French Dictionary of
Business, Commerce and Finance

Dictionnaire anglais des affaires, du
commerce et de la finance

Routledge

French Dictionary of Business, Commerce and Finance

Dictionnaire anglais des affaires, du commerce et de la finance

French–English/English–French
Français–Anglais/Anglais–Français

London and New York

First published 1996
by Routledge
11 New Fetter Lane, London EC4P 4EE

A division of International Thomson Publishing Inc.
The ITP is a trademark under licence.

Simultaneously published in the USA and Canada
by Routledge
29 West 35th Street, New York, NY 10001

© 1996 Routledge

Typeset in Monotype Times, Helvetica Neue and Bauer Bodoni
by Routledge

Printed in England by Clays Ltd, St Ives plc

Printed on acid-free paper

British Library Cataloguing-in-Publication Data
A catalogue record for this book is available from the British Library

Library of Congress Cataloging-in-Publication Data
Applied for

ISBN 0–415–09394–5

French Dictionary of Business, Commerce and Finance
Dictionnaire anglais des affaires, du commerce et de la finance

Project Manager/Chef de projet
Rebecca Moy

Programme Manager/Direction de collection
Elizabeth White

Managing Editor/Direction éditoriale
Sinda López

Editorial/Rédaction
Martin Barr   Gemma Marren   Janice McNeillie   Jessica Ramage

Marketing
Rachel Miller   Judith Watts

Systems/Informatique
Omar Raman   Simon Thompson

Administration/Secrétariat
Kristoffer Blegvad   Amanda Brindley

Production
Nigel Marsh   Maureen James

Contributors/Collaborateurs

Martin Barr
Sarah Brickwood
Pierre Briend
Catherine Carena-Barrier
Christiane Clemencin
Yves Debaugnies
Laurence Delsol
Joao Esteves-Ferreira
Gill Ewing
Patricia Festa-Nissanoff
Catherine Geffray
Michel Gouverneur
Pat Larmar
Brigitte Lemoult-Wasserman
Aliette Le Vasseur
Elizabeth Loverde-Bagwell
Catherine Maryan Green

Alain Métro
Angela Moyon
François Parigot
Sylvie Pedrazzini
Brigitte Ponsart
Manuelle Prunier
Martine Schuwer
Philippe Schuwer
Steve Smith
Patricia Sommer
Olivier Speltdoorn
Dimitri Stoquart
Edith Trenou
Evelyne Watson
Elizabeth Wiles-Portier
John Willers

Lexicographers/Lexicographes

Tom Bartlett
Hazel Curties
Stephen Curtis
Rosalind Fergusson
Margaret Jull Costa

Sophie Marin
Duncan Marshall
Jeremy Munday
Martine Pierquin

Specialist Consultants/Consultants Spécialistes

Norman Bartlett
The Institute of European Trade and Technology
Peter Bond
Chartered Institute of Banking
Dr Karen Brewer
The Law Society of England and Wales
Robert de Bruin
Association française des banques
Jean-François Chanlat
École des hautes études commerciales du Québec
Brian Clifford
Manchester Business School
Maryline Grellier
Apple France
Norman Hart
The Chartered Institute of Marketing
Thierry Jean
Groupe école supérieure internationale de commerce

Suzannah Lansdall
The Environmental Council
Josette Mell
France Télécom
Graham Monk
Department of Trade and Industry
Robert Moran
American Graduate School of Management
Bertrand Nicholas
Centre de recherche et de gestion
Chris Nobes
University of Reading
Gordon Shenton
École supérieure de commerce de Lyon
Michel Van der Yeught
Université de Toulon et du Var
Peter Walton
Université de Genève

Proofreaders/Correcteurs

Tom Bartlett
Hazel Curties
Stephen Curtis
Susan Dunsmore
Sara Fenby
Rosalind Fergusson
Julia Harding
Sophie Marin
Duncan Marshall

Jeremy Munday
Martine Pierquin
Candice Pinchard
Fabienne Rangeard
Catherine Roux
Alisa Salamon
Claire Trocmé
Vivienne Wattenhofer

Keyboarders/Clavistes

Deborah Thomas
Suzanne Dent, Alex Fenby, Sara Fenby, Antonio Fernández Entrena, Christiane Grosskopf,
Faraz Kermani, Susannah Kingston, Marianne Pendray, Fabienne Rangeard, Alisa Salamon,
Guy Winpenny

Acknowledgements

We also wish to acknowledge the valuable contribution of Flavia Hodges and Wendy Morris during the early stages of the project.

We are particularly indebted to the following people for their assistance during the compilation of this dictionary: Frank Abate and his team for checking American coverage, and Carlos Márquez Linares for his assistance in preparing the supplementary material.

Remerciements

Nous tenons également à exprimer nos remerciements à Flavia Hodges et à Wendy Morris pour leur précieuse collaboration à la phase initiale de cet ouvrage.

Nous sommes tout particulièrement reconnaissants à ceux et à celles qui ont apporté leur concours lors de la compilation de ce dictionnaire: Frank Abate et son équipe pour leur travail de recherche sur le corpus américain, et Carlos Márquez Linares pour sa contribution aux appendices.

Contents/Table des matières

Preface/Préface

Following on from the programme of technical and specialist dictionaries launched in October 1994, the *French Dictionary of Business, Commerce and Finance* is the first of a series of specialist business dictionaries to be published by Routledge.

The two factors that have enabled us to create such completely new bilingual business dictionaries, that set new standards in their field, are the database system and the method of compilation.

It would not have been possible to compile this dictionary within a realistic timescale, and to the standard achieved, without the use of a highly sophisticated, custom-designed database.

The database's most significant feature is that it is designed as a relational database: term records for each language are held in separate files, with further files consisting only of link records. Links between terms in different language files represent translations which enable us to handle various types of one-to-many and many-to-one translation equivalences. Links between terms within a single language file represent cross-references, themselves of a wide variety of types: synonyms, antonyms, spelling variants, geographical variants and abbreviations.

The content of the database for this dictionary was created in three principal phases. A considerable proportion of the term list was gathered in-house from various specialist sources, including from a wide range of reference material and the business and financial press. The term list was then sent out to specialist translators – with current practical experience of business translation – who supplied French equivalences and expanded the basic term list to include the main relevant terminology in their particular sphere of work.

The terms in each language were then vetted by native-speaker subject specialists, working at the leading edge of their respective fields, in order

Suite au lancement de la collection de dictionnaires techniques spécialisés en octobre 1994, le *Dictionnaire anglais des affaires, du commerce et de la finance* est le premier d'une série de dictionnaires de commerce spécialisés publiés par Routledge.

Les deux facteurs qui nous ont permis de créer un dictionnaire de commerce bilingue totalement nouveau, posant des normes nouvelles, sont un système de base de données et une méthode de compilation parfaitement adaptés aux résultats souhaités.

La sortie de ce dictionnaire dans les délais et conformément aux critères prévus imposait la compilation d'une base de données spécifique extrêmement sophistiquée.

Ce système a pour caractéristique essentielle d'être conçu comme une base de données relationnelle: dans chaque langue, les termes sont stockés dans des fichiers séparés, tandis que d'autres fichiers ne se composent que de liens. Les liens entre les termes de fichiers de langues séparés représentent des traductions et nous permettent de gérer différents types d'équivalences de traduction 'un à plusieurs' et 'plusieurs à un'. Les liens entre les différents termes d'un même fichier de langue représentent des renvois, eux-mêmes de différents types: synonymes, antonymes, variantes orthographiques, variantes géographiques et abréviations.

La base de données a été créée en trois phases principales: une partie considérable de la liste de termes a été recueillie dans nos locaux à partir de diverses sources spécialisées, y compris des ouvrages de référence et la presse de la finance et des affaires. Cette liste a ensuite été envoyée à des traducteurs spécialisés dont l'expérience pratique de la traduction commerciale leur a permis de fournir des équivalents français et d'ajouter à cette liste de termes de base la terminologie appropriée de leur domaine de travail. Ces termes regroupés ont ensuite été

to ensure the currency of the terminology, the accuracy of explanations and the comprehensiveness of coverage. Finally, each language file was reviewed by regional editors to ensure coverage of geographical spelling variants so that this information could be incorporated in the dictionary entries.

The creation and editing of the database of terms was, however, only the first stage in the making of the dictionary. Within the database the distinction between source and target languages is not meaningful, but for this printed dictionary it has been necessary to format the data to produce separate French–English and English–French parts. The data was processed by a further software module to produce two alphabetic sequences, of French headwords with English translations and vice versa, each displaying the nesting of compounds, ordering of translations, style for cross-references of different types and other features according to a complex algorithm.

At this stage the formatted text was edited by a team of experienced French and English lexicographers whose task it was to eliminate duplication or inconsistency; edit the entries to ensure that all relevant information was present, correct and easily interpreted; and remove terms that were on the one hand too general, or on the other, too specialized for inclusion in a general business dictionary. This phased method of working has enabled us to set extremely high standards of quality control.

The editorial team

approuvés dans les différents pays par des spécialistes techniques de haut niveau, ayant pour mission de garantir l'actualité de la terminologie et la précision des termes, et de s'assurer que les sujets soient traités de façon exhaustive. Enfin, chaque fichier de langue a été contrôlé par des lexicographes des pays concernés, chargés de veiller au respect des variantes géographiques d'orthographe, afin d'inclure ces informations pour chaque entrée concernée.

La création et la vérification de la base de données terminologique n'ont cependant représenté que la première étape de la constitution du dictionnaire. La distinction entre les langues cible et source n'étant pas significative au niveau de la base de données, nous avons dû, pour la version imprimée, mettre les données en forme pour obtenir des parties français–anglais et anglais–français séparées. Les données ont alors été traitées par un logiciel permettant de produire deux séquences alphabétiques, des mots-clés français avec leurs traductions anglaises – et vice versa – avec, dans chaque cas, indication de l'imbrication des composants, de l'ordre des traductions, du style des renvois de différents types, et d'autres fonctions, selon un algorithme complexe.

A ce stade, le texte mis en forme a été vérifié par une équipe de lexicographes anglais et français expérimentés, qui avaient pour mission d'éliminer les doublons et les incohérences; de réviser les entrées en s'assurant que toutes les informations nécessaires soient présentes, correctes et d'interprétation aisée; et de supprimer les termes soit trop généraux, soit trop spécialisés pour être inclus dans un dictionnaire de commerce général.

Cette méthodologie nous a permis d'établir des normes de contrôle de qualité extrêmement élevées.

Les éditeurs

Features of the dictionary/
Caractéristiques du dictionnaire

The main features of the dictionary are highlighted in the text extracts on the following pages. For a more detailed explanation of each of these features, and information on how to get the most out of the dictionary, see pages xv–xvii.

Les principales caractéristiques de ce dictionnaire sont mentionnées des pages suivantes dans les éclatés. Pour une explication detaillée de chacune de ces caractéristiques, et pour tirer le meilleur parti de votre dictionnaire, reportez-vous aux pages xviii–xx.

abbreviations are expanded in both French and English

—**DEPS** *abrév (dernier entré, premier sorti)* COMPTA, RES HUM LIFO *(last in, first out)*

député[1] *m* POL ≈ congressman *(US)*

député[2] *m, f* POL ≈ Member of Parliament *(UK)*, MP *(UK)*, Rep. *(US)*, Representative *(US)*;

cultural equivalents give information on target culture equivalent

— ~ **ordinaire** POL *sans porte-feuille ministériel* backbench MP *(UK)*, backbencher *(UK)*; ~ **du Parlement Européen** POL Euro MP, European MP, European member of Parliament, member of the European Parliament, MEP

députée *f* POL ≈ congresswoman *(US)*

déqualification *f* RES HUM *de la main d'oeuvre* deskilling

dérangement: **être en** ~ *loc téléphone* COM be out of action

register of language indicated

—**dérapage** *m* ADMIN outlay creep *(jarg)*, COM slippage, COMPTA, FIN outlay creep *(jarg)*; ~ **catégoriel** RES HUM grade drift; ~ **des salaires** RES HUM earnings drift, wage drift

déraper *vi* BOURSE slip

déréglementation *f* COM *commerce international*,

subject-area labels given in alphabetical order to show appropriate translation

— ECON, POL deregulation; ~ **mondiale** ECON global deregulation

dérégler *vt* COM deregulate

dérégulation *f* POL deregulation

dérive:[1] **à la** ~ *adj* TRANSP adrift

superior numbers mark homographs

—**dérive:**[2] ~ **des salaires** *f* RES HUM earnings drift, wage drift *(jarg)*

dérivé *m* ECON, ENVIR, IND, V&M by-product

dernier[1], **-ière** *adj* COM last, V&M *most recent* latest; ~ **avertissement** RES HUM final warning; ~ **cours** BOURSE closing price; ~ **cri** COM trendy *(UK, infrml)*, IND, V&M *matériel* state-of-the-art; ~ **délai** COM at the latest, closing date, deadline; ~ **jour de cotation** BOURSE last trading day; ~ **jour de**

antonyms and synonyms cross-referred at relevant entry

— **notification** *(ANT premier jour de notification)* FIN last notice day; ~ **jour de transaction** BOURSE final trading day, last day of trading, last trading day; ~ **-né** COM *d'une gamme de produit* latest addition; ~ **prix en premier** BOURSE last in, first out price; ~ **ressort** COM last resort; ~ **transporteur** TRANSP last carrier; ◆ **de** ~ **moment** COM up-to-the-minute; **en** ~ **ressort** COM as a last resort; ~ **entré, premier sorti**

abbreviation of term given at full-form entry

— *(DEPS)* COMPTA *évaluation des stocks*, RES HUM last in, first out *(LIFO)*

dernier[2], **-ière** *m,f* COM latter

dernière:[1] **de** ~ **minute** *adj* COM last-minute

dernière:[2] ~ **cotation** *f* BOURSE closing price, closing quotation; ~ **enchère** *f* COM closing bid;

contexts give supplementary information to help locate the right translation

— ~ **entrée** *f* COM *dans une liste* tail; ~ **journée de transactions** *f* BOURSE final trading day; **la** ~ **mode** *f* COM the latest fashion; ~ **mise en vente** *f* BOURSE last sale; ~ **offre** *f* COM closing bid; ~ **quinzaine** *f* COM *du mois* last half, 1h; ~ **réprimande** *f* RES HUM final warning; ◆ **à la** ~ **place** COM in last position

dernières: ~ **volontés** *f pl* DROIT last will and testament

dérogation *f* COMPTA relief, DROIT derogation,

phrases grouped together at end of entry and preceded by lozenge

— deviation; ◆ **par** ~ COM notwithstanding; **par** ~ **aux clauses de** DROIT notwithstanding the provisions of; **par** ~ **aux dispositions de** DROIT

formes intégrales des abréviations données en français comme en anglais

les équivalents culturels procurent des informations sur les équivalents dans la culture cible

indication du registre de langue

domaines en ordre alphabétique indiquant la traduction appropriée à chaque domaine

les numéros en exposant indiquent des homographes

antonymes et synonymes renvoyés à l'entrée appropriée

abréviation d'un terme donnée à l'entrée pour la forme intégrale

contextes donnant des informations supplémentaires afin de choisir la traduction correcte

les locutions apparaissent à la fin d'une entrée et sont précédées d'un losange

formes intégrales des
abréviations données en
français comme en anglais

— **S**[1] *abbr* TRANSP *(station)* gare *f*, TRANSP *(South* — abbreviations are expanded
compass point) navigation S *(quart sud)*, TRANSP   in both French and English
(single expansion engine) *shipping* machine à
expansion simple *f*, TRANSP *(starboard side)*
shipping tribord *m*
S:[2] ~ **curve** *n* ECON courbe en S *f*

lorsque le sens d'une
abréviation varie suivant le
domaine traité, il suit
directement le code de ce
domaine

s/a *abbr* IND *(single-acting) machinery* à simple — when the meaning of an
effet, TRANSP *(safe arrival)* heureuse arrivée *f*   abbreviation differs
s.a.a.r. *abbr* *(seasonally adjusted annual rate)* ECON   according to subject area it
taux annuel corrigé des variations saisonnières   follows the subject-area
m   label

indication du registre de
langue

sack *vt infrml* HRM *employee* licencier, lourder — register of language
(*infrml*), renvoyer, vider (*infrml*), virer (*infrml*);   indicated
◆ **get the** ~ *infrml* HRM être renvoyé, être viré
(*infrml*); **give sb the** ~ *infrml* HRM flanquer qn à la
porte (*infrml*), lourder qn (*infrml*)

domaines en ordre
alphabétique indiquant la
traduction appropriée à
chaque domaine

sacking *n infrml* HRM *of worker* licenciement *m*
sacrifice *vt* INS sacrifier   subject-area labels given in
— **SAD** *abbr (single administrative document)* ADMIN, — alphabetical order show
IMP/EXP, TRANSP *EU* DAU *(document adminis-*   appropriate translation
tratif unique)

deux points indiquant un mot
dépourvu de sens technique
introduisant un mot
composé ou une locution

— **saddle:** ~ **tank** *n* TRANSP *shipping* citerne trans- — a colon introduces a
versale en hauteur *f*   compound or phrase where
s.a.e *abbr UK (stamped addressed envelope, cf*   the headword has no
s.a.s.e.) COMMS, GEN COMM enveloppe affranchie   technical value
f, enveloppe timbrée à vos nom et adresse *f*
SAEF *abbr (SEAQ Automated Execution Facility)*
STOCK système international de cotation automatisé *m*
SAF *abbr (structural adjustment facility)* FIN facilité
d'ajustement structurel *f*
SAFCON: ~ **certificate** *n* TRANSP *shipping* certificat
de sécurité de construction pour navire de
charge *m*
safe *n* BANK coffre-fort *m*; ~ **arrival** *(s/a)* TRANSP

genres indiqués après les
traductions des noms en
français

heureuse arrivée *f*; ~ **asset** FIN actif sûr *m*; ~ **berth** — genders are indicated at
TRANSP *shipping* poste d'amarrage sûr *m*; ~ **cus-**   French noun translations
tody department BANK service des coffres *m*;
~ **deposit** BANK coffre *m*, dépôt en coffre *m*,

antonymes et synonymes
renvoyés à l'entrée
appropriée

dépôt en coffre-fort *m*; ~ **-deposit box** *(SYN* — antonyms and synonyms
safety-deposit box) BANK coffre *m*, dépôt en   cross-referred at relevant
coffre *m*, dépôt en coffre-fort *m*; ~ **-deposit vault**   entry
BANK salle des coffres *f*, salle des coffres-forts *f*;
~ **estimate** GEN COMM estimation prudente *f*;

variantes orthographiques
britanniques et américaines
fournies intégralement et
signalées par des codes
géographiques

~ **harbor rule** *AmE*, ~ **harbour rule** *BrE* TAX règle — British English and American
de l'abri sûr *f*; ~ **hedge** STOCK couverture sûre *f*,   English spelling variants are
opération de couverture sûre *f*; ~ **investment**   given in full and followed by
BANK placement sûr *m*; ~ **port** TRANSP *shipping*   regional labels
port sûr *m*; ~ **working load** IND charge admissible
de fonctionnement *f*, charge de travail de sécurité
f; ◆ **be on the** ~ **side** GEN COMM par précaution,
pour plus de sûreté
safeguard[1] *n* LAW *clause* sauvegarde *f*
safeguard[2] *vt* GEN COMM *assets* sauvegarder, *secret*

les locutions apparaissent à
la fin d'une entrée et sont
précédées d'un losange

garder; ◆ ~ **against inflation** ECON se protéger — phrases grouped together at
contre l'inflation   end of entry and preceded
safekeeping *n* BANK garde des valeurs *f*, services de   by lozenge
garde *m pl*; ~ **of assets** BANK garde des valeurs
actives *f*
safety *n* WEL sécurité *f*; ~ **bank** *n* GEN COMM stock
de dépannage *m*; ~ **belt** *n* TRANSP ceinture de
sécurité *f*; ~ **-deposit box** *n* *(SYN safe-deposit box)*
BANK coffre *m*, dépôt en coffre *m*, dépôt en coffre-
fort *m*; ~ **-deposit box charges** *n pl* BANK frais de

Using the dictionary

Selection of terms

We have aimed to include the essential vocabulary of each subject area as well as including more specialized references such as organizations, legal acts and financial and accounting systems. Overlap with a general bilingual dictionary has been kept to a minimum by only including terms which can be applied in a business context. The material has been checked by leading subject experts to ensure that both the English and the French terms are accurate and current, that the translations are valid equivalents and that there are no vital gaps in coverage.

Although other variant translations would often be permissible in a particular subject area, we have given the terms most widely preferred by specialists in the area.

Coverage of the subject areas is given proportionally so that a core and wide-ranging area such as stock market has a count of around 4,345 terms whereas a developing area such as environment will have fewer terms.

Placement of terms

Terms are entered in alphabetical order. Compound terms, including hyphenated compounds, are listed alphabetically at their first element. When this first element is itself a headword with a business-related sense of its own, compound forms follow the simple form. In compounds, the headword is replaced by a swung dash (~).

farming *n* ECON, ENVIR agriculture *f*, GEN COMM culture *f*; ~ **business** GEN COMM, IND entreprise agricole *f*, exploitation agricole *f*; ~ **income** ECON, GEN COMM revenu agricole *m*; ~ **method** ECON méthode d'exploitation agricole *f*

If the first element is not itself a headword with a business sense, compounds formed from that element are entered at a dummy headword:

force:[1] ~ **majeure** *n* GEN COMM, LAW force majeure *f*; ◆ GEN COMM **be in** ~ être en vigueur; **come into** ~ GEN COMM entrer en vigueur, être applicable, LAW *act, regulation, rule* entrer en vigueur

The only exceptions to this policy are phrases which begin with highly polysemous or delexicalized elements *be, make, do,* or terms beginning with an article or preposition from the following lists:

a, all, and, any, anybody, anyone, anything, anywhere, are, as, at, be, by, during, each, every, everybody, everyone, everything, everywhere, for, from, here, if, in, is, it, my, no, nobody, no-one, nor, not, nothing, nowhere, of, off, on, or, out, over, sb, so, some, somebody, someone, something, somewhere, sth, that, the, then, there, they, thing, this, to, too, very, where, while, who, with

à, au, aux, avec, c', ça, ce, cet, cette, chose, dans, d', de, des, dont, du, en, ès, est, et, être, ici, l', la, là, laquelle, le, lequel, les, lesquelles, lesquels, ne, ni, nul, nulle, on, ou, où, par, pendant, personne, peu, pour, qch, qn, qu', que, quelqu', quelque, qui, rien, s', se, si, sont, sous, sur, tous, tout, toute, toutes, très, trop, un, une, y

In the cases mentioned above, the phrase or term will be entered at the next lexical element. In addition to this, the following are also ignored in determining the alphabetical sequence of nested terms:

a, an, and, of, the, with

à, au, aux, d', de, des, du, en, ès, l', la, le, les, pour, s', se, un, une

Note that where these words precede a nested term they then determine the alphabetical sequence:

Bourse *f* BOURSE securities exchange, stock market; ~ **de Boston** BOURSE Boston Stock

Exchange; ~ **aux céréales de Minnéapolis** BOURSE Minneapolis Grain Exchange (*US*); **la ~ de Paris** BOURSE ≈ London Stock Exchange; **la ~ de Toronto** *Canada* BOURSE TSE (*Canada*), the Toronto Stock Exchange (*Canada*) ~ **des marchandises** BOURSE ≈ Commodities Exchange (*US*)

Abbreviations and acronyms written in upper case appear after vocabulary words of the same form written in lower case:

cap. *abbr (capital letter)* ADMIN capitale *f*, haut de casse *m*, lettre capitale *f*, lettre de haut de casse *f* (*jarg*), lettre majuscule *f*, majuscule *f*, MEDIA capitale *f*, haut de casse *m*, lettre capitale *f*, lettre de haut de casse *f*, lettre majuscule *f*, majuscule *f*

CAP[1] *abbr (Common Agricultural Policy)* ECON, POL European Union PAC (*politique agricole commune*)

Terms containing figures and symbols are alphabetized according to the usual expansion when written out in full:

2Q *abbr (second quarter)* GEN COMM deuxième trimestre *m*

Phrases are grouped together at the end of the relevant entry. The symbol ◆ introduces the phrase section, for example:

scheduled[1] *adj* TRANSP régulier; ◆ **as ~** ADMIN, GEN COMM comme prévu, conformément au programme (*frml*), selon le planning; **be ~ for** GEN COMM être programmé pour, être prévu pour; **be ~ to begin in** GEN COMM devoir commencer en, être prévu pour

Parts of speech

Terms are generally accompanied by a label indicating the part of speech. (In cases where nested terms have the same part of speech as the headword, parts of speech are not repeated.) For a complete list of these labels and their expansions, please see page xxi.

When terms beginning with the same element fall into two or more part-of-speech categories, the different nests will be distinguished by a raised number immediately following the head of that nest, whether the head is an entry in its own right or a dummy. The sequence is: abbreviation, adjective, adverb, noun and verb, followed by less frequent parts of speech, for example:

maison[1] *adj* COM *traducteur, rédacteur* in-company, in-house, INFO *système* in-house
maison[2] *f* BOURSE establishment, firm, house, ECON concern, IMMOB house; **~ d'acceptation**

BANQUE acceptance house; **~ d'achat étrangère** IMP/EXP foreign buying house; **~ d'arbitrage** BOURSE arbitrage house

All forms of a verb (transitive, intransitive and reflexive) are treated in separate numbered sections under a single homograph, for example:

maintenir 1. *vt* COM abide by, *les marges* hold, COMMS maintain, DROIT uphold, ECON, FIN *les marges* hold; **2.** *v réfl*; **se ~au même niveau que** COM keep pace with, keep up with; **se ~ à la page** COM keep up to date; ◆ **~ artificiellement le prix de** COM *marchandises* valorize; **~ à flot** COM *affaire* keep afloat; **~ à jour** ADMIN *dossiers* keep up to date; **~ le marché** BOURSE make a market; **~ un profil bas** COM keep a low profile

Ordering of translations

Every term is accompanied by one or more labels indicating the area in which it is used. For a complete list of these labels and their expansions, please see page xxii.

Where the same term is used in more than one area, multiple labels are given as appropriate. These labels appear in alphabetical order.

Where a term has the same translation in more than one area, this translation is given after the sequence of labels, for example:

e-mail *n (electronic mail)* ADMIN, COMMS, COMP courrier électronique *m*, messagerie électronique *f*

When a term has different translations according to the area in which it is used, the appropriate translation is given after each label or set of labels, for example:

absorption *f* COMPTA merger accounting (*BrE*), pooling of interests (*AmE*), ECON *d'une société* absorption, acquisition, TRANSP absorption

Supplementary information

The gender is given for every French noun term. In the case of compound terms, this is the gender of the term as a whole (that is, its noun head) rather than the final element, for example:

manipulation *f* BOURSE rigging, COM, GESTION manipulation; **~ de données** INFO data handling

In many cases additional data is given about a term to show how it is used. Such contextual information can be:

(a) the typical subject or object of a verb, for example:

amortir 1. *vt* BANQUE amortize, BOURSE *action*

redeem, COM *emprunt* redeem, *son, choc* absorb, COMPTA charge off, depreciate, *actif* amortize, *dette* liquidate, ECON depreciate, FIN amortize; **2.** *v réfl* **s'~** COMPTA write off; ♦ **s'~ sur dix ans** COMPTA write off over ten years

(b) typical nouns used with an adjective, for example:

soiled *adj* GEN COMM *goods* défraîchi

(c) words indicating the reference of a noun, for example:

cession *n* GEN COMM abandon *m*, LAW *of land, territory* cession *f*; **~ of portfolio** GEN COMM, INS cession de portefeuille *f*

(d) information which supplements the subject-area label, for example:

saddle: **~ tank** *n* TRANSP *shipping* citerne transversale en hauteur *f*

(e) a paraphrase or broad equivalent, for example:

squeegee: **~ agreement** *n jarg* STOCK accord de rachat de titre à perte et à une date prédéterminée

When various different translations apply in the same subject area, contextual information is also used to show which translation is appropriate in different circumstances, for example:

bidding *n* GEN COMM *at sale* enchère *f*, *submission of bids* soumission des offres *f*, S&M enchère *f*;

Cultural equivalents are built into the entry to give the user information on the equivalent organization, system, institution, and so on, in the target culture, for example:

Stock: **~ Exchange Daily Official List** *n* UK *(SEDOL)* STOCK ≈ Bulletin officiel des cours de la Bourse *m*

Cross-references

Geographical lexical variants are shown in full at each relevant entry. American-English spelling variants are cross-referred to the British-English entry and less frequent forms are cross-referred to their more common form, for example:

color *n* AmE see *colour* BrE

Geographical variants, both spelling and lexical, are given in full when they are translations, for example:

machine: **~ à écrire les chèques** *n* BANQUE check-writing machine *(AmE)*, cheque-writing machine *(BrE)*, FIN check writer *(AmE)*, check-writer machine *(AmE)*, cheque writer *(BrE)*, cheque-writer machine *(BrE)*

district: **~ attorney** *n* US *(D/A, Director of Public Prosecutions)* LAW ≈ procureur de la République *m (France)*, ≈ procureur du Roi *m (Belgique)*

Synonyms and antonyms are fully cross-referred at the relevant entries, for example:

accepting:[2] **~ bank** *n (SYN accepting house)* BANK banque d'acceptation *f*; **~ banker** *n* BANK banquier acceptant *m*; **~ house** *n (SYN accepting bank)* BANK banque d'acceptation *f*

upturn *n (ANT downturn)* ECON amélioration *f*, amélioration sensible *f*, reprise *f*, GEN COMM, STOCK reprise *f*

Both abbreviations and their full forms are entered in the main body of the dictionary in alphabetical sequence. Full information – including translations and cross-references to the full form or abbreviation as appropriate – is given at each entry, for example:

computer:[2] **~-aided design** *n (CAD)* COMP, IND conception assistée par ordinateur *f*, création assistée par ordinateur *f (CAO)*

Where an abbreviation in the source language translates to an abbreviation in the target language, the full form is in each case given after the abbreviation in brackets and in italics, for example:

CAN *abrév (convertisseur analogique-numérique)* INFO ADC *(analog-digital converter)*

If a source-language term abbreviation does not translate to a target-language abbreviation, the translation of the abbreviation is in roman, for example:

WL *abbr (wagon-lit)* TRANSP *chemin de fer* sleeper, sleeping car

Abbreviations are also listed in a separate alphabetical sequence at the back of the dictionary to allow browsing in cases where the exact form of the abbreviation is not known.

Comment utiliser ce dictionnaire

Sélection des termes

Notre objectif a été d'inclure le vocabulaire essentiel de chaque sujet traité ainsi que des références plus spécialisées telles que des organisations, des lois et des systèmes financiers et comptables. Des termes rencontrés dans un dictionnaire bilingue général, on ne trouvera ici que ceux qui peuvent être employés dans un contexte commercial. Les termes ont été minutieusement vérifiés par des spécialistes de haut niveau, chargés de veiller à l'exactitude et à l'actualité des termes anglais et français; à la parfaite correspondance des termes, et à la cohérence de l'ensemble.

Nous avons eu pour principe de donner les traductions préférées par les spécialistes bien qu'il y ait souvent d'autres variantes possibles. Les différents sujets ont été traités de façon proportionnelle: ainsi, un domaine bien établi tel que la bourse compte à peu près 4,345 termes alors qu'un domaine en devenir tel que l'environnement en comptera moins.

Ordre des termes

Les entrées sont classées par ordre alphabétique. Les mots composés, y compris ceux qui contiennent un trait d'union, sont classés par ordre alphabétique à leur premier élément. Lorsque ce premier élément est un mot-vedette ayant un ou plusieurs sens commerciaux, les mots composés suivent la forme simple et sont classés par ordre alphabétique. Le premier élément est alors remplacé par un tilde (~). Exemple:

farming *n* ECON, ENVIR agriculture *f*, GEN COMM culture *f*; ~ **business** GEN COMM, IND entreprise agricole *f*, exploitation agricole *f*; ~**income** ECON, GEN COMM revenu agricole *m*; ~ **method** ECON méthode d'exploitation agricole *f*

Si le premier élément n'est pas traduit, ses composants sont précédés de deux-points.

force:[1] ~**majeure** *n* GEN COMM, LAW force majeure *f*; ◆ **come into** ~ GEN COMM entrer en vigueur (*pref*), être applicable, LAW *act, regulation, rule* entrer en vigueur

Les seules exceptions à cette règle sont les locutions commençant par un élément polysémique ou délexicalisé tel que *être, faire* ou *avoir*, ou par un article ou une préposition des listes suivantes:

à, au, aux, avec, c', ça, ce, cet, cette, chose, dans, d', de, des, dont, du, en, ès, est, et, être, ici, l', la, là, laquelle, le, lequel, les, lesquelles, lesquels, ne, ni, nul, nulle, on, ou, où, par, pendant, personne, peu, pour, qch, qn, qu', que, quelqu', quelque, qui, rien, s', se, si, sont, sous, sur, tous, tout, toute, toutes, très, trop, un, une, y

a, all, and, any, anybody, anyone, anything, anywhere, are, as, at, be, by, during, each, every, everybody, everyone, everything, everywhere, for, from, here, if, in, is, it, my, no, nobody, no-one, nor, not, nothing, nowhere, of, off, on, or, out, over, sb, so, some, somebody, someone, something, somewhere, sth, that, the, then, there, they, thing, this, to, too, very, where, while, who, with

Dans les cas pré-cites, la locution ou le terme sera classé à l'élément lexical qui suit. De même, les termes suivants seront ignorés pour le classement de termes.

à, au, aux, d', de, des, du, en, ès, l', la, le, les, pour, s', se, un, une

a, an, and, of, the, with

A noter que lorsque ces mots précèdent une entrée imbriquée, ils déterminent la séquence alphabétique:

Bourse *f* BOURSE securities exchange, stock market; ~ **de Boston** BOURSE Boston Stock Exchange; ~ **aux céréales de Minnéapolis** BOURSE

Minneapolis Grain Exchange (*US*); **la ~ de Paris** BOURSE ≈ London Stock Exchange; **la ~ de Toronto** *Canada* BOURSE TSE (*Canada*), the Toronto Stock Exchange (*Canada*) **~ des marchandises** BOURSE ≈ Commodities Exchange (*US*)

Les abréviations et acronymes en majuscules figurent après les termes de même forme en minuscules. Exemple:

cap. *abbr (capital letter)* ADMIN capitale *f*, haut de casse *m*, lettre capitale *f*, lettre de haut de casse *f* (*jarg*), lettre majuscule *f*, majuscule *f*, MEDIA capitale *f*, haut de casse *m*, lettre capitale *f*, lettre de haut de casse *f*, lettre majuscule *f*, majuscule *f*

CAP¹ *abbr (the Common Agricultural Policy)* ECON, POL *European Union* PAC *(la politique agricole commune)*

Les termes contenant des chiffres ou des symboles sont classés comme s'ils étaient écrits en lettres. Exemple:

aforementioned *adj* COMMS, GEN COMM précité, susdit, susmentionné

a fortiori *phr* GEN COMM a fortiori

A4 *n* ADMIN, COMMS, COMP format A4 *m*

Africa *pr n* GEN COMM Afrique *f*

Les locutions sont regroupées à la fin de l'entrée concernée et sont précédées du signe ◆ qui les introduit. Exemple:

scheduled¹ *adj* TRANSP régulier; ◆ **as ~** ADMIN, GEN COMM comme prévu, conformément au programme (*frml*), selon le planning; **be ~ for** GEN COMM être programmé pour, être prévu pour; **be ~ to begin in** GEN COMM devoir commencer en, être prévu pour

Catégories grammaticales

Les termes sont, généralement, accompagnés d'une abréviation indiquant leur fonction grammaticale. La liste complète de ces abréviations figure page xxi.

    Un terme ayant plusieurs fonctions grammaticales figure sous une entrée séparée. Ces entrées se distinguent par un chiffre en exposant qui suit immédiatement le mot-vedette. La séquence est la suivante: abréviation, adjectif, adverbe, nom, verbe, suivie des fonctions moins fréquentes. Exemple:

maison¹ *adj* COM *traducteur, rédacteur* in-company, in-house, INFO *système* in-house

maison² *f* BOURSE establishment, firm, house, ECON concern, IMMOB house; **~ d'acceptation** BANQUE acceptance house; **~ d'achat étrangère**

IMP/EXP foreign buying house; **~ d'arbitrage** BOURSE arbitrage house

Toutes les formes d'un même verbe (transitif, intransitif et réfléchi) apparaissent séparément, accompagnées d'un chiffre en exposant qui les différencie. Exemple:

maintenir 1. *vt* COM abide by, *les marges* hold, COMMS maintain, DROIT uphold, ECON, FIN *les marges* hold; **2.** *v réfl*; **se ~ au même niveau que** COM keep pace with, keep up with; **se ~ à la page** COM keep up to date ◆ **~ artificiellement le prix de** COM *marchandises* valorize; **~ à flot** COM *affaire* keep afloat; **~ à jour** ADMIN *dossiers* keep up to date; **~ le marché** BOURSE make a market; **~ un profil bas** COM keep a low profile

Ordre des traductions

Chaque terme est accompagné d'une ou plusieurs abréviations indiquant le domaine auquel il se rapporte. La liste complète de ces abréviations figure page xxii.

    Lorsqu'un terme est utilisé dans plusieurs disciplines, il est suivi des abréviations appropriées, en ordre alphabétique.

    Lorsqu'un terme est traduit de la même manière dans différentes disciplines, la traduction figure après la liste des abréviations. Exemple:

e-mail *n (electronic mail)* ADMIN, COMMS, COMP courrier électronique *m*, messagerie électronique *f*

Lorsqu'un terme peut se traduire de différentes façons, selon les disciplines, sa traduction figure après chaque abréviation ou série d'abréviations. Exemple:

absorption *f* COMPTA merger accounting (*BrE*), pooling of interests (*AmE*), ECON *d'une société* absorption, acquisition, TRANSP absorption

Informations complémentaires

Le genre de chaque nom est indiqué. Pour les expressions ou termes composés, le genre est celui du terme dans son ensemble (c'est-à-dire de son mot-vedette), et non celui de l'élément final. Exemple:

manipulation *f* BOURSE rigging, COM, GESTION manipulation; **~ de données** INFO data handling

Dans de très nombreux cas, des informations complémentaires expliquent l'utilisation du terme concerné. Exemple:

(a) le sujet ou l'objet typique d'un verbe, par exemple:

amortir 1. *vt* BANQUE amortize, BOURSE *action* redeem, COM *emprunt* redeem, *son, choc* absorb, COMPTA charge off, depreciate, *actif* amortize, *dette* liquidate, ECON depreciate, FIN amortize; **2.** *v réfl* **s'~** COMPTA write off; ♦ **s'~ sur dix ans** COMPTA write off over ten years

(b) les noms typiques utilisés avec un adjectif, par exemple:

soiled *adj* GEN COMM *goods* défraîchi

(c) les mots indiquant la référence d'un nom, par exemple:

cession *n* GEN COMM abandon *m*, LAW *of land, territory* cession *f*; **~ of portfolio** GEN COMM, INS cession de portefeuille *f*

(d) un domaine plus limité que celui indiqué par l'abréviation, par exemple:

saddle: **~ tank** *n* TRANSP *shipping* citerne transversale en hauteur *f*

(e) une paraphrase ou un équivalent d'ordre général, par exemple:

squeegee: **~ agreement** *n jarg* STOCK accord de rachat de titre à perte et à une date prédéterminée

Lorsqu'un terme peut donner lieu à différentes traductions, des informations contextuelles indiquent également la traduction appropriée. Exemple:

bidding *n* GEN COMM *at sale* enchère *f, submission of bids* soumission des offres *f*, S&M enchère *f*;

Les équivalents culturels sont pris en compte afin de donner à l'utilisateur des renseignements sur les organisations, les systèmes, les institutions, etc équivalentes dans la culture cible. Exemple:

Stock: **~ Exchange Daily Official List** *n UK (SEDOL)* STOCK ≈ Bulletin officiel des cours de la Bourse *m*

Renvois

Les variantes géographiques ou linguistiques sont toujours indiquées à chaque entrée concernée. Les variantes orthographiques de l'anglais américain sont renvoyées à l'entrée en anglais britannique, et les formes moins fréquentes sont renvoyées a leur forme plus habituelle. Exemple:

color *n AmE see* **colour** *BrE*

Les variantes géographiques, tant orthographiques que lexicales, sont indiquées intégralement lorsqu'il s'agit de traductions. Exemple:

machine: **~ à écrire les chèques** *f* BANQUE check-writing machine (*AmE*), cheque-writing machine (*BrE*), FIN check writer (*AmE*), check-writer machine (*AmE*), cheque writer (*BrE*), cheque-writer machine (*BrE*)

district: **~ attorney** *n US (D/A, Director of Public Prosecutions)* LAW ≈ procureur de la République *m (France)*, ≈ procureur du Roi *m (Belgique)*

Les synonymes et les antonymes sont toujours renvoyés aux entrées appropriées. Exemple:

accepting:[2] **~ bank** *n (SYN accepting house)* BANK banque d'acceptation *f*; **~ banker** *n* BANK banquier acceptant *m*; **~ house** *n (SYN accepting bank)* BANK banque d'acceptation *f*

upturn *n (ANT downturn)* ECON amélioration *f*, amélioration sensible *f*, reprise *f*, GEN COMM, STOCK reprise *f*

Les abréviations et leurs formes intégrales figurent dans le corps principal du dictionnaire, classées par ordre alphabétique. Les informations complètes – et notamment leurs traductions et les renvois à leur abréviation ou à leur forme intégrale, le cas échéant – sont indiquées pour chaque entrée. Exemple:

computer:[2] **~-aided design** *n (CAD)* COMP, IND conception assistée par ordinateur *f*, création assistée par ordinateur *f (CAO)*

Lorsqu'une abréviation dans la langue de départ est traduite par une abréviation dans la langue cible, sa forme intégrale apparaît dans chaque cas après l'abréviation, entre parenthèses et en italiques. Exemple:

CAN *abrév (convertisseur analogique-numérique)* INFO ADC *(analog-digital converter)*

Si une abréviation dans la langue de départ ne se traduit pas par une abréviation dans la langue cible, la traduction de cette abréviation apparaît en caractères romains. Exemple:

WL *abbr (wagon-lit)* TRANSP *chemin de fer* sleeper, sleepin-car

La liste alphabétique des abréviations contenues dans ce dictionnaire figure à la fin de ce volume.

Abbreviations used in this dictionary/
Abréviations utilisées dans ce dictionnaire

Parts of speech/Catégories grammaticales

abbr	abbreviation	abréviation
abrév	abréviation	abbreviation
adj	adjective	adjectif
adv	adverb	adverbe
conj	conjunction	conjonction
f	feminine	féminin
f pl	feminine plural	féminin pluriel
interj	interjection	interjection
loc	locution	phrase
m	masculine	masculin
mf	masculine, feminine	masculin, féminin
m, f	masculine and feminine	masculin et féminin
m pl	masculine plural	masculin pluriel
n	noun	nom
n pl	noun plural	nom pluriel
n pr	nom propre	proper noun
phr	phrase	locution
pref	prefix	préfixe
préf	préfixe	prefix
prep	preposition	préposition
prép	préposition	preposition
pr n	proper noun	nom propre
suff	suffix	suffixe
vi	intransitive verb	verbe intransitif
v pron	verbe pronominal	reflexive verb
v refl	reflexive verb	verbe pronominal
vt	transitive verb	verbe transitif
vti	transitive and intransitive verb	verbe transitif et intransitif

Geographic codes/Codes géographiques

This dictionary uses two different types of geographic codes for each territory to distinguish between lexical variants (labelled *AmE, Aus, Bel, BrE, Can, Fra, Sui*) and institutional organizations, systems, and so on, that are particular to a specific territory (labelled *Australia, Belgique, Canada, France, Suisse, UK, US*). The labels and their expansions are given below.

AmE	American English	anglais américain
Aus	Australian English	anglais australien
Australia	In Australia	En Australie
Bel	Belgian	Belge
Belgique	In Belgium	En Belgique
BrE	British English	anglais britannique
Can	Canadian English	anglais canadien
Canada	In Canada	Au Canada

Fra	French	français
France	In France	En France
Sui	Swiss	suisse
Switzerland	In Switzerland	En Suisse
UK	In the UK	Au Royaume-Uni
US	In the US	Aux États-Unis

Level codes/Registres de langage

dat	dated	vieilli
frml	formal	formel
infrml	informal	informel
jarg	jargon	jargon
obs	obsolete	obsolète
pej	pejorative	péjoratif
péj	péjoratif	pejorative
vieilli	vieilli	dated

Inflection codes/Indications grammaticales

[attr]	attributive adjective	adjectif épithète
[épith]	adjectif épithète	attributive adjective
[inv pl]	invariable plural	pluriel invariable
[pl inv]	pluriel invariable	invariable plural
[inv sg]	invariable singular	singulier invariable
[sg inv]	singulier invariable	invariable singular
[pred]	predicative adjective	adjectif attribut
[préd]	adjectif attribut	predicative adjective
[+ sing v]	takes singular verb	se conjugue au singulier

Subject-area labels/Domaines

ACC	Accountancy	Comptabilité
ADMIN	Business Administration	Administration
ASSUR	Assurance	Insurance
BANK	Banking	Banque
BANQUE	Banque	Banking
BOURSE	Bourse	Stock Market
BREVETS	Brevets	Patents
COM	Commerce	General Commerce
COMMS	Communications	Communications
COMP	Computing	Informatique
COMPTA	Comptabilité	Accountancy
DROIT	Droit	Law
ECON	Economics	Économie
ENVIR	Environment	Environnement
FIN	Finance	Finance
FISC	Fiscalité	Taxation
GEN COMM	General Commerce	Commerce
GESTION	Gestion	Management
HRM	Human Resource Management	Gestion des Ressources Humaines
IMMOB	Immobilier	Property
IMP/EXP	Import & Export	Import & Export
IND	Industry	Industrie
INFO	Informatique	Computing
INS	Insurance	Assurance

LAW	Law	Droit
LEIS	Leisure and Tourism	Loisirs
LOISIRS	Loisirs	Leisure and Tourism
MATH	Mathematics	Mathématiques
MGMNT	Management	Gestion
MEDIA	Media	Médias
PATENTS	Patents	Brevets
POL	Politics	Politique
PROP	Property	Immobilier
PROT SOC	Protection sociale	Welfare and Safety
RES HUM	Gestion des Ressources Humaines	Human Resource Management
S&M	Sales and Marketing	Vente & Marketing
STOCK	Stock Market	Bourse
TAX	Taxation	Fiscalité
TRANSP	Transport	Transport
V&M	Vente & Marketing	Sales and Marketing
WEL	Welfare and Safety	Protection sociale

Registered trademarks®

Every effort has been made to label terms which we believe constitute trademarks. The legal status of these, however, remains unchanged by the presence or absence of any such label.

Marques déposées®

Nous avons fait le maximum pour faire suivre de la mention appropriée les termes que nous estimons protégés par un dépôt de marque. Néanmoins, l'absence ou la présence de cette mention est sans effet sur leur statut légal.

A

abaissé, e *adj* INFO down

abaisser: s'~ *v pron* MATH *courbe* steepen

abandon *m* ASSUR lapse, BOURSE *d'une prime* abandonment, COM abandonment, cession, FISC release or surrender, surrender, INFO abort; **~ d'un brevet** BREVETS, DROIT surrender of a patent; **~ d'une dette** COMPTA deletion of a debt; **~ des droits conférés par un brevet** BREVETS, DROIT surrender of a patent; **~ exceptionnel** COMPTA exceptional write-off; **~ progressif** COM, INFO phasing out; ◆ **à l'~** COM in a state of neglect

abandonnataire *mf* DROIT abandonee

abandonner *vt* BOURSE *option*, BREVETS abandon, COM abandon, relinquish, scrap, COMPTA *dette* delete, INFO abort, PROT SOC drop from university; ◆ **~ une créance** COMPTA forgo collection of a debt; **~ le navire** TRANSP abandon ship; **~ prématurément** INFO abort; **~ progressivement** COM, INFO phase out

abattement: ~ pour couples mariés *m* FISC married couples' allowance (*UK*); **~ fiscal** *m* FISC allowance, concession, tax allowance (*BrE*), tax deduction (*AmE*), writing-down allowance; **~ fiscal personnel** *m* FISC personal allowance (*UK*); **~ fiscal sur les intérêts versés** *m* ECON, FISC interest relief; **~ d'impôt** *m* ECON, FIN, FISC tax abatement; **~ pour personne à charge** *m* FIN revenue dependency; **~ pour personnes seules** *m* FISC single person's allowance; **~ sur les plus-values** *m* FISC capital gains allowance, capital gains deduction (*Can*); **~ sur le prélèvement** *m* FIN abatement of the levy; **~ vieillesse** *m* FISC age allowance (*UK*)

abattre *vt* ENVIR *charbon* win

abeilles: ~ à gros rapport *f pl* FIN killer bees

ab intestat *adj* DROIT *succession* intestate

abolir *vt* ADMIN, COM abolish, DROIT abolish, annul, lift

abolition *f* ADMIN abolition, COM abolishment, DROIT annulment

abondance *f* COM abundance, affluence, ECON abundance, wealth, affluence, IND, PROT SOC affluence, RES HUM abundance, affluence

abondant, e *adj* COM, ECON abundant; **peu ~** ECON scarce

abonné: [1] **peu ~** *adj* ECON scarce

abonné [2], **e** *m,f* COM subscriber, *à une association* season ticket holder (*BrE*), INFO, MÉDIA *à un magazine* subscriber; **~ à l'essai** MÉDIA trial subscriber; **~ au téléphone** COMMS telephone subscriber

abonnement *m* COM, COMPTA, MÉDIA subscription; **~ annuel** COM, MÉDIA annual subscription; **~ à l'essai** MÉDIA trial subscription, TS; **~ à forfait** FIN flat-rate subscription; **~ gratuit** COM, MÉDIA complimentary subscription; **~ pour membres** COM association subscription

abonner: s'~ à *v pron* COM, MÉDIA subscribe to

abord *m* COM approach

abordable *adj* ECON, V&M *prix* affordable

abordage *m* TRANSP *navigation* col, coll, collision

aborder *vt* COM *problème* address, tackle

Abou-Dhabi *n pr* COM Abu Dhabi

aboutir: vt ~ à COM culminate in, result in; ◆ **~ à un compromis** COM reach a compromise

above-the-line *loc* V&M above the line

abrégé *m* BREVETS, COM, ECON, FIN abstract, summary

abréger *vt* COM abbreviate, *texte* summarize

abréviation *f* COM abbreviation

abri *m* FISC shelter; **~ fiscal** FISC tax shelter

abrogation *f* COM abolishment, DROIT abrogation, annulment

abroger *vt* DROIT abrogate, annul, repeal; ◆ **~ un impôt** FISC repeal a tax

ABSAR *abrév* (*Actions à bons de souscription d'actions avec facilité de rachat*) BOURSE shares with redeemable share warrants

absence *f* COM absence, RES HUM absence, time off; **~ d'accord** RES HUM failure to agree, FTA; **~ de communication** COM, COMMS communication gap; **~ de contrepartie** COM *contrats* absence of consideration; **~ de correspondance** TRANSP misconnection; **~ non justifiée** RES HUM absence without leave; **~ non motivée** RES HUM absence without leave; **~ ponctuelle** RES HUM time off, time off work; **~ de renoncement** DROIT nonforfeiture; **~ de responsabilité** DROIT nonliability; **~ sans permission** RES HUM absence without leave; ◆ **en l'~ de qn** COM in sb's absence

absent [1], **e** *adj* COM, RES HUM absent; ◆ **être ~ pour cause de maladie** RES HUM be absent due to sickness, be off sick (*infrml*)

absent [2], **e** *m,f* COM, RES HUM absentee

absentéisme *m* COM, RES HUM absenteeism; **~ injustifié** RES HUM malingering, unexplained absence, unjustified absence

absentéiste *mf* COM, RES HUM absentee

ABSOC *abrév* (*Actions à bons de souscription d'obligations convertibles*) BOURSE shares with convertible bond warrants carrying preferential subscription rights

absolu, e *adj* COM, INFO absolute

absorbé, e *adj* BOURSE *émission de titres*, ECON absorbed

absorber *vt* BOURSE *émission* take over, COM *une autre société* absorb, FIN *perte* cover

absorption *f* COMPTA merger accounting (*BrE*), pooling of interests (*AmE*), ECON *d'une société* absorption, acquisition, TRANSP absorption

abstenir: s'~ *v pron* POL *dans une élection* abstain; **s'~ de** COM refrain from

abstention *f* ECON abstinence, POL abstention

abus *m* BREVETS *de brevets*, COM abuse, ENVIR overuse; **~ d'autorité** COM exercise of undue authority; **~ de confiance** COM abuse of confidence, abuse of trust, breach of trust, confidence game, confidence trick; **~ de droits** FISC abuse of rights; **~ d'influence** COM undue influence; **~ de pouvoir** ADMIN, COM abuse of administrative authority, abuse of power; ♦ **remédier aux ~** COM remedy abuses

abuser *vt* DROIT mislead; **~ de** COM *privilège* abuse

abusif, -ive *adj* COM *prix* excessive, exhorbitant, prohibitive, *usage, pratique* improper

a.c. *abrév* (*avarie commune*) ASSUR GA (*general average*)

AC *abrév* (*assurance-chômage*) RES HUM UI (*unemployment insurance*)

à/c *abrév* (*à compter de*) COM A/D (*after date*)

Académie: ~ royale des arts *f* PROT SOC Royal Society of Arts (*UK*), RSA (*UK*)

acc. *abrév* (*acceptation*) BANQUE, COM, COMPTA, DROIT, IMMOB acce. (*acceptance*)

accabler *vt* COM overwhelm; ♦ **~ qn d'accusations** COM throw the book at sb

accalmie *f* COM lull

accaparement: ~ du marché *m* BOURSE, ECON, FIN, V&M cornering the market

accaparer *vt* BOURSE *marché*, ECON, FIN, V&M corner

accapareur *m* BOURSE, FIN, V&M cornerer

accéder: vt ~ à COM *grade* rise to, *requête* comply with, grant, *responsabilité* accede to, INFO *base de données, fichier, dossier* access; **~ directement à** INFO hot-key

accélérateur *m* MATH accelerator; **~ flexible** ECON flexible accelerator

accélération *f* COM acceleration, speeding-up, DROIT *immobilier*, IMMOB acceleration, RES HUM speeding-up

accéléré, e *adj* COM *formation professionnelle* accelerated, fast-track

accélérer 1. *vt* COM expedite, step up; **2.** *v pron* **s'~** COM gain momentum, COM *travail, production* accelerate, put on a spurt, speed up

accent *m* COM accent, emphasis; **~ circonflexe** INFO circumflex

acceptable *adj* COM acceptable, permissible, DROIT permissible

acceptant, e *adj* BANQUE *banquier* accepting

acceptation *f* BANQUE *d'une traite*, COM, COMPTA acceptance, DROIT admission, DROIT, IMMOB *d'une sous-location* acceptance, V&M *d'une marque* acceptance; **~ de banque** BANQUE bank acceptance, banker's acceptance; **~ de cautionnement** FIN collateral acceptance; **~ commerciale** COM, ECON trade acceptance; **~ conditionnelle** BANQUE qualified acceptance; **~ contre documents** BANQUE acceptance against documents; **~ définitive** COM final acceptance; **~ d'une hypothèque** BANQUE mortgage assumption; **~ inconditionnelle** COM unconditional acceptance, FIN unqualified acceptance; **~ par complaisance** COM accommodation acceptance; **~ par les consommateurs** V&M consumer acceptance; **~ par intervention** COM acceptance by intervention, acceptance for honour; **~ partielle** FIN *d'un effet* partial basis; **~ d'un produit** V&M product acceptance; **~ du produit par le marché** V&M market acceptance; **~ provisoire** COM provisional acceptance; **~ d'un règlement forfaitaire** COM acceptance of lump-sum settlement; **~ d'un règlement global** COM acceptance of lump-sum settlement; **~ restreinte** BANQUE qualified acceptance; **~ sans réserve** BANQUE clean acceptance, general acceptance, COM *d'un document* general acceptance; **~ sur protêt** COM acceptance supra protest; **~ d'une suroffre** DROIT gazumping (*UK*)

accepté, e *adj* COM *effet* accepted

accepter *vt* BANQUE *carte de crédit*, BOURSE *offre* accept, COM agree, agree to, take up, fall in with, *offre, traite* accept, COMMS *appel* accept; ♦ **~ un compromis** COM compromise; **ne pas ~** COM disallow; **~ de payer une communication en PCV** COMMS accept a call paid for by the receiver, accept a collect call (*AmE*), accept a reverse-charge call (*BrE*); **~ un pot-de-vin** COM accept a bribe, take bribes; **~ du travail supplémentaire** RES HUM take on extra work; **~ à vue** COM accept on presentation

accepteur *m* BANQUE *d'une traite* acceptor

accès:[1] **d'~ aisé** *adj* COM easily accessible; **d'~ facile** *adj* COM easily accessible

accès[2] *m* COM admittance, INFO access; **~ direct** INFO direct access, random access; **~ à distance** INFO remote access; **~ immédiat** INFO immediate access; **~ libre** COM unrestricted access; **~ au logement sans discrimination** PROT SOC open housing (*US*); **~ multiple** COM, INFO multiaccess; **~ en parallèle** INFO parallel access; **~ du public** COM public access; **~ sélectif** INFO direct access; **~ séquentiel** INFO sequential access, serial access; **~ vertical** TRANSP *à la cargaison* vertical access; ♦ **avoir ~ à** INFO *une base de données, un fichier, un dossier* access; **avoir ~ à l'information** COM have access to information

accessibilité *f* COM *de l'information* accessibility

accessible *adj* COM *information, données* accessible, available, *location, personne* accessible

accession *f* DROIT, IMMOB, POL *à l'Union Européenne* accession

accessoire[1] *adj* COM incidental, *avantages* accessory, ancillary, DROIT *cause* appurtenant, contributory, TRANSP, V&M accessory

accessoire[2] *m* COM adjunct, INFO attachment

accessoires *m pl* TRANSP, V&M accessories

accident *m* COM accident, TRANSP accident, crash; ~ **ayant entraîné la mort** PROT SOC fatal accident, fatality; ~ **de mer** ASSUR, TRANSP accident at sea; ~ **mortel** PROT SOC fatal accident, fatality; ~ **multiple** TRANSP multiaccident, multiple accident, pile-up (*infrml*); ~ **du travail** IND, PROT SOC, RES HUM industrial accident, occupational accident; ♦ **avoir un** ~ TRANSP crash, have an accident

accidentel, -elle *adj* COM contingent

accidentellement *adv* COM contingently

accidents: ~ **mortels de la route** *m pl* TRANSP road fatalities

accommodement *m* COM compromise, DROIT composition

accompagnateur, -trice *m,f* RES HUM *d'enfants* accompanying adult, group leader, *de touristes* guide

accompagné: ~ **de** *loc* COM accompanied by; ~ **par** *loc* COM accompanied by

accompagner *vt* COM accompany, escort

accompli, e *adj* DROIT completed

accomplir *vt* COM accomplish, execute, DROIT *contrat* discharge

accomplissement *m* COM accomplishment, DROIT *d'un contrat* discharge

accorage *m* TRANSP *de marchandises* blocking off

accord *m* BOURSE indenture, COM arrangement, compact, conformity, deal, DROIT accord, agreement; ~ **d'achat à crédit** FIN, V&M hire-purchase agreement; ~ **d'achat et vente** BOURSE, ECON, FIN buy-and-sell agreement; ~ **à l'amiable** COM, DROIT friendly agreement, gentleman's agreement, private arrangement; ~ **antidumping** ENVIR, POL antidumping agreement; ~ **d'appartenance syndicale** RES HUM union membership agreement, UMA; ~ **avec la base** RES HUM shopfloor agreement (*UK*); ~ **de base** RES HUM substantive agreement; ~ **des Bermudes** ECON, POL Bermuda Agreement; ~ **bilatéral** BREVETS, DROIT reciprocal agreement; ~ **de cession de licence** DROIT licensing agreement; ~ **de la clause** *or* TRANSP *navigation* gold clause agreement, GCA; ~ **de clearing** BANQUE agreement of clearing, ECON clearing agreement; ~ **collectif sur les salaires** RES HUM collective pay agreement; ~ **commercial** COM trade agreement, ECON, POL commercial treaty, trade agreement; ~ **commercial bilatéral** ECON, POL *commerce international* bilateral trade agreement; ~ **commercial multilatéral** ECON, POL *commerce international* multilateral trade agreement; ~ **de compensation** ECON *commerce international* barter agreement, buy-back agreement, compensation agreement; ~ **de compromis** COM compromise agreement; ~ **de compte en commun** BANQUE joint account agreement; ~ **de confidentialité** BREVETS, DROIT confidentiality agreement; ~ **consensuel** COM consensus agree-

ment; ~ **contractuel** DROIT contract agreement; ~ **de coopération** COM cooperation agreement; ~ **de crédit** BANQUE, COM, FIN credit agreement; ~ **à durée déterminée** RES HUM fixed-term agreement; ~ **d'échelonnement** BOURSE spreading agreement; ~ **écrit** DROIT written agreement; ~ **d'ensemble** RES HUM comprehensive agreement; ~ **entre les garants** BANQUE agreement among underwriters; ~ **financier à terme** BOURSE financial futures contract; ~ **de fond** RES HUM substantive agreement; ~ **de franchise** COMMS franchise agreement; ~ **de fusion** BOURSE amalgamation agreement; ~ **de garantie** BANQUE guarantee agreement; ~ **général** COM consensus; ~ **général d'emprunt et de nantissement** BOURSE general loan and collateral agreement; ~ **général de prêt et nantissement** BOURSE general loan and collateral agreement; ~ **global** COM, RES HUM blanket agreement; ~ **implicite** COM invisible handshake; ~ **d'indemnisation** DROIT compensation settlement; ~ **d'information** COM information agreement; ~ **d'information mutuelle** RES HUM mutuality; ~ **interligne** TRANSP *aviation* interline agreement; ~ **international** DROIT, POL international agreement; ~ **interne** RES HUM domestic agreement (*UK*); ~ **de libre-échange** ECON *international*, POL free-trade agreement, FTA; ~ **de libre vente** TRANSP free sale agreement; ~ **local** RES HUM local agreement; ~ **marketing** V&M marketing agreement; ~ **moratoire** COM, DROIT, FIN standstill agreement; ~ **multi-fibres** (*AMF*) ECON Multi-Fibre Arrangement (*MFA*); ~ **multilatéral** ECON, POL *commerce international* multilateral agreement; ~ **au niveau d'une région** RES HUM district agreement (*UK*); ~ **au niveau d'une société** RES HUM company-level agreement; ~ **au niveau d'usine** IND, RES HUM plant agreement; ~ **de non-recours à la grève** RES HUM no-strike agreement, strike-free agreement, strike-free deal; ~ **de normalisation** COM standardization agreement; ~ **officiel** COM formal agreement, formal arrangement; ~ **officieux** COM informal agreement, informal arrangement; ~ **de paiement différé renouvelable** BANQUE revolving charge account; ~ **par branche** RES HUM company agreement; ~ **de participation** DROIT participation agreement; ~ **patronat-syndicats** DROIT, IND, RES HUM collective agreement, collective bargaining agreement, labor agreement (*AmE*), labour agreement (*BrE*), union contract; ~ **de perception** FISC collection agreement; ~ **de prise en pension** BOURSE purchase and resale agreement, PRA; ~ **de procédure** RES HUM procedural agreement; ~ **de productivité** DROIT, IND, RES HUM productivity agreement; ~ **progressif** RES HUM staged agreement (*UK*); ~ **provisoire** COM interim agreement; ~ **quadripartite** COM quadripartite agreement; ~ **de rachat** DROIT, ECON *commerce international* buy-back agreement; ~ **de rachat et de vente** BOURSE *entre les actionnaires d'une société* buy-and-sell agreement; ~ **de réciprocité fiscale** FISC reciprocal taxation agreement; ~ **de rééchelonne-ment pluriannuel** FIN multiyear rescheduling agreement; ~ **régional** ECON *inter-étatique* regional agreement; ~ **réglementé** FIN regulated agreement (*UK*); ~ **de régulation du marché** BOURSE, ECON orderly market agreement, OMA; ~ **de rendement** DROIT, IND productivity agreement, RES HUM efficiency agreement (*UK*), productivity agreement; ~ **de répartition à terme** BOURSE forward spread agreement, FSA; ~ **reposant sur l'honneur** DROIT gentleman's agreement; ~ **de restructuration pluriannuel** FIN multiyear restructuring agreement, MYRA; ~ **de rétrocession** DROIT buy-back agreement; ~ **routier bilatéral** TRANSP bilateral road agreement; ~ **salarial** RES HUM wage agreement; ~ **de savoir-faire** DROIT *propriété intellectuelle* know-how agreement; ~ **secret** COM invisible handshake; ~ **de sécurité sur les conteneurs** TRANSP container safety convention, CSC; ~ **de séparation** DROIT separation agreement; ~ **stand-by** COM standby agreement; ~ **de subordination** COMPTA, FIN subordination agreement; ~ **supplémentaire** COM supplemental agreement; ~ **sur l'adhérence syndicale** RES HUM union membership agreement; ~ **sur étalement à terme** BOURSE forward spread agreement, FSA; ~ **sur les matières premières** ECON commodity agreement; ~ **sur polices d'assurance automobile** TRANSP automobile policies insuring agreement; ~ **sur les prix** DROIT price-fixing; ~ **sur les prix et les revenus** RES HUM prices and incomes agreement; ~ **sur le salaire initial** RES HUM threshold agreement; ~ **sur les salaires** RES HUM wage agreement, wage settlement; ~ **sur la sécurité de l'emploi** RES HUM job security agreement; ~ **sur les taux de change** ECON, FIN exchange rate agreement, ERA; ~ **syndical** RES HUM union agreement; ~ **syndical unique** RES HUM single-union agreement (*UK*), single-union deal (*UK*); ~ **de syndicat de garantie** FIN purchase group agreement; ~ **de taux futur** (*ATF*) BOURSE, FIN forward rate agreement, future rate agreement, FRA; ~ **de taux à terme** BOURSE, FIN forward rate agreement, future rate agreement, FRA; ~ **à terme fixe** RES HUM fixed-term agreement; ~ **de troc** ECON *commerce international* barter agreement; ~ **de tutelle** ECON, FIN buy-and-sell agreement; ~ **type** ECON pattern settlement; ~ **unilatéral** ECON unilateral agreement; ~ **de vente** BANQUE sale agreement; ~ **verbal** COM unwritten agreement, verbal agreement; ~ **de volonté** COM, DROIT meeting of the minds; ◆ **avec l'~ des parties** COM, DROIT by mutual agreement; **d'~ avec** COM consistent with; **donner son ~** COM agree; **en ~ avec** COM in keeping with; **être d'~** COM *(ANT ne pas être d'accord, être en désaccord)* agree, concur, DROIT *avec qn* concur; **l'~ n'est pas fait** COM the deal is off; **ne pas être d'~** *(ANT être d'accord)* COM disagree; **par ~ tacite** COM by tacit agreement

Accord: ~ **de coopération économique entre pays en voie de développement** *m* ECON Economic Cooperation among Developing Countries, ECDC; ~ **général d'emprunt** *m* ECON General Agreement to Borrow; ~ **général sur les tarifs et le commerce** *m* (*GATT*) ECON, POL General Agreement on Tariffs and Trade (*GATT*); ~ **international sur le blé** *m* (*AIB*) ECON International Wheat Agreement (*IWA*); ~ **international sur le sucre** *m* (*AIS*) ECON ≈ International Sugar Agreement (*ISA*); ~ **de la Jamaïque** *m* ECON Jamaica Agreement; ~ **de libre-échange nord-américain** *m* (*ALENA*) ECON North American Free Trade Area (*NAFTA*); ~ **du Louvre** *m* ECON, POL Louvre Accord; ~ **monétaire européen** *m* (*AME*) COM European Monetary Agreement (*EMA*); ~ **sur la passation des équipements** *m* IND equipment handover agreement; ~ **tarifaire transpacifique en direction de l'ouest** *m* TRANSP Transpacific Westbound Rate Agreement, TWRA

accorder *vt* BANQUE extend, grant, *prêt* advance, grant, COM *de l'argent* allow, *prêt* grant, *qch à qqn* confer, DROIT *des droits* confer, FIN *prêt* extend, provide, FIN *subvention* allot, grant, IMMOB *location* grant; ◆ ~ **une charte à** DROIT *compagnie* charter; ~ **un crédit** FIN grant credit; ~ **un crédit de longue durée** FIN grant extended credit; ~ **des dommages-intérêts** ASSUR award damages, DROIT adjudge damages; ~ **des dommages-intérêts considérables** DROIT award heavy damages; ~ **le droit** COM *de faire qch* give the right; ~ **le droit de vote** COM, POL enfranchise; ~ **les écritures** COM, COMPTA agree the books; ~ **des fournitures intérimaires** COMPTA grant interim supply; ~ **une journée de congé aux employés** RES HUM give the employees a day off; ~ **une licence** ADMIN, COM grant a licence (BrE), grant a license (AmE); ~ **un prêt à qn** BANQUE, FIN grant a loan to sb, make a loan to sb, provide sb with a loan; ~ **la priorité à** COM give priority to; ~ **une promotion à** RES HUM promote; ~ **à qn le droit de faire** COM give sb the right to do; ~ **à qn 8 000 livres de dommages et intérêts** ASSUR allow sb £8,000 in damages; ~ **une remise sur** COM, V&M make an allowance on

accords: ~ **d'appartenance syndicale** *m pl* RES HUM Union Membership Agreements (*UK*); ~ **de Bretton Woods** *m pl* ECON, POL Bretton Woods Agreement; ~ **commerciaux de réciprocité** *m pl* ECON *commerce international* reciprocal trading agreements; ~ **communs de l'assurance corps** *m pl* ASSUR Joint Hull Understandings; ~ **entre banques régionales** *m pl* BANQUE regional banking pacts; ~ **généraux d'emprunt** *m pl* (*AGE*) FIN general arrangements to borrow (*GAB*); ~ **interbancaires** *m pl* BANQUE banking arrangements; ~ **internationaux sur les matières premières** *m pl* BOURSE ICA's, International Commodity Agreements; ~ **internationaux sur les produits de base** *m pl* BOURSE ICA's, International Commodity Agreements; ~ **inter-**

syndicaux et d'industrie en matière de politique sociale *m pl* RES HUM custom and trade practices; **les ~ de Lomé** *m pl* ECON, POL Lomé Convention; **~ privés** *m pl* COM private terms

accore *mf* TRANSP shore

accostage *m* TRANSP *navigation* berthing

accoster: ~ des clients *loc* COM tout, tout for trade

accouplement: ~ automatique *m* TRANSP *routier* automatic coupling; **~ hydraulique** *m* TRANSP *navigation* hydraulic coupling, HC, HYC

Accra *n pr* COM Accra

accréditer *vt* COM *représentant* accredit

accréditif *m* BANQUE check credit (*AmE*), cheque credit (*BrE*)

accrochage: ~ initial *m* V&M *publicité* attention getter

accroche *f* MÉDIA *presse* slogan

accrocheur, -euse *adj* V&M *marketing* eye-catching

accroissement *m* COM accretion, *du capital* accumulation; **~ de la demande** V&M expansion of demand; **~ interne** ECON *du capital* internal expansion; **~ naturel** ECON natural increase; **~ de la valeur** COMPTA, FISC, IMMOB appreciation

accroître 1. *vt* COM augment, build up, ECON boost, IND *production* build up, MATH add to, aggregate; **2.** *v pron* **s'~** BANQUE, COMPTA accrue, ECON climb; ♦ **~ l'offre** ECON increase the supply

accroupissement *m* TRANSP *navigation* squat

accru, e *adj* COM stepped-up

accueil *m* ADMIN reception, COM, RES HUM induction; **~ favorable** MÉDIA, V&M *d'un produit* acceptance; **~ des passagers** TRANSP passenger care; **~ réservé à la marque** V&M brand acceptance

accueillir *vt* COM welcome, PROT SOC accommodate

accumulateur *m* INFO accumulator

accumulation *f* ADMIN backlog, COM accruals, backlog, FIN accruals; **~ de capital** ECON, FIN capital accumulation; **~ d'épargne non productive** ECON monetary overhang; **~ d'intérêts** BANQUE, COMPTA, FIN accrual of interest

accumuler 1. *vt* COM accumulate; **2.** *v pron* **s'~** BANQUE accrue, COM accumulate, COMPTA, FIN accrue; ♦ **~ un déficit** FIN run up a deficit

accusation *f* DROIT accusation, case for the prosecution

accusé, e *m,f* DROIT accused, *procédure pénale* defendant; **l'~** *mf* DROIT the accused, the defendant; **~ de réception** COM, COMMS, DROIT, INFO acknowledgement of receipt; **~ de réception d'une commande** COM *au client*, COMMS acknowledgement of order

accuser *vt* DROIT accuse; ♦ **~ une plus-value** COMPTA, IMMOB *actif* appreciate; **~ réception de** COM *courrier, marchandises*, COMMS *lettre* acknowledge receipt of, confirm receipt of; **~ réception par courrier** COMMS acknowledge receipt by letter

acétat *m* GESTION overhead transparency

ACG *abrév* (*adhérent compensateur général*) BOURSE GCM (*general clearing member*)

achalandage *m* COM *clientèle* clientele, custom, COMPTA *Can valeur d'un fonds de commerce* goodwill

acharné, e *adj* COM *concurrence* fierce

achat *m* BOURSE buy transaction, buyout, COM acquisition, *action* buying, purchasing, *objet* purchase, COMPTA *d'une immobilisation* addition, V&M *action* buying, purchasing, *objet* purchase; **~ adossé** BOURSE leveraged buyout, LBO; **~ avec effet de levier** BOURSE leveraged buyout, LBO; **~ en bloc** BOURSE block purchase; **~ d'un call synthétique** BOURSE synthetic long call; **~ à la clôture** BOURSE closing purchase (*UK*); **~ de compensation** ECON counter purchase; **~ au comptant** COM cash purchase; **~ à crédit** BOURSE buying on margin, COM purchase credit, term purchase; **~ dans une centrale d'achats** V&M central buying; **~ dans un centre commercial** V&M central buying; **~ à découvert** BOURSE margin buying, margin purchase; **~ en dessous du cours** BOURSE buy minus; **~ d'un écart papillon** BOURSE long butterfly; **~ d'un écart papillon sur option d'achat** BOURSE long butterfly call; **~ d'un écart papillon sur option de vente** BOURSE long butterfly put; **~ d'endettement** BOURSE leveraged buyout, LBO; **~ d'espace** (ANT *vente d'espace*) V&M *publicité* space buying; **~ et vente de blocs de titres par un spécialiste** BOURSE specialist block purchase and sale; **~ et vente par correspondance** V&M mail-order business; **~ en gros** COM, V&M bulk buying; **~ groupé** BOURSE block purchase; **~ à la hausse** (ANT *vente à la baisse*) BOURSE bull buying, bull purchase; **~ impulsif** V&M compulsive buying, impulse buy, impulse buying, impulse purchase; **~ d'impulsion** V&M impulse buying; **~ liquidatif** BOURSE closing purchase transaction; **~ de liquidation** BOURSE closing purchase transaction; **~ pour liquidation** BOURSE purchase for settlement; **~ de maison** IMMOB, V&M house purchase; **~ marginal** BOURSE margin buying, margin purchase; **~ de médias** (ANT *vente de médias*) MÉDIA, V&M *publicité* media buying; **~ à montant global** FIN lump-sum purchase; **~ mutuel entre institutions** BOURSE back-to-back placement; **~ d'une option d'achat** BOURSE call purchase, synthetic long call; **~ d'option couverte** BOURSE covered long; **~ d'une option de vente** BOURSE synthetic long put; **~ d'options de vente** (ANT *vente d'options d'achat*) BOURSE put writing; **~ précaire** BOURSE toehold purchase; **~ à un prix forfaitaire** FIN basket purchase; **~ à un prix global** FIN basket purchase; **~ public d'objets d'art** COMPTA, ECON, FIN nonmonetary investment; **~ public d'objets**

précieux COMPTA, ECON, FIN nonmonetary investment; ~ **d'un put synthétique** BOURSE synthetic long put; ~ **réfléchi** COM shopping good; ~ **réfléchi comparatif** V&M comparison shopping; ~ **renouvelé** COM repeat purchase; ~ **spontané** V&M impulse buy, impulse purchase; ~ **d'un straddle** BOURSE long straddle; ~ **d'un strangle** BOURSE long strangle; ~ **sur marge** BOURSE buying on margin; ~ **à tempérament** COM installment purchase (*AmE*), instalment purchase (*BrE*); ~ **à terme** BOURSE forward buying, purchase for settlement, ECON outright forward purchase, FIN forward buying; ~ **de valeurs** COM purchase of assets; ~ **-vente d'une valeur** BOURSE wash sale; ♦ **faire un ~** COM make a purchase; **faire un ~ à crédit** COM buy sth on credit; **faire un ~ répété** V&M rebuy

achats *m pl* COM *service* procurement department, purchasing department; ~ **nets** COM, COMPTA net purchases; ~ **de précaution** COM panic buying; ~ **publics** COM public procurement; ~ **répétés** V&M *marketing* repeat buying (*jarg*); ~ **de soutien** COM, V&M supporting purchases; ♦ **faire des ~** COM go shopping; **faire ses ~ à l'extérieur** V&M do out-of-town shopping

acheminé: ~ **directement** *adj* IMP/EXP, TRANSP directly-transported

acheminement *m* COM routing, INFO despatching, dispatching, routing, TRANSP conv, conveyance, despatching, dispatching, routing, transport, transporting; ~ **de l'envoi** TRANSP route order; ~ **intérieur** IMP/EXP, TRANSP inland haulage; ~ **par le négociant** IMP/EXP, TRANSP merchant haulage, MH; ~ **par le transporteur maritime** TRANSP carrier haulage

acheminer *vt* COM route, INFO despatch, dispatch, route, TRANSP convey, despatch, dispatch, route, transport

acheter *vt* COM bribe, *marchandises* buy, ECON buy, POL, V&M *personne* bribe; ♦ ~ **des actions en bourse** BOURSE buy shares on the open market; ~ **à la baisse** BOURSE buy on a fall, buy on a falling market; ~ **à la baisse et vendre à la hausse** BOURSE buy low and sell high; ~ **bon marché et revendre plus cher** BOURSE buy low and sell high; ~ **à la clôture** BOURSE buy on close; ~ **au cours du marché** BOURSE buy at market; ~ **à crédit** COM buy on credit, buy on tick (*BrE, infrml*); ~ **aux enchères** BOURSE buy on bid; ~ **de l'espace** MÉDIA *radio, télévision* buy airtime, V&M buy space; ~ **à l'essai** COM buy on approval; ~ **en grandes quantités** COM buy in large quantities; ~ **à la hausse** BOURSE buy for a rise, buy on a rise; ~ **l'inventaire** BOURSE buy the book; ~ **en liquidation** BOURSE buy for the account; ~ **au marché noir** ECON buy on the black market; ~ **par échelons de baisse** (*ANT acheter par échelons de hausse*) BOURSE average down; ~ **par échelons de hausse** (*ANT acheter par échelons de baisse*) BOURSE average up; ~ **en petites quantités** COM buy in small quantities; ~ **au prix**

fort V&M buy at the top of the market; ~ **qch comptant** COM buy and pay immediately; ~ **au rabais** COM buy at a reduced price; ~ **au son du canon** BOURSE buy on the bad news; ~ **sur marge** FIN buy on margin; ~ **à tempérament** COM buy on hire purchase (*BrE*), buy on the installment plan (*AmE*); ~ **à terme** BOURSE buy forward; ~ **à terme en versant un dépôt de garantie** FIN buy on margin; ~ **des titres sur gains précédents** BOURSE, IMMOB pyramid

acheteur[1], **-euse** *m,f* (*ANT vendeur*) BOURSE *d'options* buyer, giver (*jarg*), holder, option buyer, COM bargainee, buyer, procurement agent, vendee, V&M buyer; ~ **d'art** (*ANT vendeur d'art*) COM art buyer; ~ **à la baisse** (*ANT acheteur à la hausse*) BOURSE bear operator; ~ **de bonne foi** COM bona fide purchaser; ~ **d'un call** BOURSE call buyer; ~ **-cible** V&M target buyer; ~ **au comptant** V&M cash buyer; ~ **à crédit** V&M charge buyer (*BrE*), credit buyer (*AmE*); ~ **de double option** (*ANT vendeur de double option*) BOURSE straddle buyer; ~ **d'espace** MÉDIA *radio, télévision* airtime buyer, V&M space buyer; ~ **d'espace publicitaire** (*ANT vendeur d'espace publicitaire*) MÉDIA, V&M advertising space buyer; ~ **ferme** (*ANT vendeur ferme*) BOURSE firm buyer; ~ **en gros** COM, V&M bulk buyer, bulk purchaser; ~ **à la hausse** (*ANT acheteur à la baisse*) BOURSE bull, bull operator; ~ **impulsif** V&M impulse buyer; ~ **industriel** IND producer buyer; ~ **de médias** (*ANT vendeur de médias*) MÉDIA, RES HUM, V&M media buyer; ~ **multiple** V&M *vente* multiple buyer; ~ **occasionnel** V&M one-time buyer; ~ **d'option** (*ANT vendeur d'option*) BOURSE option buyer, option holder; ~ **d'une option d'achat** BOURSE giver for a call; ~ **d'option d'achat** (*ANT acheteur d'option de vente*) BOURSE call writer, put seller; ~ **d'option de vente** (*ANT acheteur d'option d'achat*) BOURSE put buyer, put writer; ~ **potentiel** IMMOB potential buyer, prospective buyer, V&M potential buyer; ~ **d'un straddle** (*ANT vendeur d'un straddle*) BOURSE straddle buyer; ~ **de temps** (*ANT vendeur de temps*) MÉDIA, V&M *publicité, radio, TV* time buyer; ~ **de temps d'antenne** MÉDIA *radio, télévision* airtime buyer

acheteur:[2] **que l'~ prenne garde** *loc* DROIT caveat emptor

achevé, e *adj* COM complete, completed

achèvement *m* COM *d'un travail, d'un projet* completion; ~ **de tâche** COM task closure (*jarg*)

achever *vt* COM complete

Achkhabad *n pr* COM Ashkhabad

acier *m* IND steel; ~ **inoxydable** IND stainless steel

aciérie *f* IND steelworks

acompte *m* BANQUE advance, advance payment, deposit, down payment, installment (*AmE*), instalment (*BrE*), COM *paiement échelonné* installment (*AmE*), instalment (*BrE*), *premier paiement* advance, advance payment, deposit, down payment, COMPTA, FIN advance, advance payment, deposit, down payment, installment (*AmE*), instalment (*BrE*), IMMOB *sur un loyer* deposit, RES HUM *sur un salaire* advance, V&M down payment; **~ non-remboursable** V&M nonrefundable deposit; **~ permanent** IMP/EXP standing deposit (*UK*); **~ provisionnel** FISC *d'impôt* tax installment (*AmE*), tax instalment (*BrE*); **~ provisionnel insuffisant** FISC deficient tax installment (*AmE*), deficient tax instalment (*BrE*); **~ remboursable** COM refundable deposit; **~ sur dividende** COMPTA interim dividend; **~ trimestriel** FISC quarterly installment (*AmE*), quarterly instalment (*BrE*); ◆ **en ~** V&M on account

acquéreur, -euse *m,f* COM acquiring company, DROIT pre-emptor, FISC *taxe de prestation de service* recipient

acquérir *vt* BOURSE *option* acquire, COM learn, *réputation* acquire, earn, IMMOB *immobilier* acquire, PROT SOC, RES HUM learn; ◆ **~ de l'expérience** RES HUM gain experience, learn the ropes

acquêt *m* COM after-marriage acquired property (*US*), DROIT acquest, after-marriage acquired property (*US*)

acquis[1], **e** *adj* COM acquired

acquis[2] *m* COM background, experience, knowledge; **~ à caution** COM excise bond

acquisition *f* BOURSE buyout, COM acquisition, COMPTA acquisition, *nouvel avoir* addition; **~ d'actions** BOURSE acquisition of shareholdings, acquisition of stock; **~ de données** ECON, INFO data acquisition; **~ d'immobilisations** COMPTA acquisition of assets; **~ nette d'actifs financiers** FIN net acquisition of financial assets, NAFA; **~ partielle** DROIT, IMMOB partial taking

acquisitions: **~ nettes** *f pl* ECON, FIN net acquisitions

acquit *m* FIN paid instrument; **~ libératoire** ASSUR no risk after discharge, NRAD; **~ de transit** IMP/EXP, TRANSP transhipment bond, transit bond note, transshipment bond; ◆ **pour ~** COM rcvd, received

acquitté, e *adj* FIN paid, pd

acquittement *m* COM clearing, *d'une dette* discharge, DROIT *d'un accusé, d'une dette* acquittal, FIN clearing, *d'une dette* discharge

acquitter 1. *vt* BREVETS *taxe* pay, COM *dette* discharge, pay off, *facture* receipt, *lettre de charge* discharge, DROIT *accusé* acquit, discharge; **2.** *v pron* **s'~ de** COM acquit, *engagement, obligation* fulfil (*BrE*), fulfill (*AmE*), DROIT *dette* acquit, FIN clear; ◆ **~ une dette intégralement** FIN pay a debt in full

acronyme *m* COM acronym

act. *abrév* (*action*) BOURSE shr. (*share*)

acte *m* ADMIN cert., certificate, DROIT act, deed, POL act; **~ ab intestat** DROIT administrator's deed; **~ d'association** DROIT deed of partnership; **~ authentique** DROIT deed, legal document, IMMOB deed; **~ de cautionnement** BANQUE guarantee deed; **~ de cession** COM act of cession, deed of assignation; **~ constitutif d'une personne morale** DROIT certificate of incorporation; **~ constitutif de société** DROIT memorandum of association; **~ de décès** COM, DROIT death certificate; **~ délictueux** DROIT actus reus; **~ dommageable** DROIT nuisance; **~ de donation** DROIT gift deed, FISC deed of covenant (*UK*); **~ de faillite** COMPTA act of bankruptcy; **~ fédéral sur les cotisations de l'assurance sociale** ASSUR Federal Insurance Contributions Act (*US*), FICA (*US*); **~ de fidéicommis** DROIT deed of trust, trust deed; **~ fiduciaire** DROIT deed of trust; **~ fiduciaire établi outre-mer** DROIT, FIN offshore trust; **~ de fiducie** DROIT deed of trust; **~ de garantie de tranquillité** DROIT, IMMOB quitclaim deed; **~ illégal** DROIT unlawful act; **~ illicite** DROIT unlawful act; **~ d'incitation** DROIT, IND, RES HUM relevant act (*UK*); **~ introductif d'instance** DROIT statement of claim, FISC originating document; **~ juridique** DROIT instrument; **~ manifeste** DROIT positive action (*jarg*); **~ de mise en faillite** COMPTA act of bankruptcy; **~ de naissance** ASSUR, COM, DROIT birth certificate; **~ de nationalisation** TRANSP *d'un navire* certificate of registry; **~ notarié de garantie générale** IMMOB general warranty deed (*US*); **~ d'opposition** BREVETS notice of opposition; **~ positif** DROIT positive action (*jarg*); **~ de procédure** DROIT proceedings; **~ de propriété** DROIT deed; **~ récognitif** DROIT act of acknowledgement; **~ de reconnaissance** DROIT act of acknowledgement; **~ de recours** BREVETS notice of appeal; **~ sous seing privé** IMMOB private treaty; **~ tenant lieu de saisie d'hypothèque** DROIT, IMMOB deed in lieu of foreclosure; **~ de tutelle** IMMOB guardian deed; **~ unilatéral** DROIT deed poll

Acte: **~ unique européen** *m* (*AUE*) DROIT, POL Single European Act (*SEA*)

actes: **~ de conférence** *m pl* GESTION conference proceedings; **~ effectués en dehors des statuts** *m pl* DROIT ultra vires activities; **~ illicites** *m pl* DROIT illegal practices

actif[1], **-ive** *adj* COM brisk, *personne* active, ECON buoyant, INFO active; **peu ~** BOURSE, FIN inactive

actif[2] *m* BOURSE, COM, ECON asset, assets; **~ amortissable** COMPTA depreciable asset; **~ bancable** BANQUE bankable assets; **~ bancaire** BANQUE, COMPTA, FIN bank assets; **~ brut** FIN gross assets; **~ circulant** COMPTA current assets; **~ circulant net** COMPTA, FIN net current assets; **~ commercial** COMPTA, ECON, FIN business assets; **~ comptabilisé net** COM, FIN net recorded assets; **~ consommable** ECON wasting assets; **~ corporel** COMPTA, ECON, FIN physical assets; **~ corporel net par action** BOURSE net tangible assets per share; **~ défective** BOURSE wasting asset, COMPTA wasting assets; **~ détenu à l'étranger** ECON, POL overseas assets; **~ disponible** COMPTA, FIN liquid assets, quick assets; **~ disponible personnel** FIN personal sector liquid assets; **~ dormant** BOURSE inactive asset; **~ escomptable** FIN eligible asset;

~ **éventuel** COMPTA contingent asset; ~ **du failli** FISC estate of bankrupt; ~ **de la faillite** DROIT, FIN bankruptcy estate; ~ **fictif** COMPTA nominal assets; ~ **financier** FIN financial asset; ~ **fongible** FIN fungible asset; ~ **gelé** FIN frozen assets; ~ **immatériel** COM, FIN intangible asset; ~ **immobilisé** COMPTA fixed assets, ECON, FIN capital assets; ~ **incorporel** (ANT *actif corporel*) COMPTA intangible asset, intangible property; ~ **investi à court terme** BOURSE short-term investment assets; ~ **latent** COMPTA concealed assets, contingent asset, hidden asset; ~ **liquide** COMPTA cash assets; ~ **à long terme** COMPTA noncurrent asset; ~ **monétaire** COMPTA monetary item; ~ **national** BANQUE domestic asset; ~ **négociable** COMPTA quick assets, FIN liquid assets, quick assets; ~ **négociable sur le marché monétaire** BANQUE assets eligible for the money market; ~ **net** BOURSE equity, COMPTA net assets, FIN net assets, residue; ~ **net réalisable** COMPTA net quick assets; ~ **net sous-jacent** FIN underlying net assets; ~ **non disponible** COMPTA illiquid assets; ~ **potentiel** COMPTA contingent asset; ~ **principal** BOURSE chief assets, COMPTA principal assets; ~ **réalisable** BOURSE realizable assets, COMPTA quick assets, realizable assets, FIN liquid assets, quick assets; ~ **réel net par action** BOURSE net tangible assets per share; ~ **de réserve** BANQUE reserve assets; ~ **sous-évalué** COMPTA hidden asset; ~ **sous-jacent** BOURSE underlying asset; ~ **subordonné** COMPTA, FIN subordinated assets; ~ **sûr** FIN safe asset; ~ **utilisé** FISC used assets

actifs: ~ **des réserves monétaires mondiales** *m pl* FIN world monetary reserve assets

action *f* BOURSE stock, value share, BOURSE *détenue par le public* share, COM action, COMPTA share, DROIT action, cause, suit, FIN share; ~ **accréditive** BOURSE flow-through share; ~ **admissible** BOURSE qualifying share; ~ **annulée** BOURSE canceled share (*AmE*), cancelled share (*BrE*); ~ **antitrust** COM trustbusting (*US, infrml*); ~ **approuvée** BOURSE approved share; ~ **attribuée** BOURSE allotted share; ~ **autodétenue** BOURSE repurchased share; ~ **d'avarie** ASSUR average claim; ~ **avec droit de vote** BOURSE voting share, voting stock; ~ **en baisse** BOURSE, ECON declining share; ~ **bêta** BOURSE beta (*US*), beta share, beta stock (*UK*); ~ **boudée** *jarg* BOURSE wallflower (*jarg*); ~ **de capital non-émise** BOURSE unissued treasury share; ~ **civile** DROIT civil action; ~ **collective** COM community action, DROIT joint action; ~ **collective de formation** RES HUM group training; ~ **collective en justice** DROIT class action; ~ **communautaire** COM community action; ~ **concertée** GESTION joint venture, JV; ~ **contre X** DROIT action against X; ~ **convertible** BOURSE convertible, convertible share, convertible stock; ~ **à la cote officielle** COM stock quoted officially; ~ **cotée** (ANT *action non-cotée*) BOURSE listed share, quoted share; ~ **cotée en bourse** BOURSE

publicly traded share; ~ **coupon zéro** BOURSE zero-coupon security; ~ **à deux sous** *infrml* BOURSE penny share, penny stock (*AmE*); ~ **diluée** BOURSE watered stock; ~ **de dividende** BOURSE junior share; ~ **à dividende différé** BOURSE deferred share, deferred stock; ~ **à dividende prioritaire** (*ADP*) BOURSE preference share (*BrE*), preferred stock (*AmE*); ~ **à dividende prioritaire non-cumulative** BOURSE noncumulative preferred stock; ~ **en dommages et intérêts** ASSUR action for damages; ~ **en dommages-intérêts** ASSUR action for damages; ~ **donnée en prime** BOURSE bonus share, bonus stock; ~ **dormante** BOURSE inactive stock; ~ **à droit d'entrée au conseil d'administration** BOURSE qualifying share; ~ **à droit réduit** BOURSE deferred share; ~ **échangée** BOURSE exchanged share; ~ **émise dans le public** BOURSE publicly traded share; ~ **entière** BOURSE full share; ~ **entièrement libérée** BOURSE fully-paid share, trader; ~ **étrangère** BOURSE foreign share, foreign stock; ~ **fictive** BOURSE phantom share; ~ **fluctuante** BOURSE yo-yo stock; ~ **fréquemment négociée** BOURSE alpha share; ~ **gamma** BOURSE gamma stock (*UK*); ~ **garantie** BOURSE guaranteed share; ~ **gratuite** BOURSE bonus share, bonus stock; ~ **inactive** BOURSE inactive stock; ~ **inscrite à la cote officielle** BOURSE listed share, quoted share; ~ **en justice** DROIT action, legal action, legal proceedings; ~ **lourde** BOURSE heavy share; ~ **minoritaire** BOURSE minority share, minority shareholding, minority stock; ~ **nécessaire** COM required action; ~ **nominative** BOURSE personal share, registered share, COMPTA registered share; ~ **non-admissible** BOURSE nonqualifying share; ~ **non-convertie** BOURSE unconverted share; ~ **non-cotée** (ANT *action cotée*) BOURSE unlisted share, unquoted share; ~ **non-échangeable en bourse** BOURSE letter stock; ~ **non-émise** BOURSE unissued stock; ~ **non-enregistrée** BOURSE unregistered stock; ~ **non-entièrement libérée** BOURSE partly-paid share; ~ **non-nominative** BOURSE unregistered stock; ~ **non-pair** BOURSE no-par stock; ~ **non-participante** BOURSE nonparticipating share; ~ **non-participative** BOURSE nonparticipating share; ~ **nouvelle** BOURSE new share; ~ **nouvellement émise très demandée** BOURSE hot stock (*jarg*); ~ **de numéraire** BOURSE share issued for cash; ~ **ordinaire** BOURSE common equity, common share (*BrE*), common stock (*AmE*), ordinary share (*BrE*), COMPTA, ECON common share (*BrE*), common stock (*AmE*), ordinary share (*BrE*); ~ **ordinaire classée** BOURSE classified stock; ~ **ordinaire entièrement libérée** BOURSE paid-up common share; ~ **ordinaire sans droit de vote** BOURSE, FIN A-share (*UK*); ~ **de participation** BOURSE equity share; ~ **payée entièrement** BOURSE fully-paid share; ~ **personnelle** DROIT actio in personam; ~ **personnelle s'éteignant avec la personne** DROIT actio personalis moritur cum persona; ~ **pétitoire incidente** DROIT interpleader; ~ **peu active**

BOURSE gamma stock (*UK*), inactive stock; ~ **peu chère** BOURSE penny share, penny stock (*AmE*); ~ **au porteur** BOURSE, COMPTA, FIN bearer share, bearer stock; ~ **possessoire** DROIT quiet title suit, replevin, IMMOB quiet title suit; ~ **de préférence** BOURSE, COMPTA, FIN preference share (*BrE*), preferred stock (*AmE*); ~ **préférentielle** BOURSE golden share, participating preference share, participating preferred stock (*AmE*), prior-preferred stock; ~ **prioritaire** BOURSE, FIN priority share; ~ **de priorité** BOURSE, COMPTA, FIN preference share (*BrE*), preferred stock (*AmE*); ~ **de priorité amortissable** BOURSE redeemable preference share; ~ **de priorité cumulative** BOURSE cumulative preference share (*BrE*), cumulative preferred stock (*AmE*); ~ **de priorité perpétuelle** BOURSE perpetual preferred share; ~ **de priorité sans participation** BOURSE nonparticipating preferred stock; ~ **de priorité à taux variable** BOURSE adjustable-rate preferred stock, ARP; ~ **privilégiée** BOURSE, COMPTA, FIN preference share (*BrE*), preferred stock (*AmE*); ~ **privilégiée amortissable** BOURSE redeemable preference share; ~ **privilégiée avec garantie** FISC collateralized preferred share; ~ **privilégiée convertible** BOURSE convertible preferred share, convertible preferred stock; ~ **privilégiée imposable** BOURSE, FISC taxable preferred share; ~ **privilégiée perpétuelle** BOURSE perpetual preferred share; ~ **privilégiée de premier rang** BOURSE first preference share, first preferred stock; ~ **privilégiée rachetable au gré de l'acheteur et de l'entrepreneur** BOURSE redeemable retractable preferred share; ~ **privilégiée à taux flottant** BOURSE floating-rate preferred share; ~ **à prix élevé** BOURSE heavy share; ~ **publique** DROIT prosecution; ~ **qui fléchit** BOURSE, ECON declining share; ~ **rachetable au gré du porteur** BOURSE retractable share; ~ **rachetée** BOURSE acquired share (*US*); ~ **en reconnaissance d'un droit** DROIT *propriété* actio in rem; ~ **réelle** DROIT actio in rem, action in rem; ~ **de remplacement** BOURSE substituted share; ~ **répartie** BOURSE allotted share; ~ **en revendication de biens** DROIT, IMMOB *immobilier* ejectment; ~ **revendicative** IND, RES HUM industrial action, job action (*jarg*), official action (*UK*); ~ **à revenu variable** BOURSE equity share; ~ **sans droit de vote** BOURSE nonvoting share, nonvoting stock; ~ **sans participation** BOURSE nonparticipating preferred stock; ~ **sans risque** BOURSE widow-and-orphan stock; ~ **sans valeur nominale** BOURSE no-par-value share; ~ **de seconde catégorie** BOURSE junior share; ~ **de société étrangère** BOURSE foreign share, foreign stock; ~ **de soutien** RES HUM sympathetic action; ~ **spécifique** BOURSE golden share; ~ **superprivilégiée** BOURSE prior-preferred stock; ~ **syndicale** RES HUM primary action; ~ **syndicale appropriée** DROIT, IND, RES HUM relevant act (*UK*); ~ **totalement libérée** BOURSE fully-paid share; ~ **transférée** BOURSE transferred share;

~ **à valeur nominale** BOURSE par stock, par value share, par value stock; ~ **visée par règlement** BOURSE prescribed share; ◆ **par** ~ BOURSE per share; **pour** ~ RES HUM for action

actionnaire *mf* BOURSE investor, *public* shareholder, stockholder, FIN investor; ~ **désigné** *m* FISC specified shareholder; ~ **déterminé** *m* FISC designated shareholder; ~ **inscrit** *m* BOURSE registered shareholder; ~ **intermédiaire** *m* BOURSE nominee shareholder; ~ **majoritaire** *m* BOURSE controlling shareholder, majority shareholder, majority stockholder; ~ **minoritaire** *m* BOURSE minority shareholder, minority stockholder; ~ **ordinaire** *m* BOURSE common shareholder, common stockholder, ordinary shareholder, ordinary stockholder; ~ **-paravent** *m* BOURSE nominee shareholder; ~ **principal** *m* BOURSE principal stockholder

actionnariat *m* BOURSE share ownership, shareholding, stock ownership; ~ **majoritaire** BOURSE majority shareholding; ~ **des salariés** BOURSE, RES HUM employee shareholding scheme; ~ **à tendance normale** BOURSE, COM, FIN holding pattern (*jarg*)

actionner *vt* COM activate

actions *f pl* BOURSE equity, shares, stock; ~ **achetées à crédit** *f pl* FIN leveraged stock; ~ **appariées** *f pl* BOURSE paired shares; ~ **d'arbitrage** *f pl* BOURSE arbitrage stocks; ~ **de base en hausse** *f pl* BOURSE rising bottoms (*jarg*); ~ **de chemin de fer** *f pl* BOURSE rail shares; ~ **en circulation** *f pl* BOURSE outstanding shares, shares outstanding; ~ **de compensation** *f pl* BOURSE *lors d'une nationalisation* compensation stocks (*UK*); ~ **de contrôle** *f pl* BOURSE control stock; ~ **déclarées** *f pl* BOURSE shares authorized; ~ **à dividende garanti** *f pl* BOURSE guaranteed stock; ~ **donnant droit aux plus-values** *f pl* BOURSE capital shares; ~ **émises** *f pl* BOURSE shares outstanding; ~ **et obligations de valeur douteuse** *f pl* BOURSE cats and dogs; ~ **fréquemment négociées** *f pl* BOURSE active shares; ~ **gratuites** *f pl* BOURSE capital bonus, capitalization shares; ~ **indexées** *f pl* BOURSE, FIN index-linked stock (*UK*); ~ **non-autorisées** *f pl* BOURSE unauthorized shares; ~ **non-entièrement libérées** *f pl* BOURSE partly paid up shares; ~ **en paire** *f pl* BOURSE paired shares; ~ **rachetables** *f pl* BOURSE redeemable stock; ~ **rachetées par la société** *f pl* BOURSE Treasury stock (*UK*), COMPTA own shares (*BrE*), treasury stock (*AmE*); ~ **remboursables** *f pl* BOURSE redeemable stock; ~ **réparties en catégories distinctes** *f pl* BOURSE classified stock; ~ **réservées aux membres du conseil d'administration** *f* BOURSE directors' shares; ~ **statutaires** *f pl* BOURSE qualifying shares; ~ **surveillées** *f pl* BOURSE watered stock; ~ **très liquides** *f pl* BOURSE active shares

Actions: ~ **à bons de souscription d'actions avec facilité de rachat** *f pl* (*ABSAR*) BOURSE shares with redeemable share warrants; ~ **à bons de sou-**

scription d'obligations convertibles *f pl* (*ABSOC*) BOURSE *en actions avec droit préférentiel de souscription* shares with convertible bond warrants carrying preferential subscription rights

activation: **~ des biens détenus sur contrat de crédit-bail** *loc* COMPTA capitalization of leases

activé, e *adj* INFO activated

activement *adv* COM actively; ◆ **~ négocié** BOURSE actively traded (*UK*), heavily traded

activer *vt* COM *production* stimulate, IND *mécanisme*, INFO activate

activiser *vt* COMPTA capitalize

activiste *mf* COM, ECON, POL activist

activité *f* BANQUE, COM activity; **~ artificielle** COM dummy activity; **~ d'audit** COMPTA, FIN audit activity (*UK*); **~ bancaire** BANQUE banking business; **~ bancaire par succursales** BANQUE branch banking; **~ bénévole** RES HUM honorary membership; **~ de bienfaisance** FISC, PROT SOC *menée par une oeuvre de charité* charitable activity; **~ boursière fictive** BOURSE daisy chain; **~ commerciale** COM trading, FISC commercial activity; **~ commerciale complémentaire** FISC related business; **~ économique** ECON economic activity; **~ écran** COM *pour en cacher une autre* dummy activity; **~ financée sur fonds publics** ECON government enterprise; **~ industrielle** IND industrial activity; **~ inventive** BREVETS inventive step; **~ d'investissement** ECON investment activity; **~ de location d'ordinateurs** INFO, V&M computer-leasing business; **~ lucrative** FIN gainful employment, money-spinner (*infrml*); **~ manufacturière** IND manufacturing activity; **~ du marché** BOURSE trading activity; **~ non rétribuée** RES HUM honorary membership; **~ principale** COM core business, principal business; **~ de report** BOURSE, FIN backwardation business (*UK*); **~ réservée** BOURSE single-capacity trading; **~ du secteur bancaire** BANQUE banking activity; ◆ **en ~** RES HUM in active employment; **être en ~** COM deal

Activité: **~ principale de l'entreprise** *f* (*APE*) COM number giving company's main business

activités *f pl* COM business, operations; **~ accessoires** FISC ancillary and incidental activities; **~ admissibles** FISC qualified activities; **~ boursières** BOURSE securities business; **~ à but lucratif non directement productives** ECON directly unproductive profit-seeking activities, DUP; **~ de construction** COM construction activities; **~ fiduciaires** DROIT fiduciary activities; **~ habituelles** FISC ordinary business; **~ passives** FISC passive activities; **~ qualifiées** FISC qualified activities; **~ quotidiennes de l'entreprise** COM business routine; **~ relevant d'emploi désigné** RES HUM scope of employment; **~ du secteur primaire** (ANT *activités du secteur secondaire, activités du secteur tertiaire*) COM, ECON, IND primary activities; **~ du secteur secondaire** (ANT *activités du secteur primaire, activités du secteur tertiaire*) COM, ECON, IND secondary

activities; **~ du secteur tertiaire** (ANT *activités du secteur primaire, activités du secteur secondaire*) COM, ECON, IND tertiary activities; **~ sur un marché** FIN market dealing

actuaire *m* ASSUR actuary

actualisation *f* COM update, updating, COMPTA *des produits et charges à venir*, ECON, FIN discounting, INFO update

actualiser *vt* COM actualize, bring up to date, update

actualité: **l'~** *f* COM current events, MÉDIA, POL current affairs

actualités *f pl* MÉDIA news

actuariat *m* ASSUR actuarial science

actuariel, -elle *adj* ASSUR actuarial

actuel[1], -elle *adj* COM current, present, ECON present

actuel:[2] ~ président *m* COM chairman elect

actuellement *adv* BANQUE currently, COM at the present time, currently; ◆ **~ en stock** COM available on a current basis

ADAC *abrév* (*avion à décollage et atterrissage courts*) TRANSP *aviation* STOL (*short take-off and landing*)

adaptabilité *f* COM adaptability; **~ fonctionnelle** RES HUM task flexibility

adaptable *adj* COM adaptable

adaptateur *m* INFO adaptor; **~ graphique couleur** INFO (*CGA*) color/graphics adaptor (*AmE*), colour/graphics adaptor (*BrE*) (*CGA*), INFO (*AGA*) enhanced graphics adaptor, enhanced graphics array (*EGA*); **~ secteur** IND, INFO current adaptor (*AmE*), mains adaptor (*BrE*); **~ série** INFO serial adaptor

adaptation *f* COM accommodation, adaptation, adjustment, INFO localization, PROT SOC fitness; **~ du produit** COM product adaptation; **~ du travail à l'homme** RES HUM human engineering

adapté, e *adj* COM adequate, tailored, DROIT fit and proper, V&M *aux exigences du client, à la demande du marché* tailored

adapter: **s'~** *v pron* COM adapt; **s'~ à** COM *situation* adjust o.s. to, adjust to

ADAV *abrév* (*avion à décollage et atterrisage vertical*) TRANSP VTOL (*vertical take-off and landing*)

addendum *m* [pl: -a] DROIT, MÉDIA addendum; **~ de renonciation** ASSUR resigning addendum

Addis-Abeba *n pr* COM Addis Ababa

additif *m* COM additive, DROIT, MÉDIA addendum; **~ budgétaire** FIN supplemental budget

addition *f* COM *restaurant* bill (*BrE*), check (*AmE*), COMPTA adding, addition, INFO addition, MATH adding, addition, footing (*US*), MÉDIA addition; **~ binaire** INFO binary addition; **~ de dividende** ASSUR dividend addition

additionner *vti* COM add, add together, tot up, COMPTA add, add together, add up, MATH add, add together, add up, tot up

additionneur *m* COMPTA, MATH adder; ~ **complet** INFO full adder

ADE *abrév (avances en devises à l'exportation)* COM advance on export contract

ADEF *abrév (agence d'évaluation financière)* FIN rating agency

Aden *n pr* COM Aden

adéquat, e *adj* COM adequate

adéquation: ~ **du capital** *f* BANQUE capital adequacy; ~ **de couverture** *f* ASSUR adequacy of coverage; ~ **des fonds propres** *f* FIN *des entreprises d'investissements et des établissements de crédit* capital adequacy

adhérent, e *m,f* RES HUM member; ~ **compensateur** FIN clearing member *(BrE)*; ~ **compensateur général** *(ACG)* BOURSE general clearing member *(GCM)*; ~ **compensateur individuel** BOURSE individual clearing member; ~ **mainteneur de marché** *(AMM)* BOURSE market maker *(UK)*

adhérer: *vt* ~ **à** COM adhere to, RES HUM *syndicat* join

adhésion *f* COM membership; ~ **jusqu'à expiration de la convention collective** RES HUM maintenance of membership; ~ **à un syndicat** RES HUM trade union membership, union affiliation; ◆ **donner son ~ à** COM *projet* agree to

ad hoc *adj* COM ad hoc, DROIT fit and proper

adjoint, e *m,f* COM assistant, asst, GESTION assistant to manager, RES HUM assistant, asst; ~ **du chef de section** RES HUM assistant head of section; ~ **au contrôleur de circulation** RES HUM, TRANSP assistant traffic supervisor, ATS; ~ **exécutif** ADMIN, RES HUM executive assistant

adjonction: ~ **de main-d'oeuvre non qualifiée** *f* RES HUM dilution of labor *(AmE)*, dilution of labour *(BrE)*

adjudicateur, -trice *m,f* COM awarder

adjudication *f* COM auction, *d'un contrat* allocation, ECON auction, GESTION award, V&M auction; ~ **de bons du Trésor** BOURSE, ECON Treasury bill tender *(UK)*, tap stock tender; ~ **de gré à gré** DROIT tender by private contract; ~ **hybride** BOURSE hybrid auction; ~ **d'obligations avant émission** BOURSE bond sold prior to issue; ~ **prioritaire** BOURSE priority allocation; ~ **au soumissionnaire le plus offrant** V&M allocation to the lowest tenderer

adjuger *vt* COM allocate, *contrat* award, *objet à une vente aux enchères* knock down, *réclamation* adjudicate, DROIT award

admettre *vt* COM *retard* acknowledge, admit, RES HUM admit; ◆ **~ le bien-fondé d'une réclamation** DROIT sustain a claim

administrateur, -trice *m,f* ADMIN administrator, *d'une fondation* trustee, COM, DROIT administrator, RES HUM administrator, *d'une société* member of the board; ~ **de biens** DROIT, FIN estate manager; ~ **chargé du développement** RES HUM development director; ~ **commercial** RES HUM sales director; ~ **des exportations** IMP/EXP, RES HUM export director, export manager; ~ **externe** GESTION, RES HUM nonexecutive director, outside director; ~ **judiciaire** COM official receiver, receiver, receiver and manager, DROIT *de faillite* official receiver, receiver, receiver and manager, *de succession* administrator, FIN administrator, official receiver, receiver, receiver and manager; ~ **non-dirigeant** GESTION, RES HUM nonexecutive director; ~ **du port** RES HUM, TRANSP port director, port manager; ~ **séquestre** DROIT custodian of property, FIN sequestrator; ~ **système** INFO system administrator; ~ **des valeurs mobilières** COM securities administrator

administratif, -ive *adj* ADMIN administrative, COM administrative, prudential *(US)*

administration *f* ADMIN admin *(infrml)*, administration, management, *gouvernementale* admin, administration, government, govt, FISC public authority, GESTION admin *(infrml)*, administration; ~ **acquéreuse** COM acquiring authority; ~ **des archives** GESTION records management; ~ **centrale** COM central government, FISC *de l'Impôt* headquarters, GESTION head office, HO; ~ **chargée de l'examen préliminaire** BREVETS international preliminary examining authority; ~ **chargée de la recherche internationale** BREVETS international searching authority; ~ **commerciale** COM, GESTION business administration; ~ **du développement industriel** ECON, IND Industrial Development Authority, IDA; ~ **des domaines** ADMIN land office; ~ **des douanes** IMP/EXP Customs and Excise *(UK)*; ~ **d'entreprise** ADMIN, COM, ECON, GESTION business management; ~ **de la faillite** COM bankruptcy committee; ~ **fédérale du logement** IMMOB Federal Housing Administration *(US)*, FHA *(US)*; ~ **fiscale** ADMIN tax administration, FISC tax administration, taxation authorities; ~ **judiciaire** DROIT receivership; l'~ COM the authorities; ~ **de liaison** COM interlocking directorship; ~ **locale** ADMIN, POL local authority; ~ **du personnel** GESTION, RES HUM personnel management, staff management; ~ **des petites entreprises** COM small business administration, SBA; ~ **publique** COM public administration; ~ **régionale de la santé publique** ADMIN, PROT SOC Health Authority *(UK)*; ~ **des ressources humaines** RES HUM human resource administration; ~ **de l'union des douanes** *(AUD)* IMP/EXP UE administration of the customs union *(ACU)*; ~ **des ventes** GESTION, V&M sales management

Administration *f* COM civil service, CS

administrer *vt* ADMIN administer

admis, e *adj* FISC *déduction* allowed; ◆ **~ à faire valoir ses droits à la retraite** RES HUM eligible for retirement

admissibilité *f* COM, FISC eligibility, PROT SOC qualification

admissible *adj* COM eligible, *idée, plan* acceptable,

DROIT *preuve, témoignage, recours* admissible; ~ **pour** COM eligible for

admission *f* COM admission, admittance, *d'étudiants* intake, DROIT admission; ~ **à la cotation** BOURSE admission to listing (*UK*), admission to quotation; ~ **à la cote** BOURSE admission to listing (*UK*), admission to quotation; ~ **en franchise officielle** IMP/EXP *douane* admission; ~ **de valeurs mobilières** FIN admission of securities

adopter *vt* COM adopt, DROIT pass; ◆ **faire** ~ ECON pass; ~ **une organisation matricielle** COM go matrix (*jarg*); ~ **une position** COM take up a position; ~ **une position commune** COM adopt a joint stance; ~ **un profil bas** COM keep a low profile; ~ **progressivement** (ANT *éliminer progressivement*) COM, INFO phase in; ~ **le système métrique** COM go metric

adoption *f* ECON adoption; ~ **progressive** COM, INFO phasing in

ADP *abrév* (*action à dividende prioritaire*) BOURSE, COMPTA, FIN preference share (*BrE*), preferred stock (*AmE*)

adr.: ~ **tél.** *abrév* (*adresse télégraphique*) COMMS TA (*telegraphic address*)

adressable *adj* COMMS, INFO addressable

adressage *m* INFO addressing; ~ **absolu** INFO absolute addressing

adresse *f* COM *du siège d'une société* residency, COMMS *d'une personne, d'une entreprise* Add., address, INFO *de données en mémoire* address; ~ **absolue** COMMS absolute address, INFO absolute address, machine address; ~ **de base** INFO base address; ~ **de branchement** BANQUE, INFO branch address; ~ **au bureau** COM, COMMS, V&M business address; ~ **commerciale** COM, COMMS, V&M business address; ~ **du destinataire** TRANSP shipping address; ~ **du domicile** COM home address; ~ **émettrice** INFO source address; ~ **d'envoi** COMMS mailing address; ~ **de l'expéditeur** COMMS return address; ~ **habituelle** COMMS permanent address; **l'~ précitée** COM the above address; ~ **à notifier** IMP/EXP, TRANSP notify address; ~ **d'origine** COMMS original address; ~ **personnelle** COM home address; ~ **postale** COMMS mailing address, postal address; ~ **professionnelle** COM, COMMS, V&M business address; ~ **de publipostage** COMMS mailing address; ~ **réelle** INFO actual address, machine address, real address; ~ **de réexpédition** COM, COMMS forwarding address; ~ **du siège social** COM, COMMS registered address; ~ **de succursale** BANQUE, INFO branch address; ~ **télégraphique** (*adr. tél.*) COMMS telegraphic address (*TA*); ~ **téléphonique** COMMS tel. add., telephone address; ~ **de transfert** INFO transfer address; ~ **translatable** INFO relocatable address; ◆ ~ **ci-dessous** (ANT *adresse ci-dessus*) COM address as below; ~ **ci-dessus** (ANT *adresse ci-dessous*) COM address as above

adresser 1. *vt* COMMS *discours, paquêt*, DROIT *directive obligatoire aux États membres* address; **2.** *v pron* **s'~ à** COM cater for, COMMS address, V&M appeal to; ◆ **s'~ à qn pour obtenir qch** COM apply to sb for sth

adressez: ~ **vos réclamations à** *loc* COM address your complaints to; ~ **-vous au bureau** *loc* COM apply at the office, inquire at the office

Adressographe® *m* COM, COMMS Addressograph®

adulte *mf* DROIT adult

ad val. *abrév* (*ad valorem*) COM, FISC ad val. (*ad valorem*)

ad valorem *adj* (*ad val.*) COM, FISC ad valorem (*frml*) (*ad val.*)

adversaire *mf* DROIT adversary

AELE *abrév* (*Association européenne de libre-échange*) ECON EFTA (*European Free Trade Association*)

aérodrome *m* TRANSP *aviation* aerodrome (*BrE*), airdrome (*AmE*)

aérogare *f* TRANSP *aéroport* passenger terminal, *en ville* air terminal

aéroglisseur *m* TRANSP air cushion vehicle, ACV, hovercraft

aérogramme *m* COMMS aerogram

aérographie *f* V&M *publicité* airbrush technique

aéronef *m* TRANSP aircraft; ~ **de passagers** *frml* TRANSP passenger aircraft

aéroport *m* TRANSP airport; ~ **d'arrivée** TRANSP destination airport; ~ **international** TRANSP international airport

aérosol *m* ENVIR aerosol

aérospatial, e *adj* IND aerospace

AFC *abrév* (*Agence française de codification*) BOURSE ≈ CUSIP (*US*) (*Committee on Uniform Securities Identification Procedures*)

affacturage *m* COMPTA, FIN, MATH factoring; ~ **d'assurance** ASSUR insurance factoring; ~ **des exportations** IMP/EXP export factoring; ~ **à forfait** ECON *commerce international*, FIN forfaiting

affaiblir *vt* ECON impair, weaken

affaiblissement *m* COM *demande* slackening

affaire *f* COM deal, matter, *commerce* business concern, concern, DROIT brief, case, ECON concern; ~ **en instance** DROIT lis pendens; ~ **jugée** DROIT res judicata (*frml*); **l'~ de la semaine** V&M super saver (*jarg*); ~ **pourrie** *infrml* BOURSE bubble (*jarg*); ~ **à saisir** COM, GESTION business opportunity; ~ **sérieuse** COM urgent matter; ~ **à traiter** COM business to be transacted; ◆ **faire l'~** COM serve the purpose; **faire une** ~ COM *avec qn* make a deal; **l'~ est annulée** COM the deal is off

affaires *f pl* COM affairs, business, business activity, commerce, GESTION business activity; ~ **d'argent** *f pl* COM money matters; ~ **commerciales** *f pl* COM mercantile affairs; ~ **courantes** *f pl* COM normal course of business, routine duties; ~ **en cours** *f pl* COM pending business; ~ **étrangères** *f pl* POL foreign affairs; ~ **européennes** *f pl* COM, POL European affairs; ~ **intérieures** *f pl* COM domestic business, POL home affairs; ~ **internationales** *f pl* POL international affairs; ~ **judiciaires** *f pl* DROIT judicial affairs; ~ **maritimes** *f pl* COM shipping business; ~ **politiques** *f pl* POL political affairs; ~ **à régler** *f* COM business to be transacted; ◆ **axé sur les** ~ COM business-orientated, business-oriented; ~ **de l'entreprise** COM company's affairs; **faire des** ~ COM do business; **les** ~ **ne marchent pas** COM business is slack; **pour** ~ COM on business

affairisme *m infrml* BOURSE wheeling and dealing (*infrml*), COM commercialism, wheeling and dealing (*infrml*), POL racketeering

affairiste *mf infrml* COM wheeler-dealer (*infrml*)

affaissement *m* BOURSE *marché* slump

affectation *f* ADMIN allocation, allotment, COMPTA *de fonds* allocation, appropriation, *de frais* apportionment, *publique* allotment, ECON *de fonds* appropriation, *de la masse monétaire* allocation, *ressources* allocation, appropriation, earmarking, FIN allocation, earmarking, *de frais* appropriation, FISC earmarking, IMMOB *à un but* apportionment, INFO allocation, assignment, RES HUM *d'un employé* appointment, *d'une équipe* deployment, posting, *ressources* allocation, *à un poste ailleurs* posting; ~ **annuelle** COMPTA annual appropriation; ~ **des bénéfices** COMPTA appropriation of income; ~ **budgétaire** COMPTA, ECON, FIN, POL budget appropriation; ~ **à but spécial** COM special-purpose allotment; ~ **de chargement** TRANSP loading allocation; ~ **des charges** COMPTA allocation of costs, cost allocation; ~ **courante** POL standard allotment; ~ **d'un coût** ECON cost application; ~ **pour dépenses en capital** FIN capital allotment; ~ **de l'équipage** TRANSP crew manning; ~ **des frais** COMPTA apportionment of costs; ~ **hypothécaire malveillante** DROIT injurious affection; ~ **pour mémoire** COM memorandum allocation; ~ **de la mémoire** INFO storage allocation; ~ **non-répartie** COM undistributed allotment; ~ **de priorité** BOURSE priority allocation; ~ **aux provisions** COMPTA allocation to provisions; ~ **quasi-législative** DROIT quasi-statutory allocation; ~ **réglementaire** POL statutory allocation; ~ **de réserve pour le rajustement des salaires** *(ARRT)* RES HUM salary adjustment reserve allotment *(SARA)*; ~ **aux réserves** COMPTA allocation to reserves; ~ **des salaires** RES HUM wage assignment; ~ **spéciale de fonds publics** ECON, FIN, FISC ring fencing; ~ **des tâches** COM, RES HUM job assignment

affectations: ~ **statutaires de crédit** *f pl* DROIT statutory appropriations

affecté, e *adj* COMPTA absorbed; ~ **négativement** COM adversely affected

affecter *vt* ADMIN allocate, allot, COMPTA allot, *fonds* allocate, appropriate, *frais* apportion, ECON *fonds* allocate, appropriate, *masse monétaire* affect, allocate, *ressources* allocate, appropriate, earmark, *à un but* hit, FIN *argent* earmark, *fonds* appropriate, INFO allocate, assign, RES HUM *employé* appoint,

ressources allocate, *équipe* deploy, post, *à un poste ailleurs* post

afférent, e *adj* FIN *revenu, dépenses* accruing

affichage *m* ADMIN posting, COM bill posting, bill sticking, posting, COMMS display, DROIT *procédure civile* posting, INFO display, V&M *publicité* poster display; ~ **sauvage** POL snipe (*US, jarg*), V&M fly posting; ~ **sur écran** INFO soft copy

affiche *f* MÉDIA, V&M *publicité par affichage* bill, poster; ~ **spéciale circulation** TRANSP special traffic notice, STN; ◆ **qui tient l'**~ **longtemps** MÉDIA leggy (*jarg*)

afficher *vt* ADMIN, BOURSE post, COM affix, air, display, post, COMMS affix, INFO, V&M display; ◆ ~ **une marge** BOURSE post margin; ~ **ses idées** COM air one's opinions, air one's views

affichette: ~ **de rue** *f* V&M guttersnipe; ~ **pour vitrine** *f* COM window bill, window sticker

affidavit *m* DROIT affidavit

affiliation *f* COM affiliation

affilié[1]**, e** *adj* COM affiliated; ◆ ~ **à** COM affiliated to

affilié[2]**, e** *m,f* COM affiliate

affilier 1. *vt* COM affiliate; ~ **à** COM affiliate to; **2.** *v pron* **s'**~ **à** COM affiliate o.s. to

affiné, e *adj* IND refined

affirmation *f* COM assertion; ~ **a priori** COM a priori statement

affirmer *vt* COM assert

affluer *vi* FIN *argent, capitaux* flow

afflux *m* COM flow; ~ **de capitaux** ECON, FIN capital inflow; ~ **de commandes** COM flow of orders; ~ **de fonds** ECON, FIN capital inflow

affourché, e *adj* TRANSP tongued and grooved, T&G

affranchir *vt* COM stamp, COMMS frank

affranchissement: ~ **supplémentaire** *m* COM, COMMS extra postage

affrètement *m* DROIT charter, TRANSP charter, chartering, *navigation* affreightment; ~ **en bloc** TRANSP *maritime* lump-sum charter; ~ **au mouillage** TRANSP *navigation* berth charter; ~ **ouvert** TRANSP *maritime* open charter, OC; ~ **partagé** TRANSP *fret aérien* split charter; ~ **spot** TRANSP spot charter; ~ **à temps** TRANSP time charter, T/C; ~ **total** TRANSP whole cargo charter; ~ **au voyage** TRANSP voyage charter, voyage fixture, *maritime* trip charter

affréter *vt* TRANSP *véhicule* charter

affréteur *m* IMP/EXP, TRANSP charterer, shipper

affrontement *m* COM *conflit* confrontation; ~ **indécis** COM standoff

affronter *vt* COM confront, face up to

affût: **être à l'**~ **de** *loc* COM be on the alert for, be on the lookout for, be watching out for

afghan[1]**, e** *adj* COM Afghan

afghan[2] *m* COM *langue* Afghan

Afghan, e *m,f* COM *habitant* Afghan

afghani *m* COM afghani

Afghanistan *m* COM Afghanistan

AFNOR *abrév (Association française de normalisation)* COM, DROIT, IND French standards authority, ≈ ANSI *(American National Standards Institute,* ≈ ASA *(American Standards Association)*, ≈ BSI *(British Standards Institution)*, ≈ National Bureau of Standards *(US)*

a fortiori *loc* COM a fortiori

AFPA *abrév (Association pour la formation professionnelle des adultes)* RES HUM ≈ TA *(UK) (Training Agency)*

africain, e *adj* COM African

Africain, e *m,f* COM *habitant* African

afrikaans *m* COM *langue* Afrikaans

afrikaner *adj* COM Afrikaner

Afrikaner *mf* COM *habitant* Afrikaner

Afrique:[1] **d'~ du Nord** *adj* COM North African; **d'~ du Sud** *adj* COM South African

Afrique[2] *f* COM Africa; **~ du Sud** COM South Africa; **~ centrale** *f* COM Central Africa; **~ du Nord** *f* COM North Africa

AFSB *abrév (Association française des sociétés de Bourse)* BOURSE French association of stock exchange member firms

ag. *abrév (agence)* ADMIN agcy, *(agency)* BANQUE branch, COM agcy, branch

AG *abrév (assemblée générale)* COM GA *(General Assembly)*, GM *(general meeting)*

AGA *abrév (adaptateur graphique couleur)* INFO EGA *(enhanced graphics adaptor)*

AGE *abrév* FIN *(accords généraux d'emprunt)* GAB *(general arrangements to borrow)*, GESTION *(assemblée générale extraordinaire)* EGM *(extraordinary general meeting)*

âge *m* COM age; **~ atteint** ASSUR attained age; **~ d'effet de la retraite** RES HUM pensionable age; **~ à l'entrée** ASSUR age at entry; **~ limite** COM age limit; **~ de la mise à la retraite** RES HUM pensionable age; **~ normal de départ à la retraite** RES HUM normal retirement age; **~ d'or** COM golden age; **~ de la retraite** RES HUM normal retirement, retirement age; **~ de retraite variable** RES HUM multiple retirement ages; **~ à terme** ASSUR age at expiry

âgée: personne ~ *f* FISC, PROT SOC senior citizen

agence *f (ag.)* ADMIN agency, bureau, BANQUE *d'une banque* branch, COM agency, branch office, BO, branch operation, *banque* branch; **~ bénévole** PROT SOC voluntary agency; **~ centrale** COM head office, HO; **~ commerciale** FIN mercantile agency, V&M mercantile agency, sales agency, sales office; **~ de commercialisation** V&M marketing board; **~ donatrice** PROT SOC *aidant une région, un pays* donor agency; **~ d'évaluation financière** *(ADEF)* FIN rating agency; **~ d'évaluation de la solvabilité** ADMIN, FIN credit agency; **~ gouvernementale** ADMIN government agency; **~ immobilière** IMMOB estate agency *(BrE)*, real estate agency *(AmE)*;

~ internationale COM international agency; **~ locale** ADMIN branch office, BO; **~ de logement** PROT SOC accommodation agency *(BrE)*, accommodations agency *(AmE)*; **~ maritime** TRANSP shipping agency, shipping office; **~ de messageries** COM express agency; **~ multilatérale** ECON, POL multilateral agency; **~ nationale** COM national agency; **~ de notation** FIN credit bureau, credit reference agency, rating agency; **~ de notation obligataire** BOURSE bond rating agency; **~ de notation des obligations** BOURSE bond rating agency; **~ de placement** COM, RES HUM employment agency, employment bureau, employment office *(UK)*; **~ de presse** COMMS news agency *(BrE)*, wire service *(AmE)*, MÉDIA news agency *(BrE)*, wire service *(AmE)*, press agency; **~ privée** COM private agency; **~ pour la protection de l'environnement** ENVIR environmental protection agency, EPA; **~ de publicité** MÉDIA, V&M advertising agency; **~ de publicité globale** MÉDIA, V&M agency with full service, full-service agency; **~ de quartier** ADMIN branch office, BO; **~ de rating** FIN credit bureau, credit reference agency; **~ régionale** BANQUE area office; **~ de relations publiques** V&M public relations agency; **~ de RP** V&M PR agency; **~ de spectacles** LOISIRS ticket agency; **~ de transit en douane** IMP/EXP customs agency; **~ de tutelle** COM regulatory agency; **~ de voyages** LOISIRS ticket agency, travel agency, travel bureau, RES HUM travel bureau, TRANSP ticket agency, travel agency, travel bureau; **~ de voyages à prix réduits** LOISIRS, TRANSP, V&M bucket shop

Agence: ~ des États-Unis pour la protection de l'environnement *f* ENVIR United States Environmental Protection Agency; **~ européenne de productivité** *f* IND European Productivity Agency, EPA; **~ française de codification** *f (AFC)* BOURSE ≈ Committee on Uniform Securities Identification Procedures *(US) (CUSIP)*; **~ monétaire d'Arabie Saoudite** *f* FIN Saudi Arabian Monetary Agency, SAMA; **~ nationale pour l'emploi** *f France (ANPE)* RES HUM ≈ Employment Service *(UK)*, ≈ Jobcentre *(UK)*; **~ nationale pour la valorisation de la recherche** *f (ANVAR)* ADMIN national development research centre; **~ de planification économique** *f* RES HUM Economic Planning Agency, EPA; **~ spatiale européenne** *f (ASE)* COM European Space Agency *(ESA)*

agencement *m* IMMOB fixture

agencements: ~ et aménagements *m pl* COMPTA alterations and improvements

agenda *m* ADMIN, COM diary

agenouillement *m* TRANSP kneeling

agent *m* RES HUM commission agent, commission merchant, commission salesman, commission salesperson, commission saleswoman, officer, ADMIN official, COM agent, agt, DROIT agent, agt, attorney *(US)*, FIN broker, dealer, factor; **~ acquisiteur** ASSUR acquisition agent;

~ **administratif** RES HUM administration officer; ~ **d'affaires** COM business agent, IND business agent (*US*); ~ **d'affrètement** TRANSP chartering agent; ~ **agréé** COM authorized representative; ~ **d'assurance** ASSUR insurance agent; ~ **d'assurance-vie agréé** *(a.v.a.)* ASSUR chartered life underwriter (*US*); ~ **d'assurances** ASSUR insurance broker; ~ **en brevet d'invention** BREVETS, DROIT patent agent; ~ **certificateur** ADMIN Certification Officer (*UK*), certifying officer, CO; ~ **de change** BOURSE agency broker, stockbroker; ~ **commercial** COM commercial agent, salesagent, RES HUM, V&M sales rep (*infrml*), sales representative; ~ **commercial exclusif** ECON, V&M sole agent; ~ **commercial salarié** RES HUM salaried agent; ~ **de compensation** BANQUE clearing agent; ~ **comptable** *Fra (cf comptable public Bel)* COMPTA, FIN paymaster; ~ **comptable des transferts** FIN registrar of transfers; ~ **comptable du Trésor** FISC ≈ Commissioner of Customs and Excise (*UK*), ≈ Commissioner of Inland Revenue (*UK*); ~ **coordinateur** TRANSP umbrella agent; ~ **de crédit** FIN credit officer; ~ **du dédouanement** IMP/EXP clearance agent, customs clearance agent; ~ **en douane** IMP/EXP clearing agent, customs officer, RES HUM customs officer; ~ **économique** ECON economic agent; ~ **encaisseur** FISC encashing agent; ~ **d'enquête** RES HUM investigation officer; ~ **à l'étranger** COM foreign agent, overseas agent; ~ **exclusif** COM sole agent; ~ **expéditeur** V&M forwarding agent; ~ **financier** BOURSE fiscal agent; ~ **financier régional** ADMIN financial officer; ~ **financier supérieur** COMPTA senior financial officer; ~ **fondé de pouvoir** COM authorized agent; ~ **de fret IATA** TRANSP IATA cargo agent; ~ **général** DROIT general agent, universal agent; ~ **immobilier** IMMOB estate agent (*BrE*), realtor (*AmE*); ~ **de l'impôt** FISC, RES HUM taxation officer; ~ **de listage** IMMOB listing agent (*US*); ~ **de la Lloyds** TRANSP *navigation* Lloyd's Agent, L/A; ~ **de maîtrise** GESTION, RES HUM first-line manager, first-line supervisor, supervisor; ~ **maritime** COM shipping agent, TRANSP shifting berth; ~ **maritime-transitaire** IMP/EXP, RES HUM, TRANSP shipping and forwarding agent, S&FA; ~ **de marques** BREVETS, DROIT *propriété intellectuelle* trademark agent; ~ **de la P.A.F.** *Fra (agent de la Police de l'air et des frontières)*, immigration officer, IO; ~ **payeur** COMPTA paymaster, FIN disburser, *de salaires* paymaster, FISC paying agent; ~ **de placement** BOURSE selling agent; ~ **de la Police de l'air et des frontières** *France (agent de la P.A.F.)* ADMIN, RES HUM immigration officer, IO; ~ **portuaire** IMP/EXP, TRANSP port agent; ~ **de prêts** BANQUE lending officer, loan officer; ~ **de projet** RES HUM project agent; ~ **du receveur** RES HUM receiver's agent; ~ **de recouvrement** FISC collection agent; ~ **de recouvrement de créances** COM, FIN debt collector; ~ **rémunéré au fixe** RES HUM salaried agent; ~ **de sécurité en vol** RES HUM, TRANSP sky

marshal; ~ **du service de l'immigration** ADMIN, RES HUM immigration officer, IO; ~ **tireur** BANQUE drawing officer; ~ **de transportation routière** RES HUM, TRANSP motor transport officer, MTO; ~ **du trésor** BOURSE government broker; ~ **de vérification** COMPTA, FIN audit officer; ~ **de voyage** LOISIRS, RES HUM, TRANSP travel agent

agents: ~ **exécutifs en exercice** *m pl* GESTION, RES HUM active corps of executives

agglo. *abrév infrml (aggloméré)* COM chipboard

agglomération *f* ECON metropolitan area, GESTION agglomeration; ~ **urbaine** COM built-up area, PROT SOC built-up area, urban area, TRANSP built-up area

aggloméré *m (agglo.)* COM chipboard

aggravation *f (*ANT *amélioration)* COM turn for the worse; ~ **unique** ASSUR unique impairment

aggraver: s'~ *v pron* COM worsen

aggrégat: ~ **de la production** *m* ECON, IND aggregate output

agio *m* BOURSE, ECON agio

agios *m* COMPTA bank interest

agiotage *m* BOURSE agiotage, stock jobbery (*UK*)

agioteur *mf* BOURSE manipulator

agir *vi* COM act; ◆ ~ **de bonne foi** DROIT act in good faith; ~ **pour le compte de qn** DROIT act on sb's behalf; ~ **dans l'exercice de ses fonctions** GESTION act in one's official capacity; **faire** ~ COM actuate; ~ **illégalement** DROIT fall foul of the law; ~ **en médiateur** COM, RES HUM mediate; ~ **au nom de qn** DROIT act on sb's behalf; ~ **sur le marché** BOURSE manipulate the market

âgisme *m* ECON ageism (*BrE*), agism (*AmE*)

agitation *f* BOURSE flurry of activity, POL, RES HUM unrest

AGO *abrév (assemblée générale ordinaire)* BOURSE, COM, GESTION OGM *(ordinary general meeting)*

agorot *m* COM agora

agrafeuse *f* COM stapler

agrandir *vt* COM *entreprise* expand

agrandissement *m* COM enlarged copy, enlargement

agréé, e *adj* ADMIN registered, ASSUR approved, COM *contrat, requête* approved, *institution, qualification* accredited, FISC approved, GESTION authorized

agréer *vt* ADMIN register, ASSUR *réclamation* allow, approve, COM allow, *contrat, requête* approve, *institution, qualification* accredit, *régime de retraite* register, DROIT *droit commercial ou immobilier* accept, FISC approve, GESTION authorize, IMMOB accept, PROT SOC accredit

agrégat *m* ECON aggregate

agrégation *f* GESTION agglomeration; ◆ ~ **des ressources** COM resource aggregation

agrégats: ~ **monétaires** *m pl (M)* ECON monetary aggregates *(M)*

agrément *m* ADMIN, ASSUR *d'un régime de retraite* registration, COM *d'une institution, d'une qualifi-*

cation accreditation, *d'un contrat, d'une requête* approval, DROIT *droit commercial ou immobilier* acce., acceptance, GESTION authorization, IMMOB acce., acceptance, PROT SOC accreditation

agréments *m pl* IMMOB amenities

agressif, -ive *adj* COM, FIN, V&M aggressive

agricole *adj* ECON, ENVIR agricultural

agriculteur, -trice *m,f* ECON, ENVIR agriculturalist, agriculturist, farmer; ~ **admissible** FISC qualifying farmer; ~ **qualifiable** FISC qualifying farmer

agriculture *f* ECON, ENVIR agriculture, farming; ~ **biologique** ECON, ENVIR organic farming; ~ **industrielle** ECON, ENVIR, IND factory farming; ~ **intensive** ECON, ENVIR intensive farming; ~ **de subsistance** ECON, ENVIR subsistence farming

agro: ~ **-industries** *f pl* ECON, ENVIR, IND agribusiness

agroalimentaire *m* ECON, ENVIR, IND agribusiness, agrifoodstuffs, food-processing industry

agrobusiness *m* ECON, ENVIR, IND agribusiness

agroforesterie *f* ENVIR agro-forestry

agronome *m* ECON, ENVIR agronomist

agronomie *f* ECON, ENVIR agronomy

AIB *abrév* (*Accord international sur le blé*) ECON IWA (*International Wheat Agreement*)

AIDA *abrév* (*attention, intérêt, désir, action*) COM, V&M AIDA (*attention, interest, desire, action*)

aide:[1] ~ **-caissier** *m,f* BANQUE assistant cashier (*BrE*), assistant teller (*AmE*); ~ **-comptable** *mf* COMPTA accounting clerk, book-keeper

aide[2] *f* BANQUE aid, COM assistance, grant, subsidy, DROIT assistance, ECON aid, assistance, FISC assistance, INFO help, support, POL aid, assistance, PROT SOC grant, subsidy; ~ **alimentaire** ECON, POL food aid; ~ **bilatérale** ECON, POL bilateral aid; ~ **communautaire** ECON Community aid; ~ **complémentaire** FIN supplementary assistance; ~ **contextuelle** INFO context-sensitive help; ~ **à la création d'entreprise** FIN enterprise allowance (*UK*); ~ **au développement** ECON, POL development aid, donor aid; ~ **à l'écran** INFO help screen, on-line help; ~ **de l'État** PROT SOC state help; ~ **à l'étranger** ECON, POL foreign aid; ~ **étrangère** ECON, POL foreign aid; ~ **extérieure** ECON, POL overseas aid; ~ **financière** ECON, FIN financial aid, financial assistance, FISC award income, POL financial aid, financial assistance; ~ **financière en capital** ECON, POL capital aid; ~ **financière sous forme d'apport de capital** ECON, POL capital aid; ~ **fiscale** FISC tax assistance; ~ **gouvernementale** FISC government assistance; ~ **d'interfinancement** FIN cross subsidy; ~ **juridique** DROIT, PROT SOC legal aid; ~ **liée** ECON, POL tied aid; ~ **en ligne** INFO help screen; ~ **locative** PROT SOC rent allowance; ~ **au logement** PROT SOC housing benefit (*UK*), housing subsidy; ~ **multilatérale** ECON, POL multilateral aid; ~ **en nature** BANQUE, ECON, POL aid in kind; ~ **non-affectée** POL nonproject aid; ~ **officielle au développement** ECON, POL official

development assistance; ~ **pécuniaire** DROIT maintenance; ~ **pécuniaire uniforme** PROT SOC flat grant; ~ **au pourcentage** PROT SOC percentage grant; ~ **-programme** ECON program aid (*AmE*), programme aid (*BrE*); ~ **-projet** ECON project aid; ~ **publique au développement** ECON, POL official development assistance; ~ **à la réinsertion** ECON workfare; ~ **sociale** RES HUM social security; ~ **spécifique à un secteur** ECON, POL sector-specific aid; ~ **d'urgence** ECON, POL emergency aid; ◆ **bénéficiant d'une ~ publique** FIN, POL government-backed

Aide: ~ **financière sélective** *f* ECON Selective Financial Assistance (*UK*)

aider *vti* BANQUE, COM, ECON, POL aid

aides: ~ **à la conception** *f pl* COM design aids; ~ **à la décision** *f pl* COM decision aids

aigle *m* FIN eagle (*US*), ten dollars

aiguillage *m* INFO switch

aiguilleur: ~ **du ciel** *m* TRANSP air-traffic controller

aiguillot *m* TRANSP *d'un navire* pintle

ailleurs: par ~ *loc* COM otherwise

aimable *adj* COM polite

aîné, e *adj* COM Snr, senior

air *m* TRANSP air; ~ **conditionné** ADMIN, COM, PROT SOC air conditioning; ~ **pollué** ENVIR polluted air

airbus *m* TRANSP airbus

aire *f* ECON, MATH area; ~ **de détente** LOISIRS recreational facility; ~ **de groupage** TRANSP bundling yard; ~ **ouverte** IMMOB *dans une zone bâtie* open space; ~ **de stationnement** TRANSP *aéroport* apron; ~ **de stationnement pour les remorques** TRANSP trailer park; ~ **de stockage** COM storage area; ~ **de stockage des conteneurs** TRANSP *port* container depot, dock container park

AIS *abrév* (*Accord international sur le sucre*) ECON ≈ ISA (*International Sugar Agreement*)

aisé, e *adj* COM easy, ECON affluent

ajournement *m* COM deferment, DROIT *d'une cause* adjournment, remand, GESTION adjournment

ajourner 1. *vt* COM defer, DROIT *cause* adjourn, remand, GESTION adjourn; **2.** *v pron* **s'~ à** GESTION adjourn to; ◆ ~ **une sentence** DROIT adjourn sentence

ajout *m* BANQUE add-on, INFO addition, MÉDIA addition, *presse* fills

ajouté: ~ **à** *adj* COM, INFO coupled with

ajouter *vt* COM add up, COMPTA add, INFO append, MATH add, add up; ~ **à** MATH add to

ajustage *m* COM adjustment

ajustement *m* COM *de prix, salaires*, COMPTA, ECON, FIN adjustment; ~ **de l'amortissement** COMPTA depreciation adjustment; ~ **budgétaire** COMPTA, ECON, FIN budgetary adjustment; ~ **d'évaluation** COMPTA valuation adjustment; ~ **d'impôt** COM, FIN, FISC tax adjustment; ~ **du marché** ECON market adjustment; ~ **monétaire** ECON monetary accommodation;

~ **multiplicateur** FIN financing adjustment; ~ **de la personne à son poste** RES HUM person-job fit; ~ **des prix** COM making-up price, M/U, V&M price-lining; ~ **de rendement** COMPTA yield adjustment; ~ **rétroactif** ECON retroactive adjustment; ~ **de la somme assurée** ASSUR adjustment of sum insured; ~ **du taux de rendement** BOURSE yield maintenance; ~ **de la valeur assurée** ASSUR adjustment of sum insured; ~ **de la valeur de l'obligation** BOURSE accretion

ajuster *vt* COM, COMPTA, ECON, FIN adjust; ~ **en fonction de la demande globale** ECON *économie* fine-tune

alarme *f* COM alarm; ◆ **donner l'**~ COM raise the alarm

albanais[1], **e** *adj* COM Albanian

albanais[2] *m* COM *langue* Albanian

Albanais, e *m,f* COM *habitant* Albanian

Albanie *f* COM Albania

aléatoire *adj* ASSUR aleatoric, aleatory, COM *hasardeux* contingent

ALENA *abrév (Accord de libre-échange nord-américain)* ECON NAFTA *(North American Free Trade Area)*

alerte *f* COM alarm, alert, danger, RES HUM danger; ~ **à la bombe** COM bomb scare; ◆ **donner l'**~ COM give the alert

algarade *f* RES HUM storming

algèbre: ~ **de Boole** *f* INFO, MATH Boolean algebra

Alger *n pr* COM Algiers

Algérie *f* COM Algeria

algérien, -enne *adj* COM Algerian

Algérien, -enne *m,f* COM *habitant* Algerian

algorithme *m* INFO *séquence d'instructions pour la résolution d'un problème*, MATH algorithm

algorithmique *adj* INFO, MATH algorithmic

alias *adv* COM a.k.a., also known as, alias, COMMS a.k.a., also known as, INFO alias

aliénable *adj* DROIT alienable

aliénataire *mf* DROIT alienee

aliénation *f* DROIT, RES HUM alienation; ~ **de titres** BOURSE security disposal; ~ **de valeurs mobilières** BOURSE security disposal

aligné: ~ **à droite** *adj* (ANT *aligné à gauche*) COMMS, INFO, MÉDIA flush right, right-justified; ~ **à gauche** *adj* (ANT *aligné à droite*) COMMS, INFO, MÉDIA flush left, left-justified

alignement *m* COM alignment, INFO array, RES HUM *des salaires* comparability; ~ **sur la concurrence** V&M competitive parity *(UK)*, defensive budgeting *(UK)*, defensive spending *(UK)*; ~ **sur les prix du marché** COM, IMMOB, V&M *estimation immobilière* market comparison approach

aligner 1. *vt* DROIT align, INFO align, aline *(AmE)*; **2.** *v pron* **s'**~ **sur** BOURSE shadow; ◆ ~ **à droite** (ANT *aligner à gauche*), COMMS, INFO, MÉDIA right-justify; ~ **à gauche** (ANT *aligner à droite*) COMMS, INFO, MÉDIA left-justify

aliment: ~ **prêt à cuire** *m* V&M convenience food; ~ **tout préparé** *m* V&M convenience food

alimentation *f* INFO feed, power, supply; ~ **auxiliaire** INFO battery backup; ~ **de base** COM basic foodstuffs; ~ **continue** INFO chain feeding; ~ **en eau** ENVIR water supply; ~ **énergétique** COM energy supply; ~ **en énergie** COM energy supply; ~ **feuille à feuille** INFO sheet feeding; ~ **non-interruptible** INFO uninterruptible power supply, UPS; ~ **du papier** INFO paper feed; ~ **de secours** INFO battery backup; ~ **secteur** IND, INFO mains *(BrE)*, supply network *(AmE)*

alimenter *vt* ECON *l'inflation* fuel, INFO *en cartes, en papier* feed, power

aliments *m pl* COM foodstuffs, DROIT alimony, maintenance, ECON, IND foodstuffs; ~ **pour bétail** ECON *agriculture* feedstuffs; ~ **biologiques** COM, ENVIR organic foodstuffs; ~ **macrobiotiques** PROT SOC health foods; ~ **naturels** PROT SOC health foods

alinéa *m* ADMIN paragraph, *espace* indent

aliquote *adj* MATH aliquot

allée *f* COM, LOISIRS aisle

allégation *f* DROIT, RES HUM allegation

allège:[1] **qui ~ le travail** *adj* RES HUM labor-saving *(AmE)*, labour-saving *(BrE)*

allège[2] *f* TRANSP barge, dumb barge, *bateau* lighter; ~ **de soutage** TRANSP *navigation* bunkering barge

allègement *m* DROIT mitigation, FISC concession, reduction; ~ **de la dette** ECON, POL debt relief; ~ **fiscal** ECON, FISC, IND tax break, tax relief; ~ **d'un prêt hypothécaire** BANQUE, FIN, FISC mortgage relief; ~ **de retraite** FISC retirement relief *(UK)*; ~ **transitoire** FISC transitional relief

allègements: ~ **fiscaux** *m pl* FISC windfall profits tax

alléger *vt* COM slim down, *procédure* simplify, ECON slim down, FISC *impôt* cut, reduce

allégué, e *adj* DROIT, RES HUM alleged

Allemagne *f* COM Germany

allemand[1], **e** *adj* COM German

allemand[2] *m* COM *langue* German

Allemand, e *m,f* COM *habitant* German

aller:[1] ~ **plein-tarif** *m* LOISIRS, TRANSP standard single; ~ **-retour** *m* BOURSE bed and breakfast deal *(jarg)*, round trip, TRANSP return ticket *(BrE)*, round-trip ticket *(AmE)*; ~ **-retour de fin de semaine** *m* TRANSP *tarif* weekend return; ~ **-retour plein-tarif** *m* LOISIRS, TRANSP standard return; ~ **simple** *m* TRANSP one-way ticket *(AmE)*, single *(BrE)*, single ticket *(BrE)*; ~ **simple plein-tarif** *m* LOISIRS, TRANSP standard single; ◆ **faire des ~ -retour** BOURSE in and out trading *(jarg)*

aller[2] *vi* COM go; ◆ ~ **contre** BOURSE go against; ~ **à contre-courant** BOURSE run back, COM go against the stream; ~ **à l'encontre de** COM *intentions* defeat, *marché, tendance* buck; ~ **à l'encontre de sa propre conscience** DROIT go against one's judgment; ~ **à l'encontre de la tendance générale** COM buck the trend; ~ **jus-**

qu'au bout de qch COM follow sth through; ~ **loin** BOURSE go long, take a long position; ~ **mal** COM *économie* go downhill; ~ **mieux** COM take a turn for the better; ~ **de pair avec** COM go hand in hand with; ~ **à un rendez-vous** COM keep an appointment; ~ **à vau-l'eau** COM *économie* go to rack and ruin; ~ **voter** POL turn out to vote; **y** ~ **au pifomètre** *infrml* COM play it by ear

alliance *f* POL alliance; ~ **de coalition** POL coalition alliance; ~ **stratégique** COM, GESTION strategic alliance

allier *vt* COM ally, unite

allocataire *mf* RES HUM recipient, welfare recipient (*AmE*)

allocation *f* ADMIN allocation, COM allowance, ECON *des ressources* allocation, appropriation, earmarking, FISC allowance, benefit, INFO allocation, PROT SOC allowance, RES HUM allowance, benefit; ~ **d'ancien combattant** FISC war veteran's allowance; ~ **du budget publicitaire** FIN, V&M assignment of advertising expenditure; ~ **chômage** ECON, PROT SOC, RES HUM dole (*BrE, infrml*), unemployment benefit (*BrE*), unemployment compensation (*AmE*), welfare (*AmE, infrml*); ~ **au conjoint** FISC spouse's allowance; ~ **du coût en capital** FISC capital cost allowance; ~ **de deuil de veuve** FISC widow's bereavement allowance; ~ **de devises** FIN foreign currency allowance; ~ **efficiente** ECON efficient allocation; ~ **d'entretien** DROIT maintenance allowance, maintenance payments; ~ **familiale** FISC, PROT SOC, RES HUM family allowance; ~ **des fonds** COMPTA, ECON budget appropriation, FIN apportionment of funds, budget appropriation, POL budget appropriation; ~ **pour frais** FISC expense allowance; ~ **pour frais de déplacement** FISC allowance for travelling expenses; ~ **pour frais personnels** FISC allowance for personal expenses; ~ **de garantie** ASSUR collateral assignment; ~ **aux grévistes** RES HUM strike pay; ~ **imposable** FISC taxable allowance; ~ **journalière** ASSUR daily allowance; ~ **logement** PROT SOC housing benefit (*UK*), housing subsidy; ~ **maladie** RES HUM sick allowance, sickness benefit; ~ **de maternité** PROT SOC, RES HUM maternity allowance, maternity benefit; ~ **de nantissement** ASSUR collateral assignment; ~ **par appel d'offre** BOURSE allocation by tender (*UK*); ~ **quotidienne** ASSUR daily allowance; ~ **des ressources** FIN resource allocation; ~ **de subsistance** FISC allowance for living expenses

allocations:[1] ~ **et avantages imposables** *m pl* FISC taxable allowances and benefits

allocations[2] *f pl* PROT SOC, RES HUM welfare payments; ~ **allouées** FIN allocated benefits (*UK*); ~ **et prestations imposables** FISC taxable allowances and benefits; ~ **familiales** ECON child benefit (*UK*), FISC family allowance payments, PROT SOC child benefit (*UK*), RES HUM family allowance payments; ~ **-grévistes** RES HUM strike

benefits; ~ **de la Sécurité sociale** RES HUM Social Security benefits, welfare benefits

allocution *f* COMMS address

allodial, e *adj* DROIT *droit féodal* allodial

allonge *f* BANQUE *sur une traite de commerce* allonge

allongement *m* TRANSP *d'un navire* jumboization

allonger *vt* BOURSE lengthen

allouer *vt* ADMIN allocate, BANQUE *prêt* grant, COM *temps* allot, allow, COMPTA, ECON allocate, FIN allot, grant, INFO allocate, assign, RES HUM allocate; ♦ ~ **des dommages et intérêts** DROIT adjudge damages

allumé, e *adj* INFO *voyant* on, up (*infrml*)

Alma-Ata *n pr* COM Alma-Ata

almanach *m* MÉDIA yearbook

alourdi, e *adj* BOURSE, FISC weighted

alphabétique *adj* COM, COMMS alphabetical

alphanumérique *adj* COM, INFO alphanumeric, A/N, MATH numeric alphabetic

altérer *vt* COM *fait, texte*, ECON distort, FIN *chiffres* distort, *monnaie* falsify

alternance: en ~ *loc* COM alternate

alternatif, -ive *adj* COM alternate

alternative *f* COM alternative; ♦ **aucune** ~ **n'est possible** COM there is no alternative, TINA; **il n'y a pas d'**~ COM there is no alternative, TINA

alterné, e *adj* COM alternate

alterner *vt* COM alternate

altruisme *m* ECON altruism

aluminium *m* ENVIR, IND alum., aluminium (*BrE*), aluminum (*AmE*)

amalgamer *vt* BOURSE merge

amarrage *m* TRANSP *d'un navire* mooring, *dans un dock* docking; ~ **sur un seul coffre** TRANSP *d'un navire* single-buoy mooring, SBM

amarré: ~ **au large** *loc* TRANSP *navire* lying off

amassé *adj* COMPTA accrued

amasser *vt* COM accumulate, amass

amateur[1], **-trice** *adj* LOISIRS *sport* amateur

amateur[2], **-trice** *m,f* LOISIRS *sport* amateur; ~ **de risques** COM risk lover

ambassade *f* COM, POL embassy

ambassadeur, -drice *m,f* POL ambassador

ambiance: ~ **à la baisse** *f* (*ANT ambiance à la hausse*) BOURSE bearish tone, bearishness; ~ **à la hausse** *f* (*ANT ambiance à la baisse*) BOURSE bullish tone, bullishness; ~ **du marché** *f* BOURSE market tone

ambigu, -ë *adj* COM nonobvious

ambitieuse: personne ~ *f* COM high-flier, high-flyer

ambitieux, -euse *adj* COM *personne* ambitious

ambition *f* COM ambition

AME *abrév* (*Accord monétaire européen*) COM EMA (*European Monetary Agreement*)

amélioration *f* COM *de la balance commerciale* improvement, COM turn for the better, ECON upturn, *des biens d'équipement* improvement,

IMMOB *apportée au bien immobilier* betterment, INFO enhancement, V&M upgrade; ~ **capitale** ECON capital improvement; ~ **de l'habitat** IMMOB home improvement; ~ **locative** FIN, IMMOB leasehold improvement; ~ **matérielle** INFO hardware upgrade; ~ **de produit** V&M product improvement; ~ **de la rentabilité** COM, FIN profit improvement; ~ **sensible** ECON upswing, upturn; ~ **des tâches** RES HUM job improvement

améliorations *f pl* IMMOB improvements

amélioré, e *adj* INFO enhanced, V&M upgraded

améliorer 1. *vt* COM upgrade, *situation, traduction* improve, INFO tweak, *machine* upgrade; **2.** *v pron* **s'~** (ANT *empirer*), COM take a turn for the better

aménagement: ~ **du commerce** *m* COM, IMMOB trade fixture; ~ **de l'environnement** *m* ENVIR environmental planning; ~ **portuaire** *m* TRANSP port layout; ~ **de poste** *m* RES HUM job enrichment; ~ **au quai** *m* TRANSP *conteneurs* quay fitting; ~ **du territoire** *m* ECON, ENVIR, PROT SOC land-use planning, town and country planning (*UK*); ~ **d'unité planifiée** *m* IMMOB planned unit development, PUD

aménagements *m pl* IMMOB amenities

aménager *vt* ENVIR landscape, IMMOB *bureau* landscape (*jarg*)

amende *f* DROIT fine, penalty, RES HUM fine; ~ **illimitée** COM, DROIT unlimited fine; ~ **non limitée** COM, DROIT unlimited fine

amendement *m* DROIT, POL amendment; ~ **provisoire** DROIT, POL draft amendment; ~ **raisonné** POL reasoned amendment

amender *vt* DROIT, POL *loi, contrat* amend

amener *vt* COM bring; ◆ ~ **à la grève** RES HUM bring out on strike

amenuisement: ~ **de la demande** *m* V&M contraction of demand

américain, e *adj* COM American

Américain, e *m,f* COM *habitant* American

Américains: **les ~** *m pl* COM the Americans

American: ~ **Stock Exchange** *m* BOURSE New York Curb Exchange (*US*), AMEX

Amérique:[1] **d'~ du Nord** *adj* COM North American; **d'~ du Sud** *adj* COM South American

Amérique[2] *f* COM America; ~ **centrale** COM Central America; ~ **du Nord** COM North America; ~ **du Sud** COM South America

AMEX *f* (*American Stock Exchange*) BOURSE, FIN AMEX, ASE

AMF *abrév* (*accord multi-fibres*) ECON MFA (*Multi-Fibre Arrangement*)

amiable[1] *adj* COM, RES HUM amicable; ◆ **à l'~** COM, DROIT amicably, by mutual consent, by private contract

amiable:[2] ~ **compositeur** *m* COM, DROIT, IND, RES HUM arbitrator

amical, e *adj* COM, RES HUM amicable

Amis: ~ **de la Terre** *m pl* ENVIR ≈ FOE, ≈ Friends of the Earth

AMM *abrév* BOURSE (*adhérent mainteneur de marché*) market maker (*UK*), V&M (*autorisation de mise sur le marché*) industrie pharmaceutique marketing authorization

Amman *n pr* COM Amman

amont: **en ~** *loc* (ANT *en aval*) COM upstream

amorçage *m* INFO booting, bootup; ~ **automatique** INFO autoboot; ~ **de pompe** ECON pump priming

amorce *f* MÉDIA standfirst (*jarg*); ~ **à capot et tige** TRANSP *marchandises dangereuses* cap-type primer

amorcer *vt* INFO boot up, bootstrap (*jarg*); ◆ ~ **un mouvement** COM set sth in motion

amorti, e *adj* BOURSE, COMPTA redeemed

amortir 1. *vt* BANQUE amortize, BOURSE *action* redeem, COM *emprunt* redeem, *son, choc* absorb, COMPTA charge off, depreciate, *actif* amortize, *dette* liquidate, ECON depreciate, FIN amortize; **2.** *v pron* **s'~** COMPTA write off; ◆ **s'~ sur dix ans** COMPTA write off over ten years

amortissable *adj* BOURSE red., redeemable, COMPTA amortizable, red., redeemable

amortissement *m* BOURSE *d'action* redemption, COM *d'emprunt* redemption, *de son, choc* absorption, COMPTA amortization, amortizement, depreciation, ECON capital consumption, depletion, depreciation, FIN amortization, amortizement; ~ **accéléré** *m* COMPTA, FIN accelerated cost recovery system, accelerated depreciation, ACRS; ~ **accumulé** *m* COMPTA accumulated depreciation; ~ **annuel** *m* COM, COMPTA annual depreciation; ~ **comptable** *m* COMPTA book depreciation; ~ **constant** *m* COMPTA straight-line amortization, straight-line depreciation; ~ **dégressif** *m* COMPTA, FIN accelerated cost recovery system, accelerated depreciation, declining balance depreciation, reducing balance, ACRS; ~ **dégressif double** *m* COMPTA double declining balance; ~ **dérogatoire** *m* COMPTA, FISC exceptional depreciation, tax-based depreciation; ~ **de l'écart de première consolidation** *m* COMPTA goodwill amortization; ~ **économique franc** *m* FIN free depreciation; ~ **d'un emprunt** *m* BANQUE, COM, COMPTA, FIN amortization of a loan; ~ **du fonds de commerce** *m* COMPTA goodwill amortization; ~ **des immobilisations** *m* COMPTA accumulated depreciation; ~ **linéaire** *m* COMPTA straight-line amortization, straight-line depreciation; ~ **négatif** *m* FIN negative amortization; ~ **par classes hétérogènes** *m* FIN composite depreciation; ~ **récupérable** *m* COMPTA recapturable depreciation

ampleur *f* BOURSE *du marché* breadth

amplification *f* ECON intensification

amplitude: ~ **de fluctuation** *f* BOURSE degree of fluctuation

ampoule *f* COM ampoule

amuser *vt* COM *client* entertain

an *m* COM year, yr; ◆ **depuis un ~ environ** COM

over the last year or so; **par ~** *(p.a.)* COM per annum *(p.a.)*; **sur un ~** COM over one year

analogie: **~ entre deux cas** *f* DROIT on all fours *(jarg)*

analogique *adj* COM analogical, INFO analog, analogical; **~ -numérique** INFO analog-digital, A/D

analogue *f* COM, INFO analog

analyse *f* COM, COMPTA, GESTION analysis, INFO scanning, RES HUM analysis; **~ d'activité** TRANSP activity analysis; **~ de l'année de base** ECON, FIN base year analysis; **~ approfondie** COM in-depth analysis; **~ des aptitudes** RES HUM skills analysis; **~ de l'arborescence des défaillances** COM fault tree analysis; **~ d'article** MATH item analysis; **~ des besoins** V&M needs analysis; **~ des besoins en formation** COM, RES HUM, V&M training needs analysis; **~ des billets** TRANSP ticket analysis; **~ budgétaire** COMPTA, ECON, FIN, POL budget analysis; **~ chartiste** BOURSE chartism; **~ du chemin critique** ECON critical path analysis, CPA; **~ chronologique** COM analysis of time series, ECON time series analysis; **~ commerciale** FIN commercial analysis; **~ comptable** COMPTA accounting analysis; **~ d'un compte** BANQUE account analysis; **~ des concurrents** V&M competitor analysis; **~ de confluence** MATH confluence analysis, CA; **~ de conjoncture** COM analysis of time series; **~ coût-rendement** ECON social profit; **~ du coût de la vie** ECON, FIN base year analysis; **~ des coûts** COMPTA, FIN cost analysis, value engineering; **~ coûts-avantages** FIN cost-benefit analysis; **~ des coûts de distribution** V&M distribution cost analysis; **~ coûts-rendements** FIN cost-benefit analysis; **~ coûts-volume-profits** COMPTA, FIN cost-volume-profit analysis; **~ de crédit** BANQUE, BOURSE credit analysis; **~ du cycle de vie** V&M life-cycle analysis; **~ de la décision** GESTION decision analysis; **~ différentielle** GESTION differential analysis; **~ de la distribution de transport** TRANSP transport distribution analysis, TDA; **~ des données passagers** TRANSP passenger analysis; **~ dynamique** COM dynamic evaluation; **~ des écarts** COMPTA variance analysis; **~ d'écarts** BANQUE gap analysis; **~ des écarts de coûts** COMPTA analysis of cost variances; **~ de l'échec** GESTION failure analysis; **~ économique** ECON, FIN economic analysis; **~ électronique des données** INFO electronic data processing; **~ d'entrée/sortie** ECON, FIN, IND, INFO, MATH input/output analysis; **~ de l'environnement** GESTION environmental analysis; **~ d'équilibre général** ECON general equilibrium analysis; **~ d'équilibre partiel** ECON partial equilibrium analysis; **~ des facteurs de profit** COM, FIN profit-factor analysis; **~ factorielle** MATH factor analysis; **~ financière** FIN financial analysis, securities analysis; **~ fonctionnelle** COM, INFO functional analysis, systems analysis; **~ fondamentale** FIN fundamental analysis; **~ des forces, des faiblesses, des**

opportunités et des menaces COM, V&M strengths, weaknesses, opportunities and threats analysis, SWOT; **~ horaire** TRANSP timetable analysis; **~ des intrants et des entrants** MATH input/output analysis; **~ des intrants et des extrants** ECON, FIN, IND, INFO input/output analysis; **~ intrants-extrants** ECON, FIN, IND, INFO, MATH input/output analysis; **~ d'investissements** BOURSE, COMPTA, ECON, FIN, V&M investment analysis; **~ des lacunes** COMPTA weakness investigation; **~ des marchandises** BOURSE commodity analysis *(UK)*; **~ de marché** BOURSE market analysis; **~ des marchés** V&M market research; **~ marginale** COM incremental analysis, COMPTA incremental analysis, marginal analysis, ECON, FIN *de la valeur marchande* marginal analysis, FISC, GESTION incremental analysis; **~ des matières premières** BOURSE commodity analysis *(UK)*; **~ matricielle** ECON matrix analysis; **~ des médias** MÉDIA, V&M media analysis; **~ des méthodes** COM process analysis; **~ modulée** GESTION differential analysis; **~ morphologique** FIN, MATH morphological analysis; **~ de motivation** V&M motivational analysis; **~ des motivations** RES HUM motivational analysis; **~ d'opérations** IND, RES HUM operational analysis; **~ organique** INFO systems design; **~ par poste de travail** RES HUM job analysis; **~ par secteur d'activité** COM business segment reporting, COMPTA business segment reporting, segmental reporting, GESTION business segment reporting; **~ par segments** V&M *étude de marché* cluster analysis; **~ de Pareto** COM Pareto analysis; **~ du point mort** BOURSE, COMPTA, ECON, FIN, V&M break-even analysis; **~ de poste** RES HUM job analysis, job study; **~ de poste professionnel** RES HUM occupational analysis; **~ pourcentuelle** MATH percentage analysis; **~ préalable** INFO feasibility report; **~ de problèmes** GESTION, MATH problem analysis; **~ de produit** V&M product analysis; **~ en profondeur** GESTION depth analysis; **~ de qualification** RES HUM skills analysis; **~ qualitative** GESTION, IND, MATH, V&M *étude de marché* qualitative analysis; **~ quantitative** GESTION, IND, MATH, V&M *étude de marché* quantitative analysis; **~ quantitative du travail** COM, RES HUM work measurement; **~ de rapport** MATH ratio analysis; **~ du rapport coût-efficacité** BOURSE, COMPTA, ECON, FIN, V&M cost-effectiveness analysis; **~ de régression** MATH regression analysis; **~ de régression multiple** ECON, FIN, MATH multiple regression analysis, MRA; **~ de régularité** TRANSP punctuality analysis; **~ relationnelle** RES HUM relations analysis; **~ de rentabilité** BOURSE, COMPTA, ECON, FIN, V&M break-even analysis, cost-effectiveness analysis, profitability analysis; **~ de réseau** GESTION, INFO network analysis; **~ rétrospective** INFO audit trail; **~ des revenus** COMPTA fee split; **~ des risques** FIN risk analysis; **~ des risques commerciaux** FIN commercial risk analysis *(UK)*; **~ des risques liés au portefeuille** FIN

Standard Portfolio Analysis of Risk, SPAR; **~ de route** TRANSP route analysis; **~ sectorielle** COM circulation breakdown, sector analysis; **~ de sensibilité** FIN, MATH sensitivity analysis; **~ de la sensibilité du résultat** COMPTA profit sensitivity analysis; **~ séquentielle** FIN, MATH, V&M sequential analysis; **~ de la situation** FIN horizon analysis; **~ d'une situation comptable** COMPTA statement analysis; **~ sociale** PROT SOC, V&M social analysis; **~ des systèmes** COM, INFO systems analysis; **~ des tâches** RES HUM job analysis, operations analysis; **~ technique** BOURSE technical analysis; **~ de tendance** ECON trend analysis; **~ du trafic** TRANSP traffic analysis; **~ des trajets** TRANSP trip analysis; **~ transactionnelle** BANQUE, COM, COMPTA, ECON, FIN, GESTION transactional analysis, TA; **~ du travail** RES HUM operations analysis; **~ à travers plusieurs exercices** COMPTA horizontal analysis; **~ des utilisateurs de conteneur** TRANSP container user analysis; **~ de valeur** COMPTA, FIN value analysis, VA, value engineering, V&M *marketing* value analysis, VA; **~ de variance** COMPTA, MATH *statistique* variance analysis; **~ de variance à deux sens** MATH two-way variance analysis; **~ à variantes multiples** MATH multivariate analysis; **~ des ventes** V&M sales analysis; **~ des ventes au détail** V&M retail sales analysis; **~ verticale** COMPTA vertical analysis; ◆ **faire l'~ de** COM analyse (*BrE*), analyze (*AmE*)

analyser *vt* COM *ventes, coûts, résultats* analyse (*BrE*), analyze (*AmE*)

analyseur *m* INFO analyser (*BrE*), analyzer (*AmE*)

analyste *mf* BANQUE, BOURSE credit analyst, GESTION analyst, INFO analyst, problem solver, programmer, RES HUM analyst, programmer; **~ commercial** *m* RES HUM sales analyst; **~ de l'environnement** *m* ENVIR environmental scanner; **~ d'investissements** *m* BOURSE, FIN investment analyst; **~ -marché** *m* BOURSE, RES HUM, V&M market analyst; **~ pétrolier** *m* IND oil analyst; **~ de placements** *m* BOURSE, FIN investment analyst; **~ -programmeur** *m* INFO program analyst; **~ des risques maritimes** *m* RES HUM marine risk analyst; **~ système confirmé** *m* INFO senior systems analyst; **~ de systèmes** *m* INFO systems analyst; **~ des ventes** *m* RES HUM sales analyst

analytique *adj* COM, IND, INFO, MATH analytic, analytical

anarchie: **~ de la production** *f* POL anarchy of production

anarchisme *m* POL anarchism

anarcho-communisme *m* POL anarcho-communism

anarcho-syndicalisme *m* POL anarcho-syndicalism

ancêtre *mf* COM ancestor

ancien[1], **-enne** *adj* COM old, quondam (*frml*)

ancien:[2] **~ affrètement** *m* TRANSP *maritime* old charter, OC; **~ client** *m* V&M former customer;

~ droit *m* DROIT old law; **~ employé** *m* RES HUM ex-employee; **~ numéro** *m* MÉDIA *édition* back issue, back number

ancienne: **~ loi** *f* DROIT old law

ancienneté *f* RES HUM seniority, seniority system; ◆ **avoir de l'~** RES HUM be senior

ancrage *m* TRANSP anchorage

ancre *f* TRANSP *d'un navire* anchor; **~ à draguer** TRANSP *d'un navire* dredging anchor; **~ flottante** TRANSP *d'un navire* drag anchor, sea anchor

andorran, e *adj* COM Andorran

Andorran, e *m,f* COM *habitant* Andorran

Andorre[1] *f* COM Andorra

Andorre:[2] **~ -la-Vieille** *n pr* COM Andorra la Vella

anecdotique *adj* DROIT *preuve, témoignage*, PROT SOC anecdotal

ange: **~ déchu** *m* BOURSE fallen angel

anglais[1], **e** *adj* COM English

anglais[2] *m* COM *langue* English; **~ du Canada** COM *langue* Canadian English; **~ comme langue étrangère** PROT SOC English as a Foreign Language, EFL

Anglais *m* COM *habitant* Englishman; **les ~** *m pl* COM the English

Anglaise *f* COM *habitant* Englishwoman

angle *m* MATH angle; **~ d'attaque** COM line of attack; **~ de dégagement** TRANSP *manutention* included angle; **~ naturel de repos** TRANSP angle of repose; **~ de repos** TRANSP angle of repose

Angleterre *f* COM England

anglo: **~ -français** *adj* COM Anglo-French

Angola *m* COM Angola

angolais, e *adj* COM Angolan

Angolais, e *m,f* COM *habitant* Angolan

animateur, -trice *m,f* GESTION mover and shaker (*infrml*), MÉDIA front (*jarg*), *radio, télévision* announcer; **~ de groupe** RES HUM accompanying adult, group leader

animation: **~ à bord** *f* LOISIRS, TRANSP on-board entertainment; **~ des ventes** *f* V&M sales drive

animaux: **~ vivants à bord** *loc* TRANSP *aviation* live animals on board, LAB

animé, e *adj* BOURSE *marché* active, COM *marché* brisk, ECON *currency* buoyant

animer *vt* COM, RES HUM motivate

Ankara *n pr* COM Ankara

anneau: **~ de saisissage** *m* TRANSP *arrimage* lashing eye

année[1] *f* COM year, yr; **~ d'acquisition** COMPTA year of acquisition; **~ de base** ECON, FIN base year; **~ de base de calcul** BOURSE base date; **~ bissextile** COM leap year; **~ budgétaire** ECON, FIN, FISC, POL financial year, fiscal year, FY; **~ civile** COM calendar year; **~ complète d'imposition** FISC full taxation year; **~ en cours** COM current year; **~ difficile** ECON lean year; **~ d'émission** BOURSE year of issue; **~ d'étalement** FISC year of averaging; **~ d'évaluation** FISC year of assessment;

~ **exceptionnelle** COM banner year, bumper year; ~ **fiscale** COM natural business year, tax year; ~ **d'imposition** FISC taxable year, taxation year; ~ **d'imposition antérieure** FISC preceding taxation year; ~ **à imposition restreinte** FISC short taxation year; ~ **initiale** FISC initial year; **l'~ considérée** COM the year under review; ~ **non-imposable** FISC nontaxable year; ~ **de l'obligation** FISC bond year basis; ~ **précédente** COM preceding year, previous year; ~ **privilégiée à court terme** FISC short taxation year; ~ **de référence** ECON, FIN base year; ~ **sans revenu imposable** FISC nontaxable year; ~ **de vaches maigres** ECON lean year; ♦ **chaque** ~ COM annually, each year, every year; **d'une** ~ **à l'autre** COM year-to-year; **d'une** ~ **sur l'autre** COM year-to-year; **dans l'~ précédent** COM in the year to; **dans les dix** ~s **qui ont précédé 1995** COM in the decade to 1995; **depuis les dix dernières** ~s COM over the last decade; **une** ~ **accomplie** COM one year completed

année:[2] **l'~ dernière à la même époque** *loc* COM this time last year

années:[1] ~ **accomplies** *f pl* FISC whole years; ~ **complètes** *f pl* FISC whole years; ~ **limites du plan** *f pl* ECON planning horizon

années:[2] **pendant les** ~ **soixante** *loc* COM in the sixties

annexe[1] *adj* DROIT appurtenant

annexe[2] *f* COM appendix, *bâtiment, document* annex (*AmE*), annexe (*BrE*), COMPTA notes to the financial statements, DROIT addendum, annex (*AmE*), annexe (*BrE*), MÉDIA addendum, appendix; ~ **à porter sur les comptes** COMPTA notes to the accounts; ♦ **en** ~ COMMS joined (*AmE*), subjoined

annexer *vt* COM annex, append, INFO append

anniversaire *m* COM, COMMS, MÉDIA anniversary

annonce *f* COM ad (*infrml*), advert (*infrml*), *information* announcement, MÉDIA, V&M *publicité* ad (*infrml*), advert (*infrml*), advertisement; ~ **d'apparence rédactionnelle** V&M *publicité dans la presse* advertorial (*jarg*); ~ **attrape-nigaud** V&M bait advertising (*US*); ~ **classée** MÉDIA, V&M classified ad (*infrml*), classified advert (*infrml*), classified advertisement; ~ **à énigme** V&M teaser ad; ~ **mensongère** V&M false advertising claim; ~ **par voie de presse** V&M press advertisement; ~ **publicitaire** COM ad (*infrml*), advert (*infrml*), MÉDIA, V&M ad (*infrml*), advert (*infrml*), advertisement; ~ **radiophonique** MÉDIA radio announcement

annoncé: comme ~ *loc* MÉDIA as reported

annoncer *vt* COM *réduction* announce, MÉDIA *télévision* trail, V&M *bill*; ♦ ~ **la nouvelle** MÉDIA break the news

annonceur, -euse *m,f* MÉDIA *radio, télévision* announcer, V&M advertiser

annoter *vt* ADMIN annotate, write sth in the margin of

annuaire *m* COM, INFO directory, MÉDIA yearbook; ~ **du commerce** COM, V&M trade directory; ~ **de données commerciales de base** ECON Trade Data Elements Directory, TDED; ~ **électronique spécialisé** BOURSE Specialist Electronic Book (*US*), SEB (*US*); ~ **général des annonceurs** V&M standard directory of advertisers; ~ **par profession ou par entreprise** FIN Red Book (*US, infrml*); ~ **de statistiques** ECON, MATH annual abstract of statistics; ~ **téléphonique** COMMS phone book, telephone book, telephone directory

annualiser *vt* COM annualize

annuel, -elle *adj* BANQUE annual, COM annual, yearly, COMPTA, FIN annual

annuellement *adv* BANQUE, COM, COMPTA, FIN annually, on an annual basis, yearly

annuité *f* COM, COMPTA, FIN annual installment (*AmE*), annual instalment (*BrE*), RES HUM annuity; ~ **d'amortissement** ASSUR annual amortization; ~ **d'assurance** ASSUR insurance annuity; ~ **complémentaire** FIN wraparound annuity; ~ **conditionnelle** FIN qualifying annuity; ~ **différée à prime unique** FIN single-premium deferred annuity; ~ **non-statutaire** FIN nonqualifying annuity; ~ **de remboursement** BANQUE, COM annual repayment

annulable *adj* DROIT voidable

annulation *f* ASSUR avoidance, BOURSE cancellation, COM write-off, *d'une décision* annulment, *d'une commande, d'un ordre, d'un projet* cancellation, *d'un accord, d'un contrat* invalidation, voidance, COMPTA *d'une dette* deletion, write-off, writing off, DROIT *d'un contrat* annulment, invalidation, *d'une ordonnance, d'un verdict* quashing, *d'un jugement* quashing, *d'une loi* rescission, FIN revocation, FISC *d'une amende* abatement, GESTION overruling, INFO cancellation, POL *d'une décision* overruling, TRANSP avoidance, V&M cancellation; ~ **de crédits** COMPTA lapsing appropriation; ~ **partielle** BREVETS, COM, DROIT part cancellation; ~ **de prime** ASSUR cancellation of premium; ~ **de titres** BOURSE securities cancellation

annule: qui ~ *adj* COM annulling

annuler 1. *vt* BOURSE cancel, COM override, write off, *accord, contrat* invalidate, void, *commande, ordre, projet* cancel, COMPTA *dette* delete, write off, DROIT *acte* abate, *contrat* annul, invalidate, *décision* annul, *loi* repeal, rescind, *ordonnance, verdict* quash, FIN revoke, FISC *amende* abate, GESTION overrule, INFO cancel, POL *décision* overrule, TRANSP avoid, V&M cancel; **2.** *v pron* **s'~** COM cancel out

anomalie *f* COM anomaly, fault, irregularity, INFO fault, trouble

anomie *f* RES HUM anomie

anonymat *m* COM anonymity

anonyme *adj* COM *don* anonymous

anormal, e *adj* COM abnormal

ANPE *abrév* France (*Agence nationale pour*

l'emploi) RES HUM ≈ Employment Service (*UK*), ≈ Jobcentre (*UK*)

ANSEA *abrév* (*Association des nations du Sud-Est asiatique*) ECON ASEAN (*Association of South-East Asian Nations*)

Antananarivo *n pr* COM Tananarivo

antécédents *m pl* ADMIN track record, COM, PROT SOC, RES HUM previous history, track record; ~ **financiers** FIN financial history; ~ **en matière de crédit** BANQUE credit history

antémémoire *f* INFO cache, cache buffer, cache memory, cache storage, cache store

antenne: ~ **financière** *f* BANQUE money desk; ~ **sur le terrain** *f* COM field organization

anticipation *f* COM, ECON anticipation, expectation, V&M anticipation; ~ **des prix** ECON, V&M anticipatory pricing; ~ **stratégique** COM, ECON anticipatory response

anticipations: ~ **exogènes** *f pl* ECON exogenous expectations; ~ **inflationnistes** *f pl* ECON inflationary expectations; ~ **keynésiennes** *f pl* ECON Keynes' expectations; ~ **par extrapolation** *f pl* ECON extrapolative expectations; ~ **rationnelles** *f pl* ECON rational expectations, RE

anticipé, e *adj* BOURSE before due date, COM in advance

anticiper *vt* COM *paiement* anticipate; ♦ ~ **l'action de** COM second-guess (*infrml*)

anticoncurrentiel, -elle *adj* COM anticompetitive

anticyclique *adj* ECON anticyclical

antidatation *f* COM *officiel* antedating, backdating, predating

antidaté, e *adj* COM antedated, backdated, predated

antidater *vt* COM antedate, backdate, predate

antidumping *m* ENVIR, POL antidumping

Antigua:[1] **d'~** *adj* COM Antiguan

Antigua[2] *f* COM Antigua; ~ **et Barbuda** COM Antigua and Barbuda

anti-inflationniste *adj* ECON, POL anti-inflationary

antiréfléchissant, e *adj* INFO glare-free

antirequins *m pl* FIN porcupine provisions, shark repellents

antisélection *f* ASSUR adverse selection

antisyndicalisme *m* RES HUM union-bashing (*infrml*)

antivol *m* COM, TRANSP antitheft device

ANU *abrév* (*Association des Nations Unies*) ADMIN UNA (*United Nations Association*)

ANVAR *abrév* (*Agence nationale pour la valorisation de la recherche*) ADMIN national development research centre

AOC *abrév* (*appellation d'origine contrôlée*) COM guaranteed quality label

août *m* COM Aug., August

AP *abrév* (*l'Assistance publique*) PROT SOC authority which manages state-owned hospitals and Social Services

apaiser *vt* COM, POL, RES HUM conciliate, pacify

apathie *f* COM sluggishness

apatride *adj* ADMIN, POL nationless, stateless

APE *abrév* (*Activité principale de l'entreprise*) COM number giving company's main business

aperçu *m* COM outline, overview; ~ **avant impression** INFO print preview; ~ **du marché** BOURSE market view; ~ **stratégique** POL strategic overview

apériteur *m* ASSUR leader, BANQUE managing underwriter, FIN leading underwriter

aphorisme *m* COM aphorism

aplanir *vt* COM *difficultés* iron out, smooth out

aplatir: **s'~** *v pron* MATH flatten

a posteriori *loc* COM a posteriori

appareil *m* COM apparatus, appliance, COMMS phone, telephone, IND apparatus, appliance; ~ **de chauffage** COM heater, htr; ~ **électrique** COM electrical appliance; ~ **de forage** ENVIR *machinery* tour de forage (*frml*); ~ **de levage droit** TRANSP *manutention* straight lift; ~ **ménager** COM household appliance, white good, V&M household appliance; ~ **de mise à niveau** TRANSP *manutention* dock leveler (*AmE*), dock leveller (*BrE*); ~ **de surveillance** INFO monitor; ♦ ~ **en service** INFO busy

appareillage: ~ **audiovisuel** *m* V&M audiovisual goods

appareiller *vi* TRANSP leave port

apparentée: **personne** ~ *f* FISC *actions privilégiées imposables* specified person

apparié: ~ **à** *adj* COM, INFO coupled with

appartement *m* IMMOB apartment (*AmE*), flat (*BrE*); ~ **occupé** IMMOB immediate occupancy; ~ **en rez-de-jardin** IMMOB garden apartment (*AmE*), garden flat (*BrE*); ~ **-témoin** IMMOB show flat

appartenance: ~ **non obligatoire à un syndicat** *f* RES HUM open shop

appartenir: *vt* ~ **à** COM belong to, RES HUM belong

appauvri, e *adj* FIN impoverished

appauvrissement: ~ **paradoxal** *m* ECON, PROT SOC poverty trap

appel *m* COM appeal, COMMS call, DROIT appeal, FIN *de fonds, d'offre* call, INFO *d'un sous-programme* call, polling; ~ **argenté** BOURSE in-the-money call; ~ **en attente** COMMS, INFO call waiting, cw; ~ **automatique** COMMS direct call; ~ **avec préavis** COMMS personal call; ~ **de capitaux** BOURSE capital raising, FIN capital raising, capital-raising operation; ~ **carte de crédit** COMMS credit card call; ~ **de départ** COMMS outgoing call; ~ **de l'extérieur** COMMS incoming call; ~ **de fonds** FIN appeal for funds, fund-raising; ~ **à frais virés** Can (*cf appel en PCV Fra*) COMMS collect call (*AmE*), reverse charge call (*BrE*), transfer charge call; ~ **gratuit** (*cf appel sans frais Can*) COMMS Freefone call® (*BrE*), toll-free call (*AmE*); ~ **d'impôts** FISC tax appeal;

~ **international** COMMS international call; ~ **international automatique** COMMS international direct dialing (*AmE*), international direct dialling (*BrE*), IDD; ~ **interurbain** COMMS long-distance call, toll call (*US*); ~ **interurbain gratuit** (*cf appel sans frais Can*) COMMS Freefone call® (*BrE*), toll-free call (*AmE*); ~ **local** COMMS local call; ~ **longue distance** COMMS long-distance call, toll call (*US*); ~ **de marge** BOURSE margin, margin call, margin maintenance; ~ **de marge du jour** BOURSE mark to market, value to the market; ~ **de marge-réapprovisionner au niveau initial** BOURSE *négoce de devise* margin call-replenish to initial level; ~ **de marge pour reconstituer l'apport initial** BOURSE *négoce de devises* margin call-replenish to initial level; ~ **d'offres** ADMIN, COM *pour un marché* appeal for tenders, call for bids, call for tenders, DROIT invitation to tender; ~ **d'offres ouvert** V&M advertised bidding; ~ **en PCV** *Fra* (*cf appel à frais virés Can*) COMMS collect call (*AmE*), reverse charge call (*BrE*), transfer charge call; ~ **de personnes** COMMS paging; ~ **à prix partagé** COMMS local charge rate call, local charge rate trunk call; ~ **public à l'épargne** BOURSE public issue; ~ **publicitaire générique** V&M generic appeal; ~ **publicitaire de masse** V&M mass appeal; ~ **au rachat** BOURSE redemption call; ~ **de rendez-vous** COMMS reminder call; ~ **resté sans réponse** COMMS unanswered call; ~ **sans frais** *Can* (*SYN appel gratuit, appel interurbain gratuit*) COMMS Freefone call® (*BrE*), toll-free call (*AmE*); ~ **sans réponse** COMMS unanswered call; ~ **sélectif numérique** COMMS digital selective calling, DSC; ~ **téléphonique** COMMS phone call, telephone call; ~ **à trois** COMMS three-way call (*AmE*); ~ **d'urgence** COMMS emergency call; ◆ **à l'~ du marché** BOURSE at the market call; ~ **automatique longue distance** COMMS DDD (*AmE*), direct distance dialing (*AmE*), STD (*BrE*), subscriber trunk dialling (*BrE*); **faire ~** DROIT appeal, enter an appeal; **faire ~ au marché pour** BOURSE tap the market for; **faire ~ d'une décision** DROIT appeal against a judgement; **faire ~ public à l'épargne** BOURSE go public; **faire un ~ d'offres** COM appeal for tenders; **faire un ~ de fonds** COM appeal for funds; **sur ~** INFO on a per call basis

appeler *vt* COMMS call, call up, phone, LOISIRS *théâtre* call (*jarg*); ~ **à frais virés** *Can* (*cf appeler en PCV, téléphoner en PCV Fra*) COMMS make a collect call (*AmE*), make a reverse charge call to sb (*BrE*); ~ **en PCV** (*cf appeler à frais virés Can*) COMMS make a collect call (*AmE*), make a reverse charge call to sb (*BrE*); ◆ ~ **à la grève** RES HUM call a strike; ~ **d'un jugement** DROIT appeal against a judgement; ~ **qn par l'interphone** COMMS call sb over the intercom; ~ **qn par numéro vert** COMMS call sb toll-free (*AmE*), make a freephone call to sb (*BrE*); ~ **qn en PCV** COMMS call sb collect (*AmE*); ~ **au remboursement** BAN-

QUE call; ~ **des valeurs au remboursement** COMPTA call securities for redemption

appellation: ~ **d'origine contrôlée** *f* (*AOC*) COM *of wine* label guaranteeing quality

appendice *m* COM, MÉDIA appendix

applicabilité *f* COM appropriateness

applicable *adj* (*ANT inapplicable*) DROIT enforceable; ◆ ~ **à** COM applicable to; **être ~** COM come into force

applicatif *m* INFO *programme* applications program

application *f* COM application, DROIT application, *d'une loi* admin, administration, INFO application, *programme* applications program; ~ **à une année antérieure** COMPTA, FISC *déduction* carry-back; ~ **des cours cotés hors de la séance précédente** BOURSE put through; ~ **extraterritoriale** DROIT extraterritorial enforcement; ~ **industrielle** BREVETS, IND exploitation in industry, industrial application; ~ **du label écologique communautaire** ENVIR ecolabeling (*AmE*), ecolabelling (*BrE*); ~ **logicielle** INFO software application; ~ **des stratégies** COM, GESTION strategy implementation; ◆ **pour l'~** FISC *en début de paragraphe* in applying

applique: **ne s'~ pas** *loc* COM n/a, not applicable

appliquer 1. *vt* COM, COMPTA apply, DROIT *loi* apply, enforce; **2.** *v pron* **s'~** COM apply; **s'~ à** COM concentrate on, INFO apply to

appoint *m* COM *monnaie* exact change; ◆ **faire l'~** COM make up, make up the odd money; **faire l'~ à** COM *économies, finances* top up (*UK*)

apport *m* COM *financier, personnel* contribution, FIN capital contribution, GESTION benefit; ~ **de capital** FIN capital contribution, contribution of capital; ~ **chimique** ENVIR chemical input; ~ **commercial** COM patronage; ~ **en espèces** COMPTA *investissement* cash contribution; ~ **de gestion** FIN, GESTION management buy-in; ~ **de main-d'oeuvre** RES HUM additional labor (*AmE*), additional labour (*BrE*); ◆ **faire un ~** COM *en capital* make a contribution

apporter *vt* COM *fonds* contribute, DROIT *preuve* adduce; ◆ ~ **une aide à** BANQUE, ECON, POL *pays* aid; ~ **une contribution à** COM *oeuvre, programme* make a contribution to; ~ **des éléments sur** COM carry information on

apporteur, -euse *m,f* ASSUR acquisition agent; ~ **de capitaux** COM contributor of capital

apposer *vt* COM affix, append (*frml*), COMMS affix; ◆ ~ **la date au tampon** ADMIN stamp the date; ~ **sa signature** COM append (*frml*), sign, subscribe; ~ **son sceau sur qch** COM put one's seal to sth

appréciable *adj* COM appreciable

appréciation *f* COM assessment; ~ **d'une devise** ECON, FIN currency appreciation; ~ **des investissements** BOURSE, COMPTA, ECON, FIN investment appraisal; ~ **limitée** BOURSE limited discretion; ~ **du mérite** COM, RES HUM merit rating; **~ monétaire** ECON, FIN currency appreciation; **~ d'une monnaie** ECON, FIN currency appreciation; **~ du personnel** GESTION staff appraisal, RES HUM personnel rating, staff appraisal; **~ restreinte** BOURSE *ordre* limited discretion; **~ des risques** FIN risk assessment

apprécier *vt* COM appreciate

apprendre *vti* COM, PROT SOC, RES HUM learn; ◆ **~ qch de manière indirecte** COM hear sth through the grapevine; **~ que** COM receive notice of

apprenti, e *m,f* RES HUM apprentice; **~-programmeur** INFO trainee programmer

apprentissage *m* RES HUM apprenticeship; **~ à distance** PROT SOC distance learning; **~ à une épreuve** PROT SOC one-trial learning; **~ des langues assisté par ordinateur** INFO, PROT SOC computer-aided language learning, computer-assisted language learning, CALL; **~ pratique** RES HUM hands-on training; **~ de produit** V&M product initiation; **~ sur le tas** ECON learning-by-doing; ◆ **être en ~ chez qn** RES HUM be apprenticed to sb

apprentissages: ~ communs *m pl* PROT SOC common learnings

approbation *f* COM acceptance, approval, COMPTA *des comptes* approval, ECON adoption, V&M endorsement; **~ de comptes** COMPTA, FIN accounts certification; **~ modérée** COM qualified approval; **~ de projet** COM project approval; ◆ **pour ~** COM for approval

approche *f* COM *client, problème* approach; **~ bayesienne à la prise de décision** GESTION Bayesian approach to decision-making; **~ bouddhiste de l'économie** ECON Buddhist economics; **~ des excédents** ECON surplus approach, surplus value; **~ monétariste** ECON monetarist approach; **~ par les coûts** FIN, IMMOB cost approach; **~ par l'enquête** FISC *des vérifications sur place* investigative approach; **~ par la théorie des systèmes** INFO systems approach; **~ du produit** V&M *marketing* commodity approach; **~ pyramidale d'investissement** FIN bottom-up approach to investing, breakpoint sale; **~ qualitative** BOURSE qualitative approach; **~ quantitative** ADMIN quantification; **~ de rendement** IMMOB income approach; **~ systématique du développement** ECON world systems perspective

approcher *vt* MATH approximate; **~ de** MATH approximate

approfondi, e *adj* COM in-depth

approfondir *vt* COM *recherches, étude* extend

appropriation *f* DROIT *de fonds,* FIN appropriation

approprié, e *adj* COM appropriate

approprier: s'~ *v pron* DROIT, FIN appropriate

approuvé, e *adj* ADMIN, ASSUR, COM approved

approuver *vt* ADMIN approve, COM adopt, agree, approve, be in favor of (*AmE*), be in favour of (*BrE*), POL approve, pass; ◆ **~ les comptes** COM, COMPTA agree the books

approvisionnement *m* COM procurement, purchasing, sourcing, V&M purchasing; **~ auprès de deux sources** COM dual sourcing; **~ auprès d'une source unique** COM single sourcing; **~ à l'extérieur** GESTION outsourcing; **~ invisible** COM invisible supply

approvisionnements *m pl* COM, ECON, V&M supplies

approvisionner 1. *vt* BANQUE *compte* pay money into, COM stock, V&M supply; **2.** *v pron* **s'~ en** COM buy in, stock up on

approvisionneur: ~ de la marine *m* TRANSP ship's chandler

approximation *f* COM approximation, rough guide

approximativement *adv* COM approx., approximately

appui *m* COM, FIN backing, backup, support; **~ financier** ECON, FIN, POL financial backing; **~ populaire** POL grass-roots support

appuyer *vt* ECON sustain; **~ sur** INFO press

âpre *adj* COM, ECON harsh; **~ au gain** COM acquisitive, grasping, greedy

après:[1] **d'~ -guerre** *adj* ECON postwar; **par ~** *adj* DROIT ex post facto (*frml*); **~ -vente** *adj* V&M after-sales

après[2] *adv* COM afterwards

après:[3] **~ impôts** *m pl* ECON, FIN, FISC after-profits tax

après[4] *prép* COM after; ◆ **~ bourse** BOURSE after-hours, after-market; **d'~** COM according to; **d'~ les règles** BOURSE under the rule (*US, jarg*); **~ examen** COM on examination; **~ faillite** FIN post-bankruptcy; **~ impôts** FISC after-tax; **~ -midi** COM pm, post meridiem

a priori *loc* COM a priori

apte: ~ au travail *adj* RES HUM able to work, employable

aptitude *f* COM capability, competence, RES HUM *professionnelle* aptitude, capacity; **~ à la commercialisation** COM, ECON tradeability; **~ manuelle** IND, RES HUM manual skill; **~ professionnelle** RES HUM aptitude, capacity; **~ à travailler** COM capacity to work

aptitudes: ~ à la communication *f pl* RES HUM communication skills; **~ interpersonnelles** *f pl* RES HUM interpersonal skills; **~ pour le poste** *f pl* RES HUM job skills

apurer *vt* COMPTA *conduisant à la réception d'un quitus* audit, FIN audit, wipe off, TRANSP *permis de transbordement* clear

aquaculture *f* ECON seafarming

arabe[1] *adj* COM Arab, Arabian

arabe[2] *m* COM *langue* Arabic

Arabe *mf* COM *habitant* Arab

Arabie *f* COM Arabia; **~ Saoudite** COM Saudi Arabia

arbitrage *m* BANQUE arbitrage, BOURSE arbitrage trading, arbitrage, hedge, COM, DROIT arbitration, mediation, FIN arbitrage, IND, RES HUM arbitration, mediation; ~ **cash-and-carry** BOURSE cash and carry arbitrage; ~ **de change** FIN arbitration of exchange; ~ **comptant-terme** BOURSE cash and carry arbitrage; ~ **en couverture de risques** BOURSE, FIN hedging operations; ~ **dans le temps** COM time arbitrage; ~ **de la dernière chance** RES HUM last-offer arbitration; ~ **entre obligations à taux différents** BOURSE matrix trading; ~ **de fusion** BOURSE merger arbitrage; ~ **d'indice** BOURSE stock index arbitrage; ~ **interplace** BOURSE exchange arbitrage; ~ **en matière de conflits du travail** RES HUM industrial arbitration; ~ **en matière de salaires** RES HUM wage arbitration; ~ **d'obligations** BOURSE bond switch, bond switching; ~ **obligatoire** DROIT binding arbitration, RES HUM compulsory arbitration (*UK*); ~ **d'office** RES HUM compulsory arbitration (*UK*); ~ **par compensation** RES HUM pendulum arbitration; ~ **par compensations successives** RES HUM flip-flop arbitration; ~ **par médiateur interposé** DROIT, ECON final offer arbitration; ~ **de place à place** BOURSE space arbitrage; ~ **de portefeuille** BOURSE portfolio switching, stock arbitrage, switching, FIN portfolio switching; ~ **qui engage** DROIT binding arbitration; ~ **des risques** BOURSE risk arbitrage; ~ **sur actions** BOURSE stock arbitrage; ~ **sur devises** BOURSE currency arbitrage; ~ **sur titres** BOURSE arbitrage in securities (*UK*); ~ **de valeurs** BOURSE arbitrage in securities (*UK*)

arbitragiste *mf* BOURSE arb, arbitrage dealer, arbitrage trader, arbitrageur, RES HUM arb, arbitrageur; ~ **d'investissement** BOURSE investment hedger; ~ **de place en place** BOURSE shunter

arbitraire *adj* COM ad hoc, arbitrary, FISC arbitrary

arbitral, e *adj* COM arbitral

arbitre *m* BOURSE ombudsman, COM adjudicator, arbitrator, mediator, DROIT arbiter, arbitrator, IND, RES HUM arbitrator; ~ **unique** ASSUR sole arbitrator; ◆ **être ~ de** COM *concours* adjudicate

arbitrer: *vt* ~ **entre** COM mediate between, COM arbitrate, mediate, DROIT, IND arbitrate, RES HUM arbitrate, mediate

arborescence *f* INFO arborescence

arboriculture: ~ **fruitière** *f* ECON *agriculture*, IND fruit farming

arbre: ~ **à cames** *m* TRANSP *navigation* camshaft; ~ **de décision** *m* GESTION, RES HUM decision tree; ~ **généalogique** *m* COM, GESTION family tree; ~ **de pertinence** *m* GESTION pertinence tree; ~ **porte-hélice** *m* TRANSP *d'un navire* tail shaft; ~ **de transmission tubulaire** *m* TRANSP tubeshaft

arc *m* TRANSP *navigation* hogging; ~ **sinus** MATH arc sine, arcsin; ~ **tangente** MATH arc tangent, arctan

architecte *mf* IMMOB architect; ~ **naval** *m* TRANSP naval architect

architecture *f* IMMOB, INFO *conception interne d'un ordinateur* architecture; ~ **de réseau** INFO network architecture; ~ **de réseau de DEC** INFO DECnet®

archivage *m* ADMIN, INFO archiving

archive *f* ADMIN archive, COM record, INFO archive

archiver *vt* ADMIN archive, file, INFO archive

archives *f pl* ADMIN records; ~ **de l'État** COM public records

archiviste *mf* ADMIN archivist, record keeper

argent *m* COM cash, silver, ENVIR silver, FIN money, IND silver; ~ **en caisse** COM, COMPTA cash in hand; ~ **comptant** COM, V&M cash; ~ **devant soi** COM, FIN money up front; ~ **emprunté** BANQUE, FISC borrowed money; ~ **facile** *infrml* ECON easy money; ~ **frais** COM, FIN fresh money; ~ **improductif** *jarg* ECON, FIN idle money; ~ **inconvertible** ECON inconvertible money; ~ **au jour le jour** BANQUE, FIN call money, day-to-day money, demand money, federal funds (*US*), overnight money; ~ **liquide** FIN *monnaie* cash, ready cash, ready money, spot cash; ~ **non-convertible** ECON inconvertible money; ~ **non-déclaré au fisc** FISC black money; ~ **oisif** *jarg* BOURSE idle cash; ~ **personnel** FIN personal money; ~ **de poche** COM pocket money, spending money; ~ **du porte-à-porte** POL street money (*AmE, jarg*); ~ **qui dort** *jarg* ECON, FIN idle money; ~ **solide** ECON hard money; ~ **en trop** COM spare cash; ◆ **avoir de l'~ à ne plus savoir qu'en faire** *infrml* COM have money to burn (*infrml*); **avoir de l'~ disponible** FIN have cash in hand, have cash on hand; **avoir de l'~ en caisse** FIN have cash in hand, have cash on hand; **en avoir pour son ~** ECON get good value for money; **faire de l'~** COM make good (*infrml*), make money

argenté, e *adj* BOURSE in-the-money, ITM

argentin, e *adj* COM Argentine, Argentinian

Argentin, e *m,f* COM *habitant* Argentine, Argentinian

Argentine *f* COM Argentina

argument: ~ **de vente** *m* COM, V&M selling point

argumentaire *m* V&M promotion leaflet, sales portfolio; ~ **de vente** V&M sales presentation, sales talk

Ariel *m* BOURSE Ariel, Automated Real-time Investments Exchange

armateur, -trice *m,f* IMP/EXP shipowner, RES HUM master owner, TRANSP *d'un navire* owner, shipowner; ~ **disposant** TRANSP *d'un navire* disponent owner; ~ **-gérant** TRANSP *d'un navire* managing owner, ship's husband

arme: ~ **à double tranchant** *f* RES HUM whipsaw (*AmE, jarg*); ~ **publicitaire** *f* V&M advertising weapon

armement *m* TRANSP *aviation* catering, *commerce maritime* shipping trade, *d'un navire* fitting out

Arménie *f* COM Armenia

arménien[1], **-enne** *adj* COM Armenian

arménien[2] *m* COM *langue* Armenian

Arménien, -enne *m,f* COM *habitant* Armenian

armer *vt* TRANSP *navire* fit out

armes: à ~ **égales** *loc* COM on equal terms

armoire *f* INFO rack

arpent *m* *vieilli* COM acre

arrachement *m* IMMOB avulsion

arrangement *m* COM accommodation, DROIT composition; ~ **à l'amiable** COM, DROIT amicable settlement

arranger 1. *vt* COM arrange; **2.** *v pron* **s'~ à l'amiable** COM come to an amicable settlement

arrérages *m pl* COM back payment, FIN arrearage, arrears, back payment, RES HUM back payment

arrestation *f* ASSUR arrest

arrêt *m* BOURSE halt, COM *d'une machine, d'une usine* shutdown, DROIT *d'une décision* adjudication, judgment, *d'une cour* ord., order, order of the court, *des poursuites* abatement, INFO shutdown; ~ **complet** INFO deadlock (*jarg*); ~ **des comptes** COMPTA closing the accounts; ~ **d'expulsion** DROIT, IMMOB eviction order; ~ **des opérations** BOURSE halt of trading, trading halt; ~ **prématuré** INFO abort; ~ **de travail** RES HUM stoppage, work stoppage; ~ **de travail symbolique** RES HUM token stoppage

arrêté[1], **e** *adj* BANQUE, COMPTA, FIN balanced, IND idle, INFO down

arrêté:[2] ~ **de compte** *m* BANQUE settlement of account; ~ **ministériel** *m* DROIT ministerial order; ~ **municipal** *m* ADMIN bye-law, bylaw, DROIT ordinance (*US*), PROT SOC bye-law, bylaw

arrêter 1. *vt* BANQUE *compte* make up, BOURSE lock in, COM stem, COMPTA *compte* close, DROIT arrest, IND *production* discontinue, INFO stop; ~ **l'éxecution de** INFO *programme* abort; ~ **prématurément** INFO abort; ~ **de travailler** RES HUM down tools, stop work; **2.** *v pron* **s'~** INFO abort; ◆ ~ **les comptes** COMPTA balance the books; ~ **des dispositions** ADMIN lay down the rules; ~ **ses comptes** COMPTA make up one's accounts

arrêts: ~ **du secteur privé** *m pl* RES HUM private sector awards; ~ **du secteur public** *m pl* ECON private sector awards

arrhes *f pl* BANQUE advance, advance payment, BOURSE earnest money, COM advance, advance payment, IMMOB earnest money, V&M deposit

arriéré[1], **e** *adj* COM, COMPTA outstanding, overdue, past-due

arriéré[2] *m* ADMIN backlog, BOURSE arrearage, arrears, COM arrears, back payment, backlog, FIN arrearage, arrears, overdue payment, FISC reachback; ~ **de dividendes** BOURSE arrearage; ~ **d'impôt** FIN, FISC tax arrears; ~ **d'impôt établis** FIN, FISC assessed tax arrears; ~ **d'impôts** FISC back tax; ~ **d'intérêts** BANQUE arrears of interest, default interest, interest arrearage, interest on arrears, COMPTA back interest; ~ **de loyer** RES HUM back rent; ~ **de paiements** COMPTA backlog of payments; ~ **de salaire** RES HUM retrospective pay; ~ **de travail** COM, IND backlog of work, work backlog

arrière[1] *adj* TRANSP *navigation* aft

arrière[2] *m* TRANSP *d'un navire* stern; ~ **-guichet** ADMIN back office; ~ **-pays** TRANSP *maritime* hinterland; ◆ **sur l'~ de** TRANSP *navigation* abaft

arriérés: ~ **de crédit-logement** *m pl* IMMOB mortgage arrears

arrimage *m* TRANSP stowage; ~ **de la cargaison** TRANSP *navigation* cargo stowage; ~ **des marchandises** TRANSP cargo stowage; ~ **sur palettes** TRANSP palletized stowage

arrimer *vt* TRANSP *cargaison* stow

arrimeur *m* TRANSP stevedore, stvdr

arrivages *m pl* FISC *de déclarations* intake

arrivé: ~ **à échéance** *adj* BOURSE matured; ~ **à maturité** *adj* BOURSE matured

arrivée *f* COM *de nouvelles commandes* intake, TRANSP arrival; ~ **tardive** RES HUM lateness

arriver *vi* COM arrive, come; ◆ ~ **à** COM *accord* achieve; ~ **à un accord** COM come to an understanding, come to terms; ~ **à un compromis avec qn** COM reach an accommodation with sb; ~ **au compte-gouttes** COM trickle in; ~ **à destination** COM come to hand; ~ **à échéance** COM come to maturity, expire, COMPTA *engagement* become due, DROIT *contrats* cease to have effect; ~ **en même temps** COM concur; ~ **au port** TRANSP *navigation* make port; ~ **à saturation** COM reach saturation point; ~ **sur le marché** COM hit the market, ECON enter the market, V&M *produit, maison* come onto the market; ~ **sur le marché du travail** COM enter the labor market (*AmE*), enter the labour market (*BrE*)

arriviste *mf* RES HUM careerist, thruster (*dat*)

arrondir *vt* COMPTA, FIN round off, MATH round up

arrondissement *m* COM borough

ARRT *abrév* (*affectation de réserve pour le rajustement des salaires*) RES HUM SARA (*salary adjustment reserve allotment*)

art: ~ **du compromis** *m* POL art of the possible; ~ **de gagner par des astuces** *m* COM gamesmanship; ~ **de la vente** *m* V&M salesmanship

article *m* COM article, item, cmdty, commodity, COMPTA item, DROIT *d'une loi* article, section, *d'un contrat* clause, ECON, IND cmdty, commodity, MÉDIA *dans un journal* article, *découpé* cutting (*BrE*), POL section, V&M commodity; ~ **d'appel** *m* V&M loss leader, traffic builder (*jarg*); ~ **authentique** *m* COM genuine article; ~ **bouche-trou** *m* MÉDIA *presse* fills; ~ **de classification** *m* COM class object; ~ **de consommation** *m* COM article of consumption; ~ **courant** *m* POL standard object; ~ **courant de dépense** *m* POL standard object of expenditure; ~ **courant de recette** *m* POL standard object of revenue; ~ **défectueux** *m* V&M faulty good; ~ **dépareillé** *m* V&M oddment; ~ **de dessous de ligne** *m* (ANT *article de dessus de ligne*) ECON below-the-line item; ~ **de dessus de ligne** *m* (ANT *article de dessous de ligne*) ECON above-the-line item; ~ **équilibré** *m* DROIT balanced article;

~ **exceptionnel** *m* COM unusual item, TRANSP exceptional item; ~ **d'exécution** *m* ADMIN departmental line object, departmental object, line object; ~ **explosif** *m* TRANSP explosive article; ~ **fiscal privilégié** *m* FISC tax preference item; ~ **de fond** *m* MÉDIA *presse* feature, feature article, lead story; ~ **à forte rotation** *m* COM fast-moving article; ~ **générateur de pertes** *m* V&M loss-maker; ~ **à grand débit** *m* COM fast-moving article; ~ **imposable** *m* FISC taxable article; ~ **impropre à l'exportation** *m* IMP/EXP export reject; ~ **de ménage** *m* COM household commodity; ~ **d'origine** *m pl* COMPTA source object; ~ **qui fait la une** *m* MÉDIA lead story, leading article (*UK*); ~ **de rapport** *m* COM reporting object; ~ **-réclame** *m* V&M *publicité* leading article (*UK*); ~ **en réclame** *m* COM bargain, sale item, sale item, V&M bargain, sale item; ~ **référencé** *m* V&M stock line; ~ **réglementaire** *m* POL statutory item; ~ **réglementé** *m* TRANSP *aviation* restricted articles, REART; ~ **sans suite** *m* V&M closed stock; ~ **sensé** *m* DROIT balanced article; ~ **en solde** *m* COM, V&M bargain, oddment, sale item; ~ **suivi** *m* V&M stock line; ~ **de tête** *m* MÉDIA *presse* lead (*BrE*), lede (*AmE*); ~ **vedette** *m* MÉDIA *presse* feature article; ~ **vendu à perte** *m* V&M loss leader; ~ **vendu à plusieurs journaux** *m* MÉDIA syndicated column; ~ **volumineux et à faible marge** *m* V&M low-margin high-space good

articles *m pl* COM, IND, V&M gds, goods; ~ **en cuir** IND, V&M leather goods; ~ **démarqués** IND knock-offs (*infrml*); ~ **dépareillés** V&M broken lots; ~ **divers** COMPTA sundries, sundry articles; ~ **d'équipement** V&M consumer durables; ~ **de luxe** COM, V&M luxury goods; ~ **de marque** COM branded goods, proprietary goods; ~ **de mode** V&M fashion goods; ~ **en réclame** V&M leading line

artificiel, -elle *adj* COM artificial, IND man-made

artisan *m* RES HUM craftsman

artisanat: ~ **local** *m* RES HUM local handicraft

arts: ~ **du langage** *m pl* PROT SOC language arts (*jarg*); ~ **plastiques** *m pl* MÉDIA visual arts; ~ **visuels** *m pl* MÉDIA visual arts

ascendant¹**, e** *adj* (ANT *descendant*) INFO upward

ascendant² *m* COM authority, influence; ◆ **avoir de l'~ sur** COM have authority over, have influence over

ascendant³**, e** *m, f* COM ancestor

ascenseur *m* COM elevator (*AmE*), lift (*BrE*), passenger lift

ascension: ~ **professionnelle** *f* RES HUM *les échelons de la profession* career ladder; ~ **rapide** *f* RES HUM fast tracking

ASCII:¹ ~ **en** ~ *adj* INFO in ASCII

ASCII² *m* INFO *Code standard utilisé pour représenter les données sous forme binaire* American Standard Code for Information Interchange, ASCII

ascots *m pl* FISC, IMP/EXP ascots (*UK*)

ASE *abrév* (*Agence spatiale européenne*) COM ESA (*European Space Agency*)

asiatique *adj* COM Asian

Asiatique *mf* COM Asian

Asie *f* COM Asia; ~ **du Sud-Est** COM Southeast Asia

asile *m* COM, POL asylum

ASIRGD *abrév* (*Assurance santé-invalidité-retraite et garantie-décès*) ASSUR ≈ OASDHI (*US*) (*old age, survivors, disability and health insurance*)

aspect *m* COM aspect

assainir *vt* ENVIR *région* clean up

assainissement: ~ **écologique** *m* ENVIR, IND ecological recovery

assaisonné, e *adj* COM seasoned

asse. *abrév* (*assurance*) ASSUR ins. (*insurance*)

ASSEDIC *abrév France* (*Association pour l'emploi dans l'industrie et le commerce*) RES HUM ≈ Employment Service (*UK*)

assemblage *m* INFO assembly; ~ **définitif** COM final assembly

assemblée *f* COM gathering, meeting, POL assembly, conference; ~ **des actionnaires** BOURSE shareholders' meeting, COM, GESTION company meeting; ~ **extraordinaire** COM extraordinary meeting, special meeting; ~ **générale** (*AG*) COM General Assembly (*GA*), general meeting (*GM*); ~ **générale des actionnaires** BOURSE general meeting of shareholders, RES HUM shareholders' meeting; ~ **générale annuelle** COM, COMPTA, FISC, GESTION annual general meeting (*BrE*), annual meeting, AGM; ~ **générale extraordinaire** (*AGE*) GESTION extraordinary general meeting (*EGM*); ~ **générale ordinaire** (*AGO*) BOURSE, COM, GESTION ordinary general meeting (*OGM*); ~ **ordinaire annuelle des actionnaires** BOURSE annual meeting of shareholders; ~ **plénière** COM, POL full session; ~ **statutaire** DROIT statutory meeting

assembleur *m* INFO assembler; ~ **croisé** INFO cross assembler

assentiment *m* COM approval, consent, POL *de la Chambre* assent

asseoir: *vt* ~ **sur** COM base on

assertion *f* COM assertion; ~ **déterminante** ASSUR material representation

assesseurs: ~ **non juristes** *m pl* RES HUM lay members

assez:¹ ~ **important** *adj* ECON sizable, sizeable

assez:² ~ **de** *adv* COM sufficient

assiette *f* FISC basis, TRANSP *navigation* trim; ~ **fiscale** ECON tax base, tax basis, FISC basis for taxation, basis of assessment, tax base, tax basis; ~ **d'imposition** FISC *général* tax base; ~ **de l'impôt** ECON tax base, tax basis, FISC basis for taxation, basis of assessment, tax base, tax basis; ◆ **avoir son** ~ TRANSP *navigation* be in trim; **en** ~ **nulle** TRANSP *navigation* on an even keel

assignation *f* BOURSE assignment, DROIT writ of

subpoena; ~ **à comparaître** DROIT subpoena, summons

assigner vt COM *besogne*, RES HUM allocate; ◆ ~ **pour contrefaçon** DROIT sue for infringement of patent; **faire** ~ RES HUM take out a summons against; ~ **en justice pour contrefaçon** DROIT sue for infringement of patent; ~ **qch à qn** COM vest sth in sb; ~ **qn en justice** DROIT issue a writ against sb

assimilation f BOURSE, DROIT *UE* assimilation

assimilé, e adj COMPTA absorbed

assimiler: vt ~ **à fond** COM *compétence* internalize

assistance f COM, DROIT, ECON, FISC assistance, INFO aid, support, POL assistance; ~ **-annuaire** *Can (cf renseignements téléphoniques Fra)* COMMS directory assistance, directory enquiries *(BrE)*, directory information *(AmE)*; ~ **à la clientèle** COM field support; ~ **au développement** ECON, POL development assistance; ~ **en escale** TRANSP *aviation* ground handling; ~ **médicale** COM, PROT SOC medical assistance; ~ **privilégiée** ECON, POL concessional aid; ~ **publique** PROT SOC public welfare; ~ **au recrutement des cadres** GESTION executive search; ~ **régionale sélective** ECON regional selective assistance *(UK)*, RSA *(UK)*; ~ **sociale** PROT SOC, RES HUM social work; ~ **technico-commerciale** INFO systems engineering; ~ **technique** ECON consultant service, technical assistance, IND technical support, INFO backup, technical support, POL technical assistance; ~ **technique aux exportateurs** IMP/EXP technical help to exporters, THE; ~ **téléphonique** INFO hot line

Assistance: l'~ **publique** f *(AP)* PROT SOC authority which manages state-owned hospitals and Social Services

assistant, e m,f COM aide, assistant, asst, GESTION, RES HUM assistant, asst; ~ **au chef de projet** RES HUM project agent; ~ **machiniste** IND, RES HUM ordinary engineer assistant; ~ **personnel** GESTION, RES HUM P/Sec, personal secretary, PS, executive secretary, personal assistant, PA; ~ **social** PROT SOC, RES HUM social worker

assisté[1]**, e** adj RES HUM *prestations sociales* on welfare *(AmE)*, receiving benefit *(BrE)*; ~ **par ordinateur** INFO computer-aided, computer-assisted

assisté:[2] ~ **social** m RES HUM welfare recipient *(AmE)*

assister vt BANQUE aid; ~ **à** GESTION *une réunion*, RES HUM attend

association f COM association, comb, combination, interest group, partnership, DROIT combine, ECON linkage, GESTION agglomeration; ~ **pour l'assurance des obligations municipales** ASSUR municipal bond insurance association; ~ **communautaire** IMMOB community association; ~ **constituée en société commerciale** COM incorporated company *(AmE)*; ~ **coopérative de crédit** COM cooperative credit association; ~ **de crédit**

hypothécaire FIN mortgage credit association; ~ **d'employés** RES HUM employee association, staff association; ~ **limitée au résultat** COMPTA income limited partnership; ~ **de la marque** V&M brand association; ~ **du personnel** RES HUM staff association; ~ **professionnelle** COM, RES HUM trade association; ~ **des propriétaires d'habitat** IMMOB homeowners' association; ~ **de secours mutuel** FIN benefit club, benefit society *(AmE)*, friendly society *(BrE)*; ◆ **en** ~ **avec** COM in association with

Association: ~ **de défense du consommateur** f COM ≈ CA, ≈ Consumers' Association; ~ **pour l'emploi dans l'industrie et le commerce** f *France (ASSEDIC)* RES HUM ≈ Employment Service *(UK)*; ~ **européenne des agences de publicité** f V&M European Association of Advertising Agencies, EAAA; ~ **européenne de libre-échange** f *(AELE)* ECON European Free Trade Association *(EFTA)*; ~ **des exportateurs de céréales d'Amérique du Nord** f COM North American Export Grain Association, NAEGA; ~ **pour la formation professionnelle des adultes** f *(AFPA)* RES HUM ≈ Training Agency *(UK) (TA)*; ~ **française de codification** f *(AFC)* BOURSE ≈ CUSIP (Committee on Uniform Securities Identification Procedures); ~ **française de normalisation** f *(AFNOR)* COM, DROIT, IND French standards authority, ≈ American National Standards Institute *(US)*, *(ANSI)* ≈ American Standards Association, *(ASA)* ≈ British Standards Institution *(UK)*, *(BSI)* ≈ National Bureau of Standards *(US)*; ~ **française des sociétés de Bourse** f *(AFSB)* BOURSE French association of stock exchange member firms; ~ **de gestion des prêts étudiants** f FIN, PROT SOC Sallie Mae *(US)*, Student Loan Marketing Association *(US)*; ~ **internationale pour le développement** f ECON International Development Association, IDA; ~ **internationale des bourses de valeurs** f BOURSE International Securities Market Association, ISMA; ~ **internationale de la distribution des produits alimentaires** f TRANSP, V&M International Association for the Distribution of Food Products; ~ **internationale de l'hôtellerie** f LOISIRS ≈ International Hotel Association; ~ **internationale du marché primaire** f BOURSE International Primary Market Association, IPMA; ~ **internationale du marché des valeurs** f BOURSE International Securities Market Association, ISMA; ~ **internationale des opérateurs de swaps** f BOURSE International Swap Dealers' Association, ISDA; ~ **internationale des ports** f IMP/EXP International Association of Ports and Harbours, IAPH; ~ **internationale des transports aériens** f *(IATA)* TRANSP International Air Transport Association *(IATA)*; ~ **du marché de l'escompte de Londres** f BANQUE, FIN London Discount Market Association, LDMA; ~ **du marché secondaire** f BOURSE Secondary Market Association, SMA; ~ **nationale des agents**

immobiliers *f* IMMOB National Association of Realtors (*US*), NAR (*US*); ~ **nationale des entrepreneurs de logements** *f* IMMOB National Association of Home Builders (*US*), NAHB (*US*); ~ **des nations du Sud-Est asiatique** *f* (*ANSEA*) ECON Association of South-East Asian Nations (*ASEAN*); ~ **des Nations Unies** *f* (*ANU*) ADMIN United Nations Association (*UNA*); ~ **de normalisation des télécommunications** *f* COMMS European Telecommunications Standards Institute, ETSI; ~ **des organisateurs de voyages indépendants** *f* LOISIRS Association of Independent Tour Operators; ~ **de la protection et de l'indemnité** *f* ASSUR *maritime* Protection and Indemnity Association; ~ **de services de compensation des paiements** *f* ECON Association for Payment Clearing Services (*UK*), APACS (*UK*)

associé[1], **e** *adj* COM associated; ◆ **être ~ à** COM be associated with

associé[2], **e** *m,f* BOURSE associated person (*UK*), AP (*UK*), COM associate, partner, ECON partner, RES HUM *d'une association* member, shareholder; ~ **commanditaire** COM limited partner, silent partner (*AmE*), sleeping partner (*BrE*), special partner, DROIT limited partner, silent partner (*AmE*), sleeping partner (*BrE*), FIN silent partner (*AmE*), sleeping partner (*BrE*), RES HUM limited partner, silent partner (*AmE*), sleeping partner (*BrE*); ~ **commandité** GESTION acting partner; ~ **déterminé** FISC specified member; ~ **général** BOURSE, COMPTA general partner; ~ **général de service** BOURSE, COMPTA general service partner; ~ **gérant** RES HUM managing partner; ~ **majoritaire** BOURSE majority interest partner, COM senior partner; ~ **minoritaire** COM junior partner; ~ **en participation** COM limited partnership, special partner, DROIT special partner; ~ **à responsabilité illimitée** BOURSE general partner; ~ **responsable de l'audit** COMPTA, FIN audit head

associer 1. *vt* COM combine; ~ **à** COM associate with; **2.** *v pron* **s'~** COM *personnes* form a partnership, *sociétés* join together; **s'~ à** COM associate with; **s'~ avec** COM associate with

assolement *m* ECON, ENVIR crop rotation; ~ **triennal** ECON, ENVIR *agriculture* three-course rotation

assortiment: ~ **de denrées** *m* ECON basket of goods; ~ **de produits** *m* COM assortment of goods

assouplir *vt* GESTION *politique, loi* relax

assouplissement *m* GESTION *d'une loi, d'une politque* relaxation, TRANSP *des procédures commerciales* facilitation

assujetti: ~ **à** *adj* COM, FISC liable for, subject to; ◆ ~ **à l'avarie particulière** ASSUR subject to particular average, SPA; **être ~ à la règle** BOURSE go under the rule (*jarg*); ~ **à hypothèque** IMMOB subject to mortgage; ~ **à l'impôt** FISC liable for tax, taxed; **ne pas être ~ à la TVA** FISC be zerorated for VAT

assujettissement: ~ **à l'impôt** *m* FISC liability for tax

assumer *vt* COM *conséquences* abide by, *engagement* assume, *responsabilité* shoulder, take on, *risques* assume

assurance *f* (*asse.*) ASSUR insurance (*ins.*); ~ **des abonnés** COM assurance of subscribers; ~ **des abstinents** ASSUR abstainer's insurance; ~ **-accidents** *jarg* ASSUR accident insurance; ~ **-accidents collective** *jarg* ASSUR collective accident insurance; ~ **-accidents et maladies** ASSUR accident and health insurance (*US*); ~ **-accidents et risques divers** ASSUR casualty insurance; ~ **-accidents du travail** ASSUR industrial injury insurance, worker compensation insurance; ~ **achat-vente contre l'invalidité du partenaire** ASSUR disability of partner buy and sell insurance; ~ **agricole** ASSUR agricultural insurance; ~ **d'améliorations locatives** ASSUR improvements and betterments insurance; ~ **automobile** ASSUR, TRANSP automobile insurance (*AmE*), motor insurance, motor vehicle insurance; ~ **automobile affaires** ASSUR, TRANSP business automobile policy (*US*); ~ **automobile contre la responsabilité civile** ASSUR, TRANSP automobile liability insurance (*US*); ~ **avec participation aux bénéfices** ASSUR composite insurance, participating insurance; ~ **-aviation** ASSUR, TRANSP aviation insurance; ~ **des bicyclettes** ASSUR cycle insurance; ~ **des biens commerciaux** ASSUR, IMMOB commercial property policy; ~ **bris de glace** ASSUR glass insurance; ~ **bris de glace globale** ASSUR comprehensive glass insurance; ~ **à capital différé** ASSUR endowment assurance, endowment insurance, endowment policy, BANQUE endowment policy; ~ **en cas de fermeture d'exploitation** ASSUR business closure insurance; ~ **de chaudière** ASSUR, IND boiler insurance (*US*); ~ **des chaudières et machines** ASSUR, IND boiler and machinery insurance; ~ **-chômage** (*AC*) RES HUM unemployment insurance (*UI*); ~ **des colis postaux** ASSUR, COMMS parcel post insurance; ~ **collective** ASSUR collective insurance; ~ **collective contre les accidents** ASSUR collective accident insurance; ~ **collective contre la maladie** ASSUR group health insurance (*US*); ~ **combinée** ASSUR comprehensive insurance, multiperil insurance, multirisk insurance; ~ **combinée de magasins** ASSUR combined shop insurance; ~ **combinée spécifique** ASSUR special multiperil insurance, SMP; ~ **commerciale contre le vol** ASSUR mercantile robbery insurance; ~ **commerciale contre le vol par effraction de coffres-forts** ASSUR mercantile safe burglary insurance; ~ **commerciale contre le vol du stock initial** ASSUR mercantile open-stock burglary insurance; ~ **commerciale** ASSUR commercial insurance policy; ~ **commerciale maladie** ASSUR commercial health insurance (*US*); ~ **complémentaire** COM excess insurance; ~ **complémentaire ou supplémentaire aux**

conditions ASSUR difference-in-conditions insurance; ~ **conjointe** ASSUR joint insurance; ~ **de consignation** ASSUR consignment insurance; ~ **contre les accidents** ASSUR accident insurance; ~ **contre les accidents du travail** ASSUR worker compensation insurance; ~ **contre les accidents du travail et de la responsabilité civile** ASSUR worker compensation and employers liability insuring agreement (*US*); ~ **contre les actes de vandalisme et de malveillance** ASSUR vandalism and malicious mischief insurance; ~ **contre la carence des fournisseurs** ASSUR contingent business interruption insurance; ~ **contre le chantage** ASSUR extortion insurance; ~ **contre les détournements** ASSUR fidelity guarantee; ~ **contre l'enlèvement** ASSUR kidnap insurance; ~ **contre l'extorsion** ASSUR extortion insurance; ~ **contre le faux en écriture du déposant** ASSUR depositor's forgery insurance; ~ **contre la fraude informatique** ASSUR computer crime insurance; ~ **contre la grêle** ASSUR crop hail insurance; ~ **contre les inondations** ASSUR flood insurance; ~ **contre les intempéries** ASSUR qualified insurance corporation, rain insurance; ~ **contre la privation de jouissance** ASSUR additional expense insurance; ~ **contre les risques de transport** ASSUR, TRANSP transport insurance; ~ **contre les tremblements de terre** ASSUR earthquake insurance; ~ **corps aériens** ASSUR, TRANSP aircraft hull insurance; ~ **en cours** ASSUR current insurance, insurance in force; ~ **de crédit** FIN loan insurance; ~ **crédit** ASSUR credit insurance; ~ **crédit collective** ASSUR group credit insurance (*US*); ~ **crédit commercial** ASSUR commercial credit insurance (*US*); ~ **crédit des exportateurs** ASSUR, IMP/EXP export credit insurance; ~ **du crédit à l'exportation** ASSUR, IMP/EXP export credit insurance; ~ **cumulative** ASSUR double insurance; ~ **défense et recours** ASSUR legal expense insurance; ~ **dentaire** ASSUR dental insurance; ~ **de dépôts bancaires** BANQUE bank deposit insurance (*US*); ~ **de la dépréciation des biens** ASSUR property depreciation insurance; ~ **détournement et vol** ASSUR fidelity insurance; ~ **détournements et escroqueries du fait des employés** ASSUR fidelity bond; ~ **directe** ASSUR direct insurance; ~ **de distributeurs** ASSUR coin machine insurance; ~ **des documents de valeur** ASSUR valuable papers insurance; ~ **des enfants** ASSUR child's insurance; ~ **des enfants différée** ASSUR child's deferred assurance; ~ **explosion due à la nature même du risque** ASSUR inherent explosion clause; ~ **des expositions** ASSUR exhibition risks insurance; ~ **expressément consentie** ASSUR *objets personnels* personal property floater; ~ **facultative** ASSUR voluntary insurance; ~ **fluviale** ASSUR inland marine insurance; ~ **des frais d'hospitalisation** ASSUR, PROT SOC *assurance maladie* hospital care insurance plan; ~ **des frais d'incinération** ASSUR *assurance-vie* cremation expenses insurance; ~ **du fret** ASSUR freight insurance; ~ **de garantie** ASSUR *assurance caution,*

assurance vol fidelity bond; ~ **pour la garantie des rémunérations des travailleurs** ASSUR worker compensation and employers liability insuring agreement (*US*); ~ **globale** ASSUR blanket insurance; ~ **globale des frais médicaux** ASSUR blanket medical expense insurance (*US*); ~ **de groupe contre la maladie** ASSUR group health insurance (*US*); ~ **habitation** ASSUR homeowner's policy; ~ **hasard** ASSUR hazard insurance (*US*); ~ **hospitalisation** ASSUR, PROT SOC *assurance maladie* hospital care insurance plan; ~ **d'hypothèque** ASSUR, BANQUE mortgage insurance; ~ **hypothèque privée** ASSUR private mortgage insurance; ~ **I.A.R.D.** ASSUR nonlife insurance; ~ **incapacité** ASSUR disability insurance; ~ **informatique** ASSUR data processing insurance; ~ **des ingénieurs** ASSUR engineering insurance; ~ **d'intermédiaires de transport** ASSUR instrumentalities of transportation; ~ **invalidité** ASSUR disability insurance, disability cover; ~ **invalidité de groupe** ASSUR group disability insurance (*US*); ~ **invalidité groupe** ASSUR group disability insurance (*US*); ~ **invalidité rachetable** ASSUR disability buy-out insurance (*US*); ~ **des limites différentes** ASSUR difference-in-limits insurance; ~ **livraison** ASSUR consignment insurance; ~ **locative** ASSUR leasehold insurance; ~ **loisirs** ASSUR holiday and leisure insurance; ~ **machines** ASSUR machinery damage co-insurance clause; ~ **maladie** ASSUR health insurance, medical insurance, health services plan, RES HUM sickness insurance; ~ **maladie et vie risques professionnels** ASSUR business exposures life and health insurance (*US*); ~ **maladie propre à l'entreprise** ASSUR company sickness insurance scheme; ~ **de marchandise acheminée par les transports routiers** ASSUR, TRANSP motor truck cargo insurance (*US*); ~ **des marchandises transportées** ASSUR freight insurance; ~ **maritime** ASSUR marine insurance, sea insurance, TRANSP marine insurance; ~ **maritime de protection et de l'indemnité** ASSUR, TRANSP ocean marine protection and indemnity insurance; ~ **maternité** ASSUR maternity protection; ~ **médicale** ASSUR medical insurance; ~ **mixte** ASSUR endowment assurance; ~ **mixte avec participation aux bénéfices** ASSUR with-profits endowment assurance; ~ **mixte éducation** ASSUR educational endowment; ~ **montage** ASSUR erection insurance; ~ **multirisque** ASSUR comprehensive policy, multirisk insurance; ~ **de navigation intérieure** ASSUR inland marine insurance; ~ **d'obligations municipales** ASSUR municipal bond insurance; ~ **obligatoire** ASSUR compulsory insurance; ~ **des parcs automobiles** ASSUR, TRANSP fleet policy; ~ **passagers aériens** ASSUR, TRANSP aircraft passenger insurance; ~ **perte d'exploitation** ASSUR business interruption insurance, business interruption policy; ~ **perte de revenu** ASSUR loss-of-income insurance; ~ **de plan d'étage** ASSUR floor plan insurance; ~ **de portefeuille** ASSUR, BOURSE portfolio insurance; ~ **à la prime de risque** ASSUR risk-based premium; ~ **à primes fixes** ASSUR proprietary insurance; ~ **protection de crédit** ASSUR credit protection insurance (*UK*); ~ **protection de garantie** ASSUR title protection insurance; ~ **de la protection juridique** ASSUR legal expense insurance; ~ **de la qualité** GESTION, IND, V&M quality assurance, QA; ~ **RC de l'employeur** *(assurance responsabilité civile de l'employeur)* ASSUR employer's liability coverage; ~ **RC obligatoire** *(assurance responsabilité civile obligatoire, responsabilité civile)* ASSUR compulsory third-party insurance; ~ **des récoltes contre la grêle** ASSUR crop hail insurance; ~ **de rendement industriel** ASSUR manufacturer's output insurance; ~ **de rente** ASSUR annuity assurance; ~ **de rente d'invalidité** ASSUR disability income insurance (*US*); ~ **de responsabilité** ASSUR carrier's liability, liability insurance; ~ **de responsabilité automobile** ASSUR, TRANSP automobile liability insurance (*US*); ~ **responsabilité civile contre l'incendie et le vol** ASSUR third-party fire and theft; ~ **responsabilité civile** ASSUR liability insurance; ~ **responsabilité civile des administrateurs et des officiers** ASSUR directors' and officers' liability insurance; ~ **responsabilité civile après travaux** ASSUR, IMMOB completed operations insurance; ~ **responsabilité civile automobile sans égard au responsable** ASSUR liability no-fault automobile insurance (*US*); ~ **responsabilité civile des commerçants** ASSUR shopkeepers' liability insurance (*UK*), storekeepers' liability insurance (*US*); ~ **responsabilité civile complémentaire et excédentaire** ASSUR umbrella liability insurance; ~ **responsabilité civile couvrant l'ascenseur** ASSUR elevator liability insurance (*US*); ~ **responsabilité civile de l'employeur** *(assurance RC de l'employeur)* ASSUR employer's liability coverage; ~ **responsabilité civile des fabricants et des entreprises** ASSUR manufacturer's and contractor's liability insurance (*US*); ~ **responsabilité civile générale** ASSUR comprehensive liability insurance, comprehensive general liability insurance; ~ **responsabilité civile indirecte des propriétaires et entrepreneurs** ASSUR owners' and contractors' protective liability insurance; ~ **responsabilité civile obligatoire** *(assurance RC obligatoire)* ASSUR compulsory third party insurance; ~ **responsabilité civile des particuliers** ASSUR comprehensive personal liability insurance; ~ **responsabilité civile "umbrella"** ASSUR umbrella liability insurance; ~ **de responsabilité locative** ASSUR fire legal liability insurance (*US*); ~ **de responsabilité professionelle** ASSUR business liability insurance, professional liability insurance; ~ **de responsabilité professionnelle des experts comptables** ASSUR, COMPTA accountant's professional liability insurance; ~ **de revendeurs de matériel** ASSUR equipment dealers insurance; ~ **risque** ASSUR hazard insurance (*US*); ~ **risques divers** ASSUR, IMMOB business property and liability insurance

package (*US*); ~ **sociale** PROT SOC social insurance, supplementary benefit (*UK, obs*), RES HUM social insurance; ~ **société de vie et de maladie** ASSUR key person life and health insurance (*US*); ~ **soins dentaires** ASSUR dental insurance; ~ **des souscripteurs** COM assurance of subscribers; ~ **sur corps** ASSUR hull insurance; ~ **sur facultés** ASSUR *assurance maritime* MAR policy, cargo insurance, consignment insurance; ~ **sur le traitement des données** ASSUR data processing insurance; ~ **de survie** ASSUR survivorship insurance; ~ **temporaire** ASSUR term insurance; ~ **à terme renouvelable tous les ans** ASSUR annual renewable term insurance; ~ **aux tiers** ASSUR, TRANSP third-party insurance; ~ **tous risques** ASSUR all risks insurance, comprehensive insurance, comprehensive policy, multiperil insurance; ~ **tous risques de biens industriels** ASSUR manufacturer's output insurance; ~ **tous risques chantier** ASSUR contractor's all risks insurance; ~ **tous risques expositions** ASSUR exhibition risks insurance; ~ **transport aérien** ASSUR, TRANSP air transport insurance; ~ **vacances** ASSUR holiday and leisure insurance; ~ **valeur agréée** ASSUR agreed value insurance; ~ **des valeurs différentes** ASSUR difference-in-value insurance; ~ **-vie** ASSUR life assurance (*BrE*), life insurance; ~ **-vie avec option rente viagère** ASSUR annuity insurance; ~ **vie-entière** ASSUR adjustable life insurance, whole-life insurance, universal-life policy; ~ **-vie entière hypothèse courante** ASSUR current assumption whole life insurance; ~ **-vie et maladie appliquée aux affaires** ASSUR partnership life and health insurance; ~ **-vie et santé professionnelle** ASSUR business life and health insurance; ~ **-vie de groupe** ASSUR group life insurance (*US*); ~ **-vie indexée** ASSUR indexed life insurance; ~ **-vie individuelle** ASSUR individual life insurance (*US*); ~ **-vie liée à l'hypothèque** ASSUR, BANQUE mortgage life insurance (*US*); ~ **-vie à prestations variables** ASSUR variable life insurance; ~ **-vie à prime indéterminée** ASSUR indeterminate-premium life insurance; ~ **-vie à prime unique** ASSUR single-premium life insurance; ~ **-vie sur deux têtes** ASSUR survivor policy; ~ **-vie temporaire** ASSUR annual renewable term insurance, term life insurance; ~ **-vie universelle** ASSUR universal life insurance; ~ **-vie usage commercial** ASSUR business uses life insurance (*US*); ~ **-vie voyage aérien** ASSUR, LOISIRS, TRANSP aviation trip life insurance; ~ **vieillesse** FIN old age pension; ~ **en vigueur** ASSUR current insurance, insurance in force; ~ **vol sur la personne** ASSUR cash messenger insurance, messenger robbery insurance; ~ **volontaire** ASSUR voluntary insurance; ~ **voyage** ASSUR, LOISIRS, TRANSP travel insurance; ~ **voyageurs aériens** ASSUR, TRANSP aircraft passenger insurance

Assurance: ~ **santé-invalidité-retraite et garantie-décès** *f* *(ASIRGD)* ASSUR ≈ old age, survivors, disability and health insurance (*US*) *(OASDHI)*;

~ sociale *f France* PROT SOC, RES HUM ≈ NI *(UK)*, ≈ National Insurance *(UK)*

assuré, e *m,f* ASSUR policyholder, the assured, the claimant, the insured; **l'~** ASSUR the insured

assurer 1. *vt* ADMIN *l'entretien des bureaux* maintain, ASSUR insure, COM guarantee; **2.** *v pron* **s'~ de** BOURSE lock in, secure; ♦ **~ l'accueil de** RES HUM *stand* man; **~ la correspondance avec** COMMS connect; **~ la manoeuvre de** RES HUM man; **~ la permanence de** RES HUM *stand* man; **s'~ contre l'incendie** ASSUR insure o.s. against fire; **s'~ contre un risque** ASSUR insure o.s. against risk, provide against a risk; **~ la subsistance de** FISC support; **~ le suivi** COM follow up

assureur *mf* ASSUR insurance broker, insurer; **~ accidents** *m* ASSUR accident insurer; **~ de biens** *m* ASSUR property insurer; **~ direct** *m* ASSUR direct insurer; **~ immobilier** *m* ASSUR property insurer; **~ Lloyd's** *m* ASSUR Lloyd's member; **~ mutuel** *m* ASSUR mutual insurer; **~ principal** *m* ASSUR leader; **~ sur corps** *m* ASSUR *maritime* hull underwriter; **~ de la vie** *m* ASSUR life insurer; **~ -vie agréé** *m* ASSUR chartered life underwriter *(US)*

astreinte *f* RES HUM standby; ♦ **être d'~** COM be on standby

astuce: ~ publicitaire *f* V&M advertising gimmick, publicity stunt

Asunción *n pr* COM Asunción

asymétrie *f* COM asymmetry; **~ de production** ECON production asymmetry

asynchrone *adj* INFO asynchronous

atelier *m* COM *formation* workshop, IND factory floor, shop floor, workshop, RES HUM shop floor; **~ de carrosserie** TRANSP body shop; **~ fugitif** IND, RES HUM runaway shop *(jarg)*; **~ d'outillage** IND toolroom; **~ de réparation** COM repair shop; **~ de tissage** IND weaving mill

ATF *abrév (accord de taux futur)* BOURSE, FIN FRA *(forward rate agreement)*

Athènes *n pr* COM Athens

atmosphère *f* ENVIR atmosphere

atomicité *f* BOURSE atomicity

atout *m* COM asset, trump card

attaché:[1] **~ aux biens de consommation** *adj* COM *personne, société* acquisitive

attaché[2]**, e** *m,f* MÉDIA, RES HUM attaché; **~ fonctionnel** RES HUM staff assistant; **~ militaire** RES HUM defence attaché *(BrE)*, defense attaché *(AmE)*; **~ opérationnel** RES HUM line assistant; **~ de presse** MÉDIA press agent

attaché:[3] **être ~ à** *loc* COM *principe* adhere to

attacher 1. *vt* COM *étiquette*, COMMS affix; **2.** *v pron* **s'~ les services de qn** COM retain sb's services; ♦ **~ de l'importance à** COM attach importance to

attaquant *m* BOURSE raider

attaque *f* BOURSE raid; **~ à l'aube** BOURSE dawn raid; **~ des baissiers** BOURSE bear raid, bear raiding; **~ à l'ouverture** BOURSE dawn raid

attaquer 1. *vt* ASSUR contest, DROIT *testament* contest, dispute; **2.** *v pron* **s'~ à** COM *problème* address o.s. to; ♦ **~ le marché** BOURSE raid the market, tap the market; **~ qn en justice** DROIT bring a lawsuit against sb; **~ une société** BOURSE, COM, FIN raid a company

atteindre *vt* COM *le cours le plus haut* achieve, record, *toucher* affect; ♦ **~ une jolie somme** COM *rapporter* fetch a good price; **~ le point mort** COM, COMPTA, ECON break even; **~ le seuil de rentabilité** COM, COMPTA, ECON break even; **~ son maximum** ECON peak; **~ son niveau plancher** BOURSE, ECON bottom, bottom out; **~ son niveau le plus bas** BOURSE, COM, ECON bottom, bottom out; **~ son niveau record** ECON peak; **~ un total de** COM reach a total of

atteint: ~ d'incapacité *adj* FISC infirm

atteinte *f* DROIT breach, damage, derogation; **~ aux droits d'un individu** DROIT civil wrong; **~ due à des tensions répétées** ADMIN repetitive strain injury, RSI; **~ à l'environnement** COM environmental damage; **~ flagrante aux droits d'une partie** DROIT gross miscarriage of justice; **~ à la libre concurrence** DROIT, ECON restrictive practice; ♦ **qui ne porte pas ~ à l'environnement** ENVIR environmentally-benign

attelage: ~ pivotant *m* TRANSP *semi-remorque* fifth-wheel coupling; **~ pivotant coulissant** *m* TRANSP *semi-remorque* sliding fifth wheel

attenant, e *adj* COM adjoining

attendre 1. *vi* COM wait; **2.** *v pron* **s'~ à** COM anticipate, expect

attendu, e *adj* COM *résultat* anticipated, expected

attendus: les ~ *m pl* DROIT the whereas clauses

attente *f* COM anticipation; **~ signalée d'un appel automatique** INFO camp-on; ♦ **en ~** COM pending, TRANSP standby; **en ~ d'un poste d'amarrage** TRANSP waiting a berth

attentes: ~ du consommateur *f pl* COM consumer expectations; **~ professionnelles** *f pl* RES HUM career expectations; **~ régressives** *f pl* MATH regressive expectations

attention *f* COM attention, care, V&M attention; ♦ **~, intérêt, désir, action** *(AIDA)* COM, V&M attention, interest, desire, action *(AIDA)*; **~ portée aux besoins de la clientèle** V&M customer care

attention! *loc* RES HUM attention!

attentisme *m* ECON wait-and-see policy

atténuation *f* DROIT mitigation; **~ d'impôts** FISC mitigation of taxes

atterrissage *m* TRANSP *aviation* landing; **~ brutal** *(ANT atterrissage en douceur)* COM, ECON hard landing; **~ en douceur** *(ANT atterrissage brutal)* COM, ECON soft landing; **~ forcé** TRANSP *aviation* emergency landing, forced landing

attestation *f* DROIT attestation, representation, *sous serment* affidavit, FISC *dans les formules, les déclarations, etc.* certification; **~ d'assurance** ASSUR certificate of insurance, insurance certificate, CI; **~ d'assurance maritime** ASSUR marine insurance policy certificate; **~ du conjoint** FISC *crédit d'impôt pour enfants* certification by spouse; **~ écrite sous serment** DROIT affidavit; **~ d'inventaire** COMPTA inventory certificate; **l'~ ci-jointe** COMMS the affixed testimonial; **~ de prise en charge** IMP/EXP, TRANSP acceptance certificate; **~ de prise en charge du transitaire** TRANSP forwarder's certificate of receipt, freight forwarder's certificate of receipt, FCR, FFCR; **~ de satisfaction** ASSUR satisfaction note (*jarg*); **~ sous serment d'absence de privilège** DROIT no-lien affidavit; **~ de titre** COM warranty of title; **~ de valeur** IMP/EXP certificate of value (*UK*), CV (*UK*); **~ de valeur et d'origine** IMP/EXP certificate of value and origin (*UK*), CVO (*UK*); ◆ **~ de paiement d'impôt sur dividendes** BOURSE, FISC tax voucher

attester *vt* COM witness, DROIT attest, represent

attirer *vt* COM attract, *attention* attract, grab, *personne* appeal to; ◆ **~ l'attention de qn** COM attract sb's attention; **~ de nouveaux contrats** COM attract new business; **~ de nouvelles entreprises** COM attract new business; **s'~ le mécontentement de** COM fall foul of; **s'~ les bonnes grâces de qn** COM get into sb's good books, win sb's favor (*AmE*), win sb's favour (*BrE*)

attitré, e *adj* COM *agent, président* appointed

attitude *f* GESTION, RES HUM, V&M *vis-à-vis de produits, d'idées* attitude; **~ anti-inflationniste** ECON, POL anti-inflation stance; **~ des utilisateurs** V&M user attitude

attractif, -ive *adj* BOURSE, COM attractive

attraction: **~ commerciale** *f* V&M sales appeal

attrait *m* COM, V&M *d'un produit* appeal; **~ commercial** V&M sales appeal; **~ du message** V&M copy appeal; **~ visuel** V&M visual appeal

attrayant, e *adj* BOURSE, COM attractive

attribué: **~ à** *loc* COM attributed to

attribuer *vt* ADMIN allocate, BOURSE *action* allot, COM allocate, attribute, COMPTA allocate, DROIT award, grant, FIN allocate, allot, INFO, RES HUM allocate, assign; **~ 1 à la valeur du bit** INFO set; ◆ **~ qch à qn** COM ascribe sth to sb, attribute sth to sb

attribut *m* COM, INFO attribute

attributaire *mf* BOURSE allottee

attribution *f* ADMIN, COM, COMPTA allocation, DROIT award, grant, granting, FIN allocation, allotment, INFO allocation, assignment, RES HUM allocation, assignement; **~ d'actions** BOURSE allotment of shares; **~ d'actions gratuites** BOURSE bonus issue (*UK*), capitalization issue, scrip issue, FIN bonus issue (*UK*), scrip issue; **~ des charges par fonction** COMPTA functional costing; **~ de codes comptables** COMPTA coding of accounts; **~ des recettes** FISC revenue allocation; **~ de titres** BOURSE allotment of securities (*UK*); **~ de valeurs** BOURSE allotment of securities (*UK*)

attributions *f pl* COM remit, RES HUM competence; ◆ **ce n'est pas dans mes ~** COM it is outside my remit

au *prép* COM *date* as at

aube *f* TRANSP *d'un navire* paddle

AUD *abrév* (*administration de l'union des douanes*) IMP/EXP UE ACU (*administration of the customs union*)

audience *f* COM audience, DROIT hearing, MÉDIA audience, readership, V&M audience; **~ cumulée** V&M *marketing* cumulative penetration, reach; **~ héritée de l'émission précédente** MÉDIA *radio, télévision* inherited audience (*jarg*); **~ à huis clos** DROIT private hearing; **~ radiophonique** MÉDIA *radio* radio audience; ◆ **avoir une bonne ~** MÉDIA *télévision* score a good viewership

audioconférence *f* COMMS, INFO audio conference, audio-conferencing

audiotypie *f* COM audiotyping

audiovisuel, -elle *adj* COM, INFO, MÉDIA, V&M audiovisual

audit *m* COMPTA audit, auditing, FIN auditing; **~ analytique** COMPTA analytical audit, analytical auditing, analytical review, systems-based audit, systems-based auditing; **~ complet** COMPTA complete audit; **~ de conformité** COMPTA compliance audit; **~ en continu** COMPTA continuous audit; **~ de direction** GESTION, RES HUM management audit; **~ d'une étendue limitée** COMPTA limited audit; **~ d'exploitation** COMPTA, FIN operations audit; **~ externe** (*cf contrôle externe, révision externe, vérification externe Can*) COMPTA, FIN external audit, independent audit; **~ de fin d'exercice** COMPTA year-end audit; **~ à l'insu** COMPTA undercover audit; **~ intérim** COMPTA interim audit; **~ interne** COMPTA, FIN administrative audit, internal audit; **~ légal** COMPTA statutory audit; **~ de management** GESTION, RES HUM management audit; **~ de mi-année** COMPTA interim audit; **~ opérationnel** COMPTA, FIN, GESTION operational audit; **~ des opérations** COMPTA, FIN operations audit; **~ restreint** COMPTA limited audit; **~ sur site** COM site audit; ◆ **faire un ~ de** COMPTA, FIN *comptes* audit

Audit: **~ des systèmes de management environnemental** *m* ENVIR UE Eco Audit and Management System

auditabilité *f* COMPTA auditability

auditer *vt* Fra (*cf vérifier Can*), COMPTA, FIN audit

auditeur, -trice *m, f* FIN audit agent (*Can*), COMPTA *Fra* (*cf reviseur Bel, vérificateur Can*) FIN *Fra* (*cf reviseur Bel, vérificateur Can*) auditor; **~ indépendant** *Fra* (*cf reviseur indépendant Bel, vérificateur indépendant Can*) COMPTA independent auditor; **~ libre** COM *université* auditor (*US*)

auditeurs *m pl* MÉDIA *radio* radio audience

audition *f* DROIT hearing

AUE *abrév* (*Acte unique européen*) DROIT, POL SEA (*Single European Act*)

augmentation *f* COM *croissance* augmentation, *de*

prix hike, increase, raising, rise, COMPTA addition, FIN hike, rise, RES HUM *de salaires* increase, raise (*AmE*), rise (*BrE*), V&M *marketing* mark-up; **~ de capital** COMPTA capital gain, ECON capital deepening, capital gain, capital increase, FIN capital gain, capital increase; **~ des dépenses** V&M incremental spending; **~ différée des salaires** RES HUM deferred wage increase; **~ générale** *(*ANT *réduction générale)* COM, FISC, GESTION, RES HUM across-the-board increase; **~ globale** *(*ANT *réduction globale)* COM, FISC, GESTION, RES HUM across-the-board increase; **~ au mérite** RES HUM merit increase, merit pay, merit raise (*AmE*), merit rise (*BrE*); **~ du prix** V&M pricing up; **~ des prix** COM increase in prices, price increase, price rise, rise in prices, COMPTA price increase, price rise, rise in prices, ECON increase in prices, price increase, price rise, rise in prices, FIN, V&M price increase, price rise, rise in prices; **~ du prix du pétrole** ECON oil price increase, oil price rise; **~ d'un prix de vente** COM mark-up; **~ rampante** RES HUM grade creep *(jarg)*; **~ rapide de la masse monétaire** ECON helicopter money *(jarg)*; **~ de rattrapage** RES HUM catch-up increase; **~ de salaire** RES HUM salary increase, wage increase; **~ toutes catégories** *(*ANT *réduction toutes catégories)* COM, FISC, GESTION, RES HUM across-the-board increase; ♦ **par ~** INFO incremental

augmenté, e *adj* COM stepped-up, supplemented

augmenter 1. *vt* BOURSE advance, COM *capacité* add to, climb, jack up *(infrml)*, *les chances* augment, *offre* up, *prix* hike, increase, raise, *production* build up, ramp up *(infrml)*, *revenus* supplement, ECON go up, FIN advance, INFO *capacité mémoire* upgrade, V&M jack up *(infrml)*; **2.** *vi* COM increase; ♦ **~ l'offre** ECON increase the supply; **~ le ratio d'endettement** FIN leverage up; **~ la valeur** COMPTA write up; **~ en valeur** COMPTA, IMMOB appreciate

aujourd'hui: ~ en huit *loc* COM a week today

A1 *adj* TRANSP *navigation* A1

aussitôt: ~ que possible *loc* COM, COMMS a.s.a.p., as soon as possible

austérité *f* ECON austerity; **~ budgétaire** ECON fiscal austerity; **~ économique** ECON, POL economic austerity

austral *m* COM austral

Australie *f* COM Australia

australien, -enne *adj* COM Australian

Australien, -enne *m,f* COM *habitant* Australian

autarcie *f* ECON, POL autarky

auteur: ~ d'un affidavit *m* DROIT affiant; **~ de proposition** *m* COM proposer; **~ sans garantie** *m* BOURSE naked writer; **~ d'un tort** *m* COM, DROIT tort feasor

authentification *f* BOURSE authentication, COM certification, DROIT authentication, certification; **~ d'une obligation** BOURSE authentication

authentifier *vt* DROIT *signature, document* attest, notarize

auto-amortissable *adj* FIN self-liquidating

auto-assistance *f* COM self-help

auto-assurance *f* ASSUR self-insurance

autobus *m* TRANSP bus; **~ à impériale** TRANSP double-decker

autocommutateur: ~ privé *m* COMMS *téléphone* private automatic branch exchange (*UK*), private branch exchange (*UK*), PABX (*UK*), PBX (*UK*)

autoconsommation *f* ECON, ENVIR subsistence farming; **~ par l'entreprise productrice** ECON firm consumption

autocorrélation *f* ECON *économétrie* autocorrelation

autocotisation *f* FISC self-assessment

autocritique *f* RES HUM self-appraisal

autodéveloppement *m* ADMIN advancement, COM personal growth, GESTION executive advancement, RES HUM personal growth

autodidacte *adj* PROT SOC self-taught

auto-évaluation *f* FISC self-assessment

autofinance *f* COMPTA ploughback (*BrE*), plowback (*AmE*)

autofinancé *adj* COMPTA, FIN self-financing

autofinancement *m* COMPTA internally generated funds, self-financing, FIN autofinancing, internal financing, ploughback (*BrE*), plowback (*AmE*), self-financing; **~ net annuel** COMPTA, FIN annual net cash inflow

autogénéré, e *adj* COMPTA self-generated

autogestion *f* GESTION autogestion, self-management, POL industrial democracy, RES HUM autogestion, self-management, worker control

automatique[1] *adj* ADMIN, COM, COMMS, DROIT *protection*, IND, INFO, LOISIRS, MÉDIA, V&M automatic

automatique:[2] **~ interurbain** *m* COMMS DDD (*AmE*), direct distance dialing (*AmE*), STD (*BrE*), subscriber trunk dialling (*BrE*); **l'~** *m* COMMS STD (*BrE*), subscriber trunk dialling (*BrE*), *composition directe du numéro de téléphone* DDD (*AmE*), direct distance dialing (*AmE*); **l'~ international** *m* COMMS *composition directe du numéro de téléphone* international direct dialing (*AmE*), international direct dialling (*BrE*), IDD

automatiquement *adv* COM as a matter of routine, automatically

automatisation *f* COMMS, IND automation, INFO automation, computerization, MÉDIA automation

automatisé, e *adj* COM, COMMS automated, IND *production* machine-based, machine-made, INFO computer-orientated, computerized, machine-based, MÉDIA automated

automatiser *vt* COM, COMMS, IND automate, INFO automate, computerize, MÉDIA automate

automatisme: ~ industriel *m* COM, IND process control

automne *m* COM autumn (*BrE*), fall (*AmE*)

automobile *adj* IND, TRANSP automotive

automoteur *m* TRANSP *chaland* self-propelled barge

automotivation *f* COM, RES HUM self-motivation

automotrice *f* TRANSP *chemin de fer* railcar

autonome *adj* ADMIN self-governing, COM, ECON autonomous, INFO freestanding, *système, équipement* off-line, *unité* stand-alone, POL autonomous, self-governing, RES HUM *syndicat* independent, nonaffiliated, TRANSP self-governing

autonomie *f* COM autonomy, POL autonomy, self-government

autoréalisation *f* RES HUM self-actualization

autoréglementation *f* BANQUE, ECON self-regulation

autorégression: ~ **de vecteur** *f* MATH vector autoregression, VAR

autorisation *f* ADMIN licensing, BANQUE *d'un prêt* approval, COM authorization, permission, *accord d'un permis* licensing, DROIT authority, authorization, permit, *d'exercer une activité* licence (*BrE*), license (*AmE*), FIN warranty, INFO permission; ~ **d'absence** RES HUM leave of absence; ~ **d'accès** COM entry permit; ~ **d'achat** COM authority to buy; ~ **de congé** RES HUM furlough (*AmE*); ~ **conjoint** BANQUE joint authorization; ~ **en cours d'examen** COM authorization under consideration, AC; ~ **de crédit** BANQUE, FIN bank line, credit line, line of credit (*AmE*); ~ **de crédit irrévocable** BANQUE irrevocable credit line; ~ **de décharge négociable** COM marketable discharge permit, tradeable emission permit, transferable discharge permit, ECON tradeable discharge permit, TDP, ENVIR tradeable discharge permit, tradeable emission permit, TDP; ~ **de déchargement** TRANSP *au port* landing order; ~ **de découvert** BANQUE overdraft facility, overdraft protection; ~ **de dépense** COMPTA authorization for expenditure (*UK*); ~ **de dépenser** ECON, POL spending authority; ~ **d'engagement** FIN commitment authority; ~ **d'exercer un commerce** COM, V&M trading authorization; ~ **d'exercer un métier** COM, V&M trading authorization; ~ **d'exporter** IMP/EXP export permit; ~ **expresse** COM express authority; ~ **générale** COM general authorization, GA; ~ **d'importation** IMP/EXP import licensing; ~ **d'importation temporaire** IMP/EXP carnet; ~ **d'importer** IMP/EXP import permit; ~ **indirecte** BANQUE indirect authorization; ~ **judiciaire préalable** DROIT prior judicial authorization; ~ **limitée** IMP/EXP limited authorization; ~ **de mise sur le marché** (*AMM*) V&M *industrie pharmaceutique* marketing authorization; ~ **négociable de décharge de polluants** ECON tradeable discharge permit, TDP, ENVIR tradeable discharge permit, TDP; ~ **négociable d'émission de polluants** ECON, ENVIR tradeable emission permit; ~ **permanente** IMP/EXP standing authorization; ~ **de prélèvement** COM payment authorization; ~ **de prêt** BANQUE loan authorization; ~ **de prospection de gaz** ENVIR gas exploration licence (*BrE*), gas exploration license (*AmE*); ~ **de prospection pétrolière** ENVIR oil exploration licence (*BrE*), oil exploration license (*AmE*); ~ **de réimportation** ASSUR, FISC, IMP/EXP, TRANSP bill of store; ~ **de remboursement** BANQUE withdrawal warrant; ~ **de sortie** TRANSP release for shipment; ~ **de sortie de marchandises** COM gate pass; ~ **de transport de marchandises dangereuses** TRANSP dangerous goods authority form; ~ **de virement** BOURSE transfer; ◆ **qui n'est pas soumis à** ~ DROIT permit-free

autorisé, e *adj* ADMIN licensed, BANQUE *prêt* approved, BREVETS *revendication* admissible, permitted, COM authorized, entitled, permitted, *qui a un permis* licensed

autorisée: personne ~ *f* FISC authorized person

autoriser *vt* ADMIN license, BANQUE *prêt* approve, COM allow, authorize, entitle, license, permit, DROIT permit; ◆ ~ **qn à faire** COM allow sb to do, authorize sb to do, empower sb to do, entitle sb to do, permit sb to do, give sb the right to do, *par permis* license sb to do; ~ **qn à faire qch** RES HUM qualify sb to do sth

autorité *f* COM control, leadership, power, GESTION, RES HUM authority; ~ **compétente** ASSUR relevant authority; ~ **compétente pour délivrer** ADMIN issuing authority; ~ **fonctionnelle** RES HUM functional authority; ~ **fragmentée** GESTION splintered authority; ~ **hiérarchique** GESTION, RES HUM line authority; ~ **naturelle** RES HUM informal leader; ~ **de parquet** BOURSE floor official; ~ **portuaire** TRANSP harbor authority (*AmE*), harbour authority (*BrE*); ~ **portuaire de la santé** PROT SOC, TRANSP port health authority, PHA; ~ **qui s'exerce en douceur** RES HUM free-rein leadership; ~ **réglementaire** COM, DROIT regulatory authority, regulatory body, POL statutory authority; ~ **de régulation** COM, DROIT regulation authority, regulatory authority, regulatory body

Autorité: ~ **européenne de l'énergie nucléaire** *f* (*ENEA*) COM European Nuclear Energy Authority (*ENEA*)

autorités: les ~ *f pl* COM the authorities; **les** ~ **monétaires** *f pl* BANQUE monetary authorities, the authorities (*UK*); ~ **locales** *f pl* ADMIN, POL local authority, local government

autoroute *f* TRANSP expressway (*Can*), freeway (*AmE*), motorway (*BrE*), superhighway (*AmE*), throughway (*AmE*); ~ **d'informations** INFO information highway; ~ **à péage** TRANSP toll motorway (*BrE*), turnpike (*AmE*)

autosuffisance *f* ECON self-sufficiency

autosuffisant, e *adj* COM, ECON self-sufficient

autour[1] *adv* COM around

autour:[2] ~ **de** *prép* COM around

autre[1] *adj* COM alternative, other; ◆ **pour** ~ **vie** DROIT pour autre vie

autre:[2] ~ **bénéficiaire** *m* FIN other beneficiary; ~ **revenu** *m* COMPTA, FISC, PROT SOC other income

autrefois: d'~ *adj* COM quondam (*frml*)

autrement *adv* COM aliter, secus; ◆ ~ **dit** COM put it another way

autres:[1] ~ **comptes financiers** *m pl* BANQUE, COMPTA, FIN *actif* other receivables; ~ **dépôts vérifiables** *m pl* BANQUE other checkable deposits, OCD; ~ **éléments d'actif** *m pl* BANQUE, COMPTA, FIN other assets; ~ **produits** *m pl* COMPTA, FISC, PROT SOC other income; ~ **produits de gestion courante** *m pl* COM, COMPTA, IND nonoperating revenue; ◆ **et ~** COM et alii

autres:[2] ~ **dettes** *f pl* BANQUE, COMPTA, FIN other liabilities; ~ **questions à l'ordre du jour** *f pl* COM any other competent business, AOCB

autres:[3] **à d'~ égards** *loc* COM in other respects

Autriche *f* COM Austria

autrichien, -enne *adj* COM Austrian

Autrichien, -enne *m,f* COM *habitant* Austrian

auxiliaire[1] *adj* COM subsidiary, *service, opération* ancillary, INFO auxiliary

auxiliaire[2] *mf* COM, RES HUM assistant, asst, TRANSP *navigation* aux., auxiliary; ~ **clients** *m* BANQUE, COMPTA, FIN accounts receivable ledger; ~ **fournisseurs** *m* BANQUE, COMPTA, FIN accounts payable ledger; ~ **des postes** *m* RES HUM postal assistant

av: ~ **-spot** *m* MÉDIA, V&M *publicité* av-commercial

a.v.a. *abrév* (*agent d'assurance-vie agréé*) ASSUR chartered life underwriter (*US*)

aval: en ~ *loc* (*ANT en amont*) COM downstream

avaliser *vt* BANQUE guarantee, COM, FIN back

avaliseur *m* BANQUE guarantor, COM, FIN backer

avance *f* BANQUE *prêt* advance, COM advanced sum, sub (*BrE, infrml*), subvention (*BrE, frml*), *argent* advance, *technologique* advance, IND *technologique* advance, INFO feed; ~ **automatique** ADMIN, COM, INFO autofeed; ~ **bancaire** BANQUE, COMPTA, FIN bank advance; ~ **contre documents d'expédition** IMP/EXP, TRANSP *navigation* air mode container; ~ **en cours** COMPTA outstanding advance; ~ **à découvert** BANQUE unsecured advance, BOURSE uncovered advance; ~ **de déplacement permanente** COM standing travel advance; ~ **fixe** COMPTA fixed advance; ~ **de fonds à plafond** COMPTA imprest fund; ~ **de fonds de roulement** FIN, POL working capital advance; ~ **garantie** BANQUE secured advance; ~ **à justifier** COMPTA accountable advance; ~ **non garantie** BANQUE unsecured advance; ~ **permanente** BANQUE standing advance; ~ **sur les concurrents** ECON, V&M competitive edge; ~ **sur contrat** ASSUR policy loan; ~ **sur déplacement** COM travel advance, trip advance, trip travel advance; ~ **sur le fret** TRANSP advance freight, AF; ~ **sur garantie** BANQUE secured advance; ~ **sur marchandises** COM advance against goods, advance on goods; ~ **sur nantissement** COM advance against security;

~ **sur police** ASSUR policy loan; ~ **sur salaire** RES HUM advance on salary; ~ **sur titres** BOURSE advance on securities (*UK*); ~ **sur valeurs boursières** BOURSE advance on securities (*UK*); ~ **technologique** COM, IND technological edge; ~ **temporaire** FIN imprest; ~ **de trésorerie** COM cash advance; ◆ **d'~** COM in advance; **en ~** COM in advance; **en ~ sur le calendrier établi** COM ahead of schedule; **en ~ sur les prévisions** COM ahead of schedule; **faire une ~** BANQUE *d'argent* make an advance; **par ~** COM in advance

avancé, e *adj* COM advanced, INFO state-of-the-art

avancée *f* COM, IND *technologique* advance

avancement *m* ADMIN advancement, RES HUM advancement, promotion, vertical promotion; ~ **de la visite spéciale** TRANSP *navigation* advance of special survey

avancer *vt* COM *proposition* put forward, *ses opinions* air; ~ **une proposition** COM put forward a proposal; ◆ **faire ~** COM advance, INFO feed; ~ **à pas de géant** COM make quick progress

avances: ~ **en devises à l'exportation** *f pl* (*ADE*) COM advance on export contract; ~ **reçues sur commandes en cours** *f pl* COMPTA advances received

Avances: ~ **sur la caisse de la loi sur les terres destinées aux anciens** *f pl* POL Veterans' Land Act Fund advances

avant[1] *m* TRANSP *d'un navire* bows; ~ **amovible** TRANSP *remorque* detachable front end; ~ **du conteneur** TRANSP container head; ◆ **à l'~** TRANSP *navigation* forward; **d'~ -plan** INFO foreground; **de l'~ à l'arrière** TRANSP *navigation* fore-and-aft

avant[2] *prép* COM ante-, before, prior to; ◆ ~ **bourse** BOURSE before-hours; ~ **l'échéance** BOURSE before due date, before maturity; ~ **impôt** FISC before-tax; ~ **midi** COM am, ante meridiem

avantage *m* COM advantage, FISC, GESTION benefit, RES HUM perk (*infrml*), perquisite (*frml*); ~ **absolu** ECON *économie internationale* absolute advantage; ~ **commercial** COM commercial advantage; ~ **comparatif** ECON comparative advantage; ~ **concurrentiel** ECON competitive advantage, competitive edge, V&M competitive edge; ~ **déterminé** FISC designated benefit; ~ **différentiel** ECON differential advantage; ~ **économique** ECON economic benefit; ~ **en espèces** COM allowance in kind, benefit in kind; ~ **fiscal** ECON, FISC, IND tax advantage, tax break, tax incentive, tax relief; ~ **impalpable** RES HUM intangible reward; ~ **imposable** FISC taxable benefit; ~ **marginal** ECON *économétrie* differential advantage; ~ **matériel** COM allowance in kind, benefit in kind; ~ **en nature** COM allowance in kind, benefit in kind; ~ **personnel** FISC personal benefit; ~ **de prix** BOURSE price advantage; ~ **réciproque** COM mutual benefit; ~ **de rendement** BOURSE yield advantage; ~ **de salaire** RES HUM benefit; ~ **supplémentaire** COM cash benefit; ~ **tarifaire** BOURSE price advantage;

◆ **avoir l'~** COM have the upper hand; **avoir l'~ sur qn** COM have the edge on sb, have the edge over sb; **avoir un ~ concurrentiel sur qn** COM have a competitive advantage over sb; **faire partie des ~s du métier** RES HUM be a perk of the job

avantages: **~ accordés** *m pl* RES HUM plussage (*UK, infrml*); **~ acquis** *m pl* ASSUR vested benefits; **~ annexes** *m pl* RES HUM company benefits, employee benefits, fringe benefits, welfare benefits; **~ complémentaires des personnels d'encadrement** *m pl* RES HUM executive perks (*infrml*), executive perquisites (*frml*); **~ divers** *m pl* RES HUM fringe benefits; **~ et inconvénients** *m pl* COM, ECON assets and drawbacks; **~ en nature** *m pl* RES HUM employee benefits, fringe benefits; **~ sociaux** *m pl* PROT SOC benefits, social benefits, social welfare, RES HUM company benefits, employee benefits, fringe benefits, welfare benefits

avantageux, -euse *adj* COM advantageous, beneficial, concessional, value for money, DROIT beneficial

avant-faillite *f* FISC prebankruptcy

avant-garde *f* V&M leading edge; ◆ **à l'~** IND at the forefront; **d'~** COM *livre, film* advanced, avant-garde; **à l'~ technologique** COM, IND technologically advanced

avant-plan *m* INFO foreground

avant-première: **~ surprise** *f* MÉDIA sneak preview

avant-projet *m* COM draft project, tentative plan, DROIT draft

avarie *f* TRANSP damage; **~ avant embarcation** ASSUR, IMP/EXP country damage; **~ commune** *(a.c.)* ASSUR common average, general average *(GA)*; **~ commune étrangère** COM foreign general average, FGA; **~ commune intégrale** ASSUR general average in full; **~ due aux crocs** TRANSP *manutention* hook damage; **~ grosse** ASSUR general average in full; **~ aux marchandises due au mauvais temps** ASSUR, IMP/EXP country damage; **~ par l'eau douce** TRANSP *navigation* fresh water damage, FWD; **~ particulière** ASSUR *maritime* p.a., particular average; **~ partielle** ASSUR p.a., particular average; **~ à la suite d'abordage** TRANSP *navigation* contact damage

avarié, e *adj* ASSUR, COM, TRANSP damaged; ◆ **~ en cours de route** TRANSP damaged in transit; **~ par eau de mer** TRANSP sea-damaged

avaries: **avec ~** *loc* ASSUR with average, W.A.; **avec ~ particulières** *loc* ASSUR with particular average, WPA; **avec ~ simples** *loc* ASSUR with particular average, WPA

avec *prép* BOURSE cum, COM with

avenant *m* ASSUR clause, extended coverage endorsement *(US)*, DROIT additional clause; **~ concernant les garanties annexes** ASSUR extended coverage endorsement *(US)*; **~ couvrant l'inflation** ASSUR inflation endorsement; **~ au dossier d'inscription** BOURSE filing statement;

~ d'exclusion de la masse salariale ASSUR, COM ordinary payroll exclusion endorsement

avenir *m* COM future; ◆ **à l'~** COM in future, in the future; **dans l'~** COM at a given moment in the future, at some time in the future; **dans un ~ prévisible** COM in the foreseeable future; **dans un proche ~** COM in the near future; **qui regarde vers l'~** COM forward-thinking

aventure *f* ASSUR *maritime* venture

avérer: **s'~ faux** *v pron* (ANT *s'avérer vrai*) COM prove wrong; **s'~ vrai** (ANT *s'avérer faux*) COM prove right

aversion: **~ pour le risque** *f* COM, ECON risk aversion

avertir *vt* COM warn, COMMS inform; ◆ **~ qn de qch** COM acquaint sb with sth, notify sb of sth

avertissement *m* COM warning, word of warning, DROIT caution, RES HUM warning; **~ écrit** RES HUM written warning; **~ préalable** DROIT notice of intention; **~ public** COM public warning; **~ tardif** IMMOB blight notice

avertissements: **~ répétés** *m pl* INFO iterative warnings, repeated warnings

avertisseur: **~ sonore** *m* INFO buzzer

aveu *m* COM confession, DROIT admission, confession

aviation *f* TRANSP aviation; **~ civile** TRANSP civil aviation

avide: **personne ~ de réussite** *f* RES HUM eager beaver (*infrml*); **personne ~ et travailleuse** *f* RES HUM eager beaver (*infrml*)

avion *m* TRANSP aeroplane (*BrE*), airplane (*AmE*), aircraft, plane (*infrml*); **~ affrété** TRANSP chartered aeroplane (*BrE*), chartered aircraft, chartered airplane (*AmE*), chartered plane (*infrml*); **~ -cargo** IMP/EXP air freighter, TRANSP air freighter, cargo aircraft, cargo plane (*infrml*), freighter; **~ charter** TRANSP charter plane, chartered aircraft, chartered airplane (*AmE*), chartered plane (*infrml*), chartered aeroplane (*BrE*); **~ à décollage et atterrissage vertical** *(ADAV)* TRANSP vertical take-off and landing *(VTOL)*; **~ à décollage et atterrissage court** *(ADAC)* TRANSP short take-off and landing *(STOL)*; **~ de ligne** TRANSP airliner; **~ passagers** TRANSP passenger aircraft; **~ -taxi** TRANSP taxiplane *(US)*; **~ de transport régional** TRANSP commuter; ◆ **par ~** COMMS by airmail, TRANSP by air

avis *m* COM *annonce* notice, opinion, *d'arrivée, de livraison, de réception* advice, COMMS notice, DROIT notice, *émanant d'un juriste* opinion; **~ d'annulation** *m* BOURSE cancellation notice; **~ en aparté** *m* COM obiter dictum (*frml*), DROIT obiter dictum; **~ d'appel** *m* FISC notice of appeal; **~ d'arrivée** *m* COMMS advice of arrival, TRANSP *navigation* arrival notification form, ANF; **~ d'assignation** *m* BOURSE assignment notice, notice of assignment; **~ d'assignation de levée** *m* BOURSE assignment notice, notice of assignment; ~ **d'attribution** *m* BOURSE allotment letter (*UK*); ~ **d'attribution d'actions** *m* COMMS letter of allotment; ~ **bancaire** *m* BANQUE bank advice; ~ **de billet prépayé** *m* TRANSP prepaid ticket advice, PTA; ~ **de cession** *m* COM letter of assignment; ~ **du commissaire aux comptes** *m* COMPTA, FIN accounts certification; ~ **de compte** *m* BOURSE account statement; ~ **de confirmation** *m* COM confirmation notice; ~ **de congé** *m* IMMOB notice to quit; ~ **de cotisation** *m* FISC notice of assessment; ~ **de cotisation originale** *m* FISC notice of original assessment; ~ **défavorable** *m* COMPTA adverse opinion; ~ **de délaissement** *m* ASSUR notice of abandonment; ~ **divergent** *m* GESTION divergent thinking; ~ **de droit** *m* DROIT legal opinion; ~ **d'émission publié dans la presse** *m* MÉDIA, V&M tombstone (*jarg*); ~ **d'encaissement** *m* BANQUE advice of collection; ~ **d'exécution** *m* BOURSE confirmation, COM confirmation notice; ~ **d'expédition** *m* TRANSP notice of shipment; ~ **d'expiration** *m* ASSUR expiration notice; ~ **de faillite** *m* DROIT, FIN bankruptcy notice; ~ **fiscal anticipé** *m* BOURSE revenue anticipation note, RAN; ~ **inclus** *m* COM, COMMS advice enclosed, ADV; ~ **d'interdiction** *m* RES HUM prohibition notice; ~ **joint** *m* COM, COMMS advice enclosed, ADV; ~ **juridique** *m* DROIT legal opinion; ~ **de levée** *m* BOURSE exercise notice; ~ **de licenciement** *m* RES HUM termination papers; ~ **de livraison** *m* BOURSE delivery slip, COM, COMMS advice of delivery, TRANSP delivery notice, V&M advice of delivery; ~ **de mise à disposition** *m* TRANSP *maritime* notice of readiness; ~ **motivé d'un avocat** *m* DROIT legal opinion; ~ **de non-discrimination** *m* RES HUM nondiscrimination notice (*UK*); ~ **de nouvelle cotisation** *m* FISC notice of reassessment; ~ **d'offres d'emplois** *m pl* RES HUM help-wanted advertising; ~ **d'opération** *m* BOURSE advice of deal; ~ **d'opéré** *m* BOURSE confirmation, trade report; ~ **d'opposition** *m* FISC notice of objection; ~ **de prélèvement** *m* BANQUE direct debit, DD; ~ **de projet** *m* BOURSE project note; ~ **de rachat** *m* BOURSE call notice, notice of call; ~ **de refus** *m* BANQUE notice of dishonor (*AmE*), notice of dishonour (*BrE*); ~ **de règlement interministériel** *m* FIN, POL interdepartmental settlement advice; ~ **de remise à l'encaissement** *m* BANQUE remittance advice; ~ **de requête** *m* FISC notice of application; ~ **réservé sur la qualité des comptes** *m* COMPTA qualification; ~ **de résiliation à l'échéance** *m* ASSUR not-to-insure clause, notice of cancellation at anniversary date, NCAD; ~ **de résolution** *m* BOURSE cancellation notice, notice of cancellation; ~ **de révocation** *m* BOURSE notice of revocation; ~ **de transfert** *m* BOURSE assignment notice, notice of assignment; ~ **de vente** *m* MÉDIA, V&M announcement of sale; ◆ **à mon ~** COM in my estimation, in my opinion

aviser *vt* COM advise, warn, COMMS advise, inform;

◆ ~ **qn de qch** COM acquaint sb with sth, notify sb of sth

avitaillement *m* TRANSP *d'un navire* victualling; ~ **et soutage** *m pl* TRANSP *navigation* provisions and bunkering

avocat, e *m,f* DROIT attorney-at-law (*US*), counsel, csl, lawyer, trial attorney (*US*), trial lawyer (*US*), *à la cour* barrister (*UK*); ~ **commis d'office** DROIT kite (*infrml*); ~ **-conseil** DROIT legal adviser, legal advisor; ~ **de la défense** DROIT defence lawyer (*UK*), defense attorney (*US*); ~ **d'entreprise** DROIT corporate lawyer; ~ **général** DROIT counsel for the prosecution (*UK*), prosecuting attorney (*US*); ~ **marron** DROIT bent lawyer (*infrml*), crooked lawyer (*infrml*), shyster (*infrml*); ~ **principal** DROIT leader (*UK*); ~ **stagiaire** DROIT *dans un cabinet d'avocats, de notaires* articled clerk (*UK*), trainee solicitor (*UK*); ~ **subordonné à l'avocat principal** DROIT junior counsel (*UK*); ~ **véreux** *infrml* DROIT shyster (*infrml*); ◆ **être l'~ principal de la défense** DROIT lead for the defence (*UK*), lead for the defense (*US*)

avoir:[1] ~ **des actionnaires** *m* BOURSE shareholders' equity; ~ **à échéance plus longue** *m* BOURSE longer-term asset; ~ **extérieur net** *m* BANQUE, ECON net foreign assets; ~ **fiscal** *m* FISC dividend tax credit, tax concession, tax credit; ~ **horizontal** *m* (ANT *avoir vertical*) ECON, FISC horizontal equity; ~ **inactif** *m* BOURSE inactive asset; ~ **non-productif** *m* BANQUE nonperforming credit; ~ **des propriétaires** *m* BOURSE equity capital; ~ **de qualité** *m* FIN quality asset; ~ **en valeurs d'anticipation à long terme** *m* BOURSE long-term equity anticipation securities; ~ **vertical** *m* (ANT *avoir horizontal*) ECON, FISC vertical equity

avoir[2] *vt* COM have; ◆ ~ **du fil à retordre** COM get more than one bargains for

avoir:[3] ~ **trouvé le bon filon** *loc infrml* COM be on a winning streak

avoirs *m pl* BOURSE holdings; ~ **en actions** BOURSE equity holdings; ~ **en devises** BANQUE foreign exchange holdings, ECON, FIN currency holdings; ~ **dormants** ECON sleeping economy; ~ **à l'étranger** COM, COMPTA, FIN assets held abroad; ~ **étrangers** BOURSE foreign assets; ~ **extérieurs** BOURSE foreign assets, ECON, POL overseas assets; ~ **financiers libellés en dollars américains** FIN US dollar financial assets; ~ **liquides admissibles** FISC allowable liquid assets; ~ **du ministère** COMPTA departmental assets; ~ **non-productifs** BOURSE nonperforming assets; ~ **en obligations** BOURSE bond holdings

avoisinant, e *adj* COM adjoining

avouer *vt* COM admit; ◆ ~ **qu'on est dans son tort** COM, GESTION admit one is wrong, back down

avril *m* COM Apr., April

axe *m* COM axis, TRANSP axle; ~ **de la campagne** V&M copy platform; ~ **d'éjection** TRANSP knockout axle; ~ **lotharingien** ECON Lotharingian axis, Rhinelands hourglass; ~ **publicitaire** V&M advertising appeal, advertising concept, basic message; ~ **publicitaire du message** V&M copy appeal

axiomes: ~ **de préférence** *m pl* ECON axioms of preference

ayant: ~ **cause** *m* BREVETS assignee, successor in title; ~ **droit** *m* DROIT interested party; ~ **droit économique** *m* DROIT beneficial owner; ~ **au jour le jour** *m* ECON money at call

Azerbaïdjan *m* COM Azerbaijan

azerbaïdjanais, e *adj* COM Azerbaijani

Azerbaïdjanais, e *m,f* COM *habitant* Azerbaijani

azéri *m* COM *langue* Azeri

Azéri[1]**, e** *adj* COM Azeri

Azéri[2]**, e** *m,f* COM *habitant* Azeri

B

B/. *abrév* BANQUE, FIN PN

BAB *abrév (bord à bord)* IMP/EXP, TRANSP *maritime* FIO *(free in and out)*

baby: ~ **-boom** *m* ECON baby boom

baccalauréat *m* COM, PROT SOC ≈ A level *(UK)*, ≈ Advanced level *(UK)*

bâche *f* TRANSP slip sheet, *pour conteneurs* tilt; ~ **non-imperméable** TRANSP canvas cover, cc

bachelier, -ière *m,f* PROT SOC graduate

bâclé, e *adj infrml* COM slapdash

BAD *abrév* BANQUE *(Banque africaine de développement)* ADB *(African Development Bank)*, TRANSP *(bon à délivrer)* F/R *(freight release)*

badge: ~ **d'identification** *m* COM name badge

bagages *m pl* LOISIRS, TRANSP baggage, luggage; ~ **accompagnés** (ANT *bagages non-accompagnés*) TRANSP accompanied baggage; ~ **enregistrés** TRANSP baggage checked, registered baggage; ~ **non-accompagnés** (ANT *bagages accompagnés*) TRANSP unaccompanied baggage; ~ **non-enregistrés** TRANSP unchecked baggage; ~ **personnels** LOISIRS, TRANSP personal baggage

bagarrer: **se ~ pour** *v pron infrml* COM battle for, fight for

Bagdad *n pr* COM Baghdad

bagne *m infrml* RES HUM sweatshop

Bahamas *f pl* COM Bahamas

bahamien, -enne *adj* COM Bahamian

Bahamien, -enne *m,f* COM *habitant* Bahamian

Bahreïn *m* COM Bahrain, Bahrein

bahreïni, e *adj* COM Bahraini, Bahreini

Bahreïni, e *m,f* COM *habitant* Bahraini, Bahreini

baht *m* COM baht

bail *m* DROIT lease, real agreement, tenure, IMMOB lease, tenure; ~ **accéléré** FIN step-up lease; ~ **assuré** IMMOB security of tenure; ~ **avec option d'achat** IMMOB lease option, lease with option to purchase; ~ **brut** IMMOB gross lease *(AmE)*; ~ **commercial** COM commercial lease; ~ **conforme** FIN true lease; ~ **emphytéotique** BANQUE ninety-nine-year lease; ~ **d'expédition** TRANSP one-way lease; ~ **d'exploitation** FIN, TRANSP operation lease; ~ **d'exploitation à court terme** COMPTA operating lease; ~ **financier** COM, FIN, TRANSP financial lease; ~ **implicite** DROIT *immobilier*, IMMOB tenancy at will; ~ **initial** DROIT head lease; ~ **à long terme** FIN long lease; ~ **à loyer d'immeuble commercial** ASSUR, IMMOB commercial property policy; ~ **maître** IMMOB master lease; ~ **mensuel renouvelable** DROIT, IMMOB month-to-month tenancy; ~ **perpétuel** IMMOB perpetual lease; ~ **en pourcentage** IMMOB *propriété détaillée* percentage lease; ~ **préalable** IMMOB prelease; ~ **sandwich** *infrml*

IMMOB sandwich lease *(infrml)*; ~ **à terrain** IMMOB ground lease; ~ **à vie** IMMOB life tenancy, perpetual lease

bailleur, -eresse *m,f* DROIT, IMMOB lessor; ~ **de fonds** COM contributor of capital, silent partner *(AmE)*, sleeping partner *(BrE)*, *officiel* backer, FIN backer, financial backer, RES HUM sleeper *(infrml)*

bain: ~ **de foule** *m* POL where a politician walks around the streets of a town to gain votes and greet supporters, mainstreeting *(Canada)*, press flesh *(jarg)*, walkabout

baisse:[1] **à la ~** *adj* ECON deflated

baisse:[2] **à la ~** *adv* (ANT *à la hausse*) COM downward, downwards

baisse[3] *f* COM decline, downturn, drop, *des cours* decline, *prix* decrease, fall, ECON decline, downswing, drop; ~ **de clientèle** COM loss of custom; ~ **de courant** INFO brownout *(US)*; ~ **de cours** BOURSE price loss; ~ **lente** BOURSE slow decline; ~ **de la monnaie** ECON fall of currency; ~ **de la population** ECON fall in population; ~ **des prix** *jarg* ECON roll-back *(jarg)*; ~ **du prix** V&M pricing down; ~ **des prix imposée** BOURSE roll-down; ~ **des réserves en devises** BANQUE, BOURSE, ECON fall in foreign exchange reserves; ~ **de tension** INFO brownout *(US)*; ~ **de valeur** BANQUE impairment of value, BOURSE fall in value, impairment of value; ~ **de volume** COM drop; ◆ **en ~** BOURSE (ANT *en hausse*) bearish, COM *ventes* sagging, ECON depressed, *demande* flagging; **être en ~** (ANT *être en hausse*) ECON be down, decline, go down

baisser 1. *vt* COM *prix* abate, knock down, lower, reduce, V&M *prix* mark down; **2.** *vi* BOURSE drop, fall, slip, COM drop, *prix* decline, ECON decrease, drop; ◆ **faire ~** COM bring down, ECON *prix* deflate, drive down, force down; ~ **de valeur** BOURSE fall in value

baissier[1], **-ière** *adj* (ANT *haussier*) BOURSE bearish, COM downward; ◆ **être ~** (ANT *être haussier*) BOURSE be bearish

baissier[2], **-ière** *m,f* (ANT *haussier*) BOURSE bear, bear operator; ~ **à découvert** BOURSE uncovered bear

Bakou *n pr* COM Baku

balance *f* *(bce.)* BANQUE, COMPTA, ECON, FIN balance *(bal.)*; ~ **après clôture** COMPTA postclosing trial balance; ~ **chronologique** COMPTA aged trial balance; ~ **de clôture** COMPTA final balance; ~ **du commerce extérieur** ECON, IMP/EXP, POL balance of trade, trade balance; ~ **commerciale** ECON, IMP/EXP, POL balance of trade, trade balance; ~ **commerciale défavorable** COM unfavorable balance of trade *(AmE)*, unfavourable balance of trade (*BrE*), ECON adverse balance of trade; ~ **commerciale déficitaire** COM unfavorable balance of trade (*AmE*), unfavourable balance of trade (*BrE*), ECON adverse balance of trade; ~ **commerciale excédentaire** IMP/EXP favorable balance of trade (*AmE*), favourable balance of trade (*BrE*); ~ **commerciale des invisibles** ECON invisible trade balance; ~ **commerciale passive** COM unfavorable balance of trade (*AmE*), unfavourable balance of trade (*BrE*); ~ **commerciale des visibles** ECON visible trade balance; ~ **de compte courant** BANQUE, COMPTA, ECON, FIN balance on current account; ~ **dollar** ECON dollar balance; ~ **finale de vérification après inventaire** COMPTA adjusted trial balance; ~ **des financements officiels** COMPTA, ECON Balance for Official Financing, BOF; ~ **des forces** POL balance of power; ~ **hors produits pétroliers** ECON non-oil balance; ~ **impayé** COM open balance; ~ **des invisibles** FIN invisible balance; ~ **des marchandises** ECON merchandise balance of trade; ~ **matières** ECON material balance; ~ **des opérations courantes** BANQUE, COMPTA, ECON, FIN balance on current account; ~ **des paiements** BANQUE external account, ECON, POL balance of payments, external account, BOP; ~ **des paiements comptables** COMPTA, ECON accounting balance of payments; ~ **des paiements déficitaire** ECON deficit balance of payments; ~ **des paiements excédentaire** ECON favorable trade balance (*AmE*), favourable trade balance (*BrE*); ~ **par antériorité des soldes** COMPTA aged trial balance; ~ **des pouvoirs** POL balance of power; ~ **sterling** FIN sterling balance; ~ **de vérification** COMPTA trial balance; ~ **de vérification régularisée** COMPTA adjusted trial balance; ◆ **faire pencher la** ~ COM tilt the balance, tip the scales

balancer *vt* COM swing

balayage: ~ **de l'environnement** *m* ENVIR environment scan; ◆ **faire un** ~ INFO scan

balboa *m* COM balboa

balcon *m* LOISIRS *théâtre* circle

bale *m* COM bale cubic meters (*AmE*), bale cubic metres (*BrE*), BC

baleine *f* TRANSP *maritime* green sea

balise *f* TRANSP beacon; ~ **automatique LANBY** TRANSP *navigation* large automatic navigational buoy, LANBY

ballast *m* TRANSP *d'un navire* ballast space, ballast tank; ~ **séparé** TRANSP *navigation* segregated ballast tank, SBT; ~ **séparé-localisation défensive** TRANSP *pétrolier* segregated ballast tank-protective location

balle *f* TRANSP bale

ballot *m* TRANSP bdl, bundle, *navigation* ballot

BALO *abrév* France (*Bulletin des annonces légales obligatoires*) BOURSE official stock exchange bulletin where French quoted companies must disclose financial information

Bamako *n pr* COM Bamako

banal, e *adj* COM run-of-the-mill

banaliser *vt* COM vulgarize

banc: ~ **des accusés** *m* DROIT dock (*UK*); ~ **d'essai** *m* COM test bench, testbed, INFO benchmark, MÉDIA sneak preview; ~ **des membres sans portefeuille** *m* POL backbench (*UK*); ~ **de mémoire** *m* INFO memory bank

bancable *adj* BANQUE bankable, eligible

bancatique *f* BANQUE, INFO computerized banking, electronic banking

bandage: ~ **creux** *m* TRANSP cushion tire (*AmE*), cushion tyre (*BrE*)

Bandar: ~ **Seri Begawan** *n pr* COM Bandar Seri Begawan

bande *f* COMMS tape, FISC *TVA* band, INFO, MÉDIA tape; ~ **-annonce** MÉDIA *TV, cinéma* header, trailer; ~ **à arracher** COM tear strip; ~ **de base** INFO baseband; ~ **de contrôle** COM tally roll; ~ **jaune** BOURSE yellow strip; ~ **de lancement** MÉDIA *édition* blurb (*jarg*); ~ **magnétique** IND, INFO magnetic tape; ~ **de papier** INFO paper tape; ~ **perforée** INFO paper tape; ~ **à quatre pistes** TRANSP four-track band; ~ **tardive** BOURSE late tape; ~ **de téléscripteur** BOURSE ticker tape; ~ **témoin** INFO audit trail; ~ **vidéo** COMMS video-tape

Bande: ~ **des Quatre** *f* ECON Gang of Four

bandeau *m* MÉDIA *presse* ribbon (*jarg*); ~ **publicitaire** V&M *vente jumelée* band advertising

banderole *f* COM banner; ~ **tractée par un avion** V&M *publicité* aeroplane banner (*BrE*), airplane banner (*AmE*)

Bangkok *n pr* COM Bangkok

bangladais, e *adj* COM Bangladeshi

Bangladais, e *m,f* COM *habitant* Bangladeshi

Bangladesh *m* COM Bangladesh

bangladeshi, e *adj* COM Bangladeshi

Bangladeshi, e *m,f* COM *habitant* Bangladeshi

Bangui *n pr* COM Bangui

Banjul *n pr* COM Banjul

banlieue *f* COM suburbs, suburb; ◆ **en lointaine** ~ COM in the outer suburbs

banlieusard, e *m,f* TRANSP commuter

bannière *f* COM banner

banquable *adj voir* bancable

banque *f* BANQUE bank, bk; ~ **d'acceptation** BANQUE acceptance bank, acceptance house, accepting bank, accepting house; ~ **d'affaires** BANQUE, FIN investment bank (*US*), merchant bank (*UK*), merchant banking, secondary bank; ~ **d'affaires en participation** BANQUE joint-venture investment bank, joint-venture merchant bank; ~ **affiliée** BANQUE affiliated bank, member bank (*AmE*); ~ **agréée** BANQUE authorized bank; ~ **agricole** BANQUE, ECON agricultural bank; ~ **bénéficiaire** BANQUE recipient bank; ~ **cantonale** *Suisse* BANQUE cantonal bank; ~ **centrale** BANQUE Central Bank Facility (*UK*),

CBF (*UK*), central bank, ECON central bank; ~ **chargée des négociations** BANQUE negotiating bank; ~ **à charte** BANQUE chartered bank (*US*); ~ **chef de file** BANQUE lead bank; ~ **de commerce** BANQUE mercantile bank; ~ **commerciale** BANQUE, FIN commercial bank, merchant bank (*UK*), retail bank, wholesale bank; ~ **correspondante** BANQUE correspondent bank; ~ **de crédit** BANQUE borrowing bank; ~ **de crédits à long terme** BANQUE long-term credit bank; ~ **créneau** BANQUE niche bank; ~ **de dépôt** ADMIN deposit institution, depositary, depository, BANQUE, FIN clearer, clearing bank, commercial bank, deposit bank, joint-stock bank, listed bank, deposit institution, depositary, depository; ~ **de détail** BANQUE retail banking; ~ **de données** INFO computer bank, data bank; ~ **électronique** BANQUE, INFO computerized banking, electronic banking; ~ **émettrice** BANQUE issuing bank; ~ **d'émission** BANQUE bank of circulation, bank of issue; ~ **d'épargne** BANQUE savings bank, thrift institution (*US*); ~ **d'escompte** BANQUE acceptance house; ~ **d'escompte d'effets étrangers** BANQUE acceptance house; ~ **à l'étranger** BANQUE foreign banking; ~ **étrangère** BANQUE foreign bank, foreign-owned bank, nonresident bank; ~ **de gros** BANQUE wholesale banking; ~ **habilitée** BANQUE authorized bank; ~ **d'import-export** IMP/EXP Export-Import Bank (*US*); ~ **d'investissement** BANQUE investment bank (*US*), trust bank, FIN investment bank (*US*); ~ **d'investissement en participation** BANQUE joint-venture investment bank, joint-venture merchant bank; ~ **issue de la fusion** BANQUE amalgamated bank; ~ **mandataire** BANQUE agency bank (*UK*), agent bank; ~ **mère** FIN parent bank; ~ **multilatérale de développement** BANQUE, ECON, FIN, POL multilateral development bank; ~ **multinationale** BANQUE multinational bank; ~ **nationale** BANQUE domestic bank, national bank (*US*), ECON domestic bank; ~ **non-affiliée** BANQUE nonmember bank (*AmE*); ~ **non-membre** BANQUE nonmember bank (*AmE*); ~ **notificatrice** BANQUE advising bank; ~ **offshore** BANQUE, FISC offshore banking; ~ **en participation** BANQUE joint-venture bank; ~ **aux particuliers** BANQUE personal bank; ~ **payeuse** BANQUE paying bank; ~ **de placement** BANQUE opening bank, BOURSE issuing house; ~ **privée** BANQUE private bank; ~ **de recouvrement** BANQUE collecting bank; ~ **de référence** BANQUE reference bank; ~ **régionale** BANQUE regional bank; ~ **de réseau** BANQUE, FIN retail bank, wholesale bank; ~ **de réserve** BANQUE reserve bank; ~ **de réserve d'Australie** BANQUE Reserve Bank of Australia; ~ **résidente** BANQUE resident bank; ~ **secondaire** BANQUE fringe bank; ~ **semi-privée** BANQUE semiprivate bank; ~ **du sol** ECON soil bank (*US*); ~ **sous contrôle étranger** BANQUE foreign-controlled bank; ~ **à succursales** BANQUE branch bank; ~ **à succursales multiples** BANQUE chain bank

(*US*); ~ **universelle** BANQUE global bank, universal bank

Banque: ~ **africaine de développement** *f* (*BAD*) BANQUE African Development Bank (*ADB*); ~ **asiatique de développement** *f* BANQUE Asian Development Bank; ~ **centrale européenne** *f* BANQUE, ECON European Central Bank, ECB; ~ **de développement des Caraïbes** *f* BANQUE Caribbean Development Bank; ~ **européenne d'investissement** *f* (*BEI*) BANQUE European Investment Bank (*EIB*); ~ **européenne pour la reconstruction et le développement** *f* (*BERD*) BANQUE, ECON, POL European Bank for Reconstruction and Development (*EBRD*); ~ **fédérale américaine de réserve** *f* BANQUE, ECON Federal Reserve Bank (*US*); ~ **de France** *f* (*BF*) BANQUE, ECON, FIN Bank of France, ≈ Bank of England (*BE, B of E*); ~ **Inter-Américaine de développement** *f* (*BIAD*) BANQUE Inter-American Development Bank (*IADB*); ~ **internationale pour la coopération économique** *f* BANQUE International Bank for Economic Cooperation, IBEC; ~ **internationale d'investissement** *f* BANQUE international investment bank, IIB; ~ **internationale pour la reconstruction et le développement** *f* (*BIRD*) BANQUE International Bank of Reconstruction and Development (*IBRD*); ~ **Mondiale** *f* BANQUE World Bank; ~ **nationale du commerce extérieur** *f* BANQUE *Laos* National Bank for Foreign Trade; ~ **nordique d'investissement** *f* (*BNI*) BANQUE Nordic Investment Bank (*NIB*); ~ **des Règlements Internationaux** *f* (*BRI*) BANQUE Bank for International Settlements (*BIS*); ~ **de la réserve fédérale** *f* BANQUE, ECON Federal Reserve Bank (*US*)

banqueroute: ~ **frauduleuse** *f* COM, DROIT fraudulent bankruptcy

banquier, -ière *m,f* BANQUE banker; ~ **acceptant** BANQUE accepting banker; ~ **d'affaires** BANQUE investment banker (*US*), merchant banker (*UK*); ~ **émetteur** BANQUE issuing banker; ~ **en escompte** BANQUE discounting banker; ~ **hypothécaire** BANQUE, FIN mortgage banker (*US*); ~ **d'investissement** BANQUE investment banker (*US*), merchant banker (*UK*); ~ **payeur** BANQUE paying banker; ~ **prêteur** BANQUE lending banker

banquiers: **les ~** *m pl* BANQUE banking community

baraquage *m* TRANSP kneeling

baraterie *f* TRANSP *navigation* barratry

baratin: ~ **commercial** *m* infrml V&M sales pitch; ~ **publicitaire** *m* infrml V&M *publicité* blurb

baratiner *vt* infrml COM soften up

Barbade *f* COM Barbados

barbadien, -enne *adj* COM Barbadian

Barbadien, -enne *m,f* COM *habitant* Barbadian

bardage *m* TRANSP *navigation* cladding

bardis *m* TRANSP *navigation* shifting board

barème: ~ **de calculs** *m* COM ready reckoner; ~ **de commission** *m* BOURSE scale of commission;

~ **d'imposition** *m* FISC tax rate schedule, tax rate structure, tax schedule; ~ **d'invalidité** *m* ASSUR disability percentage table; ~ **par points** *m* RES HUM points rating; ~ **des prix** *m* V&M price schedule; ~ **progressif** *m* FISC progressive scale; ~ **des tarifs** *m* COM, IMP/EXP tariff schedule

barèmes: ~ **de durées de vie du matériel** *m pl* IMMOB guideline lives (*US*)

barge *f* TRANSP barge, dumb barge, lighter, ship-borne barge

bargette *f* TRANSP shipborne barge

baril *m* IND, TRANSP bar, barrel; ~ **sec** TRANSP dry barrel

barillet *m* TRANSP keg

barils: ~ **par jour** *m pl* ECON, IND, TRANSP b/d, barrels per day

baromètre *m* ECON barometer; ~ **économique** COM business barometer

barque: ~ **de pêche** *f* TRANSP smack

barre *f* TRANSP *de gouvernail* helm; ~ **d'espacement** INFO space bar; ~ **d'état** INFO status bar; ~ **d'impression** INFO typebar; ~ **des menus** INFO menu bar; ~ **oblique** INFO, MÉDIA slash; ~ **oblique inverse** INFO backslash; ~ **oblique inversée** INFO backslash; ~ **d'outils** INFO tool bar; ~ **porte-caractères** ADMIN typebar; ~ **de saisissage** TRANSP rod; ~ **de serrage** TRANSP batten

barreau *m* DROIT ≈ the Bar (*UK*)

barrer *vt* BANQUE *chèque* cross; ◆ ~ **spécialement** BANQUE cross specially

barrière *f* COM, ECON, IMP/EXP barrier; ~ **commerciale** COM, ECON, IMP/EXP, POL barrier to trade, trade barrier; ~ **douanière** (*ANT barrière non-douanière*) COM, ECON, IMP/EXP, POL custom fence, customs barrier, tariff barrier, trade barrier; ~ **d'entrée** (*ANT barrière de sortie*) ECON import-export, IMP/EXP barrier to entry, entry barrier; ~ **fiscale** ECON *commerce* fiscal barrier, FISC tax barrier; ~ **matérielle** ECON, POL material barrier; ~ **non-douanière** (*ANT barrière douanière*) COM, ECON, IMP/EXP, POL nontariff barrier, NTB; ~ **non-tarifaire** (*ANT barrière tarifaire*) COM, ECON, IMP/EXP, POL nontariff barrier, NTB; ~ **non-tarifaire au commerce** COM, ECON, IMP/EXP nontariff trade barrier; ~ **non-tarifaire à l'importation** ECON, IMP/EXP, V&M artificial barrier to entry; ~ **de sortie** (*ANT barrière d'entrée*) ECON, IMP/EXP barrier to exit, exit barrier; ~ **tarifaire** (*ANT barrière non-tarifaire*) COM, ECON, IMP/EXP tariff barrier, tariff wall, POL tariff barrier

barrique *f* TRANSP hhd, hogshead

barrot: ~ **de pont** *m* TRANSP *navigation* beam

bas[1], **se** *adj* BOURSE, COM low; **à ~ prix** BOURSE, COM low-priced; **trop ~** (*ANT trop haut*) COM *prix, devis* too low; ◆ **de ~ en haut** GESTION across-the-board; ~ **de gamme** (*ANT haut de gamme*) COM bottom-of-the-range, down-market, V&M bottom-of-the-range, *marketing* down-market

bas[2] *m* RES HUM bottom; ~ **de casse** (*ANT haut de casse*) ADMIN, INFO, MÉDIA l.c., lower case, lower-case letter; ~ **échelon** RES HUM basic grade; ~ **de gamme** BOURSE *options d'achat* low end of the range; ~ **de gamme du marché** V&M bottom end of the range, low end of the market; ~ **de laine** BANQUE, COM nest egg; ~ **niveau sans précédent** BOURSE *marché* all-time low; ~ **de page** INFO footer; ~ **prix** BOURSE low price; ~ **salaire** RES HUM low pay; ◆ **les ~ salaires** RES HUM the lower-paid

basculage *m* TRANSP tipping

bascule *f* INFO flip-flop, toggle, TRANSP *conteneurs* flip-flop; ~ **électronique** INFO flip-flop

basculer 1. *vt* COM *d'une chose à l'autre* switch, INFO toggle; **2.** *vi* INFO *touche, fonction* toggle

base *f* BOURSE basis, *d'un étalement* leg, COM, FISC basis, INFO base, RES HUM bottom; ~ **d'amortissement** COMPTA depreciable basis; ~ **annuelle** MATH annual basis; ~ **augmentée** FISC stepped-up basis; ~ **de bénéfices** FIN earnings base; ~ **de calcul** COM base of calculation, FIN basis of calculation; ~ **de calcul de prime** ASSUR basis of premium calculation; ~ **du capital** FIN source of capital; ~ **de clientèle** V&M client base; ~ **commune de données** INFO shared database; ~ **comparable** COMPTA comparable basis; ~ **de connaissance** PROT SOC knowledge base; ~ **constitutionnelle** ADMIN constitutional foundation; ~ **du contrat** BOURSE *frais de courtage* per contract basis; ~ **de coût systématique** COMPTA systematic cost basis; ~ **de crédit** COMPTA installment base (*AmE*), instalment base (*BrE*); ~ **de la déduction pour épuisement** FISC depletion base; ~ **de dépenses** FISC *recherche scientifique et développement expérimental* expenditure base; ~ **de discussion** COM basis for discussion; ~ **de données** INFO database; ~ **de données connectée** INFO on-line database; ~ **de données d'entreprise** INFO corporate database; ~ **de données graphiques** INFO graphic database; ~ **de données juridiques** DROIT Legal Exchange Information Service, LEXIS; ~ **de données en ligne** INFO on-line database; ~ **de données relationnelles** (*BDR*) INFO relational database (*RDB*); ~ **de données répartie** INFO distributed database, DDB; ~ **d'équilibre** BOURSE equilibrium basis; ~ **d'imposition** ECON *salaires*, FISC tax base, tax basis; ~ **industrielle** IND industrial base, manufacturing base; **la ~** POL the grass-roots, the rank and file; ~ **monétaire** ECON monetary base; ~ **monétaire étendue** FIN wide monetary base; ~ **partagée de données** INFO shared database; ~ **de participation** COMPTA equity base; ~ **partielle** FIN partial basis; ~ **de placement** BANQUE investment base; ~ **de pourcentage d'achèvement** COMPTA percentage-of-completion basis; ~ **de prix de revient actuel** COMPTA current cost basis; ~ **de provision partielle** COMPTA partial provision basis; ~ **régulière et continue** FISC regular and continuous basis; ~ **de réserve** BAN-

QUE reserve base; ~ **salariale** RES HUM salary base; ~ **de travail** COM base; ◆ **avoir des ~s d'opération en** COM *compagnie aérienne* be based at; **de la ~ au sommet** COM bottom-up; **en partant de la ~** COM bottom-up; **sur la ~ de** COM on the basis of; **sur la ~ du bénévolat** RES HUM honorary; **sur une ~ consolidée** FIN on a consolidated basis; **sur une ~ d'escompte** BOURSE on a discount basis; **sur une ~ de principal à principal** BOURSE on a principal-to-principal basis; **sur une ~ non consolidée** COMPTA on an unconsolidated basis

basé: ~ **sur des faits** *loc* COM factual

baser *vt* COM base

bases: **sur des ~ saines** *loc* COM on a sound footing

BASIC *m* COMP Beginner's All-Purpose Symbolic Instruction Code, BASIC

basse: ~ **mer** *f (BM)* TRANSP low water *(lw)*; ~ **mer de vive-eau** *f* TRANSP *navigation* low water ordinary spring tide, LWOST; ~ **pression** *f* COM low pressure, LP; ~ **saison** *f* COM low season, LOISIRS, TRANSP off-peak season

bassin *m* TRANSP *port* basin, dock; ~ **d'amarrage** TRANSP *port* mooring basin; ~ **de commerce** TRANSP commercial dock, CD; ~ **d'échouage** TRANSP *port* tidal dock; ~ **d'emploi** ECON, RES HUM labor pool *(AmE)*, labor shed *(AmE, jarg)*, labour pool *(BrE)*, labour shed *(BrE, jarg)*, zone of employment; ~ **d'évitage** TRANSP *port* maneuvring basin *(AmE)*, manoeuvring basin *(BrE)*, turning basin; ~ **à flot** COM, TRANSP *port* wet dock; ~ **de marée** TRANSP *port* open dock, tidal dock; ~ **méditerranéen** COM, ECON, POL Mediterranean basin; ~ **de radoub** TRANSP *navigation* dry dock

bastingage *m* TRANSP ship's rail

BAT *abrév (bon à tirer)* COM, MÉDIA final proof

batailler: *vt* ~ **pour** *infrml* COM battle for

bateau *m* TRANSP *navigation* boat; ~ **à aubes** TRANSP paddle steamer, PS; ~ **-citerne** TRANSP tanker; ~ **-citerne caboteur** TRANSP *navigation* intercoastal tanker; ~ **-citerne à moteur** TRANSP *navigation* motor tanker, tanker motor vessel, MT; ~ **-feu** TRANSP *navigation* light vessel, LTV; ~ **fluvial** TRANSP *navigation* inland waterway vessel; ~ **-pilote** TRANSP *navigation* pilot boat; ~ **à provisions** TRANSP *navigation* bumboat; ~ **à vapeur** TRANSP steamboat, steamer; ◆ **par ~ à vapeur** ASSUR, TRANSP any one steamer, AOS

bâtiment *m* IMMOB building, TRANSP *navigation* vessel; ~ **agricole** *m* ECON, IMMOB agricultural building; ~ **et travaux publics** *m pl (BTP)* COM building and public works; **le ~** *m* IND construction industry, housing industry

bâtir *vt* COM *réputation* build up, IMMOB build

bâtonnier: ~ **de l'ordre** *m* DROIT, RES HUM ≈ KC *(UK)*, ≈ QC *(UK)*, ≈ King's Counsel *(UK)*, ≈ Queen's Counsel *(UK)*

battage: ~ **publicitaire** *loc m jarg* V&M, MÉDIA *publicité* hype

battant *m* COM achiever

batterie *f* IND, INFO battery; ~ **sèche** TRANSP dry battery

battre *vt* ECON *monnaie* mint; ◆ **se ~ en pure perte contre** COM fight a losing battle against; **se ~ pour** COM battle for; ~ **son plein** POL be in full swing

baud *m* INFO baud

BBC *f (British Broadcasting Corporation)* MÉDIA *édition, radio, télévision* BBC; **la ~** MÉDIA the Beeb *(UK, infrml)*

bcbg *abrév (bon chic, bon genre)* COM yuppie *(young upwardly mobile professional)*

bce. *abrév (balance)* BANQUE, COMPTA, ECON, FIN bal. *(balance)*

B.d.C. *abrév (Brevet des Collèges)* PROT SOC ≈ GCSE *(UK) (General Certificate of Secondary Education)*

BDR *abrév (base de données relationnelles)* INFO RDB *(relational database)*

bear: ~ **call spread** *m (ANT bull call spread)* BOURSE bear call spread; ~ **spread** *m* BOURSE bearish spread

bec *m* TRANSP spout

BEI *abrév (Banque européenne d'investissement)* BANQUE EIB *(European Investment Bank)*

Beijing *n pr* COM Beijing

Belfast *n pr* COM Belfast

belge *adj* COM Belgian

Belge *mf* COM *habitant* Belgian

Belges: **les ~** *m pl* COM the Belgians

Belgique *f* COM Belgium

Belgrade *n pr* COM Belgrade

Belize *m* COM Belize

bélizien, -enne *adj* COM Belizean

Bélizien, -enne *m,f* COM *habitant* Belizean

Belmopan *n pr* COM Belmopan

bénéfice *m* COM benefit, payoff, COMPTA income, FIN earnings, GESTION benefit; ~ **accumulé** COMPTA accumulated surplus; ~ **au-dessus de la normale** FIN supernormal profit; ~ **brut** COMPTA, FIN gross profit, income; ~ **budgété** COMPTA, FIN budgeted profit; ~ **commercial** ECON, FIN, V&M profit; ~ **comptable** COMPTA accounting income, accounting profit, book profit; ~ **consolidé** COMPTA group profit; ~ **de conversion** ECON, FIN *commerce international* translation profit; ~ **dilué par action** BOURSE fully diluted earnings per share; ~ **disponible** COMPTA available cash flow; ~ **économique** ECON economic profit; ~ **énorme** BOURSE killing *(infrml)*; ~ **de l'exercice** COM, COMPTA, FIN, FISC annual net profit, net profit for the current year, profit for the financial year; ~ **de l'exercice après impôts** COMPTA *sur les sociétés*, FIN profit for the year after taxes; ~ **d'exploitation** COMPTA operating income, operating profit; ~ **d'exploitation actuel** COMPTA current operating profit; ~ **fiscal** FISC tax advantage, tax benefit; ~ **imposable** COMPTA taxable profit, FISC taxable benefit, taxable profit; ~ **inattendu** COM windfall profit; ~ **marginal** ECON marginal profit; ~ **net** COM net income, net profit, *de produits* line *(jarg)*, COMPTA net income, net profit, ECON pure profit, FIN clear profit, net profit, pure profit, net income, FISC net income, V&M net profit, pure profit; ~ **net annuel** COM, COMPTA, FIN, FISC annual net profit; ~ **net consolidé** COMPTA consolidated net profit; ~ **net d'exploitation** COMPTA *des organismes à but lucratif* net operating income; ~ **net par action** BOURSE net earnings per share; ~ **net par action ordinaire** BOURSE, COMPTA net income per share of common stock; ~ **non-dilué par action** BOURSE, FIN basic earnings per share; ~ **non-réalisé** COMPTA unrealized profit, FIN paper profit; ~ **nul** FIN zero profit; ~ **réinvesti** COMPTA, FIN ploughback *(BrE)*, plowback *(AmE)*; ~ **sectoriel** COMPTA segment margin; ~ **sur transactions** ECON *commerce international* transaction profit; ~ **théorique** FIN paper profit; ◆ **être un ~ par rapport à qch** COM be a benefit to sth; **faire un ~ de** COM clear; **faire un ~ énorme** FIN make a killing *(infrml)*; **faire un gros ~** FIN make a killing *(infrml)*; **pour un ~ de** COM at a profit of

bénéfices *m pl* ECON, FIN, V&M profit; ~ **après impôts** *m pl* COMPTA, ECON, FIN, FISC after-tax profit; ~ **attribués aux actionnaires** *m pl* COMPTA distributed profit; ~ **avant impôts** *m pl* COMPTA, FIN after-profits tax, profit before tax; ~ **distribués** *m* FIN distributed profit; ~ **élevés découlant d'un monopole** *m pl* ECON monopoly profit; ~ **de l'entreprise** *m pl* COMPTA corporate earnings; ~ **en espèces** *m pl* FIN cash earnings; ~ **à l'exportation** *m pl* ECON, IMP/EXP export earnings; ~ **de fabrication** *m pl* ECON manufacturing profits; ~ **de fabrication et de transformation** *m pl* FISC, IND manufacturing and processing profits; ~ **industriels et commerciaux** *m pl (BIC)* FIN business profits; ~ **inter-sociétés** *m pl* FIN intercompany profits; ~ **en monnaie constante** *m pl* COMPTA inflation-adjusted income; ~ **monopolistiques** *m pl* ECON monopoly profit; ~ **nets** *m pl* COM, COMPTA, FIN, FISC bottom line profit, net earnings; ~ **non-commerciaux** *m pl (BNC)* FISC non-business income; ~ **non-distribués** *m pl* BANQUE, COM undivided profits, COMPTA earned surplus, retained earnings, retained income, retained profits, undistributed profits, FIN retained earnings, retained income, retained profits, undistributed profit; ~ **non-distribués disponibles** *m pl* FIN unappropriated retained earnings; ~ **non-répartis** *m pl* COMPTA retained earnings, retained income, retained profits, undistributed income, FIN retained earnings, retained income, retained profits, undistributed profit; ~ **par action** *m pl (BPA)* BOURSE earnings per share, gilt-edged stock, per share earnings, COMPTA, FIN earnings per share *(EPS)*; ~ **premiers par action** *m pl* BOURSE primary earnings per share; ~ **prévus** *m pl* FIN anticipated profit;

~ **du producteur** *m pl* LOISIRS producer's profits; ~ **de revenus** *m pl* COMPTA income gain; ~ **de transformation** *m pl* ECON processing profits; ◆ **les ~ du premier trimestre ont dépassé les prévisions** FIN profits surpassed forecasts in the first quarter

bénéficiaire *mf* ASSUR beneficiary, BOURSE beneficial ownership, COM beneficiary, recipient, COMPTA payee, DROIT beneficiary, grantee, FIN beneficiary, *of cheque* recipient, IMMOB beneficiary, grantee; ~ **assimilé** *m* FISC designated beneficiary; ~ **étranger** *m* FISC designated beneficiary; ~ **d'une fiducie** *m* FISC beneficiary under a trust; ~ **imposable** *m* FISC taxable beneficiary; ~ **net** *m* COMPTA, ECON, FISC net gainer; ~ **non-imposable** *m* FISC nontaxable beneficiary; ~ **d'un prêt** *m* BANQUE advance holder, loan recipient; ~ **privilégié** *m* FISC preferred beneficiary; ~ **de redevances** *m* FISC royalty holder; ~ **d'une rente réversible** *m* RES HUM reversioner; ~ **à titre onéreux** *m* ASSUR *assurance-vie* creditor rights life assurance, creditor rights life insurance; ~ **du trust** *m* COM cestui que trust *(frml)*

bénéficier *vt* COM benefit; ◆ ~ **d'une aide financière** COM receive financial help; **faire ~ qn d'une remise** V&M allow sb a discount

Bénélux *m* ECON, POL Benelux

bengali *m* COM *langue* Bengali

Bénin *m* COM Benin

béninois, e *adj* COM Beninese

Béninois, e *m,f* COM *habitant* Beninese

benne: ~ **à ordures** *f* ENVIR dustbin lorry *(BrE)*, garbage truck *(AmE)*, refuse collection vehicle

béquille *f* TRANSP *de semi-remorque* landing gear

BERD *abrév (Banque européenne pour la reconstruction et le développement)* BANQUE, ECON, POL EBRD *(European Bank for Reconstruction and Development)*

Berlin *n pr* COM Berlin

Bermudes *f pl* COM Bermuda

bermudien, -enne *adj* COM Bermudan, Bermudian

Bermudien, -enne *m,f* COM *habitant* Bermudan, Bermudian

Berne *n pr* COM Bern

besoin: **avoir ~ de qch de toute urgence** *loc* COM be in urgent need of; **avoir un ~ urgent de** *loc* COM be in urgent need of

besoins *m pl* COM needs, requirements; ~ **en biens tutélaires** ECON merit wants; ~ **en capital net** BOURSE, ECON, FIN net capital requirements, net cash requirements, NCR; ~ **en capitaux** COM, COMPTA, ECON, FIN capital needs, capital requirements; ~ **de la clientèle** V&M customer needs; ~ **concurrents** COM competing requirements; ~ **des consommateurs** V&M consumer needs; ~ **de crédit** BANQUE borrowing requirement; ~ **en dividende** COMPTA dividend requirements; ~ **en financement** COM, COMPTA, ECON, FIN capital requirements; ~ **de financement du secteur public** ECON, FIN public sector borrowing requirement (*UK*), PSBR (*UK*); ~ **financiers** FIN financial requirements; ~ **financiers d'exploitation** COM, ECON operating capital requirements; ~ **fondamentaux** ECON basic needs; ~ **en formation** COM, RES HUM, V&M training needs; ~ **de liquidités** COMPTA cash needs, cash requirements; ~ **nets de trésorerie** BOURSE, ECON, FIN net cash requirements, NCR; ~ **sociaux** PROT SOC social wants; ~ **de transaction** BANQUE needs of trade

best: ~ **-seller** *m* MÉDIA best seller, page-turner, V&M best seller, best-selling book

bêta[1] *adj* BOURSE *actions, valeurs* beta

bêta:[2] ~ **test** *m* INFO beta test

bétail *m* COM livestock, ECON cattle

bétaillère *f* TRANSP cattle float (*Aus*), cattle truck, stock car (*AmE*)

bête: ~ **de travail** *f infrml* RES HUM eager beaver (*infrml*)

Beyrouth *n pr* COM Beirut

BF *abrév* (*Banque de France*) BANQUE, ECON, FIN Bank of France, ≈ BE (*Bank of England*), ≈ B of E (*Bank of England*)

Bhoutan *m* COM Bhutan

bhoutanais, e *adj* COM Bhutanese, Bhutani

Bhoutanais, e *m,f* COM *habitant* Bhutanese, Bhutani

BIAD *abrév* (*Banque Inter-Américaine de développement*) BANQUE IADB (*Inter-American Development Bank*)

biais: ~ **de sélection** *m* MATH selection bias

bibliothèque *f* COM library, library service,

Bibliothèque: ~ **Nationale** *f France* (*BN*) COM ≈ British Library (*UK*), ≈ Library of Congress (*US*) INFO library; ~ **de programmes** INFO program library

BIC *abrév* (*bénéfices industriels et commerciaux*) FIN business profits

bide: **faire un** ~ *loc* LOISIRS be a flop, be legless (*jarg*)

bidirectionnel, -elle *adj* INFO duplex, full-duplex, FDX

bidon *m* TRANSP drum

biélorusse *adj* COM Belarussian

Biélorusse *mf* COM *habitant* Belarussian

Biélorussie *f* COM Belarus

bien:[1] **trop** ~ **payé** *adj* RES HUM overpaid; ◆ ~ **approvisionné** COM well-stocked; ~ **distinct** COM clear-cut; ~ **équilibré** COM well-balanced; ~ **établi** COM well-established; **être** ~ **avisé de** COM be well advised to; ~ **ficelé** TRANSP well-packaged; ~ **fondé** COM well-grounded; ~ **informé** COM informed, knowledgeable; ~ **intentionné** COM well-meaning; ~ **placé** RES HUM well-meaning, well-off, well-positioned, *pour se lancer dans un marché* well-placed; ~ **rémunéré** RES HUM well-paid; ~ **renseigné** COM well-informed; ~ **en vue** COM *profession* high-profile

bien[2] *adv* COM well; ◆ ~ **connaître qch** COM be familiar with; ~ **connaître son client** BOURSE know your customer; **faire** ~ **de** COM be well advised to; ~ **fonctionner** COM run smoothly; ~ **insister sur** COM *point* hammer home; ~ **réagir dans des circonstances difficiles** RES HUM react well under stress; ~ **réfléchir à** COM give serious thought to

bien:[3] ~ **acquis** *m* COM purchased good; ~ **d'assurance** *m* ASSUR insurance property; ~ **certifié** *m* FISC certified property; ~ **collectif** *m* ECON club good; ~ **en communauté** *m* DROIT community property (*US*); ~ **de la concurrence** *m* COM rival good; ~ **définitivement acquis au failli** *m* BANQUE, DROIT, FIN after-acquired property; ~ **désigné** *m* FISC designated property, specified property; ~ **économique** *m* ECON economic good; ~ **étalon** *m* BOURSE standard commodity; ~ **étranger** *m* FISC foreign property; ~ **-être** *m* COM welfare; ~ **-être économique** *m* ECON, POL economic well-being, PROT SOC economic welfare; ~ **-être mondial** *m* ECON, POL world welfare; ~ **exclu** *m* FISC excluded property; ~ **-fonds** *m* IMMOB landed property; ~ **-fonds loué à bail** *m* IMMOB leasehold interest; ~ **de Giffen** *m* ECON, V&M Giffen good; ~ **immobilier** *m* IMMOB immovable estate, real estate; ~ **immobilier personnel** *m* FISC personal estate, personal property, personalty, IMMOB personal estate, personal property; ~ **en immobilisation** *m* FISC capital property; ~ **en immobilisation corporel** *m* COMPTA, IMMOB tangible capital property; ~ **d'incitation** *m* ECON inducement good; ~ **incorporel** *m* DROIT, IMMOB incorporeal property; ~ **inférieur** *m* ECON, IND inferior good; ~ **intermédiaire** *m* ECON, IND intermediate good; ~ **matériel** *m* ECON, IND material good; ~ **matériel personnel** *m* IMMOB tangible personal property; ~ **meuble** *m* DROIT chattel, FISC personal property, personalty, IMMOB chattel; ~ **normal** *m* ECON normal good; ~ **de petite entreprise** *m* FISC small business property; ~ **pris à bail** *m* COM leasehold estate; ~ **privé** *m* ECON private good; ~ **public** *m* ECON collective good, public good, social good; ~ **public impur** *m* ECON impure public good; ~ **public local** *m* ECON local public good; ~ **reçu en héritage** *m* DROIT inherited property; ~ **de remplacement** *m* FISC replacement property; ~ **semi-privé** *m* ECON mixed good; ~ **semi-public** *m* ECON mixed good; ~ **social** *m* ECON public good, social good; ~ **substitué** *m* FISC substituted property; ~ **transporté en gage** *m* BANQUE pledge; ~ **transporté en nantissement** *m* BANQUE pledge; ~ **tutélaire** *m* ECON merit good; ~ **de Veblen** *m* ECON, V&M Veblen good

bienfaisance *f* COM charity; ◆ **de** ~ GESTION, PROT SOC *organisation*, RES HUM benevolent

biennal, e *adj* COM biennial

biens *m pl* COMPTA asset, assets, DROIT *meubles, mobilier*, ECON gds, goods, FIN asset, assets, V&M property; ~ **amortissables** COMPTA depreciable property; ~ **d'assistance** IMP/EXP relief goods;

~ communs DROIT joint estate; **~ de consommation** ECON consumer goods, consumption goods, ENVIR, IND, V&M *marketing* consumer goods; **~ de consommation courante** V&M fast-moving consumer goods, FMCG; **~ de consommation durables** COM consumer hardgoods, ECON, IND consumer durables, durable household goods, V&M consumer durables; **~ de consommation non-durables** COM soft goods, ECON, IND, V&M nondurable goods; **~ corporels** COMPTA, ECON, FIN physical assets; **~ corporels transmissibles par héritage** (ANT *biens incorporels transmissibles par héritage*) DROIT corporeal hereditaments; **~ durables** V&M durables; **~ d'environnement** ENVIR environmental goods; **~ d'équipement** COM capital goods, hard goods, ECON capital goods, equipment goods, producer's goods, V&M investment goods; **~ d'équipement ménager** ECON, IND durable household goods, V&M consumer durables; **~ et services** ECON goods and services; **~ grevés d'une reversion** DROIT, IMMOB estate in reversion; **~ immeubles** BOURSE real property; **~ immobiliers** IMMOB real estate; **~ incorporels transmissibles par héritage** (ANT *biens corporels transmissibles par héritage*) DROIT incorporeal hereditaments; **~ indivisibles** IMMOB undivided property; **~ industriels** ECON, IND industrial goods; **~ intangibles** (ANT *biens tangibles*) ECON intangible wealth; **~ d'investissement** FIN investment goods; **~ jacents** IMMOB land in abeyance; **~ de location** FISC rentals; **~ de luxe** ECON, IND luxury goods; **~ matrimoniaux** COM, DROIT after-marriage acquired property (*US*); **~ ménagers durables** V&M household durables; **~ meubles** FISC goods and chattels, IMMOB movable property; **~ mis en liquidation** DROIT, FIN, IMMOB bankruptcy property; **~ mobiliers** DROIT movable property; **~ non-durables** COM expendable goods; **~ non-fongibles** COM, DROIT nonfungible goods; **~ non-marchands** ECON nontradeables; **~ passibles de droits** FISC, IMP/EXP excisable goods; **~ personnels** IMMOB chattels personal, personal property; **~ physiques** BOURSE actuals; **~ de production** COM business goods, capital goods, COMPTA business goods, ECON producer's goods, IND production goods; **~ en rente** IMMOB funded property; **~ semi-finis** ECON, IND partly-finished goods; **~ tangibles** (ANT *biens intangibles*) ECON tangible wealth; **~ taxables** FISC dutiable goods

bifédéralisme *m* POL dual federalism

BIFS *abrév* (*bon des institutions financières spécialisées*) BOURSE note issued by certain financial institutions

Big: **le ~ Bang** *m* BOURSE *de la Bourse de Londres, le 27 octobre 1986* the Big Bang (*UK*)

bigue *f* TRANSP *manutention* heavy lift mast crane, jumbo derrick

bihebdomadaire *adj* COM biweekly

bilan *m* COMPTA, FIN assets and liabilities statement, statement of assets and liabilities, statement of financial position, balance sheet, B/S; **~ bien équilibré** COMPTA ungeared balance sheet; **~ certifié** COMPTA, FIN certified financial statement; **~ comparable** COMPTA, FIN comparative financial statement; **~ consolidé** COMPTA consolidated balance sheet, FIN combined balance sheet, consolidated statement of condition (*US*); **~ à faible endettement** COMPTA ungeared balance sheet; **~ en forme de compte** COMPTA horizontal balance sheet; **~ général** COM blanket statement; **~ d'inventaire** COMPTA, FIN balance sheet, B/S; **~ de liquidation** BANQUE, COM statement of affairs; **~ en liste** COMPTA vertical balance sheet; **~ de mi-année** COMPTA, FIN interim statements; **~ périodique des chèques** BANQUE cutoff period; **~ de réalisation éventuelle** BANQUE, COM statement of affairs; **~ sans emprunts** COMPTA ungeared balance sheet; **~ du secteur public** ECON public sector balance sheet; **~ statistique** FISC Statistical Return (*UK*); **~ vertical** COMPTA vertical balance sheet; ♦ **faire le ~** ECON, GESTION debrief; **ne pas apparaître dans le ~** COMPTA be unaccounted for in the balance sheet

bilatéral, e *adj* ECON, POL bilateral

bilatérales *f pl* ECON bilaterals

bilatéralisme *m* ECON *commerce international*, POL bilateralism

billet *m* LOISIRS, TRANSP ticket; **~ aller-retour** TRANSP return ticket (*BrE*), round-trip ticket (*AmE*); **~ automatisé de transition** TRANSP transitional automated ticket, TAT; **~ de banque** BANQUE bank bill (*AmE*), banknote (*BrE*); **~ de cinq livres** FIN five-pound note (*UK*), fiver (*UK, infrml*); **~ en classe économique** LOISIRS, TRANSP economy ticket; **~ collectif** LOISIRS party ticket; **~ de complaisance** BANQUE accommodation bill, accommodation note, accommodation paper, BOURSE kite (*jarg*), COM, FIN accommodation bill, accommodation note, accommodation paper; **~ de contrôle** TRANSP control ticket; **~ de dépôts** BANQUE deposit note; **~ de dix dollars** FIN ten-dollar bill (*US*); **~ de dix livres** FIN ten-pound note (*UK*), tenner (*UK, infrml*); **~ d'entrée** COM entrance ticket; **~ à escompte** COMPTA discount bill; **~ garanti** BOURSE guaranteed bill; **~ impropre à la circulation** BANQUE unissuable note; **~ à moyen terme** BANQUE, FIN medium-term note; **~ mutilé** BANQUE mutilated note; **~ à note** BANQUE, FIN promissory note; **~ open** LOISIRS open ticket; **~ d'option de change indexé** BOURSE indexed currency option note, ICON; **~ d'option de rendement en liquide** BOURSE liquid yield option note, LYON; **~ à ordre** BANQUE, FIN bill to order, promissory note; **~ à ordre payable à vue** COM, FIN demand note; **~ à ordre à taux variable** BANQUE variable-rate demand note; **~ à payer** (*b. à p.*) COMPTA, FIN bill payable (*b.p.*); **~ plein-tarif** LOISIRS, TRANSP ordinary ticket; **~ à recevoir** (*b. à r.*) COMPTA bill receivable (*BR*); **~ sans garantie** LOISIRS wait list (*jarg*); **~ solidaire** FIN joint promissory note; ~ **stand-by** TRANSP standby ticket; ~ **de trésorerie** *(BT)* BANQUE *retail* commercial paper *(CP)*, BOURSE treasury note; ~ **de trésorerie euro** BOURSE Eurocommercial paper, ECP; ~ **de trésorerie en livres sterling** BOURSE sterling commercial paper; ~ **vert** *infrml* ECON, FIN greenback *(US, infrml)*

billets: ~ **combinés** *m pl* LOISIRS combined ticket; ~ **neufs** *m pl* BANQUE, COM, FIN hot bills

billetterie *f* LOISIRS, TRANSP *chemin de fer* booking office, ticket office; ~ **automatique** BANQUE *de billets de banque* automated cash dispenser, automatic cash dispenser, cash-dispensing machine

BIM *abrév (bon à intérêts mensuels)* BOURSE bond with monthly-paid interest

bimensuel, -elle *adj* COM bimonthly, biweekly, fortnightly, half-monthly, COMMS bimonthly

bimestriel, -elle *adj* COM, COMMS bimonthly

bimétallique *adj* ENVIR, IND bimetallic

bimétallisme *m* ECON bimetallism, ENVIR, IND bimetallic standard

binaire *adj* INFO, MATH binary

binôme *m* ECON, MATH binomial

binomial, e *adj* ECON, MATH binomial

biodégradabilité *f* ENVIR biodegradability

biodégradable *adj* ENVIR biodegradable

biodégradation *f* ENVIR biodegradation

bioéconomie *f* ECON bioeconomics

bioingénierie *f* IND bioengineering

biopuce *f* INFO biochip

biotechnologie *f* IND biotechnology

biotope *m* ENVIR biotope

bip *m* INFO beep; ◆ **faire un ~** INFO beep

BIPA *abrév (bon à intérêts payés d'avance)* BOURSE bond with interest paid in advance

bipolaire *adj* INFO bipolar

BIRD *abrév (Banque internationale pour la reconstruction et le développement)* BANQUE IBRD *(International Bank of Reconstruction and Development)*

birman[1]**, e** *adj* COM Burmese

birman[2] *m* COM *langue* Burmese

Birman, e *m,f* COM *habitant* Burmese

Birmanie *f obs* COM former name of Myanmar until 1989, Burma *(obs)*

birr *m* COM birr

bisannuel, -elle *adj* COM biennial

Bissau *n pr* COM Bissau

bit *m* INFO, MATH bit; ~ **d'arrêt** INFO stop bit; ~ **de contrôle** INFO check bit; ~ **de début** INFO start bit; ~ **de départ** INFO start bit; ~ **d'information** INFO data bit, information bit; ~ **de parité** INFO parity bit

BITD *abrév (Bureau international des tarifs douaniers)* IMP/EXP ICTB *(International Customs Tariffs Bureau)*

bits: ~ **par pouce** *m pl* INFO bits per inch, bpi; ~ **par seconde** *m pl (bps)* INFO bits per second *(bps)*

bivalence *f* RES HUM dual skilling

blanc[1] *adj* COM blank

blanc[2] *m* COM *typographie* blank; ~ **de couture** MÉDIA *typographie* gutter; ~ **-seing** BANQUE blank signature; ~ **de tête** MÉDIA *presse, édition, typographie* head, headline

blanchiment *m* COM *de l'argent* laundering; ~ **de capitaux** FIN money laundering

blanchir *vt* COM whitewash *(infrml)*, *argent* launder, FIN launder

blanchissement *m* COM *de l'argent* laundering; ~ **de l'argent** BANQUE laundering money

blé *m infrml* COM bread *(infrml)*

blessure *f* RES HUM injury; ~ **corporelle** ASSUR bodily injury; ~ **indépendante** ASSUR injury independent of all other means; ~ **liée à l'exercice d'une profession** RES HUM job-related injury

bleu *m* ADMIN, MÉDIA blueprint

blind: ~ **-test** *m* V&M *marketing* blind test

bloc *m* ECON block, INFO block, pad, POL bloc; ~ **d'actions** BOURSE block of shares; ~ **d'alimentation** TRANSP *porte-conteneurs* power pack; ~ **de butée** TRANSP *navire, hélice* thrust block; ~ **commercial** ECON, POL trading bloc; ~ **de contrôle** BOURSE control block, controlling interest; ~ **de l'Est** POL Eastern Bloc; ~ **de mémoire** INFO memory bank; ~ **monétaire** ECON monetary bloc; ~ **-notes** ADMIN writing pad; ~ **de papier** ADMIN writing pad; ~ **de touches numériques** INFO numeric keypad; ◆ ~ **demandé au comptant** BOURSE wanted for cash

blocage *m* BOURSE pegging, ECON *des prix, salaires* freeze, FIN freezing, INFO deadlock *(jarg)*, TRANSP *conteneurs* locking; ~ **complet** INFO deadlock *(jarg)*; ~ **de différentiel** TRANSP *véhicule routier* differential lock; ~ **des prix** COM, ECON price freeze; ~ **des salaires** RES HUM pay pause, wage freeze, wage stop; ~ **de titres** FIN escrow; ◆ **faire ~** COM *projet de loi* block

blocus *m* RES HUM blacking, blockade

bloqué, e *adj* BOURSE locked in *(US)*, ECON, FIN, FISC frozen, INFO deadlocked *(jarg)*

bloquer *vt* BANQUE *compte* block, COM obstruct, squeeze, *concurrence* block, *projet de loi* block, ECON *devise* block, freeze, FIN block, INFO inhibit; ◆ ~ **un chèque** BANQUE stop a check *(AmE)*, stop a cheque *(BrE)*; ~ **un compte** BANQUE freeze an account, place a hold on an account; ~ **un cours** BOURSE lock in a rate; ~ **les fonds pour un chèque** BANQUE hold funds for a check *(AmE)*, hold funds for a cheque *(BrE)*

BM[1] *abrév (basse mer)* TRANSP *maritime* lw *(low water)*

BM.[2] ~ **moyenne** *f* TRANSP *maritime* mean lw

BMT *abrév (bon des maisons de titres)* BOURSE securities houses bond

BMTN *abrév (bon à moyen terme négociable)* FIN MTN *(medium-term note)*

BN *abrév (Bibliothèque Nationale)* COM ≈ LC

(US) (Library of Congress), ≈ British Library (UK)

BNC abrév (bénéfices non-commerciaux) FISC non-business income

BNI abrév (Banque nordique d'investissement) BANQUE NIB (Nordic Investment Bank)

bobine f INFO reel; ~ **réceptrice** INFO take-up reel; ~ **thermique** TRANSP navigation heating coil, HC

BOCB abrév France (Bulletin officiel des cours de la Bourse) BOURSE ≈ SEDOL (UK) (Stock Exchange Daily Official List)

bogie m TRANSP bogie

Bogotá n pr COM Bogotá

bogue f INFO bug, program bug

boire: ~ **la tasse** loc infrml BOURSE take a bath (jarg)

bois m COM woodlands, ECON, ENVIR, IND forest, TRANSP w, wood; ~ **blanc et tasseaux** m pl IND bois deals and battens; ~ **blanc, tasseaux, planches** m pl IND dbb, deals, battens, boards; ~ **de fardage** m TRANSP arrimage dunnage; ~ **en lots** m TRANSP packaged timber; ~ **d'oeuvre** m IND lumber (AmE)

boisson: ~ **alcoolique** f COM alcoholic drink; ~ **non-alcoolisée** f COM soft drink

boîte f V&M shop; ~ **en carton dur** TRANSP fiberboard can (AmE), fibreboard can (BrE); ~ **de dialogue** INFO dialog box (AmE), dialogue box (BrE); ~ **à idées** COM suggestion box; ~ **aux lettres** ADMIN mailbox (AmE), postbox (BrE), COMMS accommodation address (BrE), mailbox (AmE), postbox (BrE), INFO mailbox ~ **métallique** TRANSP metal can; ~ **noire** INFO, TRANSP black box; ~ **postale** (BP) COMMS post office box (POB); ~ **de vitesses** TRANSP gearbox

boîtier: ~ **d'amarrage** m TRANSP lashing cage; ~ **à double rangée de connexions** m INFO dual-in-line package, DIP

bolivar m COM bolivar

Bolivie f COM Bolivia

bolivien, -enne adj COM Bolivian

Bolivien, -enne m,f COM habitant Bolivian

bollard m TRANSP navigation bollard

bombe: ~ **aérosol** f ENVIR aerosol

bôme f TRANSP navigation boom, BM

bon¹, ne adj BANQUE, FIN good; **d'un ~ rendement énergétique** adj ENVIR machine energy-efficient; ~ **marché** adj [inv] COM cheap; ♦ ~ **pour acceptation** ADMIN accepted; **au ~ vouloir de** COM at the discretion of; **aux ~s soins de** COM, COMMS c/o, care of; ~ **pour la casse** infrml COM pour les voitures, en plaisantant pour d'autres objects be a write-off (infrml); ~ **chic, bon genre** infrml (bcbg) COM yuppie (young upwardly mobile professional); **en ~ état** fonctionnement COM in good working order; **si vous le jugez ~** COM if you think it advisable

bon² m BOURSE bond, COM coupon, FIN bond; ~ **d'acquittement** IMMOB satisfaction piece (jarg);

~ **d'administration locale** BOURSE local authority bond; ~ **argent** BANQUE fonds du Trésor encaissables le jour même good money (US); ~ **de caisse** BANQUE, BOURSE, COM dans un magasin, ECON certificate of deposit, FIN bank certificate, cash certificate; ~ **de cautionnement** BOURSE guaranty bond; ~ **de chargement** IMP/EXP, TRANSP maritime mate's receipt, MR; ~ **de commande** COMPTA purchase order, V&M marketing direct order form, ventes manufacturing order; ~ **de commande de réassortiment** COM reorder form; ~ **à délivrer** (BAD) TRANSP marchandises freight release (F/R); ~ **de développement industriel** BOURSE industrial development bond; ~ **émis en robinet continu** BOURSE tap bill; ~ **d'enlèvement du navire** TRANSP ship's delivery order; ~ **d'épargne** BANQUE National Savings Certificate (UK), savings bond (US), BOURSE savings certificate; ~ **état apparent des marchandises** TRANSP apparent good order of goods; ~ **d'État à court terme** jarg BOURSE short; ~ **de financement anticipé** BOURSE bond anticipation note, BAN; ~ **fonctionnement** COM smooth running; ~ **des institutions financières spécialisées** (BIFS) BOURSE note issued by certain financial institutions; ~ **à intérêts mensuels** (BIM) BOURSE bond with monthly-paid interest; ~ **à intérêts payés d'avance** (BIPA) BOURSE bond with interest paid in advance; ~ **de liquidation bancaire** BANQUE bank settlement voucher; ~ **de livraison** COMPTA delivery note, TRANSP delivery note, delivery order, DO; ~ **à longue échéance** BOURSE long bond; ~ **des maisons de titres** (BMT) BOURSE securities houses bond; ~ **de marché monétaire** BOURSE rescription; ~ **à moyen terme** BOURSE medium-term bond; ~ **à moyen terme négociable** (BMTN) FIN medium-term note (MTN); ~ **municipal imposable** FISC taxable municipal bond; ~ **nid d'abeilles** BOURSE d'un bon de courtier, FIN honeycomb slip; ~ **normalisé** TRANSP Lloyd's standard slip; ~ **à ordre négociable** (BON) BOURSE tradable promissory note; ~ **de réception** COMPTA goods received note; ~ **de réduction** V&M publicité coupon; ~ **de remboursement** COM credit voucher; ~ **rendement** COMPTA good return; ~ **risque** ASSUR good risk; ~ **risque de crédit** BANQUE good credit risk; ~ **sens** COM common sense; ~ **pour services divers** TRANSP aviation miscellaneous charges order, MCO; ~ **des sociétés financières** France (BSF) BOURSE note issued by certain financial institutions; ~ **de sortie de stock** IND issue voucher; ~ **de souscription** BOURSE stock purchase warrant, subscription warrant, warrant; ~ **de souscription d'actions** BOURSE equity warrant, stock purchase warrant; ~ **de souscription d'actions détachable** BOURSE detachable warrant; ~ **de souscription détaché** BOURSE ex-warrant; ~ **de souscription non coté en bourse** BOURSE unlisted warrant; ~ **de souscription d'obligation** BOURSE bond warrant; ~ **de souscription d'obligations d'État** BOURSE sterling warrant into gilt edged stock (*UK*), SWING (*UK*); ~ **de souscription au porteur** BOURSE, COMPTA, FIN bearer warrant; ~ **de souscription à des titres d'État** BOURSE warrant into government securities; ~ **à taux annuel** *(BTA)* BOURSE annual rate bond; ~ **à taux annuel normalisé** *France (BTAN)* BOURSE French government bond; ~ **à taux fixe** *(BTF)* BOURSE fixed-rate bond; ~ **à taux mensuel** *(BTM)* BOURSE monthly rate note; ~ **à taux trimestriel** *(BTT)* BOURSE quarterly rate bond; ~ **à taux variable** *(BTV)* BOURSE floating rate bond; ~ **à tirer** *(BAT)* COM, MÉDIA final proof; ~ **titre** DROIT, IMMOB good title; ~ **titre de propriété** DROIT, IMMOB good title; ~ **de transfert de marchandise** COM commercial value movement order, CVMO; ~ **de transfert de matériel** COM materials transfer note; ~ **de travail** RES HUM job ticket; ~ **du Trésor** BOURSE government bond, rescription; ~ **du Trésor américain à long terme** BOURSE US Treasury Bonds; ~ **du Trésor pour la construction immobilière** BOURSE project note; ~ **du Trésor à court terme** BANQUE T-bill *(US)*, Treasury bill bonds *(US)*, BOURSE, ECON T-bill *(US)*, Treasury bill *(US)*; ~ **du Trésor indexé** BOURSE retirement issue certificate *(UK)*; ~ **du Trésor à long terme** BOURSE T-bond, Treasury bond, federal government bond *(US)*, long-term government bond, ECON T-bond, Treasury bond; ~ **du Trésor négociable** *(BTN)* BOURSE tradable treasury bond; ~ **de voyage** TRANSP travel voucher

BON *abrév (bon à ordre négociable)* BOURSE tradable promissory note

bonbonne *f* TRANSP carboy

bonde *f* TRANSP *d'un tonneau* bung

bonification *f* ASSUR experience refund, BANQUE, ECON, FIN *d'intérêt* rebate, TRANSP *navire, chargement/déchargement* despatch money, dispatch money, despatch, dispatch; ~ **d'ancienneté** RES HUM seniority premium; ~ **d'assurance libérée** ASSUR paid-up addition; ~ **d'intérêt** BANQUE, ECON, FISC interest rebate; ~ **payable au chargement et au déchargement pour temps gagné** TRANSP dispatch payable both ends on laytime saved, DBELTS, *navigation* despatch payable both ends all time saved, dispatch payable both ends all time saved, DBEATS; ~ **de police** ASSUR policy dividend; ~ **du taux d'intérêt** BANQUE, ECON, FISC interest rate rebate; ◆ ~ **au chargement** TRANSP *navigation* dispatch loading only, DLO; ~ **au déchargement** TRANSP *navigation* dispatch discharging only, DDO; ~ **payable au chargement et au déchargement** TRANSP *navigation* despatch money payable both ends, dispatch money payable both ends, DBE; ~ **payable pour temps gagné au chargement** TRANSP *navigation* dispatch loading only, dispatch money payable on time saved during loading, DLO

bonne ~ **affaire** *f* COM bargain, good bargain, V&M bargain; ~ **couverture** *f* (ANT *couverture*

médiocre) MÉDIA *informations* full coverage; ~ **délivrance** *f* BOURSE *d'un certificat* good delivery; ~ **expérience des affaires** *f* COM good business background; ~ **foi** *f* COM good faith, DROIT bona fides *(frml)*; ~ **foi absolue** *f* ASSUR utmost good faith; ~ **gestion** *f* GESTION good housekeeping; ~ **monnaie** *f* ECON good money; ◆ **de** ~ **foi** ASSUR in good faith; **en** ~ **santé** WEL *person* healthy; **être en** ~ **voie** ECON be under way

bonnes: ~ **feuilles** *f pl* MÉDIA advance copy; ~ **nouvelles** *f pl* COM good news

bons: ~ **de caisse** *m pl* BANQUE corporate debt securities; ~ **de caisse nationaux supplémentaires** *m pl* BOURSE add-on CDs *(UK)*, add-on domestic certificates of deposit *(UK)*; ~ **de collectivités locales sans certificat** *m pl* BOURSE certificateless municipals; ~ **de grand-mères** *m pl* BOURSE granny bonds *(UK, infrml)*; ~ **livrables** *m pl* BOURSE deliverable bills; ~ **du Trésor** *m pl* BANQUE T-bill *(US)*, Treasury bill bonds *(US)*, government obligations *(US)*, government securities *(US)*, BOURSE, ECON T-bill *(US)*, Treasury bill bonds *(US)*, government obligations *(US)*; ~ **du Trésor à court terme** *m pl* BOURSE shorts *(UK, jarg)*

bonus: ~ **pour non sinistre** *m* ASSUR no-claim bonus *(UK)*, no-claims bonus *(UK)*; ~ **réversible** *m* ASSUR, ECON, FIN reversionary bonus, terminal bonus

bookmaker *m* LOISIRS *sport* bookie *(infrml)*, bookmaker, turf accountant *(frml)*

booléen, -enne *adj* INFO Boolean

boom *m* ECON boom; ~ **économique** COM, ECON, POL economic boom

bord: **à** ~ *prép* COM aboard; ~ **à** *prép* TRANSP *navigation, bord à quai* alongside, A/S; **à** ~ *prép* TRANSP on-board; ◆ **à** ~ **de** COM aboard; ~ **arrimé** TRANSP free in and stowed, FIAS; ~ **à bord** IMP/EXP Nt, net terms, IMP/EXP *(BAB)* free in and out *(FIO)*, TRANSP Nt, net terms, TRANSP *(BAB) maritime* free in and out *(FIO)*; ~ **à bord arrimage et choulage** TRANSP free in, out, stowed and trimmed; ~ **à bord et arrimage** TRANSP *maritime* FIO and stowed, free in, out and stowed; ~ **à bord et choulage** TRANSP *maritime* FIO and trimmed, free in, out and trimmed; **être au** ~ **de** COM *la faillite* be on the verge of

bordé: ~ **extérieur** *m* TRANSP *navigation* shell plating

bordereau *m* COM bordereau, invoice, note, slip, statement; ~ **d'acceptation** ASSUR acceptance slip; ~ **d'achat** BOURSE bought contract, bought note, contract note; ~ **d'achat différé périodique** FIN periodic purchase deferred contract; ~ **d'acheminement** TRANSP *marchandises* routing order, RO; ~ **de caisse** COMPTA cash statement; ~ **de cargaison soumise aux droits de douane** IMP/EXP dutiable cargo list; ~ **de charge** TRANSP load sheet; ~ **de chèque de guichet** BANQUE counter check form *(AmE)*, counter cheque form *(BrE)*; ~ **de colisage** IMP/EXP, TRANSP packaging list, packing list; ~ **de comptabilité de la cargaison** TRANSP cargo-accounting device; ~ **de dépôt** BANQUE deposit slip, pay-in slip (*AmE*), paying-in slip (*BrE*); ~ **d'enlèvement** IMP/EXP removal note; ~ **d'expédition** TRANSP consignment note, CN, despatch note, dispatch note; ~ **d'instruction** TRANSP transport instruction, transport instruction form; ~ **d'instruction de l'expéditeur pour l'émission d'une lettre de transport aérien** IMP/EXP, TRANSP shipper's letter of instruction for issuing air waybills; ~ **de livraison** TRANSP release note, RN; ~ **de marchandises dangereuses** TRANSP dangerous goods note, DGN; ~ **de paiement** COM remittance slip; ~ **de retrait** BANQUE withdrawal slip; ~ **de signature** COMPTA signing slip; ~ **de sortie de frais** IMP/EXP out-of-charge note; ~ **de vente** BOURSE contract note; ~ **de versement** BANQUE deposit slip, pay-in slip (*AmE*), paying-in slip (*BrE*)

borne *f* DROIT landmark; ~ **d'appel d'urgence** COMMS call box (*AmE*)

bosniaque *adj* COM Bosnian

Bosniaque *m,f* COM *habitant* Bosnian

Bosnie *f* COM Bosnia

Bosnie-Herzégovine *f* COM Bosnia-Herzegovina

bosnien, -enne *adj* COM Bosnian

Bosnien, -enne *m,f* COM *habitant* Bosnian

bossoir *m* TRANSP *navigation* davit

Botswana:[1] **de ~** *adj* COM Botswana

Botswana[2] *m* COM Botswana

Bottin® *m France* COMMS phone book, telephone book, telephone directory

bouchain *m* TRANSP *d'un navire* bilge

bouche: ~ **-trou** *m* MÉDIA *imprimé* filler advertisement

boucher: *vt* ~ **le trou** ECON, FIN bridge the gap

bouchon *m* TRANSP bottleneck

bouclage *m* INFO wraparound; ~ **rapide** COM quick fix

boucle: ~ **de courant** *f* INFO current loop; ◆ **la ~ est bouclée** COM the wheel has come full circle

Bouclier: ~ **Bleu** *m* ASSUR Blue Shield (*US*)

bouge *f* TRANSP *d'un navire* camber

bouger: **ne pas ~** *loc* COM sit tight, stand firm, stand one's ground

boulanger: **être ~** *loc* COM trade as a baker

boule: ~ **de commande** *f* INFO trackball; ~ **IBM**® *f* ADMIN typewriter ball; ~ **de pointeur** *f* INFO trackball; ~ **roulante** *f* INFO trackball; ◆ **faire ~ de neige** COM snowball

bouleversement *m* COM *dans organisation* upheaval

bourgeoisie *f* ECON bourgeoisie, middle class, POL bourgeoisie

bourrage *m* INFO *dans imprimante* jam

bourreau: ~ **de travail** *m* COM, RES HUM workaholic

bourse *f* BOURSE exch., exchange, securities house, PROT SOC grant; ~ **du commerce** BOURSE ≈ Commodities Exchange (*US*); ~ **de commerce** BOURSE commodity market, mercantile exchange; ~ **à découvert** BOURSE short; ~ **d'études** FISC scholarship; ~ **aux grains** BOURSE grain exchange; ~ **internationale des produits pétroliers** BOURSE International Petroleum Exchange (*UK*), IPE (*UK*); **la ~ de Toronto** *Canada* BOURSE Toronto Stock Exchange (*Canada*); ~ **de marchandises** BOURSE commodity exchange (*US*), commodity market, mercantile exchange; ~ **régionale** BOURSE regional stock exchange; ~ **réglementée par les autorités fédérales** BOURSE federally-regulated exchange (*US*); ~ **du travail** COM, RES HUM labour exchange; ~ **de valeurs mobilières** BOURSE stock exchange; ◆ **dénouer les cordons de sa ~** FIN loosen one's purse strings; **en ~** BOURSE on the stock exchange

Bourse *f* BOURSE securities exchange, stock market; ~ **de Boston** BOURSE Boston Stock Exchange; ~ **aux céréales de Minnéapolis** BOURSE Minneapolis Grain Exchange (*US*); ~ **de commerce de l'Amex** BOURSE Amex Commodities Exchange, ACE; ~ **de commerce de Paris** BOURSE the Paris Stock Exchange, ≈ London Stock Exchange, ≈ the LSE; ~ **du coton de New York** BOURSE New York Cotton Exchange (*US*); ~ **des grains de Minnéapolis** BOURSE Minneapolis Grain Exchange (*US*); **la ~ de Paris** BOURSE ≈ London Stock Exchange, ≈ the LSE, the Paris Stock Exchange; **la ~ de Toronto** *Canada* BOURSE TSE (*Canada*), the Toronto Stock Exchange (*Canada*); ~ **des marchandises** BOURSE ≈ Commodities Exchange (*US*); ~ **des marchandises Mid-America de Chicago** BOURSE Mid-America Commodity Exchange; ~ **de matières premières de Londres** BOURSE LCE (*obs*), London Commodity Exchange (*obs*); ~ **des métaux de Londres** BOURSE London Metal Exchange, LME; ~ **du Midwest** BOURSE Midwest Stock Exchange (*US*); ~ **d'options européenne** BOURSE European Options Exchange, EOE; ~ **des options négociables de Londres** BOURSE London Trader Options Market, LTOM; ~ **du Trésor** FISC Treasury's purse (*UK*)

boursicotage *m* BOURSE punt

boursicoter 1. *vt* BOURSE scalp (*US, infrml*); **2.** *vi* BOURSE have a flutter (*UK, infrml*)

boursicoteur, -euse *m,f* BOURSE ≈ scalper (*US*), piker (*jarg*), punter, small speculator

boursier: ~ **new-yorkais** *m* BOURSE Wall-Streeter

boursiers: ~ **néophytes** *m* BOURSE lambs (*infrml*)

bousculer *vt* COM hustle

bout: ~ **-dehors** *m* TRANSP *navigation* boom, BM; ~ **d'essai** *m* MÉDIA film test, *télévision, cinéma* screen test

bouteille *f* COM, V&M bottle

boutique *f* COM shop (*BrE*); ~ **hors taxes** FISC duty-free shop, tax-free shop, LOISIRS duty-free shop, tax-free shop, TRANSP duty-free shop, tax-free shop; ~ **de proximité** V&M convenience shop (*BrE*), convenience store (*AmE*)

bouton *m* INFO button, knob; ~ **bleu** *jarg* BOURSE blue button (*UK, jarg*); ~ **de remise à zéro** INFO reset button; ~ **rouge** *jarg* BOURSE red button (*UK, jarg*)

boxe: ~ **téléphonique** *m* BOURSE phone desk

boycott *m* RES HUM boycott; ~ **complémentaire** RES HUM secondary boycott; ~ **primaire** RES HUM primary boycott; ~ **vert** RES HUM green ban (*Australia*)

boycottage *m* ECON, LOISIRS *sport* boycott, RES HUM *en grève* blacking

boycotter *vt* COM, ECON boycott, RES HUM black, boycott

b. de p. *abrév* (*bureau de poste*) COMMS PO (*post office*)

BP *abrév* (*boîte postale*) COMMS POB (*post office box*)

b. à p. *abrév* (*billet à payer*) COMPTA, FIN b.p. (*bill payable*)

BPA *abrév* (*bénéfices par action*) BOURSE, COMPTA, FIN EPS (*earnings per share*)

bps *abrév* (*bits par seconde*) INFO bps (*bits per second*)

b. à r. *abrév* (*billet à recevoir*) COMPTA BR (*bill receivable*)

brader *vt* ECON, V&M *prix* cut

braderie: ~ **d'objets usagés** *f* V&M jumble sale (*BrE*), rummage sale (*AmE*)

brainstorming *m* GESTION brainstorming; ◆ **faire du** ~ GESTION brainstorm

branche *f* INFO *d'organigramme* path; ~ **d'activité** COM activity, field of activity; ~ **d'assurance** ASSUR class of insurance; ~ **technique d'assurance** ASSUR engineering insurance

branché *adj* COM trendy (*UK, infrml*)

branchement *m* INFO branch; ~ **conditionnel** INFO conditional branch

brancher *vt* COM, INFO plug in

branlant, e *adj* COM shaky

braquer: se ~ *v pron* COM dig in one's heels (*infrml*)

bras *m* ECON arm

Brasilia *n pr* COM Brasilia

brassage: ~ **d'affaires louches** *m* BOURSE, COM wheeling and dealing (*infrml*)

brasse *f* COM fathom, fm, *maritime* 216 cubic feet, fathom

brasseur: ~ **d'affaires** *m* COM wheeler-dealer (*infrml*); ~ **de capitaux** *m* COM moneymaker

Bratislava *n pr* COM Bratislava

Brazzaville *n pr* COM Brazzaville

Brésil *m* COM Brazil

brésilien, -enne *adj* COM Brazilian

Brésilien, -enne *m,f* COM *habitant* Brazilian

brève: ~ **montée des prix** *f* BOURSE bulge

brevet *m* BREVETS pat., patent, COM pat., patent, trademark, COMPTA trademark, DROIT pat., patent; ~ **antérieur** BREVETS prior patent; ~ **d'aptitude** TRANSP *navigation* certificate of competency; ~ **de capitaine** TRANSP *navigation* master's certificate; ~ **dépendant** BREVETS dependent patent; ~ **déposé** BREVETS, DROIT pat. pend., patent pending; ~ **européen** BREVETS European patent; ~ **d'invention** BREVETS, DROIT patent of invention; ~ **national** BREVETS national patent; ~ **de perfectionnement** BREVETS improvement patent; ~ **régional** BREVETS regional patent

Brevet: ~ **des Collèges** *m* (*B.d.C.*) PROT SOC ≈ General Certificate of Secondary Education (*UK*) (*GCSE*)

brevetabilité *f* BREVETS patentability

brevetable *adj* BREVETS *propriété intellectuelle*, DROIT patentable

breveté, e *adj* BREVETS, DROIT licensed; ◆ **qui peut être** ~ BREVETS, DROIT patentable

BRI *abrév* (*Banque des Règlements Internationaux*) BANQUE BIS (*Bank for International Settlements*)

brick *m vieilli* TRANSP *navigation* b/g (*dat*), brig (*dat*)

bricolage *m* COM do-it-yourself, DIY

Bridgetown *n pr* COM Bridgetown

briefer *vt* COM brief

briefing *m* COM, GESTION briefing, briefing session; ~ **d'équipe** ECON, GESTION team briefing

brigade: ~ **de production agricole** *f jarg* ECON, POL production brigade (*jarg*)

brise: ~ **-glace** *m* TRANSP *navigation* icebreaker

briseur: ~ **de grève** *m* RES HUM blackleg (*UK*), scab (*pej*), strikebreaker

britannique *adj* COM Brit (*infrml*), British

Britannique *mf* COM Brit (*infrml*), British person, Briton

brocante *f* COM second-hand market

brochure *f* COM, COMMS booklet, brochure, LOISIRS brochure; ~ **commerciale** V&M sales literature

bromure: ~ **de méthyle** *m* TRANSP methyl bromide

brouillage *m* COMMS signal jamming

brouiller: se ~ **avec** *v pron* COM fall foul of

brouillon *m* COM draft, scrap paper, DROIT rough draft, FISC *d'une déclaration* working copy, INFO draft, scratch

broyeur *m* ADMIN shredder

bruit *m* INFO noise; ~ **blanc** MATH noise, white noise

bruitage *m* MÉDIA sound effects

brun: le ~ *m* V&M brown goods

Brunei *m* COM Brunei

brusquement *adv* COM sharply

brut, e *adj* COMPTA gross, INFO, MATH raw

brutalement *adv* COMPTA sharply

Bruxelles *n pr* COM Brussels

BSF *abrév France* (*bon des sociétés financières*) BOURSE note issued by certain financial institutions

BT *abrév* (*billet de trésorerie*) BANQUE CP (*commercial paper*), BOURSE treasury note

BTA *abrév (bon à taux annuel)* BOURSE annual rate bond

BTAN *abrév France (bon à taux annuel normalisé)* BOURSE French government bond

BTF *abrév (bon à taux fixe)* BOURSE fixed-rate bond

BTM *abrév (bon à taux mensuel)* BOURSE monthly rate note

BTN *abrév (bon du Trésor négociable)* BOURSE tradable treasury bond

BTP *abrév (bâtiment et travaux publics)* COM building and public works

BTT *abrév (bon à taux trimestriel)* BOURSE quarterly rate bond

BTV *abrév (bon à taux variable)* BOURSE floating rate bond

Bucarest *n pr* COM Bucharest

Budapest *n pr* COM Budapest

budget *m* COM, COMPTA, ECON, FIN budget, MÉDIA, V&M *de publicité* account, budget; ~ **d'achat d'espaces** COMPTA, MÉDIA media budget; ~ **en baisse** FIN soft budget; ~ **de base** COMPTA base budget; ~ **base zéro** COMPTA, FIN zero-base budget, zero-base budgeting, ZBB; ~ **commercial** V&M sales budget; ~ **conjoncturel** FIN contingent budget; ~ **de la défense** POL government defence appropriations (*BrE*), government defense appropriations (*AmE*); ~ **des dépenses** COM expenditure budget, COMPTA expense budget; ~ **des dépenses supplémentaires** FIN, POL Supplementaries; ~ **directeur** FIN comprehensive budget; ~ **équilibré** COMPTA, ECON, FIN balanced budget; ~ **d'équipement** ECON, FIN capital budget; ~ **d'exploitation** COMPTA, FIN operating budget, operational budget; ~ **flexible** ECON variable budget; ~ **fonctionnel** FIN performance budget; ~ **général** FIN comprehensive budget; ~ **des immobilisations** ECON, FIN capital budget; ~ **d'investissement** COMPTA, ECON, FIN capital budget, investment budget; ~ **des investissements** COMPTA capital expenditure budget; ~ **à long terme** FIN long-term budget; ~ **de marketing** COMPTA, V&M marketing budget; ~ **neutre** ECON, POL neutral budget; ~ **perpétuel** FIN continuous budget; ~ **de plein emploi** COMPTA, ECON *calculs économiques*, POL actual budget, full-employment budget; ~ **principal** COMPTA master budget; ~ **-promotion** V&M percentage of product price spent on promotion; ~ **de la publicité** FIN advertising allocation budget, appropriation of advertising, advertising budget, *chez l'annonceur* advertising appropriation, promotional allowance, promotional budget, V&M advertising allocation budget, appropriation of advertising, advertising appropriation, promotional allowance, promotional budget, *chez l'annonceur* advertising budget; ~ **de recettes** COMPTA income budget, revenue budget; ~ **de recherche** COMPTA research budget;

~ **réel** COMPTA, ECON *calculs économiques*, POL actual budget; ~ **serré** FIN tight budget; ~ **de trésorerie** COMPTA cash budget, ECON cash budgeting; ~ **variable** ECON flexible budget, variable budget; ~ **de ventes** COMPTA revenue budget

Budget: ~ **communautaire** *m* ECON, FIN, POL Community budget, European Community Budget; ~ **de la Communauté** *m* ECON, FIN, POL Community budget; ~ **des dépenses** *m* FIN estimates of expenditure; **le** ~ *m* ECON, POL the Budget (*UK*)

budgétaire *adj* COM, COMPTA, ECON, FIN, POL budget, budgetary, fiscal

budgétisation *f* COMPTA, FIN budgeting; ~ **base zéro** COMPTA, FIN zero-base budgeting, ZBB; ~ **en fonction de la gestion** COMPTA responsibility budgeting; ~ **des immobilisations** COMPTA capital budgeting; ~ **des investissements** COMPTA capital budgeting; ~ **de programmes** COMPTA, FIN, GESTION, RES HUM program budgeting (*AmE*), programme budgeting (*BrE*)

budgétiser *vt* COM, COMPTA, ECON, FIN, POL budget

Buenos Aires *n pr* COM Buenos Aires

bug *m* INFO bug

bugalet *m* TRANSP *navigation* h, hoy

Bujumbura *n pr* COM Bujumbura

bulbe: ~ **d'étrave** *m* TRANSP *navigation* bulbous bow, BB

bulgare[1] *adj* COM Bulgarian

bulgare[2] *m* COM *langue* Bulgarian

Bulgare *mf* COM *habitant* Bulgarian

Bulgarie *f* COM Bulgaria

bull: ~ **call spread** *m* (*ANT bear call spread*) BOURSE bull call spread; ~ **spread** *m* BOURSE bull spread, bullish spread

bulle: ~ **financière** *f* BOURSE bubble (*jarg*); ~ **spéculative** *f* BOURSE bubble (*jarg*)

bulletin *m* COM bulletin, *d'informations* newsletter, COMMS bulletin, newsletter, V&M bulletin; ~ **de bagages** LOISIRS, TRANSP baggage check; ~ **blanc** COM *lors d'une élection ou d'un scrutin* spoiled voting paper; ~ **de commande détachable** COM tear-off coupon; ~ **de consigne** COM, DROIT *commercial*, IMP/EXP, TRANSP, V&M warehouse warrant, WW; ~ **de dépôt** DROIT, IMP/EXP, TRANSP *port* dock warrant, D/W; ~ **d'expédition** TRANSP despatch note, dispatch note; ~ **financier** FIN market review; ~ **de gage agricole** ECON agricultural warrant; ~ **d'informations** COMMS, MÉDIA bulletin, news bulletin; ~ **de livraison** TRANSP delivery note; ~ **météorologique** COM weather report; ~ **de paie** RES HUM pay bill (*AmE*), pay sheet, payslip (*BrE*); ~ **de pesage** COM weight note; ~ **de quittance des marchandises** IMP/EXP, TRANSP goods received note; ~ **de salaire** RES HUM pay bill (*AmE*), pay sheet, payslip (*BrE*); ~ **de salaire analytique** RES HUM itemized pay statement; ~ **scolaire** COM school report; ~ **de souscription** ADMIN application form, COM application form, subscription form; ~ de **versement** COM credit slip, credit voucher, refund slip, FIN credit memorandum; ~ de **vote** POL ballot paper, RES HUM ballot paper, voting paper; ~ de **vote blanc** COM *lors d'une élection ou d'un scrutin* spoiled voting paper; ~ de **vote nul** POL spoilt ballot paper

Bulletin: ~ **des annonces légales obligatoires** *m France (BALO)* BOURSE official stock exchange bulletin where French quoted companies must disclose financial information; ~ **international d'assistance et prêts** *m* BANQUE International Aid and Loan Bulletin; ~ **officiel des cours de la Bourse** *m France (BOCB)* BOURSE ≈ Stock Exchange Daily Official List *(UK) (SEDOL)*

bureau *m* ADMIN agency, bureau, office, BANQUE office, COM agency, office, *espace bureaux* accommodation, *meuble* desk, COMPTA, DROIT office; ~ **d'aide sociale** RES HUM dole office *(BrE, infrml)*, welfare office *(AmE)*; ~ **des autorisations d'exportation** IMP/EXP export licensing branch, ELB; ~ **d'avocats** DROIT law firm, law practice; ~ **du cadastre** DROIT, IMMOB land registry; ~ **du caissier** ADMIN, COMPTA, FIN cash office; ~ **de la caissière** ADMIN, COMPTA, FIN cash office; ~ **central** ADMIN front office; ~ **central de réservation de transport aérien** TRANSP central freight booking office; ~ **central des réservations** LOISIRS central reservation office; ~ **central de transport** TRANSP central freight bureau, CFB; ~ **de change** BANQUE bureau de change, exchange office, foreign exchange office; ~ **commercial** ADMIN business office; ~ **consultatif sur le marché national** BOURSE national market advisory board; ~ **des contributions** FISC revenue office; ~ **de cotation** FIN credit bureau, credit reference agency; ~ **de courtier marron** BOURSE, FIN bucket shop; ~ **de dédouanement ferroviaire intérieur** IMP/EXP, TRANSP inland rail depot, IRD; ~ **de dédouanement de l'intérieur** IMP/EXP inland clearance depot, ICD; ~ **de design** COM *dessin, graphisme, maquettes* design office; ~ **de dessin** COM design office; ~ **du directeur** ADMIN, GESTION manager's office; ~ **de la direction** RES HUM executive suite; ~ **de la direction et du personnel** ADMIN, GESTION management and personnel office, MPO; ~ **de distribution** TRANSP *lieu* distribution office, DO; ~ **électronique** ADMIN, COM electronic office; ~ **d'enregistrement** ADMIN registration office, LOISIRS reception point; ~ **de l'enregistrement** ADMIN registry, registry office *(UK)*; ~ **d'enregistrement des actes** ADMIN, DROIT, IMMOB registry of deeds; ~ **de l'état civil** ADMIN register office, registrar's office, registry office *(UK)*; ~ **d'étude** COM design office, engineering and design department, research department, engineering firm; ~ **exécutif du consortium** RES HUM Group Executive Board, GEB; ~ **exécutif du groupe** RES HUM Group Executive Board, GEB; ~ **d'exportation** IMP/EXP export office; ~ **d'imposition** FISC taxation office; ~ **d'information** COM enquiry desk, inquiry desk;

~ **d'inscription** cadastre des ventes immobilières interétat IMMOB Office of Interstate Land Sales Registration *(US)*, OILSR *(US)*; ~ **d'investigation des fraudes graves** BOURSE ≈ SFO *(UK)*, ≈ Serious Fraud Office *(UK)*; ~ **local pour l'emploi** RES HUM ≈ Jobcentre *(UK)*; ~ **de location** LOISIRS *d'un théâtre* box office; ~ **de locations** LOISIRS booking office; ~ **de médiateur en matière d'assurance** ASSUR Insurance Ombudsman Bureau *(UK)*, IOB *(UK)*; ~ **de messageries** COM receiving office, RO; ~ **paysager** ADMIN open-plan office; ~ **de placement** COM, RES HUM employment agency, employment bureau, employment office *(UK)*; ~ **de planification économique** ECON economic planning unit, EPU; ~ **de poste** ADMIN post office, COMMS post office; ~ **de poste annexe** COMMS subpost office; ~ **de poste auxiliaire** COMMS subpost office; ~ **de prêteur sur gages** FIN pawnshop; ~ **privé** ADMIN private office; ~ **de réception** COM *des marchandises* receiving office, RO; ~ **du receveur** IMP/EXP collector's office; ~ **de recouvrement de créances** FIN debt collection agency, DCA; ~ **de recrutement** RES HUM recruiting office; ~ **régional** COM branch office, regional office, BO; ~ **de relations actionnaires** BOURSE, FIN investors service bureau; ~ **des relations avec les investisseurs** BOURSE, FIN investors service bureau; ~ **de renseignements** ADMIN enquiry office, inquiry office, COM enquiry desk, information bureau, information desk, inquiry desk; ~ **des réservations** LOISIRS booking office; ~ **de service actionnaires** BOURSE, FIN investors service bureau; ~ **des services nationaux de l'emploi** RES HUM ≈ Jobcentre *(UK)*; ~ **de services de secrétariat** V&M *dans aéroport* business center *(AmE)*, business centre *(BrE)*; ~ **télégraphique** COMMS telegraphic office; ~ **de transitaires** TRANSP forwarding agency; ~ **de vote** POL polling station; ◆ de ~ INFO desktop

Bureau: ~ **d'analyse économique** *m* ECON Bureau of Economic Analysis, BEA; ~ **du budget du Congrès** *m* POL Congressional Budget Office *(US)*, CBO *(US)*; ~ **central de l'information** *m* ADMIN Central Office of Information, COI; ~ **de commerce international** *m* COM Office of International Trade, OIT; ~ **de comptabilité générale** *m* COMPTA General Accounting Office *(US)*, GAO *(US)*; ~ **européen pour l'environnement** *m* ENVIR European Environmental Bureau, EEB; ~ **international des expositions** *m* ADMIN Organization for International Exhibitions; ~ **international des tarifs douaniers** *m (BITD)* IMP/EXP International Customs Tariffs Bureau *(ICTB)*; ~ **maritime international** *m* TRANSP International Maritime Bureau, IMB; ~ **de marque de fabrique** *m* BREVETS *de la Communauté européenne* Community Trade Mark Office; ~ **des télécommunications** *m* COMMS Office of Telecommunications *(UK)*, Oftel *(UK)*; ~ **de véri-**

fication de la publicité *m* *(BVP)* MÉDIA, V&M ≈ Advertising Standards Authority (*UK*) *(ASA)*

bureaucrate *mf* ADMIN, POL, RES HUM bureaucrat

bureaucratie *f* ADMIN, POL, RES HUM bureaucracy

bureaucratique *adj* ADMIN, POL, RES HUM bureaucratic

bureaucratisation *f* ADMIN, POL, RES HUM bureaucratization

bureautique *f* ADMIN office automation, office technology, OA, IND, INFO office automation, OA

bureaux: ~ **transférés à** *m pl* COM business transferred to; ~ **à vendre** *m pl* IMMOB offices for sale

Burkina Faso:[1] **du** ~ *adj* COM Burkinabe

Burkina Faso[2] *m* COM Burkina Faso

burundais, e *adj* COM Burundian

Burundais, e *m,f* COM *habitant* Burundian

Burundi *m* COM Burundi

bus *m* INFO bus, busbar; ~ **d'adresses** INFO address bus; ~ **de données** INFO data bus; ~ **fluvial** TRANSP river bus

but *m* COM aim, purpose; ~ **de l'entreprise** COM company goal, corporate goal; ♦ **à** ~ **non-lucratif** COM non-profit-making (*BrE*), not-for-profit (*AmE*)

butane *m* ENVIR butane

Butskellisme *m* ECON Butskellism (*UK*)

butterfly: ~ **spread** *m* BOURSE butterfly spread

BVP *abrév (Bureau de vérification de la publicité)* MÉDIA, V&M ≈ ASA (*UK*) *(Advertising Standards Authority)*

C

c *abrév (carré)* COM sq *(square)*

c. *abrév* COM *(centime)* c. *(centime)*, COM *(coupon)* c., CP *(coupon)*

ca *abrév (courant alternatif)* IND alternating current, INFO AC *(alternating current)*

CA *abrév* ADMIN *(conseil d'administration) d'une société* administrative board, board of directors, directorate, executive board, *d'une organisation internationale* governing board, COM *(chiffre d'affaires)* sales, trade figures, trading results, turnover, COMPTA *(conseil d'administration)* administrative board, board of directors, executive board, *d'une organisation internationale* governing board, COM *(chiffre d'affaires)* sales, turnover, ECON *(chiffre d'affaires)* output, trade figures, FIN *(chiffre d'affaires)* sales, turnover, GESTION, *(conseil d'administration) d'une société* RES HUM *(conseil d'administration)* administrative board, board of directors, directorate, executive board, *d'une organisation internationale* governing board, V&M *(chiffre d'affaires)* sales figures, sales revenue, sales volume, turnover

CA:[2] **~ tournant** *m* ADMIN, COM, GESTION, RES HUM staggered board of directors

cabestan *m* TRANSP *navigation* capstan

cabine *f* TRANSP *avion, navire* cabin; **~ de conduite** TRANSP driver's cab; **~ à deux personnes** TRANSP *navire* two-berth cabin; **~ de luxe** TRANSP *navire* de luxe cabin; **~ pour une personne** TRANSP *navire* single-berth cabin; **~ à quatre personnes** TRANSP *navire* four-berth cabin; **~ téléphonique** COMMS call box *(BrE)*, telephone booth *(AmE)*

cabinet *m* COM firm, practice, DROIT *d'un juge* barrister chamber *(UK)*, chambers, POL cabinet; **~ d'affaires** COM, GESTION business consultancy; **~ d'assurances** ASSUR insurance agency, insurance firm; **~ d'avocats** DROIT law firm, law practice; **~ -conseil** COM, GESTION consultancy; **~ de conseil en gestion** GESTION management consultancy; **~ d'expertise comptable** COMPTA accounting firm, accounting practice; **~ d'experts** COM consulting firm; **~ d'experts-comptables** COMPTA accounting firm, accounting practice; **~ fantôme** POL shadow cabinet *(UK)*; **~ d'immobilier** IMMOB estate agents *(BrE)*, real estate agents *(AmE)*; **~ juridique** DROIT law firm, law practice; **~ ministériel** POL minister's advisers; **~ de placement** RES HUM outplacement agency; **~ de placement en dehors de l'entreprise** RES HUM outplacement agency; **~ de recrutement des cadres** RES HUM executive search firm, recruitment agency

câble *m* BOURSE cable, COMMS cable, cablegram *(frml)*; **~ en acier de première qualité** TRANSP *maritime* extra-special-quality steel cable;

~ coaxial INFO coaxial cable; **~ de fer forgé** TRANSP wrought-iron cable; **~ à fibre optique** IND fiber optic cable *(AmE)*, fibre optic cable *(BrE)*; **~ en fils d'acier** TRANSP steel wire rope, SWR; **~ de saisissage** TRANSP wire lashing; **~ souple en fils d'acier** TRANSP *manutention* flexible steel wire rope; **votre ~** TRANSP y/c, your cable

câbler *vt* COMMS cable

câblogramme *m* COMMS cable, cablegram *(frml)*

cabotage *m* TRANSP *maritime* coasting, short sea shipping, *navigation* cabotage, coasting trade; ♦ **de ~** TRANSP *navigation* intercoastal

caboteur, -euse *m,f* TRANSP coaster, coasting broker

CAC *abrév* BOURSE *(cotation assistée en continu)* automated quotation, FIN *(Compagnie des agents de change)* Institute of stockbrokers

cacher *vt* COM conceal, cover up, V&M *cinéma, télévision* mask

cachet *m* COM *d'une société* seal; **~ pour colis de titres** BANQUE remittance seal; **~ de numéraire** BANQUE remittance seal; **~ de la poste** COMMS postmark

CAD *abrév (Ctrl-Alt-Del)* INFO CAD *(Control-Alt-Delete)*

c-à-d *abrév (c'est-à-dire)* COM i.e. *(id est)*

cadastre *m* FISC *administration* land registry *(BrE)*, real estate registry *(AmE)*, *registre* cadastre, land register *(BrE)*, real estate register *(AmE)*

cadeau: ~ de bienvenue *m* V&M traffic builder *(jarg)*; **~ de création de trafic** *m* V&M traffic builder *(jarg)*

cadence *f* COM, ECON, IND *de production*, RES HUM *de travail* rate; **~ de frappe** ADMIN, INFO keystroke rate; **~ maximale de chargement** TRANSP *navigation* as fast as the vessel can receive; **~ maximale de déchargement** TRANSP *navigation* as fast as the vessel can deliver

cadre *m* COM context, *institutionnel* framework, INFO frame, ADMIN, COMPTA, RES HUM exec., executive; **~ adjoint** ADMIN, RES HUM executive assistant; **~ de banque** BANQUE, RES HUM bank officer; **~ chargé des contrats** ADMIN, RES HUM contracts officer; **~ chargé de la formation** COM, RES HUM training officer; **~ commercial** GESTION, RES HUM, V&M commercial manager, sales executive; **~ conceptuel** COMPTA conceptual framework; **~ conceptuel de la comptabilité** COMPTA conceptual framework; **~ d'échantillonnage** MATH sampling frame; **~ d'entreprise** ADMIN, COM, GESTION, RES HUM company executive; **~ d'exploitation** INFO operational environment; **~ en formation** GESTION, RES HUM trainee manager; **~ à haut potentiel** COM high-flier, high-flyer; ~ **de haut vol** COM high-flier, high-flyer; ~ **hiérarchique** GESTION, RES HUM line manager; ~ **à l'information** RES HUM information officer; ~ **juridique** DROIT legal framework; ~ **à moindre potentiel** GESTION low-flier, low-flyer; ~ **moyen** GESTION, RES HUM middle manager; ~ **du plan opérationnel** FIN operational plan framework; ~ **sup** *infrml* GESTION, RES HUM executive officer, high executive, senior executive, senior manager, top executive, EO; ~ **supérieur** GESTION, RES HUM executive officer, high executive, senior executive, senior manager, top executive, EO; ~ **supérieur en mission à l'étranger** COM, RES HUM expatriate executive; ~ **d'utilisation** INFO operational environment; ◆ **dans le ~ de** COM in the framework of; **dans le ~ de l'exploitation d'une entreprise** FISC in the course of carrying on a business

cadrer *vi* COM correspond, tally

cadres *m pl* COM, GESTION, RES HUM cadre, management, managerial staff; ~ **moyens** GESTION, RES HUM middle management; ~ **sup** *infrml* GESTION, RES HUM senior management, top management; ~ **supérieurs** GESTION, RES HUM senior management, top management

CAF[1] *abrév (coût, assurance, fret)* IMP/EXP, TRANSP *livraison de cargaison* CIF *(cost, insurance and freight)*

CAF:[2] ~ **à quai** *loc* IMP/EXP CIF landed

cahier: ~ **des charges** *m* IND bill of materials; ~ **de queue** *m* COM back section

Caire: **Le ~** *n pr* COM Cairo

caisse *f* ADMIN *bureau* cash office, BANQUE cash desk, counter, COM fund, *coffre où l'on dépose l'argent* cash box, *comptoir dans un magasin* cash desk, counter, *dans un supermarché* counter, *fonds* funds, *machine* cash register, till, COMPTA *argent* cash, *bureau* cash office, FIN *bureau* cash office, TRANSP *case, CS, grande boîte pour le transport de marchandises* case, crate, packing case, V&M *d'un magasin* cash desk, *d'un supermarché* cash register, checkout, till; ~ **d'assiette** TRANSP *navigation* trimming tank; ~ **d'assurance maladie contributive** PROT SOC, RES HUM contributory sickness fund; ~ **à claire-voie** TRANSP crate; ~ **à un compartiment** TRANSP one-piece box; ~ **de crédit** BANQUE, FIN credit union; ~ **de crédit mutuelle** BANQUE mutual savings bank *(US)*; ~ **enregistreuse** V&M cash register; ~ **d'épargne** BANQUE guaranty savings bank, savings bank, thrift institution *(US)*, BOURSE savings bank; ~ **d'épargne de la poste** BANQUE post office savings bank; ~ **de financement des députés du monde ouvrier** RES HUM Labour Representation Committee, LRC; ~ **d'une firme de courtage** BOURSE cage *(US)*; ~ **de garantie** BOURSE compensation fund *(UK)*; ~ **maladie propre à l'entreprise** ASSUR company sickness insurance scheme; ~ **de manutention** TRANSP tote bin; ~ **noire** POL slush fund, RES HUM yellow-dog fund *(US)*; ~ **politique** RES HUM political fund;

~ **populaire** BANQUE, FIN credit union; ~ **de prévoyance** FIN contingency fund, provident fund, reserve fund, welfare fund; ~ **de prévoyance du personnel** RES HUM staff provident fund; ~ **privée d'assurance maladie** PROT SOC, RES HUM private health fund; ~ **profonde** TRANSP ballast tank, deep tank, DT; ~ **de règlement des sinistres** ASSUR claims settlement fund; ~ **de retraite** ASSUR, COMPTA, FIN, RES HUM pension fund, retirement fund, superannuation fund; ~ **de retraite agréée** ASSUR registered retirement income fund, RRIF; ~ **de retraite avec cotisation salariale** *(ANT caisse de retraite sans cotisation salariale)* FIN, PROT SOC, RES HUM contributory pension fund; ~ **de retraite sans cotisation salariale** *(ANT caisse de retraite avec cotisation salariale)* FIN, PROT SOC, RES HUM noncontributory pension fund; ~ **de secours** FISC, PROT SOC charity funds; ~ **de solidarité patronale** RES HUM indemnity fund; ~ **de solidarité du personnel** PROT SOC, RES HUM staff welfare fund; ~ **de sortie** V&M *dans un supermarché* checkout, checkout lane; ~ **syndicale de grève** RES HUM strike fund; ~ **à trois compartiments** TRANSP three-piece box; ◆ **faire la ~** COMPTA balance the cash

Caisse: ~ **d'épargne** *f* BOURSE ≈ National Savings *(UK)*; ~ **nationale d'épargne** *f (CNE)* BANQUE ≈ National Savings Bank *(UK) (NSB)*

caisses *f pl* BANQUE the Thrifts *(US, infrml)*

caissier, -ère *m,f* BANQUE cashier, teller, V&M cashier, checker *(AmE)*, checkout assistant *(BrE)*, checkout clerk *(AmE)*; ~ **adjoint** BANQUE assistant cashier, assistant teller

caisson: ~ **de compensation** *m* TRANSP *navigation* feeder

calage *m* TRANSP *de marchandises* blocking off

calcul *m* COMPTA calculation, reckoning, INFO calculation, computation, number crunching; ~ **en cercle fermé** FISC circular calculation; ~ **comptable** COMPTA, FIN, INFO number crunching; ~ **détaillé de l'impôt** FISC detailed tax calculation; ~ **double** FIN double counting; ~ **de la jauge** TRANSP tonnage calculation; ~ **de probabilités** MATH calculus of probabilities; ~ **de satisfaction des utilitaristes** ECON felicific calculus; ~ **du temps passé** RES HUM rate fixing; ~ **de la valeur des stocks** COM inventory computation

calculable *adj* MATH calculable

calculateur *m* INFO computer; ~ **analogique** INFO analog computer; ~ **numérique** INFO digital computer; ~ **de quantité** IND quantity surveyor; ~ **sériel** INFO serial computer

calculatrice *f* COM, INFO, MATH calculator; ~ **de poche** MATH pocket calculator; ~ **à poche** COM pocket calculator

calculé: ~ **annuellement** *adj* COM annualized

calculer *vt* COM gage *(AmE)*, gauge *(BrE)*, INFO compute, MATH calculate; ◆ ~ **les intérêts** FIN work out the interest; ~ **les intérêts courus** BANQUE work out the accrued interest

calculette *f* COM calculator, hand calculator, pocket calculator, INFO calculator, MATH calculator, hand calculator, pocket calculator

calculs: ~ **d'intérêts** *m pl* COMPTA *profits et pertes* interest operations

cale *f* TRANSP *d'un navire* Lw, ho, hold, lower hold, *placé sous un objet* quoin, wedge; ~ **de construction** TRANSP *dans un port* slipway; ~ **à eau** TRANSP *navigation* deep tank, DT; ~ **à eau d'arrière** TRANSP *navigation* DTa, deep tank aft; ~ **à eau d'avant** TRANSP *navigation* DTf, deep tank forward; ~ **de lancement** TRANSP *dans un port* slipway; ~ **sèche** TRANSP *dans un port* graving dock, *navigation* dry dock

calendrier *m* COM calendar, timing, FIN, GESTION schedule; ~ **d'amortissement** BANQUE repayment schedule; ~ **de campagne** MÉDIA media schedule; ~ **de contrôle** COMPTA, FIN audit schedule; ~ **détachable** COM tear-off calendar; ~ **d'encaissement** COMPTA encashment schedule; ~ **d'expirations** COMPTA lapsing schedule; ~ **de remboursement** BANQUE, FIN repayment schedule; ~ **de remboursement d'achat à crédit** BANQUE, FIN installment repayment schedule (*AmE*), instalment repayment schedule (*BrE*); ~ **de remboursement d'emprunt** BANQUE, FIN loan repayment schedule; ~ **de remboursement par versements** BANQUE, FIN installment repayment schedule (*AmE*), instalment repayment schedule (*BrE*); ~ **des travaux** ADMIN work schedule

calibre *m* COM *perçage, forage*, IND *de moulage*, INFO template, RES HUM *des cadres* caliber (*AmE*), calibre (*BrE*), V&M grade

calibrer *vt* COM grade, MÉDIA, V&M *publicité* cast off

call *m* (ANT *put*) BOURSE call

calme *adj* BOURSE *marché* flat, sideways market, inactive, COM quiet, *approche* level-headed, *demande* slack

calomnier *vt* DROIT defame

calomnieux, -euse *adj* DROIT *écrit* libellous (*BrE*), libelous (*AmE*)

camarade: ~ **de travail** *mf* COM, RES HUM workmate

cambiste *mf* BANQUE, BOURSE, FIN cambist, foreign exchange broker, foreign exchange dealer, foreign exchange trader

Cambodge *m* COM Cambodia

cambodgien, -enne *adj* COM Cambodian

Cambodgien, -enne *m,f* COM *habitant* Cambodian

cambriolage *m* DROIT burglary

camelote *f infrml* COM, V&M trashy goods

camembert *m* COM, INFO, MATH pie chart

caméra: ~ **vidéo** *f* COMMS, MÉDIA video camera

Cameroun *m* COM Cameroon

camerounais, e *adj* COM Cameroonian

Camerounais, e *m,f* COM *habitant* Cameroonian

camion *m* TRANSP lorry (*BrE*), truck (*AmE*); ~ **-benne** TRANSP tipper, tipper lorry (*BrE*), tipper truck (*AmE*); ~ **à benne basculante** TRANSP tipper, tipper lorry (*BrE*), tipper truck (*AmE*); ~ **-citerne** TRANSP tank truck (*AmE*), tanker lorry (*BrE*); ~ **de déménagement** TRANSP moving van, removal van; ~ **frigorifique** TRANSP refrigerated lorry (*BrE*), refrigerated truck (*AmE*); ~ **-grue** TRANSP lorry-mounted crane (*BrE*), truck-mounted crane (*AmE*); ~ **isotherme** TRANSP refrigerated lorry (*BrE*), refrigerated truck (*AmE*); ~ **de messageries** TRANSP parcels van; ~ **roulant à vide** TRANSP deadhead (*AmE, infrml*), empty vehicle; ~ **pour transport d'automobiles** TRANSP car transporter

camionnage *m* TRANSP cartage, haulage, truckage

camionneur *m* TRANSP *chauffeur* hauler (*AmE*), haulier (*BrE*), lorry driver (*BrE*), teamster (*AmE*), truck driver (*AmE*), trucker (*AmE*), *entrepreneur* carrier, haulage contractor, haulier (*BrE*), trucking company (*AmE*), trucking contractor

camp: ~ **écologique** *m* ENVIR conservation camp

campagne *f* COM *de ventes, publicitaire*, V&M campaign, drive; ~ **arrêt buffet** POL whistlestop campaign; ~ **d'assainissement** ENVIR cleanup campaign; ~ **centrée sur un secteur** V&M zoned campaign; ~ **centrée sur une zone** V&M zoned campaign; ~ **diffamatoire** POL dirty tricks campaign; ~ **d'efficacité** COM, RES HUM efficiency drive; ~ **électorale** POL election campaign; ~ **institutionnelle** V&M corporate campaign; ~ **de matraquage** V&M *publicité* burst campaign; ~ **de modernisation de la Chine** ECON, POL Chinese modernization drive; ~ **de nettoyage** ENVIR cleanup campaign; ~ **de presse** MÉDIA press campaign; ~ **de productivité** COM, IND, V&M productivity campaign, productivity drive; ~ **promotionnelle** V&M *marketing* promotional exercise; ~ **publicitaire agressive** MÉDIA, V&M hype; ~ **de publicité** MÉDIA, V&M advertising campaign; ~ **régionale** V&M zoned campaign; ~ **de saturation** V&M *publicité* saturation campaign; ~ **teasing** V&M teaser campaign; ~ **de vente** V&M sales campaign, sales drive; ◆ **faire une** ~ **arrêt buffet** POL whistlestop

CAN *abrév* (*convertisseur analogique-numérique*) INFO ADC (*analog-digital converter*)

Canada *m* COM Canada

canadien, -enne *adj* COM Canadian

Canadien, -enne *m,f* COM *habitant* Canadian

Canadiens: **les** ~ *m pl* COM the Canadians

canal *m* COMMS, MÉDIA *Fra* (*cf chaîne Can*) *télévision* channel, TRANSP *cours d'eau* canal; ~ **de communication** ADMIN, COM, GESTION, RES HUM channel of communication; ~ **de distribution** ADMIN, COM, V&M channel of distribution, marketing channel; ~ **éclusé** TRANSP *navigation* locked canal; ~ **maritime** TRANSP *navigation* maritime canal; ~ **publicitaire** MÉDIA, V&M advertising channel, advertising medium; ~ **de**

retour INFO reverse channel; ~ **unique d'information** RES HUM single channel (*UK*)

canaliser *vt* COM *fonds, informations* channel, funnel

canard *m* infrml MÉDIA *journal* rag (*infrml*); ~ **boiteux** infrml BOURSE *spéculateur*, COM *société* lame duck

Canberra *n pr* COM Canberra

candidat, e *m,f* ADMIN, BOURSE *à l'inscription*, COM *à une bourse* applicant, POL candidate, RES HUM *à un poste* applicant, interviewee; ~ **entrepreneur** COM applicant entrepreneur; ~ **à inscrire** POL write-in candidate (*US*); ~ **présidentiel favori** POL point (*US, jarg*); ~ **prisonnier** POL *de groupes d'intérêt* captive candidate (*jarg*); ~ **retenu** COM, RES HUM appointee

candidature *f* ADMIN, COM, RES HUM application, candidacy, candidature, job application; ~ **spontanée** RES HUM unsolicited application; ◆ **faire acte de ~** COM file an application, RES HUM put in an application

cannibalisation *f* COM, COMPTA, FIN asset stripping

canot: ~ **à moteur** *m* TRANSP *navigation* ml, motor launch; ~ **de sauvetage** *m* TRANSP *navigation* lifeboat; ~ **de sauvetage hyperbare autopropulsé** *m* TRANSP self-propelled hyperbaric lifeboat, SPHL

cantine *f* RES HUM canteen

canton *m Suisse* POL canton

CAO *abrév (conception assistée par ordinateur, création assistée par ordinateur)* IND, INFO CAD (*computer aided design, computer assisted design*), D/A (*design automation*)

cap[1] *abrév (capital)* COM cap (*capital*)

cap[2] *m* FIN cap, restriction

Cap: **Le ~** *n pr* COM Cape Town

capable *adj* COM capable; ◆ ~ **de faire qch** COM capable of doing sth

capacitance *f* INFO capacitance

capacité *f* COM *compétence* ability, capability, capacity, competence, *qualification* qualification, IND capacity, INFO *de la mémoire* capacity, size, RES HUM capacity; ~ **d'absorption** BOURSE *du marché* absorbing capacity, ECON absorptive capacity; ~ **en balles** TRANSP bale capacity, B; ~ **bénéficiaire** COM, COMPTA, RES HUM earning capacity, earning power; ~ **de charge** TRANSP *d'un navire* carrying capacity; ~ **de chargement** TRANSP *d'un navire* cargo capacity, cargo tonnage, cc; ~ **contributive** FISC ability to pay; ~ **de crédit** BANQUE, COM, COMPTA, ECON, FIN borrowing power; ~ **de distribution** TRANSP distributive ability; ~ **double** BOURSE dual capacity; ~ **d'emprunt** BANQUE, COM, COMPTA, ECON, FIN borrowing power; ~ **d'emprunt de titres** BOURSE borrowing power; ~ **à être transféré** BOURSE transferability; ~ **excédentaire** ECON, IND excess capacity; ~ **financière** BANQUE, COM, COMPTA, ECON, FIN financial capacity; ~ **fiscale** FISC tax

capacity; ~ **de fonctionnement** ECON, IND operating capacity; ~ **frigorifique** TRANSP *d'un conteneur* insulated capacity, refrigerated capacity; ~ **de gain** COM earning capacity; ~ **d'imposition** ECON, FISC tax base, taxable capacity, taxation capacity, taxing capacity; ~ **d'intégration** ECON absorptive capacity; ~ **inutilisée** ECON, IND excess capacity, idle capacity, spare capacity; ~ **isotherme** TRANSP *d'un conteneur* insulated capacity, refrigerated capacity; ~ **maximale** ECON ideal capacity, IND maximum capacity; ~ **maximale de production** ECON maximum practical capacity; ~ **de mémoire** INFO core size, memory capacity; ~ **multiple** BOURSE dual capacity; ~ **optimale** ECON, IND optimum capacity; ~ **optimum** ECON, IND optimum capacity; ~ **de paiement** RES HUM *des salaires* ability to pay; ~ **de pénétration** V&M capacity of penetration; ~ **de production** IND manufacturing capacity, production capacity; ~ **de production pour une année donnée** ECON, IND planned capacity; ~ **de production normale** ECON, IND normal capacity; ~ **réelle prévue** ECON expected actual capacity; ~ **de remboursement** BANQUE, COM, COMPTA, ECON, FIN ability to repay; ~ **de route** TRANSP route capacity; ~ **simple** BOURSE single capacity; ~ **de stockage** COM storage capacity; ~ **de stockage des données** INFO information storage capacity; ~ **théorique** COM theoretical capacity, ECON ideal capacity, IND theoretical capacity; ~ **de traitement** INFO throughput; ~ **de traitement des passagers** TRANSP passenger throughput; ~ **de transport** COM *navigation* stowage factor; ~ **unique** BOURSE single capacity; ~ **de l'usine** COM, IND plant capacity; ~ **utile** TRANSP cargo capacity, cargo tonnage, cc; ~ **de vente** V&M *press/communications* syndication capacity; ~ **volumétrique en céréales** TRANSP *d'un navire* grain capacity, grain cubic, GC; ~ **volumétrique du navire** TRANSP ship's cubic capacity

capacités *f pl* COM skills; ~ **locales** RES HUM local skills

CAPAFE *abrév (comptes à payer à la fin de l'exercice)* COMPTA PAYE (*AmE*) (*Payables at Year-End*)

CAPES *abrév (≈ Certificat d'aptitude au professorat d'enseignement du second degré)* PROT SOC ≈ PGCE (*UK*) (*Postgraduate Certificate of Education*)

capitaine *mf* RES HUM *d'un navire de commerce*, TRANSP captain, master; ~ **d'armes** *m* RES HUM, TRANSP master-at-arms; ~ **d'industrie** *m* COM, IND captain of industry; ~ **de port** *m* RES HUM harbor master (*AmE*), harbour master (*BrE*)

capital *m* COM, COMPTA, ECON, FIN cap, capital, capital funds, capital sum; ~ **actif** FIN active capital; ~ **actions** BOURSE, COMPTA, ECON, FIN capital stock, equity capital, share capital; ~ **actions autorisé** BOURSE, COMPTA, FIN authorized share capital; ~ **actions moyen** BOURSE average equity; ~ **actions ordinaire** BOURSE common equity; ~ **actions remboursable** BOURSE redeemable stock; ~ **appelé** (ANT *capital non-appelé*) FIN called-up capital; ~ **d'apport** BOURSE contributed capital, paid-in capital, FIN initial capital, seed money, start-up capital; ~ **assuré** ASSUR capital assured, BANQUE assured sum; ~ **autorisé** BOURSE authorized share, authorized stock, COMPTA authorized share capital, FIN authorized capital; ~ **bancaire** ECON, FIN primary capital; ~ **de base** BANQUE, ECON, FIN alpha stage, base capital, capital base; ~ **de base consolidé** BANQUE, COM, ECON, FIN consolidated base capital; ~ **de base net** BANQUE, COM, COMPTA, ECON, FIN net base capital; ~ **constitutif** ASSUR consideration; ~ **de courtage** BOURSE broker fund; ~ **décès** ASSUR death benefit; ~ **de départ** BOURSE initial capital, FIN seed money; ~ **dilué** FIN watered capital; ~ **diminué** FIN impaired capital; ~ **échu** ASSUR matured endowment, FIN due capital; ~ **émis** BOURSE issued capital; ~ **d'emprunt** COMPTA, FIN loan capital; ~ **engagé** COM capital invested; ~ **exigible** BANQUE callable capital; ~ **à faible taux d'endettement** FIN low-geared capital; ~ **fictif** BOURSE phantom capital; ~ **financier** FIN financial capital; ~ **fixe** ECON constant capital, FIN fixed capital; ~ **humain** ECON, FIN, IND human capital, RES HUM human capital, labor power (*AmE*), labour power (*BrE*), V&M human capital; ~ **immobilisé** COMPTA tied-up capital, FIN capital employed equity, capital funds, fixed capital; ~ **imposable** FISC taxable capital; ~ **initial** BOURSE, FIN initial capital, start-up capital; ~ **investi** COM, COMPTA capital employed, capital invested; ~ **libéré** FIN paid-up capital; ~ **liquide** BOURSE liquid capital; ~ **net requis** BOURSE, ECON, FIN net capital requirements; ~ **nominal** ASSUR *assurance-vie* face amount, face of policy, BOURSE shares authorized, ECON, FIN authorized capital; ~ **non-appelé** BOURSE nil paid, FIN uncalled capital; ~ **non-distribuable** FIN undistributable capital; ~ **non-émis** BOURSE unissued capital stock, unissued stock; ~ **non-souscrit** BOURSE subscription receivable; ~ **obligataire** BOURSE bond principal, capital bonds; ~ **obligations** BOURSE bond capital, debenture capital, loan capital, loan stock, COMPTA, FIN loan capital, loan stock; ~ **d'origine** FIN original capital; ~ **permanent** COM capital invested; ~ **pourvu dans les statuts** COMPTA nominal capital; ~ **remboursé** FIN capital paid out, paid-out capital; ~ **risque** BANQUE, COM *capitalisme*, FIN *argent* risk capital, venture capital; ~ **à risque** BANQUE, COM *argent*, FIN risk capital, venture capital; ~ **social** BOURSE capital base, capital stock, share capital, COMPTA capital stock, share capital, stated capital, ECON authorized capital, share capital, social capital, FIN authorized capital, share capital, social overhead capital; ~ **social autorisé** BOURSE, FIN authorized capital stock, authorized capital share; ~ **social souscrit** FIN issued share capital; ~ **soumis au risque de**

position BOURSE position-risk capital; ~ **souscrit** BOURSE issued capital, subscribed capital, COMPTA issued share capital; ~ **utilisé** COMPTA capital employed, FIN capital employed equity; ~ **variable** FIN variable capital; ~ **versé** BOURSE paid-in capital; ~ **versé nominal** BOURSE nominal paid-up capital

capitale *f* ADMIN, INFO, MÉDIA cap, capital, capital letter, u.c., upper case, upper-case letter

capitalisation *f* COM, COMPTA, ECON capitalization; ~ **boursière** BOURSE market capitalization, stock market capitalization; ~ **fiscale** ECON tax capitalization; ~ **globale** FIN total capitalization; ~ **des intérêts** FIN capitalization of interest; ~ **minimale** COMPTA, FISC thin capitalization

capitalisé: **sur-~** *adj* (ANT *sous-capitalisé*) COM, IND overcapitalized

capitaliser *vt* COM, ECON, FIN capitalize, convert into capital

capitalisme *m* ECON, POL capitalism; ~ **d'affaires** ECON, POL merchant capitalism; ~ **bénévole** ECON, POL benevolent capitalism, caring capitalism; ~ **de boutiquier** *infrml* ECON lemonade-stand capitalism (*jarg*); ~ **d'état** ECON, POL state capitalism; ~ **individuel** IND personal capitalism; ~ **industriel** ECON, IND industrial capitalism; ~ **de monopole** ECON, POL monopoly capitalism; ~ **de monopole d'État** ECON state monopoly capitalism; ~ **monopolistique** ECON, POL monopoly capitalism; ~ **noir** ECON, POL black capitalism; ~ **périphérique** ECON, POL peripheral capitalism; ~ **populaire** ECON, POL popular capitalism; ~ **pur** ECON, POL pure capitalism

capitaliste[1] *adj* ECON, POL capitalist, capitalistic

capitaliste[2] *mf* ECON, POL capitalist

capitalistes: **les ~** *m pl* ECON, POL capitalist class

capitalistique *adj* COM, IND, POL capital-intensive

capitation *f* ECON, FISC capitation tax

capitaux *m pl* ECON, FIN capital; ~ **d'amorçage** FIN seed capital, seed money; ~ **circulants** ECON, FIN circulating capital; ~ **empruntés** BANQUE, FIN borrowed capital; ~ **empruntés convertibles** BOURSE convertible loan stock; ~ **et réserves** COMPTA capital and reserves; ~ **fébriles** ECON, FIN hot money; ~ **fixes** ECON, FIN capital assets; ~ **flottants** ECON, FIN hot money; ~ **de lancement** FIN seed money; ~ **malléables** ECON malleable capital; ~ **permanents** FIN capital funds; ~ **productifs** ECON, FIN productive capital; ~ **propres** BOURSE common stockholders' equity, equity capital, shareholders' equity, stockholders' equity, COMPTA equity, equity capital base, equity funds, net equity, stockholders' equity; ~ **roulants** ECON, FIN circulating capital; ~ **spéculatifs** FIN refugee capital

capot *m* INFO cover, hood

capter *vt* COM *communication téléphonique* tap into, MÉDIA pick up

car: ~ **-ferry** *m* TRANSP car ferry, passenger-vehicle ferry, vehicular ferry, *navigation* car carrier

Caracas *n pr* COM Caracas

caractère *m* COM character, nature, INFO *impression* type, *lettre, symbole* character, MÉDIA *lettre, symbole* character, RES HUM *d'une personne* character, nature, personality; ~ **alphanumérique** INFO alphanumeric character; ~ **approprié** COM appropriateness; ~ **blanc** INFO blank character; ~ **de commande** INFO control character; ~ **de contrôle** INFO check character; ~ **distinctif** BREVETS distinctiveness; ~ **d'échappement** INFO escape character; ~ **écologique** ENVIR, IND ecological character; ~ **d'effacement** INFO delete character, DEL; ~ **Esc** INFO escape character; ~ **d'espacement arrière** INFO backspace character; ~ **exécutoire d'une convention collective** RES HUM legal enforceability; ~ **de fin de ligne** INFO end-of-line character; ~ **frauduleux** DROIT fraudulence; ~ **futile de la cause** DROIT de minimis; ~ **graphique** INFO graphic character; ~ **gras** INFO, MÉDIA *impression* bold type, boldface character; ~ **interdit** INFO, MÉDIA *impression* illegal character; ~ **de mise en page** INFO layout character; ~ **en mode points** INFO bit-mapped character; ~ **non formalisé** RES HUM informality; ~ **numérique** INFO, MATH numeric character; ~ **de présentation** INFO layout character; ~ **de retour arrière** INFO backspace character; ~ **sans empattement** INFO, MÉDIA sans serif; ~ **spécial** INFO, MÉDIA impression, optional character; ~ **de tabulation** ADMIN, INFO tabulation character

caractéristique[1] *adj* COM characteristic; ◆ **être ~ de** COM typify

caractéristique[2] *f* BREVETS feature, COM attribute, trait, feature, INFO feature, V&M characteristic, *d'un lieu, d'un produit* feature; ~ **additionnelle** BREVETS additional feature, additional matter, V&M additional feature; ~ **clé** COM key feature; ~ **essentielle** BREVETS essential feature; ~ **optionnelle** BOURSE optional feature

caractéristiques: ~ **de l'obligation** *f pl* BOURSE bond features, bond terms; ~ **du personnel** *f pl* RES HUM personnel specification; ~ **du poste** *f pl* RES HUM job spec (*infrml*), job specification; ~ **du produit** *f pl* V&M product performance; ~ **du risque** *f pl* ASSUR description of risk; ~ **du risque d'exploitation** *f pl* ASSUR description of operational risk

carat *m* COM carat

carburant *m* ENVIR, IND, TRANSP gas (*AmE*), gasoline (*AmE*), petrol (*BrE*); ~ **à coupe longue** TRANSP wide-cut gas (*AmE*), wide-cut gasoline (*AmE*), wide-cut petrol (*BrE*); ~ **de large coupe** TRANSP wide-cut gas (*AmE*), wide-cut gasoline (*AmE*), wide-cut petrol (*BrE*); ~ **privé** ENVIR *utilisé par un employé* private fuel

carcasse: ~ **diagonale** *f* TRANSP *d'un pneumatique* diagonal ply; ~ **de navire** *f* TRANSP *maritime* hulk

Cardiff *n pr* COM Cardiff

carence *f* COM, COMPTA, DROIT, IND insolvency

cargaison *f* TRANSP cargo, freight, frt, *dans un* *navire* boatload, *dans un camion* lorryload (*BrE*), truckload (*AmE*), *dans un train* trainload; ~ **d'aller** IMP/EXP, TRANSP outward cargo; ~ **commerciale** TRANSP commercial cargo; ~ **en douane** COM, FISC, IMP/EXP, IND, TRANSP bonded cargo; ~ **exclue** TRANSP cargo shut-out; ~ **fractionnée** TRANSP break bulk, break bulk cargo; ~ **à grouper** TRANSP assembly cargo; ~ **isolée** TRANSP cargo in isolation; ~ **mixte** TRANSP general cargo, GC; ~ **au mouillage** TRANSP *navigation* berth cargo; ~ **névralgique** TRANSP hot cargo; ~ **non-commerciale** TRANSP noncommercial cargo; ~ **non-déclarée** TRANSP unmanifested cargo; ~ **de retour** TRANSP return cargo, RC; ~ **soumise aux droits de douane** FISC, IMP/EXP, TRANSP dutiable cargo; ~ **TECH** (*cargaison toxique, explosive, corrosive, hasardeuse*) TRANSP TECH cargo (*toxic, explosive, corrosive, hazardous cargo*); ~ **toxique, explosive, corrosive, hasardeuse** (*cargaison TECH*) TRANSP toxic, explosive, corrosive, hazardous cargo (*TECH cargo*); ~ **traditionnelle** TRANSP conventional cargo; ~ **très importante** TRANSP very important cargo, VIC; ◆ ~, **surestaries et défense** ASSUR, TRANSP freight, demurrage and defence (*BrE*), freight, demurrage and defense (*AmE*), FD&D

cargo *m* TRANSP *navire* cargo boat, cargo vessel, freighter; ~ **charbonnier** TRANSP *navire* collier; ~ **de divers** TRANSP *navire* general cargo ship; ~ **frigorifique** TRANSP refrigerated ship, refrigerated vessel, *navire* reefer carrier, reefer ship, ref.; ~ **fruitier** TRANSP *navire* fruit carrier; ~ **de ligne régulière** TRANSP *navire* cargo liner; ~ **de marchandises diverses** TRANSP *navire* general cargo ship; ~ **mixte** TRANSP *navire* cargo liner, combi ship; ~ **polyvalent** TRANSP *navire* omnicarrier

carlingue *f* TRANSP *de navire* girder

carnet *m* BOURSE book; ~ **d'adresses** COMMS *livre* address book; ~ **d'agent de change** BOURSE bargain book; ~ **ATA** IMP/EXP ATA carnet; ~ **de banque** FIN bankbook; ~ **de chèques** BANQUE checkbook (*AmE*), chequebook (*BrE*); ~ **de commandes** COM order book; ~ **de commandes fermes** COM final orders; ~ **de dépôt** BANQUE deposit book, deposit passbook; ~ **d'échéances** BOURSE bill diary; ~ **électronique spécialisé** BOURSE Specialist Electronic Book (*US*), SEB (*US*); ~ **de quittances** COM receipt book; ~ **TIR** (*carnet de transport international routier*) TRANSP international customs transit document; ~ **de transport international routier** (*carnet TIR*) TRANSP international customs transit document; ~ **de versement** BANQUE paying-in book; ~ **de vol** TRANSP log, log book

carré[1], **e** *adj* (*c*) COM square (*sq*)

carré[2] *m* COM, MATH square; ~ **chi** MATH chi square; ~ **magique** ECON magic quadrilateral; ~ **de panneau** TRANSP *navigation* square of the hatch

carrière *f* RES HUM career, sit., situation

carriériste *adj* RES HUM career-orientated, career-oriented, careerist

carte *f* COM card, INFO board, card; ~ **d'abonnement** *f* COM commutation ticket *(AmE)*, season ticket *(BrE)*; ~ **accélératrice** *f* INFO accelerator card; ~ **d'achat** *f* BANQUE charge card; ~ **additionnelle** *f* INFO add-on board, add-on card; ~ **avec réponse payée** *f* COMMS reply-paid card; ~ **d'avis** *f pl* ASSUR advice card; ~ **bancaire** *f* BANQUE bank card, debit card, plastic money, V&M debit card; ~ **à bande magnétique** *f* INFO service card; ~ **bleue**® *f* BANQUE credit card ~ **-client** *f* COM client card; ~ **consulaire** *f* ADMIN, IMP/EXP consular declaration, CD; ~ **de crédit** *f* BANQUE credit card, *utilisée dans les billetteries* cash card, COMPTA credit card; ~ **de crédit professionnelle** *f* BANQUE, FIN company credit card, corporate credit card; ~ **de débarquement** *f* TRANSP landing card; ~ **disque dur** *f* INFO hard card; ~ **d'échantillons** *f* COM sample card; ~ **d'embarquement** *f* COM embarkation card, TRANSP boarding card, boarding pass; ~ **d'émulation** *f* INFO emulation board, emulation card; ~ **d'entrée** *f* COM entrance card; ~ **d'extension** *f* INFO add-on board, add-on card, expansion board, expansion card; ~ **d'extension mémoire** *f* INFO memory expansion board; **famille nombreuse** *f* family railcard *(UK)*; ~ **de garantie** *f* BANQUE warranty card; ~ **graphique** *f* INFO graphics board, graphics card; ~ **de guichet automatique** *f* BANQUE autobank card, automated teller card, bank teller card; ~ **d'identité** *f* ADMIN identity card, ID; ~ **d'identité bancaire** *f* BANQUE banker's card, check card *(AmE)*, cheque card *(BrE)*; ~ **infographique** *f* INFO computer map; ~ **magnétique** *f* BANQUE, INFO magnetic card, smart card; ~ **maîtresse** *f* INFO master card; ~ **mécanographique** *f* INFO data card; ~ **de membre** *f* COM membership card; ~ **à mémoire** *f* BANQUE smart card, INFO chip card, chip-based card, smart card; ~ **mémoire** *f* INFO memory card; ~ **à mémoire** *f* COM smart card, COMMS swipe card; ~ **mère** *f* INFO motherboard, mothercard; ~ **à microprocesseur** *f* INFO smart card; ~ **nationale d'identité** *f* ADMIN national identity card; ~ **normalisée de spécimen de signature** *f* BANQUE standard specimen signature card; ~ **or** *f* BANQUE gold card; ~ **de parenté par alliance** *f* PROT SOC affinity card; ~ **perforée** *f* INFO punch card, punched card; ~ **de pointage** *f* IND clock card; ~ **privative** *f* FIN company-specific card; ~ **à puce** *f* BANQUE, COM smart card, INFO chip card, chip-based card, smart card; ~ **-réponse** *f* COM, COMMS business reply card, mailing card, BRC, ≈ Business Reply Mail® *(AmE)*, ≈ BRM *(AmE)*, V&M order card, reply vehicle; ~ **-réponse payée** *f* COMMS reply-paid card; ~ **de retrait bancaire** *f* BANQUE cash card; ~ **de séjour** *f* ADMIN, PROT SOC, RES HUM alien registration card *(US)*, green card *(US)*, residence permit, residence visa; ~ **de signature** *f* BANQUE signature card; ~ **de sortie de stock** *f* IND issue card; ~ **spécimen** *f* BANQUE signature card; ~ **de spécimen de signature** *f* BANQUE specimen signature card; ~ **de téléphone** *f* COMMS phone card; ~ **de transit** *f* TRANSP transit card; ~ **d'urgence de transport** *f* TRANSP transport emergency card, trem card; ~ **vermeil**® *f* TRANSP senior citizen's railcard *(UK)*; ~ **verte** *f (ASSVR)* TRANSP *automobile* green card; ~ **VGA** *f* INFO VGA card, video graphics adaptor card, video graphics array card, VGA; ~ **vidéo** *f* INFO video card; ~ **vidéographique** *f* INFO VGA card; ~ **de visite** *f* COM visiting card; ~ **de visite professionnelle** *f* COM, GESTION business card

cartel *m* DROIT combine, ECON cartel, RES HUM *concentration industrielle* cartel, consortium; ~ **international** ECON international cartel; ~ **des matières premières** ECON commodity cartel; ~ **des taux d'intérêt** BANQUE interest rate cartel

carter *m* INFO cover

carton *m* COM *papier épais* cardboard *(BrE)*, tagboard *(AmE)*, TRANSP *boîte* cardboard box, carton; ~ **contrecollé** IND pasteboard; ~ **couché** V&M *publicité* art board; ~ **dur** IND fiberboard *(AmE)*, fibreboard *(BrE)*; ~ **paille** IND strawboard

cartonné, e *adj* MÉDIA *livre* casebound, hardback, hardcover

cartouche *f* COMMS, INFO tape cartridge, TRANSP cartouche, cartridge; ~ **de bande** COMMS, INFO tape cartridge; ~ **de ruban** INFO ribbon cartridge

cas *m* COM matter, DROIT case; ~ **de défaut** BANQUE event of default; ~ **de discordance** FISC mismatch case; ~ **de figure le plus pessimiste** ECON worst-case projection; ~ **-limite** COM borderline case; ~ **qui a une incidence considérable** FISC high-impact case; ◆ **dans le ~ présent** COM in this case, in this instance; **en aucun ~** COM on no account; **en ~ d'empêchement** COM if anything should crop up; **en ~ de non-distribution prière de renvoyer à l'expéditeur** COMMS if undelivered please return to sender; **faire ~ de son avis** COM air one's views; **le ~ échéant** COM should the occasion arise

case *f* INFO *de tableur* cell; ~ **à cocher** INFO check box *(US)*, tick box; ~ **à code** IMP/EXP code box; ~ **de réception** INFO card bin

cash: ~ **-flow** *m* COMPTA cash flow; ~ **-flow négatif** *m (ANT cash-flow positif)* COMPTA, FIN negative cash flow, FISC before-tax cash flow; ~ **-flow positif** *m (ANT cash-flow négatif)* COMPTA, FIN positive cash flow, FISC after-tax cash flow; ~ **marginal** *m* COMPTA, FIN incremental cash flow

casier: ~ **judiciaire** *m* DROIT police record; ~ **judiciaire vierge** *m* DROIT clean record

casino *m* LOISIRS casino

casque: ~ **de chantier** *m* IND, RES HUM hard hat

casquer *vi infrml* COM cough up *(BrE, infrml)*, shell out *(infrml)*, stump up *(BrE, infrml)*; ◆ **faire ~** *infrml* COM bleed *(infrml)*

cassage: ~ **des prix** *m* V&M underselling

cassation *f* DROIT *d'un jugement* annulment, invalidation, quashing

casse *f* MÉDIA *impression* case

casser *vt* COM *prix* cut, undercut, DROIT *jugement* annul, invalidate, *ordonnance, verdict* quash, ECON *monopole* break; ~ **les prix** RES HUM cut the rates

cassette *f* COMMS, INFO cassette; ~ **audio** COMMS audio cassette; ~ **vidéo** COMMS video cassette

Castries *n pr* COM Castries

catalan *m* COM *langue* Catalan

catalogue *m* COM catalog (*AmE*), catalogue (*BrE*), INFO catalog, directory; ~ **de vente par correspondance** V&M mail-order catalog (*AmE*), mail-order catalogue (*BrE*)

catalyseur *m* COM catalyst

catastrophe: ~ **naturelle** *f* ASSUR, DROIT, FIN act of God

catégorie *f* BOURSE *d'option* class, BREVETS category, class, COM category, league, RES HUM *niveau de responsabilité*, V&M grade; ~ **de bâtiment** ASSUR class of construction; ~ **de biens** FISC, IMMOB class of property; ~ **de coûts** FIN type of costs; ~ **d'emploi** FISC class of employment; ~ **d'entreprise** FISC class of business; ~ **d'imposition** FISC tax category; ~ **d'options** BOURSE class of options, option class; ~ **de paiements** FISC class of payments; ~ **de risques** ASSUR class of risk; ~ **sociale** POL social class, V&M *étude de marché* social category; ~ **socio-professionnelle** *(CSP)* COM socioprofessional group; ~ **de tarif** TRANSP rate class; ◆ **de ~ supérieure** COM *hôtel* high-class

catégories: ~ **sociales défavorisées** *f pl* PROT SOC hardship categories

catégoriquement *adv* COM *refuser* flatly

catégorisation *f* COM categorization

catégoriser *vt* COM categorize

CATIF *abrév (contrat à terme d'instrument financier)* BOURSE financial futures contract

cause *f* ASSUR consideration, DROIT case, POL cause; **à ~ de** COM o/a, on account of; ~ **déterminante** DROIT procuring cause; ~ **de doublage** DROIT metaling (*AmE*), metalling (*BrE*); ~ **de résiliation** ASSUR cause of cancellation; ~ **du sinistre** ASSUR cause of loss

causer *vt* COM cause

causes *f pl* COM causes; ~ **de chômage** RES HUM causes of unemployment

caution *f* ASSUR bond, BANQUE *document* letter of indemnity, *garantie* guarantee, guaranty, COM *argent* deposit, security, *document* letter of indemnity, *garantie* caution money, credit guarantee, COMPTA deposit, DROIT caution money, *argent* bail, deposit, *document* bail bond, *garantie* guarantee, guaranty; ~ **bancaire** BANQUE bank guarantee, bank guaranty; ~ **garantissant le paiement en nature de la main-d'oeuvre** FIN PIK bond, payment-in-kind bond; ~ **judiciaire** DROIT judicial bond; ~ **en numéraire** DROIT surety in cash; ~ **de participation à une adjudication** BOURSE bid bond; ~ **personnelle** BANQUE, FIN personal guarantee; ~ **solidaire** FIN joint guarantee

cautionnement *m* ASSUR security, surety, COM deposit, security, surety, DROIT caution money, FIN security, surety; ~ **pour avarie commune** ASSUR GA dep, general average deposit; ~ **judiciaire** DROIT judicial bond; ~ **perdu** ASSUR forfeited security; ~ **réciproque** BANQUE cross guarantee

cautionner *vt* BANQUE *personne* guarantee; ◆ ~ **qn** BANQUE *personne* stand surety for sb

CBV *abrév (Conseil des bourses de valeurs)* BOURSE regulatory body of the Paris Stock Exchange, ≈ TSA (*UK*), (*The Securities Association*), ≈ Council of the Stock Exchange (*UK*)

cc *abrév* COM *(cylindrée)* cc *(cubic centimetre)*, DROIT *(convention collective)*, IND *(convention collective)*, RES HUM *(convention collective)* collective agreement, collective bargaining agreement, labor agreement (*AmE*), labour agreement (*BrE*), union contract

c/c *abrév (compte courant, compte créditeur)* BANQUE C/A *(credit account)*, COM C/A *(checking account)*, COMPTA C/A *(credit account)*, FIN C/A *(checking account AmE, current account BrE)*

CCAA *abrév (Conseil de coordination des associations aéroportuaires)* LOISIRS ≈ AACC *(Airport Associations Co-ordinating Council)*

CCI *abrév (Certificats coopératifs d'investissement)* BOURSE investment certificates reserved to cooperative and mutual companies

CCIFP *abrév (Chambre de compensation des instruments financiers de Paris)* BOURSE clearing house for financial instruments in Paris

CCR *abrév (coefficient de capitalisation des résultats)* BOURSE, COMPTA, FIN PER *(price-earnings ratio)*

CD *abrév* BANQUE *(certificat de dépôt)*, BOURSE *(certificat de dépôt)*, ECON *(certificat de dépôt)* CD *(certificate of deposit)*, INFO *(disque compact)* CD *(compact disk)*

CDC *abrév (compte de dividende en capital)* FISC CDA *(capital dividend account)*

CDD *abrév (contrat à durée déterminée)* RES HUM fixed-term contract, fixed-term deal, TRANSP *maritime* time agreement

CDI *abrév* INFO *(disque compact interactif)* CD-I *(compact disk interactive)*, RES HUM *(contrat à durée indéterminée)* permanent contract

CDN *abrév (certificat de dépôt négociable)* BANQUE, BOURSE NCD *(negotiable certificate of deposit)*

CD-ROM *m (disque CD-ROM)* INFO CD-ROM *(compact disk read-only memory)*

CE *abrév* ECON *(Communauté européenne)* EC *(European Community)*, POL *(Conseil de l'Europe)* CE *(Council of Europe)*, RES HUM *(comité*

d'entreprise) joint consultative committee, works committee (*UK*), works council (*UK*)

CEA *abrév* BOURSE *(compte d'épargne en actions)* equity savings account, ENVIR *(Commissariat à l'énergie atomique)* ≈ AERE *(Atomic Energy Research Establishment)*

CEAO *abrév (Communauté économique de l'Afrique de l'Ouest)* ECON *customs* ECOWAS *(Economic Community of West African States)*

CECA *abrév (Communauté européenne du charbon et de l'acier)* ECON ECSC *(European Coal and Steel Community)*

ceci: **à ~** *adv* COM, COMMS, DROIT hereto

cédant, e *m,f* ASSUR assignor, cedant, BREVETS assignor, DROIT assignor, cedant, transferor, transferrer

céder 1. *vt* ASSUR *transférer* cede, BOURSE *perdre* give up, shed, COM *vendre* sell, DROIT *transférer* assign, cede, convey; **2.** *vi* COM back down, give in; ◆ **~ la propriété** IMMOB transfer ownership

CEDEX *abrév (courrier d'entreprise à distribution exceptionnelle)* ADMIN business mail service

cédi *m* COM cedi

CEE *abrév (Commission économique européenne)* ECON ECE *(Economic Commission for Europe)*

CEEA *abrév (Communauté européenne de l'énergie atomique)* IND EAEC *(European Atomic Energy Community)*

CEI *abrév (Communauté des États indépendants)* COM, ECON, POL CIS *(Commonwealth of Independent States)*

ceinture: **~ de sécurité** *f* TRANSP safety belt, seat belt; **~ verte** *f* ENVIR *autour d'une ville* green belt

cela: **à ~** *adv* COM, COMMS, DROIT hereto; ◆ **~ laisse à désirer** COM there is scope for improvement

célèbre *adj* COM famous, renowned, well-known

célébrité *f* COM renown

célérité: **~ habituelle** *f* TRANSP customary despatch, customary dispatch

célibataire[1] *adj* ADMIN, DROIT, FIN single, unmarried

célibataire[2] *mf* ADMIN, DROIT, FISC single man, single woman, V&M *statistiques* single-person household

cellule *f* INFO, TRANSP *fixation des conteneurs* cell; **~ de guidage** TRANSP *fixation des conteneurs* cell guide; **~ de réflexion** COM think-tank *(infrml)*

Celsius *m* COM Celsius

CEN *abrév (Centre européen de normalisation)* ECON European Committee for Standardization

censure *f* COMMS, MÉDIA censorship, POL managed news, word engineering

cent *m* BANQUE *unité monétaire*, COM cent, MATH hundred; ◆ **pour ~** *(p. cent, p.)* MATH per cent *(pc)*

centigrade *adj* COM centigrade

centile *m* MATH percentile

centilitre *m (cl)* COM centiliter (*AmE*), centilitre (*BrE*) *(cl)*

centime *m (c.)* COM centime *(c.)*

centimètre *m (cm)* COM centimeter (*AmE*), centimetre (*BrE*) *(cm)*; **~ cube** *(cm3)* COM cubic centimeter (*AmE*), cubic centimetre (*BrE*) *(cc)*

centrafricain, e *adj* COM Central African

central *m* COMMS *téléphone* exchange

centrale: **~ d'achat** *f* COM quantity buyer; **~ d'achat pour indépendants** *f* V&M buying house; **~ d'achats d'espaces** *f* MÉDIA *publicité, radio, télévision* airtime buyer; **~ en charge de base** *f* IND baseload power station; **~ électrique** *f* ENVIR, IND generating station, power station; **~ électrique de chauffage urbain** *f* ENVIR, IND district heating power station; **~ hydro-électrique** *f* ENVIR hydro, hydroelectric power station, IND hydroelectricity plant, hydroelectric power station; **~ mixte** *f* TRANSP *navigation* combined cycle power station; **~ nucléaire** *f* ENVIR, IND nuclear plant, nuclear power station; **~ téléphonique** *f* COMMS telephone exchange; **~ thermique** *f* ENVIR, IND thermal power station; **~ usine hydro-électrique** *f* ENVIR, IND hydroelectric power station

centralisation *f* COM centralization

centralisé, e *adj* COM centralized

centraliser *vt* COM centralize

centralisme: **~ démocratique** *m* POL democratic centralism

centraméricain, e *adj* COM Central American

centre *m* COM, COMMS, IND center (*AmE*), centre (*BrE*), TRANSP hub; **~ d'activité** *m* COM hub of activity; **~ administratif** *m* ADMIN administrative center (*AmE*), administrative centre (*BrE*); **~ d'affaires** *m* COM, V&M business center (*AmE*), business centre (*BrE*); **~ d'affaires international** *m* ECON, V&M world trade center (*AmE*), world trade centre (*BrE*); **~ d'affaires d'une ville** *m* ECON central business district, CBD; **~ d'autorisation** *m* BANQUE authorization center (*AmE*), authorization centre (*BrE*); **~ de bilan professionnel** *m* RES HUM assessment center (*AmE*), assessment centre (*BrE*); **~ de calcul** *m* INFO computer center (*AmE*), computer centre (*BrE*), computing center (*AmE*), computing centre (*BrE*); **~ céréalier** *m* TRANSP *dans un port* grain terminal; **~ de chargement** *m* TRANSP cargo center (*AmE*), cargo centre (*BrE*); **~ de commerce** *m* COM, IMMOB, V&M mart, retail center (*AmE*), retail centre (*BrE*); **~ commercial** *m* COM one-stop shopping center (*AmE*), one-stop shopping centre (*BrE*), shopping center (*AmE*), shopping centre (*BrE*), shopping mall (*AmE*), V&M commercial center (*AmE*), commercial centre (*BrE*); **~ commercial suburbain** *m* COM, V&M out-of-town center (*AmE*), out-of-town centre (*BrE*); **~ de compensation** *m* BANQUE clearing center (*AmE*), clearing centre (*BrE*); **~ des congrès internationaux** *m* V&M international convention center (*AmE*), international convention centre (*BrE*); **~ de coût** *m* COMPTA burden center (*AmE*), burden centre (*BrE*), cost center (*AmE*), cost centre (*BrE*); ~ **de coûts** *m* COMPTA expense center (*AmE*), expense centre (*BrE*); ~ **culturel** *m* COM cultural center (*AmE*), cultural centre (*BrE*); ~ **de dégroupage** *m* TRANSP *navigation* break bulk center (*AmE*), break bulk centre (*BrE*); ~ **de distribution** *m* TRANSP distribution center (*AmE*), distribution centre (*BrE*); ~ **double fond** *m* TRANSP *navigation* dbc, double bottom center (*AmE*), double bottom centre (*BrE*); ~ **d'enseignement postscolaire** *m* PROT SOC college of further education (*UK*), CFE (*UK*); ~ **d'évaluation** *m* RES HUM assessment center (*AmE*), assessment centre (*BrE*); ~ **d'évaluation de la qualité** *m* RES HUM assessment center (*AmE*), assessment centre (*BrE*); ~ **financier** *m* ECON, FIN financial center (*AmE*), financial centre (*BrE*); ~ **financier international** *m* ECON, FIN global financial center (*AmE*), global financial centre (*BrE*); ~ **de formation** *m* RES HUM training center (*AmE*), training centre (*BrE*); ~ **de gestion par responsabilité** *m* COMPTA, GESTION management by responsibility center (*AmE*), management by responsibility centre (*BrE*); ~ **de gravité** *m* TRANSP center of gravity (*AmE*), centre of gravity (*BrE*); ~ **de groupage** *m* TRANSP groupage depot; ~ **industriel** *m* IND industrial center (*AmE*), industrial centre (*BrE*); ~ **d'informations économiques et sociales** *m* PROT SOC Centre for Economic and Social Information, CESI; ~ **informatique** *m* INFO computer center (*AmE*), computer centre (*BrE*); ~ **informatique d'entreprise** *m* INFO corporate data center (*AmE*), corporate data centre (*BrE*); ~ **d'innovation** *m* IND innovation center (*AmE*), innovation centre (*BrE*); ~ **d'investissement** *m* BOURSE, FIN investment center (*AmE*), investment centre (*BrE*); ~ **de loisirs** *m* LOISIRS leisure center (*AmE*), leisure centre (*BrE*); ~ **médicosocial** *m* PROT SOC health center (*AmE*), health centre (*BrE*); ~ **du navire** *m* TRANSP m, midship; ~ **offshore** *m* BANQUE offshore center (*AmE*), offshore centre (*BrE*); ~ **-périphérie** *m* ECON core-periphery; ~ **de préscolarisation** *m* PROT SOC preschool center (*AmE*), preschool centre (*BrE*); ~ **de profit** *m* COM, COMPTA, ECON, FIN profit center (*AmE*), profit centre (*BrE*); ~ **régional** *m* COM regional center (*AmE*), regional centre (*BrE*); ~ **de rentabilité** *m* BOURSE, FIN investment center (*AmE*), investment centre (*BrE*); ~ **de responsabilité** *m* COMPTA, FIN, GESTION responsibility center (*AmE*), responsibility centre (*BrE*); ~ **de responsabilité principale** *m* COMPTA, FIN, GESTION prime responsibility center (*AmE*), prime responsibility centre (*BrE*); ~ **de traitement à façon** *m* INFO service bureau; ~ **de traitement de texte** *m* INFO word-processing center (*AmE*), word-processing centre (*BrE*); ~ **de transbordement des marchandises en vrac** *m* TRANSP bulk transshipment center (*AmE*), bulk transshipment centre (*BrE*); ~ **de transit international** *m* COMMS, TRANSP gateway; ~ **-ville** *m* [inv] COM city center (*AmE*), city centre (*BrE*), town center (*AmE*), town centre (*BrE*); ~ **de la ville** *m* COM city center (*AmE*), city centre (*BrE*), town center (*AmE*), town centre (*BrE*); ~ **-ville** *m* [inv] ENVIR, PROT SOC inner city; ◆ **de ~ gauche** POL left-of-center (*AmE*), left-of-centre (*BrE*), liberal

Centre: ~ **de documentation pour entreprises** *m* COM business library; ~ **d'emploi du Canada** *m* RES HUM Canada Employment Centre; ~ **des études politiques** *m* ECON Centre for Policy Studies (*UK*), CPS (*UK*); ~ **européen de normalisation** *m (CEN)* ECON European Committee for Standardization; ~ **européen pour la recherche nucléaire** *m (CERN)* IND European Organization for Nuclear Research; ~ **de formalités d'entreprise** *m (CFE)* COM centre for registering new businesses; ~ **international de contrôle du crédit** *m* COM International Control Centre, ICC

centré: ~ **sur l'enfant** *adj* PROT SOC child-centered (*AmE*), child-centred (*BrE*)

cercle *m* COM circle; ~ **des intimes** POL loop (*US*); ~ **de qualité** GESTION, IND, RES HUM quality circle; ~ **vicieux** ECON vicious circle; ~ **vicieux du chômage** ECON, PROT SOC unemployment trap; ~ **vicieux de la pauvreté** ECON, PROT SOC poverty trap

cerf-volant *m* BOURSE kite (*jarg*)

CERN *abrév (Centre européen pour la recherche nucléaire)* IND European Organization for Nuclear Research

certain *adj* BANQUE good, COM certain, FIN good

certif. *abrév (certificat)* ADMIN, BREVETS, COM, FIN, PROT SOC cert. *(certificate, certification)*

certificat *m (certif.)* ADMIN, BREVETS, COM, FIN, PROT SOC certificate, certification *(cert.)*; ~ **d'acheminement** TRANSP routing certificate; ~ **d'action** BOURSE share certificate (*BrE*), stock certificate (*AmE*); ~ **d'actions ordinaires** BOURSE common share certificate (*BrE*), common stock certificate (*AmE*); ~ **actuariel** ASSUR actuarial certificate; ~ **d'agrément** FISC certificate of registration; ~ **d'amélioration réciproque** FIN mutual improvement certificate; ~ **d'analyse** TRANSP certificate of analysis; ~ **d'aptitude** TRANSP *navigation* certificate of competency; ~ **d'assurance** ASSUR certificate of insurance, CI; ~ **d'audit** COMPTA, FIN accounts certification; ~ **d'authenticité de l'équipement** TRANSP equipment trust certificate; ~ **d'avarie commune** ASSUR general average certificate, GAC; ~ **bancaire** BANQUE bank certificate; ~ **de bord** IMP/EXP, TRANSP *maritime* mate's receipt, MR; ~ **de brevet** BREVETS patent certificate; ~ **de chargement en pontée** TRANSP deck cargo certificate; ~ **de circulation** IMP/EXP movement certificate; ~ **de classification** TRANSP *d'un navire* classification certificate; ~ **de commerce international** ECON international trading certificate, ITC; ~ **du commissaire aux comptes** COMPTA, FIN accounts certification, auditor's certificate, auditor's opinion; ~ **de conditionnement** TRANSP certificate of conditioning; ~ **de contrôle** TRANSP certificate of inspection; ~ **de croissance des investissements du Trésor** BOURSE Treasury Investment Growth Receipt, TIGR; ~ **de débarquement** TRANSP landing certificate; ~ **de dédouanement d'entrée** IMP/EXP jerque note; ~ **de dépôt** BANQUE, BOURSE, ECON, FIN certificate of deposit, investment certificate; ~ **de dépôt négociable** *(CDN)* BANQUE, BOURSE negotiable CD, negotiable certificate of deposit *(NCD)*; ~ **de dépôt négociable sur le marché secondaire** BOURSE seasoned certificate of deposit; ~ **de dératisation** TRANSP *d'un navire* derating certificate, rodent control certificate; ~ **de dette renouvelable amortie** FIN certificate of amortized revolving debt *(UK)*, CARD *(UK)*; ~ **de dividende** BOURSE dividend voucher; ~ **d'empotage** TRANSP *d'un conteneur* packaging certificate; ~ **d'empotage du conteneur** TRANSP container packing certificate; ~ **d'emprunt** FIN loan certificate; ~ **d'emprunt cessible** FIN transferable loan certificate, TLC; ~ **d'enregistrement** BREVETS, DROIT certificate of registration; ~ **d'entrée trop perçue** IMP/EXP overpaid entry certificate, OEC; ~ **d'entrepôt** COM warehouse warrant, WW, DROIT dock warrant, D/W, *commercial* warehouse warrant, WW, IMP/EXP dock warrant, D/W, TRANSP *port* dock warrant, D/W, V&M warehouse warrant, WW; ~ **d'épargne** BOURSE savings certificate; ~ **d'épargne cumulative** BANQUE growth savings certificate; ~ **d'exemption** FISC certificate of exemption; ~ **d'exonération** FISC certificate of exemption; ~ **d'expédition** TRANSP *de marchandises* certificate of shipment; ~ **d'expédition/ d'origine** IMP/EXP certificate of consignment/origin, CC/O; ~ **d'expertise** COM survey certificate; ~ **de fabrication** IND certificate of manufacture; ~ **de franc-bord** TRANSP *d'un navire* load line certificate; ~ **garanti par hypothèque** FIN mortgage-backed certificate; ~ **hypothécaire de résidence mobile** BANQUE, BOURSE mobile home certificate *(US)*; ~ **d'immatriculation** TRANSP *d'un navire* certificate of registry; ~ **d'indépendance** RES HUM certificate of independence; ~ **international de franc-bord** TRANSP *d'un navire* international load line certificate; ~ **d'investissement** *(CI)* BOURSE investment certificate, share certificate *(BrE)*, stock certificate *(AmE)*; ~ **d'investissement prioritaire** *(CIP)* BOURSE preferred investment certificate; ~ **de marché monétaire** BOURSE, ECON, FIN money-market certificate, MMC; ~ **médical de bonne santé** PROT SOC certificate of health; ~ **de nombre de passagers** TRANSP passenger number certificate; ~ **obligataire** BOURSE bond certificate; ~ **d'obligation** BOURSE bond certificate, debenture bond; ~ **d'occupation** IMMOB certificate of occupancy; ~ **d'option** ASSUR warrant; ~ **d'origine** IMP/EXP c/o, certificate of origin; ~ **d'origine et d'expédition** IMP/EXP certificate of origin and

consignment, C/OC; ~ **de participation** BOURSE participation certificate; ~ **pour une période déterminée** FIN term certificate; ~ **de placement** BANQUE, FIN investment certificate; ~ **de placement garanti** BANQUE, FIN guaranteed investment certificate; ~ **de poids** TRANSP certificate of weight; ~ **de pontée** TRANSP *navigation* deck cargo certificate; ~ **au porteur** BOURSE, FIN bearer certificate; ~ **de pratique** IMP/EXP certificate of pratique; ~ **de prêt** FIN loan certificate; ~ **de prêt transférable** FIN transferable loan certificate; ~ **de propriété** COM, DROIT, IMMOB certificate of ownership, land certificate; ~ **de protection renforcée** BREVETS supplementary protection certificate, SPC; ~ **de protection supplémentaire** BREVETS supplementary protection certificate, SPC; ~ **provisoire** BOURSE interim certificate; ~ **de qualité** IMP/EXP, TRANSP certificate of quality, quality certificate; ~ **de radiation** COM certificate proving an action has been struck off; ~ **radio** TRANSP wireless certificate; ~ **du receveur général** FIN receiver's certificate; ~ **de sécurité de construction pour navire de charge** TRANSP *navigation* SAFCON certificate, cargo ship safety construction certificate; ~ **de sécurité du matériel d'armement** TRANSP *maritime* safety equipment certificate *(UK)*; ~ **de sécurité du matériel d'armement pour navire de charge** TRANSP *navigation* cargo ship safety equipment certificate; ~ **de sécurité pour navire à passagers** TRANSP passenger safety certificate; ~ **de transport de passagers** TRANSP passenger certificate *(UK)*, PC *(UK)*; ~ **d'utilisation** IMMOB certificate of use; ~ **d'utilité** BREVETS utility certificate; ~ **de validité d'un titre** DROIT, IMMOB *de propriété* opinion of title; ~ **vétérinaire** IMP/EXP veterinary certificate; ~ **de vie** ASSUR certificate of existence; ~ **de visite** TRANSP *d'un navire* certificate of survey; ~ **de vote fiduciaire** BOURSE voting trust certificate; ~ **de vote groupé** BOURSE voting trust certificate

Certificat: ≈ ~ **d'aptitude au professorat d'enseignement du second degré** m *(CAPES)* PROT SOC ≈ Postgraduate Certificate of Education *(UK)* *(PGCE)*

certification f BREVETS *d'un produit* acknowledgement, certification, COM certification, COMPTA *procédure* auditing, *résultat* auditor's opinion, DROIT *d'un acte notarié, d'une attestation officielle* acknowledgement, *d'une signature* attestation, witnessing, *d'un document* authentication, *d'un produit* certification, FIN auditing, auditor's opinion, IND *d'un produit* certification, TRANSP *d'un avion* airworthiness certification, V&M *d'un acte notarié, d'une attestation officielle* acknowledgement; ~ **de signature** BANQUE guarantee of signature

Certificats: ~ **coopératifs d'investissement** m pl *(CCI)* BOURSE investment certificates reserved to cooperative and mutual companies; ~ **d'investissement à bons de souscriptions d'actions** m pl *(CIBSA)* BOURSE investment certificates with share warrants; ~ **d'investissement préférés à bons de souscription d'actions** m pl (CIPBSA) BOURSE preferred investment certificates with share warrants; ~ **pétroliers** m pl (CP) BOURSE oil company investment certificates exclusive to Total and Elf-Erap

certifier vt BREVETS certificate, COM certificate, produit guarantee, DROIT document authenticate, produit certificate, guarantee, signature attest, witness, IND produit certificate, guarantee, TRANSP avion certificate; ~ **conforme** DROIT notarize

certitude f COM certainty

CES abrév France (contrat d'emploi-solidarité) RES HUM ≈ YTS (UK) (Youth Training Scheme)

cessation f COM termination, de paiements stoppage, stopping, suspension, RES HUM de fonctions termination; ~ **d'activité** COM d'une personne retirement, d'une entreprise termination of business; ~ **de commerce** COM winding-up; ~ **de fonctions avec préavis** RES HUM termination of employment with notice; ~ **de paiement des primes** ASSUR cessation of payment of premiums

cesser vt COM break off, cease; ♦ ~ **de cotiser à qch** COM contract out of sth; ~ **d'exister** FISC cease to be extant; ~ **ses activités** COM cease trading; ~ **de soutenir un cours** jarg BOURSE pull the plug (infrml); ~ **le travail** RES HUM définitivement down tools, knock off (infrml), stop work, stop working, à cause d'une grève go on strike, strike, walk out

cessible adj COM assignable, negotiable, transferable

cession f BOURSE disposal, BREVETS d'un brevet, d'une marque déposée abandonment, assignment, COMPTA d'une créance assignment, DROIT assignment, conveyance, disposal, d'un bien abandonment, d'un droit assignment, cession, FIN disposal; ~ **d'actifs** COMPTA, FIN asset sale; ~ **de bail** DROIT, IMMOB assignment of lease; ~ **-bail** DROIT, IMMOB leaseback, sale and leaseback; ~ **d'éléments d'actif** BOURSE, COMPTA realization of assets; ~ **horizontale** IND horizontal divestiture; ~ **au pair** BOURSE par delivery; ~ **de portefeuille** ASSUR, COM cession of portfolio, portfolio transfer; ~ **de titres** BOURSE disposal of securities, security disposal; ~ **de valeurs mobilières** BOURSE disposal of securities, security disposal; ♦ **faire ~ de** DROIT assign

cessionnaire mf BANQUE assignee, endorsee, indorsee, transferee, BREVETS assignee, transferee, COMPTA assignee, endorsee, transferee, DROIT assignee, transferee

cessure f BOURSE break-out

césure f INFO, MÉDIA impression hyphenation

C&A abrév (coût et assurance) IMP/EXP c&i, C&I (cost and insurance)

C&F abrév (coût et fret) IMP/EXP, TRANSP C&F (cost and freight)

CETI abrév (contrat d'échange de taux d'intérêts) BOURSE interest rate swap

CFAO abrév (conception et fabrication assistées par ordinateur) IND, INFO CAD/CAM (computer-aided design and computer-aided manufacturing, computer-assisted design and computer-assisted manufacturing)

CFC abrév (chlorofluorocarbone) ENVIR CFC (chlorofluorocarbon)

CFE abrév (Centre de formalités d'entreprise) COM centre for registering new businesses

CGA abrév (adaptateur graphique couleur) INFO CGA (color/graphics adaptor AmE, colour/ graphics adaptor BrE)

CGT abrév (Confédération générale du travail) RES HUM ≈ CIO (US) (Congress of Industrial Organizations), ≈ TUC (UK) (Trades Union Congress)

chacun, e adj COM apiece

chaînage m INFO concatenation

chaîne f COM de magasins chain, INFO de caractères, de données string, MÉDIA Can (cf canal Fra) de télévision channel, TRANSP manutention, V&M de supermarchés chain; ~ **d'activités** COM, ECON business system; ~ **affiliée** V&M affiliated chain; ~ **alimentaire** ECON, ENVIR food chain; ~ **de bits** INFO bit string; ~ **de caractères** INFO character string; ~ **de grands magasins** COM, V&M department store chain; ~ **de montage** IND, RES HUM assembly line; ~ **de production** IND chain of production, production chain, production line; ~ **de télévision** MÉDIA television channel; ~ **de valeur** FIN value chain; ~ **volontaire de distribution** COM voluntary chain

chaîner vt INFO link

chaland m TRANSP bateau barge; ~ **automoteur** TRANSP self-propelled barge; ~ **de mer** TRANSP seagoing barge, navigation low-profile coaster; ~ **sans moteur** TRANSP navigation dumb craft

chalandage: ~ **fiscal** m FISC treaty shopping; ~ **d'opinion** m COMPTA opinion shopping

chalutier m TRANSP trawler

chambre:[1] ~ **de commerce français pour le Royaume-Uni** m COM French Chamber of Commerce for the United Kingdom, FCCUK

chambre[2] f DROIT chambers, LOISIRS dans un hotel bedroom, room, POL chamber; ~ **de compensation** BANQUE clearing corporation (US), clearing house; ~ **de compensation internationale** BANQUE international clearing house; ~ **à deux lits** LOISIRS twin room; ~ **pour deux personnes** LOISIRS double room; ~ **double** LOISIRS double room; ~ **forte** BANQUE strongroom; ~ **frigorifique** IND, TRANSP cold storage; ~ **froide** IND, TRANSP cold storage; ~ **d'hôte** LOISIRS b&b, bed and breakfast; ~ **individuelle** LOISIRS single room; ~ **internationale de compensation pour les produits de base** BOURSE International Commodities Clearing House (UK), ICCH (UK); ~ **des machines** TRANSP dans un navire engine room, ER; ~ **des métiers** COM trade chamber; ~ **pour une personne** LOISIRS single room; ~ **syndicale des agents de change** BOURSE stock exchange committee

Chambre: ~ **de commerce** *f* ECON Board of Trade (*UK*), BOT, Chamber of Commerce, CC; ~ **de commerce britannique au Nigéria** *f* COM Nigerian British Chamber of Commerce, NBCC; ~ **de commerce canadienne** *f* ECON Canadian Chamber of Commerce, CCC; ~ **de commerce et d'industrie de Londres** *f* COM London Chamber of Commerce & Industry, LCCI; ~ **de commerce française** *f* COM French Chamber of Commerce, FCC; ~ **de commerce française en Grande-Bretagne** *f* COM French Chamber of Commerce in Great Britain; ~ **de compensation des instruments financiers de Paris** *f France (CCIFP)* BOURSE clearing house for financial instruments in Paris; ~ **de compensation interbancaire internationale** *f* BANQUE Clearing House Automatic Payments System (*US*), Clearing House Interbank Payments System (*US*), CHAPS (*US*), CHIPS (*US*); ~ **des métiers** *f* ECON, POL Chamber of Trade; ~ **des représentants** *f* POL House of Representatives (*US*)

champ *m* COM area, INFO field; ~ **d'activité** COM field of activity, sphere of activity; ~ **d'adresse** INFO address field; ~ **d'application de la couverture** ASSUR scope of coverage; ~ **de données** INFO data field; ~ **de fond** INFO background field; ~ **d'imposition** FISC field of taxation; ~ **pétrolifère en mer** IND offshore oil-field

chance *f* COM lucky break; ~ **sur un marché** COM break in the market; ◆ **avoir une bonne** ~ **de** COM stand a good chance of; **ne pas avoir la moindre** ~ RES HUM not stand a chance

chanceler *vi* ECON falter

chancelier: ~ **de l'Échiquier** *m* ECON, POL Chancellor of the Exchequer (*UK*); ~ **de l'Échiquier fantôme** *m* POL shadow chancellor (*UK*)

chandelier *m* TRANSP *navigation* stanchion

change *m* BANQUE, BOURSE, ECON, FIN ex., exch., exchange, foreign exchange, FX, RES HUM *échange* trade-off; ~ **inégal** COM unequal exchange; ~ **de structure** GESTION structural change; ~ **à terme** ECON forward exchange

changé, e *adj* COM alt., altered

changement *m* COM, ECON *de l'offre, de la demande*, INFO change; ~ **d'adresse** COMMS change of address; ~ **de banque de mémoire** INFO bank switching; ~ **de bloc de mémoire** INFO bank switching; ~ **de cours à terme** BOURSE futures price change; ~ **de date d'échéance** BANQUE, BOURSE, ECON, FIN maturity transformation; ~ **fréquent d'emplois** RES HUM job hopping; ~ **de ligne** INFO lf, line feed; ~ **de ligne automatique** INFO word wrap; ~ **de page** INFO form feed, page break, FF; ~ **de page obligatoire** INFO hard page break; ~ **politique** COM, POL political change; ~ **de prix** BOURSE price change; ~ **de prix à terme** BOURSE futures price change; ~ **de propriétaire** ECON under new ownership;

~ **technologique** COM, IND technological change; ◆ ~ **de propriétaire** GESTION under new management

changements: ~ **d'avis successifs** *m pl* RES HUM flip-flop arbitration

changer 1. *vt* COM alter, change; **2.** *vi* COM change, *orientation* switch over; ◆ ~ **d'avion** TRANSP transfer; ~ **d'avis** COM have second thoughts; ~ **de direction** COM veer; ~ **l'image de** V&M reimage; ~ **de logement** IMMOB move house; ~ **de main** V&M change hands; ~ **de propriétaire** V&M change hands; ~ **de train** TRANSP transfer

chantage *m* COM blackmail, shakedown (*US, infrml*); ~ **financier** BOURSE greenmail (*US*)

chantier *m* IMMOB *construction* yard, IND site; ~ **de construction** IMMOB building lot; ~ **de ferraille** COM scrap yard; ~ **de matériaux de construction** IMMOB contractor's yard; ~ **qui admet les ouvriers non-syndiqués** COM, RES HUM open shop

chapardage *m* COM grazing (*jarg*)

chapeau: ~ **du capitaine** *m* FIN, FISC, TRANSP *maritime* primage

chapitre *m* COM section, COMPTA heading; ~ **du tarif** TRANSP sectional rate

charbon *m* ENVIR, IND coal; ~ **de bois** ENVIR, IND charcoal

charbonnage *m* IND *action* coal mining, *mine* coal mine, colliery

charbonnier *m* TRANSP *navire* coal carrier, collier

charcutage: ~ **électoral** *m* POL gerrymandering

charge *f* ADMIN administrative burden, COM burden, responsibility, DROIT encumbrance, ECON burden, responsibility, FIN charge, liability, POL encumbrance, TRANSP ld, load; ~ **admissible de fonctionnement** IND safe working load; ~ **binomiale** ECON binomial charge; ~ **commune** ECON common cost; ~ **complète d'un conteneur** TRANSP container load; ~ **constatée par régularisation** COMPTA accrued expense; ~ **au départ** BOURSE front-end load; ~ **directe** COMPTA, FIN direct cost, direct expense; ~ **directe de structure** ECON, FIN direct overhead; ~ **exceptionnelle** COMPTA extraordinary charge; ~ **explosive** TRANSP *marchandises dangereuses* booster, burster; ~ **externe** COMPTA external cost; ~ **extrême** TRANSP breaking load; ~ **financière** FIN financial burden, financial encumbrance, interest charge; ~ **fiscale** ECON, FISC tax burden, tax charge; ~ **fixe** COM, COMPTA, ECON fixed charge, fixed cost, fixed expense; ~ **incomplète** TRANSP part load; ~ **indirecte** COMPTA, FIN indirect cost, indirect expense; ~ **limite** TRANSP maximum load; ~ **maximale** TRANSP maximum load; ~ **non-courante** COMPTA nonrecurring charge; ~ **payable d'avance** COM upfront cost; ~ **payée d'avance** COMPTA prepayment; ~ **à payer** COMPTA accrued expense, accrued liability; ~ **de la preuve** DROIT burden of proof; ~ **à répartir sur plusieurs exercices** COMPTA deferred charge; ~ **de rupture** TRANSP breaking load; ~ **de**

servitude COMPTA user charge; ~ **supplémentaire** ECON prime cost; ~ **sur un bien-fonds** FISC charge on land; ~ **sur le plancher** TRANSP *navigation* floor loading; ~ **sur le toit** TRANSP *conteneurs* roof load; ~ **de travail** GESTION, IND, RES HUM working load, workload; ~ **de travail de sécurité** IND safe working load; ~ **utile** *(CU)* TRANSP carrying capacity, payload; ~ **utile dans les cales en nombre et longueur** TRANSP *d'un navire* CHo, carrying capacity in number and length in holds; ~ **utile réelle** TRANSP *poids net* actual payload; ~ **utile sur le pont en nombre et longueur** TRANSP *navigation* carrying capacity in number and length on deck, CDK; ~ **variable** COM variable charge, VC; ◆ **à ~** COM dependent; **en ~** TRANSP under load

chargé:[1] ~ **en poids et en cubage** *adj* TRANSP *navigation* full and down; ~ **en vrac** *adj* TRANSP laden in bulk; ◆ **être ~ de** COM *projet* be in charge of

chargé:[2] ~ **de courrier** *mf* ADMIN, COMMS mail clerk; ~ **de cours** *mf* PROT SOC, RES HUM adjunct professor *(US)*, lecturer, university lecturer; ~ **d'études média** *mf* MÉDIA, V&M *publicité* media planner; ~ **du marketing** *mf* RES HUM, V&M marketing officer; ~ **de la mercatique** *mf* RES HUM, V&M marketing officer; ~ **de prêts** *mf* BANQUE lending officer, loan officer

chargement *m* INFO ldg, loading, TRANSP *action* lading, ldg, loading, *marchandises* cargo, load; ~ **d'aller** IMP/EXP, TRANSP outward cargo; ~ **automatique** IND *machine* self-loading, INFO autoloading; ~ **du conteneur** TRANSP container load; ~ **encombrant** COM, TRANSP bulky cargo; ~ **liquide** TRANSP liquid bulk cargo; ~ **manuel** INFO manual feed; ~ **par allèges** TRANSP *d'un navire* loading overside, overside loading; ~ **partiel** TRANSP part load; ~ **partiel du conteneur** TRANSP container part load; ~ **en pontée** TRANSP *d'un navire* deck cargo; ~ **préélingué** TRANSP *navigation* presling; ~ **de retour** IMP/EXP inward cargo, TRANSP back load, inward cargo, return load; ~ **sous palan** TRANSP *d'un navire* loading overside, overside loading; ~ **trop élevé** TRANSP overheight cargo; ~ **volumineux** COM, TRANSP bulky cargo; ~ **en vrac** TRANSP loose cargo; ◆ ~ **et déchargement exclus** IMP/EXP, TRANSP exclusive of loading and unloading, xl & ul; ~ **et livraison** TRANSP ldg & dly, loading and delivery

charger *vt* INFO *programme* load, TRANSP *marchandises* lade, load, ship

charges *f pl* COM, COMPTA, FIN charges, expenses; ~ **associées** *f pl* COMPTA add-on costs; ~ **constatées d'avance** *f pl* BANQUE accrued charges; ~ **courantes** *f pl* COM running costs; ~ **exceptionnelles** *f pl* COMPTA *bilan* exceptional expenses; ~ **d'exploitation** *f pl* COMPTA operating costs, operating expenses, running expenses; ~ **fixes moyennes** *f pl* COMPTA average fixed cost; ~ **fixes à terme** *f pl* COMPTA times fixed charges;

~ **générales d'exploitation** *f pl* RES HUM general administrative expenses; ~ **imprévues** *f pl* COMPTA contingency payments; ~ **d'intérêts** *f pl* BANQUE, COMPTA interest charge, interest charges; ~ **latentes** *f pl* COMPTA contingent expenses; **les ~ salariales constatées** *f pl* COMPTA the accruals of wages; ~ **liées à la PAC** *f pl* ECON CAP charges; ~ **de main-d'oeuvre directes** *f pl* COMPTA direct labor costs *(AmE)*, direct labour costs *(BrE)*; ~ **payées d'avance** *f pl* COMPTA prepaid expenses, short-term prepayments; ~ **de personnel** *f* RES HUM staff cost; ~ **prévues** *f pl* COMPTA estimated charges, estimated costs; ~ **semi-variables** *f pl* COMPTA, ECON, FIN semi-variable costs; ~ **sociales** *f pl* FISC payroll taxes; ~ **supplémentaires** *f pl* COMPTA add-on costs

chargeur[1] *m* INFO *de disques* disk pack, IMP/EXP, RES HUM, ~ **feuille à feuille** INFO *machine* sheet feeder; ◆ ~ **et transporteur** TRANSP s&c, shipper and carrier

chargeur,[2] **euse** *m, f* TRANSP *personne* charterer, loading agent, loading broker, shipper; ~ **transitaire** IMP/EXP, RES HUM, TRANSP *personne* shipping and forwarding agent, S&FA

chariot *m* TRANSP cart *(AmE)*, trolley *(BrE)*; ~ **à bagages** TRANSP baggage cart *(AmE)*, baggage trolley *(BrE)*, luggage trolley *(BrE)*, self-help passenger luggage trolley; ~ **cavalier** TRANSP *manutention des conteneurs* straddle carrier; ~ **élévateur à fourche** TRANSP fork-lift truck, FLT; ~ **élévateur à grue** TRANSP *manutention* crane-jib-type fork-lift truck; ~ **élévateur pour palettes** TRANSP *manutention* pallet truck; ~ **élévateur à roues jumelées** TRANSP *manutention* dual-wheel fork lift truck; ~ **élévateur totalement libre** TRANSP *manutention* full free fork-lift truck; ~ **de manutention** TRANSP yard dolly

charognard *m* BOURSE bottom fisher

charte *f* DROIT charter; ~ **bancaire** BANQUE bank charter; ~ **communautaire des droits sociaux fondamentaux des travailleurs** RES HUM Community Charter of Fundamental Social Rights of Workers; ~ **constitutive** DROIT *d'une société* memorandum of association; ~ **de création** COM copy platform; ~ **graphique** MÉDIA *identité de l'entreprise* house style; ~ **-partie** COM charta partita *(frml)*, TRANSP *maritime* charter party, CP; ~ **-partie avec indication de quai** TRANSP *maritime* dock charter; ~ **-partie bord à bord** TRANSP *maritime* FIO charter, free-in-and-out charter; ~ **-partie coque nue** TRANSP *maritime* bare-boat charter party, bare-boat consignee; ~ **-partie nette** TRANSP *maritime* net-form charter; ~ **-partie à temps** TRANSP *avec remise totale de la gestion commerciale* demise charter party, *maritime* time C/P, time charter party, *sans remise totale de la gestion commerciale* nondemise charter party; ~ **-partie en travers** TRANSP *maritime* lump-sum charter; ~ **-partie au voyage** TRANSP *maritime* voyage C/P, voyage charter party; ~ **-partie au voyage avec désignation du poste à**

quai TRANSP *maritime* berth charter; ~ **sociale** COM social charter

Charte: ~ **européenne de l'énergie** *f* COM European Energy Charter; ~ **de la Havane** *f* ECON Havana Charter; ~ **sociale européenne** *f* POL European Social Charter

charter *m* TRANSP charter; ~ **ouvert** TRANSP open charter, OC

chartiste *mf* BOURSE chartist

chasse-marée *m* TRANSP *d'un navire* Lr, lugger

chasser: ~ **ses ancres** *loc* TRANSP *navire* drag her anchors; ~ **les têtes** *loc* RES HUM headhunt

chasseur: ~ **de centimes** *m jarg* BOURSE chase eighths (*jarg*); ~ **de têtes** *m* RES HUM headhunter

châssis: ~ **des molettes mobile** *m* TRANSP *mines* mobile lift frame

château: ~ **-dunette** *m* TRANSP *d'un navire* poop and bridge, PB; ~ **-gaillard** *m* TRANSP *d'un navire* bridge-forecastle, BF

chaud: **tout** ~ *adj* COM hot

chaudière *f* IND *dans une usine*, TRANSP *d'un navire* boiler, BLR; ~ **auxiliaire** TRANSP *d'un navire* aux. B, auxiliary boiler, AXB, donkey boiler, DKY; ~ **auxiliaire aquatubulaire** TRANSP *d'un navire* water tube auxiliary boiler; ~ **auxiliaire mixte** TRANSP *d'un navire* composite auxiliary boiler, CAXB; ~ **auxiliaire à tubes d'eau** TRANSP *d'un navire* water tube auxiliary boiler; ~ **cylindrique aquatubulaire** TRANSP *d'un navire* cylindrical water tube boiler; ~ **cylindrique ignitubulaire** TRANSP *d'un navire* cylindrical fire tube boiler, CFTB; ~ **cylindrique à tubes d'eau** TRANSP *d'un navire* cylindrical water tube boiler; ~ **cylindrique à tubes de fumée** TRANSP *d'un navire* cylindrical fire tube boiler, CFTB; ~ **domestique aquatubulaire** TRANSP *d'un navire* water tube domestic boiler, WTDB; ~ **domestique à tubes d'eau** TRANSP *d'un navire* water tube domestic boiler, WTDB; ~ **à eau chaude** TRANSP *d'un navire* hot water boiler, HWB; ~ **ignitubulaire** TRANSP *d'un navire* fire tube boiler, FTB; ~ **ordinaire** TRANSP *d'un navire* single-ended boiler, SEB; ~ **principale verticale** TRANSP *d'un navire* vertical main boiler; ~ **de récupération** TRANSP *d'un navire* waste heat boiler, WHB; ~ **de récupération aquatubulaire** TRANSP *d'un navire* waste heat water tube boiler, WHWTB; ~ **de récupération ignitubulaire** TRANSP *d'un navire* waste heat fire tube boiler; ~ **de récupération à tubes d'eau** TRANSP *d'un navire* waste heat water tube boiler, WHWTB; ~ **de récupération à tubes de fumée** TRANSP *d'un navire* waste heat fire tube boiler; ~ **à tubes de fumée** TRANSP *d'un navire* fire tube boiler, FTB

chaudronnier, -ière *mf* IND boiler manufacturer

chaufferie *f* TRANSP boiler room

chauffeur *mf* RES HUM driver; ~ **de camion** *m* TRANSP lorry driver (*BrE*), teamster (*AmE*), truck driver (*AmE*), trucker (*AmE*)

chavirer *loc* TRANSP *navire* capsize, overturn, turn over, turn turtle

ch. de f. *abrév (chemin de fer)* TRANSP rail, railroad (*AmE*), railway (*BrE*)

check-list *m* COM check list

chécographe *m* BANQUE check writer (*AmE*), check-writer machine (*AmE*), check-writing machine (*AmE*), cheque writer (*BrE*), cheque-writer machine (*BrE*), cheque-writing machine (*BrE*)

chef *m* ADMIN boss (*infrml*), chief, head, senior, GESTION *supérieur* boss (*infrml*), chief, head, senior, GESTION manager, mgr, RES HUM manager, mgr, *supérieur* boss (*infrml*), chief, head, senior; ~ **d'accusation** (SYN *chef d'inculpation*) DROIT charge, count of indictment; ~ **des achats** COM, RES HUM, V&M chief buyer, head buyer, purchasing manager; ~ **d'agence** COM, GESTION branch office manager; ~ **d'approvisionnement** COM, RES HUM, V&M chief buyer, head buyer, procurement manager; ~ **d'atelier** COM departmental head, GESTION line manager, supervisor, RES HUM head foreman, *de cols-bleus* line manager, supervisor; ~ **de bureau** ADMIN, GESTION, RES HUM chief clerk, head clerk, office manager, senior clerk; ~ **du bureau des exportations** RES HUM senior export clerk; ~ **du bureau des importations** RES HUM senior import clerk; ~ **de chantier** RES HUM site foreman; ~ **de la circulation** RES HUM, TRANSP *chemin de fer* chief traffic controller, traffic manager, TM, traffic superintendent, TS; ~ **comptable** COMPTA Accountant General, chief accountant, chief accounting officer, group chief accountant, head accountant, AG; ~ **de conception** COM copy chief; ~ **de département** GESTION, RES HUM departmental head, departmental manager, division manager, divisional head; ~ **du département juridique** RES HUM general counsel, head of the legal department; ~ **direct** GESTION, RES HUM line manager; ~ **de distribution** GESTION, TRANSP distribution manager; ~ **de division** GESTION, RES HUM division manager, divisional head, divisional manager; ~ **d'entreprise** ADMIN business manager, COM *gérant* business manager, company manager, *propriétaire* company director, GESTION business manager, company director, company manager, RES HUM business manager; ~ **d'équipe** GESTION team leader, RES HUM charge hand, foreman, overseer, team leader, ganger, *de cols-bleus* supervisor; ~ **d'établissement** COM, IND, RES HUM plant manager, works manager; ~ **d'état** POL head of state; ~ **d'exploitation** COM, GESTION, RES HUM operational manager, operations manager; ~ **de fabrication** IND, MÉDIA *édition, presse*, RES HUM production director, production manager; ~ **de famille** ECON, PROT SOC breadwinner; ~ **de gare** TRANSP station manager, stationmaster; ~ **hiérarchique** GESTION, RES HUM line manager; ~ **d'inculpation** (SYN *chef d'accusation*) DROIT charge, count of indictment; ~ **-lieu de comté**

COM county seat (*AmE*), county town (*BrE*);
~ **magasinier** COM, IND warehouse supervisor;
~ **de marque** COM, GESTION, RES HUM, V&M brand
manager; ~ **mécanicien** RES HUM, TRANSP chief
engineer; ~ **du personnel** GESTION, RES HUM head
of personnel department, personnel director,
personnel manager, staff manager; ~ **des
pointeurs** TRANSP *maritime* ship's clerk; ~ **de
production** IND, MÉDIA, RES HUM production
director, production manager; ~ **de produit** COM,
GESTION, RES HUM, V&M brand manager, product
manager; ~ **de projet** RES HUM project leader,
project manager; ~ **de publicité** MÉDIA account
executive, account manager, advertising director,
advertising manager, agency representative, publicity manager, RES HUM, V&M *chez un annonceur*
account manager, advertising director, advertising manager, agency representative, publicity
manager; ~ **de publicité d'agence** MÉDIA, RES
HUM, V&M account executive, account manager,
agency representative; ~ **de rayon** RES HUM
department manager, departmental manager,
V&M department manager, departmental manager, *dans un grand magasin* departmental head;
~ **de rédaction** COM copy chief; ~ **de région**
GESTION, RES HUM, V&M area manager, regional
manager, territory manager; ~ **de secteur**
GESTION, RES HUM area manager, division head,
divisional manager; ~ **de service** COM chief operating officer, departmental head, departmental
manager, COO, GESTION department head,
department manager, supervisor, RES HUM chief
operating officer, department head, department
manager, COO, *de cols-blancs* supervisor; ~ **du
service achats** COM, RES HUM, V&M chief buyer,
head buyer; ~ **du service consommateurs**
GESTION, RES HUM, V&M consumer relations
manager; ~ **du service étranger** MÉDIA foreign
editor; ~ **du service immigration** RES HUM chief
immigration officer; ~ **du service personnel**
GESTION, RES HUM head of the personnel department, personnel director, personnel manager,
staff manager; ~ **du service politique** MÉDIA
political editor; ~ **du service publicité** MÉDIA,
RES HUM, V&M *chez un annonceur* advertising
director, publicity manager; ~ **du service des
réclamations** ASSUR, RES HUM claims manager;
~ **du service des relations publiques** RES HUM,
V&M director of public relations, public relations
officer, DPR, PRO; ~ **du service des
renseignements** RES HUM information officer;
~ **du service des sports** MÉDIA sports editor;
~ **du service des ventes** GESTION, RES HUM, V&M
sales manager; ~ **de terrain** RES HUM field sales
manager; ~ **d'unité adjoint** RES HUM assistant
head of section
chemin *m* INFO path; ~ **d'accès** INFO pathway;
~ **critique** INFO critical path; ~ **de fer** *(ch. de f.)*
TRANSP rail, railroad (*AmE*), railway (*BrE*); ~ **de
papier** INFO paper track

cheminée *f* TRANSP *d'un navire* funnel, smokestack; ~ **d'usine** IND smokestack
cheminot *m* RES HUM, TRANSP railroad worker
(*AmE*), railroader (*AmE*), railway worker (*BrE*),
railwayman (*BrE*)
chenal *m* TRANSP *dans un cours d'eau* fairway
chèque *m* BANQUE check (*AmE*), cheque (*BrE*);
~ **bancaire** BANQUE bank bill, bank check (*AmE*),
bank cheque (*BrE*), treasurer check (*AmE*),
treasurer cheque (*BrE*), *tiré par une banque sur
une autre* B/Dft, bank draft (*BrE*); ~ **de banque**
BANQUE, FIN bank check (*AmE*), bank cheque
(*BrE*), banker's check (*AmE*), banker's cheque
(*BrE*), banker's draft; ~ **barré** BANQUE cross
check (*AmE*), cross cheque (*BrE*), crossed check
(*AmE*), crossed cheque (*BrE*); ~ **en blanc** BANQUE
blank check (*AmE*), blank cheque (*BrE*); ~ **en
bois** *infrml* BANQUE NSF check (*AmE*), NSF
cheque (*BrE*), bounced check (*AmE*), bounced
cheque (*BrE*), bum check (*AmE, infrml*), bum
cheque (*BrE, infrml*), bad check (*AmE*), bad
cheque (*BrE*), dud check (*AmE, infrml*), dud
cheque (*BrE, infrml*), not-sufficient-funds check
(*AmE*), not-sufficient-funds cheque (*BrE*), rubber
check (*AmE, infrml*), rubber cheque (*BrE,
infrml*); ~ **-cadeau** COM gift token, gift voucher,
V&M gift token, gift voucher, *à changer contre un
livre* book token; ~ **certifié** BANQUE certified
check (*AmE*), certified cheque (*BrE*); ~ **en
circulation** BANQUE outstanding check (*AmE*),
outstanding cheque (*BrE*); ~ **compensé** BANQUE
cleared check (*AmE*), cleared cheque (*BrE*);
~ **-déjeuner** RES HUM LV (*BrE*), luncheon voucher (*BrE*), meal ticket (*AmE*); ~ **à encaisser**
BANQUE uncashed check (*AmE*), uncashed cheque (*BrE*); ~ **falsifié** BANQUE forged check (*AmE*),
forged cheque (*BrE*); ~ **frappé d'opposition** BAN-
QUE stopped check (*AmE*), stopped cheque
(*BrE*); ~ **de guichet** BANQUE counter check
(*AmE*), counter cheque (*BrE*); ~ **impayé** BANQUE
dishonored check (*AmE*), dishonoured cheque
(*BrE*); ~ **d'intérêt** BANQUE interest check (*AmE*),
interest cheque (*BrE*); ~ **-livre** COM *à changer
contre un livre* book token; ~ **marqué** BANQUE
marked check (*AmE*), marked cheque (*BrE*);
~ **d'un montant de** BANQUE check in the amount
of (*AmE*), cheque to the amount of (*BrE*); ~ **non-
barré** BANQUE open check (*AmE*), open cheque
(*BrE*), uncrossed check (*AmE*), uncrossed cheque
(*BrE*); ~ **non-encaissé** BANQUE uncashed check
(*AmE*), uncashed cheque (*BrE*); ~ **non-
endossable** BANQUE account payee; ~ **non-
livrable** BANQUE undeliverable check (*AmE*),
undeliverable cheque (*BrE*); ~ **non-présenté**
BANQUE *à l'encaissement* unpresented check
(*AmE*), unpresented cheque (*BrE*); ~ **oblitéré**
BANQUE canceled chech (*AmE*), cancelled cheque
(*BrE*); ~ **officiel** BANQUE official check (*AmE*),
official cheque (*BrE*); ~ **omnibus** BANQUE counter
check (*AmE*), counter cheque (*BrE*); ~ **ouvert**
BANQUE open check (*AmE*), open cheque (*BrE*);

~ par procuration BANQUE preauthorized check *(AmE)*, preauthorized cheque *(BrE)*; **~ payable à l'ordre de qn** BANQUE check in favor of sb *(AmE)*, cheque in favour of sb *(BrE)*; **~ payable au porteur** BANQUE bearer check *(AmE)*, bearer cheque *(BrE)*, check made to cash *(AmE)*, cheque made to cash *(BrE)*; **~ payé** BANQUE canceled chech *(AmE)*, cancelled cheque *(BrE)*; **~ périmé** BANQUE stale check *(AmE)*, stale cheque *(BrE)*, stale-dated check *(AmE)*, stale-dated cheque *(BrE)*; **~ personnalisé** BANQUE personalized check *(AmE)*, personalized cheque *(BrE)*; **~ à porter en compte** BANQUE account-only check *(AmE)*, account-only cheque *(BrE)*, collection-only check *(AmE)*, collection-only cheque *(BrE)*; **~ au porteur** BANQUE bearer check *(AmE)*, bearer cheque *(BrE)*, check made to cash *(AmE)*, cheque made to cash *(BrE)*; **~ postdaté** BANQUE post-dated check *(AmE)*, postdated cheque *(BrE)*; **~ préautorisé** BANQUE preauthorized check *(AmE)*, preauthorized cheque *(BrE)*; **~ refusé** BANQUE returned check *(AmE)*, returned cheque *(BrE)*; **~ de règlement de salaire** BANQUE pay check *(AmE)*, pay cheque *(BrE)*, salary check *(AmE)*, salary cheque *(BrE)*; **~ -repas** RES HUM LV *(BrE)*, luncheon voucher *(BrE)*, meal ticket *(AmE)*; **~ réservé** BANQUE earmarked check *(AmE)*, earmarked cheque *(BrE)*; **~ retourné** BANQUE returned check *(AmE)*, returned cheque *(BrE)*; **~ de salaire** RES HUM pay check *(AmE)*, pay cheque *(BrE)*, pay packet *(BrE)*, salary check *(AmE)*, salary cheque *(BrE)*; **~ sans provision** BANQUE NSF check *(AmE)*, NSF cheque *(BrE)*, bounced check *(AmE)*, bounced cheque *(BrE)*, bum check *(AmE, infrml)*, bum cheque *(BrE, infrml)*, bad check *(AmE)*, bad cheque *(BrE)*, dud check *(AmE, infrml)*, dud cheque *(BrE, infrml)*, not-sufficient-funds check *(AmE)*, not-sufficient-funds cheque *(BrE)*, rubber check *(AmE, infrml)*, rubber cheque *(BrE, infrml)*; **~ visé** COMPTA certified check *(AmE)*, certified cheque *(BrE)*; **~ de voyage** BANQUE, LOISIRS traveler's check *(AmE)*, traveller's cheque *(BrE)*; ◆ **faire un ~** BANQUE draw a check *(AmE)*, draw a cheque *(BrE)*, make out a cheque *(BrE)*, raise a check *(AmE)*, write a check *(AmE)*, write a cheque *(BrE)*, write out a check *(AmE)*, write out a cheque *(BrE)*

chéquier *m* BANQUE checkbook *(AmE)*, chequebook *(BrE)*

cher, -ère *adj* COM dear, expensive; **peu ~** COM cheap, inexpensive; **trop ~** COM overpriced

chercher *vt* COM search for, *approbation* seek, *emploi* look for, seek, INFO *piste* search; ◆ **~ la contre-partie** BOURSE seek a market; **~ les défauts de l'adversaire** POL, V&M go negative *(jarg)*; **~ un emploi** RES HUM look for a job, seek a job; **~ à faire baisser** BOURSE *cours* bear; **~ une location** IMMOB look for a property to rent

chercheur, -euse *m,f* COM, PROT SOC, V&M research worker, researcher; **~ de marchés avantageux**

BOURSE bargain hunter; **~ d'occasion** V&M bargain hunter

chérot *adj infrml* BOURSE, COM, FIN pricey *(infrml)*, pricy *(infrml)*

cheval *m* TRANSP *puissance* horsepower; **~ pur sang** *m pl* TRANSP bloodstock; **~ -vapeur** *m (CV)* TRANSP horsepower *(HP)*; **~ -vapeur indiqué** *m* COM ihp, indicated horsepower; ◆ **à ~ sur** COM between

chevalet: **~ à feuilles mobiles** *m* COM, V&M *pour campagne publicitaire* flip chart; **~ de rampe** *m* TRANSP ramp stillage

chevalier: **~ blanc** *m* BOURSE, FIN white knight; **~ d'industrie** *m* COM wheeler-dealer *(infrml)*

chez *prép* COM, COMMS c/o, care of

chicaner: *vt* **~ sur** COM, V&M haggle about, haggle over

chien: **~ de garde** *m* COM watchdog

chiffre *m* COM amount, AMT, ECON figure, FIN amount, figure, AMT, INFO digit, MATH figure, number, V&M figure; **~ d'affaires** *(CA)* COM *résultats d'une société* sales, trade figures, trading results, turnover, COMPTA accounting income, business volume, gross income, sales, turnover, ECON output, trade figures, FIN turnover, V&M sales figures, sales revenue, sales volume, turnover; **~ d'affaires d'une agence de publicité** MÉDIA agency billing; **~ d'affaires de l'exercice** COMPTA, FIN annual turnover; **~ d'affaires à l'exportation** IMP/EXP export turnover; **~ d'affaires moyennes** COMPTA, FIN average revenue; **~ d'affaires publicitaires** COMPTA, FIN, V&M advertising turnover; **~ approximatif** MATH approximate figure, approximate number, ballpark figure *(infrml)*; **~ binaire** INFO binary digit, MATH binary number; **~ de contrôle** COM, INFO check digit; **~ décimal** INFO decimal digit, MATH decimal number; **~ rond** COM level money *(jarg)*, round figure, round number; **~ sans précédent** COM *le plus haut* all-time high, *le plus bas* all-time low; **~ de ventes** COM, V&M sales, sales figures; ◆ **le ~ le plus bas jamais atteint** COM *prix, niveau, taux* all-time low

chiffré: **être ~ à** *loc* COM amount to

chiffrement *m (ANT déchiffrement)* COMMS, INFO encryption

chiffrer: **se ~ à** *v pron* COM amount to, come to

chiffres *m pl* ECON figures; **~ du chômage** ECON, POL unemployment figures; **~ de commerce** COM *extérieur ou intérieur*, ECON trade figures; **~ consolidés** COMPTA consolidated figures; **~ corrigés** COM revised figures; **~ de l'emploi** ECON, POL employment figures; **les ~ réels pour le mois** COMPTA this month's actuals; **~ manquants** BOURSE digits deleted; **~ officiels** BANQUE, COM, ECON, FIN, POL official figures; **~ parus aujourd'hui** COM figures out today; **~ réels** ECON actual figures; **~ de tirage** MÉDIA *d'un journal* circulation figures; ◆ **en ~ ronds** COM in round figures

chiffrier *m* COMPTA work sheet

Chili *m* COM Chile

chilien, -enne *adj* COM Chilean

Chilien, -enne *m,f* COM *habitant* Chilean

chimiquier *m* TRANSP *navire* chemical carrier, chemical tanker

Chine *f* COM China; ~ **communiste** COM Communist China; ~ **nationaliste** COM Nationalist China; ~ **rouge** COM Red China

chinois[1]**, e** *adj* COM Chinese

chinois[2] *m* COM *langue* Chinese

Chinois, e *m,f* COM *habitant* Chinese

chirographaire *adj* BANQUE *créance, obligation* unsecured

chlorofluorocarbone *m* *(CFC)* ENVIR *pollution* chlorofluorocarbon *(CFC)*

choc *m* COM, ECON, FIN shock; ~ **culturel** COM culture shock; ~ **externe** ECON external shock; ~ **d'offre** ECON supply shock, supply-side shock; ~ **d'offre négatif** ECON adverse supply shock; ~ **de la pénurie des approvisionnements** ECON adverse supply shock; ~ **pétrolier** ECON *1973 & 1979* oil crisis; ~ **sur l'offre** ECON supply shock, supply-side shock

choisir 1. *vt* COM elect, pick, select, POL, RES HUM elect; **2.** *vi* COM choose, take one's pick

choix *m* COM *alternative* alternative, choice, option, FISC election, GESTION adoption, POL election; ~ **du consommateur** V&M *marketing* consumer choice; ~ **de marchandises** COM assortment of goods, choice of goods; ~ **d'une marque** V&M branding; ~ **des médias** MÉDIA, V&M media selection; ~ **optimal** COM best alternative; ~ **des supports** MÉDIA, V&M media selection; ~ **tacite** COM negative option *(jarg)*; ~ **des termes d'un contrat** COM wording; ◆ **au ~ du vendeur** BOURSE, COM seller's option; **faire son ~** COM take one's pick

chômage *m* ECON, PROT SOC, RES HUM nonemployment, unemployment; ~ **en augmentation** ECON, PROT SOC rising unemployment; ~ **caché** ECON, RES HUM concealed unemployment, hidden unemployment; ~ **conjoncturel** ECON, RES HUM cyclical unemployment; ~ **cyclique** ECON, RES HUM cyclical unemployment; ~ **déclaré** ECON, RES HUM registered unemployment; ~ **déguisé** ECON, RES HUM disguised unemployment, hidden unemployment; ~ **entraîné par l'immigration** ECON migration-fed unemployment; ~ **frictionnel** ECON, RES HUM frictional unemployment; ~ **à grande échelle** ECON, RES HUM mass unemployment; ~ **en hausse** ECON, PROT SOC rising unemployment; ~ **involontaire** ECON, RES HUM involuntary unemployment; ~ **de longue durée** ECON, RES HUM long-term unemployment; ~ **de masse** ECON, RES HUM mass unemployment; ~ **partiel** ECON, RES HUM partial unemployment, short-time working; ~ **saisonnier** ECON, RES HUM seasonal unemployment; ~ **structurel** ECON, RES HUM structural unemployment; ~ **technique** RES HUM dead time, down time, lay-off; ~ **technique automatique** ECON, RES HUM automatic check-off *(US)*; ~ **volontaire** RES HUM voluntary unemployment; ◆ **au ~** PROT SOC on the dole *(UK, infrml)*, RES HUM idle, out of a job, out of work, unemployed

chômedu *m* ECON unemployment, *indemnités* dole *(BrE, infrml)*, welfare *(AmE, infrml)*, PROT SOC *indemnités* dole *(BrE, infrml)*, welfare *(AmE, infrml)*, RES HUM unemployment, *indemnités* dole *(BrE, infrml)*, welfare *(AmE, infrml)*; ◆ **au ~** *infrml* PROT SOC on the dole *(UK, infrml)*

chômeur, -euse *m,f* COM jobless person, unemployed person; ~ **de longue durée** ECON, RES HUM hard-core unemployed *(AmE)*, long-term unemployed *(BrE)*, LTU

chômeurs: les ~ *m pl* ECON, RES HUM the jobless, the unemployed, the unwaged; **les ~ inscrits à l'Agence nationale pour l'emploi** *m* PROT SOC, RES HUM the registered unemployed *(UK)*

chopine *f* COM bottle, COM *Can* pint, pt, V&M bottle

chose *f* DROIT *effet personnel* chose

choses: les ~ étant ce qu'elles sont *loc* COM in the present state of affairs; **toutes ~ égales** *loc* COM all things being equal, other things being equal; **toutes ~ étant égales** *loc* COM all things being equal, ceteris paribus *(frml)*, other things being equal; **toutes ~ étant égales par ailleurs** *loc* COM all else being equal, all things being equal, ceteris paribus *(frml)*, other things being equal

chroniqueur, -euse *m,f* MÉDIA columnist

chronogramme *m* ADMIN time chart

chronométrage *m* COM, MATH time study; ~ **des travaux administratifs** ADMIN, RES HUM clerical work measurement, CWM

chronomètre *m* INFO timer

Chronopost® *m* *France* COMMS French postal service for urgent packages, express mail service, ≈ Datapost® *(UK)*

chronoval *m* BOURSE ≈ RNS *(UK)*, ≈ Regulatory News Service *(UK)*

chute *f* BOURSE, COM, ECON, V&M drop, fall; ~ **brutale** COM collapse; ~ **de courant** INFO brownout *(US)*; ~ **rapide** BOURSE fast decline; ~ **de tension** INFO brownout *(US)*; ~ **verticale** COM, ECON tailspin *(infrml)*

chuter *vi* BOURSE, COM, ECON, V&M drop, fall, tumble

Chypre *f* COM Cyprus

chypriote *adj* COM Cypriot

Chypriote *mf* COM *habitant* Cypriot

CI *abrév* BOURSE *(certificat d'investissement)* investment certificate, share certificate *(BrE)*, stock certificate *(AmE)*, INFO *(circuit intégré)* IC *(integrated circuit)*

CIB *abrév (Conseil international du blé)* COM IWC *(International Wheat Council)*

ciblage *m* COM, ECON, MÉDIA, V&M targeting;

~ **négatif** POL negative targeting (*jarg*); ~ **des prix** COM, V&M target pricing

cible *f* COM, INFO target, MÉDIA target, target audience, V&M market objective, *de la publicité* target, target audience; ~ **intermédiaire** POL intermediate target

cibler *vt* COM, MÉDIA, V&M *un public* target

CIBSA *abrév (Certificats d'investissement à bons de souscriptions d'actions)* BOURSE investment certificates with share warrants

ci-dessous *adv* COM hereunder, COM below, COMMS hereunder, COMMS below, DROIT hereunder; ◆ **comme** ~ (ANT *comme ci-dessus*) COMMS as below

ci-dessus *adv* (ANT *ci-dessous*) COM *mentionné plus haut, dans une lettre, un document*, COMMS above; ◆ **comme** ~ (ANT *comme ci-dessous*) COMMS as above

Cie *abrév (compagnie)* COM, ECON Co. (*company*); **et** ~ *abrév (et compagnie)* COM and Co (*and company*)

CII *abrév (crédit d'impôt à l'investissement)* FISC ITC (*investment tax credit*)

ci-inclus, e *adj* COM, COMMS appended, attached, enc., encl., enclosed, herein, herewith, DROIT affixed, annexed, appended, herein

ci-joint, e *adj* COM, COMMS appended, attached, enc., encl., enclosed, herein, herewith, DROIT affixed, annexed, appended, herein

cinéaste *mf* MÉDIA *cinéma, télévision* film-maker

cinéma *m* LOISIRS, MÉDIA *art* cinema (*BrE*), motion pictures (*AmE*), pictures (*BrE*), *production* cinema (*BrE*), film-making, movie-making (*AmE*), *salle* cinema (*BrE*), movie theater (*AmE*)

cingalais *m* COM *langue* Sinhalese

cinquante: ~ **et quelques** *loc infrml* COM fifty odd (*infrml*)

cinquième: **un** ~ *m (1/5)* COM, MATH one-fifth (*1/5*)

CIP *abrév (certificat d'investissement prioritaire)* BOURSE preferred investment certificate

CIPBSA *abrév (Certificats d'investissement préférés à bons de souscription d'actions)* BOURSE preferred investment certificates with share warrants

circonscription *f* DROIT circuit; ~ **judiciaire** DROIT, POL jurisdiction

circonspection *f* COM caution, circumstance

circonstance *f* COM occasion

circonstances *f pl* COM circumstances, ECON, V&M conditions; ~ **atténuantes** DROIT extenuating circumstances, mitigating circumstances; ~ **hypothétiques** COM hypothetical circumstances; ~ **imprévues** COM unforeseen circumstances; ~ **matérielles** ASSUR material circumstance; ~ **particulières** COM special circumstances; ◆ **dans ces** ~ COM under the circumstances; **dans des** ~ **semblables** COM in similar circumstances, on a similar occasion

circonstanciel, -elle *adj* COM ad hoc

circuit *m* INFO circuit; ~ **de commande** INFO driver; ~ **de commandes** V&M channel for orders; ~ **commercial** COM trade channel, V&M marketing channel; ~ **de commercialisation** COM distribution network; ~ **de distribution** COM, IND chain of distribution, distribution network, V&M channel of distribution, marketing channel; ~ **fermé** INFO closed circuit; ~ **intégré** (*CI*) INFO integrated circuit (*IC*); ~ **de vente** V&M channel of sales

circulaire *f* ADMIN memo, memorandum, COM, COMMS circular, newsletter; ~ **du conseil d'administration** COM directors' circular

circulation *f* BANQUE, ECON circulation, INFO flow, MÉDIA readership; ~ **aérienne** TRANSP air traffic; ~ **des données** INFO data flow; ~ **de la main-d'oeuvre** ECON, RES HUM movement of labor (*AmE*), movement of labour (*BrE*); ~ **des marchandises** COM commodity flow; ~ **routière** TRANSP road traffic; ◆ **en** ~ BANQUE *effets* in circulation, in transit, BOURSE outstanding

cire *f* COM wax; ~ **à cacheter** COMMS sealing wax; ~ **de paraffine** IND paraffin wax

CIRM *abrév (Comité international radio-maritime)* COMMS CIRM (*International Radio-Maritime Committee*)

cisaillé: ~ **par le marché** *loc* BOURSE whipsawed (*jarg*)

citation *f* DROIT citation, statement of claim; ~ **à comparaître** DROIT *adressée à un témoin* subpoena, *adressée à l'accusé* writ of subpoena

cité: ~ **ouvrière** *f* IMMOB, PROT SOC housing development (*AmE*), housing estate, housing project (*AmE*)

citer *vt* DROIT cite, *accusé* summons, *témoin* subpoena; ~ **comme témoin** DROIT call as a witness; ◆ ~ **à comparaître** DROIT *accusé* summons, *témoin* subpoena

citerne *f* TRANSP tank; ~ **à ballast propre** TRANSP *d'un navire* clean ballast tank, CBT; ~ **en cale** TRANSP *d'un navire* UnDk, under deck tank; ~ **à cargaison** ENVIR, TRANSP *d'un navire* cargo tank, CT; ~ **de cargo** ENVIR, TRANSP *d'un navire* cargo tank, CT; ~ **centrale de cargaison** TRANSP *d'un navire* cargo tank center (*AmE*), cargo tank centre (*BrE*), CTC; ~ **d'entrepont** TRANSP *d'un navire* 'tween deck tank; ~ **latérale** TRANSP *d'un navire* cargo tank wing, side tank, wing tank, CTW, SDT, ST; ~ **latérale de cargaison** TRANSP *d'un navire* cargo tank wing; ~ **sous le pont** TRANSP *d'un navire* UnDk, under deck tank; ~ **standard** TRANSP *d'un navire* cargo tank common, CTX; ~ **de stockage** ENVIR, TRANSP storage tank; ~ **transversale en hauteur** TRANSP *d'un navire* saddle tank

citoyen, -enne *m,f* POL citizen; ~ **de seconde classe** COM second-class citizen

citoyenneté *f* POL citizenship

City: **la** ~ *f* FIN *à Londres* the City (*UK*)

cl *abrév (centilitre)* COM cl (*centiliter AmE, centilitre BrE*)

clair, e *adj* COM straightforward; ◆ **en ~** COM in plain language

clairvoyant, e *adj* COM far-seeing, far-sighted

clandestin, e *adj* COM *affaire* clandestine, secret, under-the-counter, *travailleur* illegal, unregistered

clapet: **~ de dépression** *m* TRANSP vacuum relief valve; **~ non-retour** *m* TRANSP non return valve; **~ de non-retour blocable** *m* TRANSP screw-down non return valve

claquer *vt infrml* COM *son fric* blow (*infrml*), blue (*infrml*); ◆ **~ du fric** COM go on a spending spree, lash out (*infrml*), splash out (*infrml*)

clarifier *vt* COM *problème* shed light on, *situation* clarify

classe *f* BOURSE *d'actions, d'options*, BREVETS class, COM bracket, class, league, POL social class, TRANSP class; **~ d'actifs moins liquides** BOURSE Tier Two assets; **~ d'actifs plus liquides** BOURSE Tier One assets; **~ d'actions** BOURSE class of shares, share class; **~ affaires** TRANSP *aviation* business class, club class, executive class; **~ club** TRANSP *aviation* business class, club class, executive class; **~ dirigeante** POL ruling class; **~ économique** LOISIRS, TRANSP *aviation* economy class; **~ d'investissement** BOURSE investment grade; **la ~ dirigeante** POL the Establishment (*UK*); **la ~ ouvrière** ECON, POL the laboring class (*AmE*), the labouring class (*BrE*), the working class; **~ d'options** BOURSE class of options, option class; **~ possédante** ECON, POL capitalist class; **~ touriste** LOISIRS, TRANSP economy class, tourist class; **~ unique** LOISIRS, TRANSP one class; ◆ **de ~ mondiale** COM world-class

classé: **~ AAA** *loc* BOURSE, COM triple-A-rated; **~ par catégorie** *loc* COM graded by size

classement *m* COM *de documents* filing, *rang* ranking, RES HUM *rang* ranking; **~ d'avaries** ASSUR, TRANSP average statement; **~ chronologique des comptes** COMPTA ageing schedule (*BrE*), aging schedule (*AmE*); **~ chronologique des comptes clients** COMPTA ageing of accounts receivable (*BrE*), ageing of receivables (*BrE*), aging of accounts receivable (*AmE*), aging of receivables (*AmE*); **~ divergent** FIN split rating; **~ au mérite** RES HUM merit rating; **~ numérique** ADMIN, COM numerical filing; **~ par antériorité des comptes clients** COMPTA ageing of accounts receivable (*BrE*), ageing of receivables (*BrE*), aging of accounts receivable (*AmE*), aging of receivables (*AmE*); **~ par matières** COM subject filing; **~ par pourcentage** MATH percentile ranking; **~ en rayonnages** ADMIN open-shelf filing; **~ rétroactif** POL retroactive classification; **~ standard du commerce de marchandises** TRANSP standard freight trade classification, SFTC

classer 1. *vt* ADMIN *attribuer un rang à* class, grade, *classifier* categorize, classify, *ranger* file, file away, COM grade, *attribuer un rang à* class, grade, *classifier* categorize, classify, *ranger* file, file away; **~ confidentiel** ADMIN classify; **~ par ancienneté** COMPTA age; **~ par antériorité** COMPTA age; **~ par**

catégories COM categorize; **~ secret** ADMIN *document* classify; **~ le stock par date d'entrée** COMPTA age inventories, age stocks; **2.** *v pron* **se ~** COM, ECON rank

classes: **les ~ sociales défavorisées** *m pl infrml* PROT SOC hardship categories

classeur *m* ADMIN *meuble*, COM *meuble* filing cabinet, *portefeuille* binder, document holder, file, folder

classicisme: **~ économique** *m* ECON classical economics

classification *f* COM, RES HUM classification; **~ AAA** BOURSE, COM triple-A rating; **~ des emplois** RES HUM job classification; **~ des fonctions** RES HUM job classification; **~ industrielle standard** IND standard industrial classification, SIC; **~ mondiale de marchandises de fret aérien** TRANSP Worldwide Air Cargo Commodity Classification, WACCC; **~ des normes du commerce international** COM, ECON Standard International Trade Classification, SITC; **~ par activité** COMPTA activity classification; **~ par objet** COM classification by object; **~ par responsabilité** COMPTA responsibility classification; **~ de produit** COM product classification; **~ des risques** ASSUR classification of risks; **~ des tâches** RES HUM work classification

classifier *vt* COM classify

clause *f* ASSUR clause, COM provision, DROIT article, clause, provision, RES HUM clause; **~ d'abandon** ASSUR waiver clause; **~ d'abordage** ASSUR *maritime* running down clause, RDC; **~ abrogatoire** DROIT annulling clause; **~ d'accélération** BANQUE, DROIT, FIN, IMMOB acceleration clause premium; **~ accélératrice** BANQUE, DROIT, FIN, IMMOB *hypothèques* acceleration clause; **~ d'actes malveillants** ASSUR malicious acts clause; **~ additionnelle** DROIT additional clause; **~ d'ajustabilité** ASSUR adjustment clause; **~ ambiguë** DROIT joker (*US*); **~ d'annulation** DROIT *contrat* cancellation clause; **~ d'antériorité** DROIT grandfather clause; **~ d'arbitrage** COM, DROIT, IND, RES HUM arbitration clause; **~ d'assurance refusée** ASSUR not-to-insure clause; **~ d'attestation** ASSUR attestation clause; **~ attrayante** (*SYN incitation*) FIN incentive, sweetener (*infrml*); **~ avarie** ASSUR average clause; **~ du bénéficiaire** ASSUR beneficiary clause; **~ bris** ASSUR breakage clause; **~ de catastrophe** ASSUR disaster clause; **~ de collision** ASSUR collision clause; **~ compromissoire** COM, DROIT, IND, RES HUM arbitration clause; **~ concernant les salariés** RES HUM labor clause (*AmE*), labour clause (*BrE*); **~ de condition générale** DROIT blanket clause; **~ conditionnelle** DROIT conditional clause; **~ contestable** ASSUR contestable clause; **~ contre l'augmentation de prix** ASSUR escalation clause; **~ -couperet** DROIT sunset provision; **~ de couverture** BOURSE hedge clause; **~ de décès simultanés** ASSUR common disaster clause (*US*); ~ **déductible** ASSUR deductible clause; ~ **de délaissement** ASSUR *maritime* abandonment clause; ~ **dérogatoire** ASSUR *maritime* deviation clause, DC, DROIT escape clause; ~ **de déviation** ASSUR deviation clause, DC; ~ **de dommages par acte malveillant** ASSUR malicious damage clause; ~ **de doublage** ASSUR *maritime* metaling clause (*AmE*), metalling clause (*BrE*), MC; ~ **de double assurance** ASSUR *maritime* American clause; ~ **de double évaluation** ASSUR dual valuation clause; ~ **de droits acquis** DROIT grandfather clause; ~ **d'écroulement de bâtiment** ASSUR fallen building clause; ~ **d'erreurs et d'omissions** ASSUR errors and omissions clause; ~ **d'évaluation** ASSUR valuation clause, VC; ~ **d'exclusion** ASSUR, COM exclusion clause; ~ **d'exclusion générale** ASSUR, COM general exclusion clause; ~ **d'exonération** ASSUR waiver clause, COM exclusion clause, exemption clause, DROIT, TRANSP *charte-partie* exceptions clause; ~ **d'exonération pour installation électrique** ASSUR electrical exemption clause; ~ **de franchise** ASSUR deductible clause; ~ **de fret bord** TRANSP *maritime* free-in clause; ~ **de guerre** ASSUR war clause; ~ **d'habilitation** DROIT enabling clause; ~ **d'incontestabilité** ASSUR incontestable clause; ~ **incontestable** ASSUR incontestable clause; ~ **inopérante** DROIT inoperative clause; ~ **d'insolvabilité** ASSUR insolvency clause; ~ **de l'institut** ASSUR institute clause; ~ **limitative de responsabilité** TRANSP *navigation* cesser clause; ~ **de mobilité** RES HUM mobility clause (*UK*); ~ **de nantissement négative** BANQUE negative pledge, negative pledge clause; ~ **de la nation la plus favorisée** DROIT, ECON, POL most-favored nation clause (*AmE*), most-favoured nation clause (*BrE*); ~ **de négligence** ASSUR Inchmaree clause, neglect clause, negligence clause, DROIT, TRANSP *charte-partie* negligence clause; ~ **New Jason** TRANSP *charte-partie* New Jason clause, NJ; ~ **de non-contestabilité** ASSUR noncontestability clause; ~ **de non-contribution** ASSUR noncontribution clause; ~ **de non-déchargement** TRANSP hot cargo clause; ~ **de non-incommodement** BANQUE *d'un contrat d'hypothèque*, IMMOB *droits miniers*, IND nondisturbance clause (*US*); ~ **de non-recours à la grève** RES HUM no-strike clause; ~ **de paiement par anticipation** ASSUR, FIN prepayment clause; ~ **de paiements équivalents** ASSUR, FIN simultaneous payments clause; ~ **de parité** ASSUR parity clause; ~ **pénale** ASSUR, DROIT penalty clause; ~ **de pertes inconnues** DROIT, FIN undiscovered loss clause; ~ **de pluralité d'assurance** ASSUR other insurance clause; ~ **de porte-à-porte** ASSUR door-to-door clause; ~ **au porteur** BOURSE, FIN bearer clause; ~ **de post-acquisition** BANQUE, FIN after-acquired clause; ~ **de prolongation** ASSUR cc, continuation clause; ~ **provisoire** DROIT draft clause; ~ **de rachat** BOURSE call feature, DROIT, ECON buy-back clause; ~ **de recours et de conservation** ASSUR sue and labor clause (*AmE*), sue and labour

clause (*BrE*), S/LC; ~ **de réexamen avant terme** RES HUM reopener clause; ~ **de régularisation** ASSUR adjustment clause; ~ **de remplacement** ASSUR replacement clause; ~ **de renonciation** DROIT contracting-out clause; ~ **de réouverture de la négociation** RES HUM reopener clause; ~ **de report** ASSUR cc, continuation clause; ~ **de représentation du personnel par les seuls** RES HUM union-only clause (*UK*); ~ **de résiliation** ASSUR cancellation provision clause, DROIT anulling clause, canceling clause (*AmE*), cancellation clause, cancelling clause (*BrE*), termination clause; ~ **résolutoire** ASSUR cancellation provision clause, DROIT annulling clause, avoidance clause, canceling clause (*AmE*), cancellation clause, cancelling clause (*BrE*), resolutive clause, termination clause; ~ **de la responsabilité civile professionnelle** ASSUR errors and omissions clause; ~ **de responsabilité financière** ASSUR financial responsibility clause (*US*); ~ **de responsabilité réciproque en cas d'abordage** ASSUR *maritime* both-to-blame collision clause; ~ **restrictive d'un acte** DROIT, IMMOB deed restriction; ~ **restrictive d'un contrat** DROIT, IMMOB deed restriction; ~ **de rotation** BANQUE rotation clause; ~ **rouge** BANQUE, TRANSP red clause, red-line clause; ~ **de sauvegarde** ASSUR disaster clause, BOURSE *dans un contrat* hedge clause, DROIT escape clause, RES HUM escalator clause; ~ **de séquestre** TRANSP *maritime* escrow clause; ~ **sérieuse** COM, FIN bona fide clause; ~ **de signature** ASSUR attestation clause; ~ **de simple reconnaissance de la représentation** RES HUM recognition-only clause (*UK*); ~ **subrogatoire** DROIT subrogation clause; ~ **de surenchère** ASSUR escalation clause; ~ **de survie** ASSUR survivorship clause (*US*); ~ **tout ou rien** BOURSE AON clause, all-or-nothing clause; ~ **traitant des droits de l'assuré** ASSUR duty of assured clause; ~ **de transport** ASSUR, TRANSP transit clause; ~ **valeur agréée** ASSUR *maritime* agreed valuation clause; ~ **de la valeur vénale** ASSUR, IMMOB market value clause; ~ **de variation des prix** V&M price variation clause; ~ **de vente de navire** ASSUR, TRANSP sale of vessel clause; ~ **de vétusté** ASSUR obsolescence clause

clauses: ~ **et conditions d'emploi** *f pl* RES HUM terms and conditions of employment

clavier *m* INFO keyboard, *plus petit* keypad; ~ **aveugle** INFO blind keyboard; ~ **AZERTY** INFO azerty keyboard; ~ **de commande du curseur** INFO cursor control pad; ~ **numérique** INFO digital keyboard, digital keypad; ~ **personnalisé** INFO customized keyboard; ~ **programmable** INFO soft keyboard; ~ **QWERTY** INFO QWERTY keyboard; ~ **de saisie** INFO input keyboard; ~ **tactile** INFO tactile keyboard; ~ **à touches programmables** INFO soft keyboard

claviste *mf* INFO keyboard operator, keyboarder

clé *f* INFO key; ~ **d'accès** INFO key; ~ **électronique de protection** INFO dongle; ~ **d'enregistrement**

INFO record key; ~ **numérique de contrôle** INFO
check digit; ~ **principale** INFO master key; ~ **de
recherche** INFO search key; ~ **de voûte** ECON *de
l'économie* backbone, keystone

clearing *m* BANQUE, ECON clearing

clerc *m* DROIT *de notaire* clerk

clés: ~ **en main** *f pl* COM, IMMOB *projet, usine,* IND,
INFO turnkey

cliché: ~ **agrandi** *m* COM enlarged copy

client, e *m,f* COM client, customer, punter, V&M
customer, shopper, *d'une agence de publicité*
client; ~ **d'un auditeur** *Fra (cf client d'un reviseur
Bel, client d'un vérificateur Can)* COMPTA, FIN
audit client; ~ **d'un commissaire aux comptes**
*Fra (cf client d'un reviseur Bel, client d'un vérifi-
cateur Can)* COMPTA, FIN audit client; ~ **difficile**
COM, V&M difficult customer, problem customer;
~ **emprunteur** BANQUE, COM, COMPTA, ECON, FIN
borrowing customer; ~ **étranger** IMP/EXP, V&M
overseas customer; ~ **éventuel** COM, V&M prospect, prospective customer; ~ **important** COM,
V&M big customer; **le ~ roi** ECON, V&M consumer
sovereignty; ~ **mystère** COM, V&M mystery shopper *(jarg)*; ~ **nommément désigné** DROIT named
client; ~ **d'outre-mer** IMP/EXP, V&M overseas customer; ~ **à la papa** *jarg* BOURSE blue-chip
customer; ~ **potentiel** COM, V&M prospect, prospective customer; ~ **de premier ordre** BOURSE
blue-chip customer; ~ **principal** COM, V&M principal customer; ~ **d'un reviseur** *Bel (cf client d'un
auditeur Fra, client d'un commissaire aux comptes
Fra, client d'un réviseur Fra)* COMPTA, FIN audit
client; ~ **d'un réviseur** *Fra (cf client d'un reviseur
Bel, client d'un vérificateur Can)* COMPTA, FIN
audit client; ~ **sûr** BOURSE blue-chip customer;
~ **d'un vérificateur** *Can (cf client d'un auditeur
Fra, client d'un commissaire aux comptes Fra,
client d'un réviseur Fra)* COMPTA, FIN audit client

clientèle *f* COM *clients* clientele, clients, customers,
commerce custom, goodwill, V&M customer base;
~ **privée conseillée** FIN advisory account; ~ **privée
gérée** FIN discretionary account; ◆ **axé sur la ~**
COM customer-orientated, customer-oriented

clients *m pl* COMPTA, ECON receivables, trade
accounts receivable, trade receivables

client/serveur *m* INFO client/server

clignotant *m* COM performance indicator, ECON
indicator, GESTION, IND, RES HUM performance
indicator; ~ **économique** ECON *économétrie* economic indicator

clignotement: ~ **des indicateurs économiques** *m*
ECON signaling *(AmE)*, signalling *(BrE)*

clignoter *vi* INFO blink

climat *m* COM, ECON, POL atmosphere, background; ~ **économique** COM, ECON, POL
economic climate; ~ **économique favorable** ECON
favorable economic climate *(AmE)*, favourable
economic climate *(BrE)*; ~ **financier** ECON, FIN
financial climate; ~ **fiscal** FISC tax environment;
~ **d'investissement** ECON investment climate;

~ **politique** COM, POL political climate; ~ **socio-
économique** ECON socioeconomic climate

climatisation *f* ADMIN, COM, PROT SOC air conditioning

climatisé, e *adj* ADMIN, COM, PROT SOC air-condi-
tioned

clinique: ~ **privée** *f* PROT SOC private hospital

cliquer *vt* INFO click; ~ **deux fois** INFO double-click

cloison *f* ADMIN *d'un bureau* partition, TRANSP
d'un avion, d'un navire bulkhead, BH;
~ **d'abordage** TRANSP *d'un navire* collision bulkhead; ~ **partielle** TRANSP *d'un navire* partial
bulkhead, PBH; ~ **du peak arrière** TRANSP *d'un
navire* afterpeak bulkhead, APBH; ~ **du presse-
étoupe** TRANSP *d'un navire* afterpeak bulkhead,
APBH

cloisonnement *m* COM compartmentalization,
departmentalization

cloisonner *vt* COM compartmentalize, departmentalize

clone *m* COM, INFO clone

cloner *vt* COM, INFO clone

clôture *f* BOURSE, COM close, closing, closure; ~ **de
compte** IMMOB closing statement; ~ **des comptes**
BANQUE accounts close-off; ~ **à découvert** ASSUR,
BOURSE short closing; ~ **de l'exercice** COMPTA
year end, year-end closing; ~ **de marché** BOURSE
close of the market, market close; ~ **à minuit** COM
midnight deadline; ~ **des offres** BOURSE bid closing; ◆ **à la ~** BOURSE at closing, at the close; **en ~**
BOURSE at closing, at the close

clôturer *vt* COM *comptes* wind up, *séance* close

club: ~ **d'actionnaires** *m* BOURSE subscription club;
~ **des exportateurs** *m* IMP/EXP export club;
~ **d'investissement** *m* BOURSE investment club;
~ **de remise en forme** *m* LOISIRS health club; ~ **de
souscripteurs** *m* BOURSE subscription club

Club: ~ **de Rome** *m* ECON Club of Rome

cluster *m* INFO cluster

cm *abrév* COM *(centimètre)* cm *(centimeter AmE,
centimetre BrE)*, COMPTA *(coût moyen)* average
cost, mean cost

cm³ *abrév (centimètre cube)* COM cc *(cubic centimeter AmE, cubic centimetre BrE)*

CMT *abrév (Conseil des marchés à terme)* BOURSE
futures exchange council

CNA *abrév (convertisseur numérique-analogique)*
INFO DAC *(digital-analog converter)*

CNE *abrév (Caisse nationale d'épargne)* BANQUE
≈ NSB *(UK) (National Savings Bank)*

CNPF *abrév (Conseil national du patronat français)*
COM, IND ≈ CBI *(Confederation of British
Industry)*

CNUCED *abrév (Conférence des Nations Unies sur
le commerce et le développement)* ECON
UNCTAD *(United Nations Conference on Trade
and Development)*

CNUED *abrév (Conférence des Nations Unies sur
l'environnement et le développement)* COM, ENVIR

UNCED *(United Nations Conference on Environment and Development)*

coalition *f* COM coalition, comb, combination, POL *dans gouvernement* coalition

coassociation *f* COM joint partnership

coassurance *f* ASSUR coinsurance

coassuré, e *adj* ASSUR coinsured

coassureur *mf* ASSUR coinsurer

COB *abrév (Commission des opérations de Bourse)* BOURSE French stock exchange watchdog, ≈ FOMC *(US) (Federal Open Market Committee)*, ≈ SEC *(US) (Securities and Exchange Commission)*, ≈ SIB *(UK) (Securities Investment Board)*

Cobb-Douglas: fonction de production de ~ *f* ECON Cobb Douglas production function

COBOL® *abrév (langage COBOL)* INFO COBOL *(Common Ordinary Business-Oriented Language)*

cocher *vt* COM check, check off, tick, tick off; ♦ **~ la case** COM *sur un formulaire* check box *(AmE)*, put a check in the box *(AmE)*, put a tick in the box *(BrE)*, tick the box *(BrE)*

co-commissaire *mf* COMPTA joint auditor

cocontractant, e *m,f* DROIT contracting party

codage *m* BANQUE *d'un chèque* encoding, COMMS *(ANT décodage)* INFO *(ANT décodage)* coding, encryption; **~ binaire** INFO binary coding; **~ par activités** COMPTA activity coding

code: **~ de l'AFC** *m (numéro CUSIP)* BOURSE ≈ CUSIP number, COMMS code, DROIT code, statute book *(UK)*, INFO code; **~ d'arbitrage** *m* BOURSE code of arbitration; **~ d'article courant** *m* POL standard object code; **~ d'article de rapport** *m* COMPTA reporting object code; **~ d'autorisation** *m* BANQUE authorization code, authorization number; **~ bancaire de tri** *m* BANQUE *des chèques* bank code, bank sort code *(UK)*; **~ barres** *m* V&M bar code marking; **~ à barres** *m* INFO bar code *(BrE)*, bar graphics *(AmE)*; **~ barres** *m* INFO bar code marking; **~ à barres** *m* V&M bar code *(BrE)*, bar graphics; **~ du bâtiment et des travaux publics** *m* IMMOB building code; **~ de bonne conduite** *m* COM code of practice; **~ de caractères** *m* INFO code set; **~ de commerce** *m* COM, DROIT commercial code; **~ de commerce uniforme** *m* DROIT uniform commercial code; **~ de compensation foncière** *m* IMMOB land compensation code; **~ comptable** *m* COMPTA chart of accounts; **~ de comptes** *m* COMPTA code of accounts; **~ de conduite** *m* COM, TRANSP *à bord* code of conduct; **~ de conduite des conférences maritimes** *m* TRANSP *maritime* liner conference code; **~ de la devise** *m* BANQUE currency code; **~ de document** *m* INFO document code; **~ emballage** *m* V&M *étude de marché* package code; **~ des impôts** *m* FISC Internal Revenue code *(US)*, revenue ruling, tax code; **~ d'interclassement** *m* INFO collator code; **~ d'interclassement provisoire** *m* COM suspense collator; **~ d'intervention** *m* INFO action code; **~ du logement** *m* DROIT, IMMOB housing

code; **~ machine** *m* INFO computer code, machine code; **~ ONU** *m* IMP/EXP code UN; **~ de pays** *m* BANQUE country code; **~ de perforation** *m* INFO punch code; **~ personnel** *m* BANQUE personal identification number; **~ postal** *m* COMMS code, postal code *(BrE)*, postcode *(BrE)*, zip code *(AmE)*; **~ de pratique publicitaire** *m* V&M code of advertising practice; **~ de procédure** *m* BOURSE code of procedure; **~ publicitaire** *m* DROIT, V&M advertising code; **~ de responsabilité professionnelle** *m* DROIT code of professional responsibility *(US)*; **~ source** *m* INFO source code; **~ supplémentaire des douanes** *m* IMP/EXP, TRANSP customs additional code, CAC; **~ de transaction des douanes** *m* IMP/EXP, TRANSP customs transaction code, CT; **~ uniforme** *m* COM standard code; **~ des usages** *m* BOURSE rules of fair practice, uniform practice code *(US)*; **~ des valeurs** *m* BOURSE stock symbol; **~ des valeurs sur téléscripteur** *m* BOURSE ticker symbol

Code: **~ maritime** *m* DROIT, TRANSP navigation laws; **~ maritime international des marchandises dangereuses** *m* TRANSP *navigation* International Maritime Dangerous Goods Code, IMDGC

co-débiteur, -trice *m,f* FIN joint debtor; **~ hypothécaire** DROIT co-mortgagor *(US)*

codec *abrév (codeur-décodeur)* INFO codec *(coder-decoder)*

codéposant, e *m,f* BREVETS joint applicant

codet *m* INFO code element

codétenteur, -trice *m,f* BOURSE joint holder

codétermination *f* RES HUM codetermination

codeur-décodeur *m (codec)* INFO coder-decoder *(codec)*

codicille *m* DROIT codicil

codification *f* COM codification; **~ des comptes** COMPTA classification of accounts

codirecteur, -trice *m,f* COM, GESTION, RES HUM co-director, co-manager, joint director, joint manager

coefficient *m* COM factor, COMPTA ratio, MATH coefficient; **~ d'arrimage bas** TRANSP *navigation* low stowage factor; **~ d'arrimage élevé** TRANSP *navigation* high stowage factor; **~ de bénéfice brut** COMPTA gross profit ratio; **~ bêta** BOURSE, FIN beta coefficient *(AmE)*, beta factor *(BrE)*; **~ de capital** BANQUE capital ratio; **~ de capitalisation des résultats** *(CCR)* BOURSE, COMPTA, FIN price-earnings multiple, price-earnings ratio; **~ de confiance** MATH confidence coefficient; **~ de conversion** BOURSE price factor; **~ de corrélation** MATH coefficient of correlation; **~ de corrélation multiple** MATH coefficient of multiple correlation; **~ delta** BOURSE, FIN delta coefficient *(AmE)*, delta factor *(BrE)*; **~ de détermination** MATH coefficient of determination; **~ de détermination multiple** MATH coefficient of multiple determination; **~ de discrimination du marché** ECON market discrimination coefficient; **~ d'écart** MATH coefficient of variation; **~ d'employés** RES HUM employee ratio; **~ d'encombrement bas** TRANSP *navigation* low stowage factor; **~ d'encombrement élevé** TRANSP *navigation* high stowage factor; **~ d'Engel** ECON Engel coefficient; **~ d'évaluation** IMMOB assessment ratio; **~ d'exploitation** COMPTA working ratio; **~ financier** FIN financial ratio; **~ gamma** BOURSE, FIN gamma coefficient (*AmE*), gamma factor (*BrE*); **~ de Gini** ECON *économétrie* Gini coefficient; **~ d'imposition** FISC tax ratio; **~ des impôts directs-indirects** ECON, FISC direct-indirect taxes ratio, tax structure; **~ de liquidité** BANQUE, BOURSE, COMPTA, FIN current ratio, liquidity ratio; **~ de perte** BANQUE loss ratio; **~ de remplissage** TRANSP *d'un navire* block coefficient, *d'un conteneur, d'un avion* load factor; **~ de réserve** BANQUE reserve rate, reserve ratio; **~ de réserves obligatoires** BANQUE required reserve ratio; **~ rompus-ventes à découvert** BOURSE odd-lot short-sale ratio; **~ de trésorerie** BANQUE, COMPTA, ECON, FIN cash deposits ratio, cash ratio; **~ d'utilisation de la capacité** COM, MATH load factor; **~ véga** BOURSE, FIN vega coefficient (*AmE*), vega factor (*BrE*); **~ des ventes à découvert des spécialistes** BOURSE specialist's short-sale ratio

coentreprise *f* BOURSE *action*, COM *action*, COMPTA joint venture, JV, *société* joint-venture company, ECON joint venture, JV, joint-venture company, GESTION *action* joint venture, JV, *société* joint-venture company; **~ avec création de société commune** *f* COM equity joint venture; **~ sans création de société** *f* COM contract joint venture

coercitif, -ive *adj* COM coercive, compulsory

coeur *m* COM core

COFACE *abrév* (*Compagnie française d'assurance pour le commerce extérieur*) IMP/EXP ≈ ECGD (*UK*) (*Export Credit Guarantee Department*)

cofferdam *m* TRANSP *d'un navire* cofferdam

coffre *m* BANQUE safe deposit, safe-deposit box, safety-deposit box, TRANSP *de navire* well deck, *de voiture* boot (*BrE*), trunk (*AmE*); **~ d'amarrage** TRANSP *en mer* mooring buoy; **~ -fort** BANQUE safe; **~ de nuit** BANQUE night safe

cofinancement *m* COM, ECON, FIN cofinancing

cofinancer *vt* COM, ECON, FIN cofinance

cogérance *f* COM, GESTION, RES HUM joint management

cogérant, e *m,f* COM, GESTION, RES HUM joint manager

cogestion *f* COM, GESTION, RES HUM employee involvement and participation, joint management

cohabitation *f* FISC joint occupancy, shared accommodation

cohérence *f* COM coherence, coherency, consistency

cohérent, e *adj* COM coherent, consistent

cohéritier, -ère *m,f* DROIT joint heir, party to an estate

cohésion *f* COM cohesion

coiffe: ~ d'extrémité *f* TRANSP *d'un conteneur* header bar

coin *m* TRANSP *cale* quoin; **~ des bonnes affaires** COM, V&M bargain basement

coincé, e *adj* COM stuck, stymied

coincer: se ~ *v pron* IND *partie d'une machine* bind, jam, stick

coïncider: *vt* **~ avec** COM coincide with, COM *chiffres* agree, concur, *événements* coincide

coinculpé, e *m,f* DROIT co-accused, codefendant

col: ~ blanc *m* RES HUM white-collar worker; **~ bleu** *m* RES HUM blue-collar worker

colbertisme *m* POL Colbertism

colis *m* COMMS package, parcel, pkg; **~ confié** *m* IMP/EXP, TRANSP non-negotiable bill of lading; **~ en instance de livraison** *m pl* COM parcels awaiting delivery; **~ lourd** *m* TRANSP *manutention* heavy lift, H/L

colistier, -ière *m,f* POL fellow candidate (*BrE*), running mate (*AmE*)

collaborateur, -trice *m,f* MÉDIA *personne qui contribue à un journal* contributor, RES HUM *personne qui travaille avec un autre* associate, co-worker, collaborator, colleague

collaboration *f* COM collaboration, cooperation; **~ technique** COM, ECON, POL technical cooperation; ◆ **de ~** COM collaborative; **en ~** COM *action, entreprise* collaborative

collaborer: *vt* **~ à** MÉDIA *journal, magazine* contribute to, COM collaborate, cooperate

collage *m* MÉDIA, V&M *publicité* paste-up

collar *m* BOURSE collar

collecte: ~ de bienfaisance *f* PROT SOC charity fundraising; **~ de données** *f* INFO data collection, data gathering; **~ électronique d'informations** *f* INFO, MÉDIA electronic news gathering; **~ de fonds** *f* FIN fund-raising, PROT SOC fund-raising project; **~ des impôts par fermage** *f* ECON, FISC goal system, tax farming; ◆ **faire une ~** PROT SOC make a collection

collecteur *m* TRANSP *navire* feeder ship, feeder vessel, mother ship

collectif[1], -ive *adj* COM collective

collectif:[2] ~ de travailleurs *m* RES HUM workers' collective

collection: ~ de produits *f* COM, IND product line, V&M *publicité* array of products, product line

collectivement *adv* COM collectively

collectivisation *f* ECON *de l'économie, de l'industrie* collectivization, IMMOB *de la propriété, de la terre* collectivization, communization

collectiviser *vt* ECON *économie, industrie* collectivize, IMMOB *propriété, terre* collectivize, communize

collectivisme *m* POL collectivism; **~ libéral** POL liberal collectivism

collègue *mf* RES HUM co-worker, colleague

coller *vt* COM *timbre*, COMMS affix, *étiquette* affix, stick

colleter: **se ~ avec** *v pron* COM grapple with

collision *f* TRANSP col, coll, collision

colloque *m* COM, GESTION conference, convention, symposium

Colloque: **~ européen des organisations de contrôle** *m* IND European Symposium on Inspection and Control

collusion *f* ECON collusion

colocataire *mf* IMMOB cotenant

colocation *f* IMMOB cotenancy

Colombie *f* COM Colombia

colombien, -enne *adj* COM Colombian

Colombien, -enne *m,f* COM *habitant* Colombian

Colombo *n pr* COM Colombo

colon *m* COM colon

colonie *f* COM colony

colonne *f* COM *de chiffres*, MÉDIA *impression* col, column; **~ créditrice** COMPTA, FIN credit column; **~ des crédits** COMPTA, FIN credit column; **~ débitrice** COMPTA, FIN debit column; **~ des débits** COMPTA, FIN debit column; **~ de droite** (ANT *colonne de gauche*) COM right-hand column, COMPTA right column; **~ de gauche** (ANT *colonne de droite*) COM left-hand column, COMPTA left column; **~ Morris** *Fra* V&M advertising tower; **~ publicitaire** V&M advertising tower

colporter *vt* COM hawk, peddle

colporteur, -euse *m,f* COM hawker, pedlar, street trader (*BrE*), street vendor (*AmE*)

com *abrév* COM (*commission*) com. (*committee*), GESTION (*comité*), POL (*comité*), RES HUM (*comité*) board, com. (*committee*)

combat *m* COM battle, contest, *lutte, bagarre* gaming

combattre *vt* COM *inflation, crime* combat, fight

combinaison *f* COM comb, combination, INFO *de bits* configuration, MATH combination, COMB; **~ d'écarts verticaux** BOURSE box spread; **~ de straddle** BOURSE straddle combination; **~ de valeurs** BOURSE unit

combiné, e *adj* COM composite

combiner: *vt* **~ avec** COM combine with, COM combine

combines *f pl* BOURSE, COM wheeling and dealing (*infrml*)

combler *vt* ECON, FIN *déficit, écart* make up; ♦ **~ le déficit** ECON, FIN close the gap, make up the deficit; **~ l'écart** ECON, FIN bridge the gap, make up the difference

combustible: **~ fossile** *m* ENVIR, IND fossil fuel; **~ lourd** *m* ENVIR heavy fuel; **~ non-fumigène** *m* ENVIR, IND *pollution* smokeless fuel; **~ sans plomb** *m* ENVIR lead-free fuel

combustion: **~ spontanée** *f* TRANSP *des marchandises* spontaneous combustion

COMECON *abrév* (*Conseil de l'aide économique mutuelle*) ECON CMEA, COMECON (*Council for Mutual Economic Aid*)

COMEX: **la ~** *f* BOURSE ≈ COMEX (*US*), ≈ Commodities Exchange (*US*)

comité *m* (*com*) GESTION, POL, RES HUM board, committee (*com.*); **~ d'accueil** COM welcoming party; **~ d'aide au développement** ECON Development Aid Committee, Development Assistance Committee, DAC; **~ d'audit** *Fra* (*cf comité de révision Bel, comité de vérification Can*) COMPTA, FIN audit committee; **~ central d'arbitrage des litiges** BOURSE Central Arbitration Committee, CAC; **~ consultatif** ADMIN, COM, RES HUM advisory board, advisory committee, advisory group, consultative committee; **~ consultatif du marché national** BOURSE national market advisory board; **~ de coordination** COM umbrella committee; **~ de coordination pour le contrôle multilatéral des exportations** IMP/EXP Cocom, Coordinating Committee for Multilateral Export controls; **~ de développement social** POL Social Development Committee; **~ directeur** COM, POL management committee; **~ de direction** GESTION executive committee, management committee; **~ d'entreprise** COMPTA employees' committee, RES HUM joint consultative committee, joint production committee, works committee (*UK*), works council (*UK*); **~ d'entreprise du consortium** RES HUM combine committee; **~ exécutif** RES HUM executive committee; **~ de financement des sociétés** FIN corporate financing committee; **~ de gestion** COM, GESTION board of management, prudential committee (*US*); **~ de grève** RES HUM strike committee; **~ de l'immobilier** IMMOB board of estate agents (*BrE*), board of realtors (*AmE*); **~ d'inspection** DROIT committee of inspection; **~ régulateur** POL regulatory committee; **~ de restructuration** BANQUE, COM, FIN advisory committee, steering committee; **~ de révision** *Bel* (*cf comité d'audit Fra*) COMPTA, FIN audit committee; **~ de stratégie d'investissement** BOURSE, FIN investment strategy committee; **~ de surveillance** COM, POL watchdog committee, RES HUM vigilance men (*jarg*); **~ d'usagers du port** TRANSP port users' committee; **~ de vérification** *Can* (*cf comité d'audit Fra*) COMPTA, FIN audit committee; ♦ **être membre d'un ~** COM be on a committee, serve on a committee

Comité: **~ des conseillers économiques** *m* ECON Council of Economic Advisers, CEA; **~ consultatif latino-américain des échanges commerciaux** *m* COM Latin American Trade Advisory Group, LATAG; **~ économique et social** *m* ECON Economic and Social Committee, ESC; **~ européen des assurances** *m* ASSUR European Insurance Committee; **~ européen de coopération juridique** *m* DROIT European Committee of Legal Cooperation; **~ international des normes de comptabilité** *m* COMPTA International Accounting Standards Committee, IASC; **~ international**

radio-maritime *m (CIRM)* COMMS International Radio-Maritime Committee *(CIRM)*; **~ maritime international** *m* TRANSP International Maritime Committee, IMC; **~ des priorités et de la planification** *m* ADMIN Priorities and Planning Committee; **~ pour la simplification des procédures du commerce international** *m* ADMIN Committee for the Simplification of International Trade Procedures, SIPROCOM; **~ des Vingt** *m* COM Committee of Twenty, C-20

commandant, e *m,f* RES HUM, TRANSP captain, chief officer, master; **~ de bord** RES HUM, TRANSP *d'un avion* aircraft commander, captain, pilot-in-command

commande *f* COM com., commission, order, COMPTA purchase order, DROIT ord., order, INFO command, control, V&M *marchandises et services* order; **~ annuelle** COM annual order; **~ en attente** COM back order, outstanding order, backlog order, V&M back order, outstanding order; **~ automatique** INFO automatic control; **~ automatique certifiée** TRANSP automatic control certified, ACC; **~ de contrôle** INFO control command; **~ à crédit** V&M credit order; **~ à distance** COMMS remote control; **~ d'exportation de marchandises** IMP/EXP export of goods order; **~ ferme** V&M firm order; **~ de flux** INFO flow control; **~ globale** COM, V&M blanket order; **~ importante** COM, V&M large order; **~ intégrée** INFO embedded command; **~ des majuscules** INFO character pitch; **~ numérique** FIN, MATH numerical control; **~ par correspondance** COM, COMMS order by post, V&M mail order; **~ précédée d'un point** INFO dot command; **~ provisoire** DROIT draft order; **~ reçue** V&M incoming order; **~ de remplacement** COM, V&M alternative order; **~ renouvelée** COM repeat business; **~ de réservation** COM, V&M booking order; **~ en retard** COM, V&M back order; **~ en souffrance** COM, V&M back order; **~ urgente** COM, V&M rush order, urgent order; ♦ **à ~ par effleurement** INFO touch-activated; **à ~ vocale** INFO voice-activated, voice-actuated; **~ de** COM O/o, order of; **en ~** V&M on order

commandé, e *adj* INFO remote-controlled; **~ par clavier** INFO keyboard-operated; **~ par souris** INFO mouse-driven

commandement *m* COM command, leadership, DROIT summons, writ, GESTION, RES HUM command, leadership; **~ de saisie** DROIT writ of attachment

commander *vt* COM *marchandises* order, *personnel* be in charge of, be in command of, command; ♦ **~ qch par correspondance** COMMS send away for sth, send off for sth

commandes: ~ en cours *f pl* COM, V&M orders on hand; **~ futures** *f pl* COM, V&M future orders; **~ non satisfaites** *f pl* COM, V&M unfilled orders; **~ par quantité** *f pl* COM, V&M bulk orders; **~ en suspens** *f pl* COM, V&M backlog of orders

commanditaire *mf* COM backer, financial backer, limited partner, silent partner *(AmE)*, sleeping partner *(BrE)*, DROIT limited partner, silent partner *(AmE)*, sleeping partner *(BrE)*, FIN backer, financial backer, silent partner *(AmE)*, sleeping partner *(BrE)*, MÉDIA sponsor, *monde du théâtre* angel *(infrml)*, backer, financial backer, RES HUM limited partner, silent partner *(AmE)*, sleeping partner *(BrE)*

commandite *m* RES HUM general partner

commencement: ~ de preuve *m* DROIT prima-facie evidence

commencer *vi* COM begin, start, start up; ♦ **~ le déchargement** TRANSP *d'un navire* break bulk; **devoir ~ en** COM be scheduled to begin in; **~ à faire** COM begin doing, begin to do, set about doing, start doing, start to do; **~ la production** IND *industrie pétrolière* come on stream

commentaire *m* COM comment, commentary; **~ sur image** V&M *television, film* voice-over; ♦ **faire des ~s** COM comment

commerçant[1], **e** *adj* COM businesslike; **peu ~** COM unbusinesslike

commerçant[2], **e** *m,f* COM, V&M shopkeeper *(BrE)*, storekeeper *(AmE)*, trader; **~ en exercice** V&M active trader; **~ inscrit à la TVA** FISC VAT registered trader *(UK)*

commerçantes *f pl* COM, V&M tradeswomen, tradespeople

commerçants *m pl* COM, V&M tradesmen, tradespeople

commerce *m* COM business, commerce, trade, trading, shop *(BrE)*, store *(AmE)*, ECON, IMP/EXP trade, trading, V&M *activité* business, commerce, trade, trading, *magasin* shop *(BrE)*, store *(AmE)*; **~ affilié** FISC *par rapport à une oeuvre caritative* related business; **~ alimentaire de détail** V&M food retailing, retail food business, retail food trade; **~ avec l'Europe continentale** V&M continental trade, cross-Channel trade; **~ de banque** BANQUE banking business; **~ de banque à l'étranger** BANQUE foreign banking; **~ de billets de banque** BANQUE banknote trading; **~ de cabotage** TRANSP *maritime* coasting trade; **~ de la chaussure** COM shoe trade; **~ de compensation** ECON counter trade; **~ concurrentiel** ECON, V&M competitive trading; **~ cyclique** COM, ECON, V&M cyclical trade; **~ de détail** V&M retail business, retail trade; **~ dominical** COM Sunday trading; **~ d'échanges compensés** ECON barter trade; **~ des excédents** COM black trading; **~ des exportations indirectes** IMP/EXP indirect export trading; **~ extérieur** COM, ECON, IMP/EXP foreign trade; **~ familial** V&M family business, mom-and-pop store *(AmE)*; **~ frontalier** COM, IMP/EXP border trade, cross-border trading; **~ de gros** V&M wholesale trade; **~ historique** TRANSP historical trade; **~ horloger** IND watch trade; **~ illicite** COM, DROIT unfair trade, unfair trading; **~ d'importation** ECON, IMP/EXP import trade; **~ incestueux d'actions** BOURSE incestuous share dealing; **~ intégré** *(SYN grande surface)* COM combined trade, hypermarket, one-stop shopping center (*AmE*), one-stop shopping centre (*BrE*); ~ **intercommunautaire** ECON, V&M intercommunity trade; ~ **intérieur** COM, ECON, IMP/EXP domestic trade, home trade; ~ **international** COM, ECON, IMP/EXP, IND, V&M international trade; ~ **intracommunautaire** ECON, POL intra-Community trade, intra-EU trade; ~ **d'invisibles** ECON invisible trade; ~ **de la laine** COM wool trade; ~ **maritime** COM, ECON, IMP/EXP, TRANSP maritime trade, seagoing trade; ~ **maritime trans-manche** TRANSP short sea trade; ~ **mondial** ECON, POL world trade; ~ **multinational** ECON, IMP/EXP multinational trading; ~ **parallèle** COM parallel trading; ~ **personnel de services** FISC personal services business; ~ **planifié** COM, ECON, IND managed trade; ~ **de produits pharmaceutiques** IND, V&M drug trade; ~ **de proximité** V&M local shop (*BrE*), local store (*AmE*), neighborhood store (*AmE*), neighbourhood shop (*BrE*), *dans un village* village shop (*BrE*), village store (*AmE*); ~ **réciproque** COM reciprocal trading; ~ **rural** V&M village shop (*BrE*), village store (*AmE*); ~ **sensible à la conjoncture** ECON cyclical trade; ~ **spécialisé** COM, V&M niche trading; ~ **des surplus** COM black trading; ~ **à tempérament** COM, RES HUM tally trade; ~ **à terme** BOURSE futures trading, futures transaction; ~ **traditionnel** V&M over-the-counter retailing; ~ **trans-Manche** ECON, V&M continental trade, cross-Channel trade; ~ **transfrontalier** ECON cross-border trade; ~ **transitaire** IMP/EXP, TRANSP transit trade; ~ **de troc** ECON *international* barter trade, counter trade; ♦ **faire le ~ de** COM traffic in, ECON trade in

commercer *vi* COM, ECON, V&M trade; ♦ ~ **une chose contre une autre** COM, ECON trade one thing against another, trade one thing for another

commerciabilité *f* BOURSE marketability, negotiability

commercial[1], **e** *adj* COM commercial

commercial[2] *m* RES HUM, V&M salesman

commercial[3], **e** *m, f* RES HUM, V&M salesperson

commerciale *f* RES HUM, V&M saleswoman, salesperson

commercialement *adv* COM, V&M commercially

commercialisable *adj* COM, V&M marketable, merchantable

commercialisation *f* COM, V&M commercialization, marketing, merchandising, product marketing

commercialiser *vt* COM, V&M commercialize, market

commis *m* ADMIN clerk, BOURSE waiter (*jarg*), RES HUM clerk, office boy; ~ **de bourse** BOURSE unauthorized clerk, blue button (*UK, jarg*); ~ **aux communications** BOURSE pink button (*UK, jarg*); ~ **à la compensation** BOURSE red button (*UK, jarg*); ~ **aux comptes créditeurs** COMPTA accounts payable clerk; ~ **aux comptes**

fournisseurs COMPTA accounts payable clerk; ~ **de magasin** COM, RES HUM sales clerk (*AmE*), shop assistant (*BrE*); ~ **principal** RES HUM chief clerk, senior clerk

commissaire *m* ADMIN, COM *membre d'une commission* commissioner, ADMIN, COM *membre d'un comité* committee member; ~ **de bord** RES HUM, TRANSP *d'un avion, d'un navire* purser; ~ **aux comptes** *Fra (cf reviseur Bel, vérificateur Can)* COMPTA accountant, auditor, qualified accountant, FIN auditor; ~ **aux comptes coresponsable** COMPTA joint auditor; ~ **aux comptes en double mandat** COMPTA joint auditor; ~ **aux comptes indépendant** *Fra (cf reviseur indépendant Bel, vérificateur indépendant Can)* COMPTA independent auditor; ~ **aux faillites** COM, DROIT Superintendent of Bankruptcy; ~ **-priseur** COM auctioneer; ~ **spécial** FISC special commissioner (*UK*)

Commissariat: ~ **à l'énergie atomique** *m (CEA)* ENVIR ≈ Atomic Energy Research Establishment (*AERE*)

commission *f* ADMIN, BANQUE com., commission, COM errand, COM board, committee, ECON com., commission, GESTION, POL *réunion de personnes* board, committee, RES HUM, V&M *pourcentage* com., commission; ~ **d'acceptation** BANQUE acceptance fee, commission for acceptance; ~ **d'achat** BOURSE sales charge, V&M buying commission; ~ **d'acquisition** ASSUR acquisition commission; ~ **ad hoc** COM ad hoc committee; ~ **d'adresse** TRANSP *maritime* address commission; ~ **d'affacturage** FIN factorage; ~ **d'agent** V&M agent's commission; ~ **d'aller-retour** BOURSE round turn; ~ **anti-monopole** ECON antitrust commission; ~ **d'arbitrage** BOURSE conciliation board, COM arbitration board, arbitration committee, board of conciliation (*UK*), conciliation board, DROIT, IND arbitration board, arbitration committee, board of conciliation (*UK*), RES HUM arbitration board, arbitration committee, board of conciliation (*UK*), conciliation board; ~ **d'arbitrage centrale** BOURSE Central Arbitration Committee (*UK*), CAC (*UK*); ~ **bancaire** BANQUE bank commission, banking commission; ~ **de la bourse de Londres** BOURSE ≈ London Stock Exchange Board; ~ **Brady** BOURSE Brady Commission (*US*); ~ **des cartels** COM cartel commission; ~ **de chef de file** BANQUE management fee; ~ **clandestine** POL, RES HUM kickback; ~ **de codification des titres** BOURSE ≈ Committee on Uniform Securities Identification Procedures (*US*); ~ **des conflits sociaux** RES HUM disputes committee; ~ **consultative** COM, POL *Commission Européenne* advisory board, advisory committee, consultative committee; ~ **de courtage** BOURSE broker's commission, brokerage allowance (*US*), brokerage commission, brokerage fee; ~ **de créanciers** FIN creditors' committee; ~ **de démarcheur** COM finder's fee; ~ **d'encaissement** COM collection charge; ~ **d'engagement** BANQUE commitment fee; ~ **d'enquête** DROIT investigating committee, tribunal of enquiry, POL committee of inquiry, select committee (*UK*), RES HUM commission of inquiry, court of inquiry (*UK*); ~ **exécutive** RES HUM executive committee; ~ **exécutive principale** RES HUM *d'un syndicat* principal executive committee; ~ **faible** BOURSE soft commission; ~ **fixe** BANQUE flat fee; ~ **forfaitaire** FIN flat fee; ~ **de garantie** BANQUE underwriting fee, FIN underwriting commission, underwriting fee; ~ **de gestion** BANQUE agency fee, COM, MÉDIA agency fund; ~ **indépendante de révision des salaires et des conventions** RES HUM independent review committee (*UK*); ~ **d'inspection** DROIT committee of inspection; ~ **d'investissements** COM board of investment, BOI; ~ **des investissements** FIN *de l'association des assureurs britanniques* Investment Committee (*UK*), IC (*UK*); ~ **de mise sur le marché** BOURSE selling concession; ~ **mixte** RES HUM joint committee; ~ **de montage** BANQUE *d'un prêt* arrangement fee, loan fee, loan origination fee, set-up fee; ~ **de mouvement** BANQUE *perçue par l'institution financière* activity charge; ~ **de mouvement de compte** BANQUE activity charge; ~ **en nature** BOURSE soft commission; ~ **d'organisation** BANQUE, COM, FIN steering committee; ~ **de l'organisation internationale des valeurs** BOURSE International Organization of Securities Commission, IOSCO; ~ **paritaire** RES HUM joint committee; ~ **paritaire consultative** RES HUM joint consultative committee; ~ **partagée** POL split commission; ~ **de participation** BANQUE participation fee; ~ **payable d'avance** BOURSE front-end load; ~ **permanente** POL standing committee; ~ **de placement** BANQUE, FIN underwriting fee; ~ **de la planification d'urbanisme** IMMOB planning commission, planning department; ~ **de politique générale** ADMIN general policy committee; ~ **pour les procédures de mouvement de cargaisons** COM, TRANSP cargo traffic procedures committee, CTPC; ~ **de reconduction** BANQUE extension fee; ~ **des salaires agricoles** ECON, RES HUM agricultural wages board; ~ **sur débours** COM disbursement commission; ~ **sur le montant d'un prêt non-utilisé** BANQUE commitment fee; ~ **sur prêt** COM, FIN procuration fee; ~ **sur vente immobilière** IMMOB real estate commission; ~ **de tenue de compte** BANQUE *perçue par l'institution financière* account operation charge, *pour l'institution financière* account maintenance charge, account maintenance fee; ~ **du transitaire** TRANSP fac, forwarding agent's commission; ~ **unique** BOURSE single commission; ~ **de vente** V&M sale commission; ~ **des voies et moyens** *Bel* POL supply committee, ways and means committee (*US*); ◆ **faire une ~** COM run an errand

Commission: ~ **canadienne d'examen d'exportation de biens culturels** *f* IMP/EXP Canadian Cultural Property Export Review Board; ~ **des communautés européennes** *f* ECON Commission of the European Community; ~ **de contrôle des marchés de matières premières** *f* BOURSE Commodity Futures Trading Commission (*US*), CFTC (*US*); ~ **économique pour l'Afrique occidentale** *f* ECON Economic Commission for Western Africa, ECWA; ~ **économique européenne** *f* (*CEE*) ECON Economic Commission for Europe (*ECE*); ~ **de l'égalité de traitement** *f* RES HUM Equal Opportunities Commission (*UK*), EOC (*UK*); ~ **européenne** *f* ECON European Commission; ~ **européenne du commerce** *f* COM European Trade Committee, ETC; ~ **des finances** *f* FIN Congressional Budget Office (*US*), CBO (*US*); ~ **de la fonction publique** *f* ADMIN ≈ CSC, ≈ Civil Service Commission; ~ **de groupage** *f* TRANSP ≈ Joint Cargo Committee (*UK*); ~ **intergouvernementale des migrations européennes** *f* PROT SOC Intergovernmental Committee for European Migration, ICEM; ~ **océanographique intergouvernementale** *f* COMMS *basée à Paris* Intergovernmental Oceanographic Commission, IOC; ~ **des opérations de Bourse** *f* (*COB*) BOURSE French stock exchange watchdog, ≈ Federal Open Market Committee (*US*) (*FOMC*), ≈ Securities and Exchange Commission (*US*) (*SEC*), ≈ Securities and Investments Board (*UK*) (*SIB*); ~ **des opérations à terme sur les marchandises** *f* BOURSE Commodity Futures Trading Commission (*US*), CFTC (*US*); ~ **permanente des comptes publics** *f* POL Standing Committee on Public Accounts; ~ **permanente d'estimations diverses** *f* POL Standing Committee on Miscellaneous Estimates; ~ **permanente des prévisions budgétaires en général** *f* POL Standing Committee on Miscellaneous Estimates; ~ **de sécurité** *f* PROT SOC Safety Commission (*US*), Safety Committee (*US*); ~ **sur l'énergie et l'environnement** *f* ENVIR Commission on Energy and the Environment, CENE

commissionnaire *m* RES HUM commission agent, commission merchant, commission salesman, commission salesperson, commission saleswoman, COM agent, agt, broker, messenger, COMMS messenger, DROIT agent, agt, broker, messenger; ~ **chargé du recouvrement des droits de douane** FISC, IMP/EXP ≈ Commissioner of Customs and Excise (*UK*); ~ **en douane** IMP/EXP *navigation* customs broker; ~ **ducroire** COM, V&M del credere agent; ~ **exportateur** IMP/EXP, RES HUM export agent; ~ **exportateur du fabricant** IMP/EXP manufacturer's export agent; ~ **de groupage** IMP/EXP, TRANSP groupage operator; ~ **groupeur** IMP/EXP, TRANSP groupage operator; ~ **en marchandises** RES HUM commission agent; ~ **de transport** TRANSP forwarding agent, forwarding company, freight forwarder; ~ **de transport combiné** TRANSP combined transport operator; ~ **de transport international** TRANSP international freight forwarder

commissionnaires: ~ **en douane et transitaires** *m*

pl IMP/EXP ≈ REDS (*UK*), ≈ Registered Excise Dealers and Shippers (*UK*)

Commonwealth *m* ECON, POL British Commonwealth of Nations (*obs*), Commonwealth

commuabilité *f* DROIT commutability

commuable *adj* DROIT commutable

commuer *vt* COM, DROIT *en* commute

commun, e *adj* COM common, communal, joint, mutual; ◆ **d'un ~ accord** COM, DROIT by common consent, by mutual agreement, by mutual consent

communautaire *adj* COM communal, community, *concernant la Communauté Européenne* Community

communauté *f* COM community; **~ de biens** COM community of goods, DROIT joint estate; **~ d'intérêts** COM community of interests; **~ rurale** ECON rural community

Communauté: ~ économique de l'Afrique de l'Ouest *f* (*CEAO*) ECON Economic Community of West African States (*ECOWAS*); **~ des États indépendants** *f* (*CEI*) COM, ECON, POL Commonwealth of Independent States (*CIS*); **~ européenne** *f* (*CE*) ECON European Community (*EC*); **~ européenne du charbon et de l'acier** *f* (*CECA*) IND European Coal and Steel Community (*ECSC*); **~ européenne des coopératives de consommateurs** *f* COM Euro Co-op, European Community of Consumers' Co-operatives; **~ européenne de l'énergie atomique** *f* (*CEEA*) IND European Atomic Energy Community (*EAEC*)

commune *f* ECON, POL commune

Communes: les ~ *f pl* POL the Commons (*UK*)

communicateur, -trice *m,f* COMMS communicator

communication *f* COM communication, COMMS communication, *action* communication, *coup de téléphone* call, *câblogramme, fac-similé, lettre* communication, DROIT, GESTION, INFO, POL UE, RES HUM communication; **~ avec la base** GESTION downward communication; **~ avec préavis** COMMS *coup de téléphone* person-to-person call (*AmE*); **~ de données** COMMS, INFO data communications; **~ hiérarchique** COMMS formal communication; **~ horizontale** (*ANT communication verticale*) COM horizontal communication; **~ interne** COM, COMMS, GESTION internal communication, RES HUM employee communications, internal communication; **~ interurbaine** COMMS long-distance call, toll call (*US*), trunk call (*UK*); **~ à longue distance** COMMS *coup de téléphone* long-distance call, toll call (*US*), trunk call (*UK*); **~ de masse** MÉDIA mass communication; **~ non-verbale** COM, GESTION, RES HUM nonverbal communication; **~ officieuse** POL oral note; **~ par satellite** COMMS satellite communication; **~ en PCV** COMMS *coup de téléphone* collect call (*AmE*), reverse charge call (*BrE*); **~ de pièces** DROIT discovery; **~ téléphonique** COMMS phone call, telephone call; **~ verbale** COM, GESTION, RES HUM verbal communication; **~ verticale** (*ANT communication horizontale*) COM vertical communication; ◆ **en ~ directe avec** COM, INFO coupled with; **être en ~ avec** COMMS be through to

communiqué *m* COM, COMMS bulletin, communiqué, statement, MÉDIA news advisory (*jarg*), pick-up (*jarg*), V&M bulletin, communiqué, statement; **~ d'agence** MÉDIA pony (*US, jarg*); **~ officiel** COM official statement; **~ de presse** COMMS, MÉDIA news release, press release

communiquer *vt* COM communicate, release, COMMS communicate

communisant, e *m,f* POL fellow traveler (*AmE*), fellow traveller (*BrE*)

communisme *m* ECON, POL communism

commutateur *m* COMMS, INFO switch; **~ DIP** INFO DIP switch; **~ privé** COMMS private branch exchange (*UK*)

commutatif, -ive *adj* DROIT commutative

commutation *f* ASSUR commutation, COMMS switching, DROIT commutation, INFO switching; **~ de messages** COMMS message switching

commuter *vt* COM *courant électrique* commutate, switch, switch over

Comores *f pl* COM Comoros

comorien, -enne *adj* COM Comoran, Comorian

Comorien, -enne *m,f* COM *habitant* Comoran, Comorian

compagnie *f* (*Cie*) COM, ECON company, firm; **~ aérienne** TRANSP airline, airline company; **~ aérienne domestique** TRANSP domestic airline, domestic airline company; **~ aérienne internationale** TRANSP international airline, international airline company; **~ aérienne nationale** LOISIRS, TRANSP national airline; **~ agréée d'assurance** ASSUR qualified insurance corporation; **~ d'assurance captive** ASSUR captive insurance company; **~ d'assurance des valeurs** BOURSE stock insurance company; **~ d'assurance-vie** ASSUR life insurance company, life insurance corporation; **~ d'assurance-vie réserve légale** ASSUR legal reserve life insurance company; **~ d'assurances** ASSUR insurance company, insurance corporation, insurer; **~ de cars** LOISIRS, TRANSP bus company, coach company, *qui fait des voyages touristiques* tour operator, tour organizer; **~ cédante** ASSUR ceding company; **~ à charte** COMPTA chartered company; **et ~** (*et Cie*) COM and company (*and Co*); **~ fiduciaire** FIN trust company; **~ financière** FIN financial company; **~ du gaz** ENVIR gas company; **~ hydraulique** IND water company; **~ importatrice de thé** IMP/EXP tea-importing company; **~ d'investissement à revenu fixe** FIN fixed income investment company (*UK*); **~ limitée** COM limited company (*UK*); **~ maritime** TRANSP ferry company, ferry line; **~ minière** IND mining company; **~ mixte** FIN mixed activity holding company; **~ mutuelle** ASSUR mutual insurance company;

~ **mutuelle d'assurance** ASSUR mutual insurance company; ~ **de navigation** TRANSP shipping company, shipping line; ~ **pétrolière** IND oil company; ~ **proche** COM close company (*BrE*), close corporation (*AmE*), closed company (*BrE*), closed corporation (*AmE*); ~ **de réassurance** ASSUR reinsurance company; ~ **régionale** TRANSP commuter airline, regional airline, regional airline company; ~ **rentable** COM profit-making enterprise; ~ **de téléphone** COMMS telco (*AmE, infrml*), telephone company; ~ **de transport régional** TRANSP commuter airline, regional airline, regional airline company

Compagnie: ~ **des agents de change** *f (CAC)* FIN Institute of stockbrokers; ~ **française d'assurance pour le commerce extérieur** *f France (COFACE)* IMP/EXP ≈ Export Credit Guarantee Department (*UK*) (*ECGD*)

compagnon: ~ **de route** *m* POL fellow traveler (*AmE*), fellow traveller (*BrE*)

comparabilité *f* RES HUM comparability; ~ **des salaires** RES HUM pay comparability

comparable *adj* COM comparable

comparaison *f* COM comparison; ~ **inter-entreprises** COM intercompany comparison, interfirm comparison; ~ **de rendement** BOURSE yield comparison; ◆ **en** ~ **avec** COM compared with

comparaisons: ~ **croisées** *f pl* COM paired comparisons; ~ **internationales** *f pl* ECON international comparisons

comparaître *vi* DROIT *personne* appear; ◆ ~ **devant** DROIT appear before, come before

comparatif, -ive *adj* COM comparative

comparer 1. *vt* COM compare; ~ **à** COM compare to; **2.** *v pron* **se** ~ COM compare; ◆ ~ **avec** COM compare with; ~ **les prix** COM, V&M shop around

compartiment *m* TRANSP compartment; ~ **moteur** TRANSP *d'un navire* engine room, ER

compartimenter *vt* ADMIN, GESTION compartmentalize

compas: ~ **gyroscopique** *m* TRANSP *navigation* gyrocompass, GC

compatibilité *f* IND *entre des produits*, INFO compatibility; ~ **ascendante** (*ANT compatibilité descendante*) INFO upward compatibility; ~ **avec l'environnement** ENVIR environmental compatibility; ~ **descendante** (*ANT compatibilité ascendante*) INFO downward compatibility; ~ **du matériel** INFO hardware compatibility; ~ **PC** INFO PC-compatibility; ~ **-produit** ECON, IND product compatibility

compatible *adj* INFO compatible; ◆ ~ **avec** COM compatible with, consistent with; ~ **IBM** INFO IBM-compatible

compensation *f* ASSUR compensation, BANQUE set-off, settlement per contra, *d'un chèque* clearing, BOURSE mark to mark (*jarg*), offset, COM quid pro quo (*frml*), COMPTA *de pertes* making up, DROIT indemnity, ECON compensation,

commerce international barter trade, clearing, counter purchase, FISC compensation, V&M reciprocal buying; ~ **-aller** BANQUE onward clearing; ~ **bancaire** BANQUE bank clearing; ~ **de chèques** BANQUE check clearing (*AmE*), cheque clearing (*BrE*); ~ **de couverture** BOURSE offset; ~ **dollar contre dollar** BOURSE dollar-for-dollar offset; ~ **des dommages** ASSUR compensation for damage; ~ **financière** FIN compensatory financial facility, CFF, FISC fiscal offset; ~ **fiscale** FISC tax offset; ~ **interbancaire** BANQUE bank clearing, clearing; ~ **particulière** BANQUE special clearing (*UK*); ~ **des pertes** ASSUR compensation for loss; ~ **des risques** ASSUR balancing of portfolio; ~ **sur place** BANQUE, ECON town clearing; ~ **triangulaire** ECON *commerce international* triangular compensation

compensations: ~ **des risques de change** *f pl* BOURSE, FIN hedging operations; ~ **de valeurs élevées** *f pl* BANQUE high-value clearings

compensatoire *adj* BOURSE, COM, FIN compensating, compensatory

compensé, e *adj* BANQUE cld, cleared

compenser 1. *vt* BANQUE *chèque* clear, BOURSE *perte* offset, set off, COM compensate, compensate for, even up, make up for, *revers* counteract, COMPTA *perte* offset, set off, ECON make up, FIN offset, set off; **2.** *v pron* **se** ~ COMPTA balance each other out, balance out; ◆ ~ **une chute de la demande** COM compensate for a fall in demand; ~ **un débit par un crédit** COMPTA offset a debit against a credit, set off a debit against a credit; ~ **les pertes** BOURSE offset a loss

compétence *f* COM ability, competence, efficiency, *d'un tribunal, d'une juridiction* appropriateness, *expertise* expertise, *qualification* qualification, DROIT competence, jurisdiction, ECON ability, competence, efficiency, POL jurisdiction, RES HUM *professionnelle* capacity; ~ **dans le service** RES HUM service qualification; ~ **dans le travail** RES HUM job competence; ~ **fiscale** DROIT, FISC tax jurisdiction; ~ **de gestion** GESTION management skills; ~ **de management** GESTION executive competence, management competence; ~ **d'un tribunal** DROIT competence of court

compétences: ~ **en matière de secrétariat** *f pl* RES HUM secretarial skills; ~ **professionnelles** *f pl* RES HUM professional qualifications; ◆ **donner à qn les** ~ **pour faire qch** RES HUM qualify sb to do sth

compétent, e *adj* COM able, efficient, *qualifié* qualified, ECON efficient; ◆ ~ **à juger** DROIT entitled to adjudicate

compétiteur, -trice *m,f* COM, ECON, V&M competitor

compétitif, -ive *adj* COM, ECON, V&M competitive; **très** ~ COM, ECON, V&M *marché* highly competitive

compétition *f* BREVETS, COM, ECON, IND, RES HUM, V&M competition; ~ **avec épreuves éliminatoires** COM knockout competition

compétitivité *f* COM, ECON, V&M competitiveness;

~ **internationale** ECON, IND, V&M international competitiveness; ~ **des prix** BOURSE, COM, V&M price competitiveness

compilateur *m* INFO compiler

compiler *vt* COM *recueil*, INFO compile

complément *m* ASSUR excess, BREVETS supplement, COM complement, supplement, COMPTA complement, INFO supplement; ~ **proportionnel aux ressources** PROT SOC income-tested supplement; ~ **de salaire** RES HUM benefit, company benefit, employee benefit, fringe benefit

complémentaire *adj* BREVETS supplementary, COM complementary, supplementary, COMPTA supplementary, INFO complementary

complet, -ète *adj* COM *hôtel* booked up, fully booked, *étude* complete, comprehensive

complètement *adv* COM completely; ◆ ~ **désassemblé** TRANSP completely knocked down, CKD

compléter *vt* ADMIN *formulaire* complete, fill in, fill out, COM *formation, série* complete, top up (*UK*), *somme* round off; ◆ ~ **l'effectif de qch** COM bring sth up to strength

complexe[1] *adj* COM complex

complexe[2] *m* COM, IMMOB complex; ~ **immobilier** IMMOB housing complex, housing development (*AmE*), housing estate, housing project (*AmE*), PROT SOC housing development (*AmE*), housing estate, housing project (*AmE*); ~ **industriel** IMMOB, IND, V&M industrial complex, industrial estate (*BrE*), industrial park (*AmE*); ~ **de loisirs** LOISIRS entertainment complex; ~ **militaro-industriel** IND, POL military industrial complex; ~ **d'ordinateurs** COMMS, INFO computer network; ~ **de production** IND production complex

complexité *f* ECON, V&M *du marché* sophistication

complication *f* COM complication

complice *mf* DROIT accessory; ◆ **être le ~ de** DROIT aid and abet

compliments *m pl* COMMS *féliciter* compliments, *saluer* greetings

compliquer *vt* COM complicate; ◆ ~ **la vie** COM complicate matters, complicate things; ~ **la vie en formalités** ADMIN spin red tape (*jarg*)

complot *m* COM plot

comportement *m* GESTION, RES HUM attitude, behavior (*AmE*), behaviour (*BrE*), conduct; ~ **d'achat** V&M buying behavior (*AmE*), buying behaviour (*BrE*); ~ **de l'acheteur** V&M buyer behavior (*AmE*), buyer behaviour (*BrE*); ~ **du consommateur** V&M consumer behavior (*AmE*), consumer behaviour (*BrE*); ~ **des cours** BOURSE price behavior (*AmE*), price behaviour (*BrE*); ~ **étudié** COM affective behavior (*AmE*), affective behaviour (*BrE*); ~ **de l'homme dans l'organisation** GESTION, RES HUM, V&M organizational behavior (*AmE*), organizational behaviour (*BrE*); ~ **informatif** V&M cognitive behavior (*AmE*), cognitive behaviour (*BrE*); ~ **du marché** V&M *marketing* market behavior (*AmE*), market

behaviour (*BrE*); ~ **des ménages** ECON household behavior (*AmE*), household behaviour (*BrE*); ~ **non-conforme aux règles de la profession** RES HUM nonprofessional behavior (*AmE*), nonprofessional behaviour (*BrE*); ~ **opportuniste** ECON opportunistic behavior (*AmE*), opportunistic behaviour (*BrE*); ~ **du prix** BOURSE price behavior (*AmE*), price behaviour (*BrE*); ~ **du produit** V&M *marketing* product performance

comporter *vt* BOURSE *risque* carry, COM *comprendre* comprise, include

composant[1], **e** *adj* COM component, constituent

composant[2] *m* COM, ECON, IND, INFO component, component part; ~ **électronique** INFO electronic component; ~ **de l'impôt** FISC tax component

composante *f* COM component, component part; ~ **du capital** FIN capital component

composants: ~ **de conditionnement** *m pl* V&M packaging materials

composé: ~ **de** *loc* COM composed of; **être ~ de** *loc* COM be comprised of

composer *vt* COMMS *numéro* dial, DROIT compound

composite *adj* COM composite

composition *f* COM *structure* composition, *typographie* typesetting, INFO typesetting; ~ **de l'actif** COMPTA, FIN asset mix; ~ **axiale** COM axial composition; ~ **en devises** BANQUE currency mix; ~ **organique du capital** ECON organic composition of capital; ~ **sans plomb** ADMIN cold type; ~ **du trafic** TRANSP traffic mixture

compréhensible: ~ **par la machine** *adj* INFO machine-readable

compréhension *vt* COM understanding

comprendre *vt* COM *inclure* comprise, include, *intellectuellement* understand

compression *f* FIN cutting, INFO *de données* compression, packing, RES HUM *de salaire* compression, reduction, TRANSP compression; ~ **budgétaire** COMPTA, ECON, FIN, POL budget cut, budget cutting, budget reduction, budgetary constraint, budgetary cut; ~ **de données** INFO data compression; ~ **de fichiers** INFO file compression; ~ **des liquidités** FIN liquidity squeeze; ~ **de personnel** RES HUM downsize (*jarg*), staff cutback, staff reduction; ~ **du prix de revient** ECON, FIN cost containment

compressions: **faire des ~ de personnel** *loc* RES HUM trim the workforce

comprimé, e *adj* COM bottled-up

comprimer *vt* FIN cut, INFO *des données* compress, pack, RES HUM *personnel* compress, cut back, cut down, reduce, TRANSP compress

compris, e *adj* COM incl., included, inclusive; **tout ~** COM all told, all-inclusive, *prix* all told, all-in, all-inclusive, all-round, inclusive, V&M all-in; ◆ **y ~** COM incl., including

compromettre *vt* COM compromise, *situation* jeopardize

compromis *m* COM accommodation, composition, compromise, trade-off, DROIT *avec le créancier* composition, ECON, RES HUM trade-off; **~ d'avaries** ASSUR average bond; ♦ **faire un ~** COM, ECON trade off

comptabilisation *f* COMPTA posting; **~ en coûts standards** COM, COMPTA standard costing; **~ par processus** COMPTA, IND process costing; **~ des participations à la méthode de la mise en équivalence** COMPTA equity accounting; **~ à la valeur d'acquisition** COMPTA *investissements inter-entreprises* cost method

comptabiliser *vt* COM account for, COMPTA book, post, FIN carry; ♦ **~ au journal** COMPTA journalize

comptabilité *f* COMPTA accountancy, accy, accounting, book-keeping, FIN book-keeping; **~ analytique** COMPTA, FIN, GESTION analytic accounting, cost accounting, management accountancy, management accounting, managerial accounting; **~ analytique standardisée** COM, COMPTA, FIN standard cost accounting, standard cost system; **~ assouplie** COMPTA creative accounting; **~ budgétaire** COMPTA, FIN budgeting; **~ de caisse** COMPTA cash accounting, cash basis, cash basis of accounting, cash flow accounting; **~ des charges sociales ou comptes publics** COMPTA social accounting; **~ client** COMPTA receivable basis, receivable method; **~ consolidée** COMPTA consolidated accounting (*UK*); **~ de coûts courants** COMPTA current cost accounting, inflation accounting, CCA; **~ de coûts par produit** COMPTA product costing; **~ aux coûts de remplacement** COMPTA current cost accounting, inflation accounting, CCA; **~ créative** COMPTA creative accounting; **~ de croissance** COMPTA, ECON growth accounting; **~ démographique** ECON demographic accounting; **~ différée limitée** IMP/EXP limited postponed accounting; **~ des effets de l'inflation** COMPTA accounting for inflation; **~ d'engagements** COMPTA accrual accounting, accrual basis, accrual method; **~ d'une entreprise sans but lucratif** COMPTA non-profit accounting; **~ d'exercice** COMPTA accrual basis, accrual method; **~ financière** FIN financial accounting; **~ générale** FIN financial accounting; **~ de gestion** COMPTA, FIN financial accounting, managed account, management accountancy, management accounting, managerial accounting, GESTION management accountancy, management accounting, managerial accounting; **~ de gestion stratégique** COMPTA, FIN, GESTION managerial accounting, strategic management accounting; **~ indexée** COMPTA price level accounting; **~ indexée sur le niveau général des prix** COMPTA general price level accounting, price level accounting, GPLA; **~ industrielle** COMPTA cost accounting; **~ d'inflation** ECON inflation accounting; **~ informatisée** COMPTA, INFO computer accounting; **~ de magasin** COMPTA store accounting; **~ marginale** COMPTA, ECON, FIN marginal costing;

~ des matières COMPTA store accounting; **~ des matières premières** COMPTA materials accounting; **~ mécanographique** COMPTA machine accounting; **~ nationale** COMPTA national accounting; **~ par centres de profits** COMPTA, FIN profit center accounting (*AmE*), profit centre accounting (*BrE*); **~ par coûts historiques** COMPTA acquisition accounting; **~ par fabrication** COMPTA, IND process costing; **~ par fonds** COMPTA fund accounting; **~ en partie double** COMPTA double-entry book-keeping, double-entry accounting; **~ en partie simple** COMPTA single-entry book-keeping; **~ au prix de remplacement** COMPTA replacement cost accounting, replacement costing; **~ prudente** COMPTA conservative accounting; **~ publique** COMPTA, POL government accounting, governmental accounting; **~ des sections** FIN responsibility accounting; **~ des stocks** COMPTA store accounting; **~ de trésorerie** COMPTA cash basis of accounting, cash flow accounting, receivable basis, receivable method; **~ uniforme** COMPTA uniform accounting; **~ de la valeur actuelle** COMPTA current value accounting

comptable *mf* COM number cruncher, COMPTA, RES HUM accountant, accounting officer, AO, *d'une petite société* book-keeper; **~ adjoint** *m* COMPTA, RES HUM accounting officer, AO; **~ général agréé** *m* COMPTA certified general accountant; **~ public** *m Bel (cf agent comptable Fra)* COMPTA, FIN paymaster

comptage *m* COM counting, meter rate *(AmE)*, metre rate *(BrE)*, meterage *(AmE)*, metering; **~ de la circulation** TRANSP, V&M *publicité* traffic counts; **~ de mots** INFO word count; **~ du nombre de personnes présentes** COM head count

comptant[1] *adv* COM f/c, for cash

comptant[2] *m* COM, V&M *espèces* cash; **~ à l'expédition** TRANSP cash on shipment, cos; ♦ **au ~** BOURSE *achat, vente* spot; **~ contre documents** IMP/EXP cash against documents, CAD

compte *m* BANQUE, COM a/c, account, acct, COMPTA *calcul* a/c, account, acct, reckoning, FIN a/c, account, acct; **~ d'acceptations** BANQUE acceptance account; **~ d'achats à crédit** BANQUE, COMPTA charge account, credit account; **~ actif** BANQUE active account; **~ d'actif** COMPTA, FIN asset account; **~ d'affaires** BANQUE business account; **~ d'affectation des bénéfices** COMPTA, FIN appropriation account; **~ agence** COMPTA agency account; **~ d'agios** BOURSE, ECON agio account; **~ anonyme** BANQUE numbered account; **~ arrêté** BANQUE settlement account; **~ associé** BANQUE associated account; **~ d'assurance-chômage** RES HUM unemployment insurance account; **~ assuré** ASSUR insured account; **~ d'attente** COMPTA contra account, suspense account; **~ d'avances** BANQUE loan account, COMPTA advance account; **~ d'avances à montant fixe** COMPTA imprest account; **~ bancaire** BANQUE, COMPTA, FIN bank account, banking account; **~ bancaire en commun** BANQUE joint account, joint bank account, J/A; ~ **bancaire de ministère** ADMIN, BANQUE departmental bank account; ~ **bancaire à vue** BANQUE call account; ~ **en banque** BANQUE bank account, banking account, COMPTA bank account, FIN bank account, banking account; ~ **bloqué** BANQUE, COMPTA, FIN blocked account; ~ **de caisse** BANQUE cash account; ~ **de capital** COMPTA, ECON *balance internationale des paiements*, FIN capital account, C/A; ~ **de charges** COMPTA expense account; ~ **chèques postal** BANQUE ≈ Post Office Giro account (*UK*); ~ **-chèques rémunéré** BANQUE, BOURSE NOW Account (*US*), negotiable order of withdrawal, NOW; ~ **de clearing** ECON clearing account; ~ **client** FIN client account, customer account; ~ **clients** COMPTA, ECON, FIN book debt; ~ **clos** FIN closed account; ~ **collectif** BANQUE, BOURSE reconciliation account, COMPTA controlling account; ~ **de commission** BANQUE commission account; ~ **en commun** BANQUE joint account, joint bank account, J/A; ~ **compensatoire cumulatif** FISC cumulative offset account; ~ **au comptant** BANQUE cash account; ~ **en compte** *jarg* BOURSE long (*jarg*); ~ **conjoint** BANQUE joint account, joint bank account, J/A; ~ **de contrôle** COMPTA control account; ~ **courant** *(c/c)* BANQUE, COM, COMPTA, FIN checking account (*AmE*), current account (*BrE*) *(C/A)*; ~ **courant postal** BANQUE Post Office Giro account (*UK*), postal checking account (*US*); ~ **de courtage** BOURSE brokerage account; ~ **de couverture** BOURSE margin account; ~ **créance** COM trade debtors, COMPTA, ECON, FIN book debt, trade debtors; ~ **crédit** FIN budget account; ~ **créditeur** *(c/c)* BANQUE, COM, COMPTA, FIN above the line; ~ **débiteur** BANQUE, COMPTA debit account; ~ **à découvert** BOURSE short account; ~ **des déductions cumulatives** FISC cumulative deduction account; ~ **de dépôt** BANQUE deposit account (*UK*), D/A (*UK*); ~ **de dépôt de droits douaniers** IMP/EXP duty deposit account, DDA; ~ **de dépôt à intérêts supérieurs** BANQUE super now account; ~ **de dépôt du marché monétaire** FIN money-market deposit account (*US*), MMDA (*US*); ~ **de dépôt de titres** BANQUE custodianship account, custody account, securities account; ~ **de dépôts monétaires** BANQUE money-market savings account (*US*); ~ **en devises** BANQUE, FIN foreign exchange account; ~ **discrétionnaire** FIN discretionary account; ~ **de divers** BOURSE special miscellaneous account, SMA; ~ **de dividende en capital** *(CDC)* FISC capital dividend account *(CDA)*; ~ **double** COMPTA double account; ~ **d'épargne** BANQUE savings account, savings deposit; ~ **d'épargne en actions** *(CEA)* BOURSE equity savings account; ~ **d'épargne courant** BANQUE current savings account; ~ **d'épargne à intérêt quotidien** BANQUE daily interest savings account; ~ **d'épargne-placement** BANQUE investment savings account; ~ **d'épargne à taux bonifié** BANQUE bonus savings account, premium savings account; ~ **d'espèces** BANQUE

cash account; ~ **étranger** BANQUE *non-résident* foreign account; ~ **à l'étranger** BANQUE foreign account; ~ **d'exploitation** BANQUE, COMPTA operating account, trading account, working account; ~ **fermé** BANQUE, COMPTA closed account; ~ **fiduciaire** BANQUE fiduciary account; ~ **en fiducie** BANQUE fiduciary account, trust account; ~ **des flux financiers** ECON, FIN flow-of-funds account; ~ **en fonds propres de propriétaires de maisons** BANQUE homeowner's equity account; ~ **fournisseur** COMPTA creditor; ~ **des gains cumulatifs d'une petite entreprise** FISC cumulative small business gains account; ~ **en garantie** BANQUE assigned account; ~ **gelé** BANQUE frozen account; ~ **géré** COMPTA managed account; ~ **de gestion de fonds** FIN cash management account, CMA; ~ **de grand livre** COMPTA ledger account; ~ **hors bilan** COMPTA memo account, memorandum account; ~ **d'immobilisations** BANQUE capital account, capital asset account; ~ **inactif** BANQUE dead account, dormant account, inactive account; ~ **d'indemnisation d'acheteurs de titres de placement** BANQUE investors' indemnity account; ~ **insuffisamment débité** BANQUE undercharged account; ~ **à intérêt quotidien** BANQUE daily interest account; ~ **d'intermédiaire** BOURSE nominee account; ~ **d'investissement de la Caisse d'épargne** BANQUE National Savings investment account (*UK*); ~ **d'investissement national d'épargne** BANQUE National Savings investment account (*UK*); ~ **joint** BANQUE joint account, joint bank account, J/A; ~ **limité** BOURSE restricted account; ~ **maison** BOURSE house account; ~ **de mandataire** COMPTA a/c, account current; ~ **à marge** BOURSE margin account, undermargined account; ~ **de marge en débit** BOURSE restricted account; ~ **à marge insuffisante** BOURSE undermargined account; ~ **marginal** BANQUE marginal account; ~ **pour mémoire** COMPTA memo account, memorandum account; ~ **de ministère** ADMIN departmental account; ~ **de mise en main tierce** BANQUE escrow account; ~ **mixte** BOURSE mixed account; ~ **de non-résident** BANQUE, ECON, POL external account; ~ **nostro** BANQUE nostro account; ~ **numérique** BANQUE numbered account; ~ **omnibus** BANQUE catch-all account; ~ **d'opérations de change** BANQUE, FIN foreign exchange account; ~ **d'options** FIN option account; ~ **ordinaire** BANQUE ordinary account; ~ **ouvert** COM open account, open credit; ~ **particulier** BANQUE, COMPTA, FIN private account; ~ **de péréquation des impôts** FISC tax equalization account; ~ **de pertes et profits** COMPTA P&L account, income statement, profit and loss account, profit and loss statement; ~ **de placement** BANQUE delta stock, investment account; ~ **de position** BOURSE position account; ~ **à préavis** BANQUE notice account; ~ **de prêt hypothécaire** BANQUE mortgage account; ~ **prête-nom** BOURSE nominee account; ~ **de prêts** BANQUE loan account; ~ **prévisionnel**

d'exploitation FIN estimated trading account; **~ de recettes en fiducie** FIN revenue trust account; **~ de régularisation** BANQUE accruals, COMPTA accruals, accrued receivable and pre-paid expenses, contra account, *comptabilité d'engagements* adjustment account, FIN accruals; **~ de remise non soldé** BANQUE remittance account; **~ -rendu** COM debriefing, report, DROIT *d'une séance* minutes, POL position paper; **~ -rendu de conférence** V&M conference report; **~ -rendu de contact** V&M contact report; **~ -rendu de l'impact environnemental** DROIT, ENVIR environmental impact statement; **~ -rendu non-négociable** COM non-negotiable report of findings, NNRF; **~ -rendu des opérations de consignation** COMPTA account sales, A/S; **~ -rendu de passif net** BANQUE exposed net liability position; **~ -rendu de réunion** V&M call report; **~ -rendu de séance** DROIT minutes; **~ -rendu sur l'état d'avancement des travaux** COM progress report; **~ de réserve** BANQUE reserve account; **~ de résultat** COMPTA income statement, operating statement, profit and loss account, profit and loss statement; **~ de résultats en liste** COMPTA vertical profit and loss account format; **~ de retenues sur la paie** COMPTA payroll deductions account; **~ de retour** BANQUE banker's ticket; **~ de retraite individuel au nom de l'épouse** BANQUE spousal ira *(frml)*; **~ de retraits** BANQUE drawing account; **~ sans privilège de chèques** BANQUE noncheckable account *(AmE)*, nonchequable account *(BrE)*; **~ sans ségrégation** *(SYN compte à titulaire non-désigné)* BOURSE nonsegregated account; **~ sans tirage de chèques** BANQUE noncheckable account *(AmE)*, nonchequable account *(BrE)*; **~ soldé** FIN closed account; **~ à solde nul** BANQUE zero-balance account, BOURSE matched book; **~ sous-débité** BANQUE undercharged account; **~ de souscripteur** ASSUR u/a, underwriting account; **~ spécial d'arbitrage** BOURSE special arbitrage account; **~ spécial d'épargne exonéré d'impôts** BANQUE, ECON, FISC tax-exempt special savings account *(UK)*, TESSA *(UK)*; **~ sur livret** BANQUE deposit account *(UK)*, D/A *(UK)*; **~ de survie** BANQUE survivorship account; **~ en T** BANQUE, COMPTA T-account; **~ en tandem** BANQUE tandem account; **~ à titulaire non-désigné** *(SYN compte sans ségrégation)* BOURSE nonsegregated account; **~ de ventes** V&M sales account; **~ de virement** BANQUE transfer account; **~ vostro** BANQUE vostro account; **~ à vue** BANQUE demand account; ◆ **au ~ de** COM to the order of; **avoir son ~ bancaire à** BANQUE bank with; **faire mettre qch sur le ~ de qn** BANQUE charge sth to sb's account; **pour ~** COM on account; **pour le ~ de** BANQUE, COM, COMPTA, FIN account of, AO

compter *vt* COM, INFO, MATH count, count up, reckon, reckon up; ◆ **à ~ de** COM *(à/c)* after date *(A/D)*, COMPTA reckoning by; **~ comme per-**

sonne à charge FISC claim as a dependant; **~ sur** COM depend on, rely on

comptes *m pl* FIN *d'une société* accounting year then ended; **~ analytiques** COMPTA, FIN, GESTION management accounts; **~ annuels** COM, COMPTA, FIN annual accounts; **~ annuels abrégés** COMPTA limited annual statements; **~ de bilan** COMPTA permanent account; **~ du budget** COMPTA, ECON, FIN budgetary accounts; **~ certifiés** COMPTA certified accounts; **~ clients** COMPTA, ECON accounts receivable, debtors, receivables, trade accounts receivable, trade creditors, trade receivables; **~ commerciaux** COMPTA commercial accounts; **~ consolidés** COMPTA consolidated accounts, group accounts; **~ créditeurs** COMPTA, ECON accounts payable; **~ débiteurs** COMPTA, ECON trade accounts receivable, trade receivables; **~ de dépôt et de fiducie** BANQUE deposit and trust accounts; **~ de divers** COMPTA sundry accounts; **~ d'entreprise individuelle** COMPTA individual company accounts; **~ de l'état** COMPTA public accounts; **~ de fin d'exercice** COMPTA final accounts; **~ à fins déterminées** *Canada* COMPTA, POL specified-purpose accounts *(Canada)*; **~ fournisseurs** COM trade accounts payable *(AmE)*, COMPTA, ECON accounts payable, trade accounts payable *(AmE)*; **~ frappés d'imposition** COMPTA, FISC tax-assessed accounts; **~ de groupe** COMPTA group accounts; **~ légales** COMPTA statutory accounts; **~ de mi-année** COMPTA interim accounts; **~ à payer à la fin de l'exercice** *(CAPAFE)* COMPTA Payables at Year-End *(AmE)* *(PAYE)*; **~ de pension de retraite** ASSUR, COMPTA, FIN superannuation accounts; **~ publics** COMPTA public accounts; **~ de recettes et dépenses** COMPTA income accounts; **~ de résultats** COMPTA P&L account, statement of income *(US)*; **~ de revenu et de produits nationaux** ECON National Income and Product Accounts, NIPA; **~ semestriels** COMPTA interim accounts; **~ sociaux** COM, COMPTA, FIN annual accounts, company accounts, individual company accounts, statutory account; **~ sociaux audités** COMPTA individual company audited accounts; **~ spéciaux** COMPTA special accounts; **~ statutaires** COMPTA statutory accounts; **~ de trésorerie et opérations interbancaires** BANQUE *bilan* Treasury and interbank operations; **~ vérifiés consolidés** COMPTA consolidated audited accounts; **~ vérifiés d'entreprise individuelle** COMPTA individual company audited accounts

compteur *m* COM meter *(AmE)*, metre *(BrE)*; **~ additif** INFO adding counter

comptoir *m* BANQUE, COM *magasin* counter; **~ de liquidation** BOURSE clearing house

comté *m* COM ≈ county *(UK)*

Conakry *n pr* COM Conakry

concaténation *f* INFO concatenation

concédant, e *m, f* IMMOB, DROIT grantor

concentration *f* ECON concentration, GESTION agglomeration, IND concentration; **~ absolue**

ECON absolute concentration; ~ **complète** COM aggregate concentration; ~ **globale** COM aggregate concentration; ~ **horizontale** (ANT *concentration verticale*) COM, ECON horizontal business combination; ~ **industrielle** IND concentration of industry, industrial concentration; ~ **du marché** ECON market concentration; ~ **maximale admissible** ENVIR occupational MAC, occupational maximum allowable concentration, occupational TLV, occupational threshold limit value; ~ **de métaux lourds** ENVIR heavy metal concentration; ~ **relative** MATH relative concentration; ~ **tripartite** RES HUM tripartism; ~ **verticale** (ANT *concentration horizontale*) COM, ECON vertical business combination

concentrer 1. *vt* COM concentrate, focus; **2.** *v pron* **se ~ sur** COM concentrate on, concentrate upon, focus on, focus upon; ◆ **~ son attention sur** COM concentrate one's attention on, focus one's attention on

concept *m* COM concept; ~ **de base** COM basic concept; ~ **du client séparé** BOURSE separate customer; ~ **d'écoulement** BOURSE flow concept; ~ **marketing** V&M marketing concept; ~ **publicitaire** V&M advertising concept; ~ **des styles de vie** V&M *marketing* lifestyle concept; ~ **de valeur** FIN value concept

concepteur *m* COM, V&M ideas man; ~ **de moteurs** RES HUM *maritimes* engine designer; ~ **-rédacteur** V&M *publicité* copywriter; ~ **sur papier** ADMIN desk planner

conception¹ *f* COM *formation d'une idée* design, V&M *publicité* copywriting; ~ **assistée par ordinateur** (*CAO*) IND, INFO computer-aided design (*CAD*), computer-assisted design (*CAD*), design automation (*D/A*); ~ **de base** COM basic concept; ~ **de l'emballage** V&M *étude de marché* package design; ~ **de l'enfant total** PROT SOC whole-child concept (*jarg*); ~ **et fabrication assistées par ordinateur** (*CFAO*) IND, INFO computer-aided design and computer-aided manufacturing, computer-assisted design and computer-assisted manufacturing (*CAD/CAM*); ~ **globale** PROT SOC unitary approach; ~ **graphique** V&M *publicité* graphic design; ~ **d'un paquet promotionnel** V&M *publipostage* package design; ~ **de produit** V&M product conception, product design; ~ **de programmes assistée par ordinateur** (*CPAO*) INFO computer-aided software engineering, computer-assisted software engineering (*CASE*); ~ **de système** INFO computer design, system design; ~ **de tâche** RES HUM job design; ◆ **de ~ ergonomique** INFO ergonomically-designed

conception² : ~ **et agencement** *m pl* V&M *d'un grand magasin* design and layout; ~ **et dessin assistés par ordinateur** *m pl* IND, INFO computer-aided design and drafting, computer-assisted design and drafting, CADD

conceptrice *f* COM, V&M ideas woman

concernant *prép* COM about, concerning, re, reference, regarding, with reference to, with regard to, with respect to

concerne: **en ce qui ~** *loc* COM about, concerning, re, reference, regarding, with reference to, with regard to, with respect to; **en ce qui ~ votre lettre** *loc* COMMS with reference to your letter

concession *f* BOURSE *action, droit concédé*, COM *action, droit concédé* concession, DROIT *action* concession, grant, granting, licence (*BrE*), license (*AmE*), V&M concession; ~ **de crédit** BANQUE credit granting, granting of credit; ~ **d'exploitation** TRANSP operation lease; ~ **gazière et pétrolière** DROIT, IND oil and gas lease; ~ **réciproque de licences** COM, DROIT cross licensing; ~ **de vente** BOURSE selling concession; ◆ **de ~** COM concessional

concessionnaire¹ *adj* COM concessionary

concessionnaire² *mf* COM agency, concessionaire, concessionary, concessioner, dealer, *d'une marque de voitures* agent, dealer; ~ **exclusif** *m* COM sole agent; ~ **d'une licence** *m* BREVETS, DROIT licensee; ◆ **être ~** COM *dans une grande surface* run a concession

concessions: ~ **mineures** *f pl* COM, POL small change (*infrml*); ~ **mutuelles** *f pl* COM, RES HUM trade-off

concevoir *vt* COM *idée, plan* conceive; ◆ **~ l'inconcevable** COM think the unthinkable

conciliateur, -trice *m,f* RES HUM conciliation officer, conciliator; ~ **unique** RES HUM single arbitrator

conciliation *f* COM, DROIT, RES HUM conciliation; ~ **collective** RES HUM collective conciliation; ~ **privée** RES HUM individual conciliation; ~ **prud'homale** RES HUM grievance arbitration; ~ **volontaire** RES HUM voluntary arbitration

concilier *vt* COM, DROIT *des intérêts opposés*, RES HUM conciliate

concluant, e *adj* COM, DROIT conclusive, decisive

conclure 1. *vt* COM *accord* reach, *contrat, transaction* conclude, finalize, wrap up (*infrml*), *terminer* end, finish, *vente* close, make, FIN pull off, V&M *accord* reach, *contrat, transaction* conclude, finalize, wrap up (*infrml*), *vente* close, make; **2.** *v pron* **se ~** COM come to an end; ◆ **~ une affaire** BOURSE make a market, COM, V&M clinch a deal, reach a deal, strike a bargain, strike a deal; ~ **un marché** COM, V&M *avec qc* clinch a deal, make a deal, pull off a deal, reach a deal, strike a bargain, strike a deal; ~ **sa plaidoirie** DROIT rest one's case; ~ **son plaidoyer** DROIT rest one's case

conclusion *f* COM conclusion, DROIT *d'un tribunal* finding, IMMOB closing; ~ **de vente immobilière** IMMOB real estate closing (*AmE*)

conclusions *f pl* DROIT *d'un tribunal* findings, *d'un document* wherefore clauses; ~ **nettes** TRANSP clean report of findings

concomitant, e *adj* COM collateral, concomitant

concordance *f* COMPTA account reconciliation,

reconciliation, reconciliation of accounts; ~ **bancaire** COMPTA bank reconciliation

concordat *m* DROIT legal settlement, *d'une banqueroute* winding-up arrangements; ~ **incendie risque** ASSUR fire insuring agreement (*US*); ~ **judiciaire** DROIT legal settlement

concorder *vi* COM *chiffres*, COMPTA *chiffres* agree, be in agreement; ◆ **ne pas** ~ COM be at variance

concourir *vi* COM compete, DROIT concur, ECON, V&M compete

concours *m* COM *circonstance* conjunction, *compétition* contest, *coopération* cooperation, support; ~ **à court terme** BANQUE short-term advance

concret, -ète *adj* COM concrete, hard

concrétiser 1. *vt* COM consolidate; **2.** *v pron* **se** ~ COM *projet* eventuate, materialize, take shape

concubin, e *m,f* DROIT common-law spouse

concubinage *m* DROIT common-law marriage

concurrence *f* BREVETS, COM, ECON, IND, RES HUM, V&M competition; ~ **acharnée** COM, ECON, IND, RES HUM, V&M bitter competition, cutthroat competition, predatory competition; ~ **atomistique** (SYN *concurrence parfaite*) ECON, V&M atomistic competition; ~ **déloyale** (ANT *concurrence loyale*) BREVETS, COM, DROIT, ECON, IND, V&M unfair competition; ~ **destructive** ECON destructive competition; ~ **entre le secteur primaire et secondaire** ECON, IND interindustry competition; ~ **féroce** COM, ECON, IND, RES HUM, V&M bitter competition, cutthroat competition, predatory competition; ~ **imparfaite** (ANT *concurrence parfaite*) ECON, V&M imperfect competition; ~ **inter-industries** ECON, IND interindustry competition; ~ **libre** COM, ECON, V&M arm's-length competition, free competition; ~ **loyale** (ANT *concurrence déloyale*) BREVETS, COM, DROIT, ECON, IND, V&M fair competition; ~ **monopolistique** ECON monopolistic competition; ~ **parfaite** (ANT *concurrence imparfaite*) ECON, V&M perfect competition; ~ **pure** ECON pure competition; ~ **sauvage** COM, ECON, IND, RES HUM, V&M bitter competition, cutthroat competition, destructive competition, predatory competition; ◆ **en** ~ **étroite** COM, ECON, V&M in close competition; **être en** ~ COM be in competition, compete, ECON, V&M be in competition, compete, compete with; **être en** ~ **avec** COM be in competition with, compete against, compete with, ECON be in competition with, compete against, V&M compete against

concurrencer *vt* COM, ECON, V&M compete against, compete with

concurrent, e *m,f* COM, ECON, V&M competitor; ~ **dangereux** COM, ECON, V&M tough competitor; ~ **étranger** COM, ECON, V&M foreign competitor; ◆ **être** ~**s** COM, ECON compete, V&M be competitors, compete

concurrentiel, -elle *adj* COM, ECON, V&M competitive; **très** ~ COM, ECON, V&M highly competitive

concussion *f* DROIT graft (*infrml*), misappropriation

condamnation *f* COM *reproche* condemnation, DROIT *au tribunal* sentence, *inculpation* conviction, IMMOB *d'une porte, d'une voie* condemnation

condamner *vt* COM *reprocher* condemn, DROIT *au tribunal* sentence, *inculper* convict, IMMOB *porte, voie* condemn; ◆ ~ **qn à une amende** DROIT fine sb, impose a fine on sb

condition *f* COM qualification, *état* condition, DROIT *stipulation* condition, term; ~ **d'admissibilité** COM eligibility requirement; ~ **de conversion d'assurance-vie** ASSUR convertible term life insurance (*US*); ~ **d'éligibilité** COM, RES HUM eligibility requirement; ~ **expresse** COM express condition; ~ **légale requise** DROIT legal requirement; ~ **d'obtention d'une licence** IMP/EXP licensing requirement; ~ **au plus haut** BANQUE topping-up clause; ~ **préalable** COM prerequisite; ~ **de résidence** FISC residence status; ~ **résolutoire** DROIT condition subsequent (*US*), resolutory condition; ~ **suspensive** DROIT condition precedent (*US*), suspensive condition; ~ **tacite** COM implied condition, DROIT *d'un contrat* implied term; ◆ **à** ~ **de** COM on condition that, providing that; **à la** ~ **expresse que** COM on the stipulation that; **à** ~ **que** COM on condition that, provided that, providing that; ~ **sine qua non** COM causa sine qua non (*frml*)

conditionnel: ~ **ou non** *loc* FISC absolutely or contingently

conditionnement *m* TRANSP *action, matériaux d'emballage*, V&M packaging, packing, pkg.; ~ **d'air** ADMIN, COM, PROT SOC air conditioning; ~ **en gros** TRANSP, V&M bulk package; ~ **en métal** ENVIR, V&M metal packaging; ~ **sous vide** V&M vacuum packaging; ~ **en vrac** TRANSP, V&M bulk package

conditions *f pl* DROIT *d'un contrat* conditions, terms, ECON *du marché*, V&M *du marché* conditions; ~ **ambiantes** ENVIR environmental conditions; ~ **antagonistes de la distribution** POL antagonistic conditions of distribution; ~ **bancaires** BANQUE bank requirements; ~ **de banque** BANQUE bank requirements; ~ **de carburant** TRANSP ft, fuel terms; ~ **commerciales** COM, ECON business conditions; ~ **commerciales d'échanges compensés nets** ECON, IMP/EXP net barter terms of trade; ~ **complémentaires** ASSUR additional conditions; ~ **contractuelles** TRANSP conditions of contract; ~ **d'un contrat** TRANSP conditions of contract; ~ **convenues** COM private terms; ~ **de crédit** BANQUE, ECON, FIN, V&M credit conditions, credit requirements, terms of credit; ~ **de déclaration** FISC reporting requirements; ~ **défavorables pour le commerce** ECON adverse trading conditions, unfavorable trading conditions (*AmE*), unfavourable trading conditions (*BrE*); ~ **économiques** COM, ECON, POL economic conditions; ~ **économiques favorables** ECON favorable economic conditions (*AmE*), favourable economic conditions (*BrE*); ~ **d'embauche** RES HUM conditions of employment; ~ **d'émission d'une obligation** BOURSE bond terms; ~ **d'envoi** IMP/EXP, TRANSP terms of shipment; ~ **européennes** ECON, POL European terms; ~ **de faveur** COM concessional terms; ~ **hypothétiques** COM hypothetical conditions; ~ **implicites** RES HUM implied terms; ~ **intéressantes** COM attractive terms; ~ **des lignes régulières** TRANSP *maritime, taux de fret* liner terms; ~ **de livraison des marchandises** TRANSP cargo delivery terms; ~ **de livraison de la vente** IMP/EXP delivery terms of sale; ~ **nécessaires pour concourir** COM bidding requirements; ~ **normales** COM normal conditions; ~ **de l'offre** COM conditions of tender, terms of tender; ~ **de paiement** BANQUE terms of payment; ~ **de pleine concurrence** COM arm's-length competition; ~ **de règlement** FIN settlement discount; ~ **requises au listage** BOURSE listing requirements; ~ **de soumission** COM conditions of tender, terms of tender; ~ **spéciales** COM *prix* special terms; ~ **supplémentaires** ASSUR additional conditions; ~ **sur les frais du poste** TRANSP *maritime* berth terms; ~ **de transport** TRANSP conditions of carriage; ~ **de travail** RES HUM working conditions; ~ **d'utilisation** COM conditions of use; ~ **de vente** COM, ECON, IMP/EXP, V&M conditions of sale, terms of sale, trade terms; ~ **de vente à l'exportation** IMP/EXP terms of export sale; ~ **de vie** PROT SOC living conditions; ♦ **aux** ~ **américaines** ECON in American terms; **aux** ~ **habituelles** COM on the usual terms

conducteur, -trice *m,f* COM driver; ~ **de camion** TRANSP lorry driver (*BrE*), teamster (*AmE*), truck driver (*AmE*), trucker (*AmE*); ~ **de travaux** RES HUM *sur un chantier de construction* clerk of works

conduire *vt* COM *entreprise* conduct, manage, run, RES HUM conduct

conduite *f* COM conduct, *d'une entreprise* management, managing, running, supervision, RES HUM conduct; ~ **contraire au code professionnel** COM unprofessional conduct; ~ **à un seul agent** TRANSP single manning

cône *m* TRANSP locator; ~ **d'empilage** TRANSP *fixation des conteneurs* pinlock; ~ **d'empilage réversible** TRANSP reversible stacking cone

confection *f* IND *industrie des vêtements* clothing business, clothing industry, rag trade (*infrml*), *production* making

confectionné, e *adj* COM, IND made, made up

confectionner *vt* COM, IND make, make up

confédération *f* POL confederation

Confédération: ~ **générale du travail** *f* (*CGT*) RES HUM ≈ Congress of Industrial Organizations (*US*) (*CIO*) ≈ *Trades Union Congress* (*UK*) (*TUC*); ~ **syndicale européenne** *f* RES HUM European Trade Union Confederation, ETUC

conférence *f* GESTION conference; ~ **annuelle de la force de vente** GESTION, V&M annual sales conference; ~ **de Bretton Woods** ECON, POL Bretton Woods Conference; ~ **de harmonisation** TRANSP harmonization conference; ~ **maritime** COM conference system, TRANSP conference line, liner conference; ~ **nord-atlantique** TRANSP North Atlantic Conference, NAC; ~ **de presse** MÉDIA news conference, press conference; ~ **au sommet** COM, POL summit conference; ~ **téléphonique** COMMS conference call, three-way call; ♦ **faire une** ~ PROT SOC deliver a lecture

Conférence: ~ **mondiale administrative radio-maritime** *f* TRANSP World Maritime Administrative Radio Conference, WMARC; ~ **mondiale sur l'énergie** *f* ENVIR World Power Conference; ~ **des Nations Unies sur le commerce et le développement** *f* (*CNUCED*) ECON United Nations Conference on Trade and Development (*UNCTAD*); ~ **des Nations Unies sur l'environnement et le développement** *f* (*CNUED*) COM, ENVIR United Nations Conference on Environment and Development (*UNCED*)

conférencier, -ière *m,f* COM lecturer, speaker

conférer *vt* COM *privilège*, DROIT *droit*, PROT SOC *diplôme* confer; ♦ ~ **à** BOURSE vest; ~ **un privilège à qn** COM confer a privilege on sb

confiance *f* COM confidence, reliance, trust, MATH confidence; ~ **de la clientèle** V&M *dans les produits* customer confidence; ~ **du marché** BOURSE market confidence

confidentialité *f* DROIT, FISC confidentiality; ~ **des données** INFO data privacy (*BrE*), data security (*AmE*)

confidentiel, -elle *adj* COM, DROIT, FISC confidential

confier *vt* DROIT place in trust; ~ **une cause à** DROIT brief; ♦ ~ **qch à qn** COM *dire* confide sth to sb, tell sb sth in confidence, *donner* entrust sb with sth

config *abrév* (*configuration*) INFO config (*configuration*)

configuration *f* (*config*) INFO arrangement, configuration (*config*), pattern; ~ **de base** INFO base configuration; ~ **binaire** INFO bit configuration; ~ **du chargement** TRANSP cargo configuration; ~ **matérielle** INFO computer environment, hardware configuration, hardware requirements; ~ **nécessaire** INFO system requirements

configurer *vt* INFO configure, set up

confirmation *f* COM *d'une commande* acknowledgement, ACK, *d'un projet* confirmation, DROIT confirmation, recognition; ~ **d'une commande** COM, V&M confirmation of order; ~ **d'un ordre** COM, V&M confirmation of order; ~ **positive** COMPTA positive confirmation; ~ **de renouvellement** ASSUR confirmation of renewal; ~ **de réservation** COM, TRANSP booking confirmation, reservation form

confirmer 1. *vt* COM *vérifier* confirm, DROIT *verdict* uphold; **2.** *v pron* **se** ~ COM *rumeur* be confirmed

confirmez: ~ **par télex SVP** *loc* COMMS please telex your confirmation

confiscation *f* COM confiscation, DROIT impounding

confisquer *vt* COM confiscate, DROIT impound

conflit *m* COM, POL, RES HUM conflict, dispute; ~ **de compétence** RES HUM jurisdiction dispute; ~ **des générations** PROT SOC generation gap; ~ **d'identité** RES HUM demarcation dispute (*UK*); ~ **d'intérêts** COM conflict of interest; ~ **intersyndical** RES HUM interunion dispute; ~ **de loi** DROIT *droit international* conflict of law; ~ **social** ECON industrial conflict, industrial dispute, RES HUM industrial conflict, industrial dispute, industrial strife; ~ **du travail** ECON, RES HUM industrial conflict, industrial dispute, labor dispute (*AmE*), labour dispute (*BrE*), trade dispute; ◆ **en** ~ RES HUM in dispute

conforme: ~ **à** *loc* COM congruent with, in accordance with, in line with; ~ **à l'échantillon** *loc* COM true to sample, up-to-sample

conformément: ~ **à** *loc* COM according to, in accordance with, in conformity with, COMPTA in conformity with, DROIT *réglementation en vigueur* in compliance with; ~ **à l'article 120** *loc* DROIT pursuant to article 120; ~ **à la loi** *loc* DROIT by law; ~ **à la norme** *loc* DROIT according to the norm; ~ **au programme** *loc frml* ADMIN, COM as scheduled; ~ **à vos instructions** *loc* COM in accordance with your instructions

conformer 1. *vt* COM agree; **2.** *v pron* **se** ~ **à** COM act on, conform to, *règle, décision* abide by, DROIT *accord, décision, règlement* abide by, comply with, conform to, obey; ◆ ~ **les écritures** COM, COMPTA agree the books

conformité *f* COM compliance, conformity, congruence, DROIT compliance; ~ **au contrat** DROIT, RES HUM contract compliance; ~ **aux normes de la C.E** IND *normes de sécurité pour jouets* EC-mark; ◆ **être en** ~ **avec** COM be in compliance with, conform to

confrère *m* RES HUM colleague

confrontation *f* COM confrontation

confronter *vt* COM confront

congé *m* COM, LOISIRS, RES HUM holiday (*BrE*), leave, vacation (*AmE*), TRANSP *de navigation* sea letter; ~ **annuel** RES HUM annual holiday (*BrE*), annual leave, annual vacation (*AmE*), holiday leave; ~ **pour fonctions syndicales** RES HUM union leave; ~ **de formation rémunéré** PROT SOC, RES HUM day release; ~ **de maladie** PROT SOC, RES HUM sick leave; ~ **de maternité** PROT SOC, RES HUM maternity leave; ~ **de navigation** TRANSP sea letter; ~ **parental** PROT SOC, RES HUM parental leave, paternity leave; ~ **de récupération** RES HUM compensatory time; ~ **spécial** COM, RES HUM leave of absence; ◆ **en** ~ **du parti** POL off the reservation (*AmE, jarg*)

congédier *vt* COM pay off

congés: ~ **payés** *m pl* RES HUM holiday pay (*BrE*), holidays with pay (*BrE*), paid holiday (*BrE*), paid leave, paid vacation (*AmE*), vacation pay (*AmE*), vacation with pay (*AmE*)

conglomérat *m* ECON, FIN conglomerate; ~ **financier** FIN financial conglomerate; ~ **industriel japonais** ECON, IND zaibatsu

Congo *m* COM Congo

congolais, e *adj* COM Congolese

Congolais, e *m,f* COM *habitant* Congolese

congrès *m* GESTION, POL conference, congress, convention; ~ **commercial** COM business convention

Congrès *m* POL Congress (*US*); ~ **national des syndicats** RES HUM national trade union council (*UK*), NTUC (*UK*); ◆ **du** ~ POL Congressional (*US*)

congressiste *mf* GESTION, POL conference delegate, conference member, convention participant

conjecturer *vt* ECON conjecture, speculate

conjoint[1], **e** *adj* DROIT, FISC joint

conjoint[2], **e** *m,f* DROIT, FISC spouse; ~ **divorcé** DROIT divorced spouse; ~ **de fait** DROIT common-law spouse; ~ **au foyer** PROT SOC, RES HUM nonworking spouse; ~ **survivant** FISC surviving spouse

conjointement *adv* FISC jointly; ~ **et solidairement** COM, DROIT jointly and severally; ◆ ~ **avec** COM, DROIT in conjunction with; ~ **et solidairement responsable de** COM, DROIT jointly and severally liable for

conjoncture *f* COM, ECON, POL business conditions, business environment, business outlook, business trend, current economic trend, economic climate, economic conditions; ~ **actuelle** COM, ECON, POL business conditions, business environment, business outlook, business trend, current economic trend, economic climate, economic conditions; ~ **économique** COM, ECON business situation, economic trend; ~ **favorable** ECON current economic trend, favorable business conditions (*AmE*), favorable business outlook (*AmE*), favorable economic conditions (*AmE*), favourable business conditions (*BrE*), favourable business outlook (*BrE*), favourable economic conditions (*BrE*); ~ **du marché** COM, V&M market conditions; ~ **mondiale** ECON shape of the world economy; ~ **politique** COM, POL political business cycle, political climate

conjoncturel, -elle *adj* ECON *policy* anticyclical

conjoncturiste *mf* BOURSE chartist, economic analyst, market analyst, RES HUM, V&M economic analyst, market analyst

connaissance *f* COM knowledge, *personne* acquaintance, GESTION cognition; ~ **des coûts** COM, V&M cost awareness; ~ **figée** IND *production* locked-in knowledge; ~ **de la fiscalité** FISC taxmanship; ~ **d'office** DROIT judicial notice; ~ **présumée des faits** DROIT constructive notice (*US*); ~ **du produit** V&M product knowledge; ~ **subtile** COM *d'un élément du problème* acute awareness; ◆ **faire la ~ de qn** COM make sb's acquaintance

connaissances: ~ **en informatique** *f pl* INFO computer knowledge, computer literacy; ~ **techniques non-transférables** *f pl* ECON locked-in knowledge, tacit knowledge; ~ **techniques non-transposables** *f pl* ECON locked-in knowledge, tacit knowledge; ◆ **avoir de bonnes ~ de** PROT SOC have a working knowledge of; **ayant des ~ en informatique** INFO computer literate, computerate

connaissement *m (connt)* IMP/EXP, TRANSP bill of lading *(B/L)*; ~ **abrégé** *(ANT connaissement intégral)* IMP/EXP, TRANSP short form, short form bill of lading; ~ **ad valorem** IMP/EXP, TRANSP ad valorem bill of lading; ~ **avec réserves** IMP/EXP, TRANSP *maritime* claused bill of lading, dirty bill, dirty bill of lading, foul bill of lading; ~ **brut** IMP/EXP, TRANSP *maritime* claused bill of lading, dirty bill, dirty bill of lading, foul bill of lading; ~ **charte-partie** IMP/EXP, TRANSP *maritime* C/P bill of lading, charter party bill of lading; ~ **clausé** IMP/EXP, TRANSP *maritime* claused bill of lading, dirty bill, dirty bill of lading, foul bill of lading; ~ **délivré à un tiers désigné** IMP/EXP, TRANSP bill of lading issued to a named party; ~ **direct** IMP/EXP, TRANSP *maritime* direct bill of lading, through bill of lading; ~ **embarqué** IMP/EXP, TRANSP *maritime* shipped bill, shipped bill of lading; ~ **d'entrée** IMP/EXP, TRANSP inward bill of lading; ~ **de l'expéditeur** IMP/EXP, TRANSP forwarder's bill of lading; ~ **de groupage** IMP/EXP, TRANSP groupage bill of lading, house bill, house bill of lading, GBL; ~ **intégral** *(ANT connaissement abrégé)* IMP/EXP, TRANSP long form; ~ **manquant** IMP/EXP, TRANSP *maritime* missing bill of lading, mslb; ~ **minimum** IMP/EXP, TRANSP min. B/L, minimum bill of lading; ~ **négociable** IMP/EXP, TRANSP negotiable bill of lading; ~ **net** IMP/EXP, TRANSP clean b/l, clean bill of lading; ~ **nominatif** IMP/EXP, TRANSP *maritime* straight bill of lading; ~ **non-négociable** IMP/EXP, TRANSP *maritime* non-negotiable bill of lading; ~ **à ordre** IMP/EXP, TRANSP ocean bill of lading, order bill of lading; ~ **périmé** IMP/EXP, TRANSP stale bill of lading; ~ **à personne désignée** IMP/EXP, TRANSP *maritime* straight bill of lading; ~ **public** IMP/EXP, TRANSP *maritime* government bill of lading, GBL; ~ **reçu pour embarquement** IMP/EXP, TRANSP *maritime* container bill, received-for-shipment bill of lading; ~ **reçu à quai** IMP/EXP, TRANSP alongside bill of lading; ~ **sans réserves** IMP/EXP, TRANSP clean b/l, clean bill of lading; ~ **shortform** IMP/EXP, TRANSP short form, short form bill of lading; ~ **sur le pont** IMP/EXP on deck bill of lading, TRANSP *maritime* on-deck bill of lading; ~ **de transbordement** IMP/EXP, TRANSP *maritime* transhipment bill of lading, transshipment bill of lading; ~ **du transitaire** IMP/EXP, TRANSP forwarding agent's bill of lading; ~ **de transport combiné** IMP/EXP, TRANSP combined

transport bill of lading, CTBL; ~ **de transport combiné du transitaire** IMP/EXP, TRANSP forwarder's certificate of transport, freight forwarder's combined transport bill of lading, FCT

connaître *vt* COM experience, *personne* be acquainted with, know; ◆ ~ **une croissance rapide** ECON experience rapid growth; **faire ~** COM *détails* announce, *opinions* air

connecté, e *adj (ANT non-connecté)* COM on-line, INFO *à l'ordinateur* active, on, on-line; ◆ **être ~** COM, INFO interface; **être ~ à** COM, INFO interface with

connecter 1. *vt* COM, INFO attach, connect, hook, hook up, interface, link, *brancher* plug in; **2.** *v pron* **se ~** INFO *composant, élément* attach, *personne* log in, log on

connexion *f* INFO *fiche* attachment, plug

connt *abrév (connaissement)* IMP/EXP, TRANSP B/L *(bill of lading)*

connu, e *adj* COM known; ◆ **aussi ~ sous le nom de** COM a.k.a., also known as; ~ **de nom** COM known by name

consacrer *vt* COM, GESTION *du temps* allot, commit, devote, give

conscience *f* COM consciousness; ~ **des coûts** COM cost consciousness; ~ **du marché** V&M market awareness; ◆ **faire prendre ~ de** ENVIR raise awareness of

conscient, e *adj* COM aware

consécration *f* IMMOB *d'un édifice* dedication

consécutif, -ive *adj* COM consecutive, subsequent; ◆ ~ **à** COM successive

conseil *m* ADMIN *expertise* consultancy, consultancy work, COM *avis* hint, piece of advice, tip, word of advice, *expertise* consultancy, consultancy work, *réunion* board, committee, council, COMPTA *personne* adviser, advisor, consultant, DROIT *avec avocat* counsel, csl, GESTION *expertise* consultancy, consultancy work, *personne* adviser, advisor, consultant, *réunion* board, committee, council, INFO *personne* adviser, advisor, consultant, RES HUM *expertise* consultancy, consultancy work, *personne* adviser, advisor, consultant, *réunion* board, committee, council; ~ **d'administration** *(CA)* ADMIN, COM, GESTION, RES HUM *d'une société* administrative board, board of directors, directorate, executive board, *d'une organisation internationale* governing board; ~ **d'administration indépendant** DROIT interlocking directorate; ~ **d'administration tournant** ADMIN, COM, GESTION, RES HUM staggered board of directors; ~ **d'arbitrage** BOURSE, RES HUM board of arbitration, conciliation board; ~ **arbitral** BOURSE board of arbitration; ~ **en business plan** COM, GESTION business plan consulting; ~ **du développement commercial** ECON trade development board, TDB; ~ **de direction** GESTION board of directors, governing body, management board; ~ **en direction** GESTION management consultant; ~ **de direction** ADMIN,

COM, COMPTA, RES HUM board of directors, governing body, management board; ~ **des employés** RES HUM employee counseling (*AmE*), employee counselling (*BrE*); ~ **fiscal** FISC, GESTION tax consultant; ~ **général** COM ≈ CC (*UK*), ≈ county council (*UK*); ~ **en gestion** GESTION management consultant; ~ **en gestion d'entreprise** GESTION, INFO business consultant, management consultant; ~ **d'immatriculation des courtiers d'assurance** ASSUR Insurance Brokers' Registration Council (*UK*), IBRC (*UK*); ~ **en informatique** INFO computer consultant; ~ **juridique** DROIT legal advice; ~ **des ministres** POL cabinet; ~ **municipal** ADMIN, POL council; ~ **en placements** BOURSE, FIN investment counseling (*AmE*), investment counselling (*BrE*); ~ **en recrutement** RES HUM recruitment consultant; ~ **de surveillance** COM, COMPTA, GESTION, RES HUM supervisory board; ~ **syndical** RES HUM trade union council

Conseil: ~ **d'affaires européen/ANASE** *m* COM European/ASEAN Business Council, EABC; ~ **des affréteurs français** *m* IMP/EXP French Shippers' Council, FSC; ~ **de l'aide économique mutuelle** *m (COMECON)* ECON Council for Mutual Economic Aid *(CMEA, COMECON)*; ~ **des armateurs européens** *m* TRANSP European Shippers Council; ~ **de la bourse de Londres** *m* BOURSE ≈ London Stock Exchange Board; ~ **des bourses de valeurs** *m (CBV)* BOURSE regulatory body of the Paris Stock Exchange, ≈ Council of the Stock Exchange (*UK*), ≈ The Securities Association (*UK*) (TSA); ~ **commercial d'Europe de l'Est** *m* COM East European Trade Council; ~ **de coordination des associations aéroportuaires** *m (CCAA)* TRANSP ≈ Airport Associations Co-ordinating Council *(AACC)*; ~ **d'État** *m* POL Council of State; ~ **de l'Europe** *m (CE)* POL Council of Europe *(CE)*; ~ **industriel pour la technologie en matière d'éducation et de formation** *m* PROT SOC Industrial Council for Educational & Training Technology (*UK*), ICETT (*UK*); ~ **d'information financière** *m* COMPTA Financial Reporting Council (*UK*); ~ **international du blé** *m (CIB)* COM International Wheat Council *(IWC)*; ~ **international du sucre** *m* IND International Sugar Council, ISC; ~ **des marchés à terme** *m (CMT)* BOURSE futures exchange council; ~ **des ministres** *m* ECON Council of Ministers; ~ **national du patronat français** *m (CNPF)* COM, IND ≈ Confederation of British Industry *(CBI)*; ~ **des prud'hommes** *m* DROIT, IND, RES HUM ≈ Labour Relations Agency (*UK*), ≈ LRA (*UK*), labor court (*AmE*), labour court (*BrE*), ≈ Central Arbitration Committee (*UK*), ≈ CAC (*UK*), ≈ Industrial Tribunal (*UK*), ≈ IT (*UK*), ≈ industrial court (*UK*); ~ **de sécurité de l'ONU** *m* POL UN Security Council; ~ **du trésor** *m* POL Treasury Board

conseillé, e *adj* COM advisable

conseiller[1], **-ère** *m,f* ADMIN councillor, COM adviser, advisor, consultant, counsel, counsellor, COMPTA, GESTION, INFO adviser, advisor, consultant, POL *membre d'un conseil* councillor, RES HUM adviser, advisor, consultant, counsel, counsellor; ~ **en crédit** FIN credit adviser, credit advisor, credit counsellor; ~ **économique** ADMIN, ECON, POL economic adviser; ~ **financier** FIN financial agent; ~ **fiscal** FISC, GESTION tax adviser, tax advisor, tax consultant; ~ **en fiscalité** FISC, GESTION tax adviser, tax advisor; ~ **en gestion d'entreprise** GESTION, INFO business consultant, management consultant; ~ **juridique** DROIT legal adviser, legal advisor, legal officer, solicitor (*UK*); ~ **juridique d'une entreprise** COM, DROIT company attorney (*AmE*), company lawyer (*BrE*); ~ **en matière de défense** RES HUM defence advisor (*BrE*), defence attaché (*BrE*), defense advisor (*AmE*), defense attaché (*AmE*), D/A; ~ **en matière fiscale** FISC, GESTION tax adviser, tax advisor; ~ **municipal** ADMIN, POL town councillor; ~ **en organisation** INFO management consultant; ~ **-orientateur** PROT SOC careers officer; ~ **d'orientation** PROT SOC careers adviser, careers officer, vocational guide, RES HUM careers adviser, vocational guide; ~ **d'orientation professionnelle** PROT SOC careers adviser, careers officer, vocational guide, RES HUM careers adviser, vocational guide; ~ **en placements** BOURSE investment adviser, investment advisor, investment consultant, investment counsel; ~ **en planification financière** BOURSE financial planner

conseiller[2] *vt* COM advise, DROIT counsel, GESTION advise; ◆ ~ **qn sur qch** COM, GESTION advise sb on sth

conseils *m pl* ADMIN, BOURSE, COM, GESTION, RES HUM advice, counseling (*AmE*), counselling (*BrE*), guidance; ~ **aux exportateurs** IMP/EXP hints to exporters; ~ **en investissements** BOURSE, FIN investment advice, investment counseling (*AmE*), investment counselling (*BrE*); ◆ **donner des ~ à** COM, GESTION advise; **sur les ~ de** COM as per advice from, as per advice of, on the advice of

consensus *m* COM consensus

consentement *m* COM acce., acceptance, assent, compliance, consent, DROIT, IMMOB acce., acceptance; ~ **et règlement** FIN accord and satisfaction; ~ **implicite** DROIT implied consent; ~ **souscrit** FISC consent executed; ◆ **par ~ mutuel** COM, DROIT by mutual consent

consentir *vt* BANQUE accommodate, advance, allot, extend, grant, BOURSE *option* grant, COM agree, FIN *prêt* accommodate, advance, allot, extend, grant, provide; ~ **à** COM consent to, *remise* agree to; ◆ ~ **un prêt** FIN provide a loan; ~ **un prêt à qn** BANQUE, FIN accommodate sb with a loan, grant a loan to sb, make a loan to sb, provide sb with a loan; ~ **une remise à qn** V&M allow sb a discount, give sb a discount

conséquence *f* COM consequence; ~ **fiscale** FISC tax incidence; ◆ **en ~** COM accordingly, as a consequence, as a result, consequently, in consequence

conséquences *f pl* COM, POL consequences, fallout (*infrml*), implications; **~ indirectes** DROIT *d'une action en justice* consequential effect

conséquent, e *adj* COM considerable, sizeable, consistent, GESTION consistent; ◆ **par ~** COM as a consequence, as a result, consequently, in consequence

conservateur[1], **-trice** *adj* POL conservative

conservateur[2] *m* IND *traitement des aliments* preservative

conservateur[3], **-trice** *m, f* POL conservative, V&M laggard; **~ des hypothèques** IMMOB registrar of mortgages; **~ de titres** BOURSE custodian

conservation *f* BOURSE *de titres* custody, COM *matériel, bâtiments* maintenance, ENVIR conservation, IND *matériel, bâtiments* maintenance; **~ d'actions** BOURSE custody of shares; **~ financièrement rentable des ressources** ENVIR conservation of natural resources, economic conservation; **~ globale** FIN *d'actions* global custody; **~ internationale** FIN *d'actions* global custody; **~ locale** FIN local custody, subcustody; **~ des ressources compatible avec l'économie** ENVIR economic conservation; **~ des ressources naturelles** ENVIR economic conservation

conservatisme *m* COM, POL conservatism

conserver *vt* IND preserve, INFO keep

conserverie: ~ de viande *f* IND meat packing

conserves *f pl* COM preserved foods

considérable *adj* COM, ECON *demande* considerable, heavy, substantial, *prix* considerable, hefty (*infrml*)

considérablement *adv* COM considerably, significantly, substantially

considérants: les ~ *m pl* DROIT the whereas clauses

considération *f* COM consideration; **~ de prudence** BANQUE prudential consideration

considéré, e *adj* COM considered, deemed

considérer *vt* COM consider, take into consideration, deem

consignataire *mf* TRANSP cnee, consignee; **~ douanier** *m* IMP/EXP, TRANSP customs consignee; **~ de navires** *m* IMP/EXP, TRANSP ship's agent

consignateur, -trice *m,f* IMP/EXP, TRANSP consigner, consignor, shipper

consignation *f* DROIT *somme* deposit, TRANSP *action* cnmt, consgt, consignation, consignment; ◆ **en ~** TRANSP *marchandises* cnmt, on consignment

consigne *f* COM, TRANSP *lieu* baggage checkroom (*AmE*), cloakroom, left-luggage office (*BrE*), *somme* deposit; **~ automatique** COM baggage locker (*AmE*), left-luggage locker (*BrE*)

consigné, e *adj* COM *bouteille, caisse*, ENVIR *bouteille, caisse* returnable

consigner *vt* COM record, TRANSP *marchandises* consign; ◆ **~ qch par écrit** COM put sth down in writing, put sth on record

consignes: ~ officielles d'une compagnie d'aviation *f pl* TRANSP official airline guide, OAG

consoeur *f* RES HUM colleague

consolidation *f* BANQUE consolidation, COM consolidation, strengthening, COMPTA consolidation, ECON strengthening, FIN consolidation, funding, RES HUM consolidation; **~ du capital** ECON, FIN capital consolidation; **~ initiale** FIN initial funding; **~ interne** COMPTA, FIN internal funding; **~ par intégration totale** COMPTA acquisition accounting

consolidé, e *adj* BANQUE, COM, COMPTA, ECON, FIN, RES HUM consolidated

consolider *vt* BANQUE consolidate, COM consolidate, strengthen, COMPTA consolidate, ECON strengthen, FIN consolidate, *dette* fund, RES HUM consolidate; ◆ **~ un emprunt** BANQUE, FIN fund a loan

consolidés *m pl* COM cons (*UK*), consols (*UK*)

consommables *m pl* COM consumables, INFO *papier* expendables

consommateur, -trice *m,f* COM, ECON, ENVIR, IND, V&M consumer; **~ final** ENVIR, IND end consumer; **~ individuel** COM, V&M individual consumer; **~ de main-d'oeuvre non-capitalistique** ECON, RES HUM labor intensive (*AmE*), labour intensive (*BrE*); **~ précoce** V&M early adapter; **~ qui change de marque** *jarg* COM, V&M switcher (*jarg*)

consommation *f* ECON consumption, C, ENVIR, IND consumption, V&M consumer spending, consumption; **~ autonome** ECON autonomous consumption; **~ de capital** ECON capital consumption; **~ d'électricité** COM, ENVIR, IND electricity consumption; **~ humaine** COM, ENVIR, V&M human consumption; **~ intérieure** ECON domestic consumption, internal consumption; **~ ménagère** COM, ECON domestic consumption; **~ des ménages** COM private consumption, ECON household consumption, private consumption; **~ mondiale** ECON world consumption; **~ nationale** ECON domestic consumption, national consumption; **~ ostentatoire** ECON, V&M conspicuous consumption; **~ par tête** ECON consumption per capita, per capita consumption; **~ des services publics** ECON public consumption

consommer *vt* COM *accord* consummate, *combustible* consume, ECON, ENVIR, IND, V&M *utiliser* consume

consonance: ~ cognitive *f* ECON cognitive consonance

consortialiser: vt ~ d'habitation BANQUE syndicate a loan; **~ un prêt** FIN syndicate a loan

consortium *m* BANQUE consortium, syndicate, BOURSE syndicate, COM affiliated group, consortium, syndicate, ECON pool, FIN affiliated group, consortium, syndicate; **~ bancaire** BANQUE banking syndicate, consortium bank, FIN consortium bank; **~ de banques** BANQUE group banking; **~ de**

compagnies de ligne TRANSP *maritime* liner consortium

constant, e *adj* COM constant, *investissement* continuing, *préoccupation* ongoing

constante *f* INFO, MATH constant; **~ annuelle d'hypothèque** BANQUE, FIN, IMMOB annual mortgage constant

constatation *f* COM ascertainment; **~ d'une perte** COMPTA recognition of loss

constater *vt* COM ascertain, note, COMPTA *transaction* recognize; ◆ **~ une perte** COMPTA recognize a loss, report a loss; **~ un profit** COMPTA report a profit

constituant[1]**, e** *adj* COM component, constituent

constituant[2]**, e** *m,f* DROIT settlor (*UK*)

constitué, e *adj* DROIT *institution* incorporated (*UK*), *trust* constituted

constituer *vt* ADMIN constitute, COM *problème* constitute, pose, *société* incorporate, DROIT *jury* empanel, strike, RES HUM *comité* appoint, set up; ◆ **~ une contrefaçon** DROIT constitute an infringement; **~ un quorum** ADMIN, COM, GESTION constitute a quorum, form a quorum, have a quorum

constitution *f* BOURSE *d'un établissement*, COM *d'un établissement* constitution, incorporation, *d'une société* formation, DROIT constitution, incorporation, POL *principes fondamentaux* constitution; **~ d'une rente** DROIT settling of an annuity; **~ en société** COM, DROIT incorporation; **~ en société par actions** COM incorporation

constitutionnel, -elle *adj* DROIT, POL constitutional

constructeur, -trice *m,f* IND, RES HUM maker, manufacturer; **~ automobile** IND car manufacturer; **~ de machines** IND *maritime* engine builder; **~ de navires** IND naval constructor, shipbuilder; **~ d'ordinateurs** INFO computer company, computer vendor, hardware firm

construction *f* COM *production* constr, construction, making, IMMOB building, constr, construction, IND constr, construction, making; **~ avec rachat** DROIT, ECON buy-back construction; **~ à l'épreuve du feu** ASSUR, ENVIR, IND fire-resistant construction, fire-resistive construction; **~ et utilisation** DROIT legal restrictions covering construction and use of vehicles in UK, construction and use (*UK*), IND legal restrictions covering construction and use of vehicles, construction and use (*UK*); **~ ignifuge** ASSUR, ENVIR, IND fire-resistant construction, fire-resistive construction; **~ navale** IND naval construction, shipbuilding; **~ de routes** ECON road building

construire *vt* COM construct, make, IMMOB build

construit, e *adj* IMMOB built, constructed; **~ sur mesure** IMMOB *immeuble*, TRANSP purpose-built

consul *m* COM, POL consul

Consul: **~ général** *m* COM, POL Consulate-General

consulage *m* IMP/EXP consulage

consulat *m* POL consulate

Consulat: **~ général** *m* COM, POL Consulate-General

consultant, e *m,f* COMPTA, GESTION, INFO, RES HUM adviser, advisor, consultant; **~ de deuxième ordre** RES HUM second-rank consultant; **~ financier agréé** FIN chartered financial consultant (*US*); **~ en investissement** BOURSE investment consultant, investment counsel; **~ junior** (*ANT consultant senior*) RES HUM second-rank consultant

consultatif, -ive *adj* COM *comité, titre*, RES HUM advisory, consultative

consultation *f* COM consultation, DROIT *avec un avocat* counsel, csl, INFO query, *d'un fichier* inquiry, lookup, RES HUM *avec un expert, d'un livre* consultation; **~ bilatérale** COM joint consultation; **~ paritaire** GESTION joint consultation; **~ en vue de reconversion** RES HUM redundancy consultation; ◆ **en ~ avec** COM in consultation with

consulter *vt* COM consult; ◆ **à ~ sur place** COM *livre, journal* do not remove; **~ un avocat** DROIT consult a lawyer, take legal advice; **~ un conseiller juridique** DROIT seek legal advice; **~ qn sur qch** COM consult sb about sth

consumérisme *m* ECON, V&M consumerism

consumériste *mf* ECON, V&M consumerist

contact *m* COM contact, V&M *publicité* exposure; **~ visuel** V&M *marketing* eye contact

contacter *vt* COM approach, contact, get in touch with; ◆ **~ qn au sujet de qch** COM approach sb about sth, contact sb about sth, get in touch with sb about sth

container *m voir* conteneur

contamination *f* ENVIR, IND contamination, pollution

contaminé, e *adj* ENVIR, IND contaminated, polluted

contaminer *vt* ENVIR, IND contaminate, pollute

contenance *f* COM, TRANSP capacity; **~ en vrac** TRANSP bulk capacity; ◆ **faire bonne ~** COM put on a bold front

conteneur *m* TRANSP container; **~ aéré** TRANSP ventilated container; **~ en alliage** TRANSP a, alloy container; **~ bâché** TRANSP soft-top container, top-loader container; **~ à bestiaux** TRANSP cattle container; **~ de boîtes en aluminium** ENVIR aluminium can bank (*BrE*), aluminum can bank (*AmE*); **~ de boîtes de conserve à recycler** ENVIR can bank; **~ calorifique** TRANSP heated container; **~ -citerne** TRANSP bulk liquid container, tank container, tanktainer; **~ -citerne isotherme** TRANSP insulated tank container, insulated tanktainer, IT; **~ à claire-voie** TRANSP lattice-sided container; **~ de collecte** ENVIR bank; **~ de collecte de verre usé** ENVIR bottle bank; **~ complet** TRANSP container load, full container load, FCL; **~ découvert** TRANSP open container; **~ demi-hauteur** TRANSP half height, H/H; **~ démontable** TRANSP collapsible container, coltainer; **~ de**

détail TRANSP container part load; **~ fermé** TRANSP *maritime* closed container; **~ de fret** TRANSP freight container; **~ pour fret aérien** TRANSP air freight container, AC; **~ frigorifique** TRANSP reefer, reefer container, refrigerated container, R; **~ frigorifique à toit ouvert** TRANSP open-top reefer, open-topped reefer; **~ de groupage** TRANSP less than container load, LCL; **~ hors-cotes** *(HC)* TRANSP high cube *(HC)*; **~ hors-normes** TRANSP high cube, HC; **~ intégral** TRANSP integral; **~ interchangeable** TRANSP interchange container; **~ intermédiaire** TRANSP intermediate container; **~ intermodal** TRANSP intermodal container; **~ isotherme** TRANSP insulated container; **~ multimodal** TRANSP intermodal container; **~ ondulé** TRANSP corrugated container; **~ ordinaire** TRANSP closed box container; **~ ouvert** TRANSP open container; **~ à paroi latérale ouvrante** TRANSP open-sided container, open-wall container; **~ plat** TRANSP gondola flat; **~ plate-forme** TRANSP flat container, flat rack; **~ pliant** TRANSP collapsible container, coltainer; **~ pour pont inférieur** TRANSP *aviation* belly container, lower deck container; **~ à pulvérulents** TRANSP bin-type container, dry bulk container, D; **~ repliable** TRANSP collapsible container, coltainer; **~ roll-on** TRANSP roll-on container; **~ sec** TRANSP box container, bx; **~ sec fermé** TRANSP covered dry container; **~ semi-bâché** TRANSP half-tilt container, HT; **~ semi-rigide** TRANSP semi-rigid receptacle; **~ sous contrôle étranger** TRANSP foreign-owned container; **~ spécial hors-cotes** *(SHC)* TRANSP super high cube *(SHC)*; **~ sur wagon découvert à bords plats** *vieilli voir conteneur sur wagon plat* ; **~ sur wagon plat** TRANSP *chemin de fer* container on flat car *(AmE)*, container on flat wagon *(BrE)*; **~ thermique** TRANSP thermal container; **~ à toit amovible** TRANSP hard-top container; **~ à toit ouvert** TRANSP open-top container, open-topped container, OT; **~ pour transport aérien** IMP/EXP, TRANSP air mode container; **~ pour le transport intérieur** TRANSP inland container, IC; **~ en treillis** TRANSP lattice-sided container; **~ -trémie** TRANSP hoppertainer; **~ pour usage général** TRANSP g, general purpose freight container, universal container, U; **~ ventilé** TRANSP mechanically ventilated container; **~ de vrac** TRANSP bk, bulk freight container, bulktainer; **~ en vrac et intermédiaire articulé** TRANSP flexible intermediate and bulk container, FIBC; **~ de vrac intermédiaire** TRANSP intermediate bulk container, IBC; **~ LD-3** TRANSP *aviation* belly container, lower deck container

conteneurisation *f* TRANSP containerization

conteneurisé, e *adj* TRANSP containerized

conteneuriser *vt* TRANSP containerize

contenir *vt* COM *récipient* contain, hold, take, ECON *l'inflation* contain, hold in check, keep down, TRANSP accommodate, hold, take; ◆ **~ un rapport**

COM *journal* carry a report; **~ des renseignements sur** COM carry information on

contenter: se ~ de *v pron* COM be satisfied with

contentieux *m* COM bone of contention, DROIT *département* legal department, *litige* litigation

contenu *m* ADMIN index, COM *d'un récipient* content, contents, *d'un document, d'un livre* subject matter, DROIT *de l'abrégé* content, INFO contents; **~ indivisible** TRANSP no explosion of the total contents, NETC; **~ du travail** COM work content, RES HUM job content; ◆ **qui ne peut pas être ~** COM uncontrollable

contestable *adj* COM *question* arguable, debatable, DROIT *allégation, fait* traversable

contestation *f* DROIT traverse

contester *vt* ASSUR contest, DROIT litigate, *droit* challenge, deny, dispute, question, *testament* contest, dispute, RES HUM repudiate

contextuel, -elle *adj* INFO context-sensitive

contigu, -uë *adj* COM adjoining, contiguous, INFO contiguous

continent *m* COM continent; **~ européen** COM continent of Europe

continental, e *adj* COM continental

contingent *m* COM, ECON, IMP/EXP quota; **~ d'importation** ECON, IMP/EXP import quota; **~ libre** COM unrestricted quota; **~ tarifaire** COM, ECON, IMP/EXP tariff quota; **~ de transport** TRANSP transport quota; **~ des versements** FISC *fondations de charité privées et publiques* disbursement quota

contingenté, e *adj* COM, ECON, IMP/EXP subject to quota

contingentement *m* COM, ECON, IMP/EXP quota fixing, quota system

contingenter *vt* COM, ECON, IMP/EXP establish quotas for, subject to quota

continu, e *adj* COM continuous, ongoing

continuer *vt* COM continue; ◆ **~ à courir** FIN run on; **~ à faire** COM continue doing, continue to do

continuité *f* COMPTA *des méthodes* consistency, V&M *d'un thème dans une campagne de publicité* continuity; **~ de l'emploi** RES HUM continuity of employment *(UK)*; **~ d'exploitation** COMPTA going concern

contractant, e *m,f* ASSUR proposer, DROIT contracting party, contractor, covenantor, IMMOB contracting party, contractor, RES HUM contractor

contracter 1. *vt* COM *dette* contract, incur; **2.** *v pron* **se ~** ECON contract out; ◆ **~ un crédit** FIN take accommodation, take out a loan; **~ des dettes** COMPTA, FIN incur debts; **~ un emprunt** FIN contract a loan, take accommodation, take out a loan; **~ une police d'assurance** ASSUR take out a policy

contraction *f* ECON contraction; **~ des bénéfices** ECON, FIN profit squeeze; **~ de l'offre** ECON fall in supplies

contradiction: ~ de l'État-providence *f* PROT SOC welfare trap

contraignant, e *adj* COM compulsory, restricting

contraindre *vi* COM compel, constrain, force, obligate, oblige; ♦ ~ qn à faire qch COM compel sb to do sth, constrain sb to do sth, force sb to do sth, oblige sb to do sth

contrainte *f* COM, COMPTA constraint, DROIT duress, *par corps* constraint, ECON, RES HUM constraint; ~ **budgétaire** COMPTA, FIN budget constraint; ~ **horaire** RES HUM time constraint; ~ **de limite** MATH boundary constraint

contraire[1] *adj* COM *direction* opposite, *intérêts* conflicting; ~ **à** COM alien to, contrary to; ~ **à la loi** DROIT against the law, unlawful

contraire[2] *m* COM contrary, opposite, MATH inverse; ♦ **au ~** COM aliter, on the contrary, secus

contrarier *vt* COM defeat

contraste *m* INFO contrast

contrasté, e *adj* INFO highlighted

contraster *vt* INFO highlight

contrat *m* ADMIN bond, COM agreement, bond, compact, contract, DROIT contract, covenant, FIN contract, IMMOB bargain and sale, V&M contract; ~ **d'abonnement** ASSUR floater (*US*), floating policy; ~ **d'achat à terme** COM forward purchase contract; ~ **à acompte obligatoire** BOURSE take-or-pay contract; ~ **d'acquisition** FISC acquisition contract; ~ **d'adhésion** DROIT adhesion contract; ~ **-adjudication de l'État** COM, DROIT government contract; ~ **d'affrètement** TRANSP charter contract; ~ **d'affrètement aérien** DROIT, TRANSP aircraft charter agreement; ~ **d'affrètement aller-retour** TRANSP *maritime* round C/P, round charter party; ~ **d'affrètement de céréales** TRANSP *maritime* grain charter party; ~ **d'affrètement par volume** TRANSP volume contract of affreightment; ~ **d'affrètement au quai** TRANSP *maritime* wharf charter; ~ **d'agence** DROIT agency agreement; ~ **d'agence exclusive** DROIT exclusive agency agreement; ~ **aléatoire** ASSUR aleatory contract; ~ **d'assurance** ASSUR insurance contract; ~ **d'assurance automobile** ASSUR automobile policies insuring agreement; ~ **d'assurance maladie** ASSUR commercial sickness insurance policy; ~ **d'assurance responsabilité civile** ASSUR liability insuring agreement; ~ **avec primes de rendement** COM incentive contract; ~ **de bail** DROIT, IMMOB lease; ~ **-bidon** (SYN *contrat de complaisance*) IND, RES HUM sweetheart agreement, sweetheart contract; ~ **bilatéral** BREVETS, DROIT *propriété intellectuelle* bilateral contract, reciprocal agreement; ~ **caduc entre courtiers** BOURSE aged fail; ~ **CAF** IMP/EXP CIF contract; ~ **de cession** COM, DROIT deed of assignation; ~ **clé en main** COM, IMMOB turnkey contract; ~ **collectif** COM group contract; ~ **commercial** COM, DROIT commercial contract; ~ **de complaisance** (SYN *contrat-bidon*) IND, RES HUM sweetheart agreement, sweetheart contract;

~ **conditionnel** DROIT conditional contract (*US*); ~ **contre le faux et usage de faux** ASSUR commercial forgery policy; ~ **à court terme** RES HUM short-term contract; ~ **de courtier sélectionné** BOURSE selected dealer agreement; ~ **de crédit** BANQUE, FIN installment plan (*AmE*), instalment contract (*BrE*); ~ **de crédit-bail** COMPTA finance lease, FIN leasing agreement; ~ **de crédit à la consommation** V&M hire-purchase agreement; ~ **définitif** ECON recontract; ~ **de dépôt** DROIT deposit agreement, escrow agreement; ~ **double** DROIT dual contract; ~ **à durée déterminée** (*CDD*) RES HUM fixed-term contract, fixed-term deal, TRANSP *maritime* time agreement; ~ **à durée indéterminée** (*CDI*) RES HUM permanent contract; ~ **d'échange** DROIT exchange contract; ~ **d'échange de taux d'intérêts** (*CETI*) BOURSE interest rate swap; ~ **à échéance la plus courte** BOURSE nearly contract; ~ **écrit** COM, DROIT written agreement; ~ **d'embauche** RES HUM employment contract, shop's articles, TRANSP *maritime, aviation* crew agreement (*UK*); ~ **d'emploi** DROIT, RES HUM contract of employment; ~ **d'emploi à l'essai** RES HUM placement test; ~ **d'emploi-solidarité** *France* (*CES*) RES HUM ≈ Youth Training Scheme (*UK*) (*YTS*); ~ **d'État** COM, DROIT government contract; ~ **d'exclusivité** COM sole agency, DROIT agreement for exclusiveness, IMMOB exclusive agency listing, sole agency; ~ **exécuté** DROIT executed contract; ~ **à exécution échelonnée** DROIT installment contract (*AmE*), instalment contract (*BrE*); ~ **exécutoire** DROIT, ECON tying contract; ~ **explicite** DROIT explicit contract, express contract; ~ **ferme et définitif** DROIT binding agreement; ~ **financier normalisé** BOURSE financial future, financial futures contract; ~ **financier à terme** BOURSE financial future, financial futures contract; ~ **foncier** DROIT, IMMOB land contract; ~ **au forfait** RES HUM lump-sum contract; ~ **de franchisage** COM franchise; ~ **de frappe** ECON typing contract; ~ **de gage** DROIT bailment; ~ **de garantie** BOURSE underwriting agreement; ~ **général** BOURSE blanket bond; ~ **global** ASSUR blanket contract, blanket policy, COM package deal, ECON interlinked transaction, package deal, LOISIRS, RES HUM, TRANSP package deal; ~ **à la grosse aventure** ASSUR bottomry bond; ~ **d'heures à l'année** RES HUM annual hours contract; ~ **d'indemnisation** ASSUR contract of indemnity; ~ **d'indemnité** ASSUR contract of indemnity; ~ **d'investissement** BOURSE investment contract; ~ **irrévocable** DROIT binding agreement; ~ **léonin** DROIT unconscionable bargain, unfair contract; ~ **à livraison différé** BOURSE forward contract; ~ **de location** BANQUE lease agreement, COM rental agreement, IMMOB lease agreement, rental agreement; ~ **de location-acquisition** COM capital lease agreement; ~ **de location-financement** ECON direct financial leasing agreement; ~ **de maintenance** COM, INFO service agreement, service contract; ~ **du management** GESTION management contract; ~ **de marchandises** BOURSE commodity contract; ~ **de mariage** DROIT marriage contract; ~ **non-exécutoire** DROIT unenforceable contract; ~ **de non-recours à la grève** RES HUM no-strike agreement, no-strike deal, sweetheart agreement, sweetheart contract; ~ **obligataire** BOURSE bond indenture; ~ **obligataire à terme** BOURSE bond futures contract; ~ **d'occupation partielle** DROIT, IMMOB limited occupancy agreement; ~ **d'option** BOURSE option contract, stock contract; ~ **d'option d'achat** *(*ANT *contrat d'option de vente)* BOURSE call option; ~ **d'option sur contrat à terme** BOURSE futures option contract; ~ **d'option sur devises** BOURSE currency option, currency options contract; ~ **d'option à terme** BOURSE futures option contract; ~ **d'option de vente** *(*ANT *contrat d'option d'achat)* BOURSE put option; ~ **par contrat** BOURSE per contract basis; ~ **de placement garanti** COM guaranteed investment contract (*UK*), GIC (*UK*); ~ **premier** DROIT prime contract; ~ **prénuptial** DROIT prenuptial agreement, prenuptial contract; ~ **prescrit** COM prescribed contract; ~ **de prêt** BANQUE loan agreement; ~ **principal** DROIT prime contract; ~ **de prise ferme** BOURSE underwriting agreement; ~ **prix fixe** V&M fixed-price contract; ~ **de programme** ECON program deal (*AmE*), programme deal (*BrE*); ~ **public** COM, DROIT government contract; ~ **qui engage** DROIT binding agreement; ~ **qui lie** DROIT binding agreement; ~ **de rente** FISC annuity contract; ~ **de rente viagère** ASSUR annuity policy; ~ **de répartition** DROIT apportioned contract; ~ **de représentation** DROIT agency agreement; ~ **de représentation exclusive** DROIT exclusive agency agreement; ~ **de revenus garantis** ASSUR guaranteed income contract, GIC; ~ **sans ambiguïté** DROIT explicit contract; ~ **sans effet juridique** DROIT nudum pactum; ~ **de sauvetage** TRANSP *maritime* salvage agreement; ~ **de savoir-faire** BREVETS, DROIT *propriété intellectuelle* know-how agreement; ~ **de service** RES HUM contract for services, service contract; ~ **de service général** TRANSP *maritime* general service contract (*UK*); ~ **de services** DROIT contract for services, service contract; ~ **social** POL, RES HUM social compact, social contract; ~ **de société** DROIT deed of partnership; ~ **sous seing privé** COM, DROIT private contract; ~ **de sous-traitance** COM, IND subcontract; ~ **de souscription et de mise sur le marché** BOURSE selected dealer agreement; ~ **standard** COM standard agreement, standard contract; ~ **sur devise** BOURSE currency contract; ~ **sur l'indice des cours** BOURSE stock index contract; ~ **sur mesure** DROIT tailor-made contract; ~ **sur place renouvelé** RES HUM recurrent spot contracting; ~ **sur les taux d'intérêt des opérations à court terme** BOURSE short-term interest rate futures contract; ~ **synallagmatique** DROIT bilateral contract; ~ **syndical** DROIT, IND, RES HUM union contract; ~ **de syndicat unique** RES HUM single-union agreement (*UK*), single-

union deal (*UK*); ~ **tacite** DROIT implied contract, implied in fact contract; ~ **de taux d'intérêt** BOURSE, FIN interest rate contract; ~ **de taux d'intérêt à terme** BOURSE, FIN interest-rate futures contract; ~ **à tempérament** DROIT installment contract (*AmE*), instalment contract (*BrE*); ~ **à terme** BOURSE, FIN forward contract, futures contract; ~ **à terme de bons du Trésor** BOURSE, FIN T-bill futures, T-bill futures contract, Treasury bill futures, Treasury bill futures contract; ~ **à terme de fret** BOURSE, FIN freight futures contract; ~ **à terme gré à gré** BOURSE, FIN forward contract; ~ **à terme d'instrument financier** (*CATIF*) BOURSE, FIN financial futures contract; ~ **à terme de marchandises** BOURSE, FIN commodity futures, commodity futures contract; ~ **à terme de marchandises agricoles** BOURSE agricultural futures contract (*UK*), FIN agricultural futures contract; ~ **à terme non-disponible** BOURSE, FIN sold-out market; ~ **à terme normalisé** BOURSE, FIN financial future, financial futures contract; ~ **à terme reporté** BOURSE, FIN forward-forward contract; ~ **à terme sous-jacent** BOURSE, FIN underlying futures, underlying futures contract; ~ **à terme sous option** BOURSE, FIN underlying futures, underlying futures contract; ~ **à terme sur dépôt en eurodollars** BOURSE, ECON, FIN Eurodollar time deposit futures, Eurodollar time deposit futures contract; ~ **à terme sur eurodollars** BOURSE, ECON, FIN ED future, Eurodollar future; ~ **à terme sur indice** BOURSE, FIN stock index future; ~ **à terme sur indice boursier** BOURSE, FIN stock index future; ~ **à terme sur obligation** BOURSE, FIN bond futures contract; ~ **à terme sur taux d'intérêt** BOURSE, FIN interest rate contract, interest-rate future, interest futures contract; ~ **à terme sur taux d'intérêt à court terme** BOURSE, FIN short-term interest rate futures contract; ~ **à terme sur TIOL** BOURSE, FIN LIBOR futures contract; ~ **à terme de taux d'intérêt** BOURSE, FIN financial futures contract; ~ **terme-terme** BOURSE, FIN forward-forward contract; ~ **à termes de change** BOURSE, FIN currency futures, currency futures contract; ~ **à termes de devises** BOURSE, FIN currency futures, currency futures contract; ~ **à titre gratuit** COM bare contract; ~ **de travail** COM labor contract (*AmE*), labour contract (*BrE*), service contract, works contract, RES HUM agreement of service, employment contract; ~ **de travail indépendant** RES HUM freelance contract; ~ **très avantageux** COM golden handcuffs; ~ **type** COM skeleton contract, standard agreement; ~ **valide** DROIT contract that can be upheld; ~ **validé** DROIT executed contract; ~ **de vente** BANQUE *biens*, DROIT, V&M agreement of sale, contract of sale, sale agreement, sales contract; ~ **de vente de biens** DROIT, V&M contract for the sale of goods; ~ **de vente à réméré** BOURSE REPO (*AmE*), repurchase agreement, reverse repurchase agreement, RP, FIN REPO (*AmE*), repurchase agreement (*AmE*), reverse repurchase agreement,

RP; ~ **de vente à tempérament** DROIT installment contract (*AmE*), instalment contract (*BrE*); ~ **de vente à terme** COM forward sales contract; ~ **verbal** DROIT oral contract; ◆ **être sous ~** COM be on a retainer

contrats: ~ **avec primes de rendement** *m pl* COM incentive contracting; ~ **à terme différés** *m pl* BOURSE, FIN deferred futures; ~ **à terme indexés** *m pl* BOURSE, FIN index futures, stock index futures; ~ **à terme sur actions** *m pl* BOURSE, FIN equity-related futures; ~ **à terme sur matières premières** *m pl* BOURSE, FIN commodity futures

contravention *f* COM infringement, DROIT breach, infringement, violation; ~ **à la loi** DROIT infringement of the law

contre:[1] ~ **-arc** *m* TRANSP *maritime* sagging; ~ **-espionnage industriel** *m* IND, RES HUM industrial espionage, industrial security; ~ **-ordre** *m* BANQUE stop payment; ~ **-plaqué** *m* IND plywood

contre:[2] ~ **-mesure** *f* COM countermeasure; ~ **-offre** *f* V&M counteroffer; ~ **-offre publique d'achat** *f* (*contre-OPA*) BOURSE Pac-Man defense (*US*), ECON, FIN merger, reverse takeover, reversed takeover, takeover; ~ **-OPA** *f* (*contre-offre publique d'achat*) BOURSE Pac-Man defense (*US*), ECON reverse takeover, reversed takeover, FIN merger, reverse takeover, reversed takeover, takeover; ~ **-passation** *f* COMPTA contra entry, reversal, reversing, writing back, FIN *action* reversal, reversing, writing back, *écriture* contra entry; ~ **-proposition** *f* COM, GESTION alternative proposal; ~ **-solution** *f* COM alternative solution; ~ **-valeur** *f* ECON value in exchange; ~ **-valeur de biens expropriés** *f* FISC expropriation asset

contre:[3] **le pour et le ~** *loc* COM pros and cons; **faire une ~ -performance** *loc* BOURSE, ECON underperform

contre:[4] *vt* ~ **-passer** BANQUE *lettre de change* endorse back, COMPTA *écriture* contra, reverse, write back; ◆ ~ **-passer un crédit croisé** BOURSE reverse a swap; ~ **-passer une écriture** COMPTA reverse an entry; ~ **-passer une hypothèque** BANQUE reverse a mortgage

contre[5] *prép* COM against; ◆ ~ **documents** COM against documents; ~ **espèces** COM f/c, for cash; ~ **paiement** COM against payment; ~ **une personne déterminée** DROIT in personam; ~ **remise du connaissement** IMP/EXP, TRANSP on surrender of the bill of lading; ~ **texte** V&M *même page*, *publicité* against text; ~ **tous les risques** ASSUR against all risks, AAR

contrebalancer *vt* COM balance, compensate, counterbalance

contrebande *f* FISC *activité, marchandises*, IMP/EXP contraband, smuggling

contrecarrer *vt* COM counteract, DROIT *projet* interfere with

contrecoup *m* COM consequence, repercussions, ECON backwash effect

contrefaçon *f* BANQUE *activité, copie* forgery,

BREVETS *activité* infringement, COM *copie* copy, DROIT forgery, *activité* counterfeiting, *copie* counterfeit

contrefacteur, -trice *m,f* BANQUE forger, BREVETS infringer, DROIT counterfeiter

contrefaire *vt* BANQUE, COM, COMPTA, DROIT *pièce de monnaie, signature* counterfeit, forge

contremaître:[1] *m* RES HUM foreman

contremaître:[2] **-esse** *m,f* GESTION line manager, line supervisor, overseer, petty officer, line manager, line supervisor, TRANSP petty officer

contremaîtresse *f* RES HUM forewoman

contremarque *f* COM countermark

contrepartie *f* BOURSE counterparty (*UK*), offset, COMPTA contra, contra, offset, DROIT consideration, ECON *commerce international* counterpart, FIN offset; ~ **conditionnelle** COM contingent consideration; ~ **exclue** FISC excluded consideration; ◆ **en ~** COM in compensation, in exchange; **pour une ~ valable** COM valuable consideration

contreparties: ~ **commerciales** *f pl* COM commercial considerations

contrepartiste *mf* BOURSE dealer, dealer in securities, jobber (*UK, dat*), market maker, stockjobber (*UK, dat*); ~ **occulte** *m* BOURSE market rigger; ~ **reporteur** *m* BOURSE jobber in contangos

contrepoids *m* ECON countervailing power

contrer *vt* COM *attaque* counter

contresigner *vt* COM witness sb's signature, *document* countersign

contrevenir: *vt* ~ **à** COM, DROIT contravene, infringe; ~ **à la loi** DROIT infringe the law

contribuable *mf* FISC ratepayer, taxpayer; ~ **contrevenant** *m* FISC delinquent taxpayer; ~ **à faible revenu** *m* (*ANT contribuable à revenu moyen, contribuable à revenu élevé*) FISC low-income taxpayer; ~ **à revenu élevé** *m* (*ANT contribuable à faible revenu, contribuable à revenu moyen*) FISC high-income taxpayer; ~ **à revenu moyen** *m* (*ANT contribuable à faible revenu, contribuable à revenu élevé*) FISC middle-income taxpayer

contribuant: ~ **à** *adj* COM conducive to

contribue: **qui ~ à** *loc* COM conducive to

contribuer *vt* ECON contribute; ~ **à** BANQUE *progrès, redressement* aid, COM *croissance* be conducive to, COM contribute

contributeur, -trice *m,f* ECON *UE* contributor

contribution *f* COM contribution, FISC contribution, tax, GESTION benefit; ~ **déductible** PROT SOC soft money; ~ **incorporelle** COM intangible contribution; ~ **neutre** FISC revenue neutral; ~ **du personnel** FISC, RES HUM staff levy; ~ **politique** POL political contribution; ~ **privée** ECON, FIN private contribution; ~ **sociale de solidarité** FISC social contributions tax

contributions: ~ **directes** *f pl* FISC direct taxation, direct taxes; ~ **indirectes** *f pl* FISC excise, excise duty, indirect taxation, indirect taxes; **les**

~ **directes** *f pl* FISC the Inland Revenue (*UK*), the Internal Revenue (*US*); ~ **des salariés** *f pl* RES HUM employee contributions; ~ **de sécurité sociale** *f pl* RES HUM social security contributions; ~ **volontaires** *f pl* FISC voluntary contributions (*UK*)

contrôlabilité *f* COMPTA auditability

contrôle *m* COM *d'un produit* control, inspection, COMPTA auditing, DROIT regulation, ECON control, regulation, FIN audit, auditing, IMP/EXP control, IND test, *d'un produit* inspection, INFO check (*AmE*), service, POL control; ~ **d'accès** INFO access control; ~ **adaptatif** GESTION adaptive control; ~ **anti-serpent** POL snake check (*infrml*); ~ **des appartenances religieuses du personnel** RES HUM religious monitoring; ~ **après expédition** TRANSP post-shipment inspection; ~ **automatique** INFO built-in check; ~ **avant chargement** TRANSP preloading inspection; ~ **avant expédition** TRANSP preshipment inspection; ~ **avant livraison** TRANSP predelivery inspection, PDI; ~ **des bagages** TRANSP baggage check; ~ **budgétaire** COMPTA, ECON, FIN budget control, budgetary control, budgeting control, BC; ~ **de caisse** COMPTA cash control; ~ **des changes** ECON, POL exchange control; ~ **de la circulation aérienne** TRANSP air traffic control, ATC; ~ **de cohérence** COM consistency check; ~ **comptable** COMPTA, FIN accounting control; ~ **des comptes analytique** COMPTA analytical audit, analytical auditing, analytical review, systems-based audit, systems-based auditing; ~ **du conseil d'administration** GESTION board control; ~ **des conteneurs** TRANSP cc, container control; ~ **continu** COMPTA continuous audit, PROT SOC, RES HUM continuous assessment; ~ **continu de l'acquisition des connaissances** *frml* PROT SOC, RES HUM continuous assessment; ~ **du crédit** BANQUE, ECON, FIN, POL credit control; ~ **des crédits** COMPTA appropriation control; ~ **des dépenses publiques** ECON public expenditure control; ~ **de direction** GESTION management control; ~ **effectif** COM working control; ~ **d'efficience** COMPTA efficiency audit; ~ **d'embarquement** TRANSP final check-in; ~ **des engagements** DROIT commitment control; ~ **de l'environnement** ENVIR environmental control, pollution control; ~ **d'État** ECON, POL state control; ~ **d'état** TRANSP *entretien d'un navire* cm, condition monitoring; ~ **étatique** ECON, POL state control; ~ **des exportations** ECON, IMP/EXP export control; ~ **externe** *(cf audit externe, révision externe, vérification externe Can)* COMPTA, FIN external audit, independent audit; ~ **de fabrication** IND manufacturing control; ~ **de fait** FIN effective control; ~ **financier** FIN financial control; ~ **de flux** INFO flow control; ~ **frontalier** ECON, IMP/EXP frontier control; ~ **aux frontières** ECON frontier control, IMP/EXP *de marchandises* border control, frontier control, POL border control; ~ **de gestion** COMPTA, FIN, GESTION management audit, management control; ~ **de l'immigration** ADMIN immigration control; ~ **interne** COM internal check, internal control, COMPTA, FIN accounting control, internal control; ~ **interne de l'administration et de l'organisation** COMPTA, FIN administrative and organizational controls (*UK*); ~ **limité** DROIT limited check; ~ **local des exportations** IMP/EXP local export control; ~ **local des importations** IMP/EXP local import control; ~ **de la masse monétaire** BANQUE, ECON, FIN, POL corset (*infrml*); ~ **des matières dangereuses pour la santé** IND, RES HUM control of substances hazardous to health (*UK*), COSHH (*UK*); ~ **national** FIN home-country control; ~ **de l'offre** ECON supply control; ~ **des opérations** COM operational control; ~ **optimal** ECON optimal control; ~ **ouvrier** RES HUM workers' control; ~ **par lots** IND batch control; ~ **par redondance** INFO redundancy check; ~ **par sélection aléatoire** MATH random check; ~ **par sondage** MATH random check; ~ **par sondages** COM, COMPTA test audit; ~ **de parité** INFO parity check; ~ **partiel** DROIT limited check; ~ **des passeports** ADMIN passport check, passport control; ~ **de la performance** COM, ECON, GESTION, RES HUM performance monitoring; ~ **physique** COM physical examination; ~ **des points de vente** V&M *marketing* retail audit; ~ **de la pollution atmosphérique** ENVIR, IND air pollution control; ~ **portuaire** TRANSP port control; ~ **des prix** ECON, FIN price control, price supervision, price-fixing, public pricing, V&M *par le producteur ou le distributeur* price control, price supervision, public pricing; ~ **de la production** COM, GESTION, IND progress control; ~ **de programmation** INFO code check; ~ **de la qualité** GESTION, IND, V&M quality assurance, quality control, QA, QC; ~ **de la qualité globale** *(QG)* COM, GESTION, IND, V&M total quality control *(TQC)*; ~ **de risques** GESTION risk monitoring; ~ **de routine** COM routine check; ~ **des salaires** ECON, RES HUM wage control; ~ **de sécurité** COM *d'un candidat, d'un visiteur* security check, vetting; ~ **au sol** TRANSP *aviation* ground control; ~ **du son** COMMS sound check; ~ **souple** GESTION adaptive control; ~ **statistique** MATH statistical control; ~ **statistique de l'outil de production** MATH statistical process control; ~ **statistique de qualité** MATH statistical quality control, SQC; ~ **du stock** COM reserve-stock control; ~ **des stocks** BOURSE, COMPTA, ECON, FIN inventory control (*AmE*), stock control (*BrE*); ~ **des substances présentant un danger pour la santé** IND *des employés*, RES HUM control of substances hazardous to health (*UK*), COSHH (*UK*); ~ **-surprise** COM spot check; ~ **du trafic aérien** TRANSP air traffic control, ATC; ~ **du trafic portuaire** TRANSP port traffic control; ~ **d'uniformité** COM consistency check; ~ **de validité** FISC validity check; ~ **végétatif** ECON vegetative control; ♦ **de** ~ COM, GESTION, INFO, RES HUM supervisory

contrôlé: ~ **par souris** *adj* INFO mouse-driven

contrôler *vt* COM check, control, oversee, supervise, verify, *performance* monitor, COMPTA audit, DROIT, ECON regulate, FIN audit, *marché* control, GESTION *performance* monitor, INFO audit, RES HUM *performance* monitor; ◆ ~ **au hasard** COM spot-check

contrôles: ~ **organisationnels et administratifs** *m pl* COMPTA, FIN administrative and organizational controls (*UK*); ~ **qualitatifs** *m pl* BANQUE qualitative controls; ~ **quantitatifs** *m pl* BANQUE quantitative controls; ~ **sévères** *m pl* DROIT tight controls; ~ **stricts** *m pl* DROIT tight controls; ~ **vétérinaires** *m pl* IMP/EXP veterinary controls

contrôleur, -euse *m,f* COM inspector, FIN comptroller, controller, FISC inspector, TRANSP ticket collector; ~ **adjoint** RES HUM *maritime* assistant controller, AC; ~ **aérien** TRANSP air-traffic controller; ~ **de la circulation** TRANSP traffic controller; ~ **des droits et taxes** FISC, RES HUM tax inspector, taxman; ~ **financier** COMPTA controller, financial controller, POL comptroller; ~ **de gestion** COMPTA comptroller, controller, management accountant, FIN, GESTION management accountant, POL comptroller, controller; ~ **de grappe** INFO cluster controller; ~ **de présence** COM, RES HUM timekeeper; ~ **de pression des pneus** TRANSP tire gage (*AmE*), tyre gauge (*BrE*); ~ **des prix** ECON price supervisor; ~ **des transports** RES HUM, TRANSP transport controller

controverse *f* COM controversy; ~ **d'addition** ECON adding-up controversy

conv. *abrév* (*converti*) COM, IMMOB conv (*converted*)

convaincre *vt* COM win over

convenable *adj* COM *somme* acceptable, adequate, decent, respectable, satisfactory, DROIT fit and proper

convenance *f* COM convenience, expediency, leisure; ◆ **à la ~ de qn** COM at sb's convenience, at sb's leisure

convenant: ~ **a qch** *loc* COM appropriate for sth

convenir: *vt* ~ **d'une entrevue** RES HUM arrange an interview, fix up an interview, COM be adequate, be suitable for; ◆ ~ **à** COM be appropriate for, suit, INFO apply to; ~ **de** COM *prix, conditions* agree on, agree upon, decide on, decide upon; ~ **de faire** COM agree to do, decide to do

convention *f* COM accord, agreement, compact, written agreement, convention, DROIT accord, compact, convention, written agreement, agreement, covenant; ~ **d'arbitrage** COM, DROIT, IND, RES HUM arbitration agreement; ~ **d'assurance du risque de guerre des facultés maritimes** ASSUR waterborne agreement; ~ **de bail avec option d'achat** IMMOB lease option; ~ **collective** (*cc*) DROIT, IND, RES HUM collective agreement, collective bargaining agreement, labor agreement (*AmE*), labour agreement (*BrE*), union contract; ~ **de crédit** COM credit agreement; ~ **douanière**

sur le transit international des marchandises IMP/EXP customs convention on the international transit of goods, ITI; ~ **de double imposition** FISC double taxation agreement; ~ **de fiducie** COM, DROIT trust agreement; ~ **à finalité variable** RES HUM open-ended agreement; ~ **fiscale** FISC tax agreement, tax treaty; ~ **généralisée à tout le secteur** IND, RES HUM industry-wide agreement; ~ **internationale** DROIT, POL international agreement; ~ **de non-concurrence** DROIT covenant not to compete; ~ **de présentation** FIN reporting policy; ~ **un programme-un crédit** FIN one-program-to-one-vote convention (*AmE*), one-programme-to-one-vote convention (*BrE*); ~ **de protection** FIN protective covenant; ~ **salariale** RES HUM wage agreement; ~ **de souscripteur principal** ASSUR leading underwriter agreement; ~ **sur les lignes de charge** TRANSP load line convention; ~ **sur les nouvelles technologies** RES HUM new technology agreement (*UK*); ~ **sur le transport modal de la CNUCED** ECON UNCTAD multi modal-transport convention, UNCTAD MMO; ~ **à syndicat unique** RES HUM single-union agreement (*UK*), single-union deal (*UK*); ~ **de transport multimodal de la CNUCED** ECON *commerce international* UNCTAD multi modal-transport convention, UNCTAD MMO; ~ **verbale** COM simple contract, verbal agreement, DROIT oral contract

Convention: ~ **européenne des droits de l'homme** *f* PROT SOC European Convention on Human Rights; ~ **européenne sur les brevets** *f* BREVETS *propriété intellectuelle*, DROIT European Patent Convention; ~ **de Lomé** *f* ECON, POL Lomé Convention; ~ **sur les droits d'auteur** *f* BREVETS, DROIT Copyright Act; ~ **pour le trafic international des marchandises** *f* TRANSP *chemin de fer* Agreement on International Goods Traffic by Rail; ~ **de Varsovie** *f* TRANSP Warsaw Convention

conventionnel, -elle *adj* COM, DROIT *clause* contractual

conventions: ~ **comptables** *f pl* COMPTA accounting conventions

Conventions: ~ **de La Haye** *f pl* TRANSP The Hague Rules

convenu, e *adj* COM *heure, endroit, montant* agreed; ◆ **avoir ~ de qch** COM be agreed on sth; **comme ~** COM as agreed, as per agreement

convergence *f* (*ANT divergence*) BOURSE convergence, COM confluence, convergence, ECON, POL *d'opinions, de résultats* convergence

convergent, e *adj* COM confluent, convergent, ECON, POL *opinions, résultats* convergent; ◆ **être ~** COM converge

converger 1. *vt* DROIT concur; **2.** *vi* COM converge

conversationnel, -elle *adj* INFO interactive

conversion *f* BOURSE, COM *de titres* conversion, ECON *de devises*, FIN *de devises* conversion, translation, IMMOB *d'immeubles*, INFO *d'un mode à un autre* conversion, MATH decimalization;

~ **accélérée** BANQUE *d'obligations* accelerated conversion; ~ **de binaire en décimale** INFO binary-to-decimal conversion; ~ **binaire-décimale** INFO binary-to-decimal conversion; ~ **de bons** BOURSE bond conversion; ~ **de décimale en binaire** INFO decimal-to-binary conversion; ~ **décimale-binaire** INFO decimal-to-binary conversion; ~ **de devises** ECON foreign currency translation; ~ **de données** INFO data conversion; ~ **de fichiers** INFO file conversion; ~ **inverse** BOURSE reverse conversion; ~ **involontaire** IMMOB involuntary conversion; ~ **d'obligations** BOURSE bond conversion

converti, e *adj (conv.)* COM, IMMOB converted *(conv)*

convertibilité *f* BOURSE, FIN convertibility

convertible *adj* BOURSE, FIN convertible

convertir *vt* COM commute, convert, ECON, FIN *de devises* convert, translate, INFO *d'un mode à un autre* convert; ◆ ~ **en espèces** COM change into cash, convert into cash, turn into cash

convertissement *m* BOURSE liquidation, ECON, FIN *de devises* conversion, translation

convertisseur: ~ **analogique-numérique** *m (CAN)* INFO analog-digital converter *(ADC)*; ~ **numérique-analogique** *m (CNA)* INFO digital-analog converter *(DAC)*

conviction *f* COM firm belief, *publicité* belief, V&M *publicité* belief

convivial, e *adj (ANT non-convivial)* INFO, V&M friendly, user-friendly

convivialité *f* INFO, V&M user-friendliness

convocation *f* COM, GESTION *d'une réunion* calling, convening, convocation, convoking

convoquer *vt* COM, GESTION *réunion* call, convene, convoke

coop *f (coopérative)* COM coop, cooperative society

coopé *f (coopérative)* COM coop, cooperative store

coopérateur, -trice *m,f* COM, IND cooperator, joint operator

coopératif, -ive *adj* COM, RES HUM collaborative

coopération *f* COM collaboration, cooperation; ~ **avec un pays tiers** ECON *commerce international* third country cooperation; ~ **économique internationale** ECON, POL international economic cooperation; ~ **industrielle** IND industrial cooperation; ~ **politique** ADMIN, POL political cooperation; ~ **technique entre pays en voie de développement** ECON, POL technical co-operation amongst developing countries, TCDC; ~ **technologique** COM, IND technology cooperation

Coopération: ~ **économique en Asie-Pacifique** *f* ECON, POL Asia-Pacific Economic Co-operation, APEC; ~ **économique européenne** *f* ECON, POL European Monetary Cooperation; ~ **européenne en matière de science et de technologie** *f* IND European Cooperation in Science and Technology, COST

coopérative *f (coop, coopé)* COM cooperative, cooperative society *(coop)*; ~ **agricole** ECON, POL cooperative farm; ~ **de détaillants** V&M retail coop, retail cooperative; ~ **de gros** COM Cooperative Wholesale Society, wholesale coop, wholesale cooperative, CWS; ~ **ouvrière** RES HUM workers' cooperative; ~ **de vente en gros** COM wholesale coop, wholesale cooperative, *magasin* cooperative, cooperative store

coopérer *vi* COM collaborate, cooperate

coopter *vt* COM, RES HUM admit, coopt

coordinateur^1, -trice *adj* COM coordinating

coordinateur^2, -trice *m,f* COM, GESTION, RES HUM coordinator; ~ **des exportations** IMP/EXP, RES HUM export coordinator

coordination *f* COM, GESTION, TRANSP coordination; ~ **négociée** ECON negotiated coordination

coordonné, e *adj* COM, TRANSP coordinated

coordonnées *f pl* ADMIN personal details, personal particulars; ~ **bancaires** BANQUE bank details

coordonner *vt* COM coordinate, *ressources* pool, TRANSP coordinate

Copenhague *n pr* COM Copenhagen

copie *f* ADMIN facsimile, fax, COM copy, reproduction, *contrefaçon* copy, COMMS facsimile, fax, INFO copy; ~ **antenne** MÉDIA *télévision* master; ~ **carbone** ADMIN, COMMS carbon copy, cc; ~ **certifiée conforme** DROIT certified true copy; ~ **conforme** ADMIN *d'un document* certified copy, true copy, COM transcription, DROIT *d'un document légal* certified copy, conformed copy, true copy; ~ **d'enregistrement** INFO duplicated record; ~ **imprimée** ADMIN, COMMS, INFO hard copy; ~ **prête à filmer** MÉDIA *impression* camera-ready copy, CRC; ~ **prête à la reproduction** MÉDIA *impression* camera-ready copy, CRC; ~ **prête à reproduire** MÉDIA *impression* camera-ready copy, CRC; ~ **de sauvegarde** INFO backup copy, security backup, security copy; ~ **de secours** INFO backup copy, security backup, security copy; ~ **de travail** FISC *d'une déclaration* working copy; ~ **type** COM specimen copy; ◆ **faire une ~ de sauvegarde** INFO back up

copier *vt* COM copy, duplicate, INFO copy, dump, duplicate

copieur *m* ADMIN, COM, COMMS copier, photocopier, photocopying machine

copolymère: ~ **autolisseur** *m* TRANSP self-polishing copolymer, SPC

coprocesseur *m* INFO coprocessor

copropriétaire *mf* FISC, IMMOB, RES HUM co-owner, joint owner

copropriété *f* DROIT communal ownership, joint ownership, res communis, IMMOB co-ownership, communal ownership, part ownership, res communis *(frml)*; ~ **non-solidaire** DROIT, IMMOB tenancy in severalty

COPS *abrév (créances comptables émises continuellement en francs suisses)* BOURSE COPS

(continuously offered payment rights in Swiss francs)

copyright *m* BREVETS, DROIT copyright

coque *f* TRANSP *d'un navire* hull; **~ intérieure** TRANSP *d'un navire, d'un avion* fuselage, skin; ◆ **bordé de ~** TRANSP *navigation* shell plating

coqueron: **~ arrière** *m* TRANSP *d'un navire* aft peak tank, afterpeak, APT; **~ avant** *m* TRANSP *d'un navire* forepeak, *matière sèche* fore peak tank, FPT

coquille *f* INFO typo, typographical error, MÉDIA *impression* literal, literal error, typo, typographical error

corbeille *f jarg* BOURSE pit, ring, trading floor, trading pit *(jarg)*, trading post *(jarg)*; **à la ~** *jarg* BOURSE on the stock exchange; **~ des affaires en cours** COM pending tray; **~ de rangement** COM filing basket

cordoba *f* COM Cordoba, cordoba

Corée: **~ du Nord** *f* COM Democratic People's Republic of Korea, North Korea; **~ du Sud** *f* COM South Korea

coréen[1], **-enne** *adj* COM Korean

coréen[2] *m* COM *langue* Korean

Coréen, -enne *m,f* COM *habitant* Korean

co-régulation *f* RES HUM joint regulation

coresponsabilité *f* DROIT joint liability

corne: **~ d'abondance** *f* ECON cornucopia

corporation *f* ADMIN public body, COM corp., corporation, public body, DROIT combine, RES HUM guild; **~ acheteuse** FISC corporate purchaser; **~ agricole familiale** FISC family farm corporation; **~ assurant la continuation** FISC continuing corporation; **~ bénéficiaire** FISC corporate beneficiary; **~ à capital de risque visée par règlement** FIN prescribed venture capital corporation; **~ contrôlée** BOURSE controlled company, controlled corporation; **~ coopérative** FISC cooperative corporation; **~ dispensée** FISC exempt corporation; **~ dominante** BOURSE controlling corporation; **~ exclue** FISC *crédit d'impôt à l'investissement remboursable* excluded corporation; **~ exonérée d'impôt** COM, FISC tax-exempt corporation; **~ exploitant une petite entreprise admissible** FISC qualifying small business corporation; **~ fusionnée** FISC amalgamated corporation; **~ imposable** COM, FISC taxable corporation; **~ issue d'une fusion** FISC amalgamated corporation; **~ de logement** FISC housing corporation; **~ mère** BOURSE parent corporation; **~ mutuelle** ASSUR mutual corporation; **~ de placement** BOURSE, FIN investment corporation; **~ de portefeuille** COM, DROIT, FISC, IMMOB holding corporation; **~ publique** COM, FISC public corporation *(UK)*

corporations: **~ associées** *f pl* COM, FISC associated corporations

corporatisme *m* COM, POL corporatism, RES HUM guild socialism *(UK)*

corporel, -elle *adj* (ANT *incorporel*) COM, COMPTA, DROIT, ECON, FIN corporeal, tangible

corps: **~ constitués** *m pl* COM public authority; **~ du délit** *m* DROIT actus reus; **~ législatif** *m* DROIT legislative body, legislature; **~ de métier** *m* COM trade association, RES HUM guild, trade association; **~ -mort traditionnel** *m* TRANSP *navigation* conventional mooring buoy, CBM; **~ de navire** *m* TRANSP hull; **~ professionnel reconnu** *m* FIN recognized professional body *(UK)*, RPB *(UK)*

corpus *m* DROIT corpus

correct, e *adj* COM, DROIT above board, correct, fair

correctement *adv* COM correctly

correcteur, -trice *m,f* MÉDIA *d'épreuves* proofreader, *édition* editor, RES HUM editor; **~ d'orthographe** INFO spellcheck, spellchecker, word speller; **~ orthographique** INFO spellcheck, spellchecker, word speller; **~ -rédacteur** MÉDIA copyreader *(US)*

correction *f* BOURSE correction, market correction, COM contractual liability, corrective action, *cours* correction, COMPTA adjustment, DROIT contractual liability, correction; **~ à la baisse** BOURSE downward correction; **~ pour eau douce** TRANSP *navigation* fresh water allowance, FWA

corrections: **~ de fin d'exercice des dépenses constatées d'avance** *f pl* FIN year-end adjustments for accrued expenses

corrélation *f* MATH correlation, interrelation; **~ multiple** MATH multiple correlation; **~ négative** MATH negative correlation; **~ non-linéaire** MATH nonlinear correlation; **~ positive** MATH positive correlation; **~ proche** MATH close correlation; **~ de rang** MATH rank correlation; **~ sérielle** MATH serial correlation

corresp. *abrév (correspondance)* COM, COMMS corr. *(correspondence)*

correspondance *f* COM *communication, lettres* correspondence, COMMS *lettres* mail, post *(BrE)*, COMMS correspondence, TRANSP *par avion* connecting flight, connection; **~ en gros** COMMS bulk mail

correspondant[1], **e** *adj* COM corresponding

correspondant[2], **e** *m,f* BANQUE, FIN, MÉDIA correspondent; **~ à l'étranger** MÉDIA foreign correspondent; **~ financier** MÉDIA financial correspondent; **~ hypothécaire** BANQUE, FIN mortgage correspondent; **~ local** MÉDIA *presse*, RES HUM stringer *(jarg)*; **~ en valeurs du Trésor** *(CVT)* BOURSE reporting dealer

correspondre *vi* COMMS correspond; **~ à un poste inoccupé** RES HUM fill a manpower gap; ◆ **~ à** COM correspond, match, correspond to, correspond with

corrigé: **~ en fonction des variations saisonnières** *adj* COM *chiffres*, ECON seasonally adjusted

corriger *vt* COM read, *erreurs, épreuves* correct, DROIT amend, INFO edit, MÉDIA *copie* sub (*infrml*), subedit, *épreuves* correct; ◆ ~ **des épreuves** MÉDIA proofread

corroborer *vt* COM confirm, corroborate

corrompre *vt* COM bribe, give bribes, DROIT graft (*infrml*), POL, V&M *personne* bribe, corrupt

corrosion *f* IND corrosion

corruption *f* COM, POL, V&M bribery, corruption; ~ **active** *(*ANT *corruption passive)* COM, POL giving bribes; ~ **de fonctionnaire** DROIT graft (*infrml*); ~ **passive** *(*ANT *corruption active)* COM, POL taking bribes

cos *abrév (cosinus)* MATH *symbole* cos *(cosine)*

cosignataire[1] *adj* COM, DROIT cosignatory

cosignataire[2] *mf* COM, DROIT cosignatory

cosignature *f* COM, DROIT joint signature

cosigner *vt* COM, DROIT cosign

cosinus *m (cos)* MATH cosine *(cos)*

Costa: ~ **Rica** *m* COM Costa Rica

costaricien, -enne *adj* COM Costa Rican

Costaricien, -enne *m,f* COM *habitant* Costa Rican

cotable *adj* BOURSE quotable

cotation *f* ASSUR quotation, BOURSE listing, quotation, DROIT listing, FIN *valeur à l'origine* marking, TRANSP voyage estimate; ~ **assistée en continu** *(CAC)* BOURSE automated quotation; ~ **au-dessus du pair** BOURSE premium quotation; ~ **au-dessus de la valeur nominale** BOURSE premium quotation; ~ **boursière** BOURSE security rating; ~ **complète** BOURSE full quotation; ~ **du disponible** BOURSE spot quotation; ~ **ferme** BOURSE firm quote; ~ **Hulbert** FIN Hulbert rating; ~ **nominale** BOURSE nominal quotation; ~ **officielle** ASSUR, COM official quotation; ~ **à l'ouverture** BOURSE opening quotation; ~ **sans intérêt** BOURSE flat quotation; ~ **suspendue** BOURSE suspended trading; ~ **d'un taux d'intérêt** BANQUE, ECON interest rate quotation

cote *f* BOURSE quotation, quote, *des cours de Bourse* price list, FIN quotation, quote; ~ **d'alerte** COM danger point; ~ **en Bourse** BOURSE security rating; ~ **boursière** BOURSE official list, securities listing, stock exchange list; ~ **longue** BOURSE long exercise price, long strike price; ~ **officielle** BOURSE official list, securities listing, stock exchange list; ~ **de popularité** COM, POL popularity rating

Côte: ~ **-d'Ivoire** *f* COM Ivory Coast

coté, e *adj* BOURSE listed, quoted, listed; ~ **en bourse** BOURSE listed, quoted; ◆ ~ **à** BOURSE listed at, quoted at, valued at; **comme si ~** BOURSE when distributed

côte *f* TRANSP shore

côté: ~ **du crédit** *m* COMPTA, FIN credit side; ~ **du débit** *m* COMPTA, FIN debit side

coter *vt* BOURSE *au pair* list, quote; ◆ ~ **le stock** COMPTA mark stock

cotisant, e *m,f* FISC contributor

cotisation *f* ASSUR *à la Sécurité sociale* contribution, COM *à une collecte* contribution, *à un club*

subscription, FISC assessing action, assessment, RES HUM dues; ~ **des adhérents** COM association subscription; ~ **allocation familiale** FISC family benefit contribution; ~ **arbitraire** FISC arbitrary assessment; ~ **à une association** COM association subscription; ~ **d'assurance contre le chômage** ASSUR unemployment insurance premium; ~ **assurance maladie** FISC health insurance contribution; ~ **au civil** FISC civil assessment; ~ **express** FISC walk-through assessment; ~ **aux frais funéraires** ASSUR contribution to funeral expenses; ~ **aux frais des obsèques** ASSUR contribution to funeral expenses; ~ **d'impôt** FISC assessed tax; ~ **initiale** FISC initial assessment; ~ **originale** FISC original assessment; ~ **patronale** COMPTA, FISC, RES HUM employer's contribution; ~ **politique** POL political contribution; ~ **de protection** FISC jeopardy assessment; ~ **retraite** FISC retirement contribution; ~ **supplémentaire** FISC additional assessment; ~ **syndicale** RES HUM affiliation fee, dues, trade union subscription *(UK)*, trade union contribution *(UK)*, trade union dues *(UK)*, union fees

cotisations: ~ **d'employé** *f pl* FISC *pensions* contributions through employment; ~ **de membre** *f pl* FISC membership dues; ~ **à payer sur le revenu d'un travail indépendant** *f pl* FISC *retraite* contribution payable on self-employed earnings; ~ **à régime de retraite** *f pl* FIN, FISC, RES HUM pension contributions; ~ **pour la retraite** *f pl* RES HUM superannuation contribution; ~ **de Sécurité sociale** *f pl* FISC payroll taxes; ~ **sociales** *f pl* FISC payroll taxes, social security contributions

cotiser **1.** *vt* ASSUR *à la Sécurité sociale*, COM *à une collecte* contribute; **2.** *vi* COM *à un club* subscribe

cotitulaire *mf* BOURSE joint holder

cotitulaires: ~ **avec droit de survivance** *m pl* BOURSE joint tenants

coton *m* BOURSE, IND cotton; ~ **disponible immédiatement** IND spot cotton

cotre *m* TRANSP *navire* ctr, cutter

couche *f* INFO layer, PROT SOC *de société* stratum; ~ **d'ozone** ENVIR ozone layer

couches: ~ **sociales** *f pl* PROT SOC social strata, social stratification

couchette *f* TRANSP *dans un navire, un train* couchette

coulage *m* TRANSP leakage; ~ **des nappes** ENVIR oil slick sinking; ◆ ~ **et casse** TRANSP leakage and breakage, lkg & bkg

coulée: ~ **du navire** *f* TRANSP run of the ship

couler **1.** *vt infrml* COM *société* bankrupt, bring down, ruin, *stocks* work down; **2.** *vi* COM *société* go bankrupt, go to the wall *(infrml)*, go under *(infrml)*

couleur *f* INFO color *(AmE)*, colour *(BrE)*; ~ **de fond** INFO background color *(AmE)*, background colour *(BrE)*; ~ **du titre** IMMOB color of title *(AmE)*, colour of title *(BrE)*

couloir *m* COM *dans un bureau*, TRANSP *dans un*

avion, dans un train aisle; **~ aérien** TRANSP air corridor

coup *m* COM *affaire* deal, *choc* blow, knock (*infrml*), RES HUM rigging (*jarg*); **~ de bélier** *infrml* COM cash flow squeeze; **~ de bol** *infrml* COM lucky break; **~ de chance** COM lucky break; **~ de fil** *infrml* COMMS bell (*infrml*), call, phone call; **~ porté à la productivité** ECON productivity shock; **~ de pot** *infrml* COM lucky break; **~ de pouce publicitaire** V&M plug (*infrml*); **~ de téléphone** COMMS bell (*infrml*), call, phone call; ♦ **donner un ~ de collier** COM put one's back into it; **tenter le ~** *infrml* COM buy sth on spec (*infrml*)

coup. *abrév* BOURSE *(coupure)* subshare, COM *(coupon)* c., CP *(coupon)*, ECON *(coupure)* billet de banque denom. *(denomination)*

coupable[1] *adj* DROIT culpable, guilty; ♦ **~ du délit d'outrage à la cour** DROIT in contempt of court; **~ du délit d'outrage à magistrat** DROIT in contempt of court

coupable[2] *mf* DROIT guilty party

coupe:[1] **~ -feu** *adj* COM fire-resistant, fire-resistive

coupe:[2] **~ de carburant** *f* TRANSP wide-cut gas (*AmE*), wide-cut gasoline (*AmE*), wide-cut petrol (*BrE*); **~ sombre** *f* COM, COMPTA, ECON, FIN cutback, drastic cut, severe reduction; **~ transversale** *f* COM cross section

couper *vt* COM, INFO cut; ♦ **~ -coller** INFO cut and paste; **~ l'herbe sous le pied de qn** COM pull the rug out from under sb, take the wind out of sb's sails; **~ les liens avec** ECON sever links with; **~ la poire en deux** COM split the difference; **~ les vivres à qn** COM stop sb's allowance

couplage: **~ extensible** *m* TRANSP slip coupling, SC

couple *m* TRANSP *navire* frame

couplé: **~ et perdu** *loc* BOURSE matched and lost

couples: **~ longitudinaux** *m pl* TRANSP *navire* longitudinal framing

coupon *m* BOURSE bond coupon, coupon, nominal yield, COM coupon, FIN coupon; **~ attaché** BOURSE *avec le dividende* cd, cum coupon, cum dividend; **~ à court terme** BOURSE short coupon; **~ détaché** BOURSE, COM ex-coupon; **~ de dividende** BOURSE dividend coupon; **~ échu** BOURSE matured coupon; **~ émis depuis plus de trois mois** BOURSE seasoned certificate of deposit; **~ d'intérêt** FIN interest coupon; **~ obligataire** BOURSE bond coupon; **~ au porteur** BOURSE bearer coupon; **~ -réponse** V&M *vente par correspondance* reply coupon, reply device; **~ de vol** TRANSP flight coupon (*jarg*), flight ticket

couponnage: **~ croisé** *m* V&M cross couponing

coups: **à ~ d'accordéon** *loc* ECON stop-and-go

coupure *f* BOURSE subshare, ECON *billet de banque* denomination, MÉDIA *presse* clipping (*AmE*), cutting (*BrE*); **~ d'alimentation** INFO power fail, power failure; **~ de courant** INFO blackout; **~ de journal** MÉDIA clipping (*AmE*), cutting (*BrE*), press clipping (*AmE*), press cutting (*BrE*); **~ de**

presse MÉDIA clipping (*AmE*), cutting (*BrE*), press clipping (*AmE*), press cutting (*BrE*); **~ publicitaire** MÉDIA *télévision, radio* commercial break

cour *f* DROIT court; **~ d'appel** DROIT Court of Appeal, appeal court, appeals court, appellate court, CA; **~ d'arbitrage** DROIT court of arbitration; **~ de la chancellerie** DROIT ch, chancery; **~ de justice** DROIT court of law; **~ du travail** DROIT, RES HUM labor court (*AmE*), labour court (*BrE*)

Cour:[1] **~ de cassation** *m* France DROIT Court of Appeal, final Court of Appeal, CA

Cour:[2] **~ des comptes** *f* COMPTA Court of Auditors; **~ européenne** *f* DROIT, POL European Court; **~ internationale de justice** *f* DROIT, POL International Court of Justice, ICJ; **~ de justice** *f* DROIT, POL *de l'Union européenne* Court of Justice; **~ de justice européenne** *f* DROIT, POL European Court of Justice; **la ~** *f* DROIT the Bench (*infrml*); **~ suprême** *f* DROIT Supreme Court, *Angleterre et Pays de Galles* the High Court (*UK*)

courant:[1] **e** *adj* COM common, current, routine; ♦ **votre courrier du 5 ~** *frml* COMMS your letter of 5th instant

courant[2] *m* IND *électrique*, INFO current, electrical current, electricity, power; **~ alternatif** *(ca)* IND alternating current, INFO alternating current *(AC)*; **~ continu** IND, INFO direct current, DC; **~ électrique** IND, INFO current, electrical current, electricity, power; ♦ **au ~ de** COM abreast of, in the know about (*infrml*), in the picture about, informed about, up to date on; **être au ~ de** COM be acquainted with

courbe *f* ECON, MATH curve; **~ d'accoutumance** ECON, PROT SOC, RES HUM learning curve; **~ d'apprentissage** ECON, PROT SOC, RES HUM learning curve; **~ d'augmentation de salaire** RES HUM salary progression curve; **~ des bénéfices** COMPTA, FIN profit graph; **~ en cloche** MATH bell-shaped curve; **~ de consommation déterminée par le prix** ECON price consumption curve, PCC; **~ des coûts marginaux** ECON marginal cost curve; **~ de demande compensée** ECON compensated demand curve; **~ de demande coudée** ECON kinked demand curve; **~ de demande** ECON demand curve; **~ de demande par rapport aux revenus du consommateur** ECON income-consumption curve, ICC; **~ d'enveloppe** ECON envelope curve; **~ d'expérience** ECON, PROT SOC, RES HUM experience curve, learning curve; **~ en forme de cloche** MATH bell-shaped curve; **~ de fréquence** MATH frequency curve; **~ de fréquence bimodale** MATH bimodal frequency curve; **~ de fréquence embrochée** MATH skewed frequency curve; **~ de fréquence en forme de J** MATH J-shaped frequency curve; **~ de fréquence en J renversé** MATH reverse J-shaped frequency curve; **~ à fréquence multinomiale** MATH multimodal frequency curve; **~ de fréquence symétrique** MATH symmetrical frequency curve;

~ **d'indifférence** ECON behavior line (*AmE*), behaviour line (*BrE*), indifference curve; ~ **isoquante** ECON equal product curve, isoproduct curve; ~ **en J** ECON J curve; ~ **de Laffer** ECON Laffer curve; ~ **LM** ECON LM curve; ~ **de Lorenz** ECON Lorenz curve; ~ **du marché** COM market line; ~ **négative d'offre de main-d'oeuvre** ECON backward-bending labor supply curve (*AmE*), backward-bending labour supply curve (*BrE*); ~ **négative des offres** ECON backward-bending supply curve; ~ **d'offre inversée** ECON backward-bending supply curve; ~ **d'offre de main-d'oeuvre inversée** ECON backward-bending labor supply curve (*AmE*), backward-bending labour supply curve (*BrE*); ~ **de Phillips** ECON Phillips curve; ~ **en profil de buste** ECON head and shoulders; ~ **de rapport inversée** BANQUE, BOURSE, ECON inverted yield curve, negative yield curve; ~ **de recettes** ECON revenue curve; ~ **de régression** MATH regression curve; ~ **de rendement** BANQUE, BOURSE, ECON yield curve; ~ **de rentabilité** COMPTA, FIN profit graph; ~ **en S** ECON S curve; ~ **des taux** BOURSE yield gap; ~ **des taux d'intérêt** BANQUE, BOURSE, ECON yield curve; ~ **des taux inversée** BANQUE, BOURSE, ECON inverted yield curve, negative yield curve, reverse yield gap; ~ **des taux positive** BANQUE, BOURSE, ECON positive yield curve; ~ **de vie** V&M *d'un produit* life cycle

courir *vi* BANQUE *intérêts* accrue, run, COMPTA accrue; ◆ ~ **le risque de** BOURSE bear the risk of, COM run the risk of

courrier *m* COM *lettres* correspondence, COMMS mail, post (*BrE*), RES HUM runner; ~ **affranchi à la machine** COMMS metered mail (*AmE*); ~ **à l'arrivée** COMMS incoming mail (*AmE*), incoming post (*BrE*); ~ **au départ** COMMS outgoing mail; ~ **départ** ADMIN out-tray; ~ **électronique** ADMIN, COMMS, INFO computer mail, e-mail, electronic mail; ~ **d'entreprise à distribution exceptionnelle (*CEDEX*)** ADMIN business mail service; ~ **à expédier** COMMS outgoing mail; ~ **exprès** COM express mail service; ~ **express** COMMS express mail service, ≈ Datapost® (*UK*); ~ **en gros** COMMS bulk mail; ~ **gros usagers** COMMS bulk mail; ~ **du jour** COMMS day's mail (*AmE*), day's post (*BrE*), incoming mail (*AmE*), incoming post (*BrE*); ~ **non-standard** COMMS nonstandard mail (*UK*); ~ **en partance** COMMS outgoing mail; ~ **personnalisé** INFO mail merge; ~ **rapide par voie de surface** COMMS accelerated surface mail (*AmE*), accelerated surface post (*BrE*); ~ **recommandé** COMMS certified mail (*AmE*), certified post (*BrE*), registered mail, registered post (*BrE*); ~ **au tarif normal** COMMS first-class mail (*AmE*), first-class post (*BrE*); ~ **à tarif réduit** COMMS second-class mail (*AmE*), second-class post (*BrE*); ~ **urgent** COMMS priority mail (*AmE*), urgent mail (*AmE*), urgent post (*BrE*); ◆ **par** ~ **ordinaire** COMMS by surface mail

courroies *f pl* TRANSP *pour palettes* strapping

cours *m* BOURSE *d'une valeur mobilière* pr., price, quotation, quote, COM *enseignement* course, *prix* rate, ECON *de devises* rate, FIN quotation, quote, *de devises* rate, PROT SOC lecture, *enseignement* course; ~ **d'achat** *m* BOURSE buying rate; ~ **acheteur** *m* BANQUE *d'une devise* buying rate of exchange, BANQUE buyer's rate, buying rate, BOURSE bid price, buyer's rate, buying rate, COM buyer's rate, buying rate, ECON *d'une devise* buying rate of exchange, ECON buyer's rate, buying rate, FIN *d'une devise* buying rate of exchange, FIN buyer's rate, buying rate; ~ **acheteur et vendeur** *m* BOURSE bid-and-asked price, bid-and-offered price; ~ **acheteur ferme** *m* BOURSE firm bid price; ~ **de l'action** *m* GESTION course of action; ~ **d'action indicateur** *m* BOURSE bellwether (*jarg*); ~ **des actions** *m* BOURSE stock quotation; ~ **après bourse** *m* BOURSE street price; ~ **après clôture** *m* BOURSE price after hours; ~ **après l'heure de fermeture** *m* BOURSE price after hours; ~ **avantageux** *m* BOURSE favorable exchange (*AmE*), favourable exchange (*BrE*); ~ **en baisse** *m* ECON falling price; ~ **bancaire** *m* BANQUE *du taux de change* bank selling rate; ~ **bas** *m* BOURSE low price; ~ **de base** *m* BOURSE basis price; ~ **en Bourse** *m* BOURSE stock exchange quotation; ~ **de la Bourse** *m* BOURSE market price, stock list, V&M market rating; ~ **de change historique** *m* ECON historical exchange rate; ~ **de change d'origine** *m* ECON historical exchange rate; ~ **du change à terme** *m* BOURSE forward exchange rate; ~ **des changes au comptant** *m* ECON cash exchange rate, spot exchange rate; ~ **des choses** *m* COM trend of events; ~ **de clôture** *m* BOURSE close, closing price, closing quotation, daily settlement price; ~ **de compensation** *m* BOURSE daily settlement price, settlement price, COM making-up price, M/U; ~ **au comptant** *m* BOURSE spot price, spot rate; ~ **à court terme** *m* BOURSE short futures position, short option position; ~ **demandé et offert** *m* BOURSE asked and bid, bid-and-asked price, bid-and-offered price; ~ **des denrées** *m* BOURSE commodity price; ~ **directeur** *m* COM guide price; ~ **effectif** *m* BOURSE actual quotation; ~ **estimatif** *m* BOURSE valuation price; ~ **estimé** *m* BOURSE nominal quotation; ~ **d'une eurodevise** *m* ECON Eurocurrency rate; ~ **de l'eurodollar** *m* BOURSE, ECON, FIN Eurodollar Rate; ~ **d'exercice moyen** *m* BOURSE middle strike price; ~ **d'exercice de l'option d'achat** *m* (ANT *cours d'exercice de l'option de vente*) BOURSE call's strike; ~ **d'exercice de l'option de vente** *m* (ANT *cours d'exercice de l'option d'achat*) BOURSE put's strike; ~ **extrêmes** *m pl* BOURSE high and low prices; ~ **ferme** *m* BOURSE firm quotation, firm quote; ~ **forcé** *m* BOURSE, ECON, FIN forced currency; ~ **de formation professionnelle** *m* RES HUM training course; ~ **de gestion** *m* COM, PROT SOC business school, business studies; ~ **habituel de l'entreprise** *m* COM normal course of business; ~ **hors Bourse** *m* BOURSE price after hours, price in the streets; ~ **inférieur au cours précédent** *m* (ANT *cours* *supérieur au cours précédent)* BOURSE downtick, minus tick; **~ initial** *m* BOURSE starting price; **~ inscrit à la cote officielle** *m* BOURSE quoted price; **~ justifié** *m* BOURSE justified price; **~ légal** *m* FIN legal tender; **~ légal couvert** *m* BOURSE *de change* hedged tender; **~ limite** *m* BOURSE price limit; **~ de liquidation** *m* BOURSE exchange delivery settlement price, final settlement price, COM making-up price, M/U; **~ de liquidation du contrat final** *m* BOURSE final contract settlement price; **~ du livrable** *m* BOURSE terminal price; **~ du marché** *m* BOURSE current market price, market price, overall market price coverage, prevailing market price, V&M current market price; **~ minimal** *m* BOURSE minimum quote size (*UK*), MQS (*UK*); **~ moyen** *m* BOURSE average price, mid price, middle price, V&M average price; **~ normal des affaires** *m* COM normal course of business; **~ normal de l'entreprise** *m* COM normal course of business; **~ de l'obligation** *m* BOURSE bond price; **~ de l'option d'achat** *m* (ANT *cours de l'option de vente*) BOURSE call option premium; **~ de l'option de vente** *m* (ANT *cours de l'option d'achat*) BOURSE put option premium; **~ d'ouverture** *m* BOURSE opening price; **~ particulier** *m* PROT SOC private lesson, private tuition; **~ plancher** *m* BOURSE bottom, bottom price; **~ le plus bas** *m* BOURSE, COM bottom price, lowest price; **~ le plus haut** *m* BOURSE, COM highest price, top price; **~ pratiqué** *m* V&M ruling price; **~ prédéterminé** *m* BOURSE predetermined price; **~ des produits de base** *m pl* BOURSE primary commodity prices; **~ de recyclage professionnel** *m* RES HUM job retraining course; **~ de référence** *m* BOURSE mark (*jarg*); **~ en repli** *m* ECON falling price; **~ du soir** *m* COM, PROT SOC evening class; **~ supérieur au cours précédent** *m* (ANT *cours inférieur au cours précédent*) BOURSE plus tick, uptick; **~ à terme** *m* BANQUE price for the account, BOURSE forward rate, future price, ECON forward rate; **~ de la transaction** *m* BOURSE entry price; **~ vendeur** *m* (ANT *cours acheteur*) BANQUE offer price, seller's rate, BOURSE asked price, offer price, price offered, seller's rate, COM, ECON, FIN offer price, seller's rate; **~ vendeur et d'achat** *m* BOURSE asked and bid, bid-and-asked price, bid-and-offered price; **~ vendeur ferme** *m* BOURSE firm offer price; **~ de vente ferme** *m* BOURSE firm offer price; **~ en vigueur** *m* V&M ruling price; ◆ **au ~ d'une certaine période** COM over a period of time; **au ~ de la Bourse** BOURSE at the market price; **au ~ des dernières années** COM in recent years; **au ~ des négociations** COM during the negotiations, in the course of negotiations; **au ~ du marché** BOURSE at market; **avoir ~** COM obtain; **avoir un ~ faible** BOURSE run low; **dans le ~** BOURSE in-the-money, ITM; **dans le ~ d'une entreprise** FISC in the course of a business; **en ~** BANQUE *valeur, chèque, billet, lingot* in transit, under way, BOURSE outstanding, COM *affaires* current, ongoing, outstanding, *négociations, réunion, travail* in process, in progress; **en**

~ de construction IND under construction; **en ~ de discussion** COM under discussion; **en ~ de réalisation** COM *projet* in the pipeline; **en ~ de révision** COM under review; **en ~ de traitement** COMMS *commandes* in the pipeline; **en ~ de validité** ADMIN *passeport* valid; **faire ~** PROT SOC deliver a lecture; **les ~ peuvent aussi bien baisser que monter** BOURSE prices can go down as well as up; **les ~ peuvent aussi bien descendre que monter** BOURSE prices can go down as well as up

Cours: **~ des comptes** *f France* COMPTA ≈ Committee of Public Accounts (*UK*)

course *f* COM errand; **~ d'essai** TRANSP test drive; ◆ **faire une ~** COM run an errand; **ne plus être dans la ~** COM be out of the running

courses: **les ~** *f pl* COM shopping

coursier, -ière *m,f* BOURSE runner, waiter (*jarg*), COMMS courier, messenger

court[1], **e** *adj* COM short; ◆ **à ~ d'argent** ECON, short of money, strapped for cash (*infrml*); **à ~ d'une devise** BANQUE short in a currency; **à ~ de** COM low on, short of, *stock, article* in short supply; **à ~ de liquidité** FIN cash-strapped; **à ~ de main d'oeuvre** RES HUM short-handed, short-staffed; **à ~ de main-d'oeuvre** (ANT *ayant un excédent de main-d'oeuvre*) RES HUM under-manned; **à ~ de personnel** RES HUM short-handed, short-staffed; **à ~ en** *infrml* COM *valeurs* low in; **à ~ terme** (ANT *à long terme, à moyen terme*) BANQUE short-range, short-term, BOURSE *obligation, dette* short-dated, short-term, COM, COMPTA, FIN short-range, short-term; **être à ~ d'argent** ECON feel the pinch (*infrml*)

court:[2] **~ -circuit** *m* IND *électrique* short circuit

court:[3] *vt* **~ -circuiter** IND *électrique* short-circuit

courtage *m* BOURSE *activité* brokerage, brokerage allowance (*US*), brokerage commission, brokerage fee, brokering, broking, com., commission, jobbing, COM disagio, RES HUM jobbing; **~ d'assurance** ASSUR insurance broking; **~ d'obligations** BOURSE bond dealings; **~ réduit** BOURSE discount brokerage; ◆ **faire le ~** BOURSE broker

courte: **à ~ distance** *loc* TRANSP short-haul; **à ~ échéance** *loc* BOURSE short-term; **de ~ durée** *loc* COM short-lived, short-term, *répercussions* short-run

courtier[1] *m* RES HUM commission salesman

courtier[2], **ière** *m, f* BOURSE agency broker, broker, stockbroker, *firme de courtage* account executive, FIN agent, broker, RES HUM commission agent, commission merchant, commission salesperson; **~ d'affrètement** TRANSP *navigation* charter broker, chartering broker; **~ d'affrètement à la cueillette** TRANSP liner broker; **~ d'affrètement maritime** TRANSP s&c, shipper and carrier; **~ de l'armateur** TRANSP *maritime* owner's broker; **~ associé** BOURSE allied member; **~ d'assurance** ASSUR insurance broker; **~ attitré** BOURSE registrant; **~ ayant pignon sur rue** BOURSE high-street share shop (*UK*); ~ **de Bourse** BOURSE stock-broker; ~ **de change** BOURSE bill broker, bill merchant; ~ **à la commission** BOURSE commission broker (*US*); ~ **à la cueillette** TRANSP liner broker; ~ **de détail** BOURSE retail broker; ~ **en devises** BANQUE, BOURSE, FIN foreign exchange broker, foreign exchange dealer; ~ **en douane** IMP/EXP, RES HUM customs broker; ~ **d'escompte** BOURSE bill broker, bill merchant; ~ **exécutant** BOURSE discount broker, discount stockbroker; ~ **en exercice** BOURSE running broker; ~ **en fichiers** COM list broker; ~ **du gouvernement** BOURSE government broker; ~ **hypothécaire** BANQUE, FIN mortgage broker (*US*); ~ **en immobilier commercial** COM, IMMOB commercial broker (*US*); ~ **indépendant** BOURSE independent broker; ~ **internégociants** BANQUE IDB (*BrE*), interdealer broker (*BrE*); ~ **livreur** BOURSE delivery broker; ~ **en logiciel** BOURSE software broker; ~ **au long cours** RES HUM deep sea broker; ~ **mandataire** BOURSE agency broker; ~ **en marchandises** BOURSE commodity broker, FIN, V&M commodity broker, merchandise broker; ~ **du marché primaire** BOURSE primary market dealer; ~ **de marine** RES HUM deep sea broker; ~ **maritime** RES HUM, TRANSP loading broker, ship-broker, vessel broker; ~ **en matières premières** BOURSE, FIN, V&M commodity broker; ~ **membre du parquet** BOURSE floor broker; ~ **monétaire** BANQUE money broker; ~ **non-agréé** BOURSE unlicensed broker; ~ **non membre** BOURSE outsider broker; ~ **obligataire** BOURSE bond broker; ~ **en obligations** BOURSE bond broker, bond dealer; ~ **d'options agréé** BOURSE registered options broker; ~ **en options non-agréé** BOURSE put broker; ~ **payé au pourcentage** BOURSE value broker; ~ **en publicité** V&M space broker; ~ **de quartier** BOURSE high-street share shop (*UK*); ~ **à service complet** BOURSE full-service broker; ~ **spéculateur** BOURSE spectail; ~ **sur contrats à terme agréé** BOURSE futures-registered broker; ~ **tous services** BOURSE full-service broker; ~ **en transports pétroliers** BOURSE, TRANSP tanker broker; ~ **en valeurs** BOURSE jobber (*UK, dat*), market maker, stockbroker, stockjobber (*UK, dat*); ~ **en valeurs mobilières** BOURSE broker, investment dealer, stockbroker, FIN investment dealer; ~ **en valeurs de sociétés de logiciel** BOURSE software broker

courtière *f* RES HUM commission saleswoman, commission salesperson

coussin: ~ **de devises** *m* ECON monetary reserve

coût *m* ECON, FIN, V&M cost; ~ **accessoire** COM soft cost; ~ **d'achat** COMPTA acquisition cost, purchase cost; ~ **d'achat des marchandises vendues** ECON, V&M cost of sales; ~ **d'acquisition** COMPTA, ECON, FISC acquisition cost; ~ **d'acquisition comptable** COMPTA book cost; ~ **d'adaptation sociale** RES HUM social adjustment cost; ~ **admissible d'un bien** FISC eligible asset cost; ~ **affecté** COMPTA, ECON, FIN applied cost;

~ **aller-retour** TRANSP round-trip cost; ~ **amorti** COMPTA depreciated cost, FISC amortized cost; ~ **amortissable** COMPTA depreciable cost, FISC amortized cost; ~ **d'assurance** ASSUR insurance cost; ~ **en augmentation** ECON rising cost; ~ **de base** FIN hard cost; ~ **de base ajusté** COMPTA adjusted cost base (*Canada*); ~ **brut** FISC *d'un bien* gross cost; ~ **brut d'extraction de gaz** IND wellhead cost; ~ **brut d'extraction pétrolière** IND wellhead cost; ~ **budgété** COMPTA, ECON, FIN budgeted cost; ~ **du capital** BOURSE capital cost; ~ **des capitaux** BANQUE, FIN cost of funds; ~ **d'une communication téléphonique** COMMS charge, rate, toll (*US*); ~ **contrôlable** COMPTA controllable cost; ~ **contrôlé** ECON, FIN managed cost; ~ **courant** COMPTA current cost; ~ **de couverture** BOURSE hedge cost; ~ **différentiel du capital** FIN incremental cost of capital; ~ **direct** COMPTA, ECON, FIN direct cost, direct expense; ~ **discrétionnaire** ECON discretionary cost; ~ **économique** ECON economic cost; ~ **effectif** FISC actual cost, real cost; ~ **d'emballage** IND packaging cost; ~ **de l'emprunt** BANQUE, COM, COMPTA, ECON, FIN borrowing cost; ~ **d'entrée** COMPTA initial outlay, input cost; ~ **estimé** COMPTA estimated cost; ~ **évitable** COM avoidable cost; ~ **explicite** ECON explicit cost; ~ **d'exploitation** TRANSP *d'une charte-partie* running cost; ~ **des facteurs** COMPTA, ECON, IND factor cost; ~ **de facture** COMPTA invoice cost; ~ **aux fins de l'impôt** FISC tax cost; ~ **fixe** COMPTA, ECON fixed cost; ~ **de fret** TRANSP cost of freight; ~ **d'habitation** FISC, IMMOB occupancy cost; ~ **en hausse** ECON rising cost; ~ **historique** COMPTA historical cost; ~ **d'immobilisation** BOURSE capital cost; ~ **implicite** ECON implicit cost; ~ **de l'impôt** FISC tax cost; ~ **imputé** COMPTA, ECON, FIN applied cost; ~ **indiqué** FISC cost amount; ~ **indirect** (*ANT coût direct*) COMPTA, ECON, FIN indirect cost, indirect expense; ~ **irrécupérable** FIN sunk cost; ~ **limite** ECON cost objective; ~ **de location** FISC *d'un bien* rental cost; ~ **de main-d'oeuvre** ECON, FISC, RES HUM labor cost (*AmE*), labour cost (*BrE*); ~ **de main d'oeuvre par unité** RES HUM unit labor cost (*AmE*), unit labour cost (*BrE*); ~ **maîtrisable** COMPTA controllable cost, managed cost; ~ **maîtrisé** COMPTA controllable cost, managed cost; ~ **majoré des fonds** FIN cost of funds plus; ~ **des marchandises produites** COMPTA, ECON, IND cost of goods manufactured; ~ **marginal** COMPTA, ECON, FIN marginal cost; ~ **marginal moyen** COMPTA, ECON, FIN average incremental cost; ~ **médias** V&M above the line; ~ **de mise en conformité** ENVIR cost of compliance; ~ **moyen** (*cm*) COMPTA average cost, mean cost; ~ **moyen pondéré** COMPTA weighted average cost; ~ **moyen des sinistres** ASSUR average cost of claims; ~ **net** COMPTA net cost; ~ **d'obligation** BOURSE *taux d'intérêt à terme* liability cost; ~ **d'observation** FISC compliance cost; ~ **d'occupation** FISC, IMMOB occupancy cost; ~ **d'opportunité** COMPTA, ECON, FIN alternative cost, opportunity cost; ~ **d'option** FIN opportunity cost; ~ **à l'origine** COMPTA replacement cost; ~ **de passation de commande** COM, FIN procurement cost; ~ **périphérique** COM soft cost; ~ **permanent** COMPTA continuing cost; ~ **personnel du chômage** ECON, PROT SOC, RES HUM private cost of unemployment; ~ **de portage** FIN carrying cash, cost of carry; ~ **d'un prêt** BANQUE cost of a loan; ~ **privé** RES HUM private cost; ~ **privé marginal** ECON marginal private cost; ~ **de production** COMPTA, FIN, IND cost of production, production cost; ~ **de la production vendue** COMPTA, ECON, IND cost of goods sold, cost of sales; ~ **du produit** V&M product cost; ~ **de produits liés** COMPTA joint product cost; ~ **de la recherche appliquée** COM applied research cost; ~ **du recouvrement** COM collection cost; ~ **réel** COMPTA, FISC actual cost, real cost; ~ **réellement engagé** COMPTA actual cost, real cost; ~ **de remplacement** ASSUR, COMPTA, ECON current cost, replacement cost; ~ **réparti** COMPTA, ECON, FIN applied cost; ~ **d'une reprise d'un bien à bail** FIN lease acquisition cost; ~ **de revient standard** COM standard cost; ~ **de rupture de stock** COM stockout cost; ~ **salarial** ECON, FISC, RES HUM labor cost *(AmE)*, labour cost *(BrE)*, payroll cost; ~ **semi-fixe** COMPTA semifixed cost; ~ **semi-variable** COMPTA mixed cost, semivariable expense; ~ **social** ECON private cost, social cost; ~ **social du chômage** PROT SOC, RES HUM social cost of unemployment; ~ **social marginal** ECON marginal social cost; ~ **social d'un monopole** ECON social cost of monopoly; ~ **standard** COM, COMPTA, ECON, FIN budgeted cost, cost standard, standard cost; ~ **de substitution** COMPTA, ECON opportunity cost; ~ **supplétif** ECON imputed cost; ~ **total** COM, COMPTA, ECON total cost; ~ **total du crédit au consommateur** COM, FIN, V&M total cost of the credit to the consumer; ~ **total moyen** COM averge total cost, COMPTA, ECON average total cost; ~ **toujours valide** ECON unexpired cost; ~ **de transformation** COMPTA conversion cost; ~ **unitaire de la main-d'oeuvre** ECON, IND, RES HUM unit labor cost *(AmE)*, unit labour cost *(BrE)*; ~ **unitaire moyen** COM, COMPTA, V&M average unit cost; ~ **unitaire du personnel** COMPTA, RES HUM unit labour cost *(AmE)*, unit labour cost *(BrE)*; ~ **utile de base** FISC relevant cost base; ~ **utilisateur** FIN user cost; ~ **variable** COMPTA, ECON, FIN, TRANSP variable cost; ~ **variable des ventes** COM, V&M direct cost of sales; ~ **de la vie** COM, ECON cost of living; ~ **du voyage** COMPTA, TRANSP voyage expenses; ◆ ~, **assurance et fret/guerre** IMP/EXP cost, insurance and freight/war, CIFW; ~, **assurance, fret** *(CAF)* IMP/EXP, TRANSP *livraison de cargaison* cost, insurance and freight *(CIF)*; ~, **assurance, fret, commission et change** IMP/EXP cost, insurance, freight, commission and exchange, CIFC&E; ~, **assurance, fret, commission et intérêt** IMP/EXP cost, insurance, freight, commission and interest, CIFC&I; ~, **assurance, fret et commission** IMP/EXP cost, insurance,

freight and commission, CIF&C; ~, **assurance, fret et intérêt** IMP/EXP cost, insurance, freight and interest, CIF&I; ~, **assurance, fret, intérêt et change** IMP/EXP cost, insurance, freight, interest and exchange, CIFI&E; ~, **assurance, fret à quai** TRANSP *livraison des marchandises* cost, insurance, freight landed; ~ **et assurance** *(C&A)* IMP/EXP cost and insurance *(C&I)*; ~ **et fret** *(C&F)* IMP/EXP, TRANSP cost and freight *(C&F)*

coûte: qui ~ cher *loc* COM costly

coûteux, -euse *adj* BOURSE pricey *(infrml)*, pricy *(infrml)*, COM costly, dear, expensive, pricey *(infrml)*, pricy *(infrml)*, FIN pricey *(infrml)*, pricy *(infrml)*

coûts *m pl* ECON *prix*, FIN, V&M *prix* costs; ~ **budgétaires** ECON, FIN, POL budgetary costs; ~ **en capital** ECON, FIN capital costs; ~ **à la clôture** FIN closing costs; ~ **de commercialisation** ECON *commerce international* front-end costs; ~ **conjoints** ECON joint costs; ~ **de couverture supplémentaire** ASSUR extension costs; ~ **de démolition** IMMOB demolition costs; ~ **de distribution** COMPTA, TRANSP distribution costs; ~ **engagés** COMPTA committed costs; ~ **essentiels** FIN hard costs; ~ **d'exploitation** TRANSP *d'un navire* operating expenses; ~ **de fabrication** COMPTA *feuilles comptables*, ECON, IND manufacturing costs; ~ **en fin d'exercice** FIN closing costs; ~ **fixes de fabrication** COMPTA, ECON, FIN, IND manufacturing overheads; ~ **indirects de main-d'oeuvre** COMPTA, ECON, RES HUM indirect labor costs *(AmE)*, indirect labour costs *(BrE)*; ~ **d'investissement** ECON, FIN capital costs; ~ **irrécupérables** FIN sunk costs; ~ **de la main-d'oeuvre** IND *production* direct labor costs *(AmE)*, direct labour costs *(BrE)*; ~ **maîtrisés** FIN managed costs; ~ **marketing** V&M marketing cost; ~ **mixtes** COMPTA mixed cost; ~ **d'opération** BANQUE, BOURSE, COMPTA transactions costs; ~ **de promotion** V&M below the line; ~ **salariaux directs** IND *production* direct labor costs *(AmE)*, direct labour costs *(BrE)*; ~ **de soumission** COMPTA compliance costs; ~ **standards** FIN standard costs

coutume *f* DROIT custom, practice

coutumier, -ière *adj* DROIT customary

couturier, -ière *m,f* COM, IND fashion designer

couvercle: ~ d'acier *m* TRANSP steel covers, SC

couvert, e *adj* ASSUR *créancier*, BOURSE *option d'achat, de vente* covered; ◆ ~ **par l'assurance** ASSUR covered by insurance

couverture *f* ASSUR cover *(BrE)*, coverage *(AmE)*, BOURSE hedge, hedging, margin, margin, *du dividende* C'vr, cover, FIN hedging, MÉDIA *d'un magazine* front, V&M *publicitaire* exposure; ~ **d'assurance** ASSUR insurance cover *(BrE)*, insurance coverage *(AmE)*; ~ **d'assurance tiers** ASSUR third-party insurance cover *(BrE)*, third-party insurance coverage *(AmE)*; ~ **avaries comprises** ASSUR W.A. cover; ~ **bancaire** BANQUE bank reserve; ~ **de cargaison, surestaries et**

défense ASSUR, TRANSP FD&D cover, freight, demurrage and defence cover (*BrE*), freight, demurrage and defense cover (*AmE*); **~ de change** COMPTA foreign exchange hedge; **~ complète** ASSUR, MÉDIA *d'un événement* full cover, full coverage; **~ contre l'inflation** ASSUR, FIN hedge against inflation; **~ à court terme** BOURSE short hedge; **~ courte** BOURSE short hedge; **~ croisée** BOURSE cross hedge, cross hedging; **~ delta** FIN delta hedging, dynamic hedging; **~ directe** ASSUR held or direct covered; **~ du dividende privilégié par le bénéfice** COMPTA preferred dividend coverage; **~ des dividendes** BOURSE dividend coverage; **~ des dividendes par l'actif** BOURSE asset coverage; **~ d'un événement** MÉDIA news coverage; **~ fixe** BOURSE fixed hedge; **~ fractionnaire** BANQUE fractional cash reserve, fractional reserve; **~ des frais généraux** COMPTA, FIN overheads recovery; **~ générale du prix du marché** BOURSE overall market price coverage; **~ globale** ASSUR blanket cover, blanket coverage; **~ de l'insolvabilité des participants au projet** ASSUR project participants' insolvency cover; **~ d'investissement** BOURSE investment hedger; **~ des investissements extérieurs** ASSUR overseas investment cover; **~ longue** BOURSE buying hedge, purchasing hedge, long hedge; **~ de maintien** BOURSE maintenance margin; **~ du marché** V&M sales coverage; **~ maximale** BOURSE maximum coverage; **~ médiatique** MÉDIA news coverage; **~ médiocre** (*ANT bonne couverture*) MÉDIA *informations* scant coverage; **~ minimale obligatoire** BOURSE minimum margin requirement; **~ minimum** BOURSE minimum maintenance; **~ d'une option** BOURSE option coverage; **~ or** ECON gold cover; **~ par achat d'option** BOURSE option-buying hedge; **~ par achat d'options de vente** BOURSE put buying hedge; **~ par l'actif** BOURSE asset coverage; **~ par anticipation** BOURSE anticipatory hedge; **~ par vente d'option** BOURSE option-selling hedge; **~ parfaite** BOURSE perfect hedge; **~ pour personne à charge** ASSUR dependent coverage; **~ de pointe** ASSUR catastrophe cover; **~ de position** BOURSE short covering; **~ d'une position acheteur** BOURSE buying hedge; **~ de presse** MÉDIA press coverage; **~ publicitaire** MÉDIA, V&M advertising coverage; **~ sélective** BOURSE selective hedge; **~ sûre** BOURSE safe hedge; **~ à terme** BOURSE forward cover; **~ totale** ASSUR full cover, full coverage; **~ tous risques** ASSUR all risks cover; **~ de vente** BOURSE selling hedge, short hedge; ◆ **faire une ~ croisée** BOURSE cross-hedge

couvrir 1. *vt* ASSUR cover, BOURSE cover, insulate, hedge, COM cover, defray, FIN cover, hedge, defray; **2.** *v pron* **se ~** BOURSE hedge, COM hedge one's bets, FIN hedge; ◆ **~ les frais de** COM cover the cost of, defray the cost of, defray the expenses of

covariance *f* MATH *statistiques* covariance

covoiturage *m* TRANSP car pool

cow-boy *m infrml* IND cowboy (*infrml*)

CP *abrév* (*Certificats pétroliers*) BOURSE oil company investment certificates exclusive to Total and Elf-Erap

CPAO *abrév* (*conception de programmes assistée par ordinateur*) INFO CASE (*computer-aided software engineering, computer-assisted software engineering*)

cr. *abrév* (*crédit*) COM, COMPTA, FIN Cr (*credit*)

crapaudine *f* TRANSP *saisissage* pot; **~ pour pied d'éléphant** TRANSP *saisissage* star fitting; **~ pour saisissage** TRANSP *arrimage* lashing pot

crayon: **~ -lecteur** *m* IND, INFO, V&M bar code reader, bar code scanner; **~ -lecteur optique** *m* IND, INFO, V&M optical wand; **~ optique** *m* IND bar code reader, bar code scanner, INFO, V&M bar code reader, bar code scanner, stylus

créance *f* COMPTA, FIN claim, debt, receivable; **~ admissible** FISC qualifying debt obligation; **~ de deuxième rang** COMPTA secondary claim; **~ douteuse** BANQUE, COMPTA, ECON, FIN bad debt, doubtful debt; **~ financière** COMPTA financial claim; **~ en garantie** BANQUE assigned account; **~ garantie** BANQUE secured debt; **~ hypothécaire à taux d'intérêt variable** FIN open-end mortgage; **~ hypothécaire à taux variable** BANQUE, FIN open mortgage; **~ irrécouvrable** BANQUE bad debt, doubtful debt, irrecoverable debt, COM bad debt, credit loss, irrecoverable debt, COMPTA bad debt, uncollectable account, ECON, FIN bad debt, doubtful debt, irrecoverable debt; **~ irrévocable** BANQUE, COMPTA, ECON, FIN bad debt; **~ légitime** DROIT legal claim; **~ litigieuse** FIN contested claim; **~ nantie par des marchandises** BOURSE commodity paper; **~ prioritaire** BANQUE senior debt; **~ à recouvrir** COMPTA outstanding debt; **~ en retard** COMPTA past-due claim; ◆ **~ due depuis** COMPTA debt due from

créances *f pl* COMPTA accounts receivable, receivables, trade accounts receivable, trade receivables, trading debts, ECON accounts receivable, receivables, trade accounts receivable, trade receivables; **~ assorties de recours limités** BANQUE limited recourse debt; **~ commerciales** COMPTA trading debts; **~ comptables émises continuellement en francs suisses** (*COPS*) BOURSE continuously offered payment rights in Swiss francs (*COPS*); **~ douteuses** BANQUE bad and doubtful debts, B&D, COMPTA dubious accounts; **~ fiscales** FISC tax claims; **~ gelées** FIN frozen receivables; **~ immobilisées** FIN *bilan* frozen receivables; **~ privilégiées du fisc** FISC liens for taxes; **~ rattachées à des participations** COMPTA loans to related companies; **~ sur l'étranger** BOURSE foreign assets

créancier, -ière *m,f* ADMIN, BANQUE creditor, DROIT creditor, obligee, FIN creditor; **~ bénéficiaire** ASSUR *assurance-vie* creditor rights life assurance, creditor rights life insurance; **~ garanti** COMPTA secured creditor;

~ **hypothécaire** BANQUE mortgagee; ~ **non-garanti** COMPTA general creditor, unsecured creditor; ~ **non-prioritaire** BANQUE junior creditor; ~ **obligataire** BOURSE bond creditor; ~ **ordinaire** COMPTA unsecured creditor; ~ **privilégié** COM preferential creditor, preferred creditor; ~ **sur hypothèque** BANQUE mortgagee

créateur: ~ **d'entreprises** *m,f* COM venturer; ~ **de marchés** *m,f* BOURSE market maker (*UK*); ~ **publicitaire** *m,f* RES HUM, V&M commercial artist, commercial designer

création *f* COM creation, making; ~ **assistée par ordinateur** *(CAO)* IND, INFO computer-aided design *(CAD)*, computer-assisted design *(CAD)*, design automation *(D/A)*; ~ **commerciale** ECON, IMP/EXP, RES HUM trade creation; ~ **d'entreprise** COM, ECON business creation, business start-up; ~ **de licence croisée** INFO cross licensing; ~ **de marché** V&M market creation; ~ **d'une mode** COM trendsetting; ~ **de poste** RES HUM job creation; ~ **de produit** V&M product creation, product generation; ~ **de réseaux** COM network building; ~ **d'une zone piétonnière** V&M pedestrianization

créativité *f* COM creativeness, creativity; ~ **commerciale** V&M *marketing* creative marketing

crédibilité *f* COM *d'une entreprise* credibility; ~ **de la source** V&M *marketing* source credibility; ~ **au tiers** V&M *relations publiques* third-party credibility (*jarg*)

crédit *m* BANQUE accommodation, COM, COMPTA credit, FIN accommodation, FIN credit; ~ **accordé avec clause rouge** *m* BANQUE, TRANSP *maritime* red clause credit; ~ **d'achat** *m* COM cash credit, purchase credit; ~ **acheteur** *m* BANQUE buyer credit; ~ **agricole** *m* COM agricultural credit; ~ **d'ajustement structurel** *m* ECON structural adjustment loan; ~ **autorisé** *m* BANQUE, FIN authorized credit, bank line, credit line, line of credit (*AmE*); ~ **-bail** *m* BANQUE leasing, COMPTA capital lease, IMMOB leasing; ~ **-bail de biens d'équipement** *m* IMMOB equipment leasing; ~ **-bail pour cadre** *m* GESTION executive leasing; ~ **-bail de conteneurs** *m* TRANSP container leasing; ~ **-bail financier** *m* BANQUE, FIN financial leasing; ~ **-bail immobilier** *m* IND equipment leasing; ~ **bancaire** *m* BANQUE, FIN bank credit; ~ **de base** *m* FISC basic credit allowance; ~ **bon marché coûteux** *m* FIN expensive easy money; ~ **budgétaire** *m* ECON, FIN, POL budgetary appropriation; ~ **de caisse** *m* COM cash advance, cash credit; ~ **commercial** *m* BANQUE, COM, COMPTA, ECON trade credit; ~ **de complaisance** *m* COMPTA accommodating credit; ~ **confirmé** *m* BANQUE confirmed credit; ~ **à la consommation** *m* BANQUE consumer lending, ECON, FIN consumer credit; ~ **à court terme** *m* BANQUE short-term credit; ~ **de courtier** *m* BOURSE broker's loan; ~ **créant un fond** *m* COMPTA fund appropriation; ~ **croisé** *m* BOURSE swap, FIN cross-currency swap; ~ **déductible** *m* FISC allowable credit; ~ **de dépen-**

ses en capital *m* POL capital expenditure vote; ~ **pour dépenses de fonctionnement** *m* COMPTA operating expenditure vote; ~ **documentaire** *m* FIN documentary credit, IMP/EXP DOC credit, documentary credit; ~ **pour dons de charité** *m* FISC, PROT SOC charitable donations credit; ~ **des droits et taxes** *m* COMPTA extended deferment; ~ **endossé** *m* BANQUE, FIN back-to-back loan; ~ **d'enlèvement** *m* COMPTA simple deferment; ~ **aux entreprises** *m* BANQUE commercial lending, corporate credit; ~ **pour études** *m* FISC education credit; ~ **pour éventualités** *m* FIN contingencies vote; ~ **pour éventualités du Conseil du Trésor** *m* POL Treasury Board contingencies vote; ~ **exceptionnel** *m* FIN backstop loan facility; ~ **à l'exportation** *m* BANQUE, ECON, IMP/EXP export credit, export loan; ~ **à l'exportation bénéficiant d'un soutien public** *m* FIN, IMP/EXP official supported export credit; ~ **extraordinaire** *m* FIN nonrecurring appropriation; ~ **de face à face** *m* BANQUE, FIN back-to-back credit; ~ **foncier** *m* BANQUE, FIN, IMMOB land bank; ~ **foncier étalé** *m* BANQUE, IMMOB building loan agreement; ~ **fournisseur** *m* IMP/EXP supplier credit; ~ **pour frais médicaux** *m* FISC medical expense credit; ~ **garanti** *m* BANQUE secured credit, FIN guaranteed facility; ~ **global** *m* BANQUE packaging credit; ~ **aux grandes entreprises** *m* BANQUE corporate credit; ~ **hypothécaire** *m* BANQUE mortgage loan; ~ **hypothécaire remboursable par mensualités fixes** *m* FIN level-payment mortgage (*US*); ~ **à l'importation pour le redressement économique** *m* ECON, FIN rehabilitation import credit, RIC; ~ **d'impôt** *m* ECON, FISC tax credit; ~ **d'impôt pour contributions politiques** *m* FISC political contribution tax; ~ **d'impôt des corporations** *m* FISC corporate tax credit; ~ **d'impôt pour le coût de la vie** *m* FISC cost-of-living tax allowance, cost-of-living tax credit (*Canada*); ~ **d'impôt pour dividendes** *m* FISC dividend tax credit; ~ **d'impôt d'emploi** *m* FISC employment tax credit; ~ **d'impôt pour emploi à l'étranger** *m* FISC overseas employment tax credit; ~ **d'impôt pour enfants** *m* FISC child tax credit; ~ **pour impôt étranger** *m* FISC foreign tax credit (*Canada*); ~ **d'impôt fédéral pour dividendes** *m* FISC federal dividend tax credit (*Canada*); ~ **d'impôt individuel sur le revenu** *m* FISC personal income tax allowance, personal income tax credit (*Canada*); ~ **d'impôt à l'investissement** *m (CII)* FISC investment tax credit *(ITC)*; ~ **d'impôt à l'investissement commercial** *m* FISC business investment tax credit (*Canada*), business investment tax allowance; ~ **d'impôt aux locataires** *m* *Can* FISC renter's tax credit (*Canada*); ~ **d'impôt minimum** *m* FISC minimum tax allowance, minimum tax credit (*Canada*); ~ **d'impôt pour pension** *m* FISC pension income credit; ~ **d'impôt personnel** *m* FISC personal income tax allowance, personal income tax credit (*Canada*), personal tax allowance, personal tax credit (*Canada*); ~ **d'impôt pour personnes handicapées** *m* FISC disability tax allowance, disability tax credit (*Canada*); ~ **d'im-**

pôt aux petites entreprises pour capital de risque *m* FISC small business venture capital tax credit; ~ **d'impôt pour petits producteurs** *m* FISC small producer's tax credit (*Canada*); ~ **d'impôt remboursable** *m* FISC refundable tax credit; ~ **d'impôt sur le capital risque des petites entreprises** *m* FISC small business venture capital tax credit; ~ **de l'impôt sur les pensions** *m* FISC pension income credit; ~ **d'impôt au titre des dépenses d'exploration et d'aménagement** *m* FISC exploration and development expense tax credit; ~ **d'impôt de travail à l'étranger** *m* FISC overseas employment tax credit; ~ **d'impôts fonciers** *m Can* FISC property tax allowance, property tax credit (*Canada*); ~ **international** *m* BANQUE international credit; ~ **inutilisé** *m* FISC unused credit (*Canada*); ~ **irrévocable** *m* BANQUE irrevocable credit; ~ **irrévocable confirmé** *m* BANQUE confirmed irrevocable credit; ~ **librement négociable** *m* ECON *commerce international*, FIN freely negotiable credit; ~ **maximum** *m* BANQUE, FIN *pour fournisseur, client* high credit; ~ **mixte** *m* FIN mixed credit; ~ **à moyen terme** *m* BANQUE, FIN intermediate credit, intermediate-term credit; ~ **multinational à l'exportation** *m* ECON, FIN, IMP/EXP multinational export credit; ~ **net** *m* BOURSE net credit; ~ **net de position** *m* BOURSE position net credit; ~ **non-utilisé** *m* FISC unused credit (*Canada*); ~ **des obligations cautionnées** *m* COMPTA extended deferment; ~ **en or** *m* BOURSE gold credit; ~ **par acceptation** *m* BANQUE acceptance credit, acceptance facility, acceptance line of credit; ~ **parlementaire** *m* COMPTA, FIN parliamentary appropriation, parliamentary vote; ~ **permanent** *m* BANQUE, FIN revolving credit; ~ **permanent non-confirmé** *m* BANQUE, FIN evergreen, evergreen credit; ~ **pour personne à charge** *m* FISC dependant tax credit; ~ **de personne vivant seule** *m* FISC single tax credit (*Canada*); ~ **personnel** *m* BANQUE, FISC personal allowance (*UK*), personal credit (*Canada*), personal exemption (*US*); ~ **pour personnes handicapées** *m* FISC disability allowance, disability credit (*Canada*); ~ **ponctuel** *m* BANQUE, FIN spot credit; ~ **de préfinancement** *m* BANQUE prefinancing credit; ~ **de refinancement** *m* BANQUE refinance credit; ~ **réglementaire** *m* POL statutory appropriation; ~ **de relais** *m* BANQUE bridging advance, interim loan; ~ **-relais** *m* BANQUE bridge loan (*AmE*), bridging advance, bridging facility, bridging loan (*BrE*), interim loan; ~ **de relais** *m* FIN bridging advance, interim loan; ~ **-relais** *m* FIN bridge loan (*AmE*), bridging advance, bridging facility, bridging loan (*BrE*), interim loan; ~ **-relais entre partenaires commerciaux** *m* ECON swing credits (*jarg*); ~ **remboursable payé d'avance** *m* FISC refundable prepaid credit; ~ **remboursable à terme** *m* BANQUE, FIN installment credit (*AmE*), instalment credit (*BrE*); ~ **renouvelable** *m* BANQUE, FIN revolving credit; ~ **-rentier** *m* FISC annuitant; ~ **restreint** *m* BANQUE restricted credit; ~ **de restructuration** *m* BANQUE, BOURSE new money; ~ **pour revenu de pension** *m* FISC pension

income credit; ~ **révocable** *m* BANQUE revocable credit, unconfirmed credit; ~ **revolving** *m* BANQUE, FIN revolving credit; ~ **de sécurité** *m* FIN swing line; ~ **de soutien** *m* BANQUE standby credit, standby facility, standby line of credit, ECON, FIN backdoor lending; ~ **standby** *m* BANQUE standby credit; ~ **syndical** *m* BANQUE, FIN participation loan, syndicated loan; ~ **à taux privilégié** *m* FIN soft loan; ~ **à taux révisable** *m* BANQUE roll-over credit, roll-over loan; ~ **à taux variable** *m* BOURSE roll-over credit facility; ~ **pour taxe fédérale sur les ventes** *m* FISC federal sales tax credit (*Canada*); ~ **de taxe sur intrants** *m (CTI)* FISC input tax credit (*Canada*) (*ITC*); ~ **pour taxe sur les produits et services** *m (crédit pour TPS)* FISC goods and services tax credit (*Canada*) (*GST credit*); ~ **de taxe sur les ventes** *m* FISC sales tax credit (*US*); ~ **pour TPS** *m (crédit pour taxe sur les produits et services)* FISC GST credit (*goods and services tax credit*); ~ **transférable** *m* BANQUE transferable credit, COMPTA assignable credit; ~ **transitaire** *m* BANQUE transit credit; ~ **unifié** *m* FISC unified credit; ~ **à usance** *m* BANQUE usance credit; ◆ **à ~** FIN on hire purchase, on tick (*UK*); **à votre ~** BANQUE balance in your favor (*AmE*), balance in your favour (*BrE*); **donnant droit à un ~** FISC creditable

créditer *vt* BANQUE, COMPTA, FIN credit

créditeur, -trice *m,f* BANQUE, COMPTA, FIN, RES HUM Cr, creditor

créditeurs: ~ **à court terme** *m pl* COMPTA, FIN short-term liabilities

crédits *m pl* POL supply; ~ **bloqués** FIN frozen credits; ~ **commerciaux** BANQUE commodity credit; ~ **en cours** COMPTA credit outstanding, outstanding credit; ~ **gelés** FIN frozen credits; ~ **d'impôts à venir** COMPTA future tax credits; ~ **nets du secteur public** ECON, POL net lending by the public sector; ~ **permanents** FIN continuing appropriation authorities; ~ **supplémentaires** FIN supplementary estimates

créer *vt* COM *agence, projet* create, *entreprise* float, form, launch, set up, start, start up, *filiale* form, *possibilités d'emploi* create, ECON *demande* create, INFO generate, V&M *marché* create; ◆ ~ **une provision pour dépréciation** COMPTA depreciate, write down; ~ **une sûreté sur un bien** FISC create a charge on a property

créneau *m* COM window of opportunity, *dans le marché* business opportunity, *dans le temps* niche, slot, GESTION business opportunity, V&M market gap, market opening, market opportunity, niche; ~ **après les heures de grande écoute** MÉDIA *télévision* late fringe (*US, jarg*), late night; ~ **commercial** V&M market niche, market opportunity, sales opportunity; ~ **favorable** COM, V&M window of opportunity; ~ **horaire** COM time slot, MÉDIA *radio, télévision* airtime; ~ **porteur** V&M niche

créole *m* COM *langue* Creole

creuse *adj* COM *saison* slack

creux *m* ECON bottom, trough; ~ **sans précédent** BOURSE *du marché* all-time low; ~ **sur quille** TRANSP *architecture navale* dm/d, molded depth (*AmE*), moulded depth (*BrE*)

criée *f* COM, ECON, V&M auction; ◆ **à la ~** BOURSE open outcry

crime *m* DROIT crime; ~ **économique** DROIT, ECON, POL economic crime; ~ **organisé** DROIT organized crime

criminalité: ~ **d'affaires** *f* DROIT white-collar crime; ~ **en col blanc** *f* DROIT white-collar crime

criminel, -elle *adj* DROIT criminal, felonious

crise *f* BANQUE, ECON, FIN crisis, slump; ~ **des banques d'affaires** BANQUE secondary banking crisis; ~ **économique** ECON depression, economic crisis, recession; ~ **énergétique** ECON, IND energy crisis; ~ **de l'énergie** ECON, IND energy crisis; ~ **financière** BANQUE, ECON, FIN financial crisis; ~ **manifeste** POL *déclarée par le Conseil de l'Europe* manifest crisis; ~ **des opérations bancaires secondaires** BANQUE fringe banking crisis; ~ **structurelle** ADMIN *UE* structural crisis

critère *m* COM criterion, *du progrès de l'économie* yardstick; ~ **de l'actif d'une entreprise exploitée activement** FISC active business asset test; ~ **d'appréciation** COM yardstick; ~ **d'évaluation** COM yardstick; ~ **de propriété croisée** FISC cross-ownership test; ~ **de recettes** COMPTA revenue test; ~ **de recettes brutes** FISC gross revenue requirement; ~ **de rentabilité** FIN profit requirement, profitability requirement; ~ **de tri** INFO sort key; ~ **de valeur** FISC value test

critères: ~ **économiques** *m pl* ECON economic criteria; ~ **d'évaluation** *m pl* COMPTA valuation criteria; ~ **d'investissement** *m pl* FIN investment criteria; ~ **de publicité** *m pl* V&M advertising criteria; ~ **de qualité** *m pl* COM quality standards; ~ **de qualité minima** *m pl* V&M minimum quality standards

critique[1] *adj* COM, INFO critical

critique[2] *m* COM *personne* critic; ~ **en chambre** COM armchair critic; ~ **littéraire** COM, MÉDIA book reviewer, literary critic; ~ **de théâtre** LOISIRS, MÉDIA aisle sitter (*jarg*), drama critic, theater critic (*AmE*), theatre critic (*BrE*)

critiquer *vt* COM censure, criticize, hammer (*jarg*), level criticism at

croate *adj* COM Croatian

Croate *mf* COM *habitant* Croat

Croatie *f* COM Croatia

croc: ~ **à échappement** *m* TRANSP *arrimage* pelican hook

crochets *m pl* INFO, MÉDIA *impression* square brackets

croire *vti* COM believe; ◆ ~ **qn sur parole** COM take sb's word for it

croisement: ~ **d'actifs** *m* BANQUE, FIN asset swap

croissance *f* COM, ECON *des bénéfices*, INFO, V&M growth; ~ **annuelle globale** ECON, FIN compound annual growth; ~ **du capital** BOURSE capital growth; ~ **contraire** ECON antagonistic growth; ~ **démographique nulle** ECON, POL zero population growth, ZPG; ~ **démographique zéro** ECON, POL zero population growth, ZPG; ~ **économique** ECON economic growth; ~ **effective** ECON real growth; ~ **effective du PIB** ECON real GDP growth; ~ **entraînée par les exportations** ECON, IMP/EXP export-led growth; ~ **de l'entreprise** COM corporate growth; ~ **équilibrée** ECON, FIN balanced growth; ~ **exponentielle** MATH exponential growth; ~ **génératrice de conflits** ECON antagonistic growth; ~ **horizontale** ECON horizontal expansion; ~ **induite par la demande** COM, ECON demand-led growth; ~ **interne** ECON internal expansion; ~ **mal équilibrée** ECON, FIN unbalanced growth; ~ **nominale** ECON nominal growth; ~ **non-inflationniste soutenue** ECON sustained non-inflationary growth, SNIG; ~ **organique** COM, ECON organic growth; ~ **par autofinancement** ECON internal expansion; ~ **paupérisante** ECON immiserizing growth; ~ **rapide** ECON, IND rapid growth; ~ **réelle** ECON real growth; ~ **réelle du PIB** ECON real GDP growth; ~ **à un rythme soutenable** ECON sustainable development, sustainable growth, ENVIR sustainable development, POL sustainable development, sustainable growth; ~ **verticale** ECON vertical expansion; ~ **zéro** ECON zero growth; ◆ **à ~ rapide** COM, ECON fast-growing; **de ~ nulle** ECON no-growth; **de ~ zéro** ECON no-growth; **en ~ constante** COM, ECON ever-increasing

croissant, e *adj* COM growing, increasing, mounting, rising

croître *vi* COM, ECON grow, increase

Croix: ~ **Bleue** *f* ASSUR Blue Cross (*US*)

cruzeiro *m* COM cruzeiro

cryptage *m* (ANT *décryptage*) COMMS, INFO encryption

CSP *abrév* (*catégorie socio-professionnelle*) COM socioprofessional group

CTI *abrév* (*crédit de taxe sur intrants*) FISC ITC (*Canada*) (*input tax credit*)

Ctrl-Alt-Del *loc* (*CAD*) INFO Control-Alt-Delete (*CAD*)

CU *abrév* (*charge utile*) TRANSP PL (*payload*)

Cuba *f* COM Cuba

cubage *m* TRANSP *volume* cubage, cubature, cubic contents, measure, measurement, volume

cubain, e *adj* COM Cuban

Cubain, e *m,f* COM *habitant* Cuban

cube *adj* COM cu, cubic, cubic

cueillette: ~ **à la ferme** *f* COM *fruits* pick-your-own, PYO

cueillir *vt* COM pick

cuisine *f* TRANSP *d'un avion, d'un navire* galley

cuivre *m* ENVIR copper

cul:[1] ~ **-de-sac** *m* IMMOB, TRANSP *rue* cul-de-sac

cul:[2] **sur le ~** *loc* TRANSP *maritime* trimmed by the stern

culée: **~ d'ancrage** *f* TRANSP *fixation des conteneurs* buttress

culte: **~ aveugle du produit** *m* ECON, V&M commodity fetishism

culture *f* COM *agriculture* agriculture, farming, *ensemble d'idées* culture, ECON *de céréales* cultivation, *végétal cultivé* crop, LOISIRS, MÉDIA culture; **~ commerciale** ECON cash crop; **~ de dépendance** *jarg* PROT SOC dependency culture *(jarg)*; **~ d'entreprise** COM corporate culture; **~ informatique** INFO computer literacy; **~ de l'organisation** GESTION organization culture; **~ de rapport** ENVIR cash crop; **~ de la vigne** ECON vine growing

culturel, -elle *adj* COM, LOISIRS, MÉDIA cultural

cultures: **~ extensives** *f pl* ECON, ENVIR extensive farming; **~ vivrières de base** *f pl* ECON *agriculture* subsistence crops

cum. *abrév (cumulatif)* BOURSE *dividendes*, COMPTA cum. *(cumulative)*

cumul *m* COM roll-up, running total, RES HUM double-dipping *(jarg)*; **~ de l'année** COMPTA, FISC year to date; **~ annuel jusqu'à ce jour** COMPTA, FISC year to date; **~ d'emploi** RES HUM double-dipping *(jarg)*, dual job holding, moonlighting; **~ d'inscriptions** BOURSE dual listing; **~ jusqu'à ce jour** COMPTA, FIN total to date; **~ de responsabilités** RES HUM dual responsibility; **~ de risques** ASSUR accumulation of risk

cumulard, e *m,f* RES HUM double-dipper *(jarg)*

cumulatif, -ive *adj (cum.)* BOURSE *dividendes*, COMPTA cumulative *(cum.)*

cumulé, e *adj* COMPTA accrued, FIN *dividendes, amortissement* accumulated; ◆ **~ sur l'exercice en cours** COMPTA, FISC year to date

cumuler *vi* RES HUM double-dip *(infrml)*, have two jobs, hold two jobs

cupidité *f* COM acquisitive instinct, cupidity, greed

cuprifères *m pl* BOURSE coppers

curatelle *f* ADMIN administration, IMMOB admin, administration

curateur, -trice *m,f* DROIT, FIN, IMMOB curator, *successions* administrator, trustee

curriculum: **~ vitae** *m (CV)* ADMIN, COM curriculum vitae *(CV)*, RES HUM curriculum vitae *(CV)*, résumé *(AmE)*

curseur *m* INFO cursor, pointer

cursus: **~ national** *m* PROT SOC National Curriculum *(UK)*

cuve: **~ autoporteuse** *f* TRANSP *transporteur de gaz naturel liquéfié* independent tank, IT; **~ autoporteuse latérale** *f* TRANSP *transporteur de gaz*

naturel liquéfié independent tank wing, ITW; **~ autoporteuse standard** *f* TRANSP *transporteur de gaz naturel liquéfié* independent tank common, ITX; **~ indépendante** *f* TRANSP *transporteur de gaz naturel liquéfié* independent tank, IT; **~ indépendante latérale** *f* TRANSP *transporteur de gaz naturel liquéfié* independent tank wing, ITW; **~ indépendante standard** *f* TRANSP *transporteur de gaz naturel liquéfié* independent tank common, ITX; **~ sphérique indépendante en aluminium** *f* TRANSP *transporteur de gaz naturel liquéfié* independent spherical aluminium tank *(BrE)*, independent spherical aluminum tank *(AmE)*, IS

CV *abrév* ADMIN *(curriculum vitae)*, COM *(curriculum vitae)*, RES HUM *(curriculum vitae)* CV *(curriculum vitae)*, TRANSP *(cheval-vapeur)* HP *(horsepower)*

CVP *abrév (cycle de vie d'un produit)* ECON, IND, V&M PLC *(product life cycle)*

CVT *abrév (correspondant en valeurs du Trésor)* BOURSE reporting dealer

cybernétique *f* INFO cybernetics

cycle *m* BOURSE, COM, COMPTA, ECON, FIN, IMP/EXP, IND cycle; **~ comptable** COMPTA accounting cycle; **~ de conversion de liquidités** FIN capital-raising operation, cash conversion cycle; **~ court lié aux fluctuations des stocks** BOURSE inventory cycle; **~ de développement d'un produit** ECON, IND, V&M product cycle; **~ d'échéances** BOURSE expiration cycle; **~ économique** COM, ECON, IMP/EXP business cycle, economic cycle, trade cycle; **~ d'enquête permanent** COM continuous survey cycle, CSC; **~ d'exploitation** COMPTA operating cycle; **~ de facturation** COM billing cycle; **~ d'inflation en sinusoïde** ECON stop-go cycle of inflation; **~ logistique** ECON logistic cycle; **~ long** ECON long wave; **~ de longue durée** ECON long-wave cycle; **~ du marché** BOURSE stock market cycle, COM, ECON market cycle; **~ de référence** ECON reference cycle; **~ de travail** COM, RES HUM work cycle; **~ de l'Uruguay** ECON *de négociations* Uruguay Round; **~ de vie** V&M *d'une entreprise, d'un produit* life cycle; **~ de vie familiale** V&M family life cycle; **~ de vie d'un investissement** BOURSE investment life cycle; **~ de vie d'un produit** *(CVP)* ECON, IND, V&M product cycle, product life cycle *(PLC)*

cyclique *adj (ANT non-cyclique)* BOURSE, COM, ECON, FIN cyclical

cylindre *m* INFO cylinder, TRANSP cylinder, CY

cylindrée *f (cc)* COM *automobile* cubic capacity *(cc)*

cymogène *m* IND, TRANSP cymogene

cypriote *adj* COM Cypriot

Cypriote *mf* COM *habitant* Cypriot

D

D *abrév (directeur)* GESTION, RES HUM D *(director)*

DAB *abrév (distributeur automatique de billets)* BANQUE ACD *(automated cash dispenser, automatic cash dispenser)*

Dacca *n pr* COM Dhaka

dactylo: ~ **intérimaire** *f* RES HUM temporary secretary

dactylographié, e *adj frml* ADMIN, BREVETS typewritten

dactylographier *vt* ADMIN typewrite

Dakar *n pr* COM Dakar

dalasi *m* COM dalasi

Damas *n pr* COM Damascus

dame: ~ **-jeanne** *f* TRANSP demijohn

Danemark *m* COM Denmark

danger *m* COM danger, hazard, RES HUM danger; ◆ **en ~ de** COM in danger of

Danger! *m* RES HUM Danger!

danois[1]**, e** *adj* COM Danish

danois[2] *m* COM *langue* Danish

Danois, e *m,f* COM *habitant* Dane

dans *prép* COM in, within

DAP *abrév (distributeur automatique de produits)* COM, V&M automatic vending machine, vending machine

Dar es Salaam *n pr* COM Dar es Salaam

dari *m* COM *langue* Dari

date *f* COM date; ~ **d'achèvement** COM completion date; ~ **d'annulation** TRANSP *navigation* canceling date *(AmE)*, cancelling date *(BrE)*; ~ **d'arrivée** TRANSP *d'un envoi* arrival date; ~ **d'attribution** BOURSE *d'actions* date of grant; ~ **de base** BOURSE base date; ~ **butoir** BANQUE, FIN cutoff date; ~ **de clôture** IMMOB closing date *(US)*; ~ **de conversion** BOURSE conversion date; ~ **de délivrance** BREVETS date of grant; ~ **de départ** TRANSP *d'un navire* S/D, sailing date; ~ **de dépôt** BREVETS date of filing; ~ **de distribution** BOURSE release date; ~ **d'échéance** BANQUE maturity date, BOURSE contract delivery date *(UK)*, date of maturity, dd, due date, expiry date, maturity date, COM dd, due date, expiry date, ECON, FIN maturity date; ~ **échéance** ECON maturity date; ~ **d'échéance à court terme** BOURSE short-range maturity date; ~ **d'échéance fixe** BOURSE fixed expiration date; ~ **d'écoulement de l'intérêt** BANQUE interest roll-over date; ~ **d'effet** ASSUR attachment date, COM effective date; ~ **d'effet de couverture** ASSUR commencement of coverage; ~ **d'émission** ASSUR date of issue, BOURSE issue date; ~ **d'enregistrement** BOURSE date of record, BREVETS date of registration, COM record date; ~ **d'entrée en vigueur** COM effective date; ~ **d'entrée en vigueur de l'intérêt** FISC effective interest

date; ~ **ex-dividende** BOURSE ex dividend date; ~ **ex-droits** BOURSE ex-rights date; ~ **d'exercice** BOURSE, COM *droit* exercise date; ~ **d'expédition** TRANSP day of shipment; ~ **d'expiration** BOURSE expiration date, expiry date, COM expiration date, expiry date, retention date; ~ **d'expiration de licence d'exportation** IMP/EXP export licence expiry date *(BrE)*, export license expiry date *(AmE)*; ~ **d'expiration d'une obligation** RES HUM expiry of agreement; ~ **de facturation** COM billing date *(US)*; ~ **de facture** COM date of invoice; ~ **fixée par proclamation** FISC date fixed by proclamation; ~ **d'installation d'une nouvelle chaudière** TRANSP *navigation* date new boilers fitted, NB; ~ **de levée** BOURSE *prime* date of exercise, exercise date; ~ **de libération** BOURSE release date; ~ **limite** COM closing date, deadline, latest date; ~ **limite de consommation** V&M use-by date; ~ **limite d'exercice** BOURSE exercise deadline; ~ **limite de levée** BOURSE exercise deadline; ~ **limite des offres** BOURSE bid closing date; ~ **limite de production** FISC *de la déclaration d'impôt* due date of filing; ~ **limite de remise des documents** COM copy date, copy deadline, V&M copy date; ~ **limite de la remise d'un texte** MÉDIA *presse, édition* copy deadline; ~ **limite de vente** V&M *alimentation* sell-by date; ~ **de livraison** BOURSE delivery date, COM delivery time; ~ **de mise à prix d'emprunt** BOURSE *couverture de taux d'emprunt à terme* loan-pricing date; ~ **de mise sur le marché** BOURSE offering date; ~ **de mise en vente** MÉDIA *imprimé* on-sale date *(AmE)*; ~ **de l'opération** BANQUE transaction date, BOURSE trade date, transaction date, COM transaction date; ~ **de paiement** BOURSE, COM date of payment, payment date; ~ **de paiement des intérêts courus** COMPTA, FIN accrual date; ~ **de parution** MÉDIA on-sale date *(AmE)*, publication date; ~ **de premier appel** BOURSE first call date; ~ **prescrite de production** FISC *de la déclaration d'impôt* due date of filing; ~ **de la présentation officielle** FIN formal submission date; ~ **prévue** COM expected date, target date; ~ **de priorité** BREVETS *propriété intellectuelle*, DROIT priority date; ~ **probable d'arrivée** LOISIRS estimated arrival time, EAT, TRANSP *navigation* estimated arrival time, estimated time of arrival, EAT, ETA; ~ **de publication** MÉDIA publication date; ~ **de réception des marchandises** TRANSP *maritime* receiving date; ~ **de règlement** BOURSE redemption date, settlement date, value date; ~ **de règlement variable** BANQUE roll-over date; ~ **du relevé périodique des chèques** BANQUE cutoff date; ~ **de remboursement** BOURSE redemption date; ~ **de remboursement en espèces** BOURSE cash refunding date; ~ **de rem-**

boursement par anticipation BANQUE call date; **~ de résiliation** TRANSP *navigation* canceling date *(AmE)*, cancelling date *(BrE)*; **~ de retour** MÉDIA *presse* off-sale date; **~ de révision du taux** BANQUE roll-over date; **~ de révision du taux d'intérêt** BANQUE interest roll-over date, roll-over date; **~ de versement** BOURSE, COM date of payment; ◆ **à la ~ d'échéance** BOURSE, COM, FIN at due date; **à une ~ ultérieure** COM at a subsequent date, at some future date; **la ~ la moins rapprochée étant prise en considération** *(ANT la date la plus rapprochée étant prise en considération)* COM whichever is the later; **la ~ la plus rapprochée étant prise en considération** *(ANT la date la moins rapprochée étant prise en considération)* COM whichever is the sooner; **par ~** INFO by date

DAU *abrév (document administratif unique)* ADMIN, IMP/EXP, TRANSP SAD *(single administrative document)*

db *abrév (décibel)* COM db *(decibel)*

DCPE *abrév (document-cadre de politique économique)* BOURSE, ECON PFP *(policy framework paper)*

DDD *f* BOURSE Standard & Poor's notation for a high-risk bond, DDD

D.E. *abrév (demandeur d'emploi)* COM job seeker, registered applicant for work

dealer *m* BOURSE dealer, dealer in securities

déballer *vt* COM unpack

débandade *f* COM stampede

débarcadère *m* TRANSP *navigation* discharging wharf, landing stage

débardeur *m* RES HUM docker *(BrE)*, longshoreman *(AmE)*

débarqué: **~ en moins** *adj* TRANSP *marchandises* short-landed

débarquement *m* TRANSP disembarkation, unshipment; **~ de l'avion** TRANSP de-planing *(AmE)*

débarquer *vt* TRANSP *marchandises, personnes* disembark, off-load

débarrasser: **se ~ de** *v pron* COM get rid of

débat *m* COM discussion; **~ final** POL adjournment debate *(UK)*

débats *m pl* DROIT court proceedings, proceedings; **~ de conférence** GESTION conference proceedings

débattre *vt* COM debate, discuss; ◆ **à ~** COM by arrangement, MÉDIA, V&M ono, or nearest offer

débauchage *m* RES HUM poaching

débenture: **~ bancaire** *f* BANQUE bank debenture

débit *m* BANQUE *relevé de compte*, COM debit, COMPTA charge, debit, expenses, ECON *production* capacity, FIN debit, throughput, IMMOB debit, IND capacity, INFO baud rate, speed; **~ en bauds** INFO baud rate; **~ binaire** INFO bit rate; **~ de boissons lié à une brasserie** ECON tied house *(UK)*; **~ net** BOURSE net debit; **~ du terminal** TRANSP terminal throughput; **~ de transfert des données** INFO data transfer rate

débité: **être ~ de** *vt* COMPTA be debited to

débiter *vt* BANQUE *compte*, COMPTA, FIN debit; **~ de** BANQUE net against; ◆ **~ le compte de qn** COMPTA make an entry against sb

débiteur, -trice *m,f* ADMIN, COM, COMPTA, DROIT, FIN Dr, debtor; **~ douteux** BANQUE, COMPTA, FIN bad debtor; **~ externe** COMPTA external debtor; **~ fiscal** FISC tax debtor; **~ hypothécaire** BANQUE mortgager; **~ principal** FIN, V&M principal debtor; **~ sans adresse** BANQUE skip; **~ sur hypothèque** BANQUE mortgager

débiteurs *m pl* COM trade debtors, COMPTA, ECON accounts receivable, receivables, trade accounts receivable, trade debtors, trade receivables; **~ douteux** COMPTA doubtful debtors

débits *m pl* BOURSE debits

débloquer *vt* COM *compte bancaire* unblock, FIN, INFO unlock; ◆ **~ la situation** COM break the stalemate

débogage *m* INFO debugging

déboguer *vt* INFO debug *(infrml)*

débogueur *m* INFO debugger

déboisement *m* ENVIR deforestation

débouché *m* COM opening, ENVIR *pour déchets dangereux* outlet, RES HUM job opportunity, V&M *marché* outlet

débours *m* BANQUE cash disbursement, disbursement, outgoings, COM cash advance, COMPTA, FIN cash disbursement, disbursement, outgoings, TRANSP *navigation* advanced charge, advanced disbursement; **~ bilatéral** *m* BANQUE, ECON, POL bilateral disbursement; **~ effectif** *m* COMPTA actual cash disbursement; **~ nets** *m pl* ECON net disbursement; **~ ou dépenses** *m pl* COMPTA outlays or expenses; **~ de port** *m pl* IMP/EXP, TRANSP port disbursements

déboursable *adj* COMPTA, FIN disbursable

déboursement: **~ bilatéral** *m* BANQUE, ECON, POL *assistance au développement* bilateral disbursement

débourser *vt* COMPTA disburse, pay out, FIN disburse

débriefer *vt* ECON, GESTION debrief

debriefing *m* GESTION debriefing

débris *m* ENVIR residue

débrouiller 1. *vt* COM unscramble; **2.** *v pron* **se ~** COM scrape along *(infrml)*

débroussailler *vt infrml* COM gin out *(infrml)*, do the groundwork on

début *m* INFO start; **~ de l'exercice** COMPTA beginning of the year; **~ de séance** COM opening

débuter *vi* COM start up

débuts: **~ de l'industrialisation** *m pl* RES HUM protoindustrialization

dec. *abrév (décembre)* COM Dec. *(December)*

décade *f* COM decade

décaissement *m* (ANT *encaissement*) BANQUE, COMPTA, FIN cash disbursement, cash outflow, outward payment; **~ effectif** COMPTA actual cash disbursement

décaisser *vt* COMPTA pay out

décalage *m* COM lag, lag response, stagger, COMPTA mismatch, ECON lag, lag response, time lag, INFO indentation, shift, MÉDIA indentation; ~ **à droite** *(ANT décalage à gauche)* INFO right shift; ~ **fiscal** FISC fiscal drag; ~ **à gauche** *(ANT décalage à droite)* INFO left shift; ~ **horaire** TRANSP time lag; ~ **d'impôts** FISC shifting of taxes; ~ **négatif de taux d'intérêt** BOURSE negative interest rate gap; ~ **du poids de l'impôt** FISC shifting of the tax burden; ~ **des salaires** RES HUM wage lag; ◆ **souffrir du ~ horaire** COM, TRANSP *aviation* be jetlagged

décaler *vt* COM *frais* stagger

décédé, e *adj* DROIT deceased

décédée: personne ~ *f* DROIT deceased person

décembre *m (dec.)* COM December *(Dec.)*

décennie *f* COM decade

décentralisation *f* COM, GESTION, IND, POL decentralization; ~ **économique** ECON, POL economic devolution

décentralisé, e *adj* INFO distributed

décentraliser *vt* COM, GESTION, IND, POL decentralize

décerner *vt* COM *un prix* adjudicate

décevant, e *adj* COM disappointing

décharge *f* DROIT acquittance, ENVIR dumping, dumping ground; ~ **brute** ENVIR open dump; ~ **contrôlée** ENVIR landfill site; ~ **de déchets** ENVIR waste dump; ~ **d'effluent** ENVIR effluent discharge; ~ **illégale** ENVIR fly tipping; ~ **d'importation** IMP/EXP import release note, IRN; ~ **municipale** ENVIR municipal dump; ~ **non contrôlée** ENVIR indiscriminate dumping; ~ **partielle** DROIT, IMMOB partial release; ~ **sauvage** ENVIR uncontrolled dump site

déchargement *m* TRANSP unloading, unshipment, *de marchandises* off-loading; ~ **sous palan** TRANSP *maritime* overside discharge; ~ **sur allèges** TRANSP *maritime* overside discharge, *navigation* barge forwarding; ~ **sur rade** TRANSP *navigation* discharge afloat, D/A; ◆ ~ **et livraison** TRANSP *des marchandises* landing and delivering

décharger *vt* COM, TRANSP *marchandises* off-load; ◆ **se ~ d'un paquet d'actions** BOURSE unload stocks on the market

déchéance *f* ASSUR, DROIT lapse; ~ **du terme** BANQUE *France*, FIN event of default

déchet *m* COM spoilage, ENVIR waste product; ~ **de fabrication** ENVIR *recyclage* waste product; ~ **de route** TRANSP loss in transit; ~ **sous forme gazeuse** ENVIR gaseous waste; ~ **toxique** ENVIR toxic waste

déchets *m pl* ENVIR garbage *(AmE)*, refuse, rubbish *(BrE)*, waste; ~ **dangereux** ENVIR dangerous waste; ~ **encombrants** ENVIR bulky waste; ~ **de faible activité** ENVIR low-level waste; ~ **de faible et moyenne activité** ENVIR indeterminate waste; ~ **de forte activité** ENVIR high-level waste; ~ **huileux** ENVIR oil waste; ~ **industriels** ECON, ENVIR, IND industrial refuse, industrial waste; ~ **ménagers** ENVIR domestic waste; ~ **nucléaires** ENVIR nuclear waste; ~ **plastiques** ENVIR, IND plastic waste; ~ **solides** ENVIR solid waste; ~ **textiles liquides** TRANSP *marchandise dangereuse* textile waste-wet

déchetterie *f* ENVIR disposal facility

déchiffrement *m (ANT chiffrement)* COMMS, INFO decryption

déchiffreur: ~ de code barres *m* IND, INFO, V&M bar code scanner

déchiqueteuse *f* ADMIN paper shredder, shredder, INFO paper shredder

décibel *m (db)* COM decibel *(db)*

décidé: ~ à *adj* COM intent on

décider 1. *vt* COM *une affaire, une réclamation* adjudicate; **2.** *v pron* **se ~** GESTION opt; ◆ ~ **contre l'avis de** COM second-guess *(infrml)*; ~ **du montant** DROIT *de l'indemnité* settle the figure; **se ~ tout d'un coup** *infrml* COM make a snap decision

décideur, -euse *m,f* COM policymaker, GESTION policymaker, INFO decision maker, POL policymaker; ~ **de politique** COM, GESTION, POL policymaker

décimal: ~ codé binaire *m* INFO binary-coded decimal; ~ **non condensé** *m* INFO zoned decimal

décimalisation *f* ECON decimal currency, decimalization

décimaliser *vt* ECON decimalize

décisif, -ive *adj* COM critical, decisive

décision *f* COM decision, resolution, resolve, DROIT adjudication, judgment, ruling, *d'un tribunal* finding, FISC determination, GESTION resolution, resolve; ~ **d'achat** COM purchase decision; ~ **anticipée en matière d'impôt sur le revenu** FISC advance income tax ruling; ~ **arbitrale** RES HUM award; ~ **cachée** COM hidden decision; ~ **commerciale** COM, GESTION business decision; ~ **de compromis** COM compromise decision; ~ **de dernière minute** COM last-minute decision; ~ **facile** GESTION easy option; ~ **globale** GESTION decision package; ~ **interlocutoire** DROIT interlocutory decree; ~ **judiciaire** DROIT court order, determination; ~ **de justice** DROIT court order; ~ **de principe** COM, GESTION, POL policy decision; ~ **prise à haut niveau** COM high-level decision; ~ **prise à la majorité** COM *des voix* majority decision; ~ **raisonnable** COM rational decision; ~ **unilatérale d'en référer aux prud'hommes** RES HUM unilateral reference

décisions: ~ exceptionnelles *f pl* COM, GESTION nonroutine decisions

déclarant, e *m,f* FISC filer *(Canada)*, taxfiler *(Canada)*, taxpayer; ~ **irrégulier** FISC gap filer *(Canada)*; ~ **retardataire** FISC late filer

déclaration *f* COM declaration, DROIT declaration, representation, statement; ~ **d'achat et de vente** *jarg* BOURSE purchase and sale statement; ~ **d'avarie** ASSUR average claim; ~ **d'avaries**

TRANSP *maritime* protest; ~ **avec remboursement** FISC refund return; ~ **avec solde dû** FISC debit return; ~ **avec versement** FISC remittance return; ~ **de chargement** TRANSP cargo declaration; ~ **classifiée** FISC classified return; ~ **commune** COM joint statement; ~ **comportant une pénalité** FISC penalty return; ~ **conjointe d'intérêts** BANQUE joint declaration of interest, JDI; ~ **consulaire** ADMIN, IMP/EXP consular declaration, CD; ~ **de dédouanement d'entrée** IMP/EXP, TRANSP inward clearing bill; ~ **de dividende** BOURSE declaration of dividend, dividend announcement, dividend declaration; ~ **en douane** IMP/EXP customs declaration, CD, customs entry, TRANSP customs declaration, CD; ~ **en douane avant exportation** IMP/EXP customs pre-entry exports; ~ **en douane avant importation** IMP/EXP customs pre-entry imports; ~ **en douane de navire** IMP/EXP clearance of ship; ~ **douanière** IMP/EXP entry; ~ **écrite** DROIT written declaration, RES HUM written notice; ~ **écrite sous serment** DROIT affidavit; ~ **d'emballage de cargaison exportée** IMP/EXP, TRANSP export cargo packing declaration, ECPD; ~ **d'entrée en douane** IMP/EXP bill of entry, clearance inwards, entry inwards, B/E; ~ **d'entrée ou de sortie faite** ASSUR entered ship; ~ **d'équipage** TRANSP *navigation* crew manifest; ~ **erronée d'âge** ASSUR misstatement of age; ~ **de faillite** COM, COMPTA, DROIT, FIN adjudication of bankruptcy; ~ **fausse** FISC false return, false statement; ~ **fausse ou trompeuse** FISC false or deceptive statement; ~ **fiscale** COMPTA income tax return; ~ **formelle de fidéicommis** DROIT declaration of trust; ~ **frauduleuse de cubage** TRANSP *navigation* cubecutting; ~ **d'impôt séparée** FISC separate tax return; ~ **d'impôt sur les dons** FISC gift tax return; ~ **d'impôt sur le revenu** ECON Ten-Forty (*US*), FISC tax return; ~ **d'impôt sur le revenu des particuliers** FISC individual income tax return; ~ **d'impôts** FISC tax form; ~ **imprimée** FISC printed return; ~ **d'initié** BOURSE, FIN insider report; ~ **d'intention** COM memorandum of intent; ~ **d'intérêts en commun** BANQUE *dans une société commerciale* joint declaration of interest, JDI; ~ **de marchandises entreposées** IMP/EXP *douane*, TRANSP *douane* warehouse entry; ~ **mise au point** FISC dressed return, edited return; ~ **non standard** FISC off-profile return; ~ **d'objectifs** COM, GESTION, POL policy statement; ~ **officielle de vente** FIN official notice of sale; ~ **d'origine** IMP/EXP declaration of origin; ~ **d'origine certifiée** IMP/EXP certified declaration of origin; ~ **par écrit** DROIT written declaration; ~ **patronale** COMPTA, FISC employer's return; ~ **préalable** IMP/EXP pre-entry; ~ **principale** IMP/EXP *UK* prime entry; ~ **pro forma** FIN, FISC pro forma return; ~ **de procuration** DROIT proxy statement; ~ **provisoire d'importation** ASSUR, IMP/EXP, TRANSP bill of sight; ~ **réchappée** FISC salvaged return; ~ **rejetée réglée** FISC cleared reject; ~ **de renseignements** FISC information

return; ~ **de revenu** FISC reporting of income; ~ **de revenus** FISC income tax return, return of income; ~ **de revenus distincts** FISC separate tax return; ~ **sauvée** FISC salvaged return; ~ **segmentée** FISC segmented return; ~ **de sinistre** ASSUR insurance claim; ~ **de sinistre tardif** ASSUR belated claim; ~ **sommaire** COM, DROIT summary statement; ~ **sommaire de culpabilité** DROIT summary conviction; ~ **de sortie de douane** IMP/EXP clearance outwards, entry outwards; ~ **de sortie de navire** IMP/EXP clearance outward of a vessel; ~ **sous serment d'un témoin** DROIT deposition; ~ **supplémentaire** IMP/EXP, TRANSP *maritime* postentry; ~ **en suspens** FISC suspense return; ~ **de transbordement** IMP/EXP, TRANSP transhipment entry, transshipment entry; ~ **de TVA** FISC VAT return (*UK*); ◆ **faire une ~** DROIT make a statement

déclarations: ~ **dénigrantes** *f pl* DROIT disparaging statements; ~ **simultanées** *f pl* FISC concurrent returns

déclaré: ~ **insolvable** *adj* BOURSE hammered (*jarg*); ◆ ~ **entré** IMP/EXP *en douane, bateaux* entered in

déclarer *vt* BOURSE, COMMS declare, DROIT adjudge, claim, represent, FISC, IMP/EXP, INFO declare; ~ **insolvable** BOURSE hammer; ◆ ~ **catégoriquement** COM state categorically; ~ **illégal** DROIT outlaw; ~ **des marchandises pour l'entreposage** COM enter goods for warehousing; ~ **un montant** FISC claim an amount; ~ **nul** BREVETS revoke; ~ **par écrit** DROIT swear on affidavit; ~ **une perte** COMPTA report a loss; ~ **un profit** COMPTA report a profit; ~ **qn en faillite** COM, COMPTA, DROIT, FIN adjudicate sb bankrupt; ~ **à sa charge** FISC claim as a dependant; ~ **sous serment** DROIT declare on oath, swear on affidavit

déclassement *m* ENVIR, IND decommissioning

déclasser *vt* ENVIR decommission, GESTION downscale, IND decommission, RES HUM *un emploi* downgrade

déclencher *vt* COM spark off, touch off, trigger, GESTION activate

déclin *m* ECON decline, downturn, IND decline; ~ **rapide de la prime** BOURSE rapid premium decay; ◆ **en ~** ECON depressed

décliner *vi* COM recede, wane, ECON decline

décloisonnement *m* BOURSE decompartmentalization, opening up

DECnet® *m* INFO DECnet®

décodage *m* (ANT *codage*) COMMS, INFO decryption

décodeur *m* INFO decoder

décollage *m* COM, ECON, TRANSP takeoff

décoller *vi* TRANSP take off

décommander *vt* COM cancel, countermand

décomposer *vt* COM analyse (*BrE*), analyze (*AmE*)

décomposition: ~ **des tâches** *f* COM, GESTION, IND operations breakdown, RES HUM job breakdown, operations breakdown

décompte *m* COM detailed account; ~ **de prime** FIN premium statement

décompter *vt* POL count

déconcentration *f* COM, ECON demerger

déconcentrations: ~ **transfrontières** *f pl* ECON cross-border demergers

déconnecté, e *adj* INFO inactive

déconnecter 1. *vt* COM unplug; **2.** *v pron* **se** ~ INFO log off, log out

déconseillé, e *adj* COM unadvisable

déconseiller: ~ **à qn de faire qch** *loc* COM warn sb against doing sth

décontaminer *vt* ENVIR clean up

décote *f* BOURSE undervalue, *actions* discount; ◆ **avec une** ~ BOURSE at a discount, AAD; **avec une** ~ **de deux pour cent** BOURSE at a two per cent discount

découler:[1] ~ **de** *vi* COM stem from

découper:[2] ~ **un projet en tranches** *loc* COM, FIN, GESTION chunk a project (*jarg*)

décourager *vt* COM deter, discourage

découvert *m* BANQUE bank overdraft, overdraft, O/D, BOURSE shorts (*UK, jarg*), FIN gap, overdraft, uncovered balance; ~ **autorisé** COM credit ceiling, credit limit; ~ **bancaire** BANQUE bank overdraft, overdraft, O/D; ~ **en blanc** BANQUE unsecured overdraft; ◆ **à** ~ BANQUE in the red, overdrawn, O/D, BOURSE going short, COMPTA below the line, FIN below the line, in the red, on margin, V&M below the line; **être à** ~ **sur contrat à terme** BOURSE be short in futures; **faire la chasse au** ~ *jarg* BOURSE squeeze the bears (*jarg*), squeeze the shorts (*jarg*)

décrémenter *vt* INFO decrement

décret *m* COM edict, POL enactment; ~ **d'application** DROIT statutory instrument; ~ **irrévocable** DROIT decree absolute

décréter *vt* DROIT, POL enact

décriminaliser *vt* DROIT decriminalize

décrire *vt* COM describe

décrochage: ~ **local** *m* MÉDIA opt-out

décroître *vi* COM tail away, ECON taper off

décrutement *m* COM, RES HUM outplacement

décryptage *m* (ANT *cryptage*) COMMS, INFO decryption

décupler *vt* COM increase tenfold

dedans: **très en** ~ *loc* BOURSE *option* deep in the money

dédié, e *adj* INFO dedicated

dédit: ~ **de rupture de contrat** *m* DROIT penalty for breach of contract

dédomiciliation *f* COM, FISC dedomiciling

dédommagement *m* ASSUR compensation, indemnity, DROIT indemnity, FISC compensation

dédommager 1. *vt* DROIT compensate; **2.** *v pron* **se** ~ COM recoup oneself; ◆ ~ **qn pour qch** COM compensate sb for sth

dédouané: ~ **ou non** *loc* IMP/EXP wccon, whether cleared customs or not

dédouanement *m* IMP/EXP clearance, customs clearance, CCL; ~ **de cargaison** IMP/EXP clearance of cargo goods; ~ **de chargement** IMP/EXP cargo clearance; ~ **sans inspection** IMP/EXP cleared without examination, CWE

déductibilité *f* FISC deductibility

déductible *adj* FIN, FISC *du revenu imposable* deductible; ~ **fiscalement** FISC tax-deductible; ~ **d'impôts** FISC tax-deductible

déduction:[1] ~ **accordée aux petites entreprises** *f* FISC small business deduction; ~ **pour amortissement** *f Can (DPA)* FISC capital cost allowance *(CCA)*; ~ **pour amortissement accéléré** *f* FISC accelerated capital cost allowance, ACCA; ~ **annuelle** *f* FISC yearly allowance; ~ **avant impôt** *f* FISC allowance; ~ **combinée** *f* FISC combined total claim; ~ **complémentaire** *f* FISC top-up deduction; ~ **pour dépenses** *f* FISC deduction for expenses; ~ **discrétionnaire** *f* FISC discretionary deduction; ~ **pour dons** *f* FISC deduction for gifts; ~ **pour épuisement** *f* FISC depletion allowance; ~ **fiscale** *f* FISC tax deduction; ~ **fiscale pour amortissement** *f* COMPTA capital allowance; ~ **fiscale pour investissement** *f* FISC capital allowance; ~ **fiscale unique** *f* FISC single tax credit (*Can*); ~ **forfaitaire** *f* FISC standard deduction; ~ **pour frais de garde d'enfant** *f* FISC child care expense deduction; ~ **des frais réels** *f* FISC itemized deductions; ~ **pour gains en capital** *f Can* FISC capital gains allowance, capital gains deduction; ~ **d'impôt** *f* FISC tax deduction; ~ **d'impôt à l'emploi** *f* FISC employment tax deduction; ~ **pour inventaire** *f* FIN inventory allowance; ~ **maximale** *f* FISC maximum claim; ~ **maximale admissible** *f* FISC maximum allowable deduction; ~ **pour pertes sur prêts** *f* FISC deduction for loan losses; ~ **aux petites entreprises** *f* FISC small business deduction; ~ **pour placements** *f* FIN investment allowance; ~ **statistique** *f* MATH statistical inference; ~ **de taxe immobilière** *f* FISC property tax allowance, property tax credit (*Can*); ~ **au titre des revenus salariaux** *f* RES HUM earned income allowance; ~ **du vieux au neuf** *f* ASSUR deduction new for old; ◆ ~ **faite de** FIN net of

déduction:[2] **ne pas admettre une** ~ *loc* FISC disallow a deduction

déductions: ~ **estimatives** *f pl* FISC *retenues d'impôt d'un employé* estimated deductions; ~ **fiscales aux petits producteurs** *f* FISC small producer's tax credit (*Can*)

déduire *vt* COM deduce, deduct, COMPTA set against, MATH deduct; ~ **de** COM charge against, conclude from; ◆ ~ **un montant** FISC claim an amount

déduplication *f* ADMIN merge and purge, COMMS, V&M *publicité directe* merge and purge (*jarg*)

de facto *abrév* DROIT de facto

défaillance *f* COM, IND malfunction, INFO breakdown, failure, fault; ~ **matérielle** INFO hardware failure

défaire 1. *vt* COM unwrap, *accord* disaffirm; **2.** *v pron* **se ~ de** COM shake off, shed, FISC divest o.s. of

défalquer *vt* COMPTA *les frais d'envoi* make allowance for

défaut *m* BOURSE fail position, failed delivery, COM absence, bug, deficiency, flaw, DROIT absence, INFO bug, default; ~ **d'acceptation** BANQUE non-acceptance; ~ **d'acceptation de paiement** BANQUE dishonor (*AmE*), dishonour (*BrE*); ~ **caché** DROIT, IMMOB latent defect; ~ **de comparution** DROIT failure to appear; ~ **de se conformer** FISC failure to comply; ~ **croisé** BANQUE, FIN cross default; ~ **de livraison** BOURSE fail position, failed delivery; ~ **de paiement** BANQUE default of payment, nonpayment, COM delinquency, failure in payment, FIN delinquency; ~ **de paiement de prêt** BANQUE loan default; ~ **de provision** BANQUE insufficient funds, COM no funds, NF, FIN absence of consideration; ♦ **à ~ de renseignements précis** COM in the absence of detailed information; **faire ~ de paiement** COM default; **par ~** COM, INFO by default

défavorable¹ *adj* COM *facteur, rapport, conditions* adverse, *prix, conditions* unfavorable (*AmE*), unfavourable (*BrE*), COM *taux d'échange*, COMPTA unfavorable (*AmE*), unfavourable (*BrE*)

défavorable:² **être ~ à** *vi* BOURSE go against

défectueux, -euse *adj* COM defective, faulty, V&M defective

défendeur, -eresse *m,f* DROIT *procédure civile* defendant, respondent

défendre *vt* COM bar, forbid, stick up for (*infrml*), *accès, entrée* ban, *personne, intérêts* defend, stand up for

défense *f* COM defence (*BrE*), defense (*AmE*), DROIT ban, POL defence (*BrE*), defense (*AmE*); ~ **des consommateurs** ECON, V&M consumerism; ~ **de l'environnement** ENVIR nature conservation; ~ **des intérêts du consommateur** DROIT, V&M consumer protection; **la ~** DROIT case for the defence (*BrE*), case for the defense (*AmE*), the defence (*BrE*), the defense (*AmE*); ~ **du Pac Man** BOURSE Pac-Man defense (*US*); ♦ ~ **d'afficher** V&M stick no bills; ~ **d'entrer** COM, DROIT no trespassing; ~ **d'entrer sous peine de poursuites** DROIT trespassers will be prosecuted; ~ **de fumer** COM no smoking, smoking is not permitted, smoking is prohibited

défenseur: ~ **des consommateurs** *m* ECON, V&M consumerist

défi *m* COM challenge

déficience *f* FISC impairment; ~ **mentale ou physique** FISC mental or physical impairment

déficient, e *adj* COM deficient

déficit *m* COM shortfall, COMPTA deficit, shortfall, ECON, FIN deficit, FISC deficiency, TRANSP short-

fall; ~ **accumulé** FISC accumulated deficit; ~ **actuariel** ASSUR actuarial deficit, actuarial loss, experience deficiency, experience loss, FIN experience deficiency, experience loss; ~ **de la balance commerciale** COM, COMPTA, ECON trade deficit; ~ **de la balance des paiements** (*ANT excédent de la balance des paiements*) ECON BOP deficit, balance of payments deficit; ~ **budgétaire** (*ANT excédent budgétaire*) COM, COMPTA, ECON, FIN, POL budget deficit, budgetary deficit, fiscal deficit; ~ **budgétaire fédéral** ECON federal deficit (*US*); ~ **de caisse** COMPTA cash deficit, teller's shortage; ~ **corrigé pour tenir compte de l'inflation** ECON inflation-adjusted deficit; ~ **effectif** ECON primary deficit; ~ **exonéré** FISC exempt deficit; ~ **extérieur** COM, COMPTA, ECON trade deficit; ~ **fédéral** ECON federal deficit (*US*); ~ **financier** COMPTA fiscal deficit, FIN funding gap; ~ **net d'exploitation** COM, COMPTA, IND net operating loss; ~ **réel** ECON actual deficit; ~ **reportable sur les années suivantes** COMPTA carry-over loss; ~ **du secteur public** ECON, FIN public sector deficit; ~ **structurel** ECON structural deficit; ~ **de trésorerie** COMPTA cash deficit; ♦ **avoir un ~** (*ANT avoir un excédent*) ECON run a deficit

déficitaire *adj* COM *budget* adverse, COMPTA, FIN non-profit-making (*BrE*), nonprofit (*AmE*), FISC non-profit-making, nonprofit (*AmE*)

défier *vt* COM challenge

défiguration: ~ **de titres** *f* BOURSE bad delivery

défilé: ~ **de mode** *m* COM fashion show

défilement *m* INFO scrolling; ~ **vers le bas** INFO scrolling down; ~ **vers le haut** INFO scrolling up

définir *vt* COM work out; ♦ ~ **des règles** COM set rules

définitif, -ive *adj* DROIT absolute

définition *f* COM definition, INFO resolution; ~ **des articles** ASSUR definition of items; ~ **de base** COM basic definition, core definition; ~ **de fonction** RES HUM job description; ~ **des limites** ASSUR definition of limits; ~ **de marché** V&M market base; ~ **de la mission** GESTION mission statement; ~ **des objectifs** COM, GESTION, V&M objective setting; ~ **de politique** COM, GESTION, POL policy-making; ~ **de poste** RES HUM generic job title

déflation *f* ECON deflation

déforestation *f* ENVIR deforestation

défraîchi, e *adj* COM soiled

défunt¹, **e** *adj* COM defunct, DROIT deceased

défunt², **e** *m,f* DROIT deceased person

défusionner *vt* COM demerger, unbundle, INFO unbundle

dégagement *m* BOURSE sell-off

dégager 1. *vt* BOURSE unwind a tape, COM unblock, *créneaux* create; **2.** *v pron* **se ~** COM *d'une obligation, d'un contrat* back off, contract out; **se ~ de** COM back out of; ♦ ~ **sa responsabilité de** *frml* COM *documents de garantie* assume no responsibility for

dégâts *m pl* ASSUR, COM damage; ~ **aux biens loués** *m pl* ASSUR damage to rented property; ~ **causé par un incendie** *m* ASSUR damage caused by fire; ~ **des eaux** *m pl* COM water damage; ~ **matériels** *m pl* ASSUR damage to property

dégradation *f* COM *d'un immeuble* wear and tear, ENVIR degradation; ~ **biologique** ENVIR biodegradation; ~ **écologique** ENVIR, IND ecological damage; ~ **des performances** INFO software rot; ~ **des sols** ENVIR land degradation

dégrader *vt* COM *confiance commerciale* erode

dégraissage *m* RES HUM demanning, downsizing (*jarg*), redundancy, shake-out; ~ **d'actifs** ECON, FIN asset stripping; ~ **de main-d'oeuvre** RES HUM labor shedding (*AmE*), labour shedding (*BrE*)

dégraisser *vt* COM, ECON slim down, RES HUM *personnel* downsize; ◆ ~ **le personnel** RES HUM trim the workforce

degré *m* COM, RES HUM degree; ~ **de certitude** COMPTA, FIN audit assurance; ~ **de dommage** ASSUR degree of damage; ~ **des dommages** ASSUR extent of damage; ~ **d'incapacité** ASSUR degree of disablement; ~ **d'invalidité** ASSUR degree of disablement; ~ **de risque** BOURSE degree of exposure; ~ **de solvabilité** FIN credit rating; ~ **de volatilité du cours** BOURSE price volatility

degrés: ~ **Celsius** *m pl* COM degrees Centigrade; ~ **Fahrenheit** *m pl* COM degrees Fahrenheit

dégressif: ~ **sur le temps acheté** *loc* V&M time discount

dégression *f* MATH degression

dégrèvement *m* FISC abatement, refund, relief; ~ **pour l'emploi précaire** RES HUM interim relief; ~ **fiscal** ECON, FISC, IND tax break, tax relief; ~ **d'impôt** FISC tax rebate, tax relief; ~ **d'impôt sur les véhicules commerciaux** FISC tax relief for business vehicles; ~ **non-utilisé** FISC unused relief; ~ **par effilage** FISC *sur successions, dons à vie* taper relief (*UK*); ~ **roll-over** FISC roll-over relief; ~ **sur biens commerciaux** FISC relief on business assets; ~ **total** FISC full exemption

dégrever *vt* FISC relieve

dégringolade *f* COM collapse, plunge; ~ **du marché** BOURSE market slump

dégringoler *vi* COM plunge

dégroupage *m* COM unbundling; ~ **des marchandises** TRANSP cargo disassembly

dégrouper *vt* COM demerger, unbundle, INFO unbundle, TRANSP *contenu d'un conteneur* disseminate; ◆ ~ **un chargement** TRANSP break bulk; ~ **une livraison** TRANSP break bulk

dégroupeur, -euse *m,f* TRANSP break bulk agent

déhalage: ~ **du navire d'un poste à l'autre** *loc* TRANSP shifting berth

dehors: **très en** ~ *adj* BOURSE *option* deep out of the money; ◆ **en** ~ BOURSE out-of-the-money, OTM; **en** ~ **des pouvoirs** DROIT ultra vires; **en** ~ **de la ville** V&M *magasin, restaurant* out of town

déhouillement *m* IND mining

déjeuner: ~ **d'affaires** *m* COM business lunch

déjouer *vt* COM defeat

de jure *adv* DROIT de jure

DEL *abrév (diode électroluminescente)* INFO LED (*light-emitting diode*)

délabrement *m* IMMOB dilapidation

délai *m* BANQUE deadline, term, BOURSE deadline, time to market, COM days of grace, deadline, time frame, time to market, timescale, *de livraison* time limit, ECON deadline, period, timescale, FIN deadline, timescale, GESTION deadline, time frame, timescale, RES HUM deadline, timescale, V&M time to market; ~ **absolu** COM absolute limit; ~ **administratif** ECON administration lag; ~ **aller-retour** COM turnaround period, turnround period; ~ **d'attente** BOURSE waiting period, INFO delay, timeout; ~ **de base** COM basic time limit; ~ **de démarrage** V&M *d'un produit nouveau* lead time; ~ **d'exécution** COM run time, turnaround time, ECON, FIN, IND turnaround time; ~ **de fabrication** IND lead time; ~ **fixe** RES HUM allowed time, standard time; ~ **de franchise** COMPTA, DROIT grace period; ~ **de grâce** COMPTA grace period, DROIT grace period, period of grace; ~ **d'identification** ECON recognition lag; ~ **de livraison** COM delivery time, delivery turnround, IND, TRANSP, V&M *de stock* lead time; ~ **de mise en oeuvre** COM lead time, ECON implementation lag, recognition lag; ~ **de mise en production** V&M *d'un nouveau produit* lead time; ~ **de mise sur le marché** BOURSE, COM, V&M time to market; ~ **moyen de recouvrement des créances** BANQUE, COMPTA average collection period, collection ratio; ~ **de paiement** BANQUE period of payment, time for payment, term of payment; ~ **de placement** BOURSE period of digestion; ~ **de préavis** DROIT statutory notice, RES HUM notice period; ~ **de préavis légal** DROIT statutory notice; ~ **de prescription** COM term of limitation; ~ **prescrit** COM prescribed time; ~ **de réaction** COM, ECON lag, lag response; ~ **de réalisation** IND, V&M *d'un projet* lead time; ~ **de réapprovisionnement** COM *stock* lead time; ~ **de recouvrement** (*DR*) BOURSE debt recovery period; ~ **de récupération** RES HUM payback period; ~ **de redressement** ECON, FIN, IND turnaround time; ~ **de réflexion** COM time span of discretion, *avant de signer un contrat* cooling-off period; ~ **de remboursement** FIN repayment term; ~ **de rigueur** COM deadline; ~ **de suite** IND, TRANSP, V&M *d'un projet* lead time; ~ **supplémentaire** BREVETS period of grace, COM extension of time; ~ **supplémentaire de paiement** BANQUE extended payment; ~ **de vue** COM time after sight; ◆ **dans les meilleurs** ~**s** COM, COMMS a.s.a.p., as soon as possible; **dans les** ~**s prescrits** COM within the prescribed time, DROIT within prescribed limits; **dans un** ~ **de** COM within a period of; **dans un** ~ **de sept jours** COM at a week's notice, within a week

délaisser *vt* DROIT relinquish, IMP/EXP abandon

DELD *abrév (demandeur d'emploi de longue durée)* ECON, RES HUM LTU *(long-term unemployed)*

délégation *f* COM *de personnes* delegation; ~ **d'autorisation** COM delegation of authorization; ~ **de pouvoir** COM delegation of authority, ECON proxy; ~ **de la qualité de fondé de pouvoir** COM delegation of signing authority; ~ **de signature** COM delegation of signing authority; ~ **de solde** TRANSP *navigation* allotment

délégué[1], **e** *m,f* COM *(dl.)* delegate *(DEL)* GESTION conference delegate, conference member, convention participant; ~ **d'atelier** GESTION, IND shop steward; ~ **en bourse** BOURSE trader; ~ **commercial** RES HUM trade representative; ~ **du personnel** GESTION staff representative; ~ **aux questions de sécurité** GESTION safety representative; ~ **syndical** IND agent, business agent *(US)*, shop steward, RES HUM lay official, shop steward, trade union representative, union representative

délégué:[2] **être** ~ *vi* COM be in charge

déléguer *vt* GESTION delegate; ◆ ~ **son autorité à** COM give vicarious authority to

délibération: ~ **du Conseil du Trésor** *f* POL Treasury Board minute

délibérations *f pl* DROIT proceedings

délinquant *adj* COM delinquent

délit *m* DROIT crime, criminal offence, delict, offence, tort; ~ **d'abstention** DROIT *d'agir* nonfeasance; ~ **grave** DROIT misdemeanour *(UK)*; ~ **d'initié** BOURSE, FIN insider dealing; ~ **mineur** DROIT misdemeanor *(US)*

délivraison *f* TRANSP redelivery

délivrance *f* BOURSE delivery, BREVETS grant, COM *passeport, reçu* delivery, dely, FISC *formule, avis, certificat* issuance; ~ **de crédit** BANQUE credit granting, granting of credit

délivrer *vt* BREVETS *brevet* grant; ◆ ~ **un mandat à qn** COM serve sb with a warrant

delta:[1] ~ **neutre** *adj* BOURSE *options* delta-neutral

delta[2] *m* BOURSE, FIN delta; ~ **hedging** FIN delta hedging, dynamic hedging; ~ **net de position** BOURSE position net delta; ~ **d'une option d'achat** *(*ANT *delta d'une option de vente)* BOURSE call delta; ~ **d'une option de vente** *(*ANT *delta d'une option d'achat)* BOURSE put delta

demain: ~ **en huit** *m* COM tomorrow week

demande *f* BREVETS *de brevet* application, COM application, demand, desire to purchase, application, query, request, DROIT *par-devant un tribunal* petition, ECON demand, V&M *pour un produit* call, demand; ~ **accumulée** ECON, V&M pent-up demand; ~ **active** COM brisk demand; ~ **d'admission** BOURSE *à la bourse* application for admission *(UK)*; ~ **antérieure** BREVETS earlier application; ~ **attendue** ECON, V&M anticipated demand; ~ **en augmentation** ECON growing demand; ~ **de biens** ECON demand for goods; ~ **de brevet** BREVETS patent application; ~ **de brevet déposée** BREVETS pat. pend., patent pend-

ing; ~ **de brevet européen** BREVETS European patent application; ~ **de chèque** COMPTA check requisition *(AmE)*, cheque requisition *(BrE)*; ~ **de commanditaire** ECON option demand; ~ **concurrente** V&M competitive demand; ~ **conjointe** ECON joint demand; ~ **considérable** ECON heavy demand; ~ **des consommateurs** V&M *étude de marché* consumer demand; ~ **de crédit** BANQUE loan demand; ~ **cyclique** ECON cyclical demand; ~ **de décharger** TRANSP request to off-load; ~ **de dépôt de brevet** BREVETS, DROIT patent specifications; ~ **dérivée** ECON derived demand; ~ **de dommages et intérêts** DROIT claim for damages; ~ **effective** COM, ECON, V&M effective demand, effectual demand; ~ **élastique** ECON, V&M elastic demand; ~ **d'emploi** RES HUM job application; ~ **d'emploi non satisfaite** RES HUM unsuccessful job application; ~ **escomptée** ECON, V&M anticipated demand; ~ **et offre globale** ECON, FIN aggregate demand-aggregate supply, AD-AS; ~ **étrangère** ECON, V&M foreign demand; ~ **excédentaire** ECON, V&M excess demand; ~ **d'exemption personnelle** FISC claim for personal exemption; ~ **ferme** BOURSE firm bid; ~ **finale** ECON, FISC, V&M final demand; ~ **formelle** FISC demand; ~ **globale** ECON, FIN aggregate demand; ~ **globale-offre globale** ECON, FIN aggregate demand-aggregate supply, AD-AS; ~ **en hausse** ECON growing demand; ~ **importante** ECON, V&M active demand; ~ **d'indemnisation** ASSUR claim for indemnification; ~ **d'indemnité** COM claim for indemnification, DROIT compensation claim, PROT SOC claim; ~ **industrielle** IND industrial demand; ~ **inélastique** ECON inelastic demand; ~ **d'inscription à la cote** BOURSE application for listing, listing application; ~ **intérieure** ECON domestic demand; ~ **internationale** BREVETS international application; ~ **d'introduction en bourse** BOURSE application for quotation; ~ **introductive d'instance** DROIT bill, *droit civil* complaint; ~ **de main-d'oeuvre** ECON, RES HUM labor demand *(AmE)*, labour demand *(BrE)*; ~ **du marché** ECON market demand; ~ **de marge initiale** BOURSE initial margin requirement; ~ **de monnaie** ECON demand for money; ~ **de monnaie à titre de précaution** ECON precautionary demand for money; ~ **non encore satisfaite** ECON, V&M backlog demand; ~ **d'option** ECON option demand, sponsor demand; ~ **de paiement** COMPTA payment requisition, requisition for payment, FIN prompt note, request for payment; ~ **péremptoire** FISC requirement; ~ **de prêt** BANQUE loan application; ~ **prévue** ECON, V&M anticipated demand; ~ **de propositions** FIN request for proposals; ~ **de radiation de dettes** BANQUE submission for deletion of debts; ~ **reconventionnelle** DROIT counterclaim, FISC cross demand; ~ **en réduction de dommages-intérêts** DROIT mitigation of damages; ~ **réglementaire** POL statutory requirement; ~ **de remboursement** FISC claim for refund; ~ **de remboursement anticipé** BANQUE *d'un prêt* acceleration of maturity; ~ **de remboursement de** frais de déplacement COM travel claim, travel expense claim; **~ de remboursement de frais de voyage** COM travel claim, travel expense claim; **~ renouvelée** COM repeat demand; **~ de renseignements** V&M *avant un achat particulier* sales inquiry; **~ de réservation** COM booking order; **~ en retard** COM backlog demand; **~ de retenue** FISC retention requirement; **~ rétroactive de déduction** ASSUR retrospective claim; **~ de souscription** BOURSE *pour les actions* application; **~ de souscription d'actions** BOURSE application for shares; **~ spéculative** ECON *d'argent* speculative demand; **~ de vérification** COMPTA confirmation; **~ vive** COM brisk demand; ◆ **à la ~ de** COM at the request of; **à la ~ générale** COM by popular request; **faire une ~** ASSUR file a claim, COM make a request, RES HUM put in an application, *d'emploi* apply; **faire une ~ de** PROT SOC claim; **faire une ~ d'adhésion** COM apply for membership; **faire une ~ auprès des autorités compétentes** COM make a request to the appropriate authority; **faire une ~ d'emploi** RES HUM apply for, put in an application for a job, submit an application for a job; **faire une ~ par écrit** COM send a written request; **faire une ~ de prêt** BANQUE apply for a loan; **faire une ~ de remboursement** RES HUM claim expenses; **faire une ~ de souscription d'actions** BOURSE apply for shares; **la ~ est pendante** BREVETS application is pending; **sur ~** COMPTA on demand

demandé: **~ en espèces** *loc* BOURSE wanted for cash

demander *vt* COM demand, request, order, *conseil* seek, *honoraires* charge, *objet* ask for, *passeport, permis* apply for, *personne* call for, COMMS *télécommunications* page, TRANSP *taxi* order; ◆ **~ de l'aide sociale** RES HUM go on welfare (*US*); **~ l'avis d'un expert** COM take expert advice; **~ un avis d'expert** COM ask for an expert opinion; **~ des comptes à qn** COM call sb to account; **~ un conseil juridique** DROIT seek legal advice; **~ une déduction** FISC claim a deduction; **~ des dommages et intérêts** ASSUR, DROIT claim damages; **~ moins cher que** COM bargain down; **~ le point de vue d'un spécialiste** COM ask for an expert opinion; **~ le remboursement de** COM call in; **~ des renseignements** COM make enquiries; **~ réparation** DROIT claim compensation, seek redress

demanderesse: **~ fictive** *f* DROIT ≈ Jane Doe (*US*)

demandes: **~ non exécutées** *f pl* ECON, V&M backlog demand; ◆ **faire face aux ~** GESTION *d'un syndicat* meet the demands

demandeur, -euse *m,f* BREVETS, COM *d'un brevet* applicant, DROIT applicant, claimant, plaintiff; **~ d'emploi** COM job seeker, registered applicant for work, RES HUM job hunter; **~ d'emploi de longue durée** *(DELD)* ECON hard-core unemployed (*AmE*), long-term unemployed (*BrE*) *(LTU)*; **~ fictif** DROIT ≈ John Doe (*US*)

démantèlement *m* COM break-up, ECON dismantling; **~ de l'actif** COMPTA, FIN asset stripping

démanteler *vt* COM, FIN wind down; ◆ **~ progressivement** COM wind down

démarcation *f* RES HUM demarcation

démarchage *m* V&M door-to-door selling, house-to-house selling, solicitation; **~ par téléphone** V&M *par un représentant* cold calling; **~ téléphonique** FIN phoning

démarche *f* COM approach, step; **~ collective** COM, GESTION, RES HUM joint representation; **~ descendante pour investir** FIN top-down approach to investing; **~ fonctionnelle** COM, IND functional approach; **~ marketing** V&M marketing concept; ◆ **faire des ~s** COM, GESTION take action; **faire les ~s nécessaires et appropriées** DROIT take such steps as are considered necessary

démarcheur, -euse *m,f* COM business canvasser, canvasser, V&M *ventes* business canvasser, knocker (*infrml*); **~ à domicile** COM, RES HUM door-to-door salesman

démarque *f* COM markdown

démarrage *m* COM, ECON start-up, INFO start; **~ à froid** COM cold start, INFO cold boot, cold start; ◆ **de ~** COM start-up

démarrer *vt* COM start up, *affaire* get off the ground, ECON start up; ◆ **faire ~ qn en qualité de** RES HUM start sb off as

dématérialisation *f* ECON dematerialization; **~ des transferts de fonds** BANQUE truncation

dématérialisé, e *adj* BOURSE dematerialized, paperless

démembrement *m* BOURSE Separate Trading of Registered Interest and Principal Securities, STRIPS, COM break-up; **~ de l'actif** COMPTA asset stripping; **~ de dividendes** FIN, FISC dividend stripping; **~ hypothécaire** FIN mortgage strip

déménagement *m* COM removal; **~ en chaîne** COM chain migration

déménager *vi* IMMOB move out

démenti *m* ASSUR disclaimer

demi:[1] **~ -format** *adj* MÉDIA *journal* tabloid

demi:[2] **~ -additionneur** *m* INFO half adder; **~ -gaillard** *m* TRANSP *navigation* raised foredeck, RFD; **~ -hectare** *m* COM acre; **~ -produits** *m pl* COM intermediary goods, semiprocessed products, IND semiprocessed products; **~ -tarif** *m* TRANSP half fare; **un ~ -m** *(1/2)* COM, MATH one-half *(1/2)*

demi:[3] **~ -douzaine** *f* COM half a dozen; **~ -dunette** *f* TRANSP *navigation* raised quarterdeck, RQD; **~ -paire** *f* COM odd one; **~ -pension** *f* LOISIRS half board; **~ -purge** *f* BOURSE half-life (*infrml*); **~ -teinte** *f* MÉDIA halftone

de minimis *adv* DROIT de minimis

démission *f* ADMIN, RES HUM resignation; **~ forcée** RES HUM constructive dismissal; **~ provoquée** RES HUM constructive dismissal; ◆ **donner sa ~** RES HUM terminate one's appointment

démissionner *vi* ADMIN hand in one's resignation, RES HUM hand in one's resignation, quit

démocratie *f* COM democracy, POL democracy, majority rule; **~ d'entreprise** RES HUM industrial democracy, social ownership; **~ industrielle** COM industrial democracy; **~ populaire** POL people's democracy

démocratique *adj* COM, POL democratic; **~ consultatif** GESTION consultative-democratic

démocratiquement *adv* COM democratically

démodé, e *adj* COM old-fashioned, out of fashion, V&M *idée, produit* outdated

démographie *f* ECON demography

démolition *f* IMMOB demolition

démonétisation *f* ECON demonetization; **~ de l'or** ECON gold demonetization

démonétiser *vt* ECON demonetize

démontage *m* COM reverse engineering

démoraliser *vt* RES HUM demoralize

démotivation *f* RES HUM demotivation

démotiver *vt* RES HUM demotivate

démunis: les ~ *m pl* ECON the destitute, underclass

dénationalisation *f* ECON, POL denationalization

dénationaliser *vt* ECON, POL denationalize

dénégation *f* DROIT traverse

déni: ~ de justice flagrant *m* DROIT gross miscarriage of justice

deniers: les ~ de l'État *m pl* ECON public purse

dénombrement *m* COM census

dénominateur *m* COM denominator; **~ commun** COM *pour prendre une décision* common denominator

dénomination *f* BANQUE name

dénominations *f pl* BANQUE, BOURSE, FIN names

dénoncer *vt* COM *contrat* disaffirm

dénonciateur, -trice *m,f* COM whistle-blower (*infrml*), FISC informant

dénonciation *f* FISC information; **~ d'opération** BOURSE transaction exposure

de novo *adv* DROIT de novo, once more

denrée *f* BOURSE physical commodity, COM, ECON, IND cmdty, commodity; **~ au taux zéro** FISC zero-rated good

denrées: ~ alimentaires *f pl* COM, ECON produce; **~ alimentaires de base** *f pl* COM basic foodstuffs; **~ périssables** *f pl* ECON, IND nondurable goods, V&M nondurable goods, perishable goods, perishables; **~ de première nécessité** *f pl* COM essential foodstuffs

densité *f* IMMOB density; **~ binaire** INFO bit density; **~ de caractères** INFO character density; **~ de la circulation** TRANSP traffic density; **~ d'enregistrement** INFO character density, packing density; **~ de peuplement** ECON, POL population density; **~ de la population** ECON, POL population density; **~ du trafic** TRANSP traffic density

déontologie *f* COM approved code of practice, ACOP, business ethics, code of ethics, code of practice, professional code of ethics, professional ethics, DROIT code of practice (*UK*); **~ des affaires** COM business ethics; **~ commune** COM common code of practice

dépannage *m* COM correction maintenance, troubleshooting, INFO troubleshooting

dépanner *vt* INFO debug (*infrml*); ◆ **~ qn** BANQUE tide sb over

dépanneur, -euse *m,f* COM troubleshooter

dépanneuse *f* TRANSP recovery vehicle (*BrE*), towtruck (*AmE*)

dépareillé, e *adj* BOURSE unmatched, COM odd

départ *m* COM departure, start, TRANSP *navigation* departure, sailing; **~ d'entrepôt** COM ex warehouse, x-warehouse; **~ navire** IMP/EXP, TRANSP ExS, ex ship; **~ non-publié** TRANSP *d'un navire* Q-sailing; **~ plantation** IMP/EXP, TRANSP ex plantation; **~ principal** TRANSP *navigation* parent sailing; **~ en retraite à l'âge normal** RES HUM normal retirement; **~ usine** COM ex factory, IMP/EXP ex mill, ex works, x-mill, EXW, TRANSP ex mill, x-mill; **~ volontaire** RES HUM voluntary redundancy; **~ volontaire à la retraite** RES HUM voluntary retirement; ◆ **de ~** BOURSE start-up; **dès le ~** COM at the outset; **être avantagé dès le ~** COM have a head start

département *m* COM ≈ county (*UK*), department; **~ du change** BOURSE exchange department; **~ commercial** V&M sales department; **~ gouvernemental** ADMIN Bureau (*US*), government department; **~ d'ingénierie** COM engineering department; **~ d'Outre-Mer** (*DOM*) COM overseas department; **~ des périodiques** MÉDIA morgue (*infrml*); **~ de relations actionnaires** BOURSE *grandes sociétés publiques*, FIN investor relations department

Département: ~ du service diplomatique *m* COM, POL diplomatic service department

départementalisation *f* COM departmentalization

dépassé, e *adj* COM no longer valid, obsolete

dépassement *m* ECON overrun; **~ de budget** FIN overspending; **~ des coûts** ECON cost overrun; **~ d'opérations financières** BOURSE overtrading; **~ de risques** ASSUR passing of risk; **~ de souscription** BOURSE oversubscription

dépasser *vt* COM exceed, overshoot, outpace, surpass, ECON exceed, outpace, IND outpace; ◆ **~ le cubage** TRANSP cube out

dépendances *f pl* ASSUR appurtenant structures

dépendant, e *adj* FISC dependent

dépendre: ~ de *vt* COM hinge on, be dependent on

dépens *m pl* DROIT *juridique*, ECON, FIN, V&M costs

dépense *f* COM expenditure, COMPTA expense, expense item, ECON, FIN expenditure; **~ acceptable** FISC qualified expenditure; **~ admissible** FISC qualified expenditure; **~ avant fabrication** FIN preproduction expenditure; **~ budgétaire** COMPTA, ECON, FIN, POL budget expenditure; **~ déductible** FISC allowable expense;

~ **déductible de l'impôt sur les sociétés** FISC tax write-off; ~ **effective** COMPTA actual expenditure; ~ **effectuée** COMPTA actual expenditure; ~ **d'entreprise** COM, COMPTA business expense, FIN, FISC business expenses, business expense; ~ **exceptionnelle** COMPTA extraordinary expenditure; ~ **excessive** COMPTA overspend; ~ **fiscale accrue** FISC enriched tax expenditure; ~ **fiscale négative** COMPTA, FISC negative tax expenditure; ~ **initiale** FIN initial expenditure; ~ **d'investissement** BOURSE, COM, FIN investment spending; ~ **des ménages** V&M consumer spending; ~ **payée d'avance** COMPTA prepaid expense; ~ **publicitaire** FIN, V&M advertising expenditure, advertising expense; ~ **de publicité** FIN, V&M advertising expenditure, advertising expense; ~ **réelle** COMPTA actual expenditure, actual expense; ~ **réglementaire** ECON, FIN, POL statutory expenditure; ~ **régulière** FIN regular expenditure; ~ **sensible au loyer de l'argent** FIN interest-sensitive expenditure; ~ **tarifaire** COMPTA tariff expenditure; ~ **en trop** COMPTA overspend; ◆ **faire la ~ de** COM go to the expense of

dépenser: ne pas ~ **totalement** *loc* COM underspend

dépenses *f pl* COM, ECON, FIN expenditure; ~ **des administrations publiques** ECON, FIN, POL general governmental expenditure, GGE; ~ **autonomes** ECON autonomous expenditure; ~ **autorisées** COMPTA authorization for expenditure; ~ **autorisées jusqu'à un plafond de** COMPTA authorized expenditure to the amount of; ~ **budgétaires** COMPTA budgetary expenditure, ECON, FIN, POL budgetary expenditure, budgetary spending; ~ **en capital** COM, ECON, FIN capex, capital expenditure; ~ **de consommation** ECON consumer expenditure, V&M consumer expenditure, consumer spending; ~ **courantes** ADMIN *de la fonction publique* running costs, COM running costs, running expenses, ECON *de la fonction publique* current spending; ~ **en cours** ECON current spending; ~ **effectuées** COMPTA expenses incurred; ~ **encourues** COM, COMPTA, FISC incurred expenses; ~ **engagées** COM, COMPTA, FISC incurred expenses; ~ **des entreprises** FISC corporate spending; ~ **d'exploitation** COMPTA, IND operating expenditure; ~ **fiscales** ECON, FISC tax expenditure; ~ **de fonctionnement** ADMIN running costs, COMPTA, FIN running expenses; ~ **de grande consommation** ECON high-street spending (*UK*); ~ **du grand public** ECON high-street spending (*UK*); ~ **imprévues** COMPTA contingent expenses; ~ **incompressibles** FIN uncontrollable expenditures; ~ **indivises** IND oncosts; ~ **inutiles** FIN wasteful expenditure; ~ **d'investissement** COM, COMPTA, ECON, FIN, IND outlay; ~ **mineures** COMPTA, FIN petty expenses; ~ **nationales brutes** ECON gross national expenditure; ~ **nettes d'investissement** BOURSE, ECON, FIN net capital expenditure, net capital spending; ~ **non-obligatoires** ECON non-compulsory expenditure; ~ **obligatoires** ECON compulsory expenditure; ~ **publicitaires** V&M publicity expenses; ~ **publiques** ECON, FIN, POL general governmental expenditure, public expenditure, public spending, GGE; ~ **publiques globales** ECON total public spending; ~ **de recherche scientifique et de développement expérimental** FISC scientific research and experimental development expenditure; ~ **sociales** FIN social spending; ~ **de substitution** ASSUR substituted expenses; ~ **en subventions** FIN grants expenditures; ~ **de R&D** FISC R&D expenditures; ◆ **de folles ~** COM spending spree

dépensier, -ère *m,f* COM spendthrift

déperdition: ~ **d'actif** *f* ENVIR wasting asset; ~ **naturelle** *f* ENVIR natural wastage

dépérissement *m* COMPTA physical depreciation, physical deterioration, IND *d'un produit* pollution

dépeuplement *m* COM depopulation

déphasé, e *adj* ECON out of sync

déplacement *m* COM relocation, *des voix* shift; ~ **de bloc** INFO block move; ~ **en charge** TRANSP *d'un navire* displacement loaded, displacement tonnage; ~ **de colonne** INFO column move; ~ **léger** TRANSP *navigation* light displacement; ~ **professionnel** COM, LOISIRS, TRANSP business trip; ◆ **être en ~** COM be on a business trip; **faire des ~s fréquents** COM be on a business trip

déplacements: ~ **internationaux** *m pl* COM, TRANSP international travel

déplacer *vt* COM relocate, RES HUM transfer; ~ **à vide** TRANSP *train* deadhead (*AmE, infrml*), *empty vehicle* drive

dépliant *m* COM brochure, pamphlet, COMMS brochure

déploiement *m* COM deployment

déployer *vt* COM deploy

dépollué, e *adj* ENVIR *eau* depolluted

dépolluer *vt* ENVIR *plage, rivière* clean up

déport *m* BOURSE backwardation (*UK*), discount, ECON discount; ~ **de change** BOURSE exchange discount; ◆ **avec un ~** FIN at a discount, AAD

déposant, e *m,f* BANQUE depositor, *de biens sous contrat* bailor, BREVETS *d'un brevet* applicant, COM applicant, bailor, FIN depositor; ~ **distinct** BOURSE separate customer

déposer *vt* BANQUE deposit, COM deposit, table, DROIT give evidence, *amendement* table, *demande* file, *réclamation* file, FIN deposit; ~ **de nouveau** BANQUE redeposit; ◆ ~ **le bilan** COMPTA file for bankruptcy; ~ **une demande** ASSUR file a claim; ~ **une demande de** COM make an application for; ~ **une marge** BOURSE deposit margin; ~ **une plainte** COM lodge a complaint; ~ **plainte contre qn** DROIT bring an accusation against sb; ~ **une réclamation** DROIT put in a claim, set up; ~ **son bilan** COM go into voluntary liquidation, FIN submit a statement of one's affairs; ~ **sous la foi du serment** DROIT give evidence on oath

dépositaire *mf* ADMIN, BANQUE depositary, depository, BOURSE custodian, COM dealer, DROIT bailee, FIN depositary, depository; ~ **agréé** *m* BANQUE approved depository; ~ **de biens** *mf* DROIT bailee; ~ **d'enjeux** *m* COM stakeholder; ~ **intermédiaire agréé** *m* BOURSE authorized dealer; ~ **officiel** *m* MÉDIA *presse, édition* official depository

déposition *f* DROIT evidence; ~ **sous serment** DROIT deposition; ~ **sur la foi d'autrui** DROIT hearsay; ~ **du témoin** DROIT answer, statement of witness; ~ **volontaire** DROIT unsolicited testimony

déposséder *vt* DROIT, IMMOB dispossess

dépossession *f* DROIT divestiture

dépôt *m* ADMIN repository, BANQUE deposit, BOURSE margin, BREVETS *d'une demande* deposit, COM bailment, deposit, tabling, DROIT deposit, *d'une demande* filing, FIN deposit, IMMOB yard, TRANSP depot, warehouse, *chemin de fer* railway yard (*BrE*), railyard (*AmE*); ~ **à** BANQUE deposit with; ~ **bancaire** BANQUE bank deposit; ~ **en banque** BANQUE bank deposit; ~ **de banque à banque** BANQUE interbank deposit; ~ **de bilan** FIN voluntary bankruptcy; ~ **de bonne foi** BOURSE good-faith deposit; ~ **en coffre** (SYN *dépôt en coffre-fort*) BANQUE safe deposit, safe-deposit box, safety-deposit box; ~ **en coffre-fort** (SYN *dépôt en coffre*) BANQUE safe deposit, safe-deposit box, safety-deposit box; ~ **de conteneurs** TRANSP container yard, CY; ~ **contrôlé de déchets** ENVIR controlled dumping; ~ **à court terme** BANQUE short-term deposit; ~ **de couverture** BOURSE margin deposit; ~ **de couverture bancaire** ECON reserve deposit, RD; ~ **de déchets** ENVIR dumping, tipping, waste dump; ~ **de détail** BOURSE retail deposit; ~ **de distribution** TRANSP distribution depot; ~ **à échéance fixe** BANQUE fixed-term deposit, term deposit; ~ **effectué par une entreprise** BANQUE corporate account deposit; ~ **en euromonnaie** ECON Euromoney deposit; ~ **exceptionnel** BANQUE special deposit; ~ **de garantie** BOURSE earnest money, initial margin, COM caution money, conduct money, deposit, retention money; ~ **de groupage** TRANSP consolidation depot, groupage depot; ~ **d'huile végétale** TRANSP vegetable oil tank farm; ~ **initial** BOURSE good-faith deposit, initial margin; ~ **interbancaire** BANQUE interbank deposit; ~ **à intérêt quotidien** BANQUE daily interest deposit; ~ **LCL** TRANSP LCL depot; ~ **légal** ADMIN, BANQUE, FIN deposit institution, depositary, depository; ~ **de marge** BOURSE margin deposit; ~ **de matériaux de construction** IMMOB contractor's yard; ~ **de mazout** TRANSP fuel oil tank farm; ~ **moyen** FIN average deposit; ~ **non-encaissable** BANQUE noncashable deposit; ~ **non-productif d'intérêt** BANQUE non-interest-bearing deposit; ~ **non-réclamé** BANQUE unclaimed deposit; ~ **non-rémunéré** BANQUE non-interest-bearing deposit; ~ **non-transférable par chèque** BANQUE nonchequable deposit; ~ **de**

nuit BANQUE overnight deposit; ~ **obligatoire** BOURSE compulsory margin (*UK*), margin requirement; ~ **à période fixée** BANQUE fixed-period deposit; ~ **pétrolier** TRANSP tank farm; ~ **à préavis** BANQUE notice deposit; ~ **quotidien** BANQUE daily deposit; ~ **de résidus** ENVIR refuse dump; ~ **sans intérêt** BANQUE interest-free deposit, non-interest-earning deposit; ~ **sans tirage de chèques** BANQUE nonchequable deposit; ~ **des signatures** BANQUE signing authority; ~ **à taux flottant** BOURSE floating-rate deposit; ~ **à taux variable** BOURSE floating-rate deposit; ~ **à terme** BANQUE fixed deposit, savings account, term deposit, time deposit; ~ **à terme en eurodollars** BOURSE, ECON, FIN Eurodollar time deposit; ~ **à terme en eurodollars à trois mois** BOURSE three-month Eurodollar time deposit; ~ **à terme fixe** BANQUE term deposit; ~ **à terme à intérêt flexible** BANQUE flexible-rate term deposit; ~ **à terme à intérêt variable** BANQUE flexible-rate term deposit; ~ **à vue** BANQUE call deposit, demand deposit, sight deposit; ◆ **en** ~ TRANSP on consignment; **en** ~ **fiduciaire** COM in escrow

dépotage *m* IMP/EXP stripping, TRANSP container unstuffing, devanning, *conteneur* stripping

dépoter *vt* TRANSP *conteneur* strip

dépôts: ~ **acides** *m pl* ENVIR acid deposit, acid pollution; ~ **bancaires** *m pl* BANQUE *pour compte courant ou d'épargne* retail deposits; ~ **bancaires retraitables** *m pl* BANQUE bank demand deposits; ~ **en devises** *m pl* FIN credit scoring, cross subsidization, currency deposits; ~ **étrangers** *m pl* BOURSE foreign assets; ~ **de gros** *m pl* BANQUE wholesale deposits; ~ **portant intérêts** *m pl* BANQUE interest-bearing deposits

dépouillement *m* COM analysis; ~ **de l'actif** ECON, FIN asset stripping; ~ **des surplus** FISC surplus stripping

dépouiller *vt* COM *examiner* go through; ◆ ~ **le courrier** COMMS open the mail

dépourvu: ~ **de** *adj* COM void of

dépréciation *f* BOURSE, COM write-down, COMPTA depreciation, write-down, ECON debasement, depreciation, FIN, IMMOB depreciation; ~ **de l'actif** COMPTA loss in value of assets; ~ **économique** ECON, IMMOB *immobilier* economic depreciation; ~ **irrémédiable** IMMOB incurable depreciation; ~ **matérielle** COMPTA physical depreciation; ~ **monétaire** ECON, FIN currency depreciation; ~ **d'une monnaie** ECON, FIN currency depreciation; ~ **non-irrémédiable** ECON curable depreciation; ~ **rapide de prime** BOURSE rapid premium decay

déprécier 1. *vt* ECON *monnaie* depreciate; **2.** *v pron* **se** ~ ECON depreciate

dépression *f* COM *météorologie* low pressure, LP, ECON depression; ~ **post-achat** V&M post-purchase remorse (*jarg*)

déprimé, e *adj* BOURSE depressed

DEPS *abrév (dernier entré, premier sorti)* COMPTA, RES HUM LIFO *(last in, first out)*

député[1] *m* POL ≈ congressman *(US)*

député[2] *m,f* POL ≈ Member of Parliament *(UK)*, MP *(UK)*, Rep. *(US)*, Representative *(US)*; ~ **ordinaire** POL *sans porte-feuille ministériel* backbench MP *(UK)*, backbencher *(UK)*; ~ **du Parlement Européen** POL Euro MP, European MP, European member of Parliament, member of the European Parliament, MEP

députée *f* POL ≈ congresswoman *(US)*

déqualification *f* RES HUM *de la main d'oeuvre* deskilling

dérangement: être en ~ *loc téléphone* COM be out of action

dérapage *m* ADMIN outlay creep *(jarg)*, COM slippage, COMPTA, FIN outlay creep *(jarg)*; ~ **catégoriel** RES HUM grade drift; ~ **des salaires** RES HUM earnings drift, wage drift

déraper *vi* BOURSE slip

déréglementation *f* COM *commerce international*, ECON, POL deregulation; ~ **mondiale** ECON global deregulation

dérégler *vt* COM deregulate

dérégulation *f* POL deregulation

dérive:[1] **à la ~** *adj* TRANSP adrift

dérive:[2] ~ **des salaires** *f* RES HUM earnings drift, wage drift

dérivé *m* ECON, ENVIR, IND, V&M by-product

dernier[1], **-ière** *adj* COM last, V&M *most recent* latest; ~ **avertissement** RES HUM final warning; ~ **cours** BOURSE closing price; ~ **cri** COM trendy *(UK, infrml)*, IND, V&M *matériel* state-of-the-art; ~ **délai** COM at the latest, closing date, deadline; ~ **jour de cotation** BOURSE last trading day; ~ **jour de notification** *(ANT premier jour de notification)* FIN last notice day; ~ **jour de transaction** BOURSE final trading day, last day of trading, last trading day; ~ **-né** COM *d'une gamme de produit* latest addition; ~ **prix en premier** BOURSE last in, first out price; ~ **ressort** COM last resort; ~ **transporteur** TRANSP last carrier; ♦ **de ~ moment** COM up-to-the-minute; **en ~ ressort** COM as a last resort; ~ **entré, premier sorti** *(DEPS)* COMPTA *évaluation des stocks*, RES HUM last in, first out *(LIFO)*

dernier[2], **-ière** *m,f* COM latter

dernière:[1] **de ~ minute** *adj* COM last-minute

dernière:[2] ~ **cotation** *f* BOURSE closing price, closing quotation; ~ **enchère** *f* COM closing bid; ~ **entrée** *f* COM *dans une liste* tail; ~ **journée de transactions** *f* BOURSE final trading day; **la ~ mode** *f* COM the latest fashion; ~ **mise en vente** *f* BOURSE last sale; ~ **offre** *f* COM closing bid; ~ **quinzaine** *f* COM *du mois* last half, 1h; ~ **réprimande** *f* RES HUM final warning; ♦ **à la ~ place** COM in last position

dernières: ~ **volontés** *f pl* DROIT last will and testament

dérogation *f* COMPTA relief, DROIT derogation, deviation; ♦ **par ~** COM notwithstanding; **par ~ aux clauses de** DROIT notwithstanding the provisions of; **par ~ aux dispositions de** DROIT notwithstanding the provisions of

dérogatoire *adj* COM overriding

déroulement *m* INFO flow; ~ **de l'achat** COM buying process; ~ **de carrière** RES HUM career advancement, career development; ~ **des opérations** INFO work flow; ~ **de programme** INFO program flow

dérouleur: ~ **de bande** *m* INFO deck, tape drive

déroutement *m* TRANSP route diversion; ~ **frauduleux** TRANSP *navigation* deviation fraud

derrick *m* ENVIR *structure*, IND oil rig

désaccord *m* BOURSE *des comptes d'une société de courtage* break, COM contention, disagreement, dispute, friction, *entre des déclarations, versions* discrepancy; ♦ **être en ~** *(ANT être d'accord)* COM conflict, disagree; **être en ~ avec qn sur qch** COM be at variance with sb about sth

désactivé, e *adj* INFO inactive

désagréable *adj* COM unpalatable

désaisonnalisé, e *adj* COM, ECON seasonally adjusted

désarmé, e *adj* TRANSP *navigation* idle, laid-up

désarmement *m* PROT SOC disarmament

désavantage *m* COM drawback, *position* disadvantage

désavantagé, e *adj* ECON, POL disadvantaged

désavantageux, -euse *adj* COM disadvantageous

descendance: ~ **en ligne directe** *f* DROIT issue

descendant, e *adj* *(ANT ascendant)* INFO downward

descente *f* TRANSP *navigation* companionway; ~ **en spirale** COM downward spiral

descriptif[1], **-ive** *adj* BREVETS descriptive

descriptif[2] *m* BREVETS *imprimé* specifications; ~ **des marchandises à vendre** V&M *publicité* trade description; ♦ **sur ~** COM on spec *(infrml)*, on speculation

description *f* BREVETS description, COM description, write-up, DROIT, IMMOB, V&M description; ~ **de brevet** BREVETS *imprimé* patent specifications; ~ **de fonction** RES HUM job profile; ~ **juridique** DROIT legal description; ~ **légale** DROIT legal description; ~ **de poste** RES HUM job description, job profile, job title; ~ **de la propriété à vendre** IMMOB particulars of sale; ~ **du risque** ASSUR description of risk; ~ **du risque d'exploitation** ASSUR description of operational risk

déséconomie *f* ECON diseconomy; ~ **d'échelle** *(ANT économie d'échelle)* ECON, IND diseconomy of scale; ~ **urbaine** *(ANT économie urbaine)* ECON agglomeration diseconomy

désélectionner *vt* INFO deselect

désendettement *m* BOURSE, FIN defeasance; ~ **de fait** COMPTA in substance defeasance

désengagement *m* BOURSE withdrawal, COMPTA decommitment

désengager: **se ~** *v pron* ECON withdraw

désengorger *vt* ECON debottleneck

désépargne *f* ECON dissaving

déséquilibre *m* COMPTA imbalance, ECON disequilibrium; **~ des commandes** BOURSE imbalance of orders; **~ commercial** COM trade gap, trade imbalance, ECON trade gap, *entre pays* imbalance of trade, trade imbalance, IMP/EXP trade gap, trade imbalance; **~ des ordres** BOURSE imbalance of orders

désertification *f* ENVIR desertification

déshérence *f* DROIT, IMMOB bona vacantia, escheat

déshérité, e *adj* COM underprivileged

désignation *f* BREVETS designation, COM *d'une personne* appointment, DROIT *d'un immeuble* description, FISC identification, V&M description; **~ conjointe** BREVETS joint designation; **~ de l'emploi** RES HUM job title

désigné, e *adj* COM designated

désignée: **personne ~** *f* COM nominee

désigner *vt* COM designate, nominate, single out, RES HUM appoint

désincitation *f* ECON disincentive

désincorporation *f* ECON, POL disintegration

désindustrialisation *f* ECON, IND, POL deindustrialization

désinflation *f* ECON deflation, disinflation

désinformation *f* POL disinformation

désintégration *f* COM disintegration

désintensification: **~ des cultures** *f* ENVIR deintensified farming

désintéressement *m* FIN *d'un individu* buyout; **~ pour endettement** BOURSE leveraged buyout, FIN leveraged buyout, LBO

désintéresser *vt* BANQUE pay off creditors, COM, FIN *qn* buy out

désintermédiation *f* BANQUE, ECON disintermediation

désinvestissement *m* FIN disinvestment

désir: **~ de réalisation personnelle** *m* RES HUM achievement motive

désistement *m* DROIT disclaimer; **~ d'action** DROIT abandonment of action; **~ d'un appel** FISC withdrawal of an appeal; **~ d'une plainte** FISC withdrawal of an appeal

désister: **se ~** *v pron* POL stand down; **se ~ d'un appel** FISC discontinue an appeal

désolé, e *adj* COMMS sorry; ◆ **~ de vous avoir fait attendre** COMMS sorry to have kept you waiting, sorry to keep you waiting

désolidariser: **se ~** *v pron* RES HUM break ranks

dessaisissement *m* DROIT divestiture

desserrer *vt* ECON ease

desserte: **~ inaugurale** *f* TRANSP inaugural schedule

dessin *m* BREVETS design, COM drawing; **~ héliographique** ADMIN, MÉDIA blueprint; **~ de produit** V&M product design

dessinateur: **~ de publicité** *m* RES HUM, V&M commercial artist, commercial designer

dessous:[1] **~ -de-table** *m* COM, DROIT, FIN, POL, RES HUM, V&M bribe, bribe money, kickback, undercover payment

dessous[2] *prép* COM below; **au-~ de** *prép* (ANT *en-dessus de*) COM below; ◆ **au-~ de la barre de 5%** COM below the 5% mark; **au-~ de la ligne** (ANT *au-dessus de la ligne*) COMPTA, FIN, V&M below the line; **au-~ de la moyenne** (ANT *au-dessus de la moyenne*) COM below-average; **au-~ de la norme** (ANT *au-dessus de la norme*) COM below the norm; **au-~ de la valeur** COM underpriced; **au-~ du cours** (ANT *au-dessus du cours*) BOURSE below-market price; **au-~ du pair** (ANT *au-dessus du pair*) BOURSE *prix d'actions*, COM, COMPTA below par; **au-~ du quota** (ANT *au-dessus du quota*) ECON UE below quota

dessus *prép* COM above; **au-~ de** *prép* (ANT *en-dessous de*) COM above; ◆ **au-~ de la ligne** (ANT *au-dessous de la ligne*) COMPTA, FIN, V&M above the line; **au-~ de la moyenne** (ANT *au-dessous de la moyenne*) COM above-average; **au-~ de la norme** (ANT *au-dessous de la norme*) COM above the norm; **au-~ du cours** (ANT *au-dessous du cours*) BOURSE above-market price; **au-~ du pair** BOURSE *obligation, action* at a premium, BOURSE *prix d'actions*, COM, COMPTA above par; **au-~ du quota** (ANT *au-dessous du quota*) ECON UE above quota; **avoir le ~** COM have the upper hand; **être au-~ de sa valeur nominale** BOURSE stand at a discount, stand at a premium

destinataire *mf* COMMS addressee, INFO target, RES HUM receiver, TRANSP cnee, consignee; **~ d'une offre** *m* COM, DROIT, FIN offeree

destination *f* INFO, TRANSP destination; ◆ **à ~ de** TRANSP bound for; **à ~ est** TRANSP *envoi de marchandises* eastbound; **à ~ nord** TRANSP *envoi de marchandises* northbound, NB; **à ~ ouest** TRANSP *envoi de marchandises* westbound; **à ~ sud** TRANSP *envoi de marchandises* southbound

destiner *vt* COM aim, ECON, FIN earmark

destruction *f* ENVIR destruction; **~ créatrice** ECON creative destruction; **~ involontaire** ASSUR involuntary conversion

désuétude *f* COM, V&M obsolescence; **~ calculée** COMMS, ECON, IND, V&M built-in obsolescence, planned obsolescence

désutilité *f* ECON disutility

désynchronisation: **~ des entrées/sorties** *f* INFO spooling

désyndicalisation *f* RES HUM de-unionization (*UK*)

détachement *m* RES HUM secondment

détacher *vt* COM alienate

détail *m* COM *facture* itemization; **~ technique** COM technicality; ◆ **au ~** V&M retail; **de ~** V&M retail

détaillant *m* V&M retail trader, retailer; ~ **affilié** V&M affiliated retailer; ~ **spécialisé** V&M specialty retailer (*AmE*)

détaillé, e *adj* COM *rapport, étude, réponse* comprehensive, COMPTA itemized

détailler 1. *vt* V&M retail; **2.** *v pron* **se** ~ V&M retail

détails: ~ **administratifs** *m pl* ADMIN, GESTION administrative point of view, APV; **tous les** ~ *m pl* COM full particulars

détaxe *f* FISC remission of charges

détaxé, e *adj* IMP/EXP *marchandises* duty-free

détecteur: ~ **de requin** *m* BOURSE shark watcher

détection: ~ **des erreurs** *f* GESTION faults diagnosis clinic

détendre *vt* ECON ease

détenir *vt* BOURSE *marché* hold, *obligations, actions* hold; ~ **en garantie** ASSUR hold as security

détente *f* ECON easing

détenteur, -trice *m,f* BOURSE buyer, holder, option buyer; ~ **d'actions** BOURSE equity holder; ~ **de bon de souscription** BOURSE warrant holder; ~ **de bonne foi** BOURSE bona fide holder; ~ **de carte** BANQUE, COM cardholder; ~ **contre valeur** BANQUE *d'une lettre de change* holder for value; ~ **de débentures** BOURSE debenture holder; ~ **de droits d'auteur** FISC royalty holder; ~ **d'une licence** COM licence holder (*BrE*), license holder (*AmE*); ~ **d'obligations** BOURSE bondholder; ~ **d'options** BOURSE option holder; ~ **d'un prêt** FIN loan holder; ~ **de redevances** FISC royalty holder; ~ **de titres** BOURSE stockholder; ~ **d'unité** BOURSE unit holder

détention *f* BOURSE holding, withholding, TRANSP *navires* libeling (*AmE*), libelling (*BrE*); ◆ **en** ~ **préventive** DROIT on remand

détérioration *f* COM deterioration, ENVIR degradation; ~ **de l'environnement** COM environmental damage; ~ **matérielle** COMPTA physical deterioration; ~ **des prix** ECON price deterioration; ~ **du sol** ENVIR soil degradation

détériorer: **se** ~ *v pron* COM deteriorate

déterminant, e *adj* COM decisive

détermination *f* BOURSE fixation, FISC determination; ~ **de l'assiette d'imposition** COM assessment; ~ **conjointe** RES HUM codetermination; ~ **du lieu de résidence** FISC residence status; ~ **des prix** COM, ECON, V&M price determination; ~ **des prix à parité** ECON parity pricing; ~ **de la résidence** FISC residence status; ~ **des salaires entre initiés** ECON, RES HUM insider wage setting

déterminé: ~ **par règlement** *adj* COM prescribed

déterminer *vt* BOURSE *prix des options* shape, ECON determine; ◆ ~ **l'équilibre** BOURSE find the balance; ~ **l'impôt à payer** FISC assess tax; ~ **l'origine d'un appel** COMMS trace a call; ~ **le prix de** COM, ECON, FIN, V&M price

déterminisme: ~ **du milieu** *m* ENVIR environmental determinism

détonateur *m* TRANSP detonator, *marchandises dangereuses* igniter

détour *m* COM detour; ~ **commercial dû à une union douanière** ECON, IMP/EXP, RES HUM trade diversion

détournement *m* COM misappropriation, *de fonds* embezzlement, peculation, COMPTA misappropriation, DROIT *de fonds* defalcation, embezzlement, peculation, FIN misappropriation, *de fonds* embezzlement, peculation; ~ **d'impôts** FISC defraudation; ~ **d'itinéraire** TRANSP rerouting; ~ **de main-d'oeuvre** RES HUM labor piracy (*AmE*), labour piracy (*BrE*); ~ **des objectifs d'une réglementation** ECON regulatory capture

détourner *vt* COM alienate, deter, *fonds* embezzle, *sommes d'argent* siphon off, DROIT embezzle, FIN misappropriate, *fonds* embezzle

détriment: **au** ~ **de** *loc* COM to the detriment of

détritus *m* ENVIR garbage (*AmE*), rubbish (*BrE*)

détroit *m* TRANSP *navigation* narrows, straits

détruire *vt* TRANSP write off

dette *f* COM, FIN debt, indebtedness; ~ **active** COMPTA debt owed to, outstanding debt; ~ **actuarielle** ASSUR actuarial liability; ~ **brute** FIN gross debt; ~ **consolidée** BOURSE, ECON, FIN funded debt; ~ **à court terme** BANQUE current liability, short-term debt, COMPTA, FIN subordinate debt; ~ **de deuxième rang** FIN junior debt; ~ **éventuelle** DROIT, FIN contingent liabilities; ~ **extérieure** ECON, POL external debt; ~ **fiscale** FISC tax liability; ~ **flottante** FIN floating debt, unfunded debt; ~ **garantie** BANQUE secured debt; ~ **garantie par nantissement** BOURSE bonded debt; ~ **garantie par obligations** BOURSE bonded debt; ~ **hypothécaire** BANQUE mortgage debt; ~ **indépendante** FIN self-supporting debt; ~ **liquide** FIN liquid debt; ~ **à long terme** COMPTA *inventaire comptable* long-term liability, FIN long-term debt, long-term liability; ~ **mezzanine** BOURSE mezzanine debt; ~ **nationale brute** ECON gross national debt; ~ **non-garantie** FIN unsecured debt; ~ **obligataire** BOURSE bond debt, bond liability, bond payable, bonded debt; ~ **par habitant** ECON per capita debt; ~ **à plus court terme** BOURSE shorter-term liability; ~ **publique** ECON internal debt, national debt, public debt, POL national debt; ~ **publique globale** ECON total public debt; ~ **publique totale** ECON total public debt; ~ **de rang inférieur** BOURSE subordinated debt; ~ **recouvrable** COMPTA recoverable debt; ~ **réelle** BANQUE effective debt; ~ **remboursée par un fonds** BOURSE funded debt; ~ **satisfaite** COMPTA liquidated debt; ~ **de second rang** COMPTA, FIN subordinate debt; ~ **solvable** BANQUE solvent debt; ~ **sous-jacente** FIN underlying debt; ~ **subordonnée** BOURSE subordinated debt, COMPTA, FIN subordinate debt; ~ **testamentaire** DROIT, FISC testamentary debt; ◆ ~ **due à** COMPTA *personne, société* debt due to; ~ **échue**

le COMPTA *date* debt due by; **~ exigible le** COMPTA debt due by

dettes:[1] **~ et engagements** *m pl* COMPTA claims and liabilities

dettes[2] *f pl* FIN arrearage; **~ admissibles portant intérêts** BANQUE interest-bearing eligible liabilities (*UK*), IBELS (*UK*); **~ bancaires** BANQUE, FIN bank debts; **~ commerciales** COM, DROIT, FIN business exposures liability; **~ escomptables** FIN eligible liability; **~ fiscales** COMPTA tax creditor, taxation creditor, FISC tax creditor; **~ sociales** COMPTA social security creditor; ◆ **criblé de ~** BANQUE badly in debt

DEUG *m (diplôme d'études universitaires générales)* PROT SOC university diploma taken after two years of study

deutsche: ~ Mark *m* COM Deutsche Mark

deux:[1] **à ~ hélices** *adj* TRANSP *navigation* twin-screw, T; **à ~ niveaux** *adj* RES HUM two-tier; **à ~ revenus** *adj* ECON double-income

deux:[2] **tous les ~** *loc* COM alternate; **tous les ~ jours** *loc* COM every other day

deuxième:[1] **~ jour de liquidation** *m* BOURSE name day, ticket day (*UK*); **~ rang** *m* ECON second best; **~ semestre** *m* COM second half of the year; **~ transporteur** *m* TRANSP second carrier; **~ trimestre** *m* COM second quarter, 2Q

deuxième:[2] **~ base des acomptes provisionnels** *f* FISC second installment base (*BrE*), second instalment base (*AmE*); **~ de couverture** *f* MÉDIA inside front, inside front cover; **~ démarque** *f* COM *vente au détail* double reduction, DR; **~ génération** *f* MÉDIA second generation; **~ guerre mondiale** *f* COM Second World War; **~ lecture** *f* DROIT, POL second reading; **~ mise sur le marché** *f* BOURSE secondary offering; **~ société** *f* COM second largest company

deuxièmement *adv* COM secondly

dévalorisation *f* ECON depreciation, devalorization

dévaloriser 1. *vt* ECON depreciate; **2.** *v pron* **se ~** ECON depreciate

dévaluation *f* ECON devaluation; **~ monétaire** ECON currency devaluation; **~ d'une monnaie** ECON currency devaluation

dévaluer *vt* ECON devaluate, devalue

devant: ~ les tribunaux *loc* DROIT sub judice

devanture: ~ de magasin *f* COM shop front

développé, e *adj* COM advanced

développement:[1] **du ~** *adj* IMMOB, IND, PROT SOC developmental

développement[2] *m* COM, ECON, IND, POL, V&M *d'un produit* development, expansion; **~ des affaires** GESTION business development; **~ en bande** COM strip development; **~ de carrière** RES HUM career development; **~ commercial** COM business development, commercial development; **~ du crédit intérieur** ECON domestic credit expansion, DCE; **~ écologique** COM, ENVIR environmental development; **~ économique** COM, ECON, POL economic advancement, eco-

nomic development; **~ d'équipe** GESTION, INFO, RES HUM team building; **~ d'une gestion officielle** GESTION formal management development; **~ horizontal** (ANT *développement vertical*) ECON horizontal expansion; **~ maintenable** ECON, ENVIR, POL sustainable development; **~ du marché** V&M market expansion; **~ de la marque** V&M brand development; **~ organisationnel** GESTION organization development, organizational development; **~ pédagogique** COM, PROT SOC educational development; **~ personnel** COM, RES HUM personal growth; **~ de produits nouveaux** V&M new product development; **~ régional** ECON regional development; **~ des ressources humaines** RES HUM human resource development, HRD; **~ de système** INFO system development; **~ vertical** (ANT *développement horizontal*) ECON vertical expansion

développer 1. *vt* COM develop, *ses activités* expand, *son entreprise* build up, ECON boost, IND, INFO, TRANSP develop; **2.** *v pron* **se ~** COM build up, shape up

devenir *vi* COM become; ◆ **~ caduc** DROIT *contrats* cease to have effect; **~ effectif** DROIT come into effect

déverrouiller *vt jarg* FIN, INFO unlock

déversement: ~ accidentel *m* ENVIR, IND spillage; **~ de pétrole** *m* ENVIR, IND oil spill, oil spillage

déverser *vt* ENVIR dump

déversoir: ~ d'égout *m* ENVIR outfall pipe, outfall sewer

déviation: ~ moyenne *f* MATH average deviation; **~ quartile** *f* ECON quartile deviation

devis *m* COM quotation, quote; **~ approximatif** COM rough estimate; **~ estimatif** COM cost estimate, preliminary estimate; **~ de participation** V&M lowball (*jarg*), underestimation; **~ le plus récent** COM latest estimate, L/E

devise *f* ECON, FIN currency, foreign currency, CY; **~ apatride** *jarg* ECON stateless currency; **~ clé** ECON, FIN key currency; **~ comptable** FIN reporting currency; **~ contrôlée** ECON, FIN managed currency; **~ convertible** ECON, FIN convertible currency; **~ étrangère** COM, FIN foreign currency; **~ exotique** ECON exotic currency; **~ d'exploitation** ECON functional currency; **~ faible** COM, ECON soft currency; **~ flottante** ECON, FIN floating currency, fluctuating currency; **~ forte** ECON hard currency; **~ à haute puissance** ECON, FIN managed currency; **~ d'intervention** ECON, FIN intervention currency; **~ de pays tiers** IMP/EXP third-party currency; **~ de référence** ECON reference currency; **~ saine** COM sound currency; **~ sous-évaluée** ECON undervalued currency; **~ surévaluée** ECON overvalued currency

devises *f pl* BANQUE foreign exchange, forex, BOURSE foreign exchange, futures, FX, ECON *commerce international* trading currencies; **~ en circulation** *f* ECON currency in circulation

dévoiler *vt* COM *plans, propositions* unveil; ◆ **~ une**

politique POL unveil a policy; ~ **ses intentions** COM show one's hand

devoir[1] *m* DROIT duty

devoir[2] *vt* COM *argent* owe; ◆ ~ **qch à qn** COM owe sth to sb

dévolu, e *adj* FISC passing, *à un syndic, à un bénéficiaire* vested

dévolution: ~ **de responsabilité syndicale** *f* RES HUM transfer of engagement

dévoué *m* GESTION organization man

dévouée *f* GESTION organization woman

DG *abrév (directeur général)* COMPTA, GESTION, RES HUM CEO (*US*) (*chief executive officer*), DG (*director-general*), GM (*general manager*), MD (*UK*) (*managing director*)

DGA *abrév (directeur général adjoint)* GESTION, RES HUM ADG (*assistant director general*)

DGAC *abrév France (Direction générale de l'aviation civile)* TRANSP ≈ ATA (*US*) (*Air Transport Association*), ≈ CAA (*UK*) (*Civil Aviation Authority*)

DGF *abrév (dotation globale de fonctionnement)* POL block grant (*UK*)

diable *m* TRANSP *manutention des bagages* handbarrow

diabolo *m* TRANSP *semi-remorque* dolly (*jarg*)

diagnostic *m* COM diagnosis; ~ **financier** FIN financial analysis

diagnostique *m* INFO diagnostic

diagramme *m* COM chart, GESTION flow chart, INFO chart; ~ **circulaire** COM, INFO, MATH pie chart; ~ **de circulation** GESTION, MATH flow diagram, flow process chart; ~ **croisé de Keynes** ECON Keynesian cross diagram; ~ **de dispersion** GESTION, MATH scatter diagram; ~ **de Gantt** INFO Gantt chart; ~ **SIMO** ADMIN SIMO chart; ~ **en Z** MATH Z chart

dialogue *m* COM, INFO dialog (*AmE*), dialogue (*BrE*)

diamètre: ~ **du mandrin** *m* ADMIN *fax* roll centre diameter

dichotomie: ~ **classique** *f* ECON classical dichotomy

dicter *vt* ADMIN, COM dictate

dictionnaire *m* INFO dictionary

dictum meum pactum *loc frml* COM dictum meum pactum (*frml*)

diesel:[1] ~ **-électrique** *adj* TRANSP *mécanique* diesel-electric, D-E

diesel:[2] ~ **marin** *m* TRANSP marine diesel oil

dif. *abrév (différé)* COM def. (*deferred*)

diffamation *f* DROIT action for libel, defamation, libel, *édition* libel, MÉDIA *édition* libel

diffamatoire *adj* DROIT defamatory, *geste, parole* slanderous, *texte* libellous (*BrE*), libelous (*AmE*)

diffamer *vt* DROIT defame, *oral* slander, *écrit* libel

différé[1]**, e** *adj* COM *action* deferred, INFO off-line; **en** ~ INFO off-line, MÉDIA *sport* prerecorded, recorded

différé:[2] ~ **composé** *m* France IMP/EXP compound deferment

différence *f* COM difference, distinction; ~ **de caisse** COMPTA cash short; ~ **de conversion** COMPTA translation difference; ~ **offert-demandé** BOURSE turn; ~ **à peine sensible** ADMIN just noticeable difference; ~ **de prix** COM, RES HUM, V&M price differential; ◆ **en** ~ **négative** TRANSP *navigation* trimmed by the head, trimmed by the stern; **en** ~ **positive** TRANSP *navigation* trimmed by the head, trimmed by the stern; **faire la** ~ **entre** COM differentiate between, make a distinction between

différences: ~ **de calendrier** *f pl* COMPTA, FISC timing differences; ~ **de change** *f pl* ECON, FIN exchange differences

différenciation *f* V&M *marketing* differentiation; ~ **des prix** V&M differential pricing; ~ **de produits** V&M product differentiation

différencier *vt* COM differentiate

différend *m* COM disagreement, discrepancy

différent, e *adj* COM diverse

différentiel *m* COM *rendement*, RES HUM, TRANSP *véhicule routier* differential; ~ **d'accès** ECON access differential; ~ **de qualifications** RES HUM skill differential; ~ **de revenu** ECON income differential; ~ **de taux** BOURSE rate differential; ~ **de taux d'intérêt** BANQUE, ECON interest rate differential

différentiels: ~ **de salaires** *m* ECON wage differentials

différer 1. *vt* COM defer, DROIT adjourn; **2.** *vi* COM differ; ◆ ~ **le paiement de l'impôt** FISC postpone tax

difficile *adj* COM difficult, hard

difficulté *f* COM difficulty, trouble; ◆ **avoir des** ~**s** COM be in trouble; **avoir des** ~**s de trésorerie** COMPTA have cash flow problems

difficultés: ~ **indues** *f pl* FISC undue hardship

diffuser *vt* COMMS broadcast, *télévision* broadcast, MÉDIA *télévision, radio* broadcast

diffusion *f* COM dissemination, COMMS *radio* broadcasting, *télévision* broadcasting, MÉDIA circulation, readership, *radio* broadcasting, *télévision* broadcasting; ~ **des augmentations de salaires dans une économie** ECON wage diffusion; ~ **de données** COMMS data broadcasting; ~ **de l'information** MÉDIA information broadcast; ~ **en larges bandes de fréquence** COMMS, INFO, MÉDIA broadband; ~ **radiophonique** MÉDIA *radio* radio broadcasting; ~ **simultanée** MÉDIA *radio-télévision* simulcast, simultaneous broadcast; ◆ **pour** ~ **immédiate** COM *presse* for immediate release

digital, e *adj* INFO digital

digne: ~ **de confiance** *adj* COM trustworthy

digue *f* TRANSP pier

dilatoire *adj* COM evasive

dilemme: ~ **des deux prisonniers** *m* ECON prisoners' dilemma

diligence: ~ **des intermédiaires** *f* DROIT procuring cause; ~ **normale** *f* FIN due diligence

diligenter *vt* COM expedite, hasten

diluer *vt* COM *idée, politique* water down

dilution *f* BOURSE, RES HUM dilution; ~ **de l'avoir des actionnaires** BOURSE dilution of equity, equity dilution; ~ **du bénéfice par action** BOURSE dilution of equity; ~ **des revenus** COM revenue dilution; ~ **des tarifs** TRANSP rate dilution

dim. *abrév (dimanche)* COM Sun. *(Sunday)*

dimanche *m (dim.)* COM Sunday *(Sun.)*; ◆ **~s et jours fériés compris** TRANSP *charte-partie* Sundays and holidays included, SHINC; **~s et jours fériés exceptés** TRANSP *charte-partie* S&H/exct, Sundays and holidays excepted, SHEX

dimension *f* MATH measurement, met; ~ **immédiatement inférieure** COM next size down

diminué, e *adj* COM reduced

diminuer 1. *vt* COM decrease, diminish, lower, reduce, run down, shrink, *dépenses* reduce, ECON impair, weaken, FIN impair; **2.** *vi* COM dwindle, fall away, *demande* ease off, *ventes* tail away, ECON decrease, ECON decline, go down, shrink; ◆ ~ **progressivement** COM *prix* shade

diminution *f* BANQUE *d'intérêt* rebate, COM decrease, *d'effectifs, de coûts* pruning, COMPTA *d'effectifs, de coûts* pruning, ECON *d'intérêt*, FIN *d'intérêt* rebate; ~ **d'impôt** FISC tax discounting; ~ **des impôts** FISC lowering of taxation; ~ **d'intérêt** BANQUE, ECON, FISC interest rebate; ~ **de loyer** PROT SOC rent rebate; ~ **de marge** COMPTA margin shrinkage; ~ **de l'ozone** ENVIR ozone depletion; ~ **du risque** ASSUR decrease of risk; ~ **du taux d'intérêt** BANQUE, ECON, FISC interest rate rebate; ~ **du temps de réalisation** IND reduced lead time; ~ **de valeur** COM decrease in value

dinar *m* COM dinar

dîner:[1] ~ **officiel** *m* COM formal dinner

dîner:[2] ~ **dehors** *vi* LOISIRS eat out

diode *f* INFO diode; ~ **électroluminescente** *(DEL)* INFO light-emitting diode *(LED)*

dioxyde: ~ **de soufre** *m* ENVIR sulphur dioxide

diplomatie *f* GESTION diplomacy; **la** ~ ADMIN ≈ the Diplomatic Service *(UK)*

diplôme *m* PROT SOC Dip., cert., certificate, degree, diploma, RES HUM Dip., diploma; ~ **d'administration de l'état** PROT SOC DipPA, Diploma in Public Administration; ~ **d'administration publique** PROT SOC DipPA, Diploma in Public Administration; ~ **d'études de commerce** PROT SOC DipCom, Diploma of Commerce; ~ **d'études commerciales** PROT SOC DipCom, Diploma of Commerce; ~ **d'études universitaires générales** *(DEUG)* PROT SOC university diploma taken after two years of study; ~ **de gestion des entreprises** PROT SOC Diploma in Industrial Management, DIM; ~ **national supérieur** PROT SOC Higher National Diploma *(UK)*, HND *(UK)*; ~ **en sciences économiques** PROT SOC DipEcon, Diploma of Economics; ~ **universitaire de technologie** *(DUT)* PROT SOC Diploma in Technology Dip-Tech,

diplômé[1] *adj* COM qualified

diplômé[2], **e** *m,f* PROT SOC, RES HUM graduate; ~ **en administration des entreprises** PROT SOC Bachelor of Business Administration; ~ **de l'université** PROT SOC postgraduate

dire: **c'est-à-~** *conj (c-à-d)* COM id est *(i.e.)*, that is to say

direct[1], **e** *adj* RES HUM *expérience, formation* hands-on, TRANSP *trajet* dir., direct; **en** ~ LOISIRS *sport*, MÉDIA live; ◆ ~ **ou présumé couvert** ASSUR direct or held covered

direct[2] *m* MÉDIA spot coverage

directement *adv* COM *(ANT indirectement)* MATH directly; ◆ **être** ~ **intéressé par** COM have a vested interest in; ~ **exploitable** INFO machine-readable; ~ **lié à** COM directly related to; ~ **responsable vis-à-vis de** COM directly responsible to; ~ **transporté** IMP/EXP *UE*, TRANSP *UE* directly-transported

directeur, -trice *m,f* GESTION executive, manager, mgr, GESTION director, D, RES HUM manager, mgr, D, RES HUM director; ~ **des achats** COM, RES HUM, V&M chief buyer, head buyer, purchasing manager; ~ **adjoint** BANQUE assistant manager, GESTION, RES HUM assistant director, assistant manager, deputy director, deputy manager; ~ **administratif diplômé** RES HUM certified administration manager; ~ **d'agence** BANQUE, FIN, GESTION bank manager, branch manager; ~ **artistique** GESTION, RES HUM, V&M art manager; ~ **des assurances** ASSUR Superintendent of Insurance; ~ **de banque** BANQUE, FIN, GESTION bank manager; ~ **de bureau** ADMIN, GESTION, RES HUM office manager; ~ **de chantier** IND, RES HUM site manager; ~ **chargé des contrats** ADMIN, RES HUM contracts manager; ~ **de la circulation ferroviaire** RES HUM, TRANSP traffic manager, TM; ~ **clientèle** GESTION, RES HUM, V&M consumer relations manager; ~ **de collection** MÉDIA *presse, radio, TV* editor; ~ **commercial** GESTION commercial manager, marketing director, marketing manager, merchandising director, sales manager, MÉDIA business manager, RES HUM, V&M commercial manager, marketing director, marketing manager, merchandising director, sales manager; ~ **de compagnie maritime** RES HUM ferry line manager; ~ **de comptabilité** COMPTA Accountant General, AG, chief accountant, chief accounting officer, group chief accountant; ~ **de comptabilité générale** COMPTA General Accounting Officer *(US)*; ~ **des comptes** BANQUE account manager; ~ **du contrôle des changes** RES HUM exchange control officer; ~ **du crédit aux entreprises** BANQUE corporate credit manager; ~ **de département** GESTION, RES HUM department head; ~ **du développement** GESTION, RES HUM development manager; ~ **de division** GESTION, RES HUM division head; ~ **exécutif** ADMIN, RES HUM executive director, executive manager;

~ **export** IMP/EXP, RES HUM export director, export manager; ~ **des exportations** IMP/EXP, RES HUM export director, export manager; ~ **de fabrication** IND, MÉDIA *édition, presse*, RES HUM production director, production manager; ~ **financier** FIN, RES HUM chief financial officer, financial director, financial manager, CFO; ~ **de la flotte** RES HUM fleet manager; ~ **de formation** RES HUM training officer; ~ **général** *(DG)* COMPTA *société anonyme par actions* managing director *(UK) (MD)*, GESTION, RES HUM chief executive, chief executive officer *(US) (CEO)*, director-general *(DG)*, general manager *(GM)*, managing director *(UK) (MD)*; ~ **général adjoint** *(DGA)* GESTION assistant director-general *(ADG)*, deputy chief executive, deputy managing director, RES HUM assistant director-general *(ADG)*, deputy chief executive, deputy managing director *(UK)*; ~ **hiérarchique** GESTION, RES HUM line manager; ~ **des importations** IMP/EXP, RES HUM import manager; ~ **de journal** MÉDIA newspaper publisher; ~ **du marketing** GESTION, RES HUM, V&M marketing director, marketing manager; ~ **marketing des exportations** IMP/EXP, RES HUM export marketing manager; ~ **de merchandising** GESTION, RES HUM, V&M merchandising director; ~ **des opérations** COM, GESTION, RES HUM operational manager, operations manager; ~ **par intérim** GESTION acting director; ~ **du parc** RES HUM fleet manager; ~ **du parc automobile** RES HUM fleet manager; ~ **du personnel** GESTION, RES HUM head of the personnel department, personnel director; ~ **du port** RES HUM, TRANSP port director, port manager; ~ **de la production** IND, MÉDIA, RES HUM production director, production manager; ~ **de produit** COM, GESTION, RES HUM product manager; ~ **de projet** RES HUM project manager; ~ **de la publication** MÉDIA editor, newspaper publisher; ~ **de la publicité** MÉDIA, RES HUM, V&M advertising director, advertising manager, publicity manager; ~ **de la recherche** RES HUM research director; ~ **du recrutement** GESTION recruitment manager; ~ **de la rédaction** MÉDIA *presse, radio, TV* editor; ~ **régional** BANQUE area manager, RES HUM district manager; ~ **régional de circulation** RES HUM, TRANSP district traffic superintendent, DTS; ~ **régional de la formation professionnelle** RES HUM district training officer, DTO; ~ **régional des transports** RES HUM, TRANSP district traffic superintendent, DTS; ~ **des relations avec la clientèle** GESTION consumer relations manager, RES HUM consumer relations manager, customer relations manager; ~ **des relations humaines** RES HUM industrial relations director, industrial relations manager; ~ **des relations industrielles** RES HUM industrial relations director, industrial relations manager; ~ **des relations professionnelles** RES HUM industrial relations director, industrial relations manager; ~ **des relations publiques** RES HUM, V&M director of public relations, public relations officer, DPR, PRO; ~ **des relations syndicales** RES HUM industrial relations director, industrial relations manager; ~ **résident** IMMOB resident manager; ~ **des ressources humaines** *(DRH)* GESTION head of the personnel department, personnel director, RES HUM head of the personnel department, personnel director; ~ **de la santé publique** PROT SOC, RES HUM medical officer of health, MOH; ~ **SAV** *(directeur du service après-ventes)* RES HUM after-sales manager; ~ **du service** GESTION, RES HUM department head; ~ **du service après-ventes** *(directeur SAV)* RES HUM after-sales manager; ~ **du service des ventes** MÉDIA, RES HUM *presse* circulation manager; ~ **des services du fret** RES HUM, TRANSP cargo superintendent; ~ **de succursale** BANQUE branch manager, COM branch office manager, GESTION branch manager, branch office manager; ~ **technique** GESTION technical director, technical manager, IND production director, production manager, INFO technical director, technical manager, MÉDIA *édition, presse* production director, production manager, RES HUM engineering manager, technical director, technical manager, production director, production manager; ~ **de terminal** GESTION, TRANSP terminal manager; ~ **du train** RES HUM fleet manager; ~ **des transports** RES HUM, TRANSP traffic manager, TM; ~ **d'usine** COM plant manager, IND, RES HUM plant manager, works manager; ~ **des ventes** GESTION, RES HUM, V&M sales manager; ~ **des ventes-clientèle** RES HUM field sales manager; ~ **des ventes intérieures** RES HUM indoor sales manager; ~ **des ventes sédentaires** RES HUM indoor sales manager; ~ **de zone** BANQUE area manager

Directeur: ~ **des Affaires Sociales** *m* RES HUM Director of Labor Relations *(AmE)*, Director of Labour Relations *(BrE)*; ~ **général de la Concurrence et des prix** *m* COM Director General of Fair Trading *(UK)*

direction *f* ADMIN management, *bureau* manager's office, COM management, DROIT steering, GESTION direction, leadership, manager's office, IMMOB steering, RES HUM directorship, leadership, TRANSP steering system; ~ **assistée** TRANSP power steering; ~ **autoritaire** GESTION, RES HUM authoritarian management; ~ **centrale** ADMIN, RES HUM headquarters, HQ; ~ **commerciale** GESTION, V&M sales management; ~ **du courant** TRANSP *navigation* set; ~ **démocratique** GESTION, RES HUM democratic management; ~ **efficace** GESTION effective management; ~ **d'entreprise** GESTION corporate management; ~ **générale** ADMIN general management, GESTION general management, main office; ~ **hiérarchique** GESTION line management; ~ **intriquée** COM, GESTION interlocking directorate; ~ **multiple** GESTION multiple management; ~ **opérationnelle** GESTION operating management; ~ **par objectifs** *(DPO)* GESTION management by objectives *(MBO)*; ~ **par programmes** GESTION programmed management; ~ **participative** GESTION participative management; ~ **du personnel** GESTION personnel management, staff management, RES HUM personnel department, personnel management, staff management; ~ **de planning** COM, GESTION planning department; ~ **des ressources humaines** *(DRH)* RES HUM personnel department; ~ **des salaires et des traitements** RES HUM wage and salary administration; ~ **de service** COM departmental management; ~ **en structure mixte** GESTION, RES HUM line and staff management; ~ **d'un syndicat** RES HUM union government; ~ **systématisée** GESTION, INFO systems management; ~ **du travail et de l'emploi** ADMIN labor administration *(AmE)*, labour administration *(BrE)*; ~ **des ventes** GESTION sales management, V&M sales department, sales management; ◆ **de ~** COM, GESTION managerial

Direction: ~ **de l'aménagement du territoire** *f* ADMIN ≈ City and Regional Planning; ≈ ~ **de la concurrence, de la consommation et de la répression de fraudes** *f Fra* ECON ≈ OFT *(UK)*, ≈ Office of Fair Trading *(UK)*, ≈ Trading Standards Office *(US)*; ~ **générale de l'aviation civile** *f France (DGAC)* TRANSP ≈ Air Transport Association *(US)* *(ATA)*, ≈ Civil Aviation Authority *(UK)* *(CAA)*

directive *f* ADMIN, BOURSE, COM guideline, DROIT directive, GESTION guideline, POL directive, RES HUM guideline; ~ **commune** DROIT, POL common directive; ~ **des dix pour cent** FISC ten percent guideline; ~ **européenne** DROIT, POL EU Directive; ~ **préliminaire** DROIT, POL draft directive; ~ **de l'Union européenne** DROIT, POL EU Directive

Directive: ~ **d'égalité des salaires** *f* RES HUM Equal Pay Directive

directives:[1] ~ **et objectifs ministériels** *m pl* ADMIN departmental line object, departmental object, line object

directives:[2] ~ **financières** *f pl* FISC tax guidelines; ~ **en matière de salaires et de prix** *f pl* RES HUM wage-and-price guidelines

directoire *m* COM, GESTION board of management, management board; ~ **interdépendant** DROIT interlocking directorate

directorial, e *adj* COM, GESTION managerial

directrice *f* GESTION, RES HUM manageress

dirham *m* COM dirham

dirigeant[1]**, e** *adj* ADMIN, GESTION, RES HUM managing

dirigeant[2]**, e** *m,f* BANQUE *d'une banque* officer, COM *d'une corporation* insider, leader, GESTION director, manager, mgr, D, RES HUM director, D, RES HUM manager, mgr; ~ **d'une corporation** GESTION corporate manager; ~ **d'entreprise** ADMIN, COM, GESTION, RES HUM business manager, company executive; ~ **opérationnel** RES HUM line executive; ~ **de société** GESTION corporate executive

dirigeants: **les ~** *m pl* RES HUM the men at the top *(infrml)*

diriger *vt* COM carry on, channel through, funnel, *entreprise, réunion* conduct, GESTION direct, lead, RES HUM lead; ◆ ~ **les débats** GESTION, RES HUM be in the chair

disaggio *m* BOURSE discount

disciple *m* COM follower

discipline *f* COM, RES HUM discipline

discipliner *vt* DROIT discipline

disciplines: ~ **affinitaires** *f pl* PROT SOC cognate disciplines; ~ **voisines** *f pl* PROT SOC cognate disciplines

discompte *m* COM disc., discount

discompter *vt* FIN discount

discompteur *m* FIN discounter

discontinuer *vt* FIN *fonds* terminate

discours *m* COMMS address; ~ **de clôture** POL wrap-up *(US, jarg)*; ~ **de présentation du Budget** POL Budget speech *(UK)*; ~ **du président** GESTION chairman's brief; ◆ **faire un ~** GESTION make a speech

discret, -ète *adj* COM low-key, low-profile

discrétion *f* COM discretion; ◆ **à la ~ de** COM at the discretion of; **à notre ~** COM at our discretion

discrétionnaire *adj* COM, ECON discretionary

discrimination *f* COM, ECON, PROT SOC discrimination; ~ **s'appliquant à l'âge** DROIT, RES HUM age discrimination; ~ **après l'accès au marché du travail** ECON post-entry discrimination; ~ **entre hommes et femmes** DROIT, RES HUM gender discrimination, sex discrimination, sexual discrimination; ~ **horizontale** *(ANT discrimination verticale)* ECON horizontal discrimination; ~ **indirecte** RES HUM indirect discrimination; ~ **inverse** PROT SOC reverse discrimination; ~ **masquée** RES HUM indirect discrimination; ~ **en matière d'âge** DROIT, RES HUM age discrimination; ~ **pour motifs religieux** RES HUM religious discrimination; ~ **par les prix** COM third-degree price discrimination; ~ **parfaite par les prix** ECON perfect price discrimination; ~ **positive** *(SYN mesures anti-discriminatoires, politique anti-discriminatoire)* POL, PROT SOC, RES HUM *à l'embauche* affirmative action *(AmE)*, positive action *(BrE)*, positive discrimination *(BrE)*; ~ **de prix** COM, V&M price discrimination; ~ **qui bloque l'accès au marché du travail** ECON pre-entry discrimination; ~ **raciale** RES HUM racial discrimination; ~ **sexuelle** DROIT, RES HUM gender discrimination, sex discrimination, sexual discrimination; ~ **sexuelle à l'embauche** RES HUM job segregation; ~ **verticale** *(ANT discrimination horizontale)* ECON vertical discrimination

discriminer *vt* COM discriminate

disculpe: qui ~ *loc* BANQUE, DROIT exculpatory

disculper *vt* DROIT clear

discussion *f* COM discussion; ~ **approfondie** COM in-depth discussion; ~ **en prise directe** POL hands-on session; ◆ **soumis à ~** COM under discussion

discussions: ~ **franches** *f pl* COM, POL frank discussions *(jarg)*; ~ **au plus haut niveau** *f pl*

GESTION, POL top-level talks; **~ sur l'intéresse- ment à la productivité** *f pl* ECON productivity bargaining

discutable *adj* COM controversial

discuter *vt* ASSUR contest, COM debate, discuss; **~ du** COM, V&M haggle about, haggle over; **~ à fond** COM thrash out

dispacheur *m* ASSUR *maritime*, TRANSP *maritime* average adjuster, AA

disparate *adj* COM odd

disparité *f* COM disparity

disparition *f* ENVIR extinction

dispense *f* DROIT dispensation; **~ de paiement de la prime** ASSUR exemption from payment of premium

disperser: se ~ *v pron* COM break up, split up

dispersion: ~ des logements *f* PROT SOC scattered site housing (*BrE, jarg*), scattersite housing (*AmE, jarg*); **~ des risques** *f* ASSUR distribution of risks

disponibilité *f* BOURSE spot position, INFO avail- ability; **~ des ressources** FIN resource availability

disponibilités *f pl* BANQUE available cash, COM abilities, COMPTA available cash, available funds, cash, cash holdings, liquid assets, liquid funds, FIN cash

disponible *adj* COM available, free, obtainable, *personne* accessible, INFO available, free, unallo- cated, MÉDIA in print; ◆ **~ sans délai** COM available at short notice

disposé: peu ~ à faire qch *loc* COM reluctant to do sth

disposer: ~ de *vt* FISC dispose of; ◆ **ne pas ~ de fonds suffisants** FIN be undercapitalized; **~ des piquets de grève** IND, RES HUM picket

dispositif *m* INFO device; **~ d'accrochage** TRANSP *pièces de saisissage* securing pad; **~ d'alarme** COM warning device; **~ d'alimentation de document** INFO document feeder; **~ antivol** COM, TRANSP antitheft device; **~ d'arrimage transversal** TRANSP *navigation* transversal lashing system; **~ câblé** INFO hardware device; **~ de CO²** TRANSP *navigation* carbon dioxide system, CAR DI SYS; **~ de déclenchement** COM trigger mechanism; **~ de gréement pour utilisation en colis volant** TRANSP *manutention* union purchase; **~ pour la mise en oeuvre de** BREVETS apparatus for carry- ing out; **~ de protection électronique** INFO dongle; **~ de recherche de personne** COMMS, INFO paging device; **~ de réfrigération** ENVIR, IND cooling system; **~ de séparation du trafic** TRANSP *maritime* traffic separation scheme; **~ de serrage** TRANSP *manutention* squeeze clamp

dispositifs: ~ de mise en commun des ressources *m pl* COM pooling arrangements; **~ de stabilisa- tion des prix des matières premières** *m pl* ECON commodity stabilization schemes

disposition *f* ADMIN layout, COM arrangement, paste-up, *d'une loi* provision, *d'une personne* tendency, DROIT provision, FISC disposal, disposi-

tion, provision, INFO *d'un clavier* arrangement, RES HUM clause; **~ de l'année courante** FISC current year disposition; **~ anti-évitement** BOURSE, DROIT, FIN, FISC anti-avoidance rule; **~ contractuelle** DROIT contractual provision; **~ financière complémentaire** FIN Supplementary Financing Facility; **~ fiscale** FISC tax provision; **~ légale stipulant une date d'expiration** DROIT sunset provision; **~ obligatoire** ASSUR mandatory provision; **~ présumée** FISC deemed disposition; **~ de récupération** FISC clawback; **~ réglementaire stipulant une date d'expiration** DROIT sunset provision; **~ réputée** FISC deemed disposition; ◆ **à ~ à l'arrivée** TRANSP *maritime, charte-partie* always accessible, always accessible on arrival, always reachable on arrival, reachable on arrival

dispositions *f pl* DROIT *d'une loi* provisions; **~ en cas d'imprévu** COM contingency arrangements; **~ concernant la fraction à risques** FISC *de l'intérêt d'un commanditaire* at-risk rules; **les ~ des présentes** COMMS the provisions hereof; **~ particulières** COM special arrangements; **~ sur les biens restreints** FISC carve-out rules

disputé, e *adj* V&M *marché* contested

disque: ~ CD-ROM *m (CD-ROM)* INFO compact disk read-only memory *(CD-ROM)*; **~ compact** *m (CD)* INFO compact disk *(CD)*; **~ compact interactif** *m (CDI)* INFO compact disk interactive *(CD-I)*; **~ double face** *m* INFO double-sided disk; **~ dur** *m* INFO fixed disk, hard disk; **~ fixe** *m* INFO fixed disk; **~ de franc-bord** *m* TRANSP *navigation* plimsoll line; **~ d'initialisation** *m* INFO boot disk; **~ magnétique** *m* INFO magnetic disk; **~ monoface** *m* INFO single-sided disk, SSD; **~ d'or** *m* MÉDIA gold disc; **~ de platine** *m* MÉDIA platinum disc; **~ simple face** *m* INFO single-sided disk, SSD; **~ souple** *m* ADMIN, INFO disk, diskette, floppy, floppy disk, microdisk; **~ source** *m* INFO source disk; **~ système** *m* INFO system disk; **~ de travail** *m* INFO scratch disk; **~ virtuel** *m* INFO RAM disk, random access memory disk; **~ Winchester** *m* INFO Winchester disk

disquette *f* ADMIN, INFO disk, diskette, floppy, floppy disk, microdisk; **~ double densité** INFO double-density disk; **~ double face** INFO double- sided diskette; **~ à haute densité** INFO high- density disk, HDD; **~ d'installation** INFO installa- tion diskette; **~ protégée** INFO copy-protected disk

dissimulation *f* DROIT concealment; **~ de pertes** BOURSE, COMPTA concealment of losses

dissimuler *vt* COM *des faits, la vérité* conceal, cover up; ◆ **~ des faits** DROIT withhold

dissolution *f* COM, DROIT *droit des sociétés*, POL *du parlement*, RES HUM dissolution; **~ du syndicat d'enchères** BOURSE breaking the syndicate

dissonance: ~ cognitive *f* ECON cognitive disso- nance

dissoudre *vt* COM dissolve

dissuader *vt* COM deter

distance: à ~ *adj* INFO remote, remote-controlled

distancer *vt* COM leave behind

distant, e *adj* INFO remote

distillation *f* COM distilling

distinctif, -ive *adj* BREVETS distinctive

distinction *f* COM distinction; ◆ **faire une ~ entre** COM draw a distinction between

distinguer *vt* COM single out; ◆ **~ entre** COM make a distinction between

distorsion *f* COM, ECON, FIN distortion; **~ commerciale** ECON trade distortion; **~ du marché** ECON market distortion, market failure

distractions: **~ en vol** *f pl* TRANSP in-flight entertainment

distribuer *vt* COM share out, *information* distribute, RES HUM allocate, V&M *marketing* market

distributeur, -trice *m,f* IMP/EXP, TRANSP, V&M distributor; **~ automatique** COM, V&M automatic vending machine, vending machine; **~ automatique de billets** *(DAB)* BANQUE automated cash dispenser, automatic cash dispenser *(ACD)*, cash-dispensing machine; **~ automatique de produits** *(DAP)* COM, V&M automatic vending machine, vending machine; **~ de billets** BANQUE automated cash dispenser, automatic cash dispenser, cash-dispensing machine; **~ de crédit** BANQUE credit grantor; **~ d'eau** ENVIR, IND water supplier; **~ de monnaie** BANQUE change dispenser

distribution *f* COM, DROIT, TRANSP, V&M distribution; **~ d'actions** BOURSE share allotment; **~ automatique** COM vending; **~ bimodale** MATH bimodal distribution; **~ en carré chi** MATH chi-squared distribution; **~ d'échantillons gratuits en porte à porte** V&M house-to-house sampling; **~ équitable** COM equitable distribution; **~ en une fois** BOURSE lump-sum distribution; **~ des fréquences** MATH frequency distribution; **~ de masse** TRANSP open distribution; **~ de montant global** BOURSE lump-sum distribution; **~ multinomiale** MATH multimodal distribution; **~ normale** MATH normal distribution, unimodal distribution; **~ ouverte** TRANSP open distribution; **~ par âge** ECON age distribution; **~ par grandeur** MATH size distribution; **~ de plus-values** BOURSE capital gains distribution; **~ restreinte** TRANSP limited distribution; **~ du revenu des particuliers** ECON personal income distribution; **~ des revenus entre les générations** ECON intergenerational distribution of income; **~ de la richesse** ECON wealth distribution; **~ sélective** COM selective distribution; **~ spatiale** COM, MATH spatial distribution; **~ du travail** GESTION, RES HUM allocation of work

dit *adv* COMMS a.k.a., also known as

div. *abrév* *(dividende)* BOURSE, FIN div. *(dividend)*

divergence *f* *(ANT convergence)* BOURSE, COM, ECON, POL *d'opinions, de résultats* divergence; **~ de points de vue** GESTION division of thought; ◆ **avoir des ~s d'opinion avec qn** COM be at variance with sb about sth; **avoir des ~s de vue**

sur qch avec qn COM be at variance with sb about sth

diverger *vi* COM *opinions*, ECON diverge

divers[1]**, e** *adj* COM, COMPTA misc., miscellaneous

divers[2] *m pl* COMPTA sundries, TRANSP general cargo, GC

diversification *f* BOURSE, ECON, GESTION, RES HUM diversification; **~ de l'actif** FIN asset diversification; **~ des affaires** COM, GESTION business diversification; **~ commerciale** COM, GESTION business diversification; **~ excessive** BOURSE overdiversification; **~ en fonction de la liquidité** BOURSE liquidity diversification; **~ des liquidités** BOURSE liquidity diversification; **~ de produits** V&M product diversification; **~ de type conglomérat** ECON, FIN conglomerate diversification

diversifié: très ~ *adj* COM broadly diversified

diversifier *vt* COM diversify; ◆ **~ les risques** BOURSE diversify risk

diversion: **~ commerciale** *f* ECON, IMP/EXP, RES HUM trade diversion

diversité *f* COM, V&M *magasins* diversity

divertir *vt* COM entertain

divertissement *m* COM entertainment

dividende *m* *(div.)* BOURSE *action*, FIN dividend *(div.)*; **~ en actions** BOURSE, COMPTA stock dividend *(US)*; **~ -actions** BOURSE, COMPTA stock dividend *(US)*; **~ d'actions** BOURSE share dividend; **~ annuel** COM annual dividend, yearly dividend; **~ après impôt** COMPTA, ECON, FIN, FISC after-tax dividend; **~ attaché** BOURSE cd, cum dividend; **~ brut** COMPTA gross dividend; **~ en capital** BOURSE capital dividend; **~ cumulatif** BOURSE cumulative dividend; **~ cumulé** BOURSE accrued dividend, accumulated dividend; **~ déclaré** BOURSE declared dividend; **~ à découvert** FIN times uncovered; **~ détaché** BOURSE ex-div., ex-dividend; **~ différé** FIN scrip dividend; **~ donnant droit à la déduction pour revenus en intérêts et en dividendes** BOURSE dividend eligible for interest and dividends income deduction; **~ en espèces** BOURSE, FIN cash dividend; **~ exceptionnel** ASSUR capital bonus, BOURSE bonus, bonus payment, extra dividend, extraordinary dividend, FIN bonus; **~ exclu** FISC excluded dividend; **~ exonéré d'impôt** BOURSE exempt dividend; **~ fictif** BOURSE unearned dividend; **~ de filiale** BOURSE subsidiary dividends; **~ de fin d'exercice** COMPTA year-end dividend; **~ illicite** DROIT illegal dividend *(US)*; **~ impayé** FIN unpaid dividend; **~ imposable** FISC taxable dividend; **~ intérimaire** BOURSE interim dividend; **~ de liquidation** COMPTA liquidation dividend, FIN liquidating dividend; **~ majoré** BOURSE, FIN grossed-up dividend; **~ de mi-année** BOURSE interim dividend; **~ en nature** BOURSE dividend in kind; **~ net** BOURSE net dividend, COMPTA dividend net; **~ non-déclaré** COMPTA passed dividend; **~ non-réclamé** COMPTA unrequired dividend; ~ **omis** COMPTA omitted dividend, passed dividend; ~ **ordinaire** BOURSE common dividend, common share dividend (*BrE*), common stock dividend (*AmE*); ~ **par action** *(DPA)* BOURSE, COMPTA *bilan* dividend per share; ~ **passé** COMPTA omitted dividend; ~ **à payer** COMPTA accrued dividend, dividend payable; ~ **de portefeuille** BOURSE portfolio dividend; ~ **prélevé sur le capital** BOURSE capital dividend; ~ **semestriel** BOURSE half-yearly dividend, semi-annual dividend; ~ **de la société mère** COMPTA parent company dividend; ~ **sur actions ordinaires** BOURSE common dividend, common share dividend (*BrE*), common stock dividend (*AmE*); ~ **sur actions privilégiées** COMPTA preference dividend (*BrE*), preferred dividend (*AmE*); ~ **sur les gains en capital** FISC capital gains dividend; ~ **sur obligations** COMPTA liability dividend; ~ **à terme échu** BOURSE dividend in arrears; ~ **trimestriel** BOURSE quarterly dividend; ◆ **avec ~** BOURSE cd, cum dividend

dividendes: ~ **étrangers** *m pl* BOURSE foreign dividends; ~ **imposables admissibles** *m pl* FISC qualifying taxable dividends; ~ **négociés** *m pl* BOURSE trading dividends; ~ **de la paix** *m pl* POL peace dividend; ~ **de la société mère** *m pl* BOURSE parent dividends

divisé: ~ **par** *loc* MATH divided by

diviser *vt* INFO divide

division *f* COM department, division; ~ **d'actions** BOURSE share split, stock split (*AmE*); ~ **administrative** ADMIN, GESTION organizational unit; ~ **cinq pour une** BOURSE five-for-one split; ~ **de la commission économique pour le commerce européen et** ADMIN Economic Commission for Europe for Trade and Technology Division, ECOCOM; ~ **en deux** COM two-way split; ~ **opérationnelle** COM operating division; ~ **du travail** ECON division of labor (*AmE*), division of labour (*BrE*); ~ **du travail entre hommes et femmes** RES HUM sexual division of labor (*AmE*), sexual division of labour (*BrE*); ~ **du trésor public** DROIT tax jurisdiction, FISC tax district (*UK*), tax jurisdiction; ~ **en trois** COM three-way split

divulgation: ~ **complète** *f* ASSUR, DROIT full disclosure; ~ **exclusive** *f* POL exclusive distribution, exdis (*jarg*); ~ **financière** *f* FIN financial disclosure; ~ **d'information** *f* RES HUM disclosure of information; ~ **notée en bas de page** *f* COMPTA footnote disclosure; ~ **restreinte** *f* POL limdis (*jarg*), limited distribution; ~ **sur le marché** *f* BOURSE market disclosure

divulguer *vt* COM *informations* leak, *secret* disclose, MÉDIA *informations* leak; ◆ **ne pas ~** COM conceal

dixième: **un ~** *m (1/10)* COM, MATH one-tenth *(1/10)*

Djakarta *n pr* COM Jakarta

Djibouti *n pr* COM Djibouti

Djibutien, -enne *m,f* COM *habitant* Djibuti, Djibutian

dl. *abrév* COM, RES HUM DEL

dock *m* TRANSP dock; ~ **fermé** TRANSP enclosed dock; ~ **flottant** TRANSP floating dock; ~ **pour la manutention des conteneurs** TRANSP container dock

docker *m* RES HUM docker (*BrE*), longshoreman (*AmE*), stevedore, stvdr, TRANSP stevedore, stvdr

docteur *m (Dr)* COM, PROT SOC, RES HUM Doctor *(Dr)*; ~ **en droit** DROIT, PROT SOC Doctor of Laws, LLD; ~ **en droit commercial** DROIT, PROT SOC DComL, Doctor of Commercial Law; ~ **en science commerciale** PROT SOC, RES HUM DCom, Doctor of Commerce; ~ **en sciences économiques** COM, ECON DEcon, Doctor of Economics

doctorat *m* PROT SOC DPhil, Doctor of Philosophy, PhD, doctorate

doctrine: ~ **de l'exécution substantielle d'un contrat** *f* DROIT doctrine of substantial performance; ~ **du pragmatisme juridique** *f* DROIT realism

doctrines: ~ **comptables** *f pl* COMPTA accounting doctrines

document *m* ADMIN document, paper, COM, INFO document; ~ **accompagnateur** ADMIN, COMMS accompanying document; ~ **administratif unique** *(DAU)* ADMIN, IMP/EXP, TRANSP single administrative document *(SAD)*; ~ **authentique** DROIT legal document; ~ **de base** ADMIN master document, COMPTA source document, INFO master document; ~ **-cadre de politique économique** *(DCPE)* BOURSE, ECON policy framework paper *(PFP)*; ~ **ci-joint** ADMIN, COMMS accompanying document; ~ **d'engagement** DROIT commitment document; ~ **d'exécution** COM, V&M artwork; ~ **expert** INFO intelligent document; ~ **externe** COM external document; ~ **financier prévisionnel** FIN estimated financial report; ~ **fret rapide** TRANSP *navigation* data freight receipt, DFR; ~ **d'information** FIN background paper; ~ **intelligent** INFO intelligent document; ~ **joint** ADMIN, COMMS accompanying document; ~ **justificatif** MATH supporting data; ~ **maître** ADMIN, INFO master document; ~ **multiutilisateur** INFO multiuser document; ~ **officiel** ADMIN official document; ~ **originaire** FISC originating document; ~ **de transit** IMP/EXP, TRANSP transit document; ~ **de transport** TRANSP transportation document, *maritime* transport document; ~ **de transport combiné** TRANSP combined transport document, CTD; ~ **de travail** POL working paper; ~ **de voyage** LOISIRS travel document

documentaire *m* MÉDIA documentary

documentaliste *mf* MÉDIA researcher

documentation *f* ADMIN documentation, reference material, COM backup material, documentation, material, MAT, INFO documentation;

~ exportation IMP/EXP export documentation; **~ publicitaire** V&M sales literature

documents: **~ d'accompagnement** *m pl* COM backup material; **~ de bord** *m pl* DROIT *navigation*, TRANSP *navigation* ship's papers; **~ budgétaires** *m pl* COMPTA Budget Papers *(Canada)*; **~ contre acceptation** *m pl* COM documents against acceptance, D/A; **~ contre paiement** *m pl (DP)* COM documents against payment *(DP, DAP)*; **~ établissant le droit de propriété** *m pl* DROIT documents of title; **~ d'expédition** *m pl* IMP/EXP shipping documents; **~ de transport maritime** *m pl* TRANSP shipping documents

Dodoma *n pr* COM Dodoma

Doha *n pr* COM Doha

doit: **~ s'adapter** *loc* BREVETS must fit, must match

dol *m* DROIT fraud; **~ d'assurance maritime** ASSUR marine insurance fraud

dol. *abrév (dollar)* COM dol. *(dollar)*

dollar *m* COM buck *(US, infrml)*, dollar, greenback *(US, infrml)*, COM dollar, ECON, FIN buck *(US, infrml)*, dollar, greenback *(US, infrml)*; **~ au comptant et à terme** FIN dollar spot and forward

dollarisation *f* ECON dollarization

dollars: **~ constants** *m pl* ECON constant dollars *(US)*; **~ courants** *m pl* COMPTA, ECON current dollars; **~ indexés** *m* COM, FIN, IMP/EXP common dollars; **~ offshore** *m pl* BANQUE offshore dollars

DOM *abrév (département d'Outre-Mer)* COM overseas department

domaine *m* COM area, IND *de recherche* field, MATH domain; **~ d'activité** FISC field of endeavour *(BrE)*, field of endeavor *(AmE)*; **~ d'activité stratégique** COM, ECON, GESTION strategic business unit; **~ des affaires** COM business sector; **~ d'attributions** POL jurisdiction; **~ éminent** IMMOB eminent domain; **~ d'expertise** COM area of expertise; **~ financier** FIN financial field; **~ fiscal** FISC field of taxation, tax field; **~ d'imposition** FISC field of taxation; **~ problématique** COM, GESTION problem area; **~ public** MÉDIA public domain; **~ de responsabilité** GESTION, RES HUM area of responsibility; **~ de spécialisation** COM area of expertise; **~ technique** BREVETS technical field; ♦ **dans ce ~** COM in this respect; **dans le ~ public** COM in the public sphere

domestique *mf* GESTION servant

domicile:[1] **à ~** *adj* TRANSP door-to-door

domicile:[2] **à ~** *adv* TRANSP door to door

domicile[3] *m* COM dwelling, DROIT domicile, place of abode; **~ d'imposition** FISC tax domicile; **~ légal** DROIT legal residence; ♦ **avoir ~ et travail** DROIT, FISC, IMMOB reside and work; **à ~** domicile IMP/EXP house to house, TRANSP house-to-house; **~/dépôt** IMP/EXP, TRANSP house/depot

domicilié, e *adj* DROIT domiciled

dominant, e *adj* COM dominant

dominer *vt* ECON *marché* dominate; ♦ **~ son travail** RES HUM be on top of one's job

dominicain, e *adj* COM Dominican

Dominicain, e *m,f* COM *habitant* Dominican

dominiquais, e *adj* COM Dominican

Dominiquais, e *m,f* COM *habitant* Dominican

Dominique *f* COM Dominica

dommage *m* ASSUR damage, DROIT damage, nuisance, TRANSP damage; **~ causé par un incendie** ASSUR damage caused by fire; **~ indirect** TRANSP consequential damage, sympathetic damage; **~ irréparable** DROIT irreparable damage; **~ matériel** IMMOB property damage; ♦ **~ causé avec intention** ASSUR insured loss caused deliberately, DROIT malicious damage

dommages: **~ aux biens loués** *m pl* ASSUR damage to rented property; **~ connus** *m pl* ASSUR known loss; **~ consécutifs** *m pl* ASSUR consequential damage; **~ corporels** *m pl* PROT SOC physical injury; **~ et intérêts** *m pl* ASSUR, DROIT damages; **~ imputables à la corrosion** *m pl* ASSUR corrosion damages; **~ indirects** *m pl* ASSUR consequential damage; **~ -intérêts** *m pl* ASSUR, DROIT damages; **~ -intérêts accessoires** *m pl* DROIT incidental damages; **~ -intérêts compensatoires** *m pl* DROIT compensatory damages; **~ -intérêts doubles** *m pl* DROIT *sentence arbitrale* double damages; **~ -intérêts indirects** *m pl* DROIT consequential damages; **~ -intérêts infligés à titre de pénalité** *m pl* DROIT vindictive damages; **~ -intérêts liquidés** *m pl* DROIT liquidated damages; **~ -intérêts punitifs** *m pl* ASSUR punitive damages; **~ -intérêts en réparation d'un préjudice moral** *m pl* DROIT vindictive damages; **~ -intérêts symboliques** *m pl* DROIT nominal damages; **~ -intérêts à titre exemplaire** *m pl* ASSUR punitive damages; **~ lors du chargement et du déchargement** *m pl* ASSUR damage whilst loading and unloading; **~ aux marchandises en entrepôt** *m pl* ASSUR damage to goods in custody; **~ d'ordre physique** *m pl* PROT SOC physical injury; **~ partiels** *m pl* ASSUR partial loss, PL; **~ peu importants** *m pl* ASSUR small damage

domotique *f* V&M home automation

don *m* COM donation, FISC donation, gift; **~ de biens** FISC gift of property; **~ de charité** FISC, PROT SOC charitable donation, charitable gift; **~ désigné** FISC specified gift; **~ net** FISC outright gift; **~ à une oeuvre de charité** FISC, PROT SOC charitable donation; **~ par testament** FISC gift by will; **~ promis** FISC donation pledged; **~ en soutien aux activités politiques** RES HUM political donation

donataire *mf* FISC donee

donateur, -trice *m,f* COM donor, DROIT settlor *(UK)*, FISC contributor, donor, PROT SOC sponsor

donateurs: **~ bilatéraux** *m pl* BANQUE, ECON, POL *d'assistance au développement* bilateral donors; **~ multilatéraux** *m pl* ECON, POL multilateral donors

donation: **~ à cause de mort** *f* DROIT gift causa mortis; **~ entre vifs** *f* DROIT gift inter vivos; **~ faite**

dans la perspective d'un décès imminent *f* DROIT gift causa mortis; ◆ **faire une ~ en faveur de qn** COM make a settlement on sb

donations: **~ statutaires** *f pl* DROIT statutory appropriations

dong *m* COM dong

donné: **~ en garantie** *adj* DROIT cautionary

donnée: **~ de tableau** *f* MATH chart point

données *f pl* COM data, figures, ECON, INFO data; **~ d'acceptation de saisie** *f pl* INFO entry acceptance data; **~ antérieures** *f pl* COM emission data, historical data, MATH historical data; **~ de base** *f pl* INFO source data; **~ brutes** *f pl* INFO, MATH raw data; **~ clés** *f pl* COM key data; **~ comptables** *f pl* COM, COMPTA, FIN accounting data, accounting records; **~ de contrôle** *f* INFO control data; **~ corrigées des variations saisonnières** *f pl* FIN seasonally adjusted figures; **~ croisées** *f pl* ECON *économétrie* cross section data, CSD; **~ cumulées** *f pl* COMPTA aggregate data; **~ désaisonnalisées** *f pl* FIN seasonally adjusted figures; **~ économiques** *f pl* ECON economic data; **~ empiriques** *f pl* ECON, MATH empirical data; **~ d'ensemble** *f pl* COMPTA aggregate data; **~ d'entrée** *f pl* INFO input data; **~ en entrée** *f pl* INFO incoming data; **~ globales** *f pl* COMPTA aggregate data; **~ justificatives** *f pl* MATH supporting data; **~ longitudinales** *f pl* MATH longitudinal data; **~ de mouvement** *f pl* INFO transaction data; **~ non traitées** *f pl* INFO, MATH raw data; **~ numériques** *f pl* INFO digital data; **~ de sortie** *f pl* INFO output data; **~ statistiques de base** *f pl* MATH bench mark statistics; **~ statistiques comparatives** *f pl* MATH bench mark statistics; **~ statistiques de référence** *f pl* MATH bench mark statistics; **~ techniques** *f pl* COM technical data; **~ à traiter** *f pl* INFO, MATH raw data; **~ type** *f pl* INFO sample data; ◆ **~ corrigées en fonction des variations saisonnières** COM figures adjusted for seasonal variations; **en ~ brutes non corrigées** COM in unadjusted figures; **en ~ corrigées** COM adjusted

donner *vt* COM give; ◆ **~ congé** IMMOB give notice to quit; **~ congé à un locataire** IMMOB give notice to quit; **~ le la** GESTION set the standards; **~ libre cours à** COM *colère, émotion* give free rein to; **~ à la petite cuillère** COM spoon-feed; **~ un pourboire à** COM, LOISIRS tip; **~ du pouvoir à** POL empower; **~ qch à tirer** MÉDIA pass sth for press; **~ à qn le droit de faire qch** RES HUM qualify sb to do sth; **se ~ beaucoup de mal** COM go to a lot of trouble; **~ spontanément** COM *informations* volunteer; **~ un ultimatum à qn** COM give sb an ultimatum; **~ une valeur à** INFO set

donneur: **~ d'achat d'encore à prime** *m* BOURSE giver for a call of more; **~ à bail** *m* DROIT, IMMOB lessor; **~ de double option** *m* BOURSE giver for a put and call; **~ d'une licence** *m* BREVETS licensor; **~ d'option d'achat** *m* BOURSE giver for a call; **~ d'une option de vente** *m* BOURSE giver for a put; **~ d'ordres** *m* BANQUE principal; **~ de primes** *m*

BOURSE giver of option money; **~ de stellage** *m* BOURSE taker for a put and call; **~ en valeurs** *m* BOURSE giver on stock

dons: **~ spéciaux en argent** *m pl* FISC one-off cash gifts

dormant, e *adj* BOURSE, FIN *argent* inactive

dos *m* MÉDIA *édition* backstrip

DOS® *abrév* (*système d'exploitation à disques*) INFO DOS® (*disk operating system*)

dose: **~ fatale** *f* ENVIR *pollution* lethal dose; **~ de rayonnement** *f* ENVIR radiation dose

dossier *m* ADMIN dossier, file, records, COM case file, case notes, record, *sur une affaire* brief, DROIT brief; **~ d'audit** COMPTA, FIN audit file, audit working papers; **~ commercial** ECON trade brief; **~ de coût** BOURSE cost records (*UK*); **~ de la déclaration** FISC income tax package; **~ de demande de subvention** COM application for subsidies; **~ de formation** GESTION, RES HUM training pack; **~ d'impôt** FISC tax record; **~ médical** PROT SOC health record; **~ personnel** COM case history; **~ de premier palier** FISC prime range file; **~ de premier rang** FISC prime range file; **~ de presse** MÉDIA *imprimé* press kit, *publicité* background paper; **~ principal** FISC principal file

dot *f* IMMOB dowry

dotation *f* COMPTA appropriation, DROIT endowment, ECON, FIN appropriation; **~ aux amortissements** COMPTA allowance for depreciation (*US*), amortization expense, depreciation allowance, provision for depreciation, ECON capital consumption allowance, FIN amortization expense; **~ annuelle aux amortissements** COMPTA annual depreciation charge; **~ en facteurs de production** ECON, IND factor endowment; **~ globale de fonctionnement** (*DGF*) POL block grant (*UK*); **~ aux investissements** ECON capital consumption allowance; **~ en personnel** RES HUM staffing; **~ à une provision** COMPTA allocation to a provision

dotations: **~ aux amortissements** *f pl* BANQUE depreciation of fixed assets; **~ budgétaires affectées au marketing** *f pl* V&M marketing appropriation; **~ budgétaires affectées à la publicité** *f pl* FIN, V&M advertising appropriation

douaire *f* DROIT dower

douane *f* LOISIRS customs

douanier, -ière *m,f* IMP/EXP, RES HUM customs officer; **~ affecté aux opérations d'import/export** IMP/EXP, TRANSP shipping officer; **~ responsable d'un entrepôt sous douane** IMP/EXP, TRANSP warehouse officer

double:[1] **à ~ action** *adj* IND double-acting; **à ~ effet** *adj* IND double-acting; **à ~ façade** *adj* TRANSP *chaudière* db, double-ended; **à ~ face** *adj* INFO *disquette* double-sided; **à ~ précision** *adj* INFO double-precision; **~ face** *adj* INFO *disquette* two-sided

double[2] *m* COM, INFO dup., duplicate; **~ aigle** FIN double eagle (*US*), twenty dollars; ~ **-clic** INFO double-click; ~ **corps de caractères** ADMIN dual pitch; ~ **étalon** COM parallel standard; ~ **fond** TRANSP *navigation* db, double bottom; ~ **interligne** INFO double space, double spacing; ~ **marché du travail** ECON dual labor market (*AmE*), dual labour market (*BrE*); ~ **page centrale** MÉDIA centrefold (*BrE*); ~ **taux de change** ECON dual exchange rate

double:[3] ~ **assurance** *f* ASSUR double insurance; ~ **commission** *f* BOURSE each way; ~ **couverture** *f* ASSUR duplication of benefits; ~ **densité** *f* INFO double density; ~ **frappe** *f* INFO double strike; ~ **imposition** *f* FISC double taxation, duplicate taxation; ~ **option** *f jarg* BOURSE double option, put and call; ~ **page centrale** *f* MÉDIA *publicité* center spread (*AmE*), centerfold (*AmE*), centre spread (*BrE*); ~ **réduction** *f* COM double reduction, DR; ~ **résidence** *f* FISC dual residence

double:[4] **faire un** ~ **clic** *loc* INFO double-click

double:[5] ~ **cliquer** *vi* INFO double-click

doublé, e *adj* TRANSP *navire, pont* WS, wood-sheathed; ~ **en bois** TRANSP *navire, pont* wood-sheathed, WS

doubler 1. *vi* MATH double; **2.** *vti* COM increase twofold

doublon *m* INFO duplicate

doucher *vt infrml* COM *enthousiasme* dampen

doué, e *adj* PROT SOC gifted

douteux, -euse *adj* COM shady

douz. *abrév* (*douzaine*) COM doz. (*dozen*)

douzaine *f* (*douz.*) COM dozen (*doz.*)

Dow: ~ **Jones** *m* FIN Dow Jones (*US*)

doyen, -enne *m,f* COM *d'un pays* eldest citizen, oldest citizen, *d'une organisation* most senior member; **le** ~ **des officiers** RES HUM the senior officer

DP *abrév* (*documents contre paiement*) COM DAP, DP (*documents against payment*)

DPA *abrév* BOURSE (*dividende par action*), COMPTA (*dividende par action*) dividend per share, FISC *Can* (*déduction pour amortissement*) CCA (*capital cost allowance*)

DPO *abrév* (*direction par objectifs*) GESTION MBO (*management by objectives*)

Dr *abrév* (*docteur*) COM, PROT SOC, RES HUM Dr (*Doctor*)

DR *abrév* (*délai de recouvrement*) BOURSE debt recovery period

drachme *m* COM Drachma

dragage *m* TRANSP *navigation* dredging

draguer *vt* TRANSP dredge

dragueur *m* TRANSP dredger

drainage: ~ **de l'impôt** *m* FISC tax drain

drapeau *m* INFO flag; ~ **de tête** MÉDIA *presse* lead (*BrE*), lede (*AmE*)

dresser *vt* COM compile, erect, *liste* make out, make up, *programme* schedule, POL, RES HUM *liste de candidats* draw up; ◆ ~ **des barrières contre**

COM wall out (*AmE*); ~ **un budget** COM, COMPTA, ECON, FIN, POL budget; ~ **les états financiers** FIN prepare the financial statements; ~ **l'inventaire** ADMIN, COM, COMPTA, V&M take stock; ~ **l'ordre du jour** GESTION draw up the agenda

DRH *abrév* GESTION (*directeur des ressources humaines*) *personne* head of the personnel department, personnel director, RES HUM (*directeur des ressources humaines*) *personne* head of the personnel department, personnel director, RES HUM (*direction des ressources humaines*) *service* personnel department

droit *m* ASSUR claim, DROIT entitlement, jurisprudence, law, right, title, FISC duty; ~ **d'accès** DROIT access right; ~ **d'accise** FISC excise duty, excise tax; ~ **d'acconage** TRANSP lighterage charge; ~ **acquis** COM *dans une entreprise* vested interest; ~ **d'acquisition** BOURSE acquisition fee, load; ~ **d'action** DROIT *pour dettes* cause of action; ~ **administratif** ADMIN, DROIT administrative law; ~ **d'administration** ADMIN, FIN processing fee; ~ **des affaires** DROIT business law; ~ **afférent à une action** BOURSE right of interest in a share; ~ **d'affouage** DROIT, IMMOB estovers; ~ **à un allègement d'impôts** FISC eligibility for tax relief; ~ **ancien** DROIT old law; ~ **d'anticipation** DROIT, IMMOB anticipation; ~ **d'appel** DROIT right of appeal; ~ **d'auteur** BREVETS copyright, COM, MÉDIA book royalty; ~ **de bail** COMPTA leasehold; ~ **bancaire** BANQUE, DROIT banking law; ~ **de bénéficiaire** FISC beneficial interest; ~ **au brevet** BREVETS, DROIT right to a patent; ~ **au capital** FISC capital interest; ~ **civil** DROIT civil law; ~ **à la clientèle** COM goodwill; ~ **commercial** COM, DROIT business law, commercial law, mercantile law; ~ **de compensation** BANQUE right of offset; ~ **composé** FISC *douane*, IMP/EXP compound duty; ~ **de la comptabilité** COMPTA, DROIT, FIN accounting law; ~ **comptable** COMPTA, DROIT, FIN accounting law; ~ **à congé** RES HUM holiday entitlement; ~ **consacré par la prescription** IMMOB prescription (*US*), prescriptive right; ~ **consacré par l'usage** IMMOB prescription (*US*), prescriptive right; ~ **de conversion** BOURSE conversion right, right to convert; ~ **de courtage** BOURSE brokerage, brokerage fee, com., commission; ~ **coutumier** DROIT common law; ~ **dérogatoire** COM overriding interest; ~ **détaché** BOURSE ex-rights; ~ **à des dommages-intérêts** DROIT right of recovery; ~ **d'échange gratuit** BOURSE free right of exchange; ~ **d'échange libre** BOURSE free right of exchange; ~ **écrit** DROIT statute law; ~ **d'émission** ENVIR emission fee; ~ **d'entrée** COM admission fee, IMP/EXP import duty, ID; ~ **des entreprises** COM, DROIT, IND corporate law; ~ **de l'environnement** DROIT, ENVIR environmental law; ~ **d'établissement** DROIT right of establishment; ~ **exclusif** DROIT exclusive right; ~ **exclusif de vente** IMMOB exclusive right to sell listing; ~ **d'exécution** DROIT, MÉDIA performing rights; **~ d'exploitation** BREVETS rental right, COM operating interest, DROIT rental right; **~ fiscal** FISC fiscal law, law of taxation, tax law; **~ de gage** DROIT lien; **~ de grève** RES HUM right to strike; **~ incorporel** DROIT chose in action; **~ d'indemnisation** DROIT right of recovery; **~ à l'information** POL right to know; **~ de l'informatique** DROIT, INFO computer law; **~ d'inscription** COM entrance fee, FISC registrar fee; **~ d'interdire** BREVETS prohibition right; **~ international** DROIT, POL international law; **~ international commercial** DROIT, ECON, POL, V&M international trade law; **~ jurisprudentiel** DROIT case law; **~ légal** DROIT legal right; **~ du locataire** DROIT, IMMOB *compensation foncière* tenant's right (*UK*); **~ maritime** DROIT, TRANSP maritime law, navigation laws, sea law; **~ de la mer** DROIT, TRANSP maritime law, sea law; **~ mixte** FISC *douane*, IMP/EXP compound duty; **~ moral** DROIT moral law; **~ de mutation** DROIT, IMMOB transfer tax; **~ national** DROIT national law; **~ non revendiqué** DROIT unclaimed right; **~ particulier** FISC specified right; **~ de passage** DROIT access right, right of way, IMMOB access right; **~ d'un pays** DROIT national law; **~ à pension d'ancienneté** FIN retirement pension rights; **~ positif** DROIT substantive law; **~ de poursuite** DROIT, V&M stoppage in transit; **~ de préemption** BOURSE pre-emption right, pre-emptive right; **~ préférentiel de souscription** BOURSE pre-emption right, pre-emptive right, DROIT rights issue; **~ de prendre possession** DROIT right of entry; **~ prescrit** FISC specified right; **~ prévu par la loi** DROIT statutory right (*UK*); **~ de priorité** BREVETS, DROIT priority right; **~ privé** DROIT private law; **~ de procédure** DROIT adjective law; **~ proportionné** COM commensurate charge; **~ de propriété** COM, IMMOB proprietorship, sole proprietorship; **~ à la propriété industrielle** DROIT design right; **~ public** DROIT public law; **~ reconnu légalement** DROIT legal right; **~ de recours** DROIT power of recourse, right of appeal; **~ régissant le pouvoir et l'autorité** DROIT control law; **~ de réinvestissement automatique** BOURSE reinvestment privilege; **~ relatif à la novation de créance** DROIT substitution law; **~ de remboursement** FIN right of redemption; **~ de remorquage** TRANSP *navigation* towage charges, towage dues; **~ à réparation** DROIT right of recovery, right of redress; **~ de réponse** DROIT right of reply; **~ de reprise** DROIT right of resumption; **~ de rescision** DROIT right of rescission; **~ de résidence** ADMIN right of residence; **~ résultant d'un contrat** DROIT legal right; **~ résultant de la loi** DROIT legal right; **~ de rétention bancaire** BANQUE bank lien; **~ de retour** COM right of return; **~ de séjour** ADMIN right of residence; **~ social** DROIT, POL, RES HUM employment law, labor law (*AmE*), labour law (*BrE*); **~ des sociétés** COM, DROIT, IND company law, corporate law, corporation law; **~ de souscription** BOURSE application right, right on share issue, stock right, subscrip-

tion right; **~ de souscription négociable** *Fra* BOURSE allotment letter (*UK*); **~ de souscription prioritaire** BOURSE subscription privilege; **~ spécifique** FISC specific duty, IMP/EXP specific duty, specific tax; **~ statutaire** COM lex scripta (*frml*), DROIT statutory right (*UK*); **~ des successions** DROIT succession law; **~ successoral** DROIT succession law; **~ sur les biens transmis par décès** FISC inheritance duty; **~ sur la valeur globale de la succession** FISC estate duty; **~ du survivant** DROIT right of survivorship; **~ syndical** DROIT right of combination; **~ à du temps libre pour activités syndicales** RES HUM time-off rights (*UK*); **~ du tenancier** DROIT, IMMOB tenant's right (*UK*); **~ de tenure à bail** IMMOB leasehold interest; **~ de timbre** DROIT probate duty, FISC stamp duty, stamp tax; **~ de timbre sur les successions** DROIT probate duty; **~ de traiter les options du marché donné** BOURSE trading right; **~ au travail** DROIT, RES HUM right to work; **~ du travail** DROIT, POL, RES HUM employment law, labor law (*AmE*), labour law (*BrE*); **~ d'usufruit** DROIT beneficial interest; **~ d'utilisation** DROIT, IMMOB licence (*BrE*), license (*AmE*); **~ de vote** POL right to vote, voting right; ◆ **avec ~ de souscription** BOURSE cum warrant; **avoir ~ à** COM be eligible for sth, qualify for, DROIT, PROT SOC, RES HUM *des congés payés* qualify for; **ayant ~ à** COM eligible for; **ayant un ~ sur** FISC beneficially interested in; **de ~** DROIT de jure; **être en ~ de faire** DROIT be justified in doing; **faire ~ à** COM admit, allow; **faire ~ à une demande** DROIT sustain a claim; **faire son ~** PROT SOC read law

droite: **de ~** *adj* [épith] (ANT *de gauche*) POL right-wing

droitisme *m* (ANT *gauchisme*) POL rightism

droits *m pl* BREVETS *propriété intellectuelle* rights, DROIT fee, *propriété intellectuelle* rights; **~ d'accès** INFO access rights; **~ acquis** FISC grandfathering; **~ ad valorem** COMPTA, FISC, IMP/EXP, TRANSP ad valorem duty; **~ d'adaptation cinématographique** DROIT, MÉDIA film rights; **~ d'adhésion** FISC initiation dues, initiation fees; **~ annuels de maintien d'un brevet** COM patent renewal fees; **~ attachés** BOURSE cum rights; **~ d'auteur** DROIT copyright, performing rights, royalties, royalty, FISC, MÉDIA performing rights, royalties, royalty; **~ de bassin** TRANSP *navigation* dock charges, *port* dock dues; **~ de canal** TRANSP *navigation* canal dues; **~ cinématographiques** DROIT, MÉDIA film rights; **~ civils** DROIT civil rights; **~ civiques** DROIT civil rights; **~ de codétermination** BOURSE codetermination rights; **~ compensatoires** IMP/EXP countervailing duties; **~ conférés par qn** BREVETS rights afforded by sb; **~ consulaires** IMP/EXP consulage; **~ de conversion** BOURSE rights of conversion; **~ de demande** BANQUE application fee; **~ de développement de cession** DROIT, IMMOB transfer development rights; **~ de douane** FISC customs, IMP/EXP customs duty; ~ **d'échange** BOURSE rights of exchange; ~ **et actions** BREVETS, DROIT rights and actions; ~ **exclusifs d'exploitation** BREVETS *de l'invention brevetée*, DROIT *de l'invention brevetée* patent rights; ~ **de fabrication** BREVETS, DROIT, IND manufacturing rights; ~ **fondamentaux** DROIT natural rights; ~ **de garde** BANQUE custodian account fee, custodian fee, custody account charge, custody charge; ~ **de l'homme** DROIT human rights; ~ **individuels** RES HUM individual rights; ~ **d'inscription** PROT SOC tuition fees; ~ **miniers** DROIT, IMMOB, IND mineral rights; ~ **de mouillage** TRANSP anchorage charges; ~ **de mutation** FISC capital transfer tax (*UK, dat*), inheritance tax (*UK*), CTT; ~ **naturels** DROIT natural rights; ~ **d'objection** BOURSE appraisal rights (*US*); ~ **de l'occupant de fait** DROIT, IMMOB squatter's rights; ~ **de l'occupant sans titre** DROIT, IMMOB squatter's rights; ~ **particuliers de retrait** BANQUE special drawing rights, SDR; ~ **de phare** TRANSP *navigation* light dues; ~ **de pilotage** TRANSP *port* pilotage; ~ **de port** FISC harbor dues (*AmE*), harbour dues (*BrE*), IMP/EXP, TRANSP pd, port dues; ~ **de port supplémentaires** IMP/EXP, TRANSP port surcharge; ~ **à position de négociateur unique** RES HUM sole bargaining rights (*UK*); ~ **de propriété** BOURSE proprietary rights, DROIT, IMMOB property rights; ~ **de propriété collectifs** ECON common ownership; ~ **de propriété garantis par assurance vie** ASSUR ownership rights under life insurance; ~ **de propriété intellectuelle** BREVETS, DROIT, MÉDIA intellectual property rights; IPR; ~ **protecteurs** FISC protective duties; ~ **de quai** IMP/EXP quayage, TRANSP quayage, wharfage dues, *tarifs* wharf dues; ~ **de représentation** DROIT, MÉDIA performing rights; ~ **de retransmission** COMMS, DROIT air rights, broadcasting rights, LOISIRS *sport* coverage fees, MÉDIA air rights, broadcasting rights; ~ **des riverains** DROIT riparian rights; ~ **de succession** DROIT probate duty, FISC death duties (*BrE, dat*), death tax (*AmE*), legacy duty (*BrE*), legacy tax (*AmE*), succession duty (*BrE*), succession tax (*AmE*), estate tax (*US*), inheritance tax (*UK*); ~ **syndicaux** RES HUM union rights; ~ **à taux fixe** COM flat-rate fee; ~ **de tirage spéciaux** (*DTS*) DROIT special drawing rights (*SDR*); ~ **de trafic** TRANSP traffic rights; ~ **de transit** IMP/EXP, TRANSP transit rights; ~ **d'utilisation** BANQUE *de la carte* cardholder fee, user fee; ~ **de vote** BOURSE voting rights; ◆ **avec** ~ BOURSE cum rights; **ayant des** ~ **sur** FISC beneficially interested in; **tous** ~ **réservés** BREVETS, DROIT all rights reserved, copyright reserved

dry: ~ **quart américain** *m* COM dry quart (*US*)

DTS *abrév* (*droits de tirage spéciaux*) DROIT SDR (*special drawing rights*)

Dublin *n pr* COM Dublin

duc: ~ **d'Albe** *m* TRANSP *navigation* dolphin

Duchambe *n pr* COM Dushanbe

ducroire *adv* COM del credere

dûment: ~ **signé** *loc* COM duly signed

dumping *m* COM, INFO dumping

dunette *f* TRANSP *navigation* poop; ~ **et passerelle** *f pl* TRANSP *navigation* poop and bridge, PB

duopole *m* ECON duopoly; ~ **local** ECON spatial duopoly

duplex[1] *adj* INFO duplex; ~ **intégral** INFO full-duplex, FDX

duplex[2] *m* IMMOB duplex

duplicata *m* DROIT dup., duplicate

duplicateur, -trice *adj* COM duplicatory

duplication *f* COM copying; ~ **de main d'oeuvre** RES HUM double manning

dupliquer *vt* INFO copy, duplicate

dur[1]**, e** *adj* COM harsh, tough, ECON harsh; ◆ **être** ~ **en affaires** COM drive a hard bargain

dur:[2] ~ **travail** *m* RES HUM graft (*infrml*)

durabilité *f* ECON, ENVIR sustainability

durable *adj* COM long-standing

durcir *vt* COM stiffen

durée *f* BOURSE term to maturity, *d'une option* life, COM duration, *de temps* time span, INFO timing, POL *de traité, de fonctions* term; ~ **d'actionnariat** BOURSE holding period; ~ **aller-retour** TRANSP round-trip time; ~ **du brevet** BREVETS term of patent; ~ **d'un brevet** BREVETS, DROIT patent life; ~ **de crédit initiale** BOURSE original maturity; ~ **à échéance** BOURSE term to maturity; ~ **d'exécution** INFO execution time; ~ **de l'exécution** INFO run time; ~ **de fonctionnement** COM operation time; ~ **forfaitaire** RES HUM allowed time, standard time; ~ **garantie** BANQUE guaranteed term; ~ **de la garantie** ASSUR duration of benefits, COM duration of guaranty; ~ **d'immobilisation** COM, ECON, IND, INFO down time; ~ **d'indisponibilité** INFO down time; ~ **limitée** ASSUR limited term; ~ **moyenne de règlement des comptes clients** BANQUE, COMPTA average collection period, collection ratio; ~ **d'option** BOURSE option period; ~ **de perturbation** MATH disturbance term; ~ **probable** COM life expectancy; ~ **de réalisation** COM operation time; ~ **de rotation** TRANSP *chargement/déchargement* aircraft turnround time, turnaround time (*AmE*), turnround time (*BrE*); ~ **de rotation du véhicule** TRANSP vehicle turnaround time (*AmE*), vehicle turnround time (*BrE*); ~ **de service** RES HUM length of service; ~ **stochastique** MATH stochastic term; ~ **de transport** TRANSP transit time; ~ **d'utilisation de ressources** COM resource time; ~ **de validité d'un brevet** BREVETS, DROIT patent life; ~ **de vie** BOURSE life, lifetime, trading life, COM useful life, V&M shelf life; ~ **de vie comptable** ECON, FISC depreciable life; ~ **de vie dans l'atmosphère** ENVIR atmospheric lifetime; ~ **de vie économique** COMPTA useful economic life, FIN, V&M economic life; ~ **de vie de l'immobilisation** COMPTA asset life; ~ **de vie moyenne** COM average life; ~ **de vie prévue** COMPTA predictable life; ~ **de vie utile** COMPTA *d'un* *avoir* useful life; ◆ **pendant la ~ des stocks** V&M while stocks last; **pour la ~ de** COM for the duration of

durement: **~ touché** *loc* COM hard-hit

durer *vi* COM last, run, DROIT run

DUT *abrév (diplôme universitaire de technologie)* PROT SOC DipTech *(Diploma in Technology)*

dynamique[1] *adj* COM upwardly mobile, *croissance, caractère* dynamic, RES HUM upwardly mobile

dynamique:[2] **~ de groupe** *f* RES HUM group dynamics; **~ des groupes** *f* COM, MATH methetics; **~ industrielle** *f* IND industrial dynamics; **~ des machines** *f* ADMIN machine dynamics; **~ de marché** *f* V&M market dynamics; **~ des produits** *f* V&M product dynamics

dynamisme *m* COM dynamism

dysfonctionnel *adj* GESTION dysfunctional

E

E *abrév (quart est)* TRANSP *navigation* E *(East compass point)*

EAO *abrév (enseignement assisté par ordinateur)* INFO, PROT SOC CAI *(computer-aided instruction, computer-assisted instruction)*, CAL *(computer-aided learning, computer-assisted learning)*, CAT *(computer-aided training, computer-assisted training)*, CBT *(computer-based training)*

eau: ~ **à boire** *f* ENVIR drinking water; ~ **douce** *f* ENVIR fresh water, F, FW; ~ **potable** *f* ENVIR drinking water; ~ **résiduaire** *f* ENVIR industrial wastewater, wastewater; ~ **salée** *f* TRANSP salt water; ~ **usée** *f* ENVIR wastewater

eaux: ~ **territoriales** *f pl* DROIT *droit international,* POL, TRANSP territorial waters; ~ **usées** *f pl* ENVIR sewage

Eaux: les ~ et Forêts *f pl* ENVIR, IND ≈ Forestry Commission *(UK)*

ébauche *f* V&M *publicité* scamp *(jarg)*

ébauché, e *adj* COM, DROIT, POL drafted

ébaucher *vt* COM, DROIT, POL draft

EBE *abrév (excédent brut d'exploitation)* COMPTA, ECON, FIN GM *(gross margin)*

écart *m* BOURSE gap, option spread, turn, COM disparity, gap, variance, *rendement* differential, *statistique* discrepancy, COMPTA variance, ECON *entre taux d'intérêt* margin, FIN gap, MATH variance, RES HUM differential; ~ **acheteur-vendeur** BOURSE bid-offer spread; ~ **d'acquisition négatif** COMPTA negative goodwill; ~ **d'acquisition positif** COMPTA goodwill; ~ **d'ajustement** ECON adjustment gap; ~ **alligator** BANQUE, BOURSE, FIN alligator spread; ~ **baissier** *(ANT écart haussier)* BOURSE bear call spread, bear spread, bearish spread; ~ **budgétaire** COMPTA, ECON, FIN, POL budget variance; ~ **de caisse** COMPTA cash short; ~ **d'un call à la baisse** *(ANT écart d'un call à la hausse)* BOURSE bear call spread; ~ **d'un call à la hausse** *(ANT écart d'un call à la baisse)* BOURSE bull call spread; ~ **d'un pour cent** BOURSE one-percent spread; ~ **composite** BANQUE composite spread; ~ **de confiance** MATH confidence interval; ~ **de conversion** COM translation differential, COMPTA foreign currency translation reserve; ~ **de cours** BOURSE quotation spread; ~ **des coûts marketing** V&M marketing cost variance; ~ **déflationniste** *(ANT écart inflationniste)* ECON deflationary gap, recessionary gap; ~ **diagonal** BOURSE diagonal spread; ~ **entre les cours acheteur-vendeur** BOURSE bid-ask spread; ~ **entre les cours du comptant** BOURSE spot rate spread; ~ **entre les cours du terme** COM forward rate spread; ~ **entre équipes** RES HUM shift differential; ~ **entre les taux d'intérêt** BANQUE, ECON interest rate differ-

ential; ~ **entre taux d'intérêt négatif** BOURSE negative interest rate gap; ~ **favorable** COMPTA favorable variance *(AmE)*, favourable variance *(BrE)*; ~ **haussier** *(ANT écart baissier)* BOURSE bull call spread, bull spread, bullish spread; ~ **important à l'ouverture** BOURSE wide opening; ~ **inférieur à zéro** BOURSE zero-minus tick; ~ **d'inflation en diminution** ECON narrowing inflation gap; ~ **inflationniste** *(ANT écart déflationniste)* ECON inflationary gap; ~ **interquartile** MATH semi-interquartile range; ~ **inverse sur ratio d'options d'achat** *(ANT écart inverse sur ratio d'options de vente)* BOURSE call ratio backspread; ~ **inverse sur ratio d'options de vente** *(ANT écart inverse sur ratio d'options d'achat)* BOURSE put ratio backspread; ~ **LIBOR-eurodollar** BOURSE Eurodollar spread; ~ **Macmillan** FIN Macmillan gap; ~ **maximal de cours** BOURSE daily limit, fluctuation limit, maximum price change, maximum price fluctuation; ~ **maximal de cours quotidien** BOURSE daily price limit, daily trading limit; ~ **maximal hauts-bas** BOURSE maximal market spread, maximum market spread, range; ~ **maximum des cours du marché** BOURSE tick; ~ **minimum de fluctuation** BOURSE minimum price fluctuation; ~ **monétaire** BOURSE, FIN money spread; ~ **moyen** FIN, MATH mean deviation; ~ **net** BOURSE *cours* net change; ~ **d'option** BOURSE option spread; ~ **perpendiculaire** BOURSE perpendicular spread; ~ **positif entre les taux d'intérêt** ECON positive interest-rate gap; ~ **de première consolidation** COMPTA *survaleur* goodwill on consolidation; ~ **de prix** BOURSE, COM, COMPTA, FIN, RES HUM, V&M cost variance, price differential, price gap; ~ **de réajustement** ECON adjustment gap; ~ **récessionniste** ECON *économétrie* contractionary national income gap, deflationary gap, recessionary gap; ~ **de rémunération** RES HUM earnings differential; ~ **de rendement** COM, FIN efficiency variance, yield variance; ~ **de rendement inverse** BANQUE, BOURSE, ECON reverse yield gap; ~ **de Robertson** ECON Robertsonian lag; ~ **des salaires** RES HUM compensating wage differential, differential wage, differential pay, pay differential, wage differential; ~ **salarial** RES HUM compensating wage differential, pay differential, wage differential; ~ **supérieur à zéro** BOURSE zero-plus tick; ~ **sur budget** COMPTA, ECON, FIN, POL budget variance; ~ **sur les prix** COM price variance; ~ **sur puts à la baisse** *(ANT écart sur puts à la hausse)* BOURSE bear put spread; ~ **sur puts à la hausse** *(ANT écart sur puts à la baisse)* BOURSE bull put spread; ~ **sur stock** COM, ECON inventory shortage, inventory shrinkage; ~ **de taux** BOURSE rate differential; ~ **type** FIN, MATH mean deviation, standard

deviation; ~ **type de l'échantillon** MATH sampling
deviation; ~ **vertical baissier** *(*ANT *écart vertical
haussier)* BOURSE bear spread, bearish spread;
~ **vertical haussier** *(*ANT *écart vertical baissier)*
BOURSE bull spread, bullish spread; ~ **vertical sur
ratio d'options d'achat** *(*ANT *écart vertical sur
ratio d'options de vente)* BOURSE ratio put spread;
~ **vertical sur ratio d'options de vente** *(*ANT *écart
vertical sur ratio d'options d'achat)* BOURSE ratio
call spread; ~ **vide** BOURSE price gap; ◆ **à l'~** COM
aloof

écarter *vt* BOURSE lock out, COM rule out, scrap,
concurrence stave off, *d'une liste* exclude; ◆
s'~ de son sujet COM get sidetracked

écarts: ~ **de répartition** *m pl* BOURSE splitting
spreads

échange *m* COM ex., exch., exchange, ECON barter,
ex., exch., exchange, trade, trade-off, IMP/EXP,
V&M trade; ~ **d'actifs** BANQUE, FIN asset swap;
~ **de brevets** BREVETS, COM patent trading;
~ **cambiste** FIN treasury swap; ~ **de contrats**
COM, DROIT exchange of contracts; ~ **de
créances** FIN debt swap; ~ **de créances contre
actifs** FIN debt-equity swap; ~ **de devises** FIN
currency swap; ~ **de documents informatisés**
(EDI) COMMS, INFO electronic document interchange *(EDI)*; ~ **de données informatisées**
(EDI) COMMS, INFO electronic data interchange
(EDI); ~ **financier** BOURSE, FIN swap; ~ **financier
à terme** BOURSE, FIN forward swap;
~ **d'information** COM exchange of information;
~ **d'informations commerciales** ECON Trade Data
Interchange, TDI; ~ **de lettres** COMMS interchange of letters; ~ **moteur** TRANSP engine
transplant *(jarg)*; ~ **réglementé par les autorités
fédérales** BOURSE federally-regulated exchange
(US); ~ **renouvelable** FIN roller swap; ~ **standard**
COM replacement; ~ **syndiqué** FIN syndicated
swap; ~ **de taux d'intérêt** BOURSE, FIN interest
rate swap; ~ **à terme** BOURSE, FIN forward swap;
~ **à terme de devises** BOURSE, FIN currency swap;
~ **à terme de types d'emprunts** BOURSE, FIN loan
swap; ~ **de titres** BOURSE exchange of securities;
~ **de valeurs** BOURSE ex., exch., exchange; ◆ **en
~ de** COM in return for, COMPTA in exchange for;
faire un ~ COM trade off, ECON barter, trade off

échanger *vt* COM commute, COMMS exchange,
ECON barter; ◆ ~ **une chose contre une autre**
COM, ECON trade one thing against another, trade
one thing for another; ~ **qch contre qch d'autre**
COM, ECON exchange one thing for another; **s'~ à**
BOURSE trade at

échanges: ~ **commerciaux** *m pl* ECON, IMP/EXP,
V&M commercial trade, trade; ~ **entre industries**
m pl IND interindustry trade; ~ **aux frontières** *m pl*
IMP/EXP cross-border trading; ~ **industriels** *m pl*
COM industrial trade, IMP/EXP, IND trade-in indus-
trial goods; ~ **à l'intérieur du Commonwealth** *m pl*
COM trade within the Commonwealth; ~ **inter-
nationaux autorisés** *m pl* BOURSE Registered

International Exchange *(UK)*, RIE *(UK)*;
~ **d'options** *m pl* BOURSE options exchanges

échangeur: ~ **thermique intermédiaire** *m (ETI)*
TRANSP intercooler

échantillon *m* COM sample, swatch, INFO, MATH
sample, TRANSP *navigation* scantling; ~ **aléatoire**
MATH random sample; ~ **d'estimation** MATH estimation sampling; ~ **d'exploration** MATH discovery
sampling; ~ **gratuit** COM free sample; ~ **par quota**
V&M quota sample; ~ **de population** MATH statistical population; ~ **probabiliste** MATH probability
sample; ~ **représentatif** COM cross section, fair
sample, COMPTA, FIN attribute sampling;
~ **segmental** V&M *étude de marché* cluster sample;
~ **statistique** MATH statistical sampling; ~ **type**
MATH representative sample, sample mean

échantillonnage *m* COM, MATH sampling, RES HUM
work sampling, TRANSP *navigation* scantling;
~ **d'activités** MATH *statistique* activity sampling;
~ **aléatoire** MATH, V&M convenience sampling,
random sampling, statistical sampling; ~ **aléatoire par tranche** MATH, V&M stratified random
sampling; ~ **d'attribut** MATH attribute sampling;
~ **de distribution** MATH *statistique* attribute sampling; ~ **multiphase** MATH multistage sampling;
~ **multiple** COMPTA, FIN block sampling, block
testing; ~ **par attributs** MÉDIA, V&M attribute
sampling; ~ **par couches** MATH, V&M stratified
sampling; ~ **par tranche** MATH, V&M stratified
sampling; ~ **séquentiel** MATH sequential sampling; ~ **statistique** MATH statistical sampling;
~ **successif** MATH sequential sampling;
~ **systématique** MATH systematic sampling; ~ **de
variables** MATH variables sampling

Echap *abrév* (SYN *touche Echap*) INFO Esc, escape

échappatoire *f* DROIT joker *(US)*; ~ **fiscale** FISC
tax loophole

échappement: ~ **accidentel** *m* ENVIR, IND *pollution*
accidental discharge

échapper: ~ **à l'attention** *loc* COM escape notice

échéance *f* BANQUE term, BOURSE dd, due date,
expiration *(AmE)*, expiry *(BrE)*, COM dd, deadline, due date, expiration *(AmE)*, expiry *(BrE)*,
d'un effet, d'un billet date, FIN maturity, tenor,
usance, GESTION time horizon; ~ **de contrat à
terme** BOURSE futures expiration date *(AmE)*,
futures expiry date *(BrE)*; ~ **décalée** BANQUE
mismatched maturity; ~ **fixée** BANQUE fixed
maturity; ~ **modifiée** COMPTA modified accrual;
~ **moyenne** BOURSE *des titres* average maturity;
~ **à terme** BANQUE time bill; ~ **d'une traite** COMP-
TA currency of a bill; ◆ **à ... d'~** COM after date; **à
l'~** BOURSE at maturity, when due; **à l'~ prescrite**
COM at the specified tenor; **à ~ proche** BOURSE
short-dated; ~ **lointaine** BOURSE farther out;
~ **proche** BOURSE farther in

échéancier *m* BANQUE tickler file, BOURSE bill
diary; ~ **de dette** BANQUE, BOURSE, ECON, FIN
maturity structure of debt; ~ **d'effets** COMPTA bill
book

échec *m* COM failure, setback, INFO failure; ~ **du mariage** DROIT marriage breakdown; ~ **d'une société** COM company failure

échelle *f* COM scale, MATH range; ~ **d'attitudes** V&M *étude de marché* attitude scale; ~ **de Beaufort** COM Beaufort scale; ~ **de commission** BOURSE scale of commission; ~ **de cotation des emplois** RES HUM job evaluation scale; ~ **de croissance des salaires** RES HUM incremental scale; ~ **des effectifs** TRANSP manning scale; ~ **d'évaluation** COM rating scale; ~ **de grandeur** MATH ratio scale; ~ **de gris** INFO grayscale (*AmE*), greyscale (*BrE*); ~ **d'intervalle** COM interval scale; ~ **inversée** BOURSE inverted scale; ~ **minimale d'efficience** ECON minimum efficient scale, MES; ~ **mobile** COM, COMPTA sliding scale; ~ **mobile des salaires** RES HUM sliding wage scale; ~ **nominale** COM nominal scale; ~ **nominale mondiale d'affrètement** TRANSP *navigation* worldscale; ~ **de notation du personnel** RES HUM scale of points value; ~ **d'offre** BOURSE offering scale; ~ **de participation** POL ladder of participation (*jarg*); ~ **des prix** ECON, V&M price range; ~ **progressive** FISC progressive scale; ~ **des promotions** RES HUM promotion ladder; ~ **des salaires** RES HUM scaler (*jarg*), wage scale; ♦ **à l'~ internationale** COM on an international scale; **à l'~ mondiale** COM globally, on a worldwide scale; **sur une ~ gigantesque** COM on a mammoth scale; **sur une grande ~** COM on a large scale; **sur une petite ~** COM on a small scale

échelon *m* GESTION, RES HUM echelon, grade, level; ~ **de cotation** BOURSE price tick; ~ **de cotation inférieur** (ANT *échelon de cotation supérieur*) BOURSE downtick, minus tick; ~ **de cotation supérieur** (ANT *échelon de cotation inférieur*) BOURSE plus tick, uptick; ~ **minimal de cotation** BOURSE tick size (*infrml*); ~ **de négociation minimal** BOURSE minimum price change; ♦ **à l'~ international** COM at international level; **gravir les ~s de la hiérarchie** RES HUM climb the promotion ladder

échelonnement: ~ **brut** *m* BOURSE gross spread; ~ **des échéances** *m* BOURSE staggering maturities

échelonner *vt* FIN spread

Échiquier *m* BANQUE Exch., Exchequer

échoir *vi* BOURSE mature, COMPTA *engagement* become due; ♦ **à ~** FIN *intérêts* accruing

échouage *m* TRANSP *d'un navire* beaching

échoué, e *adj* COM *discussions* collapsed, TRANSP *navigation* aground

échouer 1. *vt* TRANSP *navigation* run aground; **2.** *vi* COM break down, fail, INFO fail, RES HUM *négociations, relations* break down; ♦ **faire ~** COM *plan* abort, *projets* defeat

échu, e *adj* BOURSE matured, COM delinquent, COMPTA overdue, past-due, FIN delinquent, mature; ~ **et impayé** FISC due and unpaid

éclair: ~ **de génie** *m* COM flash of inspiration

éclairer *vt* COM *question, situation* clarify, throw light on

éclatement *m* POL break-up

éclater 1. *vt* COMMS break; **2.** *vi* COM flare up

éclateur *m* INFO burster

école *f* COM, PROT SOC school; ~ **autrichienne** ECON Austrian Economics, Austrian School of Economics; ~ **autrichienne de pensée économique** ECON Austrian Economics, Austrian School of Economics; ~ **de Cambridge** ECON Cambridge School; ~ **cambrienne** ECON Cambridge School; ~ **de Chicago** ECON Chicago School; ~ **classique** ECON classical economics; ~ **de commerce** COM, PROT SOC, RES HUM business college, business school; ~ **d'État** COM state school; ~ **libre** COM, PROT SOC independent school, private school (*US*), public school (*UK*); ~ **de Manchester** ECON Manchester School (*UK*); ~ **mixte** PROT SOC co-ed (*UK, infrml*), coeducational school (*UK*); ~ **monétariste** ECON Currency School (*UK*); ~ **de pensée de Cambridge** ECON Cambridge School; ~ **privée** COM, PROT SOC private school (*US*), public school (*UK*); ~ **professionnelle** PROT SOC vocational school; ~ **publique** COM public school (*US*), state school (*UK*), *système* public education (*US*), state education (*UK*), PROT SOC public school (*US*), state school (*UK*); ~ **de la régulation** ECON Regulation School; ~ **supérieure** COM college, polytechnic (*UK*); ~ **supérieure de commerce** PROT SOC graduate school of business

École: ~ **Nationale d'Administration** *f* (*ENA*) PROT SOC School of Public Management; ~ **Supérieure d'Économie de Londres** *f* ECON London School of Economics (*UK*), LSE (*UK*)

écolo *mf infrml* ENVIR conservationist, environmentalist

écologie *f* ENVIR ecology

écologique *adj* ENVIR, POL ecological, green

écologiquement *adj* ENVIR ecologically

écologisation *f* ENVIR greening (*jarg*)

écologisme *m* ENVIR environmentalism

écologiste[1] *adj* ENVIR green, green-conscious

écologiste[2] *mf* ENVIR conservationist, environmentalist

économat *m* ADMIN bursarship, stewardship

économe[1] *adj* COM thrifty

économe[2] *m* ADMIN bursar, steward, FIN comptroller

économétricien *m* COM, ECON econometrician

économétrie *f* COM, ECON econometrics

économétrique *adj* COM, ECON econometric

économie *f* ECON, POL economy, PROT SOC economics; ~ **d'abondance** ECON economy of abundance; ~ **d'actionnariat** BOURSE, ECON share economy; ~ **analytique** ECON, MATH mathematical economics; ~ **appliquée** ECON applied economics; ~ **d'armement permanente** ECON, POL permanent arms economy; ~ **autarcique** ECON self-sufficient economy; ~ **autofinancée** ECON autoeconomy;

~ **autosuffisante** ECON self-sufficient economy; ~ **à base de réseaux informatiques** ECON networking economy; ~ **du bien-être** ECON welfare economics; ~ **de blocus** ECON siege economy; ~ **bouddhiste** ECON Buddhist economics; ~ **de champ** ECON, IND economy of scope; ~ **collectiviste** ECON revenue economy; ~ **communale** ECON communal economy; ~ **complexe** ECON complex economy; ~ **du crime** ECON economics of crime; ~ **dépendante** ECON depletable externality; ~ **développée** COM, ECON, POL advanced economy; ~ **du développement** COM, ECON, POL development economics; ~ **dimensionnelle** ECON, IND economy of size; ~ **dirigée** ECON controlled economy; ~ **dominante** ECON core economy; ~ **de la drogue** ECON drug economy; ~ **du droit** DROIT, ECON economics of law; ~ **duale** ECON, IND dual economy; ~ **d'échelle** (ANT *déséconomie d'échelle*) ECON, IND economy of scale; ~ **d'échelle effective** ECON, IND real economy of scale; ~ **d'échelle externe** ECON, IND external economy of scale; ~ **d'échelle financière** ECON, FIN, IND pecuniary economy of scale; ~ **à l'échelle humaine** ECON human-scale economics; ~ **d'échelle interne** ECON, IND internal economy of scale; ~ **enclavée** ECON enclave economy; ~ **de l'énergie** ENVIR energy conservation; ~ **d'engorgement** ECON agglomeration economy; ~ **d'entreposage** ECON warehouse economy; ~ **d'entreprise** COM, ECON business economics; ~ **équilibrée à l'optimum de premier rang** ECON first best economy; ~ **et psychologie** ECON, PROT SOC economics and psychology; ~ **extérieure** (ANT *économie intérieure*) ECON external economy; ~ **externe financière** ECON, FIN pecuniary external economy; ~ **fermée** (ANT *économie ouverte*) ECON, POL closed economy; ~ **de filiales** ECON branch economy; ~ **financière** ECON, FIN financial economy; ~ **fondée sur l'exploitation de minerais** ECON, IND mineral-based economy; ~ **industrielle** ECON, IND industrial economics; ~ **inflationniste non-contrôlée** ECON unchecked inflationary economy; ~ **informelle** ECON informal economy, underground economy; ~ **interdépendante** ECON, POL interdependent economy; ~ **intérieure** (ANT *économie extérieure*) ECON internal economy; ~ **de laissez-faire** ECON, POL laissez-faire economy; ~ **libérale** ECON, POL free economy; ~ **de libre entreprise** ECON, POL free enterprise economy; ~ **de main-d'oeuvre** ECON bootblack economy (*infrml*), labor-intensive economy (*AmE*), labour-intensive economy (*BrE*); ~ **manufacturière** ECON manufacturing-based economy; ~ **de marché** ECON, POL market economy; ~ **de marché décentralisée** ECON decentralized market economy, DME; ~ **de marché intégrale** ECON, POL pure market economy; ~ **de marché parallèle** ECON, POL parallel market economy; ~ **marxiste** ECON, POL Marxian economics; ~ **mature** ECON mature economy;

~ **minéralière** ECON, IND mineral-based economy; ~ **mixte** ECON, POL mixed economy; ~ **moderne** ECON, POL modern economy; ~ **mondiale** ECON, POL world economy; ~ **monétaire** ECON monetary economics; ~ **de monoculture** ECON, IND one-crop economy; ~ **des mouvements** ECON motion economy; ~ **nationale** ECON, POL national economy; ~ **néo-classique** ECON new classical economics; ~ **noire** ECON, FIN black economy; ~ **normative** ECON normative economics; ~ **obligatoire** FIN compulsory saving (*UK*); ~ **de l'occupation des sols** ECON land economy; ~ **officielle** ECON blue economy (*UK*); ~ **officiellement répertoriée** ECON formal economy; ~ **de l'offre** ECON supply-side economics; ~ **organisationnelle** ECON organizational economics; ~ **ouverte** (ANT *économie fermée*) ECON, POL open economy; ~ **parallèle** ECON, FIN black economy; ~ **de partenariat** ECON wider share ownership; ~ **de pénurie** ECON Soviet-type economy, shortage economy; ~ **planifiée** ECON, POL centrally-planned economy, command economy, managed economy, planned economy, CPE; ~ **de plein emploi** ECON full employment economy; ~ **politique** ECON, POL, PROT SOC political economy, villa economy; ~ **positive** ECON *économétrie* positive economics; ~ **préindustrielle** ECON advanced organic economy; ~ **première** ECON, POL first economy; ~ **primitive** ECON primitive economy; ~ **protéenne** ECON protean economy; ~ **psychologique** ECON psychological economy; ~ **qui périclite** ECON, POL ailing economy; ~ **régionale** ECON regional economics; ~ **réglementée** ECON controlled economy; ~ **rurale** ECON rural economy; ~ **du sans facture** ECON cash economy; ~ **de la santé** ECON, PROT SOC health economics; ~ **de siège** ECON siege economy; ~ **sociale de marché** ECON social market economy; ~ **socialiste** ECON, POL socialist economy; ~ **souterraine** ECON, FIN black economy, moonlight economy, shadow economy, underground economy; ~ **de subsistance** ECON subsistence economy; ~ **de succursale** ECON branch economy; ~ **en surchauffe** ECON overheated economy; ~ **de télétravail** ECON networking economy; ~ **totalement fondée sur le crédit** ECON pure credit economy; ~ **transactionnelle** ECON transaction cost economics; ~ **des transferts** ECON grants economics; ~ **des transports** ECON, TRANSP transport economics; ~ **de troc** ECON barter economy; ~ **de type soviétique** ECON Soviet-type economy, shortage economy; ~ **urbaine** (ANT *déséconomie urbaine*) ECON agglomeration economy, urban economics; ♦ **faire une ~ de** BANQUE save

économies *f pl* BANQUE, COMPTA savings; ~ **contractuelles** FIN contractual savings; ~ **nouvellement industrialisées** ECON, IND NIEs, newly-industrializing economies; ~ **de pays à industrialisation récente** ECON, IND NIEs, newly-industrializing economies; ◆ **faire des écono-miess d'énergie** COM save energy;

économique *adj* COM cheap, economic, economical, ECON, FIN economic, V&M budget

économiquement *adv* COM, ECON, FIN, V&M economically

économiser *vt* BANQUE save, COM economize on, save, ENVIR *énergie* conserve, FIN save

économisme *m* ECON economism

économiste *mf* ECON, POL economist; ~ **en chef** *m* COM, ECON chief economist; ~ **d'entreprise** *m* COM, ECON business economist; ~ **vulgaire** *m* ECON vulgar economist

écophile *adj* ENVIR environmentally-friendly

écoproduit *m* ENVIR clean product

écossais, e *adj* COM Scottish

Écossais, *m* COM *habitant* Scot, Scotsman

Écossaise, *f habitant* Scot, Scotswoman

Écosse *f* COM Scotland

écosystème *m* ENVIR ecosystem

écotoxicologique *adj* ENVIR ecotoxicological

écoulé, e *adj* COM *du mois dernier* ult., ultimo (*frml*)

écouler *vt* V&M *stock* dispose of

écoute: ~ **familiale** *f* MÉDIA *radio, télévision* family audience

écouteurs *m pl* COM *radio* earphones, headphones

écoutille *f* TRANSP *d'un navire* ha, hatchway, *navigation* hatch; ~ **arrière** TRANSP *d'un navire* after hatch, ah

écran *m* COM monitor, screen, COMMS display, INFO display, monitor, screen; ~ **d'aide** INFO help screen; ~ **de cheminée** COM fire screen; ~ **couleur** INFO color display (*AmE*), colour display (*BrE*); ~ **divisé** INFO split screen; ~ **fractionné** INFO split screen; ~ **informatique** INFO computer screen; ~ **d'ordinateur** INFO computer screen; ~ **principal** INFO main screen; ~ **publicitaire** MÉDIA *télévision, radio* commercial break; ~ **de sécurité** COM protective safety screen; ~ **tactile** INFO touch-sensitive screen; ~ **de télévision** MÉDIA television screen; ~ **de terminal** INFO terminal screen; ~ **de transactions** BOURSE exchange screen; ~ **VGA** INFO video graphics array card; ~ **vidéo** COMMS video display; ~ **de visualisation** INFO display device, display monitor, view screen

écrasement *m* INFO, TRANSP *aviation* crash; ~ **de la tête** INFO head crash (*jarg*)

écraser: **s'~** *v pron* TRANSP *aviation* crash

écrémage: ~ **du marché** *m* V&M *politique des prix* market skimming

écrémer *vt* COM cream off

écrire *vt* COM record, write; ◆ ~ **de nouveau** INFO rewrite

écrit[1]**, e** *adj* MÉDIA *presse* published; ◆ **par ~** COM, COMMS in writing

écrit:[2] ~ **diffamatoire** *m* DROIT libel; **l'~** *m* COMMS the printed word

écriture *f* COMPTA, FIN accounting entry, entry, item; ~ **d'annulation** COMPTA reversing entry; ~ **d'attente** COMPTA suspense entry; ~ **de clôture** COMPTA closing entry; ~ **de compensation** BANQUE clearing entry, COMPTA, FIN contra, contra entry, offsetting entry; ~ **complémentaire** COMPTA, FIN supplementary entry; ~ **comptable** COMPTA, FIN accounting entry, book entry, journal entry; ~ **de contre-passement** COMPTA reserve entry; ~ **de contrepartie** COMPTA, FIN contra entry; ~ **de contrepassation** COMPTA reversing entry; ~ **de correction** *Can* COMPTA adjusting entry, correcting entry; ~ **d'extourne** COMPTA adjusting entry, correcting entry; ~ **au grand livre** COMPTA ledger posting; ~ **informatique** BANQUE, INFO paperless entry; ~ **d'inventaire** COMPTA adjusting entry, correcting entry; ~ **du journal multiple** COMPTA, FIN compound journal entry; ~ **pour mémoire** COMPTA memo item, memorandum item; ~ **multiple** COMPTA compound entry; ~ **non-réglée** COMPTA outstanding entry; ~ **originale** COMPTA original entry; ~ **passée au crédit** COMPTA credit entry; ~ **passée au débit** COMPTA debit entry; ~ **rectificative** COMPTA adjusting entry, correcting entry; ~ **de redressement** COMPTA adjusting entry, correcting entry; ~ **de régularisation** COMPTA adjusting entry, correcting entry

écritures *f pl* COMPTA account movements, books, books of account; ~ **extraordinaires** COM unusual items

écrivain: ~ **indépendant** *m* MÉDIA, RES HUM freelance writer; ~ **payé à la pige** *m* MÉDIA, RES HUM freelance writer

ECU *abrév* (*unité monétaire européenne*) BANQUE, ECON, FIN ECU (*European Currency Unit*)

écuadorien, -enne *adj* COM Ecuadorian

Écuadorien, -enne *m,f* COM *habitant* Ecuadoran, Ecuadorian

éd. *abrév* (*édition*) COM, INFO, MÉDIA ed. (*edition*)

EDI *abrév* COMMS (*échange de documents informatisés*) EDI (*electronic document interchange*), COMMS (*échange de données informatisées*) EDI (*electronic data interchange*), INFO (*échange de documents informatisés*) EDI (*electronic document interchange*), INFO (*échange de données informatisées*) EDI (*electronic data interchange*)

édicté: ~ **par** *adj* DROIT, FISC enacted by

édicter *vt* DROIT decree, enact, FISC degree, enact

Édimbourg *n pr* COM Edinburgh

édit. *abrév* (*édition*) COM, INFO, MÉDIA ed. (*edition*)

éditer *vt* INFO edit, MÉDIA publish

éditeur, -trice *m,f* MÉDIA *édition*, RES HUM publisher; ~ **d'écran** INFO screen editor; ~ **de ligne** INFO line editor; ~ **ligne à ligne** INFO line editor; ~ **plein écran** INFO full-screen editor; ~ **pleine page** INFO full-screen editor; ~ **de texte** INFO, MÉDIA text editor

édition *f* COM (*éd., édit.*) INFO (*éd., édit.*) edition (*ed.*) MÉDIA editing, publishing, MÉDIA (*éd.,* *édit.) livre* edition *(ed.)*; ~ **augmentée** COM enlarged edition; ~ **commémorative** MÉDIA anniversary publication; ~ **corrigée et augmentée** MÉDIA revised edition; ~ **électronique** INFO, MÉDIA electronic publishing; ~ **graphique** MÉDIA graphical editing; ~ **du matin** MÉDIA *presse* bulldog edition *(AmE)*, early edition *(BrE)*, first edition *(BrE)*; ~ **revue et corrigée** MÉDIA revised edition; ~ **spécialisée** MÉDIA vertical publication *(jarg)*; ~ **de texte** INFO, MÉDIA text editing; ~ **à tirage limité** MÉDIA limited edition

éditorial *m* MÉDIA *presse* editorial; ~ **vendu à plusieurs journaux** MÉDIA *presse* syndicated column

éditorialiste *mf* COM editorialist, MÉDIA editorial writer, leader writer

éducation *f* PROT SOC education; ~ **de la sensibilité** COM, RES HUM sensitivity training

effacement *m* INFO blanking, erasion

effacer *vt* COM *bande* wipe, INFO delete, *bande* wipe, *memoire* blank, erase, *écran* clear

effectif[1], **-ive** *adj* COM actual, INFO *contribution* effective

effectif[2] *m* ECON labor force *(AmE)*, labour force *(BrE)*, RES HUM labor force *(AmE)*, labour force *(BrE)*, manning, manpower; ~ **de série économique** ECON, GESTION, IND economic batch quantity; ♦ **à ~ pléthorique** RES HUM overstaffed

effectivement *adv* COM effectively

effectuer *vt* COM *paiement* effect, *étude, enquête* conduct, COMPTA carry out, FIN *versement partiel* pay; ♦ ~ **un achat spéculatif** COM buy sth on spec *(infrml)*; ~ **des démarches** COM take steps; ~ **un paiement** COM make a payment; ~ **une vente** BOURSE make a sale; ~ **un versement** COM make a payment

effet *m* ASSUR, BANQUE, COMPTA, DROIT, FIN *à payer, à recevoir*, FISC *d'une perte* attachment, bill, impact, instrument, note; ~ **à l'acceptation** BANQUE acceptance bill; ~ **accepté** COM, FIN accepted bill; ~ **d'annonce** POL announcement effect; ~ **avalisé** BOURSE guaranteed bill; ~ **bancable** BANQUE bankable bill, eligible paper; ~ **bancaire** BANQUE bank acceptance, bank bill, bank draft *(BrE)*, banker's acceptance; ~ **de bien-être** ECON Pigou effect; ~ **de capacité** ECON capacity effect; ~ **en cascade** ECON ripple effect; ~ **en circulation** COMPTA outstanding item; ~ **de cliquet** ECON ratchet effect; ~ **de commerce** BANQUE, BOURSE bill of exchange, COM commercial paper, CP, FIN, IMP/EXP bill of exchange; ~ **de complaisance** BANQUE, COM, FIN accommodation bill, accommodation note, accommodation paper; ~ **de contagion** ECON spread effect; ~ **décourageant** ECON disincentive; ~ **de désincitation** ECON disincentive effect; ~ **dissuasif** COM deterrent, ECON disincentive effect; ~ **à double usance** COM bill at double usance; ~ **douteux** FIN unsafe paper; ~ **d'éloignement** V&M *publicité* alienation effect; ~ **à l'encaissement** BANQUE bill for collection,

draft for collection; ~ **à encaisser** BANQUE bill for collection, draft for collection; ~ **d'endettement** BANQUE, BOURSE, COMPTA, FIN gearing *(BrE)*, leverage *(AmE)*; ~ **d'entraînement** ECON spillover effect, third-party effect; ~ **escomptable** BANQUE eligible bill; ~ **escompté** BANQUE discounted bill; ~ **à l'escompte** BANQUE bill for discount; ~ **d'éviction** ECON, FIN crowding out; ~ **externe** ECON externality; ~ **financier** FIN finance paper, financial paper; ~ **Fisher** ECON Fisher effect; ~ **de halo** COM halo effect; ~ **d'impact** ECON impact effect; ~ **d'un impôt sur la capitalisation** ECON, FISC capitalization effect of a tax; ~ **d'incitation** ECON incentive effect; ~ **d'inertie** POL inertial effect; ~ **irréductible** ENVIR undepletable externality; ~ **juridique** FISC legal effect; ~ **Keynes** ECON Keynes' effect; ~ **de levier** BANQUE, BOURSE, COMPTA, FIN financial gearing *(BrE)*, financial leverage *(AmE)*, gearing *(BrE)*, leverage *(AmE)*; ~ **de levier élevé** BANQUE, BOURSE, COMPTA, FIN high gearing *(BrE)*, high leverage *(AmE)*; ~ **de levier de l'exploitation** COMPTA operating gearing *(BrE)*, operating leverage *(AmE)*; ~ **de levier de la marge** BOURSE margin gearing *(BrE)*, margin leverage *(AmE)*; ~ **de levier négatif** COMPTA, FIN reverse gearing *(BrE)*, reverse leverage *(AmE)*; ~ **de levier positif** COMPTA, FIN positive gearing *(BrE)*, positive leverage *(AmE)*; ~ **libre** ECON, FIN clean bill; ~ **menace** ECON threat effect; ~ **multiplicateur** ECON *économétrie* multiplier effect; ~ **de nantissement** BOURSE collateral bill; ~ **négociable** *(ANT effet non-négociable)* BANQUE negotiable instrument; ~ **nocif** ENVIR *pollution* harmful effect; ~ **non-acceptable** BANQUE ineligible paper; ~ **non-admis à la compensation** BANQUE nonclearing item; ~ **non-négociable** *(ANT effet négociable)* BANQUE nonnegotiable instrument; ~ **nuisible** ENVIR *pollution* harmful effect; ~ **d'osmose** ECON backwash effect, spread effect; ~ **papillon** BOURSE butterfly effect; ~ **payable à vue** COMPTA bill payable at sight; ~ **à payer** *(e. à p)* COMPTA, FIN bill payable, note payable; ~ **périmé** BANQUE expired bill; ~ **pervers du prix** ECON perverse price; ~ **Pigou** ECON Pigou effect; ~ **placé de gré à gré** BOURSE tap bill; ~ **d'une police** ASSUR commencement of a policy; ~ **au porteur** BOURSE, FIN bearer bill; ~ **des primes syndicales** FIN union wage effect; ~ **de prix** ECON price effect; ~ **de rappel** MÉDIA *publicité* carry-over effect; ~ **de rattrapage** RES HUM catch-up effect; ~ **à recevoir** *(e. à r)* COMPTA, FIN bill receivable, note receivable; ~ **en recouvrement** BANQUE draft for collection; ~ **refusé** COM dishonored bill *(AmE)*, dishonoured bill *(BrE)*; ~ **de règlement** BANQUE settlement draft; ~ **de rémanence** COM holdover effect, MÉDIA carry-over effect; ~ **de remous** ECON backwash effect; ~ **de retombées** ECON spillover effect, third-party effect; ~ **rétroactif sur salaire** RES HUM back pay; ~ **de revenu** ECON income effect; ~ **Ricardo** ECON Ricardo effect; ~ **richesse** ECON wealth effect; ~ **sans risque** BOURSE risk-free debt instrument;

~ **secondaire** COM side effect; ~ **de serre** ENVIR greenhouse effect; ~ **Slutsky** ECON Slutsky effect; ~ **de substitution** ECON substitution effect; ~ **tiré** ECON drawn bill; ~ **tiré d'avance** FIN advance bill; ~ **tiré à l'étranger** ECON made bill (*jarg*); ~ **toxique** ENVIR *pollution* toxic effect; ~ **à usance** FIN tenor bill, usance bill; ◆ **avec** ~ **à compter du** COM wef, with effect from; **avec** ~ **rétroactif** COM back-dated; **avoir un** ~ **sur** COM, DROIT affect; **en** ~ COM in effect

effets: ~ **externes dans la consommation** *m pl* ECON consumption externality; ~ **fiscaux régionaux** *m pl* COMPTA regional tax effects; ~ **personnels** *m pl* COM personal effects; ~ **de revenu et de substitution** *m pl* ECON income and substitution effects; ~ **sonores** *m pl* MÉDIA sound effects; ~ **en transit** *m pl* COMPTA cash in transit; ~ **à usage personnel** *m pl vieilli* IMP/EXP articles for personal use

efficace *adj* ADMIN efficient, COM effective, efficient, ECON efficient

efficacement *adv* COM effectively

efficacité *f* COM effectiveness, efficiency; ~ **de l'affectation** ECON *des facteurs de production et de distribution*, FIN allocative efficiency; ~ **d'allocation** ECON, FIN allocative efficiency; ~ **de la direction** GESTION managerial effectiveness; ~ **d'exploitation** TRANSP operating efficiency; ~ **marginale du capital** ECON marginal efficiency of capital, MEC; ~ **marginale des investissements** ECON marginal efficiency of investment; ~ **maximale** ECON, IND maximum efficiency; ~ **maximum** ECON, IND maximum efficiency; ~ **organisatrice** GESTION organizational effectiveness; ~ **publicitaire** V&M advertising effectiveness; ~ **technique** ECON, IND technical efficiency

efficience *f* COM, ECON, IND efficiency, productivity, V&M efficiency; ~ **des échanges** ECON, FIN exchange efficiency; ~ **maximale** ECON top-level efficiency; ~ **au sens de Pareto** ECON Pareto efficiency; ~ **X** ECON X efficiency

efficient, e *adj* COM, ECON efficient

effiler *vt* FISC taper

effleurement: **à** ~ *loc* INFO touch-sensitive

effluence *f* ENVIR effluence

effluent *m* ENVIR effluent; ~ **gazeux** ENVIR exhaust gas, waste gas; ~ **industriel** ECON, ENVIR, IND industrial waste; ~ **liquide** ENVIR liquid waste; ~ **toxique** ENVIR toxic effluent

effondrement *m* BOURSE collapse, *soudain* break, COM *des cours* collapse; ~ **du cours plancher** BOURSE bottom dropped out (*jarg*), BDO; ~ **du marché** BOURSE stock market collapse; ~ **du prix plancher** BOURSE bottom dropped out (*jarg*), BDO

effondrer: **s'**~ *v pron* BOURSE collapse, crash, COM collapse, fall down

effort: ~ **concerté** *m* COM concerted effort; ~ **fiscal**

m ECON, FISC tax effort; ~ **de travail optimal** *m* ECON, IND, RES HUM optimal work effort

effraction *f* DROIT forcible entry; ~ **informatique** INFO hacking

effréné, e *adj* COM uncurbed

égal, e *adj* MATH equal; ◆ **à** ~ **tirant d'eau** TRANSP *navigation* on an even keel; **être l'**~ **de** COM match up to

également: ~ **appelé** *loc* COMMS a.k.a., also known as

égaler *vt* MATH equal, V&M match

égalisation: ~ **inter-régionale** *f* ECON regional policy

égaliser 1. *vt* COM equalize; **2.** *v pron* **s'**~ COM *prix* even out

égalitarien, -enne *adj* POL egalitarian

égalitarisme *m* POL egalitarianism; ~ **spécifique** ECON specific egalitarianism

égalité *f* COM equal footing, RES HUM equality, parity; ~ **des chances** RES HUM equal opportunity; ~ **des chances face à l'emploi** RES HUM equal employment opportunity; ~ **des droits des travailleurs** RES HUM fair employment; ~ **des droits de vote** COM, DROIT, GESTION equal voting rights; ~ **des salaires** RES HUM equal pay; ~ **salariale** RES HUM equal pay; ~ **salariale entre hommes et femmes** RES HUM Equal Value Amendment (*UK*)

égard: **à cet** ~ *loc* COM on that score

égaux: ~ **et opposés** *loc* COM equal and opposite

Égypte *f* COM Egypt

égyptien, -enne *adj* COM Egyptian

Égyptien, -enne *m,f* COM *habitant* Egyptian

éjecter *vt* INFO eject

éjection *f* INFO ejection

élaboration: ~ **de l'image** *f* V&M imaging; ~ **de programmes** *f* COM, INFO programming; ~ **des stratégies** *f* COM, ECON strategy formulation; ~ **des tarifs** *f* TRANSP rates formulation

élaboré: **peu** ~ *adj* IND, INFO low-tech

élaborer *vt* COM *plan, stratégie* develop

élan *m* ECON, MATH momentum

élancement *m* TRANSP *navigation* rake

élargir *vt* COM broaden, expand, extend, widen, FISC widen

élargissement *m* COM widening; ~ **de l'assiette fiscale** ECON, FISC tax base broadening; ~ **de l'assiette de l'impôt** ECON, FISC tax base broadening; ~ **de la gamme** V&M line extension; ~ **du travail** RES HUM job enlargement

élasticité *f* ECON elasticity; ~ **des anticipants** ECON elasticity of expectations; ~ **d'anticipation** ECON elasticity of anticipation; ~ **d'arc** ECON arc elasticity; ~ **croisée de la demande** ECON, V&M cross elasticity of demand; ~ **croisée de la demande par rapport au prix** ECON, V&M cross price elasticity of demand; ~ **de la demande** ECON, V&M elasticity of demand; ~ **de la demande et de l'offre** ECON, V&M elasticity of demand and supply; ~ **de la demande**

par rapport au revenu ECON, V&M income-elasticity of demand; **~ fiscale** ECON, FISC tax buoyancy, tax elasticity; **~ -intérêts de l'épargne** ECON interest elasticity of savings; **~ négative** ECON negative elasticity; **~ de l'offre** ECON, V&M elasticity of supply; **~ ponctuelle** ECON point elasticity; **~ -prix** COM, ECON, V&M price elasticity, price flexibility, price sensitivity; **~ -revenu de la demande** ECON, V&M income-elasticity of demand; **~ de substitution** ECON elasticity of substitution; **~ unitaire** ECON unitary elasticity; ◆ **à l'~ égale à 1** ECON unitary elastic

élastique[1] *adj* ECON *demande* elastic; ◆ **~ par rapport au revenu** ECON income-elastic

élastique[2] *m* COM rubber band

électeur, -trice *m,f* POL constituent, elector, voter; **~ girouette** *infrml* POL floating voter, swing voter (*jarg*); **~ indécis** POL floating voter

électeurs: les ~ *m pl* COM, POL the electorate

élection *f* COM poll, POL election; **~ échelonnée** POL staggered election; **~ éliminatoire** POL runoff election (*US*); **~ fédérale** POL federal election (*US*); **~ locale** COM local election; **~ partielle** POL by-election (*UK*)

élections: ~ législatives *f pl* POL general election; **~ présidentielles** *f pl* POL presidential election

électrification *f* TRANSP *des chemins de fer* electrification

électronique *f* IND electronics

élément *m* COM component, element, ECON *composante* component, INFO item; **~ d'actif** COMPTA, FIN asset, corporate asset; **~ d'actif corporel** COM, COMPTA, FIN tangible asset; **~ d'actif couvert** COMPTA hedged asset; **~ d'actif national** BANQUE domestic asset; **~ d'activité** COMPTA activity element; **~ d'activité administrative** COMPTA administrative activity element; **~ des administrations centrales** FIN central government item; **~ d'arrêt** INFO stop bit; **~ du capital** FIN capital instrument; **~ au choix** BOURSE optional feature; **~ commun** IMMOB *dans une copropriété* common element (*US*); **~ constitutif** COM component part; **~ constitutif de l'impôt** FISC tax component; **~ du coût** COMPTA cost factor; **~ éligible** FIN qualifying item; **~ encastré** COM fitment; **~ exceptionnel** FISC extraordinary item; **~ extraordinaire** COM extraordinary item; **~ de fixation sur le pont** TRANSP *navigation* deck fitting; **~ de la loi** DROIT piece of legislation; **~ de passif couvert** COMPTA hedged liability; **~ du passif-dépôts** BANQUE deposit liabilities; **~ pondérateur** ECON balancing item

élevage: ~ de bétail intensif *m* ECON, ENVIR intensive livestock farming; **~ industriel** *m* ENVIR factory farming; **~ piscicole** *m* ECON, IND fish farm; **~ de volailles** *m* ECON poultry farm

élévateur: ~ à godets *m* TRANSP *manutention* bucket elevator; **~ de grain** *m* TRANSP *manutention* grain elevator

élévation: ~ du plan des formes *f* TRANSP *navigation* profile

élevé, e *adj* BOURSE, COM high; **trop ~** COM too high

élève *mf* PROT SOC pupil, student, RES HUM apprentice; **~ -programmeur** *m* INFO trainee programmer

élever: s'~ à *v pron* COM add up to, amount to, work out to, run into, tot up to (*infrml*), *offre, prix* stand at

éleveur, -euse *m,f* COM stockbreeder; **~ de bestiaux** COM stockperson

éligible *adj* DROIT eligible

élimination: ~ d'actifs non-rentables *f* COMPTA asset stripping; **~ des déchets** *f* ENVIR waste disposal; **~ des ordures ménagères** *f* ENVIR refuse disposal; **~ progressive** *f* COM, INFO phasing out

éliminatoire *f* POL runoff (*US*)

éliminer *vt* COM eliminate, weed out, INFO suppress; **~ à la présélection** RES HUM screen out; ◆ **~ progressivement** (ANT *adopter progressivement*), COM, INFO phase out

élingue *f* TRANSP *manutention* sling; **~ araignée** TRANSP *manutention* multilegged sling; **~ en chaîne** TRANSP chain sling; **~ perdue** TRANSP *matériel de manutention* one-trip sling; **~ à sacs** TRANSP *manutention* canvas sling; **~ sans fin en fils d'acier** TRANSP *manutention* endless sling; **~ à véhicules** TRANSP *manutention* vehicle sling

élire *vt* COM, POL elect; ◆ **~ qn au conseil d'administration** COM elect sb to the board

élite *f* COM elite

éloigné, e *adj* INFO remote; **~ de** COM alien from

éloignement *m* COM absence

éluder *vt* COM fend off, FISC *impôt* avoid

émancipation *f* DROIT, POL emancipation

emballage *m* COM, TRANSP, V&M packaging, packing, pkg.; **~ biodégradable** ENVIR biodegradable packaging; **~ blister** V&M blister packaging; **~ bulle** COM bubblewrap, V&M blister packaging; **~ en caisses** TRANSP case packaging, C/-; **~ en carton** TRANSP carton; **~ composite** TRANSP composite packaging; **~ export-départ usine** IMP/EXP, TRANSP *livraison* ex works export packing; **~ familial** V&M family-size pack, family-size package; **~ imperméable** TRANSP siftproof packaging; **~ intermodal** TRANSP intermodal packaging; **~ métallique** ENVIR metal packaging; **~ primaire** COM primary package; **~ sous film rétractable** COM, TRANSP shrink-packaging, shrink-wrapping; **~ transparent** V&M blister packaging; **~ trompeur** V&M deceptive packaging

emballé, e *adj* COM, V&M wrapped

emballer *vt* COM, TRANSP, V&M *dans un carton* pack up, *dans du papier* wrap up

emballeur, -euse *m,f* COM packer; **~ d'exportations** IMP/EXP export packer

embarcadère *m* TRANSP *port* pier

embarcation: ~ **de sauvetage** *f* TRANSP *navigation* lifeboat; ~ **de service** *f* TRANSP *port* service boat

embargo *m* COM, IMP/EXP *sur l'importation de qch* ban, MÉDIA gag order (*US, jarg*), reporting restrictions (*UK*), TRANSP embargo; ~ **commercial** COM stoppage of trade

embarqué, e *adj* IMP/EXP shipped on board, INFO on-board, TRANSP *connaissement* shipped on board; ~ **à bord** IMP/EXP, TRANSP shipped aboard

embarquement *m* TRANSP *sur un navire* embarkation

embarquer *vt* COM take aboard, TRANSP *cargaison* load, *passagers* board, embark

embauchage *m* COM, RES HUM hiring; ~ **et renvoi** RES HUM hiring and firing

embauche *f* COM hiring, ECON contracting, RES HUM hiring, recruitment; ~ **préférentielle** RES HUM direct discrimination (*UK*)

embaucher *vt* COM hire, RES HUM *personnel* hire, take on; ◆ ~ **et renvoyer** RES HUM hire and fire

emboîtage *m* TRANSP *manutention* nesting

emboîté, e *adj* MÉDIA *édition* hardback, hardcover

emboîter *vt* INFO nest

embourgeoisement *m* ECON, PROT SOC gentrification (*UK*)

embouteillage *m* TRANSP bottleneck, traffic congestion, traffic jam

embranchement *m* TRANSP *chemin de fer* branch line; ~ **particulier** TRANSP *chemin de fer* siding (*BrE*)

embrasser *vt* COM comprise

embrayage: ~ **à plaque sèche** *m* TRANSP *unique, double* dry plate clutch; ~ **à plateau sec** *m* TRANSP *unique, double* dry plate clutch; ~ **de renversement de marche** *m* TRANSP reversing gear clutch, RC

embrochage *m* MATH skewness

embrouillamini *m infrml* COM jungle (*infrml*)

émetteur[1], **-trice** *adj* BANQUE, BOURSE issuing, COM *poste*, COMMS transmitting, FIN issuing, MÉDIA transmitting

émetteur[2], **-trice** *m,f* BOURSE issuer, COM, COMMS transmitter, FIN carrier, issuer, MÉDIA transmitter; ~ **de cartes** BANQUE, COM card issuer; ~ **de cartes de crédit** BANQUE, COM credit card issuer; ~ **de dette** BOURSE liability issuer; ~ **d'engagement** BOURSE liability issuer

émettre *vt* BOURSE *obligation* bring out, issue, launch, COMMS *radio* broadcast, transmit, *télévision* broadcast, FIN issue, launch, INFO issue, *signal* generate, MÉDIA *radio* broadcast, transmit, *télévision* broadcast; ◆ ~ **des actions à l'escompte** BOURSE issue shares at a discount; ~ **un bip** INFO beep; ~ **un chèque** BANQUE draw a check (*AmE*), draw a cheque (*BrE*), write a check (*AmE*), write a cheque (*BrE*); ~ **dans le public** BOURSE *actions* go public; ~ **un emprunt** BANQUE float a loan, raise a loan; ~ **une lettre de crédit** BOURSE issue a letter of credit; ~ **de nouveau**

BOURSE reissue; ~ **un nouvel emprunt** BANQUE refloat a loan; ~ **une objection** COM make an objection, raise an objection; ~ **des obligations** BOURSE launch a bond issue; ~ **par adjudication** FIN issue by tender; ~ **un signal sonore** INFO beep

émeute *f* POL cc, civil commotion

émeutes: ~ **et troubles de l'ordre public** *m pl* PROT SOC riots and civil commotions, R&CC; ~, **troubles de l'ordre public et grèves** *m pl* PROT SOC riots, civil commotions and strikes, RCC & S

éminent, e *adj* COM, RES HUM distinguished

Émirats: ~ **Arabes Unis** *m pl* COM United Arab Emirates, UAE

émis, e *adj* BOURSE, FIN issued; ◆ ~ **et en circulation** BOURSE issued and outstanding

émission *f* BOURSE floating, flotation, rating, *actions* issue, COMMS broadcast, ENVIR emission, MÉDIA broadcast, broadcasting, program (*AmE*), programme (*BrE*), transmission; ~ **d'actions** BOURSE stock issue; ~ **d'actions aux ayants-droit** COMPTA rights issue; ~ **d'actions gratuites** BOURSE, FIN bonus issue (*UK*), scrip issue; ~ **d'actions de numéraire** BOURSE share issue for cash; ~ **d'actions souscrites** BOURSE takeup of shares; ~ **d'agence fédérale** FIN federal agency issue (*US*), federal agency security (*US*); ~ **des autorités locales** BOURSE corporation loan (*UK*); ~ **de bon de souscription subordonné** BOURSE subordinated warrant issue; ~ **de bons** BOURSE bond issue, bond issue operation; ~ **brûlante** BOURSE hot issue (*US, jarg*); ~ **de capital** BOURSE equity issue; ~ **de chèque sans provision** BANQUE check-kiting (*AmE*), cheque-kiting (*BrE*); ~ **de chèque sur l'étranger** BANQUE foreign check issue (*AmE*), foreign cheque issue (*BrE*); ~ **de chèques** COMPTA check issue (*AmE*), cheque issue (*BrE*); ~ **de conversion** BOURSE, FIN conversion issue; ~ **convertible** FIN convertible issue; ~ **en différé** MÉDIA *radio, télévision* prerecorded broadcast; ~ **à diffusion restreinte** BOURSE private issue; ~ **de dioxyde de carbone** ENVIR carbon dioxide emission; ~ **en direct** MÉDIA live broadcast, live program (*AmE*), live programme (*BrE*), spot coverage; ~ **de droits préférentiels de souscription** BOURSE rights issue; ~ **enregistrée à l'avance** MÉDIA *radio, télévision* prerecorded broadcast; ~ **étrangère** ENVIR, IND *pollution* foreign emission; ~ **d'euro-obligations** BOURSE Eurobond issue; ~ **d'euro-obligations en dollars canadiens** BOURSE Euro-Canadian dollar issue; ~ **excédentaire** BANQUE overissue; ~ **fiduciaire** BANQUE fiduciary issue, note issue; ~ **garantie** BOURSE guaranteed issue; ~ **de gaz carbonique** ENVIR carbon dioxide emission, carbon emission; ~ **de gaz d'échappement** ENVIR, TRANSP exhaust emission; ~ **globale** ENVIR, IND *pollution* global emission; ~ **à grand succès** LOISIRS, V&M blockbuster; ~ **hasardeuse** BOURSE sticky deal; ~ **initiale** BOURSE primary issue; ~ **à ligne ouverte** COMMS, MÉDIA phone-in, phone-in program (*AmE*), phone-in programme (*BrE*); ~ **locale**

ENVIR, IND *pollution* local emission; ~ **d'une obligation à court terme** BOURSE short-term note issuance facility, SNIF; ~ **d'une obligation subordonnée** BOURSE subordinated bond issue; ~ **d'une obligation subordonnée convertible** BOURSE subordinated convertible bond issue; ~ **d'obligations** BOURSE bond issue, bond issue operation; ~ **de polluants atmosphériques** ENVIR, IND air pollution emission; ~ **pré-enregistrée** MÉDIA *radio, télévision* prerecorded broadcast; ~ **publique** BOURSE public issue, *titres* public distribution; ~ **de radio** MÉDIA radio broadcast, radio program (*AmE*), radio programme (*BrE*); ~ **radiophonique** MÉDIA radio broadcast, radio program (*AmE*), radio programme (*BrE*); ~ **de reportages** MÉDIA longform (*US, jarg*), news report; ~ **secondaire** BOURSE junior issue (*US*); ~ **sonore** ENVIR noise emission; ~ **sulfureuse** ENVIR sulphur emission; ~ **sur chaîne câblée** COMMS, MÉDIA cable program (*AmE*), cable programme (*BrE*); ~ **sur l'euromarché des capitaux** BOURSE Eurocapital market issue; ~ **d'une télécopie** ADMIN, COMMS facsimile transmission, fax transmission; ~ **de télévision** MÉDIA television broadcast, television program (*AmE*), television programme (*BrE*); ~ **de titres** FIN *par société commerciale* corporate issue; ~ **de titres nationaux** BOURSE domestic issue; ~ **totalement écoulée** BOURSE pot is clean (*jarg*); ~ **très attendue** BOURSE hot issue (*US, jarg*); ~ **d'une valeur vedette** BOURSE glamor issue (*AmE*), glamour issue (*BrE, jarg*); ~ **de valeurs d'État** BOURSE tap issue; ~ **de warrants** FIN warrant issue; ◆ **faire une** ~ COMMS, MÉDIA broadcast

émissions: ~ **assorties d'options de change** *f pl* BOURSE issues with currency options; ~ **prévues à trente jours** *f pl* BOURSE thirty-day visible supply; ~ **des villes** *f pl* BANQUE municipal bonds (*US*)

emmagasinage *m* COM, IND, TRANSP storage, warehousing

emmagasiner *vt* TRANSP store

emménager *vi* COM move in; ◆ ~ **dans des locaux plus grands** ADMIN move to larger premises

empan: ~ **visuo-manuel** *m* ADMIN eye-hand span; ~ **visuo-vocal** *m* ADMIN eye-voice span

emparer: **s'~ de** *v pron* COM capture, snatch

empattement *m* INFO serif

empêchement *m* COM bar, difficulty, obstacle; ◆ **avoir un ~ de dernière minute** COM be unavoidably detained at the last minute

empêcher *vt* BOURSE lock out, COM prevent, *concurrence* block, *croissance* hamper; ◆ ~ **d'exercer** BOURSE bar, INFO inhibit, prohibit

emphatique *adj* COM emphatic

empiétement *m* DROIT encroachment

empiéter *vt* DROIT encroach on, encroach upon; ~ **sur** DROIT *droits de qn* impinge on

empilage *m* TRANSP stack; ~ **double** TRANSP *conteneurs* double stack, double stacking

empiler *vt* TRANSP stack; ◆ ~ **en double piles** TRANSP *conteneurs* double-stack

empirer *vi* (*ANT s'améliorer*) COM deteriorate, get worse, take a turn for the worse

empirique *adj* COM empirical, hit-or-miss (*infrml*), MATH empirical

emplacement *m* COM, INFO site; ~ **imposé** MÉDIA, V&M *publicité* appointed space; ~ **indéterminé** MÉDIA, V&M *presse* run of paper, ROP; ~ **isolé** MÉDIA *presse* solus position, V&M *dans un magasin* island site (*jarg*), *presse* solus position; ~ **le long d'une route** V&M *pour un panneau publicitaire* roadside site; ~ **de premier choix** IMMOB prime location; ~ **de la signature** COMMS letterfoot

emplanture *f* TRANSP *de mât* mast step

emploi *m* ECON, POL employment, RES HUM employment, job, sit., situation; ~ **agricole** ECON, RES HUM agricultural job; ~ **annexe** RES HUM sideline job; ~ **assuré** RES HUM secure job; ~ **de bureau** ADMIN, RES HUM clerical worker, clerk; ~ **civil** RES HUM civilian employment; ~ **dans la fonction publique** RES HUM public service employment, PSE; ~ **de départ** RES HUM entry-level job; ~ **donnant droit à la retraite** ASSUR, RES HUM pensionable employment; ~ **de fonds** COMPTA use of funds; ~ **intérimaire** RES HUM temporary employment, temporary job; ~ **involontaire** ECON, RES HUM involuntary employment; ~ **à mi-temps** COM, RES HUM part-time employment; ~ **permanent** RES HUM permanent employment; ~ **à plein temps** RES HUM full-time employment; ~ **principal** RES HUM central occupation; ~ **protégé** RES HUM sheltered employment; ~ **sans avenir** RES HUM blind-alley job (*AmE*), dead-end job (*BrE*); ~ **secondaire** RES HUM sideline job; ~ **temporaire** RES HUM temporary employment, temporary job; ~ **du temps** COM schedule, GESTION, RES HUM timetable; ~ **à temps partiel** COM, RES HUM part-time employment; ~ **à vie** RES HUM lifetime employment

emplois *m pl* COMPTA application of funds; ~ **précédents** RES HUM work history; ~ **du secteur tertiaire** RES HUM service jobs; ~ **des services** RES HUM service jobs; ~ **successifs** COM, RES HUM employment record

employé[1], **e** *m,f* RES HUM employee, office worker; ~ **de banque** BANQUE bank clerk; ~ **de bureau** RES HUM white-collar worker; ~ **chargé des importations** IMP/EXP, RES HUM import clerk; ~ **des contributions indirectes** FISC, IMP/EXP exciseman, exciseperson; ~ **de débarquement** RES HUM, TRANSP landing officer (*UK*); ~ **aux déclarations en douane** IMP/EXP, RES HUM, TRANSP manifest clerk; ~ **aux droits de port** RES HUM, TRANSP rates clerk; ~ **à l'essai** RES HUM probationary employee; ~ **d'expédition** RES HUM, TRANSP forwarding clerk; ~ **à l'exportation** IMP/EXP, RES HUM export clerk; ~ **de ferme** RES HUM farm laborer (*AmE*), farm labourer (*BrE*), farmhand; ~ **du lamanage** RES HUM, TRANSP lasher, rigger; ~ **de magasin** COM, RES HUM sales assistant, sales clerk (*AmE*), shop assistant (*BrE*); ~ **membre du conseil d'administration** GESTION, RES HUM worker director; ~ **à mi-temps** COM, RES HUM part-time employee; ~ **modèle** COM model worker; ~ **occasionnel** RES HUM casual laborer (*AmE*); ~ **à plein temps** COM, RES HUM full-timer; ~ **au pointage** RES HUM, TRANSP tally clerk; ~ **des postes** RES HUM postal assistant, postal worker; ~ **de production** IND, RES HUM production worker; ~ **temporaire** RES HUM casual worker; ~ **à temps partiel** COM, RES HUM part-time employee

employé:[2] être ~ *loc* FISC, RES HUM be employed

employée: ~ **des contributions indirectes** *f* FISC, IMP/EXP exciseperson, excisewoman

employer *vt* COM, RES HUM employ; ♦ ~ **la manière forte** COM use strong-arm tactics

employeur, -euse *m,f* RES HUM employer; ~ **désigné** FISC specified employer; ~ **membre d'un syndicat patronal** RES HUM associated employer; ~ **respectant l'égalité des chances** RES HUM equal opportunities employer

emporté: ~ **et livré** *loc* COM collected and delivered, C&D

emportements *m pl* RES HUM storming

emporter: **l'~ sur** *vt* ECON outperform; ♦ ~ **le morceau** *infrml* COM swing a deal (*infrml*)

empotage *m* IMP/EXP, TRANSP *conteneur* stuffing; ♦ TRANSP container stuffing; ~ **et dépotage** IMP/EXP, TRANSP stuffing and stripping

empoter *vt* TRANSP *conteneur* stuff (*BrE*), van (*AmE*)

empreint: ~ **d'une autorité bienveillante** *loc* GESTION benevolent-authoritative

emprise *f* DROIT, IMMOB expropriation

emprisonnement *m* DROIT imprisonment

emprunt *m* BANQUE, BOURSE, COM, COMPTA, ECON, FIN borrowing, loan; ~ **d'actions** BOURSE share borrowing, stock borrowing; ~ **auprès des établissements de crédit** BANQUE bank loan; ~ **bancaire** BANQUE bank loan; ~ **à la banque** BANQUE bank loan; ~ **boursier** BANQUE securities borrowing; ~ **de cadres** GESTION executive leasing; ~ **de capitaux étrangers** BOURSE, COM, ECON borrowing abroad; ~ **consolidé** BANQUE, FIN consolidation loan; ~ **de conversion** BANQUE, FIN conversion loan; ~ **à court terme** BANQUE short-term loan; ~ **de la défense nationale** FIN war loan; ~ **d'État** FIN government loan, public loan; ~ **d'État indexé** BOURSE retirement issue certificate (*UK*); ~ **à faible intérêt** BANQUE low-interest loan; ~ **de fonds externes** BANQUE, COM, COMPTA, ECON, FIN borrowing of external funds; ~ **garanti** BANQUE collateral loan, secured loan; ~ **gigogne** FIN piggyback loan; ~ **hors compétences** BANQUE ultra vires borrowing; ~ **hypothécaire** BANQUE, IMMOB mortgage loan; ~ **hypothécaire plafonné** BANQUE, IMMOB closed-end mortgage; ~ **indexé** BANQUE, ECON, FIN index-tied loan, indexed loan; ~ **industriel** BOURSE industrial loan; ~ **irrécouvrable** BANQUE

loan loss; ~ **au jour le jour** BANQUE, FIN call money; ~ **lié** BANQUE, ECON tied loan; ~ **-logement** IMMOB housing bond; ~ **municipal** BOURSE municipal bond (*US*); ~ **non-garanti** BANQUE, COMPTA unsecured loan; ~ **obligataire** BANQUE, BOURSE bond issue, bond issue operation, bond loan; ~ **-obligation** BOURSE bond liability, bond payable; ~ **parallèle** BANQUE, ECON, FIN parallel loan; ~ **à plus d'un an** FIN long-term debt; ~ **en plusieurs monnaies** BANQUE multicurrency loan; ~ **à prime** BANQUE premium loan; ~ **public** FIN public loan; ~ **de recours** FIN recourse loan; ~ **de redressement** FIN rehabilitation import loan, RIL; ~ **de redressement sectoriel** FIN sector adjustment loan, SECAL; ~ **remboursable in fine** BANQUE bullet (*jarg*); ~ **remboursable sur demande** BANQUE, FIN call money; ~ **à risque** FIN problem loan; ~ **à risques** BANQUE nonaccruing loan; ~ **sans intérêt** BANQUE, FIN interest-free loan; ~ **subordonné** FIN subordinated loan; ~ **subordonné convertible** FIN convertible subordinated loan; ~ **sur le marché européen des capitaux** BOURSE, COM, ECON, FIN borrowing in the Euromarket; ~ **sur le marché monétaire** BOURSE, COM, ECON, FIN borrowing in the money market; ~ **à taux fixe** BANQUE fixed-rate loan; ~ **à taux flottant** BANQUE floating-rate loan; ~ **à taux nul** BANQUE, FIN interest-free loan; ~ **à taux variable** BANQUE floating-rate loan, roll-over loan; ~ **à terme** BANQUE time loan; ~ **de titres** *(ANT prêt de titres)* FIN security borrowing

emprunter *vt* BANQUE borrow, BOURSE borrow, take a deposit, COM, COMPTA, FIN borrow; ~ **à** BANQUE borrow from; ♦ ~ **de l'argent** BANQUE borrow money, FIN hire money (*jarg*); ~ **de l'argent sur qch** COM raise money on sth; ~ **à court terme** *(ANT emprunter à long terme)* BOURSE borrow short; ~ **en fonction de** FIN borrow against; ~ **à intérêt** BANQUE borrow at interest; ~ **à long terme** *(ANT emprunter à court terme)* BOURSE borrow long; ~ **sans intérêt** BANQUE borrow interest-free; ~ **sur titres** BOURSE borrow on securities; ~ **à vue** BANQUE borrow at call

emprunteur, -euse *m,f* BANQUE, FIN borrower; ~ **de premier ordre** BANQUE, FIN premier borrower (*BrE*), prime borrower (*AmE*); ~ **public** BANQUE sovereign borrower; ~ **du secteur privé** BANQUE private sector borrower; ~ **très solvable** BANQUE, FIN premier borrower (*BrE*), prime borrower (*AmE*)

emprunts *m pl* BANQUE, FIN borrowed funds; ~ **bancaires** BANQUE borrowing by banks; ~ **et dettes à courte terme** COMPTA, FIN short-term liabilities; ~ **et dettes subordonnés** COMPTA, FIN subordinated liabilities; ~ **étrangers** BANQUE foreign borrowing; ~ **extérieurs** FIN external borrowings; ~ **des municipalités locales** BANQUE municipal notes; ~ **obligatoires convertibles** COMPTA convertible bonds; ~ **portant intérêts**

BANQUE interest-bearing liabilities; **~ de référence** BANQUE qualified borrowing

émulateur *m* INFO emulator; **~ de terminal** INFO terminal emulator

émulation *f* INFO emulation

émuler *vt* COM, INFO emulate

émulsion: **~ de pétrole brut** *f* ENVIR, TRANSP *eau de mer* crude oil emulsion

ENA *abrév (École Nationale d'Administration)* PROT SOC School of Public Management

ENBAMM *abrév (entreprise non-bancaire admise au marché monétaire)* BANQUE, BOURSE nonbank bank, nonbank financial institution

encablure *f Fra* COM *navigation* cable *(US)*

encadrement *m* COM, GESTION, RES HUM management; **~ autoritaire** GESTION, RES HUM authoritarian management; **~ du crédit** BANQUE, ECON, FIN, POL corset *(infrml)*, credit control, credit restriction, credit squeeze

encaissable *adj* BANQUE cashable, encashable; ◆ **~ par anticipation** BOURSE retractable

encaisse *f* BANQUE *disponibilités* till money, COMPTA *sommes, valeurs* cash, ECON till money, FIN *sommes, valeurs* cash; **~ fractionnaire** BANQUE fractional cash reserve, fractional reserve; **~ -or** BANQUE bullion

encaissement *m (*ANT *décaissement)* BANQUE, COMPTA, FIN collection, encashment, inward payment; **~ de comptes clients** COMPTA collection of accounts; **~ des créances** COMPTA, FIN collection; **~ d'un effet** COMPTA collection of a bill; **~ des machines** TRANSP *navigation* engine casing; **~ par anticipation** BOURSE retraction; **~ de primes** ASSUR collection of premiums; **~ d'une traite** COMPTA collection of a bill; **~ d'une tranche de prêt** BANQUE drawdown

encaisser *vt* BANQUE *chèque* cash, BOURSE, COM redeem, FIN *paiement* collect

encaisseur, -euse *m,f* BANQUE bank messenger, bank runner, RES HUM runner; **~ de loyers** IMMOB rent collector

encart *m* MÉDIA insert, inset; **~ broché** MÉDIA *presse, édition* tip-in; **~ dépliant** MÉDIA gatefold; **~ à volets** MÉDIA gatefold

enceinte: **~ des bookmakers** *f jarg* FIN, LOISIRS silver ring *(jarg)*

enchaînement *m* INFO concatenation; **~ arrière** *(*ANT *enchaînement avant)* ECON, IND backward linkage; **~ avant** *(*ANT *enchaînement arrière)* ECON, IND forward linkage

enchère *f* BOURSE tender documents, COM bid, bidding, FIN tender documents, V&M bid, bidding; **~ à la criée** BOURSE open-outcry auction market; **~ décroissante** V&M Dutch auction; **~ hybride** BOURSE hybrid auction; **~ initiale** V&M opening bid; **~ au rabais** V&M Dutch auction; ◆ **faire une ~** BOURSE, COM make a bid

enchérir *vt* COM, V&M bid; **~ sur** COM, FIN, V&M outbid, BOURSE hit the bid

enchérisseur, -euse *m,f* COM bidder

enclavé, e *adj* IMMOB landlocked

enclos: **~ avec habitation** *m* DROIT, IMMOB curtilage

encoder *vt* INFO encode

encollage: **~ du dos des livres** *m* MÉDIA pasting sides

encombrant, e *adj* COM, COMMS, TRANSP bulky

encombré, e *adj* COM encumbered by

encombrement *m* COM, COMMS congestion, INFO *en mémoire* storage requirements, TRANSP congestion, traffic congestion, traffic jam; **~ du marché** COM, ECON glut on the market

encourageant, e *adj* COM encouraging

encouragement *m* COM encouragement, FISC incentive; **~ à l'investissement** BANQUE investment incentive; **~ du personnel** RES HUM staff incentive; **~ à la production** IND, RES HUM production incentive

encourager *vt* COM encourage, promote, *idées nouvelles* buck up *(infrml)*, *soutien, participants* stimulate, ECON stimulate

encourir *vt* COM *dette* incur, *frais* incur; ◆ **~ des dépenses** COM, COMPTA, FIN, FISC incur cost, incur expenses; **~ des dettes** COMPTA, FIN incur debts

encours *m* BANQUE, COMPTA outstanding; **~ de crédit** *m* COMPTA credit outstanding, outstanding credit; **~ de la dette** *m* COMPTA outstanding debt; **~ de pension minimum** *m* FIN minimum pension liability; **~ de prêts** *m pl* BANQUE outstanding loans; **~ des prêts hypothécaires** *m* BANQUE mortgage loans outstanding, outstanding mortgage loans; **~ sous forme d'acceptation** *m* BANQUE acceptance liability

encre *f* ADMIN, INFO toner

endémique *adj* COM endemic

en-dessous: **~ de** *prép (*ANT *au-dessus de, en-dessus de)* COM below

en-dessus: **~ de** *prép (*ANT *au-dessous de, en-dessous de)* COM above

endetté, e *adj* COM, ECON, FIN indebted; **~ envers** COM, ECON, FIN indebted to

endettement *m* COM, ECON, FIN debt; **~ du consommateur** BANQUE, FIN consumer leveraging

endetter: **s'~** *v pron* COM, COMPTA, FIN get into debt

endogénisation: **~ des variables exogènes** *f* ECON endogenizing the exogenous

endommagé: **~ en cours de route** *loc* TRANSP damaged in transit; **~ à l'origine** *loc* IMP/EXP country-damaged

endos *m* BANQUE endorsement, indorsement; **~ conditionnel** BANQUE qualified endorsement, qualified indorsement

endossataire *mf* BANQUE endorsee, indorsee

endossé: **~ par la banque** *loc* BANQUE bank-endorsed, bank-indorsed

endossement *m* BANQUE endorsement, indorsement; **~ en blanc** BOURSE blank endorsement, blank indorsement; **~ de bon nid d'abeilles** ASSUR, BOURSE *annexé au bon de courtier,* FIN honeycomb slip endorsement, honeycomb slip indorsement; **~ de complaisance** BANQUE, FIN accommodation endorsement, accommodation indorsement; **~ conditionnel** FIN conditional endorsement, conditional indorsement; **~ spécial** BANQUE special endorsement, special indorsement

endosser *vt* BANQUE endorse, indorse, COM shoulder, *garantie* endorse, indorse

endosseur *m* BANQUE endorser, endorsor, indorser, indorsor; **~ par complaisance** FIN accommodation maker, accommodation party

endroit: **à l'~ des travaux** *loc* IMP/EXP ex works, EXW

endurance *f* FIN staying power

ENEA *abrév (Autorité européenne de l'énergie nucléaire)* COM ENEA *(European Nuclear Energy Authority)*

énergie *f* ENVIR, IND energy, power; **~ éolienne** ENVIR, IND wind power; **~ hydro-électrique** ENVIR hydroelectric power, IND hydro *(Can),* hydroelectric power; **~ marémotrice** ENVIR, IND tidal power; **~ nouvelle** ENVIR, IND alternative energy; **~ nucléaire** ENVIR, IND nuclear energy; **~ solaire** ENVIR, IND solar power; **~ de substitution** ENVIR, IND alternative energy; **~ thermique** ENVIR, IND thermal energy; **~ des vagues** ENVIR, IND wave power; **~ verte** ENVIR, IND green energy

énergivore *adj* ENVIR, IND wasteful

enfant *m* COM child; **~ à charge** FISC dependent child; **~ déclaré à charge** FISC child claimed; **~ visé par une déduction** FISC child claimed

enfermé: **~ dans les terres** *loc* ENVIR landlocked

enficher *vt* INFO plug in

enfoncer *vt* RES HUM leapfrog *(jarg);* ◆ **~ une porte ouverte** COM state the obvious

enfourchement: **~ d'impôt** *m* FISC tax straddle

enfreindre *vt* BREVETS, DROIT infringe, violate; ◆ **~ la loi** DROIT breach the law, break the law, infringe the law, violate the law

enfuir: **s'~** *v pron* DROIT abscond

engagement *m* ADMIN bond, COM bond, commitment, enrollment *(AmE),* enrolment *(BrE),* engagement, DROIT commitment; **~ d'acheter** BOURSE take-or-pay contract; **~ actuariel** ASSUR actuarial liability; **~ actuel** COMPTA undischarged commitment; **~ antérieur** COM previous engagement; **~ à la baisse** *(ANT engagement à la hausse)* BOURSE bear commitment; **~ en cours** COMPTA outstanding commitment, undischarged commitment; **~ de dépenses** ECON hypothecation; **~ de dette qualifiée** FISC qualifying debt obligation; **~ écrit** DROIT bond; **~ excédentaire** FIN overcommitment; **~ ferme** BOURSE firm commitment; **~ formel** DROIT covenant; **~ de fret** TRANSP booking note; **~ du gabarit** TRANSP out of gage *(AmE),*

out of gauge *(BrE),* OOG; **~ de garantie** BANQUE, BOURSE *actions privilégiées* guarantee agreement; **~ à la hausse** *(ANT engagement à la baisse)* BOURSE bull commitment; **~ hypothécaire** BANQUE, FIN mortgage commitment; **~ d'hypothèque générale** BOURSE G-O bond *(US),* general obligation bond *(US);* **~ d'investissement** COMPTA capital commitment; **~ obligataire moral** BOURSE moral obligation bond; **~ permanent** COM continuing commitment; **~ du personnel** RES HUM staff commitment; **~ personnel de la caution** DROIT bail bond; **~ potentiel** COM potential commitment; **~ de prêt** BANQUE loan commitment; **~ de prise ferme** BOURSE firm commitment, firm commitment underwriting; **~ spécifique** COM specific commitment

engagements: **~ éventuels** *m pl* COMPTA, DROIT, FIN contingent liabilities; **~ excédentaires** *m pl* ASSUR excess liabilities; **~ hors bilan** *m pl* COMPTA, FIN off-balance-sheet commitments; **~ de retraite** *m pl* COMPTA pension liabilities

engager 1. *vt* COM hire, *dépenses* incur, DROIT bind, RES HUM appoint, hire, take on, engage; **2.** *v pron* **s'~ à** COM commit o.s. to; **s'~ dans** COM embark on; ◆ **~ des dépenses** COM, COMPTA, FIN, FISC incur cost, incur expenses; **~ des frais** COM, COMPTA, FIN, FISC incur cost, incur expenses; **~ des poursuites** DROIT take legal action; **~ des poursuites judiciaires** DROIT bring an action, file a lawsuit; **s'~ à faire qch** COM undertake to do sth; **s'~ à payer** COM promise to pay; **s'~ par contrat** DROIT sign a legal agreement; **s'~ par contrat à faire qch** COM contract to do sth

engendre: **qui ~** *loc* COM conducive to

engendrer *vt* COM *croissance* be conducive to, ECON *confiance* breed

engin: **~ moteur** *m* TRANSP *chemin de fer* tractive unit; **~ de sauvetage** *m* TRANSP *navigation* lifesaving apparatus, LSA

englober *vt* COM comprise

engrais *m* ECON *agriculture,* ENVIR fertilizer; **~ azoté** ENVIR nitrogen fertilizer; **~ chimique** ENVIR chemical fertilizer

engrenage *m* TRANSP gears, GRS; **~ épicycloïdal** TRANSP planetary gear; **~ planétaire** TRANSP planetary gear

enjeu *m* COM, FIN stake; ◆ **l'~ est très important** COM the stakes are high

enlevé: **~ par la mer** *loc* TRANSP washed overboard, wob

enlèvement *m* COM removal; **~ de l'excédent** FISC surplus stripping; **~ par route** TRANSP collection on wheels, COW

enlever *vt* COM remove; ◆ **à ~ à bord** IMP/EXP ExS, ex ship, x-ship

enliser: **s'~ dans** *v pron* COM get bogged down in

ennemis: **~ de la Couronne** *m pl* DROIT King's enemies *(UK),* Queen's enemies *(UK);* **~ de la Reine** *m pl (SYN ennemis du Roi)* DROIT Queen's enemies (*UK*); **~ du Roi** *m pl* (SYN *ennemis de la Reine*) DROIT King's enemies (*UK*)

ennui *m* COM trouble; ◆ **avoir des ~s** COM be in trouble; **avoir des ~s avec l'administration fiscale** FISC run foul of the tax authorities; **avoir des ~s avec le fisc** FISC fall foul of the tax authorities

énoncé *m* COM statement; **~ des clauses et conditions** RES HUM statement of terms and conditions; **~ des objectifs** GESTION statement of objectives

énorme *adj* COM mammoth

enquête *f* COM fact-finding mission, investigation, DROIT fact-finding mission, inquiry, investigation, FISC inquiry, IMMOB survey, V&M research, survey; **~ d'attitude** V&M *étude de marché* attitude survey; **~ auprès des consommateurs** V&M consumer survey; **~ auprès des lecteurs** V&M readership survey; **~ autonome** DROIT independent inquiry; **~ d'autorisation** COM, DROIT licensing examination; **~ exhaustive** FISC full-scale investigation; **~ indépendante** DROIT independent inquiry; **~ de marché** COM, V&M survey; **~ de motivations** V&M motivational research; **~ d'opinion** V&M attitude survey, opinion survey; **~ par échantillonnage** DROIT judgment sample; **~ par sondage** V&M *étude de marché* sample survey; **~ permanente** V&M continuous survey; **~ préliminaire** DROIT preliminary investigation; **~ sans mandat** POL warrantless investigation (*jarg*); **~ sur les antécédents** RES HUM background investigation; **~ sur les dépenses de consommation** COMPTA, ECON consumer expenditure survey (*US*); **~ sur les dépenses publiques** ECON public expenditure survey; **~ sur les occupations journalières** ECON, RES HUM time budget survey; **~ sur des produits industriels** V&M industrial research; **~ sur le terrain** V&M *étude de marché* field survey; **~ tous azimuts** COMPTA, FIN across-the-board investigation (*UK*); ◆ **faire une ~** COM make enquiries; **faire une ~ au sujet de** COM vet

enquêter *vt* COM, DROIT investigate, V&M conduct a survey; **~ sur** COM make investigations into, DROIT *crime* investigate

enquêteur, -euse ou -trice *m,f* RES HUM investigation officer, V&M *étude de marché* field investigator, interviewer; **~ sur le terrain** V&M *étude de marché* field worker

enrayer *vt* ECON *inflation* stamp out

enregistré, e *adj* COM on tape; ◆ **à l'avance** MÉDIA prerecorded; **~ sur les livres** COM, COMPTA in the books

enregistrement *m* ADMIN register of companies, registration, registry, BOURSE incorporation, BREVETS registration, COM booking, recording, COMMS recording, tape recording, DROIT registration, INFO record; **~ des archives** INFO archival storage; **~ de commande** V&M order entry; **~ d'émissions de titres à date indéterminée** BOURSE shelf registration (*US*); **~ d'un fonds d'information** BANQUE jogging (*jarg*);

~ international BREVETS international registration; **~ net** FIN net register; **~ quotidien des transactions** BOURSE street book (*jarg*); **~ de société** BOURSE incorporation; **~ témoin** MÉDIA *radio, télévision* air check, air check tape; **~ témoin d'une émission** MÉDIA *radio, télévision* air check, air check tape

enregistrements: **~ des coûts** *m pl* BOURSE cost records (*UK*)

enregistrer *vt* BOURSE *légère hausse* add, COM record, *gains* account for, announce, COMMS record, tape-record, DROIT register, FIN carry, LOISIRS *à l'aéroport*, TRANSP *à l'aéroport* check in; ◆ **un bénéfice** COMPTA show a surplus; **faire ~** COM register; **~ des gains sur** FIN gain entry to; **~ une hausse** BOURSE *à la Bourse* register a high; **~ une perte** COMPTA, FIN carry a loss; **~ une perte de** COMPTA, FIN show a loss of; **~ une provision contre** COMPTA write off; **~ sur bande vidéo** COMMS videotape

enregistreur: **~ à tambour** *m* INFO drum plotter

enrichi, e *adj* INFO enhanced

enrichir: **s'~** *v pron* COM get rich

enrichissement *m* COM *des tâches* enrichment; **~ des emplois** RES HUM job enrichment

ensachage *m* IND, TRANSP *des marchandises* bagging

enseigne *f* COM, V&M trade sign; **~ lumineuse** COM, V&M neon sign

enseignement *m* PROT SOC education; **~ alterné** PROT SOC cooperative education (*US*); **~ assisté par ordinateur** (*EAO*) INFO, PROT SOC computer-aided instruction (*CAI*), computer-aided learning (*CAL*), computer-aided teaching (*CAT*), computer-assisted instruction (*CAI*), computer-assisted learning (*CAL*), computer-assisted teaching (*CAT*), computer-based training (*CBT*); **~ de l'hygiène** PROT SOC health education; **~ programmé** PROT SOC programmed instruction, programmed learning; **~ secondaire** PROT SOC secondary education; **~ supérieur** PROT SOC advanced education, tertiary education, higher education

ensemble[1] *adv* FISC jointly

ensemble[2] *m* COM complex, ECON aggregate, *de réformes* package, pkg, FIN, GESTION package, pkg, IMMOB complex, INFO *de données* set, MATH aggregate, set, POL package, pkg; **~ des attributions** GESTION role set; **~ de biens mobiliers** FISC set of chattels; **~ de données** INFO data set; **~ d'états financiers** COMPTA set of accounts; **~ des informations** MÉDIA coverage; **~ de marchandises** TRANSP cargo mix, commodity mix; **~ de produits** V&M product mix; **~ de produits financiers** FIN financial package; **~ des risques** FIN risk package; **~ des salaires versés** RES HUM total payroll

ensuite *adv* COM afterwards

entamer *vt* COM *fonds* eat into, *projet* embark on, *réserves* draw, FIN raid; ◆ **~ des poursuites** DROIT take legal action; ~ **une procédure contre qn** DROIT bring a lawsuit against sb

entendre 1. *vt* COM *comprendre* understand; **2.** *v pron* COM concur; ♦ **s'~** DROIT; **s'~ avec qn** COM have an understanding with sb

entente *f* COM compact, understanding; ~ **d'éche-lonnement du traitement** RES HUM salary deferral arrangement; ~ **illicite entre enchérisseurs** FIN, V&M *vente aux enchères* knockout, knockout agreement; ~ **illicite en matière de prix** COM common pricing; ~ **illicite sur les prix** DROIT, FIN, V&M price-fixing; ~ **sur les prix** ECON pricing arrangement

ententes *f pl* DROIT *commercial* restrictive practices

entérinement *m* DROIT *d'une décision* confirmation

entériner *vt* DROIT confirm

enterrer *vt* RES HUM remit

en-tête *m* ADMIN header, heading, COMMS caption, INFO header, header-block, heading, MÉDIA head-er, heading

entier[1], **-ère** *adj* COM complete

entier:[2] ~ **naturel** *m* INFO, MATH natural number

entièrement *adv* COM completely; ♦ ~ **à charge** FISC wholly dependent; ~ **distribué** BOURSE fully distributed; ~ **et exclusivement** DROIT wholly and exclusively; ~ **expertisé** BOURSE fully valued; ~ **réservé** COM booked up

entité *f* DROIT entity; ~ **constituée** FISC corporate entity; ~ **juridique** BREVETS, DROIT legal entity; ~ **soumise à l'audit** COMPTA, FIN auditee

entraide: ~ **entre politiciens** *f* POL logrolling (*US*)

entraîné: ~ **par ergots** *adj* INFO tractor-fed; ~ **par picots** *adj* INFO tractor-fed

entraînement: ~ **d'embrayage** *m* TRANSP *naviga-tion* clutch drive, CD; ~ **par ergots** *m* INFO tractor feed; ~ **par friction** *m* INFO friction feed; ~ **par picots** *m* INFO tractor feed; ~ **à la prise de parole** *m* PROT SOC, RES HUM assertiveness training

entraîner *vt* COM result in, *frais* involve

entrave *f* ADMIN hindrance, COM, COMPTA, DROIT, RES HUM constraint; ~ **au commerce** COM, ECON, IMP/EXP, POL barrier to trade; ~ **à la liberté du commerce** ECON restraint of trade; ~ **technique au commerce** ECON technical barrier to trade

entraver *vt* COM block, obstruct, DROIT *contrat* interfere with

entraves: ~ **au commerce** *f pl* DROIT *juridique* restrictive practices

entre:[1] ~ **-temps** *adv* COM in the interim

entre:[2] ~ **autres** *loc* COM inter alia (*frml*); ~ **états** *loc* COM *commerce* interstate (*US*); ~ **eux** *loc* COM inter se (*frml*); ~ **les mains de** *loc* COM in the hands of; ~ **les personnes présentes** *loc* COM inter praesentes (*frml*); ~ **vifs** *loc* DROIT inter vivos (*frml*)

entrée *f* ADMIN entry, BANQUE (ANT *sortie*) *de fonds* inflow, BOURSE entry, COM admission, entrance, ingress, input, COM (ANT *sortie*) COMPTA (ANT *sortie*) ECON (ANT *sortie*) FIN (ANT *sortie*) *de fonds* inflow, INFO (ANT *sortie*) input, LOISIRS gate, TRANSP (ANT *sortie*) entrance; ~ **de caisse** FIN cash collection; ~ **de capitaux** ECON, FIN capital inflow; ~ **directe commerçant** IMP/EXP direct trader input, DTI; ~ **de données** INFO data input; ~ **de l'entrepôt des douanes** ADMIN home use entry; ~ **en fonction** COM taking up office; ~ **des fournisseurs** COM trade entrance; ~ **de l'ordinateur** INFO computer input; ~ **du port** IMP/EXP, TRANSP port access; ~ **en possession anticipée** DROIT, IMMOB acceleration; ~ **de service** COM tradesman's entrance; ~ **en vigueur** DROIT entry into force; ♦ ~ **gratuite** LOISIRS admission-free; ~ **interdite** COM, DROIT no admit-tance, no trespassing; ~ **libre** LOISIRS *théâtre* admission-free, V&M no obligation to buy

entrée/sortie *f* (*E/S*) INFO input/output (*I/O*)

entremise *f vieilli* COM agency; ♦ **par l'~ de** COM through the agency of

entrepont *m* TRANSP *navigation* 'tween deck, 'tween deck space, TWD

entreposage *m* COM, IND, TRANSP storage, ware-housing; ~ **frigorifique** TRANSP cold storage; ~ **en vrac** COM bulk storage

entreposer *vt* TRANSP store

entrepôt *m* COM storehouse, IMP/EXP warehouse, whse, TRANSP godown (*infrml*), warehouse, whse; ~ **de céréales** TRANSP granary; ~ **des domaines** IMP/EXP King's warehouse; ~ **en douane** COM bond store, bonded warehouse, FISC, IMP/EXP bonded warehouse; ~ **des douanes** ADMIN approved place; ~ **frigorifique** COM cold storage plant, refrigerated warehouse, TRANSP *navigation* cold store; ~ **de fruits** TRANSP fruit terminal; ~ **des marchandises** COM, TRANSP goods depot; ~ **de marchandises dangereuses** TRANSP danger-ous cargo compound; ~ **public** ADMIN approved place; ~ **de réception** TRANSP reception depot; ~ **de vente au détail** V&M retail warehouse; ~ **à vin** IMP/EXP wine warehouse; ♦ **à prendre en ~** COM x-warehouse; **en ~ sous douane** FISC, IMP/EXP in bond, IB

entreprenant, e *adj* COM enterprising

entreprendre *vt* COM undertake, venture on; ♦ ~ **la production de qch** IND put sth into produc-tion

entrepreneur, -euse *m,f* COM entrepreneur, general contractor, ECON enterpriser, entrepreneur, IMMOB, IND, RES HUM contractor; ~ **général de transports** IND, TRANSP common carrier; ~ **de remorquage** TRANSP towage contractor; ~ **sur mesure** IMMOB custom builder; ~ **de transport combiné** (*ETC*) TRANSP combined transport operator (*CTO*); ~ **de transports** TRANSP com-mon carrier, haulage contractor, hauler (*AmE*), haulier (*BrE*), trucking contractor; ~ **de trans-ports routiers** TRANSP haulage contractor, hauler (*AmE*), haulier (*BrE*), trucking contractor

entrepreneurial *adj* COM, ECON entrepreneurial

entreprise *f* COM business, company, firm, concern, enterprise, undertaking, *projet* undertaking, venture, *société* business, company, concern, firm, ECON company, concern, enterprise, firm, venture, *projet* enterprise, undertaking, venture, *société* business, company, concern, firm, GESTION business venture, commercial venture, *projet* enterprise, undertaking, venture, *société* business, company, concern, firm; **~ absorbante** ECON absorbing company; **~ acquise** ECON acquired company; **~ acquisitrice** ECON absorbing company; **~ agricole** COM, IND farming business; **~ d'assurance** ASSUR insurance business; **~ à but non-lucratif** ECON nonprofit enterprise, NPE; **~ de camionnage** TRANSP carrier, haulage company, haulier (*BrE*), trucking company (*AmE*); **~ cible** COM, V&M target company; **~ cliente** BANQUE corporate client, corporate customer; **~ commerciale** COM, ECON business concern, business corporation, business enterprise, commercial concern, enterprise, trading company, GESTION business venture, commercial venture, trading company, V&M trading company; **~ commerciale risquée** COM, GESTION business venture, commercial venture; **~ compétitive** COM competitive business; **~ concurrentielle** COM competitive business; **~ conjointe** GESTION joint venture, joint-venture company, JV; **~ cyclique** BOURSE cyclical company; **~ dirigée de façon systématisée** COM, GESTION system-managed company; **~ diversifiée** COM, ECON diversified company; **~ dominante** COM, ECON core firm, dominant firm; **~ d'État** ECON state enterprise; **~ étrangère** COM foreign firm; **~ familiale** ECON closed company (*BrE*), closed corporation (*AmE*); **~ financière** FIN financial enterprise; **~ flexible** ECON flexible firm; **~ fortement endettée** COMPTA leveraged company; **~ de gros** COM bulk business; **~ habituelle** FISC ordinary business; **~ à haut risque** COM high-risk venture; **~ illimitée** COM unlimited company; **~ individuelle** COM individual firm, proprietorship, sole proprietorship, sole proprietor, sole trader, IMMOB proprietorship, sole proprietorship; **~ industrielle lourde** IND heavy industrial plant; **~ internationale** GESTION cross-border joint venture; **~ d'investissement** BOURSE, FIN investment firm; **~ d'investissement reconnues de pays tiers** FIN recognized third-world investment firm; **~ leader** COM market leader; **~ leader pour les coûts** ECON cost leader; **~ locale** COM, FIN local firm; **~ marginale** ECON marginal firm; **~ de messageries** COMMS courier firm; **~ à monopole syndical** IND, RES HUM preferential shop; **~ multinationale** COM, ECON, IND multinational enterprise, MNE; **~ nationale** COM, ECON domestic corporation; **~ non-admissible** COM, FISC nonqualifying business; **~ non-bancaire admise au marché monétaire** *(ENBAMM)* BANQUE, BOURSE nonbank bank, nonbank financial institution; **~ non-constituée en société** COM unincorporated business; **~ optimum** ECON optimum firm; **~ en participation** BOURSE joint venture, joint-venture company, JV; **~ périphérique** ECON periphery firm; **~ à préférence syndicale** RES HUM preferential shop; **~ de premier ordre** BOURSE blue-chip company; **~ de prestation de services personnels** FISC personal services business; **~ principale** COM principal business; **~ privée** *(ANT entreprise publique)* ECON private enterprise; **~ à propriétaire unique** COM, IMMOB proprietorship, sole proprietorship; **~ prospère** COM going concern; **~ publique** *(ANT entreprise privée)* ECON public enterprise, publicly owned company, state enterprise; **~ qui marche bien** COM active business; **~ réglementée** ECON regulated firm; **~ rentable non-imposable** COM, FISC nontaxable profitable firm; **~ réputée** COM big name; **~ risquée** COM wildcat venture; **~ sans but lucratif** COM non-profit-making organization (*BrE*), nonprofit organization (*AmE*); **~ du secteur privé** COM, ECON private sector enterprise; **~ du secteur public** ECON public sector enterprise; **~ de services** COM service enterprise; **~ de services bancaires auxiliaires** BANQUE, FIN auxiliary banking services undertaking; **~ sous contrôle étranger** COM foreign-controlled enterprise; **~ soutenue par l'État** FIN government-sponsored enterprise, GSE; **~ au stade du développement** ECON, POL development stage enterprise; **~ transnationale** COM, ECON, POL transnational corporation, TNC; **~ de transport** TRANSP haulage company, haulier (*BrE*), transport company, trucking company (*AmE*); **~ de transport public** IND common carrier; **~ de transports routiers** TRANSP carrier, haulage company, haulier (*BrE*), trucking company (*AmE*); **~ de travaux sur commandes** RES HUM job shop; **~ unipersonnelle** COM sole proprietor, sole trader; **~ de vente par correspondance** V&M mail-order business; ♦ **d'~ à entreprise** COM, V&M business-to-business

entreprises: **~ à la marge** *f* ECON competitive fringe; **~ marginales** *f* ECON competitive fringe

entrer *vt* INFO *données* enter, input, *données, texte* key, key in; ♦ **~ en contact avec** COM come into contact with; **~ dans le champ d'application de** DROIT fall within the scope of; **~ dans le cours** BOURSE move into the money; **~ dans les détails** COM get down to specifics; **faire ~** COM admit; **faire ~ qn** COM show sb in; **~ en guerre** COM go to war; **~ en jeu** COM come into play; **~ en ligne de compte** COM be a factor; **~ en liquidation** DROIT, FIN liquidate; **~ en récession** ECON enter recession; **~ en relation avec** COM come into contact with; **~ sans autorisation dans une propriété privée** DROIT trespass on private property; **~ en service** IND *pétrolière* come on stream; **~ en vigueur** COM come into force, DROIT come into force, come into operation, come into effect, take effect, *loi* enter into force; **~ en vigueur à partir de** COM take effect from

entretenir *vt* ADMIN *bureau* maintain, COM *confiance* sustain, COMMS *relations, correspondance* maintain, ECON *inflation* fuel; ♦ ~ **des relations commerciales à l'intérieur du Commonwealth** COM trade within the Commonwealth

entretien *m* COM *matériel, bâtiments,* DROIT *de la famille,* IND maintenance, INFO servicing, RES HUM interview; ~ **différé** IMMOB *estimation* deferred maintenance; ~ **de l'équipement** COM, IND plant maintenance; ~ **d'évaluation** RES HUM performance appraisal interview, PAI; ~ **de gestion du stress** RES HUM stress interview; ~ **informel** MÉDIA, RES HUM informal interview, unstructured interview; ~ **préventif** ADMIN, COM, GESTION, IND preventative maintenance, preventive maintenance; ~ **prévu par le contrat** COM contract maintenance; ~ **productif** ADMIN, IND productive maintenance; ~ **en profondeur** V&M depth interview; ~ **de reconversion** RES HUM redundancy consultation; ~ **de réorientation de carrière** RES HUM redundancy consultation; ~ **de routine** COM routine maintenance; ~ **sporadique** COM sporadic maintenance; ~ **systématique** ADMIN planning maintenance; ~ **total de l'équipement** COM, IND total plant maintenance; ♦ **faire passer un** ~ **à** RES HUM interview; ~**, réparation et révision** TRANSP maintenance, repair and overhaul, MRO

entretoise *f* TRANSP spacer

entrevue *f* RES HUM interview; ~ **de départ** RES HUM exit interview; ~ **structurée** RES HUM structured interview

énumération *f* COM enumeration

énumérer *vt* COM enumerate

envahir *vt* COM swamp

enveloppe *f* ADMIN, COMMS envelope, RES HUM *argent* envelope, pay check (*AmE*), pay packet (*BrE*); ~ **adhésive** ADMIN adhesive envelope; ~ **affranchie** COM, COMMS s.a.e (*BrE*), s.a.s.e. (*AmE*), self-addressed stamped envelope (*AmE*), stamped addressed envelope (*BrE*); ~ **autocollante** ADMIN adhesive envelope; ~ **budgétaire pluriannuelle** FIN multiyear resource envelope; ~ **de défense** FIN defence envelope (*BrE*), defense envelope (*AmE*); ~ **de dépenses directes** FIN direct spending envelope; ~ **de la dette publique** FIN public debt envelope; ~ **de développement social** POL social development envelope; ~ **à fenêtre** ADMIN, COM, COMMS panel envelope, window envelope; ~ **globale** ADMIN block grant (*UK*); ~ **pluriannuelle de dépenses** FIN multiyear spending envelope; ~ **rembourrée** COMMS jiffy bag®; ~ **-réponse** COM, COMMS business reply envelope, BRE; ~ **des services de l'État** ADMIN services-to-government envelope; ~ **timbrée à vos nom et adresse** COM, COMMS s.a.e (*BrE*), s.a.s.e. (*AmE*), self-addressed stamped envelope (*AmE*), stamped addressed envelope (*BrE*); ~ **à vos nom et adresse** COMMS self-addressed envelope

envergure *f* ECON *d'une économie, d'une entreprise* size, RES HUM caliber (*AmE*), calibre (*BrE*)

Envireg *m* ENVIR Envireg

environ[1] *adv* COM approx., approximately, in the region of

environ[2] *prép* COM *prix, quantité* about, around

environnement *m* ENVIR, INFO environment; ~ **de l'entreprise** COM, ECON, POL business environment; ~ **fiscal** FISC tax environment; ~ **du marché** V&M market environment; ~ **professionnel** RES HUM working environment; ~ **professionnel agréable** RES HUM pleasant working environment; ~ **stabilisé** ENVIR controlled atmosphere, CA

environnementalisme *m* ENVIR environmentalism

environs *m pl* COM surroundings

envisager *vt* COM envisage, envision; ♦ ~ **la situation sous un jour pessimiste** COM take a gloomy view of the situation

envoi *m* TRANSP cnmt, consgt, consignation, consignment, shipment; ~ **avec avis de réception** COMMS recorded delivery; ~ **de détail** TRANSP less than carload, part load, LCL; ~ **d'échantillons** COMMS sample mailing; ~ **de fonds** BANQUE remittance; ~ **de marchandises d'exposition** IMP/EXP exhibition forwarding; ~ **mixte** TRANSP mixed consignment; ~ **en nombre** COMMS bulk mail, INFO bus mailing; ~ **en nombre par avion** COMMS bulk air mail, BAM; ~ **par la poste** INFO, V&M mailing; ~ **par télécopie** ADMIN, COMMS facsimile transaction; ~ **de prospectus** COMMS mailing shot; ~ **publicitaire par le mailing** COMMS mailing shot; ~ **publicitaire par la poste** COMMS mailing shot, V&M mailing; ~ **recommandé** COMMS certified mail (*AmE*), certified post (*BrE*), registered mail, registered post (*BrE*)

envol: ~ **de courte durée** *m* BOURSE bulge

envolée: ~ **du marché** *f* BOURSE bulge

envoyé, e *m,f* MÉDIA correspondent; ~ **permanent à l'étranger** MÉDIA *presse, radio, télévision* foreign correspondent; ~ **spécial** MÉDIA on-the-spot reporter, special correspondent

envoyer *vt* COMMS *par la poste* mail (*AmE*), post (*BrE*), INFO send, TRANSP consign; ♦ ~ **avant la date limite** COM send in; ~ **une déclaration d'impôts** FISC file a tax return; ~ **par fax** ADMIN, COMMS *document, contrat* fax, send by fax; ~ **par la poste** COMMS mail, post (*BrE*), send by mail (*AmE*), send by post (*BrE*); ~ **par télécopie** ADMIN, COMMS *document, contrat* fax, send by fax; ~ **promener qn** *infrml* COM give a dusty answer (*infrml*), give sb a dusty response (*infrml*); ~ **qch par colis postal** COMMS send sth by parcel post; ~ **qch par l'intermédiaire d'un agent** COM send sth via an agent; ~ **qch en recommandé** COMMS send sth by certified mail (*AmE*), send sth by registered post (*BrE*); ~ **qn chercher qch** COM send sb for sth; ~ **qn sur les roses** *infrml* COM give a dusty answer (*infrml*), give sb a dusty response (*infrml*); ~ **sous pli**

discret COMMS send under plain cover; ~ **à temps** COM send in

e. à p *abrév (effet à payer)* COMPTA, FIN bill payable, note payable

épargnant, e *m,f* FIN investor, retail investor, saver

épargne *f* BANQUE, COMPTA savings, thrift (*US*); ~ **brute** FIN gross savings; ~ **contractuelle** FIN contractual savings; ~ **des entreprises** FIN corporate savings; ~ **forcée** ECON, FIN forced savings; ~ **liquide** FIN liquid savings; ~ **mensuelle** RES HUM monthly savings; ~ **nationale** BOURSE ≈ National Savings (*UK*); ~ **négative** FIN negative saving; ~ **obligatoire** FIN compulsory saving (*UK*); ~ **des particuliers** BANQUE personal savings; ~ **de précaution** ECON precautionary saving; ~ **d'une vie** BANQUE life savings

épargner *vt* BANQUE save

épauler *vt* COM back up

épave *f* TRANSP *maritime* wreck; ~ **flottante** TRANSP *maritime* flotsam; ~ **marquée par une bouée** TRANSP *navigation* lagan; ~ **rejetée** TRANSP *maritime* jetsam

épaves *f pl* ASSUR stranded goods

éphéméralisation *f jarg* ECON ephemeralization (*jarg*)

éphémère *adj* COM short-lived

épontille *f* TRANSP *navigation* prop, stanchion

époque *f* COM, ECON period

épouse *f* DROIT spouse, wife; ~ **séparée** DROIT estranged spouse; ◆ **et** ~ DROIT et ux (*frml*)

époutiage *m* TRANSP pickings

époux *m* DROIT husband, spouse; ~ **divorcé** DROIT divorced spouse; ~ **séparé** DROIT estranged spouse

épreuve *f* INFO hard copy, MÉDIA proof; ~ **de force** COM showdown, tug-of-war; ~ **à la pierre de touche** COM acid test; ~ **en placard** MÉDIA galley; ~ **sur papier couché** V&M *publicité* art pull; ~ **de vérité** COM acid test

EPROM *abrév (mémoire morte programmable électroniquement)* INFO EPROM (*electronically programmable read only memory*)

épuisé, e *adj* COM, ECON o.s., out of stock, MÉDIA out of print, OP, V&M o.s., out of stock; ◆ **être** ~ FIN run out

épuisement *m* ECON depletion, FISC burnout, depletion, RES HUM burnout; ~ **accumulé** COMPTA accumulated depletion; ~ **gagné** FISC earned depletion

épuiser *vt* COM exhaust; ◆ **s'**~ COM run low, run out, RES HUM burn out

épuration *f* ENVIR purification, removal, IND *des eaux* purification, *des matières huileuses dans des séparateurs* removal

Équateur *m* COM Ecuador

équation *f* COM, MATH equation; ~ **comptable** COMPTA accounting equation; ~ **de différence** ECON *économétrie* difference equation; ~ **de**

forme réduite ECON reduced form equation; ~ **de Slutsky** ECON Slutsky equation

équatorien, -enne *adj* COM Ecuadorian

Équatorien, -enne *m,f* COM *habitant* Ecuadoran, Ecuadorian

équilibre *m* COM *compte* balance, ECON equilibrium; ~ **autarcique** ECON no-trade equilibrium; ~ **de la balance des paiements** ECON, POL balance of payments equilibrium, external balance; ~ **des consommateurs** ECON consumer equilibrium; ~ **fondamental** ECON fundamental equilibrium; ~ **des forces** POL balance of power; ~ **général** ECON general equilibrium, GE; ~ **général du marché** ECON general market equilibrium; ~ **interne** ECON, POL internal balance; ~ **keynésien** ECON Keynesian equilibrium; ~ **du marché** ECON market equilibrium; ~ **partiel** ECON partial equilibrium; ~ **permanent** ECON steady-state equilibrium; ~ **planétaire** ENVIR global balance; ~ **de portefeuille** FIN portfolio balance; ~ **des pouvoirs** POL balance of power; ~ **des recettes et des dépenses** FIN equalization of revenue and expenditure; ~ **stable** ECON stable equilibrium; ~ **temporaire** ECON temporary equilibrium; ~ **à toute épreuve** ECON strong equilibrium

équilibré, e *adj* COM well-balanced; ◆ **être** ~ COMPTA balance, TRANSP be in trim

équilibrer 1. *vt* COM, COMPTA balance, FIN balance, *coûts, bénéfices* average out; **2.** *v pron* **s'**~ COMPTA balance; ◆ ~ **les comptes** FIN agree the accounts

équipage *m* TRANSP crew; ~ **d'un avion** LOISIRS, TRANSP aircrew; ~ **multinational** TRANSP *d'un navire* multinational crew

équipe[1] *f* GESTION team, RES HUM alternating shift, team; ~ **d'audit** COMPTA, FIN audit group, audit team; ~ **de chercheurs** V&M research team; ~ **de contrôle** COMPTA, FIN audit group, audit team; ~ **de débardeurs** RES HUM, TRANSP stevedoring gang; ~ **dédoublée** RES HUM split shift; ~ **de direction** GESTION, RES HUM management team; ~ **de dockers** RES HUM, TRANSP stevedoring gang; ~ **d'entretien** IND, RES HUM maintenance crew; ~ **d'experts** POL tiger team (*US, jarg*); ~ **à horaires adaptables** RES HUM gliding shift (*jarg*), gliding time (*jarg*); ~ **de jour** RES HUM day shift; ~ **de nuit** RES HUM graveyard shift (*AmE*), night shift, twilight shift (*BrE*); ~ **opérationnelle** COM operational staff; ~ **de rédaction** MÉDIA editorial staff; ~ **au sol** TRANSP ground crew; ~ **suppléante** RES HUM relief shift; ~ **tournante** RES HUM relief shift, swing shift; ~ **de travail à long terme** PROT SOC long-term team; ~ **de travail posté** RES HUM rotating shift; ~ **de vente** V&M sales force; ~ **de vérification** COMPTA, FIN audit group, audit team; ◆ ~ **de vérité** POL truth squad (*infrml*); ◆ ~ **chargée d'un nouveau produit** V&M venture team

équipé[2] ~ **d'une pile auxiliaire** *loc* INFO battery-backed; ~ **d'une pile de secours** *loc* INFO battery-backed

équipement *m* COM accessories, equipment, IND

equipment, plant, INFO equipment, hardware; ~ **agricole** ECON farm equipment; ~ **de bureau** ADMIN, COM office equipment; ~ **terminal de traitement de données** *(ETTD)* INFO data terminal equipment *(DTE)*; ~ **de termination de circuit de données** INFO circuit terminating equipment, data communications equipment, DCE; ~ **pour tests** INFO test equipment

équipements: ~ **collectifs** *m pl* PROT SOC public amenities

équiper *vt* COM fit out

équipier, -ère *m,f* GESTION, RES HUM team player

équitable *adj* COM, DROIT equitable, fair

équité *f* DROIT, FIN, IMMOB equity; ~ **fiscale** FISC tax fairness; ~ **horizontale** *(ANT équité verticale)* ECON, FISC horizontal equity; ~ **verticale** *(ANT équité horizontale)* ECON, FISC vertical equity

équivalence *f* COM, IMP/EXP equivalence; ~ **des charges fiscales** FISC commensurate taxation; ~ **par anticipation** IMP/EXP anticipation equivalence; ~ **de rendement** BOURSE yield equivalence; ~ **de valeur** V&M cash equivalence

équivalent[1]**, e** *adj* COM equivalent; ◆ **à peu près ~** COM roughly equivalent; **être ~ à** COM correspond to, correspond with

équivalent:[2] ~ **en actions ordinaires** *m* BOURSE common shares equivalent *(BrE)*, common stock equivalent *(AmE)*; ~ **clavier** *m* INFO keyboard equivalent; ~ **d'un conteneur de vingt pieds** *m* TRANSP twenty foot equivalent unit, TEU; ~ **de trésorerie** *m* FIN cash equivalent; ~ **vingt pieds** *m (EVP)* TRANSP twenty foot equivalent unit *(TEU)*

e. à r *abrév (effet à recevoir)* COMPTA, FIN bill receivable, note receivable

ère: l'~ **de l'informatique** *f* INFO computer age; l'~ **de l'ordinateur** *f* INFO computer age

Erevan *n pr* COM Yerevan

ergonome *m* COM, RES HUM ergonomist

ergonomie *f* ADMIN, COM, INFO, RES HUM ergonomics, human engineering; ~ **cognitive** ADMIN cognitive ergonomics; ~ **de l'information** ADMIN cognitive ergonomics

ergonomique *adj* ADMIN, COM, INFO, RES HUM ergonomic

ergophobie *f* COM, RES HUM ergophobia

ériger *vt* COM erect

érosion *f* BOURSE, ECON, ENVIR erosion; ~ **fiscale** ECON, FISC tax erosion; ~ **du sol** ENVIR soil erosion

erratum *m* COM erratum

erreur *f* COM, DROIT error, mistake, INFO bug, error, fault, MATH error; ~ **acceptable** COM permissible error; ~ **aléatoire** MATH random error; ~ **d'arrondi** MATH rounding error; ~ **bilatérale** COM bilateral mistake; ~ **bloquante** INFO fatal error; ~ **de calcul** INFO computational error; ~ **de classement** INFO sequence error; ~ **de compensation** COMPTA compensating error; ~ **de comptabilisation** COMPTA posting error; ~ **comptable** COMPTA, FIN account-

ing error; ~ **de date d'échéance** BANQUE, BOURSE, ECON, FIN maturity mismatch; ~ **de droit** DROIT error of law, mistake of law; ~ **d'échantillon** MATH sampling error; ~ **d'échantillonnage** MATH sampling error; ~ **d'écriture** ADMIN clerical error, COMPTA clerical error, posting error; ~ **fatale** INFO fatal error; ~ **intermittente** INFO soft error; ~ **d'inversion** COM transposition error; ~ **judiciaire** DROIT miscarriage of justice; ~ **judiciaire flagrante** DROIT gross miscarriage of justice; ~ **matérielle** INFO hard error; ~ **probable** MATH probable error; ~ **de programmation** INFO coding error, miscoding, program bug; ~ **récurrente** INFO hard error; ~ **relative** INFO relative error; ~ **résiduelle** ECON residual error; ~ **sur les faits** COM factual error; ~ **temporaire** INFO soft error; ~ **type** MATH standard error; ~ **type d'estimation** MATH standard error of estimate; ~ **de type I** ECON, MATH type-I error; ~ **de type II** ECON, MATH type-II error; ~ **type de moyenne** MATH standard error of the mean; ◆ **faire une ~** COM make an error

erreurs: ~ **et omissions** *f pl* ECON errors and omissions

erroné, e *adj* COM erroneous, mistaken, wrong

E/S *abrév (entrée/sortie)* INFO I/O *(input/output)*

esc. *abrév (escompte)* COM disc. *(discount)*

ESC *abrév (escudo)* COM *Portugal* ESC *(escudo)*

escale *f* TRANSP stopover; ◆ **faire une ~** TRANSP stop over

escalier: ~ **roulant** *m* COM escalator; ~ **de secours** *m* RES HUM fire escape, fire exit

escomptable *adj* BANQUE bankable

escompte *m* BANQUE bank discount, *effets* discount, BOURSE discount, COM discount; ~ **de banque** BANQUE banker's discount; ~ **de caisse** V&M cash discount; ~ **d'effets de commerce** COMPTA discounting of bills *(BrE)*, discounting of notes *(AmE)*; ~ **d'émission d'obligations** BOURSE bond discount; ~ **non-amorti des bons du Trésor** BOURSE unamortized discount on Treasury bills; ~ **non-amorti d'obligations** BOURSE bond discount; ~ **d'obligation non-amorti** BOURSE unamortized bond discount; ~ **de première émission** BOURSE, FIN original issue discount, OID; ~ **sur ventes** V&M sales discount; ◆ **à ~** BOURSE, FIN at a discount, AAD

escompter *vt* BANQUE, BOURSE discount

escorter *vt* COM accompany, escort

escroc *m* COM con artist *(infrml)*, con man *(infrml)*, confidence man, confidence trickster, embezzler, swindler, DROIT crook *(infrml)*, embezzler, FIN embezzler

escroquer *vt* COM short-change, swindle, DROIT defraud

escroquerie *f* COM confidence game, confidence trick, swindle, FIN churning, twisting *(jarg)*, V&M churning; ~ **à l'assurance** ASSUR fraudulent misrepresentation

escudo *m (ESC)* COM *Portugal* escudo *(ESC)*

espace *m* COMMS, INFO *de mémoire*, MÉDIA space;
~ **bureau** ADMIN, COM office accommodation;
~ **disponible** INFO *en mémoire, sur disque* available
space; ~ **disque** INFO disk space; ~ **habitable**
IMMOB floor space; ~ **perdu** TRANSP *arrimage*
broken stowage; ~ **publicitaire** MÉDIA, V&M
advertising space, *radio, télévision* airtime; ~ **de**
travail RES HUM working area, workspace; ~ **de**
vente V&M selling space; ~ **vital** PROT SOC living
space

espacement *m* INFO pitch; ~ **arrière** INFO backspace; ◆ **faire un ~ arrière** INFO backspace

Espagne *f* COM Spain

espagnol¹, **e** *adj* COM Spanish

espagnol² *m* COM *langue* Spanish

Espagnol, e *m,f* COM *habitant* Spaniard

Espagnols: les ~ *m pl* COM *habitant* the Spanish

espar: ~ vertical *m* TRANSP *navigation* vertical spar

espèce: ~ menacée *f* ENVIR endangered species;
~ **en voie d'extinction** *f* ENVIR endangered species

espèces *f pl* COM *paiement* specie, ECON hard cash,
FIN hard cash, *argent, monnaie* cash; ◆ **en ~** COM
paiement in specie

espérance: ~ mathématique *f* ASSUR actuarial
expectation; ~ **moyenne de vie** *f* ASSUR average
duration of life; ~ **de vie** *f* COM life expectancy;
~ **de vie d'un produit** *f* V&M product life expectancy

esperluette *f* COM ampersand

espionnage *m* COM espionage; ~ **industriel** COM,
IND industrial espionage

espoirs: ~ d'adaptations *m pl* ECON adaptive
expectations

esprit: ~ commercial *m* FIN commercialism;
~ **communautaire** *m* COM community spirit;
~ **de corps** *m* COM esprit de corps;
~ **d'entreprise** *m* COM, GESTION entrepreneurial
spirit, entrepreneurship; ~ **d'équipe** *m* GESTION,
RES HUM team spirit

esquisse *f* COM sketch

esquissé, e *adj* COM, DROIT, POL drafted; ◆ **~ dans**
ses grandes lignes POL broad-brush

esquisser *vt* DROIT, POL draft

esquiver *vt* COM sidestep

essai *m* COM test, testing, trial, IND test run, test,
testing, trial, INFO test, V&M test, testing, trial;
~ **de fiabilité** COM reliability test; ~ **filmé** MÉDIA
screen test; ~ **d'hypothèse** MATH *statistique*
hypothesis testing; ~ **en laboratoire** INFO alpha
test; ~ **de marché** V&M market testing; ~ **non-**
destructif IND nondestructive testing; ~ **pilote**
INFO beta test; ~ **de programme** INFO program
testing; ~ **radio** MÉDIA air check, air check tape;
~ **de réception** IND, V&M acceptance test, acceptance trial; ~ **sur route** TRANSP test drive, test run,
trial run; ~ **sur le terrain** V&M field testing; ~ **de**
transport TRANSP *distribution* test transit; ~ **de**
vente V&M market testing; ~ **de vérification des**
performances COM, GESTION, IND, RES HUM

performance testing; ◆ **à l'~** COM on appro
(*infrml*), on approval, MÉDIA at proof stage

essaimage *m* COM outplacement, spin-off, ECON,
FIN spin-off, RES HUM outplacement

essaimer *vt* COM hive off, spin off

essayer *vt* COM test, try out, INFO test, TRANSP test
drive, V&M test, try out

essence *f* ENVIR, IND, TRANSP gas (*AmE*), gasoline
(*AmE*), petrol (*BrE*); ~ **avion** TRANSP aviation
spirit; ~ **blanche** IND white spirit; ~ **industrielle**
IND industrial spirit; ~ **pour moteurs** TRANSP
motor spirit; ~ **sans plomb** ENVIR lead-free petrol
(*BrE*), unleaded gas (*AmE*), unleaded petrol
(*BrE*); ~ **verte** ENVIR green petrol

essentiel¹, **-elle** *adj* COM main

essentiel² *m* COM basics, core, *d'une conversation*
gist; **l'~** COM the bottom line, the essentials

essentiellement *adv* COM primarily

essieu: ~ à denture hélicoïdale *m* TRANSP spiral
bevel axle; ~ **de remorquage** *m* TRANSP towing
dolly (*jarg*); ~ **simple** *m* TRANSP dolly (*jarg*)

essieux: ~ en tandem *m pl* TRANSP tandem axle

essor *m* COM, ECON, IND, POL advancement, boom,
expansion; ~ **Barber** ECON Barber boom (*UK*);
~ **économique** COM, ECON, POL economic
advancement, economic boom

essuyer: ~ un revers *loc* COM suffer a setback

est *m* COM east, E; ◆ **de l'~** COM eastern

estaries: ~ gagnées *f pl* TRANSP *navigation* all
laytime saved, all working time saved, working
time saved; ~ **moyennes** *f pl* TRANSP *navigation*
average laytime

estimateur: ~ de probabilité maximale *m* MATH
maximum likelihood estimator, MLE

estimatif *m* COM cost estimate

estimation *f* COM appraisal, valuation, cost estimate, DROIT assessment, FIN appraisal,
appraisement, estimate, IMMOB assessment, *d'un*
bien immobilier appraisal, valuation, INFO computation, MATH, V&M estimate; ~ **approximative**
COM guesstimate (*infrml*), tentative estimate;
~ **des coûts** COM cost estimate; ~ **d'écart** MATH
interval estimate; ~ **interne** IMMOB in-house
valuation; ~ **au jugé** COM guesstimate (*infrml*),
tentative estimate; ~ **monétaire** FIN money measurement; ~ **au pifomètre** *infrml* COM guesstimate
(*infrml*), tentative estimate; ~ **du prix de revient**
par commande IND job order costing; ~ **du prix**
de revient d'un produit V&M product costing;
~ **prudente** COM safe estimate; ~ **supplémentaire**
FIN, POL supplementary estimate; ~ **de la valeur**
patrimoniale COMPTA net worth assessment;
~ **des ventes** V&M sales estimate; ◆ **faire une**
~ **des besoins futurs** COM make an appraisal of
future needs; **faire une ~ au jugé** COM guesstimate
(*infrml*)

estime: avoir beaucoup d'~ pour qn *loc* COM have a
high regard for sb

estimé *adj* COM valued

estimer *vt* COM appraise, assess, deem, estimate,

FIN appraise, estimate, assess, IMMOB value, INFO compute; ◆ ~ **nécessaire** COM deem necessary; ~ **au pifomètre** *infrml* COM guesstimate (*infrml*); ~ **en reconnaissant une marge d'erreur** COMPTA allow for a margin of error

estompé, e *adj* INFO dimmed

Estonie *f* COM Estonia

estonien[1], **-enne** *adj* COM Estonian

estonien[2] *m* COM *langue* Estonian

Estonien, -enne *m,f* COM *habitant* Estonian

estrope *f* TRANSP strop

estuaire *m* TRANSP *navigation* estuary; ~ **à marée** TRANSP tidal river estuary

établi, e *adj* COM constituted, est., established, *société* based; ◆ ~ **depuis longtemps** COM long-established

établir 1. *vt* BANQUE *compte* make up, COM draw up, *comité* form, *facture* make out, *fait, date* establish, *liste* make out, make up, *prix* ascertain, *record* set, *réputation* build up, *société* establish, DROIT lay down; **2.** *v pron* **s'~** COM *dans un nouvel emploi* settle; ◆ ~ **le bien-fondé d'une demande** DROIT substantiate a claim; ~ **le bien-fondé d'une réclamation** DROIT substantiate a claim; ~ **le bilan** BOURSE find the balance; ~ **un budget** COM, COMPTA, ECON, FIN, POL budget; ~ **un chèque à l'ordre de qn** BANQUE make a check payable to sb (*AmE*), make a cheque payable to sb (*BrE*), make out a cheque to sb (*BrE*), raise a check to sb (*AmE*); ~ **une comptabilité de qch** COMPTA render an accounting for sth; ~ **une cotisation à l'égard d'un contribuable** FISC assess a taxpayer; ~ **une cotisation d'impôt** FISC assess tax; ~ **une créance** COMPTA prove a debt; ~ **une discrimination envers** COM discriminate against; ~ **le dossier de** DROIT brief; ~ **une liaison directe avec** COMMS establish a direct link with; ~ **une liaison entre** MÉDIA link; ~ **un lien avec** COM forge a link with; ~ **des liens avec** COM build links with; ~ **une liste restreinte** COM, RES HUM shortlist; ~ **un nouveau record à la hausse** ECON set a new high; ~ **l'ordre du jour** GESTION draw up the agenda; ~ **le procès-verbal d'une réunion** COM record a meeting; ~ **des quotas** IMP/EXP *d'importations* fix quotas; ~ **des règlements** DROIT make regulations; ~ **la valeur nette de** FIN net

établissement *m* BOURSE *cours* fixing, COM establishment, institution, *d'un rapport* drawing up, IND works, RES HUM establishment; ~ **d'un budget** COMPTA budgeting; ~ **du budget** COMPTA, ECON, FIN budget preparation; ~ **du budget d'investissement** ECON capital budgeting; ~ **de catégorie particulière** BANQUE special-bracket firm; ~ **certifié** FISC certified institution; ~ **commercial** COM commercial establishment, place of business; ~ **à court terme** BOURSE short-termism; ~ **du coût de production** COMPTA costing; ~ **de crédit** BANQUE, FIN credit institution, lending institution; ~ **de crédit de la zone A** FIN Zone A credit institution; ~ **de crédit de la**

zone B FIN Zone B credit institution; ~ **de cure** PROT SOC health farm; ~ **de dossier** COM, GESTION briefing; ~ **éducatif** FISC, PROT SOC educational establishment, educational institution; ~ **d'enseignement** FISC, PROT SOC educational establishment, educational institution; ~ **d'enseignement par correspondance** PROT SOC correspondence school; ~ **d'enseignement technique** PROT SOC ≈ British Technical Education Certificate; ~ **des états financiers** COMPTA compilation; ~ **fixe** DROIT, FISC fixed place of business; ~ **fixe d'affaires** DROIT, FISC fixed place of business; ~ **des frais** BOURSE fixing of costs; ~ **industriel** IND industrial plant; ~ **membre d'une bourse** BOURSE member corporation; ~ **d'une moyenne** COMPTA block averaging; ~ **de la moyenne générale** FISC *du revenu* general averaging; ~ **de la moyenne du revenu** FISC income averaging; ~ **national** COM state school; ~ **non-bancaire admis au marché monétaire** BANQUE, BOURSE nonbank bank, nonbank financial institution; ~ **non-membre** BOURSE nonmember firm; ~ **de normes comptables** COMPTA accounting standard setting; ~ **d'objectifs** COM goal setting, target setting, V&M target setting; ~ **des plannings** COM planning; ~ **principal** COM, COMPTA chief place of business, principal place of business; ~ **des prix** BOURSE fixing of costs, COM, ECON, V&M price determination, pricing; ~ **des prix de cession** FIN transfer pricing; ~ **des prix de revient** COMPTA costing; ~ **des prix à terme** BOURSE forward pricing; ~ **public** ADMIN departmental corporation, public body, COM public body, public corporation (*UK*), FISC public corporation (*UK*); ~ **de réseaux** BANQUE networking; ~ **responsable de l'émission** BOURSE issuing house; ~ **scolaire** FISC, PROT SOC educational establishment, educational institution

étain *m* IND tin

étalage *m* COM, V&M display, window display

étale: ~ **de courant** *m* TRANSP *navigation* slack water; ~ **du flot** *m* TRANSP *navigation* slack water

étalement *m* BOURSE spread trading, FISC *du revenu* forward averaging, RES HUM spreadover (*jarg*); ~ **interlivraison** BOURSE *change à terme* interdelivery spread; ~ **des revenus** FIN income spread; ~ **statistique** MATH statistical spread; ~ **sur les années précédents** FISC backward averaging; ~ **des vacances** RES HUM staggered holidays (*BrE*), staggering of vacations (*AmE*)

étaler *vt* COM flaunt, *coûts* spread; ◆ ~ **son revenu** FISC forward-average

étalon *m* COM Std, standard, yardstick; ~ **argent** BOURSE, FIN silver standard; ~ **de change or** COM, ECON, FIN gold exchange standard; ~ **devise** BOURSE currency standard; ~ **dollar** ECON dollar standard; ~ **de lingots d'or** COM, ECON, FIN gold bullion standard; ~ **marchandises** BOURSE commodity standard; ~ **de mesure** ECON bench mark; ~ **monétaire** ECON monetary standard; ~ **-or**

BANQUE, ECON, FIN gold standard; ~ -or de change COM, ECON, FIN gold exchange standard

étanche *adj* COM watertight, TRANSP moisture-proof, watertight; ~ **à l'air** COM airtight; ~ **aux hydrocarbures** TRANSP oiltight, OT; ~ **au pétrole** TRANSP oiltight, OT; ◆ **totalement ~** TRANSP *emballage* effectively closed

étant: ~ **donné les circonstances** *loc* COM given the circumstances, in the present state of affairs; ~ **entendu que** *loc* COM on the understanding that

étape *f* COM stage; ~ **de transition** ECON stage of transition; ~ **de la vérification** COM verification phase; ~ **de vol** TRANSP flight stage; ◆ **par ~s** COM in stages

état *m* COM *civil* status, *les États-Unis* ≈ state (*US*), COMPTA statement, INFO state, status; ~ **acceptable d'un conteneur** TRANSP *navigation* acceptable container condition, ACC; ~ **des achats et des ventes** BOURSE purchase and sale statement, P&S; ~ **annuel** COMPTA annual return; ~ **d'avancement** COM, GESTION status report; ~ **d'avancement des opérations** COM, IND, V&M transaction status; ~ **de banque** BANQUE bank statement; ~ **budgétaire** ECON, FIN, POL budgetary statement; ~ **de caisse** COMPTA cash statement; ~ **civil** DROIT civil status, marital status; ~ **comparatif** COMPTA, FIN comparative financial statement, comparative statement; ~ **de compte de prêt hypothécaire** BANQUE mortgage statement; ~ **de concordance** COMPTA reconciliation statement; ~ **consolidé** COMPTA aggregate statement; ~ **contractant** DROIT contracting state; ~ **corporatif** POL corporate state; ~ **de dédouanement** IMP/EXP customs clearance status, CCS; ~ **de droit** DROIT rule of law; ~ **de l'économie** ECON state of the economy; ~ **des émissions publiques de titres** BOURSE registration statement; ~ **des enregistrements** BOURSE registration statement; ~ **financier** COMPTA, FIN financial statement; ~ **financier certifié** COMPTA, FIN certified financial statement; ~ **financier consolidé** COMPTA, FIN combined financial statement, consolidated financial statement; ~ **financier récapitulatif** COM, FIN financial summary; ~ **financier semestriel** COMPTA, FIN interim statements; ~ **de flux de trésorerie** COMPTA source and application of funds; ~ **des frais** FIN bill of costs; ~ **isolé** ECON, POL isolated state; ~ **du marché à double prime à court terme** BOURSE short straddle position; ~ **matrimonial** DROIT marital status; ~ **-membre** POL member state, MS; ~ **mensuel** COMPTA monthly return; ~ **de navigabilité** TRANSP seaworthiness; ~ **de non-croissance** ECON stationary state economy, steady-state economy; ~ **de produits et de charges** COMPTA statement of income and expenses; ~ **-providence** POL welfare state; ~ **de rapprochement** COMPTA reconciliation statement; ~ **de rapprochement bancaire** BANQUE, COMPTA bank reconciliation statement; ~ **de rapprochement de banque** BANQUE, COMPTA bank

reconciliation statement; ~ **des rémunérations versées** RES HUM pay statement; ~ **des résultats** COMPTA statement of earnings (*US*); ~ **des résultats consolidé** COMPTA combined statement of income; ~ **des risques** BOURSE risk position; ~ **sous forme de tableau** ADMIN, COM tabular report; ~ **stationnaire** ECON stationary state economy, steady-state economy; ~ **tampon** POL buffer state; ~ **de la technique** BREVETS prior art, state of the art; ~ **de la technique antérieure** BREVETS background art; ~ **de la valeur ajoutée** COMPTA value-added statement; ~ **de variations de trésorerie** COMPTA source and application of funds; ~ **zéro** INFO zero state; ◆ **à l'~ de projet** DROIT in draft form; **en ~ livrable** DROIT in a deliverable state; **en ~ de navigabilité** TRANSP *avion* airworthy; **en bon ~** COM in good repair, in good trim (*infrml*); **en l'~** COM as is; **en l'~ actuel de la législation** DROIT as the law stands at present; **en mauvais ~** COM beyond repair, in a bad state, in a bad state of repair; **être en ~ d'alerte** COM *danger* be on the alert for; **être en ~ de cessation de paiement** COM default

État: ~ **du droit au travail** *m* DROIT right to work state (*US*); ~ **-hyperprotecteur** *m* ECON, POL nanny state (*infrml*); ~ **d'immatriculation** *m* TRANSP *d'un navire* state of registry; ~ **-providence** *m* ECON nanny state (*infrml*), welfare state, POL state; ~ **des recettes et dépenses** *m* COMPTA Statement of Revenue and Expenditure; ◆ **d'~ à État** POL government-to-government

états: ~ **financiers** *m pl* COMPTA published accounts; ~ **de service** *m pl* RES HUM credentials, service in employment

États: **les ~ du sud des États-Unis** *m pl* IND sunbelt (*US*)

États-Unis *m pl* COM United States, US; ~ **d'Amérique** COM United States of America, USA

étayer *vt* ECON underpin

ETC *abrév* (*entrepreneur de transport combiné*) TRANSP CTO (*combined transport operator*)

été *m* COM summer

éteindre *vt* BANQUE *hypothèque* pay off, INFO switch off, turn off

éteint, e *adj* INFO *voyant* off

étendre *vt* COM extend, *activités* expand

étendu, e *adj* COM *effet* widespread

étendue *f* BREVETS *de la protection*, COM extent, scope; ~ **du contrôle** COM span of control, COMPTA, FIN audit coverage, audit scope; ~ **des dégâts** ASSUR extent of damage; ~ **de la garantie** ASSUR scope of coverage; ~ **de garantie** BOURSE underwriting spread; ~ **de l'indemnité** ASSUR measure of indemnity; ~ **de la négociation** RES HUM bargaining scope; ~ **des responsabilités** COM span of control; ~ **de la vérification** COM scope

Éthiopie *f* COM Ethiopia

éthiopien, -enne *adj* COM Ethiopian

Éthiopien, -enne *m,f* COM *habitant* Ethiopian

éthique *f* COM, GESTION code of ethics, ethics; ~ **du travail** RES HUM work ethic

ETI *abrév (échangeur thermique intermédiaire)* TRANSP intercooler

étiquetage *m* V&M labeling (*AmE*), labelling (*BrE*); ~ **informatif** V&M descriptive labeling (*AmE*), descriptive labelling (*BrE*), informative labeling (*AmE*), informative labelling (*BrE*)

étiquette *f* COM label, INFO label, tag, TRANSP *emballage* label, *identification des marchandises* tag, V&M label, price label; ~ **adhésive** ADMIN, COMMS adhesive label, stick-on label; ~ **-adresse** COMMS address label; ~ **à bagages** LOISIRS, TRANSP baggage tag, luggage label; ~ **de marchandises** TRANSP cargo tag; ~ **à oeillet** COM, LOISIRS tie-on label; ~ **de prix** V&M price sticker, price tag, price ticket; ~ **promotionnelle** V&M shelf-talker (*jarg*)

étoffe *f* COM fabric, material; ♦ **avoir l'~ de** COM have the makings of

étouffer *vt* ECON dampen

étranger¹, -ère *adj* COM alien, foreign, overseas, DROIT alien; ♦ ~ **à** COM alien from; ~ **au sujet** BREVETS irrelevant

étranger², -ère *m,f* COM foreigner, DROIT alien; ~ **en situation irrégulière** DROIT illegal alien; ♦ **à l'~** COM abroad, overseas

étrangère: personne ~ *f* COM nonmember

étranglement: ~ des vendeurs à découvert *m* BOURSE short squeeze (*jarg*)

étrangler: ~ les baissiers à découvert *loc jarg* BOURSE squeeze the bears (*jarg*), squeeze the shorts (*jarg*)

étrave *f* TRANSP *d'un navire* stem; ~ **à bulbe** TRANSP *d'un navire* bulbous bow, BB

étreinte: ~ fatale *f* INFO deadlock (*jarg*)

étroit, e *adj* BOURSE narrow, COM *coopération, rapport* close

ETTD *abrév (équipement terminal de traitement de données)* INFO DTE (*data terminal equipment*)

étude *f* COM investigation, study, RES HUM background check, background processing (*US*), V&M research, survey; ~ **d'aménagement des locaux** INFO site planning; ~ **d'avocats** DROIT law firm; ~ **de bandes** V&M *étude de marché* tracking study; ~ **des besoins de la clientèle** V&M *étude de marché* customer research; ~ **du budget** COMPTA, FIN, POL budget review; ~ **de cas** COM, V&M case study; ~ **de conception** COM design engineering; ~ **de consommation** V&M consumer research, consumer survey; ~ **des débouchés** V&M market survey; ~ **détaillée** COM in-depth study; ~ **des écarts** COM, V&M gap study; ~ **de l'expérience professionnelle d'un candidat** RES HUM employee's job history; ~ **de faisabilité** COM, INFO feasibility report, feasibility study, feasibility survey; ~ **globale** INFO systems approach; ~ **de l'impact** V&M impact study; ~ **des implantations** COM, IND plant layout study; ~ **d'investissement** BOURSE, FIN investment review; ~ **de marché** V&M consumer research, market analysis, market research, market report, market study, market survey, marketing research, tracking study; ~ **de marché à l'exportation** IMP/EXP, V&M export market research; ~ **des méthodes** COM methods engineering, methods study; ~ **des méthodes de travail** COM work study; ~ **de motivations** V&M motivational research; ~ **des mouvements** COM, ECON, MATH motion study; ~ **multiclients** V&M *étude de marché* omnibus survey; ~ **des périodes** COM, ECON, IND, RES HUM time and motion study; ~ **pilote** COM pilot study; ~ **de point mort** BOURSE, COMPTA, ECON, FIN, V&M break-even analysis; ~ **préalable** COM, INFO feasibility report, feasibility study, feasibility survey; ~ **prévisionnelle** COM, COMPTA, ECON, FIN, MATH, V&M forecast; ~ **de produit** V&M product engineering, product research; ~ **de projet** COM, ECON, FIN, GESTION project analysis, project appraisal, project assessment; ~ **de projet d'investissement** ECON, FIN capital project evaluation; ~ **de la provenance et de la destination** V&M *étude de marché* origin and destination study; ~ **de rappel** COM recall study; ~ **du rendement écologique** ENVIR production ecology; ~ **de rentabilité** BOURSE, COMPTA, ECON, FIN, V&M investment analysis, profitability analysis; ~ **des salaires et des traitements** RES HUM wage and salary survey; ~ **des sciences humaines** PROT SOC social studies; ~ **des sciences sociales** PROT SOC social studies; ~ **témoin** V&M *étude de marché* sample study; ~ **des temps** COM, MATH time study; ~ **des temps et des méthodes** COM, ECON, RES HUM time and methods study; ~ **des temps et des mouvements** COM, ECON, IND, RES HUM time and motion study; ~ **du travail** COM, GESTION, RES HUM work study; ♦ **à l'~** COM under examination; **faire une ~ de** COM *projet, terrain, situation* survey

études *f pl* PROT SOC studies; ~ **chronométriques** GESTION stopwatch studies; ~ **commerciales** COM, ECON, PROT SOC business studies; ~ **comparatives de la population** ECON ≈ CPS (*US*), ≈ current population survey (*US*); ~ **économiques** ECON, V&M economic research; ~ **de gestion** COM, ECON, PROT SOC business studies; ~ **publicitaires** V&M advertising research; ♦ **faire des études d'ingénieur** COM study engineering; **faire des études de comptabilité** COMPTA study accountancy

étudiant, e *m,f* PROT SOC student, *avant la licence* undergraduate; ~ **-chercheur** COM, PROT SOC research student; ~ **étranger** FISC, RES HUM foreign student

étudier *vt* COM *question* investigate, look into, PROT SOC study

euro- *préf* COM Euro-

Eurocard® *f* BANQUE Eurocard®

eurocentrique *adj* COM eurocentric

eurochèque *m* BANQUE, ECON Eurocheque

eurocontrol *m* TRANSP Eurocontrol

eurodevise *f* BANQUE, ECON Eurocurrency, Euro-money; **~ à moyen terme** BOURSE medium-term Euronote

eurodollar *m* BOURSE, ECON, FIN Eurodollar, ED

euro-emprunt *m* BANQUE Eurobond

eurofranc *m* ECON Eurofranc

euromarché *m* ECON Euromarket

euromonnaie *f* BANQUE, ECON Eurocurrency, Euromoney

Euronet *m* COMMS Euronet

euro-obligation *f* BOURSE Eurobond; **~ à moyen terme** BOURSE medium-term Euronote

europalette *f* COM Europallet

europapier: **~ commercial** *m* FIN Eurocommercial paper, ECP

Europe *f* COM Europe; **~ continentale** COM Continent; **~ de l'Est** POL Eastern Europe; **~ occidentale** COM Western Europe; **~ de l'Ouest** COM Western Europe

européen, -enne *adj* COM European

europhile *adj* COM Europhiliac

europhobe *adj* COM Europhobic

eurorebelle *m* COM Eurorebel, Eurosceptic

eurosceptique *m* COM Eurorebel, Eurosceptic

eurotaux *m pl* BANQUE Euro-rates

eurovaleur: **~ mobilière** *f* FIN Euro-security

Eurovision *f* ADMIN Eurovision

évacuation: **~ des déchets** *f* ENVIR waste disposal

évaluateur, -trice *m,f* RES HUM examiner

évaluation *f* BOURSE *titres* valuation, COM appraisal, evaluation, pricing, *d'une situation, d'un choix* assessment, *du personnel* appraisal, DROIT *du dédommagement, de l'indemnité* assessment, IMMOB appraisal, valuation, INFO computation, RES HUM appraisal (*BrE*), testing, report card (*AmE*), V&M pricing; **~ a posteriori** FISC hindsight; **~ de l'apporteur** COM vendor rating; **~ basée sur une activité** COMPTA activity-based costing (*UK*); **~ de biens immobiliers** IMMOB property valuation (*BrE*), real estate appraisal (*AmE*); **~ boursière** BOURSE market valuation; **~ du capital humain** ECON, FIN, IND, RES HUM, V&M human asset accounting; **~ des comptes** COMPTA, FIN accounts appraisal; **~ du coût d'un poste** RES HUM job costing; **~ des coûts** COMPTA costing; **~ des coûts de la santé publique** ECON, PROT SOC health economics; **~ des coûts de systèmes** COMPTA, FIN estimating systems costs; **~ du crédit** FIN credit rating, credit scoring; **~ du cycle de vie** ENVIR life cycle assessment, LCA; **~ des dégâts** COM appraise damages; **~ de la demande** ECON demand assessment; **~ des dépenses en capital** ECON, FIN capital expenditure appraisal; **~ des dépenses d'investissement** ECON, FIN capital expenditure appraisal; **~ du dommage** ASSUR appraisal of damage; **~ douanière** IMP/EXP customs valuation; **~ de l'emploi** RES HUM job appraisal, job evaluation,

job review; **~ erronée du prix** FIN mispricing; **~ de l'état des revenus** FISC income test; **~ financière** FIN financial appraisal; **~ immobilière** IMMOB property valuation (*BrE*), real estate appraisal (*AmE*); **~ des immobilisations** COMPTA, FIN asset valuation, fixed asset assessment; **~ de l'impact sur l'environnement** ENVIR environmental impact assessment; **~ d'impôts** FISC tax assessment; **~ interne** COM, PROT SOC internal assessment; **~ d'investissement** BOURSE, COMPTA, ECON, FIN capital investment appraisal, investment appraisal; **~ d'investissement sur budget** BOURSE, COMPTA, ECON, FIN capital investment appraisal; **~ du marché** COM, V&M *étude de marché* market appraisal, market evaluation; **~ marginale des prix de revient** COMPTA, ECON, FIN marginal costing; **~ d'une moyenne de revenus** FIN income averaging; **~ obligataire** BOURSE bond valuation; **~ d'une obligation** BOURSE bond rating, bond valuation; **~ d'origine** FISC original assessment; **~ des performances** COM, GESTION, IND, RES HUM performance appraisal, performance evaluation, performance review; **~ du personnel** GESTION, RES HUM staff appraisal; **~ du point** MATH point estimate; **~ des postes** RES HUM job appraisal, job evaluation, job review; **~ des problèmes** COM, GESTION problem assessment; **~ de produit** V&M product evaluation; **~ de projet** COM, ECON, FIN, GESTION project analysis, project appraisal, project assessment; **~ prudente** COM conservative estimate; **~ de la qualité** COM, GESTION, IND quality assessment; **~ des réserves** ENVIR stock inventory, stocktaking; **~ des ressources** ECON resource appraisal; **~ des ressources humaines** RES HUM human resource accounting; **~ des résultats** COM, GESTION, IND, RES HUM performance appraisal, performance evaluation, performance review; **~ du risque de baisse** BOURSE downside risk; **~ spéciale** FISC special assessment; **~ standard des dépenses** ECON standard spending assessment, SSA; **~ des stocks** COMPTA stock valuation; **~ des tâches** RES HUM job appraisal, job review

évalué: **~ à** *loc* BOURSE valued at

évaluer *vt* COM assess, estimate, evaluate, weigh, weigh up, *besoins* make an appraisal of, *du regard* size up, FIN appraise, GESTION appraise, assess, IMMOB value, INFO compute; **~ pour l'homologation d'un testament** DROIT value for probate; ◆ **~ les performances de** INFO bench mark; **~ en police maritime** ASSUR value as marine policy, VMP

évaporation *f* ENVIR, IND steam emission

évasif, -ive *adj* COM *réponse* evasive

évasion: **~ de capitaux** *f* ECON capital flight; **~ fiscale** *f* ECON, FIN tax avoidance, *illégale* tax evasion, FISC tax evasion, *illégale* tax avoidance; **~ monétaire** *f* ECON capital flight

événement *m* COM, INFO event; **~ d'actualité** COM current event; **~ après clôture des comptes** COMPTA post balance sheet event; **~ imprévu**

COM contingency; ~ **inattendu** COM contingency; ~ **médiatique** MÉDIA media event; ~ **postérieur à la date du bilan** COMPTA subsequent event; ~ **sportif** COM, LOISIRS sports event

événements: ~ **mutuellement alternatifs** *m pl* COM disjoint events; ~ **mutuellement exclusifs** *m pl* COM disjoint events; ~ **postérieurs à la date de clôture** *m pl* COMPTA events subsequent to the closing date; ◆ **en attendant la suite des** ~ COM waiting for the other shoe to drop (*infrml*)

éventail: ~ **de contrôle** *m* COM span of control; ~ **des négociations** *m* BOURSE trading range; ~ **des prix** *m* ECON, V&M price range; ~ **des produits** *m* COM, IND, V&M product range; ~ **des produits en vente** *m* V&M product mix, sales mix; ~ **des salaires** *m* RES HUM wage spread

éventualité *f* COM contingency, eventuality; ~ **peu probable** COM remote possibility

éventuel, -elle *adj* COM proposed, *responsabilité, obligation* contingent, prospective, FISC proposed, V&M prospective

évidence: ~ **de** *loc* COM evidence of

évident, e *adj* COM evident, obvious

évincer *vt* ECON, FIN crowd out, RES HUM oust

éviter *vt* COM, FISC *impôt*, TRANSP *espace perdu* avoid

évolué, e *adj* GESTION, INFO, POL advanced, high-level

évoluer *vi* COM evolve; ◆ ~ **en parallèle** BOURSE move in tandem; **qui peut** ~ COM upgradeable

évolutif, -ive *adj* COM, INFO expandable, open-ended, upgradeable

évolution *f* COM evolution, *prix* change, ECON trend, INFO growth; ~ **économique** ECON economic trend; ~ **d'un investissement** BOURSE, FIN investment history; ~ **du marché** V&M market development; ~ **matérielle** INFO hardware upgrade; ~ **de la situation économique** ECON economic trend

EVP *abrév* (*équivalent vingt pieds*) TRANSP TEU (*twenty foot equivalent unit*)

ex *adv* (ANT *avec*) BOURSE ex.

ex. *abrév* (*exemple*) COM ex. (*example*)

exact, e *adj* COM correct, faithful, *chiffres* accurate, *intention, but* express

exactement *adv* COM correctly

exactitude *f* COM, COMPTA accuracy

exagéré, e *adj* COM exaggerated

examen *m* COM investigation, *médical* vetting, *produit, compte* inspection, DROIT consideration, examination, GESTION review, IND *produit* inspection, PROT SOC, RES HUM examination, test; ~ **annuel des ventes** FIN, V&M annual sales review; ~ **approfondi** COM close examination; ~ **des besoins** FISC, PROT SOC needs test; ~ **du budget publicitaire** COMPTA, FIN, V&M advertising budget review; ~ **des débouchés** COM, V&M market study; ~ **de la demande d'assurance** ASSUR examination of proposal; ~ **d'entrée** COM

entrance examination; ~ **financier** COM, FIN financial review; ~ **médical** PROT SOC medical examination; ~ **préliminaire** BREVETS preliminary examination; ~ **de proposition** ASSUR examination of proposal; ~ **public** COM public examination; ~ **des ressources** ECON resource appraisal, FISC means test, GESTION resource appraisal; ~ **de revenu** FISC earnings test; ~ **de soumission** ASSUR examination of proposal; ~ **systématique** COMPTA, FIN across-the-board investigation (*UK*)

examinateur, -trice *m,f* COM, DROIT, PROT SOC, RES HUM examiner

examiné, e *adj* COM ex., examined, exd; ◆ **être** ~ COM come under scrutiny

examiner *vt* COM *candidature* examine, *question* adjudicate, investigate, look into, IMMOB survey; ~ **de nouveau** COM re-examine, FISC *cotisation* reconsider; ◆ ~ **les chiffres** COM look at the figures

ex ante *adj* ECON ex ante

ex-bon: ~ **de souscription** *m* BOURSE ex-warrant

ex-c *abrév* (*ex-coupon*) BOURSE, COM ex.cp., XC (*ex-coupon*)

excédent *m* BOURSE overhang, FISC excess amount, IMMOB *baux commerciaux* overage; ~ **de l'actif sur le passif** COMPTA, ECON, FIN surplus of assets over liabilities; ~ **agricole** ECON farm surplus; ~ **alimentaire** ECON food surplus; ~ **d'argent** RES HUM, V&M push money; ~ **de bagages** LOISIRS, TRANSP excess baggage; ~ **de la balance des paiements** (ANT *déficit de la balance des paiements*) ECON BOP surplus, balance of payments surplus; ~ **brut d'exploitation** (*EBE*) COMPTA, ECON, FIN gross margin (*GM*); ~ **budgétaire** (ANT *déficit budgétaire*) COM, COMPTA, ECON, FIN, POL budget surplus, budgetary surplus; ~ **de caisse** COMPTA cash surplus, excess cash; ~ **du commerce extérieur** ECON, IMP/EXP external trade surplus, foreign trade surplus; ~ **commercial** ECON, IMP/EXP, POL trade balance, trade surplus; ~ **commercial étranger** ECON, IMP/EXP external trade surplus, foreign trade surplus; ~ **du compte courant** BANQUE, ECON checking account surplus (*AmE*), current account surplus (*BrE*); ~ **d'exportation** ECON, IMP/EXP export surplus; ~ **financier** FIN, FISC fiscal surplus; ~ **d'importation** ECON, IMP/EXP import surplus; ~ **de main-d'oeuvre** RES HUM overmanning; ~ **net quotidien** TRANSP *charte-partie* net daily surplus; ~ **des opérations courantes** BANQUE, ECON checking account surplus (*AmE*), current account surplus (*BrE*); ~ **au poids pivot** TRANSP *aviation* overpivot weight; ~ **de prix** BOURSE premium; ~ **de production** IND overrun; ~ **de réévaluation** COM, COMPTA appraisal increment; ~ **des sinistres** ASSUR excess of loss; ~ **de trésorerie** COMPTA cash surplus, excess cash; ◆ **avoir un** ~ (ANT *avoir un déficit*) ECON run a surplus; **ayant un** ~ **de main-d'oeuvre** (ANT *à court de main-d'oeuvre*) RES HUM overmanned;

en ~ COM, ECON in surplus; **en ~ financier** ECON, FIN in financial surplus

excédentaire *adj* COM, ECON in surplus; ◆ **~ dans une devise donnée** ECON *commerce international* long in a currency

Excellence: **Son ~** *f* RES HUM Her Excellency, His Excellency, HE; **Son ~ Madame l'Ambassadrice** *f* RES HUM Her Excellency, HE; **Son ~ Monsieur l'Ambassadeur** *f* RES HUM His Excellency, HE

excepté, e *prép* COM ex., excl., excluding, exclusive of, except

exception *f* COM exception; **l'~ dans le groupe** RES HUM the odd one out; **~ péremptoire** DROIT demurrer; ◆ **à l'~ de** COM ex., except, excl., excluding, exclusive of, with the exception of; **faire une ~** COM make an exception

exceptionnel, -elle *adj* COM exceptional, COMPTA, FIN, V&M *dépenses* below the line

excès *m* COM excess; **~ de formalités administratives** ADMIN red tape; **~ d'indemnisation** RES HUM overcompensation; **~ de publicité** V&M advertising overkill; **~ de réglementation légale** RES HUM juridification; **~ d'urbanisation** ECON overurbanization; ◆ **en ~** FIN over

excessif, -ive *adj* COM excessive, unreasonable

excessivement *adv* COM excessively

exclu, e *adj* COM excluded

exclure *vt* COM exclude, rule out; **~ d'avance** COM preclude; ◆ **~ qn d'une société** COM bar sb from a company

exclus: les ~ *m pl* PROT SOC social outcasts

exclusif, -ive *adj* BANQUE sole, COM exclusive

exclusion *f* ASSUR exception, exclusion, COM, FISC exclusion, exemption, RES HUM dismissal; **~ de garantie** COM exclusion clause, exemption clause; **~ par voie d'achats** BOURSE *d'un actionnaire* buying out; **~ des risques d'entreprise** ASSUR business risk exclusion; **~ des risques professionnelles** ASSUR business risk exclusion; **~ statutaire** ASSUR statutory exclusion; ◆ **à l'~ de** COM excluding, exclusive of, to the exclusion of

exclusivement *adv* COM *non-compris* exclusively

exclusivité *f* MÉDIA *presse* scoop, V&M *médias* franchise

ex-conjoint, e *m,f* DROIT former spouse

ex-coup *abrév* (*ex-coupon*) BOURSE, COM ex.cp., XC (*ex-coupon*)

ex-coupon *adj* (*ex-c, ex-coup*) BOURSE, COM ex-coupon (*ex.cp., XC*)

excursion *f* LOISIRS *tourisme* tour; **~ en train** LOISIRS rail tour; **~ en train avec guide** LOISIRS rail guided tour

excuse *f* COM apology

excuser: **s'~** *v pron* COM apologize; **s'~ de** COM apologize for; ◆ **s'~ de qch auprès de qn** COM apologize to sb for sth

excuses: faire ses ~ à qn pour qch *loc* COM apologize to sb for sth

ex-d *abrév* (*ex-dividende*) BOURSE ex. div., XD (*ex dividend*)

ex-div. *abrév* (*ex-dividende*) BOURSE ex. div., XD (*ex dividend*)

ex-dividende[1] *adj* (*ex-d, ex-div.*) BOURSE ex-dividend (*ex. div., XD*)

ex-dividende[2] *m* (*ex-d, ex-div.*) BOURSE ex dividend (*XD*)

ex droit *m* DROIT ex claim

ex-droit *adj* BOURSE ex-rights

exécuter *vt* BOURSE *client* buy in, *ordre* execute, COM act on, carry out, *contrat* implement, *ordre* fill, *travaux* perform, DROIT discharge, execute, *jugement* execute, INFO *programme* execute, process, run; **~ ou annuler** BOURSE fill-or-kill, FOK; **~ sous tension** INFO bootstrap (*jarg*); ◆ **faire ~** DROIT enforce

exécuteur, -trice *m,f* DROIT estate executor, exec., executor, exor, *femme* executrix; **~ testamentaire** DROIT estate executor, exec., executor, exor, *femme* executrix

exécutif, -ive *adj* GESTION, POL, RES HUM executive

exécution *f* BOURSE execution, COM *d'une tâche* accomplishment, *d'un contrat* implementation, *de travaux* performance, DROIT admin, enforcement, ENF, execution, *d'une loi* administration, *d'un contrat* performance, GESTION execution, INFO processing, V&M fulfillment (*AmE*), fulfilment (*BrE*); **~ bon marché** BOURSE cheap execution (*UK*); **~ en Bourse** BOURSE buy-in; **~ intégrale du contrat par décision de justice** DROIT specific performance; **~ de la livraison** TRANSP delivery performance; **~ de la politique** COM, GESTION, POL policy execution; **~ pure et simple** DROIT *d'un contrat* specific performance; **~ de services** COM *de services* performance

exécutoire *adj* (ANT *non-exécutoire*) DROIT enforceable, executory

exemplaire *m* COM copy; **~ d'archives** ADMIN file copy; **~ en prépublication** MÉDIA advance copy; **~ de presse** MÉDIA press copy; **~ en service de presse** MÉDIA presentation copy, press copy; **~ témoin** MÉDIA advance copy; ◆ **en quatre ~s** COM in quadruplicate; **en trois ~s** COM in triplicate

exemple *m* (*ex.*) COM ex., example, INFO *programme* sample; **~ bien connu** COM classic example; **~ modèle** COM textbook case; **~ -type** COM classic example; **~ typique** COM textbook case, V&M case history; ◆ **par ~** COM exempli gratia (*frml*), for example (*e.g.*)

exempt, e *adj* (ANT *non-exempté*) COM, FISC exempt; ◆ **~ de droit de douane** IMP/EXP *marchandises* duty-free; **~ d'erreur** INFO error-free; **~ d'impôts** FISC tax-exempt, tax-free; **~ de loyer** FISC rent-free; **~ de tout impôt** FISC free of all taxation

exempter *vt* COM, FISC exempt

exemption *f* COM exemption, freedom, DROIT immunity, FISC exemption; **~ de base** FISC basic exemption; **~ pour dividendes** FISC dividend allowance; **~ pour enfants à charge** FISC exemption for dependent children; **~ d'impôts** ECON, FIN, FISC *légale* tax avoidance; **~ de marié** FISC married exemption; **~ maximale pour redevances** FISC royalty exemption limit; **~ personnelle** BANQUE, FISC personal allowance (*UK*), personal credit (*Canada*), personal exemption (*US*); **~ en raison d'âge** FISC age exemption; **~ statutaire** DROIT statutory exemption, statutory immunity; **~ de la TVA** FISC zero rating

ex-épouse *f* DROIT former spouse

ex-époux *m* DROIT former spouse

exercer *vt* BOURSE *droit* exercise, *option* exercise, COM exert, DROIT *droit* exercise; ◆ **~ une influence sur** COM have influence over; **~ de la pression à la baisse sur le marché** BOURSE raid the market; **~ une pression sur** COM bring pressure to bear on, POL lobby

exercice *m* COM business year, exercise, trading year, COMPTA financial year, fiscal year, trading year, FY, DROIT practice, ECON accounting period, financial year, fiscal year, trading year, FY, FIN financial year, fiscal year, trading year, FY, FISC financial year, fiscal year, tax year, FY, IND business year, POL financial year, fiscal year, FY; **~ antérieur** COMPTA prior period; **~ anticipé** BOURSE early exercise; **~ anticipé d'un droit** DROIT, IMMOB anticipation; **~ budgétaire** COMPTA, ECON, FIN, POL budget year; **~ clos** FISC financial year ended, fiscal year ended, year ended; **~ clos à cette date** COMPTA, FIN accounting year then ended, fiscal year then ended, FISC year then ended; **~ comptable** BOURSE accounting period, COMPTA accounting period, accounting year, financial period, financial year, fiscal year, FY, FIN accounting period, accounting year; **~ courant** FISC current fiscal year; **~ en cours** COM *année fiscale* current year, COMPTA, FIN, FISC current business year; **~ écoulé** COM past year; **~ d'évacuation** RES HUM fire drill; **~ financier** COM business year, COMPTA accounting period, accounting year, financial year, fiscal year, FY, ECON financial year, fiscal year, FY, FIN accounting period, accounting year, financial year, fiscal period, fiscal year, FY, FISC financial year, fiscal year, FY, IND business year, POL financial year, fiscal year, FY; **~ fiscal** FISC tax year; **~ de poursuites judiciaires** DROIT conduct of law suit; **~ social** COM, COMPTA, ECON, FIN trading year; **~ suivant** FISC upcoming fiscal year; ◆ **en ~** COM, DROIT practising, POL *ministre* incumbent

exercices: **~ militaires** *m pl* COM war games

exhaustif, -ive *adj* COM exhaustive, *rapport, étude* comprehensive

exhorbitant, e *adj* COM exhorbitant

exigeant, e *adj* COM exacting; **~ une grande qualification** RES HUM skill-intensive; ◆ **~ beaucoup de personnes** RES HUM people-intensive

exigence *f* COM, FISC requirement; **~ des**

consommateurs V&M consumer requirement; **~ de dépôt initial** BOURSE initial margin requirement; **~ juridique** DROIT legal requirement; **~ préalable à l'inspection** BANQUE preinspection requirement; **~ de publication** BOURSE disclosure requirement; **~ de rentabilité** FIN profit requirement, profitability requirement

exigences: **~ pour la cotation** *f pl* BOURSE listing requirements; **~ de déclaration** *f pl* FISC reporting requirements; **~ de poste** *f pl* GESTION, RES HUM job challenge, job requirements; **~ relatives aux déclarations** *f pl* FISC reporting requirements; **~ de sécurité** *f pl* IND safety requirements

exiger *vt* COM exact, require, FISC *paiement* demand; **~ qch de qn** COM require sth of sb

exigibilité: **~ anticipée** *f* BANQUE *du remboursement d'un prêt* acceleration of maturity

exigible: **~ d'avance** *loc* COM payable in advance

exil: **~ fiscal** *m* FISC tax exile

existant[1]**, e** *adj* COM actual

existant[2] *m* TRANSP actuals

ex navire *m* IMP/EXP, TRANSP x-ship

exode: **~ des cerveaux** *m* RES HUM brain drain (*infrml*)

ex officio *adj frml* DROIT, RES HUM ex officio (*frml*)

exonération *f* COM exemption, DROIT immunity, FISC exemption; **~ des gains en capital** FISC capital gains exemption; **~ d'impôts** FISC tax exemption, tax immunity; **~ d'impôts fiscale** ECON tax immunity; **~ mutuelle** ASSUR *à la suite de collision* knock-for-knock agreement; **~ de paiement de la prime** ASSUR exemption from payment of premium; **~ statutaire** DROIT statutory exemption, statutory immunity

exonéré, e *adj* COM, FISC exempt; ◆ **~ d'impôts** FISC tax-exempt, tax-free

exonérer *vt* COM, FISC exempt

expansion *f* COM development, expansion, ECON development, expansion, growth, IND, POL development, expansion; **~ des affaires** COM, GESTION business expansion; **~ commerciale** COM, GESTION business expansion; **~ diagonale** ECON diagonal expansion; **~ économique** ECON economic expansion; **~ de faible amplitude** ECON boomlet; **~ horizontale** (*ANT expansion verticale*) COM horizontal expansion; **~ verticale** (*ANT expansion horizontale*) COM vertical expansion; ◆ **en ~** ECON buoyant

expansionniste *adj* ECON expansionary

ex parte *adj* DROIT ex parte

expatrié, e *m,f* COM expatriate

expectative *f* COM anticipation

expédier *vt* COM expedite, COMMS forward, *par la poste* mail (*AmE*), post (*BrE*), INFO despatch, dispatch, TRANSP consign, despatch, dispatch, *marchandises* ship; **~ par avion** COMMS *lettre, colis* airmail; **~ par la poste** COMMS send by mail (*AmE*), send by post (*BrE*); **~ par le train** TRANSP ship by rail

expéditeur, -trice *m,f* COMMS addresser, forwarder, fwdr, IMP/EXP, TRANSP consigner, consignor, forwarder, fwdr, dispatcher, shipper

expédition *f* BOURSE forwarding, TRANSP cnmt, consgt, consignation, consignment, despatching, dispatching, despatch, dispatch, shipment, shipping; **~ en conteneur** TRANSP *navigation* containerized shipping; **~ groupée** TRANSP forwarding in bulk; **~ ordinaire** TRANSP customary despatch, customary dispatch; **~ par chemin de fer** TRANSP rail shipment; **~ partielle** IMP/EXP TRANSP *maritime* part shipment; **~ en volume** IMP/EXP, TRANSP volume shipping; **~ en vrac** IMP/EXP, TRANSP bulk shipment

expéditionnaire *mf* TRANSP shipping clerk

expérience *f* COM *en laboratoire* experiment, *travail* experience; **~ d'agence** V&M *publicité* agency experience; **~ professionnelle** COM, RES HUM business experience, employment record, professional achievements, work experience; **~ de terrain** RES HUM hands-on experience; ◆ **ayant de l'~** RES HUM experienced; **faire l'~ de** COM experience

expérimenté, e *adj* RES HUM experienced

expert[1]**, e** *adj* COM expert

expert[2]**, e** *m,f* ASSUR adjuster, assessor, official valuer, COM expert, specialist, DROIT official valuer, FIN, IMMOB appraiser, INFO troubleshooter, RES HUM adjuster; **~ d'assurance** ASSUR independent adjuster; **~ cité comme témoin** DROIT expert witness; **~ -comptable** COMPTA accountant, certified accountant (*UK*), certified public accountant (*US*), chartered accountant (*UK*), qualified accountant, CA (*UK*), CPA (*US*); **~ -conseil** GESTION consultant; **~ désigné par les tribunaux** ASSUR, DROIT official valuer; **~ en fiscalité** FISC tax expert; **~ indépendant** ASSUR independent adjuster, RES HUM independent expert; **~ maritime** RES HUM surveyor; **~ en marketing** RES HUM, V&M marketeer

expertise *f* COM appraisal, consultancy work, GESTION consultancy work; **~ des avaries** ASSUR damage survey; **~ comptable** COMPTA accountancy, accy; **~ des dégâts** ASSUR damage survey; **~ des dommages** ASSUR appraisal of damage; **~ intermédiaire** ASSUR int., intermediate survey; **~ quadriennale** FISC quadriennal survey

expertiser *vt* COM value; ◆ **~ les dommages** COM appraise damages; **~ qch** COM make a valuation of sth

expiration *f* COM *date* expiration (*AmE*), expiry (*BrE*), DROIT lapse; **~ d'affectation** COMPTA lapsing resources; **~ du bail** IMMOB termination of tenancy; **~ du contrat à terme** BOURSE futures expiration date (*AmE*), futures expiry date (*BrE*)

expirer *vi* COM expire; **~ dans le cours** BOURSE expire in-the-money; **~ sans valeur** BOURSE expire worthless

explicite *adj* COM explicit

expliquer *vt* COM explain, *en démontrant* demonstrate; ◆ **~ point par point** COM spell out; **s'~ une**

bonne fois pour toutes avec qn COM have it out for good with sb (*infrml*)

exploitable: **~ par la machine** *adj* INFO machine-readable

exploitant, e *m,f* COM operator, TRANSP aircraft operator; **~ individuel** COMPTA sole trader

exploitation *f* BREVETS use, working, COM sweated trade, ECON, ENVIR exploitation, RES HUM sweated trade; **~ agricole** COM, IND farming business; **~ à ciel ouvert** IND opencast mining (*BrE*), strip mining (*AmE*), *production* opencast method; **~ des contacts d'affaires** COM networking; **~ déséquilibrée** TRANSP imbalanced working; **~ économique des ressources** ENVIR economical use of resources; **~ forestière** COM logging; **~ à grande échelle** ECON, IND *agriculture* large-scale farming; **~ intensive** ECON, IND intensive production; **~ mesurée des ressources** ENVIR economical use of resources; **~ portuaire** TRANSP port operation; **~ d'un site** ENVIR *décharge* site operation

exploiter *vt* COM milk (*infrml*), operate, *entreprise* carry on, *minerai, terre, talent* exploit, *ressources, marché* tap, ENVIR *ressources en pétrole* tap, FIN cash in on, IND *minerai, terre, talent*, RES HUM exploit

explosif *m* TRANSP explosive; **~ d'amorçage** TRANSP *marchandises dangereuses* initiating explosive; **~ déflagrant** TRANSP *marchandises dangereuses* deflagrating explosive; **~ à déflagration** TRANSP *marchandises dangereuses* deflagrating explosive; **~ détonant** TRANSP *marchandises dangereuses* detonating explosive; **~ primaire** TRANSP *marchandises dangereuses* primary explosive; **~ secondaire** TRANSP *marchandises dangereuses* secondary explosive

explosion: **~ du contenu total** *f* TRANSP explosion of total contents, ETC; **~ démographique** *f* ECON, POL population explosion; **~ des salaires** *f* RES HUM wage explosion

expomarché *m* COM, V&M trade mart

exportateur[1]**, -trice** *adj* IMP/EXP exporting

exportateur[2]**, -trice** *m,f* IMP/EXP exporter; **~ net** (*ANT importateur net*) ENVIR net donator

exportation *f* IMP/EXP exp., export, exportation; **~ concessionnaire** IMP/EXP, POL concessional export; **~ envoyée par la poste** IMP/EXP postal export; **~ indivisible** IMP/EXP indivisible export; **~ invisible** ECON, IMP/EXP invisible export; **~ mondiale** IMP/EXP world export; **~ principale** IMP/EXP staple export; **~ subventionnée** ECON, IMP/EXP subsidized export; **~ visible** ECON, IMP/EXP visible export

exporté, e *adj* IMP/EXP exported

exposant *m* INFO superscript, MATH exponent, MÉDIA superscript

exposé[1] *m* COM *oral* brief, DROIT statement; **~ de l'élément de planification** FIN planning element memorandum; **~ de l'invention** BREVETS *partie d'une description* disclosure of the invention;

~ -sondage COMPTA exposure draft; ~ **sur un sujet publicitaire** V&M advertising talk

exposé:[2] **être ~ à un risque** *loc* BOURSE, COM face a risk

exposer *vt* BOURSE expose, COM exhibit, set forth; ◆ ~ **à** COM *pression* expose to; ~ **qch en détail** COM expose sth in detail; ~ **ses arguments** DROIT argue one's case

exposition *f* BREVETS, COM exhibition, V&M exhibition, *salon professionnel* trade show; ~ **agricole** ECON, V&M agricultural show; ~ **d'artisanat** COM, V&M artisan fair; ~ **itinérante** TRANSP traveling fair (*AmE*), travelling fair (*BrE*); ~ **réelle totale** V&M *publicité* total effective exposure; ~ **aux risques** COMPTA risk exposure; ~ **de taux d'intérêt** BOURSE interest rate exposure

ex post *adj frml* ECON ex post (*frml*); ~ **facto** *frml* DROIT ex post facto (*frml*)

express *m* TRANSP *service de transport* express

expression *f* COM, INFO expression; ~ **de la politique** COM, GESTION, POL policy formulation

exprimer *vt* COM *idée, opinion* air, *remerciement* express

expropriation *f* COM, DROIT compulsory purchase; ~ **pour cause d'utilité publique** IMMOB condemnation

exproprier *vt* IMMOB dispossess

expulser *vt* DROIT, IMMOB evict, PROT SOC deport

expulsion *f* COM *d'un bénéfice* voidance, DROIT, IMMOB *d'un locataire* eviction, PROT SOC deportation; ~ **constructive** IMMOB constructive eviction; ~ **effective** DROIT, IMMOB actual eviction; ~ **partielle** IMMOB partial eviction; ~ **de représailles** IMMOB retaliatory eviction

ex répartition *f* FIN ex allotment

extensible *adj* COM, INFO *système* expandable, open, open-ended, upgradeable

extensif, -ive *adj* COM, INFO expandable

extension *f* ECON intensification, INFO extension, upgrading; ~ **de convention** RES HUM scope of agreement; ~ **d'échelle** COM scale-up; ~ **de la gamme** V&M brand extension; ~ **matérielle** INFO hardware upgrade; ~ **mémoire** INFO memory extension, memory upgrade; ~ **de négociation** RES HUM scope of bargaining; ~ **à des risques annexes** ASSUR extended cover, extended coverage; ~ **des tâches** RES HUM job enlargement

extérieur: de l'~ *loc* COM visiting

extérieure: personne ~ *f* COM outsider

externalité *f* ECON externality; ~ **contemporaine** ECON contemporaneous externality; ~ **séquentielle** ECON sequential externality; ~ **spatiale** ECON neighborhood effect (*AmE*), neighbourhood effect (*BrE*)

externe *adj* COM out-house

externer *vt* COM farm out, ECON externalize

extinction *f* DROIT *d'un contrat* discharge, ENVIR extinction; ~ **d'une action** DROIT *en justice* extinction of an action; ~ **d'un gage** DROIT discharge of lien; ~ **d'une instance** DROIT extinction of an action; ~ **d'un privilège** DROIT discharge of lien

extorquer *vt* COM extort

extra:[1] ~ **-budgétaire** *adj* COMPTA nonbudgetary; ~ **-plat** *adj* INFO slim-line

extra[2] *m* COM ex., extra

extraction *f* COM extraction, INFO retrieval; ~ **de données** INFO data retrieval; ~ **de l'information** INFO information retrieval

extraire *vt* COM, ENVIR *charbon* extract, INFO remove, retrieve

extrait *m* COM *document* extract, DROIT *d'un acte* abstract; ~ **de comptes** BANQUE abstract of accounts; ~ **des comptes clients** COMPTA, FIN accounts receivable statement; ~ **de minute** DROIT *tribunal* abstract of record; ~ **de naissance** ASSUR, COM, DROIT birth certificate; ~ **d'un rapport officiel** DROIT abstract of record; ~ **du registre** DROIT extract from the register; ~ **du répertoire des mutations de propriété** DROIT abstract of title; ◆ ~, **liquide aromatique ou parfum** TRANSP aromatic liquid or flavoring extract (*AmE*), aromatic liquid or flavouring extract (*BrE*)

extrapolation *f* MATH extrapolation

extraterritorial, e *adj* BANQUE, COM, FIN offshore

extrême: ~ **neutralité** *f* ECON, POL superneutrality

F

FAB[1] *abrév (franco à bord)* TRANSP *livraison de marchandises* FOB *(free on board), FOS (free on ship, free on steamer)*

FAB:[2] ~ **aéroport** *m (franco à bord aéroport)* TRANSP *livraison de marchandises* FOB airport, FOA *(free on aircraft)*

fabricant *m* COM manufacturer, IND maker, manufacturer, producer, RES HUM fabricator; ~ **automobile** IND car manufacturer; ~ **d'engrenages** TRANSP gear manufacturer, GR; ~ **de lainages** IND woollen manufacturer

fabricants *m pl* COM, IND manufacturers, mfrs

fabrication:[1] **de ~ française** *adj* COM French-made

fabrication[2] *f* COM make, IND making, manufacturing; ~ **assistée par ordinateur** *(FAO)* IND, INFO computer-aided manufacture, computer-aided manufacturing, computer-assisted manufacture, computer-assisted manufacturing *(CAM)*; ~ **à la chaîne** IND flow production; ~ **en entrepôt sous douane** IMP/EXP in-bond manufacturing; ~ **en grandes séries** IND mass production; ~ **intégrée par ordinateur** *(FIO)* IND, INFO computer-integrated manufacture, computer-integrated manufacturing *(CIM)*; ~ **modulaire** IND, MATH modular production; ~ **par lots** IND batch production; ~ **en petites séries** IND batch production; ~ **pilote** COM, GESTION, IND pilot production; ~ **en série** IND mass production, wholesale manufacture; ~ **sous licence** IND manufacturing under licence *(BrE)*, manufacturing under license *(AmE)*; ~ **standardisée** IND standardized production; ~ **sur commande** IND jobbing

fabrique: ~ **de papier** *f* ENVIR, IND paper mill; ~ **de produits chimiques** *f* IND chemical works

fabriqué, e *adj* COM, IND made, manufactured, mfd; ◆ ~ **en France** COM, IND made in France; ~ **en grandes séries** IND *production* mass-produced; ~ **sur commande** COM, IND custom-made; ~ **sur demande** IMMOB, TRANSP purpose-built

fabriquer *vt* COM fabricate, make, IND manufacture; ◆ ~ **qch sous licence** IND *production* manufacture under licence *(BrE)*, manufacture under license *(AmE)*; ~ **sur mesure** IND *production* customize

fac: ~ **-similé** *m* ADMIN, COMMS facsimile, fax

FAC *abrév* COM *(franc d'avaries communes)* FGA *(free of general average)*, ECON *(frais d'aménagement au Canada)* CDE *(Canadian development expense)*

façade *f* ASSUR fronting, IMMOB frontage, *d'un immeuble* facade

facile *adj* COM easy, simple; ~ **à utiliser** INFO, V&M user-friendly

facilitation *f* TRANSP transport facilitation, *de trafic marchandises* facilitation

facilité *f* COM facility, TRANSP ease; ~ **d'accès** COM *pour les handicapés et les personnes âgées* accessibility; ~ **d'ajustement structurel** FIN structural adjustment facility, SAF; ~ **bancaire internationale** BANQUE international banking facility, IBF; ~ **de caisse** BANQUE bank accommodation, bank advance, overdraft facility, COMPTA, FIN bank advance, overdraft facility; ~ **commerciale** ECON *commerce international* trade facilitation; ~ **complémentaire** ECON additional facility; ~ **de crédit** BANQUE borrowing facility, credit facility; ~ **d'émission d'achat** BOURSE purchase issue facility, PIF; ~ **d'émission garantie** FIN issuance facility; ~ **d'emprunt cessible** FIN transferable loan facility, TLF; ~ **de financement multi-options** BOURSE multioption financing facility, MOFF; ~ **de financement à options multiples** BOURSE multioption financing facility, MOFF; ~ **de livraison approuvée** BOURSE approved delivery facility *(UK)*; ~ **de manutention** TRANSP ease of handling; ~ **multi-options** BOURSE multioption facility, MOF; ~ **à options multiples** BOURSE multioption facility, MOF; ~ **d'organisation** COM organizational convenience; ~ **de paiement** BANQUE easy payment, easy terms, overdraft facility; ~ **de prêt transférable** FIN transferable loan facility, TLF; ~ **renouvelable à prise ferme** FIN note issuance facility, NIF; ~ **renouvelable à prise ferme transférable** BOURSE transferable revolving underwriting security; ~ **de soutien de programme d'émission d'effets** BOURSE short-term note issuance facility, SNIF, FIN note issuance facility, NIF; ~ **de trésorerie** BANQUE advance

faciliter *vt* COM facilitate

facilités: ~ **à communiquer** *f pl* RES HUM communication skills; ~ **en vol** *f pl* TRANSP in-flight facilities

façon *f* COM *production* way, IND *production* making; ~ **de penser** COM thinking; ◆ **de ~ aléatoire** COM, INFO, MATH randomly; **de ~ cohérente** COM consistently; **de ~ multinationale** COM multinationally; **de ~ objective** DROIT on its merits; **de ~ pragmatique** COM pragmatically; **de ~ systématique** COM across the board

façonner *vt* COM shape, tailor, MÉDIA *opinion* model, mold *(AmE)*, mould *(BrE)*

factage *m* TRANSP carriage, cartage, forwarding

facteur *m* COM factor, COMMS mail carrier *(AmE)*, mailman *(AmE)*, postman *(BrE)*; ~ **d'actualisation** ASSUR annuity due, annuity factor, FIN present value factor; ~ **aléatoire** COM, ECON random factor; ~ **d'attention** MÉDIA, V&M *publicité* attention factor; ~ **bêta** BOURSE, FIN beta coefficient (*AmE*), beta factor (*BrE*); ~ **de charge** COM, ECON, IMP/EXP, IND, MATH, TRANSP load factor; ~ **commun de distinction** COM, RES HUM common distinguishing factor; ~ **de contrainte** ECON, IND, V&M constraining factor; ~ **de conversion** BOURSE, MATH conversion factor; ~ **de conversion de cotisations salariales** ASSUR conversion factor for employee contributions; ~ **coût** COMPTA cost factor; ~ **décisif** COM ratio decidendi (*frml*); ~ **de déflation** MATH deflator; ~ **delta** BOURSE, FIN delta coefficient (*AmE*), delta factor (*BrE*); ~ **d'entrée** FIN input factor; ~ **d'équilibre** ECON balancing item; ~ **d'équivalence** ASSUR, FIN, FISC pension adjustment; ~ **gamma** BOURSE, FIN gamma coefficient (*AmE*), gamma factor (*BrE*); ~ **humain** RES HUM human factor; ~ **Inwood d'annuité** ASSUR Inwood Annuity Factor; ~ **de non-discrimination** COM no discrimination factor; ~ **de production** ECON, IND factor, factor of production, input; ~ **quasi-fixe** ECON quasi-fixed factor; ~ **de réversion** MATH reversionary factor; ~ **risque** COM element of risk; ~ **saisonnier** ECON seasonal factor; ~ **de stabilisation** ECON steadying factor; ~ **stress** RES HUM stress factor; ~ **d'usure** V&M wearout factor; ~ **véga** BOURSE, FIN vega coefficient (*AmE*), vega factor (*BrE*)

factice *adj* COM artificial, blue-sky (*AmE*)

factieux *adj* RES HUM factious

faction *f* RES HUM faction

factorage *m* MATH factoring

factoriel, -elle *adj* MATH factorial

factoring *m* MATH factoring; ~ **d'assurance** ASSUR insurance factoring

factotum *m* RES HUM handyman, odd-job man

facturation *f* COM billing, COMPTA billing, invoicing; ~ **anticipée** V&M prebill; ~ **binomiale** ECON binomial charge; ~ **des clients** COMPTA customer billing; ~ **différée** V&M deferred billing; ~ **globale** V&M *publicité* gross billing (*US*); ~ **par anticipation** COMPTA advance billing, proforma billing; ~ **au temps passé** COM billing for the time spent

facture *f* (*fre*) BANQUE account, invoice (*inv.*) COM account, bill, invoice (*inv.*), COMPTA account, invoice (*inv.*), FIN invoice (*inv.*); ~ **d'achat** COM purchase invoice; ~ **d'avitaillement** TRANSP *navigation* victualing bill (*AmE*), victualling bill (*BrE*); ~ **certifiée** COMPTA certified invoice; ~ **commerciale** COMPTA commercial invoice; ~ **de douane** IMP/EXP customs invoice; ~ **d'électricité** IND electricity bill (*BrE*), hydro bill (*Can*); ~ **établie dans la devise de l'acheteur étranger** COMPTA, IMP/EXP invoice in the currency of the overseas buyer; ~ **établie dans la devise du vendeur étranger** COMPTA, IMP/EXP invoice in the currency of the overseas seller; ~ **établie en devise indépendante** COMPTA invoice

in a third currency; ~ **établie en devise tierce** COMPTA invoice in a third currency; ~ **établie en shillings ougandais** BANQUE Uganda shilling invoice; ~ **de l'étranger** BANQUE foreign bill; ~ **d'expédition** IMP/EXP, TRANSP *maritime* shipping invoice; ~ **d'exportation** IMP/EXP export invoice; ~ **originale** COM, COMPTA original invoice; ~ **pro forma** COM, FIN, IMP/EXP pro forma invoice; ~ **provisoire** COM provisional invoice; ~ **rectificative** FIN corrected invoice; ~ **de transport** IMP/EXP, TRANSP shipping invoice; ~ **valide** COM valid invoice

facturer *vt* COM, COMPTA invoice, FIN bill, invoice; ◆ ~ **les coûts et charges** COMPTA invoice cost and charges; ~ **qch à qn** COM invoice sb for sth

facturier[1] *m* COM *livre* invoice book

facturier[2], **-ière** *m,f* COM *employé* biller, invoice clerk

facultatif, -ive *adj* COM facultative, noncompulsory, optional, DROIT nonmandatory; ~ **obligatoire** ASSUR factoblig, facultative/obligatory

faculté *f* PROT SOC *université* faculty; ~ **d'achat et de revente** BOURSE purchase and resale agreement, PRA; ~ **d'adaptation** COM adaptability; ~ **contributive** ECON tax base, taxable capacity, taxation capacity, taxing capacity, FISC ability to pay, tax base, taxable capacity, taxation capacity, taxing capacity; ~ **de distribution des biens conférée à un légataire** DROIT power of appointment; ~ **de droit** PROT SOC law school; ~ **de rachat** ASSUR commutation right; ~ **de rachat au jour le jour** BOURSE overnight repurchase; ~ **de recours** DROIT power of recourse; ~ **de souscription à aliments** ASSUR *clients déterminés* line slip

Fahrenheit *m (F)* COM Fahrenheit, F

faible[1] *adj* COM *intérêt, opérations* light, *marché, commerce* sluggish, *prix, somme* low, small, *rendement, revenu* low, DROIT *protection* weak, ECON *demande* poor, weak; ◆ **à ~ rendement** BOURSE low-yielding

faible[2] *m* COM soft spot, weak point; ~ **coefficient d'arrimage** TRANSP *marchandises* low stowage factor; ~ **niveau de vie** PROT SOC low standard of living

faible:[3] ~ **aptitude à l'abstraction** *f* RES HUM low abstraction (*jarg*)

faiblement: ~ **peuplé** *adj* ECON sparsely populated

faille *f* DROIT loophole; ~ **dans la législation** DROIT loophole in the law

failli[1], **e** *adj* BANQUE, FIN, RES HUM bankrupt

failli[2] *m* BANQUE, FIN, RES HUM bankrupt, bkpt

faillibilité *f* COM fallibility

faillible *adj* COM fallible

faillite *f* BANQUE, COM, COMPTA, FIN bankruptcy, bkcy, business failure; ~ **de banque** BANQUE bank failure; ~ **d'entreprise** COM bankruptcy, business failure; ~ **forcée** COM, COMPTA, DROIT, FIN involuntary bankruptcy; ~ **frauduleuse** COM, DROIT fraudulent bankruptcy; ~ **prononcée à la**

demande des créanciers COM, COMPTA, DROIT, FIN involuntary bankruptcy; ♦ au bord de la ~ COM on the verge of bankruptcy; être en ~ COM *entreprise* be on the rocks; faire ~ BANQUE fail, COM fail, go bust (*infrml*), go toes up (*infrml*), *société* go to the wall, go under, COMPTA go bankrupt, FIN go toes up (*infrml*)

faire *vt* COM make, *demande* send in, *enquête* hold, *liste* make out, *offre* submit, *plan* draw up, *réclamation* submit, *étude* conduct, DROIT *réclamation* file; ♦ ~ un bond par rapport à RES HUM leapfrog (*jarg*); ~ circuler COM *effets* keep afloat; ~ concurrence à COM, ECON, V&M compete against, compete with; ~ déborder MÉDIA bleed; ~ une découverte COM break new ground; ~ défiler INFO *bande* advance, *écran* scroll; ~ défiler vers le bas (ANT *faire défiler vers le haut*) INFO scroll down; ~ défiler vers le haut (ANT *faire défiler vers le bas*) INFO scroll up; ~ face à COM confront, cover, face, face up to; ~ une faveur à qn COM oblige so; ~ des folies COM go on a spending spree, splash out (*infrml*); ~ une jolie somme COM fetch a good price; ~ de même COM do the same, follow suit; ~ naître ECON *confiance* breed; ~ part de COM *détails* announce, *griefs* air; ~ part de qch à qn COM, COMMS advise sb of sth; ~ part à qn que COM, COMMS advise sb that; ~ partie intégrante de qch COM be part and parcel of sth; ~ prêter serment avec devoir de réserve à qn COM swear sb to secrecy; ~ de la réclame COM, MÉDIA, V&M advertise; ~ de la réclame pour V&M *produit* advertise; se ~ *infrml* COM earn; se ~ avoir *infrml* COM be taken in; se ~ domicilier ADMIN, DROIT take up legal residence; se ~ enregistrer COM book in; se ~ envoyer qch COMMS send away for sth, send off for sth; se ~ excuser COM be excused; se ~ juge des actes d'autrui DROIT sit in judgment over; se ~ rapidement du fric *infrml* COM earn a fast buck (*infrml*); se ~ rembourser BOURSE *obligations* cash in; se ~ £100 par semaine *infrml* COM, RES HUM make £100 a week; ~ suivre SVP COMMS please forward; ~ le yoyo COM yo-yo

faire-part: ~ de fiançailles *m* COM announcement of an engagement

fair-play *m* COM fair play

faisable *adj* COM feasible, manageable

faisant: ~ l'objet de l'option *adj* BOURSE *devise* underlying

faiseur: ~ de moyennes *m* BOURSE averager; ~ de prix *m* ECON price maker

fait[1], e *adj* COM, IND made; ♦ ~ pour durer COM, IND made to last; ~ à la main IND handmade; qui ~ courir les foules LOISIRS *théâtre* be a box office hit (*jarg*); qui ~ gagner du temps COM, INFO time-saving; qui ~ mieux que le marché BOURSE market outperformer; ~ en série COM machine-made; ~ sur mesure COM custom-made, tailor-made, IND made to measure, V&M *publicité* tailor-made

fait[2] *m* COM, DROIT fact; ~ accompli COM fait accompli; ~ établi COM ascertained fact; ~ d'être

acceptable COM adequacy; ~ d'être suffisant COM adequacy; ~ de ne pas livrer un titre à la date de règlement BOURSE failure to deliver a security on value date; ~ pertinent COM material fact; ~ schématisé pour les besoins de l'abstraction ECON stylized fact; ♦ au ~ COM au fait; ce n'est pas de mon ~ COM non est factum (*frml*); de ~ DROIT de facto; ~ de dénoncer *infrml* DROIT whistle-blowing (*infrml*); être au ~ de COM be abreast of, be familiar with

faits: les ~ et les chiffres *m pl* COM facts and figures; ~ matériels d'une affaire *m pl* DROIT achievements, res gestae (*frml*)

falsification *f* COM *de comptes*, COMPTA falsification, forgery, DROIT adulteration, falsification, forgery

falsifier *vt* BANQUE, COM *comptes, signature*, COMPTA falsify, forge, DROIT adulterate, falsify, forge

familier, -ière *adj* COM familiar

famille *f* COM family; ~ de caractères INFO, MÉDIA font family; ~ de fonds de placement BOURSE family of funds; ~ immédiate BOURSE immediate family; ~ monoparentale FISC, PROT SOC single-parent family

fanzine *m* MÉDIA fanzine

FAO *abrév* (*fabrication assistée par ordinateur*) IND, INFO CAM (*computer-aided manufacturing, computer-aided manufacture, computer-assisted manufacture, computer-assisted manufacturing*)

FAP[1] *abrév* (*franc d'avarie particulière*) ASSUR *assurance maritime* FPA (*free of particular average*)

FAP:[2] ~ sauf *loc* ASSUR *assurance maritime* FPA unless

FAQ *abrév* (*franco à quai*) TRANSP *maritime* F/d (*free dock*), FAQ (*free alongside quay*), FD (*free dock*), FOQ (*free on quay*)

fardage *m* TRANSP *arrimage* dunnage; ~ gonflable TRANSP inflatable dunnage

fardeau *m* COM, ECON, POL *dette* burden; ~ fiscal ECON, FISC tax burden; ~ de la preuve DROIT burden of proof

fascicule *m* COM installment (*AmE*), instalment (*BrE*); ~ horaire TRANSP working timetable

fascisme *m* POL fascism

fauché[1], e *adj infrml* RES HUM bankrupt

fauché[2] *m infrml* BANQUE, FIN, RES HUM bankrupt, bkpt

fausse: ~ alerte *f* COM false alarm; ~ déclaration délibérée *f* DROIT wilful misrepresentation of facts; ~ déclaration intentionnelle *f* ASSUR fraudulent misrepresentation; ~ démonstration ne nuit pas *f frml* COM falsa demonstratio non nocet (*frml*); ~ économie *f* COM, ECON false economy; ~ écriture *f* COMPTA, DROIT fraudulent entry; ~ quille *f* TRANSP *navigation* rubbing keel, RK; ~ signature *f* BANQUE forgery

faute[1] *f* COM error, DROIT misdeed; ~ de copiste ADMIN clerical error; ~ de frappe ADMIN clerical error, mistype, COM, INFO, MÉDIA typing error, typo; ~ **grave** DROIT criminal negligence, RES HUM gross misconduct, misconduct; ~ **d'impression** MÉDIA literal (*jarg*), literal error, misprint; ~ **lourde** DROIT gross negligence; ~ **non-intentionnelle** DROIT mistake; ~ **professionnelle** COM breach of professional etiquette, DROIT malpractice, wrongdoing; ~ **de syntaxe** INFO, MÉDIA syntax error; ~ **de la victime** DROIT contributory negligence

faute:[2] ~ **de** *loc* COM *nouvelles* in the absence of; ~ **de détails** *loc* COM in the absence of detailed information; ~ **de renseignements** *loc* COM in the absence of information

faux[1], **-sse** *adj* COM forged, wrong

faux[2] *m* DROIT *d'une signature* forgery; ~ **accessoires** *m pl* COMPTA incidental expenses, incidentals allowance; ~ **appel** *m* COMMS wrong connection; ~ **chèque** *m* BANQUE forged check (*AmE*), forged cheque (*BrE*); ~ **énoncé** *m* FISC false declaration; ~ **frais** *m pl* COM, COMPTA incidental allowances, incidental expenses; ~ **fret** *m* TRANSP *navigation* deadfreight, DF; ~ **numéro** *m* COMMS wrong connection, wrong number; ~ **pas** *m* COM faux pas; ~ **-pont** *m* TRANSP *d'un navire* orlop; ~ **serment** *m* DROIT perjury; ~ **témoin** *m* DROIT false witness

faveur: **de** ~ *loc* COM concessional

favorabilité *f* V&M favorability (*AmE*), favourability (*BrE*)

favorable *adj* COM beneficial, concessional, *balance, commerciale* positive, COM (ANT *défavorable*) *prix, conditions, taux d'échange*, COMPTA (ANT *défavorable*) *écart* favorable (*AmE*), favourable (*BrE*), DROIT beneficial; ~ **à** COM *projet, suggestion* conducive to, in favor of (*AmE*), in favour of (*BrE*)

favorisant *adj* COM conducive to

favoriser *vt* COM be conducive to, favor (*AmE*), favour (*BrE*), *environnement, relations* foster, promote; ◆ ~ **l'efficacité** COM promote efficiency

favoritisme *m* RES HUM nepotism

fax *m* ADMIN *machine* facsimile, fax, fax machine, COMMS *document* facsimile, fax, *machine* fax machine

fco *abrév* (*franco*) TRANSP fco. (*franco*)

FCP *abrév* (*fonds commun de placement*) BOURSE, FIN OEIC (*open-end investment company*)

FDE *abrév* (*Fonds de développement européen*) ECON, POL EDF (*European Development Fund*)

FEC *abrév* (*frais d'exploration au Canada*) FISC CEE (*Canadian exploration expense*)

fed. *abrév* (*fédéral*) COM fed. (*federal*)

FEDER *abrév* (*Fonds européen de développement régional*) ECON ERDF (*European Regional Development Fund*)

Federal: ~ **Express** *m* TRANSP *messagerie* Federal Express

fédéral, e *adj* (*fed.*) COM federal (*fed.*)

fédéralisme *m* POL federalism; ~ **coopératif** POL cooperative federalism; ~ **créateur** POL creative federalism; ~ **fiscal** ECON, POL fiscal federalism, top-sided federalism

fédération *f* POL federation; ~ **internationale des syndicats** RES HUM IFTU (*AmE*), International Federation of Trade Unions (*AmE*)

Fédération: ~ **internationale des associations de transitaires et assimilés** *f* (*FIATA*) TRANSP International Federation of Forwarding Agents' Associations, International Federation of Freight Forwarders' Associations; ~ **internationale des bourses de valeurs** *f* (*FIBV*) BOURSE International Federation of Stock Exchanges, World Federation of Stock Exchanges (*IFSE*); ~ **internationale de documentation** *f France* (*FID*) COM International Federation for Documentation (*IFD*); ~ **internationale de la navigation** *f* TRANSP International Shipping Federation, ISF; ~ **internationale des ouvriers du transport** *f* (*FIOT*) TRANSP ≈ International Transport Workers' Federation (*ITF*); ~ **internationale des producteurs agricoles** *f* (*FIPA*) IND International Federation of Agricultural Producers (*IFAP*); ~ **mondiale des associations des Nations Unies** *f* ADMIN World Federation of United Nations Associations, WFUNA; ~ **russe** *f* COM Russian Federation; ~ **syndicale internationale** *f* RES HUM IFTU, International Federation of Trade Unions; ~ **syndicale mondiale** (*FSM*) RES HUM World Federation of Trade Unions (*WFTU*)

feedback *m* COM feedback

feeder *m* TRANSP *navigation* feeder

FELIN *abrév* BOURSE, FIN (*Fonds d'État libres d'intérêt nominal*) government-issued certificates which can be exchanged for bonds, ≈ COUGRs (*Certificates of Government Receipts*)

félin *m* BOURSE strip bond, stripped bond

fémelot *m* TRANSP *navigation* gudgeon

femme: ~ **active** *f* RES HUM working woman; ~ **d'affaires** *f* COM businesswoman; ~ **député** *f* POL ≈ Member of Parliament (*UK*), ≈ woman MP (*UK*); ~ **mariée** COM married woman

fenêtre *f* INFO *sur un écran* window; ~ **active** INFO active window; ~ **d'alerte** INFO alert box; ~ **de contrôle** COMPTA, FIN, INFO audit window; ~ **de dialogue** INFO dialog box (*AmE*), dialogue box (*BrE*)

fente *f* INFO *pour introduire une carte* slot

féodalisme *m* POL *histoire* feudalism

féodalité *f* POL *histoire* feudalism

fer *m* ENVIR, IND iron, IRN; ~ **de lance** COM spearhead; ◆ **au** ~ **à droite** (ANT *au fer à gauche*) COMMS, INFO, MÉDIA flush right, right-justified; **au** ~ **à gauche** (ANT *au fer à droite*) COMMS, INFO, MÉDIA flush left, left-justified

ferblanterie *f* COM tinware

ferme[1] *adj* BOURSE *marché* buoyant, firm, COM *commande* firm, ECON buoyant

ferme:[2] ~ **laitière** *f* ECON *agriculture* dairy farm

fermé, e *adj* COM, INFO closed

fermer 1. *vt* COM seal off, *entreprise, usine* close,

shut down, INFO close; ~ **une position de stellage** BOURSE lift a leg (*jarg*); **2.** *vi* ~ **définitivement** COM close down, shut down; ◆ ~ **boutique** COM go out of business

fermeté *f* BOURSE *du marché* buoyancy, COM *d'ure* firmness, ECON, FIN *du marché* buoyancy

fermeture *f* COM, ECON, IND *du marché, d'une machine, usine*, INFO shutdown; ~ **des ateliers** RES HUM *sur décision patronale* lockout; ~ **en cas de grève** RES HUM strike clause; ~ **d'usine** COM lockout, plant interruption, IND plant interruption

ferraille *f* COM, ENVIR scrap metal

ferrailleur *m* COM, RES HUM scrap dealer

ferreux, -euse *adj* ENVIR *agriculture* ferrous

ferroutage *m* TRANSP piggyback traffic (*AmE, jarg*), road-rail transport (*BrE*)

ferrouter *vt* TRANSP piggyback (*jarg*)

ferry *m* TRANSP ferry, ferry boat, train ferry, passenger ferry

fertiliser *vt* ECON *agriculture*, ENVIR fertilize

fesses *f pl* TRANSP *d'un navire* run-in

festival: ~ **du cinéma** *m* MÉDIA *cinéma, télévision* film festival; ~ **cinématographique** *m* MÉDIA *cinéma, télévision* film festival; ~ **du film** *m* MÉDIA *cinéma, télévision* film festival

F&A *abrév (fusions et acquisitions)* BOURSE, ECON M&A (*mergers and acquisitions*)

fête: ~ **légale** *f* COM bank holiday (*BrE*), public holiday; ~ **publique** *f* RES HUM general holiday, public holiday

fétichisme *m* ECON, V&M commodity fetishism

feu: ~ **vert** *m* COM green light

feuille *f* BREVETS sheet, MÉDIA, V&M *publicité* leaf; ~ **bamboche** MÉDIA *impression* badly imposed page; ~ **de calcul électronique** ADMIN, COMPTA, FIN, INFO spreadsheet; ~ **de chou** (*infrml*) MÉDIA *presse* rag (*infrml*); ~ **de couverture** MÉDIA *édition* base sheet; ~ **de pointage** RES HUM tally sheet, time card; ~ **de présence** ADMIN work schedule, RES HUM time sheet; ~ **de programmation** INFO code sheet, work sheet; ~ **rose** COM pink sheet (*US*); ~ **de route** IMP/EXP waybill, TRANSP consignment note, waybill, CN; ~ **de style** INFO style sheet; ~ **de tôle** IND tin plate; ~ **de travail** COMPTA, FIN audit working papers, working papers; ◆ **à ~s mobiles** COM loose-leaf

fév. *abrév (février)* COM Feb. (*February*)

février *m* (*fév.*) COM February (*Feb.*)

FF *abrév (franc français)* COM FF (*French franc*)

FG *abrév (frais généraux)* COMPTA overhead charges, overheads

fiabilité *f* COM, V&M reliability; ~ **du produit** V&M product reliability

fiable *adj* COM reliable; **peu ~** COM unreliable

FIATA *abrév (Fédération internationale des associations de transitaires et assimilés)* TRANSP International Federation of Forwarding Agents' Associations, International Federation of Freight Forwarders' Associations

fibre: ~ **optique** *f* COMMS, IND fiber optics (*AmE*), fibre optics (*BrE*); ~ **synthétique** *f* IND man-made fiber (*AmE*), man-made fibre (*BrE*); ~ **de verre** *f* IND fiberglass (*AmE*), fibreglass (*BrE*)

FIBV *abrév (Fédération internationale des bourses de valeurs)* BOURSE IFSE (*International Federation of Stock Exchanges*), WFSE (*World Federation of Stock Exchanges*)

ficelles: ~ **du métier** *f pl* COM tricks of the trade

fichage *m* ADMIN filing system

fiche *f* BOURSE ticket, COM index card, INFO plug, RES HUM card file; ~ **de client** COMPTA customer card; ~ **des communs** ASSUR aggregate liability index; ~ **initiale de souscription** ASSUR original slip; ~ **d'instructions de transport** TRANSP transport instruction, transport instruction form; ~ **d'inventaire** COM stock sheet; ~ **d'ordre** BOURSE trade ticket; ~ **de paie** RES HUM pay bill (*AmE*), pay sheet, payslip (*BrE*); ~ **de poste** RES HUM job card; ~ **de prix de revient** ECON job cost sheet; ~ **de recherche** COM tracer; ~ **-signature** BANQUE signature card; ~ **de spécimen de signature** BANQUE signature card; ~ **de suivi** COM checklist

fichier *m* ADMIN *collection de fiches* card index, *meuble* file, filing cabinet, COM catalog (*AmE*), catalogue (*BrE*), index file, COMMS mailing list, INFO file, RES HUM card file, card index, index-card file; ~ **actif** INFO active file; ~ **d'adresses** INFO address file; ~ **d'archives** INFO archive file; ~ **ASCII** INFO ASCII file; ~ **avec labels** INFO labeled file (*AmE*), labelled file (*BrE*); ~ **de base** INFO father file, master file; ~ **binaire** INFO binary file; ~ **caché** INFO hidden file; ~ **de caractères** INFO font file; ~ **central** INFO computer bank, data bank; ~ **de commande** INFO command file; ~ **de commandes** INFO batch file; ~ **confidentiel** INFO character card, character file; ~ **de consignation** INFO log file; ~ **de contrôle positif** BANQUE positive file; ~ **en cours** INFO active file; ~ **créateur** INFO father file; ~ **de dessins** INFO drawing file; ~ **de données** INFO data file; ~ **d'édition** INFO report file; ~ **graphique** INFO display file, drawing file, graphics file; ~ **d'index** INFO index file; ~ **informatique** INFO computer file; ~ **informatisé** INFO computerized file; ~ **Lisez-Moi** INFO ReadMe file; ~ **maître** INFO main file; ~ **de mise à jour** INFO change files, transaction file; ~ **mouvements** INFO change files, transaction file; ~ **des oppositions** BANQUE negative file; ~ **père** INFO father file, master file; ~ **principal** COM, INFO main file, master file; ~ **de programme** ADMIN program file (*AmE*), programme file (*BrE*); ~ **programme** INFO program file; ~ **résultant** INFO output file; ~ **de sauvegarde** INFO backup file; ~ **séquentiel** INFO batch file; ~ **de sortie** INFO output file; ~ **source** INFO source file; ~ **de stock** COM inventory file; ~ **sur bande** INFO tape file; ~ **sur ordinateur** INFO computer file; ~ **système** INFO system file; ~ **à**

traitement différé INFO spool file; ~ **de transactions** INFO transaction file; ~ **de travail** INFO scratch file; ~ **de tri** INFO sort file; ~ **vidéo** INFO image file; ~ **de visualisation** INFO display file; ◆ ~ **introuvable** INFO file not found

fictif, -ive *adj* COM fictitious, FIN notional

FID *abrév France (Fédération internationale de documentation)* COM IFD *(International Federation for Documentation)*

fidéicommis *m* DROIT trusteeship; ~ **complexe** DROIT complex trust *(US)*; ~ **de concédant** DROIT, IMMOB grantor trust; ~ **entre vifs** DROIT inter vivos trust; ~ **institué par testament** DROIT testamentary trust; ~ **institué sans document formel** DROIT involuntary trust *(US)*; ~ **irrévocable** DROIT irrevocable trust

fidéjusseur *m* ASSUR surety, DROIT guarantor

fidèle *adj* COM accurate, faithful, trustworthy, COMPTA true and fair; ◆ ~ **à son parti** POL on the reservation *(AmE, jarg)*

fidélisation *f* V&M *publicité* continuous promotion

fidélité *f* COM faithfulness, loyalty, fidelity; ~ **du consommateur** V&M consumer loyalty; ~ **à une marque** V&M *publicité* brand loyalty

Fidji *n pr* COM Fiji

fidjien, -enne *adj* COM Fijian

Fidjien, -enne *m,f* COM *habitant* Fijian

fiduciaire *m* DROIT fiduciary, trustee

fiduciairement *adv* DROIT fiduciarily

fiducie *f* BANQUE *testaments et droits de succession* trust, BOURSE trustee status; ~ **commerciale** FISC commercial trust; ~ **d'employés** FISC employee trust; ~ **offshore** DROIT, FIN offshore trust

figure *f* COM *d'un dessin* figure; ~ **en flamme** BOURSE pennant

figurer *vi* COM appear; ◆ ~ **en tête d'affiche** LOISIRS get top billing

file *f* BOURSE line *(jarg)*; ~ **d'attente** COM *de personnes* line *(AmE)*, queue *(BrE)*, ECON queueing system, rationing, INFO queue; ~ **d'attente à l'Agence nationale pour l'emploi** *France (file d'attente à l'ANPE)* RES HUM ≈ job queue; ~ **d'attente à l'ANPE** *France (file d'attente à l'Agence nationale pour l'emploi)* RES HUM ≈ job queue; ~ **d'attente de travaux** INFO job queue

filer: ~ **à l'anglaise** *loc* COM take French leave *(infrml)*

filet: ~ **de chargement** *m* TRANSP *manutention* basket hitch; ~ **d'élingue** *m* TRANSP *manutention* cargo net; ~ **à palettes** *m* TRANSP pallet net

filiale *f* COM *agence, grande surface, banque* branch, suboffice, *compagnie, firme* affiliate, affiliated company, affiliated firm, associated company, corporate affiliate, subsidiary, subsidiary company, subsidiary firm, COMPTA subsidiary company, ECON corporate affiliate, RES HUM subsidiary company; ~ **bancaire** BANQUE bank subsidiary, banking subsidiary; ~ **à cent pour cent** BOURSE wholly-owned subsidiary; ~ **à**

l'étranger COM associated company abroad; ~ **étrangère** BANQUE foreign branch, BOURSE foreign affiliate; ~ **intérieure** ECON domestic subsidiary; ~ **en propriété exclusive** BOURSE wholly-owned subsidiary

filiales *f pl* COM, DROIT registered offices

filigrane *m* BANQUE watermark

filigrané *adj* BANQUE watermarked

filler *m* MÉDIA *imprimé* fills; ~ **advertisement** MÉDIA *imprimé* filler advertisement

film *m* LOISIRS, MÉDIA film, motion picture *(AmE)*, movie; ~ **de série B** LOISIRS B-movie; ~ **supplémentaire** LOISIRS supporting film; ~ **en vol** TRANSP in-flight film

filon: ~ **riche** *m* IND *en minerai* bonanza *(AmE)*

fils *m* COM jnr, jr, junior, son

filtre *m* INFO filter

fin *f* COM tail end, *groupe industriel, société* break-up, end; ~ **admise** FISC specified purpose; ~ **de l'année d'imposition** FISC end of the tax year, end of the taxation year; ~ **des émissions** MÉDIA *radio, télévision* close-down; ~ **d'exercice** COM year end; ~ **de l'exercice** COMPTA end of financial year, year end; ~ **de fichier** INFO end of file, EOF; ~ **de message** INFO end of message, EOM; ~ **de mois** COMPTA end of month; ~ **de non-recevoir** DROIT demurrer; ~ **de série** V&M end-of-line goods; ~ **de trimestre** COMPTA quarter end; ◆ **à cette** ~ COM with this in view; **de** ~ **d'année** COM, COMPTA, ECON year-end; **en** ~ **de compte** COM at the end of the day; **en** ~ **de journée** COM at the end of the day

final, e *adj* COM final, MÉDIA camera-ready

finalement *adv* COM eventually, finally

finalité *f* COM, ECON, GESTION, V&M aim, objective

finance *f* FIN *dépenses d'investissement en capital* finance; ~ **d'entreprise** FIN corporate finance; ~ **fédérale** ECON federal finance *(US)*, revenue sharing *(US)*; ~ **globale** ECON, FIN outside finance; ~ **industrielle** FIN industrial finance; ~ **d'ouverture** FIN front-end finance

financé: ~ **par l'État** *loc* ECON, FIN, POL government-financed, government-funded

financement *m* COMPTA financing, FIN financing, funding; ~ **d'une acquisition** FIN acquisition financing; ~ **d'actifs** FIN active financing; ~ **d'amorçage** FIN seed capital; ~ **d'apport** FIN vendor finance; ~ **après taxe** COMPTA, ECON, FIN, FISC after-tax financing; ~ **de base** FIN core funding; ~ **de baux financiers** BANQUE lease financing; ~ **du commerce extérieur** BANQUE, FIN trade finance, trade financing; ~ **des comptes clients** COMPTA, FIN accounts receivable financing; ~ **conjoint** COM, ECON, FIN cofinancing; ~ **contractuel unique** FIN single-contract finance; ~ **des créances** COMPTA, FIN accounts receivable financing; ~ **de croissance** ECON, FIN expansion; ~ **du déficit** FIN gap financing; ~ **déguisé** ECON, FIN backdoor financing; ~ **de démarrage** FIN start-up capital; ~ **à l'exportation** ECON, FIN,

IMP/EXP export finance; ~ **des exportations nationales** ECON, IMP/EXP domestic export financing; ~ **externe** FIN external financing; ~ **fédéral** ECON, FIN federal finance (*US*); ~ **fonctionnel** FIN functional financing; ~ **à forfait** BANQUE, FIN nonrecourse finance, nonrecourse financing; ~ **de franchise** FIN franchise financing; ~ **garanti par l'actif** ECON, FIN asset-backed finance; ~ **global** COMPTA, FIN, FISC block funding; ~ **hors bilan** COMPTA, FIN off-balance-sheet finance, off-balance-sheet financing; ~ **d'immobilisations** FIN capital financing, capital funding; ~ **industriel** FIN industrial finance; ~ **initial** FIN front-end financing; ~ **institués de programmes** FIN established programmes financing (*BrE*), established programs financing (*AmE*), EPF; ~ **intérieur** COM domestic financing; ~ **intérimaire** FIN interim financing; ~ **intermédiaire** BANQUE intermediate financing; ~ **interne** ECON internal financing, FIN self-financing; ~ **de lancement** FIN start-up financing; ~ **à long terme** FIN long-term financing; ~ **mezzanine** FIN mezzanine finance, mezzanine funding; ~ **négatif** BANQUE, FIN negative financing; ~ **non durable** ADMIN soft funding (*jarg*); ~ **obligataire** BOURSE bond financing; ~ **officiel** ECON, FIN official financing; ~ **des opérations commerciales** BANQUE, FIN trade finance, trade financing; ~ **par capital risque** FIN risk-bearing capital; ~ **par capital sans risque** FIN risk-avoiding capital; ~ **par crédit relais** FIN bridge financing; ~ **par le déficit** ECON compensatory finance, deficit financing, pump priming; ~ **par émission d'obligations** FIN debt financing; ~ **par emprunt** COMPTA loan capital; ~ **par l'emprunt** ECON deficit spending; ~ **par emprunt bancaire** FIN debt financing; ~ **par le moyen de la banque** BANQUE, FIN bank financing; ~ **par obligation** BOURSE bond financing; ~ **permanent** FIN permanent financing; ~ **d'un plan de retraite** FIN pension plan funding; ~ **des programmes établis** FIN established programmes financing (*BrE*), established programs financing (*AmE*), EPF; ~ **de projets** FIN project financing; ~ **provisoire** FIN interim financing; ~ **à recours limité** BANQUE, FIN limited recourse finance, limited recourse financing; ~ **de redressement** FIN turnaround, turnround; ~ **de remplacement** FIN alternate funding, replacement capital; ~ **à rendement élevé** FIN high-yield financing; ~ **reposant sur l'actif** FIN asset-based financing; ~ **sans recours** BANQUE, FIN nonrecourse finance, nonrecourse financing; ~ **de sociétés** FIN corporate financing; ~ **de stocks** COMPTA inventory financing; ~ **sur fonds propres** FIN equity capital, equity financing; ~ **véreux** ECON, FIN backdoor financing; ◆ **disposant d'un ~ suffisant** COM adequately funded

financer *vt* BANQUE bankroll (*US, jarg*), COM back, FIN *projet* back, finance, fund; ◆ ~ **la différence** ECON finance the difference; ~ **directement** FIN finance directly

finances *f pl* COM finances; ~ **des collectivités locales** POL local government finance; ~ **publiques** FIN government finance, public finance

Financial: ~ **Times** *m* MÉDIA *presse* Financial Times (*UK*), FT (*UK*)

financier[1], **-ière** *adj* FIN financial

financier[2], **-ière** *m,f* BANQUE financier; ~ **à risque** COM, FIN venture capitalist

fine: **la ~ fleur** *f* RES HUM the cream of the crop (*infrml*)

fini, e *adj* COM completed, concluded, finished, V&M concluded

finir 1. *vt* COM complete, conclude, finish, V&M conclude; **2.** *vi* COM end, finish; ◆ ~ **par être payant** BOURSE finish in the money; ~ **le travail** COM finish work, knock off (*infrml*)

finlandais, e *adj* COM Finnish

Finlandais, e *m,f* COM *habitant* Finn; **les ~** *m pl* COM the Finnish, the Fins

Finlande *f* COM Finland

finnois *m* COM *langue* Finnish

Finnois: **les ~** *m pl* COM *Finlande* the Finnish, the Fins

fins: ~ **charitables** *f pl* FISC, PROT SOC charitable purposes; ~ **fiscales** *f pl* COMPTA, FISC tax purposes; ~ **d'imposition** *f pl* COMPTA, FISC tax purposes; ~ **de série** *f pl* V&M broken lots, oddments; ◆ **à des ~ comptables** COMPTA for book purposes

FIO *abrév* (*fabrication intégrée par ordinateur*) IND, INFO CIM (*computer-integrated manufacture, computer-integrated manufacturing*)

FIOT *abrév* (*Fédération internationale des ouvriers du transport*) TRANSP ≈ ITF (*International Transport Workers' Federation*)

fioul *m* TRANSP fuel oil

FIPA *abrév* (*Fédération internationale des producteurs agricoles*) IND IFAP (*International Federation of Agricultural Producers*)

firme *f* COM business concern, concern, company, firm, ECON company, concern, firm; ~ **affiliée** BOURSE member firm; ~ **de courtiers** BOURSE brokerage firm, brokerage house, stock brokerage firm; ~ **dominante** COM core firm, ECON core firm, dominant firm; ~ **étrangère** COM foreign firm; ~ **non-affiliée** BOURSE nonmember firm; ~ **souple et mobile** COM flexible firm; **une ~ sous contrôle étranger** COM foreign-owned company

Fisc: **le ~** *m* FISC the Inland Revenue (*UK*), the Internal Revenue (*US*), the Internal Revenue Service (*US*), IR (*UK*), IRS (*US*)

fiscal, e *adj* COM budgetary, COMPTA, ECON, FIN, POL budgetary, fiscal

fiscaliste *mf* FISC fiscalist, tax expert

fiscalité *f* ECON tax system, taxation, taxation system, FIN taxation, FISC tax system, taxation, taxation system; ~ **excessive** FISC excessive taxation, overtaxation; ~ **latente passive** COMPTA,

FISC deferred tax liabilities; **~ à taux zéro** FISC zero rate taxation

fixage *m* BOURSE fixation, fixing

fixation *f* BOURSE pegging, COM fastening, DROIT, IMMOB *du dédommagement, de l'indemnité* assessment; **~ administrative des prix** ECON administered pricing; **~ conventionnelle des prix** ECON administered pricing; **~ forfaitaire des prix** ECON basing point pricing; **~ d'impôt** FISC assessing tax; **~ marginale du prix** COMPTA, ECON, FIN, V&M marginal pricing; **~ d'objectifs** COM goal setting; **~ des objectifs** COM target setting, targeting, ECON targeting, V&M target setting, targeting; **~ d'objectifs de travail** COM task setting; **~ du point de base** ECON basing point pricing; **~ des prix** COM price determination, pricing, ECON price determination, FIN price-fixing, V&M price determination, pricing, *par un commerçant* price-fixing; **~ du prix d'appel** COM penetration pricing; **~ d'un prix de déclenchement** COM, IND trigger pricing; **~ de prix différentiels** ECON differential pricing; **~ d'un prix élevé** V&M premium pricing; **~ des prix étalée** ECON price bunching, price staggering; **~ des prix en fonction du coût marginal** ECON marginal cost pricing; **~ d'un prix fort** V&M premium pricing; **~ d'un prix majoré** V&M premium pricing; **~ des prix à des niveaux compétitifs** COM, V&M competitive pricing; **~ des prix au niveau du point mort** ECON, V&M break-even pricing; **~ du prix de l'or à Londres** BANQUE London gold fixing; **~ des prix par anticipation** ECON, V&M anticipatory pricing; **~ des prix par une entreprise leader** ECON, V&M price leadership; **~ des prix par le jeu du marché** BOURSE commodity pricing; **~ des prix de transfert** ECON, V&M *multinationales* transfer pricing; **~ des salaires par une personne extérieure** ECON, RES HUM outsider wage setting; **~ synchronisée des prix** ECON price bunching, price staggering; **~ des tâches** RES HUM job spec (*infrml*), job specification; **~ des tarifs** COM fare pricing

fixe *adj* COM fixed, flat

fixé, e *adj* COM *attaché avec un rivet* riveted, R, *taux, tarif, forfait* flat; **~ au sol** FISC *bâtiment construction* affixed to land

fixer *vt* BOURSE *cours* peg, COM *date, endroit* appoint, ECON determine, set, FIN fix; **~ le prix de** ECON price; ◆ **~ la cotisation d'impôt** FISC assess tax; **~ une date** COM set a date; **~ le montant** DROIT *de l'indemnité* settle the figure; **~ une nouvelle cotisation pour** FISC reassess; **~ les paramètres** MATH set parameters; **~ un plafond de** COM cap; **~ le prix de** COM, FIN price, V&M fix the price of, price; **~ un prix forfaitaire** ECON set a price-point

fixeur: ~ de prix *m* ECON price maker

fixing *m* BOURSE fixing, gold fixing

flamand *m* COM *langue* Flemish

flambage *m* TRANSP *navigation* buckling

flambant: ~ neuf *adj* COM brand-new

flambée *f* COM *prix* explosion, jump, surge, ECON boom; **~ des prix** ECON price escalation

flamber *vi* ECON boom

flâneuse *f* IMMOB rambler (*jarg*)

flanquer: ~ qn à la porte *loc infrml* RES HUM boot sb out (*infrml*), give sb the sack (*infrml*), throw sb out (*infrml*)

flash: ~ info *m* COMMS, MÉDIA *TV, radio* news bulletin, news flash; **~ d'information** *m* COMMS, MÉDIA *TV, radio* news flash

FLB *abrév* (*franco le long du bord*) TRANSP *maritime, livraison* FAS (*free alongside ship*), FFA (*free from alongside*)

flèche: ~ de défilement *f* INFO scroll arrow; **~ de retour arrière** *f* INFO back arrow; **~ verticale** *f* INFO down arrow

fléchir *vi* BOURSE sag, COM *prix, tendance du marché etc* dip

fléchissement *m* BOURSE sag, COM *cours* decline, ECON downswing; **~ de la hausse** BOURSE topping out

flémarder *vi* RES HUM goldbrick (*US, infrml*)

flexibilité *f* COM flexibility; **~ des emplois** RES HUM job flexibility; **~ entre services** RES HUM interdepartmental flexibility, IDF; **~ des horaires** RES HUM flexibility of time, flexible time, flexible working hours, flexitime, flextime; **~ des prix** COM, ECON, V&M price flexibility; **~ des salaires** ECON, RES HUM wage flexibility; **~ des tarifs** ECON, TRANSP rate flexibility

flexible *adj* COM flexible, *heure, date* adjustable

flip: ~ -chart *f* COM, V&M flip chart

florin *m* COM florin, guilder

florissant, e *adj* COM flourishing, thriving; ◆ **être ~** COM flourish, thrive

flot *m* INFO flow; ◆ **à ~** COM afloat

flottage: ~ en amont *m* COM upstream float; **~ en aval** *m* COM downstream float

flottant¹, e *adj* BANQUE *taux d'intérêt* floating

flottant² *m* BANQUE bank float, debit float, BOURSE floating stock, floating supply

flotte *f* TRANSP fleet

flottement: ~ impur *m* ECON dirty float; **~ pur** *m* ECON clean float

fluctuation *f* COM fluctuation, movement, swing, ECON fluctuation, move; **~ des cours** BOURSE price move; **~ défavorable** BOURSE *des prix des obligations* adverse movement; **~ défavorable des cours** ECON adverse price movement; **~ du niveau des prix** COM price level change; **~ de prix** price tick; **~ saisonnière** COM seasonal swing

fluctuations: ~ journalières *f pl* BOURSE mark-to-the-market, marking-to-market; **~ des taux de change** *f pl* ECON, FIN exchange rate fluctuations, exchange rate movements

fluctuer *vi* BANQUE float, BOURSE fluctuate, COM fluctuate, yo-yo (*infrml*), ECON move together

fluide: ~ de dégivrage *m* TRANSP de-icing fluid

fluorure: ~ **de sulfuryle** *m* TRANSP sulfuryl fluoride (*AmE*), sulphuryl fluoride (*BrE*)

flux *m* COM flow, flux, COMPTA, ECON, FIN, TRANSP flow; ~ **d'affaires** *m* COM, ECON business stream; ~ **de capitaux** *m* ECON, FIN capital flow, flow of funds; ~ **circulaire** *m* ECON circular flow; ~ **commercial** *m* ECON, IMP/EXP trade flow; ~ **de données** *m* COM data stream; ~ **de l'encaisse** *m* COMPTA cash flow; ~ **financier** *m* COMPTA, ECON, FIN financial flow, flow of funds; ~ **de l'information** *m* COM *dans une société*, INFO information flow; ~ **monétaire** *m* ECON, FIN flow of money; ~ **monétaires internationaux** *m pl* ECON international money flow; ~ **net total** *m* ECON total net flow; ~ **des revenus** *m* ECON income stream; ~ **de travail** *m* COM work flow; ~ **de trésorerie** *m* COMPTA cash flow, flow of funds, ECON, FIN flow of funds; ~ **de trésorerie avant impôts** *m* COMPTA before-tax cash flow, FISC after-tax cash flow; ~ **de trésorerie disponible** *m* COMPTA available cash flow; ◆ **à ~ tendus** IND, MÉDIA, RES HUM just-in-time, JIT

FM *abrév* (*modulation de fréquence*) COMMS FM (*frequency modulation*)

FME *abrév* (*Fonds monétaire européen*) ECON, POL EMF (*European Monetary Fund*)

FMEC *abrév* (*Fonds monétaire européen de coopération*) ECON, POL EMCF (*European Monetary Cooperation Fund*)

FMI *abrév* (*Fonds monétaire international*) BANQUE, ECON, FIN IMF (*International Monetary Fund*)

FN *abrév* (*Front National*) POL ≈ NF (*UK*) (*National Front*)

focaliser *vt* COM focus

foi: ~ **aveugle** *f* COM blind faith; ~ **du charbonnier** *f* COM blind faith; **en ~ de quoi** DROIT in witness whereof

foire *f* V&M *de l'automobile, des arts ménagers, etc* exhibition; ◆ ~ **de l'artisanat** COM, V&M artisan fair; ~ **commerciale** V&M *ouverte au public* trade exhibition, trade fair, trade show; ~ **d'empoigne** COM free-for-all (*infrml*), rat race, V&M free-for-all (*infrml*)

fois *f pl* MATH times; **une ~ et demie** *f* RES HUM time and a half

foncier: ~ **non bâti** *m* IMMOB vacant land; ~ **à perpétuité** *m* IMMOB freeholder

fonction *f* COM activity, *rôle* function, INFO facility, feature, function, MATH function; ~ **bergsonienne de bien-être social** ECON, PROT SOC Bergson social welfare function; ~ **de bien-être social** ECON, PROT SOC social welfare function; ~ **de consommation** ECON consumption function; ~ **consultative** RES HUM advisory function, advisory work; ~ **de déperdition** MATH loss function; ~ **de direction** GESTION managerial function; ~ **élevée** RES HUM high office, important office; ~ **d'emploi** ECON employment function; ~ **d'épargne** ECON savings function;

~ **exponentielle** INFO, MATH exponential function; ~ **de micro-production** ECON microproduction function; ~ **objective** MATH objective function; ~ **d'offre** ECON supply function; ~ **de l'offre de Lucas** ECON Lucas supply function; ~ **de production** ECON production function; ~ **programmable** INFO programmable function; ~ **de pseudo-production** ECON pseudo production function; ~ **publique** COM civil service, public service, CS; ~ **de réaction** ECON reaction function; ~ **de recherche et remplacement** INFO search and replace; ~ **de surprise** ECON surprise function; ~ **d'utilité** ECON utility function; ◆ **avoir une ~ de** RES HUM perform the office of; **de par ses ~s** RES HUM by virtue of one's position, ex officio (*frml*); **en ~** RES HUM in charge, in office; **en ~ de** COM as a function of, in terms of; **en ~ des informations à connaître** COM, GESTION on a need-to-know basis; **en ~ du revenu** FISC income-tested

fonctionnaire *mf* ADMIN *d'État* civil servant, official, PROT SOC *d'État*, RES HUM civil servant; ~ **boursier** *m* BOURSE floor official; ~ **de l'immigration** *m* ADMIN, RES HUM immigration officer, IO; ~ **de l'ordre judiciaire** *m* DROIT legal officer; ~ **titulaire** *m* ADMIN, RES HUM senior civil servant

fonctionnel, -elle *adj* COM functional

fonctionnement *m* ADMIN, COM functioning, DROIT machinery; ~ **par ateliers** PROT SOC multiple-track plan (*jarg*); ~ **en réseau** COM networking; ◆ **en ~** COM at work

fonctionner *vi* COM function, operate; ◆ ~ **en tandem** GESTION operate in tandem

fonctions: ~ **complémentaires** *f pl* COM, GESTION, INFO support activities

fond *m* COM core, TRANSP *d'un navire* bottom, btm; ~ **de cale** TRANSP *navigation* bilge; ~ **de garantie** BOURSE compensation fund (*UK*); ~ **de panier** INFO cage card, motherboard, mothercard; ~ **perdu** MÉDIA bleed (*infrml*); ~ **rond** TRANSP *d'un navire* round bottom, RDBTN; ~ **en V** TRANSP *navigation* vee bottom, VEE BTM; ◆ **à ~ en V** TRANSP *navigation* vee built (*US*), VBLT (*US*); **sur le ~** DROIT on its merits

fondamental, e *adj* COM fundamental

fondateur, -trice *m,f* DROIT settlor (*UK*)

fondation *f* COM establishment, foundation, TRANSP *navigation* foundation; ~ **de charité** FISC, PROT SOC charitable foundation; ~ **privée** FISC private foundation; ~ **publique** FISC public foundation; ~ **d'utilité publique** FISC, PROT SOC charitable trust

Fondation: ~ **européenne** *f* COM European Foundation, EF

fondé[1]**, e** *adj* COM est., established, justified; ◆ **être ~ à faire** DROIT be justified in doing

fondé:[2] ~ **de pouvoir** *mf* DROIT attorney (*US*), authorized agent, private attorney, proxyholder, COM authorized representative

Fondé: ~ **de pouvoir supérieur** *m* RES HUM officer with statutory authority

fondement *m* COM basis; ~ **d'une action** DROIT cause of action

fonder *vt* COM base, establish, *agence* create

fonderie *f* IND smelting works

fondre *vt* FIN *métal* fuse, IND smelt

fonds *m pl* BANQUE bankroll (*US*), trade finance, trade financing, COM *caisse* capital funds, fund, funds, COMPTA cash, FIN cash, financial means, funds, trade finance, trade financing; ~ **accumulés** *m pl* FISC accumulating fund; ~ **d'actions ordinaires** *m* BOURSE common shares fund (*BrE*), common stock fund (*AmE*); ~ **d'affectation spéciale** *m* DROIT, ECON, FIN trust fund; ~ **d'aide au développement** *m* BANQUE, ECON aid money (*UK*), POL aid money; ~ **d'amortissement** *m* BOURSE sinking fund, COMPTA, FIN amortization fund, sinking fund; ~ **d'amortissement de la dette publique** *m* ECON, FIN, FISC consolidated fund (*UK*); ~ **pour amortissement des obligations** *m* BOURSE bond sinking fund; ~ **d'arbitrage** *m* BOURSE hedge fund (*jarg*); ~ **autogénérés** *m pl* COMPTA cash flow, FIN self-generated funds; ~ **autogénérés par action** *m pl* BOURSE cash flow per share; ~ **cadre** *m* FIN umbrella fund; ~ **de caisse** *m* COM, COMPTA cash in hand, petty cash fund; ~ **de capital et d'emprunt** *m* COMPTA, FIN capital fund; ~ **de cautionnement** *m* BANQUE guaranty fund; ~ **des changes** *m* BOURSE exchange fund; ~ **de cohésion** *m* ECON cohesion fund; ~ **de commerce** *m* COM business concern, COMPTA goodwill money; ~ **commercial** *m* COM goodwill, goodwill money, COMPTA goodwill; ~ **commun de l'énergie** *m* ENVIR energy mutual fund; ~ **commun de placement** *m* *(FCP)* BOURSE, FIN investment trust, mutual fund (*AmE*), open-end investment company, unit trust (*BrE*); ~ **commun de placement du marché monétaire** *m* FIN money-market mutual fund (*US*), MMMF (*US*); ~ **de compensation** *m* ASSUR equalization fund; ~ **compensés** *m pl* BANQUE clearing house funds; ~ **de consolidation** *m* FIN umbrella fund; ~ **consolidés** *m pl* FIN cons (*UK*), consols (*UK*), consolidated annuities (*UK*), consolidated stock (*UK*); ~ **de coordination** *m* FIN umbrella fund; ~ **courants** *m pl* FIN general fund; ~ **de courtage** *m* BOURSE broker fund (*UK*); ~ **de croissance** *m* BOURSE growth fund; ~ **de dépôt en eurodollars** *m pl* BOURSE, ECON, FIN Eurodollar time deposit funds; ~ **pour le développement de la conscience sociale** *m* ECON social conscience fund; ~ **disponibles** *m pl* COMPTA available funds, liquid funds; ~ **disponibles en banque** *m pl* BANQUE cash in bank; ~ **de dividendes** *m* BOURSE dividend fund; ~ **dominant** *m* IMMOB dominant tenement; ~ **empruntés** *m pl* BANQUE borrowed funds, BOURSE bear hug takeover, bond washing, other peoples' money, OPM; ~ **d'escompte** *m* FIN discount market loan; ~ **d'État** *m pl* BOURSE gilt (*UK*), FIN federal agency issue (*US*), federal

agency security (*US*), BOURSE cons (*UK*), consols (*UK*); ~ **à l'étranger** *m pl* BANQUE funds abroad; ~ **de l'étranger** *m pl* FISC offshore funds; ~ **pour éventualités** *m* FIN contingency fund; ~ **exceptionnels** *m pl* FIN Superfund (*US*); ~ **externes** *m pl* FIN external funds; ~ **en fidéicommis** *m pl* DROIT agency fund, trust fund, ECON, FIN trust fund; ~ **de garantie bancaire** *m* FIN bank insurance fund; ~ **de garantie des investisseurs** *m* BOURSE Investors' Compensation Scheme (*UK*); ~ **de garantie des salaires** *m* FISC national salary guarantee fund; ~ **gelés** *m pl* FIN frozen assets; ~ **géré en devises** *m* ECON, FIN managed currency fund; ~ **hautement spéculatif** *m* FIN go-go fund (*jarg*); ~ **indice** *m* BOURSE index fund; ~ **indiciel** *m* BOURSE index fund; ~ **insuffisants** *m pl* BANQUE, COM n.s.f., not sufficient funds, FIN insufficient funds; ~ **investi au marché monétaire** *m* BOURSE, ECON, FIN money-market fund (*US*), MMF (*US*); ~ **d'investissement en actions** *m* BOURSE equity investment fund; ~ **d'investissement à capital fixe** *m* BOURSE closed-end mutual fund (*US*); ~ **d'investissement diamantaire** *m* BOURSE diamond investment trust; ~ **d'investissement en options** *m* BOURSE option mutual fund; ~ **d'investissement en valeurs aurifères** *m* BOURSE gold mutual fund; ~ **du jour au lendemain** *m pl* BANQUE federal funds (*US*), overnight funds; ~ **de liquidation** *m* ASSUR clean-up fund; ~ **mis de côté** *m pl* FIN impound account; ~ **mixtes** *m pl* BOURSE mixed funds; ~ **monétaire** *m* BOURSE, ECON, FIN money-market fund (*US*), MMF (*US*); ~ **mutuel d'entraide sociale** *m* FIN social consciousness mutual fund; ~ **national** *m* BOURSE country fund (*UK*); ~ **nets disponibles** *m pl* BANQUE, FIN net liquid funds; ~ **non-agréés** *m pl* FIN unapproved funds; ~ **non-collectés** *m pl* BANQUE uncollected funds; ~ **non-engagés** *m pl* FIN uncommitted funds; ~ **obligataire** *m* BOURSE bond fund; ~ **obligataire municipal** *m* FIN single-state municipal bond fund; ~ **occultes** *m pl* FIN secret reserve; ~ **offshore** *m pl* FIN offshore funds; ~ **périmés** *m pl* COMPTA lapsed funds; ~ **de placement** *m* BOURSE investment trust, *qui prélève une commission* load fund, FIN investment trust, load fund; ~ **de placement en actions** *m* BOURSE investment fund for shares; ~ **de placement en actions ordinaires** *m* BOURSE common shares fund (*BrE*), common stock fund (*AmE*); ~ **de placement en biens immobiliers** *m* COMPTA real estate fund (*US*); ~ **de placement aux investissements équilibrés** *m* BOURSE balanced mutual fund; ~ **de placement à plus-values maximales** *m* BOURSE maximum capital gains mutual fund; ~ **de placement suivant un indice** *m* FIN index-tracking fund; ~ **de placements immobiliers** *m* BANQUE real estate investment trust (*US*), REIT (*US*); ~ **prédateur** *m* FIN vulture fund; ~ **prêtables** *m pl* BANQUE lendable funds; ~ **de prévoyance** *m* FIN contingency fund, GESTION contingency reserve; ~ **propres** *m pl* BOURSE equity capital, shareholders' equity, COMPTA, FIN capital employed, equity, equity funds; **~ de provenance inconnue** *m pl* PROT SOC soft money *(jarg)*; **~ publics** *m pl* ECON *budget des pouvoirs publics* federal funds *(US)*; **~ publics à taux favorable** *m pl* ADMIN soft funding *(jarg)*; **~ de rachat** *m* COM purchase fund; **~ de règlement des sinistres** *m* ASSUR claims settlement fund; **~ de régularisation** *m* ASSUR equalization fund; **~ renouvelable** *m* FIN revolving fund; **~ renouvelable des approvisionnements** *m* ECON supply revolving fund; **~ renouvelable d'indemnisation pétrolière** *m* FIN Petroleum Compensation Revolving Fund; **~ renouvelable de la production de défense** *m* FIN defence production revolving fund *(BrE)*, defense production revolving fund *(AmE)*; **~ de réserve** *m* BANQUE *d'une banque* bank reserve, rest fund, BOURSE rest account, FIN contingency reserve; **~ de la réserve fédérale** *m pl* BANQUE *marché* Fed funds *(US)*, Federal funds *(US)*; **~ de retraite** *m* ASSUR, COMPTA, FIN, RES HUM pension fund; **~ de roulement** *m* COM working capital, ECON circulating capital, FIN circulating capital, working capital; **~ de roulement négatif** *m* COMPTA negative working capital; **~ de roulement net** *m* COMPTA, FIN net current assets, net working capital; **~ sans frais** *m* BOURSE no-load fund *(US)*; **~ de sauvegarde** *m* BOURSE hedge fund *(jarg)*; **~ servant aux activités politiques** *m* RES HUM political fund; **~ soutenu** *m* POL hard money *(jarg)*; **~ spéculatifs** *m pl* BOURSE performance fund, speculative fund; **~ de stabilisation** *m* FISC stabilization fund; **~ de stabilisation des changes** *m* FIN Exchange Equalization Account, EEA; **~ structurels** *m pl* ECON structural funds; **~ venant d'opérations** *m pl* COMPTA funds from operations; ♦ **à ~ publics** COM publicly-funded; **avec ~ bancaires** BANQUE bank-financed; **injecter des ~ dans** FIN pump funds into

Fonds: **~ agricole européen** *m* ECON, FIN, POL European Agricultural Fund, UAF; **~ d'aide aux projets à l'exportation** *m* ECON *commerce international* overseas project fund; **~ de développement européen** *m (FDE)* ECON, POL European Development Fund *(EDF)*; **~ d'État libres d'intérêt nominal** *m pl (FELIN)* BOURSE, FIN government-issued certificates which can be exchanged for bonds, ≈ Certificates of Government Receipts *(COUGRs)*; **~ européen de coopération monétaire** *m* BANQUE European Monetary Cooperation Fund; **~ européen de développement régional** *m (FEDER)* ECON European Regional Development Fund *(ERDF)*; **~ mondial pour la nature** *m* ENVIR World Wide Fund, WWF; **~ monétaire européen** *m (FME)* ECON, POL European Monetary Fund *(EMF)*; **~ monétaire européen de coopération** *m (FMEC)* ECON, POL European Monetary Cooperation Fund *(EMCF)*; **~ monétaire international** *m (FMI)* BANQUE, ECON, FIN International Monetary Fund *(IMF)*; **~ national de**

prévoyance *m* ECON National Contingency Fund, FIN national contingency fund; **~ de rétablissement du conseil de l'Europe** *m (FRCE)* BANQUE Council of Europe Resettlement Fund *(CERF)*; **~ social européen** *m (FSE)* ECON, POL European Social Fund *(ESF)*

fongibles *m pl* ECON fungibles

fonte *f* FIN *d'un métal* fusion, INFO, MÉDIA font; **~ froide** MÉDIA *imprimerie* cold type

forage: **~ d'exploration** *m* ENVIR wildcat drilling; **~ d'exploration contrôlé** *m* ENVIR controlled wildcat drilling; **~ sauvage** *m* ENVIR wildcat drilling; **~ sauvage sous contrôle** *m* ENVIR controlled wildcat drilling; **~ en terrain vierge** *m* ENVIR wildcat drilling

force *f* BOURSE, COM strength; **~ d'appui** POL leverage; **~ contenue** COM pent-up energy; **~ financière** FIN financial strength; **~ de loi** DROIT legal force; **~ majeure** COM, DROIT force majeure; **~ de serrage** TRANSP *manutention* clamping force; **~ de tirage** TRANSP *au bollard* b.p., bollard pull; **~ de vente** V&M sales force; ♦ **avoir ~ de loi** DROIT have statutory effect; **avoir ~ réglementaire** DROIT have statutory effect

forcé, e *adj* COM compulsory

forcer *vt* COM force; ♦ **~ qn à faire qch** COM force sb to do sth, oblige sb to do sth

forces: **~ du marché** *f pl* ECON, POL, V&M market forces

forclusion *f* DROIT foreclosure; **~ fiscale** FISC tax foreclosure; **~ légale** DROIT statutory foreclosure

fordisme *m* ECON Fordism

forêt *f* ECON, ENVIR, IND forest; **~ ombrophile** ENVIR rainforest; **~ tropicale ombrophile** ENVIR tropical rainforest

forfait *m* BOURSE fixed price, flat sum, COM agreed sum, COMPTA fixed price, LOISIRS package deal, package holiday *(BrE)*, package tour *(BrE)*, package vacation *(AmE)*, TRANSP *fret* ls, lump sum; **~ de sous-traitance** RES HUM lump; **~ volcroisière** LOISIRS fly-cruise; ♦ **à ~** BOURSE at a flat price, COM *contrat* at an agreed price

forfaitaire *adj* ASSUR flat-rate, COM *imposition* flat-rate, *prix* all-inclusive, ECON, V&M flat-rate

forint *m* COM forint

formaliser *vt* COM formalize

formalité *f* COM formality

formalités: **~ douanières** *f pl* IMP/EXP clearance, customs formalities; **~ douanières d'une cargaison** *f pl* IMP/EXP customs cargo clearance; **~ juridiques** *f pl* DROIT legal formalities; **~ légales** *f pl* DROIT legal formalities

format *m* INFO format, *d'un document* size; **~ de l'écran** COM, INFO, MÉDIA aspect ratio; **~ d'enregistrement** INFO record format; **~ à la française** INFO, MÉDIA *presse, édition* portrait format; **~ en hauteur** INFO, MÉDIA *imprimé* portrait format; **~ horizontal** COM landscape format, INFO, MÉDIA *impression* landscape format, landscape mode; **~ à l'italienne** COM landscape format, INFO, MÉDIA landscape format, landscape mode; ~ **portrait** INFO, MÉDIA portrait format; ~ **standard** COM basic size, standard size, INFO standard size; ~ **vertical** INFO, MÉDIA portrait format; ~ **A4** ADMIN, COMMS, INFO A4; ~ **B5** ADMIN, COMMS, INFO B5 letter, B5

Format: ~ **2** *m (*SYN *Format 1)* COMPTA Format 2 *(BrE)*; ~ **1** *m (*SYN *Format 2)* COMPTA Format 1 *(BrE)*

formatage *m* ADMIN *de disquette, vidéo* format, INFO *de disque, disquette* formatting

formater[1] *vt* INFO *disque, disquette* format

formateur[1], **-trice** *adj* COM *influence* formative, RES HUM *stage* instructive; ◆ **être** ~ RES HUM train

formateur[2], **-trice** *m,f* RES HUM trainer

formation *f* COM training, PROT SOC educational background, RES HUM training, *expérience* background, *éducation* ET *(BrE)*, employment training *(BrE)*; ~ **brute de capital fixe** COMPTA, ECON gross fixed capital formation; ~ **des cadres** GESTION executive training, management training, RES HUM executive training; ~ **de capital** COMPTA, ECON capital formation; ~ **continue** RES HUM day release or evening classes paid for or provided by companies to their employees; ~ **dans l'entreprise** IND in-plant training, training within industry, TWI, RES HUM in-house training, in-plant training, TWI, on-the-job training, OJT, training within industry; ~ **en dehors de l'entreprise** RES HUM off-the-job training; ~ **à l'emploi** RES HUM ET *(BrE)*, employment training *(BrE)*; ~ **en entreprise** RES HUM on-the-job training, OJT; ~ **extérieure** RES HUM off-the-job training; ~ **de formateurs** RES HUM training of trainers; ~ **générale** RES HUM general training; ~ **hors de l'entreprise** RES HUM off-the-job training; ~ **des jeunes** RES HUM youth training *(UK)*, YT *(UK)*; ~ **au management** COM, GESTION management development; ~ **par alternance** PROT SOC sandwich course; ~ **par étapes** COM part-analysis training, GESTION analytical training, RES HUM analytical training, part-analysis training; ~ **permanente** PROT SOC further education; ~ **du personnel** RES HUM staff training; ~ **plurimédiatique** INFO, MÉDIA, PROT SOC, RES HUM multimedia training; ~ **pratique** RES HUM hands-on training; ~ **professionnelle** RES HUM industrial training, job training, vocational training; ~ **professionnelle continue** COMPTA, PROT SOC continual professional education; ~ **programmée** INFO computer-based training; ~ **spécifique** RES HUM specific training; ~ **supérieure** PROT SOC advanced education; ~ **sur site** RES HUM in-house training, on-the-job training, OJT; ~ **sur le tas** RES HUM on-the-job training, OJT; ~ **sur le terrain** RES HUM on-the-job training, OJT; ~ **verticale** COM vertical formation; ◆ **ayant une ~ en informatique** INFO computer literate, computerate; **faire de la** ~ RES HUM train

formats: ~ **postaux normalisés** *m pl* COMMS post office preferred, POP

forme *f* COM form, make, ECON, MATH *d'une courbe* shape; ~ **de l'économie mondiale** ECON shape of the world economy; ~ **négociée** RES HUM bargaining form; ~ **organisationnelle** COM organizational shape; ~ **de propriété** DROIT, IMMOB ownership form *(US)*; ~ **de radoub** TRANSP *port* graving dock; ◆ **en ~ de M** ECON M-form; **en ~ provisoire** DROIT, POL in draft form; **pour la** ~ COM pro forma

former *vt* COM *comité* form, *nouvelle entreprise* establish, form, MÉDIA mold *(AmE)*, mould *(BrE)*, RES HUM train; ~ **un recours** DROIT appeal

formidable *adj* COM tremendous *(infrml)*, TRANSP A-1 *(jarg)*

formulaire *m* BREVETS *imprimé*, INFO form; ~ **commercial** ASSUR commercial form, COM, RES HUM business form, TRANSP commercial form; ~ **de déclaration de sinistre** ASSUR claim form; ~ **de demande de licence d'exportation** IMP/EXP export licence application form *(BrE)*, export license application form *(AmE)*; ~ **de demande de renseignements** COM enquiry form, inquiry form; ~ **d'inscription** ADMIN, RES HUM application form; ~ **normalisé** ADMIN aligned form; ~ **prescrit** FISC prescribed form; ~ **réglementaire** FISC prescribed form; ~ **à remplir** COM blank form; ~ **sensible** FISC sensitive form; ~ **standardisé** ADMIN, TRANSP aligned form; ~ **T** IMP/EXP T form; ~ **de transfert** BOURSE transfer; ~ **de transit CEE** TRANSP EU transit form; ~ **de transport d'actions** BOURSE stock transfer form; ~ **de versement** FISC remittance return; ~ **10K** BOURSE form 10K; ~ **10Q** BOURSE form 10Q; ~ **8K** BOURSE form 8K; ~ **4** BOURSE form 4

formulation *f* COM, GESTION formulation; ~ **de la politique** POL policy lag

formule *f* MATH formula; ~ **de calcul d'intérêt** BANQUE, FIN interest formula; ~ **de chèque** BANQUE blank check *(AmE)*, blank cheque *(BrE)*, check form *(AmE)*, cheque form *(BrE)*; ~ **Du Pont** FIN Du Pont formula; ~ **de l'établissement du prix de l'option** BOURSE option-pricing formula; ~ **d'étalement** BANQUE averaging formula; ~ **d'évaluation des options** BOURSE option-pricing formula; ~ **expressément utilisée par l'employeur** RES HUM employer express term; ~ **fiscale** FISC tax form; ~ **gravée** BANQUE engraved form; ~ **magique** RES HUM golden formula *(UK)*; ~ **de marketing** V&M marketing mix; ~ **de moment de produit** MATH product moment formula; ~ **de politesse** COMMS complimentary close; ~ **au porteur** BOURSE, FIN, FISC bearer form; ~ **préférentielle** BOURSE preferential form; ~ **quinquennale** BANQUE five-year formula; ~ **à usage restreint** FISC sensitive form

formuler *vt* COM *conditions* set out, *demande* formulate; ◆ ~ **une demande de renseignements** COM make enquiries

fort, e *adj* COM heavy, ECON heavy, steep, stiff,

devise strong; ◆ **à ~ coefficient de main-d'oeuvre** ECON, IND, RES HUM labor-intensive (*AmE*), labour-intensive (*BrE*); **à ~ coefficient de recherche** IND *production* research-intensive; **~ coefficient d'arrimage** TRANSP *marchandises* high stowage factor

forte: **~ augmentation** *f* ECON sharp rise; **~ baisse** *f* ECON sharp drop; **~ concurrence** *f* COM tough competition; **~ demande** *f* ECON active demand, heavy demand, V&M active demand; **~ expansion** *f* COM boom; **~ hausse** *f* ECON boom, sharp rise; **~ progression** *f* COM boom; ◆ **à ~ image de marque** V&M high-profile; **à ~ intensité capitalistique** IND capital-intensive; **à ~ intensité de capitaux** IND capital-intensive; **à ~ intensité de connaissances** COM knowledge-intensive; **à ~ intensité de main-d'oeuvre** ECON, IND, RES HUM labor-intensive (*AmE*), labour-intensive (*BrE*); **à ~ proportion de capital** ECON, IND capital-intensive; **à ~ utilisation d'acier** IND *production* steel-intensive; **être en ~ hausse** ECON boom

fortement: **~ peuplé** *adj* ECON densely-populated; ◆ **être ~ présent** COM be in evidence

forteresse: **~ Europe** *f jarg* POL *UE* fortress Europe (*jarg*)

fortuit, e *adj* COM chance, contingent

fortune *f* COM fortune; **~ de mer** ASSUR accident at sea, maritime peril, sea damage, SD, *assurance maritime* perils of the sea, TRANSP sea damage, SD, *maritime* accident at sea, *navigation* perils of the sea; ◆ **faire ~** COM strike it rich (*infrml*)

fortuné, e *adj* COM well-to-do

forum *m* POL forum

fossé: **~ entre les salaires** *loc* RES HUM wage gap

fouille *f* IMP/EXP *douane* examination; **~ et perquisition** *f pl* FISC search; **~ au hasard** *f* IMP/EXP spot check; **~ incontestée** *f* POL UPS (*jarg*), uncontested physical search (*jarg*)

fouiller *vt* COM search for, IMP/EXP *douane* examine, frisk (*infrml*), search

fourche: **~ à palettes** *f* TRANSP *manutention* pallet fork; **~ à rallonge** *f* TRANSP extension fork

fourchette *f* BOURSE *marché à terme* range, COM *de prix*, FISC bracket; **~ des cours en fin de séance** BOURSE closing range; **~ de point fixe** TRANSP anchor bracket; **~ de prix** BOURSE accumulation area, price range, ECON, V&M price range; **~ de prix du jobber** BOURSE jobber's spread; **~ des prix limites de transaction** BOURSE trading range; **~ de variation du cours** BOURSE distribution area; **~ visée** ECON target range

fourgon *m* TRANSP freight car (*AmE*), goods wagon (*BrE*); **~ frigorifique** TRANSP refrigerated box van; **~ isotherme** TRANSP insulated van; **~ postal** COMMS mail van (*BrE*), mailcar (*AmE*), mailcoach (*BrE*)

fourguer *vt infrml* COM *marchandises* flog (*BrE, infrml*), hustle (*infrml*)

fourni, e *adj* COM abundant; **~ avec** INFO bundled with

fournir *vt* COM *documents* provide, supply, *marchandises, renseignements* provide, *service* accommodate, deliver, DROIT *preuve* adduce, FIN provide; ◆ **~ une assistance technique** COM provide technical assistance; **~ des directives à** COM brief; **~ des marchandises à crédit** COM supply goods on credit, supply goods on trust; **~ un marché pour** BOURSE provide a market for; **~ du personnel à** RES HUM man; **~ des preuves à l'appui d'une demande** DROIT substantiate a claim; **~ un soutien technique** COM provide technical assistance

fournissant: **personne ~ le soutien** *f* FISC supporting person

fournisseur *m* COM provider, purveyor, supplier, trade creditor, COMPTA, ECON trade creditor, INFO vendor, V&M dealer, retailer, stockist (*UK*); **~ d'alimentation fine** COM purveyor of fine foods; **~ de crédit** BANQUE credit grantor; **~ de matériaux** IND material man; **~ de navires** TRANSP ship's chandler; **~ d'ordinateurs** INFO computer vendor; **~ de système** FIN system-provider

fourniture *f* COM provision, supply, DROIT provision, V&M provision, supply; **~ publique** COM public procurement

fournitures *f pl* COM, ECON, V&M supplies; **~ de bureau** ADMIN office requisites, office stationery, office supplies, COM office requisites, office supplies; **~ consommables** COMPTA factory supplies; **~ au taux zéro** FISC zero-rated supplies (*UK*)

foyer *m* ADMIN *d'un immeuble, d'un bureau* reception area, *maison* home (*frml*); **~ à caractère d'incendie** ASSUR hostile fire; **~ à faible revenu** V&M low-income household; **~ fiscal** ECON, FISC tax unit; **~ à parois ondulés** TRANSP *navigation* ribbed furnace; **~ récalcitrant** PROT SOC residual family

FPP *abrév (frontière des possibilités de production)* ECON production possibility frontier

fraction *f* FIN portion, MATH fraction; **~ d'action** BOURSE fractional share; **~ d'une action** BOURSE subshare; **~ convenue** FISC agreed portion; **~ inutilisée** FISC unused part; **~ non amortie du coût** COMPTA, FIN undepreciated cost; **~ non amortie du coût en capital** COMPTA undepreciated cost, FIN undepreciated capital cost; **~ non-amortie des insuffisances actuarielles** COMPTA, FIN unamortized portion of actuarial deficiencies; **~ à risques** FISC *de l'intérêt d'un commanditaire* at-risk amount; **~ simple** MATH simple fraction

fractionnement: **~ d'actions** *m* BANQUE roll-over loan, stock split (*AmE*); **~ de portefeuille** *m* BOURSE, FIN portfolio split; **~ du revenu** *m* FISC income splitting

fractionner *vt* COM divide up, MATH fractionalize; ◆ **~ un chargement** TRANSP break bulk; **~ une livraison** TRANSP break bulk

fragile *adj* COM *sur les paquets* handle with care, TRANSP fragile

fragmentation *f* COM, ECON *du marché* fragmenta-tion, market fragmentation, INFO fragmentation
fragmenter *vt* COM break up, chunk down *(jarg)*
frais *m pl* BANQUE borrowing fee, fee, BOURSE fee, COM borrowing fee, charge, charges, COMPTA borrowing fee, expenses, DROIT, ECON *dépense* costs, FIN borrowing fee, costs, V&M costs; ~ **accessoires** COM incidental allowances, COMP-TA incidental allowances, incidental charges; ~ **accumulés** BANQUE accrued charges; ~ **d'achat** COM purchasing costs, COMPTA original cost; ~ **d'acquisition** ASSUR, BOURSE acquisition fee, COMPTA acquisition cost; ~ **d'adaptation** ADMIN administrative costs of regulation, com-pliance costs; ~ **administratifs** ADMIN administrative charge, administrative costs, ASSUR administrative charge, COM administrative costs, COMPTA administrative expense; ~ **d'administration** ADMIN administration costs, administrative charge, administrative costs, ser-vice charge, administrative costs of regulation, compliance costs, ASSUR administrative charge, COM administrative costs, business charges, office expenses, COMPTA administration expenses, administrative expense, business charges, office expenses; ~ **admissibles** FISC eligible expense; ~ **d'agence** BOURSE agency cost *(UK)*, COM agency fee, booking fee; ~ **d'allège** TRANSP light-erage; ~ **d'aménagement au Canada** *(FAC)* ECON Canadian development expense *(CDE)*; ~ **amortis** FIN sunk cost; ~ **d'annulation** COM cancellation fee; ~ **anticipés** TRANSP advanced charge, advanced disbursement; ~ **d'assurance** ASSUR insurance charge, insurance cost; ~ **d'audit** COMPTA, FIN audit costs; ~ **bancaires** BANQUE bank charges, bank commission, bank-ing charges, charges on banking transactions, COMPTA, FIN bank charges; ~ **de banque** BANQUE bank charges, bank commission, banking charges, charges on banking transactions, COMPTA, FIN bank charges; ~ **du barème** FISC scale charge; ~ **de bureau à domicile** FISC home office expenses; ~ **de camionnage** TRANSP truck-ing charges; ~ **de case de coffre-fort** BANQUE safety-deposit box charges; ~ **à la charge de qn** FISC costs taxable to sb; ~ **de chargement, déchargement et d'arrimage en sus du fret** TRANSP free in, out and stowed, free in, out and trimmed, free in, out, stowed and trimmed; ~ **de chargement et d'arrimage en sus du fret** TRANSP free in and stowed, FIAS; ~ **de chargement en sus du fret** TRANSP fi, free in; ~ **de commercialisation** COMPTA front-end costs, sell-ing expenses; ~ **commerciaux** V&M sale charges; ~ **commerciaux ordinaires et nécessaires** FISC ordinary and necessary business expenses; ~ **de commission** BOURSE load; ~ **comptables** COMPTA, FIN accounting costs, accounting fees; ~ **de conservation** ASSUR sue and labor charges *(AmE)*, sue and labour charges *(BrE)*; ~ **consulaires** IMP/EXP consulage; ~ **de**

contentieux DROIT legal charges; ~ **de courtage** BOURSE agency cost *(UK)*, brokerage, brokerage allowance *(US)*, brokerage fee, com., commis-sion; ~ **de couverture** BOURSE carrying charge, carrying cost, hedge cost; ~ **de débarquement** TRANSP *dans un port* landing account, landing charge, L/A; ~ **de déblaiement** ASSUR costs of clearance of debris; ~ **de déchargement en sus du fret** TRANSP fo, free out terms; ~ **déductibles** FISC allowable expense; ~ **de démarrage** COMPTA, FIN start-up costs; ~ **de démolition** IMMOB demolition costs; ~ **de déplacement** COM, FISC, RES HUM travel expenses, traveling expenses *(AmE)*, travel-ling expenses *(BrE)*; ~ **de développement** COMPTA development expenditure; ~ **différés** COMPTA deferred charge; ~ **directs** *(ANT frais indirects)* COMPTA, FIN direct cost, direct expense; ~ **de distribution** COMPTA, TRANSP distribution costs; ~ **divers** COMPTA miscellaneous expenses, sundries, sundry expenses *voyage d'affaires* sub-sistence allowance; ~ **pour droit d'accès** BANQUE standby charges; ~ **pour droit d'usage** BANQUE standby charges; ~ **d'emballage et d'envoi non compris** COM exclusive of post and packing; ~ **d'émission** BOURSE flotation cost; ~ **d'emprunt** BANQUE cost of borrowing; ~ **d'encaissement** BANQUE exchange charge, COM collection charge; ~ **encourus pendant une période donnée** COM period cost, period expense; ~ **d'engagement** BOURSE liability cost; ~ **engagés** COM incurred expenses, COMPTA incurred costs, incurred expenses, FISC incurred expenses; ~ **engagés à l'extérieur** FISC away from home expenses; ~ **d'enlèvement** TRANSP collection charge; ~ **à l'entrée** IMP/EXP *navigation*, TRANSP inward charges; ~ **d'entreposage à l'exportation** IMP/EXP export depot charges; ~ **d'entreposage à l'importation** IMP/EXP import depot charges; ~ **d'entrepôt** IMP/EXP depot charges, warehouse charges, TRANSP warehouse charges; ~ **d'entretien** COM maintenance charges, maintenance expenses; ~ **d'envoi** COM dispatching charge; ~ **d'escompte** COMPTA discount charges; ~ **d'essence** FISC gasoline expenses; ~ **et dépens** DROIT legal costs; ~ **d'établissement** COMPTA preliminary expenses, set-up costs, setting-up costs, start-up costs, FIN set-up costs, start-up costs; ~ **d'étude de base** COM basic research cost; ~ **d'expédition** COM dispatching charge; ~ **d'expertise** ASSUR loss adjustment expense; ~ **d'exploitation** COM business expenses, COMPTA business expenses, operating costs, operating expenses, FIN business expenses, TRANSP *d'un navire* operating expenses, *d'une charte-partie* running cost; ~ **d'exploitation actuels** FIN current expenditure; ~ **d'exploration au Canada** *(FEC)* FISC Canadian exploration expense *(CEE)*; ~ **d'extension** ASSUR extension costs; ~ **extraordinaires** COMPTA extraordinary expenses; ~ **de fabrication** COMPTA manufactur-ing expenses; ~ **financiers** BANQUE finance charge; ~ **fiscalement déductibles** COMPTA allowable expense; ~ **fixes** COM, COMPTA, ECON fixed charge, fixed charges, fixed expense, FIN *(SYN frais généraux)* fixed costs; ~ **de fonctionnement** COM running costs, running expenses; ~ **de fonctionnement auxiliaire** COM, COMPTA, IND nonoperating expense; ~ **de fret** TRANSP *navigation* cargo dues; ~ **de garde d'enfants** FISC, PROT SOC childcare expenses; ~ **généraux** COM general expense, general expenses, overhead charge, overheads, COMPTA general expense, overhead charges, overheads, FIN overhead charge, overheads, IND oncosts; ~ **généraux d'administration** ADMIN, COMPTA, FIN administrative overheads; ~ **généraux de fabrication** COMPTA, ECON, FIN, IND factory overheads, manufacturing overheads; ~ **généraux fixes** COMPTA, FIN fixed overheads; ~ **généraux imputés** COMPTA, FIN applied overhead; ~ **généraux sous-imputés** COMPTA, FIN underapplied overheads; ~ **généraux variables** COMPTA, FIN variable overhead cost; ~ **de gestion** ADMIN administration costs, administrative costs, handling charge, BANQUE, BOURSE *pour gestion de portefeuille* management fee, COM administrative costs, handling charge, COMPTA administration expenses, administrative expense, management expenses, GESTION management expenses, V&M handling charge; ~ **de gestion de compte** BANQUE bank charges, bank commission, COMPTA, FIN bank charges; ~ **de gestion de comptes** BANQUE service charge; ~ **hors-site** IMMOB off-site cost; ~ **d'hospitalisation** ASSUR, FISC hospital expenses; ~ **imputés** COMPTA applied overhead, imputed cost, FIN applied overhead; ~ **incorporels de forage et développement** COMPTA intangible drilling and development cost; ~ **indirects** COMPTA *(ANT frais directs)*, ECON *(ANT coût direct)* indirect cost, indirect expense, FIN, (ANT *frais directs)* indirect costs, indirect expense, FIN *(ANT coût direct)* indirect cost; ~ **indirects imputés par produits** COMPTA, FIN applied overhead; ~ **d'inscription** BOURSE, COM, FIN registration fee; ~ **de jouissance** IMMOB carrying charge; ~ **judiciaires** DROIT legal charges, legal expenses; ~ **de justice** DROIT legal charges, legal expenses; ~ **de lancement** BOURSE flotation cost; ~ **de liquidation** COM closing-down costs; ~ **de livraison** TRANSP delivery charge; ~ **de magasinage** COM storage charges, IMP/EXP, TRANSP warehouse charges; ~ **de main-d'oeuvre** COM employment expenses; ~ **de maintenance** COM maintenance charges, maintenance expenses; ~ **de manutention** ADMIN, COM handling charge, TRANSP cargo-handling charge, CHC, V&M handling charge; ~ **de manutention à la charge de la marchandise** TRANSP *maritime* port liner terms charge, PLTC; ~ **de manutention des marchandises** TRANSP cargo-handling charge, CHC; ~ **médicaux** ASSUR, COM medical costs, FISC medical expenses; ~ **mensuels** COM, COMPTA, FIN monthly expenses; ~ **de mise en conformité** ADMIN, COMPTA administrative costs

of regulation, compliance costs; ~ **de mise à quai** TRANSP *tarif* wharfage, wharfage charges; ~ **de mise à terre** TRANSP *dans un port* landing account, landing charge, L/A; ~ **de montage** BANQUE *pour l'emprunteur* arrangement fee, loan fee, loan origination fee, set-up fee; ~ **de mouvement** BANQUE *à payer par le client* account activity charge, activity charge; ~ **de mouvement de compte** BANQUE *perçus par l'institution financière* account activity charge, activity charge; ~ **moyens** COM, COMPTA, ECON average costs; ~ **de négociation** BANQUE negotiation fee; ~ **d'option** FIN option fee; ~ **de la PAC** ECON CAP charges, Common Agricultural Policy charges; ~ **par opération** BANQUE transaction cost; ~ **particuliers** ASSUR particular charge; ~ **de passage** ADMIN pass-through charge *(AmE)*, throughput charge *(BrE)*; ~ **à payer** COM accrued expenses; ~ **payés d'avance** IMP/EXP charges prepaid, TRANSP charges prepaid, prepaid charges; ~ **de personnel** COMPTA manpower costs, personnel expenses, RES HUM personnel overheads; ~ **personnels** FISC personal expenses; ~ **de placement** FISC investment expense; ~ **de port** IMP/EXP, TRANSP carriage charge, carriage expenses, port charge; ~ **de port et d'emballage** COMMS p&p, postage and packing; ~ **de portage** BOURSE carrying charge, carrying cost, cost of carry; ~ **de possession** BOURSE carrying charge, carrying cost, TRANSP *marchandises* carrying charge; ~ **de premier établissement** COMPTA formation expense, FIN organization cost, promotion cost; ~ **prioritaires** GESTION expense preference; ~ **de procédure** COM cost of proceedings; ~ **de production** ECON, IND capacity charge; ~ **professionnels** COM, COMPTA business charges, business expenses, FIN, FISC business expenses; ~ **progressifs** FIN step cost; ~ **de protêt** DROIT protest charges; ~ **de publicité par vente de produit** COMPTA, FIN, V&M advertising cost per product sale; ~ **de quarantaine** IMP/EXP quarantine dues; ~ **de rachat** ASSUR surrender charge, BOURSE redemption fee; ~ **raisonnables** COM reasonable expense; ~ **de ramassage** TRANSP pick-up cost; ~ **rattachés à une dette** COMPTA debt charges; ~ **de recherche appliquée** COM *comptabilité* applied research cost; ~ **de recherche fondamentale** COM *marketing* basic research cost; ~ **de recherche scientifique** FISC scientific research expenditure *(UK)*; ~ **de recours et de conservation** ASSUR sue and labor charges *(AmE)*, sue and labour charges *(BrE)*; ~ **de recouvrement** COM collecting charge, collection charge, collection cost; ~ **de règlement** ASSUR adjustment costs, claims expenses; ~ **relatifs à un emploi** FISC employment expense; ~ **de remise en état** IMMOB *d'un bien immobilier pour la vente* fixing-up expense *(infrml)*; ~ **de remorquage** TRANSP towage charges, towage dues; ~ **de remplacement** ASSUR cost of replacement; ~ **de repas et de logement** FISC cost of meals and lodging; ~ **reportés** COMPTA deferred charge; **~ de représentation** COM entertainment allowance, COMPTA expense account, FISC entertainment expense, RES HUM expense account; **~ de réservation** COM booking fee; **~ de retrait** BOURSE back-end load; **~ rétroactifs** BOURSE billback (*US*); **~ de révision** COMPTA, FIN audit costs; **~ de sauvetage** TRANSP *maritime* salvage charges; **~ de séjour** COM living expenses; **~ semi-variables** COMPTA semivariable costs; **~ de service** BANQUE service charge; **~ de subsistance** FISC living expenses; **~ superflus** COM avoidable cost; **~ de taxi** TRANSP taxi charge; **~ de tenue de compte** BANQUE account maintenance charge, account maintenance fee, account operation charge, maintenance fee; **~ de traitement** ADMIN passthrough charge (*AmE*), throughput charge (*BrE*), ASSUR cost of treatment; **~ de transaction** BANQUE, BOURSE transaction fee, transactions costs, COM transaction costs, transaction fee, COMPTA transaction fee, transactions costs; **~ de transfert international** COMMS, ECON *commerce international* cable rate; **~ de transmission** COMPTA transmission expenses; **~ de transport** TRANSP transportation expenses; **~ de transport non compris** COM transportation charges not included, TRANSP transportation charges not allowed for; **~ de transport au prorata** TRANSP pro rata freight; **~ d'utilisation** BANQUE *d'une carte* cardholder fee, user fee; **~ variables** COMPTA, ECON, FIN variable expenses; **~ de vente** BOURSE sales charge, COMPTA selling expenses; **~ de voyage** COM, FISC, RES HUM travel expenses, traveling expenses (*AmE*), travelling expenses (*BrE*); ◆ **en être pour ses ~** COM be out of pocket; **faire face à des ~** COM, COMPTA, FIN meet costs; **tous ~ payés** COM all expenses paid

franc[1], **-che** *adj* COM absolute, clear-cut, unequivocal; ◆ **~ d'avarie grosse** COM free of general average; **~ d'avarie particulière** (*FAP*) ASSUR *assurance maritime* free of particular average (*FPA*); **~ d'avaries communes** (*FAC*) COM free of general average (*FGA*); **~ de capture et de saisie** ASSUR free of capture and seizure, FC&S; **~ de capture, de saisie et émeutes et mouvements** ASSUR fcsrcc, free of capture, seizure and riots, and civil commotions; **~ de réclamation pour accident signalé** ASSUR free of claim for accident reported, FCAR; **~ de sinistre pour l'accident constaté** ASSUR free of claim for accident reported, FCAR; **~ de toute avarie** COM f.a.a., free of all average; **~ de toute charge** DROIT, IMMOB free and clear (*US*)

franc[2] *m* COM franc; **~ -bord** TRANSP *navigation* freeboard, FBD; **~ CFA** COM CFA franc; **~ français** (*FF*) COM French franc (*FF*); **~ -jeu** COM fair play; **~ or** COM French gold franc, ECON gold franc

français[1], **e** *adj* COM French

français[2] *m* COM *langue* French; **~ du Canada** COM *langue* Canadian French

Français *m* COM *habitant* Frenchman; **les ~** *m pl* COM the French

française: à la ~ *adj* COM, INFO, MÉDIA portrait

Française *f* COM *habitante* Frenchwoman

France:[1] **~ Telecom** *m* COMMS French Telecom, ≈ British Telecom

France[2] *f* COM France

franchement *adv* COM straightforwardly

franchir *vt* COM overstep, top

franchisage *m* COM franchising

franchise *f* ASSUR excess, COM *contrat* franchise, franchising, *de bagages* allowance, free allowance, *de caractère* straightforwardness, TRANSP *de bagages* allowance, free allowance, V&M franchise; **~ pour bagages** TRANSP free baggage allowance (*BrE*), free luggage allowance (*AmE*); **~ de bagages** LOISIRS, TRANSP baggage allowance; **~ bancaire** BANQUE free banking; **~ obligatoire** COM compulsory deduction; **~ la plus parfaite** COM *juridique* uberrimae fides (*frml*), DROIT uberrimae fides; **~ de poids** COM weight allowed free; ◆ **en ~ douanière** IMP/EXP *marchandises* duty-free

franchisé, e *m,f* V&M franchisee

franchiseur *m* V&M franchisor

francisation *f* TRANSP registration as French

franco:[1] **~ -anglais** *adj* COM Franco-English; **~ -britannique** *adj* COM Franco-English

franco[2] *adv* COM free of charge, FOC, TRANSP *libraison de marchandise* carriage-paid, franco; ◆ **~ allège** TRANSP *navigation* free into barge, FIB; **~ assurance et transport** TRANSP free insurance and carriage, FIC; **~ à bord** (*FAB*) TRANSP *livraison de marchandises* free on board, free on ship, free on steamer (*dat*), free on (*FOS*); **~ à bord aéroport** (*FAB aéroport*) TRANSP *livraison de marchandises* free on aircraft, free on board airport (*FOB airport*); **~ à bord et arrimé** TRANSP free on board and trimmed, FOB & T; **~ chargement** TRANSP fi, free in; **~ déchargement** IMP/EXP landed terms, TRANSP fd, free discharge, landed terms; **~ domicile** TRANSP *livraison de marchandises* fd, free domicile, free house; **~ gare** TRANSP f.o.r., free on rail; **~ le long du bord** (*FLB*) TRANSP *maritime, livraison* free alongside ship, free alongside steamer (*dat*), free from alongside (*FFA*); **~ le long du quai** TRANSP *navigation* free alongside quay; **~ le long du vapeur** *vieilli* TRANSP *livraison* free alongside ship, free alongside steamer (*dat*); **~ de port** IMP/EXP carriage-free; **~ à port** TRANSP *maritime* fih, free in harbor (*AmE*), free in harbour (*BrE*); **~ à quai** (*FAQ*) TRANSP *maritime* ex docks, free alongside quay, free dock, free on quay, free on wharf; **~ à quai - franco à quai** TRANSP *maritime* free on quay to free on quay, FOQ-FOQ; **~ sous palan** TRANSP fo, free overboard, free overside, *maritime, livraison* free alongside ship, free alongside steamer (*dat*); **~ soutes** TRANSP *maritime* free into bunkers,

FIB; ~ **sur rail** TRANSP f.o.r., free on rail; ~ **transporteur** TRANSP free carrier, FRC; ~ **transporteur maritime** TRANSP *maritime, livraison de marchandises* free sea carrier; ~ **wagon** TRANSP f.o.r., free on rail, f.o.t., free on truck, fiw, free into wagon

frappe *f* ECON *de monnaie* mintage; ~ **répétée** INFO double strike; ~ **d'une touche** INFO keystroke

frappé: ~ **de panique** *loc* COM panic-stricken

frapper *vt* COM strike, INFO *touches* hit

fraude *f* DROIT fraud; ~ **d'assurance maritime** ASSUR marine insurance fraud; ~ **documentaire** COM documentary fraud; ~ **étendue** COM long fraud; ~ **fiscale** COM skimming, ECON tax evasion, tax on income, FIN tax evasion, FISC tax dodging, tax evasion, tax fraud; ~ **informatique** DROIT, INFO computer fraud; ~ **maritime** DROIT, TRANSP maritime fraud

frauder *vt* DROIT defraud, FISC *le fisc* evade

fraudeur: ~ **du fisc** *m* ECON, FISC tax dodger, tax evader; ~ **fiscal** *m* ECON tax evader, FISC tax dodger, tax evader; ~ **de l'impôt** *m* ECON, FISC tax dodger, tax evader

frauduleusement *adv* DROIT fraudulently

frayer: ~ **le chemin à qch** *loc* COM pave the way for sth

FRCE *abrév (Fonds de rétablissement du conseil de l'Europe)* BANQUE CERF *(Council of Europe Resettlement Fund)*

fre *abrév (facture)* BANQUE, COM, COMPTA, FIN inv. *(invoice)*

free:[1] ~ **-lance** *adj* MÉDIA, RES HUM freelance

free:[2] ~ **-lance** *mf* MÉDIA, RES HUM freelance

Freetown *n pr* COM Freetown

freiner *vt* ECON dampen, reduce; ◆ ~ **les coûts** COM control costs

freins: ~ **à air comprimé** *m pl* TRANSP full air brakes; ~ **à l'investissement** *m pl* ECON investment restriction

freinte: ~ **de route** *f* TRANSP loss in transit; ~ **de stock** *f* COM, ECON inventory shortage, inventory shrinkage

fréquemment: **personne qui change** ~ **d'emplois** *f* RES HUM job hopper, job jumper

fréquence *f* MATH, MÉDIA *radio* frequency; ~ **de base** INFO clock rate

fréquentation *f* COM attendance; ~ **à plein temps** FISC full-time attendance

fret *m* TRANSP freight, frt, goods; ~ **ad valorem** IMP/EXP, TRANSP ad valorem freight; ~ **aérien** IMP/EXP, TRANSP air cargo, air freight; ~ **aller** *(ANT fret de retour)* TRANSP *navigation* cargo outward; ~**, assurance et frais d'expédition** IMP/EXP, TRANSP *maritime* freight, insurance and shipping charges, FIS; ~ **de charte-partie** TRANSP charter party freight; ~ **de distance** TRANSP *maritime* distance freight; ~ **et surestarie** ASSUR, TRANSP freight and demurrage, F&D; ~ **à forfait** TRANSP *maritime* lump-sum freight; ~ **au long cours** TRANSP mar-*itime* ocean freight; ~ **payable à destination** COM, TRANSP freight forward, frt fwd; ~ **payé à** IMP/EXP, TRANSP *lieu désigné* DCP *(dat)*, freight paid to; ~ **payé d'avance** TRANSP advance freight, AF, freight prepaid, frt ppd; ~ **payé à l'expédition** TRANSP freight prepaid, frt ppd; ~ **payé jusqu'à** IMP/EXP, TRANSP *lieu désigné* DCP *(dat)*, freight paid to; ~ **de retour** *(ANT fret aller)* TRANSP *navigation* back freight, cargo homeward, return freight; ~ **sec** TRANSP dry freight; ~ **sur le vide** TRANSP *navigation* deadfreight, DF; ~ **à temps** TRANSP time freight; ~ **de transbordement** IMP/EXP, TRANSP transhipment freight, transshipment freight; ~ **à l'unité payante** TRANSP *maritime* liner rate; ◆ ~ **et assurance payés à** ASSUR, TRANSP *lieu désigné* freight and insurance paid

fric *m infrml* COM bread *(infrml)*

frigo *m infrml* MÉDIA morgue *(infrml)*, TRANSP reefer

friperie *f* COM thrift shop *(AmE)*, *vêtements, meubles* second-hand market

friser: ~ **l'illégalité** *loc* COM sail close to the wind

front: **sur le** ~ **de l'emploi** *loc* RES HUM on the employment front

Front: ~ **National** *m (FN)* POL National Front *(UK) (NF)*

frontal[1], **e** *adj* INFO front-end *(jarg)*

frontal[2] *m* INFO front-end computer

frontière *f* COM, ECON border, frontier, IMMOB boundary, IMP/EXP border, frontier; ~ **commune** IMP/EXP, POL mutual border; ~ **extérieure** COM *d'un pays* external border; ~ **fiscale** ECON, POL fiscal frontier; ~ **nationale** COM national border, national boundary, *d'un pays* external border, IMP/EXP, POL national border, national boundary; ~ **des possibilités de production** *(FPP)* ECON production possibility frontier

fruits: ~ **naturels annuels** *m pl* DROIT *agriculture* emblements

FSE *abrév (Fonds social européen)* ECON, POL ESF *(European Social Fund)*

FSI *abrév (Fédération syndicale internationale)* RES HUM IFTU *(International Federation of Trade Unions)*

FSM *abrév (Fédération syndicale mondiale)* RES HUM WFTU *(World Federation of Trade Unions)*

FTSE *abrév (indice FTSE des 100 valeurs)* BOURSE FT-SE *(UK) (Financial Times Stock Exchange index)*

fuit: **qui** ~ *adj* POL *seau* leaky *(infrml)*

fuite *f* COM *d'eau* leak, leakage, seepage, *d'information* leak, leakage, security leak, ECON leakage; ~ **de capitaux** ECON capital flight, capital outflow, flight of capital; ~ **de cerveaux** RES HUM brain drain *(infrml)*; ~ **devant la monnaie** ECON flight from money; ~ **vers la qualité** BOURSE flight to quality

fumées *f pl* ENVIR fumes

fumoir *m* COM smoke room, smoking room

fur: **au** ~ **et à mesure** *loc* COM in a series, one after the other, seriatim (*frml*); **au ~ et à mesure que le paiement est reçu** *loc* COMPTA on a cash received basis

fuseau: **~ horaire** *m* COM time zone

fusion *f* BOURSE amalgamation, merger, COM consolidation, merger, COMPTA merger accounting (*BrE*), pooling of interests (*AmE*), ECON merger, FIN takeover, INFO merge; **~ avec une entreprise étrangère** BOURSE, COM foreign merger; **~ avec un fichier d'adresses** INFO mail merge; **~ de capitaux** DROIT commingling of funds; **~ conforme aux statuts** DROIT statutory merger; **~ dans un conglomérat** ECON conglomerate merger, FIN conglomerate, conglomerate merger; **~ horizontale** (*ANT fusion verticale*) COM horizontal amalgamation, ECON horizontal merger; **~ légale** DROIT statutory merger; **~ syndicale** RES HUM amalgamation; **~ transfrontière** BOURSE, ECON cross-border merger; **~ transnationale** COM, ECON *concentration industrielle* cross-border merger; **~ triangulaire** COM, ECON triangular merger; **~ triangulaire inversée** COM, ECON reverse triangular merger; **~ verticale** (*ANT fusion horizontale*) COM vertical amalgamation, ECON vertical merger

fusionnement *m* BOURSE amalgamation

fusionner 1. *vi* ADMIN, COM; **2.** *vti* ADMIN, BOURSE merge, COM *sociétés, groupements industriels* amalgamate, consolidate, incorporate, COMMS merge, ECON amalgamate, INFO merge; ◆ **~ en** COM merge into

fusions: **~ et acquisitions** *f pl* (*F&A*) BOURSE, ECON mergers and acquisitions (*M&A*)

fût *m* IND bar, barrel, TRANSP bar, barrel, cask, ck

fuyant: **personne ~ le fisc** *f* FISC tax exile

G

g *abrév (gramme)* COM g *(gram)*

GAB *abrév (guichet automatique de banque)* BANQUE automated teller machine, automatic teller, automatic telling machine

gabarit *m* COM, IND, INFO template; **~ de surface** COM, IND, INFO template

Gabon *m* COM Gabon

gabonais, e *adj* COM Gabonese

Gabonais, e *m,f* COM *habitant* Gabonese

Gabrone *n pr* COM Gaborone

gâchage: **~ des prix** *m* V&M price cutting

gâcheur, -euse *m,f* POL spoiler *(jarg)*

gâchis *m* COM waste; **~ d'emploi** RES HUM job wastage

gadget *m* COM gadget

gaffe *f infrml* COM blunder, boob, faux pas

gage *m* BANQUE pledge, security, COM pawn, ECON, FIN collateral; **~ de second rang** DROIT junior lien

gages *m pl* COM pay, wages

gagnant¹, e *adj* COM winning

gagnant², e *m,f* COM winner

gagne: **~ -pain** *m* COM bread-and-butter, ECON, PROT SOC breadwinner

gagner 1. *vt* COM *client* win, MATH add, RES HUM *de l'argent* earn; **2.** *vi* COM gain, make a benefit; ◆ **~ de l'argent rapidement** COM earn a fast buck *(infrml)*; **~ facilement** COM sail through; **~ le gros lot** COM hit the jackpot, win the jackpot; **~ qn à son point de vue** COM win sb over to one's point of view; **~ sa vie** COM earn a living, earn one's keep, make a living; **~ un salaire de** RES HUM earn a salary of; **~ du terrain** COM gain ground; **~ en valeur** BOURSE gain in value, gain value; **~ de la valeur** BOURSE gain in value, gain value; **~ £100 par semaine** RES HUM earn £100 a week, make £100 a week; **~ 40.000** RES HUM earn 40 K, earn 40,000

gaillard *m* TRANSP *d'un navire* forecastle; **~ d'arrière** TRANSP *d'un navire* quarterdeck; **~ -château-dunette** TRANSP *d'un navire* poop, bridge and forecastle, PBF; **~ -dunette** TRANSP *d'un navire* poop and forecastle, PF

gain *m* BOURSE, COMPTA, ECON, FIN, FISC gain; **~ aléatoire** COMPTA, ECON, FIN gain contingency; **~ en capital** COMPTA, ECON, FIN, FISC capital gain; **~ en capital après impôt** COMPTA, ECON, FIN, FISC after-tax capital gain, net capital gain; **~ en capital immédiat** COMPTA, ECON, FIN, FISC immediate capital gain; **~ en capital imposable** COMPTA, ECON, FIN, FISC taxable capital gain; **~ en capital imposable admissible net** COMPTA, ECON, FIN, FISC net eligible taxable capital gain; **~ en capital imposable net** COMPTA, ECON, FIN, FISC net taxable capital gain; **~ en capital impo-**sable net cumulatif FISC cumulative net taxable capital gain; **~ en capital imposé** COMPTA, ECON, FIN, FISC taxed capital gain; **~ en capital net** COMPTA, ECON, FIN, FISC after-tax capital gain, net capital gain; **~ exceptionnel** ECON windfall gain; **~ immobilier** IMMOB real estate gain; **~ de mortalité** FISC mortality gain; **~ net** COMPTA, ECON, FIN, FISC net gain; **~ net imposable** COMPTA, ECON, FIN, FISC taxable net gain; **~ net de trésorerie** COMPTA net cash flow; **~ normal** FISC ordinary gain; **~ reconnu** FISC recognized gain; **~ ou perte à court terme** BOURSE short-term gain or loss; **~ ou perte sur titres** BOURSE paper profit or loss

gainage: **~ chargé de verre** *m* TRANSP *conteneurs ISO* glass-reinforced cladding

gaine *f* TRANSP *de palette* snood; **~ en toile à voile** TRANSP canvas cover, cc

gains *m pl* RES HUM earnings, payoff; **~ avant imposition** COM, ECON, FIN, FISC pretax earnings; **~ cotisables d'un emploi** FISC *pension* contributory earnings from employment; **~ cotisables d'un travail indépendant** FISC *pension* contributory self-employed earnings; **~ exonérés** FISC exempt earnings; **~ à l'exportation** ECON, IMP/EXP export earnings; **faire des ~** BOURSE, COMPTA, FIN make gains; **~ à l'importation** ECON, IMP/EXP import earnings; **~ invisibles** ECON, FIN invisible earnings; **~ de loterie** FIN, FISC lottery winnings; **~ non-réalisés** COMPTA, FIN, FISC unrealized gains; **~ d'opportunité** ECON transfer earnings; **~ de productivité** COM, IND productivity gains; **~ réalisés** COMPTA, FIN, FISC realized gains

galée *f* MÉDIA *typographie* galley, galley proof

galère *f* TRANSP *navire* galley

galerie *f* COM, V&M gallery; **~ marchande** COM, V&M arcade, mall, precinct, shopping mall *(AmE)*, shopping precinct *(BrE)*

galiote *f* TRANSP *navire* g, galliot

gallois¹, e *adj* COM Welsh

gallois² *m* COM *langue* Welsh

Gallois *m* COM *habitant* Welshman; **les ~** *m pl* COM *habitant* the Welsh

Galloise *f* COM *habitante* Welshwoman

gallon *m* COM gal, gallon; **~ américain** COM 3,785 litres, American gallon; **~ impérial** COM 4,546 litres, imperial gallon

Gambie *f* COM Gambia

gambien, -enne *adj* COM Gambian

Gambien, -enne *m,f* COM *habitant* Gambian

gamin: **être un ~** *loc infrml* RES HUM be wet behind the ears *(infrml)*

gamma *m* BOURSE gamma

gamme *f* COM, V&M *de produits* line, range; ~ **d'amortissement d'actif** COMPTA, FIN, IMMOB asset depreciation range, ADR; ~ **étendue** COM, V&M wide range; ~ **d'ordinateurs** INFO computer line, computer range; ~ **de prix** ECON, V&M price range; ~ **de produits** COM, IND, V&M product line, product range, range of products; ~ **qui rapporte à l'entreprise de quoi se maintenir à flot** COM bread-and-butter line *(infrml)*; ◆ **de haute** ~ INFO high-end

gap *m* BOURSE price gap

GAP *abrév (gestion actif-passif)* BANQUE, COMPTA, FIN, GESTION ALM *(assets and liabilities management)*

garage *m* BOURSE garage, TRANSP *d'autobus* depot; ~ **à deux voies** TRANSP *d'un roulier* two-lane deck

garant, e *m,f* BOURSE security dealer, COM guarantor, DROIT warranter, warrantor

garanti, e *adj* ASSUR W/d, warranted, BOURSE underwritten, COM guar, guaranteed

garantie *f* ASSUR guarantee, guaranty, warranty, BANQUE guarantee, guaranty, security, BOURSE C'vr, backing, cover, COM guarantee, guaranty, maintenance bond, security, warranty, DROIT appeal bond, bail, guarantee, guaranty, maintenance bond, warranty, FIN warranty; ~ **annexe** ASSUR extended cover, extended coverage; ~ **anticipée** BOURSE advance guaranty *(UK)*, advanced guarantee *(UK)*; ~ **d'assurabilité** ASSUR guaranteed insurability *(AmE)*; ~ **d'assurance** ASSUR insurance cover *(BrE)*, insurance coverage *(AmE)*, title insurance; ~ **d'avarie commune** ASSUR general average guarantee; ~ **bancaire** BANQUE bank guarantee; ~ **bancaire globale** BANQUE comprehensive bank guarantee; ~ **bancaire globale de longue durée** BANQUE comprehensive extended-term banker's guarantee, CXBG; ~ **de bonne exécution** BOURSE performance guarantee, DROIT, IMMOB completion bond *(US)*, V&M performance guarantee; ~ **en bonne fin** BOURSE, V&M performance guarantee; ~ **de bonne fin** COM contract bond, performance bond; ~ **de commerce extérieur** ASSUR external trade guarantee; ~ **contre l'échouement** ASSUR cover against stranding; ~ **contre la hausse des prix** ASSUR cost escalation cover *(UK)*; ~ **contre le risque de remboursement anticipé** BOURSE call protection; ~ **de dépôt** ASSUR surety; ~ **d'émission négociée** BOURSE negotiated underwriting; ~ **d'émission obligataire** BOURSE bond underwriting; ~ **d'émission renouvelable** ASSUR revolving underwriting facility, RUF; ~ **d'engagement ferme** BOURSE firm commitment underwriting; ~ **expresse** COM express warranty; ~ **fidélité** ASSUR fidelity guarantee; ~ **fiduciaire** DROIT fiduciary bond; ~ **générale** ASSUR blanket bond; ~ **générale d'assurance de responsabilité civile** ASSUR general liability insurance; ~ **générale de commerce** ASSUR commercial blanket bond; ~ **générale commerciale** ASSUR commercial blanket bond; ~ **implicite** DROIT implied warranty; ~ **inassurable**

ASSUR uninsurable title; ~ **invalidité** ASSUR disability annuity, PROT SOC disability annuity, disability benefit; ~ **matérielle** BANQUE physical collateral; ~ **du moins disant** COM bid bond; ~ **non-assurable** ASSUR uninsurable title; ~ **d'option** BOURSE option coverage; ~ **de paiement** COM payment bond, COMPTA payment guarantee, DROIT payment bond; ~ **de permis** DROIT permit bond; ~ **de prêt** FIN loan guarantee; ~ **de provisions** COM, IMP/EXP advance payment guarantee; ~ **de la qualité marchande** COM warranty of merchantability; ~ **des recettes** FISC revenue guarantee; ~ **remboursable par anticipation** FIN accelerable guarantee *(UK)*; ~ **de revenu** FISC revenue guarantee; ~ **de solidarité professionnelle** ASSUR external trade guarantee; ~ **de soumission** FIN bid security; ~ **de stocks supplémentaires** IMP/EXP supplementary stocks guarantee; ~ **supplémentaire** ASSUR additional security; ~ **sur déménagement** FIN removal bond; ~ **de taux plafond** BANQUE interest rate capping, BOURSE, ECON, FIN cap; ~ **de taux plancher** BOURSE, ECON, FIN floor; ~ **à tous endroits** ASSUR floater *(US)*; ◆ **avoir des** ~**s** ASSUR be covered

garantir *vt* BANQUE back, guarantee, warrant, *prêt* secure, BOURSE secure, COM accredit, guarantee; ◆ ~ **une dette par hypothèque** BANQUE secure a debt by mortgage; ~ **par nantissement** BANQUE collateralize; ~ **un placement** BANQUE secure an investment

garçon: ~ **de bureau** *m* COM, RES HUM office boy; ~ **de courses** *m* COMMS, RES HUM messenger boy

garde:[1] ~ **-côte** *m* RES HUM coastguard, CG; ~ **-magasin** *m* COM warehouse keeper, warehouseman; ~ **-meubles** *m* COM depository, furniture depot

garde[2] *f* DROIT ward, *d'un enfant* custody, PROT SOC *d'un enfant* custody; ~ **conjointe** BANQUE *d'un coffre-fort*, DROIT *d'un enfant* joint custody; ~ **et surveillance** DROIT, PROT SOC *d'un enfant* custody and control; ~ **des valeurs** BANQUE safekeeping; ~ **des valeurs actives** BANQUE safekeeping of assets

garder *vt* BOURSE retain, COM keep, *en lieu sûr* safeguard, RES HUM *stand* man; ◆ ~ **une poire pour la soif** COM save for a rainy day; ~ **qch présent à l'esprit** COM bear sth in mind; ~ **en réserve** COM keep in reserve; ~ **secret** COM keep under wraps; ~ **une trace écrite de** COM keep a note of

gardeur: ~ **de bestiaux** *m,f* COM stockperson

gardien, -enne *m,f* DROIT, PROT SOC custodian, RES HUM guard, watchman; ~ **de nuit** RES HUM night watchman

gare *f* TRANSP depot, station, S, rail terminal, railroad station *(AmE)*, railway station *(BrE)*, train station *(BrE)*; ~ **aéroglisseur** TRANSP *navigation* hoverport; ~ **de destination** TRANSP *chemin de fer* receiving station; ~ **d'expédition** TRANSP *chemin de fer* forwarding station; ~ **routière** TRANSP *pour autobus* bus station, *pour cars* bus station, coach station, *pour camions* haulage depot

garniture: ~ **du conteneur** *f* TRANSP container stuffing

garnitures *f pl* COM trimmings

gasohol *m* ENVIR, IND, TRANSP green petrol

gas-oil *m* ENVIR, IND, TRANSP diesel oil, DO, diesel-engined road vehicle fuel *(BrE)*, DERV *(BrE)*, gas oil

gaspillage *m* COM squandering, wastage, waste, ENVIR waste

gaspiller *vt* COM squander, waste, ENVIR waste

GATT *abrév (Accord général sur les tarifs et le commerce)* ECON, POL GATT *(General Agreement on Tariffs and Trade)*

gauche:[1] **de ~** *adj* [épith] *(ANT de droite)* POL left-wing

gauche:[2] **la ~ caviar** *f infrml* POL champagne socialism *(infrml)*, limousine liberals *(infrml)*

gauchisme *m (ANT droitisme)* POL leftism

gauchissement: ~ **oblique** *m* TRANSP racking

gaz *m* COM, ENVIR gas; ~ **brûlé** ENVIR, TRANSP exhaust gas; ~ **d'échappement** ENVIR, TRANSP exhaust gas, vehicle exhaust emissions; ~ **à effet de serre** ENVIR greenhouse effect gas, greenhouse gas; ~ **de la mer du Nord** IND North Sea gas; ~ **naturel** ENVIR, IND natural gas; ~ **naturel liquéfié** *(GNL)* ENVIR, IND, TRANSP liquefied natural gas *(LNG)*; ~ **de pétrole liquéfié** *(GPL)* ENVIR, IND, TRANSP liquid petroleum gas *(LPG)*; ~ **toxique** ENVIR, IND noxious gas

Gaz: ~ **de France** *m (GDF)* IND ≈ British Gas

gazoduc *m* IND gas main, gas pipeline

gazole *m* ENVIR, IND, TRANSP diesel oil, DO, diesel-engined road vehicle fuel *(BrE)*, DERV *(BrE)*, gas oil

GDF *abrév (Gaz de France)* IND ≈ British Gas

gel *m* BANQUE, COM, ECON, FIN, FISC freeze, freezing; ~ **de l'emploi** ECON, RES HUM job freeze; ~ **des loyers** IMMOB rent freeze; ~ **des prix** COM, ECON price freeze; ~ **des salaires** ECON, RES HUM pay freeze; ~ **des salaires et des prix** ECON squeeze and freeze *(jarg)*; ~ **successoral** FISC estate freezing *(Can)*

gelé, e *adj* BANQUE, COM, ECON, FIN, FISC frozen

geler *vt* BANQUE, COM, ECON, FIN, FISC freeze

gendarme: ~ **maritime** *m* RES HUM coastguard, CG

gendarmerie *f* DROIT police, police force; ~ **maritime** RES HUM *organisation* coastguard, CG

gêne *f* BANQUE, COM, ECON, FIN financial difficulty

gêné, e *adj* BANQUE, COM, ECON, FIN in financial difficulty, short of money

gêner *vt* COM hamper, hinder, obstruct

général, e *adj* COM *accord*, GESTION across-the-board, general

généralisé, e *adj* COM across-the-board, generalized

généraliser *vi* COM generalize

généraliste *mf* COM, RES HUM generalist; ~ **de l'entreprise** *m* COM business generalist

généralités *f pl* COM background information, overview

générateur: ~ **de nombres aléatoires** *m* MATH random-number generator; ~ **de recettes** *m* ECON revenue earner; ~ **à vapeur** *m* TRANSP *d'un navire* steam-heated generator

génération *f* COM *de profits*, FIN, IND, INFO generation, V&M *copie vidéo d'une publicité destinée à la télévision et envoyée aux différentes chaînes* G-spool *(jarg)*; ~ **du baby-boom** ECON, V&M *public ciblé* baby-boomers; ~ **d'électricité** IND electricity generation; ~ **d'états** INFO report generation; ~ **de nombres aléatoires** MATH randomization; ~ **de programmes d'édition** INFO report generation

généré: ~ **par le premier achat** *adj* V&M *marketing* after-sales

générer *vt* BOURSE *profits*, COM *déchets, profits* generate, ECON *confiance* breed, generate, INFO *programme* generate

générique[1] *adj* COM, V&M *marketing* generic

générique[2] *m* MÉDIA masthead

génie *m* COM *personne* genius, wizard; ~ **biologique** IND bioengineering; ~ **électrique** IND electrical engineering; ~ **de la finance** FIN *personne* financial wizard; ~ **industriel** IND industrial engineering; ~ **informatique** INFO computer engineering; ~ **de l'informatique** INFO *personne* computer wizard; ~ **logiciel** INFO software engineering; ♦ **avoir le ~ de** COM be a wizard at *(infrml)*

géodémographie *f* V&M *étude de marché* geodemography

géographie *f* COM geography; ~ **économique** ECON economic geography

géographique *adj* COM geographic, geographical

géomètre *m* IMMOB surveyor; ~ **expert** IMMOB surveyor

géopolitique *adj* POL geopolitical

Georgetown *n pr* COM Georgetown

Géorgie *f* COM Georgia

géorgien, -enne *adj* COM Georgian

Géorgien, -enne *m,f* COM *habitant* Georgian

gérance *f* COM management

gérant, e *m,f* GESTION manager, mgr, IMMOB administrator, RES HUM administrator, manager, mgr; ~ **général** RES HUM general administrator; ~ **d'hôtel** RES HUM hotel manager; ~ **de société** COM *à responsabilité limitée* managing director; ~ **de succursale** BANQUE, COM branch manager

gérante *f* GESTION, RES HUM manageress

gerbage *m* TRANSP *manutention* stacking; ~ **du chargement** TRANSP stacking of cargo; ~ **double** TRANSP *conteneurs* double stack, double stacking; ~ **des marchandises** TRANSP stacking of cargo

gerber: ~ **en doubles piles** *loc* TRANSP *conteneurs* double-stack

géré: ~ **par ordinateur** *adj* INFO computer-controlled, computer-operated; ~ **par le système central** *adj* INFO host-driven

gérer *vt* ADMIN administer, COM manage, *entreprise, hôtel, magasin, projet* manage, run, *situation* handle, GESTION *entreprise, hôtel, magasin, projet* manage, run, IMMOB administer, V&M *franchise* exercise; ◆ ~ **de grosses sommes d'argent** FIN handle large sums of money; ~ **par ordinateur** INFO computerize

gestion *f* ADMIN administration, management, *d'une propriété, d'un patrimoine* admin, administration, COM management, GESTION admin, administration, management, IMMOB *d'une propriété, d'un patrimoine* admin, administration, INFO control; ~ **de l'actif** BANQUE, BOURSE, COMPTA, FIN, GESTION asset management; ~ **actif-passif** *(GAP)* BANQUE, COMPTA, FIN, GESTION asset and liability management, assets and liabilities management; ~ **d'actions** BOURSE management of shares; ~ **active** COM, GESTION active management; ~ **d'agenda** GESTION calendar management; ~ **automatisée** GESTION, INFO, V&M computerized management; ~ **de bas en haut** GESTION bottom-up management; ~ **du bilan** BANQUE, COMPTA, FIN, GESTION asset and liability management, assets and liabilities management, ALM; ~ **de bon père de famille** BOURSE prudent-man rule *(US)*; ~ **à bord** TRANSP *d'un navire* shipboard management; ~ **des canaux de communication** GESTION channel management; ~ **de capitaux internationaux** ECON, FIN international financial management; ~ **de carrière** RES HUM career management; ~ **cellulaire** GESTION divisional management; ~ **du changement** GESTION, RES HUM change management; ~ **commerciale** GESTION, V&M market management; ~ **des comptes** BANQUE, COMPTA, FIN account management; ~ **de la configuration** INFO configuration control; ~ **consultative** GESTION bottom-up management; ~ **de la contingence** GESTION contingency management; ~ **de couverture** BOURSE hedge management; ~ **de créances** COMPTA, FIN credit management; ~ **des crises** GESTION crisis management; ~ **décentralisée** GESTION decentralized management; ~ **de déchets** COM, ENVIR waste management; ~ **du déplacement des navires** TRANSP ship management; ~ **du développement** COM, GESTION development management; ~ **de disque dur** INFO hard disk management; ~ **de la distribution physique** GESTION, TRANSP physical distribution management, PDM; ~ **des documents essentiels** GESTION vital records management; ~ **de données** INFO data management, database management; ~ **des effectifs** GESTION, RES HUM manpower management; ~ **d'entreprise** ADMIN, COM, ECON, GESTION business management, corporate governance; ~ **de fichiers** INFO file management; ~ **des finances** ADMIN, COM, COMPTA, FIN financial administra-

tion, financial management, GESTION financial management; ~ **financière des entreprises** COM, COMPTA, FIN business finance; ~ **financière internationale** FIN international financial management; ~ **de la flotte** TRANSP *d'avions, de navires* fleet planning; ~ **des flux de travail** V&M traffic planning; ~ **fonctionnelle** ADMIN systems management; ~ **de fonds** BANQUE fund management; ~ **immobilière** GESTION, IMMOB property management; ~ **des immobilisations** COMPTA, FIN fixed asset management; ~ **de l'imprévu** GESTION contingency management; ~ **informatisée** GESTION, INFO, V&M computerized management; ~ **intégrée de projet** FIN, GESTION integrated project management, IPM; ~ **d'investissements** BOURSE, FIN investment management; ~ **macroéconomique** ECON *de la demande* fine-tuning; ~ **des marchandises** V&M merchandise control; ~ **de la marque** V&M brand management; ~ **des opérations** COM, GESTION operations management; ~ **par département** GESTION departmental management, divisional management; ~ **par exception** GESTION management by exception; ~ **par fonctions** GESTION functional management, horizontal specialization; ~ **par ordinateur** GESTION, INFO, V&M computerized management; ~ **par les systèmes** GESTION, INFO systems management; ~ **du parc** TRANSP *de véhicules* fleet planning; ~ **du passif** BANQUE, BOURSE, COMPTA, FIN, GESTION liability management; ~ **du personnel** GESTION, RES HUM personnel management, staff management; ~ **d'une petite entreprise** COM small business administration, SBA; ~ **de portefeuille** BANQUE, BOURSE, COM, FIN, GESTION portfolio management; ~ **portuaire** TRANSP port management; ~ **prévisionnelle de l'emploi** RES HUM human resource planning, manpower planning, HRP; ~ **prévisionnelle des stocks** BOURSE, COMPTA, ECON, FIN inventory planning; ~ **de processus industriel** COM, IND process control; ~ **de la production** COM, GESTION, IND production control, production management; ~ **de produit** GESTION, V&M product management; ~ **programmée** GESTION programmed management; ~ **du projet** FIN, GESTION, RES HUM project management; ~ **de la QG** *(gestion de la qualité globale)* GESTION, IND, V&M TQM *(total quality management)*; ~ **de la qualité** GESTION, IND, V&M quality management; ~ **de la qualité absolue** GESTION, IND, V&M total quality management; ~ **de la qualité globale** *(gestion de la QG)* GESTION, IND, V&M total quality management *(TQM)*; ~ **rationnelle** GESTION rational management; ~ **de réseau** MÉDIA networking; ~ **des ressources** ENVIR resources management, GESTION policy and resource management, resources management, IND resources management; ~ **des ressources humaines** *(GRH)* RES HUM human resource management *(HRM)*; ~ **du risque** BOURSE risk management; ~ **des risques** ASSUR risk management, COM venture management, FIN risk management, GES-

TION venture management; **~ scientifique** GESTION, IND, MATH scientific management; **~ de la sécurité** GESTION, RES HUM safety management; **~ de service** COM departmental management; **~ des stocks** BOURSE inventory control (*AmE*), stock control (*BrE*), COMPTA inventory control (*AmE*), inventory management, stock control (*BrE*), store audit, ECON, FIN inventory control (*AmE*), inventory management, stock control (*BrE*), GESTION, IND inventory management, V&M stock management; **~ systématisée** ADMIN, GESTION, INFO systems management; **~ des tâches** GESTION, INFO task management; **~ du temps** GESTION calendar management; **~ du temps de travail** GESTION, RES HUM time management; **~ tenant compte des imprévus** GESTION contingency management; **~ transactionnelle** INFO transaction management; **~ du travail** GESTION energy management; **~ des travaux** INFO job control; **~ de trésorerie** COMPTA, FIN, GESTION cash management; **~ d'usine** COM, GESTION, IND plant management; **~ de la vente au détail** V&M retail management; **~ des ventes** GESTION, V&M sales management; ♦ **de ~** COM, GESTION managerial

gestionnaire *mf* GESTION manager, mgr, IMMOB *d'une propriété, d'un patrimoine*, INFO administrator, RES HUM administrator, manager, mgr; **~ de l'actif** *m* BANQUE, BOURSE, COMPTA, FIN, GESTION, RES HUM asset manager; **~ de centre de responsabilité** *m* COMPTA responsibility-center manager (*AmE*), responsibility-centre manager (*BrE*); **~ de couverture** *m* BOURSE hedge manager; **~ de la dette** *m* BOURSE liability manager, RES HUM debt manager; **~ de fait** *m* GESTION de facto manager; **~ de fonds** *m* FIN fund manager; **~ du passif** *m* BANQUE, BOURSE, COMPTA, FIN, GESTION liability manager; **~ de périphérique** *m* INFO device driver, driver; **~ de portefeuille** *m* BANQUE, BOURSE, COM, FIN, GESTION portfolio manager; **~ des risques** *m* ASSUR risk manager

Ghana *m* COM Ghana

ghanéen, -enne *adj* COM Ghanaian

Ghanéen, -enne *m,f* COM *habitant* Ghanaian

Gibraltar *n pr* COM Gibraltar

GIEE *abrév (Groupement d'intérêt économique européen)* ECON, POL EEIG (*European Economic Interest Grouping*)

gigaoctet *m (Go)* INFO gigabyte (*Gb*)

gisement *m* BOURSE bond pool, list of deliverable bonds, IND *de minerai* deposit; **~ de charbon** IND coal deposit; **~ de houille** IND coal deposit; **~ de pétrole** IND oil deposit; **~ pétrolifère** IND oil deposit

GL *abrév (grande ligne)* TRANSP *chemin de fer* main line

glasnost *f* POL glasnost

glissement: **~ d'une tranche d'imposition à l'autre** *m* ECON, FISC bracket creep, tax-bracket creep

glisser *vi* COM *prix*, ECON slide, slip; ♦ **~ un mot en faveur de qn** COM put in a good word for sb, put in a word for sb

global, e *adj* COM global, overall, ECON *montant, valeur, demande*, MATH aggregate

globalement *adv* COM globally, overall

globalisation *f* COM, ECON globalization

globaliser *vt* COM, ECON globalize

GLOBEX *m* BOURSE GLOBEX

gloire *f* COM glory, kudos

glossaire *m* COM glossary

GMT *abrév (heure de Greenwich)* COM GMT (*Greenwich Mean Time*)

GNL *abrév (gaz naturel liquéfié)* ENVIR, IND, TRANSP LNG (*liquefied natural gas*)

Go *abrév (gigaoctet)* INFO Gb (*gigabyte*)

goélette *f* TRANSP *navire* Sr, schooner

gondole *f* V&M *présentoir* gondola

gonflement *m* COM *de la note* padding

gonfler *vt* COM *chiffres, prix* inflate, *compte* swell; **~ qn** *infrml* COM get sb's back up (*infrml*)

goulet *m* TRANSP *navigation* narrows

goulot: **~ d'étranglement** *m* ECON, IND bottleneck

goupille *f* TRANSP *navigation* actuator pole

gourde *f* COM gourde

gourmand: **~ en mémoire** *adj* INFO memory-hungry (*infrml*)

goût: **~ de la propriété** *m* COM acquisitiveness

gouvernement *m* POL government, govt; **~ de coalition** POL coalition government; **~ donateur** POL, PROT SOC donor government; **~ étranger** POL foreign government, overseas government; **~ fédéral** POL federal government

gouvernemental, e *adj* POL governmental

gouverner *vt* POL govern

gouverneur *m* ADMIN governor; **~ général** ADMIN, POL governor general

GPL *abrév (gaz de pétrole liquéfié)* ENVIR, IND, TRANSP LPG (*liquid petroleum gas*)

gradé: **~ de banque** *m* BANQUE bank officer

gradin *m* LOISIRS *bancs* tier

gradué, e *adj* COM graduated

graduel, -elle *adj* COM gradual

graduellement *adv* COM gradually, in graduated stages

graisser *vt* IND grease, oil; ♦ **~ la patte à qn** *infrml* COM grease sb's palm (*infrml*), oil sb's palm (*infrml*)

grammage *m* INFO paper weight

gramme *m (g)* COM gram (*AmE*) (*g*), gramme (*BrE*) (*g*)

grand[1], **e** *adj* COM, ECON large, large-scale; **~ public** MÉDIA popular

grand:[2] **~ capital** *m* (ANT *petit capital*) BOURSE, FIN big investors; **~ commis de l'État** *m* RES HUM high-flier, high-flyer; **~ compte** *m* BANQUE, COM, COMPTA major account; **~ ensemble** *m* IMMOB housing complex; **~ film** *m* MÉDIA feature film; **le ~ public** *m* COM the general public, the public at large; ~ **livre** m BANQUE *comptabilité générale* book of accounts, book of final entry, COMPTA book of accounts, general ledger, ledger, nominal ledger, private ledger, FIN book of accounts; ~ **livre auxiliaire** m BANQUE, COMPTA, FIN subsidiary ledger; ~ **livre auxiliaire des clients** m BANQUE, COMPTA, FIN accounts receivable ledger, clients' ledger, customers' ledger; ~ **livre auxiliaire des fournisseurs** m BANQUE, COMPTA, FIN accounts payable ledger; ~ **livre des clients** m BANQUE, COMPTA, FIN accounts receivable ledger, sales ledger; ~ **livre des comptes clients** m BANQUE, COMPTA, FIN accounts receivable ledger, sales ledger; ~ **livre des comptes fournisseurs** m BANQUE, COMPTA, FIN accounts payable ledger; ~ **livre des fournisseurs** m BANQUE, COMPTA, FIN accounts payable ledger; ~ **livre des ventes** m BANQUE, COMPTA, FIN clients' ledger, customers' ledger, sales ledger; ~ **magasin** m COM, V&M chain store, department store, emporium, multivariety store; ~ **panneau** m TRANSP *d'un navire* main hatch, MH; ~ **reportage** m MÉDIA feature; ~ **réseau** m GESTION, INFO wide area network, WAN; ~ **risque** m FIN large exposure; ~ **sac** m TRANSP *cargaison* big bag; ~ **sac souple** m TRANSP *cargaison* big bag

grand:[3] **-rue** f COM, IMMOB, V&M high street (*BrE*), main street (*AmE*)

grande: ~ **annonce** f MÉDIA display advertisement; ~ **banlieue** f COM commuter belt (*UK*); ~ **banque de dépôt** f BANQUE high-street bank (*UK*); ~ **entreprise** f COM megacorp (*jarg*), megacorporation; ~ **industrie** f IND large-scale industry; ~ **informatique** f INFO high-end computing, macrocomputing; ~ **ligne** f (*GL*) TRANSP *chemin de fer* main line; ~ **poche** f TRANSP *cargaison* big bag; ~ **presse** f MÉDIA national press; ~ **rareté** f ECON absolute scarcity; ~ **société** f COM big company; ~ **surface** f (*SYN commerce intégré*) COM hypermarket, one-stop shopping center (*AmE*), one-stop shopping centre (*BrE*); ~ **valeur industrielle** f BOURSE blue-chip industrial; ◆ à ~ **échelle** COM *projet*, ECON large-scale; à très ~ **échelle** COM, ECON very large-scale, VLS; de ~ **consommation** V&M admass; de ~ **envergure** COM wide-ranging; de ~s **lignes** TRANSP *gare* mainline; en ~ **banlieue** COM in the outer suburbs; en ~ **partie** COM largely, to a large extent; en ~s **quantités** COM in large quantities

Grande-Bretagne f COM Brit, Britain, Great Britain, GB

grandeur f COM size, MATH magnitude

grands: ~ **pays industrialisés** m pl ECON, POL First World, big industrialized countries

graphe m INFO, MATH graph

graphiciel m INFO graphic software

graphique[1] *adj* INFO, MATH graphic

graphique[2] m COM chart, INFO, MATH chart, graph; ~ **d'acheminement** GESTION, MATH flow chart, flow process chart; ~ **des activités** GESTION activity chart; ~ **en barres** MATH bar chart, bar graph;

~ **à bâtons** MATH bar chart, bar graph; ~ **camembert** COM, INFO, MATH pie chart; ~ **des chiffres et des points** BOURSE point and figure chart; ~ **circulaire** COM, INFO, MATH pie chart; ~ **de circulation** GESTION, MATH flow chart, flow process chart; ~ **en dents de scie** MATH Z chart; ~ **des étapes critiques** MATH milestone chart; ~ **d'évolution** GESTION, MATH flow chart, flow process chart; ~ **en point et figure** BOURSE point and figure chart; ~ **en tuyaux d'orgue** MATH bar chart, bar graph

graphique[3] f INFO, MÉDIA *technique, art* graphics

graphiques m pl INFO, MÉDIA graphics; ~ **de gestion** COM, COMPTA, FIN, INFO business graphics; ~ **de Hicks** ECON Hicks Charts

graphisme m INFO, MÉDIA graphics; ~ **maison** MÉDIA *identité de l'entreprise* house style

graphiste mf RES HUM, V&M art designer, commercial artist, commercial designer, graphic designer

grappe f INFO *de terminaux* cluster

grappin m TRANSP *matériel de manutention* grab

gras, se *adj* MÉDIA *caractère* bold

gratifiant, e *adj* COM, RES HUM *travail* rewarding

gratification f COM bonus, ECON incentive, FISC gratuity, RES HUM incentive; ~ **collective** *jarg* ECON, RES HUM synthetic incentive; ~ **psychologique** ECON, RES HUM psychic income (*jarg*)

gratis[1] *adj* COM at no charge, free, gratis, w.c., without charge

gratis[2] *adv* COM foc, free, free of charge, gratis, w.c., without charge, FOC

gratuit, e *adj* COM at no charge, foc, free, free of charge, gratis, w.c., without charge, FOC, *prêt* gratuitous, COMMS *appel, numéro* Freefone® (*BrE*), toll-free® (*AmE*), TRANSP *autoroute* free

gratuitement *adv* COM at no charge, foc, free, free of charge, gratis, w.c., without charge, FOC

grave[1] *adj* BOURSE, COM, FISC, INFO *erreur* serious

grave:[2] ~ **question** f COM big issue

gravure f MÉDIA lettering

gré: de ~ à gré *loc* COM, DROIT by mutual agreement, by mutual consent, by private contract

grec[1], **-que** *adj* COM Greek

grec[2] m COM *langue* Greek

Grec, -que m,f COM *habitant* Greek

Grèce f COM Greece

Greenpeace m ENVIR Greenpeace

gréeur m RES HUM, TRANSP *dans un port* lasher, rigger

greffier, -ière m,f DROIT *d'un tribunal* clerk

Grenade f COM Grenada

grenadin, e *adj* COM Grenadian

Grenadin, e m,f COM *habitant* Grenadian

grève f IND, RES HUM industrial action, job action (*jarg*), lockout, strike, walkout; ~ **des achats** ECON boycott; ~ **approuvée par le syndicat** DROIT *droit du travail*, IND, RES HUM official strike; ~ **avec occupation des locaux** RES HUM sit-down strike, sit-in, stay-in strike; ~ **avec préavis** RES HUM official strike; ~ **d'avertissement** RES HUM token strike; ~ **des cheminots** RES HUM, TRANSP rail strike; ~ **des chemins de fer** RES HUM, TRANSP rail strike; ~ **éclair** RES HUM hit-and-run strike, lightning strike; ~ **générale** RES HUM all-out strike, general strike; ~ **illicite** DROIT, IND, RES HUM illegal strike, unconstitutional strike; ~ **légale** DROIT, IND, RES HUM constitutional strike, legal strike; ~ **officielle** DROIT, IND, RES HUM official action (*UK*), official strike; ~ **par le travail** RES HUM work-in; ~ **perlée** RES HUM go-slow (*BrE*), slowdown (*AmE*); ~ **politique** POL, RES HUM political strike; ~ **revendicative** RES HUM protest strike, strike action; ~ **sans occupation des locaux** RES HUM stay-out strike; ~ **sans préavis** RES HUM unofficial strike; ~ **sauvage** RES HUM unofficial strike, wildcat strike; ~ **de solidarité** RES HUM sympathetic strike, sympathy strike; ~ **de soutien** RES HUM sympathetic strike, sympathy strike; ~ **sur le tas** RES HUM sit-down strike, sit-in strike, stay-in strike; ~ **surprise** IND walkout, RES HUM lightning strike, snap strike, walkout, wildcat strike; ~ **symbolique** RES HUM token strike; ~ **du zèle** RES HUM work-to-rule; ◆ **en** ~ RES HUM on strike; **faire** ~ RES HUM hit the bricks (*AmE*), strike, take industrial action; **faire une** ~ **surprise** RES HUM stage a walkout; ~**s, émeutes et insurrections civiles** DROIT strikes, riots and civil commotions, SR ~**s tournantes** RES HUM rolling strikes (*jarg*)

grever: ~ **d'une hypothèque** *loc* BANQUE *bien immeuble* mortgage

gréviste *mf* IND, RES HUM picket, striker

GRH *abrév* (*gestion des ressources humaines*) RES HUM HRM (*human resource management*)

grief *m* COM grievance; ◆ **avoir un** ~ **contre qn** COM have a grievance against sb

griffe *f* TRANSP *matériel de manutention* claw, V&M label

griffonnage *m* COM *d'un accord* scratching

grille *f* COM *de prix, tarifs, salaires* scale, INFO *sur écran*, MATH grid; ~ **d'échantillonnage** MATH sampling grid; ~ **de gestion** GESTION managerial grid; ~ **de produits** V&M product group; ~ **des salaires** RES HUM salary scale

grimper *vi* ECON climb; ◆ ~ **dans la hiérarchie** RES HUM climb the ladder, scale the ladder; ~ **en flèche** *infrml* COM *prix* rocket (*infrml*), skyrocket (*infrml*), soar

gros[1], **se** *adj* COM, ECON big, large, large-scale; ~ **calibre** RES HUM high-caliber (*AmE*), high-calibre (*BrE*)

gros:[2] **en** ~ *adv* COM by wholesale, wholesale

gros:[3] ~ **bénéfice** *m* BOURSE killing (*infrml*); ~ **bonnet** *m infrml* COM big wheel (*infrml*); ~ **bonnets** *m pl infrml* COM brass (*jarg*), top brass (*infrml*); ~ **budget** *m* ECON big budget, sizeable budget; ~ **client** *m* COM, V&M big customer; ~ **dommages** *m pl* ASSUR *maritime* hidden damage; ~ **employeur** *m* RES HUM big employer, large employer; ~ **exportateur** *m* ECON, IMP/EXP, V&M big exporter, large-scale exporter; ~ **importateur** *m* ECON, IMP/EXP, V&M big importer, large-scale importer; ~ **ordinateur** *m* INFO mainframe; ~ **-porteur** *m* TRANSP heavy jet, jumbo (*infrml*), jumbo jet (*infrml*), wide-body aircraft; ~ **producteur** *m* ECON, IND big producer, large producer, major producer; ~ **revenus** *m pl* FISC upper income; ~ **risque** *m* COM big risk, shot in the dark; ~ **système** *m* INFO mainframe; ~ **titre** *m* MÉDIA *presse, radio, télévision* banner headline, head, headline; ~ **titres** *m pl* MÉDIA *presse, radio, télévision* heads; ~ **transporteur** *m* TRANSP *véhicule* high loader; ~ **utilisateur** *m* INFO heavy user; ~ **utilisateur industriel** *m* IND big industrial user; ◆ **personne à** ~ **revenus** COM big income earner, high earner

grosse *f* COM, MATH, V&M *douze douzaines* gross; ~ **affaire** COM *contrat* big business, *entreprise* big business, big company; ~ **chaudronnerie** IND *production* industrial boilers; ~ **entreprise** COM big business, big company; ~ **quantité** COM bulk, large quantity; ~ **remise** FIN hard discount

grossiste *m* BOURSE, ECON wholesaler, V&M, COM wholesale dealer, wholesale merchant, wholesale trader, wholesaler; ~ **affilié** V&M affiliated wholesaler

grouillot *m* BOURSE blue button (*UK, jarg*)

groupage *m* MATH grouping, TRANSP consolidation, groupage, V&M bundling, mixed bundling; ~ **des frais** TRANSP combination of charges; ~ **de fret aérien** IMP/EXP, TRANSP air freight consolidation; ~ **des marchandises** TRANSP cargo assembly; ~ **par conteneur** TRANSP bulk unitization; ~ **des tarifs** TRANSP combination of rates

groupe *m* COM *de pays, de personnes, de sociétés* bracket, cluster, consortium, group, COMPTA group; ~ **affilié** COM affiliate; ~ **d'audit** COMPTA, FIN audit group, audit team; ~ **bancaire** BANQUE bank group (*AmE*), banking group; ~ **de bits** INFO packet; ~ **du Cairn** ECON Cairns' Group; ~ **cible** POL, V&M *étude de marché* focus group; ~ **de clients liés** FIN group of connected clients; ~ **concurrentiel** COM, RES HUM, V&M competing group; ~ **de cotation** BOURSE pit, pitch (*UK*); ~ **de diagnostic** RES HUM T-group training; ~ **de distribution** V&M store group; ~ **électrogène portable** TRANSP *porte-conteneurs* power pack; ~ **électrogène de secours** IND standby power plant; ~ **d'éléments d'actif** COMPTA, FIN group of assets; ~ **d'emplois** ECON, RES HUM job cluster; ~ **filiale** COM affiliated group; ~ **frigorifique amovible** TRANSP *navigation* clip-on unit, COU; ~ **HLM** IMMOB, PROT SOC housing development (*AmE*), housing estate, housing project (*AmE*); ~ **d'intérêt** COM interest group; ~ **d'intervention** POL, RES HUM task force; ~ **d'investissement en commun** BOURSE, FIN investment club; ~ **d'investisseurs** BOURSE, FIN investor group; **le** ~ **dirigeant** COM the establishment; ~ **lié** FISC related group; ~ **de négociation** BOURSE crowd; ~ **de négociation peu actif** BOURSE inactive post; ~ **de niveau** PROT SOC ability grouping; ~ **nonconcurrentiel** COM, RES HUM, V&M noncompeting group; ~ **d'options** BOURSE set of options; ~ **politique** POL political group; ~ **de portefeuille financier** FIN financial holding group; ~ **de pression** POL lobby group, pressure group; ~ **de pression agricole** POL farm lobby, farm lobby group, farm pressure group; ~ **de pression écologique** ENVIR, POL environmental lobby, environmental lobby group, environmental pressure group; ~ **de pression des écologistes** ENVIR, POL ecology lobby group, ecology pressure group, green lobby; ~ **de produits** V&M product group; ~ **de référence** COM reference group; ~ **de réflexion** COM think-tank (*infrml*), working group, working party, WP, POL, RES HUM task force; ~ **séparatiste** POL splinter group; ~ **de sociétés** COM group of companies; ~ **témoin** V&M consumer panel, consumers' panel; ~ **de travail** POL, RES HUM study group, task force, working group, working party; ~ **de travail autonome** RES HUM autonomous work group; ~ **de travail paritaire** RES HUM joint working party, JWP; ~ **d'utilisateurs** INFO user group

Groupe: ~ **de la Banque mondiale** *m* BANQUE, ECON, FIN World Bank Group; ~ **des Sept** *m* *(G7)* ECON Group of Seven *(G7)*

groupement *m* BOURSE trading party, COM *de pays, de personnes, de sociétés* group, *de ressources* pool, FIN pool, TRANSP consolidation; ~ **d'acheteurs** V&M buyer concentration; ~ **aveugle** FIN blind pool; ~ **bancaire** BANQUE bank group (*AmE*), group of banks; ~ **d'entreprises** COM consortium, group of companies; ~ **d'intérêt** COM interest group; ~ **professionnel** COM professional body

Groupement: ~ **de coopération européen** *m* DROIT, POL European Cooperation Grouping, ECG; ~ **d'intérêt économique européen** *m* *(GIEE)* ECON, POL European Economic Interest Grouping *(EEIG)*

grouper *vt* COM *ressources* pool, MATH group, TRANSP consolidate, group, V&M bundle

groupeur, -euse *m,f* TRANSP consolidator, forwarding agent, groupage agent

grue *f* TRANSP Cr, crane; ~ **de déchargement** TRANSP unloader crane; ~ **fixe** TRANSP fixed crane; ~ **kangourou** TRANSP kangaroo crane; ~ **mobile** TRANSP mobile crane, MC; ~ **plateforme** TRANSP pc, platform crane; ~ **à portée variable** TRANSP luffing crane; ~ **portique** TRANSP gantry, gantry crane, portal crane; ~ **roulante** TRANSP mobile crane, MC; ~ **semi-portique** TRANSP semi-portal crane; ~ **sur camion** TRANSP lorry-mounted crane (*BrE*), truck-mounted crane (*AmE*)

grumier *m* TRANSP *navire* timber ship

grutier, -ière *m,f* TRANSP crane driver, crane operator

G7 *abrév (Groupe des Sept)* ECON G7 *(Group of Seven)*

Guatemala[1] *m* COM Guatemala

Guatemala:[2] ~ **City** *n pr* COM Guatemala City

guatémaltèque *adj* COM Guatemalan

Guatémaltèque *mf* COM *habitant* Guatemalan

guerre *f* COM, ECON, POL, V&M war; ~ **commerciale** COM, ECON, V&M trade war; ~ **du Golfe** COM, ECON, POL Gulf War; ~ **des prix** COM, ECON, V&M price war; ~ **des tarifs** COM, ECON tariff war, TRANSP fare war, rate war

guetter *vt* COM be on the lookout for, be watching out for

gui *m* TRANSP *d'un navire* boom, BM

guichet *m* BANQUE, FIN counter, LOISIRS *d'un théâtre* booking office, box office, ticket office, wicket (*US*), TRANSP booking office, ticket office; ~ **automatique** BANQUE automated teller machine, automatic teller, automatic telling machine; ~ **automatique de banque** *(GAB)* BANQUE automated teller machine, automatic teller, automatic telling machine; ~ **bancaire** BANQUE automated teller machine, automatic teller, automatic telling machine; ~ **des billets** LOISIRS *d'un théâtre* booking office, box office, ticket office, wicket (*AmE*), TRANSP booking office, ticket office; ~ **fermé** BANQUE, COM position closed; ~ **de vente des billets** LOISIRS *d'un théâtre* booking office, box office, ticket office, wicket (*AmE*), TRANSP booking office, ticket office

guichetier, -ière *m,f* BANQUE bank teller, teller

guide *m* COM, LOISIRS *brochure, livre, personne* guide; ~ **aérien** TRANSP airline guide; ~ **d'audit** COMPTA, FIN auditing manual; ~ **du business plan** COM, GESTION business plan guide; ~ **de contrôle** COMPTA, FIN auditing manual; ~ **d'entretien** COM service handbook, service manual; ~ **d'entrevue** RES HUM interview guide; ~ **gastronomique** IND, LOISIRS good food guide; ~ **de l'utilisateur** COM instruction book, instruction manual, instructions, INFO user manual; ~ **d'utilisation** COM instruction book, instruction manual, instructions

guillemets *m pl* INFO, MÉDIA *typographie* inverted commas

Guinée *f* COM Guinea; ~ **équatoriale** COM Equatorial Guinea

Guinée-Bissau *f* COM Guinea-Bissau

guinéen[1]**, -enne** *adj* COM Guinean; ~ **équatorial** COM Equatorial Guinean

guinéen[2] *m* COM *langue* Guinean

Guinéen, -enne *m,f* COM *habitant* Guinean; ~ **équatorial** COM *habitant* Equatorial Guinean

gulden *m* COM *Pays-Bas* florin, guilder

guyanais, e *adj* COM Guyanese

Guyanais, e *m,f* COM *habitant* Guyanese

Guyane *f* COM Guyana

gyrocompas *m* TRANSP *navigation* gyrocompass, GC

H

h *abrév (heure)* COM, TRANSP h, hr *(hour)*

ha *abrév (hectare)* COM ha *(hectare)*

habeas corpus *m* DROIT habeas corpus

habendum *m* DROIT, IMMOB habendum *(frml)*

habileté *f* COM, RES HUM skill

habilité: ~ **à juger** *adj* DROIT entitled to adjudicate

habillage *m jarg* MÉDIA *typographie* run-around; ~ **de bilan** BANQUE, BOURSE, COM, COMPTA, FIN window-dressing

habillement *m* COM apparel

habiller: ~ **le bilan** *loc* BOURSE, COMPTA, FIN massage the figures

habitant, e *m,f* COM, DROIT, POL citizen, inhabitant; ♦ **par ~** COM per capita

habitat *m* ENVIR habitat

habitation: ~ **à loyer modéré** *f (HLM)* IMMOB, PROT SOC council block *(UK)*, council flats *(UK)*, public housing unit *(US)*

habitations: ~ **en grappe** *f pl* IMMOB cluster housing

habitudes: ~ **d'achat** *f pl* COM, V&M buying habits, spending patterns; ~ **des consommateurs** *f pl* COM, V&M consumer patterns; ~ **de consommation** *f pl* COM, V&M consumer habits; ~ **d'écoute** *f pl* MÉDIA *radio* listeners' habits; ~ **et accords d'industrie** *f pl* IND, RES HUM custom and practice; ~ **du métier** *f pl* COM trade custom; ~ **des téléspectateurs** *f pl* MÉDIA *télévision* listeners' habits

habituel, -elle *adj* COM usual

habituellement: ~ **domicilié** *adj* DROIT ordinarily resident

habituer *vt* IMMOB inure

Haïti *m* COM Haiti

haïtien, -enne *adj* COM Haitian

Haïtien, -enne *m,f* COM *habitant* Haitian

halo *m* V&M halo *(jarg)*

Hamilton *n pr* COM Hamilton

handicap *m* RES HUM disability; ~ **physique ou mental** PROT SOC physical or mental handicap

handicapé, e *m,f* RES HUM handicapped person

hangar: ~ **des exportations** *m* IMP/EXP export shed; ~ **des importations** *m* IMP/EXP import shed; ~ **de transit** *m* IMP/EXP, TRANSP transit shed

Hanoi *n pr* COM Hanoi

hantise: ~ **du travail** *f* COM, RES HUM ergophobia

Harare *n pr* COM Harare

harcèlement: ~ **sexuel** *m* RES HUM sexual harassment

hardware *m* INFO hardware

harmonisation *f* COMPTA, DROIT, ECON, IMP/EXP, POL harmonization; ~ **comptable** COMPTA accounting harmonization *(UK)*; ~ **du droit** DROIT, POL legal harmonization; ~ **fiscale** ECON tax harmonization; ~ **globale** COMPTA, ECON, FIN global harmonization; ~ **juridique** DROIT, POL legal harmonization; ~ **au niveau mondial** COMPTA, ECON, FIN global harmonization; ~ **de la politique** ECON policy harmonization; ~ **salariale** RES HUM salary harmonization

harmoniser *vt* COM, DROIT, ECON, IMP/EXP, POL harmonize

hasard: **au ~** *loc* COM, INFO, MATH at random

hasardeux *adj* COM risky, touch and go

hausse:[1] **à la ~** *adj (ANT à la baisse)* COM upward, upwards

hausse[2] *f* BOURSE *actions, monnaie* appreciation, run-up, running ahead, COM, COMPTA, ECON advance, hike, increase, rise, V&M *des prix* mark-up; ~ **brutale** BOURSE spike *(jarg)*; ~ **lente** BOURSE slow rise; ~ **maximum** BOURSE limit up; ~ **d'une monnaie** BOURSE, ECON appreciation of currency; ~ **du prix** V&M pricing up; ~ **des prix** COM, COMPTA, ECON, FIN, V&M increase in prices, price increase, price rise, rise in prices; ~ **du prix du pétrole** ECON oil price increase, oil price rise; ~ **rapide** BOURSE fast rise; ~ **sans effet** COM dead rise, DR; ~ **de prix de 0,25%** BOURSE quarter-up price *(jarg)*; ♦ **à la ~** BOURSE bullish; **en ~** BOURSE bullish, COM, ECON rising; **en ~ de 14%** BOURSE up 14%; **être en ~** *(ANT être en baisse)* ECON go up

haussier[1]**, -ière** *adj (ANT baissier)* BOURSE bullish, COM upward; ♦ **être ~** *(ANT être baissier)* BOURSE be bullish

haussier[2]**, -ière** *m,f (ANT baissier)* BOURSE bull, bull operator; ~ **et baissier** BOURSE bull and bear

haut:[1] ~ **placé** *adj* COM top-ranking; ~ **risque** *adj* BOURSE high-risk; **trop ~** *adj (ANT trop bas)* COM *prix, devis* too high; ♦ **à ~ profil** *(ANT à profil bas)* COM *profession, compagnie*, V&M high-profile; ~ **de gamme** COM, INFO high-end, top-of-the-range, up-market, V&M high-end, top-of-the-range, up-market, *produits* high-end, top-of-the-range, up-market; **de ~ en bas** COM top-down

haut:[2] **en ~** *adv* COM *de l'échelle* at the top end, TRANSP aloft

haut:[3] ~ **de casse** *m (ANT bas de casse)* ADMIN, INFO capital letter, u.c., upper case, upper-case letter, MÉDIA *lettre d'alphabet* ~ **-comité britannique** *m* ADMIN British High Commission, BHC; ~ **commissariat** *m* COM high commission; ~ **fonctionnaire** *m* ADMIN top-ranking official, RES HUM high-flier, high-flyer; ~ **de gamme dans la série** *m* V&M top end of the range; ~ **de gamme du marché** *m* V&M top end of the market; **le ~ de la gamme** *m* COM the top of the line; ~ **niveau sans précédent** *m* BOURSE all-time high

haute:[1] **~ résolution** *adj* INFO high-resolution; ◆ **à ~ résolution** INFO high-resolution; **à ~ technologie** IND, INFO hi-tech, high-tech, high-technology

haute:[2] **~ densité** *f (HD)* INFO high density *(HD)*; **~ direction** *f* GESTION top management; **~ finance** *f* FIN high finance; **~ saison** *f* ECON peak season; **~ saison des importations** *f* IMP/EXP peak importing season; **très ~ fréquence** *f (VHF)* COM very high frequency *(VHF)*; ◆ **à très ~ résistance** IND extra high strength, EHS

hautement: **~ perfectionné** *adj* IND high-stream *(jarg)*; **~ qualifié** *adj* RES HUM highly skilled

hauteur *f* COM height, hgt; **~ du châssis** TRANSP *véhicule routier* frame height; **~ fermée** TRANSP *chariot-élévateur à fourches* closed height; **~ métacentrique** COM metacentric height; **~ de page** INFO page depth; ◆ **être à la ~** COM be up to scratch *(infrml)*; **qui n'est pas à la ~** COM wanting

hauts: **~ et bas** *m pl* BOURSE ups and downs

Havane: La ~ *n pr* COM Havana

havre *m* COM haven

Haye: La ~ *n pr* COM The Hague

HC *abrév (conteneur hors-cotes)* TRANSP HC *(high cube)*

HD *abrév (haute densité)* INFO HD *(high density)*

hebdomadaire *adj* COM weekly

hébergement *m* IMMOB, PROT SOC accommodation *(BrE)*, accommodations *(AmE)*

héberger *vt* PROT SOC accommodate

hectare *m (ha)* COM hectare *(ha)*

hégémonie *f* POL hegemony

hélice *f* TRANSP *navigation, aviation* propeller; **~ en acier inoxydable** TRANSP *navigation, aviation* stainless-steel propeller, SSP; **~ cycloïdale** TRANSP *navigation, aviation* cycloidal propeller, CYCLD; **~ monobloc en fonte d'acier** TRANSP *navigation, aviation* solid cast-steel propeller, SCSP; **~ monobloc en fonte de fer** TRANSP *navigation, aviation* solid cast-iron propeller, SCIP; **~ monobloc non-ferreuse** TRANSP *navigation, aviation* solid non-ferrous propeller, SBP; **~ à moyeu en fonte et à pales en acier** TRANSP *navigation, aviation* cast-iron hub steel blades propeller, CIHSB; **~ à moyeu en fonte et à pales non-ferreuses** TRANSP *navigation, aviation* cast-iron hub non-ferrous blades propeller, CIHBB

hélicoptère *m* TRANSP helicopter

héliport *m* TRANSP heliport

hélistation *f* TRANSP helistop

Helsinki *n pr* COM Helsinki

hémorragie *f* ECON drain

héritage *m* DROIT inheritance, legacy

hériter *vt* DROIT inherit; ◆ **~ qch de qn** DROIT inherit sth from sb

héritier, -ière *m,f* DROIT, IMMOB heir, heiress, legatee; **~ légitime** DROIT, IMMOB rightful heir; **~ testamentaire** DROIT, IMMOB devisee

héritiers: **~ et ayants droit** *m pl* DROIT, IMMOB *actes, testaments* heirs and assigns

hermétique *adj* COM airtight, watertight

hésitant, e *adj* BOURSE hesitant, COM hesitant, wobbly

hétérogène *adj (* ANT *homogène)* COM heterogeneous

hétéroscédasticité *f* MATH heteroscedasticity

heure *f (h)* COM TRANSP hour, time; **~ d'arrivée prévue** LOISIRS estimated arrival time, EAT, TRANSP estimated arrival time, estimated time of arrival, EAT, ETA; **~ comptée double** RES HUM double time; **~ courante** TRANSP *charte-partie* running hour; **~ de départ prévue** COM, TRANSP estimated time of departure, estimated time of sailing, ETD, ETS; **~ d'écoute** MÉDIA *radio, télévision* listening time, viewing time; **~ d'écoute maximale** MÉDIA *radio, télévision* peak hour, prime listening time, prime time, prime viewing time; **~ d'émission** MÉDIA *radio, télévision* airtime; **~ de l'Est** COM Eastern Standard Time *(US)*, EST *(US)*; **~ d'été** COM daylight saving; **~ de l'Europe centrale** COM Central European Time, CET; **~ de l'Europe de l'Est** COM Eastern European Time, EET; **~ de fermeture** COM closing time; **~ de grande écoute** MÉDIA *radio, télévision* family hour *(jarg)*, peak hour, prime listening time, prime time, prime viewing time, V&M peak time, traffic time; **~ de Greenwich *(GMT)*** COM Greenwich Mean Time *(GMT)*; **l'~ dite** COM the appointed time; **l'~ fixée** COM the appointed time; **~ légale française** COM French Standard Time, ≈ British Standard Time; **~ locale** COM local time, MÉDIA local time, station time *(US)*; **~ normale des États du centre des États-Unis** COM Central Standard Time *(US)*, CST *(US)*; **~ de pointe** COM rush hour, MÉDIA peak hour, V&M drivetime; **~ précise** TRANSP *navigation* right time; **~ de travail socialement nécessaire** RES HUM socially necessary labor time *(AmE)*, socially necessary labour time *(BrE)*; **~ du triple sabbat** BOURSE triple witching hour *(US)*; **~ des trois sorcières** BOURSE triple witching hour *(US)*; **~ universelle** COM universal time coordinated, UTC; ◆ **à l'~** COM on schedule; **à l'~ convenue** COM at the appointed time; **à une ~ déterminée** COM at a given time; **être à l'~** COM be on schedule

heures: **~ d'affluence** *f pl* TRANSP peak period; **~ annualisées** *f pl* RES HUM annualized hours; **~ de bourse** *f pl* BOURSE market hours, stock exchange hours, trading hours; **~ de bureau** *f pl* COM business hours, h.b., hours of business, office hours, V&M business hours; **~ du dernier jour** *f pl* BOURSE *boursier* last-day hours; **~ indues** *f pl* RES HUM unsocial hours; **~ inemployées** *f pl* RES HUM idle time; **~ machines** *f pl* INFO computer time; **~ de négociation** *f pl* BOURSE market hours, stock exchange hours, trading hours; **~ normales** *f pl* COM regular hours; **~ d'ouverture** *f pl* COM business hours, h.b., hours of business, opening hours, V&M business hours; ~ **d'ouverture de la banque** *f pl* BANQUE banking hours; ~ **ouvrables** *f pl* COM business hours, h.b., hours of business, V&M business hours; ~ **de pointe** *f pl* TRANSP peak period; ~ **de réception de clientèle** *f pl* COM business hours, h.b., hours of business, V&M business hours; ~ **récupérées** *f pl* RES HUM compensatory time; ~ **supp'** *f pl infrml (heures supplémentaires)* RES HUM OT *(overtime)*; ~ **supplémentaires** *f pl (HS, heures supp')* RES HUM overtime *(OT)*, overtime hours; ~ **de travail** *f pl* COM working time, RES HUM working hours; ~ **d'utilisation** *f pl* COM service hours; ◆ **à 7 ~ précises** COM at 7 o'clock sharp

heureuse: ~ **arrivée** *f* TRANSP s/a, safe arrival

heureux: **être ~ d'avoir l'opinion de qn sur** *loc* COM welcome sb's opinion on

heuristique[1] *adj* COM, GESTION, INFO heuristic

heuristique[2] *f* COM, GESTION, INFO heuristics

hiérarchie *f* COM, GESTION, RES HUM chain of command, hierarchy, managerial structure; ~ **des besoins** RES HUM hierarchy of needs; ~ **de commandement** GESTION, RES HUM chain of command; ~ **des effets** V&M *marketing* hierarchy of effects; ~ **des objectifs** COM hierarchy of objectives; ~ **salariale** RES HUM pay differential; ◆ **en remontant la ~** COM, GESTION up the line

hiloire: ~ **de cale** *f* TRANSP *navigation* hatch coaming; ~ **d'écoutille** *f* TRANSP *navigation* hatch coaming; ~ **de panneau** *f* TRANSP *navigation* coaming; ~ **renversée** *f* TRANSP *navigation* girder; ~ **sous barrots** *f* TRANSP *navigation* girder

hindi[1] *adj* COM Hindi

hindi[2] *m* COM *langue* Hindi

hindoustani[1] *adj* COM Hindi

hindoustani[2] *m* COM *langue* Hindi

hinterland *m* TRANSP hinterland

hipothèque: ~ **à taux réglable** *f* FIN adjustable-rate mortgage, ARM

histogramme *m* MATH bar chart, bar graph, histogram

historique[1] *adj* COM, COMPTA, ECON historical

historique[2] *m* COM case history, *commercial* background paper; ~ **d'un investissement** BOURSE, FIN investment history

hiver *m* COM winter

HLM *abrév (habitation à loyer modéré)* IMMOB, PROT SOC council block *(UK)*, council flats *(UK)*, public housing unit *(US)*

holding *m* COM holding company; ~ **à activité mixte** BOURSE mixed-activity holding company; ~ **bancaire** BANQUE, COM bank holding company

hollandais[1], **e** *adj* COM Dutch, Netherlandish, of the Netherlands

hollandais[2] *m* COM *langue* Dutch

Hollandais *m* COM *habitant* Dutchman, COM *habitant* Netherlander

Hollandaise *f* COM *habitante* Dutchwoman

homicide: ~ **au premier degré** *m* DROIT murder one *(infrml)*

homme: ~ **actif** *m* RES HUM working man; ~ **d'affaires** *m* COM businessman; ~ **de confiance** *m* COM confidential clerk; ~ **économique** *m* ECON economic man; ~ **de garde** *m* RES HUM watchman; ~ **de loi** *m* DROIT legal practitioner; ~ **marié** *m* ADMIN, DROIT, FISC married man; ~ **du métier** *m* BREVETS person skilled in the art; ~ **de paille** *m* DROIT dummy; ~ **de peine** *m* RES HUM handyman, odd-job man; ~ **politique** *m* COM, POL politician; ~ **de terrain** *m* COM field operator; ~ **à tout faire** *m* RES HUM handyman, odd-job man; ◆ **l'~ de la rue** COM the man in the street

homo economicus *m frml* ECON homo economicus *(frml)*

homogène *adj* (ANT *hétérogène*) COM homogeneous

homologation *f* BREVETS *d'un produit* certification, COM approval, seal of approval, IMP/EXP homologation, IND certification, RES HUM certification mark

homologue *m* RES HUM *personne* opposite number

homologuer *vt* COM approve, DROIT *testament* confirm, grant

homoscédasticité *f* MATH homoscedasticity

homo sovieticus *m frml* ECON homo sovieticus *(frml)*

Honduras *m* COM Honduras

hondurien, -enne *adj* COM Honduran

Hondurien, -enne *m,f* COM *habitant* Honduran

Hong Kong *n pr* COM Hong Kong

Hongrie *f* COM Hungary

hongrois[1], **e** *adj* COM Hungarian

hongrois[2] *m* COM *langue* Hungarian

Hongrois, e *m,f* COM *habitant* Hungarian

honnête *adj* COM above board, fair, honest, DROIT fair

honnêteté *f* COM honesty, trustworthiness

honneur *m* COM honor *(AmE)*, honour *(BrE)*

honorable: **très ~** *adj* POL Right Honourable, Rt Hon *(UK)*

honoraire *adj* RES HUM honorary

honoraires *m pl* COM honorarium *(frml)*, *professions libérales* fee, DROIT, MÉDIA fee; ~ **annuels** COM, COMPTA annual fee; ~ **d'avocat** DROIT legal expenses, legal fees; ~ **comptables** COMPTA, FIN accounting fees; ~ **consulaires** IMP/EXP consular fees; ~ **dérogatoires** RES HUM override; ~ **d'encouragement** V&M incentive fee; ~ **éventuels** COM contingent fee; ~ **d'expertise** COM, FIN, PROT SOC survey fee; ~ **d'expertise comptable** COMPTA, FIN accounting fees; ~ **de gestion** IMMOB management fee; ~ **non-remboursables** V&M nonrefundable fee; ~ **de recherche** V&M finder's fee *(US)*; ~ **de registraire** FISC registrar fee; ~ **supplémentaires** DROIT refresher *(UK)*

honorariat *m* RES HUM honorary membership

honorer *vt* BANQUE *chèque, lettre de change* honor (*AmE*), honour (*BrE*), BOURSE *emprunt* take up, COM honor (*AmE*), honour (*BrE*), *engagements, obligations* fulfil (*BrE*), fulfill (*AmE*), meet, FIN *effet* take up; ◆ **ne pas ~** BANQUE, FIN dishonor (*AmE*), dishonour (*BrE*); **ne pas ~ ses échéances** COM default

honorifique *adj* RES HUM honorary

hôpital: ~ public *m* PROT SOC public hospital

horaire[1] *adj* COM hourly

horaire[2] *m* COM schedule, timetable, FIN, GESTION schedule, RES HUM working hours, TRANSP timetable, TT, *d'exploitation* operating schedule; **~ flexible** RES HUM flexible schedule; **~ des trains** TRANSP railroad timetable (*AmE*), railway timetable (*BrE*); ◆ **à ~ variable** RES HUM numerical flexibility (*UK*)

horaires: ~ aménagés *m pl* RES HUM flexible working hours, flexitime, flextime; **~ à la carte** *m pl* RES HUM flexible working hours, flexitime, flextime; **~ de travail à la carte** *m pl* RES HUM flexible working hours, flexitime, flextime; **~ variables** *m pl* RES HUM gliding shift (*jarg*); **~ des vols** *m pl* TRANSP flight time information

horizon: ~ temporel *m* ECON time span

horizontal, e *adj* (ANT *vertical*) BOURSE, COM, ECON, FISC, IND, MÉDIA horizontal

horloge: ~ -calendrier *f* INFO clock-calendar; **~ pointeuse** *f* IND, RES HUM time clock

hors:[1] **~ bilan** *adj* COMPTA, FIN off-balance-sheet, OBS; **~ -bord** *adj* TRANSP *navigation, moteur* outboard, O; **~ bourse** *adj* BOURSE after-hours, after-market; **~ CE** *adj* COM extra-EU; **~ cote** *adj* BOURSE off-the-board, over-the-counter (*US*), OTC (*US*); **~ du cours** *adj* BOURSE out-of-the-money, OTM; **~ impôts** *adj* COM, COMPTA, FISC net of taxes; **~ -jeu** *adj* BOURSE out-of-the-money, OTM; **~ ligne** *adj* INFO off-line; **~ marché** *adj* BOURSE *transactions entre courtiers* away from the market; **~ -média** *adj* MÉDIA below-the-line; **~ -saison** *adj* COM off-season; **~ séance** *adj* BOURSE after-hours, after-market; **~ série** *adj* COM ungraded; **~ -série** *adj* COM one-off, ungraded; **~ service** *adj* INFO disabled; **~ taxes** *adj* ECON, FIN, FISC exclusive of tax, tax-free, IMP/EXP duty-free, net of taxes

hors:[2] **~ -bord** *m* TRANSP outboard; **~ -texte** *m* MÉDIA tip-in

hors:[3] **~ saison** *f* COM off season

hors:[4] **~ de compétence** *loc* DROIT ultra vires; **~ du cadre légal** *loc* DROIT ex-legal; **~ de la compétence de** *loc* COM, DROIT outside the reference of; **~ conférence** *loc* TRANSP *maritime* no liner, NL; **~ contingent** *loc* ECON above quota; **être ~ de portée** *loc* COM be out of range; **être ~ d'usage** *loc* COM be out of order

hostile *adj* FIN unfriendly

hôte *m* INFO host; **~ payant** COM paying guest, PG

hôtel *m* COM, LOISIRS hotel; **~ d'aéroport** LOISIRS, TRANSP airport hotel; **~ de congrès** COM, GESTION, IMMOB convention hotel; **~ international** LOISIRS international-standard hotel; **~ recevant des congrès** COM, GESTION, IMMOB convention hotel; **~ trois-étoiles** COM, LOISIRS three-star hotel

Hôtel: ~ de la Monnaie *m* ECON ≈ Royal Mint (*UK*)

hôtesse: ~ de l'air *f* TRANSP *avion* air hostess, flight attendant

houille *f* ENVIR, IND coal; **~ blanche** ENVIR, IND white coal

houillère *f* IND coal mine

housse *f* INFO cover, dust cover, TRANSP *palettes* snood

HS *abrév (heures supplémentaires)* RES HUM OT (*overtime*)

hub: ~ d'éclatement *m* GESTION nerve center (*AmE*), nerve centre (*BrE*)

huile *f* ENVIR, TRANSP oil; **~ de carter** TRANSP *navigation* c/o, cargo oil, case oil; **~ combustible** TRANSP burning oil; **~ résiduaire** ENVIR waste oils

huis: à ~ clos *loc* DROIT in camera, POL in camera (*frml*)

huissier *m* DROIT *de justice* bailiff

huitième: un ~ *m (1/8)* COM, MATH one-eighth (1/8)

humeur *f* COM, RES HUM frame of mind

hybride *adj* COM, INFO hybrid

hydrocarbure *m* ENVIR, IND hydrocarbon

hydroélectrique *adj* ENVIR hydro, hydroelectric, IND hydroelectric

hydrofoil *m* TRANSP hovercraft, hydrofoil, jetfoil

hydroglisseur *m* TRANSP hovercraft, jetfoil, hydrofoil

hydromètre *m* ENVIR hydrometer

hydroptère *m* TRANSP hovercraft, hydrofoil, jetfoil

hygiène: ~ de l'environnement *f* ENVIR environmental hygiene; **~ et sécurité du travail** *f* RES HUM health and safety; **~ du travail** *f* PROT SOC, RES HUM industrial hygiene, occupational health

hygroscopique *adj* ENVIR hygroscopic

hyp. *abrév (hypothèque)* BANQUE, FIN, IMMOB mortg. *(mortgage)*

hyperfréquence *f* COM very high frequency

hyperinflation *f* ECON hyperinflation, runaway inflation; **~ de la monnaie** ECON helicopter money

hypermarché *m* COM, V&M hypermarket, superstore

hypothèque *f (hyp.)* BANQUE, FIN, IMMOB mortgage *(mortg.)*; **~ auto-amortissable** BANQUE, IMMOB self-amortizing mortgage; **~ à capital croissant** BANQUE growing-equity mortgage (*US*), GEM (*US*); **~ de deuxième rang** BANQUE, IMMOB junior mortgage (*US*), second mortgage; **~ à évaluation partagée** BANQUE, IMMOB shared-appreciation mortgage; **~ fiduciaire** BANQUE trust mortgage; **~ à frais modérés** BANQUE budget mortgage (*US*); **~ garantie** BANQUE guaranteed mortgage; **~ garantie par nantissement** BANQUE,

FIN collateralized mortgage obligation, CMO; ~ **générale** BANQUE blanket mortgage, general mortgage; ~ **immobilière** BANQUE, IMMOB house mortgage; ~ **intégrante** BANQUE wraparound mortgage; ~ **investie en actions** FIN equity-linked mortgage; ~ **à paiements croissants** BANQUE growing-equity mortgage (*US*), GEM (*US*); ~ **à paiements échelonnés** BANQUE graduated-payment mortgage; ~ **de premier rang** BANQUE, IMMOB first mortgage; ~ **à règlements variables** IMMOB flexible-payment mortgage, FPM; ~ **à remboursements fixes** FIN level-payment mortgage (*US*); ~ **sans date limite** BANQUE open-ended mortgage; ~ **sous-jacente** BANQUE, IMMOB underlying mortgage; ~ **sur bien loué** IMMOB leasehold mortgage; ~ **sur biens meubles** BANQUE chattel mortgage (*US*); ~ **à taux fixe** BANQUE fixed-rate mortgage; ~ **à taux réglable** BANQUE adjustable-rate mortgage, ARM; ~ **à taux renégocié** BANQUE, IMMOB renegotiated rate mortgage

hypothéquer *vt* BANQUE mortgage, DROIT hypothecate, FIN mortgage out

hypothèse *f* COM assumption, hypothesis, scenario, ECON hypothesis, scenario; ~ **alternative** MATH alternative hypothesis; ~ **de la convergence** ECON convergence hypothesis; ~ **du cycle de vie** ECON life-cycle hypothesis, LCH; ~ **de l'écart de valeur** ECON value discrepancy hypothesis; ~ **de Fisher** ECON Fisher theorem; ~ **nulle** MATH null hypothesis; ~ **optimiste** (ANT *hypothèse pessimiste*) COM, ECON, POL best-case scenario; ~ **de la permanence du revenu** ECON permanent income hypothesis; ~ **pessimiste** (ANT *hypothèse optimiste*) COM, ECON, POL worst-case scenario; ~ **du rattrapage économique** ECON catching-up hypothesis; ~ **du renversement de la relation de cause à effet** ECON reverse causation hypothesis; ~ **de revenu absolu** ECON absolute income hypothesis; ~ **du revenu relatif** ECON relative income hypothesis; ~ **des salaires réels** ECON real-wage hypothesis; ~ **de Tiebout** ECON Tiebout hypothesis; ~ **de travail** COM working hypothesis; ~ **en U** ECON U-hypothesis; ~ **d'uniformité** ECON uniformity assumption; ~ **de Wagner** ECON Wagner's law; ◆ **dans l'~ où** COM on the premise that

hypothétique *adj* COM hypothetical

hystérèse *f* ECON hysteresis

hystérésis *f* ECON hysteresis

I

I *abrév (important indice du marché, indice du marché principal)* BOURSE MMI *(Major Market Index)*

IA *abrév (intelligence artificielle)* INFO AI *(artificial intelligence)*

IAO *abrév (ingénierie assistée par ordinateur)* IND, INFO CAE *(computer-aided engineering, computer-assisted engineering)*

IATA *abrév (Association internationale des transports aériens)* TRANSP IATA *(International Air Transport Association)*

ibid. *abrév (ibidem)* COM ibid. *(ibidem)*

ibidem *adv (ibid.)* COM ibidem *(ibid.)*

IBM® *abrév* INFO IBM® International Business Machines®

IC *abrév (intérêts courus, intérêts cumulés)* BANQUE, BOURSE, COM, COMPTA, FIN AI *(accrued interest)*, IA *(interest accrued)*

ici: d'~ *adj* ADMIN patrial *(UK, dat)*

icône *f* COM, INFO icon; ◆ **par ~** INFO by icon

id. *abrév (idem)* COM id. *(idem)*

ID *abrév (identification)* COM, FISC, V&M ID *(identification)*

idée: ~ **de base** *f* COM basic concept; ~ **directrice** *f* COM governing principle; ~ **dominante** *f* COM governing principle; ~ **générale du marché** *f* COM feel of the market; ~ **personnelle** *f* COM brainchild *(infrml)*

idem *adj (id.)* COM idem *(id.)*

identifiable *adj* FISC ascertainable

identificateur *m* INFO identifier

identification *f (ID)* COM, FISC, V&M identification *(ID)*; ~ **d'incident** INFO problem determination; ~ **de la marque** V&M brand identification, brand recognition

identité: ~ **fondamentale** *f* COMPTA accounting identity

IDP *abrév (indication de durée et de prix)* COM ADC *(advice of duration and/or charge)*

IEP *abrév (Institut d'études politiques)* POL ≈ Centre for Political Studies

IES *abrév (prêt d'investissement et d'entretien sectoriel)* FIN SIM *(sector investment and maintenance loan)*

IGF *abrév (impôt sur les grandes fortunes)* FISC tax aimed at very rich people

igloo *m* TRANSP *aviation* igloo

il: dont ~ **s'agit** *loc* COM at issue; ~ **est contraire à notre politique d'accorder des remises** *loc* COM it is against our policy to grant discounts; ~ **est interdit de fumer** *loc* COM no smoking, smoking is not permitted, smoking is prohibited; ~ **est raisonnable de considérer** *loc* COM it may

reasonably be considered; **là où ~ y a un droit** *loc* DROIT ubi remedium ibi jus; ~ **n'a pas un rond** *loc infrml* COM he hasn't got a bean *(infrml)*; **qu'~ soit à quai ou non** *loc* TRANSP *charte-partie* whether in berth or not; **s'~ vous plaît** *loc* COMMS please

Ile: ~ **Maurice** *f* COM Mauritius; ~ **de la Réunion** *f* COM Reunion Island

Iles:[1] ~ **Sous-le-Vent** *f pl* COM Leeward Islands; ~ **Vierges** *f pl* COM Virgin Islands

Iles:[2] ~ **Canaries** *n pr* COM Canary Islands; ~ **du Vent** *n pr* COM Windward Islands

illégal, e *adj* DROIT illegal, unlawful

illégalement *adv* DROIT illegally, unlawfully

illicite *adj* DROIT illegal, unlawful

illimité, e *adj* BOURSE unlimited, ENVIR *ressources* infinite; ~ **à la hausse** BOURSE unlimited on the upside; ~ **vers le haut** BOURSE unlimited on the upside

illusion: ~ **du coût engagé indifférent** *f* FIN sunk cost fallacy; ~ **inflationniste** *f* ECON inflation illusion; ~ **monétaire** *f* ECON money illusion, price perception

illustration *f* COM, MÉDIA illustration

illustré[1]**, e** *adj* COM, MÉDIA illustrated; ~ **à grand renfort de détails** COM, MÉDIA graphically illustrated

illustré[2]**, e** *m* MÉDIA illustrated magazine

illustrer *vt* COM, MÉDIA illustrate

îlot *m* V&M island

image *f* COM image, picture, INFO image, *de film* frame, MÉDIA image, picture, V&M image; ~ **clip art** INFO clip art; ~ **de l'entreprise** COM corporate image; ~ **fidèle** COMPTA fair presentation *(AmE)*, true and fair view *(BrE)*; ~ **de fond** INFO background picture; ~ **globale** V&M global image; ~ **graphique** INFO clip art; ~ **de marque** COM *de l'entreprise* corporate image, V&M brand label, *d'un produit* brand image, product image; ~ **rémanente** V&M *publicité* afterimage; ◆ **donner une ~ fidèle de qch** COMPTA present sth fairly

images *f pl* MÉDIA graphics

imagination *f* COM, GESTION creative thinking

imbrication *f* INFO nesting

imbriqué, e *adj* INFO embedded, nested

imbriquer *vt* INFO nest

IMC *abrév (impôt minimum complémentaire)* FISC add-on minimum tax

imitation *f* COM copy

immatriculation *f* COM enrollment *(AmE)*, enrolment *(BrE)*, FISC registration, TRANSP *d'une voiture* car registration, registration; ~ **fiscale d'employeur** FISC taxation employer number

(Canada); ~ **maritime** TRANSP nautical registration; ~ **des navires** TRANSP registry of shipping

immatriculé *adj* FISC *-e*, TRANSP registered; ~ **au Canada** DROIT, FISC *navigation*, TRANSP registered in Canada

immatriculer *vt* COM, FISC, TRANSP register; ◆ **faire** ~ ADMIN, COM license

immédiat, e *adj* COM immediate; ◆ **dans l'**~ COM in the short term

immeuble *m* COM accommodation, building, IMMOB apartment building *(AmE)*, block of flats *(BrE)*, tenement; ~ **de bureaux** COM, IMMOB office block, office building; ~ **commercial** COM, IMMOB trading estate; ~ **construit pour une fonction** IMMOB *d'appartements* purpose-built block; ~ **en copropriété** IMMOB condominium *(AmE)*, cooperative *(BrE)*; ~ **d'habitation** IMMOB residential occupancy; ~ **résidentiel à logements multiples** ADMIN, IMMOB multiple-unit residential building

immeubles: ~ **à usage d'habitation** *m pl* IMMOB residential accommodation

immigration *f* ADMIN, DROIT, ECON immigration; ~ **clandestine** DROIT illegal immigration

immigré, e *m,f* ADMIN immigrant; ~ **clandestin** DROIT illegal immigrant

immiscer: **s'**~ **dans** *v pron* COM interfere in

immixtion: ~ **du patronat dans les affaires syndicales** *f* RES HUM employer interference

immobilier *m* COM, IMMOB property; ~ **acquis** IMMOB property acquired; ~ **commercial** COM, IMMOB commercial property; ~ **détaillé** IMMOB retail property; ~ **de placement** IMMOB investment property; ~ **de rapport** IMMOB income property *(AmE)*; ~ **de spéculation** IMMOB spec house; ~ **sujet à dépréciation** FIN, IMMOB depreciable real estate; ~ **en viager** IMMOB life estate

immobilisation *f* ECON, FIN, IND capital investment, shutdown; ~ **corporelle** *(*ANT *immobilisation incorporelle)* COM, COMPTA, FIN tangible asset, tangible fixed asset; ~ **incorporelle** *(*ANT *immobilisation corporelle)* COM, COMPTA, FIN intangible asset, intangible fixed asset

immobilisations *f pl* COM capex, capital expenditure, fixed assets, COMPTA, FIN fixed assets; ~ **amortissables** COMPTA depreciable property; ~ **en cours** COMPTA, FIN assets under construction; ~ **défectibles** ECON wasting assets; ~ **défectives** COMPTA wasting assets; ~ **financières** COMPTA long-term financial investments, FIN capital assets

immobilité: ~ **en matière salariale** *f* RES HUM wage standstill

immunisation *f* FIN immunization

immunité *f* DROIT immunity; ~ **fiscale** FISC tax immunity; ~ **légale** DROIT legal immunity, statutory immunity; ~ **statutaire** DROIT statutory immunity

immunités: ~ **légales** *f pl* DROIT *droit syndical*, RES HUM statutory immunities; ~ **syndicales** *f pl* DROIT *droit syndical*, RES HUM statutory immunities, trade union immunities *(UK)*

imp. *abrév (importation)* IMP/EXP imp. *(import)*

impact *m* COM, ENVIR impact, RES HUM loading *(jarg)*; ~ **environnemental** ENVIR environmental impact; ~ **sur l'environnement** ENVIR environmental impact; ~ **visuel** COM visual impact

impair, e *adj* COM, INFO odd

imparfait, e *adj* COM flawed

impartial, e *adj* COM impartial

impasse *f* COM deadlock *(jarg)*, impasse, stalemate, standoff; ~ **budgétaire** ECON deficit spending; ~ **professionnelle** RES HUM blind-alley job *(AmE)*, dead-end job *(BrE)*; ◆ **dans l'**~ COM stalemated; **dans une** ~ COM stymied; **être dans une** ~ COM have reached a stalemate

impayé[1], e *adj* COMPTA outstanding

impayé[2] *m* COMPTA unpaid bill

impenses *f pl* FISC maintenance expenditures, upkeep

impératif, -ive *adj* DROIT mandatory

impératifs: ~ **de la dette** *m pl* ECON, POL debt obligations

imperfection *f* COM flaw

impérialisme *m* POL imperialism; ~ **capitaliste** ECON, POL capitalist imperialism

imperméable *adj* COM waterproof

implantation *f* ENVIR *décharge* site development, IND siting; ~ **à l'étranger** COM foreign venture; ~ **fonctionnelle** COM functional layout; ~ **d'usine** COM, IND plant location

implémentation *f* INFO *de système* implementation

implémenter *vt* INFO implement

implication: ~ **des ouvriers** *f* RES HUM workers' involvement; ~ **du personnel** *f* RES HUM involvement of employees

implicite *adj* BOURSE implied, COM defaulting, implied, tacit, DROIT, FIN implied, INFO by default, defaulting

impliquer *vt* BREVETS *activité inventive*, COM *frais* involve

impopulaire *adj* COM unpopular

import: ~ **-export** *m* IMP/EXP import-export

importance: ~ **d'un droit** *f* DROIT magnitude of a right; ~ **relative** *f* COMPTA materiality; ~ **d'un tirage moyen** *f* MÉDIA *presse* run of paper, ROP

important[1], e *adj* COM large-scale, massive, material, prominent, *achat* large, *gain* substantial, *personne* high-powered, ECON large, large-scale, substantial; **peu** ~ COM small

important[2]: ~ **indice du marché** *f (I)* BOURSE Major Market Index *(MMI)*

importateur[1], -trice *adj* IMP/EXP importing

importateur[2], -trice *m,f* IMP/EXP importer; ~ **net** *(*ANT *exportateur net)* ENVIR net receiver

importation *f (imp.)* IMP/EXP import, importation *(imp.)*; ~ **invisible** ECON, IMP/EXP invisible import; ~ **parallèle** IMP/EXP parallel import; ~ **temporaire**

IMP/EXP temporary importation; ~ **visible** IMP/EXP visible import

importations: ~ **communautaires** *f pl* IMP/EXP community imports

importé, e *adj* ECON, IMP/EXP imported

importer *vt* IMP/EXP, INFO import

importun, e *adj* V&M *publicité* intrusive

imposable[1] *adj* COM ratable, COMPTA, FIN taxable, FISC chargeable to tax, subject to taxation, taxable; ♦ ~ **comme revenu de** FISC taxable in the hands of

imposable:[2] **personne** ~ *f* FISC person liable to tax

imposé, e *adj* FISC taxed; ♦ ~ **par** COM driven by; ~ **à la source** FISC taxed at source

imposer *vt* COM *restriction* impose, DROIT *limite, restriction* impose, *loi* lay down, FISC *pénalité* assess, levy, GESTION enjoin; ♦ ~ **une amende à qn** DROIT impose a fine on sb; ~ **des règles** ADMIN lay down the rules; ~ **une taxe** FISC raise a tax

imposition *f* COM assessment, imposition, DROIT imposition, ECON taxation, FIN levy, taxation, FISC taxation, *d'une pénalité* assessment, tax assessment; ~ **d'après le domicile** FISC domicile taxation; ~ **arbitraire** FISC arbitrary taxation; ~ **directe** ECON, FISC direct tax, direct taxation; ~ **directe et indirecte** ECON, FISC direct and indirect taxation; ~ **discriminatoire des étrangers** FISC discriminatory taxation of foreigners; ~ **exclusive** FISC exclusive taxation; ~ **indirecte** ECON, FISC indirect tax, indirect taxation; ~ **moyenne à long terme** ECON, FISC lifetime averaging; ~ **multiple** FISC multiple taxation; ~ **optimale** FISC optimal taxation; ~ **présomptive** FISC presumptive tax; ~ **régressive** FISC regressive taxation; ~ **du Royaume-Uni** FISC UK taxation

impossibilité: ~ **d'exécuter un contrat** *f* DROIT frustration of contract

impossible: ~ **à trafiquer** *loc infrml* COM tamperproof

impôt *m* COMPTA, ECON, FIN tax, FISC duty, imposition, levy, tax, IMP/EXP levy; ~ **accumulé** FISC accrual tax; ~ **ad valorem** *frml* COMPTA ad valorem tax, FISC ad valorem tax *(frml)*; ~ **affecté à une fin spéciale** FISC earmarked tax; ~ **agricole** ECON, FISC agricultural levy; ~ **de base** FISC basic tax; ~ **de Bourse** BOURSE, FISC transaction tax; ~ **de capitation** ECON, FISC capitation tax; ~ **contesté** FISC disputed tax; ~ **correctif** FISC, POL corrective subsidy, corrective tax; ~ **déduit** FISC tax deduction *(AmE)*; ~ **dégressif** FISC decreasing tax, degressive tax; ~ **déguisé** FISC hidden tax; ~ **différé** COMPTA, FISC deferred tax; ~ **éludé** FISC defrauded tax; ~ **établi** FISC assessed tax; ~ **de l'État** FISC state tax; ~ **étranger** FISC foreign tax; ~ **étranger accumulé** FISC foreign accrual tax; ~ **excessif** FISC overtax; ~ **exigible** FISC tax payable; ~ **fédéral net** FISC net federal tax; ~ **fictif** FISC phantom tax; ~ **fixé** FISC assessed tax; ~ **foncier** FISC real-property tax; ~ **forfaitaire**

FISC basic-rate tax, flat-rate tax, standard-rate tax; ~ **général sur le revenu** FISC general income tax; ~ **de guerre** FISC war tax; ~ **individuel sur le revenu** FISC personal income tax; ~ **latent** COMPTA, FISC deferred tax; ~ **minier** FISC, IND mining tax; ~ **minimum** FISC *sur le revenu* minimum income tax, minimum tax; ~ **minimum complémentaire** *(IMC)* FISC add-on minimum tax; ~ **minimum de remplacement** FISC alternative minimum tax *(Can)*; ~ **minimum sur le revenu des particuliers** FISC minimum personal income tax; ~ **moyen** FISC average tax; ~ **municipal** FISC local tax; ~ **négatif sur le revenu** FISC negative income tax, social dividend scheme, NIT; ~ **noncumulatif** FISC noncumulative tax; ~ **non-payé** FISC unpaid tax; ~ **des non-résidents** FISC non-resident tax; ~ **normal** FISC standard tax; ~ **normal sur le revenu des particuliers** FISC standard individual income tax; ~ **ordinaire** FISC standard tax; ~ **par tête** FISC capitation; ~ **par unité** FISC per unit tax; ~ **payable par ailleurs** FISC tax otherwise payable; ~ **à payer** FISC tax liability, tax payable; ~ **programmé** FISC schedular tax; ~ **de progrès social** FISC social development tax *(Canada)*; ~ **progressif** FISC graduated tax, progressive tax; ~ **progressif sur le revenu** FISC graduated income tax; ~ **proportionnel** FISC proportional tax; ~ **proportionnel sur le revenu** FISC proportional income tax; ~ **rajusté à payer** FISC adjusted tax payable; ~ **de redressement** FISC compensation tax; ~ **réduit** FISC reduced tax; ~ **réellement versé** COMPTA, FISC taxes actually paid; ~ **régressif** FISC regressive tax; ~ **régulier** FISC standard tax; ~ **de remplacement** FISC replacement tax; ~ **reporté** FISC deferred profit-sharing plan; ~ **répressif** FISC repressive tax; ~ **retenu** FISC tax deduction *(AmE)*; ~ **retenu à la source** FISC source tax; ~ **selon Pigou** ECON, FISC Pigouvian tax; ~ **sinon exigible** FISC tax otherwise payable; ~ **de sortie** FISC output tax; ~ **à la source** FISC source tax; ~ **sous-déclaré** FISC underdeclared tax; ~ **spécifique** FISC earmarked tax; ~ **standard** FISC standard tax; ~ **standard sur le revenu des particuliers** FISC standard individual income tax; ~ **superposé** FISC superimposed tax; ~ **de superposition** FISC superimposed tax; ~ **supplémentaire** FISC incremental tax; ~ **sur les bénéfices** COMPTA, FISC profits tax; ~ **sur les bénéfices exceptionnels** FISC excess profits tax, windfall-profit tax; ~ **sur les bénéfices non distribués** FISC undistributed-profits tax; ~ **sur le capital** FISC capital tax *(Canada)*; ~ **sur le chiffre d'affaires** FISC turnover tax; ~ **sur les dividendes** FISC dividend tax; ~ **sur les dons** FISC gifts tax; ~ **sur l'exploitation minière** FISC, IND mining tax; ~ **sur la fortune** FISC wealth tax; ~ **sur les gains exceptionnels** FISC windfall tax; ~ **sur les grandes fortunes** *(IGF)* FISC tax aimed at very rich people; ~ **sur les mines** FISC, IND mining tax; ~ **sur les plus-values** ECON CGT *(dat)*, capital gains tax *(dat)*, FISC betterment tax, capital gains tax, CGT; ~ **sur le revenu**

ECON, FISC income tax; ~ **sur le revenu des corporations** FISC corporate income tax; ~ **sur le revenu inversé** FISC reverse income tax; ~ **sur le revenu ne provenant pas d'une entreprise** FISC nonbusiness income tax; ~ **sur le revenu des particuliers** FISC individual income tax; ~ **sur le revenu de placements** FISC investment income tax; ~ **sur le revenu de production** FISC production revenue tax; ~ **sur le revenu reporté** FISC deferred income tax; ~ **sur le revenu des valeurs mobilières** FISC securities tax; ~ **sur les revenus pétroliers** FISC oil revenue tax, petroleum revenue tax, PRT; ~ **sur les revenus pétroliers supplémentaires** FISC incremental oil revenue tax, IORT; ~ **sur les sociétés** COMPTA, FISC taxes due, FISC business income tax (*Canada*), company tax, corporate tax, corporation tax (*BrE*); ~ **sur les successions** FISC death duties (*BrE, dat*), death tax (*AmE*), legacy duty (*BrE*), legacy tax (*AmE*), succession duty (*BrE*), succession tax (*AmE*); ~ **sur le travail sélectif** FISC selective employment tax; ~ **sur la valeur** COMPTA ad valorem tax, FISC ad valorem tax (*frml*); ~ **sur la valeur cadastrale** FISC land-value tax; ~ **sur les valeurs** FISC securities tax; ~ **à taux standard** FISC standard-rate tax; ~ **uniforme** FISC flat tax, normal tax; ~ **unitaire** FISC unit tax; ~ **versé** COMPTA, FISC taxes actually paid; ♦ **frappé d'~** FISC taxed

impôts *m pl* ECON, FIN, FISC revenue, taxation; ~ **déduits** FISC after-tax; ~ **différés** COMPTA, FISC deferred taxation; ~ **excessifs** FISC excessive taxation; ~ **irrécouvrables** FISC uncollectable taxes; ~ **latents actifs** COMPTA, FISC deferred tax assets; ~ **locaux** *France* FISC, PROT SOC ≈ council tax (*UK*), ≈ poll tax (*UK, obs*), ≈ rates (*UK, obs*)

impraticable *adj* COM *projet* unworkable

impression *f* COM impression, INFO printing, MÉDIA impression, printing; ~ **artistique** V&M *publicité* art print; ~ **du contenu de la mémoire** INFO memory print-out; ~ **de droite à gauche** INFO reverse printing; ~ **en gras** INFO, MÉDIA bold printing; ~ **au verso** MÉDIA *édition* backing up; ♦ **avoir une ~ défavorable** COM be unfavorably impressed (*AmE*), be unfavourably impressed (*BrE*)

impressionnant, e *adj* COM impressive; **peu ~** COM unimpressive

impressionner *vt* COM impress, make an impression on

imprévisible *adj* COM unforeseeable, unpredictable

imprévoyant, e *adj* COM short-sighted

imprévu[1]**, e** *adj* COM contingent, unanticipated, unforeseen

imprévu[2] *m* COM contingency

imprimante *f* COM, INFO, MÉDIA printer, printing unit; ~ **aller-retour** *f* INFO bidirectional printer; ~ **bidirectionnelle** *f* INFO bidirectional printer; ~ **caractère par caractère** *f* INFO character-at-a-time printer; ~ **à cartes** *f* BANQUE credit-card

imprinter, COM credit-card imprinter, imprinter; ~ **électrostatique** *f* INFO electrostatic printer; ~ **à entraînement par friction** *f* INFO friction-feed printer; ~ **graphique** *f* INFO graphics printer; ~ **à impact** *f* INFO impact printer; ~ **à jet d'encre** *f* INFO ink-jet printer; ~ **à laser** *f* ADMIN, INFO laser printer; ~ **ligne par ligne** *f* INFO line printer; ~ **à marguerite** *f* INFO, MÉDIA daisywheel printer; ~ **matricielle** *f* INFO dot printer, dot-matrix printer, matrix printer; ~ **PostScript**® *f* INFO PostScript printer®; ~ **qualité courrier** *f* INFO letter-quality printer; ~ **qualité pseudo-courrier** *f* ADMIN, INFO near letter-quality printer; ~ **rapide** *f* INFO high-speed printer; ~ **série** *f* INFO serial printer; ~ **à tambour** *f* INFO drum printer

imprimé[1]**, e** *adj* ADMIN, INFO, MÉDIA printed; ~ **en caractères gras** INFO, MÉDIA *impression* printed in bold type

imprimé[2] *m* COM printed form, INFO form, MÉDIA printed matter; ~ **à remplir** COM blank form

imprimer 1. *vt* ADMIN, INFO, MÉDIA print; **2.** *vti* ~ **à la française** MÉDIA print in portrait; ~ **à l'italienne** MÉDIA print in landscape

imprimerie *f* IND, MÉDIA *presse, édition* printing works

Imprimerie: ~ **nationale** *f* ADMIN, COM ≈ HMSO (*UK*), ≈ Her Majesty's Stationery Office (*UK*), ≈ His Majesty's Stationery Office (*UK*)

imprimés *m pl* COM printed matter (*BrE*), third-class matter (*AmE*); ~ **publicitaires** COMMS junk mail

imprimeur *m* COM, INFO, MÉDIA printer

impropre: ~ **à la consommation** *loc* COM unfit for consumption; ~ **à faire** *loc* COM unfit to do

improviser *vt* COM play it by ear

improviste: à l'~ *adv* COM contingently, without warning

impulsion *f* COM impetus, INFO pulse

imputable *adj* COM chargeable; ♦ ~ **à** COM attributable to

imputation: ~ **des charges** *f* COMPTA allocation of costs; ~ **d'un coût** *f* ECON cost application

imputer *vt* COMPTA apply, *frais* assign; ~ **à** COM charge against, *dépense* charge to; ♦ ~ **une dépense à un compte** BANQUE, FIN charge an expense to an account; ~ **à l'exercice** COMPTA charge off; ~ **qch à qn** COM attribute sth to sb

inaccessible *adj* COM unattainable

inachevé, e *adj* COM incomplete, incompleted

inactif, -ive *adj* BOURSE inactive, COM idle, FIN inactive, INFO idle, inactive

inadapté, e *adj* COM unsuited

inadéquat, e *adj* COM unfit

inadvertance: par ~ *adv* COM inadvertently

inaliénable *adj* DROIT unassignable, *droit* inalienable

inanimé, e *adj* BOURSE lifeless

inapplicable *adj* (ANT *applicable*) DROIT unenforceable

inappliqué, e *adj* DROIT in abeyance

inapte *adj* COM unfit; **~ à travailler** RES HUM unemployable

inaptitude: **~ au travail** *f* RES HUM unemployability

inassurable *adj* ASSUR uninsurable

inassuré, e *adj* ASSUR unassured, uninsured

inattaquable *adj* COM unimpeachable

inattendu, e *adj* COM unforeseen

INC *abrév (Institut national de la consommation)* COM ≈ CA *(Consumers' Association)*

incapable *adj* COM, DROIT, ECON, IND, RES HUM incompetent

incapacité *f* COM, DROIT, FISC, PROT SOC incapacity; **~ de travailler** FISC, PROT SOC inability to work

incarcération *f* DROIT imprisonment

incendie *m* ASSUR fire, hostile fire; **~ et vol au tiers** ASSUR third-party fire and theft; **~ volontaire** ASSUR, DROIT arson, incendiarism

incertitude *f* BOURSE, COM, ECON, V&M uncertainty

incessant, e *adj* COM *soutien* continuing

incessible *adj* BOURSE untransferable, DROIT unassignable, untransferable

inchangé, e *adj* COM unaltered, unchanged

incidence *f* COM effect, ECON incidence; **~ budgétaire** ECON budget incidence; **~ comptable** COMPTA accounting effect; **~ fiscale** FISC tax incidence; **~ statutaire** FISC statutory incidence; **~ sur le profit** COM, FIN profit impact; ◆ **avoir une ~ sur** COM, DROIT affect

incident *m* INFO trouble; **~ machine** INFO hardware failure; **~ technique** COM technical hitch; **~ au travail** RES HUM industrial incident

incinérateur *m* ENVIR, IND incinerator

incinération *f* ENVIR, IND incineration

incitant *m* FIN kicker *(US, infrml)*

incitation *f* COM encouragement, impetus, incentive, DROIT *à enfreindre la loi* inducement, FIN incentive, sweetener *(infrml)*, FISC incentive, RES HUM encouragement, impetus, incentive, V&M incentive; **~ économique** ECON economic incentive; **~ fiscale** FISC tax incentive; **~ monétaire** FIN monetary inducement; **~ au rendement** IND, RES HUM production incentive; **~ à la vente** V&M sales incentive; **~ à voyager** V&M travel incentive *(UK)*

inciter *vt* COM actuate; **~ au crime** DROIT counsel; ◆ **~ qn à faire** COM urge sb to do

inclure *vt* COM add in, comprise, encompass, *joindre* enclose, include, INFO embed

inclus, e *adj* COM enc., encl., incl., included, inclusive, INFO embedded

inclusion *f* COM inclusion

inclusive *adj* ECON flat-rate

inclusivement *adv* COM *date* bdi, both dates inclusive

incomber: **~ à** *vt* DROIT lie with

incombustible *adj* COM fireproof

incomparable *adj* COM unparalleled

incompatible *adj* COM incompatible, mutually exclusive

incompatibles: **être ~** *loc* COM conflict

incompétence *f* COM, ECON, IND, RES HUM incompetence, inefficiency

incompétent, e *adj* COM, ECON, IND, RES HUM incompetent

incomplet, -ète *adj* COM incomplete, DROIT inchoate

inconditionnel, -elle *adj* DROIT *contrat* absolute, unconditional, INFO unconditional

inconnu, e *adj* COM not known; ◆ **~ à cette adresse** COMMS unknown at this address

incontestable *adj* COM unquestionable, *contrat* unimpeachable

inconvenable *adj* COM unsuitable

inconvénient *m* COM drawback, pitfall, snag *(infrml)*, *problème* disadvantage

inconvertibilité *f* BOURSE *d'une devise* block

incopiable *adj* INFO copy-protected

incorporation *f* IMMOB embodiment

incorporé, e *adj* COM incorporated, ECON built-in, INFO built-in, embedded

incorporel, -elle *adj (*ANT *corporel)* COM, COMPTA, DROIT, ECON, FIN incorporeal, intangible

incorporer *vt* COM incorporate, integrate, ECON, FIN, GESTION, IND integrate, INFO embed, integrate, RES HUM, TRANSP integrate

incorrectement *adv* COM wrongly

INCOTERME *abrév (terme commercial international)* ECON INCOTERM *(international commercial term)*

incrémentiel, -elle *adj* INFO incremental

incrimination *f* DROIT accusation

incriminer *vt* DROIT accuse

incroyable *adj* COM staggering

inculper *vt* DROIT charge

incursion *f* COM raid

Inde *f* COM India

indéchirable *adj* TRANSP tear-proof

indécis, e *adj* COM undecided

indécomposabilité *f* ECON indecomposability

indemnisation *f* ASSUR indemnity, COM, DROIT compensation, FIN indemnity, IMMOB judgment, RES HUM compensation; **~ des accidentés du travail** RES HUM compo *(infrml)*, workers' compensation; **~ des accidents du travail** RES HUM compo *(infrml)*, workers' compensation; **~ des dommages** ASSUR reparation for damage; **~ de maladie** COM, PROT SOC, RES HUM sickness pay; **~ pétrolière** FIN petroleum compensation; **~ des victimes d'accidents de travail** RES HUM compo *(infrml)*, workers' compensation

indemniser *vt* ASSUR indemnify, COM recoup, DROIT compensate; ◆ **~ qn pour qch** COM compensate sb for sth

indemnité *f* ASSUR indemnity, COM allowance, DROIT compensation, indemnity, FIN weighting,

RES HUM compensation; ~ **absolue** ASSUR aggregate indemnity; ~ **en cas de perte** COMMS compensation fee; ~ **de cessation d'emploi** RES HUM severance pay, severance wage; ~ **-chômage** ECON, PROT SOC, RES HUM unemployment compensation (*AmE*), unemployment pay; ~ **de chômage** ECON, PROT SOC, RES HUM unemployment benefit (*BrE*), unemployment compensation (*AmE*), unemployment pay; ~ **complémentaire** PROT SOC income support (*UK*); ~ **de déménagement** RES HUM removal allowance; ~ **de départ** FIN *dans le cadre d'une OPA* golden parachute (*infrml*); ~ **de déplacement** COM car allowance, traveling allowance (*AmE*), travelling allowance (*BrE*); ~ **différée** RES HUM deferred compensation; ~ **d'emploi régional** RES HUM regional employment premium, REP; ~ **équitable** DROIT, IMMOB just compensation; ~ **fixe** COM fixed benefits; ~ **de fonction** COM acting allowance; ~ **de frais accessoires** COM, COMPTA incidentals allowance; ~ **individuelle** BANQUE, FISC personal allowance (*UK*), personal credit (*Canada*), personal exemption (*US*); ~ **journalière** ASSUR daily allowance, daily compensation; ~ **juste** DROIT, IMMOB just compensation; ~ **kilométrique** COM car allowance, FISC mileage allowance, motor mileage allowance (*UK*); ~ **de licenciement** RES HUM dismissal wage, redundancy benefit, redundancy pay, redundancy payment, *de personnel en surnombre* push money, redundancy severance pay, redundancy severance payment, severance pay, severance wage, V&M push money; ~ **de logement** COM, PROT SOC, RES HUM accommodation allowance (*BrE*), accommodations allowance (*AmE*), housing allowance; ~ **de maladie** COM, PROT SOC, RES HUM sickness benefit, sickness pay; ~ **de manutention** BOURSE handling allowance; ~ **de maternité** PROT SOC, RES HUM maternity pay; ~ **non-imposable** FISC tax-free allowance; ~ **parlementaire** POL lulu (*US*); ~ **pécuniaire** RES HUM compensation money; ~ **de porte à porte** RES HUM portal-to-portal pay; ~ **professionnelle des experts comptables** ASSUR, COMPTA accountant's professional liability insurance; ~ **quotidienne** ASSUR daily compensation; ~ **réajustée** BANQUE, ECON, FIN adjusted claim; ~ **de repas** RES HUM meal allowance; ~ **de résidence Londres** COM, PROT SOC, RES HUM London weighting (*UK*); ~ **de subsistance** PROT SOC, RES HUM subsistence allowance, subsistence wage; ~ **sur fret** FIN, FISC, TRANSP *maritime* primage; ~ **de travail salissant** TRANSP *manutention* dirty money; ~ **de vie chère** COM, PROT SOC, RES HUM cost-of-living allowance, weighting

indemnités: ~ **de cessation** *f pl* FIN *EU* retirement payments; ~ **de départ** *f pl* RES HUM termination benefits; ~ **sommes rondes** *f pl* FISC round sum allowances; ~ **de subsistance** *f pl* COM living expenses; ~ **de subsistance sur assurance-vie** *f pl* ASSUR living benefits of life insurance

indépendance *f* COM, COMPTA, FIN independence; ~ **des exercices** COMPTA accrual accounting

indépendant, e *adj* COM independent, self-sufficient, *appartement, industrie* self-contained, *financièrement* self-supporting, ECON self-sufficient, INFO stand-alone, MÉDIA, RES HUM freelance; ◆ ~ **de** COM independent of; ~ **du type d'unité** INFO device-independent

indéterminé, e *adj* COM indefinite

index *m* ADMIN, COM, ECON, FIN, INFO index

indexation *f* BANQUE, BOURSE, ECON, FIN indexation, indexing, RES HUM indexation, indexing, threshold (*jarg*); ~ **légale** FISC formal indexation; ~ **des salaires** COMPTA, ECON *économétrie* cost-of-living adjustment (*US*), COLA (*US*), RES HUM cost-of-living adjustment (*US*), wage indexation, COLA (*US*); ~ **sur le coût de la vie** ECON cost-of-living adjustment (*US*), COLA (*US*), RES HUM cost-of-living adjustment (*US*), index linking, COLA (*US*)

indexé, e *adj* BANQUE index-linked, indexed, BOURSE index-linked, linked, ECON, FIN index-linked, indexed, MATH indexed, RES HUM index-linked, indexed

indexer *vt* ECON, FIN peg

indicateur *m* BOURSE indicator, COM pointer, timetable, *de tendances* gage (*AmE*), gauge (*BrE*), ECON indicator, FIN timetable, INFO flag, POL, V&M indicator; ~ **avancé composite** BOURSE composite leading indicator; ~ **avancé de tendance** ECON leading indicator; ~ **du commerce extérieur** ECON *commerce international* external trade indicator; ~ **composite principal** BOURSE composite leading indicator; ~ **de conjoncture** COM, ECON business indicator; ~ **de divergence** ECON *UE* divergence indicator; ~ **écologique** ENVIR, IND ecological indicator; ~ **économique** ECON, POL economic indicator; ~ **de marché** COM, V&M market indicator; ~ **du niveau d'huile** ENVIR, TRANSP oil gage (*AmE*), oil gauge (*BrE*); ~ **de performance** COM performance-related indicator, performance indicator, GESTION, IMMOB, IND, RES HUM performance indicator, performance-related indicator; ~ **principal** MATH leading indicator; ~ **de prospérité** ECON prosperity indicator; ~ **retardé d'activité** ECON *économétrie* lagging indicator; ~ **de tendance** COM business barometer, ECON *économétrie* leading indicator

indicateurs: ~ **d'objectif** *m pl* COM, GESTION, V&M objective indicators; ~ **de service de la dette** *m pl* ECON, POL debt service indicators; ~ **simultanés** *m pl* ECON *économétrie* coincident indicators

indicatif[1], **-ive** *adj* COM indicative; ◆ ~ **de** COM indicative of

indicatif[2] *m* ADMIN answerback code, COM, COMMS code, dialing code (*AmE*), dialling code (*BrE*); ~ **d'appel** TRANSP *navigation, aviation* call sign; ~ **interurbain** COMMS area code; ~ **musical** MÉDIA signature tune, theme tune; ~ **de zone** COMMS area code

indication: ~ **additionnelle** *f* BREVETS additional matter; ~ **de durée et de prix** *f (IDP)* COM advice of duration and/or charge *(ADC)*; ~ **de provenance** *f* BREVETS indication of source; ~ **technique** *f* BOURSE *de mouvement, de reprise* technical sign

indice *m* BOURSE index, COM factor, ECON Nikkei average, index, index number, FIN index, INFO subscript, MATH index number, RES HUM grade; ~ **des actions** BOURSE share index, stock exchange price index; ~ **avancé composite** BOURSE composite leading index; ~ **de Barron** BOURSE Barron's confidence index *(US)*; ~ **de base** ECON economic base, MATH *calcul de rapport* index basis; ~ **de base total** ENVIR total base number, TBN; ~ **des bons du trésor du Marché monétaire international** *(indice des bons du trésor* BOURSE International Monetary Market Treasury-bill index *(IMM T-bill index)*; ~ **des bons du trésor du MMI** *(indice des bons du trésor du Marché monétaire international)* BOURSE IMM T-bill index *(International Monetary Market Treasury-bill index)*; ~ **de la Bourse de Londres** *m* BOURSE FT-SE *(UK)*; ~ **boursier** BOURSE average, index, market index, share index, stock exchange price index, stock market index, stock market price index, stock price index; ~ **boursier mondial Morgan Stanley** BOURSE Morgan Stanley Capital International World Index; ~ **boursier "Value Line"** BOURSE Value Line Stock Index; ~ **CAC 40** BOURSE ≈ FT-SE *(UK)*; ~ **des certificats de dépôt du Marché monétaire international** *(indice des certificats de dépôt du MMI)* BOURSE International Monetary Market Certificate of Deposit index *(IMM CD index)*; ~ **des certificats de dépôt du MMI** *(indice des certificats de dépôt du Marché monétaire international)* BOURSE IMM CD index *(International Monetary Market Certificate of Deposit index)*; ~ **de charge** COM, ECON, IND, MATH load factor; ~ **Comit** BOURSE Comit index; ~ **composé** ECON, FIN composite index; ~ **composé de la Bourse de New York** BOURSE New York Stock Exchange composite index *(US)*; ~ **composite** ECON, FIN composite index; ~ **composite du New York Stock Exchange** BOURSE New York Stock Exchange composite index *(US)*; ~ **composite principal** BOURSE composite leading index; ~ **composite "Value Line"** BOURSE Value Line Composite Index *(US)*; ~ **des cours des actions** BOURSE share index, stock exchange price index; ~ **du coût de la construction** BOURSE construction cost index *(UK)*; ~ **du coût de la vie** ECON, PROT SOC cost-of-living index; ~ **du Crédit suisse** BOURSE Credit suisse index; ~ **de croissance** ECON growth index; ~ **de décompte trimestriel du Marché monétaire international** *(indice de décompte trimestriel du MMI)* BOURSE International Monetary Market Three-Month Discount Index *(IMM Three-Month Discount Index)*; ~ **de décompte trimestriel du MMI** *(indice de décompte trimestriel du*

Marché monétaire international) BOURSE IMM Three-Month Discount Index *(International Monetary Market Three-Month Discount Index)*; ~ **de diffusion** ECON diffusion index; ~ **Donoghue des fonds monétaires** *m* BOURSE Donoghue's Money Fund average *(US)*; ~ **Dow-Jones** BOURSE Dow-Jones index, Dow-Jones-average; ~ **Dow-Jones des 30 valeurs industrielles** *m* BOURSE Dow-Jones industrial average; ~ **de l'eurodollar** BOURSE, ECON, FIN Eurodollar index; ~ **d'évaluation du bruit** ENVIR, PROT SOC weighted noise level indicator; ~ **Footsie** *(indice FTSE des 100 valeurs)* BOURSE Footsie *(UK)* *(FT-SE 100 Share index)*; ~ **des grandes valeurs** BOURSE index of leading indicators; ~ **Hang Seng** BOURSE Hang Seng index; ~ **Hong Kong** BOURSE Hang Seng index; ~ **d'inconfort** ECON discomfort index; ~ **des indicateurs à courte durée** FIN index of shorter leading indicators; ~ **des indicateurs à longue durée** FIN index of longer leading indicators; ~ **des indicateurs retardés d'activité** FIN index of lagging indicators; ~ **des indicateurs simultanés** FIN index of coincident indicators; ~ **des indicateurs de tête** BOURSE, FIN index of leading indicators; ~ **d'intérêt** BOURSE indication of interest; ~ **de Laspeyre** ECON *économétrie* Laspeyres index; ~ **des marchandises** BOURSE commodities index *(UK)*; ~ **du marché principal** *(I)* BOURSE Major Market Index *(MMI)*; ~ **des matières premières** BOURSE commodities index *(UK)*; ~ **MMI** BOURSE Major Market Index, MMI; ~ **mondial des bourses de valeurs** *m* BOURSE Capital International World Index; ~ **moyen des services publics** BOURSE utility average; ~ **Nikkei** *m* BOURSE Nikkei average, Nikkei index; ~ **des obligations** BOURSE bond index; ~ **de Paasche** ECON Paasche index; ~ **pondéré** BOURSE, COM weighted index; ~ **pondéré des cours** BOURSE price-weighted index; ~ **pondéré par la capitalisation boursière** BOURSE market value-weighted index; ~ **pondéré par les prix** BOURSE price-weighted index; ~ **pondéré de valeur marchande** BOURSE market value-weighted index; ~ **des principales valeurs industrielles** BOURSE, IND Thirty Share Index; ~ **des prix** COMPTA, ECON, FIN price index; ~ **des prix à la consommation** *(IPC)* COMPTA, ECON consumer price index *(CPI)*; ~ **des prix de détail** COM, ECON retail price index, RPI; ~ **des prix de gros** MATH wholesale price index; ~ **des prix à la production** COMPTA, ECON producer price index, PPI; ~ **de rareté** ECON scarcity index; ~ **de traitement** RES HUM salary grade; ~ **d'utilité** ECON revealed preference, util; ~ **des valeurs unitaires** ECON unit value index, UVI; ~ **du volume** COM volume index; ~ **Z** MATH Z score; ~ **FTSE 100** BOURSE FT-SE 100 Share index *(UK)*; ~ **FTSE des 100 valeurs** *(FTSE, indice Footsie)* BOURSE FT-SE 100 Share index *(UK)*, Financial Times Stock Exchange index *(UK)* *(FT-SE, Footsie)*;

~ **FTSE des 200 valeurs** BOURSE FT-SE Eurotrack 200 index (*UK*)

indices: ~ **boursiers** *m pl* BOURSE stock indexes and averages

indien, -enne *adj* COM Indian

Indien, -enne *m,f* COM *habitant* Indian

indigent, e *m,f* COM pauper

indiquer *vt* COM set out, *prix* quote, FISC *montant* claim, INFO flag; ◆ ~ **pour mention** COM mention; ~ **en passant** COM mention

indirectement *adv* (ANT *directement*) COM indirectly

indiscutable *adj* COM watertight

indispensable[1] *adj* COM vital

indispensable[2] *m* V&M necessity

indisponibilité *f* COM unavailability

indisponible *adj* COM, INFO unavailable

individu *m* COM individual

individualisme *m* RES HUM individualism

individuel, -elle *adj* COM individual, INFO stand-alone, LOISIRS *chambre* single

individuellement *adv* COM individually; ◆ ~ **mais non-conjointement** BOURSE severally but not jointly

indivisibilité *f* ECON, MATH indivisibility

indivision *f* IMMOB joint tenancy

Indonésie *f* COM Indonesia

indonésien[1]**, -enne** *adj* COM Indonesian

indonésien[2] *m* COM *langue* Indonesian

Indonésien, -enne *m,f* COM *habitant* Indonesian

induire: ~ **en erreur** *vt* DROIT mislead

industrialisation *f* ECON, IND, POL development, industrialization

industrialisé, e *adj* ECON, IND, POL industrialized

industrie *f* ECON, IND industry; ~ **aéronautique** COM, IND, TRANSP aircraft industry; ~ **affaiblie** ECON, IND ailing industry, declining industry; ~ **agro-alimentaire** ECON, ENVIR, IND agrifood industry; ~ **alimentaire** IND food-processing industry; ~ **artisanale** IND cottage industry, high-stream industry (*jarg*); ~ **des assurances** ASSUR insurance industry; ~ **de base** IND basic industry; ~ **basée sur la connaissance** IND knowledge-based industry; ~ **basée sur le savoir** IND knowledge-based industry; ~ **du bâtiment** IND construction industry; ~ **de capital** ECON, IND capital-intensive industry; ~ **capitale** ECON, IND essential industry; ~ **capitalistique** ECON, IND capital-intensive industry; ~ **cinématographique** LOISIRS, MÉDIA film industry, motion picture industry (*AmE*); ~ **clé** IND key industry; ~ **en croissance rapide** (ANT *industrie en déclin*) ECON, IND growth industry, sunrise industry; ~ **cyclique** ECON, IND cyclical industry; ~ **en déclin** (ANT *industrie en croissance rapide*) ECON, IND ailing industry, declining industry, sunset industry; ~ **diversifiée** IND runaway industry; ~ **extractive** IND basic industry, resource industry; ~ **figée** IND locked-in industry; ~ **à forte**

intensité de capitaux ECON, IND capital-intensive industry; ~ **de la fringue** *infrml* IND clothing business, clothing industry, rag trade (*infrml*); ~ **du gaz** ENVIR, IND gas industry; ~ **gazière** ENVIR, IND gas industry; ~ **à haute technologie** IND high-technology industry; ~ **horlogère** IND watch trade; ~ **houillère** ENVIR, IND coal industry; ~ **intérieure** IND domestic industry; ~ **légère** IND light industry; ~ **libre** IND footloose industry; ~ **locale** IND local industry, native industry; ~ **des loisirs** IND, LOISIRS amusement industry, leisure industry; ~ **lourde** COMPTA capital-intensive industry, IND heavy engineering, heavy industry; ~ **manufacturière** IND manufacturing industry, processing industry; ~ **mécanique légère** IND light engineering; ~ **minière** ENVIR coal industry, mining industry, mineral industry, IND *houille* coal industry, mining industry, *minerai* mineral industry; ~ **naissante** IND infant industry; ~ **nationalisée** ECON, IND nationalized industry, public interest company; ~ **nucléaire** ENVIR, IND nuclear industry; ~ **obsolescente** IND sunset industry; ~ **du papier** ENVIR, IND paper industry; ~ **du passé** IND sunset industry; ~ **patrimoniale** IND patrimonial industry; ~ **pétrolière** IND oil industry, petroleum industry; ~ **pharmaceutique** IND drug industry, pharmaceutical industry; ~ **plastique** IND plastics industries; ~ **primaire** COM, ECON, IND primary industry; ~ **principale** IND key industry; ~ **réglementée** IND regulated industry; ~ **sans entraves** IND footloose industry; ~ **secondaire** ECON, IND nonbasic industry; ~ **du secteur primaire** COM, ECON, IND primary industry; ~ **de service** ECON, IND service industry; ~ **du spectacle** IND, LOISIRS amusement industry; ~ **technologique** IND technology-based industry; ~ **textile** IND rag trade (*infrml*), textile industry; ~ **du tissage** IND weaving trade; ~ **traditionnelle** COM smokestack industry; ~ **de transformation** IND manufacturing industry, processing industry, transformation industry; ~ **à trois chiffres** ECON *dans la nomenclature* three-digit industry; ~ **viticole** COM, IND wine industry

industriel[1]**, -elle** *adj* BOURSE *titre, valeur*, ECON, IND industrial

industriel[2]**, -elle** *m,f* ECON, IND industrialist

industries: ~ **agroalimentaires** *f pl* ECON, ENVIR, IND agribusiness; ~ **connexes** *f pl* IND allied industries; ~ **extractives** *f pl* COM, IND extractive industries; ~ **minières** *f pl* COM, IND extractive industries; ~ **de pointe** *f pl* IND leading industries; ~ **protégées de la concurrence étrangère** *f pl* IND sheltered industries

inéchangeable *adj* COM, V&M unexchangeable

inéconomique *adj* COM, ECON, IND, V&M uneconomic

inédit, e *adj* COM, MÉDIA unpublished

inefficacité *f* COM, ECON, IND, RES HUM inefficiency; ~ **sur le marché** BOURSE inefficiency in the market

inefficience *f* COM, ECON, IND, RES HUM inefficiency

inégalité *f* DROIT, ECON, POL, RES HUM inequality

inélasticité *f* ECON inelasticity; **~ de la demande** ECON inelasticity of demand; **~ de l'offre** ECON inelasticity of supply; **~ des prix** ECON price inelasticity

inemployé, e *adj* TRANSP idle

inépuisable *adj* ENVIR inexhaustible, infinite

inertie *f* COM sluggishness; **~ industrielle** IND industrial inertia

inescomptable *adj* BANQUE indiscountable

inestimable *adj* COM invaluable

inévitable *adj* COM inevitable, unavoidable

inévitablement *adv* COM inevitably

inexactitude *f* COM, MATH inaccuracy

inexécution *f* DROIT nonexecution; **~ du contrat** DROIT nonfulfillment of contract (*AmE*), nonfulfilment of contract (*BrE*)

inexpliqué, e *adj* COM unaccounted-for

inexploitable *adj* INFO unprocessable

inexploité, e *adj* COM untapped

infaillible *adj* COM unfailing

inférer: ~ de *vt* COM conclude from

inférieur, e *adj* COM second-grade, V&M *qualité* low-grade; **~ à** *adj* (*ANT supérieur à*) COM below, under; ◆ **être ~ à** COM fall short of; **~ à la moyenne** (*ANT supérieur à la moyenne*) COM below-average; **~ au taux de base** *Fra* (*cf inférieur au taux préférentiel Can*) ECON off-prime; **~ au taux préférentiel** *Can* (*cf inférieur au taux de base Fra*) ECON off-prime

infiltration *f* COM *eau* seepage

infini: à l'~ *adv* COM ad infinitum (*frml*)

infirmation *f* DROIT *d'un jugement* invalidation

infirmer *vt* DROIT *jugement* invalidate

inflation *f* ECON inflation; **~ administrée** ECON administered inflation, mark-up inflation; **~ bouchon** ECON, IND bottleneck inflation; **~ cachée** ECON hidden inflation; **~ contenue** ECON suppressed inflation; **~ déguisée** ECON hidden inflation; **~ à deux chiffres** ECON, FIN double-digit inflation, two-digit inflation; **~ dirigée** ECON administered inflation; **~ fiscale** ECON, FISC taxflation (*jarg*); **~ générée par augmentation de coûts** ECON cost-push inflation; **~ importée** ECON imported inflation; **~ induite par les chocs externes** ECON shock inflation; **~ larvée** ECON creeping inflation; **~ mondiale** ECON world inflation; **~ monétaire** ECON monetary inflation; **~ par les coûts** ECON cost-push inflation; **~ par la demande** COM, ECON demand-pull inflation; **~ par les prix** ECON price inflation; **~ par les prix de revient** ECON cost-push inflation; **~ par les salaires** ECON wage-push inflation; **~ du prix de l'actif** ECON, FIN asset price inflation; **~ des prix de gros** ECON wholesale price inflation; **~ pure** ECON pure inflation; **~ rampante** ECON creeping inflation; **~ réglementée** ECON administered

inflation; **~ des salaires** ECON wage inflation; **~ sous-jacente** ECON inertial inflation, underlying inflation; **~ structurelle** ECON core inflation, structural inflation; **~ structurelle des prix à la consommation** ECON core consumer price inflation

inflationniste *adj* ECON inflationary

infliger *vt* COM *amende* impose; ◆ **~ une sanction à** DROIT penalize

influence *f* COM impact, influence; **~ fiscale** COMPTA, FISC tax influence; **~ des marchés des capitaux** COMPTA capital market influence; **~ des marchés financiers** COMPTA capital market influence; **~ personnelle** COM personal influence; ◆ **avoir de l'~** COM be influential

influencer *vt* COM bring pressure to bear on, sway, DROIT affect

influent, e *adj* COM influential

influer: ~ sur *vt* COM affect, have an impact on, *coûts* influence

infographie *f* INFO computer graphics, graphic data processing, graphics; **~ à adressage binaire** INFO bit-mapped graphics; **~ par points binaire** INFO bit-mapped graphics

informaticien, -enne *m,f* INFO computer engineer, computer expert, computer scientist, information scientist

information *f* COM piece of information, COMMS, MÉDIA news item; **~ après-vol** TRANSP post-flight information; **~ asymétrique** ASSUR asymmetric information; **~ commerciale** V&M market intelligence; **~ comptable** COMPTA reporting; **~ de contrôle** COM control information; **~ contrôlée** POL managed news; **~ économique** ECON economic intelligence; **~ erronée ou trompeuse** DROIT false or misleading information; **~ financière** COMPTA reporting; **~ d'initié** BOURSE, FIN inside information; **~ à jour** COM up-to-date information; **~ de marché enregistrée** BOURSE recorded market information; **~ d'organisation de la gestion** GESTION, INFO management information; **~ probante** COMPTA, FIN audit evidence; **~ en retour** COM feedback; **~ voyageurs** TRANSP journey planner; ◆ **pour ~** BOURSE for your information, FYI

Information: ~ et transmission d'ordres *loc* BOURSE ≈ DOT (*US*), ≈ Designated Order Turnaround (*US*)

informations *f pl* COM data, inf., info (*infrml*), information, material, news, MAT, COMMS advice, MÉDIA bulletin, news; **~ boursières par MINITEL** BOURSE ≈ TOPIC (*UK*), ≈ Teletex Output of Price Information by Computer (*UK*); **~ en bref** MÉDIA news roundup; **~ confidentielles** DROIT confidential information; **~ économiques** ECON economic news; **~ éparses** INFO garbage; **~ financières** COMPTA accounting data, FIN, MÉDIA financial news; **~ nécessaires à l'admission à la cote** BOURSE listing particulars; **~ non-communiquées au public** COM, COMMS nonpublic information (*US*); ~ **parasites** INFO garbage; ~ **segmentaires** COM segment information; ~ **spécialisées** COM specialist information; ~ **de vol** TRANSP flight information

informatique *f* ADMIN data processing, COM computing, data processing, INFO computer science, computing, data processing, informatics, information processing, information technology, IT; ~ **de gestion** COM business computing, business data processing, GESTION management information system, INFO business data processing, management information system; ~ **graphique** INFO computer graphics; ~ **individuelle** INFO end-user computing; ~ **interactive** INFO interactive computing; ~ **professionnelle** COM, INFO business computing; ~ **répartie** INFO distributed computing; ~ **théorique** INFO computer science

informatisation *f* INFO computerization

informatisé, e *adj* INFO computer-based, computerized

informatiser *vt* INFO computerize

informé, e *adj* COM informed; ♦ **être ~** COM keep up to date

informel, -elle *adj* COM informal

informer *vt* COM, COMMS advise, inform; ♦ ~ **qn de qch** COM, COMMS advise sb of sth; ~ **qn que** COM, COMMS advise sb that

infra *adv* (ANT *supra*) COM infra

infraction *f* DROIT breach, infringement, offence; ~ **fiscale** DROIT, FISC tax offence; ~ **à la loi** DROIT infringement of the law; ~ **mineure** DROIT misdemeanor (*US*); ~ **pénale** DROIT criminal offence; ~ **aux règles de sécurité** DROIT safety violation

infrastructure *f* COM, ECON infrastructure, substructure; ♦ **d'~** COM, ECON infrastructural

infructueux, -euse *adj* COM unrewarding

ingénierie: ~ **assistée par ordinateur** *f* (*IAO*) IND, INFO computer-aided engineering, computer-assisted engineering (*CAE*); ~ **financière** *f* FIN financial engineering; ~ **informatique** *f* INFO computer engineering; ~ **logicielle assistée par ordinateur** *f* IND computer-aided software engineering, computer-assisted software engineering; ~ **médicale** *f* IND medical engineering; ~ **de pointe** *f* IND advanced engineering

ingénieur *m* COM, IND, RES HUM engineer; ~ **agronome** ENVIR agricultural engineer; ~ **de chantier** IND, RES HUM site engineer; ~ **en chef** RES HUM, TRANSP chief engineer; ~ **commercial** RES HUM sales engineer; ~ **-conseil** COM consultant engineer, consulting engineer, engineering consultant, GESTION management consultant, IND consultant engineer, consulting engineer, engineering consultant, RES HUM efficiency engineer; ~ **des constructions navales** TRANSP naval architect; ~ **électricien** COM electrical engineer; ~ **électronicien** COM electronic engineer; ~ **d'entretien** IND, RES HUM maintenance engineer; ~ **d'études** INFO design engineer; ~ **expert** RES HUM surveyor; ~ **du génie maritime** TRANSP

naval architect; ~ **informatique** INFO computer engineer; ~ **logiciel** INFO software engineer; ~ **maritime** RES HUM, TRANSP marine engineer; ~ **de produit** IND, RES HUM product engineer; ~ **programmeur** INFO software engineer; ~ **projet** COM, GESTION, IND project engineer; ~ **système** INFO systems engineer

ingéniosité *f* COM ingenuity

ingérable *adj* COM unmanageable

ingérence *f* COM *dans les affaires*, DROIT interference

ingérer: **s'~ dans** *v pron* COM interfere in

inhospitalier, -ère *adj* COM inhospitable

initial, e *adj* BOURSE *investissement* initial, *opération* opening, COM *coût*, COMPTA, FIN *intérêt*, FISC initial

initiale *f* COM initial

initialisation *f* INFO initialization

initialiser *vt* INFO boot up, bootstrap (*jarg*), initialize, set up

initiateur, -trice *m,f* BANQUE originator, POL initiator

initiative *f* GESTION initiative

initié, e *m,f* BOURSE, FIN insider; ~ **à l'informatique** INFO computer literate; ~ **membre d'une société** COM corporate insider

injection *f* ECON, FIN injection; ~ **de capitaux** FIN capital injection

injonction *f* DROIT injunction, *d'un tribunal* ord., order, order of the court; ~ **donnée par un tribunal** DROIT mandatory injunction; ~ **provisoire** BREVETS, DROIT interim injunction, interlocutory

injuste *adj* COM unjust

injustice *f* DROIT wrongdoing

injustifié, e *adj* COM unjustified, unwarranted, DROIT unjustified

innocente: **qui ~** *loc* BANQUE, DROIT exculpatory

innocenter *vt* DROIT clear

innovateur[1], **-trice** *adj* COM innovative, trailblazing

innovateur[2], **-trice** *m,f* COM innovator, V&M market leader, *marketing* innovator

innovation *f* COM breakthrough, innovation, ECON breakthrough, IND breakthrough, innovation, V&M pioneer product; ~ **technologique** COM, IND technological innovation

innover 1. *vt* COM pioneer; **2.** *vi* COM innovate

inobservation *f* DROIT failure to comply, noncompliance; ~ **des conditions** COM nonobservance of conditions

inoccupé, e *adj* IMMOB untenanted

inonder *vt* COM *marché*, ECON glut

inopportun, e *adj* COM unseasonable, untimely

in pari delicto *loc* DROIT in pari delicto

in personam *loc* DROIT in personam

input *m* COM, IND input, inputs; ~ **de l'ordinateur** INFO computer input

inquiétant, e *adj* COM unsettling

inquiétude *f* COM unrest

in rem *loc* DROIT in rem

inscription *f* ADMIN registration, registry, BREVETS, COM, DROIT registration, FIN listing, IMMOB registration; ~ **aux ASSEDIC** *(inscription à l'Association pour l'emploi dans l'industrie et le commerce)* PROT SOC, RES HUM signing-on; ~ **à l'Association pour l'emploi dans l'industrie et le commerce** *(inscription aux ASSEDIC)* PROT SOC, RES HUM signing-on; ~ **au budget** COMPTA, FIN budgeting; ~ **au cadastre** DROIT, IMMOB land registration; ~ **comptable** COMPTA, FIN accounting entry; ~ **fausse ou trompeuse** FISC false or deceptive entry; ~ **gigogne** BOURSE piggyback registration; ~ **au registre foncier** DROIT, IMMOB land registration

inscrire 1. *vt* COM book in, LOISIRS, TRANSP *hôtel* check in; ~ **au barreau** DROIT admit to the bar *(US)*, call to the bar; ~ **au budget** COM, COMPTA, ECON, FIN budget, budget for, POL budget; ~ **des charges à payer** COMPTA accrue previously unrecorded expenses; ~ **à la cote** BOURSE *en bourse* list; ~ **à l'heure de sortie** COM book out; ~ **des informations dans un registre** COM enter information onto a register; ~ **des produits à recevoir** COMPTA accrue previously unrecorded revenues; ~ **au registre** BREVETS record in the register; **2.** *v pron* **s'~** COM *pour un stage de formation* sign up; ♦ **s'~ au chômage** PROT SOC sign on

inscrit, e *adj* BOURSE listed; ~ **au compte de résultat** COMPTA, FIN above the line; ~ **à la cote** BOURSE listed; **être ~ à** LOISIRS belong

INSEE *abrév (Institut national de la statistique et des études économiques)* ECON ≈ CSO *(UK)* *(Central Statistical Office)*

insensible *adj* BOURSE, COM unresponsive; ♦ ~ **aux défaillances** INFO fault-tolerant; ~ **aux pannes** INFO fault-tolerant

insérer *vt* COM insert, INFO insert, slot in, paste, MÉDIA, V&M insert; ♦ ~ **une annonce dans le journal** V&M run an ad in the paper; ~ **une annonce pour un poste dans le journal** MÉDIA, RES HUM, V&M advertise a job in the paper; ~ **qch dans un contrat** DROIT build sth into a contract

insert: ~ **de pont** *m* TRANSP *pour conteneurs* bushing, keyhole socket

insertion: ~ **sauvage** *f* MÉDIA *presse* run of paper, ROP

insignifiant, e *adj* COM trifling

insister: ~ **sur** *vt* COM lay the emphasis on, stress

insoluble *adj* COM insoluble

insolvabilité *f* COM, COMPTA, DROIT, IND insolvency

insolvable *adj* COM, COMPTA, DROIT, IND insolvent

inspecter *vt* COM supervise, IMMOB survey, IMP/EXP examine, RES HUM inspect, supervise

inspecteur, -trice *m,f* IMP/EXP examiner, RES HUM inspector, supervisor *(AmE)*; ~ **adjoint chargé de la circulation** RES HUM, TRANSP assistant traffic supervisor, ATS; ~ **de banque** BANQUE bank examiner *(US)*; ~ **en chef** RES HUM chief inspec-

tor, CI; ~ **de la circulation** RES HUM, TRANSP traffic supervisor; ~ **des contributions directes** FISC inspector of taxes *(UK)*; ~ **des documents d'importation** IMP/EXP, RES HUM import documentation supervisor; ~ **du fret** RES HUM, TRANSP cargo inspector, cargo surveyor; ~ **général des banques** BANQUE inspector general of banks; ~ **des impôts** FISC, RES HUM revenue officer, tax inspector, taxation officer, taxman; ~ **maritime** RES HUM, TRANSP marine superintendent; ~ **des plaintes** RES HUM claims inspector; ~ **principal** RES HUM chief inspector, CI; ~ **régleur** ASSUR claims adjuster; ~ **des services de santé** PROT SOC, RES HUM health officer; ~ **du travail** IND factory inspector *(UK)*, labor inspector *(AmE)*, labour inspector *(BrE)*, PROT SOC factory inspector *(UK)*, labor inspector *(AmE)*

inspection *f* COM inspection, ENVIR inspectorate, IND inspection; ~ **des connaissements** TRANSP *au port* sighting bills of lading; ~ **du dossier** BREVETS *demande de brevet* inspection of files; ~ **officielle des banques** BANQUE bank examination *(US)*; ~ **du personnel** RES HUM staff inspection

Inspection: ~ **du travail** *f* PROT SOC Factory Inspectorate *(UK)*, Health and Safety Inspectorate *(UK)*

inspections: ~ **renforcées** *f pl* DROIT tight controls

inspectorat *m* IND, PROT SOC inspectorate

inspirer: **s'~ de l'original** *loc* COM copy from the original

instabilité: ~ **du marché** *f* COM market sensitivity

instable *adj* BOURSE sensitive, POL *gouvernement* unstable

installation *f* COM, INFO facility, installation; ~ **à bord** LOISIRS, TRANSP shipboard facility; ~ **de chaudières pour le chauffage urbain** IND district heating boiler plant; ~ **de combustion** ENVIR, IND combustion plant; ~ **défectueuse** ASSUR faulty installation; ~ **d'élimination des déchets** ENVIR disposal facility; ~ **fixe** *(ANT installation flexible)* ECON, IND fixed plant; ~ **flexible** *(ANT installation fixe)* ECON, IND flexible plant; ~ **de forage** ENVIR, IND oil rig; ~ **illégale de piquets de grève** RES HUM unlawful picketing; ~ **de loisirs** COM, LOISIRS leisure facility; ~ **en mer** TRANSP offshore installation; ~ **offshore** TRANSP offshore installation; ~ **de secours** COM, INFO backup facility; ~ **de stockage** ENVIR *déchets* storage facility

installations *f pl* IMMOB amenities, RES HUM facilities; ~ **et agencements** COM fittings and fixtures; ~ **industrielles** COMPTA, IND plant; ~ **portuaires** IMP/EXP, TRANSP harbor facilities *(AmE)*, harbour facilities *(BrE)*, port facilities; ~ **techniques** COMPTA plant, IND plant, production goods

installé, e *adj* INFO inst., installed

installer 1. *vt* COM set up, INFO instal *(AmE)*, install *(BrE)*, set up; **2.** *v pron* **s'~** COM *dans une résidence, dans un pays* settle; ♦ ~ **le siège de** ADMIN headquarter *(AmE)*

instance:[1] **~ d'arbitrage** *f* COM, DROIT, IND, RES HUM arbitration board

instance:[2] **en ~** *loc* COM, RES HUM outstanding, pending

instances: ~ dirigeantes *f pl* RES HUM executive

instaurer *vt* INFO set

instinct: ~ de possession *m* COM acquisitive instinct, acquisitiveness

institué, e *adj* DROIT constituted

institut *m* COM inst., institute; **~ des affaires économiques** ECON Institute of Economic Affairs (*UK*), IEA (*UK*); **~ des prêts à la consommation** BANQUE, FIN consumer loan institute; **~ de recherche agréé** FISC approved research institute

Institut: ~ Adam Smith *m* POL Adam Smith Institute (*UK*); **~ des banquiers** *m* BANQUE Institute of Bankers, IOB; **~ canadien des comptables agréés** *m* COMPTA Canadian Institute of Chartered Accountants, CICA; **~ du développement outre-mer** *m* ECON, POL Overseas Development Institute (*UK*), ODI (*UK*); **~ d'études politiques** *m (IEP)* POL ≈ Centre for Political Studies; **~ d'études sur la main d'oeuvre** *m* RES HUM Institute of Manpower Studies, IMS; **~ de finances internationales** *m* FIN Institute for International Finance, IIF; **~ de la gestion administrative** *m* GESTION ≈ IAM (*UK*), ≈ Institute of Administrative Management (*UK*); **~ de gestion du personnel** *m* GESTION Institute of Personnel Management (*UK*), IPM (*UK*); **~ international de finance** *m* FIN Institute for International Finance, IIF; **~ international pour l'unification du droit privé** *m* DROIT ≈ International Institute for Unification of Private Law; **~ monétaire européen** *m* ECON, POL European Monetary Institute, EMI; **~ national de la consommation** *m (INC)* COM ≈ Consumers' Association *(CA)*; **~ national de la statistique et des études économiques** *m (INSEE)* ECON ≈ Central Statistical Office (*UK*) *(CSO)*; **~ des Nations Unies pour la formation et la recherche** *m* RES HUM United Nations Institute for Training and Research, UNITAR; **~ des produits tropicaux** *m* ECON Tropical Products Institute, TPI; **~ de Recherche des Nations Unies pour le développement social** *m (IRNUDS)* PROT SOC United Nations Research Institute for Social Development *(UNRISD)*

institution *f* BANQUE, BOURSE, COM, ECON, FIN institution; **~ bancaire** BANQUE, FIN banking institution; **~ centralisée** COM centralized institution; **~ coopérative de crédit** COM cooperative credit institution; **~ de crédit** BANQUE, FIN lending institution; **~ de dépôts** ADMIN, BANQUE, FIN deposit institution, depositary, depository; **~ économique** ECON economic institution; **~ financière** FIN financial institution; **~ financière désignée** FIN, FISC specified financial institution; **~ financière para-bancaire** BANQUE, BOURSE non-bank bank; **~ du marché monétaire** BOURSE, ECON, FIN money-market institution; **~ politique** POL political institution; **~ de prêt** BANQUE, FIN lending institution; **~ privée** COM private institution

institutionnalisme *m* ECON institutional economics (*US*)

instruction *f* DROIT preliminary investigation, INFO command, instruction, statement; **~ d'arrêt** INFO breakpoint instruction; **~ effective** INFO actual instruction; **~ machine** INFO computer instruction; **~ relative à l'emballage** TRANSP packing instruction, pkg. instr.; **~ de renvoi** INFO breakpoint instruction; **~ de transport de cargaison exportée** IMP/EXP, TRANSP export cargo shipping instruction, ECSI; ◆ **pour toute ~ complémentaire** COM for further instructions, FFI

instructions *f pl* COM, COMMS, TRANSP instructions; **~ d'expédition** COMMS forwarding instructions, TRANSP forwarding instructions, shipping instructions; ◆ **pour ~** COM fo, for orders

instruire *vt* COM warn, DROIT *affaire* conduct the investigation

instruit, e *adj* RES HUM educated, well-educated

instrument *m* BANQUE, BOURSE instrument, COM instrument, tool, DROIT, FIN instrument; **~ créateur d'un fidéicommis** DROIT trust instrument; **~ de dépôt** BANQUE deposit instrument; **~ dérivé** BOURSE, FIN derivative instrument; **~ dérivé hors bourse** BOURSE, FIN over-the-counter derivative instrument (*US*); **~ d'emprunt cessible** FIN transferable loan instrument, TLI; **~ financier** FIN financial instrument; **~ financier dérivé** BOURSE, FIN derivative; **~ financier à intérêt** BOURSE, FIN interest-bearing instrument; **~ financier résiduel** FIN residual financial instrument; **~ hors change** FIN off-exchange instrument; **~ du marché monétaire** BOURSE, ECON, FIN money-market certificate, money-market instrument, money-market paper, MMC; **~ du marché monétaire à court terme** BOURSE short-term money-market instrument; **~ à moyen terme** BOURSE medium-term instrument; **~ négociable** *(ANT instrument non-négociable)* BANQUE marketable instrument, negotiable instrument; **~ non-compensable** BANQUE nonclearing item; **~ non-enregistré** COM unrecorded deed; **~ non-négociable** *(ANT instrument négociable)* BANQUE nonmarketable instrument, nonnegotiable instrument; **~ obligatoire sans risque** BOURSE risk-free debt instrument; **~ de paiement privilégié** BANQUE priority payment instrument; **~ de participation différent** BOURSE alternative participation instrument (*UK*), API (*UK*); **~ portant intérêt** BOURSE interest-bearing instrument; **~ de prêt transférable** FIN transferable loan instrument; **~ de taux d'intérêt** BOURSE, FIN interest rate instrument

instrumentalité *f* FIN instrumentality (*US*)

insuffisamment: ~ ciblé *adj* V&M *public* untargeted; **~ financé** *adj* FIN underfunded

insuffisance *f* COM shortage, shortfall, COMPTA shortfall, FIN deficiency, TRANSP shortfall; **~ actuarielle** ASSUR actuarial deficit, actuarial loss, experience deficiency, experience loss, FIN experience deficiency, experience loss; **~ de capital** COM, COMPTA, DROIT, IND insolvency; **~ d'effectifs** RES HUM undermanning; **~ de provision** BANQUE, COM n.s.f., not sufficient funds

insuffisant, e *adj* BANQUE insufficient, COM deficient, FIN insufficient

insurgé, e *adj* COM insurgent

insurrection: **~ populaire** *f* ASSUR, COM, POL cc, civil commotion

int. *abrév (intérêt)* BANQUE, BOURSE, COM, COMPTA, ECON, FIN int. *(interest)*

intact, e *adj* COM free of damage, FOD

intégral, e *adj* COM unabridged

intégralement *adv* COM in full

intégralité *f* COMPTA *des informations comptables* completeness

intégrateur *m* IMP/EXP, TRANSP integrator

intégration *f* COM integration, *du personnel* induction, COMPTA consolidation, ECON, FIN, GESTION, IND, INFO, RES HUM, TRANSP integration; **~ en amont** *(ANT intégration en aval)* ECON, GESTION, IND backward integration; **~ en arrière** *(ANT intégration en avant)* ECON, GESTION, IND backward integration; **~ en aval** *(ANT intégration en amont)* ECON, GESTION, IND forward integration; **~ en avant** *(ANT intégration en arrière)* ECON, GESTION, IND forward integration; **~ économique** ECON economic integration; **~ horizontale** *(ANT intégration verticale)* COM, ECON, IND horizontal integration, lateral integration; **~ horizontale-verticale** ECON horizontal-vertical amalgamation; **~ latérale** COM, ECON, IND horizontal integration, lateral integration; **~ à la sécurité sociale** RES HUM *de pension* integration with social security; **~ verticale** *(ANT intégration horizontale)* COM vertical integration, vertical merger, ECON vertical combination, vertical integration, IND vertical integration; **~ verticale en amont** *(ANT intégration verticale en aval)* ECON, GESTION, IND backward vertical integration; **~ verticale en arrière** *(ANT intégration verticale en avant)* ECON, GESTION, IND backward vertical integration; **~ verticale en aval** *(ANT intégration verticale en amont)* ECON, GESTION, IND forward vertical integration; **~ verticale en avant** *(ANT intégration verticale en arrière)* ECON, GESTION, IND forward vertical integration

intégré, e *adj* COM integrated, ECON absorbed, built-in, integrated, FIN, GESTION, IND integrated, INFO built-in, embedded, integrated, RES HUM, TRANSP integrated; ♦ **~ à** COM integrated into

intégrer *vt* COM, ECON, FIN, GESTION, IND integrate, INFO embed, integrate, RES HUM, TRANSP integrate; ♦ **~ au revenu** COMPTA add to income

intégrité *f* COM integrity; **~ de données** INFO data integrity

intelligence: **~ artificielle** *f (IA)* INFO artificial intelligence *(AI)*; **~ subtile** *f* COM *d'un problème* acute awareness

intelligent, e *adj* COM, INFO intelligent

intendance *f* ADMIN stewardship, COM commissary *(US)*

intendant, e *m,f* ADMIN comptroller, IMMOB bailiff

intense *adj* COM concentrated

intensif, -ive *adj* COM intensive

intensification *f* ECON intensification; **~ de l'apport en capital** ECON capital deepening

intensifié, e *adj* COM *activité* stepped-up

intensifier 1. *vt* COM heighten, *effort* intensify; **2.** *v pron* **s'~** COM *concurrence* intensify

intensité: **~ de la circulation** *f* TRANSP traffic flow; **~ du trafic** *f* TRANSP traffic flow; **~ de l'utilisation des sols** *f* ENVIR land-use intensity

intenter: **~ une action** *vt* DROIT bring an action, take legal action; **~ une action en justice contre qn** DROIT bring a lawsuit against sb, bring an action against sb; **~ un procès** DROIT file a lawsuit; **~ un procès à** DROIT sue; **~ un procès contre qn** DROIT bring an action against sb, take legal action against sb; **~ un procès en diffamation** DROIT sue for libel; **~ un procès en diffamation à qn** DROIT *pour texte injurieux* bring an action for libel against sb, *pour paroles injurieuses* bring an action for slander against sb; **~ un procès en dommages-intérêts** DROIT file a claim for damages; **~ un procès à qn** DROIT bring an action against sb, take legal action against sb

intention *f* COM intention; ♦ **avec ~ de nuire** DROIT maliciously; **avec une ~ frauduleuse** DROIT fraudulently; **dans l'~ de faire** COM with a view to doing

intentions: **~ cachées** *f pl* COM hidden agenda

interactif, -ive *adj* COM, INFO interactive, on-line

interaction *f* COM interplay

intercaler *vt* INFO embed

interchangeabilité *f* COM commutability

interchangeable *adj* COM commutable, DROIT, RES HUM fungible

interclassement *m* INFO collation

interclasseuse *f* INFO collator

interconnecter *vt* INFO network

interconnexion *f* COM interconnection, INFO networking; **~ portuaire** TRANSP port interchange; **~ de systèmes ouverts** *(ISO)* INFO open-systems interconnection *(OSI)*

intercontinental, e *adj* TRANSP intercontinental

interdépartemental, e *adj* ADMIN, COM, RES HUM interdepartmental

interdépendance *f* COM, ECON, POL interdependence; **~ des stratégies** COM, GESTION strategic interdependence

interdépendant, e *adj* COM, ECON, POL interdependent

interdiction *f* COM, DROIT, IMP/EXP ban, prohibition; **~ d'aliénation** DROIT restraint of alienation;

~ **générale** COM blanket ban; ~ **d'opérations** BOURSE cease-trading order; ~ **de publier les débats** DROIT gag order (*US, jarg*), gagging order (*UK, jarg*); ~ **de rapporter les débats** MÉDIA gag order (*US, jarg*), reporting restrictions (*UK*)

interdire *vt* COM bar, prohibit, DROIT outlaw, prohibit, IMP/EXP prohibit, INFO inhibit, prohibit; ~ **l'accès à** COM shut off

interdit: ~ **de séjour** *adj* ADMIN nonpatrial (*UK, dat*)

intéressant, e *adj* COM advantageous; ◆ **sembler** ~ COM look promising

intéressé, e *adj* COM concerned, interested; ◆ **être** ~ **dans** COM have a vested interest in

intéressement *m* COM share of production plan, FIN financial involvement, IND share of production plan; ~ **aux bénéfices** COMPTA, FIN profit-sharing; ~ **par option de souscription d'actions** BOURSE incentive stock option, ISO; ~ **du personnel** RES HUM labor force participation rate (*AmE*), labour force participation rate (*BrE*), LFPR; ~ **du personnel aux bénéfices** RES HUM profit-sharing

intéressés *m pl* COM persons concerned

intérêt *m* BANQUE i, interest, rate of interest, BANQUE (*int.*) BOURSE (*int.*) interest (*int.*) COM concern, COM (*int.*) COMPTA (*int.*) interest (*int.*) ECON i, interest, rate of interest, ECON (*int.*) interest (*int.*) FIN concern, i, interest, rate of interest, FIN (*int.*) interest (*int.*); ~ **assurable** *m* ASSUR insurable interest; ~ **d'assurance** *m* ASSUR insurable interest; ~ **bancaire** *m pl* BANQUE bank interest; ~ **capitalisé** *m* BOURSE capitalized interest; ~ **commercial** *m* COM, ECON business interest, commercial interest; ~ **complémentaire** *m* BANQUE, COMPTA, FIN additional interest; ~ **composé** *m* BANQUE, COM, ECON, FIN compound interest; ~ **composé mensuellement** *m* BANQUE monthly compounding of interest; ~ **à courir** *m* BANQUE unearned interest; ~ **dans des biens immeubles** *m* BOURSE interest in real property; ~ **de deuxième rang** *m* COMPTA, FIN subordinated interest; ~ **direct** *m* FISC *dans une corporation* direct equity; ~ **économique** *m* ECON economic benefit; ~ **exonéré** *m* FISC exempt interest; ~ **gagné** *m* COMPTA earned interest; ~ **important** *m* BANQUE substantial interest; ~ **d'investissement à terme** *m* BOURSE forward investment return; ~ **matériel** *m* BOURSE *dans une société* material interest; ~ **minoritaire** *m* BOURSE minority interest, minority stake; ~ **national** *m* POL national interest; ~ **négatif** *m* BANQUE negative interest; ~ **nominal** *m* BOURSE, FIN nominal interest; ~ **non gagné** *m* BANQUE unearned interest; ~ **non réparti** *m* FIN undivided interest; ~ **obligataire** *m* BOURSE bond interest, interest on bonds; ~ **d'obligation** *m* BOURSE bond interest, interest on bonds; ~ **ordinaire** *m* FIN ordinary interest; ~ **de participation** *m* BOURSE participating interest; ~ **payé d'avance** *m* FIN prepaid interest; ~ **perçu** *m* BANQUE interest received;

~ **personnel opposé et divergent** *m* COM conflicting interest; ~ **quotidien** *m* BANQUE daily interest; ~ **réel nul** *m* FIN zero real interest; ~ **de report** *m* BOURSE contango rate (*UK*); ~ **simple** *m* BANQUE ordinary interest, simple interest, COM simple interest; ~ **de subordination** *m* BANQUE, BOURSE subordination interest, COM concern, COMPTA, ECON subordination interest, FIN concern, subordination interest; ~ **supplémentaire** *m* BANQUE add-on interest, COM extra interest; ~ **sur arriérés** *m* BANQUE arrears of interest, default interest, interest arrearage, interest on arrears; ~ **sur les dépôts** *m* BANQUE deposit interest; ~ **sur obligation** *m* BOURSE bond interest, interest on bonds; ~ **des tâches** *m* RES HUM job interest; ~ **visuel** *m* V&M visual appeal; ◆ **à** ~ **non-comptabilisé** BANQUE nonaccrual; **avec** ~ BOURSE and interest; **avoir de l'**~ **sur des actions** BOURSE have an equity interest; **détenant un** ~ **dans** FISC beneficially interested in

inter-État *adj* COM *loi* interstate (*US*)

intérêts *m pl* BANQUE, COM, COMPTA, FIN int., interest; ~ **composés** BANQUE, COM, ECON, FIN compound interest; ~ **composés courus** BANQUE accrued compound interest; ~ **en cours** BANQUE running interest; ~ **courus** (*IC*) BANQUE, BOURSE, COM, COMPTA, FIN accrued interest (*AI*), interest accrued (*IA*); ~ **courus à payer** BANQUE, COMPTA accrued interest payable; ~ **courus à recevoir** BANQUE, COMPTA accrued interest receivable; ~ **cumulés** (*IC*) BANQUE, BOURSE, COM, FIN accrued interest (*AI*), interest accrued (*IA*); ~ **cumulés à payer** BANQUE, COMPTA accrued interest payable; ~ **cumulés à recevoir** BANQUE accrued interest receivable; ~ **débiteurs** FIN debit interest; ~ **échelonnés** FIN graduated interest; ~ **imputés** FISC imputed interest; ~ **moratoires** BANQUE postmaturity interest; ~ **de retard** BANQUE postmaturity interest; ~ **en souffrance** BANQUE arrears of interest, default interest, interest arrearage, interest on arrears; ~ **versés** COMPTA interest paid; ◆ **avoir des** ~ **dans une affaire** COM have a share in a business

interface *f* COM, INFO interface; ~ **parallèle** *f* INFO parallel interface; ~ **parallèle Centronics®** *f* INFO Centronics interface®; ~ **technologie-marché** *f* COM, V&M technology-and-market interface; ~ **utilisateur** *f* INFO user interface

interfacer *vt* COM, INFO interface

interférence: ~ **avec le contrat** *f* RES HUM interference with contract (*UK*)

interfinancement *m* COM cross subsidization

interfonctionnement *m* INFO interoperability

intergouvernemental, e *adj* COM *sommet* intergovernmental

intergroupal, e *adj* RES HUM intergroup

intérieur, e *adj* ECON, TRANSP *réseau de transport* domestic; ◆ **à l'**~ **de l'État** COM intrastate (*US*)

intérieurisation *f* BOURSE internalization

intérim *m infrml* COM interim, RES HUM temping;

◆ **par ~** COM acting, ad interim (*frml*); **pendant l'~** COM in the interim

intérimaire[1] *adj* COM acting, interim

intérimaire[2] *mf* RES HUM casual laborer (*AmE*), casual labourer (*BrE*), temp (*infrml*), temporary, temporary worker

interjeter: **~ appel** *vt* DROIT appeal, lodge an appeal, FISC institute an appeal, lodge an appeal

interligne *m* MÉDIA line space; **~ simple** INFO single spacing

interlocuteur, -trice *m,f* COM contact

intermédiaire[1] *adj* COM intermediate, INFO midrange

intermédiaire[2] *m* COM agency, COM broker, intermediary, go-between, FIN intermediary; **~ de Bourse** BOURSE agency broker; **~ en cession de navires** DROIT, RES HUM, TRANSP sale and purchase broker; **~ des échanges** ECON, FIN medium of exchange; **~ entre courtiers** BANQUE IDB (*BrE*), interdealer broker (*BrE*); **~ financier** FIN financial intermediary; **~ en gros** V&M drop shipping (*US*); ◆ **par l'~ de** COM through the agency of

intermédiation *f* BOURSE agency, FIN intermediation; **~ financière** FIN financial intermediation; **~ ratée** FIN misintermediation

intermittent, e *adj* COM, IND intermittent

intermittents: **~ du spectacle** *m pl* RES HUM casual show-business labor (*AmE*), casual show-business labour (*BrE*)

intermodal, e *adj* TRANSP intermodal

internalisation *f* ECON internalizing

international, e *adj* (*intl*) COM, COMMS, ECON, POL international (*intl*)

International: **~ Standard Book Number** *m* (*ISBN*) MÉDIA *édition* International Standard Book Number (*ISBN*); **~ Standard Serial Number** *m* (*ISSN*) MÉDIA *édition* International Standard Serial Number (*ISSN*)

internationalisation *f* COM, ECON internationalization

internationaliser *vt* COM, ECON internationalize

internationalisme *m* POL internationalism; **~ prolétarien** ECON, POL proletarian internationalism

interne *adj* COM internal, INFO in-house, on-board; **en ~** RES HUM in-house

Internet *m* COMMS Internet

interopérabilité *f* FIN, IND *production* interoperability

interphone *m* COMMS buzzer, intercom

interpolation *f* COM, MATH interpolation

interprétation *f* COM interpretation, COMMS interpretation, *langues* interpreting; ◆ **donner une ~ peu rigoureuse de qch** COM give a loose interpretation of sth

interprète *mf* COMMS interpreter

interpréter *vt* COM, COMMS interpret

interpréteur *m* INFO interpreter

interpropriété *f* COM, MÉDIA crossownership

interrogation *f* COM debriefing, INFO inquiry, polling, query

interrogatoire *m* DROIT hearing; **~ écrit** DROIT interrogatories; **~ pendant la garde à vue** DROIT judges' rules (*UK*)

interrogée: **personne ~** *f* V&M respondent

interrompre *vt* COM abort, interrupt, *activité commerciale* suspend, INFO *programme* abort, interrupt, stop

interrupteur *m* INFO button, switch; **~ à bascule** INFO toggle switch; **~ à positions multiples** INFO DIP switch, dual-in-line package switch

interruption *f* COM disruption, interruption, INFO *de programme* interruption; **~ des émissions** MÉDIA blackout; **~ matérielle** INFO hardware interrupt; **~ publicitaire** MÉDIA *télévision* commercial break; **~ de service** TRANSP *relation ferroviaire* breakdown; **~ du voyage** LOISIRS break of journey

intersaison *f* COM *sommet* shoulder period

interurbain *adj* COMMS long-distance

intervalle: **~ d'un demi-point** *m* BOURSE half a strike price interval

intervenant, e *m,f* BOURSE *sur un marché* participant, COM *dans des négociations*, GESTION player

intervenir: **~ dans** *vt* COM interfere in, COM intervene, step in; ◆ **~ en Bourse pour son propre compte** BOURSE trade for one's account

intervention *f* COM intervention, *volontaire* interference, ECON intervention, INFO servicing, POL intervention; **~ après protêt** DROIT *droit commercial* act of honor (*AmE*), act of honour (*BrE*); **~ de l'État** ADMIN, ECON, POL government intervention, state intervention; **~ minimale de l'État** ADMIN, ECON, POL minimal state intervention; **~ d'un tiers** COM novus actus interveniens (*frml*), RES HUM third-party intervention

interventionniste[1] *adj* ECON, POL *UE* interventionist

interventionniste[2] *mf* ECON, POL *UE* interventionist (*jarg*)

intervertir *vt* COM invert

interview *f* COM, MÉDIA, RES HUM, V&M interview; **~ collective** COM group interview; **~ dirigée** V&M *étude de marché* directed interview; **~ d'évaluation des performances** RES HUM performance appraisal interview, PAI; **~ par téléphone** V&M *étude* telephone interviewing; **~ en profondeur** PROT SOC, RES HUM, V&M in-depth interview

interviewé, e *m,f* MÉDIA, RES HUM interviewee

intervieweur, -euse *m,f* MÉDIA interviewer

intestat *adj* DROIT *succession* intestate

intimidation *f* RES HUM intimidation; **~ injustifiée** DROIT unjustified threat

intitulé *m* COM, COMPTA title; **~ de colonne** COMPTA column heading; **~ de compte** BANQUE, COMPTA account name, name of an account, title of an account; ~ **de crédit** FIN budget heading; ~ **de l'emploi** RES HUM generic job title

intl *abrév (international)* COM, COMMS, ECON, POL intl *(international)*

intraministériel, -elle *adj* ADMIN intradepartmental

intransigeant, e *adj* COM uncompromising

introducteur: ~ **feuille à feuille** *m* INFO single-sheet feeder

introduction *f* BOURSE introduction *(jarg)*, COM institution, introduction, FISC *d'un appel* institution; ~ **automatique des documents** ADMIN automatic feeder; ~ **à la cote** BOURSE introduction *(jarg)*; ~ **de données** INFO data entry; ~ **progressive** COM, INFO phasing in; ~ **du système métrique** COM, MATH metrication

introduire *vt* COM, DROIT *modifications* introduce, INFO *données* enter, input, punch in, tap in; ~ **progressivement** COM phase in; ♦ ~ **en Bourse** BOURSE *nouvelle émission* float; ~ **globalement** V&M roll out; ~ **qch dans un contrat** DROIT build sth into a contract; **s'~ dans le marché** COM gain a toehold in the market; **s'~ en Bourse** BOURSE go public, take public, FIN take public; ~ **sur le marché** BOURSE bring out

introduit: **être ~ en Bourse** *loc* BOURSE go public

intrus, e *m,f* DROIT trespasser; **l'~** RES HUM the odd one out

intrusion *f* DROIT interference; ~ **illicite sur la propriété d'autrui** DROIT unlawful trespass

inutilisé, e *adj* BANQUE lying idle, COM redundant, unused

invalidation *f* COM *d'un accord, d'un contrat*, DROIT *d'un document* invalidation

invalider *vt* COM *document, vote* invalidate, DROIT *document* invalidate, render null and void

invalidité *f* COM disablement, RES HUM disability; ~ **répétée** RES HUM recurrent disability

invendable *adj* COM, V&M unmarketable, unsalable *(AmE)*, unsaleable *(BrE)*

invendu¹, **e** *adj* COM, V&M unsold

invendu² *m* MÉDIA *presse, édition* returned book

invendus *m pl* COM unsold goods, V&M dead stock, sales returns

inventaire *m* ASSUR, COM inventory, COMPTA inventory costing, inventory evaluation, inventory valuation, stock valuation, inventory, stocks, IND inventory, stocks; ~ **de cabine** TRANSP cage inventory record, CIR; ~ **de clôture** COMPTA ending inventory, entity convention; ~ **comptable** BOURSE book inventory; ~ **continu** COM continuous inventory; ~ **en cours** COM continuous inventory, continuous stocktaking, CS; ~ **des effectifs** COMPTA, RES HUM manpower audit, staff audit; ~ **matériel** COMPTA materials accounting, store accounting; ~ **permanent** COM continuous stocktaking, CS, continuous inventory, COMPTA perpetual inventory, ECON continuous stocktaking, CS, V&M continuous process; ~ **perpétuel** COMPTA perpetual inventory;

~ **physique** COMPTA physical inventory; ~ **du prix d'exercice** COMPTA closing inventory; ~ **des produits frais** COM, COMPTA, V&M merchandise inventory; ~ **des réserves** ENVIR stock inventory, stocktaking; ~ **des stocks** COM, ECON, V&M stocktaking; ~ **tournant** FIN perpetual inventory

inventer *vt* BREVETS, COM, IND invent; ♦ ~ **le fil à couper le beurre** *infrml* COM reinvent the wheel

inventeur, -trice *m,f* BREVETS, COM, IND inventor

inventif, -ive *adj* COM inventive

invention *f* BREVETS, COM, IND invention; ~ **brevetable** BREVETS patentable invention; ~ **personnelle** COM brainchild *(infrml)*

inverse¹ *adj* MATH inverse

inverse² *m* MATH inverse

inversement *adv* COM conversely, MATH inversely

inverser *vt* COM, ECON *tendance* reverse, INFO invert; ♦ ~ **une position** FIN close a position, liquidate a position; ~ **un swap** BOURSE reverse a swap; ~ **une transaction par compensation** BOURSE unwind a trade

inversion *f* ECON inversion, INFO case shift; ~ **de la courbe des taux** ECON yield-curve inversion; ~ **des courbes de taux** ECON yield-curve inversion

investir *vt* BANQUE, BOURSE, COMPTA, ECON, FIN, IND, V&M invest; ~ **qn de qch** COM, DROIT vest sb with sth, BANQUE, BOURSE, COMPTA, ECON, FIN, IND, V&M invest; ♦ ~ **en actions** BOURSE, FIN invest in shares; ~ **en obligations** BOURSE, FIN invest in bonds; ~ **en valeurs** BOURSE, FIN invest in shares

investissement *m* BANQUE, BOURSE, COMPTA, ECON, FIN, IND, V&M investment; ~ **actif** BOURSE active investment; ~ **en actions** COM equity investment; ~ **en actions ordinaires** BOURSE common share investment *(BrE)*, common stock investment *(AmE)*; ~ **adapté** BOURSE fit, fit investment; ~ **agressif** FIN aggressive investment; ~ **autonome** ECON autonomous investment; ~ **de base** FISC expenditure base; ~ **basé sur l'actif** BANQUE, FIN asset-based investment; ~ **brut** COMPTA gross investment; ~ **en capital** ECON capital investment, *pour maintenir le rapport capital-travail* capital widening, FIN capital investment; ~ **de capitaux** ECON, FIN capital investment; ~ **collectif** BANQUE real investment; ~ **commercial** ECON trade investments; ~ **à court terme** BOURSE short-term investment assets; ~ **direct** BOURSE direct investment; ~ **à l'étranger** COM, BOURSE, FIN foreign investment, investment abroad; ~ **étranger** COM foreign investment, FIN inward investment; ~ **étranger direct** ECON direct foreign investment; ~ **d'exploitation** COMPTA operational investment; ~ **extérieur net** COMPTA, ECON net foreign investment; ~ **extraterritorial** FIN offshore investment; ~ **fiduciaire** BANQUE, FIN fiduciary investment; ~ **financier** ECON, FIN, IND, V&M financial investment; ~ **garanti par des actifs** FIN asset-backed investment; ~ **initial** FIN seed money; ~ **intérieur net** COMPTA, ECON net domestic investment; ~ **involontaire** BANQUE unintended investment, FIN involuntary investment; ~ **légal** FIN statutory investment; ~ **licite** BOURSE legal investment; ~ **minoritaire** BOURSE minority interest, minority investment; ~ **négatif** ECON, FIN negative investment; ~ **de portefeuille** BOURSE, FIN portfolio investment; ~ **en prêt** FIN loan investment; ~ **de qualité** BOURSE legal investment; ~ **réel** BANQUE actual investment (*UK*); ~ **à rendement fixe** BANQUE straight investment; ~ **à revenu fixe** BOURSE fixed-income investment; ~ **sain** BOURSE fit investment; ~ **du secteur privé** BOURSE private investment, ECON private sector investment, FIN private investment; ~ **à taux flottant** BOURSE floating-rate investment; ~ **à taux variable** BOURSE floating-rate investment; ◆ **susceptible d'~** BOURSE, FIN investible

investissements *m pl* COM capex, capital expenditure; ~ **à capacité fiscale** FIN, FISC tax-efficient investments (*UK*); ~ **de l'État** FIN government investment; ~ **nationaux** ECON domestic investments; ~ **de rationalisation** ECON capital deepening; ~ **des sociétés** FIN corporate investment; ~ **à valeur constante en dollars** BOURSE dollar cost averaging

investisseur *m* BOURSE, ECON, FIN, IND investor; ~ **accrédité** BOURSE accredited investor; ~ **actif** BOURSE active investor; ~ **en actions** BOURSE equity investor; ~ **averti** BOURSE experienced investor; ~ **chevronné** BOURSE experienced investor; ~ **commercial** BOURSE corporate investor (*UK*); ~ **à contre-courant** BOURSE contrarian; ~ **à contre-tendance** BOURSE contrarian; ~ **étranger** ECON inbound investor, FIN foreign investor, inward investor, overseas investor; ~ **éventuel** BOURSE potential investor; ~ **individuel** BOURSE individual investor; ~ **institutionnel** BOURSE institutional investor; ~ **passif** FIN passive investor; ~ **potentiel** BOURSE potential investor; ~ **privé** BOURSE, FIN private investor; ~ **public** FIN public investor; ~ **à la recherche d'une bonne affaire** BOURSE bargain hunter

investisseurs: les ~ les plus importants *m pl* BOURSE the largest investors

inviolable *adj* COM theft-proof

invisible *adj* ECON, FIN invisible

invisibles *m pl* COM, ECON, IMP/EXP invisibles

invitation *f* COM invitation, LOISIRS *théâtre* punched paper (*US*)

invite: ~ du DOS *m* INFO DOS prompt

inviter *vt* COM *suggestions* welcome

invoquer *vt* COM *loi* invoke; ◆ **~ son ignorance** COM plead ignorance

iota *m* COM iota

IPC *abrév* (*indice des prix à la consommation*) COMPTA, ECON CPI (*consumer price index*)

ipso facto *adv frml* COM ipso facto (*frml*)

Irak *m* COM Irak, Iraq

irakien[1], **-enne** *adj* COM Iraki, Iraqi

irakien[2] *m* COM *langue* Iraki, Iraqi

Irakien, -enne *m,f* COM *habitant* Iraki, Iraqi

Iran *m* COM Iran

iranien[1], **-enne** *adj* COM Iranian

iranien[2] *m* COM *langue* Iranian

Iranien, -enne *m,f* COM *habitant* Iranian

Iraq *m* COM Irak, Iraq

iraquien[1], **-enne** *adj* COM Iraki, Iraqi

iraquien[2] *m* COM *langue* Iraki, Iraqi

Iraquien, -enne *m,f* COM *habitant* Iraki, Iraqi

irlandais, e *adj* COM Irish

Irlandais *m* COM *habitant* Irishman; **les ~** *m pl* COM *habitant* the Irish; **les ~ du Nord** *m pl* COM *habitant* the Northern Irish

Irlandaise *f* COM *habitante* Irishwoman

Irlande:[1] **de l'~ du Nord** *adj* COM Northern Irish

Irlande[2] *f* COM Ireland; **~ du Nord** COM Northern Ireland

IRNUDS *abrév* (*Institut de Recherche des Nations Unies pour le développement social*) PROT SOC UNRISD (*United Nations Research Institute for Social Development*)

irréalisable *adj* COM unfeasible, unworkable

irréductible *adj* COM irreducible

irréfutable *adj* COM *réputation* irrefutable, unassailable

irrégularité *f* COM irregularity

irrégulier, -ière *adj* COM unsteady, *résultats* erratic, *tendance* uneven

irrémédiable *adj* INFO unrecoverable

irremplaçable *adj* COM irreplaceable

irréparable *adj* COM beyond repair, irreparable; ◆ **être ~** COM be a write-off (*infrml*)

irréprochable *adj* COM faultless

irrésistible *adj* COM uncontrollable

irrésolu, e *adj* COM, GESTION *problème, question* unresolved

irréversible *adj* COM *stratégie* irreversible

irrévocable *adj* COM *décision* irreversible, DROIT binding, irrevocable

IS *abrév* (*impôt sur les sociétés*) FISC business income tax (*Canada*), company tax, corporate tax, corporation tax (*BrE*)

ISBN *abrév* (*International Standard Book Number*) MÉDIA *édition* ISBN (*International Standard Book Number*)

Islamabad *n pr* COM Islamabad

islandais[1], **e** *adj* COM Icelandic

islandais[2] *m* COM *langue* Icelandic

Islandais, e *m,f* COM *habitant* Icelander

Islande *f* COM Iceland

ISO *abrév* (*interconnexion de systèmes ouverts*) INFO OSI (*open-systems interconnection*)

isocoût *m* ECON isocost

isolation: ~ acoustique *f* COMMS, ENVIR sound insulation; **~ en bas de page** *f* MÉDIA *typographie* orphan; **~ en haut de page** *f* MÉDIA *typographie* widow; ~ **phonique** *f* COM noise insulation, COMMS sound insulation, ENVIR noise insulation, sound insulation

isolationniste[1] *adj* POL isolationist

isolationniste[2] *mf* POL isolationist

isolé, e *adj* COM isolated, segregated

isoler *vt* BOURSE insulate, COM isolate

isoloir *m* POL polling booth, voting booth

isoquant *m* ECON isoquant

isotherme *adj* TRANSP ins., insulated

Israël *m* COM Israel

israélien, -enne *adj* COM Israeli

Israélien, -enne *m,f* COM *habitant* Israeli

ISSN *abrév (International Standard Serial Number)* MÉDIA *édition* ISSN *(International Standard Serial Number)*

issue: ~ **positive** *f* COM successful outcome; ~ **probable** *f* COM likely outcome

Italie *f* COM Italy

italien[1], **-enne** *adj* COM Italian

italien[2] *m* COM *langue* Italian

Italien, -enne *m,f* COM *habitant* Italian

italienne: à l'~ *adj* COM, INFO, MÉDIA landscape

italique[1] *adj* INFO, MÉDIA italic

italique[2] *m* INFO, MÉDIA italics; ◆ **en** ~ INFO, MÉDIA in italics

itération *f* INFO iteration

itinéraire *m* LOISIRS, TRANSP itinerary; ~ **détourné** TRANSP indirect route; ~ **direct** TRANSP direct route, through route; ~ **à escales multiples** TRANSP *navigation* multiport itinerary

ivoirien, -enne *adj* COM Ivorian

Ivoirien, -enne *m,f* COM *habitant* Ivorian

J

jable *m* TRANSP *d'un tonneau* chime

jachère: en ~ *loc* ECON *agriculture* fallow

jalon *m* COM bench mark

jamaïcain, e *adj* COM Jamaican

Jamaïcain, e *m,f* COM *habitant* Jamaican

jamaïquain, e *adj* COM Jamaican

jamaïquain, e *m,f* COM *habitant* Jamaican

Jamaïque *f* COM Jamaica

jambe *f* BOURSE *d'un écart* leg

janv. *abrév (janvier)* COM Jan. *(January)*

janvier *m (janv.)* COM January *(Jan.)*

japanisation *f* ECON japanization

Japon *m* COM Japan

japonais[1]**, e** *adj* COM Japanese

japonais[2] *m* COM *langue* Japanese; **les ~** *m pl* COM the Japanese

Japonais, e *m,f* COM *habitant* Japanese

jaquette *f* INFO jacket

jargon *m* COM jargon; **~ administratif** ADMIN, COMMS officialese

j'atteste: ~ par la présente que *loc* DROIT I, the undersigned hereby testify that

jauge *f* TRANSP *d'un navire* carrying capacity, tonnage; **~ brute** TRANSP *d'un navire* gross registered tonnage; **~ sous le pont** TRANSP *d'un navire* under-deck tonnage

jaugeage *m* TRANSP tonnage measurement, *maritime* measurement

jaune *m,f péj* RES HUM blackleg *(pej)*, scab *(UK)* *(pej)*

je: ~ ne souhaite pas contester *loc* DROIT nolo contendere *(frml)*; **~ soussigné certifie que** *loc* DROIT I the undersigned hereby testify that; **~ soussigné déclare que** *loc* ASSUR, DROIT I the undersigned declare that; **~ vous demande pardon** *loc* COM I beg your pardon; **~ vous prie d'agréer, Madame/Monsieur, l'expression de mes sentiments les meilleurs** *loc* COMMS Sincerely yours *(AmE)*, Yours faithfully, Yours sincerely *(BrE)*, Yours truly; **~ vous saurais gré** *loc frml* COM I should be much obliged *(frml)*

Jérusalem *n pr* COM Jerusalem

jet: ~ à la mer *m* TRANSP *navigation* jettison; **~ à la mer et enlèvement par une lame** *m* ASSUR jettisoning and washing overboard, J&WO

jeter *vt* ENVIR dump; ◆ **~ les bases de** COM lay the basis for; **~ un froid sur** COM put a damper on; **~ un oeil** COM browse; **~ par-dessus bord** TRANSP jettison; **~ son argent par les fenêtres** *infrml* COM throw one's money about *(infrml)*

jeton *m* COM, INFO token

jetons: ~ de présence *m pl* RES HUM attendance fees, attendance money, directors' fees

jeu *m* BOURSE play, COM, ECON, GESTION game, INFO *de caractères* set, POL game; **~ à la baisse** *(ANT jeu à la hausse)* BOURSE strong bearish play *(jarg)*; **~ de caractères** INFO character array, character set, code set, font, MÉDIA font; **~ d'entreprise** COM, ECON business game, GESTION business game, management game, RES HUM business game; **~ d'essai** INFO testdeck; **~ à la hausse** *(ANT jeu à la baisse)* BOURSE strong bullish play *(jarg)*; **~ de revendications** BREVETS set of claims; **~ de rôles** COM, ECON business game, GESTION *formation d'affaires* business game, role-playing, RES HUM business game; **~ à somme négative** ECON negative sum game; **~ à somme non-nulle** ECON non-zero-sum game; **~ à somme nulle** ECON, GESTION, POL zero-sum game; **~ à somme positive** *jarg* ECON positive sum game *(jarg)*; ◆ **au ~** BOURSE at-the-money; **en ~** BOURSE in-the-money, ITM, COM at stake

jeudi *m* COM Thurs., Thursday

Jeudi: le ~ d'argent *m* BOURSE silver Thursday

jeune[1] *adj* COM jnr, jr, junior, young

jeune:[2] **~ cadre** *m* RES HUM junior manager; **~ cadre dynamique** *m* COM young upwardly mobile professional, yuppie *(infrml)*; **~ prodige** *m* COM whizz kid *(infrml)*; **~ turc** *m* COM whizz kid *(infrml)*

jeunes: les ~ *m pl* COM young people; **~ travailleurs** *m pl* RES HUM young workers

jeunot: être un peu ~ *loc infrml* RES HUM be wet behind the ears *(infrml)*

jeux:[1] **~ d'hypothèses** *m pl* COM what-if games *(jarg)*

jeux:[2] **par ~ de** *loc* COM in sets of

jingle *m* MÉDIA signature tune, V&M jingle; **~ sonal** MÉDIA, V&M advertising jingle

jl *abrév (journal)* COM db *(daybook)*, COMPTA db *(daybook)*, MÉDIA mag *(magazine)*

JO *abrév (Journal officiel)* ECON UE OJ *(Official Journal)*

jobber *m* BOURSE jobber *(UK, dat)*, market maker, stockjobber *(UK, dat)*

joindre *vt* COM *notes, liste, document* append, COMMS append, attach, enclose

joint[1] *adj* COM, COMMS enc., encl., enclosed

joint:[2] **~-venture** *m* COM joint equity venture company, joint venture, JV, joint-venture company, ECON joint venture, JV; **~-venture avec création de société commune** *m* COM equity joint venture; **~-venture sans création de société** *m* COM contract joint venture

joker *m* INFO wild card

jonction *f* COM connection, interface; **~ des appels** FISC joinder of appeals

Jordanie *f* COM Jordan

jordanien, -enne *adj* COM Jordanian

Jordanien, -enne *m,f* COM *habitant* Jordanian

jouer *vt* COM *rôle* perform, play; ♦ ~ **à la baisse** BOURSE bear; ~ **à la bourse** BOURSE gamble on the stock exchange; ~ **gros jeu** BOURSE take a flier; ~ **à guichets fermés** LOISIRS *pièce de théâtre* be a sellout (*infrml*); ~ **le marché** BOURSE play the market; ~ **un rôle dans** COM play a part in, play a role in

jouir: ~ **de** *vt* COM *droits, allocation, bonne réputation* enjoy

jouissance: ~ **anticipée** *f* COM, DROIT, IMMOB anticipation; ~ **immédiate** *f* DROIT vacant possession, IMMOB immediate possession, vacant possession, PROT SOC immediate possession; ~ **tranquille** *f* IMMOB quiet enjoyment; ♦ **avec** ~ **au** FIN payable on

jour *m* BANQUE, BOURSE, COM, FIN, RES HUM, TRANSP day; ~ **d'assignation** BOURSE *de l'option* assignment day; ~ **de bourse** BOURSE market day; ~ **du calendrier** DROIT calendar day; ~ **de chargement** TRANSP *maritime* loading date; ~ **civil** COM calendar day; ~ **de compensation** BANQUE clearing day; ~ **de congé** RES HUM day off; ~ **courant** TRANSP *charte-partie* Rd, running day; ~ **courant de travail** TRANSP *charte-partie* running working day; ~ **creux** COM off-peak day; ~ **de déclaration** TRANSP *maritime* reporting day; ~ **de départ** TRANSP *d'un navire* sailing date, S/D; ~ **d'échéance de la prime** ASSUR due date of premium; ~ **d'échéance de renouvellement** ASSUR due date of renewal; ~ **des élections** POL polling day; ~ **de l'évaluation** FISC valuation day; ~ **de facturation** COMPTA billing day; ~ **férié** COM bank holiday (*UK*), statutory holiday, legal holiday (*US*), public holiday, DROIT, ECON tax holiday, FISC legal holiday (*US*), IND legal holiday (*US*), tax holiday; ~ **de fermeture avancée** COM early-closing day (*UK*); ~ **de fête légale** COM legal holiday (*US*); ~ **fixé** COM appointed day; ~ **de liquidation** BOURSE, FIN account day; ~ **de livraison** BOURSE delivery day; ~ **de livraison du contrat** BOURSE contract delivery date (*UK*); ~ **des opérations au compte de réserve** BANQUE reservable day; ~ **ouvrable** COM, IND, RES HUM business day, workday (*AmE*), working day (*BrE*); ~ **ouvrable temps permettant** TRANSP *déchargement* weather working day; ~ **de paie** RES HUM payday; ~ **de planche** TRANSP *maritime* layday; ~ **de la présentation du Budget** POL budget day (*UK*); ~ **de règlement** BOURSE settlement date, settlement day, value date; ~ **des reports** BOURSE contango day (*UK*), continuation day, preliminary day; ~ **du terme** COM, FIN term day; ~ **de transfert des biens** BOURSE assignment day; ~ **de travail** COM, IND, RES HUM business day, workday (*AmE*), working day (*BrE*); ♦ **à** ~ COM up-to-date, RES HUM in benefit; **à ce** ~ COM to date; **à** ~ **de sa cotisation** RES HUM in benefit; **au** ~ **le jour** COM on a day-to-day basis; **de** ~ **en jour**

COM de die in diem, from day to day; **du** ~ **au lendemain** TRANSP *livraison* next-day; **être à** ~ **de** COM *paiements* be up to date with, keep up with; **le** ~ **et l'heure sont essentiels** DROIT time is of the essence; **le** ~ **même** TRANSP *livraison* same-day; **par** ~ COM per diem

journal *m* ADMIN log, log book, COM daybook, magazine, COMMS news bulletin, COMPTA account book, book of first entry, book of original entry, book of prime entry, daybook, journal, FISC log, log book, INFO log, MÉDIA *d'un institut, d'une société* journal, *radio, télévision* bulletin, news, MÉDIA magazine, news bulletin, newspaper, paper, TRANSP log, log book; ~ **des achats** COMPTA purchases journal, purchases ledger, V&M purchase book; ~ **auxiliaire** COMPTA special journal; ~ **de banque** FIN bankbook; ~ **de bord** TRANSP *navigation* ship's log; ~ **économique** ECON, MÉDIA economic journal; ~ **d'entreprise** MÉDIA house journal, house magazine; ~ **grand format** MÉDIA *presse* broadsheet; ~ **gratuit** MÉDIA *presse* free newspaper, free paper, freesheet; ~ **local** MÉDIA local newspaper, local paper; ~ **de marche** INFO computer log; ~ **de mode** MÉDIA fashion magazine; ~ **national** MÉDIA *presse* national newspaper; ~ **petit format** MÉDIA *presse* tabloid, tabloid newspaper, tabloid paper; ~ **plein format** MÉDIA *presse* broadsheet; ~ **professionnel** COM, MÉDIA trade journal; ~ **de qualité** MÉDIA *presse* quality newspaper, quality paper; ~ **radio** COMMS *d'un navire* radio log, wireless logbook; ~ **des recettes au comptant** COMPTA cash receipts journal; ~ **réglementaire** TRANSP *d'un navire* official log, official logbook, OLB; ~ **des rentrées de fonds** COMPTA cash receipts journal; ~ **sérieux** MÉDIA *presse* quality newspaper, quality paper; ~ **des sorties de caisse** COMPTA cash payments journal; ~ **des ventes** COM sold daybook, V&M sales book, sales journal

Journal: ~ **officiel** *m (JO)* ECON UE Official Journal *(OJ)*

journalier[1], **-ière** *adj* COM daily, IND per day

journalier[2], **-ère** *m,f* RES HUM casual laborer *AmE*, casual labourer (*BrE*)

journalisme *m* MÉDIA journalism; ~ **à sensation** MÉDIA checkbook journalism (*AmE, pej*), chequebook journalism (*BrE, pej*)

journaliste *mf* MÉDIA, RES HUM correspondent, journalist; ~ **indépendant** *m,f* MÉDIA *presse, radio, télévision*, RES HUM freelance correspondent, freelance journalist, stringer (*jarg*), ~ **payé à la pige** *m,f* MÉDIA, RES HUM *presse, radio, télévision* freelance correspondent, freelance journalist, stringer (*jarg*); ~ **radio** *m,f* MÉDIA *qui présente les actualités* newscaster, radio journalist; ~ **à sensation** *m,f* MÉDIA, COM muckraker; ~ **de télévision** *m,f* MÉDIA *qui présente les actualités* newscaster, television journalist

journée: ~ **d'étude** *f* PROT SOC study day; ~ **à tarif réduit** *f* COM off-peak day

journées: ~ **de remplacement** *f pl* RES HUM lieu days

jours: ~ **après acceptation** *m pl* COM days after acceptance, D/A; ~ **d'attente** *m pl* COM wait days; ~ **consécutifs** *m pl* COM consecutive days, TRANSP Rd, running day; ~ **de franchise** *m pl* COMPTA, DROIT days of grace, grace days; ~ **francs** *m pl* TRANSP *navigation* clear days; ~ **de grâce** *m pl* COMPTA, DROIT days of grace, grace days; ~ **ouvrables temps permettant, dimanches et jours fériés exceptés** *m pl* TRANSP *charte-partie* weather working days, Sundays and holidays excluded; ~ **ouvrables temps permettant, vendredis et jours fériés exceptés** *m pl* TRANSP *charte-partie* weather working days, Fridays and holidays excluded; ~ **de planche gagnés** *m pl* TRANSP *navigation* all working time saved, working time saved; ~ **de planche réversibles** *m pl* TRANSP *maritime, charte-partie* reversible lay days; ~ **restant jusqu'à échéance** *m pl* BOURSE days to maturity; ~ **restant jusqu'à livraison** *m pl* BOURSE days to delivery; ~ **successifs** *m pl* COM consecutive days; ~ **de suite** *m pl* COM consecutive days; ~ **de travail à la mine de houille** *m pl* IND colliery working days; ~ **de valeur** *m pl* BANQUE, IMP/EXP float time; ~ **de vue** *m pl* COM days after sight; ◆ **tous les** ~ COM daily, every day

joyau *m* COM showpiece

joyaux: ~ **de la couronne** *m pl* ECON crown jewels (*infrml*)

judiciaire *adj* DROIT judicial, legal

judicieux, -euse *adj* COM advisable

juge *m* COM adjudicator, DROIT judge, magistrate, J; ~ **-arbitre** DROIT judicial arbitrator; ~ **d'instance** RES HUM justice of the peace, JP; ~ **médiateur** DROIT trial examiner; ~ **de paix** RES HUM justice of the peace, JP; ~ **des référés** DROIT summary judge; ◆ **être** ~ **de** COM *concours* adjudicate

jugé, e *adj* COM deemed; ◆ **être** ~ **par un jury** DROIT have a jury trial

jugement *m* COM adjudication, judgment, DROIT *d'un tribunal* ord., order, order of the court, ruling, *règlement d'une controverse* adjudication, judgment, IMMOB judgment; ~ **d'allure** FIN, RES HUM performance rating; ~ **avant dire** DROIT interlocutory decree; ~ **compensatoire** DROIT deficiency judgment; ~ **déclaratif de faillite** COM, COMPTA, DROIT, FIN adjudication of bankruptcy; ~ **déclaratif de liquidation judiciaire** COM, COMPTA, DROIT, FIN adjudication of bankruptcy order; ~ **entérinant un accord** DROIT consent decree; ~ **gracieux** DROIT special case; ~ **gracieux sur requête** DROIT special case; ~ **par défaut** DROIT default judgment; ~ **de valeur** COM value judgment

juger *vt* COM size up, *concours* adjudicate, *réclamation* adjudicate, DROIT judge, sit in judgment over; ◆ ~ **en chambre du conseil** DROIT hear a case in chambers; ~ **nécessaire** COM deem necessary; ~ **en référé** DROIT hear a case in chambers

juges *m pl* DROIT judges, JJ; ~ **compétents** DROIT magistrates entitled to adjudicate

juguler *vt* ECON control, *l'inflation* stamp out

juil. *abrév* (*juillet*) COM Jul. (*July*)

juillet *m* (*juil.*) COM July (*Jul.*)

juin *m* COM Jun., June

jumbo: ~ **-jet** *m* TRANSP jumbo (*infrml*), jumbo jet (*infrml*), wide-body aircraft

jumboïsation *f infrml* TRANSP *d'un navire* jumboization

jurer *vt* DROIT swear

juridiction *f* DROIT, POL jurisdiction; ~ **d'arbitrage** DROIT court of arbitration; ~ **compétente** DROIT court entitled to adjudicate; ~ **fiscale** DROIT, FISC tax jurisdiction

juridictions: ~ **compétentes** *f pl* DROIT tribunals entitled to adjudicate

juridique *adj* DROIT legal

juridiquement:[1] ~ **tenu** *adj* DROIT legally binding

juridiquement[2] *adv* DROIT legally; ◆ **être** ~ **contraignant** DROIT legally bind

juridisme *m* RES HUM juridification

jurisprudence *f* DROIT case law, jurisprudence, RES HUM case law

juriste *mf* DROIT paralegal; ~ **d'entreprise** COM, DROIT, IND company lawyer (*UK*), corporate lawyer, RES HUM company lawyer (*UK*)

jury *m* DROIT jury, trial jury (*US*); ~ **d'accusation** DROIT grand jury (*US*); ~ **ad hoc** DROIT special jury; ~ **d'opinion exécutive** MATH jury of executive opinion; ~ **populaire** DROIT trial jury (*US*); ~ **de présélection** RES HUM screening board; ~ **de sélection** RES HUM selection board; ~ **spécial** DROIT special jury

jusqu'à *loc* COM up to; ~ **concurrence de** *loc* COM up to a maximum of; ~ **nouvel avis** *loc* COM until countermanded, until further notice; ~ **nouvel ordre** *loc* COM until countermanded, T/C, until further notice; ~ **preuve du contraire** *loc* DROIT in the absence of evidence to the contrary

jusqu'ici *adv* COM, COMMS, DROIT heretofore

juste[1] *adj* COM *estimation, évaluation, prévision* correct, *jugement, raisonnement* accurate, *prix, salaire, valeur marchande* fair, DROIT equitable, fair; ◆ ~ **en** *frml* COM low in; ~ **à temps** IND, MÉDIA, RES HUM just-in-time, JIT; ~ **valeur** BOURSE fair value; ~ **valeur locative** IMMOB fair rental value; ~ **valeur marchande** COM fair market value

juste:[2] ~ **prix** *m* ECON just price; ~ **salaire** *m* ECON, RES HUM just wage

justesse *f* COM *d'un jugement* accuracy

justice *f* DROIT justice, J; ~ **fiscale entre générations** ECON intergenerational equity; ~ **fiscale inter-pays** ECON inter-nation equity; ~ **de paix** DROIT court of petty session; ~ **rawlsienne** ECON Rawlsian justice, utilitarianism

justices *f pl* DROIT justices, JJ

justifiable *adj* COM justifiable

justificatif *m* BANQUE, COMPTA, V&M voucher; ~ **de caisse** COMPTA petty cash voucher; ~ **de compte créditeur** BANQUE credit account voucher; ~ **de guichet automatique** BANQUE automated teller machine statement, automatic telling machine statement

justification *f* COM justification, COMPTA explanation, FIN warranty, INFO justification; ~ **de dette** FIN proof of debt, POD; ~ **de livraison** COM, TRANSP proof of delivery, POD; ~ **de perte** ASSUR proof of loss; ~ **de titre** DROIT, IMMOB proof of title

justificatives: ~ **pour contrôle** *f pl* COMPTA, FIN audit evidence

justifié, e *adj* COM, COMMS, INFO justified; ~ **à droite** *(*ANT *justifié à gauche)* COMMS, INFO, MÉDIA flush right, right-justified; ~ **à gauche** *(*ANT *justifié à droite)* COMMS, INFO, MÉDIA flush left, left-justified

justifier *vt* COM *action, dépense, résultats* account for, *affirmation* substantiate, *opinion, actions, droits* vindicate, COMMS, INFO *texte* justify; ♦ ~ **à droite** *(*ANT *justifier à gauche)*, COMMS, INFO, MÉDIA right-justify; ~ **à gauche** *(*ANT *justifier à droite)* COMMS, INFO, MÉDIA left-justify; ~ **de son identité** DROIT prove one's identity

K

Kaboul *n pr* COM Kabul

Kampala *n pr* COM Kampala

Katmandu *n pr* COM Kathmandu

kazakh *adj* COM Kazak, Kazakh

Kazakh *mf* COM *habitant* Kazak, Kazakh

Kazakhstan *m* COM Kazakhstan

keiretsu *f* COM *schéma de la structure hiérarchique d'une compagnie* keiretsu

Kenya *m* COM Kenya

kényan, -enne *adj* COM Kenyan

Kényan, -enne *m,f* COM *habitant* Kenyan

kérosène: ~ **aviation** *m* TRANSP aviation fuel, aviation turbine fuel

ketch *m* TRANSP *navire* ketch

keynésianisme *m* ECON, POL Keynesian economics, Keynesianism; ~ **abâtardi** ECON bastard Keynesianism; ~ **militaire** ECON, POL military Keynesianism

keynésien, -enne *adj* ECON Keynesian

Keynésien: ~ **éclectique** *m,f* ECON Eclectic Keynesian

kg *abrév (kilogramme)* COM kg *(kilogram)*

Khartoum *n pr* COM Khartoum

khmer *m* COM *langue* Khmer

Kichinev *n pr* COM Kishinev

Kiev *n pr* COM Kiev

Kigali *n pr* COM Kigali

kilo *m (kilogramme)* COM kilo *(kilogram)*; ~ **-octet** *(ko)* INFO kilobyte *(kb)*

kilogramme *m (kg, kilo)* COM kilogram ~ **au centimètre carré** COM kilogram per square centimeter *(AmE)*, kilogramme per square centimetre *(BrE)*, KC

kilolitre *m (kl)* COM kiloliter *(AmE)*, kilolitre *(BrE)* *(kl)*

kilométrage *m* TRANSP mileage; ~ **illimité** TRANSP *location de voitures* unlimited mileage; ~ **réparti au prorata** TRANSP *aviation* ≈ proration mileage

kilomètre *m (km)* COM kilometer *(AmE)*, kilometre *(BrE)* *(km)*; ~ **carré** *(km²)* COM square kilometer *(AmE)*, square kilometre *(BrE)* *(km²)*; ~ **-passager** TRANSP *avion, voiture, bateau* passenger mile; ~ **-voyageur** TRANSP *autobus, train* passenger mile; ◆ **au** ~ INFO unjustified

kilomètre/heure *m (km/h)* COM kilometers per hour *(AmE)*, kilometres per hour *(BrE)* *(km/h)*

kilomètres: ~ **-avion** *m pl* TRANSP aircraft kilometers *(AmE)*, aircraft kilometres *(BrE)*; ~ **au cent** *m pl (km au cent)* COM ≈ miles per gallon *(mpg)*; ~ **-passagers par heure de circulation du véhicule** *m pl* TRANSP *avion, voiture, bateau* passenger miles per vehicle hour; ~ **-voyageurs par heure de circulation du véhicule** *m pl* TRANSP *autobus, train* passenger miles per vehicle hour

kilotonne *f (kt)* COM kiloton *(kt)*

kilowatt *m (kW)* COM kilowatt *(kW)*; ~ **-heure** *(kWh)* COM kilowatt-hour *(kWh)*

kina *m* COM kina

Kingston *n pr* COM Kingston

Kingstown *n pr* COM Kingstown

Kinshasa *n pr* COM Kinshasa

kip *m* COM *Laos* kip

kl *abrév (kilolitre)* COM kl *(kiloliter AmE, kilolitre BrE)*

km *abrév (kilomètre)* COM km *(kilometer AmE, kilometre BrE)*

km au cent *abrév (kilomètres au cent)* COM ≈ mpg *(miles per gallon)*

km/h *abrév (kilomètre/heure)* COM km/h *(kilometers per hour AmE, kilometres per hour BrE)*

km² *abrév (kilomètre carré)* COM km² *(square kilometer AmE, square kilometre BrE)*

ko *abrév (kilo-octet)* INFO kb *(kilobyte)*

koruna *f* COM koruna

Koweït[1] *m* COM Kuwait

Koweït:[2] ~ **City** *n pr* COM Kuwait City

koweïtien, -enne *adj* COM Kuwaiti

Koweïtien, -enne *m,f* COM *habitant* Kuwaiti

krach *m* BOURSE crash; ◆ **le** ~ **de Wall Street** BOURSE the Wall Street crash

krona *f* COM krona

krone *f* COM krone

krugerrand *m* ECON Krugerrand

kt *abrév (kilotonne)* COM kt *(kiloton)*

Kuala: ~ **Lumpur** *n pr* COM Kuala Lumpur

kuna *m* COM kuna

kurtose *m* MATH kurtosis

kW *abrév (kilowatt)* COM kW *(kilowatt)*

kwancha *m* COM kwacha

kwanza *m* COM *Angola* kwanza

kWh *abrév (kilowatt-heure)* COM kWh *(kilowatt-hour)*

kyat *m* COM *Birmanie* kyat

Kyrghyzstan *m* COM Kyrgyzstan

L

l *abrév (litre)* COM l *(liter AmE, litre BrE)*

label *m* INFO, MÉDIA *compagnie de disques*, V&M label; **~ de qualité** COM, V&M quality label; **~ syndical** RES HUM union label

laboratoire *m* IND lab *(infrml)*, laboratory; **~ de recherche** IND research laboratory

lacune *f* DROIT loophole in the law

Lagos *n pr* COM Lagos

laine *f* COM, IND wool; **~ d'habillement** IND apparel wool; **~ mérinos** IND merino wool; **~ de verre** IND glass wool; **~ à vêtements** IND apparel wool

laïque *adj* COM lay

laisse: **~ de haute mer** *f* TRANSP *maritime* high-water mark, HWM; **~ de mer** *f* DROIT foreshore

laisser:[1] **~ -faire** *m* [pl inv] ECON, POL laissez-faire

laisser[2] **1.** *vt* DROIT leave; **2.** *v pron* **se ~ corrompre** COM take bribes; ◆ **~ de côté** COM put on the back burner; **~ à entendre à qn que** COM give sb to understand that; **~ entrer** COM admit; **~ un espace** INFO leave a space; **~ flotter** BOURSE float; **~ grossir une dette** BANQUE run up a debt; **~ la question en suspens** COM leave the matter open; **~ tomber** COM drop, scrap; **tout ~ en plan** *infrml* RES HUM drop everything, *personne* leave in the lurch *(infrml)*

laissez: **~ général** *m* IMP/EXP general transire; **~ -passer** *m* [pl inv] COM pass, IMP/EXP transire

lamanage *m* TRANSP *maritime* boatage

lamaneur *m* RES HUM, TRANSP lasher, rigger

lame *f* IND blade, TRANSP blade, chisel fork

lancement *m* BOURSE *d'une entreprise* flotation, promotion, COM release, INFO *d'un logiciel* booting, bootup, release, MÉDIA launch, launching, TRANSP *d'un navire* launch, V&M *d'un nouveau produit* launch, launching; **~ d'un appel d'offres** COM opening of tenders; **~ automatique** INFO autoboot, autostart; **~ dans la presse** MÉDIA *publicité* press launch; **~ d'entreprise** BOURSE company flotation, company promotion; **~ d'une mode** COM trendsetting; **~ de produit** V&M product introduction, product launch; **~ de tâche** INFO task initiation; **~ -test** V&M pilot launch

lancer 1. *vt* BOURSE *entreprise, nouvelle émission* float, INFO *programme* initiate, release, *système* activate, boot, boot up, bootstrap *(jarg)*, MÉDIA *prospectus* issue, TRANSP *navire*, V&M *produit, campagne* launch; **2.** *v pron* **se ~ dans de grosses dépenses** COM go to great expense; **se ~ dans les affaires** COM set up in business, start in business, start up in business; ◆ **~ un appel** COM launch an appeal; **~ un appel d'offres** COM put out for tender; **~ une campagne nationale** V&M *publicité* launch a national campaign; **~ un mandat** DROIT issue a warrant; **~ une mode** COM set a trend,

start a fashion; **~ la mode de** COM set the fashion for, start a fashion for; **~ un mot d'ordre de grève** RES HUM call a strike; **~ une OPA contre une société** BOURSE raid a company, COM launch a takeover bid for a company, mount a takeover bid for a company, raid a company, FIN raid a company; **~ sur le marché** V&M launch, launch on the market

lanceur: **~ d'OPA** *m* BOURSE raider

langage *m* INFO, V&M *publicité* language; **~ COBOL (COBOL)** INFO Common Ordinary Business-Oriented Language *(COBOL)*; **~ commun** COM common language; **~ corporel** GESTION, RES HUM body language; **~ évolué** INFO advanced language, high-order language, high-level language, HLL; **~ gestuel** GESTION, RES HUM body language; **~ de haut niveau** INFO advanced language, high-level language, high-order language, HLL; **~ informatique** INFO computer language; **~ d'interrogation** INFO query language, QL; **~ machine** INFO computer language; **~ objet** INFO target language; **~ d'ordinateur** INFO computer language; **~ de programmation** INFO computer language, program language, programming language, software language, APL; **~ de requête** INFO query language, QL

langue: **~ d'arrivée** *f* INFO target language; **~ commune** *f* COM common language; **~ étrangère** *f* COM foreign language; **~ source** COM, INFO source language

Laos *m* COM Laos

laotien[1], **-enne** *adj* COM Laotian

laotien[2] *m* COM *langue* Lao

Laotien, -enne *m,f* COM *habitant* Laotian

laps: **~ de temps** *m* COM lapse of time; ◆ **dans le ~ de temps imparti** COM within the allotted time frame

larbin *m infrml* RES HUM peon *(jarg)*

largage: **~ des amarres** *m* TRANSP *maritime* casting off, unmooring

large:[1] **à ~ bande** *adj* COMMS, INFO, MÉDIA broadband

large:[2] **au ~** *adv* TRANSP *maritime* to windward, windward

large:[3] **~ coalition** *f* POL big tent *(US, jarg)*

largement: **~ diversifié** *adj* COM *gamme de produits* broadly diversified; **~ reconnu** *adj* COM widely recognized

largeur *f* INFO *de zone* width, TRANSP *d'un navire* beam; **~ de bande** COMMS, INFO, MÉDIA bandwidth; **~ totale** TRANSP overall width

larguer: **~ les amarres** TRANSP *maritime* unmoor

lat. *abrév (latitude)* COM lat. *(latitude)*

latéral, e *adj* COM *mouvement* lateral

latex *m* IND latex

latitude *f (lat.)* COM latitude *(lat.)*

latte *f* TRANSP batten

lavage: ~ **au brut** *m* TRANSP *pétroliers* crude oil washing, COW

lazaret *m* IMP/EXP lazaretto

lb *abrév (livre)* COM lb *(pound)*

l/c *abrév (lettre de change)* BANQUE, BOURSE, FIN, IMP/EXP B/E *(bill of exchange)*

L/C *abrév (lettre de crédit)* BANQUE, FIN L/C *(letter of credit)*

leader *m* COM leader, top of the league, MÉDIA *article* lead story, leading article *(UK)*, *éditorial* leader *(UK)*, leading article *(UK)*, V&M *produit* leader, top of the league; ~ **du marché** V&M market leader; ~ **naturel** RES HUM informal leader, natural leader; ~ **né** COM, GESTION, RES HUM born leader; ~ **au niveau des prix** V&M price leader; ~ **d'opinion** V&M opinion leader; ~ **spontané** RES HUM informal leader

leasing *m* IMMOB leasing

lèche: ~ **-vitrines** *m* [pl inv] COM window-shopping; ◆ **faire du** ~ COM be window-shopping, go window-shopping

lecteur[1] *m* INFO *dispositif* reader, stylus; ~ **de bande** INFO tape drive; ~ **de cartes** INFO card reader; ~ **de cartouche** INFO tape drive; ~ **de cassette** INFO cassette player; ~ **de codes barres** IND, INFO, V&M bar code reader, bar code scanner; ~ **de disques** INFO disk drive; ~ **de disques souples** ADMIN, INFO floppy disk drive; ~ **de disquettes** ADMIN floppy disk drive, INFO diskette drive, floppy disk drive; ~ **de documents** INFO document reader; ~ **d'étiquettes** INFO tag reader; ~ **laser** INFO, MÉDIA laser scanner; ~ **optique** IND, INFO, V&M optical scanner; ~ **par défaut** INFO default drive; ~ **série** INFO serial reader

lecteur[2] **-trice** *m,f* MÉDIA *personne* proofreader, reader

lectorat *m* COM audience, MÉDIA *d'un journal* readership; ~ **secondaire** V&M pass-along readership *(jarg)*

lecture *f* COM reading, INFO read, reading, scanning

lecture/écriture *f* INFO read/write

légal, e *adj* DROIT lawful, legal, statutory

légalement *adv* DROIT lawfully, legally; ◆ ~ **contraignant** DROIT legally binding; **être** ~ **obligé de** DROIT be under a legal obligation to

légalisation *f* DROIT *d'une signature* attestation, authentication, *d'un contrat, d'un document* legalization

légaliser *vt* DROIT decriminalize, *contrat, document* legalize, notarize, *signature* attest, authenticate

légaliste *adj* DROIT legalistic

légalité *f* DROIT lawfulness, legality

légataire *mf* DROIT, IMMOB devisee, legatee; ~ **universel** *m* DROIT sole legatee

légende *f* MÉDIA caption

léger, -ère *adj* COM slight

légèrement: ~ **inférieur à** *adj* COM a little under, slightly less than

légiférer *vi* DROIT bring in legislation, introduce legislation, legislate

Légion: **la** ~ **d'honneur** *f* POL the Legion of Honour

législateur, -trice *m,f* DROIT, POL legislator

législatif, -ive *adj* DROIT legislative

législation *f* DROIT legislation; ~ **anti-évasion fiscale** BOURSE, DROIT, FIN, FISC anti-avoidance legislation; ~ **anti-monopoles** COM, DROIT, ECON, V&M antimonopoly laws, antimonopoly legislation; ~ **antitrust** DROIT antitrust law and legislation; ~ **douanière** DROIT, FISC, IMP/EXP tariff legislation; ~ **nationale** DROIT national legislation; ~ **relative à l'alimentation** DROIT food law; ~ **relative au contrat d'agence** DROIT agency law; ~ **relative au contrat de licence** DROIT licensing laws; ~ **relative au contrat de représentation** DROIT agency law; ~ **relative à la liquidation judiciaire** COM, DROIT, IND insolvency legislation; ~ **relative à la protection des consommateurs** DROIT, V&M consumer protection legislation; ~ **relative au transport multimodal** DROIT, TRANSP multimodal transport law; ~ **réprimant la dissimulation fiscale** BOURSE, DROIT, FIN, FISC anti-avoidance legislation; ~ **secondaire** DROIT, POL piggyback legislation, secondary legislation; ~ **sociale** RES HUM welfare legislation, welfare services; ~ **sur la faillite** COM, DROIT, IND insolvency legislation; ~ **sur les faillites** DROIT, FIN bankruptcy law, bankruptcy legislation; ~ **du travail** DROIT employment law, job legislation, POL employment law, RES HUM employment law, job legislation, labor laws *(AmE)*, labour laws *(BrE)*; ◆ **faire passer une** ~ DROIT bring in legislation, introduce legislation

légitime *adj* DROIT justifiable, legal

legs *m* DROIT bequest, devise, legacy, IMMOB devise; ~ **de biens immobiliers** DROIT, IMMOB devise

léguer *vt* DROIT bequeath, devise, leave

lek *m* COM lek

lempira *m* COM lempira

lendemain *m* COM following day, next day; ◆ **au** ~ **de** COM in the aftermath of

lent, e *adj* COM, ECON slow; ~ **déclin** BOURSE slow decline; ◆ ~ **à répondre** COM slow to reply

lente: ~ **remontée** *f* BOURSE slow rise

leone *m* COM leone

L.E.P. *abrév (lycée d'enseignement professionnel)* PROT SOC seconary school for vocational training

LEP *abrév (livret d'épargne populaire)* BANQUE *populaire* savings account passbook, savings bankbook, savings book, savings passbook

leptokurtique *m* MATH leptokurtic

lésiner: ~ **sur** *vt* COM *finition, qualité* skimp on *(infrml)*, COM scrimp and save

lésion: ~ **corporelle** *f* DROIT personal injury

Lesotho *m* COM Lesotho

lest *m* TRANSP ballast; ~ **d'eau** TRANSP water ballast; ~ **d'eau fixe** TRANSP *maritime* permanent water ballast, PWB; ~ **fixe** TRANSP *navigation* permanent ballast, PB; ~ **liquide** TRANSP water ballast; ~ **liquide permanent** TRANSP *maritime* permanent water ballast, PWB; ~ **permanent** TRANSP *navigation* permanent ballast, PB

letton[1], **e** *adj* COM Latvian

letton[2] *m* COM *langue* Latvian

Letton, e *m,f* COM *habitant* Latvian

Lettonie *f* COM Latvia

lettrage *m* MÉDIA lettering

lettre *f* ADMIN *de l'alphabet* letter, BOURSE bill, COMMS letter, FIN bill; ~ **d'accompagnement** COMMS accompanying letter, transmittal letter; ~ **d'accord** COM letter of comfort; ~ **d'accord du client** FIN client agreement letter (*UK*); ~ **d'accord présumé** FIN comfort letter; ~ **d'accréditation** DROIT procuratory letter; ~ **aérienne** COMMS airmail letter; ~ **d'affaires** ADMIN, COM, COMMS business letter; ~ **alimentaire** COM, COMMS bread-and-butter letter (*infrml*); ~ **d'approbation** FISC award letter; ~ **d'attribution** BOURSE letter stock; ~ **d'autorité** COM letter of authority, L/A; ~ **d'aval** BOURSE guarantee letter; ~ **d'avis** COM, COMMS advice note, letter of advice; ~ **d'avis navire prêt à charger** TRANSP *maritime* notice of readiness; ~ **de bas de casse** (ANT *lettre de haut de casse*) ADMIN, INFO, MÉDIA l.c., lower case, lower-case letter; ~ **de candidature** COMMS letter of application; ~ **capitale** ADMIN, INFO, MÉDIA cap, capital, capital letter, u.c., upper case, upper-case letter; ~ **de change** *(l/c)* BANQUE bill of exchange *(B/E)*, negotiable bill of exchange, term draft, BOURSE, FIN IOU money, bill of exchange *(B/E)*, negotiable bill of exchange, term draft, IMP/EXP bill of exchange *(B/E)*; ~ **de change avalisée** BOURSE, FIN backed bill of exchange; ~ **de change garantie** BOURSE, FIN backed bill of exchange; ~ **de change négociable** BANQUE, BOURSE, FIN negotiable bill, negotiable bill of exchange; ~ **de change de premier ordre** BOURSE gilt-edged bill of exchange; ~ **commerciale** ADMIN, COM, COMMS business letter; ~ **de complaisance** IMP/EXP facility letter; ~ **confirmative** ADMIN, COMMS covering letter; ~ **de consentement** COM, COMMS letter of consent; ~ **de coopération** COM letter of cooperation; ~ **de couverture** ADMIN covering letter, ASSUR binder (*US*), cover note, CN, COMMS covering letter; ~ **de créance** COMMS letter of subrogation; ~ **de créance à l'importation** IMP/EXP import credit, import letter of credit; ~ **de crédit** *(L/C)* BANQUE, FIN letter of credit *(L/C)*; ~ **de crédit confirmée** BANQUE confirmed letter of credit; ~ **de crédit garantie** BANQUE guaranteed letter of credit; ~ **de crédit illimité** BANQUE unrestricted letter of credit; ~ **de crédit pour l'importation** IMP/EXP import credit, import letter of credit; ~ **de**

crédit irrévocable BANQUE irrevocable letter of credit, ILOC; ~ **de crédit limitée** BANQUE restricted letter of credit; ~ **de crédit payée d'avance** BANQUE prepaid letter of credit; ~ **datée du six** COMMS letter dated the sixth; ~ **de déclaration d'intention** COM letter of intent; ~ **de demande de renseignements** COMMS letter of inquiry; ~ **de démission** COM, COMMS letter of resignation, resignation letter; ~ **d'engagement** BOURSE guarantee letter, COM letter of commitment; ~ **d'engagement d'audit** COMPTA, FIN audit brief; ~ **d'excuse** COMMS letter of apology; ~ **d'exemption des droits de douane** ASSUR, IMP/EXP, TRANSP bill of sufferance; ~ **de garantie** BANQUE, COM letter of indemnity, L/I; ~ **de groupage aérien** IMP/EXP, TRANSP house air waybill, HAWB; ~ **de haut de casse** (ANT *lettre de bas de casse*) ADMIN, INFO, MÉDIA cap, capital, capital letter, u.c., upper case, upper-case letter; ~ **hypothécaire** BANQUE letter of hypothecation; ~ **d'information aux investisseurs** BOURSE market letter (*US*); ~ **d'instruction** COM letter of direction; ~ **d'instruction du chargeur** IMP/EXP *maritime*, TRANSP *maritime* shipper's letter of instruction; ~ **d'intention** BOURSE letter of intent; ~ **d'introduction** ADMIN covering letter, COMMS covering letter, letter of introduction; ~ **de licenciement** COMMS, RES HUM pink slip (*AmE, infrml*), redundancy letter (*BrE*); ~ **majuscule** (ANT *lettre minuscule*) ADMIN, INFO, MÉDIA cap, capital, capital letter, u.c., upper case, upper-case letter; ~ **minuscule** (ANT *lettre majuscule*) ADMIN, INFO, MÉDIA l.c., lower case, lower-case letter; ~ **mise au rebut** COMMS dead letter; ~ **négociable** BANQUE, BOURSE, FIN negotiable bill; ~ **de nomination** COMMS, RES HUM letter of appointment; ~ **de nuit** COMMS night letter (*US*); ~ **par avion** COMMS airmail letter; ~ **de procuration** DROIT procuratory letter; ~ **publicitaire** V&M sales letter; ~ **de rappel** COMMS follow-up letter; ~ **de recommandation** COMMS letter of introduction, RES HUM letter of recommendation; ~ **de relance** COMMS, V&M follow-up letter; ~ **de remerciement** COM, COMMS bread-and-butter letter (*infrml*), thank-you letter; ~ **de renoncement** BOURSE letter of renunciation; ~ **de renonciation** BOURSE letter of renunciation; ~ **de renvoi** COMMS, RES HUM pink slip (*AmE, infrml*), redundancy letter (*BrE*); ~ **de réponse** COMMS ≈ Business Reply Mail® (*AmE*), ≈ BRM® (*AmE*); ~ **retournée** COMMS dead letter; ~ **en souffrance** COMMS unclaimed letter; ~ **de souscription** FIN letter of application; ~ **de soutien** COMPTA comfort letter; ~ **de subordination** COMMS letter of subordination; ~ **subrogatoire** COMMS letter of subrogation; ~ **de transmission** ADMIN letter of transmittal, transmittal letter; ~ **de transport aérien** *(LTA)* IMP/EXP, TRANSP air bill, air bill of lading, air consignment note, air waybill *(AWB)*, waybill; ~ **de transport aérien de bout en bout** IMP/EXP, TRANSP through air waybill, TAWB; ~ **de transport aérien groupé** IMP/EXP, TRANSP master air

waybill, MAWB; ~ **de transport aérien IATA** IMP/
EXP, TRANSP IATA air waybill; ~ **de transport
aérien du transitaire** IMP/EXP, TRANSP forwarder
air waybill, FAB; ~ **de transport aérien
universelle** *(LTAU)* IMP/EXP, TRANSP universal
air waybill *(UAWB)*; ~ **de transport maritime**
IMP/EXP, TRANSP sea waybill; ~ **de voiture** IMP/
EXP bill of freight, trucking bill of lading, waybill,
TRANSP *chemin de fer* consignment note, CN;
~ **de voiture ferroviaire** TRANSP railroad bill
(AmE), railroad consignment note *(AmE)*, railway bill *(BrE)*, railway consignment note *(BrE)*;
♦ **à la** ~ COM by the book, to the letter

Lettre: ~ **Lehman sur les investissements** *m*
BOURSE LIONs, Lehman Investment Opportunity Notes; ~ **de Lehman sur les opportunités
d'investissement** *m* BOURSE LIONs, Lehman
Investment Opportunity Notes

lettres: ~ **bâtardes** *f pl* ADMIN, MÉDIA *typographie*
bastard face; ~ **en nombre par avion** *f pl* COMMS
bulk air mail, BAM

leu *m* COM leu

lev *m* COM lev

levable *adj* BOURSE exercisable

levé: ~ **aérien** *m* TRANSP aerial survey

lève: ~ **-bogie** *m* TRANSP *essieu de camion* bogie lift

levée *f* BOURSE *d'une option* exercise, COM lifting,
raising, COMMS *de la poste* collection, DROIT *d'un
embargo, d'une peine* lifting, raising, FISC raising,
d'un impôt collection, levy, levying; ~ **d'impôts**
FISC levy of taxes, levying of taxes; ~ **d'une
nouvelle émission** BOURSE takeup; ~ **de l'option**
BOURSE exercise of an option, option exercise

lever 1. *vt* BOURSE *option, prime* exercise, take up,
COM *sanction, embargo* lift, raise, COMMS *courrier*
collect, DROIT *sanction, embargo* lift, raise, FISC
impôt levy, raise; **2.** *vi* POL *session du Parlement*
adjourn, rise; ♦ ~ **des capitaux** BOURSE raise
capital; ~ **une option** BOURSE tender notice; ~ **la
séance** COM adjourn the meeting, break up, close
the meeting; ~ **une taxe** FISC raise a tax

levier: ~ **financier** *m* BANQUE financial gearing
(BrE), financial leverage *(AmE)*, gearing *(BrE)*,
leverage *(AmE)*, BOURSE capital leverage, financial gearing *(BrE)*, financial leverage *(AmE)*,
gearing *(BrE)*, leverage *(AmE)*, COM lever,
COMPTA, FIN financial gearing *(BrE)*, financial
leverage *(AmE)*, gearing *(BrE)*, leverage *(AmE)*

LHT *abrév (longueur hors tout)* TRANSP LOA
(length overall)

liaison *f* COM communication, connection, link,
linkage, COMMS communication, liaison, INFO
communication, interface, link, MÉDIA, TRANSP
link; ~ **avec la clientèle** COM, V&M customer
liaison; ~ **dans l'entreprise** ADMIN, GESTION, RES
HUM channel of communication; ~ **de données**
INFO data link; ~ **ferroviaire** TRANSP rail link;
~ **par modem** INFO modem link; ~ **train-avion**
TRANSP rail-air link; ♦ **en** ~ **avec** COMMS *travailler* in association with, in liaison with

liaisons: ~ **fonctionnelles** *f pl* COM, GESTION functional relations; ~ **hiérarchiques** *f pl* COM line
relations

liasse *f* BANQUE *de billets* bundle, wad *(infrml)*,
COM *de papiers* bundle, MÉDIA batch; ~ **fiscale**
COMPTA income tax return

lib. *abrév (libéré)* COM FP *(fully paid)*

Liban *m* COM Lebanon

libanais, e *adj* COM Lebanese

Libanais, e *m,f* COM *habitant* Lebanese

libellé *m* BANQUE *d'un crédit* wording, COM *d'une
lettre* terms, wording; ~ **d'un crédit** POL vote
wording; ~ **d'une obligation** BOURSE bond
denomination

libeller *vt* ECON denominate, FIN *chèque* make out;
♦ ~ **un chèque** BANQUE write a check *(AmE)*,
write a cheque *(BrE)*, write out a check *(AmE)*,
write out a cheque *(BrE)*

libéral[1], **e** *adj* COM, POL liberal, RES HUM professional

libéral[2] *m* POL Liberal

libéralisation *f* COM, DROIT, ECON liberalization;
~ **du commerce** ECON *commerce international*
liberalization of trade, trade liberalization

libéraliser *vt* COM, DROIT, ECON liberalize

libéralisme *m* ECON liberalism; ~ **économique**
ECON laissez-faire economy, libertarian economics, POL laissez-faire economy; ~ **social** ECON, POL
social liberalism

libération:[1] ~ **ou rachat** *m pl* FISC release or
surrender

libération[2] *f* BANQUE release, COM *des prix* deregulation, DROIT *d'un prisonnier*, PROT SOC
discharge, release; ~ **du fidéicommissaire** DROIT
en matière de faillite discharge of the trustee;
~ **d'hypothèque** BANQUE discharge of mortgage;
~ **à la participation** FIN payment in full on allotment; ~ **partielle** DROIT, IMMOB partial release;
~ **des prix** COM price deregulation; ~ **sous caution**
DROIT release of recognizance; ~ **à titre onéreux**
FIN *d'une obligation* accord and satisfaction

libéré, e *adj* BOURSE *titre* freed up, COM fully paid

libérer 1. *vt* COM *prix* deregulate, DROIT *prisonnier*,
PROT SOC *prisonnier* discharge, release; ~ **sous
caution** DROIT release on bail; **2.** *v pron* **se** ~
COM contract out

Libéria *m* COM Liberia

libérien, -enne *adj* COM Liberian

Libérien, -enne *m,f* COM *habitant* Liberian

liberté *f* COM, DROIT freedom, liberty; ~ **d'action**
COM freedom of action; ~ **d'association** COM
freedom of association, POL freedom of association, right to associate, RES HUM right to
associate; ~ **de choix** POL freedom of choice;
~ **de circulation** POL freedom of movement; ~ **de
concurrence** ECON, POL freedom of competition;
~ **de direction** RES HUM right to manage; ~ **de
dissociation** RES HUM right to dissociate *(UK)*;
~ **économique** ECON, POL economic freedom;

~ **d'établissement** POL freedom of establishment; ~ **syndicale** RES HUM right to organize; ◆ **en** ~ DROIT at liberty, *prisonnier* discharged, released, PROT SOC discharged; **faire mettre en** ~ **provisoire sous caution** DROIT bail, bail out

libertés: ~ **publiques** *f pl* DROIT civil rights, human rights

liberty: ~ ~ **ship** *m* TRANSP *navire* liberty ship

libre[1] *adj* COM free, ECON clean, INFO free; ◆ ~ **de dettes** FIN clean, clear of debts; ~ **à l'entrée** IMP/EXP uncustomed; ~ **d'hypothèque** BANQUE, IMMOB unmortgaged

libre:[2] ~ **accès** *m* PROT SOC open admissions; ~ **-échange** *m* ECON, POL free trade; ~ **-échange réciproque** *m* V&M *établissement des prix* fair trade; ~ **-service** *m* COM free access and choice, self-service, LOISIRS self-service; ~ **-service bancaire** *m* BANQUE self-service banking

libre:[3] ~ **circulation** *f* ECON *des biens, des services* free movement, ENVIR free circulation; ~ **circulation de la main d'oeuvre** *f* DROIT, ECON free movement of labor (*AmE*), free movement of labour (*BrE*); ~ **entreprise** *f* ECON, POL free enterprise, private enterprise; ~ **immatriculation** *f* TRANSP *de navires* open registry, OR; ~ **possession** *f* DROIT vacant possession

Libreville *n pr* COM Libreville

Libye *f* COM Libya

libyen, -enne *adj* COM Libyan

Libyen, -enne *m,f* COM *habitant* Libyan

licence *f* BREVETS *droits d'auteur* licence (*BrE*), license (*AmE*), COM *diplôme*, PROT SOC bachelor's degree, DROIT *pour une activité* licence (*BrE*), license (*AmE*); ~ **contractuelle** IMP/EXP contract licence (*BrE*), contract license (*AmE*); ~ **de droit** PROT SOC ≈ LLB, ≈ Bachelor of Laws; ~ **d'enseignement** PROT SOC, RES HUM ≈ BEd, ≈ Bachelor of Education; ~ **d'ensemble** DROIT blanket licence (*BrE*), blanket license (*AmE*); ~ **en études d'administration des entreprises** PROT SOC ≈ BSBA, ≈ Bachelor of Science in Business Administration; ~ **exclusive** BREVETS exclusive licence (*BrE*), exclusive license (*AmE*); ~ **d'exportation** IMP/EXP export licence (*BrE*), export license (*AmE*); ~ **générale** DROIT blanket licence (*BrE*), blanket license (*AmE*); ~ **globale** DROIT blanket licence (*BrE*), blanket license (*AmE*), IMP/EXP bulk licence (*BrE*), bulk license (*AmE*); ~ **d'homologation** DROIT, IND certification mark; ~ **d'importation** IMP/EXP import licence (*BrE*), import license (*AmE*), I/L; ~ **d'importation individuelle** IMP/EXP individual import licence (*BrE*), individual import license (*AmE*); ~ **individuelle** IMP/EXP individual licence (*BrE*), individual license (*AmE*); ~ **individuelle ouverte** IMP/EXP open individual licence (*BrE*), open individual license (*AmE*); ~ **informatique** INFO computer software licence (*BrE*), computer software license (*AmE*); ~ **de lettres** PROT SOC ≈ BA, ≈ Bachelor of Arts; ~ **obligatoire** BREVETS,

DROIT compulsory licence (*BrE*), compulsory license (*AmE*); ~ **ouverte d'importation générale** IMP/EXP open general import licence (*BrE*), open general import license (*AmE*), OGIL; ~ **de portée générale** DROIT *autorisations* blanket licence (*BrE*), blanket license (*AmE*); ~ **de prospection de gaz** IND gas exploration licence (*BrE*), gas exploration license (*AmE*); ~ **de prospection pétrolière** IND oil exploration licence (*BrE*), oil exploration license (*AmE*); ~ **sans mention** PROT SOC third-class degree (*UK*); ~ **de sciences** PROT SOC, RES HUM ≈ BSc, ≈ Bachelor of Science; ~ **en sciences des relations humaines** PROT SOC ≈ BSIR, ≈ Bachelor of Science in Industrial Relations; ~ **sur site** INFO site licence (*BrE*), site license (*AmE*); ~ **de surveillance** IMP/EXP surveillance licence (*BrE*), surveillance license (*AmE*), SL; ~ **temporaire d'exportation** IMP/EXP sample licence (*BrE*), sample license (*AmE*)

licencié[1]**, e** *adj* RES HUM *renvoyé* redundant; ◆ **être** ~ RES HUM be made redundant

licencié[2]**, e** *m,f* COM, PROT SOC, RES HUM graduate; ~ **en dessin industriel** PROT SOC, RES HUM ≈ BID, ≈ Bachelor of Industrial Design; ~ **en droit** PROT SOC ≈ LLB, ≈ Bachelor of Laws; ~ **d'enseignement** PROT SOC ≈ BEd, ≈ Bachelor of Education; ~ **en études d'administration des entreprises** PROT SOC ≈ BSBA, ≈ Bachelor of Science in Business Administration; ~ **en études commerciales** PROT SOC, RES HUM ≈ BCom, ≈ Bachelor of Commerce; ~ **ès lettres** PROT SOC ≈ BA, ≈ Bachelor of Arts; ~ **en sciences économiques** PROT SOC, RES HUM ≈ BEcon, ≈ Bachelor of Economics; ~ **ès Sciences** PROT SOC, RES HUM ≈ BSc, ≈ Bachelor of Science; ~ **en sciences des relations humaines** PROT SOC ≈ BSIR, ≈ Bachelor of Science in Industrial Relations

licenciement *m* RES HUM dehiring (*AmE*), dismissal, downsizing (*jarg*), firing (*infrml*), lay-off, laying off, redundancy, sacking (*infrml*), termination; ~ **abusif** RES HUM unfair dismissal; ~ **arbitraire** RES HUM wrongful dismissal; ~ **collectif** RES HUM collective dismissal (*UK*), mass redundancy; ~ **justifié** RES HUM fair dismissal; ~ **régulier** RES HUM fair dismissal; ~ **sec** RES HUM compulsory redundancy; ~ **sommaire** COM, RES HUM summary dismissal

licencier *vt* COM pay off, RES HUM dehire (*AmE*), dismiss, fire (*infrml*), lay off, make redundant, sack (*BrE, infrml*); ◆ ~ **qn** RES HUM terminate sb's appointment, terminate sb's employment

lié, e *adj* BOURSE *à un investissement, à une indexation* linked; ~ **à l'environnement** ENVIR environmental; ~ **à l'épargne** COM savings-linked; ~ **juridiquement** DROIT legally binding

Liechtenstein:[1] **du** ~ *adj* COM Liechtensteiner

Liechtenstein[2] *m* COM Liechtenstein

lien *m* COM connection, link, tie; ~ **contractuel** COM contractual relationship; ~ **de parenté** FISC relationship; ◆ **avec ~ de dépendance** BANQUE, FISC non-arm's-length

liens: **~ en amont** *m pl* (ANT *liens en aval*) ECON, IND backward linkage; **~ en aval** *m pl* (ANT *liens en amont*) ECON, IND forward linkage

lier 1. *vt* BOURSE *taux* link, COM link, tie; **2.** *vi* IND *mécanisme* bind; **~ juridiquement** DROIT legally bind

lieu *m* COM *événement* place, venue; **~ du congrès** GESTION conference venue; **~ de destination** TRANSP place of destination; **~ d'emploi** RES HUM place of employment; **~ d'entrée** COM point of entry; **~ d'essai pilote** INFO beta site; **~ d'immersion** IND *en mer* dumping ground; **~ de livraison** TRANSP place of delivery, POD; **~ d'origine** TRANSP place of origin, point of origin; **~ de paiement** BANQUE place of payment; **~ de réception** TRANSP place of acceptance, POA; **~ de résidence** FISC place of residence; **~ de réunion** COM venue; **~ de travail** ADMIN workplace, RES HUM place of work, work location, workplace; **~ de vente** *(LV)* V&M point of sale *(POS)*; ◆ **au ~ de** COM in lieu of, instead of; **avoir ~** COM take place

lieudit *m* IMMOB locality

lieux *m pl* IMMOB premises; **~ de pêche** IND fishing grounds

lignage *m jarg* MÉDIA *presse* linage, lineage

ligne *f* BOURSE line *(jarg)*, COM *de chiffres* row, COMMS *téléphonique*, INFO, MÉDIA *impression* line, TRANSP *compagnie, route* line, *service* service, V&M *de produits* line, *publicité* line; **~ aérienne** TRANSP airline; **~ aérienne intérieure** TRANSP domestic airline; **~ aérienne internationale** TRANSP international airline; **~ affluente** TRANSP feeder line; **~ de base** INFO baseline; **~ de charge** TRANSP *d'un navire* load line, LL; **~ de charge tropicale en eau douce** *(TD)* TRANSP *maritime* tropical fresh water load line *(TF)*; **~ de code** INFO code line; **~ de commande** INFO command line; **~ commune** COMMS party line; **~ de comportement** ECON *microéconomie* behavior line *(AmE)*, behaviour line *(BrE)*; **~ de conduite** GESTION course of action; **~ continue** MATH *d'un graphique* solid line; **~ de crédit** *(cf marge de crédit Can)* BANQUE, FIN bank line, credit line, line of credit *(AmE)*; **~ de crédit ouverte par l'émission de titres à court** FIN note issuance facility, NIF; **~ de crédit par acceptation** BANQUE acceptance bank line, acceptance credit line, acceptance line of credit; **~ de crédit renouvelable** FIN revolving bank line, revolving credit line, revolving line of credit; **~ de crédit spéciale** BANQUE special credit facility; **~ de crédits croisés** FIN swap bank line, swap credit line, swap line of credit; **~ de creux haussière** BOURSE rising bottoms *(jarg)*; **~ de découvert** *(cf marge de crédit Can)* BANQUE, FIN bank line, credit line, line of credit *(AmE)*; **~ directe** COMMS direct line; INFO hot line; **~ directrice** ADMIN blueprint, BREVETS leading line, reference line; **~ d'état** INFO status line; **~ de** **fond** MATH *d'un graphique* baseline; **~ à imprimer** INFO print line; **~ interurbaine** COMMS trunk line; **~ de liaison** TRANSP *de palettes* flow line; **~ de lotissement zéro** IMMOB zero lot line; **~ louée** INFO leased line; **~ maritime** TRANSP *route* shipping line; **~ de moindre résistance** COM line of least resistance; **~ multipoint** COMMS party line; **~ d'obligeance** ASSUR oblige line; **~ ouverte vingt-quatre heures sur vingt-quatre** COMMS hot line; **~ partagée** COMMS party line; **~ du parti** POL party line; **~ pointillée** MÉDIA *impression* dotted line; **~ de pointillés** INFO dashed line; **~ de pont** TRANSP *d'un navire* deck line; **~ à postes groupés** COMMS party line; **~ principale** TRANSP *chemin de fer* main line; **~ de production** COM, MATH flow line; **~ de produits** COM, IND, V&M product line; **~ de programmation** INFO code line; **~ régulière** LOISIRS, TRANSP scheduled service; **~ secondaire** TRANSP *chemin de fer* branch line; **~ de sommets baissière** BOURSE descending tops; **~ de sommets haussière** BOURSE ascending tops; **~ de substitution** BANQUE backup line; **~ de tendance ascendante** BOURSE ascending tops; **~ de tendance descendante** BOURSE descending tops; **~ transconteneur** TRANSP container line; **~ zéro** MATH *d'un diagramme* baseline; ◆ **dans la ~ du parti** POL on the reservation *(AmE, jarg)*; **en ~** COM, INFO on-line; **être en ~ avec** COMMS be through to; **par ~ familiale** DROIT per stirpes; **rester en ~** COMMS hold the line

Lilongwe *n pr* COM Lilongwe

Lima *n pr* COM Lima

limitation *f* COM limitation, DROIT limit; **~ du crédit** FIN restriction of credit; **~ des dégâts** COM damage limitation; **~ des dommages** COM damage limitation; **~ d'impôt** FISC tax restriction; **~ du nombre de passagers** TRANSP passenger control; **~ des pertes** FIN loss limitation; **~ de poids** COM weight limit; **~ des salaires** RES HUM wage restraint

limitations: **~ à la planification** *f pl* ADMIN, DROIT, ENVIR, IMMOB planning restrictions; **~ de sous-traitance aux salariés** *f pl* RES HUM labor-only sub-contracting *(AmE)*, labour-only sub-contracting *(BrE)*; **~ aux valorisations** *f pl* ECON valuation restrictions

limite *f* BOURSE *d'un cours* limit, COM limit, limitation, ECON cap; **~ d'âge** COM age limit; **~ de construction** IMMOB building line; **~ de crédit** COM credit ceiling, credit limit; **~ de dépenses** FISC expenditure limit; **~ discrétionnaire** BANQUE discretionary limit; **~ des disponibilités de trésorerie** FIN, RES HUM cash limit; **~ du disponible** FIN, RES HUM cash limit; **~ d'émission** ENVIR *de gaz polluant* emission limit; **~ d'emprise** BOURSE position limit; **~ d'exonération de droits d'auteur** FISC royalty exemption limit; **~ de financement externe** FIN external financing limit, EFL; **~ de fluctuation** BOURSE fluctuation limit, price fluctuation limit; **~ de fluctuation quotidienne** BOURSE daily price limit; **~ d'humidité transportable** TRANSP transportable moisture limit; **~ de levée** BOURSE exercise limit; **~ de prix** BOURSE price limit; **~ supérieure** BOURSE upper limit; **~ de trésorerie** ECON cash limit; **~ de l'utilité possible** ECON utility possibility frontier; **~ de variation** BOURSE fluctuation limit, price fluctuation limit; **~ de variation des cours** BOURSE fluctuation limit; **~ de variation quotidienne** BOURSE daily price limit, daily trading limit; **~ d'une zone de chalandise** ECON ideal limit

limité, e *adj* COM limited, DROIT restricted, ENVIR *ressources énergétiques* finite

limiter *vt* BOURSE limit, COM, DROIT limit, restrict; ◆ **~ le nombre de** COM limit the number of

limites *f pl* IMMOB *d'un terrain* boundary; **~ fondamentales de la garantie** *f* ASSUR basic limits of liability; **~ de propriété** *f pl* IMMOB property line; **~ spatiales à l'utilisation des biens sociaux locaux** *f pl* ECON spatial benefit limitation

linéaire *m* COM shelf space, V&M facing, shelf space

liner *m* TRANSP *avion* airliner, *navire* boat, liner

lingot *m* COM ingot

lingots: ~ d'or *m pl* COM gold bullion

lingua: ~ franca *f* COM lingua franca

liquidateur, -trice *m,f* COMPTA, DROIT, FIN liquidator, receiver

liquidation *f* BANQUE clearing, BOURSE liquidization, COMPTA *d'une société* liquidation, winding-up, DROIT liquidation, FIN liquidation, sellout (*infrml*), *d'une dette* satisfaction, GESTION winding-up, V&M *liquidation du stock* clearance, clearance sale; **~ en continu** BOURSE continuous net settlement (*UK*), CNS (*UK*); **~ d'un contrat à terme avant maturité** BOURSE ringing out (*jarg*); **~ en espèces** BOURSE, FIN cash settlement; **~ fictive quotidienne** BOURSE daily settlement, settlement to the market; **~ de fin d'année** COMPTA yearly settlement; **~ de fin de mois** BANQUE end-of-month account; **~ forcée** COM, COMPTA, DROIT, FIN compulsory liquidation; **~ involontaire** COM, COMPTA, DROIT, FIN involuntary liquidation; **~ judiciaire** COM, COMPTA, DROIT, FIN involuntary liquidation; **~ des positions** BOURSE book squaring; **~ de sinistres** ASSUR runoff; **~ suivante** FIN succeeding account; **~ volontaire** COM *d'une société* voluntary liquidation, voluntary winding up

liquide¹ *adj* BANQUE, FIN liquid, TRANSP *cargaison* wet

liquide² *m* FIN cash, readies (*infrml*), ready cash, ready money, IND *fluide*, TRANSP *fluide* liquid; **~ cryogénique** TRANSP cryogenic, cryogenic liquid; **~ pyrophorique** TRANSP *marchandises dangereuses* pyrophoric liquid

liquidé, e *adj* BOURSE closed-out, liquidated

liquider *vt* BOURSE *opération* close, sell off, *position* close, liquidate, *société* sell out, sell up, COM *biens* sell off, *dette* clear, liquidate, pay off, satisfy, *société* sell out, sell up, DROIT *société* boot off

(*infrml*), liquidate, wind up (*infrml*), FIN *biens* sell off, sell up, *dette* clear, liquidate, pay off, satisfy; **~ avant fermeture** COM *marchandises* close out; ◆ **~ une opération** BOURSE close a deal; **~ une position** (*ANT ouvrir une position*) BOURSE close a position, liquidate a position

liquidité *f* BANQUE, BOURSE, COMPTA, FIN available cash, liquidity; **~ bancaire** BANQUE bank liquidity; **~ internationale** BANQUE, ECON, FIN international liquidity; **~ d'ouverture** FIN front money, front-end money; **~ du secteur privé** ECON PSL, private sector liquidity; **~ de la société** FIN company liquidity

liquidités *f pl* COMPTA liquid assets, liquidities, liquidity adequacy, FIN cash, liquid assets, ready cash, ready money; **~ et titres d'État** FIN liquid assets and government securities, LGS; ◆ **regorgeant de ~** COM awash with cash (*infrml*)

lire¹ *f* COM lira

lire² *vt* COM read, INFO read, scan; ◆ **~ le téléscripteur** BOURSE read the tape

Lisbonne *n pr* COM Lisbon

lisible: ~ par la machine *adj* INFO machine-readable

lisitng *m* ADMIN print-out

lissage *m* MATH *technique de prévision* smoothing; **~ exponentiel** ECON, MATH *technique de prévision* exponential smoothing

lisse: ~ de plat-bord *f* TRANSP *d'un navire* gunwale

lisser *vt* MATH smooth

listage *m* ADMIN print-out, COM listing, INFO computer print-out, listing, print-out; **~ informatique** INFO computer print-out; **~ multiple** IMMOB multiple listing (*US*); **~ d'ordinateur** INFO computer print-out

liste *f* BOURSE listing, COM *d'erreurs* catalog (*AmE*), catalogue (*BrE*), *de noms* list, IMMOB list (*US*), listing, INFO list, POL ticket (*US*); **~ d'adresses** COMMS, V&M mailing list; **~ agréée** BOURSE approved list; **~ d'attente** COM waiting list, TRANSP wait list; **~ des candidats** POL list of candidates, slate (*US*); **~ -cible** V&M hit list (*infrml*); **~ de colisage** IMP/EXP, TRANSP packaging list, packing list; **~ de commissions** COM shopping list; **~ de contrôle** COM check list; **~ de contrôle des commandes d'exportation** IMP/EXP export order check list; **~ de correspondances** INFO cross reference listing; **~ des cours** BOURSE price list, price quotation list, COM price quotation list; **~ de départs** TRANSP *maritime* sailing schedule; **~ de diffusion** V&M mailing list; **~ électorale** COM, POL electoral register, electoral roll; **~ immobilière** IMMOB list (*US*), listing; **~ d'indésirables** ADMIN lookout book (*jarg*); **~ d'investissement agréée** BOURSE approved list; **~ des investissements authentiques** BOURSE legal list (*US*); **~ kangourou** COM kangaroo ticket (*US, infrml*); **~ de modifications** INFO punch list; **~ des navires en partance** TRANSP sailing card; **~ nette** IMMOB net listing; **~ noire** COM *des sociétés non-fréquentables ou douteuses*, FIN, IND *du personnel* *syndiqué d'une entreprise de mauvais employeurs*, RES HUM blacklist; ~ **officielle des taux d'imposition** FISC tax rate schedule, tax rate structure; ~ **d'oppositions** BANQUE hot card list, hot list, warning list; ~ **ouverte** IMMOB open listing; ~ **partagée** POL split ticket (*US*); ~ **des passagers** TRANSP passenger list, passenger manifest; ~ **du personnel** RES HUM payroll; ~ **des points à contrôler** COM check list; ~ **des points à perfectionner** RES HUM gap sheet (*jarg*); ~ **des priorités** COM, POL hit list (*infrml*), list of priorities; ~ **des prix** COM, V&M price list; ~ **des produits** BREVETS specification of goods; ~ **restreinte** COM, RES HUM shortlist; ~ **des services** BREVETS specification of services; ~ **de surveillance** BANQUE watch list; ~ **des valeurs les plus actives** BOURSE most active list; ~ **de valeurs sous surveillance** BOURSE watch list; ♦ **être sur ~ d'attente** TRANSP be on standby; **faire une ~** COM make a list; **sur la ~ rouge** COMMS ex-directory (*BrE*), unlisted (*AmE*), XD

lister *vt* COM list

listing *m* COM listing, INFO computer print-out, listing, print-out; ~ **informatique** INFO computer print-out

listings: ~ **pré-imprimés** *m pl* COM continuous forms

litige *m* DROIT litigation, RES HUM grievance

litiges: ~ **de moindre intérêt** *m pl* DROIT small claims

litispendance *f* DROIT lis pendens, pendency

litre *m* (*l*) COM liter (*AmE*), litre (*BrE*) (*l*)

Lituanie *f* COM Lithuania

lituanien, -enne *adj* COM Lithuanian

Lituanien, -enne *m,f* COM *habitant* Lithuanian

livr. *abrév* (*livraison*) BOURSE, COM, COMMS, TRANSP D (*delivery*)

livrable *adj* BOURSE, COM, IMP/EXP deliverable; ♦ ~ **à quai** IMP/EXP, TRANSP ExQ, ex quay, x-quay, x-wharf

livraison *f* (*livr.*) BOURSE, COM, COMMS, TRANSP delivery, dely (*D*) ~ **au comptant** BOURSE spot delivery; ~ **correcte** BOURSE good delivery; ~ **dans la journée** COM same-day delivery; ~ **différée** BOURSE delayed delivery; ~ **directe** TRANSP direct delivery; ~ **garantie** BOURSE, COM guaranteed delivery; ~ **gratuite** TRANSP free delivery; ~ **au gré du vendeur** BOURSE, COM *dans un délai convenu* s.o., seller's option; ~ **en gros** COM wholesale delivery; ~ **groupée** TRANSP consolidated delivery; ~ **immédiate** BOURSE spot delivery, COM immediate delivery; ~ **matérielle** BOURSE physical delivery; ~ **multiple** TRANSP multidelivery; ~ **ordinaire** BOURSE regular way delivery; ~ **au pair** BOURSE par delivery; ~ **par route** TRANSP delivery on wheels, DOW; ~ **par voie ordinaire** COM regular way delivery; ~ **partielle** BOURSE partial delivery, short delivery; ~ **physique** BOURSE physical delivery; ~ **à quai** IMP/EXP, TRANSP *navigation* delivered at docks,

DD; ~ **tardive** COM late delivery; ~ **à terme** BOURSE forward delivery, COM tender; ~ **à 5+5** BOURSE regular way delivery; ♦ ~ **contre remboursement** IMP/EXP, V&M cash on delivery, COD; ~ **dès réception du paiement** COM, V&M cash before delivery, CBD; ~ **droits non payés** IMP/EXP delivered duty unpaid; ~ **et re-livraison** TRANSP delivery and redelivery, dely and re-dely; **faire une ~ de** BOURSE make delivery of; ~ **franco de douane** IMP/EXP delivered duty paid, DDP; ~ **franco de douane à quai** IMP/EXP delivered ex quay, DEQ; ~ **à la frontière** IMP/EXP, TRANSP delivered at frontier, DAF; ~ **au navire** IMP/EXP, TRANSP delivered ex ship, DES

livre[1] *m* BOURSE, COM book, COMPTA book, ledger, POL paper; ~ **des acceptations** BANQUE acceptance ledger, acceptance register, FIN acceptance ledger; ~ **des achats** COMPTA bought book, bought day book, bought journal, bought ledger, V&M purchase book; ~ **d'achats** COM sold ledger; ~ **de balance** BANQUE, COMPTA, FIN balance book; ~ **de banque** COMPTA cashbook; ~ **blanc** POL white paper; ~ **bleu** POL bluebook (*Canada*); ~ **de bord** TRANSP *d'un avion, d'un navire* log, log book, official log, official logbook, OLB; ~ **brun** POL brown book (*UK, jarg*); ~ **de caisse** COMPTA cash journal, cashbook, petty cash book; ~ **cartonné** MÉDIA *édition* casebound book, hardback, hardback book, hardbound book, hardcover, hardcover book; ~ **des chèques** COMPTA check register (*AmE*), cheque register (*BrE*); ~ **à colonnes** COMPTA columnar journal; ~ **de comptabilité** COMPTA, FIN book; ~ **de comptes** BANQUE, COMPTA, FIN account book, analysis book, book of accounts, books; ~ **à couverture souple** MÉDIA *édition* soft-cover, soft-cover book; ~ **des créditeurs** COMPTA creditors' ledger; ~ **des effets** COMPTA *à payer et à recevoir* bill book; ~ **emboîté** MÉDIA *édition* casebound book, hardback, hardback book, hardbound book, hardcover, hardcover book; ~ **d'entrepôt** IMP/EXP, TRANSP *contrôle des stocks* warehouse book; ~ **des fournisseurs** COMPTA bought book, bought day book, bought journal, bought ledger; ~ **à gros succès** MÉDIA *édition* best seller, best-selling book; ~ **d'inventaire** BANQUE balance book, COMPTA balance book, inventory book, FIN balance book; ~ **-journal général** COMPTA general journal; ~ **d'or** COM business visitors' memorandum, visitors' book, BVM; ~ **de paie** RES HUM payroll; ~ **de poche** MÉDIA *édition* paperback, paperback book, soft-cover, soft-cover book; ~ **relié en dur** MÉDIA *édition* casebound book, hardback, hardback book, hardbound book, hardcover, hardcover book; ~ **de rendement** COM yield book; ~ **des ventes** COM sold ledger, V&M sales book

livre[2] *f* COM pound, quid (*UK, infrml*), ECON *devise* pound; ~ **irlandaise** COM punt; ~ **maltaise** COM Maltese pound, MTA; ~ **sterling** COM pound sterling; ~ **verte** ECON green pound

livré, e *adj* COM dd, delivered

livrer *vt* BOURSE make delivery of, tender, *actions* deliver, COM *marchandises* deliver, MÉDIA *presse* issue; **~ à terme** BOURSE tender; ◆ **ne pas pouvoir ~** BOURSE fail to deliver

livres:[1] **~ de base** *m pl* FIN basic books; **~ comptables** *m pl* COM accounting records, COMPTA accounting records, books of account, FIN accounting records; **~ de fond** *m pl infrml* COM *industrie de l'édition* furniture; **~ jaunes** *m pl* POL yellow books *(jarg)*; **~ noirs** *m pl* ECON black books

livres:[2] **~ par pouce carré** *f pl* TRANSP pounds per square inch, PSI

livret *m* COM, COMMS, MÉDIA booklet; **~ de banque** BANQUE bankbook, book, passbook; **~ de compte** BANQUE bankbook, book, passbook; **~ de compte d'épargne** BANQUE bankbook, savings account passbook, savings book; **~ de dépôt** BANQUE deposit book, deposit passbook; **~ d'épargne populaire** *(LEP)* BANQUE *populaire* savings bankbook, savings book, savings passbook; **~ de marche** TRANSP *chemin de fer* working timetable

livreur *m* COM delivery man

livreuse *f* COM delivery woman

Ljubljana *n pr* COM Ljubljana

lobby *m* POL lobby, lobby group; **~ écologiste** ENVIR, POL ecology lobby, green lobby

lobbying *m* POL lobbying

lobbyiste *mf* POL lobbyist

local[1], **e** *adj* ADMIN local, COM home-grown, local, INFO local

local[2], **e** *m,f* BOURSE local *(jarg)*

localisation *f* COM *lieu* location, INFO localization; **~ défensive** TRANSP *pétrolier* protective location, PL; **~ de l'usine** COM, IND plant location

localiser *vt* COM *repérer* locate, INFO *panne* troubleshoot, TRANSP *envoi* trace

locataire *mf* DROIT lessee, IMMOB lessee, renter, tenant; **~ agricole** *m* IMMOB agricultural tenant; **~ à bail** *m* DROIT, IMMOB lessee; **~ débordant** *m* IMMOB holdover tenant *(AmE)*, sitting tenant *(BrE)*; **~ à vie** *m* IMMOB life tenant

locataires: **~ en commun** *m pl* BOURSE joint tenants

location *f* COM hire, IMMOB *d'un appartement par le locataire* let *(UK)*, tenancy, *d'une voiture* rent, rental, renting, *par le propriétaire d'un appartement* letting, letting out, renting out, TRANSP *d'une voiture* hire, hiring; **~ -acquisition** COM capital lease; **~ commerciale** IMMOB commercial letting *(UK)*; **~ en commun** DROIT, IMMOB tenancy in common; **~ de conteneurs** TRANSP container leasing; **~ contractuelle** COM contract hire; **~ à durée indéterminée** DROIT, IMMOB tenancy at will; **~ endettée** IMMOB leveraged lease; **~ d'équipement** COM, IND plant hire; **~ fermière** IMMOB farm tenancy; **~ foncière** IMMOB land lease; **~ groupée** COM *de places de*

théâtre block booking; **~ immobilière** IMMOB let property; **~ indexée** FIN leverage lease; **~ intégrale** DROIT, IMMOB tenancy by the entirety; **~ longue durée** RES HUM contract hire; **~ de matériel** COM equipment leasing; **~ au mois** IMMOB month-to-month tenancy, monthly tenancy; **~ par carte de crédit** COM credit card booking; **~ par téléphone** COM telephone booking; **~ sous contrat** COM contract hire; **~ de véhicules** TRANSP vehicle leasing; **~ -vente** FIN HP *(BrE)*, hire purchase *(BrE)*, sales type lease, V&M HP *(BrE)*, hire purchase *(BrE)*, installment plan *(AmE)*; **~ de voitures** TRANSP auto rental *(AmE)*, car hire *(BrE)*; ◆ **en ~** IMMOB self-catering

locations *f pl* FISC rentals

locaux *m pl* COM, IND premises; **~ à bail** IMMOB demised premises; **~ de bureaux** COM, IMMOB office premises, office space; **~ commerciaux** COM business premises, office premises, office space, IMMOB business premises, commercial premises, office space; **~ homologués** IMP/EXP approved premises

lock: **~ -out** *m* COM, RES HUM lockout

logement *m* IMMOB accommodation *(BrE)*, accommodations *(AmE)*, dwelling, housing, housing accommodation, *bâtiment* apartment *(AmE)*, flat *(BrE)*, PROT SOC accommodation *(BrE)*, accommodations *(AmE)*, dwelling, housing, housing accommodation; **~ pour cadres** IMMOB executive-style housing; **~ pour une famille** IMMOB, PROT SOC one-family home, single-family dwelling, single-family housing; **~ d'une famille** IMMOB single-family dwelling, single-family housing, PROT SOC one-family home; **~ de fonction** IMMOB *appartement* company apartment *(AmE)*, company flat *(BrE)*, *maison* company house, tied cottage *(UK)*, tied house *(UK)*, RES HUM job-related accommodation *(BrE)*, job-related accommodations *(AmE)*; **~ gratuit** FISC free lodging; **~ à l'hôtel** COM hotel accommodation; **~ modulaire** IMMOB modular housing *(US)*; **~ occupé par le propriétaire** FISC owner-occupied home; **~ partagé** FISC shared accommodation; **~ plurifamilial** IMMOB, PROT SOC multifamily housing; **~ préfabriqué** IMMOB prefabricated housing; **~ de type propriétaire-occupant** FISC owner-occupied home; **~ de vacances** IMMOB, LOISIRS holiday accommodation

loger *vt* PROT SOC accommodate, lodge

logiciel *m* INFO computer software, software; **~ antivirus** INFO antivirus software; **~ d'application** INFO applications package, applications program, applications software; **~ d'audit** COMPTA, FIN, INFO audit software; **~ de base** INFO systems software; **~ de calcul fiscal** FISC, INFO tax software; **~ de commande** INFO driver; **~ de comptabilité** COMPTA, FIN, INFO accounting package, accounting software; **~ contributif** INFO shareware; **~ à contribution** INFO shareware; **~ de**

dessins INFO drawing software; **~ du domaine public** INFO public domain software; **~ d'émulation** INFO emulation software; **~ d'enseignement assisté par ordinateur** INFO, PROT SOC computer-aided learning program, computer-assisted learning program; **~ fourni en lot** INFO bundled software; **~ de gestion** COM business software, COMPTA, FIN, INFO business package; **~ de gestion des investissements** BOURSE, FIN, INFO investment software; **~ de gestion de réseau** INFO networking software; **~ de gestion transactionnelle** INFO transaction management software; **~ graphique** INFO drawing software, graphic software; **~ inclus à l'achat d'un ordinateur** INFO bundled software; **~ informatique** INFO computer package, computer software, software; **~ intégré** INFO bundled software, integrated software; **~ livré avec le matériel** INFO bundled software; **~ maison** INFO in-house software, proprietary software; **~ paramétrable** INFO parameter-driven software; **~ personnel de planification financière** FIN, INFO personal financial planning software; **~ de pilotage** INFO driver; **~ piloté par paramètres** INFO parameter-driven software; **~ prêt à l'emploi** INFO packaged software; **~ propre à un constructeur** INFO proprietary software; **~ propriétaire** INFO proprietary software; **~ de reconnaissance de la parole** INFO speech recognition software; **~ de reconnaissance vocale** INFO speech recognition software; **~ de simulation financière** FIN, INFO financial simulation software; **~ statistique** INFO, MATH statistical software; **~ système** INFO system software, systems software; **~ de télétexte** INFO telesoftware, tsw; **~ de traitement de texte** INFO word-processing software; **~ de transition** INFO bridgeware, bridging software; **~ de vérification** COMPTA, FIN, INFO audit software

logique[1] *adj* COM, GESTION consistent, logical; ◆ **c'est ~** COM it makes sense, it's logical

logique[2] *f* COM, GESTION consistency, logic, INFO logic

logis *m* FISC dwelling

logistique[1] *adj* COM, COMMS, INFO, MATH, TRANSP logistical

logistique[2] *f* COM, INFO, MATH, TRANSP logistics

logistiquement *adv* COM, INFO, MATH, TRANSP logistically

logo *m* COM logo, motif, organizational symbol, V&M logo

logotype *m* COM, V&M logo, logotype; **~ de la société** COM, V&M company logo, company logotype

loi *f* BREVETS legislation, statute law, DROIT law, piece of legislation, statute, POL act; **~ d'airain des salaires** ECON iron law of wages, subsistence theory of wages; **~ amendée** DROIT amended act; **~ anti-gogos** BOURSE, DROIT blue-sky law (*US*); **~ antitrust** COM, DROIT, ECON, V&M antitrust act, antitrust law; **~ d'assistance sociale**

RES HUM welfare legislation; **~ de l'avantage comparatif** ECON *commerce international* law of comparative advantage; **~ du bon sens** COM law 29 (*jarg*); **~ -cadre** COM, DROIT blanket statute; **~ Clayton** ECON Clayton Act (*US*); **~ des coûts croissants** ECON, FIN law of increasing costs; **~ des coûts d'opportunité croissants** ECON, FIN increasing opportunity costs law; **~ de la demande réciproque** ECON law of reciprocal demand; **~ de Dennison** ECON Dennison's law; **~ de disposition** COM jus disponendi (*frml*); **~ d'Engel** ECON Engel's Law; **~ de finances** COMPTA, DROIT, ECON, FIN ≈ Appropriation Act (*UK*), ≈ Appropriation Bill (*US*), ≈ finance act (*UK*), ≈ reconciliation bill (*US*); **~ de gestion financière** DROIT financial administration act; **~ de Goodhart** ECON Goodhart's law; **~ des grands nombres** MATH law of large numbers; **~ de Gresham** ECON Gresham's law; **~ de l'impôt sur le revenu** FISC income tax act; **~ MacFadden** BANQUE, DROIT McFadden Act (*US*); **~ de Malthus sur la population** ECON, POL Malthusian law of population; **~ modifiée** DROIT amended act; **~ de Monnet** ECON Monnet's law; **~ de l'offre et de la demande** ECON, V&M law of supply and demand; **~ d'Okun** ECON Okun's law (*US*); **~ de Pareto** ECON Pareto's law; **~ du pavillon** COM, DROIT law of the flag; **~ de Petty** ECON Petty's law; **~ du prix unique** DROIT, ECON one-price law; **~ des proportions variables** ECON law of variable proportions; **~ protégeant les données** DROIT, INFO data protection act (*UK*); **~ de redressement industriel national** DROIT, IND National Industrial Recovery Act (*US*); **~ du reflux** ECON law of reflux; **~ de réforme fiscale** DROIT, ECON, FISC tax reform act; **~ relative à l'avarie commune** ASSUR general average act; **~ relative à l'avarie grosse** ASSUR general average act; **~ relative à la novation de créance** DROIT substitution law; **~ relative à la subrogation** DROIT substitution law; **~ relative à la substitution** DROIT substitution law; **~ relative aux titres et valeurs mobilières** DROIT securities act; **~ relative au transport multimodal** DROIT, TRANSP multimodal transport law; **~ relative aux valeurs mobilières** DROIT securities act; **~ des rendements décroissants** ECON, FIN diminishing returns law; **~ révisée** DROIT amended act; **~ de Say** ECON Say's law; **~ des séries** COM Murphy's law (*infrml*), Sod's law (*infrml*); **~ somptuaire** DROIT sumptuary law; **~ de substitution** DROIT substitution law; **~ sur les administrations locales** BOURSE local authority bill, LAB; **~ sur l'agriculture** DROIT agriculture act (*UK*); **~ sur les banques nationales** BANQUE, DROIT National Banking Act (*US*); **~ sur les coalitions** RES HUM combination acts (*UK*); **~ sur les conseillers en investissements** FIN investment advisers' act, investment advisors' act; **~ sur les consultants en placements** FIN investment advisers' act, investment advisors' act; **~ sur le crédit à la consommation** DROIT consumer credit act (*UK*); **~ sur les droits** civiques DROIT civil rights act (*US*); ~ sur l'égalité des salaires DROIT, RES HUM EqPA (*UK*), Equal Pay Act (*UK*); ~ sur les faillites DROIT, FIN bankruptcy act; ~ sur l'indemnisation des travailleurs DROIT, RES HUM workers' compensation act; ~ sur la marine marchande DROIT *navigation*, TRANSP *navigation* merchant shipping Act (*UK*), MSA (*UK*); ~ sur les opérations bancaires internationales BANQUE international banking act; ~ sur l'ordre public DROIT, RES HUM public order act (*UK*); ~ sur la protection de l'emploi DROIT, RES HUM Employment Protection Act (*UK*), EPA (*UK*); ~ sur les rapports patrons-ouvriers DROIT Labor Management Relations Act (*US*); ~ sur le recouvrement provisoire de l'impôt FISC provisional collection of taxes act; ~ sur les salaires DROIT wages act; ~ sur la sécurité des revenus des employés en retraite DROIT, RES HUM employee retirement income security act; ~ sur la sécurité des revenus des personnes retraitées DROIT, RES HUM retirement income security act; ~ sur la sécurité sociale DROIT social security act; ~ sur les sociétés COM, DROIT, IND companies act (*UK*); ~ sur les sociétés commerciales et industrielles COM, DROIT, IND companies act (*UK*); ~ sur les sociétés d'investissement BOURSE, DROIT, FIN investment company act; ~ sur les syndicats DROIT, ECON, IND, POL, RES HUM trade union act (*UK*), TUA (*UK*); ~ sur les taux réels de prêt DROIT, ECON truth in lending act; ~ sur les taxes à l'importation IMP/EXP import duty act, IDA; ~ sur la transparence du crédit BANQUE, COM, DROIT, FIN truth in lending law; ~ sur les transports DROIT, TRANSP Transport Act (*UK*); ~ sur les ventes de marchandises DROIT, V&M sales of goods law; ~ de temporalisation DROIT, POL sunset act; ~ de l'utilité marginale décroissante ECON diminishing marginal utility law, law of diminishing marginal utility; ~ de la valeur ECON law of value; ~ de la valeur de Ricardo ECON Ricardian theory of value; ~ **Verdoorn** DROIT Verdoorn's law; ~ **Wagner 1935** ECON Wagner Act 1935; ~ de **Walras** ECON Walras' law; ~ de **1940** sur les sociétés d'investissement BOURSE, DROIT, FIN investment company act of 1940; ~ de **1986** sur les salaires RES HUM Wages Act 1986; ~ **405** FIN rule 405 (*US*); ♦ au regard de la ~ DROIT in the eyes of the law; ne pas observer la ~ DROIT fail to observe the law

loin:[1] ~ d'être parfait *adj* COM less-than-perfect

loin:[2] ~ du but *adv* COM wide of the mark (*infrml*); ~ du marché *adv* BOURSE away from the market

lois: ~ anti-monopoles *f pl* COM, DROIT, ECON, V&M antimonopoly laws, antimonopoly legislation; ~ de l'arrivage *f pl* COM packaging laws; ~ contre la diffamation *f pl* DROIT libel laws; ~ économiques *f pl* DROIT, ECON economic laws; ~ fixant la prescription d'une action en justice *f pl* DROIT statutes of limitation of action; ~ relatives à l'arrivage *f pl* DROIT packaging laws; ~ relatives

à l'étiquetage *f pl* DROIT labeling laws (*AmE*), labelling laws (*BrE*); ~ relatives à l'octroi de licences *f pl* DROIT licensing laws; ~ sur la concurrence *f pl* POL competition acts

loisir *m* COM, LOISIRS leisure

Lomé *n pr* COM Lomé

Londres *n pr* COM London

long[1] *adj* COM long; au ~ cours TRANSP *maritime* ocean-going; ~ **-courrier** TRANSP long-haul, long-range, *navire* foreign-going, ocean-going; ♦ à ~ terme (ANT *à court terme, à moyen terme*) BANQUE long-term, BOURSE *effet* long-dated, long-term, COM *programme, prévision* in the long term, long-term, COMPTA, FIN long-term

long:[2] ~ **califourchon** *m* BOURSE long straddle; ~ **call** *m* BOURSE call purchase, long call; ~ **coupon** *m* BOURSE *d'intérêts* long coupon; ~ **-courrier** *m* TRANSP *avion* long-haul aircraft, long-range aircraft, *navire* foreign-going ship, foreign-going vessel, ocean vessel, ocean-going ship, ocean-going vessel; ~ **-courrier à passagers** *m* TRANSP *avion* long-haul passenger aircraft, long-range passenger aircraft, *navire* foreign-going passenger ship, foreign-going passenger vessel, ocean-going passenger ship, ocean-going passenger vessel; ~ **étranglement** *m* BOURSE long strangle; ~ **hedge** *m* BOURSE buying hedge, long hedge, purchasing hedge; ~ **put** *m* BOURSE long put, put purchase; ~ **week-end** *m* COM long weekend

long:[3] le ~ de *prép* TRANSP *navire* alongside, A/S

longeron: ~ de toit *m* TRANSP *d'un conteneur* roof rail

longitudinal, e *adj* COM longitudinal

longs *m pl* BOURSE longs

longue:[1] à ~ distance *adj* COMMS *communication* long-distance

longue[2] *f* MÉDIA long; ~ **couverture** BOURSE long hedge; ~ **durée** ASSUR long term; ~ **salle** IMP/EXP long room (*UK*)

longueur *f* COM length, INFO *d'un enregistrement* size, TRANSP length; ~ **entre perpendiculaires** (*LPP*) TRANSP *de la coque d'un navire* length between perpendiculars (*LBP*); ~ **envahissable** TRANSP *d'un navire* floodable length; ~ **hors tout** (*LHT*) TRANSP *d'un navire* length overall, overall length; ~ **de mot** INFO word length; ~ **totale** TRANSP length overall, overall length; ♦ sur la même ~ d'onde COM on the same wavelength

lot *m* COM batch, lot, IMMOB *de terrain* plot, IND lot, INFO batch, V&M batch, packaging, pkg.; ~ **d'articles divers** COM job lot; ~ **de fabrication** IND batch; ~ **fractionnaire** COM fractional lot, uneven lot; ~ **de marchandises composites** V&M pure bundling; ~ **de marchandises pures** V&M bundling, mixed bundling, pure bundling; ~ **régulier** BOURSE, COM round lot (*US, jarg*), COMPTA *Fra* (*cf quotité Can*) full lot (*AmE, jarg*)

loterie *f* COM, LOISIRS lottery; ~ **du gaz et du**

pétrole ENVIR oil and gas lottery; **~ nationale** ECON, LOISIRS national lottery

lotir *vt* IMMOB *terrain* apportion, divide into plots

lotissement *m* IMMOB apportionment, housing complex, housing development (*AmE*), housing estate, housing project (*AmE*), PROT SOC housing development (*AmE*), housing estate, housing project (*AmE*); **~ et pâté** IMMOB lot and block (*US*); **~ interne** IMMOB inside lot

loto: **~ sportif** *m France* LOISIRS *football* ≈ pools (*UK*)

louage *m* COM hiring; **~ de services** COM work contract

loué: **~ à bail** *adj* COM leased

louer *vt* COM hire, IMMOB *logement* let (*UK*), rent, rent out, TRANSP hire; **~ à l'avance** COM, LOISIRS book in advance; **~ à bail** IMMOB lease; ◆ **à ~** IMMOB for rent (*AmE*), to let (*BrE*), to rent

loueur, -euse *m,f* IMMOB renter, *d'un logement* letter, *de bateaux* hirer; **~ de voitures** COM car hire operator, car rental firm

lougre *m* TRANSP *navire* Lr, lugger

loup *m* BOURSE, COM stag

lourd, e *adj* BOURSE *marché* heavy (*jarg*), slack, sluggish, stale, COM *charge, impôt, perte* heavy; ◆ **trop ~ du haut** COM *structuration, organisation, prix* top-heavy

lourdement *adv* COM *taxé* heavily

lourder: **~ qn** *vt infrml* RES HUM fire (*infrml*), give sb his/her cards (*infrml*), give sb the sack (*infrml*), sack (*BrE, infrml*)

loyal, e *adj* COM *personne* above board, fair, honest, trustworthy, DROIT fair

loyauté *f* COM *d'une personne* honesty, trustworthiness

loyer *m* BREVETS, DROIT rental right, IMMOB rent, rental, renting; **~ de base** IMMOB base rent (*US*); **~ brut** FISC gross rent; **~ contractuel** IMMOB contract rent; **~ économique** ECON economic rent; **~ équitable** IMMOB fair rent; **~ hebdomadaire** IMMOB weekly rent; **~ indexé** IMMOB index lease; **~ industriel** IMMOB, IND industrial rent; **~ du marché** ECON, IMMOB, POL market rent; **~ mensuel** IMMOB monthly rent, rent pcm (*BrE*), rent per calendar month (*BrE*); **~ mis aux enchères** IMMOB bid rent; **~ modéré** IMMOB fair market rent, fair rental value; **~ au mois** IMMOB monthly rent, rent pcm (*BrE*), rent per

calendar month (*BrE*); **~ monopolisé** ECON, IMMOB monopoly rent; **~ notionnel** IMMOB notional rent; **~ progressif** IMMOB graduated lease; **~ réduit** IMMOB retainer; **~ de la terre** IMMOB ground rent

loyers *m pl* FISC rentals

LPP *abrév* (*longueur entre perpendiculaires*) TRANSP *d'un navire* LBP (*length between perpendiculars*)

LTA *abrév* (*lettre de transport aérien*) IMP/EXP, TRANSP AWB (*air waybill*)

LTAU *abrév* (*lettre de transport aérien universelle*) IMP/EXP, TRANSP UAWB (*universal air waybill*)

Luanda *m* COM Luanda

lucratif, -ive *adj* COM *emploi, métier, travail* gainful, lucrative

luddisme *m* RES HUM Luddism (*UK*)

luddite *mf* RES HUM luddite

lugubre *adj* COM, ECON bleak

lumière: **~ des projecteurs** *f* COM spotlight

luminosité *f* INFO *de l'écran* brightness

lundi *m* COM Mon., Monday; **~ noir** BOURSE Black Monday

Lusaka *n pr* COM Lusaka

lutte *f* COM battle, contest, ENVIR *contre la pollution atmosphérique, des eaux, du bruit* prevention; **~ antipollution** ENVIR pollution control; **~ antipollution intégrée** ENVIR integrated pollution control, IPC; **~ biologique** ENVIR biocontrol; **~ des classes** ECON, POL class struggle; **~ contre les odeurs** ENVIR odor control (*AmE*), odour control (*BrE*); **~ pour le pouvoir** POL power struggle

lutter: **~ contre** *vt* COM *chômage, trafic de stupéfiants* combat, fight; **~ pour** COM *survie d'une société* battle for

luxe *m* V&M *marchandises* luxury; ◆ **de ~** V&M *marchandises* luxury

Luxembourg[1] *m* COM Luxembourg

Luxembourg[2] *n pr* COM Luxembourg

luxembourgeois, e *adj* COM Luxemburgian

Luxembourgeois, e *m,f* COM *habitant* Luxemburgian

LV *abrév* (*lieu de vente*) V&M POS (*point of sale*)

lycée: **~ d'enseignement professionnel** *m* (*L.E.P.*) PROT SOC secondary school for vocational training; **~ mixte** *m* PROT SOC coeducational high school

M

m *abrév (mètre)* COM m *(meter AmE, metre BrE)*

M *abrév (agrégats monétaires)* ECON M *(monetary aggregates)*

M. *abrév (Monsieur)* COM Mr *(Mister)*

Macédonie *f* COM Macedonia

macédonien, -enne *adj* COM Macedonian

Macédonien, -enne *m,f* COM *habitant* Macedonian

mâcher: ~ **le travail à** *loc* COM spoon-feed

machine *f* COM, IND, INFO machine; ~ **à additionner** COM adding machine; ~ **à adresser** COM, COMMS addressing machine; ~ **à affranchir** COMMS franking machine *(BrE)*, postage meter *(AmE)*, postal meter *(AmE)*, stamping machine; ~ **de bureau** COM business machine; ~ **à calculer** COM adding machine, calculating machine, calculator, number cruncher; ~ **à calculer électronique** INFO electronic calculator; ~ **à calculer à imprimante** COM add lister, add listing machine; ~ **de compilation** INFO source computer; ~ **comptable** COM business machine; ~ **à écrire** COM typewriter; ~ **à écrire automatique** COM automatic typewriter; ~ **à écrire les chèques** BANQUE check-writing machine *(AmE)*, cheque-writing machine *(BrE)*, FIN check writer *(AmE)*, check-writer machine *(AmE)*, cheque writer *(BrE)*, cheque-writer machine *(BrE)*; ~ **à écrire électronique** COM electronic typewriter; ~ **à écrire à mémoire** COM memory typewriter; ~ **à enseigner** PROT SOC teaching machine; ~ **à expansion mixte** TRANSP *maritime* compound expansion engine, C; ~ **à expansion simple** TRANSP *navigation* single expansion engine, S; ~ **à facturer** COM biller; ~ **de gestion** COM business machine; ~ **à imprimer les adresses** COM, COMMS addressing machine; ~ **-outil** IND machine tool; ~ **à photocopier** ADMIN, COM, COMMS copier, photocopier, photocopying machine; ~ **à quadruple expansion** TRANSP *maritime* quadruple expansion engine, Q; ~ **à signer** COM check signer *(AmE)*, check-signing machine *(AmE)*, cheque signer *(BrE)*, cheque-signing machine *(BrE)*; ~ **totalisatrice** COM totalizator, totalizer; ~ **à traitement de texte** COM, INFO word processor, WP

machines *f pl* COM, IND, INFO machinery, TRANSP *navigation* machinery, mchy; ~ **d'arrière** TRANSP *navigation* machinery aft, mchy aft; ~ **d'avant** TRANSP *navigation* machinery forward, mchy fwd

machiniste *m* RES HUM engine-room boy, junior motorman

macro:[1] ~ **-modèle économique** *m* ECON *économétrie* large-scale model

macro[2] *f* INFO macro

macro-[3] *préf* COM macro-

macrodéchet *m* ENVIR macrowaste

macroéconomie *f* (ANT *microéconomie*) ECON macroeconomics

macroéconomique *adj* (ANT *microéconomique*) ECON macroeconomic

macroenvironnement *m* COM macroenvironment

macroinformatique *f* (ANT *micro-informatique*) INFO macrocomputing

macromarketing *m* V&M macromarketing

Madagascar *f* COM Madagascar

Madame *f* COM Mrs, COMMS *en début de lettre* Dear Madam; ~ **Dupont** DROIT ≈ Jane Doe *(US)*

Mademoiselle *f* COM Miss, COMMS *en début de lettre* Dear Madam

Madrid *n pr* COM Madrid

magasin *m* COM *entrepôt* store, storehouse, warehouse, *salle pour entreposer* shop *(BrE)*, store *(AmE)*, storeroom, V&M *pour vendre* shop *(BrE)*, store *(AmE)*; ~ **d'alimentation** INFO card bin, feed bin, V&M food store; ~ **de brocante** V&M second-hand shop *(BrE)*, thrift shop *(AmE)*; ~ **au centre-ville** V&M in-town store; ~ **en dehors de la ville** V&M out-of-town store; ~ **discompte** V&M discount center *(AmE)*, discount centre *(BrE)*, discount house, discount shop *(BrE)*, discount store; ~ **discount** V&M discount center *(AmE)*, discount centre *(BrE)*, discount house, discount shop *(BrE)*, discount store; ~ **de groupage** TRANSP *conteneurs* CB *(BrE)*, container base *(BrE)*, CFS *(AmE)*, container freight station *(AmE)*; ~ **indépendant** V&M independent store; ~ **mini-marge** V&M discount house, discount shop *(BrE)*, discount store; ~ **de prestige** V&M flagship store; ~ **de proximité** V&M convenience shop *(BrE)*, convenience store *(AmE)*, corner shop *(BrE)*, corner store *(AmE)*, local shop *(BrE)*, local store *(AmE)*, neighborhood store *(AmE)*, neighbourhood shop *(BrE)*; ~ **à succursales multiples** V&M chain store; ~ **d'usine** V&M factory shop; ◆ **en** ~ COM, ECON, V&M in stock

magasinage *m* COM, IND, TRANSP storage, warehousing

magasinier *m* COM storeman, RES HUM stockman *(AmE)*, warehouseman *(AmE)*, TRANSP warehouse keeper

magazine *m* COM, MÉDIA magazine; ~ **de grande diffusion** COM *pour le grand public* consumer magazine; ~ **gratuit** MÉDIA give-away magazine; ~ **illustré** MÉDIA illustrated magazine; ~ **de luxe** MÉDIA glossy mag *(infrml)*, glossy magazine

magistrat *m* DROIT magistrate

magistrats: ~ **compétents** *m pl* DROIT magistrates entitled to adjudicate

magnat *m* COM big wheel *(infrml)*, magnate, RES

HUM tycoon; ~ **de la finance** FIN financial magnate

magnétocassette *m* COM cassette recorder

magnétophone *m* COM magnetic tape recorder, tape recorder; ~ **à cassettes** INFO cassette recorder

magnétoscope *m* COM video recorder, videocassette recorder, videotape recorder

magnétothèque *f* COM tape library

magouille *f infrml* FIN graft (*infrml*), POL graft (*infrml*), pork barrel (*US, infrml*), whipsaw (*US, jarg*)

mai *m* COM May

maigres: ~ **diversions** *f pl* COM trickle diversions (*jarg*)

mailing *m* COMMS mailing, mailing shot, mailshot, mass mailing, INFO mailing, mass mailing, V&M direct mail shot, mailing, mailing shot, mailshot, mass mailing; ◆ **faire un** ~ COMMS do a mailshot

maille: ~ **sèche** *f* TRANSP *entre deux varangues étanches* cofferdam

main: ~ **courante** *f* COM, COMPTA daybook; ~ **invisible** *f* ECON invisible hand (*jarg*); ~ **mise à court terme** *f* BOURSE short strangle; ~ **-d'oeuvre** *f* ECON, IND, RES HUM labor (*AmE*), labor force (*AmE*), labour (*BrE*), labour force (*BrE*), manpower, workforce; ~ **-d'oeuvre abstraite** *f* (ANT *main-d'oeuvre concrète*) RES HUM abstract labor (*AmE*), abstract labour (*BrE*); ~ **-d'oeuvre concrète** *f* (ANT *main-d'oeuvre abstraite*) RES HUM concrete labor (*AmE*), concrete labour (*BrE*); ~ **-d'oeuvre contractuelle** *f* RES HUM contract labor (*AmE*), contract labour (*BrE*); ~ **-d'oeuvre à coût élevé** *f* RES HUM high-cost labor (*AmE*), high-cost labour (*BrE*); ~ **-d'oeuvre directe** *f* (ANT *main-d'oeuvre indirecte*) COMPTA, ECON, RES HUM direct labor (*AmE*), direct labour (*BrE*); ~ **-d'oeuvre expérimentée** *f* RES HUM experienced workforce; ~ **-d'oeuvre exploitée** *f* RES HUM sweated labor (*AmE*), sweated labour (*BrE*); ~ **-d'oeuvre immigrée** *f* ECON migrant labor (*AmE*), migrant labour (*BrE*); ~ **-d'oeuvre improductive** *f* ECON, RES HUM unproductive labor (*AmE*), unproductive labour (*BrE*); ~ **-d'oeuvre indirecte** *f* (ANT *main-d'oeuvre directe*) COMPTA, ECON, RES HUM indirect labor (*AmE*), indirect labour (*BrE*); ~ **-d'oeuvre locale** *f* RES HUM local labor (*AmE*), local labour (*BrE*); ~ **-d'oeuvre migrante** *f* ECON migrant labor (*AmE*), migrant labour (*BrE*); ~ **-d'oeuvre non-déclarée** *f* RES HUM unregistered labor (*AmE*), unregistered labour (*BrE*); ~ **-d'oeuvre non-qualifiée** *f* ECON unskilled labor (*AmE*), unskilled labour (*BrE*), RES HUM common labor (*AmE*), common labour (*BrE*), unskilled labour (*BrE*); ~ **-d'oeuvre non-réduite** *f* RES HUM unrestricted labor (*AmE*), unrestricted labour (*BrE*); ~ **-d'oeuvre non-spécialisée** *f* ECON, RES HUM unskilled labor (*AmE*), unskilled labour (*BrE*); ~ **-d'oeuvre non-syndiquée** *f* RES

HUM nonunion labor (*AmE*), nonunion labour (*BrE*); ~ **-d'oeuvre occasionnelle** *f* RES HUM casual labor (*AmE*), casual labour (*BrE*); ~ **-d'oeuvre productive** *f* ECON, RES HUM productive labor (*AmE*), productive labour (*BrE*); ~ **-d'oeuvre professionnelle** *f* ECON, RES HUM skilled labor (*AmE*), skilled labour (*BrE*); ~ **-d'oeuvre qualifiée** *f* RES HUM skilled labor (*AmE*), skilled labour (*BrE*); ~ **-d'oeuvre de remplacement** *f* RES HUM replacement labor force (*AmE*), replacement labour force (*BrE*); ~ **-d'oeuvre sans emploi** *f* RES HUM unemployed labor force (*AmE*), unemployed labour force (*BrE*); ~ **-d'oeuvre spécialisée** *f* ECON semiskilled labor (*AmE*), semiskilled labour (*BrE*), RES HUM skilled labor (*AmE*), skilled labour (*BrE*); ~ **-d'oeuvre syndiquée** *f* RES HUM organized labor (*AmE*), organized labour (*BrE*); ~ **-d'oeuvre temporaire** *f* RES HUM casual labor (*AmE*), casual labour (*BrE*); ~ **visible** *f* ECON visible hand; ◆ **à la** ~ COM, INFO manually; **en** ~ COM in hand; **en** ~ **tierce** COM in the hands of a third party

mainlevée: ~ **de saisie** *f* DROIT replevin

mains: **en** ~ **propres** *f pl* COM clean hands (*jarg*); ~ **propres** *f pl* COM clean hands (*jarg*)

maintenance *f* COM, IND, INFO maintenance, service; ~ **préventive** ADMIN, COM, GESTION, IND preventative maintenance, preventive maintenance

mainteneur: ~ **de marché** *m* BOURSE market maker (*UK*)

maintenir 1. *vt* COM abide by, *les marges* hold, COMMS maintain, DROIT uphold, ECON, FIN *les marges* hold; **2.** *v pron* **se** ~ **à la page** COM keep up to date, COM *normes* keep up with; ◆ ~ **artificiellement le prix de** COM *marchandises* valorize; ~ **à flot** COM *affaire* keep afloat; ~ **à jour** ADMIN *dossiers* keep up to date; ~ **le marché** BOURSE make a market; ~ **un profil bas** COM keep a low profile; **se** ~ **au même niveau que** COM keep pace with, keep up with

maintien *m* FISC upkeep; ~ **artificiel** COM *des prix* valorization; ~ **des prix** COM, V&M price maintenance; ~ **du prix de revente** ECON, FIN resale price maintenance, RPM, V&M retail price maintenance, RPM

mairie *f* ADMIN, POL town hall

maison¹ *adj* COM *traducteur, rédacteur* in-company, in-house, INFO *système* in-house

maison² *f* BOURSE establishment, firm, house, ECON concern, IMMOB house; ~ **d'acceptation** BANQUE acceptance house; ~ **d'achat étrangère** IMP/EXP foreign buying house; ~ **d'arbitrage** BOURSE arbitrage house; ~ **bancaire** BANQUE, FIN banking house; ~ **de banque** BANQUE banking establishment; ~ **de commerce** COM business concern, business house, commercial establishment; ~ **de commission** BOURSE commission house; ~ **de courtage** BOURSE brokerage firm, brokerage house, broking house, commission house, stock brokerage firm, *profession* brokerage; ~ **de couture** COM fashion house; ~ **de début** IMMOB starter home; ~ **de disque** MÉDIA label (*jarg*), record company; ~ **d'édition** MÉDIA publishing company, publishing firm, publishing house; ~ **d'exportation** IMP/EXP export company, export firm, export house; ~ **de gros** COM wholesale business, wholesale company, wholesale firm; ~ **individuelle** *Can (cf maison unifamiliale Fra)* COM single-family home (*AmE*), single-family house (*BrE*); ~ **jumelée** *(SYN maisonnette)* IMMOB duplex (*AmE*), semi-detached house (*BrE*); ~ **mère** ADMIN front office, COM main branch; ~ **mobile** IMMOB mobile home; ~ **de santé** PROT SOC nursing home; ~ **témoin** IMMOB show house; ~ **de titres** BOURSE house, securities company, securities firm, securities house; ~ **unifamiliale** *Fra (cf maison individuelle Can)* COM single-family home (*AmE*), single-family house (*BrE*); ~ **de vente par correspondance** V&M *entreprise* mail-order business, mail-order company, mail-order firm

maisonnette *f (SYN maison jumelée)* IMMOB duplex (*AmE*), semi-detached house (*BrE*)

maistrance *f* RES HUM, TRANSP petty officers

maître: ~ **d'hôtel** *m* RES HUM *dans restaurant* head waiter, *dans maison privée* porter; ~ **d'oeuvre** *m* COM prime contractor

maîtrise *f* COM first-line management, master's degree, GESTION, RES HUM first-line management, middle management, supervision, supervisory management; ~ **des coûts** COMPTA cost control; ~ **de gestion des entreprises** PROT SOC ≈ MBA, ≈ Master of Business Administration; ~ **de sciences** COM ≈ MSc, ≈ Master of Science; ~ **en sciences économiques** COM ≈ MCom, ≈ Master of Commerce, *diplôme* ≈ MEcon, ≈ Master of Economics; ~ **technique** COM technical mastery

maîtriser *vt* COM *demande, inflation* contain, ECON bring under control, hold in check; ♦ ~ **les coûts** COM control costs, keep costs under control

Major: le ~ **Market Index** *m* BOURSE Major Market Index

majoration *f* COM overcharge, OC, COMPTA grossing up, FISC gross-up, V&M overcharge, OC, *hausse du prix* increase, mark-up; ~ **d'âge** ASSUR addition to age; ~ **de dividende** ASSUR dividend addition; ~ **des dividendes** BOURSE dividend gross-up; ~ **exorbitante des prix** COM banker's ramp (*jarg*), ramp (*UK, infrml*); ~ **de prix** COM, COMPTA, ECON, FIN, V&M increase in prices, price increase, price rise, rise in prices; ~ **de retard** FISC penalty for late tax payment

majorer *vt* ASSUR load, COM *prix* hike, increase, jack up (*infrml*), mark up, V&M *prix* increase, jack up (*infrml*), mark up

majorité *f* COM *des voix*, DROIT *âge*, POL majority; ~ **absolue** POL absolute majority; ~ **innovatrice** V&M *marketing* early majority (*jarg*); ~ **qualifiée** COM, POL qualified majority; ~ **silencieuse** POL

silent majority; ~ **simple** POL simple majority; ~ **tardive** V&M *marketing* late majority (*jarg*)

majuscule *f (*ANT *minuscule)* ADMIN, INFO capital letter, u.c., upper case, upper-case letter

makuta *m pl* COM makuta

mal:[1] ~ **payé** *adj* RES HUM badly paid, low-paid, poorly paid

mal[2] *adv* COM badly

mal:[3] ~ **des organisations** *m* GESTION, RES HUM organizational pathology; ~ **tutélaire** *m* ECON demerit good, merit bad

mal:[4] ~ **administrer** *vt* FIN, GESTION mismanage; ~ **appliquer** DROIT misapply; ~ **calculer** COM, COMPTA, ECON, FIN, MATH, V&M miscalculate; ~ **classer** COM misfile; ~ **gérer** FIN, GESTION mismanage; ~ **représenter** COM, FISC misrepresent

Malabo *n pr* COM Malabo

maladie: ~ **hollandaise** *f* ECON Dutch disease; ~ **professionnelle** *f* RES HUM industrial disease, occupational disease, occupational illness; ~ **de travail** *f* RES HUM industrial disease, occupational disease, occupational illness

malais[1]**, e** *adj* COM Malaysian

malais[2] *m* COM *langue* Malay

malaise: ~ **social** *m* RES HUM industrial unrest, labor unrest (*AmE*), labour unrest (*BrE*)

Malaisie *f* COM Malaysia

Malaisien, -enne *m,f* COM *habitant* Malaysian

Malawi *m* COM Malawi

malawien, -enne *adj* COM Malawian

Malawien, -enne *m,f* COM *habitant* Malawian

Maldives[1] *f pl* COM Maldives

Maldives:[2] **des** ~ *adj* COM Maldivian

Malé *n pr* COM Malé

malentendu *m* COM misapprehension, misunderstanding

malfaçon *f* COM *défaut* bad deal, defect, fault

malgache[1] *adj* COM Madagascan

malgache[2] *m* COM *langue* Malagasy

Malgache *mf* COM *habitant* Madagascan

malgré: ~ **mes/tes/ses préférences** *loc* COM contra preferentem (*frml*)

malheureusement *adv* COM regretfully, unfortunately

malhonnête *adj* COM dishonest

Mali *m* COM Mali

malien, -enne *adj* COM Malian

Malien, -enne *m,f* COM *habitant* Malian

malle: ~ **diplomatique** *f* ADMIN Diplomatic Service Post

maltais[1]**, e** *adj* COM Maltese

maltais[2] *m* COM *langue* Maltese

Maltais, e *m,f* COM *habitant* Maltese

Malte *f* COM Malta

management *m* ADMIN, COM, ECON, GESTION business management, management; ~ **baladeur** GESTION management by walking around,

MBWA; ~ **directif** GESTION, V&M lead management; ~ **intuitif** GESTION intuitive management; ~ **participatif** GESTION, RES HUM multiple-management plan

manager *m* GESTION, RES HUM manager, mgr

Managua *n pr* COM Managua

Manama *n pr* COM Manama

manat *m* COM manat

manche: ~ **à balai** *m* INFO joystick

manchette *f* MÉDIA *journaux* banner headline, head, headline, heads, splash, streamer

mandarin *m* COM *langue* Mandarin; ~ **politique** POL mandarin

mandat *m* BANQUE money order (*AmE*), postal note (*Aus*), postal order (*BrE*), COM com., commission, mandate, *d'un comité* terms of reference, COMPTA order to pay, payment order, written order to pay, DROIT authority, mandate, FIN money order (*AmE*), postal note (*Aus*), postal order (*BrE*), POL warrant; ~ **apparent** DROIT apparent authority; ~ **d'audit** COMPTA, FIN audit engagement; ~ **de banque** BANQUE bank postbill; ~ **de l'étranger** BANQUE foreign money order; ~ **international** BANQUE international money order, world money order; ~ **de paiement international** BANQUE international money draft; ~ **de perquisition** DROIT search warrant; ~ **postal** (*MP*) BANQUE, FIN money order (*AmE*), postal note (*Aus*), postal order (*BrE*); ~ **postal télégraphe** FIN telegraph money order, telegraphic money order, TMO; ~ **postal télégraphique** BANQUE, FIN telegraph money order, telegraphic money order, TMO; ~ **spécial** POL special warrant

mandataire *mf* BREVETS representative, COM authorized agent, DROIT attorney (*US*), authorized agent, proxy, representative, RES HUM authorized representative, V&M agent; ~ **spécial** *m* DROIT attorney-in-fact (*US*)

mandater *vt* ADMIN, BANQUE, COM commission; ♦ ~ **des frais** BANQUE, FIN pay expenses by money order

manette: ~ **de jeux** *f* INFO joystick

manier *vt* COM *objets* handle

manière: ~ **d'opérer** *f* COM modus operandi (*frml*); ♦ **c'est la** ~ **habituelle de procéder** COM it is standard practice, it is standard practice to do so; **de** ~ **prononcée** COM *monter, tomber* sharply

manifestation *f* COM demonstration; ~ **d'intérêt** BOURSE indication of interest

manifeste[1] *adj* COM obvious, *signal* strong

manifeste[2] *m* IMP/EXP manifest, TRANSP manifest, ship's manifest; ~ **d'entrée** IMP/EXP clearance inwards; ~ **de fret** TRANSP freight manifest; ~ **de marchandises** IMP/EXP, TRANSP cargo manifest, manifest of cargo; ~ **de marchandises pour conteneurs** IMP/EXP, TRANSP container import cargo manifest; ~ **des passagers** TRANSP passenger manifest; ~ **de sortie** IMP/EXP clearance

outwards; ~ **de transfert** TRANSP transfer manifest

manille *f* TRANSP *manutention* clutch hook, shackle

Manille *n pr* COM Manila

manipulateur, -trice *m,f* BOURSE, COM manipulator

manipulation *f* BOURSE rigging, COM, GESTION manipulation; ~ **de données** INFO data handling; ~ **de l'information** INFO information handling; ~ **de marchés** BOURSE market rigging; ~ **des prix** BOURSE stock jobbery (*UK*)

manipulé, e *adj* BOURSE whipsawed (*jarg*)

manipuler *vt* COM, COMPTA manipulate; ♦ ~ **les chiffres** COMPTA, FIN manipulate the figures, massage the figures; ~ **les cours à la hausse** BOURSE kite; ~ **le marché** BOURSE rig the market

mannequin *m* COM fashion model, model

manoeuvre[1] *m* RES HUM laborer (*AmE*), labourer (*BrE*), unskilled worker

manoeuvre[2] *f* COM maneuver (*AmE*), manoeuvre (*BrE*); ~ **frauduleuse** FISC *fraude fiscale* scheme

manoeuvres[1] *m pl* RES HUM simple labor (*AmE*), simple labour (*BrE*)

manoeuvres:[2] ~ **dilatoires** *f pl* COM delaying tactics; ~ **frauduleuses** *f pl* DROIT illegal practices

manomètre: ~ **pour pneus** *m* TRANSP tire gage (*AmE*), tyre gauge (*BrE*)

manquant[1] *adj* COM *marchandises* missing, *personnel* absent; ~ **à l'embarquement** TRANSP short-shipped

manquant[2] *m* FIN, IMP/EXP ullage

manquant[3] **-e** *m,f* COM *personne* absentee

manquants *m pl* COM, COMPTA *marchandises* shortages

manque[1] *m* COM deficiency, shortfall, *de capital ou de fonds* absence, COMPTA shortfall, RES HUM *de main-d'oeuvre* shortage, TRANSP shortfall; ~ **de bol** *infrml* COM bad break (*infrml*), bad luck; ~ **de communication** COM, COMMS communication gap; ~ **de dollars** BOURSE dollar shortage; ~ **à gagner** COM shortfall in earnings; ~ **de liquidités** BANQUE, COM liquidity crisis; ~ **en magasin** V&M o.s., out of stock; ~ **de main-d'oeuvre** RES HUM undermanning; ~ **de personnel** COM shortage of staff, staff shortage, RES HUM undermanning, understaffing; ~ **de pot** *infrml* COM bad break (*infrml*), bad luck

manque:[2] **qui** ~ **de personnel** *loc* RES HUM understaffed

manquement *m* DROIT breach; ~ **au devoir** DROIT breach of duty, dereliction of duty; ~ **à la discipline** RES HUM misconduct; ~ **grave à la discipline** RES HUM gross misconduct

manquer *vt* COM *occasion, rendez-vous* miss; ~ **de** COM be lacking in, be short of, low on, lack, COM be unaccounted for, FIN be wanting; ♦ ~ **de cohérence** COM be lacking in consistency, lack consistency; ~ **d'expérience** RES HUM be unfledged, be wet behind the ears (*infrml*), lack experience; ~ **de personnel** RES HUM be short-staffed, be undermanned, be understaffed; ~ **à une règle** COM break a rule, violate a rule; ~ **à son devoir** COM fail in one's duty

manuel[1], **-elle** adj COM, IND, RES HUM manual

manuel[2] m COM guide, handbook, manual, MÉDIA textbook; ~ **du code des comptes** COMPTA coding manual; ~ **d'utilisation** COM instruction book, instruction manual, instructions

manuellement adv COM, INFO manually

manufacturé, e adj COM, IND manufactured, mfd

manuscrit[1], **e** adj COMMS handwritten

manuscrit[2] m COMMS handwriting, FISC manuscript

manutention f COM, TRANSP des marchandises handling, hdlg, materials handling; ~ **des bagages** TRANSP baggage handling; ~ **horizontale** TRANSP ro/ro, roll on/roll off; ~ **horizontale et verticale** TRANSP ro/lo, roll on/roll off-lift on/lift off; ~ **modulaire et automatisée de conteneurs** TRANSP modular automated container handling, MACH; ~ **par chariot latéral** TRANSP side frame handling; ~ **verticale** TRANSP lift on/lift off, lo/lo

manutentionnaire mf RES HUM checker

Maputo n pr COM Maputo

maquette f V&M publicité model, visual

maquignonnage m IND, POL horse trading, sharp practice

maquillage m BANQUE d'un chèque falsification, falsifying, COM d'un document faking, COMPTA de chiffres, DROIT d'un témoignage falsification, falsifying; ~ **du bilan** BANQUE, COM, COMPTA, FIN window-dressing; ~ **des comptes** BOURSE window-dressing

maquiller vt BANQUE chèque falsify, COM document fake, COMPTA chiffres, DROIT témoignage falsify

maraîchage m ECON market gardening (BrE), truck farming (AmE)

maraîcher, -ère m,f ECON market gardener (BrE), truck farmer (AmE)

marasme m ECON slack, slump, stagnation; ♦ **dans le ~** COM, ECON in the doldrums

marathon: ~ **budgétaire** m POL Budget purdah (UK)

marchand[1], **e** adj COM commercial, tradeable, ECON tradeable, V&M marketable

marchand[2], **e** m,f RES HUM mcht, merchant, V&M dealer, trader; ~ **ambulant** COM hawker, pedlar, street trader (BrE), street vendor (AmE); ~ **de biens** IMMOB estate agent (BrE), realtor (AmE); ~ **de fonds** IMMOB estate agent (BrE), realtor (AmE); ~ **de journaux** V&M dans la rue news vendor, dans un magasin newsagent; ~ **de journaux-buraliste** V&M confectioner, newsagent and tobacconist, CTN; ~ **de produits d'utilisation finale** IMP/EXP end use trader; ~ **de vins** RES HUM wine merchant

marchandage m COM, V&M bargaining, haggling

marchander 1. vt COM, V&M bargain over, haggle about, haggle over; ~ **sur** COM, V&M haggle about, haggle over, COM, V&M bargain, bargain down, haggle; **2.** vi ~ **avec qn** COM bargain with sb, haggle with sb

marchandisage m V&M merchandising

marchandise f BOURSE, COM, ECON, IND cmdty, commodity; ~ **disponible** BOURSE spot commodity; ~ **non-essentielle** ECON nonbasic commodity; ~ **réglementée** BOURSE controlled commodity (UK), regulated commodity

marchandises f pl COM, ECON commodities, goods, wares, TRANSP cargo, freight, frt, goods, V&M merchandise; ~ **à l'arrivée** COM incoming goods; ~ **commerciales** TRANSP commercial cargo; ~ **communautaires** IMP/EXP Community goods; ~ **consignées** COM returnable goods; ~ **de consommation ou services** FISC consumer goods or services; ~ **de contrebande** FISC, IMP/EXP contraband; ~ **couvertes par un certificat** COM goods covered by warrant; ~ **au cubage** TRANSP measurement goods; ~ **dangereuses** TRANSP dangerous cargo, hazardous cargo; ~ **à densité élevée** (ANT marchandises à faible densité) TRANSP high cube, high-density cargo, high-density freight; ~ **détaxées** FISC duty-free goods (UK); ~ **diverses** TRANSP general cargo, GC; ~ **diverses non-unitisées** TRANSP break bulk, break bulk cargo; ~ **emballées** TRANSP package goods; ~ **encombrantes** TRANSP bulky cargo; ~ **d'encombrement** TRANSP measurement goods; ~ **entreposées sous douane** COM, FISC, IMP/EXP, IND, TRANSP b/g, bonded cargo, bonded goods; ~ **à l'essai** COM goods on approval; ~ **exclues** TRANSP cargo shut-out, shut-out, shut-out cargo; ~ **à faible densité** (ANT marchandises à densité élevée) TRANSP low cube, low-density cargo, low-density freight; ~ **à faibles droits douaniers** IMP/EXP commissary goods; ~ **de gros** COM wholesale goods; ~ **en gros** COM wholesale goods; ~ **homogènes** TRANSP homogeneous cargo; ~ **hors taxes** FISC duty-free goods (UK); ~ **importées** IMP/EXP imported goods; ~ **isolées** TRANSP cargo in isolation; ~ **légères** TRANSP measurement freight, cargaison light cargo; ~ **liquides** BOURSE wet goods; ~ **livrables à terme** COM future goods; ~ **lourdes** COM, TRANSP deadweight cargo; ~ **manquantes** TRANSP missing cargo, msca, short shipment; ~ **mixtes** TRANSP general merchandise; ~ **non-conteneurisables** TRANSP uncontainerable goods, UNCON; ~ **non-déclarées** TRANSP unmanifested cargo; ~ **non-homogènes** TRANSP heterogeneous cargo; ~ **périssables** ECON, IND, V&M nondurable goods; ~ **physiques** BOURSE actuals; ~ **prohibées** COM, DROIT, IMP/EXP prohibited goods; ~ **de provenance étrangère** COM goods of foreign origin; ~ **de qualité** COM quality goods; ~ **à la réception** COM incoming goods; ~ **à réexporter** IMP/EXP goods for re-export; ~ **reprises** COM returned goods; ~ **retournées** COM returned goods;

~ **sèches** TRANSP dry cargo, dry freight; ~ **sous douane** COM, FISC, IMP/EXP, IND, TRANSP b/g, bonded cargo, bonded goods; ~ **à terme** BOURSE commodity futures; ~ **vérifiées** COM ascertained goods; ~ **volumineuses** TRANSP bulky cargo; ~ **en vrac** TRANSP bulk cargo, loose cargo, bulk commodity, bulk goods, V&M bulky goods

marche: ~ **arrière** *f* COM back-pedaling (*AmE*), back-pedalling (*BrE*), backtracking; ~ **erratique** *f* BOURSE random walk; ~ **d'essai** *f* TRANSP test drive; ◆ **en** ~ COM under way, INFO *machine* up (*infrml*); **faire** ~ **arrière** COM *plan, engagement* backtrack

marché *m* BOURSE market, sideways market, COM commercial market, market, *contrat* bargain, deal, ECON market, V&M bargain, market; ~ **accéléré** BOURSE fast market; ~ **des acceptations** BANQUE acceptance market; ~ **acheteur** (ANT *marché vendeur*) BOURSE, ECON, IMMOB, V&M buyer's market; ~ **actif** BOURSE brisk trading, broad market, swimming market, ECON swimming market; ~ **des actions** BOURSE, FIN equity market; ~ **des actions nationales** BOURSE Domestic Equities Market, DEM; ~ **des adjudications** BOURSE auction market; ~ **ample** BOURSE broad market; ~ **animé** BOURSE active dealings, active market, active trading, brisk market, brisk trading; ~ **après bourse** BOURSE evening trade; ~ **arrivé à la maturité** V&M mature market; ~ **artificiellement soutenu** BOURSE technical market; ~ **de l'assurance** ASSUR insurance market; ~ **des assurances** ASSUR insurance market; ~ **atone** BOURSE, ECON shallow market; ~ **à la baisse** (ANT *marché à la hausse*) BOURSE bear market, bearish market, buyer's market, ECON, IMMOB buyer's market; ~ **en baisse** BOURSE declining market, soft market, weak market; ~ **baissier** (ANT *marché haussier*) BOURSE bear market, bearish market, buyer's market; ~ **baissier sans issue** BOURSE graveyard market; ~ **blanc** ECON white market; ~ **bloqué** BOURSE locked market; ~ **boursier** BOURSE securities exchange, stock market; ~ **des capitaux** BOURSE, FIN capital market, financial market; ~ **captif** V&M captive market; ~ **des certificats de dépôt** BANQUE certificate of deposit market; ~ **des changes** FIN currency market, foreign exchange market; ~ **cible** V&M target market; ~ **ciblé sur les jeunes** V&M teenage market; ~ **de compensation** ECON clearing market; ~ **au comptant** BOURSE cash bargain, cash market, option bargain, physical market, spot market; ~ **conditionnel** ASSUR contingent market; ~ **confus et non-transparent** BOURSE disorderly market; ~ **de la consommation** V&M consumer market; ~ **des conteneurs** TRANSP container market; ~ **en continu** BOURSE continuous market; ~ **continu** BOURSE all-day trading; ~ **des contrats à terme sur indice** BOURSE stock index futures market; ~ **à court terme** BOURSE short, short market; ~ **du**

crédit COM credit market, FIN loan market; ~ **du crédit à la consommation** BANQUE, FIN consumer credit market; ~ **à découvert** BOURSE short market; ~ **en déport** BOURSE inverted market; ~ **des devises au comptant** ECON, FIN spot currency market; ~ **des devises principales** ECON, FIN major foreign exchange market; ~ **des disponibilités** BOURSE liquid market; ~ **à double prime à court terme** BOURSE short straddle; ~ **à double tendance** BOURSE two-sided market; ~ **d'échanges croisés** BOURSE swap market; ~ **des effets acceptés** BANQUE acceptance market; ~ **efficient** ECON efficient market; ~ **des émissions** BOURSE issue market; ~ **de l'emploi** ECON, RES HUM labor market (*AmE*), labour market (*BrE*); ~ **des emplois non déclarés** RES HUM secondary labor market (*AmE*), secondary labour market (*BrE*); ~ **aux enchères** BOURSE auction market; ~ **épuisé** BOURSE sold-out market; ~ **d'escompte** FIN discount market; ~ **de l'escompte** BOURSE bill market; ~ **étranger** BOURSE foreign section, COM external market, ECON, V&M foreign market, overseas market; ~ **étroit** BOURSE narrow market, thin market, tight market, ECON, V&M limited market; ~ **des euro-obligations** ECON Eurobond market; ~ **des eurodevises** BOURSE Eurocurrency market; ~ **de l'eurodollar** BOURSE, ECON, FIN Eurodollar market; ~ **exploité** V&M developed market; ~ **à l'exportation** ECON, IMP/EXP export market; ~ **extérieur** COM external market, ECON overseas market, V&M foreign market, overseas market; ~ **des facteurs de production** ECON, IND factor market; ~ **falsifié** (SYN *marché sophistiqué*) BOURSE sophisticated market; ~ **favorable aux vendeurs** ECON seller's market; ~ **ferme** COM firm deal; ~ **figé** BOURSE locked market; ~ **financier** BOURSE, FIN capital market, equity market, financial market, financial marketplace; ~ **financier international** ECON, FIN global financial market; ~ **financier à terme** BOURSE financial futures market; ~ **à fort volume** BOURSE broad market; ~ **fragmenté** COM, ECON fragmented market; ~ **du fret** BOURSE freight market; ~ **du fret à terme** BOURSE freight futures market; ~ **de futures et d'options de marchandises** BOURSE commodity market; ~ **générique** V&M generic market; ~ **des gilts** BOURSE gilt-edged market; ~ **de gré à gré** BOURSE, ECON OTC market (*US*), over-the-counter market (*US*), OTCM (*US*); ~ **gris** BOURSE gray market (*AmE*), grey market (*BrE*); ~ **grisâtre** BOURSE gray market (*AmE*), grey market (*BrE*); ~ **de gros** COM wholesale market; ~ **à la hausse** (ANT *marché à la baisse*) BOURSE bull market, bullish market, seller's market, ECON, IMMOB, V&M seller's market; ~ **haussier** (ANT *marché baissier*) BOURSE bull market, bullish market, seller's market; ~ **hésitant** BOURSE hesitant market; ~ **homogène** V&M homogeneous market; ~ **hors bourse** BOURSE curb market (*AmE*), kerb market (*BrE*), BOURSE after-hours market; ~ **hors cote** BOURSE OTC market (*US*), over-the-counter market (*US*), OTCM (*US*), no market, ECON OTC market (*US*), over-the-counter market (*US*), OTCM (*US*); ~ **hors séance** (SYN *marché hors bourse*) BOURSE after-hours market; ~ **hypothécaire** COM mortgage market; ~ **de l'immobilier** IMMOB property market, real estate market; ~ **imparfait** ECON, V&M imperfect market; ~ **indécis** BOURSE sideways market; ~ **inégal** ECON *commerce international* unequal trade; ~ **instable** BOURSE sensitive market, unsettled market; ~ **interbancaire** ECON interbank market; ~ **intérieur** ECON domestic market, home market, internal market, V&M domestic market; ~ **intérieur des valeurs mobilières** BOURSE domestic securities market; ~ **des intermédiaires** BOURSE intercompany market; ~ **international des actions** BOURSE International Equities Market, IEM; ~ **international des capitaux** BOURSE International Equities Market, IEM; ~ **international des options** BOURSE International Options Market, IOM; ~ **international du pétrole** BOURSE International Petroleum Exchange (*UK*), IPE (*UK*); ~ **interne du travail** ECON, POL internal labor market (*AmE*), internal labour market (*BrE*); ~ **d'investissement agréé** BOURSE designated investment exchange (*UK*), recognized investment exchange, RIE; ~ **irrégulier** BOURSE irregular market; ~ **libre** BOURSE open position, COM, ECON, POL, V&M free market, open market; ~ **de libre entreprise** ECON, POL, V&M free enterprise market; ~ **libre et ouvert** ECON, V&M free and open market; ~ **liquide** BOURSE liquid market; ~ **du logement** IMMOB, V&M housing market; ~ **manipulé** BOURSE rigged market; ~ **manquant** ECON missing market; ~ **marginal** BOURSE, V&M fringe market; ~ **de matières premières** BOURSE commodity market; ~ **des messageries** COMMS, TRANSP parcels market; ~ **des métaux** BOURSE metal market; ~ **des métaux précieux** BOURSE bullion market; ~ **à moitié au noir** ECON semiblack market; ~ **mondial** ECON, POL world market; ~ **monétaire** BOURSE money market, money mart, short-term market, ECON money market, money mart, open market, FIN money market, money mart, POL open market; ~ **monétaire à court terme** BOURSE short-term money market; ~ **monétaire de gros** FIN wholesale money market; ~ **monétaire national** ECON, FIN domestic money market; ~ **morose** BOURSE, ECON soft market; ~ **mort** BOURSE graveyard market; ~ **noir** ECON, V&M black market; ~ **non-homogène** COM, ECON fragmented market; ~ **obligataire** BOURSE bond market; ~ **des obligations nationales** (SYN *marché des obligations Yankee*) BOURSE Yankee bond market (*US*); ~ **des obligations à taux fixe** FIN straights market; ~ **des obligations Yankee** (SYN *marché des obligations nationales*) BOURSE Yankee bond market (*US*); ~ **de l'occasion** COM *marché de revente* second-hand market; ~ **officiel** ECON controlled market, official market; ~ **des opérations de change à terme** BOURSE forward

exchange market; ~ **à options** BOURSE options market, OM; ~ **à options international** BOURSE International Options Market, IOM; ~ **des options sur obligations** BOURSE bond options market; ~ **de l'or** ECON, FIN gold market; ~ **ordonné** *jarg* BOURSE, ECON orderly market; ~ **orienté à la baisse** (ANT *marché orienté à la hausse*) BOURSE bear market, bearish market, buyer's market; ~ **orienté à la hausse** (ANT *marché orienté à la baisse*) BOURSE bull market, bullish market, seller's market; ~ **ouvert 24 heures sur 24** BOURSE twenty-four hour trading; ~ **parallèle** BOURSE gray market (*AmE*), grey market (*BrE*); ~ **parfait** ECON perfect market; ~ **peu actif** BOURSE, ECON shallow market, soft market; ~ **en pleine maturité** BOURSE mature market; ~ **des prêts aux entreprises** BANQUE, FIN corporate lending market; ~ **primaire** BOURSE, ECON primary market, primary market area; ~ **à prime** BOURSE cash bargain, option bargain; ~ **à primes international** BOURSE International Options Market, IOM; ~ **privé** COM, DROIT private contract; ~ **des produits de grande consommation** V&M consumer market; ~ **public** COM, DROIT, ECON public contract, public procurement contract; ~ **de qualité** V&M *marketing* quality market; ~ **qui se raffermit** COM, V&M hardening market; ~ **qui se rétrécit** COM shrinking market; ~ **régional** V&M regional market; ~ **réglementé** FIN regulated market; ~ **de remplacement** COM replacement market; ~ **restreint** ECON restricted market; ~ **de la revente** V&M resale market, reseller market; ~ **secondaire** BOURSE after market, secondary market, ECON secondary market; ~ **sensible** BOURSE sensitive market; ~ **serré** BOURSE tight market; ~ **des services** ASSUR residential service contract; ~ **des services publics** COM public service contract; ~ **sophistiqué** (SYN *marché falsifié*) BOURSE sophisticated market; ~ **des swaps** BOURSE swap market; ~ **technique** BOURSE technical market; ~ **tendanciel** V&M market potential; ~ **à terme** BOURSE *bourse* account market, futures market, settlement market, terminal market, forward market, *contrat* bargain for the account, settlement bargain, time bargain; ~ **à terme de devises** BOURSE currency futures market, forward exchange market; ~ **à terme d'instruments financiers de Paris** FIN Paris financial futures market; ~ **à terme des matières premières** BOURSE commodity futures market; ~ **à terme sur les valeurs de transport** BOURSE freight futures market; ~ **à terme de titres financiers** BOURSE financial futures market; ~ **-test** V&M market test; ~ **trafiqué à la hausse** BOURSE rigged market; ~ **de transit** ECON, FIN transit market; ~ **du travail** ECON, RES HUM job market, labor market (*AmE*), labour market (*BrE*); ~ **du travail externe** ECON external labor market (*AmE*), external labour market (*BrE*); ~ **du travail primaire** ECON primary labor market (*AmE*), primary labour market (*BrE*); ~ **du travail**

régional ECON local labor market (*AmE*), local labour market (*BrE*); ~ **unique** BOURSE, ECON, POL *de l'UE*, V&M Single Market; ~ **unique du travail** RES HUM single labor market (*AmE*), single labour market (*BrE*), SLM; ~ **des valeurs en espèces** BOURSE bullion market; ~ **de valeurs mobilières** FIN securities market; ~ **des valeurs non-cotées** BOURSE Unlisted Securities Market (*UK*), USM (*UK*); ~ **des valeurs de premier ordre** BOURSE gilt-edged market, gilts market; ~ **des valeurs à revenu fixe** COM fixed income securities market; ~ **des valeurs de transport** BOURSE freight market; ~ **vendeur** (ANT *marché acheteur*) BOURSE, ECON, IMMOB, V&M seller's market; ~ **de vente à la criée** BOURSE outcry market; ~ **des voyages d'affaires** COM, TRANSP business travel market; ~ **voyageurs** TRANSP passenger market; ◆ ~ **effondré** BOURSE bottom dropped out (*jarg*), BDO; **faire des ~s à court terme** BOURSE be short in futures; **faire des ~s à long terme** BOURSE be long in futures; **faire mieux que le ~** BOURSE outperform the market; **faire un ~ au comptant** BOURSE bargain for cash; **faire un ~ à terme** BOURSE bargain for account; **le ~ s'est effondré** COM the bottom has dropped out of the market, the bottom has fallen out of the market; **le ~ est rompu** COM the deal is off

Marché: ~ **des bons du Trésor américain** BOURSE US Treasury bond market; ~ **boursier de Kansas City** BOURSE Kansas city board of trade, KCBT; ~ **commercial à options de Londres** BOURSE London Traded Options Market, London Trader Options Market; ~ **commun** *m* ECON Common Market, CM; ~ **commun d'Amérique centrale** *m* (*MCAC*) ECON Central American Common Market (*CACM*); ~ **Commun Andin** *m* ECON Andean Common Market, ACM; ~ **commun des Caraïbes orientales** *m* ECON East Caribbean Common Market, ECCM; ~ **commun du cône sud** *m* ECON *commerce international* Mercosur; ~ **du coton de New-York** *m* BOURSE New York Cotton Exchange (*US*); ~ **en coulisse** BOURSE, FIN Third Market (*UK, obs*); ~ **hors cote de New York** *m* BOURSE New York Curb Exchange (*US*); ~ **interbancaire des options sur devises de Londres** BOURSE London Interbank Currency Options Market, LICOM; ~ **interprofessionnel européen** *m* BOURSE European Interprofessional Market, EIM; ~ **monétaire international** *m* (*MMI*) BOURSE, ECON International Monetary Market (*IMM*); ~ **des obligations du Trésor américain** BOURSE US Treasury bond market; ~ **des options négociables de Paris** *m* (*MONEP*) BOURSE Paris traded options exchange, ≈ Chicago Board Options Exchange (*US*), ≈ London International Financial Futures Exchange (*UK*); ~ **des options négociants de Londres** *m* BOURSE London Traded Options Market, London Trader Options Market, LTOM; ~ **à terme d'instruments financiers** *m* (*MATIF*) *France* BOURSE financial futures market, ≈ Australian Financial Futures Market, ≈ Chicago Board of Trade (*US*), ≈ London International Financial Futures Exchange (*UK*); ~ **à terme de New-York** *m* BOURSE New York Futures Exchange (*US*), NYFE (*US*); ~ **des transactions à terme de New York** *m* BOURSE New York Futures Exchange (*US*), NYFE (*US*); ~ **du Trésor américain** FIN US Treasury market; ~ **unique européen** *m* BOURSE, ECON, POL, V&M European Single Market, Single European Market

marcher *vi* COM go well; ◆ ~ **avec son temps** COM be abreast of the times, keep abreast of the times; **faire ~** COM actuate, carry on; **faire ~ l'affaire** COM run the show

marchés: ~ **d'options** *m pl* BOURSE options exchanges; ~ **organisés** *m pl* COM, ECON, V&M organized markets; ~ **publics** *m pl* COM public procurement

mardi *m* COM Tues., Tuesday

marée: ~ **basse** *f* TRANSP low tide, low water, lw; ~ **descendante** *f* TRANSP ebb tide; ~ **de ME** *f* (*marée de morte-eau*) TRANSP neap tide; ~ **de morte-eau** *f* (*marée de ME*) TRANSP neap tide; ~ **noire** *f* ENVIR, IND oil spill, oil spillage; ~ **de VE** *f* (*marée de vive-eau*) TRANSP ost (*ordinary spring tide*); ~ **de vive-eau** *f* (*marée de VE*) TRANSP ordinary spring tide (*ost*), spring tide

marge *f* ADMIN margin, BANQUE, BOURSE margin, spread, BREVETS, COMPTA, ECON, MÉDIA *impression, sur une page* margin, V&M *marketing* mark-up; ~ **amont** COM upstream float; ~ **d'arbitrage** BOURSE arbitrage margin (*UK*); ~ **aval** COM downstream float; ~ **bancaire** BANQUE banker's turn; ~ **bénéficiaire** COMPTA, ECON, FIN margin of profit, profit margin, V&M margin of profit margin, *d'un détaillant* margin, mark-up; ~ **bénéficiaire brute** COMPTA gross profit margin; ~ **bénéficiaire nette** COM, COMPTA net profit margin; ~ **bénéficiaire du résultat net** COM, COMPTA, FIN bottom-line profit margin; ~ **brute** BOURSE gross spread, COMPTA, ECON, FIN gross margin, GM; ~ **brute d'autofinancement** (*MBA*) COMPTA cash flow; ~ **brute d'autofinancement annuelle** COMPTA, FIN annual cash flow; ~ **brute d'autofinancement marginale** COMPTA, FIN incremental cash flow; ~ **brute d'autofinancement négative** (ANT *marge brute d'autofinancement positive*) COMPTA, FIN negative cash flow; ~ **brute d'autofinancement par action** BOURSE cash flow per share; ~ **brute d'autofinancement positive** (ANT *marge brute d'autofinancement négative*) COMPTA, FIN positive cash flow; ~ **commerciale** V&M return on sales; ~ **complémentaire** BOURSE additional margin; ~ **d'un contrepartiste** BOURSE *fourchette de prix* jobber's spread, jobber's turn; ~ **de crédit** *Can* (SYN *ligne de crédit, ligne de découvert*) BANQUE, FIN bank line, credit line, line of credit; ~ **de départ** BOURSE original margin; ~ **de détail** V&M retail margin; ~ **en-tête** ADMIN header, INFO header, header-block, MÉDIA *d'une* *page* header; ~ **entre produits** BOURSE intra-commodity spread; ~ **d'entretien** BOURSE *transactions à terme* maintenance margin; ~ **d'erreur** COM, COMPTA margin of error; ~ **étroite** COMPTA narrow margin; ~ **eurodollar** BOURSE Eurodollar spread; ~ **de flottement** ECON *taux de change* band of fluctuation, fluctuation band; ~ **de fluctuation** ECON *taux de change* band of fluctuation, fluctuation band; ~ **de fluctuation étroite** ECON narrow fluctuation band; ~ **de fond** ADMIN, INFO, MÉDIA *d'une page* back margin; ~ **initiale** BOURSE initial margin, original margin; ~ **d'intérêt** BANQUE interest margin, interest spread; ~ **de maintenance** BOURSE maintenance margin; ~ **de manoeuvre** FIN tolerance level; ~ **minimale** BOURSE minimum margin; ~ **minimum** BOURSE minimum margin; ~ **nette** COMPTA, ECON, FIN net margin; ~ **nette sur les intérêts** COMPTA, ECON net interest margin; ~ **obligatoire** BOURSE compulsory margin (*UK*); ~ **de petits fonds** ADMIN, INFO, MÉDIA *d'une page* back margin; ~ **des produits de base** BOURSE intercommodity spread; ~ **de profit finale** COM, COMPTA, FIN bottom-line profit margin; ~ **de sécurité** BOURSE margin security, margin, margin maintenance, COM safety margin, security margin, COMPTA, FIN margin of safety, safety margin, IND, RES HUM margin of safety; ~ **de solvabilité** FIN solvency margin; ~ **supérieure** ADMIN header, top margin, INFO header-block, header, top margin, MÉDIA *d'une page* header, top margin; ~ **sur coûts variables** COMPTA contribution margin, contribution profit, net contribution; ~ **à terme** ECON *commerce international* forward margin; ~ **de tolérance** COM allowance; ~ **de variation** BOURSE variation margin; ♦ **de ~** COM marginal; **sur ~** FIN on margin

margeur *m* ADMIN margin stop

marginal[1], **e** *adj* COM marginal, ECON *coût*, INFO incremental

marginal[2] *m* MATH outlier

marginalement *adv* COM marginally

marginaliser *vt* COM, COMPTA, ECON, FIN marginalize

marginalisme *m* ECON marginalism

marginalistes *m pl* ECON marginalists

marginaux *m pl* MÉDIA, V&M *relations publiques* peripherals

marguerite *f* INFO, MÉDIA daisywheel; ~ **d'impression** INFO, MÉDIA daisywheel

marie: ~ **-salope** *f* TRANSP *navire* deslopping barge

marier *vt* V&M *vente aux enchères* marry up

marine: ~ **marchande** *f* TRANSP commercial marine (*dat*), mercantile marine, merchant marine, merchant navy, merchant service

maritime *adj* TRANSP marine, maritime

mark *m* COM mark; ~ **allemand** FIN mark; ~ **-to-the-market** BOURSE value to the market

market: ~ **maker** *m* BOURSE market maker (*UK*)

marketing *m* V&M marketing; ~ **de bouche à oreille** V&M word-of-mouth marketing; ~ **de comportement** V&M performance marketing; ~ **de création** V&M creative marketing; ~ **du créneau** V&M niche marketing; ~ **de destination** V&M destination marketing; ~ **de différenciation** V&M differentiated marketing; ~ **direct** V&M direct marketing; ~ **dynamique** V&M aggressive marketing; ~ **global** V&M global marketing; ~ **de la marque** V&M brand marketing; ~ **de masse** V&M mass marketing; ~ **-mix** V&M marketing mix; ~ **multiniveau** V&M multilevel marketing, MLM; ~ **à niveaux multiples** V&M multilevel marketing, MLM; ~ **de produit** V&M product marketing; ~ **des produits de grande consommation** V&M consumer marketing; ~ **des produits industriels** V&M industrial marketing; ~ **de relance** V&M remarketing; ~ **symbiotique** V&M symbiotic marketing; ~ **téléphonique** FIN, V&M telemarketing

markka *m* COM markka

marnage *m* TRANSP tidal fall, *maritime* tidal range

Maroc *m* COM Morocco

marocain, e *adj* COM Moroccan

Marocain, e *m,f* COM *habitant* Moroccan

MARPOL *abrév* (*Pollution maritime*) ENVIR *Convention 1978* MARPOL (*Maritime Pollution*)

marquage *m* V&M branding, marking; ~ **de la date de péremption** V&M *sur marchandises* date marking; ~ **des marchandises** TRANSP cargo marking symbol

marque *f* BREVETS *d'un produit* mark, trademark, COM brand, make, trademark, *contre un nom* check (*AmE*), tick (*BrE*), COMPTA check (*AmE*), tick (*BrE*), *d'un produit* trademark, DROIT *d'un produit* mark, trademark, V&M label, *d'un produit* brand, make, trademark; ~ **associée** BREVETS associated mark; ~ **de certification** BREVETS certification mark; ~ **collective** BREVETS collective mark; ~ **combinée** BREVETS combined mark, composite mark, figurative device, word and device mark; ~ **de contrôle** COM *d'un produit* brand, check mark (*AmE*), make, tick mark (*BrE*), trademark, COMPTA trademark; ~ **dénominative** BREVETS work mark; ~ **déposée** BREVETS registered mark, registered trademark, COM proprietary brand, registered trademark, DROIT registered mark, registered trademark; ~ **de distributeur** V&M own brand, private brand, store brand; ~ **d'essai** BANQUE, COM, IND assay mark, certification mark; ~ **du fabricant** V&M manufacturer's brand, name brand, producer's brand; ~ **de fabrique** BREVETS, COM, COMPTA, DROIT *propriété intellectuelle* trademark, V&M brand name, trademark; ~ **figurative** BREVETS device mark; ~ **de fin de fichier** INFO end-of-file mark; ~ **de franc-bord** TRANSP *d'un navire* plimsoll line; ~ **générique** V&M generic brand; ~ **grand public** V&M consumer brand; ~ **de haute renommée** BREVETS mark with high reputation; ~ **d'homologation** TRANSP *d'un véhicule* approval mark; ~ **de jauge** TRANSP *d'un navire* tonnage mark; ~ **loyale et marchande** IND good merchantable brand, GMB; ~ **non déposée** BREVETS unregistered mark, COM unregistered trademark; ~ **notoire** BREVETS well-known mark; ~ **de pointage** COMPTA check mark (*AmE*), tick mark (*BrE*), vouch mark; ~ **de prestige** COM status symbol; ~ **de qualité** COM seal of quality, *d'un produit* quality brand, V&M quality brand; ~ **réputée** COM big name, reputable brand, V&M name brand; ~ **de service** BREVETS service mark; ~ **verbale** BREVETS work mark; ♦ **de** ~ COM proprietary; **de** ~ **déposée** COM proprietary

marqué, e *adj* COM *déclin, différence, prix* marked

marquer *vt* COM score, *marchandises* mark; ~ **un prix** COMPTA mark off

marqueur *m* ADMIN, COM *stylo* marker, marker pen

mars *m* COM Mar., March

marteau *m* COM *d'un commissaire-priseur* gavel

martingale *f* MATH martingale

marxisme *m* POL Marxism

marxiste[1] *adj* POL Marxist

marxiste[2] *mf* POL Marxist

mascaret *m* TRANSP *d'une rivière* bore

Mascate *n pr* COM Muscat

Maseru *n pr* COM Maseru

masque *m* INFO form; ~ **d'étrave** TRANSP *d'un roulier* bow visor

masquer *vt* INFO hide

mass: ~ **-média** *m pl* COMMS mass media, MÉDIA information broadcast

masse *f* COM *majorité* bulk; ~ **brute** COM gross mass; ~ **brute réelle** COM actual gross weight; ~ **créancière** ASSUR *maritime* amount to be made good; ~ **des créditeurs** COMPTA, FIN body of creditors; ~ **critique** COM, ECON, V&M critical mass; ~ **de la faillite** DROIT, FIN bankruptcy estate; ~ **des fournisseurs** COMPTA, FIN body of creditors; ~ **indivisible** TRANSP *de marchandises* indivisible load; ~ **indivisible anormale** TRANSP *de marchandises* abnormal indivisible load; ~ **monétaire** ECON Divisia money index, money supply; ~ **salariale** RES HUM payroll, wage bill; ~ **successorale** COM deceased estate; ♦ **de** ~ COM *culture, vie* admass

masses: **les** ~ *f pl* POL the masses; **les** ~ **laborieuses** *f pl* POL the working masses

massif *adj* COM *quantité* huge, massive, RES HUM *licenciements* huge, massive, wholesale

mastodonte *m* TRANSP *camion* juggernaut

mât *m* TRANSP *d'un navire* mast; ~ **de charge** TRANSP *d'un navire* cargo derrick, der, derrick; ~ **de charge pour colis lourds** TRANSP *manutention* heavy lift mast crane; ~ **de charge à rotation de 270°** TRANSP scotch derrick

matelot *m* TRANSP sailor, seaman; ~ **breveté** TRANSP able seaman, able-bodied seaman, ABS; ~ **de pont** RES HUM, TRANSP deck hand; ~ **de première classe** RES HUM, TRANSP leading seaman, seaman grade I; ~ **qualifié** TRANSP able seaman, able-bodied seaman, ABS; ~ **de seconde**

classe RES HUM, TRANSP able seaman, able-bodied seaman, seaman grade II, ABS; ~ **de troisième classe** RES HUM, TRANSP ordinary seaman

mâtereau *m* TRANSP *d'un navire* Samson post, king post

matérialiser *vi* COM materialize

matérialisme *m* ECON, POL materialism

matériau *m* ECON material; ~ **de base** ECON basic material; ~ **combustible** ENVIR, IND combustible material; ~ **récupérable** ENVIR recoverable material; ~ **résistant à la corrosion** IND, TRANSP corrosion-resistant material

matériaux *m pl* COM material, materials, ECON materials, IND material, materials; ~ **de construction** IND building materials; ~ **en gros** COM bulk material

matériel *m* COM *documents* material, *machines, outils* equipment, COMPTA industrial equipment, IND equipment, *machines, outils* plant, INFO equipment, hardware; ~ **agricole** ECON farm implements; ~ **audiovisuel** INFO audiovisual aid; ~ **de bureau** ADMIN, COM office aid, office equipment; ~ **complémentaire** GESTION add-on equipment; ~ **d'entretien** COM, IND maintenance equipment; ~ **humain** RES HUM labor power (*AmE*), labour power (*BrE*); ~ **de manutention** TRANSP cargo-handling equipment; ~ **de manutention mécanique** TRANSP mechanical handling equipment, MHE; ~ **pédagogique** COM *documents* backup material; ~ **périphérique** INFO peripheral equipment; ~ **publicitaire** V&M publicity material; ~ **de publicité sur le lieu de vente** V&M point-of-sale material; ~ **réservé** COM allocated material; ~ **roulant** TRANSP *chemin de fer* rolling stock; ~ **de sauvetage** TRANSP life-saving apparatus, LSA; ~ **supplémentaire** GESTION add-on equipment; ~ **de transport** TRANSP transportation equipment; ~ **de transport admissible** TRANSP qualified transportation equipment

matière *f* COM *sujet* matter, subject, subject matter, ECON, IND *substance* material; ~ **brute** IND raw material; ~ **explosive** TRANSP *marchandises dangereuses* explosive substance; ~ **grise** COM, GESTION creative thinking; ~ **imposable** FISC taxable article; ~ **minérale** ENVIR, IND mineral resource; ~ **plastique** ENVIR, IND plastic; ~ **polymérisable** TRANSP *marchandises dangereuses* polymerizable material; ~ **première** BOURSE cmdty, commodity, physical commodity, COM, ECON cmdty, commodity, IND cmdty, commodity, raw material, unmanufactured material; ~ **première agricole** BOURSE soft commodity; ~ **première au comptant** BOURSE spot commodity; ~ **première contrôlée** BOURSE controlled commodity (*UK*); ~ **première directe** ECON direct material; ~ **première échangée sur les marchés internationaux** ECON *commerce international* commodity trades; ~ **première réglementée** BOURSE regulated commodity; ~ **pyrotechnique** TRANSP *marchandises dangereuses* pyrotechnic substance;

~ **récupérable** ENVIR *recyclage* recoverable material; ~ **résistante à la corrosion** IND, TRANSP corrosion-resistant material

matières: ~ **plastiques** *f pl* IND plastics

MATIF *abrév France (Marché à terme d'instruments financiers)* BOURSE ≈ AFFM *(Australian Financial Futures Market)*, ≈ CBT *(US) (Chicago Board of Trade)*, ≈ LIFFE *(UK) (London International Financial Futures Exchange)*

matin: **du ~** *adv* COM am, ante meridiem

matinée *f* COM *spectacle* matinée

matraquage: ~ **publicitaire** *m* V&M burst advertising

matrice *f* INFO, MATH matrix

mature *adj* COM, RES HUM *candidat* mature

mâture *f* TRANSP *d'un navire* masts; ◆ **dans la ~** TRANSP *d'un navire* aloft

maturer *vi* BOURSE *effet* mature

maturité *f* RES HUM maturity; ~ **moyenne** BOURSE average maturity; ◆ **à ~** BOURSE *effet* at maturity

mauricien, -enne *adj* COM Mauritian

Mauricien, -enne *m,f* COM *habitant* Mauritian

Mauritanie *f* COM Mauritania

mauritanien, -enne *adj* COM Mauritanian

Mauritanien, -enne *m,f* COM *habitant* Mauritanian

mauvais: ~ **achat** *m* COM bad buy; ~ **alignement** *m* COM misalignment; ~ **calcul** *m* COM, COMPTA, ECON, FIN, MATH, V&M miscalculation; ~ **état de navigabilité** *m* TRANSP *d'un navire* unseaworthiness; ~ **fonctionnement** *m* COM, IND *d'une machine* malfunction, malfunctioning, RES HUM dysfunction; ~ **papier** *m* BANQUE bad paper *(infrml)*; ~ **payeur** *m* V&M deadbeat; ~ **risque** *m* COM bad risk, unsound risk; ~ **travail** *m* COM bad deal, bad workmanship; ~ **usage** *m* ENVIR misuse

mauvaise: ~ **administration** *f* GESTION bad management, mismanagement; ~ **affaire** *f* COM bad bargain, bad deal; ~ **approche** *f* COM mishandling; ~ **créance** *f* BANQUE bad debt, COMPTA bad debt, uncollectable account, ECON, FIN bad debt; ~ **gestion** *f* GESTION bad management, mismanagement; ~ **nouvelle** *f* COM bad news; ~ **réputation** *f* COM bad name, bad reputation; ~ **volonté** *f* COM, RES HUM bad will, ill will; ◆ **de ~ foi** DROIT mala fide *frml*

MAV *abrév (mercatique après-vente)* V&M after-sales marketing

max. *abrév (maximal, maximum)* COM all-out, max. *(maximum)*, MATH max. *(maximum)*

maxi: ~ **-discompte** *m* FIN hard discount; ~ **-discompteur** *m* FIN hard discounter

maximal, e *adj (max.)* COM maximal, maximum *(max)*, MATH maximal *(max)*

maximalisation *f* COMPTA maximation, maximization; ~ **des profits** ECON, V&M profit maximization

maximaliser *vt* BOURSE, COM, COMPTA, FIN maximize

maximin *m* ECON maximin

maximisation: ~ **des bénéfices** *f* FIN profit maximization; ~ **du profit** *f* COM, FIN profit maximization; ~ **des recettes** *f* ECON revenue maximization, V&M revenue maximization, sales maximization

maximiser *vt* COM, COMPTA, FIN maximize

maximum[1] *adj (max.)* COM all-out, maximum *(max.)*, MATH maximum *(max.)*

maximum[2] *m* COM, MATH maximum; ◆ **le ~ que vous puissiez perdre** BOURSE the most you can lose

mazout *m* TRANSP fuel oil; ~ **de soute** TRANSP *d'un navire* bunker fuel oil, BFO

MBA *abrév (marge brute d'autofinancement)* COMPTA cash flow

Mbabane *n pr* COM Mbabane

MCAC *abrév (Marché commun d'Amérique centrale)* ECON CACM *(Central American Common Market)*

mécanicien, -enne *m,f* IND, RES HUM machine operator, mechanic, petty officer

mécanique *f* IND mechanical engineering; ~ **de précision** IND precision engineering

mécanisation *f* IND mechanization; ~ **de la manutention** TRANSP mechanization of cargo handling

mécanisé, e *adj* COM, IND *production* mechanized, INFO machine-based

mécaniser *vt* COM, IND mechanize

mécanisme *m* COM device, mechanism, ECON machinery, mechanism, IND device, mechanism; ~ **d'alimentation automatique** ADMIN automatic feeder; ~ **automatique de stabilisation** ECON built-in stabilizer; ~ **de coupe-circuit** BOURSE circuit breaker mechanism *(US)*; ~ **d'entraînement de bande** INFO tape feed; ~ **d'escompte** FIN discount mechanism; ~ **de garantie d'achat** ASSUR, FIN purchase underwriting facility, PUF; ~ **d'indexation** ECON pegging device; ~ **du marché** ECON market mechanism; ~ **pour minimiser les pertes** BANQUE stop-loss rules; ~ **de mouvement en numéraire** BANQUE specie flow mechanism; ~ **de négociation** RES HUM negotiating machinery; ~ **des prix** ECON price mechanism; ~ **des retombées technologiques par incitation** ECON inducement mechanism; ~ **de taux de change** *(MTC)* ECON exchange rate mechanism *(ERM)*; ~ **de transmission** ECON Friedman, transmission mechanism

mécanographe *m* ADMIN punch card operator, punch operator, tab operator, tabulator operator

mécénat *m* V&M sponsorship; ~ **d'entreprise** V&M *publicité* corporate sponsorship

méconnu, e *adj* COM unrecognized

mécontentement: ~ **sur le lieu de travail** *m* RES HUM discontent in the workplace

MEDAF *abrév (modèle d'équilibre des actifs financiers, modèle d'évaluation des actifs financiers)* BOURSE, ECON, FIN CAPM *(capital asset pricing model)*

médecin *m* PROT SOC, RES HUM doctor, medical officer, MO; ~ **départemental** PROT SOC, RES HUM medical officer of health, MOH; ~ **long-courrier** PROT SOC flying doctor (*Australia*); ~ **volant** PROT SOC flying doctor (*Australia*)

média *m* COM, COMMS, MÉDIA medium; ~ **de base** *m* MÉDIA basic medium; ~ **éphémère** *m* MÉDIA, V&M transient medium; ~ **planning** *m* MÉDIA, V&M media planning; ~ **publicitaires** *m pl* MÉDIA advertising media

médian, e *adj* MATH median

médiane *f* FISC median amount, MATH median

médiaplanneur *m* MÉDIA, V&M media planner

médias *m pl* COMMS, MÉDIA, V&M communication media, mass media, media; ~ **classiques** MÉDIA basic media; **les ~** COMMS, MÉDIA, V&M the media; ~ **de presse écrite** MÉDIA print media; ~ **publicitaires** V&M advertising media

médiateur, -trice *m,f* COM arbitrator, mediator, DROIT arbiter, arbitrator, IND arbitrator, honest broker, POL *entre des groupes qui se disputent* honest broker, *entre citoyens et gouvernement* ombudsman, RES HUM arbitrator, mediator

médiation *f* COM, DROIT, IND arbitration, mediation, POL mediation, RES HUM arbitration, mediation

médiatique *adj* MÉDIA media

médiatiser *vt* MÉDIA *événement* give a lot of media coverage to

médical, e *adj* COM, PROT SOC medical

médicament *m* COM drug, medicament, medicine; ~ **grand-public** V&M over-the-counter medicine; ~ **sans ordonnance** V&M over-the-counter medicine; ~ **vendu sous marque** COM, PROT SOC proprietary drug

Medspa *m* ENVIR Medspa

méfait *m* DROIT misdemeanor (*AmE*), misdemeanour (*BrE*), misfeasance; ~ **prémédité** DROIT malicious mischief

méga: ~ **-électron-volt** *m* COM MeV, mega electron volt; ~ **-octet** *m* (*Mo*) INFO megabyte (*Mb*)

mégabit *m* INFO megabit

mégadimension *f* V&M mammoth size

mégalomane *mf* RES HUM megalomaniac

mégalomanie *f* RES HUM megalomania

mégawatt *m* (*MW*) COM megawatt (*MW*)

meilleur[1], e *adj* COM *perspective* better, brighter; ~ **marché** *adj* COM cheaper; ◆ ~ **moyen pratique** COM best practical means, bpm; **ou à ~ prix** BOURSE or better still; ~ **prix** COM best price; ~ **que la moyenne** COM better than average; ~ **que prévu** COM *résultat* better than expected

meilleur:[2] ~ **des cas** *m* (ANT *le pire des cas*) COM, ECON, POL best-case scenario

meilleure: ~ **offre** *f* COM best bid; ~ **option** *f* COM best alternative

mélange *m* COM, V&M mix; ~ **dosé** ENVIR blending; ~ **de politiques** GESTION policy mix

membre *mf* COM, RES HUM member; ~ **adhérent** *m* BANQUE direct clearer, direct clearing member, IND, POL card-carrying member; ~ **affilié** *m* COM affiliate member; ~ **de l'Association des Comptables d'entreprise certifiés** *m* COMPTA ≈ FCCA, ≈ Fellow of the Chartered Association of Certified Accountants; ~ **de la Bourse des valeurs** *m* BOURSE trading member; ~ **d'une chambre de compensation** *m* BOURSE clearing member; ~ **d'un comité** *m* COM member of a committee; ~ **d'une commission** *m* COM committee member, member of a commission, member of a committee; ~ **compensateur** *m* BOURSE, FIN clearing member; ~ **du conseil de surveillance** *m* RES HUM member of the supervisory board; ~ **du directoire** *m* RES HUM member of the board of management; ~ **d'équipage** *m* TRANSP *d'un avion, d'un navire* crew member; ~ **de l'équipe d'audit** *m* COMPTA, FIN audit officer; ~ **fondateur** *m* COM founder member; ~ **de la gendarmerie maritime** *m* RES HUM coastguard, CG; ~ **de la haute société** *m* POL socialite; ~ **de l'IATA** *m* TRANSP IATA member; ~ **non-compensant** *m* BOURSE nonclearing member; ~ **de non-compensation** *m* BOURSE nonclearing member; ~ **d'office** *m* COM, RES HUM ex officio member (*frml*); ~ **opérateur** *m* BOURSE trading member; ~ **du Parlement Européen** *m* POL *UE* Euro MP, European MP, European Member of Parliament, Member of the European Parliament, MEP; ~ **à part entière** *m* COM full member; ~ **du personnel** *m* RES HUM member of staff, staffer; ~ **du public** *m* COM member of the public; ~ **spécifié** *m* FISC specified member; ~ **suppléant du directoire** *m* GESTION, RES HUM deputy member of the board of management; ~ **d'un syndicat** *m* RES HUM member of a union, union member

membres *m pl* COM, RES HUM members rank and file

membrures *f pl* TRANSP *d'un navire* frame, framing, FRMG; ~ **longitudinales** TRANSP *d'un navire* longitudinal framing

même:[1] ~ **langue** *f* COM same language; ◆ **de la ~ façon** COM in the same terms, in the same way

même:[2] **être à ~ de faire** *loc* COM be in a position to do; **être du ~ avis** *loc* COM agree; **être du ~ avis que** *loc* COM agree with

mémoire[1] *m* COM *d'un compte* bill, *rapport* report, DROIT memorandum, statement; ~ **descriptif** BREVETS specifications; ~ **descriptif de brevet** BREVETS patent specifications; ~ **de vente** FIN prompt note

mémoire[2] *f* COM *d'une personne* memory, INFO memory, storage, store; ~ **additionnelle externe** INFO add-on memory; ~ **d'archivage** INFO archival storage; ~ **auxiliaire** INFO archival storage; ~ **auxiliaire d'entrée/sortie** INFO bulk input/output; ~ **basse** INFO low memory; ~ **à bulles** INFO bubble memory; ~ **cache** INFO cache, cache buffer, cache memory, cache storage, cache store; ~ **centrale** INFO core, core memory; ~ **commune** INFO global memory; ~ **étendue** INFO expanded memory, extended memory; **~ d'expansion** INFO expanded memory, extended memory; **~ fixe** INFO read only memory, ROM; **~ de grande capacité** INFO bulk storage, mass memory, mass storage, mass storage device; **~ intermédiaire** INFO buffer, buffer storage, buffer store; **~ interne** INFO internal storage; **~ magnétique** IND, INFO magnetic storage; **~ de masse** INFO mass memory, mass storage, mass storage device; **~ de masse auxiliaire** INFO auxiliary memory, auxiliary storage; **~ morte** INFO read only memory, ROM; **~ morte programmable électroniquement** *(EPROM)* INFO electronically programmable read only memory *(EPROM)*; **~ d'ordinateur** INFO computer memory; **~ principale** INFO core storage; **~ RAM** INFO random access memory, RAM; **~ réelle** INFO real storage; **~ ROM** INFO read only memory, ROM; **~ de sauvegarde** INFO backup memory; **~ supplémentaire** INFO add-on memory; **~ tampon** INFO buffer, buffer storage, buffer store; **~ à tores** INFO core storage, magnetic core; **~ de travail** INFO scratch pad, working storage; **~ ultra-rapide** INFO high-speed memory; **~ vive** INFO random access memory, RAM; **~ vive dynamique** INFO dynamic RAM, dynamic random access memory

mémorandum *m* ADMIN memo, memorandum, COM aide-mémoire, COMMS *note* memo, memorandum, DROIT memorandum

mémorisation *f* INFO *de données* storage, V&M *de produits par le client* customer awareness; **~ assistée** V&M aided recall; **~ de données** INFO data storage

mémoriser *vt* COM memorize, INFO *données* store

menace: ~ de grève *f* RES HUM strike threat; **~ injustifiée** *f* DROIT unjustified threat

menacé, e *adj* BOURSE at risk

ménage *m* ECON household, private household; **~ agricole** ECON agricultural household; **~ d'agriculteurs** ECON agricultural household; **~ sans enfants** ECON, IMMOB *marché de l'immobilier* childless couple, empty nesters *(infrml)*

ménager: ~ la chèvre et le chou *loc* COM sit on the fence *(infrml)*

ménagère *f* ECON, V&M housewife

mener *vt* COM *campagne* wage, *vente, commerce* conduct, GESTION, RES HUM lead, V&M carry out; ◆ **~ une affaire à bien** COM bring off a deal, swing a deal *(infrml)*, pull off a deal; **~ à bien** FIN pull off; **~ une campagne** POL, V&M wage a campaign; **~ une campagne négative** POL *pour chercher les défauts de l'adversaire*, V&M go negative *(jarg)*, wage a negative campaign; **~ qch à terme** COM follow sth through; **~ la vie dure à qn** COM make things hard for sb, make things rough for sb *(infrml)*

meneur, -euse *m,f* COM leader, IMMOB lead *(jarg)*, IND, POL *chef* leader; **~ mondial** POL world leader

meneurs: ~ et traînards *m pl* BOURSE leads and lags

mensualité *f* BANQUE, COMPTA, FIN installment *(AmE)*, instalment *(BrE)*, monthly installment *(AmE)*, monthly instalment *(BrE)*

mensualités: par ~ *loc* COMPTA, FIN in monthly installments *(AmE)*, in monthly instalments *(BrE)*

mensuel[1], **-elle** *adj* COM, COMPTA, FIN monthly, MÉDIA monthly, published monthly

mensuel[2] *m* MÉDIA monthly, monthly magazine

mensuel[3] **-elle** *m,f* COM employee who is paid monthly

mensuellement *adv* COM, COMPTA, FIN monthly

mentionné: ~ ci-dessous *loc* (ANT *mentionné ci-dessus*) COM undermentioned, COMMS as mentioned below, below; **~ ci-dessus** *loc* (ANT *mentionné ci-dessous*) COM, COMMS above, above-mentioned, as mentioned above; **~ plus bas** *loc* (ANT *mentionné plus haut*) COMMS as mentioned below, below; **~ plus haut** *loc* (ANT *mentionné plus bas*) COMMS above, above-mentioned, as mentioned above

mentionner *vt* COM bring up, mention

menu *m* COM *dans un restaurant*, INFO menu; **~ déroulant** INFO pop-down menu, pull-down menu; **~ édition** INFO edit menu; **~ fichier** INFO file menu; **~ hiérarchique** INFO hierarchical menu; **~ principal** INFO main menu; **~ surgissant** INFO pop-up menu

menue: ~ monnaie *f* COMPTA, FIN, RES HUM pc, petty cash

méprise: ~ non-intentionnelle *f* DROIT mistake

mer *f* TRANSP sea; ◆ **en ~** COM, IND *plate-forme* afloat, offshore

mercantile *adj* COM, ECON mercantile

mercantilisme *m* ECON mercantilism

mercantiliste[1] *adj* ECON mercantilist

mercantiliste[2] *mf* ECON mercantilist

mercaphonie *f* V&M phone marketing

mercateur *m* RES HUM, V&M marketeer

mercatique *f* V&M marketing; **~ après-vente** *(MAV)* V&M after-sales marketing; **~ téléphonique** V&M phone marketing, reporting

mercatis *adj* COM market-driven

merchandiser *m* RES HUM merchandiser

merchandising *m* V&M merchandising

merci: ~ de votre lettre *loc* COMMS thank you for your letter, thanks for your letter *(infrml)*

Mercosur: le ~ *m* ECON *commerce international* Mercosur

mercredi *m* COM Wed., Wednesday

méridien *m* COM meridian

méritocratie *f* RES HUM meritocracy

Mesdames:[1] **~ et Messieurs** *m pl* COM ladies and gentlemen

Mesdames[2] *f pl* COM ladies

Mesdemoiselles *f pl* COM ladies

mésoéconomie *f* ECON mesoeconomy

mesokurtique *m* MATH mesokurtic

message *m* COMMS, INFO, V&M *publicité* message; ~ **d'alerte** INFO alert box; ~ **de bienvenue** INFO welcome message; ~ **brouillé** COMMS scrambled message; ~ **codé** COMMS coded message; ~ **concernant le mouvement des aéronefs** TRANSP aircraft movement message, MVT; ~ **de diagnostique** INFO diagnostic message; ~ **d'entrée** INFO input message; ~ **d'erreur** INFO error message; ~ **d'erreur d'entrée/sortie** INFO I/O error message, input/output error message; ~ **d'état** INFO status message; ~ **de faute de syntaxe** INFO syntax error message; ~ **guide-opérateur** INFO prompt; ~ **d'intervention** INFO action code, action message; ~ **publicitaire** V&M *TV, radio* advertising message; ~ **publicitaire à la radio** V&M radio commercial; ~ **publicitaire télévisé** MÉDIA, V&M TV commercial, television commercial; ~ **téléphonique** COMMS telephone message; ~ **de vente** TRANSP *aviation* sold message

messager, -ère *m,f* COM runner, COMMS courier, messager

messagerie *f* COMMS bulletin board system, courier service, BBS; ~ **électronique** ADMIN, COMMS e-mail, electronic mail, INFO bulletin board, e-mail, electronic mail; ~ **vocale** INFO voice mail

messages: ~ **contradictoires** *m pl* COM mixed signals

Messieurs *m pl* COM gentlemen

mesure *f* COM measure, RES HUM degree; ~ **de banc d'essai** ECON bench mark; ~ **de bien-être économique** ECON, PROT SOC *économétrie*, RES HUM measure of economic welfare, MEW; ~ **de capacité liquide** COM liquid measure; ~ **du coefficient bêta d'un portefeuille** BOURSE portfolio beta score; ~ **de compensation** COM countermeasure; ~ **de conservation** ASSUR sue and labor (*AmE*), sue and labour (*BrE*); ~ **de contrôle** ECON measure of control; ~ **de cotisation** FISC assessing action; ~ **de degrés** MATH degree measure; ~ **dissuasive** COM deterrent; ~ **d'exécution** FISC *prise par le Ministère* enforcement action; ~ **fiscale** FISC tax measure; ~ **fiscale d'incitation** FISC tax incentive; ~ **linéaire** COM linear measure; ~ **de mobilité géographique** ECON mobility status; ~ **par pieds-planches** IND board measure, BM; ~ **de performances** COM, GESTION, IND, RES HUM performance measurement; ~ **de postcotisation** FISC postassessing; ~ **de précaution** COM precautionary measure; ~ **de précotisation** FISC preassessing; ~ **préventive** COM precautionary measure; ~ **de la productivité** COM, IND productivity measurement; ~ **pour produits secs** COM dry measure; ~ **de la quantité** IND quantity surveying; ~ **de relance** ECON stimulative measure; ~ **du rendement** COM, GESTION, IND, RES HUM performance measurement; ~ **du revenu** ECON income measure; ~ **de sécurité** COM safety measure, safety precaution, security measure;

~ **du travail** GESTION, IND work measurement; ~ **du travail par sondage** GESTION, MATH, V&M *étude de marché* activity sampling; ~ **unilatérale** ENVIR unilateral measure; ◆ **dans cette** ~ COM pro tanto *frml*; **dans la** ~ **où** COM in so far as (*BrE*), insofar as (*AmE*); **dans la** ~ **de ses mérites** COM quantum meruit *frml*; **être en** ~ **de faire** COM be in a position to do; **par** ~ **d'économie** COM as an economy measure; **par** ~ **de précaution** COM as a precautionary measure; **par** ~ **préventive** COM as a precautionary measure

mesurer *vt* COM gage (*AmE*), gauge (*BrE*), measure, ECON measure, RES HUM assess, measure; ◆ ~ **le rendement de qn** RES HUM measure sb's performance

mesures: ~ **anti-discriminatoires** *f pl* (SYN *discrimination positive, politique anti-discriminatoire*) POL, PROT SOC, RES HUM *à l'embauche* affirmative action (*AmE*), positive action (*BrE*), positive discrimination (*BrE*); ~ **d'arbitrage** *f pl* COM, DROIT, IND, RES HUM arbitration proceedings; ~ **en cas d'urgence** *f pl* COM contingency arrangements; ~ **disciplinaires** *f pl* DROIT disciplinary measures; ~ **draconiennes** *f pl* ECON drastic measures; ~ **drastiques** *f pl* ECON drastic measures; ~ **et limites** *f pl* IMMOB metes and bounds; ~ **d'incitation économique** *f pl* ECON compensatory finance, deficit financing, pump priming; ~ **particulières pour l'emploi** *f pl* RES HUM special employment measures, SEM; ~ **réglementaires** *f pl* DROIT regulatory measures; ~ **de réglementation** *f pl* DROIT regulatory measures; ~ **de représailles** *f pl* COM retaliatory measures; ~ **de sécurité contre incendie** *f pl* ASSUR, IND, RES HUM fire prevention; ~ **de superficie** *f pl* COM square measures; ~ **de surface** *f pl* COM square measures; ~ **d'urgence** *f pl* COM, POL emergency measures

méta *m* ENVIR white coal

métal *m* [pl: -aux] ENVIR, IND metal; ~ **affiné** IND refined metal; ~ **jaune** IND yellow metal; ~ **lourd** ENVIR *pollution* heavy metal; ~ **précieux** ENVIR precious metal

métaldéhyde *m* ENVIR white coal

métalliste *mf* ECON metallist

métallo *m infrml* IND metalworker, steelworker, RES HUM metalworker, steelworker

métallurgiste *mf* IND metallurgist, *ouvrier* metalworker, steelworker, RES HUM metallurgist

métayer, -ère *m,f* ECON agricultural tenant, tenant farmer, sharecropper (*US*)

méthode:[1] ~ **de l'amortissement linéaire** *m* FISC method of depreciation, straight-line method of amortization

méthode[2] *f* COM, GESTION approach, method, system; ~ **ABC** COMPTA, GESTION ABC method; ~ **d'achat au prix coûtant** COMPTA purchase method; ~ **de l'achèvement des travaux** COMPTA completed contract method; ~ **d'actualisation** COMPTA, ECON, FIN present value method; ~ **d'ali-**

gnement sur la concurrence V&M competitive-parity method; ~ **d'amarrage sur un seul point fixe** TRANSP *d'un pétrolier* single-point mooring, SPM; ~ **d'amortissement** COMPTA, FIN amortization method, payback method; ~ **d'amortissement linéaire** COMPTA, FIN amortization on a straight-line basis, straight-line method of depreciation; ~ **basée sur le pourcentage des ventes** V&M percentage-of-sales method; ~ **Bayesienne** MATH Bayesian method; ~ **du bénéfice brut** COMPTA gross profit method; ~ **de la carotte et du bâton** GESTION carrot and stick, carrot and stick approach, carrot and stick method; ~ **du chemin critique** COM, ECON, MATH critical path method, critical path theory, CPM; ~ **de la comptabilisation de la mise en équivalence** COMPTA equity method of accounting; ~ **de la comptabilité d'exercice** COMPTA accrual basis, accrual method; ~ **de la comptabilité de trésorerie** COMPTA receivable basis, receivable method; ~ **comptable** COMPTA, FIN accounting method, accounting procedure; ~ **comptable du passif** COMPTA, FIN liability method; ~ **de consolidation par intégration globale** COMPTA purchase method; ~ **du coût complet** COMPTA absorption costing, full-cost method; ~ **du coût de revient complet** COMPTA absorption costing, full-cost method; ~ **du coût de revient standard** COM, COMPTA standard cost accounting, standard cost system; ~ **des coûts complets** FIN full-cost method; ~ **des coûts directs** COMPTA direct costing; ~ **des coûts marginaux** COMPTA, ECON, FIN marginal costing; ~ **des coûts moyens** COMPTA overall expenses method; ~ **des coûts moyens annuels** COMPTA overall expenses method; ~ **des coûts standards** FIN standard costing; ~ **des coûts variables** FIN contribution analysis; ~ **du crédit net** FIN net voting, vote netting; ~ **de croissance régulière** COM steady-growth method; ~ **des dépenses globales** COMPTA overall expenses method; ~ **de détermination des coûts de fabrication par lot** COMPTA job cost system; ~ **empirique** COM rule of thumb; ~ **des essais et des erreurs** ECON, MATH trial and error method; ~ **de l'étude de cas** GESTION case study method; ~ **d'évaluation des stocks au prix coûtant** COMPTA *inventaire* cost method; ~ **d'exploitation agricole** ECON farming method; ~ **de financement préétablie** FIN formula funding; ~ **de l'impôt exigible** FISC flow-through basis, tax payable basis; ~ **de l'impôt reporté** FISC deferred tax accounting; ~ **de l'indice-chaîne** COMPTA, ECON chain index method; ~ **d'inventaire périodique** COMPTA periodic inventory method; ~ **d'investissement de Graham et Dodd** BOURSE Graham and Dodd method of investing; ~ **d'investissement préétablie** BOURSE formula investing; ~ **linéaire** COMPTA *d'amortissement annuel* straight-line method; ~ **manuelle** MATH manual mode; ~ **de la mise en équivalence** COMPTA equity method; ~ **des moindres carrés** MATH least squares method; ~ **des moindres carrés en**

trois phases ECON three-stage least squares; ~ **des observations instantanées** GESTION, MATH, V&M random observation method; ~ **de paiement** COM, COMPTA method of payment, FIN, V&M method of payment, payment method, payment type; ~ **par échelles** BANQUE daily balance interest calculation; ~ **par paliers** BANQUE daily balance interest calculation; ~ **à partie double** COMPTA double-entry method; ~ **PERT** *(méthode de programmation optimale)* GESTION PERT *(program evaluation and review technique)* *(AmE)*, PERT *(programme evaluation and review technique)* *(BrE)*; ~ **de pourcentage d'achèvement** COMPTA percentage-of-completion method; ~ **de prélèvement des frais d'achat sur les premiers versements** FIN front-end loading; ~ **de préparation** COMPTA method of preparation; ~ **du prix d'achat** BOURSE purchase price method; ~ **du prix de revient complet** COMPTA absorption costing, ECON, V&M full-cost pricing; ~ **de programmation optimale** *(méthode PERT)* GESTION program evaluation and review technique *(AmE)*, programme evaluation and review technique *(BrE)* *(PERT)*; ~ **progressive** INFO steps method; ~ **de qualification par points** COM, GESTION, MATH points-rating method; ~ **de reconnaissance en fin de contrat** COMPTA completed contract method; ~ **de recyclage** COM recycling method; ~ **de référence** FIN bench mark method; ~ **de réserve d'investissement** FIN investment reserve system; ~ **statique** COMPTA static method; ~ **temporelle** COMPTA temporal method; ~ **des temps prédéterminés** *(PMTS)* ECON, FIN, GESTION predetermined motion time system *(PMTS)*; ~ **de transfert de technologie** ECON transfer of technology method; ~ **des unités de production** COMPTA units-of-production method

méthodes: ~ **administratives** *f pl* ADMIN, COM, INFO systems and procedures; ~ **économiques** *f pl* ECON economic methods; ~ **et règles relatives aux enveloppes** *f pl* COM envelope procedures and rules

méthodologie *f* ECON, GESTION, V&M methodology; ~ **économique** ECON economic methodology; ~ **qualitative** V&M *étude de marché* qualitative methodology; ~ **quantitative** V&M *étude de marché* quantitative methodology

metical *m* COM metical

méticuleusement *adv* COM meticulously, painstakingly

méticuleux, -euse *adj* COM meticulous, painstaking

métier *m* RES HUM job, occupation, trade, vocation; ~ **de base** ECON core business; ~ **à tisser** IND *machine* weaving loom; ♦ **ayant du ~** RES HUM experienced

métiers: ~ **analogues** *m pl* IND allied trades

métrage *m* COM ≈ yardage; ~ **carré** IMMOB *d'un immeuble* square footage; ~ **de planche** IND board measure, BM

mètre *m* COM meter *(AmE)*, metre *(BrE)*, tape

measure; ~ **de couturière** COM tape measure; ~ **cube** *(m³)* COM cubic meter *(AmE)*, cubic metre *(BrE) (cbm)*; **le** ~ **carré** IMMOB *loyer* ≈ psf, ≈ per square foot; ~ **à ruban** COM measuring tape

mètres: ~ **par seconde** *m pl (m/s)* COM meters per second *(AmE)*, metres per second *(BrE) (m/s)*

métro *m* TRANSP *à Londres* underground, *à New York* subway, *à Paris, Montréal* metro

métropole *f* COM metropolis, metropolitan town

métropolitain, e *adj (*ANT *non-métropolitain)* COM metropolitan

mettre 1. *vt* COM place, put; **2.** *v pron* **s'en ~ plein les poches** *infrml* COM make a killing *(infrml)*; **se ~ à** COM *une tâche* address o.s. to, begin, start; **se ~ d'accord** COM *deux ou plusieurs personnes* agree; **se ~ dans l'illégalité** DROIT fall foul of the law; **se ~ en évidence** COM come to the fore; **se ~ en grève** RES HUM come out on strike *(UK)*, down tools *(infrml)*, go on strike, take industrial action; **se ~ en grève de solidarité** RES HUM strike in sympathy; **se ~ en guerre** COM go to war; **se ~ qn à dos** COM alienate; **se ~ à son compte** COM set up in business on one's own, set up on one's own account; **se ~ au travail** COM begin work, get down to work, start work; ◆ **~ l'accent sur** COM place emphasis on; **~ l'adresse sur** COM put the address on, COMMS address, MÉDIA, V&M put the address on; **~ une annonce** COM, MÉDIA, V&M advertise; **~ une annonce dans le journal** V&M put an advert in the paper, run an ad in the paper; **~ une annonce pour vendre** COM, MÉDIA advertise; **~ en application** DROIT enforce, INFO implement; **~ en apprentissage chez qn** RES HUM apprentice to sb; **~ en balance** COM weigh up; **~ au banc d'essai** INFO bench mark; **~ en chômage partiel** RES HUM *personnel* stand off; **~ en chômage technique** RES HUM *personnel* lay off; **~ les choses au point** COM get sth straight; **~ en commun** ECON *ressources* pool; **~ en communication avec** COMMS connect, put through to; **~ un compte à découvert** BANQUE overdraw an account; **~ un compte à jour** BANQUE post up an account; **~ en contact** COM bring together, COMMS *deux ou plusieurs personnes* put in touch; **~ en conteneurs** TRANSP containerize; **~ à la corbeille** COM bin, MÉDIA spike; **~ en corrélation** MATH correlate; **~ de côté** BANQUE *de l'argent* put away, save, ECON set aside; **~ au courant** COM brief, update; **~ en danger** COM *emploi* compromise, endanger, jeopardize, put in danger; **~ la dernière main à** COM put the final touches to, put the finishing touches to; **~ en détention préventive** DROIT remand in custody; **~ à disposition** COM make available; **~ en doute** COM query; **~ à l'eau** TRANSP *navire* launch; **~ en eau** TRANSP impound; **~ un embargo sur** COM lay an embargo on, place an embargo on, put an embargo on; **~ une enchère** COM bid, put in a bid; **~ à l'épreuve** COM put to the test; **~ à l'essai** COM *machine, produit* test out; **~ en**

évidence INFO *zone, caractère* highlight; **~ à exécution** COM carry out, execute, put into execution; **~ en faillite** BANQUE, COM, COMPTA, FIN, RES HUM bankrupt; **~ en fidéicommis** DROIT place in trust; **~ en file d'attente** INFO *programmes* queue; **~ fin à** ADMIN abolish, bring to an end, eradicate, set a term to, COM set a term to; **~ fin à une session** INFO log off, log out; **~ en fonction** INFO *système* activate; **~ en forme** *jarg* INFO edit, format, MÉDIA *presse* edit, rewrite; **~ en fourrière** DROIT impound; **~ les gaz** *infrml* COM put on a spurt; **~ une histoire à la une** MÉDIA lead with a story; **~ hors tension** INFO power off, turn off; **~ un impôt sur qch** FISC impose a tax on, put a tax on sth; **~ à l'index** COM, FIN, RES HUM blacklist; **~ en jachère** ECON *terre* set aside; **~ à jour** COM bring up to date, update, INFO update; **~ en liberté provisoire sous caution** DROIT release on bail; **~ en ligne** INFO align *(BrE)*, aline *(AmE)*; **~ en liquidation** DROIT put into receivership; **~ en lumière** COM bring to light; **~ en manchette** *jarg* MÉDIA *presse nouvelle* splash *(jarg)*; **~ en marche** COM actuate, INFO activate, switch on, turn on; **~ à la mode** COM bring into fashion; **~ un nouveau produit à l'essai** COM carry out a trial on a new product; **~ en oeuvre** BREVETS *brevet* work, COM *politique* carry out, *projet, plan, décision, article* implement, INFO implement; **~ en ordre** COM *en ordre alphabétique* put in order, put into order; **~ de l'ordre dans ses affaires** COM put one's affairs in order; **~ par écrit** COM set down in writing; **~ en péril** COM *emploi* compromise, jeopardize; **~ un piquet de grève devant** IND, RES HUM picket; **~ en place** COM instal *(AmE)*, install *(BrE)*, put in place, put in position, INFO instal *(AmE)*, install *(BrE)*; **~ en place progressivement** INFO phase in; **~ au point** COM adjust, finalize, fine-tune, *projet* formulate, INFO debug *(infrml)*, fine-tune, tweak, MÉDIA *texte* sub *(infrml)*, subedit; **~ à la poste** COMMS *lettre* mail *(AmE)*, post *(BrE)*; **~ en pratique** COM carry out, put into practice; **~ en préretraite obligatoire** RES HUM force into early retirement; **~ la pression sur qn** COM put pressure on sb; **~ en priorité** ADMIN, COM, GESTION prioritize; **~ un prix trop bas à** *(*ANT *mettre un prix trop élevé à)* V&M underprice; **~ un prix trop élevé à** *(*ANT *mettre un prix trop bas à)* V&M overprice; **~ au propre** COM write a fair copy of; **~ qn en apprentissage chez qn** RES HUM apprentice sb to sb; **~ qn en colère** COM get sb's back up *(infrml)*; **~ qn au courant** COM put sb in the picture; **~ qn au courant de** COM update sb on; **~ qn au courant de qch** COM brief sb on sth, bring sb up to date on sth, update sb on sth; **~ qn au courant de la situation** COM acquaint sb with the situation; **~ qn dehors** *infrml* RES HUM give sb his/her cards *(infrml)*; **~ qn à l'essai** COM give sb a trial; **~ qn au pied du mur** COM corner sb, push sb to the wall; **~ qn à la porte** *infrml* RES HUM give sb his/her cards *(infrml)*; **~ une question à l'ordre du jour** COM, GESTION place a question on the agenda, put a question on the agenda; **~ en**

relation COMMS *personnes* put in touch; ~ **en relief** COM outline; ~ **à la retraite** FIN, RES HUM pension off, retire, superannuate; ~ **en route** INFO set up; ~ **en service** INFO enable, TRANSP commission; ~ **son veto à** COM put a veto on, veto; ~ **sous forme de tableau** ADMIN, COM tabulate; ~ **sous tension** INFO power on, power up, turn on; ~ **en soute** TRANSP bunker; ~ **sur la liste noire** COM, FIN, RES HUM blacklist; ~ **sur le marché** INFO release; ~ **sur ordinateur** INFO computerize; ~ **sur le tapis** COM *idée, suggestion* air, bring up; ~ **en surnombre** ADMIN surplus; ~ **une taxe sur qch** FISC impose a tax on, put a tax on sth; ~ **à la terre** INFO, TRANSP earth (*BrE*), ground (*AmE*); ~ **tout sur la table** RES HUM work through; ~ **en tutelle** PROT SOC place under guardianship; ~ **à 1** INFO *bit* set; ~ **à la une** MÉDIA lead with; ~ **en valeur** ENVIR reclaim; ~ **en vente** IMMOB put on the market, put up for sale; ~ **en vigueur** COM put into effect, DROIT enforce, put into force; ~ **aux voix** POL *résolution* put to the vote, take a vote on, vote on; ~ **à zéro** INFO zero

meunier, -ière *m,f* IND, RES HUM miller

meurtre: ~ **avec préméditation** *m* DROIT murder one (*infrml*); ~ **au premier degré** *m* DROIT murder one (*infrml*)

mévente *f* COM slump in sales, V&M sales slump

mexicain, e *adj* COM Mexican

Mexicain, e *m,f* COM *habitant* Mexican

Mexico *n pr* COM Mexico City

Mexique *m* COM Mexico

mi: **à ~ -temps** *adj* COM, RES HUM part-time

micro:[1] ~ **-électronique** *adj* IND microelectronic

micro[2] *m* COMMS *(microphone)* microphone, INFO *(micro-ordinateur)* micro; ~ **-interrupteur** INFO DIP switch; ~ **-ordinateur** INFO *(micro)* microcomputer

micro:[3] ~ **-électronique** *f* IND microelectronics; ~ **-informatique** *f* (ANT *macroinformatique*) INFO microcomputing

micro:[4] ~ **-éditer** *vt* MÉDIA desktop-publish

microcoupure *f* INFO brownout (*US*)

microdisquette *f* INFO microdisk

microéconomie *f* (ANT *macroéconomie*) ECON microeconomics

microéconomique *adj* (ANT *macroéconomique*) ECON microeconomic

microfiche *f* ADMIN, COM, COMMS, INFO microfiche

microfilm *m* ADMIN, COM, COMMS, INFO microfilm

microlecteur *m* ADMIN, COM, COMMS, INFO microfiche reader

micrologiciel *m* INFO firmware

micromarketing *m* V&M micromarketing

microphone *m* *(micro)* COMMS microphone

microplaquette *f* INFO chip, microchip

microprocesseur *m* INFO microprocessor

microprogramme *m* INFO firmware, microprogram

microseconde *f* COM microsecond

Midwest: le ~ Stock Exchange *m* BOURSE Midwest Stock Exchange (*US*)

mieux[1] *adj* COM better; **au ~** *adj* BOURSE at the market, COM at best; ◆ **il vaudrait ~ vendre maintenant** COM you'd be better-off selling now; **ou ~** BOURSE, COM or better still; ~ **qu'attendu** COM better than expected; ~ **que la moyenne** COM better than average; ~ **que prévu** COM better than predicted

mieux:[2] ~ **disant** *m* COM best bidder, highest bidder, highest tender, highest tenderer

migration *f* ECON migration; ~ **circulaire** ECON circular migration

migrations: ~ **alternantes** *f pl* TRANSP commutation (*AmE*), commuting

mile *m* COM mile; ~ **carré** COM square mile; ~ **marin** COM *navigation* nautical mile; ~ **nautique** COM *navigation* nautical mile

miles/heure *m pl* COM miles per hour, mph

milice: ~ **anti-grèves** *f* RES HUM goon squad (*US, jarg*); ~ **patronale** *f* RES HUM goon squad (*US, jarg*)

milieu *m* COM circle; ~ **aménagé** ENVIR planned environment; ~ **constant** ENVIR controlled atmosphere, CA; ~ **naturel** ENVIR natural environment; ~ **du navire** TRANSP m, midship; ◆ **au ~** *jarg* BOURSE at-the-money; **au ~ du navire** TRANSP amidships, midships; **de ~ de gamme** INFO midrange

milieux: ~ **d'affaires** *m pl* COM business circles, business quarters; ~ **financiers** *m pl* FIN financial circles; ~ **industriels** *m pl* COM industrial circles; ~ **informatiques** *m pl* INFO computer circles, computer world

militant, e *m,f* POL activist, militant

mille: ~ **dollars** *m pl* COM one thousand dollars

millésime *m* ECON *d'un vin* vintage

milliard *m* BANQUE, COM billion, milliard, thousand million, BN

milliardaire *mf infrml* COM billionaire, multimillionaire; ~ **rouge** *m infrml* POL champagne communist (*infrml*)

millicurie *m* COM mCi, millicurie

millième *m* FISC millage rate (*US*); ~ **d'un dollar** FISC mill (*US*)

milligramme *m* COM mg, milligram

millilitre *m* *(ml)* COM milliliter (*AmE*), millilitre (*BrE*) *(ml)*

millimètre[1] *m* *(mm)* COM millimeter (*AmE*), millimetre (*BrE*) *(mm)*

millimètre:[2] ~ **carré par seconde** *loc* (mm^2/s) COM square millimeter per second (*AmE*), square millimetre per second (*BrE*) (mm^2/s)

million *m* MATH million

millionnaire *mf* COM millionaire; ~ **en actions** *m* COM millionaire on paper, paper millionaire

millions: ~ **de dollars** *m pl* COM megabucks (*infrml*)

millirem: ~ **par heure** m *(millirem/h, mrem/h)* COM *radioactivité* millirem per hour *(mrem/h)*

millirem/h m *(millirem par heure)* COM *radioactivité* mrem/h *(millirem per hour)*

milliröntgen: ~ **par heure** m *(mr/h)* COM milliroentgen per hour *(mr/h)*

milliröntgen/heure m *(mr/h)* COM milliroentgen per hour *(mr/h)*

milliseconde f COM millisecond

min. *abrév (minimum)* COM min. *(minimum)*

mine f IND mine; ~ **de charbon** IND coal mine; ~ **d'or** COM gold mine, money-spinner *(infrml)*, ECON cash cow *(jarg)*

miner vt COM erode

minerai m IND ore; ~ **argentifère** IND silver ore; ~ **argileux** IND clay ore; ~ **de cuivre** IND copper ore; ~ **d'étain** IND tin ore; ~ **de fer** IND iron ore; ~ **lourd** ECON, IND hard commodity; ~ **métallique** IND metalliferous ore; ~ **d'or** IND gold ore; ~ **de plomb** IND lead ore; ~ **de zinc** IND zinc ore

minéralier m TRANSP *navigation* iron-ore carrier, ore carrier

mineur¹, **e** *adj* COM, DROIT minor

mineur² **-e** m,f IND miner, DROIT minor

mini¹ *adj* COM mini, INFO slim-line

mini:² ~ **-feuilleton** m MÉDIA *télévision* miniseries; ~ **-ordinateur** m INFO minicomputer

miniaturisé, e *adj* COM miniaturized, subcompact

minibus m TRANSP minibus; ~ **de transport en commun** TRANSP public service minibus

minimal, e *adj* COM, MATH minimal

minimax m ECON minimax

minimiser vt COM soft-pedal *(infrml)*, FIN *risques* minimize, POL *résultats* soft-pedal *(infrml)*

minimum¹ *adj (min.)* COM minimum *(min.)*

minimum² m COM bottom line, FISC minimum amount; ~ **imposable** ECON, FIN, FISC tax threshold; ~ **vital** PROT SOC living wage, RES HUM minimum living wage

minipage f MÉDIA, V&M *publicité, presse* minipage

ministère m ADMIN government department, POL department, ministry; ~ **des Affaires étrangères** POL ≈ MFA, ≈ Ministry of Foreign Affairs; ~ **des Affaires étrangères et du Commonwealth** ADMIN ≈ FCO *(UK)*, ≈ Foreign and Commonwealth Office *(UK)*; ~ **des Affaires sociales** POL, PROT SOC ≈ DSS *(UK)*, ≈ Department of Social Security *(UK)*; ~ **de l'Agriculture, de la Pêche et de l'Alimentation** ADMIN ≈ MAFF *(UK)*, ≈ Ministry of Agriculture, Fisheries and Food *(UK)*; ~ **du Commerce** COM, POL ≈ Department of Commerce *(US)*, ≈ Department of Trade *(UK)*; ~ **du Commerce et de l'Industrie** COM, ECON, POL ≈ Board of Trade *(UK)*, ≈ BOT *(UK)*, ≈ DTI *(UK)*, ≈ Department of Trade and Industry *(UK)*; ~ **du Commerce et de l'Industrie international** IND *Japon* ≈ MITI, ≈ Ministry of International Trade and Industry; ~ **créancier** ADMIN creditor department;

~ **débiteur** ADMIN debtor department; ~ **de la Défense** ADMIN ≈ MOD *(UK)*, ≈ Ministry of Defence *(UK)*; ~ **de la Défense nationale** POL ≈ Department of Defense *(US)*, ≈ DOD *(US)*, ≈ Ministry of Defence *(UK)*, ≈ MOD *(UK)*, ≈ Defence Department *(UK)*, ≈ Defense Ministry *(US)*; ~ **de l'Éducation nationale** PROT SOC ≈ DES *(UK, obs)*, ≈ Department for Education *(UK, obs)*, ≈ Department of Education *(US)*, ≈ Department of Education and Science *(UK, obs)*; ~ **de l'Énergie** POL ≈ DOE *(US)*, ≈ Department of Energy *(US)*; ~ **de l'Environnement** ENVIR, POL ≈ DOE *(UK)*, ≈ Department of the Environment *(UK)*; ~ **des Finances** ECON ≈ Ministry of Finance, ≈ Treasury *(UK)*, ≈ Treasury Department *(US)*; ~ **de l'Industrie** IND ≈ DI *(US)*, ≈ DOI *(US)*, ≈ Department of Industry *(US)*; ~ **de la Justice** DROIT ≈ Ministry of Justice, ≈ justice ministry; ~ **du Logement et de l'Urbanisme** POL, PROT SOC ≈ Department of Housing and Urban Development *(US)*; ~ **de la Planification industrielle** IND ≈ Industrial Planning Department *(US)*; ~ **public** DROIT prosecution, public prosecutor; ~ **de la Santé** POL, PROT SOC ≈ DOH *(UK)*, ≈ Department of Health *(UK)*, ≈ Department of Health and Human Services *(US)*; ~ **de la Santé et des Affaires sociales** PROT SOC has now been split into the Department of Health (DoH) and the Department of Social Security (DSS), ≈ DHSS *(UK, obs)*, ≈ Department of Health and Social Security *(UK, obs)*; ~ **du Tourisme** LOISIRS ≈ Ministry of Transport *(UK)*, ≈ MOT *(UK)*, ≈ Ministry of Tourism *(UK)*; ~ **des Transports** COMMS, IND, TRANSP ≈ DTp *(UK)*, ≈ Department of Transport *(UK)*, ≈ MOT *(UK)*, ≈ Ministry of Transport *(UK)*; ~ **du Travail** ADMIN ≈ Department of Labor *(US)*, ≈ Ministry of Employment; ~ **du Travail et de l'Emploi** ECON, RES HUM ≈ DEE *(UK)*, ≈ Department of Education and Employment *(UK)*, ≈ DE *(UK)*, ≈ Department of Employment *(UK, obs)*

ministre mf ADMIN, POL Secretary of State *(UK)*, minister, secretary *(US)*; ~ **des Affaires étrangères** m POL ≈ Foreign Secretary *(UK)*, ≈ Secretary of State *(US)*, foreign minister, minister for foreign affairs, minister of foreign affairs; ~ **de la Défense nationale** m POL ≈ Defence Minister *(UK)*, ≈ Defense Secretary *(US)*; ~ **délégué** m ADMIN, POL deputy minister; ~ **de l'Environnement** m COM, POL Minister for the Environment, Minister of the Environment; ~ **d'État** m ADMIN, POL Secretary of State *(UK)*; ~ **des Finances** m FIN ≈ Chancellor of the Exchequer *(UK)*, ≈ Secretary of the Treasury *(US)*, Minister of Finance, finance minister; ~ **de l'Industrie** m COM industry minister; ~ **de la Justice** m RES HUM ≈ LC *(UK)*, ≈ Attorney General *(US)*, ≈ Lord Chancellor *(UK)*; ~ **titulaire d'un portefeuille** m ADMIN departmental

minister; ~ **des Transports** *m* POL, TRANSP
≈ Secretary of State for Transport (*UK*),
≈ Transportation Secretary (*US*), Minister of
Transport, transport secretary

ministres: ~ **des finances de la communauté
européenne** *m pl* ECON, FIN, POL European Community Finance Ministers, ECOFIN

minoration *f* COM, FISC underreporting

minorer *vt* COM, FISC underreport

minorité: ~ **ethnique** *f* POL, PROT SOC ethnic minority

Minsk *n pr* COM Minsk

minuscule *f* (ANT *majuscule*) ADMIN, INFO, MÉDIA
l.c., lower case, lower-case letter

minutage *m* COM timing

minuties *f pl* COM minutiae

miracle *m* COM miracle; **le ~ économique allemand**
ECON the German economic miracle

mire *f* COMMS, MÉDIA test card

mis:[1] ~ **à l'index** *adj* COM, FIN, RES HUM blacklisted

mis:[2] ~ **en attente** *loc* INFO camp-on; **être ~ au
chômage** *loc* RES HUM be made redundant, join
the dole queue (*BrE*); **être ~ en minorité** *loc* COM
be outvoted; **être ~ en règlement judiciaire** *loc*
COM, FIN, IND go into receivership; ~ **en évidence**
loc INFO highlighted; ~ **au point** *loc* COM perfected; ~ **en réserve** *loc* COM *bateau, voiture* laid-
up

mise *f* FIN *argent* outlay; ~ **en accusation** DROIT
indictment; ~ **en administration judiciaire** COM,
COMPTA, DROIT, FIN receivership; ~ **en application**
DROIT enforcement, ENF, INFO implementation;
~ **en attente** BOURSE parking; ~ **en balles** TRANSP
de marchandises baling; ~ **à bord** TRANSP lading;
~ **en bouteille du vin** IND wine-bottling; ~ **en cale
sèche** TRANSP *d'un navire* dry docking, DD; ~ **en
chômage temporaire** RES HUM furlough (*US*),
lay-off, laying off, short-time working; ~ **en
commun** ASSUR, FIN pool, pooling; ~ **en commun
des risques** ASSUR risk pooling; ~ **en conteneurs**
TRANSP containerization; ~ **au courant** RES HUM
du personnel induction, teach-in; ~ **en couverture**
ASSUR commencement of cover; ~ **en décharge**
ENVIR dumping; ~ **en décharge de déchets** ENVIR
waste dumping; ~ **en demeure** COM enforcement
order, DROIT notice; ~ **en demeure avec garantie**
DROIT injunction bond; ~ **en disponibilité** RES
HUM *d'un employé* secondment; ~ **à disposition
de crédit** BANQUE credit granting, granting of
credit; ~ **à disposition de main-d'oeuvre** POL, RES
HUM manpower aid; ~ **en eau** TRANSP *d'un bassin*
impounding; ~ **en évidence** INFO *de texte* highlighting; ~ **en file d'attente** INFO queueing; ~ **de
fonds** ECON, FIN capex, capital expenditure,
capital outlay; ~ **de fonds initiale** COM, COMPTA,
ECON initial outlay, outlay, FIN initial capital,
initial outlay, outlay, start-up capital, IND initial
outlay, outlay; ~ **de fonds nette** BOURSE, ECON,
FIN net capital expenditure, net capital spending;
~ **en forme** INFO *d'une disquette* formatting; ~ **en**

forme juridique RES HUM formalization; ~ **en
fourrière** DROIT impounding; ~ **en gage** BANQUE
pledging; ~ **en gage préjudiciable** DROIT injurious
affection; ~ **en garde** COM caution; ~ **hors tension**
INFO powering off, turning off; ~ **initiale** COMPTA
initial outlay; ~ **à jour** COM, INFO update, updating; ~ **à jour automatique** INFO automatic
updating; ~ **en liquidation** COMPTA receivership;
~ **en main tierce** FIN escrow; ~ **à niveau** INFO
upgrade, upgrading; ~ **en oeuvre** BREVETS *du
brevet* carrying-out, COM application, implementation, *d'un article, plan* implementation, INFO
implementation; ~ **en oeuvre du domaine public**
IMMOB public development; ~ **en oeuvre de la
politique** COM, GESTION policy execution, POL
policy execution, policy lag; ~ **en page** ADMIN,
INFO layout, MÉDIA *de texte* page layout, page
setting; ~ **en pension** BOURSE REPO (*AmE*),
repurchase agreement, RP; ~ **en pension inverse**
FIN reverse repurchase; ~ **en pension du jour au
lendemain** BOURSE overnight repurchase; ~ **à pied**
RES HUM *de personnel* lay-off, laying off, standing
down; ~ **à pied pour motif disciplinaire** RES HUM
disciplinary lay-off; ~ **en place de piquets de
grève** IND, RES HUM picketing; ~ **en place
progressive** COM, INFO phasing in; ~ **au point**
COM adjustment, formulation, GESTION formulation, INFO debugging, fine-tuning; ~ **au point des
objectifs** GESTION goal setting; ~ **au point du
produit** V&M product development; ~ **au point
de programme** INFO program testing; ~ **à prix**
COM floor price, *ventes aux enchères* reservation
price, reserve, reserve price (*BrE*), upset price
(*AmE*), V&M *ventes aux enchères* floor price,
reservation price, reserve, reserve price (*BrE*),
upset price (*AmE*); ~ **à prix au point mort** ECON,
V&M break-even pricing; ~ **à prix prévisionnelle**
ECON, V&M anticipatory pricing; ~ **en réseau**
BANQUE networking; ~ **en retrait** INFO *traitement
de texte*, MÉDIA *impression* indentation; ~ **à la
retraite d'office** RES HUM compulsory retirement
(*BrE*), mandatory retirement (*AmE*); ~ **en route**
INFO start; ~ **en sac** IND, TRANSP *de marchandises*
bagging; ~ **en service** TRANSP commissioning;
~ **sous tension** INFO powering on, powering up,
turning on; ~ **sur écoute téléphonique** COMMS
telephone tapping, wiretapping; ~ **sur le marché**
INFO release, V&M market entry; ~ **sur ordinateur**
INFO computerization; ~ **à la terre** INFO earthing
(*BrE*), grounding (*AmE*); ~ **à terre** TRANSP *maritime, d'une cargaison* landing; ~ **à la terre** TRANSP
earthing (*BrE*), grounding (*AmE*); ~ **en valeur**
ENVIR reclaiming; ~ **en vigueur** DROIT ENF, *d'une
loi* enforcement; ◆ ~ **à terre, magasinage et
livraison** IMP/EXP, TRANSP landing storage delivery, LSD

miser 1. *vt* FIN *argent* bet, gamble, stake; **2.** *vi* COM
gamble

mission *f* COM mission, *charge* assignment, brief;
~ **commune** COM joint assignment;
~ **diplomatique** POL diplomatic mission;

~ économique ECON, GESTION economic mission; **~ d'enquête** COM fact-finding mission; **~ d'entreprise** GESTION corporate mission; **~ à l'étranger** IMP/EXP, TRANSP outward mission

mix *m* V&M mix; **~ de produits** V&M mix, product mix; **~ des produits en vente** V&M sales mix

mixage *m* MÉDIA *enregistrement* mix, mixing

mixte *adj* PROT SOC *école* co-ed, coeducational, TRANSP *navires, cales* comb, combined

ml *abrév (millilitre)* COM ml *(milliliter AmE, millilitre BrE)*

Mlle *abrév (Mademoiselle)* COM Miss

mm *abrév (millimètre)* COM mm *(millimeter AmE, millimetre BrE)*

mm²/s *abrév (millimètre carré par seconde)* COM mm²/s *(square millimeter per second AmE, square millimetre per second BrE)*

Mme *abrév (Madame)* COM Mrs

MMI *abrév (Marché monétaire international)* BOURSE, ECON IMM *(International Monetary Market)*

m/o *abrév (mon ordre)* COM m/o *(my order)*

Mo *abrév (méga-octet)* INFO Mb *(megabyte)*

mobile *m* COM, GESTION, RES HUM motivator, motive; **~ d'achat** V&M purchasing motivator

mobilier *m* COM furniture; **~ domestique** TRANSP household effects

mobilisation *f* DROIT liquidation, FIN liquidation, *de fonds* capital raising, raising; **~ de fonds** BOURSE capital raising, FIN raising of capital, raising of funds

mobiliser *vt* DROIT *actif* liquidate, FIN *capitaux* liquidate, mobilize, raise; ◆ **~ des capitaux** BOURSE raise capital; **~ des fonds extérieurs** COM raise external funds

mobilité *f* ECON mobility; **~ efficiente de la main d'oeuvre** ECON, RES HUM efficient job mobility; **~ fiscale** ECON fiscal mobility; **~ de la main-d'oeuvre** ECON, RES HUM labor mobility *(AmE)*, labour mobility *(BrE)*, mobility of labor *(AmE)*, mobility of labour *(BrE)*; **~ du personnel** RES HUM staff mobility; **~ professionnelle** ECON occupational mobility, RES HUM job mobility; **~ du travail** ECON occupational mobility; **~ verticale** RES HUM vertical mobility

modalité *f* COM method, mode; **~ de paiement** COM, COMPTA, FIN, V&M method of payment

modalités *f pl* BANQUE terms, BOURSE *d'une émission*, COM terms and conditions; **~ de consolidation** COMPTA consolidation method; **~ en dollars** ECON American terms; **~ de paiement** BANQUE terms of payment, FIN terms and conditions

mode¹ *m* COM method, INFO, MATH mode; **~ aide** INFO help mode; **~ bloc** INFO block mode; **~ brouillon** INFO draft mode; **~ continu** INFO burst mode; **~ conversationnel** INFO conversational mode; **~ dialogué** INFO conversational mode; **~ discontinu** INFO byte mode; **~ document** INFO document mode; **~ d'édition** INFO edit mode;

~ d'emploi COM directions for use, instructions, MÉDIA instruction leaflet; **~ d'exploitation normal** COM s.o.p., standard operating procedure; **~ de fonctionnement** COM operating instructions; **~ graphique** INFO graphics mode; **~ d'imposition** FISC method of taxation; **~ interactif** INFO interactive mode; **~ listage** INFO draft mode; **~ opératoire** COM modus operandi *(frml)*, MO; **~ de paiement** COM, COMPTA, FIN, V&M method of payment; **~ de production asiatique** ECON, IND Asiatic mode of production; **~ de rémunération** RES HUM wage system; **~ réponse** INFO answer mode; **~ texte** INFO text mode; **~ de transmission de données par paquets** INFO burst mode; **~ de transmission de données par rafales** INFO burst mode; **~ de transport** TRANSP mode of transport, transport mode; **~ de vie** COM way of life

mode² *f* COM, ECON, V&M fashion; **~ passagère** COM, ECON, V&M fad; ◆ **en ~ conversationnel** INFO conversationally; **à la ~** COM in fashion; **qui crée la ~** COM trendsetter

modelage: **~ statistique** *m* MATH statistical modeling *(AmE)*, statistical modelling *(BrE)*

modèle *m* BREVETS design, COM *copie* model, *illustrations* artwork, version, MATH model, V&M artwork; **~ d'analyse cobweb** ECON cobweb; **~ auto-régressif à moyenne mobile** MATH autoregressive moving-average model; **~ auto-régressif à moyenne mobile intégrée** MATH autoregressive integrated moving-average model; **~ de Black-Scholes** BOURSE Black-Scholes Option Pricing Model; **~ classique** ECON classical model; **~ comptable** COMPTA, FIN accounting model; **~ de consommation** ECON consumption pattern; **~ de convention** ADMIN boilerplate; **~ de décision** GESTION decision model; **~ déposé** BREVETS, DROIT registered design; **~ duopole de Bertrand** ECON Bertrand duopoly model; **~ du duopole de Cournot** ECON Cournot's duopoly model; **~ duopolistique de Stackelberg** ECON Stackelberg duopoly model; **~ dynamique de gestion** GESTION dynamic management model; **~ économique** ECON economic model; **~ économique dynamique** ECON dynamic economics; **~ économique à moyen terme pour la communauté européenne** ECON *économétrie* Common Market Medium Term Model, COMET; **~ de l'entreprise** COM, COMPTA, FIN company model, corporate model; **~ de l'épargne selon Ramsey** ECON Ramsey savings model; **~ d'équilibre des actifs financiers *(MEDAF)*** BOURSE, ECON, FIN capital asset pricing model *(CAPM)*; **~ d'évaluation des actifs financiers *(MEDAF)*** BOURSE, ECON, FIN capital asset pricing model *(CAPM)*; **~ d'évaluation d'un prix** BOURSE pricing model; **~ de facture** COM specimen invoice; **~ global** PROT SOC unitary model; **~ Hermès** ECON Hermes model; **~ intégré de moyenne mobile régressive** MATH autoregressive integrated moving-average model; **~ de lettre** ADMIN lettertype; **~ de liaison ascendante** ECON bottom-up linkage model; **~ de liaison**

descendante ECON top-down linkage model; ~ **de lien dessus-dessous** ECON bottom-up linkage model; ~ **de moyenne mobile régressive** MATH autoregressive moving-average model; ~ **de Mundell et Fleming** ECON Mundell-Fleming model; ~ **de présentation de formulaires nouveaux** ADMIN forms design sheet; ~ **de simulation** ECON simulation model; ~ **statique** ECON static model; ~ **structure-conduite-performance** ECON structure-conduct-performance model, SCP; ~ **structurel** ECON structural model; ~ **de Tobit** ECON Tobit model; ~ **d'utilité** BREVETS utility model

modèles: ~ **d'exploitation** *m pl* RES HUM working patterns; ~ **macroéconomiques comparatifs** *m pl* ECON *économétrie* linkage models

modélisation *f* MATH modeling (*AmE*), modelling (*BrE*); ~ **discrète** ECON soft modeling (*AmE*), soft modelling (*BrE*); ~ **de simulation** ECON simulation modeling (*AmE*), simulation modelling (*BrE*)

modéliser *vt* MATH model

modem *m* (*modulateur-démodulateur*) COMMS, INFO modem (*modulator-demodulator*); ~ **à connexion directe** COMMS, INFO direct-connect modem

modéré, e *adj* ECON moderate, modest

modérément *adv* COM moderately, modestly

modérer *vt* COM contain, moderate

modérés *m pl* POL moderates, wets (*UK, infrml*)

modern: ~ **portfolio theory** *m* BOURSE modern portfolio theory, MPT

modernisation *f* COM modernization, revamping, ECON capital improvement, modernization, rejuvenation, IND, POL modernization

moderniser *vt* COM modernize, revamp, ECON modernize, rejuvenate, IND, POL modernize

modes: ~ **facultatifs de règlement** *m pl* ASSUR optional modes of settlement

modeste *adj* COM *augmentation, salaire*, ECON modest

modification *f* COM alteration, modification, variation, DROIT amendment, revision, ECON *de la courbe de la demande* shift, FISC alteration, IMMOB *d'un immeuble* modification, INFO change, POL amendment; ~ **du capital** COM, FIN alteration of capital; ~ **de la clause d'attribution du bénéficiaire** ASSUR *assurance-vie* change of beneficiary provision; ~ **du comportement** RES HUM behavior modification (*AmE*), behaviour modification (*BrE*); ~ **comptable** COMPTA accounting change; ~ **de la consommation** V&M shift in consumption; ~ **de la disposition du bénéficiaire** ASSUR *assurance-vie* change of beneficiary provision; ~ **d'itinéraire** TRANSP change of itinerary, rerouting; ~ **provisoire** DROIT, POL draft amendment

modifié, e *adj* COM alt., altered, modified, FISC amended

modifier *vt* BREVETS amend, COM alter, modify, vary, DROIT amend, revise, INFO edit, POL amend

modulaire *adj* COM, MATH modular

modularité *f* COM, MATH modularity

modulateur: ~ **-démodulateur** *m* (*modem*) COMMS, INFO modulator-demodulator (*modem*)

modulation *f* COMMS modulation; ~ **de fréquence** (*FM*) COMMS frequency modulation (*FM*)

module *m* COM, MATH module; ~ **d'alarme** TRANSP *navigation* automatic watch keeper; ~ **de décision** FIN decision package

moduler *vt* COMMS modulate

Mogadiscio *n pr* COM Mogadischu

moindre: ~ **coût** *m* COMPTA least-cost; ◆ **à un ~ degré** COM to a lesser extent

moindres: ~ **carrés généralisés** *m pl* MATH generalized least squares, GLS

moins:[1] ~ **cher** *adj* COM cheaper; ~ **onéreux** *adj* COM cheaper

moins[2] *adv* COM less

moins[3] *m* MATH *signe* minus, minus sign; ~ **-disant** COM lowest bidder, lowest tender, lowest tenderer; ~ **non réalisé sur titres** BOURSE paper loss; ~ **sur titres** BOURSE paper loss

moins:[4] ~ **nette** *f* COM, COMPTA, ECON, FIN, FISC net capital loss; ~ **-value** *f* BOURSE write-down, COM, COMPTA, ECON, FIN capital loss, write-down, FISC capital loss

moins[5] *prép* COMPTA, FIN, MATH less, minus; ~ **de** *prép* COM under; **de ~ de** *prép* (*ANT de plus de*) COM below; **un peu ~ de** *prép* COM *cent kilos, vingt ans* a bit less than, a little under

mois[1] *m* COM m, month, MTH; ~ **du calendrier** COM calendar month; ~ **civil** COM calendar month; ~ **d'échéance** BOURSE contract delivery month (*BrE*), contract month, delivery month, expiration month, expiry month, COM months after date; ~ **d'échéance le plus proche** BOURSE nearest month; ~ **d'exercice** FISC fiscal month; ~ **d'expiration** BOURSE expiration month, expiry month; ~ **de livraison** BOURSE contract month, delivery month, spot month, COM *d'un contrat* contract month; ~ **de livraison du contrat** BOURSE contract delivery month (*BrE*); ~ **de livraison immédiate** BOURSE spot delivery month, spot month; ~ **prochain** BOURSE nearest month, COM next month; ◆ **du ~ dernier** COM ult., ultimo (*frml*); **un ~ à l'avance** COM a month in advance

mois:[2] ~ **après date** *loc* COM months after date; ~ **de transaction** *loc* BOURSE months traded; ~ **à vue** *loc* BANQUE m/s, months after sight

moitié *f* COM, MATH half; ~ **de vie** BOURSE half-life

moldave *adj* COM Moldovan

Moldave *mf* COM *habitant* Moldovan

Moldavie *f* COM Moldova

môle *m* TRANSP mole, *dans un port* breakwater

moment *m* COM moment; ~ **nécessaire pour faire varier l'assiette** TRANSP *dans un navire* moment to change trim, MCT; ◆ **à tout ~** COM at all times, constantly; **à un ~ donné** COM at a given moment, at some stage; **à un ~ donné dans le futur** COM at a given moment in the future, at some time in the future; **pour le ~** COM for the time being

moments *m pl* MATH moments

mon: **~ compte** *m* COM m/a, my account; **~ ordre** *m* *(m/o)* COM my order *(m/o)*

Monaco *n pr* COM Monaco

monde *m* COM world; **~ des affaires** COM business community, business world; **~ anglophone** COM English-speaking world; **~ du commerce** COM business world, commercial world; **~ de la finance** FIN financial world, world of finance; **~ francophone** COM French-speaking world; **~ de la publicité** V&M advertising world; **~ du spectacle** COM show business; ◆ **dans le ~ entier** COM all over the world, in the whole world

mondial *adj* [pl: -aux] COM global, world, world-wide

mondialement *adv* COM globally, worldwide

mondialisation *f* COM, ECON *marchés* globalization

mondialiser *vt* COM, ECON *marchés* globalize

monégasque *adj* COM Monegasque

Monégasque *mf* COM *habitant* Monegasque

MONEP *abrév (Marché des options négociables de Paris)* BOURSE Paris traded options exchange, ≈ CBOE *(Chicago Board Options Exchange)*, ≈ LIFFE *(London International Financial Futures Exchange)*

monétaire *adj* COM, ECON monetary

monétarisme *m* ECON monetarism, quantity theory of money, POL monetarism; **~ global** ECON, POL global monetarism; **~ gradualiste** ECON gradualist monetarism; **~ instantané** ECON instant monetarism

monétariste[1] *adj* ECON, POL monetarist

monétariste[2] *mf* ECON, POL monetarist

monétisation *f* ECON monetization

monétiser *vt* ECON monetize

mongol, e *adj* COM Mongolian

Mongol, e *m,f* COM *habitant* Mongolian

Mongolie *f* COM Mongolia

moniteur *m* COM *dispositif*, INFO *matériel* monitor; **~ analogique** INFO *matériel* analog monitor; **~ d'eau** TRANSP *navigation* water monitor; **~ vidéo** INFO *matériel* video monitor

monkey *m* FIN monkey *(US, infrml)*

monnaie *f* BANQUE coinage, currency, money, CY, COM *argent/espèces* cash, money, *pièces de faible valeur* change, loose change, odd change, *pièces de monnaie* coin, ECON, FIN coinage, currency, money, CY; **~ de banque** BANQUE bank deposit money, bank money, deposit money; **~ de base** TRANSP basic currency; **~ bloquée** FIN, IMP/EXP blocked currency; **~ centrale** BANQUE centralized money; **~ circulante** FIN active money; **~ en circulation** ECON currency in circulation, FIN active money; **~ clé** ECON, FIN key currency;

~ commune ECON, FIN common currency; **~ composite** BANQUE, ECON, FIN composite currency; **~ dominante** BANQUE, ECON, FIN major currency; **~ d'échange** FIN circulating medium; **~ étrangère** COM, ECON, FIN foreign currency; **~ externe** ECON, FIN outside money; **~ fiduciaire** BANQUE, FIN credit money, fiat money *(US)*, fiduciary currency, paper money, token money; **~ fiduciaire d'appoint** BANQUE, FIN fiat money *(US)*; **~ forte** ECON hard money; **~ à haute puissance** BANQUE centralized money, ECON high-powered money; **~ inconvertible** ECON inconvertible money; **~ légale** *(SYN pouvoir libératoire)* FIN legal tender; **~ locale** FIN, IMP/EXP lc, local currency; **~ marchandise** BOURSE commodity currency; **~ nationale** FIN national currency; **~ en or** BANQUE gold currency; **~ parallèle** ECON parallel currency; **~ principale** BANQUE, ECON, FIN major currency; **~ de réserve** COM reserve currency; **~ scripturale** BANQUE bank deposit money, bank money, deposit money; **~ de singe** *infrml* BOURSE Chinese money *(UK, jarg)*, COM quasi-money; **~ surévaluée** ECON overvalued currency; **~ unique** COM, ECON, FIN common currency, single currency; **~ unique européenne** ECON single European currency; **~ verte** ECON green currency; ◆ **ne pas rendre assez de ~ à** COM short-change

Monnaie *f* BANQUE mint

monochrome *adj* INFO, MÉDIA monochrome

monoéconomie *f* ECON monoeconomics

monogramme *m* COM monogram

monomère: **~ chloruré vinylique** *m* IND vinyl chloride monomer

monométallisme *m* ECON monometallism

monométalliste[1] *adj* ECON monometallic

monométalliste[2] *mf* ECON monometallist

monopole *m* COM corner, monopoly, ECON, V&M monopoly; **~ absolu** ECON absolute monopoly, perfect monopoly, FIN, V&M absolute monopoly; **~ bilatéral** ECON bilateral monopoly; **~ discriminatoire** ECON discriminating monopoly; **~ exclusif** ECON exclusive monopoly; **~ intégral** ECON pure monopoly; **~ légal** ECON legal monopoly; **~ local** ECON spatial monopoly; **~ en matière de brevets** IND patent monopoly; **~ naturel** ECON natural monopoly; **~ parfait** ECON perfect monopoly; **~ partagé** ECON oligopoly, shared monopoly, POL oligopoly; **~ pur** ECON pure monopoly; **~ régional** ECON local monopoly; **~ syndical** RES HUM closed shop; **~ syndical après l'embauche** RES HUM post-entry closed shop; **~ syndical de l'embauche** RES HUM union shop; **~ syndical préalable à l'embauche** RES HUM pre-entry closed shop; ◆ **avoir le quasi-~ du marché** ECON, V&M have a stranglehold on the market

monopolisation *f* COM, ECON, V&M monopolization

monopoliser *vt* COM, ECON, V&M monopolize

monopoliste[1] *adj* ECON, V&M monopolistic

monopoliste^2 *mf* ECON, V&M monopolist

monopsone *m* ECON monopsony

monorail *m* TRANSP *chemin de fer* monorail

monospace *m* TRANSP minivan

monotone *adj* COM monotonous

monoxyde: ~ **de carbone** *m* ENVIR carbon monoxide

Monrovia *n pr* COM Monrovia

monsieur: ~ **tout-le-monde** *m* COM the man in the street

Monsieur *m (M.)* COM Mister *(Mr)*; ~ **Dupont** DROIT ≈ John Doe *(US)*

montage *m* COM, IND assembling, assembly, INFO set-up, MÉDIA, V&M *publicité* paste-up; ~ **financier** FIN financing package; ~ **financier multi-options** BOURSE multioption facility, multioption financing facility; ~ **financier à options multiples** BOURSE multioption facility, multioption financing facility; ~ **préalable** V&M *publicité* rough

montagne *f* ECON mountain; ~ **de beurre** ECON *UE* butter mountain; ~ **de viande** ECON meat mountain

montant *m* COM amount, AMT, *d'une facture* total amount; ~ **de l'adjudication** COM tender price; ~ **amortissable** COMPTA depreciable amount; ~ **d'angle** TRANSP *d'un conteneur* corner post; ~ **annuel de la rente** FISC annual annuity amount; ~ **arrondi** COM round sum; ~ **attribué** FISC designated amount; ~ **des avaries** ASSUR amount of damage; ~ **de base** COM basic amount, FISC base amount; ~ **brut** COMPTA gross amount; ~ **en capital** FIN principal amount; ~ **de la communication téléphonique** COMMS call charge; ~ **compensatoire** ECON compensatory amount; ~ **compensatoire monétaire** ECON, FIN monetary compensation amount, monetary compensatory amount, MCA; ~ **compensatoire monétaire négatif** *(ANT montant compensatoire monétaire positif)* ECON, FIN negative monetary compensatory amount; ~ **compensatoire monétaire positif** *(ANT montant compensatoire monétaire négatif)* ECON, FIN positive monetary compensatory amount; ~ **d'un compte douteux** COMPTA delinquency; ~ **du contrat** BOURSE contract value; ~ **convenu** COM agreed sum; ~ **cumulatif des immobilisations admissibles** FISC cumulative eligible capital; ~ **cumulatif imputé** FISC cumulative imputed amount; ~ **à découvert** BANQUE uncovered amount; ~ **déductible** FISC allowable deduction; ~ **déterminant** FISC threshold amount; ~ **déterminé** COM specific amount; ~ **différé** FISC deferred amount; ~ **du dommage** ASSUR amount of damage; ~ **dû** COM, FIN amount due, invoice amount, invoicing amount; ~ **échu** COMPTA *qui a dépassé son échéance* amount overdue; ~ **estimatif** FISC estimate, estimated amount; ~ **étalé** FISC averaging amount; ~ **d'étalement** FISC averaging amount; ~ **d'étalement accumulé** FISC accumulated averaging amount; ~ **éventuel** COM, FIN amount if any; ~ **des gains** FISC earnings amount;

~ **garanti** FISC amount secured; ~ **garanti par une sûreté sur un bien** FIN, IMMOB amount secured by a charge upon property; ~ **global** FISC combined amount, RES HUM lump sum; ~ **impayé** COMPTA amount outstanding; ~ **d'investissement de petite entreprise** FISC small business investment amount; ~ **locatif** FISC rental cost; ~ **de la masse salariale** COMPTA *bilan* total wages and salaries; ~ **moyen en dépôt** ASSUR mean amount on deposit; ~ **moyen** COM average amount; ~ **net de l'actif** COMPTA, FIN net asset amount; ~ **net de l'ajustement de la réserve** COMPTA net reserve adjustment amount; ~ **net des emprunts** ECON, FIN net borrowing; ~ **net de l'inclusion de la réserve** COMPTA net reserve inclusion amount; ~ **net des placements** BANQUE net investment position; ~ **net des prêts** BANQUE net lending; ~ **de l'offre** BOURSE bid value; ~ **payable** FISC amount payable; ~ **payable à terme** COMPTA amount payable on settlement; ~ **payé par acomptes** FISC amount paid by installments *(AmE)*, amount paid by instalments *(BrE)*; ~ **à payer** COM amount charged, amount to pay; ~ **d'un placement dans des petites entreprises** FISC small business investment amount; ~ **pour provision nette** COMPTA net reserve inclusion amount; ~ **de redressement pour provision nette** COMPTA net reserve adjustment amount; ~ **réel** COMPTA actual amount; ~ **remboursable** COMPTA amount repayable; ~ **reporté** COMPTA amount brought forward; ~ **du sinistre** ASSUR amount of loss; ~ **des sommes versées à la sécurité sociale** COMPTA, PROT SOC *bilan* total social charges; ~ **du transfert** COM transfer fee, *pour un footballeur* transfer fee; ~ **versé** COM amount paid, COMPTA amount paid out

monte:^{1} **qui** ~ *adj* COM upwardly mobile; **qui** ~ **en flèche** *adj* COM *prix* soaring

monte:^{2} ~ **-charge à ciseaux** *m* TRANSP scissor lift

montée *f* COM rise; ~ **des enchères** BOURSE bidding up; ~ **en flèche** COM *des prix* boom, jump; ~ **de l'impôt sur les salaires** ECON, FISC wage-tax spiral; ~ **soudaine des dépenses** COM, ECON spending surge; ~ **en spirale** COM, ECON upward spiral

monténégrin, e *adj* COM Montenegrin

Monténégrin, e *m,f* COM *habitant* Montenegrin

Monténégro *m* COM Montenegro

monter 1. *vt* COM *affaire, machine, système* set up, V&M *campagne* mount; **2.** *vi* COM *prix* be advancing, rise, ECON climb, *prix* rise; **3.** *v pron* **se** ~ **à** COM amount to, *charges, frais* add up to; **se** ~ **en affaires** COM set up in business, start in business; ◆ **faire** ~ COM escalate, *prix* bid up, inflate; ~ **en flèche** COM *prix* escalate, soar, *prix, activité boursière* shoot up, ECON boom, *prix* soar; ~ **lentement** ECON edge up; ~ **à nouveau** COM, ECON rise again; ~ **un stage de formation** RES HUM hold an in-service training *(jarg)*

Montevideo *n pr* COM Montevideo

montrer 1. *vt* COM show; **2.** *v pron* **se** ~ **discret** COM keep a low profile; **se ~ à la hauteur** COM be up to scratch (*infrml*), come up to scratch (*infrml*); **se ~ irréductible sur** COM adhere to, stick to; ◆ **~ une hausse des exportations** COM, IMP/EXP show a rise in exports

Montserrat *n pr* COM Montserrat

monument *m* IMMOB monument (*US*); **~ classé** IMMOB listed building (*UK*)

moral[1], **e** *adj* GESTION, PROT SOC ethical, moral

moral[2] *m* RES HUM *des grévistes, du personnel* morale

morale: **personne ~** *f* BREVETS legal entity, legal person, natural person, DROIT juridical person, legal entity, legal person; **personne ~ en cours de fusion** *f* COM amalgamating body corporate; **personne ~ issue de la fusion** *f* COM amalgamated body corporate

moratoire *m* COM, DROIT, FIN moratorium (*frml*)

moratorium *m frml* COM, DROIT, FIN moratorium (*frml*), standstill agreement

morceler *vt* DROIT, IMMOB *terrain* break up, parcel out, parcel up

morcellement: **~ de terrain** *m* DROIT partition, IMMOB breaking up, parceling out (*AmE*), parceling up (*AmE*), parcelling out (*BrE*), parcelling up (*BrE*), partition

morgue *f jarg* MÉDIA morgue (*infrml*)

morne *adj* COM *avenir, perspective*, ECON bleak

Moroni *n pr* COM Moroni

morose *adj* BOURSE, COM sluggish

morosité *f* BOURSE, COM *du marché* sluggishness

mortalité *f* ASSUR, PROT SOC mortality; **~ infantile** PROT SOC infant mortality; **~ présumée** ASSUR expected mortality; **~ probable** ASSUR expected mortality

morte: **~ saison** *f* COM off season, slack period

morts: **~ vivants** *m pl* BOURSE living dead (*jarg*)

Moscou *n pr* COM Moscow

mot *m* COM, INFO word; **~ branché** *infrml* COM buzz word (*infrml*); **~ clé** COM, INFO key word; **~ à la mode** COM buzz word (*infrml*); **~ d'ordre** COM watchword; **~ d'ordre de grève** RES HUM strike call; **~ de passe** INFO password; **~ du président** GESTION chairman's brief; ◆ **avoir son ~ à dire dans qch** COM have a say in sth

moteur *m* COM, ECON driving force, IND, TRANSP engine, motor, ENG, MOT; **~ de croissance** ECON engine of growth; **~ diagonal** TRANSP diagonal engine, D; **~ diesel-électrique** TRANSP diesel-electric engine; **~ principal** TRANSP *d'un navire* main engine, ME; **~ de rechange** COM replacement engine; **~ à triple expansion** TRANSP triple expansion engine, T

motif *m* ASSUR, COM *raison* motive, grounds, DROIT motive, *d'opposition, de nullité* grounds, INFO pattern; **~ de prévention** COM precautionary motive; **~ de renvoi** RES HUM grounds for dismissal; **~ de résiliation** ASSUR cause of cancellation

motion *f* POL motion; **~ de censure** POL motion of censure

motivant, **e** *adj* COM, GESTION, RES HUM motivational

motivateur *m* COM, GESTION, RES HUM motivator

motivation *f* COM, GESTION, RES HUM motivation; **~ de l'actif** ECON *économie monétaire* asset motive; **~ d'équipe** GESTION, INFO, RES HUM team building; **~ extrinsèque** RES HUM extrinsic motivation; **~ intrinsèque** RES HUM intrinsic motivation; **~ par les prix** ECON, V&M price incentive; **~ par le profit** ECON, FIN, V&M profit motive

motivé, **e** *adj* COM driven, RES HUM well-motivated, *personne* motivated; **~ par le profit** ECON profit-motivated

motiver *vt* COM, GESTION, RES HUM motivate

mots: **~ à la minute** *loc* ADMIN words per minute, wpm

moufle *mf* TRANSP *appareil de levage* purchase

mouillage *m* TRANSP anchorage; **~ réservé à la marine** TRANSP accommodation berth, naval anchorage

mourir *vi* COM die; ◆ **~ intestat** DROIT die intestate

mousse *m* RES HUM deck boy

moutons *m pl* BOURSE lambs (*infrml*)

mouvement *m* BANQUE *d'un compte* activity, BOURSE move, movement, COM, POL movement; **~ anormal** BOURSE *du cours d'une action, vers le haut ou vers le bas* break-out; **~ à la baisse** (*ANT mouvement à la hausse*) BOURSE bearish movement, bearish tendency, downward movement, downward trend; **~ brusque** BOURSE sharp movement; **~ comptable** BANQUE, COMPTA, FIN account turnover; **~ de compte** BANQUE account activity; **~ contraire** BOURSE *de prix des obligations* adverse movement; **~ du cours** BOURSE price move; **~ à la hausse** (*ANT mouvement à la baisse*) BOURSE bullish movement, bullish tendency, upward movement, upward trend; **~ d'imposition unique** FISC single tax movement; **~ de longue durée** ECON logistic cycle, long wave; **~ des marchandises** TRANSP movement of freight; **~ ouvrier** RES HUM labor movement (*AmE*), labour movement (*BrE*); **~ du personnel** RES HUM staff turnover; **~ planifié** TRANSP disciplined movement; **~ populaire** COM, POL grass-roots movement; **~ qui part de la base** COM, POL grass-roots movement; **~ de solidarité** RES HUM solidarity action, sympathy action; **~ soudain** BOURSE sharp movement; **~ de soutien** RES HUM go out in sympathy with; **~ des stocks** BOURSE, COMPTA, ECON, IND stock turnover; **~ syndical** RES HUM labor union movement (*US*), trade union movement (*UK*), union movement; **~ des taux d'intérêt** BANQUE, ECON interest rate movement; **~ vers le bas** (*ANT mouvement vers le haut*) BOURSE bearish movement, bearish tendency, downward movement, downward trend; **~ vers le haut** (*ANT mouvement vers le bas*) BOURSE bullish movement, bullish tendency, upward movement, upward trend; **~ de virement automatique** BANQUE direct deposit transaction (*Can*); ◆ **être dans le ~** COM be abreast of the times, be in the swim (*infrml*), be up-to-date, keep up-to-date

mouvements: **~ de l'actif** *m pl* COMPTA, FIN asset turnover; **~ des cours** *m pl* BOURSE swings; **~ de l'encaisse** *m pl* COMPTA cash flow; **~ de fonds** *m pl* BOURSE, COMPTA flow of funds; **~ sociaux** *m pl* IND, RES HUM industrial action; **~ de trésorerie** *m pl* COMPTA cash flow; **~ de trésorerie annuels** *m pl* COMPTA, FIN annual cash flow

moyen[1], **-enne** *adj* ASSUR, BOURSE, COM, COMPTA, FIN, FISC, INFO, MATH average; ◆ **à ~ terme** (ANT *à court terme, à long terme*) BANQUE medium-term, BOURSE *valeurs* medium-dated, medium-term, COM *planification* in the medium term, medium-term, COMPTA, FIN medium-term

moyen[2] *m* COM, ECON, FIN means; **~ audiovisuel** COMMS, MÉDIA audiovisual aid; **~ de communication** COMMS communications, means of communication, medium; **~ de communication secrète** POL back-channel (*US*); **~ d'échange** ECON, FIN medium of exchange; **~ d'échange généralisé** ECON, FIN generalized medium; **~ d'évaluation** COM yardstick; **~ de paiement** ECON medium of exchange, FIN medium of exchange, payment device; **~ de production** COM factor; **~ de rachat** ECON, FIN medium of redemption; **~ de souscription renouvelable** ASSUR revolving underwriting facility, RUF; **~ terme** BANQUE, COM, FIN intermediate term, medium term; **~ de transport** TRANSP means of conveyance, means of transport, transport mode

moyennant: **~ contrepartie valable** *loc* DROIT for good and valuable consideration

moyenne *f* COM, COMPTA, MATH av., average, mean; **~ arithmétique** MATH arithmetic mean; **~ d'un compte** COMPTA medium of account, unit of account; **~ de l'échantillon** MATH sample mean; **~ générale** MATH general average, GA; **~ géométrique** MATH geometric mean, GM; **~ harmonique** MATH harmonic mean; **~ journalière** BOURSE average equity; **~ mobile** MATH moving average; **~ nationale** ECON national average; **~ pondérée** COM, ECON, MATH weighted average; **~ tous secteurs confondus** ECON all-sector average; ◆ **en ~** COM at an average; **faire une ~** BOURSE *à la hausse ou à la baisse*, FIN average out, MATH take an average; **faire une ~ à la baisse** (ANT *faire une moyenne à la hausse*) BOURSE average down; **faire une ~ à la hausse** (ANT *faire une moyenne à la baisse*) BOURSE average up

moyens *m pl* COM means, ECON, FIN means, medium; **~ d'action promotionnelle** V&M *publicité* promotion mix, promotional mix; **~ de communication** COMMS, MÉDIA communication media, mass media, TRANSP communications; **~ d'échange standard** TRANSP *aviation* Standard

Interchange Facilities; **~ financiers** FIN financial means; **~ légaux** DROIT lawful means; **les ~ de communication** MÉDIA information broadcast, the media; **~ de paiement** BANQUE, COM, ECON, FIN means of payment; **~ privés** FIN private means; **~ de production** ECON, IND inputs; **~ de production asiatiques** ECON, IND Asiatic mode of production; **~ de transport** TRANSP transport facilities; ◆ **avoir les ~ de** COM have the means to, ECON afford; **avoir les ~ d'acheter qch** ECON be able to afford to buy sth; **ne pas être doté de ~ de financement suffisants** FIN be underfunded

moyeu *m* TRANSP hub

mozambicain, e *adj* COM Mozambican

Mozambicain, e *m,f* COM *habitant* Mozambican

Mozambique *m* COM Mozambique

MP *abrév* (*mandat postal*) BANQUE, FIN MO (*AmE*) (*money order*), PO (*BrE*) (*postal order*)

mrem/h *abrév* (*millirem par heure*) COM *radioactivité* mrem/h (*millirem per hour*)

mr/h *abrév* (*milliröntgen par heure, milliröntgen/heure*) COM mr/h (*milliroentgen per hour*)

m/s *abrév* (*mètres par seconde*) COM m/s (*meters per second AmE, metres per second BrE*)

MS *abrév* (*manuscrit*) FISC MS (*manuscript*)

MS-DOS® *m* INFO Microsoft Disk Operating System®, MS-DOS®

MTC *abrév* (*mécanisme de taux de change*) ECON ERM (*exchange rate mechanism*)

m³ *abrév* (*mètre cube*) COM cbm (*cubic meter AmE, cubic metre BrE*)

multi: **~ -fonction** *adj* COM multipurpose, MP; **~ -route** *adj* TRANSP multiroute

multicolinéarité *f* MATH multicollinearity

multicorrélation *f* ECON multicollinearity

multidevise *f* BANQUE, ECON, FIN multicurrency

multijuridictionnel, -elle *adj* DROIT multijurisdictional

multilatéral, e *adj* ECON, POL multilateral

multilatéralisme *m* ECON, POL multilateralism

multimédia *adj* INFO, MÉDIA, V&M multimedia

multimodal, e *adj* TRANSP multimodal

multinational, e *adj* COM, ECON, IND multinational

multinationale *f* COM, ECON, IND multinational, multinational company, multinational corporation, MNC

multiple[1] *adj* COM, MATH multiple

multiple[2] *m* MATH multiple

multiplet *m* INFO byte

multiplicateur *m* ECON multiplier; **~ du budget équilibré** COMPTA, ECON, FIN balanced budget multiplier; **~ du commerce extérieur** ECON foreign trade multiplier; **~ de crédit** FIN credit multiplier, credit scoring; **~ de l'emploi** ECON employment multiplier; **~ fiscal** ECON fiscal multiplier; **~ d'impact** ECON impact multiplier; **~ d'investissement** ECON *économétrie* investment multiplier; **~ de Keynes** ECON *économétrie* Keynesian multiplier; **~ de loyer brut** IMMOB gross rent multiplier, GRM; ~ **monétaire** ECON money multiplier; ~ **régional** ECON regional multiplier; ~ **des réserves bancaires** ECON deposit multiplier

multiplication *f* COM, MATH multiplication

multiplier 1. *vt* MATH multiply; **2.** *v pron* **se ~** MATH multiply; ◆ ~ **les transactions fictives** BOURSE paint the tape (*jarg*)

multipostage *m* ECON, FIN bus mailing

multiprocesseur *m* INFO multiprocessor

multiprogrammation *f* INFO multiprogramming

multipropriété *f* IMMOB time share, time sharing, unitization, time-share property

multiracial, e *adj* COM multiracial

multirisque *adj* ASSUR *police d'assurance automobile* comprehensive

multitraitement *m* INFO multiprocessing

multiutilisateur *m* INFO multiuser

M1: ~ **non porteur d'intérêts** *m* ECON non-interest-bearing M1, NIBM1

municipal *adj* ADMIN local, COM, POL municipal

municipalité *f* ADMIN borough, local council, local government, municipal borough, municipal government, municipality, ≈ council (*UK*), ≈ local authority (*UK*), COM municipality, POL ≈ council (*UK*), ≈ local authority (*UK*), borough, local council, local government, municipal borough, municipal government, municipality, ≈ local authority (*UK*)

munie: personne ~ d'un billet *f* COM, LOISIRS, TRANSP ticket holder

mur: ~ **mitoyen** *m* DROIT, IMMOB party wall

muraille: ~ **de Chine** *f* BANQUE, FIN Chinese wall

musique: ~ **en vol** *f* TRANSP in-flight music

mutation *f* DROIT, IMMOB, RES HUM transfer; ~ **de personnel** ECON, RES HUM labor turnover (*AmE*), labour turnover (*BrE*), staff transfer; ~ **du personnel** RES HUM staff turnover; ~ **des structures** GESTION organizational change

mutatis mutandis *loc* DROIT mutatis mutandis, the necessary changes having been made

muter *vt* RES HUM post, transfer

mutuel, -elle *adj* ASSUR knock-for-knock

mutuelle *f* ASSUR mutual insurance company

MW *abrév (mégawatt)* COM MW *(megawatt)*

Myanmar *m* COM Myanmar

mystique *f* COM mystique

N

n *abrév (nominal)* COM n. *(nominal)*

N *abrév* COM *(nord)* N *(north)*, TRANSP *(quart nord) navigation* N *(North compass point)*

N/A *abrév (numérique-analogique)* INFO D/A *(digital-analog)*

naira *m (NR)* COM naira *(NR)*

Nairobi *n pr* COM Nairobi

Namibie *f* COM Namibia

namibien, -enne *adj* COM Namibian

Namibien, -enne *m,f* COM *habitant* Namibian

nantir *vt* DROIT hypothecate

nantissement *m* BANQUE pledge, pledging, DROIT lien, ECON collateral, collateral security, FIN collateral security, collateral; **~ pour acompte** *m* BOURSE security bond for down payment; **~ de crédit** *m* BANQUE perfected security; **~ hypothécaire** *m* BANQUE, DROIT, IMMOB mortgage lien; **~ de prêt** *m pl* FIN lending securities; **~ d'un prêt par titres** *m* BOURSE rehypothecation; ◆ **donner un bien en ~** BANQUE supply collateral

nappe *f* ENVIR, IND *de pétrole* slick; **~ d'hydrocarbures** ENVIR, IND hydrocarbon slick; **~ de pétrole** ENVIR, IND oil slick

narcodollars *m pl* ECON narcodollars

NAS *abrév (numéro d'assurance sociale)* FISC, PROT SOC SIN *(social insurance number)*

NASA *f* TRANSP *administration nationale de l'aéronautique et de l'espace aux Etats-Unis* NASA *(US)*

Nassau *n pr* COM Nassau

nat. *abrév (national)* COM nat. *(national)*

natif, -ive *m,f* COM native

nation: **~ industrialisée** *f* ECON, POL industrial nation; **~ la plus favorisée** *f* ECON most-favored nation *(AmE)*, most-favoured nation *(BrE)*, MFN

national, e *adj* COM *(nat.)* national, nationwide *(nat.)*, ECON domestic

nationalisation *f* ECON, POL nationalization

nationalisé: **être ~** *loc* ECON come under public ownership

nationaliser *vt* COM nationalize

nationalisme *m* POL nationalism

nationalité *f* COM, POL nationhood

Nations: **~ Unies** *f pl* ECON, POL United Nations

nature *f* COM nature; **~ baissière** *(ANT nature haussière)* BOURSE *du marché* bearish tone, bearishness; **~ d'un call** BOURSE call feature; **~ haussière** *(ANT nature baissière)* BOURSE *du marché* bullish tone, bullishness; **~ de l'invention** BREVETS nature of the invention; **~ des obligations** BOURSE bond features; ◆ **de**

~ semblable COM ejusdem generis *(frml)*; **en ~** COM *paiement* in kind

navet *m infrml* LOISIRS *théâtre, cinéma* flop *(infrml)*

navette *f* TRANSP ground transportation, *vol* shuttle; **~ autobus** TRANSP bus shuttle; **~ spatiale** TRANSP space shuttle; ◆ **faire la ~** COM commute

navetteur *m Bel* TRANSP commuter

navigabilité *f* TRANSP seaworthiness

navigation *f* TRANSP *maritime* navigation, sailing; **~ en fleuve à marée** TRANSP tidal river navigation; **~ fluviale** TRANSP river navigation; **~ sur lest** TRANSP *navigation* ballast sailing; **~ à vue** TRANSP window-guidance

naviguer *vt* INFO browse

navire *m* TRANSP boat, vessel; **~ d'apport** TRANSP feeder ship, mother ship, feeder vessel; **~ cargo sans ligne régulière** TRANSP coaster, tramp; **~ charbonnier** TRANSP coal carrier; **~ de charge** TRANSP freighter; **~ -citerne** TRANSP tanker; **~ -citerne à moteur** TRANSP motor tanker, tanker motor vessel, MT; **~ collecteur** TRANSP feeder ship, feeder vessel, mother ship; **~ de commerce** TRANSP merchant ship, merchant vessel, trading vessel; **~ couvert** TRANSP arrived ship; **~ dépollueur** ENVIR, TRANSP depolluting ship, oil clearance vessel, oil recovery vessel; **~ à deux classes** TRANSP two-class vessel; **~ disparu** TRANSP missing vessel; **~ de divers** TRANSP general trader; **~ d'éclatement** TRANSP feeder ship, feeder vessel, mother ship; **~ de forte stabilité** TRANSP stiff vessel; **~ frigorifique** TRANSP refrigerated ship, refrigerated vessel; **~ de grand cabotage** TRANSP home trade ship; **~ hors-conférence** TRANSP non-conference line vessel; **~ inférieur aux normes** TRANSP substandard ship; **~ de ligne** TRANSP liner; **~ de ligne continue** TRANSP cl, continuous liner; **~ de ligne à escales** TRANSP noncontinuous liner, NC; **~ long-courrier** TRANSP ocean vessel; **~ au long cours** TRANSP ocean-going vessel; **~ à manutention horizontale** *(ro/ro)* TRANSP ro/ro vessel, roll on/roll off, roll on/roll off ship *(ro/ro ship)*; **~ à manutention horizontale et verticale** *(ro/lo)* TRANSP roll on/roll off-lift on/lift off ship *(ro/lo)*; **~ à manutention verticale** TRANSP lift on/lift off, lo/lo; **~ marchand** TRANSP merchant ship, merchant vessel, trading vessel; **~ marchand à moteur** TRANSP motor merchant vessel, MV; **~ du même type** TRANSP sister ship; **~ à moteur** TRANSP m, motor ship, motor vessel, motorship, MS, MV; **~ à passagers de grand cabotage** TRANSP home trade passenger ship; **~ pétrolier** ENVIR, TRANSP crude carrier; **~ pétrolier à long cours continu** IND, TRANSP oil-bearing continuous liner; **~ polytherme** TRANSP reefer carrier, reefer ship, ref., refrigerated ship, refrigerated vessel; ~ **polyvalent** TRANSP multipurpose vessel; ~ **à pont-abri couvert** TRANSP closed-shelter deck, CSD; ~ **à pont-abri ouvert** TRANSP open-shelter deck, OSD; ~ **porte-barges** TRANSP lighter aboard ship, lighter carrier, LASH; ~ **porte-conteneurs** TRANSP boxer class, container ship; ~ **porte-conteneurs spécialisé** TRANSP cellular container ship, fully cellular container ship, FCC; ~ **poseur d'oléoducs** TRANSP pipe-laying ship; ~ **de production au large** TRANSP floating production vessel, FPV; ~ **de production, stockage et déchargement au large** TRANSP floating production, storage and off-loading vessel, FPSO; ~ **en quarantaine** TRANSP infected ship; ~ **qui rappelle dur** TRANSP stiff vessel; ~ **qui se redresse doucement** TRANSP stiff vessel; ~ **régulier** TRANSP liner; ~ **régulier à escales** TRANSP noncontinuous liner, NC; ~ **sous normes** TRANSP substandard ship; ~ **sous pavillon national** TRANSP national flagship; ~ **sous pavillon tiers** TRANSP third flag carrier; ~ **spécial** TRANSP purpose-built tonnage; ~ **sucrier** TRANSP sugar ship; ~ **supplémentaire** TRANSP *service régulier* duplicate sailing, relief sailing; ~ **transbordeur** TRANSP car ferry, ferry boat, train ferry; ~ **de transport** TRANSP freighter; ~ **à trois superstructures** TRANSP three-island ship; ~ **à turbines à gaz** TRANSP gas turbine ship, GT; ~ **type trois îles** TRANSP three-island ship; ~ **à vapeur** TRANSP steamer, steamship; ~ **à voiles** TRANSP sailing vessel, SV; ◆ **d'un bord à l'autre du** ~ TRANSP *arrimage des conteneurs* thwartship; **par** ~ ASSUR, TRANSP any one bottom, any one vessel, AOB, AOV; ~ **perdu ou non-perdu** ASSUR *maritime* ship lost or not lost, SL/NL

navires: ~ **de commerce** *m pl* TRANSP merchant shipping; ~ **désarmés** *m pl* TRANSP idle shipping, laid-up tonnage; ~ **inemployés** *m pl* TRANSP idle shipping

n'ayant: ~ **pas un caractère obligatoire** *loc* DROIT nonmandatory

NB *abrév (nota bene)* COM NB *(nota bene)*

N'Djamena *n pr* COM N'Djamena

NE *abrév (nord-est)* COM NE *(north east)*

nécessaire *adj* COM necessary

nécessitant: ~ **beaucoup de personnel** *loc* RES HUM personnel-intensive; ~ **une licence** *loc* IMP/EXP licensable

nécessité: ~ **de couverture** *f* BANQUE margin requirements

nécessiter *vt* COM necessitate, require

nécessiteux: **les** ~ *m pl* PROT SOC the needy

néerlandais[1], **e** *adj* COM Dutch

néerlandais[2] *m* COM *langue* Dutch

Néerlandais[1], *m* COM *habitant* Dutchman

Néerlandais[2], **e** *m,f* COM *habitant* Netherlander

Néerlandaise *f* COM *habitante* Dutchwoman

négatif, -ive *adj* COM adverse

négativement *adv* COM negatively

négligé *adj* COM *travail* slack

négligeant *adj* COM *travailleur* slack

négligemment *adv* DROIT negligently

négligence *f* DROIT laches, negligence; ~ **coupable** DROIT laches; ~ **dans le chef de la victime** DROIT contributory negligence; ~ **professionnelle** DROIT malpractice; ◆ **par** ~ DROIT negligently

négliger: ~ **de faire qch** *vt* COM omit to do sth

négoce *m* COM trade, ECON merchant trading; ~ **d'entrée et sortie** BOURSE in and out trading *(jarg)*; ~ **du frigorifique** ECON reefer trade; ~ **marginal** BOURSE margin trading; ~ **de titres sauvegardés** BOURSE hedge trading; ~ **du vin** COM trading in wine

négociabilité *f* BOURSE marketability, negotiability

négociable *adj* BANQUE negotiable, BOURSE negotiable, *titres* marketable, COM marketable, negotiable; ~ **en banque** BANQUE bankable

négociant, e *m,f* BOURSE bond trader, dealer, V&M dealer, *sur une grande échelle* trader; ~ **en bloc de titres** BOURSE block positioner; ~ **-courtier** BOURSE broker-dealer; ~ **courtier de parquet** BOURSE floor trader; ~ **exportateur** IMP/EXP, RES HUM export merchant; ~ **en laine** COM wool merchant; ~ **du parquet** BOURSE floor trader; ~ **en titres** BOURSE dealer in securities, jobber *(UK, dat)*, market maker, security dealer, stock-jobber *(UK, dat)*; ~ **en titres agréé** BOURSE authorized dealer; ~ **en valeurs** BOURSE trader in securities; ~ **en valeurs mobilières** BOURSE, FIN investment dealer; ~ **en vins** COM, RES HUM vintner, wine merchant

négociateur, -trice *m,f* BOURSE trader, COM bargainer, GESTION negotiator; ~ **agréé** BOURSE registered competitive trader; ~ **de blocs d'actions** BOURSE block stock trader; ~ **individuel de parquet** *(NIP)* BOURSE floor trader, local *(jarg)*; ~ **d'obligations** BOURSE bond trader; ~ **d'options agréé** BOURSE registered options trader; ~ **de positions à long terme** BOURSE position trader; ~ **aux pupitres** BOURSE desk trader; ~ **sur le marché hors cote** BOURSE unlisted trader; ~ **sur le marché primaire** BOURSE primary market dealer; ~ **sur rompus de titres** BOURSE odd-lot dealer; ~ **unique** RES HUM sole bargaining agent *(UK)*; ~ **en valeurs mobilières** BOURSE broker, jobber *(UK, dat)*, market maker, stockjobber *(UK, dat)*

négociation *f* COM, RES HUM bargaining, negotiation; ~ **d'actions** BOURSE equity trading; ~ **assistée par ordinateur** BOURSE program trading *(AmE)*, programme trading *(BrE)*, INFO program trading; ~ **avec association patronale** RES HUM association bargaining, multiemployer bargaining; ~ **avec la base** RES HUM shop-floor bargaining *(UK)*; ~ **avec employeur unique** RES HUM single-employer bargaining *(UK)*; ~ **bidon** *jarg* (ANT *négociation sérieuse*) IND, RES HUM blue-sky bargaining; ~ **collective** RES HUM Boulwareism *(US)*, collective bargaining, association bargaining, multiemployer bargaining; ~ **collec-**

tive sur le lieu de travail RES HUM workplace bargaining; ~ **commerciale multilatérale** ECON, POL *commerce international* multilateral trade negotiation, MTN; ~ **continue** BOURSE all-day trading; ~ **des contrats de productivité** DROIT, RES HUM productivity bargaining; ~ **à un cours inférieur** (ANT *négociation à un cours supérieur*) BOURSE downtick, minus tick; ~ **à un cours supérieur** (ANT *négociation à un cours inférieur*) BOURSE plus tick, upstairs market, uptick; ~ **individuelle** RES HUM individual bargaining; ~ **modèle** RES HUM pattern bargaining (*jarg*); ~ **au niveau d'un atelier** RES HUM workshop bargaining; ~ **au niveau de l'établissement** RES HUM establishment-level bargaining (*UK*); ~ **au niveau local** COM, IND, RES HUM plant bargaining; ~ **au niveau de l'usine** COM, IND, RES HUM plant bargaining; ~ **d'obligations** BOURSE bond trading; ~ **par branche** RES HUM company bargaining; ~ **par établissement** RES HUM establishment-level bargaining (*UK*); ~ **par tranches** RES HUM fragmented bargaining; ~ **paritaire** COM, GESTION, RES HUM joint negotiation; ~ **à perte** RES HUM whipsaw (*US, jarg*); ~ **plurisyndicale** RES HUM multiunion bargaining (*UK*); ~ **à plusieurs employeurs** RES HUM multiemployer bargaining; ~ **à plusieurs usines** RES HUM multiplant bargaining; ~ **de la productivité** DROIT productivity bargaining; ~ **salariale au plan régional** RES HUM regional wage bargaining; ~ **sérieuse** (ANT *négociation bidon*) IND, RES HUM good-faith bargaining; ~ **à un seul niveau** RES HUM single table bargaining (*UK*); ~ **sur positions à long terme** BOURSE position trading; ~ **sur le salaire** ECON, RES HUM wage round; ~ **des valeurs non cotées** BOURSE unlisted trading; ~ **24 heures sur 24** BOURSE twenty-four hour trading

négociations: ~ **avant l'ouverture** *f pl* BOURSE before-hours dealings; ~ **de blocs d'actions** *f pl* BOURSE volume trading; ~ **commerciales** *f pl* ECON round, trade talks, POL trade talks; ~ **Dillon** *f pl* ECON Dillon Round; ~ **paritaires** *f pl* BOURSE, RES HUM joint negotiation; ~ **salariales** *f pl* RES HUM contract bargaining, pay talks, wage negotiations, wage talks; ~ **serrées** *f pl* COM hard bargaining; ~ **d'Uruguay** *f pl* ECON Uruguay Round

négocié: ~ **massivement** *loc* BOURSE heavily traded

négocier 1. *vt* BANQUE *emprunt* negotiate, BOURSE negotiate, trade in; ~ **en bourse** BOURSE deal, COM negotiate, RES HUM bargain, bargain down, negotiate; **2.** *v pron* **se ~ à** BOURSE be trading at, trade at; ◆ ~ **pour le compte de** COM trade under the name of; ~ **en position de force** COM negotiate from strength

neige: ~ **acide** *f* ENVIR acid snow

néo: ~ **-capitalisme** *m* ECON late capitalism; ~ **-corporatisme** *m* ECON, POL neo-corporatism; ~ **-fédéralisme** *m* POL new federalism (*US*); ~ **-keynésianisme** *m* ECON new economics;

~ **-keynésien** *m* ECON, POL neo-Keynesian, new Keynesian; ~ **-malthusien** *m* ECON, POL neo-Malthusian; ~ **-marxiste** *mf* ECON, POL neo-Marxist; ~ **-mercantilisme** *m* ECON neo-mercantilism, new protectionism; ~ **-protectionnisme** *m* ECON neo-mercantilism, new protectionism; ~ **-ricardien** *m* ECON neo-Ricardian

néo-zélandais, e *adj* COM New Zealand
Néo-Zélandais, e *m,f* COM *habitant* New Zealander

Népal *m* COM Nepal
népalais¹, e *adj* COM Nepalese
népalais² *m* COM *langue* Nepali
Népalais, e *m,f* COM *habitant* Nepalese
népotisme *m* RES HUM nepotism
nerveux *adj* ECON *marché* jumpy
n'est: **nul ~ censé ignorer la loi** *loc* DROIT ignorance of the law is no excuse, ignorantia juris neminem excusat (*frml*)
net, -ette *adj* COM clear-cut, *prix* all-in, all-inclusive, V&M *prix* all-in; ◆ ~ **d'impôt** FISC after-tax
nettement *adv* COM substantially
nettoyage: ~ **des citernes** *m* TRANSP tank cleaning
nettoyer *vt* ENVIR clean up
nettoyeur *m* TRANSP *dans un navire* donkeyman
neuf, neuve *adj* COM hot, new, N; **tout ~** COM brand-new
neutraliser *vt* COM cancel out, counteract
neutralisme *m* COM neutralism
neutralité *f* POL neutrality; ~ **monétaire** ECON neutrality of money; ~ **positive** POL positive neutrality
neutre: **de ~ à baissier** *adj* (ANT *de neutre à haussier*) BOURSE neutral to bearish; **de ~ à haussier** *adj* (ANT *de neutre à baissier*) BOURSE neutral to bullish
neuvième: **un ~** *m* (*1/9*) COM one-ninth (*1/9*)
New:¹ ~ **Deal** *m* POL *1933* New Deal (*US*)
New:² ~ **Delhi** *n pr* COM New Delhi
n'excédant: ~ **pas** *loc* COM not exceeding
nez: **sur le ~** *loc* TRANSP *navigation* trimmed by the head
Niamey *n pr* COM Niamey
Nicaragua *m* COM Nicaragua
nicaraguayen, -enne *adj* COM Nicaraguan
Nicaraguayen, -enne *m,f* COM *habitant* Nicaraguan
niche *f* V&M market niche, niche
Nicosie *n pr* COM Nicosia
nier *vt* DROIT deny, RES HUM repudiate
Niger *m* COM Niger
Nigéria *m* COM Nigeria
nigérien, -enne *adj* COM Nigerian
Nigérien, -enne *m,f* COM *habitant* Nigerian
NIP *abrév* BANQUE (*numéro d'identification personnel*) PIN (*personal identification number*), BOURSE (*négociateur individuel de parquet*) floor trader, local (*jarg*)

niveau *m* COM, ECON, GESTION, INFO *de code*, RES HUM level; ~ **d'acidité** ENVIR *pollution* acidity level; ~ **d'activité** COM activity ratio; ~ **d'aptitude** PROT SOC ability level; ~ **bas** BOURSE, COM, ECON low; ~ **de base** RES HUM basic grade; ~ **budgétaire** COMPTA, ECON, FIN budget level; ~ **cadre** RES HUM executive grade; ~ **de commandes** V&M level of orders; ~ **de concurrence réalisable** ECON workable competition; ~ **de confiance** MATH confidence level; ~ **de croissance à un rythme soutenable** ECON sustainable level; ~ **de dépenses** COM spending level, ECON level of expenditure; ~ **du dépôt initial** BOURSE initial margin level; ~ **effectif du chômage** ECON, POL actual level of unemployment; ~ **des effectifs** RES HUM manning level, staffing level; ~ **élevé** COM high standards; ~ **de l'enveloppe** COM envelope level; ~ **de fluctuation** BOURSE degree of fluctuation; ~ **historique** COM all-time high; ~ **de l'indice des cours** BOURSE price index level; ~ **de l'indice des prix** BOURSE price index level; ~ **d'investissement** COM level of investment; ~ **locatif** IMMOB rental level; ~ **de marge initiale** BOURSE initial margin level; ~ **maximum** BOURSE peak level, ECON peak; ~ **mezzanine** FIN mezzanine level; ~ **moyen de la marée** TRANSP *maritime* mean tidal level, MTL; ~ **moyen de la mer** TRANSP *maritime* mean sea level, MSL; ~ **de négociation** RES HUM bargaining level; ~ **de notoriété** V&M awareness level; ~ **d'occupation** IMMOB occupancy level; ~ **de prix** ECON price level; ~ **de prix relatifs** ECON relative price level; ~ **de qualification** PROT SOC ability level; ~ **record** BOURSE all-time high, peak level, ECON peak; ~ **de référence** COM standard grade, FIN reference level; ~ **de résistance** BOURSE resistance level; ~ **de revenu équilibré** COMPTA, ECON, FIN break-even level of income; ~ **de risque** COM degree of risk; ~ **des salaires** RES HUM wage level; ~ **sans précédent** COM all-time high; ~ **seuil** COM threshold level; ~ **de signification** MATH level of significance; ~ **sonore** ENVIR noise level; ~ **de soutien** ECON level of support; ~ **tarifaire** ECON, FISC, IMP/EXP tariff level; ~ **de vie** ECON standard of living; ~ **de vie bas** PROT SOC low standard of living; ~ **de vie élevé** PROT SOC high standard of living; ◆ **à un ~ record** ECON record-high; **au ~ fédéral** COM federal-level; **au ~ international** COM at international level; **au ~ régional** COM regionally; **être au ~** RES HUM be up to standard; **personne qui n'a pas le ~** PROT SOC underachiever

niveaux: ~ **internationaux des salaires** *m pl* ECON, RES HUM international wage levels

nivellement *m* COM, FIN leveling (*AmE*), leveling-out (*AmE*), levelling (*BrE*), levelling-out (*BrE*)

NO *abrév* (*nord-ouest*) COM NW (*north west*)

nocturne: ~ **le vendredi** *f* COM late opening Friday

noeud *m* COM knot, INFO node

noir: **au ~** *loc* COM *acheter, vendre* on the black market, *réparation, travaux* on the side

nolisement *m* TRANSP *navire, avion* chartering

noliser *vt* TRANSP *navire, avion* charter

nom *m* COM name; ~ **de code** INFO code name; ~ **commercial** BREVETS, COM trading name; ~ **d'un compte** BANQUE, COMPTA account name, name of an account, title of an account; ~ **de document** INFO document name; ~ **d'emprunt** BOURSE nominee name; ~ **et prénoms** COM full name; ~ **de guerre** COM, INFO alias; ~ **de l'intermédiaire** BOURSE nominee name; ~ **légal** ADMIN, DROIT legal name; ~ **de marque** V&M brand name, household name; ~ **d'ours** MÉDIA masthead; ~ **patronymique** ADMIN surname; ~ **de plume** COM, INFO alias; ◆ **au ~ de** COM on behalf of; ~ **et adresse** COMMS name and address; **exercer sous le ~ de** COM do business as, DBA

nombre *m* COM, COMPTA, FIN amount, AMT, MATH *de francs* no., number; ~ **d'actions émises** BOURSE number of shares issued, *retraité d'auto-contrôle* outstanding capital stock; ~ **aléatoire** INFO, MATH random number; ~ **binaire** INFO, MATH binary number; ~ **de bits par pouce** INFO bits per inch, bpi; ~ **de bits par seconde** INFO bits per second; ~ **de chômeurs en données non corrigées des variations saisonnières** RES HUM seasonally unadjusted employment figures; ~ **décimal** INFO decimal number; ~ **entier** INFO, MATH natural number; ~ **indice** ECON index number; ~ **de lignes par page** INFO page length; ~ **de lignes d'une petite annonce** MÉDIA linage, lineage; ~ **à précision déterminée** MATH fixed-point number; ~ **réel** INFO, MATH real number; ~ **de salariés** COMPTA, RES HUM number of employees; ~ **de spectateurs** LOISIRS *sport* gate; ~ **en virgule flottante** MATH floating-point number; ◆ **en ~ pair** COM even-numbered; ~ **moyen d'exemplaires vendus** COM average number of copies sold

n° *abrév* (*numéro*) COM no. (*number*); ~ **tél.** *abrév* (*numéro de téléphone*) COMMS tel. no. (*telephone number*)

nomenclature *f* IND *des composants et des matières premières* bill of materials

nominal, e *adj* (*n*) COM nominal (*n.*)

nominatif, -ive *adj* COM nominal

nomination *f* COM nomination, *d'une personne* appointment, RES HUM posting

nommé, e *adj* COM designated, *président* appointed

nommée: **personne ~** *f* COM, GESTION, RES HUM appointee

nommément: **personne ~ désignée** *f* DROIT named person

nommer *vt* COM designate, RES HUM appoint

non: **personne ~ -déclarante** *f* FISC nonfiler; **personne ~ -déclarée** *f* FISC unregistered person

non:[3] **et ~** *loc* COM et non (*frml*); **nul et ~ avenu** *loc* DROIT null and void

non-abrogé, e *adj* COM unrepealed

non-acceptation *f* COM nonacceptance

non-accepté, e *adj* COM unaccepted

non-acquitté, e *adj* COM unreceipted, FIN unliquidated

non-adhésion *f* RES HUM nonmembership

non-admis, e *adj* BOURSE unlisted, unquoted

non-affecté, e *adj* COM unappropriated, INFO unallocated

non-affilié, e *adj* COM, RES HUM *syndicat* unaffiliated

non-amélioré, e *adj* COM *situation, travail* unimproved

non-amorti, e *adj* COMPTA unamortized, undepreciated

non-amortissable *adj* BANQUE, BOURSE unredeemable

non-appelable *adj* FIN uncallable

non-applicable *adj* COM n/a, not applicable

non-approuvé, e *adj* BOURSE nonapproved

non-assujetti: ~ **à l'impôt** *adj* FISC nontaxable; ~ **à la TVA** *adj* FISC zero-rated

non-assurable *adj* ASSUR uninsurable

non-assurance-vie *f* ASSUR nonlife insurance

non-assuré, e *adj* ASSUR bare, unassured, uninsured

non-attribué, e *adj* BOURSE unallotted

non-audité, e *adj* COMPTA unaudited

non-authentifié, e *adj* DROIT unauthenticated

non-bancable *adj* ASSUR not negotiable

non-barré, e *adj* BANQUE uncrossed

non-biodégradable *adj* COM non-biodegradable

non-breveté, e *adj* BREVETS, COM unpatented

non-budgétaire *adj* COMPTA nonbudgetary

non-cadré, e *adj* INFO unjustified

non-cloisonné, e *adj* COM open-plan

non-communiste *adj* POL non-Communist

non-comparution *f* DROIT absence, failure to appear, nonappearance

non-compensé, e *adj* BANQUE uncleared

non-compris, e *adj* COM extra

non-comptabilisable *adj* COMPTA unpostable

non-comptabilisé, e *adj* COM off the books

non-concordance *f* COMPTA mismatch

non-confirmé, e *adj* COM unsupported

non-conformité *f* DROIT nonconformity

non-connecté, e *adj* (ANT *connecté*) COM, INFO off-line

non-consolidé, e *adj* COMPTA nonconsolidated

non-contaminé, e *adj* INFO virus-free

non-contribuable *mf* FISC non-taxpaying

non-contrôlé, e *adj* COMPTA unaudited

non-converti, e *adj* BANQUE unconverted

non-convertible *adj* BOURSE nonconvertible

non-convivial, e *adj* (ANT *convivial*) INFO, V&M user-hostile, user-unfriendly

non-coté, e *adj* BOURSE unlisted, unquoted

non-couvert, e *adj* BOURSE undersubscribed, unhedged

non-cumulatif, -ive *adj* BOURSE noncumulative

non-cyclique *adj* (ANT *cyclique*) BOURSE, COM, ECON, FIN noncyclical

non-débogué, e *adj* INFO nondebugged

non-déchargé, e *adj* COM *maritime* undischarged

non-déductibilité *f* FISC, RES HUM nondeductibility

non-dépensé, e *adj* COM *argent* unspent, FIN unexpended

non-déposé, e *adj* BREVETS *propriété intellectuelle*, DROIT unregistered

non-déprécié, e *adj* COMPTA undepreciated

non-déprimé, e *adj* BOURSE undepressed

non-détenu, e *adj* BOURSE not held

non-devise *f* ECON artificial currency

non-dirigeant, e *adj* GESTION, RES HUM nonexecutive

non-disponible *adj* INFO disabled, down

non-divulgable *adj* MÉDIA, POL not for attribution (*AmE, jarg*), on lobby terms (*BrE, jarg*)

non-divulgation *f* ASSUR nondisclosure, DROIT concealment

non-échu, e *adj* BOURSE unmatured

non-écoulé, e *adj* COM undisposed of

non-efficience: ~ **du marché** *f* BOURSE inefficiency in the market

non-élasticité: ~ **des prix** *f* ECON price inelasticity

non-émis, e *adj* BOURSE *capital* unissued

non-encaissé, e *adj* COM uncashed

non-endommagé, e *adj* COM undamaged

non-endossé, e *adj* BANQUE unendorsed

non-enregistré, e *adj* COM unrecorded

non-exécution *f* DROIT nonexecution, nonfulfillment (*AmE*), nonfulfilment (*BrE*), nonperformance; ~ **du contrat** DROIT nonfulfillment of contract (*AmE*), nonfulfilment of contract (*BrE*)

non-exécutoire *adj* (ANT *exécutoire*) DROIT unenforceable

non-exempté, e *adj* (ANT *exempt*) COM, FISC nonexempt

non-expiré, e *adj* DROIT *contrat* unexpired

non-expressément: ~ **prévu** *loc* COM not specially provided for, nspf

non-fondé, e *adj* COM groundless, unsubstantiated

non-formaté, e *adj* INFO unformatted

non-formé, e *adj* PROT SOC untrained

non-fourni: ~ **par ailleurs** *adj* COM nop, not otherwise provided

non-garanti, e *adj* BANQUE unsecured, COM unvouched for

non-grevé, e *adj* DROIT, IMMOB *titre de propriété* free and clear (*US*); ~ **d'hypothèque** IMMOB unencumbered

non-imposable *adj* FISC nontaxable

non-imposé, e *adj* FISC unassessed

non-inscrit:[1] ~ **à la cote** *adj* BOURSE unlisted, unquoted

non-inscrit[2], **e** *m,f* FISC unregistered person, POL Independent

non-intervention *f* ECON, POL nonintervention

non-interventionniste *adj* COM hands-off; ~ **privilégié** *adj* COM, COMPTA, FISC *relations entretenues entre les parties* arm's-length

non-investi, **e** *adj* BANQUE uninvested

non-justifié, **e** *adj* COM groundless, INFO unjustified

non-légalisé, **e** *adj* DROIT unauthenticated

non-lié, **e** *adj* ECON, POL untied

non-limité, **e** *adj* BOURSE unlimited

non-liquide *adj* COMPTA illiquid

non-livraison *f* COM failure to deliver

non-marketing *m* V&M *publicité* demarketing

non-membre *mf* COM nonmember

non-métropolitain, **e** *adj* (ANT *métropolitain*) COM nonmetropolitan

non-négligeable *adj* COM considerable

non-négociable *adj* ASSUR not negotiable, COM unnegotiable

non-nuisible: ~ **à l'environnement** *loc* ENVIR ecologically sound

non-obligatoire *adj* DROIT *directives* nonmandatory

nonobstant, **e** *adv* COM notwithstanding; ◆ ~ **les autres dispositions** COM notwithstanding any other provision

non-officiel, **-elle** *adj* COM *nomination* unofficial, *rapport* unofficial

non-paiement *m* FIN default

non-payé, **e** *adj* BOURSE nil paid, COM, FIN delinquent

non-périmé, **e** *adj* ADMIN *passeport* valid

non-placé, **e** *adj* BANQUE uninvested

non-planifié, **e** *adj* COM unscheduled, RES HUM nonscheduled

non-polluant, **e** *adj* ENVIR clean, unpolluted

non-pondéré, **e** *adj* COM unweighted

non-précisé: ~ **par ailleurs** *adj* COM not elsewhere specified, NES

non-présentation *f* LOISIRS no-show

non-prévu: ~ **par ailleurs** *adj* COM nop, not otherwise provided

non-productif, **-ive** *adj* BOURSE, COM, GESTION, IND nonproductive, unproductive

non-production *f* FISC nonfiling

non-programmé, **e** *adj* COM unprogrammed

non-protesté, **e** *adj* FIN unprotested

non-qualifié, **e** *adj* RES HUM unqualified, unskilled

non-rachet *m* BOURSE *disposition, clause* noncallable feature

non-rachetable *adj* BOURSE *obligation* noncallable

non-recouvrable *adj* FISC uncollectable, unrecoverable

non-recyclable *adj* ENVIR nonrecyclable

non-redressé, **e** *adj* COM uncorrected

non-réglé: ~ **à l'échéance** *adj* COM past-due

non-rémanent, **e** *adj* INFO volatile

non-remboursable *adj* BANQUE *obligation* noncallable, unredeemable, BOURSE nonrefundable, unredeemable

non-remboursement *m* COM default

non-remplacement: ~ **des départs** *m* ECON, IND, RES HUM natural wastage

non-rempli, **e** *adj* COM unfulfilled

non-renouvelable *adj* ENVIR finite

non-résident[1], **e** *adj* FISC nonresident

non-résident[2], **e** *m,f* COM nonresident

non-résiliation *f* DROIT nonforfeiture

non-respect: ~ **des conditions** *m* COM nonobservance of conditions; ~ **du contrat** *m* DROIT nonfulfillment of contract (*AmE*), nonfulfilment of contract (*BrE*); ~ **de la règle de priorité** *m* BOURSE frontrunning, running ahead

non-responsabilité *f* DROIT nonliability

non-ressortissant: ~ **de l'UE** *m* COM, POL non-EU national

non-réutilisable *adj* COM expendable

non-révélé, **e** *adj* FIN undisclosed

non-satisfait, **e** *adj* COM unexecuted

non-signé, **e** *adj* COM unsigned

non-soldé, **e** *adj* BANQUE unbacked

non-sollicité, **e** *adj* COM unsolicited

non-souscrit, **e** *adj* FIN undersubscribed

non-spécialisé, **e** *adj* RES HUM unskilled

non-spécifié: ~ **par ailleurs** *adj* COM not elsewhere specified, not otherwise specified, NES

non-statutaire *adj* DROIT nonstatutory

non-structuré, **e** *adj* COM unstructured, INFO unformatted

non-subventionné, **e** *adj* COM unsubsidized

non-testé, **e** *adj* COM untested, untried, unverified

non-titulaire: ~ **du type d'unité** *adj* INFO device-independent

non-traité, **e** *adj* INFO, MATH raw, unprocessed

non-transférable *adj* BOURSE not transferable

non-transmissible *adj* (ANT *transmissible* BOURSE not transferable

non-trié, **e** *adj* COM u/s, unscreened, unsorted

non-utilisé, **e** *adj* COM nonutilized, unused

non-valable *adj* BOURSE not held

non-variable *adj* BANQUE nonvariable

non-vérification *f* COMPTA, FISC nonaudit

non-vérifié, **e** *adj* COM unchecked, unverified, COMPTA unaudited

non-versé, **e** *adj* BOURSE *dividende* unpaid

nord[1] *adj* TRANSP *route, ligne de métro* northbound, NB; ~ **-africain** COM North African; ~ **-américain** COM North American; ~ **-coréen** COM North Korean

nord[2] *m* (*N*) COM north (*N*); ~ **-est** (*NE*) COM north east (*NE*); ~ **-ouest** (*NO*) COM north west (*NW*); ◆ **du** ~ COM northern

Nord-Africain, e *m,f* COM *habitant* North African

Nord-Américain, e *m,f* COM *habitant* North American

Nord-Coréen, -enne *m,f* COM *habitant* North Korean

normalisation *f* COM, COMPTA, DROIT, V&M standardization; **~ comptable** COMPTA accounting standard setting; **~ quantitative** COM, ECON variety reduction

normalisé, e *adj* COM standardized

normaliser *vt* DROIT, V&M standardize

normalité *f* COM normalcy (*AmE*), normality (*BrE*)

norme *f* COM norm, DROIT, INFO standard; **~ AFNOR** *(norme de l'Association française de normalisation)* DROIT, IND ≈ BSS *(British Standards Specification)*; **~ de l'Association française de normalisation** *(norme AFNOR)* DROIT, IND ≈ British Standards Specification *(BSS)*; **~ comptable** COMPTA Financial Reporting Standard, Statement of Standard Accounting Practice *(UK)*, FRS, SSAP *(UK)*; **~ écologique** ENVIR environmental standard; **~ d'émission** ENVIR emission standard; **~ environnementale** ENVIR environmental standard; **~ financière** COM, FIN financial standard; **~ d'hygiène** PROT SOC standard of hygiene; **~ industrielle** ECON, IND industry standard; **~ opérationnelle d'audit** COMPTA, FIN Auditor's Operational Standard; **~ de péréquation** COM standard of equalization; **~ de prix de revient** COM, FIN cost standard; **~ de production** COM, IND production standard; **~ d'un produit** V&M product standard; **~ de pureté de l'air** ENVIR ambient standard *(US)*, *pour la protection de la végétation* secondary standard; **~ de rejet d'effluent** ENVIR effluent standard; **~ relative à la qualité** ENVIR *de l'air* ambient quality standard; **~ de rendement** COMPTA, RES HUM performance standard

normes: ~ acoustiques nationales *f pl* ENVIR national noise standards; **~ d'audit** *f pl* COMPTA, FIN audit standards, auditing standards; **~ d'audit généralement acceptées** *f pl* COMPTA Generally Accepted Auditing Standards *(US)*, GAAS *(US)*; **~ commerciales** *f pl* COM trading standards; **~ comptables** *f pl* COMPTA accounting standards, accounting conventions; **~ de déversement** *f pl* ENVIR dumping standards; **~ et pratiques** *f pl* DROIT, MÉDIA *TV* standards and practices *(US)*; **~ d'exploitation** *f pl* ENVIR licensing standards; **~ internationales** *f pl* ENVIR international standards; **~ internationales de comptabilité** *f pl* COMPTA international auditing standards; **~ de présentation de l'information** *f pl* COM reporting standards; **~ de produit** *f pl* DROIT, IND product standards; **~ de qualité** *f pl* COM quality standards; **~ de qualité de l'environnement** *f pl* ENVIR environmental quality standards; **~ de rejet** *f pl* ENVIR dumping standards; **~ de sécurité** *f pl* COM, IND safety standards; **~ techniques** *f pl* IND technical standards

Norvège *f* COM Norway

norvégien, -enne *adj* COM Norwegian

Norvégien, -enne *m,f* COM *habitant* Norwegian

nos[1] *abrév (numéros)* MATH nos. *(numbers)*; **~ rf.** *abrév (nos références)* COM our ref. *(our reference)*

nos:[2] **~ références** *f pl (nos rf.)* COM our reference *(our ref.)*

nota bene *loc (NB)* COM nota bene *(NB)*

notaire *m* DROIT notary public

notation *f* BOURSE rating, FIN credit score, rating; **~ exponentielle** INFO, MATH exponential notation; **~ de la main-d'oeuvre** RES HUM personnel rating, workforce rating; **~ polonaise** MATH Polish notation; **~ des résultats** FIN performance rating; **~ d'une valeur** BOURSE security rating

note *f* ADMIN memorandum, COM nota bene, *facture* account, *hôtel* bill *(BrE)*, check *(AmE)*, COMPTA account; **~ en bas de page** INFO footnote; **~ de chargement** TRANSP *maritime* shipping note, S/N; **~ de chargement nationale standard** IMP/EXP, TRANSP national standard shipping note, NSSN; **~ de chargement normalisée** IMP/EXP, TRANSP *maritime* standard shipping note; **~ de couverture** ASSUR binder *(US)*, cover note, CN; **~ de crédit** COM, FIN credit note, CN; **~ de débit** BANQUE debit memorandum *(US)*, COM charge ticket, debit note, D/N; **~ de frais** COMPTA *bordereau de frais de représentation* expense report; **~ de garantie d'avaliste** BOURSE GUN, guarantor underwritten note; **~ en marge** ADMIN marginal note; **~ marginale** ADMIN marginal note, COM side note; **~ d'option sur rendement disponible** BOURSE liquid yield option note, LYON; **~ la plus basse** PROT SOC, RES HUM minimum grade; **~ de service** ADMIN memo, memorandum; **~ de téléphone** COMMS telephone bill

notebook *m* INFO notebook

notice: ~ d'emballage *f* TRANSP packing instruction; **~ d'entretien** *f* COM service manual; **~ explicative** *f* COM instructions, MÉDIA instruction leaflet

notification *f* COM, COMMS, DROIT notice, FISC notification; **~ d'exercice** BOURSE exercise notice; **~ requise par la loi** DROIT legal notice

notifier *vt* DROIT *un arrêt à qn* notify, serve

notions: ~ générales *f pl* COM background information

notoriété: ~ de la marque *f* COM, V&M brand awareness; **~ d'un produit** *f* V&M product awareness

notre: ~ proposition reste valable *f* COM our proposal still stands; **~ propre marque** *f* V&M our own make; **~ référence** *f (n/réf)* COM our reference *(our ref.)*

Nouakchott *n pr* COM Nouakchott

nourriture: ~ peu diététique *f* PROT SOC junk food

nous: ~ avons les mains liées *loc* COM our hands are tied; **en ~ référant à** *loc* COMMS with reference to; **en ~ référant à votre demande** *loc* COMMS with reference to your enquiry

nouveau[1], **-elle** *adj* COM new, N

nouveau:[2] **de ~** *adv* DROIT de novo, once more

nouveau:[3] **~ mécanisme économique** *m* ECON New Economic Mechanism; **~ pays industrialisé** *m* (*NPI*) ECON, IND newly industrialized country (*NIC*); **~ placement** *m* BOURSE, COM reinvestment; **~ pont** *m* TRANSP *navigation* new deck, ND; **~ réalisme** *m* RES HUM new realism (*UK*); **~ tirage** *m* MÉDIA *presse, édition* new edition

Nouveau: **~ Commonwealth** *m* POL New Commonwealth

nouveauté *f* BREVETS novelty, COM breakthrough, innovation, ECON breakthrough, IND innovation, V&M novelty

nouveautés *f pl* COM fancy goods

nouveaux: **~ clients** *m pl* COM new business

nouvel: **~ affrètement** *m* TRANSP *maritime* new charter; **~ an** *m* COM new year; **~ aval** *m* BANQUE re-endorsement; **~ examen** *m* COM re-examination; **~ examen d'une cotisation** *m* FISC reconsideration of an assessment; **le ~ état industriel** *m* ECON new industrial state; **~ ordre économique international** *m* ECON New International Economic Order, NIEO; **~ ordre mondial** *m* POL new world order

nouvelle: **~ autorité de placement** *f* BOURSE New Investment Authority, NIA; **~ charte-partie** *f* TRANSP *maritime* new charter; **~ cotisation** *f* FISC reassessment; **~ cotisation à l'égard de l'impôt, des intérêts ou des pénalités** *f pl* FISC reassessment of tax, interest or penalties; **~ division internationale du travail** *f* ECON new international division of labor (*AmE*), new international division of labour (*BrE*), NIDL; **~ droite** *f* ECON, POL New Right; **~ économie classique** *f* ECON new classical economics; **~ édition** *f* MÉDIA new edition; **~ émission** *f* BOURSE new issue, offering, reissue; **~ flambée des prix** *f* COM resurgence in prices; **~ gauche radicale** *f* ECON, POL New Left; **~ inscription hypothécaire** *f* BOURSE rehypothecation; **~ loi** *f* DROIT new law; **~ microéconomie** *f* ECON new microeconomics; **~ offre** *f* BOURSE retendering; **~ politique économique** *f* (*NPE*) ECON New Economic Policy (*NEP*); **~ récolte** *f* ECON new crop, NC; **~ vague** *f* MÉDIA, POL new wave

nouvellement: **~ élu** *adj* COM newly-elected

nouvelles: **~ activités** *f pl* COM new business; **~ technologies** *f pl* IND new technology

Nouvelle-Zélande *f* COM New Zealand

nov. *abrév* (*novembre*) COM Nov. (*November*)

novateur[1], **-trice** *adj* COM innovative

novateur[2], **-trice** *m,f* COM innovator

novation *f* COM, DROIT novation

novembre *m* (*nov.*) COM November (*Nov.*)

novice *m* RES HUM prime age worker; ◆ **être un ~** RES HUM be wet behind the ears (*infrml*)

noyau *m* INFO core; **~ dur** COM hard core

NPE *abrév* (*nouvelle politique économique*) ECON NEP (*New Economic Policy*)

NPI *abrév* (*nouveau pays industrialisé*) ECON, IND NIC (*newly industrialized country*)

NR *abrév* (*naira*) COM NR (*naira*)

n/réf *abrév* (*notre référence*) COM our ref. (*our reference*)

nu[1], **e** *adj* ASSUR bare

nu:[2] **~ -propriétaire** *m* IMMOB bare owner

nuage: **~ sur titre** *m* IMMOB cloud on title (*US*)

nuancer *vt* COM, POL nuance

nucléaire *adj* IND nuclear

nue: **~ -propriété** *f* IMMOB bare ownership, bare property

nuisance *f* COM, DROIT nuisance

nuisances: **~ acoustiques** *f pl* ENVIR noise pollution

nuit:[1] **d'une ~** *adj* COM *séjour* overnight; **de ~** *adj* COM overnight

nuit:[2] **de ~** *adv* COM overnight

nul, le *adj* DROIT, MATH null

nullité *f* BREVETS revocation

numération *f* PROT SOC number facts; **~ décimale** INFO decimal notation

numérique *adj* COM, COMMS digital, ECON numeric, INFO digital, numeric, MATH numeric; **~ -analogique** (*N/A*) INFO digital-analog (*D/A*)

numérisation *f* INFO scanning

numériser *vt* COM digitize, INFO scan

numériseur *m* INFO scanner

numéro *m* COM copy, COM number; **~ d'annonce** COMMS, MÉDIA *presse* box number; **~ antérieur** MÉDIA *édition* back issue, back number; **~ d'assurance sociale** (*NAS*) FISC, PROT SOC social insurance number (*SIN*); **~ d'autorisation** BANQUE authorization code, authorization number; **~ de commande** V&M order number; **~ de compte** BANQUE, COMPTA, FIN account number; **~ de compte pour le règlement** FISC remittance account number; **~ de compte de versements** FISC remittance account number; **~ couplé** MÉDIA *presse* combined issue; **~ CUSIP** BOURSE ≈ CUSIP number; **~ de l'employeur aux fins de l'impôt** FISC taxation employer number (*Canada*); **~ d'enregistrement** COM registration number; **~ d'enregistrement de l'organisme de charité** FISC, PROT SOC charity number; **~ de l'étiquette de contrôle du bordereau d'expédition** TRANSP consignment note control label number, CCLN; **~ gratuit** COMMS Freefone number (*BrE*), toll-free number (*AmE*); **~ hors série** MÉDIA *presse* anniversary publication; **~ d'identification** INFO ID number, identification number; **~ d'identification en code barres** INFO, V&M bar-coded identification number; **~ d'identification personnel** (*NIP*) BANQUE personal identification number (*PIN*); **~ d'immatriculation** COM registration number, TRANSP license plate (*AmE*), number plate (*BrE*), *d'un navire* official no., official number, on; **~ d'immatriculation sécurité sociale** FISC, PROT SOC social insurance number; **~ d'inscription**

douanière IMP/EXP customs registered number, CRN; ~ **d'inscription à la TVA** FISC VAT registration number (*UK*); ~ **d'interclassement** INFO collator number; ~ **intra** ADMIN intra number; ~ **de licence d'exportation** IMP/EXP export licence number (*BrE*), export license number (*AmE*); ~ **un mondial** IND world leader; ~ **d'obligation** BANQUE, BOURSE bond number; ~ **officiel** TRANSP *d'un navire* official no., official number, on; ~ **d'ordre** COM running number, INFO sequence number, MATH sequence number, sequential number; ~ **de page** COM page number; ~ **de porte** TRANSP *aéroport* gate number; ~ **de référence** COMMS, MÉDIA *presse* box number, reference number; ~ **de référence unique** ADMIN unique reference number, URN; ~ **de série** BREVETS, COM, INFO serial number; ~ **spécial anniversaire** MÉDIA *presse* anniversary publication; ~ **de succursale** BANQUE branch number; ~ **de téléphone** *(n° tél.)* COMMS phone number, telephone number *(tel. no.)*; ~ **de train** TRANSP train number; ~ **UN** TRANSP UN number; ~ **vert** COMMS *Minitel* Freefone number (*BrE*), toll-free number (*AmE*); ~ **de vol** TRANSP flight number

numéros *m pl (nos)* MATH numbers *(nos.)*

numérotation *f* BREVETS, COM numbering, INFO call, MATH numbering

numéroter *vt* BREVETS, COM, MATH number; ~ **consécutivement** BREVETS number consecutively; ~ **de façon continue** BREVETS number consecutively

O

O *abrév (quart ouest)* TRANSP *navigation* W *(West compass point)*

OACI *abrév (Organisation de l'aviation civile internationale)* TRANSP ICAO *(International Civil Aviation Organization)*

OAT *abrév (obligation assimilable du Trésor)* BOURSE French government bond, French treasury bond

obéir: ~ **à** *vt* COM, DROIT comply with, obey

objecter *vi* COM object

objectif[1], **-ive** *adj* COM impartial, objective

objectif[2] *m* COM aim, goal, objective, object, target, ECON *des entreprises*, GESTION objective, V&M objective, target; ~ **d'arbitrage** BOURSE, FIN hedging goal; ~ **d'une campagne publicitaire** V&M advertising program objectives *(AmE)*, advertising programme objectives *(BrE)*; ~ **commercial** V&M sales objective; ~ **à court-terme** COM short-term objective; ~ **de couverture** BOURSE, FIN hedging goal; ~ **de l'entreprise** COM company objective, corporate objective; ~ **immédiat** COM immediate aim; ~ **à long terme** COM long-term objective; ~ **de marché** V&M market aim; ~ **de performance** COM, GESTION, IND, RES HUM performance target; ~ **de placement** FIN investment objective; ~ **de production** COM, IND production target; ~ **de profit** COMPTA, FIN profit goal, profit target; ~ **de recherche** COM research objective; ~ **de vente** V&M sales goal, sales target; ~ **visé** ECON target variable; ◆ **avec pour ~ de faire** COM with the sole object of doing

objectifs: ~ **commerciaux** *m pl* COM commercial targets; ~ **globaux de l'entreprise** *m pl* COM overall company objectives; ~ **professionnels** *m pl* RES HUM career goals

objection *f* COM objection; ◆ ~ **admise** *loc* DROIT objection sustained; **faire une** ~ COM make an objection; ~ **rejetée** *loc* DROIT objection overruled

objectivité: **en toute** ~ *loc* DROIT on its merits

objet *m* BREVETS subject matter, COM aim, object, *accord, contrat, réunion* subject, *d'une société* purpose, DROIT chose; ~ **de collection** COM collectible; ~ **très important** TRANSP very important object, VIO

objets: ~ **de valeur** *m pl* COM valuables

obl. *abrév (obligation)* BOURSE db *(debenture)*

obligataire *mf* BOURSE bondholder, DROIT obligee

obligation *f* ASSUR investment bond, BOURSE bond, *payable en livres sterling* BOURSE debenture, COM obligation, DROIT commitment, obligation, FIN bond; ~ **d'acceptation** BANQUE acceptance duty; ~ **d'adaptation** BREVETS *propriété intellectuelle* must fit, must match; ~ **d'administration locale ou régionale** BOURSE local authority bill, local authority bond, LAB; ~ **amortie** BOURSE callable bond, redeemable bond, redeemed debenture; ~ **amortissable** BOURSE callable bond, redeemable bond, redeemed debenture; ~ **à un an** ECON government bond, yearling *(BrE)*; ~ **anticipée de nouvelles mesures sociales** RES HUM projected benefit obligation; ~ **assimilable du Trésor** *(OAT)* BOURSE French government bond, French treasury bond; ~ **d'assurance** ASSUR compulsory insurance; ~ **au-dessous du pair** BOURSE discount bond, discounted bond; ~ **autorisée** BOURSE authorized bond; ~ **avec bon de souscription détachable** BOURSE bond with detachable warrant; ~ **bancaire** BANQUE bank bond; ~ **à bon de souscription** BOURSE bond cum warrant, bond with warrant, bond with warrant attached; ~ **à bons de souscription en actions** *(OBSA)* BOURSE bond cum warrant; ~ **à bons de souscription en actions rachetables** *(OBSAR)* BOURSE bonds with redeemable share warrants; ~ **à bons de souscription d'obligations** *(OBSO)* BOURSE bond with bond-buying warrant; ~ **bull-and-bear** BOURSE bull-and-bear bond *(UK)*; ~ **en circulation** BOURSE bond outstanding; ~ **co-émise** BOURSE joint bond; ~ **de collectivité locale** BOURSE municipal bond *(US)*; ~ **de collectivité locale garantie** BOURSE moral obligation bond; ~ **des collectivités locales financée par impôt** BOURSE special district bond; ~ **des collectivités locales garantie** BOURSE G-O bond *(US)*, general obligation bond *(US)*; ~ **conditionnelle** FISC contingent obligation; ~ **conjointe** BOURSE joint bond; ~ **conjointe et solidaire** DROIT joint and several obligation; ~ **contractuelle** COM contractual liability, DROIT contractual obligation, contractual liability; ~ **contrôlée** BOURSE, ECON managed bond; ~ **de conversion** BOURSE redemption bond; ~ **convertible** BOURSE *en actions* convertible, convertible bond, convertible debenture, FIN convertible bond; ~ **convertible en action** BOURSE equity kicker; ~ **convertible à haut rendement** BOURSE high-premium convertible debenture; ~ **convertible à prime élevée** BOURSE high-premium convertible debenture; ~ **à coupon différé** BOURSE zero-coupon bond; ~ **à coupon à long terme et à échéance courte** BOURSE super sinker bond; ~ **à coupon zéro** BOURSE strip, strip bond, stripped bond, zero-coupon bond; ~ **à coupons** FIN coupon bond; ~ **à coupons détachés** BOURSE strip, strip bond, stripped bond, zero-coupon bond; ~ **à cours non-limité** BOURSE unlimited tax bond; ~ **à court terme** BOURSE short-term bond; ~ **démembrée** BOURSE strip, strip bond, stripped bond; ~ **de deuxième rang** FIN second debenture; ~ **de développement**

industriel BOURSE industrial development bond; ~ **pour le développement de la petite entreprise** *(ODPE)* COM small business development bond *(SBDB)*; ~ **à échéance** BOURSE drawn bond; ~ **à échéance prorogeable** BOURSE extendible bond; ~ **échéant par tranches** BOURSE serial bond; ~ **échéant en série** BOURSE serial bond; ~ **émise depuis plus de trois mois** BANQUE seasoned loan; ~ **émise au pair** BOURSE parity bond; ~ **émise par une collectivité locale** BOURSE municipal bond *(US)*; ~ **émise par une société privée** BOURSE corporate bond *(US)*; ~ **encaissable par anticipation** BOURSE retractable bond; ~ **à escompte** BOURSE discount bond, discounted bond; ~ **à escompte important** BOURSE deep discount bond; ~ **essentiellement nominative** BOURSE fully registered bond; ~ **d'État** BOURSE gilt *(UK)*, government bond, state bond; ~ **d'État indexée** BOURSE index-linked gilt; ~ **étrangère** BOURSE, ECON, FIN foreign bond; ~ **en eurodollars** BOURSE, ECON, FIN Eurodollar bond; ~ **éventuelle** DROIT, FIN contingent liabilities; ~ **exclue** FISC excluded obligation *(Can)*; ~ **fiduciaire** COMPTA accountability; ~ **fiscale** FISC tax liability; ~ **garantie** BOURSE, FIN guaranteed bond, secured bond, secured debenture, warranty bond; ~ **de garantie** BOURSE retention bond, salvage bond, COMPTA guarantee liability, ECON retention bond, salvage bond; ~ **garantie pour acompte** BOURSE security bond for down payment; ~ **garantie par nantissement de titres** BOURSE collateral trust bond; ~ **du gouvernement fédéral** BOURSE federal government bond *(US)*; ~ **hypothécaire** FIN mortgage bond; ~ **hypothèque générale** BOURSE general mortgage bond; ~ **immatriculée** BOURSE registered bond; ~ **immobilière** FIN, IMMOB property bond; ~ **implicite** COM implied obligation; ~ **imposable** FISC taxable obligation; ~ **imposable spéciale** BOURSE special tax bond; ~ **d'impôts anticipés** FISC tax anticipation bill *(US)*, tax anticipation note, TAB *(US)*, TAN; ~ **inactive** BOURSE inactive bond; ~ **indexée** BANQUE, BOURSE, FIN indexed bond; ~ **d'information** COM disclosure requirement; ~ **à intérêt différé** BOURSE deferred interest bond; ~ **à intérêt élevé** BOURSE full coupon bond; ~ **à intérêts composés** FIN compound interest bond; ~ **juridique** DROIT legal obligation, perfect obligation; ~ **légale** DROIT legal obligation, legal requirement, statutory obligation; ~ **légale de cotiser au système de retraite** RES HUM employer's legal obligation to fund; ~ **de limiter le dommage** DROIT mitigation of damages; ~ **à long terme** BOURSE long bond, long coupon, long-term bond, stock; ~ **à long terme émise par une collectivité** FIN hospital revenue bond, utility revenue bond; ~ **à lots** FIN prize bond; ~ **à maturité courte** BOURSE short coupon; ~ **à mode de paiement optionnel** BOURSE optional payment bond; ~ **morale** DROIT imperfect obligation; ~ **à moyen terme** BOURSE medium-term bond; ~ **municipale** BOURSE corpo-

rate bond *(US)*, municipal bond *(US)*; ~ **municipale à revenu** BOURSE municipal revenue bond *(US)*; ~ **nantie** BOURSE collateral trust bond; ~ **ne portant pas d'intérêt** BOURSE passive bond; ~ **négociable** BOURSE marketable bond; ~ **négociable au porteur** FISC bearer marketable bond; ~ **négociée bien en dessous du pair** BOURSE deep discount bond; ~ **nominative** BOURSE registered bond; ~ **nominative à coupons** FIN coupon registered bond; ~ **non-amortissable des building sociétés** BOURSE PIBs, permanent income-bearing share; ~ **non-convertible** BOURSE straight bond; ~ **non-garantie** BOURSE debenture, unsecured bond; ~ **non-imposable** FISC nontaxable obligation; ~ **non-remboursable** BOURSE noncallable bond; ~ **notée AAA** BOURSE AAA bond, triple-A bond; ~ **officielle** COM public engagement; ~ **de pacotille** BOURSE junk bond; ~ **de paiement** BANQUE, FIN payment commitment; ~ **à paiement anticipé** BOURSE advance payment bond; ~ **participante** BOURSE dividend bond, participating bond, profit-sharing bond; ~ **perpétuelle** BOURSE perpetual bond; ~ **pour petite entreprise** COM small business bond; ~ **peu active** BOURSE inactive bond; ~ **à plus court terme** BOURSE shorter-term liability; ~ **au porteur** BOURSE, FIN bearer bond, bearer debenture, FISC bearer debenture; ~ **pourrie** *infrml* BOURSE junk bond; ~ **de premier ordre** BOURSE high-grade bond; ~ **de première qualité** BOURSE high-grade bond; ~ **prévue par la loi** DROIT statutory obligation; ~ **à prime complète** BOURSE full coupon bond; ~ **à primes** BOURSE premium bond; ~ **prioritaire** BOURSE prior-lien bond; ~ **provisoire** BOURSE provisional bond; ~ **rachetable** BOURSE callable bond, redeemable bond, redeemed debenture; ~ **rapportant gros** BOURSE killer bond; ~ **réditionnelle** COMPTA accountability; ~ **remboursable** BOURSE callable bond, redeemable bond, redeemed debenture; ~ **remboursable au pair** BOURSE par bond; ~ **remboursable par anticipation** BOURSE callable preferred stock *(US)*; ~ **remboursable à périodes déterminées** BOURSE put bond; ~ **de remplacement** BOURSE replacement bond; ~ **de rente** BOURSE annuity bond; ~ **à revenu variable** BOURSE income bond, income debenture; ~ **samouraï** BOURSE samurai bond; ~ **sans bon de souscription** BOURSE bond ex warrant; ~ **sans bon de souscription d'actions** BOURSE bond ex warrant; ~ **sans intérêt** BOURSE flat bond, passive bond; ~ **sans valeur** BOURSE junk bond; ~ **sans warrant** BOURSE bond ex warrant; ~ **du secteur privé** BOURSE corporate loan; ~ **de société** BOURSE corporate debenture; ~ **solidaire** FISC joint liability; ~ **sous-jacente** BOURSE underlying bond; ~ **sous-option** BOURSE underlying bond; ~ **spéciale à coupons à réinvestir** *(OSCAR)* BOURSE bunny bond *(jarg)*; ~ **spéculative à haut risque** BOURSE junk bond; ~ **statutaire** DROIT statutory obligation; ~ **subordonnée** BOURSE subordinated debenture; ~ **sur demande** BANQUE on demand bond; ~ **synthétique** BOURSE synthetic bond; ~ **à taux fixe** BOURSE fixed-rate bond; ~ **à taux flottant** BOURSE floating-rate debenture, floating-rate note; ~ **à taux glissant** BOURSE, FIN rolling rate, rolling-rate note; ~ **à taux variable** BOURSE floater (*US*), floating-rate debenture, rolling-rate note, BOURSE floating-rate note, FIN rolling rate, rolling-rate note; ~ **du Trésor** BOURSE, ECON T-bond, Treasury bond; ~ **vendue au-dessous du pair à l'émission** BOURSE, FIN OID bond, original issue discount bond; ~ **vendue avant l'émission** BOURSE bond sold prior to issue; ~ **à warrant** BOURSE bond cum warrant, bond with warrant, bond with warrant attached; ~ **Yankee** BOURSE Yankee bond (*US*); ♦ **être dans l'~ de faire qch** COM to be obligated to do sth, to be tied to doing sth, DROIT to be obliged to do sth, to be tied to doing sth; **être dans l'~ légale de** DROIT be under a legal obligation to; ♦ ~ **la moins chère à livrer** *(OMCL)* BOURSE cheapest to deliver *(CTD)*

obligations *f pl* BOURSE, COMPTA, FIN loan stock; ~ **d'arbitrage** BOURSE arbitrage bonds (*US*); ~ **assimilables à des actions** BOURSE equity-related bonds; ~ **convertibles à bons de souscription en actions** *f pl (OCBSA)* BOURSE convertible bonds with share warrants; ~ **à échéance** *f* BOURSE matured bond; ~ **échues** BOURSE matured bonds; ~ **en Eurosterling à coupon zéro** BOURSE ZEBRAs, zero coupon Eurosterling bearer-registered accruing securities; ~ **à lots** BOURSE, FIN Premium Bonds (*UK*), Premium Savings Bonds (*UK*); ~ **nominatives** BANQUE nontransferable debentures; ~ **non-estampillées** BOURSE unstamped debentures; ~ **non-garanties** BOURSE debenture stock; ~ **non-garanties consolidées** BOURSE consolidated debenture stock (*UK*); ~ **particulières non-négociables** BOURSE special non-marketable bonds; ~ **à plus de 15 ans** BOURSE longs; ~ **en portefeuille** BOURSE bond holdings; ~ **produisant des intérêts** BANQUE interest-bearing eligible liabilities (*UK*), IBELS (*UK*); ~ **remboursables en actions** *(ORA)* BOURSE bonds redeemable in shares; ~ **spéciales non-négociables** BOURSE special non-marketable bonds; ~ **subordonnées à durée indéterminée à bons de souscription en actions rachetables** *(OSDIBSAR)* BOURSE subordinated perpetual bonds with redeemable share warrants; ~ **à terme** BOURSE, FIN Premium Bonds (*UK*), Premium Savings Bonds (*UK*); ~ **du Trésor américain** BOURSE US Treasury Bonds

obligatoire *adj* COM compulsory, obligatory, enforced, DROIT mandatory, *décision* binding; ♦ **être ~** DROIT bind

obligé[1]**, e** *m,f* DROIT obligor

obligé:[2] **être ~ de faire qch** *vt* COM to be obligated to do sth, DROIT to be obliged to do sth

obliger *vt* COM oblige; ♦ ~ **qn à faire qch** COM force sb to do sth, oblige sb to do sth

OBSA *abrév (obligation à bons de souscription en actions)* BOURSE bond cum warrant

OBSAR *abrév (obligation à bons de souscription en actions rachetables)* BOURSE bonds with redeemable share warrants

observateur, -trice *m,f* COM, POL observer

observation *f* COM comment, observation, DROIT compliance; ~ **fiscale** FISC tax compliance; ~ **volontaire** FISC voluntary compliance; ♦ **faire des ~s** COM comment

observatoire *m* COM observatory

observer *vt* COM remark, DROIT *loi* observe

OBSO *abrév (obligation à bons de souscription d'obligations)* BOURSE bond with bond-buying warrant

obsolescence *f* COM, V&M obsolescence; ~ **économique** ECON economic obsolescence; ~ **fonctionnelle** V&M functional obsolescence; ~ **programmée** COM, ECON, IND, V&M built-in obsolescence, planned obsolescence

obsolète *adj* COM obsolete

obstacle *m* COM bar, hurdle, obstacle, ECON barrier; ~ **au commerce maritime** TRANSP *navigation* barrier to trade; ~ **à la communication** COM, COMMS communication barrier

obtenir *vt* BREVETS *consentement* obtain, COM get, obtain, *résultat* achieve, DROIT *autorisation*, FIN obtain; ~ **le baccalauréat** PROT SOC graduate (*US*); ~ **la communication avec qn** COMMS get through to sb; ~ **frauduleusement** DROIT obtain by fraud; ♦ ~ **l'accord officiel de** COM gain formal approval from; ~ **l'approbation de** COM have the approval of; ~ **une augmentation de salaire** RES HUM get a pay rise; ~ **de bons résultats** RES HUM get results; ~ **gain de cause** DROIT get justice; ~ **une majorité sur** COM outvote; ~ **de nouvelles commandes** COM secure new orders; ~ **la permission par écrit** COMMS obtain permission in writing; ~ **un prêt** BOURSE take out loan; ~ **une réponse** COM get an answer; ~ **sa licence** PROT SOC graduate (*UK*); ~ **son diplôme** COM qualify, PROT SOC graduate (*UK*)

obtention *f* COM obtainment, V&M procurement

obtenu: ~ **par nomination** *adj* COM appointive (*AmE*), elective

OCAMM *abrév (Organisation commune africaine, malgache et mauricienne)* COM AASMM *(Associated African States, Madagascar and Mauritius)*

OCBSA *abrév (obligations convertibles à bons de souscription en actions)* BOURSE convertible bonds with share warrants

occasion *f* COM, GESTION business opportunity, occasion, opportunity; ~ **d'investissement** BANQUE investment opportunity; ♦ **avoir l'~ de** COM have the opportunity to; **donner à qn l'~ de** COM give sb the opportunity to; **si l'~ se présente** COM should the occasion arise

occasionnel, -elle *adj* COM occasional

occasionner *vt* COM cause

occasions: beaucoup d'~ *f* COM *pour faire qch*

wealth of opportunities; ~ **d'entendre** *f pl* MÉDIA, V&M *publicité, radio* opportunities to hear (*jarg*), OTH; ~ **de voir** *f pl* MÉDIA, V&M *publicité, télévision* opportunities to see (*jarg*), OTS

occidentaliser: **s'~** *v pron* COM become westernized

occupant, -e *m,f* DROIT, FISC occupant, IMMOB occupant, occupier

occupation *f* DROIT occupancy, occupation, IMMOB occupancy, POL, RES HUM tenure; ~ **commerciale** COM, IMMOB commercial occupancy; ~ **industrielle** IMMOB, IND industrial occupancy; ~ **des locaux** RES HUM occupation; ~ **par le propriétaire** IMMOB owner occupation; ~ **des sols** ENVIR *niveau local* land use

occupations *f pl* COM business

occupé, e *adj* COM engaged, COMMS busy (*AmE*), engaged (*BrE*), INFO busy; ◆ **être ~ à faire** COM be engaged in doing

occuper 1. *vt* IMMOB, RES HUM occupy; **2.** *v pron* **s'~ de** COM run, *magasin* attend to, *projet* be in charge of, GESTION run, *d'une tâche quelconque* be engaged in, V&M deal with; ◆ **~ un créneau dans le marché** COM, V&M bridge a gap in the market; **s'~ de la nourriture** COM cater for; **~ le devant de la scène** COM hold the stage

OCDE *abrév* (*Organisation de coopération et de développement économique*) ECON OECD (*Organization for Economic Cooperation and Development*)

oct. *abrév* (*octobre*) COM Oct. (*October*)

octet *m* INFO byte

octobre *m* (*oct.*) COM October (*Oct.*)

octroi *m* IMMOB grant; ~ **de crédit** BANQUE credit granting, granting of credit; ~ **de dommages-intérêts** DROIT awarding of damages; ~ **d'un emprunt** BANQUE, COM, COMPTA, ECON, FIN borrowing allocation; ~ **de licence** ECON, IMP/EXP licensing; ~ **de subventions** COM, FIN subsidization

octroyer *vt* COM award, grant

odeur *f* ENVIR odor (*AmE*), odour (*BrE*)

ODPE *abrév* (*obligation pour le développement de la petite entreprise*) COM SBDB (*small business development bond*)

OECE *abrév* (*Organisation européenne de coopération économique*) ECON OEEC (*Organization for European Economic Cooperation*)

oeuvre: ~ **accomplie** *f* RES HUM accomplishment; ~ **de bienfaisance** *f* FISC, PROT SOC charitable organization, charity; ~ **caritative reconnue** *f* FISC registered charity; ~ **de charité** *f* FISC, PROT SOC charitable organization

oeuvrer *vi* RES HUM labor (*AmE*), labour (*BrE*)

offensive: ~ **commerciale** *f* V&M sales offensive

offert, e *adj* BOURSE offered

office: ~ **désigné** *m* BREVETS designated office; ~ **élu** *m* POL elected office; ~ **européen des marques** *m* DROIT *de la Communauté européenne*

Community Trade Mark Office; ~ **de logement** *m* PROT SOC accommodations bureau (*AmE*); ~ **récepteur** *m* BREVETS receiving office, RO; ~ **de régularisation** *m* V&M marketing board; ~ **du tourisme** *m* LOISIRS Tourist Board (*UK*)

Office: ~ **international des épizooties** *m* (*OIE*) TRANSP International Office of Epizootics (*IOE*); ~ **de justification de la diffusion** *m* COMPTA, V&M ≈ Audit Bureau of Circulation; ~ **de secours et de travaux des Nations Unies pour les réfugiés** *m* ECON, POL United Nations Relief and World Agency, UNRWA

officialiser *vt* COM formalize

officiel, -elle *adj* COM formal, official

officiellement *adv* COM officially, RES HUM ex officio (*frml*)

officier: ~ **chargé des passagers** *m* RES HUM, TRANSP *d'un vaisseau* staff captain; ~ **d'intendance** *m* RES HUM, TRANSP catering officer; ~ **mécanicien** *m* IND, RES HUM petty officer; ~ **mécanicien adjoint 1ère classe** *m* TRANSP *navigation* Motorman Grade I; ~ **mécanicien adjoint 2ème classe** *m* TRANSP *navigation* Motorman Grade II; ~ **payeur** *m* FIN disburser; ~ **de police du service de l'immigration** *m* ADMIN, RES HUM immigration officer, IO; ~ **radio** *m* RES HUM, TRANSP radio officer; ~ **de recrutement** *m* RES HUM recruiting officer; ~ **de santé** *m* PROT SOC, RES HUM medical officer of health, MOH; ~ **de service** *m* RES HUM duty officer, DO; ~ **supérieur** *m* RES HUM senior officer, SO; ~ **supérieur à la P.A.F.** *m* RES HUM chief immigration officer, CIO; ~ **supérieur de la police des frontières** *m* RES HUM chief immigration officer, CIO

officieux, -euse *adj* COM off-the-record, unofficial

offrant *m* COM bidder, offerer

offre[1] *f* BOURSE offer, offering, *pour l'achat d'actions ou d'une participation* bid, COM bid, offer, supply, tender, tendering, ECON tendering, FIN *pour l'achat d'actions ou d'une participation* bid, GESTION bid, tendering, V&M offer; ~ **d'achat** BOURSE bid, tender offer, buyout proposal, hedged tender, tender, ECON tender, FIN bid; ~ **d'achat d'actions** BOURSE, PROT SOC, RES HUM share scheme; ~ **d'acquisition** BOURSE buyout proposal; ~ **auto-payante** V&M self-liquidator, *marketing* premium offer; ~ **de base** COM basic submission, basic tender; ~ **de biens** ECON supply of goods; ~ **demandée** BOURSE offer wanted; ~ **au détail** BOURSE retail offer; ~ **en dollars** BOURSE dollar bid; ~ **écrite** COM written offer; ~ **élastique** ECON, V&M elastic supply; ~ **d'emploi** RES HUM job advertisement, job offer; ~ **d'essai** COM sampling offer; ~ **essai** COM trial offer; ~ **et acceptation** COM, DROIT offer and acceptance; ~ **excédentaire** ECON, V&M excess supply; ~ **excédentaire de dollars** FIN, IMP/EXP dollar overhang; ~ **ferme** BOURSE firm offer, COM bona fide offer; ~ **fixe** ECON fixed supply; ~ **flottante** BOURSE floating stock, floating supply; ~ **forfaitaire**

BOURSE fixed-price offering; **~ globale** ECON aggregate supply; **~ indexé** BOURSE leveraged bid; **~ inélastique** ECON inelastic supply; **~ irrévocable** COM binding offer; **l'~ et la demande** BOURSE bid-and-asked price, bid-and-offered price, COM supply and demand; **~ de lancement** V&M introductory offer; **~ de main-d'oeuvre** ECON labor supply (*AmE*), labour supply (*BrE*); **~ non-concurrentielle** BOURSE noncompetitive bid; **~ d'obligations municipales** BANQUE municipal bond offering; **~ originale** COM original bid; **~ ouverte** GESTION open bid; **~ plus avantageuse** COM better offer; **~ la plus élevée** BOURSE highest bid; **~ plus intéressante** COM better offer; **~ de prix** BOURSE price bid; **~ promotionnelle** COM bargain offer, V&M bargain offer, *pour l'acheteur* sales incentive, *publicité* special purchase; **~ publique d'achat** *(OPA)* BOURSE, COM, COMPTA takeover bid *(TOB)*; **~ publique d'achat hostile** BOURSE hostile take-over bid; **~ publique d'échange** *(OPE)* BOURSE exchange offer; **~ publique d'enchère** COM public invitation to bid; **~ publique initiale** BOURSE IPO (*AmE*), initial public offering (*AmE*); **~ publique de vente** *(OPV)* BOURSE offer for sale, public offering; **~ rampante** BOURSE, FIN creeping tender; **~ reçue** COM bid is received; **~ régressive** ECON regressive supply; **~ de répartition** BOURSE split offering; **~ sérieuse** COM bona fide offer; **~ de services** ECON supply of services; **~ spéciale** COM bargain offer, premium offer, special offer, V&M bargain offer, special offer; **~ de valeur** COMPTA, FIN value proposal; **~ variable** COM soft offer; **~ verbale** COM verbal offer; ◆ **faire une ~** BOURSE bid, COM make a bid, make an offer, FIN, GESTION bid; **faire une ~ d'argent pour régler une dette** DROIT tender money in discharge of debt; **faire une ~ ferme** BOURSE make a firm bid; **faire une ~ pour** GESTION *marché* tender for

offres: ~ d'emploi *f pl* RES HUM *dans le journal* appointments vacant, sits. vac. (*BrE*), situations vacant (*BrE*); **~ d'emploi non satisfaites** *f pl* RES HUM unfilled vacancies; **~ sur deuxième marché** *f pl* BOURSE secondary offering

offrir 1. *vt* COM offer; **~ des conditions plus avantageuses** COM underbid, BOURSE, FIN bid; **2.** *v pron* **s'~** ECON *sac, livre* afford; ◆ **~ beaucoup de possibilités** COM offer considerable scope; **pouvoir s'~ qch** ECON be able to afford to buy sth; **s'~ le restaurant** ECON treat oneself to a meal out (*infrml*)

offshore[1] *adv* ENVIR offshore

offshore[2] *adj* COM offshore

OIE *abrév* (*Office international des épizooties*) TRANSP IOE (*International Office of Epizootics*)

OIML *abrév* (*Organisation internationale de métrologie légale*) DROIT International Organization for Legal Metrology

OIT *abrév* (*Organisation internationale du travail*) RES HUM ILO (*International Labour Organization*)

Old: ~ Lady of Threadneedle Street *f* BANQUE Old Lady of Threadneedle Street (*UK*)

oléoduc *m* ENVIR oil pipeline, IND oil pipeline, pipeline

oligopole *m* ECON oligopoly, shared monopoly, IND, POL oligopoly; **~ collusif** ECON collusive oligopoly; **~ homogène** ECON homogeneous oligopoly; **~ local** ECON spatial oligopoly

oligopolistique *adj* ECON, POL oligopolistic

oligopsone *f* ECON oligopsony

OM *abrév* (*organisation et méthodes*) COM, GESTION, RES HUM O&M (*organization and methods*)

Oman *m* COM Oman

omanais, e *adj* COM Omani

Omanais, e *m,f* COM *habitant* Omani

ombrage *m* INFO shading

ombre *f* COM shadow

ombrelle: ~ fiscale *f* FISC tax umbrella

OMCL *abrév* (*obligation la moins chère à livrer*) BOURSE CTD (*cheapest to deliver*)

omettre *vt* COM omit, INFO skip; ◆ **~ les détails** COM *dans un rapport* skip the details; **~ le paiement** FIN *d'un dividende* pass

omission *f* COM omission; **~ coupable** ASSUR, DROIT negligence; **~ volontaire** FISC wilful default

omnibus *m* TRANSP *chemin de fer* accommodation train (*AmE*), slow train (*AmE*)

OMS *abrév* (*Organisation mondiale de la santé*) ADMIN, PROT SOC WHO (*World Health Organization*)

once *f* COM ounce, oz; **~ liquide** COM fl.oz, fluid ounce; **~ troy** ECON *d'or* troy ounce

on-dit *m* COM *principalement négatif* hearsay

onéreux, -euse *adj* COM costly; **peu ~** COM cheap

ONG *abrév* (*organisation non-gouvernementale*) COM NGO (*nongovernmental organization*)

ONU *abrév* (*Organisation des Nations Unies*) ECON, POL UN (*United Nations*), UNO (*United Nations Organization*)

OP *abrév* (*ordinateur personnel*) INFO PC (*personal computer*)

OPA[1] *abrév* (*offre publique d'achat*) BOURSE, COM, COMPTA TOB (*takeover bid*)

OPA:[2] **~ amicale** *f* ECON agreed takeover; **~ hostile** *f* BOURSE hostile takeover bid; **~ négociée à l'amiable** *f* ECON agreed takeover; **~ à rebours** *f* ECON, FIN reverse takeover, reversed takeover

OPCVM *abrév* (*organisme de placements collectifs en valeurs mobilières*) FIN UCITS (*undertakings for collective investment in transferables*)

OPE *abrév* (*offre publique d'échange*) BOURSE exchange offer

opéable[1] *adj* BOURSE raidable

opéable:[2] **société ~** *f* BOURSE sleeping beauty

OPEP *abrév* (*Organisation des pays exportateurs de pétrole*) ECON, ENVIR, POL OPEC (*Organization of Petroleum Exporting Countries*)

opérateur^1 *m* MATH operand

opérateur^2 **-trice**, *m,f* BOURSE *en bourse* trader, *sur le marché obligataire* dealer, COM operator, COMMS telephone operator; ~ **binaire** INFO binary operator; ~ **de conteneurs** TRANSP container operator; ~ **en couverture** BOURSE hedger; ~ **des groupages import** RES HUM import groupage operator; ~ **de machine** IND, RES HUM machine operator; ~ **multi-transports** TRANSP multimodal transport operator, MTO; ~ **en obligations** BOURSE bond trader; ~ **principal du marché (OPM)** BOURSE bill broker, discount house; ~ **professionnel** ECON professional trader; ~ **de saisie de données** INFO data entry keyboarder; ~ **sur graphique** BOURSE chartist; ~ **sur le marché monétaire** BOURSE, ECON, FIN money-market trader; ~ **sur ordinateur** INFO computer operator; ~ **de terminal** INFO terminal operator; ~ **d'usine** IND plant operator; ◆ être ~ **en Bourse** BOURSE trade in stocks and bonds

opération *f* BANQUE transaction, BOURSE dealing, transaction, COM agency, operation, transaction, COMPTA, ECON, FIN transaction, GESTION operation, INFO process, transaction; ~ **d'achat** BOURSE buy transaction; ~ **d'achat et de vente sur le marché des changes à terme** ECON forward-forward currency deal; ~ **d'achat-vente compensée** BOURSE matched sale-purchase transaction; ~ **d'arbitrage** BOURSE arbitrage, arbitration transaction; ~ **d'arrière-boutique** ECON, FIN backdoor operation; ~ **d'assainissement** ENVIR cleaning-up operation; ~ **au-dessous de ligne** (ANT *opération au-dessus de ligne*) ECON below-the-line item; ~ **au-dessus de ligne** (ANT *opération au-dessous de ligne*) ECON above-the-line item; ~ **bancaire** BANQUE, COMPTA, FIN banking operation, banking transaction; ~ **bancaire de terre** BANQUE, FIN, IMMOB land banking; ~ **de banque** BANQUE, COMPTA, FIN banking transaction; ~ **de Bourse** BOURSE stock exchange transaction; ~ **boursière** BOURSE stock exchange transaction; ~ **de caisse** COM cash transaction, COMPTA cash operation, cash transaction; ~ **de change** BANQUE foreign exchange, BOURSE foreign exchange deal, ECON, FIN foreign exchange; ~ **de change à terme** BANQUE *contrat d'échange de devises* forward exchange contract; ~ **commerciale** COM business transaction; ~ **de compensation** BOURSE offsetting transaction, ECON *commerce international* barter transaction; ~ **compensatrice** BOURSE offsetting transaction; ~ **comptable** BANQUE, COMPTA, FIN account transaction; ~ **au comptant** BOURSE cash bargain, COM cash transaction, spot business; ~ **conjointe** COM joint-venture company, *action* joint venture, JV; ~ **de contre-achats** ECON switch dealing (*jarg*); ~ **à un cours fictif** BOURSE wash sale; ~ **de couverture** BOURSE, FIN hedging; ~ **de couverture sûre** BOURSE safe hedge; ~ **de couverture à terme** BOURSE hedge, hedging, FIN hedging; ~ **à la criée** BOURSE open-outcry action; ~ **en dollars** BANQUE dollar transaction; ~ **d'émission obligataire** BOURSE bond issue operation; ~ **à escales multiples** TRANSP *navigation* multiport operation; ~ **de face à face** BANQUE, FIN back-to-back transaction; ~ **fictive** BOURSE shell operation; ~ **fictive par achat et vente simultanés** BOURSE wash sale; ~ **fiduciaire** BANQUE fiduciary operation; ~ **de financement quotidienne** FIN day-to-day funding activity; ~ **aux frais de la princesse** *jarg* BOURSE free ride (*infrml*), free-riding; ~ **intégrée** BOURSE embedded option; ~ **interdite** INFO illegal operation; ~ **interne** BOURSE in-house operation; ~ **liée** BOURSE straddle; ~ **liée sur option à delta neutre** BOURSE delta-neutral straddles, delta-neutral strangle; ~ **de liquidation** BOURSE closing trade, closing transaction; ~ **liquidative** BOURSE closing trade, closing transaction; ~ **machine** INFO computer operation; ~ **menée dans les règles de l'art** COM textbook operation; ~ **mixte** BOURSE spread, spreading; ~ **mixte à la baisse** (ANT *opération mixte à la hausse*) BOURSE bear spread, bearish spread; ~ **mixte baissière** (ANT *opération mixte haussière*) BOURSE bear spread, bearish spread; ~ **mixte à la hausse** (ANT *opération mixte à la baisse*) BOURSE bull spread, bullish spread; ~ **mixte haussière** (ANT *opération mixte baissière*) BOURSE bull spread, bullish spread; ~ **mixte horizontale** BOURSE calendar spread, horizontal spread, time spread; ~ **mixte du papillon** BOURSE butterfly spread; ~ **mixte sur options d'achat** (ANT *opération mixte sur options de vente*) BOURSE call spread; ~ **mixte sur options avec dates d'échéance** BOURSE calendar spread; ~ **mixte sur options avec dates d'échéance différentes** BOURSE time spread, vertical spread; ~ **mixte symétrique** BOURSE box spread; ~ **mixte sur options de vente** (ANT *opération mixte sur options d'achat*) BOURSE put spread; ~ **mixte verticale** BOURSE money spread, price spread, vertical spread, FIN money spread; ~ **mixte verticale à la hausse sur options d'achat** BOURSE bullish vertical call spread; ~ **mixte verticale à la hausse sur options de vente** BOURSE bullish vertical put spread; ~ **de nettoyage** ENVIR cleaning-up operation; ~ **non valide** INFO illegal operation; ~ **de pleine concurrence** COMMS arm's-length transaction; ~ **de prêt** BANQUE lending power; ~ **de protection** BOURSE, FIN hedging; ~ **rapide** BOURSE wash sale; ~ **ratée** COM minus advantage (*jarg*); ~ **de renflouement** BANQUE lifeboat operation (*infrml*); ~ **de report** BOURSE contango business (*UK*); ~ **sans bourse délier** BOURSE free ride (*infrml*), free-riding; ~ **sans lien de dépendance** COMMS arm's-length transaction; ~ **de scalpage** BOURSE scalp (*US, infrml*); ~ **en série** FISC step transaction, INFO serial operation; ~ **de soutien du cours de l'action** BOURSE share support operation; ~ **de spread** BOURSE spreading; ~ **sur actions** BOURSE equity trading; ~ **sur le capital** FIN capital transaction; ~ **sur carte de crédit** COM credit card transaction; ~ **sur des**

devises BOURSE foreign exchange deal; ~ **sur double option** BOURSE double option; ~ **sur titres** BOURSE securities dealing, securities transaction; ~ **sur valeurs mobilières** BOURSE securities dealing, securities transaction; ~ **à terme** BOURSE forward operation; ~ **à terme sur les marchandises** BOURSE commodity futures trading; ~ **de transport combiné** TRANSP combined transport operation; ~ **de trésorerie** COMPTA cash operation, cash transaction; ~ **triangulaire** ECON triangular operation; ~ **de troc** ECON *commerce international* barter transaction; ~ **twist** ECON price twist; ~ **vente-rachat** *jarg* FISC quick flip; ◆ **faire des ~s symétriques** BOURSE marry; **faire une** ~ COM make a transaction

opérationnel[1], **-elle** *adj* COM, GESTION operational
opérationnel[2], **-elle** *m,f* GESTION, IND, RES HUM operative
opérationnels *m pl* RES HUM line
opérations *f pl* COM operations; ~ **d'arbitrage** *f pl* BOURSE arbitrage dealings, arbitrage trading; ~ **d'assurance sur la vie** *f pl* ASSUR life insurance business; ~ **bancaires** *f pl* BANQUE banking, bkg; ~ **bancaires à distance** *f pl* BANQUE *par téléphone* telebanking; ~ **bancaires effectuées à partir du territoire national** *f pl* BANQUE onshore banking; ~ **bancaires étrangères** *f pl* BANQUE foreign banking; ~ **bancaires en eurodevises** *f pl* BANQUE Eurobanking; ~ **bancaires fiduciaires** *f pl* BANQUE fiduciary banking; ~ **bancaires intérieures** *f pl* BANQUE in-home banking; ~ **bancaires internationales** *f pl* BANQUE international banking, international banking facility, IBF; ~ **bancaires islamiques** *f pl* BANQUE Islamic banking; ~ **bancaires laser** *f pl* BANQUE *voir banque guichet* laser banking; ~ **bancaires sur le marché intérieur** *f pl* BANQUE home banking; ~ **de banque** *f pl* BANQUE banking, bkg; ~ **de banque d'affaires** *f pl* BANQUE, FIN merchant banking; ~ **de banque sur la réserve fractionnaire** *f pl* BANQUE fractional reserve banking; ~ **des banques commerciales** *f pl* BANQUE commercial banking; ~ **en Bourse** *f pl* BANQUE, BOURSE trading operations; ~ **boursières** *f pl* BOURSE securities business; ~ **boursières au pair** *f pl* BOURSE par trading; ~ **clientèles** *f pl* BANQUE transactions with customers; ~ **commerciales** *f pl* COM, GESTION business dealings; ~ **commerciales compensées** *f pl* BOURSE matched trade; ~ **en compte courant** *f pl* COM open-account business; ~ **de couverture** *f pl* BOURSE hedge trading; ~ **de couverture à terme** *f pl* BOURSE, FIN hedging operations; ~ **de crédit commercial** *f pl* BANQUE commercial lending; ~ **en devises** *f pl* BANQUE forex trading; ~ **de dividendes** *f pl* BOURSE trading dividends; ~ **d'initié** *f pl* BOURSE self-dealing; ~ **d'initiés** *f pl* BOURSE, FIN insider dealing, insider trading; ~ **interbancaires** *f pl* BANQUE interbank business, interbank transactions; ~ **internes** *f pl* COMPTA internal transactions; ~ **de liquidation** *f pl* FIN dealings

for the account; ~ **de marché** *f pl* BOURSE market operations; ~ **nettes** *f pl* BOURSE net transaction; ~ **portuaires** *f pl* TRANSP dock operations, DO; ~ **de prêt** *f pl* BANQUE lending business; ~ **spéculatives** *f pl* BOURSE speculative trading; ~ **sur blocs d'actions** *f pl* BOURSE volume trading; ~ **sur marchandises** *f pl* BOURSE commodities trading, commodity trading; ~ **sur le marché hors cote** *f pl* FIN over-the-counter trading (*US*); ~ **sur le marché monétaire** *f pl* ECON *commerce international* open-market operations, open-market trading; ~ **sur le marché à options** *f pl* BOURSE option bargains; ~ **sur obligations** *f pl* BOURSE bond trading; ~ **sur valeurs de placement** *f* BANQUE business bank, investment banking (*US*), merchant banking (*UK*); ~ **à terme** *f pl* BOURSE futures, FIN dealings for the account; ~ **24 heures sur 24** *f pl* BOURSE twenty-four hour trading; ◆ **faire des ~ boursières** BOURSE deal

opérer: ~ **une déduction** *vt* FISC *d'un salaire* make a deduction; ~ **en dehors de son lieu de travail** RES HUM free-ride (*infrml*); ~ **une retenue** FISC make a deduction; ~ **un retour** COM make a comeback; ~ **une saisie-arrêt** DROIT garnish; ~ **une transaction** COM transact

ophélimité *f* ECON Pareto optimality

opinion *f* COM opinion, view, DROIT *émanant d'un juriste* opinion; ~ **avec réserve** COM qualified opinion; ~ **défavorable** *Can* COMPTA adverse opinion; ~ **publique** COM public opinion; ~ **sans réserve** COMPTA clean opinion (*infrml*), unqualified opinion

OPM *abrév* (*opérateur principal du marché*) BOURSE bill broker, discount house

opportun, e *adj* COM advisable

opportunisme *m* POL lifeboat ethics (*infrml*), opportunism

opportunité *f* FIN timeliness; ~ **commerciale** COM, GESTION business opportunity; ~ **sur un marché** COM break in the market

opposé, e *adj* COM *effets* adverse; ~ **à** COM alien to; ~ **au risque** COM, ECON risk averse

opposer: **s'~ à** *v pron* COM disagree, oppose, *une proposition* object to; **s'~ à une cotisation** FISC object to an assessment; **s'~ à une évaluation** FISC object to an assessment; ◆ ~ **le règlement à qn** COM throw the book at sb; **s'~ résolument à une décision** COM make a stand against a decision

opposition *f* BANQUE stop payment, BREVETS, COM opposition, DROIT adverse claim, FISC objection, POL opposition; ~ **du débiteur** BANQUE payment stopped; ~ **au paiement** BANQUE payment stopped; ◆ **faire ~ à** COM counter; **faire ~ à un chèque** BANQUE stop a check (*AmE*), stop a cheque (*BrE*), stop payment of a check (*AmE*), stop payment of a cheque (*BrE*), stop payment on a check (*AmE*), stop payment on a cheque (*BrE*)

opter: ~ **pour** *vt* COM opt for, COM elect
optimal, e *adj* COM optimum

optimalité *f* ECON optimality; ~ **de Pareto** ECON Pareto optimality

optimisation *f* COM maximization, optimization, ECON, IND optimization; ~ **du profit** ECON, FIN profit optimization; ~ **des revenus** ECON revenue maximization, V&M revenue maximization, sales maximization; ~ **des ventes** ECON, V&M revenue maximization

optimiser *vt* COM, ECON, FIN, IND optimize, INFO *machine* upgrade; ♦ ~ **la fonction objective** COM optimize the objective function

optimiste *adj* COM *attitude, prévision* upbeat, COM *(ANT pessimiste)* optimistic

optimum: ~ **de Pareto** *m* ECON Pareto improvement, Pareto optimum; ~ **de premier rang** *m* BOURSE first best

option *f* BOURSE option contract, stock contract, option, privilege *(US)*, COM alternative, option, FIN option, INFO feature, option, TRANSP *distribution* ship's option; ~ **d'achat** BOURSE buyer's option, call, call option, COM, ECON buyer's option, IMMOB *accord de contrat* binder; ~ **d'achat d'actions** BOURSE share option, stock option; ~ **d'achat d'actions accordée à des employés** BOURSE, RES HUM employee stock option; ~ **d'achat argenté** BOURSE in-the-money call option; ~ **d'achat couverte** *(ANT option d'achat à découvert)* BOURSE covered call *(UK)*, covered call option, covered call write; ~ **d'achat dans l'argent** BOURSE in-the-money call, in-the-money call option; ~ **d'achat dans le cours** BOURSE in-the-money call, in-the-money call option; ~ **d'achat à découvert** *(ANT option d'achat couverte)* BOURSE covered put write, naked call, naked call option, uncovered call, uncovered call option; ~ **d'achat découverte** *(ANT option de vente à découvert)* BOURSE naked call option, uncovered call, uncovered call option; ~ **d'achat en dedans** BOURSE in-the-money call option; ~ **d'achat en dehors** *(ANT option de vente en dehors)* BOURSE out-of-the-money call; ~ **d'achat hors du cours** *(ANT option de vente hors du cours)* BOURSE out-of-the-money call; ~ **d'achat au jeu** *jarg (ANT option de vente au jeu)* BOURSE at-the-money call, at-the-money call option; ~ **d'achat de juin** *(ANT option de vente de juin)* BOURSE *ou de tout autre mois* June call; ~ **d'achat au milieu** *(ANT option de vente au milieu)* BOURSE at-the-money call, at-the-money call option; ~ **d'achat de papillon long** BOURSE long butterfly call; ~ **d'achat à parité** *(ANT option de vente à parité)* BOURSE at-the-money call, at-the-money call option; ~ **d'achat sans garantie** BOURSE naked call; ~ **d'achat sur devises** *(ANT option de vente sur devises)* BOURSE currency call option; ~ **d'achat sur obligation** *(ANT option de vente sur obligation)* BOURSE bond call option; ~ **d'achat sur titres détenus** BOURSE covered call *(UK)*; ~ **d'achat à trois mois** BOURSE three-month call; ~ **d'achat vendue** *(ANT option de vente vendue)* BOURSE written call; ~ **d'action à prime**

BOURSE incentive stock option, ISO; ~ **américaine** BOURSE American option; ~ **à l'argent** BOURSE at-the-money option; ~ **at-the-money** BOURSE at-the-money option; ~ **de change** BOURSE FX option, currency option, forex option; ~ **de contrat à terme** IMP/EXP, V&M option forward contract; ~ **cotée** BOURSE listed option; ~ **cotée en Bourse** BOURSE exchange traded option, listed option; ~ **couplée** BOURSE *d'achat et de vente* matched book; ~ **au cours** BOURSE at-the-money option; ~ **à cours moyen** BOURSE middle strike option; ~ **couverte** BOURSE covered option; ~ **dans le cours** BOURSE in-the-money option; ~ **dans la monnaie** BOURSE in-the-money option; ~ **à découvert** BOURSE naked option, uncovered option; ~ **en dehors** BOURSE out-of-the-money option; ~ **donnant lieu à un règlement en espèces** BOURSE cash delivery option, cash-settled option; ~ **du double** BOURSE double option; ~ **du double pour livrer** BOURSE put of more option; ~ **d'échange** FIN swap option; ~ **à échéance dépassée** BOURSE lapsed option; ~ **à échéance plus courte** BOURSE longer-term option; ~ **à échéance plus longue** BOURSE longer-term option; ~ **écrite** BOURSE written call, written option, written put; ~ **d'entrée sur le marché** IMP/EXP market entry option; ~ **euro-américanisée** BOURSE Americanized-European option; ~ **européenne** BOURSE European option, European-style option; ~ **européenne-américanisée** BOURSE Americanized-European option; ~ **expirée** BOURSE lapsed option; ~ **hors du cours** BOURSE out-of-the-money option; ~ **hors la monnaie** BOURSE out-of-the-money option; ~ **d'immobilisation** BOURSE, FIN *prise de contrôle de société* lock-up option; ~ **in-the-money** BOURSE in-the-money option; ~ **d'indexation** BOURSE index option, stock index option; ~ **inscrite à la cote** BOURSE exchange traded option, listed option; ~ **-médias** MÉDIA, V&M *publicité* media options; ~ **de mise sur indice** BOURSE index option, stock index option; ~ **à la monnaie** BOURSE at-the-money option; ~ **de monnaies** FIN currency linked; ~ **négociable** BOURSE exchange traded option, listed option, traded option; ~ **négociée de gré à gré** BOURSE OTC option *(US)*, over-the-counter option *(US)*; ~ **négociée hors Bourse** BOURSE OTC option *(US)*, over-the-counter option *(US)*; ~ **négociée hors cote** BOURSE OTC option *(US)*, over-the-counter option *(US)*; ~ **d'obligation à long terme** BOURSE long-term bond option; ~ **out-of-the-money** BOURSE out-of-the-money option; ~ **de paiement par anticipation** FIN prepayment privilege; ~ **par défaut** INFO default option; ~ **à parité** BOURSE at-the-money option; ~ **à plus court terme** BOURSE shorter-term option; ~ **à plus long terme** BOURSE longer-term option; ~ **produire ou acheter** COM make-or-buy decision; ~ **de rachat** BOURSE buy-back option; ~ **de reconduction** IMMOB renewal option; ~ **rente viagère** ASSUR annuity plan; ~ **de repli** GESTION fall-back option;

~ **à risques limités** BOURSE *achat ou vente* stellage straddle option; ~ **de route** TRANSP route option; ~ **sans garantie** BOURSE naked option; ~ **de souscripteurs d'actions sans impôt** BOURSE qualifying stock option; ~ **de souscription à des actions fictives** BOURSE phantom share option, phantom stock plan; ~ **sur action** BOURSE equity option; ~ **sur actions** BOURSE stock option; ~ **sur devises** BOURSE FX option, currency option, forex option, currency options contract; ~ **sur obligations** BOURSE bond option; ~ **sur swap** BOURSE swap option; ~ **sur valeurs mobilières** BOURSE equity option; ~ **à taux d'intérêt** BOURSE interest rate option; ~ **de titre fictif** BOURSE phantom share option; ~ **de type européen** BOURSE European option, European-style option; ~ **vendue** BOURSE written option; ~ **de vente** *(ANT option d'achat)* BOURSE put, put option, seller's option, COM seller's option; ~ **de vente d'argenté** BOURSE in-the-money put option; ~ **de vente dans l'argent** BOURSE in-the-money put option; ~ **de vente dans le cours** BOURSE in-the-money put, in-the-money put option; ~ **de vente à découvert** *(ANT option d'achat découverte)* BOURSE naked put, naked put option, uncovered put; ~ **de vente découverte** BOURSE naked put option, uncovered put; ~ **de vente en dedans** BOURSE in-the-money put option; ~ **de vente en dehors** *(ANT option d'achat en dehors)* BOURSE out-of-the-money put; ~ **de vente garantie** BOURSE qualifying stock option; ~ **de vente garantie par un dépôt en liquide** BOURSE writing cash-secured put; ~ **de vente hors du cours** *(ANT option d'achat hors du cours)* BOURSE out-of-the-money put; ~ **de vente au jeu** *(ANT option d'achat au jeu)* BOURSE at-the-money put, at-the-money put option; ~ **de vente de juin** *(ANT option d'achat de juin)* BOURSE *ou de tout autre mois* June put; ~ **de vente au milieu** *(ANT option d'achat au milieu)* BOURSE at-the-money put, at-the-money put option; ~ **de vente de papillon long** BOURSE long butterfly put; ~ **de vente à parité** *(ANT option d'achat à parité)* BOURSE at-the-money put, at-the-money put option; ~ **de vente sans garantie** BOURSE naked put; ~ **de vente sur devises** *(ANT option d'achat sur devises)* BOURSE currency put option; ~ **de vente sur obligation** *(ANT option d'achat sur obligation)* BOURSE bond put option; ~ **de vente vendue** *(ANT option d'achat vendue)* BOURSE short put, written put

options[1] *m pl* INFO settings

options:[2] ~ **de longue durée** *f pl* BOURSE *de plus de neuf mois* long-term equity anticipation securities, LEAPS; ~ **sur contrat à terme sur devises** *f pl* BOURSE options on currency futures; ~ **sur contrats à terme** *f pl* BOURSE options on currency futures; ~ **sur indice** *f pl* BOURSE index options; ~ **de vente et d'achat** *f pl* BOURSE put and call

optique: ~ **de la direction générale** *f* GESTION top

management approach; ~ **des fibres** *f* INFO fiber optics *(AmE)*, fibre optics *(BrE)*

OPV *abrév (offre publique de vente)* BOURSE offer for sale, public offering

or *m* FIN gold; ~ **d'importation** IMP/EXP import gold; ~ **massif** ENVIR solid gold; ~ **monétaire** FIN gold bullion; ~ **noir** ENVIR black gold; ~ **-papier** BANQUE paper gold

ORA *abrév (obligations remboursables en actions)* BOURSE bonds redeemable in shares

orateur *m* COM speaker

orchestre *m* LOISIRS *théâtre* stalls

ordinaire *adj jarg* BOURSE ordinary, COM standard

ordinateur *m* INFO computer, system; ~ **analogique** INFO analog computer, digital computer; ~ **de bureau** COM business computer, INFO business computer, desktop computer, desktop unit; ~ **de calcul** INFO number cruncher; ~ **central** INFO mainframe; ~ **cible** INFO target computer; ~ **de cinquième génération** INFO fifth-generation computer; ~ **civil** INFO commercial computer; ~ **de compilation** INFO source computer; ~ **connecté** INFO active computer; ~ **dédié** INFO applications terminal; ~ **domestique** INFO home computer; ~ **frontal** INFO front-end computer; ~ **de gestion** COM business computer, INFO business computer, commercial computer; ~ **hybride** INFO hybrid computer; ~ **individuel** INFO personal computer; ~ **numérique** INFO digital computer; ~ **personnel** *(OP)* INFO personal computer *(PC)*; ~ **de poche** INFO pocket computer; ~ **portable** INFO laptop computer, portable computer; ~ **de première génération** INFO first-generation computer; ~ **principal** INFO host, number cruncher; ~ **professionnel** COM, INFO business computer; ~ **de quatrième génération** INFO fourth-generation computer; ~ **sans clavier** INFO pen-based computer; ~ **satellite** INFO peripheral computer, satellite computer, terminal computer; ~ **sériel** INFO serial computer; ~ **en service** INFO active computer; ~ **spécialisé** INFO applications terminal; ~ **de traitement par lots** INFO batch computer; ~ **de troisième génération** INFO third-generation computer

ordinatique *f* INFO computer science

ordinogramme *m* INFO block diagram, flow chart

ordinophobe[1] *adj* INFO computerphobic

ordinophobe[2] *mf* INFO computer phobic

ordonnance *f* ADMIN administration order, org., organization, COM arrangement, org., organization, DROIT court order, decree, ruling, *d'un tribunal* ord., order, order of the court, *d'une autorité locale* ordinance *(US)*, FIN authorization, order, POL enactment, PROT SOC prescription; ~ **de la cour** DROIT court order; ~ **émanant du pouvoir exécutif** DROIT ministerial order; ~ **instituant l'administration judiciaire** DROIT administration order; ~ **de libération** FISC order of discharge; ~ **libératoire** FISC order of discharge; ~ **de mise en liquidation** DROIT winding-up order;

~ **de mise sous séquestre** TRANSP receiving order, RO; ~ **de paiement** COM warrant for payment, FIN dividend warrant; ~ **de saisie-arrêt** DROIT writ of attachment; ~ **du tribunal** DROIT court order; ~ **de zonage** IMMOB zoning ordinance

ordonnancement *m* GESTION, IND *production* scheduling; ~ **de la production** COM, GESTION, IND production schedule

ordonner *vt* COM command, DROIT enact, prescribe, POL enact

ordre *m* COM command, DROIT court order, ord., order, order of the court, INFO command, sequence; ~ **d'achat** BOURSE buy order, buying order, order; ~ **d'achat obligatoire** DROIT, IMMOB compulsory purchase order (*UK*); ~ **d'achat préalable** BOURSE presale order; ~ **annuel** COM annual order; ~ **d'annulation** BOURSE cancel order; ~ **d'arrimage** TRANSP stowage order; ~ **en attente** BOURSE resting order; ~ **des avocats** DROIT ≈ the American Bar Association (*US*), ≈ the Bar (*UK*); ~ **bivalent** BOURSE alternative order; ~ **de cession de vente** BOURSE sell-stop order; ~ **de classement des caractères** INFO collating sequence; ~ **conditionnel** BOURSE conditional market order (*UK*); ~ **au cours exact** BOURSE MIT order, market-if-touched order; ~ **à cours limité** BOURSE limit, limit order, limited order; ~ **au cours du marché** BOURSE market order; ~ **de courtage** BOURSE broker's order; ~ **de courtier** COM broker's order (*UK*); ~ **décroissant** INFO decreasing order; ~ **d'écart** BOURSE spread order; ~ **d'exécution** RES HUM work order; ~ **d'expropriation** DROIT, IMMOB compulsory purchase order (*UK*); ~ **de fabrication** IND job order, RES HUM work order; ~ **good-till-cancelled** BOURSE open order; ~ **de grandeur** MATH order of magnitude; ~ **immédiat** BOURSE fill-or-kill, FOK, BOURSE *(ordre IOC)* hit order, immediate-or-cancel order *(IOC order)*; ~ **immédiat ou annuler** *(ordre IOC)* BOURSE hit order, immediate-or-cancel order *(IOC order)*; ~ **IOC** *(ordre immédiat ou annuler, ordre immédiat)* BOURSE IOC order *(immediate-or-cancel order)*; ~ **du jour** GESTION agenda; ~ **jour** BOURSE day order; ~ **du jour provisoire** COM tentative agenda; ~ **lexicographique** INFO collating sequence; ~ **lié** BOURSE contingent order, matched order, straddle; ~ **lié un contre un** BOURSE one-to-one straddle; ~ **lié un pour un** BOURSE one-way protection; ~ **limité** BOURSE limit order; ~ **limité inversé** BOURSE stop-loss order; ~ **limite ou mieux** BOURSE at or better; ~ **de liquidité croissante** COMPTA increasing liquidity order; ~ **de liquidité décroissante** COMPTA decreasing liquidity order; **l'~ de** COM O/o, order of; ~ **au mieux** BOURSE market order; ~ **au mieux à la clôture** BOURSE market order on the close, MOC; ~ **au mieux conditionnel** BOURSE conditional market order (*UK*); ~ **mixte** BOURSE spread order; ~ **ouvert** BOURSE open order; ~ **de paiement** COMPTA order to pay, payment order,

written order to pay; ~ **de paiement international** BANQUE international payment order, IPO; ~ **de paiement permanent** BANQUE s.o. (*UK*), standing order (*UK*); **par ~** *(p.o.)* COM by order; ~ **permanent** BANQUE s.o. (*UK*), standing order (*UK*); ~ **préalable à la vente** BOURSE presale order; ~ **au prix du marché en fin de séance** BOURSE market order on the close, MOC; ~ **de rang** MATH rank order; ~ **de reconduction** BOURSE roll-over order; ~ **de recouvrement de créances** FIN debt collection order, DCO; ~ **de réexpédition** COMMS, TRANSP forwarding instructions; ~ **de report de position** BOURSE roll-over order; ~ **de retrait de fonds négociable** BANQUE, BOURSE negotiable order of withdrawal, NOW; ~ **de retrait négociable** BANQUE, BOURSE negotiable order of withdrawal, NOW; ~ **à révocation** BOURSE GTC order, good-till-canceled order (*AmE*), good-till-cancelled order (*BrE*), open order; ~ **semaine** BOURSE week order; ~ **sous condition** BOURSE contingency order; ~ **stop** BOURSE stop loss, stop order, stop-limit order, stop-loss order; ~ **sur le marché** BOURSE, ECON orderly market; ~ **de suspendre les paiements** BANQUE stop-payment order; ~ **de transfert** BANQUE, FIN transfer order; ~ **de transfert monétaire** BANQUE, FIN money transfer order; ~ **de transfert permanent** BANQUE s.o. (*UK*), standing order (*UK*); ~ **valable jusqu'à annulation** BOURSE GTC order, good-till-canceled order (*AmE*), good-till-cancelled order (*BrE*); ~ **valable tout le mois** BOURSE month order; ~ **de vente** BOURSE order, resting order; ~ **de vente stop** BOURSE sell-stop order; ~ **de virement** BANQUE, FIN transfer order; ~ **de virement bancaire** FIN banker's order; ◆ **à l'~ de** BANQUE, DROIT to the order of; **en ~ croissant** COM in ascending order; **être à l'~ du jour** ADMIN be on the agenda; **par ~ de** COM per procuration, per procurationem *(frml)*; **par ~ alphabétique** COM in alphabetical order; **par ~ d'importance** COM in order of importance; **par ~ de priorité** COM in order of priority

ordres: ~ **couplés** *m pl* BOURSE *d'achat et de vente* matched securities; ~ **similaires** *m pl* BOURSE matched orders

ordures *f pl* ENVIR garbage (*AmE*), refuse (*BrE*), rubbish (*BrE*), waste; ~ **ménagères** ENVIR household waste, refuse (*BrE*)

organe: ~ **consultatif** *m* COM advisory body, consultative bodies, GESTION advisory body; ~ **de dépôt de titres** *m* BOURSE ≈ DTC (*US*), ≈ Depository Trust Company (*US*)

organigramme *m* COM flow chart, organization chart, GESTION organization chart, organizational chart, INFO block diagram, flow chart, process chart, MATH flow diagram; ~ **de données** GESTION, MATH data flow chart

organisateur, -trice *m,f* FIN arranger; ~ **de transport combiné** TRANSP combined transport operator; ~ **de voyages** LOISIRS, TRANSP package operator, package tour operator, tour operator, tour organizer

organisation *f* COM management, set-up; **~ d'aide aux exportations** IMP/EXP export facilitation organization; **~ autonome** BOURSE self-regulating organization (*UK*), SRO (*UK*); **~ à base de produits** COM product organization; **~ des bureaux** ADMIN, GESTION office management; **~ à caractère éducatif** FISC educational organization; **~ caritative** FISC, PROT SOC charitable organization, charity; **~ cellulaire** IND *production cell organization*; **~ de centrales des intermédiaires financiers** COM self-regulatory organization (*UK*), SRO (*UK*); **~ des déplacements** TRANSP journey planning; **~ de l'entreprise** COM business organization; **~ et méthodes** *(OM)* COM, GESTION, RES HUM organization and methods *(O&M)*; **~ fonctionnelle** COM, GESTION, RES HUM functional organization, staff organization; **~ hiérarchique** GESTION, RES HUM line organization; **~ horizontale** COM, GESTION, RES HUM functional organization, staff organization; **~ humanitaire** BANQUE, ECON, POL aid donor; **~ indépendante** COM self-regulatory organization (*UK*), SRO (*UK*); **~ industrielle** IND industrial organization, IO; **~ informelle** COM *gestion* informal organization; **~ internationale** COM international organization; **~ des inventaires** BOURSE, ECON inventory planning; **~ en matrices** GESTION, MATH matrix management; **~ de médecine préventive et curative** ASSUR health maintenance organization (*US*), HMO (*US*); **~ mixte** GESTION, RES HUM line and staff organization; **~ non-gouvernementale** *(ONG)* COM nongovernmental organization *(NGO)*; **~ non-officielle** COM *association* informal organization; **~ des objectifs** GESTION goal programming; **~ opérationnelle** GESTION line organization; **~ par région** GESTION regional organization; **~ par secteurs d'activité** COM functional organization; **~ de la production** COM, GESTION, IND production engineering, production management; **~ professionnelle** COM, RES HUM trade organization; **~ professionnelle non-répertoriée** RES HUM nonofficial trade organization, NOTO; **~ professionnelle sans existence officielle** RES HUM nonofficial trade organization, NOTO; **~ réglementaire relative à une succession** DROIT, FIN, IMMOB *testaments* estate planning; **~ sans but lucratif** FISC nonprofit organization; **~ scientifique** GESTION, MATH scientific management; **~ scientifique du travail** COM organization and methods, O&M, GESTION organization and methods, O&M, scientific management, MATH scientific management, RES HUM O&M, organization and methods; **~ serrée** COM, GESTION tight ship (*infrml*); **~ sur le terrain** IMP/EXP *d'une société* field organization; **~ de surveillance des gestionnaires d'investissement** BOURSE Investment Managers' Regulatory Organization (*UK*), IMRO (*UK*); **~ du temps** GESTION, RES HUM time management; **~ du trafic** TRANSP *maritime* routing; **~ du travail** COM work organization; **~ tripartite** COM three-ply organization (*jarg*); **~ uniforme** GESTION flat organization; **~ des ventes** GESTION, V&M sales management; **~ verticale** GESTION line organization, vertical organization

Organisation: **~ pour l'alimentation et l'agriculture** *f* ECON Food and Agriculture Organization, FAO; **~ de l'aviation civile internationale** *f (OACI)* TRANSP International Civil Aviation Organization *(ICAO)*; **~ commune africaine, malgache et mauricienne** *f (OCAMM)* COM Associated African States, Madagascar and Mauritius *(AASMM)*; **~ pour la coopération commerciale** *f* ECON *commerce international* Organization for Trade Co-operation, OTC; **~ de coopération et de développement économique** *f (OCDE)* ECON Organization for Economic Cooperation and Development *(OECD)*; **~ de défense des consommateurs** *f* COM ≈ CA, ≈ Consumers' Association; **~ des états américains** *f* COM, PROT SOC Organization of American States, OAS; **~ des états de l'Amérique Centrale** *f* ECON Organization of Central American States, OCAS; **~ européenne de brevets** *f* DROIT European Patent Organization, EPO; **~ européenne pour le contrôle de qualité** *f* ADMIN European Organization for Quality Control, EOQC; **~ européenne de coopération économique** *f (OECE)* ECON Organization for European Economic Cooperation *(OEEC)*; **~ européenne de transport** *f* TRANSP European Transport Organization, ETO; **~ internationale de métrologie légale** *f (OIML)* DROIT International Organization for Legal Metrology; **~ internationale de normalisation** *f* COM International Standards Organization, ISO; **~ internationale de satellites maritimes** *f* COMMS International Maritime Satellite Organization, INMARSAT; **~ internationale du sucre** *f* IND International Sugar Organization, ISO; **~ internationale du travail** *f (OIT)* RES HUM International Labour Organization (*BrE*) *(ILO)*; **~ météorologique mondiale** *f* TRANSP World Meteorological Organization, WMO; **~ mondiale du commerce** ECON, POL *commerce international* Multilateral Trade Organization; **~ mondiale pour la propriété intellectuelle** *f* DROIT World Intellectual Property Organization, WIPO; **~ mondiale de la santé** *f (OMS)* ADMIN, PROT SOC World Health Organization *(WHO)*; **~ nationale des femmes** *f* FIN National Organization for Women (*US*), NOW (*US*); **~ des Nations Unies** *f (ONU)* ECON, POL United Nations *(UN)*, United Nations Organization *(UNO)*; **~ des pays exportateurs de pétrole** *f (OPEP)* ECON, ENVIR, POL Organization of Petroleum Exporting Countries *(OPEC)*; **~ de surveillance pour les valeurs internationales** *f* BOURSE International Securities Regulatory Organization, ISRO; **~ du**

Traité de l'Atlantique Nord *f (OTAN)* POL North Atlantic Treaty Organization *(NATO)*; ~ **de l'unité africaine** *f (OUA)* ECON Organization of African Unity *(OAU)*

organiser *vt* BANQUE *prêt* arrange, COM organize, *referendum* hold, GESTION *conférence* stage; ~ **une grève** RES HUM stage a strike; ~ **une grève perlée** RES HUM stage a go-slow; ~ **par paliers** RES HUM staging; ~ **un stage de formation** RES HUM hold an in-service training *(jarg)*; ~ **le trafic** TRANSP route

organisme *m* ADMIN org., organization, COM org., organization, *de l'état* agency, body, FIN agency, LOISIRS org., organization; ~ **assurant un service public** DROIT statutory body; ~ **auto-réglementé** BOURSE self-regulating organization *(UK)*, SRO *(UK)*; ~ **autorégulateur** COM self-regulatory organization *(UK)*, SRO *(UK)*; ~ **bancaire de crédit aux agriculteurs** BANQUE, ECON agricultural bank; ~ **de charité** FISC, PROT SOC charity; ~ **de charité enregistré** FISC registered charity; ~ **consultatif** COM advisory body, consultative bodies, GESTION advisory body; ~ **de défense des consommateurs** V&M consumer organization; ~ **de défense des intérêts** COM, POL watchdog; ~ **émetteur de cartes de crédit** BANQUE, COM credit card issuer; ~ **fédéral d'assurance et des dépôts bancaires** ASSUR Federal Deposit Insurance Corporation *(US)*, FDIC *(US)*; ~ **de garantie des prêts étudiants** BOURSE Student Loan Marketing Association *(US)*, SLMA *(US)*; ~ **intergouvernemental** ADMIN intergovernmental organization; ~ **municipal** FISC municipal body; ~ **officiel** DROIT statutory body; ~ **de placement collectif** FIN collective investment undertaking; ~ **de placements collectifs en valeurs mobilières** *(OPCVM)* FIN undertakings for collective investment in transferablcs *(UCITS)*; ~ **privé de formation** PROT SOC teaching company; ~ **professionnel** FIN recognized professional body *(UK)*, RPB *(UK)*; ~ **public** ADMIN government agency, public body, COM public body, FISC public authority; ~ **de réglementation** COM regulatory authority, regulatory body, DROIT regulator, regulatory authority, regulatory body; ~ **régulateur des assurances-vie et des SICAV** FIN Lautro *(UK)*, Life Assurance and Unit Trust Regulatory Organization *(UK)*; ~ **religieux** FISC religious organization; ~ **de révision des salaires élevés** GESTION, RES HUM top salaries review body *(UK)*; ~ **du secteur public** ECON, FISC public sector body; ~ **de services communs** ADMIN common service agency; ~ **de services publics** COM public service body; ~ **spécialisé accrédité** FIN recognized professional body *(UK)*, RPB *(UK)*; ~ **de tutelle** COM, DROIT regulatory authority, regulatory body; ~ **volontaire** PROT SOC voluntary body

Organisme: ~ **de compensation des options pour tous les marchés** *m* BOURSE Option Clearing Corporation *(US)*; ~ **du développement outre-**

mer *m* ECON, POL ≈ ODA *(UK)*, ≈ Overseas Development Administration *(UK)*; ~ **européen de contrôle et certification** *m* COM European Organization for Testing and Certification, EOTC; ~ **européen pour la promotion du commerce** *m* COM European Trade Promotion Organization, ETPO; ~ **de recherche spatiale européenne** *m* COM European Space Research Organization, ESRO; ~ **régulateur des titres internationaux** *m* BOURSE International Securities Regulatory Organization, ISRO

oriental, e *adj* COM eastern

orientation *f* COM guidance, ECON direction, POL orientation; ~ **à la baisse** *(ANT orientation à la hausse)* ECON downtrend; ~ **à la hausse** *(ANT orientation à la baisse)* ECON uptrend; ~ **du marché** COM, ECON, V&M market trend; ~ **professionnelle** RES HUM career guidance, vocational guidance; ~ **vers le client** V&M customer orientation; ~ **vers le consommateur** V&M consumer orientation

orienté: ~ **à la baisse** *loc* BOURSE bearish; **être** ~ **vers** *loc* GESTION be geared towards; ~ **grand public** *loc* INFO consumer-orientated; ~ **par le marché** *loc* ECON, V&M market-orientated; ~ **vers la clientèle** *loc* COM customer-orientated; ~ **vers l'exportation** *loc* IMP/EXP export-orientated; ~ **vers la recherche** *loc* IND research-orientated

orienter *vt* COM funnel

original[1]**, e** *adj* COM, INFO original; ~ **de reproduction** MÉDIA camera-ready

original[2] *m* ADMIN, COM, INFO master copy, original, original document; ♦ **un** ~ **et trois copies** COM one top and three copies

origine *f* COM onset; **d'**~ **hydrique** ENVIR water-generated

orphelin *m* MÉDIA *typographie* orphan

O.S. *abrév (ouvrier spécialisé)* RES HUM skilled worker

OSCAR *abrév (obligation spéciale à coupons à réinvestir)* BOURSE bunny bond *(jarg)*

oscillation *f* COM swing

oscillations: ~ **des cours** *f pl* COM swings; ~ **du marché** *f pl* BOURSE ups and downs

osciller *vi* COM swing; ~ **autour de** COM hover around

OSDIBSAR *abrév (obligations subordonnées à durée indéterminée à bons de souscription en actions rachetables)* BOURSE subordinated perpetual bonds with redeemable share warrants

oseille *m infrml* FIN bread *(infrml)*

Oslo *n pr* COM Oslo

OST *abrév (organisation scientifique du travail)* GESTION, MATH scientific management

OTAN *abrév (Organisation du Traité de l'Atlantique Nord)* POL NATO *(North Atlantic Treaty Organization)*

ôter: ~ **7 de 49** *loc* COM take 7 away from 49

Ottawa *n pr* COM Ottawa

OTV *abrév (obligation à taux variable)* BOURSE FRN *(floating-rate note)*

OUA *abrév (Organisation de l'unité africaine)* ECON OAU *(Organization of African Unity)*

Ouagadougou *n pr* COM Ouagadougou

ouest[1] *adj* TRANSP *route, ligne de métro* westbound

ouest[2] *m* COM west

Ouganda *m* COM Uganda

ougandais, e *adj* COM Ugandan

Ougandais, e *m,f* COM *habitant* Ugandan

ouguiya *m* COM Ouguiya

ouï: ~ **-dire** *m* COM hearsay

Oulan Bator *n pr* COM Ulan Bator

ourdi *m* COM *langue* Urdi

ours *m* MÉDIA *imprimé* masthead

outil *m* COM, INFO tool; ~ **de production** IND production implement

outillage: ~ **industriel** *m* COMPTA industrial equipment

outiller *vt* IND tool up

outilleur *m* COM, IND toolmaker

outils: ~ **du métier** *m pl* COM tools of the trade; ~ **de programmation** *m pl* COM, INFO programming aid

outplacement *m* COM, RES HUM outplacement

output *m* ECON output

outrage: ~ **à la cour** *m* DROIT contempt of court; ~ **à magistrat** *m* DROIT contempt of court

outre: en ~ *adv* COMMS further

outrepasser *vt* COM override

ouvert, e *adj* BOURSE open, COM open-ended, INFO open-ended, *fichier* open; ~ **sur l'extérieur** COM outward-looking; ♦ ~ **à l'achat** V&M open-to-buy

ouverture[1] *f* COM window of opportunity, INFO slot; ~ **automatique de session** INFO autologin, autologon; ~ **du concours** COM bid opening; ~ **des frontières** COM *commerciales* abolition of trade controls; ~ **en nocturne** COM late-night opening; ~ **préventive** BOURSE pre-emptive bid; ~ **de séance** COM opening; ~ **de tonnage** TRANSP *d'un navire* tonnage opening; ♦ **à l'**~ BOURSE at the opening

ouverture:[2] ~ **à** *loc* COM *exposition* doors open at; ~ **des magasins le dimanche** *loc* COM Sunday trading

ouvrage: ~ **approuvé** *m* FISC approved project; ~ **à ciel ouvert** *m* IND opencast mining *(BrE)*, strip mining *(AmE)*, *production* opencast method; ~ **d'intérêt général** *m* MÉDIA trade book

ouvrant:[1] ~ **droit à pension** *adj* FIN, RES HUM pensionable

ouvrant:[2] **s'**~ **à l'extrémité** *loc* ADMIN *enveloppe* open-end

Ouvrez: ~ **-moi** *m* INFO ReadMe document

ouvrier, -ière *m,f* IND, RES HUM manual worker, worker; ~ **agricole** ECON farmhand, RES HUM farm laborer *(AmE)*, farm labourer *(BrE)*; ~ **du bâtiment** IND construction worker; ~ **de l'équipe de jour** RES HUM dayworker; ~ **de l'industrie automobile** IND, TRANSP car worker; ~ **membre du conseil d'administration** GESTION, RES HUM worker director; ~ **métallurgiste** RES HUM metalworker; ~ **non-syndiqué** RES HUM nonunion worker; ~ **à part entière** RES HUM journeyman; ~ **payé à l'heure** RES HUM hourly worker; ~ **de la production** IND, RES HUM production worker; ~ **professionnel** RES HUM skilled worker; ~ **qualifié** RES HUM skilled worker; ~ **sans travail fixe** RES HUM casual labourer *(BrE)*, casual laborer *(AmE)*; ~ **sidérurgiste** IND steelworker; ~ **spécialisé** *(O.S.)* RES HUM skilled worker; ~ **d'usine** RES HUM factory hand

ouvriers *m pl* IND shop floor, RES HUM members rank and file, shop floor; **les** ~ **indépendants** FISC, RES HUM the Lump *(UK)*; ~ **non-qualifiés** RES HUM unskilled labor *(AmE)*, unskilled labour *(BrE)*; ~ **non-spécialisés** RES HUM unskilled labor *(AmE)*, unskilled labour *(BrE)*; ~ **spécialisés** ECON semiskilled labor *(AmE)*, semiskilled labour *(BrE)*, RES HUM skilled labor *(AmE)*, skilled labour *(BrE)*

ouvrir[1] *vt* BANQUE open, COM open up, INFO open; ~ **un dossier** ADMIN open a file; ~ **une session** INFO log in, log on; ♦ ~ **à la baisse** BOURSE open a short position; ~ **un compte** BANQUE open an account; ~ **un compte bancaire avec** BANQUE open a bank account with; ~ **le courrier** COMMS deal with the mail, open the mail; ~ **des crédits provisoires** COMPTA grant interim supply; ~ **une écriture** COMPTA start an entry; ~ **à la hausse** BOURSE open a long position; ~ **le marché à la concurrence** COM open the market up to competition; ~ **la porte** COM open the door; ~ **la porte à** COM open the door to; ~ **une position** *(ANT déboucler une position, liquider une position)* BOURSE open a position; ~ **une position courte** BOURSE open a short position; ~ **une position longue** BOURSE open a long position; ~ **une souscription pour** COM invite subscriptions for; ~ **les transactions** BOURSE open trading; ~ **la voie** COM break new ground

ouvrir:[2] ~ **ici** *loc* COMMS open here

ouzbek[1], **-èke** *adj* COM Uzbek

ouzbek[2] *m* COM *langue* Uzbek

Ouzbek, -èke *m,f* COM *habitant* Uzbek

Ouzbékistan *m* COM Uzbekistan

oxyde: ~ **de carbone** *m* ENVIR carbon monoxide

P

p. *abrév* COM *(page)* pg. *(page)*, COM *(poids)* wt *(weight)*, INFO *(page)* pg. *(page)*, MATH *(pour cent)* pc *(per cent)*; ~ **cent** *(pour cent)* MATH pc *(per cent)*

p.a. *abrév (par an)* COM p.a. *(per annum)*

pa'anga *m* COM pa'anga

PAC *abrév (la politique agricole commune)* ECON, POL CAP *(the Common Agricultural Policy)*

pack: ~ **de trois** *m* COM, V&M tripack

pacte *m* DROIT accord, POL accord, alliance; ~ **d'aide mutuelle** ECON, POL *commerce international* mutual aid pact

Pacte: ~ **andin** *m* ECON Andean Pact

P.A.F. *abrév (Police de l'Air et des Frontières)* RES HUM border police

page *f (p.)* COM page *(pg.)* INFO frame, page *(pg.)*; ~ **de garde** MÉDIA flyleaf; ~ **à l'italienne** *(SYN placard)* MÉDIA landscape page; ~ **mal imposée** MÉDIA *impression* badly imposed page; ~ **de publicité** MÉDIA *radio* station break, *télévision, radio* commercial break; ~ **de titre** MÉDIA face page; ◆ **être à la** ~ COM keep up to date

pages *f pl (p.p.)* COM pages *(p.p.)*; ~ **économiques** *f pl* MÉDIA economic section; ~ **jaunes** *f pl* BOURSE *de la Bourse de Londres* yellow sheets

Pages: ~ **Jaunes**® *f pl* COM *annuaire*, COMMS Yellow Pages® *(UK)*

pagination *f* ADMIN, INFO pagination

paginer *vt* ADMIN, INFO *document* paginate

paie: ~ **de départ** *f* RES HUM payoff; ~ **hebdomadaire** *f* COM weekly pay packet, RES HUM weekly pay packet, weekly wage, weekly wage packet; ~ **tenant lieu de préavis** *f* RES HUM pay in lieu of notice

paiement *m* COM, FIN *d'une dette* discharge; ~ **anticipé** COMPTA advance payment, payment in advance; ~ **en arriérés** COMPTA payment in arrears; ~ **d'assistance sociale** FISC social assistance payment *(Can)*, PROT SOC social assistance payment *(Can)*, social security payment *(BrE)*; ~ **automatique** FIN automatic withdrawal; ~ **en avance** COMPTA payment in advance; ~ **d'avance en espèces** COMPTA cash in advance; ~ **avant la livraison** COM, V&M cash before delivery, CBD; ~ **budgétaire** ECON, POL budget payment; ~ **à la commande** COM, FIN, V&M cash with order, CWO; ~ **de complaisance** BANQUE, COM, FIN, V&M accommodation payment; ~ **comptant** BANQUE cash payment, BOURSE paydown, COMPTA cash drawdown, cash payment; ~ **pour le compte d'autrui** COMPTA payment on behalf of others; ~ **contractuel** COMPTA contract payment, contractual payment; ~ **contre son gré** COM, DROIT payment under protest; ~ **à date due** BOURSE payment in due course; ~ **déterminé** COM specific payment; ~ **différé** COM deferred payment; ~ **différentiel** ECON deficiency payment; ~ **direct** ECON direct payment; ~ **à dix jours de vue** RES HUM ten days after sight pay; ~ **électronique** FIN electronic payment; ~ **en espèces** BANQUE cash payment; ~ **en fonction des résultats** RES HUM payment by results, PBR *(UK)*; ~ **au fur et à mesure** V&M pay-as-you-go; ~ **incitatif** FISC inducement payment; ~ **d'intérêts supplémentaires** FIN bonus interest payment; ~ **international** ECON international payment; ~ **à la livraison** IMP/EXP, V&M cash on delivery, COD; ~ **locatif** IMMOB rental payment; ~ **multilatéral** ECON multilateral disbursement; ~ **en nature** COM payment in kind, RES HUM noncash rewards; ~ **par anticipation** COMPTA advance payment; ~ **par avis de prélèvement** BANQUE preauthorized payment; ~ **par carte** BANQUE credit card payment; ~ **par chèque** BANQUE check payment *(AmE)*, cheque payment *(BrE)*; ~ **par étape** FIN stage payment; ~ **par versements échelonnés** COMPTA deferred payment; ~ **par virement bancaire** BANQUE Bank Giro *(UK)*; ~ **partiel** COMPTA partial consideration, FIN part payment; ~ **de péréquation** FISC equalization payment; ~ **de perte d'habitat** IMMOB home loss payment; ~ **de prélèvement** BANQUE preauthorized payment; ~ **rapide** FIN prompt payment; ~ **reçu** BANQUE, COMPTA, FIN inward payment; ~ **de redevances par anticipation** FISC advance royalty payment; ~ **réel** COMPTA actual cash disbursement; ~ **de rente** FISC annuity payment; ~ **reporté** COM deferred payment; ~ **sans contrepartie** FIN nugatory payment; ~ **sous réserve** FIN payment under reserve; ~ **sur décision de justice** RES HUM overaward payment *(Australia)*; ~ **symbolique** COM *en reconnaissance d'une dette*, FIN token payment; ~ **tardif** FIN late payment; ~ **en temps voulu** BOURSE payment in due course; ~ **en timbres-poste** COM postage stamp remittance; ~ **à titre d'exemple** FIN ex gratia payment *(frml)*; ~ **à titre de faveur** ASSUR, RES HUM ex gratia payment *(frml)*; ~ **de transfert** BANQUE, FIN transfer payment; ~ **en trop** COMPTA, FIN overpayment; ~ **unique** FIN single payment; ◆ ~ **contre livraison** BOURSE delivery versus payment; **en** ~ **de** COMPTA in satisfaction of; ~ **fait à** COM payment made to; ~ **à la livraison** TRANSP paid on delivery, POD

paiements: ~ **d'achat à crédit** *m pl* BANQUE, FIN installment payments *(AmE)*, instalment payments *(BrE)*; ~ **en cours** *m pl* FIN progress payments; ~ **de loyer minimum** *m pl* IMMOB *loyer du capital* minimum lease payments; ~ **réguliers** *m pl* COM regular payments; ~ **de terminaison** *m* *pl* FISC, PROT SOC *à la retraite*, RES HUM termination payments; **~ de TVA** *m pl* FISC VAT payments (*UK*)

pair[1]**, e** *adj* INFO, MATH even; ◆ **au ~** BANQUE, COM at par

pair[2] *m* BOURSE par, parity, COM par; **~ du change** ECON, FIN mint par of exchange; **~ intrinsèque** ECON, FIN mint par of exchange; **~ métallique** ECON, FIN mint par, mint par of exchange; ◆ **de ~ avec** COM, DROIT *aller* pari passu (*frml*)

Pakistan *m* COM Pakistan

pakistanais, e *adj* COM Pakistani

Pakistanais, e *m,f* COM *habitant* Pakistani

PAL *m* MÉDIA phase alternation line, PAL

palais: ~ des expositions *m* COM exhibition center (*AmE*), exhibition centre (*BrE*); **~ de justice** *m* DROIT court of law

Palais: ~ Grognard *m* BOURSE ≈ London FOX, ≈ London Futures and Options Exchange; **le ~** *m* BOURSE the Paris Stock Exchange, ≈ the House (*infrml*), ≈ the Stock Exchange, ≈ the Stock Market; **le ~ Brongniart** *m* BOURSE ≈ London Stock Exchange, ≈ the LSE, ≈ the Stock Exchange, ≈ the Stock Market

palan *m* TRANSP *appareil de levage* purchase, *manutention* hoist, *matériel de levage* tackle; ◆ **sous ~** (ANT *sur palan*) TRANSP *navigation* below bridges, BB, under ship's derrick; **sur ~** (ANT *sous palan*) TRANSP above bridges, AB

pale *f* TRANSP *d'un navire* paddle

palette *f* TRANSP pallet; **~ à ailes** TRANSP winged pallet; **~ de bois** TRANSP wooden pallet; **~ -caisse** TRANSP box pallet; **~ à démontage automatique** TRANSP self-demounting pallet; **~ à double plancher** TRANSP double-decked pallet; **~ à montants** TRANSP post pallet; **~ non-réutilisable** TRANSP expendable pallet; **~ perdue** TRANSP expendable pallet; **~ principale** TRANSP master pallet; **~ à quatre entrées** TRANSP four-way entry pallet, four-way pallet; **~ réversible** TRANSP reversible pallet; **~ à ridelles** TRANSP post pallet; **~ à véhicules** TRANSP *navigation* car pallet

palettisable *adj* TRANSP palletizable

palettisation *f* TRANSP palletization

palettiser *vt* TRANSP *marchandises* palletize

palier: ~ en milieu de carrière *m* RES HUM midcareer plateau; **~ de mise à niveau** *m* TRANSP *fixation des conteneurs* leveling pedestal (*AmE*), levelling pedestal (*BrE*), pedestal; **~ de résistance** *m* BOURSE resistance level; **~ de revenu** *m* FISC income range, range; **~ supérieur de revenu** *m* FISC upper income

palonnier *m* TRANSP spreader; **~ rectangulaire** TRANSP spreader

panachage: ~ à court terme *m* BOURSE current blend

Panama[1] *m* COM Panama

Panama:[2] **~ City** *n pr* COM Panama City

panamax *m* TRANSP *navigation* Panamax vessel

panaméen, -enne *adj* COM Panamanian

Panaméen, -enne *m,f* COM *habitant* Panamanian

panaméricain *adj* COM Pan-American

Pan-American: ~ système de tracement et des réservations *m* TRANSP Pan-American Tracing and Reservations System, PANTRAC

pancarte *f* COM show card

panel: ~ de consommateurs *m* V&M consumer panel

paneuropéen, -enne *adj* COM Pan-European

panier *m* COM basket, LOISIRS package deal; **~ de denrées** ECON basket of goods; **~ de devises** ECON, FIN basket of currencies, currency basket; **~ de la ménagère** COM, ECON shopping basket; **~ de monnaies** ECON, FIN basket of currencies; **~ de produits** ECON basket of products; **~ de rebut** COM reject bin; **~ de taux** IND basket of rates

panique: ~ bancaire *f* BANQUE, BOURSE run on the banks; **~ financière** *f* ECON, FIN financial panic

paniquer *vi* COM get into a tailspin, panic

panne *f* INFO breakdown, crash, failure, trouble; **~ d'appareil** COM *bureau* equipment failure; **~ de courant** INFO blackout, power fail, power failure; **~ d'électricité** INFO blackout, power fail, power failure; **~ machine** INFO hardware failure; **~ de machine** COM *usine* equipment failure; **~ d'oreiller** *infrml* RES HUM malingering; **~ de secteur** INFO blackout, power fail, power failure; **~ système** INFO system failure; ◆ **en ~** COM out of action, INFO down; **être en ~** COM be out of action, be out of order

panneau *m* INFO *de commande* panel, TRANSP *d'un navire* ha, hatch, hatchway; **~ d'affichage** COM, COMMS, INFO, RES HUM *électronique* bulletin board (*AmE*), notice board (*BrE*), BB, V&M display, stand (*jarg*); **~ d'affichage portatif** V&M poster site; **~ en aggloméré** COM chipboard; **~ à arrimage automatique** TRANSP *navigation* self-trimming hatch; **~ auto-arrimeur** TRANSP *navigation* self-trimming hatch; **~ avertisseur** COM warning sign; **~ de commande** INFO control panel; **~ de copeaux** COM chipboard; **~ d'écoutille** TRANSP *navigation* hatch covering; **~ géant animé** V&M spectacular (*jarg*); **~ de particules** COM chipboard; **~ de signalisation** TRANSP traffic sign; **~ utilisable** TRANSP *chartepartie* workable hatch, WH; ◆ **par ~ et par jour** TRANSP *maritime* per hatch per day; **par ~ utilisable et par jour** TRANSP *maritime* per workable hatch per day, per working hatch per day

panneaux: ~ en aluminium *m pl* TRANSP *navigation* aluminium covers (*BrE*), aluminum covers (*AmE*); **~ de cale en acier** *m pl* TRANSP *navigation* steel covers, SC; **~ de cale en bois** *m pl* TRANSP wood covers; **~ de cale en fibre de verre** *m pl* TRANSP *navigation* fiberglass covers (*AmE*), fibreglass covers (*BrE*), FC

panoplie: ~ d'options *f* COM range of options

panorama *m* MÉDIA *radio, télévision* take-out (*US, jarg*)

PAO *abrév (publication assistée par ordinateur)* INFO DTP *(desktop publishing)*

paperasserie *f infrml* ADMIN paperwork

papeterie *f* ADMIN, COM stationery, ENVIR, IND paper industry, *usine* paper mill

papetier, -ère *m,f* COM stationer

papier *m* ADMIN paper, FIN paper (*infrml*), INFO form; ~ **d'affaires** COM business paper, trade paper; ~ **d'ambiance** MÉDIA background story; ~ **anticipant une obligation** BOURSE bond anticipation note, BAN; ~ **avalisé par la banque** BANQUE bank paper; ~ **bancable** BANQUE bankable paper; ~ **baryté** ADMIN baryta paper; ~ **bitumé** IND waterproof paper; ~ **brillant** COM, COMMS, MÉDIA glossy paper; ~ **buvard** ADMIN blotting paper; ~ **carbone** COMMS carbon paper; ~ **commercial** COM, FIN commercial paper, CP; ~ **commercial en livres sterling** BOURSE sterling commercial paper, SCP; ~ **commercial de premier ordre** BOURSE, FIN prime paper, P-1; ~ **en continu** ADMIN, INFO continuous stationery; ~ **couché mat** V&M art matt paper; ~ **d'emballage** COM wrapper; ~ **à en-tête** COMMS printed writing paper; ~ **eurocommercial** BOURSE Eurocommercial paper, ECP; ~ **feuille à feuille** INFO cut paper; ~ **de financement** FIN finance paper, financial paper; ~ **financier** FIN finance paper, financial paper; ~ **glacé** COM, COMMS, MÉDIA glossy paper; ~ **informatique** INFO computer paper; ~ **monétaire** BOURSE, ECON, FIN money-market paper; ~ **ordre** BANQUE order paper; ~ **par avion** COMMS airmail paper; ~ **à polycopier** COM manifold; ~ **recyclé** COM, ENVIR recycled paper; ~ **réglé** COM ruled paper; ~ **rose** POL Pink Paper (*UK*); ~ **support** MÉDIA base sheet; ~ **à terme offert en permanence** BOURSE Continuously Offered Longer-Term Securities

papillon *m* ASSUR attachment; ~ **long** BOURSE long butterfly

Papouasie-Nouvelle-Guinée *f* COM Papua New Guinea

paquebot *m* TRANSP boat, ocean liner, passenger ship, *navigation* freighter; ~ **de ligne** TRANSP ocean liner

paquet *m* BOURSE *d'actions* parcel, COM pack, packet, pkt., COMMS package, parcel, pkg, COMPTA batch, FIN *d'actions* block, INFO packet, MÉDIA *journaux, lettres* batch, TRANSP bdl, bundle; ~ **économique** COM, V&M economy pack; ~ **familial** V&M family-size pack, family-size package; ~ **de mer** TRANSP *maritime* green sea; ~ **promotionnel** V&M *publipostage* package, pkg; ~ **de trois** COM, V&M tripack

paquetage *m* TRANSP *arrimage des marchandises* baling

par *prép* COM per, COMMS, TRANSP *voiture, train* via

paradigme: ~ **économique** *m* ECON economic paradigm

paradis: ~ **fiscal** *m* ECON, FISC tax haven

paradoxe: ~ **de l'épargne** *m* ECON paradox of thrift; ~ **de Giffen** *m* ECON Giffen paradox; ~ **de Saint-Pétersbourg** *m* ECON St Petersburg paradox; ~ **de la valeur** *m* ECON paradox of value, water and diamonds paradox; ~ **du vote** *m* ECON paradox of voting

paraffine: ~ **dure** *f* IND paraffin wax

paragraphe *m* ADMIN, DROIT paragraph; ~ **passe-partout** COM boilerplate; ~ **de tête** MÉDIA *presse* lead (*BrE*), lede (*AmE*); ◆ **décrit au ~ 1** COM referred to in paragraph 1

Paraguay *m* COM Paraguay

paraguayen, -enne *adj* COM Paraguayan

Paraguayen, -enne *m,f* COM *habitant* Paraguayan

paraît: **qui ~ tous les mois** *loc* MÉDIA published monthly

paraître *vi* MÉDIA come out; ◆ **faire ~** MÉDIA *édition* issue; **faire ~ une annonce pour** COM, MÉDIA, V&M advertise for

paralégal, e *adj* DROIT paralegal

parallèle *adj* COM parallel, MATH collateral; ◆ **en ~** COM in parallel; **en ~ avec** COM in parallel with

parallèlement: ~ **à** *loc* COM in parallel with

paralysé: ~ **par une grève** *loc* RES HUM strikebound

Paramaribo *n pr* COM Paramaribo

paramètre *m* COM, INFO, MATH parameter; ~ **d'évaluation d'option** BOURSE option-pricing parameter; ~ **temps** COM time component

paramètres *m pl* INFO settings

paramétrique *adj* INFO, MATH parametric

parasite *m* ECON *économétrie* noise, white noise, INFO noise

parasites *f pl* INFO interference

paravent *m* COM screen

parc *m* COM *de biens d'équipement* stock; ~ **d'affaires** ECON, IMMOB, IND, RES HUM enterprise zone; ~ **d'attractions** LOISIRS amusement park, *autour d'un thème* theme park; ~ **automobile** TRANSP fleet of cars; ~ **à bestiaux** COM stockyard; ~ **de conteneurs** TRANSP container park, container pool; ~ **de dissuasion** TRANSP park and ride; ~ **européen de palettes** TRANSP European pallet pool; ~ **d'expositions** COM exhibition center (*AmE*), exhibition centre (*BrE*); ~ **immobilier** IMMOB housing stock; ~ **relais** (*P.R.*) TRANSP park and ride (*P&R*); ~ **à réservoirs de stockage** TRANSP tank farm; ~ **scientifique** IND science park; ~ **de stationnement** COM car park (*BrE*), parking lot (*AmE*); ~ **technologique** IND technology park; ~ **à thème** LOISIRS theme park; ~ **de véhicules** TRANSP pool of vehicles; ~ **de voitures** TRANSP car pool

parcage: ~ **automatique** *m* INFO *des têtes de lecture, écriture* autopark

parcelle *f* IMMOB *de terre* parcel

parcelliser *vt* COM chunk down (*jarg*), IMMOB *terrain* parcel out

parcourir *vt* INFO browse

parcours: ~ **professionnel** *m* ADMIN, COM, PROT SOC, RES HUM track record; ~ **rapide** *m* COM fast track

pardonner: ~ qch à qn *vt* COM forgive sb sth

pare: ~ -chocs *m* TRANSP buffer (*AmE*), bumper (*BrE*)

pareil: du ~ au même *loc* COM a similibus ad similia (*frml*)

parent *m* DROIT parent; ~ **unique** FISC single parent

parental, e *adj* COM parental

parenthèse *f* ADMIN parenthesis

parenthèses *f pl* INFO, MÉDIA round brackets

parents: ~ **proches** *m pl* BOURSE immediate family

parfaire *vt* COM consummate

parfait, e *adj* TRANSP A-1 (*jarg*); ◆ **en ~ accord** COM *en négociations, réunions* ad idem (*frml*)

pari *m* COM gamble

parier *vt* COM bet, *courses de chevaux* gamble, have a flutter (*UK, infrml*)

parieur, -euse *m,f* COM punter

paris *m pl* FISC, LOISIRS betting

Paris *n pr* COM Paris

parité *f* BOURSE p.v., par value, ECON, FIN parity, INFO even parity, parity, MATH, PROT SOC, RES HUM parity; ~ **de change** BANQUE parity of exchange; ~ **de conversion** BOURSE conversion parity (*UK*); ~ **à crémaillère** ECON crawling peg; ~ **croisée** ECON, FIN cross rate, exchange cross rate; ~ **glissante** BOURSE sliding parity; ~ **indexée optimale** ECON, FIN optimal peg; ~ **en légère baisse** BOURSE sliding parity; ~ **du pouvoir d'achat** (*PPA*) ECON purchasing power parity (*PPP*); ~ **des taux** TRANSP parity on rates; ◆ **à ~** BOURSE at-the-money

parjure *m* DROIT perjury

parking *m* BOURSE parking, COM car park (*BrE*), parking lot (*AmE*); ~ **courte durée** TRANSP short-term vehicle park, STVP

parle: la chose ~ d'elle-même *loc* COM, DROIT res ipsa loquitur (*frml*); qui ~ de soi-même *loc* COM ex hypothesi (*frml*)

parlement *m* COM, POL parliament; ~ **fédéral** POL Federal Parliament

Parlement: ~ **européen** *m* ECON European Parliament, EP

parlementaire *adj* POL parliamentary

parler *vi* COM talk; ◆ ~ **affaires** COM talk business; ~ **métier** COM talk shop (*infrml*)

paroi: ~ **de cale** *f* TRANSP *navigation* wing

parquet *m* BOURSE *de la Bourse* dealing floor, floor, trading floor; ◆ **sur le ~** BOURSE on the stock exchange

parrain *m* COM proposer, sponsor; ~ **politique** POL rabbi (*US, jarg*)

parrainage *m* V&M sponsorship; ~ **de bienfaisance** PROT SOC charity sponsorship

parrainer *vt* MÉDIA sponsor

part *f* COM *marché, bénéfices* share; ~ **de la Couronne** FISC Crown share; ~ **discrétionnaire** BOURSE discretionary share; ~ **éditeur** MÉDIA remit rate; ~ **équitable** COM fair share; ~ **de fiducie** BOURSE trust unit; ~ **de marché** ECON, V&M market share, share of market, slice of market; ~ **de marché de la marque** V&M brand share; ~ **nette** ASSUR net line; ~ **d'un organisme de placement collectif** FIN unit of a collective investment undertaking; ~ **de responsabilité imputée à la victime dans l'accident** DROIT contributory negligence; ~ **de responsabilité relative** DROIT *accidents* comparative negligence; ~ **du résultat revenant aux intérêts minoritaires** COMPTA minority interests in profit; ~ **du revenu national qui revient à la main d'oeuvre** ECON labor's share of national income (*AmE*), labour's share of national income (*BrE*); ~ **sociale** COMPTA share; ~ **souscrite** ASSUR written line; ◆ **de la ~ de** COM on behalf of; **faire la ~ du feu** COM cut one's losses; **faire sa ~ de travail** RES HUM do one's stint; **la ~ du lion** COM the lion's share; **pour ma ~** COM for my part

partage *m* DROIT partition, *Droit des successions* distribution, IMMOB apportionment, partition; ~ **d'actions cinq pour une** BOURSE five-for-one split; ~ **de commission** IMMOB coop (*US*); ~ **de données** INFO data sharing; ~ **de l'emploi** RES HUM job share, job sharing; ~ **de fichiers** INFO file sharing; ~ **de poste** RES HUM job splitting; ~ **de risque** ASSUR risk sharing; ~ **des risques** ASSUR risk sharing; ~ **de temps** INFO time sharing; ~ **du travail** RES HUM job share, job sharing, work sharing

partager *vt* COM share, share out, IMMOB apportion, INFO share; ~ **proportionnellement** COM *finances* prorate; ◆ ~ **la différence** COM split the difference; ~ **les frais avec** COM go shares with

partenaire *mf* COM, ECON partner; ~ **actif** *m* GESTION active partner; ~ **actif commandite** *m* GESTION active partner; ~ **commercial** *m* ECON, POL, V&M trading partner; ~ **étranger** *m* COM associated company abroad

partenaires: ~ **sociaux** *m pl* IND union and management

partenariat *m* POL *entre nations* partnership

parti: le ~ **écologiste** *m* ENVIR, POL the Green Party; ~ **politique** *m* COM, POL political party; ~ **politique reconnu** *m* FISC recognized political party, registered political party, POL recognized political party; ~ **pris** *m* COM bias

Parti: ~ **conservateur** *m* POL Conservative Party (*UK*); ~ **travailliste** *m* POL Labour Party (*UK*); ~ **travailliste socialiste** *m* POL Socialist Labor Party (*US*)

partial, e *adj* COM partial

partialité: ~ **de l'enquêteur** *f* MÉDIA, V&M interviewer bias

participant[1], **e** *adj* COM participating

participant[2], **e** *m,f* BOURSE participant, GESTION

conference delegate, conference member, convention participant; **~ du marché** BOURSE market participant

participatif, -ive *adj* GESTION participative

participation *f* BOURSE equity ownership, participating interest, stake, COM involvement, participation, *affaire* int., interest, *électorale* turnout, COMPTA participation, FIN int., interest, RES HUM employee involvement (*UK*), EI (*UK*); **~ de l'assuré à l'assurance** ASSUR coinsurance; **~ aux bénéfices** COMPTA profit-sharing, RES HUM incentive scheme, profit-sharing; **~ aux bénéfices de l'entreprise** RES HUM profit-sharing; **~ au capital** FISC *d'une fiducie* capital interest; **~ croisée** BOURSE cross holdings between companies; **~ dans une banque** BANQUE holding in a bank; **~ déterminante** COM working control; **~ différée aux bénéfices** RES HUM deferred contribution plan; **~ différée aux bénéfices de l'entreprise** RES HUM deferred profit-sharing; **~ directe** FIN working interest; **~ électorale** POL voter turnout; **~ des employés** COM organicity; **~ des employés aux bénéfices** RES HUM employee profit-sharing; **~ de la main-d'oeuvre** RES HUM labor force participation rate (*AmE*), labour force participation rate (*BrE*), LFPR; **~ majoritaire** BOURSE (ANT *participation minoritaire*) majority holding, majority interest, majority shareholding, majority stake, RES HUM controlling interest; **~ minoritaire** BOURSE (ANT *participation majoritaire*) minority holding, minority interest, minority shareholding, minority stake, COM minority holding, minority interest, COMPTA minority participation; **~ ouvrière** RES HUM shop-floor participation, worker participation, workers' participation; **~ partielle** GESTION trust share; **~ permanente** COMPTA permanent participation; **~ de police** ASSUR policy dividend; **~ qualifiée** FIN qualifying holding; **~ des travailleurs à la gestion** RES HUM worker participation; ◆ **avoir une ~ en actions** BOURSE have an equity interest

participations *f pl* BOURSE holdings, COMPTA share investments in other companies; **~ actuelles** BOURSE current holdings; ◆ **avoir des ~ dans une entreprise** COM, V&M have holdings in a company

participer 1. *vi* COM participate; **2.** *vti* **~ à** COM play a part in, play a role in; **~ à qch** COM *détenir une part* take a share in sth; **~ à un travail d'équipe** RES HUM work as part of a team

particularité *f* COM detail

particulier[1], **-ière** *adj* ASSUR particular

particulier[2], **-ière** *m,f* COM private individual; **~ admissible** FISC eligible individual

partie:[1] **tout ou ~** *adv* COM wholly or in substantial part

partie[2] *f* ADMIN part, DROIT *dans un contrat* party, FIN portion; **~ adverse** DROIT *litige* adversary; **~ associée** COM related party; **~ ayant capacité à contracter** DROIT competent party; **~ caractérisante** BREVETS characterizing portion; **~ contractante** DROIT contract party, contracting party, covenantor, party to a contract; **~ convenue** FISC agreed portion; **~ gagnante** DROIT prevailing party; **~ inférieure de la mémoire** INFO low memory; **~ intégrante** COM *d'un contrat* integral part; **~ intéressée** COM, DROIT interested party; **~ juridique** DROIT legal section; **~ lésée** DROIT injured party; **~ en litige** DROIT litigant; **~ non-utilisée** FISC unused part; **~ par million** (*p.p.m.*) COM parts per million (*ppm*); **~ plaignante** DROIT prosecution; **~ prenante dans une convention** RES HUM party to an agreement; **~ requérante** DROIT claimant; **~ réservée d'une émission** BOURSE preferential form; **~ souscrite** ASSUR written line

partiel, -elle *adj* COM partial

partiellement *adv* COM partially, partly; ◆ **~ déchargé** TRANSP *un envoi* partially knocked down, PKD; **~ démonté** TRANSP semiknocked down, SKD; **~ libéré** BOURSE partly paid

parties: **~ communes** *f pl* IMMOB common area

partir: **~ en bateau** *vt* TRANSP set sail; **~ en retraite** RES HUM go into retirement; **~ de zéro** COM build up from scratch, start from scratch; ◆ **à ~ de** COM starting from, wef, with effect from

partisan *m* COM supporter; **~ convaincu de** POL strong supporter of; **~ de l'État-providence** POL welfarist; **~ de l'inflation** ECON inflationist; **~ d'un retour à l'étalon or** ECON goldbug

partition *f* INFO *de mémoire* partition

partout: **~ dans le monde** *loc* COM worldwide

parts:[1] **~ fractionnaires** *f pl* BOURSE fractional share

parts:[2] **à ~ égales** *loc* COM in equal proportions

parution *f* MÉDIA publication

parvenir: **~ à un accord** *loc* COM come to an understanding, come to terms, reach an agreement; **~ à un accord avec** *loc* COM *ses fournisseurs* come to an arrangement with; **faire ~** *loc* COM *lettre, document* send

pas:[1] **~ assez cher** *adj* V&M underpriced; **~ coté** *adj* FIN not rated; **~ à pas** *adj* INFO step-by-step; **~ prévu** *adj* infrml COM scarcely scheduled

pas[2] *m* COM step; **~ de porte** IMMOB *appartement* key money; **~ de siège** TRANSP seat pitch; ◆ **donner le ~** COM set the pace; **faire le premier ~** COM make the first move

pas:[3] **à ne ~ dédaigner** *loc* COM *offre* not to be sneezed at (*infrml*); **~ de bonne livraison** *loc* BOURSE not in good delivery; **~ de compte** *loc* BANQUE n/a, no-account; **~ de marché** *loc* BOURSE no market; **~ de nom** *loc* BOURSE no-name; **~ prévu** *loc* BANQUE not provided for; **~ de rabais** *loc* V&M no discount, ND; **~ de remède** ASSUR no-cure-no-pay; **~ de risque avant confirmation** *loc* ASSUR no risk until confirmed, NR; **~ spécialement prévu** *loc* COM not specially provided for; **~ suffisamment affranchi** *loc* COMMS insufficiently stamped;

~ toujours à flot *loc* TRANSP *charte-partie* not always afloat, NAA; **~ toujours à flot mais échoué en sécurité** *loc* TRANSP *charte-partie* not always afloat but safe aground

passage *m* COM switchover; **~ automatique à la ligne** INFO word wrap; **~ de fourche** TRANSP *dans un conteneur* fork pocket; **~ imprimé en petits caractères** DROIT *dans un contrat* small print; **~ à la ligne** INFO lf, line feed; **~ en machine** INFO computer run, machine run, TRANSP machine run; **~ de production** IND production run; **~ d'une tranche d'imposition à une autre** ECON, FISC tax-bracket creep

passager, -ère *m,f* TRANSP *bateau, avion, automobile* passenger, passr; **~ clandestin** TRANSP free rider (*infrml*); **~ transféré d'une compagnie aérienne à une autre** LOISIRS interliner (*jarg*)

passagers: **~ à l'arrivée** *m pl* TRANSP inbound passengers; **~ au retour** *m pl* TRANSP inbound passengers

passant, e *m,f* COM passer-by

passation *f* COM conclusion, COMPTA reversal, writing back; **~ autoritaire de contrat** RES HUM authoritative contracting

passavant *m* IMP/EXP carnet, transire; **~ général** IMP/EXP general transire

passe *f* TRANSP *navigation* fairway, narrows; **~ de caisse** COM cashier's error allowance

passé¹, e *adj* COM passed; ◆ **~ de mode** COM out of fashion

passé:² **par le ~** *adv* COM historically

passeport *m* ADMIN passport, TRANSP sea letter; **~ valable** ADMIN valid passport

passer *vt* COM *commande* place, COMPTA *une écriture* pass, INFO skip; **~ une annonce** COM, MÉDIA, V&M advertise; **~ en charges** COMPTA charge off; **~ aux comptes de résultat** COMPTA write off; **~ un coup de fil à** *infrml* COMMS phone; **~ outre** COM, POL *à un veto* override; **~ aux profits et pertes** FIN write off; ◆ **cela se passe de commentaires** COM, DROIT res ipsa loquitur (*frml*); **~ un accord** COM enter into an agreement; **~ en assises** DROIT have a jury trial; **~ un avis d'appel d'offres** V&M *publicité* advertise for bids; **~ une commande par télégramme** COMMS send an order by wire; **~ un contrat avec** COM enter into a contract with, let out a contract to; **~ en contrebande à la douane** DROIT, FISC, IMP/EXP smuggle through customs; **~ au crible** COM, RES HUM screen; **~ au crible la candidature de qn** RES HUM screen sb for a job; **~ une écriture dans le grand livre** COM enter an item in the ledger; **~ de l'épargne publique à l'épargne privée** ECON go private; **~ l'éponge** COM wipe the slate clean; **faire ~** COM pass off, DROIT pass; **faire ~ clandestinement** IMP/EXP smuggle; **faire ~ en premier** ADMIN, COM, GESTION prioritize; **faire ~ au premier plan** INFO bring to front; **~ en fraude à la douane** DROIT, FISC, IMP/EXP smuggle through customs; **~ par pertes et profits** BANQUE write off,

COM be a write-off (*infrml*); **~ par la voie hiérarchique** COM go through the proper channels; **~ qch sous silence** COM pass sth over in silence; **~ au secteur privé** PROT SOC *médecine* go private (*infrml*); **~ sous presse** MÉDIA *édition, presse* go to press

passerelle *f* COMMS gateway; **~ couverte** TRANSP *navigation* covered gangway; **~ de débarquement** TRANSP *maritime* bridge, gangway, *navigation* portable gangway; **~ double** TRANSP *navigation* double-width gangway, double-width passenger gangway; **~ haute** TRANSP *d'un navire* flying bridge; **~ hydraulique** TRANSP *navigation* hydraulically operated gangway; **~ simple** TRANSP single-width gangway; **~ surélevée** TRANSP *navigation* raised bridge, RB; **~ télescopique** TRANSP *aviation* jetway

passible: **~ d'amende** *loc* DROIT liable to a fine; **~ d'une pénalité** *loc* DROIT liable to a penalty; **~ de poursuites** *loc* DROIT actionable; **~ de prosécution** *loc* DROIT liable to prosecution

passif¹, -ive *adj* V&M *affiche* passive

passif² *m* COMPTA, FIN liabilities; **~ à court terme** BANQUE short-term debt; **~ -dépôts** BANQUE deposit liabilities; **~ éventuel** DROIT, FIN contingent liabilities; **~ exigible** BANQUE short-term debt; **~ exigible à terme** FIN fixed liabilities; **~ national** BANQUE domestic liabilities; **~ de réserve** ASSUR reserve liability; **~ subordonné** COMPTA, FIN subordinated liabilities

passionné: **-e ~ d'informatique** *m,f* INFO hacker (*infrml*)

pastille *f* INFO chip

pâte: **~ à papier** *f* ENVIR paper pulp

patente *f* FISC franchise tax (*US*), PROT SOC bill of health, BH; **~ de santé** *frml* PROT SOC bill of health, BH; **~ de santé brute** PROT SOC foul bill of health; **~ de santé nette** COM, PROT SOC clean bill of health; **~ de santé suspecte** COM *maritime* touched bill of health, PROT SOC suspected bill of health, TRANSP *maritime* touched bill of health

patenté, e *adj* BREVETS, DROIT licensed

paternalisme *m* GESTION paternalism

patient: **~ privé** *m* PROT SOC private patient; **~ titre privé** *m* PROT SOC private patient

patin *m* TRANSP *manutention* skid

patrimoine *m* COMPTA assets, net equity, stockholders' equity; **~ naturel** ENVIR natural heritage

patron, ne *m,f* RES HUM master owner, TRANSP master; **~ de paille** IMMOB straw boss (*infrml*); ◆ **être son propre ~** RES HUM be one's own boss

patronat: **~ et travailleurs** *loc* GESTION, RES HUM managers and workers

patronné: **~ par l'État** *loc* FIN, POL government-sponsored

patte: **~ à futailles** *f* TRANSP *manutention* barrel hook, can hook

paupérisation *f* ECON immiseration; **~ de l'habitat** IMMOB filtering down (*US*)

pause *f* RES HUM *au travail* break *(UK)*; ~ -café RES HUM coffee break

pauvre *adj* ECON, PROT SOC poor; ~ **en liquidité** *(ANT riche en liquidité)* COMPTA, FIN cash-poor; ◆ **être ~ en** COM *calories* be low in

pauvreté *f* PROT SOC hardship, poverty; ~ **absolue** ECON absolute poverty

pavé: ~ **numérique** *m* INFO keypad, numeric keypad; ~ **de touches** *m* INFO keypad

pavillon *m* TRANSP *maritime* flag; ~ **de complaisance** TRANSP *navigation* convenience flag, flag of convenience; ~ **étranger** TRANSP *navigation* foreign flag; ~ **de foire** COM exhibition center *(AmE)*, exhibition centre *(BrE)*

pavois *m* TRANSP *d'un navire* bulwark

payable *adj* COM payable; ◆ ~ **à l'avance** COM payable in advance; ~ **à la commande** COM, FIN, V&M cash with order, CWO; ~ **à échéance** COM, FIN payable at maturity; ~ **mensuellement à terme échu** FIN payable monthly in arrears; ~ **à préavis** FIN payable after notice; ~ **sur demande** FIN payable at sight, payable on demand, payable on presentation; ~ **à vue** BANQUE cashable, FIN payable at sight, payable on demand, payable on presentation

payback *m* RES HUM payback

payé, e *adj* COM, FIN, RES HUM paid, pd; ◆ ~ **d'avance** COM paid in advance, pp., prepaid, upfront; ~ **comptant à l'avance** COMPTA cash in advance; ~ **à l'heure** RES HUM paid by the hour, paid hourly; ~ **intégralement** COM fully paid, FP; ~ **à la livraison** TRANSP paid on delivery; ~ **à la pièce** RES HUM paid by the piece, paid piece rate

payements: ~ **échelonnés** *m pl* FIN graduated payments

payer 1. *vt* COM *qn* pay; **2.** *v pron* se ~ ECON *des vacances, le restaurant* afford; ◆ ~ **à l'année** COM pay by the year; ~ **cash** *infrml* COM, FIN pay cash, pay in cash; ~ **au comptant** COM, FIN pay cash, pay in cash; ~ **les dépenses de** COM defray the expenses of; ~ **en** BANQUE pay in; ~ **en espèces** COM, FIN pay cash, pay in cash, pay in specie; ~ **et classer** FISC *impôt sur les sociétés* pay and file; ~ **la facture** COM pay a bill, settle the bill; **faire ~** COM *customes* charge; **faire ~ Marianne** *infrml* PROT SOC bulk billing *(Australia, jarg)*; ~ **le fret au cubage** TRANSP *maritime* pay for cargo by measurement; ~ **le fret au volume** TRANSP *maritime* pay for cargo by measurement; ~ **en liquide** COM, FIN pay cash, pay in cash; ~ **en nature** FIN pay in kind; ~ **la note** COM pay a bill, settle the bill; ~ **à l'ordre de** BANQUE pay to the order of; ~ **par trimestre** COM pay by the quarter; ~ **par virement bancaire** BANQUE pay by giro; ~ **qch au prix fort** COM pay over the odds for sth, pay top dollar for sth *(AmE)*; ~ **qn au forfait** COM pay sb a flat rate; ~ **rubis sur l'ongle** COM pay on the line *(jarg)*; ~ **à la semaine** RES HUM pay by the week; ~ **trimestriellement** COM pay by the quarter

payeur, -euse *m,f* COM payer

pays *m* COM country; ~ **d'accueil** *m* COM host country; ~ **de l'ACP** *m pl* ECON, POL ACP countries, ACPs; ~ **d'Afrique, des Caraïbes et du Pacifique** *m pl* ECON, POL African, Caribbean and Pacific countries; ~ **alpins** *m pl* COM, POL Alpine countries; ~ **autonome** *m* POL self-governing nation; ~ **bailleur de fonds** *m* ECON, POL donor country; ~ **du bloc de l'Est** *m* POL Eastern-bloc country; ~ **destinataire** *m* IMP/EXP country of destination; ~ **développé** *m* ECON, POL developed country, DC; ~ **donateur** *m* ECON, POL donor country; ~ **emprunteur** *m* ECON borrower country; ~ **et territoires d'outre-mer associés** *m pl* ECON, POL AOCTs, associated overseas countries and territories; ~ **d'expédition** *m* TRANSP country whence consigned, CWC; ~ **exportateurs de pétrole** *m pl* COM, IND, POL oil-exporting countries; ~ **à faible revenu modérément endetté** *m* FIN moderately indebted low-income country; ~ **à haut risque** *m* COM country of ultimate risk; ~ **hôte** *m* LOISIRS host country; ~ **industrialisé** *m* ECON, IND, POL advanced country, industrial country, industrialized country, AC; ~ **industrialisés occidentaux** *m pl* ECON industrialized countries of the West; **les ~ développés** *m pl* COM the developed world; **les ~ occidentaux** *m pl* COM the Western World; **les ~ socialistes** *m pl* ECON, POL Second World; ~ **limitrophe** *m* COM neighboring country *(AmE)*, neighbouring country *(BrE)*; ~ **méditerranéens** *m pl* COM, ECON, POL Mediterranean bloc; ~ **moins avancé** *m (PMA)* COM, ECON, POL developing country, less developed country; ~ **non-producteur de pétrole** *m* ENVIR non-oil country; ~ **nouvellement industrialisé** *m* ECON, IND newly industrialized country; ~ **d'origine** *m* COM, IMP/EXP country of origin, home country, COO; ~ **producteur de pétrole** *m* ECON, ENVIR, POL oil-producing country; ~ **au revenu bas sévèrement endetté** *m* FIN severely indebted low-income country, SILIC; ~ **à revenu intermédiaire modérément endetté** *m* ECON, FIN, POL moderately indebted middle-income country, MIMIC; ~ **à revenu moyen et à fort endettement** *m* FIN heavily indebted middle-income country, HIC; ~ **au revenu moyen sévèrement endetté** *m* FIN severely indebted middle-income country, SIMIC; ~ **scandinaves** *m pl* COM, POL Nordic countries; ~ **sous-développé** *m* COM, ECON, POL underdeveloped country; ~ **technologiquement avancé** *m* ECON, IND, POL advanced country, AC; ~ **tiers** *m* ECON *commerce international* third country; ~ **du tiers monde** *m* ECON third world country; ~ **en voie de développement** *m (PVD)* COM, ECON, POL developing country, less developed country, underdeveloped country; ◆ **du ~** ADMIN patrial *(UK, dat)*, COM *légumes* home-grown; **un ~, deux systèmes économiques** ECON *Hong Kong après 1997* one country, two systems

Pays: ~ **de Galles** *m* COM Wales

paysage: ~ **informatique** *m* INFO computer environment

Pays-Bas: **Les** ~ *m pl* COM The Netherlands

Paz: **La** ~ *n pr* COM La Paz

PBR *abrév (prix de base rajusté)* COMPTA ACB (*Canada*) *(adjusted cost base)*

PC: **pour** ~ *adj* INFO PC-based

PCGA *abrév (Principes comptables généralement admis)* COMPTA GAAP (*US*) *(Generally Accepted Accounting Principles)*

p.d. *abrév (port dû)* COM, TRANSP carr fwd, CF *(carriage forward)*, frt fwd *(freight forward)*

PDG *abrév (président-directeur général)* GESTION, RES HUM CEO (*US*) *(chief executive officer)*, DG *(director-general)*, GM *(general manager)*, MD (*UK*) *(managing director)*

péage *m* TRANSP road toll; ~ **automatique** TRANSP automatic fare collection; ~ **d'autoroute** TRANSP toll; ~ **sur voies** FISC road tax; ~ **du tunnel** TRANSP tunnel toll

peak: ~ **arrière** *m* TRANSP *d'un navire* afterpeak; ~ **avant** *m* TRANSP *d'un navire* forepeak

peaufiner *vt* INFO tweak

pêche *f* ECON, IND fishing

pêcherie *f* COM, ECON, IND fishery

pécuniaire *adj* COM, DROIT, FIN pecuniary

peine *f* DROIT penalty; ~ **contractuelle** DROIT penalty clause; ~ **pécuniaire civile** DROIT civil penalty (*US*)

Pékin *n pr* COM Peking

pénalisation: ~ **fiscale** *f* FISC tax penalty; ~ **importante pour fausse déclaration** *f* FISC serious misdeclaration penalty (*UK*); ~ **pour manque de ponctualité** *f* RES HUM quartering (*jarg*); ~ **pour récidive** *f* FISC second or further occurrence penalty

pénaliser *vt* DROIT penalize

pénalité *f* BANQUE, DROIT penalty; ~ **fiscale** FISC tax penalty; ~ **pour infraction** DROIT penalty for noncompliance; ~ **d'intérêt** BANQUE interest penalty; ~ **pour première contravention** FISC first occurrence penalty; ~ **pour récidive** FISC second or further occurrence penalty; ~ **de remboursement anticipé** BANQUE prepayment penalty; ~ **pour retrait anticipé** BOURSE, FIN early-withdrawal penalty; ~ **de retrait de fonds** BOURSE back-end load

pence *m* COM p, pence (*UK*)

pénétration *f* V&M *publicité* penetration; ~ **du marché** V&M market penetration

pénétrer *vt* COM make inroads, penetrate; ◆ ~ **le marché** V&M penetrate the market

péniche *f* TRANSP peniche

penny *m* COM penny

pensée: ~ **créatrice** *f* COM, GESTION creative thinking; ~ **latérale** *f* COM, COMMS, GESTION lateral thinking; ~ **politique** *f* POL political thinking

penser *vt* COM think

pension *f* FIN pension; ~ **anticipée** *Bel* (SYN

retraite anticipée) RES HUM early retirement, early retirement annuity; ~ **complète** LOISIRS full board, single-room supplement; ~ **différée** RES HUM deferred retirement credit; ~ **d'invalidité** FIN, PROT SOC disablement pension; ~ **livrée** BOURSE REPO (*AmE*), repurchase agreement, RP; ~ **non-contributive** FIN, PROT SOC, RES HUM noncontributory pension plan, noncontributory pension scheme; ~ **de retraite** ASSUR, FIN, PROT SOC old age pension, retirement pay, retirement pension, retiring allowance; ~ **de retraite anticipée** FIN, RES HUM early retirement scheme; ~ **vieillesse** ASSUR, PROT SOC old age pension

pensionnaire *m* COM paying guest, PG

pensionné, e *m,f* FIN, PROT SOC, RES HUM pension-holder

pente *f* COM slope; ~ **de substitution** ECON substitution slope

pentiolite *m* TRANSP pentiolite

pénurie *f* ECON shortage; ~ **de dollars** ECON dollar gap; ~ **de logements** PROT SOC housing shortage; ~ **de main-d'oeuvre** RES HUM labor shortage (*AmE*), labour shortage (*BrE*); ~ **de matières premières** ENVIR lack of raw material; ~ **de moyens de paiement** FIN liquidity famine; ~ **d'or** ECON gold shortage; ~ **de pétrole** ECON, IND oil shortage

PEPS *abrév (premier entré, premier sorti)* COMPTA FIFO *(first in, first out)*

percé, e *adj* POL leaky (*infrml*)

percée *f* COM breakthrough, *technologique* advance, ECON breakthrough, IND *technologique* advance; ~ **commerciale** ECON, V&M competitive thrust; ~ **dans un marché** COM break in the market; ◆ **faire une** ~ **dans le marché** COM breach the market

percepteur, -trice *m,f* FISC, RES HUM tax collector, tax inspector, taxman; ~ **des droits de port** RES HUM, TRANSP rates officer

Percepteur: ~ **des impôts** *m* FISC ≈ Commissioner of Inland Revenue (*UK*)

perception *f* COM perception, FIN levy, FISC collection, PROT SOC take-up; ~ **claire** COM clear thinking; ~ **des deniers publics** FISC collection of public money; ~ **des droits de douane** FISC collection of customs duties; ~ **de l'impôt** FISC tax collection; ~ **du prix** ECON price perception; ~ **standard à l'exportation** FISC, IMP/EXP standard export levy

percer: *vti* ~ **sur un marché** COM break into a market

percevoir *vt* FISC levy, RES HUM draw; ~ **un salaire horaire de** RES HUM be paid a rate of

perdre *vt* COM, DROIT *procès*, POL *élections* lose; ~ **par confiscation** COM forfeit; ◆ ~ **la partie** COM *individu* go to the wall; ~ **son emploi** RES HUM lose one's job; ~ **son travail** RES HUM lose one's job; ~ **du terrain** COM lose ground; ~ **de la valeur** BOURSE go down in value

perdu, e *adj* ENVIR *emballage* nonreusable

perdurer *vi* COM last

père[1] *adj* BANQUE senior

père[2] *m* INFO parent; ♦ **un ~ de famille** *jarg* BOURSE blue-chip customer

péremption: ~ prévue *f* COMPTA estimated lapse, lapsing

péremptoire *adj* COM, DROIT conclusive

pérennité *f* ECON, ENVIR sustainability

péréquation *f* FISC equalization, fiscal equalization; **~ fiscale** FISC equalization; **~ des impôts** FISC equalization of taxes, tax equalization

perestroïka *f* POL perestroika

perfectionné, e *adj* INFO enhanced

perfectionnement *m* COM training, *système* improvement, INFO enhancement, RES HUM training; **~ des cadres** COM, GESTION development management, executive development, management development

perforage *m* TRANSP puncturing

perforateur *m* INFO punch; **~ de bande** INFO tape punch; **~ de cartes** COM card punch

perforation *f* COM paper punch, INFO hole

perforations: ~ d'entraînement *f pl* INFO feed holes

perforatrice *f* INFO keypuncher, punch; **~ à clavier** INFO keypunch

performance *f* BOURSE, RES HUM *au travail*, V&M performance; **~ à l'exportation** IMP/EXP export performance; **~ du prix des actions** BOURSE, FIN share price performance; **~ supérieure** BOURSE outperformance

performances: ~ de la société *f pl* COM, FIN company results

performant, e *adj* INFO efficient

péricliter *vi* COM *société* go downhill

péril *m* ASSUR *maritime* peril; **~ de la mer** ASSUR maritime peril

périls: tous ~ *adj* ASSUR all-risk

périmé, e *adj* COM obsolete

périmer: se ~ *v pron* COM become obsolete

perimètre: ~ de consolidation *m* COMPTA companies included within consolidation

période *f* BANQUE *d'un prêt* term, COM period, time frame, ECON period; **~ d'accueil** COM orientation; **~ d'admissibilité** PROT SOC qualification period; **~ admissible** FISC qualifying period; **~ d'amortissement de l'actif** COMPTA, FIN, IMMOB asset depreciation range, ADR; **~ applicable** FISC relevant period; **~ d'après-guerre** ECON postwar period; **~ d'attente** COM vestibule period, waiting time; **~ avec droits** BOURSE cum rights period; **~ de base** FISC base period; **~ budgétaire** COMPTA budget period, ECON, FIN budget period, budgetary period, POL budgetary period; **~ de chômage** RES HUM unemployment spell; **~ complémentaire** FISC supplementary period; **~ comptable** BOURSE, COMPTA, FIN accounting period; **~ de cotation obligatoire** BOURSE mandatory quote period; **~ de couverture** ASSUR time on risk, BOURSE hedge period; **~ creuse** COM slack period,

MÉDIA *télévision* closed season; **~ de déclaration** FISC reporting period; **~ de demande maximum de la soirée** COM, ENVIR *en électricité* evening peak; **~ de détente** RES HUM cooling-off period; **~ de détention** BOURSE holding period; **~ d'essai** ECON trial period, RES HUM employment test, probation period, probationary period, trial period, V&M trial period; **~ d'étalement du revenu** FISC averaging period; **~ ex-droits** BOURSE ex-rights period; **~ d'exclusion** FISC excluded period; **~ d'exonération** FISC exempt period; **~ d'exonération fiscale** FISC tax holiday; **~ de gains** FISC earnings period; **~ de garantie** BANQUE *pendant laquelle on se porte garant pour qn* bail-out period; **~ de gestation** ECON gestation period; **~ gratuite** IMMOB *location* rent-free period; **~ d'imposition** FISC taxation period; **~ de jouissance foncière** DROIT, IMMOB tenure in land; **~ de latence** BOURSE waiting period; **~ de livraison** BOURSE delivery period; **~ de location** FIN tenancy period, FISC rental period, IMMOB tenancy period; **~ longue** ECON long period; **~ de maintien** BOURSE retention period; **~ moyenne d'encaissement** BANQUE, COMPTA average collection period, collection ratio; **~ moyenne de recouvrement** COMPTA collection period; **~ obligatoire d'affichage des prix** BOURSE mandatory quote period; **~ de l'option** BOURSE option period; **~ de paie** FISC pay period; **~ de pointe** ENVIR *électricité* peak period, MÉDIA *radio, télévision* prime listening time, prime time, prime viewing time; **~ porteuse pour le marché** BOURSE market timing; **~ de programmation** V&M time segment; **~ de prospérité** ECON boom; **~ de prospérité économique** COM, ECON, POL economic boom; **~ de qualification** FISC qualifying period; **~ de récupération** COM payout period, RES HUM payback period; **~ de réflexion** BOURSE cooling-off period; **~ de remboursement** COMPTA, RES HUM payback period; **~ de rodage** COM running in period; **~ de transition** COM transitional period; **~ transitoire** COM transition period; **~ utile** FISC relevant period; **~ de vacances** LOISIRS holiday period; **~ de validité** COM validity period; ♦ **en ~ de creux** COM, TRANSP off-peak; **pendant la ~ précédant** COM *élections* in the run-up to; **pour la ~ considérée** COMPTA for the period

périodes: ~ d'échéance *f pl* BANQUE, BOURSE, ECON, FIN maturity bands

périodique[1] *adj* COM periodic, periodical

périodique[2] *m* COM magazine, MÉDIA magazine, periodical

périphérique[1] *adj* COM peripheral, INFO add-on, peripheral

périphérique[2] *m* INFO device, peripheral, unit, TRANSP *route* ring road; **~ d'entrée** INFO input device; **~ de sortie** INFO output device; **~ de stockage** INFO storage device

périphériques *m pl* COM peripherals, INFO add-on equipment

péripole: ~ technologique *m* IND technology park

périssable *adj* V&M perishable

permanence *f* ADMIN manned service, COMPTA *des méthodes comptables* consistency; **~ téléphonique** INFO hot line

permanent[1], **e** *adj* COM ongoing, permanent

permanent[2], **e** *m,f* RES HUM full-time official (*BrE*), FTO (*BrE*), official, union officer, union official

permettant *adj* COM qualifying

permettre 1. *vt* COM allow, authorize; **2.** *v pron* **se ~** ECON afford; ◆ **~ à qn d'accéder à** COM give sb access to

permis[1], **e** *adj* FISC *déduction* allowed

permis[2] *m* BANQUE licence (*BrE*), license (*AmE*), COM authorization, DROIT *d'exercer une activité* licence (*BrE*), license (*AmE*), permit, TRANSP licence (*BrE*), license (*AmE*); **~ CEMT** TRANSP *acheminement par route* ECMT permit; **~ de conduire** TRANSP *document* driver's licence (*BrE*), driver's license (*AmE*), *examen* driving test; **~ de conduire international** ADMIN, TRANSP international driver's licence (*BrE*), international driver's license (*AmE*), international driving permit; **~ de conduire international pour transports routiers** ADMIN, TRANSP international road haulage permit; **~ de construire** ADMIN, ENVIR, IMMOB building permit (*AmE*), planning approval, planning permission (*BrE*); **~ de débarquement** TRANSP landing permit; **~ d'entrée** IMP/EXP clearance inwards; **~ international de conduite d'un véhicule de transport** ADMIN, TRANSP international road haulage permit; **~ multilatéral** TRANSP *UE* multilateral permit; **~ de résidence** ADMIN residence permit, residence visa; **~ de séjour** ADMIN residence permit, residence visa; **~ de séjour limité** ADMIN, DROIT, FISC temporary residence permit, temporary residence visa; **~ de sortie** IMP/EXP clearance outwards; **~ spécifique individuel** IMP/EXP, TRANSP specific individual licence (*BrE*), specific individual license (*AmE*), SIL; **~ de transbordement** IMP/EXP, TRANSP transhipment delivery order, transshipment delivery order; **~ de travail** RES HUM work permit; ◆ **qui ne nécessite pas un ~** DROIT permit-free

permutabilité *f* COM commutability

permutable *adj* COM commutable

permutation *f* MATH permutation

Pérou *m* COM Peru

perpendiculaire: **~ arrière** *f* (*PPAR*) TRANSP *navigation* aft perpendicular *(AP)*; **~ avant** *f* (*PPAV*) TRANSP *navigation* forward perpendicular *(FP)*

perpétuel, **-elle** *adj* BOURSE *obligation*, COM perpetual

perpétuité:[1] **à ~** *adv* COM in perpetuity

perpétuité[2] *f* BOURSE perpetuity

perquisition *f* DROIT *de la police* forcible entry; **~ à domicile** DROIT house search; **~ et saisie** COM search and seizure

persécution: **~ des syndicats** *f* *infrml* RES HUM union-bashing (*infrml*)

personnage: **~ de marque** *m* COM very important person, VIP

personnalisable *adj* COM tailorable

personnalisation *f* COM tailoring, PROT SOC individualization, V&M tailoring, *publicité* personalization

personnalisé, **e** *adj* COM customized, tailor-made, INFO customized, user-orientated, user-oriented, V&M customized

personnaliser *vt* IND *production*, INFO customize

personne: *f* ADMIN, COM, DROIT person; **~ à charge** *f* DROIT, FISC dependant

personnel *m* RES HUM human resources, manning, personnel, staff; **~ administratif** ADMIN, RES HUM administrative staff; **~ de bureau** ADMIN, RES HUM clerical personnel, clerical staff, office staff; **~ de cabine** TRANSP cabin staff; **~ à charge** RES HUM chargeable staff; **~ chargé de négocier** RES HUM bargaining agent; **~ de contrôle** *Fra (cf personnel de révision Bel)* COMPTA, FIN audit staff (*UK*); **~ de direction** GESTION, RES HUM managerial staff; **~ dirigeant** GESTION, RES HUM management staff; **~ d'encadrement** GESTION management staff, RES HUM management, management staff; **~ d'entretien** IND, RES HUM maintenance personnel, maintenance staff; **~ de fabrication** IND, RES HUM manufacturing workforce; **~ financier de soutien** FIN financial support staff; **~ intérimaire** RES HUM casual labor (*AmE*), casual labour (*BrE*); **~ de maîtrise** RES HUM supervisory personnel; **~ navigant commercial** TRANSP *avion* cabin staff; **~ non-syndiqué** RES HUM nonunion labor (*AmE*), nonunion labour (*BrE*); **~ pléthorique** RES HUM overstaffing; **~ de production** GESTION, IND, RES HUM manufacturing workforce, operative; **~ de réception** ADMIN front-office personnel; **~ réduit** RES HUM skeleton staff; **~ de révision** *Bel (cf personnel de contrôle Fra)* COMPTA, FIN audit staff (*UK*); **~ salarié** RES HUM salaried staff; **~ de secrétariat** ADMIN, RES HUM clerical staff, secretarial staff; **~ de service et de remplacement** RES HUM indirect workers; **~ subalterne** RES HUM down-the-line personnel; **~ sur le terrain** RES HUM front-line employees; **~ de surveillance** RES HUM supervisory personnel; **~ de terrain** RES HUM field staff; **~ titulaire** RES HUM tenured staff; **~ trop nombreux** RES HUM overstaffing; **~ de vente** V&M sales personnel; ◆ **à ~ non-syndiqué** RES HUM nonunion; **faire partie du ~** RES HUM be on the payroll, be on the strength

personnellement: **~ responsable** *adj* DROIT personally liable, personally responsible

personnes: **~ apparentées** *f pl* FISC related persons; **~ liées** *f pl* FISC related persons

perspective *f* COM, ECON outlook; **~ de profit** ECON, FIN profit outlook

perspectives: **~ d'avenir** *f pl* RES HUM future

prospects; ~ **de carrière** *f pl* RES HUM career prospects, job expectations, job prospects; ~ **commerciales** *f pl* V&M market prospects; ~ **économiques** *f pl* COM, ECON, POL economic outlook, economic prospects; ~ **financières** *f pl* ECON, FIN financial perspective; ~ **du marché** *f pl* V&M market prospects; ~ **professionnelles** *f pl* RES HUM career prospects; ~ **de travail** *f pl* COM, RES HUM work prospects

persuasion *f* COM persuasion

perte *f* ASSUR, BANQUE, FIN *capital* loss; ~ **actuarielle** ASSUR actuarial loss; ~ **agricole** FISC farm loss; ~ **agricole déductible** FISC deductible farm loss; ~ **apparente** COM, FIN superficial loss; ~ **d'un bien par confiscation** DROIT forfeiture; ~ **en capital** COM capital loss; ~ **en capital déductible** BOURSE, COMPTA, FIN, FISC allowable capital loss; ~ **en capital nette cumulative** FISC cumulative net capital loss; ~ **catastrophique** COM catastrophic loss; ~ **censée totale** ASSUR constructive total loss, CTL; ~ **censée totale uniquement** ASSUR constructive total loss only, CTLO; ~ **de clientèle** COM, V&M attrition; ~ **commerciale** COM, COMPTA, FIN business loss; ~ **compensatoire** BOURSE compensating loss (*UK*); ~ **comptable** COMPTA book loss; ~ **de conversion** ECON, FIN *commerce international* translation loss; ~ **courante** COM net operating loss, COMPTA net operating loss, revenue loss, IND net operating loss; ~ **à découvert** BOURSE uncovered hedge loss; ~ **déductible au titre d'un placement d'entreprise** COM, COMPTA, FIN, FISC allowable business investment loss; ~ **du droit à l'indemnité** DROIT loss of claim; ~ **d'un droit pour inexécution d'une obligation** DROIT forfeiture, loss of claim; ~ **du droit à revendication** DROIT loss of claim; ~ **économique** ECON economic loss; ~ **effective** COMPTA actual loss; ~ **d'embarcation** TRANSP *navigation* cl, craft loss; ~ **énorme** COM catastrophic loss; ~ **exceptionnelle** COMPTA extraordinary loss, ECON windfall loss; ~ **d'exploitation** COM business loss, COMPTA business loss, operating loss, revenue loss, FIN business loss; ~ **finale** COMPTA terminal loss; ~ **fortuite** ASSUR fortuitous loss; ~ **d'information** INFO dropout; ~ **à long-terme** FISC long-term loss; ~ **de marché** COM loss of market; ~ **de mortalité** FISC mortality loss; ~ **nette** COMPTA, ECON, FISC net loss; ~ **nette cumulative sur placement** FISC cumulative net investment loss; ~ **nette d'exploitation** COM, COMPTA, IND net operating loss; ~ **nette quotidienne** TRANSP *charte-partie* net daily loss; ~ **non-réalisée** COMPTA unrealized loss; ~ **normale** FISC ordinary loss; ~ **à l'origine** COMPTA historical loss; ~ **partielle** ASSUR partial loss, PL; ~ **partielle ou totale** ASSUR partial/total loss, PTL; ~ **primitive d'acquisition** COMPTA historical loss; ~ **de la priorité** BREVETS loss of priority; ~ **de récolte** ECON, ENVIR *agriculture* crop failure; ~ **réelle sur prêts** BANQUE actual loan loss, actual loan loss experience; ~ **de réinvestissement** COM

reinvestment loss; ~ **réprimée totale seulement** ASSUR constructive total loss only, CTLO; ~ **réputée totale** ASSUR *sinistre d'assurance* constructive total loss, CTL; ~ **de salaire** RES HUM loss of pay; ~ **de sauvetage** ASSUR salvage loss; ~ **sèche** COM, FIN clear loss, outright loss, write-off; ~ **sèche de l'impôt** FISC tax write-off; ~ **sèche sur prêt** BANQUE loan write-off; ~ **simple** ASSUR elementary loss; ~ **subie** COMPTA actual loss; ~ **sur des biens amortissables** COMPTA loss on depreciable property; ~ **sur créance** COM credit loss; ~ **sur investissement** BOURSE investment loss; ~ **sur prêts** BANQUE loan loss; ~ **sur transactions** ECON *commerce international* transaction loss; ~ **au titre d'un placement d'entreprise (PTPE)** FISC business investment loss (*BIL*); ~ **totale** ASSUR total loss, T/L, COM total loss; ~ **totale effective** ASSUR *cause de délaissement* actual total loss; ~ **totale relative** ASSUR *sinistre d'assurance* constructive total loss, CTL; ~ **totale transigée** ASSUR arranged total loss, *assurance transport maritime* comprised total loss; ~ **totale uniquement** ASSUR total loss only, TLO; ~ **de valeur** COM decrease in value

pertes: ~ **accumulées** *f pl* COMPTA accumulated deficit; ~ **et bénéfices de change** *f pl* FIN premium and discount on exchange; ~ **et profits** *f pl* (*P et P*) COMPTA profit and loss (*P&L*); ~ **d'exploitation** *f pl* COM, COMPTA trading losses; ~ **indirectes** *f pl* ASSUR consequential loss; ~ **occasionnées par créances douteuses** *f pl* BANQUE, COMPTA, ECON, FIN bad debt losses; ~ **réalisées** *f pl* FIN realized losses; ~ **reportées** *f pl* COMPTA losses carried forward; ~ **subies** *f pl* DROIT losses suffered; ~ **sur créances** *f pl* BANQUE, COMPTA, ECON, FIN bad debt losses

perturbation *f* COM disruption

perturbé, e *adj* RES HUM hot (*jarg*)

perturber *vt* COM unsettle

péruvien, -enne *adj* COM Peruvian

Péruvien, -enne *m,f* COM *habitant* Peruvian

pèse: ~ **-papier** *m* COM basic weight scales

peser *vt* COM weigh; ♦ ~ **contre** DROIT *nouvelle loi* bring to bear against; ~ **le pour et le contre** COM weigh the pros and cons, weigh up the pros and cons; ~ **lourdement sur** COM rest heavily on; ~ **la situation pour savoir s'il faut dire oui ou non** COM weigh up whether to say yes or no

peseta *f* (*pta.*) COM peseta (*pta.*)

peso *m* COM peso

pessimisme *m* BOURSE bearishness, gloom

pessimiste *adj* (*ANT optimiste*) COM pessimistic

pesticide *m* ENVIR, IND pesticide

petit: ~ **actionnaire** *m* BOURSE, FIN private investor; ~ **boulot** *m* RES HUM menial job; ~ **capital** *m* (*ANT grand capital*) BOURSE, FIN small investors; ~ **commerçant** *m* COM, V&M shopkeeper (*BrE*), storekeeper (*AmE*), trader; ~ **cultivateur** *m* ECON *agriculture* smallholder; ~ **employeur** *m* RES HUM small employer; ~ **fonctionnaire** *m* RES HUM petty

official; ~ **fond** *m* MÉDIA *édition* back margin;
~ **gain rapide** *m* FISC quick flip; ~ **génie de
l'informatique** *m* INFO computer whizz kid
(*infrml*); ~ **joueur** *m* *jarg* BOURSE piker (*jarg*);
~ **prodige** *m* COM whizz kid (*infrml*); ~ **profit** *m*
BOURSE scalp (*US, infrml*)

petite: ~ **annonce** *f* *infrml* COM *journaux, magazines* ad (*infrml*), advert, MÉDIA, V&M classified
ad (*infrml*), classified advert, classified advertisement, small ads, smalls (*jarg*), *journaux,
magazines* ad (*infrml*), advert, advertisement;
~ **annonce classée** *f* MÉDIA, V&M classified advertisement; ~ **caisse** *f* COMPTA, FIN, RES HUM pc,
petty cash; ~ **coupure** *f* BANQUE small denomination; ~ **entreprise** *f* COM small business, small
firm, FISC small business; ~ **entreprise commerciale qualifiable** *f* FISC qualifying small business
corporation; **la ~ épargne** *f* BANQUE, FIN small
savings; ~ **série** *f* IND batch, short run, SR; ♦ **de
~ taille** ECON small-scale

petites: ~ **et moyennes entreprises** *f pl* (*PME*)
COM small and medium-sized companies, small
and medium-sized enterprises (*SME*); ~ **et
moyennes industries** *f pl* (*PMI*) COM small and
medium-sized manufacturing companies
(*SMME*)

pétition *f* COM petition, COMMS *lettre* round robin

petits: ~ **boulots** *m pl* RES HUM odd jobs;
~ **caractères** *m pl* DROIT *dans un contrat* small
print; ~ **dragons** *m pl* *infrml* ECON, POL little
dragons (*infrml*); ~ **fonds** *m pl* MÉDIA backs,
gutter; **les ~ salaires** *m pl* PROT SOC, RES HUM
the low-paid; ~ **prix** *m pl* V&M budget prices

P et P *abrév* (*pertes et profits*) COMPTA P&L (*profit
and loss*)

pétrin *m* *infrml* COM jam (*infrml*); ♦ **dans le ~**
infrml COM in a jam (*infrml*)

pétro: ~ **-obligation** *f* BOURSE petrobond

pétrodevise *f* ECON petrocurrency, FIN, IMP/EXP
petrochemical currency

pétrodollar *m* ECON petrodollar, FIN, IMP/EXP
petrochemical currency

pétrole *m* ENVIR black gold, oil, IND oil; ~ **brut**
ENVIR, IND crude oil, crude petroleum; ~ **carburant pour tracteurs** IND vaporizing oil (*AmE*),
vapourizing oil (*BrE*)

pétrolier *m* IND, TRANSP *navigation* oil carrier, oil
tanker; ~ **de ligne sans escales** IND, TRANSP
navigation oil-bearing continuous liner, OC;
~ **-minéralier** TRANSP *navigation* O/o, combination carrier, ore-oil ship; ~ **-vraquier-minéralier-
transporteur de produits** TRANSP *navigation* pro-
duct/oil/bulk/ore carrier, PROBO; ~ **-vraquier-
roulier** TRANSP *navigation* bulk-oil and roll-on/
roll-off vessel, BORO

pétrolifère *adj* IND oil-bearing

pfennig *m* COM pfennig

pharmaceutique *adj* IND pharmaceutical

phase *f* COM *dans les négociations* stage, *mise en
oeuvre d'un projet* phase; ~ **d'alerte** MÉDIA *pub-

licité advance publicity; ~ **clé** COM key stage; ~ **de
démarrage** COM start-up; ~ **initiale** ADMIN phase
zero (*jarg*); ~ **intermédiaire** FIN intermediate
stage; ~ **d'introduction** PROT SOC introductory
course; ~ **de lancement** V&M *marketing* introductory stage; ~ **de mise en train** GESTION warm-up
session; ~ **préliminaire** DROIT, POL draft stage;
~ **de production** IND processing stage;
~ **provisoire** DROIT, POL draft stage; ~ **de
récession** ECON recessionary phase;
~ **récessionniste** ECON recessionary phase; ~ **de
traitement** INFO computer run; ~ **de vérification**
COM verification phase; ♦ **en ~ d'achèvement**
COM near completion

philippin, e *adj* COM Philippine

Philippin, e *m,f* COM *habitant* Filipino

Philippines *f pl* COM Philippines

philosophie *f* COM philosophy; ~ **de l'entreprise**
COM company philosophy

Phnom Penh *n pr* COM Phnom Penh

photocalque *m* ADMIN, MÉDIA blueprint

photocomposeuse *f* MÉDIA filmsetter

photocomposition *f* MÉDIA filmsetting (*BrE*),
photocomposition (*AmE*)

photocopie *f* ADMIN, COM, COMMS Photostat®,
Xerox®, photocopy; ♦ **faire une ~ de** ADMIN,
COM, COMMS Xerox®, photocopy

photocopier *vt* ADMIN, COM, COMMS Xerox®,
photocopy

photocopieur, -euse *m,f* ADMIN, COM, COMMS
photocopier

photocopieuse *f* ADMIN, COM, COMMS Xerox®,
copier, photocopier, photocopying machine

photographe: ~ **de presse** *mf* MÉDIA *presse* press
photographer

photographie: ~ **en dégradé** *f* V&M *publicité* vignette (*jarg*)

photograveur, -euse *m,f* RES HUM process worker

Photostat® *m* ADMIN, COM, COMMS Photostat®

photostyle *m* INFO light pen, stylus

phrase: ~ **d'appel** *f* MÉDIA *presse* blurb (*jarg*)

physicien, nne ~ atomiste *m,f* IND, RES HUM nuclear physicist; ~ **nucléaire** *m,f* IND, RES HUM
nuclear physicist

physiocrate *mf* ECON physiocrat

physique: **personne ~** *f* BREVETS natural person,
COM, RES HUM persona

physiquement *adv* COM physically

piastre *f* COM piastre

PIB[1] *abrév* (*produit intérieur brut*) ECON GDP
(*gross domestic product*), GNP (*gross national
product*)

PIB[2] ~ **d'équilibre** *m* ECON equilibrium GNP;
~ **nominal** *m* ECON nominal GDP; ~ **par
habitant** *m* ECON GDP per capita, GDP per head,
per capita GDP

picot: ~ **d'entraînement** *m* INFO pin

pictogramme *m* COM logoptics, MATH pictogram

pièce *f* COM pc, piece, IND component; ~ **biconique**

de saisissage TRANSP *manutention des conteneurs* stacking fitting; **~ de caisse** COMPTA cash voucher; **~ de coin** TRANSP *conteneur* corner casting; **~ comptable** BANQUE, COMPTA voucher; **~ de dix cents** FIN dime (*US*); **~ de dix dollars** FIN eagle (*US*), ten dollars; **~ fiscale** BOURSE, FISC tax voucher; **~ de gerbage** TRANSP stacker; **~ de gerbage double** TRANSP double stacker; **~ de gerbage quadruple** TRANSP quadruple stacker; **~ jointe** ADMIN accompanying document, COM enclosure, COMMS accompanying document; **~ justificative** BANQUE, COM, COMPTA voucher, DROIT supporting document, FISC voucher; **~ justificative de caisse** COMPTA cash voucher; **~ justificative de virement de fonds** BANQUE transfer of funds voucher; **~ de monnaie** COM coin; **~ en or** BANQUE gold coin; **~ d'or d'investissement** FIN investment gold coin; **~ de rechange** COM replacement part, spare part; **~ de règlement bancaire** BANQUE bank settlement voucher; **~ de vingt dollars** FIN double eagle (*US*), twenty dollars; **~ de virement de fonds** BANQUE transfer of funds voucher; ◆ **la ~** COM apiece; **la ~ ci-jointe** ADMIN, COMMS the affixed document

pièces: **~ détachées** *f pl* IND spares; **~ d'un dossier** *f pl* COM case papers; **~ d'embarquement** *f pl* IMP/EXP shipping documents; ◆ **en ~ détachées** TRANSP completely knocked down, CKD

pied *m* COM foot, ft; **~ carré** COM square foot; **~ cube** COM cu ft, cubic feet, CF; **~ d'éléphant** TRANSP elephant's foot; **~ de façade** IMMOB front foot (*US*); **~ de page** INFO footer; ◆ **sur le même ~** COM on the same footing

piège: **~ de la liquidité** *m* ECON liquidity trap; **~ de la mobilité** *m* ECON mobility trap

pierre: **~ d'achoppement** *f* COM stumbling block; **~ angulaire** *f* COM cornerstone

piéton *m* COM pedestrian

pige *f* MÉDIA *pour journalistes* fee

pigiste *mf* MÉDIA, RES HUM freelance correspondent, freelance journalist, freelance writer, *imprimé* piece-rate typographer, space writer, *presse* stringer (*jarg*)

pignon *m* TRANSP pinion

pile *f* IND battery, INFO stack, TRANSP *numérotage des conteneurs* row; **~ auxiliaire** INFO battery backup; **~ de conteneurs** TRANSP container stack; **~ de secours** INFO battery backup

pilier *m* ECON *de l'économie* backbone, keystone

pillage *m* BOURSE corporate raiding, COM piracy

pilotage *m* INFO control, TRANSP pilotage

pilote¹ *adj* COM pilot

pilote² *m* INFO driver, MÉDIA *télévision, radio* pilot, TRANSP *de l'air* pilot, *navigation* pilot; **~ automatique** TRANSP autopilot; **~ d'écran** INFO screen driver; **~ d'émission** MÉDIA *télévision* anchor; **~ d'impression** INFO print driver; **~ de ligne** TRANSP pilot; **~ de périphérique** INFO device driver; **~ de souris** INFO mouse driver

piloté: **~ par logiciel** *adj* INFO software-driven; **~ par menus** *adj* INFO menu-driven; **~ par ordinateur** *adj* INFO computer-driven; **~ par souris** *adj* INFO mouse-driven

pilule: **~ empoisonnée** *f jarg* FIN poison pill (*jarg*)

pince: **~ à levier** *f* TRANSP *manutention* pinch bar

pinces *f pl* TRANSP *matériel de manutention* dog hooks, tongs

pint *m* COM pint, pt

pinte *f* COM pint, pt

pionnier¹ IND pioneer, V&M *marketing* early adapter

pionnier², **-ière** *m,f* IND pioneer

pipeline *m* COMMS, ENVIR, IND pipeline

piqué, e *adj infrml* COM hot (*infrml*)

piquet: **~ de grève** *m* IND, RES HUM picket, picket line, strike picket; **~ de grève devant une autre entreprise** *m* RES HUM secondary picketing

piquets: **~ de grève** *m pl* RES HUM flying pickets; **~ de grève pacifiques** *m pl* RES HUM peaceful picketing

piratage *m* INFO, MÉDIA piracy; **~ de films vidéo** DROIT, MÉDIA video piracy; **~ informatique** INFO computer hacking, hacking; **~ de logiciel** INFO software piracy

pirate: **~ informatique** *m* INFO computer hacker, hacker (*infrml*)

pirater *vt* INFO hack, hack into, pirate, MÉDIA pirate

piraterie *f* TRANSP *maritime* marine piracy

pire: **le ~ des cas** *m* (ANT *meilleur des cas*) COM, ECON, POL worst-case scenario

pisciculture *f* ECON, IND fish farming

piste *f* TRANSP carriageway, *aéroport* runway; **~ d'audit** COMPTA, FIN audit trail; **~ de bande magnétique** INFO channel; **~ de révision** COMPTA, FIN audit trail; **~ de roulement** TRANSP *aéroport* taxiway; **~ sonore** COMMS soundtrack

piston *m infrml* RES HUM nepotism

pistonné, e *m,f* RES HUM pork chop (*US*)

pistonner: **~ qn** *vt infrml* COM pull strings for sb (*infrml*), pull wires for sb (*AmE, infrml*)

pit *m* BOURSE pit

piton: **~ à oeil** *m* TRANSP *conteneurs* eye bolt, *saisissage* pad eye

pivot *m* TRANSP hub; **~ d'attelage réversible** TRANSP reversible kingpin

pixel *m* INFO pixel

p.j. *abrév* (*pièce jointe*) COM enclosure

PL *abrév* (*port en lourd*) TRANSP *navigation* D/W (*deadweight*), DWC (*deadweight capacity*), DWCC (*deadweight cargo capacity*), DWT (*deadweight tonnage*)

placard *m* MÉDIA bill, *typographie* broadsheet, MÉDIA *typographie* galley, galley proof, V&M bill; **~ publicitaire** MÉDIA, V&M large display advertisement, *pleine page* full-page advertisement

place *f* COM accommodation, LOISIRS seat;

~ bancable BANQUE bank place, banking center (*AmE*), banking centre (*BrE*); **~ bancaire** BANQUE bank place, banking center (*AmE*), banking centre (*BrE*), financial center (*AmE*), financial centre (*BrE*); **~ extraterritoriale** BANQUE, FIN offshore center (*AmE*), offshore centre (*BrE*), offshore place; **~ financière** BOURSE financial market, ECON financial center (*AmE*), financial centre (*BrE*), financial market, FIN financial market, financial center (*AmE*), financial centre (*BrE*); **~ financière internationale** ECON, FIN global financial center (*AmE*), global financial centre (*BrE*); **~ isolée** LOISIRS *théâtre* single; **~ -kilomètre utilisée** LOISIRS seat kilometers used (*AmE*), seat kilometres used (*BrE*); **~ du marché** COM, V&M marketplace; **~ -mille** LOISIRS seat mile; **~ -milles par heure-moteur** LOISIRS seat miles per engine hour; **~ séparée** LOISIRS *théâtre* single; ♦ **à la ~ de** COM in lieu of; **sur ~** COM on the spot

placé: **être ~ sous administration judiciaire** *loc* DROIT go into receivership

placement *m* BOURSE distribution, investment, placement, ECON, FIN investment; **~ acceptable** FISC acceptable investment; **~ actif** BOURSE active investment; **~ en actions** COM equity investment; **~ en actions ordinaires** BOURSE common share investment (*BrE*), common stock investment (*AmE*); **~ admissible** BOURSE qualified investment; **~ d'un bloc de contrôle** BOURSE secondary-primary distribution; **~ direct** BOURSE direct investment; **~ éthique** ENVIR ethical investment; **~ étranger** COM foreign investment; **~ excessif** BANQUE overplacing; **~ facultatif** ASSUR facultative placing; **~ de fonds commun d'options** BOURSE option mutual fund; **~ garanti** COM guaranteed investment; **~ initial** BOURSE *titres* primary distribution, primary offering; **~ privé** BANQUE private placement, private placing, FIN private placing, private placement; **~ qui ne rapporte pas** BANQUE, COMPTA, FIN bad investment; **~ sûr** BANQUE safe investment; ♦ **faire des ~s** BOURSE, FIN invest; **faire un ~ immobilier** FIN, IMMOB invest in property

placements: **~ sûrs du Royaume-Uni** *m pl* BOURSE gilt-edged stocks (*UK*)

placer 1. *vt* COMPTA, FIN invest **2.** *v pron* **se ~** BOURSE take a position; ♦ **~ de l'argent en viager** ASSUR invest in an annuity; **~ un dépôt** BOURSE place a deposit; **~ qn comme apprenti chez qn** RES HUM apprentice sb to sb; **~ qn dans une situation financière extrêmement difficile** FISC, PROT SOC impose extreme hardship on sb; **~ en report** BOURSE lend; **se ~ à cheval** BOURSE take a straddle position; **~ ses petits copains** *infrml* RES HUM get jobs for the boys (*infrml*); **~ sous administration judiciaire** DROIT put into receivership; **~ sous garde** DROIT *documents saisis* place in custody

places: **~ couchées** *f pl* TRANSP berth, berth accommodation

placier *m* COM business tout, canvasser

plafond[1] *adj* BOURSE high

plafond[2] *m* BOURSE ceiling, upper limit, COM cap, upper limit, ECON cap, ceiling, FIN cutoff point, FISC cutoff point, upper cap (*BrE*), RES HUM ceiling, wage ceiling, V&M ceiling; **~ de ballast** TRANSP *navigation* tank top, TT; **~ des bénéfices retraite** FISC pension earnings cap; **~ budgétaire** COMPTA, ECON, FIN, POL budget ceiling; **~ de crédit** COM credit ceiling, credit limit; **~ des dépenses** ECON cash limit, FISC expenditure limit; **~ des emprunts** BANQUE, COM, COMPTA, ECON, FIN borrowing ceiling, borrowing limit; **~ des gains cumulatifs** FISC cumulative gains limit; **~ d'hypothèque** BANQUE, IMMOB mortgage ceiling; **~ des investissements à l'étranger** FIN foreign investment limit; **~ maximal de la période d'amortissement** COMPTA, FIN, IMMOB asset depreciation range, ADR; **~ d'un prêt** COM lending ceiling; **~ de prix** ECON price ceiling; **~ sur les taux d'intérêt** BANQUE, ECON interest rate ceiling; **~ des taux** BANQUE, ECON, FIN rate ceiling; ♦ **à concurrence d'un ~ de** COM up to a maximum of; **crever le ~** BOURSE, FIN break the ceiling

plafonnement: **~ des bénéfices** *m* ECON, FIN profit ceiling; **~ des salaires** *m* RES HUM wage ceiling

plafonner 1. *vt* BANQUE *taux d'intérêt* cap; **2.** *vi* COM top out

plage: **~ avant** *f* TRANSP forecastle; **~ disponible** *f* MÉDIA *radio* availabilities on radio; **~ fixe** *f* RES HUM core time; **~ horaire** *f* MÉDIA, TRANSP time band

plages: **~ horaires fixes** *f pl* IND core hours

plagiat: **~ de brevets d'entreprise** *m* BREVETS, COM corporate plagiarism

plaider 1. *vt* COM plead; **2.** *vi* DROIT litigate, plead, put in a plea; ♦ **~ coupable** DROIT plead guilty; **~ sa cause** DROIT argue one's case

plaideur, -euse *m,f* DROIT litigant

plaidoirie *f* DROIT pleading

plaidoyer *m* DROIT pleading

plaignant, e *m,f* DROIT plaintiff

plaindre: **se ~** *v pron* COM complain

plainte *f* DROIT *droit pénal* accusation, complaint; **~ contre X** DROIT action against X

plaire: *vti* **~ à** COM, V&M appeal to

plaisant, e *adj* COM, RES HUM amicable

plan *m* COM blueprint, draft, plan, planning, ECON, GESTION, IMMOB plan; **~ d'accession au logement** IMMOB, PROT SOC housing scheme; **~ d'accroissement de capital volontaire** FIN voluntary accumulation plan; **~ d'achat d'actions** BOURSE stock purchase plan; **~ d'action** COM action plan, game plan, RES HUM action plan; **~ d'affaires** COM, GESTION business plan; **~ d'aménagement d'une zone** COM zone improvement plan (*US*), ZIP (*US*); **~ d'amortissement** COMPTA amortization schedule, depreciation schedule, FIN amortization schedule; **~ annuel de vérification** COMPTA annual audit plan (*UK*); **~ d'arrimage**

TRANSP *d'un navire* cargo plan, ship planning, stowage plan; ~ **d'assurance** ASSUR insurance plan, insurance scheme; ~ **d'audit** COMPTA, FIN audit plan; ~ **d'audit annuel** COMPTA annual audit plan (*UK*); ~ **Baker** ECON, FIN Baker Plan; ~ **de base** COM ground plan; ~ **budgétaire** ECON, FIN, POL budgetary planning; ~ **de carrière** RES HUM career path, career planning; ~ **de carrière ambitieux** RES HUM fast tracking; ~ **en chaîne** COM daisy-chain scheme (*jarg*); ~ **de charge** TRANSP load plan; ~ **de chargement** TRANSP *d'un navire* cargo plan, stowage plan; ~ **comptable** COMPTA, FIN accounting plan, chart of accounts; ~ **de désengagement** BOURSE withdrawal plan; ~ **de développement pluriannuel** FIN multiyear operational plan, MYOP; ~ **directeur** ECON master plan; ~ **de divisions** COM, GESTION departmental plan; ~ **en dollar constant** COM constant dollar plan; ~ **d'économies sur la masse salariale** RES HUM payroll savings plan; ~ **d'encouragement** RES HUM incentive plan; ~ **d'ensemble** GESTION master plan; ~ **d'entreprise** BANQUE *d'une banque* business plan; ~ **d'entreprise détaillé** COM in-depth business plan; ~ **d'entreprise générique** COM generic business plan; ~ **d'épargne en actions** BOURSE, FIN personal equity plan (*UK*), PEP (*UK*); ~ **d'épargne avec capitalisation** BOURSE automatic reinvestment, dividend reinvestment plan; ~ **d'épargne-retraite** BANQUE, FIN, RES HUM retirement savings plan, retirement savings program (*AmE*), retirement savings programme (*BrE*); ~ **d'étage** IMMOB *des chambres* floor plan; ~ **d'évaluation annuel** FIN annual evaluation plan; ~ **d'évaluation de programme** COM program evaluation plan (*AmE*), programme evaluation plan (*BrE*); ~ **d'expansion économique** BOURSE BES (*UK, obs*), Business Expansion Scheme (*UK, obs*), Enterprise Investment Scheme (*UK*); ~ **d'exploitation** TRANSP operating plan; ~ **de financement** FIN financing plan; ~ **financier** FIN, GESTION financial planning; ~ **financier de l'exercice courant** FISC current fiscal plan; ~ **de formation** RES HUM training scheme; ~ **de garantie de pénétration de marché** V&M market entry guarantee scheme; ~ **de garantie de prêts** FIN loan guarantee scheme; ~ **de groupe** MATH bunch map; ~ **d'hospitalisation** ASSUR hospitalization plan; ~ **d'intéressement aux bénéfices** FIN profit-sharing plan (*US*), profit-sharing scheme (*UK*); ~ **d'intéressement des employés** BOURSE, PROT SOC, RES HUM share participation scheme, share scheme; ~ **d'investissement** FIN investment plan; ~ **d'investissement en actions pour cadres** BOURSE executive share option scheme; ~ **d'investissement pour cadres** BOURSE executive option scheme; ~ **d'investissement contractuel** BOURSE contractual plan; ~ **d'investissement mensuel** BOURSE monthly investment plan; ~ **d'investissement du personnel** BOURSE employee share ownership plan (*BrE*), employee stock ownership plan (*AmE*), ESOP; ~ **d'investisse-**ment en titres indexés BOURSE Indexed Security Investment Plan; ~ **de Keynes** ECON Keynes' Plan; ~ **à longue échéance** COM forward planning; ~ **de lot** IMMOB plot plan (*US*); ~ **de marché** V&M *processus de planification* market plan, market planning; ~ **marketing** V&M marketing plan; ~ **marketing et ventes** V&M marketing and sales plan; ~ **média** MÉDIA, V&M media plan, media planning, media schedule; ~ **du navire** TRANSP ship plan; ~ **d'occupation des sols** ECON *local*, ENVIR, PROT SOC land-use planning; ~ **opérationnel de l'année budgétaire** COMPTA budget year operational plan; ~ **opérationnel pluriannuel** FIN multiyear operational plan, MYOP; ~ **d'options d'achat d'actions** BOURSE, RES HUM employee stock option plan, stock option plan; ~ **-paquet** V&M pack shot; ~ **de participation aux bénéfices** FIN profit-sharing plan (*US*), profit-sharing scheme (*UK*); ~ **personnel de capitalisation** BOURSE, FIN personal equity plan (*UK*), PEP (*UK*); ~ **pilote** COM, IND *production* pilot plan; ~ **professionnel** COMPTA sectoral accounting plan; ~ **de projet** COM, FIN, GESTION project planning; ~ **quinquennal** COMPTA five-year plan; ~ **de rachat des actions** BOURSE share repurchase plan; ~ **de redressement** ECON recovery plan; ~ **de réduction des salaires** RES HUM salary reduction plan; ~ **de réinvestissement des dividendes** BOURSE dividend reinvestment plan; ~ **de relance** COM recovery scheme; ~ **de remboursement** COMPTA redemption table; ~ **de remboursement périodique** FIN periodic payment plan; ~ **de réservation** V&M booking system; ~ **de réserve** COM, GESTION plan B; ~ **de retrait systématique** BOURSE systematic withdrawal plan; ~ **de retraite basée sur les primes d'assurance** ASSUR benefit-based pension plan; ~ **de retraite financé par avance** FIN advance-funded pension plan (*UK*), PROT SOC, RES HUM advanced funded pension plan (*UK*); ~ **de retraite professionnelle de l'employeur** FISC, RES HUM employer's occupational pension scheme (*UK*); ~ **de sauvetage d'hypothèque** BANQUE, IMMOB mortgage rescue scheme (*UK*); ~ **de secours** COM contingency plan, fall-back, GESTION contingency plan; ~ **de souscription à des actions** BOURSE, RES HUM employee stock option plan, stock option plan; ~ **stratégique** COM strategic plan, strategic planning; ~ **sur titre fictif** BOURSE phantom stock plan; ~ **tactique** COM tactical plan, tactical planning; ~ **de travail** FIN, GESTION schedule; ~ **de trésorerie** COMPTA, FIN cash forecast; ~ **d'urgence** COM, GESTION contingency plan; ~ **de vérification** COMPTA, FIN audit work schedule; ◆ **sur le ~ international** COM at international level

Plan: ~ **Marshall** *m* ECON Marshall Plan; ~ **national** *m* POL National Plan (*UK*)

plancher *m* BOURSE, COM, ECON, FIN, IND bottom, bottom line, floor, lower limit; ~ **des prix** ECON price floor; ~ **des salaires** RES HUM wage floor; ~ **des taux** BANQUE, ECON, FIN rate floor

planchette *f* BANQUE planchette

planificateur: ~ **financier agréé** *m* FIN certified financial planner

planification *f* COM planning; ~ **administrative** *f* COM, GESTION business planning; ~ **de base** *f* BANQUE floor planning, flooring; ~ **des bénéfices** *f* FIN, GESTION profit planning; ~ **des bureaux** *f* ADMIN, COM office planning; ~ **d'une campagne de publicité** *f* MÉDIA, V&M account planning; ~ **centralisée** *f* GESTION central planning; ~ **à court terme** *f* COM, FIN, GESTION short-range planning, short-term planning; ~ **de distribution** *f* COM, TRANSP distribution planning; ~ **économique** *f* ECON, ENVIR, POL economic planning; ~ **des effectifs** *f* GESTION staff planning, RES HUM human resource planning, manpower planning, staff planning, HRP; ~ **de l'emploi** *f* RES HUM human resource planning, manpower planning, HRP; ~ **d'entreprise** *f* COM, GESTION organization planning; ~ **de l'entreprise** *f* COM company planning, corporate planning; ~ **du financement d'immobilisations** *f* FIN capital-funding planning; ~ **fiscale** *f* FISC tax planning; ~ **indicative** *f* ECON indicative planning (*jarg*); ~ **à long terme** *f* COM, FIN long-range planning, long-term planning; ~ **des opérations** *f* COM operational planning; ~ **de l'organisation** *f* COM, GESTION organization planning; ~ **préliminaire** *f* COM preplanning; ~ **de produit** *f* V&M product planning; ~**, programmation, budgétisation** *f pl* POL planning, programming, budgeting (*US*), PPB; ~ **du remplacement** *f* COMPTA replacement planning; ~ **des ressources humaines** *f* RES HUM human resource planning, manpower planning, HRP; ~ **stratégique d'entreprise** *f* GESTION corporate strategic planning, strategic planning; ~ **stratégique de l'impôt** *f* FISC strategic tax planning; ~ **des systèmes** *f* COM, INFO systems planning; ~ **à terme** *f* FIN forward planning; ~ **des ventes** *f* V&M sales planning; ~ **verticale** *f* COM vertical planning

planifier *vt* COM plan

planning *m* COM planning; ~ **des cabines** TRANSP *navigation* cabin allocation; ~ **de distribution** COM, TRANSP distribution planning; ~ **financier** FIN, GESTION financial planning; ~ **de la production** COM, GESTION, IND production planning

planque: **c'est la** ~ *loc infrml* COM it's a cushy number (*infrml*)

plans: ~ **comptables obligatoires** *m pl* COMPTA mandatory accounting plans; ~ **de remplacement** *m pl* GESTION management succession planning; ~ **de succession** *m pl* GESTION management succession planning

plantage *m* INFO crash

plantation *f* ECON, IND plantation; ~ **nationale** IND state-owned plantation

planter: **se** ~ *v pron infrml* INFO crash

plaque *f* COM *de porte* nameplate; ~ **d'accrochage de saisine** TRANSP *arrimage* lashing plate; ~ **d'accrochage de saisine rabattable** TRANSP folding lashing plate; ~ **de base** TRANSP breech base; ~ **indicatrice** TRANSP consolidated data plate, data plate

plaquer: **tout** ~ *loc infrml* RES HUM ankle (*jarg*)

plaquette: ~ **publicitaire** *f* MÉDIA, V&M tombstone ad (*jarg*)

plaquettes *f pl* COMPTA published accounts

plastique¹ *adj* ENVIR, IND plastic

plastique² *m* ENVIR, IND plastic; ~ **biodégradable** ENVIR biodegradable plastic

plat¹, **e** *adj* COM flat

plat:² ~ **tout préparé** *m* V&M convenience food

plate: ~ **-forme** *f* IND *pétrole*, INFO *matérielle, logicielle* platform, TRANSP *chemin de fer* flat car (*US*); ~ **-forme de chargement** *f* TRANSP tail lift; ~ **-forme de forage** *f* ENVIR, IND oil platform, oil rig; ~ **-forme pétrolière** *f* ENVIR, IND oil platform

plateau: ~ **de cargaison** *m* TRANSP cargo tray

platykurtique *m* MATH platykurtic

plein¹, **e** *adj* COM full; ◆ **à** ~ **régime** COM at full capacity; **à** ~ **rendement** COM at full capacity; ~ **d'avenir** COM up-and-coming; **de** ~ **droit** DROIT, RES HUM ex officio (*frml*); ~ **et chargé à ses marques** TRANSP *navigation* full and down; ~ **ouvert** TRANSP open full, OF

plein:² ~ **écran** *m* INFO full-screen; ~ **emploi** *m* ECON, POL full employment; ~ **propriétaire** *m* IMMOB freehold owner, freeholder; ~ **tarif** *m* LOISIRS adult fare, TRANSP adult fare, full fare

pleine: ~ **confiance et crédit** *f* BOURSE full faith and credit (*US*); ~ **garantie** *f* ASSUR full cover, full coverage; ~ **mer de vive-eau** *f* TRANSP *maritime* high-water ordinary spring tide, HWOST; ~ **mer de vive-eau moyenne** *f* (*PM de VE moyenne*) TRANSP *maritime* mean high water at springs (*MHWS*); ~ **page** *f* INFO full-screen; ~ **propriété** *f* IMMOB freehold, freehold property; ◆ **de** ~ **concurrence** COM, COMPTA, FISC arm's-length

plénier, -ère *adj* POL plenary

pléthore: ~ **de l'offre** *f* ECON oversupply

pli: ~ **accordéon** *m* MÉDIA, V&M *publicité* accordion folding

pluies: ~ **acides** *f pl* ENVIR acid rain

pluralisme *m* RES HUM pluralism

pluri: ~ **-annuel** *adj* COM multiyear

plus:¹ ~ **grand** *adj* COM greater, larger; ~ **riche** *adj* COM better-off

plus² *adv* COM *avantage* plus; **au** ~ **tard** COM at the latest; ~ **bas** (*ANT plus haut*) COMMS below; **de** ~ COMMS further; **de** ~ **en plus** COM increasingly; ~ **haut** (*ANT plus bas*) COMMS above; **le** ~ **élevé** COM top of the tree (*infrml*); ~ **ou moins** COM more or less

plus:³ ~ **amples renseignements** *m pl* COM further

information; ~ **haut niveau** *m* COM peak rate; **les ~ gros investisseurs** *m pl* BOURSE the largest investors; ~ **offrant** *m* BOURSE highest bidder, COM best profferer, highest bidder; ~ **petit dénominateur commun** *m* COM lowest common denominator, LCD

plus:[4] ~ **-value** *f* COMPTA appreciated surplus, capital gain, surplus, holding gain, *de bien* appreciation, DROIT unearned premium, ECON capital gain, FIN capital gain, capital profit, increase in value, increased value, iv, unearned increment, unearned premium, FISC appreciation, IMMOB appreciation, betterment; ~ **-value absolue** *f* ECON absolute surplus value; ~ **-value de capital** *f* ECON, FIN capital appreciation; ~ **-value constatée par expertise** *f* COM, COMPTA appraisal increment; ~ **-value éventuelle** *f* BOURSE potential profit; ~ **-value foncière** *f* FIN, IMMOB unearned increment of land; ~ **-value globale** *f* ECON absolute surplus value; ~ **-value imposable** *f* FISC taxable capital gain; ~ **-value imposée** *f* COMPTA, ECON, FIN, FISC taxed capital gain; ~ **-value à long-terme** *f* FISC long-term gain; ~ **-value nette réalisée par action** *f* BOURSE net realized capital gains per share; ~ **-value de prime** *f* FISC unearned premium; ~ **-value relative** *f* ECON relative surplus value, surplus value; ~ **-value sur la réalisation d'actifs immobilisés** *f* FIN capital profit

plus:[5] **la ~ basse entre le coût d'entrée et la valeur actuelle** *loc* COMPTA lower of cost or market; **le ~ que vous puissiez perdre** *loc* BOURSE the most you can lose; **le ~ tôt possible** *loc* COM, COMMS a.s.a.p., as soon as possible; **pour ~ de sûreté** *loc* COM to be on the safe side

plus[6] *prép* COM, MATH plus; ◆ **avec ~ ou moins de** COM with varying degrees of; **de ~ de** (ANT *de moins de*) COM *âge, poids, quantité* above; **en ~ de** COM in addition to

plusieurs: **à ~ étages** *adj* IMMOB multistorey

PLV *abrév (publicité sur le lieu de vente)* MÉDIA *publicité*, V&M point-of-sale advertising, point-of-sale promotion

PM: ~ **de VE moyenne** *abrév (pleine mer de vive-eau moyenne)* TRANSP *maritime* MHWS *(mean high water at springs)*

PMA *abrév (pays moins avancé)* COM, ECON, POL developing country, LDC *(less developed country)*

PME[1] *abrév (petites et moyennes entreprises)* COM SME *(small and medium-sized enterprises)*

PME:[2] ~ **existante** *f* COM existing SME

PMH *abrév (point mort haut)* TRANSP TDC *(top dead center AmE, top dead centre BrE)*

PMI *abrév (petites et moyennes industries)* COM SMME *(small and medium-sized manufacturing companies)*

PMTS *abrév (méthode des temps prédéterminés)* ECON, FIN, GESTION PMTS *(predetermined motion time system)*

PNB[1] *abrév (produit national brut)* ECON GNP *(gross national product)*

PNB:[2] ~ **augmenté** *m (PNBA)* ECON, POL augmented GNP *(AGNP)*

PNBA *abrév (PNB augmenté)* ECON, POL AGNP *(augmented GNP)*

pneu *m* TRANSP tire *(AmE)*, tyre *(BrE)*

PNN *abrév (produit national net)* ECON n.n.p. *(net national product)*

p.o. *abrév (par ordre)* COM by order

poche *f* ECON pocket; ◆ **en être de sa ~** COM be out of pocket

pochette *f* INFO jacket

pognon *m infrml* COM bread *(infrml)*, FIN wampum *(US, infrml)*

poids *m* COM weight, FISC burden, INFO, MATH weight, TRANSP weight, wgt; ~ **brut** *m* COM g, gr.wt., gross weight; ~ **de calcul** *m* TRANSP *aviation* design weight; ~ **de cargaison** *m* TRANSP weight of cargo; ~ **du commerce** *m* COM avdp., avoirdupois; ~ **constaté** *m* COM weight ascertained; ~ **constructeur** *m* TRANSP *véhicule* design weight; ~ **de la dette** *m* ECON, POL debt burden; ~ **d'équilibre** *m* TRANSP break-even weight; ~ **de l'essieu** *m* COM axle weight; ~ **et mesures** *m pl* COM weights and measures; ~ **garanti** *m* TRANSP *gestion des stocks* weight guaranteed, wg; ~ **de l'impôt** *m* ECON tax burden, FISC tax burden, tax load; ~ **juste** *m* COM full weight; ~ **lourd** *m* TRANSP heavy goods vehicle, road haulage vehicle, HGV, RHV; ~ **des marchandises** *m* TRANSP weight of cargo; ~ **maximal d'un train routier** *m* TRANSP gross train weight, GTW; ~ **maximal d'un véhicule articulé** *m* TRANSP gross combination weight, GCW; ~ **-média** *m* MÉDIA, V&M media weight; ~ **mort** *m* COM dead load; ~ **net** *m* COM net weight; ~ **en ordre de marche** *m* TRANSP *véhicule* kerb weight; ~ **des pertes** *m* COM burden of losses; ~ **pivot** *m* TRANSP *aviation* pivot weight; ~ **de la preuve** *m* DROIT burden of proof; ~ **prévu** *m* TRANSP *véhicule routier* design weight; ~ **à sec** *m* TRANSP dry weight; ~ **spécifique** *m* COM specific gravity, SG; ~ **total en charge** *m (PTC)* TRANSP *véhicule routier* gross vehicle weight *(GVW)*; ~ **transitaire** *m* TRANSP shipper weight, SW; ~ **troy** *m* COM troy weight; ~ **du véhicule à vide** *m* TRANSP vehicle unladen weight; ~ **à vide** *m* COM tare weight, unladen weight, weight when empty, TRANSP tare weight, unladen weight; ~ **à vide de la remorque** *m* COM trailer unladen weight; ◆ **de ~** COM forceful; **donner du ~ à** COM *argument* lend weight to; ~ **et capacité à charge complète** TRANSP *conteneur* full loaded weight and capacity, FWC; ~ **et/ou cubage à l'avantage du navire** TRANSP weight and/or measurements at ship's option, W/M; ~ **ou cubage** TRANSP *tarif* weight/measurement

poignée *f* INFO handle

point *m* BOURSE point, COM item, point, FIN point *(US)*, INFO dot, MATH point, MÉDIA news roundup, POL plank; ~ **d'accès** INFO access, port, TRANSP *aviation* gateway; ~ **d'accès international** TRANSP *aviation* international gateway; ~ **d'ancrage soudé** TRANSP *sur un navire* fixed lashing plate; ~ **d'appui** COM fulcrum; ~ **d'arrêt** COM sticking point, INFO breakpoint, TRANSP break point, break weight; ~ **bas** BOURSE, COM low, ECON bottom, low, *d'un graphe, d'une courbe* trough; ~ **de base** BOURSE, FIN, MATH basis point; ~ **butoir** ECON cutoff point; ~ **-cadeau** V&M coupon; ~ **central** COM *débat* focal point, POL, V&M focus group; ~ **chaud** MÉDIA, POL front line *(jarg)*; ~ **de combustion en degrés Celsius** COM FP-°C, flash point in degrees centigrade; ~ **de combustion en degrés fahrenheit** COM FP-°F, flash point in degrees fahrenheit; ~ **de combustion spontanée** COM spontaneous ignition temperature; ~ **de comparaison** COM baseline; ~ **de contrôle** INFO, TRANSP checkpoint; ~ **critique** ECON, IMP/EXP peril point; ~ **décisif** COM turning point; ~ **de déclenchement** COM trigger point; ~ **de départ** COM starting point, IMP/EXP point of departure; ~ **de discussion** POL bargaining chip *(infrml)*; ~ **de droit** DROIT point of law; ~ **d'ébullition initial** COM initial boiling point; ~ **d'équilibre** BOURSE, COM, COMPTA, ECON, FIN, IMMOB break-even point; ~ **essentiel** COM key point; ~ **d'exportation** IMP/EXP point of export; ~ **fixe du saisissage** TRANSP *arrimage* lashing point; ~ **focal** COM focus; ~ **d'impact** COM ground zero; ~ **d'indice** BOURSE index point; ~ **d'interrogation clignotant** INFO blinking question mark; ~ **d'interruption** INFO breakpoint; ~ **en litige** DROIT issue; ~ **mort** BOURSE, COM, COMPTA, ECON, FIN break-even point, GESTION break-even quantity, IMMOB break-even point, IND break-even quantity; ~ **mort à la baisse** BOURSE downside break-even, downside break-even point; ~ **mort haut** *(PMH)* TRANSP top dead center *(AmE)*, top dead centre *(BrE)* *(TDC)*; ~ **mort en quantité** ECON break-even quantity; ~ **mort vers le haut** BOURSE upside break-even, upside break-even point; ~ **noir** COM trouble spot; ~ **d'or** COM gold point, specie point; ~ **de pourcentage** FIN percentage point; ~ **de ralliement** COM, TRANSP rallying point; ~ **de référence** COM bench mark; ~ **de repère** COM bench mark, reference point, landmark, DROIT landmark; ~ **de reprise** INFO *d'un programme* checkpoint; ~ **de rosée** COM dew point; ~ **de satisfaction maximale** ECON, PROT SOC bliss point; ~ **de saturation** COM, V&M saturation point; ~ **de vente** V&M outlet, outlet store, V&M *(PV)* point of sale *(POS)*; ~ **de vente électronique** COM electronic point of sale, EPOS; ~ **de vente de services de détail** V&M retail outlet; ~ **-virgule** COM semicolon; ~ **de vue** COM point of view, position, viewpoint; ~ **de vue administratif** ADMIN administrative point of view, APV; ♦ **avoir gagné un ~** BOURSE be a one point winner; **du ~ de vue de l'emploi** RES HUM on the employment front; **du ~ de vue ergonomique** INFO ergonomically; **du ~ de vue historique** COM historically; **faire le ~ d'un compte** COMPTA reconcile an account

pointage *m* RES HUM clocking-in; ~ **des emplacements disponibles** V&M *publicité* available sites list

pointe:[1] **de ~** *adj* INFO state-of-the-art

pointe[2] *f* BOURSE spike *(jarg)*; ~ **de puissance** IND, INFO power surge; ♦ **à la ~** IND at the forefront; **à la ~ du progrès** COM in the vanguard of progress, state-of-the-art

pointer *vi* IND, RES HUM punch the time clock, TRANSP *chargement, déchargement d'un navire* tally; ♦ ~ **en arrivant** IND clock in, clock on, RES HUM clock in, clock on, sign in; ~ **en sortant** IND, RES HUM clock off, clock out, sign off

pointeur *m* INFO pointer, RES HUM checker, tally clerk, TRANSP tally clerk

pointillés *m pl* ADMIN, MÉDIA points of suspension

points: ~ **divers** *m pl* COM any other business, AOB; ~ **expressément formulés** *m pl* RES HUM express terms; ~ **par pouce** *m pl (ppp)* INFO dots per inch *(dpi)*; ~ **de suspension** *m pl* ADMIN, MÉDIA points of suspension; ♦ ~ **sur lesquels il convient de revenir** *loc* COM matters to be followed up

polarisation *f* COMMS, FIN polarization

pôle: ~ **de croissance** *m* ECON, IND growth pole

polémique *f* COM controversy

poli, e *adj* COM polite

police *f* DROIT police, police force, INFO, MÉDIA font; ~ **d'abonnement** ASSUR floating policy, open policy, open-cargo insurance policy, OP, TRANSP open policy, open-cargo insurance policy, OP; ~ **annulable** ASSUR voidable policy; ~ **d'assurance** ASSUR insurance policy; ~ **d'assurance contre le manque à gagner** ASSUR profits policy; ~ **d'assurance hypothèque** ASSUR mortgage insurance policy; ~ **d'assurance incendie accidents risques divers** ASSUR property and casualty policy insuring agreement; ~ **d'assurance maritime** ASSUR, TRANSP marine insurance policy, MIP; ~ **d'assurance mixte** ASSUR mixed policy; ~ **d'assurance sur la vie** ASSUR life insurance policy; ~ **d'assurance temporaire** ASSUR term insurance policy; ~ **d'assurance tiers** ASSUR third-party insurance policy; ~ **d'assurance tous risques** ASSUR comprehensive insurance policy, fully comprehensive insurance policy; ~ **d'assurance-vie** ASSUR life assurance policy; ~ **d'assurance-vie agréée** ASSUR registered life insurance policy; ~ **d'assurance-vie entière** ASSUR straight life insurance policy, whole life insurance policy; ~ **d'assurance-vie indexée sur le cours des valeurs boursières** BOURSE equity-linked policy; ~ **avec participation aux bénéfices** ASSUR participating policy; ~ **de base** ASSUR master policy *(US)*; ~ **de caractères** ADMIN typeface, INFO font, type font, typeface, MÉDIA font, typeface; ~ **de caractères qualité courrier** INFO letter-quality fonts; ~ **de caractères téléchangeable** INFO downloadable font; **~ de catastrophe** ASSUR catastrophe policy; **~ contre catastrophe** ASSUR catastrophe policy; **~ commerciale** *f* ASSUR commercial form; **~ contre le vol intérieur** ASSUR interior robbery policy; **~ évaluée** ASSUR valued policy; **~ flottante** ASSUR, TRANSP floating cargo policy, floating marine policy, open policy, open-cargo insurance policy, FP, OP; **~ flotte** ASSUR fleet policy; **~ forfaitaire** ASSUR block policy; **~ de fret** ASSUR freight policy; **~ globale** ASSUR blanket policy; **~ imprimante** INFO printer font; **~ incendie normalisée** ASSUR standard fire policy *(US)*; **~ incendie type** ASSUR standard fire policy *(US)*; **~ de justification d'intérêt** ASSUR PPI policy, policy proof of interest, PPI; **~ limitée** ASSUR limited policy; **~ maritime flottante** ASSUR, TRANSP *navigation* floating cargo policy, floating marine policy, open policy, open-cargo insurance policy, FP, OP; **~ multirisque** ASSUR comprehensive insurance policy; **~ multirisque spéciale** ASSUR special multiperil insurance, SMP; **~ non-évaluée** ASSUR unvalued policy; **~ nulle** ASSUR void policy; **~ ouverte** ASSUR open cover, OC; **~ payée intégralement** ASSUR fully-paid policy; **~ perte d'exploitation** ASSUR business interruption insurance, business interruption policy; **~ pertes indirectes** ASSUR consequential-loss policy, *assurance de dommages* pay as cargo; **~ pertes indirectes sur facultés** ASSUR pay as cargo; **~ au porteur** FISC policy to bearer; **~ preuve de l'intérêt assuré** ASSUR PPI policy, policy proof of interest, PPI; **~ pour propriétaires d'entreprise** ASSUR business owner's policy; **~ provisoire** ASSUR binder *(US)*, cover note, provisional policy, CN; **~ de rente individuelle** ASSUR individual annuity policy; **~ de la responsabilité civile des propriétaires et des locataires** ASSUR owners' landlords' and tenants' liability policy; **~ revenu familial garanti** ASSUR family income policy; **~ risque énuméré** ASSUR named peril policy; **~ aux risques désignés** ASSUR named peril policy; **~ sans effet légal** DROIT honor policy *(AmE)*, honour policy *(BrE)*; **~ à taille variable** INFO, MÉDIA variable-size font; **~ tarifée** ASSUR rated policy; **~ à temps** ASSUR time policy; **~ à terme** ASSUR, BANQUE term policy; **~ tous riques d'argent et des valeurs** ASSUR money and securities broad-form policy; **~ en valeur agrée** ASSUR valued policy; **~ vie modifiée** ASSUR modified life insurance; **~ au voyage** ASSUR voyage policy

Police: **~ de l'Air et des Frontières** *f (P.A.F.)* RES HUM border police

politique[1] *adj* COM, POL political

politique[2] *f* COM, ECON, GESTION, POL policy; **~ d'acquisition** BOURSE acquisition policy; **~ agricole** ECON, ENVIR, POL agricultural policy, farm policy; **~ d'ajustement structurel** ECON structural adjustment policy; **~ anti-discriminatoire** *(SYN discrimination positive, mesures anti-discriminatoires)* POL, PROT SOC, RES HUM *à l'embauche* affirmative action

(AmE), positive action *(BrE)*, positive discrimination *(BrE)*; **~ de l'argent à bon marché** BANQUE cheap money policy; **~ de l'argent cher** ECON tight monetary policy; **~ d'argent facile** ECON easy money policy; **~ attentiste** ECON wait-and-see policy; **~ budgétaire** ECON budgetary policy, fiscal policy, FISC fiscal policy, POL budgetary policy, fiscal policy; **~ commerciale** COM, ECON, GESTION, IMP/EXP, POL business policy, commercial policy, trade policy; **~ commune** COM, POL common policy; **~ comptable** COMPTA, FIN accounting policy; **~ conjoncturelle** ECON stabilization policy; **~ contractuelle** RES HUM Social Contract *(UK)*, voluntarism *(jarg)*; **~ contractuelle en matière de salaires** RES HUM bargaining theory of wages; **~ du coup de force** POL power politics; **~ des coups d'accordéon** ECON stop-go policy *(UK)*; **~ de crédit** COM credit policy; **~ du crédit à bon marché** BANQUE cheap money policy; **~ de défense du consommateur** COM consumer policy; **~ de déficit budgétaire** FISC compensatory fiscal policy; **~ démographique** ECON, POL population policy; **~ de développement** POL development policy; **~ déviationniste** GESTION deviation policy; **~ dictée par les besoins de la clientèle** V&M client-led marketing policy; **~ dictée par les besoins des consommateurs** V&M consumer-led marketing policy; **~ discrétionnaire** ECON, POL discretionary policy; **~ de distribution** COM, TRANSP distribution policy; **~ de dividendes** BOURSE, FIN dividend policy; **~ dynamiquement incohérente** POL dynamically inconsistent policy; **~ économique des ressources et de l'environnement** ECON resource economics; **~ d'écrémage** V&M *marketing* skimming policy; **~ de l'égalité des chances** RES HUM Equal Opportunity Policy *(EOP) (UK)*; **~ de l'égalité de traitement** RES HUM Equal Opportunity Policy *(UK)*, EOP *(UK)*; **~ à l'égard des remises de dettes** COM remittance policy; **~ de l'emploi** POL labor market policy *(AmE)*, labour market policy *(BrE)*; **~ d'encadrement du crédit** ECON tight monetary policy; **~ énergétique** COM, POL energy policy; **~ de l'énergie** COM, POL energy policy; **~ d'entreprise** ECON technical policy; **~ de l'entreprise** COM company policy, corporate policy; **~ de l'environnement** ENVIR, POL environment policy, environmental policy; **~ environnementale** ENVIR, POL environmental policy; **~ de l'escarpolette** ECON stop-go policy *(UK)*; **~ d'expédients** POL practical politics; **~ extérieure** ECON, POL external government policy; **~ financière** FIN financial policy; **~ fiscale** ECON, FISC, POL fiscal policy, tax policy; **~ fiscale discrétionnaire** ECON, FISC discretionary fiscal policy; **~ fiscale restrictive** FISC tight fiscal policy; **~ fiscale serrée** FISC tight fiscal policy; **~ de la force** POL machtpolitik *(jarg)*; **~ générale de l'entreprise** COM, ECON, GESTION business policy; **~ de gestion** COM, ECON, GESTION business policy; **~ du gros bâton** POL policy of the big stick;

~ **d'immigration** DROIT, POL immigration policy; ~ **d'immobilisation** COMPTA fixed asset policy; ~ **industrielle** ECON, IND industrial policy; ~ **intérieure** ECON, POL internal policy; ~ **d'intimidation** POL power politics; ~ **d'investissement** BOURSE, ECON, FIN, POL investment policy; ~ **keynésienne** ECON, POL Keynesian policy; **la ~ agricole commune** *(PAC)* ECON, POL *UE* the Common Agricultural Policy *(CAP)*; ~ **de limitation de l'expansion** POL *du communisme* containment; ~ **macroéconomique** ECON, POL macroeconomic policy; ~ **de la main d'oeuvre** RES HUM manpower policy; ~ **de marketing** V&M marketing policy; ~ **en matière de technique** ECON technical policy; ~ **monétaire** ECON, FIN, POL monetary policy; ~ **monétaire restrictive** ECON restrictive monetary policy, tight monetary policy; ~ **de non-intervention** COM, ECON hands-off policy; ~ **des organisations** POL organizational politics; ~ **du parti** POL party line; ~ **du personnel** RES HUM personnel policy; ~ **des petits pas** *infrml* POL gradualism; ~ **de la porte ouverte** COM, GESTION, POL open-door policy; ~ **du possible** POL possibilism; ~ **de prêt** BANQUE lending policy; ~ **de prêts bancaires** BANQUE, ECON bank lending policy; ~ **de prise en compte globale** ENVIR bubble policy; ~ **des prix** ECON, FIN price control, price supervision, prices policy, profit squeeze, public pricing, V&M pricing policy, pricing strategy, *par le producteur ou le distributeur* price control, price supervision, prices policy, public pricing; ~ **de prix agressive** V&M aggressive pricing; ~ **de prix différentiels** ECON differential pricing; ~ **de prix d'écrémage** V&M prestige pricing; ~ **des prix et des revenus** ECON, POL prices and incomes policy; ~ **de prix de pénétration par la base** V&M penetration pricing; ~ **de promotion** COM, V&M promotional policy; ~ **de promotion agressive** V&M hard sell tactics; ~ **de providence** POL popularism *(jarg)*; ~ **de prudence** BANQUE prudent policy; ~ **publicitaire** V&M advertising policy; ~ **de rachat** FIN, FISC retirement annuity policy *(UK)*; ~ **régionale** ECON, IND regional policy, spatial equalization; ~ **règlementaire** RES HUM statutory policy *(UK)*; ~ **de relance par le déficit budgétaire** COMPTA deficit spending policy; ~ **de la rémunération des services** ADMIN fee-for-service policy; ~ **de resserrement budgétaire** FISC tight fiscal policy; ~ **de resserrement des dépenses** ECON tight fiscal policy; ~ **des revenus** ECON, FIN, RES HUM incomes policy, pay policy, wage policy, wages policy; ~ **salariale** POL, RES HUM incomes policy, pay policy, wage policy, wages policy; ~ **salariale des syndicats** RES HUM union wage policy; ~ **sociale** COM social policy; ~ **de soutien** ECON pump priming; ~ **de vente** COM, V&M sales policy, selling policy; ~ **des ventes** COM, ECON, GESTION business policy; ~ **de versement des dividendes** BOURSE, FIN dividend policy; ~ **vis-à-vis de la concurrence** POL, V&M competition policy; ~ **visant à l'affaiblissement du voisin** COM beggar-my-neighbor

policy *(AmE)*, beggar-my-neighbour policy *(BrE)*; ~ **volontariste en matière de revenus** RES HUM voluntary policy

politiquement *adv* COM, POL politically

politiser *vt* POL politicize

polluant:[1] **peu ~** *adj* ENVIR low-polluting

polluant[2] *m* ENVIR pollutant; ~ **atmosphérique** ENVIR air pollutant; ~ **des eaux** ENVIR water pollutant

pollué, e *adj* ENVIR, IND polluted

polluer *vt* ENVIR, IND contaminate

pollueur, -euse *m,f* ENVIR polluter

pollution *f* ENVIR contamination, pollution; ~ **atmosphérique** ENVIR air pollution; ~ **des côtes** ENVIR coastal pollution; ~ **côtière** ENVIR coastal pollution; ~ **des cours d'eau** ENVIR river pollution; ~ **diffuse** ENVIR background pollution; ~ **des eaux** ENVIR water pollution; ~ **de fond** ENVIR background pollution; ~ **du littoral** ENVIR coastal pollution; ~ **marine** ENVIR marine pollution; ~ **par les hydrocarbures** ENVIR, IND oil pollution; ~ **par les neiges acides** ENVIR acid snow pollution; ~ **par le pétrole** ENVIR, IND oil pollution; ~ **par les pluies acides** ENVIR acid rain pollution; ~ **par les rayonnements** ENVIR radiation pollution; ~ **radioactive** ENVIR radioactive pollution

Pollution: ~ **maritime** *f (MARPOL)* ENVIR Maritime Pollution *(MARPOL)*

Pologne *f* COM Poland

polonais[1]**, e** *adj* COM Polish

polonais[2] *m* COM *langue* Polish

Polonais, e *m,f* COM *habitant* Pole

polycentrisme *m* POL polycentrism

polycopie *f* COM manifold

polycopier *vt* ADMIN stencil

polyculture *f* ECON mixed farming

polyglotte *adj* COM multilingual

polygone: ~ **de fréquence** *m* MATH frequency polygon

polyvalence *f* INFO versatility, RES HUM dual skilling, functional flexibility, multiskilling; ~ **de la production** ECON, IND economy of scope

polyvalent, e *adj* COM all-purpose

ponction: ~ **fiscale** *f* FISC tax take

ponctionnement: ~ **des réserves** *m* ECON draining reserves

ponctualité *f* COM, TRANSP punctuality

ponctuel, -elle *adj* COM, TRANSP *chargement* prompt

pondération *f* BOURSE *d'un portefeuille* indexing, FIN, MATH, V&M weighting; ~ **du risque** FIN risk weighting

pondérer *vt* BOURSE weight

pont *m* TRANSP *d'un navire* deck, DK; **à ~ unique** TRANSP *navire* single-deck; ~ **-abri** TRANSP *d'un navire* S d/k, shelter deck; ~ **-abri fermé** TRANSP *d'un navire* closed shelter deck, CSD; ~ **-abri surélevé** TRANSP *d'un navire* raised shelter deck,

RSD; ~ **aérien** TRANSP airlift; ~ **arrière surélevé** TRANSP *navigation* raised afterdeck, RAD; ~ **-bascule** TRANSP *marchandises* weighbridge; ~ **découvert** TRANSP *d'un navire* open deck, weather deck; ~ **doublé de teck** TRANSP *d'un navire* teak-sheathed deck; ~ **exposé** TRANSP *d'un navire* weather deck; ~ **inférieur** TRANSP *d'un avion, navire* lower deck; ~ **ouvert** TRANSP *d'un navire* open deck; ~ **à péage** TRANSP toll bridge; ~ **promenade** TRANSP *d'un navire* prom dk, promenade deck; ~ **ras** TRANSP *d'un navire* flush deck; ~ **supérieur** TRANSP *d'un navire* Udk, upper deck; ~ **surélevé** TRANSP *d'un navire* Rdk, raised deck; ~ **-tente** TRANSP *d'un navire* Adk, awning deck, AWD; ~ **terrestre** TRANSP landbridge; ~ **de tonnage** TRANSP *d'un navire* tonnage deck; ~ **wagons** TRANSP *transbordeur* train ferry deck; ◆ **faire le** ~ COM take an extra day off; **faire un** ~ **d'or à qn** RES HUM pay sb a fortune; **sur le** ~ *(ANT sous le pont)* TRANSP *navigation* above deck, A/D

pontée *f* TRANSP *navigation* deck cargo, deck load; ◆ **en** ~ TRANSP *cargaison* above deck, A/D

pontet: ~ **d'hiloire** *m* TRANSP *navigation, fixation des conteneurs* coaming bridge fitting; ~ **en os de chien** *m* TRANSP *manutention* dog bone bridge

ponton *m* TRANSP *maritime* hulk, pon, pontoon; ~ **-grue** TRANSP *maritime* floating crane

ponts: ~ **et chaussées** *m pl* COM, IND structural engineering

pool *m* ADMIN *dactylos*, ASSUR, BOURSE, ECON, FIN pool; ~ **bancaire** BANQUE, FIN consortium of banks

pop: ~ **-up** *m jarg* V&M pop-up *(jarg)*

populaire *adj* COM popular

population *f* ECON, V&M population; ~ **active** ECON, IND labor force *(AmE)*, labour force *(BrE)*, RES HUM active population; ~ **adulte** COM adult population; ~ **de droit** ECON de jure population; ~ **de facto** ECON de facto population; ~ **de fait** ECON de facto population; ~ **fermée** *(ANT population ouverte)* ECON closed population; ~ **de jure** ECON de jure population; ~ **optimale** ECON, PROT SOC optimum population; ~ **ouverte** *(ANT population fermée)* ECON open population; ~ **ouvrière** RES HUM working population; ~ **résidente** ECON resident population; ~ **-seuil** ECON threshold population; ~ **vieillissante** ECON ageing population *(BrE)*, aging population *(AmE)*

port *m* TRANSP port, *maritime* harbor *(AmE)*, harbour *(BrE)*; ~ **d'accès** *m* INFO port; ~ **d'aéroglisseurs** *m* TRANSP *maritime* hoverport; ~ **d'armement** *m* TRANSP port of registry; ~ **d'arrivée** *m* IMP/EXP port of arrival, port of entry, TRANSP port of arrival, port of entry, *navigation* destination port; ~ **d'attache** *m* TRANSP port of registry; ~ **autonome** *m* TRANSP self-governing port; ~ **de charge** *m* TRANSP port of shipment; ~ **de chargement** *m* IMP/EXP port of loading, TRANSP lading port, load port, port of

loading, shipping port; ~ **de commerce** *m* TRANSP commercial port, trading port, *navigation* commercial dock, CD; ~ **de conteneurs** *m* TRANSP container port; ~ **de déchargement** *m* IMP/EXP port of discharge, TRANSP discharge port, port of discharge; ~ **de destination** *m* IMP/EXP, TRANSP port of destination; ~ **direct** *m* TRANSP *navigation* direct port, DP; ~ **dû** *m* *(p.d.)* COM, TRANSP carriage forward, freight forward *(frt fwd)*; ~ **en eau profonde** *m* TRANSP *navigation* deepwater harbor *(AmE)*, deepwater harbour *(BrE)*; ~ **d'embarquement** *m* COM embarkation port, TRANSP lading port; ~ **entrepôt** *m* IMP/EXP free port; ~ **et emballage** *m pl* COMMS p&p, postage and packing; ~ **fermé** *m* TRANSP *maritime* enclosed port; ~ **franc** *m* IMP/EXP free port; ~ **intérieur** *m* TRANSP *maritime* inner harbor *(AmE)*, inner harbour *(BrE)*; ~ **en lourd** *m* COM dead weight, TRANSP *(PL) d'un navire* dead weight, deadweight capacity, deadweight cargo capacity, deadweight tonnage *(DWT)*; ~ **en lourd total** *m* TRANSP *d'un navire* deadweight all told, DWAT; ~ **à marée** *m* TRANSP open port; ~ **maritime** *m* TRANSP sea port, seaport; ~ **de mer** *m* TRANSP sea port, seaport; ~ **ouvert au commerce international** *m* TRANSP treaty port *(dat)*; ~ **payé** *m* *(p.p.)* COM, COMMS post-paid, postage paid, prepaid *(p.p.)*, ≈ Business Reply Mail® *(AmE)*, ≈ Freepost® *(BrE)*, TRANSP *marchandises* carriage paid *(carr pd)*, freight prepaid; ~ **de pêche** *m* ECON, IND fishing port; ~ **de refuge** *m* IMP/EXP, TRANSP port of necessity; ~ **série** *m* INFO serial port; ~ **de soutage** *m* TRANSP *navigation* bunker port; ~ **sûr** *m* TRANSP safe port; ◆ ~ **et assurance payés jusqu'à** IMP/EXP *lieu de destination* carriage and insurance paid to, CIP; ~ **payé assurance comprise jusqu'à** IMP/EXP carriage and insurance paid to, CIP; ~ **payé jusqu'à** IMP/EXP *lieu nommé de destination* carriage paid to, CPT; ~ **à port** IMP/EXP, TRANSP p to p, port to port

Port: ~ **-au-Prince** *n pr* COM Port-au-Prince; ~ **Louis** *n pr* COM Port Louis; ~ **Moresby** *n pr* COM Port Moresby; ~ **of Spain** *n pr* COM Port of Spain

portabilité *f* INFO portability

portable[1] *adj* INFO laptop, portable

portable[2] *m* INFO laptop, portable, portable computer

portage *m* INFO porting

portant: ~ **intérêt** *adj* BANQUE, COMPTA interest-bearing

portatif, -ive *adj* ADMIN *machine à écrire* portable, INFO hand-held

porte:[1] ~ **à porte** *adj* TRANSP door-to-door

porte:[2] ~ **-barges** *m* TRANSP *navigation* Baco Liner, barge carrier, barge-carrying vessel, lighter aboard ship, lighter carrier, BCV, LASH; ~ **-barils,** *m* TRANSP barrel handler; ~ **-conteneurs** *m* TRANSP *navigation* container ship; ~ **-conteneurs entièrement cellulaire** *m*

TRANSP cellular container ship, fully cellular container ship, FCC; ~ -**étiquettes** *m* COM price marker; ~ -**monnaie** *m* ECON pocket; ~ -**parole** *m* MÉDIA spokesperson; ~ **à porte** *m* V&M door-to-door selling

porte:[3] ~ **coupe-feu** *f* RES HUM fire door; ~ **à dépôt** *f* TRANSP door-to-depot; ~ **d'embarquement** *f* LOISIRS, TRANSP boarding gate; ~ **d'entrée** *f* TRANSP *aviation* gateway; ~ **d'entrée internationale** *f* TRANSP *aviation* international gateway; ~ **d'imprimante** *f* INFO printer port; ~ **LCL** *f* TRANSP LCL door

porté: ~ **au crédit de** *loc* FIN credited to

portée *f* BREVETS scope; ~ **de commandement** *f* GESTION, RES HUM chain of command; ~ **et fréquence** *f pl* V&M *publicité* reach and frequency; ~ **du plancher** *f* TRANSP *navigation* floor bearing; ~ **statistique** *f* MATH statistical spread; ♦ **à la ~ de tous** COM accessible; **d'une ~ considérable** COM far-reaching; **être à ~ de main** COM be within reach

portefeuille *m* BOURSE, COM, POL portfolio; ~ **d'actifs** BOURSE, FIN asset portfolio; ~ **d'actions** BANQUE trading portfolio, BOURSE equity holdings, stock portfolio, trading portfolio, FIN stock portfolio; ~ **d'activités** BOURSE, COM, ECON, FIN business portfolio; ~ **d'affaires portant intérêt** BOURSE interest-bearing trading portfolio; ~ **effets** BANQUE bill holding, bill portfolio; ~ **effets de change** BANQUE bill holding, bill portfolio; ~ **efficient** BOURSE efficient portfolio; ~ **équilibré** BOURSE, FIN balanced portfolio; ~ **hypothécaire** BANQUE mortgage portfolio; ~ **d'investissement** BANQUE, BOURSE, FIN investment portfolio; ~ **d'investissement à court terme** BOURSE short-term investment portfolio; ~ **de marques** BOURSE, FIN, V&M brand portfolio; ~ **de négociation** FIN *d'un établissement* trading book; ~ **d'obligations** BOURSE bond portfolio; ~ **des prêts** BANQUE loan portfolio; ~ **des prêts hypothécaires** BANQUE mortgage portfolio; ~ **de produits** BOURSE, FIN, V&M product portfolio; ~ **de titres** BOURSE securities portfolio; ~ **de valeurs portant intérêt** BOURSE interest-bearing trading portfolio

porter 1. *vt* COM *toast* propose, COMPTA post, DROIT lay; ~ **au compte de** V&M charge; **2.** *vti* ~ **sur** COM be concentrated on; ♦ ~ **un coup très dur à l'économie** ECON throw a wrench into the economy (*infrml*); ~ **la date du** COM bear the date; ~ **au débit d'un compte** COM charge to an account; ~ **une écriture** COMPTA post an entry; ~ **indûment préjudice** FISC *à contribuable* cause undue hardship; ~ **un intérêt de** COMPTA bear an interest of; ~ **plainte contre qn** DROIT bring an accusation against sb; ~ **en réduction sur** COM charge against; ~ **au revenu** COMPTA add to income; **se ~ aval pour qn** FIN stand as guarantor for sb; **se ~ candidat à un poste** COM apply for a job; **se ~ caution pour qn** BANQUE stand surety for sb; **se ~ contrepartiste** BOURSE make a mar-ket; **se ~ garant de** COM answer for, vouch for, attest to; **se ~ garant de qn** BANQUE stand surety for sb, COM stand as guarantor for sb; ~ **son attention à** COM turn one's attention to; ~ **sur un compte** COMPTA post

portes: ~ **ouvertes** *f pl* IMMOB open day (*BrE*), open house (*AmE*)

porteur:[1] ~ **d'une notation** *adj* COM notational

porteur[2]**, -euse** *m,f* BANQUE bearer, BOURSE bearer, *de titres d'une société* holder of record, FIN bearer, carrier, FISC bearer; ~ **d'actions** BOURSE equity holder; **au ~** BOURSE, FIN bearer form; ~ **de bonne foi** DROIT holder in due course; ~ **de carte** BANQUE, COM cardholder; ~ **de débentures** BOURSE bona fide holder, debenture holder; ~ **de droits de souscription** BOURSE rights holder; ~ **d'obligations** BOURSE bondholder; ~ **d'obligations non garanties** BOURSE debenture holder; ~ **de titres** BOURSE security holder; ~ **de valeurs** BOURSE security holder

porteuse *f* INFO carrier

portier, -ière *m,f* LOISIRS *d'un hôtel*, RES HUM commissionaire (*UK*)

portillon *m* TRANSP barrier

portique *m* TRANSP *manutention* gantry, gantry crane, portal crane; ~ **pour colis lourds** TRANSP *manutention* heavy lifting beam; ~ **à conteneurs** TRANSP *manutention* portainer crane; ~ **sur pneus** TRANSP *manutention* travelift; ~ **sur quai** TRANSP shore-based gantry crane; ~ **sur rails** TRANSP *manutention* travelift

Porto:[1] ~ **Rico** *f* COM Puerto Rico

Porto:[2] ~ **Novo** *n pr* COM Porto Novo

portoricain, e *adj* COM Puerto Rican

Portoricain, e *m,f* COM *habitant* Puerto Rican

portrait *m* INFO, MÉDIA *presse, édition* portrait; ~ **complet** COM cross section

ports: ~ **de cueillette** *m pl* TRANSP picked ports, pp

portugais[1]**, e** *adj* COM Portuguese

portugais[2] *m* COM *langue* Portuguese

Portugais, e *m,f* COM *habitant* Portuguese

Portugal *m* COM Portugal

pose: ~ **de tabulations** *f* INFO tab setting

poser *vt* COM, COMMS affix; ♦ ~ **sa candidature à une élection** POL stand for election; ~ **sa candidature pour un emploi** RES HUM apply for, put in an application for a job

positif, -ive *adj* COM plus, *rendement* positive

position *f* BOURSE position, COM status, *sur une question* position, stance; ~ **acheteur** (*ANT position vendeur*) BOURSE *pour options* bull account, bull position, long position; ~ **acheteur initiale** BOURSE open long position; ~ **acheteur sur options d'achat** BOURSE call purchase, long call; ~ **acheteur sur options de vente** BOURSE long put, put purchase; ~ **anti-inflationniste** ECON, POL anti-inflation stance; ~ **à la baisse** (*ANT position à la hausse*) BOURSE bear account, bear position; ~ **binaire** INFO bit location; ~ **de choix** V&M *sur le* *marché* prime position; ~ **de compensation** BANQUE clearing position, valued position, COMPTA *à découvert* value position; ~ **de compensation en compte** BOURSE long value position; ~ **compensée** BOURSE long leg; ~ **au comptant** BOURSE spot position; ~ **en compte** BOURSE long position; ~ **du compte** COM account statement; ~ **d'un compte à découvert** BOURSE short account position; ~ **concurrentielle** COM, ECON competitive position; ~ **courte** (ANT *position longue*) BOURSE, FIN short position; ~ **courte assignée** FIN assigned short position; ~ **courte sur contrat à terme** BOURSE short futures position; ~ **courte sur option** BOURSE short option position; ~ **couverte** (ANT *position à découvert*) BOURSE bull account, bull position, bull purchase, covered position (*UK*); ~ **de couverture** BOURSE offset; ~ **à découvert** (ANT *position couverte*) BOURSE bear account, bear position, naked position, short position; ~ **dominante** ECON dominant position; ~ **économique** ECON economic position; ~ **exposée** COM in an exposed position; ~ **fermée** BANQUE evened-out position; ~ **fiscale** FISC tax position; ~ **de force** COM bargaining position; ~ **à la hausse** (ANT *position à la baisse*) BOURSE bull account, bull position; ~ **inflexible** COM tough stance; ~ **initiale** BOURSE opening position; ~ **inverse** BOURSE offset; ~ **isolée** V&M *PLV* island display; ~ **liquidée** BOURSE closed position; ~ **de long califourchon** BOURSE long straddle position; ~ **longue** (ANT *position courte*) BOURSE, FIN long position; ~ **de longue option d'achat** BOURSE long call position; ~ **de longue option de vente** BOURSE long put position; ~ **longue d'un straddle** BOURSE long straddle position; ~ **longue sur contrat à terme** BOURSE long futures position; ~ **de marché** BOURSE market position; ~ **mixte** BOURSE spread position; ~ **au mouillage** TRANSP *navigation* anchor position; ~ **de négociation** FIN negotiating position; ~ **nette** BOURSE net position; ~ **nette débitrice** COM exposed net asset position; ~ **nette à terme** BANQUE net forward position; ~ **non-dénouée** BOURSE, FIN closed position; ~ **ouverte** BOURSE, FIN open contract, open interest, open position, open-ended position; ~ **à l'ouverture** BOURSE opening position; **personne en** ~ **longue** *jarg* BOURSE long (*jarg*); ~ **de place** BOURSE, FIN open interest; ~ **de repli** POL fall-back position; ~ **à risque** BOURSE risk position; ~ **sociale** PROT SOC social standing; ~ **à terme** BOURSE forward position, futures position; ~ **à terme long** BOURSE long futures position; ~ **de titres en garde** BOURSE segregated free position; ~ **trading** BOURSE position trading; ~ **vendeur** (ANT *position acheteur*) BOURSE bear account, bear position, short position; ~ **vendeur couverte** BOURSE covered short position; ~ **vendeur initiale** BOURSE open short position; ~ **vendeur sur option d'achat** BOURSE short call, short call position; ~ **vendeur sur option de vente** BOURSE short put position, short put; ~ **de vente de straddle** BOURSE short straddle position; ~ **de**

numéro 1 V&M market leadership; ♦ **avoir une** ~ **longue sur contrat à terme** BOURSE be long in futures; **déboucher une** ~ *jarg* BOURSE unwind a trade; **déboucler une** ~ (ANT *ouvrir une position*) BOURSE close a position, liquidate a position

positionnement *m* BOURSE, COM, V&M positioning; ~ **dynamique** COM dynamic positioning, DP; ~ **de la marque** V&M brand positioning

positionner 1. *vt* BOURSE, COM, V&M position; **2.** *v pron* **se** ~ COM position oneself

positions: ~ **croisées** *f pl* MATH *feuille de calculs* cross-footing; ~ **de roulement variable** *f pl* BOURSE rolling options positions

positivement *adv* COM positively

possédants: les ~ *m pl* IMMOB propertied class

possession *f* COM ownership, DROIT, IMMOB possession; ~ **d'actions** BOURSE shareholding, stockholding; ~ **effective de terres** DROIT, IMMOB occupation; ~ **de fait** DROIT, IMMOB adverse possession; ~ **immédiate** IMMOB immediate occupancy; ~ **sommaire** DROIT summary possession

possibilité *f* COM alternative, possibility, window of opportunity; ~ **d'écoulement des excédents** ECON vent for surplus; ~ **d'emprunt** BANQUE, COM, COMPTA, ECON, FIN borrowing power; ~ **de rachat** BOURSE buy-back option; ~ **de virement** BOURSE transferability

possibilités: ~ **d'adaptation** *f pl* COM adaptability; ~ **d'emploi** *f pl* RES HUM job opportunities; ~ **d'épargne** *f pl* ECON savings ratio; ~ **offertes** *f pl* RES HUM facilities

possible: dès que ~ *loc* COM, COMMS a.s.a.p., as soon as possible; **tout est** ~ *loc* COM the sky's the limit

post:[1] ~ **-communiste** *adj* COM post-Communist; ~ **-électoral** *adj* COM post-election

post:[2] ~ **-keynésiens** *m pl* ECON post-Keynesians; ~ **-marché** *m* ADMIN operations department, BOURSE back office, operations department; ~ **-scriptum** *m (PS)* COMMS postscript *(PS)*

postacheminement *m* TRANSP on-carriage

Postclair® *m France* COMMS ≈ Intelpost®

postdaté, e *adj* COMMS pd, postdated

postdater *vt* COMMS postdate

poste[1] *m* COM appointment, COMMS telephone extension, X, COMPTA item, INFO station, RES HUM position, post; ~ **d'acconage** *m* TRANSP *port* lighterage berth; ~ **d'actif** *m* COMPTA asset item; ~ **d'amarrage sûr** *m* TRANSP *port* safe berth; ~ **annexe** *m* COMMS subpost office; ~ **auxiliaire** *m* COMMS subpost office; ~ **du bilan** *m* COMPTA balance item, balance sheet item, FIN balance sheet item; ~ **de chalandage** *m* TRANSP *port* lighterage berth; ~ **clients** *m* COM trade creditors, COMPTA, ECON accounts payable, trade creditors; ~ **de commandement** *m* RES HUM position of authority; ~ **de débutant** *m* RES HUM junior position; ~ **de déchargement** *m* TRANSP *port* discharging berth; ~ **de désarmement** *m* TRANSP *port* lay-up berth; ~ **de direction** *m* GESTION, RES HUM managerial position; ~ **de douane** *m* IMP/EXP customs station; ~ **douanier frontalier** *m* IMP/EXP frontier customs post; ~ **en eau profonde** *m* TRANSP *port* deepwater berth; ~ **exceptionnel** *m* COM extraordinary item; ~ **facultatif** *m* FIN optional item; ~ **flottant** *m* TRANSP *port* floating berth; ~ **fournisseurs** *m pl* COMPTA, ECON, COM trade accounts payable (*AmE*); ~ **hors bilan** *m* COMPTA memo item, memorandum item; ~ **inactif** *m* BOURSE inactive post; ~ **libre** *m* RES HUM vacancy; ~ **à marchandises diverses** *m* TRANSP *port* general cargo berth; ~ **à marchandises diverses et conteneurs** *m* TRANSP *port* general cargo and container berth; ~ **pour mémoire** *m* COMPTA memo item, memorandum item; ~ **opérationnel** *m* RES HUM line position; ~ **de passif** *m* COMPTA liability item; ~ **de péage** *m* TRANSP tollbooth; ~ **polyvalent** *m* TRANSP *poste* general purpose berth; ~ **à pourvoir** *m* RES HUM job vacancy; ~ **à quai pour navires porte-conteneurs** *m* TRANSP *port* container berth; ~ **qui se libère** *m* RES HUM job opportunity; ~ **de radio** *m* COMMS, MÉDIA radio set; ~ **de relève** *m* RES HUM relief shift, swing shift; ~ **réservé aux transbordeurs** *m* TRANSP *maritime* ferry berth; ~ **à temps partiel** *m* COM, RES HUM part-time job; ~ **de travail** *m* ADMIN workstation, INFO terminal, workstation; ~ **à vracs liquides** *m* TRANSP *port* bulk liquid berth; ~ **à vracs secs** *m* TRANSP *port* bulk dry cargo berth; ~ **à vracs secs et liquides** *m* TRANSP *navigation* bulk dry and wet cargo berth

poste[2] *f* COMMS *service* mail, post (*BrE*); ~ **aérienne** COMMS airmail; ~ **de négociation** BOURSE trading pit (*jarg*), trading post (*jarg*)

poste:[3] **être en** ~ *loc* RES HUM be posted; **par la** ~ *loc* COMMS through the mail (*AmE*), through the post (*BrE*)

Poste: ~ **des États-Unis** *f* COMMS United States Postal Service, USPS

poster *vt* COMMS *lettre* mail (*AmE*), post (*BrE*)

postes: ~ **d'accueil** *m pl* ADMIN front-of-house jobs; ~ **du budget des dépenses** *m pl* FIN items in the estimates; ~ **fonctionnels** *m pl* ADMIN back-of-house jobs; ~ **à pourvoir** *m pl* RES HUM sits. vac. (*BrE*), situations vacant (*BrE*); ~ **vacants non pourvus** *m pl* RES HUM unfilled vacancies

postévaluation *f* FISC postassessing

postier *m* COMMS postman (*BrE*)

postréponse *f* COM, COMMS BRM (*AmE*), ≈ Business Reply Mail® (*AmE*)

postulant, e *m,f* RES HUM applicant

postulats: ~ **comptables** *m pl* COMPTA accounting conventions

postuler: ~ **pour un emploi** *loc* RES HUM apply for

pot: ~ **catalytique** *m* ENVIR catalytic converter; ~ **-de-vin** *m* COM bribe money, hush money (*infrml*), inducement, bribe, DROIT kickback, FIN kickback, sweetener (*infrml*), POL bribe, bribe money, kickback, graft (*infrml*), pork (*US, infrml*), RES HUM kickback, V&M bribe, bribe money, payola (*US, infrml*); ~ **de lancement** *m* infrml MÉDIA *d'un livre* launch party

poteau: ~ **indicateur** *m* TRANSP signpost; ~ **télégraphique** *m* COMMS telegraph pole

potentiel[1], **-elle** *adj* COM potential, prospective, V&M *client* prospective

potentiel[2] *m* COM capability, potential; ~ **de bénéfice** FIN profit potential; ~ **de bénéfices à la hausse** BOURSE upside profit potential; ~ **des cadres** COM, GESTION management potential; ~ **de croissance** COM, ECON growth potential; ~ **de croissance de production** ECON, IND potential output, productive potential; ~ **de développement** COM development potential; ~ **d'emprunt** BANQUE, COM, COMPTA, ECON, FIN borrowing potential; ~ **d'expansion** COM development potential; ~ **à la hausse** FIN upside potential; ~ **inemployé** ECON, IND spare capacity, surplus capacity; ~ **du marché** V&M market potential; ~ **de production** ECON productive potential, IND manufacturing capacity, production capacity, productive potential; ~ **de production utilisé** IND utilized capacity; ~ **de profit à la hausse** BOURSE upside profit potential; ~ **sous-utilisé** ECON, IND idle capacity, surplus capacity; ~ **de trafic** TRANSP traffic potential; ~ **de vente** V&M sales potential; ♦ **avoir du** ~ COM have potential

potentiellement *adv* COM potentially

poubelle *f* COM round file (*jarg*)

pouce: ~ **cube** *m* COM cu in, cubic inch

poudre: ~ **de mine** *f* ENVIR black powder; ~ **sans fumée** *f* TRANSP *marchandises dangereuses* smokeless powder

poulailler *m* [sing inv] LOISIRS *théâtre* gods

poulie *f* TRANSP *manutention* block

poupée *f* TRANSP *manutention* gypsy

pourboire *m* COM gratuity, tip, LOISIRS tip

pourcentage *m* COM, MATH percentage, MÉDIA royalty, RES HUM com., commission; ~ **d'actions de priorité** BOURSE preferred stock ratio; ~ **du bénéfice net distribué en dividende** COMPTA dividend payout ratio; ~ **de clients perdus** COM, V&M attrition rate; ~ **de dépréciation** TRANSP *maritime* percentage of depreciation; ~ **déterminé** FISC specified percentage; ~ **d'exonération** FISC exempt percentage; ~ **de frais** BOURSE expense ratio; ~ **d'intérêt** FISC *dans le revenu ou la propriété d'un trust* percentage interest; ~ **sur les recettes** MÉDIA back end (*jarg*); ~ **de variation** FIN percentage change; ♦ **comme** ~ **de** COM, MATH as a percentage of, as a proportion of; **en guise de** ~ MATH percentagewise

pourparlers *m pl* GESTION negotiations

poursuite: ~ **contre assuré** *f* ASSUR defence of suit against insured (*BrE*), defense of suit against insured (*AmE*); ~ **en dommages et intérêts** *f* ASSUR action for damages

poursuites *f pl* DROIT action, prosecution, proceedings; ~ **en diffamation** DROIT libel proceedings; ~ **judiciaires** DROIT court proceedings, judicial proceedings, law suit, legal proceedings, proceedings

poursuivre *vt* BANQUE continue, COM follow up, pursue, DROIT *en justice* prosecute, GESTION follow up; ◆ ~ **en contrefaçon** DROIT prosecute for forgery; ~ **devant les tribunaux** DROIT sue; ~ **pour diffamation** DROIT sue for libel; ~ **pour dommages-intérêts** DROIT file a claim for damages, sue for damages; ~ **pour faux** DROIT prosecute for forgery; ~ **jusqu'au bout** COM follow sth through; ~ **en justice** DROIT sue; ~ **qn en justice** DROIT bring an action against sb; ~ **ses remboursements hypothécaires** FIN keep up payment on one's mortgage

pourvoi *m* DROIT appeal

pourvoir: ~ **à** *vt* COM cater for; ~ **de capital** COM, FIN capitalize; ~ **de fonds** COM, FIN capitalize; ◆ ~ **en personnel** RES HUM man, staff; ~ **un poste** RES HUM fill a vacancy; **se** ~ **en appel** DROIT appeal, FISC lodge an appeal

pourvu:[1] ~ **en personnel** *adj* RES HUM staffed

pourvu:[2] ~ **que** *conj* COM provided that

poussée *f* COM *d'activité* upsurge; ~ **récessionniste** ECON contractionary pressure

pousser *vt* COM boost, drive, push, *à l'achat* prompt; ~ **à la baisse** (ANT *pousser à la hausse*) BOURSE bear; ~ **à la hausse** (ANT *pousser à la baisse*) BOURSE bull; ◆ ~ **qn à bout** COM push sb to the limit; ~ **à la vente** BOURSE hammer the market

pousseur: ~ **-barge** *m* TRANSP push-tow barge; ~ **-barge intégré** *m* TRANSP *navigation* integrated tug-barge, ITB

poussière: ~ **de charbon** *f* ENVIR coal dust

pouvoir[1] *m* COM power, DROIT authority, authorization, warrant of attorney; ~ **d'achat** BOURSE buying power, COM buying power, purchasing power, spending power, ECON purchasing power; ~ **d'achat courant** ECON current purchasing power, CPP; ~ **d'achat discrétionnaire** ECON, POL discretionary spending power; ~ **d'un acheteur sur le marché** ECON market power; ~ **administratif** ADMIN, COM administrative authority; ~ **budgétaire** ECON, POL budgetary power; ~ **compensatoire** ECON countervailing power; ~ **de crédit commercial** BANQUE commercial lending power; ~ **discrétionnaire** BANQUE discretionary authority; ~ **électoral** FISC voting power; ~ **d'emprunt des titres** BOURSE borrowing power of securities; ~ **exécutif** POL, RES HUM cadre; ~ **judiciaire** DROIT judiciary; ~ **législatif** DROIT legislative power; ~ **libératoire** ECON *de l'argent* acceptability, FIN legal tender; ~ **en matière de crédit commercial** BANQUE commercial lending power; ~ **de monopole** ECON monopoly power; ~ **de négociation** COM, GESTION, RES HUM bargaining power; ~ **policier**

DROIT, POL police power; ~ **de prêt** BANQUE lending power; ~ **de signer les documents financiers** FIN financial signing authority; ~ **de vendre** DROIT power of sale; ~ **de vente** DROIT, IMMOB power of sale; ◆ **au** ~ POL *gouvernement* in power; **avoir le** ~ **de** COM have the power to; **être au** ~ POL hold power

pouvoir:[2] ~ **se servir de qch** *loc* COM have the use of sth

pouvoirs: ~ **donnés par l'expérience** *m pl* GESTION expert power; ~ **d'enquête** *m pl* DROIT investigatory powers; ~ **d'exception** *m pl* POL, RES HUM emergency powers; ~ **d'instruction** *m pl* DROIT investigatory powers; **les** ~ **publics** *m pl* COM the authorities

p.p. *abrév* COM (*port payé*) p.p. (*postage paid*), COM (*par procuration*) p.p. (*postage paid*), per pro. (*frml*) (*per procurationem*), COM (*pages*) p.p. (*pages*), COM (*prépayé*) p.p. (*prepaid*), COMMS (*port payé*) p.p. (*postage paid*), ≈ Freepost® (*BrE*) (*Business Reply Mail*), TRANSP (*port payé*) carr pd (*carriage paid*), frt ppd (*freight prepaid*)

PPA *abrév* (*parité du pouvoir d'achat*) ECON PPP (*purchasing power parity*)

PPAR *abrév* (*perpendiculaire arrière*) TRANSP *navigation* AP (*aft perpendicular*)

PPAV *abrév* (*perpendiculaire avant*) TRANSP *navigation* FP (*forward perpendicular*)

p.p.m. *abrév* (*partie par million*) COM ppm (*parts per million*)

ppp *abrév* (*points par pouce*) INFO dpi (*dots per inch*)

P.R. *abrév* (*parc relais*) TRANSP P&R (*park and ride*)

pragmatique *adj* COM pragmatic

Prague *n pr* COM Prague

pratique[1] *adj* RES HUM *expérience, formation* hands-on

pratique[2] *f* DROIT practice; ~ **abusive** V&M *du vendeur* abusive practice; ~ **des cinq pour cent** BOURSE five per cent rule; ~ **comptable** COMPTA accounting firm; ~ **déloyale en matière de relations** RES HUM unfair labor practice (*AmE*), unfair labour practice (*BrE*); ~ **de discrimination par les prix** ECON third-degree price discrimination; ~ **d'embauche sur le marché interne du travail** ECON *d'une grande entreprise* internal labor market contracting (*AmE*), internal labour market contracting (*BrE*); ~ **de fabrication sous licence** ECON, IMP/EXP licensing; ~ **d'investissement normale** FIN normal investment practice; ~ **politique** POL political practice; ~ **des prix magiques** V&M odd-value pricing; ~ **de prix sauvage** ECON predatory pricing; ~ **professionnelle** COM working practice; ~ **d'un ratio d'endettement élevé** ECON, FIN trading on the equity; ~ **restrictive** IND restrictive practice; ◆ **en** ~ COM in practice

pratiquer *vt* COM, DROIT practice (*AmE*), practise (*BrE*); ◆ ~ **le charcutage électoral** POL gerrymander; ~ **une déduction** FISC make a deduction; ~ **un électrochoc** *jarg* RES HUM goose *(jarg)*; ~ **un prix d'appel** ECON set a price-point; ~ **une retenue** FISC make a deduction; ~ **une saisie-arrêt** DROIT garnish

pratiques: ~ **anticoncurrentielles** *f pl* ECON, POL anticompetitive practices; ~ **commerciales** *f pl* ADMIN trade practices, COM business practices, trade practices, ECON business practices, GESTION business practices, trade practices; ~ **commerciales déloyales** *f pl* COM unfair trading practices; ~ **commerciales honnêtes** *f pl* COM fair business practices; ~ **commerciales loyales** *f pl* COM fair business practices, DROIT, ECON fair trading; ~ **commerciales respectant la libre concurrence** *f pl* COM fair business practices; ~ **comptables** *f pl* COMPTA accounting practices; ~ **déloyales** *f pl* ECON, POL anticompetitive practices; ~ **et conventions du secteur** *f pl* ADMIN, COM, GESTION trade practices; ~ **illégales** *f pl* DROIT *commerce* illegal practices; ~ **restrictives** *f pl* DROIT, IND *industrielles* restrictive practices

praxéologie *f* ECON praxeology

pré:[1] ~ **-budgétaire** *adj* ECON pre-budget; ~ **-défini** *adj* INFO preset; ~ **-enregistré** *adj* MÉDIA prerecorded

pré:[2] ~ **-élingage** *m* TRANSP *manutention* preslinging; ~ **-projet** *m* COM draft project

pré:[3] ~ **-impression** *f* COM, COMMS, IMP/EXP postage-paid impression, PPI

préalable *adj* COM prior

préambule *m* BREVETS preamble, precharacterizing portion, COM label clause, lc, preamble, precondition

préavis *m* COM, COMMS notice, DROIT advance notice, notice, notice of intention; ~ **de clause de résiliation** ASSUR notice of cancellation clause; ~ **légal** DROIT legal notice; ~ **en règle** COM formal notice; ◆ **donner 5 jours de** ~ COM give 5 days notice, RES HUM give 5 days notice

précaution: **par** ~ *loc* COM to be on the safe side

précautionneux, -euse *adj* COM cautious

précédent, e *adj* COM preceding

précéder *vt* COM antedate, precede

précipitation: ~ **acide** *f* ENVIR acid precipitation

précis, e *adj* COM express, *rapport* accurate

précisé, e *adj* COM specified

préciser *vt* COM make clear, *forme d'un contrat* formalize, qualify

précision *f* COM detail, *de rapport, de document* accuracy, COMPTA accuracy; ~ **à la seconde près** COM split-second timing

précisions: ~ **sur la personne à charge** *f pl* FISC details of dependant

précité, e *adj* COM aforementioned, COMMS above, above-mentioned, aforementioned, as mentioned above

préconiser *vt* COM advocate

prédateur, -trice *m,f* BOURSE corporate raider, raider, COM predator, FIN corporate raider, V&M predator

prédécesseur *m* COM predecessor; ~ **en droit** BREVETS legal predecessor, predecessor in title, DROIT legal predecessor

prédéterminé, e *adj* COM prearranged, predetermined

prédéterminer *vt* COM prearrange, predetermine

prédiction: ~ **auto-réalisée** *f* COM self-fulfilling prophecy

prédire *vt* COM foresee

prédominant, e *adj* COM on stream, prevailing

prédominer *vi* COM prevail

préemballé, e *adj* V&M *marketing* prepackaged

prééminent, e *adj* COM, RES HUM pre-eminent

préétablir *vt* FIN precompute

préévaluation *f* FISC preassessing

préf. *abrév (préférence)* COM pref. *(preference)*

préfabriqué, e *adj* IMMOB prefabricated

préférence *f (préf.)* COM preference *(pref.)*, ECON, V&M taste; ~ **du consommateur** COM consumer preference, V&M consumer choice; ~ **pour la liquidité** ECON liquidity preference; ~ **pour une marque** V&M brand preference; ~ **révélée** ECON revealed preference

préfet: ~ **maritime** *m* RES HUM, TRANSP naval superintendent

préfigurer *vt* COM anticipate

préfinancement *m* FIN bridge financing

préjudice *m* COM prejudice; ~ **indu** FISC undue hardship; ~ **irréparable** DROIT irreparable harm; ~ **subi** DROIT losses suffered; ◆ **au** ~ **de** COM to the detriment of

préjudiciable *adj* COM prejudicial

préjugé *m* COM bias

préjugés: ~ **liés au sexe des employés** *m pl* MÉDIA sex stereotyping; ~ **sexistes** *m pl* RES HUM sex stereotyping

prélèvement *m* BANQUE *sur emprunt* drawing, FISC deduction, IMP/EXP levy, RES HUM holdback; ~ **agricole** ECON, FISC agricultural levy; ~ **automatique** BANQUE direct debit, DD, COM demand draft, DD, ECON, RES HUM automatic check-off *(US)*; ~ **autorisé** BANQUE direct debit, DD; ~ **compensatoire à l'exportation** IMP/EXP compensatory levy; ~ **de la cotisation syndicale** RES HUM check-off; ~ **de droits** COMMS cc, charges collect; ~ **forfaitaire** FISC flat-rate withholding, standard deduction; ~ **obligatoire** COM compulsory deduction; ~ **PAC** ECON *UE* CAP levy; ~ **à la source** RES HUM salary deduction; ~ **sur le salaire** RES HUM payroll deduction; ~ **sur stocks** COM withdrawal from stocks; ~ **temporaire** RES HUM holdback pay

prélever *vt* BANQUE *des fonds* withdraw, COM cream off, FISC levy; ~ **un intérêt** BANQUE charge interest; ~ **sur** RES HUM draw from

préliminaires: ~ **d'absorption** *m pl* ECON absorption approach; **~ d'intégration** *m pl* ECON absorption approach

prématuré, **e** *adj* COM premature

préméditation: avec ~ *loc* DROIT maliciously

premier[1], **-ère** *adj* COM main, primary; **de ~ ordre** BANQUE top-rated, BOURSE investment-grade (*US*), COM top-flight; **de ~ plan** COM front-running, INFO foreground; **de ~ rang** BANQUE senior; ◆ **en ~ lieu** COM in the first instance; **~ entré, premier sorti** *(PEPS)* COMPTA *évaluation des stocks* first in, first out *(FIFO)*

premier[2], **-ère** *m,f* COM first; **~ avertissement** RES HUM verbal warning; **~ clerc** DROIT head clerk, senior clerk; **~ commis** RES HUM head clerk; **~ coupon** BOURSE long coupon; **~ cours** BOURSE opening price, opening quotation; **~ détenteur des droits d'auteur** BREVETS, DROIT *propriété intellectuelle* first owner of copyright; **~ jour de notification** *(ANT dernier jour de notification)* FIN first notice day; **~ jour des opérations** BOURSE first dealing day; **~ maître** RES HUM *maritime*, TRANSP chief petty officer, CPO; **~ navire disponible** TRANSP *maritime* firavv, first available vessel; **~ plan** INFO foreground; **~ privilège** IMMOB first lien; **~ projet** DROIT rough draft; **~ semestre** COM first half; **~ transporteur** TRANSP first carrier; **~ trimestre** COM first quarter, 1Q, COMPTA, FIN first quarter; **~ vice-président** RES HUM first vice president; **~ voyage** TRANSP maiden voyage; ◆ **être le ~ à faire qch** COM take the lead in doing sth

Premier: ~ ministre *m* POL prime minister, PM

première:[1] **de ~ classe** *adj* COM first-rate; **de ~ génération** *adj jarg* IND, INFO first-generation; **de ~ qualité** *adj* TRANSP *navigation* A-1 *(jarg)*

première:[2] **~ classe** *f* LOISIRS, TRANSP first class; **~ commande** *f* V&M original order; **~ date de remboursement** *f* BOURSE first call date; **~ décennie de développement** *f* POL First Development Decade; **~ écriture** *f* COMPTA prime entry; **~ édition matinale** *f* MÉDIA *presse* bulldog edition (*AmE*), early edition (*BrE*), first edition (*BrE*); **~ émission publique** *f* BOURSE IPO (*AmE*), initial public offering (*AmE*); **~ épreuve** *f* V&M *publicité* pull; **~ génération** *f* IND, INFO first generation; **~ mise de fonds** *f* COMPTA initial outlay; **~ mouture** *f* INFO draft; **~ offre** *f* V&M opening bid; **~ page** *f* MÉDIA title page; **~ qualité** *f* COM premium grade; **~ quinzaine** *f* COM *du mois* fh, first half; **~ sortie** *f* TRANSP *véhicule* roll-out; ◆ **à ~ vue** COM prima facie *(frml)*

premières: ~ actions privilégiées *f pl* BOURSE first preferred stock

1er: ~ quartile *m* MATH lower quartile

prémisse *f* COM premise

premium: ~ de l'option d'achat *m* (*ANT premium de l'option de vente*) BOURSE call option premium; **~ de l'option de vente** *m* (*ANT premium de l'option d'achat*) BOURSE put option premium

prémunir: se ~ contre *v pron* COM provide against

prendre 1. *vt* BOURSE take, COM *abonnement, brevet* take out, *associé* take, *le pouvoir,le commandement* assume, take on, DROIT pass, RES HUM *emploi* take, TRANSP *marchandises* pick up; **~ en compte** BOURSE discount; **2.** *vi* **~ de l'âge** COM age; **~ ferme** BOURSE *émission* underwrite; ◆ **~ de l'avance** COM forge ahead; **~ de l'avance petit à petit** ECON edge ahead; **~ un bon départ** COM get off to a flying start; **~ une chambre** COM, LOISIRS *dans un hôtel* book in; **~ en charge** COM assume responsibility for; **~ des commandes** COM take orders; **~ congé** RES HUM take leave; **~ conscience de** COM realize; **~ contact avec** COM come into contact with; **~ à contre-pied** COM wrong-foot; **~ le contrôle administratif** COM *d'une société* take administrative control; **~ le contrôle** COM take control; **~ le contrôle de** COM take over; **~ un créneau dans le marché** COM, V&M bridge a gap in the market; **~ une décision** COM, GESTION make a decision, take a decision; **~ un dépôt** BOURSE take a deposit; **~ les devants** GESTION take the lead; **~ un échantillon** MATH take a sample; **~ effet** DROIT take effect; **~ effet le...** COM take effect from; **~ fin** COM break up, cease, come to an end, DROIT *contrats* cease to have effect; **~ forme** COM *idée* take shape; **~ les frais à sa charge** COM bear the costs; **~ des garanties** BOURSE obtain security; **~ l'initiative** GESTION take the initiative; **~ livraison** BOURSE take delivery, take up; **~ livraison de** COM accept delivery of; **~ livraison des titres** BOURSE take up stocks; **~ la mer** TRANSP set sail; **~ des mesures** COM make arrangements, take steps, DROIT, RES HUM take measures; **~ des mesures pour faire** COM take steps to do; **~ les mesures qui sont jugées nécessaires** DROIT take such steps as are considered necessary; **~ en note** COM take down; **~ note de** COM jot down, *arrivée* acknowledge; **~ note de qch** COM make a note of sth; **~ l'offensive** COM take the offensive; **~ les paroles de qn pour argent comptant** COM take sb's word at face value; **~ part à** COM take part in; **~ parti pour qn** COM take sides with sb; **~ une participation en actions dans** BOURSE take an equity stake in; **~ une participation dans** COM acquire an interest in; **~ le passif à sa charge** COMPTA take over liabilities; **~ une position** COM take up a position; **~ une position longue** BOURSE go long, take a long position; **~ une position de straddle** BOURSE take a straddle position; **~ possession** IMMOB take possession; **~ qch en compte** COM take sth into account; **~ qch en considération** COM take sth into account; **~ qch en sténo** COM take sth down in shorthand; **~ rendez-vous avec qn** COM make an appointment with sb; **~ des renseignements sur qn** RES HUM take up sb's references; **~ une réservation** TRANSP make a reservation; **~ la responsabilité de qch** COM take responsibility for sth; **~ du retard** COM fall behind schedule; **~ une retraite anticipée** RES HUM take early retirement; **~ un risque** COM take a risk; **~ le risque de** BOURSE bear the risk of; **~ des risques**

COM take a gamble; ~ **sa retraite** RES HUM retire; ~ **des sanctions** DROIT discipline, take measures, RES HUM take measures; ~ **soin de** COM make a point of; ~ **la succession de** COM take over from; ~ **le taux** BOURSE take the rate; ~ **un tournant** COM take a turn; ~ **toutes les mesures nécessaires** DROIT take such steps as are considered necessary; ~ **des vacances** LOISIRS, RES HUM go on holiday (*BrE*), take a holiday (*BrE*), take a vacation (*AmE*); ~ **de la valeur** COMPTA *bien*, IMMOB appreciate; ~ **de la vitesse** COM gather speed; ~ **un weekend prolongé** COM take a long weekend

preneur, -euse *m,f* COM bargainee, COMPTA payee, DROIT, IMMOB lessee; ~ **à bail** DROIT, IMMOB lessee; ~ **de prix** ECON price taker

preneurs: ~ **d'offre** *m pl* BOURSE takers-in

prénom *m* ADMIN Christian name (*BrE*), first name, forename, given name (*AmE*), RES HUM first name, forename; ~ **usuel** DROIT usual first name

préoccuper *vt* COM cause concern

PREP *abrév* (*prêt au redressement des entreprises publiques, prêt à la rationalisation des entreprises publiques, prêt à la réforme des entreprises publiques*) FIN PERL (*public enterprise rationalization loan*)

préparateur: ~ **de copie** *m* MÉDIA copy editor, sub, subeditor

préparation *f* COM preparation, COMPTA *d'un bilan* making up; ~ **du budget** COMPTA budget preparation, budgeting, ECON budget preparation, FIN budget preparation, budgeting; ~ **des budgets de trésorerie** COMPTA cash budgeting; ~ **de copie** MÉDIA *composition* mark-up; ~ **des données** ADMIN, INFO data preparation

préparer *vt* COM plan, prepare; ◆ ~ **un budget** COM, COMPTA, ECON, FIN, POL budget; ~ **qch** COM *à l'avance* plan ahead for sth; ~ **qch pour qn** COM lay sth on for sb; ~ **le terrain pour qch** COM lay the ground for sth, pave the way for sth

prépayé, e *adj* (*p.p.*) COM prepaid, p.p.

prépension *f Bel* (SYN *préretraite*) RES HUM early retirement

prépensionné, e *m,f Bel* RES HUM preretiree

préposé:[1] ~ **à plein temps** *m* FISC full-time attendant; ~ **aux prêts** *m* BANQUE lending officer, loan officer

préposé:[2] **être** ~ *vi* COM be in charge

préretraite *f* (*cf prépension Bel*) RES HUM early retirement, early retirement pension; ~ **obligatoire** RES HUM early retirement

préretraité, e *m,f* RES HUM person who has taken early retirement, preretiree

prérogative *f* DROIT prerogative

prérogatives: ~ **de la direction** *f pl* RES HUM managerial prerogative

près: **à peu** ~ *adv* COM in the region of

prescripteur *m* COM adviser

prescription *f* DROIT statute of limitations, time bar

prescrire *vt* DROIT prescribe

prescrit, e *adj* COM prescribed, DROIT time-barred

préséance *f* COM precedence; ◆ **avoir la** ~ **sur** COM take precedence over, take priority over

présélection *f* COM screening, RES HUM screening, screening process

présence: ~ **sur un marché** *f* V&M market presence

présentateur, -trice *m* MÉDIA *télévision* front man, presenter, talking head (*jarg*), MÉDIA *radio, télévision* announcer; ~ **-réalisateur** MÉDIA *télévision, journal diffusé* anchor, anchorman; ~ **vedette** MÉDIA *télévision* anchor, anchorman

présentation *f* BANQUE *d'une lettre de change* presentment, COM tender, COMPTA layout, GESTION presentation, TRANSP *véhicule* roll-out, V&M presentation; ~ **de bilan en compte** COMPTA account form, account format; ~ **budgétaire** COMPTA budgetary submission; ~ **de collections** COM fashion parade; ~ **des comptes annuels** COMPTA reporting treatment; ~ **de documents** IMP/EXP presentation of documents; ~ **erronée des faits** COM, FISC misrepresentation; ~ **de feuille** INFO form feed, FF; ~ **graphique en disposition verticale** BOURSE vertical line charting; ~ **horizontale** COMPTA *bilan* account form; ~ **d'informations par voie de notes** COM note disclosure; ~ **à l'italienne** COM landscape format, INFO, MÉDIA landscape format, landscape mode; ~ **du plan opérationnel pluriannuel de printemps** POL spring multi-year operational plan submission; ~ **verticale du compte de résultat** COMPTA vertical profit and loss account format; ~ **visuelle** INFO soft copy; ~ **volontairement déformée des faits** DROIT wilful misrepresentation of facts; ◆ **sur** ~ BANQUE, BOURSE, COM at sight, A/S, COMPTA on demand, FIN at sight, A/S

présentatrice: ~ **-réalisatrice** *f* MÉDIA *télévision, journal diffusé* anchorwoman; ~ **vedette** *f* MÉDIA anchorwoman

présenté: ~ **par année** *adj* COM annualized; ~ **sur l'année** *adj* COM annualized

présenter 1. *vt* COM *candidature* submit, *objectifs d'un projet* set forth, *rapport* present, MÉDIA anchor, POL propose; **2.** *v pron* **se** ~ COM apply in person; ◆ ~ **avec parti pris** COM slant; ~ **un chèque au paiement** BANQUE present a check for payment (*AmE*), present a cheque for payment (*BrE*); ~ **les conditions requises pour** *frml* COM be eligible for sth; ~ **un déficit** (ANT *présenter un excédent*) ECON run a deficit; ~ **un effet à l'escompte** BANQUE present a bill for discount; ~ **un excédent** (ANT *présenter un déficit*) ECON run a surplus; ~ **une facture pour réception** BANQUE present a bill for reception; ~ **une facture pour remise** BANQUE present a bill for discount; ~ **peu d'attrait pour les consommateurs** V&M have little consumer appeal; ~ **une proposition** COM, GESTION submit a proposal; ~ **qch sous un jour**

favorable COM put sth in the window; **se ~ aux élections** POL stand for election; **se ~ à l'enregistrement** LOISIRS, TRANSP check in; **se ~ à la réception** LOISIRS, TRANSP *hôtel* check in; **~ ses excuses** COM apologize; **~ un solde de** COMPTA show a balance of; **~ sur écran** INFO display; **~ une traite à l'acceptation** BANQUE present a draft for acceptance

présentoir *m* COM showcase, MÉDIA display stand; **~ -géant** RES HUM merchandiser; **~ de gondole** V&M shelf display; **~ en vrac** COM, V&M dump bin

présérie *f* COM pilot production, pilot run, GESTION, IND pilot production

préservation *f* ENVIR conservation, preservation; **~ de l'environnement compatible avec l'économie** ENVIR economic conservation; **~ financièrement rentable de l'environnement** ENVIR economic conservation; **~ du portefeuille** COM conservation of portfolio

préserver *vt* COM *opportunité*, ENVIR preserve

présidence *f* COM, POL presidency

président[1], *m* RES HUM chairman

président[2], **-e** *f* COM president, POL *d'état* Pres., President, RES HUM chair, chairperson; **~ adjoint** RES HUM vice-president; **~ du bureau exécutif** GESTION President of the Group Executive Board (*US*); **~ du comité exécutif** RES HUM chairman of the executive committee; **~ du conseil** RES HUM chairman of the board; **~ du conseil d'administration** GESTION chairman of the administrative board, RES HUM chairman, chairman of the administrative board; **~ du conseil de surveillance** RES HUM chairman of the supervisory board; **~ du Conseil du Trésor** FIN President of the Treasury Board (*US*); **~ -directeur général** (*PDG*) GESTION, RES HUM chairman and chief executive (*US*), chairman and managing director (*UK*), chairman of the board of directors, chairman of the board of management, chief executive officer (*US*), director-general, managing director (*UK*), president; **~ du directoire** GESTION, RES HUM chairman of the board of management; **~ élu** COM chairman elect; **~ de la Haute Cour de Justice** *France* RES HUM ≈ LCJ (*UK*), ≈ Lord Chief Justice (*UK*); **~ d'honneur** RES HUM honorary chairman, honorary president; **~ de syndicat financier** BANQUE syndicate manager; **~ de tribunal** DROIT presiding judge

Président: **~ de la cour des comptes** *m* COMPTA, POL Comptroller General (*US*)

présidente *f* RES HUM chairwoman, chairperson, chair

présider *vt* COM preside over, GESTION, RES HUM chair

présidium *m* RES HUM presidium

présomption *f* BREVETS *d'innocence*, COM presumption

presse:[1] **~ -papier** *m* INFO clipboard®

presse[2] *f* MÉDIA press; **~ financière** ECON, FIN financial journalism; **~ imprimante de cartes magnétiques** BANQUE credit-card imprinter, COM credit-card imprinter, imprinter; **~ à imprimer** MÉDIA *impression* printing press; **la ~ populaire** MÉDIA tabloid press; **~ nationale** MÉDIA national press; **~ parallèle** MÉDIA alternate press; **~ à scandale** MÉDIA the gutterpress; **~ à sensation** MÉDIA the gutterpress; **~ spécialisée** MÉDIA trade press

pressé: **être ~ par le temps** *loc* COM be under time pressure

pressenti: **être ~ pour** *loc* RES HUM be considered for

pression *f* COM pressure; **~ de citerne** TRANSP tank pressure; **~ effective moyenne** COM mean effective pressure, mep; **~ effective moyenne de frein** TRANSP bmep, brake mean effective pressure; **~ fiscale** ECON, FISC tax burden; **~ de fluage** TRANSP yield load; **~ à la hausse** ECON upward pressure; **~ indirecte** POL leverage; **~ inflationniste** ECON downward pressure, upward pressure, inflationary pressure; **~ morale** BANQUE moral persuasion; **~ de service** TRANSP working pressure, WP; **~ sur les prix** ECON price pressure; ♦ **faire ~ sur** POL jawbone (*US*); **faire ~ sur qn** COM bring pressure to bear on sb

pressions: **~ déflationnistes** *f pl* ECON deflationary pressures; **~ gouvernementales** *f pl* POL jawboning (*US*)

prestataire *m* RES HUM *de l'aide sociale* recipient, welfare recipient (*AmE*); **~ de services** COM service enterprise

prestation *f* ASSUR benefit, RES HUM benefit, *au travail* performance; **~ accessoire** V&M accessorial service; **~ d'assistance** FISC welfare payment; **~ d'assistance sociale** FISC social assistance payment (*Can*), PROT SOC social assistance payment (*Can*), social security payment (*BrE*); **~ d'attribution de droits de retraite** FIN past service benefit (*US*); **~ bénévole** ASSUR, FIN, RES HUM ex gratia payment (*frml*); **~ de bien-être social** FISC welfare payment; **~ en cas de maladie** RES HUM sickness benefit; **~ de décès** ASSUR death benefit; **~ d'entretien** IMMOB maintenance fee; **~ en espèces** ASSUR, COM cash benefit; **~ de gestion** BOURSE *de portefeuille* management fee; **~ pour incapacité** ASSUR disability annuity, PROT SOC disability annuity, disability benefit; **~ maladie réglementaire** ASSUR statutory sick pay (*UK*), SSP (*UK*); **~ en nature** COM allowance in kind; **~ de service** BANQUE fee-based service; **~ de service bancaire** BANQUE bank service charge; **~ de services** COM performance, performance of services, provision of services, rendering of services, service delivery; **~ supplémentaire** FIN supplementary assistance

prestations *f pl* COM services; **~ bancaires** BANQUE banking services; **~ maladie** PROT SOC health benefits; **~ de préretraite** RES HUM early retirement benefits; **~ de la Sécurité Sociale** RES HUM Social Security benefits, welfare benefits; **~ de**

services COMPTA income from services; ~ **sociales** RES HUM Social Security benefits, welfare benefits; ~ **sociales imposables** FISC, PROT SOC taxable social security benefits

prestigieux, -euse adj COM prestigious

prêt[1], **e** adj COM ready; ~ **-à-porter** COM, V&M off-the-peg, ready-to-wear; ~ **à filmer** MÉDIA camera-ready; ~ **pour la reproduction** MÉDIA camera-ready; ◆ ~ **pour l'expédition** TRANSP ready for shipment; **~, volontaire et capable** COM ready, willing and able

prêt[2] m BANQUE accommodation, loan, FIN accommodation, lending; ~ **accordé au taux de base** Fra (cf prêt accordé au taux préférentiel Can) BANQUE prime rate loan; ~ **accordé au taux préférentiel** Can (cf prêt accordé au taux de base Fra) BANQUE prime rate loan; ~ **pour achat de titres** BOURSE purpose loan; ~ **agricole** BANQUE, ECON agricultural loan, farm loan; ~ **aux agriculteurs** BANQUE, ECON farm loan; ~ **à l'agriculture** BANQUE, ECON agricultural loan; ~ **d'aide au développement** BANQUE, ECON, POL aid development loan (UK); ~ **d'ajustement de politique industrielle et commerciale** FIN ITPAL, industrial and trade policy adjustment loan; ~ **d'ajustement structurel** ECON structural adjustment loan; ~ **d'amélioration résidentielle** BANQUE, PROT SOC home improvement loan; ~ **d'amortissement** BANQUE, COMPTA, FIN amortization loan; ~ **de l'argent emprunté** FIN on-lending; ~ **d'assistance technique** FIN technical assistance loan, TAL; ~ **au-dessus du pair** FIN lending at a premium; ~ **automobile** BANQUE car loan; ~ **-bail** IMMOB lease-lend; ~ **bancaire** BANQUE bank loan; ~ **de banque** BANQUE bank loan; ~ **bilatéral** BANQUE, ECON, POL bilateral loan; ~ **bonifié** ECON soft loan; ~ **boursier** BANQUE securities lending, BOURSE securities loan; ~ **capitalisé à l'échéance** BANQUE interest-only loan; ~ **certifié** BANQUE truth in lending; ~ **commercial** BANQUE commercial loan; ~ **aux conditions commerciales** BANQUE hard loan; ~ **aux conditions du marché** BANQUE hard loan; ~ **à conditions particulièrement favorables** ECON soft loan; ~ **conjoint** BANQUE joint loan; ~ **consenti pour l'achat d'une maison** BANQUE home purchase loan; ~ **à la consommation** BANQUE, FIN consumer lending, consumer loan, personal loan; ~ **à la consommation remboursable par versements échelonnés** BANQUE consumer installment loan (AmE), consumer instalment loan (BrE); ~ **à la construction** BANQUE, IND construction loan; ~ **à la construction de logement** BANQUE house-building loan; ~ **de conversion** BANQUE, FIN conversion loan; ~ **de courtage** BOURSE broker's loan; ~ **à décaissement rapide** BANQUE quick-disbursing loan; ~ **déguisé** ECON, FIN backdoor lending; ~ **destiné à l'amélioration de l'habitat** BANQUE, PROT SOC home improvement loan; ~ **de développement de carrière** BANQUE, PROT SOC, RES HUM Career

Development Loan (UK), CDL (UK); ~ **en devises étrangères** ECON, FIN foreign currency loan; ~ **à durée fixe** BANQUE fixed-term loan; ~ **à échéance fixée** BANQUE fixed-term loan; ~ **entièrement productif** BANQUE fully performing loan; ~ **à l'entreprise** BANQUE, COM, FIN business loan; ~ **escompté** BANQUE discounted loan; ~ **d'État** FIN government loan; ~ **étudiant** BANQUE student loan; ~ **de façade** FIN fronting loan; ~ **à faible intérêt** BANQUE low-interest loan; ~ **à faible taux** BANQUE low-cost loan; ~ **financier intermédiaire** FIN financial intermediary loan, FIL; ~ **fixe** BANQUE fixed loan; ~ **au fonds d'amortissement** COMPTA sinking fund loan; ~ **à forfait** BANQUE, FIN nonrecourse loan; ~ **garanti** BANQUE collateral loan, secured loan; ~ **garanti par l'État** FIN sovereign loan; ~ **garanti à terme fixe** BANQUE secured fixed-term loan; ~ **géré** BANQUE managed loan; ~ **global** FIN package mortgage, whole loan; ~ **à l'habitation** BANQUE housing loan; ~ **d'honneur** BANQUE loan on trust; ~ **hypothécaire** BANQUE mortgage loan; ~ **hypothécaire autre qu'à l'habitation** BANQUE nonresidential mortgage; ~ **hypothécaire avec participation à la plus-value** BANQUE shared-appreciation mortgage; ~ **hypothécaire classique** BANQUE conventional mortgage; ~ **hypothécaire à court terme à taux d'intérêt renégociable** BANQUE roll-over mortgage; ~ **hypothécaire de deuxième rang** FIN second mortgage lending; ~ **hypothécaire différent** BANQUE alternative mortgage instrument; ~ **hypothécaire à l'habitation** BANQUE home mortgage, home mortgage loan, residential mortgage, residential mortgage loan; ~ **hypothécaire investi en actions** FIN equity-linked mortgage; ~ **hypothécaire de premier rang** BANQUE first mortgage, first mortgage loan; ~ **hypothécaire à remboursements périodiques** BANQUE, COMPTA, FIN amortized mortgage loan; ~ **hypothécaire résidentiel** BANQUE home mortgage, home mortgage loan, residential mortgage, residential mortgage loan; ~ **hypothécaire sur un immeuble non résidentiel** BANQUE nonresidential mortgage; ~ **hypothécaire à taux réglable** IMMOB adjustable-rate mortgage, ARM; ~ **hypothécaire variable** BANQUE, FIN, IMMOB adjustable mortgage loan, AML; ~ **immobilier** BANQUE home loan, home purchase loan; ~ **impayé** BANQUE outstanding loan; ~ **de l'importation pour le redressement économique** FIN rehabilitation import loan, RIL; ~ **indexé** BANQUE index-tied loan, indexed loan, ECON indexed loan, resource allocation, FIN indexed loan, INFO resource allocation; ~ **initial** FIN front-end loan, start-up loan; ~ **à intérêt fixe** FIN fixed interest loan; ~ **intermédiaire** FIN pass-through loan; ~ **d'intermédiaire financier** FIN financial intermediary loan, FIL; ~ **d'investissement et d'entretien sectoriel** (IES) FIN sector investment and maintenance loan (SIM); ~ **irrécouvrable** BANQUE, COMPTA, FIN bad loan; ~ **irrévocable** BANQUE uncallable loan; ~ **au jour le jour** BANQUE call loan, daily loan, day loan, day-to-day loan; ~ **lié** BANQUE, ECON tied loan; ~ **-logement gigogne** FIN piggyback loan; ~ **à long terme** BANQUE long-term loan; ~ **maritime** FIN maritime loan; ~ **minimum** FIN floor loan; ~ **à moyen terme** BANQUE intermediate loan, medium-term loan, MTL, FIN intermediate loan; ~ **multidevises** BANQUE multicurrency loan; ~ **multiple** BANQUE back-to-back loan; ~ **à la navigation** BANQUE shipping loan; ~ **non-garanti** COMPTA unsecured loan; ~ **non-productif** BANQUE nonperforming loan, nonproductive loan; ~ **non-remboursé** BANQUE outstanding loan; ~ **obligataire** BOURSE debenture loan; ~ **parallèle** BANQUE, ECON, FIN parallel loan; ~ **participant** BANQUE, FIN participation loan; ~ **en participation** BANQUE, FIN syndicated loan; ~ **personnel** BANQUE, FIN consumer loan, personal loan; ~ **personnel garanti** BANQUE secured personal loan; ~ **à prime** FIN lending at a premium; ~ **principal** BANQUE senior loan; ~ **de production** BANQUE, FIN production loan; ~ **-programme d'ajustement** FIN program adjustment loan (*AmE*), programme adjustment loan (*BrE*), PAL; ~ **progressif** BANQUE step-up loan; ~ **de qualité** BANQUE quality loan; ~ **quasi-productif** BANQUE quasi-performing loan; ~ **à la rationalisation des entreprises publiques** (*PREP*) FIN public enterprise rationalization loan (*PERL*); ~ **recouvré** BANQUE loan recovery; ~ **au redressement des entreprises publiques** (*PREP*) FIN public enterprise rehabilitation loan (*PERL*); ~ **à la réforme des entreprises publiques** (*PREP*) FIN public enterprise reform loan (*PERL*); ~ **-relais** BANQUE, FIN bridge loan (*AmE*), bridging loan (*BrE*), gap loan, interim loan; ~ **remboursable en monnaie forte** BANQUE hard loan; ~ **remboursable par versements** BANQUE installment loan (*AmE*), instalment loan (*BrE*); ~ **remboursable sur demande** BANQUE call loan; ~ **à remboursement régulier** BANQUE constant-payment loan (*UK*); ~ **restructuré** BANQUE restructured loan; ~ **révocable** BANQUE callable loan; ~ **à risque souverain** BANQUE sovereign risk loan; ~ **sans intérêt** BANQUE, FIN interest-free loan; ~ **sans recours** BANQUE, FIN nonrecourse loan; ~ **de secours** BANQUE, ECON, POL aid loan; ~ **simple** BANQUE straight loan; ~ **à une société** BANQUE, FIN corporate loan; ~ **aux sociétés** FIN corporation loan (*UK*); ~ **en souffrance** BANQUE noncurrent loan; ~ **soumis à fluctuations** BANQUE swing loan; ~ **de soutien** FIN standby loan; ~ **spécial à l'investissement** FIN specific investment loan, SIL; ~ **sur hypothèque** BANQUE mortgage loan; ~ **sur hypothèque à taux variable** BANQUE variable-rate mortgage; ~ **sur nantissement** COM advance against security; ~ **sur la valeur nette d'une maison** BANQUE home equity loan; ~ **à taux de base** *Fra* (*cf prêt à taux préférentiel Can*) BANQUE prime rate loan; ~ **à taux de financement plafonné** BOURSE cap rate loan; ~ **à taux fixe** BANQUE fixed-rate loan; ~ **à taux nul** BANQUE, FIN interest-free loan; ~ **à taux**

plafonné BOURSE cap rate loan; ~ **à taux préférentiel** *Can* (*cf prêt à taux de base Fra*) BANQUE prime rate loan; ~ **à taux révisable** BANQUE roll-over credit, roll-over loan; ~ **à taux usuraires** FIN loan shark (*infrml*); ~ **à taux variable** BOURSE roll-over credit facility; ~ **à tempérament** BANQUE installment loan (*AmE*), instalment loan (*BrE*); ~ **à tempérament aux consommateurs** BANQUE consumer installment loan (*AmE*), consumer instalment loan (*BrE*); ~ **à terme** BANQUE term loan; ~ **à terme fixe** BANQUE fixed-term loan; ~ **à terme fixe non garanti** BANQUE unsecured fixed-term loan; ~ **aux termes mal définis** BANQUE fuzzy loan; ~ **à titre gratuit** FIN gratuitous loan; ~ **de titres** BOURSE securities loan, FIN security lending; ~ **d'une très grande somme** BANQUE jumbo loan; ~ **à vue** BANQUE demand loan, BOURSE call loan; ♦ **faire un ~** FIN take accommodation, take out a loan

prêtable *adj* BANQUE lendable

prête: ~ **-nom** *m* DROIT dummy

prétendre *vti* DROIT claim; ~ **à** DROIT lay claim to

prétendu, e *adj* DROIT, RES HUM alleged

prétentions: **avoir des ~ à** *loc* DROIT lay claim to

prêter *vt* BANQUE *de l'argent* accommodate, lend, BOURSE lend, FIN accommodate, lend; ♦ ~ **contre titre** BOURSE lend against security; ~ **de l'importance à** COM attach importance to; ~ **en participation** BANQUE, FIN syndicate a loan; ~ **sur gage** BOURSE lend on security; ~ **sur nantissement** BOURSE lend against security, lend on security

prêteur, -euse *m,f* BANQUE lender, FIN creditor; ~ **de dernier ressort** BANQUE lender of last resort; ~ **hypothécaire** BANQUE mortgage lender; ~ **institutionnel** FIN institutional lender; ~ **privé** FIN private lender; ~ **résiduel** FIN residual lender; ~ **sur gages** FIN money lender, pawnbroker

prétexter: ~ **l'ignorance** *vt* COM plead ignorance

Pretoria *n pr* COM Pretoria

prêts: ~ **agricoles** *m pl* BANQUE, ECON agricultural lending; ~ **en amont** *m pl* FIN upstream loans (*jarg*); ~ **bancaires** *m pl* BANQUE, ECON bank lending; ~ **commerciaux** *m pl* BANQUE commercial lending; ~ **en cours** *m pl* BANQUE outstanding loans; ~ **aux entreprises** *m pl* BANQUE, FIN corporate lending; ~ **hypothécaires en cours** *m pl* BANQUE mortgage loans outstanding, outstanding mortgage loans; ~ **hypothécaires aux vétérans** *m pl* BANQUE Veterans Administration mortgage (*US*); ~ **interbancaires** *m pl* BANQUE bank-to-bank lending; ~ **par découvert** *m pl* BANQUE overdraft lending; ♦ ~, **dotations en capital et avances aux organismes internationaux** COMPTA loans, investments and advances to international organizations; ~, **participations et avances** COMPTA loans, investments and advances

preuve *f* DROIT evidence, proof; ~ **d'audit** COMPTA, FIN audit evidence; ~ **concluante** DROIT conclusive evidence; **~ contradictoire** DROIT conflicting evidence; **~ de créance** FISC evidence of indebtedness; **~ documentaire** COM documentary evidence; **~ écrite** DROIT documentary evidence, written evidence; **~ factuelle** DROIT factual evidence; **~ indirecte** DROIT circumstantial evidence; **~ irréfragable** DROIT conclusive evidence; **~ matérielle** DROIT concrete evidence; **~ péremptoire** DROIT conclusive evidence; **~ prima facie** DROIT prima-facie evidence; **~ du titre** DROIT, IMMOB evidence of title; **~ de l'utilisation** BREVETS evidence of use; ◆ **ayant fait ses ~s** RES HUM experienced; **~ de** COM *intelligence* evidence of; **faire ses ~s** COM win one's spurs

prévaloir *vi* COM obtain; **~ sur** COM outweigh

prévarication *f* COM breach of trust

prévenir *vt* COM warn

préventif, -ive *adj* COM precautionary

prévention: **~ des accidents** *f* RES HUM *de travail* accident prevention; **~ des fraudes** *f* DROIT fraud prevention; **~ des fraudes maritimes** *f* DROIT, TRANSP maritime fraud prevention; **~ du gaspillage** *f* ENVIR waste prevention; **~ de sinistre** *f* ASSUR claims prevention

prévisible *adj* COM foreseeable, predictable

prévision *f* COM forecast, prediction, COMPTA forecasting, forecast, ECON anticipation, forecast, forecasting, FIN, MATH forecast, forecasting, V&M anticipation, forecasting, forecast; **~ de bénéfices** COM, FIN earnings forecast; **~ des bénéfices** FIN, GESTION profit planning; **~ de bénéfices et de performances** FIN, GESTION profit and performance planning, PPP; **~ de caisse** COMPTA, FIN cash forecast; **~ de coûts** COMPTA cost forecast; **~ dans l'entreprise** COM, ECON business forecasting; **~ de la demande** V&M demand forecasting; **~ des dépenses d'investissement** COMPTA capital budgeting; **~ des effectifs** RES HUM staff forecasting; **~ de l'emploi** COM, RES HUM manpower forecast, manpower forecasting; **~ de ligne de crédit financée par plusieurs contrats** FIN multiple-contract-finance projected line of credit; **~ à long terme** COM long-range forecast; **~ de main-d'oeuvre** COM, RES HUM manpower forecasting; **~ de programme** COM program forecast (*AmE*), programme forecast (*BrE*); **~ des réponses** V&M *publicité* response projection; **~ technologique** COM, IND technological forecast, technological forecasting; **~ de trafic** TRANSP traffic forecast; **~ de trésorerie** COMPTA cash flow forecast, cash forecast, FIN cash forecast; **~ de ventes** ECON, V&M sales forecast, sales projection; ◆ **en ~ de** COM in expectation of; **en ~ d'une chute du cours** BOURSE in anticipation of a fall in the price

prévisionniste *mf* COM forecaster

prévisions: **~ commerciales** *f pl* COM, ECON business forecasting; **~ de dépenses publiques** *f pl* ECON, FIN, POL public spending plans; **~ détaillées** *f pl* COM, V&M brick by brick forecasting; **~ économiques** *f pl* COM business forecasts, ECON Treasury model, economic fore-

casting, business forecasts; **~ financières** *f pl* ECON, FIN financial forecasts, FISC fiscal projections; **~ du marché** *f pl* COM, V&M market forecast; **~ normatives** *f pl* COM normative forecasting; **~ rationnelles** *f pl* ECON rational expectations, RE; **~ sur l'environnement** *f pl* ENVIR environmental forecasting

prévisualiser *vt* INFO preview

prévoir *vt* COM anticipate, envisage, predict; ◆ **~ une baisse de cours** (ANT *prévoir une hausse de cours*), BOURSE be bearish; **~ des frais de** COM, COMPTA, ECON, FIN budget for; **~ une hausse de cours** (ANT *prévoir une baisse de cours*) BOURSE be bullish; **~ une marge d'erreur** COM allow for a margin of error

prévoyance: **~ inoffensive** *f* POL hold-harmless provision (*jarg*); **~ pour pertes** *f* FIN *feuille de bilan, inventaire comptable* loss contingency

prévu, e *adj* COM anticipated, expected, on the horizon, predicted; **~ par la loi** DROIT statutory; **~ par réglement** COM prescribed; ◆ **comme ~** ADMIN, COM according to plan, as scheduled; **être ~ pour** COM be scheduled for, be scheduled to begin in; **qui n'est pas ~ par un texte de loi** DROIT nonstatutory

prière: **~ de faire suivre** *loc* COMMS please forward; **~ d'insérer immédiatement** *loc* MÉDIA for immediate release

primage *m* FIN, FISC, TRANSP *maritime* primage

primaire *adj* COM primary

prime:[1] **~ -time** *m jarg* MÉDIA prime listening time, prime viewing time

prime[2] *f* ASSUR, BANQUE *pour les prêts* premium, BOURSE bounty, option premium, option price, premium, *marché à terme* premium, COM bonus, DROIT, FIN premium, RES HUM bonus, bonus payment, premium, V&M *publicité* premium; **~ absorbée** ASSUR earned premium; **~ d'achat** (ANT *prime de vente*) BOURSE call option price, call premium; **~ acheteur** (ANT *prime vendeur*) BOURSE, COM, ECON buyer's option; **~ acquise** ASSUR earned premium; **~ additionnelle** ASSUR additional premium, AP; **~ d'adieu** RES HUM golden handshake; **~ d'ancienneté** RES HUM seniority bonus; **~ annuelle** ASSUR annual premium; **~ en argent** BOURSE cash bonus; **~ d'assurance** ASSUR insurance premium; **~ d'assurance automobile** TRANSP motor premium; **~ d'assurance maladie** ASSUR, PROT SOC, RES HUM sickness insurance premium; **~ d'assurance-vie** ASSUR life insurance premium; **~ automobile** ASSUR, TRANSP motor premium; **~ pour bons et loyaux services** RES HUM golden handshake; **~ de célérité** TRANSP *navire, chargement/déchargement* despatch money, dispatch money, despatch, dispatch; **~ de célérité au déchargement** TRANSP *navigation* discharging only, DDO; **~ de célérité payable au chargement et au déchargement** TRANSP *navigation* despatch money payable both ends, dispatch money payable both ends, DBE; **~ de célérité**

payable au chargement et au déchargement pour temps gagné TRANSP *navigation* despatch payable both ends all time saved, dispatch payable both ends all time saved, DBEATS; ~ **de célérité payable au taux de la demi-surestarie** TRANSP *navire, chargement/déchargement* d1/2D, dispatch half demurrage; ~ **de célérité payable pour temps gagné au chargement** TRANSP *navigation* dispatch money payable on time saved during loading; ~ **collective** ECON synthetic incentive, RES HUM group bonus, group incentive; ~ **collective d'incitation au rendement** RES HUM group incentive scheme (*UK*); ~ **conditionnement** V&M *marketing* container premium; ~ **constante** ASSUR level premium; ~ **à la construction** TRANSP *naval* construction subsidy; ~ **à la construction ou à l'exploitation d'un navire** TRANSP ship subsidy; ~ **de conversion** BOURSE conversion premium; ~ **dégressive** ASSUR premiums reducing; ~ **de départ** RES HUM golden handshake; ~ **de dépôt** ASSUR deposit premium; ~ **en dollars** BOURSE dollar premium; ~ **emballage** V&M *marketing* container premium; ~ **d'émission** BOURSE bond discount, bond premium, issue premium, original issue discount, paid-in surplus (*AmE*), share premium (*BrE*), OID, COMPTA additional paid-in capital, capital contributed in excess of par value (*US*), capital surplus, paid-in surplus (*AmE*), share premium (*BrE*), stock issue bonus, FIN additional paid-in capital, original issue discount, paid-in surplus (*AmE*), share premium (*BrE*), OID; ~ **d'émissions d'obligations** BOURSE bond premium; ~ **à l'emploi régional** RES HUM regional employment premium, REP; ~ **d'encouragement** RES HUM incentive bonus, V&M incentive commission; ~ **d'encouragement pour le négociant** V&M dealer incentive; ~ **d'équipe** RES HUM group bonus, group incentive; ~ **essentielle** ASSUR basic premium; ~ **à l'exportation** IMP/EXP export subsidy; ~ **de fidélité** BOURSE loyalty bonus; ~ **de fin d'année** RES HUM Christmas bonus; ~ **de fin de contrat** ASSUR, ECON, FIN reversionary bonus, terminal bonus; ~ **fixe** ASSUR fixed premium; ~ **forfaitaire** ASSUR fixed premium, RES HUM flat-rate bonus; ~ **d'heures supplémentaires** RES HUM overtime premium; ~ **de licenciement** RES HUM lay-off pay, redundancy pay, redundancy payment; ~ **moyenne** ASSUR average premium; ~ **multirisque** ASSUR combined premium; ~ **nette** ASSUR Net Abs, BOURSE net premium; ~ **nette modifiée** ASSUR modified net premium; ~ **nivelée** ASSUR level premium; ~ **non-amortie des investissements** BOURSE unamortized premiums on investments; ~ **non-hiérarchisée** RES HUM flat-rate bonus; ~ **en options sur actions** BOURSE compensatory stock option (*UK*); ~ **organique** ECON organic premium; ~ **payée d'avance** ASSUR advance premium, DROIT, FIN unearned premium; ~ **de ponctualité** RES HUM attendance bonus; ~ **de présence** RES HUM attendance bonus; ~ **de production** IND production bonus; ~ **de**

productivité IND acceleration premium; ~ **provisionnelle** ASSUR deposit premium; ~ **de reconversion** RES HUM redundancy pay, redundancy payment; ~ **de recrutement** RES HUM golden hello, recruitment bonus; ~ **de régularisation** ASSUR adjustment premium; ~ **de remboursement** BOURSE redemption bond, COMPTA redemption premium; ~ **de remboursement des obligations** BOURSE, COMPTA bond redemption premium; ~ **de rendement** IND output bonus, production bonus, RES HUM acceleration premium, output bonus; ~ **de rentabilité** RES HUM incentive pay; ~ **de réorientation** RES HUM redeployment premium; ~ **de risque** ASSUR risk premium, risk-related premium; ~ **de risque de marché** BOURSE market risk premium; ~ **salariale** RES HUM wage bonus; ~ **sur réserve capitalisée** COM bonus reserve; ~ **sur taux d'intérêt** FIN interest rate subsidy; ~ **sur valeur de conversion** BOURSE premium over conversion value; ~ **sur valeur de l'obligation** BOURSE premium over bond value; ~ **à taux fixe** RES HUM flat-rate bonus; ~ **au temps** BOURSE time premium; ~ **de terme** ECON term premium; ~ **en trop** FISC excess contribution; ~ **unique** RES HUM single premium; ~ **au vendeur** RES HUM, V&M push money; ~ **vendeur** (ANT *prime acheteur*) BOURSE, COM, ECON seller's option; ~ **à la vente** V&M *publicité* push incentive; ~ **de vente** (ANT *prime d'achat*) BOURSE put option price, put premium; ♦ **à ~** COM, FIN at a premium

primé: être ~ par *loc* BOURSE rank after

primes: ~ non-amorties sur investissements *f pl* BOURSE unamortized premiums on investments; ~ **de retraite** *f pl* COMPTA pension charges, pension costs

primeur: avoir la ~ de l'information *loc* MÉDIA be the first one to hear the news

principal[1]**, e** *adj* BOURSE principal, COM main, major, *hiérarchie* Snr, senior, RES HUM *hiérarchie* Snr, senior

principal[2] *m* DROIT head clerk, senior clerk, FIN principal amount; ~ **marché des changes** FIN major foreign exchange market; ~ **d'une obligation** BOURSE bond principal; ~ **producteur** ECON, IND major producer; ~ **rajusté** FISC adjusted principal amount

principalement *adv* COM principally

principaux: ~ partenaires commerciaux *m pl* ECON, POL main trading partners

principe *m* COM principle, COMPTA convention, MATH principle; ~ **de l'accélérateur** ECON, FIN acceleration principle, accelerator principle; ~ **d'ancienneté** RES HUM seniority principle; ~ **d'audit** COMPTA, FIN auditing principles; ~ **de compensation** ECON compensation principle; ~ **de compensation de Kaldor-Hicks** ECON Kaldor-Hicks' compensation principle; ~ **de la continuité de l'exploitation** COMPTA going-concern concept, going-concern principle; ~ **du corps unique** RES HUM broad banding (*UK*); ~ **de diffé-**

rence de **Rawls** ECON Rawlsian difference principle; ~ **directeur** COM guiding principle; ~ **de l'échelle des salaires** RES HUM scalar principle; ~ **de l'égalité devant la loi** DROIT, POL Equal Protection of the Laws (*US*); ~ **d'exclusion** ECON exclusion principle; ~ **d'invariance de Ricardo** ECON Ricardian equivalence theorem, Ricardo invariance principle; ~ **marginal d'attribution** ECON MPA, marginal principle of allocation; ~ **multiplicateur** ECON *économétrie* multiplier principle; ~ **de l'observation volontaire** FISC principle of voluntary compliance; ~ **de la péréquation** FISC principle of equalization; ~ **de la permanence** COMPTA consistency principle; ~ **pollueur-payeur** DROIT, ENVIR, PROT SOC polluter pays principle; ~ **de précaution** ENVIR precautionary principle; ~ **du prix de pleine concurrence** COM arm's-length principle; ~ **de prudence** COMPTA conservatism principle, principle of conservatism; ~ **de rattachement à l'exercice** COMPTA accrual concept, accrual principle, concept of accrual, principal of accrual; ~ **de la réciprocité contractuelle** DROIT mutuality of contract; ~ **de répartition égalitaire** ECON needs standard; ◆ **en** ~ COM in theory; **par** ~ COM on principle

principes: ~ **comptables** *m pl* COMPTA accounting conventions, accounting principles; ~ **du coût historique** *m pl* COMPTA historical cost principles; ~ **d'évaluation** *m pl* COMPTA valuation principles; ~ **fondamentaux** *m pl* COM heads of agreement

Principes: ~ **comptables généralement admis** *m pl* (*PCGA*) COMPTA Generally Accepted Accounting Principles (*US*) (*GAAP*)

printemps *m* COM spring

prioritaire *adj* COM priority

priorité *f* BREVETS, COM priority; ~ **absolue** COM number one priority; ~ **antérieure** BREVETS earlier priority; ◆ **avoir la** ~ **sur** COM take precedence over, take priority over

prioritiser *vt* ADMIN, COM, GESTION prioritize

pris: ~ **en charge par l'entreprise** *adj* COMPTA absorbed; ~ **par** *adj* FISC *règlement* enacted by

prise *f* INFO, TRANSP *saisissage* plug; ~ **de bénéfices** ECON, FIN, GESTION profit taking; ~ **en charge totale des soins médicaux** PROT SOC comprehensive health-care system; ~ **en compte de l'inflation** COMPTA allowance for inflation (*UK*); ~ **de conscience écologiste** ENVIR greening; ~ **de contrôle** BOURSE, COM takeover, ECON repurchase, reverse takeover, reversed takeover, takeover, FIN reverse takeover, reversed takeover; ~ **de contrôle adossée** BOURSE leveraged buyout, LBO; ~ **de contrôle amicale** BOURSE friendly takeover; ~ **de contrôle convenue** ECON agreed takeover; ~ **de courant** INFO plug; ~ **de décision** GESTION decision making; ~ **d'échantillon** MATH sample drawing; ~ **d'effet du contrat d'assurance** ASSUR commencement of coverage; ~ **ferme** BOURSE bought deal, underwriting; ~ **de force** TRANSP *véhicule* power takeoff; ~ **d'images** INFO

imaging; ~ **de livraison** BOURSE taking delivery; ~ **de mouvement** TRANSP *véhicule* power takeoff; ~ **en pension** BOURSE REPO (*AmE*), repurchase agreement, reverse repurchase agreement, RP, purchase and resale agreement, PRA; ~ **de possession** DROIT, IMMOB *d'un lieu* occupation; ~ **de possession anticipée** DROIT, IMMOB acceleration

prises: ~ **en pension** *f pl* FIN discount window (*AmE*); ~ **totales autorisées** *f pl* ENVIR *pêche* TACs, total allowable catches; ◆ **être aux** ~ **avec un problème** COM grapple with a problem

priseur *m* FIN pricer

privation *f* PROT SOC *deprivation* hardship; ~ **de liberté** COM, COMPTA, DROIT, RES HUM constraint; ~ **sensorielle** GESTION sensory deprivation

privatisation *f* COM, ECON privatization

privatisé, e *adj* COM, ECON privatized; ~ **de fraîche date** ECON newly-privatized

privatiser *vt* COM, ECON privatize

privé, e *adj* COM private, private-sector, proprietary, DROIT *biens par séquestre* deprived, ECON private-sector

privilège *m* DROIT lien, IMMOB licence (*BrE*), license (*AmE*); ~ **du constructeur** IMMOB, IND mechanic's lien; ~ **d'exemption de paiement** FIN skip-payment privilege; ~ **fiscal** FISC tax lien, tax privilege; ~ **général** IMMOB general lien; ~ **hypothécaire** BANQUE, DROIT, IMMOB mortgage lien; ~ **judiciaire** DROIT judgment lien (*US*); ~ **maritime** DROIT, TRANSP maritime lien; ~ **obligatoire** DROIT involuntary lien; ~ **de pavillon** TRANSP *navigation* flag discrimination; ~ **de réinvestissement** BOURSE reinvestment privilege; ~ **de second rang** DROIT junior lien; ~ **du transporteur** TRANSP carrier's lien; ~ **du voiturier** TRANSP carrier's lien

privilèges: ~ **fiscaux** *m pl* FISC liens tax; ~ **en garantie d'impôt** *m pl* FISC liens tax; ~ **sur biens imposés** *m pl* FISC liens tax

privilégié, e *adj* DROIT *en droit* privileged

prix *m* COM charge, prize, COM price, ECON *option* premium, price, FIN prize; ~ **acceptable** *m* COM, V&M acceptable price; ~ **d'achat** *m* BOURSE bid price, purchase price, trade price, COM buying price, cost price, trade price, FIN acquisition price, purchase price, V&M purchase price, trade price; ~ **achat garanti hypothécairement** *m* BANQUE, FIN, IMMOB purchase money mortgage; ~ **acheteur** *m* BOURSE bid price; ~ **actualisé de l'action** *m* BOURSE discounted share price; ~ **affiché** *m* ECON, V&M displayed price; ~ **d'un aller-retour** *m* TRANSP return fare (*BrE*), round-trip fare (*AmE*); ~ **approuvé** *m* COM, V&M approved price; ~ **approximatif** *m* BOURSE approximate price; ~ **au-dessus du pair** *m* BOURSE premium; ~ **avant chargement sur wagon** *m* TRANSP track price; ~ **en baisse** *m pl* ECON falling price; ~ **de base** *m* BOURSE basis price, COM base price, basic price, FISC base price, cost base, V&M base price, basic price; ~ **de base approprié** *m* FISC *d'un bien* relevant cost base; ~ **de base rajusté** *m* *(PBR)* COMPTA adjusted cost base *(Canada)* *(ACB)*; ~ **de base rajusté total** *m* FISC aggregate of the adjusted cost bases; ~ **du billet** *m* TRANSP passenger fare, *train* train fare; ~ **du billet d'avion** *m* LOISIRS, TRANSP air fare; ~ **à bord** *m* BOURSE afloat price; ~ **de bout en bout** *m* TRANSP through fare; ~ **bradé après faillite** *m* BOURSE hammer price *(jarg)*; ~ **budgétaires** *m pl* COM, COMPTA, FIN budget prices; ~ **de la cabine** *m* TRANSP *navigation* cabin charge; ~ **cassé** *m* *infrml* COM, V&M bargain price; ~ **de catalogue** *m* COM catalog price *(AmE)*, catalogue price *(BrE)*, list price, V&M *ventes* catalog price *(AmE)*, catalogue price *(BrE)*, list price; ~ **catalogue** *m* COM catalog price *(AmE)*, catalogue price *(BrE)*, list price, V&M *ventes* catalog price *(AmE)*, catalogue price *(BrE)*, list price; ~ **de cession** *m* COM transfer price; ~ **de cession interne** *m* COM transfer price; ~ **cible** *m* COM, ECON *UE agriculture*, V&M target price; ~ **de clôture** *m* COM shutdown price; ~ **du commerce** *m pl* COM high-street prices *(UK)*; ~ **de la communication téléphonique** *m* COMMS call charge; ~ **de compensation du marché** *m* ECON market clearing price; ~ **compétitif** *m* ECON, V&M competitive price; ~ **comptable** *m* BANQUE, COMPTA accounting price; ~ **au comptant** *m* BOURSE spot price; ~ **de conclusion** *m* IMMOB *de transaction* closing cost; ~ **concurrentiel** *m* ECON, V&M competitive price; ~ **conseillé** *m* V&M recommended retail price, RRP; ~ **à la consommation** *m* V&M consumer price; ~ **constants** *m pl* ECON, V&M constant prices; ~ **contractuel** *m* FISC contract price *(US)*; ~ **des contrats à terme sur taux d'intérêt** *m* BOURSE, FIN interest-rate futures prices; ~ **contrôlé** *m* ECON pegged price; ~ **convenu** *m* COM, V&M agreed price; ~ **de conversion** *m* BOURSE, FIN conversion price; ~ **coté** *m* BOURSE quoted price; ~ **courant** *m* COM average market price, ECON current price, FIN current price, V&M average market price; ~ **courant du marché** *m* BOURSE current market price, prevailing market price, V&M current market price; ~ **coûtant** *m* ECON prime cost, supplementary cost; ~ **de début de négociations** *m* BOURSE arm's-length price; ~ **défiant toute concurrence** *m* COM knock *(infrml)*; ~ **demandé** *m* COM *ventes aux enchères* reservation price, reserve, reserve price *(BrE)*, upset price *(AmE)*, IMMOB asked price, V&M *ventes aux enchères* reservation price, reserve, reserve price *(BrE)*, upset price *(AmE)*; ~ **des denrées** *m* BOURSE commodity price; ~ **de départ** *m* COM asking price, reservation price, reserve, reserve price *(BrE)*, upset price *(AmE)*, V&M *ventes aux enchères* reservation price, reserve, reserve price *(BrE)*, upset price *(AmE)*; ~ **au départ du Golfe** *m* ECON Gulf Plus; ~ **départ quai** *m* IMP/EXP *livraison* ex-wharf price; ~ **départ usine** *m* COM, V&M price ex-works; ~ **dernier entré, premier sorti** *m* COMP-

TA last in, first out price; ~ **de déséquilibre** *m* ECON disequilibrium price; ~ **au détail conseillé** *m* V&M suggested retail price; ~ **différentiel** *m* ECON, V&M differential price; ~ **directeur** *m* V&M price leader; ~ **discompte** *m* FIN discount price; ~ **discompté** *m* FIN discount price; ~ **discriminatoires** *m pl* COM price discrimination, third-degree price discrimination, V&M price discrimination; ~ **du dollar** *m* BOURSE dollar price; ~ **élevé** *m* BOURSE, COM high price, V&M premium price; ~ **d'émission** *m* BOURSE issue price; ~ **d'émission obligataire** *m* BOURSE bond issuing price; ~ **d'émission d'une obligation** *m* BOURSE bond issuing price; ~ **d'entrée** *m* COM admission fee; ~ **d'entrée actuel** *m* COMPTA current entry price; ~ **d'entrée en possession** *m* BANQUE acceptance price; ~ **d'équilibre** *m* ECON equilibrium price; ~ **estimatif** *m* BOURSE valuation price; ~ **exceptionnel** *m* COM, V&M bargain price; ~ **excessif** *m* ECON overshooting price; ~ **d'exercice** *m* BOURSE call price, exercise price, strike price, striking price; ~ **d'exercice ajusté** *m* BOURSE adjusted exercise price *(UK)*; ~ **d'exercice d'une option d'achat** *m* *(ANT prix d'exercice d'une option de vente)* BOURSE call strike price, call's strike; ~ **d'exercice d'une option de vente** *m* *(ANT prix d'exercice d'une option d'achat)* BOURSE option strike price, put strike, put's strike; ~ **à l'exportation** *m pl* ECON, IMP/EXP export prices; ~ **de fabrique** *m* V&M manufacturer's price; ~ **de facture** *m* BOURSE invoice price; ~ **ferme** *m* COM bona fide price; ~ **fixe** *m* BOURSE, V&M fixed price; ~ **flexible** *m* COM, ECON flexprice; ~ **à flot** *m* BOURSE *bourse de marchandises* afloat price; ~ **forfaitaire** *m* COM all-inclusive price, flat-rate price, lump-sum price, FISC contract price *(US)*, RES HUM lump sum, TRANSP through fare, V&M flat-rate price; ~ **forfaitaire contractuel final** *m* BOURSE *contrats à terme* final contract settlement price; ~ **fort** *m* V&M premium price; ~ **garanti** *m* FIN guaranteed price; ~ **de gros** *m* COM, V&M bulk price, wholesale price; ~ **homologué** *m* BOURSE probate price; ~ **hors séance** *m* BOURSE after-hours price; ~ **immobiliers** *m pl* IMMOB, V&M house prices; ~ **à l'importation** *m* ECON, IMP/EXP import price; ~ **imposé** *m* COM prescribed price, V&M administered price; ~ **indexé** *m* COM, ECON pegged price; ~ **de l'indice** *m* BOURSE index price; ~ **initial** *m* BOURSE arm's-length price, COMPTA original cost; ~ **intérieur américain** *m* ECON, FIN, IMP/EXP American selling price; ~ **d'intervention** *m* ECON, FIN intervention price; ~ **justifié** *m* BOURSE justified price; ~ **du kilomètre-véhicule** *m* TRANSP cost per vehicle mile; ~ **de lancement** *m* V&M introductory price; ~ **de levée** *m* BOURSE exercise price, strike price; ~ **de levée à la baisse** *m* *(ANT prix de levée à la hausse)* BOURSE bear strike price; ~ **de levée à la hausse** *m* *(ANT prix de levée à la baisse)* BOURSE bull strike price; ~ **de levée de l'option d'achat** *m* *(ANT prix de levée de l'option de vente)* BOURSE call exercise price, call option exercise price, call strike price; ~ **de levée d'option global** *m* BOURSE aggregate exercise price; ~ **de levée d'option rajusté** *m* BOURSE adjusted exercise price (*UK*); ~ **de levée de l'option de vente** *m* (*ANT prix de levée de l'option d'achat*) BOURSE put exercise price, put option exercise price, put strike price; ~ **libellé en dollars** *m* BOURSE dollar price; ~ **de location** *m* IMMOB rent, rental; ~ **majoré** *m* V&M premium price; ~ **marchand** *m* V&M market price; ~ **de marchandises** *m* BOURSE commodity price; ~ **du marché** *m* BOURSE market price, market value, COM average market price, market price, COMPTA arm's-length price, ECON, V&M average market price, market price; ~ **de marché négocié** *m* ECON, V&M negotiated market price; ~ **marqué** *m* V&M marked price; ~ **maximum** *m* BOURSE peak price, IND, V&M maximum price; ~ **maximums** *m pl* COM top prices; ~ **minimal de l'offre de main-d'oeuvre** *m* ECON, RES HUM minimum supply price of labor (*AmE*), minimum supply price of labour (*BrE*); ~ **minimum** *m* COM, V&M *ventes aux enchères* reservation price, reserve, reserve price (*BrE*), upset price (*AmE*); ~ **minimum à l'importation** *m* IMP/EXP trigger price; ~ **modiques** *m pl* V&M budget prices; ~ **mondial** *m* ECON world price; ~ **de monopole** *m* ECON, V&M monopoly price; ~ **moyen** *m* BOURSE mid price, ECON, V&M mean price; ~ **moyen pratiqué** *m pl* COM, V&M average market price; ~ **naturel** *m* ECON natural price; ~ **négocié** *m* ECON, V&M negotiated price; ~ **normal** *m* COM normal price, COMPTA arm's-length price, ECON, V&M normal price; ~ **offert** *m* BOURSE offer price, price offered, *par l'intermédiaire d'un courtier* bid price, COM price offered; ~ **offert et demandé** *m* BOURSE bid-and-asked price; ~ **d'offre** *m* BOURSE offering price; ~ **de l'offre** *m* ECON supply price; ~ **d'option** *m* BOURSE option premium, option price, premium; ~ **d'option d'achat** *m* (*ANT prix d'option de vente*) BOURSE call option premium, call premium; ~ **de l'option de vente** *m* BOURSE put premium; ~ **d'option de vente** *m* (*ANT prix d'option d'achat*) BOURSE put option premium, put premium; ~ **de l'or** *m* BOURSE gold price; ~ **ouvert** *m* BOURSE open price; ~ **au pair** *m* COM parity price; ~ **pervers** *m* ECON perverse price; ~ **pour petits ordres** *m* BOURSE green stripe price; ~ **peu flexible** *m* ECON sticky price; ~ **des places** *m* COM admission fee; ~ **plafond** *m* ECON ceiling price, limit price; ~ **plancher** *m* BOURSE floor price, COM rock-bottom price, ECON, FIN floor price; ~ **plancher accepté pour une adjudication de bons du Trésor** *m* BOURSE stop-out price (*US*); ~ **de pleine concurrence** *m* COMPTA arm's-length price; ~ **le plus avantageux** *m* COM best price; ~ **plus bas** *m* BOURSE lower price; ~ **le plus bas** *m* BOURSE lowest price; ~ **le plus bas de l'offre de main-d'oeuvre** *m* ECON, RES HUM minimum supply price of labor (*AmE*), minimum supply price of labour (*BrE*); ~ **le plus élevé** *m* BOURSE, COM highest price; ~ **du point** *m* BOURSE point price; ~ **pratiqué entre entreprises indépendants** *m*

COMPTA arm's-length price; ~ **prédéterminé** *m* BOURSE predetermined price; ~ **à la production** *m* ECON, ENVIR producer price; ~ **des produits de base** *m pl* BOURSE primary commodity prices; ~ **promotionnels** *m pl* V&M budget prices; ~ **psychologique** *m* V&M *marketing* psychological price, psychological pricing; ~ **public** *m* COM catalog price (*AmE*), catalogue price (*BrE*), published price, V&M catalog price (*AmE*), catalogue price (*BrE*), published price, *ventes* manufacturer's recommended price, MRP; ~ **publicitaire** *m* FIN, V&M advertising price; ~ **publié** *m* TRANSP *billet, trajet* published fare; ~ **à quai** *m* IMP/EXP, TRANSP landed cost; ~ **de rachat** *m* BOURSE call price, redemption price, ECON buying-in price; ~ **à raie verte** *m* BOURSE green stripe price; ~ **raisonnable** *m* COM reasonable price; ~ **Ramsey** *m pl* ECON Ramsey prices; ~ **-réclame** *m* COM, V&M bargain price; ~ **recommandé par le fabriquant** *m* V&M *ventes* manufacturer's recommended price, MRP; ~ **record** *m* BOURSE peak price; ~ **réduit** *m* BOURSE lower price, COM bargain price, knockdown price, V&M bargain price, reduced price; ~ **réel** *m* COM, COMPTA, ECON, FIN, V&M actual price; ~ **de référence** *m* FISC base price; ~ **réglementé** *m* ADMIN, V&M administered price; ~ **relatif** *m* ECON relative price; ~ **de remplacement** *m* COM replacement price; ~ **de réserve** *m* COM, V&M *ventes aux enchères* reservation price, reserve, reserve price (*BrE*), upset price (*AmE*); ~ **de revente** *m* BOURSE (*ANT prix de rachat*) put price, V&M resale price; ~ **de revient** *m* COM cost price; ~ **de revient calculé au plus juste** *m* COMPTA strict cost price; ~ **de revient initial** *m* ECON prime cost, supplementary cost; ~ **de revient standard** *m* COM standard cost; ~ **de revient unitaire** *m* COMPTA unit cost; ~ **sacrifié** *m* V&M mammoth reduction; ~ **selon la demande** *m* ECON demand price; ~ **selon le tarif** *m pl* COM scheduled prices; ~ **de seuil** *m* COM threshold price; ~ **de solde** *m* COM sale price; ~ **soldé** *m* COM, V&M bargain price; ~ **de sortie** *m* BOURSE exit price; ~ **à la source** *m* COM wellhead prices; ~ **de souscription** *m* BOURSE, COM subscription price, FIN allotment price; ~ **de soutien** *m* ECON *agriculture* support price; ~ **stabilisé** *m* ECON stabilized price; ~ **standard** *m* COM, ECON, V&M standard price; ~ **standards** *m pl* COM, COMPTA, FIN budget prices; ~ **sur la base zéro** *m* COM zero-priced; ~ **sur demande** *m pl* COM prices on application; ~ **sur linéaire** *m* V&M shelf price; ~ **sur place** *m* IMP/EXP, TRANSP loco; ~ **sur wagon** *m* TRANSP price on rail; ~ **de taux d'intérêt à terme** *m pl* BOURSE, FIN interest-rate futures prices; ~ **à terme** *m* BOURSE future price, terminal price; ~ **théorique** *m* COMPTA nominal price; ~ **tout compris** *m* COM all-inclusive price, inclusive terms; ~ **de la transaction** *m* BOURSE, COM, V&M trade price; ~ **de transfert** *m* COMPTA transfer pricing; ~ **unique** *m* COM, ECON, V&M uniform price; ~ **unitaire** *m* COM unit price; ~ **à l'unité** *m* COM, V&M unit pricing; ~ **variable** *m* COM variable charge; ~ **de vente** *m* COM consideration for sale, sale price, selling price; ~ **de vente imposé** *m* ECON, FIN resale price maintenance, RPM, V&M retail price maintenance, RPM; ~ **de vente rajusté** *m* COMPTA adjusted selling price; ~ **virtuel** *m* COMPTA shadow price; ♦ **à** ~ COM at price; **à** ~ **coûtant** COM at cost; **à des** ~ **allant de** COM at prices ranging from; **à** ~ **réduit** COM concessionary, low-cost; **au** ~ **actuel** COM at current prices; **au** ~ **de revient** COM at cost; **deux pour le** ~ **d'un** V&M one-cent sale (*US*); **dont le** ~ **n'est pas marqué** COM unpriced; **en** ~ **constants** COM at constant prices; **faire baisser le** ~ COM beat the price down; **les** ~ **se sont inscrits en baisse** BOURSE prices have been marked down; **soumis à des contrôles de** ~ ECON subject to price controls; ♦ ~ **en gare de départ** COM, TRANSP at station price; **pour un** ~ **convenu** COM at an agreed price

Prix: ~ **Nobel d'économie** *m* ECON Nobel Prize for Economics

pro *m* COM, LOISIRS pro (*infrml*)

proactif, -ive *adj* COM, GESTION, POL proactive

proaméricain, e *adj* POL pro-American

probabilité *f* COM likelihood, probability, GESTION, MATH probability; ~ **corrigée** FIN, MATH corrected probability

probable *adj* COM likely, probable

probant, e *adj* COM conclusive, DROIT conclusive, evident

probité: ~ **de l'entreprise** *f* COM corporate morality

problématique *adj* COM problematic

problème *m* COM problem, snag (*infrml*), trouble, DROIT issue; ~ **des agrégats** COMPTA, ECON aggregation problem; ~ **concernant la protection de l'environnement** ENVIR, POL green issue; ~ **de la dette mondiale** ECON, POL world debt problem; ~ **écologique** ENVIR, POL environmental issue, environmental problem, green issue; ~ **d'identification** ECON *économétrie* identification problem; ~ **de liquidité** COMPTA cash flow problem; ~ **majeur** COM big issue; ~ **d'optimisation** MATH optimization problem; ~ **préoccupant** RES HUM concern; ~ **quotidien** POL, PROT SOC bread-and-butter issue (*infrml*); ~ **relevant des conventions collectives** RES HUM negotiable issue; ~ **technique** INFO glitch; ~ **test** COM test problem; ~ **de totalisation** COMPTA, ECON aggregation problem; ~ **de transfert de capitaux** ECON transfer problem; ~ **de transformation** ECON transformation problem; ~ **de trésorerie** COMPTA cash flow problem

problèmes: ~ **humains** *m pl* COM, RES HUM people-related problems; ~ **de liquidité** *m pl* COMPTA liquidity problems; ~ **relatifs aux consommateurs** *m pl* V&M consumer issues; ~ **sociaux** *m pl* RES HUM labor troubles (*AmE*), labour troubles (*BrE*); ♦ **avoir beaucoup de** ~ COM have a lot of trouble; **avoir des** ~ COM be in trouble

procédé *m* IND process; ~ **analytique** GESTION, RES HUM analytic process; ~ **comptable** COMPTA, FIN accounting procedure; ~ **de contrôle de gestion** ADMIN administrative control procedure; ~ **de fabrication** COM engineering process, IND production process; ~ **de fabrication en continu** ECON, IND continuous process; ~ **industriel** ENVIR, IND industrial process; ~ **original** COM original device; ~ **de répartition aléatoire** MATH randomization

procéder *vi* COM proceed; ♦ ~ **à une désintermédiation** ECON disintermediate; ~ **à un vote scrutin** RES HUM take a ballot

procédural, e *adj* ADMIN, COM, DROIT, GESTION, RES HUM procedural

procédure *f* ADMIN procedure, BREVETS *devant l'Organisation européenne de Brevets* proceedings, COM procedure, DROIT practice, proceedings, procedure, RES HUM procedure; ~ **d'appel** DROIT appeal proceedings, appeals procedure, RES HUM appeals procedure; ~ **d'arbitrage** COM, DROIT, IND, RES HUM arbitration proceedings; ~ **en cas de conflit** COM, RES HUM dispute procedure; ~ **de choix d'investissement** ECON capital budgeting; ~ **coercitive** COM enforcement procedure; ~ **de commande** INFO control procedure; ~ **de conciliation** DROIT, RES HUM conciliation procedure (*UK*); ~ **contradictoire** COM audita altera parte procedure (*frml*); ~ **de contrôle** COMPTA, FIN auditing procedure; ~ **courante** COM standing procedure; ~ **de dédouanement simplifiée** IMP/EXP simplified clearance procedure, SCP; ~ **de dépôt de plainte** DROIT complaints procedure; ~ **disciplinaire** RES HUM disciplinary procedure; ~ **de documentation exportation** IMP/EXP export documentation procedure; ~ **douanière** IMP/EXP customs procedure; ~ **électorale** POL voting procedure; ~ **d'essai** IND testing procedure; ~ **d'éviction** DROIT, IMMOB ejectment; ~ **d'exercice** BOURSE exercise procedure; ~ **d'expropriation** BREVETS, DROIT *immobilier* dispossess proceedings; ~ **externe** TRANSP *transit* external procedure; ~ **de faillite** DROIT, FIN bankruptcy proceedings; ~ **interne** TRANSP *transit* internal procedure; ~ **judiciaire** DROIT court procedure; ~ **de levée** BOURSE exercise procedure; ~ **de licenciement** RES HUM redundancy procedure; ~ **de négociation** RES HUM negotiating procedure; ~ **normale à suivre** COM s.o.p., standard operating procedure; ~ **d'opposition** BREVETS opposition proceedings; ~ **orale** BREVETS oral proceedings; ~ **parlementaire** GESTION parliamentary procedure; ~ **prud'hommale** RES HUM grievance procedure; ~ **prud'hommale collective** RES HUM collective grievance procedure (*UK*); ~ **prud'hommale privée** RES HUM individual grievance procedure; ~ **de réclamation** ASSUR claims procedure; ~ **de réclamation concernant les marchandises** TRANSP cargo claims procedure; ~ **de règlement des conflits** COM, RES HUM dispute procedure, grievance and disciplinary procedure; ~ **de renvoi** RES HUM dismissal procedure; ~ **pour résoudre des griefs** RES HUM grievance procedure; ~ **simplifiée pour marchandises transportées par chemin de fer** TRANSP simplified procedure for goods carried by rail, SPGER

procédures: ~ **de clôture des comptes** *f pl* COMPTA cutoff procedures; ~ **de fin d'exercice** *f pl* COMPTA cutoff procedures; ~ **de gestion** *f pl* GESTION management practices; ~ **d'inventaire** *f pl* COM year-end procedures; ~ **de recouvrement de protection** *f pl* FISC jeopardy collection procedures

procédurier, -ère *adj* ADMIN, COM, DROIT, GESTION, RES HUM procedural

procès *m* DROIT action, case, law suit, legal proceedings, suit, trial; ~ **à l'amiable** DROIT friendly suit; ~ **avec jury** DROIT jury trial; ~ **civil** DROIT civil proceedings; ~ **en diffamation** DROIT action for libel, libel proceedings, slander action; ~ **-verbal** ADMIN minutes; ♦ **faire un ~ à qn** DROIT take sb to court

processeur *m* INFO processor; ~ **central** INFO central processing unit, mainframe; ~ **d'entrée/ sortie** INFO input/output processor; ~ **vectoriel** INFO array processor, AP

processus *m* COM, INFO process; ~ **d'achat** COM buying process; ~ **d'adoption** DROIT *enfant*, V&M *d'un produit* adoption process; ~ **analytique** GESTION, RES HUM analytic process; ~ **d'autorisation** BANQUE approval process; ~ **de compensation** BANQUE clearing process; ~ **compétitif** ECON competitive process; ~ **de la décision** GESTION decision process; ~ **de décision des ménages** ECON household decision-making; ~ **de fabrication** IND manufacturing process; ~ **de fabrication en continu** IND process engineering; ~ **d'harmonisation** COM, DROIT, ECON, IMP/EXP, POL harmonization process; ~ **industriel** ENVIR, IND industrial process; ~ **logistique** IND, MATH logistic process; ~ **de prise de décision** GESTION decision-making process; ~ **de production** IND production process; ~ **de survie** ECON survival process

prochain[1], **e** *adj* COM forthcoming, next

prochain:[2] ~ **exercice fiscal** *m* COM, FISC upcoming fiscal year; ~ **mois de livraison** *m* BOURSE spot delivery month

proche[1] *adj* COM close, near, nearby

proche:[2] ~ **admissible** *m* FISC qualified relation; ~ **avenir** *m* COM near future

procommuniste *adj* POL pro-communist

procuration *f* ADMIN power of attorney, PA, DROIT letter of attorney, proxy statement, warrant of attorney, power of attorney, PA, ECON proxy; ~ **autorisant le transfert d'actions** BOURSE stock power; ~ **en blanc** BOURSE bearer proxy; ♦ **par ~** *(p.p.)* COM per procuration, per procurationem *(frml)* *(per pro.)*

procurer 1. *vt* COM, FIN obtain; **2.** *v pron* **se ~** COM, FIN obtain; ♦ **se ~ de l'argent** COM, FIN raise

funds, raise money; **se ~ des capitaux** BOURSE raise capital, COM, FIN raise funds, raise money

procureur: ~ **général** *m* DROIT ≈ Attorney General *(US)*, public prosecutor; ~ **de la République** *m France* DROIT ≈ D/A *(US)*, ≈ district attorney *(US)*, ≈ DPP *(UK)*, ≈ Director of Public Prosecutions *(UK)*, ≈ Attorney General *(US)*; ~ **du Roi** *m Belgique* DROIT ≈ D/A *(US)*, ≈ district attorney *(US)*, ≈ DPP *(UK)*, ≈ Director of Public Prosecutions *(UK)*, ≈ Attorney General *(US)*

producteur, -trice *m,f* ECON producer; ~ **de fruits** ECON, IND *agriculture* fruit farmer; ~ **marginal** ECON, IND marginal producer; ~ **d'or** IND gold producer; ~ **de réserve** IND swing producer

productif, -ive *adj* COM *capital* instrumental, COMPTA cost-effective, FIN active, RES HUM productive; ~ **d'intérêts** BANQUE interest-bearing

production *f* COMPTA output, yield, ECON output, production, yield, FIN yield, FISC *d'une déclaration* filing *(Canada)*, IND output, production, yield; ~ **agricole** COM, ECON, IMP/EXP, IND agricultural production; ~ **à la chaîne** IND chain production, line production; ~ **ciblée pour audience spécialisée** MÉDIA *édition* vertical publication *(jarg)*; ~ **en continu** IND continuous process production, continuous production; ~ **continue** IND continuous-flow production; ~ **dans les délais impartis** IND, RES HUM just-in-time production, JIT; ~ **directe** ECON direct production; ~ **à domicile** ECON, IND home production; ~ **à flux tendus** IND, RES HUM just-in-time production, JIT; ~ **de gaz naturel** ENVIR gas recovery; ~ **globale** ECON, IND aggregate output, aggregate production; ~ **à grande échelle** IND large-scale production; ~ **groupée** IND process equipment layout; ~ **hâtive** FISC *d'une déclaration* early filing; ~ **industrielle** ECON, IND industrial production; ~ **intégrée par ordinateur** IND, INFO computer-integrated manufacturing; ~ **en masse** IND mass production; ~ **nationale** ECON, IND domestic output; ~ **nette** ECON, IND, POL net output; ~ **par lots** IND batch production; ~ **en petites séries** IND batch production; ~ **de revenus** COM, ECON revenue production; ~ **de sucre** IND sugar production; ~ **tardive** FISC *d'une déclaration* late filing; ~ **d'usine** IND plant manufacturing

productivité *f* COM, ECON earning performance, efficiency, productivity, *rendement* output, yield, IND *rendement* output, productivity; ~ **des facteurs de production** ECON, IND factor productivity; ~ **marginale** ECON, IND marginal productivity

produire *vt* BANQUE *des intérêts* earn, yield, BOURSE *bénéfice, perte* yield, COM *des idées* generate, DROIT *preuve* adduce, ECON generate, produce, IND grow, produce; ~ **une déclaration** FISC file a return; ~ **en grandes séries** IND mass-produce; ~ **un revenu** BOURSE generate income

produit[1], **e** *adj* COM, IND made; ♦ ~ **en France**

COM, IND made in France; ~ **en grandes séries** IND mass-produced; ~ **en série** COM machine-made

produit² *m* BANQUE avails, COM avails, cmdty, commodity, proceeds, product, ECON cmdty, commodity, product, FIN avails, proceeds, IND cmdty, commodity, produce, product, INFO facility, V&M commodity, cmdty, product; ~ **agricole** COM, ECON, IMP/EXP agricultural commodity, agricultural produce, agricultural product; ~ **agricole de base** ECON, IMP/EXP agricultural commodity; ~ **agrochimique** ENVIR agrochemical product; ~ **alimentaire industriel** IND processed food; ~ **d'appel** COM appeal product, V&M sell up (*jarg*), sell up product, *marketing* loss leader; ~ **d'appel bon marché** V&M leader (*US*), product leader; ~ **en baisse** BOURSE soft commodity; ~ **banal** ECON, IND homogeneous goods; ~ **bas de gamme** V&M down-market product; ~ **de base** BOURSE primary commodity, COM cmdty, commodity, ECON basic commodity, cmdty, commodity, primary commodity, primary product, IND base product, cmdty, commodity, primary commodity, tertiary product, V&M basic commodity; ~ **biologique** ENVIR organic material; ~ **brut** FIN gross cash flow; ~ **compensatoire** IMP/EXP compensating product; ~ **composite** ECON composite commodity; ~ **de consommation** COM article of consumption, ECON, IND, V&M consumer product; ~ **constaté d'avance** COMPTA accrued credit, accrued income; ~ **constaté par régularisation** COMPTA accrued revenue; ~ **dérivé** ECON, ENVIR by-product, IND, V&M by-product, derivative product; ~ **de deuxième génération** V&M second-generation product; ~ **écologique** ENVIR clean product, environmentally-friendly product; ~ **de l'emploi alternatif** FIN opportunity cost; ~ **d'excellente qualité** V&M high-quality product; ~ **exceptionnel** COMPTA, ECON below-the-line revenue; ~ **d'exploitation commun** COMPTA, ECON common revenue; ~ **de la ferme** ECON farm produce; ~ **final** COM end product; ~ **à forte rentabilité** COM cash cow product; ~ **à forte valeur ajoutée** ECON, IND, V&M high added-value product; ~ **grand public** IND, V&M consumer-oriented product; ~ **haut de gamme** V&M up-market product; ~ **de l'impôt** FISC tax proceeds; ~ **d'intérêts** BANQUE interest income; ~ **intérieur brut** *(PIB)* ECON gross domestic product *(GDP)*; ~ **intérieur brut au coût des facteurs** ECON gross domestic product at factor cost; ~ **intérieur brut de l'État** ECON gross state product; ~ **intérieur brut aux prix du marché** ECON gross domestic product at market prices; ~ **leader** V&M brand leader, core product; ~ **lié** ECON, V&M complement; ~ **locomotive** V&M star product; ~ **marginal** IND, V&M marginal product; ~ **marginal de la main-d'oeuvre** ECON marginal product of labor (*AmE*), marginal product of labour (*BrE*); ~ **marginal physique** ECON marginal physical product, MPP; ~ **marginal du travail** ECON marginal pro-

duct of labor (*AmE*), marginal product of labour (*BrE*); ~ **-mix** V&M *marketing* product mix; ~ **national brut** *(PNB)* ECON gross national product *(GNP)*; ~ **national net** *(PNN)* ECON net national product *(n.n.p.)*; ~ **net** COM, IMMOB net proceeds, np; ~ **non-essentiel** ECON nonbasic commodity; ~ **pétrolier** ENVIR petroleum product; ~ **potentiel** ECON, IND potential output; ~ **pourvu d'un code barres** INFO, V&M bar-coded product; ~ **de première catégorie** COM top-rank product; ~ **de première qualité** COM top-rank product; ~ **de privatisation** COM, ECON privatization proceeds; ~ **à recevoir** COMPTA accrued asset, accrued revenue; ~ **recherche et développement** IND, V&M research and development product; ~ **de récupération** ENVIR waste product; ~ **de remplacement** ECON, IND substitute product; ~ **de la revente** COM, IMMOB proceeds from resale; ~ **secondaire** ECON nonbasic commodity; ~ **semi-fini** IND semifinished product; ~ **social** ECON national income, social product; ~ **social brut** ECON gross social product; ~ **de substitution** ECON, IND substitute product; ~ **tertiaire** ECON staple commodity, tertiary product, IND tertiary product, V&M staple commodity, tertiary product; ~ **vache à lait** COM cash cow product; ~ **vedette** V&M star product; ~ **de la vente** COM proceeds of sales, sale proceeds; ~ **vert** ENVIR environmentally-friendly product; ♦ ce ~ **est en vente à un prix inférieur à sa vraie valeur** COM this product is underpriced; ~ **fictif ou moins-value** BOURSE paper profit or loss

produits *m pl* COM, IND gds, goods, produce, V&M gds, goods; ~ **d'achat courant** V&M convenience goods; ~ **agro-alimentaires** ECON agrifoodstuffs; ~ **alimentaires** COM, ECON, IND foodstuffs; ~ **d'appel** V&M impulse goods; ~ **d'assurance** ASSUR insurance proceeds; ~ **audiovisuels** V&M brown goods; ~ **blancs** V&M white goods; ~ **bruns** V&M brown goods; ~ **bruts** COM crude goods; ~ **budgétés** COMPTA, FIN budgeted income; ~ **chimiques** IND chemicals; ~ **chimiques dangereux** TRANSP hazardous chemicals, hazchem; ~ **de choc** V&M impulse goods; ~ **conditionnés** V&M packaged goods; ~ **de consommation courante** COM convenience products, ECON consumer products, IND basic consumer products, V&M consumer products, convenience goods; ~ **de consommation durables** V&M consumer durables; ~ **constatés d'avance** COMPTA deferred credit, deferred income; ~ **en cours** COM work-in-process (*AmE*), work-in-progress (*BrE*); ~ **dangereux** COM, IND, TRANSP, V&M dangerous goods; ~ **dangereux à bord** TRANSP dangerous goods on board, DGB; ~ **différenciés** V&M differentiated goods, differentiated products; ~ **divers** COMPTA, FISC, PROT SOC other income; ~ **divers de gestion courante** COM, COMPTA, IND nonoperating revenue; ~ **à durée de vie moyenne** V&M orange goods; ~ **entreposés en douanes** COM, FISC, IMP/

EXP, IND, TRANSP b/g, bonded goods; ~ **d'épicerie** V&M dry goods; ~ **et charges** COMPTA revenue and expenses; ~ **financiers** COMPTA income from interest, *compte de pertes et profits* interest earned; ~ **finis** COM, ECON, IND final goods, final products, finished goods, finished products; ~ **frais** IND live food, V&M fresh food, fresh goods; ~ **de grande consommation** V&M consumer brands, convenience goods, red goods (*jarg*); ~ **de grande consommation à forte rotation** V&M fast-moving consumer goods, FMCG; ~ **de grande diffusion** V&M convenience goods; ~ **des immobilisations financières** BOURSE, COMPTA income from securities; ~ **industriels** IND industrial products; ~ **intermédiaires** COMPTA semifinished goods; ~ **jaunes** COM yellow goods (*jarg*); ~ **laitiers** COM dairy products, milk products; ~ **libres** COM unbranded goods; ~ **liés** ECON joint products; ~ **manufacturés** ECON, IND manufactured goods, manufactures; ~ **nationaux** COM, ECON home products; ~ **PAC** ECON CAP goods; ~ **de participations** COMPTA income from participations; ~ **pétroliers** FISC, IND mineral oil products; ~ **pharmaceutiques** IND pharmaceuticals; ~ **de qualité inférieure** COM inferior goods; ~ **de services** ECON tertiary products; ~ **soumis à l'accise** FISC, IMP/EXP excisable goods; ~ **du tabac** FISC, IND tobacco products; ~ **d'utilisation finale** IMP/EXP end use goods

prof *abrév (professeur)* RES HUM Prof *(Professor)*

professeur *m (prof)* RES HUM Professor *(Prof)*; ~ **vacataire** PROT SOC, RES HUM adjunct professor *(US)*

profession *f* IMMOB occupation, RES HUM occupation, profession; ~ **bancaire** BANQUE banking circles; ~ **comptable** COMPTA accountancy profession, accountancy; ~ **connexe** RES HUM closely connected profession; ~ **de courtier en bourse** BOURSE stockbroking; ~ **libérale** FISC self-employment, RES HUM profession

professionnalisation *f* RES HUM professionalization

professionnalisme *m* COM professionalism

professionnel[1], **-elle** *adj* RES HUM occupational, professional

professionnel[2], **-elle** *m,f* COM *(pro)* professional *(pro)*, LOISIRS *sport* pro *(infrml)*, professional

professionnellement: personne ~ instable *f* RES HUM *personne* job hopper, job jumper

profil *m* COM contour, cross section, outline, profile; ~ **d'acquisition** BANQUE acquisition profile; ~ **de la clientèle** V&M customer profile; ~ **de compétences** RES HUM personnel specification; ~ **du consommateur** V&M *marketing* consumer profile; ~ **démographique** PROT SOC, V&M demographics; ~ **de l'emploi** RES HUM job profile; ~ **de l'entreprise** COM company profile; ~ **du lectorat** V&M *étude de marché* readership profile; ~ **d'un marché** V&M market profile; ~ **marketing** V&M marketing profile; ~ **du poste** RES HUM job spec *(infrml)*, job specification; ~ **du produit** V&M

product profile; ~ **de profit** FIN profit profile; ~ **des ressources** COM resource profile; ~ **de risque** ASSUR risk profile, FIN profile risk; ~ **des salaires** RES HUM wage contour; ~ **du salarié** RES HUM employee profile; ~ **selon l'âge et les revenus** RES HUM age-earnings profile; ~ **technique** COM technical profile; ~ **type** COM model profile; ~ **de l'utilisateur** V&M user profile; ◆ **à ~ bas** *(ANT à haut profil)* COM, V&M low-profile; **avoir le ~ de l'emploi** RES HUM have the right qualifications for the job; **le candidat n'a pas le ~ requis pour le poste** RES HUM this candidate is not suited to the job; **ne pas avoir le ~ voulu pour le poste** RES HUM be unsuited to the job

profit *m* COM benefit, gain, ECON, FIN gain, profit, V&M profit; ~ **exceptionnel** COMPTA extraordinary gain, extraordinary item FIN extraordinary item; ~ **fictif** COMPTA, FIN illusory profit; ~ **illusoire** COMPTA, FIN illusory profit; ~ **non matérialisé** COMPTA, FIN paper profit; ~ **non-réalisé** COMPTA, FIN unrealized profit; ~ **normal** COM, ECON, V&M normal profit; ~ **personnel** FISC personal benefit, personal profit; ~ **potentiel** BOURSE potential profit; ~ **sectoriel** COMPTA segment profit; ~ **social** ECON social profit

profitable *adj* COM advantageous, beneficial, DROIT beneficial

profiter: ~ **à** *vt* COM, FIN benefit; ~ **de** COM *situation, vente, employé* take advantage of, FIN cash in on; ~ **à qn** COM be of benefit to sb, be to sb's advantage; ◆ ~ **d'une occasion pour faire** COM take advantage of an opportunity to do

profiteur *m* FIN profiteer; ~ **de grève** RES HUM free rider *(infrml)*

profond, e *adj* BOURSE profound, COM *problèmes* deep-seated, profound

profondément *adv* BOURSE *hors du cours*, COM deep, deeply, profoundly; ◆ ~ **ancré** COM deep-rooted, deep-seated; ~ **structurel** COM *problèmes, difficultés* deep-rooted, deep-seated

profondeur:[1] **en ~** *adv* COM in depth

profondeur:[2] ~ **au quai** *f* TRANSP *navigation* depth alongside

pro forma *adj* COM pro forma

profusion *f* COM abundance, profusion

progiciel *m* INFO package, pkg, program package *(AmE)*, programme package *(BrE)*, software, software package; ~ **de comptabilité** COMPTA, FIN, INFO accounting package, accounting software; ~ **logique** INFO graphic software

prognostiquer *vt* COM prognosticate

programmateur: ~ **de vol** *m* TRANSP flight scheduler

programmation *f* COM programming, GESTION, IND *production* scheduling, INFO coding, computer programming, programming; ~ **dynamique** COM, INFO, MATH dynamic programming; ~ **économique** ECON economic programming; ~ **horaire** TRANSP timetable planning;

~ **d'itinéraires** TRANSP route planning; ~ **linéaire** ECON *économétrie*, INFO, MATH linear programming; ~ **mathématique** MATH mathematical programming, scientific programming; ~ **non-linéaire** ECON, INFO, MATH nonlinear programming; ~ **paramétrique** INFO, MATH parametric programming; ~ **de la production** COM, GESTION, IND production planning, production scheduling; ~ **progressive** *(*ANT *programmation régressive)* GESTION forward scheduling; ~ **régressive** *(*ANT *programmation progressive)* GESTION backward scheduling; ~ **structurée** INFO structured programming; ~ **systèmes** INFO systems programming; ~ **des tâches** COM task scheduling

programme *m* ADMIN scheme, COM program *(AmE)*, programme *(BrE)*, routine, schedule, *de placements* playbook *(US, jarg)*, ECON program *(AmE)*, programme *(BrE)*, FIN schedule, GESTION agenda, program *(AmE)*, programme *(BrE)*, schedule, INFO driver, program, MÉDIA program *(AmE)*, programme *(BrE)*, PROT SOC curriculum, *scolaire* syllabus; ~ **ACE** ENVIR ACE program *(AmE)*, ACE programme *(BrE)*; ~ **d'action** COM action plan, action program *(AmE)*, action programme *(BrE)*, ECON, POL action program *(AmE)*, action programme *(BrE)*, RES HUM action plan; ~ **d'action communautaire pour l'environnement** ENVIR ACE program *(AmE)*, ACE programme *(BrE)*, action by the community relating to the environment programme; ~ **d'action environnemental** ECON environmental action program *(AmE)*, environmental action programme *(BrE)*; ~ **d'aide** BANQUE, ECON, POL aid program *(AmE)*, aid programme *(BrE)*, aid scheme; ~ **alimentaire mondial** ECON World Food Program *(AmE)*, World Food Programme *(BrE)*, WFP; ~ **d'amélioration de la manutention des bagages** TRANSP baggage improvement program *(AmE)*, baggage improvement programme *(BrE)*, BIP; ~ **d'analyse** INFO analyser *(BrE)*, analyzer *(AmE)*; ~ **des annonces** MÉDIA, V&M advertising schedule; ~ **d'appel** INFO calling program; ~ **d'application** INFO applications program, applications software; ~ **d'assemblage** COM, IND assembly program *(AmE)*, assembly programme *(BrE)*, INFO assembler, RES HUM assembly program *(AmE)*, assembly programme *(BrE)*; ~ **d'audit annuel** COMPTA annual audit plan *(UK)*; ~ **de base** PROT SOC core curriculum; ~ **chargé** COM, GESTION, RES HUM busy schedule; ~ **communautaire** POL, RES HUM Community Programme *(UK*; ~ **compilateur** INFO translator; ~ **de complétion** ENVIR completion program *(AmE)*, completion programme *(BrE)*; ~ **de contrôle** COMPTA, FIN audit program *(AmE)*, audit programme *(BrE)*, INFO control program; ~ **de dépenses directes** COMPTA direct spending program *(AmE)*, direct spending programme *(BrE)*; ~ **de développement** ECON development program *(AmE)*, development programme *(BrE)*, development planning, FIN, GESTION, POL devel-

opment planning, development program *(AmE)*, development programme *(BrE)*; ~ **de diagnostic** COM diagnostic routine; ~ **en direct** MÉDIA *radio, télévision* live program *(AmE)*, live programme *(BrE)*; ~ **d'édition** INFO editor; ~ **élargi** COM enriched program *(AmE)*, enriched programme *(BrE)*; ~ **d'entretien** COM maintenance schedule; ~ **d'étiquetage des produits écologiques** ENVIR, V&M green labeling scheme *(AmE)*, green labelling scheme *(BrE)*; ~ **d'études** COM curriculum, PROT SOC curriculum, *scolaire* syllabus; ~ **d'exploitation** TRANSP operating schedule; ~ **de fabrication** COM, GESTION, IND production schedule; ~ **financé par l'administration centrale** COMPTA centrally-financed program *(AmE)*, centrally-financed programme *(BrE)*; ~ **de forage** ENVIR drilling program *(AmE)*, drilling programme *(BrE)*; ~ **de formation** COM, RES HUM training program *(AmE)*, training programme *(BrE)*; ~ **à frais partagés** POL cost-shared program *(AmE)*, cost-shared programme *(BrE)*, shared-cost program *(AmE)*, shared-cost programme *(BrE)*; ~ **des immobilisations** COMPTA capital program *(AmE)*, capital programme *(BrE)*; ~ **imposé aux télévisions par l'IBA** MÉDIA mandated programme *(UK)*; ~ **informatique** INFO computer program; ~ **intensifié** COM extended program *(AmE)*, extended programme *(BrE)*; ~ **d'interprétation** INFO translator; ~ **d'interrogation** INFO enquiry program, inquiry program; ~ **d'investissement** BOURSE, FIN investment program *(AmE)*, investment programme *(BrE)*; ~ **linéaire** ECON *économétrie* linear program *(AmE)*, linear programme *(BrE)*, INFO linear program, MATH linear program *(AmE)*, linear programme *(BrE)*; ~ **machine** INFO computer program; ~ **de matériel roulant** FIN rolling program *(AmE)*, rolling programme *(BrE)*; ~ **ministériel** ADMIN departmental program *(AmE)*, departmental programme *(BrE)*; ~ **de mise à jour** COM maintenance schedule; ~ **de mise en valeur d'anciens forages** ECON developmental drilling program *(AmE)*, developmental drilling programme *(BrE)*; ~ **de négoce** COM, FIN trading program *(AmE)*, trading programme *(BrE)*; ~ **d'options ouvert à tous les employés** BOURSE all-employee option scheme *(UK)*; ~ **d'ordinateur** INFO computer program; ~ **d'origine** INFO source program; ~ **de participation boursière** BOURSE, PROT SOC, RES HUM share participation scheme; ~ **de participation directe** FIN direct participation program *(AmE)*, direct participation programme *(BrE)*; ~ **portable** INFO canned program; ~ **de primes d'encouragement** RES HUM bonus scheme; ~ **de primes de rendement** RES HUM bonus scheme; ~ **prioritaire** INFO foreground program; ~ **de privatisations** COM, ECON privatization program *(AmE)*, privatization programme *(BrE)*; ~ **de rachat d'actions** BOURSE share repurchase plan; ~ **de rationalisation** COM, ECON rationalization program *(AmE)*, rationalization programme *(BrE)*; ~ **de recherche** IND, PROT SOC research

program (*AmE*), research programme (*BrE*); ~ **de**
réformes ECON, POL reform program (*AmE*),
reform programme (*BrE*); ~ **réglementaire** POL
statutory program (*AmE*), statutory programme
(*BrE*); ~ **de relance** INFO restart program; ~ **de**
remboursements BANQUE schedule of repayments; ~ **de salaires au rendement** RES HUM
incentive wage plan; ~ **sans endettement** FIN
unleveraged program (*AmE*), unleveraged programme (*BrE*); ~ **secret** GESTION, POL hidden
agenda; ~ **source** INFO source program; ~ **spécial**
de relance des projets d'investissement COM
SRCPP (*Canada*), Special Recovery Capital Projects Program (*Canada*); ~ **de stimulants**
salariaux RES HUM incentive scheme, incentive
wage plan; ~ **symbolique** INFO source program;
~ **tenant compte des imprévus** GESTION, POL
contingency planning; ~ **de traduction** INFO
translator; ~ **transportable** INFO canned program;
~ **de travail** ADMIN, GESTION work schedule; ~ **de**
travaux publics COM public works program
(*AmE*), public works programme (*BrE*);
~ **utilitaire** INFO utility, utility program; ~ **d'utilité**
publique POL, RES HUM Community Programme
(*UK*); ~ **de vérification** COMPTA, FIN audit program (*AmE*), audit programme (*BrE*); ~ **de**
vérification annuelle COMPTA annual audit plan
(*UK*); ◆ **par** ~ INFO programmatic

programmé: être ~ **pour** *loc* COM be scheduled for
programmer *vt* COM program (*AmE*), programme
(*BrE*), *rendez-vous* schedule, GESTION schedule,
INFO encode, program
programmeur, -euse *m,f* INFO computer programmer; ~ **d'applications** INFO applications
programmer; ~ **sur ordinateur** INFO computer
programmer; ~ **système** INFO systems programmer
progrès *m* COM, IND advance, progress;
~ **commercial** GESTION business development;
~ **technique** ECON, IND technical progress; ~ **tech-**
nique augmentant les facteurs IND factor-
augmenting technical progress; ~ **technique fac-**
teur d'accroissement de la main d'oeuvre ECON
labor-augmenting technical progress (*AmE*),
labour-augmenting technical progress (*BrE*);
~ **technique facteur d'augmentation du capital**
ECON capital-augmenting technical progress;
~ **technique incorporé** IND embodied technical
progress; ~ **technique induit** ECON induced technical progress; ~ **technique mis en application**
IND embodied technical progress; ~ **technique**
neutre ECON neutral technical progress; ~ **tech-**
nologique rapide ECON, IND rapid technological
progress; ◆ **faire des** ~ BOURSE make solid
ground, COM advance, come along, make headway
progresser *vi* BOURSE move ahead, COM *entreprise*
make progress, *inflation, salaires* rise, *pouvoir*
d'achat increase; ~ **lentement** ECON edge up; ◆
faire ~ COM advance, *travail* advance

progressif, -ive *adj* COM gradual, progressive, FISC
graduated
progression *f* BOURSE advance, ECON growth;
~ **arithmétique** MATH arithmetic progression;
~ **géométrique** ECON *de chômage, d'inflation,*
MATH geometric progression
progressivement *adv* COM in graduated stages,
progressively
prohibitif, -ive *adj* COM prohibitive
projecteur *m* COM *diapositive, film* projector; ~ **de**
diapositives COM slide projector; ~ **sonore** COM
sound projector
projectile *m* IND missile, TRANSP *marchandises*
dangereuses projectile
projection *f* COM, ECON, MATH projection;
~ **catastrophe** COM, ECON worst-case projection;
~ **d'image de marque** V&M image projection;
~ **des profits** COM, ECON, FIN profit projection
projet *m* ADMIN blueprint, COM blueprint, design,
plan, project, proposal, ECON, GESTION, IMMOB
plan; ~ **d'accroissement des revenus** COM revenue project; ~ **d'acte** DROIT draft; ~ **de budget**
COMPTA budget proposal, draft budget, FIN budget proposal; ~ **cadre** COM umbrella project;
~ **cahotique** COM rolling plan; ~ **commercial**
COM, GESTION business plan, business planning;
~ **de contrat** COM, DROIT draft contract; ~ **de**
développement ECON, POL development project;
~ **de directive** DROIT, POL *UE* draft directive; ~ **en**
dollar constant COM, ECON constant dollar plan
(*UK*); ~ **d'essai** COM, GESTION pilot project; ~ **et**
contrôle de la production COM, GESTION, IND
production planning and control; ~ **d'expédition**
TRANSP project forwarding; ~ **d'exploitation**
pluriannuel FIN multiyear operational plan,
MYOP; ~ **financé par des bons** POL aid-financed
project; ~ **de financement de grandes entreprises**
FIN corporate financing project; ~ **inutile** RES
HUM boondoggle (*US, infrml*);
~ **d'investissement** BOURSE, COMPTA, ECON, FIN
capital project; ~ **d'investissement sur budget**
BOURSE, COMPTA, ECON, FIN capital project;
~ **de loi** DROIT bill; ~ **de loi éventreur** POL ripper
bill (*US, jarg*); ~ **de loi de finances** COMPTA,
DROIT, ECON Appropriation Act (*UK*), Appropriation Bill (*US*), reconciliation bill (*US*); ~ **de**
loi des finances POL finance bill, supply bill; ~ **de**
lotissement IMMOB, PROT SOC housing project;
~ **management** FIN, GESTION, RES HUM project
management; ~ **mise à l'étude** COMPTA exposure
draft; ~ **de norme** COMPTA exposure draft;
~ **pilote** COM pilot scheme; ~ **de placement**
BOURSE, FIN investment project; ~ **de promotion**
immobilière IMMOB property development project; ~ **de prospectus** BOURSE draft prospectus;
~ **réalisé** COM, RES HUM accomplishment; ~ **de**
réforme POL reform package; ~ **de résolution**
DROIT draft resolution; ~ **sans valeur** BOURSE
bubble (*jarg*); ~ **de stabilisation monétaire** ECON
currency stabilization scheme
projeté, e *adj* COM projected

projeter *vt* COM plan, project

prolétariat *m* ECON, POL proletariat

prolétarisation *f* ECON, POL proletarianization

prolifération *f* COM, V&M *de magasins* spread

prolongation *f* MÉDIA road show; **~ d'échéance** BANQUE extended terms

prolongé, e *adj* COM len., lengthened, prolonged

promesse *f* COM commitment, promise, undertaking; **~ solidaire** COM binding promise; **~ unique de vente** V&M unique selling point, unique selling proposition, USP; ◆ **faire une ~ de vente** V&M promise to sell

prometteur: être ~ *loc* COM have potential

promettre *vt* COM promise, shape up

promo *abrév infrml (promotion)* V&M promo *(infrml), (promotion)*

promoteur, -trice *m,f* COM land developer, *de régimes* promoter, ENVIR land developer, FIN sponsor, FISC promoter, IMMOB developer, land developer, developer; **~ d'abris fiscaux** FISC promoter; **~ commercial** COM, IMMOB commercial developer; **~ immobilier** IMMOB property developer; **~ de programmes en multipropriété** IMMOB, RES HUM time-share developer; **~ de projet** COM, FIN project sponsor

promotion *f (promo)* ADMIN advancement, COM special offer, RES HUM advancement, promotion *(promo)*, V&M promotion *(promo)*, special offer; **~ auprès des détaillants** V&M trade promotion; **~ -cadeau** V&M *publicité* gift promotion; **~ des cadres** GESTION, RES HUM executive advancement, executive promotion; **~ concertée** V&M *fabricant et détaillant* tie-in promotion *(US)*; **~ discrète** V&M *de vente* soft sell; **~ des exportations** IMP/EXP export promotion, EP; **~ immobilière** IMMOB property development; **~ jumelée** V&M tie-in display *(US)*, tie-in promotion *(US)*; **~ au mérite** RES HUM meritocracy; **~ produit** V&M brand promotion; **~ rapide** RES HUM fast tracking; **~ -réseau** V&M trade promotion; **~ sur le lieu de vente** V&M point-of-sale promotion; **~ des ventes** V&M sales promotion; ◆ **avoir une ~** RES HUM be promoted

promotionnel, -elle *adj* COM promotional, V&M on special offer, promotional

promouvoir *vt* COM, RES HUM, V&M further, promote

promu: être ~ *loc* RES HUM be promoted

promulgation *f* DROIT, POL enactment

promulguer *vt* DROIT, POL enact

prononcer 1. *vt* COM *discours* deliver, DROIT *condamnation, jugement* pass; 2. *v pron* **se ~ sur** COM adjudicate; ◆ **~ une condamnation** DROIT pass sentence; **~ un jugement sous toutes réserves** DROIT reserve judgment; **~ quelques mots de bienvenue** COM say a few words of welcome

pronostic *m* COM prognosis, prognostication, LOISIRS forecast; **~ relatif au marché** COM, V&M market forecast; ◆ **faire des ~s** COM, FIN, LOISIRS make forecasts

propager *vt* COM disseminate, propagate, COMMS circulate, POL disseminate, propagate

propane *m* COM, TRANSP propane

propension *f* COM, ECON propensity; **~ à consommer** ECON propensity to consume; **~ à épargner** ECON propensity to save; **~ à investir** BANQUE, ECON, FIN propensity to invest; **~ marginale à consommer** ECON marginal propensity to consume, MPC; **~ marginale à épargner** BANQUE, ECON, FIN marginal propensity to save, MPS; **~ marginale à investir** BANQUE, ECON, FIN marginal propensity to invest; **~ moyenne à consommer** ECON average propensity to consume, APC; **~ moyenne à économiser** ECON average propensity to save, propensity to save, savings ratio; **~ moyenne à épargner** ECON average propensity to save, savings ratio; **~ à travailler** ECON propensity to work

prophète: ~ de malheur *m* COM doomwatcher

propice *adj* COM favorable *(AmE)*, favourable *(BrE)*, suitable

proportion *f* COM *share* part, proportion, MATH proportion; **~ de chiffon** ENVIR, IND rag content; **~ de travailleurs handicapés** RES HUM disabled quota; ◆ **comme ~ de** COM, MATH as a proportion of; **en ~** COM proportionate

proportionalité *f* COM proportionality

proportionné, e *adj* COM commensurate

proportionnel, -elle *adj* COM ad valorem *(frml)*, pro rata *(frml)*, proportional, FISC ad valorem *(frml)*, RES HUM pro rata *(frml)*

proportionnellement *adv* COM proportionately, proportionally

propos *m* COM suggestion; ◆ **à ~** COM appropriateness, relevance, *de votre travail* re, regarding; **à ce ~** COM in this respect

proposé, e *adj* COM, FISC proposed

proposer *vt* COM offer, propose, put forward, RES HUM *emploi, situation* offer, suggest; **~ à l'examen** COM air; ◆ **~ qn pour un poste** RES HUM put sb forward for a job, put sb up for a job; **~ sa candidature** RES HUM apply, put in an application; **~ ses services** COM offer one's services

proposition *f* COM business proposition, proposal, proposition, ECON *d'affaires* business proposition, GESTION approach, *d'affaires* business proposition, proposal; **~ alléchante** COM attractive offer; **~ fiscale** ECON, FISC tax proposal; ◆ **faire une ~ à qn** V&M make an approach to sb

propre[1] *adj* COM own, ENVIR clean; **~ à une unité** INFO device-specific; ◆ **~ à** COM appropriate for sth, characteristic of

propre:[2] **~ assurance** *f* ASSUR self-insurance

propriétaire *mf* ASSUR homeowner, BOURSE beneficial owner, BREVETS *propriété intellectuelle* proprietor, COM owner, proprietor, FISC beneficial owner, homeowner, GESTION proprietor, sole proprietor, IMMOB landlord, *d'un bien* homeowner, owner, PROT SOC landlord, RES HUM proprietor; ~ **absentéiste** *m* DROIT, IMMOB absentee owner; ~ **pour compte** *m* BANQUE nominee; ~ **-exploitant** *m* COM owner-operator; ~ **exploitant** *m* COM, GESTION, RES HUM proprietor; ~ **-gérant** *m* GESTION, RES HUM owner-manager; ~ **d'hôtel** *m* IMMOB, RES HUM hotel proprietor; ~ **immatriculé** *m* BOURSE registered owner; ~ **immobilier** *m* IMMOB property owner; ~ **initial** *m* FISC original owner; ~ **inscrit au registre du cadastre** *m* DROIT, IMMOB registered proprietor; ~ **légitime** *m* DROIT rightful owner, true owner, IMMOB true owner; ~ **majoritaire** *m* BOURSE majority holding, majority interest, majority ownership; ~ **non-occupant** *m* DROIT, IMMOB nonoccupying owner; ~ **d'obligations** *m* BANQUE bondowner; ~ **obligé** *m* COM, FISC original owner; ~ **-occupant** *m* IMMOB owner-occupier; ~ **d'origine** *m* COM, FISC original owner; ~ **de ranch** *m* IMMOB rancher; ~ **de restaurant** *m* RES HUM restaurant proprietor; ~ **terrien** *m* IMMOB landowner; ~ **usufruitier** *m* DROIT, IMMOB limited owner

propriété *f* BOURSE beneficial ownership, COM attribute, property, IMMOB homestead (*US*), ownership, property, V&M property; ~ **absolue** IMMOB outright ownership; ~ **à bail** IMMOB leasehold property; ~ **bénéficiaire** FISC beneficial ownership; ~ **conjointe** BANQUE, IMMOB joint ownership; ~ **d'État** ECON, POL state ownership; ~ **foncière** ECON, ENVIR land ownership; ~ **foncière libre** IMMOB freehold, freehold property; ~ **d'habitat** IMMOB home ownership; ~ **immobilière** IMMOB immovable property; ~ **individuelle** IMMOB estate in severalty; ~ **indivise** DROIT *immobilier* tenancy in severalty, IMMOB joint tenancy, property held in joint names, tenancy in severalty; ~ **industrielle** BREVETS industrial property, patent rights, DROIT patent rights, IMMOB, IND industrial property; ~ **intellectuelle** BREVETS, DROIT, MÉDIA intellectual property; ~ **louée** IMMOB leasehold property; ~ **marginale** IMMOB marginal property; ~ **de même type** FISC like-kind property (*US*); ~ **mobilière** ASSUR, COM, IMMOB personal property; ~ **non-grevée** IMMOB unencumbered estate; ~ **de petite entreprise** FISC small business property; ~ **privée** COM, DROIT no trespassing, IMMOB private property; ~ **publique** ECON, FIN public ownership, RES HUM industrial democracy, social ownership; ~ **résiduaire** DROIT, FISC, IMMOB residuary estate; ~ **résiduelle** DROIT, FISC, IMMOB residuary estate; ~ **saisie** IMMOB distressed property; ◆ ~ **foncière, habitations et biens immobiliers hérités** DROIT, IMMOB land, tenements, and hereditaments

propulseur *m* TRANSP thruster; ~ **avant et arrière** TRANSP *d'un navire* bow and stern thruster; ~ **de babord et de tribord** TRANSP paddle steamer, port and starboard thruster, PS; ~ **d'étrave** TRANSP *navigation* bow thruster; ~ **hydraulique** TRANSP *navigation* hydraulic propulsion unit, HYD

PRO UN; ~ **latéral** TRANSP *navigation* transverse propulsion unit; ~ **latéral arrière** TRANSP *navigation* stern thruster

propulsion: ~ **à charbon** *f* TRANSP *navigation* coal propulsion; ~ **par hélice** *f* TRANSP *navigation* screw propulsion; ~ **au vent** *f* TRANSP *navigation* wind-assisted ship propulsion

prorata: **au** ~ *adv* COM on a pro rata basis, pro rata (*frml*)

prorogation *f* DROIT adjournment, deferment, extension; ~ **des délais** DROIT extension of time limits; ~ **de délais pour les déclarations** FISC extension for returns; ~ **d'échéance** BANQUE extended terms

proroger *vt* COM defer, put back, put off, DROIT *réglementations* extend

proscrire *vt* COM ban, prohibit, DROIT outlaw

prospect *m* COM, V&M prospect, prospective customer

prospecter *vt* ENVIR prospect, V&M canvass, prospect

prospecteur, -trice *m,f* ENVIR prospector, V&M missionary salesperson, prospector

prospection *f* COM business development, ENVIR prospecting, V&M canvassing, prospecting; ~ **à l'improviste** COM, V&M cold canvass; ~ **d'un marché étranger potentiel** ECON market selection overseas; ~ **des marchés** V&M market exploration

prospective *f* ECON *à long terme* forecasting

prospectus *m* BOURSE prospectus, COM brochure, COMMS brochure, circular, handbill, FIN prospectus, MÉDIA *publicité* flier, flyer; ~ **d'admission** BOURSE prospectus; ~ **d'émission définitif** BOURSE final prospectus; ~ **modifié** BOURSE amended prospectus; ~ **préliminaire** BOURSE preliminary prospectus; ~ **provisoire** BOURSE red herring, red-herring prospectus; ~ **provisoire avant une nouvelle émission d'actions** BOURSE red herring, red-herring prospectus; ~ **de vente** V&M sales leaflet

prospère *adj* ECON prosperous

prospérer *vi* COM *affaire, concurrence* flourish, *entreprise, personne* thrive

prospérité *f* ECON prosperity; ~ **d'après-guerre** ECON postwar boom

protecteur: ~ **de chèque** *m* BANQUE check protector (*AmE*), cheque protector (*BrE*)

protection *f* BREVETS, COM, DROIT, ECON protection, ENVIR conservation, protection, preservation, IND backstop; ~ **cathodique** TRANSP *navigation* cathodic protection; ~ **conditionnelle** BREVETS conditional protection; ~ **conférée par un brevet** BREVETS, DROIT patent protection; ~ **du consommateur** DROIT, V&M consumer protection; ~ **contre la copie** INFO copy protection; ~ **contre les rayonnements** ENVIR radiation protection; ~ **du cours** BOURSE price protection; ~ **des données** INFO data protection; ~ **douanière** ECON, IMP/EXP tariff protection; ~ **de l'environnement** ENVIR environmental control, environmental protection; ~ **de fichiers** INFO file protection; ~ **fiscale** FISC tax shield; ~ **de l'investisseur** BOURSE investor protection; ~ **de la nature** ENVIR nature conservation; ~ **perdue** BOURSE one-way protection; ~ **des placements** BOURSE, FIN hedging; ~ **pleine et entière** BREVETS full protection; ~ **de la propriété industrielle** BREVETS, IMMOB, IND industrial property protection; ~ **provisoire** BREVETS provisional protection; ~ **tarifaire** ECON, IMP/EXP tariff protection; ◆ ~ **requise contre le soleil** COM, LOISIRS, TRANSP *pour conteneurs* sun protection required; **soucieux de la ~ de l'environnement** ENVIR green-conscious

protectionnisme *m* ECON protectionism; ~ **commercial** ECON, IMP/EXP trade protectionism

protégé, e *adj* FIN privileged; ◆ ~ **contre la copie** INFO copy-protected; ~ **contre les pirates** INFO *piratage informatique* hacker-proof (*infrml*); ~ **en écriture** INFO write-protected

protéger 1. *vt* BOURSE insulate, BREVETS protect, COM protect, shield, DROIT, ECON protect, ENVIR preserve, protect, INFO write-protect; **2.** *v pron* **se ~** COM protect oneself; ◆ ~ **contre la copie** INFO copy-protect; ~ **les intérêts de** COM protect the interests of; **se ~ contre** COM protect oneself against; **se ~ contre l'inflation** ECON safeguard against inflation; **se ~ de qch** COM protect o.s. from sthg

protestation *f* COM outcry

protester 1. *vt* COM make a protest; **2.** *vi* COM protest

protocole *m* COM, INFO etiquette, protocol; ~ **d'accord** COM draft agreement, DROIT memorandum of agreement; ~ **des affaires** COM business etiquette

protoprolétariat *m* PROT SOC protoproletariat

prototype *m* COM, V&M prototype

prouvé, e *adj* COM well-tried

prouver *vt* COM prove, substantiate; ◆ ~ **son identité** DROIT prove one's identity

provenance *f* COM *de marchandises* country of origin, IND, V&M origin; ~ **des fonds** COMPTA *marchandises, capitaux* sources of funds; ◆ **en ~ de** TRANSP *marchandises, personne* from

provenir: 1. *vt* COM *situation, déséquilibre* stem from; **2.** *vi* ~ **de** COM come from

providentiel *m* POL popularist

provincial, e *adj* COM provincial

provision *f* COM advance payment, COMPTA payment on account; ~ **pour amortissements** COMPTA, FIN amortization reserve; ~ **en aval** COM downstream float; ~ **pour créances douteuses** BANQUE allowance for bad debts, bad debt provision, provision for bad debts, provision for loan loss, COMPTA allowance for bad debts, bad debt provision, provision for bad debts, FIN bad debt provision, doubtful debt provision; ~ **pour créances irrécouvrables** BANQUE, COMPTA, FIN bad debt provision; ~ **pour**

dépréciation BANQUE depreciation reserve, provision for depreciation, COMPTA accumulated depreciation, depreciation reserve, depreciation reserve fund, provision for depreciation, replacement investment, FIN depreciation reserve, provision for depreciation; ~ **pour épuisement** COMPTA depletion reserve; ~ **pour évaluation** COMPTA, ECON *comptabilité gouvernementale* allowance for inflation (*UK*); ~ **pour évaluation d'actifs** COMPTA valuation allowance; ~ **pour fluctuations du change** BOURSE, ECON, FIN allowance for exchange fluctuations; ~ **pour impôts différés** COMPTA, FISC deferred tax liabilities; ~ **pour imprévus** FIN contingency reserve; ~ **pour inflation** COMPTA, ECON allowance for inflation (*UK*); ~ **d'une lettre de change** BANQUE bill cover; ~ **mathématique** ASSUR policy reserve; ~ **pour moins-value** COMPTA valuation allowance; ~ **pour perte sur prêt** BANQUE, FIN loan loss provision; ~ **pour pertes sur risques de crédit** BANQUE reserve for credit risk losses; ~ **pour plus-values** COMPTA, ECON, POL allowance for inflation (*UK*); ~ **pour prêts irrécouvrables** BANQUE, COMPTA, FIN bad loan provision; ~ **réglementaire** ASSUR mandatory provision; ~ **pour risques** COMPTA provision for contingency; ~ **pour risques et changes** COMPTA, ECON loss provision; ~ **pour sinistres à payer** ASSUR unpaid claim reserve; ~ **spéciale pour pertes sur créances hors frontières** BANQUE special provision for losses on transborder claims; ~ **transitoire** FISC transitional provisions; ◆ **être sans ~** COM *chèque* bounce (*infrml*); **faire ~ pour** COM make provision for

provisions: ~ **d'amortissement** *f pl* FIN payback provisions; ~ **pour amortissement** *f pl* ECON capital consumption allowance; ~ **de crédit** *f pl* FIN credit reserves; ~ **pour éventualités** *f pl* FISC appropriations for contingencies; ~ **générales pour risques** *f pl* COMPTA general provisions; ~ **pour impôts** *f pl* COMPTA, FISC tax provisions; ~ **pour sinistre à payer** *f pl* ASSUR reserve for unpaid claims; ~ **spécifiques** *f pl* BANQUE specific provisions, specifics

provisoire *adj* COM acting, interim, temporary, DROIT *jugement* ad interim

provisoirement *adv* COM for the time being, provisionally, DROIT ad interim

provoqué: ~ **par** *loc* COM driven by

provoquer *vt* COM cause, spark off, *la chute de l'inflation* prompt; ◆ ~ **la déflation** ECON deflate; ~ **l'échéance de qch** COM extend the time limit for sth; ~ **une hausse fictive du marché** BOURSE rig the market; ~ **un lourd bilan de faillites** FIN, RES HUM take a heavy toll of bankruptcies

prudemment *adv* COM carefully, prudently

prudence *f* COM caution; ◆ **avec ~** COM prudently; **de ~** COM prudential

prudent, e *adj* COM cautious, prudent, prudential, *évaluation, dépenses* conservative

PS *abrév* (*post-scriptum*) COMMS PS (*postscript*)

pseudo: ~ **fonction de production** *f* ECON pseudo production function

pseudonyme *m* COM, INFO alias

psychologie *f* ECON, RES HUM, V&M psychology; ~ **d'entreprise** GESTION, RES HUM personnel psychology; ~ **industrielle** GESTION, IND industrial psychology; ~ **de marché** COM, V&M market psychology; ~ **d'organisation** GESTION organizational psychology; ~ **du travail** IND, RES HUM industrial psychology

psychométrie *f* RES HUM psychometrics

psychose: ~ **de guerre** *f* COM war fever

pta. *abrév (peseta)* COM pta. *(peseta)*

PTC *abrév (poids total en charge)* TRANSP *véhicule routier* GVW *(gross vehicle weight)*

PTPE *abrév (perte au titre d'un placement d'entreprise)* FISC BIL *(business investment loss)*

pub *f* infrml *(publicité)* COM ad *(infrml)*, advert, advertisement, commercial, MÉDIA *radio, télévision* ad, advert, advertisement, commercial, V&M advertising, advertising industry, publicity, *radio, TV* ad, advert, advertisement, commercial; ◆ **faire de la ~ pour** infrml MÉDIA plug *(infrml)*

public[1], **-que** *adj* COM communal, public, *entreprise* government-owned, POL government-owned, public

public:[2] ~ **bien informé** *m* COM informed public; ~ **captif** *m* V&M captive audience; **le ~** *m* COM, V&M *relations publiques* the public; ~ **de la première** *m* LOISIRS *théâtre* jury *(jarg)*; ◆ **du ~** COM popular

publication *f* BOURSE disclosure, COM magazine, MÉDIA magazine, publication, publishing; ~ **agricole** ECON, MÉDIA agricultural publication; ~ **anniversaire** MÉDIA anniversary publication; ~ **assistée par ordinateur** *(PAO)* INFO desktop publishing *(DTP)*; ~ **d'entreprise** MÉDIA house journal, house magazine; ~ **horizontale** jarg MÉDIA horizontal publication *(jarg)*; ~ **précoce** BREVETS, MÉDIA early publication; ~ **trimestrielle** MÉDIA quarterly; ~ **verticale** jarg MÉDIA vertical publication *(jarg)*; ◆ **pour ~ immédiate** MÉDIA *presse* for immediate release

publications *f pl* COM published information

publiciste *mf* RES HUM, V&M adman *(infrml)*

publicitaire *m* RES HUM adman *(infrml)*, publicity man, V&M adman *(infrml)*, *qui travaille pour la radio et la télévision* huckster *(AmE)*

publicité *f (pub)* COM advert, advertising, COM *(pub)* commercial, MÉDIA *radio, TV* advert, commercial, V&M advert, advertising, advertising industry, publicity, *radio, TV* commercial; ~ **aérienne** V&M aerial advertising; ~ **d'aéroport** MÉDIA, TRANSP, V&M airport advertising; ~ **d'amorçage** MÉDIA advance publicity; ~ **anticyclique** V&M anticyclic advertising; ~ **de bouche à oreille** V&M word-of-mouth advertising; ~ **bouche-trou** MÉDIA *presse* filler advertisement; ~ **centrée sur une zone** V&M zoned advertising; ~ **au cinéma** MÉDIA, V&M cinema advertising;

~ **cinématographique** LOISIRS, MÉDIA film advertising, motion picture advertising *(AmE)*, V&M screen advertising; ~ **collective** V&M coop advertising, cooperative advertising; ~ **pour compagnies aériennes** TRANSP, V&M airline advertising; ~ **comparative** V&M comparative advertising; ~ **de complément** V&M accessory advertising; ~ **dans les moyens de transport** TRANSP, V&M transport advertising, transportation advertising; ~ **directe** ADMIN direct mail, V&M direct mail, direct mail advertising, direct mailing, direct response; ~ **directe par correspondance** V&M direct mail, direct mail advertising, direct mailing, direct response; ~ **d'embauche** V&M direct action advertising, direct response advertising; ~ **d'entreprise à entreprise** COM, V&M business-to-business advertising; ~ **du fabricant** V&M producer advertising; ~ **financière** V&M financial advertising; ~ **foncière** IMMOB publication of sale of property; ~ **à frais partagés** V&M coop advertising, cooperative advertising; ~ **grand public** V&M consumer advertising; ~ **groupée** V&M coop advertising, cooperative advertising; ~ **industrielle** V&M industrial advertising; ~ **informative** V&M informative advertising; ~ **institutionnelle** V&M corporate advertising, image advertising, institutional advertising; ~ **intensive** V&M heavy advertising; ~ **de liaison** V&M tie-in advertising *(US)*; ~ **médias** V&M above the line; ~ **mensongère** COM misleading advertising, V&M deceptive advertising, false advertising, misleading advertising; ~ **mystère** V&M teaser ad; ~ **par affichage** V&M poster advertising; ~ **par ballons** V&M balloon advertising; ~ **par cadeaux-primes** V&M speciality advertising; ~ **par correspondance** V&M direct action advertising, direct response advertising; ~ **par coupon-réponse** V&M direct action advertising, direct response advertising; ~ **PLV** V&M POS advertising; ~ **-presse** MÉDIA newspaper advertising, V&M newspaper advertising, press advertising; ~ **de prestige** V&M corporate advertising, prestige advertising; ~ **de produit** V&M product advertising; ~ **produit** V&M brand advertising; ~ **quart de page** MÉDIA, V&M quarter-page advertisement; ~ **radiophonique** MÉDIA, V&M radio advertising; ~ **rédactionnelle** jarg COM editorial advertising, MÉDIA *presse* reader *(jarg)*, reading notice *(jarg)*; ~ **subliminale** MÉDIA, V&M subliminal advertising; ~ **sur comptoir** V&M counter-advertising; ~ **sur double page** MÉDIA, V&M double spread, double spread advertising; ~ **sur le lieu de vente** *(PLV)* MÉDIA *publicité*, V&M point-of-sale advertising, point-of-sale promotion; ~ **tapageuse** V&M stunt advertising; ~ **télévisée** COMMS, MÉDIA, V&M television advertising; ◆ **dans la ~** V&M in advertising; **faire de la ~** COM, MÉDIA, V&M advertise; **faire de la ~ pour** V&M promote, *produit* advertise

publié: **être ~** *loc* MÉDIA come out

publier *vt* BREVETS publish, COM *des gains* announce, MÉDIA publish, *édition, presse* issue; ◆ ~ **une déclaration** COM put out a statement; ~ **une offre d'emploi dans un journal** MÉDIA, RES HUM, V&M *publicité* advertise a job in the paper

publipostage *m* ADMIN mail merge, mailing, COMMS mail merge, mailing, mailing shot, mail-shot, mass mailing, INFO bus mailing, mail merge, mailing, mass mailing, V&M direct mailing, mailing, mailing shot, mailshot, *publicité* direct mail advertising, mailing; ~ **frauduleux** COMMS, V&M mail fraud; ~ **-test** V&M test mailing; ◆ **faire un** ~ COMMS do a mailshot

publi-reportage *m* MÉDIA reader (*jarg*), *presse* reading notice (*jarg*)

puce *f* INFO bullet, chip, microchip; ~ **électronique** IND silicon chip, INFO chip, silicon chip; ~ **mémoire** INFO memory chip; ~ **de silicon** IND, INFO silicon chip

puisard *m* TRANSP *d'un navire* well

puiser: ~ **dans** *loc* BOURSE raid; ~ **dans ses économies** *loc* FIN draw on one's savings

puissance *f* IND power; ~ **d'achat** BOURSE, COM buying power; ~ **arrière** TRANSP *d'un navire* astern power; ~ **de calcul** INFO computing power; ~ **en chevaux** TRANSP horsepower; ~ **au frein** TRANSP bhp, brake horsepower; ~ **des médias** MÉDIA power of media; ~ **nominale** COM nominal horsepower, NHP; ~ **réelle** IND effective horsepower, ehp; ~ **sur l'arbre** TRANSP *d'une turbine* shaft horsepower, shp

puissant, e *adj* COM powerful

puits *m* TRANSP *d'un navire* well; ~ **en exploitation** ENVIR *de pétrole, etc* commercial well; ~ **en mer** ENVIR, IND offshore well; ~ **sous-marin** ENVIR, IND subsea well

pula *m* COM pula

punir *vt* DROIT discipline

pupitre *m* COM desk; ~ **de commande** INFO control panel; ~ **de négociation** BOURSE trading desk

pur:[1] ~ **et dur** *adj* POL hardline

pur:[2] ~ **et dur** *m* POL hardliner

pure: ~ **économie de crédit** *f* ECON pure credit economy

purge: ~ **d'un privilège** *f* DROIT discharge of lien

purger *vt* BANQUE *hypothèque* pay off, FIN clear, IMMOB *hypothèque* lift (*AmE*), pay off, redeem

purification *f* ENVIR, IND purification

pur-sang *m* [pl inv] TRANSP bloodstock

pushtu *m* COM *langue* Pushtu

put *m* (*ANT call*) BOURSE put; ~ **couvert** BOURSE covered put

PV *abrév* (*point de vente*) V&M POS (*point of sale*)

PVD *abrév* (*pays en voie de développement*) COM, ECON, POL developing country, underdeveloped country, LDC (*less developed country*)

px *abrév* (*prix*) COM, ECON pr. (*price*)

Pyongyang *n pr* COM Pyongyang

pyramidal, e *adj* COM pyramidal

pyramide: ~ **des âges** *f* ECON age pyramid; ~ **financière** *f* FIN financial pyramid

pyromètre *m* COM pyrometer

Q

Qatar *m* COM Qatar

qatarien, -enne *adj* COM Qatari

Qatarien, -enne *m,f* COM *habitant* Qatari

QG *abrév (contrôle de la qualité globale)* COM, GESTION, IND, V&M TQC *(total quality control)*

qté *abrév (quantité)* COM, MATH qnty, qt. *(quantity)*

quadriade *f* ECON quadriad *(US)*

quai *m* TRANSP wharf, *au port* quay; ~ **de chargement** TRANSP charging wharf, despatch bay, dispatch bay, loading dock; ~ **à conteneurs** TRANSP *au port* container berth; ~ **de déchargement** TRANSP *au port* discharging wharf, landing stage, *chemin de fer* unloading platform; ~ **de la douane** TRANSP sufferance wharf; ~ **à manutention horizontale** TRANSP portal berth; ~ **mis à disposition** TRANSP *au port* ready berth; ~ **polyvalent** TRANSP *au port* multiproduct berth, multiuser berth; ~ **réservé aux bateaux de pêche** TRANSP *au port* fish dock; ~ **réservé aux charbonniers** TRANSP *au port* coal berth; ~ **réservé aux exportations** IMP/EXP, TRANSP *au port* export berth; ~ **réservé aux importations** IMP/EXP, TRANSP *au port* import berth; ~ **réservé à la manutention du diesel marin** TRANSP *au port* marine oil berth; ~ **réservé aux phosphatiers** TRANSP *au port* phosphate berth; ~ **Ro/Ro** TRANSP ro/ro berth; ~ **de roulage** TRANSP *au port* ramped cargo berth; ~ **subsidiaire** TRANSP *chemin de fer* bay; ♦ **à ~** IMP/EXP ExQ, ex quay, x-quay, x-wharf, TRANSP *livraison* ExQ, ex quay, x-quay, x-wharf, *navire* alongside; **à ~ ou non** TRANSP *charte-partie* whether in berth or not, *navigation* berth no berth; **à prendre à ~** IMP/EXP, TRANSP ExQ, ex quay, x-quay, x-wharf; ~ **à domicile** IMP/EXP, TRANSP pier to house; ~ **à quai** IMP/EXP, TRANSP pier to pier, quay to quay

quaiage *m* IMP/EXP, TRANSP quayage

qualification *f* COM qualification, RES HUM job title, qualification; ~ **des comptes** COMPTA qualification; ~ **financière** BOURSE, FIN financial reward; ~ **professionnelle véritable** RES HUM BFOQ *(AmE)*, bona fide occupational qualification *(AmE)*, genuine occupational qualification *(BrE)*, GOQ *(BrE)*; ~ **du travail** RES HUM job evaluation

qualifications: ~ **professionnelles** *f pl* RES HUM professional qualifications; ♦ **avoir les ~ nécessaires pour le poste** RES HUM have the right qualifications for the job

qualifié, e *adj* COM qualified, RES HUM skilled; ♦ ~ **pour faire qch** COM qualified to do sth

qualifier *vt* COM, RES HUM qualify

qualitatif, -ive *adj* COM qualitative

qualitativement *adv* COM qualitatively

qualité *f* V&M grade, quality; ~ **des bénéfices** FIN quality of earnings; ~ **brouillon** INFO draft printing; ~ **commerciale** COM fair average quality, FAQ; ~ **de conseil** RES HUM advisory capacity; ~ **courrier** INFO letter quality, LQ; ~ **de l'eau** ENVIR, PROT SOC quality of water; ~ **des éléments d'actif** FIN asset quality; ~ **des immobilisations** FIN quality of assets; ~ **listing** INFO draft printing; ~ **de la main-d'oeuvre** ECON, RES HUM quality of the labor force *(AmE)*, quality of the labour force *(BrE)*; ~ **marchande** DROIT, V&M merchantable quality; ~ **la meilleure** COM top quality; ~ **de membre** COM membership; ~ **physique de l'indice de vie** ECON *économétrie* physical quality of life index, PQLI; ~ **supérieure** BOURSE Prime 1, COM top quality, FIN Prime 1; ~ **de vie** ECON, PROT SOC, RES HUM quality of life; ~ **de la vie active** RES HUM quality of working life, QWL; ~ **de la vie professionnelle** RES HUM quality of working life, QWL; ~ **de la vie au travail** RES HUM quality of working life, QWL; ♦ **de ~ acceptable** COM of acceptable quality; **de ~ inférieure** COM substandard; **de ~ marchande** COM marketable; **de ~ suffisante** COM of acceptable quality; **de ~ supérieure** BOURSE investment-grade *(US)*, COM top-quality; **en ~ de** COM in the capacity of

qualités: ~ **de chef** *f pl* COM leadership qualities

quand: ~ **on fait faire qch par un tiers on le fait soi-même** *loc* COM, DROIT qui facit per alium facit ipse *(frml)*, qui facit per alium facit per se *(frml)*

quant: ~ **à** *loc* COM in respect of, re, reference, regarding, with reference to

quantifier *vt* MATH quantify

quantitatif, -ive *adj* COM quantitative

quantité *f* COM *(qté)* quantity *(qt., qnty)* COMPTA amount, AMT, MATH *(qté)* quantity *(qt., qnty)*; ~ **autorisée** IMP/EXP quantity permitted; ~ **à l'avantage du navire** TRANSP Qco, quantity at captain's option; ~ **économique à commander** ECON, GESTION, IND, MATH economic order quantity, EOQ; ~ **économique de fabrication** ECON, GESTION, IND economic manufacturing quantity; ~ **économique de production** ECON, GESTION, IND economic manufacturing quantity; ~ **économique de réapprovisionnement** ECON, GESTION, IND, MATH economic order quantity, EOQ; ~ **d'équilibre** ECON equilibrium quantity; ~ **optimale de commande** ECON, GESTION, IND, MATH economic order quantity, EOQ; ~ **optimale de réapprovisionnement** ECON, GESTION, IND, MATH economic order quantity, EOQ

quantités: ~ **autorisées de produits hors taxe** *f pl* IMP/EXP duty-free allowance *(UK)*

quantum *m* COM, MATH quantum

quarantaine *f* COM, IMP/EXP quarantine

quarante: les ~ à cinquante ans *m pl* ECON forty-to fifty-year-olds, the forty to fifty age group

quarantième *adj* COM fortieth, in the fortieth place

quart *m* COM qt., quart, qtr, quarter; ~ **américain** COM dry quart *(US)*; ~ **britannique** COM 1.136 litre, British quart *(UK)*; ~ **est** *(E)* TRANSP *navigation* East compass point *(E)*; ~ **liquide** COM 0.946 litre, liquid quart *(US)*; ~ **de livre** COM quarter of a pound; ~ **-monde** ECON, POL Fourth World; ~ **nord** *(N)* TRANSP *navigation* North compass point *(N)*; ~ **ouest** *(O)* TRANSP *navigation* West compass point *(W)*; ~ **sud** *(S)* TRANSP *navigation* South compass point *(S)*; **un ~** *(1/4)* COM, MATH one-quarter *(1/4)*

quartier *m* COM, ENVIR *d'une ville* area, district; ~ **central d'affaires** ECON central business district; ~ **disciplinaire** PROT SOC adjustment center *(AmE)*, adjustment centre *(BrE)*; ~ **général** ADMIN, RES HUM headquarters, HQ; ~ **locatif** IMMOB rentable area; ~ **-maître** TRANSP boatswain, bosun; ~ **surpeuplé** FISC impacted area; ~ **vétuste** ENVIR, PROT SOC blighted area

quartiers: ~ déshérités *m pl* ENVIR, PROT SOC *à l'intérieur d'une ville* inner-city areas

quartile: ~ inférieur *m* MATH lower quartile; ~ **supérieur** *m* MATH upper quartile

quasi:[1] ~ **-contrat** *m* DROIT implied contract, quasi-contract; ~ **-fabricant** *m* IND quasi-manufacturer

quasi:[2] ~ **-certitude** *f* COM likelihood; ~ **-espèces** *f pl* FIN cash equivalent; ~ **-indépendance** *f* COM quasi-independence; ~ **-monnaie** *f* BOURSE near cash *(jarg)*, ECON near money; ~ **-rente** *f* ECON quasi-rent

quasi-[3] *préf* COM quasi-

quatre: les ~ libertés *f pl* ECON four freedoms

quatrième:[1] ~ **marché** *m* BOURSE fourth market; ~ **trimestre** *m* COM fourth quarter, 4Q

quatrième:[2] ~ **de couverture** *f* MÉDIA back cover, fourth cover, V&M fourth cover; ~ **directive de la Communauté Européenne** *f* COMPTA, POL Fourth European Community Directive; ~ **directive européenne** *f* COMPTA, POL Fourth European Directive; ~ **directive sur le droit des sociétés** *f* COM Fourth Company Law Directives, DROIT Fourth Company Law Directive

quelconque *adj* COM run-of-the-mill

quelques: ~ francs *loc* COM a few francs

question *f* COM *demande* query, question, *sujet* issue, item, DROIT issue; ~ **clé** COM key issue; ~ **de compétence** DROIT question of jurisdiction; ~ **controversée** COM vexed question; ~ **dont l'inclusion a été approuvée** COM item approved for inclusion; ~ **écologique** ENVIR, POL environmental issue, environmental question; ~ **fermée** *(ANT question ouverte)* COM, V&M *étude de marché* closed question; ~ **hypothétique** COM hypothetical question; ~ **d'intérêt secondaire** COM side issue; ~ **d'opinion** COM matter of opinion; ~ **ouverte** *(ANT question fermée)* COM, V&M *étude*

de marché open-ended question; ~ **politique** COM, POL political issue, political question; ~ **de procédure** ADMIN, COM procedural issue, DROIT technical point, technicality; ~ **de stratégie** GESTION strategic issue; ~ **touchant au portefeuille** POL, PROT SOC bread-and-butter issue *(UK, infrml)*, pocketbook issue *(US, infrml)*; ~ **très débattue** COM vexed question; ♦ **brusquer la ~** COM force the issue; **en ~** COM at hand, at issue, in question

questionnaire *m* COM, V&M questionnaire; ~ **directif** *(ANT questionnaire non-directif)* COM open-ended questionnaire, V&M *étude de marché* closed questionnaire; ~ **d'évaluation** COM evaluation questionnaire; ~ **non-directif** *(ANT questionnaire directif)* COM closed questionnaire, V&M *étude de marché* open-ended questionnaire

questionner *vt* COM question; ♦ ~ **discrètement** COM sound out

questions: ~ diverses *f pl* COM any other competent business, AOCB; ~ **à l'ordre du jour** *f pl* COM items on the agenda; ~ **en suspens** *f pl* COM outstanding matters

quête *f* TRANSP *d'un navire* rake

quêter *vt* COM *l'approbation de qn* seek

quetzal *m* COM quetzal

queue *f* COM line *(AmE)*, queue *(BrE)*; ~ **de castor** TRANSP beavertail; ~ **de portefeuille** ASSUR runoff; ♦ **faire la ~** COM queue up *(BrE)*, stand in line, wait in line *(AmE)*, INFO stand in line, wait in line *(AmE)*

quick: ~ -tite® *m* TRANSP *conteneurs* quick tite®

quille: ~ caisson *f* TRANSP *navigation* box K, box keel, duct keel, DK; ~ **massive** *f* TRANSP *d'un navire* bar keel, bk

quintal *m* COM quintal

Quito *n pr* COM Quito

quittance *f* COM acknowledgement, receipt, receipt for payment, receipt slip, recpt, rept, DROIT acquittance; ~ **comptable** COMPTA accountable receipt; ~ **de loyer** IMMOB rent receipt; ~ **des services exportation** IMP/EXP export services voucher

quitter *vt* COM, RES HUM leave; ♦ ~ **sa chambre** COM, LOISIRS book out, check out; ~ **son travail** RES HUM terminate one's appointment; ~ **la table des négociations** RES HUM fail to agree

quittez: ne ~ pas, s'il vous plaît *loc* COMMS hang on, please *(infrml)*

quorum *m* COM quorum

quota *m* COM, ECON, IMP/EXP quota; ~ **à l'importation** ECON, IMP/EXP import quota; ~ **imposable** FISC taxable quota; ~ **national** ECON national quota; ~ **régional** ECON regional quota; ~ **de ventes** V&M sales quota

quote: ~ -part *f* FISC percentage interest; ~ **-part du capital détenu** *f* COMPTA percentage of capital held; ~ **-part dans les résultats** *f* COMPTA share

quotidien[1] **-enne** *adj* COM *dépense, tâche* daily

quotidien[2] *m* MÉDIA daily, daily newspaper, daily publication

quotidiennement *adv* COM daily

quotient *m* MATH quotient; ~ **de réussite** COM achievement quotient

quotité *f* BOURSE round lot (*US, jarg*), trading unit, unit of trading, COM quota, COMPTA *Can (cf lot régulier Fra)* full lot (*AmE, jarg*); ~ **du contrat** BOURSE contract size; ~ **imposable** COM taxable quota; ~ **inférieure** *jarg* BOURSE odd lot; ~ **minimale** BOURSE minimum quote size (*UK*), MQS (*UK*); ~ **normale** BOURSE NMS, normal market size; ~ **normale de transaction** BOURSE normal trading unit

quo warranto *loc* DROIT quo warranto

R

r. *abrév* COMMS *(recommandé)* regd. *(registered)*, TRANSP *(route, rue)* Rd. *(road)*

rabais *m* COM abatement, allowance, price cut, ECON price cut, FIN discount, price cut, rebate, V&M *prix* discount, markdown, price cut; **~ différé** *m* TRANSP *navigation* deferred rebate; **~ de gros** *m* COM, COMPTA, V&M trade discount; **~ immédiat** *m* TRANSP *navigation* immediate rebate; **~ importants** *m pl* FISC deep discounts; **~ des prix** *m* COM, ECON, FIN, V&M price cutting; **~ sur marchandise** *m* V&M merchandise allowance

Rabat *n pr* COM Rabat

rabatteur, -euse *m,f* LOISIRS tout

rabattre *vt* COM bargain down

raccordé: ~ à *adj* COM, INFO coupled with

raccordement: ~ privé *m* Bel TRANSP *chemin de fer* siding

raccorder *vt* COM, INFO connect, hook, hook up

raccourci: ~ clavier *m* INFO keyboard shortcut

raccourcir *vt* BOURSE shorten, COM abbreviate, shorten

raccourcissement *m* COM *programme* curtailment

raccrocher *vi* COMMS hang up, replace the receiver, ring off

rachat *m* ASSUR surrender, BOURSE merger, redemption amount, short covering, COM merger, takeover, COMPTA redemption, ECON, FIN merger, takeover; **~ d'actions** BOURSE buy-back, share redemption; **~ anticipé** FIN early redemption; **~ de direction endettée** BOURSE, COM, FIN, GESTION management buy-out; **~ d'entreprise** BOURSE buy-out; **~ d'entreprise financé par l'endettement** BOURSE, COM leveraged buy-out, LBO; **~ d'entreprise financé par un fort endettement** BOURSE, COM high-geared takeover *(BrE)*, high-leveraged takeover *(AmE)*, HLT; **~ d'une entreprise par des investisseurs** *(REI)* BOURSE, COM, FIN, GESTION leveraged management buy-out *(LMBI)*; **~ d'une entreprise par ses employés** FIN, RES HUM worker buy-out; **~ d'une entreprise par ses salariés** *(RES)* BOURSE, COM, FIN, GESTION leveraged management buy-out *(LMBO)*, management buy-out *(MBO)*; **~ modifié** V&M modified rebuy *(jarg)*; **~ d'office** BOURSE buy-in; **~ par anticipation** BOURSE retraction; **~ par levier** BOURSE leveraged buy-out, LBO; **~ de parts de gestionnaires** BOURSE, COM, FIN, GESTION management buy-out; **~ de parts de gestionnaires endettés** BOURSE, COM, FIN, GESTION leveraged management buy-out *(LMBO)*; **~ d'une société** BOURSE corporate raiding, *par une autre plus grande* bear hug *(jarg)*, FIN bear hug *(jarg)*, corporate raid-

ing; **~ au titre des gains en capital** Can FISC capital gains refund; **~ des vendeurs à découvert** BOURSE bear closing, bear covering, short covering

rachetable *adj* BOURSE callable, *par anticipation* red., redeemable, COMPTA *par anticipation* red., redeemable; **~ au gré du porteur** BOURSE retractable

racheté, e *adj* BOURSE, COMPTA *action* redeemed

rachetée *f* BOURSE recall

racheter *vt* BOURSE buy back, recall, redeem, retire, COM buy back, redeem, retire, take over, *enchères* buy in, DROIT buy back, ECON, FIN buy back, redeem, retire, take over; ♦ **~ un emprunt obligataire** BANQUE, BOURSE call bonds; **~ qch de moins cher** COM trade down

racheteur, -trice *m,f* FIN bagman *(US, infrml)*; **~ de sociétés** BOURSE, FIN *par offre publique d'achat et offre publique d'échange* corporate raider

racine *f* INFO root

racisme: ~ à l'envers *m* PROT SOC reverse discrimination

rack *m* TRANSP stillage

racket *m infrml* COM shakedown *(US, infrml)*

racoler *vt* LOISIRS *des clients* tout

radar *m* TRANSP *navigation* radar

rade *f* TRANSP *maritime* roads

radeau: ~ pneumatique *m* TRANSP *navigation* inflatable raft; **~ de sauvetage pneumatique** *m* TRANSP *navigation* inflatable life raft

radiation *f* BREVETS *d'une inscription au registre* cancellation, COMPTA write-off, writing off; **~ de la cote** BOURSE delisting; **~ de dette** COMPTA deletion of a debt; **~ partielle** COMPTA partial write-off

radical, e *adj* COM radical, *changements* sweeping, POL radical

radicalisme: ~ économique *m* ECON radical economics

radier[1] *m* TRANSP *d'un quai* apron, *d'une porte d'écluse* sill

radier[2] *vt* BREVETS cancel, COM delete, COMPTA write off

radin: être ~ sur *loc infrml* COM skimp on *(infrml)*

radio *f* COM, COMMS, MÉDIA radio; **~ cellulaire** COMMS cellular radio; **~ commerciale** COM, MÉDIA commercial radio; **~ locale indépendante** COM, MÉDIA independent local radio; **~ pirate** MÉDIA pirate radio

radiodiffuser *vt* COMMS, MÉDIA broadcast

radiodiffusion *f* COMMS, MÉDIA broadcasting; **~ par satellite** MÉDIA satellite broadcasting

radiogoniomètre *m* TRANSP *navigation* direction finder, DF, position-finding instrument, PFI, radio direction finder, RDF

radiotélégramme *m* COMMS radiotelegram

radiotélégraphie *f* COMMS radiotelegraphy, RT

radiotéléphone *m* COMMS radiophone, RP, radiotelephone, RT; **~ haute fréquence** TRANSP *navigation* RTh, high frequency radiotelephone; **~ moyenne fréquence** TRANSP *navigation* RTm, medium frequency radiotelephone; **~ très haute fréquence** TRANSP *navigation* RTv, very high frequency telephone

radiotéléphonie *f* COMMS radiotelephony, RT; **~ haute fréquence** TRANSP *navigation* RTh, high frequency radiotelephony; **~ moyenne fréquence** TRANSP *navigation* RTm, medium frequency radiotelephony; **~ très haute fréquence** TRANSP *navigation* RTv, very high frequency radiotelephony

radis: ne pas avoir un ~ *m infrml* COM not to have a bean (*infrml*)

raffermi, e *adj* COM consolidated

raffermir 1. *vt* COM consolidate; **2.** *v pron* **se ~** COM, V&M firm, harden

raffinage *m* IND refining

raffiné, e *adj* IND refined

raffinement *m* COM refinement

raffinerie *f* IND refinery; **~ de pétrole** ENVIR, IND oil refinery; **~ de pétrole brut** ENVIR, IND crude-oil refinery

raffineur *m* IND refiner

rafiot *m infrml* TRANSP *navigation* rust bucket (*infrml*)

rafraîchir *vt* INFO refresh, V&M revamp

rafraîchissement *m* V&M revamping

raid *m* BOURSE bear raiding, COM raid

raider *m* BOURSE raider

rail *m* TRANSP rail

raison *f* COM reason; **~ propre à une industrie naissante** IND infant industry argument; **~ sociale** COM business name, corporate name, trade name, V&M trade name; **~ spécifiée** FISC specified purpose; ♦ **à ~ de** COM at a rate of; **en ~ de** COM by virtue of, o/a, on account of; **pour quelque ~ que ce soit** COM for any reason

raisonnable[1] *adj* COM rational, reasonable

raisonnable:[2] **personne ~** *f* COM reasonable person

raisonnement *m* COM rationale, reasoning; **~ déductif** DROIT, GESTION, MATH deductive reasoning; **~ par déduction** DROIT, GESTION, MATH deductive reasoning

raisons:[1] **~ médicales** *f pl* PROT SOC, RES HUM medical grounds

raisons:[2] **pour ~ de santé** *loc* RES HUM on the grounds of ill health; **pour des ~ d'opportunité** *loc* COM on grounds of expediency

rajeunir *vt* ECON rejuvenate

rajeunissement *m* ECON rejuvenation

rajouter: ~ la différence *loc* COM make up the difference

rajusté, e *adj* COM, COMPTA, ECON, FISC adjusted

rajustement *m* COM, COMPTA, ECON, FISC, RES HUM *de salaires* adjustment; **~ annuel** COMPTA, FISC annual adjustment; **~ sans pénalité** FISC nonpenalized adjustment; **~ de taux d'intérêt** BANQUE, ECON, FIN interest rate adjustment

rajuster *vt* ECON, FISC adjust

ralentir 1. *vt* BOURSE *activité* scale down, COM *le travail de qn, une affaire, la demande* slack off, ECON adjust, deflate, reduce; **2.** *vi* COM decelerate, ECON decelerate, slacken; **3.** *v pron* **se ~** ECON slow down

ralentissement *m* COM deceleration, downswing, slowdown, *d'activité* slack, ECON deceleration, downswing, slowdown, TRANSP *navigation* slow steaming; **~ économique** COM, ECON business slowdown, economic slowdown

rallonge *f* COM *de temps* extension

rallongé, e *adj* COM len., lengthened

RAM: ~ dynamique *f* INFO dynamic RAM, DRAM

ramassage: ~ des ordures ménagères *m* COM garbage collection (*AmE*), refuse collection (*BrE*); ♦ **~ et livraison** COM collection and delivery, C&D

ramasser *vt* BOURSE collect, COM collect, rake in

rame: ~ de wagons *f* TRANSP *chemin de fer* rake of wagons

ramener *vt* BOURSE bring back; ♦ **~ qn dans une fourchette imposable** FISC bring sb within the tax net

rampe *f* TRANSP ramp; **~ d'accès réglable** TRANSP *navigation* adjustable shore ramp; **~ d'appontement** TRANSP *navigation* link span; **~ d'appontement amovible** TRANSP *transbordeur, roulier* movable-link span; **~ d'appontement fixe** TRANSP *transbordeur, roulier* fixed-link span; **~ mécanique** V&M *dans grands magasins* travelscator; **~ de transbordeur** TRANSP *navigation* ferry ramp

ranch *m* IMMOB rancher (*jarg*)

rand *m* COM rand

rang *m* COM rank; ♦ **de ~ supérieur** COM top-flight

rangée *f* INFO array

Rangoon *n pr* COM Rangoon

rangs: sur les ~ pour *loc* COM in the running for

ranimer *vt* COM revive

rapatriement *m* ECON repatriation; **~ de bénéfices** ECON repatriation of profits; **~ de capitaux** ECON repatriation of funds; **~ de capitaux détenus à l'étranger** ECON repatriation of overseas funds; **~ de fonds** ECON repatriation of funds; **~ de fonds étrangers** ECON repatriation of overseas funds

rapatrier *vt* ECON *profits* repatriate, INFO *données* retrieve

rapetisseur, -trice *m jarg* BOURSE lowballer (*jarg*)

rapide[1] *adj* COM fast, quick, speedy, rapid

rapide² *m* TRANSP *train* InterCity (*UK*)

rapidité: ~ **de changement** *f* COM pace of change

rappel *m* BOURSE recall, COM back payment, follow-up, recall, FIN arrears; ~ **automatique** COMMS automatic redialing (*AmE*), automatic redialling (*BrE*); ~ **d'impôts** FISC back tax; ~ **de salaire** RES HUM back pay; ~ **de traitement** RES HUM back pay

rappeler *vt* BOURSE, COM recall, COMMS call back, phone back; ◆ ~ **un numéro de référence** COMMS quote a reference number

rapport *m* COM connection, link, relation, report, COMPTA certificate, ratio, report, DROIT statement, ECON payoff, report, FIN certificate, ratio, report, MATH ratio, POL position paper (*jarg*), TRANSP ratio; ~ **annuel** COM annual report, directors' report, COMPTA *audit*, FIN annual certificate, annual report; ~ **annuel des commissaires aux comptes** COMPTA, FIN annual certificate; ~ **annuel de statistiques économiques** ECON, MATH annual abstract of statistics; ~ **d'audit** COMPTA, FIN audit report, auditor's report; ~ **d'audit favorable** COMPTA clean; ~ **d'audit sans réserve** COMPTA clean; ~ **d'avaries** ASSUR damage report; ~ **de bureau de douane** IMP/EXP customs house report; ~ **du capital à l'actif** COMPTA capital-to-asset ratio; ~ **capital-travail** ECON, FIN, IND capital-labor ratio (*AmE*), capital-labour ratio (*BrE*); ~ **chiffre d'affaires-immobilisations** COM, COMPTA turnover ratio; ~ **du commissionnaire aux comptes** COMPTA, FIN audit report, auditor's report; ~ **comptable** COMPTA, FIN accounting report; ~ **de compte nouveau** BOURSE new-account report; ~ **de conférence** V&M call report; ~ **contractuel** DROIT privity; ~ **cours-bénéfice** BOURSE, COMPTA, FIN price-earnings multiple, price-earnings ratio; ~ **coût-efficacité** COMPTA, FIN cost-effectiveness; ~ **coûts-avantages** FIN cost-benefit analysis; ~ **curviligne** MATH curvilinear relationship; ~ **détaillé** COM detailed account; ~ **dettes-actions** FIN debt-equity ratio; ~ **dividende-prix** FIN dividend-price ratio; ~ **documentaire** MÉDIA background paper; ~ **économique** ECON economic report; ~ **emprunt-valeur** BANQUE, FIN loan-to-value ratio, LTV; ~ **d'entrée de navire** IMP/EXP, TRANSP ship's inward report; ~ **d'erreurs** INFO error report; ~ **d'évaluation** COM valuation report; ~ **d'exercice** COM annual report, COMPTA, FIN *audit* annual certificate, annual report; ~ **d'expertise** ASSUR damage report, survey report, COM appraisal report; ~ **externe** COM external report; ~ **financier** ECON pecuniary return, FIN earnings report, financial statement, pecuniary return, treasurer's report; ~ **financier annuel détaillé** ECON, FIN, GESTION comprehensive annual financial report, CAFR; ~ **des flux financiers** COMPTA, FIN application of funds statement; ~ **de gestion financière** FIN, GESTION financial management report; ~ **indiqué** BOURSE indicated yield; ~ **d'intervention** INFO call report;

~ **d'irrégularité** TRANSP irregularity report; ~ **maximum** BOURSE maximum return; ~ **de mer** DROIT ship's protest, TRANSP noting protest, ship's protest, voyage report; ~ **moyen** BOURSE *analyse de valeurs* mean return; ~ **d'opération** BOURSE trade report; ~ **d'ouverture de compte** BOURSE new-account report; ~ **de parité** BOURSE parity ratio; ~ **parlementaire** COM, POL government report; ~ **passif-réserves** COMPTA, FIN reserve-assets ratio; ~ **pays** ECON country report; ~ **périodique** COMPTA interim report; ~ **plancher** BOURSE floor return; ~ **de prêt** BANQUE, BOURSE loan yield; ~ **prêt-garantie** BANQUE loan value; ~ **prêt-valeur** BANQUE, FIN loan-to-value ratio, LTV; ~ **prix-performance** COM price-performance ratio; ~ **profit et changement de quantités vendues** COMPTA, FIN profit/volume ratio, P/V; ~ **profit sur ventes** COMPTA, FIN profit/volume ratio, P/V; ~ **puissance-poids** TRANSP power-to-weight ratio; ~ **qualité-prix** COM, V&M *marketing* quality-price ratio; ~ **de recherche** BREVETS search report; ~ **réciproque** MATH reciprocal ratio; ~ **de réexamen** POL sunset report; ~ **réservé** COMPTA qualified report; ~ **du réviseur** COMPTA, FIN audit report, auditor's report; ~ **risque-bénéfice** COMPTA risk-reward ratio; ~ **risque-bénéfit** COMPTA risk reward; ~ **sinistres-primes** ASSUR burning cost, loss ratio; ~ **de situation** COM sitrep, situation report; ~ **sol-terrain** MATH *immobilier* floor-area ratio; ~ **de solvabilité** COM, COMPTA credit report; ~ **sommaire** COM summary report; ~ **sur l'état des marchés étrangers** IMP/EXP overseas status report; ~ **sur la solvabilité** COM, GESTION status report; ~ **de synthèse** FIN conspectus; ~ **valeur élevée-poids faible** (ANT *rapport valeur faible-poids élevé*) TRANSP *charbon* high value to low weight ratio; ~ **valeur faible-poids élevé** (ANT *rapport valeur élevée-poids faible*) TRANSP low value to high weight ratio; ~ **valeur-poids** TRANSP value-to-weight ratio; ◆ **en** ~ **étroit avec** COM in close touch with; **en** ~ **indirect avec** COM indirectly related to; ~ **financier utilisé comme prospectus** BOURSE statement in lieu of prospectus (*UK*); **par** ~ **à** COM by reference to, compared with, in proportion to, in relation to

rapportant: **se** ~ **à** *loc* COM pertaining to

rapporte: **qui** ~ *adj* FIN *capital, avoirs* active

rapporter 1. *vt* BANQUE *intérêts* earn, BOURSE *bénéfice, perte* yield, COM clear, FIN pull in (*jarg*); **2.** *v pron* **se** ~ **à** COM pertain to; ◆ ~ **un intérêt de** COMPTA bear an interest of; ~ **ses conclusions** COM report one's conclusions

rapports *m pl* GESTION, RES HUM dealings, relations; ~ **entre groupes** RES HUM intergroup relations; ~ **au sein du groupe** RES HUM intragroup relations

rapprochement *m* BANQUE, COMPTA reconciliation, POL rapprochement, *des politiques* approximation; ~ **bancaire** BANQUE bank reconciliation, bank summary and agreement;

~ bancaire de contrôle BANQUE cutoff bank reconciliation; **~ de banque** BANQUE bank reconciliation, bank summary and agreement; **~ de comptes** COMPTA account reconciliation, reconciliation of accounts

rapprocher *vt* BANQUE, COMPTA reconcile

rare *adj* COM, ECON scarce

raréfaction: **~ de l'ozone** *f* ENVIR ozone depletion

rassemblement: **~ de données** *m* INFO data collection, data gathering

rassembler *vt* COM collect, compile

râtelier *m* INFO *pour bande magnétique* rack

ratification *f* COM, DROIT confirmation, ratification

ratifié, e *adj* COM approved, DROIT ratified

ratifier *vt* COM approve, ratify, FISC *cotisation* confirm

ratio *m* BANQUE, BOURSE, COMPTA, ECON, FIN ratio; **~ d'actifs** COMPTA asset coverage; **~ d'actifs disponibles** FIN quick assets ratio; **~ d'actifs et passifs monétaires à court terme** BANQUE, COMPTA, FIN quick ratio; **~ administration-production** ADMIN, FIN, IND administration-production ratio; **~ des bénéfices d'exploitation sur le capital employé** ECON primary ratio; **~ de capital** BANQUE, ECON, FIN capital ratio; **~ du capital de base** BANQUE, ECON, FIN base capital leverage ratio, base capital ratio; **~ de capital redressé** BANQUE, ECON, FIN adjusted capital ratio; **~ de capital total redressé** BANQUE, ECON, FIN adjusted total capital ratio; **~ de capitalisation** FIN capitalization ratio; **~ comptable** COMPTA, FIN accounting ratio; **~ de concentration** ECON concentration ratio, leading firms ratio; **~ de concentration à n entreprises** ECON n-firm concentration ratio; **~ de conversion** BOURSE conversion ratio; **~ corrélatif** BOURSE correlation ratio (*UK*); **~ de corrélation** BOURSE correlation ratio (*UK*); **~ cours-bénéfice** BOURSE, COMPTA, FIN price-earnings multiple, price-earnings ratio; **~ coût-chiffre d'affaires** ECON expense ratio; **~ de couverture** BOURSE hedge ratio; **~ de couverture des dividendes** BOURSE dividend coverage ratio; **~ débiteur** FIN debit ratio; **~ des dépenses publiques sur le produit intérieur brut** ECON, FIN public spending ratio; **~ de la dette extérieure sur les exportations** ECON, IMP/EXP ratio of external debt to exports; **~ d'efficience** ECON efficiency ratio; **~ d'emprunt** BANQUE, FIN borrowing ratio; **~ d'endettement** BANQUE, BOURSE, COMPTA, FIN debt ratio, gearing ratio (*BrE*), leverage ratio (*AmE*); **~ d'endettement bas** BANQUE, BOURSE, COMPTA, FIN low gearing ratio (*BrE*), low leverage ratio (*AmE*); **~ d'endettement élevé** BANQUE, BOURSE, COMPTA, FIN high gearing ratio (*BrE*), high leverage ratio (*AmE*); **~ d'endettement extérieur** ECON, POL external debt ratio; **~ d'endettement financier** FIN financial leverage ratio; **~ épargne-revenus** BANQUE, FIN savings-to-income ratio; **~ fonds engagements** BANQUE capital cover; **~ fonds propres** BANQUE capital cover; **~ du fonds de roulement** COMPTA current ratio, working-capital ratio; **~ de gestion** FIN, GESTION management ratio; **~ d'immobilisations et chiffre d'affaires** COMPTA, FIN asset turnover; **~ d'intensité** ECON, FIN capital-outlay ratio, capital-output ratio; **~ d'intensité de capital** ECON, FIN capital-outlay ratio, capital-output ratio; **~ de levier** BANQUE, BOURSE, COMPTA, FIN gearing ratio (*BrE*), leverage ratio (*AmE*); **~ de liquidité** BANQUE liquidity ratio, BOURSE current ratio, liquidity ratio, COMPTA liquidity ratio, FIN current ratio, liquidity ratio; **~ de liquidité générale** BANQUE, COMPTA current ratio; **~ de liquidité immédiate** BANQUE, COMPTA, FIN acid-test ratio, quick ratio; **~ de liquidité immédiate des banques** BANQUE bank cash ratio; **~ de liquidités** BANQUE, BOURSE, COMPTA, FIN liquid assets ratio; **~ de placement** BANQUE, FIN placement ratio; **~ prêt sur valeur** BANQUE, FIN loan-to-value ratio, LTV; **~ du prix coûtant au prix de détail** COMPTA cost ratio; **~ de recouvrement** BANQUE, COMPTA average collection period, collection ratio; **~ de rentabilité** ECON, FIN profitability ratio; **~ de rentabilité du capital** ECON, FIN capital-outlay ratio, capital-output ratio; **~ du résultat aux capitaux propres** COMPTA net income to net worth ratio; **~ de solvabilité** FIN *établissements de crédit* solvency ratio; **~ de solvabilité à court terme** COMPTA current ratio; **~ de trésorerie** BANQUE, COMPTA, ECON, FIN cash deposits ratio, cash ratio; **~ des ventes** V&M sales ratio; **~ de versement** V&M *marketing* payout ratio; **~ de volume de bénéfices** COMPTA, FIN profit/volume ratio, P/V; ♦ **à ~ d'endettement élevé** BOURSE highly-geared; **~ entre le chiffre d'affaires et la masse des actions ordinaires** BOURSE equity turnover; **le ~ de x à y** COMPTA the ratio of x to y

rationalisation *f* COM rationalization, ECON, FIN capital improvement, rationalization, streamlining, GESTION rationalization, IND capital improvement, rationalization, streamlining, TRANSP rationalization; **~ des choix budgétaires (*RCB*)** COMPTA, FIN, GESTION, RES HUM output budgeting, performance budgeting, planning, programming, budgeting system, program budgeting (*AmE*), programme budgeting (*BrE*); **~ de la flotte** TRANSP fleet rationalization; **~ du parc** TRANSP fleet rationalization; **~ du parc automobile** TRANSP fleet rationalization

rationaliser *vt* COM rationalize, ECON, FIN rationalize, streamline, GESTION rationalize, IND rationalize, streamline, TRANSP rationalize

rationalité: **~ limitée** *f* MATH bounded rationality

rationnement *m* ECON queuing system, rationing; **~ du capital** ECON, FIN capital rationing; **~ des fonds** ECON, FIN capital rationing

rationner *vt* COM, ECON, FIN put on short allowance, ration

ratrapper *vt* COM catch up

rattaché: ~ à *loc* COM, FISC connected with

rattachement: ~ **des charges et des produits** *m* COMPTA *bilans, coûts et revenus* matching principle (*US*)

rattacher: ~ **des charges à un exercice** *loc* COMPTA apply expenses to a period; ~ **des produits à un exercice** *loc* COMPTA apply revenues to a period

rattrapage: ~ **de la demande** *m* ECON catch-up demand; ~ **de salaire** *m* RES HUM make-up pay

rattraper: ~ **son retard** *vi* COM catch up for lost time, make up for lost time; ~ **le temps perdu** COM catch up for lost time, make up for lost time

ravitaillement *m* TRANSP refueling (*AmE*), refuelling (*BrE*), *aviation* catering

ravitailler 1. *vt* ECON refuel; ~ **en carburant** ECON refuel; **2.** *v pron* **se ~** TRANSP refuel; ◆ **se ~ en carburant** TRANSP refuel

ravitailleur, -euse *m* TRANSP tender

rayé, e *adj* TRANSP *navigation* expunged

rayer *vt* COM delete, scratch out; ◆ ~ **qn de la liste** COM strike sb off the list

rayon *m* COM, V&M department, section, shelf; ~ **des bonnes affaires** COM, V&M bargain basement; ~ **de braquage** TRANSP turning circle; ~ **hommes** COM, V&M men's department; ~ **laser** IND laser beam; ~ **des soldes** COM, V&M bargain counter

rayonnage *m* COM, V&M shelf space, *action* shelving

rayonnement *m* ENVIR, IND radiation, RES HUM job depth

RCB *abrév* (*rationalisation des choix budgétaires*) COMPTA, FIN, GESTION, RES HUM PPBS (*planning, programming, budgeting system*)

RCI *abrév* (*rentabilité des capitaux investis*) COMPTA, ECON, FIN ROCE (*return on capital employed*)

RCS *abrév* (*Registre du commerce et des services*) COM, DROIT ≈ CRO (*Companies Registration Office*)

réabonnement *m* MÉDIA renewal of a subscription

réabonner: **se ~** *v pron* MÉDIA renew one's subscription

réacteur: ~ **nucléaire** *m* ENVIR, IND nuclear reactor, NR; ~ **thermique** *m* IND thermal reactor

réactif, -ive *adj* COM reactive

réaction *f* COM feedback, reaction; ~ **de l'acheteur** V&M buyer response; ~ **d'anticipation** COM, ECON anticipatory response; ~ **en chaîne** COM knock-on effect; ~ **des consommateurs** V&M consumer response; ~ **négative** COM, ECON negative feedback; ~ **positive** COM, ECON positive feedback

réactionnaire[1] *adj* POL reactionary

réactionnaire[2] *mf* POL reactionary

réadressable *adj* INFO relocatable

réadressage *m* INFO relocation

réaffectation *f* COMPTA, FIN, INFO reallocation, reassignment

réaffecter *vt* COMPTA, FIN, INFO reallocate, reassign

réaffirmer *vt* COM reaffirm

reaganomie: **la ~** *f* ECON, POL Reaganomics

réagir *vi* COM react

réajustement *m* COMPTA, ECON, FISC adjustment; ~ **après inventaire** COMPTA inventory valuation adjustment; ~ **de pension** FISC pension adjustment; ~ **du prix de base** FISC adjustment to cost base

réajuster *vt* COMPTA, ECON, FISC adjust; ~ **en baisse** MATH adjust downwards; ~ **en hausse** MATH adjust upwards

réalisable *adj* BOURSE realizable, COM achievable, feasible, realizable, COMPTA, FIN realizable

réalisateur, -trice *m,f* MÉDIA *radio, télévision* director, film-maker

réalisation *f* COM accomplishment, achievement, COMPTA, FIN *d'un bénéfice* making, MÉDIA *télévision, radio* direction; ~ **d'éléments d'actif** BOURSE, COMPTA realization of assets

réalisations: ~ **comparées aux projets** *f pl* GESTION, RES HUM performance against objectives

réaliser 1. *vt* BOURSE realize, sell out, *obligations* cash in, BREVETS *invention* carry out, make, COM bring into operation, implement, proceed with, realize, execute, *objectif* achieve, COMPTA realize, FIN realize, sell out, MÉDIA *télévision, radio* direct, V&M sell out; **2.** *v pron* **se ~** COM come off, come to fruition; ◆ ~ **des actifs** BOURSE, COMPTA realize assets; ~ **un bénéfice** BOURSE, COM, COMPTA, FIN make a profit, take a profit; ~ **des éléments d'actif** BOURSE, COMPTA realize assets; ~ **des gains** BOURSE, COMPTA, FIN make gains; ~ **une plus-value** BOURSE, COM, COMPTA, FIN make a capital gain; ~ **une première pénétration du marché** COM, V&M get a toehold in the market

réalisme *m* COM, DROIT, POL realism

réaliste *adj* COM realistic

réalité *f* COM actuality; ~ **des objectifs** GESTION goal congruence

realpolitik *f* POL realpolitik

réaménagement *m* BANQUE *d'une dette* rescheduling, COM dating, rescheduling, ECON redevelopment, FIN rescheduling, IMMOB redevelopment, TRANSP *aviation* change request, request for change, CR, RFC; ~ **des devises** FIN, IMP/EXP currency reordering

réaménager *vt* BANQUE, COM reschedule, ECON redevelop, FIN reschedule, IMMOB redevelop

réamorçage *m* INFO rebooting

réamorcer *vt* INFO reboot

réapprovisionner 1. *vt* BANQUE *compte*, FIN replenish, V&M restock; **2.** *v pron* **se ~** COM replenish one's stocks

réarmement *m* TRANSP *navigation* ship conversion

réarrimage *m* TRANSP restowage

réassortisseur *m* V&M shelf filler

réassurance *f* ASSUR reinsurance; ~ **effective** ASSUR active reinsurance; ~ **en excédent brut de sinistre** ASSUR gross excess reinsurance policy; ~ **en excédent de pertes** ASSUR stop-loss reinsurance; ~ **en excédent de sinistres** ASSUR excess of loss reinsurance; ~ **générale** ASSUR treaty reinsurance; ~ **de portefeuille** ASSUR portfolio reinsurance

réattribution *f* BOURSE reallowance

reboisement *m* ENVIR reafforestation

rebut *m* ENVIR garbage (*AmE*), rubbish (*BrE*), INFO garbage; ~ **à l'entrée et à la sortie** INFO garbage in, garbage out, GIGO

recalculer 1. *vt* MATH recalculate; **2.** *vi* ~ **a posteriori** BOURSE job backwards (*jarg*)

récapituler *vt* COM summarize

recensement *m* COM, ECON, IND, MATH, V&M census; ~ **de l'activité économique** ECON census of business (*US*); ~ **du commerce de détail** ECON, V&M census of retail trade (*US*); ~ **de fabrications** ECON, IND census of manufactures (*US*); ~ **de la population** ECON, MATH population census

récent, e *adj* COM recent

recentrage *m* COM refocusing

récépissé *m* COM receipt, recpt, rept, *paiement* acknowledgement, FIN acknowledgement of receipt, cash acknowledgment, TRANSP, V&M receipt, recpt, rept; ~ **de dépôt** BANQUE deposit receipt, DR; ~ **de documents** BREVETS receipt for documents; ~ **d'entrepôt** COM warehouse receipt, WR, warehouse warrant, WW, DROIT, IMP/EXP, TRANSP dock warrant, warehouse receipt, warehouse warrant, D/W, WR, WW, V&M warehouse receipt, warehouse warrant, WR, WW; ~ **d'un envoi** COMMS, TRANSP certificate of posting; ~ **de livraison** TRANSP delivery receipt; ~ **du transitaire** TRANSP forwarding agent's receipt; ~ **-warrant** COM, DROIT, IMP/EXP, TRANSP, V&M warehouse receipt, warehouse warrant, WR, WW

récepteur, -trice *m,f* COM, ENVIR receptor; ~ **de papier** INFO paper stacker; ~ **téléphonique** COMMS telephone receiver

réceptif: ~ **précoce** *m* V&M *marketing* early adapter

réception *f* ADMIN front desk, front office, reception, COM acceptance, reception, TRANSP place of delivery, POD; ~ **et chargement des marchandises** TRANSP *maritime* receiving and loading cargo; ~ **favorable** MÉDIA acceptance; ~ **des marchandises** TRANSP receipt of goods, ROG; ~ **officielle** COM, GESTION function; ~ **organisée pour le lancement d'un livre** MÉDIA launch party; ◆ **dès** ~ **de** COM on receipt of; **sur** ~ COM on receipt

réceptionnaire *mf* ADMIN, COM, RES HUM receptionist

réceptionner *vt* COM *livraison, marchandises* accept delivery of

réceptionniste *mf* ADMIN, COM, RES HUM receptionist

réceptivité *f* COM acceptance, receptiveness; ~ **des consommateurs** V&M consumer acceptance; ~ **du marché** BOURSE market receptiveness

récession *f* COM, ECON, POL crisis, depression, recession, slump, RES HUM crisis, recession, slump; ~ **conjuguée à l'inflation** ECON slumpflation (*jarg*); ~ **provoquée par l'inflation** ECON infession (*jarg*)

récessionniste *adj* ECON, POL recessionary

recette *f* COM takings, LOISIRS box office takings; ~ **marginale** ECON, FIN marginal revenue; ~ **de primes** ASSUR premium income; ~ **totale** COMPTA, ECON, FIN, FISC total revenue; ◆ **faire** ~ LOISIRS be a success (*jarg*); **faire la** ~ FIN collect sums due

recettes *f pl* BOURSE receipts, COMPTA cash receipt, ECON income, revenue, FIN cash receipt, FISC income, revenue, V&M *des ventes* sales returns; ~ **budgétaires** ECON, FIN, POL budgetary revenue; ~ **au comptant** COMPTA, FIN cash receipt; ~ **courantes** COMPTA, FIN current revenues; ~ **effectives** COMPTA, FIN, RES HUM actual takings; ~ **effectuées** COMPTA, FIN monies paid in; ~ **en espèces** COMPTA, FIN cash receipt; ~ **fiscales** ECON, FISC tax receipts, tax revenue; ~ **d'honoraires** COMPTA fee income; ~ **liquides** BANQUE, COM, COMPTA, ECON, FIN cash inflow; ~ **moyennes** COMPTA, FIN average revenue; ~ **nettes** COMPTA net receipts; ~ **nettes en commun** TRANSP net receipts pool; ~ **nettes en vertu d'un crédit** COMPTA, FIN vote-netted revenue; ~ **non-fiscales** FIN, FISC nontax revenue; ~ **obligataires** BOURSE bond proceeds; ~ **de privatisation** COM, ECON privatization proceeds; ~ **publicitaires** COMPTA, FIN, V&M advertising revenue; ~ **publicitaires par média** COMPTA, FIN, MÉDIA, V&M advertising revenue by media; ~ **à valoir sur le crédit** COMPTA, FIN receipts credited to the fund, vote-netting revenue; ~ **de ventes** V&M sales revenue

recevabilité *f* COM acceptability, DROIT *d'une demande, d'une action* admissibility

recevable *adj* COM actionable, DROIT *preuve, témoignage, recours* admissible

receveur, -euse *m,f* COM warrantee, IMP/EXP collector, RES HUM customs officer (*UK*), TRANSP warrantee; ~ **des douanes** IMP/EXP customs collector; ~ **de l'enregistrement** ADMIN, DROIT registrar of deeds; ~ **des épaves** RES HUM, TRANSP receiver of wrecks; ~ **général du Canada** ADMIN, FIN Receiver General for Canada; ~ **des impôts** FISC, RES HUM collector of taxes; ~ **des loyers** IMMOB rent collector; ~ **de la prime** BOURSE taker of a rate

recevoir *vt* COM entertain, receive, *lettre, paiement* be in receipt of, PROT SOC accommodate; ◆ ~ **un agrément après contrôle technique** DROIT pass inspection; ~ **contre paiement** FIN receive versus payment; **ne pas pouvoir** ~ BOURSE fail to receive; ~ **un visa d'inspection favorable** DROIT pass inspection

rechange: **de ~** *adj* COM, GESTION alternative

RECHAR *abrév (reconversion charbon)* ECON European Union scheme introduced in 1990 to help the revitalization of areas hit by coal pit closures

recharger *vt* INFO, TRANSP reload

réchauffement: **~ de l'atmosphère** *m* ENVIR global warming

recherche *f* BREVETS search, COM, GESTION, IND research, search, INFO search, RES HUM research, search; **~ action** GESTION action research; **~ active** GESTION action research; **~ appliquée** COM, GESTION applied research, V&M *étude de marché* industrial research; **~ des besoins des consommateurs** V&M consumer research; **~ binaire** INFO binary search; **~ des buts** COM, GESTION goal-seeking; **~ de cadres** RES HUM executive search; **~ commerciale** COM commercial research, V&M marketing research; **~ dichotomique** INFO binary search; **~ documentaire** INFO document retrieval, information retrieval, V&M *étude de marché* desk research; **~ documentaire intelligente** INFO intelligent information retrieval; **~ en économie** ECON, V&M economic research; **~ d'emploi** RES HUM employment search, job hunting, job search; **~ d'erreurs** BANQUE tick-up; **~ et développement** *(R&D)* IND research and development *(R&D)*; **~ expérimentale** GESTION applied research; **~ fondamentale** COM basic research, PROT SOC academic research; **~ globale** INFO global search; **~ d'informations** INFO information retrieval; **~ marketing** V&M marketing research; **~ de motivations** V&M motivational research; **~ d'objectifs** COM, GESTION goal-seeking; **~ opérationnelle** *(RO)* COM operational research, operations research, GESTION, V&M operational research, operations research *(OR)*; **~ par dichotomie** INFO binary search; **~ par mot clé** INFO keyword search; **~ de produit** V&M product research; **~ du profit** ECON, FIN, V&M profit motive; **~ qualitative** V&M *étude de marché* qualitative research; **~ quantitative** V&M *étude de marché* quantitative research; **~ scientifique** IND scientific research; **~ sur le terrain** V&M *étude de marché* field research; **~ universitaire** PROT SOC academic research; ◆ **être à la ~ de** COM be in search of; **faire une ~ de** INFO search; **personne à la ~ d'un emploi** RES HUM job hunter

recherché, e *adj* COM, RES HUM in demand, sought-after; ◆ **être ~ par les chasseurs de têtes** RES HUM be headhunted; **être très ~** RES HUM be in great demand

rechercher *vt* COM *de l'aide* seek, INFO find, RES HUM headhunt, search out, seek; ◆ **~ un marché** BOURSE seek a market; **~ qch dans un fichier** COM search a file for sth

recherches: **~ éditées** *f pl* MÉDIA published research; **~ sans applications immédiates** *f pl* IND, RES HUM blue-sky research

Recherches: **~ et secours internationaux** *m pl* PROT SOC ≈ International SAR, ≈ International Search & Rescue

rechute *f* ECON double dip *(jarg)*

récidive *f* DROIT second offence *(BrE)*, second offense *(AmE)*

récipiendaire *m* FISC recipient

récipient: **~ non-poreux** *m* TRANSP siftproof receptacle; **~ semi-rigide** *m* TRANSP semi-rigid receptacle

réciprocité *f* COM, ECON reciprocity

réciproque[1] *adj* COM reciprocal

réciproque[2] *f* MATH reciprocal

réciproquement *adv* COM conversely, reciprocally

réclamation *f* ASSUR claim, COM claim, complaint, complaints procedure, DROIT, FISC, TRANSP claim; **~ acceptable** COM valid claim; **~ admissible** ASSUR allowable claim; **~ de l'assureur** ASSUR insurer's claim; **~ concernant les marchandises** TRANSP cargo claim; **~ faite par un tiers** DROIT, IND third-party claim; **~ de frais de déplacement** COM travel claim, travel expense claim; **~ de frais de voyage** COM travel claim, travel expense claim; **~ potentielle** COMPTA, FIN contingent claim; **~ recevable** ASSUR allowable claim; **~ de remboursement** FISC repayment claim; **~ d'un tiers** ASSUR, DROIT third-party claim; ◆ **faire une ~** DROIT put in a claim, set up

réclamations: **~ fiscales** *f pl* FISC tax claims

réclamer *vt* DROIT claim; ◆ **~ un dédommagement** DROIT claim compensation; **~ des dommages et intérêts** ASSUR, DROIT claim damages

reclassement *m* COM, RES HUM *de main-d'oeuvre* outplacement, reclassification, redeployment, upgrading; **~ en amont d'un prêt** BANQUE upgrading of a loan

reclasser *vt* COM redeploy, *compte* reclassify, RES HUM redeploy

reclassification *f* COM *des comptes*, RES HUM reclassification; **~ continue** TRANSP *navigation* continuous survey, CS

réclusion *f* DROIT *criminelle* imprisonment

récolte *f* COM, ECON, ENVIR crop, vintage, yield; **~ de céréales** ECON, ENVIR grain crop; **~ destinée à la vente** ECON, ENVIR cash crop; **~ de rapport** ECON, ENVIR cash crop

récolter *vt* COM, FIN reap; ◆ **~ les bénéfices** BOURSE, FIN reap the benefits; **~ les récompenses** BOURSE, FIN reap the rewards; **~ les rémunérations** BOURSE, FIN reap the rewards

recommandataire *m* BANQUE referee in case of need

recommandation *f* COM recommendation; **~ générale** BOURSE blanket recommendation

recommandations: **~ professionnelles** *f pl* COMPTA, FIN audit guide

recommandé, e *adj (r.)* COMMS registered *(regd.)*

recommander *vt* COM advocate, recommend, *lettre* register, DROIT counsel

récompense: ~ **financière** *f* BOURSE, FIN financial reward; ◆ **en** ~ **de** COM as a reward for

recompiler *vt* INFO recompile

réconcilier *vt* COM reconcile

reconditionnement *m* V&M repackaging

reconditionner *vt* V&M *marketing* repackage

reconduction *f* BANQUE, BOURSE roll-over, COM renewal, FIN roll-over; ~ **tacite** COM tacit renewal

reconduire *vt* BANQUE, BOURSE roll over, COM renew, show out, IMMOB renew

reconfiguration *f* COM reconfiguration, INFO remapping

reconnaissance *f* BANQUE, COM acknowledgement, DROIT *d'une obligation* recognition, *de dette* acknowledgement, FIN acknowledgement, GESTION, RES HUM *des syndicats* recognition, V&M acknowledgement; ~ **de dépôt** FIN cash acknowledgment, cash deposit acknowledgment; ~ **de dette** BANQUE, COM, FIN I owe you, acknowledgement of debt, IOU, TRANSP I owe you, acknowledgement of debt, due bill (*AmE*), IOU; ~ **d'endettement** BANQUE acknowledgement of indebtness; ~ **du fait syndical** RES HUM syndicalism; ~ **en fin de transaction** COMPTA completion basis; ~ **légale** DROIT legal recognition; ~ **mutuelle** DROIT, POL *lois nationales dans l'UE* mutual recognition; ~ **optique des caractères** (*ROC*) INFO optical character recognition (*OCR*); ~ **de la parole** INFO speech recognition, voice recognition; ~ **d'une perte** COMPTA recognition of loss; ~ **des syndicats** RES HUM trade union recognition (*UK*); ~ **vocale** INFO speech recognition, voice recognition

reconnaître *vt* COM *erreur, dette* acknowledge, admit, recognize, *fait* understand, FIN acknowledge, RES HUM recognize; ◆ ~ **qn coupable** DROIT find sb guilty; ~ **qn non-coupable** DROIT find sb not guilty

reconnu, e *adj* COM recognized

reconsidération: ~ **d'une évaluation** *f* FISC reconsideration of an assessment

reconsidérer *vt* COM reconsider

reconsigner *vt* TRANSP reconsign

reconstituer *vt* BOURSE, COM, ECON reconstruct, INFO *fichier* rebuild

reconstitution *f* BOURSE *d'une société*, COM, ECON reconstruction

reconstruction *f* BOURSE *d'une société*, COM, ECON reconstruction

reconstruire *vt* BOURSE reconstruct, COM rebuild, reconstruct, ECON reconstruct, INFO *machine* rebuild

reconstruit, e *adj* COM rebuilt, RBT

reconversion *f* ECON *devise* retranslation, *usine* reconversion, IND *usine*, INFO reconversion; ~ **charbon** (*RECHAR*) ECON European Union scheme introduced in 1990 to help the revitalization of areas hit by coal pit closures

reconvertir *vt* ECON, IND, INFO reconvert

recopie: ~ **d'écran** *f* INFO screen copy

record *m* COM record; ~ **absolu** COM all-time high, all-time record; ~ **le plus élevé** COM all-time high; ~ **de vente** BOURSE, V&M selling climax

recouper: **se** ~ *v pron* COM, POL add up

recours *m* ASSUR claim of recourse, COM recourse, DROIT appeal; ~ **en annulation** DROIT action for cancellation; ~ **bilatéral à l'arbitrage** RES HUM bilateral reference; ~ **collectif en justice** DROIT class action; ~ **entre coassurés** ASSUR cross liability; ~ **à l'impasse budgétaire** ECON compensatory finance, deficit financing, pump priming; ~ **des tiers** ASSUR, DROIT third-party claim; ◆ **avec** ~ ASSUR with recourse; **avoir** ~ **à** ASSUR, COM fall back on, have recourse to; **avoir** ~ **à la capitalisation boursière** BOURSE, ECON capitalize; **avoir** ~ **à la justice** DROIT take legal action; ~ **et conservation** ASSUR sue and labor (*AmE*), sue and labour (*BrE*)

recouvrement *m* COM *of assets*, COMPTA, FIN, FISC collection, recovery; ~ **de base** FISC recovery of basis; ~ **complexe** FISC advanced collection; ~ **de créances** COM, COMPTA, FIN collection of debts, debt collection; ~ **des créances** COM *agence spécialisée*, COMPTA, FIN collection; ~ **des dépenses** COM, COMPTA, FIN recovery of expenses; ~ **de dettes** COM, COMPTA, FIN collection of debts, debt collection; ~ **de l'impôt** FISC tax collection; **pour** ~ BOURSE *valeur mobilière* for collection; ~ **de prêt** BANQUE loan recovery; ~ **sur créance radiée** BANQUE, COMPTA, FIN bad debt recovery, bad debtor

recouvrer *vt* FIN *paiement dans un établissement de crédit* collect

recouvrir *vt* COM *créance* collect, recover, COMPTA recover, FIN *créance* collect, recover

récrire *vt* COM, INFO, MÉDIA rewrite

recrutement *m* RES HUM recruitment; ~ **interne** RES HUM internal search; ~ **du personnel** RES HUM staffing; ~ **syndical** RES HUM union recruitment; ◆ ~ **et gestion des effectifs** RES HUM human resource planning, manpower planning, staff resourcing, HRP

recruter *vt* COM *gestion du personnel* absorb, RES HUM headhunt, recruit; ◆ ~ **des cadres** RES HUM headhunt; ~ **du personnel** RES HUM staff up

recruteur, -euse *m,f* BOURSE canvasser, RES HUM recruiting officer

rectification *f* BANQUE adjustment, BOURSE market correction, COM rectification, *cours* correction, COMPTA adjustment, DROIT correction, POL rectification; ~ **comptable** COMPTA accounting adjustment

rectifier *vt* BANQUE adjust, COM correct, rectify, COMPTA adjust, DROIT amend, MATH *chiffres, erreurs* adjust, POL rectify

recto *m* (*ANT verso*) COM *d'un page, d'une médaille*, MÉDIA recto

recto-verso *adj* MÉDIA duplex

reçu[1], **e** *adj* COM rcvd, received

reçu² *m* BANQUE, BOURSE receipt, recpt, rept, COM acknowledgement, receipt, recpt, rept, FIN, TRANSP receipt, recpt, rept, V&M receipt, recpt, rept, sales receipt; **~ d'action** BOURSE stock receipt; **~ à l'appui** COM, V&M supporting receipt; **~ en blanc** COM blank receipt; **~ en bonne et due forme** COM formal receipt; **~ de bord** IMP/EXP, TRANSP *maritime* mate's receipt, MR; **~ de caisse** BANQUE till receipt; **~ de chargement** TRANSP *maritime* data freight receipt, DFR; **~ de dépôt** BANQUE deposit receipt, DR; **~ de livraison** TRANSP delivery receipt; **~ officiel** FISC official receipt; **~ provisoire** TRANSP *maritime* dock receipt

reçue: personne ~ *f* RES HUM interviewee

recueil: ~ de données *m* INFO data collection, data gathering; **~ des lois** *m* DROIT statute book (*UK*)

recueillir *vt* COM collect, gather; ◆ **~ des informations** COM gather information, gather intelligence; **~ des renseignements** COM gather information, gather intelligence

recul *m* COM stepback

reculer *vi* COM recede, slip back, step back

récupérateur: ~ de pétrole *m* ENVIR, IND oil recovery skimmer

récupération *f* COM, COMPTA recovery, FIN clawback, recovery, INFO *de données* recovery, retrieval, RES HUM *d'une entreprise, du capital investi* payback, TRANSP *des marchandises, des bagages* reclaiming; **~ de l'amortissement** COMPTA, FISC depreciation recapture; **~ de la déduction pour épuisement** COMPTA depletion recapture; **~ de l'énergie** ENVIR *recyclage* energy recovery; **~ des frais** COM, COMPTA, FIN recovery of expenses; **~ de l'information** INFO information retrieval; **~ primaire** FISC primary recovery

récupérer *vt* COM recoup, recover, ENVIR recover, INFO recover, retrieve; ◆ **~ du temps sur un autre travail** RES HUM time off the cuff (*jarg*)

récusation *f* COM denial of opinion

recyclable *adj* ENVIR recyclable

recyclage *m* ENVIR recycling, RES HUM booster training, retraining, upskilling; **~ des déchets** ENVIR recycling of waste, waste recycling; **~ professionnel** RES HUM vocational rehabilitation

recycler *vt* ENVIR recycle

rédacteur, -trice *m,f* ADMIN preparer, COMMS news editor, MÉDIA news editor, *édition* editor, RES HUM *édition* editor; **~ en chef** MÉDIA *journaux* editor; **~ en chef adjoint** MÉDIA *journaux* deputy editor; **~ d'édition** MÉDIA associate editor; **~ de mode** MÉDIA fashion editor; **~ publicitaire** V&M copy adapter, copywriter

rédaction *f* COM, MÉDIA edition, editorship

reddition: ~ de comptes *f* FIN rendering of accounts

redéfinition *f* INFO remapping; **~ du contenu d'un poste** RES HUM job regulation

redémarrage *m* ECON, INFO restart; **~ automatique** INFO autorestart, warm restart; **~ soutenu** ECON sustained resurgence

redémarrer *vt* ECON, INFO restart

redéploiement *m* COM, RES HUM redeployment

redéployer *vt* COM, RES HUM redeploy

redéposer *vt* BANQUE redeposit

redevance *f* BREVETS rental right, COM royalty, DROIT rental right, FISC royalty, MÉDIA licence (*BrE*), license (*AmE*), royalty; **~ à la Couronne** FISC Crown royalty; **~ fixe** COM fixed fee; **~ foncière** IMMOB, PROT SOC rent charge; **~ forfaitaire** COM flat-rate fee; **~ de pollution** ENVIR pollution charge, pollution tax; **~ au profit de l'environnement** ENVIR environmental tax; **~ de télévision** DROIT, MÉDIA television licence (*UK*)

redevances *f pl* DROIT fee; **~ d'émission** ENVIR emission charges

rédigé, e *adj* COM, DROIT, POL drafted

rédiger *vt* COM write up, *rapport* draft, draw up, DROIT, POL *projet* draft, *rapport* draw, draw up

rédigeur, -euse *m,f* DROIT maker

redistribution: ~ partielle des recettes de l'État *f* ECON federal finance (*US*), revenue sharing (*US*); **~ des revenus** *f* ECON income redistribution

redondance *f* INFO redundancy

redonner: ~ confiance à qn *loc* COM bolster up sb's confidence

redoublé, e *adj* COM *activité, efforts* renewed

redressement *m* BOURSE rally, rallying, COM adjustment, *du marché* recovery, COMPTA *comptabilité d'engagements* adjustment, ECON rally, rallying, upswing, MATH *dans l'évaluation de la valeur de biens assujettis* adjustment; **~ affecté aux exercices antérieurs** COMPTA prior period adjustment, prior year adjustment; **~ pour amortissement** ASSUR, COMPTA, FIN amortization adjustment; **~ comptable** COMPTA accounting adjustment; **~ des comptes clients** COMPTA adjustment of accounts receivable; **~ économique** ECON recovery; **~ économique lié aux exportations** ECON, IMP/EXP export-led economic recovery; **~ économique tiré par les exportations** ECON, IMP/EXP export-led economic recovery; **~ d'entreprises** ECON, GESTION corporate turnaround; **~ financier** FIN gearing adjustment (*BrE*), leverage adjustment (*AmE*); **~ fiscal** COM, FIN, FISC tax adjustment; **~ du marché** COM market recovery; **~ modéré de la conjoncture** ECON modest cyclical recovery; **~ du taux d'endettement** FIN gearing adjustment (*BrE*), leverage adjustment (*AmE*)

redresser 1. *vt* COM *bilan* right, *corriger* adjust, COMPTA *bilan* right, ECON, FIN turn around; **2.** *v pron* **se ~** BOURSE rally, COM recover, straighten out, turn around, ECON rally, recover; ◆ **~ l'équilibre** COM, COMPTA redress the balance

réducteur: ~ simple *m* TRANSP *navigation* Sr, single-reduction gearing

réduction *f* BOURSE write-down, COM, COMPTA

abatement, allowance, concession, discount, reduction, slackening, write-down, *d'effectifs, de coûts* pruning, DROIT mitigation, ECON, FIN retrenchment, IMMOB concession, RES HUM retrenchment, V&M discount, markdown; ~ **pour achat en gros** COM, COMPTA, V&M bulk discount; ~ **budgétaire** COMPTA, ECON, FIN, POL budget cut, budget reduction, budgetary constraint, budgetary cut; ~ **de capital** BOURSE reduction in capital; ~ **des coûts** COM, COMPTA, ECON, FIN cost reduction, cutback; ~ **du délai d'exécution** DROIT, IMMOB acceleration; ~ **d'effectifs** RES HUM downsizing *(jarg)*; ~ **d'emplois secondaires** RES HUM reduction in force, RIF; ~ **générale** *(ANT augmentation générale)* COM, FISC, GESTION, RES HUM across-the-board cut; ~ **globale** *(ANT augmentation globale)* COM, FISC, GESTION, RES HUM across-the-board cut; ~ **d'impôt** ECON, FISC, IND tax break, tax cut, tax reduction, tax relief; ~ **du nombre d'actions** BOURSE stock split-down; ~ **pour personne âgée** FISC reduction for senior citizen; ~ **du personnel** RES HUM shakedown *(infrml)*, staff cutback, staff reduction; ~ **du point central** TRANSP *véhicules routiers* hub reduction; ~ **des prix** COM, ECON, FIN, V&M price cut, price cutting; ~ **du risque** COM risk minimizing; ~ **sur le loyer** PROT SOC rent rebate; ~ **des tarifs** COM, TRANSP rate cutting; ~ **du taux d'escompte** BANQUE, ECON fall in the bank rate; ~ **toutes catégories** *(ANT augmentation toutes catégories)* COM, FISC, GESTION, RES HUM across-the-board cut; ~ **de valeur** BANQUE, BOURSE impairment of value

réduire 1. *vt* BOURSE *activité* scale down, COM decrease, *dépenses* reduce, *effectif, stocks* shed, *personnel* shake out, *prix* abate, reduce, *écart* narrow, ECON, FIN reduce, run down, trim, *coûts* retrench, GESTION discount, RES HUM *coûts* retrench; ~ **de moitié** COM halve; ~ **peu à peu** COM *frais, commissions, capital* whittle down; ~ **la valeur** COMPTA write down; **2.** *v pron* **se ~** ECON contract out, taper off; ◆ ~ **les frais de crédit** BANQUE buy down; ~ **le personnel** RES HUM trim the workforce; ~ **les pertes** COM cut one's losses; ~ **à la portion congrue** COM, ECON, FIN put on short allowance

réduit, e *adj* COM reduced

rééchelonnement *m* BANQUE rescheduling, COM dating, rescheduling, FIN rescheduling; ~ **de la dette** BANQUE, COM, COMPTA, FIN debt rescheduling

rééchelonner *vt* BANQUE, COM, FIN reschedule

réécouter *vt* INFO *message* replay

réécrire *vt* COM, INFO, MÉDIA rewrite

rééditer *vt* MÉDIA republish

réel, -elle *adj* COM, COMPTA, ECON, FIN actual, real, tangible

réélection *f* COM, POL re-election

réembauche *f* RES HUM re-employment, re-engagement

réembaucher *vt* RES HUM re-employ, re-engage

réémettre *vt* BOURSE reissue

réemploi *m* RES HUM re-employment, re-engagement

réemployer *vt* RES HUM re-employ, re-engage

réengagement *m* RES HUM re-employment, re-engagement

réengager *vt* RES HUM re-employ, re-engage

réescomptable *adj* COMPTA, FIN rediscountable

réescompte *m* COMPTA, FIN rediscount, rediscounting

réescompteur *m* COMPTA, FIN rediscounter

réévaluation *f* COMPTA, ECON, FIN revaluation, FISC reassessment; ~ **des actifs** COMPTA, FIN revaluation of assets; ~ **d'impôt, d'intérêts ou de pénalisations** FISC reassessment of tax, interest or penalties; ~ **légale** COMPTA, DROIT legal revaluation; ~ **monétaire** ECON currency revaluation; ~ **d'une monnaie** ECON currency revaluation; ~ **des salaires** RES HUM salary review; ~ **du taux de change** ECON revaluation of exchange rate; ~ **des traitements** RES HUM salary review

réévaluer *vt* COMPTA, ECON, FIN revalue, FISC reassess

réexamen *m* COM re-examination

réexaminer *vt* COM re-examine, FISC reconsider; ◆ ~ **une évaluation** FISC reconsider an assessment; ~ **les termes d'une transaction** BOURSE clear the market *(jarg)*

réexécuter *vt* COM, INFO *programme* rerun

réexécution *f* INFO *d'un programme* rerun

réexpédié, e *adj* TRANSP reforwarded, reshipped

réexpédier *vt* TRANSP reforward, reship

réexpédition *f* TRANSP reforwarding, reshipping

réexportateur *m* IMP/EXP re-exporter

réexportation *f* IMP/EXP re-export, re-exportation

réfaction *f* COM allowance for loss, V&M allowance

référence[1] *f* COM reference, ECON bench mark, INFO label, RES HUM reference, testimonial; ~ **bancaire** BANQUE banker's reference; ~ **croisée** INFO cross reference; ◆ ~ **à** BREVETS reference to; **avoir d'excellentes ~s** RES HUM have excellent references, have excellent testimonials; **en ~ à** COM reference, with reference to, COMMS with reference to; ~ **notre télex** COMMS reference our telex, ROT; **par ~ à** COM by referral to, referring to

référence:[2] **votre ~** *loc (V/réf.)* COMMS your reference *(yr ref.)*

référendum *m* COM, POL referendum

référer: se ~ à *v pron* COM refer to

refinancement *m* BANQUE, FIN refinancing; ~ **d'obligations** BOURSE bond refunding

refinancer *vt* BANQUE, FIN refinance

refixation: ~ de taux *f* BOURSE rate resetting, RR

refléter *vt* COM reflect

réflexion: à la ~ *loc* COM upon further consideration

refondre *vt* FIN *dette* recast

reformater *vt* INFO reformat

réforme *f* COM, ECON, POL reform; ~ **agraire** ECON, ENVIR land reform; ~ **économique** ECON, POL economic reform; ~ **fiscale globale** ECON, FISC comprehensive tax reform; ~ **de fiscalité** ECON, FISC tax reform; ~ **monétaire** ECON currency reform; ~ **des tarifs douaniers** COM, IMP/EXP tariff reform

réformer *vt* COM, ECON, POL reform

réformisme *m* POL gradualism, reformism

refoulement *m* TRANSP *avion* pushback

refouler *vt* TRANSP *avion* push back

refrain *m* MÉDIA *télévision* theme tune; ~ **publicitaire** MÉDIA, V&M advertising jingle

refrapper *vt* INFO re-enter, retype

réfrigération *f* COM, TRANSP refrigeration, R

réfrigéré, e *adj* COM, TRANSP refrigerated, R

refroidir *vt* COM *enthousiasme* dampen

refroidisseur: ~ **intermédiaire** *m* TRANSP intercooler

refuge *m* COM haven; ~ **fiscal** ECON, FISC tax haven

réfugié, e *m,f* COM refugee; ~ **politique** POL political refugee

refus *m* BREVETS refusal, COM failure to accept, refusal; ~ **de certifier** COMPTA adverse opinion; ~ **d'effectuer des heures supplémentaires** RES HUM overtime ban; ~ **d'exprimer une opinion** COMPTA disclaimer of opinion; ~ **de faire grève** RES HUM strikebreaking; ~ **des heures supplémentaires** RES HUM overtime ban; ~ **d'obtempérer** DROIT *à un ordre* noncompliance; ~ **de reconnaissance** RES HUM derecognition (*UK*)

refuser *vt* COM refuse; ♦ ~ **d'accepter une traite** BANQUE refuse acceptance of a draft; ~ **de décharger** IND, RES HUM, TRANSP black containers (*UK*); ~ **une déduction** FISC disallow a deduction; ~ **pour défaut de provision** BANQUE *chèque* bounce (*infrml*); ~ **de mettre qn en liberté sous caution** DROIT refuse sb bail; ~ **pour non-provision** BANQUE *chèque* bounce (*infrml*); ~ **de payer un chèque** BANQUE dishonor a check (*AmE*), dishonour a cheque (*BrE*); ~ **de prendre part à** RES HUM repudiate

regarder 1. *vt* COM look at; **2.** *vi* COM browse; ♦ ~ **les choses en face** COM face the facts; ~ **vers l'avenir** COM look ahead

régénération *f* ENVIR reclaiming

régénérer *vt* ENVIR reclaim, INFO refresh

régie *f* IMP/EXP C&E (*UK*), Customs & Excise (*UK*); ~ **d'État** FISC public corporation (*UK*)

Régie: la ~ de Sa Majesté *f* IMP/EXP Her Majesty's Customs and Excise (*UK*)

régime *m* COM arrangement, regime; ~ **d'actionnariat compensatoire** BOURSE compensatory stock option (*UK*); ~ **d'assurance** ASSUR insurance plan, insurance scheme; ~ **d'assurance-hospitalisation** ASSUR, PROT SOC hospital care insurance plan; ~ **d'assurance maladie** ASSUR, PROT SOC medical care insurance plan; ~ **commercial** ECON trade regime; ~ **complémentaire interprofessionnel de prévoyance** FIN, RES HUM supplementary intercompany pension scheme; ~ **complémentaire professionnel de prévoyance** FIN, RES HUM supplementary company pension scheme; ~ **de croisière** COM on stream; ~ **douanier** COM, IMP/EXP customs arrangements; ~ **enregistré d'épargne-retraite** ASSUR registered retirement savings plan, RRSP; ~ **d'épargne** BANQUE savings plan; ~ **fiscal** ECON, FISC tax system, taxation system; ~ **de libre accès aux besoins d'assurance** ASSUR FAIR plan (*US*), Fair Access To Insurance Requirements Plan (*US*); ~ **de parité à crémaillère** ECON crawling peg system; ~ **de participation des employés aux bénéfices** BOURSE, RES HUM employee profit sharing plan; ~ **de pension d'employés** RES HUM employee pension plan; ~ **de pensions du Canada** FISC Canada Pension Plan; ~ **plein** COMPTA full basis; ~ **de préretraite** FIN, PROT SOC, RES HUM bridging pension scheme; ~ **de prestations aux employés** RES HUM employee benefit plan; ~ **privé d'assurance maladie** ASSUR, PROT SOC private health services plan; ~ **de redevances** FISC royalty system; ~ **de retraite** ASSUR, FIN, PROT SOC, RES HUM pension plan, retirement plan, retirement scheme; ~ **de retraite agréé** ASSUR registered pension plan; ~ **de retraite basé sur les avantages salariaux** ASSUR benefit-based pension plan; ~ **de retraite entièrement financé par l'employeur** (ANT *régime de retraite mixte, système de retraite par répartition*) FIN, PROT SOC, RES HUM noncontributory pension plan, noncontributory pension scheme; ~ **de retraite indépendant** ASSUR personal pension plan; ~ **de retraite mixte** (ANT *régime de retraite entièrement financé par l'employeur*) FIN, PROT SOC, RES HUM contributory pension plan, contributory pension scheme; ~ **de retraite non-agréé** FIN nonapproved pension scheme; ~ **de retraite des ouvriers** PROT SOC, RES HUM cloth cap pensions; ~ **de retraite personnelle** FIN, FISC personal pension scheme (*UK*); ~ **de retraite professionnel** FIN, PROT SOC, RES HUM occupational pension plan (*UK*); ~ **de retraite proportionnel** RES HUM graduated pension scheme; ~ **de retraite sans capitalisation** RES HUM unfunded pension scheme; ~ **de retraite vieillesse** FIN old-age pension plan, old-age pension scheme; ~ **de taux de change** ECON, FIN exchange rate regime

région *f* COM area, region, ECON area, INFO *de mémoire* region, POL area, region; ~ **assistée** ECON, POL, PROT SOC assisted area; ~ **centrale** ECON core region; ~ **en crise** ECON depressed region; ~ **en déclin** ECON depressed region; ~ **désignée** FISC designated region; ~ **à développer** ECON, POL development region; ~ **des industries en déclin** IND rustbelt (*US*); ~ **sinistrée** ECON depressed region; ~ **viticole**

COM vine-growing district, wine industry, wine-producing-area, IND vine-growing district, wine industry, wine-producing area

régional, e adj COM regional

régions: ~ **neigeuses** f pl ECON snowbelt (US); ~ **les plus défavorisées** f pl ECON least-favored regions (AmE), least-favoured regions (BrE)

régir vt DROIT, POL govern

régisseur, -euse m,f DROIT, FIN estate manager, IMMOB bailiff

registre m ADMIN log, log book, register, ASSUR register, BOURSE book, BREVETS, COM, DROIT, INFO d'un programme register; ~ **des actionnaires** COM, DROIT livre statutaire d'une société register of members; ~ **des actions** BOURSE share register, stock register; ~ **des Caisses Nationales d'Épargne** BOURSE National Savings Register (UK); ~ **des chèques** COMPTA check register (AmE), cheque register (BrE); ~ **des commandes en attente** COM backlog order books; ~ **du commerce** ADMIN office, COM register of companies, trade register; ~ **de comptabilité** COMPTA account book; ~ **comptable auxiliaire** COMPTA subsidiary accounting record; ~ **de comptage** COM tally register; ~ **de contrôle de caisse** COMPTA cash control record; ~ **des créances** FIN liability ledger; ~ **des délibérations** COM, DROIT d'une société minute book; ~ **des engagements** DROIT commitment record; ~ **foncier** DROIT, IMMOB land registry, plat book (US); ~ **de l'hôtel** COM, LOISIRS hotel register; ~ **d'immatriculation** TRANSP shipping register; ~ **du Lloyd's** ASSUR Lloyd's Register, TRANSP maritime Register Book; ~ **de navigation du Lloyd's** ASSUR Lloyd's Register of Shipping; ~ **du personnel** RES HUM payroll; ~ **de pointage** RES HUM time book; ~ **des sociétés** ADMIN register of companies; ~ **des titres de la Caisse d'épargne** BOURSE National Savings Register (UK); ~ **des transferts** BOURSE transfer register; ~ **des véhicules du commissionnaire de transport** TRANSP agent's vehicle record, AVR; ~ **des ventes** V&M sales record; ~ **des visiteurs** COM business visitors' memorandum, BVM

Registre: ~ **du commerce et des services** m (RCS) COM, DROIT geré par le "Centre de formalités des entreprises (C.F.E)" ≈ Companies Registration Office (CRO); ~ **du commerce européen** m COM European Registry of Commerce, ERC; ~ **international des substances chimiques potentiellement toxiques** m (RISCPT) ENVIR, IND International Register of Potentially Toxic Chemicals (IRPTC)

registres m pl ADMIN, COM, COMPTA books, records; ~ **comptables** COMPTA books of account; ~ **et pièces comptables** COM books, in the books, records, COMPTA books, records; ~ **statutaires** DROIT statutory books

réglable vt COM adjustable

réglage m COM adjustment, tuning, ECON fine-tuning; ~ **de l'affichage** INFO display setting

réglé, e adj FISC clean-assessed; ~ **en espèces** COM cash-settled; ♦ ~ **par l'agent** TRANSP maritime paid by agent, PBA

règle f BOURSE, BREVETS rule, COM rule, ruler, DROIT, ECON, FIN, FISC, GESTION rule; ~ **de l'abri sûr** FISC safe harbor rule (AmE), safe harbour rule (BrE); ~ **d'admissibilité** FISC eligibility rule; ~ **anti-évitement** BOURSE, DROIT, FIN, FISC anti-avoidance rule; ~ **du bâillon** POL gag rule (US); ~ **de la blouse blanche** V&M publicité white coat rule (jarg); ~ **à calcul** COM, MATH slide rule, slide ruler; ~ **de calcul au prorata** FISC apportionment rule; ~ **des cinq pour cent** BOURSE five per cent rule; ~ **des cinq cents dollars** BOURSE five hundred dollar rule; ~ **de la demi-année** FISC half-year rule; ~ **disciplinaire** RES HUM disciplinary rule; ~ **de l'épargne selon Ramsey** ECON Ramsey saving rule; ~ **de l'homme prudent** BOURSE prudent-man rule (US); ~ **du lessivage à trente jours** FISC thirty-day wash rule (US); ~ **majoritaire** POL majority rule; ~ **de la médiane** COM, MATH median rule; ~ **de mise en service** FISC put-in-use rule; ~ **de modération** COM prudent-man rule (US); ~ **des neuf obligations** BOURSE nine bond rule; ~ **d'or** COM, ECON golden rule; ~ **de priorité absolue** FIN absolute priority rule; ~ **proportionnelle** ASSUR average clause; ~ **405** FIN rule 405 (US); ~ **de rattachement à l'exercice** COMPTA accrual concept, accrual principle; ~ **des 78** FIN rule of the 78s; ~ **du 72** FIN rule of 72; ~ **de la vente à découvert** BOURSE short-sale rule; ♦ **personne qui suit la ~ de modération** COM reasonable person

règlement m ASSUR des pertes adjustment, BANQUE, BOURSE settlement, COM regulation, rule book, set of rules, d'une dette discharge, settlement, DROIT regulation, settlement, ECON regulation, FIN d'une dette discharge, settlement, FISC regulation; ~ **administratif** ADMIN, COM bye-law, bylaw; ~ **à l'amiable** DROIT out-of-court settlement; ~ **anticipé** BOURSE ringing out (jarg); ~ **applicable aux marchandises dangereuses** TRANSP dangerous goods regulations; ~ **d'assurance** ASSUR insurance settlement; ~ **d'avaries** ASSUR, TRANSP average adjustment; ~ **de commande et de contrôle** ADMIN, DROIT command and control regulation; ~ **en continu** BOURSE continuous net settlement (UK), CNS (UK); ~ **de dettes** BANQUE settlement of debts; ~ **disciplinaire** RES HUM disciplinary rule; ~ **en espèces** BOURSE, FIN cash settlement; ~ **graduel** BOURSE rolling settlement; ~ **intérieur** RES HUM rule book, works regulations; ~ **intérieur du syndicat** RES HUM union rule book; ~ **intérieur de l'usine** RES HUM works rules (UK); ~ **interministériel** DROIT, POL interdepartmental settlement; ~ **judiciaire** DROIT legal settlement; ~ **livraison en continu** BOURSE rolling settlement; ~ **mensuel** BANQUE monthly installment (AmE), monthly instalment (BrE), BOURSE account (UK); ~ **de neuf garanties** BOURSE nine bond rule; ~ **par avis de prélèvement** BANQUE pre-authorized payment; ~ **par carte** BANQUE credit card payment; ~ **par chèque** BANQUE check payment (*AmE*), cheque payment (*BrE*); ~ **de sinistre** ASSUR claim payment, claim settlement, claims adjustment; ~ **syndical** RES HUM union rules; ~ **à terme** BOURSE settlement; ~ **du transport combiné** TRANSP intermodal transport law; ~ **-type** RES HUM pattern settlement; ~ **des ventes à terme** BOURSE short-sale rule; ◆ **en ~** COM in settlement; **en ~ de** COMPTA in satisfaction of; **en ~ partiel** RES HUM in part payment; **être en ~ judiciaire** COM, DROIT, IND be in the hands of the receiver

réglementaire *adj* COM prescribed, DROIT statutory

réglementation *f* COM, DROIT, ECON regulation; ~ **des banques** BANQUE, DROIT banking regulation; ~ **des commandes** TRANSP order regulation; ~ **commerciale** COM, DROIT, ECON trade regulations; ~ **comptable** COMPTA accounting standard setting; ~ **D** FIN Regulation D (*US*); ~ **des exportations** IMP/EXP export regulations; ~ **foncière** DROIT, IMMOB land-use regulation; ~ **des importations** IMP/EXP import regulations; ~ **K** FIN Regulation K (*US*); ~ **privée** FISC private ruling; ~ **des prix** ECON, POL price regulation; ~ **Q** FIN *sur la rémunération des dépôts* Regulation Q (*US*); ~ **relative à la construction** DROIT, IMMOB building regulations; ~ **relative au lotissement des propriétés foncières** DROIT, FIN, IMMOB estate planning; ~ **relative à la santé publique** DROIT, PROT SOC, RES HUM health regulations; ~ **stricte** DROIT tight controls; ~ **T** FIN Regulation T (*US*); ~ **du tarif extérieur** IMP/EXP overseas tariff regulations; ~ **des transactions** COM, ECON dealing restriction; ~ **unilatérale** RES HUM unilateral regulation; ~ **vieux pour neuf** TRANSP *navires* scrap-and-build regulation; ~ **Z** FIN Regulation Z (*US*)

réglementé: ~ **par l'État** *loc* POL government-regulated

réglementer *vt* COM, DROIT, ECON regulate

règlements *m pl* COM, DROIT, FISC regulations; ~ **commerciaux** COM, DROIT, ECON business regulations; ~ **douaniers** IMP/EXP customs regulations; ~ **et usages** DROIT code of practice (*UK*); ~ **de l'impôt sur le revenu** FISC income tax regulations; ~ **de l'impôt sur le revenu à la source** FISC PAYE remittances (*UK*); ~ **en matière d'incendie** IND, RES HUM fire regulations; ~ **sanitaires** DROIT, PROT SOC, RES HUM health regulations; ~ **tracassiers** COM, FIN petty regulations

régler *vt* BANQUE discharge, pay off, settle, BREVETS *taxe* pay, COM pay, regulate, settle, *dette* discharge, liquidate, pay off, *différends* resolve, DROIT regulate, *dette* discharge, liquidate, ECON regulate, FIN liquidate, IND regulate, INFO tweak; ◆ **à ~** ADMIN in-basket situation (*jarg*), in-tray exercise (*jarg*); ~ **à l'amiable** DROIT, RES HUM settle amicably; ~ **avec précision** ECON fine-tune; ~ **au comptant** BOURSE, FIN settle in cash; ~ **un**

compte BANQUE, FIN, IND settle an account; ~ **des comptes** COM settle old scores; ~ **un conflit** COM, DROIT, IND, RES HUM settle a dispute; ~ **un conflit par arbitrage** COM, DROIT, IND, RES HUM settle a dispute by arbitration; ~ **une dette à l'amiable** BANQUE, DROIT, FIN compound a debt; ~ **en espèces** BOURSE, FIN settle in cash; ~ **la facture** COM pay a bill, settle the bill; ~ **la note** COM pay a bill, pick up the tab (*infrml*), settle the bill; ~ **des problèmes** COM troubleshoot; ~ **un sinistre** ASSUR adjust a claim

règles: ~ **absolues** *f pl* COM hard and fast rules; ~ **adaptées** *f pl* FIN suitability rules; ~ **anti-discrétionnaires** *f pl* ECON rules versus discretion; ~ **applicables aux successeurs** *f pl* FISC successor rules; ~ **d'attribution** *f pl* FISC attribution rules; ~ **d'attribution de revenu** *f pl* FISC income attribution rules (*Canada*); ~ **de base** *f pl* COM ground rules; ~ **concernant les corporations remplaçantes** *f pl* FISC successor rules; ~ **d'encaissement normalisées** *f pl* BANQUE uniform rules for collections; ~ **fiscales** *f pl* FISC tax rules; ~ **de Hambourg** *f pl* TRANSP *maritime* Hamburg Rules; ~ **de La Haye** *f pl* TRANSP *maritime* Hague Rules; ~ **de La Haye et de Visby** *f pl* TRANSP *maritime* Hague Visby Rules; ~ **de pratique équitable** *f pl* BOURSE rules of fair practice; ~ **de procédure** *f pl* DROIT adjective law; ~ **de prudence** *f pl* BOURSE prudent-man rule (*US*); ~ **quantitatives** *f pl* BOURSE quantitative rules; ~ **de sécurité** *f pl* COM, IND, RES HUM safety regulations

régleur, -euse *m,f* ASSUR, RES HUM adjuster; ~ **d'avaries communes** ASSUR, RES HUM loss adjuster

règne *m* COM, POL reign

régner *vi* COM, POL prevail, reign

régresser *vi* ECON retrogress

régressif, -ive *adj* COM, MATH regressive

régression *f* ECON retrogression, MATH regression, RES HUM takeback bargaining; ~ **linéaire** COMPTA, MATH linear regression; ~ **multiple** ECON, FIN, MATH multiple regression; ~ **simple linéaire** COMPTA, MATH simple linear regression

regret *m* COM regret; ◆ **avoir le ~ d'informer qn que** COM regret to inform sb that

regroupement: ~ **d'actions** *m* BOURSE, FIN consolidation of shares, reverse split; ~ **économique mondial** *m* ECON world economic grouping; ~ **d'entreprises** *m* COMPTA, GESTION business combination; ~ **régional** *m* ECON regional grouping; ~ **de zone statistique métropolitaine** *m* ADMIN Consolidated Metropolitan Statistical Area (*US*), CMSA (*US*)

regrouper *vt* COM regroup; ◆ ~ **aux arrêts** BOURSE gather in the stops

régularisation *f* COMPTA *comptabilité d'engagements* adjustment

régulariser *vt* BANQUE *compte bancaire* put in order

régularité *f* COM punctuality, COMPTA conformity to accounting rules, TRANSP punctuality

régulateur[1], **-trice** *adj* DROIT regulatory

régulateur[2], **-trice** *m,f* FISC regulator, TRANSP *aviation* despatcher, dispatcher; **~ de tension** ENVIR voltage regulator

régulation *f* COM, ECON, IND control, TRANSP *aviation* despatching, dispatching; **~ de la circulation** TRANSP traffic control; **~ employeur-employé** COM, RES HUM master-servant rule; **~ de processus** COM, IND process control; **~ de production** COM, GESTION, IND production control; **~ du trafic** TRANSP traffic control

réguler *vt* TRANSP *trafic* despatch, dispatch

régulier, -ière *adj* COM regular, *affaire* above board, *personne* above board, TRANSP scheduled

régulièrement *adv* COM steadily

réhabilitation *f* COM rehabilitation, DROIT *d'un failli* discharge, ENVIR rehabilitation, FIN discharge; **~ du failli** DROIT, FIN discharge in bankruptcy; **~ de faillite** DROIT, FIN discharge of bankruptcy; **~ des quartiers défavorisés** ENVIR, PROT SOC greenlining (*jarg*)

réhabiliter *vt* COM re-educate, rehabilitate, DROIT discharge, rehabilitate, ENVIR rehabilitate, RES HUM re-educate

rehausser *vt* ECON enhance

REI *abrév* (*rachat d'une entreprise par des investisseurs*) BOURSE, COM, FIN, GESTION LMBI (*leveraged management buy-out*)

réimplantation *f* COM resettlement

réimplanter *vt* COM resettle

réimposer *vt* COM reimpose

réimputation *f* BANQUE charge-back (*US*)

réincorporation *f* RES HUM *personnel* re-employment, re-engagement

réincorporer *vt* MATH add back, RES HUM *personnel* re-engage

réinitialisation *f* INFO rebooting, reset; **~ automatique** INFO automatic rebooting, automatic reset

réinitialiser *vt* INFO reboot, reset

réinjection *f* FIN reinfusion

réintégration *f* COM reinstatement, RES HUM re-employment, re-engagement

réintégré, e *adj* COM recmd, recommissioned, reinstated

réintégrer *vt* COM reinstate, MATH add back, RES HUM re-employ, re-engage

réinvestir *vt* BOURSE plow back (*AmE*), plough back (*BrE*), reinvest, COM *bénéfices de l'entreprise* plough back (*BrE*), plow back (*AmE*), reinvest

réinvestissement *m* BOURSE, COM reinvestment; **~ automatique** BOURSE automatic reinvestment; **~ des dividendes** BOURSE dividend reinvestment, reinvestment of dividends

réitérer *vt* COM reiterate

rejet *m* BREVETS refusal, rejection, COM quashing, rejection, DROIT rejection, ENVIR dumping, *dans*

l'air, dans l'eau effluent; **~ accidentel** ENVIR, IND *pollution* accidental discharge; **~ industriel** ENVIR, IND industrial discharge; **~ intentionnel** ENVIR, IND *pollution* intentional discharge; **~ en mer** ENVIR, IND *pollution* discharge at sea

rejeter *vt* COM disallow, quash, turn away, reject, DROIT *demande* ignore, ENVIR dump, FISC *déduction* disallow, GESTION overrule, MÉDIA *imprimé* spike, POL *décision* overrule

relâché, e *adj* COM *contrôle* slack

relâchement *m* COM relaxation

relâcher 1. *vt* COM relax, slacken; **2.** *vi* TRANSP *navigation* put into port; **3.** *v pron* **se ~** RES HUM *dans son travail* be slack; ◆ **~ la bride** ECON slacken the reins; **~ les rênes** ECON slacken the reins

relais *m* BANQUE accommodation, bridging, COM bridging, FIN accommodation, bridging

relance *f* COM follow-up, ECON boost, *par augmentation de la masse monétaire* reflation (*jarg*), INFO rebooting, reloading, restart; **~ en route** INFO autorestart

relancement *m* COM, V&M relaunch

relancer *vt* COM boost, dun, relaunch, ECON inflate, reflate, *inflation* refuel, *économie* boost, FIN dun, INFO restart, *programme* re-enter, reactivate, reload, V&M boost, dun, relaunch; ◆ **~ un secteur affaibli** ECON take up the slack (*infrml*)

relatif, -ive *adj* COM relative, *valeur* comparative; **~ au commerce** ECON trade-related; ◆ **~ à** COM relative to; **~ à l'exercice du droit de propriété** DROIT *action satisfaisant une prétention* in rem; **~ à une personne déterminée** DROIT in personam

relation *f* COM acquaintance, connection, link, relation, relationship, *personne* contact, ECON, FIN link, relationship; **~ d'affaires** COM business acquaintance, business connection; **~ contractuelle** COM contractual relationship; **~ linéaire** RES HUM linear relationship; **~ mandataire** COMPTA agency relationship; **~ normale** BOURSE normal relationship; **~ patronat-syndicat au point mort** RES HUM cooling-off period; **~ qualifiée** FISC qualified relation; **~ rendement d'une valeur** BOURSE security market line

relations *f pl* COM, ECON, GESTION, RES HUM relations; **~ d'affaires** BOURSE *avec une société* material interest, COM, ECON, GESTION business relations; **~ avec les employés** RES HUM employee relations; **~ avec la presse** MÉDIA press relations; **~ commerciales et exportations** IMP/EXP Commercial Relations and Exports (*UK*), CRE (*UK*); **~ commerciales officielles** COM, ECON formal trade links; **~ directes patronat-employés** RES HUM positive labor relations (*AmE*), positive labour relations (*BrE*); **~ entre groupes** RES HUM intergroup relations; **~ extérieures** COM, GESTION external relations; **~ gouvernementales** POL government relations; **~ humaines** COM, RES HUM human relations; **~ humaines dans l'entreprise** RES HUM industrial relations, IR; **~ industrielles**

RES HUM industrial relations, IR; ~ **intergroupales** RES HUM intragroup relations; ~ **normales** BOURSE normal relationship; ~ **ouvrières** RES HUM employee relations, labor relations *(AmE)*, labour relations *(BrE)*; ~ **professionnelles** RES HUM industrial relations, IR; ~ **publiques** *(RP)* V&M public relations *(PR)*; ~ **sociales** RES HUM labor relations *(AmE)*, labour relations *(BrE)*; ~ **syndicales** RES HUM industrial relations, IR; ~ **du travail** RES HUM industrial relations, staff relations; ~ **de travail** RES HUM employment relationship; ♦ **avoir des ~ commerciales** ECON trade

relativement:[1] ~ **important** *adj* COM considerable

relativement[2] *adv* COM comparatively, relatively; ♦ ~ **à** COM re, reference, regarding, with reference to

relativités *f pl* RES HUM relativities

relaxer *vt* DROIT acquit

relevé: ~ **bancaire** *m* BANQUE bank statement; ~ **de compensation** *m* BANQUE clearing report; ~ **de compte** *m* BANQUE account statement, bank statement, BOURSE account statement, purchase and sale statement, COM, COMPTA account statement, bank statement; ~ **de compte de liquidation** *m* BOURSE, COM broker's statement; ~ **de compte mensuel** *m* BANQUE, FIN monthly statement; ~ **de comptes** *m* BANQUE abstract of accounts; ~ **des comptes clients** *m* COMPTA, FIN accounts receivable statement; ~ **de courtage** *m* BOURSE brokerage statement; ~ **des effets émis** *m* BANQUE statement of instruments issued; ~ **d'erreurs** *m* FIN notice of default; ~ **de frais** *m* RES HUM expense account; ~ **général** *m* COM *de comptes*, COMPTA general statement; ~ **de modalités d'émission** *m* FIN statement of condition; ~ **des opérations avec solde** *m* COMPTA transaction balance report; ~ **d'opérations de courtage** *m* BOURSE brokerage statement; ~ **périodique des chèques** *m* BANQUE cutoff period; ~ **de la position nette** *m* BOURSE net position report; ~ **quotidien des opérations** *m* COM daily activity report; ~ **quotidien de la situation** *m* COMPTA daily position statement; ~ **de solde de compensation** *m* BANQUE clearing balance statement; ~ **des taxes de tonnage** *m* FISC, IMP/EXP, TRANSP *maritime* tonnage dues slip, tonnage slip; ~ **des varangues** *m* TRANSP *navigation* dead rise, rf, rise of floor; ♦ **faire un ~ de compte** BANQUE draw up a statement of account

relever *vt* COM *défi* take up, ECON, FIN put up, RES HUM *équipe* relieve; ♦ ~ **de la compétence de** ADMIN, DROIT come under the jurisdiction of; ~ **conformément à l'inflation** ECON *prix* raise in line with inflation; ~ **les indications d'un compteur** COM take a reading; ~ **de la juridiction de** ADMIN, DROIT come under the jurisdiction of

relevés: ~ **réguliers** *m pl* COM regular statements

relié: ~ **en dur** *loc* MÉDIA *édition* hardback, hardcover; **être ~** *loc* INFO interface; **être ~ à** *loc* INFO interface with

relier *vt* COMMS connect, INFO link, MÉDIA *édition* bind

reliquat *m* BOURSE overhang, FIN residue

relire *vt* INFO *bande* replay

remake *m* LOISIRS remake

remaniement: ~ **de capital** *m* FIN reorganization of capital; ~ **de l'équipe dirigeante** *m* GESTION management reshuffle; ~ **ministériel** *m* POL cabinet reshuffle

remanier *vt* COM, MÉDIA rewrite

remarquable *adj* COM, RES HUM distinguished, pre-eminent

remarque *f* COM comment, observation, remark, nota bene; ♦ **faire des ~s** COM comment

remarquer *vt* COM note, remark

remb. *abrév (remboursable)* BOURSE, COMPTA red. *(redeemable)*

remballage *m* COM, IMP/EXP repacking

remballer *vt* COM, IMP/EXP repack

rembarquer 1. *vt* TRANSP; **2.** *vti* COM re-embark

rembaucher *vt* RES HUM re-engage

rembobiner *vt* INFO, MÉDIA rewind

remboursable *adj* BANQUE refundable, repayable, BOURSE *(remb.)* callable, redeemable *(red.)*, COM, COMPTA refundable, repayable, COMPTA *(remb.)* redeemable *(red.)* ECON, FISC refundable, repayable; ~ **par anticipation** BOURSE callable; ~ **sur demande** COM repayable on demand

remboursé, e *adj* BOURSE, COMPTA redeemed

remboursement *m* BANQUE repayment, BOURSE refund, COM liquidation, refund, reimbursement, repayment, COMPTA redemption, ECON repayment, FIN liquidation, redemption, *prêt* amortization, FISC refund; ~ **admissible** FISC allowable refund; ~ **anticipé** BOURSE advance refunding, COM accelerated redemption, accelerated repayment, advance repayment, COMPTA anticipated redemption, anticipated repayment, FIN anticipated redemption, anticipated repayment, redemption before due date; ~ **avant la date d'échéance** FIN redemption before due date; ~ **des bons du Trésor** FIN take-up of Treasury bills; ~ **de dette** COMPTA debt retirement; ~ **de la dette de l'État** ECON public sector debt repayment *(UK)*, PSDR *(UK)*; ~ **de la dette publique** ECON public sector debt repayment *(UK)*, PSDR *(UK)*; ~ **des droits de douane** COM, IMP/EXP Dbk, drawback; ~ **échelonné sur 2 ans** BANQUE repayment over 2 years; ~ **d'une émission obligataire par une autre** BOURSE refund; ~ **des emprunts** FIN debt financing; ~ **final** BANQUE payout; ~ **d'un hypothèque** BANQUE, FIN mortgage servicing; ~ **d'impôt** FISC tax refund; ~ **de l'impôt sur le revenu** FISC income tax refund; ~ **in fine** BANQUE bullet repayment; ~ **de loyer** PROT SOC rent rebate; ~ **d'une obligation par une nouvelle émission** BOURSE paydown; ~ **d'un paiement en trop** FISC refund; ~ **par déchéance du terme** DROIT repayment by acceleration; ~ **d'une partie du principal** BOURSE paydown; ~ **périodique** BANQUE,

COMPTA, FIN amortization payment; ~ **de prêt** BANQUE, COM, COMPTA, FIN loan repayment; ~ **d'un prêt** BANQUE, COM, COMPTA, FIN amortization of a loan; ~ **prioritaire** BOURSE, FIN senior refunding; ~ **en retour** FISC refund return; ~ **de second rang** BOURSE, FIN junior refunding; ~ **sur impôt** FISC tax refund; ~ **de taxe** FISC tax rebate; ~ **au titre des gains en capital** *Can* FISC capital gains refund; ~ **total net** BANQUE total net redemption; ~ **en tranches égales** BANQUE level payment, level repayment; ~ **trimestriel** COMPTA quarterly installment (*AmE*), quarterly instalment (*BrE*); ♦ **au ~** BOURSE at call; **dont le ~ est demandé** BOURSE called-away

rembourser *vt* BANQUE pay off, pay off creditors, refund, repay, BOURSE redeem, retire, COM clear, repay, defray, refund, redeem, reimburse, COMPTA redeem, refund, ECON refund, *dette* pay off, *emprunt* repay, FIN defray, FISC refund; ♦ **à ~** COMPTA outstanding; ~ **des obligations** BANQUE, BOURSE call bonds

remède *m* COM remedy, GESTION prescription

remédier: ~ **à** *vt* COM *situation* remedy

remembrement *m* ENVIR, IMMOB *de terrains* assemblage

remerciant: **en vous ~ d'avance** *loc* COMMS thanking you in advance, thanking you in anticipation; **en vous ~ par avance** *loc* COMMS thanking you in advance, thanking you in anticipation

remettre 1. *vt* COM adjourn, postpone, shelve, table, *rapport* put in, DROIT abate, adjourn, remit, GESTION adjourn; ~ **en activité** INFO reactivate; ~ **à neuf** COM recondition, refurbish, renovate; **2.** *v pron* **se ~ à** COM brush up on; ♦ **l'accent sur** COM re-emphasize; ~ **en bon état** COM recondition, refurbish, renovate, INFO restore; ~ **aux calendes grecques** RES HUM remit; ~ **une dette** COM, FIN forego a debt, forgo a debt; ~ **en état** ENVIR *décharge* clean up, rehabilitate; ~ **en forme** INFO reformat; ~ **à plus tard** COM hold off, postpone, put into cold storage (*infrml*); ~ **qch à une huitaine** COM adjourn sth for a week; ~ **sa démission** ADMIN, RES HUM hand in one's resignation; ~ **en valeur** ENVIR reclaim; ~ **à zéro** INFO reset, zero

remis: ~ **à neuf** *loc* COM reconditioned, renovated, R

remise *f* COM abatement, allowance, concession, deferment, discount, postponement, rebate, surrender, trade discount, DROIT *de peine, de dette* remittal, FIN discount, rebate, FISC *d'un impôt* remission, GESTION adjournment, V&M discount, markdown; ~ **absolue** FIN unconditional remission; ~ **bancaire** BANQUE bank remittance; ~ **de capital à la société mère** FIN, GESTION repatriation of capital; ~ **de charges** FISC remission of charges; ~ **en compensation** BANQUE onward clearing; ~ **consentie avec effet rétroactif** TRANSP retrospective rebate; ~ **au détaillant pour mise en avant des produits** V&M retail-display allowance; ~ **de dette** FIN debt forgiveness; ~ **de distribution** V&M distribution allowance; ~ **à l'encaissement** BANQUE remittance for collection; ~ **en état** ENVIR rehabilitation, GESTION, IND, TRANSP overhaul; ~ **à l'état initial** INFO reset; ~ **de fonds complémentaires** COMPTA, FIN additional paid-in capital; ~ **gracieuse d'impôt** FISC forgiveness of tax; ~ **hypothécaire** BANQUE, FIN mortgage discount; ~ **d'impôt** FISC forgiveness of tax, remission of tax, tax remission; ~ **pour manutention** BOURSE handling allowance; ~ **à neuf** COM reconditioning, refurbishment, renovation; ~ **à plus tard** COM postponement; ~ **à la profession** COM trade allowance; ~ **quantitative** V&M volume merchandise allowance; ~ **en recouvrement** BANQUE remittance for collection; ~ **en route** INFO autorestart; ~ **en sac** TRANSP rebagging; ~ **sur la quantité** COM, COMPTA, V&M bulk discount, quantity discount; ~ **sur volume** COM, COMPTA, V&M bulk discount, quantity discount; ~ **totale** BANQUE payout; ~ **en valeur** ENVIR reclaiming; ~ **à zéro** INFO reset; ♦ **faire une ~ de** COM discount; **pour ~** BOURSE for surrender

remisier *m* BOURSE intermediate broker

remodelage *m* TRANSP lifting

remontée: ~ **de l'information** *f* INFO feedback

remonter *vi* COM bounce back, rise again, ECON rise again; ♦ ~ **jusqu'à l'origine de** COM trace back

remorquage *m* TRANSP tow, towing

remorque *f* TRANSP drawbar trailer, trailer; ~ **autochargeable** TRANSP self-loading trailer; ~ **à benne basculante** TRANSP tilt trailer; ~ **de chargement par rampe arrière** TRANSP rear-ramp-loading trailer; ~ **composée** TRANSP composite trailer; ~ **fourgon** TRANSP box trailer; ~ **nue** TRANSP skeletal trailer; ~ **à plate-forme surbaissée** TRANSP lo, low loader; ~ **à ridelles** TRANSP curtain-sided trailer, CS; ~ **sur wagon plat** TRANSP *chemin de fer* trailer on flat car; ~ **surbaissée** TRANSP lo, low loader; ~ **à timon** TRANSP drawbar trailer; ~ **vide rentrant de la livraison** TRANSP single back

remorquer *vt* TRANSP tow

remorqueur *m* TRANSP anchor-handling tug, towboat, tug, AHT, T; ~ **pilote** TRANSP *navigation* pilotage tug; ~ **de sauvetage** TRANSP anchor-handling salvage tug, AHST

rempaquetage *m* COM, IMP/EXP repacking

rempaqueter *vt* COM, IMP/EXP repack

remplaçant, e *m,f* COM alternate, RES HUM fill-in

remplacement *m* COM replacement, RES HUM stand-in, substitution (*jarg*); ~ **du revenu** ASSUR income replacement

remplacer *vt* COM replace, substitute, take over from, *objet, idée, méthode* supersede, LOISIRS *sport* substitute, RES HUM stand in for; ♦ ~ **les membres du conseil d'administration** GESTION unseat the board

remplir *vt* COM *conditions* fit, meet, *formulaire*

complete, fill in, fill out, DROIT discharge, IMP/EXP fill in, RES HUM carry out; ◆ à ~ ADMIN blank; ~ les conditions ADMIN qualify for; ~ une déclaration FISC prepare a return; se ~ les poches COM make a killing (*infrml*); ~ ses obligations COM meet one's obligations; ~ un vide COM fill the vacuum

remplissage: ~ truqué m V&M *marketing* slack fill (*jarg*)

remploi m ENVIR reuse, RES HUM re-employment, re-engagement

remployer vt ENVIR reuse, RES HUM re-employ, re-engage

remporter: ~ un grand succès loc COM score a hit

remue-méninges m GESTION brainstorming

rémunérateur, -trice adj COM gainful, remunerative; peu ~ COM unprofitable, unremunerative

rémunération f BOURSE fee, COM compensation, earnings, pay, remuneration, salaries and wages, DROIT consideration, RES HUM compensation, earnings, pay, remuneration, salaries and wages; ~ de l'affréteur TRANSP *navigation* charterer's pay dues, cpd; ~ des cadres GESTION, RES HUM executive remuneration; ~ des heures supplémentaires RES HUM overtime pay; ~ aux honoraires MÉDIA fee system; ~ occulte RES HUM secret payment; ~ de service COM, RES HUM service fee; ~ total du personnel COMPTA, RES HUM total wages and salaries; ◆ ~ accordée pour un travail payé au temps RES HUM pay for work at time rates

rémunérations: ~ commerciales f pl COM commercial considerations; ~ et charges sociales f pl RES HUM salaries, wages and fringe benefits

rémunéré, e adj BANQUE interest-bearing, COM, RES HUM paid, pd

rémunérer vt COM, RES HUM compensate, pay

renantissement m FIN remarging

renchérissement m COM increase in prices, price increase, price rise, rise in prices, COMPTA price increase, price rise, rise in prices, ECON increase in prices, price increase, price rise, rise in prices, FIN, V&M price increase, price rise, rise in prices

rencontrer vt COM meet, *problème* encounter

rendement m BOURSE performance, COM productivity, return, COMPTA return, yield, ECON capacity, efficiency, output, productivity, yield, FIN earnings yield, profit performance, return, throughput, yield, FISC *d'un impôt* yield, IND capacity, efficiency, output, productivity, RES HUM output, V&M efficiency; ~ de l'actif BOURSE, COMPTA, FIN asset return, return on assets; ~ de l'actif net BOURSE, COMPTA, FIN return on net assets; ~ de l'actif net employé BOURSE, COMPTA, FIN return on net assets employed; ~ des actifs BOURSE earnings on assets, COMPTA earnings on assets, return on investment, ROI, FIN return on investment, ROI; ~ d'une action BOURSE stock yield; ~ de l'action BOURSE, COMPTA, FIN return on equity,

ROE; ~ des actions BOURSE dividend yield, earnings yield; ~ des actions brut BOURSE, ECON Y'ld-Gr's, gross dividend yield; ~ actualisé BANQUE, BOURSE yield to maturity, YTM; ~ actuel BOURSE current return, current yield; ~ annuel COMPTA, ECON, FIN annual yield; ~ après impôt COMPTA, ECON, FIN, FISC after-tax yield; ~ après impôt d'une obligation COMPTA, ECON, FIN, FISC after-tax bond yield; ~ d'un bon BOURSE bond yield; ~ boursier BOURSE dividend yield, earnings yield; ~ boursier brut BOURSE, ECON Y'ld-Gr's, gross dividend yield; ~ brut COM, COMPTA, ECON, FIN, FISC gross yield, pretax yield; ~ du capital COMPTA, ECON, FIN return on capital, ROC; ~ du capital investi COMPTA, ECON, FIN return on invested capital, ROIC; ~ des capitaux propres BOURSE, COMPTA, FIN return on equity, ROE; ~ du combustible ENVIR fuel efficiency; ~ composite BANQUE composite yield; ~ comptable COMPTA, FIN accounting return; ~ coupon BOURSE coupon yield; ~ courant BOURSE current return, current yield; ~ direct BOURSE direct yield; ~ de dividende brut BOURSE, ECON Y'ld-Gr's, gross dividend yield; ~ à l'échéance BANQUE, BOURSE, ECON, FIN yield to maturity, YTM; ~ économique ECON commercial efficiency, economic efficiency, ENVIR energy efficiency; ~ effectif BOURSE *d'un investissement* actual yield, effective yield; ~ équitable COMPTA, FIN fair rate of return, fair return, IMMOB fair rental value; ~ équivalent obligataire BOURSE bond equivalent yield; ~ équivalent à l'obligation à trois mois BOURSE three-month bond equivalent yield; ~ équivalent sur obligation BOURSE bond equivalent yield; ~ factoriel ECON, IND factor productivity; ~ des fonds propres BOURSE, COMPTA earnings on assets, return on equity, ROE, FIN return on assets, return on equity, ROA, ROE; ~ global ECON aggregate output, FIN compound yield, IND aggregate output; ~ à l'hectare ECON *agriculture* yield per acre; ~ historique BOURSE historical yield; ~ horaire IND, RES HUM output per hour; ~ de l'impôt FISC tax yield; ~ indiqué BOURSE indicated yield; ~ des investissements COMPTA, FIN return on investment, ROI; ~ à la levée BOURSE strike yield; ~ du marché des capitaux BOURSE capital market yield; ~ du marché financier BOURSE capital market yield; ~ marginal sur le capital BOURSE, FIN marginal return on capital; ~ maximal ECON, IND maximum efficiency; ~ maximum BOURSE maximum return, ECON, IND maximum efficiency, maximum output; ~ minimum COM yield to call, yield to worst; ~ minimum réalisé BOURSE realized minimum return; ~ moyen BOURSE average yield, mean return, FIN, IND average yield, RES HUM standard performance; ~ négatif à trois mois BOURSE three-month discount yield; ~ net BOURSE, COMPTA, ECON, FIN, FISC after-tax yield, net yield; ~ net des intérêts BANQUE, FIN net interest yield; ~ de l'obligation BOURSE bond yield; ~ par ouvrier IND, RES HUM output per head; ~ **de Pareto** ECON Pareto efficiency; ~ **de placement** BANQUE, BOURSE, FIN investment yield; ~ **portant intérêt** BOURSE interest-bearing yield; ~ **positif à trois mois** BOURSE three-month add-on yield; ~ **d'un prêt** BANQUE, BOURSE loan yield; ~ **propulsif** TRANSP *moteur* quasi-propulsive coefficient, QPC; ~ **raisonnable** BOURSE fair rate of return, IND, RES HUM reasonable output; ~ **réel** BOURSE effective yield; ~ **simple** BOURSE simple yield; ~ **standard** COM, IND, RES HUM standard performance; ~ **supplémentaire** BOURSE add-on yield; ~ **sur investissement à terme** BOURSE forward investment return; ~ **sur remboursement** BOURSE redemption yield; ~ **du trafic** TRANSP traffic yield; ~ **au travail** RES HUM job performance; ♦ **à ~ élévé** BOURSE, FIN high-return, high-yield, high-yielding

rendements: ~ **d'échelle** *m pl* BOURSE, ECON, FIN returns to scale; ~ **d'échelle constants** *m pl* BOURSE, ECON, FIN constant returns to scale; ~ **d'échelle croissants** *m pl* BOURSE, ECON, FIN increasing returns to scale; ~ **d'échelle décroissants** *m pl* BOURSE, ECON, FIN diminishing returns to scale; ~ **du marché monétaire** *m pl* BOURSE, ECON, FIN money-market returns

rendez-vous *m* COM appointment, engagement; ♦ **donner ~ à qn** COM make an appointment with sb; **sur ~ uniquement** COM by appointment only

rendre 1. *vt* COM render, yield, DROIT *jugement* pass; 2. *v pron* **se ~ coupable d'un faux** DROIT commit forgery; ♦ ~ **compte de** COM account for; ~ **compte des résultats** COM report one's findings; ~ **les coups** COM fight back; ~ **désuet** COM render obsolete; ~ **exigible immédiatement** COM *dette* call in; ~ **indépendant** COM *filliale* hive off; ~ **un jugement en faveur de qn** COM give a ruling in favor of sb (*AmE*), give a ruling in favour of sb (*BrE*); ~ **nul** COM make void; ~ **nul et non avenu** DROIT abate, render null and void; ~ **périmé** COM render obsolete; **se ~ compte de** COM realize; ~ **service à** COM oblige; ~ **supportable** COM alleviate; ~ **un verdict de culpabilité** DROIT find sb guilty; ~ **un verdict de non culpabilité** DROIT find sb not guilty; ~ **visite à qn** COM call on sb, pay a call on sb, pay a visit to sb

rendu, e *adj* TRANSP dd, delivered; ♦ ~ **à domicile** TRANSP *marchandises* delivered domicile; ~ **droits acquittés** IMP/EXP delivered duty paid, DDP; ~ **droits non-acquittés** IMP/EXP delivered duty unpaid, DDU; ~ **ex ship** IMP/EXP, TRANSP delivered ex ship, DES; ~ **à la frontière** IMP/EXP delivered at frontier, DAF, TRANSP delivered at frontier, DAF; ~ **à quai** IMP/EXP, TRANSP delivered at docks, DD; ~ **à quai droits acquittés** IMP/EXP delivered ex quay, DEQ

renégociation *f* COM renegotiation

renégocier *vt* COM renegotiate

renfermé, e *adj* BOURSE locked in (*US*), COM locked-in

renfermer *vt* BOURSE, COM lock in

renflouement *m* COM bail-out, ECON refloating, FIN bail-out

renflouer *vt* COM bail out, ECON refloat, FIN bail out

renforcé, e *adj* COM, ECON consolidated, strengthened

renforcement *m* COM consolidation, reinforcement, ECON strengthening; ~ **en cours** RES HUM continuous reinforcement

renforcer *vt* COM consolidate, reinforce, *règlement, consignes* stiffen, DROIT tighten up, ECON consolidate, reinforce; ♦ ~ **la confiance de** COM bolster the confidence of

rengagement *m* RES HUM re-employment, re-engagement

rengager *vt* RES HUM re-employ, re-engage

renom: de ~ *loc* COM *entreprise* renowned

renommée *f* COM renown

renommer *vt* INFO *fichier* rename

renoncer: ~ **à** *vt* COM forego, renounce, *projet, plainte* abandon, DROIT, FISC waive; ♦ ~ **à une succession** DROIT relinquish an inheritance; ~ **à toute prétention** DROIT abandon any claim

renonciation *f* BREVETS waiving, COM abandonment, DROIT disclaimer, *à un droit* abandonment, waiver, FISC waiver; ~ **à un droit** ASSUR disclaimer, DROIT quitclaim; ~ **aux droits conférés par un brevet** BREVETS, DROIT surrender of a patent

renouvelé, e *adj* COM *bail* renewed

renouveler 1. *vt* BANQUE reissue, roll over, BREVETS, COM, FIN renew; 2. *v pron* **se ~** RES HUM turn over

renouvellement *m* BANQUE *d'une lettre de change* reissue, BREVETS, COM, FIN renewal; ~ **d'hypothèque** BANQUE renewal of mortgage

rénovation *f* COM reconditioning, refurbishment, renovation, revamping, IMMOB reconditioning, refurbishment, POL, PROT SOC renewal; ~ **urbaine** COM urban renewal; ~ **de vieux quartiers** ENVIR, PROT SOC greenlining (*jarg*)

rénové, e *adj* COM, IMMOB reconditioned, renovated, R

rénover *vt* COM recondition, refurbish, renovate, revamp, IMMOB recondition, refurbish, renovate

renseignements *m pl* COM, COMPTA, ECON, FISC, TRANSP details, inf., info (*infrml*), information; ~ **commerciaux** COM status information; ~ **d'initié** ECON price-sensitive information; ~ **de listage** BOURSE listing particulars; ~ **prescrits** FISC prescribed information; ~ **réglementaires** FISC prescribed information; ~ **sur crédit** COMPTA credit information; ~ **téléphoniques** Fra (*cf assistance-annuaire Can*) COMMS directory enquiries (*BrE*), directory information (*AmE*); ~ **en vol** TRANSP in-flight information

renseigner: ~ **qn sur qch** *loc* COM acquaint sb with sth

rentabilité *f* BANQUE rate of return, BOURSE break-even point, cost-effectiveness, COM cost-effectiveness, profitability, COMPTA cost-effectiveness, profitability, rate of return, earning power, earnings performance, ECON cost-effectiveness, profitability, FIN cost-effectiveness, profitability, rate of return, *d'une valeur* earnings performance, IMMOB break-even point, cost-effectiveness, RES HUM earning power, payoff, V&M break-even point, cost-effectiveness; **~ des actifs** COMPTA, FIN return on investment, ROI; **~ des capitaux investis** *(RCI)* COMPTA, ECON, FIN return on capital employed *(ROCE)*; **~ des entreprises** ECON corporate earning power; **~ à la hausse** BOURSE upside break-even; **~ d'investissements** COMPTA, FIN return on investment, ROI; **~ de produit** COMPTA, FIN, V&M product profitability; **~ des ventes** FIN, V&M return on sales

rentable *adj* COM cost-effective, profitable, *entreprise* gainful, COMPTA cost-effective, *entreprise* profitable, ECON, FIN profitable; ◆ **être ~** FIN pay back; **peu ~** COM underperforming, unprofitable, COMPTA, ECON, FIN unprofitable, IND underperforming

rente *f* ASSUR annuity, COM annuity fund; **~ anticipée** FIN early retirement annuity; **~ certaine** ASSUR annuity certain; **~ conjointe au dernier survivant** ASSUR joint and survivor annuity *(US)*; **~ en cours** ASSUR current annuity; **~ en cours de paiement** ASSUR current annuity; **~ différée** ASSUR deferred annuity, deferred payment annuity; **~ économique** ECON economic rent; **~ économique pure** ECON pure economic rent; **~ d'État** BOURSE cons *(UK)*, consols *(UK)*; **~ fixe** ASSUR fixed annuity; **~ d'invalidité** ASSUR disability annuity, PROT SOC disability annuity, disability benefit; **~ d'invalidité en remplacement de revenu** ASSUR income replacement; **~ de monopole** ECON, IMMOB monopoly rent; **~ ordinaire** ASSUR ordinary annuity; **~ à paiement différé** ASSUR deferred annuity, deferred payment annuity; **~ payable d'avance** ASSUR annuity due, annuity factor, annuity in advance; **~ payable à terme échu** ASSUR annuity in arrears; **~ perpétuelle** BANQUE bank annuities, BOURSE perpetuity, COM cons *(UK)*, consols *(UK)*; **~ réversible** ASSUR annuity in reversion, reversionary annuity, joint and survivor annuity *(US)*; **~ sur l'État** FIN government annuity; **~ de survie** ASSUR reversionary annuity; **~ technologique** ECON technological rent; **~ viagère avec réversion** IMMOB survivorship annuity

rentes *f pl* FIN unearned income, velvet; **~ consolidées** FIN consolidated annuities *(UK)*, consolidated stock *(UK)*; **~ et paiements différés** ASSUR deferred benefits and payments

rentier, -ère *m,f* COM person of independent means, FISC annuitant, IMMOB rentier; **~ viager** IMMOB life annuitant

rentrée: **~ d'argent** *f* BANQUE, COM, COMPTA, ECON, FIN cash inflow; **~ de fonds** *f (ANT sortie de fonds)* BANQUE, COM, COMPTA, ECON, FIN cash inflow, inflow of funds; **~ sur créance passée en**

charges *f* BANQUE, COMPTA, FIN bad debt recovery; **~ sur créance radiée** *f* BANQUE, COMPTA, FIN bad debt recovery

rentrées *f pl* BOURSE, COMPTA, FIN receipts; **~ d'argent** COMPTA cash receipt, FIN cash receipt, earning streams; **~ de fonds** COMPTA cash receipt, FIN cash receipt, cash streams; **~ de fonds rapides** FIN quick returns; **~ minimales réalisées** BOURSE realized minimum return; **~ publiques** COMPTA, FIN, V&M *publicité* advertising revenue

rentrer: **~ dans ses frais** *loc* COM, COMPTA, ECON break even

renversement *m* COM reversing, REV; **~ de la tendance** COM retracement, trend reversal

renvoi *m* COM footnote, DROIT *à une instance inférieure* remand, remittal, RES HUM dismissal, firing *(infrml)*; **~ automatique d'un appel** COMMS *Can* automatic call transfer, call forwarding, INFO call forwarding; **~ pur et simple** RES HUM summary dismissal; **~ en révision** DROIT writ of error

renvoyé: **être ~** *loc* RES HUM get the sack *(infrml)*

renvoyer[1] *abrév* RES HUM discharge, dismiss, fire *(infrml)*, sack *(BrE, infrml)*

renvoyer[2] *vt* COM pay off, return, COMMS *paquet* return, DROIT remand, remit, *procès* adjourn, V&M *marchandises* return; **~ l'ascenseur** POL logroll *(US)*; **~ devant** DROIT refer to

réorganisation *f* BOURSE reorganization, COM redeployment, reorganization, FIN, GESTION, IND reorganization, RES HUM redeployment, reorganization; **~ du capital** BOURSE, ECON, FIN capital reorganization; **~ de structure** GESTION structural adjustment

réorganiser *vt* BOURSE reorganize, COM redeploy, reorganize, ECON, FIN, GESTION, IND reorganize, RES HUM redeploy, reorganize

réorientation *f* COM, RES HUM redeployment

réorienter *vt* COM redeploy, IND *production* switch, RES HUM deselect, redeploy

répandre: **se ~** *v pron* COM spill over, COMMS break

répandu, e *adj* COM widespread

réparateur, m COM repairman

réparation *f* ASSUR compensation, DROIT redress, IMMOB repair; **~ du dommage** ASSUR compensation for damage; **~ d'immeuble** IMMOB building repair; **~ en justice** DROIT legal redress; **~ légale** DROIT legal redress, redress; **~ locative** PROT SOC tenant's repair

réparatice *f* COM repairwoman

réparer *vt* COM make good, repair, redress, DROIT *erreurs* redress

réparti, e *adj* INFO distributed; **~ uniformément** COM evenly spread

repartir *vi* COM recover, resume, ECON pick up, recover; **~ à la hausse** COM bounce up; ◆ **faire ~** ECON reflate

répartir *vt* ASSUR adjust, spread, BANQUE split, BOURSE *action* allot, *actions* apportion, COM *bénéfices*, FIN distribute, IMMOB *terrain, propriété* apportion, INFO assign, RES HUM allocate, TRANSP despatch, dispatch; ~ **au prorata** COM prorate; ◆ ~ **les avaries** ASSUR *maritime* apportion the average; ~ **le risque** ASSUR spread the risk

répartiteur, -trice *m,f* FISC assessor, TRANSP *aviation* despatcher, dispatcher; ~ **d'avaries** ASSUR, TRANSP *maritime* average adjuster, AA

répartition *f* ASSUR adjustment, BOURSE allocation, allotment, BREVETS apportionment, COM distribution, COMPTA *des risques* allocation, apportionment, DROIT, ECON, FIN distribution, GESTION breakdown, IMMOB apportionment, RES HUM allocation, allotment, TRANSP *aviation* despatching, dispatching, *de la charge* distribution; ~ **des actifs** BOURSE asset allocation; ~ **de bonus** ASSUR allotment of bonus; ~ **de capital** ECON, FISC distribution of capital; ~ **de capitaux** ECON, FIN capital structure; ~ **des charges** COMPTA apportionment of costs, cost apportionment; ~ **conditionnelle** COMPTA qualifying distribution; ~ **des coûts** COMPTA allocation of costs; ~ **équitable** COM equitable distribution; ~ **fonctionnelle des charges d'exploitation** COMPTA functional analysis of costs; ~ **de fréquence** MATH frequency distribution; ~ **immobilière** IMMOB estate distribution; ~ **des impôts de l'exercice** COMPTA intra-period tax allocation; ~ **par âge** ECON age distribution; ~ **par nature des charges d'exploitation** COMPTA analysis of costs by nature; ~ **par voie d'adjudication** BOURSE allocation by tender (*UK*); ~ **des pouvoirs** COM, POL division of powers; ~ **au prorata** COM proration; ~ **des recettes** COM, TRANSP *revenus du service de transport* revenue allocation; ~ **de la réserve d'ajustement des salaires** RES HUM salary adjustment reserve allotment; ~ **des responsabilités** COM, FIN, GESTION, RES HUM allocation of responsibilities; ~ **des ressources** FIN resource allocation; ~ **du résultat** COMPTA annual appropriation; ~ **du résultat net** COMPTA distribution of net profit; ~ **du revenu** ECON, FISC income distribution; ~ **du revenu national entre les facteurs de production** ECON functional income distribution; ~ **du revenu des particuliers** ECON personal income distribution; ~ **des revenus** RES HUM allocation of earnings; ~ **des richesses** ECON, POL distribution of wealth; ~ **des risques** ASSUR distribution of risks; ~ **des tâches** COM, RES HUM job assignment

repas: ~ **d'affaires bien arrosé** *m* FISC three-martini lunch (*AmE, infrml*); ~ **tout prêt** *m* V&M ready-made meal; ~ **en vol** *m* TRANSP in-flight meal

repasser *vt* COM rerun, *leçon* brush up on, INFO rerun

repenser *vi* COM rethink

repérage: ~ **de l'environnement** *m* ENVIR environmental scanning

répercussion *f* COM aftereffect, ECON, V&M pass-along (*jarg*); ~ **de la charge de l'impôt** FISC shifting of the tax burden; ~ **éventuelle et**

tardive ASSUR long tail; ~ **sur les bénéfices** COM, FIN profit implication

répercussions *f pl* COM implications, repercussions, POL implications

répercuter *vt* COM, ECON pass on

repère *m* COM, DROIT landmark

répertoire *m* INFO directory, repertoire; ~ **d'adresses** COMMS address book; ~ **de base** INFO root directory; ~ **de fichiers** INFO file directory; ~ **à onglets** COM, MÉDIA thumb index; ~ **opérationnel des métiers et des emplois** (*ROME*) RES HUM job bank; ~ **par défaut** INFO default directory; ~ **racine** INFO root directory

répéter *vt* COM repeat

replacement *m* BOURSE reinvestment, COM reinvestment, relocation

replacer *vt* BOURSE reinvest, COM reinvest, relocate

repli *m* BOURSE *du marché* downturn, ECON downswing

réplique *f* ADMIN, COMMS carbon copy, cc, DROIT reply

répondant *m* COM guarantor, DROIT bail

répondeur *m* COM Ansaphone®, answering machine, answerphone, COMMS Ansaphone®, answering machine, answerphone, INFO Ansaphone®, answering machine, answerphone; ~ **automatique** COM Ansaphone®, answering machine, answerphone, COMMS Ansaphone®, answering machine, answerphone, INFO Ansaphone®, answering machine, answerphone; ~ **téléphonique** COM Ansaphone®, answering machine, answerphone, COMMS Ansaphone®, answering machine, answerphone, INFO Ansaphone®, answering machine, answerphone

répondez: ~ **s'il vous plaît** *loc* (*RSVP*) COMMS please reply (*RSVP*)

répondre: ~ **à** *vt* COM *besoins, conditions* meet, *demande* satisfy; ~ **de** COM answer for, be answerable for; ~ **pour qn** BANQUE stand surety for sb; ~ **de qn** BANQUE stand surety for sb, COM answer, reply, *à une lettre* write back; ◆ ~ **à un besoin** COM fill a gap; ~ **aux besoins de** COM meet the needs of; ~ **à un objectif** GESTION meet a goal; ~ **par retour du courrier** COMMS reply by return; ~ **à une prime** BOURSE declare an option; ~ **au téléphone** COMMS answer the phone

réponse *f* COM answer, reply, response, INFO answer; ~ **affirmative** COM positive response; ~ **à un appel d'offre** V&M competitive bid; ~ **du défendeur** DROIT answer; ~ **du demandeur** DROIT reply; ~ **directe** V&M direct response; ~ **payée** COMMS reply paid; ◆ **donner une** ~ COM answer; **en** ~ **à** COM in response to; **en** ~ **à votre appel** COMMS further to your telephone call; **en** ~ **à votre lettre** COMMS further to your letter

report *m* BOURSE backwardation (*UK*), balance brought forward, contango (*UK*), COMPTA, FIN carry-over, contango (*UK*), FISC deferral; ~ **en amont** COMPTA, FISC carry-back; ~ **en aval** COMPTA, FISC carry-forward; ~ **de l'impôt** FISC deferral of taxes, tax deferral; ~ **d'impôt étranger** FISC foreign tax carry-over; ~ **d'impôt minimum** FISC minimum tax carry-over; ~ **de l'impôt sur le revenu** FISC income tax deferral; ~ **négatif** COMPTA, FIN negative carry; ~ **à nouveau** BOURSE b/d, balance brought down, balance brought forward, balance carried forward, COMPTA accumulated profits, amount carried forward, balance brought down, b/d, balance carried forward, profit carried forward, balance brought forward, FIN b/d, balance brought down, balance brought forward, balance carried forward, profit carried forward; ~ **à nouveau de perte fiscale** FISC tax loss carry-back; ~ **de perte** COMPTA *inventaire comptable* loss carry-forward; ~ **d'une perte en amont** COMPTA, FIN loss carry-back; ~ **d'une perte sur une année ultérieure** COMPTA loss carry-forward; ~ **des pertes** COMPTA losses carried forward; ~ **de position** BOURSE roll-over, rolling in; ~ **de position à la baisse** BOURSE roll-down, rolling down; ~ **d'une position d'une échéance sur une autre** BOURSE switch trading; ~ **de position à la hausse** BOURSE rolling up; ~ **prospectif** COMPTA, FISC carry-forward; ~ **rétrospectif** COMPTA, FISC carry-back; ~ **rétrospectif d'une perte** COMPTA, FIN loss carry-back; ~ **sur une année antérieure** COMPTA, FISC *d'une perte* carry-back; ~ **sur une année ultérieure** COMPTA, FISC carry-forward; ~ **sur exercice suivant** BOURSE carry-over business; ~ **sur les exercices précédents** COMPTA, FISC carry-back; ~ **sur les exercices suivants** COMPTA, FISC carry-forward

reportage *m* MÉDIA action, take-out (*US, jarg*), *émission* report; ~ **financier** FIN financial reporting; ~ **photographique** MÉDIA news pictures; ~ **sur place** MÉDIA spot coverage

reporté, e *adj* COM deferred

reporter[1] *m* MÉDIA reporter; ~ **à la tâche** MÉDIA assignment man; ~ **à toutes mains** *infrml* MÉDIA assignment man

reporter[2] **1.** *vt* BANQUE borrow, BOURSE borrow, *titres* take in, COM adjourn, *décision* defer, COMPTA borrow, bring forward, carry down, DROIT adjourn, *décision* defer, FIN borrow, bring forward, carry down, GESTION adjourn, *décision* defer; **2.** *vi* BOURSE take the rate; ◆ **à ~** COMPTA *sur un bilan* carried down, cd, carried forward, CF, def., deferred; ~ **en amont** COMPTA, FISC carry back; ~ **en arrière** COMPTA, FIN carry down; ~ **en avant** COMPTA, FISC carry back; ~ **l'impôt** FISC defer tax; ~ **un paiement** COMPTA, FIN defer payment; ~ **prospectivement** COMPTA, FIN carry forward; ~ **qch jusqu'à la semaine prochaine** COM adjourn sth for a week; ~ **le remboursement d'une dette** COMPTA, FIN defer a debt; ~ **sur un exercice ultérieur** COMPTA, FIN carry forward

repos: de tout ~ *loc* ECON secure

reposer: ~ sur *vt* COM base on; ◆ ~ **essentiellement sur** COM depend on

repositionnement *m* V&M *marketing* repositioning

reprendre 1. *vt* COM resume, RES HUM re-employ, re-engage; **2.** *vi* BOURSE rally, COM pick up, take back, recover, ECON rally, recover; ◆ ~ **à sa charge** COM *dettes* take over

représailles *f pl* RES HUM victimization; ◆ **de ~** COM tit-for-tat; **en ~** COM in retaliation

représentant[1] *m* RES HUM *à domicile*, V&M salesman, traveling salesman (*AmE*), travelling salesman (*BrE*),

représentant[2]**, e** *m,f* COM agent, agt, rep, representative, DROIT agent, agt, fiduciary, *dûment désigné* attorney (*US*), POL Rep. (*US*), Representative (*US*), RES HUM drummer (*AmE, infrml*), *de commerce* sales rep (*infrml*), sales representative, *à domicile* salesperson, V&M *de commerce* agent, drummer (*AmE, infrml*), sales rep (*infrml*), sales representative; ~ **accrédité** COM authorized representative; ~ **agréé** BOURSE registered representative; ~ **de commerce** COM, V&M commercial traveler (*AmE*), commercial traveller (*BrE*); ~ **à la commission** RES HUM commission representative; ~ **à l'étranger** COM overseas agent; ~ **en fret** COM freight sales representative (*UK*); ~ **général** DROIT general agent, universal agent, RES HUM Agent General (*UK*), AG (*UK*); ~ **légal** DROIT legal representative; ~ **d'une marque de fabrique** BREVETS, DROIT trademark agent; ~ **permanent du Royaume-Uni à la Communauté Européenne** ECON, POL United Kingdom Permanent Representative to the European Community, UKREP; ~ **du personnel** GESTION, RES HUM staff representative; ~ **au pourcentage** RES HUM commission representative; ~ **régional** COM, V&M area salesman, area salesperson; ~ **du service clientèle** RES HUM customer-service representative

représentante *f* RES HUM *à domicile*, V&M saleswoman, traveling saleswoman (*AmE*), travelling saleswoman (*BrE*), salesperson, traveling salesperson *(AmE)*, travelling salesperson *(BrE)*; ~ **régionale** COM, V&M area salesperson

représentation *f* COM representation; ~ **analogique** INFO analog representation; ~ **pour les besoins de la cause** DROIT agency of necessity (*US*); ~ **de bienfaisance** LOISIRS benefit; ~ **commerciale** COM, V&M commercial representation; ~ **internationale** COM international representation; ~ **par ratification** DROIT agency by ratification; ~ **paritaire** RES HUM joint representation; ~ **du personnel** RES HUM worker representation; ~ **plurisyndicale** RES HUM multi-unionism; ~ **proportionnelle** *(RP)* POL proportional representation *(PR)*; ~ **régionale** V&M *d'une chaîne de magasins* regional representation; **sur-~** (ANT *sous-représentation*) V&M *sur marché* overrepresentation

représentations: ~ graphiques *f pl* MÉDIA graphics

représenter *vt* COM represent

répression: ~ des fraudes *f* DROIT fraud prevention; ~ **des fraudes maritimes** *f* DROIT, TRANSP maritime fraud prevention

reprise *f* BOURSE rally, rallying, upturn, COM part exchange, rerun, upturn, *du marché* recovery, COMPTA fixtures and fittings, DROIT premium, ECON rally, rallying, recovery, upswing, upturn, FIN purchase acquisition, IMMOB *appartement* key money, INFO *d'un travail* recovery, *du traitement* rerun, LOISIRS *théâtre* revival, RES HUM re-employment, re-engagement; **~ des affaires** COM, ECON business recovery; **~ après clôture** BOURSE after-hours rally, **~ boursière** BOURSE market recovery; **~ économique** ECON recovery; **~ à fort effet de levier** BOURSE, COM high-geared takeover (*BrE*), high-leveraged takeover (*AmE*), HLT; **~ du marché obligataire** BOURSE bond market rally; **~ offshore** FIN offshore takeover; **~ sur erreur** INFO error recovery; **~ sur provisions** COMPTA writing back; **~ technique** BOURSE technical rally

reproductible *adj* MÉDIA camera-ready

reproduction *f* COM copy, ECON reproduction, INFO copy; **~ automatique** INFO autoduplication; **~ des bénéfices** ASSUR duplication of benefits

reproduire *vt* COM, INFO copy; ♦ **~ d'après l'original** COM copy from the original

reprogrammer *vt* INFO reprogram

reprographie *f* COM copying, MÉDIA reprography

réprouver *vt* COM censure

republier *vt* MÉDIA republish

République: **~ centrafricaine** *f* COM Central African Republic; **~ dominicaine** *f* COM Dominican Republic; **~ d'Irlande** *f* COM Irish Republic, Republic of Ireland; **~ du Niger** *f* COM Niger Republic; **~ populaire de Chine** *f* COM People's Republic of China; **~ populaire de Corée** *f* COM Democratic People's Republic of Korea, North Korea; **~ tchèque** *f* COM Czech Republic

répudiation *f* DROIT, FISC *loi de l'impôt sur le revenu* disclaimer

répudier *vt* DROIT, FISC disclaim

réputation *f* COM reputation; **~ bien établie** COM, RES HUM proven track record; **~ de solvabilité** FIN, V&M credit rating, credit standing

requalifier *vt* RES HUM *emploi* upgrade

requérant, e *m,f* BREVETS applicant, DROIT applicant, claimant

requête *f* BREVETS petition, COM request; **~ ex parte** FISC ex parte application (*frml*); **~ formulée par le client** *(RFC)* TRANSP *aviation* change request *(CR)*, request for change *(RFC)*; **~ sommaire** DROIT summary application; **~ unilatérale** FISC ex parte application (*frml*)

réquisitionner *vt* DROIT levy

réquisitoire *m* DROIT statement of prosecution

RES *abrév (rachat d'une entreprise par ses salariés)* BOURSE, COM, FIN, GESTION LMBO *(leveraged management buy-out)*, MBO *(management buy-out)*

rescinder *vt* DROIT rescind

rescision *f* DROIT rescission

rescription *f dat* BOURSE rescription

réseau[1] *m* BANQUE, BOURSE, COM, COMMS, GESTION, INFO, TRANSP, V&M network; **~ bancaire** BANQUE banking network; **~ de chemin de fer** TRANSP rail network, railroad system (*AmE*), railway system (*BrE*); **~ de communication** INFO communications network; **~ de contrepartistes** BOURSE dealer network; **~ de détaillants** V&M retail network; **~ de distribution** COM, INFO distribution network; **~ de données** INFO data network; **~ d'eau** COM water system; **~ d'échanges croisés** BOURSE swap network; **~ d'entreprise** INFO corporate network; **~ étendu** INFO wide area network, WAN; **~ en étoile** INFO star network; **~ d'experts** COM expert network; **~ express régional** TRANSP rapid transit system; **~ ferroviaire** TRANSP rail network, railroad system (*AmE*), railway system (*BrE*); **~ ferroviaire de transport collectif** TRANSP *réseau urbain* mass transit railroad (*AmE*), mass transit railway (*BrE*), MTR; **~ d'information** INFO information network; **~ d'information relatif aux brevets d'invention** BREVETS *propriété intellectuelle*, DROIT patent information network (*UK*); **~ informatique** COMMS, INFO computer network, data network, information network; **~ d'interconnexion** IND national grid (*UK*); **~ local** INFO local area network; **~ local d'entreprise** *(RLE)* INFO local area network *(LAN)*; **~ longue distance** INFO wide area network, WAN; **~ mondial** ADMIN global network; **~ numérique à intégration de services** *(RNIS)* COMMS integrated services digital network *(ISDN)*; **~ d'ordinateurs** COMMS, INFO computer network; **~ ouvert** INFO open network; **~ de points de vente** V&M network of sales outlets; **~ routier** TRANSP road network; **~ de spécialistes** COM expert network; **~ de succursales** BANQUE, COM branch network; **~ de succursales bancaires** BANQUE branch banking system; **~ de swap** BOURSE swap network; **~ de télécommunications** COMMS telecommunication network; **~ de télévision** COMMS TV network, television network; **~ de télévision par câble** COMMS community network; **~ transeuropéen** COM, COMMS, INFO, TRANSP transeuropean network; **~ de transmission** COMMS communication network; **~ à valeur ajoutée** INFO value-added network, VAN; **~ de vente** V&M sales network

réseau:[2] **~ téléphonique de transmission de donnés par paquets** *f* COM packet switching telephone network

réseau:[3] **faire partie des ~x** *loc* COM, INFO networked

réservation *f* COM, LOISIRS, TRANSP, V&M advance booking, booking, reservation; **~ à l'avance** COM, LOISIRS, TRANSP, V&M advance booking; **~ de cargaison** TRANSP reservation of cargo; **~ directe** LOISIRS direct booking; **~ d'espace conteneur** TRANSP container space allocation; **~ groupée** LOISIRS, V&M block booking; **~ de vol**

ouverte LOISIRS, TRANSP open-ended flight reservation

réserve *f* BANQUE reserve, COM qualification, stockpile, *ventes aux enchères* reservation price, reserve, reserve price (*BrE*), upset price (*AmE*), COMPTA, ECON, ENVIR, FIN, FISC reserve, V&M stock, *ventes aux enchères* reservation price, reserve, reserve price (*BrE*), upset price (*AmE*); ~ **pour amortissement des obligations** BOURSE bond sinking fund; ~ **apportée à un rapport d'audit** COMPTA qualification of opinion; ~ **d'argent** FIN smart money; ~ **bancaire** BANQUE bank reserve; ~ **pour catastrophe** ASSUR catastrophe reserve; ~ **pour dépassement des crédits législatifs** COMPTA reserve for statutory overruns; ~ **d'emprunt** BANQUE borrowed reserve; ~ **en espèces** BANQUE cash reserve, vault cash; ~ **pour éventualités** FIN contingency reserve; ~ **excédentaire** BANQUE excess reserve, supplementary reserve; ~ **fédérale** BANQUE, ECON Federal Reserve (*US*), the Fed (*US, infrml*); ~ **de fonds commun de placement** BANQUE mutual-fund custodian; ~ **fractionnaire** BANQUE fractional cash reserve, fractional reserve; ~ **pour gains en capital** *Can* FISC capital gains reserve; ~ **générale** ECON general reserves; ~ **globale visée par règlement** BANQUE prescribed aggregate reserve, PAR; ~ **pour impôts sur le revenu reportés** FISC deferred income tax reserve; ~ **pour indemnités à liquider** ASSUR reserve for unpaid claims; ~ **internationale** ECON international reserve; ~ **légale** COMPTA legal reserve, ECON general reserves; ~ **de main-d'oeuvre** ECON, RES HUM labor pool (*AmE*), labour pool (*BrE*), reserve army of labor (*AmE*), reserve army of labour (*BrE*); ~ **métallique** BANQUE, COM stock of bullion; ~ **monétaire** BANQUE, ECON monetary reserve, money reserve; ~ **naturelle nationale** ENVIR national nature reserve; ~ **négative** COMPTA negative reserve; ~ **obligatoire** BANQUE bench mark reserve (*US*), ECON reserve deposit, RD; ~ **obligatoire des régimes de retraite** FIN pension plan liability reserve; ~ **primaire** BANQUE primary reserve; ~ **prime d'émission** BOURSE, FIN premium reserve; ~ **pour réclamations non réglées** ASSUR *assurance-vie* reserve for unpaid claims; ~ **pour sinistres** ASSUR claims reserve; ~ **spéciale** COMPTA special reserve; ~ **supplémentaire** BANQUE excess reserve, supplementary reserve; ~ **totale prescrite** *(RTP)* BANQUE prescribed aggregate reserve *(PAR)*; ~ **de trésorerie** COMPTA cash reserve; ~ **de valeur** ECON store of value; ◆ **de** ~ ADMIN backup, COM standby

réservé, e *adj* COM reserved; ◆ ~ **à l'administration** ADMIN for office use only; ~ **au personnel** ADMIN for office use only

réserver *vt* ADMIN, COM book, reserve, ECON, FIN earmark, ring-fence, FISC ring-fence, LOISIRS, TRANSP, V&M book, reserve; ◆ ~ **à l'avance** COM, LOISIRS book in advance; ~ **une chambre** COM, LOISIRS book a room, make a reservation;

~ **un jugement** DROIT reserve judgment; **se ~ le droit de faire** BANQUE, COM reserve the right to do

réserves *f pl* BANQUE reserve burden, reserves, COMPTA capital reserves, reserves, ECON, FIN reserves; ~ **bancaires** BANQUE bank capital; ~ **des banques de dépôts** BANQUE banker's deposits (*UK*); ~ **de bilan** ASSUR, COMPTA balance sheet reserves; ~ **cachées** COMPTA secret reserves; ~ **en chambre forte** BANQUE vault reserve (*US*); ~ **de change** ECON foreign exchange reserves; ~ **de charbon** ENVIR, IND coal reserves; ~ **déclarées** COMPTA disclosed reserves; ~ **en devises étrangères** ECON foreign exchange reserves; ~ **énergétiques** ENVIR, IND energy reserves; ~ **extractibles** ENVIR *ressources énergétiques* extractable reserves; ~ **à des fins spécifiques** FIN surplus reserves; ~ **de houille** ENVIR, IND coal reserves; ~ **indisponibles** COMPTA restricted surplus (*AmE*), undistributable reserves (*BrE*); ~ **latentes** COMPTA secret reserves; ~ **légales** DROIT legal reserves; ~ **légales minimales** ECON minimum reserve requirements, MRR; ~ **légales minimum** ECON minimum reserve requirements, MRR; ~ **obligatoires** BANQUE required reserves, reserve requirements; ~ **occultes** BANQUE hidden reserves; ~ **d'or** ECON gold reserves; ~ **de réévaluation** COMPTA revaluation reserves; ~ **secrètes** BANQUE hidden reserves; ~ **spéciales** FISC *contributions à la Sécurité sociale* special provisions

res gestae *loc frml* DROIT res gestae (*frml*)

résidant, e *adj* ADMIN, COM, FISC, INFO *programme* resident; ~ **habituellement** DROIT ordinarily resident

résidence *f* COM residence, DROIT place of abode, FISC, IMMOB residence; ~ **distincte** FISC separate residence; ~ **habituelle** COM, DROIT permanent residence; ~ **indépendante** FISC separate residence; ~ **légale** DROIT legal residence; ~ **principale** FISC, IMMOB main residence, principal residence; ~ **secondaire** FISC, IMMOB second home, second residence; ~ **temporaire** ADMIN, DROIT, FISC temporary residence

résident, e *m,f* ADMIN, COM, FISC resident; ~ **contribuable** FISC resident taxpayer; ~ **étranger** ADMIN resident alien; ~ **en mémoire** INFO memory resident; ~ **permanent** COM, DROIT permanent resident; ~ **temporaire** ADMIN, DROIT, FISC temporary resident

résidentiel, -elle *adj* IMMOB residential

résider *vi* DROIT reside, FISC, IMMOB reside; ◆ ~ **et travailler** DROIT, FISC, IMMOB reside and work

résidu *m* DROIT residuum, ENVIR residue; ~ **de Solow** ECON Solow residual

résignation *f* RES HUM resignation

résiliable *adj* ASSUR, COM terminable, DROIT voidable, RES HUM terminable

résiliation *f* ASSUR termination, COM annulment, DROIT *d'un contrat*, RES HUM *du contrat de travail* termination; **~ d'un contrat de location** IMMOB termination of tenancy

résilier *vt* ASSUR, COM, DROIT *contrat*, RES HUM annul, terminate

res integra *loc frml* DROIT res integra (*frml*)

res ipsa loquitur *loc frml* COM, DROIT res ipsa loquitur (*frml*)

résistance *f* COM resistance, ECON, RES HUM resilience; **~ des consommateurs** V&M consumer resistance; **~ du marché** V&M market resistance; **~ des matériaux** IND strength of materials

res judicata *loc frml* DROIT res judicata (*frml*)

res nullius *loc frml* DROIT, IMMOB res nullius (*frml*)

résolu: ~ à *adj* COM intent on; ◆ **être ~ à faire qch** COM be set on doing sth

résolution *f* BOURSE *actions* cancellation, COM, GESTION resolution, resolve, solution; **~ budgétaire** POL budget resolution (*US*); **~ de conflit** RES HUM dispute resolution; **~ de contrat** DROIT frustration of contract; **~ de problèmes** COM, GESTION, INFO, MATH problem solving; ◆ **faire accepter une ~ au niveau fédéral** POL composite a resolution, make a composite resolution, RES HUM composite a resolution, make a composite resolution

résorbé, e *adj* COMPTA *économétrie* absorbed

résorber *vt* COM absorb; **~ un surplus de véhicules d'occasion** COM absorb a used-car surplus

résoudre *vt* COM, GESTION *problème* resolve, solve

respect *m* COM, DROIT observance; **~ strict du contrat** DROIT strict adherence to the contract

respecter *vt* COM abide by, DROIT obey, respect, *disposition* comply with, *loi* observe; ◆ **ne pas ~** COM *contrat, règle* breach; **~ le règlement** COM comply with the regulations

respectivement *adv* COM respectively

respectueux, -euse *adj* COM respectful; ◆ **~ de l'environnement** ENVIR environmentally-aware, environmentally-friendly

responsabilisation: ~ des cadres supérieurs *f* GESTION accountability in management

responsabilité *f* ASSUR liability, COM accountability, responsibility, COMPTA accountability, DROIT liability, FIN accountability, FISC liability; **~ de l'architecte** ASSUR, DROIT, IMMOB architect's liability; **~ de l'armateur** ASSUR, DROIT, TRANSP shipowner's liability, SOL; **~ civile** ASSUR *(assurance RC obligatoire)* compulsory third-party insurance, DROIT civil liability, vicarious liability; **~ civile de propriétaire d'animal** ASSUR, DROIT, LOISIRS animal-keeper's liability; **~ collective** BANQUE, DROIT, FISC joint liability; **~ commerciale** COM, DROIT business liability; **~ conjointe** BANQUE, DROIT, FISC joint liability; **~ conjointe et solidaire** DROIT joint and several liability; **~ contractuelle** COM, DROIT contractual liability; **~ croisée** ASSUR cross liability; **~ cumulative** ASSUR cumulative liability; **~ délictuelle** DROIT tort liability; **~ directe** DROIT direct liability; **~ de la direction** GESTION account-

ability in management; **~ extracontractuelle** DROIT tort liability; **~ du fabricant** V&M product liability; **~ fiscale** FISC tax liability; **~ fonctionnelle** COM, GESTION functional responsibility; **~ du garant** BANQUE surety liability; **~ globale** COM comprehensive responsibility; **~ hiérarchique** COM line responsibility, GESTION, MATH linear responsibility; **~ illimitée** COM, DROIT unlimited fine, unlimited liability; **~ légale** DROIT legal liability; **~ objective** DROIT absolute liability; **~ personnelle** COM, DROIT personal liability; **~ pleine et entière** ASSUR, COM, DROIT full liability; **~ professionnelle** ASSUR, COM, DROIT professional indemnity, professional liability; **~ du propriétaire du quai** COM wharf-owner's liability, WOL, DROIT *commercial* wharf-owner's liability, WOL; **~ des sociétés** COM, GESTION corporate accountability; **~ syndicale** RES HUM trade union liability (*UK*); **~ au tiers** DROIT third-party liability

responsable[1] *adj* COM accountable, responsible, DROIT liable; **~ de** COM in charge of, COM accountable for; ◆ **~ devant** COM answerable to; **~ en droit** DROIT responsible in law; **être ~** COM be in charge; **être ~ de** COM answer for, be answerable for, *entreprise, projet* be in charge of; **~ légalement** DROIT responsible in law

responsable[2] *mf* GESTION, RES HUM manager, mgr; **~ des achats** *m* COM chief buyer, head buyer, procurement officer, RES HUM, V&M chief buyer, head buyer, purchasing officer; **~ administratif** *m* RES HUM administration officer; **~ de bassin** *m* COM, RES HUM wharfinger; **~ de budget** *m* RES HUM *finance* account executive, account manager; **~ d'un centre de gestion** *m* COMPTA responsibility-center manager (*AmE*), responsibility-centre manager (*BrE*); **~ de comptabilité analytique** *m* COMPTA, FIN, GESTION management accountant; **~ de conformité aux règlements** *m* RES HUM, TRANSP *maritime* registered manager; **~ de la création d'un consortium bancaire** *m* BANQUE syndication official; **~ de l'évaluation du prix de revient** *m* V&M estimator; **~ financier** *m* FIN, RES HUM cash manager, chief financial officer, financial director, financial manager, CFO; **~ de la formation professionnelle** *m* COM, RES HUM training officer; **~ de la gestion d'un investissement** *m* FIN jockey (*jarg*); **~ de la gestion des risques** *m* ASSUR risk manager; **~ d'hôtel** *m* RES HUM hotel manager; **~ de l'hygiène du milieu** *m* ENVIR, RES HUM Environmental Health Officer (*UK*); **~ indépendant du règlement des sinistres** *m* ASSUR, RES HUM adjuster; **~ de la mise en cale** *m* RES HUM hatchman; **~ national du budget** *m* COMPTA, FIN, RES HUM national accounts manager; **~ opérationnel** *m* GESTION, RES HUM line manager; **~ des opérations portuaires** *m* RES HUM, TRANSP port operations officer, POO; **~ en permanence** *m* RES HUM duty officer, DO; **~ des permis de transport maritime** *m* RES HUM, TRANSP registered manager;

~ **régional** *m* GESTION, RES HUM district officer, regional manager, DO; ~ **régional de la formation professionnelle** *m* RES HUM district training officer, DTO; ~ **du règlement des sinistres** *m* ASSUR, RES HUM adjuster; ~ **des relations publiques** *m* RES HUM, V&M director of public relations, public relations officer, DPR, PRO; ~ **de la salubrité de l'environnement** *m* ENVIR, RES HUM Environmental Health Officer (*UK*); ~ **de section** *m* RES HUM convenor; ~ **de la sécurité** *m* COM, RES HUM safety officer; ~ **du service de distribution** *m* MÉDIA *presse*, RES HUM circulation manager; ~ **du service de presse** *m* MÉDIA, POL, RES HUM, V&M press officer; ~ **des stocks** *m* COM, RES HUM inventory controller, stock controller; ~ **supérieur** *m* GESTION, RES HUM senior vice president (*US*); ~ **des techniques marchandes** *m* RES HUM merchandiser; ~ **en titre** *m* RES HUM titular head; ~ **du trafic** *m* RES HUM, TRANSP traffic executive; ~ **des transferts de titres** *m* BOURSE, RES HUM stock transfer agent; ~ **des transports** *m* RES HUM, TRANSP traffic superintendent, TS; ~ **des transports motorisés** *m* RES HUM, TRANSP motor transport officer, MTO; ~ **des ventes** *m* GESTION, RES HUM, V&M sales manager; ~ **des ventes d'importation** *m* RES HUM import sales executive

responsables: ~ **de l'aménagement du territoire** *m pl* ADMIN, ENVIR planning authority; ~ **opérationnels** *m pl* GESTION line management

resquilleur, -euse *m,f* COM deadhead (*AmE, infrml*), queue jumper (*BrE*)

ressemblance *f* COM conformity

resserrement: ~ **des bénéfices** *m* ECON, FIN profit squeeze; ~ **des coûts** *m* ECON, FIN cost containment; ~ **du crédit à découvert** *m* BOURSE short squeeze (*jarg*); ~ **de la politique monétaire** *m* ECON, FIN, POL snugging

resserrer *vt* COM tighten, DROIT tighten up, ECON tighten; ◆ ~ **les cordons de la bourse** FIN tighten the purse strings

ressort *m* ECON resilience; ~ **semi-elliptique** COM semielliptic spring

ressortissant, e *m,f* ADMIN national; ~ **étranger** ADMIN, RES HUM foreign national

ressource *f* BANQUE, COM, COMPTA, ECON, ENVIR, FIN, FISC, IND, RES HUM resource; ~ **en capital** ECON, FIN capital resource; ~ **économique** ECON economic resource; ~ **énergétique** ENVIR, IND energy resource; ~ **exploitée** ENVIR exploited resource; ~ **de financements** COMPTA, FIN source of funds; ~ **humaine** RES HUM human resource; ~ **minérale** ENVIR, IND mineral resource; ~ **minière** ENVIR, IND mineral resource; ~ **monétaire** BANQUE bankroll (*US*); ~ **naturelle** ECON, ENVIR, IND, POL natural resource; ~ **naturelle non-renouvelable** ECON, ENVIR nonrenewable natural resource; ~ **non-renouvelable** (*ANT ressource renouvelable*) ECON, ENVIR nonrenewable resource; ~ **primaire** ENVIR, IND primary resource; ~ **propre** ECON, ENVIR, POL own resource; ~ **propre calculée en fonction du PIB** ECON GNP-based own resource; ~ **publique** COM public resource; ~ **récupérable** ECON, ENVIR recoverable reserve; ~ **renouvelable** (*ANT ressource non-renouvelable*) ECON, ENVIR renewable resource; ~ **réutilisable** ECON, ENVIR recoverable reserve; ~ **de trésorerie** COMPTA, FIN cash resource

ressources *f pl* BANQUE, COM, ECON, FIN, RES HUM resources; ~ **et emplois de capitaux** COMPTA, FIN source and disposition of funds; ~ **humaines** RES HUM human resources, personnel

restant: **le** ~ **de la somme** *m* COM the balance, the outstanding amount

restaurant *m* COM restaurant; ~ **d'entreprise** RES HUM staff canteen; ~ **réservé aux chauffeurs de véhicules ro-ro** TRANSP ro/ro drivers' restaurant; ~ **d'usine** RES HUM works canteen

restaurateur, -trice *m,f* COM, RES HUM restaurateur

restauration *f* INFO reset, LOISIRS catering, catering trade; ~ **rapide** V&M fast food; ~ **en vol** TRANSP in-flight catering

restaurer *vt* INFO reset, restore, undelete

reste *m* DROIT residuum, MATH remainder; **le** ~ **du monde** ECON the rest of the world, ROW; ◆ ~ **à bord** TRANSP remain on board, ROB

rester *vi* COM remain, stay; ◆ ~ **dans le cours** BOURSE stay in-the-money; ~ **dans la course** COM keep in step with one's competitors; ~ **dans la légalité** DROIT keep within the law; ~ **ferme** COM *prix* stand firm; ~ **en grève** RES HUM stay out; ~ **informé** COMMS stay informed; ~ **en relation avec** COM keep in touch with; ~ **en suspens** COM remain in suspense, stand over

restitution: ~ **de la garantie** *f* COM return of guarantee; ~ **d'un trop-perçu** *f* COM return of amount overpaid

restocker *vt* V&M replenish

restreindre *vt* COM, DROIT contain, limit, restrict

restrictif, -ive *adj* COM, ECON, IND restrictive

restriction *f* COM restriction, COMPTA cap, cut, reduction, DROIT restriction, ECON, FIN cap, cut, reduction, TRANSP restriction; ~ **budgétaire** COMPTA, ECON, FIN, POL budget reduction, budgetary constraint, budgetary cut; ~ **du commerce** COM, ECON, POL dealing restriction, trade restriction; ~ **commerciale** COM *gouvernementale*, ECON, POL trade restriction; ~ **du crédit** BANQUE, ECON, FIN, POL credit squeeze; ~ **des dépenses** COMPTA, ECON, FIN, POL budget cut, budget reduction, budgetary constraint; ~ **à l'investissement** ECON investment restriction; ~ **à la liberté du commerce** ECON restraint of trade; ~ **monétaire** ECON currency restriction, monetary restriction, money restraint; ~ **au pouvoir d'aliéner un bien** DROIT restraint of alienation; ~ **quantitative** ECON, IND quantitative restriction, QR; ~ **volontaire des exportations** (*RVE*) IMP/EXP voluntary export restraint *(VER)*; ~ **de voyage** TRANSP travel restriction

restructuration *f* BOURSE, COM, ECON, FIN, GESTION, IND, RES HUM reorganization, restructuring; ~ **du capital** BOURSE, ECON, FIN capital reorganization, recapitalization; ~ **industrielle** IND restructuring of industry; ~ **du travail** COM, RES HUM work restructuring

restructuré, e *adj* BOURSE, COM, ECON, FIN, GESTION, IND, RES HUM restructured

restructurer *vt* BOURSE, COM, ECON, FIN, GESTION, IND, RES HUM reorganize, restructure

restylage *m* TRANSP lifting

résultant: ~ **de** *adj* COM subsequent to

résultat *m* COM outcome, result, *d'une discussion* bottom line, INFO output; ~ **brut d'exploitation** COM, COMPTA, ECON, FIN gross cash flow, net trading surplus; ~ **comptable** COMPTA accounting income, accounting profit; ~ **courant** COMPTA, ECON, FIN, FISC net operating profit, ordinary profit before taxation; ~ **effectif** COM actual outcome; ~ **de l'exercice** COMPTA, FISC annual earnings; ~ **final** COM end result; ~ **financier** COMPTA financial profit or loss; ~ **heureux** COM successful outcome; ~ **net** COM, COMPTA, FIN, FISC bottom line profit, net income, net profit for the current year; ~ **net de l'exercice** COMPTA distributable profit; ~ **net d'exploitation** COMPTA net operating income; ~ **des opérations** COMPTA operating profit; ~ **probable** COM likely outcome; ~ **réel** COMPTA, ECON, RES HUM actual earnings

résultats *m pl* COM results, COMPTA performance, FIN results, RES HUM payoff; ~ **-clés** COMPTA financial highlights; ~ **croisés** MATH cross tabulation; ~ **d'examen** COM exam results; ~ **mitigés** COM mixed results; ~ **prévisionnels** COM, ECON, FIN earnings forecast; ~ **record** COM record results; ~ **de régularité** TRANSP punctuality performance; ~ **du scrutin** POL election results; ~ **de la société** COM, FIN company results; ~ **statistiques** MATH statistical returns

résulter: ~ **de** *vti* COM stem from

résumé *m* BREVETS *d'un brevet* abstract, COM abstract, résumé, summary, synopsis, ECON, FIN abstract; ~ **des informations** MÉDIA news roundup; ~ **de la séance** COM, DROIT summary of the proceedings; ~ **succinct** COM brief summary

résumer *vt* COM summarize

rétablir *vt* COM re-establish, restore; ◆ ~ **l'ordre public** DROIT restore law and order

rétablissement *m* COM re-establishment

rétablisseur: ~ **de taux** *m* BOURSE rate resetter, RR

retard *m* COM delay, ECON time lag, FIN arrearage, INFO delay; ~ **extérieur** POL outside lag; ~ **d'identification** ECON recognition lag; ~ **d'introduction** COM lead-time delay; ~ **technologique** COM, IND technological gap; ◆ **en ~ économique** ECON, POL *région* economically backward; **être en ~ dans ses paiements** COM be in arrears; **être en ~ sur** COM, V&M lag behind

retarder *vt* COM defer, postpone, put back, put off

R&D *abrév (recherche et développement)* IND R&D *(research and development)*

retenir *vt* ADMIN book, BOURSE retain, COM book, detain, LOISIRS book; ◆ ~ **à l'avance** COM, LOISIRS book in advance; ~ **une chambre** COM, LOISIRS book in; ~ **dès maintenant** COM *des places*, LOISIRS book early; ~ **l'impôt** FISC deduct tax; ~ **une place** COM, LOISIRS book in, TRANSP make a reservation

rétention *f* ASSUR retention

retenu: **être ~** *loc* RES HUM *pour un poste* be shortlisted

retenue *f* BOURSE withholding, COM deduction, self-restraint, ECON *de crédit* containment, FIN deduction, self-restraint, FISC deduction, IMMOB holdback, retainage, RES HUM *sur salaire* stoppage, TRANSP *cordage* guy; ~ **fiscale** COMPTA, FISC tax withholding; ~ **de garantie** COM contract holdback; ~ **d'impôt** COMPTA tax withholding, FISC tax deduction *(AmE)*, tax withholding; ~ **d'impôt des non-résidents** FISC nonresident tax deduction *(Canada)*; ~ **de l'impôt sur le revenu à la source** COMPTA, FISC, RES HUM pay as you earn *(UK)*, PAYE *(UK)*; ~ **à la source** FIN deduction at source, salary deduction, FISC deduction at source, withholding tax; ~ **sur salaire** RES HUM retention on wages

réticence *f* ASSUR nondisclosure

retiration *f* MÉDIA *imprimé* backing up

retirer 1. *vt* BANQUE, COM *offre* withdraw; ~ **l'investiture de** POL deselect *(UK)*; **2.** *v pron* **se ~** BOURSE pull the plug *(infrml)*, COM back off, pull out, withdraw, PROT SOC opt out; **se ~ de** COM *d'une affaire* back out of, drop out FIN contract out *(UK)*,; ◆ ~ **du marché** COM, V&M take off the market; ~ **une offre** COM bid off; ~ **progressivement** COM, INFO phase out; **se ~ des affaires** COM go out of business, retire from business, shut up shop; **se ~ d'une enchère** COM bid off; **se ~ des enchères** COM stop bidding

retombée *f* COM spill-off effect, spillover effect

retombées *f pl* COM fallout *(infrml)*, ECON spillover, POL fallout *(infrml)*; ~ **acides** ENVIR acid deposit; ~ **économiques** V&M spin-off effect; ~ **de polluants** ENVIR, IND contamination fallout; ~ **radioactives** ENVIR, IND radioactive fallout

retour *m* COM, COMMS, INFO, V&M return; ~ **arrière** INFO backspace; ~ **de chariot** INFO carriage return, CR; ~ **de curseur** INFO carriage return, CR; ~ **à l'emploi** RES HUM return to work; ~ **d'information** COMMS, INFO feedback; ~ **à la ligne automatique** INFO word wrap, wraparound; ~ **à la ligne obligatoire** INFO hard return; ~ **à des méthodes d'intensité capitalistique** ECON capital reswitching; ~ **sur les avantages acquis** RES HUM giveback *(jarg)*; ~ **à vide** TRANSP deadheading *(AmE)*; ◆ ~ **à l'envoyeur** COMMS return to sender; **faire un ~ arrière** INFO backspace; **par ~ du courrier** COMMS by return of post; ~ **au port en**

attendant des instructions TRANSP return to port for orders, RP; **~ de souscription** BOURSE *avis* regret; **~ au tiroir** BANQUE refer to drawer, RD; **être de ~ dans une heure** *loc* COM be back within an hour

retournement: ~ à la baisse *m* BOURSE downturn

retourner *vt* COM, COMMS, V&M return; ◆ **~ à la case départ** COM go back to square one; **~ à l'envoyeur** COMMS return to sender

retours: ~ et réfactions sur achats *m pl* V&M purchase returns and allowances

retrait *m* BANQUE roundtripping (*jarg*), withdrawal, BOURSE roundtripping (*jarg*), COM withdrawal, FIN roundtripping (*jarg*); **~ d'agrément** FIN *d'un régime de retraite* deregistration; **~ automatique** FIN automatic withdrawal; **~ des bagages** LOISIRS, TRANSP baggage reclaim area; **~ en espèces** BANQUE cash withdrawal; **~ d'espèces** BANQUE cash withdrawal; **~ de fonds** BANQUE withdrawal of capital; **~ de l'investiture** POL deselection (*UK*); **~ massif de dépôts bancaires** BANQUE bank run; **~ du montant d'étalement accumulé** FISC accumulated averaging amount withdrawal; **~ d'une opposition** FISC withdrawal of an objection; **~ partiel** BOURSE partial withdrawal

retraite *f* FIN, PROT SOC, RES HUM pension, retirement; **~ anticipée** *(cf pension anticipée Bel)* RES HUM early retirement, early retirement annuity; **~ anticipée obligatoire** RES HUM early retirement; **~ complémentaire des cadres supérieurs** FIN, GESTION, PROT SOC, RES HUM top-hat pension (*infrml*); **~ complémentaire de prévoyance** FIN supplementary pension scheme; **~ constituée dans l'entreprise** RES HUM internally funded pension; **~ de dette** FIN retirement of debt; **~ différée** RES HUM deferred retirement; **~ de l'État** PROT SOC state pension (*UK*); **~ à indemnités différées** RES HUM deferred compensation plan (*US*); **~ obligatoire** RES HUM compulsory retirement (*BrE*), mandatory retirement (*AmE*); **~ professionnelle** PROT SOC, RES HUM occupational pension; **~ de vieillesse** FIN pension

retraité[1]**, e** *adj* FIN, RES HUM superannuated

retraité[2]**, e** *m,f* COM, PROT SOC, RES HUM OAP (*BrE*), old age pensioner (*BrE*), retired person, retiree (*AmE*)

retraitement *m* ENVIR reprocessing

retraiter *vt* ENVIR reprocess

retraites: ~ sans capitaux suffisants *f pl* RES HUM unfunded pensions (*UK*)

retrancher *vt* COM take away

retransmission *f* IMMOB reconveyance, LOISIRS *sport* coverage

rétrécir *vi* COM contract

rétrécissement *m* COM, ECON contraction; **~ de la chaussée** TRANSP bottleneck; **~ de la demande** V&M contraction of demand

rétribution *f* COM reward, DROIT consideration; **~ d'agence** TRANSP *navigation* agency fee; **~ en**

nature RES HUM noncash rewards, nonmonetary rewards

rétroactif, -ive *adj* COM retroactive

rétroaction *f* COM feedback; **~ positive** COM, ECON positive feedback

rétrocession: ~ de fonds empruntés *f* FIN onlending

rétrogradation *f* RES HUM *d'un employé* demotion, downgrading

rétroprojecteur *m* COM, GESTION overhead projector

retrousser: se ~ les manches *v pron* COM put on a spurt

retrouver *vt* COM trace, INFO retrieve

reu: ~ non-conforme *loc* COM wrongshipped

réunification *f* COM reunification

réunion *f* ADMIN, COM assembly, meeting, GESTION conference, meeting, POL assembly, RES HUM joinder, meeting; **~ des actionnaires** COM, GESTION company meeting; **~ d'affaires** COM business meeting; **~ de comité** COM committee meeting; **~ de commission** COM committee meeting; **~ du conseil d'administration** ADMIN, COM, GESTION, RES HUM board meeting; **~ extraordinaire** COM special meeting; **~ informelle** COM informal meeting; **~ en marge** POL fringe meeting; **~ marketing** V&M marketing conference; **~ de mise au point** GESTION debriefing; **~ de négociation** GESTION, POL, RES HUM negotiating table; **~ normale** COM, GESTION regular meeting; **~ de vendeurs** V&M sales conference

Réunion *f* COM Reunion Island; **~ des conseillers économiques** ECON Council of Economic Advisers, CEA

réunir *vt* COM bring together, consolidate, MATH aggregate; ◆ **~ des fonds** COM, FIN raise finance, raise funds, raise money; **~ en trust** COM, GESTION trustify

réussi, e *adj* COM successful

réussir: ~ à *vt* COM manage to, COM come off, succeed; ◆ **~ dans la vie** COM get ahead; **~ un grand coup** COM make a scoop (*infrml*); **~ qch** COM make a go of sth

réussit: qui ~ *loc* COM successful

réussite *f* COM accomplishment, success; **~ constante** COM continued success

réutiliser *vt* ENVIR reuse

revalorisation *f* COM adjustment, ECON adjustment, revalorization, RES HUM *de salaire* adjustment

revaloriser *vt* ECON adjust, RES HUM *emploi* upgrade

réveil *m* COM alarm clock; **~ par téléphone** COM, COMMS alarm call

réveille-matin *m* [pl inv] COM alarm clock

révélation: ~ de l'actif *f* BANQUE, COMPTA asset exposure

révéler 1. *vt* COM *opinion* disclose, COMMS *des informations* break; **2.** *v pron* **se ~** COM prove to be; ◆ **se ~ faux** *(ANT se révéler vrai)*, COM prove wrong; **se ~ vrai** *(ANT se révéler faux)* COM prove right

revendeur: **~ de billets** *m* LOISIRS ticket tout; **~ de systèmes à valeur ajoutée** *m* INFO value-added reseller, VAR

revendication *f* BREVETS claim, COM *de ses droits* assertion, DROIT claim, RES HUM grievance, primary action; **~ complémentaire** RES HUM secondary action; **~ dépendante** BREVETS dependent claim; **~ indépendante** BREVETS independent claim; **~ légitime** DROIT legal claim; **~ de salaire** RES HUM wage claim; **~ salariale** RES HUM wage claim; **~ syndicale** RES HUM claim; **~ d'un tiers** ASSUR, DROIT third-party claim

revendications: **~ de différentes catégories** *f pl* DROIT claims of different categories; **~ donnant lieu au paiement de redevances** *f pl* DROIT claims incurring fees; **~ de la même catégorie** *f pl* DROIT claims of the same category

revendiquer *vt* COM stand out for, DROIT claim, lay claim to, RES HUM claim, demand

revendre *vt* BOURSE sell back, COM hive off, DROIT, ECON buy back

revenir: **~ sur** *vi* COM back out of; ◆ **~ sur les avantages acquis** RES HUM give back *(jarg)*

revente *f* COM, V&M resale; **~ de titres** BOURSE secondary distribution

revenu *m* COMPTA, ECON, FIN, FISC income, revenue; **~ accessoire** FIN secondary income; **~ accumulé** FISC accumulating income; **~ accumulé tiré de biens** FISC, IMMOB accrual property income; **~ de l'actif** BOURSE, COMPTA, FIN asset return; **~ agricole** COM, ECON farming income; **~ ajusté compte tenu de l'inflation** COMPTA inflation-adjusted income; **~ pour l'année** FISC income for the year; **~ annuel** COMPTA annual return; **~ après impôt** COMPTA, ECON, FIN, FISC after-tax income; **~ arbitraire** FISC arbitrary income; **~ assujetti à l'impôt** FISC income subject to tax; **~ de biens** FIN, FISC, IMMOB property income; **~ brut** COM, COMPTA, RES HUM gross earnings, gross income, gross revenue, gross sales, trading income; **~ brut d'exploitation** COMPTA gross operating income; **~ brut de placements** FIN, FISC gross investment revenue; **~ budgété** COMPTA, FIN budgeted income; **~ compensateur** BOURSE compensating income *(UK)*; **~ compensatoire** BOURSE compensating income *(UK)*; **~ déclaré en moins** FISC understatement of income; **~ direct** FIN basic income; **~ discrétionnaire** ECON discretionary income; **~ disponible** ECON, FISC disposable income; **~ disponible pour charges fixes** COMPTA, FISC income available for fixed charges; **~ disponible des particuliers** ECON personal disposable income, PDI; **~ de distribution** FIN *fiducie* designated income; **~ de dividende** BOURSE dividend income; **~ élevé** BOURSE high return; **~ d'emploi** FISC employment income; **~ d'entreprise** FISC, GESTION business income; **~ enveloppé** FISC rolled-up income;

~ d'escompte BANQUE income from discounting; **~ estimé** COMPTA estimated revenue; **~ étalé** FISC elective income; **~ étranger net** FISC net foreign income; **~ exonéré** FISC exempt income; **~ des facteurs de production** ECON, IND factor income; **~ familial** FISC family income; **~ fantôme** FISC phantom income; **~ final** ECON final income; **~ financier** ECON, FIN pecuniary return; **~ fixe** BOURSE fixed income; **~ foncier** DROIT, FIN, IMMOB estate revenue, land rent; **~ gagné** FISC earned income; **~ garanti** FIN guaranteed income; **~ global** ECON aggregate income; **~ horaire moyen** RES HUM average hourly earnings; **~ immobilier** FIN, FISC estate income, property income, IMMOB estate income, property income, return on real estate; **~ implicite** COMPTA, ECON, FISC imputed income; **~ imposable** COMPTA, ECON, FIN, FISC taxable income; **~ imposable modifié** FISC adjusted taxable income; **~ imposable non-pénalisé** FISC nonpenalized taxable income; **~ imposé** FISC assessed income; **~ imposé à un taux inférieur** FISC income taxed at a lower rate; **~ imputé** COMPTA, ECON, FISC imputed income; **~ intermédiaire** FIN moderate income; **~ d'investissements** BOURSE, FIN investment income; **~ libéré d'impôt** FISC tax-paid income; **~ locatif** FISC, IMMOB rental income; **~ de location** FISC, IMMOB rental income; **~ de location net** FISC, IMMOB net rental income; **~ du marché de l'argent** BOURSE, ECON, FIN money-market returns; **~ marginal implicite** ECON implicit marginal income; **~ minimal attendu du capital** ECON, FIN required rental on capital; **~ modeste** FIN moderate income; **~ moyen** FIN average income, LOISIRS Average Revenue, AR, RES HUM average income; **~ national** ECON *économétrie* social product; **~ national brut** ECON gross national income, GNI; **~ national de l'épargne** BANQUE National Savings Income *(UK)*; **~ net** COM, COMPTA, FIN, FISC net income; **~ net de biens immobiliers à l'étranger** FIN, IMMOB net property income from abroad; **~ net d'emploi** FISC net employment earnings; **~ net des intérêts** BANQUE net interest income; **~ net moyen** FISC average net income; **~ net par action** BOURSE net realized capital gains per share; **~ net par action après impôt et dividende prioritaire** BOURSE primary earnings per share; **~ net relatif à des ressources** COM, COMPTA, FISC net resource income; **~ net révisé** FISC revised net income; **~ net sur commissions** COMPTA, FISC net commission income; **~ nominal** ECON, FIN, FISC money income, nominal income; **~ non-pécunier** RES HUM nonpecuniary returns; **~ normal** FISC ordinary income; **~ par habitant** ECON income per head, per capita income; **~ de pension** FISC pension income; **~ de pension admissible** FISC qualified pension income; **~ de pension designée** FISC qualified pension income; **~ personnel** COM, ECON, FISC personal income, private income; **~ personnel disponible** ECON personal disposable income, PDI; **~ des personnes physiques** ECON, FISC personal income; **~ de**

placements ASSUR, BOURSE, FIN investment income, investment revenue, portfolio income, FISC passive income; ~ **de placements étrangers** FIN, FISC foreign investment income; ~ **de portefeuille** BOURSE, COMPTA income from securities; ~ **potentiel** ECON potential income; ~ **des primes** ASSUR premium income; ~ **de production** FIN, IND production revenue; ~ **de profession libérale** FISC professional income, self-employment income; ~ **en provenance de l'étranger** ECON interest, profit and dividends, IPD; ~ **provenant d'investissements immobiliers** DROIT, FIN estate revenue; ~ **provenant du patrimoine** DROIT, FIN estate revenue; ~ **psychique** *jarg* ECON, RES HUM psychic income *(jarg)*; ~ **rajusté** FISC adjusted income; ~ **à recevoir** COMPTA accrued income; ~ **réel** COMPTA, ECON, RES HUM actual earnings, real earnings, real income; ~ **relatif à des ressources** COMPTA, FISC resource income; ~ **de rente** FISC annuity income; ~ **reporté** COMPTA, FISC deferred credit, deferred income, deferred revenue; ~ **résiduel** RES HUM residential amount; ~ **de retraite** FISC, RES HUM retirement income; ~ **de société** FISC partnership income; ~ **de source étrangère** FISC foreign income; ~ **sous-déclaré** FISC understatement of income; ~ **d'une succession** FIN, FISC, IMMOB estate income; ~ **théorique** ECON theoretical income; ~ **tiré d'une entreprise** FISC, GESTION business income; ~ **total** COMPTA, ECON, FIN, FISC total income, total revenue; ~ **de transfert** ECON transfer income; ~ **transitoire** ECON transitory income; ~ **d'un travail indépendant** FISC self-employment income; ◆ **en tirant un ~ de** FISC in the course of earning income

revenus: ~ **de l'État** *m pl* ECON public revenue; ~ **publics** *m pl* ECON public revenue

reversement *m* COM payout

réversible *adj* TRANSP *charte-partie* reversible

revêtement: ~ **intérieur** *m* TRANSP *navigation* adjusting loading wall

revirement *m* COM turnabout, POL *vers la gauche/vers la droite* swing

réviser *vt* COM brush up on, review, revise, COMPTA audit, DROIT review, revise, ECON *prix* adjust, FIN audit, GESTION review, INFO edit, RES HUM review; ◆ ~ **à la baisse** ECON *prix* adjust downwards; ~ **à la hausse** ECON *prix* adjust upwards

reviseur, -euse *m,f* COMPTA *Bel (cf auditeur Fra, commissaire aux comptes Fra, réviseur Fra, vérificateur Can)* FIN *Bel (cf auditeur Fra, commissaire aux comptes Fra, réviseur Fra)* auditor; ~ **indépendant** *Bel (cf auditeur indépendant Fra, commissaire aux comptes indépendant Fra, réviseur indépendant Fra)* COMPTA independent auditor

révision *f* COM revision, DROIT amendment, revision, ECON adjustment, GESTION overhaul, review, IND overhaul, POL amendment, RES HUM review, TRANSP overhaul; ~ **analytique** COMPTA analytical audit, analytical auditing, analytical review, systems-based audit, systems-based auditing; ~ **annuelle** COMPTA annual review; ~ **annuelle des salaires** RES HUM annual salary review; ~ **à la baisse** *(ANT révision à la hausse)* COM downward revision; ~ **comptable** COMPTA audit; ~ **de conformité** COMPTA compliance audit; ~ **externe** *(cf audit externe, contrôle externe, vérification externe Can)* COMPTA, FIN external audit, independent audit; ~ **à la hausse** *(ANT révision à la baisse)* COM upvaluation, upward revision; ~ **des prix** V&M pricing review; ~ **des salaires** RES HUM pay review, salary review; ~ **des services votés** COMPTA A-base review; ~ **des tarifs** COM rates review; ~ **des traitements** RES HUM salary review

revitalisation *f* COM revitalization

révocable *adj* COM revocable

revoir *vt* BREVETS amend, COM review, DROIT amend, review, ECON *prix* adjust, GESTION review, IND overhaul, POL amend, RES HUM review, TRANSP overhaul; ◆ ~ **à la baisse** COM revise downward; ~ **à la hausse** COM revise upward

révolution *f* ECON, POL revolution; ~ **blanche** ECON white revolution; ~ **culturelle** POL cultural revolution; ~ **démographique** ECON demographic transition, vital revolution; ~ **industrielle** ECON, IND industrial revolution; ~ **managériale** GESTION, POL managerial revolution; ~ **ordinaliste** ECON ordinalist revolution; ~ **technocratique** ADMIN managerial revolution; ~ **verte** ECON, ENVIR green revolution; ~ **vitale** ECON vital revolution

revue *f* COM, MÉDIA journal, magazine; ~ **agricole** ECON, MÉDIA agricultural publication; ~ **analytique** COMPTA, FIN accounts appraisal; ~ **de la compagnie aérienne** TRANSP in-flight magazine; ~ **du consommateur** COM, MÉDIA consumer magazine; ~ **d'entreprise** COM, MÉDIA house journal, house magazine; ~ **féminine** MÉDIA women's magazine; ~ **gratuite** MÉDIA give-away magazine; ~ **illustrée** MÉDIA illustrated magazine; ~ **de mode** MÉDIA fashion magazine; ~ **professionnelle** COM, MÉDIA trade journal, trade magazine

Reykjavik *n pr* COM Reykjavik

rez-de-chaussée *m* IMMOB *aménagement tel que aire de stationnement* ground level

rezonage *m* IMMOB downzoning

rf. *abrév (référence)* COM ref. *(reference)*

RFC *abrév (requête formulée par le client)* TRANSP *aviation* CR *(change request)*, RFC *(request for change)*

rhétorique *f* COM, ECON rhetoric

Riad *n pr* COM Riyadh

rial *m* COM rial, ryal

riche *adj* COM rich, well-off, ECON affluent; ~ **en liquidité** *(ANT pauvre en liquidité)* COMPTA, FIN cash-rich; ~ **en pétrole** ECON oil-rich

riches: **les ~** *m pl* COM the rich, the wealthy, ECON, PROT SOC the wealthy

richesse *f* COM, ECON, IND, PROT SOC, RES HUM

affluence, wealth; ~ **corporelle** (ANT *richesse incorporelle*) ECON tangible wealth; ~ **incorporelle** (ANT *richesse corporelle*) ECON intangible wealth; ~ **nationale** ECON national wealth

Richesse: ~ **des nations** *f* ECON Wealth of Nations

rideau: ~ **de bambou** *m* POL bamboo curtain (*US*)

ridoir *m* TRANSP *pièces de saisissage* bottlescrew, screw, turnbuckle

riel *m* COM riel

rien: on n'a ~ **pour rien** *loc* COM there's no such thing as a free lunch

Riga *n pr* COM Riga

rigidité: ~ **des prix** *f* ECON price rigidity; ~ **des salaires** *f* ECON, RES HUM labor market rigidities (*AmE*), labour market rigidities (*BrE*), wage rigidity

rigoureusement *adv* COM stringently

rigoureux, -euse *adj* COM stringent

ringgit *m* COM Malaysian ringgit, MAL, ringgit

RISCPT *abrév* (*Registre international des substances chimiques potentiellement toxiques*) ENVIR, IND IRPTC (*International Register of Potentially Toxic Chemicals*)

risque *m* ASSUR peril, risk, BANQUE risk, BOURSE exposition, risk, COM hazard, risk, COMPTA, ECON risk, FIN risk, *de change* exposure, MATH risk; ~ **d'accident** ASSUR accident risk; ~ **d'accumulation** ASSUR accumulation risk; ~ **actuel** ECON current risk; ~ **des affaires** BOURSE, FIN businessman's risk; ~ **aléatoire** COM unsystematic risk; ~ **anormal** ASSUR abnormal risk; ~ **assumé en dernier ressort** BANQUE ultimate risk; ~ **assurable** ASSUR insurable risk; ~ **assuré** ASSUR insured peril; ~ **d'audit** COMPTA, FIN audit risk (*UK*); ~ **d'aviation** ASSUR, TRANSP aviation risk; ~ **de base** BOURSE basic risk, basis risk, COM basic risk; ~ **de bris de glace** ASSUR breakage-of-glass risk; ~ **calculé** BOURSE, COM calculated risk; ~ **de capital** FIN capital risk; ~ **de catastrophe** ASSUR catastrophe hazard, catastrophe risk; ~ **de change** ECON, FIN currency risk, exchange risk, foreign exchange risk; ~ **commercial** ASSUR, COM, IND business risk, commercial risk; ~ **considérable** ASSUR large risk; ~ **constant** ASSUR constant risk; ~ **de contrepartie** FIN credit risk; ~ **de conversion** FIN translation risk; ~ **corrigé selon le taux d'escompte** FIN risk-adjusted discount rate; ~ **à cotisation et à prestations déterminées** ASSUR target risk; ~ **couvert sous réserve d'acceptation** ASSUR subject approval no risk, SANR; ~ **du crédit** FIN loan exposure; ~ **de crédit** V&M credit risk; ~ **de décès** ASSUR death risk; ~ **de déchargement** COM, TRANSP unloading risk; ~ **diver** ASSUR mixed peril; ~ **encouru** COMPTA risk exposure; ~ **envisageable** BOURSE foreseeable risk; ~ **financier** BOURSE, FIN financial risk; ~ **global** COM aggregate risk; ~ **de guerre** ASSUR war risk; ~ **de guerre exclusivement** ASSUR war risk only,

wro; ~ **de guerre uniquement** ASSUR war risk only, wro; ~ **à la hausse** BOURSE upside risk; ~ **illimité** BOURSE unbounded risk; ~ **imminent** ASSUR imminent peril; ~ **important** ASSUR large risk; ~ **d'incendie** ASSUR, IND, RES HUM fire hazard; ~ **d'incendie sur fret** TRANSP fire risk on freight, frof; ~ **indirect** ASSUR consequential loss; ~ **inhérent** BOURSE inherent risk; ~ **d'insolvabilité de l'État emprunteur** FIN sovereign risk; ~ **lié** ASSUR allied peril; ~ **lié aux initiatives économiques** COM entrepreneurial risk; ~ **lié à l'intérêt** FIN interest risk; ~ **lié à la marge** BOURSE spread risk; ~ **lié au pays** FIN country risk; ~ **lié à la politique** COM, POL political risk; ~ **lié au taux d'intérêt** BANQUE, BOURSE interest rate exposure, interest rate risk; ~ **lié au taux d'intérêt à court terme** BOURSE short-term interest-rate risk; ~ **lié à la transaction** BOURSE transaction exposure, transaction risk; ~ **de litige** COMPTA *arrhes* litigation risk; ~ **du marché** BOURSE market risk; ~ **maritime** ASSUR maritime risk; ~ **de masse** ASSUR mass risk; ~ **maximum** BOURSE *options* maximum risk; ~ **ménager** ASSUR domestic risk; ~ **de mer** TRANSP sea risk; ~ **du métier** ASSUR, COM, RES HUM occupational hazard; ~ **moral** ASSUR moral hazard; ~ **de non-remboursement** BANQUE risk of nonrepayment; ~ **d'opération en Bourse** BOURSE transaction risk; ~ **ouvert** BOURSE open-ended risk; ~ **des parités croisées** ECON *commerce international*, FIN cross-currency exposure; ~ **-pays** ECON country exposure, FIN country risk; ~ **portant sur les marchandises** DROIT, TRANSP risk in the goods; ~ **prévisible** BOURSE foreseeable risk; ~ **prévus** *m pl* ASSUR expected perils; ~ **privilégié** ASSUR preferred risk; ~ **professionnel** ASSUR, COM, RES HUM occupational hazard; ~ **de recours au tiers** ASSUR third-party risk; ~ **de refinancement** BANQUE refinancing risk; ~ **de retard** BANQUE lag risk; ~ **sanitaire** PROT SOC health hazard; ~ **pour la santé** PROT SOC health hazard, health risk; ~ **pour la sécurité** COM safety hazard; ~ **souverain** FIN sovereign risk; ~ **statistique** MATH statistical risk; ~ **subjectif** ASSUR moral hazard; ~ **substantiel** BOURSE substantial risk; ~ **sur les taux d'intérêt à court terme** BOURSE short-term interest-rate risk; ~ **systématique** BOURSE systematic risk; ~ **de taux** BANQUE rate risk; ~ **de taux d'intérêt** BANQUE, BOURSE interest rate exposure, interest rate risk; ~ **à terme** ASSUR time risk; ~ **au tiers** ASSUR third-party risk; ~ **de transport aérien** ASSUR, TRANSP aviation risk; ~ **du transporteur** TRANSP carrier's risk, CR; ~ **trésorien** BOURSE cash risk; ~ **ultime** BANQUE ultimate risk; ~ **de vol** ASSUR theft risk; ◆ **à ~ élevé** BOURSE high-risk; **à ses ~ et périls** COM at one's own risk; **à vos ~s** BOURSE at risk; **aux ~s de l'acheteur** (ANT *aux risques du vendeur*) BOURSE at buyer's risk, DROIT caveat emptor; **aux ~s du destinataire** COM at receiver's risk; **aux ~s du propriétaire** COM at owner's risk; **aux ~s du vendeur** (ANT *aux risques de l'acheteur*) BOURSE at seller's risk, DROIT caveat venditor; **aux ~s et périls du freteur** ASSUR, TRANSP *navigation* owner's risk, OR; **aux ~s et périls du propriétaire** COM at owner's risk; **aux ~s et périls du transporteur** TRANSP carrier's risk, CR; **ne pas prendre de ~** COM play safe; **qui tient compte du ~** COM risk-orientated; **tous ~** ASSUR against all risks, AAR, all risks, all-in, all-loss, all-risk, AR, fully comp (*infrml*), fully comprehensive

risqué, e *adj* COM risky, venturesome; **peu ~** BOURSE risk-minimizing; **très ~** COM touch and go

ristourne *f* ASSUR no-claim bonus (*UK*), COM discount, volume discount, FIN kickback, rebate, V&M discount, volume discount; **~ de mise en rade** ASSUR lay-up return; **~ de participation** ASSUR experience refund; **~ pour résiliation** ASSUR canceling return (*AmE*), cancelling return (*BrE*); **~ sur quantité** TRANSP *marchandises* volume rebate

rivage *m* TRANSP shore

rivaliser: **~ avec** *vi* COM vie with

riverain[1]**, e** *adj* DROIT riparian

riverain[2]**, e** *m,f* DROIT riparian, riverside resident

riveraineté *f* DROIT riparian rights

riveté, e *adj* COM riveted, R; **~ et soudé** TRANSP *navigation* riveted and welded, RW

Riyad *n pr* COM Riyadh

riyal *m* COM riyal

RLE *abrév* (*réseau local d'entreprise*) INFO LAN (*local area network*)

RNIS *abrév* (*réseau numérique à intégration de services*) COMMS ISDN (*integrated services digital network*)

RO *abrév* (*recherche opérationnelle*) COM, GESTION, V&M OR (*operational research*)

robot *m* IND robot, RES HUM steel-collar worker

robotique *f* IND robotics

robotiser *vt* IND robotize

robuste *adj* COM robust, ECON buoyant

ROC *abrév* (*reconnaissance optique des caractères*) INFO OCR (*optical character recognition*)

rocade *f* TRANSP ring road

rogner: **~ sur** *vt* ECON whittle down

rôle *m* COM, RES HUM function, role; **~ consultatif** RES HUM advisory function; **~ dominant en matière de prix** ECON, V&M price leadership; **~ d'équipage** TRANSP articles of agreement, ship's articles; **~ du gouvernement** POL government role

roll-over *m* BANQUE, FIN roll-over

ro/lo *m* (*navire à manutention horizontale et verticale*) TRANSP *navigation* ro/lo (*roll on/roll off-lift on/lift off ship*)

Rome *n pr* COM Rome

ROME *abrév* (*répertoire opérationnel des métiers et des emplois*) RES HUM job bank

rompre *vt* COM *négociations, pourparlers* break off, DROIT *contrat* break; ♦ **~ un contrat** DROIT contract out of an agreement; **~ les liens avec** ECON sever links with

rompu *m* BOURSE broken amount, broken lot; **~ de titres** BOURSE broken amount, broken lot, odd lot

rond: **ne pas avoir un ~** *m infrml* COM not to have a bean (*infrml*)

rond-point *m* COM, TRANSP roundabout (*BrE*), traffic circle (*AmE*)

ronger *vt* COM erode

ro/ro *m* (*navire à manutention horizontale*) TRANSP *navigation* ro/ro ship (*roll on/roll off ship*)

Roseau *n pr* COM Roseau

rotation *f* COM, COMPTA, ECON, FIN, IND, RES HUM turnover, TRANSP *d'un navire* turnaround (*AmE*), turnround (*BrE*); **~ de l'actif** COMPTA, FIN asset turnover; **~ des cultures** ECON, ENVIR crop rotation; **~ des éléments d'actif** COMPTA, FIN asset turnover; **~ du personnel** ECON, RES HUM labor turnover (*AmE*), labour turnover (*BrE*), staff turnover; **~ des postes** RES HUM job rotation; **~ des stagiaires** RES HUM trainee turnover; **~ des stocks** BOURSE stock turnover, COM stock turn, COMPTA, ECON, FIN inventory turnover, stock turnover, IND stock turnover, V&M stock rotation

rotonde *f* IMMOB roundhouse

rouages *m pl* DROIT, ECON machinery; **~ administratifs** ADMIN, ECON machinery; **les ~ du gouvernement** POL the wheels of government

rouble *m* COM rouble, ruble

roue: **~ arrière** *f* TRANSP *navigation* stern wheel; **~ latérale** *f* TRANSP side wheel, SDW

rouge *adj* COM red

rouillé, e *adj* COM rusty

roulage *m* TRANSP haulage; **~ de bûches** *infrml* POL logrolling (*US*)

rouleau: **~ compresseur** *m* IND steamroller

roulement *m* FISC roll-over, RES HUM job rotation; **~ en arrière** BOURSE *options* rolling in; **~ en avant** BOURSE *options* rolling out; **~ à la baisse** BOURSE *options* rolling down; **~ en caoutchouc** TRANSP rubber bearing, RB; **~ de gains en capital** *Can* FISC capital gains rollover; **~ à la hausse** BOURSE *options* rolling up

rouler *vt infrml* COM short-change, take in (*infrml*)

roulier *m* TRANSP ro/ro vessel, roll on/roll off, roll on/roll off ship

roumain[1]**, e** *adj* COM Romanian, Rumanian

roumain[2] *m* COM *langue* Romanian, Rumanian

Roumain, e *m,f* COM *habitant* Romanian, Rumanian

Roumanie *f* COM Romania, Rumania

round *m* ECON round

roupie *f* COM rupee

routage *m* COM, INFO, TRANSP routing, V&M bundling, mixed bundling

route *f* LOISIRS itinerary, TRANSP (*r.*) Rd., road, route; **~ commerciale** ECON, IMP/EXP, TRANSP trade route; **~ commerciale transocéanique**

TRANSP world trade route; ~ **de desserte** TRANSP accommodation road; ~ **directe** TRANSP *navigation, aviation* direct route; ~ **en eau profonde** TRANSP deepwater route; ~ **maritime** TRANSP sea route; ~ **de navigation en eau profonde** TRANSP deep-sea shipping lane; ~ **principale** TRANSP major road, trunk road; ~ **à usage restreint** TRANSP accommodation road; ~ **à utilisateurs multiples** TRANSP multiuser route; ◆ **en** ~ COM en route; **faire** ~ COM be under way; **faire fausse** ~ COM be on the wrong track

router *vt* COM, TRANSP route

routeur *m* INFO router

routier *m* TRANSP lorry driver (*BrE*), teamster (*AmE*), truck driver (*AmE*), trucker (*AmE*)

routiers: **les** ~ *m pl* RES HUM *syndicat* the Teamsters (*US*)

routine *f* COM routine

royalties *f pl* COMPTA fee, MÉDIA royalties; ~ **dues par le concessionnaire d'un brevet** FIN patent royalties

Royaume-Uni[1] *m* COM United Kingdom, UK

Royaume-Uni:[2] ~ **ou Continent** *n pr* TRANSP *ports* UK/Cont, United Kingdom or Continent

RP *abrév* POL *(représentation proportionnelle)* PR *(proportional representation)*, V&M *(relations publiques)* PR *(public relations)*

RSVP *abrév (répondez s'il vous plaît)* COMMS RSVP *(please reply)*

RTP *abrév (réserve totale prescrite)* BANQUE PAR *(prescribed aggregate reserve)*

Ruanda *n pr* COM Rwanda

ruandais, e *adj* COM Rwandan

Ruandais, e *m,f* COM *habitant* Rwandan

rubrique *f* COM section, COMPTA heading, MÉDIA col, column, section; ~ **économique** MÉDIA economic section; ~ **économique et financière** COM, MÉDIA business pages

rue *f* COM street, TRANSP *(r.)* road *(Rd.)*; ~ **à double sens** TRANSP two-way street; ◆ **de la** ~ V&M *mode* high-street (*UK*)

ruée: ~ **sur les banques** *f* BANQUE, BOURSE run on the banks; ~ **sur le dollar** *f* BANQUE, BOURSE run on the dollar, rush on the dollar; ~ **vers l'or** *f* COM gold rush

ruiné, e *adj* BANQUE *e*, COMPTA, FIN, RES HUM bankrupt

ruiner *vt* BANQUE, COM, COMPTA, FIN, RES HUM *personne, société* bankrupt

rumeur *f* COM hearsay, rumor (*AmE*), rumour (*BrE*)

runner *m* BOURSE runner

rupiah *f* COM rupiah

rupteur *m* INFO burster

rupture *f* BOURSE break, DROIT breach, RES HUM breakdown; ~ **anticipée de contrat** DROIT anticipatory breach of contract; ~ **de contrat** DROIT, RES HUM breach of contract; ~ **de garantie** DROIT, IND breach of warranty; ~ **du lien conjugal** DROIT marriage breakdown; ~ **du mariage** DROIT marriage breakdown; ~ **de stock** COM, V&M stock shortage; ◆ **en** ~ **de stock** COM, V&M o.s., out of stock, unstocked

rusé, e *adj* COM *campagne de vente, personne* slick

russe[1] *adj* COM Russian

russe[2] *m* COM *langue* Russian

Russe *mf* COM *habitant* Russian

Russie *f* COM Russia

RVE *abrév (restriction volontaire des exportations)* IMP/EXP VER *(voluntary export restraint)*

Rwanda *m* COM Rwanda

rwandais, e *adj* COM Rwandan

Rwandais, e *m,f* COM *habitant* Rwandan

rythme *m* COM pace; ~ **de facturation** COM billing cycle; ~ **de production** IND throughput

S

s. *abrév* COM *(seconde)* sec. *(second)*, COMMS *(signé)* sgd *(signed)*

S *abrév (quart sud)* TRANSP *navigation* S *(South compass point)*

SA *abrév (société anonyme)* COM plc *(UK) (public limited company)*, limited company *(UK)*, public company

sabordage *m* TRANSP *navigation* scuttling

saborder *vt* TRANSP *navigation* scuttle

sac: ~ **gonflable** *m* TRANSP air bag; ~ **à provisions** *m* COM shopping bag; ~ **textile** *m* TRANSP textile bag; ~ **textile doublé kraft** *m* TRANSP textile bag-paper lined; ~ **de voyage** *m* COM valise

sacrifier *vt* ASSUR sacrifice

sacs: ~ **gonflables** *m pl* TRANSP *arrimage* inflatable dunnage

saignée *f* TRANSP bleeding

saigner *vt* COM bleed *(infrml)*; ◆ ~ **qn à blanc** *infrml* COM bleed sb dry *(infrml)*

sain, e *adj* COM *concurrence* healthy, ECON buoyant, INFO *virus informatique* uninfected, RES HUM healthy

Saint-Denis *n pr* COM Saint-Denis

Sainte-Lucie *f* COM St Lucia

Saint-George's *n pr* COM St George's

Saint-Jean *n pr* COM St John's

Saint-John's *n pr* COM St John's

Saint-Vincent *m* COM St Vincent

saisie *f* COM confiscation, DROIT distraint, distraint of property, foreclosure, IMMOB distraint, distraint of property, INFO *de données* capture, TRANSP *de navire, de marchandises* detention; ~ **-arrêt** DROIT *d'une créance* garnishment; ~ **-arrêt sur salaire** RES HUM wage withholding; ~ **d'un bien hypothéqué** DROIT foreclosure; ~ **codée de données** INFO coded data entry; ~ **directe** INFO direct data entry, DDE; ~ **de données** INFO data capture, data entry, data input; ~ **de données ordinales** INFO ordinal data entry; ~ **d'écran** INFO screen capture; ~ **-exécution** DROIT, IMMOB distraint; ~ **d'hypothèque sans faculté de rachat** DROIT strict foreclosure; ~ **légale d'une hypothèque** DROIT statutory foreclosure; ~ **en ligne** INFO direct data entry, DDE; ~ **masquée** INFO blind keyboard; ~ **en mode conversationnel** INFO conversational entry; ~ **unique des données concernant le pays d'origine** ADMIN single-country data capture

saisine: ~ **à chaîne** *f* TRANSP *manutention* chain lashing

saisir *vt* COM grab, snap up, DROIT foreclose, impound, levy, FIN foreclose, INFO *données, entrées* input, key, key in, *texte* enter, tap in; ◆ ~ **un bien hypothéqué** FIN foreclose a mortgage;

faire ~ COM *liquidation ordonnée par tribunal* sell up

saisissage *m* TRANSP lashing, *des conteneurs* tie-down

saisisseur *m* RES HUM, TRANSP *arrimeur* lasher, rigger

saison *f* LOISIRS season; ~ **touristique** ECON, LOISIRS tourist season

saisonnalité: ~ **de la demande** *f* ECON seasonality of demand

saisonnier[1], **-ère** *adj* COM seasonal

saisonnier[2], **-ère** *m,f* RES HUM seasonal worker

salaire *m* COM, ECON wage, RES HUM pay, salary, wage, wages; ~ **annuel** *m* RES HUM annual salary, annual wage; ~ **annuel garanti** *m* RES HUM guaranteed annual wage, GAW; ~ **d'appoint** *m* COM pin money; ~ **de base** *m* RES HUM base pay *(AmE)*, base salary *(AmE)*, basic pay, basic salary, basic wage; ~ **basé sur le rendement** *m* RES HUM payment by results, PBR *(UK)*; ~ **bonifié** *m* RES HUM premium pay; ~ **brut** *m* RES HUM gross pay, gross wage; ~ **cotisable** *m* ASSUR, FISC, RES HUM pensionable earnings; ~ **de croissance** *m* RES HUM incremental payment; ~ **de départ** *m* RES HUM commencing salary *(frml)*, starting salary, starting wage, threshold rate *(AmE)*; ~ **différentiel** *m* RES HUM differential pay; ~ **efficient** *m* ECON, RES HUM efficiency wage; ~ **élevé** *m* RES HUM top wages; ~ **d'embauche** *m* RES HUM commencing salary *(frml)*, starting salary, starting wage; ~ **et avantages complémentaires** *m pl* RES HUM remuneration package; ~ **et conditions de travail** *m pl* RES HUM pay and conditions; ~ **fixe** *m* RES HUM fixed salary; ~ **en fonction des résultats** *m* RES HUM payment by results, PBR; ~ **garanti** *m* RES HUM guaranteed wage; ~ **de garantie** *m* RES HUM guarantee pay; ~ **hebdomadaire** *m* RES HUM weekly pay packet, weekly wage, weekly wage packet; ~ **horaire** *m* ECON price rate, time rate, RES HUM hourly wage, price rate, time rate; ~ **initial** *m* RES HUM starting salary, threshold rate *(AmE)*; ~ **lié aux bénéfices** *m* COMPTA, RES HUM profit-related pay, PRP; ~ **lié aux résultats** *m* RES HUM performance-related pay; ~ **mensuel** *m* RES HUM monthly salary, monthly wage; ~ **minimum** *m* DROIT, ECON, PROT SOC, RES HUM minimum wage; ~ **minimum agricole garanti** *m (SMAG)* ECON guaranteed minimum agricultural wage; ~ **minimum garanti** *m* COM fall-back pay, RES HUM guaranteed minimum wage, statutory minimum wage; ~ **minimum interprofessionnel de croissance** *m (SMIC)* RES HUM guaranteed minimum wage, statutory minimum wage; ~ **minimum interprofessionnel garanti** *m*

(SMIG) RES HUM guaranteed annual wage *(GAW)*, guaranteed minimum wage, statutory minimum wage; ~ **modulé** *m* RES HUM graduated wage; ~ **moyen** *m* COMPTA average compensation, RES HUM average pay, average wage; ~ **moyen d'une journée** *m* RES HUM fair day's pay *(UK)*; ~ **net** *m* RES HUM net pay, take-home pay; ~ **nominal** *m* COM, RES HUM nominal pay, nominal wage, nominal wages; ~ **d'offre minimum** *m* RES HUM reservation wage, supply price; ~ **payé en espèces** *m frml* RES HUM pay check *(AmE)*, pay packet *(BrE)*; ~ **du personnel d'astreinte** *m* RES HUM standby rate; ~ **à la pièce** *m* RES HUM piece rate, piece wage; ~ **aux pièces** *m* RES HUM piece rate, piece wage; ~ **plafond** *m* RES HUM earnings ceiling; ~ **à prime de rendement** *m* BOURSE, RES HUM premium bonus; ~ **proposé pour l'emploi** *m* RES HUM rate for the job; ~ **proposé par les syndicats** *m* RES HUM union rate; ~ **réel** *m* COMPTA, ECON, RES HUM actual wage, real pay, real wage; ~ **réel efficient** *m* ECON efficient real wage, RES HUM efficiency real wage; ~ **au rendement** *m* RES HUM incentive wage, payment by results, PBR, performance-related pay, PRP; ~ **du secteur public** *m* ECON public sector pay; ~ **selon l'ancienneté dans le poste** *m* RES HUM longevity pay; ~ **unique** *m* RES HUM single income; ◆ ~ **à débattre** RES HUM salary to be negotiated; ~ **égal** RES HUM of comparable worth

salaires: ~ **et charges sociales** *m pl* RES HUM salaries, wages and fringe benefits

salariat *m* RES HUM salariat

salarié[1], **e** *adj* RES HUM employed

salarié[2], **e** *m,f* RES HUM employee, salaried employee, salary earner

salle: ~ **des coffres** *f* BANQUE safe-deposit vault, safety vault; ~ **des coffres-forts** *f* BANQUE safe-deposit vault, safety vault; ~ **du conseil** *f* ADMIN, GESTION, RES HUM boardroom; ~ **des cotations** *f* BOURSE boardroom; ~ **des dépêches** *f* BOURSE boardroom; ~ **d'embarquement** *f* TRANSP airport lounge, departure lounge; ~ **d'embarquement Classe Club** *f* TRANSP *aérien et maritime* executive lounge; ~ **d'exposition** *f* COM exhibition room; ~ **forte** *f* BANQUE vault; ~ **des machines** *f* INFO computer room, computing room; ~ **des machines sans surveillance** *f* IND *production* unattended machinery spaces, unmanned machinery spaces; ~ **de marché** *f* BANQUE trading room; ~ **des marchés** *f* BOURSE trading room, dealing floor, front office; ~ **d'opération** *f* BOURSE trading room; ~ **des ordinateurs** *f* INFO computer room; ~ **de projection** *f* MÉDIA viewing room; ~ **de rédaction** *f* MÉDIA *presse* newsroom; ~ **de stockage** *f* COM storeroom; ~ **des ventes** *f* COM auction room

salon *m* V&M *des arts ménagers* show; ~ **de l'aéronautique** TRANSP air show; ~ **de l'agriculture** ECON, V&M agricultural show; ~ **d'attente** TRANSP *embarquement* passenger lounge; ~ **Classe Club** TRANSP executive lounge; ~ **d'essayage** COM fitting room; ~ **informatique** INFO computing show; ~ **interprofessionnel** V&M trade show; ~ **non-fumeur** LOISIRS, TRANSP non-smoking lounge; ~ **passagers** TRANSP *à bord* passenger lounge; ~ **professionnel** V&M trade exhibition, trade fair

salons: ~ **professionnels et séminaires à l'étranger** *m pl* IMP/EXP overseas trade fairs and seminars

salutaire *adj* COM, DROIT beneficial

salutations *f pl* COMMS greetings

Salvador *m* COM El Salvador

salvadorien, -enne *adj* COM Salvadoran, Salvadorean, Salvadorian

Salvadorien, -enne *m,f* COM *habitant* Salvadoran, Salvadorean, Salvadorian

samedi *m* COM Sat., Saturday

Sanaa *n pr* COM Sanaa

sanction *f* COM sanction, DROIT penalty, V&M endorsement

sanctionner *vt* DROIT penalize, sanction

sanctions: ~ **commerciales** *f pl* ECON, IMP/EXP, POL trade sanctions; ~ **économiques** *f pl* ECON, POL economic sanctions

San José *n pr* COM San José

San Juan *n pr* COM San Juan

sans *prép* BOURSE ex, COM without; ◆ ~ **accès à la mer** ENVIR landlocked; ~ **accroc** COM without a reach; ~ **additifs** COM, ENVIR free of all additives; ~ **adresse** TRANSP *maritime* free of address; ~ **appel** DROIT with no right of appeal; ~ **arôme artificiel** COM no flavoring *(AmE)*, no flavouring *(BrE)*; ~ **ascenseur** IMMOB walk-up *(US, infrml)*; ~ **avaries** ASSUR free of damage, FOD; **avec et** ~ BOURSE cum and ex; ~ **bénéfice du sauvetage** ASSUR wbs, without benefit of salvage; ~ **bonification pour temps gagné** TRANSP *maritime, chargement/déchargement* fd, free dispatch; ~ **but lucratif** COMPTA, FIN, FISC non-profit-making *(BrE)*, nonprofit *(AmE)*; ~ **cesse** COMMS *travail* without respite; ~ **condensation** TRANSP noncondensing; ~ **condition** DROIT unconditional; ~ **conditions** COM no strings attached; ~ **conditions restrictives** COM no strings attached; ~ **conservateur** IND no preservatives; ~ **conservateur ni additif** IND no preservatives or additives; ~ **constituer de précédent** ASSUR without prejudice, WP; ~ **couverture suffisante** BANQUE insufficient funds; ~ **date** COM undated; ~ **déduction pour dépréciation** ASSUR new for old; ~ **dettes** COMPTA clean; ~ **différence** TRANSP *navigation* on an even keel; ~ **droit** BOURSE ex-rights; ~ **effet** COM no effects, NE; ~ **égard à la responsabilité** ASSUR *assurance dommages* no fault; ~ **emballage** COM unpacked; ~ **émeutes ou troubles civils** TRANSP fr & cc, free of riots and civil commotions; ~ **emploi** ECON jobless, RES HUM jobless, out of work; ~ **endettement** COMPTA clear of debts; ~ **engagement de notre part** COM without any liability on our part; ~ **engage-**

ment de votre part V&M without obligation; ~ **expérience** COM unfledged; ~ **faille** COM *soutien* continuing; ~ **fiche** COMMS cordless; ~ **fioriture** COM with no trimmings; ~ **fondement** COM unfounded; ~ **frais** COM w.c., without charge; ~ **garantie** COM without engagement; ~ **garantie du fournisseur** DROIT caveat emptor *(frml)*; ~ **indication de prix** COM unpriced; ~ **intérêt** FIN interest-free, x-interest; ~ **intermédiaire** COM across the counter; ~ **lien de dépendance** COM, COMPTA, FISC arm's-length; ~ **liquidité** FIN cash-strapped; ~ **littoral** IMMOB landlocked; ~ **locataire** IMMOB untenanted; ~ **la mention "pour acquit"** COM unreceipted; ~ **nom** INFO *fichier sans nom* unnamed; ~ **objet** COM n/a, not applicable; ~ **ordonnance** PROT SOC *médicament* over-the-counter, OTC; ~ **papier** BOURSE paperless; ~ **pareil** COM second to none; ~ **péage** TRANSP free; ~ **plomb** ENVIR lead-free, unleaded; ~ **préavis** COM n/a, no advice, without previous warning, without prior notice; ~ **précédent** COM unprecedented; ~ **préjudice** COM without prejudice, WP; ~ **preuves** COM unsupported; ~ **prime de célérité** TRANSP *maritime, chargement/déchargement* fd, free dispatch; ~ **privilège** COM without privileges, x pri; ~ **problèmes** COM trouble-free; ~ **publicité** COM unadvertised; ~ **recours** ASSUR, BANQUE without recourse, COM accept no liability, without recourse, FIN nonrecourse; ~ **relâche** COMMS *travail* without respite; ~ **répit** COMMS *travail* without respite; ~ **réponse** COM unacknowledged; ~ **réserve** DROIT absolute, unconditional; ~ **ressort** COM listless; ~ **restriction** COM uncurtailed; ~ **retard sur l'horaire** RES HUM on schedule; ~ **risque** BOURSE risk-free, COM riskless; ~ **risque sous réserve d'acceptation des conditions** ASSUR subject approval no risk, SANR; ~ **rival** COM unrivalled; ~ **scintillement** INFO flicker-free; ~ **scrupules** COM unscrupulous; ~ **tarif** IMP/EXP tariff-free; ~ **tenir compte de** COM irrespective of; ~ **terme particulier** TRANSP *maritime, affrètement* free of term; ~ **titre** INFO untitled; ~ **travail** RES HUM workless; ~ **valeur** COM valueless; ~ **valeur commerciale** COM n.c.v., no commercial value; ~ **valeur déclarée** IMP/EXP no value declared, NVD; ~ **valeur douanière** IMP/EXP n.c.v., no customs value; ~ **valeur nominale** *(SVN)* BOURSE no-par value *(NPV)*

sans-abri *mf* [inv pl] PROT SOC homeless person; **les** ~ *m pl* PROT SOC the homeless

San Salvador *n pr* COM San Salvador

sans-emplois *mf* [inv pl] ECON, RES HUM unemployed person; **les** ~ *m pl* [inv pl] ECON, RES HUM the jobless, the unemployed, the unwaged

sans-logis *mf* [inv pl] PROT SOC homeless person; **les** ~ *m pl* PROT SOC the homeless

santé *f* COM health; ~ **publique** COM public health; ~ **sur le lieu de travail** PROT SOC, RES HUM industrial health

Santiago *n pr* COM Santiago

Santo Domingo *n pr* COM Santo Domingo

saoudien, -enne *adj* COM Saudi, Saudi Arabian

Saoudien, -enne *m,f* COM *habitant* Saudi, Saudi Arabian

saper *vt* COM undermine

Sarajevo *n pr* COM Sarajevo

SARL *abrév (société à responsabilité limitée)* BOURSE plc *(private limited company)*, COM Inc. *(US) (incorporated company)*, Ltd *(UK) (limited liability company)*

sas *m* TRANSP *canal* lock-chamber

satellite *m* COMMS, MÉDIA satellite; ~ **de communication** COMMS communications satellite; ♦ **par ~** INFO remote

satisfaction *f* COM satisfaction; ~ **du consommateur** V&M consumer satisfaction; ~ **non-financière** *jarg* ECON, RES HUM nonfinancial reward; ~ **psychologique apportée par le travail** *jarg* ECON, RES HUM psychic income *(jarg)*; ~ **au travail** RES HUM job satisfaction

satisfaire *vt* COM cater for, *besoins* accommodate, satisfy, *revendication, exigences* meet; ♦ ~ **à** COM *désir* gratify; ~ **au contrôle** DROIT pass inspection

satisfaisant, e *adj* COM satisfactory

satisfait: ~ **de** *adj* COM satisfied with; ♦ **être ~ de** COM be satisfied with

saturation *f* COMMS congestion, INFO, V&M *du marché* saturation; ~ **du marché** COM, V&M market saturation

saturer *vt* COM, ECON, V&M *marché* glut, saturate

sauf *prép* COM except, TRANSP *navigation* excepted; ♦ ~ **avarie commune** ASSUR unless general; ~ **avis contraire** COM unless otherwise agreed; ~ **causé par** ASSUR unless caused by; ~ **dimanches et jours fériés** COM Sundays and holidays excepted; ~ **disposition contraire** ASSUR unless general, FISC except as otherwise provided, unless otherwise provided; ~ **dispositions contraires du présent** COM eohp, except otherwise herein provided; ~ **erreur** COM unless I'm mistaken; ~ **erreur ou omission** *(SEO)* COM errors and omissions excepted *(E&OE)*; ~ **s'ils ont été utilisés** TRANSP *charte-partie* unless used; ~ **indication contraire** COM unless otherwise required; ~ **stipulation contraire** COM unless otherwise agreed, unless otherwise specified; ~ **vendredis et jours fériés** COM FHEx, Fridays and holidays excepted; ~ **vendredis et périodes de congé** COM FHEx, Fridays and holidays excepted; ~ **vente** COM subject unsold

saut *m* INFO skip; ~ **de page** INFO form feed, FF, line feed, lf; ~ **de papier** INFO paper throw

sauter *vt* INFO skip; ♦ ~ **les détails** COM skip the details; ~ **un paiement** BANQUE skip a payment

sauvegarde *f* DROIT safeguard, INFO backup; ~ **automatique** INFO autosave; ~ **fixe** INFO timed backup; ♦ **de ~** INFO backup

sauvegarder *vt* COM safeguard, INFO back up, *données* save

sauvetage *m* COM, FIN bail-out, TRANSP *du navire et des biens* salvage

sauveteur *m* TRANSP *maritime* salvor

savant *m* RES HUM scientist

savoir:[1] ~ **figé** *m* IND *production* locked-in knowledge; ~ **de spécialiste** *m* RES HUM expert knowledge, specialist knowledge

savoir[2] *vt* COM know

savoir-faire *m* BREVETS, COM know-how, *commercial, professionnel* ability

SBF *abrév France (Société des bourses françaises)* BOURSE ≈ ISE *(International Stock Exchange)*

scalpage *m* BOURSE day trading, scalping *(US, infrml)*

scalper *m* BOURSE day trader, scalper *(US, infrml)*

scalping *m* BOURSE scalping *(US, infrml)*

scandale *m* COM scandal

scandinave *adj* COM Scandinavian

Scandinave *mf habitant* COM Scandinavian

Scandinavie *n pr* COM Scandinavia

scanner *vt* INFO scan

scanneur *m* INFO scanner; ~ **de prix** V&M price scanner

SCC *abrév Canada (système central de comptabilité)* COMPTA CAS *(Canada) (Central Accounting System)*

sceau: ~ **d'approbation** *m* COM seal of approval; ~ **de la banque** *m* BANQUE corporate seal; ~ **légal** *m* COM company seal, DROIT *d'une société* common seal, company seal

scellé, e *adj* COM sealed

scénario *m* COM scenario, MÉDIA film script; ~ **de message publicitaire** V&M storyboard

scepticisme *m* COM scepticism

schéma *m* COM diagram, outline, *d'un projet* work design; ~ **d'activité économique** ECON pattern of economic activity; ~ **de consommation** ECON consumption pattern; ~ **de la demande** ECON demand pattern; ~ **directeur** ADMIN blueprint; ~ **de dispersion** MATH scatter diagram, scattergram; ~ **fonctionnel** INFO block diagram; ~ **de présentation typographique d'une lettre** ADMIN layout chart

schilling *m* COM schilling

scie: ~ **à ruban** *f* IND band saw

science: ~ **du comportement** *f* GESTION behavioral science *(AmE)*, behavioural science *(BrE)*; ~ **et technologie pour la protection de l'environnement programme** *f* ENVIR science and technology for environmental protection programme; ~ **de la gestion** *f* GESTION, MATH management science

sciences: ~ **économiques** *f pl* PROT SOC economics

scinder *vt* COM demerge

scintillement *m* INFO flicker

scintiller *vi* INFO flick

scission *f* COM, ECON demerger; ~ **d'actif** FIN divestment

SCMC *abrév (Société de compensation des marchés conditionnels)* BOURSE ≈ LOCH *(UK) (London Options Clearing House)*

SCN *abrév (spécification de changement notifié)* TRANSP *aviation* MC *(master change)*, SCN *(specification change notice)*

scoop *m jarg* MÉDIA *presse* scoop

score *m* COM score; ~ **bêta de portefeuille** BOURSE portfolio beta score

SCPI *abrév (société civile de placement immobilier)* BOURSE REIT *(US) (real estate investment trust)*

SCRA *abrév (système de compensation et de règlement automatisé)* BANQUE ACSS *(Automated Clearing Settlement System)*

scripophilie *f* BOURSE scripophily

scrutation *f* COM scanning

scrutin *m* COM poll, POL *vote*, RES HUM ballot

SDT *abrév (simplification des tâches)* GESTION, RES HUM job simplification, work simplification

SE *abrév (système expert)* COM, INFO ES *(expert system)*

séance *f* POL *parlementaire* assembly, session, V&M *en publicité, de photos* shoot; ~ **d'affectation de fonds** BANQUE auction, banking day *(Can)*, COMPTA auction, banking day *(Can)*; ~ **de bourse** BOURSE trading session; ~ **de clôture** BOURSE closing session; ~ **extraordinaire** COM special meeting; ~ **d'information** COM, GESTION briefing, briefing session; ~ **de négociation** BOURSE trading session; ~ **des questions** POL *parlement* question time *(UK)*; ~ **de travail** COM business meeting, COMPTA working meeting, working session

seau *m* TRANSP pail

sec: **être à** ~ *loc infrml* ECON feel the pinch *(infrml)*

sécheresse *f* ENVIR drought

second *m* RES HUM chief mate, first mate; ~ **degré** PROT SOC secondary education; ~ **marché** BOURSE Unlisted Securities Market *(UK)*, USM *(UK)*, kerb market, unlisted market, ECON second market

seconde *f (s.)* COM second *(sec.)*; ~ **lecture** DROIT, POL *d'un projet de loi, d'une directive* second reading

secouer *vt* COM shake up

secourir *vt* COM aid

secours: **de** ~ *adj* COM backup, standby, INFO *appareil* backup

secousse: ~ **sur l'offre** *f* ECON supply-side shock

secret[1]**, e** *adj* COM secret, POL restricted

secret[2] *m* COM *bancaire* secrecy; ~ **commercial** COM trade secret; ~ **professionnel** COM, professional secrecy

secrétaire *mf* ADMIN, GESTION, RES HUM sec., secretary, typist; ~ **de direction** *m* GESTION, RES HUM P/Sec, personal secretary, PS, executive secretary, personal assistant, PA; ~ **d'État** *m* ADMIN, POL minister, Secretary of State *(UK)*; ~ **général** *m* ADMIN company secretary *(UK)*, RES HUM *d'une société* company secretary *(UK)*, general secretary; ~ **par intérim** *m* RES HUM temporary secretary; ~ **particulier** *m* GESTION P/Sec, personal secretary, PS, executive secretary, personal assistant, PA, RES HUM P/Sec, personal secretary, PS, executive secretary, private secretary, personal assistant, PA; ~ **privé** *m* RES HUM confidential secretary, private secretary; ~ **de rédaction** *m,f* MÉDIA chief sub (*UK, infrml*), copy editor, MÉDIA *presse* chief sub-editor, sub, sub-editor; ~ **de section** *m* RES HUM father of the chapel (*UK*); ~ **social** *m* RES HUM social secretary; ~ **-stagiaire** *m* ADMIN trainee typist

Secrétaire: ~ **général** *m* RES HUM General Executive Manager

secrétariat *m* ADMIN secretary's office, POL *gouvernement*, RES HUM secretariat; ~ **d'État** POL State Secretariat

Secrétariat: ~ **du conseil du trésor** *m* POL Treasury Board Secretariat; ~ **d'État du gouvernement** *m* POL Government State Secretariat

secteur *m* COM area, zone, *industriel, de représentation* sector, IND *de recherche* field, INFO cluster, sector; ~ **agricole** ECON agricultural sector, rural sector, ENVIR agricultural sector, IND agricultural sector, rural sector; ~ **bancaire** BANQUE, FIN banking industry, banking sector; ~ **défectueux** INFO bad sector; ~ **électrique** IND electricity sector; ~ **exclu** IND excluded sector, utilities sector; ~ **exportateur** IMP/EXP export sector; ~ **exposé** COM exposed sector; ~ **financier** ECON financial sector, FIN financial industry, financial sector; ~ **à fort coût de main-d'oeuvre** IND, RES HUM labor-intensive industry (*AmE*), labour-intensive industry (*BrE*); ~ **du gaz** ENVIR, IND gas industry; ~ **géographique desservi** TRANSP *par un navire* plying limit; ~ **individuel** ECON personal sector; ~ **industriel** IND industrial sector; ~ **des investissements** BOURSE, FIN investment business; le ~ **privé** ECON the private sector; ~ **des marchandises de base** COM basic goods sector; ~ **de marché** V&M market sector; ~ **nationalisé** IND nationalized sector; ~ **non-bancaire** FIN non-bank sector; ~ **non-manufacturier** IND nonmanufacturing sector; ~ **non-marchand** ECON nonmarket sector; ~ **des particuliers** ECON personal sector; ~ **pétrolier** ECON oil sector, petroleum sector; ~ **primaire** ECON, IND primary sector; ~ **de production** ECON, IND manufacturing sector; ~ **des produits de base** COM basic goods sector; ~ **public** COM public enterprise, ECON public sector, IND utilities sector; ~ **du représentant** V&M *publicité* agent's territory; ~ **à risque** COM exposed sector; ~ **sanitaire** IND, PROT SOC health care industry, health sector; ~ **de la santé** IND, PROT SOC health care industry, health sector; ~ **secondaire** ECON, IND secondary sector; ~ **des services** ECON, IND service sector; ~ **des services financiers** FIN financial services industry; ~ **des sociétés privées** ECON company sector; ~ **tertiaire** ECON services, tertiary sector, service industry, IND service industry; ~ **de vente** COM trading

area, V&M *zone géographique* sales area; ◆ **du** ~ **privé** COM, ECON private-sector

secteurs: ~ **d'activités abandonnés** *m pl* COMPTA discontinued operations

section *f* COM *d'une organisation* branch, DROIT, POL section, RES HUM chapel (*UK*); ~ **Économie** MÉDIA *presse* economic section; ~ **étrangère** BOURSE foreign section; ~ **homogène** COMPTA burden center (*AmE*), burden centre (*BrE*); ~ **d'investissement** COMPTA, FIN *collectivités locales* capital fund; ~ **juridique** DROIT legal section; ~ **nouveaux syndicats de métiers** RES HUM modified union shop (*US*); ~ **syndicale** RES HUM agency shop, local

sectoriel, -elle *adj* ECON sectoral

sectorisation *f* RES HUM divisionalization; ~ **logicielle** INFO soft sectoring

sectoriser *vt* INFO sector

Sécu *abrév infrml* France (*Sécurité sociale*) PROT SOC, RES HUM ≈ NHS (*UK*) (*National Health Service*)

sécurité *f* ADMIN, COM, INFO security, PROT SOC safety; ~ **de l'emploi** RES HUM job security; ~ **industrielle** PROT SOC, RES HUM industrial safety; ~ **informatique** INFO computer security; ~ **machine** IND, PROT SOC machine safety; ~ **du matériel** INFO hardware security; ~ **routière** TRANSP road safety

Sécurité: ~ **sociale** *f* France (*SS, Sécu*) PROT SOC, RES HUM ≈ National Health Service (*UK*) (*NHS*)

segment *m* INFO, V&M segment; ~ **de base** INFO root segment; ~ **ciblé** V&M target segment; ~ **du marché** V&M *marketing* market area, market segment, segment of the market

segmentation *f* V&M breakdown, division, segmentation, *marketing* clustering; ~ **des bénéfices** V&M *publicité* benefit segmentation; ~ **du marché** V&M market segmentation; ~ **des médias** MÉDIA, V&M media fragmentation; ~ **des styles de vie** V&M *marketing* lifestyle segmentation

segmenter *vt* COM, GESTION *politique*, V&M *marché* segment

ségrégation *f* COMMS segregation; ~ **professionnelle** ECON, RES HUM occupational segregation; ~ **au travail** ECON, RES HUM occupational segregation

seigneuriage *m* COM seigniorage

sélection *f* INFO, RES HUM selection; ~ **aléatoire** MATH random selection; ~ **et recrutement** *m pl* RES HUM recruitment and selection; ~ **des médias** MÉDIA, V&M media selection; ~ **de portefeuille** BOURSE, FIN portfolio selection; ~ **d'un site** ENVIR *pour une décharge* site selection

sélectionné, e *adj* COM selected; ◆ **être** ~ **pour** COM *avancement* be earmarked for

sélectionner *vt* COM screen, shortlist, *selon des critères* select, RES HUM screen, shortlist

self *m* COM, LOISIRS self-service; ~ -**service** COM, LOISIRS self-service

sellette: ~ **d'attelage** *f* TRANSP *convoi semi-remorque* fifth wheel, *semi-remorque* fifth-wheel coupling; ~ **coulissante** *f* TRANSP *semi-remorque* sliding fifth wheel; ◆ **sur la** ~ RES HUM in the hot seat

selon *prép* COM according to, *normes, règlement* in accordance with; ◆ ~ **le calendrier** GESTION, TRANSP, V&M according to schedule; ~ **l'estimation la plus basse** COM at the lowest estimate; ~ **l'estimation la plus élevée** COM at the highest estimate; ~ **l'horaire** GESTION, TRANSP, V&M according to schedule; ~ **la loi** DROIT by statute; ~ **la norme** DROIT according to the norm; ~ **les normes** GESTION normative; ~ **les normes de la compagnie** COM by the company's standards; ~ **le planning** ADMIN, COM as scheduled; ~ **le programme** GESTION, TRANSP, V&M according to schedule; ~ **les termes du contrat** DROIT under the terms of the contract; ~ **la valeur de la marchandise** COM, FISC ad valorem (*frml*)

SEM *abrév* (*société à économie mixte*) ECON partially-privatized company, semi-public company

semaine *f* COM week, wk.; ~ **commerciale** COM, V&M trade week; ~ **garantie** RES HUM guaranteed week; ~ **record** IND, RES HUM bull week (*jarg*); ~ **de travail** RES HUM working week (*BrE*), work-week (*AmE*); ~ **de travail moyenne** RES HUM average working week (*BrE*), average workweek (*AmE*); ~ **très productive** IND, RES HUM bull week (*jarg*); ◆ **dans deux ~s** COM fortnight tomorrow; **dans une** ~ COM within a week; **en** ~ COM on weekdays; **une** ~ **à l'avance** COM a week in advance

semaque *m vieilli* TRANSP smack

semblable *adj* COM similar

semer: ~ **la pagaille** *vt* COM rock the boat

semestre *m* COM half year

semestres *m pl* COM six-monthly periods

semestriel, -elle *adj* BOURSE *dividende* half-yearly, semiannual, COM biannual, half-yearly

semestriellement *adv* COM half-yearly

semi-conducteur *m* IND, INFO semiconductor

semi-duplex *adj* INFO full-duplex, FDX, half-duplex, HDX

semi-durable *adj* COM semidurable

semi-fini, e *adj* COM, IND semifinished

semi-industrialisé, e *adj* ECON, POL semi-industrialized

séminaire *m* GESTION seminar

semi-portique *m* TRANSP *manutention* semi-portal crane

semi-remorque *f* TRANSP articulated lorry, semi-trailer

sénat *m* POL senate (*US*)

Sénégal *m* COM Senegal

sénégalais, e *adj* COM Senegalese

Sénégalais, e *m,f* COM *habitant* Senegalese

sens: ~ **des affaires** *m* COM business sense; ~ **aigu des affaires** *m* COM, GESTION business acumen; ~ **du commerce** *m* COM commercial acumen; ~ **des responsabilités** *m* COM sense of responsibility

sensibilisation *f* PROT SOC, V&M awareness

sensibiliser *vt* COM sensitize

sensibilité: ~ **aux coûts** *f* COM cost awareness, cost consciousness, V&M cost awareness; ~ **envers les coûts** *f* V&M cost awareness; ~ **aux taux d'intérêt** *f* ECON interest rate sensitivity, interest sensitivity

sensible *adj* BOURSE sensitive, COM, ECON responsive; ~ **au coût** COM, ECON, V&M *client* cost-sensitive; ~ **au marché** V&M market-sensitive; ~ **au niveau des coûts** COM, ECON, V&M *client* cost-sensitive; ~ **au prix** V&M price-sensitive

sentence: ~ **arbitrale** *f* COM arbitral award; ~ **arbitrale de protection** *f* RES HUM protective award

sentier: ~ **de croissance** *m* COM growth path

sentiment: ~ **de bien-être** *m* COM, POL feelgood factor; ~ **de culpabilité** *m* COM mens rea (*frml*)

SEO *abrév* (*sauf erreur ou omission*) COM E&OE (*errors and omissions excepted*)

Séoul *n pr* COM Seoul

séparateur *m* INFO separator, *de feuilles* burster

séparation *f* IMMOB *de la terre* severance; ~ **de corps** DROIT judicial separation; ~ **judiciaire** DROIT judicial separation; ~ **légale** DROIT legal separation

séparé, e *adj* COM segregated

séparément *adv* COM singly

séparer: **se** ~ *v pron* COM break up

sept. *abrév* (*septembre*) COM Sept. (*September*)

Sept: **les** ~ **Moyens** *m pl* COMPTA Middle Seven; ~ **d'Or** *m* MÉDIA award for television programmes and people, ≈ Bafta (*UK*), ≈ British Academy of Film and Television Awards

septembre *m* (*sept.*) COM September (*Sept.*)

septième: **un** ~ *m* (*1/7*) COM, MATH one-seventh (*1/7*)

Septième: ~ **directive relative au droit de sociétés** *f* COM, DROIT, POL *UE* Seventh Company Law Directive; ~ **directive de l'UE** *f* COMPTA Seventh EU Directive

séquence *f* COM, INFO sequence; ~ **de classement** INFO collating sequence; ~ **d'échappement** INFO escape sequence; ~ **Esc** INFO escape sequence; ~ **de touches** INFO key sequence

séquentiel, -elle *adj* COM, INFO sequential

séquestration *f* FIN sequestration

séquestre: ~ **judiciaire** *m* DROIT writ of sequestration

serbe[1] *adj* COM Serb, Serbian

serbe[2] *m* COM *langue* Serb, Serbian

Serbe *mf* COM *habitant* Serb, Serbian

Serbie *f* COM Serbia

serbo:[1] ~ -**croate** *adj* COM Serbo-Croat, Serbo-Croatian

serbo:[2] ~ -**croate** *m* COM *langue* Serbo-Croat

Serbo: ~ -**croate** *mf* COM *habitant* Serbo-Croat, Serbo-Croatian

série *f* INFO set, V&M production; ~ **chronologique** ECON seasonal variations, MATH time series; ~ **économique de fabrication** ECON, GESTION, IND economic manufacturing quantity; ~ **de mesures** COM set of measures; ~ **de négociations salariales** ECON wage round, RES HUM pay round, wage round; ~ **d'obligations à intérêt identique mais progressif** BOURSE stepped bond; ~ **d'options** BOURSE option series, series of options; ~ **de produits** COM, IND, V&M product line; ◆ **de** ~ IND standard design, SD; **en** ~ INFO serial; ~ -**parallèle** INFO serial-parallel

sériel, -elle *adj* INFO serial

séries: par ~ **de** *loc* COM in sets of

sérieux, -euse *adj* COM bona fide

serment *m* DROIT oath

serpent *m* ECON UE snake; ~ **dans le tunnel** ECON snake in the tunnel; ~ **monétaire** ECON UE snake

serpentin: ~ **de réchauffage** *m* TRANSP *navigation* heating coil, HC; ~ **de réchauffage dans les soutes** *m* TRANSP *navigation* HE Cls B, heating coil in bunkers

serré, e *adj* ECON stiff

serrurier: ~ -**mécanicien** *m* IND engine builder

serv. *abrév (service)* ADMIN, COM, POL, RES HUM, V&M dept. *(department)*

serveur *m* INFO server; ~ **de fichiers** INFO file server; ~ **télématique** INFO bulletin board service, BBS, on-line data service

service *m (serv.)* ADMIN department *(dept.)*, COM favor *(AmE)*, favour *(BrE)*, service, COM department *(dept.)*, FIN *d'une dette* servicing, INFO service, RES HUM department *(dept.)*; ~ **d'accueil** ADMIN front-of-house jobs; ~ **des achats** COM procurement department, purchasing department; ~ **administratif** ADMIN admin *(infrml)*, administration, administrative service, back office, COM, GESTION admin *(infrml)*, administration, administrative service; ~ **annuel de la dette** BANQUE, ECON annual debt service *(UK)*; ~ **d'appel gratuit** COMMS Freefone number *(BrE)*, toll-free number *(AmE)*; ~ **d'appoint** TRANSP *navigation* backup service; ~ **d'apport** TRANSP *navigation* feeder service; ~ **après-vente** COM backup service, client department, V&M after-sales service, backup service; ~ **d'arrimage** TRANSP stevedoring department; ~ **d'assistance annuaire** COMMS directory assistance, directory enquiries *(BrE)*, directory information *(AmE)*; ~ **d'assistance technique par téléphone** INFO support hotline; ~ **assuré** ADMIN manned service; ~ **d'astreinte** RES HUM standby duty; ~ **d'audit** COMPTA, FIN auditing department; ~ **d'audit interne** ADMIN, COMPTA auditing department; ~ **bancaire d'investissement** BANQUE bank trust

department; ~ **bas de gamme** V&M down-market service; ~ **de la caisse** COM cash department; ~ **des chambres** LOISIRS *dans hôtel* room service; ~ **du change** BANQUE, BOURSE, FIN foreign exchange department; ~ **chargé des malfaçons et défauts de fabrication** COM defective services; ~ **des chèques postaux** BANQUE ≈ Girobank *(UK)*; ~ **à la clientèle** V&M customer service; ~ **clientèle** COM client department, customer service; ~ **des coffres** BANQUE safe custody department; ~ **de colis postaux** COMMS parcel post; ~ **commercial** COM business service, V&M sales department; ~ **commun** TRANSP joint service; ~ **de la comptabilité** ADMIN, COM, COMPTA, FIN accounting department, accounting office, accounts department; ~ **conseil** COM consulting service, ECON consultant service; ~ **conseil au consommateur** V&M consumer advisory service; ~ **de conseil des devises** BANQUE, BOURSE, FIN foreign exchange advisory service; ~ **conseil en investissements** BOURSE Investment Advisory Service *(US)*; ~ **de conseil en matière de recherche sur le bâtiment** IMMOB, IND Building Research Advisory Service, BRAS; ~ **conseil en placements** BOURSE Investment Advisory Service *(US)*; ~ **conteneur commun** TRANSP joint container service, JCS; ~ **conteneurs** TRANSP container service; ~ **du contentieux** DROIT legal department; ~ **des contributions** FISC revenue department; ~ **de contrôle interne** BOURSE compliance department; ~ **création** ADMIN art department, V&M *publicité* art department, creative department; ~ **du crédit** BANQUE credit department, FIN loan department; ~ **de dépôt** ADMIN deposit facility; ~ **de la dette** COMPTA debt service; ~ **de la dette publique** FIN public debt service; ~ **de la diffusion** MÉDIA *presse* circulation department; ~ **de distribution** TRANSP distribution service; ~ **de documentation** COM advisory service; ~ **des douanes** IMP/EXP Customs and Excise department *(UK)*, customs service; ~ **de l'emploi** RES HUM ≈ Job Centre *(UK)*; ~ **encaissement** FIN cashiering department *(UK)*; ~ **d'endettement stabilisé** FISC *charte municipale* level debt service *(US)*; ~ **d'enregistrement des valeurs** BOURSE stock record; ~ **aux entreprises** COM business service; ~ **d'entretien** IND maintenance department; ~ **d'escale** TRANSP *aviation* ground handling; ~ **d'expédition** TRANSP despatch department, dispatch department; ~ **facturation** COM billing department *(US)*, invoicing department, COMPTA invoicing department; ~ **feeder** TRANSP *navigation* feeder service; ~ **ferroviaire** TRANSP railroad service *(AmE)*, railway service *(BrE)*; ~ **du fret à l'arrivée** IMP/EXP, TRANSP inward freight department; ~ **du fret de sortie** IMP/EXP, TRANSP outward freight department; ~ **des garanties** BOURSE margin department; ~ **de gestion** ADMIN, GESTION admin *(infrml)*, administration; ~ **de gestion de portefeuille** BANQUE, BOURSE, FIN, GESTION portfolio management service; ~ **gouvernemental**

ADMIN Bureau (*US*); ~ **de groupage** TRANSP consolidate-cargo service, CCS; ~ **de groupage conteneurs** TRANSP consolidate-cargo container service; ~ **haut de gamme** V&M up-market service; ~ **informatique** INFO computer department; ~ **d'investissement** BOURSE, FIN investment service; ~ **juridique** DROIT legal department, legal section; ~ **de ligne maritime sans navire** TRANSP non-vessel-operating carrier, NVOC, non-vessel-operating common carrier, NVOCC, non-vessel-owning carrier, non-vessel-owning common carrier; ~ **de listage multiple** IMMOB Multiple Listing Service (*US*), MLS (*US*); ~ **de livraison** TRANSP delivery service; ~ **de livraisons gratuites en zone rurale** COMMS rural delivery service (*US*), RDS (*US*); ~ **de location de voitures** TRANSP car hire service; ~ **logistique** COM, RES HUM support service; ~ **des marchandises** COM goods department; ~ **du marché monétaire** BOURSE money-market department; ~ **maritime** TRANSP maritime service; ~ **marketing** ADMIN, V&M marketing department; ~ **du matériel** COM central supplies depot; ~ **mécanographique** ADMIN tabulating department; ~ **médiocre** V&M poor service; ~ **de merchandising** V&M merchandising service; ~ **de messageries** COMMS parcel post; ~ **multi-usagers** COM common user facility; ~ **de navette** TRANSP shuttle service; ~ **non-compris** COM *au restaurant, à l'hôtel* service not included; ~ **des opérations** ADMIN, BOURSE operations department; ~ **des opérations sur marge** BOURSE margin department; ~ **des opérations sur obligations** BOURSE bond trading department; ~ **payant** BANQUE fee-based service; ~ **de permanence** TRANSP skeleton service; ~ **personnalisé** V&M customized service; ~ **du personnel** RES HUM personnel department, staff department; ~ **des perspectives du marché** V&M market prospects service; ~ **de planification** COM, GESTION planning department; ~ **planning** COM, GESTION planning department; ~ **pont** TRANSP *d'un navire* deck department; ~ **portuaire fluvial** TRANSP *navigation* estuarial service; ~ **de positionnement précis** TRANSP *navigation par satellites* precise positioning service, PPS; ~ **de post-marché** BOURSE back office; ~ **postal** COMMS postal service; ~ **de presse** MÉDIA press relations; ~ **principal** TRANSP parent service; ~ **de la production** IND production department; ~ **public** ADMIN, COM, ECON, FISC public utility; ~ **public non-étatisé** ADMIN public service corporation (*US*); ~ **de publicité** V&M publicity department; ~ **publicité** MÉDIA, V&M *d'annonceur* advertising department; ~ **radio telex maritime automatique** COMMS, TRANSP *navigation* automatic maritime radio telex service; ~ **de ramassage** TRANSP pick-up service, *aviation* service pick up; ~ **de réception** COM, TRANSP *des marchandises* receiving department; ~ **des recettes et des dépenses** FIN cashiering department (*UK*); ~ **de recherche** COM research department; ~ **de rédaction** COM copy department; ~ **des**

règlements BANQUE settlements department; ~ **régleur** ASSUR claims department; ~ **régulier** LOISIRS, TRANSP interval service, regular service, scheduled service; ~ **des relations avec les investisseurs** BOURSE, FIN investor relations department; ~ **des relations publiques** V&M public relations department; ~ **de remplacement** ECON, IND substitute product; ~ **de renseignements** BOURSE *au sujet des titres, des matières premières* broad tape (*US*), COM advisory service, FIN *au sujet des titres, des matières premières* broad tape (*US*); ~ **de renseignements de la police** DROIT police intelligence; ~ **de la rente** FISC annuity payment, payment of annuity, pension payment; ~ **de réseau à valeur ajoutée** ECON value-added network service; ~ **des réservations** COM, LOISIRS, TRANSP advance booking office, reservation counter; ~ **de routage** TRANSP routes section; ~ **des sinistres** ASSUR claims department; ~ **social** RES HUM welfare department; ~ **sporadique** TRANSP sporadic service; ~ **de substitution** ECON, IND substitute product; ~ **de surveillance des opérations de bourse** BOURSE surveillance department of exchanges; ~ **de surveillance des titres** BOURSE stock watcher; ~ **technique** COM engineering and design department; ~ **télégraphique** COMMS telegraphic office, TO; ~ **téléphonique** COMMS wire service; ~ **des titres** BOURSE securities department; ~ **tour-du-monde** TRANSP *maritime* Rws, round the world service; ~ **transconteneurs** TRANSP container service; ~ **de transport multimodal** TRANSP multimodal transport service; ~ **triangulaire** TRANSP triangle service; ~ **d'urgence** PROT SOC emergency service; ~ **Value Line d'évaluation des investissements** FIN Value Line Investment Survey; ~ **veillant au respect de la déontologie** DROIT, MÉDIA *TV* standards and practices; ~ **des ventes** MÉDIA *presse* circulation department, V&M sales department; ~ **de virement automatique** BANQUE automatic transfer service (*UK*), ATS (*UK*); ~ **en vol** TRANSP in-flight service; ~ **voyageurs** TRANSP passenger service; ~ **24 heures sur 24** COM around-the-clock service (*AmE*), round-the-clock service; ◆ **au ~ de sa Majesté** COM, COMMS On Her Majesty's Service, OHMS; **être au ~ de la société** RES HUM serve the company

Service: ~ **de messagerie des éditeurs et libraires** *m* MÉDIA ≈ PBDS (*UK*), ≈ Publishers and Booksellers Delivery Service (*UK*); ~ **national des poids et mesures** *m* COM ≈ Namas, ≈ National Measurement Accreditation Service; ~ **de protection du consommateur et de l'environnement** *m* ENVIR Environment and Consumer Protection Service, ECPS; ~ **social international** *m* PROT SOC ≈ ISS, ≈ International Social Service

services *m pl* BREVETS, ECON services; ~ **accessoires** COM ancillary services; ~ **des administrations publiques** ECON general government services; ~ **d'assistance sociale** RES HUM welfare department; ~ **auxiliaires** COM ancillary operations; ~ **bancaires** BANQUE, COMPTA bank facilities; ~ **bancaires commerciaux** BANQUE commercial banking; ~ **bancaires au consommateur** BANQUE consumer banking; ~ **bancaires de détail** BANQUE retail banking; ~ **bancaires aux entreprises** BANQUE corporate banking; ~ **bancaires de fiducie** BANQUE fiduciary banking; ~ **bancaires de gros** BANQUE wholesale banking; ~ **bancaires d'investissement** BANQUE, FIN merchant banking; ~ **bancaires aux particuliers** BANQUE personal banking services, private banking; ~ **de banque d'affaires** BANQUE, FIN merchant banking; ~ **de banque d'investissement** BANQUE, FIN merchant banking; ~ **comptables** ADMIN, COM, COMPTA, FIN accounting department, accounting office, accounts department; ~ **de conseil** FIN *interne* advisory services, management services; ~ **de conseil interne** COM advisory services, GESTION advisory services, management services; ~ **de direction** FIN management services; ~ **aux entreprises** BANQUE commercial banking; ~ **d'état-major** GESTION management services; ~ **d'expertise comptable** COMPTA accountancy services; ~ **financiers** FIN financial services, financial services industry; ~ **fiscaux** COM revenue center (*AmE*), revenue centre (*BrE*); ~ **fonctionnels** ADMIN back-of-house jobs, FIN, GESTION management services; ~ **de garde** BANQUE safekeeping; ~ **industriels** IND industrial services; ~ **en informatique** INFO computer services; ~ **d'intendance** GESTION ancillary operations; ~ **juridiques** DROIT legal services; ~ **logistiques** COM, FIN, GESTION extension services; ~ **permanents du fond d'amortissement** ECON consolidated fund standing services (*UK*); ~ **primaires** (ANT *services secondaires, services tertiaires*) COM, ECON, IND primary activities; ~ **professionnels** COM professional services; ~ **publics** COM public service; ~ **rendus** COM rendering of services; ~ **de santé** COM health care; ~ **secondaires** (ANT *services primaires, services tertiaires*) COM, ECON, IND secondary activities; ~ **de sécurité** ADMIN security services; ~ **de soutien** BOURSE back office; ~ **tertiaires** (ANT *services primaires, services secondaires*) COM, ECON, IND tertiary activities; ~ **de trafic des navires** TRANSP vessel traffic services; ~ **de transports** ECON, TRANSP travel services; ~ **votés** *Can* COMPTA A-base (*Canada*); ◆ **pour ~ rendus** COM for services rendered

Services: ~ **d'études de marché industriel** *m pl* V&M Industrial Market Research Services, IMRS

servir *vt* COM serve, tend (*US*), *marché* service, V&M *marché* serve; ◆ ~ **les intérêts** FIN service a loan; **pour ~ cet objectif** COM in furtherance of this goal

servitude *f* DROIT encumbrance, IMMOB easement,

POL encumbrance; ~ **implicite** DROIT implied easement; ~ **touristique** IMMOB scenic easement

session *f* INFO, POL *parlementaire* session; ~ **ininterrompue** BOURSE twenty-four hour trading; ~ **parlementaire de l'été** COM, POL summer recess (*UK*); ~ **de travail** COM business meeting, COMPTA working meeting, working session; ◆ **la ~ fut levée** COM the meeting broke up

seuil *m* BOURSE threshold point, ENVIR, FISC threshold, INFO level, threshold; ~ **du bien-être** ECON, PROT SOC bliss point; ~ **de commande** COMPTA reorder point; ~ **critique** COM critical level; ~ **de divergence** ECON divergence threshold; ~ **d'enregistrement** FISC registration threshold; ~ **d'importance relative** COMPTA materiality level; ~ **d'imposition minimum** ECON, FIN, FISC tax threshold; ~ **d'intervention** ECON support level; ~ **de pauvreté** PROT SOC poverty line; ~ **de propriété croisée** FISC cross-ownership threshold; ~ **de réajustement** FISC adjustment limit; ~ **de réajustement automatique** RES HUM automatic adjustment point; ~ **de réapprovisionnement** COMPTA reorder point; ~ **de rentabilité** BOURSE, COM break-even point, COMPTA, ECON, FIN break-even level of income, break-even point, IMMOB break-even point; ~ **de rentabilité à la hausse** BOURSE upside break-even point; ~ **de revenu** FISC income threshold; ~ **de revenu familial** FISC family income threshold

seul: ~ **dépositaire** *m* COM sole agent; ~ **inventeur** *m* BREVETS sole inventor; ~ **propriétaire** *m* IMMOB sole owner; ◆ **en un ~ lieu** ASSUR, TRANSP any one location, AOLOC

seule: ~ **de change** *f* BANQUE sole of exchange; ◆ **à ~ fin de faire** COM with the sole object of doing

sévère *adj* COM harsh, ECON harsh, stiff

sexisme *m* DROIT, RES HUM gender discrimination, sex discrimination, sexual discrimination

Seychelles *f pl* COM Seychelles

SFI *abrév* (*société financière internationale*) FIN IFC (*international finance corporation*)

SGBD *abrév* (*système de gestion de bases de données*) INFO DBMS (*database management system*)

SGF *abrév* (*système de gestion financière*) FIN financial management system

SGTP *abrév* (*système généralisé des tarifs et préférences*) IMP/EXP GSTP (*generalized system of tariffs and preferences*)

shareware *m* INFO shareware

SHC *abrév* (*conteneur spécial hors-cotes*) TRANSP SHC (*super high cube*)

shekel *m* COM shekel

shift *m* INFO shift

shilling *m* COM shilling

shipchandler *m* TRANSP ship's chandler

shopping: **le ~** *m* COM shopping

short *m* BOURSE short; ~ **call** *m* BOURSE short call; ~ **hedge** *m* BOURSE selling hedge, short hedge; ~ **put** *m* BOURSE short put

shunto *m* RES HUM shunto

SIAM *abrév (système des intermédiaires entre courtiers)* BOURSE IDBS *(interdealer broker system)*

SICAF *abrév (société d'investissement à capital fermé ou fixe)* FIN CEIC *(closed-end investment company)*

SICAV[1] *abrév (société d'investissement à capital variable)* BOURSE, FIN OEIC *(open-end investment company)*

SICAV:[2] **~ éthique** *f* ECON ethical unit trust; **~ en mines d'or** *f* BOURSE gold mutual fund; **~ à plus-value maximum** *f* BOURSE maximum capital gains mutual fund

SICOVAM *abrév (≈ société interprofessionnelle pour la compensation des valeurs mobilières)* BOURSE ≈ DTC *(US) (Depository Trust Company)*

siège *m* POL *à la Chambre* seat; **~ bancaire** BANQUE bank address; **~ du conseil de conté** COM County Hall *(UK)*; **~ social** ADMIN headquarters, HQ, BANQUE head office, HO, COM head office, main office, HO, principal place of business, *d'une société* registered office, COMPTA head office, HO, principal place of business, DROIT *d'une société* registered office, GESTION head office, HO, RES HUM headquarters, HQ; **~ à suspension** TRANSP suspension seat; ◆ **dont le ~ est** COM based

siéger *vi* POL *à la Chambre* sit

sierra-léonais, e *adj* COM Sierra Leonean

Sierra-Léonais, e *m,f* COM *habitant* Sierra Leonean

Sierra Leone *f* COM Sierra Leone

SIG *abrév (système intégré de gestion)* GESTION, INFO MIS *(management information system)*

sigle *m* COM acronym

signal: **~ d'alarme** *m* COM alarm signal, warning indicator; **~ d'arrêt** *m* INFO stop signal; **~ de baisse** *m (ANT signal de hausse)* BOURSE bearish signal information; **~ de hausse** *m (ANT signal de baisse)* BOURSE bullish signal information; **~ d'horloge** *m* INFO clock signal; **~ d'occupation** *m* COMMS busy signal *(AmE)*, engaged tone *(BrE)*; **~ sonore** *m* INFO beep; **~ technique** *m* BOURSE technical sign; **~ transitoire** *m* INFO glitch

signalement *m* DROIT, V&M description

signaler *vt* COM show, COMMS *Can numéro* dial, INFO flag

signataire *mf* DROIT *d'un contrat, d'un traité* signatory; **~ autorisé** *m* BANQUE signing officer; ◆ **être ~ de** ENVIR be a signatory to

signature *f* COMMS acknowledgement, INFO signature; **~ collective** BANQUE joint signature; **~ des contrats** COM exchange of contracts; **~ en fac-similé** COM facsimile signature; **~ non-authentifiée** DROIT unauthenticated signature; **~ sans réserve** COM clean signature; **~ témoin** BANQUE specimen signature; **~ d'une vente** IMMOB completion of sale; ◆ **~ pour**

acceptation COMPTA signing and accounting; **avoir la ~** BANQUE be authorized to sign; **pour ~** COM for signature

signe *m* COM signal, *indication* sign, MATH sign; **~ moins** MATH minus sign; **~ plus** COM, MATH plus sign; **~ de référence** BREVETS reference sign; ◆ **en ~ de reconnaissance** DROIT tokenism

signé, e *adj (s.)* COMMS signed *(sgd)*

signer *vt* COM *accord* sign, DROIT subscribe; ◆ **à ~** COM for signature; **~ un contrat légal** DROIT sign a legal agreement; **~ les contrats** COM, DROIT, IMMOB exchange contracts; **~ en partant** ADMIN, COM, GESTION book out; **~ à la sortie** ADMIN, COM, GESTION book out; **~ sur les pointillés** ADMIN sign on the dotted line

significatif, -ive *adj* COM material, significant

signification *f* BREVETS notification, DROIT *d'un acte, d'une demande, d'un avis* service; **~ statistique** MATH statistical significance

signifier *vt* COM stand for, *indiquer* signify, DROIT *arrêt* notify, *avis* serve; ◆ **~ un acte judiciaire à qn** DROIT issue a writ against sb; **~ une assignation** DROIT enter a writ; **~ un avis contraire** DROIT serve counternotice

silo: **~ en douane** *m* COM bonded elevator

SIM *abrév* GESTION, INFO *(système d'information de management)* MIS *(management information system)*, V&M *(système d'information de marketing)* MIS *(marketing information system)*

similitude *f* BREVETS similarity; **~ de cas** *jarg* DROIT on all fours *(jarg)*

simple[1] *adj* COM simple; **à ~ effet** TRANSP *mécanisme* s/a, single-acting; **~ densité** INFO *disquette* single-density; **~ face** INFO single-sided; ◆ **~ face-double densité** INFO *disquette* single-sided double density, SSDD; **~ face-simple densité** INFO *disquette* single-sided single density, SSSD

simple[2] *m* TRANSP *chemin de fer* single

simple:[3] **~ précision** *f* INFO *calculs* single precision

simplex *m* INFO simplex

simplification: **~ des tâches** *f (SDT)* GESTION, RES HUM job simplification, work simplification

simplifié, e *adj* COM simplified

simplifier *vt* COM *instructions, mode opératoire* simplify; ◆ **~ les choses** COM simplify matters

simulation *f* COM, INFO simulation; **~ de gestion** COM, ECON business game, GESTION business game, management game, RES HUM business game; **~ de maladie** RES HUM malingering; **~ par ordinateur** INFO computer simulation; **~ de privatisation** ECON, POL market testing; **~ sur ordinateur** INFO computer simulation; **~ de voyage en navire de ligne** TRANSP *navigation* liner voyage simulation

simulé *m* INFO computer simulation

simuler *vt* COM, INFO simulate

simultané[1]**, e** *adj* COM simultaneous, INFO full-duplex, FDX

simultané^2 *m* MÉDIA simulcast, simultaneous broadcast

simultanées *f pl* FISC concurrent returns

sincérité *f* COMPTA application of accounting rules in good faith, *des comptes* truthfulness

sinécure *f* RES HUM sinecure

sine die *loc frml* DROIT sine die *(frml)*

Singapour *m* COM Singapore

singapourien, -enne *adj* COM Singaporean

Singapourien, -enne *m,f* COM *habitant* Singaporean

sinistre *m* ASSUR loss; ~ **d'assurance** ASSUR insurance claim; ~ **au comptant** ASSUR cash loss; ~ **partiel** ASSUR partial loss, PL; ~ **payé** ASSUR claim paid; ~ **réglé** ASSUR claim paid; ~ **tardif** ASSUR belated claim

sinistré, e *m,f* ASSUR the claimant

sis *adj juridique* COM located

sister-ship *m* TRANSP sister ship

site *m* INFO site; ~ **contaminé** ENVIR contaminated site; ~ **de décharge** ENVIR dump site, dumping ground, landfill, tip; ~ **de décharge contrôlée** ENVIR landfill site; ~ **industriel** IMMOB industrial estate *(BrE)*, industrial park *(AmE)*, IND industrial estate *(BrE)*, industrial park *(AmE)*, industrial site, V&M industrial estate *(BrE)*, industrial park *(AmE)*; ~ **de premier choix** IMMOB *surtout en logement individuel* prime site; ~ **touristique** LOISIRS tourist attraction; ~ **vedette** COM, V&M *magasin, salle d'exposition, garage, hôtel* flagship site; ♦ **sur** ~ RES HUM inhouse

Site: ~ **d'intérêt scientifique spécial** *m* ENVIR Site of Special Scientific Interest, SSSI

situation *f* BANQUE position, COM location, state of affairs, COMPTA position; ~ **de banque** BANQUE bank return, bank statement; ~ **de blocage** BOURSE living dead *(jarg)*, RES HUM standoff; ~ **budgétaire** COMPTA, FIN budgetary position; ~ **de caisse** COMPTA cash position; ~ **des dettes dues aux fournisseurs** COMPTA creditor position; ~ **de l'économie** ECON state of the economy; ~ **économique** COM, ECON, POL economic situation; ~ **de l'emploi** COM employment situation; ~ **épineuse** COM sticky situation *(infrml)*; ~ **de famille** DROIT marital status, FISC, RES HUM, WEL family circumstances; ~ **financière** COMPTA financial position, financial situation, FIN *d'une entreprise* financial standing; ~ **financière extrêmement difficile** FISC extreme hardship; ~ **fiscale** ADMIN, FISC tax status; ~ **hebdomadaire** BANQUE weekly return; ~ **hypothétique** COM hypothetical situation; ~ **juridique** DROIT juridical position, legal standing; ~ **nette** BOURSE shareholders' equity, FIN net position; ~ **nette du gouvernement** POL general government net worth; ~ **particulière** COM special situation; ~ **permettant de négocier** COM bargaining position; ~ **politique** COM, POL political situation; ~ **à terme** BOURSE forward position; ~ **de trésorerie** COMPTA

cash position; ♦ **avoir la** ~ **bien en main** COM have the situation well in hand; **avoir une** ~ BOURSE hold a position; ~ **de la caisse et de la dette** BANQUE cash and debt position; **être dans une** ~ **financière difficile** FIN be in financial straits

situé, e *adj* COM located

situer: **se** ~ **à** *v pron* COM stand at

sixième: **un** ~ *m (1/6)* MATH one-sixth *(1/6)*

Skopje *n pr* COM Skopje

slogan *m* V&M *publicitaire* slogan, tagline; ~ **publicitaire** V&M advertising slogan, catch line

sloop *m* TRANSP Sp, sloop

slovaque *adj* COM Slovak, Slovakian

Slovaque *mf* COM *habitant* Slovak, Slovakian

Slovaquie *f* COM Slovak Republic, Slovakia

slovène^1 *adj* COM Slovene, Slovenian

slovène^2 *m* COM *langue* Slovene

Slovène *mf* COM *habitant* Slovene, Slovenian

Slovénie *f* COM Slovenia

SM *abrév (système métrique)* COM, MATH metric system

smack *m* TRANSP smack

SMAG *abrév (salaire minimum agricole garanti)* ECON guaranteed minimum agricultural wage

smart: ~ **card** *m* IMP/EXP, TRANSP smart card

SME *abrév (Système monétaire européen)* ECON UE EMS *(European Monetary System)*

SMIC *abrév (salaire minimum interprofessionnel de croissance)* RES HUM guaranteed minimum wage, statutory minimum wage

SMIG *abrév (salaire minimum interprofessionnel garanti)* RES HUM GAW *(guaranteed annual wage)*

SNCF *abrév (Société nationale des chemins de fer français)* TRANSP ≈ BR *(UK)* *(British Rail)*

SNJ *abrév (Syndicat national des journalistes)* MÉDIA ≈ NUJ *(UK)* *(National Union of Journalists)*

social, e *adj* COM social

social-démocratie *f* ECON, POL social democracy

socialisation *f* PROT SOC socialization

socialisme *m* ECON, POL socialism; ~ **autogestionnaire** ECON third way

socialiste *mf* ECON, POL socialist

société *f (Sté)* COM association, company, firm, ECON company, firm; ~ **absorbante** ECON absorbing company; ~ **absorbée** BANQUE amalgamating corporation; ~ **acquise** COM purchased company; ~ **à activité unique** BOURSE pure play *(jarg)*; ~ **d'affacturage** FIN factoring company; ~ **affiliée** BOURSE member corporation, member firm, COM affiliate company, associate company, associated company, corporate affiliate, ECON associate company, corporate affiliate; ~ **altruiste** ECON, POL caring society; ~ **annexe** COMPTA subsidiary company; ~ **anonyme** *(SA)* COM limited company *(UK)*, public company, public limited company *(UK)* *(plc)*; ~ **apparentée** COM associate company, corporate affiliate, COMPTA affiliated company, ECON associate company, corporate affiliate; ~ **apporteuse** COM vendor company; ~ **d'assistance en escale** TRANSP *aviation* ground handling agent; ~ **d'assistés** PROT SOC dependency culture *(jarg)*; ~ **associée** COM associated company, COMPTA affiliated company; ~ **d'assurance toutes branches** ASSUR composite insurance company; ~ **d'assurances** ASSUR insurance company, insurance corporation; ~ **autoritaire** ECON, POL authoritarian society; ~ **auxiliaire** COM intermediary company; ~ **de biens de grande consommation** COM consumer goods company; ~ **de bourse** BOURSE member firm, *depuis 1988* brokerage firm, brokerage house; ~ **à la campagne** RES HUM greenfield site company *(UK)*; ~ **de capital-risque** FIN venture capital corporation, venture capital company; ~ **à capital variable** BOURSE, FIN open-end fund; ~ **de capitaux à risque** FIN venture capital company, venture capital corporation; ~ **captive** COM daughter company; ~ **cédante** COM transferor company; ~ **cessionnaire** COM transferee company; ~ **civile de placement immobilier** *(SCPI)* BOURSE real estate investment trust *(US)* *(REIT)*; ~ **cliente** BANQUE corporate client, corporate customer, V&M client firm; ~ **en commandite** BOURSE limited partnership, public limited partnership, COM master limited partnership; ~ **en commandite de capital à risque** FIN venture capital limited partnership; ~ **en commandite par actions** BOURSE public limited partnership; ~ **en commandite de recherche et de développement** FIN research and development limited partnership; ~ **de commerce** COM, ECON, V&M trading company; ~ **commerciale** COM business corporation, corp., corporation, trading company, ECON business corporation, trading company, V&M trading company; ~ **commerciale de droit étranger** COM, DROIT alien corporation; ~ **commerciale non-cotée** COM, ECON, V&M unquoted trading company; ~ **de commercialisation des services** COM service provider; ~ **de compensation d'actions** BOURSE options clearing corporation, OCC; ~ **de compensation des options** BOURSE options clearing corporation, OCC; ~ **concessionnaire** COM statutory company; ~ **de conseil** COM consulting company; ~ **de conseil juridique** DROIT law firm; ~ **de consommation** ECON, POL consumer society; ~ **constituante** BOURSE constituent company; ~ **constituée** COM incorporated company *(US)*; ~ **contrôlée par l'État** ADMIN government-controlled corporation; ~ **coopérative** COM cooperative society; ~ **coopérative de consommation** COM Cooperative Wholesale Society, CWS; ~ **coquille** BOURSE shell operation; ~ **cotée** BOURSE, FIN listed company; ~ **cotée en bourse** BOURSE, FIN listed company, publicly listed company, publicly traded company, quoted company; ~ **de courtage** FIN retail house; ~ **de crédit** FIN finance company, finance house *(UK)*, loan company; ~ **de crédit-bail** FIN leasing cor-

poration, IMMOB leasing company; ~ **déclarante** COM reporting corporation; ~ **des détenteurs d'obligations étrangers** BOURSE Corporation of Foreign Bondholders *(UK)*, CFBH; ~ **de deuxième ordre** COM second-tier company; ~ **dissoute** COM, ECON defunct company; ~ **dominante** COM controlling company; ~ **dont les actions sont cotées en bourse** BOURSE, FIN publicly listed company, publicly traded company; ~ **de droit étranger** COM, DROIT foreign corporation; ~ **à économie mixte** *(SEM)* ECON partially-privatized company, semi-public company; ~ **écran** COM shell company, shell corporation; ~ **émettrice** BOURSE issuing company; ~ **enregistrée** COM incorporated company *(US)*; ~ **entièrement cotée** BOURSE fully quoted company; ~ **d'État** ADMIN Crown corporation; ~ **d'État mère** COM parent Crown corporation; ~ **d'État provinciale** ADMIN provincial Crown corporation; ~ **étrangère** COM, DROIT foreign company, foreign corporation, foreign firm, non-resident company, out-of-state corporation, FISC nonresident company; ~ **exonérée d'impôts** COM, FISC tax-exempt corporation; ~ **d'exploitation en commun** GESTION joint venture, joint-venture company, JV; ~ **d'exportation** COM indent house; ~ **d'extraction de l'or** ENVIR, IND gold-mining company; ~ **de fait** COM, ECON de facto corporation; ~ **fantôme** COM bogus company; ~ **favorable à l'autorité** ECON, POL authoritarian society; ~ **fédérale d'assurance épargne et crédit** BANQUE ≈ FSLIC *(US)*, ≈ Federal Savings and Loan Insurance Corporation *(US)*; ~ **fédérale des prêts hypothécaires** FIN, IMMOB Federal Home Loan Mortgage Corporation *(US)*, Freddie Mac *(US, infrml)*, FHLMC *(US)*; ~ **fédérée** RES HUM federated company; ~ **fermée** COM private company, ECON closely held corporation; ~ **fictive** COM bogus company, FISC shell company *(jarg)*; ~ **de fiducie** FIN trust company; ~ **filiale à cent pour cent** BOURSE wholly-owned subsidiary; ~ **de financement** FIN finance company, finance house *(UK)*, funding agency, promotary company *(US)*; ~ **de financement à l'exportation** FIN, IMP/EXP export finance house; ~ **financière** FIN financial company, financial firm; ~ **financière de portefeuille** FIN financial holding company; ~ **financière satellite** ECON captive finance company; ~ **fondatrice** COM founding company; ~ **de gestion** ADMIN, COMPTA, FIN, GESTION administrative management society *(US)*, asset management company; ~ **de gestion à capital fixe** FIN closed-end management company *(UK)*; ~ **de gestion d'exportations** GESTION, IMP/EXP export management company; ~ **de gestion de portefeuille à capital non-variable** FIN closed-end investment trust; ~ **de gestion des redevances** ENVIR royalty trust; ~ **de gestion de retraite** ASSUR pension corporation; ~ **de holding** COM holding company, parent company, proprietary company; ~ **holding bancaire** FIN pure holding company; ~ **humanitaire** ECON, POL caring society; ~ **iceberg** COM iceberg company; ~ **immatriculée** ADMIN registered company; ~ **immobilière** COM property company, IMMOB property company, real estate company; ~ **d'import-export** IMP/EXP trading company; ~ **importante** COM big company; ~ **d'importation** IMP/EXP trading company; ~ **imposable** COM, FISC taxable corporation; ~ **individuelle de portefeuille** FISC personal holding company (*US*), PHC (*US*); ~ **industrielle** ECON, IND manufacturing company; ~ **industrielle et commerciale** COM, ECON industrial and commercial company, ICC; ~ **industrielle de premier qualité** BOURSE blue-chip industrial; ~ **informatique** INFO computer company, computing company; ~ **inscrite au registre du commerce** ADMIN registered company; ~ **intégrée** COM integrated company; ~ **d'intérêt public** ECON, IND nationalized industry, public interest company; ~ **d'intérim** RES HUM temping agency; ~ **intermédiaire** BANQUE, BOURSE nominee company, COM intermediary corporation, nominee company; ~ **intermédiaire pour la compensation des titres** BOURSE Stock Exchange Pool Nominees (*UK*), SEPON (*UK*); ≈ ~ **interprofessionnelle pour la compensation des valeurs mobilières** *France (SICOVAM)* BOURSE ≈ Depository Trust Company (*US*) *(DTC)*; ~ **d'investissement** BOURSE, FIN investment company, investment corporation, investment firm, investment fund; ~ **d'investissement à capital fermé ou fixe** *(SICAF)* FIN closed-end fund, closed-end investment company, closed-end investment fund; ~ **d'investissement à capital variable** *(SICAV)* BOURSE, FIN mutual fund (*AmE*), open-end fund, open-end investment company (*OEIC*), open-end investment trust, unit trust (*BrE*); ~ **d'investissement équilibrée** BOURSE balanced mutual fund *(AmE)*; ~ **d'investissement et de crédit immobiliers** BANQUE ≈ building and loan association (*AmE*), ≈ building society (*BrE*); ~ **d'investissement immobilier à vie** FIN finite life real estate investment trust; ~ **d'investissement immobilière** FIN, IMMOB property investment company; ~ **d'investissement innovatrice** BOURSE rocket scientist *(jarg)*; ~ **d'investissement ouverte** BOURSE, FIN mutual fund *(AmE)*, open-end investment company, unit trust (*BrE*); ~ **d'investissement réglementée** FIN regulated investment company; ~ **d'investissement de revenus** FIN income investment company; ~ **d'investissement révocable** FIN revocable trust; **la ~ d'abondance** COM, ECON the affluent society; **la ~ Best** ASSUR Best's Rating (*US*); **la ~ de gaspillage** COM the waste society; **la ~ IBM**® INFO Big Blue *(infrml)*; ~ **leader** COM pacesetter; ~ **de leasing** COM lease company; ~ **limitée en matière de pétrole et gas** COM oil and gas limited partnership; ~ **de location d'ordinateurs** INFO, V&M computer-leasing firm; ~ **en logiciel** INFO software company, software house; ~ **mandataire** COMPTA agent corporation; ~ **membre** BOURSE corporate member, member firm; ~ **mère** COM parent company, proprietary company; ~ **mère holding** COMPTA holding company; ~ **mixte** COM joint equity venture company, joint venture, JV, joint-venture company; ~ **multinationale** COM, ECON, IND multinational company, multinational corporation, MNC, multinational enterprise, MNE; ~ **mutualiste** ASSUR mutual corporation; ~ **mutuelle** ASSUR mutual benefit society, COM cooperative society, PROT SOC mutual benefit society; ~ **mutuelle de crédit** COM cooperative credit institution; ~ **nationale** FISC public corporation (*UK*); ~ **nationale de compensation de titres** BOURSE National Securities Clearing Corporation (*US*); ~ **nationale de compensation des valeurs** BOURSE National Securities Clearing Corporation (*US*); ~ **en nom collectif** COM, FIN partnership; ~ **à nombre d'actionnaires réduit** BOURSE closely held corporation; ~ **non-inscrite à la cote** BOURSE, COM unlisted company; ~ **non-résidente** COM, DROIT nonresident company, out-of-state corporation, FISC nonresident company; ~ **non-responsabilité** COM nonliability company; ~ **par actions** BOURSE joint-stock company; ~ **en participation** COM joint equity venture company, joint venture, JV, joint-venture company; ~ **pétrolière** ENVIR, IND oil company; ~ **de placement** BOURSE, FIN investment company, investment firm; ~ **de placement à capital variable** BOURSE, FIN open-end fund, open-end investment company, open-end investment trust; ~ **plagiaire** V&M me-too firm; ~ **de portefeuilles** BOURSE investment company, investment firm, COM, DROIT holding company, FIN investment company, investment firm, FISC, IMMOB holding company; ~ **de portefeuilles à activité mixte** BOURSE mixed-activity holding company; ~ **de portefeuilles à capital variable** BOURSE, FIN open-end investment company, open-end investment trust; ~ **de portefeuilles privée** BOURSE private holding corporation; ~ **post-industrielle** ECON, POL post-industrial society; ~ **de premier ordre** BOURSE blue-chip company; ~ **preneuse** COM purchasing company; ~ **de prêt hypothécaire** BANQUE mortgage company, mortgage loan company, mortgage loan corporation; ~ **de prêt hypothécaire immobilier** BANQUE GNMA (*US*), Ginnie Mae (*US, infrml*), FIN Ginnie Mae (*US, infrml*), GNMA (*US*), Government National Mortgage Association (*US*), GNMA (*US*), IMMOB GNMA (*US*), Ginnie Mae (*US, infrml*); ~ **prête-nom** BANQUE, BOURSE, COM nominee company; ~ **de prévoyance** FIN benefit club, benefit society (*AmE*), friendly society (*BrE*); ~ **privée** COM private company, privately owned company; ~ **publique** FISC public corporation (*UK*); ~ **de réassurance** ASSUR reinsurance company; ~ **à responsabilité limitée** *(SARL)* BOURSE private limited company, COM incorporated company (*US*), limited liability company (*UK*), plc (*UK*), private company, private limited company, private sector company, public limited company (*UK*); **~ resyndicataire en commandite** IMMOB resyndication limited partnership; **~ sans argent** COM cashless society; **~ sans représentation syndicale** RES HUM nonunion firm; **~ de secours mutuel** ASSUR mutual benefit society, FIN benefit club, benefit society (*AmE*), friendly society (*BrE*), PROT SOC mutual benefit society; **~ du secteur privé** COM, ECON private sector company; **~ de service** INFO service company; **~ de service d'escale** TRANSP *aviation* ground handling agent; **~ de services et de conseils en informatique** *(SSCI)* INFO software and computer services company, computer consultancy firm; **~ de services d'ingénierie informatique** *(SSII)* INFO computer services company; **~ -soeur** COM sister company; **~ en tête au baromètre** ECON barometric firm leadership; **~ tiroir** COM off-the-shelf company; **~ transnationale** COM, ECON, POL transnational corporation, TNC; **~ très fermée** ECON closed company (*BrE*), closed corporation (*AmE*); **~ au vert** RES HUM greenfield site company (*UK*); **~ vieillissante** ECON gray society (*AmE*), grey society (*BrE*); ◆ **~ née d'une fusion** FIN merger company

Société: **~ des bourses françaises** *f France (SBF)* BOURSE ≈ International Stock Exchange *(ISE)*; **~ de compensation des marchés conditionnels** *f (SCMC)* BOURSE ≈ London Options Clearing House *(UK) (LOCH)*; **~ pour le développement urbain** *f* ECON Urban Development Corporation *(UK)*; **~ financière internationale** *f (SFI)* FIN International Finance Corporation *(IFC)*; **~ internationale de télécommunications financières interbanques** *f* BANQUE, COMMS Society for Worldwide Interbank Financial Telecommunications, SWIFT; **~ nationale des chemins de fer français** *f (SNCF)* TRANSP ≈ British Rail *(UK) (BR)*

socio-économique *adj* ECON, V&M socioeconomic

socioculturel, -elle *adj* V&M sociocultural

sociométrique *adj* MATH, V&M sociometric

socle *m* TRANSP *fixation des conteneurs* deck socket; **~ à plat pont** TRANSP *navire, fixation des conteneurs* flush deck socket; **~ en queue d'aronde** TRANSP *fixation des conteneurs* dovetail socket; **~ en saillie** TRANSP *sur le pont d'un navire* raised deck socket

Sofia *n pr* COM Sofia

soi: **en ~** *loc* COM per se

soi-disant *adj* COM so-called

soif: **~ de possession** *f* COM acquisitiveness

soin *m* COM care

soins: **~ en clinique** *m pl* PROT SOC private hospital treatment; **~ et prévention** *m pl* PROT SOC care and control; **~ gratuits** *m pl* PROT SOC free medical treatment

soirée: **~ de bienfaisance** *f* COM benefit

sol *m* COM sol; **~ naturel** ENVIR, IND unspoilt land; **~ sans perturbation artificielle** ENVIR, IND unspoilt land

solde *m* BANQUE bal., balance, *d'un bilan, d'un compte* account balance, amount outstanding, balance of account, BOURSE square, COM account balance, balance of account, *vente* sale, COMPTA account balance, balance of account, amount outstanding, *d'un bilan, d'un compte* bal., balance, ECON bal., balance, FIN account balance, amount outstanding, bal., balance, balance of account, V&M *vente* sale; **~ accumulé** FISC accumulated balance; **~ d'amortissement** IMMOB hang-out *(infrml)*; **~ à l'arrêté des comptes** BANQUE, COMPTA, FIN closing balance, ending balance; **~ bancaire** BANQUE, COMPTA, FIN balance in bank; **~ de banque** BANQUE, COMPTA, FIN bank balance; **~ de caisse** COMPTA cash balance; **~ de caisse non-dépensé** COMPTA unspent cash balance; **~ de clôture** *(ANT solde d'ouverture)* BANQUE, COMPTA, FIN closing balance, ending balance; **~ commercial** COM, ECON trade account; **~ compensateur** BANQUE compensating balance; **~ comptable** BANQUE, COM, COMPTA, FIN account balance, balance of account; **~ de compte** BANQUE, COM, COMPTA, FIN account balance, balance of account; **~ de compte d'attente** BANQUE suspense balance; **~ de compte bancaire** BANQUE, COMPTA, FIN bank balance; **~ de compte courant** BANQUE, COM checking account balance *(AmE)*, current account balance *(BrE)*; **~ d'un compte du grand livre** COMPTA ledger balance; **~ des comptes** FIN make-up *(jarg)*; **~ créditeur** BANQUE, FIN balance due to creditor, credit balance; **~ créditeur minimum** BANQUE minimum balance, minimum credit balance; **~ créditeur de votre compte** BANQUE amount standing to your account; **~ débiteur** BANQUE balance due to debitor, debit balance, COMPTA debit balance, FIN balance due to debitor, debit balance; **~ débiteur net des clients** BOURSE customers' net debit balance; **~ de dépôt** BANQUE deposit balance; **~ disponible** BANQUE, COMPTA available balance; **~ de dividende** BOURSE final dividend, FIN liquidating dividend; **~ dû** FISC balance due; **~ d'exploitation** BANQUE operational balance; **~ extérieur** ECON, IMP/EXP, POL trade balance; **~ de facture** COMPTA balance of invoice; **~ de fin de saison** COM, V&M end-of-season sale; **~ générale** COMPTA aggregate balance; **~ d'hypothèque** BANQUE, FIN final mortgage payment; **~ impayé** COMPTA outstanding balance; **~ inemployé** FIN *d'un crédit* unexpended balance; **~ initial** BANQUE, COMPTA, FIN opening balance; **~ minimal** BANQUE minimum balance, minimum credit balance; **~ minimum de titres exigé** BOURSE house maintenance requirement; **~ moyen** BANQUE average balance; **~ non-grevé** COMPTA unencumbered balance; **~ non-mouvementé** FIN idle balance; **~ non-réclamé** BANQUE unclaimed balance; **~ non-réparti** COMPTA undistributed balance; **~ à nouveau** BOURSE, COMPTA, FIN account rendered, b/d, balance brought down, balance brought forward, balance carried forward; **~ d'ouverture** (ANT *solde de clôture*) BANQUE, COMPTA, FIN opening balance; **~ à payer du principal** COMPTA outstanding principal balance; **~ quotidien à la fermeture** COMPTA daily closing balance; **~ à régler** FISC balance due; **~ reporté** BOURSE b/d, balance brought down, balance brought forward, balance carried forward, COMPTA b/d, balance brought forward, balance brought down, balance carried forward, FIN b/d, balance brought down, balance brought forward, balance carried forward; **~ à reporter** BOURSE, COMPTA, FIN account rendered, b/d, balance brought down, balance brought forward, balance carried forward; **~ de titres minimum en compte** BOURSE minimum maintenance; **~ de trésorerie** COMPTA cash balance; ♦ **à ~ nul** BOURSE at a flat price; **pour ~ de tout compte** COMPTA in full settlement

solder 1. *vt* COM sell off, COMPTA *compte* balance, V&M discount; **2.** *v pron* **se ~ par** COM culminate in

soldes *m pl* BOURSE differences, COM bargain sale, sale goods, V&M bargain sale, clearance, clearance sale; **~ à l'étranger** BANQUE balances abroad; **~ des grands magasins** V&M department store sale; **~ de janvier** V&M January sales

soldeur, -euse *m,f* FIN remainderman

solidairement:[1] **~ responsable** *adj* DROIT severally liable; **~ tenu** *adj* DROIT severally liable

solidairement[2] *adv* FISC jointly

solidarité *f* ECON, POL, RES HUM solidarity

solide[1] *adj* COM hard, robust, *réputation* strong, *société, personne* sound; ♦ **financièrement ~** COM financially sound

solide:[2] **~ en suspension** *m* IND suspended solid

solidement *adv* COM steadily

solidité *f* COM *marché, monnaie* firmness

sollicitations *f pl jarg* POL *d'un groupe de pression* lobbying

solliciter *vt* COM invite, petition, solicit

solution *f* BREVETS *d'un problème* solution, COM remedy; **~ de compromis** COM compromise solution; **~ de fortune** COM makeshift solution

solvabilité *f* COM creditworthiness, COMPTA solvency, DROIT ability to pay, FIN creditworthiness

solvable *adj* COM, FIN creditworthy, solvent

somali *m* COM *langue* Somali

Somalie *f* COM Somalia

somalien, -enne *adj* COM Somali, Somalian

Somalien, -enne *m,f* COM *habitant* Somali, Somalian

sombre *adj* COM, ECON bleak

sommaire *m* COM summary, synopsis

Sommaire: **~ des facteurs d'intrant** *m* ECON *Formule du SGSD* Summary of Input Factors

somme *f* BANQUE, COM sum; **~ en capital** ASSUR, FIN principal sum; **~ en chiffres ronds** COM round

sum; **~ considérable** FIN vast sum; **~ de contrôle** INFO checksum; **~ due** COM amount due; **~ exonérée** FISC exempted sum; **~ forfaitaire** ASSUR lump sum, COM agreed sum, TRANSP *fret ls*, lump sum; **~ globale** ASSUR lump sum, COM blanket amount, FIN lump sum; **~ investie** COMPTA, FIN, FISC amount invested; **~ à investir** BANQUE amount to be invested; **~ jointe** COMMS, FIN amount enclosed; **~ nulle** ECON zero sum; **~ payable** FISC amount payable; **~ reportée** COMPTA amount brought forward; **~ totale** BANQUE, COM grand total, total sum; **~ en toutes lettres** COM sum at length; **~ versée** COM amount paid; **~ versée à l'avance** FIN retainer; **~ à verser** COM amount charged

sommelier, -ière *m,f* RES HUM wine waiter

sommes: **~ déclarées comme revenu** *f pl* FISC income amounts; **~ périodiques** *f pl* FISC periodic amounts; **~ versées** *f pl* COMPTA, FIN monies paid in

sommet *m* POL summit, RES HUM top; **~ économique** ECON, POL economic summit; **~ de l'iceberg** COM tip of the iceberg; ♦ **du ~ à la base** GESTION top-down

Sommet: **~ de Maastricht** *m* COM Maastricht Summit

son *m* INFO sound

sonal *m* MÉDIA signature tune

sondage *m* COM poll, survey; **~ aléatoire** MATH, V&M random sampling; **~ Gallup** POL, V&M *étude de marché* Gallup poll; **~ d'opinion** V&M *étude de marché* opinion poll, opinion polling, straw poll, straw vote; **~ par grappes** V&M cluster sampling; **~ par quota** V&M quota sampling; **~ par segments** V&M *études de marché* cluster sampling; **~ par téléphone** COMMS phone-in poll; **~ en profondeur** POL depth polling

sonder *vt* IND spot-check

sondeur *m* TRANSP depth sounder, *navigation* depth sounder, DS; **~ par ultrasons** (*sondeur U.S.*) TRANSP *navigation* echo sounder, echo-sounding device; **~ U.S.** (*sondeur par ultrasons*) TRANSP *navigation* echo sounder, ESD (*echo-sounding device*)

sonnerie *f* COM alarm; **~ d'alarme** COM alarm bell, burglar alarm

sophisme: **~ de la main d'oeuvre au forfait** *m* RES HUM lump of labor fallacy (*AmE*), lump of labour fallacy (*BrE*)

sophistication *f* COM sophistication

sophistiqué, e *adj* COM sophisticated, INFO advanced

sorte *f* DROIT description; ♦ **de ~ que** COM with the result that

sortie *f* BANQUE (ANT *entrée*) *de fonds* outflow, COM egress, release, COM (ANT *entrée*) COMPTA (ANT *entrée*) ECON (ANT *entrée*) *de fonds*, FIN (ANT *entrée*) *de fonds* outflow, INFO (ANT *entrée*) output, TRANSP (ANT *entrée*) exit; **~ d'argent** BANQUE, COM, COMPTA, ECON, FIN cash outflow;

~ de capitaux ECON capital outflow; **~ de devises étrangères** ECON foreign currency outflow; **~ de données** INFO data output; **~ éducative** PROT SOC field trip; **~ de fonds** (ANT *rentrée de fonds*) BANQUE cash disbursement, cash outflow, outflow of funds, COM outflow of funds, COMPTA cash disbursement, cash outflow, outflow of funds, ECON outflow of funds, FIN cash disbursement, cash outflow, outflow of funds; **~ d'imprimante** ADMIN, INFO print-out; **~ imprimée** ADMIN print-out, INFO computer print-out, print-out; **~ d'ordinateur** INFO computer output; **~ papier** INFO hard copy; **~ de pavillon** TRANSP *navigation* flagging out; **~ de secours** RES HUM emergency exit, fire escape, fire exit; **~ de session** INFO timeout; **~ sur imprimante** INFO computer print-out; **~ sur papier** INFO computer print-out; **~ de trésorerie** BANQUE, COMPTA, FIN cash outflow; ◆ **~ à** IMP/EXP *livraison*, TRANSP *livraison* ex mill, x-mill

sortir *vt* INFO output; ◆ **~ d'affaire** COM, FIN bail out; **~ de l'auberge** COM be out of the woods; **~ dîner** LOISIRS eat out; **~ de l'impasse** COM break the stalemate; **~ du pays** ECON flow out of the country; **~ sur imprimante** ADMIN, INFO print out, ECON flow out, INFO quit, *d'un programme* exit, MÉDIA come out; **~ du système** INFO log off, log out; **~ du tunnel** COM be out of the woods

sou: ne pas avoir un ~ *m infrml* COM not to have a bean (*infrml*)

souche *f* BANQUE stub, LOISIRS passenger coupon; ◆ **par ~** DROIT *descente* per stirpes (*frml*)

souci: ~ du client *m* V&M customer care

soucoupe *f* MATH saucer

Soudan *m* COM Sudan

soudanais[1]**, e** *adj* COM Sudanese

soudanais[2] *m* COM *langue* Sudanese

Soudanais, e *m,f* COM *habitant* Sudanese

soudoyer *vt infrml* COM bribe, POL bribe, buy over, V&M bribe

soudoyeur *m infrml* POL intermediary in any form of political payoff or corruption, bagman (*Canada, pej*)

souffrance: en ~ *loc* COM in abeyance, COMPTA overdue, past-due

souffrant, e *adj* COM ailing

souffrir *vi* ECON suffer

soulager *vt* COM alleviate

soulever *vt* COM bring up

soulignement *m* INFO underline, underscore

souligner *vt* COM highlight, outline, point to, underscore, INFO underline, underscore

soumettre 1. *vt* BREVETS submit, COM file, *application, qch pour approbation* submit, *article* contribute, POL lay, *motion, proposition* propose, table, *opinion* deliver; **~ à** DROIT refer to; **2.** *v pron* **se ~ à** DROIT abide by; ◆ **~ à l'approbation** COM submit for approval; **~ un différend à arbitrage** DROIT, IND submit a dispute to arbitration; **~ une proposition à un comité** COM put a suggestion before a committee; **~ une proposition à une**

commission COM lay a proposal before a committee; **se ~ à la loi** DROIT comply with the law

soumis: ~ à l'impôt *adj* FISC chargeable to tax, taxable; **~ à un rabais** *adj* TRANSP rebateable; **~ aux réserves** *adj* BANQUE reservable; ◆ **être ~ à** COM be subjected to

soumission *f* COM bid, *achat* tender, GESTION bid, POL submission, V&M competitive bid; **~ à un appel d'offres** BOURSE, ECON tap stock tender; **~ cachetée** COMMS sealed tender; **~ concurrentielle** COM, ECON competitive tendering; **~ contraignante** COM binding tender; **~ de couverture de contrat** ASSUR tender to contract cover; **~ d'offre** COM *pour un marché* tender to contract, TTC; **~ des offres** COM bidding, submission of bids; **~ ouverte** COM open tendering; **~ de travaux** INFO job entry; ◆ **faire une ~** COM put up for tender, tender; **~ obligatoire en vue d'adjudication** COM, POL compulsory competitive tendering (*UK*)

soumissionnaire *mf* COM, FIN bidder; **~ le moins disant** *m* BOURSE lowest bidder

soumissionner 1. *vt* COM tender, tender for; **2.** *vi* GESTION bid

soupape: ~ de sûreté du bidon *f* TRANSP drum safety valve, DSV; **~ de sûreté du surchauffeur** *f* TRANSP superheater safety valve, SHSV

souple *adj* COM flexible

souplesse *f* COM adaptability, flexibility

sourçage *m* V&M sourcing

source *f* INFO source; **~ d'emprunts** BANQUE borrowing facility; **~ de l'énergie** COM energy source; **~ de financement** FIN funding source; **~ industrielle** ENVIR industrial source; **~ de pollution** ENVIR, IND pollution emitter, pollution source; **~ de revenus** COMPTA, FISC resource income, source of income; ◆ **de ~ confidentielle** MÉDIA *presse*, POL not for attribution (*AmE, jarg*), on lobby terms (*BrE, jarg*); **de ~ officieuse** MÉDIA *presse*, POL not for attribution (*AmE, jarg*), on lobby terms (*BrE, jarg*); ◆ **à la ~** FISC at source

sourceur, -euse *m,f* V&M sourcing expert

souriant, e *adj* COM *perspective* rosy

souris *f* INFO mouse

sous:[1] **~ -armé** *adj* TRANSP undermanned; **~ -capitalisé** *adj* (ANT *sur-capitalisé*) COM, IND undercapitalized; **~ -divisé** *adj* COM subdivided; **~ -employé** *adj* RES HUM underemployed; **~ -évalué** *adj* FIN undervalued; **~ -jacent** *adj* BOURSE underlying; **~ -mentionné** *adj* (ANT *susmentionné*) COMMS as mentioned below, below; **~ -peuplé** *adj* COM underpopulated

sous:[2] **~ -proportionnellement** *adv* COM under-proportionately

sous:[3] **~ -agent** *m* COM subagent; **~ -caissier** *m* BANQUE assistant cashier (*BrE*), assistant teller (*AmE*); **~ -chapitre m** *m* FISC subchapter m; **~ -chapitre s** *m* FISC subchapter s; **~ -chef** *mf* GESTION, RES HUM assistant manager; **~ -compte**

m COMPTA subsidiary account; ~ **-développement** *m* ECON underdevelopment; ~ **-directeur** *m* BANQUE assistant manager, GESTION assistant manager, deputy director, deputy manager, submanager, POL vice-president, RES HUM assistant manager, deputy director, deputy manager, junior manager, submanager; ~ **-effectif** *m* RES HUM undermanning; ~ **-emploi** *m* (ANT *suremploi*) COM underemployment, ECON subemployment (*jarg*), underemployment, RES HUM underemployment; ~ **-ensemble** *m* COM subset; ~ **-entendu** *m* COM invisible handshake; ~ **-fichier** *m* ADMIN subfile; ~ **-groupe** *m* COM subgroup; ~ **-investissement** *m* BANQUE underinvestment; ~ **-jacent** *m* BOURSE underlying asset; ~ **-locataire** *mf* COM, DROIT, IMMOB sublessee, subtenant, underlessee; ~ **-ministre** *m* ADMIN, POL deputy minister; ~ **-officier** *m* RES HUM, TRANSP petty officer; ~ **-produit** *m* ECON, ENVIR by-product, IND by-product, *produit secondaire* spin-off, V&M by-product; ~ **-programme** *m* INFO routine, subprogram, subroutine; ~ **-receveur général** *m* ADMIN, FIN *Can* Deputy Receiver General; ~ **-répertoire** *m* INFO subdirectory; ~ **-secrétaire** *mf* RES HUM under-secretary; ~ **-secteur** *m* IND subsector; ~ **-titre** *m* MÉDIA *presse* caption; ~ **-total** *m* MATH subtotal; ~ **-traitant** *m* COM, RES HUM subcontractor

sous:[4] ~ **-absorption** *f* COMPTA underabsorption; ~ **-activité** *f* ECON subactivity; ~ **-affectation** *f* POL suballotment; ~ **-capacité** *f* (ANT *surcapacité*) COM, ECON, IND undercapacity; ~ **-consommation** *f* ECON underconsumption; ~ **-déclaration** *f* FISC underdeclaration; ~ **-estimation** *f* BOURSE overwriting, COM underestimation; ~ **-évaluation** *f* COM, ECON undervaluation, FISC underassessment; ~ **-hypothèque** *f* BANQUE submortgage; ~ **-imposition** *f* FISC underassessment; ~ **-imputation** *f* COMPTA underabsorption; ~ **-imputation des frais généraux** *f* COMPTA underrecovery of overhead costs; ~ **-licence** *f* BREVETS, COM sublicence (*BrE*), sublicense (*AmE*); ~ **-location** *f* COM, DROIT, IMMOB sublease, subleasing, sublet, subletting, subtenancy; ~ **-optimisation** *f* COM, ECON, FIN suboptimization; ~ **-production** *f* (ANT *surproduction*) ECON, IND underproduction; ~ **-représentation** *f* (ANT *sur-représentation*) V&M *sur marché* underrepresentation; ~ **-rubrique** *f* INFO subentry; ~ **-traitance** *f* COM contracting out, subcontract, subcontracting, PROT SOC *de services au secteur privé* contracting out, RES HUM distancing, subcontracting; ~ **-utilisation** *f* FIN *des crédits* underrun; ~ **-valeur** *f* (ANT *survaleur*) COMPTA negative goodwill

sous:[5] ~ **-absorber** *vt* COMPTA underabsorb; ~ **-affréter** TRANSP subcharter; ~ **-employer** COM underuse, COMPTA underspend; ~ **-entendre** COM imply; ~ **-estimer** COM underestimate; ~ **-évaluer** COMPTA underassess; ~ **-imposer** FISC undertax;

~ **-imputer** COMPTA underabsorb; ~ **-payer** COM underpay; ~ **-produire** (ANT *surproduire*) ECON, IND underproduce; ~ **-rémunérer** COM underpay; ~ **-représenter** V&M underrepresent; ~ **-traiter** COM contract out, subcontract, farm out, DROIT, RES HUM subcontract; ~ **-utiliser** COM underutilize

sous[6] *prép* (ANT *sur*) COM under; ◆ ~ **l'angle de** COM in terms of; ~ **aucune condition** COM not on any terms; ~ **caution** DROIT on bail; ~ **contrôle étranger** COM foreign-controlled, foreign-owned; ~ **forme de projet** DROIT in draft form; ~ **forme provisoire** DROIT in draft form; ~ **forme de subvention** FIN in grant form; ~ **forme de tableau** ADMIN, COM in tabulated form; ~ **garantie** COM under guarantee; ~ **la forme de** COM in the form of; ~ **la main** COM ready to hand; ~ **le pont** (ANT *sur le pont*) TRANSP *navigation* b/d, below deck; ~ **les auspices de** COM under the umbrella of; ~ **les réserves d'usage** BOURSE if, as and when, DROIT with the usual proviso; ~ **licence** BREVETS, DROIT licensed, under licence (*BrE*), under license (*AmE*); ~ **pli cacheté** COM in a sealed envelope; ~ **pli séparé** COMMS under separate cover; ~ **réglementation fédérale** FISC federally regulated; ~ **réserve d'approbation** COM, V&M subject to approval; ~ **réserve de changement** COM subject to change; ~ **réserve de** COM subject to; ~ **réserve d'émission** BOURSE when distributed; ~ **réserve que** COM provided that; ~ **serment** DROIT under oath; ~ **60 jours** COM under 60 days; ~ **tension** INFO *ligne* up (*infrml*); ~ **toutes réserves** ASSUR without prejudice, WP

souscripteur, -trice *m,f* ASSUR policyholder, proposer, underwriter, U/W, BANQUE drawer, BOURSE *d'actions* applicant, COM contributor of capital, subscriber; ~ **d'action à découvert** BOURSE uncovered call writer, uncovered writer; ~ **par complaisance** FIN accommodation maker, accommodation party; ~ **de soutien** FIN standby underwriter

souscripteurs: ~ **de second rang** *m pl* BOURSE mezzanine bracket

souscription *f* BOURSE, MÉDIA, POL subscription; ~ **d'actions** BOURSE application for shares, subscription for shares; ~ **à des actions** BOURSE subscription for shares; ~ **excédentaire** BOURSE oversubscription; ~ **négociée** BOURSE negotiated underwriting; ~ **d'obligations** BOURSE bond underwriting; ~ **privilégiée** BOURSE subscription privilege; ~ **surpassée** BOURSE oversubscription; ◆ ~ **à** COM application for

souscrire *vt* ASSUR write business, *assurance* take out, BOURSE *à des actions* subscribe, FIN *prêt* apply for; ~ **à** BOURSE, DROIT *à un accord de confidentialité* subscribe; ◆ ~ **un billet à ordre** FIN make a promissory note; ~ **à une émission** FIN subscribe to an issue; ~ **à un emprunt** BANQUE, COM apply for a loan, subscribe for a loan; ~ **à une police d'assurance** ASSUR take out a policy

souscrit, e *m* BOURSE underwritten; ◆ **totalement ~** BOURSE *émission* fully distributed

soustracteur: **~ de valeur** *m* ECON value subtractor

soustraire 1. *vt* MATH subtract; **2.** *vi* COM contract out; **3.** *v pron* **se ~ à** COM back out of, FISC *impôt* evade; **se ~ à la justice** DROIT abscond

soutage *m* TRANSP bunkering

soute *f* TRANSP *navigation* bunker; **~ à bagages** TRANSP *avion* belly hold; **~ fixe** TRANSP *navigation* permanent bunker, PB; **~ permanente** TRANSP *maritime* permanent bunker, PB

soutenir *vt* BANQUE aid, BOURSE *marché* hold, COM back up, *pour défendre* back, bolster, DROIT uphold, ECON aid, *devise* support, *livre* prop up, *prix* buy, sustain, POL aid, back

soutenu, e *adj* BOURSE *marché* buoyant, COM *intérêt* continuing, ECON buoyant, undamped, FIN buoyant; ◆ **~ financièrement par les pouvoirs publics** FIN, POL government-supported; **~ par l'État** FIN, POL government-backed, government-supported

soutien *m* COM backing, backup, *financier, moral* support, FISC, INFO support; **~ à l'encadrement** GESTION, RES HUM management support; **~ de famille** ECON, PROT SOC breadwinner; **~ financier** ECON, FIN, POL financial assistance, financial backing, financial support; **~ au management** GESTION, RES HUM management support; **~ du marché** V&M market support; **~ des prix** BOURSE pegging, FIN price support; **~ des prix agricoles** ECON agricultural price support; **~ publicitaire** V&M advertising support; **~ au revenu** PROT SOC income support *(UK)*

soutirer: **~ des renseignements de qn** *loc* COM wring information out of sb *(infrml)*

souverain *m* COM, POL sovereign

souveraineté: **~ du consommateur** *f* ECON, V&M consumer sovereignty

speaker, -erine *m* MÉDIA *radio, télévision* announcer

spécial, e *adj* COM ad hoc, one-off

spécialement *adv* COM esp., especially

spécialisation *f* COM, RES HUM specialization; **~ des exercices** COMPTA accrual accounting; **~ du poste** RES HUM job specialization; **~ réussie** RES HUM niche; **~ verticale** COM vertical specialization

spécialisé, e *adj* COM *pour usage particulier* dedicated, IND specialized, INFO dedicated, RES HUM semiskilled

spécialiser: **se ~ dans** *v pron* COM specialize in

spécialiste *mf* COM specialist; **~ en débogage** *m* INFO troubleshooter; **~ de l'environnement** *m* ENVIR environmental scanner; **~ du marché automobile** *m* COM car market watcher; **~ en marketing** *m* RES HUM, V&M marketeer; **~ du matériel** *m* INFO hardware specialist; **~ en obligations** *m* BOURSE bond specialist; **~ d'obligations** *m* BOURSE bond specialist; **~ des questions financières** *m* FIN financial sophisti-

cate; **~ des services de banque d'affaires** *m* BANQUE investment banker *(US)*, merchant banker *(UK)*; **~ des services de banque d'investissement** *m* BANQUE investment banker *(US)*, merchant banker *(UK)*; **~ technique des ventes à l'exportation** *m* IMP/EXP company technical specialist export salesman; **~ de la valeur** *m* BOURSE specialist

spécialistes: **~ en valeurs du Trésor** *m pl* *(SVT)* BOURSE gilt-edged market makers *(GEMMS)*

spécialité *f* COM speciality; **~ boursière** BOURSE security market line

spécification *f* MATH specification; **~ de changement notifié** *(SCN)* TRANSP *aviation* master change, specification change notice *(SCN)*; **~ du navire** TRANSP ship specification

spécificité: **~ de l'actif** *f* ECON, FIN asset specificity

spécifié, e *adj* COM specified

spécifiée: **personne ~** *f* FISC specified person

spécifier *vt* COM *compte* state

spécifique *adj* COM specific; **~ à un pays** ECON *aide* country-specific

spécimen *m* COM specimen copy, MÉDIA *presse, édition* presentation copy, press copy; **~ gratuit** COM, MÉDIA complimentary copy; **~ de signature** BANQUE specimen signature

spéculateur, -trice *m,f* BOURSE speculator, FIN gunslinger; **~ à la baisse** *(ANT spéculateur à la hausse)* BOURSE bear, bear operator, bear speculator; **~ expérimenté** BOURSE wolf *(jarg)*; **~ habituel** BOURSE trader; **~ à la hausse** *(ANT spéculateur à la baisse)* BOURSE bull, bull operator, bull speculator; **~ immobilier** IMMOB property speculator; **~ en obligations** BOURSE bond trader; **~ sur la journée** BOURSE scalper *(US, infrml)*

spéculatif, -ive *adj* BOURSE speculative

spéculation *f* BOURSE *prix des actions* speculation, staggism, COM *vague* speculation; **~ à la baisse** *(ANT spéculation à la hausse)* BOURSE bear campaign, bear speculation, bearing the market; **~ à la hausse** *(ANT spéculation à la baisse)* BOURSE bull buying, bull campaign, bull speculation; **~ à la journée** BOURSE day trading

spéculer *vi* BOURSE take a flier, BOURSE buy a bull *(jarg)*, COM speculate; ◆ **~ à la baisse** *(ANT spéculer à la hausse)*, BOURSE bear, go a bear; **~ au comptant** BOURSE bargain for cash; **~ à la hausse** *(ANT spéculer à la baisse)* BOURSE bull, go a bull; **~ à terme** BOURSE bargain for account

sphère *f* COM *d'activité, d'influence* sphere of activity; **~ d'impression** ADMIN typewriter ball

spirale *f* ECON spiral; **~ ascendante** COM upward spiral; **~ descendante** COM downward spiral; **~ inflationniste** ECON galloping inflation, runaway inflation, spiralling inflation, inflationary spiral; **~ inflationniste prix-salaires** ECON wage-price inflation spiral; **~ prix-impôts** ECON wage-tax spiral; **~ prix-salaires** ECON wage-price spiral; **~ des salaires et des prix** ECON wage-price spiral

spiritueux: **les ~** *m pl* COM wet stock

sponsor *m* COM, LOISIRS, MÉDIA sponsor

sponsoring *m* FIN, LOISIRS *sport* sponsorship

sponsorisation *f* V&M sponsorship

sponsoriser *vt* COM, LOISIRS *sport*, MÉDIA sponsor

spontané, e *adj* RES HUM on spec (*infrml*), on speculation

spooling *m* INFO spooling; ◆ **faire un ~** INFO spool

sporadique *adj* COM sporadic

sport *m* COM sport

spot *m* COM ad, advert, advertisement, commercial, MÉDIA, V&M *radio, TV* ad, advert, advertisement, commercial; **~ publicitaire** COM ad, advert, advertisement, commercial, MÉDIA, V&M *radio, TV* ad, advert, advertisement, commercial

spouling *m* INFO spooling

spread *m* BOURSE spread; **~ baissier** (*ANT spread haussier*) BOURSE bear spread, bearish spread; **~ calendaire** BOURSE calendar spread, horizontal spread, time spread; **~ haussier** (*ANT spread baissier*) BOURSE bull spread, bullish spread; **~ horizontal** BOURSE calendar spread, horizontal spread, time spread; **~ TED** BOURSE TED spread; **~ vertical** BOURSE price spread, vertical spread

spreader *m* TRANSP spreader

square *m* BOURSE square

Sri Lanka *m* COM Sri Lanka

sri-lankais *adj* COM Sri Lankan

Sri-Lankais, e *m,f* COM *habitant* Sri Lankan

SS *abrév France* (*Sécurité sociale*) PROT SOC, RES HUM ≈ NHS (*UK*) (*National Health Service*)

SSCI *abrév* (*société de services et de conseils en informatique*) INFO computer consultancy firm, software and computer services company

SSII *abrév* (*société de services d'ingénierie informatique*) INFO computer services company

stabilisateur *m* ECON, TRANSP *navigation* stabilizer; **~ à ailerons** TRANSP *navigation* fin-type stabilizer, FIN; **~ automatique** ECON *dépenses publiques* automatic stabilizer, built-in stabilizer, POL automatic stabilizer; **~ incorporé** ECON built-in stabilizer; **~ à réservoir** TRANSP *navigation* tank-type stabilizer

stabilisation *f* BOURSE pegging, ECON leveling-off (*AmE*), levelling-off (*BrE*), stabilization; **~ des prix** ECON price stabilization; **~ des salaires** RES HUM wage stabilization

stabiliser 1. *vt* ECON peg, stabilize, FIN peg; **2.** *v pron* **se ~** COM *tendance, graphique* flatten out, ECON level off, level out, stabilize, RES HUM level out

stabilité *f* ECON, POL, TRANSP *d'un navire* stability; **~ financière** ECON, FIN financial stability; **~ politique** COM, POL political stability; **~ des prix** ECON price stability; **~ walrassienne** ECON Walrasian stability

stable *adj* BOURSE *marché* flat, COM stable

stade *m* COM stage; ◆ **au ~ des épreuves** MÉDIA at proof stage

stage *m* PROT SOC vocational training, RES HUM placement; **~ d'accueil** COM, RES HUM induction course; **~ d'assertivité** PROT SOC, RES HUM assertiveness training; **~ en centre de formation** RES HUM on-the-job training, OJT; **~ de direction d'entreprise** RES HUM management training; **~ en entreprise** RES HUM traineeship; **~ de formation dans l'entreprise** RES HUM in-service training; **~ de formation sur le lieu de travail** RES HUM in-service training; **~ de formation sur site** RES HUM in-service training; **~ de perfectionnement** RES HUM advanced training; **~ de recyclage** RES HUM booster training, retraining course; **~ à temps complet** RES HUM residential course

stagflation *f* ECON stagflation

stagiaire *mf* ADMIN, RES HUM trainee

stagnant, e *adj* BOURSE *marché* sluggish, ECON stagnant

stagnation *f* ECON stagnation

stagner *vi* ECON stagnate

stand *m* V&M *dans une foire, une exposition* stand

standard¹ *adj* COM *modèle* standard

standard² *m* COM, DROIT standard; **~ budgétaire** COM, COMPTA, FIN budget standard; **~ D2MAC** COM D2-MAC standard; **~ d'égalité** POL equality standard; **~ téléphonique** COMMS switchboard; **~ de vie** ECON standard of living

standardisation *f* COM, COMPTA, DROIT standardization, IND commonality, V&M standardization

standardiser *vt* DROIT, V&M standardize

standardiste *mf* RES HUM switchboard operator

standing *m* ECON standard of living, FIN credit rating, PROT SOC social status

stands *m pl* BOURSE stands

star *f* *infrml* COM high-flier, high-flyer; **~ du moment** MÉDIA star

starie *f* TRANSP *maritime* layday

staries: **~ définies** *f pl* TRANSP *navigation* definite laytime; **~ gagnées** *f pl* TRANSP *maritime* laytime saved, *navigation* all working time saved, working time saved; **~ habituelles** *f pl* TRANSP *navigation* normal laytime; **~ moyennes** *f pl* TRANSP *navigation* average laytime; **~ non-définies** *f pl* TRANSP *maritime* indefinite laytime; **~ non-réversibles** *f pl* TRANSP nonreversible laytime; **~ réversibles** *f pl* TRANSP *maritime, charte-partie* reversible lay days

station: **~ balnéaire** *f* COM seaside resort; **~ d'épuration** *f* ENVIR purification plant; **~ d'épuration des eaux d'égout** *f* ENVIR sewage treatment works, wastewater treatment works; **~ d'épuration des eaux usées** *f* ENVIR sewage treatment plant, wastewater treatment plant; **~ de montagne** *f* LOISIRS mountain resort; **~ de radio** *f* MÉDIA radio station; **~ de radio commerciale** *f* MÉDIA *radio* commercial radio station; **~ -service** *f* TRANSP gas station (*AmE*), petrol station (*BrE*), service station; **~ de taxis** *f* TRANSP taxi rank, taxi stand (*AmE*); **~ de traitement des déchets** *f*

ENVIR waste treatment plant; **~ de travail** *f* INFO workstation

stationnaire *adj* ECON stagnant, static

stationnement *m* COM car parking

statique[1] *adj* ECON static

statique:[2] **~ comparative** *f* ECON comparative statics

statisticien, -enne *m,f* MATH statistician

statistique[1] *adj* MATH statistical

statistique:[2] **~ -test** *m* ECON test statistic

statistique[3] *f* MATH statistics; **~ déductive** MATH inferential statistics; **~ démographique** MATH, POL population statistics; **~ descriptive** MATH descriptive statistics; **~ Durbin-Watson** MATH DW statistic, Durbin-Watson statistic; **~ F** MATH F statistic; **~ paramétrique** MATH parametric statistics

statistiquement: **~ significatif** *adj* MATH statistically significant

statistiques: **~ de banc d'essai** *f pl* MATH benchmark statistics; **~ du chômage** *f pl* RES HUM unemployment statistics; **~ commerciales** *f pl* COM trade returns; **~ de l'emploi** *f pl* ECON, POL employment figures; **~ non-paramétriques** *f pl* MATH nonparametric statistics; **~ officielles** *f pl* MATH statistical returns; **~ portuaires** *f pl* IMP/EXP, TRANSP port statistics; **~ de publicité** *f pl* V&M advertising statistics; **~ sur les ventes** *f pl* V&M sales returns

Statistiques: **~ du commerce extérieur** *f pl* ECON, POL Overseas Trade Statistics (*UK*), OTS (*UK*)

stature *f* RES HUM caliber (*AmE*), calibre (*BrE*)

statut *m* COM bye-law, bylaw, status, DROIT statute, INFO status; **~ de cadre** RES HUM staff status; **~ d'entreprise** RES HUM corporate status (*UK*); **~ fiduciaire** BOURSE trustee status; **~ fiscal** ADMIN, FISC tax status; **~ des immigrés** DROIT migrant status; **~ légal** DROIT legal status; **~ personnel** RES HUM personal statute; **~ professionnel** RES HUM professional status; **~ résidentiel** BANQUE *d'un déposant* residency; **~ socio-économique** ECON socioeconomic status; **~ de solde minime** COMPTA minor balance status; **~ temporaire** DROIT temporary status; **~ unique** RES HUM single status

statutaire *adj* DROIT intra vires, statutory

statuts *m pl* DROIT memorandum and articles, memorandum of association, *société à responsabilité limitée* articles of association, *société commerciale* articles of incorporation, POL constitution; **~ et règlements** DROIT rules and regulations

Sté *abrév* (*société*) COM, ECON Co. (*company*)

stellage *m* BOURSE call and put option, put and call

sténo *abrév infrml* ADMIN (*sténographe*) shorthand writer, stenographer, ADMIN (*sténographie*) shorthand, stenography

sténodactylo *mf* ADMIN shorthand typist

sténographe *mf* (*sténo*) ADMIN shorthand writer, stenographer

sténographie *f* (*sténo*) ADMIN shorthand, stenography

ster. *abrév* (*sterling*) COM stg (*sterling*)

stérile *adj* COM fruitless

stérilisation *f* FIN sterilization

sterling *m* (*ster.*) COM sterling (*stg*); **~ M3** FIN sterling M3

steward *m* TRANSP flight attendant, steward

stimulant[1], **e** *adj* RES HUM stimulating

stimulant[2] *m* COM booster, incentive, stimulus, RES HUM, V&M incentive; **~ compétitif** ECON, V&M competitive stimulus; **~ salarial** RES HUM wage incentive

stimulants *m pl* RES HUM staff incentive

stimulation: **~ financière** *f* FIN financial incentive

stimuler *vt* COM *confiance, support, demande* stimulate, *efficacité* boost, ECON stimulate; ◆ **~ les exportations** IMP/EXP be a stimulus for exports

stimuli: **~ fiscaux** *m pl* FISC tax stimuli

stipulation *f* COM, DROIT provision; **~ dérogatoire** DROIT derogatory stipulation

stipulations *f pl* DROIT provisions; **~ contractuelles** DROIT contract specifications; **~ d'un contrat** DROIT contract specifications

stipuler *vt* COM *condition* stipulate, DROIT *dans un acte, un contrat* lay down

stock *m* COM stockpile, V&M *en magasin* stock; **~ de base** COM baseload; **~ comptable** BOURSE book inventory; **~ conjoncturel** BOURSE, ECON cyclical stock; **~ en cours** BOURSE current stock; **~ au début de l'exercice** COMPTA beginning inventory, initial inventory, opening inventory; **~ de dépannage** COM safety bank; **~ disponible** COM stock in hand; **~ de fabrication** IND manufacturing inventory; **~ fermé** V&M closed stock; **~ en fin d'exercice** BOURSE closing stock; **~ final** BOURSE closing stock; **~ initial** COMPTA beginning inventory, initial inventory, opening inventory; **~ de marchandises** COM, COMPTA, V&M merchandise inventory; **~ minimal** COM baseload; **~ -outil** BOURSE base stock; **~ d'ouverture** COMPTA beginning inventory, initial inventory, opening inventory; **~ à l'ouverture de l'exercice** COMPTA beginning inventory, initial inventory, opening inventory; **~ de précaution** BOURSE, COM, ECON, IND safety stock; **~ principal** COM staple stock; **~ réel** COM actual inventory (*AmE*), actual stock (*BrE*); **~ de régularisation** ECON, TRANSP buffer stock; **~ régulateur** ECON buffer stock; **~ de sécurité** BOURSE, COM, ECON, IND safety stock; **~ tampon** BOURSE, COM safety stock, ECON buffer stock, safety stock, IND safety stock; **~ volé** COM hot stock (*infrml*); ◆ **avoir en ~** COM stock; **en ~** COM, ECON, V&M in stock

stockage *m* COM stockpiling, INFO, TRANSP storage; **~ des archives** ADMIN archive storage; **~ commercial** TRANSP commercial storage; **~ de données** INFO data storage; **~ d'informations**

INFO information storage; **~ de réduction des émissions** ENVIR emission reductions banking; **~ en vrac** COM bulk storage

stocker *vt* COM stockpile, INFO store, *bandes* save, TRANSP store

Stockholm *n pr* COM Stockholm

stockiste *mf* BOURSE stockist (*UK*); **~ attitré** *m* V&M appointed stockist

stocks *m pl* COMPTA, IND inventory, stocks; **~ existants** TRANSP goods on hand, GDH, GOH; **~ marchands** COM commercial stocks; **~ de report** COM carry-over stocks; **~ reportés** COM carry-over stocks

store *m* COM awning

straddle *m* BOURSE straddle

strangle *m* BOURSE strangle; **~ sur option à delta neutre** BOURSE delta-neutral straddles, delta-neutral strangle

strap *m* BOURSE strap, strap option

strapontins *m pl* LOISIRS *théâtre* whiskey seats (*US, infrml*)

stratagème: **~ frauduleux** *m* FISC *fraude fiscale* scheme

strate: **~ de marché** *f* V&M market segment

stratégie *f* COM game plan, strategy; **~ d'acheter et de conserver** BOURSE *des actions, des titres* buy-and-hold strategy; **~ d'acheter et de vendre** BOURSE *d'une participation* buy-and-write strategy; **~ des affaires** COM, ECON, GESTION business strategy; **~ d'arbitrage inversée** BOURSE reverse conversion; **~ de bas prix** V&M *marketing* penetration pricing; **~ des cadres** GESTION, RES HUM executive manpower strategy; **~ commerciale** COM, ECON business strategy, commercial strategy, trade strategy, GESTION business strategy, V&M marketing, marketing strategy, trade strategy; **~ de communication** COMMS communication strategy, V&M *publicité* copy strategy; **~ de conception** TRANSP *d'un navire* ship design strategy; **~ concurrentielle** COM, ECON, V&M competitive strategy; **~ de couverture** BOURSE, FIN hedging strategy; **~ de création** V&M *publicité* creative strategy; **~ de croissance** COM, ECON expansion strategy, growth strategy; **~ de défense** COM defensive strategy; **~ défensive** COM defensive strategy; **~ de différenciation** V&M differentiation strategy (*UK*); **~ de diversification** V&M diversification strategy; **~ d'écart sur livraisons** BOURSE interdelivery spread; **~ d'écart sur matières premières** BOURSE intercommodity spread, intra-commodity spread; **~ économique** COM, ECON, POL economic strategy; **~ économique de rechange** ECON, POL alternative economic strategy; **~ d'ensemble** COM global strategy; **~ de l'entreprise** COM company strategy, corporate strategy, GESTION corporate strategic planning; **~ d'entreprise** COM, ECON business strategy, GESTION business strategy, strategic planning; **~ d'expansion** COM, ECON expansion strategy; **~ d'exploitation** TRANSP operating strat-

egy; **~ financière** COM, FIN financial strategy; **~ financière à moyen terme** ECON medium-term financial strategy; **~ fiscale** FISC tax strategy; **~ de fret** TRANSP freight strategy; **~ informatique** INFO computer strategy; **~ d'investissement** BOURSE investment strategy, FIN capital investment strategy, capital strategy, investment strategy; **~ d'investissement à long terme** BOURSE buy-and-hold strategy; **~ des investissements** BOURSE, FIN investment mix; **~ de marché** V&M marketing strategy; **~ marketing** V&M marketing strategy; **~ de marque** FIN, V&M brand strategy; **~ de milking** V&M milking strategy; **~ -minimax** ECON minimax strategy; **~ de la monnaie parallèle** ECON parallel currency strategy; **~ de négociation** BOURSE, COM, RES HUM negotiation strategy; **~ d'option** BOURSE option spread; **~ d'option alligator** BANQUE, BOURSE, FIN alligator spread; **~ Pac-Man** FIN Pac-Man strategy (*US*); **~ de participation** ECON, FIN, GESTION profit-taking strategy; **~ passagers** TRANSP passenger strategy; **~ du potentiel humain** RES HUM staff strategy; **~ de prise de bénéfices** ECON, FIN, GESTION profit-taking strategy; **~ proactive** COM, GESTION, POL proactive strategy; **~ de produit** COM, V&M product strategy; **~ de profit** FIN, GESTION profit strategy; **~ publicitaire** V&M advertising tactics; **~ réactive** COM reactive strategy; **~ sectorielle** GESTION sectoral strategy; **~ de segmentation** V&M segmentation strategy (*UK*); **~ de survie** COM survival strategy; **~ tarifaire** TRANSP rates strategy; **~ de l'utilisateur** COM, V&M user strategy; **~ de vol** TRANSP flight strategy; **~ voyageurs** TRANSP passenger strategy

stratégique *adj* GESTION strategic

stratification: **~ sociale** *f* PROT SOC social stratification

stress: **le ~ des cadres** *m* RES HUM executive stress

strip *m* BOURSE strip

structuration *f* COM structuring

structure *f* COM structure; **~ arborescente** INFO tree structure; **~ en arbre** INFO tree structure; **~ d'autorité** COM authority structure; **~ du capital** COM capitalization, ECON capital structure, capitalization; **~ en capital complexe** ECON complex capital structure; **~ du commerce extérieur par type de produit** ECON commodity trade structure; **~ commerciale** COM business organization; **~ du conteneur** TRANSP container frame; **~ des coûts** COM, COMPTA, FIN cost structure; **~ des crédits** COMPTA, POL vote structure; **~ de données** INFO data structure; **~ de l'entreprise** COM company structure, corporate structure; **~ du financement de l'entreprise** COMPTA capital structure; **~ financière** COM, FIN financial structure; **~ fiscale** ECON, FISC tax structure; **~ fonctionnelle** COM line function; **~ géographique du commerce extérieur** ECON geographical trade structure; **~ de gestion** GESTION management structure; **~ en grille** COM, FIN grid structure; **~ de groupe** COM group structure;

~ hiérarchique COM authority structure, line organization, GESTION, RES HUM managerial structure; **~ du marché** COM structure of the market, ECON market form, market structure, V&M market structure; **~ matricielle** GESTION, MATH matrix organization; **~ mixte** GESTION, RES HUM line and staff organization; **~ nationale des filiales** COM *au sein d'une société* national subsidiary structure; **~ de la négociation** RES HUM bargaining structure; **~ d'organisation** COM, GESTION organization structure; **~ du passif financier** FIN financial leverage ratio; **~ de prix** ECON, FIN, V&M price structure; **~ de programme** COM program structure (*AmE*), programme structure (*BrE*); **~ en pyramide** COM pyramiding; **~ des salaires** ECON salary structure, RES HUM salary structure, wage structure; **~ staff and line** RES HUM staff and line structure; **~ syndicale** RES HUM union structure; **~ tarifaire** TRANSP rates structure; **~ temporelle des taux d'intérêts** ECON term structure of interest rates; ◆ **à ~ non-imposée** INFO free-format

structuré, e *adj* COM structured

structurer *vt* COM structure; **~ en holdings** COM pyramid

studio *m* COM studio; **~ de création** V&M hot shop (*jarg*)

stupéfiant, e *adj* FIN staggering

style *m* GESTION *de gestion*, INFO style; **~ de direction** COM leadership, GESTION managerial style; **~ directorial** COM, GESTION management style; **~ de l'entreprise** COM house style; **~ de gestion** COM, GESTION management style; **~ maison** COM house style; **~ managérial** COM, GESTION management style; **~ de vie** COM life-style; ◆ **de ~ occidental** ECON western-style

styliser *vt* COM stylize

styliste *mf* COM stylist

stylo: **~ à bille** *m* ADMIN ball point; **~ optique** *m* IND, INFO, V&M bar code reader, bar code scanner; **~ à plume** *m* COM fountain pen

subalterne *m* RES HUM underling, COM adjunct, jnr, jr, junior

subdivisé, e *adj* COM subdivided

subdivision *f* COM subdivision

subir *vt* BREVETS *dommage* suffer, COM undergo, DROIT *perte, dommage* sustain, ECON suffer; ◆ **~ une perte** BOURSE take a loss, DROIT suffer loss; **~ un préjudice** DROIT suffer loss; **~ la pression de** COM come under pressure from

subjectif, -ive *adj* COM subjective

subordonné[1]**, e** *adj* COM down-the-line

subordonné[2]**, e** *m,f* COM junior, subordinate

subordonner *vt* COM subordinate

subsides *m pl* BOURSE subsidiary dividends

subsidiaire *adj* COM subsidiary, FIN collateral

subsidiarité *f* COM, ECON, POL subsidiarity

subsistance *f* FISC support, PROT SOC, RES HUM subsistence

substance *f* IND substance; **~ biodégradable** ENVIR biodegradable substance; **~ dangereuse** ENVIR dangerous substance, hazardous substance; **~ hygroscopique** ENVIR hygroscopic substance; **~ nocive** ENVIR hazardous substance; **~ polluante dangereuse** TRANSP hazardous polluting substance, HPS; **~ radioactive** ENVIR radioactive substance; **~ toxique** ENVIR dangerous substance

substantiellement *adv* COM substantially

substituer *vt* COM substitute; ◆ **~ une chose à une autre** COM substitute one thing for another

substitut *m* ECON, IND substitute product

substitution *f* ECON substitution; **~ d'importation** IMP/EXP import substitution

subterfuge *m* FISC gimmick; **~ fiscal** FISC tax gimmick

subvenir: **~ aux besoins de** *loc* FISC support

subvention *f* BOURSE bounty, ECON grant, FIN grant, subsidy; **~ accordée par la ville** *f* COM City Grant (*UK*); **~ agricole** *f* ECON agricultural subsidy; **~ aux agriculteurs** *f* ECON, POL farm subsidy; **~ à l'agriculture** *f* ECON agricultural subsidy; **~ d'aide** *f* POL proportionate grant; **~ catégorique** *f* POL categorical grant; **~ à un chantier naval** *f* TRANSP *de l'État* shipyard subsidy; **~ à la construction ou à l'exploitation d'un navire** *f* TRANSP ship subsidy; **~ de contrepartie** *f* FIN matching grant; **~ corrective** *f* ECON, POL corrective subsidy; **~ démographique** *f* RES HUM demogrant; **~ de l'État** *f* ECON government grant, state subsidy, POL grant-in-aid; **~ de l'État aux collectivités locales** *f* ECON rate support grant (*UK*), RSG (*UK*); **~ de l'État à l'éducation** *f pl* POL, PROT SOC hard money (*jarg*); **~ d'exploitation** *f* COMPTA operating grant, TRANSP operating subsidy; **~ à l'exportation** *f* IMP/EXP export subsidy; **~ à l'exportation agricole** *f* ECON, IMP/EXP agricultural export subsidy; **~ à l'exportation de produits agricoles** *f* ECON, IMP/EXP agricultural export subsidy; **~ financière** *f* ECON grant-in-aid, proportionate grant; **~ à la formation dans l'industrie** *f* FIN industrial training grant; **~ à une industrie** *f* ECON, RES HUM featherbedding; **~ d'investissement** *f* COMPTA investment grant; **~ à la production** *f* ECON *agricole* producer subsidy; **~ proportionnelle** *f* ECON grant-in-aid, proportionate grant; **~ publique pour la recherche** *f* FIN government research grant; **~ pour la recherche** *f* FISC research grant; **~ de recherches** *f* FISC research grant; **~ remboursable sous condition** *f* FIN forgivable loan; **~ des salaires** *f* ECON wage subsidy; **~ sans condition** *f* FIN federal finance (*US*), unconditional grant; **~ selon Pigou** *f* ECON Pigouvian subsidy; **~ de soutien** *f* POL sustaining grant; **~ de soutien de taux** *f* ECON rate support grant (*UK*), RSG (*UK*)

subventionné, e *adj* COM, FIN subsidized; **~ par l'État** ECON, POL grant-aided, grant-maintained, state-aided; ◆ **~ par les pouvoirs publics** ECON,

FIN, POL government-financed, government-funded

subventionnement *m* ECON, RES HUM featherbedding

subventionner *vt* BANQUE *industrie, entreprise* aid

succédané *m* COM ersatz, ECON, IND *souvent péjoratif* substitute product; ~ **parfait** ECON perfect substitute

succéder: ~ à *vt* COM take over from

succès: ~ **constant** *m* COM continued success; ~ **d'estime** *m* LOISIRS *théâtre* critical success; ~ **ininterrompu** *m* COM continued success; ~ **de librairie** *m* MÉDIA best seller, page-turner; ~ **permanent** *m* COM continued success; ◆ à ~ MÉDIA leggy (*jarg*)

successeur *m* COM successor

successif, -ive *adj* COM consecutive, successive

succession *f* DROIT inheritance, FISC estate; ~ **ab intestat** DROIT intestacy; ~ **consécutives** *f pl* FISC quick successions; ~ **ordinale** MATH ordinal scale; ~ **d'utilisation des sols** IMMOB land-use succession; ~ **vacante** COM estate in abeyance

successivement *adv* COM seriatim (*frml*)

succursale *f* ADMIN branch office, BO, BANQUE *d'une banque* agency, branch, *d'un établissement de crédit* branch, COM branch office, suboffice, BO, branch operation, *magasin, banque* branch; ~ **bancaire** BANQUE bank branch; ~ **de banque** BANQUE bank branch, unit banking; ~ **centrale** BANQUE central branch, hub branch; ~ à **l'étranger** IMP/EXP *commerce direct à l'exportation* overseas branch; ~ **extraterritoriale** BANQUE, FIN, FISC offshore banking unit, OBU; ~ **offshore** BANQUE, FIN, FISC offshore banking unit, OBU; ~ **principale** BANQUE main branch

sucre *m* COM sucre

sud[1] *adj* TRANSP *route, ligne de métro* southbound; ~ **-africain** COM South African; ~ **-américain** COM South American; ~ **-coréen** COM South Korean; ~ **-est** TRANSP southeast, southeastern

sud[2] *m* COM south; ~ **-est** COM, TRANSP southeast, SE; ~ **-ouest** COM, TRANSP southwest, SW; ◆ **du** ~ COM southern

Sud-Africain, e *m,f* COM *habitant* South African

Sud-Américain, e *m,f* COM *habitant* South American

Sud-Coréen, -enne *m,f* COM *habitant* South Korean

Suède *f* COM Sweden

suédois[1], **e** *adj* COM Swedish

suédois[2] *m* COM *langue* Swedish

Suédois, e *m,f* COM *habitant* Swede

suffire: se ~ à soi-même *v pron* COM be self-sufficient

suffisamment: ~ **financé** *adj* COMPTA adequately funded

suffisance: ~ **du capital** *f* BANQUE capital adequacy

suffisant, e *adj* COM adequate, sufficient

suffrage *m* POL suffrage, RES HUM vote; ~ **universel** POL universal suffrage

suggestion *f* COM suggestion; ◆ **faire une** ~ COM make a suggestion

suisse[1] *adj* COM Swiss

suisse:[2] ~ **allemand** *m* COM *langue* Swiss German; ~ **français** *m* COM *langue* Swiss French

Suisse[1] *mf* COM *habitant* Swiss

Suisse[2] *f* COM Switzerland

Suisses: les ~ *m pl* COM the Swiss

suite *f* COM aftereffect, result; ~ **rapide** FISC quick successions; ◆ ~ à COM in response to; à la ~ **de** COM in the wake of; **comme** ~ COM, COMMS as follows; **comme** ~ à **votre demande** COMMS with reference to your inquiry; **donner** ~ à COM *demande* follow up, *décision* act on; **faire** ~ à COM *lettre* act upon; ~ à **votre appel** COMMS further to your telephone call; ~ à **votre lettre** COMMS further to your letter, in answer to your letter, with reference to your letter

suites *f pl* COM consequence

suivant[1], **e** *adj* COM succeeding

suivant[2] *prép* COM according to; ◆ ~ **avis de** COM as per advice from, as per advice of; ~ **l'ordre indiqué** BREVETS in the order specified; ~ **l'ordre prévu** BREVETS in the order specified; ~ **relevé** BANQUE as per statement

suivi *m* ASSUR, BOURSE tail, COM follow-up, tracking; ~ **d'enquêtes** V&M research survey; ~ **d'études de marché** V&M research survey; ~ **de marché** FIN middle office; ~ **de la production** COM, GESTION, IND progress control; ◆ **faire le** ~ **de** COM track

suivisme *m* BOURSE tailgating

suivre *vt* COM act on, follow, follow up, *progrès* be abreast of, MATH *courbe similaire* follow; ◆ à ~ COM cont'd, continued, matters to be followed up; ~ **le développement de quelque chose** COM keep track of sth; **faire** ~ COMMS forward; ~ **les fortunes** ASSUR follow the fortunes; ~ **un modèle similaire** COM follow a similar pattern; ~ **le mouvement** RES HUM go with the flow; ~ **la trace de** COM trace; ~ **la voie de** COM follow the path of

sujet:[1] ~ à *adj* COM liable to, subject to; ◆ ~ à **la casse** ASSUR subject to breakage; ~ à **controverse** COM controversial; ~ à **discussion** COM open to debate

sujet[2] *m* COM matter, *discours, exposition* subject, DROIT issue; ~ **doué** (ANT *sujet peu doué*) COM high achiever; ~ **peu doué** (ANT *sujet doué*) COM low achiever; ◆ **au** ~ **de** COM about, re, reference, regarding, with reference to

super *m* ENVIR four-star petrol (*BrE*), premium-grade gasoline (*AmE*), premium-grade petrol (*BrE*); ~ **multiplicateur** ECON super multiplier; ~ **-ordinateur** INFO supercomputer

supercarburant *m* ENVIR four-star petrol (*BrE*), premium-grade gasoline (*AmE*), premium-grade petrol (*BrE*)

supercommission *f* ASSUR overriding commission

superdividende *f* FIN surplus dividend

superficie *f* COM acreage, surface area, ECON, MATH area, surface area; ~ **cultivée** FISC cultivated acreage

superflu, e *adj* COM unwanted

supérieur, e *adj* COM Snr, senior; ◆ ~ **à** COM above, COM in excess of; **être ~ à** COM rank above; **~ à la moyenne** *(ANT inférieur à la moyenne)* COM above-average

supermarché *m* V&M supermarket; ~ **de produits financiers** FIN financial supermarket; ~ **à succursales multiples** V&M chain superstore *(UK)*

superpétrolier *m* ENVIR supertanker

superpuissance *f* COM, POL superpower

superstructure *f* COM superstructure

superviseur *m* INFO supervisor; ~ **de premier niveau** GESTION, RES HUM line supervisor

supplanter *vt* COM *qn* supersede

suppléant, e *m,f* COM alternate

supplément *m* COM ex., extra, COMPTA additional charge, extra charge, LOISIRS, TRANSP excess fare; ~ **couleur** MÉDIA *presse* color supplement *(AmE)*, colour supplement *(BrE)*; ~ **pour excédent de bagages** LOISIRS, TRANSP excess baggage charge; ~ **d'impôt** FISC additional tax; ~ **publicitaire** MÉDIA, V&M advertising supplement; ~ **de revenu garanti** FISC guaranteed income supplement; ~ **de salaire** RES HUM additional pay; ◆ **avec ~** COM add-on basis; **en ~** COM extra

supplémentaire *adj* ADMIN backup, COM add-on, additional, extra

support *m* TRANSP *navigation* girder, stanchion, V&M *radio, TV* medium; ~ **audiovisuel** COMMS, INFO, MÉDIA audiovisual aid; ~ **central** TRANSP *d'un navire* center girder *(AmE)*, centre girder *(BrE)*; ~ **client** V&M customer support; ~ **publicitaire** MÉDIA advertising medium, V&M advertising medium, advertising support; ~ **de stockage** INFO storage medium; ~ **supplémentaire** BOURSE backup support; ~ **technique** IND, INFO technical support; ~ **TV** COMMS, MÉDIA television support

supporter *vt* COM *conséquences* abide by, *responsabilité* bear; ◆ ~ **les conséquences** COM *de ses actions* suffer the consequences; ~ **le coût de** COM stand the cost of, COMPTA bear the cost of; ~ **les coûts de** COM bear the costs; ~ **les coûts indirects** COMPTA absorb overheads; ~ **les frais de** COM pay for the expenses of, COMPTA bear the cost of; ~ **les frais généraux** COMPTA absorb overheads; ~ **une perte** COM stand a loss, COMPTA sustain losses; ~ **des pertes** COMPTA sustain losses

supports *m pl* V&M media; ~ **de communication** COMMS communication media, mass media; ~ **comptables** COMPTA accounting papers; **les ~ de communication** MÉDIA communication media, information broadcast, the media; ~ **publicitaires** MÉDIA advertising media; ~ **visuels** COM visuals

supposition *f* COM assumption; ~ **éclairée** RES HUM educated guess

suppression *f* ADMIN abolition, COM abolishment, deletion, lifting, *des barrières tarifaires* removal, DROIT *de dispositions des statuts* deletion, lifting; ~ **des barrières douanières** COM abolition of trade controls; ~ **des déformations d'imposition** FISC removal of tax distortions; ~ **de la double imposition** FISC double taxation relief, DTR; ~ **d'emplois** RES HUM reduction in force, RIF; ~ **progressive** COM, INFO phasing out

supprimer *vt* ADMIN abolish, COM discontinue, eradicate, remove, DROIT abolish, *restrictions* lift, INFO blank, delete, deselect, remove, suppress, MÉDIA suppress, PROT SOC discontinue; ~ **progressivement** COM, INFO phase out

supra *adv* *(ANT infra)* COM supra

supranational, e *adj* COM supranational

suprématie: ~ **du droit** *f* DROIT rule of law

sur *prép* *(ANT sous)* COM above

sûr, e *adj* BOURSE good, COM certain, sound, ECON riskless, secure, FIN good; **peu ~** COM unreliable

surabondance *f* COM, ECON glut; ~ **de l'offre** ECON oversupply; ~ **de personnel** RES HUM overstaffing; ~ **de pétrole** ECON, ENVIR, IND oil glut

suraccumulation *f* ECON overaccumulation

suracheté, e *adj* BOURSE overbought

suractivé: être ~ *loc* ECON be overstimulated

suramélioration *f* IMMOB overimprovement

surapprentissage *m* PROT SOC overlearning

surassuré *m* ASSUR overinsured

surbaissé, e *adj* INFO slim-line

surbooké, e *adj* LOISIRS, TRANSP *transports aériens* overbooked

surcapacité *f* *(ANT sous-capacité)* COM, ECON, IND excess capacity, overcapacity; ~ **de cales** TRANSP *maritime* shipping overcapacity, *navigation* overtonnaging

surcharge *f* BANQUE *argent* penalty, COM overcharge, OC, surcharge, FISC overtax, V&M overcharge, OC; ~ **monétaire** TRANSP *navigation* currency adjustment factor, CAF; ~ **monétaire et de soutage** TRANSP *navigation* currency and bunker adjustment factor, CABAF; ~ **sensorielle** GESTION sensory overload; ~ **de soutage** TRANSP *navigation* bunker adjustment factor, bunkering adjustment factor, bunkering surcharge, BAF; ◆ **ni ~, ni rature** COM no addition, no correction

surchauffe *f* ECON overheating

surchauffé: être ~ *loc* ECON be overheated, be overstimulated

surchauffeur *m* TRANSP superheater, SH

surcommission *f* ASSUR overriding commission

surconsolidation *f* ECON overfunding

surcroît *m* COM boom; ~ **de capacité** TRANSP spare capacity; ◆ **donner un ~ de travail à** GESTION overstretch

surdépendance *f* COM overdependence

surdoué, e *m,f* PROT SOC overachiever; ~ **de l'informatique** INFO computer wizard

sureffectif *m* RES HUM overmanning, overstaffing

sureffectifs: en ~ *adj* RES HUM overstaffed

surémission *f* BANQUE overissue

suremploi *m* (ANT *sous-emploi*) COM excess employment, overemployment, ECON, RES HUM overemployment

surenchère *f* RES HUM leapfrogging; ~ **salariale** RES HUM leapfrogging; ◆ **faire l'objet d'une** ~ COM *prix* leapfrog

surenchérir *vi* RES HUM leapfrog (*jarg*), V&M *vente aux enchères* outbid

surendettement *m* BANQUE overindebtedness

suréquiper: ~ **en personnel** *vt* RES HUM overman, overstaff

surestaries *f pl* TRANSP demurrage

surestimer *vt* FIN overestimate

sûreté *f* BOURSE security interest, COM security, FIN surety; ~ **sur un bien** FISC charge upon a property

surévaluation *f* BOURSE, COMPTA, ECON overvaluation; ~ **d'actif** BOURSE watered stock

surévalué, e *adj* BOURSE overvalued, COM *claim* exaggerated, COMPTA, ECON overvalued

surévaluer *vt* BOURSE, COMPTA, ECON overvalue

surexploitation *f* ENVIR, IND overexploitation

surface *f* BREVETS *utile, utilisée* surface; ~ **d'appui** TRANSP *rampe d'accès* bearing surface; ~ **brute louable** IMMOB gross leasable area (*AmE*); ~ **de charge** COM loading space; ~ **consacrée à la vente au détail** V&M retail floorspace; ~ **financière** RES HUM financial muscle; ~ **industrielle** RES HUM industrial muscle; ~ **de présentation** V&M facing; ~ **au sol** IMMOB floor space; ~ **de stockage** COM storage area; ~ **totale des sols** IMMOB *d'un immeuble* net leasable area; ~ **de vente** V&M *dans un magasin* sales area

surfacturation *f* COMPTA extra-billing

surfourniture *f* ECON overprovision

surfrappe *f* INFO strikeover

surfret *m* COM extra freight

surimposition *f* FISC excessive taxation, overtax

Surinam *m* COM Suriname

surinamais, e *adj* COM Surinamese

Surinamais, e *m,f* COM *habitant* Surinamese

surintendant: ~ **des assurances** *m* ASSUR Superintendent of Insurance; ~ **des faillites** *m* COM, DROIT Superintendent of Bankruptcy

surmenage *m* RES HUM industrial fatigue

surmonter *vt* ECON *récession* weather

surmortalité *f* ASSUR excess mortality

surmultiplication *f* TRANSP overdrive

surnombre: en ~ *loc* RES HUM redundant

surnuméraire *adj* RES HUM supernumerary

suroffre *f* COM better offer, IMMOB gazumping (*UK*)

surpaiement *m* COMPTA, FIN overpayment

surpasser *vt* COM surpass

surpâturage *m* ENVIR overgrazing

surplus *m* COM overage, ECON *agriculture* surplus; ~ **acquis** FIN acquired surplus (*US*); ~ **de capital en main** FISC capital surplus on hand; ~ **du consommateur** ECON consumer's surplus; ~ **désigné** FISC designated surplus; ~ **disponible** COM unappropriated surplus; ~ **exonéré** FISC exempt surplus; ~ **de main-d'oeuvre** RES HUM overmanning; ~ **net** COM, FIN net surplus; ~ **de personnel** RES HUM overmanning; ~ **du plein emploi** ECON, RES HUM high employment surplus; ~ **du producteur** ECON producer's surplus; ◆ **être en** ~ ADMIN to be in surplus; **qui souffre d'un** ~ **de personnel** RES HUM overstaffed

surproduction *f* (ANT *sous-production*) ECON, IND overproduction

surproduire *vt* (ANT *sous-produire*) ECON, IND overproduce

surremplissage *m* TRANSP overstuffing

surreprésenter *vt* V&M overrepresent

surréservation *f* LOISIRS, TRANSP overbooking

sursalaire *m* RES HUM extra pay

sursis *m* COM deferment, DROIT suspended sentence; ~ **simple** FIN simple deferment

sursouscrit, e *adj* BOURSE oversubscribed

surtare *f* COM extra tare

surtarifé, e *adj* V&M overpriced

surtaxe *f* FISC overtax, surtax; ~ **pour combustibles** TRANSP *maritime* fuel surcharge; ~ **des corporations** FISC corporate surtax; ~ **d'encombrement** FISC congestion surcharge; ~ **d'encombrement portuaire** TRANSP *navigation* congestion surcharge; ~ **postale** COMMS additional postage

surtension *f* IND, INFO power surge

surtout *adv* COM esp., especially

survaleur *m* (ANT *sous-valeur*) COMPTA goodwill

surveillance *f* COM monitoring, supervision, DROIT surveillance, FIN monitoring; ~ **de la bourse** BOURSE surveillance department of exchanges; ~ **des établissements de crédit** FIN supervision of credit institutions; ~ **maximale** BOURSE radar alert; ~ **des origines du personnel** RES HUM ethnic monitoring; ~ **de la production** COM, GESTION, IND production control, production planning and control, progress control; ◆ **de** ~ COM, GESTION, INFO, RES HUM supervisory

surveillant, e *m,f* GESTION, RES HUM supervisor; ~ **de circulation** RES HUM, TRANSP traffic superintendent, TS; ~ **d'entrepôt** COM warehouse keeper; ~ **de premier niveau** GESTION, RES HUM line manager, line supervisor

surveiller *vt* BOURSE watch, COM monitor, supervise, *quelqu'un* put a guard on, GESTION, RES HUM supervise, TRANSP *taux*, V&M *marché* monitor; ◆ ~ **de près** COM keep a close watch on; ~ **ses arrières** COM watch one's back

survendu, e *adj* BOURSE oversold

survie *f* DROIT, IMMOB survivorship

survivre *vi* COM survive

survol *m* INFO browsing

survoler *vt* INFO browse

susceptible: **~ de** *adj* COM *explication, augmentation* capable of; ◆ **~ d'application industrielle** BREVETS susceptible of industrial application; **~ d'interprétations diverses** COM open to several interpretations

susciter *vt* COM *intérêt, soupçon* give rise to

susdit, e *adj* COM, COMMS aforementioned

susmentionné, e *adj* COM aforementioned, COMMS above, above-mentioned, aforementioned, as mentioned above

susnommé, e *adj* COMMS above-named

suspendre *vt* COM *autorisation* suspend, *procédure de faillite* stop; ◆ **~ les cotations** BOURSE suspend trading; **~ le paiement d'un chèque** BANQUE stop a check (*AmE*), stop a cheque (*BrE*); **~ les transactions** BOURSE suspend trading

suspens: **en ~** *adv* ADMIN in-basket situation (*jarg*), in-tray exercise (*jarg*), COM in abeyance

suspension *f* DROIT remise, *d'une action* abatement, GESTION adjournment, RES HUM *d'un employé* suspension; **~ des affaires** COM business interruption; **~ d'affrètement** TRANSP *maritime* off hire; **~ antiroulis** TRANSP anti-roll suspension; **~ d'appel** DROIT stay of appeal; **~ de droits** IMP/EXP duty suspension; **~ d'intérêt** BANQUE cessation of interest (*UK*); **~ de paiement des primes** ASSUR cessation of payment of premiums; **~ des transactions** BOURSE halt of trading, trading halt

Suva *n pr* COM Suva

SVN *abrév (sans valeur nominale)* BOURSE NPV *(no-par value)*

SVT *abrév* BOURSE, ECON *(spécialistes en valeurs du Trésor)* GEMMS *(gilt-edged market makers)*

swahili *m* COM *langue* Swahili

swap *m* BOURSE swap; **~ simple** FIN plain vanilla swap

Swazi, e *m,f* COM *habitant* Swazi

Swaziland *m* COM Swaziland

switch *m jarg* COM switch trading

syli *m* COM Syli

sylviculture *f* ENVIR, IND forestry

sylvo-agriculture *f* ENVIR agro-forestry

symbole *m* COM symbol; **~ monétaire** INFO currency symbol; **~ de pointage** BOURSE ticker symbol

symbolique *adj* COM, INFO symbolic

symétrie *f* MATH symmetry

symétrique *adj* BOURSE, MATH symmetric

symmétallisme *m* COM symmetallism

sync *abrév infrml (synchronisation)* COM sync (*infrml*) *(synchronization)*

synchrone *adj* INFO synchronous

synchronisation *f (sync)* COM synchronization *(sync)*, INFO timing

syndic *m* BANQUE trustee; **~ de faillite** BANQUE assignee in bankruptcy, trustee in bankruptcy, COM, DROIT, FIN receiver and manager

syndicalisation *f* RES HUM union certification, unionization

syndicalisé, e *adj* RES HUM unionized

syndicalisme *m* RES HUM trade unionism; **~ international** BANQUE international syndication

syndicaliste *m* RES HUM union man; **~ indépendant** RES HUM Certification Officer (*UK*)

syndicat *m* BOURSE syndicate, *d'investisseurs* syndicate, COM *financier* syndicate, RES HUM labor union (*US*), trade union (*UK*), TU (*UK*), *ouvrier* syndicate, union; **~ américain** RES HUM US labor union; **~ de banque** BANQUE banking syndicate; **~ de banques** BANQUE group banking; **~ bidon** *infrml* RES HUM yellow union; **~ de bonne foi** RES HUM bona fide trade union (*UK*); **~ dissident** RES HUM breakaway union, splinter union; **~ de distribution** MÉDIA syndicate (*AmE*); **~ d'émission** ASSUR underwriting syndicate, BOURSE syndicate; **~ d'employés** RES HUM non-manual union, white-collar union; **~ d'enchères** FIN tender panel; **~ d'entreprise** RES HUM enterprise union; **~ exerçant un monopole de l'embauche** RES HUM closed union; **~ financier** BANQUE syndicate; **~ de garantie** FIN purchase group; **~ général** RES HUM general union; **~ indépendant** RES HUM independent trade union, independent union; **~ d'industrie** PROT SOC, RES HUM industrial union; **~ d'initiative** LOISIRS tourist information bureau, tourist information office, tourist office; **~ international** ECON, RES HUM international union; **~ local** RES HUM local union; **~ maison** RES HUM company union, yellow union; **~ de métier** RES HUM craft union; **~ national** RES HUM national union; **~ non-officiel** RES HUM nonofficial trade organization, NOTO; **~ ouvert** RES HUM open union; **~ d'ouvriers qualifiés** RES HUM skilled union (*UK*); **~ du personnel de production** RES HUM blue-collar union; **~ de placement** BOURSE distributing syndicate, syndicate; **~ de prise ferme** BOURSE syndicate; **~ professionnel** RES HUM horizontal union, vertical union, occupational union (*UK*); **~ reconnu** RES HUM recognized trade union (*UK*); **~ regroupant les adhérents par métier** RES HUM vertical union; **~ regroupant les adhérents par niveau** RES HUM horizontal union; **~ de travailleurs manuels** RES HUM manual union (*UK*); **~ vertical** RES HUM vertical union

Syndicat: **~ des employés de la distribution et assimilés** *m* RES HUM Union of Shop, Distributive & Allied Workers (*UK*), USDAW (*UK*); **~ international des cheminots** *m* TRANSP International Union of Railways, IUR; **~ international des organisations officielles de voyages** *m* TRANSP International Union of Official Travel Organizations, IUOTO; **~ international des transporteurs routiers** *m* TRANSP International Road Transport Union, IRU; **~ de la Lloyd**

ASSUR Lloyd's Corporation (*UK*); ~ **national des journalistes** *m (SNJ)* MÉDIA ≈ National Union of Journalists (*UK*) *(NUJ)*; ~ **national des mineurs** IND, RES HUM National Union of Mineworkers (*UK*), NUM (*UK*); ~ **des transports et des travailleurs confédérés** IND, RES HUM Transport and General Workers' Union (*UK*), TGWU (*UK*)

syndicataire *m* RES HUM member of a syndicate

syndication *f* BANQUE, FIN syndication

syndicats: ~ **affiliés** *m pl* RES HUM affiliated trade unions; ~ **patronaux** *m pl* RES HUM scab unions (*pej*); ◆ **les ~ et le patronat** RES HUM unions and management

syndiqué, e *m,f* RES HUM member of a trade union, member

syndiquer *vt* RES HUM syndicate, *ouvriers* organize

syndrome: ~ **des bâtiments insalubres** *m* ADMIN sick building syndrome; ~ **de rejet** *m* ENVIR NIMBY syndrome

synergie *f* COM, ECON synergism, synergy

syntaxe *f* INFO syntax

synthèse *f* COM synthesis

synthétique *adj* BOURSE, COM synthetic, IND manmade

Syrie *f* COM Syria

syrien, -enne *adj* COM Syrian

Syrien, -enne *m,f* COM *habitant* Syrian

systématique *adj* COM across-the-board, systematic

systématiquement *adv* COM across the board

systématiser *vt* COM systematize

système *m* ADMIN scheme, system, COM *hi-fi, informatique* set-up, system, INFO system; ~ **d'accueil des idées** *m* GESTION *du personnel* suggestion scheme; ~ **d'administration financière** *m* FIN system of financial administration; ~ **d'aide à la décision** *m* GESTION decision support system, DSS; ~ **allodial** *m* DROIT allodial system; ~ **d'amarrage à propulsion** *m* TRANSP *navigation* thruster-assisted mooring system, TAMS; ~ **d'amortissement dégressif** *m* COMPTA declining balance method, reducing balance method; ~ **d'analyse des tendances assisté par ordinateur** *m* BOURSE, INFO computerized market timing system; ~ **anti-fraude de l'industrie du crédit** *m* FIN Credit Industry Fraud Avoidance System (*UK*), CIFAS (*UK*); ~ **antifouling** *m* TRANSP *navigation* antifouling system; ~ **d'appel d'offres** *m* COM competitive bidding; ~ **d'arrimage au cadre fixe** *m* TRANSP *conteneurs* solid-frame securing system; ~ **d'assurance maladie** *m* RES HUM health insurance scheme; ~ **d'attribution de codes comptables** *m* COMPTA coding system; ~ **autex** *m* BOURSE autex system; ~ **d'autocotisation** *m* FISC self-assessing system; ~ **d'autoévaluation** *m* FISC self-assessing system; ~ **autonome** *m* INFO stand-alone system; ~ **autoritaire** *m* ECON, POL authoritarian society; ~ **d'avance de fonds à plafond** *m* COMPTA imprest

system; ~ **bancaire** *m* BANQUE, FIN banking system; ~ **bancaire fédéral de prêts hypothécaires** *m* FIN Federal Home Loan Bank System (*US*); ~ **bancaire de l'orfèvrerie** *m* BANQUE goldsmith banking system; ~ **de banque à succursales** *m* BANQUE branch banking system; ~ **BIOS** *m* (SYN *système d'exploitation des entrées/sorties*) INFO basic input/output operating system, BIOS; ~ **de bons** *m* V&M voucher system; ~ **budgétaire** *m* COMPTA, ECON, FIN, POL budget system; ~ **à carnet** *m* IMP/EXP carnet system; ~ **carrousel** *m* TRANSP circuit working; ~ **central de comptabilité** *m Canada (SCC)* COMPTA Central Accounting System (*Canada*) *(CAS)*; ~ **centralisé de cotation** *m* BOURSE consolidated quotation system; ~ **centre périphérie** *m* ECON center periphery system (*AmE*), centre periphery system (*BrE*); ~ **de chargement sur résidus** *m* TRANSP *pétrolier* load-on-top system; ~ **de classe unique** *m* PROT SOC mainstreaming; ~ **de classement des fiches** *m* ADMIN filing system; ~ **de classification des emplois** *m* RES HUM job evaluation scheme; ~ **de classification industrielle standard** *m* IND standard industrial classification system; ~ **commercial** *m* COM, ECON business system; ~ **commercial inter-marché** *m* BOURSE Intermarket Trading System (*US*), ITS (*US*); ~ **à la commission** *m* RES HUM commission system; ~ **de communication interréseau** *m* COMMS gateway; ~ **de compensation** *m* BOURSE clearing system; ~ **de compensation des actionnaires** *m* BOURSE Investors' Compensation Scheme (*UK*); ~ **de compensation de chèques** *m* BANQUE check-clearing system (*AmE*), cheque-clearing system (*BrE*); ~ **de compensation et de règlement automatisé** *m (SCRA)* BANQUE Automated Clearing Settlement System *(ACSS)*; ~ **de compensation mutuelle** *m* BOURSE Mutual Offset System; ~ **de comptabilité** *m* COMPTA, FIN accounting system; ~ **de comptabilité nationale** *m* COMPTA System of National Accounts, SNA; ~ **de comptabilité supplémentaire** *m* COMPTA supplementary accounting system; ~ **de comptabilité sur ordinateur** *m* COMPTA, INFO computerized accounting system; ~ **comptable** *m* COMPTA accounting system, system of accounts, FIN accounting system; ~ **comptable auxiliaire** *m* COMPTA subsidiary accounting system; ~ **comptable électronique** *m* COMPTA electronic accounting system; ~ **comptable principal** *m* COMPTA principal accounting system; ~ **connecté** *m* INFO on-line system; ~ **de contrôle de la caisse** *m* COMPTA cash control system; ~ **de contrôle de la circulation aérienne** *m* TRANSP air traffic control system; ~ **de contrôle des départs** *m* TRANSP *aviation* departure control system, DCS; ~ **de contrôle de la radioactivité d'effluent** *m* ENVIR effluent monitor; ~ **de convoyeur et d'élévateur à bord** *m* TRANSP *navigation* shipboard conveyor belt and elevator system; ~ **de cotation automatisé** *m* BOURSE Stock Exchange Automated Quotation, SEAQ; ~ **de cotation** électronique *m* BOURSE computer-assisted trading system, CATS; ~ de crédit agricole fédéral *m* ECON Federal Farm Credit System *(US)*; ~ de crédits d'impôt *m* FISC tax credit system; ~ à la criée *m* BOURSE open-outcry system; ~ décentralisé *m* INFO distributed system; ~ de déductions sociales *m* FISC *pour les dons aux institutions caritatives* payroll deduction scheme; ~ dégressif *m* RES HUM tapering; ~ démontable *m* TRANSP *véhicules routiers* demountable system; ~ de dépôts spécial complémentaire *m* BANQUE, FIN supplementary special deposits scheme; ~ des dépouilles *m* POL spoils system *(US)*; ~ à deux niveaux *m* COM two-tier system; ~ à deux taux *m* FISC two-rate system; ~ de direction *m* GESTION management system, TRANSP steering system; ~ de direction continu *m* GESTION ongoing management system; ~ de dividende social *m* ECON social dividend scheme; ~ des droits d'auteur *m* FISC royalty system; ~ duplex *m* INFO duplex computer; ~ d'économie mixte *m* ECON, POL mixed economic system; ~ économique *m* ECON, POL economic system; ~ économique national *m* ECON domestic economy, domestic system; ~ énergétique *m* COM energy system; ~ de l'entreprise privée *m* ECON private enterprise system; ~ d'évaluation des risques *m* BANQUE risk asset system, risk-based banking standards; ~ d'évaluation de la solvabilité *m* COM, FIN credit rating system; ~ expert *m* COM expert system, INFO knowledge-based system, KBS, INFO expert system; ~ d'exploitation *m* INFO o.s., operation system; ~ d'exploitation à disques® *m (DOS)* INFO disk operating system® *(DOS)*; ~ d'exploitation des entrées/sorties *m* (SYN *système BIOS)* INFO basic input/output operating system, BIOS; ~ de fabrication *m* IND manufacturing system; ~ des files d'attente *m* ECON rationing; ~ financier *m* COM, FIN financial system; ~ fiscal *m* ECON, FISC tax system, taxation system; ~ de garantie *m* BOURSE backup system; ~ généralisé des tarifs et préférences *m (SGTP)* IMP/EXP generalized system of tariffs and preferences *(GSTP)*; ~ de gestion *m* GESTION management system; ~ de gestion de bases de données *m (SGBD)* INFO database management system *(DBMS)*; ~ de gestion de caisse *m* BANQUE cash management system; ~ de gestion financière *m (SGF)* FIN financial management system; ~ de gestion informatisé *m* GESTION, INFO management information system; ~ de gestion des secteurs de dépenses *m* FIN Policy and Expenditure Management System; ~ de gestion de trafic maritime *m* TRANSP vessel traffic management system; ~ de gestion de trésorerie *m* BANQUE cash management system; ~ hectométrique *m* TRANSP people mover; ~ des heures-années *m* RES HUM annualized hours system; ~ d'heures annualisées *m* RES HUM annualized hours system; ~ homme-machine *m* ADMIN man-machine system; ~ d'impôt progressif *m* FISC progressive income tax system,

progressive tax system; ~ de l'impôt progressif sur le revenu *m* FISC progressive income tax system; ~ d'indemnité de maladie *m* PROT SOC, RES HUM sick-pay scheme *(UK)*; ~ d'indexation *m* ECON pegging system; ~ industriel *m* IND industrial system; ~ d'information *m* INFO information system; ~ d'information comptable *m* FIN reporting system; ~ d'information de management *m (SIM)* GESTION, INFO management information system *(MIS)*; ~ d'information de marketing *m (SIM)* V&M marketing information system *(MIS)*; ~ informatique *m* INFO computer system, information system; ~ informatique embarqué *m* TRANSP *navigation* loadmate; ~ insensible aux défaillances *m* INFO fault-tolerant system; ~ insensible aux pannes *m* INFO fault-tolerant system; ~ intégré de gestion *m* GESTION, INFO *(SIG)* integrated management system, management information system *(MIS)*; ~ interactif *m* INFO interactive system, on-line system; ~ d'interaction économique *m* COM, ECON business system; ~ des intermédiaires entre courtiers *m (SIAM)* BOURSE interdealer broker system *(IDBS)*; ~ international de cotation automatisé *m* BOURSE SEAQ Automated Execution Facility *(UK)*, SAEF *(UK)*; ~ interne *m* INFO in-house system; ~ judiciaire *m* DROIT judiciary; ~ juridique *m* DROIT legal system; ~ de libre entreprise *m* ECON, POL free enterprise system; ~ en ligne *m* INFO on-line system; ~ de livraison *m* BOURSE delivery system; ~ de livraison agréé *m* BOURSE approved delivery facility *(UK)*; ~ longitudinal *m* TRANSP *navigation* longitudinal framing; ~ maison *m* INFO in-house system; ~ majoritaire *m* POL majority rule; ~ manuel *m* TRANSP *navigation* manual system, MS; ~ de marché *m* ECON market system; ~ de marché national *m* BOURSE National Market System, NMS; ~ des marchés financiers mondiaux *m* BOURSE Capital Markets System, CMS; ~ de métayage *m* ECON sharecropping *(US)*; ~ métrique *m (SM)* COM, MATH metric system; ~ de mise en commun *m* TRANSP *fonds commun* pooling system; ~ monétaire *m* ECON coinage system; ~ monétaire international *m* ECON international monetary system; ~ monétaire mondial *m* FIN world monetary system; ~ multiutilisateur *m* INFO multiuser system; ~ national du marché *m* BOURSE National Market System, NMS; ~ d'option sur les bénéfices *m* FISC, PROT SOC, RES HUM *avantages des employés* share option scheme; ~ d'organisation *m* COM, RES HUM organization behavior *(AmE)*, organization behaviour *(BrE)*; ~ de paiement *m* ECON payment system; ~ de paiement non-financier *m* BANQUE noncash payment system; ~ de paiement sans argent *m* BANQUE *par carte de crédit* cashless payment system; ~ de partage des bénéfices *m* FIN *avantage aux employés* profit-sharing plan *(US)*, profit-sharing scheme *(UK)*; ~ de partage du travail *m* RES HUM job share scheme; ~ de participation *m* RES HUM employee stock ownership plan *(US)*; ~ de participation financière *m*

RES HUM financial participation scheme (*UK*); ~ **de péréquation des impôts** *m* FISC *maintenu par les employeurs étrangers* tax equalization scheme; ~ **de planning, de budget et de programmation** *m* COMPTA, FIN, GESTION, RES HUM planning, programming, budgeting system; ~ **de point de réapprovisionnement** *m* TRANSP order point system; ~ **politique** *m* COM, POL political system; ~ **de positions automatisées de téléphonistes** *m* COMMS operator system; ~ **de préférences généralisé** *m* ECON generalized system of preferences; ~ **de primes d'encouragement** *m* IND factory incentive scheme, plant incentive scheme, RES HUM factory incentive scheme, incentive payment system, plant incentive scheme, incentive scheme; ~ **de primes Halsey** *m* RES HUM Halsey Premium Plan (*US*); ~ **des primes moyennes** *m* ASSUR average premium system; ~ **privé d'assurance maladie** *m* PROT SOC, RES HUM private health scheme (*UK*); ~ **de prix** *m* ECON price system; ~ **de production et d'entreposage sur allège** *m* TRANSP *navigation* barge-mounted production and storage system, BPSS; ~ **de production au large** *m* TRANSP *maritime* floating production system, FPS; ~ **de production à tourelle d'ancrage** *m* TRANSP turret anchored production system, TAPS; ~ **de protection par programme informatique** *m* BOURSE program trading (*AmE*), programme trading (*BrE*), INFO program trading; ~ **de quotas** *m* COM, IMP/EXP quota system; ~ **des quotes-parts** *m* TRANSP *tarifs aériens* proration; ~ **de radiation direct** *m* COMPTA direct charge-off method; ~ **de rapports ministériels** *m* ADMIN Departmental Reporting System; ~ **de recherche documentaire** *m* INFO document retrieval system, information retrieval system; ~ **récursif** *m* ECON *économétrie* recursive system; ~ **de règlement bancaire** *m* BANQUE bank settlement system; ~ **de règlement des chèques** *m* BANQUE check payment system (*AmE*), cheque payment system (*BrE*); ~ **de règlement des comptes marchandises** *m* TRANSP Cargo Accounts Settlement System, CASS; ~ **réglementaire** *m* DROIT regulatory system; ~ **de rémunération** *m* RES HUM commission system, salary scheme; ~ **de répartition du coût des services communs** *m* COMPTA common service cost distribution system; ~ **de repérage** *m* COM tracking system; ~ **de réservation** *m* COM, TRANSP reservation system; ~ **de réservation central** *m* LOISIRS central reservation system; ~ **de réservation des places** *m* LOISIRS seat reservation system; ~ **de retenue à la source** *m* RES HUM pay-as-you-go (*AmE*); ~ **de retraite** *m* RES HUM funded pension plan (*US*); ~ **de retraite par accumulation** *m* RES HUM funded pension plan (*US*), funded retirement plan (*US*); ~ **de retraite par répartition** *m* (ANT *régime de retraite entière-*

ment financé par l'employeur) FIN, PROT SOC, RES HUM contributory pension plan, contributory pension scheme; ~ **de retraite à prestation définie** *m* FIN, RES HUM defined-benefit pension plan; ~ **de retraite professionnelle** *m* FIN, PROT SOC, RES HUM occupational pension scheme (*UK*); ~ **rouge et vert** *m* IMP/EXP red and green system; ~ **routier** *m* TRANSP road network; ~ **du sacrifice salarial** *m* FISC salary sacrifice scheme (*UK*); ~ **des salaires** *m* RES HUM wage system; ~ **de séparation des sens de circulation** *m* TRANSP traffic separation scheme; ~ **de seuil de réapprovisionnement** *m* TRANSP order point system; ~ **simplifié de retraite des employés** *m* PROT SOC, RES HUM simplified employee pension plan; ~ **social** *m* PROT SOC social system; ~ **socio-technique** *m* ADMIN sociotechnical system; ~ **de sonorisation** *m* COMMS PA system, public address system; ~ **de soumission** *m* COM competitive bidding; ~ **stabex** *m* ECON stabex system; ~ **de suggestion** *m* COM suggestion scheme; ~ **synchrone** *m* TRANSP *navigation* synchronous system; ~ **des taux de clôture** *m* COMPTA closing rate method (*BrE*), current rate method (*AmE*); ~ **de télévirement** *m* BANQUE electronic funds transfer system, EFTS; ~ **de terminal pour articles réglementés** *m* TRANSP Restricted Articles Terminal System, RATS; ~ **de traitement de texte** *m* INFO word-processing system; ~ **de transaction inter-marchés** *m* BOURSE Intermarket Trading System (*US*), ITS (*US*); ~ **de transactions automatisées** *m* ECON, INFO computer trading (*US*); ~ **de transfert** *m* TRANSP *aéroport* people mover; ~ **de transport** *m* TRANSP transportation system; ~ **de transport combiné** *m* TRANSP intermodal transport system; ~ **de transport contractuel** *m* TRANSP *navigation* contract system; ~ **de transport direct** *m* TRANSP through transport system; ~ **de transport urbain automatique** *m* TRANSP people mover; ~ **de travail à la pièce** *m* RES HUM piecework system; ~ **de travail aux pièces** *m* RES HUM piecework system; ~ **unique de changes flottants** *m* ECON managed floating system; ~ **de virements bancaires** *m* BANQUE banking transfer system

Système: ~ **de management environnemental** *m* ENVIR Environmental Management System; ~ **mondial de détresse et de sécurité en mer** *m* TRANSP *navigation* Global Maritime Distress and Safety System, GMDSS; ~ **mondial de surveillance continue de l'environnement** *m* ENVIR Global Environment Monitoring System; ~ **monétaire européen** *m* (*SME*) ECON *UE* European Monetary System (*EMS*)

systèmes: ~ **d'information financière et budgétaire** *m pl* FIN financial information and budgeting systems, FIBS

T

t. *abrév* BOURSE *(titre)* security, COM *(tare)* t. *(tare)*, COM *(tonne)* t. *(ton)*, TRANSP *(tare)* t. *tare)*

tabac *m* COM tobacco

table *f* COM, INFO table; ~ **agrégée** ASSUR aggregate table; ~ **d'allocation des fichiers** INFO file, file allocation table, FAT; ~ **de change** ECON desk; ~ **de conférence** GESTION conference table; ~ **de décision** INFO decision table; ~ **de fréquence** MATH frequency table; ~ **d'invalidité** ASSUR disability percentage table; ~ **des matières** ADMIN index, COM table of contents, *d'un livre, catalogue, manuel* contents; ~ **de mortalité** ASSUR mortality table; ~ **de négociations** COM, GESTION, RES HUM bargaining table; ~ **de paiements hypothécaires** BANQUE mortgage table; ~ **de parités** BOURSE table of par values; ~ **de référence** INFO lookup table; ~ **ronde** COM round table; ~ **traçante** COM plotting table, INFO plotting board; ♦ **sur la ~ des négociations** COM on the table

tableau *m* COM chart, *d'une situation* picture, *des chiffres de l'année* table, COMPTA work sheet, GESTION drawing board, INFO array, chart, panel, table; ~ **d'activités multiples** INFO multiple-activity chart; ~ **d'affichage** COM, COMMS, INFO, RES HUM bulletin board *(AmE)*, notice board *(BrE)*, BB; ~ **d'affichage électronique** BOURSE electronic posting board, COMMS bulletin board system, BBS, INFO bulletin board; ~ **d'appel** BOURSE annunciator board *(US)*; ~ **de bord** ADMIN management chart, COM control panel, COMPTA, FIN management accounts, GESTION management accounts, management chart, MATH management chart; ~ **de concordance** COMPTA reconciliation table; ~ **de cotation** BOURSE quotation board; ~ **de données** COM array; ~ **d'échanges interindustriels** ECON, FIN, IND, MATH input/output table; ~ **économique** ECON Quesnay; ~ **économique d'ensemble** ECON financial balance; ~ **électronique** INFO spreadsheet program; ~ **électronique de cotations** BOURSE Stock Exchange Alternative Trading Service *(UK)*, SEAT *(UK)*; ~ **des emplois et des ressources de finance** COMPTA source and application of funds; ~ **d'entrées/sorties** ECON, FIN, IND, INFO input/output table; ~ **à feuilles mobiles** COM, V&M flip chart; ~ **de financement** FIN source and applications of funds statement; ~ **de financement consolidé** COMPTA consolidated cash flow statement; ~ **macroéconomique de la demande** ECON macroeconomic demand schedule; ~ **des opérations financières** *(TOF)* FIN flow-of-funds table; ~ **de remboursement** COMPTA redemption table; ~ **de service** RES HUM roster; ~ **des tarifs** COM scale of charges; ~ **de variation des capitaux propres**

COMPTA movements on shareholders' equity; ~ **des variations de fonds** COMPTA funds statement; ~ **de ventilation** BOURSE spread sheet

Tableau: ~ **de calcul** *m* COMPTA Derivation Schedule

tabler: ~ **sur** *vi* COM bank on

tableur *m* ADMIN, COMPTA, FIN spreadsheet, INFO spreadsheet, spreadsheet program

tabloïd, e *adj jarg* MÉDIA *presse* tabloid

tabulaire *adj* ADMIN, COM tabular

tabulation *f* ADMIN tabulation, INFO tab, *horizontale, verticale* tabulation; ♦ **faire une ~** INFO tab

tabulatrice *f* ADMIN tabulating machine

tâche *f* ADMIN administrative burden, COM job, task, INFO, POL task; ~ **de fond** INFO background task; ~ **non prioritaire** INFO background task; ♦ **à la ~** RES HUM at piece rate

Tachkent *n pr* COM Tashkent

tachygraphe *m* TRANSP tachograph

tacite *adj* BOURSE implied, COM implied, tacit, DROIT, FIN implied

tactile *adj* INFO touch-sensitive

tactique: ~ **concurrentielle** *f* ECON, GESTION, V&M competitive tactics

Tadjikistan *m* COM Tajikistan

taille *f* ECON *d'une économie, d'une entreprise* size; ~ **au-dessous** COM next size down; ~ **économique** V&M economy size; ~ **des lots** IND batch size; ~ **normale du marché** BOURSE NMS *(BrE)*, normal market size *(BrE)*; ~ **d'une organisation** COM organizational size; ~ **peu courante** IND *production* odd size; ~ **des séries** IND batch size; ~ **standard** COM *général* basic size; ~ **standard d'une affiche** V&M sheet *(UK, jarg)*

tailles: ~ **tout-venant** *f pl* COM random sizes

Taipeh *n pr* COM Taipei

Taipei *n pr* COM Taipei

taire *vt* DROIT withhold

Taiwan *m* COM Taiwan

taiwanais, e *adj* COM Taiwanese

Taiwanais, e *m,f* COM *habitant* Taiwanese

takka *m* COM taka

talent *m* RES HUM accomplishment

talisman *m* BOURSE Talisman

talkie-walkie *m* COMMS walkie-talkie

Tallinn *n pr* COM Tallinn

talon *m* BANQUE stub, BOURSE talon; ~ **de chèque** BANQUE check counterfoil *(AmE)*, check stub *(AmE)*, cheque counterfoil *(BrE)*, cheque stub *(BrE)*

TAM *abrév (taux annuel monétaire)* FIN annual monetary rate

tambour *m* INFO drum; ~ **en contreplaqué** TRANSP plywood drum

tamoul *m* COM *langue* Tamil

tampon *m* ASSUR line stamp (*UK*), COM rubber stamp, INFO, TRANSP buffer; ~ **encreur** COM stamp pad; ~ **d'entrée** IMP/EXP *à l'arrivée dans un nouveau pays* entry stamp

tandem *m* TRANSP tandem

tangon *m* TRANSP *de spinnaker* boom

tank: ~ **de peak arrière** *m* TRANSP *d'un navire* aft peak tank, APT

tant: **en** ~ **que moyen de** *loc* COM as a means of; **en** ~ **que multipropriété** *loc* IMMOB on a time sharing basis

tantième *m* GESTION fee

Tanzanie *f* COM Tanzania

tanzanien, -enne *adj* COM Tanzanian

Tanzanien, -enne *m,f* COM *habitant* Tanzanian

TAO *abrév* INFO *(traduction assistée par ordinateur)* CAT *(computer-assisted translation, computer-aided translation)*, MAT *(machine-assisted translation, machine-aided translation)*, INFO, PROT SOC *(test assisté par ordinateur)* CAT *(computer-aided testing, computer-assisted testing)*

tapé: ~ **à la machine** *adj* ADMIN, BREVETS typewritten

taper: ~ **à la machine** *vi* ADMIN typewrite, INFO type; ~ **sans regarder le clavier** ADMIN, COM, COMMS, INFO touch-type; ~ **au toucher** ADMIN, COM, COMMS, INFO touch-type

tapis: ~ **roulant** *m* COM moving pavement (*BrE*), travolator (*AmE*), LOISIRS conveyor belt, moving pavement (*BrE*), travolator (*AmE*), TRANSP conveyor belt; ~ **de souris** *m* INFO mouse mat

taquet: ~ **d'hiloire** *m* TRANSP *navigation, fixation des conteneurs* coaming chock

tarage *m* COM taring

tare *f (t.)* COM tare *(t.)*, TRANSP tare *(t.)*, tare weight, unladen weight; ~ **brute** TRANSP gross tare weight; ~ **nette** COM net tare weight; ~ **d'usage** FISC customary tare

tarif *m* COM *liste des prix* price list, rate, tariff, ECON *de devises* rate, FIN current price, p.c., *de devises* rate, FISC, IMP/EXP tariff, V&M price list, price schedule; ~ **d'abonnement** TRANSP *fret* incentive rate (*AmE*); ~ **d'affranchissement** COMMS postage; ~ **aller-retour** TRANSP round-trip rate; ~ **applicable aux marchandises dangereuses** TRANSP dangerous goods rate; ~ **bibliothèque** COMMS library rate (*US*); ~ **à la boîte** TRANSP box rate; ~ **de bout en bout** IMP/EXP, TRANSP through charge; ~ **cabine** TRANSP *navigation* cabin charge; ~ **charge complète** TRANSP carload rate; ~ **des chevaux de pur sang** TRANSP bloodstock rate; ~ **en classe économique** LOISIRS, TRANSP economy fare; ~ **de classification avec réduction** TRANSP *fret aérien* reduce class rate, R; ~ **commun** TRANSP joint charge, joint fare, joint rate; ~ **commun compensatoire** ECON compensating common tariff, CCT; ~ **complet** RES HUM full

rate; ~ **concurrentiel** V&M competitive rate; ~ **de construction** TRANSP construction rate; ~ **à déterminer** TRANSP rate to be agreed, RTBA; ~ **direct** IMP/EXP, TRANSP through charge, through rate; ~ **discriminatoire** COM, V&M price discrimination; ~ **discriminatoire de second ordre** COM second-degree price discrimination; ~ **douanier** IMP/EXP customs tariff; ~ **douanier commun** IMP/EXP *UE* common customs tariff, CCT; ~ **douanier communautaire** IMP/EXP *UE* common customs tariff, CCT; ~ **des échantillons** COM sample rate; ~ **excursion** LOISIRS excursion fare; ~ **extérieur commun** ECON common external tariff, CET; ~ **familles** TRANSP family fare; ~ **fixe** V&M flat rate; ~ **forfaitaire** IMP/EXP through charge, through rate, TRANSP through charge, through rate, *maritime* fixture rate; ~ **fret à perte** TRANSP *distribution* under cost freight rate; ~ **fret spécial weekend** TRANSP weekend freight tariff; ~ **global** COM blanket rate; ~ **de groupage** TRANSP groupage rate; ~ **groupé** TRANSP combination charge, combination rate, consolidated rate; ~ **de groupe** COM blanket rate; ~ **des importations** ECON, IMP/EXP import tariff; ~ **intérieur** TRANSP domestic rate; ~ **au kilo excédant le poids pivot** TRANSP *aviation* overpivot area; ~ **lent** COM third-class mail (*US*); ~ **à la ligne** MÉDIA *presse* linage, lineage; ~ **local** TRANSP *aviation* local charge; ~ **marchandises** TRANSP freight tariff; ~ **marchandises demandé** TRANSP required freight rate, RFR; ~ **marchandises diverses** TRANSP general cargo rate; ~ **minimum** TRANSP minimum charge; ~ **non-dégressif** V&M flat rate; ~ **non-répertorié** TRANSP rate not reported, RNR; ~ **normal** TRANSP normal rate; ~ **optimal** ECON, IMP/EXP optimal tariff; ~ **par poids** TRANSP weight charge; ~ **par wagon** TRANSP *chemin de fer* carload rate; ~ **passagers** TRANSP passenger tariff; ~ **à perte** TRANSP rate below cost; ~ **pont terrestre** TRANSP landbridge rate; ~ **portuaire** IMP/EXP, TRANSP port tariff; ~ **postal réduit spécial** COMMS special fourth-class mail; ~ **préférentiel** TRANSP commodity rate; ~ **promotionnel** RES HUM golden rate, V&M bargain rate; ~ **proportionnel** FIN *aviation* proportional rate; ~ **publicitaire** FIN, V&M adrate, advertising rates; ~ **publié** FIN published charge, published rate; ~ **de recouvrement** IMP/EXP collection tariff; ~ **réduit** COM concession, LOISIRS concessionary rate, off-peak fare, TRANSP off-peak fare, reduced fare; ~ **réduit aux heures creuses** COM off-peak charges; ~ **séparant coûts variables et coûts fixes** ECON two-part tariff; ~ **du service conteneur** TRANSP container service tariff, CST; ~ **de services supplémentaires** TRANSP supplementary service tariff, SST; ~ **de soudure** TRANSP *chemin de fer* combination of rates; ~ **spécial pour les membres de la profession** COM special terms for the trade; ~ **spécifié** TRANSP specified rate; ~ **stable** TRANSP stable rate; ~ **sur réseau** TRANSP *tarif de transport aérien* on-line rate; ~ **télégraphique** COMMS, ECON *commerce international* cable rate; ~ **touriste**

LOISIRS, TRANSP tourist fare; **~ uniforme** COM blanket rate; **~ variable** IMP/EXP swinging tariff; **~ pour vol domestique** TRANSP internal fare; **~ pour vol intérieur** TRANSP internal fare; **~ voyageurs** TRANSP passenger fare, passenger tariff; ♦ **et réglementations extérieurs** IMP/EXP overseas tariff and regulations, OTAR

tarification *f* COM pricing, FIN, FISC tarification, V&M pricing; **~ de Best** ASSUR Best's Rating (*US*); **~ en charge maximum** ECON peak-load pricing; **~ envisagée** ASSUR prospective rating; **~ en fonction du marché** FIN, V&M market pricing; **~ non-linéaire** ECON nonlinear pricing; **~ parallèle** ECON parallel pricing; **~ personnalisée** ASSUR experience rating; **~ de pointe** ECON peak-load pricing; **~ en pointe de consommation** ECON peak-load pricing; **~ de prestige** V&M prestige pricing; **~ sauvage** ECON predatory pricing; **~ selon la statistique** ASSUR experience rating; **~ des transferts** COM transfer pricing; **~ à l'unité** COM, V&M unit pricing

tarifs: ~ conjoints *m pl* LOISIRS, TRANSP spouse fare; **~ différents** *m pl* TRANSP multiquote; **~ d'espace** *m pl* V&M *publicité* space rates; **~ et classifications** *m pl* COMMS rates and classifications (*US*); **~ d'insertion** *m pl* V&M *publicité* space rates; **~ postaux** *m pl* COMMS postage, postage rates; **~ préferentiels** *m pl* IMP/EXP, TRANSP *fret aérien* specific commodity rates; **~ ro-ro** *m pl* TRANSP ro/ro rates; **~ soudés** *m pl* TRANSP *chemin de fer* combination of rates; ♦ **aux ~ en vigueur** COM at ruling prices

tarte: ~ à la crème *f infrml* COM classic example

tas: sur le ~ *loc* RES HUM hands-on

taux:[1] **~ zéro** *adj* FISC *TVA* zero-rated

taux[2] *m* COM *pourcentage* level, ECON level, rate of increase, INFO rate; **~ d'absentéisme** *m* COM, RES HUM absentee rate; **~ d'absorption** *m* V&M absorption rate; **~ d'accroissement** *m* ECON rate of increase; **~ acheteur** *m* (ANT *taux vendeur*) COMPTA buyer's rate; **~ d'action préférentiel** *m* BOURSE preferred stock ratio; **~ d'activité** *m* RES HUM activity rate; **~ d'activité constant** *m* FIN Uniform Business Rate, UBR; **~ d'actualisation** *m* FIN hurdle rate of return; **~ actuariel** *m* BANQUE yield to maturity, YTM, BOURSE current yield, redemption yield, yield to maturity, YTM; **~ actuel** *m* COM current rate, CR; **~ ad valorem** *m* COMPTA ad valorem rate (*frml*); **~ d'amortissement** *m* COMPTA rate of depreciation; **~ pour un an** *m* BANQUE, FIN annualized rate; **~ annualisé** *m* BANQUE, COM, FIN annual percentage rate, annualized percentage rate, APR; **~ annuel** *m* BANQUE, COM, ECON, FIN annual rate; **~ annuel composé** *m* BANQUE compound annual rate (*UK*), CAR (*UK*); **~ annuel corrigé des variations saisonnières** *m* ECON s.a.a.r., seasonally adjusted annual rate; **~ annuel monétaire** *m* (*TAM*) FIN annual monetary rate; **~ applicable aux journées de remplacement** *m* RES HUM lieu rate; **~ d'argent au jour le jour** *m*

(*TJJ*) BANQUE call money rate, daily money rate; **~ d'assistance effectif** *m* ECON, IND effective rate of assistance; **~ d'Atlantique sud** *m pl* TRANSP South Atlantic rates; **~ d'augmentation** *m* ECON rate of increase; **~ en augmentation** *m* BANQUE, ECON, FIN rising interest rate; **~ bancaire moyen** *m* BANQUE, ECON average interest rate; **~ de base** *m* France (*cf taux préférentiel Canada*) BOURSE, ECON, FIN base lending rate (*UK*), base rate (*UK*), prime lending rate (*US*), prime rate (*US*); **~ de base bancaire** *m* (*TBB*) BANQUE, ECON, FIN bank base rate, bank rate; **~ de base à long terme** *m* FIN long-term prime rate, LTPR; **~ de bénéfice au chiffre d'affaires** *m* COMPTA return on sales; **~ bonifié** *m* BANQUE preferential interest rate; **~ de bons du Trésor** *m* BOURSE, ECON Treasury bill rate, TBR; **~ brut** *m* TRANSP gross rate; **~ de capacité de la main-d'oeuvre** *m* ECON, IND, RES HUM capacity ratio; **~ de capitalisation** *m* COMPTA, ECON capitalization rate; **~ de change** *m* BANQUE, ECON, FIN currency value, exchange rate, rate of exchange; **~ de change acheteur** *m* BANQUE, FIN buying rate; **~ de change artificiel** *m* ECON artificial exchange rate; **~ de change en données corrigées des changes** *m* ECON trade-weighted exchange rate; **~ de change effectif** *m* ECON, FIN effective exchange rate; **~ de change fixe** *m* ECON fixed exchange rate; **~ de change flexible** *m* ECON flexible exchange rate; **~ de change flottant** *m* ECON floating currency exchange rate, floating exchange rate; **~ de change indexé** *m* ECON, FIN pegged exchange rate, pegged rate of exchange; **~ de change mal aligné** *m* ECON misaligned rate of exchange; **~ de change multiple** *m* ECON multiple exchange rate; **~ de change officiel** *m* BANQUE, ECON, FIN official exchange rate; **~ de change pondéré en fonction des échanges commerciaux** *m* ECON trade-weighted exchange rate; **~ de change réel** *m* BOURSE real exchange rate; **~ de change réglementé** *m* ECON, FIN controlled rate; **~ de change réservé aux touristes** *m* ECON, FIN, LOISIRS tourist exchange rate; **~ de change de soutien** *m* ECON, FIN pegged exchange rate, pegged rate of exchange; **~ de change spécial appliqué au commerce** *m* ECON special commercial exchange rate; **~ de change à terme** *m* BOURSE, ECON forward exchange rate; **~ de charge** *m* COM, ECON, IND, MATH load factor; **~ de chômage** *m* ECON, PROT SOC unemployment rate, RES HUM jobless rate; **~ cible** *m* BOURSE target rate; **~ de clientèle** *m* COM switching-in rate; **~ de commission** *m* BANQUE commission rate; **~ composite** *m* COM composite rate; **~ de comptant** *m* BOURSE spot rate; **~ contractuel du prêt** *m* BOURSE contractual loan rate; **~ de conversion** *m* BANQUE, ECON, FIN conversion rate, translation rate; **~ courant** *m* COM current rate, CR; **~ à court terme de spécialiste** *m* BOURSE specialist's short-sale ratio; **~ des coûts à long terme tous frais mélangés** *m* FIN long-term blended cost rate, LTB; **~ de couverture** *m*

COMPTA, FIN cover ratio; ~ **de couverture de la dette** *m* COMPTA, FIN debt coverage ratio; ~ **de couverture du dividende** *m* COMPTA, FIN dividend cover; ~ **de couverture des frais financiers fixes** *m* COMPTA, FIN fixed-charge coverage; ~ **de crédit variable** *m* FIN variable lending rate, VLR; ~ **de croissance** *m* BOURSE growth rate, growth stock, COM, ECON, INFO growth rate; ~ **de croissance économique** *m* ECON economic growth rate; ~ **de croissance économique soutenable** *m* ECON, POL sustainable economic growth rate; ~ **de croissance garantie** *m* ECON warranted rate of growth; ~ **de croissance global** *m* ECON, FIN compound growth rate; ~ **de croissance naturel** *m* ECON natural rate of growth; ~ **de déclin** *m* BOURSE rate of decay; ~ **dégressif** *m* FIN decreasing rate; ~ **de dégrèvement** *m* FISC rate of relief; ~ **demandé** *m* BOURSE rate asked; ~ **de départs** *m* ECON exit-voice, quit rate, RES HUM quit rate; ~ **de départs naturels** *m* COM, V&M attrition rate; ~ **de dépendance** *m* PROT SOC dependency ratio; ~ **de déport** *m* BOURSE, FIN backwardation rate; ~ **de dépréciation** *m* BOURSE rate of decay; ~ **de diffusion** *m* IND *production* diffusion rate; ~ **directeur** *m* ECON, FIN key rate; ~ **des disponibilités** *m* COMPTA liquid ratio; ~ **disponible** *m* COMPTA liquid ratio; ~ **du dollar** *m* BOURSE dollar rate; ~ **d'échecs** *m* COM failure rate; ~ **effectif global** *m* BANQUE, COM, FIN annual percentage rate, annualized percentage rate, APR; ~ **d'emprunt** *m* BANQUE, FIN borrowing ratio; ~ **d'emprunt interbancaire de Londres** *m* BOURSE London Interbank Bid Rate, LIBID; ~ **d'emprunt à terme** *m* BOURSE forward borrowing rate; ~ **emprunteur** *m* BANQUE, BOURSE bid rate; ~ **des emprunts à terme** *m* BOURSE *devises à terme* forward borrowing rate; ~ **d'encadrement** *m* RES HUM management ratio; ~ **d'endettement** *m* BANQUE, BOURSE, COMPTA, FIN gearing ratio (*BrE*), leverage ratio (*AmE*); ~ **d'endettement élevé** *m* BANQUE, BOURSE, COMPTA, FIN high gearing (*BrE*), high leverage (*AmE*); ~ **d'endettement financier** *m* FIN financial leverage ratio; ~ **d'épargne bonifié** *m* BANQUE bonus savings rate; ~ **d'épargne des ménages** *m* ECON savings ratio; ~ **d'érosion** *m* COM, V&M attrition rate; ~ **d'erreurs** *m* INFO error rate; ~ **d'escompte** *m* BANQUE, FIN discount rate, rate of discount; ~ **de l'escompte** *m* BANQUE, ECON, FIN bank lending rate, bank rate; ~ **d'escompte attendu** *m* ECON test rate of discount; ~ **d'escompte bancaire** *m* BANQUE bank discount rate; ~ **d'escompte interne** *m* COMPTA internal rate of discount; ~ **d'escompte du marché** *m* COM market rate of discount; ~ **d'escompte social** *m* FIN social rate of discount; ~ **d'exploitation** *m* ECON rate of exploitation; ~ **des exportations** *m* IMP/EXP export figures; ~ **favorable** *m* ECON favorable rate (*AmE*), favourable rate (*BrE*); ~ **de financement** *m* BOURSE financing rate; ~ **de financement à court terme** *m* BOURSE short-date financing rate; ~ **de financement effectif** *m* BOURSE effective

funding rate; ~ **fixe de l'impôt** *m* FISC fixed tax rate; ~ **flottant** *m* BANQUE, ECON floating interest rate, floating rate, variable rate; ~ **des fonds fédéraux** *m* BANQUE *marché monétaire* federal funds rate (*US*); ~ **de gain** *m* COM switching-in rate; ~ **général des matières premières** *m* BOURSE general commodity rate, GCR; ~ **glissant** *m* BOURSE gliding rate; ~ **global de fertilité** *m* ECON total fertility rate, TRF; ~ **horaire** *m* RES HUM hourly rate; ~ **hors banque** *m* BANQUE, ECON open-market rate, private rate of discount; ~ **d'imposition** *m* FISC rate of tax, rate of taxation, tax rate; ~ **d'imposition apparent** *m* FISC apparent tax rate; ~ **d'imposition de base des corporations** *m* FISC basic corporate tax rate; ~ **d'imposition effectif** *m* FISC effective tax rate; ~ **d'imposition prévu par la loi** *m* FISC statutory tax rate; ~ **d'imposition réel** *m* FISC actual tax rate; ~ **d'imposition spécial** *m* FISC special tax rate; ~ **d'impôt** *m* FISC rate of tax, rate of taxation, tax rate; ~ **de l'impôt foncier** *m* FISC residential tax rate; ~ **de l'impôt sur le revenu** *m* FISC income tax rate; ~ **d'inclusion** *m* FISC *des gains et des pertes en capital* inclusion rate; ~ **incrémental de dépenses en capital** *m* FIN incremental capital-output ratio, ICOR; ~ **d'inflation** *m* ECON inflation rate; ~ **d'inflation apparent** *m* ECON headline rate; ~ **d'inflation sous-jacente** *m* ECON underlying inflation rate; ~ **de l'inflation structurelle** *m* ECON core inflation rate; ~ **interbancaire** *m* BANQUE federal funds rate (*US*), interbank exchange rate, interbank rate, ECON interbank exchange rate, interbank rate; ~ **interbancaire moyen de Londres** *m* BOURSE London Interbank Mean Rate, LIMEAN; ~ **interbancaire offert** *m* BANQUE, BOURSE, ECON interbank offered rate, IBOR; ~ **interbancaire offert à Londres** *m* (*TIOL*) BANQUE, BOURSE London Interbank Offered Rate (*LIBOR*); ~ **interbancaire offert à Paris** *m* (*TIOP*) BANQUE Paris Interbank Offered Rate (*PIBOR*); ~ **interbancaire offert à Singapour** *m* (*TIOS*) BANQUE Singapore Interbank Offered Rate (*SIBOR*); ~ **interbancaire offert à Tokyo** *m* (*TIOT*) ECON Tokyo Interbank Offered Rate (*TIBOR*); ~ **interbancaire proposé** *m* BANQUE, BOURSE, ECON interbank offered rate, IBOR; ~ **d'intérêt annuel** *m* BANQUE, COM, FIN annual percentage rate, annualized percentage rate, APR; ~ **d'intérêt en baisse** *m* BANQUE, ECON, FIN declining interest rate; ~ **d'intérêt bancaire** *m* BANQUE, FIN banking interest; ~ **d'intérêt de base** *m* BANQUE prime rate of interest; ~ **d'intérêt bonifié** *m* BANQUE bonus rate of interest; ~ **d'intérêt brut** *m* ECON, FIN pure interest rate; ~ **d'intérêt composé** *m* BANQUE compound annual rate (*UK*), CAR (*UK*); ~ **d'intérêt comptable** *m* (*TIC*) BANQUE, COMPTA, FIN accounting rate of interest (*ARI*); ~ **d'intérêt de compte d'épargne bancaire** *m* BANQUE banker's deposit rate; ~ **d'intérêt à la consommation** *m* FIN consumption rate of interest (*UK*), CRI (*UK*); ~ **d'intérêt contractuel** *m* BOURSE coupon rate;

~ d'intérêt à court terme *m* ECON short-term interest rate; ~ d'intérêt créditeur *m* BANQUE deposit rate; ~ d'intérêt pour crédits aux courtiers *m* BOURSE broker call-loan rate (*US*); ~ d'intérêt des dépôts bancaires *m* BANQUE bank deposit rates; ~ d'intérêt d'un emprunt bancaire *m* BANQUE bank loan rate; ~ d'intérêt des emprunts *m* BANQUE, ECON, FIN borrowing rate; ~ d'intérêt flottant *m* BANQUE, ECON floating interest rate, variable interest rate; ~ d'intérêt généralement coté du marché *m* ECON generally quoted market interest rate; ~ d'intérêt en hausse *m* BANQUE, ECON, FIN rising interest rate; ~ d'intérêt du marché *m* ECON, FIN market rate of interest; ~ d'intérêt mélangé *m* BANQUE blended rate; ~ d'intérêt net de toutes charges *m* FIN interest rate net of all charges; ~ d'intérêt nominal *m* BOURSE coupon rate, nominal interest rate, FIN nominal interest rate; ~ d'intérêt obligataire *m* BOURSE bond rate; ~ d'intérêt plafond *m* BANQUE, ECON, FIN cap, cap rate; ~ d'intérêt préférentiel *m* *Canada* BANQUE prime rate of interest; ~ d'intérêt d'un prêt à vue *m* BOURSE call loan rate; ~ d'intérêt propre *m* ECON own rate of interest; ~ d'intérêt réel *m* BANQUE effective interest rate, FIN real interest rate; ~ d'intérêt variable *m* BANQUE, ECON floating interest rate, variable interest rate; ~ des intérêts courus *m* BANQUE, COMPTA, FIN accrual interest rate; ~ internationaux de liquidité *m pl* BANQUE, ECON, FIN international liquidity ratios; ~ interne de rentabilité *m* COMPTA, FIN internal rate of return, IRR; ~ d'investissement élevé *m* ECON, FIN high rate of investment; ~ au jour le jour *m* BANQUE call money rate, daily money rate, call rate, ECON, FIN call rate; ~ kilométrique *m* TRANSP *taxis* per kilometer rate (*AmE*), per kilometre rate (*BrE*); ~ de liquidation du contrat à terme *m* BOURSE futures liquidation rate; ~ de liquidation d'opération à terme *m* BOURSE futures liquidation rate; ~ de liquidité *m* BANQUE liquid ratio, liquidity ratio, BOURSE current ratio, liquid ratio, liquidity ratio, COMPTA liquid ratio, liquidity ratio, FIN current ratio, liquid ratio, liquidity ratio; ~ de liquidité immédiate *m* BANQUE, COMPTA, FIN acid-test ratio, quick ratio; ~ de liquidités *m* BANQUE, BOURSE, COMPTA, FIN liquid assets ratio; ~ locatif *m* COMPTA rental/turnover ratio, IMMOB rental rate; ~ Lombard *m* BANQUE Lombard rate; ~ du marché *m* BOURSE market rate; ~ du marché au comptant *m* BOURSE cash market rates; ~ du marché monétaire *m* BOURSE, ECON, FIN money-market rate; ~ de marché obligataire *m* (*TMO*) BOURSE bond market rate; ~ de marge brute *m* V&M return on sales; ~ marginal *m* FISC marginal rate; ~ marginal d'impôt *m* FISC marginal tax rate; ~ marginal de substitution *m* ECON marginal rate of substitution, MRS; ~ marginal de substitution décroissant *m* ECON diminishing marginal rate of substitution; ~ marginal de transformation *m* ECON marginal rate of transformation; ~ mi-Atlantique *m pl* TRANSP *aviation*

mid-Atlantic rates; ~ mobile *m* BOURSE gliding rate; ~ de mortalité *m* COM death rate; ~ moyen *m* COMPTA average rate; ~ moyen interbancaire des eurobanques de Londres *m* BOURSE London Interbank Mean Rate, LIMEAN; ~ moyen interbancaire de Londres *m* BOURSE London Interbank Mean Rate, LIMEAN; ~ moyen mensuel du marché monétaire *m* (*T4M, TMMMM*) BOURSE average monthly money market rate; ~ moyen pondéré *m* (*TMP*) BOURSE average weighted rate; ~ mystère *m* FIN teaser rate; ~ de natalité *m* COM birth rate; ~ naturel de chômage *m* ECON natural rate of unemployment, nonaccelerating inflation rate of unemployment; ~ naturel de croissance *m* ECON warranted rate of growth; ~ naturel d'emploi *m* ECON natural rate of employment; ~ naturel d'intérêt *m* ECON natural rate of interest; ~ net *m* BANQUE net rate; ~ nominal *m* BOURSE nominal yield; ~ nominal d'emprunt *m* FIN nominal loan rate; ~ non-rajustable *m* BANQUE nonadjustable rate; ~ nord-atlantique *m pl* TRANSP North Atlantic rates; ~ normalisé d'activités *m* FIN Uniform Business Rate, UBR; ~ nul d'imposition *m* FISC zero rate of tax; ~ nul de taxe *m* FISC zero rate of tax; ~ d'obligation *m* BOURSE liability rate; ~ d'occupation *m* TRANSP *cabines et couchettes* berth user rate, *d'un train* load factor; ~ officiel d'escompte *m* BANQUE, ECON minimum lending rate (*UK*), official rate, MLR (*UK*), FIN official rate; ~ de l'offre interbancaire de Londres *m* BOURSE London Interbank Bid Rate, LIBID; ~ pour les opérations à terme *m* ECON forward rate; ~ optimal de pollution *m* ECON, ENVIR optimal rate of pollution; ~ de l'option d'achat *m* (ANT *taux de l'option de vente*) BOURSE call rate; ~ de l'option de vente *m* (ANT *taux de l'option d'achat*) BOURSE put rate; ~ de participation *m* RES HUM participation rate; ~ de pénalisation *m* DROIT penalty rate; ~ de pénétration *m* V&M *marketing* penetration rate; ~ de pénétration des importations *m* IMP/EXP import penetration ratio; ~ de perte de clientèle *m* COM switching-out rate; ~ pivot *m* ECON central rate; ~ plafond *m* BANQUE cap, cap rate, maximum rate, BOURSE ceiling rate, ECON cap rate, FIN cap, cap rate; ~ plafond d'imposition *m* FISC top rate of tax; ~ plafond de l'impôt *m* FISC ceiling tax rate; ~ plancher *m* BOURSE floor rate; ~ préférentiel *m* BANQUE preferential rate, BOURSE, ECON, FIN *Canada (cf taux de base France)* base lending rate (*UK*), base rate (*UK*), prime lending rate (*US*), prime rate (*US*); ~ préférentiel de New York *m* BANQUE New York prime loan rate, NYPLR; ~ de prélèvement fiscal *m* ECON, FISC tax burden; ~ prescrit *m* FISC prescribed rate; ~ de prêt *m* BANQUE lending rate; ~ de prêt contractuel *m* BOURSE contractual loan rate; ~ de prêt hypothécaire *m* BANQUE mortgage rate; ~ de prêt préférentiel de New York *m* BANQUE New York prime loan rate (*US*), NYPLR (*US*); ~ de prêt à vue *m* BOURSE call loan rate;

~ **de prime** *m* ASSUR, BOURSE premium rate; ~ **des prises en pension** *m* BANQUE repurchase rate; ~ **privé de l'escompte** *m* BANQUE, ECON private rate of discount; ~ **privilégié** *m* COM concessionary rate, preferred rate; ~ **de production** *m* BOURSE, IND production rate; ~ **de protection effectif** *m* ECON, IND effective rate of protection; ~ **publié** *m* TRANSP *fret* published rate; ~ **de rachat** *m* V&M *marketing* repeat rate; ~ **de réclamation** *m* PROT SOC take-up rate; ~ **de reclamation** *m* PROT SOC take up rate; ~ **réduit** *m* COM, FISC reduced rate; ~ **réel** *m* COMPTA effective rate; ~ **de réescompte** *m* COMPTA rediscount rate; ~ **de référence** *m* BOURSE target rate; ~ **de référence suffisant** *m* COMPTA adequate target rate; ~ **de réinvestissement** *m* BOURSE, COM reinvestment rate; ~ **de remplacement** *m* PROT SOC replacement ratio; ~ **de remplissage** *m* ECON load factor; ~ **de rémunération** *m* RES HUM salary rate; ~ **de rendement** *m* BANQUE rate of return, BOURSE return, yield, COM utilization percent, COMPTA rate of return, ECON capacity ratio, FIN rate of return, IND, RES HUM capacity ratio; ~ **de rendement approximatif** *m* COMPTA approximate rate of return; ~ **de rendement après-impôts** *m* COMPTA, ECON, FIN, FISC after-tax rate of return; ~ **de rendement avant imposition** *m* COM, ECON, FIN, FISC pretax rate of return; ~ **de rendement du capital différentiel** *m* FIN incremental capital-output ratio, ICOR; ~ **de rendement des capitaux investis** *m* ECON, FIN rate of return on capital employed, RORCE; ~ **de rendement comptable** *m* COMPTA accounting rate of return, book rate of return; ~ **de rendement pour une durée de vie moyenne** *m* BOURSE yield to average life; ~ **de rendement de la gestion financière** *m* FIN financial management rate of return, FMRR; ~ **de rendement implicite** *m* FIN implied repo rate (*US, infrml*); ~ **de rendement minimal** *m* ECON hurdle rate; ~ **de rendement moyen** *m* BOURSE, IND average yield; ~ **de rendement réel** *m* BANQUE real rate of return, RRR; ~ **de rendement requis** *m* FIN required rate of return; ~ **de rendement sur le capital employé** *m* ECON, FIN rate of return on capital employed, RORCE; ~ **de rentabilité** *m* COMPTA overall rate of return; ~ **de rentabilité des actifs nets utilisés** *m* BOURSE, COMPTA, FIN return on net assets employed; ~ **de rentabilité des actifs utilisés** *m* BOURSE, COMPTA, FIN return on assets; ~ **de rentabilité intérieur** *m* COMPTA, FIN internal rate of return, IRR; ~ **de rentabilité interne** *m* COMPTA, FIN internal rate of return, IRR; ~ **de rentabilité d'un investissement** *m* (*TRI*) COMPTA, FIN return on investment (*ROI*); ~ **de répartition au prorata** *m* TRANSP *aviation* proration rate; ~ **de réponse** *m* V&M *marketing* response rate; ~ **de reproduction** *m* ECON reproduction rate; ~ **de réussite** *m* V&M *d'un vendeur* strike rate (*jarg*); ~ **révisable annuellement** *m* (*TRA*) FIN interest rate subject to modification every year; ~ **de rotation des comptes clients** *m* COMPTA, FIN accounts recei-

vable turnover; ~ **de roulement** *m* BOURSE rate of rolling; ~ **de salaire d'équilibre** *m* ECON equilibrium wage rate; ~ **de salaire horaire** *m* RES HUM base pay rate; ~ **de salaire de référence** *m* ECON, FIN key rate; ~ **servi sur les dépôts** *m* BANQUE deposit rate; ~ **de solvabilité** *m* COMPTA solvency ratio; ~ **sous-jacent** *m* ECON underlying rate; ~ **de souscription** *m* BOURSE subscription ratio, COM, PROT SOC take-up rate; ~ **standard** *m* FISC standard rate (*UK*); ~ **statutaire d'imposition** *m* FISC statutory tax rate; ~ **de succès** *m* V&M *publicité* advertising conversion rate; ~ **de syndicalisation** *m* RES HUM union density; ~ **tarifaire** *m* IMP/EXP tariff rate; ~ **à terme** *m* BOURSE, FIN forward rate; ~ **à terme à la hausse** *m* BOURSE, ECON, FIN cap; ~ **de trois mois** *m* FIN three-months' rate; ~ **uniforme** *m* COMPTA blanket rate, FISC flat rate; ~ **uniforme de salaire** *m* RES HUM flat rate of pay; ~ **d'utilisation des capacités** *m* ECON, IND capacity utilization rate; ~ **d'utilisation de la main-d'oeuvre** *m* ECON, IND, RES HUM capacity ratio; ~ **d'utilisation du potentiel de production** *m* ECON, IND capacity utilization rate; ~ **d'utilisation d'un quai** *m* TRANSP *installations portuaires* berth user rate; ~ **de la valeur excédentaire** *m* BANQUE rate of surplus value; ~ **variable** *m* BANQUE, ECON floating interest rate, floating rate, roll-over ratio, variable rate; ~ **vendeur** *m* (*ANT taux acheteur*) COMPTA seller's rate; ~ **en vigueur** *m* COM, FIN, RES HUM the going rate; ~ **zéro** *m* COMPTA zero rating, FISC zero rate, IMP/EXP zero rating; ◆ **à ~ fixe** BOURSE at a flat rate; **au ~ annuel** COM, FIN at an annual rate; **au ~ de** COM at; **aux ~ standard** FISC standard-rated; **faire grimper les ~ d'intérêts** FIN give an upward thrust to interest rates; **faire monter les ~ artificiellement** BOURSE kite

taxation *f* ECON taxation, FIN levy, taxation, FISC taxation; ~ **à la valeur** TRANSP valuation charge; ~ **au volume** TRANSP volume charge; ~ **zéro** FISC zero rating

taxe *f* COMPTA, ECON, FIN tax, FISC duty, imposition, levy, tax, IMP/EXP levy; ~ **d'aéroport** FISC airport tax, departure tax, TRANSP airport tax; ~ **d'affaires** COM, FISC business tax; ~ **annuelle** BREVETS renewal fee; ~ **d'apprentissage** FISC training tax; ~ **compensatrice** FISC compensation tax; ~ **de consommation** FISC consumption tax; ~ **de débarquement** IMP/EXP, TRANSP *port* port tax; ~ **directe** FISC open tax; ~ **à l'exportation** FISC, IMP/EXP export tax; ~ **fédérale sur les ventes au détail** FISC federal retail sales tax; ~ **fixe** FISC fixed duty; ~ **forfaitaire** COM flat-rate fee; ~ **franche** FISC open tax; ~ **d'habitation** FISC roof tax; ~ **immobilière** FISC property tax; ~ **à l'importation** IMP/EXP import duty, ID; ~ **locale** FISC local tax, TRANSP local charge; ~ **nationale** FISC national tax; ~ **passager** LOISIRS passenger dues, TRANSP *maritime* passenger toll; ~ **postale** COMMS postage due; ~ **de prestation de service** (*TPS*) FISC goods and services tax (*GST*);

~ professionnelle COM, FISC business tax; **~ de séjour** FISC tourist tax, visitor's tax, LOISIRS tourist tax; **~ de succession** FISC transfer tax; **~ superposée** FISC superimposed tax; **~ sur les achats** FISC purchase tax; **~ sur les articles de luxe** FISC luxury tax; **~ sur le capital** FISC capital tax (*Canada*); **~ sur les carburants** FISC fuel tax; **~ sur la consommation** ECON, FISC commodity tax, expenditure tax; **~ sur la construction de logements** FISC housing construction tax; **~ sur les dépenses du consommateur** ECON, FISC expenditure tax; **~ sur les effluents** ECON, ENVIR effluent fee; **~ sur l'emploi** FISC employment tax; **~ sur un facteur de production** ECON, FISC factor tax; **~ sur la formation professionnelle** FISC continuing education tax; **~ sur le gaz naturel et les liquides extraits du gaz** FISC gas and natural gas liquids tax; **~ sur intrants donnant droit à un crédit** FISC creditable input tax; **~ sur le transport aérien** *(TTA)* FISC air transportation tax *(ATT)*; **~ sur la valeur** COMPTA, FISC ad valorem tax *(frml)*; **~ sur la valeur ajoutée** *(TVA)* FISC value-added tax *(UK)* *(VAT)*; **~ sur les véhicules de société** FISC tax on company cars; **~ sur les ventes** FISC, V&M sales tax; **~ de Tobin** ECON, FISC Tobin tax; **~ de transport** FISC transport tax; **~ à la valeur** TRANSP value surcharge; **~ de vente fédérale** FISC federal sales tax; **~ de vente nationale** FISC national sales tax *(US)*; **~ de vente de Quebec** *(TVQ)* FISC Quebec sales tax *(QST)*

taxer *vt* FISC impose a tax

taxes: **~ et droits sur les conteneurs** *f pl* FISC, TRANSP container dues; **~ terminales** *f pl* FIN terminal charges; **~ de tonnage** *f pl* TRANSP delivery charge, tonnage dues

taxi *m* TRANSP taxi

taxiway *m* TRANSP *aéroport* taxiway

taylorisme *m* ECON, RES HUM Taylorism *(UK)*

TBB *abrév (taux de base bancaire)* BANQUE, ECON, FIN bank base rate, bank rate

Tbilissi *n pr* COM Tbilisi

Tchad *m* COM Chad

tchadien, -enne *adj* COM Chadian

Tchadien, -enne *m,f* COM *habitant* Chadian

tchécoslovaque *adj obs* COM Czechoslovak *(obs)*, Czechoslovakian *(obs)*

Tchécoslovaque *mf* COM *habitant* Czechoslovak *(obs)*, Czechoslovakian *(obs)*

Tchécoslovaquie *f obs* COM now called Czech Republic since 1989, Czechoslovakia *(obs)*

tchèque[1] *adj* COM Czech

tchèque[2] *m* COM *langue* Czech

Tchèque *mf* COM *habitant* Czech

TD *abrév (ligne de charge tropicale en eau douce)* TRANSP TF *(tropical fresh water load line)*

tech. *abrév (technicien)* RES HUM technical assistant

technicien, -enne *m,f (tech.)* RES HUM technical assistant; **~ d'entretien** IND, RES HUM maintenance engineer; **~ de hardware** INFO hardware specialist; **~ informatique** INFO troubleshooter; **~ de maintenance** RES HUM service engineer

technico:[1] **~ -commercial** *m* GESTION technical salesman, RES HUM sales engineer

technico:[2] **~ -commerciale** *f* GESTION technical saleswoman, RES HUM sales engineer

technique[1] *adj* COM, IND *agent* technical

technique[2] *f* IND engineering; **~ de l'appât** V&M *destinée à tromper le client* bait and switch advertising *(US)*; **~ d'audit** COMPTA, FIN auditing technique *(UK)*; **~ du budget base zéro** COMPTA, FIN zero-base budgeting, ZBB; **~ de contrôle** COMPTA, FIN audit technique *(UK)*; **~ courante** COM bread-and-butter technique *(infrml)*; **~ des enchères** COM, ECON, V&M bidding technique; **~ de gestion** GESTION management technique; **~ informatique** INFO computer technology; **~ de mise au courant** GESTION Delphi technique; **~ de pointe** IND advanced engineering; **~ du prix d'appel** V&M *marketing* loss pricing *(jarg)*; **~ de production** COM, IND production technique; **~ publicitaire** V&M advertising technique; **~ de vente** V&M sales technique

techniques: **~ de l'abréaction** *f pl* COMMS, GESTION, RES HUM abreaction channels; **~ de gestion de trésorerie** *f pl* GESTION cash management techniques; **~ de laboratoire** *f pl* V&M *marketing* laboratory techniques *(jarg)*; **~ marchandes** *f pl* V&M merchandising; **~ de la production** *f pl* COM, GESTION, IND production engineering

technocratique *adj* COM, POL technocratic

technologie *f* COM, ECON, IND, INFO technology; **~ adaptée** ECON, ENVIR, IND appropriate technology; **~ appropriée** ECON, ENVIR, IND appropriate technology; **~ de bureau** ADMIN office technology; **~ de communication** COMMS communication technology; **~ complémentaire** COM complementary technology, incremental technology, supplemental technology; **~ douce** ECON, ENVIR, IND alternative technology, soft technology; **~ écologique** ENVIR clean technology; **~ énergétique** ENVIR, IND energy technology; **~ idoine** ECON, ENVIR, IND appropriate technology; **~ incrémentielle** COM complementary technology, incremental technology, supplemental technology; **~ de l'information** INFO information technology, IT; **~ informatique** INFO computer technology; **~ intermédiaire** IND *production* intermediate technology; **~ en mer** IND offshore technology; **~ non-polluante** ENVIR clean technology; **~ de pointe** IND, INFO advanced technology, hi tech, high technology; **~ propre** ENVIR clean technology; **~ de remplacement** COM replacement technology, ECON, ENVIR, IND alternative technology

technologiquement: **~ avancé** *adj* IND high-stream *(jarg)*; **~ rétrogradé** *adj* IND low-stream *(jarg)*

Tegucigalpa *n pr* COM Tegucigalpa

Téhéran *n pr* COM Teheran, Tehran

TEI *abrév (traitement électronique de l'information)* INFO EDP *(electronic data processing)*

tel: ~ **écran, tel écrit** *loc* INFO WYSIWYG *(jarg)*, what you see is what you get

tél. *abrév (téléphone)* COMMS tel. *(telephone)*

télé *abrév (télévision)* COM, COMMS, MÉDIA telly *(BrE, infrml)*, TV *(television)*

téléachat *m* FIN teleshopping, INFO electronic shopping, V&M teleshopping

télé-assistance *f* INFO remote support

téléautographie *f* ADMIN telewriting

Télécarte® *f* COMMS phone card

télécharger *vt* INFO download, upload

télécommande *f* COMMS remote control

télécommandé, e *adj* INFO remote-controlled

télécommunications *f pl* COMMS telecommunications; ~ **numériques sans fil** COMMS cordless digital telecommunications

télécommuniquer *vt* COMMS telecommunicate

téléconférence *f* COMMS conference call, three-way call, INFO, V&M teleconference; ~ **informatisée** COMMS, INFO computer conferencing

téléconsultation *f* INFO remote access

télécopie *f* ADMIN, COMMS facsimile, fax

télécopier *vt* ADMIN, COMMS fax

télécopieur *m* ADMIN, COMMS facsimile, fax, fax machine

télédiffusion *f* COMMS, MÉDIA broadcasting

téléenregistrement *m* COMMS telerecording

télé-enseignement *m* PROT SOC distance learning

télégramme *m* COMMS cable, cablegram *(frml)*, night letter *(US)*

télégraphier *vt* COMMS cable

télé-impression *f* INFO remote printing

téléimprimeur *m* ADMIN, INFO tape machine *(BrE)*, ticker *(AmE)*, teleprinter *(BrE)*, teletypewriter *(AmE)*

télélogiciel *m* INFO telesoftware, tsw

télémaintenance *f* INFO remote maintenance

télémarché *m* FIN, V&M telemarket

télémarketing *m* FIN, V&M telemarketing

télématique *f* COM telematics, COMMS, INFO computer communication, telematics

télémessage *m* COMMS telemessage, TMESS

téléphone *m (tél.)* COMMS phone, telephone; ~ **arabe** COM the grapevine; ~ **automatique** COMMS direct dialing *(AmE)*, direct dialling *(BrE)*; ~ **automatique international** COMMS international subscriber dialing *(AmE)*, international subscriber dialling *(BrE)*, ISD; ~ **cellulaire** COM cellphone, COMMS cellphone, cellular phone; ~ **à clavier** COMMS push-button telephone, touch-tone phone; ~ **mobile** ADMIN, COM, COMMS mobile phone, mobile telephone; ~ **de police secours** COMMS call box *(AmE)*; ~ **portable** ADMIN, COM, COMMS mobile phone, mobile tele-

phone; ~ **portatif** COMMS cellphone, cellular phone; ~ **à poussoirs** *Can* COMMS key telephone set; ~ **public** COMMS pay phone *(BrE)*, pay station *(AmE)*; ~ **rouge** COMMS hot line; ~ **sans fil** COM cellphone; ~ **à touches** COMMS key telephone set, push-button telephone, touch-tone phone; ◆ **au** ~ COMMS *parler* on the phone, *réservation* over the telephone

téléphoner *vti* COMMS phone; ~ **à** COMMS phone, telephone; ◆ ~ **en PCV** *Fra (cf appeler à frais virés Can)*, COMMS call collect *(AmE)*, make a collect call *(AmE)*, make a reverse charge call to sb *(BrE)*, reverse the charges *(BrE)*, transfer the charges; ~ **à qn en PCV** COMMS call sb collect *(AmE)*

téléphonie *f* COMMS telephony

téléphonique *adj* COMMS telephonic

téléscripteur *m* ADMIN tape machine *(BrE)*, teleprinter *(BrE)*, teletypewriter *(AmE)*, ticker *(AmE)*, BOURSE consolidated tape, INFO tape machine *(BrE)*, teleprinter *(BrE)*, teletypewriter *(AmE)*, ticker *(AmE)*; ~ **en retard** BOURSE late tape

téléspectateur, -trice *m,f* MÉDIA televiewer, viewer; ~ **assidu** V&M heavy viewer

Télétel® *m France* COMMS viewdata service operated by France Telecom, ≈ Prestel® *(UK)*

Télétex® *m* COMMS teletex®

télétexte *m* INFO, MÉDIA teletext® *(UK)*

télétraitement *m* INFO remote processing, teleprocessing; ~ **par lots** INFO remote batch processing

télétravail *m* ECON telecommuting, telework, teleworking, RES HUM telework, teleworking

télétravailleur, -euse *m,f* ECON networker, teleworker, RES HUM teleworker

Télétype® *m* INFO Teletype®

télévendeur, -euse *m,f* FIN, V&M telesales person

télévente *f* FIN, V&M telesales, teleselling

télévirement *m* BANQUE, FIN electronic funds transfer, EFT; ~ **au point de vente** BANQUE electronic funds transfer at point of sale, EFT-POS

télévirer *vt* BANQUE transfer by wire

téléviser *vt* COMMS, MÉDIA broadcast, televise

télévision *f (télé)* COM, COMMS, MÉDIA television *(TV)*; ~ **commerciale** MÉDIA *télévision* commercial television; ~ **par satellite** MÉDIA *télévision* satellite television

télévisuel, -elle *adj* COMMS, MÉDIA televisual

télex *m* COMMS telex, tx.

telle: ~ **entrée, telle sortie** *loc* INFO garbage in, garbage out, GIGO

témoignage *m* DROIT evidence, testimony, *d'un témoin* statement of witness; ~ **contradictoire** DROIT conflicting evidence; ~ **en justice consigné par écrit** DROIT deposition; ~ **spontané** DROIT unsolicited testimony; ◆ **en** ~ **de quoi** DROIT in witness whereof

témoigner *vi* COM witness, DROIT attest, testify,

give evidence; ◆ ~ **en faveur de** DROIT give witness on behalf of

témoin *m* DROIT witness, V&M *marketing direct* control; ~ **à charge** DROIT witness for the prosecution; ~ **à décharge** DROIT witness for the defence (*BrE*), witness for the defense (*AmE*); ~ **défaillant** DROIT defaulting witness; ~ **de la défense** DROIT witness for the defence (*BrE*), witness for the defense (*AmE*); ~ **oculaire** DROIT eye witness

tempérament: **à ~** *adv* BANQUE in installments (*AmE*), in instalments (*BrE*)

température *f* ENVIR, TRANSP temperature; ~ **ambiante** COM room temperature; ~ **minimale** COM minimum temperature, MT

temporaire *adj* COM temporary, transient, *accord, travail* interim

temporairement *adv* COM provisionally, temporarily

temps *m* COM *durée* time, *météo* weather, DROIT time, TRANSP weather; ~ **d'accès** *m* INFO access time; ~ **d'accès à l'information** *m* INFO retrieval time; ~ **d'accès moyen** *m* INFO average access time; ~ **d'antenne** *m* MÉDIA *radio, télévision* airtime, viewing time, *télévision* airtime, station time (*US*), V&M *télévision* airtime; ~ **d'antenne disponible** *m* MÉDIA *radio* availabilities on radio, *radio, TV* availability, V&M *radio, TV* availability; ~ **d'arrêt** *m* INFO down time, stop time, RES HUM standoff; ~ **cale à cale** *m* TRANSP *aviation* block time; ~ **de connexion** *m* INFO connection time; ~ **défavorable** *m* COM adverse weather; ~ **disponible** *m* INFO available time; ~ **écoulé** *m* INFO elapsed time; ~ **émission** *m* MÉDIA *télévision* station time (*US*); ~ **forts** *m pl* COM highlights; ~ **gagné** *m* TRANSP *navigation* all time saved; ~ **d'inactivité** *m* INFO idle time; ~ **de latence** *m* ADMIN reaction time, IND *plan* lead time; ~ **de lecture** *m* MÉDIA *radio* needle time; ~ **libre** *m* COM spare time; ~ **de loisirs** *m* COM, LOISIRS leisure time; ~ **machine** *m* INFO computer time; ~ **minimum de correspondance** *m* TRANSP *aviation* minimum connecting time, MCT; ~ **mort** *m* COM, ECON, IND, INFO down time; ~ **moyen** *m* COM mean time, MT, RES HUM allowed time; ~ **moyen de bon fonctionnement** *m* TRANSP mean time between failures, MTBF; ~ **partagé** *m* INFO, RES HUM time sharing; ~ **de planche** *m* TRANSP *maritime* laytime; ~ **de planche gagné** *m* TRANSP *navigation* all working time saved, laytime saved, working time saved; ~ **de planche non-réversible** *m* TRANSP nonreversible laytime; ~ **de planche réversible** *m* TRANSP *maritime, charte-partie* reversible laytime; ~ **publicitaire** *m* V&M advertising time; ~ **de réaction** *m* ADMIN reaction time; ~ **réel** *m* COM, COMPTA, ECON, INFO real time; ~ **de référence** *m* COM standard time; ~ **de réponse** *m* COM, ECON *administration* lag, lag response; ~ **réservé aux émissions du network** *m* MÉDIA station time (*US*); ~ **de rotation** *m* COM turnaround time; ~ **de rotation du navire** *m*

TRANSP ship turnaround time (*AmE*), ship turnround time (*BrE*); ~ **standard** *m* COM standard time; ~ **pour tout louer** *m* IMMOB rent-up period; ~ **de vol** *m* TRANSP flight time; ~ **de vol réel** *m* TRANSP airborne time; ~ **vrai local** *m* (*TVL*) TRANSP *navigation* apparent time at ship (*ATS*); ◆ **à ~ complet** RES HUM full-time; **à ~ partiel** COM, RES HUM part-time; **à ~ plein** RES HUM full-time; **en ~ opportun** COM timely; **en ~ réel** INFO real-time; **être dans les ~** COM be on schedule; **qui prend beaucoup de ~** COM, GESTION time-consuming

Temps: ~ **universel** *m* (*TU*) COM universal time coordinated (*UTC*)

tendance *f* COM pattern, tendency, ECON direction, RES HUM *à la hausse* trend; ~ **à** RES HUM leaning towards; ~ **à la baisse** (*ANT tendance à la hausse*) BOURSE bearish movement, bearish tendency, downward movement, downward trend, ECON downtrend; ~ **baissière** (*ANT tendance haussière*) BOURSE falling trend, BOURSE bearish movement, bearish tendency, downward movement, downward trend; ~ **de base** COM basic trend; ~ **centrale** MATH central tendency; ~ **de la circulation** TRANSP traffic trend; ~ **commerciale** COM, ECON, POL business trend; ~ **du cours** FIN price trend; ~ **dominante** COM major trend; ~ **économique** ECON economic trend; ~ **économique actuelle** COM, ECON, POL current economic trend; ~ **exponentielle** COM exponential trend; ~ **du flux des commandes** V&M *publipostage* order flow pattern; ~ **fondamentale** COM basic trend; ~ **à la hausse** BOURSE *du marché* buoyancy, rising tendency, rising trend, BOURSE (*ANT tendance à la baisse*) bullish movement, bullish tendency, upward movement, upward trend, ECON *du marché* buoyancy, ECON (*ANT tendance à la baisse*) uptrend, FIN *du marché* buoyancy; ~ **à la hausse des salaires** RES HUM earnings drift, wage drift (*jarg*); ~ **haussière** (*ANT tendance baissière*) BOURSE bullish movement, bullish tendency, upward movement, upward trend; ~ **inflationniste** ECON inflationary trend; ~ **à long terme** COM long-term trend, ECON secular trend; ~ **du marché** BOURSE trading pattern, COM, ECON, V&M market trend; ~ **marginale à importer** (*TMI*) ECON, IMP/EXP marginal propensity to import (*MPI*); ~ **moyenne de la consommation** ECON average propensity to consume, APC; ~ **moyenne à économiser** COMPTA, ECON *statistique économique* average propensity to save, APS; ~ **nationale** COM national trend; ~ **profonde** COM underlying tendency; ~ **régionale** V&M regional trend; ~ **sous-jacente** COM underlying trend; ~ **tarifaire** TRANSP rate trend; ◆ **avoir ~ à** COM tend to; ~ **en faveur des familles moins nombreuses** COM trend towards smaller families; **ne pas aller contre la ~** BOURSE don't fight the tape (*jarg*)

tendances: ~ **de la consommation** *f pl* V&M consumer trends; ~ **futures** *f pl* COM future trends; ~ **du marché** *f pl* ECON, POL, V&M market forces

tendeur: ~ **de chaîne** *m* TRANSP chain tensioner; ~ **à déclenchement rapide** *m* TRANSP quick-release tensioner; ~ **à détente brusque** *m* TRANSP *saisissage* overcentre tensioner; ~ **de levier** *m* TRANSP lever tensioner; ~ **pneumatique** *m* TRANSP pneumatic tensioner

tendre *vti* COM *direction* tend; ~ **à** COM tend to, tend towards; ~ **vers** COM tend to, tend towards

tendu, e *adj* COM strained, FIN stringent, RES HUM hot (*jarg*)

teneur:¹ ~ **de marché** *m* BOURSE market maker (*UK*); ~ **de marché d'actions nominatives** *m* BOURSE registered equity market maker; ~ **de marché agréé** *m* BOURSE registered competitive market maker; ~ **de marché agréé pour les actions** *m* BOURSE registered equity market maker

teneur² *f* BANQUE assay, COM assay, content, DROIT tenor, IND assay; ~ **en alcool insuffisante** COM under proof

tenir 1. *vt* RES HUM *stand* man; **2.** *vi* COM last; ♦ ~ **bon** COM hold one's ground, stand firm, stand one's ground; ~ **bon en sachant que** COM stand firm in the belief that; ~ **une boulangerie** COM trade as a baker; ~ **la bride serrée de la politique monétaire** ECON tighten the monetary reins; ~ **compte de** COM allow for, make allowances for, take account of sth, take into consideration, TIC, keep tally of; ~ **compte de l'imprévu** COM contingency planning; ~ **compte de qch** COM take sth into account; ~ **les cordons de la bourse** *infrml* ECON control the purse strings (*infrml*), hold the purse strings (*infrml*); ~ **le filon** *infrml* COM strike it rich (*infrml*); ~ **le marché** BOURSE make a market; ~ **qn au courant** COM, COMMS keep sb informed; ~ **qn responsable de qch** COM hold sb responsible for sth; **se** ~ **au courant de** COM be abreast of, *événements* keep abreast of, keep up with

tension: ~ **due au travail** *f* GESTION, RES HUM work stress; ~ **nerveuse** *f* RES HUM stress

tentative *f* COM endeavor (*AmE*), endeavour (*BrE*); ~ **d'offre publique d'achat** BOURSE, COM, FIN takeover attempt; ~ **d'OPA** BOURSE, COM, FIN takeover attempt; ~ **d'OPA surprise** FIN Saturday night special (*jarg*), dawn raid; ~ **de prise de contrôle inamicale** BOURSE hostile takeover bid; ~ **de prise de contrôle sauvage** BOURSE hostile takeover bid

tenu: ~ **par la loi** *adj* DROIT legally bound; ~ **de par la loi** *adj* DROIT legally bound; ♦ **être** ~ **de** COM be obliged to; **être** ~ **de faire** COM be under an obligation to do; ~ **de payer des dommages et intérêts** DROIT liable for damages

tenue *f* RES HUM conduct; ~ **des barèmes d'imposition** COMPTA asset, DROIT *immobilier* run of schedule, FIN asset; ~ **de compte** BANQUE account operation; ~ **des comptes** COMPTA, FIN book-keeping; ~ **des livres comptables** COMPTA, FIN book-keeping

tenure *f* BOURSE, DROIT *droit commercial et immobilier* holding; ~ **à bail** IMMOB leasehold, leasehold interest

terme:¹ **à** ~ *adj* COM future; **à** ~ **moyen** *adj* BOURSE medium-dated; ~ **à terme** *adj* BOURSE, ECON forward-forward

terme² *m* BANQUE *temps* term, COMMS term; ~ **branché** *infrml* COM buzz word (*infrml*); ~ **commercial international** *(INCOTERME)* ECON international commercial term *(INCOTERM)*; ~ **d'échéance** BANQUE period of payment, term of payment, time for payment; ~ **locatif** IMMOB rental term; ~ **de rigueur** COM strict time limit

termes *m pl* COM, DROIT *d'un accord* terms; ~ **de l'échange** ECON commodity terms of trade, single factorial terms of trade, terms of trade; ~ **de l'échange par rapport aux revenus des exploitations** ECON income terms of trade; ~ **et conditions** ASSUR terms and conditions; ~ **factoriels de l'échange** ECON factorial terms of trade; **les** ~ **de l'alternative** COM alternatives; ~ **précisés** RES HUM *d'un contrat* express terms; ♦ **en** ~ **absolus** ECON in absolute terms; **aux** ~ **du contrat** DROIT under the terms of the contract; **en** ~ **de pourcentage** COM in percentage terms; **en** ~ **réels** ECON in real terms; **en** ~ **relatifs** COM in relative terms

terminal *m* INFO station, terminal, visual display terminal, visual display unit, VDT, VDU, TRANSP passenger terminal, terminal; ~ **acier** TRANSP steel terminal; ~ **d'aéroglisseurs** TRANSP *navigation* hoverport; ~ **autonome** *(ANT terminal non-autonome)* INFO smart terminal; ~ **à conteneurs** TRANSP *maritime* container terminal; ~ **à écran de visualisation** INFO video display unit, visual display terminal, visual display unit, VDT, VDU; ~ **d'édition** INFO report terminal; ~ **éloigné** INFO report terminal; ~ **de fret** TRANSP freight terminal; ~ **de fret international de Londres** TRANSP London International Freight Terminal, LIFT *(UK)*; ~ **de fret international de Manchester** TRANSP Manchester International Freight Terminal, MIFT *(UK)*; ~ **frigo** TRANSP *navigation* cold store terminal; ~ **graphique** INFO graphic display terminal; ~ **informatique** INFO computer terminal; ~ **intelligent** *(ANT terminal non-intelligent)* INFO intelligent terminal, smart terminal; ~ **intérieur** ENVIR, IND onshore terminal; ~ **maritime** TRANSP *pour la réception et l'expédition des conteneurs* container terminal, maritime terminal; ~ **muet** INFO dumb terminal; ~ **non-autonome** *(ANT terminal autonome)* INFO dumb terminal; ~ **non-intelligent** *(ANT terminal intelligent)* INFO dumb terminal; ~ **d'ordinateur** INFO computer terminal; ~ **de paiement électronique** *(TPE)* FIN electronic payment terminal *(EPT)*; ~ **passif** INFO dumb terminal; ~ **pétrolier** ENVIR, IND oil terminal; ~ **plein écran**

INFO full-screen terminal; ~ **point de vente** V&M POS machine, POS terminal, point-of-sale terminal; ~ **vidéo** INFO video terminal

terminé, e *adj* COM completed

terminer 1. *vt* COM complete, conclude, finish, INFO close, V&M conclude; **2.** *v pron* **se ~** COM break up, wind up, finish; ◆ **~ dans le cours** BOURSE finish in the money; **~ les émissions** COM close down; **~ une session** INFO log out

terminologie *f* COM *traité*, COMMS, INFO terminology

terne *adj* COM flat

terrain *m* IMMOB property; **~ entourant la maison d'habitation** DROIT, IMMOB curtilage; **~ non-bâti** IMMOB vacant lot (*AmE*); **~ pétrolifère** IND oil field; **~ remis en valeur** ENVIR, IMMOB reclaimed area; **~ vague** IMMOB wasteland; ◆ **en ~ sûr** COM on solid ground

terrains *m pl* COMPTA freehold property

terre:[1] **à ~** *adj* COM *banks* onshore

terre[2] *f* ECON, ENVIR, IMMOB land; **~ agricole** ECON agricultural land, farmland, ENVIR, FISC agricultural land; **~ agricole occupée par le propriétaire** IMMOB owner-occupied farmland; **~ améliorée** IMMOB improved land; **~ blanche** IMMOB white land (*jarg*); **~ rurale** IMMOB rural land; **~ vierge** IMMOB raw land

terre-plein *m* TRANSP open storage, *port* standage area

terres: **~ cultivées** *f pl* ECON *agriculture* farmland; **~ inondables** *f* IMMOB flood plain; **~ en jachère** *f pl* DROIT land in abeyance, ECON redundant farmland

terrestre *adj* COMMS terrestrial

territoire *m* BOURSE pitch (*UK*), COM, POL, V&M territory; **~ de vente** COM trading area, V&M *zone* sales area, sales territory, trading area

territorial, e *adj* POL patrimonial

terrorisme *m* POL terrorism

test *m* INFO check, test, V&M test; **~ d'admissibilité** BANQUE eligibility test; **~ alpha** INFO alpha test; **~ anonyme** V&M *marketing* blind test; **~ d'aptitude** RES HUM, V&M aptitude test; **~ assisté par ordinateur** (*TAO*) INFO, PROT SOC computer-aided testing, computer-assisted testing (*CAT*); **~ aveugle** V&M *marketing* blind test; **~ en aveugle** V&M blind test; **~ de bonne répartition** MATH goodness-of-fit test; **~ du carré chi** MATH chi square test; **~ comparatif** COM comparison test; **~ de concept** V&M concept test; **~ de conformité** COM compliance test; **~ de consommation** V&M consumer test; **~ dans un édifice public** V&M hall test; **~ à deux issues** MATH two-tailed test; **~ d'essai des performances** INFO benchmark test; **~ d'évaluation** INFO benchmark; **~ d'évaluation des performances** INFO benchmark test; **~ intégré** INFO built-in test; **~ à une issue** MATH one-tailed test; **~ de marché** V&M test marketing; **~ de mémorisation assistée** V&M *étude de marché*

aided recall test; **~ de niveau** COM achievement test; **~ d'observation** COMPTA, FIN observation test; **~ des performances** INFO benchmark; **~ pilote** INFO beta test; **~ de produit** V&M product testing; **~ psychologique** RES HUM psychological test; **~ psychométrique** MATH, RES HUM, V&M psychometric test; **~ publicitaire** V&M advertising test; **~ de rentabilité** COMPTA, FIN profit test; **~ de signification** MATH significance test; **~ statistique** MATH test statistic; **~ sur un panel** V&M *étude de marché* panel testing; **~ t** MATH T-test; **~ de vente** V&M *sur une région* market test

testamentaire *adj* DROIT testamentary

testé, e *adj* DROIT testate

tester *vt* COM, INFO test

testimonial *m* V&M testimonial advertisement

tête *f* COM head; **~ fixe** TRANSP fixed head; **~ de lecture** INFO read head; **~ de lecture/écriture** INFO read/write head; **~ de ligne** TRANSP railhead; **~ de liste minimale** IND minimum list heading (*UK*), MLH (*UK*); ◆ **être à la ~** COM top the list

Tetra Pack® *m* V&M Tetra Pack®

texte *m* COM copy, MÉDIA text; **~ d'écran** INFO soft copy; **~ intégral** COM text in full; **~ législatif** DROIT legal enactment, POL enactment; **~ de présentation** MÉDIA blurb (*jarg*); **~ promulgué** DROIT legal enactment; **~ publicitaire** MÉDIA, V&M advertising copy, advertising text; **~ publicitaire obligatoire** V&M mandatory copy

textes: **~ d'application** *m pl* DROIT, POL *UE* secondary legislation

textiles *m pl* IND textiles

textuellement *adv* COM verbatim

TGD *abrév* (*transport à grande distance*) ENVIR long-range transport

TGDPA *abrév* (*transport à grande distance des polluants aéroportés*) ENVIR long-range transport of air pollutants

TGV *abrév* (*train à grande vitesse*) TRANSP ≈ HST (*high-speed train*)

thaï *m* COM *langue* Thai

thaïlandais, e *adj* COM Thai

Thaïlandais, e *m,f* COM *habitant* Thai

Thaïlande *f* COM Thailand

Thatchérisme *m* COM, POL Thatcherism (*UK*)

théâtre *m* LOISIRS, MÉDIA theater (*AmE*), theatre (*BrE*)

thème *m* POL plank; **~ musical** MÉDIA *télévision* theme tune; **~ publicitaire** V&M advertising appeal, advertising theme

théonomie *f* ECON theonomy

théorème: **~ de la baignoire** *m* ECON bathtub theorem; **~ d'équivalence de Ricardo** *m* ECON Ricardian equivalence theorem, Ricardo invariance principle, overlapping generations model, OLG; **~ d'Euler** *m* ECON Euler's Theorem; **~ du péage** *m* ECON turnpike theorem; **~ de la surcapacité** *m* ECON excess capacity theorem

théoricien: ~ **d'option** *m* BOURSE option theorist; ~ **des options** *m* BOURSE option theorist

théorie *f* COM theory; ~ **administrative** ADMIN, GESTION administrative theory; ~ **de l'agence** BOURSE agency theory; ~ **de l'analyse préalable de la main-d'oeuvre** RES HUM labor process theory (*AmE*), labour process theory (*BrE*); ~ **du capital** ECON, FIN, IND, V&M capital theory; ~ **des caractéristiques** ECON *de la demande* characteristics theory; ~ **catastrophe** MATH catastrophe theory; ~ **du chaos** BOURSE chaos theory; ~ **du choix politique des gouvernants** ECON public choice theory; ~ **du choix social** ECON social choice theory; ~ **classique** ECON classical economics; ~ **classique de l'épargne** ECON *économétrie* classical savings theory; ~ **des clubs** ECON theory of clubs; ~ **du commerce international** ECON international trade theory; ~ **de la communication** COMMS, GESTION, RES HUM communications theory; ~ **des comourants** ASSUR common disaster clause (*US*); ~ **de la concentration géographique** ECON location theory; ~ **de la contingence** GESTION contingency theory; ~ **du contrat implicite** ECON implicit contract theory; ~ **des coûts comparatifs** ECON theory of comparative costs; ~ **de croissance de l'entreprise** ECON growth theory of the firm; ~ **du cycle des élections présidentielles** BOURSE presidential election cycle theory; ~ **des décisions** GESTION, RES HUM decision theory; ~ **de la dépendance** ECON, POL dependency theory; ~ **de la désutilité de la main-d'oeuvre** ECON labor disutility theory (*AmE*), labour disutility theory (*BrE*); ~ **différentielle de la rente** ECON differential theory of rent; ~ **de Dow** BOURSE Dow theory; ~ **économique** ECON economic theory; ~ **économique du déséquilibre** ECON disequilibrium economics; ~ **économique dominante** ECON mainstream economics; ~ **des effets commerciaux d'Adam Smith** ECON Banking School (*UK*), real bills doctrine; ~ **de l'entreprise** ECON Coase, theory of the firm; ~ **des équipes** ECON team theory; ~ **de l'établissement du prix de l'option** BOURSE option-pricing theory; ~ **des étapes** ECON stages theory; ~ **de l'évaluation d'arbitrage** BOURSE arbitrage pricing theory, APT; ~ **d'évaluation des options** BOURSE option-pricing theory; ~ **évolutionniste** ECON *de firme* evolutionary theory; ~ **du facteur général de Spearman** MATH Spearman's rank correlation formula; ~ **des files d'attente** COM waiting-line theory, ECON, INFO, MATH queueing theory; ~ **des fonds prêtables** FIN loanable funds theory; ~ **du fonds salarial** ECON wages fund theory; ~ **générale** *f* ECON General Theory; ~ **générale de Keynes** ECON Keynes' General Theory; ~ **de la gestion de l'entreprise** GESTION management theory; ~ **de gestion moderne de portefeuille** BOURSE modern portfolio theory, MPT; ~ **de gestion de portefeuille** BANQUE, BOURSE, FIN portfolio management theory; ~ **de l'implantation**

centrale des villes dans une région ECON central place theory; ~ **de l'information** GESTION, INFO, MATH information theory; ~ **de l'intérêt des agios** BOURSE, ECON agio theory of interest; ~ **des jeux** ECON, GESTION, RES HUM game theory; ~ **libertaire de l'économie** ECON libertarian economics; ~ **du lieu préféré** FIN preferred habitat theory; ~ **des marchés ouverts à la concurrence** ECON contestable markets thesis; ~ **des mini et maxijupes** BOURSE hemline theory; ~ **de la motivation par les attentes** RES HUM expectancy theory of motivation; ~ **de la motivation par le terrain** RES HUM field theory of motivation; ~ **de la négociation en matière de salaires** RES HUM bargaining theory of wages; ~ **néo-ricardienne** ECON neo-Ricardian theory; ~ **néo-classique de l'économie** ECON neoclassical economics; ~ **de l'organisation** ECON, GESTION organization theory; ~ **organisationnelle** COM, ECON, GESTION organization theory, organizational theory; ~ **du plus faible chaînon** COM weakest link theory; ~ **de portefeuille** BANQUE, BOURSE, FIN portfolio theory; ~ **de la position de place vendeur** BOURSE short interest theory; ~ **des probabilités** GESTION, MATH probability theory; ~ **de la productivité marginale** ECON marginal productivity theory; ~ **quantitative de la monnaie** ECON quantity theory of money; ~ **des relations humaines** RES HUM human relations; ~ **des rompus de titres** BOURSE odd-lot theory; ~ **des salaires** ECON wage theory; ~ **de la segmentation du marché de la main-d'oeuvre** ECON segmented labor market theory (*AmE*), segmented labour market theory (*BrE*); ~ **sur l'épargne des classes** ECON *économétrie* class savings theory; ~ **des systèmes** GESTION systems theory; ~ **des taches solaires** ECON sunspot theory; ~ **du taux de salaire de subsistance** ECON subsistence theory of wages; ~ **de la vague** COM wave theory; ~ **des vagues** COM wave theory; ~ **de la valeur travail** ECON labor theory of value (*AmE*), labour theory of value (*BrE*); ~ **des variations aléatoires** BOURSE, ECON random walk theory; ~ **X** RES HUM theory X (*jarg*); ~ **Y** RES HUM theory Y (*jarg*); ~ **Z** RES HUM theory Z (*jarg*)

théorique *adj* COM theoretical

thermomètre: ~ **publicitaire** *m* V&M advertising thermometer

thésauriser *vi* BOURSE hoard

thèse: ~ **de la continuité** *f* ECON continuity thesis; ~ **de la convergence** *f* POL convergence thesis; ~ **des disponibilités** *f* ECON availability thesis

Thimbu *n pr* COM Thamphu

THS *abrév* (*transaction hors séance*) BOURSE THS transaction

TIC *abrév* (*taux d'intérêt comptable*) BANQUE, COMPTA, FIN ARI (*accounting rate of interest*)

tick *m* BOURSE tick

ticket: ~ **de caisse** *m* COM sales slip; ~ -**repas** *m* RES HUM LV (*BrE*), luncheon voucher (*BrE*), meal ticket (*AmE*); ~ -**restaurant** *m* RES HUM LV

(*BrE*), luncheon voucher (*BrE*), meal ticket (*AmE*)

tient: ça se ~ *loc infrml* COM it makes sense

tierce: ~ collision *f* ASSUR collision coverage, collision insurance; **~ personne** *f* ASSUR, BREVETS third party, TP, COM third person, DROIT third party, TP

tiers *m* ASSUR, BREVETS third party, TP, COM *police d'assurance* third person, DROIT third party, TP; **~ monde** ECON, POL Third World; **~ responsable de titres bloqués** FIN escrow agent; **~ saisi** DROIT garnishee; **un ~** (*1/3*) COM, MATH one-third (*1/3*)

Tiers: le ~ Monde *m* COM the Third World

tige: ~ à caractères *f* ADMIN typebar

timbre *m* COMMS postage stamp; **~ d'endos** BANQUE endorsement stamp; **~ -épargne** *vieilli* V&M coupon; **~ fiscal** FISC Inland Revenue stamp (*UK*); **~ -poste** COMMS postage stamp; **~ -prime** COM trading stamp; **~ de quittance** COMMS receipt stamp; **~ -taxe** COMMS postage-due stamp

timonerie *f* TRANSP *d'un navire* wheelhouse

TIOL[1] *abrév* (*taux interbancaire offert à Londres*) BANQUE, BOURSE LIBOR (*London Interbank Offered Rate*)

TIOL:[2] **~ moyen** *m* BOURSE average LIBOR

TIOP *abrév* (*taux interbancaire offert à Paris*) BANQUE PIBOR (*Paris Interbank Offered Rate*)

TIOS *abrév* (*taux interbancaire offert à Singapour*) BANQUE SIBOR (*Singapore Interbank Offered Rate*)

TIOT *abrév* (*taux interbancaire offert à Tokyo*) ECON TIBOR (*Tokyo Interbank Offered Rate*)

TIR *abrév* (*transport international routier*) TRANSP convention on the contract for the international carriage of goods by road

tirage *m* BANQUE drawdown, *d'un effet, d'un chèque* drawing, INFO hard copy, MÉDIA *presse* circulation, print run, *édition* impression; **~ en l'air** BANQUE kiting; **~ à découvert** BANQUE kiting; **~ forcé** TRANSP *navire, contrôle de chauffe* fd, forced draft (*AmE*), forced draught (*BrE*); **~ au sort** BANQUE draw

Tirana *n pr* COM Tirana

tirant: ~ d'eau *m* TRANSP *d'un navire* draft (*AmE*), draught (*BrE*); **~ d'eau maximal** *m* TRANSP *d'un navire* design draft (*AmE*), design draught (*BrE*), scantling draft (*AmE*), scantling draught (*BrE*)

tire-au-flanc *m* COM shirker (*infrml*), RES HUM malingerer

tiré, e *m,f* BANQUE drawee, *d'une traite* acceptor

tirer 1. *vt* BANQUE draw, COM *conclusion* draw, *information* extract, DROIT *sonnette d'alarme* blow; **~ à découvert** BANQUE overdraw; **2.** *v pron* **s'en ~ de justesse** COM scrape through; ◆ **~ avantage** COM benefit; **~ beaucoup de profit de** COM *des biens* make a good deal by; **~ le bon numéro** COM spot the winner; **~ les ficelles pour qn** *infrml* COM pull strings for sb (*infrml*), pull wires for sb (*AmE, infrml*); **~ au flanc** RES HUM goldbrick (*US, infrml*); **~ parti de** COM make full

use of; **~ profit de** COM benefit, capitalize on, take advantage of, ECON capitalize on, FIN cash in on; **se ~ d'affaire** COM get out of trouble; **~ la sonnette d'alarme** DROIT blow the whistle (*infrml*); **~ les vers du nez à qn** *infrml* COM wring information out of sb (*infrml*)

tiret *m* MÉDIA dash; **~ cadratin** MÉDIA dash, em dash, em space; **~ court** MÉDIA en dash; **~ demi-cadratin** MÉDIA en dash; **~ long** MÉDIA em dash

tireur[1] *m* BANQUE drawer, DROIT *d'un effet* maker

tireur[2]**, -euse** *m,f* COM payer

tiroir: ~ classeur *m* COM filing drawer

tissé: ~ à la main *adj* IND hand-woven

tissu: ~ d'entreprises *m* COM corporate veil (*jarg*)

Titograd *n pr* COM Titograd

titre *m* BOURSE security, share, stock, BOURSE security, BREVETS *de l'invention* title, COMPTA heading, DROIT instrument, FIN bond, cert., certificate, paper, stock, MÉDIA *imprimé* head, headline, *revues, périodiques* title; **~ acquis sur marge** BOURSE margin security; **~ d'action** BOURSE share certificate (*BrE*), stock certificate (*AmE*); **~ appelé au remboursement** BOURSE called security; **~ assurable** ASSUR insurable title; **~ avec bons de souscription** BOURSE stock with subscription rights; **~ avec droit de vote** BOURSE voting security; **~ avec rétrocession immédiate** FIN pass-through security; **~ de bas de page** INFO footer; **~ bêta** BOURSE beta (*US*), beta share, beta stock (*UK*); **~ boudé** BOURSE, FIN, IND out-of-favor stock (*AmE*), out-of-favour stock (*BrE*); **~ en caractères d'affiche** MÉDIA *impression* banner headline; **~ de chevalier** ECON K (*UK*), knighthood (*UK*), POL knighthood (*UK*), K; **~ commercial** BANQUE, FIN *détail* commercial bill (*AmE*), trade bill; **~ du compte** BANQUE, COMPTA account name, name of an account, title of an account; **~ du compte de placement** BANQUE investment account security; **~ constitutif de propriété sur la marchandise** COM, DROIT, IMMOB title to the goods; **~ contestable** DROIT defective title; **~ convertible** FIN convertible security; **~ court neutre garanti** BOURSE neutral covered short; **~ de créance** BOURSE credit instrument, COM *pour le créancier* debt instrument, debt security, indebtedness, COMPTA debt obligation, FIN debt instrument, FISC certificate of indebtedness; **~ de créance hypothécaire** BOURSE mortgage-backed security, MBS; **~ de créance principale** BANQUE, FIN primary instrument of indebtedness; **~ de créances** FIN proof of debt, POD; **~ démembré** BOURSE stripped security; **~ déposé en garantie** ECON, FIN collateral security; **~ déprécié** BOURSE wallflower (*jarg*); **~ détenu** BOURSE security holding; **~ détenu sans profit** BOURSE stale bull (*jarg*); **~ de deuxième ordre** FIN second-class paper; **~ d'emprunt** COM *pour l'emprunteur* debt security; **~ essentiellement nominatif** BOURSE fully registered security; **~ d'État** BOURSE government bond, government stock; **~ fictif** BOURSE phantom share;

~ **flamboyant** MÉDIA *presse* streamer; ~ **de fonction** RES HUM job title; ~ **garanti** BOURSE guaranteed security; ~ **du gouvernement fédéral américain** BOURSE US federal government paper; ~ **de hors-cote** BOURSE over-the-counter (*US*), OTC (*US*); ~ **hors marché** BOURSE municipal bond (*US*); ~ **imparfait** DROIT defective title; ~ **incontestable** DROIT clear title (*US*); ~ **indexé** BANQUE, BOURSE, FIN indexed security; ~ **d'investissement** BOURSE security; ~ **irréfragable** DROIT clear title (*US*); ~ **irréfutable** DROIT clear title (*US*), IMMOB absolute title; ~ **du jour au lendemain** BOURSE overnight security; ~ **long neutre garanti** BOURSE neutral covered long; ~ **mutilé** BOURSE mutilated security; ~ **négociable** (ANT *titre non-négociable*) IMMOB marketable title, merchantable title (*AmE*); ~ **nominatif** BOURSE registered security; ~ **non-négociable** (ANT *titre négociable*) IMMOB nonmerchantable title (*AmE*); ~ **d'obligataire** FIN obligation bond; ~ **d'une option couverte** BOURSE covered option securities, COPS; ~ **participatif** BOURSE participating security; ~ **de participation** BOURSE equity investment, equity security, participating security, participation certificate; ~ **de placement** BANQUE investment account security, BOURSE marketable bond; ~ **portant intérêt** BOURSE interest-bearing security; ~ **au porteur** BOURSE bearer certificate, bearer security, FIN bearer certificate; ~ **pouvant faire l'objet d'options** BOURSE option eligible security; ~ **préférentiel** BOURSE prior-lien bond; ~ **de prêt** FIN loan certificate; ~ **prioritaire** BOURSE senior security; ~ **privilégié** BOURSE senior security; ~ **privilégié à taux variable** BOURSE adjustable-rate preferred stock, ARP; ~ **de propriété** BOURSE proof of ownership, COM certificate of ownership, DROIT abstract of title, documents of title, proof of title, title deed, IMMOB certificate of ownership, certificate of title, proof of title, title deed; ~ **de propriété inscrit au registre du cadastre** ADMIN registered title; ~ **de propriété invalide** DROIT, IMMOB bad title; ~ **de propriété non-valable** DROIT, IMMOB bad title; ~ **de propriété non-valide** DROIT, IMMOB bad title; ~ **de propriété sur la marchandise** COM, DROIT, IMMOB title to the goods; ~ **de référence** BOURSE bellwether (*jarg*); ~ **subordonné à durée indéterminée** (*TSDI*) BOURSE subordinated perpetual bond; ~ **subordonné remboursable** (*TSR*) BOURSE subordinated redeemable bond; ~ **transporté en gage** BANQUE pledge security; ~ **transporté en nantissement** BANQUE pledge security; ~ **trou d'air** BOURSE air pocket stock (*jarg*); ♦ **à ~ consultatif** COM in an advisory capacity; **à ~ gracieux** COM ex gratia (*frml*); **à ~ honoraire** RES HUM in an honorary capacity; **à ~ indicatif** COM for your information, FYI; **à ~ d'information** COM for your information, FYI; **à ~ non-officiel** COM in an unofficial capacity; **à ~ onéreux** COM valuable consideration; **à ~ de renseignement** COM for your information, FYI; **en ~** COM n., nominal

titrer: ~ **en gros caractères** *vt* MÉDIA *presse* screamline (*jarg*)

titres *m pl* BOURSE securities, COMPTA stocks, MÉDIA heads, PROT SOC paper qualifications; ~ **de l'actualité** COMMS, MÉDIA *presse, radio, télévision* news headline; ~ **admis à la cote officielle** BOURSE quoted securities; ~ **avec certification informatique** BOURSE book-entry securities; ~ **de chemin de fer** BOURSE railroad securities (*AmE*), railway securities (*BrE*); ~ **en compte** BOURSE securities long; ~ **cotés** BOURSE listed securities; ~ **à découvert** BOURSE securities short; ~ **demandés** BOURSE securities wanted; ~ **détenus en fiducie** BOURSE *GETC* securities held in trust; ~ **détenus par un courtier pour un client** BOURSE street name; ~ **émis par l'État** ECON governments (*US, infrml*); ~ **empruntés** BOURSE borrowed stock; ~ **de l'établissement Lehman Brothers** BOURSE LIONs, Lehman Investment Opportunity Notes; ~ **d'État** ECON, POL government securities; ~ **exemptés d'impôts** FISC tax-exempt securities; ~ **exonérés d'impôts** FISC tax-exempt securities; ~ **formant rompus** BOURSE broken amount, broken lot; ~ **frappés d'opposition** FIN stopped bonds; ~ **garantis par actif financier** FIN asset-backed securities; ~ **garantis par le nantissement du matériel** FIN equipment trust bond; ~ **à long terme offerts en continu** BOURSE Continuously Offered Longer-Term Securities; ~ **négociables** BOURSE negotiable securities; ~ **non-achetés** BOURSE floating securities; ~ **non-remboursables** BOURSE noncallable securities, NCS; ~ **non-rémunérés** BOURSE non-interest-bearing securities; ~ **partiellement payés** BOURSE partly paid up shares; ~ **en pension** BOURSE pawned stock; ~ **de placement** BOURSE marketable securities; ~ **de propriété** DROIT, IMMOB muniments, muniments of title; ~ **très liquides** BOURSE near cash (*jarg*); ~ **vendus en pension livrée** BOURSE securities sold under repurchase agreement; ~ **vendus à réméré** BOURSE securities sold under repurchase agreement; ♦ **faire les gros ~ des journaux** COM hit the headlines

Titres: ~ **participatifs à bons de souscription de titres participatifs** *m pl* (*TPBSTP*) BOURSE equity loans with equity loans warrants; ~ **participatifs convertibles en certificats d'investissement privilégiés** *m pl* (*TPCCIP*) BOURSE equity loans convertible into preference investment certificates; ~ **subordonnés remboursables avec bons de souscription d'obligations remboursables en actions** *m pl* (*TSRBSORA*) BOURSE subordinated redeemable notes with warrants that can be converted into bonds or shares

titrisation *f* BOURSE, FIN securitization

titriser *vt* BOURSE, FIN securitize

titulaire[1] *adj* ADMIN incumbent

titulaire[2] *mf* ADMIN incumbent, BOURSE buyer,

holder, option buyer, option holder, BREVETS owner, proprietor, POL incumbent, RES HUM occupant; ~ **du brevet** *m* BREVETS patent proprietor; ~ **de carte** *m* BANQUE, COM cardholder; ~ **d'un compte** *m* BANQUE account holder; ~ **d'un compte courant** *m* BANQUE checking account customer (*AmE*), checking account holder (*AmE*), current account customer (*BrE*), current account holder (*BrE*); ~ **contractant** *m* FIN contracting holder; ~ **d'une licence** *m* BREVETS *propriété intellectuelle*, DROIT licensee; ~ **d'une maîtrise de gestion** *m* PROT SOC ≈ MBA, ≈ Master of Business Administration; ~ **d'une maîtrise de sciences** *m* COM *diplôme* ≈ MSc, ≈ Master of Science; ~ **d'une maîtrise en sciences économiques** *m* COM ≈ MCom, ≈ Master of Commerce, ≈ MEcon, ≈ Master of Economics; ~ **d'un passeport** *m* ADMIN passport holder

titularisation *f* RES HUM permanent appointment

titularisé: **être** ~ RES HUM have security of tenure

TJJ *abrév (taux d'argent au jour le jour)* BANQUE call money rate, daily money rate

tk *abrév (tonne-kilomètre)* TRANSP ≈ TM *(ton mile)*

TMI *abrév (tendance marginale à importer)* ECON, IMP/EXP MPI *(marginal propensity to import)*

TMM *abrév (taux du marché monétaire)* BOURSE, ECON, FIN money-market rate

TMMMM *abrév (taux moyen mensuel du marché monétaire)* BOURSE average monthly money market rate

TMO *abrév (taux de marché obligataire)* BOURSE bond market rate

TMP *abrév (taux moyen pondéré)* BOURSE average weighted rate

TOF *abrév (tableau des opérations financières)* FIN flow-of-funds table

Togo *m* COM Togo

togolais, e *adj* COM Togolese

Togolais, e *m,f* COM *habitant* Togolese

toile: ~ **de fond** *f* COM backdrop

toile-ballon *f* COM balloon linen

toilettes *f pl* COM lavatory (*BrE*), rest room (*AmE*), toilet (*BrE*), washroom (*AmE*)

Tokyo *n pr* COM Tokyo

tôle: ~ **noire** *f* TRANSP *navigation* black plate

tolérable *adj* COM, DROIT permissible

tolérance *f* COM tolerance, IMP/EXP quantity permitted, IND tolerance; ~ **à l'importation** ECON, IMP/EXP import allowance; ~ **maximale** COM absolute limit; ◆ **à** ~ **de pannes** INFO fault-tolerant

tolérant: ~ **à l'acide** *adj* ENVIR acid-resistant

tollé: ~ **général** *m* COM public outcry

tombée *f* MÉDIA copy deadline

tomber: ~ **sur** *infrml vi* COM be down on, COM tumble; ◆ ~ **d'accord** COM agree; ~ **au-dessous du minimum** BOURSE, COM, ECON bottom out; ~ **au-dessous du plancher** BOURSE, COM, ECON bottom out; ~ **dans le champ d'application de** DROIT fall within the scope of; ~ **en deçà d'un objectif** ECON undershoot a target; ~ **en désuétude** DROIT fall into abeyance; ~ **à l'eau** *infrml* COM come unstuck, fall apart, fall through; ~ **en panne** COM *machine* break down, INFO break down, crash, fail; ~ **sous le coup de la loi** DROIT fall foul of the law

tonalité *f* COMMS dial tone (*AmE*), dialling tone (*BrE*); ~ **d'occupation** COMMS busy signal (*AmE*), engaged tone (*BrE*)

toner *m* ADMIN, INFO toner

tonnage *m* TRANSP *d'un navire* carrying capacity, tonnage; ~ **brut** COM gross tonnage, GT; ~ **brut complet** TRANSP *train* gross train weight, GTW; ~ **de cargaison** TRANSP cargo tonnage; ~ **cube** COM cubic tonnage, CT; ~ **désarmé** TRANSP *navigation* idle tonnage; ~ **inemployé** TRANSP *navigation* idle tonnage; ~ **de jauge** COM register tonnage; ~ **de jauge net** COM net registered tonnage, NRT; ~ **en lourd** TRANSP dead weight, deadweight capacity, deadweight cargo capacity, deadweight tonnage; ~ **net** COM net tonnage; ~ **de portée en lourd** COM dead weight tonnage; ~ **sous pavillon national** TRANSP *navires* national flag tonnage

tonne *f* COM ton, tonne, weight ton *(t.)*; ~ **d'arrimage** *f* COM measurement tonne; ~ **connaissement** *f* COM B/L ton, bill of lading ton; ~ **courte américaine** *f* COM American short ton; ~ **d'encombrement** *f* TRANSP *maritime* measurement ton; ~ **d'équivalent pétrole** *f* ENVIR ton of oil-equivalent; ~ **forte** *f* COM *maritime* gross ton, long ton; ~ **de jauge** *f* COM registered ton; ~ **de jauge brute** *f* COM gross register ton, GRT; ~ **de jauge nette** *f* COM net register ton, NRT; ~ **-kilomètre** *f (tk)* TRANSP ≈ ton mile, ≈ tonne mile; ~ **-kilomètres fret complètes** *f pl* TRANSP cargo tonne kilometers used (*AmE*), cargo tonne kilometres used (*BrE*); ~ **kilométrique** *f* COM freight ton, frt ton, ft, ton kilometer (*AmE*), tonne kilometre (*BrE*); ~ **métrique** *f* COM metric ton, mton; ~ **milliaire** *f* TRANSP ≈ ton mile, ≈ tonne mile; ~ **par mile** *f* TRANSP ≈ ton mile, ≈ tonne mile

Tonne: ~ **Port en Lourd** *f (TPL)* TRANSP *maritime* tons deadweight *(TDW)*

tonneau *m* IND bar, barrel, TRANSP bar, barrel, cask, ck; ~ **d'affrètement** TRANSP shipping ton; ~ **de jauge brute** COM gross register ton, GRT; ~ **de jauge nette** COM net register ton, NRT

tonnelet *m* TRANSP keg

tonnellerie *f* TRANSP cooperage

tonnes: ~ **au centimètre** *f pl* COM tonnes per centimeter (*AmE*), tonnes per centimetre (*BrE*), TPC; ~ **-kilomètres par heure de circulation du véhicule** *f pl* TRANSP ≈ tonne miles per vehicle hour

tontine *f* ECON tontine

tonture *f* TRANSP *d'un navire* camber

topogramme *m* INFO map; ~ **de mémoire** INFO storage map

topographie *f* INFO map; ~ **de mémoire** INFO storage map

torchon *m infrml* MÉDIA *presse* rag (*infrml*)

tore *m* INFO core; ~ **magnétique** INFO magnetic core

tort:[1] **à** ~ *adv* COM unduly

tort:[2] ~ **causé à autrui** *m* DROIT nuisance

torts: à ~ **partagés** *loc* ASSUR knock-for-knock

total[1], **e** *adj* COM complete, o/a, overall, ECON aggregate

total[2] *m* COM, COMPTA, ECON, FIN total, MATH aggregate, total; ~ **de l'actif** COMPTA, FIN asset value, total assets; ~ **annuel mobile** MATH moving annual total, MAT; ~ **du budgétaire** FIN total budgetary; ~ **de contrôle** INFO checksum; ~ **des créditeurs** BANQUE, COMPTA total liabilities; ~ **cumulé** COMPTA, FIN total to date; ~ **cumulé de l'année** COMPTA, FISC year to date; ~ **de la dette publique** ECON total public debt; ~ **des emprunts et dettes** BANQUE, COMPTA total liabilities; ~ **des feuilles de paie** RES HUM total payroll; ~ **des fonds fournis** FIN total funds provided; ~ **des fonds imputés** FIN total funds applied; ~ **général** BANQUE, COM grand total; ~ **du non-budgétaire** FIN total nonbudgetary; ~ **par activité** COM activity total; ~ **partiel** COMPTA subtotal; ~ **des prévisions** FIN total estimates; ~ **de suffrages exprimés** COM *lors d'un scrutin, d'une élection* total votes cast

totalisateur *m* INFO accumulator

totalisation *f* COM totalling

totaliser *vt* COM add up, totalize, COMPTA add, add up, add, MATH add, add together, add up

totalité *f* COM entirety; ~ **des dépenses publiques** ECON total public spending; ◆ **dans sa** ~ COM in its entirety; **en** ~, **ou presque** COM wholly or in substantial part

touchant: ~ **l'ensemble de l'économie** *adj* ECON economy-wide

touche *f* BOURSE touch, INFO *de clavier* key; ~ **d'activation** INFO hot key; ~ **d'aide** INFO help key; ~ **Alt** COM, INFO Alt key, Alternate key; ~ **barre oblique inverse** INFO backslash key; ~ **de commande de curseur** INFO arrow key; ~ **de commande** INFO command key, control key; ~ **de contrôle** (*touche CTRL*) INFO control key (*CTRL key*); ~ **CTRL** (*touche de contrôle*) INFO CTRL key (*control key*); ~ **de déplacement du curseur** INFO arrow key; ~ **de direction** INFO arrow key; ~ **Echap** (SYN *Echap*) INFO escape; ~ **d'échappement** INFO escape key (*Esc*); ~ **à effleurement** INFO touch key; ~ **Entrée** INFO enter key; ~ **F** (*touche de fonction*) INFO F-key (*function key*); ~ **de fonction** (*touche F*) INFO function key (*F-key*); ~ **majuscule** INFO shift key; ~ **morte** INFO dead key; ~ **option** ADMIN dead key; ~ **rapide** INFO hot key; ~ **de remise à zéro** INFO

reset button; ~ **Retour** INFO enter key; ~ **souris** INFO mouse key; **sur la** ~ INFO on the touchline

touché: être ~ **par la limite d'âge** *loc* COM reach the age limit

toucher *vt* BANQUE *chèque* cash, BOURSE *prime* collect, ECON *cours le plus bas* hit, record, PROT SOC take up; ◆ ~ **des allocations** PROT SOC, RES HUM be on benefit (*UK*), be on welfare (*US*), receive benefit (*UK*); ~ **le cours offert** BOURSE hit the bid; ~ **un mot à qn au sujet de qch** COM have a word with sb about sth; ~ **des pots-de-vin** COM be on the take (*infrml*); ~ **des prestations sociales** PROT SOC, RES HUM be on benefit (*BrE*), be on welfare (*AmE*), receive benefit (*UK*); ~ **une retraite** RES HUM retire on a pension; ~ **un salaire de** RES HUM earn a salary of

toujours *adv* DROIT always; ◆ **être** ~ **en train de chercher des combines** COM wheel and deal; ~ **à flot** TRANSP *navigation* always afloat; **ne** ~ **pas être livré** COM remain undelivered; **ne** ~ **pas être réglé** COM remain undecided; ~ **en vigueur** DROIT *contrat* unexpired

tour[1] *m* LOISIRS tour; ~ **de mise à quai** TRANSP *port* turn time; ~ **de rôle** TRANSP port turnaround time (*AmE*), port turnround time (*BrE*), turn time; ~ **de table** BOURSE pool; ◆ **à** ~ **de rôle** COM in rotation; **faire un** ~ **d'horizon de la situation** COM survey the situation

tour:[2] ~ **de contrôle** *f* TRANSP *aéroport, port maritime* air traffic control, traffic control tower, ATC; ~ **d'habitation** *f* IMMOB high rise, tower block

tourbillon: ~ **d'activité** *m* COM hustle and bustle

Touring: ~ **Club de France** *m France* TRANSP ≈ American Automobile Association, ≈ Automobile Association (*UK*)

tourisme *m* LOISIRS tourism, tourist trade; ~ **étranger** COM, LOISIRS overseas tourism

touriste *mf* LOISIRS tourist; ~ **étranger** *m* COM, LOISIRS overseas tourist

tournage *m* V&M *publicité, d'un film* shoot

tournant *m* COM watershed

tourné: ~ **vers l'action** *adj* COM action-orientated, action-oriented; ~ **vers l'avenir** *adj* COM forward-looking; ~ **vers le commerce** *adj* COM business-orientated; ~ **vers l'entreprise** *adj* COM business-orientated, business-oriented

tournée: ~ **électorale** *f* POL whistlestop campaign; ~ **de présentation** *f* FIN road show; ~ **publicitaire** *f* V&M advertising tour; ◆ **en** ~ LOISIRS *théâtre* on tour; **faire une** ~ **électorale** POL whistlestop

tourner 1. *vi* COM veer; **2.** *v pron* **se** ~ **vers qn pour qch** COM look to sb for sth; ◆ ~ **bien** (ANT *tourner mal*), COM take a turn for the better; **faire** ~ BANQUE churn; ~ **mal** (ANT *tourner bien*) COM take a turn for the worse; ~ **à plein régime** IND go full steam

tournez: ~ **s'il vous plaît** *loc* (*TSVP*) COMMS please turn over (*PTO*)

tournure: ~ **des événements** *f* COM trend of events

tout va *loc* COM the sky's the limit

toxicité *f* ENVIR toxicity

toxicologique *adj* ENVIR toxicological

toxique *adj* ENVIR toxic

TPBSTP *abrév (Titres participatifs à bons de souscription de titres participatifs)* BOURSE equity loans with equity loans warrants

TPCCIP *abrév (Titres participatifs convertibles en certificats d'investissement privilégiés)* BOURSE equity loans convertible into preference investment certificates

TPE *abrév (terminal de paiement électronique)* FIN EPT *(electronic payment terminal)*

TPL *abrév (Tonne Port en Lourd)* TRANSP *maritime* TDW *(tons deadweight)*

TPS *abrév (taxe de prestation de service)* FISC GST *(goods and services tax)*

TPV *abrév (terminal point de vente)* V&M POST *(point-of-sale terminal)*

T4M *abrév (taux moyen mensuel du marché monétaire)* BOURSE average monthly money market rate

TRA *abrév (taux révisable annuellement)* FIN interest rate subject to modification every year

trabac *m* TRANSP trabaccolo

trace: ~ **écrite** *f* INFO hard copy

tracer *vt* IMMOB, MATH *graphique* plot; ◆ ~ **une courbe** COM chart; ~ **une voie nouvelle** COM break new ground

traceur *m* INFO plotting pen; ~ **de courbes** ADMIN X-Y plotter, INFO, MATH graph plotter, plotter; ~ **à tambour** INFO drum plotter

trackball *m jarg* INFO trackball

tract *m* MÉDIA flier, flyer

tractage *m* TRANSP *aviation* towing

tracteur *m* TRANSP *routier* tractive unit; ~ **de terminal** TRANSP *ports* tugmaster

tradition *f* COM tradition

traditionnel, -elle *adj* COM traditional

traducteur, -trice *m,f* COM, INFO translator

traduction *f* COMMS translation; ~ **assistée par ordinateur** *(TAO)* INFO computer-aided translation, computer-assisted translation *(CAT)*, machine-aided translation, machine-assisted translation *(MAT)*; ~ **automatique** INFO machine translation, MT; ~ **simultanée** COM simultaneous translation

traduire 1. *vt* COMMS translate; **2.** *v pron* **se** ~ **par** COM be reflected in

trafic *m* TRANSP traffic, V&M traffic, *de drogue, d'antiquités* dealing; ~ **aérien** TRANSP air traffic; ~ **de drogue** IMP/EXP drug trafficking; ~ **ferroviaire** TRANSP rail traffic; ~ **international** TRANSP international traffic; ~ **marchandises** TRANSP freight traffic; ~ **maritime** TRANSP maritime shipping; ~ **de poids lourds** TRANSP heavy goods traffic; ~ **portuaire** IMP/EXP, TRANSP port throughput, port traffic; ~ **de remplissage** TRANSP *marchandises* filler traffic; ~ **réservé**

TRANSP booked traffic; ~ **sur pneus** TRANSP rubber-tired traffic *(AmE)*, rubber-tyred traffic *(BrE)*; ~ **à tarif passagers** TRANSP passenger-rated traffic; ~ **à tarif voyageurs** TRANSP passenger-rated traffic; ~ **de terminal** TRANSP terminal traffic; ~ **de transit** TRANSP transit traffic; ◆ **faire du** ~ **de** IMP/EXP smuggle

trafiquant, e *m,f* COM *de drogue* trafficker

trafiquer *vt infrml* COM fiddle *(infrml)*

trafiqueur *m* BOURSE scalper *(US, infrml)*

train *m* ECON *de réformes* package, pkg; ~ **-bloc de conteneurs** TRANSP F/L® *(BrE)*, freightliner® *(BrE)*; ~ **direct** TRANSP through train; ~ **électrique** TRANSP electric train; ~ **-ferry** TRANSP train ferry; ~ **à grande vitesse** *(TGV)* TRANSP ≈ high-speed train *(HST)*; ~ **de marchandises** TRANSP freight train *(AmE)*, goods train *(BrE)*; ~ **roulant à vide** TRANSP deadhead *(AmE, infrml)*; ~ **routier** TRANSP drawbar combination, road train *(Australia)*, triback; ~ **de voyageurs** TRANSP passenger train; ~ **voyageurs** TRANSP passenger train

trainard *f infrml* BOURSE laggard

traîne: **être à la** ~ *loc* COM fall behind, lag behind

traîner: ~ **derrière** *vt* COM lag behind; ◆ ~ **en justice** DROIT take sb to court

traite *f* BANQUE bill, bill of exchange, dft, draft, BOURSE bill of exchange, COMPTA bill, FIN bill, bill of exchange, dft, draft, FISC bill, IMP/EXP bill of exchange; ~ **à l'acceptation** BANQUE acceptance bill; ~ **acceptée** BANQUE accepted draft; ~ **en l'air** *jarg* BOURSE kite *(jarg)*; ~ **avisée** BANQUE, FIN advised bill; ~ **bancaire** BANQUE B/Dft, bank draft *(BrE)*, cashier's check *(AmE)*, cashier's cheque *(BrE)*; ~ **de complaisance** BANQUE, COM, FIN accommodation draft, convenience bill; ~ **à courte échéance** TRANSP short bill, SB; ~ **en devises** BANQUE currency draft; ~ **documentaire** IMP/EXP, TRANSP *maritime* documentary draft; ~ **à échéance** BANQUE usance bill; ~ **à échéance fixe** COM date draft; ~ **impayée** IMP/EXP dishonored bill of exchange *(AmE)*, dishonoured bill of exchange *(BrE)*; ~ **induite** FIN induced draft; ~ **nantie par des titres** BOURSE stock draft; ~ **à payer** COMPTA, FIN bill payable; ~ **à recevoir** COMPTA, FIN bill receivable, note receivable; ~ **à vue** BANQUE at sight draft *(AmE)*, sight draft, stock check *(AmE)*, stock cheque *(BrE)*, SD, COM demand draft, DD, sight draft, SD, FIN sight bill; ◆ **donner avis d'une** ~ BANQUE advise a draft

traité *m* COM treaty, DROIT *international* accord, POL treaty, *entre pays* accord; ~ **commercial** ECON, POL trade agreement; ~ **commercial bilatéral** ECON, POL *commerce international* bilateral trade agreement; ~ **de coopération relatif aux brevets d'invention** BREVETS *propriété intellectuelle*, DROIT Patent Cooperation Treaty, PCT; ~ **de réassurance** ASSUR stop-loss reinsurance

Traité: ~ **de Rome** m ECON, POL Treaty of Rome; ~ **de l'Union européenne** m COM European Union Treaty

traitement m BANQUE *des chèques*, BREVETS *de demande d'un brevet*, FISC, IND processing, INFO process, processing; ~ **en arrière-plan** INFO background processing; ~ **automatique des données** INFO automatic data processing, ADP; ~ **automatique de l'information** INFO automatic data processing, ADP; ~ **de base** ASSUR, ECON, FIN, FISC, RES HUM basic rate; ~ **biologique** ENVIR, IND biological treatment; ~ **communautaire** IMP/EXP *de marchandises* Community treatment; ~ **comptable** COMPTA, FIN accounting treatment; ~ **concurrent** INFO concurrent processing; ~ **décentralisé** INFO distributed computing; ~ **des déchets** ENVIR waste treatment; ~ **des denrées alimentaires** IND food processing; ~ **différé** INFO batch processing; ~ **différé des entrées/sorties** INFO spooling; ~ **en direct des opérations bancaires** BANQUE on-line banking; ~ **des données** INFO data processing; ~ **des eaux** ENVIR water treatment; ~ **des eaux usées** ENVIR sewage treatment, wastewater treatment; ~ **électronique des données** INFO electronic data processing; ~ **électronique de l'information** *(TEI)* INFO electronic data processing *(EDP)*; ~ **des entrées** IMP/EXP, TRANSP inward processing; ~ **des erreurs** INFO error control; ~ **de faveur** COM preferential treatment; ~ **fiscal** FISC tax treatment; ~ **de fond** INFO background processing; ~ **de l'information** COM information handling, INFO data processing, information handling, information processing; ~ **informatique** INFO computer processing; ~ **interactif** INFO interactive processing; ~ **de messages** COMMS, INFO message handling; ~ **de mouvements** INFO transaction processing; ~ **multitâche** INFO multitasking; ~ **multitravail** INFO multijobbing; ~ **de la nation la plus favorisée** ECON, POL *commerce international* most-favored nation treatment *(AmE)*, most-favoured nation treatment *(BrE)*; ~ **non-prioritaire** INFO background processing; ~ **par lots** INFO batch job, batch processing; ~ **par ordinateur** INFO computer processing, computerization; ~ **par paquets** INFO batch processing; ~ **en parallèle** INFO parallel processing; ~ **de la parole** INFO speech processing; ~ **du personnel** COMPTA payroll; ~ **préliminaire** ENVIR pretreatment; ~ **série** INFO serial processing; ~ **simultané** INFO concurrent processing; ~ **en simultanéité** INFO parallel processing; ~ **en tâche de fond** INFO background processing; ~ **de texte** ADMIN, INFO text processing, word processing, word processor, WP; ~ **transactionnel** INFO transaction processing; ~ **vocal** INFO speech processing

traitements: ~ **et salaires** *loc* RES HUM salaries and wages

traiter *vt* BANQUE process, COM process, transact, treat, ENVIR *égouts* treat, IND, INFO process; ~ **de** COM, COMMS *courrier* deal with; ~ **par ordinateur** INFO computerize

trajet: ~ **direct** m TRANSP direct route; ~ **à escales multiples** m TRANSP *routier* multiple drop; ~ **d'essai** m TRANSP test drive; ~ **fixe** m TRANSP fixed route; ~ **de retour** m TRANSP *expédition* back haul; ~ **à la zone de travail** m COM travel-to-work area

trajets: ~ **journaliers** m pl TRANSP commutation *(AmE)*, commuting

trame f INFO raster, *de télécommunication* frame

tramp m *vieilli* TRANSP *navigation* tramp

tramping m *vieilli* TRANSP tramping

tranche f COM band, *d'imposition* bracket, FISC *d'imposition* bracket, MATH *d'un graphique camembert* segment; ~ **d'âge** COM, V&M *étude de marché* age bracket, age group; ~ **d'âge du consommateur** V&M consumer age group; ~ **de crédit** ECON credit tranche facility, FIN credit rating, credit tranche, currency accounts; ~ **horaire** MÉDIA, TRANSP time band; ~ **horaire de fin de soirée** MÉDIA late fringe *(US, jarg)*; ~ **horaire du soir** MÉDIA *télévision* early fringe; ~ **horizontale de cellule** TRANSP *porte-conteneurs* slot; ~ **d'imposition** FISC tax band, tax bracket; ~ **inférieure de revenus** ECON lower income bracket; ~ **matinale** *jarg* MÉDIA early fringe *(jarg)*; ~ **mezzanine** BOURSE mezzanine bracket; ~ **moyenne du marché** V&M middle range of the market; ~ **moyenne de revenus** ECON middle income bracket; ~ **de la nuit** MÉDIA late night; ~ **de revenu** FISC income band, income bracket, range, V&M *étude de marché* income group; ~ **de salaires** RES HUM wage bracket; ~ **supérieure de revenus** ECON higher income bracket

trancher *vti* COM, DROIT, IND, RES HUM arbitrate

transaction f BANQUE account transaction, transaction, BOURSE bargain, transaction, COM compromise, transaction, COMPTA account transaction, transaction, DROIT posting, ECON transaction, FIN account transaction, transaction, INFO transaction; ~ **d'achat** BOURSE bought deal; ~ **aller et retour** BOURSE bed and breakfast deal *(jarg)*; ~ **à la baisse** *(* ANT *transaction à la hausse)* BOURSE bear operation, bear transaction; ~ **de clôture** BOURSE closing trade, closing transaction; ~ **commerciale** COM business transaction; ~ **complexe** BANQUE complex transaction *(UK)*; ~ **au comptant** BOURSE spot transaction, COMPTA cash deal; ~ **croisée** BOURSE crossed trade; ~ **en devises** BANQUE, ECON, FIN foreign currency transaction; ~ **à l'échelon de cotation inférieur** BOURSE zero-minus tick; ~ **à l'échelon de cotation supérieur** BOURSE zero-plus tick; ~ **expédiée** BOURSE bundled deal; ~ **fictive** BOURSE sham trading; ~ **financière transfrontalière** FIN cross-border financial transaction; ~ **à la hausse** *(* ANT *transaction à la baisse)* BOURSE bull operation, bull transaction; ~ **hors corbeille** BOURSE ex-pit transaction; ~ **hors parquet** BOURSE upstairs market; ~ **hors**

séance *(THS)* BOURSE THS transaction; ~ **d'initié** BOURSE, FIN insider dealing, insider trading; ~ **inverse** COM opposite transaction; ~ **nette de frais** BOURSE net transaction; ~ **au pair** BOURSE par trading; ~ **de plusieurs millions libellés en livres sterling** FIN multimillion pound deal; ~ **à prix garanti remise à plus tard** BOURSE stopped stock; ~ **au prix du marché** COM arm's-length transaction; ~ **programmée par ordinateur** COM program trade *(AmE)*, programme trade *(BrE)*; ~ **sans lien de dépendance** COMMS arm's-length transaction; ~ **sans risque** BOURSE riskless transaction; ~ **sur bloc de titres** BOURSE block trade; ~ **sur contrat à terme** BOURSE futures transaction; ~ **sur rompu** BOURSE odd lot; ~ **à terme** BOURSE forward transaction, settlement transaction; ~ **transfrontières** ECON cross-border transaction; ♦ **faire une ~** COM make a transaction

transactionnel, -elle *adj* BANQUE, BOURSE, COM, COMPTA, ECON, FIN, INFO transactional

transactions: ~ **d'arbitrage** *f pl* BOURSE arbitrage transactions *(UK)*; ~ **automatisées** *f pl* ECON computer trading *(US)*, INFO paperless trading; ~ **avant-bourse** *f pl* BOURSE before-hours dealings; ~ **de la banque centrale** *f pl* BANQUE, ECON central bank transactions; ~ **en capacité unique** *f pl* BOURSE single-capacity trading; ~ **en continu** *f pl* BOURSE twenty-four hour trading; ~ **excessives** *f pl* BOURSE overtrading; ~ **hors bourse** *f pl* BOURSE after-hours dealing, after-hours trading, street dealings, FIN after-hours dealing, after-hours trading; ~ **hors séance** *f pl* BOURSE, FIN after-hours dealing, after-hours trading; ~ **informatisées** *f pl* INFO paperless trading; ~ **de portefeuille** *f pl* BANQUE, BOURSE, FIN portfolio trade; ~ **spéculatives** *f pl* BOURSE speculative trading; ~ **sur contrats à terme** *f pl* BOURSE futures trading; ~ **sur marge** *f pl* BOURSE margin trading; ~ **sur obligations** *f pl* BOURSE bond dealings; ~ **sur valeurs non-cotées** *f pl* BOURSE unlisted trading; ~ **suspendues** *f pl* BOURSE suspended trading; ~ **24h/24** *f pl* BOURSE twenty-four hour trading

transbordement *m* TRANSP transhipment, transshipment; ~ **direct** TRANSP direct transhipment; ~ **de marchandises** TRANSP cargo transfer; ~ **de véhicule** IMP/EXP vehicle transhipment

transborder *vt* TRANSP tranship, transship

transbordeur *m* TRANSP car ferry, ferry boat, train ferry, passenger ferry, vehicular ferry; ~ **de passagers et véhicules** TRANSP *navigation* passenger-vehicle ferry

transcoder *vt* COMMS transcode

transcodeur *m* COMMS transcoder

transcripteur *m* COMMS transcriber

transcription *f* COM, INFO transcription

transcrire *vt* INFO transcribe

transducteur *m* COMMS transducer

transeuropéen, -enne *adj* COM, TRANSP transeuropean

transférabilité *f* INFO *des données* import-export

transférable *adj* BOURSE transferable, COM assignable, RES HUM portable

transférer *vt* BANQUE transfer, COM relocate, DROIT assign, convey, ECON *fonds* transfer, INFO dump; ♦ ~ **par endossement** BANQUE transfer by endorsement

transfert *m* BANQUE tr., transfer, BREVETS transfer, COM relocation, *de responsabilité* transfer, DROIT *de propriété* assignment, conveyance, FISC *d'un compte, de dividendes* flow-through *(US)*, IMMOB assignment, INFO migration, transfer, TRANSP transfer, TFR; ~ **d'actif** COMPTA transfer of assets; ~ **d'actions** BOURSE legal transfer, share transfer; ~ **d'appel** COMMS call forwarding; ~ **d'argent** BANQUE money transmission; ~ **d'argent immédiat** BANQUE immediate money transfer, IMT; ~ **de bloc** INFO block move, block transfer; ~ **de données** INFO data transfer; ~ **électronique de fonds** BANQUE FIN electronic funds transfer, EFT; ~ **électronique de fonds au point de vente** BANQUE electronic funds transfer at point of sale, EFTPOS; ~ **entre dépôts** TRANSP interdepot transfer; ~ **entre frontières** TRANSP *de déchets dangereux* cross-frontier transfer; ~ **aux entreprises** COM transfer to business; ~ **et enregistrement automatisé de titres non certifiés** BOURSE Taurus *(UK)*, Transfer & Automated Registration of Uncertified Stock *(UK)*; ~ **financier télégraphique express** FIN express telegraphic money transfer; ~ **de fonds** BANQUE cash transfer, funds transfer, tr., transfer, FIN funds transfer; ~ **d'information** INFO information transfer; ~ **interne** BOURSE internalization; ~ **légal** BOURSE *de valeurs* legal transfer; ~ **libre d'impôt** FISC roll-over; ~ **de marchandises** TRANSP cargo transfer; ~ **minimum** COM minimum transfer, MT; ~ **par courrier** BANQUE mail transfer, MT; ~ **pécuniaire** COMPTA cash transfer; ~ **de personnel** ECON, RES HUM staff transfer; ~ **de portefeuille** ASSUR, COM portfolio transfer; ~ **de prime** ASSUR premium transfer; ~ **social** BANQUE payment transfer; ~ **de technologie** COM, COMMS technology transfer, ECON technology transfer, transfer of technology, IND, INFO technology transfer; ~ **technologique** COM technological transfer, technology transfer, COMMS, ECON technology transfer, IND technological transfer, technology transfer, INFO technology transfer; ~ **télégraphique** *(TT)* BANQUE, COMMS telegraphic transfer *(TT)*; ~ **de vote** POL crossover vote *(US)*

transferts: ~ **courants vers les particuliers** *m pl* ECON current grants to persons; ~ **multiples** *m pl* BANQUE, FIN back-to-back transfers; ~ **potentiellement exonérés** *m pl* FISC PETs *(UK)*, potentially exempt transfers *(UK)*

transformation *f* COM revamping, *de locaux* conversion, IND *acier* processing; ~ **de créances en**

participation FIN debt-equity swap; ~ **des déchets** ENVIR waste processing; ~ **de la monnaie en marchandises** ECON commodification of money

transformer 1. *vt* COM change, revamp, transform, ECON transform, IND process; **2.** *v pron* **se** ~ COM change; ◆ **se** ~ **en société ouverte** BOURSE go public

transfrontalier, -ère *adj* COM, IMP/EXP transfrontier

transiger 1. *vt* BOURSE trade in, DROIT compound; **2.** *vi* COM compromise; ◆ ~ **sur une dette** BANQUE, DROIT, FIN compound a debt

transistor: ~ **bipolaire** *m* INFO bipolar transistor

transistorisé, e *adj vieilli* COM solid-state

transit *m* IMP/EXP, LOISIRS, TRANSP transit; ~ **communautaire** IMP/EXP, TRANSP *pour les marchandises à l'intérieur de l'UE* Community transit, CT; ~ **contrôlé** TRANSP controlled transit; ~ **inaugural** TRANSP inaugural transit; ~ **de marchandises** TRANSP cargo transit; ◆ **en** ~ COM in transit

transitaire *mf* IMP/EXP forwarder, fwdr, TRANSP forwarding agent, forwarding company, freight forwarder, transport agent, V&M forwarding agent

transition: ~ **démographique** *f* ECON demographic transition

transitionnel, -elle *adj* COM transitional

translatable *adj* INFO relocatable

translation *f* INFO relocation

transmetteur, -trice *adj* COM *fil*, COMMS, MÉDIA transmitting

transmettre *vt* COM communicate, COMMS communicate, transmit, DROIT assign, convey, INFO send, MÉDIA transmit

transmis, e *adj* FISC passing

transmissible *adj Can* (ANT *non-transmissible*) BOURSE transferable

transmission *f* COMMS communication, transmission, DROIT *de propriété* conveyance, INFO communication, transmission; ~ **de capital** FIN capital transfer; ~ **de données** COMMS, INFO data communications; ~ **de l'information par voie hiérarchique** COMMS formal communication; ~ **d'octets en série** INFO byte mode; ~ **par engrenages réducteurs** TRANSP *navigation* clutch drive, CD; ~ **simultanée** MÉDIA *radio-télévision* simulcast, simultaneous broadcast; ~ **de titres au porteur ordinaire** BOURSE regular way delivery; ~ **unidirectionnelle** INFO simplex

transnational, e *adj* COM cross-border, transnational, ECON, IND, POL transnational

transpalette *m* TRANSP pallet truck, *manutention* hand pallet-transporter

transparence *f* COM transparency (*jarg*), COMPTA transparency, FIN visibility; ~ **bancaire en matière de prêts** BANQUE, COM, DROIT *commercial*, FIN truth in lending (*jarg*); ~ **financière** FIN financial visibility; ~ **fiscale** FISC tax transparency; ~ **de l'information** POL transparency of information

(*jarg*); **la** ~ POL glasnost, openness; ~ **du marché** COM market transparency; ~ **en matière de crédits** BANQUE, COM, DROIT *commercial*, FIN truth in lending (*jarg*); ~ **à trente jours** BOURSE thirty-day visible supply

transparent[1]**, e** *adj* COM, INFO transparent

transparent[2] *m* ADMIN overlay, COM, GESTION overhead transparency

transport *m* TRANSP carriage, conv, conveyance, transport, transportation; ~ **aérien** IMP/EXP air freight, TRANSP air freight, air transport; ~ **de bout à bout** TRANSP through shipment; ~ **de colis lourds** TRANSP *navigation* belship; ~ **collectif rapide** TRANSP mass rapid transit, MRT; ~ **combiné** TRANSP combined transport, intermodal transport, CT; ~ **de l'eau** TRANSP water transportation; ~ **ferroviaire** TRANSP rail transport; ~ **à grande distance** (*TGD*) ENVIR long-range transport; ~ **à grande distance des polluants aéroportés** (*TGDPA*) ENVIR long-range transport of air pollutants; ~ **international** TRANSP carriage international, international carriage, international traffic; ~ **international routier** (*TIR*) TRANSP convention on the contract for the international carriage of goods by road; ~ **de marchandises** TRANSP conveyance of goods, freight transport, movement of freight; ~ **maritime** ECON sea transport; ~ **maritime à la demande** TRANSP tramping; ~ **multimodal** TRANSP combined transport, multimodal transport, CT; ~ **de nuit** TRANSP Nt, night trunk; ~ **par chemin de fer** TRANSP rail freight; ~ **par conteneurs** TRANSP container transport; ~ **par service rapide** COM expressage; ~ **par terre** TRANSP land carriage; ~ **par voie d'eau** TRANSP water transportation; ~ **privé du client** TRANSP customer's own transport, COT; ~ **routier** TRANSP haulage, motor freight, road transport; ~ **à température contrôlée** IMP/EXP, TRANSP temperature-controlled transport; ~ **terrestre** TRANSP ground transportation, land carriage, overland transport; ~ **thermorégulé** IMP/EXP, TRANSP temperature-controlled transport

transportable *adj* TRANSP transportable

transporté: ~ **par mer** *adj* TRANSP *marchandises* seaborne

transporter *vt* COMPTA *créance* transfer, TRANSP carry, convey, transport; ◆ ~ **par avion** TRANSP transport by air

transporteur *m* TRANSP carrier, common carrier, hauler (*AmE*), haulier (*BrE*), forwarding company, haulage contractor, trucking contractor; ~ **aérien** IMP/EXP air carrier, TRANSP air carrier, carrier; ~ **aérien pour le contrôle de la capacité des routes** TRANSP route capacity control airline, RCCA; ~ **automatique** TRANSP conveyor belt; ~ **d'automobiles** TRANSP *navigation* car carrier, pure car carrier, PCC; ~ **d'automobiles et de camions** TRANSP *navigation* pure car and truck carrier, PCTC; ~ **à bande** TRANSP conveyor belt; ~ **de brut géant** TRANSP ultra large crude carrier;

~ de colis lourds TRANSP *navigation* heavy lift ship; **~ pour compte propre** TRANSP industrial carrier; **~ contractuel** TRANSP contract carrier; **~ destinataire** TRANSP receiving carrier; **~ direct** TRANSP through transport operator; **~ de données** INFO data carrier; **~ émetteur** TRANSP issuing carrier; **~ de gaz naturel liquéfié** TRANSP *navigation* liquefied natural gas carrier; **~ de gaz de pétrole liquéfié** TRANSP *navigation* liquid petroleum gas carrier; **~ de GNL** TRANSP *navigation* liquefied natural gas carrier; **~ de GPL** TRANSP *navigation* liquid petroleum gas carrier; **~ intégral** IMP/EXP, TRANSP integrator; **~ intérieur** IMP/EXP, TRANSP *entreprise* inland carrier; **~ interligne** TRANSP *aviation* interline carrier; **~ livrant** TRANSP delivering carrier; **~ maritime** TRANSP sea carrier; **~ mixte** TRANSP *navigation* combi carrier; **~ multimodal** TRANSP multimodal transport operator, MTO; **~ participant** TRANSP participating carrier; **~ principal** TRANSP principal carrier; **~ de produits** TRANSP *navigation* product tanker; **~ qui assure la correspondance** TRANSP connecting carrier; **~ réel** TRANSP actual carrier; **~ routier** TRANSP forwarding company, freight forwarder; **~ substitué** TRANSP actual carrier; **très gros ~ de brut** TRANSP *pétrolier* very large crude carrier, VLCC; **~ de voitures** TRANSP car transporter; **~ en vrac** TRANSP *navigation* bulk carrier, BLK CAR

transports: **~ en commun** *m pl* TRANSP mass transit system (*AmE*), public transport, public transport system (*BrE*), public transportation; **~ routiers** *m pl* TRANSP road haulage

transposer *vt* MATH decimalize

transposition *f* DROIT, POL UE transposal

Transsibérien *m* TRANSP *chemin de fer* Trans-Siberian Railway, TSR

transversal, e *adj* COM transverse, TRANS

transverse *f* TRANSP *d'un conteneur* cross member, transverse member

travail *m* COM job, work, IND labor (*AmE*), labour (*BrE*), INFO job, RES HUM job, labor (*AmE*), labour (*BrE*); **~ abstrait** (ANT *travail concret*) RES HUM abstract labor (*AmE*), abstract labour (*BrE*); **~ administratif** ADMIN administrative work, paperwork; **~ agricole** ECON, RES HUM agricultural job; **~ d'audit** COMPTA, FIN audit activity (*UK*); **~ de bureau** ADMIN, RES HUM clerical work, office job, office work; **~ clandestin** RES HUM moonlighting; **~ en colis volant** TRANSP *manutention* union purchase; **~ compté** RES HUM measured daywork, MDW; **~ concret** (ANT *travail abstrait*) RES HUM concrete labor (*AmE*), concrete labour (*BrE*); **~ en continu** RES HUM continuous labor (*AmE*), continuous labour (*BrE*); **~ courant de bureau** ADMIN, COM office routine; **~ détestable** COM bad deal; **~ à domicile** ECON, RES HUM homework, networking, outwork; **~ à domicile par réseau informatique** ECON telecommuting; **~ d'équipe** GESTION, RES HUM teamwork; **~ d'équipe à la**

pièce RES HUM gang piecework, group piecework; **~ à forfait** RES HUM contract work, work by contract; **~ de groupe** RES HUM group working; **~ à l'heure** RES HUM time work; **~ indépendant** FISC self-employment; **~ intermittent** RES HUM casual work; **~ de jour** RES HUM daywork; **~ à la journée** RES HUM measured daywork, MDW; **~ manuel** IND, RES HUM manual work; **~ matérialisé** RES HUM materialized labor (*AmE, jarg*), materialized labour (*BrE, jarg*); **~ à mi-temps** COM, RES HUM part-time employment, part-time work; **~ moyen d'une journée** RES HUM fair day's work (*UK*); **~ nécessaire** RES HUM indispensable labor (*AmE*), indispensable labour (*BrE*), necessary labor (*AmE*), necessary labour (*BrE*); **~ au noir** RES HUM moonlighting; **~ non-déclaré** RES HUM secondary employment; **~ de nuit** RES HUM night work; **~ occasionnel** RES HUM casual work; **~ par équipes** IND, RES HUM shift work; **~ par relais** RES HUM shift work; **~ pénible** RES HUM slog; **~ à la pièce** RES HUM piecework; **~ aux pièces** RES HUM piecework, task work; **~ posté** IND, RES HUM shift work; **~ préparatoire** COM groundwork; **~ de prospection** V&M missionary work; **~ en réseau** ECON, RES HUM homework, networking; **~ en retard** IND work backlog; **~ sans valeur** RES HUM boondoggle (*US, infrml*); **~ de secrétariat** ADMIN, RES HUM clerical work; **~ en simultanéité** RES HUM time sharing; **~ temporaire** RES HUM casual work, temporary work; **~ à temps partiel** COM, RES HUM part-time employment, part-time work; **~ d'urgence** COM rush job; **~ volontaire** RES HUM voluntary work; **♦ à ~ égal, salaire égal** RES HUM same job, same pay; **c'est du beau ~** COM workmanship; **~ en cours** COM work in progress, WIP; **être dans le ~ jusqu'au cou** *infrml* RES HUM be up to one's neck in work (*infrml*); **qui facilite le ~** RES HUM labor-saving (*AmE*), labour-saving (*BrE*); **~ en souffrance** COM work for abeyance

travailler *vi* COM, RES HUM work; **♦ ~ d'arrache-pied** COM work flat out, RES HUM work like a beaver (*infrml*); **~ en association avec** GESTION work in partnership with; **~ en collaboration avec** COM to work in tandem with; **~ comme une brute** *infrml* RES HUM work like a beaver (*infrml*); **~ de concert** COM work together; **~ côte à côte avec** RES HUM work alongside sb; **devoir ~ un weekend sur deux** COM work alternate weekends; **~ dur** RES HUM graft (*infrml*), labor (*AmE*), labour (*BrE*); **~ ensemble** COM work together; **~ en étroite collaboration avec** COM work closely with; **~ en free-lance** MÉDIA work freelance; **~ pour gagner sa vie** PROT SOC work for a living; **~ à horaire réduit** RES HUM be on short time; **~ en indépendant** MÉDIA work freelance; **~ à mi-temps** COM, RES HUM be on half-time, work part-time; **~ au noir** RES HUM moonlight (*infrml*); **~ par équipes** RES HUM work in shifts; **~ pendant ses vacances** COM do holiday work (*BrE*), do vacation work (*AmE*); **~ à plein temps**

RES HUM work full-time; ~ **qn** *infrml* COM bring pressure to bear on sb; ~ **à reculons** BOURSE job backwards (*jarg*); ~ **selon un horaire strictement minuté** COM work to a very tight schedule; ~ **sous pression** COM be under time pressure; ~ **sur** COM work on; ~ **à temps partiel** RES HUM work part-time

travailleur, -euse *m,f* RES HUM worker; ~ **à la chaîne** IND, RES HUM assembly line worker, production worker; ~ **clandestin** DROIT, RES HUM undocumented worker; ~ **à domicile** RES HUM homeworker; ~ **étranger** PROT SOC, RES HUM foreign worker; ~ **frontalier** RES HUM frontier worker; ~ **immigré** RES HUM guestworker, immigrant worker; ~ **indépendant** FISC self-employed person, self-employed worker, MÉDIA freelance, freelance worker, freelancer, RES HUM freelance, freelance worker, freelancer, self-employed person, self-employed worker; ~ **intermittent** RES HUM casual worker; ~ **itinérant** RES HUM mobile worker; ~ **manuel** IND manual worker, RES HUM blue-collar worker, manual worker; ~ **marginal** RES HUM marginal worker; ~ **à mi-temps** COM, RES HUM part-time worker, part-timer; ~ **migrant** RES HUM migrant worker, migratory worker; ~ **mobile** RES HUM mobile worker; ~ **au noir** RES HUM moonlighter; ~ **non-syndiqué** RES HUM free rider (*infrml*); ~ **occasionnel** RES HUM occasional worker; ~ **payé à l'heure** RES HUM hourly worker, wage worker; ~ **posté** IND, RES HUM shift worker; ~ **au salaire initial** RES HUM threshold worker (*US, jarg*); ~ **sans papiers** DROIT, RES HUM undocumented worker; ~ **social** PROT SOC social worker, welfare worker, RES HUM social worker; ~ **temporaire** RES HUM casual worker; ~ **à temps partiel** COM, RES HUM part-time worker, part-timer; ~ **volontaire pour le développement** COM volunteer development worker

travailleurs: ~ **atypiques** *m pl* RES HUM atypical workers; ~ **démotivés** *m pl* RES HUM discouraged workers; ~ **handicapés** *m pl* RES HUM disabled workers; ~ **manuels** *m pl* IND, RES HUM manual labor (*AmE*), manual labour (*BrE*); ~ **migrants** *m pl* RES HUM transient workers; ~ **périphériques** *m pl* RES HUM peripheral workers; ~ **sous contrat à court terme** *m pl* RES HUM short-term workers; ~ **unifié de l'automobile** *m pl (TUA)* RES HUM United Automobile Workers (*US*) (*UAW*)

travaillistique *adj* ECON, IND, RES HUM labor-intensive (*AmE*), labour-intensive (*BrE*)

travaux *m pl* TRANSP road works; ~ **de conférence** GESTION conference proceedings; ~ **en cours** COMPTA, ECON work-in-process (*AmE*), work-in-progress (*BrE*); ~ **de fin d'exercice** COMPTA year-end adjustment; ~ **menus** RES HUM odd jobs; ~ **publics** ECON public works; ~ **de transformation** COM alterations; ~ **d'utilité collective** *(TUC)* ECON, POL, PROT SOC, RES HUM ≈ Youth Training Scheme *(YTS)*, Community Programme (*UK*) *(CP)*

travers: **en** ~ **de** *loc* TRANSP *du navire* athwart; **en** ~ **de barque** *loc* TRANSP thwartship; **par le** ~ *loc* TRANSP *navigation* abeam

traverse *f* TRANSP grade crossing, level crossing

traversée: ~ **d'un navire** *f* TRANSP vessel crossing

traverser *vt* IMP/EXP *frontière*, LOISIRS, TRANSP cross; ◆ ~ **un cordon de grévistes** RES HUM cross a picket line

traversier *m* Can TRANSP ferry boat

TRC *abrév (tube à rayons cathodiques)* INFO CRT *(cathode ray tube)*

trémie *f* TRANSP hopper tank, *récipient* hopper; ~ **latérale** TRANSP hopper side tank, HSDT

trente: **les** ~ **glorieuses** *f pl* ECON Long Boom

très *adv* BOURSE *en dehors*, COM deep

trésor: ~ **de guerre** *m* COM war chest (*US*); ~ **de nuit** *m* BANQUE night depository; ~ **permanent** *m* BANQUE night depository

Trésor *m* FIN Consolidated Revenue Fund *(Canada)*; **le** ~ **Public** ECON public purse

trésorerie *f* ADMIN, COMPTA, FIN cash, cash office; ◆ **en brèche de** ~ COMPTA illiquid

trésorier, -ère *m,f* FIN, RES HUM cash manager, treasurer; ~ **d'entreprise** RES HUM corporate treasurer; ~ **de société** RES HUM corporate treasurer

treuil *m* TRANSP winch

tri *m* INFO sort; ~ **des déchets** ENVIR waste sorting; ~ **numérique** INFO digital sort; ~ **par permutation de paires de bulles** INFO bubble sort; ◆ **faire le** ~ **de** COM sort out

TRI *abrév (taux de rentabilité d'un investissement)* COMPTA, FIN ROI *(return on investment)*

triade *f* COM triad

triangle: **le** ~ **d'or** *m* ECON golden triangle

triangulaire *adj* COM triangular

triangulation *f* IMP/EXP triangulation

tribord *m* TRANSP *navigation* sor, starboard, starboard side, S

tribunal *m* DROIT court, trib., tribunal, FISC tax court; ~ **d'arbitrage** COM, DROIT, IND, RES HUM arbitration tribunal; ~ **chargé de l'application des lois antitrusts** COM R.P.Ct. (*UK*), Restrictive Practices Court (*UK*); ~ **civil** DROIT county court; ~ **de commerce** DROIT, FIN bankruptcy court; ~ **compétent** DROIT court of competent jurisdiction; ~ **des faillites** DROIT, FIN bankruptcy court; ~ **fédéral** DROIT, RES HUM federal tribunal; ~ **fédéral de première instance** DROIT district court (*US*); ~ **du gouvernement d'état** RES HUM state government tribunal; ~ **de grande instance** DROIT, POL *de l'Union européenne* Court of First Instance; ~ **d'instance** DROIT county court, magistrates court, small claims court; ~ **de première instance** DROIT, POL *de l'Union européenne* Court of First Instance; ~ **réglant les litiges douaniers** DROIT, IMP/EXP customs court (*US*); ~ **statuant sur toute atteinte à la libre concurrence** COM, DROIT R.P.Ct. (*UK*), Restrictive Practices

Court (*UK*); ~ **des successions** DROIT probate court; ~ **des successions et des tutelles** DROIT probate court; ~ **du travail** DROIT, RES HUM labor court (*AmE*), labour court (*BrE*); ◆ **le ~ est en cours d'audience** DROIT court is now in session; **le ~ est en séance** DROIT court is now in session

Tribunal: le ~ *m* DROIT the Bench (*infrml*)

tribunaux: ~ **compétents** *m pl* DROIT tribunals entitled to adjudicate

tributaire: ~ **des clients** *adj* INFO customer-driven

tricher: ~ **sur les prix** *loc* BOURSE fake the marks (*jarg*)

trieur, -euse *m,f* COM sorter

trieuse: ~ **de cartes** *f* INFO card sorter

trimestre *m* COM quarter; ~ **civil** COM calendar quarter; ~ **d'exercice** FISC fiscal quarter; ◆ **chaque ~** COM every quarter

trimestres: tous les ~ *loc* COM every quarter

trimestrialité *f* COMPTA quarterly instalment (*BrE*)

trimestriel, -elle *adj* COM, MÉDIA *presse* quarterly

trimestriellement *adv* COM, MÉDIA quarterly

trinidadien, -enne *adj* COM Trinidadian

Trinidadien, -enne *m,f* COM *habitant* Trinidadian

Trinité: ~ **-et-Tobago** *f* COM Trinidad and Tobago

triple *adj* COM treble; ◆ **à ~ expansion** TRANSP triple-expansion, TE; **en ~ exemplaire** COM *courrier, facture* in triplicate; ~ **exemption d'impôt** FISC triple tax exempt; ~ **réduction** COM triple reduction, TR

tripler *vt* MATH triple

Tripoli *n pr* COM Tripoli

tripotage *m pl* POL graft (*infrml*)

tripotages *m pl* BOURSE *cours* manipulation

troc *m* COM swop, ECON barter; ◆ **faire un ~** ECON barter

trocquer *vt* ECON barter

troïka *f* POL troika (*jarg*)

trois: à ~ hélices *adj* TRANSP triple-screw; **à ~ mois** *adj* BOURSE, COM three-month

troisième:[1] **de ~ classe** *adj* TRANSP *place* third-class; **de ~ ordre** *adj* COM third-rate

troisième:[2] ~ **âge** *m* ECON third age; ~ **bloc** *m* POL third force (*jarg*); ~ **marché** *m* BOURSE, FIN Third Market (*UK, obs*); ~ **transporteur** *m* TRANSP *distribution par voie aérienne* third carrier; ~ **trimestre** *m* COM third quarter, 3Q

troisième:[3] ~ **classe** *f* TRANSP third-class; ~ **de couverture** *f* MÉDIA inside back cover; ~ **devise** *f* COM third currency; ~ **monnaie** *f* COM third currency; ~ **voie** *f* ECON market socialism, third way, POL market socialism

troisièmement *adv* COM thirdly

trois-quarts *m pl* MATH three quarters

tromper 1. *vt* DROIT mislead; **2.** *v pron* **se ~** COM err; ◆ **se ~ dans les calculs** COM have the sum wrong; **se ~ dans les chiffres** COM get the figures wrong

tromperie: ~ **sur la charte-partie** *f* DROIT, TRANSP charter party fraud; ~ **sur le connaissement** *f* IMP/EXP, TRANSP bill of lading fraud

trompeur, -euse *adj* BREVETS, COM misleading

tronçon: ~ **de vol** *m* TRANSP flight stage

tronquer *vt* COM, INFO truncate

tropique *adj* COM tropical, T

trop-perçu *m* COM amount overpaid

troquer: ~ **une chose contre une autre** *loc* COM, ECON trade one thing against another, trade one thing for another

trottoir: ~ **de chargement** *m* TRANSP *véhicules* loading platform; ~ **roulant** *m* COM, LOISIRS moving pavement (*BrE*), travolator (*AmE*)

trouble: ~ **-fête** *m* COM wet blanket (*infrml*); ~ **intérieur** *m* ASSUR cc, civil commotion

troubles *m pl* COM unrest

troupe: ~ **itinérante** *f* LOISIRS *théâtre* tour company; ~ **de théâtre de province** *f* LOISIRS rep, repertory, repertory company

trousse: ~ **de premiers secours** *f* PROT SOC, RES HUM first-aid kit; ~ **de réparation** *f* COM repair kit; ~ **d'urgence** *f* PROT SOC, RES HUM first-aid kit

trouvaille *f* V&M *publicité* gimmick; ~ **publicitaire** V&M advertising gimmick

trouver *vt* INFO find; ◆ ~ **un débouché pour** V&M market; ~ **des défauts à** COM fault; ~ **le juste milieu** COM strike a balance; ~ **à redire à** COM find fault with; **se ~ contraint de** COM come under pressure from; **se ~ à court de** COM run short of; ~ **un second souffle** COM get a second wind; ~ **une trace du paiement** BANQUE trace a payment

truc *m* V&M *publicité* gimmick; ~ **publicitaire** *infrml* V&M advertising gimmick, publicity stunt

trucages: ~ **sonores** *m pl* MÉDIA sound effects

truquage *m* COMPTA *comptes* falsification; ~ **du bilan** BANQUE, BOURSE, COM, COMPTA, FIN window-dressing

truquer *vt* DROIT falsify, POL gerrymander; ◆ ~ **une circulaire** ADMIN salt a memo (*US, jarg*)

trust *m* ECON trust

trusts: ~ **d'actifs disponibles** *m pl* BOURSE ready assets trusts, RAT

TSDI *abrév* (*titre subordonné à durée indéterminée*) BOURSE subordinated perpetual bond

TSR *abrév* (*titre subordonné remboursable*) BOURSE subordinated redeemable bond

TSRBSORA *abrév* (*Titres subordonnés remboursables avec bons de souscription d'obligations remboursables en actions*) BOURSE subordinated redeemable notes with warrants that can be converted into bonds or shares

TSVP *abrév* (*tournez s'il vous plaît*) COMMS PTO (*please turn over*)

TT *abrév* (*transfert télégraphique*) BANQUE, COMMS TT (*telegraphic transfer*)

TTA *abrév* (*taxe sur le transport aérien*) FISC ATT (*air transportation tax*)

TU *abrév (Temps universel)* COM UTC *(universal time coordinated)*

TUA *abrév (travailleurs unifié de l'automobile)* RES HUM UAW *(US) (United Automobile Workers)*

tube: ~ **à rayons cathodiques** *m (TRC)* INFO cathode ray tube *(CRT)*

TUC *abrév (travaux d'utilité collective)* ECON, POL, PROT SOC, RES HUM ≈ YTS *(UK) (Youth Training Scheme)*, CP *(Community Programme)*

tuer *vt* V&M kill

tugrik *m* COM tugrik

tuile: **la ~ de Groningue** *f* ECON Dutch disease

Tunis *n pr* COM Tunis

Tunisie *f* COM Tunisia

tunisien, -enne *adj* COM Tunisian

Tunisien, -enne *m,f* COM *habitant* Tunisian

tunnel *m jarg* ECON tunnel *(jarg)*; ~ **de l'arbre** TRANSP *navire, hélice* shaft tunnel; ~ **sous la Manche** TRANSP Channel Tunnel, fixed link; ~ **de taux** BOURSE collar

turbine *f* TRANSP turbine; ~ **basse pression** TRANSP *navigation* low-pressure turbine, LPTB; ~ **BP** TRANSP *navigation* low-pressure turbine, LPTB; ~ **à condensation** TRANSP *navigation* condensing turbine; ~ **à gaz** TRANSP *navigation* gas turbine; ~ **haute pression** TRANSP *navigation* high-pressure turbine, HPTB; ~ **à vapeur** TRANSP steam turbine

turbo-électrique *adj* TRANSP turbo-electric

turc[1], **-que** *adj* COM Turkish

turc[2] *m* COM *langue* Turkish

Turc, -que *m,f* COM *habitant* Turk

Turkménistan *m* COM Turkmenistan

Turquie *f* COM Turkey

tutelle *f* DROIT ward, IMMOB administration

tuteur, -trice *m,f* DROIT guardian, IMMOB administrator

tuyau *m infrml* BOURSE wrinkle *(infrml)*, COM gratuity, tip, hint, tip-off, GESTION pointer; ~ **de couplage de l'amenée d'air** TRANSP susie *(jarg)*

tuyaux: ~ **boursiers** *m pl* BOURSE stock tips

TVA *abrév (taxe sur la valeur ajoutée)* FISC VAT *(UK) (value-added tax)*

TVL *abrév (temps vrai local)* TRANSP *navigation* ATS *(apparent time at ship)*

TVQ *abrév (taxe de vente de Quebec)* FISC QST *(Quebec sales tax)*

type: ~ **d'activité économique** *m* ECON pattern of economic activity; ~ **d'assurance** *m* ASSUR class of insurance; ~ **de construction** *m* ASSUR class of construction; ~ **deuxième génération** *m* IMMOB *d'entrepôt* second-generation type; ~ **de données** *m* INFO data type; ~ **d'écart** *m* BOURSE *stratégie d'option* backspread; ~ **de législation particulier** *m* DROIT piece of legislation; ~ **d'organisation interne** *m* RES HUM management organization; ~ **de paiement** *m* V&M payment method; ~ **spécial** *m* TRANSP *véhicule* special type

typiquement *adj* COM typically

typographe *mf* COM, MÉDIA typographer

typologie *f* COM typology, V&M cluster analysis

U

UC *abrév* *(unité centrale, unité centrale de traitement)* INFO CPU *(central processing unit)*

UCE *abrév* *(unité de compte européenne)* BANQUE, ECON, FIN EUA *(European unit of account)*

UDEAC *abrév* *(Union douanière et économique de l'Afrique centrale)* IMP/EXP UDEAC *(Central African Customs and Economics Union)*

UE *abrév* *(Union européenne)* ECON, POL EU *(European Union)*

UEBL *abrév* *(Union économique Belgique-Luxembourg)* ECON, POL BLEU *(Belgium-Luxembourg Economic Union)*

UEM *abrév* *(Union économique et monétaire)* ECON, POL EMU *(Economic and Monetary Union)*

UEO *abrév* *(Union de l'Europe occidentale)* POL WEU *(Western European Union)*

UEP *abrév* *(Union européenne des paiements)* COM EPU *(European Payments Union)*

UER *abrév* *(Union européenne de radiodiffusion)* COMMS, MÉDIA EBU *(European Broadcasting Union)*

UICF *abrév* *(Union internationale des chemins de fer)* ADMIN IUR *(International Union of Railways)*

UIP *abrév* *(Union interparlementaire)* POL IPU *(Inter-Parliamentary Union)*

UIT *abrév* *(Union internationale des télécommunications)* COMMS ITU *(International Telecommunications Union)*

Ukraine *f* COM Ukraine

ukrainien, -enne *adj* COM Ukrainian

Ukrainien, -enne *m,f* COM *habitant* Ukrainian

ultérieur, e *adj* COM later, subsequent

ultérieurement *adv* COM at a later date

ultimatum *m* COM ultimatum

ultimo *adv frml* COM ult., ultimo *(frml)*

ultra-secret *adj* COM top-secret

UME *abrév* *(Union monétaire européenne)* ECON, POL EMU *(European Monetary Union)*

un: ~ **pour un** *adj* BOURSE one-for-one

unanime *adj* COM unanimous

unanimement *adv* COM unanimously

unanimité *f* COM unanimity; ◆ **à l'~** COM, RES HUM *voter* unanimously

1/5 *m* *(un cinquième)* COM, MATH 1/5 *(one-fifth)*

1/2 *m* *(un demi)* COM, MATH 1/2 *(one-half)*

1/10 *m* *(un dixième)* COM, MATH 1/10 *(one-tenth)*

une: être à la ~ *loc* MÉDIA be front-page news

UNEDIC *abrév* *(Union nationale pour l'emploi dans l'industrie et le commerce)* ECON, PROT SOC, RES HUM ≈ Unemployment Benefit Office *(UK)*

1/8 *m* *(un huitième)* MATH 1/8 *(one-eighth)*

uni, e *adj* COM united; ~ **par les liens du sang** FISC connected by blood relationship

unicité: ~ **du brevet européen** *f* BREVETS unity of European patent

unidirectionnel, -elle *adj* INFO one-way

unification *f* BANQUE *d'un prêt* consolidation, COM *de l'Allemagne, d'un parti politique* unification, *de poids et mesures* standardization, FIN *d'un prêt* consolidation; ~ **étrangère** BOURSE, COM foreign merger; ~ **des pratiques et coutumes pour les crédits documentaire** ECON *commerce international* Uniform Customs and Practice for Documentary Credits, UC&P

unifier *vt* COM *parti politique, pays* unify, *poids, mesures* standardize, POL merge

uniforme¹ *adj* COM steady, uniform

uniforme² *m* COM *vêtement* uniform

uniformisation *f* COM, DROIT, V&M standardization; ~ **des salaires** RES HUM flat scale, standardization of salaries

uniformiser *vt* COM, DROIT, V&M standardize

uniformité *f* COM uniformity

unilatéral, e *adj* COM unilateral, DROIT ex parte, ECON, POL unilateral

unilatéralement *adv* COM, ECON, POL unilaterally

union *f* COM union, DROIT joinder, union, IND union, POL alliance, union, PROT SOC union, RES HUM joinder, union; ~ **douanière** ECON, IMP/EXP, RES HUM customs union; ~ **économique** ECON, POL economic union; ~ **de fait** DROIT common-law marriage; ~ **monétaire** FIN, POL monetary union; ~ **patronale** RES HUM employers' association; ~ **politique** POL *Communauté européenne* political union

Union: ~ **des annonceurs** *f France* V&M ≈ Advertising Association *(UK)*; ~ **de Berne** *f* ASSUR Berne Union; ~ **de clearing internationale** *f* POL International Clearing Union, ICU; ~ **douanière et économique de l'Afrique centrale** *f (UDEAC)* IMP/EXP Central African Customs and Economics Union *(UDEAC)*; ~ **économique Belgique-Luxembourg** *f (UEBL)* ECON, POL Belgium-Luxembourg Economic Union *(BLEU)*; ~ **économique et monétaire** *f (UEM)* ECON, POL Economic and Monetary Union *(EMU)*; ~ **de l'Europe occidentale** *f (UEO)* POL Western European Union *(WEU)*; ~ **européenne** *f (UE)* ECON, POL European Union *(EU)*; ~ **européenne des paiements** *f (UEP)* COM European Payments Union *(EPU)*; ~ **européenne de radiodiffusion** *f (UER)* COMMS, MÉDIA European Broadcasting Union *(EBU)*; ~ **internationale des chemins de fer** *f (UICF)* ADMIN International Union of Railways *(IUR)*; ~ **internationale des**

télécommunications *f (UIT)* COMMS International Telecommunications Union *(ITU)*; ~ **interparlementaire** *f (UIP)* POL Inter-Parliamentary Union *(IPU)*; ~ **du Maghreb arabe** *f* ECON, POL Arab Common Market, Arab Maghreb Union, AMU; ~ **monétaire européenne** *f (UME)* ECON, POL European Monetary Union *(EMU)*; ~ **nationale pour l'emploi dans l'industrie et le commerce** *f* ECON, PROT SOC, RES HUM *(UNEDIC)* ≈ Unemployment Benefit Office *(UK)*; ~ **postale universelle** *f (UPU)* COMMS, COMPTA Universal Postal Union *(UPU)*; ~ **des Républiques Socialistes Soviétiques** *f obs (URSS)* COM now called the Commonwealth of Independent States, Union of Soviet Socialist Republics *(obs)*; ~ **soviétique** *f* COM Soviet Union

unique[1] *adj* COM unique

unique:[2] ~ **inventeur** *m* BREVETS sole inventor

unir *vt* COM join, link, unite

unité *f* BOURSE, COM, ECON unit; INFO device, facility, unit; ~ **d'affichage** INFO display unit; ~ **agricole** ECON agricultural unit; ~ **de bande magnétique** COM tape unit; ~ **de base** COM basic unit; ~ **boursière** BOURSE trading unit; ~ **centrale** *(UC)* INFO central processing unit, processor; ~ **centrale de traitement** *(UC)* INFO central processing unit *(CPU)*, mainframe; ~ **de charge** TRANSP unit load, U; ~ **de chargement** TRANSP unit load, U; ~ **de chargement aérienne** TRANSP unit load device, ULD; ~ **de chargement stakrak** TRANSP stakrak cargo unit; ~ **commerciale** COM *bâtiments* business unit; ~ **commerciale normale** BOURSE normal trading unit; ~ **de compte** COMPTA unit of account; ~ **de compte étrangère** BANQUE, ECON, FIN foreign currency unit; ~ **de compte européenne** *(UCE)* BANQUE, ECON, FIN European unit of account *(EUA)*; ~ **de décision** COM decision unit; ~ **de disque** INFO disk drive, disk unit; ~ **de disque dur** INFO hard disk drive, hard disk unit, HDD; ~ **de disque souple** ADMIN, INFO floppy disk drive; ~ **de disquette** ADMIN, INFO diskette drive, floppy disk drive; ~ **d'élevage** COM stockkeeping unit; ~ **d'entrée** INFO input device; ~ **d'exploitation agricole** ECON agricultural unit; ~ **implicite** INFO default device; ~ **d'invention** BREVETS unity of invention; ~ **locale** RES HUM local; ~ **de mémoire de masse** INFO bulk storage; ~ **minimale de transaction** BOURSE unit of trading; ~ **mobile de drainage pétrolier offshore** IND mobile offshore drilling unit, MODU; ~ **monétaire** BANQUE, ECON, FIN currency unit, monetary unit; ~ **monétaire composite** BANQUE, ECON, FIN composite currency unit; ~ **monétaire européenne** *(ECU)* BANQUE, ECON, FIN European Currency Unit *(ECU)*; ~ **de négociation** RES HUM bargaining unit; ~ **périphérique** INFO peripheral device; ~ **principale** IMMOB prime unit; ~ **de prise de décision** V&M decision-making unit; ~ **de production** IND plant, production, production plant, production unit; ~ **de saisie** INFO data

entry terminal; ~ **salariale** RES HUM wage unit; ~ **en stock** COM inventory item; ~ **de stockage** COM, IND storage facility; ~ **de traitement** INFO computer run; ~ **de traitement des déclarations** IMP/EXP entry processing unit, EPU; ~ **de transaction** BOURSE trading unit; ~ **de transport** TRANSP transport unit; ~ **de visualisation** INFO display device, visual display unit, VDU; ◆ **à l'~ de chargement** TRANSP *tarification* freight all kinds, FAK

Unité: ~ **internationale de recrutement** *f* RES HUM International Recruitment Unit, IRU

unités: ~ **indexées liées à la croissance** *f pl* BOURSE index growth linked units, IGLU; ~ **périphériques** *f pl* IND peripheral equipment

univers *m* V&M *marketing, publicité* universe; **l'~ d'une enquête** V&M *marketing, publicité* total field of a survey

universalisme *m* PROT SOC universalism *(jarg)*

universel, -elle *adj* COM *ordinateur, appareil* all-purpose, *suffrage, système* universal

universitaire *adj* COM *honneur* academic, *études, ville* university, PROT SOC academic

université *f* COM, PROT SOC university

1/9 *m (un neuvième)*, COM, MATH 1/9 *(one-ninth)*

1/4 *m (un quart)* COM, MATH 1/4 *(one-quarter)*

1/7 *m (un septième)* COM, MATH 1/7 *(one-seventh)*

1/6 *m (un sixième)* COM, MATH 1/6 *(one-sixth)*

1/3 *m (un tiers)* COM, MATH 1/3 *(one-third)*

UPU *abrév (Union postale universelle)* COMMS, COMPTA UPU *(Universal Postal Union)*

urbain, e *adj* ECON urban

urbanisation *f* ECON urbanization; ~ **excessive** ECON overurbanization

urbaniser *vt* ECON urbanize

urbanisme *m* ADMIN city planning *(AmE)*, town planning *(BrE)*, urban planning, ECON urban economics, POL, PROT SOC city planning *(AmE)*, town planning *(BrE)*

urbaniste *mf* ADMIN, POL, PROT SOC city planner *(AmE)*, town planner *(BrE)*, urban planner

urgence *f* COM emergency, emy

urgent, e *adj* COM for immediate attention, urgent; ◆ **quelque chose d'~** COM matter of urgency

urne *f* POL, RES HUM ballot box

URSS *abrév obs (Union des Républiques Socialistes Soviétiques)* COM now called the Commonwealth of Independent States, USSR *(obs)*

Uruguay *m* COM Uruguay; **l'~ Round** ECON Uruguay Round

uruguayen, -enne *adj* COM Uruguayan

Uruguayen, -enne *m,f* COM *habitant* Uruguayan

usage *m* COM purpose, *coutume* custom, *utilisation* use, DROIT practice; ~ **abusif** ENVIR misuse; ~ **antérieur** BREVETS, COM prior use; ~ **non-conforme** DROIT, IMMOB nonconforming use; ~ **du port** TRANSP custom of port, COP; ~ **pratique** RES HUM practical use; ~ **public** BREVETS public use; ~ **de simple reconnaissance de la**

représentation RES HUM recognition-only practice (*UK*); ◆ à ~ **général** COM general purpose, GP; **faire beaucoup d'~** COM stand up to wear

usagé, e *adj* ENVIR *huile* used

usager *m* COM *d'une route, d'un moyen de transport*, INFO user; ~ **des chemins de fer** TRANSP rail traveler (*AmE*), rail traveller (*BrE*), rail user; ~ **inscrit sur le registre** BREVETS, DROIT, INFO registered user

usages: ~ **commerciaux** *m pl* COM, ECON, GESTION business practices; ◆ à ~ **multiples** COM, INFO multipurpose

usance *f* FIN usance; ◆ à ~ **de trente jours** FIN at thirty days' usance

user: **s'~** *v pron* RES HUM *employé* burn out

usine *f* IND factory, plant, works; ~ **de base** IND baseload power station; ~ **center** COM factory shop; ~ **de composants** IND component factory; ~ **de construction mécanique** IND engineering works; ~ **d'essai** IND testing plant; ~ **et matériels** COM, IND plant and machinery; ~ **existante** ENVIR, IND existing plant; ~ **à gaz** IND gasworks; ~ **d'incinération** ENVIR, IND incineration plant; ~ **de montage** IND, RES HUM assembly plant; ~ **de papeterie** ENVIR, IND paper mill; ~ **à papier** ENVIR, IND paper mill; ~ **de pièces détachées** IND component factory; ~ **-pilote** IND advance factory; ~ **de production** IND plant, production plant; ~ **de régénération des huiles usées** ENVIR oil regeneration plant; ~ **de retraitement** ENVIR reprocessing plant; ~ **en service** ENVIR, IND existing plant; ~ **sidérurgique** IND ironworks; ~ **à syndicats multiples** RES HUM multiunion plant; ~ **thermique** IND thermal power station; ~ **thermique à houille** IND coal-fired power station; ~ **de traitement** IND processing plant; ~ **de traitement des déchets** ENVIR waste treatment plant; ~ **transplantée** IND transplant factory

usines: ~ **parallèles** *f pl* IND parallel plants

usufruit *m* DROIT beneficial ownership, life interest, usufruct

usufruitier, -ière *m,f* DROIT beneficial owner, life tenant, usufructuary

usuraire *adj* BANQUE, FIN usurious

usure *f* BANQUE usury, COM wear, wear and tear, FIN usury; ~ **normale** COM *de marchandises* fair wear and tear, COMPTA, FISC, IMMOB *du matériel* normal wear and tear

usurier, -ière *m,f* FIN loan shark (*infrml*), usurer

usurpation *f* DROIT encroachment

usurper *vt* DROIT *les droits de qn* encroach on, encroach upon

util *m* ECON revealed preference, util

utile *adj* COM useful; ◆ ~ **à qn** COM useful to sb; ~ **pour la compréhension de l'invention** BREVETS useful for understanding the invention

utilement *adv* COM *avec profit* effectively, profitably, usefully, COMPTA, ECON, FIN profitably

utilisable *adj* COM, ENVIR, IND *déchets* usable; ~ **sans restrictions** COM *fonds* expendable

utilisateur, -trice *m,f* COM *d'une machine*, INFO user; ~ **comme armateur** TRANSP *d'un navire* disponent owner; ~ **final** COM, ECON disponent user, INFO disponent user, end-user; ~ **inscrit au registre** BREVETS, DROIT, INFO registered user; ◆ **conçu en pensant à l'~** V&M user-orientated, user-oriented

utilisation *f* ENVIR *ressources naturelles* utilization; ~ **abusive d'informations privilégiées** BOURSE frontrunning, running ahead; ~ **en alternance** IMMOB alternative use; ~ **anormale** COM *d'un outil* service abuse; ~ **à bonne fin** IMP/EXP completion of end use (*UK*); ~ **des capacités** ECON, IND capacity utilization; ~ **du capital** ECON capital utilization; ~ **collective de fichier** INFO file sharing; ~ **du conteneur** TRANSP *seul conteneur* container use, container utilization; ~ **des conteneurs** TRANSP container use, container utilization; ~ **excessive** COM, ENVIR overuse; ~ **de la flotte** TRANSP fleet utilization; ~ **des fonds** BOURSE flow of funds, COMPTA application of funds; ~ **non-agricole** ENVIR, IMMOB nonagricultural use; ~ **par alternance** IMMOB alternative use; ~ **du parc** TRANSP fleet utilization; ~ **du parc automobile** TRANSP fleet utilization; ~ **la plus rentable** IMMOB *évaluation* highest and best use (*AmE*); ~ **du potentiel industriel** ECON, IND industrial capacity utilization; ~ **du potentiel de production** ECON, IND capacity utilization; ~ **préexistante** IMMOB pre-existing use; ~ **des remorques** TRANSP trailer utilization; ◆ **d'~ facile** INFO user-friendly

utiliser *vt* COM make use of, utilize, *méthode, possibilité* employ, use

utilitaire[1] *adj* COM utilitarian, utility, INFO utility

utilitaire[2] *m* INFO utility, TRANSP *véhicule* commercial vehicle; ~ **de sauvegarde** INFO backup utility program

utilitarisme *m* ECON utilitarianism

utilité *f* ECON utility; ~ **de lieu** ECON place utility; ~ **marginale** ECON marginal significance, marginal utility; ~ **marginale privée** ECON private marginal benefit; ~ **ordinale** ECON ordinal utility; ~ **primordiale** ECON cardinal utility, utilitarianism

V

V *abrév (volt)* COM V *(volt)*

vacance: ~ **de poste** *f* RES HUM job vacancy

vacances *f pl* COM, LOISIRS, RES HUM holiday (*BrE*), holidays (*BrE*), vacation (*AmE*)

vacancier, -ière *m,f* COM, LOISIRS holiday-maker (*BrE*), vacationer (*AmE*), vacationist (*AmE*)

vacation *f* DROIT, POL recess (*UK*), vacations

vaccination *f* IMP/EXP inoculation, vaccination

vacciner *vt* IMP/EXP inoculate, vaccinate

vache: ~ **à lait** *f jarg* ECON cash cow (*jarg*)

Vaduz *n pr* COM Vaduz

vague *f* COM boom, spate, wave; ~ **d'achats** COM buying surge

vaigrage *m* TRANSP *d'un navire* sparring fitting, SF

vainqueur: ~ **ramasse tout** *loc* COM winner takes all

vaisseau *m* TRANSP *d'un navire* boat, ship, vessel; ~ **auxiliaire** TRANSP *navire* aux., auxiliary

val. *abrév (valeur)* BOURSE security, stock

valable *adj* ADMIN *passeport* valid, COM applicable, *argument, excuse* valid, *document* admissible

valant *adj* COM worth; ◆ ~ **10 livres** FIN worth £10

Valette: **La** ~ *n pr* COM Valletta

valeur *f* BOURSE security, stock, COM value, worth, ECON denomination, value, *réelle* pr., price, FIN stock; ~ **d'accroche** V&M *publicité* attention value; ~ **de l'acquisition** COM acquisition value; ~ **de l'actif** COMPTA asset value, ECON capital value, FIN asset value, capital value; ~ **de l'actif net** COMPTA, FIN net asset value, NAV; ~ **de l'actif par action** BOURSE, FIN asset value per share; ~ **actualisée** FIN discounted present value; ~ **actualisée nette** COMPTA, FIN discounted cash flow, DCF; ~ **actuelle** BANQUE current value, COMPTA current value, market value, FIN current value; ~ **actuelle nette** *(VAN)* COMPTA, ECON, FIN net present value *(NPV)*; ~ **affective** ASSUR affection value; ~ **agréée** ASSUR agreed value; ~ **agricole** ECON, POL agricultural paper (*US*); ~ **ajoutée** COM added value, COMPTA, ECON, FISC value added, V&M *offre spéciale* added value; ~ **amortie** COMPTA written-down value; ~ **à amortir** COMPTA depreciable amount; ~ **de l'argent** ECON value of money; ~ **arrivant à échéance** BOURSE maturing security, maturing value; ~ **attendue** MATH expectation, expected value; ~ **attribuée** COMPTA, FIN stated value (*Canada*); ~ **autorisée** BOURSE authorized share (*UK*), authorized stock (*UK*); ~ **en baisse** BOURSE (*ANT valeur en hausse*) bearish stock, declining share, ECON declining share; ~ **bêta** BOURSE beta (*US*), beta share, beta stock (*UK*); ~ **boursière** BOURSE trading security; ~ **de caisse** COMPTA cash value; ~ **du capital** ECON, FIN capital value;

~ **capitalisée** ECON capitalized value; ~ **à certificat endommagé** BOURSE mutilated security; ~ **comptable** COMPTA *d'une action* book value, stated value, FIN book value, FISC burden; ~ **comptable brute** COMPTA gross book value; ~ **comptable globale nette** COMPTA aggregate book value; ~ **comptable d'investissement** COMPTA, FIN book value of investment; ~ **comptable nette** COMPTA, FIN amortized value, net book value; ~ **comptable du patrimoine** BOURSE, COMPTA balance sheet value of shares; ~ **du compte de placement** BANQUE investment account security; ~ **du contrat** BOURSE contract value; ~ **contributive** ASSUR contributory value; ~ **convertible** BOURSE convertible security; ~ **convertible à coupon zéro** BOURSE zero-coupon convertible security; ~ **corporelle** COM, COMPTA, FIN tangible asset; ~ **à la cote** BOURSE quote value; ~ **cotée en bourse** BOURSE listed security, quoted security; ~ **à coupon zéro** BOURSE zero-coupon security; ~ **au cours du marché** BOURSE current market value; ~ **à court terme** (*ANT valeur à long terme*) BOURSE short-term security; ~ **critique** MATH critical value; ~ **de croissance** BOURSE growth stock, performance stock, FIN leveraged stock; ~ **croissante** BOURSE growth in value; ~ **cumulative** BOURSE cumulative security; ~ **déclarée en douane** IMP/EXP, TRANSP declared value for customs; ~ **déclarée pour le transport** TRANSP declared value for carriage; ~ **delta** BOURSE delta stock (*UK*); ~ **détenue** BOURSE security holding; ~ **de dollar** BOURSE dollar value; ~ **en douane par kilo brut** IMP/EXP customs value per gross kilogram (*AmE*), customs value per gross kilogramme (*BrE*), CVGK; ~ **en douane par livre brute** IMP/EXP customs value per gross pound, CVGP; ~ **d'échange** BOURSE exchange value, ECON value in exchange; ~ **à échéance** BANQUE, BOURSE, ECON, FIN maturity value; ~ **économique** ECON economic value; ~ **de l'écu exprimée en dollars** BOURSE dollar price of the ECU; ~ **effective au comptant** BOURSE, FIN actual cash value, ACV; ~ **égale** BOURSE equal value; ~ **émise en robinet continu** *jarg* BOURSE tap (*jarg*); ~ **d'emprunt** ASSUR loan value; ~ **à l'encaissement** COMPTA value for collection; ~ **de l'entreprise en continuité d'exploitation** COMPTA going-concern value; ~ **d'une entreprise prospère** COMPTA going-concern value; ~ **équitable** COMPTA fair value; ~ **en espèces** BANQUE value in cash; ~ **estimative** ASSUR estimated value, FIN, IMMOB appraised value; ~ **estimée** ASSUR estimated value, FIN, IMMOB appraised value; ~ **d'État** BOURSE government stock; ~ **étrangère** BOURSE foreign security; ~ **d'excédent** COMPTA rate of exploitation, surplus approach, surplus value; ~ **externe** ECON extremum (*frml*); ~ **externe pondérée en fonction des échanges commerciaux** ECON trade-weighted external value; ~ **extrinsèque** BOURSE extrinsic value; ~ **faciale** BOURSE face value; ~ **de la facture** COM, FIN invoice value, iv; ~ **fixe** BOURSE locked-in value; ~ **de fonds de portefeuille** BOURSE blue chip, blue-chip security, blue-chip stock; ~ **des fonds propres** ECON, FIN capital value; ~ **garantie** BOURSE guaranteed security; ~ **garantie par hypothèque** BOURSE mortgage-backed security, MBS; ~ **de grande qualité** BOURSE gilt-edged stock; ~ **de gré à gré** BOURSE tap (*jarg*); ~ **en hausse** (ANT *valeur en baisse*) BOURSE advance, bullish stock, winner; ~ **des immobilisations incorporelles** COMPTA intangible asset worth; ~ **imposable** FISC taxable value; ~ **imputée** COMPTA imputed value; ~ **incorporelle** COM intangible asset, COMPTA intangible asset, intangible value, FIN intangible asset; ~ **indexée de premier choix** BOURSE index-linked gilt; ~ **industrielle** BOURSE industrial share, FIN industrial security; ~ **industrielle de premier ordre** BOURSE blue-chip industrial; ~ **inscrite à la cote** BOURSE listed security, quoted security; ~ **intérieure actuelle** IMP/EXP current domestic value, CDV; ~ **intrinsèque** BOURSE intrinsic value, ECON intrinsic value, value in use; ~ **d'inventaire** COMPTA stocktaking value; ~ **d'inventaire des titres détenus** BOURSE, COMPTA *bilan* balance sheet value of shares; ~ **jour** BANQUE same-day value; ~ **de liquidation** COMPTA, FIN break-up value, liquidating value; ~ **liquidative** FIN cash-in value; ~ **livrable** BOURSE deliverable security; ~ **locative** FIN leasehold value, FISC rental value, IMMOB leasehold value; ~ **à long terme** (ANT *valeur à court terme*) BOURSE lockaway (*jarg*), long-term security; ~ **marchande** BOURSE, V&M market value, sale value, marketable value; ~ **marchande actuelle** BOURSE, V&M *d'un bien* current market value; ~ **marchande contre valeur comptant réelle** IMMOB market value versus actual cash value; ~ **du marché** ASSUR, IMMOB market value, market value clause; ~ **matérielle** COM, COMPTA, FIN tangible asset; ~ **mixte** BOURSE blended value; ~ **mobilière** BOURSE security; ~ **mobilière de participation** BOURSE shareholding; ~ **mobilière transportée en gage** BANQUE pledge security; ~ **mobilière transportée en nantissement** BANQUE pledge security; ~ **moindre** BOURSE undervalue; ~ **moyenne** MATH mean value; ~ **nantie** BANQUE pledged security; ~ **négociée** BOURSE trading security; ~ **nette** BANQUE equity, equity value, COMPTA, FIN net value, net worth; ~ **nette du bien** FISC net estate (*US*); ~ **nette du déficit** ECON deficit net worth; ~ **nette déficitaire** ECON negative net worth; ~ **nette négative** ECON negative net worth; ~ **nette réelle** BANQUE equity, equity value, COMPTA effective net worth; ~ **nominale** BOURSE face value, nominal value, p.v., par value, COMPTA, FIN nominal value; ~ **nominative** BOURSE registered security;

~ **non-cotée** BOURSE unlisted security, unquoted security; ~ **de nouveauté** V&M novelty value; ~ **objective** ECON objective value; ~ **obligataire** BOURSE bond capital, bond denomination; ~ **originale de la police** ASSUR value as in original policy; ~ **au pair** BOURSE p.v., par value; ~ **au pair d'une devise** BOURSE par value of currency; ~ **patrimoniale** COMPTA, FIN net worth; ~ **patrimoniale nette** COMPTA, FIN net asset value, NAV; ~ **de père de famille** *jarg* BOURSE blue chip, one for the shelf (*jarg*); ~ **peu active** BOURSE cabinet security (*US*), delta stock (*UK*); ~ **peu dynamique** BOURSE cabinet security (*US*), delta stock (*UK*); ~ **de placement** BANQUE investment account security; ~ **d'un point** BOURSE value of one point; ~ **de pointage** BOURSE tick size (*infrml*); ~ **de la police d'origine** ASSUR value as in original policy, VOP; ~ **de premier choix** BOURSE gilt-edged security, ECON primary capital, FIN gilt-edged security, primary capital; ~ **de premier ordre** BOURSE blue chip, gilt (*UK*), gilt-edged security, gilt-edged stock, FIN gilt-edged security; ~ **principale** BOURSE principal value, COM chief value, CV; ~ **privilégiée à taux variable** BOURSE floating-rate preferred share; ~ **au prix coûtant** COMPTA value at cost; ~ **publicitaire** V&M advertising value; ~ **qui fléchit** BOURSE, ECON declining share; ~ **de rachat** ASSUR cash surrender value, BOURSE redemption value, COMPTA surrender value; ~ **de rachat d'assurance vie** ASSUR cash value life insurance (*US*); ~ **de rachat au comptant** ASSUR cash surrender value; ~ **rachetée** BOURSE called security; ~ **de rapportage** IMMOB plottage value (*US*); ~ **de rareté** ECON scarcity value; ~ **réalisable estimative** BANQUE, COMPTA, ECON, FIN estimated realizable value; ~ **réalisable nette** COMPTA, ECON, FIN, V&M *publicité* net realizable value, NRV; ~ **de réalisation nette** BANQUE equity, equity value; ~ **de réalisation réelle** BANQUE equity, equity value; ~ **de reconstruction** COMPTA reproduction cost; ~ **reçue en pension** COMPTA, FIN *bilan* bill purchased under resale agreement, note purchased under resale agreement; ~ **réelle de l'argent** ECON real money (*jarg*); ~ **réelle nette** BOURSE, FIN tangible net worth; ~ **de référence** BOURSE *de l'indicateur de tendance* barometer stock; ~ **de remplacement** BOURSE actual cash value, ACV, COMPTA replacement value, ECON economic value, FIN actual cash value, ACV; ~ **renfermée** BOURSE *d'actions attribuées au personnel* locked-in value; ~ **de reprise** COM trade-in allowance; ~ **résiduelle** FISC residual value; ~ **résiduelle de liquidation** ECON salvage value, winding-up value; ~ **de revente** V&M resale value; ~ **à revenu fixe** BOURSE fixed income, fixed income security; ~ **de réversion** IMMOB reversionary value; ~ **risquée** BANQUE risky asset; ~ **de seconde catégorie** BOURSE junior security (*US*); ~ **de second rang** BOURSE junior security (*US*); ~ **des services publics à avantages fiscaux** BOURSE qualifying utility; ~ **de seuil** INFO threshold value; ~ **de Shapley** ECON Shapley value; ~ **de société de crédit** FIN finance company paper; ~ **de société étrangère** BOURSE foreign security; ~ **en solde en fin de journée** BOURSE overnight security; ~ **sous-jacente** BOURSE underlying security; ~ **sous-option** BOURSE underlying security; ~ **spéculative** BOURSE speculative stock; ~ **spéculative d'une société surendettée** BOURSE stub equity; ~ **sûre** BOURSE blue chip; ~ **de surtaxe** IMP/EXP, TRANSP surcharge value; ~ **tangible** COM, COMPTA, FIN tangible asset; ~ **à taux fixe** BOURSE fixed-interest security, fixed-rate security; ~ **à taux flottant** BOURSE floating-rate security; ~ **à taux variable** BOURSE floating-rate security; ~ **temporelle** BOURSE time value; ~ **-temps** BOURSE time value; ~ **à terme** BOURSE forward security, short-term security; ~ **théorique au remboursement** BOURSE actual cash value, ACV; ~ **des transactions obligataires** BOURSE bond turnover; ~ **unitaire** COM unit value; ~ **de l'unité de construction** TRANSP construction unit value, CUV; ~ **d'usage** ECON use value, value in use; ~ **vedette** BOURSE glamor stock (*AmE*), glamour stock (*BrE*), leader, leading stock; ~ **vénale** COM market value; ~ **venant à échéance** BOURSE maturing security, maturing value; ~ **en vogue** BOURSE high-flier, high-flyer, high-flying stock; ~ **volatile** BOURSE high-flier, high-flyer, high-flying stock; ~ **yo-yo** *jarg* BOURSE yo-yo stock (*jarg*); ♦ **à la ~ faciale** BOURSE at face value; **à la ~ nominale** BANQUE at par, BOURSE at face value, COM at par; **à sa pleine ~** BOURSE fully valued; **de ~** COM valuable; **sur la ~** COM valuable, FISC ad valorem (*frml*)

valeurisation *f* BANQUE securitization

valeurs *f pl* BOURSE securities, stock; ~ **alpha** BOURSE alpha stock; ~ **bancaires** BANQUE bank shares; ~ **de banque** BANQUE bank securities; ~ **basées sur l'actif net** COMPTA, FIN net-asset-based values; ~ **brûlantes** *jarg* BOURSE hot stock (*jarg*); ~ **de chemin de fer** BOURSE rail shares; ~ **en compte** BOURSE securities long; ~ **cotées** BOURSE listed securities, quoted securities; ~ **à cours non-limité** BOURSE unlimited securities; ~ **cuprifères** BOURSE coppers; ~ **cycliques** BOURSE cycle stock, cyclical fluctuation; ~ **à découvert** BOURSE securities short; ~ **défensives** BOURSE defensive securities; ~ **demandées** BOURSE securities wanted; ~ **disponibles** BOURSE available assets, liquid assets; ~ **données en pension** COMPTA, FIN *bilan* notes under repurchase agreement; ~ **d'État** BOURSE tap stocks (*UK*); ~ **d'État émises en robinet continu** BOURSE government tap stocks (*UK*); ~ **fréquemment négociées** BOURSE active securities; ~ **garanties par le gouvernement** BOURSE warrant into government securities, WINGS; ~ **en hausse** BOURSE highs; ~ **haute-tech** BOURSE high-tech stock; ~ **immobilisées** COMPTA fixed assets; ~ **des industries de défense** BOURSE war babies (*jarg*); ~ **des industries de haute technologie** BOURSE high-tech stock; ~ **des industries sidérurgiques** BOURSE steel securities; ~ **du marché monétaire à court terme** BOURSE short-term money-market instrument; ~ **minières** BOURSE, IND mining shares; ~ **mobilières** BOURSE, FIN transferable securities; ~ **mobilières cessibles** BOURSE negotiable securities; ~ **mobilières négociables** BOURSE negotiable securities; ~ **mobilières de placement** COMPTA Treasury investments (*UK*); ~ **ne portant pas intérêt** BOURSE non-interest-bearing securities; ~ **nettes** COMPTA, FIN net assets; ~ **or sud-africaines** BOURSE South African gold shares; ~ **pétrolières** BOURSE oil shares; ~ **de placement** BOURSE marketable securities; ~ **au plus haut** BOURSE highs; ~ **en portefeuille** BOURSE securities in portfolio; ~ **au porteur** BOURSE, COMPTA, FIN bearer stock; ~ **de premier choix** BOURSE gilts (*UK*); ~ **sans certificat** BOURSE book-entry securities; ~ **de spéculation** BOURSE floating securities; ~ **stannifères** BOURSE tin shares; ~ **à terme sous options** BOURSE underlying futures; ~ **transférables** BOURSE, FIN transferable securities; ~ **très actives** BOURSE active securities; ~ **très liquides** BOURSE active securities; ~ **du Trésor** BANQUE, BOURSE, ECON T-bill (*US*), Treasury bill bonds (*US*), government obligations (*US*); ~ **variables** BOURSE floating securities; ~ **vedettes et titres à la traîne** BOURSE leaders and laggards; ~ **ZEBRA** BOURSE ZEBRAs, zero coupon Euro-sterling bearer-registered accruing securities

validation *f* COM ratification, validation, DROIT *d'un acte* authentication, execution, ratification, *d'un testament* granting, probate, proving, *d'un mariage* validation, FISC, INFO validation

valide *adj* COM *contrat, laissez-passer* valid

valider *vt* COM validate, DROIT *acte* authenticate, execute, ratify, *mariage* validate, *testament* grant, probate, prove, FISC validate, INFO enable

validité *f* BREVETS, COM, DROIT validity

valise *f* LOISIRS case, suitcase (*BrE*), valise (*AmE*); ~ **diplomatique** COMMS diplomatic bag (*BrE*), diplomatic pouch (*AmE*)

valoir *vt* BOURSE, COM, ECON be worth; ♦ **à ~** COM paid in advance; ~ **le coup** *infrml* COM be worthwhile; **faire ~** COM *ses droits* enforce; **faire ~ ses droits** DROIT put in a claim; **faire ~ une exception** DROIT enter a plea; ~ **la peine** COM be worthwhile; ~ **très cher** COM command a very high price

valorisation *f* ECON *d'un produit* valorization; ~ **à leur coût total** COMPTA *des produits* full costing; ~ **des stocks** COM inventory valuation, stock valuation, COMPTA inventory pricing

valoriser 1. *vt* ECON *produit* valorize; **2.** *v pron* **se ~** BOURSE gain, COM, IMMOB increase in value

valuation: ~ **de l'apporteur** *f* COM vendor rating

VAN *abrév* (*valeur actuelle nette*) COMPTA, ECON, FIN NPV (*net present value*)

vap. *abrév* (*vapeur*) TRANSP *navire* SS (*steamship*)

vapeur[1] *m* (*vap.*) TRANSP steamboat, steamer, steamship (*SS*); ~ **en cueillette** TRANSP tramp,

tramp steamer; ~ **à deux hélices** TRANSP twin-screw steamer; ~ **à hélices** TRANSP screw steamer; ~ **à turbine** TRANSP turbine steamship

vapeur^2 *f* TRANSP steam

vaquer: ~ **à ses occupations** *loc* COM go about one's business

varangue *f* TRANSP *d'un navire* floor

variabilité *f* COM, MATH variability

variable^1 *adj* ASSUR adjustable, FIN adjustable, variable

variable^2 *f* INFO, MATH variable; ~ **aléatoire** MATH random variable; ~ **auxiliaire** ECON *économétrie* dummy variable; ~ **booléenne** INFO Boolean variable; ~ **du but** POL goal variable; ~ **continue** MATH continuous variable; ~ **décalée** MATH lagged variable; ~ **discrète** MATH discrete variable; ~ **endogène** ECON *économétrie* endogenous variable; ~ **exogène** ECON *économétrie* exogenous variable; ~ **globale** INFO global variable; ~ **indépendante** MATH independent variable; ~ **indicateur** ECON indicator variable; ~ **locale** INFO local variable; ~ **t de Student-Fisher** MATH Student's t-distribution

variables: ~ **ex ante** *f pl* ECON ex ante variables *(frml)*; ~ **ex post** *frml f pl* ECON ex post variables *(frml)*

variance *f* COM, MATH variance; ~ **de l'échantillon** MATH sampling variance; ~ **des sorties** MATH output variance

variation *f* BOURSE *d'un cours, d'un prix*, COM change, fluctuation, swing, variation, COMPTA flow, ECON variation; ~ **aléatoire** BOURSE random walk, ECON random variation, random walk; ~ **boursière** BOURSE trading variation; ~ **conjoncturelle** ECON cyclic variation; ~ **de cours minimale** BOURSE minimum price change, minimum price fluctuation; ~ **maximale des cours autorisée** BOURSE maximum price change, maximum price fluctuation; ~ **minimale des cours** BOURSE minimum price fluctuation, trading variation; ~ **négative de trésorerie** *(*ANT *variation positive de trésorerie)* COMPTA, FIN negative cash flow; ~ **nette** BOURSE net change; ~ **positive de trésorerie** *(*ANT *variation négative de trésorerie)* COMPTA, FIN positive cash flow; ~ **de prix** BOURSE price change, price fluctuation, price swing, price variation

variations: ~ **à court terme** *f pl* ECON short-term fluctuations; ~ **cycliques** *f pl* COM, ECON cyclical variations; ~ **saisonnières** *f pl* ECON, MATH, POL seasonal adjustments, seasonal fluctuations, seasonal swings, seasonal variations, time series

varié, e *adj* COM diverse, varied, varying

varier *vi* COM diversify, fluctuate, vary; ~ **simultanément** ECON move together

variété *f* COM, V&M variety

variomètre *m* IND variometer

Varsovie *n pr* COM Warsaw

vaste *adj* COM far-flung; ~ **gamme** COM wide-ranging

vaut: **qui en** ~ **la peine** *loc* COM worthwhile; **qui ne** ~ **rien** *loc* COM worthless

vecteur *m* COM, MATH vector

vedette *f* MÉDIA star, TRANSP *navigation* ctr, cutter, *navire* ml, motor launch; ◆ **avoir la** ~ COM hold the stage

véga *m* BOURSE vega

véhicule *m* COM *moyen de transmission*, TRANSP vehicle; ~ **articulé** TRANSP articulated vehicle; ~ **articulé à plate-forme** TRANSP flat-bed; ~ **automobile** TRANSP motor vehicle; ~ **à bagages** TRANSP baggage vehicle; ~ **de communication** MÉDIA, V&M *publicité* advertising vehicle; ~ **composé** TRANSP built-up vehicle; ~ **construit sur commande** TRANSP *véhicule routier* purpose-built vehicle; ~ **à deux essieux** TRANSP two-axle vehicle; ~ **industriel** TRANSP industrial vehicle; ~ **de location sans chauffeur** TRANSP self-drive hire vehicle, self-drive rental vehicle; ~ **à moteur** TRANSP motor vehicle; ~ **à moteur à essence** ENVIR, TRANSP gasoline engine vehicle *(AmE)*, petrol engine vehicle *(BrE)*; ~ **d'occasion** TRANSP second-hand vehicle, used vehicle; ~ **passager** TRANSP passenger vehicle; ~ **-plateforme** TRANSP platform vehicle; ~ **ravitailleur** TRANSP tender vehicle; ~ **rigide** TRANSP rigid vehicle, supply vehicle; ~ **routier à moteur diesel** TRANSP DERV *(BrE)*, diesel-engined road vehicle *(BrE)*; ~ **simple** TRANSP rigid vehicle; ~ **sur coussin d'air** TRANSP *maritime* air cushion vehicle, ACV; ~ **de tourisme** TRANSP passenger vehicle; ~ **de transport public** TRANSP public service vehicle, PSV; ~ **à trois essieux** TRANSP three-axle vehicle; ~ **utilitaire** TRANSP commercial vehicle

veille: ~ **de la liquidation** *f* BOURSE name day, ticket day *(UK)*

veilleur *m* RES HUM night watchman, watchman

veine *f* COM good luck, luck, lucky break

vélin *m* ADMIN, IND wove paper

vélocité *f* COM, ECON velocity

vendable *adj* COM marketable, merchantable, salable *(AmE)*, saleable *(BrE)*, vendible, V&M merchantable

vendange *f* COM vine harvest, wine harvest, ECON vintage

vendeur^1 *adj* BOURSE offered

vendeur^2 *m* COM, RES HUM salesman; ~ **à commission** RES HUM commission salesman; ~ **régional** RES HUM area salesman

vendeur^2, **-euse** *m,f* BOURSE *d'options* grantor, option seller, options writer, seller, transferor, writer, COM sales clerk *(AmE)*, salesperson, seller, shop assistant *(BrE)*, vendor, RES HUM sales clerk *(AmE)*, salesagent, salesperson, shop assistant *(BrE)*, V&M salesagent, vendor; ~ **d'art** *(*ANT *acheteur d'art)* COM art seller; ~ **baratineur** V&M advertising agent, huckster; ~ **de bateaux** RES HUM, TRANSP yacht broker; ~ **de call couvert** BOURSE covered writer; ~ **de choc** *infrml* COM advertising agent; ~ **à commission** RES HUM commission salesperson; ~ **à découvert** BOURSE bear, short seller; ~ **de double option** (ANT *acheteur de double option*) BOURSE straddle seller, straddle writer; ~ **d'espace** (ANT *acheteur d'espace*) V&M space seller; ~ **d'espace publicitaire** (ANT *acheteur d'espace publicitaire*) MÉDIA, V&M advertising space seller; ~ **ferme** (ANT *acheteur ferme*) BOURSE firm seller;˙ ~ **de médias** (ANT *acheteur de médias*) MÉDIA, RES HUM, V&M media seller; ~ **d'option** (ANT *acheteur d'option*) BOURSE option seller, option writer, seller; ~ **d'option d'achat à découvert** BOURSE uncovered call writer; ~ **d'option à découvert** BOURSE naked writer, uncovered writer; ~ **d'options d'achat** (ANT *vendeur d'options de vente*) BOURSE call option writer; ~ **d'options d'achat partiellement à découvert** BOURSE ratio writer; ~ **d'options sur devises** BOURSE currency options seller, currency options writer; ~ **d'options de vente** (ANT *vendeur d'options d'achat*) BOURSE put option writer; ~ **par correspondance** V&M inertia salesman; ~ **régional** COM area salesperson; ~ **d'un straddle** (ANT *acheteur d'un straddle*) BOURSE straddle seller, straddle writer; ~ **de temps** (ANT *acheteur de temps*) MÉDIA, V&M *publicité, radio, télévision* time seller

vendeuse *f* COM, RES HUM saleswoman, commission salesperson; ~ **à commission** RES HUM commission salesperson, commission saleswoman; ~ **régionale** RES HUM area salesperson, area saleswoman

vendre 1. *vt* COM sell, FIN sell out; 2. *v pron* se ~ **au détail** V&M retail; se ~ **mal** COM undersell; ◆ ~ **au-dessous du prix normal** BOURSE *titres, valeurs* scalp (*infrml*); ~ **à la clôture** BOURSE sell on close (*jarg*); ~ **à la commission** V&M sell on commission; ~ **au comptant** BOURSE sell spot; ~ **un contrat** BOURSE short a contract; ~ **au cours du marché** BOURSE sell at market; ~ **à couvert** COM sell for delivery; ~ **à crédit** V&M sell on credit; ~ **à la criée** COM, V&M auction, auction off, sell at auction, sell by auction; ~ **à découvert** (ANT *spéculer*) BOURSE go short, sell a bear, sell short; ~ **au détail** V&M retail; ~ **aux enchères** COM, V&M auction, auction off, sell at auction, sell by auction; ~ **de gré à gré** COM sell by private treaty; ~ **en gros** V&M sell in bulk; ~ **une idée à qn** V&M sell sb an idea; ~ **en masse** BOURSE unwind a trade; ~ **meilleur marché que ses concurrents** V&M undersell one's competitors; ~ **moins cher que** COM *concurrent*, ECON undercut; **ne pas savoir se** ~ COM undersell o.s.; ~ **une option** BOURSE write a stock option; ~ **une option pour compenser une position inverse** BOURSE write an option against; ~ **une option à découvert** BOURSE write a naked option; ~ **une option en face de** BOURSE write against; ~ **des options de vente pour acquérir des actions** BOURSE write puts to acquire stock; ~ **à perte** BOURSE take a bath (*jarg*), take a loss; ~ **qch à la casse** COM sell sth

for scrap; ~ **en reprise** COM trade in; ~ **à terme** BOURSE sell for the account, sell for the settlement, sell forward, V&M sell on credit

vendredi *m* COM Fri., Friday; ~ **noir** BOURSE Black Friday; ◆ ~**s et jours fériés compris** TRANSP *charte-partie* Fridays and holidays included

vendu: ~ **avec possibilité de retour** *loc* COM on sale or return; ~ **ou repris** *loc* V&M *marchandises* on sale or return

Venezuela *m* COM Venezuela

vénézuélien, -enne *adj* COM Venezuelan

Vénézuélien, -enne *m,f* COM *habitant* Venezuelan

venir *vt* COM come; ~ **de** COM come from, originate from; ◆ **à** ~ COM forthcoming; ~ **en aide à** BANQUE aid, COM come to the rescue of; ~ **à échéance** BOURSE mature, COM come to maturity, COMPTA become due; ~ **en lecture** POL come under scrutiny; ~ **à la rescousse de** COM come to the rescue of; ~ **en tête** COM come at the top, top the list; ~ **en tête de** COM *sondages* top

Venise: ~ **Simplon Orient Express** *m* TRANSP *chemin de fer* Venice Simplon Orient Express, VSOE

vent: **un** ~ **de changement** *m* COM the winds of change; ◆ **être dans le** ~ COM be abreast of things, be up to date, keep up to date

vente *f* BOURSE *de valeurs* placement, sale, placement, COM sale, selling, V&M deal, sale, selling; ~ **agressive** V&M hard sell, hard selling, high-pressure selling; ~ **anticipée** BOURSE advance selling (*UK*), anticipated sale; ~ **d'appel** V&M impulse sale; ~ **après imposition** FISC, IMMOB tax sale; ~ **d'argenté** BOURSE in-the-money put; ~ **attrape-nigaud** V&M bait and switch selling (*US*); ~ **avant imposition** FISC, IMMOB tax selling; ~ **à la baisse** (ANT *achat à la hausse*) BOURSE bear sale; ~ **bien arrosée** COM wet sell (*jarg*); ~ **à la boule de neige** V&M pyramid selling; ~ **d'un call à découvert** BOURSE naked call, uncovered call, uncovered call option; ~ **pour cause d'inventaire** COM stock-taking sale; ~ **pour cessation de commerce** COM winding-up sale; ~ **de charité** V&M *d'objets d'occasion* bazaar, charity sale, jumble sale (*BrE*), rummage sale (*AmE*); ~ **de choc** V&M impulse sale; ~ **couplée** COM tie-in sale (*US*); ~ **à couvert** BOURSE sale for delivery; ~ **couverte** BOURSE covered option writing; ~ **à crédit** FIN HP (*BrE*), hire purchase (*BrE*), V&M HP (*BrE*), credit sale, hire purchase (*BrE*), term sale; ~ **à la criée** COM, V&M auction, auction sale, public sale, sale by auction, vendue (*US*); ~ **à découvert** BOURSE bear sale, short sale, selling short, short selling; ~ **à découvert protégée** BOURSE hedged short sale; ~ **définitive** V&M absolute sale; ~ **en dépôt** TRANSP consignment sale; ~ **au détail** V&M retail sale, retailing; ~ **directe** BOURSE *à des institutionnels* placing, V&M direct sale, direct selling, face-to-face selling; ~ **en distributeurs automatiques** COM, V&M automatic selling; ~ **à domicile** V&M door-to-door selling, speciality selling; ~ **d'un écart papillon** BOURSE short butterfly; ~ **aux enchères** BOURSE auction, COM auction, auction sale, public sale, sale by auction, vendue (*US*), ECON auction, V&M auction, auction sale, public sale, sale by auction, vendue (*US*); ~ **d'espace** (*ANT achat d'espace*) V&M *publicité* space selling; ~ **à l'essai** V&M sale on approval; ~ **et location d'une immobilisation** COMPTA sale and leaseback; ~ **à l'étranger** V&M foreign sales; ~ **expérimentale** V&M market test, sales test; ~ **facile** COM, V&M quick sale; ~ **fictive** BOURSE sham trading; ~ **fictive d'obligations** FIN bear hug takeover, bond washing, borrowed funds, other peoples' money, OPM; ~ **forcée** V&M hard sell, *imposée au vendeur* inertia selling; ~ **forcée de marchandises** COM, DROIT, V&M forced sale of stock; ~ **à forfait** IMP/EXP forfaiting; ~ **en gros** COM jobbing, V&M wholesaling; ~ **groupée** COM *marketing*, V&M banded offer, banded pack; ~ **hors magasin** V&M nonstore retailing; ~ **indirecte** V&M back-selling; ~ **irrévocable** V&M absolute sale; ~ **judiciaire** DROIT judicial foreclosure, judicial sale; ~ **jumelée** COM banded offer, banded pack, V&M *marketing* banded offer, banded pack, composite package; ~ **de liquidation** BOURSE closing sale transaction; ~ **liquidative** BOURSE closing sale transaction; ~ **pour livraison** BOURSE sale for delivery; ~ **de médias** (*ANT achat de médias*) MÉDIA, V&M media selling; ~ **nécrophage** IMMOB scavenger sale (*infrml*); ~ **d'option couverte** BOURSE covered put, covered short; ~ **d'une option de vente** BOURSE short put; ~ **d'options d'achat** (*ANT achat d'options de vente*) BOURSE call writing; ~ **d'options couvertes** BOURSE covered option writing; ~ **par appartements** ECON, FIN asset stripping; ~ **par autorité de justice** DROIT judicial foreclosure, judicial sale; ~ **par correspondance** (*VPC*) ADMIN, COMMS, INFO mail order (*MO*), V&M inertia selling, mail order (*MO*), mail-order business, mail-order selling; ~ **par distributeur automatique** V&M automatic merchandising; ~ **par ensembles** ECON pure bundling; ~ **par lots** ECON pure bundling; ~ **par des méthodes de persuasion** V&M soft sell; ~ **par réseau coopté** V&M multilevel marketing, MLM; ~ **par soumission** V&M sale by tender; ~ **par téléphone** FIN, V&M telephone sales, telephone selling, telesales, teleselling; ~ **par voie d'adjudication** V&M sale by tender; ~ **personnelle** V&M *marketing* personal selling; ~ **à perte** BOURSE dumping, V&M leader pricing, loss leader pricing; ~ **au plus haut** BOURSE, V&M selling climax; ~ **en porte-à-porte** V&M door-to-door selling; ~ **à prix** COM undercutting; ~ **à prix imposé** COM, V&M price maintenance; ~ **à des prix qui défient la concurrence** COM undercutting; ~ **à prix sacrifié** V&M leader pricing, loss leader pricing; ~ **promotionnelle** COM promotional sale; ~ **publique** COM, V&M public sale; ~ **pyramidale** V&M pyramid selling; ~ **au rabais** COM discount sale, discount selling; ~ **-rachat de titres** FISC quick flip; ~ **-réclame** COM, V&M bargain sale, sale; ~ **sous condition** V&M conditional sale, conditional sales agreement; ~ **sous réserve d'ar-**

rivée en bon état V&M sale subject to safe arrival; ~ **de straddle** BOURSE short straddle; ~ **de strangle** BOURSE short strangle; ~ **sur catalogue** V&M mail order (*MO*), mail-order business, mail-order selling; ~ **sur plans** IMMOB presale; ~ **sur saisie** V&M foreclosure sale; ~ **à tempérament** FIN, IMMOB, V&M HP (*BrE*), hire purchase (*BrE*), installment sale (*AmE*), instalment sale (*BrE*); ~ **à terme** BANQUE sale for the account; ~ **à un tiers** V&M third-party sale; ~ **de valeurs à revenu fixe** BOURSE, FIN bond washing; ◆ ~ **avec possibilité d'échanger la marchandise** COM *si elle ne convient pas* sale or exchange; **en** ~ COM, IMMOB for sale, on sale, on the market, V&M on offer, on sale; **faire une** ~ BOURSE, COM make a sale

ventes *f pl* COM sales, sales activity, COMPTA sales, V&M sales, sales activity; ~ **à découvert** COM futures sales; ~ **à l'exportation** IMP/EXP, V&M export sales; ~ **imposables** FISC, V&M taxable sales; ~ **mensuelles** V&M monthly sales; ~ **nettes** COM, COMPTA net sales; ~ **d'obligations** BOURSE bond sales; ~ **prévues** V&M anticipated sales; ~ **promotionnelles** V&M store promotion; ~ **record** V&M record sales; ~ **de renouvellement** V&M repeat sales; ~ **répétées** V&M repeat sales; ~ **sur le marché intérieur** V&M domestic sales, home sales; ~ **taxables** FISC, V&M taxable sales

ventilateur: ~ **thermostatique** *m* IND thermostatic fan

ventilation *f* BANQUE splitting, COM ventilation, COMPTA *de coûts, frais, comptes* allocation, apportionment, breakdown, breaking down, DROIT allocation, FIN allocation, distribution, spreading, INFO *d'une zone de données* exploding; ~ **des charges** COMPTA, FIN breakdown of expenses; ~ **des coûts** COMPTA apportionment of costs, cost allocation, cost apportionment; ~ **de la paie** COMPTA payroll distribution; ~ **en pourcentage** MATH percentage distribution

ventiler *vt* BANQUE split, COM ventilate, COMPTA *coûts, frais, comptes* allocate, apportion, break down, DROIT allocate, FIN allocate, distribute, INFO *zone de données* explode; ◆ ~ **les charges entre certains comptes** COMPTA allocate costs to certain accounts

ventre *m* TRANSP *d'un avion* belly

verbal, e *adj* COM verbal

verdict *m* DROIT verdict; ~ **rendu à la majorité** DROIT majority verdict

vérifiable *adj* COM verifiable, COMPTA, FIN auditable

vérificabilité *f* COMPTA, FIN auditability

vérificateur, -trice *m,f* COMPTA, FIN Can (*cf auditeur Fra, commissaire aux comptes Fra, réviseur Fra, reviseur Bel*) auditor, RES HUM, TRANSP tally clerk; ~ **des crédits** BANQUE, FIN, RES HUM Can credit controller; ~ **financier supérieur** COMPTA senior financial auditor; ~ **indépendant** Can (*cf auditeur indépendant Fra, commissaire aux* *comptes indépendant Fra, réviseur indépendant Fra)* COMPTA independent auditor; ~ **d'orthographe** INFO spellcheck, spellchecker, word speller

vérification *f* COM checking, verification, COMPTA audit, auditing, INFO check; ~ **a posteriori** COM postimplementation audit, FISC postaudit; ~ **analytique** *Can* COMPTA analytical audit, analytical auditing, analytical review, systems-based audit, systems-based auditing; ~ **anonyme** COMPTA undercover audit; ~ **du bilan** COMPTA audit; ~ **cachée** COMPTA undercover audit; ~ **comptable** COMPTA audit, verification, financial auditing, financial verification, verification of accounts, FIN audit, auditing; ~ **des comptes** *Can* COMPTA audit, verification of accounts; ~ **continue** COMPTA continuous audit; ~ **dissimulée** COMPTA undercover audit; ~ **douanière** IMP/EXP customs check, customs examination; ~ **externe** *Can* (SYN *audit externe, contrôle externe, révision externe*) COMPTA, FIN external audit, independent audit; ~ **fiscale** FIN, FISC tax audit; ~ **illimitée** BANQUE unlimited checking; ~ **à l'insu** COMPTA undercover audit; ~ **interne** *Can* COMPTA, FIN administrative audit, internal audit; ~ **du logiciel comptable** COMPTA, FIN, INFO application control; ~ **par sondages** COM, COMPTA sample audit, test audit; ~ **par un tiers** BANQUE third-party check (*US*); ~ **permanente** COMPTA continuous audit; ~ **préalable** FISC preaudit; ~ **de premier palier** *Can* COMPTA prime range audit; ~ **de routine** TRANSP routine control; ~ **sur place** FISC field audit; ♦ ~ **de l'efficacité des ventes** V&M sales effectiveness test

vérifié: **qui n'a pas été** ~ *loc* COM untried, unverified

vérifier *vt* COM ascertain, check, verify, COMPTA *Can* (*cf auditer, réviser*), FIN *comptes* audit

véritable *adj* COM bona fide

verrou: ~ **de sécurité** *m* INFO keylock; ~ **tournant** *m* TRANSP *fixation des conteneurs* twistlock

verrouillage *m* TRANSP *conteneurs* locking; ~ **d'enregistrement** INFO record locking

verrouiller *vt* BOURSE lock in, INFO *clavier, enregistrement* lock

vers:[1] ~ **le bas** *adv* (ANT *vers le haut*) COM, INFO downward, downwards; ~ **le haut** *adv* (ANT *vers le bas*) COM, INFO upward, upwards

vers[2] *prép* COM *approximativement* about, around; ♦ ~ **le milieu de l'année** COM midyear, towards the middle of the year

versé, e *adj* FIN paid, pd

versement *m* BANQUE paying, paying in, payment, remittance, PYT, *argent* installment (*AmE*), instalment (*BrE*), COM *action* paying, payment, PYT, FIN *action* paying, payment, PYT, *argent* installment (*AmE*), instalment (*BrE*), V&M *marketing* payback, payout; ~ **annuel** BANQUE, COM, COMPTA, FIN annual installment (*AmE*), annual instalment (*BrE*), annual payment; ~ **bilatéral** BANQUE, ECON, POL bilateral disbursement; ~ **différé d'annuités** RES HUM deferred group annuity; ~ **fixe** FIN fixed installment (*AmE*), fixed instalment (*BrE*); ~ **hypothécaire** BANQUE, FIN mortgage payment; ~ **illégal** DROIT, POL illegal payoff; ~ **d'impôt** FISC remittance of tax; ~ **initial** RES HUM front-end payment; ~ **d'intérêt** BANQUE, FIN interest payment; ~ **libératoire** FIN final installment (*BrE*), final instalment (*AmE*); ~ **net** FISC net remittance; ~ **postal** COMPTA postal remittance; ~ **de rente** ASSUR annuity installment (*AmE*), annuity instalment (*BrE*); ~ **de souscription** BOURSE allotment money, application money; ~ **d'une tranche de prêt** BANQUE drawdown; ~ **trimestriel** COMPTA quarterly installment (*AmE*), quarterly instalment (*BrE*); ♦ **faire un** ~ COM make a payment

versements: ~ **échelonnés** *m pl* BANQUE, FIN installment payments (*AmE*), instalment payments (*BrE*); ~ **effectués** *m pl* COMPTA, FIN monies paid out; ~ **de garantie** *m pl* RES HUM guarantee payments; ♦ **par** ~ BANQUE, FIN in installments (*AmE*), in instalments (*BrE*)

verser *vt* BANQUE, FIN *de l'argent* pay, pay in; ♦ ~ **un acompte** BANQUE make a down payment, make an advance payment, pay a deposit, pay on account, FIN make a down payment, make an advance payment, put money down; ~ **des arrhes** BANQUE make a down payment, pay a deposit, pay money down, FIN make a down payment, put a deposit, put money down; ~ **à la baisse** IMMOB buy down

version *f* COM, INFO, MÉDIA version; ~ **actualisée** MÉDIA revised version; ~ **avancée** INFO advanced version; ~ **bêta** INFO beta version; ~ **évoluée** INFO advanced version; ~ **de logiciel** INFO software release; ~ **révisée** MÉDIA *édition* revised version

verso *m* (*vo*, ANT *recto*), COM, MÉDIA *édition, d'une page* verso (*vo*)

vert, e *adj* ENVIR green, green-conscious, POL green

vertical, e *adj* (ANT *horizontal*) BOURSE, COM, ECON, FISC, IND, MÉDIA vert., vertical

verticalement *adv* COM steeply, vertically

Verts: **les** ~ *m pl* ENVIR, POL the Green Party, the Greens

vertu: **en** ~ **de** *loc* COM by virtue of, virtute officii (*frml*); **en** ~ **de l'article 120** *loc* DROIT pursuant to article 120; **en** ~ **de la loi** *loc* DROIT in accordance with the law, in compliance with the law, in the eyes of the law

vestiges *m pl* COM remnants

veto *m* COM, POL veto

veuillez: ~ **accepter nos excuses** *loc* COMMS please accept our apologies; ~ **agréer, Madame/Monsieur, l'expression de mes sentiments les plus distingués** *loc* COMMS Sincerely yours (*AmE*), Yours faithfully, Yours sincerely (*BrE*), Yours truly; ~ **m'excuser** *loc* COM I'm sorry, please excuse me; ~ **nous indiquer la date qui vous convient** *loc* COMMS please let us know which date suits you; ~ **nous indiquer vos prix** *loc* COM please let us have your prices, please submit your quotations; ~ **nous inscrire sur votre liste de diffusion** *loc* COMMS please add our name to your mailing list; ~ **répondre s'il vous plaît** *loc* COMMS please reply

veuve *f* MÉDIA *typographie* widow

VHF *abrév (très haute fréquence)* COM VHF *(very high frequency)*

via *prép* COMMS, TRANSP via

viabilisation *f* ENVIR, IMMOB land improvement; ~ **foncière** ENVIR, IMMOB land development; ~ **de terrain** ENVIR, IMMOB land improvement

viabiliser *vt* ENVIR, IMMOB *terrain* develop, improve, service

viabilité *f* COM *d'un projet* practicability, viability, ECON, ENVIR sustainability, FIN *d'un projet* practicability, viability, MATH viability; ~ **économique** ECON, FIN economic viability

viable *adj* COM *projet* practicable, viable, ENVIR sustainable, FIN *projet* practicable, viable

vice:[1] ~ **versa** *adv* COM vice versa

vice[2] *m* COM, DROIT defect; ~ **caché** *m* DROIT, IMMOB latent defect; ~ **du consentement** *m* DROIT duress; ~ **de forme** *m* DROIT irregularity, technical point, technicality; ~ **-président** *m* POL deputy leader *(UK)*, vice-president, RES HUM deputy chairman, vice-chairman, vice-president; ~ **-président des communes** *m* POL Deputy Speaker *(UK)*; ~ **-président directeur général** *m* RES HUM executive vice president; ~ **propre** *m* COM, TRANSP inherent vice

vicier *vt* DROIT *acte* contaminate, invalidate, vitiate, TRANSP *marchandises* taint

victoire: ~ **dans un fauteuil** *f* COM walkaway victory, walkover *(infrml)*; ~ **facile** *f* COM walkaway victory, walkover *(infrml)*

Victoria *n pr* COM Victoria

vidage *m* IMP/EXP turnout; ~ **d'écran** INFO screen dump; ~ **de mémoire** INFO memory dump, storage dump; ~ **de mémoire sur imprimante** INFO memory print-out; ~ **de mouvements** INFO change dump; ~ **de transfert sur disque** INFO dump, dumping

vidange: ~ **des eaux usées** *f* ENVIR sewage disposal, wastewater disposal

vide[1] *adj* COM *caisse, bouteille* empty, INFO *écran* blank, TRANSP *caisse, bouteille* empty

vide[2] *m* TRANSP ullage; ~ **-ordures** ENVIR garbage chute *(AmE)*, rubbish chute *(BrE)*

vidéo *f* MÉDIA *média* video; ~ **inverse** INFO reverse video

vidéoachat *m* V&M videoshopping

vidéocassette *f* MÉDIA video cassette

vidéoconférence *f* COMMS, INFO video conference, video conferencing

vidéodisque *f* INFO video disk

vidéographie *f* MÉDIA video graphics; ~ **diffusée**

COMMS teletex®; ~ **interactive** INFO, MÉDIA Videotex®, Viewdata®, Teletext® *(UK)*

vidéophone *m* COMMS videophone, visual telephone

vidéotex® *m* INFO, MÉDIA Videotex®, Teletext® *(UK)*; ~ **diffusé** INFO, MÉDIA Teletext® *(UK)*

vidéotext: ~ **diffusé** *m* INFO, MÉDIA Teletext® *(UK)*

vidéotexte *m* INFO videotext

vidéothèque *f* MÉDIA video library

vider *vt* COM *tiroir, boîte* empty, INFO clear, dump, RES HUM *employé* fire *(infrml)*, sack *(BrE, infrml)*

vides: ~ **d'arrimage** *m pl* TRANSP *arrimage* broken stowage

vie *f* ASSUR, COM life; ~ **active** COM working life; ~ **économique** FIN, V&M economic life; ~ **entière à primes temporaires** ASSUR limited payment life insurance *(US)*; ~ **privée** DROIT privacy; ~ **d'un produit** V&M product life; ◆ **dans la ~ politique** POL in the public sphere

vieillir *vi* COM age, grow old

vieillissement *m* COM, V&M obsolescence; ~ **programmé** COM, ECON, IND, V&M built-in obsolescence, planned obsolescence; ~ **technologique** COM, IND *production* technological obsolescence

Vienne *n pr* COM Vienna

Vientiane *n pr* COM Vientiane

vierge *adj* ADMIN *feuille, papier* blank, IMMOB *terrain* virgin, INFO *disquette* blank

Viêt Nam *m* COM Vietnam

vietnamien[1], **-enne** *adj* COM Vietnamese

vietnamien[2] *m* COM *langue* Vietnamese

Vietnamien, -enne *m,f* COM *habitant* Vietnamese

vieux: ~ **charter** *m* TRANSP old charter, OC; ~ **numéro** *m* MÉDIA back issue, back number; ~ **papiers** *m pl* ADMIN, ENVIR wastepaper; ◆ **du ~ au neuf** ASSUR new for old

vigiles *m pl* RES HUM goon squad *(US, jarg)*

vignette *f* COM *ayant valeur légale* stamp, sticker, *d'une marque de fabrique* label, FISC tax disc *(BrE)*, tax disk *(AmE)*, INFO clip art, TRANSP road-fund licence *(BrE)*, road-fund license *(AmE)*

vignoble *m* COM vineyard

vigoureux, -euse *adj* COM sharp, vigorous

vigueur *f* COM *du marché* strength; ◆ **en ~** COM applicable; **être en ~** COM *loi, mesure* be active, *situation* be in force, INFO be effective

Vikane *m* IND Vikane

villa: ~ **-économie** *f* ECON, POL, PROT SOC villa economy; ~ **style village** *f* IMMOB town house

ville *f* COM town, *plus grande* city; ~ **d'accueil** COM host city; ~ **-dortoir** RES HUM bedroom community *(AmE)*, dormitory suburb *(BrE)*; ~ **moteur** ECON generative city; ~ **nouvelle** ECON new town *(UK)*; ~ **parasite** ECON parasitic city; ~ **satellite** COM overspill town, satellite town; ~ **test** COM test town

Vilnius *n pr* COM Vilnius

vingt: ~ -cinq cents *m pl* FIN twenty-five cents (*US*), two-bits (*US, infrml*)

24h: à ~ valeur lendemain *adj* BOURSE from tomorrow to the next business day, tom/next

24: ~ heures sur 24 *adj* COM around-the-clock, round-the-clock

violation *f* BREVETS *d'un brevet* infringement, DROIT breach, infringement, offence, violation; ~ de contrat COM, DROIT breach of contract; ~ d'un droit DROIT breach of contract, infringement of the law, legal wrong, offence, violation of the law; ~ de propriété DROIT trespassing, unlawful trespass; ~ du secret COM breach of secrecy; ~ technique POL technical trespass (*US, jarg*); ◆ en ~ de COM, DROIT in breach of, in violation of

violence *f* RES HUM brutality, violence; ~ familiale PROT SOC family violence

violer *vt* BREVETS *brevet* infringe, violate, DROIT breach, break, infringe, traverse, violate, IMMOB traverse; ◆ ~ la loi DROIT breach the law, break the law, infringe the law, violate the law; ~ une propriété privée DROIT trespass on private property

virages: ~ à 180 degrés *m pl* RES HUM flip-flop arbitration

viré: être ~ *loc infrml* RES HUM get the sack (*infrml*)

virement *m* BANQUE credit transfer, giro, COMPTA *de fonds*, FIN transfer; ~ automatique BANQUE automatic funds transfer, AFT, automatic transfer, bank credit transfer, bank transfer, banker's transfer, direct deposit (*Can*), COMPTA automatic funds transfer, AFT, FIN automatic funds transfer, AFT, bank credit transfer; ~ automatique de fonds BANQUE automatic funds transfer, AFT, automatic transfer, bank credit transfer, bank transfer, banker's transfer, direct deposit (*Can*), COMPTA automatic funds transfer FIN automatic funds transfer, AFT, bank credit transfer; ~ bancaire BANQUE bank transfer, banker's transfer; ~ direct de fonds BANQUE direct fund transfer, DFT; ~ entre crédits FIN intervote transfer; ~ interbancaire BANQUE airmail transfer, interbank transfer, AMT; ~ minimum COM minimum transfer, MT; ~ en nature PROT SOC in-kind transfer; ~ par avion BANQUE airmail transfer, AMT; ~ télégraphique BANQUE telegraphic transfer, wire transfer, COMMS cable transfer, telegraphic transfer

virer **1.** *vt* BANQUE, FIN *de l'argent* transfer, RES HUM *employé* boot out (*infrml*), fire (*infrml*), sack (*BrE, infrml*); **2.** *vi* COM, POL *à droite, à gauche* swing

virgule *f* INFO, MATH comma, decimal point, point, MÉDIA *typographie* comma

virt *abrév* (*virement*) COMPTA, FIN *de fonds* tr. (*transfer*)

virtuel, **-elle** *adj* INFO virtual

virure *f* TRANSP *d'un navire* strake; ~ de galbord TRANSP *d'un navire* garboard strake

virus *m* INFO virus; ~ informatique INFO computer virus

visa *m* ADMIN *de passeport, signature officielle* visa; ~ accordé pour deux entrées ADMIN double-entry visa; ~ accordé pour une entrée ADMIN single-entry visa; ~ de certification DROIT, IND certification mark; ~ en cours de validité ADMIN working visa; ~ d'entrée ADMIN entrance visa, entry permit, entry visa; ~ multi-transit ADMIN multientry visa, multiple-entry visa; ~ permanent ADMIN multientry visa, multiple-entry visa; ~ de signification DROIT service mark; ~ de tourisme ADMIN tourist visa; ~ touristique ADMIN tourist visa; ~ de transit ADMIN visa

vis-à-vis *prép* COM vis-à-vis

viscosité *f* COM viscosity; ~ de la demande ECON viscous demand; ~ de l'offre ECON viscous supply

vise *f* COM aim

visé: ~ à l'alinéa 1 *loc* COM referred to in paragraph 1; ~ par règlement *loc* COM prescribed

visée: ~ de couverture *f* BOURSE, FIN hedging goal

viser *vt* COM affect, *diplôme* certify, V&M aim at, target

visibilité *f* COM, V&M visibility

visible *adj* ECON visible

visibles *m pl* ECON visibles

visière: ~ d'étrave *f* TRANSP *d'un roulier* bow visor

vision *f* COM, GESTION vision; ~ du monde COM outlook of the world, view of the world

visiophone *m* COMMS videophone, visual telephone

visite *f* DROIT *de la police* search, FISC survey, IMP/EXP *customs* examination, LOISIRS *tourisme* tour, TRANSP survey; ~ d'affaires COM business call; ~ annuelle TRANSP *d'un navire* year of grace survey, YGS; ~ annuelle de la centrale de navigation TRANSP *d'un navire* annual automated controls survey, AAS; ~ annuelle de la coque TRANSP *d'un navire* annual hull survey, AHS; ~ annuelle des machines TRANSP *d'un navire* annual machinery survey, AMS; ~ de la chaudière TRANSP *d'un navire* boiler survey; ~ de la chaudière auxiliaire mixte TRANSP *d'un navire* composite auxiliary boiler survey, CAXBS; ~ de la chaudière cylindrique aquatubulaire TRANSP *d'un navire* cylindrical water tube boiler survey; ~ de la chaudière cylindrique à tubes d'eau TRANSP *d'un navire* cylindrical water tube boiler survey; ~ de la chaudière ignitubulaire TRANSP *d'un navire* fire-tube boiler survey, FTBS; ~ de la chaudière à tubes de fumée TRANSP *d'un navire* fire-tube boiler survey, FTBS; ~ de la coque en vue d'une reclassification continue TRANSP continuous hull survey, continuous survey cycle hull, continuous survey of the hull quoting date, CHS, CS; ~ domiciliaire DROIT house search; ~ éclair COM flying visit; ~ à l'étranger IMP/EXP, TRANSP outward mission; ~ impromptue V&M *par un vendeur* cold call; ~ d'inspection COM inspection, visitation; ~ **des machines** TRANSP *d'un navire* machinery survey, MS; ~ **des machines en vue d'une reclassification continue** TRANSP *d'un navire* continuous survey cycle machinery; ~ **médicale** PROT SOC check-up, medical examination, physical examination; ~ **à la mi-période** TRANSP *navigation* half-time survey, HT; ~ **du navire** TRANSP ship survey; ~ **périodique** TRANSP *d'un navire* periodical survey; ~ **quadriennale** FISC quadriennal survey; ~ **de représentant** V&M sales call; ~ **à sec** TRANSP *navigation* docking survey; ~ **spéciale** TRANSP *d'un navire* ship's special survey, special survey, SS; ~ **spéciale de la coque** TRANSP *d'un navire* special survey of the hull, SSH; ~ **spéciale intermédiaire** TRANSP *d'un navire* special intermediate survey, SIS; ~ **spéciale des machines** TRANSP *d'un navire* special survey of the machinery, SSM; ♦ **en** ~ COM visiting

visiter *vt* COM call on, visit, DROIT search, IMMOB *maison à vendre* go round, look round, view, IMP/EXP examine, inspect, search, IND *tourisme* go round, TRANSP *navire* survey; ♦ **faire** ~ **l'usine à qn** COM show sb around the factory *(AmE)*, show sb round the factory *(BrE)*

visites: ~ **seulement sur rendez-vous** *loc* IMMOB viewing by appointment only

visiteur, -euse *m,f* COM representative, visitor, IMP/EXP inspector; ~ **avec permis de séjour d'étudiant** ADMIN, FISC visitor with student authorization; ~ **détenant un permis de séjour d'étudiant** ADMIN, FISC visitor with student authorization; ~ **étranger** ADMIN, COM overseas visitor

visualisation *f* COMMS display, INFO display, soft copy, visual display

visualiser *vt* INFO display, view

visuel[1], **-elle** *adj* COM, INFO visual

visuel[2] *m* INFO visual display terminal, visual display unit, VDT, VDU, POL visual *(jarg)*

vite *adv* COM fast; ♦ **aussi** ~ **que possible** COM as quickly as possible, TRANSP *maritime, chargement, déchargement* fac, faccop, fast as can

vitesse *f* COM rate, ECON rate, speed, velocity, FIN velocity, INFO speed, velocity; ~ **d'adaptation** ECON adjustment speed; ~ **d'ajustement** ECON *des prix à une offre ou une demande* adjustment speed; ~ **d'alimentation** INFO feed rate; ~ **appropriée** TRANSP *d'un navire* convenient speed; ~ **de calcul** INFO computing speed; ~ **de circulation** FIN velocity of circulation; ~ **de circulation monétaire** FIN velocity of money; ~ **de circulation de la monnaie** ECON velocity of circulation of money; ~ **de circulation revenu de la monnaie** ECON income velocity of money; ~ **du double-clic** INFO double-click speed; ~ **de frappe** COM typing speed; ~ **d'impression** INFO printing speed; ~ **de réajustement** ECON adjustment speed; ~ **de rotation** COM turnover rate; ~ **de traitement des documents** INFO document rate; ~ **de transfert** INFO transfer rate; ~ **de transformation de la monnaie en revenu** ECON income velocity of

money; ~ **de transmission de données** INFO data rate

viticulteur, -trice *m,f* COM, ECON, IND vine grower, wine grower

viticulture *f* COM, ECON, IND vine growing, wine growing

vitrine *f* COM shop window, window, V&M window

vivre *vi* COM live; ♦ ~ **de l'aide sociale** PROT SOC, RES HUM be on benefit *(BrE)*, be on welfare *(AmE)*, receive benefit *(UK)*; ~ **au-dessus de ses moyens** COM live beyond one's means

VL *abrév (voiture-lit)* TRANSP *chemin de fer* sleeper, sleeping car

vo *abrév (verso)* COM, MÉDIA vo *(verso)*

vocation *f* RES HUM calling, vocation; ~ **de la société** COM, GESTION corporate mission; ♦ **à** ~ **générale** COM general purpose, GP, FIN *compte* all-purpose

vogue *f* COM, V&M fashion, vogue; ♦ **en** ~ COM in fashion, in vogue

voie *f* ADMIN, COM, COMMS, INFO channel, TRANSP *chaussée* carriageway, lane, *chemin de fer* line, track; ~ **d'accès** INFO *aux données* path; ~ **aérienne** TRANSP airway, AWY; ~ **analogique** INFO analog channel; ~ **d'arrêt** TRANSP *chemin de fer* bay; ~ **de chargement** TRANSP *chemin de fer* siding *(BrE)*, sidetrack *(AmE)*; ~ **de circulation** TRANSP traffic lane; ~ **de communication** ADMIN, COM, GESTION, RES HUM, V&M channel of communication; ~ **d'embranchement** TRANSP *chemin de fer* branch line; ~ **ferrée** TRANSP railroad line *(AmE)*, railroad track *(AmE)*, railway line *(BrE)*, railway track *(BrE)*, *chemin de fer* railroad *(AmE)*, railway *(BrE)*; ~ **fluviale** TRANSP inland waterway; ~ **de garage** TRANSP *chemin de fer* sidetrack *(AmE)*, siding *(BrE)*; ~ **hiérarchique** GESTION chain of command, line of command; ~ **navigable** TRANSP inland waterway; ~ **de navigation** TRANSP shipping lane; ~ **privée** TRANSP accommodation road, private road; ~ **publique** ADMIN, TRANSP public highway; ~ **de raccordement** TRANSP *d'usine* siding; ~ **rapide** COM fast track, TRANSP *d'autoroute* fast lane; ~ **de retour** INFO reverse channel; ~ **de terre** COMMS surface mail; ~ **de triage** TRANSP *chemin de fer* sidetrack *(AmE)*, siding *(BrE)*; ♦ **en** ~ TRANSP *chemin de fer* on track, ot; **être sur la bonne** ~ COM be on the right track; **par** ~ **de terre** COMMS by surface mail; **par la** ~ **de** TRANSP via

voies: ~ **de droit** *f pl* DROIT legal action; ~ **et moyens** *f pl* ECON ways and means; ~ **de recours** *f pl* DROIT power of recourse

voir[1] *vti* COM see; ♦ ~ **autrement** COM *de qch* take a different view; ~ **au dos** MÉDIA *édition* see over, see overleaf; **en** ~ **de toutes les couleurs** *infrml* COM have a lot of trouble; **en** ~ **des vertes et des pas mûres** *infrml* COM have a lot of trouble; ~ **le tiré** COM refer to acceptor, R/A; ~ **le tireur** BANQUE refer to drawer, RD; ~ **au verso** MÉDIA *édition* see over, see overleaf

voir[2] *loc* COM, MÉDIA *édition* quod vide (*frml*), qv

voisin: être ~ de travail de qn *loc* RES HUM work alongside sb

voisinage *m* COM neighborhood (*AmE*), neighbourhood (*BrE*)

voit: qui ~ loin *loc* COM far-seeing, far-sighted

voiture *f* TRANSP automobile (*AmE*), car, motorcar (*BrE*), *chemin de fer* car, carriage, coach; ~ **avec la conduite à droite** (ANT *voiture avec la conduite à gauche*) TRANSP right-hand drive automobile (*AmE*), right-hand drive car (*BrE*); ~ **avec la conduite à gauche** (ANT *voiture avec la conduite à droite*) TRANSP left-hand drive automobile (*AmE*), left-hand drive car (*BrE*); ~ **désassemblée** TRANSP car knocked down; ~ **d'entreprise** COM, TRANSP company car; ~ **de fonction** COM, TRANSP company car; ~ **-lit** (*VL*) TRANSP *chemin de fer* sleeper, sleeping car; ~ **d'occasion** TRANSP pre-owned car, second-hand car, used car; ~ **de société** COM, TRANSP company car; ~ **à toit de tôle amovible** TRANSP hardtop

voix *f* POL vote; ~ **consultative** COM advisory capacity, advisory voice; ~ **contre** POL opposing vote, vote against

vol[1] *abrév* (*volume*) COM vol. (*volume*)

vol[2] *m* DROIT larceny, robbery, theft, TRANSP flight; ~ **affrété** TRANSP charter flight, chartered flight; ~ **d'arrivée** TRANSP inbound flight, incoming flight; ~ **avec effraction** DROIT burglary; ~ **camionné** TRANSP *aviation* truck service, trucking (*AmE*); ~ **charter** TRANSP charter flight, chartered flight; ~ **en classe économique** LOISIRS, TRANSP economy flight, economy-class flight; ~ **de correspondance** TRANSP connecting flight, onward flight; ~ **domestique** LOISIRS, TRANSP domestic flight, internal flight; ~ **à l'étalage** DROIT shoplifting, V&M shoplifting, shrinkage; ~ **d'inauguration** TRANSP inaugural flight; ~ **intérieur** TRANSP domestic flight, internal flight; ~ **interligne** TRANSP interchange flight; ~ **qualifié** DROIT grand larceny (*US*); ~ **régulier** LOISIRS, TRANSP scheduled flight; ~ **retardé** TRANSP delayed flight; ~ **de retour** LOISIRS, TRANSP inbound flight, incoming flight, return flight; ~ **sans escale** TRANSP nonstop flight; ♦ **en** ~ TRANSP airborne

volant *m* BANQUE, COM *carnet de tickets, de chèques* leaf, tear-off portion

volatile *adj* BOURSE, COM, ECON, INFO volatile

volatilité *f* BOURSE, COM, ECON, INFO volatility; ~ **historique** BOURSE historical volatility; ~ **implicite** BOURSE implied volatility

Volcoa *m* TRANSP *maritime* Volcoa

voler 1. *vt* DROIT *quelqu'un* rob, *quelque chose* steal; **2.** *vi* DROIT steal, TRANSP fly; ♦ ~ **de l'argent dans la caisse** COM, DROIT rob the till; ~ **qch à qn** COM rob sb of sth, DROIT rob sb of sth, steal sth from sb

voleur, -euse *m,f* DROIT robber, thief

volontaire *mf* RES HUM volunteer

volt *m* (*V*) COM volt (*V*)

volte: ~ **-face** *f* COM turnaround, turnround

volume *m* COM bulk, volume, COM volume, COMPTA, ECON volume, INFO volume, *d'un fichier* size; ~ **d'affaires** COM amount of business, business volume, volume of business; ~ **balle** TRANSP *d'un navire* bale space; ~ **des commandes** COM volume of orders; ~ **d'échanges** ECON, IMP/EXP trade flow; ~ **des échanges commerciaux** ECON trade volume; ~ **d'effets à recevoir** FIN receivables turnover; ~ **des exportations** COM amount exported, ECON volume of exports, IMP/EXP amount exported; ~ **global des contrats** billing V&M billing; ~ **grain** TRANSP *d'un navire* grain capacity, grain cubic, GC; ~ **important** BOURSE high volume; ~ **non-indiqué** BOURSE volume deleted; ~ **des opérations** COM trading volume, volume of trading; ~ **perdu** TRANSP waste cube; ~ **de production** COM, IND output volume, production volume; ~ **quotidien** BOURSE daily volume; ~ **réel** IND real volume; ~ **des transactions** BOURSE amount of business, COM trading volume, volume of trading; ~ **des transactions effacé** BOURSE volume deleted; ~ **des transactions sur obligations** BOURSE bond turnover; ~ **de ventes** COMPTA, V&M sales volume; ~ **des ventes au détail** ECON volume of retail sales; ~ **vertical réservé à la cargaison** TRANSP *d'un navire* verticalized cargo space; ♦ **à** ~ **élevé** BOURSE high-volume

volumineux, -euse *adj* COM, COMMS, TRANSP bulky, voluminous

vorace *adj* COM acquisitive

votant, e *m,f* POL, RES HUM voter

vote *m* COM, GESTION *aux réunions directionnelles*, POL, RES HUM vote, voting; ~ **à l'aveuglette** POL bullet vote; ~ **bloqué** POL *d'un syndicat* block vote; ~ **à bulletin secret** RES HUM blanket ballot (*US*), secret ballot; ~ **contre la grève** RES HUM anti-strike ballot; ~ **cumulatif** BOURSE cumulative voting; ~ **favorable à la grève** RES HUM pro-strike vote; ~ **pour la grève** RES HUM pro-strike ballot; ~ **à inscrire** POL write-in vote (*US*); ~ **à mains levées** COM, RES HUM vote by show of hands; ~ **majoritaire** COM majority vote; ~ **à la majorité** BOURSE majority rule voting; ~ **à la majorité qualifiée** COM, POL qualified majority vote; ~ **par correspondance** POL postal vote, RES HUM absentee ballot (*AmE*), postal ballot (*BrE*), postal vote; ~ **par procuration** POL proxy vote, vote by proxy; ~ **plural** POL cumulative voting; ~ **de protestation** POL protest vote; ~ **réglementaire** POL statutory vote; ~ **statutaire** DROIT statutory voting

voté: ~ **à l'unanimité** *adj* COM, RES HUM unanimously accepted

voter 1. *vt* COM, POL, RES HUM *budget* vote, *loi* vote for, vote in favour of; **2.** *vi* COM, GESTION, POL, RES HUM vote; ♦ ~ **des crédits provisoires** POL vote interim supply; ~ **la dotation totale** POL vote full supply; **faire ~** ECON pass; **~ au scrutin** RES HUM ballot, vote by ballot; **~ la totalité des crédits** POL vote full supply

votre *adj* COMMS your, yr

vouloir: **~ dire** *vt* COM *abréviation, initiale* mean, stand for

vous: **c'est à ~ de voir** *loc* COM it's up to you

voyage *m* TRANSP voyage; **~ d'affaires** COM business travel, business trip, LOISIRS, TRANSP business trip; **~ d'aller** (ANT *voyage de retour*) TRANSP outward voyage; **~ d'essai** TRANSP shakedown (*infrml*); **~ d'étude** POL facility trip (*jarg*), PROT SOC field trip, study trip; **~ d'étude sur le terrain** PROT SOC field trip; **~ de fonction** POL facility trip (*jarg*); **~ aux frais de la princesse** *infrml* TRANSP junket (*AmE, infrml*); **~ gratuit** BOURSE free ride (*infrml*), free-riding; **~ inaugural** TRANSP maiden voyage, *navigation* inaugural sailing; **~ international de courte distance** TRANSP short international voyage; **~ organisé** LOISIRS package holiday (*BrE*), package tour (*BrE*), package vacation (*AmE*); **~ par voiture tout compris** LOISIRS motorist inclusive tour; **~ professionnel** COM business travel, business trip, LOISIRS, TRANSP business trip; **~ de retour** (ANT *voyage d'aller*) TRANSP homeward voyage; **~ sur lest** TRANSP *navigation* ballast trip; **~ tout compris** LOISIRS, TRANSP inclusive tour, IT

voyager: **1.** *vt* **~ en bateau** TRANSP sail; **2. ~ aux frais de la princesse** *infrml* TRANSP junket (*AmE, infrml*)

voyages: **~ de groupe** *m pl* LOISIRS group travel; **les ~ en avion** *m pl* LOISIRS, TRANSP air travel; **~ de nuit** *m pl* LOISIRS, TRANSP overnight travel; **~ à tarif réduit** *m pl* LOISIRS discount travel; **~ tous frais payés** *m pl* LOISIRS subsidized travel

voyageur[1]: **~ de commerce** COM, RES HUM, V&M traveling salesman *(AmE)*, travelling salesman *(BrE)*

voyageur, -euse *m,f* LOISIRS traveler (*AmE*), traveller (*BrE*), TRANSP *train, autobus* passenger, passr; **~ de commerce** COM, RES HUM, V&M commercial traveler (*AmE*), commercial traveller (*BrE*), drummer (*AmE, infrml*), sales rep (*infrml*), sales representative, traveling salesperson (*AmE*), travelling salesperson (*BrE*); **~ par avion** LOISIRS, TRANSP air traveler (*AmE*), air traveller (*BrE*);

~ représentant placier *(VRP)* COM, V&M bagman, commercial traveler (*AmE*), commercial traveller (*BrE*); **~ représentant placier régional** COM area salesman, area salesperson; **~ en transit** LOISIRS, TRANSP transit passenger

voyageuse: **~ de commerce** *f* COM, RES HUM, V&M traveling salesperson (*AmE*), traveling saleswoman (*AmE*), travelling salesperson (*BrE*), travelling saleswoman (*BrE*)

voyant: **~ lumineux** *m* INFO light, signal light; **~ rouge** *m* (SYN *voyant vert*) COM adjustment trigger; **~ vert** *m* (SYN *voyant rouge*) COM adjustment trigger; **~ vert déclenchant** *m* COM adjustment trigger; **~ vert servant de déclic** *m* COM adjustment trigger

V-P *abrév* (*vice-président*) RES HUM veep (*AmE, infrml*), VP (*vice-president*)

VPC *abrév* (*vente par correspondance*) ADMIN, COMMS, INFO, V&M MO (*mail order*)

vrac *m* TRANSP *articles à transporter* bulk; **~ liquide** TRANSP wet bulk cargo; **~ sec** TRANSP dry bulk cargo; ◆ **en ~** IND *production* in bulk

vraie: **~ double** *f* MÉDIA center spread (*AmE*), centerfold (*AmE*), centre spread (*BrE*), centrefold (*BrE*)

vraquier *m* TRANSP bulk carrier, BLK CAR; **~ porte-conteneurs** TRANSP bulk container ship

V/réf. *abrév* (*votre référence*) COMMS yr ref. (*your reference*)

VRP[1] *abrév* (*voyageur représentant placier*) COM, V&M bagman, commercial traveler (*AmE*), commercial traveller (*BrE*)

VRP:[2] **~ régional** *m* COM area salesperson

vu: **~ à la télévision** *loc* MÉDIA as advertised on TV, V&M *publicité* as advertised on television

vue *f* FIN sight; **~ en coupe** COM cross section; **~ à court terme** BOURSE short-termism; **~ d'ensemble** COM conspectus; **~ générale** COM conspectus; **~ du marché** BOURSE market view; ◆ **à ~** BANQUE, BOURSE, COM at sight, A/S, COMPTA on demand, FIN at call, at sight, A/S; **de ~** COM, FIN after sight, A/S; **en ~ de** COM with a view to; **en ~ de faire** V&M with an eye to doing; **très en ~** COM *profession* high-profile

vulnérable *adj* COM vulnerable

W

wagon: ~ **à ciment** *m* TRANSP *chemin de fer* cement wagon; ~ **-citerne** *m* TRANSP tank car (*AmE*), tank wagon (*BrE*); ~ **découvert** *m* TRANSP *chemin de fer* gondola; ~ **découvert à bords plats** *m vieilli* TRANSP *chemin de fer* flat car (*US*), gondola; ~ **-lit** *m* (*WL*) TRANSP sleeper, sleeping car; ~ **de marchandises couvert** *m* TRANSP boxcar (*AmE*), goods truck (*BrE*); ~ **plat** *m* TRANSP *chemin de fer* flat car (*US*), gondola; ~ **à plate-forme surbaissée** *m* TRANSP *chemin de fer* lo, low loader; ~ **porte-conteneurs** *m* TRANSP *chemin de fer* container car (*US*); ~ **postal** *m* COMMS mail van (*BrE*), mailcar (*AmE*), mailcoach (*BrE*); ~ **-restaurant** *m* TRANSP dining car, restaurant car; ~ **pour transport d'automobiles** *m* TRANSP *chemin de fer* car transporter; ~ **voyageurs** *m* TRANSP *chemin de fer* carriage

Wait: ~ **berth** *m* TRANSP *maritime* Wait berth

Wall: ~ **Street** *n pr* FIN Wall Street (*US*)

warrant *m* BOURSE bond warrant, COM, DROIT dock warrant, D/W, warehouse warrant, WW, warrant, FIN warrant, IMP/EXP, TRANSP, V&M dock warrant, D/W, warehouse warrant, WW, warrant; ~ **à l'achat** (ANT *warrant à la vente*) BOURSE call warrant; ~ **agricole** ECON agricultural warrant; ~ **couvert** FIN covered warrant; ~ **à la vente** (ANT *warrant à l'achat*) BOURSE put warrant; ◆ **avec** ~ BOURSE cum warrant

warrantage *m* FIN warrant discounting

Washington: ~ **D.C.** *n pr* COM Washington D.C.

week-end: **un** ~ **prolongé** *m* COM long weekend

Wellington *n pr* COM Wellington

white-spirit *m* IND white spirit

Whitleyisme *m* RES HUM Whitleyism

Windhoek *n pr* COM Windhoek

WL *abrév* (*wagon-lit*) TRANSP *chemin de fer* sleeper, sleeping car

won *m* COM won

X

xénophobe[1] *adj* GEN COM xenophobic
xénophobe[2] *mf* GEN COM xenophobe
xénophobie *f* ADMIN xenophobia
xérographique *adj* ADMIN xerographic

xérographie *f* ADMIN xerography
xième *adj* GEN COM nth; ◆ **pour le ~ fois** GEN COM for the nth time

Y

Yamoussoukro *n pr* COM Yamoussoukro
Yangon *n pr* COM Yangon
Yaoundé *n pr* COM Yaoundé
yard *m* COM yard, yd
Yémen *m* COM Yemen
yéménite *adj* COM Yemeni
Yéménite *mf* COM *habitant* Yemeni

yen *m* COM yen
yougoslave *adj* COM Yugoslav, Yugoslavian
Yougoslave *mf* COM *habitant* Yugoslav, Yugoslavian
Yougoslavie *f* COM Yugoslavia
yuan *m* COM Rmb, yuan
yuppie *m* COM yuppie

Z

ZAC *abrév (zone d'aménagement concerté)* ECON, IMMOB, IND, RES HUM EZ *(enterprise zone)*

ZAD *abrév (zone d'aménagement différé)* ECON, IMMOB, RES HUM future development zone

Zagreb *n pr* COM Zagreb

zaïre *m* COM zaïre

Zaïre *m* COM Zaïre

zaïrois, e *adj* COM Zaïrian

Zaïrois, e *m,f* COM *habitant* Zaïrian

zai teku *m* FIN zai-teku

Zambie *f* COM Zambia

zambien, -enne *adj* COM Zambian

Zambien, -enne *m,f* COM *habitant* Zambian

zaòre *m* COM zaïre

zèle *m* COM zeal

zéro *m* COM, COMPTA, FIN, MATH nought, zero; **~ défaut** COM, COMPTA, FIN, MATH zero defect

Zimbabwe *m* COM Zimbabwe

zimbabwéen, -enne *adj* COM Zimbabwean

Zimbabwéen, -enne *m,f* COM Zimbabwean

zinc *m* IND zinc

zloty *m* COM zloty

zonage *m* IMMOB zoning; **~ du gaz et du pétrole** ENVIR oil and gas lottery; **~ de lieu** IMMOB spot zoning

zonation *f* RES HUM banding

zone *f* COM area, zone, INFO field, *de mémoire* area, zone; **~ A** *(ANT zone B)* FIN zone A; **~ d'accueil** ADMIN reception area; **~ d'activité économique** ECON, IMMOB, IND, RES HUM enterprise zone; **~ d'alerte** INFO alert box; **~ d'aménagement concerté** *(ZAC)* ECON, IMMOB, IND, RES HUM enterprise zone *(EZ)*; **~ d'aménagement différé** *(ZAD)* ECON, IMMOB, RES HUM future development zone; **~ d'aménagement rural** ECON rural development area *(UK)*, RDA *(UK)*; **~ d'aménagement urbain** COM Urban Programme Area *(UK)*, urban development area; **~ anti-fumée** COM *pollution*, ENVIR, RES HUM no-smoking area; **~ d'appel** V&M catchment area; **~ d'arrimage** TRANSP stowage area; **~ d'assistance** ECON, POL, PROT SOC assisted area; **~ d'attraction** V&M catchment area; **~ B** *(ANT zone A)* FIN zone B; **~ de chalandise** V&M catchment area, market area, *dans un magasin* trading area; **~ de chargement des camions** TRANSP lorry loading reception area *(BrE)*, lorry reception area *(BrE)*, truck loading reception area *(AmE)*, truck reception area *(AmE)*; **~ cible** ECON, FIN target zone; **~ cible de change** ECON, FIN exchange rate target zone; **~ commerçante** COM, V&M shopping mall *(AmE)*, shopping precinct *(BrE)*; **~ commerciale** COM, V&M retail park; **~ de comptes négociables** TRANSP transferable account area, TAA; **~ de** **conflagration** ASSUR conflagration area; **~ de cours** BOURSE ticker; **~ en crise** ECON depressed area; **~ critique** COM, GESTION problem area, MATH *test statistique* critical region; **~ en déclin** ECON depressed area; **~ défavorisée** ECON less favored area *(AmE)*, less favoured area *(BrE)*; **~ destinataire** INFO target field; **~ à deux voies de navigation** TRANSP *dans un port* two-way scheme; **~ de développement rural** ECON rural development area *(UK)*, RDA *(UK)*; **~ à développer** ECON development area *(UK)*; **~ de dialogue** INFO dialog box *(AmE)*, dialogue box *(BrE)*; **~ de diffusion** V&M *publicité* advertising zone; **~ dollar** ECON dollar area; **~ écologiquement fragile** ENVIR Environmentally-Sensitive Area *(UK)*, environmentally-sensitive zone; **~ économique européenne** ECON European economic area, EEA; **~ économique spéciale** ECON special economic zone; **~ d'enregistrement** LOISIRS, TRANSP reception area; **~ d'entreprise** ECON, IMMOB, IND, RES HUM enterprise zone; **~ à faible population** ECON sparsely populated area; **~ franc** COM zone franc; **~ franche** COM, ECON, IMP/EXP, POL free zone, free-trade area, free-trade zone, FTZ; **~ géographique** COM geographical area; **~ habitée** COM, TRANSP built-up area; **~ industrielle** COM industrial estate, industrial park, trading estate, IMMOB, IND, V&M industrial estate *(BrE)*, industrial park *(AmE)*, trading estate; **~ industrielle en déclin** ECON, IND declining industrial area; **~ industrielle nouvelle** COM, IMMOB, IND greenfield site; **~ interdite** COM off-limits area; **~ de liberté** TRANSP zone of freedom; **~ de libre-échange** COM, ECON, IMP/EXP, POL free zone, free-trade area, free-trade zone, FTZ; **~ de libre-échange latino-américaine** ECON Latin American Free Trade Association *(obs)*, Latin American Integration Association, LAIA; **~ de ligne de charge** TRANSP *navigation* load line zone; **~ limitée** TRANSP restricted area; **~ de lotissement minimum** IMMOB minimum lot area *(US)*, minimum lot size *(US)*; **~ du marché primaire** BOURSE primary market area; **~ de mémoire** INFO storage area; **~ métropolitaine** ECON metropolitan area; **~ monétaire** COM currency zone; **~ monétaire optimale** ECON, FIN optimum currency area; **~ de navigation** TRANSP trading limit; **~ de navigation côtière** TRANSP inshore traffic zone; **~ de navigation côtière de l'Angleterre** TRANSP English Inshore Traffic Zone, EITZ; **~ de non-libre-échange** COM, ECON, IMP/EXP, POL Non Free Trade Zone, NFTZ; **~ non-sterling** ECON nonsterling area, NSA; **~ de numérisation** INFO scan area; **~ peu peuplée** ECON sparsely populated area; **~ piétonnière** COM shopping mall *(AmE)*, shopping precinct *(BrE)*; **~ portuaire franche**

TRANSP *maritime* free port zone, FPZ; ~ **primaire de statistique métropolitaine** COM primary metropolitan statistical area (*US*), PMSA (*US*); ~ **de recrutement de la main-d'oeuvre** ECON, RES HUM labor force recruitment (*AmE*), labor shed (*AmE, jarg*), labour force recruitment (*BrE*), labour shed (*BrE, jarg*), recruiting area; ~ **de récupération des bagages** LOISIRS, TRANSP baggage reclaim area; ~ **réglementée** TRANSP *aviation* restricted area; ~ **de responsabilité** POL jurisdiction; ~ **rurale** ECON rural area; ~ **de salaire** RES HUM wage zone; ~ **sinistrée** ECON depressed area; ~ **de stabilité** PROT SOC stability zone; ~ **standard de statistique métropolitaine** MATH standard metropolitan statistical area, SMSA; ~ **de stationnement interdit** TRANSP no parking area, no parking zone, towaway area (*BrE*), towaway zone (*AmE*); ~ **sterling** COM, ECON, FIN, IMP/EXP sterling area, sterling zone; ~ **tampon** IMMOB, INFO buffer area, buffer zone; ~ **de tarification européenne** TRANSP European zone charge, EZC; ~ **test** V&M test area; ~ **de travail** INFO scratch area, scratch pad, working area; ~ **très fortement peuplée** ECON densely populated area; ~ **troisième âge** ECON gray belt (*AmE, jarg*), grey belt (*BrE, jarg*); ~ **à urbaniser** ECON development area (*UK*), development zone; ~ **à urbaniser en priorité** (*ZUP*) ECON, IMMOB, RES HUM priority development zone, urban development zone (*PDZ*); ~ **à vitesse limitée** TRANSP restricted speed area; ~ **vulnérable** ENVIR sensitive zone

zoom *m* INFO zooming, zoom; ♦ **faire un ~ arrière** INFO, LOISIRS zoom out; **faire un ~ avant** INFO, LOISIRS zoom in

ZUP *abrév* (*zone à urbaniser en priorité*) ECON, IMMOB, RES HUM PDZ (*priority development zone*)

Abréviations/Abbreviations

ABSAR *abrév (Actions à bons de souscription d'actions avec facilité de rachat)* BOURSE shares with redeemable share warrants

ABSOC *abrév (Actions à bons de souscription d'obligations convertibles)* BOURSE shares with convertible bond warrants carrying preferential subscription rights

a.c. *abrév (avarie commune)* ASSUR GA *(general average)*

AC *abrév (assurance-chômage)* RES HUM UI *(unemployment insurance)*

à/c *abrév (à compter de)* COM A/D *(after date)*

acc. *abrév (acceptation)* BANQUE, COM, COMPTA, DROIT, IMMOB acce. *(acceptance)*

ACG *abrév (adhérent compensateur général)* BOURSE GCM *(general clearing member)*

act. *abrév (action)* BOURSE shr. *(share)*

ADAC *abrév (avion à décollage et atterrissage courts)* TRANSP aviation STOL *(short take-off and landing)*

ADAV *abrév (avion à décollage et atterrisage vertical)* TRANSP VTOL *(vertical take-off and landing)*

ADE *abrév (avances en devises à l'exportation)* COM advance on export contract

ADEF *abrév (agence d'évaluation financière)* FIN rating agency

ADP *abrév (action à dividende prioritaire)* BOURSE, COMPTA, FIN preference share *(BrE)*, preferred stock *(AmE)*

adr.: ~ tél. *abrév (adresse télégraphique)* COMMS TA *(telegraphic address)*

ad val. *abrév (ad valorem)* COM, FISC ad val. *(ad valorem)*

AELE *abrév (Association européenne de libre-échange)* ECON EFTA *(European Free Trade Association)*

AFC *abrév (Agence française de codification)* BOURSE ≈ CUSIP *(US) (Committee on Uniform Securities Identification Procedures)*

AFNOR *abrév (Association française de normalisation)* COM, DROIT, IND French standards authority, ≈ ANSI *(US) (American National Standards Institute)*, ≈ ASA *(US) (American Standards Association)*, ≈ BSI *(UK) (British Standards Institute)*, ≈ National Bureau of Standards *(US)*

AFPA *abrév (Association pour la formation professionnelle des adultes)* RES HUM ≈ TA *(UK) (Training Agency)*

AFSB *abrév (Association française des sociétés de Bourse)* BOURSE French association of stock exchange member firms

ag. *abrév (agence)* ADMIN agcy *(agency)*, BANQUE branch, COM agcy *(agency)*, branch

AG *abrév (assemblée générale)* COM GA *(General Assembly)*, GM *(general meeting)*

AGA *abrév (adaptateur graphique couleur)* INFO EGA *(enhanced graphics adaptor)*

AGE *abrév* FIN *(accords généraux d'emprunt)* GAB *(general arrangements to borrow)*, GESTION *(assemblée générale extraordinaire)* EGM *(extraordinary general meeting)*

agglo. *abrév (aggloméré)* COM chipboard

AGO *abrév (assemblée générale ordinaire)* BOURSE, COM, GESTION OGM *(ordinary general meeting)*

AIB *abrév (Accord international sur le blé)* ECON IWA *(International Wheat Agreement)*

AIDA *abrév (attention, intérêt, désir, action)* COM, V&M AIDA *(attention, interest, desire, action)*

AIS *abrév (Accord international sur le sucre)* ECON ≈ ISA *(International Sugar Agreement)*

ALENA *abrév (Accord de libre-échange nord-américain)* ECON NAFTA *(North American Free Trade Area)*

AME *abrév (Accord monétaire européen)* COM EMA *(European Monetary Agreement)*

AMF *abrév (accord multi-fibres)* ECON MFA *(Multi-Fibre Arrangement)*

AMM *abrév* BOURSE *(adhérent mainteneur de marché)* market maker *(UK)*, V&M *(autorisation de mise sur le marché)* industrie pharmaceutique marketing authorization

ANPE *abrév* France *(Agence nationale pour l'emploi)* RES HUM ≈ Employment Service *(UK)*, ≈ Jobcentre *(UK)*

ANSEA *abrév (Association des nations du Sud-Est asiatique)* ECON ASEAN *(Association of South-East Asian Nations)*

ANU *abrév (Association des Nations Unies)* ADMIN UNA *(United Nations Association)*

ANVAR *abrév (Agence nationale pour la valorisa-*

tion de la recherche) ADMIN national development research centre

AOC *abrév (appellation d'origine contrôlée)* COM guaranteed quality label

AP *abrév (l'Assistance publique)* PROT SOC authority which manages state-owned hospitals and Social Services

APE *abrév (Activité principale de l'entreprise)* COM number giving company's main business

ARRT *abrév (affectation de réserve pour le rajuste-ment des salaires)* RES HUM SARA *(salary adjustment reserve allotment)*

ASE *abrév (Agence spatiale européenne)* COM ESA *(European Space Agency)*

ASIRGD *abrév (Assurance santé-invalidité-retraite et garantie-décès)* ASSUR ≈ OASDHI *(US) (old age, survivors, disability and health insurance)*

asse. *abrév (assurance)* ASSUR ins. *(insurance)*

ASSEDIC *abrév France (Association pour l'emploi dans l'industrie et le commerce)* RES HUM ≈ Employment Service *(UK)*

ATF *abrév (accord de taux futur)* BOURSE, FIN FRA *(forward rate agreement)*

AUD *abrév (administration de l'union des douanes)* IMP/EXP *UE* ACU *(administration of the customs union)*

AUE *abrév (Acte unique européen)* DROIT, POL SEA *(Single European Act)*

a.v.a. *abrév (agent d'assurance-vie agréé)* ASSUR chartered life underwriter *(US)*

B/. *abrév* BANQUE, FIN PN

BAB *abrév (bord à bord)* IMP/EXP, TRANSP *maritime* FIO *(free in and out)*

BAD *abrév* BANQUE *(Banque africaine de dévelop-pement)* ADB *(African Development Bank)*, TRANSP *(bon à délivrer)* F/R *(freight release)*

BALO *abrév France (Bulletin des annonces légales obligatoires)* BOURSE official stock exchange bulle-tin where French quoted companies must disclose financial information

BAT *abrév (bon à tirer)* COM, MÉDIA final proof

bcbg *abrév (bon chic, bon genre)* COM yuppie *(young upwardly mobile professional)*

bce. *abrév (balance)* BANQUE, COMPTA, ÉCON, FIN bal. *(balance)*

B.d.C. *abrév (Brevet des Collèges)* PROT SOC ≈ GCSE *(UK) (General Certificate of Secondary Education)*

BDR *abrév (base de données relationnelles)* INFO RDB *(relational database)*

BEI *abrév (Banque européenne d'investissement)* BANQUE EIB *(European Investment Bank)*

BERD *abrév (Banque européenne pour la recon-struction et le développement)* BANQUE, ÉCON, POL EBRD *(European Bank for Reconstruction and Development)*

BF *abrév (Banque de France)* BANQUE, ÉCON, FIN

Bank of France, ≈ BE, ≈ B of E *(Bank of England)*

BIAD *abrév (Banque inter-américaine de développement)* BANQUE IADB *(Inter-American Development Bank)*

BIC *abrév (bénéfices industriels et commerciaux)* FIN business profits

BIFS *abrév (bon des institutions financières spécialisées)* BOURSE note issued by certain finan-cial institutions

BIM *abrév (bon à intérêts mensuels)* BOURSE bond with monthly-paid interest

BIPA *abrév (bon à intérêts payés d'avance)* BOURSE bond with interest paid in advance

BIRD *abrév (Banque internationale pour la recon-struction et le développement)* BANQUE IBRD *(International Bank of Reconstruction and Deve-lopment)*

BITD *abrév (Bureau international des tarifs douaniers)* IMP/EXP ICTB *(International Customs Tariffs Bureau)*

BM *abrév (basse mer)* TRANSP *maritime* lw *(low water)*

BMT *abrév (bon des maisons de titres)* BOURSE securities houses bond

BMTN *abrév (bon à moyen terme négociable)* FIN MTN *(medium-term note)*

BN *abrév (Bibliothèque Nationale)* COM ≈ LC *(US) (Library of Congress)*, ≈ British Library *(UK)*

BNC *abrév (bénéfices non-commerciaux)* FISC non-business income

BNI *abrév (Banque nordique d'investissement)* BAN-QUE NIB *(Nordic Investment Bank)*

BOCB *abrév France (Bulletin officiel des cours de la Bourse)* BOURSE ≈ SEDOL *(UK) (Stock Exchange Daily Official List)*

BON *abrév (bon à ordre négociable)* BOURSE trad-able promissory note

b. à p. *abrév (billet à payer)* COMPTA, FIN b.p. *(bill payable)*

b. de p. *abrév (bureau de poste)* COMMS PO *(post office)*

BP *abrév (boîte postale)* COMMS POB *(post office box)*

BPA *abrév (bénéfices par action)* BOURSE, COMPTA, FIN EPS *(earnings per share)*

bps *abrév (bits par seconde)* INFO bps *(bits per second)*

b. à r. *abrév (billet à recevoir)* COMPTA BR *(bill receivable)*

BRI *abrév (Banque des règlements internationaux)* BANQUE BIS *(Bank for International Settlements)*

BSF *abrév France (bon des sociétés financières)* BOURSE note issued by certain financial institutions

BT *abrév (billet de trésorerie)* BANQUE CP *(commercial paper)*, BOURSE treasury note

BTA *abrév (bon à taux annuel)* BOURSE annual rate bond

BTAN *abrév France (bon à taux annuel normalisé)* BOURSE French government bond

BTF *abrév (bon à taux fixe)* BOURSE fixed-rate bond

BTM *abrév (bon à taux mensuel)* BOURSE monthly rate note

BTN *abrév (bon du Trésor négociable)* BOURSE tradeable treasury bond

BTP *abrév (bâtiment et travaux publics)* COM building and public works

BTT *abrév (bon à taux trimestriel)* BOURSE quarterly rate bond

BTV *abrév (bon à taux variable)* BOURSE floating rate bond

BVP *abrév (Bureau de vérification de la publicité)* MÉDIA, V&M ≈ ASA *(UK) (Advertising Standards Authority)*

c *abrév (carré)* sq COM *(square)*

c. *abrév* COM *(centime)* c. *(centime)*, COM *(coupon)* c., CP *(coupon)*

ca *abrév (courant alternatif)* IND INFO AC *(alternating current)*

CA *abrév* ADMIN *(conseil d'administration) d'une société* administrative board, board of directors, directorate, executive board, *d'une organisation internationale* governing board, COM *(chiffre d'affaires)* sales, trade figures, trading results, turnover, COM *(conseil d'administration)* administrative board, board of directors, directorate, executive board, *d'une organisation internationale* governing board, COMPTA *(chiffre d'affaires)* sales, turnover, ECON *(chiffre d'affaires)* output, trade figures, FIN *(chiffre d'affaires)* sales, turnover, GESTION *(conseil d'administration) d'une société*, RES HUM *(conseil d'administration)* administrative board, board of directors, directorate, executive board, *d'une organisation internationale* governing board, V&M *(chiffre d'affaires)* sales figures, sales revenue, sales volume, turnover

CAC *abrév* BOURSE *(cotation assistée en continu)* automated quotation, FIN *(Compagnie des agents de change)* Institute of stockbrokers

CAD *abrév (Ctrl-Alt-Del)* INFO CAD *(Control-Alt-Delete)*

c-à-d *abrév (c'est-à-dire)* COM i.e. *(id est)*

CAF *abrév (coût, assurance, fret)* IMP/EXP, TRANSP *livraison de cargaison* CIF *(cost, insurance and freight)*

CAN *abrév (convertisseur analogique-numérique)* INFO ADC *(analog-digital converter)*

CAO *abrév (conception assistée par ordinateur, création assistée par ordinateur)* IND, INFO CAD *(computer-aided design, computer-assisted design)*, D/A *(design automation)*

cap *abrév (capital)* COM, ECON, FIN cap *(capital)*

CAPAFE *abrév (comptes à payer à la fin de l'exercice)* COMPTA PAYE *(US) (Payables at Year-End)*

CAPES *abrév (≈ Certificat d'aptitude au professorat d'enseignement du second degré)* PROT SOC ≈ PGCE *(UK) (Postgraduate Certificate of Education)*

CATIF *abrév (contrat à terme d'instrument financier)* BOURSE financial futures contract

CBV *abrév (Conseil des bourses de valeurs)* BOURSE regulatory body of the Paris Stock Exchange, ≈ TSA *(UK) (The Securities Association)*, ≈ Council of the Stock Exchange *(UK)*

cc *abrév* COM *(cylindrée)* cc *(cubic centimetre)*, DROIT *(convention collective)*, IND *(convention collective)*, RES HUM *(convention collective)* collective agreement, collective bargaining agreement, labor agreement *(AmE)*, labour agreement *(BrE)*, union contract

c/c *abrév (compte créditeur compte courant)* BANQUE, COM, COMPTA, FIN C/A *(checking account AmE, current account BrE)*

CCAA *abrév (Conseil de coordination des associations aéroportuaires)* LOISIRS ≈ AACC *(Airport Associations Co-ordinating Council)*

CCI *abrév (Certificats coopératifs d'investissement)* BOURSE investment certificates reserved to cooperative and mutual companies

CCIFP *abrév (Chambre de compensation des instruments financiers de Paris)* BOURSE clearing house for financial instruments in Paris

CCR *abrév (coefficient de capitalisation des résultats)* BOURSE, COMPTA, FIN PER *(price-earnings ratio)*

CD *abrév* BANQUE *(certificat de dépôt)*, BOURSE *(certificat de dépôt)*, ECON *(certificat de dépôt)*, FIN *(certificat de dépôt)* CD *(certificate of deposit)*, INFO *(disque compact)* CD *(compact disk)*

CDC *abrév (compte de dividende en capital)* FISC CDA *(capital dividend account)*

CDD *abrév (contrat à durée déterminée)* RES HUM fixed-term contract, fixed-term deal, TRANSP *maritime* time agreement *(certificat de dépôt)*

CDI *abrév* INFO *(disque compact interactif)* CD-I *(compact disk interactive)*, RES HUM *(contrat à durée indéterminée)* permanent contract

CDN *abrév (certificat de dépôt négociable)* BANQUE, BOURSE NCD *(negotiable certificate of deposit)*

CD-ROM *abrév (disque CD-ROM)* INFO CD-ROM *(compact disk read-only memory)*

CE *abrév* ECON *(Communauté européenne)* EC *(European Community)*, POL *(Conseil de l'Europe)* CE *(Council of Europe)*, RES HUM *(comité d'entreprise)* joint consultative committee, works committee *(UK)*, works council *(UK)*

CEA *abrév* BOURSE *(compte d'épargne en actions)* equity savings account, ENVIR *(Commissariat à l'énergie atomique)* ≈ AERE *(Atomic Energy Research Establishment)*

CEAO *abrév (Communauté économique de l'Afrique de l'Ouest)* ECON customs ECOWAS *(Economic Community of West African States)*

CECA *abrév (Communauté européenne du charbon et de l'acier)* ECON ECSC *(European Coal and Steel Community)*

CEDEX *abrév (courrier d'entreprise à distribution exceptionnelle)* ADMIN business mail service

CEE *abrév (Commission économique européenne)* ECON ECE *(Economic Commission for Europe)*

CEEA *abrév (Communauté européenne de l'énergie atomique)* IND EAEC *(European Atomic Energy Community)*

CEI *abrév (Communauté des États indépendants)* COM, ECON, POL CIS *(Commonwealth of Independent States)*

CEN *abrév (Centre européen de normalisation)* ECON European Committee for Standardization

CERN *abrév (Centre européen pour la recherche nucléaire)* IND European Organization for Nuclear Research

certif. *abrév (certificat)* ADMIN, BREVETS, COM, FIN, PROT SOC cert. *(certificate)*

CES *abrév France (contrat d'emploi-solidarité)* RES HUM ≈ YTS *(UK) (Youth Training Scheme)*

C&A *abrév (coût et assurance)* IMP/EXP c&i, C&I *(cost and insurance)*

C&F *abrév (coût et fret)* IMP/EXP, TRANSP C&F *(cost and freight)*

CETI *abrév (contrat d'échange de taux d'intérêts)* BOURSE interest rate swap

CFAO *abrév (conception et fabrication assistées par ordinateur)* IND, INFO CAD/CAM *(computer-aided design and computer-aided manufacturing, computer-assisted design and computer-assisted manufacturing)*

CFC *abrév (chlorofluorocarbone)* ENVIR CFC *(chlorofluorocarbon)*

CFE *abrév (Centre de formalités d'entreprise)* COM centre for registering new businesses

CGA *abrév (adaptateur graphique couleur)* INFO CGA *(color/graphics adaptor AmE, colour/graphics adaptor BrE)*

CGT *abrév (Confédération générale du travail)* RES HUM ≈ CIO *(US) (Congress of Industrial Organizations)*, ≈ TUC *(UK) (Trades Union Congress)*

ch. de f. *abrév (chemin de fer)* TRANSP rail, railroad *(AmE)*, railway *(BrE)*

CI *abrév* BOURSE *(certificat d'investissement)* investment certificate, share certificate *(BrE)*, stock certificate *(AmE)*, INFO *(circuit intégré)* IC *(integrated circuit)*

CIB *abrév (Conseil international du blé)* COM IWC *(International Wheat Council)*

CIBSA *abrév (Certificats d'investissement à bons de souscriptions d'actions)* BOURSE investment certificates with share warrants

Cie *abrév (compagnie)* COM, ECON Co. *(company)*;

et ~ *abrév (et compagnie)* COM and Co *(and company)*

CII *abrév (crédit d'impôt à l'investissement)* FISC ITC *(investment tax credit)*

CIP *abrév (certificat d'investissement prioritaire)* BOURSE preferred investment certificate

CIPBSA *abrév (Certificats d'investissement préférés à bons de souscription d'actions)* BOURSE preferred investment certificates with share warrants

CIRM *abrév (Comité international radio-maritime)* COMMS CIRM *(International Radio-Maritime Committee)*

cl *abrév (centilitre)* COM cl *(centiliter AmE, centilitre BrE)*

cm *abrév* COM *(centimètre)* cm *(centimeter AmE, centimetre BrE)*, COMPTA *(coût moyen)* average cost, mean cost

cm³ *abrév (centimètre cube)* COM cc *(cubic centimeter AmE, cubic centimetre BrE)*

CMT *abrév (Conseil des marchés à terme)* BOURSE futures exchange council

CNA *abrév (convertisseur numérique-analogique)* INFO DAC *(digital-analog converter)*

CNE *abrév (Caisse nationale d'épargne)* BANQUE ≈ NSB *(UK) (National Savings Bank)*

CNPF *abrév (Conseil national du patronat français)* COM, IND ≈ CBI *(Confederation of British Industry)*

CNUCED *abrév (Conférence des Nations Unies sur le commerce et le développement)* ECON UNCTAD *(United Nations Conference on Trade and Development)*

CNUED *abrév (Conférence des Nations Unies sur l'environnement et le développement)* COM, ENVIR UNCED *(United Nations Conference on Environment and Development)*

COB *abrév (Commission des opérations de Bourse)* BOURSE French stock exchange watchdog, ≈ FOMC *(US) (Federal Open Market Committee)*, ≈ SEC *(US) (Securities and Exchange Commission)*, ≈ SIB *(UK) (Securities Investment Board)*

COBOL® *abrév (langage COBOL)* INFO COBOL *(Common Ordinary Business-Oriented Language)*

codec *abrév (codeur-décodeur)* INFO codec *(coder-decoder)*

COFACE *abrév (Compagnie française d'assurance pour le commerce extérieur)* IMP/EXP ≈ ECGD *(UK) (Export Credit Guarantee Department)*

com *abrév* COM *(commission)* com. *(committee)*, GESTION *(comité)*, POL *(comité)*, RES HUM *(comité)* board, com. *(committee)*

COMECON *abrév (Conseil de l'aide économique mutuelle)* ECON CMEA, COMECON *(Council for Mutual Economic Aid)*

config *abrév (configuration)* INFO config *(configuration)*

connt *abrév (connaissement)* IMP/EXP, TRANSP B/L *(bill of lading)*

conv. *abrév (converti)* COM, IMMOB conv *(converted)*

COPS *abrév (créances comptables émises continuellement en francs suisses)* BOURSE COPS *(continuously offered payment rights in Swiss francs)*

corresp. *abrév (correspondance)* COM, COMMS corr. *(correspondence)*

cos *abrév (cosinus)* MATH *symbole* cos *(cosine)*

coup. *abrév* BOURSE *(coupure)* subshare, COM *(coupon)* c., CP *(coupon)*, ECON *(coupure)* billet de banque denom. *(denomination)*

CP *abrév (Certificats pétroliers)* BOURSE oil company investment certificates exclusive to Total and Elf-Erap

CPAO *abrév (conception de programmes assistée par ordinateur)* INFO CASE *(computer-aided software engineering, computer-assisted software engineering)*

cr. *abrév (crédit)* COM, COMPTA, FIN Cr *(credit)*

CSP *abrév (catégorie socio-professionnelle)* COM socioprofessional group

CTI *abrév (crédit de taxe sur intrants)* FISC ITC *(Canada)* *(input tax credit)*

CU *abrév (charge utile)* TRANSP PL *(payload)*

cum. *abrév (cumulatif)* BOURSE *dividendes*, COMPTA cum. *(cumulative)*

CV *abrév* ADMIN *(curriculum vitae)*, COM *(curriculum vitae)*, RES HUM *(curriculum vitae)* CV *(curriculum vitae)*, TRANSP *(cheval-vapeur)* HP *(horsepower)*

CVP *abrév (cycle de vie d'un produit)* ECON, IND, V&M PLC *(product life cycle)*

CVT *abrév (correspondant en valeurs du Trésor)* BOURSE reporting dealer

D *abrév (directeur)* GESTION, RES HUM D *(director)*

DAB *abrév (distributeur automatique de billets)* BANQUE ACD *(automated cash dispenser, automatic cash dispenser)*

DAP *abrév (distributeur automatique de produits)* COM, V&M automatic vending machine, vending machine

DAU *abrév (document administratif unique)* ADMIN, IMP/EXP, TRANSP SAD *(single administrative document)*

db *abrév (décibel)* COM db *(decibel)*

DCPE *abrév (document-cadre de politique économique)* BOURSE, ECON PFP *(policy framework paper)*

D.E. *abrév (demandeur d'emploi)* COM job seeker, registered applicant for work

dec. *abrév (décembre)* COM Dec. *(December)*

de facto *abrév* DROIT de facto

DEL *abrév (diode électroluminescente)* INFO LED *(light-emitting diode)*

DELD *abrév (demandeur d'emploi de longue durée)* ECON, RES HUM LTU *(long-term unemployed)*

DEPS *abrév (dernier entré, premier sorti)* COMPTA, RES HUM LIFO *(last in, first out)*

DG *abrév (directeur général)* COMPTA, GESTION, RES HUM CEO *(US)* *(chief executive officer)*, DG *(director general)*, GM *(general manager)*, MD *(UK)* *(managing director)*

DGA *abrév (directeur général adjoint)* GESTION, RES HUM ADG *(assistant director general)*

DGAC *abrév France (Direction générale de l'aviation civile)* TRANSP ≈ ATA *(US)* *(Air Transport Association)*, ≈ CAA *(UK)* *(Civil Aviation Authority)*

DGF *abrév (dotation globale de fonctionnement)* POL block grant *(UK)*

dif. *abrév (différé)* COM def. *(deferred)*

dim. *abrév (dimanche)* COM Sun. *(Sunday)*

div. *abrév (dividende)* BOURSE, FIN div. *(dividend)*

dl. *(délégué)* *abrév* COM, RES HUM DEL *(delegate)*

dol. *abrév (dollar)* COM dol. *(dollar)*

DOM *abrév (département d'Outre-Mer)* COM overseas department

DOS® *abrév (système d'exploitation à disques)* INFO DOS® *(disk operating system)*

douz. *abrév (douzaine)* COM doz. *(dozen)*

DP *abrév (documents contre paiement)* COM DAP, DP *(documents against payment)*

DPA *abrév* BOURSE *(dividende par action)*, COMPTA *(dividende par action)* dividend per share, FISC Can *(déduction pour amortissement)* CCA *(capital cost allowance)*

DPO *abrév (direction par objectifs)* GESTION MBO *(management by objectives)*

Dr *abrév (docteur)* COM, PROT SOC, RES HUM Dr *(Doctor)*

DR *abrév (délai de recouvrement)* BOURSE debt recovery period

DRH *abrév* GESTION *(directeur des ressources humaines)* *personne* head of the personnel department, personnel director RES HUM *(directeur des resources humaines)* *personne* head of the personnel department, personnel director, RES HUM *(direction des ressources humaines)* *service* personnel department

DTS *abrév (droits de tirage spéciaux)* DROIT SDR *(special drawing rights)*

DUT *abrév (diplôme universitaire de technologie)* PROT SOC DipTech *(Diploma in Technology)*

E *abrév (quart est)* TRANSP *navigation* E *(East compass point)*

EAO *abrév (enseignement assisté par ordinateur)* INFO, PROT SOC CAI *(computer-aided instruction, computer-assisted instruction)*, CAL *(computer-aided learning, computer-assisted learning)*, CAT *(computer-aided training, computer-assisted training)*, CBT *(computer-based training)*

e. à p *abrév (effet à payer)* COMPTA, FIN bill payable, note payable

e. à r *abrév (effet à recevoir)* COMPTA, FIN bill receivable, note receivable

EBE *abrév (excédent brut d'exploitation)* COMPTA, ECON, FIN GM *(gross margin)*

ECU *abrév (unité monétaire européenne)* BANQUE, ECON, FIN ECU *(European Currency Unit)*

éd. *abrév (édition)* COM, INFO, MÉDIA ed. *(edition)*

EDI *abrév* COMMS *(échange de documents informatisés)* EDI *(electronic document interchange)*, COMMS *(échange de données informatisées)* EDI *(electronic data interchange)*, INFO *(échange de documents informatisés)* EDI *(electronic document interchange)*, INFO *(échange de données informatisées)* EDI *(electronic data interchange)*

édit. *abrév (édition)* COM, INFO, MÉDIA ed., edn. *(edition)*

ENA *abrév (École Nationale d'Administration)* PROT SOC School of Public Management

ENBAMM *abrév (entreprise non-bancaire admise au marché monétaire)* BANQUE, BOURSE nonbank bank, nonbank financial institution

ENEA *abrév (Autorité européenne de l'énergie nucléaire)* COM ENEA *(European Nuclear Energy Authority)*

EPROM *abrév (mémoire morte programmable électroniquement)* INFO EPROM *(electronically programmable read only memory)*

E/S *abrév (entrée/sortie)* INFO I/O *(input/output)*

esc. *abrév (escompte)* COM disc. *(discount)*

ESC *abrév (escudo)* COM Portugal ESC *(escudo)*

ETC *abrév (entrepreneur de transport combiné)* TRANSP CTO *(combined transport operator)*

ETI *abrév (échangeur thermique intermédiaire)* TRANSP intercooler

ETTD *abrév (équipement terminal de traitement de données)* INFO DTE *(data terminal equipment)*

EVP *abrév (équivalent vingt pieds)* TRANSP TEU *(twenty foot equivalent unit)*

ex. *abrév (example)* COM ex. *(example)*

ex-c *abrév (ex-coupon)* BOURSE, COM ex.cp., XC *(ex-coupon)*

ex-coup *abrév (ex-coupon)* BOURSE, COM ex.cp., XC *(ex-coupon)*

ex-d *abrév (ex-dividende)* BOURSE ex. div., XD, *(ex-dividend)*

ex-div. *abrév (ex-dividende)* BOURSE ex. div., XD, *(ex-dividend)*

FAB *abrév (franco à bord)* TRANSP livraison de marchandises FOB *(free on board)*, FOS *(free on ship, free on steamer)*

FAC *abrév* COM *(franc d'avaries communes)* FGA *(free of general average)*, ECON *(frais d'aménagement au Canada)* CDE *(Canadian development expense)*

FAO *abrév (fabrication assistée par ordinateur)* IND, INFO CAM *(computer-aided manufacture, computer-aided manufacturing, computer-assisted manufacture, computer assisted manufacturing)*

FAP *abrév (franc d'avarie particulière)* ASSUR assurance maritime FPA *(free of particular average)*

FAQ *abrév (franco à quai)* TRANSP maritime F/d *(free dock)*, FAQ *(free alongside quay)*, FD *(free dock)*, FOQ *(free on quay)*

fco *abrév (franco)* TRANSP fco. *(franco)*

FCP *abrév (fonds commun de placement)* BOURSE, FIN OEIC *(open-end investment company)*

FDE *abrév (Fonds de développement européen)* ECON, POL EDF *(European Development Fund)*

FEC *abrév (frais d'exploration au Canada)* FISC CEE *(Canadian exploration expense)*

fed. *abrév (fédéral)* COM fed. *(federal)*

FEDER *abrév (Fonds européen de développement régional)* ECON ERDF *(European Regional Development Fund)*

FELIN *abrév (Fonds d'État libres d'intérêt nominal)* BOURSE, FIN government-issued certificates which can be exchanged for bonds, ≈ COUGRs *(Certificates of Government Receipts)*

F&A *abrév (fusions et acquisitions)* BOURSE, ECON M&A *(mergers and acquisitions)*

fév. *abrév (février)* COM Feb. *(February)*

FF *abrév (franc français)* COM FF *(French franc)*

FG *abrév (frais généraux)* COMPTA overhead charges, overheads

FIATA *abrév (Fédération internationale des associations de transitaires et assimilés)* TRANSP International Federation of Forwarding Agents' Associations, International Federation of Freight Forwarders' Associations

FIBV *abrév (Fédération internationale des bourses de valeurs)* BOURSE IFSE *(International Federation of Stock Exchanges)*, WFSE *(World Federation of Stock Exchanges)*

FID *abrév (Fédération internationale de documentation)* COM IFD *(International Federation for Documentation)*

FIO *abrév (fabrication intégrée par ordinateur)* IND, INFO CIM *(computer-integrated manufacture, computer-integrated manufacturing)*

FIOT *abrév (Fédération internationale des ouvriers du transport)* TRANSP ITF *(International Transport Workers' Federation)*

FIPA *abrév (Fédération internationale des producteurs agricoles)* IND IFAP *(International Federation of Agricultural Producers)*

FLB *abrév (franco le long du bord)* TRANSP maritime, livraison FAS *(free alongside ship)*, FFA *(free from alongside)*

FM *abrév (modulation de fréquence)* COMMS FM *(frequency modulation)*

FME *abrév (Fonds monétaire européen)* ECON, POL EMF *(European Monetary Fund)*

FMEC *abrév (Fonds monétaire européen de coopération)* ECON, POL EMCF *(European Monetary Cooperation Fund)*

FMI *abrév (Fonds monétaire international)*

BANQUE, ECON, FIN **IMF** *(International Monetary Fund)*

FN *abrév (Front National)* POL **NF** *(UK) (National Front)*

FPP *abrév (frontière des possibilités de production)* ECON production possibility frontier

FRCE *abrév (Fonds de rétablissement du conseil de l'Europe)* BANQUE **CERF** *(Council of Europe Resettlement Fund)*

fre *abrév (facture)* BANQUE, COM, COMPTA, FIN inv. *(invoice)*

FSE *abrév (Fonds social européen)* ECON, POL **ESF** *(European Social Fund)*

FSI *abrév (Fédération syndicale internationale)* RES HUM **IFTU** *(International Federation of Trade Unions)*

FSM *abrév (Fédération syndicale mondiale)* RES HUM **WFTU** *(World Federation of Trade Unions)*

FTSE *abrév (indice FTSE des 100 valeurs)* BOURSE **FT-SE** *(UK) (Financial Times Stock Exchange index)*

g *abrév (gramme)* COM **g** *(gram AmE, gramme BrE)*

GAB *abrév (guichet automatique de banque)* BANQUE automated teller machine, automatic teller, automatic telling machine

GAP *abrév (gestion actif-passif)* BANQUE, COMPTA, FIN, GESTION **ALM** *(assets and liabilities management)*

GATT *abrév (Accord général sur les tarifs et le commerce)* ECON, POL **GATT** *(General Agreement on Tariffs and Trade)*

GDF *abrév (Gaz de France)* IND ≈ British Gas

GIEE *abrév (Groupement d'intérêt économique européen)* ECON, POL **EEIG** *(European Economic Interest Grouping)*

GL *abrév (grande ligne)* TRANSP chemin de fer main line

GMT *abrév (heure de Greenwich)* COM **GMT** *(Greenwich Mean Time)*

GNL *abrév (gaz naturel liquéfié)* ENVIR, IND, TRANSP **LNG** *(liquefied natural gas)*

Go *abrév (gigaoctet)* INFO **Gb** *(gigabyte)*

GPL *abrév (gaz de pétrole liquéfié)* ENVIR, IND, TRANSP **LPG** *(liquefied petroleum gas)*

GRH *abrév (gestion des ressources humaines)* RES HUM **HRM** *(human resource management)*

G7 *abrév (Groupe des Sept)* ECON **G7** *(Group of Seven)*

h *abrév (heure)* COM time, TRANSP **h, hr** *(hour)*

ha *abrév (hectare)* COM **ha** *(hectare)*

HC *abrév (conteneur hors-cotes)* TRANSP **HC** *(high cube)*

HD *abrév (haute densité)* INFO **HD** *(high density)*

HLM *abrév (habitation à loyer modéré)* IMMOB, PROT SOC council block *(UK)*, council flats *(UK)*, public housing unit *(US)*

HS *abrév (heures supplémentaires)* RES HUM **OT** *(overtime)*

hyp. *abrév (hypothèque)* BANQUE, FIN, IMMOB mortg. *(mortgage)*

I *abrév (important indice du marché, indice du marché principal)* BOURSE **MMI** *(Major Market Index)*

IA *abrév (intelligence artificielle)* INFO **AI** *(artificial intelligence)*

IAO *abrév (ingénierie assistée par ordinateur)* IND, INFO **CAE** *(computer-aided engineering, computer-assisted engineering)*

IATA *abrév (Association internationale des transports aériens)* TRANSP **IATA** *(International Air Transport Association)*

ibid. *abrév (ibidem)* COM ibid. *(ibidem)*

IC *abrév (intérêts courus, intérêts cumulés)* BANQUE, BOURSE, COM, COMPTA, FIN **AI** *(accrued interest)*, **IA** *(interest accrued)*

id. *abrév (idem)* COM id. *(idem)*

ID *abrév (identification)* COM, FISC, V&M **ID** *(identification)*

IDP *abrév (indication de durée et de prix)* COM **ADC** *(advice of duration and/or charge)*

IEP *abrév (Institut d'études politiques)* POL ≈ Centre for Political Studies

IES *abrév (prêt d'investissement et d'entretien sectoriel)* FIN **SIM** *(sector investment and maintenance loan)*

IGF *abrév (impôt sur les grandes fortunes)* FISC tax aimed at very rich people

IMC *abrév (impôt minimum complémentaire)* FISC add-on minimum tax

imp. *abrév (importation)* IMP/EXP imp. *(import)*

INC *abrév (Institut national de la consommation)* COM ≈ **CA** *(Consumers' Association)*

INCOTERME *abrév (terme commercial international)* ECON **INCOTERM** *(international commercial term)*

INSEE *abrév (Institut national de la statistique et des études économiques)* ECON ≈ **CSO** *(UK) (Central Statistical Office)*

int. *abrév (intérêt)* BANQUE, BOURSE, COM, COMPTA, ECON, FIN int. *(interest)*

intl *abrév (international)* COM, COMMS, ECON, POL intl *(international)*

IPC *abrév (indice des prix à la consommation)* COMPTA, ECON **CPI** *(consumer price index)*

IRNUDS *abrév (Institut de Recherche des Nations Unies pour le développement social)* PROT SOC **UNRISD** *(United Nations Research Institute for Social Development)*

IS *abrév (impôt sur les sociétés)* FISC business income tax *(Canada)*, company tax, corporate tax, corporation tax *(BrE)*

ISBN *abrév (International Standard Book Number)* MÉDIA édition **ISBN** *(International Standard Book Number)*

ISO *abrév (interconnexion de systèmes ouverts)* INFO OSI *(open-systems interconnection)*

ISSN *abrév (International Standard Serial Number)* MÉDIA *édition* ISSN *(International Standard Serial Number)*

janv. *abrév (janvier)* COM Jan. *(January)*

jl *abrév (journal)* COM db *(daybook)*, COMPTA db *(daybook)*, MÉDIA mag *(magazine)*

JO *abrév (Journal officiel)* ECON UE OJ *(Official Journal)*

juil. *abrév (juillet)* COM Jul. *(July)*

kg *abrév (kilogramme)* COM kg *(kilogram AmE, kilogramme BrE)*

kl *abrév (kilolitre)* COM kl *(kiloliter AmE, kilolitre BrE)*

km *abrév (kilomètre)* COM km *(kilometer AmE, kilometre BrE)*

km au cent *abrév (kilomètres au cent)* COM ≈ mpg *(miles per gallon)*

km/h *abrév (kilomètre/heure)* COM km/h *(kilometers per hour AmE, kilometres per hour BrE)*

km² *abrév (kilomètre carré)* COM km² *(square kilometer AmE, square kilometre BrE)*

ko *abrév (kilo-octet)* INFO kb *(kilobyte)*

kt *abrév (kilotonne)* COM kt *(kiloton)*

kW *abrév (kilowatt)* COM kW *(kilowatt)*

kWh *abrév (kilowatt-heure)* COM kWh *(kilowatt-hour)*

l *abrév (litre)* COM l *(liter AmE, litre BrE)*

lat. *abrév (latitude)* COM lat. *(latitude)*

lb *abrév (livre)* COM lb *(pound)*

l/c *abrév (lettre de change)* BANQUE, BOURSE, FIN, IMP/EXP B/E *(bill of exchange)*

L/C *abrév (lettre de crédit)* BANQUE, FIN LC *(letter of credit)*

L.E.P. *abrév (lycée d'enseignement professionnel)* PROT SOC secondary school for vocational training

LEP *abrév (livret d'épargne populaire)* BANQUE savings account passbook, savings bankbook, savings book, savings passbook

LHT *abrév (longueur hors tout)* TRANSP LOA *(length overall)*

lib. *abrév (libéré)* COM FP *(fully paid)*

livr. *abrév (livraison)* BOURSE, COM, COMMS, TRANSP D *(delivery)*

LPP *abrév (longueur entre perpendiculaires)* TRANSP *d'un navire* LBP *(length between perpendiculars)*

LTA *abrév (lettre de transport aérien)* IMP/EXP, TRANSP AWB *(air waybill)*

LTAU *abrév (lettre de transport aérien universelle)* IMP/EXP, TRANSP UAWB *(universal air waybill)*

LV *abrév (lieu de vente)* V&M POS *(point of sale)*

m *abrév (mètre)* COM m *(meter AmE, metre BrE)*

M *abrév (agrégats monétaires)* ECON M *(monetary aggregates)*

M. *abrév (Monsieur)* COM Mr *(Mister)*

MATIF *abrév France (Marché à terme d'instruments financiers)* BOURSE ≈ AFFM *(Australian Financial Futures Market)*, ≈ CBOT *(US)*, ≈ CBT *(US)* *(Chicago Board of Trade)*, ≈ LIFFE *(UK)* *(London International Financial Futures Exchange)*

MAV *abrév (mercatique après-vente)* V&M after-sales marketing

max. *abrév (maximal, maximum)* COM all-out, max. *(maximum)*, MATH max. *(maximum)*

MBA *abrév (marge brute d'autofinancement)* COMPTA cash flow

MCAC *abrév (Marché commun d'Amérique centrale)* ECON CACM *(Central American Common Market)*

MEDAF *abrév (modèle d'équilibre des actifs financiers, modèle d'évaluation des actifs financiers)* BOURSE, ECON, FIN CAPM *(capital asset pricing model)*

min. *abrév (minimum)* COM min. *(minimum)*

ml *abrév (millilitre)* COM ml *(milliliter AmE, millilitre BrE)*

Mlle *abrév (Mademoiselle)* COM Miss

mm *abrév (millimètre)* COM mm *(millimeter AmE, millimetre BrE)*

mm²/s *abrév (millimètre carré par seconde)* COM mm²/s *(square millimeter per second AmE, square millimetre per second BrE)*

Mme *abrév (Madame)* COM Mrs

MMI *abrév (Marché monétaire international)* BOURSE, ECON IMM *(International Monetary Market)*

m/o *abrév (mon ordre)* COM m/o *(my order)*

Mo *abrév (méga-octet)* INFO Mb *(megabyte)*

MONEP *abrév (Marché des options négociables de Paris)* BOURSE Paris traded options exchange, ≈ CBOE *(US)* *(Chicago Board Options Exchange)*, ≈ LIFFE *(UK)* *(London International Financial Futures Exchange)*

MP *abrév (mandat postal)* BANQUE, FIN MO *(AmE)* *(money order)*, PO *(BrE)* *(postal order)*

mrem/h *abrév (millirem par heure)* COM radioactivité mrem/h *(millirem per hour)*

mr/h *abrév (milliröntgen par heure, milliröntgen/heure)* COM mr/h *(milliroentgen per hour)*

m/s *abrév (mètres par seconde)* COM m/s *(meters per second AmE, metres per second BrE)*

MS *abrév (manuscrit)* FISC MS *(manuscript)*

MTC *abrév (mécanisme de taux de change)* ECON ERM *(exchange rate mechanism)*

m³ *abrév (mètre cube)* COM cbm *(cubic meter AmE, cubic metre BrE)*

MW *abrév (mégawatt)* COM MW *(megawatt)*

n *abrév (nominal)* COM n. *(nominal)*

N abrév COM *(nord)* N *(north)*, TRANSP *(quart nord) navigation* N *(North compass point)*

N/A abrév *(numérique-analogique)* INFO D/A *(digital-analog)*

NAS abrév *(numéro d'assurance sociale)* FISC, PROT SOC SIN *(social insurance number)*

nat. abrév *(national)* COM nat. *(national)*

NB abrév *(nota bene)* COM NB *(nota bene)*

NE abrév *(nord-est)* COM NE *(north east)*

NIP abrév BANQUE *(numéro d'identification personnel)* PIN *(personal identification number)*, BOURSE *(négociateur individuel de parquet)* floor trader, local *(jarg)*

NO abrév *(nord-ouest)* COM NW *(north west)*

n° abrév *(numéro)* COM no. *(number)*

nos abrév *(numéros)* MATH nos. *(numbers)*; **~ rf.** abrév *(nos références)* COM our ref. *(our reference)*

nov. abrév *(novembre)* COM Nov. *(November)*

NPE abrév *(nouvelle politique économique)* ECON NEP *(New Economic Policy)*

NPI abrév *(nouveau pays industrialisé)* ECON, IND NIC *(newly industrialized country)*

NR abrév COM NR *(naira)*

n° tél. abrév *(numéro de téléphone)* COMMS tel. no. *(telephone number)*

n/réf abrév *(notre référence)* COM our ref. *(our reference)*

O abrév *(quart ouest)* TRANSP *navigation* W *(West compass point)*

OACI abrév *(Organisation de l'aviation civile internationale)* TRANSP ICAO *(International Civil Aviation Organization)*

OAT abrév *(obligation assimilable du Trésor)* BOURSE French government bond, French treasury bond

obl. abrév *(obligation)* BOURSE db *(debenture)*

OBSA abrév *(obligation à bons de souscription en actions)* BOURSE bond cum warrant

OBSAR abrév *(obligation à bons de souscription en actions rachetables)* BOURSE bonds with redeemable share warrants

OBSO abrév *(obligation à bons de souscription d'obligations)* BOURSE bond with bond-buying warrant

OCAMM abrév *(Organisation commune africaine, malgache et mauricienne)* COM AASMM *(Associated African States, Madagascar and Mauritius)*

OCBSA abrév *(obligations convertibles à bons de souscription en actions)* BOURSE convertible bonds with share warrants

OCDE abrév *(Organisation de coopération et de développement économique)* ECON OECD *(Organization for Economic Cooperation and Development)*

oct. abrév *(octobre)* COM Oct. *(October)*

ODPE abrév *(obligation pour le développement de la petite entreprise)* COM SBDB *(small business development bond)*

OECE abrév *(Organisation européenne de coopération économique)* ECON OEEC *(Organization for European Economic Cooperation)*

OIE abrév *(Office international des épizooties)* TRANSP IOE *(International Office of Epizootics)*

OIML abrév *(Organisation internationale de métrologie légale)* DROIT International Organization for Legal Metrology

OIT abrév *(Organisation internationale du travail)* RES HUM ILO *(International Labour Organization)*

OM abrév *(organisation et méthodes)* COM, GESTION, RES HUM O&M *(organization and methods)*

OMCL abrév *(obligation la moins chère à livrer)* BOURSE CTD *(cheapest to deliver)*

OMS abrév *(Organisation mondiale de la santé)* ADMIN, PROT SOC WHO *(World Health Organization)*

ONG abrév *(organisation non-gouvernementale)* COM NGO *(nongovernmental organization)*

ONU abrév *(Organisation des Nations Unies)* ECON, POL UN *(United Nations)*, UNO *(United Nations Organization)*

OP abrév *(ordinateur personnel)* INFO PC *(personal computer)*

OPA abrév *(offre publique d'achat)* BOURSE, COM, COMPTA TOB *(takeover bid)*

OPCVM abrév *(organisme de placements collectifs en valeurs mobilières)* FIN UCITS *(undertakings for collective investment in transferables)*

OPE abrév *(offre publique d'échange)* BOURSE exchange offer

OPEP abrév *(Organisation des pays exportateurs de pétrole)* ECON, ENVIR, POL OPEC *(Organization of Petroleum Exporting Countries)*

OPM abrév *(opérateur principal du marché)* BOURSE bill broker, discount house

OPV abrév *(offre publique de vente)* BOURSE offer for sale, public offering

ORA abrév France *(obligations remboursables en actions)* BOURSE bonds redeemable in shares

O.S. abrév *(ouvrier spécialisé)* RES HUM skilled worker

OSCAR abrév *(obligation spéciale à coupons à réinvestir)* BOURSE bunny bond *(jarg)*

OSDIBSAR abrév *(obligations subordonnées à durée indéterminée à bons de souscription en actions rachetables)* BOURSE subordinated perpetual bonds with redemable share warrants

OST abrév *(organisation scientifique du travail)* GESTION, MATH scientific management

OTAN abrév *(Organisation du Traité de l'Atlantique Nord)* POL NATO *(North Atlantic Treaty Organization)*

OTV abrév *(obligation à taux variable)* BOURSE FRN *(floating-rate note)*

OUA *abrév (Organisation de l'unité africaine)* ECON OAU *(Organization of African Unity)*

p. *abrév* COM *(page)* pg. *(page)*, COM *(poids)* wt. *(weight)*, INFO *(page)* pg. *(page)*, MATH *(pour cent)* pc *(per cent)*

p.a. *abrév (par an)* COM p.a. *(per annum)*

PAC *abrév (la politique agricole commune)* ECON, POL, *UE* CAP *(the Common Agricultural Policy)*

P.A.F. *abrév (Police de l'Air et des Frontières)* RES HUM border police

PAO *abrév (publication assistée par ordinateur)* INFO DTP *(desktop publishing)*

PBR *abrév (prix de base rajusté)* COMPTA ACB *(Canada) (adjusted cost base)*

p. cent *abrév (pour cent)* MATH pc *(per cent)*

PCGA *abrév (Principes comptables généralement admis)* COMPTA GAAP *(US) (Generally Accepted Accounting Principles)*

p.d. *abrév (port dû)* COM, TRANSP carr fwd, CF *(carriage forward)*, frt fwd *(freight forward)*

PDG *abrév (président-directeur général)* GESTION, RES HUM CEO *(US) (Chief Executive Officer)*, DG *(director-general)*, MD *(UK) (managing director)*

PEPS *abrév (premier entré, premier sorti)* COMPTA FIFO *(first in, first out)*

P et P *abrév (pertes et profits)* COMPTA P&L *(profit and loss)*

PIB *abrév (produit intérieur brut)* ECON GDP *(gross domestic product)*

p.j. *abrév (pièce jointe)* COM enclosure

PL *abrév (port en lourd)* TRANSP *navigation* D/W *(dead weight)*, DWC *(deadweight capacity)*, DWCC *(deadweight cargo capacity)*, DWT *(deadweight tonnage)*

PLV *abrév (publicité sur le lieu de vente)* MÉDIA *publicité*, V&M point-of-sale advertising, point-of-sale promotion

PM: **~ de VE moyenne** *abrév (pleine mer de vive-eau moyenne)* TRANSP *maritime* MHWS *(mean high water at springs)*

PMA *abrév (pays moins avancé)* COM, ECON, POL developing country, LDC *(less-developed country)*

PME *abrév (petites et moyennes entreprises)* COM SME *(small and medium-sized enterprises)*

PMH *abrév (point mort haut)* TRANSP TDC *(top dead center AmE, top dead centre BrE)*

PMI *abrév (petites et moyennes industries)* COM SMME *(small and medium-sized manufacturing companies)*

PMTS *abrév (méthode des temps prédéterminés)* ECON, FIN, GESTION PMTS *(predetermined motion time system)*

PNB *abrév (produit national brut)* ECON GNP *(gross national product)*

PNBA *abrév (PNB augmenté)* ECON, POL AGNP *(augmented GNP)*

PNN *abrév (produit national net)* ECON n.n.p. *(net national product)*

p.o. *abrév (par ordre)* COM by order

p.p. *abrév* COM *(port payé)* p.p. *(postage paid)*, COM *(par procuration)* p.p., per pro. *(frml) (per procurationem)*, COM *(pages)* p.p. *(pages)*, COM *(prépayé)* p.p. *(prepaid)*, COMMS *(port payé)* p.p. *(postage paid)*, ≈ Freepost® *(BrE) (Business Reply Mail)*, TRANSP *(port payé)* carr pd *(carriage paid)*, frt ppd *(freight prepaid)*

PPA *abrév (parité du pouvoir d'achat)* ECON PPP *(purchasing power parity)*

PPAR *abrév (perpendiculaire arrière)* TRANSP *navigation* AP *(aft perpendicular)*

PPAV *abrév (perpendiculaire avant)* TRANSP *navigation* FP *(forward perpendicular)*

p.p.m. *abrév (partie par million)* COM ppm *(parts per million)*

ppp *abrév (points par pouce)* INFO dpi *(dots per inch)*

P.R. *abrév (parc relais)* TRANSP P&R *(park and ride)*

préf. *abrév (préférence)* COM pref. *(preference)*

PREP *abrév (prêt au redressement des entreprises publiques, prêt à la rationalisation des entreprises publiques, prêt à la réforme des entreprises publiques)* FIN PERL *(public enterprise rationalization loan)*

prof *abrév (professeur)* RES HUM Prof *(Professor)*

PS *abrév (post-scriptum)* COMMS PS *(postscript)*

pta. *abrév (peseta)* COM pta. *(peseta)*

PTC *abrév (poids total en charge)* TRANSP *véhicule routier* GVW *(gross vehicle weight)*

PTPE *abrév (perte au titre d'un placement d'entreprise)* FISC BIL *(business investment loss)*

PV *abrév (point de vente)* V&M POS *(point of sale)*

PVD *abrév (pays en voie de développement)* COM, ECON, POL developing country, LDC *(less developed country)*

px *abrév (prix)* COM, ECON pr. *(price)*

QG *abrév (contrôle de la qualité globale)* COM, GESTION, IND, V&M TQC *(total quality control)*

qté *abrév (quantité)* COM, MATH qt. *(quantity)*

r. *abrév* COMMS *(recommandé)* regd. *(registered)*, TRANSP *(route, rue)* Rd. *(road)*

RCB *abrév (rationalisation des choix budgétaires)* COMPTA, FIN, GESTION, RES HUM PPBS *(planning, programming, budgeting system)*

RCI *abrév (rentabilité des capitaux investis)* COMPTA, ECON, FIN ROCE *(return on capital employed)*

RCS *abrév (Registre du commerce et des services)* COM, DROIT ≈ CRO *(Companies Registration Office)*

RECHAR *abrév (reconversion charbon)* ECON European Union scheme introduced in 1990 to help the revitalization of areas hit by coal pit closures

REI *abrév (rachat d'une entreprise par des investisseurs)* BOURSE, COM, FIN, GESTION LMBI *(leveraged management buy-out)*

remb. *abrév (remboursable)* BOURSE, COMPTA red. *(redeemable)*

RES *abrév (rachat d'une entreprise par ses salariés)* BOURSE, COM, FIN, GESTION LMBO *(leveraged management buyout)*, MBO *(management buy-out)*

rf. *abrév (référence)* COM ref. *(reference)*

R&D *abrév (recherche et développement)* IND R&D *(research and development)*

RFC *abrév (requête formulée par le client)* TRANSP aviation CR *(change request)*, RFC *(request for change)*

RISCPT *abrév (Registre international des substances chimiques potentiellement toxiques)* ENVIR, IND IRPTC *(International Register of Potentially Toxic Chemicals)*

RLE *abrév (réseau local d'entreprise)* INFO LAN *(local area network)*

RNIS *abrév (réseau numérique à intégration de services)* COMMS ISDN *(integrated services digital network)*

RO *abrév (recherche opérationnelle)* COM, GESTION, V&M OR *(operational research)*

ROC *abrév (reconnaissance optique des caractères)* INFO OCR *(optical character recognition)*

ROME *abrév (répertoire opérationnel des métiers et des emplois)* RES HUM job bank

RP *abrév* POL *(représentation proportionnelle)* PR *(proportional representation)*, V&M *(relations publiques)* PR *(public relations)*

RSVP *abrév (répondez s'il vous plaît)* COMMS RSVP *(please reply)*

RTP *abrév (réserve totale prescrite)* BANQUE PAR *(prescribed aggregate reserve)*

RVE *abrév (restriction volontaire des exportations)* IMP/EXP VER *(voluntary export restraint)*

s. *abrév* COM *(seconde)* sec. *(second)*, COMMS *(signé)* sgd *(signed)*

S *abrév (quart sud)* TRANSP navigation S *(South compass point)*

SA *abrév (société anonyme)* COM Ltd *(UK) (limited liability company)*, plc *(UK) (public limited company)*

SARL *abrév (société à responsabilité limitée)* BOURSE private limited company, COM Inc. *(US) (incorporated company)*, Ltd *(UK) (limited liability company)*

SBF *abrév (Société des bourses françaises)* BOURSE ≈ ISE *(International Stock Exchange)*

SCC *abrév Canada (système central de comptabilité)* COMPTA CAS *(Canada) (Central Accounting System)*

SCMC *abrév (Société de compensation des marchés conditionnels)* BOURSE ≈ LOCH *(UK) (London Options Clearing House)*

SCN *abrév (spécification de changement notifié)* TRANSP aviation MC *(master change)*, SCN *(specification change notice)*

SCPI *abrév (société civile de placement immobilier)* BOURSE REIT *(US) (real estate investment trust)*

SCRA *abrév (système de compensation et de règlement automatisé)* BANQUE ACSS *(Automated Clearing Settlement System)*

SDT *abrév (simplification des tâches)* GESTION, RES HUM job simplification, work simplification

SE *abrév (système expert)* COM, INFO ES *(expert system)*

Sécu *abrév infrml France (Sécurité sociale)*, PROT SOC, RES HUM ≈ NHS *(UK) (National Health Service)*

SEM *abrév (société à économie mixte)* ECON partially-privatized company, semi-public company

SEO *abrév (sauf erreur ou omission)* COM E&OE *(errors and omissions excepted)*

sept. *abrév (septembre)* COM Sept. *(September)*

serv. *abrév (service)* ADMIN, COM POL RES HUM, V&M dept. *(department)*

SFI *abrév (Société financière internationale)* FIN IFC *(International Finance Corporation)*

SGBD *abrév (système de gestion de bases de données)* INFO DBMS *(database management system)*

SGF *abrév (système de gestion financière)* FIN financial management system

SGTP *abrév (système généralisé des tarifs et préférences)* IMP/EXP GSTP *(generalized system of tariffs and preferences)*

SHC *abrév (conteneur spécial hors-cotes)* TRANSP SHC *(super high cube)*

SIAM *abrév (système des intermédiaires entre courtiers)* BOURSE IDBS *(interdealer broker system)*

SICAF *abrév (société d'investissement à capital fermé ou fixe)* FIN CEIC *(closed-end investment company)*

SICAV *abrév (société d'investissement à capital variable)* BOURSE, FIN OEIC *(open-end investment company)*

SICOVAM *abrév (≈ société interprofessionnelle pour la compensation des valeurs mobilières)* BOURSE ≈ DTC *(US) (Depository Trust Company)*

SIG *abrév (système intégré de gestion)* GESTION, INFO MIS *(management information system)*

SIM *abrév* GESTION *(système d'information de management)*, INFO *(système d'information de management)* MIS *(management information system)*, V&M *(système d'information de marketing)* MIS *(marketing information system)*

SM *abrév (système métrique)* COM, MATH metric system

SMAG *abrév (salaire minimum agricole garanti)* ECON guaranteed minimum agricultural wage

SME *abrév (Système monétaire européen)* ECON UE EMS *(European Monetary System)*

SMIC *abrév (salaire minimum interprofessionnel de croissance)* RES HUM guaranteed minimum wage, statutory minimum wage

SMIG *abrév (salaire minimum interprofessionnel garanti)* RES HUM GAW *(guaranteed annual wage)*

SNCF *abrév (Société nationale des chemins de fer français)* TRANSP ≈ BR *(UK) (British Rail)*

SNJ *abrév (Syndicat national des journalistes)* MÉDIA ≈ NUJ *(UK) (National Union of Journalists)*

SS *abrév France (Sécurité sociale)* PROT SOC, RES HUM ≈ NHS *(UK) (National Health Service)*

SSCI *abrév (société de services et de conseils en informatique)* INFO computer consultancy firm, software and computer services company

SSII *abrév (société de services d'ingénierie informatique)* INFO computer services company

Sté *abrév (société)* COM, ECON Co. *(company)*

sténo *abrév* ADMIN *(sténographe)* shorthand writer, stenographer, ADMIN *(sténographie)* shorthand, stenography

ster. *abrév (sterling)* COM stg *(sterling)*

SVN *abrév (sans valeur nominale)* BOURSE NPV *(no-par value)*

SVT *abrév (spécialistes en valeurs du Trésor)* BOURSE, ECON GEMMS *(gilt-edged market makers)*

sync *abrév infrml (synchronisation)* COM sync *(infrml) (synchronization)*

t. *abrév* BOURSE *(titre)* security, COM *(tare)* t. *(tare)*, COM *(tonne)* t. *(ton)*, TRANSP *(tare)* t. *(tare)*

TAM *abrév (taux annuel monétaire)* FIN annual monetary rate

TAO *abrév* INFO *(traduction assistée par ordinateur)* CAT *(computer-aided translation, computer-assisted translation)*, MAT *(machine-aided translation, machine-assisted translation)*, INFO, PROT SOC *(test assisté par ordinateur)* CAT *(computer-aided testing, computer-assisted testing)*

TBB *abrév (taux de base bancaire)* BANQUE, ECON, FIN bank base rate, bank rate

TD *abrév (ligne de charge tropicale en eau douce)* TRANSP TF *(tropical fresh water load line)*

tech. *abrév (technicien)* RES HUM technical assistant

TEI *abrév (traitement électronique de l'information)* INFO EDP *(electronic data processing)*

tél. *abrév (téléphone)* COMMS tel. *(telephone)*

télé *abrév (télévision)* COM, COMMS, MÉDIA telly *(BrE, infrml)*, TV *(television)*

TGD *abrév (transport à grande distance)* ENVIR long-range transport

TGDPA *abrév (transport à grande distance des*

polluants aéroportés)* ENVIR long-range transport of air pollutants

TGV *abrév (train à grande vitesse)* TRANSP ≈ HST *(high-speed train)*

THS *abrév (transaction hors séance)* BOURSE THS transaction

TIC *abrév (taux d'intérêt comptable)* BANQUE, COMPTA, FIN ARI *(accounting rate of interest)*

TIOL *abrév (taux interbancaire offert à Londres)* BANQUE, BOURSE LIBOR *(London Interbank Offered Rate)*

TIOP *abrév (taux interbancaire offert à Paris)* BANQUE PIBOR *(Paris Interbank Offered Rate)*

TIOS *abrév (taux interbancaire offert à Singapour)* BANQUE SIBOR *(Singapore Interbank Offered Rate)*

TIOT *abrév (taux interbancaire offert à Tokyo)* ECON TIBOR *(Tokyo Interbank Offered Rate)*

TIR *abrév (transport international routier)* TRANSP convention on the contract for the international carriage of goods by road

TJJ *abrév (taux d'argent au jour le jour)* BANQUE call money rate, daily money rate

tk *abrév (tonne-kilomètre)* TRANSP ≈ TM *(ton mile)*

TMI *abrév (tendance marginale à importer)* ECON, IMP/EXP MPI *(marginal propensity to import)*

TMM *abrév (taux du marché monétaire)* BOURSE, ECON, FIN money-market rate

TMMMM *abrév (taux moyen mensuel du marché monétaire)* BOURSE average monthly money market rate

TMO *abrév (taux de marché obligataire)* BOURSE bond market rate

TMP *abrév (taux moyen pondéré)* BOURSE average weighted rate

TOF *abrév (tableau des opérations financières)* FIN flow-of-funds table

TPBSTP *abrév (Titres participatifs à bons de souscription de titres participatifs)* BOURSE equity loans with equity loans warrants

TPCCIP *abrév (Titres participatifs convertibles en certificats d'investissement privilégiés)* BOURSE equity loans convertible into preference investment certificates

TPE *abrév (terminal de paiement électronique)* FIN EPT *(electronic payment terminal)*

TPL *abrév (Tonne Port en Lourd)* TRANSP *maritime* TDW *(tons deadweight)*

TPS *abrév (taxe de prestation de service)* FISC GST *(goods and services tax)*

TPV *abrév (terminal point de vente)* V&M POST *(point-of-sale terminal)*

T4M *abrév (taux moyen mensuel du marché monétaire)* BOURSE average monthly money market rate

TRA *abrév (taux révisable annuellement)* FIN interest rate subject to modification every year

TRC *abrév (tube à rayons cathodiques)* INFO CRT *(cathode ray tube)*

TRI *abrév (taux de rentabilité d'un investissement)* COMPTA, FIN ROI *(return on investment)*

TSDI *abrév (titre subordonné à durée indéterminée)* BOURSE subordinated perpetual bond

TSR *abrév (titre subordonné remboursable)* BOURSE subordinated redeemable bond

TSRBSORA *abrév (Titres subordonnés remboursables avec bons de souscription d'obligations remboursables en actions)* BOURSE subordinated redeemable notes with warrants that can be converted into bonds or shares

TSVP *abrév (tournez s'il vous plaît)* COMMS PTO *(please turn over)*

TT *abrév (transfert télégraphique)* BANQUE, COMMS TT *(telegraphic transfer)*

TTA *abrév (taxe sur le transport aérien)* FISC ATT *(air transportation tax)*

TU *abrév (Temps universel)* COM UTC *(universal time coordinated)*

TUA *abrév (travailleurs unifié de l'automobile)* RES HUM UAW *(US)* *(United Automobile Workers)*

TUC *abrév (travaux d'utilité collective)* ECON, POL, PROT SOC, RES HUM ≈ YTS *(UK)* *(Youth Training Scheme)*, CP *(UK)* *(Community Programme)*

TVA *abrév (taxe sur la valeur ajoutée)* FISC VAT *(UK)* *(value-added tax)*

TVL *abrév (temps vrai local)* TRANSP *navigation* ATS *(apparent time at ship)*

TVQ *abrév (taxe de vente de Quebec)* FISC QST *(Quebec sales tax)*

UC *abrév (unité centrale, unité centrale de traitement)* INFO CPU *(central processing unit)*

UCE *abrév (unité de compte européenne)* BANQUE, ECON, FIN EUA *(European unit of account)*

UDEAC *abrév (Union douanière et économique de l'Afrique centrale)* IMP/EXP UDEAC *(Central African Customs and Economics Union)*

UE *abrév (Union européenne)* ECON, POL EU *(European Union)*

UEBL *abrév (Union économique Belgique-Luxembourg)* ECON, POL BLEU *(Belgium-Luxembourg Economic Union)*

UEM *abrév (Union économique et monétaire)* ECON, POL EMU *(Economic and Monetary Union)*

UEO *abrév (Union de l'Europe occidentale)* POL WEU *(Western European Union)*

UEP *abrév (Union européenne des paiements)* COM EPU *(European Payments Union)*

UER *abrév (Union européenne de radiodiffusion)* COMMS, MÉDIA EBU *(European Broadcasting Union)*

UICF *abrév (Union internationale des chemins de fer)* ADMIN IUR *(International Union of Railways)*

UIP *abrév (Union interparlementaire)* POL IPU *(Inter-Parliamentary Union)*

UIT *abrév (Union internationale des télécommunications)* COMMS ITU *(International Telecommunications Union)*

UME *abrév (Union monétaire européenne)* ECON, POL EMU *(European Monetary Union)*

UNEDIC *abrév (Union nationale pour l'emploi dans l'industrie et le commerce)* ECON, PROT SOC, RES HUM ≈ Unemployment Benefit Office *(UK)*

UPU *abrév obs (Union postale universelle)* COMMS, COMPTA UPU *(Universal Postal Union)*

URSS *abrév (Union des Républiques Socialistes Soviétiques)* COM now called the Commonwealth of Independent States, USSR *(obs)*

V *abrév (volt)* COM V *(volt)*

val. *abrév (valeur)* BOURSE security, stock

VAN *abrév (valeur actuelle nette)* COMPTA, ECON, FIN NPV *(net present value)*

vap. *abrév (vapeur)* TRANSP *navire* ss *(steamship)*

VHF *abrév (très haute fréquence)* COM VHF *(very high frequency)*

virt *abrév (virement)* COMPTA, FIN *de fonds* tr. *(transfer)*

VL *abrév (voiture-lit)* TRANSP *chemin de fer* sleeper, sleeping car

vo *abrév (verso)* COM, MÉDIA vo *(verso)*

vol *abrév (volume)* COM vol. *(volume)*

V-P *abrév (vice-président)* RES HUM veep *(AmE, infrml)*, VP *(vice-president)*

VPC *abrév (vente par correspondance)* ADMIN, COMMS, INFO, V&M MO *(mail order)*

V/réf. *abrév (votre référence)* COMMS yr ref. *(your reference)*

VRP *abrév (voyageur représentant placier)* COM, V&M bagman, commercial traveler *(AmE)*, commercial traveller *(BrE)*

WL *abrév (wagon-lit)* TRANSP *chemin de fer* sleeper, sleeping car

ZAC *abrév (zone d'aménagement concerté)* ECON, IMMOB, IND, RES HUM EZ *(enterprise zone)*

ZAD *abrév (zone d'aménagement différé)* ECON, IMMOB, RES HUM future development zone

ZUP *abrév (zone à urbaniser en priorité)* ECON, IMMOB, RES HUM PDZ *(priority development zone)*

Appendice français–anglais/

French–English appendix

Table des matières/Contents

Correspondance et situations commerciales/ Business correspondence and situations

Discuter de contrats/Discussing contracts

Conditions de vente

CLIENT: Je suis heureux de vous apprendre que nous sommes prêts à inclure votre entreprise sur la liste de nos fournisseurs. Avant de signer un contrat, nous devons nous mettre d'accord sur les termes et conditions.

FOURNISSEUR: Nous en sommes enchantés. Sur quels aspects particuliers devons-nous nous mettre d'accord?

CLIENT: Tout d'abord nos termes de règlement sont de 20% à la réception des marchandises et le solde sous 90 jours.

FOURNISSEUR: Normalement, nous préférons être réglés entièrement sous 60 jours, mais si nous avons un contrat de deux ans, nous pourrions accepter vos conditions.

CLIENT: Très bien. Nous voulons également une ristourne de 10% pour les commandes supérieures à 5 000 pièces. Les livraisons doivent être effectuées à des dates spécifiées et soumises à des amendes pour livraison tardive. Je crois que l'on vous a donné des détails à ce sujet, n'est-ce pas?

FOURNISSEUR: Oui, je peux vous garantir que nous avons l'habitude de livrer dans les délais. Je suis sûr que vous êtes tout à fait conscient que nous offrons un bon service. Nous sommes prêts à signer.

CLIENT: Parfait. Voici le contrat.

Sales conditions

CLIENT: I'm pleased to inform you that we are prepared to include your company as one of our suppliers. Before we sign an agreement, we need to agree on terms and conditions.

SUPPLIER: We're delighted. What in particular do we need to agree?

CLIENT: Firstly, our terms of payment are 20 per cent on receipt of the goods and the remainder within 90 days.

SUPPLIER: We normally expect to be paid in full within 60 days, but if we can have a two-year agreement, we could accept your conditions.

CLIENT: Fine. We also want a 10 per cent discount for orders of over 5,000 parts. Deliveries must also be made by the specified date, with penalties for late delivery. I think you've been given some details.

SUPPLIER: Yes, and I can assure you that we are accustomed to delivering in good time. I'm sure that you know already that we offer good service at a good price. We're ready to sign.

CLIENT: That's good. I have the agreement here.

Contrat de travail

Monsieur,

A la suite de nos récentes discussions, nous sommes heureux de vous offrir le poste de directeur régional au sein de notre entreprise, selon les termes et conditions suivants:

Rémunération:
Votre salaire s'élèvera à 15.000,00 livres sterling par an plus une commission relevant des points déjà discutés avec vous. Comme tout le personnel, votre salaire sera payé mensuellement le dernier jeudi de chaque mois. La première réévaluation sera en juillet 199-.

Préavis:
Comme tous nos employés, vous serez employé pendant une période initiale de six mois pendant lesquels chacune des deux parties pourra mettre un terme à son engagement en en avisant l'autre partie par écrit sept jours au préalable. Si nous sommes satisfaits de vos performances pendant le période d'essai, nous vous confirmerons, dès son échéance, votre engagement permanent et la période de préavis d'une semaine sera prolongée à un mois.

Indemnisation de maladie:
Toute absence raisonnable pour cause de maladie sera indemnisée, pour la partie non prise en charge par la sécurité sociale par nos soins à la hauteur de votre salaire normal. Toutefois, il est à noter que cette participation sera relative à votre durée de service chez nous.

Vacances:
Vous aurez droit à 20 jours ouvrables de vacances payées dans une année entière, la période normale des congés étant comprise entre le 1er janvier et le 31 décembre.

Voiture:
Nous vous fournirons une voiture d'entreprise appropriée (coût environ 14 000,00 livres sterling), qui est prévue pour un usage principalement lié à vos activités d'entreprise mais dont vous pourrez également vous servir pour votre utilisation personnelle. Nous prendrons en charge tous les coûts normaux engendrés par ce véhicule: vignette, assurance, réparations, entretien et essence.

Retraite:
L'entreprise est à même d'offrir un régime de retraite. Vous aurez ainsi la possibilité soit d'y souscrire après six mois de service lors de l'anniversaire de la mise en place de ce régime en juillet 19–, soit de choisir un régime de retraite indépendant auquel l'entreprise contribuerait.

Horaires:
Les heures de bureau normales sont de 9h00 à 17h15 du lundi au vendredi avec une heure pour le déjeuner. Il se peut cependant que vous soyez parfois amené à travailler au-delà de ces horaires.

Différends et procédures disciplinaires:
Si vous avez quelques plaintes que ce soit vous devrez les soumettre soit au Secrétaire Général, soit au Directeur Général. Les problèmes de discipline seront réglés de la manière la plus équitable et juste possible.

Santé et Sécurité sur le lieu de travail:
Un exemplaire de la "Notification au Personnel" publié suivant la loi 1974 'Santé et sécurité au Travail' vous sera donné le jour de votre prise de fonction. L'acceptation du poste vous engage également à accepter et respecter ces consignes.

Date d'entrée en fonction:
Votre date d'entrée en fonction n'a toujours pas été déterminée. Nous serions heureux de la fixer avec vous dans les plus brefs délais.

Nous vous serions reconnaissants de bien vouloir nous faire parvenir votre acceptation de cette offre d'emploi et de nous retourner un exemplaire dûment signé de cette lettre.

Nous espérons que votre association à notre entreprise sera de longue durée, heureuse et pleine de succès.

Je vous prie d'agréer, Monsieur, l'assurance de mes meilleurs sentiments.

B. Foster,
Directeur Général.

Contract of employment

Dear

Following recent discussions we are pleased to offer you employment at our Company as Area Manager on the following terms and conditions:

Remuneration
Your salary will be £15,000 per annum plus commission on the basis we have already discussed with you. As with all our staff your salary will be paid monthly on the last Thursday in each month, your first review being in July 199-.

Notice
As with all our staff, you will be employed for an initial trial period of six months, during which time either you or we may terminate your appointment at any time upon giving seven days' notice in writing to each other. Provided that we are satisfied with your performance during the trial period, we will thereafter immediately confirm your appointment as a permanent member of our staff and the seven days' period of notice referred to above will be increased to one month.

Sickness Pay
During any reasonable absence for illness the Company, at its discretion, will make up the amount of your National Insurance Benefit to the equivalent of your normal salary, although this will be essentially relative to your length of service.

Holidays
Your normal paid holiday entitlement will be 20 working days in a full year, the holiday year running from January 1st to December 31st.

Car
We will provide you with a suitable Company car (cost circa £14,000), which is to be mainly for your business use but also for your private use. We will meet all normal running expenses associated with the car such as road tax, insurance, repairs, servicing and petrol.

Pensions
The Company operates a Pension Plan. You can either decide to join the Company Scheme after 6 months' service at the Scheme's next anniversary date (July 199-), or alternatively choose a Personal Pension Plan to which the Company would contribute.

Hours
Normal office hours are from 9.00 a.m. to 5.15 p.m. from Monday to Friday with one hour for lunch. However, it is probable that additional calls will be made upon your time.

Grievance and Disciplinary Procedure
Should you wish to seek redress for any grievance relating to your employment, you should refer, as appropriate, either to the Company Secretary or to the Managing Director. Matters involving discipline will be dealt with in as fair and equitable a manner as possible.

Health and Safety at Work Act
A copy of the Staff Notice issued under the Health & Safety at Work etc. Act 1974 will be given to you on the first day of employment. Your acceptance of the appointment will be deemed to constitute your willingness to comply with these regulations.

Start date
The date on which your employment by the Company is to start remains to be agreed by us. We look forward to establishing a mutually acceptable date with you as soon as possible.

Will you kindly provide us with your acceptance of this offer of employment by signing and returning to us the enclosed duplicate copy of this letter.

We trust that you will have a long, happy and successful association with our Company.

Yours sincerely

B. Foster
Managing Director

Rupture d'un contrat

CLIENT: Bon, voici le contrat d'achat dont vous désiriez discuter.

FOURNISSEUR: Oui, merci. Le paragraphe qui m'intéresse est celui-ci, 9b.

CLIENT: Y a-t-il un problème?

FOURNISSEUR: Il est dit que si nous ne livrons pas sous les trois jours après la date indiquée, il y aura rupture de contrat et que la commande sera annulée.

CLIENT: Cela fait partie des clauses normales de nos contrats. Cela vous créera-t-il un problème?

FOURNISSEUR: J'ai rarement vu cela.

CLIENT: Il a fallu que nous prenions ce genre de mesure car il nous est arrivé d'avoir beaucoup de problèmes avec des fournisseurs qui avaient jusqu'à plusieurs semaines de retard. Nous avons perdu des clients à cause de cela. Depuis que nous avons adopté cette nouvelle clause, nous avons eu beaucoup moins de problèmes au niveau des retards.

FOURNISSEUR: Serait il possible de la modifier un petit peu?

CLIENT: Dans quel sens?

FOURNISSEUR: Eh bien, je trouve que trois jours c'est un petit peu trop restrictif. Nous serions bien plus satisfaits s'il s'agissait d'une semaine.

CLIENT: Je n'en doute pas! Avez-vous des raisons particulières? Avez-vous déjà eu des difficultés à respecter les délais imposés?

FOURNISSEUR: Rarement, mais c'est arrivé. Et c'est généralement parce qu'un fournisseur n'a pas respecté les siens. J'aimerais que ce paragraphe soit un peu modifié, pour nous donner un peu plus de temps.

CLIENT: Laissez-moi en parler avec mon directeur. Je vous contacterai d'ici vingt-quatre heures.

FOURNISSEUR: Merci.

Breach of contract

CLIENT: Well, here we have the order contract that you wanted to discuss.

SUPPLIER: Yes, thanks. The paragraph I wanted to look at was this one, 9b.

CLIENT: Is there a problem?

SUPPLIER: It indicates that unless we deliver within three days of the date indicated we are in breach of contract, and the order can be cancelled.

CLIENT: That's part of our normal contract. Would you have a problem with that?

SUPPLIER: I find it a bit unusual.

CLIENT: We've had to introduce it, because in the past we had lots of problems with suppliers missing the delivery dates by weeks. We have lost customers because of that. Since we introduced this new clause we've had far fewer problems with delay.

SUPPLIER: Is it possible to vary it a little?

CLIENT: In what way?

SUPPLIER: Well, I find three days very restrictive. We'd be much happier with one week.

CLIENT: I'm sure you would! Any particular reason? Have you had difficulties meeting dates in the past?

SUPPLIER: Only rarely, but it does happen. And it's usually because a supplier has let us down. I'd like to modify that paragraph a bit, to give us a little more time.

CLIENT: Let me check it out with my manager. I'll get back to you in the next 24 hours.

SUPPLIER: Thanks.

Conditions de paiement

CLIENT: A quelle date voulez-vous que le règlement final soit effectué pour l'installation du nouveau matériel?

FOURNISSEUR: Il y a plusieurs contrats qui offrent un maximum de souplesse au niveau des conditions. Bien sûr, vous pouvez régler la somme d'un seul coup, ce qui vous permettrait de faire pas mal d'économies car comme vous le savez, les intérêts sont toujours élevés dans le domaine du transport.

CLIENT: Supposons que je puisse vous payer 50% du montant total dès maintenant, quel genre de contrat nous conviendrait le mieux, à vous tant qu'à moi, si l'on voulait échelonner la somme restante sur deux ans?

FOURNISSEUR: Cela dépend de la façon dont nous structurerions notre propre endettement; en principe il n'y a aucune raison pour que les règlements ne puissent pas être ajustés pour convenir à vos circonstances.

CLIENT: Très bien. Pouvez-vous me donner quelques jours pour discuter de tout cela avec mon comptable? Si la banque accepte de me prêter plus que je ne le pensais au départ, je pourrais peut-être faire cet achat comptant.

FOURNISSEUR: Pourquoi pas? Avec des taux d'intérêts généraux tels qu'ils sont il vaudrait peut-être la peine de risquer une grosse dépense. Mais souvenez-vous que quelle que soit votre décision, nous pouvons vous aider car nos propres finances sont garanties par notre société-mère.

CLIENT: Je vous remercie de m'avoir rassuré. Je vous ferai connaître ma décision dès que possible.

Payment conditions

CLIENT: When will I be required to complete the payment of the instalments on the new equipment?

SUPPLIER: There are several plans under which you have maximum flexibility of conditions. Obviously, you can pay the full amount in a one-off sum, which would mean a substantial saving overall as interest costs are always high in the transport sector.

CLIENT: Suppose I could pay you 50 per cent of the total cost now, what sort of arrangements would best suit us both for the other half over a couple of years?

SUPPLIER: That would depend on how we structure our own borrowing requirement, but in principle there is no reason why payments cannot be adjusted exactly to suit your circumstances.

CLIENT: Fine. Can you give me a few days to discuss this with my accountant? If the bank is willing to lend me more money than I had first thought, I may perhaps be able to pay you outright.

SUPPLIER: Why not? With general interest rates as they are it could be worth risking a big outlay. But remember that whatever your decision, we can help as our own finances are secured by the parent company.

CLIENT: Thanks for the reassurance. I'll let you know a.s.a.p.

Informer du désir d'intenter une action en justice

Francis Designs Ltd,
114 Bestwood Park,
West Hampstead,
London

Cabinet Rossignol,
4, rue des Glaïeuls,
75009 Paris,
France.

West Hampstead, le 24 mai 199-

A l'attention de Maître Patelin.

Cher Maître,

Votre nom nous a été communiqué par Robert Mackenzie de chez Canine Crunch Ltd pour qui vous avez travaillé l'année dernière.

Nous avons une plainte à formuler contre le journal *La Gazette du Samedi* qui nous a sérieusement diffamés dans l'article que nous joignons à cette lettre concernant la fermeture de notre usine de Roissy-en-France.

Nous désirons intenter une action en justice contre ledit journal mais nous aimerions tout d'abord avoir votre avis professionnel concernant la solidité de notre cas. Pourriez-vous également nous faire savoir la durée probable de cette action et nous donner une idée du montant des frais judiciaires que cette poursuite pourrait engendrer.

Vous en remerciant par avance, nous vous prions d'agréer, cher Maître, nos salutations distinguées.

Lionel E. Bone
Président Directeur Général

Considering legal action

Francis Designs Ltd
114 Bestwood Park
West Hampstead
London

Cabinet Rossignol
4 rue des Glaïeuls
75009 Paris
France

24 May 199-

For the attention of Maître Patelin

Dear Maître Patelin

Your name was given to us by Robert Mackenzie of Canine Crunch Ltd for whom you acted last year.

We have a complaint against the newspaper *La Gazette du Samedi* who have in our opinion seriously defamed us in the enclosed article dealing with the closure of our plant at Roissy-en-France.

We would wish to take legal action against the said newspaper but first would like to have your professional advice about the strength of our case. Could you also let us know how long the case might run and the likely scale of our legal costs.

Yours sincerely

Lionel E Bone
Managing Director

Contacter des organismes publics/Contacting official agencies

La Chambre de commerce

RC: Bonjour, Monsieur. Robert Cid de chez Textiles United.

AC: Enchanté de faire votre connaissance. Arthur Collin. Ma secrétaire m'a prévenu que vous alliez venir ce matin. Que puis-je faire pour vous?

RC: Nous pensons sérieusement à agrandir notre entreprise, et nous visons principalement le marché touchant les 'trente à cinquante ans'. On m'a conseillé de venir recueillir vos conseils quant à la meilleure localisation de nos magasins pour la vente de nos produits de mode.

AC: Eh bien, M. Cid, j'espère que vous adhérerez à la Chambre de Commerce lorsque votre société sera établie dans notre ville. En attendant, je me ferai effectivement un plaisir de vous aider.

RC: Oui, je comprends. Pour le moment, nous aimerions obtenir des renseignements d'ordre général, les chiffres de ventes réalisés dans la région, des informations concernant la concurrence, la population locale, les locaux actuellement disponibles et ainsi de suite.

AC: Il n'y a aucun problème. Nous pouvons vous procurer toutes ces informations et bien plus encore. Allez-vous créer de nouveaux emplois grâce à cette nouvelle initiative?

RC: Nous aurons inévitablement besoin de personnel tant à l'usine que dans les magasins. Avez-vous de bonnes relations avec l'ANPE?

AC: Oui, bien sûr. Mais, venez plutôt dans mon bureau. Nous boirons une tasse de café et discuterons affaires plus à notre aise.

Chamber of Commerce

RC: How do you do? I'm Robert Cid, from Textiles United.

AC: Pleased to meet you. Arthur Collin. My staff told me you were going to call in this morning. How can we help?

RC: We are thinking of expanding the business, especially to focus on the '30s to 50s' market. We were advised to seek your views on how and where best to establish retail outlets for our fashion products.

AC: Well, Mr Cid. I hope you will join the Chamber as and when you set up in the city, but for the time being you are welcome to our assistance.

RC: Yes, I understand, but right now we are keen to obtain some information on local retail figures, the competition, some data on the local population, available premises and so on.

AC: That's no problem. We can provide you with what you request and much more. Are you likely to be creating any jobs through your new initiative?

RC: We will inevitably need new staff, both in the factory and in the local shops. Do you happen to have a good contact at the Job Centre?

AC: Yes, of course. If you'd like to come through to my office, we'll have a coffee and get down to discussing things.

La douane

DOUANIER: Bonjour, Monsieur.

DÉTAILLANT: Bonjour, j'ai besoin de quelques renseignements concernant l'importation de produits à base de viande. Pouvez-vous m'aider?

DOUANIER: Bien sûr. Que voulez-vous exactement?

DÉTAILLANT: Nous vendons de la viande ici à Douvres et nous aimerions importer une sélection de viandes cuites et de saucisses qui nous viendraient d'un fournisseur allemand. Jusqu'à présent, nous étions approvisionnés par des fournisseurs britanniques. Je dois donc connaître les réglementations.

DOUANIER: C'est relativement complexe et difficile à expliquer brièvement. J'ai ici tout un tas de réglementations et de restrictions à respecter. Elles figurent toutes dans nos brochures d'information. Quand comptiez-vous importer ces produits?

DÉTAILLANT: Nous devrions recevoir notre première commande d'ici deux semaines.

DOUANIER: Il faut donc se dépêcher. Alors. Je vais rassembler ces informations pour vous. La meilleure chose à faire est de les lire et de nous contacter si vous avez d'autres questions.

DÉTAILLANT: Très bien. Je vais étudier cela de près.

Customs and Excise

CUSTOMS AND EXCISE OFFICER: Good morning, Sir.

RETAILER: Hello, I have a query regarding the import of meat.

CUSTOMS AND EXCISE OFFICER: Certainly. Can you explain?

RETAILER: We're a meat retailer based here in Dover, and we're intending to import a range of cooked meats and sausages from a German supplier. So far we've only been supplied by British companies. I need to know what the regulations are.

CUSTOMS AND EXCISE OFFICER: It's rather difficult and complex to explain briefly. There is a range of regulations and restrictions. They're contained in our information brochures. When are you intending to import these products?

RETAILER: We'll get the first shipment in a couple of weeks.

CUSTOMS AND EXCISE OFFICER: Then you'd better move fast. I'll collect all the information for you. The best thing is for you to read it and then come back to us with any queries.

RETAILER: Fine. I'll get down to it.

Se faire excuser de ne pas pouvoir assister/Apologizing for non-attendance

A une réunion ultérieure

NADINE RICHARD: Allô, Nadine Richard à l'appareil.

BERNARD PÉGUY: Bonjour Nadine. C'est Bernard Péguy.

NADINE RICHARD: Bonjour Bernard, comment allez-vous?

BERNARD PÉGUY: Très bien, merci. Je viens juste d'apprendre qu'il y aura une réunion pour le service commercial mardi.

NADINE RICHARD: Oui. Y a-t-il un problème?

BERNARD PÉGUY: Oui, j'en ai peur. Il faudra que vous m'excusiez mais je me suis déjà engagé et dois me rendre à un salon professionnel.

NADINE RICHARD: D'accord. Je transmettrai. Quelqu'un d'autre pourrait-il-vous représenter?

BERNARD PÉGUY: J'ai une collègue qui pourrait probablement venir. Il s'agit de Suzanne Roger. Elle vous contactera plus tard dans la journée.

NADINE RICHARD: Très bien. Bon, faites bon voyage. Je vous verrai lors de votre retour.

At a future meeting

NANCY RICHARDS: Nancy Richards.

BILL PERKINS: Morning, Nancy. Bill Perkins here.

NANCY RICHARDS: Hello, Bill, how are you?

BILL PERKINS: Fine thanks. Look, I've just received notice of the meeting for the Sales Department next Tuesday.

NANCY RICHARDS: Yes, is there a problem?

BILL PERKINS: Afraid so. I'll have to send my apologies. I've already committed to a trade fair trip.

NANCY RICHARDS: OK. I'll pass on your apologies. Can you send someone else?

BILL PERKINS: I've a colleague who can probably come. Her name is Susie Rogerson. She'll contact you later today.

NANCY RICHARDS: Fine. Well, have a nice trip. I'll see you when you get back.

A une réunion qui a déjà eu lieu

GEORGE POISSON: Pourriez-vous me passer le directeur général s'il vous plaît?

SECRÉTAIRE: Bien sûr, Monsieur. Veuillez patienter quelques instants s'il vous plaît.

HENRI SACHS: Bonjour Georges. Tu nous as manqué hier.

GEORGE POISSON: Je te demande de m'excuser. Je n'ai pas écrit car je pensais vraiment pouvoir venir mais j'ai eu un empêchement de dernière minute.

HENRI SACHS: J'ai cru comprendre que le Golfe est à la source de quelques soucis.

GEORGE POISSON: Ah, tu es au courant. Les mauvaises nouvelles se répandent vite. Oui, nous avons un porte-conteneurs en route, et il y a rumeur de guerre à destination.

HENRI SACHS: Que vas-tu faire? L'envoyer ailleurs temporairement?

GEORGE POISSON: Oui mais ne t'inquiète pas. Je résoudrai ce problème. Et pour toi, comment s'est passée ta soirée?

HENRI SACHS: Très bien. Thierry Maréchal du Ministère m'a demandé de tes nouvelles. Je lui ai dit que tu lui passerais un coup de fil.

GEORGE POISSON: Je le ferai. Je suis vraiment désolé ne pas avoir pu venir.

At a meeting that has already been held

GEORGE PARSONS: Could you put me through to the Managing Director please.

SECRETARY: Certainly, sir. One moment please.

HENRY SACHS: Hello, George. We missed you yesterday.

GEORGE PARSONS: I am calling to apologize. I didn't write because I intended to come and was prevented at the last moment.

HENRY SACHS: I gather there's a spot of bother in the Gulf.

GEORGE PARSONS: Oh, you've heard. Bad news travels fast. Yes, we have a container ship on its way and rumours of war at its destination.

HENRY SACHS: What will you do? Send it somewhere else pro tem?

GEORGE PARSONS: Yes, but don't worry – I'll sort it out. Meanwhile how did your 'do' go?

HENRY SACHS: Very well. All the important people came. Barry Clerkenwell from the BOTB was asking for you. I said you'd give him a bell.

GEORGE PARSONS: Will do. I'm really sorry that I couldn't make it.

Titres de fonction employés dans le domaine commercial/Job titles used in commerce

en France/*in France*	au Royaume-Uni et aux États-Unis/*in the UK and US*
administrateur *m* [-trice] *f*	administrator
administrateur chargé du développement	development director
administrateur commercial	commercial director
administrateur externe	outside director, non-executive director
administrateur général	general administrator
administrateur non-dirigeant	nonexecutive director
agent *m*	
agent administratif	administration officer
agent commercial	sales representative
agent d'enquête	investigation officer
agent de maîtrise	first-line manager, first-line supervisor, supervisor
agent de transportation routière	motor transport officer
animateur de groupe *m* [-trice] *f*	group leader
associé *m* [-e] *f*	shareholder, member (*US*: shareholder, stockholder)
associé gérant *m*	managing partner
cadre *m*	
cadre chargé des contrats	training officer
cadre chargé de la formation	contracts officer
cadre commercial	commercial manager, sales executive
cadre en formation	trainee manager
cadre hiérarchique	line manager
cadre à l'information	information officer
cadre moyen	middle manager
cadre supérieur	executive officer, top executive, chief exective, senior executive, senior manager
chargé du marketing *mf*	marketing officer
chargé de la mercatique *mf*	marketing officer
chef *mf*	manager
chef d'approvisionnement	procurement manager, chief buyer, head buyer
chef d'atelier	head foreman, first-line manager
chef de bureau	office manager, chief clerk, senior clerk, head clerk
chef de bureau des exportations	senior export clerk
chef de bureau des importations	senior import clerk
chef de cabinet	chief of staff
chef de chantier	site foreman
chef de la circulation	traffic superintendent, traffic manager
chef de département	division manager, divisional manager, divisional head, department head, departmental head
chef du département juridique	head of legal department, *US* general counsel
chef direct	line manager
chef de division	division manager
chef d'équipe	charge hand, team leader, foreman
chef d'établissement	works manager, plant manager
chef de fabrication	production manager, production director
chef hiérarchique	line manager
chef du personnel	personnel manager, personnel director, staff manager
chef de production	production director, production manager
chef de produit	brand manager, product manager
chef de projet	project leader, project manager
chef de publicité	advertising director, advertising manager, agency representative, publicity manager, *chez un annonceur, agence de RP* account manager, account executive
chef de région	regional manager, territory manager, area manager
chef de service	chief operating officer, departmental manager, departmental head

en France/*in France*	au Royaume-Uni et aux États-Unis/*in the UK and US*
chef du service consommateurs	consumer relations manager
chef du service personnel	head of the personnel department, personnel director, staff manager, personnel manager
chef du service publicité	publicity manager, advertising director
chef du service des réclamations	claims manager
chef du service des relations publiques	director of public relations, public relations officer
chef du service de renseignements	information officer
chef du service des ventes	sales manager
chef de terrain	field sales manager
chef d'unité adjoint	assistant head of section *UK*
co-directeur *m* [-trice] *f*	joint director, co-manager, joint manager, co-director
co-gérant *m* [-e] *f*	joint manager
commanditaire *mf*	limited partner (*in limited partnership*)
commandité *m* [-e] *f*	general partner (*in limited partnership*)
commis principal, *m*	senior clerk, chief clerk
contremaître *m* [-esse] *f*	overseer
contrôleur des transports, [-euse] *m,f*	transport controller
coordinateur des exportations *m* [-trice] *f*	export coordinator
co-propriétaire *mf*	co-owner, joint owner
directeur *m* [-trice] *f*	director, manager, manageress
directeur des achats	purchasing manager, chief buyer, head buyer
directeur adjoint	deputy director, deputy manager *US*, assistant manager, assistant director
directeur des affaires sociales	director of labour relations *BrE*, director of labor relations *AmE*
directeur artistique	art manager, artistic director
directeur chargé des contrats	contracts manager
directeur commercial	commercial manager, marketing director, marketing manager, merchandising director, sales manager
directeur commercial et du développement	commercial and development manager
directeur de département	department head
directeur du développement	development manager
directeur de division	division head
directeur exécutif	executive director, executive manager
directeur des exportations	export director, export manager
directeur de fabrication	production director, production manager
directeur financier	chief financial officer, financial manager, financial director
directeur de formation	training officer
directeur général	chief executive, chief executive officer *US*, director-general, executive manager, general manager, managing director
directeur général adjoint	assistant general director, deputy chief executive, assistant director general, assistant general manager, deputy managing director
directeur hiérarchique	line manager
directeur des importations	import manager
directeur de marketing	marketing manager, marketing director
directeur marketing des exportations	export marketing manager
directeur des opérations	operations manager, operational manager
directeur du parc automobile	fleet manager
directeur de produit	product manager
directeur de projet	project manager
directeur de la publicité	advertising manager, advertising director, publicity manager
directeur régional de la formation professionnelle	district training officer
directeur des relations avec la clientèle	consumer relations manager, customer relations manager
directeur des relations humaines	industrial relations manager, industrial relations director
directeur des relations industrielles	industrial relations manager, industrial relations director

en France/*in France*	au Royaume-Uni et aux États-Unis/*in the UK and US*
directeur des relations professionelles	industrial relations manager, industrial relations director
directeur des relations publiques	director of public relations, public relations officier
directeur du service après-ventes	after-sales manager
directeur du service des ventes	circulation manager
directeur technique	production manager, production director, engineering manager, technical manager, technical director
directeur des transports	traffic manager, traffic superintendent
directeur d'usine	works manager, plant manager
directeur des ventes	sales manager
directeur des ventes-clientèle	field sales manager
directeur de ventes intérieures	indoor sales manager
directeur de ventes sédentaires	indoor sales manager
dirigeant *m* [-e] *f*	manager, manageress, director
dirigeant opérationnel	line executive
enquêteur *m* [-euse, -trice] *f*	investigation officer
gérant *m*, [-e] *f*	manager, manageress, managing director, *US: limited companies* general manager, administrator
gestionnaire *mf*	manager, manageress, administrator
gestionnaire de l'actif	asset manager
ingénieur *m*	
ingénieur commercial	sales engineer
inspecteur *m* [-trice] *f*	inspector
inspecteur en chef	chief inspector
inspecteur des documents d'importation	import documentation supervisor
inspecteur du mouvement	traffic supervisor
inspecteur des plaintes	claims inspector
inspecteur principal	chief inspector
jeune cadre *m*	junior manager, junior manageress
manager *m*	manager
mandataire *mf*	authorized representative
membre *m*	
membre du conseil de surveillance	*in PLCs** member of the supervisory board
membre du directoire	*in PLCs** member of the board of management
membre suppléant du directoire	*in PLCs** deputy member of the board of management
officier *m*	
officier supérieur	senior officer
patron *m*	
patron directeur	owner-manager
premier commis	head clerk
président *m* [-e] *f*	chair, chairman, chairperson, chairwoman
président du comité executif	chairman of the executive committee
président du conseil	chairman of the board
président du conseil d'administration	chairman, *in associations in* chairman of the board of directors
président du conseil de surveillance	*in PLCs** chairman of the supervisory board
président-directeur général	chairman of the board of management, chief executive officer *US*, chairman and chief executive *US*, chairman of the administrative board, chairman of the board of directors, president, chairman and managing director *UK*, managing director *UK*

en France/*in France*	au Royaume-Uni et aux États-Unis/*in the UK and US*
président du directoire	chairman of the board of management
président d'honneur	honorary president, honorary chairman, *in associations only* honorary chairman of the board of directors
propriétaire *mf*	
propriétaire exploitant	proprietor
représentant *m* [-e] *f*	sales representative
responsable *mf*	manager, manageress
responsable des achats	purchasing officer, chief buyer, head buyer
responsable administratif	administration officer
responsable de conformité aux règlements	registered manager
responsable financier	cash manager, chief financial officer, financial director, financial manager
responsable de la formation professionnelle	training officer
responsable national du budget	national accounts manager
responsable opérationnel	line manager
responsable régional	district officer
responsable des relations publiques	director of public relations, public relations officer
responsable du service de presse	press officer
responsable des stocks	stock controller, inventory controller
responsable supérieur	senior vice president
responsable du trafic	traffic executive
responsable des transports motorisés	motor transport officer
responsable des ventes d'importation	import sales executive
secrétaire *mf*	
secrétaire de direction	personal secretary, personal assistant, executive secretary
secrétaire général	company secretary, general secretary
secrétaire particulier	private secretary, personal secretary, executive secretary
secrétaire privée	confidential secretary, private secretary
sous-directeur *m* [-trice] *f*	deputy manager, deputy director, junior manager, submanager
surveillant *m* [-e] *f*	supervisor
surveillant de circulation	traffic superintendent
surveillant de premier niveau	first-line manager, first-line supervisor
technico-commercial *m* [-e] *f*	sales engineer
trésorier *m* [-ière] *f*	cash manager
trésorier-payeur général	paymaster general *UK*, treasurer
vérificateur des crédits *m* [-trice] *f*	credit controller
vice-président *m* [-e] *f*	executive vice president, deputy chairman, vice-chairman, vice president
vice-président du conseil de surveillance	*in PLCs** deputy chairman of the supervisory board
vice-président du directoire	*in PLCs** deputy chairman of the board of management
voyageur de commerce *m* [-euse] *f*	sales representative, commercial traveler *AmE*, traveling salesperson *AmE*, commercial traveller *BrE*, travelling salesperson *BrE*

* US stock corporations

Bourses des marchés et des valeurs/Stock exchanges

nom français/ *French name*	pays, ville/ *country, city*	nom anglais/ *English name*
	la France/ ***France***	
Bourse de Bordeaux *f*	Bordeaux	Bordeaux Stock Exchange
Bourse de Lille *f*	Lille	Lille Stock Exchange
Bourse de Lyon *f*	Lyon	Lyon Stock Exchange
Bourse des marchés financiers à terme de Paris *f*	Paris	Paris Financial Futures Exchange
Bourse de Marseille *f*	Marseille	Marseille Stock Exchange
Bourse de Nancy *f*	Nancy	Nancy Stock Exchange
Bourse de Nantes *f*	Nantes	Nantes Stock Exchange
Bourse de Paris *f*	Paris	Paris Stock Exchange
Marché des options négociables de Paris *m*	Paris	Paris Trader Options Exchange
	la Suisse/ ***Switzerland***	
Bourse de Bâle *f*	Bâle	Basle Stock Exchange
Bourse de Berne *f*	Berne	Berne Stock Exchange
Bourse de Genève *f*	Genève	Geneva Stock Exchange
Bourse de Lausanne *f*	Lausanne	Lausanne Stock Exchange
Bourse de Neuchâtel *f*	Neuchâtel	Neuchâtel Stock Exchange
Bourse des options et valeurs à terme suisse *f*	Zürich	Swiss Options and Financial Futures Exchange
Bourse de St. Gall *f*	St. Gall	St. Gall Stock Exchange
Bourse de Zürich *f*	Zürich	Zurich Stock Exchange
	le Royaume-Uni/ ***UK***	
Bourse internationale financière à terme de Londres *f*	Londres	London International Financial Futures Exchange
Bourse de Londres *f*	Londres	International Stock Exchange (also London Stock Exchange)
Bourse de marchés à terme et options de Londres *f*	Londres	London Futures and Options Exchange
Bourse des matières premières de Londres *f*	Londres	London Commodity Exchange
Bourse des métaux de Londres *f*	Londres	London Metal Exchange
Bourse des options négociables de Londres *f*	Londres	London Trader Options Exchange
Marché à terme baltique *m*	Londres	Baltic Futures Exchange
Marché de valeurs non-cotées *m*	Londres	Unlisted Securities Market
	les États-Unis/ ***USA***	
Amex (marché financier secondaire de New York) *m*	New York	American Stock Exchange
Bourse de Boston *f*	Boston	Boston Stock Exchange
Bourse du café, du sucre et du cacao de New York *f*	New York	New York Coffee, Sugar and Cocoa Exchange
Bourse des céréales de Minnéapolis *f*	Minnéapolis	Minneapolis Grain Exchange
Bourse du commerce de l'Amex *f*	New York	Amex Commodity Exchange
Bourse du commerce de Chicago *f*	Chicago	Chicago Mercantile Exchange
Bourse de commerce de New York *f*	New York	New York Mercantile Exchange
Bourse du commerce de la Nouvelle Orléans *f*	Nouvelle Orléans	New Orleans Commodity Exchange
Bourse des marchandises de Chicago *f*	Chicago	Mid-America Commodity Exchange

nom français/ *French name*	pays, ville/ *country, city*	nom anglais/*English name*
Bourse du Midwest *f*	Chicago	Chicago Stock Exchange (Midwest Stock Exchange)
Bourse de New York *f*	New York	New York Stock Exchange
	les États-Unis/ *USA*	
Bourse des options de Chicago *f*	Chicago	Chicago Board Options Exchange
Bourse de Philadelphie *f*	Philadelphie	Philadelphia Stock Exchange
Marché hors cote de New York *m*	New York	New York Curb Exchange
	Canada/ **Canada**	
Bourse de Toronto *f*	Toronto	Toronto Stock Exchange

Indices financiers et économiques/Financial and economic indexes

domaine/ area	indice/*index*	traduction/explication *translation/explanation*	étendue/ *coverage*
AC	indice des prix *m*	price index	générale
AC	indice des prix à la consommation *m*	consumer price index	générale
EC	balance commerciale *f*	balance of trade	générale
EC	dépenses de l'État *mpl*	national expenditure	générale
EC	indice composé/indice composite *m*	composite index	générale
EC	indice du coût de la vie *m*	cost-of-living index	générale
EC	indice de croissance *m*	growth index	générale
EC	indice de diffusion *m*	diffusion index	générale
EC	indice d'inconfort *m*	discomfort index	générale
EC	indice de Laspeyre *m*	Laspeyre's index	générale
EC	indice de Lerner *m*	Lerner index	générale
EC	indice de Paasche *m*	Paasche index	générale
EC	indice des prix *m*	price index	générale
EC	indice des prix à la consommation *m*	consumer price index	générale
EC	indice des prix de détail *m*	retail price index	générale
EC	indice des prix de gros *m*	wholesale price index	générale
EC	indice des prix à la production *m*	producer price index	générale
EC	indice de rareté *m*	scarcity index	générale
EC	indice de traitement *m*	salary grade	générale
EC	indice des valeurs unitaires *m*	unit value index	générale
EC	masse monétaire *f*	Divisia Money index	internationale
EC	produit national brut *m*	gross national product	générale
EC	produit national net *m*	net national product	générale
EC	revenu national brut *m*	gross national income	générale
EC	revenu national net *m*	net national income	générale
EC	salaire individuel *m*	income per capita	générale
EC	taux de chômage *n inv*	unemployment rate	générale
EC	taux d'inflation *m inv*	rate of inflation	générale
FI	indice composé/indice composite *m*	composite index	générale
FI	indice des indicateurs à courte durée *m*	index of shorter leading indicators	générale
FI	indice des indicateurs à longue durée *m*	index of longer leading indicators	générale
FI	indice des prix *m*	price index	générale
FI	indice des indicateurs retardés d'activité *m*	index of lagging indicators	générale
FI	indice des indicateurs simultanés *m*	index of coincident indicators	générale
FI	indice des indicateurs de tête *m*	index of leading indicators	générale
GC	indice pondéré *m*	weighted index	générale
GC	indice des prix de détail *m*	retail price index	générale
IND	indice des principales valeurs industrielles *m*	Thirty-Share Index	Royaume-Uni
IND	indice de production industrielle *m*	Index of Industrial Production	Royaume-Uni
ST	indice des actions *m*, indice des cours des actions *m*	share index, stock exchange, price index	générale
ST	indice des actions industrielles ordinaires du Financial Times *m*	Financial Times Industrial Ordinary Share index	Royaume-Uni
ST	indice de Barron *m*	Barron's confidence index	États-Unis
ST	indice des bons du trésor du Marché monétaire international *m*	International Monetary Market Treasury-bill index	internationale
ST	indice de la Bourse néo-zélandaise *m*	Barclays Index	Nouvelle Zélande
ST	indice boursier *m*	stock price index, stock market price index	générale
ST	indice boursier de la Bourse de Helsinki *m*	Unitas All Share index	Finlande

domaine/ area	indice/*index*	traduction/explication *translation/explanation*	étendue/ *coverage*
ST	indice boursier mondial Morgan Stanley *m*	Morgan Stanley Capital International World index	internationale
ST	indices boursiers *m*	stock indexes and averages	générale
ST	indice boursier "value line" *m*	Value Line Stock index	États-Unis
ST	indice des certificats de dépôt du Marché monétaire international *m*	International Monetary Market Certificate of Deposit index	internationale
ST	indice Comit *m*	Comit index	Italie
ST	indice composé de la bourse de New York *m*	New York Stock Exchange Composite index	États-Unis
ST	indice composite principal *m*	composite leading index	générale
ST	indice composite "value line" *m*	Value Line Composite index	États-Unis
ST	indice du coût de la construction *m*	construction cost index	générale
ST	indice du Crédit suisse *m*	Credit Suisse index	Suisse
ST	indice de décompte trimestriel du Marché monétaire international *m*	International Monetary Market Three-Month Discount index	internationale
ST	indice Donoghue des fonds monétaires *m*	Donoghue's Money Fund average	internationale
ST	indice Dow Jones *m*	Dow-Jones index	États-Unis
ST	indice de l'eurodollar *m*	Eurodollar Index	Europe
ST	indice du Financial Times *m*	Financial Times index (FT index)	Royaume-Uni
ST	indice du Financial Times et de l'Institut d'Actuaires *m*	Financial Times Actuaries All Share index (All Share index)	Royaume-Uni
ST	indice FTSE 100 *m*, indice des FTSE 100 valeurs *m*, indice Footsie *m*	Financial Times Stock Exchange index, FT-SE 100 Share index, Footsie	Royaume-Uni
ST	indice FTSE eurotrack des 100 européennes *m*	FT-SE Eurotrack 100 index	Europe
ST	indice FTSE eurotrack des 200 valeurs européennes *m*	FT-SE Eurotrack 200 index	Europe
ST	indice des grandes valeurs *m*, indice des indicateurs de tête *m*	index of leading indicators	générale
ST	indice Hang Seng *m*, indice Hong Kong *m*	Hang Seng index	Hong-Kong
ST	indice des marchandises *m*	commodities index	générale
ST	indice du Marché principal *m*	Major Market index	générale
ST	indice des métaux précieux *m*	golds index	générale
ST	indice mondial des bourses de valeurs *m*	Capital International World Index	internationale
ST	indice moyen des services publics *m*	utility average	générale
ST	indice Nikkei *m*	Nikkei index, Nikkei average	Japon
ST	indice des obligations *m*	bond index	générale
ST	indice pondéré *m*	weighted index	générale
ST	indice pondéré des cours *m*, indice pondéré par les prix *m*	price-weighted index	générale
ST	indice pondéré de valeur marchande *m*, indice pondéré par la capitalisation boursière *m*	market value-weighted index	générale
ST	indice des principales valeurs de la bourse d'Amsterdam *m*	CBS Tendency Index	Pays-Bas
ST	indice des principales valeurs industrielles *m*	Thirty-Share index	Royaume-Uni
ST	indice de toutes les actions ordinaires *m*	All Ordinaries Index	Australie
ST	Rajout trimestriel à l'indice du Marché monétaire international *m*	International Monetary Market Three-Month Add-On index	internationale

domaine/ indice/*index*	traduction/explication	étendue/
area	*translation/explanation*	*coverage*
WE indice du coût de la vie *m*	cost-of-living index	générale

Légende/*Key*

AC: Accountancy   EC: Economics
FI: Finance   IND: Industry
ST: Stock Market   WE: Welfare

Les pays/Countries

pays/ *country*	capitale/ *capital*	habitant/ *inhabitant*	langue/s officielle/s *official language/s*	devise/ *currency*
Afghanistan *m*	Kaboul	Afghan *m*, [-e], *f*	pushtou/dari	afghani *m*
Afghanistan	*Kabul*	*Afghan*	*Pushtu/Dari*	*afghani*
Afrique du Sud *f*	Pretoria	Sud-Africain *m* [-e] *f*	afrikaans/anglais	rand *m*
South Africa	*Pretoria*	*South African*	*Afrikaans/ English*	*rand*
Albanie *f*	Tirana	Albanais *m*, [-e] *f*	albanais	lek *m*
Albania	*Tirana*	*Albanian*	*Albanian*	*lek*
Algérie *f*	Alger	Algérien *m*, [-enne] *f*	arabe/français	dinar *m*
Algeria	*Algiers*	*Algerian*	*Arabic/French*	*dinar*
Allemagne *f*	Berlin	Allemand *m*, [-e] *f*	allemand	deutsche mark *m*
Germany	*Berlin*	*German*	*German*	*Deutsche Mark*
Andorre *f*	Andorre-la- Vieille	Andorran *m*, [-e] *f*	catalan/français/ espagnol	franc français *m*/ peseta *f*
Andorra	*Andorra la Vella*	*Andorran*	*Catalan/French/ Spanish*	*French franc/peseta*
Angleterre *f*	Londres	Anglais *m*, [-e] *f*	anglais	livre sterling *f*
England	*London*	*Englishman/woman*	*English*	*pound sterling*
Angola *m*	Luanda	Angolais *m*, [-e] *f*	portugais	kwanza *m*
Angola	*Luanda*	*Angolan*	*Portuguese*	*kwanza*
Antigua *f*	Saint-Jean	d'Antigua	anglais	dollar antillais *m*
Antigua and Barbuda	*St. John's Saint-John's*	*Antiguan/Barbudian*	*English*	*East Caribbean dollar*
Arabie Saoudite *f*	Riyad/Riad	Saoudien *m*, [-enne] *f*	arabe	riyal *m*
Saudi Arabia	*Riyadh*	*Saudi/Saudi Arabian*	*Arabic*	*riyal*
Argentine *f*	Buenos Aires	Argentin *m*, [-e] *f*	espagnol	austral *m*
Argentina	*Buenos Aires*	*Argentinian/Argentine*	*Spanish*	*austral*
Arménie *f*	Erevan	Arménien *m*, [-enne] *f*	arménien	rouble/ruble *m*
Armenia	*Yerevan*	*Armenian*	*Armenian*	*rouble*
Australie *f*	Canberra	Australien *m*, [-enne] *f*	anglais	dollar australien *m*
Australia	*Canberra*	*Australian*	*English*	*Australian dollar*
Autriche *f*	Vienne	Autrichien *m*, [-enne] *f*	allemand	schilling *m*
Austria	*Vienna*	*Austrian*	*German*	*schilling*
Azerbaïdjan *m*	Bakou	Azeri/Azerbaïdjanais *m*, [-e] *f*	azeri/russe	manat *m*
Azerbaijan	*Baku*	*Azeri/Azerbaijani*	*Azeri/Russian*	*manat*
Bahamas *f pl*	Nassau	des Bahamas	anglais	dollar des Bahamas *m*
Bahamas	*Nassau*	*Bahamian*	*English*	*Bahamian dollar*
Bahreïn *m*	Manama	Bahreïni *m*, [-e] *f*	arabe	dinar *m*
Bahrain	*Manama*	*Bahraini*	*Arabic*	*dinar*
Bangladesh *m*	Dacca	Bangladeshi, Bangladais *m* [-e] *f*	bengali	takka *m*
Bangladesh	*Dhaka*	*Bangladeshi*	*Bengali*	*taka*
Barbade *f*	Bridgetown	Barbadien *m*, [-enne] *f*	anglais	dollar de Barbade *m*
Barbados	*Bridgetown*	*Barbadian*	*English*	*Barbados dollar*
Belgique *f*	Bruxelles	Belge *mf*	français/flamand	franc belge *m*
Belgium	*Brussels*	*Belgian*	*French/Flemish*	*Belgian franc*
Bélize *m*	Belmopan	Bélizien *m*, [-enne] *f*	anglais/espagnol/ créole	dollar de Bélize *m*
Belize	*Belmopan*	*Belizean*	*English/Spanish/ Creole*	*Belize dollar*

pays/ *country*	capitale/ *capital*	habitant/ *inhabitant*	langue/s officielle/s *official language/s*	devise/ *currency*
Bermudes *f pl*	Hamilton	Bermudien *m* [-enne] *f*	anglais	dollar (dol.) *m*
Bermuda	*Hamilton*	*Bermudan/Bermudian*	*English*	*dollar (dol.)*
Bénin *m*	Porto Novo	Béninois *m*, [-e] *f*	français	franc CFA *m*
Benin	*Porto Novo*	*Beninese*	*French*	*C.F.A. franc*
Bhoutan *m*	Thimbu	Bhoutanais *m*, [-e] *f*	dzongka	ngultrum *m*/roupie de l'Inde *f*
Bhutan	*Thamphu*	*Bhutanese/Bhutani*	*Dzongka*	*ngultrum/Indian rupee*
Biélorussie *f*	Minsk	Biélorusse *mf*	biélorusse	rouble biélorusse *m*
Belarus	*Minsk*	*Belarussian*	*Belarussian*	*Belarussian rouble*
Birmanie *f*	Rangoon	Birman *m*, [-e] *f*	birman	kyat *m*
Burma	*Rangoon*	*Burmese*	*Burmese*	*kyat*
Birmanie *f*	Yangon (Rangoon)	Birman *m*, [-e] *f*	birman	kyat *m*
Myanmar	*Yangon (Rangoon)*	*Burmese*	*Burmese*	*kyat*
Bolivie *f*	La Paz	Bolivien *m*, [-enne] *f*	espagnol, langues indiennes	peso bolivien *m*
Bolivia	*La Paz*	*Bolivian*	*Spanish, Indian languages*	*Bolivian peso*
Bosnie-Herzégovine *f*	Sarajevo	Bosniaque *mf* Bosnien *m*, [-enne] *f*	serbo-croate	dinar *m*
Bosnia-Herzegovina	*Sarajevo*	*Bosnian*	*Serbo-Croat*	*dinar*
Botswana *m*	Gaborone	du Botswana	anglais/tswana	pula *m*
Botswana	*Gaborone*	*Botswanan*	*English/Setswana*	*pula*
Brésil *m*	Brasilia	Brésilien *m*, [-enne] *f*	portugais	cruzeiro *m*
Brazil	*Brasilia*	*Brazilian*	*Portuguese*	*cruzeiro*
Brunei *m*	Bandar Seri Begawan	du Brunei	malais/anglais	dollar du Brunei *m*
Brunei	*Bandar Seri Begawan*	*Brunei/Bruneian*	*Malay/English*	*Brunei dollar*
Bulgarie *f*	Sofia	Bulgare *mf*	bulgare	lev *m*
Bulgaria	*Sofia*	*Bulgarian*	*Bulgarian*	*lev*
Burkina Faso *m*	Ouagadougou	du Burkina Faso	français/mossi	franc CFA *m*
Burkina Faso	*Ouagadougou*	*Burkinabe*	*French/Mossi*	*C.F.A. franc*
Burundi *m*	Bujumbura	Burundais *m*, [-e] *f*	kirundi/français	franc du Burundi *m*
Burundi	*Bujumbura*	*Burundian*	*Kirundi/French*	*Burundi franc*
Cambodge *m*	Phnom Penh	Cambodgien *m*, [-enne] *f*	khmer	riel *m*
Cambodia	*Phnom Penh*	*Cambodian*	*Khmer*	*riel*
Cameroun *m*	Yaoundé	Camerounais *m*, [-e] *f*	français/anglais	franc CFA *m*
Cameroon	*Yaoundé*	*Cameroonian*	*French/English*	*C.F.A. franc*
Canada *m*	Ottawa	Canadien *m*, [-enne] *f*	anglais/français	dollar canadien *m*
Canada	*Ottawa*	*Canadian*	*English/French*	*Canadian dollar*
Chili *m*	Santiago	Chilien *m*, [-enne] *f*	espagnol	peso *m*
Chile	*Santiago*	*Chilean*	*Spanish*	*peso*
Chine *f*	Pékin (Beijing)	Chinois *m*, [-e] *f*	mandarin/chinois	yuan *m*
China	*Beijing (Peking)*	*Chinese*	*Mandarin/Chinese*	*yuan*
Chypre *f*	Nicosie	Cypriote/Chypriote *mf*	grec/turc	livre chypriote *f*
Cyprus	*Nicosia*	*Cypriot*	*Greek/Turkish*	*Cyprus pound*
Colombie *f*	Bogotá	Colombien *m*, [-enne] *f*	espagnol	peso *m*
Colombia	*Bogotá*	*Colombian*	*Spanish*	*peso*

pays/ country	capitale/ capital	habitant/ inhabitant	langue/s officielle/s official language/s	devise/ currency
Comores *f pl* *Comoros*	Moroni *Moroni*	Comorien *m*, [-enne] *f* *Comorian/Comoran*	français/arabe *French/Arabic*	franc comorien *m* *Comorian franc*
Congo *m* *Congo*	Brazzaville *Brazzaville*	Congolais *m*, [-e] *f* *Congolese*	français *French*	franc CFA *m* *C.F.A. franc*
Corée du Nord *f* *Korea, North*	Pyongyang *Pyongyang*	Nord-Coréen *m*, [-enne] *f* *North Korean*	coréen *Korean*	won *m* *won*
Corée du Sud *f* *Korea, South*	Séoul *Seoul*	Sud-Coréen *m*, [-enne] *f* *South Korean*	coréen *Korean*	won *m* *won*
Costa Rica *m* *Costa Rica*	San José *San José*	Costaricain *m*, [-e] *f* *Costa Rican*	espagnol *Spanish*	colón *m* *colón*
Côte d'Ivoire *f* *Côte d'Ivoire*	Yamoussoukro *Yamoussoukro*	Ivoirien *m*, [-enne] *f* *Ivorian*	français *French*	franc CFA *m* *C.F.A. franc*
Croatie *f* *Croatia*	Zagreb *Zagreb*	Croate *mf* *Croat/Croatian*	serbo-croate *Serbo-Croat*	kuna *m* *kuna*
Cuba *f* *Cuba*	La Havane *Havana*	Cubain *m*, [-e] *f* *Cuban*	espagnol *Spanish*	peso cubain *m* *Cuban peso*
Danemark *m* *Denmark*	Copenhague *Copenhagen*	Danois *m*, [-e] *f* *Dane*	danois *Danish*	krone danoise *f* *Danish krone*
Djibouti *m* *Djibouti*	Djibouti *Djibouti*	Djiboutien *m*, [-enne] *f* *Djibuti/Djibutian*	arabe/français *Arabic/French*	franc de Djibouti *m* *Djibouti franc*
Dominique *f* *Dominica*	Roseau *Roseau*	Dominicain *m*, [-e] *f* *Dominican*	anglais *English*	dollar antillais *m* *East Caribbean dollar*
Écosse *f* *Scotland*	Édimbourg *Edinburgh*	Écossais *m*, [-e] *f* *Scot, Scotsman/-woman*	anglais *English*	livre sterling *f* *pound sterling*
Égypte *f* *Egypt*	Le Caire *Cairo*	Égyptien *m*, [-enne] *f* *Egyptian*	arabe *Arabic*	livre égyptienne *f* *Egyptian pound*
Émirats Arabes Unis *m pl* *United Arab Emirates*	Abou-Dhabi *Abu Dhabi*	des Émirats Arabes Unis *from the United Arab Emirates*	arabe *Arabic*	dirham *m* *dirham*
Équateur *m* *Ecuador*	Quito *Quito*	Équadorien *m*, [-enne] *f* *Ecuadorian/Ecuadoran*	espagnol *Spanish*	sucre *m* *sucre*
Espagne *f* *Spain*	Madrid *Madrid*	Espagnol *m*, [-e] *f* *Spaniard*	espagnol *Spanish*	peseta *f* *peseta*
Estonie *f* *Estonia*	Tallinn *Tallinn*	Estonien *m*, [-enne] *f* *Estonian*	estonien *Estonian*	kroon *f* *kroon*
États-Unis d'Amérique *m pl* *United States of America*	Washington, D.C. *Washington, D.C.*	Américain *m*, [-e] *f* *American*	anglais *English*	dollar (dol.) *m* *dollar (dol.)*
Éthiopie *f* *Ethiopia*	Addis-Abeba *Addis Ababa*	Éthiopien *m*, [-enne] *f* *Ethiopian*	amharic *Amharic*	birr *m* *birr*
Fidji, les *f pl* *Fiji*	Suva *Suva*	Fidjien *m*, [-enne] *f* *Fijian*	anglais *English*	dollar fidjien *m* *Fiji dollar*
Finlande *f* *Finland*	Helsinki *Helsinki*	Finlandais *m*, [-e] *f* *Finn*	finlandais *Finnish*	markka *m* *markka*
France *f* *France*	Paris *Paris*	Français *m*, [-e] *f* *Frenchman/woman*	français *French*	franc français *m* *French franc*
Gabon *m* *Gabon*	Libreville *Libreville*	Gabonais *m*, [-e] *f* *Gabonese*	français *French*	franc CFA *m* *C.F.A. franc*
Gambie *f* *Gambia*	Banjul *Banjul*	Gambien *m*, [-enne] *f* *Gambian*	anglais *English*	dalasi *m* *dalasi*

pays/ *country*	capitale/ *capital*	habitant/ *inhabitant*	langue/s officielle/s *official language/s*	devise/*currency*
Géorgie *f*	Tbilissi	Géorgien *m*, [-enne] *f*	géorgien	lari *m*
Georgia	*Tbilisi*	*Georgian*	*Georgian*	*lari*
Ghana *m*	Accra	Ghanéen *m*, [-enne] *f*	anglais	cédi *m*
Ghana	*Accra*	*Ghanaian*	*English*	*cedi*
Grèce *f*	Athènes	Grec *m*, [-que], *f*	grec	drachme *m*
Greece	*Athens*	*Greek*	*Greek*	*drachma*
Grenade *f*	St. George's	Grenadin *m*, [-e] *f*	anglais	dollar antillais *m*
Grenada	*St. George's*	*Grenadian*	*English*	*East Caribbean dollar*
Guatemala *m*	Guatemala	Guatémaltèque *mf*	espagnol	quetzal *m*
Guatemala	*Guatemala City*	*Guatemalan*	*Spanish*	*quetzal*
Guinée *f*	Conakry	Guinéen *m*, [-enne] *f*	français	franc guinéen *m*
Guinea	*Conakry*	*Guinean*	*French*	*Guinean franc*
Guinée-Bissau *f*	Bissau	de Guinée-Bissau	espagnol	peso de Guinée-Bissau *m*
Guinea-Bissau	*Bissau*	*from Guinea-Bissau*	*Spanish*	*Guinea-Bissau peso*
Guinée équatoriale *f*	Malabo	Guinéen équatorial, *m*, [-enne, -e] *f*	espagnol	franc CFA *m*
Equatorial Guinea	*Malabo*	*Equatorial Guinean*	*Spanish*	*C.F.A. franc*
Guyana *f*	Georgetown	Guyanais *m*, [-e] *f*	anglais	dollar guyanais *m*
Guyana	*Georgetown*	*Guyanese/Guyanan*	*English*	*Guyana dollar*
Haïti *m*	Port-au-Prince	Haïtien *m*, [-enne] *f*	français	gourde *f*
Haiti	*Port-au-Prince*	*Haitian*	*French*	*gourde*
Honduras *m*	Tegucigalpa	Hondurien *m*, [-enne] *f*	espagnol	lempira *m*
Honduras	*Tegucigalpa*	*Honduran*	*Spanish*	*lempira*
Hong-Kong *f*	Victoria	d'Hong-Kong	anglais	dollar de Hong-Kong *m*
Hong Kong	*Victoria*	*from Hong Kong*	*English*	*Hong Kong dollar*
Hongrie *f*	Budapest	Hongrois *m*, [-e] *f*	hongrois	forint *m*
Hungary	*Budapest*	*Hungarian*	*Hungarian*	*forint*
Île Maurice *f*	Port Louis	Mauricien *m*, [-enne] *f*	anglais/français	roupie mauricienne *f*
Mauritius	*Port Louis*	*Mauritian*	*English/French*	*Mauritian rupee*
Inde *f*	New Delhi	Indien *m*, [-enne] *f*	hindi/anglais	roupie indienne *f*
India	*New Delhi*	*Indian*	*Hindi/English*	*Indian rupee*
Indonésie *f*	Djakarta	Indonésien *m*, [-enne] *f*	indonésien	roupie indonésienne *f*
Indonesia	*Jakarta*	*Indonesian*	*Indonesia*	*Indonesian rupiah*
Iran *m*	Téhéran	Iranien *m*, [-enne] *f*	iranien	rial *m*
Iran	*Tehran/Teheran*	*Iranian*	*Iranian*	*rial*
Iraq (*aussi* Irak) *m*	Bagdad	Iraquien/Irakien, *m*, [-enne] *f*	arabe	dinar iraquien *m* dinar irakien *m*
Iraq (also Irak)	*Baghdad*	*Iraqi/Iraki*	*Arabic*	*Iraqi dinar/Iraki dinar*
Irlande du Nord *f*	Belfast	Irlandais *m*, [-e] *f* /	gaélique irlandais/anglais	livre sterling *f*
Northern Ireland	*Belfast*	*Irishman/-woman*	*Irish Gaelic/English*	*pound sterling*
Islande *f*	Reykjavik	Islandais *m*, [-e] *f*	islandais	krona, *f*
Iceland	*Reykjavik*	*Icelander*	*Icelandic*	*krona*
Israël *m*	Jérusalem	Israélien *m*, [-enne] *f*	hébreu/arabe	shekel *m*
Israel	*Jerusalem*	*Israeli*	*Hebrew/Arabic*	*shekel*
Italie *f*	Rome	Italien *m*, [-enne] *f*	italien	lire *f*
Italy	*Rome*	*Italian*	*Italian*	*lira*

pays/ country	capitale/ capital	habitant/ inhabitant	langue/s officielle/s official language/s	devise/ currency
Jamaïque f	Kingston	Jamaïquain/Jamaïcain, m, [-e] f	anglais	dollar jamaïcain m
Jamaica	*Kingston*	*Jamaican*	*English*	*Jamaica dollar*
Japon m	Tokyo	Japonais m, [-e] f	japonais	yen m
Japan	*Tokyo*	*Japanese*	*Japanese*	*yen*
Jordanie f	Amman	Jordanien m, [-enne] f	arabe	dinar jordanien m
Jordan	*Amman*	*Jordanian*	*Arabic*	*Jordan dinar*
Kazakhstan m	Alma-Ata	Kazakh mf	kazakh	rouble/ruble m
Kazakhstan	*Alma-Ata*	*Kazakh/Kazak*	*Kazakh*	*rouble*
Kenya m	Nairobi	Kényen m, [-enne] f	swahili/anglais	shilling m
Kenya	*Nairobi*	*Kenyan*	*Swahili/English*	*shilling*
Koweït m	Koweït	Koweïtien m, [-enne] f	arabe	dinar koweïtien m
Kuwait	*Kuwait City*	*Kuwaiti*	*Arabic*	*Kuwaiti dinar*
Kyrghyzstan m	Bichkek	du Kyrghyzstan	kyrgyz	som m
Kyrgyzstan	*Bishkek*	*Kyrgyz*	*Kyrgyz*	*som*
Laos m	Vientiane	Laotien m, [-enne] f	laotien	kip m
Laos	*Vientiane*	*Laotian*	*Lao*	*kip*
Lesotho m	Masaru	du Lesotho	sotho/anglais	loti m
Lesotho	*Maseru*	*Sotho/ inh: Mosotho/ Basotho*	*Sotho/English*	*loti*
Lettonie f	Riga	Letton m, [-onne] f	letton	lats m
Latvia	*Riga*	*Latvian*	*Latvian*	*lats*
Liban m	Beyrouth	Libanais m, [-e] f	arabe	livre libanaise f
Lebanon	*Beirut*	*Lebanese*	*Arabic*	*Lebanese pound*
Libéria m	Monrovia	Libérien m, [-enne] f	anglais	dollar libérien m
Liberia	*Monrovia*	*Liberian*	*English*	*Liberian dollar*
Libye f	Tripoli	Libyen m, [-enne] f	arabe	dinar libyen m
Libya	*Tripoli*	*Libyan*	*Arabic*	*Libyan dinar*
Liechtenstein m	Vaduz	du Liechtenstein	allemand	franc suisse m
Liechtenstein	*Vaduz*	*Liechtensteiner*	*German*	*Swiss franc*
Lituanie f	Vilnius	Lituanien m, [-enne] f	lituanien	litas m
Lithuania	*Vilnius*	*Lithuanian*	*Lithuanian*	*litas*
Luxembourg m	Luxembourg	Luxembourgeois m, [-e] f	français/ allemand	franc luxembourgeois m
Luxembourg	*Luxembourg*	*Luxemburger*	*French/German*	*Luxembourg franc*
Macédoine f	Skopje	Macédonien m, [-enne] f	macédonien	dinar m
Macedonia	*Skopje*	*Macedonian*	*Macedonian*	*dinar*
Madagascar f	Tananarive	Malgache mf	malgache/ français	franc malgache m
Madagascar	*Antananarivo*	*Madagascan*	*Malagasy/French*	*Malagasy franc*
Malaisie f	Kuala Lumpur	Malaisien m, [-enne] f	malais	ringgit malaisien m
Malaysia	*Kuala Lumpur*	*Malaysian/Malay*	*Malay*	*Malaysian ringgit*
Malawi m	Lilongwe	Malawien m, [-enne] f	anglais	kwacha m
Malawi	*Lilongwe*	*Malawian*	*English*	*kwacha*
Maldives f pl	Malé	des Maldives	divehi	roupie des Maldives f
Maldives	*Malé*	*Maldivian*	*Divehi*	*Maldivian rupee*
Mali m	Bamako	Malien m, [-enne] f	français	franc CFA m
Mali	*Bamako*	*Malian*	*French*	*C.F.A. franc*
Malte f	La Valette	Maltais m, [-e] f	maltais/anglais	livre maltaise f
Malta	*Valletta*	*Maltese*	*Maltese/English*	*Maltese pound*
Maroc m	Rabat	Marocain m, [-e] f	arabe/français	dirham m
Morocco	*Rabat*	*Moroccan*	*Arabic/French*	*dirham*

pays/ *country*	capitale/ *capital*	habitant/ *inhabitant*	langue/s officielle/s *official language/s*	devise/ *currency*
Mauritanie *f*	Nouakchott	Mauritanien *m*, [-enne] *f*	arabe/français	ouguiya *m*
Mauritania	*Nouakchott*	*Mauritanian*	*Arabic/French*	*ouguija*
Mexique *m*	Mexico	Mexicain *m*, [-e] *f*	espagnol	peso *m*
Mexico	*Mexico City*	*Mexican*	*Spanish*	*peso*
Moldavie *f*	Kichinev	Moldave *mf*	roumain	leu *m*
Moldova	*Kishinev*	*Moldovan*	*Romanian*	*leu*
Monaco *m*	Monaco	Monégasque *mf*	français	franc français *m*
Monaco	*Monaco*	*Monegasque*	*French*	*French franc*
Mongolie *f*	Oulan Bator	Mongol *m*, [-e] *f*	khalkha/mongol	tugrik *m*
Mongolia	*Ulaanbaatar* *(Ulan Bator)*	*Mongolian*	*Khalkha/Mongol*	*tugrik*
Monténégro *m*	Titograd	Monténégrin *m*, [-e] *f*	serbo-croate	dinar *m*
Montenegro	*Titograd*	*Montenegrin*	*Serbo-Croat*	*dinar*
Mozambique *m*	Maputo	Mozambicain *m*, [-e] *f*	portugais	metical *m*
Mozambique	*Maputo*	*Mozambican*	*Portuguese*	*metical*
Namibie *f*	Windhoek	Namibien *m*, [-enne] *f*	anglais/afrikaans	dollar namibien *m*
Namibia	*Windhoek*	*Namibian*	*English/* *Afrikaans*	*Namibian dollar*
Népal *m*	Katmandou/ Katmandu	Népalais *m*, [-e] *f*	népalais	roupie népalaise *f*
Nepal	*Kathmandu*	*Nepalese/Nepali*	*Nepali*	*Nepali rupee*
Nicaragua *m*	Managua	Nicaraguayen *m*, [-enne] *f*	espagnol	cordoba *f*
Nicaragua	*Managua*	*Nicaraguan*	*Spanish*	*cordoba*
Niger *m*	Niamey	Nigérien *m*, [-enne] *f*	français	franc CFA *m*
Niger	*Niamey*	*Nigerian*	*French*	*C.F.A. franc*
Nigéria *m*	Abuja	Nigérien *m*, [-enne] *f*	anglais	naira *m*
Nigeria	*Abuja*	*Nigerian*	*English*	*naira*
Norvège *f*	Oslo	Norvégien *m*, [-enne] *f*	norvégien	krone norvégienne *f*
Norway	*Oslo*	*Norwegian/Norse (pl* *only)*	*Norwegian*	*Norwegian krone*
Nouvelle- Zélande *f*	Wellington	Néo-Zélandais *m*, [-e] *f*	anglais/maori	dollar néo-zélandais *m*
New Zealand	*Wellington*	*New Zealander*	*English/Maori*	*New Zealand dollar*
Oman *m*	Mascate	Omanais *m*, [-e] *f*	arabe	rial oman *m*
Oman	*Muscat*	*Omani*	*Arabic*	*Omani rial*
Ouganda *m*	Kampala	Ougandais *m*, [-e] *f*	swahili/anglais	shilling ougandais *m*
Uganda	*Kampala*	*Ugandan*	*Swahili/English*	*Uganda shilling*
Ouzbékistan *m*	Tachkent	Ouzbek *m*, [-èke], *f*	ouzbek	rouble/ruble *m*
Uzbekistan	*Tashkent*	*Uzbek*	*Uzbek*	*rouble*
Pakistan *m*	Islamabad	Pakistanais *m*, [-e] *f*	ourdi/anglais	roupie pakistanaise *f*
Pakistan	*Islamabad*	*Pakistani*	*Urdu/English*	*Pakistan rupee*
Panama *m*	Panama	Panaméen *m*, [-enne] *f*	espagnol	balboa *m*
Panama	*Panama City*	*Panamanian*	*Spanish*	*balboa*
Papouasie- Nouvelle Guinée *f*	Port Moresby	de Papouasie-Nouvelle Guinée	anglais	kina *m*
Papua New *Guinea*	*Port Moresby*	*Papuan*	*English*	*kina*
Paraguay *m*	Asunción	Paraguayen *m*, [-enne] *f*	espagnol	guarani *m*
Paraguay	*Asunción*	*Paraguayan*	*Spanish*	*guarani*

pays/ *country*	capitale/ *capital*	habitant/ *inhabitant*	langue/s officielle/s *official language/s*	devise/ *currency*
Pays Bas, Les *m* *pl* *Holland (also* *Netherlands,* *The)*	Amsterdam/ La Haye *Amsterdam/* *The Hague*	Hollandais/Néerlandais *m*, [-e] *f* *Dutchman/-woman/* *Netherlander*	hollandais/ néerlandais *Dutch*	florin *m* *guilder*
Pays de Galles *m* *Wales*	Cardiff *Cardiff*	Gallois *m*, [-e] *f* *Welshman/-woman*	anglais/gallois *English/Welsh*	livre sterling, *f* *pound sterling*
Pérou *m* *Peru*	Lima *Lima*	Péruvien *m*, [-enne] *f* *Peruvian*	espagnol/ quechua *Spanish/Quechua*	sol *m* *nuevo sol*
Philippines *f pl* *Philippines*	Manille *Manila*	Philippin *m*, [-e] *f* *Philippine/Filipino*	philippin/anglais *Philipino/English*	peso philippin *m* *Philippine peso*
Pologne *f* *Poland*	Varsovie *Warsaw*	Polonais *m*, [-e] *f* *Pole*	polonais *Polish*	zloty *m* *zloty*
Porto Rico *f* *Puerto Rico*	San Juan *San Juan*	Portoricain *m*, [-e] *f* *Puerto Rican*	espagnol/anglais *Spanish/English*	dollar US *m* *US dollar*
Portugal *m* *Portugal*	Lisbonne *Lisbon*	Portugais *m*, [-e] *f* *Portuguese*	portugais *portuguese*	escudo *m* *escudo*
Qatar *m* *Qatar*	Doha *Doha*	du Qatar *Qatari*	arabe *Arabic*	riyal *m* *riyal*
République centrafricaine *f* *Central African* *Republic*	Bangui *Bangui*	de la République centrafricaine *from the Central African* *Republic*	français/sango *French/Sango*	franc CFA *m* *C.F.A. franc*
République dominicaine *f* *Dominican* *Republic*	Santo Domingo *Santo* *Domingo*	Dominicain *m*, [-e] *f* *Dominican*	espagnol *Spanish*	peso dominicain *m* *Dominican peso*
République d'Irlande (*aussi* Eire) *f* *Republic of* *Ireland (also* *Eire)*	Dublin *Dublin*	Irlandais *m*, [-e] *f* *Irishman/woman*	gaélique irlandais/ anglais *Irish Gaelic/* *English*	livre irlandaise *f* *Irish pound (also punt)*
République tchèque *f* *Czech Republic*	Prague *Prague*	Tchèque *mf* *Czech*	tchèque *Czech*	couronne *f* *koruna*
Roumanie *f* *Romania*	Bucarest *Bucharest*	Roumain *m*, [-e] *f* *Romanian*	roumain *Romanian/*	leu roumain *m* *Romanian leu*
Royaume-Uni *m* *United Kingdom*	Londres *London*	Britannique *mf* *Briton*	anglais *English*	livre sterling *f* *pound sterling*
Ruanda/Rwanda *m* *Rwanda*	Kigali *Kigali*	Ruandais/Rwandais *m* [-e] *f* *Rwandese*	français/ kinyaruandais *French/* *Kinyarwanda*	franc ruandais *m* *Rwanda franc*
Russie *f* *Russia*	Moscou *Moscow*	Russe *mf* *Russian*	russe *Russian*	rouble/ruble *m* *rouble*
Sainte-Lucie *f* *Saint Lucia*	Castries *Castries*	de Sainte-Lucie *Saint Lucian*	anglais *English*	dollar antillais *m* *East Caribbean dollar*
Saint-Marin *m* *San Marino*	Saint-Marin *San Marino*	de Saint-Marin *San Marinese*	italien *Italian*	lire italienne *f* *Italian lira*

pays/ *country*	capitale/ *capital*	habitant/ *inhabitant*	langue/s officielle/s *official language/s*	devise/ *currency*
Saint-Vincent et Grenades *m pl*	Kingstown	de Saint-Vincent	anglais	dollar antillais *m*
Saint Vincent and the Grenadines	*Kingstown*	*Vincentian*	*English*	*East Caribbean dollar*
Salvador *m*	San Salvador	Salvadorien *m*, [-enne] *f*	espagnol	colón *m*
El Salvador	*San Salvador*	*Salvadoran/Salvadorean*	*Spanish*	*colón*
Sénégal *m*	Dakar	Sénégalais *m*, [-e] *f*	français	franc CFA *m*
Senegal	*Dakar*	*Senegalese*	*French*	*C.F.A. franc*
Seychelles *f pl*	Victoria	des Seychelles	anglais/français/ créole	roupie des Seychelles *f*
Seychelles	*Victoria*	*Seychellois/Seselwa*	*English/French/ Creole*	*Seychelles rupee*
Sierra Leone *f*	Freetown	Sierra Leonais *m*, [-e] *f*	anglais	leone *m*
Sierra Leone	*Freetown*	*Sierra Leonean*	*English*	*leone*
Singapour *m*	Singapour	Singapourien *m* [-enne] *f*	chinois/malais/ tamoul/anglais	dollar de Singapour *m*
Singapore	*Singapore*	*Singaporean*	*Chinese/Malay/ Tamil/English*	*Singapore dollar*
Slovaquie *f*	Bratislava	Slovaque *mf*	slovaque	koruna slovaque *f*
Slovakia	*Bratislava*	*Slovak*	*Slovak*	*Slovak koruna*
Slovénie *f*	Ljubljana	Slovène *mf*	slovène	tolar *m*
Slovenia	*Ljubljana*	*Slovenian/Slovene*	*Slovene*	*tolar*
Somalie *f*	Mogadiscio	Somalien *m*, [-enne] *f*	somali/anglais	shilling somalien *m*
Somalia	*Mogadishu*	*Somali/Somalian*	*Somali/Arabic*	*Somali shilling*
Soudan *m*	Khartoum	Soudanais *m*, [-e] *f*	arabe	livre soudanaise *f*
Sudan	*Khartoum*	*Sudanese*	*Arabic*	*Sudanese pound*
Sri Lanka *m*	Colombo	Sri-Lankais *m*, [-e] *f*	cingalais/tamoul/ anglais	roupie cingalaise *f*
Sri Lanka	*Colombo*	*Sri Lankan*	*English/ Sinhalese/Tamil*	*Sri Lanka rupee*
Suède *f*	Stockholm	Suédois *m*, [e] *f*	suédois	krone suédoise *f*
Sweden	*Stockholm*	*Swede*	*Swedish*	*Swedish krona*
Suisse *f*	Berne	Suisse *mf*	français/ allemand/italien	franc suisse *m*
Switzerland	*Bern*	*Swiss*	*French/German/ Italian*	*Swiss franc*
Surinam *m*	Paramaribo	Surinamais *m*, [-e] *f*	hollandais/ néerlandais/ anglais	florin du Surinam *m*
Suriname	*Paramaribo*	*Surinamese*	*Dutch/English*	*Suriname guilder*
Swaziland *m*	Mbabane	Swazi *m*, [-e] *f*	swazi/anglais	lilangeni *m*
Swaziland	*Mbabane*	*Swazi*	*Swazi/English*	*lilangeni*
Syrie *f*	Damas	Syrien *m*, [-enne] *f*	arabe	livre syrienne *f*
Syria	*Damascus*	*Syrian*	*Arabic*	*Syrian pound*
Tadjikistan *m*	Duchambe	Tadjik *mf*	tadjik	rouble/ruble *m*
Tajikistan	*Dushanbe*	*Tajik*	*Tajik*	*rouble*
Taiwan *m*	Taipei/Taipeh	Taiwanais *m*, [-e] *f*	mandarin/ chinois	dollar de Taïwan *m*
Taiwan	*Taipei*	*Taiwanese*	*Mandarin/ Chinese*	*Taiwan dollar*
Tanzanie *f*	Dar es Salaam	Tanzanien *m*, [-enne] *f*	swahili/anglais	shilling tanzanien *m*
Tanzania	*Dar es Salaam*	*Tanzanian*		*Tanzanian shilling*
Tchad *m*	N'Djamena	Tchadien *m*, [-enne] *f*	arabe/français	franc CFA *m*
Chad	*N'Djamena*	*Chadian*	*Arabic/French*	*C.F.A. franc*

pays/ *country*	capitale/ *capital*	habitant/ *inhabitant*	langue/s officielle/s *official language/s*	devise/ *currency*
Thaïlande *f*	Bangkok	Thaïlandais *m*, [-e] *f*	thaï	baht *m*
Thailand	*Bangkok*	*Thai*	*Thai*	*baht*
Togo *m*	Lomé	Togolais *m*, [-e] *f*	français	franc CFA *m*
Togo	*Lomé*	*Togolese*	*French*	*C.F.A. franc*
Trinité-et-Tobago *f*	Port of Spain	Trinidadien *m*, [-enne] *f*/ de la Trinité	anglais	dollar de Trinité-et-Tobago *m*
Trinidad and Tobago	*Port of Spain*	*Trinidadian/Tobagoan/ Tobagodian*	*English*	*Trinidad and Tobago dollar*
Tunisie *f*	Tunis	Tunisien *m*, [-enne] *f*	arabe	dinar *m*
Tunisia	*Tunis*	*Tunisian*	*Arabic*	*dinar*
Turkménistan *m*	Achkabad	Turkmène *mf*	turkmène	manat *m*
Turkmenistan	*Ashkhabad*	*Turkmen*	*Turkmen*	*manat*
Turquie *f*	Ankara	Turc *m*, [-que], *f*	turc	lire turque, *f*
Turkey	*Ankara*	*Turk*	*Turkish*	*Turkish lira*
Ukraine *f*	Kiev	Ukrainien *m*, [-enne] *f*	ukrainien	karbovanet *m*
Ukraine	*Kiev*	*Ukrainian*	*Ukrainian*	*karbovanet*
Uruguay *m*	Montevideo	Uruguayen *m*, [-enne] *f*	espagnol	peso *m*
Uruguay	*Montevideo*	*Uruguayan*	*Spanish*	*peso*
Vénézuela *m*	Caracas	Vénézuélien *m*, [-enne] *f*	espagnol	bolivar *m*
Venezuela	*Caracas*	*Venezuelan*	*Spanish*	*bolivar*
Viêt Nam *m*	Hanoï	Vietnamien *m*, [-enne] *f*	vietnamien	dong *m*
Vietnam	*Hanoi*	*Vietnamese*	*Vietnamese*	*dong*
Yémen *m*	Sanaa	Yéménite *mf*	arabe	dinar yéménite *m*
Yemen	*Sanaa*	*Yemeni*	*Arabic*	*Yemeni dinar*
Yougoslavie *f* (ex-~)	Belgrade	Yougoslave *mf*	serbo-croate	dinar *m*
Yugoslavia	*Belgrade*	*Yugoslav*	*Serbo-Croat*	*dinar*
Zaïre *m*	Kinshasha	Zaïrois *m*, [-e] *f*	français	zaïre *m*
Zaïre	*Kinshasha*	*Zaïrese/Zairean*	*French*	*zaïre*
Zambie *f*	Lusaka	Zambien *m*, [-enne] *f*	anglais	kwacha *m*
Zambia	*Lusaka*	*Zambian*	*English*	*kwacha*
Zimbabwe *m*	Harare	Zimbabwéen *m*, [-enne] *f*	anglais	dollar du Zimbabwe *m*
Zimbabwe	*Harare*	*Zimbabwean*	*English*	*Zimbabwe dollar*

Les nombres cardinaux et ordinaux/Cardinal and ordinal numbers

Cardinaux/ Cardinal	Français/ French	Anglais/ English	Ordinaux/ Ordinal	Français/ French	Anglais/ English
1	un	one	1st	premier	first
2	deux	two	2nd	deuxième	second
3	trois	three	3rd	troisième	third
4	quatre	four	4th	quatrième	fourth
5	cinq	five	5th	cinquième	fifth
6	six	six	6th	sixième	sixth
7	sept	seven	7th	septième	seventh
8	huit	eight	8th	huitième	eighth
9	neuf	nine	9th	neuvième	ninth
10	dix	ten	10th	dixième	tenth
11	onze	eleven	11th	onzième	eleventh
12	douze	twelve	12th	douzième	twelfth
13	treize	thirteen	13th	treizième	thirteenth
14	quatorze	fourteen	14th	quatorzième	fourteenth
15	quinze	fifteen	15th	quinzième	fifteenth
16	seize	sixteen	16th	seizième	sixteenth
17	dix-sept	seventeen	17th	dix-septième	seventeenth
18	dix-huit	eighteen	18th	dix-huitième	eighteenth
19	dix-neuf	nineteen	19th	dix-neuvième	nineteenth
20	vingt	twenty	20th	vingtième	twentieth
21	vingt et un	twenty-one	21st	vingt et unième	twenty-first
22	vingt-deux	twenty-two	22nd	vingt-deuxième	twenty-second
23	vingt-trois	twenty-three	23th	vingt-troisième	twenty-third
24	vingt-quatre	twenty-four	24th	vingt-quatrième	twenty-fourth
25	vingt-cinq	twenty-five	25th	vingt-cinquième	twenty-fifth
30	trente	thirty	30th	trentième	thirtieth
40	quarante	forty	40th	quarantième	fortieth
50	cinquante	fifty	50th	cinquantième	fiftieth
60	soixante	sixty	60th	soixantième	sixtieth
70	soixante-dix	seventy	70th	soixante-dixième	seventieth
80	quatre-vingts	eighty	80th	quatre-vingtième	eightieth
90	quatre-vingt-dix	ninety	90th	quatre-vingt-dixième	ninetieth
100	cent	one hundred	100th	centième	one hundredth
101	cent un	one hundred and one	101st	cent unième	one hundred and first
156	cent cinquante-six	one hundred and fifty-six	156th	cent cinquante-sixième	one hundred and fifty-sixth
200	deux cents	two hundred	200th	deux centième	two hundredth
300	trois cents	three hundred	300th	trois centième	three hundredth
400	quatre cents	four hundred	400th	quatre centième	four hundredth
1 000	mille	one thousand	1 000th	millième	one thousandth
1 001	mille un	one thousand and one	1 001st	mille et unième	one thousand and first

Cardinaux/ Cardinal	Français/ French	Anglais/ English	Ordinaux/ Ordinal	Français/ French	English/ English
1 247	mille deux cent quarante-sept	one thousand, two hundred and forty-seven	1 247th	mille deux cent quarante-septième	one thousand, two hundred and forty-seventh
2 000	deux mille	two thousand	2 000th	deux millième	two thousandth
3 000	trois mille	three thousand	3 000th	trois millième	three thousandth
10 000	dix mille	ten thousand	10 000th	dix millième	ten thousandth
20 000	vingt mille	twenty thousand	20 000th	vingt millième	twenty thousandth
100 000	cent mille	one hundred thousand	100 000th	cent millième	one hundred thousandth
200 000	deux cent mille	two hundred thousand	200 000th	deux cent millième	two hundred thousandth
325 863	trois cent vingt-cinq mille huit cent soixante-trois	three hundred and twenty-five thousand, eight hundred and sixty-three	225 863rd	deux cent vingt-cinq mille huit cent soixante troisième	two hundred and twenty-five thousand, eight hundred and sixty-third
1 000 000	un million	one million	1 000 000th	millionième	one millionth
1 739 412	un million sept cent trente-neuf mille quatre cent douze	one million, seven hundred and thirty-nine thousand, four hundred and twelve			
10 000 000	dix millions	ten million(s)			
100 000 000	cent millions	one hundred million(s)			
1 000 000 000	un milliard	one thousand million(s) (*UK*) (one billion *US*)			
1 000 000 000 000	un trillion	one billion (*UK*) (one trillion *US*)			

A

a *abbr (alloy container)* TRANSP *shipping* conteneur en alliage *m*

A:[1] **~ Inst M** *abbr (Associate of the Institute of Marketing)* HRM, S&M membre associé de l'institut de marketing

A:[2] **~ level** *n UK (Advanced level)* GEN COMM, WEL examen de niveau supérieur, ≈ baccalauréat *m*

AA *abbr* INS *(average adjuster)* marine, TRANSP *(average adjuster)* marine dispacheur *m*, répartiteur d'avaries *m*, TRANSP *UK (Automobile Association)* association automobile britannique

AAA[1] *abbr* INS *(Association of Average Adjusters)* association des répartiteurs d'avaries, TRANSP *(American Automobile Association)* association automobile américaine

AAA:[2] **~ bond** *n (SYN triple-A bond)* STOCK obligation notée AAA *f*

AAAA *abbr (American Association of Advertising Agencies)* S&M association nationale américaine des agences de publicité

AACC *abbr (Airport Associations Co-ordinating Council)* TRANSP ≈ CCAA *(Conseil de coordination des associations aéroportuaires)*

AACCA *abbr (Associate of the Association of Certified and Corporate Accountants)* ACC membre associé de l'association des comptables agréés

AAD *abbr (at a discount)* FIN *forward markets* avec un déport *loc m*, à escompte *loc m*, STOCK avec une décote *loc f*, à escompte *loc m*

AAG *abbr (Area Advisory Group)* IMP/EXP groupe consultatif de zone qui s'occupe de développer les marchés étrangers vers lesquels les sociétés anglaises veulent exporter

AAR *abbr (against all risks)* INS contre tous les risques, tous risques *loc*

AAS *abbr (annual automated controls survey)* TRANSP *of ship* visite annuelle de la centrale de navigation *f*

AASMM *abbr (Associated African States, Madagascar and Mauritius)* GEN COMM OCAMM *(Organisation commune africaine, malgache et mauricienne)*

AASO *abbr (Association of American Shipowners)* TRANSP association des armateurs américains

AB *abbr (above bridges)* TRANSP sur palan *loc m*

ABAA *abbr UK (Associate of the British Association of Accountants and Auditors)* ACC membre associé de l'association britannique des comptables et des commissaires aux comptes

abaft *prep* TRANSP *shipping* sur l'arrière de *loc m*

abandon *vt* GEN COMM abandonner, renoncer à, IMP/EXP *goods in customs* délaisser, PATENTS, STOCK *option* abandonner; ◆ **~ any claim** LAW renoncer à toute prétention; **~ ship** TRANSP abandonner le navire

abandonee *n* INS abandonnataire *mf*

abandonment *n* GEN COMM renonciation *f*, INS *marine* abandon *m*, LAW cession *f*, *of right* renonciation *f*, PATENTS cession *f*, STOCK *of option* abandon *m*; **~ of action** LAW désistement d'action *m*; **~ clause** INS *marine* clause de délaissement *f*

A-base *n Canada* ACC services votés *m pl (Can)*; **~ review** ACC révision des services votés *f*

abate *vt* GEN COMM *taxes, prices* baisser, réduire, LAW *sentence* remettre, *writ* annuler, rendre nul et non avenu, TAX annuler

abatement *n* ACC réduction *f*, GEN COMM *price* rabais *m*, remise *f*, réduction *f*, LAW *of action* arrêt *m*, suspension *f*, TAX annulation *f*, dégrèvement *m*; **~ of the levy** FIN abattement sur le prélèvement *m*

abbreviate *vt* GEN COMM abréger, raccourcir

abbreviation *n* GEN COMM abréviation *f*

ABC[1] *abbr (Australian Broadcasting Corporation)* MEDIA organisme de Radio-Télévision australien

ABC:[2] **~ method** *n* ACC *inventory management*, MGMNT *inventory management* méthode ABC *f*

ABCC *abbr* IND *(Association of British Chambers of Commerce)* association des chambres de commerce britanniques, IND *(Arab-British Chamber of Commerce)* chambre de commerce arabo-britannique

abeam *adj* TRANSP *shipping* par le travers

abeyance: in ~ *phr* GEN COMM en souffrance, en suspens, LAW *property* inappliqué

abide: ~ by *vt* GEN COMM *result* assumer, supporter, *rule, decision* respecter, se conformer à, *statement* maintenir, LAW *agreement, rule* se conformer à, se soumettre à

abilities *n pl* GEN COMM disponibilités *f pl*

ability *n* ECON compétence *f*, GEN COMM capacité *f*, compétence *f*, savoir-faire *m*; **~ grouping** WEL groupe de niveau *m*; **~ level** WEL *of students* niveau d'aptitude *m*, *of workers, students* niveau de qualification *m*; **~ to pay** HRM *salary* capacité de paiement *f*, LAW solvabilité *f*, TAX capacité contributive *f*, faculté contributive *f*; **~ to repay** ACC, BANK, ECON, FIN, GEN COMM capacité de remboursement *f*

able[1] *adj* GEN COMM compétent; ◆ **be ~ to afford to buy sth** ECON avoir les moyens d'acheter qch, pouvoir s'offrir qch; **~ to work** HRM apte au travail

able:[2] **~ -bodied seaman** *n (ABS)* HRM matelot de seconde classe *m*, TRANSP matelot breveté *m*, matelot qualifié *m*; **~ seaman** *n* TRANSP matelot breveté *m*, matelot de seconde classe *m*, matelot qualifié *m*

abnormal[1] *adj* GEN COMM anormal

abnormal:[2] ~ **indivisible load** *n* TRANSP masse indivisible anormale *f*; ~ **risk** *n* INS risque anormal *m*

aboard *adv* GEN COMM à bord, à bord de

abolish *vt* ADMIN abolir, supprimer, *frontier controls* mettre fin à, GEN COMM abolir, LAW abolir, supprimer

abolishment *n* GEN COMM abolition *f*, abrogation *f*, suppression *f*

abolition *n* ADMIN abolition *f*, suppression *f*; ~ **of trade controls** GEN COMM ouverture des frontières *f*, suppression des barrières douanières *f*

abort[1] *n* COMP abandon *m*, arrêt prématuré *m*

abort[2] **1.** *vt* COMP *program* abandonner, abandonner prématurément, arrêter l'éxecution de, arrêter prématurément, interrompre, GEN COMM *mission, trial, launch* faire échouer, interrompre; **2.** *vi* COMP *program* s'arrêter

about *prep* GEN COMM *approximately* environ, vers, *concerning* concernant, en ce qui concerne, au sujet de *loc m*

above[1] *adj* COM mentionné ci-dessus *loc*, COMMS mentionné ci-dessus *loc*, mentionné plus haut *loc*, précité, susmentionné; ~ **-average** *(ANT below-average)* GEN COMM au-dessus de la moyenne, supérieur à la moyenne; ~ **board** GEN COMM *action, deal* correct, régulier, *person* honnête, loyal, régulier, LAW correct; ~ **-mentioned** COM mentionné ci-dessus *loc*, COMMS mentionné ci-dessus *loc*, mentionné plus haut *loc*, précité, susmentionné; ~ **-named** COMMS susnommé

above[2] *adv* *(ANT below)* COMMS ci-dessus, plus haut, GEN COMM *in letter* ci-dessus; ◆ **as ~** *(ANT as below)* COMMS comme ci-dessus

above:[3] ~ **the line** *n* ACC, BANK, FIN, GEN COMM compte créditeur *m*, S&M *advertising investment* above-the-line *loc*, coût médias *m*, *advertising* publicité médias *f*; **the ~ address** *n* GEN COMM l'adresse précitée *f*; ~ **-the-line item** *n* *(ANT below-the-line item)* ECON article de dessus de ligne *m*, opération au-dessus de ligne *f*

above[4] *prep* GEN COMM au-dessus de, de plus de, dessus, en-dessous de, supérieur à; ~ **bridges** *(AB)* TRANSP sur palan; ~ **deck** *(A/D, ANT below deck)* TRANSP *shipping* en pontée, sur le pont; ◆ ~ **the line** ACC au-dessus de la ligne, inscrit au compte de résultat, FIN *profit and loss accounts* au-dessus de la ligne, inscrit au compte de résultat, S&M au-dessus de la ligne; ~ **-market price** *(ANT below-market price)* STOCK *options on currency futures* au-dessus du cours; ~ **the norm** *(ANT below the norm)* GEN COMM au-dessus de la norme; ~ **quota** *(ANT below quota)* ECON au-dessus du quota, hors contingent

ABP *abbr* *(Associated British Ports)* TRANSP ports britanniques associés

abreaction: ~ **channels** *n pl* COMMS, HRM, MGMNT techniques de l'abréaction *f pl*

abreast: **be ~ of** *phr* GEN COMM *latest developments* se tenir au courant de, suivre, être au fait de *loc m*; **be ~ of things** *phr* GEN COMM être dans le vent *loc m*; **be ~ of the times** *phr* GEN COMM marcher avec son temps, être dans le mouvement *loc m*; **keep ~ of** *phr* GEN COMM se tenir au courant de; **keep ~ of the times** *phr* GEN COMM marcher avec son temps; ~ **of** *phr* GEN COMM au courant de *loc m*

abroad *adv* GEN COMM à l'étranger *loc m*

abrogate *vt* LAW abroger

abrogation *n* LAW abrogation *f*

ABS *abbr* HRM *(able-bodied seaman)* matelot de seconde classe *m*, TRANSP *(American Bureau of Shipping)* registre américain d'immatriculation (société de classification), TRANSP *(able-bodied seaman)* matelot breveté *m*, matelot qualifié *m*

abscond *vi* LAW s'enfuir, se soustraire à la justice

absence *n* GEN COMM *being elsewhere* absence *f*, éloignement *m*, *lack* défaut *m*, manque *m*, HRM absence *f*, LAW défaut *m*; ~ **of consideration** FIN défaut de provision *m*, GEN COMM absence de contrepartie *f*; ~ **without leave** HRM absence non justifiée *f*, absence non motivée *f*, absence sans permission *f*; ◆ **in sb's ~** GEN COMM en l'absence de qn; **in the ~ of** GEN COMM *news* faute de *loc*; **in the ~ of detailed information** GEN COMM faute de détails *loc*, à défaut de renseignements précis; **in the ~ of evidence to the contrary** LAW jusqu'à preuve du contraire *loc*; **in the ~ of information** GEN COMM faute de renseignements *loc*

absent *adj* GEN COMM absent, manquant, HRM absent; ◆ **be ~ due to sickness** HRM être absent pour cause de maladie

absentee *n* GEN COMM absent *m*, manquant *m*, *habitually* absentéiste *mf*, HRM absent *m*, absentéiste *mf*; ~ **ballot** *AmE* *(cf postal ballot BrE)* HRM vote par correspondance *m*; ~ **owner** LAW, PROP propriétaire absentéiste *m*; ~ **rate** GEN COMM, HRM taux d'absentéisme *m*

absenteeism *n* GEN COMM, HRM absentéisme *m*

absolute[1] *adj* COMP absolu, GEN COMM absolu, franc, LAW *contracts* inconditionnel, sans réserve, *court order, decree* définitif; ◆ **in ~ terms** ECON en termes absolus

absolute:[2] ~ **address** *n* COMMS, COMP adresse absolue *f*; ~ **addressing** *n* COMP adressage absolu *m*; ~ **advantage** *n* ECON avantage absolu *m*; ~ **concentration** *n* ECON concentration absolue *f*; ~ **income hypothesis** *n* ECON hypothèse de revenu absolu *f*; ~ **liability** *n* LAW responsabilité objective *f*; ~ **limit** *n* GEN COMM tolérance maximale *f*, *within prescribed time-limits* délai absolu *m*; ~ **majority** *n* POL majorité absolue *f*; ~ **monopoly** *n* ECON, FIN, S&M monopole absolu *m*; ~ **poor** *n* ECON personnes en situation de pauvreté absolue; ~ **poverty** *n* ECON pauvreté absolue *f*; ~ **priority rule** *n* FIN règle de priorité absolue *f*; ~ **sale** *n* S&M

vente définitive *f*, vente irrévocable *f*; ~ **scarcity** *n* ECON grande rareté *f*; ~ **surplus value** *n* ECON plus-value absolue *f*, plus-value globale *f*; ~ **title** *n* PROP *to property* titre irréfutable *m*

absolutely: ~ **or contingently** *phr* TAX conditionnel ou non

absorb *vt* GEN COMM *costs, profits, business* absorber, *shock, impact* amortir, *staff, management* recruter, *stock* résorber; ◆ ~ **overheads** ACC supporter les coûts indirects, supporter les frais généraux; ~ **a used-car surplus** GEN COMM résorber un surplus de véhicules d'occasion

absorbed *adj* ACC assimilé, *cost accounting* affecté, pris en charge par l'entreprise, résorbé, ECON absorbé, intégré, STOCK *securities* absorbé

absorbing: ~ **capacity** *n* STOCK *security market* capacité d'absorption *f*; ~ **company** *n* ECON entreprise absorbante *f*, entreprise acquisitrice *f*, société absorbante *f*

absorption *n* GEN COMM *of business, company, costs, profit* absorption *f, of shock, impact* amortissement *m*, TRANSP absorption *f*; ~ **approach** ECON préliminaires d'absorption *m pl*, préliminaires d'intégration *m pl*; ~ **costing** ACC *cost accounting* méthode du coût complet *f*, méthode du coût de revient complet *f*, méthode du prix de revient complet *f*; ~ **rate** S&M taux d'absorption *m*

absorptive: ~ **capacity** *n* ECON capacité d'absorption *f*, capacité d'intégration *f*

abstain *vi* POL *in election* s'abstenir

abstainer's: ~ **insurance** *n* INS assurance des abstinents *f*

abstention *n* POL abstention *f*

abstinence *n* ECON abstention *f*

abstract *n* ECON *summary*, FIN *summary*, GEN COMM *of document* abrégé *m*, résumé *m*, LAW extrait *m*, PATENTS abrégé *m*, résumé *m*; ~ **of accounts** BANK extrait de comptes *m*, relevé de comptes *m*; ~ **labor** *AmE*, ~ **labour** *BrE* (ANT *concrete labour*) HRM travail abstrait *m, workers* main-d'oeuvre abstraite *f*; ~ **of record** LAW extrait d'un rapport officiel *m*, extrait de minute *m*; ~ **of title** LAW extrait du répertoire des mutations de propriété *m*, titre de propriété *m*

ABT *abbr* (*American Board of Trade*) GEN COMM bureau américain du commerce

ABTA *abbr* (*Association of British Travel Agents*) LEIS association des agents de voyage britanniques

Abu Dhabi *pr n* GEN COMM Abou-Dhabi *n pr*

abundance *n* ECON abondance *f*, GEN COMM abondance *f*, profusion *f*, HRM abondance *f*

abundant *adj* ECON abondant, GEN COMM abondant, fourni

abuse[1] *n* GEN COMM *of system*, PATENTS abus *m*; ~ **of administrative authority** ADMIN, GEN COMM abus de pouvoir *m*; ~ **of confidence** GEN COMM abus de confiance *m*; ~ **of power** ADMIN, GEN COMM abus de pouvoir *m*; ~ **of rights** TAX abus de

droits *m*; ~ **of trust** GEN COMM abus de confiance *m*

abuse[2] *vt* GEN COMM *privilege, power, trust* abuser de

abusive: ~ **practice** *n* S&M *of seller* pratique abusive *f*

a/c *abbr* ACC (*account*) compte *m*, ACC (*account current*) compte de mandataire *m*, BANK (*account*), FIN (*account*), GEN COMM (*account*) compte *m*

AC *abbr* COMP (*alternating current*) ca (*courant alternatif*), ECON (*advanced country*) pays industrialisé *m*, pays technologiquement avancé *m*, GEN COMM (*authorization under consideration*) autorisation en cours d'examen *f*, HRM (*assistant controller*) contrôleur adjoint *m*, IND (*advanced country*), POL (*advanced country*) pays industrialisé *m*, pays technologiquement avancé *m*, TRANSP (*air freight container*) conteneur pour fret aérien *m*

academic[1] *adj* GEN COMM, WEL universitaire

academic:[2] ~ **research** *n* WEL recherche universitaire *f, in science* recherche fondamentale *f*

ACAS *abbr* UK (*Advisory, Conciliation and Arbitration Service*) HRM service consultatif d'arbitrage et de conciliation

ACB *abbr* Canada (*adjusted cost base*) ACC PBR (*prix de base rajusté*)

ACC *abbr* IND (*American Chamber of Commerce*) chambre américaine de commerce, TRANSP (*automatic control certified*) commande automatique certifiée *f*, TRANSP (*acceptable container condition*) *shipping* état acceptable d'un conteneur *m*

ACCA *abbr* ACC (*Associate of the Chartered Association of Certified Accountants*) membre associé de l'association des comptables agréés, TAX (*accelerated capital cost allowance*) déduction pour amortissement accéléré *f*

acce. *abbr* (*acceptance*) ACC, BANK acc, GEN COMM acc. (*acceptation*), consentement *m*, LAW acc. (*acceptation*), agrément *m*, consentement *m*, PROP acc. (*acceptation*), agrément *m*, consentement *m*

accede: ~ **to** *vt* GEN COMM accéder à

accelerable: ~ **guarantee** *n* UK FIN garantie remboursable par anticipation *f*

accelerate *vti* GEN COMM accélérer

accelerated[1] *adj* GEN COMM *training courses* accéléré

accelerated:[2] ~ **capital cost allowance** *n* (*ACCA*) TAX déduction pour amortissement accéléré *f*; ~ **conversion** *n* BANK *debentures* conversion accélérée *f*; ~ **cost recovery system** *n* (*ACRS*) ACC, FIN *economic accounting* amortissement accéléré *m*, amortissement dégressif *m*; ~ **depreciation** *n* ACC *economic accounting*, FIN amortissement accéléré *m*, amortissement dégressif *m*; ~ **redemption** *n* GEN COMM remboursement anticipé *m*; ~ **repayment** *n* GEN COMM remboursement anticipé *m*; ~ **surface mail** *n AmE (cf accelerated surface post BrE)* COMMS courrier rapide par voie de surface *m*; ~ **surface post** *n BrE (cf accelerated surface mail AmE)* COMMS courrier rapide par voie de surface *m*

acceleration *n* GEN COMM *in rate* accélération *f*, LAW *real estate*, PROP accélération *f*, entrée en possession anticipée *f*, prise de possession anticipée *f*, *of plan, proposal* réduction du délai d'exécution *f*; ~ **clause** BANK, FIN, LAW, PROP *mortgages* clause accélératrice *f*; ~ **clause premium** BANK, FIN, LAW, PROP clause d'accélération *f*; ~ **of maturity** BANK demande de remboursement anticipé *f*, exigibilité anticipée *f*; ~ **premium** HRM prime de rendement *f*, IND prime de productivité *f*; ~ **principle** (SYN *accelerator principle*) ECON *investment*, FIN *investment* principe de l'accélérateur *m*

accelerator *n* MATH *investment* accélérateur *m*; ~ **card** COMP carte accélératrice *f*; ~ **principle** (SYN *acceleration principle*) ECON *investment*, FIN *investment* principe de l'accélérateur *m*

accent *n* GEN COMM accent *m*

accept *vt* BANK *credit card*, COMMS *call*, GEN COMM *bid* accepter, LAW, PROP agréer, STOCK *bid, tender* accepter; ♦ ~ **a bribe** GEN COMM accepter un pot-de-vin; ~ **a call paid for by the receiver** COMMS accepter de payer une communication en PCV; ~ **a collect call** *AmE (cf accept a reverse-charge call BrE)* COMMS accepter de payer une communication en PCV; ~ **delivery of** GEN COMM prendre livraison de, réceptionner; ~ **no liability** GEN COMM sans recours; ~ **on presentation** GEN COMM accepter à vue; ~ **a reverse-charge call** *BrE (cf accept a collect call AmE)* COMMS accepter de payer une communication en PCV

acceptability *n* ECON *of money* pouvoir libératoire *m*, GEN COMM recevabilité *f*

acceptable[1] *adj* GEN COMM acceptable, admissible, convenable; ♦ **of ~ quality** GEN COMM de qualité acceptable, de qualité suffisante

acceptable:[2] ~ **container condition** *n (ACC)* TRANSP *shipping* état acceptable d'un conteneur *m*; ~ **investment** *n* TAX placement acceptable *m*; ~ **price** *n* GEN COMM, S&M prix acceptable *m*

acceptance *n* ACC *(acce.)* BANK *(acce.)* acceptation *f (acc.)* GEN COMM réceptivité *f*, *of goods, invitation, offer* réception *f*, *of plan, proposal* approbation *f*, GEN COMM *(acce.)* assent consentement *m*, bill of exchange acceptation *f (acc.)*, LAW *(acce.)* contract acceptation *f (acc.)*, agrément *m*, consentement *m*, MEDIA *of product* accueil favorable *m*, réception favorable *f*, PROP *(acce.)* acceptation *f (acc.)*, agrément *m*, consentement *m*, S&M *of brand* acceptation *f*, accueil favorable *m*; ~ **account** BANK compte d'acceptations *m*; ~ **against documents** BANK acceptation contre documents *f*; ~ **bank** BANK banque d'acceptation *f*; ~ **bank line** BANK ligne de crédit par acceptation *f*; ~ **bill** BANK effet à l'acceptation *m*, traite à l'acceptation *f*; ~ **by intervention** GEN

COMM acceptation par intervention *f*; ~ **certificate** IMP/EXP, TRANSP attestation de prise en charge *f*; ~ **credit** BANK crédit par acceptation *m*; ~ **credit line** BANK ligne de crédit par acceptation *f*; ~ **duty** BANK obligation d'acceptation *f*; ~ **facility** BANK crédit par acceptation *m*; ~ **fee** BANK commission d'acceptation *f*; ~ **for honour** GEN COMM acceptation par intervention *f*; ~ **house** BANK banque d'acceptation *f*, banque d'escompte *f*, banque d'escompte d'effets étrangers *f*, maison d'acceptation *f*; ~ **ledger** BANK, FIN livre des acceptations *m*; ~ **liability** BANK encours sous forme d'acceptation *m*; ~ **line of credit** BANK crédit par acceptation *m*, ligne de crédit par acceptation *f*; ~ **of lump-sum settlement** GEN COMM acceptation d'un règlement forfaitaire *f*, acceptation d'un règlement global *f*; ~ **market** BANK marché des acceptations *m*, marché des effets acceptés *m*; ~ **price** BANK prix d'entrée en possession *m*; ~ **register** BANK livre des acceptations *m*; ~ **slip** INS bordereau d'acceptation *m*; ~ **supra protest** GEN COMM acceptation sur protêt *f*; ~ **test** IND, S&M essai de réception *m*; ~ **trial** IND, S&M essai de réception *m*

accepted[1] *adj* ADMIN *handwritten on bill* bon pour acceptation, GEN COMM accepté

accepted:[2] ~ **bill** *n* FIN, GEN COMM effet accepté *m*; ~ **draft** *n* BANK traite acceptée *f*

accepting[1] *adj* BANK *banker* acceptant

accepting:[2] ~ **bank** *n* (SYN *accepting house*) BANK banque d'acceptation *f*; ~ **banker** *n* BANK banquier acceptant *m*; ~ **house** *n* (SYN *accepting bank*) BANK banque d'acceptation *f*

acceptor *n* BANK *of bill* accepteur *m*, tiré *m*

access[1] *n* COMP accès *m*, point d'accès *m*; ~ **control** *n* COMP *auditing* contrôle d'accès *m*; ~ **differential** *n* ECON différentiel d'accès *m*; ~ **right** *n* LAW droit d'accès *m*, droit de passage *m*, PROP droit de passage *m*; ~ **rights** *n pl* COMP droits d'accès *m pl*; ~ **time** *n* COMP temps d'accès *m*; ♦ **give sb ~ to** GEN COMM permettre à qn d'accéder à; **have ~ to information** GEN COMM avoir accès à l'information

access[2] *vt* COMP *database, information, machine* accéder à, avoir accès à *loc m*

Access® *n* BANK carte de crédit britannique

accessibility *n* GEN COMM *of information* accessibilité *f*, *of public places* facilité d'accès *f*

accessible *adj* GEN COMM *file, information* accessible, à la portée de tous *loc f*, *person* accessible, disponible; **easily ~** GEN COMM d'accès aisé, d'accès facile

accession *n* LAW, POL *to the EU*, PROP accession *f*

accessorial: ~ **service** *n* S&M prestation accessoire *f*

accessories *n pl* GEN COMM équipement *m*, S&M, TRANSP accessoires *m pl*

accessory[1] *adj* GEN COMM, S&M, TRANSP accessoire

accessory[2] *n* LAW complice *mf*; **~ advertising** S&M publicité de complément *f*

accident *n* GEN COMM, TRANSP accident *m*; **~ at sea** INS, TRANSP accident de mer *m*, fortune de mer *f*; **~ and health insurance** *US* INS assurance-accidents et maladies *f*; **~ insurance** INS assurance contre les accidents *f*, assurance-accidents *f* (*jarg*); **~ insurer** INS assureur accidents *m*; **~ prevention** HRM *at work* prévention des accidents *f*; **~ risk** INS risque d'accident *m*; ◆ **have an ~** TRANSP avoir un accident

accidental: **~ discharge** *n* ENVIR, IND *pollution* rejet accidentel *m*, échappement accidentel *m*

accommodate *vt* BANK *with loan*, FIN *with loan* consentir, prêter, GEN COMM *request* satisfaire, *with supply, service* fournir, TRANSP contenir, WEL *provide room for* accueillir, héberger, loger, recevoir; ◆ **~ sb with a loan** BANK, FIN consentir un prêt à qn

accommodating: **~ credit** *n* ACC crédit de complaisance *m*

accommodation *n* BANK, FIN crédit *m*, prêt *m*, relais *m*, GEN COMM *compromise* adaptation *f*, arrangement *m*, compromis *m*, *office* bureau *m*, immeuble *m*, place *f*, PROP *BrE*, WEL *BrE* hébergement *m*, logement *m*; **~ acceptance** GEN COMM acceptation par complaisance *f*; **~ address** *BrE* COMMS boîte aux lettres *f*; **~ agency** *BrE* WEL agence de logement *f*; **~ allowance** *BrE* GEN COMM, HRM, WEL indemnité de logement *f*; **~ berth** TRANSP *shipping* mouillage réservé à la marine *m*; **~ bill** (SYN *accommodation note, accommodation paper*) BANK, FIN, GEN COMM billet de complaisance *m*, effet de complaisance *m*; **~ draft** BANK, FIN, GEN COMM traite de complaisance *f*; **~ endorsement** BANK, FIN endossement de complaisance *m*; **~ indorsement** *see accommodation endorsement*; **~ maker** (SYN *accommodation party*) FIN endosseur par complaisance *m*, souscripteur par complaisance *m*; **~ note** (SYN *accommodation bill, accommodation paper*) BANK, FIN, GEN COMM billet de complaisance *m*, effet de complaisance *m*; **~ paper** (SYN *accommodation bill, accommodation note*) BANK, FIN, GEN COMM billet de complaisance *m*, effet de complaisance *m*; **~ party** (SYN *accommodation maker*) FIN endosseur par complaisance *m*, souscripteur par complaisance *m*; **~ payment** BANK, FIN, GEN COMM, S&M paiement de complaisance *m*; **~ road** TRANSP route de desserte *f*, route à usage restreint *f*, voie privée *f*; **~ train** *AmE* (*cf slow train*) TRANSP omnibus *m*; ◆ **take ~** FIN contracter un crédit, contracter un emprunt, faire un prêt

accommodations *n AmE see accommodation BrE*

accompanied:[1] **~ baggage** *n* (ANT *unaccompanied baggage*) TRANSP bagages accompagnés *m pl*

accompanied:[2] **~ by** *phr* GEN COMM accompagné de, accompagné par

accompany *vt* GEN COMM accompagner, escorter

accompanying: **~ adult** *n* HRM accompagnateur *m*, animateur de groupe *m*; **~ document** *n* ADMIN, COMMS document accompagnateur *m*, document ci-joint *m*, document joint *m*, pièce jointe *f*; **~ letter** *n* COMMS lettre d'accompagnement *f*

accomplish *vt* GEN COMM accomplir

accomplishment *n* GEN COMM *of task* accomplissement *m*, exécution *f*, réalisation *f*, *thing accomplished* projet réalisé *m*, réussite *f*, HRM *achievement* oeuvre accomplie *f*, projet réalisé *m*, *skill* talent *m*

accord *n* GEN COMM convention *f*, LAW *formal agreement* accord *m*, convention *f*, *treaty* pacte *m*, traité *m*, POL *treaty* pacte *m*, traité *m*; **~ and satisfaction** FIN *bond, debenture* consentement et règlement *m*, libération à titre onéreux *f*

accordance: **in ~ with** *phr* GEN COMM *standards, regulations* conforme à, conformément à, selon; **in ~ with the law** *phr* LAW en vertu de la loi; **in ~ with your instructions** *phr* GEN COMM conformément à vos instructions

according: **~ to** *phr* GEN COMM conformément à, d'après, selon, suivant; **~ to the norm** *phr* LAW conformément à la norme, selon la norme; **~ to plan** *phr* ADMIN, GEN COMM comme prévu; **~ to schedule** *phr* MGMNT, S&M, TRANSP selon l'horaire, selon le calendrier, selon le programme

accordingly *adv* GEN COMM en conséquence *loc f*

accordion: **~ folding** *n* MEDIA, S&M *advertising* pli accordéon *m*

account[1] *n* ACC *bill* facture *f*, note *f*, ACC *(alc, acct)* BANK *(alc)* compte *m*, BANK *(acct)* bill facture *f (fre)* FIN *(alc, acct) money in bank; credit arrangement* compte *m*, GEN COMM *bill* note *f*, GEN COMM *(alc)* compte *m*, GEN COMM *(acct)* facture *f (fre)* MEDIA, S&M *advertising* budget *m*, STOCK *UK* règlement à la bourse de Londres, règlement mensuel *m*; **~ activity** *n* BANK mouvement de compte *m*; **~ activity charge** *n* BANK frais de mouvement *m pl*, frais de mouvement de compte *m pl*; **~ analysis** *n* BANK analyse d'un compte *f*; **~ balance** *n* ACC, BANK, FIN, GEN COMM solde *m*, solde comptable *m*, solde de compte *m*; **~ book** *n* ACC jl, journal *m*, livre de comptes *m*, registre de comptabilité *m*, BANK, FIN livre de comptes *m*; **~ current** *n (alc)* ACC compte de mandataire *m*; **~ day** *n* FIN, STOCK jour de liquidation *m*; **~ executive** *n* HRM *advertising* chef de publicité d'agence *m*, *finance* responsable de budget *m*, MEDIA *advertising*, S&M chef de publicité d'agence *m*, STOCK *brokerage firm* responsable de la gestion du compte d'un client, courtier *m*; **~ form** *n* ACC présentation de bilan en compte *f*, *balance sheet* présentation horizontale *f*; **~ format** *n* ACC présentation de bilan en compte *f*; **~ holder** *n* BANK titulaire d'un compte *m*; **~ maintenance charge** *n* (SYN *account maintenance fee*) BANK commission de tenue de compte *f*, frais de tenue de compte *m pl*; **~ maintenance fee** *n* (SYN *account maintenance charge*) BANK commission de tenue de compte *f*, frais de tenue de compte *m pl*; **~ management** *n* ACC, BANK, FIN gestion des comptes *f*; **~ manager** *n* BANK directeur des comptes *m*, HRM chef de publicité *m*, chef de publicité d'agence *m*, *finance* responsable de budget *m*, MEDIA, S&M *advertising* chef de publicité *m*, chef de publicité d'agence *m*; **~ market** *n* STOCK marché à terme *m*; **~ movements** *n pl* ACC écritures *f pl*; **~ name** *n* ACC, BANK intitulé de compte *m*, nom d'un compte *m*, titre du compte *m*; **~ number** *n* ACC, BANK, FIN numéro de compte *m*; **~ -only check** *n AmE*, **~ -only cheque** *n BrE* BANK chèque à porter en compte *m*; **~ operation** *n* BANK tenue de compte *f*; **~ operation charge** *n* BANK commission de tenue de compte *f*, frais de tenue de compte *m pl*; **~ planning** *n* MEDIA *advertising*, S&M *advertising* planification d'une campagne de publicité *f*; **~ reconciliation** *n* ACC concordance *f*, rapprochement de comptes *m*; **~ rendered** *n* ACC, FIN, STOCK solde à nouveau *m*, solde à reporter *m*; **~ sales** *n (A/S)* ACC compte-rendu des opérations de consignation *m*; **~ statement** *n* ACC, BANK relevé de compte *m*, GEN COMM relevé de compte *m*, *amount* position du compte *f*, STOCK *securities* avis de compte *m*, relevé de compte *m*; **~ transaction** *n* ACC, BANK, FIN opération comptable *f*, transaction *f*; **~ turnover** *n* ACC, BANK, FIN mouvement comptable *m*; ◆ **my ~** *(m/a)* GEN COMM mon compte *m*; **~ of** *(AO)* ACC, BANK, FIN, GEN COMM pour le compte de; **on ~** GEN COMM pour compte, S&M en acompte; **on no ~** GEN COMM en aucun cas; **on ~ of** *(o/a)* GEN COMM en raison de, à cause de *f*; **~ payee** BANK *on cheque* chèque non-endossable *m*; **rendering of ~s** FIN reddition de comptes *f*; **take ~ of sth** GEN COMM tenir compte de; **take sth into ~** GEN COMM prendre qch en compte, tenir compte de qch, prendre qch en considération

account:[2] **~ for** *vt* GEN COMM *enter in accounts* comptabiliser, *expenses* justifier, rendre compte de, *record* enregistrer

accountability *n* ACC obligation fiduciaire *f*, obligation réditionnelle *f*, responsabilité *f*, FIN, GEN COMM responsabilité *f*; **~ in management** MGMNT responsabilisation des cadres supérieurs *f*, responsabilité de la direction *f*

accountable[1] *adj* GEN COMM responsable; ◆ **~ for** GEN COMM responsable de

accountable:[2] **~ advance** *n* ACC avance à justifier *f*; **~ receipt** *n* ACC quittance comptable *f*

accountancy *n* ACC *profession* profession comptable *f*, ACC *bookkeeping* comptabilité *f*, expertise comptable *f*; **~ profession** *n* ACC profession comptable *f*; **~ services** *n pl* ACC services d'expertise comptable *m pl*

accountant *n* ACC commissaire aux comptes *m* *(Fra)*, comptable *mf*, expert-comptable *m*, HRM comptable *mf*

Accountant: **~ General** *n (AG)* ACC chef comptable *m*, directeur de comptabilité *m*

accountant's: **~ professional liability insurance** *n* ACC, INS assurance de responsabilité professionnelle des experts-comptables *f*, indemnité professionnelle des experts-comptables *f*

accounting *n* ACC comptabilité *f*; **~ adjustment** *n* ACC rectification comptable *f*, redressement comptable *m*; **~ analysis** *n* ACC analyse comptable *f*; **~ balance of payments** *n* ACC, ECON balance des paiements comptables *f*; **~ change** *n* ACC modification comptable *f*; **~ clerk** *n* ACC aide-comptable *mf*; **~ control** *n* ACC *auditing*, FIN *auditing* contrôle comptable *m*, contrôle interne *m*; **~ conventions** *n pl* ACC conventions comptables *f pl*, normes comptables *f pl*, postulats comptables *m pl*, principes comptables *m pl*; **~ costs** *n pl* ACC, FIN frais comptables *m pl*; **~ cycle** *n* ACC cycle comptable *m*; **~ data** *n pl* ACC données comptables *f pl*, *published by companies* informations financières *f pl*, FIN, GEN COMM données comptables *f pl*; **~ department** *n* ACC, ADMIN, FIN, GEN COMM service de la comptabilité *m*, services comptables *m pl*; **~ doctrines** *n pl* ACC doctrines comptables *f pl*; **~ effect** *n* ACC *of rules or change in rules* incidence comptable *f*; **~ entry** *n* ACC, FIN inscription comptable *f*, écriture *f*, écriture comptable *f*; **~ equation** *n* ACC équation comptable *f*; **~ error** *n* ACC, FIN erreur comptable *f*; **~ fees** *n pl* ACC, FIN frais comptables *m pl*, honoraires comptables *m pl*, honoraires d'expertise comptable *m pl*; **~ firm** *n (SYN accounting practice)* ACC cabinet d'expertise comptable *m*, cabinet d'experts-comptables *m*, pratique comptable *f*; **~ for inflation** *n* ACC comptabilité des effets de l'inflation *f*; **~ harmonization** *n UK* ACC harmonisation comptable *f*; **~ identity** *n* ACC identité fondamentale *f*; **~ income** *n* ACC *net profit* bénéfice comptable *m*, résultat comptable *m*, *revenue* chiffre d'affaires *m*; **~ law** *n* ACC, FIN, LAW droit comptable *m*, droit de la comptabilité *m*; **~ method** *n* ACC, FIN méthode comptable *f*; **~ model** *n* ACC, FIN modèle comptable *m*; **~ office** *n* ACC, ADMIN *of government department*, FIN, GEN COMM service de la comptabilité *m*, services comptables *m pl*; **~ officer** *n (AO)* ACC, HRM comptable *mf*, comptable adjoint *m*; **~ package** *n* ACC, COMP, FIN logiciel de comptabilité *m*, progiciel de comptabilité *m*; **~ papers** *n pl* ACC supports comptables *m pl*; **~ period** *n* ACC exercice comptable *m*, exercice financier *m*, période comptable *f*, ECON exercice *m*, FIN exercice comptable *m*, exercice financier *m*, période comptable *f*, STOCK exercice comptable *m*, période comptable *f*; **~ plan** *n* ACC, FIN plan comptable *m*; **~ policy** *n* ACC, FIN politique comptable *f*; **~ practice** *n (SYN accounting firm)* ACC cabinet d'expertise comptable *m*, cabinet d'experts-comptables *m*; **~ practices** *n pl* ACC pratiques comptables *f pl*; **~ price** *n* ACC, BANK prix comptable *m*; **~ principles** *n pl* ACC principes comptables *m pl*; **~ procedure** *n* ACC, FIN méthode comptable *f*, procédé comptable *m*; **~ profit** *n* ACC bénéfice comptable *m*, résultat comptable *m*; **~ rate of interest** *n (ARI)* ACC, BANK, FIN taux d'intérêt comptable *m (TIC)*; **~ rate of return** *n* ACC taux de rendement comptable *m*; **~ ratio** *n* ACC, FIN ratio comptable *m*; **~ records** *n pl* ACC, FIN, GEN COMM données comptables *f pl*, livres comptables *m pl*; **~ report** *n* ACC, FIN rapport comptable *m*; **~ return** *n* ACC, FIN rendement comptable *m*; **~ software** *n* ACC, COMP, FIN logiciel de comptabilité *m*, progiciel de comptabilité *m*; **~ standard setting** *n* ACC normalisation comptable *f*, réglementation comptable *f*, établissement de normes comptables *m*; **~ standards** *n pl* ACC normes comptables *f pl*; **~ system** *n* ACC, FIN système comptable *m*, système de comptabilité *m*; **~ treatment** *n* ACC, FIN traitement comptable *m*; **~ year** *n* ACC, FIN exercice comptable *m*, exercice financier *m*; **~ year then ended** *n* ACC, FIN exercice clos à cette date *m*

Accounting: **~ Principles Board** *n US (APB)* ACC bureau des principes en comptabilité; **~ Standards Board** *n UK* ACC conseil de normes comptables

accounts: **~ appraisal** *n* ACC *auditing*, FIN *auditing* revue analytique *f*, évaluation des comptes *f*; **~ certification** *n* ACC *auditing*, FIN *auditing* approbation de comptes *f*, avis du commissaire aux comptes *m*, certificat d'audit *m*, certificat du commissaire aux comptes *m*; **~ close-off** *n* BANK clôture des comptes *f*; **~ department** *n* ACC, ADMIN, FIN, GEN COMM service de la comptabilité *m*, services comptables *m pl*; **~ payable** *n* ACC, ECON comptes créditeurs *m pl*, comptes fournisseurs *m pl*, poste clients *m*; **~ payable clerk** *n* ACC commis aux comptes créditeurs *m*, commis aux comptes fournisseurs *m*; **~ payable ledger** *n* ACC, BANK, FIN auxiliaire fournisseurs *m*, grand livre auxiliaire des fournisseurs *m*, grand livre des comptes fournisseurs *m*, grand livre des fournisseurs *m*; **~ receivable** *n pl* ACC, ECON comptes clients *m pl*, créances *f pl*, débiteurs *m pl*; **~ receivable financing** *n* ACC, FIN financement des comptes clients *m*, financement des créances *m*; **~ receivable ledger** *n* ACC, BANK, FIN auxiliaire clients *m*, grand livre auxiliaire des clients *m*, grand livre des clients *m*, grand livre des comptes clients *m*; **~ receivable statement** *n* ACC, FIN extrait des comptes clients *m*, relevé des comptes clients *m*; **~ receivable turnover** *n* ACC, FIN taux de rotation des comptes clients *m*

Accra *pr n* GEN COMM Accra *n pr*

accredit *vt* GEN COMM *guarantee* garantir, *institution, qualification* agréer, *representative, official* accréditer, WEL agréer

accreditation *n* GEN COMM, WEL *institution, qualification* agrément *m*

accredited[1] *adj* GEN COMM agréé

accredited:[2] **~ investor** *n* STOCK investisseur accrédité *m*

accretion *n* GEN COMM accroissement *m*, STOCK ajustement de la valeur de l'obligation *m*

accrual: **~ accounting** *n* ACC comptabilité d'enga-

gements *f*, indépendance des exercices *f*, spécialisation des exercices *f*; **~ basis** *n* (SYN *accrual method*) ACC comptabilité d'engagements *f*, comptabilité d'exercice *f*, méthode de la comptabilité d'exercice *f*; **~ concept** *n* (SYN *accrual principle*) ACC principe de rattachement à l'exercice *m*, règle de rattachement à l'exercice *f*; **~ date** *n* ACC, FIN date de paiement des intérêts courus *f*; **~ of interest** *n* ACC, BANK, FIN accumulation d'intérêts *f*; **~ interest rate** *n* ACC, BANK, FIN taux des intérêts courus *m*; **~ method** *n* (SYN *accrual basis*) ACC comptabilité d'engagements *f*, comptabilité d'exercice *f*, méthode de la comptabilité d'exercice *f*; **~ principle** *n* (SYN *accrual concept*) ACC principe de rattachement à l'exercice *m*, règle de rattachement à l'exercice *f*; **~ property income** *n* PROP, TAX revenu accumulé tiré de biens *m*; **~ tax** *n* TAX impôt accumulé *m*

accruals *n pl* ACC, BANK compte de régularisation *m*, FIN accumulation *f*, compte de régularisation *m*, GEN COMM *interest, cost, revenue* accumulation *f*; ◆ **the ~ of wages** ACC les charges salariales constatées *f pl*

accrue *vi* ACC, BANK *expense, revenue* courir, s'accroître, s'accumuler, FIN s'accumuler; ◆ **~ previously unrecorded expenses** ACC inscrire des charges à payer; **~ previously unrecorded revenues** ACC inscrire des produits à recevoir

accrued[1] *adj* ACC cumulé, *wealth* amassé

accrued:[2] **~ asset** *n* ACC produit à recevoir *m*; **~ charges** *n pl* BANK charges constatées d'avance *f pl*, frais accumulés *m pl*; **~ compound interest** *n* BANK intérêts composés courus *m pl*; **~ credit** *n* ACC produit constaté d'avance *m*; **~ dividend** *n* ACC dividende à payer *m*, STOCK dividende cumulé *m*; **~ expense** *n* ACC charge constatée par régularisation *f*, charge à payer *f*; **~ expenses** *n pl* GEN COMM frais à payer *m pl*; **~ income** *n* ACC produit constaté d'avance *m*, revenu à recevoir *m*; **~ interest** *n (AI)* ACC, BANK, FIN, GEN COMM, STOCK intérêts courus *m pl*, intérêts cumulés *m pl (IC)*; **~ interest payable** *n* ACC, BANK intérêts courus à payer *m pl*, intérêts cumulés à payer *m pl*; **~ interest receivable** *n* ACC intérêts courus à recevoir *m pl*, BANK intérêts courus à recevoir *m pl*, intérêts cumulés à recevoir *m pl*; **~ liability** *n* ACC charge à payer *f*; **~ receivable and pre-paid expenses** *n pl* ACC compte de régularisation *m*; **~ revenue** *n* ACC produit constaté par régularisation *m*, produit à recevoir *m*

accruing *adj* FIN *expenses, revenue* afférent, *interests* à échoir

acct *abbr (account)* ACC, BANK, FIN, GEN COMM compte *m*

accumulate 1. *vt* GEN COMM *debt* accumuler, *wealth* amasser; **2.** *vi* GEN COMM *debt* s'accumuler

accumulated[1] *adj* FIN *dividends, depreciation* cumulé

accumulated:[2] **~ averaging amount** *n* TAX montant d'étalement accumulé *m*; **~ averaging amount withdrawal** *n* TAX retrait du montant d'étalement accumulé *m*; ~ **balance** *n* TAX solde accumulé *m*; ~ **deficit** *n* ACC pertes accumulées *f pl*, TAX déficit accumulé *m*; ~ **depletion** *n* ACC épuisement accumulé *m*; ~ **depreciation** *n* ACC *special write-down* amortissement des immobilisations *m pl*, provision pour dépréciation *f*, *systematic depreciation* amortissement accumulé *m*; ~ **dividend** *n* STOCK dividende cumulé *m*; ~ **profits** *n pl* ACC *on balance sheet* report à nouveau *m*; ~ **surplus** *n* ACC bénéfice accumulé *m*

accumulating: ~ **fund** *n* TAX fonds accumulés *m pl*; ~ **income** *n* TAX revenu accumulé *m*

accumulation *n* GEN COMM *of capital, wealth, interest* accroissement *m*; ~ **area** STOCK fourchette de prix *f*; ~ **of risk** INS cumul de risques *m*; ~ **risk** INS risque d'accumulation *m*

accumulator *n* COMP accumulateur *m*, totalisateur *m*

accuracy *n* ACC *of figures* exactitude *f*, *of report, document, statement* précision *f*, GEN COMM *of figures, data* exactitude *f*, *of judgement* justesse *f*, *of report, document, aim* précision *f*

accurate *adj* GEN COMM *description* fidèle, *figures, estimate* exact, *judgement* juste, *report, aim* précis

accusation *n* LAW accusation *f*, incrimination *f*, plainte *f*

accuse *vt* LAW accuser, incriminer

accused *n* LAW accusé *m*; **the** ~ LAW l'accusé *mf*

accy *abbr* (*accountancy*) ACC comptabilité *f*, expertise comptable *f*

ACD *abbr* (*automated cash dispenser, automatic cash dispenser*) BANK DAB (*distributeur automatique de billets*)

ACE[1] *abbr* (*Amex Commodities Exchange*) STOCK Bourse de commerce de l'Amex *f*

ACE:[2] ~ **program** *n* AmE, ~ **programme** *n* BrE ENVIR *EU* programme ACE *m*, programme d'action communautaire pour l'environnement *m*

ACH *abbr* (*Automated Clearing House*) BANK, FIN chambre de compensation automatisée

achievable *adj* GEN COMM réalisable

achieve *vt* GEN COMM *growth, level, objective* arriver à, atteindre, *result* obtenir, réaliser

achievement *n* GEN COMM réalisation *f*; ~ **motive** HRM désir de réalisation personnelle *m*; ~ **quotient** GEN COMM quotient de réussite *m*; ~ **test** GEN COMM test de niveau *m*

achievements *n pl* LAW faits matériels d'une affaire *m pl*

achiever *n* GEN COMM battant *m*

acid:[1] ~ -**resistant** *adj* ENVIR tolérant à l'acide

acid:[2] ~ **deposit** *n* ENVIR dépôts acides *m pl*, retombées acides *f pl*; ~ **pollution** *n* ENVIR dépôts acides *m pl*; ~ **precipitation** *n* ENVIR *snow, hail, fog* précipitation acide *f*; ~ **rain** *n* ENVIR pluies acides *f pl*; ~ **rain pollution** *n* ENVIR pollution par les pluies acides *f*; ~ **snow** *n* ENVIR neige acide *f*; ~ **snow pollution** *n* ENVIR pollution par les neiges acides *f*; ~ **test** *n* GEN COMM épreuve de vérité *f*,

épreuve à la pierre de touche *f*; ~ -**test ratio** *n* (SYN *quick ratio*) ACC, BANK, FIN ratio de liquidité immédiate *m*, taux de liquidité immédiate *m*

acidity: ~ **level** *n* ENVIR *pollution* niveau d'acidité *m*

ACIS *abbr* (*Associate of the Chartered Institute of Secretaries*) ADMIN membre de l'institut des secrétaires qualifiées

ACK *abbr* (*acknowledgement*) GEN COMM confirmation *f*

acknowledge *vt* FIN *debt* reconnaître, GEN COMM *arrival* prendre note de, *fact* admettre, *mistake, debt* reconnaître; ◆ ~ **receipt by letter** COMMS accuser réception par courrier; ~ **receipt of** COMMS *letter, cheque*, GEN COMM *mail, goods* accuser réception de

acknowledgement *n* BANK reconnaissance *f*, COMMS *on document* signature *f*, FIN reconnaissance *f*, GEN COMM reconnaissance *f*, *payment* quittance *f*, reçu *m*, récépissé *m*, GEN COMM *request for goods* confirmation *f*, LAW, S&M certification *f*, reconnaissance *f*; ~ **of debt** BANK, FIN, GEN COMM, TRANSP reconnaissance de dette *f*; ~ **of indebtness** BANK reconnaissance d'endettement *f*; ~ **of order** COMMS *to customer*, GEN COMM *to customer* accusé de réception d'une commande *m*; ~ **of receipt** COMMS, COMP accusé de réception *m*, FIN récépissé *m*, GEN COMM, LAW accusé de réception *m*

ACM *abbr* (*Andean Common Market*) ECON Marché Commun Andin *m*

ACMA *abbr* UK (*Associate of the Chartered Institute of Management Accountants*) ACC, MGMNT membre associé de l'institut des comptables de prix de revient et de gestion

ACOP *abbr* (*approved code of practice*) GEN COMM déontologie *f*

ACP: ~ **countries** *n pl* (*African, Caribbean and Pacific countries*) ECON, POL pays de l'ACP *m pl*

ACPs *abbr* (*African, Caribbean and Pacific countries*) ECON, POL pays de l'ACP *m pl*

acquaint: ~ **sb with the situation** *phr* GEN COMM mettre qn au courant de la situation; ~ **sb with sth** *phr* GEN COMM avertir qn de qch, aviser qn de qch, renseigner qn sur qch

acquaintance *n* GEN COMM connaissance *f*, relation *f*; ◆ **make sb's** ~ GEN COMM faire la connaissance de qn

acquainted: **be** ~ **with** *phr* GEN COMM *news* être au courant de *loc m*, *person* connaître

acquest *n* LAW acquêt *m*

acquire *vt* GEN COMM, PROP, STOCK *option* acquérir; ◆ ~ **an interest in** GEN COMM prendre une participation dans

acquired[1] *adj* GEN COMM acquis

acquired:[2] ~ **company** *n* ECON entreprise acquise *f*; ~ **share** *n* US STOCK action rachetée *f*; ~ **surplus** *n* US FIN surplus acquis *m*

acquiring: ~ **authority** *n* GEN COMM administration

acquéreuse *f*; ~ **company** *n* GEN COMM *in corporate takeover* acquéreur *m*

acquisition *n* ECON *of company* absorption *f*, GEN COMM achat *m*, acquisition *f*, *of company* acquisition *f*; ~ **accounting** ACC comptabilité par coûts historiques *f*, *method of consolidation* consolidation par intégration totale *f*; ~ **agent** INS agent acquisiteur *m*, apporteur *m*; ~ **of assets** ACC acquisition d'immobilisations *f*; ~ **commission** INS commission d'acquisition *f*; ~ **contract** TAX contrat d'acquisition *m*; ~ **cost** ACC coût d'achat *m*, coût d'acquisition *m*, frais d'acquisition *m pl*, TAX coût d'acquisition *m*; ~ **fee** GEN COMM frais d'acquisition *m pl*, STOCK droit d'acquisition *m*, frais d'acquisition *m pl*; ~ **financing** FIN financement d'une acquisition *m*; ~ **policy** STOCK politique d'acquisition *f*; ~ **price** FIN prix d'achat *m*; ~ **profile** BANK *merchant* profil d'acquisition *m*; ~ **of shareholdings** STOCK acquisition d'actions *f*; ~ **of stock** STOCK acquisition d'actions *f*; ~ **value** GEN COMM valeur de l'acquisition *f*

acquisitive[1] *adj* FIN *company* possédant une politique agressive de rachat, GEN COMM *person, society* attaché aux biens de consommation, vorace, âpre au gain

acquisitive:[2] ~ **instinct** *n* GEN COMM cupidité *f*, instinct de possession *m*

acquisitiveness *n* GEN COMM goût de la propriété *m*, instinct de possession *m*, soif de possession *f*

acquit *vt* GEN COMM *debt, duty* s'acquitter de, LAW *accused* acquitter, relaxer, *debt, duty* s'acquitter de

acquittal *n* LAW *of the accused, of a debt* acquittement *m*

acquittance *n* LAW *confirmation of payment* décharge *f*, quittance *f*

ACRA *abbr UK (Associate of the Corporation of Registered Accountants)* ACC membre associé de la corporation des comptables agréés

acre *n* GEN COMM arpent *m* (*vieilli*), demi-hectare *m*

acreage *n* GEN COMM superficie *f*

acronym *n* GEN COMM acronyme *m*, sigle *m*

across:[1] ~ **-the-board** *adj* GEN COMM général, généralisé, systématique, MGMNT *changes* de bas en haut, général

across:[2] ~ **the board** *adv* GEN COMM de façon systématique *loc f*, systématiquement; ~ **the counter** GEN COMM *purchases* sans intermédiaire

across:[3] ~ **-the-board cut** *n* (ANT *across-the-board increase*) GEN COMM *in prices*, HRM *in wages*, MGMNT *in taxes*, TAX réduction globale *f*, réduction générale *f*, réduction toutes catégories *f*; ~ **-the-board increase** *n* (ANT *across-the-board cut*) GEN COMM *in prices*, HRM *in wages*, MGMNT, TAX *in taxes* augmentation globale *f*, augmentation générale *f*, augmentation toutes catégories *f*; ~ **-the-board investigation** *n UK* ACC *auditing*, FIN

auditing enquête tous azimuts *f*, examen systématique *m*

ACRS *abbr (accelerated cost recovery system)* ACC, FIN amortissement accéléré *m*, amortissement dégressif *m*

ACS *abbr (Australian Container Service)* TRANSP *shipping* service transconteneur australien

ACSS *abbr (Automated Clearing Settlement System)* BANK SCRA (*système de compensation et de règlement automatisé*)

act[1] *n* LAW acte *m*, POL acte *m*, loi *f*; ~ **of acknowledgement** LAW acte de reconnaissance *m*, acte récognitif *m*; ~ **of bankruptcy** ACC acte de faillite *m*, acte de mise en faillite *m*; ~ **of cession** GEN COMM acte de cession *m*; ~ **of God** FIN, INS, LAW catastrophe naturelle *f*; ~ **of honor** *AmE*, ~ **of honour** *BrE* LAW intervention après protêt *f*

act:[2] **1.** *vt* ~ **on** GEN COMM *advice, suggestion* se conformer à, suivre, *decision* donner suite à, *order* exécuter; **2.** *vi* ~ **upon** GEN COMM agir; ♦ ~ **in good faith** LAW agir de bonne foi; ~ **in one's official capacity** MGMNT agir dans l'exercice de ses fonctions; ~ **on sb's behalf** LAW agir au nom de qn, agir pour le compte de qn

acting[1] *adj* GEN COMM intérimaire, par intérim *loc m*, provisoire

acting:[2] ~ **allowance** *n* GEN COMM indemnité de fonction *f*; ~ **director** *n* MGMNT directeur par intérim *m*; ~ **partner** *n* MGMNT associé commandité *m*

actio personalis moritur cum persona *n* LAW action personnelle s'éteignant avec la personne *f*

actio in personam *n* LAW action personnelle *f*

actio in rem *n* LAW action en reconnaissance d'un droit *f*, action réelle *f*

action:[1] ~ **-orientated** *adj* GEN COMM tourné vers l'action

action[2] *n* GEN COMM action *f*, LAW action *f*, action en justice *f*, poursuites *f pl*, procès *m*, MEDIA reportage *m*; ~ **against X** LAW action contre X *f*, plainte contre X *f*; ~ **by the community relating to the environment programme** ENVIR *EU* programme d'action communautaire pour l'environnement *m*; ~ **code** COMP code d'intervention *m*, message d'intervention *m*; ~ **for cancellation** LAW recours en annulation *m*; ~ **for damages** INS action en dommages et intérêts *f*, action en dommages-intérêts *f*, poursuite en dommages et intérêts *f*; ~ **for libel** LAW diffamation *f*, procès en diffamation *m*; ~ **in rem** LAW action réelle *f*; ~ **message** COMP message d'intervention *m*; ~ **plan** GEN COMM, HRM plan d'action *m*, programme d'action *m*; ~ **program** *AmE*, ~ **programme** *BrE* ECON *of the EU*, GEN COMM, POL *of the EU* programme d'action *m*; ~ **research** MGMNT recherche action *f*, recherche active *f*; ♦ **be out of** ~ GEN COMM *machine* être en panne, *telephone* être en dérangement; **for** ~ HRM pour action; **take legal** ~ LAW avoir recours à la justice, engager des poursuites, entamer des poursuites, intenter une action; **take legal ~ against sb** LAW intenter un procès contre qn, intenter un procès à qn

actionable *adj* GEN COMM *claim* receivable, LAW *remark, offence, allegation* passible de poursuites *loc*

activate *vt* COMP activer, lancer, mettre en fonction, mettre en marche, IND *mechanism, button, switch* actionner, activer, MGMNT *contingency plan, procedure* déclencher

activated *adj* COMP activé

active[1] *adj* COMP actif, connecté, FIN *capital, assets* productif, qui rapporte, GEN COMM *person* actif, STOCK *market* animé; ◆ **be ~** GEN COMM être en vigueur; **in ~ employment** HRM en activité

active:[2] **~ account** *n* BANK compte actif *m*; **~ bond** *n US* STOCK catégorie d'obligations faisant l'objet de forts volumes de transactions à la bourse de New York, obligation à revenu fixe; **~ bond crowd** *n US* STOCK courtiers en obligations à forts volumes de transactions; **~ business** *n* GEN COMM entreprise qui marche bien *f*; **~ business asset test** *n* TAX critère de l'actif d'une entreprise exploitée activement *m*; **~ capital** *n* FIN capital actif *m*; **~ computer** *n* COMP ordinateur connecté *m*, ordinateur en service *m*; **~ corps of executives** *n* HRM, MGMNT agents exécutifs en exercice *m pl*; **~ dealings** *n pl* STOCK marché animé *m*; **~ demand** *n* ECON, S&M demande importante *f*, forte demande *f*; **~ file** *n* COMP fichier actif *m*, fichier en cours *m*; **~ financing** *n* FIN financement d'actifs *m*; **~ investment** *n* STOCK investissement actif *m*, placement actif *m*; **~ investor** *n* STOCK investisseur actif *m*; **~ management** *n* GEN COMM, MGMNT gestion active *f*; **~ market** *n* STOCK marché animé *m*; **~ money** *n* FIN monnaie circulante *f*, monnaie en circulation *f*; **~ partner** *n* MGMNT partenaire actif *m*, partenaire actif commandite *m*; **~ population** *n* HRM population active *f*; **~ reinsurance** *n* INS réassurance effective *f*; **~ securities** *n pl* STOCK valeurs fréquemment négociées *f pl*, valeurs très actives *f pl*, valeurs très liquides *f pl*; **~ shares** *n pl* STOCK actions fréquemment négociées *f pl*, actions très liquides *f pl*; **~ trader** *n* S&M commerçant en exercice *m*; **~ trading** *n* STOCK marché animé *m*; **~ window** *n* COMP fenêtre active *f*

actively *adv* GEN COMM activement; ◆ **~ traded** *UK* STOCK activement négocié

activist *n* ECON, GEN COMM activiste *mf*, POL activiste *mf*, militant *m*

activity *n* BANK *of account* activité *f*, mouvement *m*, GEN COMM activité *f*, branche d'activité *f*, fonction *f*; **~ analysis** GEN COMM analyse d'activité *f*; **~ -based costing** *UK* ACC évaluation basée sur une activité *f*; **~ charge** BANK commission de mouvement *f*, commission de mouvement de compte *f*, frais de mouvement *m pl*, frais de mouvement de compte *m pl*; **~ chart** MGMNT graphique des activités *m*; **~ classification** ACC classification par activité *f*; **~ coding** ACC codage

par activités *m*; **~ element** ACC élément d'activité *m*; **~ rate** HRM taux d'activité *m*; **~ ratio** GEN COMM niveau d'activité *m*; **~ sampling** MATH *statistics* mesure du travail par sondage *f*, échantillonnage d'activités *m*, MGMNT, S&M *market research* mesure du travail par sondage *f*; **~ total** GEN COMM total par activité *m*

ACTU *abbr (Australian Council of Trade Unions)* HRM confédération des syndicats australiens

actual[1] *adj* ACC *figures*, ECON, FIN réel, GEN COMM *commodity* effectif, existant, réel

actual:[2] **~ address** *n* COMP adresse réelle *f*; **~ amount** *n* ACC *of outlay, expenditure* montant réel *m*; **~ budget** *n* ACC, ECON, POL budget de plein emploi *m*, budget réel *m*; **~ carrier** *n* TRANSP transporteur réel *m*, transporteur substitué *m*; **~ cash disbursement** *n* ACC débours effectif *m*, décaissement effectif *m*, paiement réel *m*; **~ cash value** *n (ACV)* FIN valeur de remplacement *f*, valeur effective au comptant *f*, STOCK valeur de remplacement *f*, valeur effective au comptant *f*, valeur théorique au remboursement *f*; **~ cost** *n (SYN real cost)* ACC coût réel *m*, coût réellement engagé *m*, TAX coût effectif *m*, coût réel *m*; **~ deficit** *n* ECON déficit réel *m*; **~ earnings** *n pl* ACC, ECON, HRM revenu réel *m*, résultat réel *m*; **~ eviction** *n* LAW, PROP expulsion effective *f*; **~ expenditure** *n* ACC dépense effective *f*, dépense effectuée *f*, dépense réelle *f*; **~ expense** *n* ACC dépense réelle *f*; **~ figures** *n pl* ECON chiffres réels *m pl*; **~ gross weight** *n* GEN COMM *transportation* masse brute réelle *f*; **~ instruction** *n* COMP instruction effective *f*; **~ inventory** *n AmE (cf actual stock BrE)* GEN COMM stock réel *m*; **~ investment** *n UK* BANK investissement réel *m*; **~ level of unemployment** *n* ECON, POL niveau effectif du chômage *m*; **~ loan loss** *n* BANK perte réelle sur prêts *f*; **~ loan loss experience** *n* BANK perte réelle sur prêts *f*; **~ loss** *n* ACC perte effective *f*, perte subie *f*; **~ outcome** *n* GEN COMM résultat effectif *m*; **~ payload** *n* TRANSP charge utile réelle *f*; **~ price** *n* ACC, ECON, FIN, GEN COMM, S&M prix réel *m*; **~ quotation** *n* STOCK cours effectif *m*; **~ stock** *n BrE (cf actual inventory AmE)* GEN COMM stock réel *m*; **~ takings** *n pl* ACC, FIN, HRM recettes effectives *f pl*; **~ tax rate** *n* TAX taux d'imposition réel *m*; **~ total loss** *n* INS *abandonment clauses* perte totale effective *f*; **~ wage** *n* ACC, ECON, HRM salaire réel *m*; **~ yield** *n* STOCK *of bond, investment* rendement effectif *m*

actuality *n* GEN COMM réalité *f*

actualize *vt* GEN COMM *represent realistically* actualiser

actuals *n pl* STOCK biens physiques *m pl*, marchandises physiques *f pl*, TRANSP *freight market* existant *m*; **this month's ~** ACC les chiffres réels pour le mois *m pl*

actuarial[1] *adj* INS actuariel

actuarial:[2] **~ certificate** *n* INS certificat actuariel *m*; **~ deficit** *n* INS déficit actuariel *m*, insuffisance actuarielle *f*; **~ expectation** *n* INS espérance mathématique *f*; ~ **liability** *n* INS dette actuarielle *f*, engagement actuariel *m*; ~ **loss** *n* INS déficit actuariel *m*, insuffisance actuarielle *f*, perte actuarielle *f*; ~ **science** *n* INS actuariat *m*

actuary *n* INS actuaire *m*

actuate *vt* GEN COMM *machine, system, device* faire marcher, mettre en marche, *person* faire agir, inciter .

actuator: ~ **pole** *n* TRANSP *shipping* goupille *f*

actus reus *n* LAW acte délictueux *m*, corps du délit *m*

ACU *abbr* (*administration of the customs union*) IMP/EXP *EU* AUD (*administration de l'union des douanes*)

acute: ~ **awareness** *n* GEN COMM *of particular factor* connaissance subtile *f*, intelligence subtile *f*

ACV *abbr* FIN (*actual cash value*), STOCK (*actual cash value*) valeur de remplacement *f*, valeur effective au comptant *f*, TRANSP (*air cushion vehicle*) aéroglisseur *m*, véhicule sur coussin d'air *m*

ad *n infrml* GEN COMM, MEDIA, S&M annonce *f*, annonce publicitaire *f*, *TV, radio* pub *f* (*infrml*), spot *m* (*infrml*), spot publicitaire *m*, *newspapers, magazines* petite annonce *f*

A/D *abbr* COMP (*analog-digital*) analogique-numérique, GEN COMM (*after date*) à/c (*à compter de*), TRANSP (*above deck*) *shipping* en pontée *loc f*, sur le pont *loc m*

Adam: ~ **Smith Institute** *n UK* POL Institut Adam Smith *m*

adapt *vi* GEN COMM s'adapter

adaptability *n* GEN COMM *of product, machine, system* adaptabilité *f*, possibilités d'adaptation *f pl*, *of person* faculté d'adaptation *f*, *of technology, procedure, project* souplesse *f*

adaptable *adj* GEN COMM adaptable

adaptation *n* GEN COMM adaptation *f*

adaptive: ~ **control** *n* MGMNT contrôle adaptatif *m*, contrôle souple *m*; ~ **expectations** *n pl* ECON espoirs d'adaptations *m pl*

adaptor *n* COMP adaptateur *m*

AD-AS *abbr* (*aggregate demand-aggregate supply*) ECON, FIN demande et offre globale *f*, demande globale-offre globale *f*

ADB *abbr* (*Asian Development Bank*) BANK Banque asiatique de développement *f*

ADC *abbr* COMP (*analog-digital converter*) *hardware* CAN (*convertisseur analogique-numérique*), GEN COMM (*advice of duration and/or charge*) IDP (*indication de durée et de prix*)

add:[1] ~ **lister** *n* (SYN *add listing machine*) GEN COMM machine à calculer à imprimante *f*; ~ **listing machine** *n* (SYN *add lister*) GEN COMM machine à calculer à imprimante *f*

add[2] **1.** *vt* ACC *column of figures* totaliser, *figures* additionner, ajouter, totaliser, GEN COMM additionner, MATH *column of figures* totaliser, *figures* additionner, ajouter, *points* gagner, STOCK *frac-*

tion on price of security enregistrer; ~ **back** MATH *sum* réincorporer, réintégrer; ~ **in** GEN COMM inclure; ~ **to** MATH accroître, ajouter à, augmenter; ~ **to income** ACC intégrer au revenu, porter au revenu; ~ **together** ACC, GEN COMM additionner, MATH *figures* additionner, totaliser; ~ **up** ACC *bill, column of figures* totaliser, *figures* additionner, GEN COMM *column of figures* totaliser, *figures* ajouter, totaliser, MATH *column of figures* totaliser, *figures* additionner, ajouter; ~ **up to** GEN COMM s'élever à, se monter à; **2.** *vi* ~ **up** GEN COMM, POL *figures, results* se recouper

Add. *abbr* (*address*) COMMS adresse *f*

added: ~ **value** *n* GEN COMM, S&M *special offer* valeur ajoutée *f*

addendum *n* [pl -da] LAW, MEDIA addendum *m*, additif *m*, annexe *f*

adder *n* ACC, MATH additionneur *m*

adding *n* ACC, MATH addition *f*; ~ **counter** COMP compteur additif *m*; ~ **machine** GEN COMM machine à additionner *f*, machine à calculer *f*; ~ **-up controversy** ECON controverse d'addition *f*

Addis: ~ **Ababa** *pr n* GEN COMM Addis-Abeba *n pr*

addition *n* ACC *new asset* achat *m*, acquisition *f*, *to fixed assets* addition *f*, augmentation *f*, COMP addition *f*, ajout *m*, MATH addition *f*, MEDIA *text amendment* addition *f*, ajout *m*; ~ **to age** INS majoration d'âge *f*; ◆ **in ~ to** GEN COMM en plus de; **no ~, no correction** GEN COMM ni surcharge, ni rature

additional[1] *adj* GEN COMM supplémentaire

additional[2] ~ **assessment** *n* TAX cotisation supplémentaire *f*; ~ **charge** *n* ACC supplément *m*; ~ **clause** *n* LAW avenant *m*, clause additionnelle *f*; ~ **conditions** *n pl* INS conditions complémentaires *f pl*, conditions supplémentaires *f pl*; ~ **expense insurance** *n* INS assurance contre la privation de jouissance *f*; ~ **facility** *n* ECON *balance of payments* facilité complémentaire *f*; ~ **feature** *n* PATENTS, S&M caractéristique additionnelle *f*; ~ **interest** *n* ACC, BANK, FIN intérêt complémentaire *m*; ~ **labor** *n AmE*, ~ **labour** *n BrE* HRM apport de main-d'oeuvre *m*; ~ **margin** *n* STOCK marge complémentaire *f*; ~ **mark-on** *n UK* S&M majoration supplémentaire du prix détaillant d'un article; ~ **matter** *n* PATENTS caractéristique additionnelle *f*, indication additionnelle *f*; ~ **paid-in capital** *n* ACC, FIN prime d'émission *f*, remise de fonds complémentaires *f*; ~ **pay** *n* HRM supplément de salaire *m*; ~ **postage** *n* COMMS surtaxe postale *f*; ~ **premium** *n* (*AP*) INS prime additionnelle *f*; ~ **security** *n* INS garantie supplémentaire *f*; ~ **tax** *n* TAX supplément d'impôt *m*; ~ **worker hypothesis** *n* HRM hypothèse de l'employé supplémentaire

additive *n* GEN COMM additif *m*

add-on[1] *adj* COMP périphérique, GEN COMM supplémentaire

add-on[2] *n* BANK ajout *m*; ~ **board** *n* COMP carte additionnelle *f*, carte d'extension *f*; ~ **card** *n* COMP carte additionnelle *f*, carte d'extension *f*; ~ **CDs** *n* pl UK (add-on domestic certificates of deposit) STOCK bons de caisse nationaux supplémentaires m pl; **~ costs** n pl ACC charges associées f pl, charges supplémentaires f pl; **~ domestic certificates of deposit** n pl UK (add-on CDs) STOCK bons de caisse nationaux supplémentaires m pl; **~ equipment** n COMP périphériques m pl, MGMNT matériel complémentaire m, matériel supplémentaire m; **~ interest** n BANK intérêt supplémentaire m; **~ memory** n COMP mémoire additionnelle externe f, mémoire supplémentaire f; **~ minimum tax** n TAX impôt minimum complémentaire m, IMC; **~ yield** n STOCK rendement supplémentaire m; ◆ **on an ~ basis** GEN COMM avec supplément

address[1] n COMMS talk, speech allocution f, discours m, COMMS of person, company, building, COMP adresse f; **~ book** COMMS carnet d'adresses m, répertoire d'adresses m; **~ bus** COMP bus d'adresses m; **~ commission** TRANSP shipping commission d'adresse f; **~ field** COMP champ d'adresse m; **~ file** COMP fichier d'adresses m; **~ label** COMMS étiquette-adresse f; ◆ **~ as above** (ANT address as below) GEN COMM adresse ci-dessus; **~ as below** (ANT address as above) GEN COMM adresse ci-dessous

address[2] vt COMMS parcel, envelope mettre l'adresse sur, person s'adresser à, speech, talk, parcel adresser, GEN COMM issue, problem aborder, LAW adresser; ◆ **~ o.s. to** GEN COMM issue, problem s'attaquer à, problem, task se mettre à; **~ your complaints to** GEN COMM adressez vos réclamations à loc

addressable adj COMMS, COMP adressable

addressee n COMMS destinataire mf

addresser n COMMS expéditeur m

addressing n COMP adressage m; **~ machine** COMMS, GEN COMM machine à adresser f, machine à imprimer les adresses f

Addressograph® n COMMS, GEN COMM Adressographe® m

adduce vt LAW proof, reason apporter, fournir, produire

Aden pr n GEN COMM Aden n pr

adequacy n GEN COMM of report, explanation, description fait d'être acceptable m, fait d'être suffisant m; **~ of coverage** INS adéquation de couverture f

adequate[1] adj GEN COMM funds, supply, explanation adéquat, convenable, suffisant, technique adapté; ◆ **be ~** GEN COMM convenir

adequate[2] **~ target rate** n ACC taux de référence suffisant m

adequately: **~ funded** adj ACC suffisamment financé, GEN COMM disposant d'un financement suffisant loc m

ADG abbr (assistant director general) HRM, MGMNT DGA (directeur général adjoint)

adhere: **~ to** vt GEN COMM contract se montrer irréductible sur, principle adhérer à, être attaché à loc

adhesion: **~ contract** n LAW contrat d'adhésion m

adhesive: **~ envelope** n ADMIN enveloppe adhésive f, enveloppe autocollante f; **~ label** n ADMIN, COMMS étiquette adhésive f

ad hoc[1] adj GEN COMM ad hoc, arbitraire, circonstanciel, spécial

ad hoc:[2] **~ committee** n GEN COMM commission ad hoc f

ad idem adv frml GEN COMM en parfait accord

ad infinitum adv frml GEN COMM à l'infini

ad interim[1] adj frml GEN COMM par intérim loc m, LAW judgement provisoire

ad interim[2] adv LAW judge provisoirement

adjective: **~ law** n LAW droit de procédure m, règles de procédure f pl

adjoining adj GEN COMM avoisinant, contigu, room, building attenant

adjourn vt GEN COMM meeting remettre, reporter, LAW case, trial ajourner, différer, remettre, renvoyer, reporter, MGMNT meeting ajourner, POL lever; **~ to** MGMNT boardroom, meeting room s'ajourner à, remettre, reporter; ◆ **~ the meeting** MGMNT lever la séance; **~ sentence** LAW ajourner une sentence; **~ sth for a week** GEN COMM remettre qch à une huitaine, reporter qch jusqu'à la semaine prochaine

adjournment n LAW ajournement m, prorogation f, MGMNT of decision remise f, of meeting ajournement m, suspension f; **~ debate** UK POL débat final m

adjudge vt LAW decree déclarer; ◆ **~ damages** LAW accorder des dommages-intérêts, allouer des dommages et intérêts

adjudicate vt GEN COMM décider, se prononcer sur, claim adjuger, examiner, juger, contest juger, être arbitre de, être juge de, prize décerner; ◆ **~ sb bankrupt** ACC, FIN, GEN COMM, LAW déclarer qn en faillite

adjudication n GEN COMM jugement m, LAW arrêt m, décision f, jugement m; **~ of bankruptcy** ACC, FIN, GEN COMM, LAW déclaration de faillite f, jugement déclaratif de faillite m; **~ of bankruptcy order** ACC, FIN, GEN COMM, LAW jugement déclaratif de liquidation judiciaire m

adjudicator n GEN COMM arbitre m, juge m

adjunct n GEN COMM accessoire m, person subalterne mf; **~ professor** US HRM, WEL chargé de cours mf, professeur vacataire m

adjust vt ACC ajuster, rectifier, réajuster, BANK rectifier, ECON price, amount, timetable ajuster, réajuster, price, salary rajuster, revoir, réajuster, réviser, wages ralentir, revaloriser, FIN ajuster, GEN COMM redresser, mechanism, component, level ajuster, mettre au point, INS average répartir, MATH figures, error rectifier, TAX rajuster, réajuster; **~ downwards** ECON prices réviser à la baisse, MATH réajuster en baisse; **~ o.s. to** GEN COMM situation s'adapter à; **~ to** GEN COMM s'adapter à; **~ upwards** ECON prices réviser à la hausse, MATH réajuster en hausse; ♦ **~ a claim** INS régler un sinistre

adjustable[1] *adj* FIN *mortgage rate, timetable* variable, GEN COMM *appliance, position, speed* réglable, *hours, rate* flexible, INS *policy* variable

adjustable:[2] **~ life insurance** *n* INS assurance vie-entière *f*; **~ mortgage loan** *n* (*AML*) BANK, FIN, PROP prêt hypothécaire variable *m*; **~ -rate mortgage** *n* (*ARM*) BANK hypothèque à taux réglable *f*, FIN hypothèque à taux réglable *f*, PROP prêt hypothécaire à taux réglable *m*; **~ -rate preferred stock** *n* (*ARP*) STOCK action de priorité à taux variable *f*, titre privilégié à taux variable *m*; **~ shore ramp** *n* TRANSP *shipping* rampe d'accès réglable *f*

adjusted[1] *adj* ACC, ECON rajusté, GEN COMM en données corrigées *loc f*, rajusté, TAX rajusté

adjusted:[2] **~ capital ratio** *n* BANK *merchant*, ECON, FIN ratio de capital redressé *m*; **~ claim** *n* BANK, ECON, FIN indemnité réajustée *f*; **~ cost base** *n* *Canada* (*ACB*) ACC coût de base ajusté *m*, prix de base rajusté *m*; **~ exercise price** *n UK* STOCK prix d'exercice ajusté *m*, prix de levée d'option rajusté *m*; **~ income** *n* TAX revenu rajusté *m*; **~ principal amount** *n* TAX principal rajusté *m*; **~ selling price** *n* ACC prix de vente rajusté *m*; **~ tax payable** *n* TAX impôt rajusté à payer *m*; **~ taxable income** *n* TAX revenu imposable modifié *m*; **~ total capital ratio** *n* BANK, ECON, FIN ratio de capital total redressé *m*; **~ trial balance** *n* ACC balance de vérification régularisée *f*, balance finale de vérification après inventaire *f*

adjuster *n* HRM, INS expert *m*, responsable du règlement des sinistres *m*, responsable indépendant du règlement des sinistres *m*, régleur *m*

adjusting: **~ entry** *n* ACC écriture d'extourne *f*, écriture d'inventaire *f*, écriture de correction *f* (*Can*), écriture de redressement *f*, écriture de régularisation *f*, écriture rectificative *f*; **~ loading wall** *n* TRANSP *shipping* revêtement intérieur *m*

adjustment *n* ACC ajustement *m*, rajustement *m*, réajustement *m, accrual accounting* redressement *m*, régularisation *f, statistics, error* correction *f*, rectification *f*, BANK rectification *f*, ECON *of prices, rates, charges* ajustement *m*, réajustement *m*, révision *f, of wages* rajustement *m*, revalorisation *f*, FIN *of prices, wages* ajustement *m*, GEN COMM ajustement *m*, redressement *m, of appliance, position, speed* ajustage *m*, mise au point *f*, réglage *m, of wages* rajustement *m*, revalorisation *f, to situation* adaptation *f*, HRM *of wages* rajustement *m*, revalorisation *f*, INS répartition *f, loss* règlement *m*, MATH *of value of subject property* redressement *m*, TAX rajustement *m*, réajustement *m*; **~ account** *n* ACC *accrual accounting* compte de régularisation *m*; **~ of accounts receivable** *n* ACC *following deletion of debts* redressement des comptes clients *m*; **~ bond** *n* STOCK obligation de transition émise par une société en situation de faillite; **~ center** *n AmE*, **~ centre** *n BrE* WEL quartier disciplinaire *m*; **~ clause** *n* INS clause d'ajustabilité *f*, clause de régularisation *f*; **~ costs** *n pl* INS frais de règlement *m pl*; **~ gap** *n* ECON écart d'ajustement *m*, écart de réajustement *m*; **~ limit** *n* TAX seuil de réajustement *m*; **~ premium** *n* INS prime de régularisation *f*; **~ speed** *n* ECON vitesse d'adaptation *f*, vitesse d'ajustement *f*, vitesse de réajustement *f*; **~ of sum insured** *n* INS ajustement de la somme assurée *m*, ajustement de la valeur assurée *m*; **~ to cost base** *n* TAX réajustement du prix de base *m*; **~ trigger** *n* GEN COMM voyant rouge *m*, voyant vert *m*, voyant vert déclenchant *m*, voyant vert servant de déclic *m*

Adk *abbr* (*awning deck*) TRANSP *shipping* pont-tente *m*

adman *n infrml* HRM publiciste *mf*, publicitaire *m*, S&M *advertising* publiciste *mf*, publicitaire *mf*

admass *adj* GEN COMM *culture, society* de grande consommation *loc f*, de masse *loc f*

admin[1] *abbr* ADMIN gestion *f*, LAW application *f*, exécution *f*, MGMNT gestion *f*, POL administration *f*, PROP curatelle *f*, gestion *f*

admin[2] *n* ADMIN administration *f*, service administratif *m*, service de gestion *m*, GEN COMM service administratif *m*, MGMNT administration *f*, service administratif *m*, service de gestion *m*

administer *vt* ADMIN administrer, gérer, PROP gérer

administered: **~ inflation** *n* ECON inflation administrée *f*, inflation dirigée *f*, inflation réglementée *f*; **~ price** *n* ADMIN prix réglementé *m*, S&M *pricing theory* prix imposé *m*, prix réglementé *m*; **~ pricing** *n* ECON fixation administrative des prix *f*, fixation conventionnelle des prix *f*

administration *n* ADMIN administration *f*, service administratif *m*, service de gestion *m*, gestion *f, of estate, inheritance* curatelle *f*, gestion *f*, GEN COMM service administratif *m*, LAW *of act* application *f*, exécution *f*, MGMNT administration *f*, service administratif *m*, service de gestion *m*, gestion *f*, POL *of government* administration *f*, PROP *of estate, inheritance* curatelle *f*, gestion *f*, tutelle *f*; **~ costs** *n pl* ADMIN frais d'administration *m pl*, frais de gestion *m pl*; **~ of the customs union** *n* (*ACU*) IMP/EXP EU administration de l'union des douanes *f* (*AUD*); **~ expenses** *n pl* ACC frais d'administration *m pl*, frais de gestion *m pl*; **~ lag** *n* ECON délai administratif *m*; **~ officer** *n* HRM agent administratif *m*, responsable administratif *m*; **~ order** *n* ADMIN ordonnance *f*, LAW ordonnance instituant l'administration judiciaire *f*; **~ -production ratio** *n* ADMIN, FIN, IND ratio administration-production *m*

administrative[1] *adj* ADMIN, GEN COMM administratif

administrative:[2] **~ activity element** *n* ACC élément d'activité administrative *m*; **~ audit** *n* ACC *auditing*, FIN *auditing* audit interne *m*, vérification interne *f* (*Can*); **~ authority** *n* ADMIN, GEN COMM pouvoir administratif *m*; **~ board** *n* GEN COMM, HRM, MGMNT conseil d'administration *m*, CA;

~ **burden** n ADMIN charge f, tâche f; ~ **center** n AmE, ~ **centre** n BrE ADMIN centre administratif m; ~ **charge** n ADMIN, INS frais administratifs m pl, frais d'administration m pl; ~ **control procedure** n ADMIN procédé de contrôle de gestion m; ~ **costs** n pl ADMIN, GEN COMM frais administratifs m pl, frais d'administration ·m pl, frais de gestion m pl; ~ **costs of regulation** n ACC frais de mise en conformité m pl, ADMIN frais d'adaptation m pl, frais d'administration m pl, frais de mise en conformité m pl; ~ **expense** n ACC frais administratifs m pl, frais d'administration m pl, frais de gestion m pl; ~ **law** n ADMIN, LAW droit administratif m; ~ **management society** n US ACC, ADMIN, FIN, MGMNT société de gestion f; ~ **and organizational controls** n pl UK ACC auditing, FIN auditing contrôle interne de l'administration et de l'organisation m, contrôles organisationnels et administratifs m pl; ~ **overheads** n pl ACC, ADMIN, FIN frais généraux d'administration m pl; ~ **point of view** n (APV) ADMIN détails administratifs m pl, point de vue administratif m, MGMNT détails administratifs m pl; ~ **service** n ADMIN, GEN COMM, MGMNT service administratif m; ~ **staff** n pl ADMIN, HRM personnel administratif m; ~ **theory** n ADMIN, MGMNT théorie administrative f; ~ **work** n ADMIN travail administratif m

administrator n ADMIN administrateur m, COMP software gestionnaire mf, FIN administrateur judiciaire m, of estate curateur m, GEN COMM administrateur m, HRM administrateur m, gestionnaire mf, gérant m, LAW administrateur m, inheritance administrateur judiciaire m, of estate curateur m, PROP of estate, inheritance curateur m, gestionnaire mf, gérant m, tuteur m; ~**'s deed** LAW acte ab intestat m

admissibility n LAW recevabilité f

admissible adj GEN COMM document valable, LAW evidence, claim admissible, recevable, PATENTS claim autorisé

admission:[1] ~ **-free** adj LEIS entrée gratuite loc f, theatre entrée libre loc f

admission[2] n GEN COMM entry admission f, entrée f, IMP/EXP customs admission en franchise officielle f, LAW of a crime acceptation f, admission f, aveu m; ~ **fee** GEN COMM droit d'entrée m, prix d'entrée m, prix des places m; ~ **of securities** FIN admission de valeurs mobilières f; ~ **to listing** UK STOCK admission à la cotation f, admission à la cote f; ~ **to quotation** STOCK admission à la cotation f, admission à la cote f

admit vt GEN COMM coopter, acknowledge admettre, avouer, reconnaître, claim faire droit à, let in faire entrer, laisser entrer, HRM new partner admettre, coopter; ♦ ~ **one is wrong** GEN COMM, MGMNT avouer qu'on est dans son tort; ~ **to the bar** US LAW inscrire au barreau

admittance n GEN COMM accès m, admission f; **no ~** loc n LAW, GEN COMM entrée interdite loc f

adopt vt GEN COMM procedures, resolution adopter, approuver; ♦ ~ **a joint stance** GEN COMM adopter une position commune

adoption n ECON of single currency adoption f, approbation f, MGMNT of a method choix m; ~ **process** LAW child, S&M of product by customer processus d'adoption m

ADP abbr (automatic data processing) COMP traitement automatique de l'information m, traitement automatique des données m

ADR abbr ACC (asset depreciation range) gamme d'amortissement d'actif f, plafond maximal de la période d'amortissement m, période d'amortissement de l'actif f, BANK (American depositary receipt), FIN (asset depreciation range) gamme d'amortissement d'actif f, plafond maximal de la période d'amortissement m, période d'amortissement de l'actif f, GEN COMM (American depositary receipt) certificat américain d'actions étrangers, PROP (asset depreciation range) gamme d'amortissement d'actif f, plafond maximal de la période d'amortissement m, période d'amortissement de l'actif f, STOCK (American depositary receipt) certificat américain d'actions étrangers

adrate n FIN, S&M tarif publicitaire m

adrift adj TRANSP à la dérive

adult n LAW adulte mf; ~ **fare** LEIS, TRANSP plein tarif m; ~ **population** GEN COMM population adulte f

adulterate vt LAW falsifier

adulteration n LAW falsification f

ADV abbr (advice enclosed) COMMS, GEN COMM avis inclus m, avis joint m

ad val. abbr (ad valorem) GEN COMM, TAX ad val. (ad valorem)

ad valorem[1] adj frml (ad val.) GEN COMM, TAX ad valorem (ad val.), proportionnel, selon la valeur de la marchandise, sur la valeur loc f

ad valorem:[2] ~ **bill of lading** n IMP/EXP, TRANSP connaissement ad valorem m; ~ **duty** n ACC, IMP/EXP, TAX, TRANSP droits ad valorem m pl; ~ **freight** n IMP/EXP, TRANSP fret ad valorem m; ~ **rate** n frml ACC taux ad valorem m; ~ **tax** n ACC, TAX impôt ad valorem m (frml), impôt sur la valeur m, taxe sur la valeur f

advance[1] n ACC increase hausse f, payment acompte m, BANK facilité de trésorerie f, down payment acompte m, arrhes f pl, on salary avance f, ECON hausse f, FIN acompte m, GEN COMM hausse f, down payment acompte m, arrhes f pl, in technology avance f, avancée f, percée f, progrès m, loan avance f, of civilization, in science progrès m, HRM acompte m, IND in technology avance f, avancée f, percée f, progrès m, STOCK of prices progression f, valeur en hausse f; ~ **account** ACC compte d'avances m; ~ **against goods** GEN COMM avance sur marchandises f; ~ **against security** GEN COMM avance sur nantissement f, prêt sur nantissement m; ~ **bill** FIN effet tiré d'avance m; ~ **billing** ACC facturation par anticipation f; ~ **booking** GEN COMM, LEIS hotel, S&M, TRANSP réservation *f*, réservation à l'avance *f*; ~ **booking office** GEN COMM, LEIS, TRANSP service des réservations *m*; ~ **copy** MEDIA *publishing* bonnes feuilles *f pl*, exemplaire en prépublication *m*, exemplaire témoin *m*; ~ **factory** IND usine-pilote *f*; ~ **freight** *(AF)* TRANSP avance sur le fret *f*, fret payé d'avance *m*; ~-**funded pension plan** *UK* FIN *personal* plan de retraite financé par avance *m*; ~ **guaranty** *UK* STOCK garantie anticipée *f*; ~ **holder** BANK bénéficiaire d'un prêt *m*; ~ **income tax ruling** TAX décision anticipée en matière d'impôt sur le revenu *f*; ~ **notice** LAW préavis *m*; ~ **on export contract** GEN COMM avances en devises à l'exportation *f pl*, ADE; ~ **on goods** GEN COMM avance sur marchandises *f*; ~ **on salary** HRM avance sur salaire *f*; ~ **on securities** *UK* STOCK avance sur titres *f*, avance sur valeurs boursières *f*; ~ **payment** ACC acompte *m*, paiement anticipé *m*, paiement par anticipation *m*, BANK acompte *m*, arrhes *f pl*, FIN acompte *m*, GEN COMM acompte *m*, arrhes *f pl*, provision *f*; ~ **payment bond** STOCK obligation à paiement anticipé *f*; ~ **payment guarantee** GEN COMM, IMP/EXP garantie de provisions *f*; ~ **premium** INS prime payée d'avance *f*; ~ **publicity** MEDIA phase d'alerte *f*, publicité d'amorçage *f*; ~ **refunding** STOCK *of government securities, municipal bonds* remboursement anticipé *m*; ~ **repayment** GEN COMM remboursement anticipé *m*; ~ **royalty payment** TAX paiement de redevances par anticipation *m*; ~ **selling** *UK* STOCK *security* vente anticipée *f*; ~ **of special survey** TRANSP *of a ship* avancement de la visite spéciale *m*; ◆ **in** ~ GEN COMM anticipé, d'avance, en avance, par avance; **make an** ~ BANK *of money* faire une avance

advance[2] **1.** *vt* BANK *loan* accorder, consentir, COMP *tape* faire défiler, FIN *loan* consentir, *prices* augmenter, GEN COMM faire avancer, faire progresser, *work* faire progresser, STOCK *prices* augmenter; **2.** *vi* GEN COMM *person, society, civilization* faire des progrès *loc m*

advanced[1] *adj* COMP *software, system* sophistiqué, évolué, GEN COMM avancé, développé, *book, film* d'avant-garde *loc f*, MGMNT, POL évolué

advanced:[2] ~ **charge** *n* *(SYN advanced disbursement)* TRANSP débours *m*, frais anticipés *m pl*; ~ **collection** *n* TAX recouvrement complexe *m*; ~ **country** *n* *(AC)* ECON, IND, POL pays industrialisé *m*, pays technologiquement avancé *m*; ~ **disbursement** *n* *(SYN advanced charge)* TRANSP débours *m*, frais anticipés *m pl*; ~ **economy** *n* ECON, GEN COMM, POL économie développée *f*; ~ **education** *n* WEL enseignement supérieur *m*, formation supérieure *f*; ~ **engineering** *n* IND ingénierie de pointe *f*, technique de pointe *f*; ~ **funded pension plan** *n* *UK* HRM *personal*, WEL *personal* plan de retraite financé par avance *m*; ~ **guarantee** *n* *UK* STOCK garantie anticipée *f*; ~ **language** *n* COMP langage de haut niveau *m*, langage évolué *m*; ~ **organic economy** *n* ECON *agricultural* économie préindus-

trielle *f*; ~ **technology** *n* COMP, IND technologie de pointe *f*; ~ **training** *n* HRM stage de perfectionnement *m*; ~ **version** *n* COMP version avancée *f*, version évoluée *f*

Advanced: ~ **level** *n* *UK (A level)* GEN COMM, WEL examen de niveau supérieur, $\approx$ baccalauréat *m*

advancement *n* ADMIN autodéveloppement *m*, avancement *m*, promotion *f*, ECON, GEN COMM essor *m*, HRM avancement *m*, promotion *f*, IND, POL essor *m*

advances: ~ **received** *n pl* ACC avances reçues sur commandes en cours *f pl*

advancing: **be** ~ *phr* GEN COMM *prices* monter

advantage *n* GEN COMM avantage *m*; ◆ **be to sb's** ~ GEN COMM profiter à qn; **take** ~ **of** GEN COMM profiter de, *situation, person* tirer profit de; **take** ~ **of an opportunity to do** GEN COMM profiter d'une occasion pour faire

advantageous *adj* GEN COMM avantageux, *lucrative* intéressant, profitable

adversary *n* LAW adversaire *mf*, partie adverse *f*

adverse[1] *adj* GEN COMM *budget* déficitaire, *consequences, influence* négatif, *effects* opposé, *reaction, factor, conditions* défavorable

adverse:[2] ~ **balance of trade** *n* ECON balance commerciale défavorable *f*, balance commerciale déficitaire *f*; ~ **claim** *n* LAW opposition *f*; ~ **movement** *n* STOCK *in price of bonds* fluctuation défavorable *f*, mouvement contraire *m*; ~ **opinion** *n* ACC avis défavorable *m*, opinion défavorable *f* *(Can)*, refus de certifier *m*; ~ **possession** *n* LAW, PROP possession de fait *f*; ~ **price movement** *n* ECON fluctuation défavorable des cours *f*; ~ **selection** *n* INS antisélection *f*; ~ **supply shock** *n* ECON choc d'offre négatif *m*, choc de la pénurie des approvisionnements *m*; ~ **trading conditions** *n pl* ECON conditions défavorables pour le commerce *f pl*; ~ **weather** *n* GEN COMM temps défavorable *m*

adversely: ~ **affected** *adj* GEN COMM affecté négativement

advert *n* GEN COMM, MEDIA, S&M *TV, radio* pub *f* *(infrml)*, publicité *f*, spot *m* *(infrml)*, spot publicitaire *m*, *newspapers, magazines* annonce *f*, annonce publicitaire *f*, petite annonce *f*

advertise 1. *vt* GEN COMM, MEDIA, S&M *house, car* mettre une annonce, mettre une annonce pour vendre, passer une annonce, *product, party, service* faire de la publicité pour, faire de la réclame pour; ~ **for** GEN COMM, MEDIA, S&M faire paraître une annonce pour **2.** *vi* GEN COMM *for product, party, service*, MEDIA *for product, party, service* faire de la publicité, faire de la réclame, *in newspaper, magazine* mettre une annonce, S&M *for product, party, service* faire de la publicité, faire de la réclame, *in newspaper, magazine* mettre une annonce; ◆ ~ **for bids** S&M passer un avis d'appel d'offres; ~ **a job in the paper** HRM, MEDIA, S&M insérer une annonce pour un poste dans le journal, publier une offre d'emploi dans un journal

advertised:[1] **~ bidding** n S&M appel d'offres ouvert m

advertised:[2] **as ~ on television** phr S&M vu à la télévision; **as ~ on TV** phr MEDIA vu à la télévision

advertisement n GEN COMM, MEDIA, S&M TV, radio pub f (infrml), spot m (infrml), spot publicitaire m, newspapers, magazines annonce f, annonce publicitaire f, petite annonce f

advertiser n S&M annonceur m

advertising n GEN COMM publicité f, S&M pub f (infrml), publicité f; **~ agency** n MEDIA, S&M agence de publicité f; **~ agent** n GEN COMM vendeur de choc m (infrml), S&M vendeur baratineur m; **~ allocation budget** n FIN, S&M budget de la publicité m; **~ appeal** n S&M axe publicitaire m, thème publicitaire m; **~ appropriation** n FIN, S&M budget de la publicité m, dotations budgétaires affectées à la publicité f pl; **~ budget** n FIN, S&M budget de la publicité m; **~ budget review** n ACC, FIN, S&M examen du budget publicitaire m; **~ campaign** n MEDIA, S&M campagne de publicité f; **~ channel** n MEDIA, S&M canal publicitaire m; **~ code** n LAW, S&M code publicitaire m; **~ concept** n S&M axe publicitaire m, concept publicitaire m; **~ conversion rate** n S&M taux de succès m; **~ copy** n MEDIA, S&M texte publicitaire m; **~ coverage** n MEDIA, S&M couverture publicitaire f; **~ criteria** n pl S&M critères de publicité m pl; **~ department** n MEDIA, S&M of magazine service publicité m; **~ director** n HRM, MEDIA, S&M chef de publicité m, chef du service publicité m, directeur de la publicité m; **~ effectiveness** n S&M efficacité publicitaire f; **~ expenditure** n FIN, S&M dépense de publicité f, dépense publicitaire f; **~ expense** n FIN, S&M dépense de publicité f, dépense publicitaire f; **~ gimmick** n S&M astuce publicitaire f, trouvaille publicitaire f, truc publicitaire m (infrml); **~ industry** n S&M pub f, publicité f; **~ jingle** n MEDIA, S&M jingle sonal m, refrain publicitaire m; **~ manager** n HRM, MEDIA, S&M chef de publicité m, directeur de la publicité m; **~ media** n pl MEDIA supports publicitaires m pl, S&M médias publicitaires m pl; **~ medium** n MEDIA, S&M canal publicitaire m, support publicitaire m; **~ message** n S&M message publicitaire m; **~ overkill** n S&M excès de publicité m; **~ policy** n S&M politique publicitaire f; **~ price** n FIN, S&M prix publicitaire m; **~ program objectives** n pl AmE, **~ programme objectives** n pl BrE S&M objectif d'une campagne publicitaire m; **~ rates** n pl FIN, S&M tarif publicitaire m; **~ research** n S&M études publicitaires f pl; **~ revenue** n ACC, FIN, S&M recettes publicitaires f pl, rentrées publiques f pl; **~ revenue by media** n ACC, FIN, MEDIA, S&M recettes publicitaires par média f pl; **~ schedule** n MEDIA, S&M programme des annonces m; **~ slogan** n S&M slogan publicitaire m; **~ space** n MEDIA, S&M espace publicitaire m;

~ space buyer n (ANT advertising space seller) MEDIA, S&M acheteur d'espace publicitaire m; **~ space seller** n (ANT advertising space buyer) MEDIA, S&M vendeur d'espace publicitaire m; **~ statistics** n pl S&M statistiques de publicité f pl; **~ supplement** n MEDIA, S&M supplément publicitaire m; **~ support** n S&M soutien publicitaire m, support publicitaire m; **~ tactics** n pl S&M stratégie publicitaire f; **~ talk** n S&M exposé sur un sujet publicitaire m; **~ technique** n S&M technique publicitaire f; **~ test** n S&M test publicitaire m; **~ text** n MEDIA, S&M texte publicitaire m; **~ theme** n S&M thème publicitaire m; **~ thermometer** n S&M thermomètre publicitaire m; **~ time** n S&M temps publicitaire m; **~ tour** n S&M tournée publicitaire f; **~ tower** n S&M colonne Morris f (Fra), colonne publicitaire f; **~ turnover** n ACC, FIN, S&M chiffre d'affaires publicitaires m; **~ value** n S&M valeur publicitaire f; **~ vehicle** n MEDIA, S&M véhicule de communication m; **~ weapon** n S&M arme publicitaire f; **~ world** n S&M monde de la publicité m; **~ zone** n S&M zone de diffusion f; ◆ **~ cost per product sale** ACC, FIN, S&M frais de publicité par vente de produit m pl; **in ~** S&M dans la publicité

Advertising: **~ Association** n UK S&M ≈ Union des annonceurs f (France); **~ Standards Authority** n UK (ASA) MEDIA, S&M ≈ Bureau de vérification de la publicité m (BVP)

advertorial n S&M annonce d'apparence rédactionnelle f

advice n ADMIN conseils m pl, COMMS informations f pl, GEN COMM notification avis m, conseils m pl, HRM, MGMNT, STOCK conseils m pl; **~ of arrival** COMMS avis d'arrivée m; **~ card** INS marine carte d'avis f pl; **~ of collection** BANK avis d'encaissement m; **~ of deal** STOCK avis d'opération m; **~ of delivery** COMMS, GEN COMM, S&M avis de livraison m; **~ of duration and/or charge** (ADC) GEN COMM indication de durée et de prix f (IDP); **~ note** COMMS, GEN COMM lettre d'avis f; ◆ **as per ~ from** GEN COMM suivant avis de, sur les conseils de; **as per ~ of** GEN COMM suivant avis de, sur les conseils de; **~ enclosed** (ADV) COMMS, GEN COMM avis inclus m, avis joint m; **no ~** (n/a) GEN COMM sans préavis; **on the ~ of** GEN COMM sur les conseils de

advisable adj GEN COMM conseillé, judicieux, opportun; ◆ **if you think it ~** GEN COMM si vous le jugez bon

advise vt COMMS inform aviser, informer, GEN COMM aviser, informer, give advice to conseiller, donner des conseils à, MGMNT conseiller, donner des conseils à; ◆ **~ a draft** BANK donner avis d'une traite; **~ sb on sth** GEN COMM, MGMNT conseiller qn sur qch; **~ sb of sth** COMMS, GEN COMM faire part de qch à qn, informer qn de qch; **~ sb that** COMMS, GEN COMM faire part à qn que, informer qn que

advised: **~ bill** n BANK, FIN traite avisée f

adviser n ACC, COMP conseil m, conseiller m,

consultant *m*, GEN COMM conseiller *m*, prescripteur *m*, HRM, MGMNT conseil *m*, conseiller *m*, consultant *m*

advising: **~ bank** *n* BANK banque notificatrice *f*

advisor *n* ACC, COMP conseil *m*, conseiller *m*, consultant *m*, GEN COMM conseiller *m*, HRM, MGMNT conseil *m*, conseiller *m*, consultant *m*

advisory¹ *adj* GEN COMM *role*, HRM *role* consultatif; ◆ **in an ~ capacity** GEN COMM à titre consultatif

advisory:² **~ account** *n* FIN clientèle privée conseillée *f*; **~ board** *n* ADMIN comité consultatif *m*, GEN COMM comité consultatif *m*, commission consultative *f*, HRM comité consultatif *m*, POL commission consultative *f*; **~ body** *n* GEN COMM, MGMNT organe consultatif *m*, organisme consultatif *m*; **~ capacity** *n* GEN COMM voix consultative *f*, HRM qualité de conseil *f*; **~ committee** *n* ADMIN comité consultatif *m*, BANK *rescheduling of debt*, FIN *rescheduling of debt* comité de restructuration *m*, GEN COMM comité consultatif *m*, comité de restructuration *m*, commission consultative *f*, HRM comité consultatif *m*, POL *European Commission* commission consultative *f*; **~ function** *n* HRM fonction consultative *f*, rôle consultatif *m*; **~ group** *n* ADMIN, GEN COMM, HRM comité consultatif *m*; **~ service** *n* GEN COMM service de documentation *m*, service de renseignements *m*; **~ services** *n pl* FIN services de conseil *m pl*, GEN COMM, MGMNT services de conseil interne *m pl*; **~ voice** *n* GEN COMM voix consultative *f*; **~ work** *n* HRM fonction consultative *f*

Advisory: **~, Conciliation and Arbitration Service** *n* UK *(ACAS)* HRM service consultatif d'arbitrage et de conciliation

advocate *vt* GEN COMM préconiser, recommander

AERE *abbr (Atomic Energy Research Establishment)* ENVIR ≈ CEA *(Commissariat à l'énergie atomique)*

aerial: **~ advertising** *n* S&M publicité aérienne *f*; **~ survey** *n* TRANSP *aviation* levé aérien *m*

aerodrome *n BrE* TRANSP *aviation* aérodrome *m*

aerogram *n* COMMS *letter* aérogramme *m*

aeroplane *n BrE (cf airplane AmE)* TRANSP avion *m*; **~ banner** *BrE* S&M *advertising* banderole tractée par un avion *f*

aerosol *n* ENVIR can bombe aérosol *f, system* aérosol *m*

aerospace *adj* IND aérospatial

AF *abbr (advance freight)* TRANSP avance sur le fret *f*, fret payé d'avance *m*

AFBD *abbr (Association of Futures Brokers and Dealers)* STOCK association des courtiers et négociants de marchandises à terme

AFDC *abbr US (Aid to Families with Dependent Children)* WEL aide aux familles ayant des enfants à charge

affairs *n pl* GEN COMM affaires *f pl*

affect *vt* ECON *supply of money* affecter, GEN COMM *business, earnings* avoir un effet sur *loc m*, avoir

une incidence sur *loc f*, influer sur, *order, restrictions* atteindre, viser, LAW *findings* avoir un effet sur *loc m*, avoir une incidence sur *loc f*, influencer

affection: **~ value** *n* INS valeur affective *f*

affective: **~ behavior** *n AmE*, **~ behaviour** *n BrE* GEN COMM comportement étudié *m*

affiant *n US* LAW auteur d'un affidavit *m*

affidavit *n* LAW affidavit *m*, attestation *f*, attestation écrite sous serment *f*, déclaration écrite sous serment *f*

affiliate¹ *n* GEN COMM *organization* groupe affilié *m, person* affilié *m, company* filiale *f*; **~ company** GEN COMM filiale *f*, société affiliée *f*; **~ member** GEN COMM membre affilié *m*

affiliate² **1.** *vt* GEN COMM affilier; **~ o.s. to** GEN COMM s'affilier à; **2.** *vi* **~ to** GEN COMM affilier à

affiliated¹ *adj* GEN COMM affilié; ◆ **~ to** GEN COMM affilié à

affiliated:² **~ bank** *n* BANK banque affiliée *f*; **~ chain** *n* S&M chaîne affiliée *f*; **~ company** *n* ACC société apparentée *f*, société associée *f*, GEN COMM filiale *f*; **~ firm** *n* GEN COMM filiale *f*; **~ group** *n* FIN consortium *m*, GEN COMM consortium *m*, groupe filiale *m*; **~ retailer** *n* S&M détaillant affilié *m*; **~ trade unions** *n pl* HRM syndicats affiliés *m pl*; **~ wholesaler** *n* S&M grossiste affilié *m*

affiliation *n* GEN COMM affiliation *f*; **~ fee** HRM cotisation syndicale *f*

affinity: **~ card** *n* WEL carte de parenté par alliance *f*

affirmative: **~ action** *n AmE (cf positive action BrE, positive discrimination BrE)* HRM, POL, WEL discrimination positive *f*, mesures anti-discriminatoires *f pl*, politique anti-discriminatoire *f*; **~ relief** *n* LAW conclusions de la défense pouvant donner lieu à une demande reconventionnelle

affix *vt* COMMS, GEN COMM *label* attacher, coller, *notice, poster* afficher, poser, *signature, seal* apposer, *stamp* coller

affixed¹ *adj* LAW *attached* ci-inclus, ci-joint; **~ to land** TAX fixé au sol

affixed:² **the ~ document** *n* ADMIN, COMMS la pièce ci-jointe *loc f*; **the ~ testimonial** *n* COMMS l'attestation ci-jointe *f*

affluence *n* ECON, GEN COMM, HRM, IND, WEL abondance *f*, richesse *f*

affluent¹ *adj* ECON *person* aisé, riche

affluent:² **the ~ society** *n* ECON, GEN COMM la société d'abondance *f*

AFFM *abbr (Australian Financial Futures Market)* STOCK ≈ MATIF *(France) (Marché à terme d'instruments financiers)*

afford *vt* ECON avoir les moyens de *loc m*, s'offrir, se payer, se permettre

affordable *adj* ECON, S&M *price* abordable

affreightment *n* TRANSP *shipping* affrètement *m*

Afghan¹ *adj* GEN COMM afghan

Afghan² *n* GEN COMM *person, language* Afghan *m*

afghani *n* GEN COMM afghani *m*

Afghanistan *pr n* GEN COMM Afghanistan *m*

AFL-CIO *abbr* (*American Federation of Labor - Congress of Industrial Organizations*) HRM confédération générale américaine du travail

afloat[1] *adj* GEN COMM *business, company* à flot, *goods from wrecked ship* en mer, IND en mer; ♦ **keep ~** GEN COMM *business* faire circuler, maintenir à flot

afloat:[2] **~ price** *n* STOCK prix à bord *m*, prix à flot *m*

aforementioned *adj* COMMS, GEN COMM précité, susdit, susmentionné

a fortiori *phr* GEN COMM a fortiori

A4 *n* ADMIN, COMMS, COMP format A4 *m*

Africa *pr n* GEN COMM Afrique *f*

African[1] *adj* GEN COMM africain

African[2] *n* GEN COMM *person* Africain *m*; **~, Caribbean and Pacific countries** (*ACP countries, ACPs*) ECON, POL pays d'Afrique, des Caraïbes et du Pacifique *m pl*; **~ Development Bank** (*ADB*) BANK Banque africaine de développement *f* (*BAD*)

Afrikaans *n* GEN COMM *language* afrikaans *m*

Afrikaner[1] *adj* GEN COMM afrikaner

Afrikaner[2] *n* GEN COMM *person* Afrikaner *mf*

aft[1] *adj* TRANSP *shipping* arrière

aft:[2] **~ peak tank** *n* (*APT*) TRANSP *of ship* coqueron arrière *m*, tank de peak arrière *m*; **~ perpendicular** *n* (*AP*) TRANSP *of ship* perpendiculaire arrière *f* (*PPAR*)

AFT *abbr* (*automatic funds transfer*) ACC, BANK, FIN virement automatique *m*, virement automatique de fonds *m*

after:[1] **~ -hours** *adj* STOCK après bourse, hors bourse, hors séance; **~ -market** *adj* STOCK après bourse, hors bourse, hors séance; **~ -sales** *adj* S&M après-vente, *revenue* généré par le premier achat; **~ -tax** *adj* TAX après impôts, impôts déduits *m pl*, net d'impôt

after:[2] **~ -acquired clause** *n* BANK *in a mortgage agreement*, FIN *in a mortgage agreement* clause de post-acquisition *f*; **~ -acquired property** *n* BANK, FIN, LAW *bankruptcy* bien définitivement acquis au failli *m*; **~ hatch** *n* (*ah*) TRANSP *shipping* écoutille arrière *f*; **~ -hours dealing** *n* FIN, STOCK transactions hors bourse *f pl*, transactions hors séance *f pl*; **~ -hours market** *n* STOCK marché hors bourse *m*, marché hors séance *m*; **~ -hours price** *n* STOCK prix hors séance *m*; **~ -hours rally** *n* STOCK reprise après clôture *f*; **~ -hours trading** *n* FIN, STOCK transactions hors bourse *f pl*, transactions hors séance *f pl*; **~ market** *n* STOCK marché secondaire *m*; **~ -marriage acquired property** *n* US GEN COMM, LAW *commercial* acquêt *m*, biens matrimoniaux *m pl*; **~ -profits tax** *n* ACC bénéfices avant impôts *m pl*, ECON après impôts *m pl*, FIN après impôts *m pl*, bénéfices avant impôts *m pl*, TAX après impôts *m pl*; **~ -sales manager** *n* HRM directeur SAV *m*, directeur du service après-ventes *m*; **~ -sales marketing** *n* S&M mercatique

après-vente *f*, MAV; **~ -sales service** *n* S&M service après-vente *m*; **~ -tax bond yield** *n* ACC, ECON, FIN, TAX rendement après impôt d'une obligation *m*; **~ -tax capital gain** *n* ACC, ECON, FIN, TAX gain en capital après impôt *m*, gain en capital net *m*; **~ -tax cash flow** *n* TAX cash-flow positif *m*, flux de trésorerie avant impôts *m*; **~ -tax dividend** *n* ACC, ECON, FIN, TAX dividende après impôt *m*; **~ -tax financing** *n* ACC, ECON, FIN, TAX financement après taxe *m*; **~ -tax income** *n* ACC, ECON, FIN, TAX revenu après impôt *m*; **~ -tax profit** *n* ACC, ECON, FIN, TAX bénéfices après impôts *m pl*; **~ -tax rate of return** *n* ACC, ECON, FIN, TAX taux de rendement après-impôts *m*; **~ -tax yield** *n* ACC, ECON, FIN rendement après impôt *m*, rendement net *m*, STOCK rendement net *m*, TAX rendement après impôt *m*, rendement net *m*

after[3] *prep* GEN COMM après; ♦ **~ date** (*A/D*) GEN COMM à ... d'échéance, à compter de; **~ sight** (*A/S*) FIN, GEN COMM de vue

aftereffect *n* GEN COMM répercussion *f*, suite *f*

afterimage *n* S&M *advertising* image rémanente *f*

aftermath: in the ~ of *phr* GEN COMM au lendemain de *loc m*

afterpeak *n* TRANSP *shipping* coqueron arrière *m*, peak arrière *m*; **~ bulkhead** (*APBH*) TRANSP *shipping* cloison du peak arrière *f*, cloison du presse-étoupe *f*

afterwards *adv* GEN COMM après, ensuite

AG *abbr* ACC (*Accountant General*) chef comptable *m*, directeur de comptabilité *m*, HRM UK (*Agent General*) représentant général *m*

against *prep* GEN COMM contre; ♦ **~ all risks** (*AAR*) INS contre tous les risques, tous risques; **~ the box** *jarg* STOCK vente de titres empruntés alors que le vendeur en est détenteur; **~ documents** GEN COMM contre documents; **it is ~ our policy to grant discounts** GEN COMM il est contraire à notre politique d'accorder des remises; **~ the law** LAW contraire à la loi; **~ payment** GEN COMM contre paiement; **~ text** S&M *advertising* contre texte

agcy *abbr* (*agency*) ADMIN, GEN COMM ag. (*agence*)

age[1] *n* GEN COMM âge *m*; **~ allowance** UK TAX abattement vieillesse *m*; **~ at entry** INS âge à l'entrée *m*; **~ at expiry** INS âge à terme *m*; **~ bracket** GEN COMM, S&M *market research* tranche d'âge *f*; **~ discrimination** HRM, LAW discrimination en matière d'âge *f*, discrimination s'appliquant à l'âge *f*; **~ distribution** ECON distribution par âge *f*, répartition par âge *f*; **~ -earnings profile** HRM profil selon l'âge et les revenus *m*; **~ exemption** TAX exemption en raison d'âge *f*; **~ group** GEN COMM *market research, statistics*, S&M *market research* tranche d'âge *f*; **~ limit** GEN COMM limite d'âge *f*, âge limite *m*; **~ pyramid** ECON pyramide des âges *f*

age[2] **1.** *vt* ACC *accounts* classer par ancienneté, classer par antériorité; **2.** *vi* GEN COMM prendre de l'âge, vieillir; ♦ ~ **inventories** ACC classer le stock par date d'entrée; ~ **stocks** ACC classer le stock par date d'entrée

aged: ~ **fail** n STOCK *contract* contrat caduc entre courtiers m; ~ **trial balance** n ACC balance chronologique f, balance par antériorité des soldes f

ageing: ~ **of accounts receivable** n BrE ACC classement chronologique des comptes clients m, classement par antériorité des comptes clients m; ~ **population** n BrE ECON population vieillissante f, ~ **of receivables** n BrE ACC classement chronologique des comptes clients m, classement par antériorité des comptes clients m; ~ **schedule** n BrE ACC classement chronologique des comptes m

ageism n BrE ECON âgisme m

agency n ADMIN agence f, bureau m, BANK succursale f, FIN *trust institutions* organisme m, GEN COMM *means* entremise f *(vieilli)*, opération f, *company* agence f, bureau m, concessionnaire mf, intermédiaire m, organisme m, STOCK intermédiation f; ~ **account** ACC compte agence m; ~ **agreement** LAW contrat d'agence m, contrat de représentation m; ~ **bank** UK BANK banque mandataire f; ~ **billing** MEDIA chiffre d'affaires d'une agence de publicité m; ~ **broker** STOCK agent de change m, courtier m, courtier mandataire m, intermédiaire de bourse m; ~ **by ratification** LAW représentation par ratification f; ~ **cost** UK STOCK frais d'agence m pl, frais de courtage m pl; ~ **experience** S&M *advertising* expérience d'agence f; ~ **fee** BANK commission de gestion f, GEN COMM frais d'agence m pl, TRANSP *shipping* rétribution d'agence f; ~ **with full service** MEDIA *advertising*, S&M *advertising* agence de publicité globale f; ~ **fund** GEN COMM commission de gestion f, LAW fonds en fidéicommis m pl, MEDIA commission de gestion f; ~ **law** LAW législation relative au contrat d'agence f, législation relative au contrat de représentation f; ~ **of necessity** US LAW représentation pour les besoins de la cause f; ~ **relationship** ACC relation mandataire f; ~ **representative** HRM, MEDIA, S&M *advertising* chef de publicité m, chef de publicité d'agence m; ~ **shop** HRM section syndicale f; ~ **theory** STOCK théorie de l'agence f; ♦ **through the** ~ **of** GEN COMM par l'entremise de, par l'intermédiaire de

agenda n MGMNT ordre du jour m, programme m; ♦ **be on the** ~ ADMIN être à l'ordre du jour

agent n FIN courtier m, GEN COMM agent mf, commissionnaire mf, concessionnaire mf, représentant m, IND délégué syndical m, LAW agent m, commissionnaire mf, représentant m, S&M mandataire mf, représentant m; ~ **bank** BANK banque mandataire f; ~ **corporation** ACC société mandataire f; ~**'s commission** S&M commission d'agent f; ~**'s territory** S&M *advertising* secteur du représentant m; ~**'s vehicle record** *(AVR)* TRANSP registre des véhicules du commissionnaire de transport m

Agent: ~ **General** n UK *(AG)* HRM représentant général m

agglomeration n MGMNT agglomération f, agrégation f, association f, concentration f; ~ **diseconomy** *(ANT agglomeration economy)* ECON déséconomie urbaine f; ~ **economy** *(ANT agglomeration diseconomy)* ECON économie d'engorgement f, économie urbaine f

aggregate[1] adj ECON *amount, demand* global, total, MATH global

aggregate[2] n ECON agrégat m, ensemble m, MATH ensemble m, total m; ~ **of the adjusted cost bases** n TAX prix de base rajusté total m; ~ **balance** n ACC solde générale m; ~ **book value** n ACC valeur comptable globale nette f; ~ **concentration** n GEN COMM concentration complète f, concentration globale f; ~ **data** n pl ACC données cumulées f pl, données d'ensemble f pl, données globales f pl; ~ **demand** n ECON, FIN demande globale f; ~ **demand-aggregate supply** n pl *(AD-AS)* ECON, FIN demande et offre globale f, demande globale-offre globale f; ~ **exercise price** n STOCK prix de levée d'option global m; ~ **income** n ECON revenu global m; ~ **indemnity** n INS indemnité absolue f; ~ **liability index** n INS fiche des communs f; ~ **output** n ECON, IND aggrégat de la production m, production globale f, rendement global m; ~ **production** n ECON, IND production globale f; ~ **risk** n GEN COMM risque global m; ~ **statement** n ACC état consolidé m; ~ **supply** n ECON offre globale f; ~ **table** n INS table aggrégée f

aggregate[3] vt MATH accroître, réunir

aggregation: ~ **problem** n ACC, ECON problème de totalisation m, problème des agrégats m

aggressive[1] adj FIN, GEN COMM, S&M *marketing, sales* agressif

aggressive:[2] ~ **investment** n FIN investissement agressif m; ~ **marketing** n S&M marketing dynamique m; ~ **pricing** n S&M politique de prix agressive f

aging: ~ **of accounts receivable** n AmE see ageing of accounts receivable BrE; ~ **population** n AmE see ageing population BrE; ~ **of receivables** n AmE see ageing of receivables BrE; ~ **schedule** n AmE see ageing schedule BrE

agio n ECON *foreign bills of exchange*, STOCK *foreign bills of exchange* agio m; ~ **account** ECON, STOCK compte d'agios m; ~ **theory of interest** ECON, STOCK théorie de l'intérêt des agios f

agiotage n STOCK *foreign bills of exchange* agiotage m

agism n AmE see ageism BrE

AGM abbr *(annual general meeting)* ACC, FIN, GEN COMM, MGMNT assemblée générale annuelle f

AGNP abbr *(augmented GNP)* ECON, POL PNBA *(PNB augmenté)*

agora n GEN COMM agorot m

agree 1. vt GEN COMM conformer; ~ **on** GEN COMM

prices, terms convenir de; ~ **to** GEN COMM *discount* consentir à, *project, plan* donner son adhésion à, *terms* accepter; ~ **upon** GEN COMM *price, terms* convenir de; ~ **with** GEN COMM être du même avis que *loc*, ACC *figures* concorder, *report, proposal* approuver **2.** *vi* GEN COMM consent donner son accord, *figures, statements* concorder, coïncider, *share opinion* accepter, consentir, se mettre d'accord, tomber d'accord, être d'accord, être du même avis *loc*; ◆ ~ **the accounts** FIN équilibrer les comptes; ~ **the books** ACC, GEN COMM accorder les écritures, approuver les comptes, conformer les écritures; ~ **to do** GEN COMM convenir de faire

agreed[1] *adj* GEN COMM *time, place, total* convenu; ◆ **as** ~ GEN COMM comme convenu; **at an** ~ **price** GEN COMM *contract* pour un prix convenu, à forfait; **be** ~ **on sth** GEN COMM avoir convenu de qch

agreed:[2] ~ **portion** *n* TAX fraction convenue *f*, partie convenue *f*; ~ **price** *n* GEN COMM, S&M prix convenu *m*; ~ **sum** *n* GEN COMM forfait *m*, montant convenu *m*, somme forfaitaire *f*; ~ **takeover** *n* ECON OPA amicale *f*, OPA négociée à l'amiable *f*, prise de contrôle convenue *f*; ~ **valuation clause** *n* INS clause valeur agréée *f*; ~ **value** *n* INS valeur agréée *f*; ~ **value insurance** *n* INS assurance valeur agréée *f*

agreement *n* GEN COMM convention *f*, LAW accord *m*, contrat *m*, convention *f*; ~ **among underwriters** BANK accord entre les garants *m*; ~ **of clearing** BANK accord de clearing *m*; ~ **for exclusiveness** LAW contrat d'exclusivité *m*; ~ **of sale** BANK, LAW, S&M contrat de vente *m*; ~ **of service** LAW contrat de travail *m*; ◆ **as per** ~ GEN COMM comme convenu; **be in** ~ ACC, GEN COMM concorder

Agreement: ~ **on International Goods Traffic by Rail** *n* TRANSP Convention pour le trafic international des marchandises *f*

agribusiness *n* ECON, ENVIR, IND agro-industries *f pl*, agroalimentaire *m*, agrobusiness *m*, industries agroalimentaires *f pl*

agricultural[1] *adj* ECON, ENVIR agricole

agricultural:[2] ~ **bank** *n* BANK, ECON banque agricole *f*, organisme bancaire de crédit aux agriculteurs *m*; ~ **building** *n* ECON, PROP bâtiment agricole *m*; ~ **commodity** *n* ECON produit agricole *m*, produit agricole de base *m*, GEN COMM produit agricole *m*, IMP/EXP produit agricole *m*, produit agricole de base *m*; ~ **credit** *n* GEN COMM crédit agricole *m*; ~ **engineer** *n* ENVIR ingénieur agronome *m*; ~ **export subsidy** *n* ECON, IMP/EXP subvention à l'exportation agricole *f*, subvention à l'exportation de produits agricoles *f*; ~ **futures contract** *n* FIN, STOCK *UK CME* contrat à terme de marchandises agricoles *m*; ~ **household** *n* ECON ménage agricole *m*, ménage d'agriculteurs *m*; ~ **insurance** *n* INS assurance agricole *f*; ~ **job** *n* ECON, HRM emploi agricole *m*, travail agricole *m*; ~ **land** *n* ECON, ENVIR, TAX terre agricole *f*;

~ **lending** *n* BANK, ECON prêts agricoles *m pl*; ~ **levy** *n* ECON, TAX impôt agricole *m*, prélèvement agricole *m*; ~ **loan** *n* BANK, ECON prêt agricole *m*, prêt à l'agriculture *m*; ~ **paper** *n US* ECON, POL valeur agricole *f*; ~ **policy** *n* ECON, ENVIR, POL politique agricole *f*; ~ **price support** *n* ECON soutien des prix agricoles *m*; ~ **produce** *n* ECON, GEN COMM, IMP/EXP produit agricole *m*; ~ **product** *n* ECON, GEN COMM, IMP/EXP produit agricole *m*; ~ **production** *n* ECON, GEN COMM, IMP/EXP, IND production agricole *f*; ~ **publication** *n* ECON, MEDIA publication agricole *f*, revue agricole *f*; ~ **sector** *n* ECON, ENVIR, IND secteur agricole *m*; ~ **show** *n* ECON, S&M exposition agricole *f*, salon de l'agriculture *m*; ~ **subsidy** *n* ECON subvention agricole *f*, subvention à l'agriculture *f*; ~ **tenant** *n* ECON métayer *m*, PROP locataire agricole *m*; ~ **unit** *n* ECON unité agricole *f*, unité d'exploitation agricole *f*; ~ **wages board** *n* ECON, HRM commission des salaires agricoles *f*; ~ **warrant** *n* ECON bulletin de gage agricole *m*, warrant agricole *m*

Agricultural: ~ **Holdings Act** *n UK* LAW concentrations d'entreprises agricoles

agriculturalist *n* ECON, ENVIR agriculteur *m*

agriculture *n* ECON, ENVIR agriculture *f*, GEN COMM culture *f*; ~ **act** *UK* LAW loi sur l'agriculture *f*

agriculturist *n* ECON, ENVIR agriculteur *m*

agrifood: ~ **industry** *n* ECON, ENVIR, IND industrie agro-alimentaire *f*

agrifoodstuffs *n pl* ECON agroalimentaire *m*, produits agro-alimentaires *m pl*, ENVIR, IND agroalimentaire *m*

agrochemical: ~ **product** *n* ENVIR produit agrochimique *m*

agro-forestry *n* ENVIR agroforesterie *f*, sylvo-agriculture *f*

agronomist *n* ECON, ENVIR agronome *m*

agronomy *n* ECON, ENVIR agronomie *f*

aground *adj* TRANSP échoué

agt *abbr* (*agent*) GEN COMM, LAW agent *mf*, commissionnaire *mf*, représentant *m*

ah *abbr* (*after hatch*) TRANSP *shipping* écoutille arrière *f*

AHC *abbr* (*Airport Handling Committee*) TRANSP comité de manutention aux aéroports

ahead: ~ **of schedule** *phr* GEN COMM en avance sur le calendrier établi *loc f*, en avance sur les prévisions *loc f*

AHM *abbr* (*Airport Handling Manual*) TRANSP manuel de la manutention aux aéroports

AHS *abbr* (*annual hull survey*) TRANSP *shipping* visite annuelle de la coque *f*

AHST *abbr* (*anchor-handling salvage tug*) TRANSP remorqueur de sauvetage *m*

AHT *abbr* (*anchor-handling tug*) TRANSP remorqueur *m*

AHTS *abbr* (*anchor-handling tug supply, anchor-handling tug supply vessel*) TRANSP remorqueur spécialisé dans la recherche et l'exploitation du pétrole

AI *abbr* ACC *(accrued interest)*, BANK *(accrued interest)* IC *(intérêts courus)*, COMP *(artificial intelligence)* IA *(intelligence artificielle)*, FIN *(accrued interest)*, GEN COMM *(accrued interest)*, STOCK *(accrued interest)* IC *(intérêts courus)*

AIA *abbr UK (Associate of the Institute of Actuaries)* INS membre associé de l'institut des actuaires

AIB *abbr (American Institute of Bankers)* BANK association professionnelle américaine des banquiers

AIBD *abbr (Association of International Bond Dealers)* STOCK association des négociants d'obligations internationales

AIBOR *abbr (Amsterdam interbank offered rate)* BANK taux interbancaire offert par Amsterdam

AICPA *abbr (American Institute of Certified Public Accountants)* ACC association professionnelle américaine des experts-comptables

AICS *abbr (Associate Institute of Chartered Shipbrokers)* HRM association des courtiers maritimes agréés

aid[1] *n* BANK *help* aide *f*, COMP *assistance f*, ECON *help*, POL *help* aide *f*; ~ **development loan** *UK* BANK, ECON, POL prêt d'aide au développement *m*; ~ **donor** BANK, ECON, POL *development* organisation humanitaire *f*; ~ **in kind** BANK, ECON, POL *development* aide en nature *f*; ~ **loan** BANK, ECON, POL *development* prêt de secours *m*; ~ **money** BANK, ECON, POL *UK development* fonds d'aide au développement *m*; ~ **program** *AmE*, ~ **programme** *BrE* BANK, ECON, POL *development* programme d'aide *m*; ~ **scheme** BANK, ECON, POL *development* programme d'aide *m*

aid[2] *vt* BANK aider, contribuer à, *company* subventionner, *development* apporter une aide à, soutenir, *person* assister, venir en aide à, ECON *development* aider, apporter une aide à, soutenir, GEN COMM *financially* aider, secourir, POL *development* aider, apporter une aide à, soutenir; ♦ ~ **and abet** LAW être le complice de

Aid: ~ **to Families with Dependent Children** *n US (AFDC)* WEL aide aux familles ayant des enfants à charge

AIDA *abbr (attention, interest, desire, action)* GEN COMM, S&M AIDA *(attention, intérêt, désir, action)*

aide *n* GEN COMM assistant *m*; ~ **-mémoire** GEN COMM mémorandum *m*

aided: ~ **recall** *n* S&M *market research* mémorisation assistée *f*; ~ **recall test** *n* S&M *market research* test de mémorisation assistée *m*

AIFTA *abbr* ECON *(Anglo-Irish Free Trade Area Agreement)* accord anglo-irlandais de zone de libre-échange, HRM *(Associate Institute Freight Trades Association)*, TRANSP *(Associate Institute Freight Trades Association)* association professionnelle des transporteurs

AIGSS *abbr (annual inert gas system survey)* ENVIR enquête annuelle sur les systèmes de gaz inertes

ailing[1] *adj* GEN COMM souffrant

ailing:[2] ~ **economy** *n* ECON, POL économie qui périclite *f*; ~ **industry** *n (SYN declining industry)* ECON, IND industrie affaiblie *f*, industrie en déclin *f*

aim[1] *n* ECON finalité *f*, GEN COMM but *m*, finalité *f*, objectif *m*, objet *m*, vise *f*, MGMNT, S&M finalité *f*

aim[2] *vt* GEN COMM *criticism, product, programme* destiner; ~ **at** S&M viser

AIMS *abbr (American Institute of Merchant Shipping)* TRANSP institut américain des navires de commerce

air:[1] ~ **-conditioned** *adj* ADMIN, GEN COMM, WEL climatisé

air[2] *n* TRANSP air *m*; ~ **bag** *n* TRANSP sac gonflable *m*; ~ **bill** *n* IMP/EXP, TRANSP lettre de transport aérien *f*; ~ **bill of lading** *n* IMP/EXP, TRANSP lettre de transport aérien *f*; ~ **cargo** *n* IMP/EXP, TRANSP fret aérien *m*; ~ **carrier** *n* IMP/EXP, TRANSP transporteur aérien *m*; ~ **check** *n* MEDIA *broadcast* enregistrement témoin *m*, enregistrement témoin d'une émission *m*, essai radio *m*; ~ **check tape** *n* MEDIA *broadcast* enregistrement témoin *m*, enregistrement témoin d'une émission *m*, essai radio *m*; ~ **conditioning** *n* ADMIN, GEN COMM, WEL air conditionné *m*, climatisation *f*, conditionnement d'air *m*; ~ **consignment note** *n* IMP/EXP, TRANSP lettre de transport aérien *f*; ~ **corridor** *n* TRANSP couloir aérien *m*; ~ **cushion vehicle** *n (ACV)* TRANSP aéroglisseur *m*, véhicule sur coussin d'air *m*; ~ **fare** *n* LEIS, TRANSP prix du billet d'avion *m*; ~ **freight** *n* IMP/EXP, TRANSP fret aérien *m*, transport aérien *m*; ~ **freight consolidation** *n* IMP/EXP, TRANSP groupage de fret aérien *m*; ~ **freight container** *n (AC)* TRANSP conteneur pour fret aérien *m*; ~ **freighter** *n* IMP/EXP, TRANSP avion-cargo *m*; ~ **hostess** *n (SYN flight attendant)* TRANSP hôtesse de l'air *f*; ~ **mode container** *n* IMP/EXP, TRANSP avance contre documents d'expédition *f*, conteneur pour transport aérien *m*; ~ **pocket stock** *n jarg* STOCK titre trou d'air *m*; ~ **pollutant** *n* ENVIR polluant atmosphérique *m*; ~ **pollution** *n* ENVIR pollution atmosphérique *f*; ~ **pollution control** *n* ENVIR, IND contrôle de la pollution atmosphérique *m*; ~ **pollution emission** *n* ENVIR, IND émission de polluants atmosphériques *f*; ~ **rights** *n pl* COMMS, LAW, MEDIA droits de retransmission *m pl*; ~ **show** *n* TRANSP salon de l'aéronautique *m*; ~ **terminal** *n* TRANSP aérogare *f*; ~ **traffic** *n* TRANSP circulation aérienne *f*, trafic aérien *m*; ~ **traffic control** *n (ATC)* TRANSP *activity* contrôle de la circulation aérienne *m*, contrôle du trafic aérien *m*, *building* tour de contrôle *f*; ~ **traffic control system** *n* TRANSP système de contrôle de la circulation aérienne *m*; ~ **-traffic controller** *n* TRANSP aiguilleur du ciel *m*, contrôleur aérien *m*; ~ **transport** *n* TRANSP transport aérien *m*; ~ **transport insurance** *n* INS, TRANSP assurance transport aérien *f*; ~ **transportation tax** *n* (*ATT*) TAX taxe sur le transport aérien *f* (*TTA*); ~ **travel** *n* LEIS, TRANSP les voyages en avion *m pl*; ~ **traveler** *n* AmE, ~ **traveller** *n* BrE LEIS, TRANSP voyageur par avion *m*; ~ **waybill** *n* (*AWB*) IMP/EXP, TRANSP lettre de transport aérien *f* (*LTA*); ◆ **by** ~ *n* TRANSP par avion *loc m*

air³ *vt* GEN COMM *idea, proposal* avancer, exprimer, mettre sur le tapis, proposer à l'examen, *opinion, view* afficher, faire connaître, faire part de; ◆ ~ **one's opinions** GEN COMM afficher ses idées; ~ **one's views** GEN COMM afficher ses idées, faire cas de son avis

Air: ~ **Transport Association** *n* US (*ATA*) TRANSP association de transport aérien des États-Unis, ≈ Direction générale de l'aviation civile *f* (*France*) (*DGAC*)

airborne¹ *adj* TRANSP en vol

airborne:² ~ **time** *n* TRANSP temps de vol réel *m*

airbrush: ~ **technique** *n* S&M *advertising* aérographie *f*

airbus *n* TRANSP airbus *m*

aircraft *n* [inv pl] TRANSP avion *m*, aéronef *m*; ~ **charter agreement** *n* LAW, TRANSP contrat d'affrètement aérien *m*; ~ **commander** *n* HRM, TRANSP commandant de bord *m*; ~ **hull insurance** *n* INS, TRANSP assurance corps aériens *f*; ~ **industry** *n* GEN COMM, IND, TRANSP industrie aéronautique *f*; ~ **kilometers** *n pl* AmE, ~ **kilometres** *n pl* BrE TRANSP kilomètres-avion *m pl*; ~ **movement message** *n* (*MVT*) TRANSP message concernant le mouvement des aéronefs *m*; ~ **operator** *n* TRANSP exploitant *m*; ~ **passenger insurance** *n* INS, TRANSP assurance passagers aériens *f*, assurance voyageurs aériens *f*; ~ **turnround time** *n* TRANSP *loading/unloading* durée de rotation *f*

aircrew *n* LEIS, TRANSP équipage d'un avion *m*

airdrome *n* AmE *see* aerodrome BrE

airlift *n* TRANSP pont aérien *m*

airline *n* TRANSP compagnie aérienne *f*, ligne aérienne *f*; ~ **advertising** S&M, TRANSP publicité pour compagnies aériennes *f*; ~ **company** TRANSP compagnie aérienne *f*; ~ **guide** TRANSP guide aérien *m*

airliner *n* TRANSP avion de ligne *m*, liner *m*

airmail¹ *n* COMMS poste aérienne *f*; ~ **letter** COMMS lettre aérienne *f*, lettre par avion *f*; ~ **paper** COMMS papier par avion *m*; ~ **transfer** (*AMT*) BANK virement interbancaire *m*, virement par avion *m*; ◆ **by** ~ COMMS par avion

airmail² *vt* COMMS *letter* expédier par avion

airplane *AmE* (*cf* aeroplane BrE) TRANSP avion *m*

airport *n* TRANSP aéroport *m*; ~ **advertising** MEDIA, S&M, TRANSP publicité d'aéroport *f*; ~ **hotel** LEIS, TRANSP hôtel d'aéroport *m*; ~ **lounge** TRANSP salle d'embarquement *f*; ~ **tax** TAX, TRANSP taxe d'aéroport *f*

Airport: ~ **Associations Co-ordinating Council** *n* (*AACC*) TRANSP ≈ Conseil de coordination des associations aéroportuaires *m* (*CCAA*); ~ **Handling Committee** *n* (*AHC*) TRANSP comité de manutention aux aéroports; ~ **Handling Manual** *n* (*AHM*) TRANSP manuel de la manutention aux aéroports

airtight *adj* GEN COMM *container, seal* hermétique, étanche à l'air

airtime *n* MEDIA *broadcast* heure d'émission *f, for advertising* espace publicitaire *m*, temps d'antenne *m, radio, TV* créneau horaire *m*, temps d'antenne *m, S&M for advertising* espace publicitaire *m*, temps d'antenne *m*; ~ **buyer** MEDIA *radio, TV* acheteur d'espace *m*, acheteur de temps d'antenne *m*, centrale d'achats d'espaces *f*

airway *n* (*AWY*) TRANSP *route* voie aérienne *f*

airworthiness: ~ **certification** *n* TRANSP certification *f*

airworthy *adj* TRANSP en état de navigabilité *loc m*

aisle *n* GEN COMM *in cinema, shop* allée *f, in train, aeroplane* couloir *m*, LEIS *in cinema* allée *f*, TRANSP *in train, aeroplane* couloir *m*; ~ **sitter** *jarg* LEIS *broadcast, theatre*, MEDIA critique de théâtre *m*

AIWM *abbr* (*American Institute of Weights and Measures*) GEN COMM institut américain des poids et mesures

a.k.a. *abbr* (*also known as*) COMMS alias, dit, également appelé, GEN COMM alias, aussi connu sous le nom de

alarm *n* GEN COMM *as warning* alarme *f*, alerte *f, in clock* sonnerie *f*; ~ **bell** GEN COMM sonnerie d'alarme *f*; ~ **call** COMMS, GEN COMM réveil par téléphone *m*; ~ **clock** GEN COMM réveil *m*, réveille-matin *m*; ~ **signal** GEN COMM signal d'alarme *m*

Albania *pr n* GEN COMM Albanie *f*

Albanian¹ *adj* GEN COMM albanais

Albanian² *n* GEN COMM *language* albanais *m, person* Albanais *m*

alcoholic: ~ **drink** *n* GEN COMM boisson alcoolique *f*

aleatoric *adj* INS aléatoire

aleatory¹ *adj* INS aléatoire

aleatory:² ~ **contract** *n* INS contrat aléatoire *m*

alert *n* GEN COMM alerte *f*; ~ **box** COMP fenêtre d'alerte *f*, message d'alerte *m*, zone d'alerte *f*; ◆ **be on the** ~ **for** GEN COMM être en état d'alerte, être à l'affût de; **give the** ~ GEN COMM donner l'alerte

Algeria *pr n* GEN COMM Algérie *f*

Algerian¹ *adj* GEN COMM algérien

Algerian² *n* GEN COMM *person* Algérien *m*

Algiers *pr n* GEN COMM Alger *n pr*

algorithm *n* COMP, MATH algorithme *m*

algorithmic *adj* COMP, MATH algorithmique

alias¹ *adv* COMP, GEN COMM alias

alias[2] *n* COMP, GEN COMM nom de guerre *m*, nom de plume *m*, pseudonyme *m*

alien[1] *adj* GEN COMM, LAW étranger; ~ **from** GEN COMM éloigné de, étranger à; ~ **to** GEN COMM contraire à, opposé à

alien[2] *n* LAW étranger *m*; ~ **corporation** GEN COMM, LAW société commerciale de droit étranger *f*; ~ **registration card** *US* ADMIN, HRM, WEL carte de séjour *f*

alienable *adj* LAW aliénable

alienate *vt person* LAW aliener; ◆ ~ **sb from sth** GEN COMM détacher qn de qch, détourner qn de qch, se mettre à dos

alienation *n* HRM, LAW aliénation *f*; ~ **effect** S&M *advertising* effet d'éloignement *m*

alienee *n* LAW aliénataire *mf*

align *vt* *BrE* COMP aligner, mettre en ligne, LAW aligner

aligned: ~ **form** *n* ADMIN formulaire normalisé *m*, formulaire standardisé *m*, TRANSP formulaire standardisé *m*

alignment *n* GEN COMM alignement *m*

alimony *n* LAW aliments *m pl*

aline *AmE see* align

aliquot *adj* MATH *parts* aliquote

aliter *adv* GEN COMM *on the contrary* au contraire *loc m*, *otherwise* autrement

All: ~ **Ordinaries Index** *n* *Australia* STOCK indice de toutes les actions ordinaires; ~ **Share Index** *n* *UK* STOCK indice du Financial Times et de l'Institut des actuaires

all-day: ~ **trading** *n* STOCK marché continu *m*, négociation continue *f*

allegation *n* HRM, LAW allégation *f*

alleged *adj* HRM, LAW allégué, prétendu

all-employee: ~ **option scheme** *n* *UK* STOCK programme d'options ouvert à tous les employés *m*

alleviate *vt* GEN COMM *problem* rendre supportable, soulager

alliance *n* POL alliance *f*, pacte *m*, union *f*

allied: ~ **industries** *n pl* IND industries connexes *f pl*; ~ **member** *n* STOCK courtier associé *m*; ~ **peril** *n* INS risque lié *m*; ~ **trades** *n pl* IND métiers analogues *m pl*

alligator: ~ **spread** *n* BANK, FIN, STOCK *of securities, options* stratégie d'option alligator *f*, écart alligator *m*

all-in *adj* GEN COMM *price* net, tout compris, INS tous risques, S&M *price* net, tout compris

all-inclusive[1] *adj* GEN COMM *price* forfaitaire, tout compris, *rate* net, tout compris

all-inclusive:[2] ~ **price** *n* GEN COMM prix forfaitaire *m*, prix tout compris *m*

all-loss *adj* INS tous risques

allocate *vt* ACC ventiler, *money, duties* affecter, allouer, attribuer, ADMIN *money, duties*, COMP affecter, allouer, attribuer, ECON *funds, resources, money, duties* affecter, allouer, attribuer, *resources*

affecter, FIN *contract* ventiler, GEN COMM *money, duties* attribuer, *work* assigner, HRM *money, duties* allouer, assigner, attribuer, *resource* affecter, *share out* distribuer, répartir, LAW *contract* adjuger, ventiler; ◆ ~ **costs to certain accounts** ACC ventiler les charges entre certains comptes

allocated: ~ **benefits** *n pl* *UK* FIN *personal* allocations allouées *f pl*; ~ **material** *n* GEN COMM matériel réservé *m*

allocation *n* ACC attribution *f*, répartition *f*, ventilation *f*, *of funds* affectation *f*, ADMIN, COMP affectation *f*, allocation *f*, attribution *f*, ECON *monetary supply* affectation *f*, *of resources* affectation *f*, allocation *f*, FIN *of money, duties* affectation *f*, attribution *f*, ventilation *f*, GEN COMM attribution *f*, *of contract* adjudication *f*, *of resources* affectation *f*, HRM attribution *f*, répartition *f*, LAW ventilation *f*, STOCK répartition *f*; ~ **by tender** *UK* STOCK allocation par appel d'offre *f*, répartition par voie d'adjudication *f*; ~ **of costs** ACC affectation des charges *f*, imputation des charges *f*, répartition des coûts *f*; ~ **of earnings** HRM répartition des revenus *f*; ~ **of responsibilities** FIN, GEN COMM, HRM, MGMNT répartition des responsabilités *f*; ~ **to the lowest tenderer** S&M adjudication au soumissionnaire le plus offrant *f*; ~ **to a provision** GEN COMM dotation à une provision *f*; ~ **to provisions** ACC affectation aux provisions *f*; ~ **to reserves** ACC affectation aux réserves *f*; ~ **of work** HRM, MGMNT distribution du travail *f*

allocative: ~ **efficiency** *n* ECON, FIN efficacité d'allocation *f*, efficacité de l'affectation *f*

allodial[1] *adj* LAW allodial

allodial:[2] ~ **system** *n* LAW système allodial *m*

allonge *n* BANK *on bill of exchange* allonge *f*

all-or-nothing: ~ **clause** *n* *(AON clause)* STOCK clause tout ou rien *f*

allot *vt* ACC, ADMIN affecter, BANK consentir, FIN *money, resources* accorder, allouer, attribuer, consentir, GEN COMM *time* allouer, consacrer, MGMNT *time* consacrer, STOCK *share* attribuer, répartir

allotment *n* ACC *public*, ADMIN affectation *f*, FIN attribution *f*, HRM, STOCK *of shares* répartition *f*, TRANSP *shipping* délégation de solde *f*; ~ **of bonus** INS répartition de bonus *f*; ~ **letter** *UK* STOCK avis d'attribution *m*, droit de souscription négociable *m* *(Fra)*; ~ **money** FIN versement de souscription *m*; ~ **price** FIN prix de souscription *m*; ~ **of securities** *UK* STOCK attribution de titres *f*, attribution de valeurs *f*; ~ **of shares** STOCK attribution d'actions *f*

allotted: ~ **share** *n* STOCK action attribuée *f*, action répartie *f*

allottee *n* STOCK attributaire *mf*

all-out[1] *adj* GEN COMM *effort* max., maximum

all-out:[2] ~ **strike** *n* HRM grève générale *f*

allow *vt* GEN COMM *action, change* autoriser, *claim* agréer, faire droit à, *money, resources* accorder, *person, organization* permettre, *time* allouer, INS *claim* agréer; **~ for** GEN COMM tenir compte de; ◆ **~ for a margin of error** ACC estimer en reconnaissant une marge d'erreur, GEN COMM prévoir une marge d'erreur; **~ sb a discount** S&M consentir une remise à qn, faire bénéficier qn d'une remise; **~ sb to do** GEN COMM autoriser qn à faire; **~ sb £8,000 in damages** INS accorder à qn 8 000 livres de dommages et intérêts

allowable: **~ business investment loss** *n* ACC, FIN, GEN COMM, TAX perte déductible au titre d'un placement d'entreprise *f*; **~ capital loss** *n* ACC, FIN, STOCK, TAX perte en capital déductible *f*; **~ claim** *n* INS réclamation admissible *f*, réclamation recevable *f*; **~ credit** *n* TAX crédit déductible *m*; **~ deduction** *n* TAX montant déductible *m*; **~ expense** *n* ACC frais fiscalement déductibles *m pl*, TAX dépense déductible *f*, frais déductibles *m pl*; **~ liquid assets** *n pl* TAX *of corporation, partnership* avoirs liquides admissibles *m pl*; **~ refund** *n* TAX remboursement admissible *m*

allowance *n* ACC réduction *f*, GEN COMM allocation *f*, indemnité *f*, rabais *m*, remise *f*, réduction *f*, franchise *f*, *tolerance* marge de tolérance *f*, HRM allocation *f*, S&M *for damaged or lost goods* réfaction *f*, TAX abattement fiscal *m*, déduction avant impôt *f*, allocation *f*, TRANSP franchise *f*, WEL allocation *f*; **~ for bad debts** ACC, BANK *(SYN provision for bad debts)* provision pour créances douteuses *f*; **~ for depreciation** US ACC dotation aux amortissements *f*; **~ for exchange fluctuations** ECON, FIN, STOCK provision pour fluctuations du change *f*; **~ for inflation** UK ACC prise en compte de l'inflation *f*, provision pour inflation *f*, provision pour plus-values *f*, provision pour évaluation *f*, ECON provision pour inflation *f*, provision pour plus-values *f*, provision pour évaluation *f*, POL provision pour plus-values *f*; **~ for living expenses** TAX allocation de subsistance *f*; **~ for loss** GEN COMM réfaction *f*; **~ for personal expenses** TAX allocation pour frais personnels *f*; **~ for travelling expenses** TAX allocation pour frais de déplacement *f*; **~ in kind** GEN COMM avantage en espèces *m*, avantage en nature *m*, avantage matériel *m*, prestation en nature *f*; ◆ **make an ~ on** GEN COMM *discount*, S&M *discount* accorder une remise sur; **make ~ for** ACC défalquer; **make ~s for** GEN COMM tenir compte de

allowed[1] *adj* TAX *deduction* admis, permis

allowed:[2] **~ time** *n (SYN standard time)* HRM *for job performance* durée forfaitaire *f*, délai fixe *m*, temps moyen *m*

alloy: **~ container** *n (a)* TRANSP *shipping* conteneur en alliage *m*

all-purpose *adj* FIN *statement* à vocation générale *loc f*, GEN COMM *computer, device* polyvalent, universel

all-risk *adj* INS tous risques *phr, policy* tous périls

all-round *adj* GEN COMM *fee, price* tout compris

all-sector: **~ average** *n* ECON *growth* moyenne tous secteurs confondus *f*

all-time: **~ high** *n* GEN COMM chiffre sans précédent *m*, niveau historique *m*, niveau sans précédent *m*, record absolu *m*, record le plus élevé *m*, STOCK haut niveau sans précédent *m*, niveau record *m*; **~ low** *n* GEN COMM chiffre sans précédent *m*, le chiffre le plus bas jamais atteint *loc m*, STOCK *market* bas niveau sans précédent *m*, creux sans précédent *m*; **~ record** *n* GEN COMM record absolu *m*

ally *vt* GEN COMM allier

ALM *abbr (assets and liabilities management)* ACC, BANK, FIN, MGMNT GAP *(gestion actif-passif)*, gestion du bilan *f*

Alma-Ata *pr n* GEN COMM Alma-Ata *n pr*

aloft *adv* TRANSP *shipping* dans la mâture *loc f*, en haut

alongside[1] *adv* TRANSP à quai *loc m*

alongside:[2] **~ bill of lading** *n* IMP/EXP, TRANSP connaissement reçu à quai *m*

alongside[3] *prep (A/S)* TRANSP *quay* bord à, le long de

aloof *adj* GEN COMM à l'écart *loc m*

alpha: **~ share** *n* STOCK action fréquemment négociée *f*; **~ stage** *n* BANK, ECON, FIN capital de base *m*; **~ stock** *n* STOCK valeurs alpha *f pl*; **~ test** *n* COMP essai en laboratoire *m*, test alpha *m*

alphabetical *adj* COMMS, GEN COMM alphabétique; ◆ **in ~ order** GEN COMM par ordre alphabétique

alphanumeric[1] *adj (A/N)* COMP, GEN COMM alphanumérique

alphanumeric:[2] **~ character** *n* COMP caractère alphanumérique *m*

Alpine: **~ countries** *n pl* GEN COMM, POL pays alpins *m pl*

also: **~ known as** *phr (a.k.a.)* COMMS alias, dit, également appelé, GEN COMM alias, aussi connu sous le nom de

alt. *abbr (altered)* GEN COMM changé, modifié

Alt: **~ key** *n (Alternate key)* COMP, GEN COMM touche Alt *f*

alter *vt* GEN COMM changer, modifier

alteration *n* GEN COMM, TAX modification *f*; **~ of capital** FIN, GEN COMM modification du capital *f*

alterations *n pl* GEN COMM travaux de transformation *m pl*; **~ and improvements** ACC *annual accounts* agencements et aménagements *m pl*

altered *adj (alt.)* GEN COMM changé, modifié

alternate[1] *adj* GEN COMM *by turns* alternatif, alterné, *successive* en alternance; ◆ **on ~ days** GEN COMM tous les deux jours

alternate[2] *n* GEN COMM remplaçant *m*, suppléant *m*; **~ funding** FIN financement de remplacement *m*; **~ press** MEDIA presse parallèle *f*

alternate[3] *vt* GEN COMM alterner

Alternate: **~ key** *n (Alt key)* COMP, GEN COMM touche Alt *f*

alternating: ~ **current** n COMP, IND courant alternatif m (ca); ~ **shift** n HRM équipe f

alternative[1] adj GEN COMM autre, de rechange, MGMNT de rechange

alternative[2] n GEN COMM alternative f, option f, from several choix m, possibilité f; ~ **cost** ACC, ECON, FIN coût d'opportunité m; ~ **economic strategy** ECON, POL stratégie économique de rechange f; ~ **energy** ENVIR, IND énergie de substitution f, énergie nouvelle f; ~ **hypothesis** MATH statistical testing hypothèse alternative f; ~ **minimum tax** Can TAX impôt minimum de remplacement m; ~ **mortgage instrument** BANK prêt hypothécaire différent m; ~ **order** GEN COMM commande de remplacement f, ordre bivalent m, S&M commande de remplacement f; ~ **participation instrument** UK (API) STOCK instrument de participation différent m; ~ **proposal** GEN COMM, MGMNT contre-proposition f; ~ **solution** GEN COMM contre-solution f; ~ **technology** ECON, ENVIR, IND technologie de remplacement f, technologie douce f; ~ **use** PROP utilisation en alternance f, utilisation par alternance f; ◆ **there is no ~** (TINA) GEN COMM aucune alternative n'est possible, il n'y a pas d'alternative

alternatives n pl GEN COMM les termes de l'alternative m pl

altruism n ECON altruisme m

alum. abbr (aluminium BrE, aluminum AmE) ENVIR, IND aluminium m

aluminium n BrE (alum.) ENVIR, IND aluminium m; ~ **can bank** n BrE ENVIR conteneur de boîtes en aluminium m; ~ **covers** n pl BrE TRANSP on a ship panneaux en aluminium m pl

aluminum n AmE see aluminium BrE

always adv LAW toujours; ◆ ~ **accessible** (SYN reachable on arrival) TRANSP à disposition à l'arrivée; ~ **accessible on arrival** (SYN always reachable on arrival) TRANSP shipping à disposition à l'arrivée; ~ **afloat** TRANSP shipping à flot; **not ~ afloat** (NAA) TRANSP pas toujours à flot; **not ~ afloat but safe aground** TRANSP pas toujours à flot mais échoué en sécurité; ~ **reachable on arrival** (SYN always accessible on arrival) TRANSP shipping à disposition à l'arrivée

am abbr (ante meridiem) GEN COMM avant midi, du matin

AMA abbr (Asset Management Account) FIN compte de gestion des actifs

amalgamate vti ECON companies, activities, shares, GEN COMM companies, activities, shares fusionner

amalgamated: ~ **bank** n BANK banque issue de la fusion f; ~ **body corporate** n GEN COMM personne morale issue de la fusion f; ~ **corporation** n TAX corporation fusionnée f, corporation issue d'une fusion f

amalgamating: ~ **body corporate** n GEN COMM personne morale en cours de fusion f; ~ **corporation** n BANK société absorbée f

amalgamation n HRM fusion syndicale f, STOCK fusion f, fusionnement m; ~ **agreement** STOCK accord de fusion m

amass vt GEN COMM money, property, goods amasser

amateur[1] adj LEIS sport amateur

amateur[2] n LEIS sport amateur m

ambassador n POL ambassadeur m

ambient: ~ **quality standard** n ENVIR of air norme relative à la qualité f; ~ **standard** n US ENVIR of air quality norme de pureté de l'air f

ambition n GEN COMM ambition f

ambitious adj GEN COMM person, plan ambitieux

amend vt LAW amender, corriger, modifier, rectifier, revoir, PATENTS modifier, revoir, POL amender, modifier, revoir

amended[1] adj TAX modifié

amended:[2] ~ **act** n LAW loi amendée f, loi modifiée f, loi révisée f; ~ **prospectus** n STOCK prospectus modifié m

amendment n LAW, POL amendement m, modification f, révision f

amenities n pl PROP appraisal agréments m pl, aménagements m pl, installations f pl

America pr n GEN COMM Amérique f

American[1] adj GEN COMM américain

American[2] n GEN COMM person Américain m; ~ **Association of Advertising Agencies** n (AAAA) S&M association nationale américaine des agences de publicité; ~ **Automobile Association** n (AAA) TRANSP association automobile américaine, ≈ Touring Club de France m (France); ~ **Bar Association** n US LAW ≈ ordre des avocats m; ~ **Board of Trade** n (ABT) GEN COMM bureau américain du commerce; ~ **Bureau of Shipping** n (ABS) TRANSP registre américain d'immatriculation (société de classification); ~ **Chamber of Commerce** n (ACC) IND chambre américaine de commerce; ~ **clause** n INS marine clause de double assurance f; ~ **depositary receipt** n (ADR) BANK, FIN, GEN COMM, STOCK certificat américain d'actions étrangers; ~ **Federation of Labor - Congress of Industrial Organizations** n (AFL-CIO) HRM confédération générale américaine du travail; ~ **Federation of Labor-Congress of Industrial Organizations** n HRM confédération Générale Américaine du Travail; ~ **gallon** n GEN COMM gallon américain m; ~ **Institute of Accountants** n ACC association professionnelle américaine des comptables; ~ **Institute of Bankers** n (AIB) BANK association professionnelle américaine des banquiers; ~ **Institute of Certified Public Accountants** n (AICPA) ACC association Professionnelle Américaine des Experts-Comptables; ~ **Institute of Merchant Shipping** n (AIMS) TRANSP institut américain des navires de commerce; ~ **Institute of Weights and Measures** n (AIWM) GEN COMM institut américain des poids et mesures; ~ **Management Association** n MGMNT association Américaine d'Administration; ~ **Marketing Association** n S&M association américaine de marketing; ~ **Merchant Marine Institute** *n (AMMI)* TRANSP institut américain de la marine marchande; ~ **National Standards Institute** *n US (ANSI)* GEN COMM, IND, LAW association américaine de normalisation, ≈ Association française de normalisation *f (AFNOR)*; ~ **Newspaper Publishers' Association** *n (ANPA)* MEDIA association américaine des Editeurs de Quotidiens; ~ **option** *n* STOCK option américaine *f*; ~ **selling price** *n* ECON, FIN, IMP/EXP prix intérieur américain *m*; ~ **short ton** *n* GEN COMM tonne courte américaine *f*; ~ **Standard Code for Information Interchange** *n (ASCII)* COMP ASCII *m*; ~ **Standards Association** *n (ASA)* GEN COMM, IND, LAW association américaine de normalisation, ≈ Association française de normalisation *f (AFNOR)*; ~ **Standards Authority** *n* IND association américaine de normalisation; ~ **Statistical Association** *n (ASA)* MATH association américaine de la statistique; ~ **Stock Exchange** *n (AMEX, ASE, the Curb)* FIN, STOCK la bourse de New York secondaire où sont listées les valeurs qui n'apparaissent pas au New York Stock Exchange; ~ **terms** *n pl* ECON modalités en dollars *f pl*; ◆ **in ~ terms** *n* ECON *currency exchange* aux conditions américaines *loc f*

Americanized-European: ~ **option** *n* STOCK option euro-américanisée *f*, option européenne américanisée *f*

Americans: **the ~** *n pl* GEN COMM les Américains *m pl*

Amex: ~ **Commodities Exchange** *n (ACE)* STOCK Bourse de commerce de l'Amex *f*

AMEX *abbr (American Stock Exchange, the Curb)* FIN, STOCK la bourse de New York secondaire où sont listées les valeurs qui n'apparaissent pas au New York Stock Exchange, AMEX *f*

AMI: ~ **Ex** *abbr (Associate Member of the Institute of Export)* HRM, IMP/EXP membre associé du groupement des exportateurs

amicable[1] *adj* GEN COMM, HRM *manner, performance* plaisant, *person* amiable, amical

amicable:[2] ~ **settlement** *n* GEN COMM, LAW arrangement à l'amiable *m*

amicably *adv* GEN COMM, LAW à l'amiable

amidships *adv* TRANSP au milieu du navire *loc m*

AMIME *abbr (Associate Member of the Institute of Marine Engineers)* HRM, IND membre associé du groupement des mécaniciens de marine

AML *abbr (adjustable mortgage loan)* BANK, FIN, PROP prêt hypothécaire variable *m*

Amman *pr n* GEN COMM Amman *n pr*

AMMI *abbr (American Merchant Marine Institute)* TRANSP institut américain de la marine marchande

amortizable *adj* ACC amortissable

amortization *n* ACC amortissement *m*, FIN *loan* amortissement *m*, remboursement *m*; ~ **adjustment** ACC, FIN, INS redressement pour amortissement *m*; ~ **expense** ACC, FIN dotation aux amortissements *f*; ~ **fund** ACC, FIN fonds

d'amortissement *m*; ~ **loan** ACC, BANK, FIN, GEN COMM prêt d'amortissement *m*; ~ **of a loan** ACC, BANK, FIN amortissement d'un emprunt *m*, remboursement d'un prêt *m*; ~ **method** ACC, FIN méthode d'amortissement *f*; ~ **on a straight-line basis** ACC, FIN méthode d'amortissement linéaire *f*; ~ **payment** ACC, BANK, FIN remboursement périodique *m*; ~ **reserve** ACC, FIN provision pour amortissements *f*; ~ **schedule** ACC, FIN plan d'amortissement *m*

amortize *vt* ACC *asset*, BANK, FIN amortir

amortized: ~ **cost** *n* TAX coût amorti *m*, coût amortissable *m*; ~ **mortgage loan** *n* ACC, BANK, FIN prêt hypothécaire à remboursements périodiques *m*; ~ **value** *n* ACC, FIN valeur comptable nette *f*

amortizement *n* ACC, FIN amortissement *m*

amount[1] *n (AMT)* ACC *of goods* quantité *f*, *of people* nombre *m*, FIN chiffre *m*, nombre *m*, GEN COMM chiffre *m*, nombre *m*, *total* montant *m*, nombre *m*; ~ **brought forward** ACC montant reporté *m*, somme reportée *f*; ~ **of business** GEN COMM volume d'affaires *m*, STOCK volume des transactions *m*; ~ **carried forward** ACC report à nouveau *m*; ~ **charged** GEN COMM montant à payer *m*, somme à verser *f*; ~ **of damage** INS montant des avaries *m*, montant du dommage *m*; ~ **due** FIN montant dû *m*, GEN COMM montant dû *m*, somme due *f*; ~ **exported** GEN COMM, IMP/EXP volume des exportations *m*; ~ **invested** ACC, FIN, TAX somme investie *f*; ~ **of loss** INS montant du sinistre *m*; ~ **outstanding** ACC montant impayé *m*, solde *m*, BANK, FIN solde *m*; ~ **overdue** ACC montant échu *m*; ~ **overpaid** GEN COMM trop-perçu *m*; ~ **paid** GEN COMM montant versé *m*, somme versée *f*; ~ **paid by installments** *AmE*, ~ **paid by instalments** *BrE* TAX montant payé par acomptes *m*; ~ **paid out** ACC montant versé *m*; ~ **payable** TAX montant payable *m*, somme payable *f*; ~ **payable on settlement** ACC montant payable à terme *m*; ~ **repayable** ACC montant remboursable *m*; ~ **secured** TAX montant garanti *m*; ~ **secured by a charge upon property** FIN, PROP montant garanti par une sûreté sur un bien *m*; ~ **standing to your account** BANK solde créditeur de votre compte *m*; ~ **to be invested** BANK somme à investir *f*; ~ **to be made good** INS *marine* masse créancière *f*; ~ **to pay** GEN COMM montant à payer *m*; ◆ ~ **enclosed** COMMS, FIN somme jointe *f*; ~ **if any** FIN, GEN COMM montant éventuel *m*

amount:[2] ~ **to** *vt* GEN COMM s'élever à, se chiffrer à, se monter à, être chiffré à

ampersand *n* GEN COMM esperluette *f*

ampoule *n* GEN COMM ampoule *f*

AMS *abbr (annual machinery survey)* TRANSP *shipping* visite annuelle des machines *f*

Amsterdam: ~ **interbank offered rate** *n UK (AIBOR)* BANK taux interbancaire offert par Amsterdam

AMT *abbr* ACC *(amount)* of goods quantité *f*, of

people nombre *m*, BANK *(airmail transfer)* virement interbancaire *m*, virement par avion *m*, FIN *(amount)* chiffre *m*, nombre *m*, GEN COMM *(amount)* chiffre *m*, nombre *m, total* chiffre *m*, montant *m*

AMTRAK *n US* TRANSP société nationale des chemins de fer américains

AMU *abbr (Arab Maghreb Union)* ECON, POL Union du Maghreb arabe *f*

amusement: ~ **industry** *n* IND, LEIS industrie des loisirs *f*, industrie du spectacle *f*; ~ **park** *n* LEIS parc d'attractions *m*

A/N *abbr (alphanumeric)* COMP, GEN COMM alphanumérique

analog[1] *adj* COMP analogique; ~ **-digital** *(A/D)* COMP analogique-numérique

analog[2] *n* COMP, GEN COMM analogue *f*; ~ **channel** COMP voie analogique *f*; ~ **computer** COMP calculateur analogique *m*, ordinateur analogique *m*; ~ **-digital converter** *(ADC)* COMP *hardware* convertisseur analogique-numérique *m (CAN)*; ~ **monitor** COMP *hardware* moniteur analogique *m*; ~ **representation** COMP représentation analogique *f*

analogical *adj* COMP, GEN COMM analogique

analyse *vt BrE* GEN COMM analyser, décomposer, faire l'analyse de *loc f*

analyser *n BrE* COMP analyseur *m*, programme d'analyse *m*

analysis *n* ACC analyse *f*, GEN COMM *account, report* analyse *f*, dépouillement *m*, HRM, MGMNT analyse *f*; ~ **book** ACC, BANK, FIN livre de comptes *m*; ~ **of cost variances** ACC analyse des écarts de coûts *f*; ~ **of costs by nature** ACC *annual accounts* répartition par nature des charges d'exploitation *f*; ~ **of time series** GEN COMM analyse chronologique *f*, analyse de conjoncture *f*

analyst *n* COMP, HRM, MGMNT analyste *mf*

analytic[1] *adj* COMP, GEN COMM, IND, MATH analytique

analytic:[2] ~ **accounting** *n* ACC, FIN, MGMNT comptabilité analytique *f*; ~ **process** *n* HRM, MGMNT processus analytique *m*, procédé analytique *m*

analytical[1] *adj* COMP, GEN COMM, IND, MATH analytique

analytical:[2] ~ **audit** *n* ACC audit analytique *m*, contrôle des comptes analytique *m*, révision analytique *f*, vérification analytique *f (Can)*; ~ **auditing** *n* ACC audit analytique *m*, contrôle des comptes analytique *m*, révision analytique *f*, vérification analytique *f (Can)*; ~ **review** *n* ACC audit analytique *m*, contrôle des comptes analytique *m*, révision analytique *f*, vérification analytique *f (Can)*; ~ **training** *n* HRM, MGMNT formation par étapes *f*

analyze *vt AmE see* analyse *BrE*

analyzer *n AmE see* analyser *BrE*

anarchism *n* POL anarchisme *m*

anarcho: ~ **-communism** *n* POL anarcho-commu-

nisme *m*; ~ **-syndicalism** *n* POL anarchosyndicalisme *m*

anarchy: ~ **of production** *n* POL anarchie de la production *f*

ancestor *n* GEN COMM ancêtre *mf*, ascendant *m*

anchor[1] *n* MEDIA *newscasting* pilote d'émission *m*, présentateur vedette *m*, présentateur-réalisateur *m*, TRANSP ancre *f*; ~ **bracket** TRANSP fourchette de point fixe *f*; ~ **-handling salvage tug** *(AHST)* TRANSP remorqueur de sauvetage *m*; ~ **-handling tug** *(AHT)* TRANSP remorqueur *m*; ~ **-handling tug supply** *(AHTS)* TRANSP remorqueur spécialisé dans la recherche et l'exploitation du pétrole; ~ **-handling tug supply vessel** *(AHTS)* TRANSP remorqueur spécialisé dans la recherche et l'exploitation du pétrole; ~ **position** TRANSP *shipping* position au mouillage *f*; ~ **tenant** PROP locataire cramponné

anchor[2] *vt* MEDIA *newscasting* présenter

anchorage *n* TRANSP *shipping* ancrage *m*, mouillage *m*; ~ **charges** *n pl* TRANSP *shipping* droits de mouillage *m pl*

anchorman *n* [pl -men] MEDIA *newscasting* présentateur vedette *m*, présentateur-réalisateur *m*

anchorwoman *n* [pl -men] MEDIA *newscasting* présentatrice vedette *f*, présentatrice-réalisatrice *f*

ancillary[1] *adj* GEN COMM *costs* accessoire, *service, operation, department* auxiliaire

ancillary:[2] ~ **and incidental activities** *n pl* TAX activités accessoires *f pl*; ~ **operations** *n pl* GEN COMM services auxiliaires *m pl*, MGMNT services d'intendance *m pl*; ~ **services** *n pl* GEN COMM services accessoires *m pl*

Andean: ~ **Common Market** *n (ACM)* ECON *international trade* Marché Commun Andin *m*; ~ **Pact** *n* ECON Pacte andin *m*

Andorra *pr n* GEN COMM Andorre *f*; ~ **la Vella** GEN COMM Andorre-la-Vieille *n pr*

Andorran[1] *adj* GEN COMM andorran

Andorran[2] *n* GEN COMM *person* Andorran *m*

anecdotal *adj* LAW *evidence*, WEL *evidence* anecdotique

ANF *abbr (arrival notification form)* TRANSP *shipping* avis d'arrivée *m*

angel *n infrml* MEDIA commanditaire *mf*

angle *n* MATH angle *m*; ~ **of repose** TRANSP *of stockpiled material* angle de repos *m*, angle naturel de repos *m*

Anglo-French *adj* GEN COMM anglo-français

Anglo-Irish: ~ **Free Trade Area Agreement** *n (AIFTA)* ECON accord anglo-irlandais de zone de libre-échange

Angola *pr n* GEN COMM Angola *m*

Angolan[1] *adj* GEN COMM angolais

Angolan[2] *n* GEN COMM *person* Angolais *m*

animal: ~ **-keeper's liability** *n* INS, LAW, LEIS responsabilité civile de propriétaire d'animal *f*

Ankara *pr n* GEN COMM Ankara *n pr*

ankle *vi jarg* HRM tout plaquer *loc (infrml)*

annex[1] *n AmE see* annexe *BrE*

annex[2] *vt* GEN COMM *territory, land, country* annexer

annexe *n BrE* GEN COMM *of building, document,* LAW annexe *f*

annexed *adj* LAW ci-inclus, ci-joint

anniversary *n* COMMS, GEN COMM, MEDIA anniversaire *m*; **~ publication** MEDIA numéro hors série *m*, numéro spécial anniversaire *m*, publication anniversaire *f*, édition commémorative *f*

annotate *vt* ADMIN annoter

announce *vt* GEN COMM *cut* annoncer, *details* faire connaître, faire part de, *profit, figures* enregistrer, publier

announcement *n* GEN COMM annonce *f*; **~ effect** POL effet d'annonce *m*; **~ of an engagement** GEN COMM faire-part de fiançailles *m*; **~ of sale** MEDIA, S&M avis de vente *m*

announcer *n* MEDIA *broadcast* animateur *m*, annonceur *m*, présentateur *m*, speaker *m*

annual[1] *adj* ACC, BANK, FIN, GEN COMM annuel; ◆ **at an ~ rate** FIN, GEN COMM au taux annuel; **on an ~ basis** ACC, BANK, FIN, GEN COMM annuellement

annual:[2] **~ abstract of statistics** *n* ECON, MATH annuaire de statistiques *m*, rapport annuel de statistiques économiques *m*; **~ accounts** *n pl* ACC, FIN, GEN COMM comptes annuels *m pl*, comptes sociaux *m pl*; **~ adjustment** *n* ACC, TAX rajustement annuel *m*; **~ amortization** *n* INS annuité d'amortissement *f*; **~ annuity amount** *n* TAX montant annuel de la rente *m*; **~ appropriation** *n* ACC affectation annuelle *f*, répartition du résultat *f*; **~ audit plan** *n UK* ACC plan annuel de vérification *m*, plan d'audit annuel *m*, programme d'audit annuel *m*, programme de vérification annuelle *m*; **~ automated controls survey** *n (AAS)* TRANSP *of ship* visite annuelle de la centrale de navigation *f*; **~ basis** *n* MATH *statistics* base annuelle *f*; **~ cash flow** *n* ACC, FIN marge brute d'autofinancement annuelle *f*, mouvements de trésorerie annuels *m pl*; **~ certificate** *n* ACC *audit*, FIN *audit* rapport annuel *m*, rapport annuel des commissaires aux comptes *m*, rapport d'exercice *m*; **~ debt service** *n UK* BANK, ECON service annuel de la dette *m*; **~ depreciation** *n* ACC, GEN COMM amortissement annuel *m*; **~ depreciation charge** *n* ACC dotation annuelle aux amortissements *f*; **~ dividend** *n* GEN COMM dividende annuel *m*; **~ earnings** *n pl* ACC, TAX résultat de l'exercice *m*; **~ evaluation plan** *n* FIN plan d'évaluation annuel *m*; **~ fee** *n* ACC, GEN COMM honoraires annuels *m pl*; **~ general meeting** *n BrE (AGM)* ACC, FIN, GEN COMM, MGMNT assemblée générale annuelle *f*; **~ holiday** *n BrE (cf annual vacation AmE)* HRM congé annuel *m*; **~ hours contract** *n* HRM contrat d'heures à l'année *m*; **~ hull survey** *n (AHS)* TRANSP *shipping* visite annuelle de la coque *f*; **~ inert gas system survey** *n (AIGSS)* ENVIR enquête annuelle sur les systèmes de gaz inertes;

~ installment *n AmE*, **~ instalment** *n BrE* ACC annuité *f*, versement annuel *m*, BANK versement annuel *m*, FIN, GEN COMM annuité *f*, versement annuel *m*; **~ leave** *n* HRM congé annuel *m*; **~ machinery survey** *n (AMS)* TRANSP *shipping* visite annuelle des machines *f*; **~ meeting** *n* ACC, FIN, GEN COMM, MGMNT assemblée générale annuelle *f*; **~ meeting of shareholders** *n* STOCK assemblée ordinaire annuelle des actionnaires *f*; **~ monetary rate** *n* FIN taux annuel monétaire *m*, TAM; **~ mortgage constant** *n* BANK, FIN, PROP constante annuelle d'hypothèque *f*; **~ net cash inflow** *n* ACC, FIN autofinancement net annuel *m*; **~ net profit** *n* ACC, FIN, GEN COMM, TAX bénéfice de l'exercice *m*, bénéfice net annuel *m*; **~ order** *n* GEN COMM commande annuelle *f*, ordre annuel *m*; **~ payment** *n* ACC, BANK, FIN, GEN COMM versement annuel *m*; **~ percentage rate** *n (APR)* BANK, FIN, GEN COMM taux annualisé *m*, taux d'intérêt annuel *m*, taux effectif global *m*; **~ premium** *n* INS prime annuelle *f*; **~ rate** *n* BANK, ECON, FIN, GEN COMM taux annuel *m*; **~ rate bond** *n* STOCK bon à taux annuel *m*, BTA; **~ renewable term insurance** *n* INS assurance à terme renouvelable tous les ans *f*, assurance-vie temporaire *f*; **~ repayment** *n* BANK, GEN COMM annuité de remboursement *f*; **~ report** *n* ACC, FIN, GEN COMM rapport annuel *m*, rapport d'exercice *m*; **~ return** *n* ACC revenu annuel *m*, état annuel *m*, LAW *document* dépôt en greffe du tribunal de commerce; **~ review** *n* ACC révision annuelle *f*; **~ salary** *n* HRM salaire annuel *m*; **~ salary review** *n* HRM révision annuelle des salaires *f*; **~ sales conference** *n* MGMNT, S&M conférence annuelle de la force de vente *f*; **~ sales review** *n* FIN, S&M examen annuel des ventes *m*; **~ subscription** *n* GEN COMM, MEDIA abonnement annuel *m*; **~ turnover** *n* ACC, FIN chiffre d'affaires de l'exercice *m*; **~ vacation** *n AmE (cf annual holiday BrE)* HRM congé annuel *m*; **~ wage** *n* HRM salaire annuel *m*; **~ yield** *n* ACC, ECON, FIN rendement annuel *m*

annualize *vt* GEN COMM annualiser

annualized[1] *adj* GEN COMM calculé annuellement, présenté par année, présenté sur l'année

annualized:[2] **~ hours** *n pl* HRM heures annualisées *f pl*; **~ hours system** *n* HRM système d'heures annualisées *m*, système des heures-années *m*; **~ percentage rate** *n (APR)* BANK, FIN, GEN COMM taux annualisé *m*, taux d'intérêt annuel *m*, taux effectif global *m*; **~ rate** *n* BANK *of interest*, FIN *of interest* taux pour un an *m*

annually *adv* ACC, BANK, FIN annuellement, GEN COMM annuellement, chaque année *loc f*

annuitant *n* TAX *life annuity* crédit-rentier *m*, rentier *m*

annuity *n* HRM annuité *f*, INS rente *f*; **~ assurance** INS assurance de rente *f*; **~ bond** STOCK obligation de rente *f*; **~ certain** INS rente certaine *f*; **~ contract** TAX contrat de rente *m*; **~ due** *(SYN annuity factor)* INS facteur d'actualisation *m*, rente payable d'avance *f*; ~ **factor** *(SYN annuity due)* INS facteur d'actualisation *m*, rente payable d'avance *f*; ~ **fund** GEN COMM rente *f*; ~ **in advance** INS rente payable d'avance *f*; ~ **in arrears** INS rente payable à terme échu *f*; ~ **in reversion** INS rente réversible *f*; ~ **income** TAX revenu de rente *m*; ~ **installment** *AmE*, ~ **instalment** *BrE* INS versement de rente *m*; ~ **insurance** INS assurance-vie avec option rente viagère *f*; ~ **payment** TAX paiement de rente *m*, paiement de rentes *m*, service de la rente *m*; ~ **plan** INS option rente viagère *f*; ~ **policy** INS contrat de rente viagère *m*

annul *vt* GEN COMM, HRM, INS *contract* résilier, LAW abolir, abroger, *contract* annuler, résilier, *decision, judgement* annuler, casser

annulling[1] *adj* GEN COMM qui annule

annulling:[2] ~ **clause** *n* LAW clause abrogatoire *f*, clause résolutoire *f*

annulment *n* GEN COMM *of contract* annulation *f*, résiliation *f*, LAW abolition *f*, abrogation *f*, cassation *f*, *of contract* annulation *f*

annunciator: ~ **board** *n* US STOCK tableau d'appel *m*

anomaly *n* GEN COMM *in a system* anomalie *f*; ~ **switch** STOCK anomalie de prix qui provoque l'achat d'un titre et la vente d'un autre

anomie *n* HRM anomie *f*

anonymity *n* GEN COMM anonymat *m*

anonymous *adj* GEN COMM anonyme

ANPA *abbr (American Newspaper Publishers' Association)* MEDIA association américaine des Editeurs de Quotidiens

Ansaphone® *n* COMMS, COMP, GEN COMM répondeur *m*, répondeur automatique *m*, répondeur téléphonique *m*

ANSI *abbr (American National Standards Institute)* GEN COMM, IND, LAW association américaine de normalisation, ≈ AFNOR *(Association française de normalisation)*

answer[1] *n* COMP, GEN COMM réponse *f*, LAW déposition du témoin *f*, réponse du défendeur *f*; ~ **mode** COMP mode réponse *m*; ♦ **get an** ~ GEN COMM obtenir une réponse; **give a dusty** ~ *infrml* GEN COMM envoyer promener qn *(infrml)*, envoyer qn sur les roses *(infrml)*; **in** ~ **to your letter** COMMS suite à votre lettre

answer:[2] **1.** *vt* ~ **for** GEN COMM *person* se porter garant de, *safety* répondre de, être responsable de **2.** *vi* GEN COMM donner une réponse, répondre; ♦ ~ **the phone** COMMS répondre au téléphone

answerable: **be** ~ **for** *phr* GEN COMM répondre de, être responsable de; ~ **to** *phr* GEN COMM responsable devant

answerback: ~ **code** *n* ADMIN indicatif *m*

answering: ~ **machine** *n* COMMS, COMP, GEN COMM répondeur *m*, répondeur automatique *m*, répondeur téléphonique *m*

answerphone *n* COMMS, COMP, GEN COMM répon-

deur *m*, répondeur automatique *m*, répondeur téléphonique *m*

antagonistic: ~ **conditions of distribution** *n pl* POL conditions antagonistes de la distribution *f pl*; ~ **growth** *n* ECON croissance contraire *f*, croissance génératrice de conflits *f*

Antananarivo *pr n* GEN COMM Antananarivo *n pr*

ante- *pref* GEN COMM avant

antedate *vt* GEN COMM *document, cheque* antidater, *event* précéder

antedated *adj* GEN COMM antidaté

antedating *n* GEN COMM antidatation *f*

ante meridiem *adv (am)* GEN COMM avant midi, du matin

anti-avoidance: ~ **legislation** *n* FIN, LAW, STOCK, TAX législation anti-évasion fiscale *f*, législation réprimant la dissimulation fiscale *f*; ~ **rule** *n* FIN, LAW, STOCK, TAX disposition anti-évitement *f*, règle anti-évitement *f*

anticipate *vt* GEN COMM *bill, debt* anticiper, *later work, development* préfigurer, *problem, delay* prévoir, s'attendre à

anticipated[1] *adj* GEN COMM attendu, prévu

anticipated:[2] ~ **demand** *n* ECON, S&M demande attendue *f*, demande escomptée *f*, demande prévue *f*; ~ **profit** *n* FIN bénéfices prévus *m pl*; ~ **redemption** *n* FIN, GEN COMM remboursement anticipé *m*; ~ **repayment** *n* FIN, GEN COMM remboursement anticipé *m*; ~ **sale** *n* STOCK vente anticipée *f*; ~ **sales** *n pl* S&M ventes prévues *f pl*

anticipation *n* ECON anticipation *f*, prévision *f*, GEN COMM attente *f*, *of profits, income* anticipation *f*, expectative *f*, jouissance anticipée *f*, LAW, PROP droit d'anticipation *m*, exercice anticipé d'un droit *m*, jouissance anticipée *f*, S&M anticipation *f*, prévision *f*; ~ **equivalence** IMP/EXP équivalence par anticipation *f*; ♦ **in** ~ **of a fall in the price** STOCK en prévision d'une chute du cours

anticipatory: ~ **breach of contract** *n* LAW rupture anticipée de contrat *f*; ~ **hedge** *n* STOCK couverture par anticipation *f*; ~ **pricing** *n* ECON, S&M anticipation des prix *f*, fixation des prix par anticipation *f*, mise à prix prévisionnelle *f*; ~ **response** *n* ECON, GEN COMM anticipation stratégique *f*, réaction d'anticipation *f*

anticompetitive[1] *adj* GEN COMM anticoncurrentiel

anticompetitive:[2] ~ **practices** *n pl* ECON, POL pratiques anticoncurrentielles *f pl*, pratiques déloyales *f pl*

anticyclic: ~ **advertising** *n* S&M publicité anticyclique *f*

anticyclical *adj* ECON *policy* anticyclique, conjoncturel

antidumping *n* ENVIR, POL antidumping *m*; ~ **agreement** ENVIR, POL accord antidumping *m*

antifouling: ~ **system** *n* TRANSP *shipping* système antifouling *m*

Antigua *pr n* GEN COMM Antigua *f*; **~ and Barbuda** GEN COMM Antigua et Barbuda *f*

Antiguan *adj* GEN COMM d'Antigua

anti-inflation: **~ stance** *n* ECON, POL attitude anti-inflationniste *f*, position anti-inflationniste *f*

anti-inflationary *adj* ECON, POL anti-inflationniste

antimonopoly: **~ laws** *n pl* ECON, GEN COMM, LAW, S&M lois anti-monopoles *f pl*, législation anti-monopoles *f*; **~ legislation** *n pl* ECON, GEN COMM, LAW, S&M lois anti-monopoles *f pl*, législation anti-monopoles *f*

anti-roll: **~ suspension** *n* TRANSP suspension anti-roulis *f*

anti-strike: **~ ballot** *n* HRM *against motion* vote contre la grève *m*

antitheft: **~ device** *n* GEN COMM, TRANSP antivol *m*, dispositif antivol *m*

antitrust: **~ act** *n* ECON, GEN COMM, LAW, S&M loi antitrust *f*; **~ commission** *n* ECON commission anti-monopole *f*; **~ law** *n* ECON, GEN COMM, LAW, S&M loi antitrust *f*; **~ law and legislation** *n pl* LAW législation antitrust *f*

antivirus: **~ software** *n* COMP logiciel antivirus *m*

any: **~ other business** *phr* (*AOB*) GEN COMM points divers *m pl*

AO *abbr* ACC (*accounting officer*) comptable *mf*, comptable adjoint *m*, ACC (*account of*), BANK (*account of*), FIN (*account of*), GEN COMM (*account of*) pour le compte de *loc m*, HRM (*accounting officer*) comptable *mf*, comptable adjoint *m*

AOB *abbr* GEN COMM (*any other business*) points divers *m pl*, INS (*any one bottom*), TRANSP (*any one bottom*) marine par navire *loc m*

AOCB *abbr* (*any other competent business*) GEN COMM autres questions à l'ordre du jour *f pl*, questions diverses *f pl*

AOCTs *abbr* (*associated overseas countries and territories*) ECON, POL *international trade* pays et territoires d'outre-mer associés *m pl*

AOLOC *abbr* (*any one location*) INS, TRANSP marine en un seul lieu *loc m*

AON: **~ clause** *n* (*all-or-nothing clause*) STOCK clause tout ou rien *f*

A-1 *adj jarg* TRANSP de première qualité, formidable, parfait

A1 *adj* TRANSP *shipping* A1

AOS *abbr* (*any one steamer*) INS, TRANSP marine par bateau à vapeur *loc m*

AOV *abbr* (*any one vessel*) INS, TRANSP marine par navire *loc m*

AP *abbr* COMP (*array processor*) processeur vectoriel *m*, INS (*additional premium*) prime additionnelle *f*, MEDIA US (*Associated Press*) les presses associées, STOCK UK (*associated person*) associé *m*, TRANSP (*aft perpendicular*) *of ship* PPAR (*perpendiculaire arrière*)

APACS *abbr* UK (*Association for Payment Clear-*

ing Services) ECON Association de services de compensation des paiements *f*

apartment *n* AmE (*cf flat BrE*) PROP appartement *m*, logement *m*; **~ building** AmE (*cf block of flats BrE*) PROP immeuble *m*

APB *abbr* US (*Accounting Principles Board*) ACC bureau des principes en comptabilité

APBH *abbr* (*afterpeak bulkhead*) TRANSP *shipping* cloison du peak arrière *f*, cloison du presse-étoupe *f*

APC *abbr* (*average propensity to consume*) ECON propension moyenne à consommer *f*, tendance moyenne de la consommation *f*

APEC *abbr* (*Asia-Pacific Economic Co-operation*) ECON, POL Coopération économique en Asie-Pacifique *f*

aphorism *n* GEN COMM aphorisme *m*

API *abbr* UK (*alternative participation instrument*) STOCK instrument de participation différent *m*

apiece *adv* GEN COMM chacun, la pièce *loc f*

APL *abbr* (*programming language*) COMP langage de programmation *m*

apologize: **~ for** *vt* GEN COMM s'excuser de, GEN COMM présenter ses excuses, s'excuser; ◆ **~ to sb for sth** GEN COMM faire ses excuses à qn pour qch, s'excuser de qch auprès de qn

apology *n* GEN COMM excuse *f*

a posteriori *phr* GEN COMM a posteriori

apparatus *n* GEN COMM, IND appareil *m*; **~ for carrying out** PATENTS dispositif pour la mise en oeuvre de *m*

apparel *n* GEN COMM habillement *m*; **~ wool** IND laine d'habillement *f*, laine à vêtements *f*

apparent: **~ authority** *n* LAW mandat apparent *m*; **~ good order of goods** *n* TRANSP bon état apparent des marchandises *m*; **~ tax rate** *n* TAX taux d'imposition apparent *m*; **~ time at ship** *n* (*ATS*) TRANSP *shipping* temps vrai local *m* (*TVL*)

appeal[1] *n* GEN COMM *of plan, idea* attrait *m*, *to public* appel *m*, LAW appel *m*, pourvoi *m*, recours *m*, S&M *of product* attrait *m*; **~ bond** *n* LAW garantie *f*; **~ court** *n* LAW cour d'appel *f*; **~ for funds** *n* FIN appel de fonds *m*; **~ for tenders** *n* ADMIN, GEN COMM appel d'offres *m*; **~ proceedings** *n pl* LAW procédure d'appel *f*; **~ product** *n* GEN COMM produit d'appel *m*

appeal[2] **1.** *vt* **~ to** GEN COMM *attract* attirer, plaire à, S&M *advertising, broadcasting* s'adresser à, *of product, flavour, colour etc* plaire à **2.** *vi* LAW faire appel, former un recours, interjeter appel, se pourvoir en appel; ◆ **~ against a judgement** LAW appeler d'un jugement, faire appel d'une décision; **~ for funds** GEN COMM faire un appel de fonds; **~ for tenders** GEN COMM faire un appel d'offres

appeals: **~ court** *n* (SYN *appellate court*) LAW cour d'appel *f*; **~ procedure** *n* HRM, LAW procédure d'appel *f*

appear: **1.** *vt* **~ before** LAW *court* comparaître devant **2.** *vi* GEN COMM *item in catalogue* figurer, LAW *person before court* comparaître

appellate: ~ **court** *n* (SYN *appeals court*) LAW cour d'appel *f*

append *vt* COMMS joindre, COMP ajouter, annexer, GEN COMM *document* annexer, joindre, *signature* apposer, apposer sa signature

appended *adj* COMMS, GEN COMM, LAW ci-inclus, ci-joint

appendix *n* GEN COMM, MEDIA annexe *f*, appendice *m*

appliance *n* GEN COMM, IND appareil *m*

applicable *adj* GEN COMM *argument* valable, *rule, requirement* en vigueur; **not** ~ *(n/a)* GEN COMM ne s'applique pas, non-applicable, sans objet; ♦ ~ **to** GEN COMM applicable à

applicant *n* ADMIN candidat *m*, GEN COMM *for grant* candidat *m, for licence* demandeur *m, for trademark* déposant *m*, HRM *for job* candidat *m*, postulant *m*, LAW demandeur *m*, requérant *m*, PATENTS demandeur *m*, déposant *m*, requérant *m*, STOCK *for registration* candidat *m, for shares* souscripteur *m*; ~ **entrepreneur** GEN COMM candidat entrepreneur *m*

application *n* ADMIN *for job* candidature *f*, COMP application *f*, GEN COMM *for job, licence* candidature *f*, demande *f, for grant* demande *f, of idea* application *f, of technique* mise en oeuvre *f*, HRM *for job* candidature *f*, LAW application *f*, PATENTS demande *f*, STOCK *for shares* demande de souscription *f*; ~ **of accounting rules in good faith** ACC sincérité *f*; ~ **control** ACC, COMP, FIN *auditing* vérification du logiciel comptable *f*; ~ **fee** BANK droits de demande *m pl*; ~ **for admission** STOCK *to the stock exchange* demande d'admission *f*; ~ **for listing** STOCK *on the stock exchange* demande d'inscription à la cote *f*; ~ **for quotation** STOCK demande d'introduction en bourse *f*; ~ **for shares** STOCK demande de souscription d'actions *f*, souscription d'actions *f*; ~ **for subsidies** GEN COMM dossier de demande de subvention *m*; ~ **form** ADMIN, HRM bulletin de souscription *m*, formulaire d'inscription *m*; ~ **of funds** ACC emplois *m pl*, utilisation des fonds *f*; ~ **of funds statement** ACC, FIN rapport des flux financiers *m*; ~ **money** STOCK versement de souscription *m*; ~ **right** STOCK droit de souscription *m*; ♦ ~ **for** GEN COMM souscription à; ~ **is pending** PATENTS la demande est pendante; **make an** ~ **for** GEN COMM déposer une demande de

applications: ~ **package** *n* COMP logiciel d'application *m*; ~ **program** *n* COMP applicatif *m*, application *f*, logiciel d'application *m*, programme d'application *m*; ~ **programmer** *n* COMP programmeur d'applications *m*; ~ **software** *n* COMP logiciel d'application *m*, programme d'application *m*; ~ **terminal** *n* COMP ordinateur dédié *m*, ordinateur spécialisé *m*

applied: ~ **cost** *n* ACC, ECON, FIN coût affecté *m*, coût imputé *m*, coût réparti *m*; ~ **economics** *n*

ECON économie appliquée *f*; ~ **overhead** *n* ACC, FIN frais généraux imputés *m pl*, frais imputés *m pl*, frais indirects imputés par produits *m pl*; ~ **research** *n* GEN COMM recherche appliquée *f*, MGMNT recherche appliquée *f*, recherche expérimentale *f*; ~ **research cost** *n* GEN COMM coût de la recherche appliquée *m*, frais de recherche appliquée *m pl*

apply 1. *vt* ACC *principle* appliquer, *sum, rent* imputer, GEN COMM *principle*, LAW appliquer; ~ **for** BANK *loan* souscrire, GEN COMM *passport, licence* demander; ~ **to** COMP convenir à, s'appliquer à **2.** *vi* GEN COMM *rule* s'appliquer, HRM *for job* faire une demande, proposer sa candidature; ♦ ~ **at the office** GEN COMM adressez-vous au bureau; ~ **expenses to a period** ACC rattacher des charges à un exercice; ~ **for a job** GEN COMM se porter candidat à un poste, HRM faire une demande d'emploi, poser sa candidature pour un emploi, postuler pour un emploi; ~ **for a loan** BANK faire une demande de prêt, souscrire à un emprunt, GEN COMM souscrire à un emprunt; ~ **for membership** GEN COMM faire une demande d'adhésion; ~ **for shares** STOCK faire une demande de souscription d'actions; ~ **in person** GEN COMM se présenter; ~ **revenues to a period** ACC rattacher des produits à un exercice; ~ **to sb for sth** GEN COMM s'adresser à qn pour obtenir qch

applying: **in** ~ *phr* TAX pour l'application *loc f*

appoint *vt* GEN COMM *date, place* fixer, HRM désigner, nommer, *committee* constituer, *date, place* désigner, *employee* affecter, engager

appointed[1] *adj* GEN COMM *agent, chairman* attitré, nommé; ♦ **at the** ~ **time** GEN COMM à l'heure convenue

appointed:[2] ~ **day** *n* GEN COMM jour fixé *m*; ~ **space** *n* MEDIA, S&M *advertising* emplacement imposé *m*; ~ **stockist** *n* S&M stockiste attitré *m*; **the** ~ **time** *n* GEN COMM l'heure dite *f*, l'heure fixée *f*

appointee *n* GEN COMM, HRM *executive* personne nommée *f, junior* candidat retenu *m*, MGMNT *executive* personne nommée *f*

appointive *adj* AmE (ANT *elective*) GEN COMM obtenu par nomination

appointment *n* GEN COMM poste *m, of someone* désignation *f*, nomination *f, with someone* rendez-vous *m*, HRM affectation *f*; ♦ **by** ~ **only** GEN COMM sur rendez-vous uniquement; **keep an** ~ GEN COMM aller à un rendez-vous; **make an** ~ **with sb** GEN COMM donner rendez-vous à qn, prendre rendez-vous avec qn

appointments: ~ **vacant** *n pl* HRM offres d'emploi *f pl*

apportion *vt* ACC ventiler, *costs* affecter, PROP *land, property* lotir, partager, répartir, STOCK *shares* répartir; ♦ ~ **the average** INS *marine* répartir les avaries

apportioned: ~ **contract** *n* LAW contrat de répartition *m*

apportionment *n* ACC affectation *f*, répartition *f*, ventilation *f*, PATENTS répartition *f*, PROP lotissement *m*, partage *m, property expenses* affectation *f*, répartition *f*; ~ **of costs** ACC affectation des frais *f*, répartition des charges *f*, ventilation des coûts *f*; ~ **of funds** FIN *government agency, project* allocation des fonds *f*; ~ **rule** TAX *input tax credit* règle de calcul au prorata *f*

appraisal *n* FIN estimation *f*, GEN COMM estimation *f*, évaluation *f, by expert* expertise *f, of job performance* évaluation *f*, HRM *BrE (cf report card AmE)* évaluation *f*, PROP estimation *f*, évaluation *f*; ~ **of damage** *n* INS expertise des dommages *f*, évaluation du dommage *f*; ~ **increment** *n* ACC, GEN COMM excédent de réévaluation *m*, plus-value constatée par expertise *f*; ~ **report** *n* GEN COMM rapport d'expertise *m*; ~ **rights** *n pl US* STOCK droits d'objection *m pl*; ♦ **make an ~ of** GEN COMM évaluer; **make an ~ of future needs** GEN COMM faire une estimation des besoins futurs

appraise *vt* FIN estimer, évaluer, GEN COMM estimer, MGMNT *project* évaluer; ~ **damages** GEN COMM expertiser les dommages, évaluation des dégâts *f*

appraised: ~ **value** *n* FIN, PROP valeur estimative *f*, valeur estimée *f*

appraisement *n* FIN estimation *f*

appraiser *n* FIN, PROP expert *m*

appreciable *adj* GEN COMM appréciable

appreciate 1. *vt* GEN COMM *significance* apprécier; **2.** *vi* ACC, PROP *asset* accuser une plus-value, augmenter en valeur, prendre de la valeur

appreciated: ~ **surplus** *n* ACC plus-value *f*

appreciation *n* ACC, PROP accroissement de la valeur *m*, plus-value *f*, STOCK *of currency, share* hausse *f*, TAX accroissement de la valeur *m*, plus-value *f*; ~ **of currency** ECON, STOCK hausse d'une monnaie *f*

apprentice[1] *n* HRM élève *mf, in arts and crafts* apprenti *m*

apprentice:[2] *phr* ~ **sb to sb** HRM mettre qn en apprentissage chez qn, placer qn comme apprenti chez qn

apprenticed: **be ~ to sb** *phr* HRM être en apprentissage chez qn *loc m*

apprenticeship *n* HRM apprentissage *m*

appro: **on ~** *phr infrml (on approval)* GEN COMM à l'essai *loc m*

approach[1] *n* GEN COMM abord *m*, approche *f*, démarche *f*, méthode *f*, MGMNT méthode *f, proposal* proposition *f*

approach[2] *vt* GEN COMM contacter; ♦ ~ **sb about sth** GEN COMM contacter qn au sujet de qch

appropriate[1] *adj* GEN COMM approprié; ♦ ~ **for sth** GEN COMM convenant a qch, propre à

appropriate:[2] ~ **technology** *n* ECON, ENVIR, IND technologie adaptée *f*, technologie appropriée *f*, technologie idoine *f*

appropriate[3] *vt* ACC *funds* affecter, ECON *funds* affecter, *resources* affecter, FIN affecter, s'approprier, LAW s'approprier; ♦ **be ~ for** GEN COMM convenir à

appropriateness *n* GEN COMM applicabilité *f*, caractère approprié *m*, compétence *f*, à propos *loc m*

appropriation *n* ACC *of funds* affectation *f*, dotation *f*, ECON *of funds* affectation *f*, dotation *f, of resources* affectation *f*, allocation *f*, FIN affectation *f*, appropriation *f*, dotation *f*, LAW *of funds* appropriation *f*; ~ **account** ACC, FIN compte d'affectation des bénéfices *m*; ~ **of advertising** FIN, S&M budget de la publicité *m*; ~ **control** ACC contrôle des crédits *m*; ~ **of income** ACC affectation des bénéfices *f*

Appropriation: ~ **Act** *n UK* ACC, ECON, FIN, LAW loi de finances *f*, projet de loi de finances *m*; ~ **Bill** *n US* ACC, ECON, FIN, LAW loi de finances *f*, projet de loi de finances *m*

appropriations: ~ **for contingencies** *n pl* TAX provisions pour éventualités *f pl*

approval *n* ACC *of accounts* approbation *f*, BANK *of loan* autorisation *f*, GEN COMM approbation *f*, assentiment *m, of contract, request* agrément *m, of machine, process* homologation *f*; ~ **mark** TRANSP *road vehicles* marque d'homologation *f*; ~ **process** BANK processus d'autorisation *m*; ♦ **for ~** GEN COMM pour approbation; **have the ~ of** GEN COMM obtenir l'approbation de; **on ~** *(on appro)* GEN COMM à l'essai

approve *vt* ADMIN approuver, BANK *loan* autoriser, GEN COMM *action, accounts* approuver, *contract, request* agréer, *decision, document, plan* homologuer, ratifier, INS agréer, POL approuver, TAX agréer

approved[1] *adj* ADMIN approuvé, BANK autorisé, GEN COMM agréé, approuvé, *decision, document* ratifié, INS *marine* agréé, approuvé, TAX agréé

approved:[2] ~ **code of practice** *n (ACOP)* GEN COMM déontologie *f*; ~ **delivery facility** *n UK* STOCK facilité de livraison approuvée *f*, système de livraison agréé *m*; ~ **depository** *n* BANK dépositaire agréé *m*; ~ **list** *n* STOCK *of investments* liste agréée *f*, liste d'investissement agréée *f*; ~ **place** *n* ADMIN entrepôt des douanes *m*, entrepôt public *m*; ~ **premises** *n pl* IMP/EXP locaux homologués *m pl*; ~ **price** *n* GEN COMM, S&M prix approuvé *m*; ~ **project** *n* TAX ouvrage approuvé *m*; ~ **research institute** *n* TAX institut de recherche agréé *m*; ~ **share** *n* STOCK action approuvée *f*

approx. *abbr (approximately)* GEN COMM approximativement, environ

approximate:[1] ~ **figure** *n* MATH chiffre approximatif *m*; ~ **number** *n* MATH chiffre approximatif *m*; ~ **price** *n* STOCK prix approximatif *m*; ~ **rate of return** *n* ACC taux de rendement approximatif *m*

approximate[2] *vt* MATH approcher, approcher de

approximately *adv (approx.)* GEN COMM approximativement, environ

approximation *n* GEN COMM approximation *f*, POL *of international policies* rapprochement *m*

appurtenant[1] *adj* LAW accessoire, annexe

appurtenant:[2] **~ structures** *n pl* INS dépendances *f pl*

Apr. *abbr (April)* GEN COMM avril *m*

APR *abbr (annual percentage rate, annualized percentage rate)* BANK, FIN, GEN COMM taux annualisé *m*, taux d'intérêt annuel *m*, taux effectif global *m*

April *n (Apr.)* GEN COMM avril *m*

a priori *phr* GEN COMM a priori

a priori statement *n* GEN COMM affirmation a priori *f*

apron *n* TRANSP *at airport* aire de stationnement *f, of road surface* radier *m*

APS *abbr (average propensity to save)* ACC, ECON tendance moyenne à économiser *f*

APT *abbr* STOCK *(arbitrage pricing theory)* théorie de l'évaluation d'arbitrage *f*, TRANSP *(aft peak tank) of ship* coqueron arrière *m*, tank de peak arrière *m*

aptitude *n* HRM *of individual* aptitude *f*, aptitude professionnelle *f*; **~ test** HRM, S&M test d'aptitude *m*

APV *abbr (administrative point of view)* ADMIN détails administratifs *m pl*, point de vue administratif *m*, MGMNT détails administratifs *m pl*

AR *abbr* INS *(all risks)* tous risques *loc*, LEIS *(Average Revenue)* revenu moyen *m*

Arab[1] *adj* GEN COMM arabe

Arab[2] *n* GEN COMM *person* Arabe *mf*; **~ -British Chamber of Commerce** *(ABCC)* IND chambre de commerce arabo-britannique; **~ Common Market** ECON, POL Union du Maghreb arabe *f*; **~ Maghreb Union** *(AMU)* ECON, POL Union du Maghreb arabe *f*

Arabia *pr n* GEN COMM Arabie *f*

Arabian *adj* GEN COMM arabe

Arabic *n* GEN COMM *language* arabe *m*

arb *abbr (arbitrageur)* HRM, STOCK arbitragiste *mf*

arbiter *n* LAW arbitre *m*, médiateur *m*

arbitrage *n* BANK, FIN arbitrage *m*, STOCK arbitrage *m*, opération d'arbitrage *f*; **~ bonds** *n pl US* STOCK obligations d'arbitrage *f pl*; **~ dealer** *n* STOCK arbitragiste *mf*; **~ dealings** *n pl* STOCK opérations d'arbitrage *f pl*; **~ house** *n* STOCK *banker, broker, FX dealer* maison d'arbitrage *f*; **~ in securities** *n UK* STOCK arbitrage de valeurs *m*, arbitrage sur titres *m*; **~ margin** *n UK* STOCK marge d'arbitrage *f*; **~ pricing theory** *n (APT)* STOCK théorie de l'évaluation d'arbitrage *f*; **~ stocks** *n pl* STOCK actions d'arbitrage *f pl*; **~ trader** *n* STOCK arbitragiste *mf*; **~ trading** *n* STOCK arbitrage *m*, opérations d'arbitrage *f pl*;

~ transactions *n pl UK* STOCK transactions d'arbitrage *f pl*

arbitrageur *n (arb)* HRM, STOCK arbitragiste *mf*

arbitral[1] *adj* GEN COMM arbitral

arbitral:[2] **~ award** *n* GEN COMM sentence arbitrale *f*

arbitrary[1] *adj* GEN COMM, TAX arbitraire

arbitrary:[2] **~ assessment** *n* TAX cotisation arbitraire *f*; **~ income** *n* TAX revenu arbitraire *m*; **~ taxation** *n* TAX imposition arbitraire *f*

arbitrate *vi* GEN COMM, HRM, IND, LAW arbitrer, trancher

arbitration *n* GEN COMM, HRM, IND, LAW arbitrage *m*, médiation *f*; **~ agreement** *n* GEN COMM, HRM, IND, LAW convention d'arbitrage *f*; **~ board** *n* GEN COMM, HRM, IND, LAW commission d'arbitrage *f*, instance d'arbitrage *f*; **~ clause** *n* GEN COMM, HRM, IND, LAW clause compromissoire *f*, clause d'arbitrage *f*; **~ committee** *n* GEN COMM, HRM, IND, LAW commission d'arbitrage *f*; **~ of exchange** *n* FIN arbitrage de change *m*; **~ proceedings** *n pl* GEN COMM, HRM, IND, LAW mesures d'arbitrage *f pl*, procédure d'arbitrage *f*; **~ transaction** *n* STOCK opération d'arbitrage *f*; **~ tribunal** *n* GEN COMM, HRM, IND, LAW tribunal d'arbitrage *m*

arbitrator *n* GEN COMM, HRM, IND, LAW amiable compositeur *m*, arbitre *m*, médiateur *m*

arborescence *n* COMP arborescence *f*

arc: **~ elasticity** *n* ECON élasticité d'arc *f*; **~ tangent** *n (arctan)* MATH *function* arc tangente *m*

arcade *n* GEN COMM, S&M *shopping* galerie marchande *f*

architect *n* PROP architecte *mf*; **~'s liability** INS, LAW, PROP responsabilité de l'architecte *f*

architecture *n* COMP, PROP architecture *f*

archival: **~ storage** *n* COMP enregistrement des archives *m*, mémoire auxiliaire *f*, mémoire d'archivage *f*

archive[1] *n* ADMIN, COMP archive *f*; **~ file** COMP fichier d'archives *m*; **~ storage** ADMIN stockage des archives *m*

archive[2] *vt* ADMIN, COMP archiver

archiving *n* ADMIN, COMP archivage *m*

archivist *n* ADMIN archiviste *mf*

arcsine *n* MATH *function* arc sinus *m*

arctan *n (arc tangent)* MATH *function* arc tangente *m*

area *n* COMP zone *f*, ECON région *f, of surface* aire *f*, superficie *f*, ENVIR *in town* quartier *m*, GEN COMM région *f, in town* quartier *m, of knowledge* champ *m*, domaine *m, scope, extent* domaine *m*, secteur *m, space* zone *f*, MATH *of surface* aire *f*, superficie *f*, POL région *f*; **~ code** COMMS *telephone* indicatif de zone *m*, indicatif interurbain *m*; **~ of expertise** GEN COMM domaine d'expertise *m*, domaine de spécialisation *m*; **~ manager** BANK directeur de zone *m*, directeur régional *m*, HRM, MGMNT chef de région *m*, chef de secteur *m*, S&M chef de région *m*; **~ office** BANK agence régionale *f*; **~ of**

responsibility HRM, MGMNT domaine de responsabilité *m*; ~ **salesman** GEN COMM VRP régional
m, représentant régional *m*, vendeur régional *m*,
voyageur représentant placier régional *m*, S&M
représentant régional *m*; ~ **salesperson** COM
voyageur représentant placier régional *m*, représentant régional *m*, représentante régionale *f*

Area: ~ **Advisory Group** *n* UK *(AAG)* IMP/EXP
groupe consultatif de zone qui s'occupe de développer les marchés étrangers vers lesquels les
sociétés anglaises veulent exporter

Argentina *pr n* GEN COMM Argentine *f*

Argentine[1] *adj* GEN COMM argentin

Argentine[2] *n* GEN COMM *person* Argentin *m*

Argentinian[1] *adj* GEN COMM argentin

Argentinian[2] *n* GEN COMM *person* Argentin *m*

arguable *adj* GEN COMM contestable

argue: ~ **one's case** *phr* LAW exposer ses arguments, plaider sa cause

ARI *abbr (accounting rate of interest)* ACC, BANK,
FIN TIC *(taux d'intérêt comptable)*

Ariel *abbr (Automated Real-time Investments
Exchange)* STOCK réseau informatique pour transactions de blocs d'actions, Ariel *m*

arithmetic: ~ **mean** *n* MATH moyenne arithmétique
f; ~ **progression** *n* MATH progression arithmétique *f*

arm *n* ECON bras *m*

ARM *abbr (adjustable-rate mortgage)* BANK, FIN
hypothèque à taux réglable *f*, PROP prêt hypothécaire à taux réglable *m*

armchair: ~ **critic** *n* GEN COMM critique en chambre
m

Armenia *pr n* GEN COMM Arménie *f*

Armenian[1] *adj* GEN COMM arménien

Armenian[2] *n* GEN COMM *language* arménien *m*,
person Arménien *m*

arm's:[1] ~ **-length** *adj* ACC, GEN COMM, TAX de
pleine concurrence *loc f*, non privilégié, sans lien
de dépendance

arm's:[2] ~ **-length competition** *n* ECON concurrence
libre *f*, GEN COMM concurrence libre *f*, conditions
de pleine concurrence *f pl*, S&M concurrence libre
f; ~ **-length price** *n* ACC prix de pleine concurrence
m, prix du marché *m*, prix normal *m*, prix
pratiqué entre entreprises indépendants *m*,
STOCK prix de début de négociations *m*, prix
initial *m*; ~ **-length principle** *n* GEN COMM principe
du prix de pleine concurrence *m*; ~ **-length
transaction** *n* COMMS opération de pleine concurrence *f*, opération sans lien de dépendance *f*,
transaction sans lien de dépendance *f*, GEN COMM
transaction au prix du marché *f*

aromatic: ~ **liquid or flavoring extract** *n* AmE,
~ **liquid or flavouring extract** *n* BrE TRANSP
classified goods extrait, liquide aromatique ou
parfum *loc m*

around:[1] ~ **-the-clock** *adj* (SYN *round-the-clock*)
GEN COMM 24 heures sur 24

around[2] *adv* GEN COMM autour

around:[3] ~ **-the-clock service** *n* (SYN *round-the-
clock service*) GEN COMM service 24 heures sur 24
m

around[4] *prep* GEN COMM autour de, *approximately*
environ, vers

ARP *abbr (adjustable-rate preferred stock)* STOCK
action de priorité à taux variable *f*, titre privilégié
à taux variable *m*

arrange *vt* BANK *loan* organiser, GEN COMM
arranger; ◆ ~ **an interview** HRM convenir d'une
entrevue

arranged: ~ **total loss** *n* INS *marine* perte totale
transigée *f*

arrangement *n* COMP configuration *f*, disposition
f, GEN COMM accord *m*, disposition *f*, ordonnance
f, régime *m*; ~ **fee** BANK commission de montage
f, frais de montage *m pl*; ◆ **by** ~ GEN COMM à
débattre; **come to an** ~ **with** GEN COMM *suppliers*
parvenir à un accord avec; **make** ~**s** GEN COMM
prendre des mesures

arranger *n* FIN organisateur *m*

array *n* COMP *of figures, data* rangée *f*, tableau *m*,
GEN COMM alignement *m*, tableau de données *m*;
~ **processor** *(AP)* COMP processeur vectoriel *m*;
~ **of products** S&M *advertising* collection de
produits *f*

arrearage *n* FIN arriéré *m*, arrérages *m pl*, dettes *f
pl*, retard *m*, STOCK arriéré *m*, arriéré de
dividendes *m*

arrears *n pl* FIN *money owed* arriéré *m*, arrérages *m
pl*, *in wages* rappel *m*, GEN COMM, STOCK arriéré
m; ~ **of interest** *n* BANK arriéré d'intérêts *m*,
intérêt sur arriérés *m*, intérêts en souffrance *m pl*;
◆ **be in** ~ GEN COMM être en retard dans ses
paiements

arrest[1] *n* INS *marine* arrestation *f*

arrest[2] *vt* LAW arrêter

arrival *n* TRANSP arrivée *f*; ~ **date** TRANSP *of
consignment* date d'arrivée *f*; ~ **notification form**
(ANF) TRANSP *shipping* avis d'arrivée *m*

arrive *vi* GEN COMM arriver

arrived: ~ **ship** *n* TRANSP *shipping* navire couvert *m*

arrow: ~ **key** *n* COMP *for moving cursor* touche de
commande de curseur *f*, touche de direction *f*,
touche de déplacement du curseur *f*

arson *n* INS, LAW incendie volontaire *m*

art: ~ **board** *n* S&M *advertising* carton couché *m*;
~ **buyer** *n* (ANT *art seller*) GEN COMM acheteur
d'art *m*; ~ **department** *n* ADMIN, S&M *advertising*
service création *m*; ~ **designer** *n* HRM, S&M
advertising graphiste *mf*; ~ **manager** *n* HRM,
MGMNT, S&M *advertising* directeur artistique *m*;
~ **matt paper** *n* S&M *advertising* papier couché mat
m; ~ **of the possible** *n* POL art du compromis *m*;
~ **print** *n* S&M *advertising* impression artistique *f*;
~ **pull** *n* S&M *advertising* épreuve sur papier
couché *f*; ~ **seller** *n* (ANT *art buyer*) GEN COMM
vendeur d'art *m*

article *n* GEN COMM article *m*, LAW article *m*, clause *f*, MEDIA article *m*; **~ of consumption** GEN COMM article de consommation *m*, produit de consommation *m*

articled: **~ clerk** *n* UK LAW avocat stagiaire *m*

articles: **~ of agreement** *n pl* TRANSP *shipping* rôle d'équipage *m*; **~ of association** *n pl* LAW statuts *m pl*; **~ for personal use** *n pl* IMP/EXP effets à usage personnel *m pl* (*vieilli*); **~ of incorporation** *n pl* LAW statuts *m pl*

articulated: **~ lorry** *n* TRANSP semi-remorque *f*; **~ vehicle** *n* TRANSP véhicule articulé *m*

artificial[1] *adj* GEN COMM artificiel, factice

artificial:[2] **~ barrier to entry** *n* ECON *trade*, IMP/EXP, S&M *trade* barrière non-tarifaire à l'importation *f*; **~ currency** *n* ECON non-devise *f*; **~ exchange rate** *n* ECON taux de change artificiel *m*; **~ intelligence** *n (AI)* COMP intelligence artificielle *f (IA)*

artisan: **~ fair** *n* GEN COMM, S&M exposition d'artisanat *f*, foire de l'artisanat *f*

Arts: **~ Council** *n* UK LEIS organisme public britannique de promotion des arts

artwork *n* GEN COMM, S&M document d'exécution *m*, modèle *m*

A/S *abbr* ACC *(account sales)* compte-rendu des opérations de consignation *m*, BANK *(at sight)* sur présentation *loc f*, à vue *loc f*, FIN *(after sight)* de vue *loc f*, FIN *(at sight)* sur présentation *loc f*, GEN COMM *(after sight)* de vue *loc f*, GEN COMM *(at sight)*, STOCK *(at sight)* sur présentation *loc f*, à vue *loc f*, TRANSP *(alongside)* *of quay* bord à, le long de

ASA *abbr* GEN COMM *(American Standards Association)*, IND *(American Standards Association)*, LAW *(American Standards Association)* association américaine de normalisation, ≈ AFNOR, MATH *(American Statistical Association)* association américaine de la statistique, MEDIA UK *(Advertising Standards Authority)*, S&M UK *(Advertising Standards Authority)* ≈ BVP *(Bureau de vérification de la publicité)*

a.s.a.p. *abbr (as soon as possible)* COMMS, GEN COMM aussitôt que possible *loc*, dans les meilleurs délais *loc m*, dès que possible *loc*, le plus tôt possible *loc*

ascending:[1] **~ tops** *n pl* STOCK ligne de sommets haussière *f*, ligne de tendance ascendante *f*

ascending:[2] **in ~ order** *phr* GEN COMM en ordre croissant *loc m*

ascertain *vt* GEN COMM *fact* constater, vérifier, *price* établir

ascertainable *adj* TAX *group, person* identifiable

ascertained: **~ fact** *n* GEN COMM fait établi *m*; **~ goods** *n pl* GEN COMM marchandises vérifiées *f pl*

ascertainment *n* GEN COMM constatation *f*

ASCII[1] *abbr (American Standard Code for Information Interchange)* COMP ASCII *m*

ASCII:[2] **~ file** *n* COMP fichier ASCII *m*; ◆ **in ~** COMP en ASCII

ascots *n pl* UK IMP/EXP, TAX ascots *m pl*

ascribe: **~ sth to sb** *vt* GEN COMM attribuer qch à qn

ASE *abbr (American Stock Exchange)* FIN, STOCK la bourse de New York secondaire où sont listées les valeurs qui n'apparaissent pas au New York Stock Exchange, AMEX *f*

ASEAN *abbr (Association of South-East Asian Nations)* ECON ANSEA *(Association des nations du Sud-Est asiatique)*

A-share *n* UK FIN, STOCK action ordinaire sans droit de vote *f*

Ashkhabad *pr n* GEN COMM Achkabad *n pr*

Asia *pr n* GEN COMM Asie *f*

Asian[1] *adj* GEN COMM asiatique

Asian[2] *n* GEN COMM *person* Asiatique *mf*; **~ Development Bank** BANK Banque asiatique de développement *f*

Asia-Pacific: **~ Economic Co-operation** *n (APEC)* ECON, POL Coopération économique en Asie-Pacifique *f*

Asiatic: **~ mode of production** *n* ECON, IND mode de production asiatique *m*, moyens de production asiatiques *m pl*

a similibus ad similia *phr frml* GEN COMM du pareil au même

ask: **~ for** *vt* GEN COMM demander; ◆ **~ for an expert opinion** GEN COMM demander le point de vue d'un spécialiste, demander un avis d'expert

asked: **~ and bid price** *n* STOCK *selling and buying* cours demandé et offert *m*, cours vendeur et d'achat *m*; **~ price** *n* PROP prix demandé *m*, STOCK cours vendeur *m*

asking: **~ price** *n* GEN COMM prix de départ *m*

ASOA *abbr (Australian Steamship Owners Association)* TRANSP association australienne des armateurs de paquebots

aspect *n* GEN COMM aspect *m*; **~ ratio** COMP, GEN COMM, MEDIA format de l'écran *m*

assay:[1] **~ mark** *n (SYN certification mark)* BANK, GEN COMM, IND *on gold and silver* marque d'essai *f*

assay[2] *vt* BANK, GEN COMM, IND *purity of metals* analyser, essayer

assemblage *n* ENVIR, PROP *of land* remembrement *m*

assembler *n* COMP *assembly language* assembleur *m*, programme d'assemblage *m*

assembling *n* GEN COMM, IND montage *m*

assembly *n* ADMIN réunion *f*, COMP assemblage *m*, GEN COMM montage *m*, réunion *f*, IND montage *m*, POL assemblée *f*, réunion *f*, séance *f*; **~ cargo** TRANSP cargaison à grouper *f*; **~ line** HRM, IND chaîne de montage *f*; **~ line worker** HRM, IND travailleur à la chaîne *m*; **~ plant** HRM, IND usine de montage *f*; **~ program** *AmE*, **~ programme** *BrE* GEN COMM, HRM, IND programme d'assemblage *m*

assent *n* GEN COMM consentement *m*, POL *of parliament* assentiment *m*

assert *vt* GEN COMM affirmer

assertion *n* GEN COMM affirmation *f*, assertion *f*, revendication *f*

assertiveness: ~ **training** *n* HRM, WEL entraînement à la prise de parole *m*, stage d'assertivité *m*

assess *vt* FIN *loss, damage* estimer, GEN COMM *person, work* estimer, évaluer, HRM mesurer, MGMNT évaluer, TAX *penalty* imposer; ♦ ~ **tax** TAX déterminer l'impôt à payer, fixer la cotisation d'impôt, établir une cotisation d'impôt; ~ **a taxpayer** TAX établir une cotisation à l'égard d'un contribuable

assessed: ~ **income** *n* TAX revenu imposé *m*; ~ **tax** *n* TAX cotisation d'impôt *f*, impôt fixé *m*, impôt établi *m*; ~ **tax arrears** *n pl* FIN, TAX arriéré d'impôt établis *m*

assessing: ~ **action** *n* TAX cotisation *f*, mesure de cotisation *f*; ~ **tax** *n* TAX fixation d'impôt *f*

assessment *n* GEN COMM imposition *f*, évaluation *f*, *evaluation* appréciation *f*, *of tax* détermination de l'assiette d'imposition *f*, LAW *of compensation* estimation *f*, fixation *f*, évaluation *f*, PROP *of compensation* estimation *f*, fixation *f*, TAX cotisation *f*, imposition *f*; ~ **center** *AmE*, ~ **centre** *BrE* HRM centre d'évaluation *m*, centre d'évaluation de la qualité *m*, centre de bilan professionnel *m*; ~ **ratio** PROP coefficient d'évaluation *m*

assessor *n* INS *marine* expert *m*, TAX répartiteur *m*

asset *n* ACC élément d'actif *m*, *balance sheet* tenue des barèmes d'imposition *f*, ECON actif *m*, FIN élément d'actif *m*, *balance sheet* tenue des barèmes d'imposition *f*, GEN COMM *strong point* actif *m*, atout *m*, STOCK actif *m*; ~ **account** *n* ACC, FIN compte d'actif *m*; ~ **allocation** *n* STOCK répartition des actifs *f*; ~ **-backed finance** *n* ECON, FIN financement garanti par l'actif *m*; ~ **-backed investment** *n* FIN investissement garanti par des actifs *m*; ~ **-backed securities** *n pl* FIN titres garantis par actif financier *m pl*; ~ **-based financing** *n* FIN financement reposant sur l'actif *m*; ~ **-based investment** *n* BANK, FIN investissement basé sur l'actif *m*; ~ **coverage** *n* ACC ratio d'actifs *m*, STOCK couverture des dividendes par l'actif *f*, couverture par l'actif *f*; ~ **depreciation range** *n* (*ADR*) ACC, FIN, PROP gamme d'amortissement d'actif *f*, plafond maximal de la période d'amortissement *m*, période d'amortissement de l'actif *f*; ~ **diversification** *n* FIN diversification de l'actif *f*; ~ **exposure** *n* ACC, BANK révélation de l'actif *f*; ~ **item** *n* ACC poste d'actif *m*; ~ **and liability management** *n* ACC, BANK, FIN, MGMNT gestion actif-passif *f*, gestion du bilan *f*; ~ **life** *n* ACC durée de vie de l'immobilisation *f*; ~ **management** *n* ACC, BANK, FIN, MGMNT, STOCK gestion de l'actif *f*; ~ **management company** *n* ACC, ADMIN, FIN, MGMNT société de gestion *f*; ~ **manager** *n* ACC, BANK, FIN, HRM, MGMNT, STOCK gestionnaire de l'actif *m*; ~ **mix** *n* ACC, FIN composition de l'actif *f*; ~ **motive** *n* ECON *monetary* motivation de l'actif *f*; ~ **portfolio** *n* FIN, STOCK portefeuille d'actifs *m*; ~ **price inflation** *n*

ECON, FIN inflation du prix de l'actif *f*; ~ **quality** *n* FIN *analysis* qualité des éléments d'actif *f*; ~ **return** *n* ACC, FIN, STOCK rendement de l'actif *m*, revenu de l'actif *m*; ~ **sale** *n* ACC, FIN cession d'actifs *f*; ~ **specificity** *n* ECON, FIN spécificité de l'actif *f*; ~ **stripping** *n* ACC cannibalisation *f*, démantèlement de l'actif *m*, démembrement de l'actif *m*, élimination d'actifs non-rentables *f*, ECON dégraissage d'actifs *m*, dépouillement de l'actif *m*, vente par appartements *f*, FIN cannibalisation *f*, dégraissage d'actifs *m*, démantèlement de l'actif *m*, dépouillement de l'actif *m*, vente par appartements *f*, GEN COMM cannibalisation *f*; ~ **swap** *n* BANK, FIN croisement d'actifs *m*, échange d'actifs *m*; ~ **turnover** *n* ACC, FIN mouvements de l'actif *m pl*, rotation de l'actif *f*, rotation des éléments d'actif *f*, ratio d'immobilisations et chiffre d'affaires *m*; ~ **valuation** *n* ACC, FIN évaluation des immobilisations *f*; ~ **value** *n* ACC, FIN total de l'actif *m*, valeur de l'actif *f*; ~ **value per share** *n* FIN, STOCK valeur de l'actif par action *f*

Asset: ~ **Management Account** *n* (*AMA*) FIN compte de gestion des actifs *m*

assets *n pl* ACC biens *m pl*, *of company* patrimoine *m*, ECON actif *m*, FIN biens *m pl*, GEN COMM, STOCK actif *m*; ~ **and drawbacks** *n pl* ECON, GEN COMM avantages et inconvénients *m pl*; ~ **eligible for the money market** *n pl* BANK actif négociable sur le marché monétaire *m*; ~ **held abroad** *n pl* ACC, FIN, GEN COMM avoirs à l'étranger *m pl*; ~ **and liabilities management** *n* (*ALM*) ACC, BANK, FIN, MGMNT gestion actif-passif *f* (*GAP*), gestion du bilan *f*; ~ **and liabilities statement** *n* ACC, FIN bilan *m*; ~ **under construction** *n pl* ACC *annual accounts*, FIN *annual accounts* immobilisations en cours *f pl*

assign *vt* ACC *costs* imputer, COMP affecter, allouer, attribuer, répartir, HRM attribuer, LAW céder, faire cession de *loc f*, transférer, transmettre

assignable[1] *adj* GEN COMM cessible, transférable

assignable:[2] ~ **credit** *n* ACC crédit transférable *m*

assigned: ~ **account** *n* BANK compte en garantie *m*, créance en garantie *f*; ~ **short position** *n* FIN position courte assignée *f*

assignee *n* ACC cessionnaire *mf*, LAW ayant cause *m*, cessionnaire *mf*, PATENTS cessionnaire *mf*; ~ **in bankruptcy** BANK syndic de faillite *m*

assignment *n* ACC *receivables* cession *f*, COMP affectation *f*, attribution *f*, GEN COMM mission *f*, HRM attribution *f*, LAW cession *f*, transfert *m*, PATENTS cession *f*, PROP transfert *m*, STOCK assignation *f*; ~ **of advertising expenditure** FIN, S&M allocation du budget publicitaire *f*; ~ **day** STOCK jour de transfert des biens *m*, *options* jour d'assignation *m*; ~ **of lease** LAW, PROP cession de bail *f*; ~ **man** MEDIA reporter à la tâche *m*, reporter à toutes mains *m* (*infrml*); ~ **notice** STOCK avis d'assignation *m*, avis d'assignation de levée *m*, avis de transfert *m*

assignor *n* INS, LAW, PATENTS cédant *m*

assimilation *n* LAW *EU*, STOCK assimilation *f*

assistance *n* ECON, GEN COMM, LAW, POL, TAX aide *f*, assistance *f*

assistant *n* (*asst*) GEN COMM, HRM adjoint *m*, assistant *m*, auxiliaire *mf*, MGMNT assistant *m*; **~ cashier** BANK aide-caissier *m*, caissier adjoint *m*, sous-caissier *m*; **~ controller** (*AC*) HRM *shipping* contrôleur adjoint *m*; **~ director** HRM, MGMNT directeur adjoint *m*; **~ director general** (*ADG*) HRM, MGMNT directeur général adjoint *m* (*DGA*); **~ head of section** HRM adjoint du chef de section *m*, chef d'unité adjoint *m*; **~ manager** BANK directeur adjoint *m*, sous-directeur *m*, HRM, MGMNT directeur adjoint *m*, sous-chef *mf*, sous-directeur *m*; **~ teller** BANK aide-caissier *m*, caissier adjoint *m*, sous-caissier *m*; **~ to manager** MGMNT adjoint *m*; **~ traffic supervisor** (*ATS*) HRM, TRANSP adjoint au contrôleur de circulation *m*, inspecteur adjoint chargé de la circulation *m*

assisted: **~ area** *n* ECON, POL, WEL région assistée *f*, zone d'assistance *f*

associate[1] *n* GEN COMM associé *m*, HRM collaborateur *m*; **~ company** ECON, GEN COMM société affiliée *f*, société apparentée *f*; **~ editor** MEDIA *print* rédacteur d'édition *m*

associate:[2] **~ with** *vt* GEN COMM associer à, s'associer avec, s'associer à

Associate: **~ of the Association of Certified and Corporate Accountants** *n* (*AACCA*) ACC membre associé de l'association des comptables agréés; **~ of the Association of International Accountants** *n* ACC membre associé de l'association des comptables internationaux; **~ of the British Association of Accountants and Auditors** *n UK* (*ABAA*) ACC membre associé de l'association britannique des comptables et des commissaires aux comptes; **~ of the Chartered Association of Certified Accountants** *n* (*ACCA*) ACC membre associé de l'association des comptables agréés; **~ of the Chartered Institute of Management Accountants** *n UK* (*ACMA*) ACC, MGMNT membre associé de l'institut des comptables de prix de revient et de gestion; **~ of the Chartered Institute of Secretaries** *n* (*ACIS*) ADMIN membre de l'institut des secrétaires qualifiées; **~ of the Corporation of Registered Accountants** *n UK* (*ACRA*) ACC membre associé de la corporation des comptables agréés; **~ of the Institute of Actuaries** *n UK* (*AIA*) INS membre associé de l'institut des actuaires; **~ Institute of Chartered Shipbrokers** *n* (*AICS*) HRM association des courtiers maritimes agréés; **~ Institute Freight Trades Association** *n* (*AIFTA*) HRM, TRANSP association professionnelle des transporteurs; **~ of the Institute of Marketing** *n* (*A Inst M*) HRM, S&M membre associé de l'institut de marketing; **~ Member of the Institute of Export** *n* (*AMI Ex*) HRM, IMP/EXP membre associé du groupement des exportateurs; **~ Member of the Institute of Marine Engineers** *n* (*AMIME*) HRM, IND membre associé du groupement des mécaniciens de marine

associated[1] *adj* GEN COMM associé; ◆ **be ~ with** GEN COMM être associé à

associated:[2] **~ account** *n* BANK compte associé *m*; **~ company** *n* GEN COMM filiale *f*, société affiliée *f*, société associée *f*; **~ company abroad** *n* GEN COMM filiale à l'étranger *f*, partenaire étranger *m*; **~ corporations** *n pl* GEN COMM, TAX corporations associées *f pl*; **~ employer** *n* HRM employeur membre d'un syndicat patronal *m*; **~ mark** *n* PATENTS marque associée *f*; **~ overseas countries and territories** *n pl* (*AOCTs*) ECON *international trade*, POL pays et territoires d'outre-mer associés *m pl*; **~ person** *n UK* (*AP*) STOCK associé *m*

Associated: **~ African States, Madagascar and Mauritius** *n pl* (*AASMM*) GEN COMM Organisation commune africaine, malgache et mauricienne *f* (*OCAMM*); **~ British Ports** *n* (*ABP*) TRANSP ports britanniques associés; **~ Press** *n US* (*AP*) MEDIA les presses associées

association *n* GEN COMM association *f*, société *f*; **~ bargaining** (SYN *multiemployer bargaining*) HRM négociation avec association patronale *f*, négociation collective *f*; **~ subscription** GEN COMM abonnement pour membres *m*, cotisation des adhérents *f*, cotisation à une association *f*; ◆ **in ~ with** COMMS en liaison avec, GEN COMM en association avec

Association: **~ of American Shipowners** *n* (*AASO*) TRANSP association des armateurs américains; **~ of Average Adjusters** *n* (*AAA*) INS association des répartiteurs d'avaries; **~ of British Chambers of Commerce** *n* (*ABCC*) IND association des chambres de commerce britanniques; **~ of British Travel Agents** *n* (*ABTA*) LEIS association des agents de voyage britanniques; **~ of European Steel Producers** *n* (*Euro Fer*) IND association des producteurs européens d'acier; **~ for Payment Clearing Services** *n UK* (*APACS*) BANK Association de services de compensation des paiements *f*; **~ of Futures Brokers and Dealers** *n* (*AFBD*) STOCK association des courtiers et négociants de marchandises à terme; **~ of Independent Tour Operators** *n* LEIS Association des organisateurs de voyages indépendants *f*; **~ of International Bond Dealers** *n* (*AIBD*) STOCK association des négociants d'obligations internationales; **~ of Scientific, Technical and Managerial Staff** *n* (*ASTMS*) HRM association des personnels scientifique, technique, et d'encadrement; **~ of Shipbrokers and Agents** *n US* TRANSP association des courtiers et agents maritimes des États-Unis; **~ of South-East Asian Nations** *n* (*ASEAN*) ECON Association des nations du Sud-Est asiatique *f* (*ANSEA*)

assortment: **~ of goods** *n* GEN COMM assortiment de produits *m*, choix de marchandises *m*

asst *abbr* (*assistant*) GEN COMM, HRM adjoint *m*, assistant *m*, auxiliaire *mf*, MGMNT assistant *m*

assume *vt* GEN COMM *commitment* assumer, *risk, power* assumer, prendre; ◆ **~ no responsibility for** GEN COMM dégager sa responsabilité de (*frml*); **~ responsibility for** GEN COMM prendre en charge

assumption *n* GEN COMM hypothèse *f*, supposition *f*

assurance: **~ of subscribers** *n* GEN COMM assurance des abonnés *f*, *insurance policy* assurance des souscripteurs *f*

assured: **the ~** *n* INS l'assuré *m*

astern: **~ power** *n* TRANSP *shipping* puissance arrière *f*

ASTMS *abbr* (*Association of Scientific, Technical and Managerial Staff*) HRM association des personnels scientifique, technique, et d'encadrement

Asunción *pr n* GEN COMM Asunción *n pr*

asylum *n* GEN COMM, POL asile *m*

asymmetric: **~ information** *n* INS information asymétrique *f*

asymmetry *n* GEN COMM asymétrie *f*

asynchronous *adj* COMP asynchrone

at *prep* GEN COMM au taux de *loc m*; **as ~** GEN COMM *date* au

ATA[1] *abbr US* (*Air Transport Association*) TRANSP association de transport aérien des États-Unis, ≈ DGAC (*France*) (*Direction générale de l'aviation civile*)

ATA:[2] **~ carnet** *n* IMP/EXP carnet ATA *m*

ATC *abbr* (*air traffic control*) TRANSP *activity* contrôle de la circulation aérienne *m*, contrôle du trafic aérien *m*, *building* tour de contrôle *f*

Athens *pr n* GEN COMM Athènes *n pr*

athwart *prep* TRANSP *shipping* en travers de

atmosphere *n* ECON climat *m*, ENVIR atmosphère *f*, GEN COMM, POL climat *m*

atmospheric: **~ lifetime** *n* ENVIR durée de vie dans l'atmosphère *f*

Atomic: **~ Energy Research Establishment** *n* (*AERE*) ENVIR ≈ Commissariat à l'énergie atomique *m* (*CEA*)

atomicity *n* STOCK atomicité *f*

atomistic: **~ competition** *n* (SYN *perfect competition*) ECON, S&M concurrence atomistique *f*

at-risk: **~ amount** *n* TAX fraction à risques *f*; **~ rules** *n pl* TAX dispositions concernant la fraction à risques *f pl*

ATS *abbr* BANK *UK* (*automatic transfer service*) service de virement automatique *m*, HRM (*assistant traffic supervisor*), TRANSP (*assistant traffic supervisor*) adjoint au contrôleur de circulation *m*, inspecteur adjoint chargé de la circulation *m*, TRANSP (*apparent time at ship*) *shipping* TVL (*temps vrai local*)

ATT *abbr* (*air transportation tax*) TAX TTA (*taxe sur le transport aérien*)

attach *vt* COMMS joindre, COMP connecter, se connecter, GEN COMM connecter; ♦ **~ importance to** GEN COMM attacher de l'importance à, prêter de l'importance à

attaché *n* HRM, MEDIA attaché *m*

attached *adj* COMMS, GEN COMM ci-inclus, ci-joint

attachment *n* ACC, BANK effet *m*, COMP accessoire

m, connexion *f*, FIN effet *m*, INS effet *m*, papillon *m*, LAW, TAX effet *m*; **~ date** INS date d'effet *f*

attained: **~ age** *n* INS âge atteint *m*

attend *vt* HRM, MGMNT *meeting* assister à; **~ to** GEN COMM *customer, problem* s'occuper de

attendance *n* GEN COMM fréquentation *f*; **~ bonus** *n* HRM prime de ponctualité *f*, prime de présence *f*; **~ fees** *n pl* (SYN *attendance money*) HRM jetons de présence *m pl*; **~ money** *n* (SYN *attendance fees*) HRM jetons de présence *m pl*

attention *n* GEN COMM, S&M attention *f*; **~ factor** MEDIA, S&M *advertising* facteur d'attention *m*; **~ getter** S&M *advertising* accrochage initial *m*; **~ value** S&M *advertising* valeur d'accroche *f*; ♦ **~, interest, desire, action** (*AIDA*) GEN COMM, S&M attention, intérêt, désir, action (*AIDA*)

attention! *phr* HRM attention!

attest *vt* LAW attester, authentifier, certifier, légaliser, témoigner; **~ to** GEN COMM se porter garant de

attestation *n* LAW attestation *f*, *of signature* certification *f*, légalisation *f*; **~ clause** INS *marine* clause d'attestation *f*, clause de signature *f*

at-the-money: **~ call** *n* (ANT *at-the-money put*) STOCK option d'achat au jeu *f* (*jarg*), option d'achat au milieu *f*, option d'achat à parité *f*; **~ call option** *n* (ANT *at-the-money put option*) STOCK option d'achat au jeu *f* (*jarg*), option d'achat au milieu *f*, option d'achat à parité *f*; **~ option** *n* STOCK option at-the-money *f*, option au cours *f*, option à l'argent *f*, option à la monnaie *f*, option à parité *f*; **~ put** *n* (ANT *at-the-money call*) STOCK option de vente au jeu *f*, option de vente au milieu *f*, option de vente à parité *f*; **~ put option** *n* (ANT *at-the-money call option*) STOCK option de vente au jeu *f*, option de vente au milieu *f*, option de vente à parité *f*

attitude *n* HRM, MGMNT attitude *f*, comportement *m*, S&M *about products, ideas* attitude *f*; **~ scale** S&M *market research* échelle d'attitudes *f*; **~ survey** S&M *market research* enquête d'attitude *f*, enquête d'opinion *f*

attorney *n US* LAW agent *mf*, fondé de pouvoir *m*, mandataire *mf*, représentant *m*; **~ -at-law** *US* LAW avocat *m*; **~ -in-fact** *US* LAW mandataire spécial *m*

Attorney: **~ General** *n* LAW ≈ ministre de la Justice *m*, ≈ procureur de la République *m* (*France*), ≈ procureur du Roi *m* (*Belgique*), ≈ procureur général *m*

attornment *n US* LAW reconnaissance des droits du nouveau propriétaire

attract *vt* GEN COMM attirer; ♦ **~ new business** GEN COMM attirer de nouveaux contrats, attirer de nouvelles entreprises; **~ sb's attention** GEN COMM attirer l'attention de qn

attractive[1] *adj* GEN COMM *for investors*, STOCK attractif, attrayant

attractive:[2] **~ nuisance** *n US* LAW, PROP source de danger pour les enfants engageant la responsabilité du propriétaire; **~ offer** *n* GEN COMM proposition alléchante *f*; **~ terms** *n pl* GEN COMM conditions intéressantes *f pl*

attributable: **~ to** *phr* GEN COMM imputable à

attribute[1] *n* COMP attribut *m*, GEN COMM attribut *m*, caractéristique *f*, propriété *f*; **~ sampling** ACC, FIN *auditing* échantillon représentatif *m*, MATH *statistics* échantillonnage d'attribut *m*, échantillonnage de distribution *m*, MEDIA *market research* échantillonnage par attributs *m*, S&M échantillonnage par atributs *m*

attribute[2] *vt* GEN COMM attribuer; ◆ **~ sth to sb** GEN COMM attribuer qch à qn, imputer qch à qn

attributed: **~ to** *phr* GEN COMM attribué à

attribution: **~ rules** *n pl* *jarg* TAX règles d'attribution *f pl*; ◆ **not for ~** *jarg AmE (cf on lobby terms BrE)* MEDIA *print*, POL de source confidentielle, de source officieuse, non-divulgable

attrition *n* GEN COMM, S&M perte de clientèle *f*; **~ rate** GEN COMM, S&M pourcentage de clients perdus *m*, taux d'érosion *m*, taux de départs naturels *m*

atypical: **~ workers** *n pl* HRM travailleurs atypiques *m pl*

auction[1] *n* ACC, BANK *Can* séance d'affectation de fonds *f*, ECON adjudication *f*, criée *f*, vente aux enchères *f*, GEN COMM, S&M adjudication *f*, criée *f*, vente aux enchères *f*, vente à la criée *f*, STOCK vente aux enchères *f*; **~ market** STOCK marché aux enchères *m*, marché des adjudications *m*; **~ room** GEN COMM salle des ventes *f*; **~ sale** GEN COMM, S&M vente aux enchères *f*, vente à la criée *f*

auction[2] *vt* GEN COMM, S&M vendre aux enchères, vendre à la criée; **~ off** GEN COMM, S&M vendre aux enchères, vendre à la criée

auctioneer *n* GEN COMM commissaire-priseur *m*

audi alteram partem *phr* GEN COMM que l'autre partie se fasse entendre

audience *n* GEN COMM audience *f, for the press* lectorat *m*, MEDIA, S&M *advertising* audience *f*

audio: **~ cassette** *n* COMMS cassette audio *f*; **~ conference** *n* COMMS, COMP audioconférence *f*

audiotyping *n* GEN COMM audiotypie *f*

audiovisual[1] *adj* COMP, GEN COMM, MEDIA, S&M audiovisuel

audiovisual:[2] **~ aid** *n* COMMS moyen audiovisuel *m*, support audiovisuel *m*, COMP matériel audiovisuel *m*, support audiovisuel *m*, MEDIA moyen audiovisuel *m*, support audiovisuel *m*; **~ goods** *n pl* S&M appareillage audiovisuel *m*

audit[1] *n* ACC audit *m*, révision comptable *f*, vérification *f*, vérification des comptes *f (Can)*, *of balance sheet* vérification du bilan *f, of tax returns* vérification comptable *f*, FIN contrôle *m*, vérification comptable *f*; **~ activity** *n UK* ACC, FIN activité d'audit *f*, travail d'audit *m*; **~ agent** *n Can* FIN auditeur *m*; **~ assurance** *n* ACC, FIN degré de certitude *m*; **~ brief** *n* ACC, FIN lettre d'engagement d'audit *f*; **~ client** *n* ACC, FIN client d'un auditeur *m (Fra)*, client d'un commissaire aux comptes *m (Fra)*, client d'un reviseur *m (Bel)*, client d'un réviseur *m (Fra)*, client d'un vérificateur *m (Can)*; **~ committee** *n* ACC, FIN comité d'audit *m (Fra)*, comité de révision *m (Bel)*, comité de vérification *m (Can)*; **~ costs** *n pl* ACC, FIN frais d'audit *m pl*, frais de révision *m pl*; **~ coverage** *n (SYN audit scope)* ACC, FIN étendue du contrôle *f*; **~ engagement** *n* ACC, FIN mandat d'audit *m*; **~ evidence** *n* ACC, FIN information probante *f*, justificatives pour contrôle *f pl*, preuve d'audit *f*; **~ file** *n* ACC, FIN dossier d'audit *m*; **~ group** *n* ACC, FIN groupe d'audit *m*, équipe d'audit *f*, équipe de contrôle *f*, équipe de vérification *f*; **~ guide** *n* ACC, FIN recommandations professionnelles *f pl*; **~ head** *n* ACC, FIN associé responsable de l'audit *m*; **~ officer** *n* ACC, FIN agent de vérification *m*, membre de l'équipe d'audit *m*; **~ plan** *n* ACC, FIN plan d'audit *m*; **~ program** *n AmE*, **~ programme** *n BrE* ACC, FIN programme de contrôle *m*, programme de vérification *m*; **~ report** *n* ACC, FIN rapport d'audit *m*, rapport du commissionnaire aux comptes *m*, rapport du réviseur *m*; **~ risk** *n UK* ACC, FIN risque d'audit *m*; **~ schedule** *n* ACC, FIN calendrier de contrôle *m*; **~ scope** *n (SYN audit coverage)* ACC, FIN étendue du contrôle *f*; **~ software** *n* ACC, COMP, FIN logiciel d'audit *m*, logiciel de vérification *m*; **~ staff** *n UK* ACC, FIN personnel de contrôle *m (Fra)*, personnel de révision *m (Bel)*; **~ standards** *n pl* ACC, FIN normes d'audit *f pl*; **~ team** *n* ACC, FIN groupe d'audit *m*, équipe d'audit *f*, équipe de contrôle *f*, équipe de vérification *f*; **~ technique** *n UK* ACC, FIN technique de contrôle *f*; **~ trail** *n* ACC piste d'audit *f*, piste de révision *f*, COMP analyse rétrospective *f*, bande témoin *f*, FIN piste d'audit *f*, piste de révision *f*; **~ window** *n* ACC, COMP, FIN fenêtre de contrôle *f*; **~ work schedule** *n* ACC, FIN plan de vérification *m*; **~ working papers** *n pl* ACC, FIN dossier d'audit *m*, feuille de travail *f*

audit[2] *vt* ACC apurer, auditer *(Fra)*, contrôler, réviser, vérifier *(Can)*, *accounts* faire un audit de *loc m*, COMP contrôler, FIN apurer, auditer, contrôler, réviser, vérifier *(Can)*, *accounts* faire un audit de *loc m*

Audit: **~ Bureau of Circulation** *n* ACC, S&M *advertising* ≈ Office de justification de la diffusion *m*

audita altera parte: **~ procedure** *n frml frml* GEN COMM procédure contradictoire *f*

auditability *n* ACC auditabilité *f*, contrôlabilité *f*, vérificabilité *f*, FIN vérificabilité *f*

auditable *adj* ACC, FIN vérifiable

auditee *n* ACC, FIN entité soumise à l'audit *f*

auditing *n* ACC audit *m*, certification *f*, contrôle *m*, vérification *f*, FIN audit *m*, certification *f*, contrôle *m*, vérification comptable *f*; **~ department** *n* ACC service d'audit *m, within company* service d'audit interne *m*, ADMIN *within company* service d'audit interne *m*, FIN service d'audit *m*; **~ manual** *n* ACC, FIN guide d'audit *m*, guide de contrôle *m*;

~ **principles** *n pl* ACC, FIN principe d'audit *m*; ~ **procedure** *n* ACC, FIN procédure de contrôle *f*; ~ **standards** *n pl* ACC, FIN normes d'audit *f pl*; ~ **technique** *n UK* ACC, FIN technique d'audit *f*

auditor *n* ACC, FIN auditeur *m* (*Fra*), commissaire aux comptes *m* (*Fra*), reviseur *m* (*Bel*), réviseur *m* (*Fra*), vérificateur *m* (*Can*), GEN COMM *US* auditeur libre *m*; ~**'s certificate** ACC, FIN certificat du commissaire aux comptes *m*; ~**'s opinion** ACC, FIN certificat du commissaire aux comptes *m*, certification *f*; ~**'s report** ACC, FIN rapport d'audit *m*, rapport du commissionnaire aux comptes *m*, rapport du réviseur *m*

Auditor's: ~ **Operational Standard** *n* ACC, FIN norme opérationnelle d'audit *f*

au fait *adj* GEN COMM au fait *loc m*

Aug. *abbr* (*August*) GEN COMM août *m*

augment *vt* GEN COMM accroître, augmenter

augmentation *n* GEN COMM augmentation *f*

augmented: ~ **GNP** *n* (*AGNP*) ECON, POL PNB augmenté *m* (*PNBA*)

August *n* (*Aug.*) GEN COMM août *m*

austerity *n* ECON austérité *f*

austral *n* GEN COMM austral *m*

Australia *pr n* GEN COMM Australie *f*

Australian[1] *adj* GEN COMM australien

Australian[2] *n* GEN COMM *person* Australien *m*; ~ **Broadcasting Corporation** (*ABC*) MEDIA organisme de Radio-Télévision australien; ~ **Conciliation and Arbitration Commission** HRM commission australienne d'arbitrage et de conciliation; ~ **Container Service** (*ACS*) TRANSP service transconteneur australien; ~ **Council of Trade Unions** (*ACTU*) HRM confédération des syndicats australiens; ~ **Financial Futures Market** *Australia* (*AFFM*) STOCK ≈ Marché à terme d'instruments financiers *m* (*MATIF*); ~ **Steamship Owners Association** (*ASOA*) TRANSP association australienne des armateurs de paquebots

Austria *pr n* GEN COMM Autriche *f*

Austrian[1] *adj* GEN COMM autrichien

Austrian[2] *n* GEN COMM *person* Autrichien *m*; ~ **Economics** ECON école autrichienne *f*, école autrichienne de pensée économique *f*; ~ **School of Economics** ECON école autrichienne *f*, école autrichienne de pensée économique *f*

autarky *n* ECON, POL autarcie *f*

autex: ~ **system** *n* STOCK système informatique qui relie les courtiers, système autex *m*

authenticate *vt* LAW certifier, légaliser, valider

authentication *n* LAW authentification *f*, certification *f*, légalisation *f*, validation *f*, STOCK authentification *f*, authentification d'une obligation *f*

authoritarian: ~ **management** *n* HRM, MGMNT direction autoritaire *f*, encadrement autoritaire *m*; ~ **society** *n* ECON, POL société autoritaire *f*, société favorable à l'autorité *f*, système autoritaire *m*

authoritative: ~ **contracting** *n* HRM passation autoritaire de contrat *f*

authorities: **the** ~ *n pl* BANK *UK* les autorités monétaires *f pl*, GEN COMM l'administration *f*, les autorités *f pl*, les pouvoirs publics *m pl*

authority *n* GEN COMM ascendant *m*, HRM *of managers* autorité *f*, LAW autorisation *f*, mandat *m*, pouvoir *m*, MGMNT *of managers* autorité *f*; ~ **bond** *US* STOCK obligation émise par une autorité locale; ~ **structure** GEN COMM structure d'autorité *f*, structure hiérarchique *f*; ~ **to buy** GEN COMM *on behalf of third party* autorisation d'achat *f*; ♦ **give vicarious** ~ **to** GEN COMM déléguer son autorité à; **have** ~ **over** GEN COMM avoir de l'ascendant sur

authorization *n* FIN ordonnance *f*, GEN COMM autorisation *f*, permis *m*, LAW autorisation *f*, pouvoir *m*, MGMNT agrément *m*; ~ **center** *AmE*, ~ **centre** *BrE* BANK centre d'autorisation *m*; ~ **code** BANK code d'autorisation *m*, numéro d'autorisation *m*; ~ **for expenditure** ACC autorisation de dépense *f*, dépenses autorisées *f pl*; ~ **number** BANK code d'autorisation *m*, numéro d'autorisation *m*; ♦ ~ **under consideration** (*AC*) GEN COMM autorisation en cours d'examen *f*

authorize *vt* GEN COMM autoriser, permettre, MGMNT agréer; ♦ ~ **sb to do** GEN COMM autoriser qn à faire

authorized[1] *adj* GEN COMM autorisé, MGMNT agréé; ♦ **be** ~ **to sign** BANK avoir la signature

authorized:[2] ~ **agent** *n* GEN COMM agent fondé de pouvoir *m*, mandataire *mf*, LAW fondé de pouvoir *m*, mandataire *mf*; ~ **bank** *n* BANK banque agréée *f*, banque habilitée *f*; ~ **bond** *n* STOCK obligation autorisée *f*; ~ **capital** *n* ECON capital nominal *m*, capital social *m*, FIN capital autorisé *m*, capital nominal *m*, capital social *m*; ~ **capital share** *n* FIN capital social autorisé *m*; ~ **capital stock** *n* FIN capital social autorisé *m*; ~ **clerk** *n* STOCK commis de bourse *m*; ~ **credit** *n* BANK, FIN crédit autorisé *m*; ~ **dealer** *n* STOCK dépositaire intermédiaire agréé *m*, négociant en titres agréé *m*; ~ **person** *n* TAX personne autorisée *f*; ~ **representative** *n* GEN COMM agent agréé *m*, fondé de pouvoir *mf*, représentant accrédité *m*, HRM mandataire *mf*; ~ **share** *n* SYN *authorized stock*) STOCK capital autorisé *m*, valeur autorisée *f*; ~ **share capital** *n* ACC capital actions autorisé *m*, capital autorisé *m*, FIN, STOCK capital actions autorisé *m*; ~ **stock** *n* (*cf authorized share*) STOCK capital autorisé *m*, valeur autorisée *f*; ♦ ~ **expenditure to the amount of** ACC dépenses autorisées jusqu'à un plafond de *f pl*

auto: ~ **rental** *n AmE* (*cf car hire BrE*) TRANSP location de voitures *f*

autobank: ~ **card** *n* BANK carte de guichet automatique *f*

autoboot *n* COMP amorçage automatique *m*, lancement automatique *m*

autocorrelation *n* ECON *econometrics* autocorrélation *f*

autoduplication *n* COMP reproduction automatique *f*

autoeconomy *n* ECON économie autofinancée *f*

autofeed *n* ADMIN, COMP, GEN COMM avance automatique *f*

autofinancing *n* FIN autofinancement *m*

autogestion *n* HRM, MGMNT autogestion *f*

autoloading *n* COMP chargement automatique *m*

autologin *n* COMP ouverture automatique de session *f*

autologon *n* COMP ouverture automatique de session *f*

automate *vt* COMMS, COMP, GEN COMM, IND, MEDIA automatiser

automated[1] *adj* COMMS, GEN COMM, MEDIA automatisé

automated:[2] ~ **cash dispenser** *n* (*ACD, automatic cash dispenser*) BANK billetterie automatique *f*, distributeur automatique de billets *m*, distributeur de billets *m*; ~ **quotation** *n* STOCK cotation assistée en continu *f*, CAC; ~ **teller card** *n* BANK carte de guichet automatique *f*; ~ **teller machine** *n* BANK GAB, guichet automatique *m*, guichet automatique de banque *m*, guichet bancaire *m*; ~ **teller machine statement** *n* BANK justificatif de guichet automatique *m*

Automated: ~ **Clearing House** *n* (*ACH*) BANK, FIN chambre de compensation automatisée; ~ **Clearing Settlement System** *n* (*ACSS*) BANK système de compensation et de règlement automatisé *m* (*SCRA*); ~ **Pit Trading** *n* STOCK vente à la corbeille automatisée; ~ **Real-time Investments Exchange** *n* (*Ariel*) STOCK réseau informatique pour transactions de blocs d'actions, Ariel *m*

automatic[1] *adj* ADMIN, COMMS, COMP, GEN COMM, IND, LAW *protection*, LEIS, MEDIA, S&M automatique; ◆ ~ **control certified** (*ACC*) TRANSP commande automatique certifiée *f*

automatic:[2] ~ **adjustment point** *n* HRM *salaries* seuil de réajustement automatique *m*; ~ **call transfer** *n* COMMS renvoi automatique d'un appel *m* (*Can*); ~ **cash dispenser** *n* (*ACD, automated cash dispenser*) BANK billetterie automatique *f*, distributeur automatique de billets *m*, distributeur de billets *m*; ~ **check-off** *n* US ECON, HRM chômage technique automatique *m*, prélèvement automatique *m*; ~ **control** *n* COMP commande automatique *f*; ~ **coupling** *n* TRANSP *road* accouplement automatique *m*; ~ **data processing** *n* (*ADP*) COMP traitement automatique de l'information *m*, traitement automatique des données *m*; ~ **fare collection** *n* TRANSP péage automatique *m*; ~ **feeder** *n* ADMIN *office equipment* introduction automatique des documents *f*, mécanisme d'alimentation automatique *m*; ~ **funds transfer** *n* (*AFT*) ACC, BANK, FIN virement automatique *m*, virement automatique de fonds *m*; ~ **maritime radio telex service** *n* COMMS *shipping, terrestrial service*, TRANSP *shipping, terrestrial service* service radio telex maritime automatique *m*;

~ **merchandising** *n* S&M vente par distributeur automatique *f*; ~ **rebooting** *n* COMP réinitialisation automatique *f*; ~ **redialing** *n* AmE, ~ **redialling** *n* BrE COMMS rappel automatique *m*; ~ **reinvestment** *n* STOCK plan d'épargne avec capitalisation *m*, réinvestissement automatique *m*; ~ **reset** *n* COMP réinitialisation automatique *f*; ~ **selling** *n* GEN COMM, S&M vente en distributeurs automatiques *f*; ~ **stabilizer** *n* ECON, POL stabilisateur automatique *m*; ~ **teller** *n* BANK GAB, guichet automatique *m*, guichet automatique de banque *m*, guichet bancaire *m*; ~ **telling machine** *n* BANK GAB, guichet automatique *m*, guichet automatique de banque *m*, guichet bancaire *m*; ~ **telling machine statement** *n* BANK justificatif de guichet automatique *m*; ~ **transfer** *n* BANK virement automatique *m*, virement automatique de fonds *m*; ~ **transfer service** *n* UK (*ATS*) BANK service de virement automatique *m*; ~ **typewriter** *n* GEN COMM machine à écrire automatique *f*; ~ **updating** *n* COMP mise à jour automatique *f*; ~ **vending machine** *n* GEN COMM, S&M distributeur automatique *m*, distributeur automatique de produits *m*, DAP; ~ **watch keeper** *n* TRANSP *shipping* module d'alarme *m*; ~ **withdrawal** *n* FIN paiement automatique *m*, retrait automatique *m*

automatically *adv* GEN COMM automatiquement

automation *n* COMMS, COMP, IND, MEDIA automatisation *f*

automobile *n* AmE (*cf car, motorcar BrE*) TRANSP voiture *f*; ~ **insurance** *AmE* INS, TRANSP assurance automobile *f*; ~ **liability insurance** *US* INS, TRANSP assurance automobile contre la responsabilité civile *f*, assurance de responsabilité automobile *f*; ~ **policies insuring agreement** INS contrat d'assurance automobile *m*, TRANSP accord sur polices d'assurance automobile *m*

Automobile: ~ **Association** *n* UK (*AA*) TRANSP ≈ Touring Club de France *m* (*France*)

automotive *adj* IND, TRANSP automobile

autonomous[1] *adj* ECON, GEN COMM, POL autonome

autonomous:[2] ~ **consumption** *n* ECON consommation autonome *f*; ~ **expenditure** *n* ECON dépenses autonomes *f pl*; ~ **investment** *n* ECON investissement autonome *m*; ~ **work group** *n* HRM groupe de travail autonome *m*

autonomy *n* GEN COMM, POL autonomie *f*

autopark *n* COMP *of heads* parcage automatique *m*

autopilot *n* TRANSP pilote automatique *m*

autoregressive: ~ **integrated moving-average model** *n* MATH *time series* modèle auto-régressif à moyenne mobile intégrée *m*, modèle intégré de moyenne mobile régressive *m*; ~ **moving-average model** *n* MATH modèle auto-régressif à moyenne mobile *m*, modèle de moyenne mobile régressive *m*

autorestart *n* COMP redémarrage automatique *m*, relance en route *f*, remise en route *f*

autosave *n* COMP sauvegarde automatique *f*

autostart *n* COMP lancement automatique *m*

autumn *n BrE (cf fall AmE)* GEN COMM *seasons* automne *m*

aux. *abbr (auxiliary)* TRANSP *shipping* auxiliaire *mf*, vaisseau auxiliaire *m*; ~ **B** *(auxiliary boiler)* TRANSP *shipping* chaudière auxiliaire *f*

auxiliary[1] *adj* COMP *memory* auxiliaire

auxiliary[2] *n (aux.)* TRANSP *shipping* auxiliaire *mf*, vaisseau auxiliaire *m*; ~ **banking services undertaking** BANK, FIN entreprise de services bancaires auxiliaires *f*; ~ **boiler** *(AXB, aux. B)* TRANSP *shipping* chaudière auxiliaire *f*; ~ **memory** COMP mémoire de masse auxiliaire *f*; ~ **storage** COMP *hardware* mémoire de masse auxiliaire *f*

av. *abbr (average)* ACC, GEN COMM, MATH moyenne *f*

availabilities: ~ **on radio** *n pl* MEDIA *broadcast* plage disponible *f*, temps d'antenne disponible *m*

availability *n* COMP disponibilité *f*, MEDIA *radio, TV*, S&M *radio, TV* temps d'antenne disponible *m*; ~ **thesis** ECON thèse des disponibilités *f*

available[1] *adj* COMP disponible, GEN COMM accessible, disponible; ~ **at short notice** GEN COMM disponible sans délai; ◆ **make** ~ GEN COMM *money* mettre à disposition; ~ **on a current basis** GEN COMM actuellement en stock

available:[2] ~ **assets** *n pl* STOCK valeurs disponibles *f pl*; ~ **balance** *n* ACC, BANK solde disponible *m*; ~ **cash** *n* ACC, BANK disponibilités *f pl*, liquidité *f*, FIN, STOCK liquidité *f*; ~ **cash flow** *n* ACC bénéfice disponible *m*, flux de trésorerie disponible *m*; ~ **funds** *n pl* ACC disponibilités *f pl*, fonds disponibles *m pl*; ~ **sites list** *n* S&M *advertising* pointage des emplacements disponibles *m*; ~ **space** *n* COMP espace disponible *m*; ~ **time** *n* COMP temps disponible *m*

avails *n pl* BANK, FIN, GEN COMM produit *m*

avant-garde *adj* GEN COMM d'avant-garde *loc f*

av-commercial *n* MEDIA, S&M av-spot *m*

avdp. *abbr (avoirdupois)* GEN COMM poids du commerce *m*

average[1] *adj* ACC, COMP, FIN, GEN COMM, INS, MATH, STOCK, TAX moyen

average[2] *n* ACC *(av.)* GEN COMM *(av.)* MATH *(av.)* moyenne *f*, STOCK *(SYN index)* indice boursier *m*; ~ **access time** *n* COMP temps d'accès moyen *m*; ~ **adjuster** *n (AA)* INS *marine*, TRANSP *marine* dispacheur *m*, répartiteur d'avaries *m*; ~ **adjustment** *n* INS, TRANSP règlement d'avaries *m*; ~ **amount** *n* GEN COMM montant moyen *m*; ~ **balance** *n* BANK solde moyen *m*; ~ **bond** *n* INS compromis d'avaries *m*; ~ **claim** *n* INS action d'avarie *f*, déclaration d'avarie *f*; ~ **clause** *n* INS clause avarie *f*, règle proportionnelle *f*; ~ **collection period** *n (SYN collection ratio)* ACC, BANK durée moyenne de règlement des comptes clients *f*, délai moyen de recouvrement des créances *m*, période moyenne d'encaissement *f*, ratio de recouvrement *m*; ~ **compensation** *n* ACC salaire moyen *m*; ~ **cost** *n* ACC cm, coût moyen *m*; ~ **cost**

of claims *n* INS coût moyen des sinistres *m*; ~ **costs** *n pl* ACC, ECON, GEN COMM frais moyens *m pl*; ~ **deposit** *n* FIN dépôt moyen *m*; ~ **deviation** *n* MATH déviation moyenne *f*; ~ **duration of life** *n* INS espérance moyenne de vie *f*; ~ **equity** *n* STOCK capital actions moyen *m*, moyenne journalière *f*; ~ **fixed costs** *n pl* ACC charges fixes moyennes *f pl*; ~ **hourly earnings** *n pl* HRM revenu horaire moyen *m*; ~ **income** *n* FIN, HRM revenu moyen *m*; ~ **incremental cost** *n* ACC, ECON, FIN coût marginal moyen *m*; ~ **interest rate** *n* BANK, ECON taux bancaire moyen *m*; ~ **laytime** *n* TRANSP *shipping* estaries moyennes *f pl*, staries moyennes *f pl*; ~ **life** *n* GEN COMM durée de vie moyenne *f*; ~ **market price** *n* ECON prix du marché *m*, GEN COMM, S&M prix courant *m*, prix du marché *m*, prix moyen pratiqué *m pl*; ~ **maturity** *n* STOCK *security* maturité moyenne *f*, échéance moyenne *f*; ~ **monthly money market rate** *n* STOCK taux moyen mensuel du marché monétaire *m*, T4M, TMMMM; ~ **net income** *n* TAX revenu net moyen *m*; ~ **pay** *n* HRM salaire moyen *m*; ~ **premium** *n* INS prime moyenne *f*; ~ **premium system** *n* INS système des primes moyennes *m*; ~ **price** *n* S&M, STOCK cours moyen *m*; ~ **propensity to consume** *n (APC)* ECON propension moyenne à consommer *f*, tendance moyenne de la consommation *f*; ~ **propensity to save** *n (APS)* ACC tendance moyenne à économiser *f*, ECON propension moyenne à économiser *f*, propension moyenne à épargner *f*, tendance moyenne à économiser *f*; ~ **rate** *n* ACC taux moyen *m*; ~ **revenue** *n* ACC, FIN chiffre d'affaires moyennes *m*, recettes moyennes *f pl*; ~ **statement** *n* INS *marine*, TRANSP *marine* classement d'avaries *m*; ~ **tax** *n* TAX impôt moyen *m*; ~ **total cost** *n* ACC, GEN COMM, ECON coût total moyen *m*; ~ **unit cost** *n* ACC, GEN COMM, S&M coût unitaire moyen *m*; ~ **wage** *n* HRM salaire moyen *m*; ~ **weighted rate** *n* STOCK taux moyen pondéré *m*, TMP; ~ **working week** *n BrE (cf average workweek AmE)* HRM semaine de travail moyenne *f*; ~ **workweek** *n AmE (cf average working week BrE)* HRM semaine de travail moyenne *f*; ~ **yield** *n* FIN rendement moyen *m*, taux de rendement moyen *m*, IND rendement moyen *m*, STOCK rendement moyen *m*, taux de rendement moyen *m*; ◆ **at an** ~ GEN COMM en moyenne; ~ **number of copies sold** GEN COMM nombre moyen d'exemplaires vendus; **take an** ~ MATH faire une moyenne; **with** ~ *(W.A.)* INS *marine* avec avaries

average:[3] **1.** *vt* ~ **down** *(ANT average up)* STOCK acheter par échelons de baisse; ~ **out** FIN équilibrer; ~ **up** *(ANT average down)* STOCK acheter par échelons de hausse; **2.** *vi* ~ **down** *(ANT average up)* STOCK faire une moyenne à la baisse *loc f*; ~ **out** FIN *cost, profit*, STOCK faire une moyenne *loc f*; ~ **up** *(ANT average down)* STOCK faire une moyenne à la hausse *loc f*

Average: ~ **Revenue** *n (AR)* LEIS revenu moyen *m*

averager *n* STOCK faiseur de moyennes *m*

averaging: ~ **amount** *n* TAX montant d'étalement *m*, montant étalé *m*; ~ **formula** *n* BANK formule d'étalement *f*; ~ **period** *n* TAX période d'étalement du revenu *f*

aviation *n* TRANSP aviation *f*; ~ **fuel** TRANSP kérosène aviation *m*; ~ **insurance** INS, TRANSP assurance-aviation *f*; ~ **risk** INS, TRANSP risque d'aviation *m*, risque de transport aérien *m*; ~ **spirit** TRANSP essence avion *f*; ~ **trip life insurance** INS, LEIS, TRANSP assurance-vie voyage aérien *f*; ~ **turbine fuel** TRANSP kérosène aviation *m*

avoid *vt* GEN COMM éviter, TAX *tax* éluder, éviter, TRANSP annuler, éviter

avoidable: ~ **cost** *n* GEN COMM coût évitable *m*, frais superflus *m pl*

avoidance *n* INS, TRANSP *marine* annulation *f*; ~ **clause** LAW clause résolutoire *f*

avoirdupois *n* *(avdp.)* GEN COMM *weight* poids du commerce *m*

AVR *abbr* *(agent's vehicle record)* TRANSP registre des véhicules du commissionnaire de transport *m*

avulsion *n* PROP arrachement *m*

award[1] *n* HRM décision arbitrale *f*, LAW attribution *f*, MGMNT *of a contract* adjudication *f*; ~ **income** TAX aide financière *f*; ~ **letter** TAX lettre d'approbation *f*

award[2] *vt* GEN COMM *contract* adjuger *(frml)*, octroyer, LAW *contract* adjuger, attribuer; ◆ ~ **damages** INS accorder des dommages-intérêts; ~ **heavy damages** LAW accorder des dommages-intérêts considérables

awarder *n* GEN COMM adjudicateur *m*

awarding: ~ **of damages** *n* LAW octroi de dommages-intérêts *m*

aware *adj* GEN COMM conscient

awareness *n* S&M, WEL sensibilisation *f*; ~ **level** S&M niveau de notoriété *m*

awash: ~ **with cash** *phr infrml* INFRML GEN COMM regorgeant de liquidités *loc f*

away: ~ **from home expenses** *n pl* TAX frais engagés à l'extérieur *m pl*

AWB *abbr* *(air waybill)* IMP/EXP, TRANSP LTA *(lettre de transport aérien)*

AWD *abbr* *(awning deck)* TRANSP *shipping* pont-tente *m*

awning *n* GEN COMM *advertising* store *m*; ~ **deck** *(AWD, Adk)* TRANSP *shipping* pont-tente *m*

AWY *abbr* *(airway)* TRANSP voie aérienne *f*

AXB *abbr* *(auxiliary boiler)* TRANSP *shipping* chaudière auxiliaire *f*

axial: ~ **composition** *n* GEN COMM *advertising* composition axiale *f*

axioms: ~ **of preference** *n pl* ECON axiomes de préférence *m pl*

axis *n* TRANSP axe *m*

axle *n* TRANSP axe *m*; ~ **weight** GEN COMM poids de l'essieu *m*

Azerbaijan *pr n* GEN COMM Azerbaïdjan *m*

Azerbaijani[1] *adj* GEN COMM azerbaïdjanais

Azerbaijani[2] *n* GEN COMM *person* Azerbaïdjanais *m*

Azeri[1] *adj* GEN COMM Azeri

Azeri[2] *n* GEN COMM *language* azeri *m, person* Azeri *m*

azerty: ~ **keyboard** *n* COMP clavier AZERTY *m*

B

B *abbr (bale capacity)* TRANSP capacité en balles *f*;
~ **of E** *(Bank of England)* BANK, ECON, FIN
banque d'Angleterre, ≈ BF *(Banque de France)*

BA *abbr (Bachelor of Arts)* WEL *degree* ≈ licence
de lettres *f, person* ≈ licencié ès lettres *m*

BAA *abbr (British Airports Authority)* TRANSP
administration des aéroports britanniques

baby: ~ **bond** *n jarg US* STOCK obligation inférieure à
$100; ~ **boom** *n* ECON baby-boom *m*; ~ **-boomers**
n pl ECON, S&M *target audience* génération du
baby-boom *f*

BACC *abbr (British-American Chamber of
Commerce)* GEN COMM chambre de commerce
anglo-américaine

Bachelor: ~ **of Arts** *n (BA)* WEL *degree* ≈ licence
de lettres *f, person* ≈ licencié ès lettres *m*; ~ **of
Business Administration** *n* WEL *person*
≈ diplômé en administration des entreprises *m*;
~ **of Commerce** *n (BCom)* HRM, WEL *person*
≈ licencié en études commerciales *f*; ~ **of
Economics** *n (BEcon)* HRM, WEL *person* ≈ licencié en sciences économiques *f*; ~ **of Education** *n
(BEd)* HRM, WEL *degree* ≈ licence d'enseignement *f, person* ≈ licencié d'enseignement *m*; ~ **of
Industrial Design** *n (BID)* HRM, WEL *person*
≈ licencié en dessin industriel *f*; ~ **of Laws** *n
(LLB)* WEL *degree* ≈ licence de droit *f, person*
≈ licencié en droit *m*; ~ **of Science** *n (BSc)* HRM,
WEL *degree* ≈ licence de sciences *f, person*
≈ licencié ès Sciences *m*; ~ **of Science in Business Administration** *n (BSBA)* WEL *degree*
≈ licence en études d'administration des entreprises *f, person* ≈ licencié en études
d'administration des entreprises *m*; ~ **of Science
in Industrial Relations** *n (BSIR)* WEL *degree*
≈ licence en sciences des relations humaines *f,
person* ≈ licencié en sciences des relations
humaines *m*

bachelor's: ~ **degree** *n* GEN COMM, WEL licence *f*

back:[1] ~ **arrow** *n* COMP flèche de retour arrière *f*;
~ **-channel** *n US* POL moyen de communication
secrète *m*; ~ **cover** *n* MEDIA quatrième de couverture *f*; ~ **end** *n jarg* MEDIA pourcentage sur les
recettes *m*; ~ **-end load** *n* STOCK frais de retrait *m
pl*, pénalité de retrait de fonds *f*; ~ **freight** *n*
TRANSP fret de retour *m*; ~ **haul** *n* TRANSP
shipping trajet de retour *m*; ~ **interest** *n* ACC
arriéré d'intérêts *m*; ~ **issue** *n* MEDIA *of newspaper, magazine* ancien numéro *m*, numéro
antérieur *m*, vieux numéro *m*; ~ **load** *n* TRANSP
chargement de retour *m*; ~ **margin** *n* ADMIN,
COMP marge de fond *f*, MEDIA *print* marge de
fond *f*, marge de petits fonds *f*, petit fond *m*;
~ **number** *n* MEDIA *of newspaper, magazine* ancien
numéro *m*, numéro antérieur *m*, vieux numéro *m*;

~ **-of-house jobs** *n pl (ANT front-of-house jobs)*
ADMIN postes fonctionnels *m pl*, services fonctionnels *m pl*; ~ **office** *n* ADMIN arrière-guichet *m*,
service administratif *m*, STOCK service de post-
marché *m*, services de soutien *m pl, settlements*
post-marché *m*; ~ **order** *n* GEN COMM, S&M
commande en attente *f*, commande en retard *f*,
commande en souffrance *f*; ~ **pay** *n* HRM effet
rétroactif sur salaire *m*, rappel de salaire *m*,
rappel de traitement *m*; ~ **payment** *n* FIN arrérages *m pl*, GEN COMM arriéré *m*, arrérages *m pl*,
rappel *m*, HRM arrérages *m pl*; ~ **-pedaling** *n
AmE*, ~ **-pedalling** *n BrE* GEN COMM marche
arrière *f*; ~ **rent** *n* HRM arriéré de loyer *m*;
~ **section** *n* GEN COMM *of magazines* cahier de
queue *m*; ~ **tax** *n* TAX arriéré d'impôts *m*, rappel
d'impôts *m*; ~ **-to-back credit** *n* BANK, FIN crédit
de face à face *m*; ~ **-to-back loan** *n* BANK crédit
endossé *m*, prêt multiple *m*, FIN crédit endossé *m*;
~ **-to-back placement** *n* STOCK achat mutuel entre
institutions *m*; ~ **-to-back transaction** *n* BANK,
FIN opération de face à face *f*; ~ **-to-back
transfers** *n pl* BANK, FIN transferts multiples *m
pl*; ◆ **get sb's** ~ **up** *infrml* GEN COMM gonfler qn
(infrml), mettre qn en colère

back[2] **1.** *vt* BANK *loan* garantir, FIN avaliser,
financer, GEN COMM *candidate* soutenir, *project,
commanditer* avaliser, financer, POL *candidate*
soutenir; ~ **out of** GEN COMM *contract, deal*
revenir sur, se dégager de, se retirer de, *obligation*
se soustraire à; ~ **up** COMP sauvegarder, GEN
COMM *claim* soutenir, *person* épauler; **2.** *vi*
~ **down** GEN COMM avouer qu'on est dans son
tort, céder, MGMNT *in dispute* avouer qu'on est
dans son tort; ~ **off** GEN COMM se dégager, se
retirer; ~ **up** COMP *file, data* faire une copie de
sauvegarde *loc f*; ◆ **be** ~ **within an hour** GEN
COMM être de retour dans un heure; **go** ~ **to
square one** GEN COMM retourner à la case départ

backbench *n UK* POL *Parliament* banc des
membres sans portefeuille *m*; ~ **MP** *UK* POL
Parliament député ordinaire *m*

backbencher *n UK* POL *Parliament* député ordinaire *m*

backbone *n* ECON *of economy* clé de voûte *f*, pilier
m

backdate *vt* GEN COMM *cheque, contract* antidater

backdated *adj* GEN COMM antidaté, avec effet
rétroactif *loc m*

backdating *n* GEN COMM antidatation *f*

backdoor: ~ **financing** *n* ECON, FIN financement
déguisé *m*, financement véreux *m*; ~ **lending** *n*
ECON, FIN crédit de soutien *m*, prêt déguisé *m*;
~ **operation** *n* ECON, FIN opération d'arrière-
boutique *f*

backdrop *n* GEN COMM *to situation, event* toile de fond *f*

backed: ~ **bill of exchange** *n* FIN, STOCK lettre de change avalisée *f*, lettre de change garantie *f*

backer *n* FIN, GEN COMM avaliseur *m*, bailleur de fonds *m*, commanditaire *mf*, MEDIA commanditaire *mf*

background *n* ECON climat *m*, GEN COMM acquis *m*, climat *m*, HRM formation *f*, POL *of event, situation* climat *m*; ~ **art** PATENTS état de la technique antérieure *m*; ~ **check** *(cf background processing US)* HRM étude *f*; ~ **color** *AmE*, ~ **colour** *BrE* COMP couleur de fond *f*; ~ **field** COMP *of screen* champ de fond *m*; ~ **information** GEN COMM généralités *f pl*, notions générales *f pl*; ~ **investigation** HRM *of applicant* enquête sur les antécédents *f*; ~ **paper** FIN document d'information *m*, MEDIA dossier de presse *m*, historique *m*, rapport documentaire *m*; ~ **picture** COMP *of screen* image de fond *f*; ~ **pollution** ENVIR pollution de fond *f*, pollution diffuse *f*; ~ **processing** COMP *of low priority tasks* traitement de fond *m*, traitement en arrière-plan *m*, traitement en tâche de fond *m*, traitement non-prioritaire *m*, HRM *US (SYN background check)* étude *f*; ~ **story** MEDIA *of print, newspaper* papier d'ambiance *m*; ~ **task** COMP *of low priority* tâche de fond *f*, tâche non prioritaire *f*

backing *n* FIN appui *m*, GEN COMM appui *m*, soutien *m*, STOCK *of currency* garantie *f*; ~ **up** MEDIA *print* impression au verso *f*, retiration *f*

backlog *n* ADMIN, GEN COMM accumulation *f*, arriéré *m*; ~ **demand** ECON demande non encore satisfaite *f*, demandes non exécutées *f pl*, GEN COMM demande en retard *f*, S&M demande non encore satisfaite *f*, demandes non exécutées *f pl*; ~ **order** GEN COMM commande en attente *f*; ~ **order books** GEN COMM registre des commandes en attente *m*; ~ **of orders** GEN COMM, S&M commandes en suspens *f pl*; ~ **of payments** ACC arriéré de paiements *m*; ~ **of work** GEN COMM, IND arriéré de travail *m*

backs *n pl* MEDIA *print* petits fonds *m pl*

backselling *n* S&M *market research* vente indirecte *f*

backslash *n* COMP barre oblique inverse *f*, barre oblique inversée *f*; ~ **key** COMP touche barre oblique inverse *f*

backspace[1] *n* COMP espacement arrière *m*, retour arrière *m*; ~ **character** COMP caractère d'espacement arrière *m*, caractère de retour arrière *m*

backspace[2] *vi* COMP faire un espacement arrière *loc m*, faire un retour arrière *loc m*

backspread *n* STOCK *options* type d'écart *m*

backstop *n* IND protection *f*; ~ **loan facility** FIN crédit exceptionnel *m*

backstrip *n* MEDIA *of book* dos *m*

backtrack *vi* GEN COMM *from plan, promise* faire marche arrière

backtracking *n* GEN COMM marche arrière *f*

backup[1] *adj* ADMIN *supplies* de réserve *loc f*,

supplémentaire, COMP de sauvegarde *loc f*, de secours *loc m*, GEN COMM *plan* de secours *loc m*

backup[2] *n* COMP assistance technique *f*, sauvegarde *f*, FIN appui *m*, GEN COMM appui *m*, soutien *m*; ~ **copy** COMP *of file, data* copie de sauvegarde *f*, copie de secours *f*; ~ **facility** COMP, GEN COMM *installations* installation de secours *f*; ~ **file** COMP *electronic copy* fichier de sauvegarde *m*; ~ **line** BANK ligne de substitution *f*; ~ **material** GEN COMM documentation *f*, documents d'accompagnement *m pl*, matériel pédagogique *m*; ~ **memory** COMP mémoire de sauvegarde *f*; ~ **service** GEN COMM, S&M service après-vente *m*, TRANSP *shipping* service d'appoint *m*; ~ **support** STOCK support supplémentaire *m*; ~ **system** STOCK *for options* système de garantie *m*; **timed** ~ COMP sauvegarde fixe *f*; ~ **utility program** COMP utilitaire de sauvegarde *m*

backward: ~ **averaging** *n (ANT forward averaging)* TAX *of income* étalement sur les années précédents *m*; ~ **-bending labor supply curve** *n AmE*, ~ **-bending labour supply curve** *n BrE* ECON courbe d'offre de main-d'oeuvre inversée *f*, courbe négative d'offre de main-d'oeuvre *f*; ~ **-bending supply curve** *n* ECON courbe d'offre inversée *f*, courbe négative des offres *f*; ~ **integration** *n (ANT forward integration)* ECON, IND, MGMNT intégration en amont *f*, intégration en arrière *f*; ~ **linkage** *n (ANT forward linkage)* ECON, IND enchaînement arrière *m*, liens en amont *m pl*; ~ **scheduling** *n (ANT forward scheduling)* MGMNT programmation régressive *f*; ~ **vertical integration** *n (ANT forward vertical integration)* ECON, IND, MGMNT intégration verticale en amont *f*, intégration verticale en arrière *f*

backwardation *n UK* STOCK déport *m*, report *m*; ~ **business** *UK* FIN, STOCK activité de report *f*; ~ **rate** FIN, STOCK taux de déport *m*

backwash: ~ **effect** *n* ECON contrecoup *m*, effet d'osmose *m*, effet de remous *m*

backyard: **not in my** ~ *phr (NIMBY)* ENVIR attitude de celui qui est un faveur d'un projet à condition que celui-ci ne soit pas effectué près de chez lui

Baco: ~ **Liner** *n* TRANSP *shipping* porte-barges *m*

bad: ~ **bargain** *n* GEN COMM mauvaise affaire *f*; ~ **break** *n infrml* GEN COMM manque de bol *m* *(infrml)*, manque de pot *m* *(infrml)*; ~ **buy** *n* GEN COMM mauvais achat *m*; ~ **check** *n AmE*, ~ **cheque** *n BrE* BANK chèque en bois *m* *(infrml)*, chèque sans provision *m*; ~ **deal** *n* GEN COMM malfaçon *f*, mauvais travail *m*, mauvaise affaire *f*, travail détestable *m*; ~ **debt** *n* ACC, BANK, ECON, FIN créance douteuse *f*, créance irrécouvrable *f*, créance irrévocable *f*, mauvaise créance *f*, GEN COMM créance irrécouvrable *f*; ~ **debt losses** *n pl* ACC, BANK, ECON, FIN pertes occasionnées par créances douteuses *f pl*, pertes sur créances *f pl*; ~ **debt provision** *n* ACC, BANK, FIN provision pour créances douteuses *f*, provision pour créances irrécouvrables *f*; ~ **debt recovery** *n* ACC, BANK,

FIN recouvrement sur créance radiée *m*, rentrée sur créance passée en charges *f*, rentrée sur créance radiée *f*; ~ **debtor** *n* ACC, BANK, FIN débiteur douteux *m*; ~ **delivery** *n* STOCK défiguration de titres *f*; ~ **and doubtful debts** *n pl* (*B&D*) BANK créances douteuses *f pl*; ~ **investment** *n* ACC, BANK, FIN placement qui ne rapporte pas *m*; ~ **loan** *n* ACC, BANK, FIN prêt irrécouvrable *m*; ~ **loan provision** *n* ACC, BANK, FIN provision pour prêts irrécouvrables *f*; ~ **luck** *n* GEN COMM manque de bol *m* (*infrml*), manque de pot *m* (*infrml*); ~ **management** *n* MGMNT mauvaise administration *f*, mauvaise gestion *f*; ~ **name** *n* GEN COMM mauvaise réputation *f*; ~ **news** *n* GEN COMM mauvaise nouvelle *f*; ~ **paper** *n* infrml BANK mauvais papier *m*; ~ **reputation** *n* GEN COMM mauvaise réputation *f*; ~ **risk** *n* GEN COMM mauvais risque *m*; ~ **sector** *n* COMP secteur défectueux *m*; ~ **title** *n* LAW, PROP titre de propriété invalide *m*, titre de propriété non-valable *m*, titre de propriété non-valide *m*; ~ **will** *n* GEN COMM, HRM mauvaise volonté *f*; ~ **workmanship** *n* GEN COMM mauvais travail *m*

badly[1] *adv* GEN COMM mal; ◆ ~ **in debt** BANK criblé de dettes; ~ **paid** HRM mal payé

badly:[2] ~ **imposed page** *n* MEDIA *print* feuille bamboche *f*, page mal imposée *f*

BAEC *abbr* (*British Agricultural Export Council*) IMP/EXP conseil britannique des exportations agricoles

BAF *abbr* (*bunker adjustment factor, bunkering adjustment factor*) TRANSP *shipping* surcharge de soutage *f*

Bafta *n* UK (*British Academy of Film and Television Awards*) MEDIA ≈ Sept d'Or *m*

baggage *n* LEIS, TRANSP bagages *m pl*; ~ **allowance** LEIS, TRANSP franchise de bagages *f*; ~ **cart** *AmE* (*cf baggage trolley BrE, luggage trolley BrE*) TRANSP chariot à bagages *m*; ~ **check** LEIS bulletin de bagages *m*, TRANSP bulletin de bagages *m*, contrôle des bagages *m*; ~ **checked** (SYN *registered baggage*) TRANSP *luggage* bagages enregistrés *m pl*; ~ **checkroom** *AmE* (*cf cloakroom, left-luggage office BrE*) GEN COMM, TRANSP consigne *f*; **excess ~** LEIS, TRANSP excédent de bagages *m*; ~ **handling** TRANSP manutention des bagages *f*; ~ **improvement program** *AmE*, ~ **improvement programme** *BrE* (*BIP*) TRANSP programme d'amélioration de la manutention des bagages *m*; ~ **locker** *AmE* (*cf left-luggage locker BrE*) GEN COMM consigne automatique *f*; ~ **reclaim area** LEIS, TRANSP retrait des bagages *m*, zone de récupération des bagages *f*; ~ **tag** LEIS, TRANSP étiquette à bagages *f*; ~ **trolley** *BrE* (*cf baggage cart AmE*) TRANSP chariot à bagages *m*; ~ **vehicle** TRANSP véhicule à bagages *m*

bagging *n* IND, TRANSP *placing into bags* ensachage *m*, mise en sac *f*

Baghdad *pr n* GEN COMM Bagdad *n pr*

bagman *n pej* [pl -men] FIN *US* racheteur *m*, GEN COMM voyageur représentant placier *m*, VRP, POL *Canada* soudoyeur *m* (*infrml*), S&M voyageur représentant placier *m*, VRP

Bahamas *pr n* [inv pl] GEN COMM Bahamas *f pl*

Bahamian[1] *adj* GEN COMM bahamien

Bahamian[2] *n* GEN COMM *person* Bahamien *m*

Bahrain *pr n* GEN COMM Bahreïn *m*

Bahraini[1] *adj* GEN COMM bahreïni

Bahraini[2] *n* GEN COMM *person* Bahreïni *m*

Bahrein *pr n* see *Bahrain*

Bahreini[1] *adj* see *Bahraini*

Bahreini[2] *n* see *Bahraini*

baht *n* GEN COMM baht *m*

bail[1] *n* LAW *guarantor* répondant *m*, *money* caution *f*, garantie *f*; ~ **bond** LAW caution *f*, engagement personnel de la caution *m*; ~ **-out** FIN, GEN COMM renflouement *m*, sauvetage *m*; ~ **-out period** BANK période de garantie *f*; ◆ **on ~** LAW sous caution

bail[2] *vt* LAW faire mettre en liberté provisoire sous caution *loc f*; ~ **out** FIN, GEN COMM renflouer, sortir d'affaire, LAW faire mettre en liberté provisoire sous caution *loc f*

bailee *n* LAW dépositaire *mf*, dépositaire de biens *mf*

bailiff *n* LAW *officer* huissier *m*, PROP *on estate, farm* intendant *m*, régisseur *m*

bailment *n* GEN COMM dépôt *m*, LAW contrat de gage *m*

bailor *n* BANK, GEN COMM déposant *m*

bait: ~ **advertising** *n* *US* S&M annonce attrape-nigaud *f*; ~ **and switch advertising** *n* *US* S&M *consumer deception* technique de l'appât *f*; ~ **and switch selling** *n* *US* S&M *consumer deception* vente attrape-nigaud *f*

Baker: ~ **Plan** *n* ECON, FIN *international aid* plan Baker *m*

Baku *pr n* GEN COMM Bakou *n pr*

bal. *abbr* (*balance*) ACC, BANK, ECON, FIN bce. (*balance*), solde *m*

balance[1] *n* ACC, BANK, ECON, FIN (*bal.*) balance *f* (*bce.*), solde *m* GEN COMM *budget* équilibre *m*; ~ **of account** *n* ACC, BANK, FIN, GEN COMM solde *m*, solde comptable *m*, solde de compte *m*; ~ **book** *n* ACC, BANK, FIN livre d'inventaire *m*, livre de balance *m*; ~ **brought down** *n* (*b/d*) ACC, FIN, STOCK report à nouveau *m*, solde reporté *m*, solde à nouveau *m*, solde à reporter *m*; ~ **brought forward** *n* ACC, FIN report à nouveau *m*, solde reporté *m*, solde à nouveau *m*, solde à reporter *m*, STOCK report *m*, report à nouveau *m*, solde reporté *m*, solde à nouveau *m*, solde à reporter *m*; ~ **carried forward** *n* ACC, FIN, STOCK report à nouveau *m*, solde reporté *m*, solde à nouveau *m*, solde à reporter *m*; ~ **due** *n* TAX solde dû *m*, solde à régler *m*; ~ **due to creditor** *n* BANK, FIN solde créditeur *m*; ~ **due to debitor** *n* BANK, FIN solde débiteur *m*; ~ **in bank** *n* ACC, BANK, FIN solde bancaire *m*; ~ **of invoice** *n* ACC solde de facture *m*; ~ **item** *n* ACC poste du bilan *m*; ~ **on current**

account *n* ACC, BANK, ECON, FIN balance de compte courant *f*, balance des opérations courantes *f*; **~ of payments** *n (BOP)* ECON, POL balance des paiements *f*; **~ of payments deficit** *n (*ANT *balance of payments surplus)* ECON déficit de la balance des paiements *m*; **~ of payments equilibrium** *n* ECON, POL équilibre de la balance des paiements *m*; **~ of payments surplus** *n (*ANT *balance of payments deficit)* ECON excédent de la balance des paiements *m*; **~ of power** *n* POL *between states* balance des forces *f*, équilibre des forces *m, in government* balance des pouvoirs *f*, équilibre des pouvoirs *m*; **~ sheet** *n (B/S)* ACC, FIN bilan *m*, bilan d'inventaire *m*; **~ sheet item** *n* ACC, FIN poste du bilan *m*; **~ sheet reserves** *n pl* ACC, INS réserves de bilan *f pl*; **~ sheet value of shares** *n* ACC, STOCK *accounting value of shareholders' equity in the company* valeur comptable du patrimoine *f, shares owned by one company in another* valeur d'inventaire des titres détenus *f*; **the ~** *n* GEN COMM le restant de la somme *m*; **~ of trade** *n* ECON, IMP/EXP, POL balance commerciale *f*, balance du commerce extérieur *f*; ◆ **~ in your favor** *AmE*, **~ in your favour** *BrE* BANK à votre crédit; **post ~ sheet event** ACC événement après clôture des comptes *m*

balance² **1.** *vt* ACC solder, équilibrer, FIN équilibrer, GEN COMM *positive with negative factors* contrebalancer, équilibrer; **2.** *vi* ACC s'équilibrer, être équilibré; **~ each other out** ACC se compenser; **~ out** ACC se compenser; ◆ **~ the books** ACC arrêter les comptes; **~ the cash** ACC faire la caisse

Balance: **~ for Official Financing** *n (BOF)* ACC, ECON *of payments* balance des financements officiels *f*

balanced¹ *adj* ACC, BANK, FIN arrêté

balanced:² **~ article** *n* LAW article sensé *m*, équilibre *m*; **~ budget** *n* ACC, ECON, FIN budget équilibré *m*; **~ budget multiplier** *n* ACC, ECON, FIN multiplicateur du budget équilibré *m*; **~ growth** *n* ECON, FIN croissance équilibrée *f*; **~ mutual fund** *n* STOCK fonds de placement aux investissements équilibrés *m*, société d'investissement équilibrée *f*; **~ portfolio** *n* FIN, STOCK portefeuille équilibré *m*

Balanced: **~ Budget and Emergency Deficit Control Act** *n US* ECON loi Gramm-Rudman-Hollings pour la réduction du déficit

balances: **~ abroad** *n pl* BANK soldes à l'étranger *m pl*

balancing: **~ item** *n* ECON facteur d'équilibre *m*, élément pondérateur *m*; **~ of portfolio** *n* INS compensation des risques *f*

balboa *n* GEN COMM balboa *m*

bale *n* TRANSP balle *f*; **~ capacity** *n (B)* TRANSP capacité en balles *f*; **~ cubic meters** *n pl AmE*, **~ cubic metres** *n pl BrE (BC)* GEN COMM bale *m*; **~ space** *n* TRANSP *shipping* volume balle *m*

baling *n* TRANSP *shipping* mise en balles *f*, paquetage *m*

ball: **~ -point** *n* ADMIN stylo à bille *m*

ballast *n* TRANSP *shipping* lest *m*; **~ sailing** TRANSP *shipping* navigation sur lest *f*; **~ space** TRANSP *shipping* ballast *m*; **~ tank** TRANSP *shipping* ballast *m*, caisse profonde *f*; **~ trip** TRANSP *shipping* voyage sur lest *m*

balloon *n* BANK versement final; **~ advertising** S&M publicité par ballons *f*; **~ interest** STOCK *on loan* retard d'intérêt; **~ linen** GEN COMM *advertising* toile-ballon *f*; **~ loan** BANK prêt avec versement final supérieur *m*; **~ payment** STOCK *bonds* intérêt accumulé payable à la maturité d'une obligation; **~ repayment** BANK remboursement avec intérêt final

ballot¹ *n* HRM, POL *vote* scrutin *m*, TRANSP *shipping* ballot *m*; **~ box** HRM, POL urne *f*; **~ paper** HRM, POL bulletin de vote *m*; ◆ **take a ~** HRM procéder à un vote scrutin

ballot² *vi* HRM voter au scrutin

ballpark: **~ figure** *n infrml* MATH chiffre approximatif *m*

Baltic: **~ Futures Exchange** *n UK (BFE)* STOCK marché à terme baltique; **~ International Freight Futures Exchange** *n UK (BIFFEX)* TRANSP bourse internationale Balte des instruments financiers à terme concernant le fret; **~ and International Maritime Conference** *n* TRANSP conférence maritime internationale des pays baltiques

BAM *abbr (bulk air mail)* COMMS envoi en nombre par avion *m*, lettres en nombre par avion *f pl*

Bamako *pr n* GEN COMM Bamako *n pr*

bamboo: **~ curtain** *n US* POL rideau de bambou *m*

ban¹ *n* GEN COMM, IMP/EXP embargo *m*, interdiction *f*, LAW défense *f*, interdiction *f*

ban² *vt* GEN COMM défendre, proscrire

BAN *abbr (bond anticipation note)* STOCK bon de financement anticipé *m*, papier anticipant une obligation *m*

B&D *abbr (bad and doubtful debts)* BANK créances douteuses *f pl*

band *n* GEN COMM *range* tranche *f*, TAX bande *f*; **~ advertising** S&M bandeau publicitaire *m*; **~ of fluctuation** ECON *currency rate* marge de flottement *f*, marge de fluctuation *f*; **~ saw** IND scie à ruban *f*

Bandar: **~ Seri Begawan** *pr n* GEN COMM Bandar Seri Begawan *n pr*

banded: **~ offer** *n* GEN COMM, S&M *different products* vente jumelée *f, same product* vente groupée *f*; **~ pack** *n* GEN COMM, S&M *different products* vente jumelée *f, same product* vente groupée *f*

banding *n* HRM zonation *f*

bandwidth *n* COMMS, COMP, MEDIA *radio* largeur de bande *f*

Bangkok *pr n* GEN COMM Bangkok *n pr*

Bangladesh *pr n* GEN COMM Bangladesh *m*

Bangladeshi¹ *adj* GEN COMM bangladais, bangladeshi

Bangladeshi[2] *n* GEN COMM *person* Bangladais *m*, Bangladeshi *m*

Bangui *pr n* GEN COMM Bangui *n pr*

Banjul *pr n* GEN COMM Banjul *n pr*

bank:[1] ~ -**endorsed** *adj* BANK endossé par la banque *loc*; ~ -**financed** *adj* BANK avec fonds bancaires *loc m*; ~ -**indorsed** *adj see bank-endorsed*

bank[2] *n* BANK banque *f*, ENVIR conteneur de collecte *m*; ~ **acceptance** *n* BANK acceptation de banque *f*, effet bancaire *m*; ~ **accommodation** *n* BANK facilité de caisse *f*; ~ **account** *n* ACC, BANK, FIN compte bancaire *m*, compte en banque *m*; ~ **address** *n* BANK siège bancaire *m*; ~ **advance** *n* ACC, BANK, FIN avance bancaire *f*, facilité de caisse *f*; ~ **advice** *n* BANK avis bancaire *m*; ~ **annuities** *n pl* BANK rente perpétuelle *f*; ~ **assets** *n pl* ACC, BANK, FIN actif bancaire *m*; ~ **balance** *n* ACC, BANK, FIN solde de banque *m*, solde de compte bancaire *m*; ~ **base rate** *n* BANK, ECON, FIN taux de base bancaire *m*, TBB; ~ **bill** *n* BANK *document* chèque bancaire *m*, effet bancaire *m*, BANK *AmE (cf banknote BrE)* billet de banque *m*; ~ **bond** *n* BANK obligation bancaire *f*; ~ **branch** *n* BANK succursale bancaire *f*, succursale de banque *f*; ~ **capital** *n* BANK réserves bancaires *f pl*; ~ **card** *n* BANK carte bancaire *f*; ~ **cash ratio** *n* BANK ratio de liquidité immédiate des banques *m*; ~ **certificate** *n* BANK bon de caisse *m*, certificat bancaire *m*; ~ **charges** *n pl* ACC, BANK, FIN frais bancaires *m pl*, frais de banque *m pl*, frais de gestion de compte *m pl*; ~ **charter** *n* BANK charte bancaire *f*; ~ **check** *n* AmE, ~ **cheque** *n* BrE BANK chèque bancaire *m*, chèque de banque *m*, FIN chèque de banque *m*; ~ **of circulation** *n* BANK banque d'émission *f*; ~ **clearing** *n* BANK compensation bancaire *f*, compensation interbancaire *f*; ~ **clerk** *n* BANK employé de banque *m*; ~ **code** *n* BANK code bancaire de tri *m*; ~ **commission** *n* BANK commission bancaire *f*, frais bancaires *m pl*, frais de banque *m pl*, frais de gestion de compte *m pl*; ~ **credit** *n* BANK, FIN crédit bancaire *m*; ~ **credit transfer** *n* BANK, FIN virement automatique *m*, virement automatique de fonds *m*; ~ **debenture** *n* BANK débenture bancaire *f*; ~ **debts** *n pl* BANK, FIN dettes bancaires *f pl*; ~ **demand deposits** *n pl* BANK dépôts bancaires retraitables *m pl*; ~ **deposit** *n* BANK dépôt bancaire *m*, dépôt en banque *m*; ~ **deposit insurance** *n* US BANK assurance de dépôts bancaires *f*; ~ **deposit money** *n* BANK monnaie de banque *f*, monnaie scripturale *f*; ~ **deposit rates** *n pl* BANK taux d'intérêt des dépôts bancaires *m*; ~ **details** *f pl* BANK coordonnées bancaires *f pl*; ~ **discount** *n* BANK escompte *m*; ~ **discount rate** *n* BANK taux d'escompte bancaire *m*; ~ **draft** *n (B/D\ft)* BANK chèque bancaire *m*, effet bancaire *m*, traite bancaire *f*; ~ **examination** *n* US BANK inspection officielle des banques *f*; ~ **examiner** *n* US BANK inspecteur de banque *m*; ~ **facilities** *n pl* ACC,

BANK services bancaires *m pl*; ~ **failure** *n* BANK faillite de banque *f*; ~ **financing** *n* BANK, FIN financement par le moyen de la banque *m*; ~ **float** *n* BANK flottant *m*; ~ **group** *n AmE* BANK groupe bancaire *m*, groupement bancaire *m*; ~ **guarantee** *n* BANK caution bancaire *f*, garantie bancaire *f*; ~ **guaranty** *n* BANK caution bancaire *f*; ~ **holding company** *n* BANK, GEN COMM holding bancaire *m*; ~ **holiday** *n BrE* GEN COMM fête légale *f*, jour férié *m*; ~ **insurance fund** *n* FIN fonds de garantie bancaire *m*; ~ **interest** *n* ACC agios *m*, BANK intérêt bancaire *m pl*; ~ **of issue** *n* BANK banque d'émission *f*; ~ **lending** *n* BANK, ECON prêts bancaires *m pl*; ~ **lending policy** *n* BANK, ECON politique de prêts bancaires *f*; ~ **lending rate** *n* BANK, ECON, FIN taux de l'escompte *m*; ~ **lien** *n* BANK droit de rétention bancaire *m*; ~ **line** *n (cf credit line, line of credit AmE)* BANK, FIN autorisation de crédit *f*, crédit autorisé *m*, ligne de crédit *f*, ligne de découvert *f*, marge de crédit *f (Can)*; ~ **liquidity** *n* BANK liquidité bancaire *f*; ~ **loan** *n* BANK emprunt auprès des établissements de crédit *m*, emprunt bancaire *m*, emprunt à la banque *m*, prêt bancaire *m*, prêt de banque *m*; ~ **loan rate** *n* BANK taux d'intérêt d'un emprunt bancaire *m*; ~ **manager** *n* BANK, FIN, MGMNT directeur d'agence *m*, directeur de banque *m*; ~ **messenger** *n* BANK encaisseur *m*; ~ **money** *n* BANK monnaie de banque *f*, monnaie scripturale *f*; ~ **officer** *n* BANK cadre de banque *m*, gradé de banque *m*, HRM cadre de banque *m*; ~ **overdraft** *n* BANK découvert *m*, découvert bancaire *m*; ~ **paper** *n* BANK papier avalisé par la banque *m*; ~ **place** *n* BANK place bancable *f*, place bancaire *f*; ~ **postbill** *n* BANK mandat de banque *m*; ~ **rate** *n* BANK, ECON, FIN taux de base bancaire *m*, taux de l'escompte *m*, TBB; ~ **reconciliation** *n* ACC concordance bancaire *f*, BANK rapprochement bancaire *m*, rapprochement de banque *m*; ~ **reconciliation statement** *n* ACC, BANK état de rapprochement bancaire *m*, état de rapprochement de banque *m*; ~ **remittance** *n* BANK remise bancaire *f*; ~ **requirements** *n pl* BANK conditions bancaires *f pl*, conditions de banque *f pl*; ~ **reserve** *n* BANK couverture bancaire *f*, fonds de réserve *m*, réserve bancaire *f*; ~ **return** *n* BANK situation de banque *f*; ~ **run** *n* BANK retrait massif de dépôts bancaires *m*; ~ **runner** *n* BANK encaisseur *m*; ~ **securities** *n pl* BANK valeurs de banque *f pl*; ~ **selling rate** *n* BANK cours bancaire *m*; ~ **service charge** *n* BANK prestation de service bancaire *f*; ~ **settlement system** *n* BANK système de règlement bancaire *m*; ~ **settlement voucher** *n* BANK bon de liquidation bancaire *m*, pièce de règlement bancaire *f*; ~ **shares** *n pl* BANK valeurs bancaires *f pl*; ~ **sort code** *n UK* BANK code bancaire de tri *m*; ~ **statement** *n* BANK relevé de compte *m*, *of bank's financer* situation de banque *f*, état de banque *m*, *of customer account* relevé bancaire *m*, relevé de compte *m*, GEN COMM *document* relevé de compte *m*; ~ **subsidiary** *n* BANK filiale bancaire *f*; ~ **summary and agreement** *n* BANK rapprochement bancaire *m*, rapprochement de banque *m*; ~ **switching** *n* COMP changement de banque de mémoire *m*, changement de bloc de mémoire *m*; ~ **teller** *n* BANK guichetier *m*; ~ **teller card** *n* BANK carte de guichet automatique *f*; ~ **-to-bank lending** *n* BANK prêts interbancaires *m pl*; ~ **transfer** *n* BANK virement automatique *m*, virement automatique de fonds *m*, virement bancaire *m*; ~ **trust department** *n* BANK service bancaire d'investissement *m*

bank:[3] ~ **with** *vt* BANK avoir son compte bancaire à; ◆ ~ **on** GEN COMM tabler sur

Bank: ~ **Charter Act** *n* UK BANK loi de la charte bancaire; ~ **of England** *n* (*B of E, BE*) BANK, ECON, FIN banque d'Angleterre, ≈ Banque de France *f* (*BF*); ~ **for International Settlements** *n* (*BIS*) BANK Banque des Règlements Internationaux *f* (*BRI*); ~ **Giro** *n* UK BANK paiement par virement bancaire *m*

bankable[1] *adj* BANK bancable, banquable, escomptable, négociable en banque

bankable:[2] ~ **assets** *n pl* BANK actif bancable *m*; ~ **bill** *n* BANK effet bancable *m*; ~ **paper** *n* BANK papier bancable *m*

bankbook *n* BANK *for customers* livret de banque *m*, livret de compte *m*, livret de compte d'épargne *m*, FIN carnet de banque *m*, journal de banque *m*

banker *n* BANK banquier *m*; ~**'s acceptance** *n* BANK acceptation de banque *f*, effet bancaire *m*; ~**'s card** *n* BANK carte d'identité bancaire *f*; ~**'s check** *n* AmE, ~**'s cheque** *n* BrE BANK, FIN chèque de banque *m*; ~**'s deposit rate** *n* BANK taux d'intérêt de compte d'épargne bancaire *m*; ~**'s deposits** *n pl* UK BANK réserves des banques de dépôts *f pl*; ~**'s discount** *n* BANK escompte de banque *m*; ~**'s draft** *n* BANK, FIN chèque de banque *m*; ~**'s order** *n* FIN ordre de virement bancaire *m*; ~**'s ramp** *n jarg* GEN COMM majoration exorbitante des prix *f*; ~**'s reference** *n* BANK référence bancaire *f*; ~**'s ticket** *n* BANK compte de retour *m*; ~**'s transfer** *n* BANK virement automatique *m*, virement automatique de fonds *m*, virement bancaire *m*; ~**'s turn** *n* BANK marge bancaire *f*

banking *n* (*bkg*) BANK opérations bancaires *f pl*, opérations de banque *f pl*; ~ **account** *n* ACC compte bancaire *m*, BANK, FIN compte bancaire *m*, compte en banque *m*; ~ **activity** *n* BANK activité du secteur bancaire *f*; ~ **arrangements** *n pl* BANK accords interbancaires *m pl*; ~ **business** *n* BANK activité bancaire *f*, commerce de banque *m*; ~ **center** *n* AmE, ~ **centre** *n* BrE BANK place bancable *f*, place bancaire *f*; ~ **charges** *n pl* BANK frais bancaires *m pl*, frais de banque *m pl*; ~ **circles** *n pl* BANK profession bancaire *f*; ~ **commission** *n* BANK commission bancaire *f*; ~ **community** *n* BANK les banquiers *m pl*; ~ **day** *n Can* ACC, BANK séance d'affectation de fonds *f*; ~ **establishment** *n* BANK maison de banque *f*; ~ **group** *n* BANK groupe bancaire *m*; ~ **hours** *n pl*

BANK heures d'ouverture de la banque *f pl*; ~ **house** *n* BANK, FIN maison bancaire *f*; ~ **industry** *n* BANK, FIN secteur bancaire *m*; ~ **institution** *n* BANK, FIN institution bancaire *f*; ~ **interest** *n* BANK, FIN taux d'intérêt bancaire *m*; ~ **law** *n* BANK, LAW droit bancaire *m*; ~ **network** *n* BANK réseau bancaire *m*; ~ **operation** *n* ACC, BANK, FIN opération bancaire *f*; ~ **regulation** *n* BANK, LAW réglementation des banques *f*; ~ **sector** *n* BANK, FIN secteur bancaire *m*; ~ **services** *n pl* BANK prestations bancaires *f pl*; ~ **subsidiary** *n* BANK filiale bancaire *f*; ~ **syndicate** *n* BANK consortium bancaire *m*, *for loans* syndicat de banque *m*; ~ **system** *n* BANK, FIN système bancaire *m*; ~ **transaction** *n* ACC, BANK, FIN opération bancaire *f*, opération de banque *f*; ~ **transfer system** *n* BANK système de virements bancaires *m*

Banking: ~ **Act** *n* US BANK, LAW loi bancaire des États-Unis; ~ **School** *n* UK BANK (SYN *law of reflux, real bills doctrine*) ECON théorie des effets commerciaux d'Adam Smith *f*; ~ **Supervision Division** *n* UK BANK *Bank of England* division de contrôle bancaire de la Banque d'Angleterre

banknote *n* BrE (*cf bank bill* AmE) BANK billet de banque *m*; ~ **trading** BANK commerce de billets de banque *m*

bankroll[1] *n* US BANK fonds *m pl*, ressource monétaire *f*

bankroll[2] *vt* US BANK financer

bankrupt[1] *adj* ACC ruiné, BANK, FIN failli, ruiné, HRM failli, *person* fauché (*infrml*), ruiné

bankrupt[2] *n* (*bkpt*) BANK, FIN, HRM failli *m*, fauché *m* (*infrml*)

bankrupt[3] *vt* ACC, BANK, FIN mettre en faillite, ruiner, GEN COMM *company* couler, mettre en faillite, ruiner, HRM mettre en faillite, ruiner

bankruptcy *n* (*bkcy*) ACC, BANK, FIN faillite *f*, GEN COMM faillite *f*, faillite d'entreprise *f*; ~ **act** *n* FIN, LAW loi sur les faillites *f*; ~ **committee** *n* GEN COMM administration de la faillite *f*; ~ **court** *n* FIN, LAW tribunal de commerce *m*, tribunal des faillites *m*; ~ **estate** *n* FIN, LAW actif de la faillite *m*, masse de la faillite *f*; ~ **law** *n* FIN, LAW législation sur les faillites *f*; ~ **legislation** *n* FIN, LAW législation sur les faillites *f*; ~ **notice** *n* FIN, LAW avis de faillite *m*; ~ **proceedings** *n pl* FIN, LAW procédure de faillite *f*; ~ **property** *n* FIN, LAW, PROP biens mis en liquidation *m pl*; ◆ **on the verge of** ~ GEN COMM au bord de la faillite

banner *n* GEN COMM banderole *f*, bannière *f*; ~ **headline** MEDIA *newspaper* gros titre *m*, manchette *f*, titre en caractères d'affiche *m*; ~ **year** GEN COMM année exceptionnelle *f*

bar[1] *abbr* (*barrel*) IND, TRANSP baril *m*, fût *m*, tonneau *m*

bar[2] *n* GEN COMM empêchement *m*, obstacle *m*; ~ **chart** *n* MATH graphique en barres *m*, graphique en tuyaux d'orgue *m*, graphique à bâtons *m*, histogramme *m*; ~ **code** *n* COMP, S&M code à barres *m*; **~ code marking** *n* COMP, S&M code barres *m*; **~ code reader** *n* COMP, IND, S&M crayon optique *m*, crayon-lecteur *m*, lecteur de codes barres *m*, stylo optique *m*; **~ code scanner** *n* COMP, IND, S&M crayon optique *m*, crayon-lecteur *m*, déchiffreur de code barres *m*, lecteur de codes barres *m*, stylo optique *m*; **~ -coded identification number** *n* COMP, S&M numéro d'identification en code barres *m*; **~ -coded product** *n* COMP, S&M produit pourvu d'un code barres *m*; **~ graph** *n* MATH graphique en barres *m*, graphique en tuyaux d'orgue *m*, graphique à bâtons *m*, histogramme *m*; **~ graphics** *n pl* COMP *AmE (cf bar code)*, S&M code à barres *m*; **~ keel** *n (bk)* TRANSP *shipping* quille massive *f*

bar[3] *vt* GEN COMM défendre, empêcher, interdire; ◆ **~ sb from a company** GEN COMM exclure qn d'une société

Bar: the ~ *n* UK LAW ≈ barreau *m*, ≈ ordre des avocats *m*

Barbadian[1] *adj* GEN COMM barbadien

Barbadian[2] *n* GEN COMM *person* Barbadien *m*

Barbados *pr n* GEN COMM Barbade *f*

Barber: ~ boom *n* UK ECON essor Barber *m*

Barclays: ~ Index *n* STOCK indice de la Bourse néo-zélandaise

bare[1] *adj* INS non-assuré, nu

bare:[2] **~ -boat charter party** *n* TRANSP *shipping* charte-partie coque nue *f*; **~ -boat consignee** *n* TRANSP charte-partie coque nue *f*; **~ contract** *n* GEN COMM contrat à titre gratuit *m*; **~ owner** *n* PROP nu-propriétaire *m*; **~ ownership** *n* PROP nue-propriété *f*; **~ property** *n* PROP nue-propriété *f*

bargain[1] *n* GEN COMM, S&M *bought at low price* article en réclame *m*, article en solde *m*, bonne affaire *f*, *contract* marché *m*, STOCK transaction *f*; **~ basement** GEN COMM, S&M *in store* coin des bonnes affaires *m*, rayon des bonnes affaires *m*; **~ book** STOCK carnet d'agent de change *m*; **~ counter** GEN COMM, S&M rayon des soldes *m*; **~ for the account** STOCK marché à terme *m*; **~ hunter** S&M chercheur d'occasion *m*, STOCK chercheur de marchés avantageux *m*, investisseur à la recherche d'une bonne affaire *m*; **~ offer** GEN COMM, S&M offre promotionnelle *f*, offre spéciale *f*; **~ price** GEN COMM, S&M prix cassé *m (infrml)*, prix exceptionnel *m*, prix réduit *m*, prix soldé *m*, prix-réclame *m*; **~ rate** S&M tarif promotionnel *m*; **~ and sale** PROP contrat *m*; **~ sale** GEN COMM, S&M soldes *m pl*, vente-réclame *f*

bargain[2] **1.** *vt* **~ down** GEN COMM marchander, *seller* demander moins cher que, rabattre, S&M marchander **2.** *vi* GEN COMM marchander, HRM négocier, S&M marchander; **~ over** GEN COMM, S&M marchander; ◆ **~ for account** STOCK faire un marché à terme, spéculer à terme; **~ for cash** STOCK faire un marché au comptant, spéculer au comptant; **~ with sb** GEN COMM marchander avec qn; **get more than one ~s for** GEN COMM avoir du fil à retordre

bargainee *n* GEN COMM acheteur *m*, preneur *m*

bargainer *n* GEN COMM négociateur *m*

bargaining *n* GEN COMM marchandage *m*, négociation *f*, HRM négociation *f*, S&M marchandage *m*; **~ agent** HRM *unions* personnel chargé de négocier *m*; **~ chip** *infrml* POL point de discussion *m*; **~ form** HRM forme négociée *f*; **~ level** HRM niveau de négociation *m*; **~ position** GEN COMM position de force *f*, situation permettant de négocier *f*; **~ power** GEN COMM, HRM, MGMNT pouvoir de négociation *m*; **~ scope** HRM étendue de la négociation *f*; **~ structure** HRM structure de la négociation *f*; **~ table** GEN COMM, HRM, MGMNT table de négociations *f*; **~ theory of wages** HRM politique contractuelle en matière de salaires *f*, théorie de la négociation en matière de salaires *f*; **~ unit** HRM unité de négociation *f*

barge *n* TRANSP *shipping* allège *f*, barge *f*, chaland *m*; **~ carrier** TRANSP *shipping* porte-barges *m*; **~ -carrying vessel** *(BCV)* TRANSP *shipping* porte-barges *m*; **~ forwarding** TRANSP *shipping* déchargement sur allèges *m*; **~ -mounted production and storage system** *(BPSS)* TRANSP *shipping* système de production et d'entreposage sur allège *m*

barometer *n* ECON *of measuring trends* baromètre *m*; **~ stock** STOCK valeur de référence *f*

barometric: ~ firm leadership *n* ECON société en tête au baromètre *f*

barratry *n* TRANSP *shipping* baraterie *f*

barrel *n (bar)* IND, TRANSP baril *m*, fût *m*, tonneau *m*; **~ handler** TRANSP *fork-lift truck* porte-barils *m*; **~ hook** TRANSP *cargo handling* patte à futailles *f*

barrels: ~ per day *phr (b/d)* IND, TRANSP barils par jour *m pl*

barrier *n* ECON barrière *f*, obstacle *m*, GEN COMM, IMP/EXP barrière *f*, TRANSP *at station* portillon *m*; **~ to entry** *(ANT barrier to exit)* ECON, IMP/EXP barrière d'entrée *f*; **~ to exit** *(ANT barrier to entry)* ECON, IMP/EXP barrière de sortie *f*; **~ to trade** ECON, GEN COMM, IMP/EXP, POL barrière commerciale *f*, entrave au commerce *f*, TRANSP *shipping* obstacle au commerce maritime *m*

barrister *n* UK LAW avocat *m*; **~ chamber** UK LAW cabinet *m*

Barron's: ~ confidence index *n* US STOCK indice de Barron *m*; **~ Group Stock Averages** *n pl* US STOCK indice des titres Barron

barter[1] *n* ECON troc *m*, échange *m*; **~ agreement** ECON *international trade* accord de compensation *m*, accord de troc *m*; **~ economy** ECON économie de troc *f*; **~ trade** ECON commerce d'échanges compensés *m*, commerce de troc *m*, compensation *f*; **~ transaction** ECON *international trade* opération de compensation *f*, opération de troc *f*

barter[2] **1.** *vt* ECON troquer, échanger; **2.** *vi* ECON faire un troc *loc m*, faire un échange *loc m*

baryta: ~ paper *n* ADMIN papier baryté *m*

base[1] *n* COMP *hardware* base *f*, GEN COMM base de travail *f*; **~ address** COMP adresse de base *f*;

~ **amount** TAX montant de base *m*; ~ **budget** ACC budget de base *m*; ~ **of calculation** GEN COMM base de calcul *f*; ~ **capital** BANK, ECON, FIN capital de base *m*; ~ **capital leverage ratio** BANK, ECON, FIN ratio du capital de base *m*; ~ **capital ratio** BANK, ECON, FIN ratio du capital de base *m*; ~ **configuration** COMP configuration de base *f*; ~ **date** STOCK *for comparison of share prices, returns, etc* année de base de calcul *f*, date de base *f*; ~ **lending rate** UK *(cf prime lending rate US)* ECON, FIN, STOCK taux de base *m* (*France*), taux préférentiel *m* (*Canada*); ~ **pay** AmE HRM salaire de base *m*; ~ **pay rate** HRM taux de salaire horaire *m*; ~ **period** TAX période de base *f*; ~ **price** GEN COMM, S&M prix de base *m*, TAX prix de base *m*, prix de référence *m*; ~ **product** IND produit de base *m*; ~ **rate** UK *(cf prime rate US)* ECON, FIN, STOCK taux de base *m* (*France*), taux préférentiel *m* (*Canada*); ~ **rent** US PROP loyer de base *m*; ~ **salary** AmE HRM salaire de base *m*; ~ **sheet** MEDIA *print* feuille de couverture *f*, papier support *m*; ~ **stock** STOCK stock-outil *m*; ~ **year** ECON, FIN année de base *f*, année de référence *f*; ~ **year analysis** ECON, FIN analyse de l'année de base *f*, analyse du coût de la vie *f*

base[2] *vt* GEN COMM baser, fonder; ~ **on** GEN COMM asseoir sur, reposer sur

baseband *n* COMP bande de base *f*

based *adj* GEN COMM dont le siège est, établi; ♦ **be ~ at** GEN COMM *airlines* avoir des bases d'opération en

baseline *n* COMP *of diagram* ligne de base *f*, GEN COMM *standard* point de comparaison *m*, MATH *of diagram* ligne de fond *f*, ligne zéro *f*

baseload *n* GEN COMM stock de base *m*, stock minimal *m*; ~ **power station** IND centrale en charge de base *f*, usine de base *f*

basic: ~ **amount** *n* GEN COMM montant de base *m*; ~ **books** *n pl* FIN livres de base *m pl*; ~ **commodity** *n* ECON, S&M produit de base *m*; ~ **concept** *n* GEN COMM concept de base *m*, conception de base *f*, idée de base *f*; ~ **consumer products** *n pl* IND produits de consommation courante *m pl*; ~ **corporate tax rate** *n* TAX taux d'imposition de base des corporations *m*; ~ **credit allowance** *n* TAX crédit de base *m*; ~ **currency** *n* ECON monnaie de base *f*; ~ **definition** *n* GEN COMM définition de base *f*; ~ **earnings per share** *n* FIN, STOCK bénéfice non-dilué par action *m*; ~ **exemption** *n* TAX exemption de base *f*; ~ **foodstuffs** *n pl* GEN COMM alimentation de base *f*, denrées alimentaires de base *f pl*; ~ **goods sector** *n* GEN COMM secteur des marchandises de base *m*, secteur des produits de base *m*; ~ **grade** *n* HRM bas échelon *m*, niveau de base *m*; ~ **income** *n* FIN revenu direct *m*; ~ **industry** *n* IND industrie de base *f*, industrie extractive *f*; ~ **input/output operating system** *n* (*BIOS*) COMP *software* système BIOS *m*, système d'exploitation des entrées/sorties *m*; ~ **limits of liability** *n pl* INS limites fondamentales de la garantie *f*; ~ **material** *n* ECON matériau de base *m*;

~ **media** *n pl* MEDIA médias classiques *m pl*; ~ **medium** *n* MEDIA média de base *m*; ~ **message** *n* S&M *advertising* axe publicitaire *m*; ~ **needs** *n pl* ECON besoins fondamentaux *m pl*; ~ **pay** *n* HRM salaire de base *m*; ~ **premium** *n* INS prime essentielle *f*; ~ **price** *n* GEN COMM, S&M prix de base *m*; ~ **rate** *n* ECON, FIN, HRM, INS, TAX traitement de base *m*; ~ **-rate tax** *n* TAX impôt forfaitaire *m*; ~ **research** *n* GEN COMM recherche fondamentale *f*; ~ **research cost** *n* GEN COMM *marketing* frais d'étude de base *m pl*, frais de recherche fondamentale *m pl*; ~ **risk** *n* GEN COMM, STOCK risque de base *m*; ~ **salary** *n* HRM salaire de base *m*; ~ **size** *n* GEN COMM format standard *m*, taille standard *f*; ~ **submission** *n* GEN COMM offre de base *f*; ~ **tax** *n* TAX impôt de base *m*; ~ **tender** *n* GEN COMM offre de base *f*; ~ **time limit** *n* GEN COMM délai de base *m*; ~ **trend** *n* GEN COMM tendance de base *f*, tendance fondamentale *f*; ~ **unit** *n* GEN COMM unité de base *f*; ~ **wage** *n* HRM salaire de base *m*; ~ **weight scales** *n pl* GEN COMM pèse-papier *m*

BASIC *abbr* (*Beginner's All-Purpose Symbolic Instruction Code*) COMP BASIC *m*

basics *n pl* GEN COMM essentiel *m*

basin *n* TRANSP *harbour* bassin *m*

basing: ~ **point pricing** *n* ECON fixation du point de base *f*, fixation forfaitaire des prix *f*

basis *n* GEN COMM base *f*, fondement *m*, STOCK base *f*, TAX assiette *f*, base *f*; ~ **of assessment** TAX assiette de l'impôt *f*, assiette fiscale *f*; ~ **of calculation** FIN base de calcul *f*; ~ **for discussion** GEN COMM base de discussion *f*; ~ **for taxation** TAX assiette de l'impôt *f*, assiette fiscale *f*; ~ **point** FIN, MATH, STOCK point de base *m*; ~ **of premium calculation** INS base de calcul de prime *f*; ~ **price** STOCK *odd-lot trading* cours de base *m*, prix de base *m*; ~ **risk** STOCK risque de base *m*; ♦ **on an unconsolidated ~** ACC sur une base non consolidée; **on the ~ of** GEN COMM sur la base de

basket *n* GEN COMM panier *m*; ~ **of currencies** ECON, FIN panier de devises *m*, panier de monnaies *m*; ~ **of goods** ECON assortiment de denrées *m*, panier de denrées *m*; ~ **hitch** TRANSP *cargo handling* filet de chargement *m*; ~ **of products** ECON panier de produits *m*; ~ **purchase** FIN achat à un prix forfaitaire *m*, achat à un prix global *m*; ~ **of rates** IND panier de taux *m*

bastard: ~ **face** *n* ADMIN, MEDIA *printing* lettres bâtardes *f pl*; ~ **Keynesianism** *n* ECON keynésianisme abâtardi *m*

batch *n* ACC *invoices* paquet *m*, COMP *group of items*, GEN COMM lot *m*, IND lot de fabrication *m*, petite série *f*, MEDIA *letters* liasse *f*, paquet *m*, S&M lot *m*; ~ **computer** COMP ordinateur de traitement par lots *m*; ~ **control** IND contrôle par lots *m*; ~ **file** COMP fichier de commandes *m*, fichier séquentiel *m*; ~ **job** COMP traitement par lots *m*; ~ **processing** COMP traitement différé *m*, traitement par lots *m*, traitement par paquets *m*;

~ **production** IND fabrication en petites séries *f*, fabrication par lots *f*, production en petites séries *f*, production par lots *f*; ~ **size** IND taille des lots *f*, taille des séries *f*

bathtub: ~ **theorem** *n* ECON théorème de la baignoire *m*

batten *n* TRANSP *shipping* barre de serrage *f*, latte *f*

battery:[1] ~ **-backed** *adj* COMP équipé d'une pile auxiliaire, équipé d'une pile de secours

battery[2] *n* COMP batterie *f*, IND *automobile* batterie *f*, *for torch, radio* pile *f*; ~ **backup** COMP alimentation auxiliaire *f*, alimentation de secours *f*, pile auxiliaire *f*, pile de secours *f*

battle[1] *n* GEN COMM combat *m*, lutte *f*

battle:[2] ~ **for** *vt* GEN COMM *contract* batailler pour (*infrml*), se bagarrer pour (*infrml*), *existence* lutter pour, *share in the market* se battre pour

baud *n* COMP baud *m*; ~ **rate** COMP débit *m*, débit en bauds *m*

bay *n* TRANSP *rail* quai subsidiaire *m*, voie d'arrêt *f*

Bayesian: ~ **approach to decision-making** *n* MGMNT approche bayesienne à la prise de décision *f*; ~ **method** *n* MATH méthode Bayesienne *f*

bazaar *n* S&M vente de charité *f*

b&b *abbr* (*bed and breakfast*) LEIS chambre d'hôte *f*

BB[1] *abbr* COMMS, COMP, GEN COMM, HRM (*bulletin board*) panneau d'affichage *m*, tableau d'affichage *m*, TRANSP (*below bridges*) sous palan *loc m* (*sur palan*), TRANSP (*bulbous bow*) *shipping* bulbe d'étrave *m*, étrave à bulbe *f*

BB:[2] ~ **Certificate** *n* IMP/EXP, TRANSP déclaration d'admission en douane d'un navire

BBA *abbr* (*British Bankers' Association*) BANK association britannique des banquiers

BBC *abbr* (*British Broadcasting Corporation*) MEDIA compagnie de télévision et de radio nationale britannique, BBC *f*

BBS *abbr* COMMS (*bulletin board system*) messagerie *f*, tableau d'affichage électronique *m*, COMP (*bulletin board service*) *hardware* serveur télématique *m*

BC *abbr* ACC (*budget control, budgetary control*), ECON (*budget control, budgetary control*), FIN (*budget control, budgetary control*) contrôle budgétaire *m*, GEN COMM (*bale cubic meters, bale cubic metres*) bale *m*

BCC *abbr* (*British Chamber of Commerce*) GEN COMM chambre de commerce britannique

BCom *abbr* (*Bachelor of Commerce*) HRM, WEL *degree* ≈ licence en études commerciales *f*, *person* ≈ licencié en études commerciales *m*

BCV *abbr* (*barge-carrying vessel*) TRANSP *shipping* porte-barges *m*

b/d *abbr* ACC (*balance brought down*), FIN (*balance brought down*) report à nouveau *m*, solde reporté *m*, solde à nouveau *m*, solde à reporter *m*, IND (*barrels per day*) barils par jour *m pl*, STOCK

(*balance brought down*) report à nouveau *m*, solde reporté *m*, solde à nouveau *m*, solde à reporter *m*, TRANSP (*barrels per day*) barils par jour *m pl*, TRANSP (*below deck*) *shipping* sous le pont (*sur le pont*)

B/Dft *abbr* (*bank draft*) BANK chèque bancaire *m*, traite bancaire *f*

bdi *abbr* (*both dates inclusive*) GEN COMM inclusivement

bdl *abbr* (*bundle*) TRANSP ballot *m*, paquet *m*

BDO *abbr* (*bottom dropped out*) STOCK effondrement du cours plancher *m*, effondrement du prix plancher *m*, marché effondré *loc m*

B/E *abbr* BANK (*bill of exchange*), FIN (*bill of exchange*) l/c (*lettre de change*), IMP/EXP (*bill of entry*) déclaration d'entrée en douane *f*, IMP/EXP (*bill of exchange*), STOCK (*bill of exchange*) l/c (*lettre de change*)

BE *abbr* (*Bank of England*) BANK, ECON, FIN banque d'Angleterre, ≈ BF (*Banque de France*)

BEA *abbr* (*Bureau of Economic Analysis*) ECON Bureau d'analyse économique *m*

beaching *n* TRANSP *shipping* échouage *m*

beacon *n* TRANSP balise *f*

beam *n* TRANSP *breadth of ship at widest part* largeur *f*, *shipping* barrot de pont *m*

bean: not to have a ~ *phr infrml* GEN COMM ne pas avoir un radis *m* (*infrml*), ne pas avoir un rond *m* (*infrml*), ne pas avoir un sou *m* (*infrml*)

bear[1] *n* (*ANT bull*) STOCK baissier *m*, spéculateur à la baisse *m*, vendeur à découvert *m*; ~ **account** (*ANT bull account*) STOCK position vendeur *f*, position à découvert *f*, position à la baisse *f*; ~ **call spread** (*ANT bull call spread*) STOCK *options* bear call spread *m*, écart baissier *m*, écart d'un call à la baisse *f*; ~ **campaign** (*ANT bull campaign*) STOCK spéculation à la baisse *f*; ~ **closing** STOCK rachat des vendeurs à découvert *m*; ~ **commitment** (*ANT bull commitment*) STOCK engagement à la baisse *m*; ~ **covering** STOCK rachat des vendeurs à découvert *m*; ~ **hug** FIN, STOCK *corporate takeover* rachat d'une société *m*; ~ **hug takeover** FIN vente fictive d'obligations *f*, STOCK fonds empruntés *m pl*; ~ **market** (*ANT bull market*) STOCK marché baissier *m*, marché orienté à la baisse *m*, marché à la baisse *m*; ~ **operation** (*ANT bull operation*) STOCK transaction à la baisse *f*; ~ **operator** (*ANT bull operator*) STOCK acheteur à la baisse *m*, baissier *m*, spéculateur à la baisse *m*; ~ **position** (*ANT bull position*) STOCK position vendeur *f*, position à découvert *f*, position à la baisse *f*; ~ **put spread** (*ANT bull put spread*) STOCK *options* écart sur puts à la baisse *m*; ~ **raid** STOCK attaque des baissiers *f*; ~ **raiding** STOCK attaque des baissiers *f*, raid *m*; ~ **sale** (*ANT bull buying, bull purchase*) STOCK vente à découvert *f*, vente à la baisse *f*; ~ **speculation** (*ANT bull speculation*) STOCK spéculation à la baisse *f*; ~ **speculator** (*ANT bull speculator*) STOCK spéculateur à la baisse *m*;

~ **spread** *(*ANT *bull spread)* STOCK opération mixte baissière *f,* opération mixte à la baisse *f,* spread baissier *m,* écart baissier *m,* écart vertical baissier *m;* ~ **strike price** *(*ANT *bull strike price)* STOCK prix de levée à la baisse *m;* ~ **transaction** *(*ANT *bull transaction)* STOCK transaction à la baisse *f*

bear[2] **1.** *vt* GEN COMM *burden, responsibility* supporter, STOCK *market, prices, shares* chercher à faire baisser, pousser à la baisse, spéculer à la baisse; **2.** *vi* STOCK jouer à la baisse; ◆ ~ **the cost of** ACC supporter le coût de, supporter les frais de; ~ **the costs** GEN COMM prendre les frais à sa charge, supporter les coûts de; ~ **the date** GEN COMM porter la date du; ~ **an interest of** ACC porter un intérêt de, rapporter un intérêt de; ~ **the risk of** STOCK courir le risque de, prendre le risque de; ~ **sth in mind** GEN COMM garder qch présent à l'esprit

bearer *n* BANK, FIN, STOCK, TAX porteur *m;* ~ **bill** FIN, STOCK effet au porteur *m;* ~ **bond** FIN, STOCK obligation au porteur *f;* ~ **certificate** FIN, STOCK certificat au porteur *m,* titre au porteur *m;* ~ **check** *AmE,* ~ **cheque** *BrE* BANK chèque au porteur *m,* chèque payable au porteur *m;* ~ **clause** FIN, STOCK clause au porteur *f;* ~ **coupon** STOCK coupon au porteur *m;* ~ **debenture** FIN, STOCK, TAX obligation au porteur *f;* ~ **form** FIN, STOCK, TAX au porteur *m,* formule au porteur *f;* ~ **marketable bond** BANK, FIN, TAX obligation négociable au porteur *f;* ~ **proxy** STOCK procuration en blanc *f;* ~ **security** STOCK titre au porteur *m;* ~ **share** ACC, FIN, STOCK action au porteur *f;* ~ **stock** ACC, FIN, STOCK action au porteur *f,* valeurs au porteur *f pl;* ~ **warrant** ACC, FIN, STOCK bon de souscription au porteur *m*

bearing: ~ **the market** *n* STOCK spéculation à la baisse *f;* ~ **surface** *n* TRANSP *shipping* surface d'appui *f*

bearish[1] *adj* *(*ANT *bullish)* STOCK baissier, en baisse, orienté à la baisse *loc;* ◆ **be** ~ *(*ANT *be bullish)* STOCK prévoir une baisse de cours, être baissier

bearish:[2] ~ **market** *n* *(*ANT *bullish market)* STOCK marché baissier *m,* marché orienté à la baisse *m,* marché à la baisse *m;* ~ **movement** *n* *(*ANT *bullish movement)* STOCK mouvement vers le bas *m,* mouvement à la baisse *m,* tendance baissière *f;* tendance à la baisse *f;* ~ **signal information** *n* *(*ANT *bullish signal information)* STOCK *in point and figure analysis* signal de baisse *m;* ~ **spread** *n* *(*ANT *bullish spread)* STOCK bear spread *m,* opération mixte baissière *f,* opération mixte à la baisse *f,* spread baissier *m,* écart baissier *m,* écart vertical baissier *m;* ~ **stock** *n* *(*ANT *bullish stock)* STOCK valeur en baisse *f;* ~ **tendency** *n* *(*ANT *bullish tendency)* STOCK mouvement vers le bas *m,* mouvement à la baisse *m,* tendance baissière *f,* tendance à la baisse *f;* ~ **tone** *n* *(*ANT *bullish tone)*

STOCK *of market* ambiance à la baisse *f,* nature baissière *f*

bearishness *n* *(*ANT *bullishness)* STOCK *of market* ambiance à la baisse *f,* nature baissière *f,* pessimisme *m*

beat: ~ **the price down** *phr* GEN COMM faire baisser le prix *loc m*

Beaufort: ~ **scale** *n* GEN COMM échelle de Beaufort *f*

beavertail *n* TRANSP *road transport* queue de castor *f*

become: 1. *vt* ~ **westernized** GEN COMM s'occidentaliser, GEN COMM devenir; **2.** *vi* ~ **due** ACC arriver à échéance, venir à échéance, échoir; ~ **obsolete** GEN COMM se périmer

BEcon *abbr (Bachelor of Economics)* HRM, WEL ≈ licencié en sciences économiques *m*

bed: ~ **and breakfast** *n (b&b)* LEIS chambre d'hôte *f;* ~ **and breakfast deal** *n jarg* STOCK aller-retour *m,* transaction aller et retour *f*

BEd *abbr (Bachelor of Education)* HRM ≈ licence d'enseignement *f,* WEL *degree* ≈ licence d'enseignement *f, person* ≈ licencié d'enseignement *m*

bedroom *n* LEIS chambre *f;* ~ **community** *AmE (cf dormitory suburb BrE)* HRM ville-dortoir *f*

Beeb: **the** ~ *n infrml UK* MEDIA *broadcasting* la BBC *f*

beep[1] *n* COMP *warning* bip *m,* signal sonore *m*

beep[2] *vi* COMP faire un bip *loc m,* émettre un bip, émettre un signal sonore

before:[1] ~ **-hours** *adj* STOCK avant bourse; ~ **-tax** *adj* TAX avant impôt

before:[2] ~ **-hours dealings** *n pl* STOCK négociations avant l'ouverture *f pl,* transactions avant-bourse *f pl;* ~ **-tax cash flow** *n* ACC flux de trésorerie avant impôts *m,* TAX cash-flow négatif *m*

before[3] *prep* GEN COMM avant; ◆ ~ **due date** STOCK anticipé, avant l'échéance; ~ **maturity** STOCK avant l'échéance

beggar: ~ **-my-neighbor policy** *n AmE,* ~ **-my-neighbour policy** *n BrE* GEN COMM politique visant à l'affaiblissement du voisin *f*

begin 1. *vt* GEN COMM commencer, se mettre à **2.** *vi* GEN COMM commencer; ◆ ~ **doing** GEN COMM commencer à faire; ~ **to do** GEN COMM commencer à faire; ~ **work** GEN COMM se mettre au travail, GEN COMM commencer

Beginner: ~'**s All-Purpose Symbolic Instruction Code** *n (BASIC)* COMP BASIC *m*

beginning: ~ **inventory** *n* ACC stock au début de l'exercice *m,* stock d'ouverture *m,* stock initial *m,* stock à l'ouverture de l'exercice *m;* ~ **of the year** *n* ACC début de l'exercice *m*

BEHA *abbr (British Export Houses' Association)* IMP/EXP association des maisons d'exportation britanniques

behalf: **on** ~ **of** *prep* GEN COMM au nom de *loc m,* de la part de *loc f*

behavior *n AmE see* **behaviour** *BrE*

behavioral: ~ **science** n AmE see behavioural science BrE

behaviour n BrE HRM, MGMNT comportement m; ~ **line** BrE ECON microeconomics courbe d'indifférence f, ligne de comportement f; ~ **modification** BrE HRM modification du comportement f

behavioural: ~ **science** n BrE MGMNT, S&M science du comportement f

Beijing pr n GEN COMM Beijing n pr

Beirut pr n GEN COMM Beyrouth n pr

Belarus pr n GEN COMM Biélorussie f

Belarussian[1] adj GEN COMM biélorusse

Belarussian[2] n GEN COMM person Biélorusse mf

belated: ~ **claim** n INS déclaration de sinistre tardif f, sinistre tardif m

Belfast pr n GEN COMM Belfast n pr

Belgian[1] adj GEN COMM belge

Belgian[2] n GEN COMM person Belge mf

Belgium pr n GEN COMM Belgique f

Belgium-Luxembourg: ~ **Economic Union** n (BLEU) ECON, POL Union économique Belgique-Luxembourg f (UEBL)

Belgo-Luxembourg: ~ **Chamber of Commerce** n (BLCC) GEN COMM chambre de commerce belgo-luxembourgeoise

Belgrade pr n GEN COMM Belgrade n pr

belief n GEN COMM, S&M advertising conviction f

believe vt GEN COMM croire

Belize pr n GEN COMM Belize m

Belizean[1] adj GEN COMM bélizien

Belizean[2] n GEN COMM person Bélizien m

bell n COMMS coup de fil m (infrml), coup de téléphone m; ~ **-shaped curve** MATH statistics courbe en cloche f, courbe en forme de cloche f

bellwether n jarg STOCK cours d'action indicateur m, titre de référence m

belly n TRANSP ventre m; ~ **container** TRANSP conteneur LD-3 m, conteneur pour pont inférieur m; ~ **hold** TRANSP soute à bagages f

Belmopan pr n GEN COMM Belmopan n pr

belong vi HRM to union appartenir à, LEIS to club, library être inscrit à; ◆ ~ **to** GEN COMM appartenir à

below[1] adj COMMS mentionné ci-dessous, mentionné plus bas, sous-mentionné, GEN COMM inférieur à; ~ **-average** (ANT above-average) GEN COMM au-dessous de la moyenne, inférieur à la moyenne; ◆ ~ **-market price** (ANT above-market price) STOCK options on currency futures au-dessous du cours; ~ **-the-line** MEDIA advertising hors-média

below[2] adv (ANT above) COMMS ci-dessous, plus bas, GEN COMM in letter ci-dessous; ◆ **as** ~ (ANT as above) COMMS comme ci-dessous

below:[3] ~ **-the-line item** n (ANT above-the-line item) ECON article de dessous de ligne m, opération au-dessous de ligne f; ~ **-the-line revenue** n ACC, ECON produit exceptionnel m

below[4] prep (ANT above) GEN COMM au-dessous de, de moins de, dessous, en-dessous de; ◆ ~ **bridges** (BB, ANT above bridges) TRANSP shipping sous palan (ANT sur palan); ~ **deck** (b/ d, ANT above deck) TRANSP shipping sous le pont (ANT sur le pont); ~ **the 5% mark** GEN COMM au-dessous de la barre de 5%; ~ **the gangway** POL sous la passerelle; ~ **the line** ACC, FIN au-dessous de la ligne, exceptionnel, à découvert, S&M advertising investment coûts de promotion m pl, S&M au-dessous de la ligne, exceptionnel, à découvert; ~ **the norm** (ANT above the norm) GEN COMM au-dessous de la norme; ~ **quota** (ANT above quota) ECON au-dessous du quota

belship n TRANSP shipping transport de colis lourds m

Bench: **the** ~ n infrml LAW la Cour f, le Tribunal m

benchmark[1] n jarg COMP test performance banc d'essai m, test d'évaluation m, test des performances m, ECON mesure de banc d'essai f, référence f, étalon de mesure m, GEN COMM jalon m, point de repère m, point de référence m; ~ **method** n FIN méthode de référence f; ~ **reserve** n US BANK réserve obligatoire f; ~ **statistics** n pl MATH données statistiques comparatives f pl, données statistiques de base f pl, données statistiques de référence f pl, statistiques de banc d'essai f pl; ~ **test** n COMP test d'essai des performances m, test d'évaluation des performances m

benchmark[2] vt COMP mettre au banc d'essai, évaluer les performances de

beneficial[1] adj GEN COMM, LAW avantageux, favorable, profitable, salutaire

beneficial:[2] ~ **interest** n LAW droit d'usufruit m, TAX droit de bénéficiaire m; ~ **owner** n LAW ayant droit économique m, usufruitier m, STOCK, TAX propriétaire mf; ~ **ownership** n LAW usufruit m, STOCK bénéficiaire mf, propriété f, TAX propriété bénéficiaire f

beneficially: ~ **interested in** phr TAX ayant des droits sur loc m, ayant un droit sur loc m, détenant un intérêt dans loc m

beneficiary n FIN, GEN COMM, INS, LAW, PROP bénéficiaire mf; ~ **clause** INS clause du bénéficiaire f; ~ **under a trust** TAX bénéficiaire d'une fiducie m

benefit[1] n GEN COMM bénéfice m, profit m, performance soirée de bienfaisance f, HRM avantage de salaire m, complément de salaire m, payment allocation f, prestation f, INS from plans prestation f, LEIS représentation de bienfaisance f, MGMNT apport m, avantage m, bénéfice m, contribution f, TAX allocation f, avantage m; ~ **-based pension plan** n INS plan de retraite basée sur les primes d'assurance m, régime de retraite basé sur les avantages salariaux m; ~ **club** n FIN association de secours mutuel f, société de prévoyance f, société de secours mutuel f; ~ **in kind** n GEN COMM avantage en espèces m, avantage en nature m, avantage matériel m;

~ **segmentation** n S&M *advertising* segmentation des bénéfices *f*; ~ **society** n *AmE (cf friendly society BrE)* FIN association de secours mutuel *f*, société de prévoyance *f*, société de secours mutuel *f*; ◆ **be a ~ to sth** GEN COMM être un bénéfice par rapport à qch; **be of ~ to sb** GEN COMM profiter à qn; **be on ~** *BrE (cf be on welfare AmE)* HRM, WEL toucher des allocations, toucher des prestations sociales, vivre de l'aide sociale; **in ~** HRM à jour, à jour de sa cotisation; **make a ~** GEN COMM gagner

benefit[2] **1.** *vt* FIN, GEN COMM profiter à; **2.** *vi* GEN COMM bénéficier, tirer avantage, tirer profit de

benefits n pl WEL avantages sociaux m pl

Benelux n ECON, POL Bénélux m

benevolent[1] *adj* HRM, MGMNT, WEL *organization, trust, fund* de bienfaisance *loc f*; ~ **-authoritative** MGMNT *leadership style* empreint d'une autorité bienveillante

benevolent:[2] ~ **capitalism** n ECON, POL capitalisme bénévole m

Bengali n GEN COMM *language* bengali m

Benin *pr n* GEN COMM Bénin m

Beninese[1] *adj* GEN COMM béninois

Beninese[2] n GEN COMM *person* Béninois m

bent: ~ **lawyer** n *infrml* LAW avocat marron m

bequeath *vt* LAW léguer

bequest n LAW legs m

Bergson: ~ **social welfare function** n ECON, WEL fonction bergsonienne de bien-être social *f*

Berlin *pr n* GEN COMM Berlin *n pr*

Bermuda:[1] ~ **Agreement** n ECON, POL accord des Bermudes m

Bermuda[2] *pr n* GEN COMM Bermudes *f pl*

Bermudan[1] *adj* GEN COMM bermudien

Bermudan[2] n GEN COMM *person* Bermudien m

Bermudian[1] *adj* GEN COMM bermudien

Bermudian[2] n GEN COMM *person* Bermudien m

Bern *pr n* GEN COMM Berne *n pr*

Berne: ~ **Union** n INS Union de Berne *f*

berth n TRANSP *ship, train* place couchée *f*, couchette *f*; ~ **accommodation** n TRANSP places couchées *f pl*; ~ **cargo** n TRANSP *shipping* cargaison au mouillage *f*; ~ **charter** n TRANSP *shipping* affrètement au mouillage m, charte-partie au voyage avec désignation du poste à quai *f*; ~ **terms** n pl TRANSP *shipping* conditions sur les frais du poste *f pl*; ~ **user rate** n TRANSP *shipping* taux d'occupation m, taux d'utilisation d'un quai m; ◆ ~ **no berth** TRANSP *shipping* à quai ou non

berthing n TRANSP *of ships* accostage m

Bertrand: ~ **duopoly model** n ECON modèle duopole de Bertrand m

BES *abbr obs UK (Business Expansion Scheme)* STOCK remplacé par Enterprise Investment Scheme en 1993, plan d'expansion économique m

best:[1] **at ~** *adj* GEN COMM, STOCK *price, order* au mieux

best:[2] ~ **alternative** n GEN COMM choix optimal m,

meilleure option *f*; ~ **bid** n GEN COMM meilleure offre *f*; ~ **bidder** n GEN COMM mieux disant m; ~ **-case scenario** n (ANT *worst-case scenario*) ECON, GEN COMM, POL hypothèse optimiste *f*, meilleur des cas m; ~ **practical means** n pl *(bpm)* GEN COMM meilleur moyen pratique; ~ **price** n GEN COMM meilleur prix, prix le plus avantageux m; ~ **profferer** n GEN COMM plus offrant m; ~ **seller** n MEDIA *book* best-seller m, livre à gros succès m, succès de librairie m, S&M best-seller m; ~ **-selling book** n MEDIA best-seller m, livre à gros succès m

Best's: ~ **Rating** n US INS la société Best *f*, tarification de Best *f*

bet *vt* FIN miser, GEN COMM parier

beta[1] *adj* STOCK bêta

beta[2] n US STOCK action bêta *f*, titre bêta m, valeur bêta *f*; ~ **coefficient** *AmE (cf beta factor BrE)* FIN, STOCK coefficient bêta m, facteur bêta m; ~ **factor** *BrE (cf beta coefficient AmE)* FIN, STOCK coefficient bêta m, facteur bêta m; ~ **share** STOCK action bêta *f*, titre bêta m, valeur bêta *f*; ~ **site** COMP lieu d'essai pilote m; ~ **stock** UK STOCK action bêta *f*, titre bêta m, valeur bêta *f*; ~ **test** COMP *software* bêta test m, essai pilote m, test pilote m; ~ **version** COMP version bêta *f*

better[1] *adj* GEN COMM meilleur; ~ **-off,** GEN COMM plus riche; ◆ ~ **than average** GEN COMM meilleur que la moyenne, mieux que la moyenne; ~ **than expected** GEN COMM meilleur que prévu, mieux qu'attendu, mieux que prévu; ~ **than predicted** GEN COMM mieux que prévu; **you'd be ~ -off selling now** GEN COMM il vaudrait mieux vendre maintenant

better[2] *adv* GEN COMM mieux; ◆ **at or ~** STOCK à la limite ou mieux, limite ou mieux; **or ~ still** GEN COMM ou mieux, STOCK ou mieux, ou à meilleur prix

better:[3] ~ **offer** n GEN COMM offre plus avantageuse *f*, offre plus intéressante *f*, suroffre *f*

betterment n PROP amélioration *f*, plus-value *f*; ~ **tax** TAX impôt sur les plus-values m

betting n LEIS, TAX paris m pl

between *prep* GEN COMM à cheval sur *loc m*

beyond: ~ **repair** *adj* GEN COMM en mauvais état *loc m*, irréparable

BF *abbr (bridge-forecastle)* TRANSP *shipping* château-gaillard m

BFE *abbr UK (Baltic Futures Exchange)* STOCK marché à terme baltique

B5 n ADMIN, COMMS, COMP format B5 m; ~ **letter** ADMIN, COMMS, COMP format B5 m

BFO *abbr (bunker fuel oil)* TRANSP *shipping* mazout de soute m

BFOQ *abbr (bona fide occupational qualification, see GOQ)* HRM qualification professionelle veritable *f*

b/g *abbr dat* GEN COMM *(bonded goods)*, IMP/EXP *(bonded goods)*, IND *(bonded goods)*, TAX *(bonded goods)*, TRANSP *(bonded goods)* marchandises entreposées sous douane *f pl*, marchandises sous douane *f pl*, produits entreposés en douanes *m pl*, TRANSP *(brig) shipping* brick *m* (*vieilli*)

BH *abbr* TRANSP *(bulkhead) shipping* cloison *f*, WEL *(bill of health)* patente *f*, patente de santé *f* (*frml*)

BHC *abbr (British High Commission)* ADMIN hautcomité britannique *m*

BHCEC *abbr (British Health-Care Export Council)* IMP/EXP conseil britannique des exportations de produits sanitaires

BHEC *abbr obs (British Hospitals Export Council)* IMP/EXP conseil britannique des exportations hospitalières

bhp *abbr (brake horsepower)* TRANSP puissance au frein *f*

BHRA *abbr (British Hotels and Restaurants Association)* LEIS association britannique d'hôtels et de restaurants *f*

Bhutan *pr n* GEN COMM Bhoutan *m*

Bhutanese[1] *adj* GEN COMM bhoutanais

Bhutanese[2] *n* GEN COMM *person* Bhoutanais *m*

Bhutani[1] *adj* GEN COMM bhoutanais

Bhutani[2] *n* GEN COMM *person* Bhoutanais *m*

biannual *adj* GEN COMM semestriel

bias *n* GEN COMM parti pris *m*, préjugé *m*

BIC *abbr (British Importers' Confederation)* IMP/EXP confédération des importateurs britanniques

bid[1] *n* FIN offre *f*, offre d'achat *f*, GEN COMM *at auction* enchère *f, for company* offre *f, for contract* soumission *f*, MGMNT *for company* offre *f, for contract* soumission *f*, S&M *at auction* enchère *f*, STOCK offre *f*, offre d'achat *f*; **~ -and-asked price** STOCK cours acheteur et vendeur *m*, cours demandé et offert *m*, cours vendeur et d'achat *m*, l'offre et la demande *f*, prix offert et demandé *m*; **~ -and-offered price** STOCK cours acheteur et vendeur *m*, cours demandé et offert *m*, cours vendeur et d'achat *m*, l'offre et la demande *f*; **~ -ask spread** STOCK écart entre les cours acheteur-vendeur *m*; **~ bond** GEN COMM garantie du moins disant *f*, STOCK caution de participation à une adjudication *f*; **~ closing** STOCK clôture des offres *f*; **~ closing date** STOCK date limite des offres *f*; **~ -offer spread** STOCK écart acheteur-vendeur *m*; **~ opening** GEN COMM ouverture du concours *f*; **~ price** STOCK cours acheteur *m*, prix acheteur *m*, prix d'achat *m*, prix offert *m*; **~ rate** BANK, STOCK taux emprunteur *m*; **~ rent** PROP loyer mis aux enchères *m*; **~ security** FIN garantie de soumission *f*; **~ value** STOCK montant de l'offre *m*; **~ vehicle** GEN COMM moyen d'effectuer une offre; ◆ **~ is received** GEN COMM offre reçue *f*; **make a ~** GEN COMM faire une enchère, faire une offre; **make a firm ~** STOCK faire une offre ferme

bid[2] **1.** *vt* **~ up** FIN faire une offre *loc f*, offrir, GEN COMM *price* faire monter **2.** *vi* MGMNT *for company* faire une offre *loc f, for contract, project* soumissionner, S&M enchérir, *at auction* enchérir,

mettre une enchère, STOCK faire une offre *loc f*, offrir; **~ off** GEN COMM retirer une offre, se retirer d'une enchère

BID *abbr (Bachelor of Industrial Design)* HRM, WEL *degree* ≈ licence en dessin industriel *f, person* ≈ licencié en dessin industriel *m*

bidder *n* FIN *in tender offer* soumissionnaire *mf*, GEN COMM enchérisseur *m*, offrant *m*, soumissionnaire *mf*

bidding *n* GEN COMM *at sale* enchère *f, submission of bids* soumission des offres *f*, S&M enchère *f*; **~ requirements** *n pl* GEN COMM conditions nécessaires pour concourir *f pl*; **~ technique** *n* ECON, GEN COMM, S&M technique des enchères *f*; **~ up** *n* STOCK montée des enchères *f*

bidirectional: ~ printer *n* COMP imprimante allerretour *f*, imprimante bidirectionnelle *f*

BIDS *abbr (British Institute of Dealers in Securities)* STOCK institut britannique des courtiers de valeurs

biennial *adj* GEN COMM biennal, bisannuel

BIF *abbr (British Industries Fair)* IND foire des industries britanniques

BIFFEX *abbr UK (Baltic International Freight Futures Exchange)* TRANSP bourse internationale balte des instruments financiers à terme concernant le fret

big[1] *adj* ECON, GEN COMM gros

big:[2] **~ bag** *n* TRANSP grand sac *m*, grande poche *f, shipping* grand sac souple *m*; **~ bank** *n* BANK banque principale de dépôt; **~ budget** *n* ECON gros budget *m*; **~ business** *n* GEN COMM grosse affaire *f*, grosse entreprise *f*, grosse affaire *f*; **~ company** *n* GEN COMM grande société *f*, grosse affaire *f*, grosse entreprise *f*, société importante *f*; **~ customer** *n* GEN COMM, S&M client important *m*, gros client *m*; **~ employer** *n* HRM gros employeur *m*; **~ exporter** *n* ECON, IMP/EXP, S&M gros exportateur *m*; **~ figure** *n* STOCK *foreign exchange* nombre entier d'un cours d'action; **~ importer** *n* ECON, IMP/EXP, S&M gros importateur *m*; **~ income earner** *n* GEN COMM personne à gros revenus *loc m*; **~ industrial user** *n* GEN COMM utilisateur industriel *m*; **~ industrialized countries** *n pl* ECON, POL grands pays industrialisés *m pl*; **~ investors** *n pl (ANT small investors)* FIN, STOCK grand capital *m*; **~ issue** *n* GEN COMM grave question *f*, problème majeur *m*; **~ name** *n* GEN COMM entreprise réputée *f*, marque réputée *f*; **~ producer** *n* ECON, IND gros producteur *m*; **~ risk** *n* GEN COMM gros risque *m*; **~ tent** *n jarg US* POL large coalition *f*; **~ wheel** *n infrml* GEN COMM gros bonnet *m (infrml)*, magnat *m*

Big: ~ Blue *n infrml* COMP la société IBM® *f*; **the ~ Bang** *n UK* STOCK *of London Stock Exchange* le Big Bang *m*; **the ~ Board** *n infrml US* STOCK la Bourse de New York; **the ~ Four** *n UK* BANK *Barclays, Lloyds, Midland, National Westminster* les quatres grandes banques anglaises

BIL *abbr (business investment loss)* TAX PTPE *(perte au titre d'un placement d'entreprise)*

bilateral[1] *adj* ECON, POL bilatéral

bilateral:[2] **~ aid** *n* (SYN *multilateral aid, tied aid*) ECON, POL *international* aide bilatérale *f*; **~ contract** *n* LAW contrat bilatéral *m*, contrat synallagmatique *m*, PATENTS contrat bilatéral *m*; **~ disbursement** *n* BANK, ECON, POL *development assistance* débours bilatéral *m*, déboursement bilatéral *m*, versement bilatéral *m*; **~ donors** *n pl* BANK, ECON, POL *of development assistance* donateurs bilatéraux *m pl*; **~ loan** *n* BANK, ECON, POL *development* prêt bilatéral *m*; **~ mistake** *n* GEN COMM erreur bilatérale *f*; **~ monopoly** *n* ECON monopole bilatéral *m*; **~ reference** *n* HRM recours bilatéral à l'arbitrage *m*; **~ road agreement** *n* TRANSP accord routier bilatéral *m*; **~ trade agreement** *n* ECON, POL accord commercial bilatéral *m*; **~ trade treaty** *n* ECON, POL traité commercial bilatéral *m*

bilateralism *n* ECON, POL *international trade* bilatéralisme *m*

bilaterals *n pl* ECON bilatérales *f pl*

bilge *n* TRANSP *shipping* bouchain *m*, fond de cale *m*

bill[1] *n* ACC *promissory note*, BANK effet *m*, traite *f*, FIN *promissory note* effet *m*, lettre *f*, traite *f*, GEN COMM facture *f*, mémoire *m*, GEN COMM *BrE (cf check AmE) account in hotel* note *f*, GEN COMM *BrE in restaurant* addition *f*, INS effet *m*, LAW demande introductive d'instance *f*, projet de loi *m*, effet *m*, MEDIA, S&M affiche *f*, placard *m*, STOCK lettre *f*, TAX effet *m*, traite *f*; **~ at double usance** GEN COMM effet à double usance *m*; **~ book** ACC livre des effets *m*, échéancier d'effets *m*; **~ broker** STOCK courtier d'escompte *m*, courtier de change *m*, opérateur principal du marché *m*, OPM; **~ of costs** FIN état des frais *m*; **~ cover** BANK provision d'une lettre de change *f*; **~ diary** STOCK carnet d'échéances *m*, échéancier *m*; **~ of entry** *(B/E)* IMP/EXP *customs* déclaration d'entrée en douane *f*; **~ of exchange** *(B/E)* BANK, FIN, IMP/EXP, STOCK effet de commerce *m*, lettre de change *f (l/c)*, traite *f*; **~ for collection** BANK effet à encaisser *m*, effet à l'encaissement *m*; **~ for discount** BANK effet à l'escompte *m*; **~ of freight** IMP/EXP lettre de voiture *f*; **~ of health** *(BH)* WEL patente *f*, patente de santé *f (frml)*; **~ holding** BANK portefeuille effets *m*, portefeuille effets de change *m*; **~ of lading** *(B/L)* IMP/EXP, TRANSP *freight* connaissement *m (connt)*; **~ of lading fraud** IMP/EXP, TRANSP *freight* tromperie sur le connaissement *f*; **~ of lading issued to a named party** IMP/EXP, TRANSP connaissement délivré à un tiers désigné *m*; **~ of lading ton** *(B/L ton)* GEN COMM tonne connaissement *f*; **~ market** STOCK marché de l'escompte *m*; **~ of materials** IND *production* cahier des charges *m*, nomenclature *f*; **~ merchant** STOCK courtier d'escompte *m*, courtier de change *m*; **~ payable** *(b.p.)* ACC, FIN billet à payer *m*, e. à p, effet à payer *m*, traite à

payer *f (effet à payer)*; **~ payable at sight** ACC effet payable à vue *m*; **~ portfolio** BANK portefeuille effets *m*, portefeuille effets de change *m*; **~ posting** GEN COMM affichage *m*; **~ purchased under resale agreement** ACC, FIN *balance sheet* valeur reçue en pension *f*; **~ receivable** ACC billet à recevoir *m*, e. à r, effet à recevoir *m*, traite à recevoir *f*, FIN e. à r, effet à recevoir *m*, traite à recevoir *f*; **~ of sight** IMP/EXP, INS, TRANSP déclaration provisoire d'importation *f*; **~ sticking** GEN COMM affichage *m*; **~ of store** IMP/EXP, INS, TAX, TRANSP autorisation de réimportation *f*; **~ of sufferance** IMP/EXP, INS, TRANSP lettre d'exemption des droits de douane *f*; **~ to order** BANK, FIN billet à ordre *m*

bill[2] *vt* FIN facturer, S&M *advertising* annoncer

billback *n US* STOCK frais rétroactifs *m pl*

biller *n* GEN COMM *machine* machine à facturer *f*, *person* facturier *m*

billing *n* ACC *of customers*, GEN COMM facturation *f*, S&M *advertising* volume global des contrats billing *m*; **~ cycle** GEN COMM cycle de facturation *m*, rythme de facturation *m*; **~ date** *US* GEN COMM date de facturation *f*; **~ day** ACC jour de facturation *m*; **~ department** *US* GEN COMM service facturation *m*; **~ for the time spent** GEN COMM facturation au temps passé *f*; ♦ **get top ~** LEIS figurer en tête d'affiche

billion *n* *(BN)* BANK, GEN COMM milliard *m*

billionaire *n* GEN COMM milliardaire *mf*

BIM *abbr (British Institute of Management)* MGMNT institut britannique de gestion

bimetallic[1] *adj* ENVIR, IND bimétallique

bimetallic:[2] **~ standard** *n* ENVIR, IND bimétallisme *m*

bimetallism *n* ENVIR, IND bimétallisme *m*

bimodal: **~ distribution** *n* MATH *statistics* distribution bimodale *f*; **~ frequency curve** *n* MATH courbe de fréquence bimodale *f*

bimonthly *adj* COMMS, GEN COMM *every two months* bimestriel, *twice a month* bimensuel

bin:[1] **~-type container** *n* TRANSP *shipping* conteneur à pulvérulents *m*

bin[2] *vt* GEN COMM mettre à la corbeille

binary[1] *adj* COMP, MATH binaire

binary:[2] **~ addition** *n* COMP *programs* addition binaire *f*; **~-coded decimal** *n* COMP décimal codé binaire *m*; **~ coding** *n* COMP codage binaire *m*; **~ digit** *n* COMP *programs* chiffre binaire *m*; **~ file** *n* COMP fichier binaire *m*; **~ number** *n* COMP *programs* nombre binaire *m*, MATH chiffre binaire *m*, nombre binaire *m*; **~ operator** *n* COMP opérateur binaire *m*; **~ search** *n* COMP *programs* recherche binaire *f*, recherche dichotomique *f*, recherche par dichotomie *f*; **~-to-decimal conversion** *n* COMP *of program* conversion binaire-décimale *f*, conversion de binaire en décimale *f*

bind 1. *vt* LAW engager, MEDIA *book* relier; **2.** *vi* IND *machinery* lier, se coincer, LAW être obligatoire

binder n ADMIN (SYN *document holder, file, folder*), GEN COMM (SYN *document holder*) classeur m, INS *US insurance contract* lettre de couverture f, note de couverture f, police provisoire f, PROP *agreement in deal* option d'achat f

binding[1] adj LAW *decision* irrévocable, obligatoire

binding:[2] ~ **agreement** n LAW contrat ferme et définitif m, contrat irrévocable m, contrat qui engage m, contrat qui lie m; ~ **arbitration** n LAW arbitrage obligatoire m, arbitrage qui engage m; ~ **offer** n GEN COMM offre irrévocable f; ~ **promise** n GEN COMM promesse solidaire f; ~ **tender** n GEN COMM soumission contraignante f

binomial[1] adj ECON, MATH binomial

binomial[2] n ECON, MATH binôme m; ~ **charge** ECON charge binomiale f, facturation binomiale f

biochip n COMP biopuce f

biocontrol n ENVIR lutte biologique f

biodegradability n ENVIR biodégradabilité f

biodegradable[1] adj ENVIR biodégradable

biodegradable:[2] ~ **packaging** n ENVIR emballage biodégradable m; ~ **plastic** n ENVIR plastique biodégradable m; ~ **substance** n ENVIR substance biodégradable f

biodegradation n ENVIR biodégradation f, dégradation biologique f

bioeconomics n ECON bioéconomie f

bioengineering n IND bioingénierie f, génie biologique m

biological: ~ **treatment** n ENVIR, IND traitement biologique m

BIOS abbr (*basic input/output operating system*) COMP *software* système BIOS m, système d'exploitation des entrées/sorties m (*système BIOS*)

biotechnology n IND biotechnologie f

biotope n ENVIR biotope m

BIP abbr (*baggage improvement program, baggage improvement programme*) TRANSP programme d'amélioration de la manutention des bagages m

bipolar[1] adj COMP bipolaire

bipolar:[2] ~ **transistor** n COMP *hardware* transistor bipolaire m

birr n GEN COMM birr m

birth: ~ **certificate** n GEN COMM, INS, LAW acte de naissance m, extrait de naissance m; ~ **rate** n GEN COMM taux de natalité m

BIS abbr (*Bank for International Settlements*) BANK BRI (*Banque des Règlements Internationaux*)

BISRA abbr (*British Iron & Steel Research Association*) IND association britannique de recherche sur le fer et l'acier

Bissau pr n GEN COMM Bissau n pr

bit n COMP *programs*, MATH bit m; ~ **configuration** COMP configuration binaire f; ~ **density** COMP densité binaire f; ~ **location** COMP position binaire f; ~ **-mapped character** COMP caractère en mode points m; ~ **-mapped graphics** COMP *graphics* infographie par points binaire f, info-

graphie à adressage binaire f; ~ **rate** COMP débit binaire m; ~ **string** COMP chaîne de bits f; ◆ **a ~ less than** GEN COMM un peu moins de

bits: ~ **per inch** n pl (*bpi*) COMP bits par pouce m pl, nombre de bits par pouce m; ~ **per second** n pl (*bps*) COMP *programs* bits par seconde m pl, nombre de bits par seconde m

bitter: ~ **competition** n ECON, GEN COMM, HRM concurrence acharnée f, concurrence féroce f, IND concurrence acharnée f, concurrence féroce f, concurrence sauvage f, S&M concurrence acharnée f, concurrence féroce f

biweekly adj GEN COMM *every two weeks* bimensuel, *twice a week* bihebdomadaire

bk abbr BANK (*bank*) banque f, TRANSP (*bulktainer*) *shipping* conteneur de vrac m, TRANSP (*bar keel*) *shipping* quille massive f

bkcy abbr (*bankruptcy*) ACC, BANK, FIN, GEN COMM faillite f

bkg abbr (*banking*) BANK opérations bancaires f pl, opérations de banque f pl

bkpt abbr (*bankrupt*) BANK, FIN, HRM failli m, fauché m (*infrml*)

B/L abbr (*bill of lading*) IMP/EXP, TRANSP connt (*connaissement*); ~ **ton** (*bill of lading ton*) GEN COMM tonne connaissement f

black:[1] ~ **books** n pl ECON *takeover bids* livres noirs m pl; ~ **box** n COMP, TRANSP boîte noire f; ~ **capitalism** n ECON, POL capitalisme noir m; ~ **economy** n ECON, FIN économie noire f, économie parallèle f, économie souterraine f; ~ **gold** n ENVIR or noir m, pétrole m; ~ **market** n ECON, S&M marché noir m; ~ **money** n TAX argent non-déclaré au fisc m; ~ **plate** n TRANSP *shipping* tôle noire f; ~ **powder** n ENVIR poudre de mine f; ~ **trading** n GEN COMM commerce des excédents m, commerce des surplus m; ◆ **on the ~ market** GEN COMM au noir

black[2] vt HRM *industrial action* boycotter; ◆ ~ **containers** UK HRM, IND, TRANSP *industrial action* refuser de décharger

Black: ~ **Friday** n STOCK vendredi noir m; ~ **Monday** n STOCK lundi noir m

blacking n HRM blocus m, boycottage m

blackleg n UK HRM briseur de grève m, jaune m

blacklist[1] n FIN, GEN COMM, HRM, IND liste noire f

blacklist[2] vt FIN, GEN COMM, HRM mettre sur la liste noire, mettre à l'index

blacklisted adj FIN, GEN COMM, HRM mis à l'index

blackmail n GEN COMM chantage m

blackout n COMP *of electrical supply* coupure de courant f, panne d'électricité f, panne de courant f, panne de secteur f, MEDIA *TV, radio* interruption des émissions f

Black-Scholes: ~ **Option Pricing Model** n STOCK modèle de Black-Scholes m

blade n IND, TRANSP *on fork-lift trucks* lame f

blank[1] adj ADMIN *form* vierge, à remplir, COMP *disk* vierge, *screen* vide, GEN COMM *paper* blanc

blank[2] *n* GEN COMM blanc *m*; ~ **character** COMP caractère blanc *m*; ~ **check** *AmE*, ~ **cheque** *BrE* BANK chèque en blanc *m*, formule de chèque *f*; ~ **endorsement** STOCK endossement en blanc *m*; ~ **form** GEN COMM formulaire à remplir *m*, imprimé à remplir *m*; ~ **indorsement** *see blank endorsement* ; ~ **order** GEN COMM, S&M commande dont le montant n'est pas spécifié; ~ **receipt** GEN COMM reçu en blanc *m*; ~ **signature** BANK blanc-seing *m*

blank[3] *vt* COMP effacer, supprimer

blanket: ~ **agreement** *n* GEN COMM, HRM accord global *m*; ~ **amount** *n* GEN COMM somme globale *f*; ~ **ballot** *n* US POL vote à bulletin secret *m*; ~ **ban** *n* GEN COMM interdiction générale *f*; ~ **bond** *n* INS garantie générale *f*, STOCK contrat général *m*; ~ **clause** *n* LAW clause de condition générale *f*; ~ **contract** *n* INS contrat global *m*; ~ **cover** *n* INS couverture globale *f*; ~ **coverage** *n* INS couverture globale *f*; ~ **fidelity bond** *n* INS assurance patronale contre les pertes occasionnées par la négligence; ~ **insurance** *n* INS assurance globale *f*; ~ **licence** *n* *BrE* LAW licence d'ensemble *f*, licence de portée générale *f*, licence globale *f*, licence générale *f*; ~ **license** *n* *AmE* *see blanket licence* *BrE*; ~ **medical expense insurance** *n* US INS assurance globale des frais médicaux *f*; ~ **mortgage** *n* BANK hypothèque générale *f*; ~ **order** *n* GEN COMM, S&M commande globale *f*; ~ **policy** *n* INS contrat global *m*, police globale *f*; ~ **rate** *n* ACC taux uniforme *m*, GEN COMM tarif de groupe *m*, tarif global *m*, tarif uniforme *m*; ~ **recommendation** *n* STOCK recommandation générale *f*; ~ **statement** *n* GEN COMM bilan général *m*; ~ **statute** *n* GEN COMM, LAW loi-cadre *f*

blanking *n* COMP effacement *m*

BLCC *abbr* (*Belgo-Luxembourg Chamber of Commerce*) GEN COMM chambre de commerce belgo-luxembourgeoise

bleak *adj* ECON, GEN COMM *outlook* lugubre, morne, sombre

bleed[1] *n* *infrml* MEDIA fond perdu *m*

bleed[2] *vt* GEN COMM faire casquer (*infrml*), saigner (*infrml*), MEDIA *printing* faire déborder; ◆ ~ **sb dry** *infrml* GEN COMM saigner qn à blanc (*infrml*)

bleeding *n* TRANSP saignée *f*

blended: ~ **rate** *n* BANK *of interest* taux d'intérêt mélangé *m*; ~ **value** *n* STOCK valeur mixte *f*

blending *n* ENVIR mélange dosé *m*

BLEU *abbr* (*Belgium-Luxembourg Economic Union*) ECON, POL UEBL (*Union économique Belgique-Luxembourg*)

blight: ~ **notice** *n* PROP avertissement tardif *m*

blighted: ~ **area** *n* ENVIR, WEL *of city* quartier vétuste *m*

blind: ~ **-alley job** *n* *AmE* (*cf dead-end job BrE*) HRM emploi sans avenir *m*, impasse professionnelle *f*; ~ **faith** *n* GEN COMM *in integrity* foi aveugle *f*, foi du charbonnier *f*; ~ **keyboard** *n* COMP clavier aveugle *m*, saisie masquée *f*; ~ **pool** *n* FIN

groupement aveugle *m*; ~ **test** *n* S&M *marketing* blind-test *m*, test anonyme *m*, test aveugle *m*, test en aveugle *m*; ~ **trust** *n* US LAW fidéicommis dont l'actif reste confidentiel

blink *vi* COMP clignoter

blinking: ~ **question mark** *n* COMP point d'interrogation clignotant *m*

bliss: ~ **point** *n* ECON, WEL point de satisfaction maximale *m*, seuil du bien-être *m*

blister: ~ **packaging** *n* S&M *of goods* emballage blister *m*, emballage bulle *m*, emballage transparent *m*

BLK: ~ **CAR** *abbr* (*bulk carrier*) TRANSP *shipping* transporteur en vrac *m*, vraquier *m*

bloc *n* POL bloc *m*

block[1] *n* COMP *section*, ECON *currency* bloc *m*, FIN *of shares* paquet *m*, STOCK inconvertibilité *f*, TRANSP *shipping* poulie *f*; ~ **averaging** ACC établissement d'une moyenne *m*; ~ **booking** LEIS réservation groupée *f*, S&M location groupée *f*, réservation groupée *f*; ~ **coefficient** TRANSP *shipping* coefficient de remplissage *m*; ~ **diagram** COMP ordinogramme *m*, organigramme *m*, schéma fonctionnel *m*; ~ **of flats** *BrE* (*cf apartment building AmE*) PROP immeuble *m*; ~ **funding** ACC, FIN, TAX *public sector* financement global *m*; ~ **grant** *UK* ADMIN enveloppe globale *f*, POL dotation globale de fonctionnement *f*, DGF; ~ **mode** COMP mode bloc *m*; ~ **move** COMP *data or word processing* déplacement de bloc *m*, transfert de bloc *m*; ~ **policy** INS police forfaitaire *f*; ~ **positioner** STOCK négociant en bloc de titres *m*; ~ **purchase** STOCK achat en bloc *m*, achat groupé *m*; ~ **sampling** ACC, FIN *auditing* échantillonnage multiple *m*; ~ **of shares** STOCK bloc d'actions *m*; ~ **stock trader** STOCK négociateur de blocs d'actions *m*; ~ **testing** ACC, FIN *auditing* échantillonnage multiple *m*; ~ **time** TRANSP *aviation* temps cale à cale *m*; ~ **trade** STOCK transaction sur bloc de titres *f*; ~ **transfer** COMP transfert de bloc *m*; ~ **vote** HRM, POL vote bloqué *m*

block[2] *vt* BANK *account*, ECON *currency*, FIN *credit, funds* bloquer, GEN COMM *competition* bloquer, empêcher, *vote, bill* bloquer, entraver, faire blocage *loc m*

blockade *n* HRM blocus *m*

blockbuster *n* LEIS, S&M émission à grand succès *f*

blockbusting *n* *infrml* US ENVIR repossession d'un ghetto/quartier défavorisé par la jeune bourgeoisie blanche, PROP procédure discriminatoire qui consiste à forcer la vente d'une maison à un membre d'une minorité ethnique de façon à dévaluer un quartier, WEL repossession d'un ghetto/quartier défavorisé par la jeune bourgeoisie blanche

blocked: ~ **account** *n* ACC, BANK, FIN compte bloqué *m*; ~ **currency** *n* FIN, IMP/EXP monnaie bloquée *f*

blocking: ~ **off** *n* TRANSP *shipping* accorage *m*, calage *m*

bloodstock *n* TRANSP cheval pur sang *m pl*, pursang *m*; ~ **rate** TRANSP tarif des chevaux de pur sang *m*

blotting: ~ **paper** *n* ADMIN papier buvard *m*

blow¹ *n* GEN COMM coup *m*

blow² *vt* GEN COMM tirer, *money* claquer (*infrml*)

blowout *n* AmE S&M article de détail vendu rapidement très bon marché

BLR *abbr* (*boiler*) IND, TRANSP *shipping* chaudière *f*

blue:¹ ~ **-sky** *adj* AmE GEN COMM factice

blue:² ~ **button** *n jarg* UK STOCK bouton bleu *m* (*jarg*), commis de bourse *m*, grouillot *m*; ~ **chip** *n* (*cf leading stock, penny stock AmE,* ANT *speculative stock*) STOCK valeur de fonds de portefeuille *f*, valeur de premier ordre *f*, valeur de père de famille *f* (*jarg*), valeur sûre *f*; ~ **-chip company** *n* STOCK entreprise de premier ordre *f*, société de premier ordre *f*; ~ **-chip customer** *n* STOCK client de premier ordre *m*, client sûr *m*, client à la papa *m* (*jarg*), un père de famille *loc m* (*jarg*); ~ **-chip industrial** *n* STOCK grande valeur industrielle *f*, société industrielle de premier qualité *f*, valeur industrielle de premier ordre *f*; ~ **-chip security** *n* STOCK valeur de fonds de portefeuille *f*; ~ **-chip stock** *n* STOCK valeur de fonds de portefeuille *f*; ~ **-collar union** *n* HRM syndicat du personnel de production *m*; ~ **-collar worker** *n* HRM col bleu *m*, travailleur manuel *m*; ~ **economy** *n* UK ECON économie officielle *f*; ~ **-sky bargaining** *n* (ANT *good-faith bargaining*) HRM, IND négociation bidon *f* (*jarg*); ~ **-sky law** *n* US LAW, STOCK législation protégeant le public contre les titres douteux, ≈ loi anti-gogos *f*; ~ **-sky research** *n* HRM, IND recherches sans applications immédiates *f pl*

blue³ *vt* GEN COMM claquer (*infrml*)

Blue: ~ **Cross** *n* US INS *hospital plan* Croix Bleue *f*; ~ **laws** *n pl* US LAW, S&M *Sunday trading* législation d'inspiration puritaine sur le repos dominical et qui limite les activités le dimanche; ~ **Shield** *n* US INS *medical-surgical plan* plan de couverture de frais médicaux, ≈ Bouclier Bleu *m*

bluebook *n Can* POL livre bleu *m*

blueprint *n* ADMIN ligne directrice *f*, projet *m*, schéma directeur *m, printing* bleu *m*, dessin héliographique *m*, photocalque *m*, GEN COMM plan *m*, projet *m*, MEDIA *printing* bleu *m*, dessin héliographique *m*, photocalque *m*

blunder *n* GEN COMM gaffe *f*

blurb *n jarg* MEDIA *print* bande de lancement *f*, phrase d'appel *f*, texte de présentation *m*, S&M *publicity* baratin publicitaire *m*

BM *abbr* IND (*board measure*) mesure par pieds-planches *f*, métrage de planche *m*, TRANSP (*boom*) *shipping* bout-dehors *m*, bôme *f*, gui *m*

BMEG *abbr* UK (*Building Materials Export Group*) IMP/EXP groupe d'exportation de matériaux de construction

bmep *abbr* (*brake mean effective pressure*) TRANSP pression effective moyenne de frein *f*

BMLA *abbr* (*British Maritime Law Association*) LAW association britannique de droit maritime

B-movie *n* LEIS film de série B *m*

BN *abbr* (*billion*) BANK, GEN COMM milliard *m*

BNC/ICC *abbr* (*British National Committee of the International Chamber of Commerce*) GEN COMM conseil national britannique de la chambre de commerce international

BNOC *abbr* (*British National Oil Corporation*) IND société nationale des pétroles britanniques

BO *abbr* ADMIN (*branch office*) agence de quartier *f*, agence locale *f*, succursale *f*, GEN COMM (*branch office*) agence *f*, bureau régional *m*, succursale *f*

BOAG *abbr* (*British Overseas Aid Group*) WEL groupe pour l'aide britannique outre-mer

board¹ *n* COMP *hardware* carte *f*, GEN COMM commission *f*, conseil *m*, HRM com, comité *m*, conseil *m*, MGMNT com, comité *m*, commission *f*, conseil *m*, POL com, comité *m*, commission *f*; ~ **of arbitration** HRM conseil d'arbitrage *m*, STOCK conseil arbitral *m*, conseil d'arbitrage *m*; ~ **of conciliation** UK GEN COMM, HRM, IND, LAW commission d'arbitrage *f*; ~ **control** MGMNT contrôle du conseil d'administration *m*; ~ **of directors** GEN COMM, HRM, MGMNT conseil d'administration *m*, conseil de direction *m*, CA; ~ **of estate agents** BrE (*cf board of realtors AmE*) PROP comité de l'immobilier *m*; ~ **of investment** *n* (*BOI*) GEN COMM *Philippines* commission d'investissements *f*; ~ **of management** GEN COMM, MGMNT comité de gestion *m*, directoire *m*; ~ **measure** (*BM*) IND *timber* mesure par pieds-planches *f*, métrage de planche *m*; ~ **meeting** ADMIN, GEN COMM, HRM, MGMNT réunion du conseil d'administration *f*; ~ **of realtors** AmE (*cf board of estate agents BrE*) PROP comité de l'immobilier *m*

board² *vt* TRANSP embarquer

Board: ~ **of Governors of the Federal Reserve System** *n* US ECON *of the 12 central banks* conseil d'administration du système fédéral de réserve; ~ **of Trade** *n* ECON UK (*BOT*) ≈ ministère du Commerce et de l'Industrie *m*, ECON UK Chambre de commerce *f*, GEN COMM UK (*BOT*), POL UK (*BOT*) ≈ ministère du Commerce et de l'Industrie *m*

boarding: ~ **card** *n* TRANSP carte d'embarquement *f*; ~ **gate** *n* LEIS, TRANSP porte d'embarquement *f*; ~ **pass** *n* TRANSP carte d'embarquement *f*

boardroom *n* ADMIN, HRM, MGMNT salle du conseil *f*, STOCK salle des cotations *f*, salle des dépêches *f*

boat *n* TRANSP bateau *m*, navire *m*, vaisseau *m*, *passenger ship* liner *m*, paquebot *m*

boatage *n* TRANSP lamanage *m*

boatload *n* TRANSP cargaison *f*

boatswain *n* TRANSP quartier-maître *m*

bodily: ~ **injury** *n* INS blessure corporelle *f*

body *n* GEN COMM organisme *m*; ~ **of creditors**

ACC, FIN masse des créditeurs *f,* masse des fournisseurs *f;* ~ **language** HRM, MGMNT langage corporel *m,* langage gestuel *m;* ~ **shop** TRANSP atelier de carrosserie *m*

BOF *abbr (Balance for Official Financing)* ACC, ECON balance des financements officiels *f*

bogged: get ~ down in *phr* GEN COMM s'enliser dans

bogie *n* TRANSP *rail* bogie *m;* ~ **lift** TRANSP lève-bogie *m*

Bogotá *pr n* GEN COMM Bogotá *n pr*

bogus: ~ **company** *n* GEN COMM société fantôme *f,* société fictive *f*

BOI *abbr (Board of Investment)* GEN COMM *Philippines* commission d'investissements *f*

boiler *n (BLR)* IND, TRANSP *shipping* chaudière *f;* ~ **insurance** US IND, INS assurance de chaudière *f;* ~ **and machinery insurance** IND, INS assurance des chaudières et machines *f;* ~ **manufacturer** IND *production* chaudronnier *mf;* ~ **room** INS US société proposant des produits financiers douteux, TRANSP *shipping* chaufferie *f;* ~ **survey** TRANSP *shipping* visite de la chaudière *f*

boilerplate *n* ADMIN modèle de convention *m,* GEN COMM *draft, contract* paragraphe passe-partout *m*

bold[1] *adj* COMP, MEDIA *printing* gras

bold:[2] ~ **printing** *n* COMP, MEDIA impression en gras *f;* ~ **type** *n* COMP, MEDIA *printing* caractère gras *m*

boldface: ~ **character** *n* COMP, MEDIA *printing* caractère gras *m*

bolivar *n* GEN COMM bolivar *m*

Bolivia *pr n* GEN COMM Bolivie *f*

Bolivian[1] *adj* GEN COMM bolivien

Bolivian[2] *n* GEN COMM *person* Bolivien *m*

bollard *n* TRANSP *shipping* bollard *m;* ~ **pull** *(b.p.)* TRANSP *shipping* force de tirage *f*

bolster *vt* GEN COMM soutenir; ♦ ~ **the confidence of** GEN COMM renforcer la confiance de; ~ **up sb's confidence** GEN COMM redonner confiance à qn

bomb: ~ **scare** *n* GEN COMM alerte à la bombe *f*

bona fide:[1] *adj* GEN COMM sérieux, véritable

bona fide:[2] ~ **clause** *n* FIN, GEN COMM *of letter of credit* clause sérieuse *f;* ~ **holder** *n* STOCK détenteur de bonne foi *m,* porteur de débentures *m;* ~ **occupational qualification** *n AmE (BFOQ, genuine occupational qualification)* HRM qualification professionnelle véritable *f;* ~ **offer** *n* GEN COMM offre ferme *f,* offre sérieuse *f;* ~ **price** *n* GEN COMM prix ferme *m;* ~ **purchaser** *n* GEN COMM acheteur de bonne foi *m;* ~ **trade union** *n* UK HRM syndicat de bonne foi *m*

bona fides *n* LAW bonne foi *f*

bonanza *n AmE* IND *mining* filon riche *m*

bona vacantia *n* LAW, PROP déshérence *f*

bond *n* ADMIN contrat *m,* engagement *m,* FIN obligation *f, certificate* bon *m,* titre *m,* GEN COMM contrat *m,* engagement *m,* INS caution *f,* LAW *guarantee* engagement écrit *m,* STOCK

obligation *f, short-term* bon *m, sterling* obligation *f;* ~ **anticipation note** *n (BAN)* STOCK bon de financement anticipé *m,* papier anticipant une obligation *m;* ~ **with bond-buying warrant** *n* STOCK obligation à bons de souscription d'obligations *f,* OBSO; ~ **broker** *n* STOCK courtier en obligations *m,* courtier obligataire *m;* ~ **call option** *n (ANT bond put option)* STOCK option d'achat sur obligation *f;* ~ **capital** *n* STOCK capital obligations *m,* valeur obligataire *f;* ~ **certificate** *n* STOCK certificat d'obligation *m,* certificat obligataire *m;* ~ **conversion** *n* STOCK conversion d'obligations *f,* conversion de bons *f;* ~ **coupon** *n* STOCK coupon *m,* coupon obligataire *m;* ~ **creditor** *n* STOCK créancier obligataire *m;* ~ **cum warrant** *n* STOCK obligation à bon de souscription *f,* obligation à bons de souscription en actions *f,* obligation à warrant *f,* OBSA; ~ **dealer** *n* STOCK courtier en obligations *m;* ~ **dealings** *n pl* STOCK courtage d'obligations *m,* transactions sur obligations *f pl;* ~ **debt** *n* STOCK dette obligataire *f;* ~ **denomination** *n* STOCK libellé d'une obligation *m,* valeur obligataire *f;* ~ **with detachable warrant** *n* STOCK obligation avec bon de souscription détachable *f;* ~ **discount** *n* STOCK escompte d'émission d'obligations *m,* escompte non-amorti d'obligations *m,* prime d'émission *f;* ~ **equivalent yield** *n* STOCK rendement équivalent obligataire *m,* rendement équivalent sur obligation *m;* ~ **ex warrant** *n* STOCK obligation sans bon de souscription *f,* obligation sans bon de souscription d'actions *f,* obligation sans warrant *f;* ~ **features** *n pl* STOCK caractéristiques de l'obligation *f pl,* nature des obligations *f;* ~ **financing** *n* STOCK financement obligataire *m,* financement par obligation *m;* ~ **fund** *n* STOCK fonds obligataire *m;* ~ **futures contract** *n* FIN contrat à terme sur obligation *m,* STOCK contrat obligataire à terme *m,* contrat à terme sur obligation *m;* ~ **holdings** *n pl* STOCK avoirs en obligations *m pl,* obligations en portefeuille *f pl;* ~ **indenture** *n* STOCK contrat obligataire *m;* ~ **index** *n* STOCK indice des obligations *m;* ~ **interest** *n* STOCK intérêt d'obligation *m,* intérêt obligataire *m,* intérêt sur obligation *m;* ~ **with interest paid in advance** *n* STOCK bon à intérêts payés d'avance *m,* BIPA; ~ **issue** *n* BANK emprunt obligataire *m,* STOCK emprunt obligataire *m,* émission d'obligations *f,* émission de bons *f;* ~ **issue operation** *n* BANK emprunt obligataire *m,* STOCK emprunt obligataire *m,* opération d'émission obligataire *f,* émission d'obligations *f,* émission de bons *f;* ~ **issuing price** *n* STOCK prix d'émission d'une obligation *m,* prix d'émission obligataire *m;* ~ **liability** *n* STOCK dette obligataire *f,* emprunt-obligation *m;* ~ **loan** *n* BANK, STOCK emprunt obligataire *m;* ~ **market** *n* STOCK marché obligataire *m;* ~ **market rally** *n* STOCK reprise du marché obligataire *f;* ~ **market rate** *n* STOCK taux de marché obligataire *m,* TMO; ~ **with monthly-paid interest** *n* STOCK bon à intérêts mensuels *m,* BIM;

~ **number** n BANK, STOCK numéro d'obligation m; ~ **option** n STOCK option sur obligations f; ~ **options market** n STOCK marché des options sur obligations m; ~ **outstanding** n STOCK obligation en circulation f; ~ **payable** n STOCK dette obligataire f, emprunt-obligation m; ~ **pool** n STOCK gisement m; ~ **portfolio** n STOCK portefeuille d'obligations m; ~ **power** n STOCK procuration autorisant le transfert d'obligations; ~ **premium** n STOCK prime d'émission f, prime d'émissions d'obligations f; ~ **price** n STOCK cours de l'obligation m; ~ **principal** n STOCK capital obligataire m, principal d'une obligation m; ~ **proceeds** n pl STOCK recettes obligataires f pl; ~ **put option** n (ANT bond call option) STOCK option de vente sur obligation f; ~ **rate** n STOCK taux d'intérêt obligataire m; ~ **rating** n STOCK évaluation d'une obligation f; ~ **rating agency** n STOCK agence de notation des obligations f, agence de notation obligataire f; ~ **redemption premium** n ACC, STOCK prime de remboursement des obligations f; ~ **refunding** n STOCK refinancement d'obligations m; ~ **sales** n pl STOCK ventes d'obligations f pl; ~ **sinking fund** n STOCK fonds pour amortissement des obligations m, réserve pour amortissement des obligations f; ~ **sold prior to issue** n STOCK adjudication d'obligations avant émission f, obligation vendue avant l'émission f; ~ **specialist** n STOCK spécialiste d'obligations m, spécialiste en obligations m; ~ **store** n GEN COMM entrepôt en douane m; ~ **switch** n STOCK arbitrage d'obligations m; ~ **switching** n STOCK arbitrage d'obligations m; ~ **terms** n pl STOCK caractéristiques de l'obligation f pl, conditions d'émission d'une obligation f pl; ~ **trader** n STOCK négociant m, négociateur d'obligations m, opérateur en obligations m, spéculateur en obligations m; ~ **trading** n STOCK négociation d'obligations f, opérations sur obligations f pl; ~ **trading department** n STOCK service des opérations sur obligations m; ~ **turnover** n STOCK valeur des transactions obligataires f, volume des transactions sur obligations m; ~ **underwriting** n STOCK garantie d'émission obligataire f, souscription d'obligations f; ~ **valuation** n STOCK évaluation d'une obligation f, évaluation obligataire f; ~ **warrant** n STOCK bon de souscription d'obligation m, warrant m; ~ **with warrant** n STOCK obligation à bon de souscription f, obligation à warrant f; ~ **with warrant attached** n STOCK obligation à bon de souscription f, obligation à warrant f; ~ **washing** n FIN vente de valeurs à revenu fixe f, vente fictive d'obligations f, STOCK fonds empruntés m pl, vente de valeurs à revenu fixe f; ~ **year basis** n TAX année de l'obligation f; ~ **yield** n STOCK rendement d'un bon m, rendement de l'obligation m; ◆ **in ~** (IB) IMP/EXP, TAX en entrepôt sous douane

bonded: ~ **cargo** n GEN COMM, IMP/EXP, IND, TAX, TRANSP cargaison en douane f, marchandises entreposées sous douane f pl, marchandises sous

douane f pl; ~ **debt** n STOCK dette garantie par nantissement f, dette garantie par obligations f, dette obligataire f; ~ **elevator** n GEN COMM silo en douane m; ~ **goods** n pl (b/g) GEN COMM, IMP/EXP, IND, TAX, TRANSP marchandises entreposées sous douane f pl, marchandises sous douane f pl, produits entreposés en douanes m pl; ~ **warehouse** n GEN COMM, IMP/EXP, TAX entrepôt en douane m

bondholder n STOCK détenteur d'obligations m, obligataire mf, porteur d'obligations m

bondowner n BANK propriétaire d'obligations m

bone: ~ **of contention** n GEN COMM contentieux m

bonus n FIN dividende exceptionnel m, GEN COMM gratification f, prime f, HRM prime f, STOCK dividende exceptionnel m; ~ **interest payment** FIN paiement d'intérêts supplémentaires m; ~ **issue** UK FIN, STOCK attribution d'actions gratuites f, émission d'actions gratuites f; ~ **payment** HRM prime f, STOCK dividende exceptionnel m; ~ **rate of interest** BANK taux d'intérêt bonifié m; ~ **reserve** GEN COMM prime sur réserve capitalisée f; ~ **savings account** BANK compte d'épargne à taux bonifié m; ~ **savings rate** BANK taux d'épargne bonifié m; ~ **scheme** HRM programme de primes d'encouragement m, programme de primes de rendement m; ~ **share** STOCK action donnée en prime f, action gratuite f; ~ **stock** STOCK action donnée en prime f, action gratuite f

boob n GEN COMM gaffe f

book[1] n ACC livre m, livre de comptabilité m, BANK livret de banque m, livret de compte m, FIN livre de comptabilité m, GEN COMM livre m, STOCK carnet m, registre m, in underwriting of securities livre m; ~ **of accounts** n ACC, BANK, FIN grand livre m, livre de comptes m; ~ **cost** n ACC coût d'acquisition comptable m; ~ **debt** n ACC, ECON, FIN compte clients m, compte créance m; ~ **depreciation** n ACC amortissement comptable m; ~ **entry** n ACC, FIN écriture comptable f; ~ **-entry securities** n pl STOCK titres avec certification informatique m pl, valeurs sans certificat f pl; ~ **of final entry** n BANK grand livre m; ~ **of first entry** n ACC jl, journal m; ~ **inventory** n STOCK inventaire comptable m, stock comptable m; ~ **-keeper** n ACC aide-comptable mf, comptable mf, HRM comptable mf; ~ **-keeping** n ACC, FIN comptabilité f, tenue des comptes f, tenue des livres comptables f; ~ **loss** n (ANT book profit) ACC perte comptable f; ~ **of original entry** n ACC jl, journal m; ~ **of prime entry** n ACC jl, journal m; ~ **profit** n (ANT book loss) ACC bénéfice comptable m; ~ **rate of return** n ACC taux de rendement comptable m; ~ **reviewer** n GEN COMM, MEDIA critique littéraire m; ~ **royalty** n GEN COMM, MEDIA droit d'auteur m; ~ **squaring** n STOCK liquidation des positions f; ~ **token** n GEN COMM chèque-livre m, S&M chèque-cadeau m; ~ **value** n ACC bookkeeping, FIN valeur comptable f; ~ **value of investment** n ACC, FIN valeur comptable d'investissement *f*; ♦ **by the** ~ GEN COMM à la lettre; **for** ~ **purposes** ACC à des fins comptables

book[2] **1.** *vt* ACC *book-keeping* comptabiliser, ADMIN, GEN COMM, LEIS retenir, réserver, S&M, TRANSP réserver; ~ **in** GEN COMM inscrire; ~ **out** GEN COMM inscrire à l'heure de sortie **2.** *vi* ~ **in** GEN COMM se faire enregistrer, *at airport* retenir une place, *at hotel* prendre une chambre, retenir une chambre, LEIS *at airport* retenir une place, *at hotel* prendre une chambre, retenir une chambre; ~ **out** ADMIN signer en partant, signer à la sortie, GEN COMM quitter sa chambre, signer en partant, signer à la sortie, LEIS *at hotel* quitter sa chambre, MGMNT signer en partant, signer à la sortie; ♦ ~ **early** GEN COMM, LEIS retenir dès maintenant; ~ **in advance** GEN COMM, LEIS louer à l'avance, retenir à l'avance, réserver à l'avance; ~ **a room** GEN COMM, LEIS réserver une chambre

booked:[1] ~ **up** *adj* GEN COMM complet, entièrement réservé

booked:[2] ~ **traffic** *n* TRANSP trafic réservé *m*

bookie *n infrml* LEIS *sport* bookmaker *m*

booking *n* GEN COMM *of orders* enregistrement *m*, *travel and tourism* réservation *f*, LEIS *theatre*, S&M *of advertising space*, TRANSP réservation *f*; ~ **confirmation** GEN COMM, TRANSP confirmation de réservation *f*; ~ **fee** GEN COMM frais d'agence *m pl*, frais de réservation *m pl*; ~ **note** TRANSP engagement de fret *m*; ~ **office** LEIS billetterie *f*, guichet *m*, guichet des billets *m*, bureau de locations *m*, bureau des réservations *m*, guichet de vente des billets *m*, TRANSP guichet *m*, guichet de vente des billets *m, rail* billetterie *f*, guichet des billets *m*; ~ **order** GEN COMM commande de réservation *f*, demande de réservation *f*, S&M commande de réservation *f*; ~ **system** S&M plan de réservation *m*

booklet *n* COMMS, GEN COMM brochure *f*, livret *m*, MEDIA livret *m*

bookmaker *n* LEIS *sport* bookmaker *m*

books:[1] **off the** ~ *adj* GEN COMM non-comptabilisé

books[2] *n pl* ACC livre de comptes *m*, registres *m pl*, registres et pièces comptables *m pl*, écritures *f pl*, ADMIN registres *m pl*, BANK, FIN livre de comptes *m*, GEN COMM registres *m pl*, registres et pièces comptables *m pl*; ~ **of account** ACC livres comptables *m pl*, registres comptables *m pl*, écritures *f pl*; ♦ **in the** ~ ACC, GEN COMM enregistré sur les livres

Boolean[1] *adj* COMP booléen

Boolean:[2] ~ **algebra** *n* COMP *program*, MATH algèbre de Boole *f*; ~ **variable** *n* COMP *program* variable booléenne *f*

boom[1] *n* ECON boom *m*, essor *m*, période de prospérité *f, in prices* flambée *f*, montée en flèche *f, in trade* forte hausse *f*, GEN COMM essor *m*, forte expansion *f*, forte progression *f, in orders* surcroît *m*, vague *f*, IND, POL essor *m*, TRANSP *shipping* bout-dehors *m*, bôme *f*, gui *m*, tangon *m*

boom[2] *vi* ECON flamber, monter en flèche, être en forte hausse *loc f*

boomlet *n* ECON expansion de faible amplitude *f*

boondoggle *n infrml US* HRM projet inutile *m*, travail sans valeur *m*

boost[1] *n* ECON relance *f*

boost[2] *vt* ECON *demand, exports* accroître, développer, *economy* relancer, GEN COMM stimuler, S&M relancer, *sales* pousser, relancer

booster *n* GEN COMM stimulant *m*, TRANSP *dangerous classified cargo movement* charge explosive *f*; ~ **training** HRM recyclage *m*, stage de recyclage *m*

boot[1] *n BrE (cf trunk AmE)* TRANSP coffre *m*; ~ **disk** COMP disque d'initialisation *m*

boot[2] *vt* COMP lancer; ~ **off** *infrml* LAW liquider; ~ **out** *infrml* HRM virer *(infrml)*; ~ **up** COMP *computer* amorcer, initialiser, lancer; ♦ ~ **sb out** *infrml* HRM flanquer qn à la porte *(infrml)*

bootblack: ~ **economy** *n infrml* ECON économie de main-d'oeuvre *f*

booting *n* COMP amorçage *m*, lancement *m*

bootstrap *vt jarg* COMP amorcer, exécuter sous tension, initialiser, lancer

bootup *n* COMP amorçage *m*, lancement *m*

BOP[1] *abbr (balance of payments)* ECON, POL balance des paiements *f*

BOP:[2] ~ **deficit** *n (ANT BOP surplus)* ECON déficit de la balance des paiements *m*; ~ **surplus** *n (ANT BOP deficit)* ECON excédent de la balance des paiements *m*

border *n* ECON, GEN COMM, IMP/EXP frontière *f*; ~ **control** IMP/EXP, POL contrôle aux frontières *m*; ~ **police** HRM Police de l'Air et des Frontières *f*, P.A.F.; ~ **trade** GEN COMM, IMP/EXP commerce frontalier *m*

bordereau *n* [*pl* -aux] GEN COMM bordereau *m*

borderline: ~ **case** *n* GEN COMM cas-limite *m*

bore *n* TRANSP *shipping* mascaret *m*

born: ~ **leader** *n* GEN COMM, HRM, MGMNT leader né *m*

BORO *abbr (bulk-oil and roll-on/roll-off vessel)* TRANSP *shipping* pétrolier-vraquier-roulier *m*

borough *n* ADMIN municipalité *f*, GEN COMM *in London* arrondissement *m*, POL municipalité *f*

borrow *vt* ACC, BANK, FIN emprunter, reporter, GEN COMM emprunter, STOCK emprunter, reporter; ~ **against** FIN *income* emprunter en fonction de; ~ **from** BANK emprunter à; ♦ ~ **at call** BANK emprunter à vue; ~ **at interest** BANK emprunter à intérêt; ~ **interest-free** BANK emprunter sans intérêt; ~ **long** *(ANT borrow short)* STOCK emprunter à long terme; ~ **money** BANK emprunter de l'argent; ~ **on securities** STOCK emprunter sur titres; ~ **short** *(ANT borrow long)* STOCK emprunter à court terme

borrowed: ~ **capital** *n* BANK, FIN capitaux empruntés *m pl*; ~ **funds** *n pl* BANK emprunts *m pl*, fonds empruntés *m pl*, FIN emprunts *m pl*, vente fictive d'obligations *f*; ~ **money** *n* BANK, FIN, TAX argent emprunté *m*; ~ **reserve** *n* BANK réserve d'emprunt *f*; ~ **stock** *n* STOCK titres empruntés *m pl*

borrower *n* BANK, FIN emprunteur *m*; ~ **country** ECON pays emprunteur *m*

borrowing *n* ACC, BANK, ECON, FIN, GEN COMM, STOCK emprunt *m*; ~ **abroad** BANK, ECON, FIN, GEN COMM, STOCK emprunt de capitaux étrangers *m*; ~ **allocation** ACC, BANK, ECON, FIN, GEN COMM octroi d'un emprunt *m*; ~ **bank** BANK banque de crédit *f*; ~ **by banks** BANK emprunts bancaires *m pl*; ~ **ceiling** ACC, BANK, ECON, FIN, GEN COMM plafond des emprunts *m*; ~ **cost** ACC, BANK, ECON, FIN, GEN COMM coût de l'emprunt *m*; ~ **customer** ACC, BANK, ECON, FIN, GEN COMM client emprunteur *m*; ~ **of external funds** ACC, BANK, ECON, FIN, GEN COMM emprunt de fonds externes *m*; ~ **facility** BANK facilité de crédit *f*, source d'emprunts *f*; ~ **fee** ACC, BANK, FIN, GEN COMM frais *m pl*; ~ **in the Euromarket** ECON, FIN, GEN COMM, STOCK emprunt sur le marché européen des capitaux *m*; ~ **in the money market** ECON, FIN, GEN COMM, STOCK emprunt sur le marché monétaire *m*; ~ **limit** ACC, BANK, ECON, FIN, GEN COMM plafond des emprunts *m*; ~ **potential** ACC, BANK, ECON, FIN, GEN COMM potentiel d'emprunt *m*; ~ **power** ACC, BANK, ECON, FIN, GEN COMM capacité d'emprunt *f*, capacité de crédit *f*, possibilité d'emprunt *f*, STOCK capacité d'emprunt de titres *f*; ~ **power of securities** STOCK pouvoir d'emprunt des titres *m*; ~ **rate** BANK, ECON, FIN taux d'intérêt des emprunts *m*; ~ **ratio** ACC, BANK, FIN ratio d'emprunt *m*, taux d'emprunt *m*; ~ **requirement** BANK besoins de crédit *m pl*

Bosnia *pr n* GEN COMM Bosnie *f*

Bosnia-Herzegovina *pr n* GEN COMM Bosnie-Herzégovine *f*

Bosnian[1] *adj* GEN COMM bosniaque, bosnien

Bosnian[2] *n* GEN COMM *person* Bosniaque *mf*, Bosnien *m*, Bosnienne *f*

boss *n infrml* (SYN *chief, head, senior*) ADMIN, HRM, MGMNT chef *m*; ◆ **be one's own ~** HRM être son propre patron

Boston: ~ **Stock Exchange** *n* STOCK Bourse de Boston *f*

bosun *n* TRANSP quartier-maître *m*

BOT *abbr UK* (*Board of Trade*) ECON Chambre de commerce *f*, ECON, GEN COMM, POL ≈ ministère du Commerce et de l'Industrie *m*

both: ~ **-to-blame collision clause** *n* INS *maritime* clause de responsabilité réciproque en cas d'abordage *f*

Botswana[1] *adj* GEN COMM de Botswana

Botswana[2] *pr n* GEN COMM Botswana *m*

bottle *n* GEN COMM, S&M bouteille *f*, chopine *f*; ~ **bank** ENVIR conteneur de collecte de verre usé *m*

bottled: ~ **-up** *adj* GEN COMM *price increase* comprimé

bottleneck *n* ECON, IND goulot d'étranglement *m*, TRANSP *in road* rétrécissement de la chaussée *m*, *of traffic* bouchon *m*, embouteillage *m*; ~ **inflation** ECON inflation bouchon *f*, IND inflation due à des goulets d'étranglement dans l'économie, inflation bouchon *f*

bottlescrew *n* (SYN *turnbuckle*) TRANSP ridoir *m*

bottom:[1] ~ **-of-the-range** *adj* (ANT *top-of-the-range*) GEN COMM, S&M bas de gamme; ~ **-up** *adj* GEN COMM de la base au sommet *loc f*, en partant de la base *loc f*

bottom[2] *n* ECON creux *m*, point bas *m*, plancher *m*, FIN, GEN COMM plancher *m*, HRM *of organization* bas *m*, base *f*, IND plancher *m*, STOCK cours plancher *m*, plancher *m*, TRANSP *of ship* fond *m*; ~ **end of the range** S&M bas de gamme du marché *m*; ~ **fisher** STOCK *investor* charognard *m*; ~ **line** ECON, FIN plancher *m*, GEN COMM minimum *m*, plancher *m*, résultat *m*, IND, STOCK plancher *m*; ~ **line profit** ACC, FIN, GEN COMM, TAX bénéfices nets *m pl*, résultat net *m*; ~ **-line profit margin** ACC, FIN, GEN COMM marge bénéficiaire du résultat net *f*, marge de profit finale *f*; ~ **price** GEN COMM cours le plus bas *m*, STOCK cours le plus bas *m*, cours plancher *m*; **the ~ line** GEN COMM *overall result* l'essentiel *m*; ~ **-up approach to investing** FIN approche pyramidale d'investissement *f*; ~ **-up linkage model** ECON modèle de liaison ascendante *m*, modèle de lien dessus-dessous *m*; ~ **-up management** MGMNT gestion consultative *f*, gestion de bas en haut *f*; ◆ **any one ~** (*AOB*) INS *marine*, TRANSP par navire; ~ **dropped out** *jarg* (*BDO*) STOCK effondrement du cours plancher *m*, effondrement du prix plancher *m*, marché effondré; **the ~ has dropped out of the market** GEN COMM le marché s'est effondré; **the ~ has fallen out of the market** GEN COMM le marché s'est effondré

bottom[3] *vi* ECON, GEN COMM, STOCK atteindre son niveau le plus bas, atteindre son niveau plancher; ~ **out** ECON atteindre son niveau plancher, *market, prices, graph* atteindre son niveau le plus bas, tomber au-dessous du minimum, tomber au-dessous du plancher, GEN COMM *market, prices, graph* atteindre son niveau le plus bas, tomber au-dessous du minimum, tomber au-dessous du plancher, STOCK *market, prices, graph* atteindre son niveau le plus bas, atteindre son niveau plancher, tomber au-dessous du minimum, tomber au-dessous du plancher

bottomry: ~ **bond** *n* INS *marine* contrat à la grosse aventure *m*

bought: ~ **book** *n* ACC livre des achats *m*, livre des fournisseurs *m*; ~ **contract** *n* STOCK bordereau d'achat *m*; ~ **day book** *n* ACC livre des achats *m*, livre des fournisseurs *m*; ~ **deal** *n* STOCK prise ferme *f*, transaction d'achat *f*; ~ **journal** *n* ACC livre des achats *m*, livre des fournisseurs *m*; ~ **ledger** *n* ACC livre des achats *m*, livre des fournisseurs *m*; ~ **note** *n* STOCK *of broker* bordereau d'achat *m*

Boulwareism *n US* HRM négociation collective *f*

bounce 1. *vt* BANK *cheque* refuser pour défaut de provision, refuser pour non-provision **2.** *vi* GEN COMM *cheque* être sans provision *loc f*; **~ back** GEN COMM *currency, prices* remonter; **~ up** GEN COMM *price* repartir à la hausse

bounced: **~ check** *n AmE*, **~ cheque** *n BrE (cf bum cheque, uncovered cheque)* BANK chèque en bois *m (infrml)*, chèque sans provision *m*

bound: **~ for** *phr* TRANSP à destination de *loc f*

boundary *n* PROP frontière *f*, limites *f pl*; **~ constraint** MATH contrainte de limite *f*

bounded: **~ rationality** *n* MATH rationalité limitée *f*

bounty *n* STOCK *shares to employees* prime *f*, subvention *f*

bourgeoisie *n* ECON, POL bourgeoisie *f*

bow: **~ and stern thruster** *n* TRANSP *shipping* propulseur avant et arrière *m*; **~ thruster** *n* TRANSP *shipping* propulseur d'étrave *m*; **~ visor** *n* TRANSP masque d'étrave *m*, visière d'étrave *f*

bows *n pl* TRANSP *shipping* avant *m*

box: **~ container** *n (bx)* TRANSP *shipping* conteneur sec *m*; **~ K** *n (box keel)* TRANSP *shipping* quille caisson *f*; **~ keel** *n (box K)* TRANSP *shipping* quille caisson *f*; **~ number** *n* COMMS, MEDIA *newspaper* numéro d'annonce *m*, numéro de référence *m*; **~ office** *n* LEIS guichet de vente des billets *m*, guichet des billets *m, theatre* bureau de location *m*, guichet *m*; **~ office takings** *n pl* LEIS recette *f*; **~ pallet** *n* TRANSP palette-caisse *f*; **~ rate** *n* TRANSP tarif à la boîte *m*; **~ spread** *n* STOCK combinaison d'écarts verticaux *f*, opération mixte symétrique *f*; **~ trailer** *n* TRANSP *shipping* remorque fourgon *f*; ◆ **be a ~ office hit** *n jarg* LEIS *theatre* faire courir les foules

boxcar *n AmE (cf goods truck BrE)* TRANSP *rail* wagon de marchandises couvert *m*

boxer: **~ class** *n* TRANSP *shipping* navire porte-conteneurs *m*

boycott[1] *n* ECON boycottage *m*, grève des achats *f*, HRM boycott *m*, LEIS *sport* boycottage *m*

boycott[2] *vt* ECON, GEN COMM, HRM boycotter

b.p. *abbr* ACC *(bill payable)*, FIN *(bill payable)* b. à p. *(billet à payer)*, TRANSP *(bollard pull) shipping* force de tirage *f*

BPA *abbr (British Ports Association)* TRANSP association des ports britanniques

bpi *abbr (bits per inch)* COMP bits par pouce *m pl*, nombre de bits par pouce *m*

bpm *abbr (best practical means)* GEN COMM meilleur moyen pratique

bps *abbr (bits per second)* COMP *programs* bps *(bits par seconde)*

BPSS *abbr (barge-mounted production and storage system)* TRANSP *shipping* système de production et d'entreposage sur allège *m*

BR *abbr* ACC *(bill receivable)* b. à r. *(billet à recevoir)*, TRANSP *UK (British Rail)* chemins de fer britanniques, ≈ SNCF *(Société nationale des chemins de fer français)*

bracket *n* GEN COMM *category* classe *f*, groupe *m*, *prices, taxes* fourchette *f*, tranche *f*, TAX *prices, taxes* fourchette *f*, tranche *f*; **~ creep** ECON, TAX glissement d'une tranche d'imposition à l'autre *m*

Bradbury *n UK* BANK billet de banque Bradbury

Brady: **~ Commission** *n US* STOCK commission Brady *f*

brain: **~ drain** *n infrml* HRM exode des cerveaux *m*, fuite de cerveaux *f*

brainchild *n infrml* GEN COMM idée personnelle *f*, invention personnelle *f*

brainstorm *vi* MGMNT faire du brainstorming *loc m*

brainstorming *n* MGMNT brainstorming *m*, remue-méninges *m*

brake: **~ horsepower** *n (bhp)* TRANSP puissance au frein *f*; **~ mean effective pressure** *n (bmep)* TRANSP pression effective moyenne de frein *f*

branch *n* BANK *of bank* ag., agence *f*, succursale *f*, *of credit institution* succursale *f*, COMP branchement *m*, GEN COMM ag., agence *f*, filiale *f*, *shop, bank* succursale *f*; **~ address** BANK, COMP adresse de branchement *f*, adresse de succursale *f*; **~ bank** BANK banque à succursales *f*; **~ banking** BANK activité bancaire par succursales *f*; **~ banking system** BANK réseau de succursales bancaires *m*, système de banque à succursales *m*; **~ economy** ECON économie de filiales *f*, économie de succursale *f*; **~ line** TRANSP *rail* embranchement *m*, ligne secondaire *f*, voie d'embranchement *f*; **~ manager** BANK *of bank* directeur d'agence *m*, directeur de succursale *m*, gérant de succursale *m*, FIN directeur d'agence *m*, GEN COMM directeur d'agence *m*, directeur de succursale *m*, gérant de succursale *m*; **~ network** BANK, GEN COMM réseau de succursales *m*; **~ number** BANK numéro de succursale *m*; **~ office** *(BO)* ADMIN agence de quartier *f*, agence locale *f*, succursale *f*, GEN COMM agence *f (ag.)*, bureau régional *m*, succursale *f*; **~ office manager** GEN COMM, MGMNT chef d'agence *m*, directeur de succursale *m*; **~ operation** GEN COMM agence *f*, succursale *f*

brand:[1] **~-new** *adj* GEN COMM flambant neuf, tout neuf

brand[2] *n* GEN COMM *of product, service* marque *f*, marque de contrôle *f*, S&M *of product, service* marque *f*; **~ acceptance** S&M accueil réservé à la marque *m*; **~ advertising** S&M publicité produit *f*; **~ association** S&M association de la marque *f*; **~ awareness** GEN COMM, S&M notoriété de la marque *f*; **~ development** S&M développement de la marque *m*; **~ extension** S&M extension de la gamme *f*; **~ identification** S&M identification de la marque *f*; **~ image** S&M image de marque *f*; **~ label** S&M image de marque *f*; **~ leader** S&M marque qui détient la plus grande part du marché, produit leader *m*; **~ loyalty** S&M *advertising* fidélité à une marque *f*; **~ management** HRM, MGMNT, S&M gestion de la marque *f*; **~ manager**

GEN COMM, HRM, MGMNT, S&M chef de marque *m*, chef de produit *m*; ~ **marketing** S&M marketing de la marque *m*; ~ **name** S&M marque de fabrique *f*, nom de marque *m*; ~ **portfolio** FIN, S&M, STOCK portefeuille de marques *m*; ~ **positioning** S&M positionnement de la marque *m*; ~ **preference** S&M préférence pour une marque *f*; ~ **promotion** S&M promotion produit *f*; ~ **recognition** S&M identification de la marque *f*; ~ **share** S&M part de marché de la marque *f*; ~ **strategy** FIN, S&M stratégie de marque *f*

branded: ~ **goods** *n pl* GEN COMM articles de marque *m pl*

branding *n* S&M choix d'une marque *m*, marquage *m*

BRAS *abbr (Building Research Advisory Service)* IND, PROP service de conseil en matière de recherche sur le bâtiment *m*

Brasilia *pr n* GEN COMM Brasilia *n pr*

brass *n jarg* GEN COMM gros bonnets *m pl* (*infrml*)

Bratislava *pr n* GEN COMM Bratislava *n pr*

Brazil *pr n* GEN COMM Brésil *m*

Brazilian[1] *adj* GEN COMM brésilien

Brazilian[2] *n* GEN COMM *person* Brésilien *m*

Brazzaville *pr n* GEN COMM Brazzaville *n pr*

BRC *abbr (business reply card)* COMMS, GEN COMM carte-réponse *f*

BRE *abbr (business reply envelope)* COMMS, GEN COMM enveloppe-réponse *f*

breach[1] *n* LAW atteinte *f*, contravention *f*, infraction *f*, manquement *m*, rupture *f*, violation *f*; ~ **of contract** GEN COMM violation de contrat *f*, HRM rupture de contrat *f*, LAW rupture de contrat *f*, violation d'un droit *f*, violation de contrat *f*; ~ **of duty** LAW manquement au devoir *m*; ~ **of professional etiquette** GEN COMM faute professionnelle *f*; ~ **of secrecy** GEN COMM violation du secret *f*; ~ **of trust** GEN COMM abus de confiance *m*, prévarication *f*; ~ **of warranty** IND, LAW rupture de garantie *f*; ♦ **in** ~ **of** GEN COMM, LAW en violation de; ~ **the law** LAW enfreindre la loi, violer la loi; ~ **the market** GEN COMM faire une percée dans le marché

breach[2] *vt* GEN COMM *contract, rule* ne pas respecter, LAW violer

bread *n infrml* GEN COMM blé *m* (*infrml*), fric *m* (*infrml*), oseille *m* (*infrml*), pognon *m* (*infrml*); ~ **-and-butter** GEN COMM gagne-pain *m*; ~ **-and-butter issue** *infrml* POL *frequently occurring* problème quotidien *m*, POL *UK concerning money* question touchant au portefeuille *f*, WEL *frequently occurring* problème quotidien *m*, WEL *UK concerning money* question touchant au portefeuille *f*; ~ **-and-butter letter** *infrml* COMMS, GEN COMM lettre alimentaire *f*, lettre de remerciement *f*; ~ **-and-butter line** *infrml* GEN COMM gamme qui rapporte à l'entreprise de quoi se maintenir à flot *f*; ~ **-and-butter technique** *infrml* GEN COMM technique courante *f*

breadth *n* STOCK *of market* ampleur *f*

breadwinner *n* ECON, WEL chef de famille *m*, gagne-pain *m*, soutien de famille *m*

break[1] *n* HRM *UK tea, coffee* pause *f*, STOCK désaccord *m*, rupture *f*, effondrement *m*; ~ **bulk** TRANSP cargaison fractionnée *f*, marchandises diverses non-unitisées *f pl*; ~ **bulk agent** TRANSP dégroupeur *m*; ~ **bulk cargo** TRANSP *shipping* cargaison fractionnée *f*, marchandises diverses non-unitisées *f pl*; ~ **bulk center** *AmE*, ~ **bulk centre** *BrE* TRANSP *shipping* centre de dégroupage *m*; ~ **-even analysis** ACC, ECON, FIN, S&M, STOCK analyse de rentabilité *f*, analyse du point mort *f*, étude de point mort *f*; ~ **-even level of income** ACC, ECON, FIN niveau de revenu équilibré *m*, seuil de rentabilité *m*; ~ **-even point** ACC, ECON, FIN, GEN COMM point d'équilibre *m*, point mort *m*, seuil de rentabilité *m*, PROP point d'équilibre *m*, point mort *m*, seuil de rentabilité *m*, rentabilité *f*, S&M rentabilité *f*, STOCK point d'équilibre *m*, point mort *m*, seuil de rentabilité *m*, rentabilité *f*; ~ **-even pricing** ECON, S&M fixation des prix au niveau du point mort *f*, mise à prix au point mort *f*; ~ **-even quantity** ECON point mort en quantité *m*, IND, MGMNT point mort *m*; ~ **-even weight** TRANSP poids d'équilibre *m*; ~ **in the market** GEN COMM chance sur un marché *f*, opportunité sur un marché *f*, percée dans un marché *f*; ~ **of journey** LEIS interruption du voyage *f*; **lucky** ~ GEN COMM chance *f*, veine *f*; ~ **-out** STOCK cessure *f*, mouvement anormal *m*; ~ **point** (SYN *break weight*) TRANSP point d'arrêt *m*; ~ **-up** GEN COMM *of company, association* démantèlement *m*, démembrement *m*, *of meeting* fin *f*, POL *of party* éclatement *m*; ~ **-up value** ACC, FIN valeur de liquidation *f*; ~ **weight** (SYN *break point*) TRANSP point d'arrêt *m*

break[2] **1.** *vt* COMMS *news* révéler, ECON *monopoly* casser, LAW violer, *contract* rompre; ~ **down** ACC *costs, expenses* ventiler; ~ **off** GEN COMM *meeting* cesser, *negotiations* rompre; ~ **up** GEN COMM fragmenter, LAW, PROP morceler, COMMS *news* se répandre, éclater; **2.** *vi* ~ **down** COMP tomber en panne, GEN COMM tomber en panne, échouer, HRM *negotiations, relations* échouer; ~ **up** GEN COMM *group* se disperser, se séparer, *meeting* lever la séance, prendre fin, se terminer; ♦ ~ **bulk** TRANSP dégrouper un chargement, dégrouper une livraison, fractionner un chargement, fractionner une livraison, *shipping* commencer le déchargement; ~ **the ceiling** FIN, STOCK crever le plafond; ~ **even** ACC, ECON, FIN, GEN COMM atteindre le point mort, atteindre le seuil de rentabilité, rentrer dans ses frais; ~ **into a market** GEN COMM percer sur un marché; ~ **the law** LAW enfreindre la loi, violer la loi; ~ **new ground** GEN COMM faire une découverte, ouvrir la voie, tracer une voie nouvelle; ~ **the news** MEDIA annoncer la nouvelle; ~ **ranks** HRM se désolidariser; ~ **a rule** GEN COMM manquer à une règle; ~ **the stalemate** GEN COMM débloquer la situation, sortir de l'impasse

breakage: ~ **clause** n INS clause bris f; ~ **-of-glass risk** n INS risque de bris de glace m

breakaway: ~ **union** n HRM syndicat dissident m

breakdown n ACC of costs ventilation f, COMP défaillance f, panne f, HRM of communications, negotiations rupture f, MGMNT for analysis répartition f, S&M segmentation f, TRANSP rail interruption de service f; ~ **of expenses** ACC, FIN ventilation des charges f

breaking: ~ **down** n ACC ventilation f; ~ **load** n TRANSP charge de rupture f, charge extrême f; ~ **the syndicate** n STOCK dissolution du syndicat d'enchères f; ~ **up** n PROP of land morcellement de terrain m

breakpoint n COMP point d'arrêt m, point d'interruption m; ~ **instruction** COMP instruction d'arrêt f, instruction de renvoi f; ~ **sale** FIN approche pyramidale d'investissement f

breakthrough n ECON, GEN COMM innovation f, nouveauté f, percée f, IND innovation f

breakwater n TRANSP shipping môle m

breech: ~ **base** n TRANSP shipping plaque de base f

breed vt ECON confidence engendrer, faire naître, générer

Bretton: ~ **Woods Agreement** n ECON, POL accords de Bretton Woods m pl; ~ **Woods Conference** n ECON, POL conférence de Bretton Woods f

bribe¹ n FIN dessous-de-table m, GEN COMM dessous-de-table m, pot-de-vin m, HRM, LAW dessous-de-table m, POL, S&M dessous-de-table m, pot-de-vin m; ~ **money** FIN dessous-de-table m, GEN COMM dessous-de-table m, pot-de-vin m, HRM, LAW dessous-de-table m, POL, S&M dessous-de-table m, pot-de-vin m; ◆ **giving ~s** (ANT taking bribes) GEN COMM, POL corruption active f; **taking ~s** (ANT giving bribes) GEN COMM, POL corruption passive f

bribe² vt GEN COMM, POL, S&M acheter, corrompre, soudoyer

bribery n GEN COMM, POL, S&M corruption f

brick: ~ **by brick forecasting** n GEN COMM, S&M prévisions détaillées f pl

bridge¹ n TRANSP shipping passerelle de débarquement f; ~ **financing** FIN financement par crédit relais m, préfinancement m; ~ **-forecastle** (BF) TRANSP shipping château-gaillard m; ~ **loan** AmE see bridging loan BrE

bridge:² ~ **the gap** phr ECON, FIN boucher le trou, combler l'écart; ~ **a gap in the market** GEN COMM, S&M occuper un créneau dans le marché, prendre un créneau dans le marché

Bridgetown pr n GEN COMM Bridgetown n pr

bridgeware n COMP logiciel de transition m

bridging n BANK, FIN, GEN COMM relais m; ~ **advance** BANK, FIN crédit de relais m, crédit-relais m; ~ **facility** BANK, FIN crédit-relais m; ~ **loan** BrE BANK, FIN crédit-relais m, prêt-relais m; ~ **pension scheme** FIN, HRM, WEL régime de préretraite m; ~ **software** COMP logiciel de transition m

brief¹ n GEN COMM dossier m, exposé m, mission f, LAW affaire f, dossier m; ~ **summary** GEN COMM résumé succinct m

brief² vt GEN COMM briefer, fournir des directives à, mettre au courant, LAW case établir le dossier de, lawyer confier une cause à; ◆ ~ **sb on sth** GEN COMM mettre qn au courant de qch

briefing n GEN COMM, MGMNT briefing m, séance d'information f, établissement de dossier m; ~ **session** GEN COMM, MGMNT briefing m, séance d'information f

brig n dat (b/g) TRANSP shipping brick m (vieilli)

brighter adj GEN COMM outlook meilleur

brightness n COMP luminosité f

bring vt GEN COMM amener; ~ **back** STOCK ramener; ~ **out** STOCK new issue introduire sur le marché, émettre; ~ **together** GEN COMM mettre en contact, réunir; ~ **up** GEN COMM mettre sur le tapis, subject mentionner, soulever; ◆ ~ **an accusation against sb** LAW déposer plainte contre qn, porter plainte contre qn; ~ **an action** LAW engager des poursuites judiciaires, intenter une action; ~ **an action against sb** LAW intenter un procès à qn, intenter une action en justice contre qn, poursuivre qn en justice; ~ **an action for libel against sb** LAW intenter un procès en diffamation à qn; ~ **an action for slander against sb** LAW intenter un procès en diffamation à qn; ~ **down** GEN COMM company couler, prices, inflation rate faire baisser; ~ **forward** ACC, FIN reporter; ~ **in legislation** LAW faire passer une législation loc f, légiférer; ~ **into fashion** GEN COMM mettre à la mode; ~ **into operation** GEN COMM réaliser; ~ **a lawsuit against sb** LAW attaquer qn en justice, entamer une procédure contre qn, intenter une action en justice contre qn; ~ **off a deal** GEN COMM mener une affaire à bien; ~ **out on strike** HRM amener à la grève; ~ **pressure to bear on** GEN COMM exercer une pression sur, influencer; ~ **pressure to bear on sb** GEN COMM faire pression sur qn loc f, travailler qn (infrml); ~ **sb up to date on sth** GEN COMM mettre qn au courant de qch; ~ **sb within the tax net** TAX ramener qn dans une fourchette imposable; ~ **sth up to strength** GEN COMM compléter l'effectif de qch; ~ **to bear against** LAW peser contre; ~ **to an end** ADMIN mettre fin à; ~ **to front** COMP faire passer au premier plan; ~ **to light** GEN COMM mettre en lumière; ~ **under control** ECON inflation, unemployment maîtriser; ~ **up to date** GEN COMM actualiser, mettre à jour

brisk¹ adj GEN COMM actif, animé

brisk:² ~ **demand** n GEN COMM demande active f, demande vive f; ~ **market** n STOCK marché animé m; ~ **trading** n STOCK marché actif m, marché animé m

Brit abbr infrml GEN COMM (Britain) Grande-Bretagne f, GEN COMM (British) britannique, GEN COMM (Briton) person Britannique mf

Britain pr n (Brit) GEN COMM Grande-Bretagne f

British[1] *adj (Brit)* GEN COMM britannique

British:[2] ~ **Academy of Film and Television Awards** *n (Bafta)* MEDIA ≈ Sept d'Or *m*; ~ **Agricultural Export Council** *n (BAEC)* IMP/EXP conseil britannique des exportations agricoles; ~ **Airports Authority** *n (BAA)* TRANSP autorité aéroportuaire britannique; ~ **-American Chamber of Commerce** *n (BACC)* GEN COMM chambre de commerce anglo-américaine; ~ **Bankers' Association** *n (BBA)* BANK association britannique des banquiers; ~ **Broadcasting Corporation** *n (BBC)* MEDIA compagnie de télévision et de radio nationale britannique; ~ **Chamber of Commerce** *n (BCC)* GEN COMM chambre de commerce britannique; ~ **Commonwealth of Nations** *n obs* ECON, POL Commonwealth *m*; ~ **Export Houses' Association** *n (BEHA)* IMP/EXP association des maisons d'exportation britanniques; ~ **Gas** *n* IND compagnie de gaz britannique, ≈ GDF, ≈ Gaz de France *m*; ~ **Health-Care Export Council** *n (BHCEC)* IMP/EXP conseil britannique des exportations de produits sanitaires; ~ **High Commission** *n (BHC)* ADMIN haut-comité britannique *m*; ~ **Hospitals Export Council** *n obs (BHEC)* IMP/EXP conseil britannique des exportations hospitalières; ~ **Hotels and Restaurants Association** *n (BHRA)* LEIS association britannique d'hôtels et de restaurants *f*; ~ **Importers' Confederation** *n (BIC)* IMP/EXP confédération des importateurs britanniques; ~ **Industries Fair** *n (BIF)* IND foire des industries britanniques; ~ **Institute of Dealers in Securities** *n (BIDS)* STOCK institut britannique des courtiers de valeurs; ~ **Institute of Management** *n (BIM)* MGMNT institut britannique de gestion; ~ **Iron & Steel Research Association** *n (BISRA)* IND association britannique de recherche sur le fer et l'acier; ~ **Library** *n UK* GEN COMM bibliothèque nationale britannique, ≈ BN, ≈ Bibliothèque Nationale *f (France)*; ~ **Maritime Law Association** *n (BMLA)* LAW association britannique de droit maritime; ~ **National Committee of the International Chamber of Commerce** *n (BNC/ICC)* GEN COMM conseil national britannique de la chambre de commerce international; ~ **National Oil Corporation** *n (BNOC)* IND société nationale des pétroles britanniques; ~ **Overseas Aid Group** *n (BOAG)* WEL groupe pour l'aide britannique outre-mer; ~ **Overseas Trade Board** *n* GEN COMM ministère britannique du commerce extérieur; ~ **person** *n* GEN COMM Britannique *mf*; ~ **Ports Association** *n (BPA)* TRANSP association des ports britanniques; ~ **quart** *n UK* GEN COMM 1.136 litre, quart britannique *m*; ~ **Rail** *n (BR)* TRANSP chemins de fer britanniques, ≈ Société nationale des chemins de fer français *f (SNCF)*; ~ **Savings Bonds** *n pl* STOCK bons d'épargne britanniques; ~ **Shippers Council** *n (BSC)* TRANSP conseil des affréteurs britanniques; ~ **Shipping Federation** *n (BSF)* TRANSP fédération britannique des compagnies maritimes; ~ **Standard Code of Practice** *n (BSCP)* IND, LAW code référentiel des standards de qualité en Grande-Bretagne; ~ **Standard Time** *n (BST)* GEN COMM heure légale britannique, ≈ heure légale française *f*; ~ **Standards Institution** *n UK (BSI)* GEN COMM association britannique de normalisation, ≈ Association française de normalisation *f (AFNOR)*, IND association britannique de normalisation, ≈ Association française de normalisation *f*, LAW association britannique de normalisation, ≈ Association française de normalisation *f (AFNOR)*; ~ **Standards Specification** *n (BSS)* IND spécification standardisée britannique, ≈ norme de l'Association française de normalisation *f*, LAW spécification standardisée britannique, ≈ norme de l'Association française de normalisation *f (norme AFNOR)*; ~ **Summer Time** *n (BST)* GEN COMM heure d'été en Grande-Bretagne; ~ **Technical Education Certificate** *n (BTEC)* WEL ≈ lycée d'enseignement professionnel *m*, ≈ établissement d'enseignement technique *m (L.E.P.)*; ~ **Telecom** *n* COMMS société britannique de télécommunications, ≈ France Telecom *m*; ~ **Tourist Authority** *n (BTA)* LEIS office de tourisme de Grande-Bretagne *m*; ~ **Travel Association** *n (BTA)* LEIS, TRANSP association britannique des voyages *f*; ~ **United Provident Association** *n (BUPA)* INS régime privé britannique d'assurance maladie; ~ **Venture Capital Association** *n* FIN association britannique de capital spéculatif; ~ **Waterways Board** *n (BWB)* TRANSP administration des voies navigables britanniques

Briton *n (Brit)* GEN COMM *person* Britannique *mf*

BRM *abbr US (Business Reply Mail)* COMMS, GEN COMM carte-réponse *f*, port payé *f*, postréponse *f*

broad:[1] ~ **-brush** *adj* POL esquissé dans ses grandes lignes

broad:[2] ~ **banding** *n UK* HRM principe du corps unique *m*; ~ **market** *n* STOCK marché actif *m*, marché ample *m*, marché à fort volume *m*; ~ **tape** *n US* FIN, STOCK *real estate, securities* service de renseignements *m*

broadband[1] *adj* COMMS, COMP, MEDIA *television, radio* à large bande

broadband[2] *n* COMMS, COMP, MEDIA *television, radio* diffusion en larges bandes de fréquence *f*

broadcast[1] *n* COMMS, MEDIA *television, radio* émission *f*

broadcast[2] **1.** *vt* COMMS *radio* diffuser, radiodiffuser, émettre, *television* diffuser, téléviser, émettre, MEDIA *radio* radiodiffuser, émettre, *television* diffuser, téléviser, émettre; **2.** *vi* COMMS *person*, MEDIA *person* faire une émission *loc f*

broadcasting *n* COMMS *radio* diffusion *f*, radiodiffusion *f*, *television* diffusion *f*, télédiffusion *f*, MEDIA émission *f*, *radio* diffusion *f*, radiodiffusion *f*, *television* diffusion *f*, télédiffusion *f*; ~ **rights** *n pl* COMMS, LAW, MEDIA droits de retransmission *m pl*

broaden *vt* GEN COMM élargir

broadening: ~ **of tax base** *n* TAX élargissement de l'assiette de l'impôt *m*

broadly: ~ **diversified** *adj* GEN COMM *range of products* largement diversifié, très diversifié

broadsheet *n* MEDIA *newspaper* journal grand format *m*, journal plein format *m, printing* placard *m*

broadtape *n jarg* STOCK agence de presse financière

brochure *n* COMMS, GEN COMM brochure *f*, dépliant *m*, prospectus *m*, LEIS brochure *f*

broken: ~ **amount** *n* STOCK rompu *m*, rompu de titres *m*, titres formant rompus *m pl*; ~ **lot** *n* STOCK rompu *m*, rompu de titres *m*, titres formant rompus *m pl*; ~ **lots** *n pl* S&M articles dépareillés *m pl*, fins de série *f pl*; ~ **stowage** *n* TRANSP *shipping* espace perdu *m*, vides d'arrimage *m pl*

broker[1] *n* FIN agent *mf*, courtier *m*, GEN COMM commissionnaire *mf*, intermédiaire *mf*, LAW commissionnaire *mf*, STOCK courtier *m*, courtier en valeurs mobilières *m*, négociateur en valeurs mobilières *m*; ~ **call-loan rate** *US* STOCK taux d'intérêt pour crédits aux courtiers *m*; ~ **-dealer** STOCK négociant-courtier *m*; ~ **fund** STOCK capital de courtage *m*, fonds de courtage *m*; ~'**s commission** STOCK commission de courtage *f*; ~'**s loan** STOCK crédit de courtier *m*, prêt de courtage *m*; ~'**s order** GEN COMM *UK* ordre de courtier *m*, STOCK ordre de courtage *m*; ~'**s statement** GEN COMM, STOCK relevé de compte de liquidation *m*

broker[2] *vi* STOCK faire le courtage *loc m*

brokerage *n* STOCK *business* maison de courtage *f*, *fee* courtage *m*, droit de courtage *m*, frais de courtage *m pl*; ~ **account** STOCK compte de courtage *m*; ~ **allowance** *US* STOCK commission de courtage *f*, courtage *m*, frais de courtage *m pl*; ~ **commission** STOCK commission de courtage *f*, courtage *m*; ~ **fee** STOCK commission de courtage *f*, courtage *m*, droit de courtage *m*, frais de courtage *m pl*; ~ **firm** STOCK firme de courtiers *f*, maison de courtage *f*, société de bourse *f*; ~ **house** STOCK firme de courtiers *f*, maison de courtage *f*, société de bourse *f*; ~ **statement** STOCK relevé d'opérations de courtage *m*, relevé de courtage *m*

brokering *n* STOCK courtage *m*

broking *n* STOCK courtage *m*; ~ **house** STOCK maison de courtage *f*

brown: ~ **book** *n jarg UK* POL livre brun *m*; ~ **goods** *n pl* S&M *television, hi-fi equipment* le brun *m*, produits audiovisuels *m pl*, produits bruns *m pl*

brownout *n US* COMP *of electrical power* baisse de courant *f*, baisse de tension *f*, chute de courant *f*, chute de tension *f*, microcoupure *f*

browse 1. *vt* COMP *document, database* naviguer, parcourir, survoler; **2.** *vi* GEN COMM jeter un oeil, *in a shop window* regarder

browsing *n* COMP survol *m*

Brunei *pr n* GEN COMM Brunei *m*

brush: ~ **up on** *vt* GEN COMM *skill* repasser, réviser, se remettre à

Brussels *pr n* GEN COMM Bruxelles *n pr*

brutality *n* HRM violence *f*

B/S *abbr (balance sheet)* ACC, FIN bilan *m*, bilan d'inventaire *m*

BSBA *abbr (Bachelor of Science in Business Administration)* WEL *degree* ≈ licence en études d'administration des entreprises *f*, *person* ≈ licencié en études d'administration des entreprises *m*

BSC *abbr (British Shippers Council)* TRANSP conseil des affréteurs britanniques

BSc *abbr (Bachelor of Science)* HRM, WEL *degree* ≈ licence de sciences *f*, *person* ≈ licencié ès Sciences *m*

BSCP *abbr (British Standard Code of Practice)* IND, LAW code référentiel des standards de qualité en Grande-Bretagne

BSF *abbr (British Shipping Federation)* TRANSP fédération britannique des compagnies maritimes

B-share *n UK* STOCK action ordinaire avec droit de vote

BSI *abbr UK (British Standards Institution)* GEN COMM, LAW association britannique de normalisation, ≈ AFNOR *(Association française de normalisation)*

BSIR *abbr (Bachelor of Science in Industrial Relations)* WEL *degree* ≈ licence en sciences des relations humaines *f*, *person* ≈ licencié en sciences des relations humaines *m*

BSS *abbr (British Standards Specification)* IND, LAW ≈ norme AFNOR *f (norme de l'Association française de normalisation)*

BST *abbr* GEN COMM *(British Standard Time)* heure légale britannique, *(British Summer Time)* heure d'été en Grande-Bretagne

BTA *abbr* LEIS *(British Travel Association)* association britannique des voyages *f*, LEIS *(British Tourist Authority)* office de tourisme de Grande-Bretagne *m*, TRANSP *(British Travel Association)* association britannique des voyages *f*

BTEC *abbr (British Technical Education Certificate)* WEL ≈ L.E.P. *(lycée d'enseignement professionnel)*

btm *abbr (bottom)* TRANSP *shipping* fond *m*

bubble *n jarg* STOCK affaire pourrie *f (infrml)*, bulle financière *f*, bulle spéculative *f*, projet sans valeur *m*; ~ **memory** COMP mémoire à bulles *f*; ~ **policy** ENVIR politique de prise en compte globale *f*; ~ **sort** COMP *programs* tri par permutation de paires de bulles *m*

bubblewrap *n* GEN COMM emballage bulle *m*

Bucharest *pr n* GEN COMM Bucarest *n pr*

buck[1] *n infrml US* ECON, FIN, GEN COMM dollar *m*

buck[2] *vt* GEN COMM *market, trend* aller à l'encontre de; ~ **up** *infrml* GEN COMM *ideas, efficiency* encourager; ◆ ~ **the trend** GEN COMM aller à l'encontre de la tendance générale

bucket: ~ **elevator** *n* TRANSP *cargo handling equipment* élévateur à godets *m*; ~ **shop** *n* FIN bureau de courtier marron *m*, LEIS, S&M agence de voyages à prix réduits *f*, STOCK bureau de courtier marron *m*, TRANSP agence de voyages à prix réduits *f*

buckling *n* TRANSP *shipping* flambage *m*

Budapest *pr n* GEN COMM Budapest *n pr*

Buddhist: ~ **economics** *n* ECON approche bouddhiste de l'économie *f*, économie bouddhiste *f*

budget[1] *adj* ACC, ECON, FIN, GEN COMM, POL budgétaire, S&M *inexpensive* économique

budget[2] *n* ACC, ECON, FIN, GEN COMM, MEDIA, S&M budget *m*; ~ **account** *n* FIN compte crédit *m*; ~ **analysis** *n* ACC, ECON, FIN, POL analyse budgétaire *f*; ~ **appropriation** *n* ACC, ECON, FIN, POL affectation budgétaire *f*, allocation des fonds *f*; ~ **ceiling** *n* ACC, ECON, FIN, POL plafond budgétaire *m*; ~ **constraint** *n* ACC, FIN contrainte budgétaire *f*; ~ **control** *n* (*BC*) ACC, ECON, FIN contrôle budgétaire *m*; ~ **cut** *n* ACC, ECON, FIN, POL compression budgétaire *f*, restriction des dépenses *f*, réduction budgétaire *f*; ~ **cutting** *n* ACC, ECON, FIN, POL *supply side* compression budgétaire *f*; ~ **day** *n* UK POL jour de la présentation du Budget *m*; ~ **deficit** *n* (*ANT budget surplus*) ACC, ECON, FIN, GEN COMM, POL déficit budgétaire *m*; ~ **expenditure** *n* ACC, ECON, FIN, POL dépense budgétaire *f*; ~ **heading** *n* FIN intitulé de crédit *m*; ~ **incidence** *n* ECON incidence budgétaire *f*; ~ **level** *n* ACC, ECON, FIN niveau budgétaire *m*; ~ **mortgage** *n* US BANK hypothèque à frais modérés *f*; ~ **payment** *n* ECON *development aid*, POL paiement budgétaire *m*; ~ **period** *n* ACC, ECON, FIN période budgétaire *f*; ~ **preparation** *n* ACC, ECON, FIN préparation du budget *f*, établissement du budget *m*; ~ **prices** *n pl* ACC, FIN, GEN COMM *used in establishing budget* prix budgétaires *m pl*, prix standards *m pl*, S&M *reduced* petits prix *m pl*, prix modiques *m pl*, prix promotionnels *m pl*; ~ **proposal** *n* ACC, FIN projet de budget *m*; ~ **reduction** *n* ACC, ECON, FIN, POL compression budgétaire *f*, restriction budgétaire *f*, restriction des dépenses *f*, réduction budgétaire *f*; ~ **resolution** *n* US POL résolution budgétaire *f*; ~ **review** *n* ACC, FIN, POL étude du budget *f*; ~ **standard** *n* ACC, FIN, GEN COMM standard budgétaire *m*; ~ **surplus** *n* (*ANT budget deficit*) ACC, ECON, FIN, GEN COMM, POL excédent budgétaire *m*; ~ **system** *n* ACC, ECON, FIN, POL système budgétaire *m*; ~ **variance** *n* ACC, ECON, FIN, POL écart budgétaire *m*, écart sur budget *m*; ~ **year** *n* ACC, ECON, FIN, POL exercice budgétaire *m*; ~ **year operational plan** *n* ACC plan opérationnel de l'année budgétaire *m*

budget[3] **1.** *vt* ACC, ECON, FIN, GEN COMM, POL budgétiser, inscrire au budget; ~ **for** ACC, ECON, FIN, GEN COMM inscrire au budget, prévoir des frais de **2.** *vi* ACC, ECON, FIN, GEN COMM, POL dresser un budget, préparer un budget, établir un budget

Budget: ~ **Papers** *n Can* ACC *government* documents budgétaires *m pl*; ~ **purdah** *n UK* POL marathon budgétaire *m*; ~ **speech** *n UK* POL discours de présentation du Budget *m*; **the** ~ *n UK* ECON, POL le Budget *m*

budgetary[1] *adj* ACC, ECON, FIN, GEN COMM, POL budgétaire, fiscal

budgetary[2] ~ **accounts** *n pl* ACC, ECON, FIN comptes du budget *m pl*; ~ **adjustment** *n* ACC, ECON, FIN ajustement budgétaire *m*; ~ **appropriation** *n* ECON, FIN, POL *governmental* crédit budgétaire *m*; ~ **constraint** *n* ACC, ECON, FIN, POL compression budgétaire *f*, restriction budgétaire *f*, restriction des dépenses *f*, réduction budgétaire *f*; ~ **control** *n* (*BC*) ACC, ECON, FIN contrôle budgétaire *m*; ~ **costs** *n pl* ECON, FIN, POL coûts budgétaires *m pl*; ~ **cut** *n* ACC, ECON, FIN, POL compression budgétaire *f*, réduction budgétaire *f*; ~ **deficit** *n* (*ANT budgetary surplus*) ACC, ECON, FIN, GEN COMM, POL déficit budgétaire *m*; ~ **expenditure** *n* ACC, ECON, FIN, POL *governmental* dépenses budgétaires *f pl*; ~ **period** *n* ACC, ECON, FIN, POL *governmental* période budgétaire *f*; ~ **planning** *n* ECON, FIN, POL *governmental* plan budgétaire *m*; ~ **policy** *n* ECON, POL politique budgétaire *f*; ~ **position** *n* ACC, FIN situation budgétaire *f*; ~ **power** *n* ECON, POL pouvoir budgétaire *m*; ~ **revenue** *n* ECON, FIN, POL recettes budgétaires *f pl*; ~ **spending** *n* ECON, FIN, POL *governmental* dépenses budgétaires *f pl*; ~ **statement** *n* ECON, FIN, POL *governmental* état budgétaire *m*; ~ **submission** *n* ACC présentation budgétaire *f*; ~ **surplus** *n* (*ANT budgetary deficit*) ACC, ECON, FIN, GEN COMM, POL excédent budgétaire *m*

budgeted: ~ **cost** *n* ACC, ECON, FIN coût budgété *m*, coût standard *m*, GEN COMM coût standard *m*; ~ **income** *n* ACC, FIN produits budgétés *m pl*, revenu budgété *m*; ~ **profit** *n* ACC, FIN bénéfice budgété *m*

budgeting *n* ACC, FIN budgétisation *f*, comptabilité budgétaire *f*, inscription au budget *f*, préparation du budget *f*, établissement d'un budget *m*; ~ **control** ACC, ECON, FIN contrôle budgétaire *m*

Buenos Aires *pr n* GEN COMM Buenos Aires *n pr*

buffer *n* COMP *circuit* tampon *m, storage area* mémoire intermédiaire *f*, mémoire tampon *f*, TRANSP *on train* tampon *m*, TRANSP *AmE (cf bumper BrE) on car* pare-chocs *m*; ~ **area** COMP, PROP zone tampon *f*; ~ **state** POL état tampon *m*; ~ **stock** ECON stock de régularisation *m*, stock régulateur *m*, stock tampon *m*, TRANSP stock de régularisation *m*; ~ **storage** COMP mémoire intermédiaire *f*, mémoire tampon *f*; ~ **store** COMP mémoire intermédiaire *f*, mémoire tampon *f*; ~ **zone** COMP, PROP zone tampon *f*

bug *n* COMP *in program* bogue *f*, bug *m*, défaut *m*, erreur *f*, GEN COMM défaut *m*

build *vt* PROP bâtir, construire; ~ **up** GEN COMM *business* développer, se développer, *production* accroître, augmenter, *reputation* bâtir, établir, IND *production* accroître; ♦ ~ **links with** GEN COMM établir des liens avec; ~ **sth into a contract** LAW *clause, guarantee, provision* insérer qch dans un contrat, introduire qch dans un contrat; ~ **up from scratch** GEN COMM partir de zéro

building *n* GEN COMM immeuble *m*, PROP bâtiment *m*, *work* construction *f*; ~ **code** *n* PROP code du bâtiment et des travaux publics *m*; ~ **line** *n* PROP limite de construction *f*; ~ **loan agreement** *n* BANK, PROP crédit foncier étalé *m*; ~ **and loan association** *n* AmE *(cf building society BrE)* BANK ≈ société d'investissement et de crédit immobiliers *f*; ~ **lot** *n* PROP chantier de construction *m*; ~ **materials** *n pl* IND matériaux de construction *m pl*; ~ **permit** *n* AmE *(cf planning approval, planning permission BrE)* ADMIN, ENVIR, PROP permis de construire *m*; ~ **and public works** *n* GEN COMM BTP, bâtiment et travaux publics *m pl*; ~ **regulations** *n pl* LAW, PROP réglementation relative à la construction *f*; ~ **repair** *n* PROP réparation d'immeuble *f*; ~ **society** *n* BrE *(cf building and loan association AmE)* BANK ≈ société d'investissement et de crédit immobiliers *f*

Building: ~ **Materials Export Group** *n* UK *(BMEG)* IMP/EXP groupe d'exportation de matériaux de construction; ~ **Research Advisory Service** *n (BRAS)* IND, PROP service de conseil en matière de recherche sur le bâtiment *m*; ~ **Societies' Act** *n* UK BANK, LAW loi des établissements de crédit foncier; ~ **Societies' Association** *n* UK BANK association des crédits fonciers

built[1] *adj* PROP construit; ~ **-in** COMP, ECON incorporé, intégré

built:[2] ~ **-in check** *n* COMP contrôle automatique *m*; ~ **-in obsolescence** *n* (SYN *planned obsolescence*) ECON, GEN COMM, IND, S&M *of product* désuétude calculée *f*, obsolescence programmée *f*, vieillissement programmé *m*; ~ **-in stabilizer** *n* ECON mécanisme automatique de stabilisation *m*, stabilisateur automatique *m*, stabilisateur incorporé *m*; ~ **-in test** *n* COMP test intégré *m*; ~ **-up area** *n* GEN COMM, TRANSP agglomération urbaine *f*, zone habitée *f*, WEL agglomération urbaine *f*; ~ **-up vehicle** *n* TRANSP véhicule composé *m*

Bujumbura *pr n* GEN COMM Bujumbura *n pr*

bulbous: ~ **bow** *n (BB)* TRANSP *shipping* bulbe d'étrave *m*, étrave à bulbe *f*

Bulgaria *pr n* GEN COMM Bulgarie *f*

Bulgarian[1] *adj* GEN COMM bulgare

Bulgarian[2] *n* GEN COMM *language* bulgare *m*, *person* Bulgare *mf*

bulge *n* STOCK brève montée des prix *f*, envol de courte durée *m*, envolée du marché *f*

bulk *n* GEN COMM *majority* masse *f, volume* grosse quantité *f*, volume *m*, TRANSP *items to be carried* vrac *m*; ~ **air mail** *n (BAM)* COMMS envoi en nombre par avion *m*, lettres en nombre par avion *f pl*; ~ **billing** *n jarg Australia* WEL consulter aux frais de la princesse, faire payer Marianne *(infrml)*;

~ **business** *n* GEN COMM entreprise de gros *f*; ~ **buyer** *n* GEN COMM, S&M acheteur en gros *m*; ~ **buying** *n* GEN COMM, S&M achat en gros *m*; ~ **capacity** *n* TRANSP *shipping* contenance en vrac *f*; ~ **cargo** *n* TRANSP marchandises en vrac *f pl*; ~ **carrier** *n (BLK CAR)* TRANSP transporteur en vrac *m*, vraquier *m*; ~ **commodity** *n* TRANSP marchandises en vrac *f pl*; ~ **container ship** *n* TRANSP vraquier porte-conteneurs *m*; ~ **discount** *n* ACC, GEN COMM, S&M remise sur la quantité *f*, remise sur volume *f*, réduction pour achat en gros *f*; ~ **dry cargo berth** *n* TRANSP *shipping* poste à vracs secs *m*; ~ **dry and wet cargo berth** *n* TRANSP *shipping* poste à vracs secs et liquides *m*; ~ **freight container** *n* TRANSP *shipping* conteneur de vrac *m*; ~ **goods** *n pl* TRANSP marchandises en vrac *f pl*; ~ **input/output** *n* COMP mémoire auxiliaire d'entrée/sortie *f*; ~ **licence** *n* BrE IMP/EXP licence globale *f*; ~ **license** *n* AmE *see bulk licence BrE*; ~ **liquid bag** *n* TRANSP *shipping* sac étanche pour vrac liquides; ~ **liquid berth** *n* TRANSP *shipping* poste à vracs liquides *m*; ~ **liquid container** *n* TRANSP *shipping* conteneur-citerne *m*; ~ **mail** *n* COMMS correspondance en gros *f*, courrier en gros *m*, courrier gros usagers *m*, envoi en nombre *m*; ~ **material** *n* GEN COMM matériaux en gros *m pl*; ~ **-oil and roll-on/roll-off vessel** *n (BORO)* TRANSP *shipping* pétrolier-vraquier-roulier *m*; ~ **orders** *n pl* GEN COMM, S&M commandes par quantité *f pl*; ~ **package** *n* S&M, TRANSP conditionnement en gros *m*, conditionnement en vrac *m*; ~ **price** *n* GEN COMM, S&M prix de gros *m*; ~ **purchaser** *n* GEN COMM, S&M acheteur en gros *m*; ~ **shipment** *n* IMP/EXP, TRANSP expédition en vrac *f*; ~ **storage** *n* COMP mémoire de grande capacité *f*, unité de mémoire de masse *f*, GEN COMM entreposage en vrac *m*, stockage en vrac *m*; ~ **transshipment center** *n* AmE, ~ **transshipment centre** *n* BrE TRANSP *shipping* centre de transbordement des marchandises en vrac *m*; ~ **unitization** *n* TRANSP *shipping* groupage par conteneur *m*; ♦ **in** ~ IND *production* en vrac

bulkhead *n (BH)* TRANSP *shipping* cloison *f*

bulktainer *n (bk)* TRANSP *shipping* conteneur de vrac *m*

bulky[1] *adj* COMMS, GEN COMM, TRANSP encombrant, volumineux

bulky:[2] ~ **cargo** *n* GEN COMM chargement encombrant *m*, chargement volumineux *m*, TRANSP chargement encombrant *m*, chargement volumineux *m*, marchandises encombrantes *f pl*, marchandises volumineuses *f pl*; ~ **goods** *n pl* S&M *specialist retailer* marchandises en vrac *f pl*; ~ **waste** *n* ENVIR déchets encombrants *m pl*

bull[1] *n* *(ANT bear)* STOCK acheteur à la hausse *m*, haussier *m*, spéculateur à la hausse *m*; ~ **account** *(ANT bear account)* STOCK position acheteur *f*, position couverte *f*, position à la hausse *f*; ~ **and bear** STOCK haussier et baissier *m*; ~ **-and-bear bond** UK STOCK obligation bull-and-bear *f*; ~ **buying** *(ANT bear sale)* STOCK achat à la hausse *m*, spéculation à la hausse *f*; ~ **call spread** (ANT *bear call spread*) STOCK *options* bull call spread *m*, écart d'un call à la hausse *m*, écart haussier *m*; ~ **campaign** (ANT *bear campaign*) STOCK spéculation à la hausse *f*; ~ **commitment** (ANT *bear commitment*) STOCK engagement à la hausse *m*; ~ **market** (ANT *bear market*) STOCK marché haussier *m*, marché orienté à la hausse *m*, marché à la hausse *m*; ~ **operation** (ANT *bear operation*) STOCK transaction à la hausse *f*; ~ **operator** (ANT *bear operator*) STOCK acheteur à la hausse *m*, haussier *m*, spéculateur à la hausse *m*; ~ **position** (ANT *bear position*) STOCK position acheteur *f*, position couverte *f*, position à la hausse *f*; ~ **purchase** (ANT *bear sale*) STOCK achat à la hausse *m*, position couverte *f*; ~ **put spread** (ANT *bear put spread*) STOCK *options* écart sur puts à la hausse *m*; ~ **speculation** (ANT *bear speculation*) STOCK spéculation à la hausse *f*; ~ **speculator** (ANT *bear speculator*) STOCK spéculateur à la hausse *m*; ~ **spread** (ANT *bear spread*) STOCK bull spread *m*, opération mixte haussière *f*, opération mixte à la hausse *f*, spread haussier *m*, écart haussier *m*, écart vertical haussier *m*; ~ **strike price** (ANT *bear strike price*) STOCK prix de levée à la hausse *m*; ~ **transaction** (ANT *bear transaction*) STOCK transaction à la hausse *f*; ~ **week** *jarg* HRM, IND semaine record *f*, semaine très productive *f*; ◆ **go a** ~ (ANT *go a bear*) STOCK spéculer à la hausse

bull[2] *vt* (ANT *bear*) STOCK *market, prices, shares* pousser à la hausse, spéculer à la hausse

bulldog: ~ **bond** *n* UK FIN obligation sterling émise par une société étrangère; ~ **edition** *n* AmE (*cf early edition BrE, first edition BrE*) MEDIA *of newspaper* première édition matinale *f*, édition du matin *f*; ~ **issue** *n* UK STOCK obligation sterling émise par une société étrangère; ~ **loan** *n* UK BANK crédit en sterling émis par une société étrangère

bullet *n* BANK emprunt remboursable in fine *m*, COMP puce *f*; ~ **repayment** BANK remboursement in fine *m*; ~ **vote** POL vote à l'aveuglette *m*, électeur indécis *m*

bulletin *n* COMMS bulletin *m*, bulletin d'informations *m*, communiqué *m*, GEN COMM bulletin *m*, communiqué *m*, MEDIA journal *m*, *news* bulletin d'informations *m*, informations *f pl*, S&M bulletin *m*, communiqué *m*; ~ **board** COMMS AmE (*BB, notice board*) panneau d'affichage *m*, tableau d'affichage *m*, COMP messagerie électronique *f*, tableau d'affichage électronique *m*, COMP, GEN COMM, HRM AmE (*BB, notice board*) panneau d'affichage *m*, tableau d'affichage *m*; ~ **board service** (*BBS*) COMP *hardware* serveur télématique *m*; ~ **board system** (*BBS*) COMMS messagerie *f*, tableau d'affichage électronique *m*

bullion *n* BANK encaisse-or *f*; ~ **market** STOCK marché des métaux précieux *m*, marché des valeurs en espèces *m*

bullish[1] *adj* (ANT *bearish*) STOCK en hausse, haussier, à la hausse; ◆ **be** ~ (ANT *be bearish*) STOCK prévoir une hausse de cours, être haussier

bullish:[2] ~ **market** *n* (ANT *bearish market*) STOCK marché haussier *m*, marché orienté à la hausse *m*, marché à la hausse *m*; ~ **movement** *n* (ANT *bearish movement*) STOCK mouvement vers le haut *m*, mouvement à la hausse *m*, tendance haussière *f*, tendance à la hausse *f*; ~ **signal information** *n* (ANT *bearish signal information*) STOCK *in the point and figure analysis* signal de hausse *m*; ~ **spread** *n* (ANT *bearish spread*) STOCK bull spread *m*, opération mixte haussière *f*, opération mixte à la hausse *f*, spread haussier *m*, écart haussier *m*, écart vertical haussier *m*; ~ **stock** *n* (ANT *bearish stock*) STOCK valeur en hausse *f*; ~ **tendency** *n* (ANT *bearish tendency*) STOCK mouvement vers le haut *m*, mouvement à la hausse *m*, tendance haussière *f*, tendance à la hausse *f*; ~ **tone** *n* (ANT *bearish tone*) STOCK *of market* ambiance à la hausse *f*, nature haussière *f*; ~ **vertical call spread** *n* STOCK opération mixte verticale à la hausse sur options d'achat *f*; ~ **vertical put spread** *n* STOCK opération mixte verticale à la hausse sur options de vente *f*

bullishness *n* (ANT *bearishness*) STOCK *of market* ambiance à la hausse *f*, nature haussière *f*

bulwark *n* TRANSP *shipping* pavois *m*

bum: ~ **check** *n* *infrml* AmE, ~ **cheque** *n* *infrml* BrE (*cf bounced cheque*) BANK chèque en bois *m* (*infrml*), chèque sans provision *m*

bumboat *n* TRANSP *shipping* bateau à provisions *m*

bumper *n* BrE (*cf buffer AmE*) TRANSP *on car* pare-chocs *m*; ~ **year** GEN COMM année exceptionnelle *f*

bunch: ~ **map** *n* MATH plan de groupe *m*

bundle[1] *n* BANK, GEN COMM *of papers, notes* liasse *f*, TRANSP ballot *m*, paquet *m*; ~ **-of-rights theory** LAW, PROP théorie exposant les prérogatives conférées par le droit de propriété

bundle[2] *vt* S&M grouper

bundled:[1] ~ **with** *adj* COMP fourni avec

bundled:[2] ~ **deal** *n* STOCK transaction expédiée *f*; ~ **software** *n* COMP logiciel fourni en lot *m*, logiciel inclus à l'achat d'un ordinateur *m*, logiciel intégré *m*, logiciel livré avec le matériel *m*

bundling *n* S&M groupage *m*, lot de marchandises pures *m*, routage *m*; ~ **yard** TRANSP aire de groupage *f*

bung *n* TRANSP *shipping* bonde *f*

bunker[1] *n* TRANSP *shipping* soute *f*; ~ **adjustment factor** (*BAF*) TRANSP surcharge de soutage *f*; ~ **fuel oil** (*BFO*) TRANSP *shipping* mazout de soute *m*; ~ **port** TRANSP *shipping* port de soutage *m*

bunker[2] *vt* TRANSP *shipping* mettre en soute

bunkering *n* TRANSP soutage *m*; ~ **adjustment factor** (*BAF*) TRANSP *shipping* surcharge de soutage *f*; ~ **barge** TRANSP *shipping* allège de soutage *f*; ~ **surcharge** TRANSP *shipping* surcharge de soutage *f*

bunny: ~ **bond** *n jarg* STOCK obligation spéciale à coupons à réinvestir *f*, OSCAR

buoyancy *n* ECON, FIN, STOCK *of market* fermeté *f*, tendance à la hausse *f*

buoyant *adj* ECON actif, animé, *currency* ferme, soutenu, *economy* en expansion *loc f*, robuste, sain, FIN *prices* soutenu, STOCK *profits, sales* ferme, soutenu

BUPA *abbr (British United Provident Association)* INS régime privé britannique d'assurance maladie

burden *n* ECON, GEN COMM *of responsibility* charge *f*, fardeau *m*, POL fardeau *m*, TAX valeur comptable *f, charge* poids *m*; ~ **center** *AmE*, ~ **centre** *BrE* ACC centre de coût *m*, section homogène *f*; ~ **of losses** GEN COMM poids des pertes *m*; ~ **of proof** LAW charge de la preuve *f*, fardeau de la preuve *m*, poids de la preuve *m*

bureau *n* ADMIN agence *f*, bureau *m*; ~ **de change** BANK bureau de change *m*

Bureau *n US* ADMIN département gouvernemental *m*, service gouvernemental *m*; ~ **of Economic Analysis** *(BEA)* ECON Bureau d'analyse économique *m*; ~ **of Labour Statistics** HRM institut statistique de l'emploi

bureaucracy *n* ADMIN, HRM, POL bureaucratie *f*

bureaucrat *n* ADMIN, HRM, POL bureaucrate *mf*

bureaucratic *adj* ADMIN, HRM, POL bureaucratique

bureaucratization *n* ADMIN, HRM, POL bureaucratisation *f*

burglar: ~ **alarm** *n* GEN COMM sonnerie d'alarme *f*

burglary *n* LAW cambriolage *m*, vol avec effraction *m*

Burkinabe *adj* GEN COMM du Burkina Faso

Burkina Faso *pr n* GEN COMM Burkina Faso *m*

Burma *pr n obs* GEN COMM appelé Myanmar depuis 1989, Birmanie *f (obs)*

Burmese[1] *adj* GEN COMM birman

Burmese[2] *n* GEN COMM *language* birman *m. person* Birman *m*

burn: ~ **out** *vi* HRM s'user, s'épuiser

burning: ~ **cost** *n* INS rapport sinistres-primes *m*; ~ **oil** *n* TRANSP huile combustible *f*

burnout *n* HRM, TAX épuisement *m*

bursar *n* ADMIN économe *m*

bursarship *n* ADMIN économat *m*

burst: ~ **advertising** *n* S&M matraquage publicitaire *m*; ~ **campaign** *n* S&M *advertising* campagne de matraquage *f*; ~ **mode** *n* COMP mode continu *m*, mode de transmission de données par paquets *m*, mode de transmission de données par rafales *m*

burster *n* COMP *for paper* rupteur *m*, séparateur *m*, éclateur *m*, TRANSP *dangerous classified cargo* charge explosive *f*

Burundi *pr n* GEN COMM Burundi *m*

Burundian[1] *adj* GEN COMM burundais

Burundian[2] *n* GEN COMM *person* Burundais *m*

bus *n* COMP *hardware* bus *m*, TRANSP autobus *m*; ~ **company** LEIS, TRANSP compagnie de cars *f*; ~ **mailing** COMP envoi en nombre *m*, publipostage *m*, ECON, FIN multipostage *m*; ~ **shuttle** TRANSP navette autobus *f*; ~ **station** TRANSP gare routière *f*

busbar *n* COMP *hardware* bus *m*

bushing *n* TRANSP *container securing* insert de pont *m*

business:[1] ~ **-orientated** *adj* GEN COMM axé sur les affaires *loc f*, tourné vers l'entreprise, tourné vers le commerce; ~ **-to-business** *adj* GEN COMM, S&M d'entreprise à entreprise *loc f*

business[2] *n* ECON entreprise *f*, GEN COMM *duties* activités *f pl*, entreprise *f*, occupations *f pl, firm* entreprise *f, trade, commerce* affaires *f pl*, commerce *m*, MGMNT entreprise *f*, S&M *trade, commerce* commerce *m*; ~ **account** *n* BANK compte d'affaires *m*; ~ **acquaintance** *n* GEN COMM relation d'affaires *f*; ~ **activity** *n* GEN COMM, MGMNT affaires *f pl*; ~ **acumen** *n* GEN COMM, MGMNT sens aigu des affaires *m*; ~ **address** *n* COMMS, GEN COMM, S&M adresse au bureau *f*, adresse commerciale *f*, adresse professionnelle *f*; ~ **administration** *n* GEN COMM, MGMNT administration commerciale *f*; ~ **agent** *n* GEN COMM agent d'affaires *m*, IND *US* agent d'affaires *m*, délégué syndical *m*; ~ **assets** *n pl* ACC, ECON, FIN actif commercial *m*; ~ **automobile policy** *n US* INS, TRANSP assurance automobile affaires *f*; ~ **bank** *n* BANK opérations sur valeurs de placement *f*; ~ **barometer** *n* GEN COMM baromètre économique *m, index* indicateur de tendance *m*; ~ **call** *n* GEN COMM visite d'affaires *f*; ~ **canvasser** *n* GEN COMM, S&M démarcheur *m*; ~ **card** *n* GEN COMM, MGMNT carte de visite professionnelle *f*; ~ **center** *n AmE*, ~ **centre** *n BrE* GEN COMM centre d'affaires *m*, S&M centre d'affaires *m, in aeroport* bureau de services de secrétariat *m*; ~ **charges** *n pl* ACC, GEN COMM frais d'administration *m pl*, frais professionnels *m pl*; ~ **circles** *n pl* GEN COMM milieux d'affaires *m pl*; ~ **class** *n* TRANSP classe affaires *f*, classe club *f*; ~ **closure insurance** *n* INS assurance en cas de fermeture d'exploitation *f*; ~ **college** *n* GEN COMM, HRM, WEL école de commerce *f*; ~ **combination** *n* ACC, MGMNT regroupement d'entreprises *m*; ~ **community** *n* GEN COMM monde des affaires *m*; ~ **computer** *n* COMP, GEN COMM ordinateur de bureau *m*, ordinateur de gestion *m*, ordinateur professionnel *m*; ~ **computing** *n* COMP informatique professionnelle *f*, GEN COMM informatique de gestion *f*, informatique professionnelle *f*; ~ **concern** *n* ECON entreprise commerciale *f*, GEN COMM affaire *f*, entreprise commerciale *f*, firme *f*, fonds de commerce *m*, maison de commerce *f*; ~ **conditions** *n pl* ECON, GEN COMM conditions commerciales *f pl*, conjoncture *f*, conjoncture actuelle *f*, POL conjoncture *f*, conjoncture actuelle *f*; ~ **connection** *n* GEN COMM relation d'affaires *f*; ~ **consultancy** *n* GEN COMM, MGMNT cabinet d'affaires *m*; ~ **consultant** *n* COMP, MGMNT conseil en gestion d'entreprise *m*, conseiller en gestion d'entreprise *m*; ~ **convention** *n* GEN COMM congrès commercial *m*; ~ **corporation** *n* ECON, GEN COMM entreprise commerciale *f*, société commerciale *f*; ~ **creation** *n* ECON, GEN COMM création d'entreprise *f*; ~ **cycle** *n* ECON, GEN COMM, IMP/EXP cycle économique *m*; ~ **data processing** *n* COMP, GEN COMM informatique de gestion *f*; ~ **day** *n* GEN COMM, HRM, IND jour de travail *m*, jour ouvrable *m*; ~ **dealings** *n pl* GEN COMM, MGMNT opérations commerciales *f pl*; ~ **decision** *n* GEN COMM, MGMNT décision commerciale *f*; ~ **development** *n* GEN COMM développement commercial *m*, prospection *f*, MGMNT développement des affaires *m*, progrès commercial *m*; ~ **diversification** *n* GEN COMM, MGMNT diversification commerciale *f*, diversification des affaires *f*; ~ **economics** *n pl* ECON, GEN COMM économie d'entreprise *f*; ~ **economist** *n* ECON, GEN COMM économiste d'entreprise *m*; ~ **enterprise** *n* ECON, GEN COMM entreprise commerciale *f*; ~ **environment** *n* ECON, GEN COMM, POL conjoncture *f*, conjoncture actuelle *f*, environnement de l'entreprise *m*; ~ **ethics** *n pl* GEN COMM déontologie *f*, déontologie des affaires *f*; ~ **etiquette** *n* GEN COMM protocole des affaires *m*; ~ **expansion** *n* GEN COMM, MGMNT expansion commerciale *f*, expansion des affaires *f*; ~ **expense** *n* ACC, FIN, GEN COMM, TAX dépense d'entreprise *f*; ~ **expenses** *n pl* ACC frais d'exploitation *m pl*, frais professionnels *m pl*, FIN dépense d'entreprise *f*, frais professionnels *m pl*, frais d'exploitation *m pl*, GEN COMM frais d'exploitation *m pl*, frais professionnels *m pl*, TAX dépense d'entreprise *f*, frais professionnels *m pl*; ~ **experience** *n* GEN COMM, HRM expérience professionnelle *f*; ~ **exposures liability** *n* FIN, GEN COMM, LAW dettes commerciales *f pl*; ~ **exposures life and health insurance** *n* US INS assurance maladie et vie risques professionnels *f*; ~ **failure** *n* ACC, BANK *of bank*, FIN faillite *f*, GEN COMM faillite *f*, faillite d'entreprise *f*; ~ **finance** *n* ACC, FIN, GEN COMM gestion financière des entreprises *f*; ~ **forecasting** *n* ECON, GEN COMM prévision dans l'entreprise *f*, prévisions commerciales *f pl*; ~ **forecasts** *n pl* ECON, GEN COMM prévisions économiques *f pl*; ~ **form** *n* GEN COMM, HRM formulaire commercial *m*; ~ **game** *n* ECON, GEN COMM, HRM, MGMNT jeu d'entreprise *m*, jeu de rôles *m*, simulation de gestion *f*; ~ **generalist** *n* GEN COMM généraliste de l'entreprise *m*; ~ **goods** *n pl* ACC, GEN COMM biens de production *m pl*; ~ **graphics** *n pl* ACC, COMP, FIN, GEN COMM graphiques de gestion *m pl*; ~ **hours** *n pl* GEN COMM, S&M heures d'ouverture *f pl*, heures de bureau *f pl*, heures de réception de clientèle *f pl*, heures ouvrables *f pl*; ~ **house** *n* GEN COMM maison de commerce *f*; ~ **income** *n* MGMNT, TAX revenu d'entreprise *m*, revenu tiré d'une entreprise *m*; ~ **income tax** *n* Canada *(cf corporation tax BrE)* TAX impôt sur les sociétés *m*, IS; ~ **indicator** *n* ECON, GEN COMM indicateur de conjoncture *m*; ~ **interest** *n* ECON, GEN COMM intérêt commercial *m*; ~ **interruption** *n* GEN COMM

suspension des affaires *f*; ~ **interruption insurance** *n* INS assurance perte d'exploitation *f*, police perte d'exploitation *f*; ~ **interruption policy** *n* INS assurance perte d'exploitation *f*, police perte d'exploitation *f*; ~ **investment loss** *n (BIL)* TAX perte au titre d'un placement d'entreprise *f (PTPE)*; ~ **investment tax allowance** *n* TAX crédit d'impôt à l'investissement commercial *m*; ~ **investment tax credit** *n Can* TAX crédit d'impôt à l'investissement commercial *m*; ~ **law** *n* GEN COMM droit commercial *m*, LAW droit commercial *m*, droit des affaires *m*; ~ **letter** *n* ADMIN, COMMS, GEN COMM lettre commerciale *f*, lettre d'affaires *f*; ~ **liability** *n* GEN COMM, LAW responsabilité commerciale *f*; ~ **liability insurance** *n* INS assurance de responsabilité professionelle *f*; ~ **library** *n* GEN COMM *public services* Centre de documentation pour entreprises *m*; ~ **life and health insurance** *n* INS assurance-vie et santé professionnelle *f*; ~ **loan** *n* BANK, FIN, GEN COMM prêt à l'entreprise *m*; ~ **loss** *n* ACC, FIN, GEN COMM perte commerciale *f*, perte d'exploitation *f*; ~ **lunch** *n* GEN COMM déjeuner d'affaires *m*; ~ **machine** *n* GEN COMM machine comptable *f*, machine de bureau *f*, machine de gestion *f*; ~ **management** *n* ADMIN, ECON, GEN COMM, MGMNT administration d'entreprise *f*, gestion d'entreprise *f*, management *m*; ~ **manager** *n* ADMIN, GEN COMM, HRM chef d'entreprise *m*, dirigeant d'entreprise *m*, MEDIA directeur commercial *m*, MGMNT chef d'entreprise *m*, dirigeant d'entreprise *m*; ~ **meeting** *n* GEN COMM réunion d'affaires *f*, session de travail *f*, séance de travail *f*; ~ **name** *n* GEN COMM raison sociale *f*; ~ **office** *n* ADMIN bureau commercial *m*; ~ **opportunity** *n* GEN COMM, MGMNT affaire à saisir *f*, créneau *m*, occasion *f*, opportunité commerciale *f*; ~ **organization** *n* GEN COMM organisation de l'entreprise *f*, structure commerciale *f*; ~ **outlook** *n* ECON, GEN COMM, POL conjoncture *f*, conjoncture actuelle *f*; ~ **owner's policy** *n* INS police pour propriétaires d'entreprise *f*; ~ **package** *n* ACC, COMP, FIN logiciel de gestion *m*; ~ **pages** *n pl* GEN COMM, MEDIA *of newspaper* rubrique économique et financière *f*; ~ **paper** *n* GEN COMM papier d'affaires *m*; ~ **plan** *n* BANK plan d'entreprise *m*, GEN COMM, MGMNT plan d'affaires *m*, projet commercial *m*; ~ **plan consulting** *n* GEN COMM, MGMNT conseil en business plan *m*; ~ **plan guide** *n* GEN COMM, MGMNT guide du business plan *m*; ~ **planning** *n* GEN COMM, MGMNT planification administrative *f*, projet commercial *m*; ~ **policy** *n* ECON, GEN COMM politique commerciale *f*, politique de gestion *f*, politique des ventes *f*, politique générale de l'entreprise *f*, IMP/EXP politique commerciale *f*, MGMNT politique commerciale *f*, politique de gestion *f*, politique des ventes *f*, politique générale de l'entreprise *f*, POL politique commerciale *f*; ~ **portfolio** *n* ECON, FIN, GEN COMM, STOCK portefeuille d'activités *m*; ~ **practices** *n pl* ECON, GEN COMM, MGMNT pratiques commerciales *f pl*, usages commerciaux *m pl*; ~ **premises** *n pl* GEN COMM, PROP locaux commerciaux *m pl*; ~ **profits** *n pl* FIN bénéfices industriels et commerciaux *m pl*, BIC; ~ **property and liability insurance package** *n US* INS, PROP assurance risques divers *f*; ~ **proposition** *n* ECON, GEN COMM, MGMNT proposition *f*; ~ **quarters** *n pl* GEN COMM *of town, city* milieux d'affaires *m pl*; ~ **recovery** *n* ECON, GEN COMM reprise des affaires *f*; ~ **regulations** *n pl* ECON, GEN COMM, LAW règlements commerciaux *m pl*; ~ **relations** *n pl* ECON, GEN COMM, MGMNT relations d'affaires *f pl*; ~ **reply card** *n* *(BRC)* COMMS, GEN COMM carte-réponse *f*; ~ **reply envelope** *n* *(BRE)* COMMS, GEN COMM enveloppe-réponse *f*; ~ **risk** *n* GEN COMM, IND, INS risque commercial *m*; ~ **risk exclusion** *n* INS exclusion des risques d'entreprise *f*, exclusion des risques profession- nelles *f*; ~ **routine** *n* GEN COMM activités quotidiennes de l'entreprise *f pl*; ~ **school** *n* GEN COMM cours de gestion *m*, école de commerce *f*, HRM école de commerce *f*, WEL cours de gestion *m*, école de commerce *f*; ~ **sector** *n* GEN COMM domaine des affaires *m*; ~ **segment reporting** *n* ACC, GEN COMM, MGMNT analyse par secteur d'activité *f*; ~ **sense** *n* GEN COMM sens des affaires *m*; ~ **service** *n* GEN COMM service aux entreprises *m*, service commercial *m*; ~ **situation** *n* ECON, GEN COMM conjoncture économique *f*; ~ **slowdown** *n* ECON, GEN COMM ralentissement économique *m*; ~ **software** *n* GEN COMM logiciel de gestion *m*; ~ **start-up** *n* ECON, GEN COMM création d'entre- prise *f*; ~ **strategy** *n* ECON, GEN COMM, MGMNT stratégie commerciale *f*, stratégie d'entreprise *f*, stratégie des affaires *f*; ~ **stream** *n* ECON, GEN COMM flux d'affaires *m*; ~ **studies** *n pl* ECON études commerciales *f pl*, études de gestion *f pl*, GEN COMM, WEL cours de gestion *m*, études commerciales *f pl*, études de gestion *f pl*; ~ **system** *n* ECON, GEN COMM chaîne d'activités *f*, système commercial *m*, système d'interaction économique *m*; ~ **tax** *n* GEN COMM, TAX taxe d'affaires *f*, taxe professionnelle *f*; ~ **to be transacted** *n* GEN COMM affaire à traiter *f*, affaires à régler *f*; ~ **-to-business advertising** *n* GEN COMM, S&M publicité d'entreprise à entreprise *f*; ~ **tout** *n* GEN COMM placier *m*; ~ **transaction** *n* GEN COMM opération commerciale *f*, transaction commerciale *f*; ~ **travel** *n* GEN COMM voyage d'affaires *m*, voyage professionnel *m*; ~ **travel market** *n* GEN COMM, TRANSP marché des voyages d'affaires *m*; ~ **trend** *n* ECON, GEN COMM, POL conjoncture *f*, conjoncture actuelle *f*, tendance commerciale *f*; ~ **trip** *n* GEN COMM, LEIS, TRANSP déplacement professionnel *m*, voyage d'affaires *m*, voyage professionnel *m*; ~ **unit** *n* GEN COMM unité commerciale *f*; ~ **uses life insurance** *n US* INS assurance-vie usage commercial *f*; ~ **venture** *n* GEN COMM entreprise commerciale risquée *f*, MGMNT entreprise *f*, entreprise commerciale *f*, entreprise commerciale risquée *f*; ~ **visitors' memorandum** *n* *(BVM)* GEN COMM livre d'or *m*, registre des visiteurs *m*; ~ **volume** *n* ACC chiffre d'affaires *m*, GEN COMM volume d'affaires *m*; ~ **world** *n* GEN COMM monde des affaires *m*, monde du commerce *m*; ~ **year** *n* GEN COMM, IND exercice *m*, exercice financier *m*; ◆ **any other competent** ~ *(AOCB)* GEN COMM autres ques- tions à l'ordre du jour *f pl*, questions diverses *f pl*; **be on a** ~ **trip** GEN COMM *salesperson* faire des déplacements fréquents, être en déplacement; **do** ~ GEN COMM faire des affaires; **do** ~ **as** *(DBA)* GEN COMM *name* exercer sous le nom de; **go about one's** ~ GEN COMM vaquer à ses occupations; **go out of** ~ GEN COMM fermer boutique, se retirer des affaires; ~ **is slack** GEN COMM les affaires ne marchent pas; **on** ~ GEN COMM *travel* pour affaires; ~ **is transferred to** GEN COMM bureaux transférés à *m pl*

Business: ~ **Expansion Scheme** *n obs UK* *(BES)* STOCK remplacé par Enterprise Investment Scheme en 1993, plan d'expansion économique *m*; ~ **Reply Mail**® *n AmE* *(BRM, cf Freepost BrE)* COMMS carte-réponse *f*, lettre de réponse *f*, port payé *m*, postréponse *f*

businesslike *adj* GEN COMM commerçant

businessman *n* [pl -men] GEN COMM homme d'affaires *m*; ~**'s risk** FIN, STOCK risque des affaires *m*

businesswoman *n* [pl -men] GEN COMM femme d'affaires *f*

bust: ~ **-up acquisition** *n* STOCK *corporate* rachat par éclatement

busy[1] *adj* COMMS *AmE (cf engaged BrE) telephone* occupé, COMP *machine* appareil en service *loc m, tone, signal* occupé

busy:[2] ~ **schedule** *n* GEN COMM, HRM, MGMNT programme chargé *m*; ~ **signal** *n AmE (cf engaged tone BrE)* COMMS *telephone* signal d'occupation *m*, tonalité d'occupation *f*

butane *n* ENVIR butane *m*

Butskellism *n UK* ECON *policy* Butskellisme *m*

butter: ~ **mountain** *n* ECON *agricultural* montagne de beurre *f*

butterfly: ~ **effect** *n* (SYN *chaos theory*) STOCK effet papillon *m*; ~ **spread** *n* STOCK butterfly spread *m*, opération mixte du papillon *f*

button *n* COMP bouton *m*, interrupteur *m*

buttress *n* TRANSP *container securing* culée d'an- crage *f*

buy:[1] ~ **-and-hold strategy** *n* STOCK stratégie d'acheter et de conserver *f*, stratégie d'investisse- ment à long terme *f*; ~ **-and-sell agreement** *n* ECON, FIN accord d'achat et vente *m*, accord de tutelle *m*, STOCK *among partners or stockholders* accord d'achat et vente *m*, accord de rachat et de vente *m*; ~ **-and-write strategy** *n* STOCK stratégie d'acheter et de vendre *f*; ~ **-back** *n* STOCK rachat d'actions *m*; ~ **-back agreement** *n* ECON *interna- tional trade* accord de compensation *m*, accord de rachat *m*, LAW *contract* accord de rachat *m*, accord de rétrocession *m*; ~ **-back clause** *n* ECON, LAW clause de rachat *f*; ~ **-back construction** *n*

ECON, LAW construction avec rachat *f*; ~ **-back option** *n* STOCK option de rachat *f*, possibilité de rachat *f*; ~ **-in** *n* STOCK exécution en Bourse *f*, rachat d'office *m*; ~ **minus** *n* STOCK achat en dessous du cours *m*; ~ **order** *n* STOCK ordre d'achat *m*; ~ **transaction** *n* STOCK achat *m*, opération d'achat *f*

buy² *vt* ECON *prices* acheter, soutenir, GEN COMM acheter; ~ **back** ECON, FIN, GEN COMM, LAW, STOCK racheter; ~ **down** BANK réduire les frais de crédit, PROP verser à la baisse; ~ **forward** STOCK acheter à terme; ~ **in** GEN COMM racheter, s'approvisionner en, STOCK exécuter; ~ **out** FIN, GEN COMM désintéresser; ~ **over** POL soudoyer; ◆ ~ **airtime** MEDIA acheter de l'espace; ~ **at market** STOCK acheter au cours du marché; ~ **at a reduced price** GEN COMM acheter au rabais; ~ **at the top of the market** S&M acheter au prix fort; ~ **the book** STOCK acheter l'inventaire; ~ **a bull** *jarg* (ANT *sell a bear*) STOCK spéculer; ~ **for the account** STOCK acheter en liquidation; ~ **for a rise** STOCK acheter à la hausse; ~ **in large quantities** (ANT *buy in small quantities*) GEN COMM acheter en grandes quantités; ~ **in small quantities** (ANT *buy in large quantities*) GEN COMM acheter en petites quantités; ~ **low and sell high** STOCK acheter bon marché et revendre plus cher, acheter à la baisse et vendre à la hausse; ~ **on approval** GEN COMM acheter à l'essai; ~ **on the bad news** STOCK acheter au son du canon; ~ **on bid** STOCK acheter aux enchères; ~ **on the black market** ECON acheter au marché noir; ~ **on close** STOCK acheter à la clôture; ~ **on credit** (*cf buy on tick BrE*) GEN COMM acheter à crédit; ~ **on a fall** STOCK acheter à la baisse; ~ **on a falling market** STOCK acheter à la baisse; ~ **on hire purchase** *BrE* (*cf buy on the installment plan AmE*) GEN COMM acheter à tempérament; ~ **on the installment plan** *AmE* (*cf buy on hire purchase BrE*) GEN COMM acheter à tempérament; ~ **on margin** FIN acheter sur marge, acheter à terme en versant un dépôt de garantie; ~ **on a rise** STOCK acheter à la hausse; ~ **on tick** *infrml BrE* (SYN *buy on credit*) GEN COMM acheter à crédit; ~ **and pay immediately** GEN COMM acheter qch comptant; ~ **shares on the open market** STOCK acheter des actions en bourse; ~ **space** S&M acheter de l'espace; ~ **sth on credit** GEN COMM faire un achat à crédit; ~ **sth on spec** *infrml* GEN COMM effectuer un achat spéculatif, tenter le coup (*infrml*)

buyer *n* GEN COMM, S&M acheteur *m*, STOCK acheteur *m*, détenteur *m*, titulaire *mf*; ~ **behavior** *AmE*, ~ **behaviour** *BrE* S&M comportement de l'acheteur *m*; ~ **concentration** S&M groupement d'acheteurs *m*; ~ **credit** BANK crédit acheteur *m*; ~ **response** S&M réaction de l'acheteur *f*; ~'s **market** (ANT *seller's market*) ECON, PROP, S&M marché acheteur *m*, marché à la baisse

m, STOCK marché acheteur *m*, marché baissier *m*, marché orienté à la baisse *m*, marché à la baisse *m*; ~'s **option** (ANT *seller's option*) ECON, GEN COMM, STOCK option d'achat *f*, prime acheteur *f*; ~'s **rate** (ANT *seller's rate*) ACC taux acheteur *m*, BANK, ECON, FIN, GEN COMM, STOCK cours acheteur *m*; ◆ **at** ~'s **risk** (ANT *at seller's risk*) STOCK aux risques de l'acheteur

buying *n* GEN COMM, S&M achat *m*; ~ **behavior** *n* AmE*, ~ **behaviour** *n* BrE* S&M comportement d'achat *m*; ~ **commission** *n* S&M commission d'achat *f*; ~ **habits** *n pl* GEN COMM, S&M habitudes d'achat *f pl*; ~ **hedge** *n* STOCK couverture d'une position acheteur *f*, couverture longue *f*, long hedge *m*; ~ **house** *n* S&M centrale d'achat pour indépendants *f*; ~ **-in price** *n* ECON *EU* prix de rachat *m*; ~ **on margin** *n* STOCK achat sur marge *m*, achat à crédit *m*; ~ **order** *n* STOCK ordre d'achat *m*; ~ **out** *n* STOCK exclusion par voie d'achats *f*; ~ **power** *n* GEN COMM, STOCK pouvoir d'achat *m*, puissance d'achat *f*; ~ **price** *n* GEN COMM prix d'achat *m*; ~ **process** *n* GEN COMM déroulement de l'achat *m*, processus d'achat *m*; ~ **rate** *n* BANK cours acheteur *m*, taux de change acheteur *m*, ECON cours acheteur *m*, FIN cours acheteur *m*, taux de change acheteur *m*, GEN COMM cours acheteur *m*, STOCK cours acheteur *m*, cours d'achat *m*; ~ **rate of exchange** *n* BANK, ECON, FIN cours acheteur *m*; ~ **surge** *n* GEN COMM vague d'achats *f*

buyout *n* FIN désintéressement *m*, STOCK achat *m*, acquisition *f*, rachat d'entreprise *m*; ~ **proposal** STOCK offre d'achat *f*, offre d'acquisition *f*

buzz: ~ **word** *n infrml* GEN COMM mot branché *m* (*infrml*), mot à la mode *m*, terme branché *m* (*infrml*)

buzzer *n* COMMS interphone *m*, COMP avertisseur sonore *m*

BVM *abbr* (*business visitors' memorandum*) GEN COMM livre d'or *m*, registre des visiteurs *m*

BWB *abbr* (*British Waterways Board*) TRANSP administration des voies navigables britanniques

bx *abbr* (*box container*) TRANSP *shipping* conteneur sec *m*

bye: ~ **-law** *n see* bylaw

by-election *n UK* POL élection partielle *f*

bylaw *n* ADMIN règlement administratif *m*, *local authority* arrêté municipal *m*, GEN COMM règlement administratif *m*, statut *m*, WEL *local authority* arrêté municipal *m*

by-product *n* ECON, ENVIR, IND, S&M dérivé *m*, produit dérivé *m*, sous-produit *m*

byte *n* COMP multiplet *m*, octet *m*; ~ **mode** COMP mode discontinu *m*, transmission d'octets en série *f*

C

c. *abbr* GEN COMM *(centime)* c. *(centime)*, GEN COMM *(coupon)* c., coup. *(coupon)*

C *abbr* ECON *(consumption)* consommation *f*, TRANSP *(compound expansion engine)* *shipping* machine à expansion mixte *f*

C/- *abbr (case packaging)* TRANSP emballage en caisses *m*

C/A *abbr* ACC *(capital account)* compte de capital *m*, ACC *(checking account, credit account, current account)* balance of payments, BANK *(checking account, credit account, current account)* c/c *(compte courant)*, ECON *(capital account)* balance of payments compte de capital *m*, FIN *(checking account, current account)* c/c *(compte courant)*, FIN *(capital account)* balance of payments compte de capital *m*, GEN COMM *(checking account, current account)* c/c *(compte courant)*

CA *abbr* ACC *UK (certified accountant, chartered accountant)* expert-comptable *m*, ENVIR *(controlled atmosphere)* environnement stabilisé *m*, milieu constant *m*, GEN COMM *(Consumers' Association)* ≈ INC *(Institut national de la consommation)*, ≈ Association de défense du consommateur *f*, ≈ Organisation de défense des consommateurs *f*, LAW *(Court of Appeal)* cour d'appel *f*, ≈ Cour de cassation *m (France)*, MATH *(confluence analysis)* analyse de confluence *f*

CAA *abbr UK (Civil Aviation Authority)* TRANSP aviation ≈ DGAC *(France) (Direction générale de l'aviation civile)*

CAB *abbr UK (Citizens Advice Bureau)* ADMIN bureau d'aide et de conseil aux citoyens

CABAF *abbr (currency and bunker adjustment factor)* TRANSP *shipping* surcharge monétaire et de soutage *f*

cabin *n* TRANSP *on ship, aircraft* cabine *f*; **~ allocation** TRANSP *shipping* planning des cabines *m*; **~ charge** TRANSP *shipping* prix de la cabine *m*, tarif cabine *m*; **~ staff** TRANSP personnel de cabine *m*, personnel navigant commercial *m*

cabinet *n* POL cabinet *m*, conseil des ministres *m*; **~ reshuffle** POL remaniement ministériel *m*; **~ security** *US* STOCK valeur peu active *f*, valeur peu dynamique *f*

Cabinet: ~ Committee on Social Development *n UK* POL commission du cabinet du développement social

cable[1] *n* COMMS *(cablegram)* câble *m*, câblogramme *m*, télégramme *m*, GEN COMM *US shipping* encablure *f (Fra)*, STOCK câble *m*; **~ program** *AmE*, **~ programme** *BrE* COMMS, MEDIA émission sur chaîne câblée *f*; **~ rate** COMMS, ECON *international trade* frais de transfert international *m pl*, tarif télégraphique *m*;

~ transfer COMMS virement télégraphique *m*; ◆ **your ~** *(y/c)* TRANSP *correspondence* votre câble *m*

cable[2] *vt* COMMS câbler, télégraphier

cablegram *n frml (cable)* COMMS câble *m*, câblogramme *m*, télégramme *m*

cabotage *n (*ANT *carriage international)* TRANSP cabotage *m*

CAC *abbr* HRM *UK (Central Arbitration Committee)* ≈ Conseil des prud'hommes *m*, IMP/EXP *(customs additional code)* code supplémentaire des douanes *m*, IND *UK (Central Arbitration Committee)*, LAW *UK (Central Arbitration Committee)* ≈ Conseil des prud'hommes *m*, STOCK *(Central Arbitration Committee)* comité central d'arbitrage des litiges *m*, commission d'arbitrage centrale *f*, TRANSP *(customs additional code)* code supplémentaire des douanes *m*, WEL *US (Consumers' Advisory Council)* Institut National de la Consommation

cache *n* COMP antémémoire *f*, mémoire cache *f*; **~ buffer** COMP antémémoire *f*, mémoire cache *f*; **~ memory** COMP antémémoire *f*, mémoire cache *f*; **~ storage** COMP antémémoire *f*, mémoire cache *f*; **~ store** COMP antémémoire *f*, mémoire cache *f*

CACM *abbr (Central American Common Market)* ECON MCAC *(Marché commun d'Amérique centrale)*

CAD *abbr* COMP *(Control-Alt-Delete)* CAD *(Ctrl-Alt-Del)*, COMP *(computer-aided design, computer-assisted design)* graphics CAO *(conception assistée par ordinateur)*, IMP/EXP *(cash against documents)* comptant contre documents *loc m*, IND *(computer-aided design, computer-assisted design)* graphics CAO *(conception assistée par ordinateur)*

cadastre *n (cf land register BrE, real estate register AmE)* TAX cadastre *m*

CAD/CAM *abbr (computer-aided design and computer-aided manufacturing, computer-assisted design and computer-assisted manufacturing)* COMP, IND *graphics* CFAO *(conception et fabrication assistées par ordinateur)*

CADD *abbr (computer-assisted design and drafting)* COMP, IND conception et dessin assistés par ordinateur *f*

cadre *n* GEN COMM cadres *m pl*, HRM cadres *m pl*, pouvoir exécutif *m*, MGMNT cadres *m pl*, POL pouvoir exécutif *m*

CAE *abbr (computer-aided engineering, computer-assisted engineering)* COMP, IND IAO *(ingénierie assistée par ordinateur)*

CAF *abbr (currency adjustment factor)* TRANSP *shipping* surcharge monétaire *f*

CAFR *abbr (comprehensive annual financial report)*

ECON, FIN, MGMNT rapport financier annuel détaillé *m*

cage *n US* STOCK caisse d'une firme de courtage *f*; **~ card** COMP fond de panier *m*; **~ inventory record (CIR)** TRANSP inventaire de cabine *m*

CAI *abbr (computer-aided instruction, computer-assisted instruction)* COMP, WEL EAO *(enseignement assisté par ordinateur)*

Cairns': **~ Group** *n* ECON *agricultural* groupe du Cairn *m*

Cairo *pr n* GEN COMM Le Caire *n pr*

CAL *abbr (computer-aided learning, computer-assisted learning)* COMP, WEL EAO *(enseignement assisté par ordinateur)*

calculable *adj* MATH calculable

calculate *vt* MATH calculer

calculated: **~ risk** *n* GEN COMM, STOCK risque calculé *m*

calculating: **~ machine** *n* GEN COMM machine à calculer *f*

calculation *n* ACC, COMP calcul *m*

calculator *n* COMP calculatrice *f*, calculette *f*, GEN COMM calculatrice *f*, calculette *f*, machine à calculer *f*, MATH calculatrice *f*, calculette *f*

calculus: **~ of probabilities** *n* MATH *theory* calcul de probabilités *m*

calendar *n* GEN COMM calendrier *m*; **~ day** GEN COMM jour civil *m*, LAW *contract* jour du calendrier *m*; **~ management** MGMNT gestion d'agenda *f*, gestion du temps *f*; **~ month** GEN COMM mois civil *m*, mois du calendrier *m*; **~ quarter** GEN COMM trimestre civil *m*; **~ spread** STOCK opération mixte sur options avec dates d'échéance *f*, opération mixte horizontale *f*, spread calendaire *m*, spread horizontal *m*; **~ year** GEN COMM année civile *f*

caliber *n AmE*, **calibre** *n BrE* HRM calibre *m*, envergure *f*, stature *f*

call:[1] **at ~** *adv* FIN à vue *loc f*, STOCK au remboursement *loc m*

call[2] *n* COMMS appel *m*, communication *f*, coup de fil *m (infrml)*, coup de téléphone *m*, COMP appel *m*, numérotation *f*, FIN *capital* appel *m*, S&M *sales* demande *f*, STOCK call *m*, option d'achat *f*; **~ account** BANK compte bancaire à vue *m*; **~ box** COMMS *AmE* borne d'appel d'urgence *f*, téléphone de police secours *m*, COMMS *BrE (cf telephone booth AmE)* cabine téléphonique *f*; **~ buyer** STOCK acheteur d'un call *m*; **~ charge** COMMS montant de la communication téléphonique *m*, prix de la communication téléphonique *m*; **~ date** BANK date de remboursement par anticipation *f*; **~ delta** *(ANT put delta)* STOCK delta d'une option d'achat *m*; **~ deposit** BANK dépôt à vue *m*; **~ exercise price** *(ANT put exercise price)* STOCK prix de levée de l'option d'achat *m*; **~ feature** STOCK clause de rachat *f*, nature d'un call *f*; **~ for bids** ADMIN, GEN COMM *for contract* appel d'offres *m*; **~ for tenders** ADMIN, GEN COMM *for contract* appel d'offres *m*; **~ forwarding**

COMMS *telephone company service* renvoi automatique d'un appel *m (Can)*, transfert d'appel *m*, COMP renvoi automatique d'un appel *m*; **~ loan** BANK prêt au jour le jour *m*, prêt remboursable sur demande *m*, STOCK prêt à vue *m*; **~ loan rate** STOCK taux d'intérêt d'un prêt à vue *m*, taux de prêt à vue *m*; **~ money** BANK, FIN argent au jour le jour *m*, emprunt au jour le jour *m*, emprunt remboursable sur demande *m*; **~ money rate** BANK taux au jour le jour *m*, taux d'argent au jour le jour *m*, TJJ; **~ notice** STOCK avis de rachat *m*; **~ option** *(ANT put option)* STOCK contrat d'option d'achat *m*, option d'achat *f*; **~ option exercise price** *(ANT put option exercise price)* STOCK prix de levée de l'option d'achat *m*; **~ option premium** *(ANT put option premium)* STOCK cours de l'option d'achat *m*, premium de l'option d'achat *m*, prix d'option d'achat *m*; **~ option price** *(ANT put option price)* STOCK prime d'achat *f*; **~ option writer** *(ANT put option writer)* STOCK vendeur d'options d'achat *m*; **~ premium** *(ANT put premium)* STOCK prime d'achat *f*, prix d'option d'achat *m*; **~ price** *(ANT put price)* STOCK prix d'exercice *m*, prix de rachat *m*; **~ protection** STOCK garantie contre le risque de remboursement anticipé *f*; **~ provision** *(ANT put provision)* STOCK provision pour le prix d'un rachat; **~ purchase** STOCK achat d'une option d'achat *m*, long call *m*, position acheteur sur options d'achat *f*; **~ and put option** STOCK stellage *m*; **~ rate** BANK, ECON *interest rates*, FIN taux au jour le jour *m*, STOCK *of stock, shares* taux de l'option d'achat *m*; **~ ratio backspread** *(ANT put ratio backspread)* STOCK options écart inverse sur ratio d'options d'achat *m*; **~ report** COMP rapport d'intervention *m*, S&M compte-rendu de réunion *m*, rapport de conférence *m*; **~ sign** TRANSP *shipping, aviation* indicatif d'appel *m*; **~ spread** *(ANT put spread)* STOCK opération mixte sur options d'achat *f*; **'s ~ strike** *n (ANT put's strike)* STOCK cours d'exercice de l'option d'achat *m*, prix d'exercice d'une option d'achat *m*; **~ strike price** *(ANT put strike price)* STOCK prix d'exercice d'une option d'achat *m*, prix de levée de l'option d'achat *m*; **~ waiting** *(cw)* COMMS *telephone*, COMP *telephone* appel en attente *m*; **~ warrant** *(ANT put warrant)* STOCK warrant à l'achat *m*; **~ writer** *(ANT put writer)* STOCK *on currency futures* acheteur d'option d'achat *m*; **~ writing** *(ANT put writing)* STOCK vente d'options d'achat *f*

call[3] *vt* BANK appeler au remboursement, COMMS appeler, GEN COMM convoquer, LEIS *theatre* appeler, MGMNT convoquer; **~ back** COMMS rappeler; **~ for** GEN COMM demander; **~ in** GEN COMM *debt* demander le remboursement de, rendre exigible immédiatement; **~ on** GEN COMM visiter; **~ up** COMMS appeler; ◆ **~ as a witness** LAW citer comme témoin; **~ bonds** BANK, STOCK racheter un emprunt obligataire, rembourser des obligations; **~ collect** *AmE (cf make a reverse charge call to sb BrE, reverse the charges BrE)* COMMS téléphoner en PCV (*Fra*); ~ **on sb** GEN COMM rendre visite à qn; ~ **sb collect** *AmE (cf make a reverse charge call to sb BrE)* COMMS appeler qn en PCV, téléphoner à qn en PCV; ~ **sb over the intercom** COMMS appeler qn par l'interphone; ~ **sb to account** GEN COMM demander des comptes à qn; ~ **sb toll-free** *AmE (cf make a freephone call to sb BrE)* COMMS appeler qn par numéro vert; ~ **securities for redemption** ACC appeler des valeurs au remboursement; ~ **a strike** HRM appeler à la grève, lancer un mot d'ordre de grève; ~ **to the bar** LAW inscrire au barreau

CALL *abbr (computer-aided language learning, computer-assisted language learning)* COMP, WEL apprentissage des langues assisté par ordinateur *m*

callable[1] *adj* STOCK rachetable, remboursable, remboursable par anticipation

callable:[2] ~ **bond** *n* STOCK obligation amortie *f*, obligation amortissable *f*, obligation rachetable *f*, obligation remboursable *f*; ~ **capital** *n* BANK capital exigible *m*; ~ **loan** *n* BANK prêt révocable *m*; ~ **preferred stock** *n* US STOCK obligation remboursable par anticipation *f*

called:[1] ~ **-away** *adj* STOCK *bonds* dont le remboursement est demandé *loc m*; **so-~** *adj* GEN COMM soi-disant

called:[2] ~ **security** *n* STOCK titre appelé au remboursement *m*, valeur rachetée *f*; ~ **-up capital** *n* FIN capital appelé *m*

calling *n* GEN COMM convocation *f*, HRM vocation *f*, MGMNT convocation *f*; ~ **program** COMP programme d'appel *m*

CAM *abbr (computer-aided manufacture, computer-aided manufacturing, computer-assisted manufacture, computer-assisted manufacturing)* COMP, IND FAO *(fabrication assistée par ordinateur)*

camber *n* TRANSP *shipping* bouge *f*, tonture *f*

cambist *n* BANK, FIN, STOCK cambiste *mf*

Cambodia *pr n* GEN COMM Cambodge *m*

Cambodian[1] *adj* GEN COMM cambodgien

Cambodian[2] *n* GEN COMM *person* Cambodgien *m*

Cambridge: ~ **School** *n* ECON école cambrienne *f*, école de Cambridge *f*, école de pensée de Cambridge *f*

CAMEL *abbr UK (capital, assets, management, earnings, liquidity)* FIN capital, actif, gestion, bénéfices et liquidité

camera:[1] **in ~** *adj frml* LAW, POL *meeting* à huis clos; ~ **-ready** *adj* MEDIA final, original de reproduction, prêt pour la reproduction, prêt à filmer, reproductible

camera:[2] ~ **-ready copy** *n (CRC)* MEDIA *print* copie prête à filmer *f*, copie prête à la reproduction *f*, copie prête à reproduire *f*

Cameroon *pr n* GEN COMM Cameroun *m*

Cameroonian[1] *adj* GEN COMM camerounais

Cameroonian[2] *n* GEN COMM *person* Camerounais *m*

camp: ~ **-on** *adj* COMP *of calls* attente signalée d'un appel automatique *f*, mis en attente *loc*

campaign *n* GEN COMM, S&M campagne *f*

camshaft *n* TRANSP *shipping* arbre à cames *m*

can: ~ **bank** *n* ENVIR conteneur de boîtes de conserve à recycler *m*; ~ **hook** *n* TRANSP *shipping* patte à futailles *f*

Canada:[1] ~ **Employment Centre** *n* HRM Centre d'emploi du Canada *m*; ~ **Pension Plan** *n* TAX régime de pensions du Canada *m*

Canada[2] *pr n* GEN COMM Canada *m*; ~ **-United Kingdom Chamber of Commerce** *n (CUKCC)* ECON chambre de commerce anglo-canadienne

Canadian[1] *adj* GEN COMM canadien

Canadian[2] *n* GEN COMM *person* Canadien *m*; ~ **Chamber of Commerce** *(CCC)* ECON Chambre de commerce canadienne *f*; ~ **Cultural Property Export Review Board** IMP/EXP Commission canadienne d'examen d'exportation de biens culturels *f*; ~ **development expense** *(CDE)* ECON frais d'aménagement au Canada *m pl (FAC)*; ~ **English** GEN COMM *language* anglais du Canada *m*; ~ **exploration expense** *(CEE)* TAX frais d'exploration au Canada *m pl (FEC)*; ~ **French** GEN COMM *language* français du Canada *m*; ~ **Institute of Chartered Accountants** *(CICA)* ACC Institut canadien des comptables agréés *m*; ~ **Pacific Railway** *(CPR)* TRANSP compagnie des chemins de fer canadienne

Canadians: **the ~** *n pl* GEN COMM les Canadiens *m pl*

canal *n* TRANSP canal *m*; ~ **dues** *n pl* TRANSP *shipping* droits de canal *m pl*

Canary: ~ **Islands** *pr n* GEN COMM Iles Canaries *n pr*

Canberra *pr n* GEN COMM Canberra *n pr*

cancel:[1] ~ **order** *n* STOCK ordre d'annulation *m*

cancel[2] *vt* COMP annuler, GEN COMM *order* annuler, décommander, PATENTS radier, S&M, STOCK annuler; ~ **out** GEN COMM neutraliser, s'annuler

canceled: ~ **check** *n AmE see* cancelled cheque *BrE*; ~ **share** *n AmE see* cancelled share *BrE*

canceling: ~ **clause** *n AmE see* cancelling clause *BrE*; ~ **date** *n AmE see* cancelling date *BrE*; ~ **return** *n AmE see* cancelling return *BrE*

cancellation *n* COMP, GEN COMM *of order, project* annulation *f*, PATENTS *of entry* radiation *f*, S&M *of order* annulation *f*, STOCK *shares* annulation *f*, résolution *f*; ~ **clause** LAW *contract* clause d'annulation *f*, clause de résiliation *f*, clause résolutoire *f*; ~ **fee** GEN COMM frais d'annulation *m pl*; ~ **notice** STOCK avis d'annulation *m*, avis de résolution *m*; ~ **of premium** INS annulation de prime *f*; ~ **provision clause** INS clause de résiliation *f*, clause résolutoire *f*

cancelled: ~ **cheque** *n BrE* BANK chèque oblitéré *m*, chèque payé *m*; ~ **share** *n BrE* STOCK action annulée *f*

cancelling: ~ **clause** *n BrE* LAW clause de résiliation *f*, clause résolutoire *f*; ~ **date** *n BrE* TRANSP *shipping* date d'annulation *f*, date de résiliation *f*; **~ return** *n BrE* INS *marine* ristourne pour résiliation *f*

C&D *abbr (collected and delivered, collection and delivery)* GEN COMM emporté et livré, ramassage et livraison *loc m*

C&E *abbr UK (Customs & Excise)* IMP/EXP régie *f*

C&F *abbr (cost and freight)* IMP/EXP, TRANSP C&F *(coût et fret)*

C&I *abbr (cost and insurance)* IMP/EXP C&A *(coût et assurance)*

candidacy *n* ADMIN, GEN COMM, HRM candidature *f*

candidate *n* POL candidat *m*; ◆ **this ~ is not suited to the job** HRM le candidat n'a pas le profil requis pour le poste

candidature *n* ADMIN, GEN COMM, HRM candidature *f*

canned: **~ program** *n* COMP programme portable *m*, programme transportable *m*

canteen *n* HRM cantine *f*

canton *n* POL canton *m* (*Suisse*)

cantonal: **~ bank** *n* BANK banque cantonale *f* (*Suisse*)

canvas: **~ cover** *n (cc)* TRANSP bâche non-imperméable *f*, gaine en toile à voile *f*; **~ sling** *n* TRANSP *shipping* élingue à sacs *f*

canvass *vt* S&M prospecter

canvasser *n* GEN COMM démarcheur *m*, placier *m*, STOCK recruteur *m*

canvassing *n* S&M prospection *f*

cap[1] *abbr* ACC (*capital*) capital *m*, ADMIN, COMP (*capital letter*) capitale *f*, lettre capitale *f*, lettre de haut de casse *f*, lettre majuscule *f*, ECON, FIN (*capital*) capital *m*, MEDIA (*capital letter*) capitale *f*, lettre capitale *f*, lettre de haut de casse *f*, lettre majuscule *f*

cap[2] *n* ACC restriction *f*, BANK taux d'intérêt plafond *m*, taux plafond *m*, ECON garantie de taux plafond *f*, taux à terme à la hausse *m*, limite *f*, plafond *m*, restriction *f*, taux d'intérêt plafond *m*, FIN cap *m*, restriction *f*, taux d'intérêt plafond *m*, taux plafond *m*, garantie de taux plafond *f*, taux à terme à la hausse *m*, GEN COMM plafond *m*, STOCK garantie de taux plafond *f*, taux à terme à la hausse *m*; **~ rate** BANK, ECON, FIN *for interest* taux d'intérêt plafond *m*, taux plafond *m*; **~ rate loan** STOCK *interest rate futures* prêt à taux de financement plafonné *m*, prêt à taux plafonné *m*; **~ -type primer** TRANSP *classified cargo* amorce à capot et tige *f*

cap[3] *vt* BANK *interest rate* plafonner, GEN COMM fixer un plafond de

CAP[1] *abbr (the Common Agricultural Policy)* ECON, POL *European Union* PAC *(la politique agricole commune)*

CAP[2]: **~ charges** *n pl* ECON charges liées à la PAC *f pl*, frais de la PAC *m pl*; **~ goods** *n pl* ECON produits PAC *m pl*; **~ levy** *n* ECON prélèvement PAC *m*

capability *n* GEN COMM aptitude *f*, capacité *f*, potentiel *m*

capable *adj* GEN COMM capable, susceptible de; ◆ **~ of doing sth** GEN COMM capable de faire qch

capacitance *n* COMP capacitance *f*

capacity *n* COMP capacité *f*, ECON *production* débit *m*, rendement *m*, GEN COMM capacité *f*, *of container* contenance *f*, HRM *personal, professional* aptitude *f*, aptitude professionnelle *f*, capacité *f*, compétence *f*, IND capacité *f*, débit *m*, rendement *m*, TRANSP contenance *f*; **~ charge** ECON, IND frais de production *m pl*; **~ effect** ECON effet de capacité *m*; **~ of penetration** S&M capacité de pénétration *f*; **~ ratio** ECON, HRM, IND taux d'utilisation de la main-d'oeuvre *m*, taux de capacité de la main-d'oeuvre *m*, taux de rendement *m*; **~ to work** GEN COMM aptitude à travailler *f*; **~ utilization** ECON, IND utilisation des capacités *f*, utilisation du potentiel de production *f*; **~ utilization rate** ECON, IND taux d'utilisation des capacités *m*, taux d'utilisation du potentiel de production *m*; ◆ **in the ~ of** GEN COMM en qualité de

Cape: **~ Town** *pr n* GEN COMM Le Cap *n pr*

capex *abbr (capital expenditure)* ECON, FIN dépenses en capital *f pl*, mise de fonds *f*, GEN COMM dépenses en capital *f pl*, immobilisations *f pl*, investissements *m pl*

capital:[1] **~ -intensive** *adj* ECON à forte proportion de capital *loc f*, GEN COMM capitalistique, IND capitalistique, à forte intensité capitalistique *loc f*, à forte intensité de capitaux *loc f*, à forte proportion de capital *loc f*, POL capitalistique

capital[2] *n (cap)* ACC capital *m*, ADMIN, COMP capitale *f*, lettre capitale *f*, lettre de haut de casse *f*, lettre majuscule *f*, ECON, FIN capital *m*, capitaux *m pl*, MEDIA lettre capitale *f*, lettre de haut de casse *f*, lettre majuscule *f*; **~ account** *n* ACC *(C/A)* compte de capital *m*, BANK compte d'immobilisations *m*, ECON *(C/A)* balance of payments, FIN *(C/A)* compte de capital *m*; **~ accumulation** *n* ECON, FIN accumulation de capital *f*; **~ adequacy** *n* BANK adéquation du capital *f*, suffisance du capital *f*, FIN *of investment firms and credit institutions* adéquation des fonds propres *f*; **~ aid** *n* ECON *development aid*, POL aide financière en capital *f*, aide financière sous forme d'apport de capital *f*; **~ allotment** *n* FIN affectation pour dépenses en capital *f*; **~ allowance** *n* ACC déduction fiscale pour amortissement *f*, TAX déduction fiscale pour investissement *f*; **~ appreciation** *n* ECON, FIN plus-value de capital *f*; **~ asset account** *n* BANK compte d'immobilisations *m*; **~ asset pricing model** *n (CAPM)* ECON, FIN, STOCK modèle d'équilibre des actifs financiers *m*, modèle d'évaluation des actifs financiers *m (MEDAF)*; **~ assets** *n pl* ECON actif immobilisé *m*, capitaux fixes *m pl*, FIN actif immobilisé *m*, capitaux fixes *m pl*, *investment* immobilisations financières *f pl*;

~ **assured** *n* INS capital assuré *m*; ~ **-augmenting technical progress** *n* ECON progrès technique facteur d'augmentation du capital *m*; ~ **base** *n* BANK, ECON, FIN capital de base *m*, STOCK capital social *m*; ~ **bonds** *n pl*> ~ **bonus** *n* INS dividende exceptionnel *m*, STOCK actions gratuites *f pl*; ~ **budget** *n* ACC budget d'investissement *m*, ECON, FIN budget d'investissement *m*, budget d'équipement *m*, budget des immobilisations *m*; ~ **budgeting** *n* ACC budgétisation des immobilisations *f*, budgétisation des investissements *f*, prévision des dépenses d'investissement *f*, ECON procédure de choix d'investissement *f*, établissement du budget d'investissement *m*; ~ **commitment** *n* ACC engagement d'investissement *m*; ~ **component** *n* FIN composante du capital *f*; ~ **consolidation** *n* ECON, FIN consolidation du capital *f*; ~ **consumption** *n* ECON amortissement *m*, consommation de capital *f*; ~ **consumption allowance** *n* ECON dotation aux amortissements *f*, dotation aux investissements *f*, provisions pour amortissement *f pl*; ~ **contributed in excess of par value** *n* US ACC prime d'émission *f*; ~ **contribution** *n* FIN apport *m*, apport de capital *m*; ~ **cost** *n* STOCK coût d'immobilisation *m*, coût du capital *m*; ~ **cost allowance** *n (CCA)* TAX allocation du coût en capital *f*, déduction pour amortissement *f (Can)*; ~ **costs** *n pl* ECON, FIN coûts d'investissement *m pl*, coûts en capital *m pl*; ~ **cover** *n* BANK ratio fonds engagements *m*, ratio fonds propres *m*; ~ **deepening** *n* ECON augmentation de capital *f*, intensification de l'apport en capital *f*, investissements de rationalisation *m pl*; ~ **dividend** *n* STOCK dividende en capital *m*, dividende prélevé sur le capital *m*; ~ **dividend account** *n (CDA)* TAX compte de dividende en capital *m (CDC)*; ~ **employed** *n* ACC capital investi *m*, capital utilisé *m*, fonds propres *m pl*, GEN COMM capital investi *m*, fonds propres *m pl*; ~ **employed equity** *n* FIN capital immobilisé *m*, capital utilisé *m*; ~ **expenditure** *n (capex)* ECON, FIN dépenses en capital *f pl*, mise de fonds *f*, GEN COMM dépenses en capital *f pl*, immobilisations *f pl*, investissements *m pl*; ~ **expenditure appraisal** *n* ECON, FIN évaluation des dépenses d'investissement *f*, évaluation des dépenses en capital *f*; ~ **expenditure budget** *n* ACC budget des investissements *m*; ~ **expenditure vote** *n* POL *governmental* crédit de dépenses en capital *m*; ~ **financing** *n* FIN financement d'immobilisations *m*; ~ **flight** *n* ECON fuite de capitaux *f*, évasion de capitaux *f*, évasion monétaire *f*; ~ **flow** *n* ECON, FIN flux de capitaux *m*; ~ **formation** *n* ACC, ECON formation de capital *f*; ~ **fund** *n* ACC, FIN fonds de capital et d'emprunt *m, local authorities* section d'investissement *f*; ~ **funding** *n* FIN financement d'immobilisations *m*; ~ **-funding planning** *n* FIN planification du financement d'immobilisations *f*; ~ **funds** *n pl* ACC, ECON capital *m*, FIN capital *m*, capital immobilisé *m, investments* capitaux permanents *m pl*, GEN COMM fonds *m pl*; ~ **gain** *n* ACC, ECON, FIN augmentation de capital *f*, gain en capital *m*, plus-value *f*, TAX gain en capital *m*; ~ **gains allowance** *n* TAX abattement sur les plus-values *m*, déduction pour gains en capital *f (Can)*; ~ **gains deduction** *n Can* TAX abattement sur les plus-values *m*, déduction pour gains en capital *f (Can)*; ~ **gains distribution** *n* STOCK distribution de plus-values *f*; ~ **gains dividend** *n* TAX dividende sur les gains en capital *m*; ~ **gains exemption** *n* TAX exonération des gains en capital *f*; ~ **gains refund** *n* TAX rachat au titre des gains en capital *m (Can)*, remboursement au titre des gains en capital *m (Can)*; ~ **gains reserve** *n* TAX réserve pour gains en capital *f (Can)*; ~ **gains rollover** *n* TAX roulement de gains en capital *m (Can)*; ~ **gains tax** *n (CGT)* ECON, TAX impôt sur les plus-values *m*; ~ **goods** *n pl* ECON biens d'équipement *m pl*, GEN COMM biens d'équipement *m pl*, biens de production *m pl*; ~ **growth** *n* STOCK croissance du capital *f*; ~ **improvement** *n* ECON amélioration capitale *f*, modernisation *f*, rationalisation *f*, FIN, IND rationalisation *f*; ~ **increase** *n* ECON, FIN augmentation de capital *f*; ~ **inflow** *n* ECON, FIN afflux de capitaux *m*, afflux de fonds *m*, entrée de capitaux *f*; ~ **injection** *n* FIN injection de capitaux *f*; ~ **instrument** *n* FIN élément du capital *m*; ~ **-intensive industry** *n* ACC industrie qui dépend des immobilisations importantes, industrie lourde *f*, ECON, IND industrie capitalistique *f*, industrie de capital *f*, industrie à forte intensité de capitaux *f*; ~ **interest** *n* TAX *in trust* droit au capital *m*, participation au capital *f*; ~ **invested** *n* ACC capital investi *m*, GEN COMM capital engagé *m*, capital investi *m*, capital permanent *m*; ~ **investment** *n* ECON, FIN immobilisation *f*, investissement de capitaux *m*, investissement en capital *m*, IND immobilisation *f*; ~ **investment appraisal** *n* ACC, ECON, FIN, STOCK évaluation d'investissement *f*, évaluation d'investissement sur budget *f*; ~ **investment strategy** *n* FIN stratégie d'investissement *f*; ~ **-labor ratio** *n AmE*, ~ **-labour ratio** *n BrE* ECON, FIN, IND rapport capital-travail *m*; ~ **lease** *n* ACC crédit-bail *m*, GEN COMM location-acquisition *f*; ~ **lease agreement** *n* GEN COMM contrat de location-acquisition *m*; ~ **letter** *n (cap)* ADMIN, COMP, MEDIA capitale *f*, lettre capitale *f*, lettre de haut de casse *f*, lettre majuscule *f*; ~ **leverage** *n* STOCK levier financier *m*; ~ **loss** *n* ACC, ECON, FIN moins-value *f*, GEN COMM moins-value *f*, perte en capital *f*, TAX moins-value *f*; ~ **market** *n* FIN, STOCK marché des capitaux *m*, marché financier *m*; ~ **market influence** *n* ACC *on accounting theory & practice* influence des marchés des capitaux *f*, influence des marchés financiers *f*; ~ **market yield** *n* STOCK rendement du marché des capitaux *m*, rendement du marché financier *m*; ~ **needs** *n pl* ACC, ECON, FIN, GEN COMM besoins en capitaux *m pl*; ~ **outflow** *n* ECON fuite de capitaux *f*, sortie de capitaux *f*; ~ **outlay** *n* ECON, FIN mise de fonds *f*; ~ **-outlay ratio** *n* ECON, FIN ratio d'intensité *m*, ratio d'intensité de capital *m*, ratio de rentabilité du capital *m*; ~ **-output ratio** *n* ECON, FIN ratio d'intensité *m*, ratio d'intensité de capital *m*, ratio de rentabilité du capital *m*; ~ **paid out** *n* FIN capital remboursé *m*; ~ **profit** *n* FIN plus-value *f*, plus-value sur la réalisation d'actifs immobilisés *f*; ~ **program** *n AmE*, ~ **programme** *n BrE* ACC programme des immobilisations *m*; ~ **project** *n* ACC, ECON, FIN, STOCK projet d'investissement *m*, projet d'investissement sur budget *m*; ~ **project evaluation** *n* ECON, FIN étude de projet d'investissement *f*; ~ **property** *n* TAX bien en immobilisation *m*; ~ **raising** *n* FIN appel de capitaux *m*, mobilisation *f*, STOCK appel de capitaux *m*, mobilisation de fonds *f*; ~ **-raising operation** *n* FIN appel de capitaux *m*, cycle de conversion de liquidités *m*; ~ **ratio** *n* BANK coefficient de capital *m*, ratio de capital *m*, ECON, FIN ratio de capital *m*; ~ **rationing** *n* ECON, FIN rationnement des fonds *m*, rationnement du capital *m*; ~ **reorganization** *n* ECON, FIN, STOCK restructuration du capital *f*, réorganisation du capital *f*; ~ **requirements** *n pl* ACC, ECON, FIN, GEN COMM besoins en capitaux *m pl*, besoins en financement *m pl*; ~ **and reserves** *n pl* ACC capitaux et réserves *m pl*; ~ **reserves** *n pl* ACC *undistributed* réserves *f pl*; ~ **resource** *n* ECON, FIN ressource en capital *f*; ~ **reswitching** *n* ECON retour à des méthodes d'intensité capitalistique *m*; ~ **risk** *n* FIN risque de capital *m*; ~ **shares** *n pl* STOCK actions donnant droit aux plus-values *f pl*; ~ **stock** *n* ACC capital actions *m*, capital social *m*, ECON, FIN capital actions *m*, STOCK capital actions *m*, capital social *m*; ~ **strategy** *n* FIN stratégie d'investissement *f*; ~ **structure** *n* ACC *arrangement of long-term funds* structure du financement de l'entreprise *f*, ECON répartition de capitaux *f*, structure du capital *f*, FIN répartition de capitaux *f*; ~ **sum** *n* ACC, ECON, FIN capital *m*; ~ **surplus on hand** *n* TAX surplus de capital en main *m*; ~ **tax** *n Canada* TAX impôt sur le capital *m*, taxe sur le capital *f*; ~ **theory** *n* ECON, FIN, IND, S&M théorie du capital *f*; ~ **-to-asset ratio** *n* ACC rapport du capital à l'actif *m*; ~ **transaction** *n* FIN opération sur le capital *f*; ~ **transfer** *n* FIN transmission de capital *f*; ~ **transfer tax** *n dat UK (CTT)* TAX droits de mutation *m pl*; ~ **utilization** *n* ECON utilisation du capital *f*; ~ **value** *n* ECON, FIN valeur de l'actif *f*, valeur des fonds propres *f*, valeur du capital *f*; ~ **widening** *n* ECON investissement en capital *m*; ◆ ~**, assets, management, earnings, liquidity** *UK (CAMEL)* FIN capital, actif, gestion, bénéfices et liquidité; **make a ~ gain** ACC, FIN, GEN COMM, STOCK réaliser une plus-value

Capital: ~ **International World Index** *n* STOCK Indice mondial des bourses de valeurs *m*; ~ **Markets System** *n (CMS)* STOCK système des marchés financiers mondiaux *m*

capitalism *n* ECON, POL capitalisme *m*

capitalist[1] *adj* ECON, POL capitaliste

capitalist[2] *n* ECON, POL capitaliste *mf*; ~ **class** ECON, POL classe possédante *f*, les capitalistes *m pl*; ~ **imperialism** ECON, POL impérialisme capitaliste *m*

capitalistic *adj* ECON, POL capitaliste

capitalization *n* ACC capitalisation *f*, ECON, GEN COMM capitalisation *f*, structure du capital *f*; ~ **effect of a tax** *n* ECON, TAX effet d'un impôt sur la capitalisation *m*; ~ **of interest** *n* FIN capitalisation des intérêts *f*; ~ **issue** *n* STOCK attribution d'actions gratuites *f*; ~ **of leases** *n* ACC activation des biens détenus sur contrat de crédit-bail *loc*; ~ **rate** *n* ACC, ECON taux de capitalisation *m*; ~ **ratio** *n* FIN ratio de capitalisation *m*; ~ **shares** *n pl* STOCK actions gratuites *f pl*

capitalize *vt* ACC activiser, ECON avoir recours à la capitalisation boursière *loc m*, capitaliser, FIN *estimate value of sth*, GEN COMM capitaliser, *provide with capital* pourvoir de capital, pourvoir de fonds, STOCK avoir recours à la capitalisation boursière *loc m*; ~ **on** ECON, GEN COMM tirer profit de

capitalized: ~ **interest** *n* STOCK intérêt capitalisé *m*; ~ **value** *n* ECON valeur capitalisée *f*

capitation *n* TAX impôt par tête *m*; ~ **tax** ECON capitation *f*, TAX capitation *f*, impôt de capitation *m*

CAPM *abbr (capital asset pricing model)* ECON, FIN, STOCK MEDAF *(modèle d'équilibre des actifs financiers)*

capsize *vi* TRANSP chavirer

capstan *n* TRANSP *shipping* cabestan *m*

captain *n* HRM, TRANSP *of aircraft* commandant de bord *m*, *ship's officer* capitaine *mf*, commandant *m*; ~ **of industry** GEN COMM, IND capitaine d'industrie *m*; ~**'s imperfect entry** *UK (CIE)* IMP/EXP entrée incomplète du capitaine

caption *n* COMMS en-tête *m*, MEDIA *heading* légende *f*, sous-titre *m*

captive: ~ **audience** *n* S&M public captif *m*; ~ **candidate** *n jarg* POL candidat prisonnier *m*; ~ **finance company** *n* ECON société financière satellite *f*; ~ **insurance company** *n* INS compagnie d'assurance captive *f*; ~ **market** *n* S&M marché captif *m*

capture[1] *n* COMP *of data* saisie *f*

capture[2] *vt* GEN COMM *market* s'emparer de

car *n* TRANSP *rail*, TRANSP *(cf automobile AmE, motorcar BrE)* voiture *f*; ~ **allowance** GEN COMM indemnité de déplacement *f*, indemnité kilométrique *f*; ~ **carrier** TRANSP *shipping* car-ferry *m*, transporteur d'automobiles *m*; ~ **ferry** TRANSP car-ferry *m*, navire transbordeur *m*, transbordeur *m*; ~ **hire** *BrE (cf auto rental AmE)* TRANSP location de voitures *f*; ~ **hire operator** GEN COMM loueur de voitures *m*; ~ **hire service** TRANSP service de location de voitures *m*; ~ **knocked down** TRANSP voiture désassemblée *f*; ~ **loan** BANK prêt automobile *m*; ~ **manufacturer** IND constructeur automobile *m*, fabricant automobile *m*; ~ **market watcher** GEN COMM spécialiste du marché automobile *m*; ~ **pallet** TRANSP *shipping* palette à véhicules *f*; ~ **park** *BrE (cf parking lot AmE)* GEN COMM parc de stationnement *m*, parking *m*; ~ **parking** GEN COMM stationnement *m*; ~ **pool** TRANSP covoiturage *m*, parc de voitures *m*; ~ **registration** TRANSP immatriculation *f*; ~ **rental firm** GEN COMM loueur de voitures *m*; ~ **transporter** TRANSP camion pour transport d'automobiles *m*, transporteur de voitures *m*, wagon pour transport d'automobiles *m*; ~ **worker** IND, TRANSP ouvrier de l'industrie automobile *m*

CAR *abbr UK (compound annual rate)* BANK *interest* taux annuel composé *m*, taux d'intérêt composé *m*; ~ **DI SYS** *(carbon dioxide system)* TRANSP *shipping* dispositif de CO_2 *m*

Caracas *pr n* GEN COMM Caracas *n pr*

carat *n* GEN COMM *of gold* carat *m*

carbon: ~ **copy** *n (cc)* ADMIN copie carbone *f*, COMMS copie carbone *f*, réplique *f*; ~ **dioxide emission** *n* ENVIR émission de dioxide de carbone *f*, émission de gaz carbonique *f*; ~ **dioxide system** *n (CAR DI SYS)* TRANSP *shipping* dispositif de CO_2 *m*; ~ **emission** *n* ENVIR émission de gaz carbonique *f*; ~ **monoxide** *n* ENVIR monoxyde de carbone *m*, oxyde de carbone *m*; ~ **paper** *n* COMMS papier carbone *m*

carboy *n* TRANSP bonbonne *f*

card *n* COMP *hardware*, GEN COMM carte *f*; ~ **bin** COMP case de réception *f*, magasin d'alimentation *m*; ~ **-carrying member** IND membre adhérent *m*; ~ **file** HRM fiche *f*, fichier *m*; ~ **index** ADMIN, HRM fichier *m*; ~ **issuer** BANK, GEN COMM émetteur de cartes *m*; ~ **punch** GEN COMM perforateur de cartes *m*; ~ **reader** COMP lecteur de cartes *m*; ~ **sorter** COMP trieuse de cartes *f*

CARD *abbr UK (certificate of amortized revolving debt)* FIN certificat de dette renouvelable amortie *m*

cardboard *n* *BrE (cf tagboard AmE)* GEN COMM carton *m*; ~ **box** TRANSP carton *m*

cardholder *n* BANK, GEN COMM détenteur de carte *m*, porteur de carte *m*, titulaire de carte *m*; ~ **fee** BANK droits d'utilisation *m pl*, frais d'utilisation *m pl*

Cardiff *pr n* GEN COMM Cardiff *n pr*

cardinal: ~ **utility** *n* ECON utilité primordiale *f*

cards: give sb his/her ~ *phr infrml* HRM lourder qn *(infrml)*, mettre qn dehors *(infrml)*, mettre qn à la porte *(infrml)*

care[1] *n* GEN COMM attention *f*, soin *m*; ◆ ~ **and control** WEL soins et prévention *m pl*

care:[2] ~ **of** *prep (c/o)* COMMS, GEN COMM aux bons soins de, chez

career:[1] ~ **-orientated** *adj* HRM carriériste

career[2] *n* HRM carrière *f*; ~ **advancement** *n* HRM déroulement de carrière *m*; ~ **development** *n* HRM déroulement de carrière *m*, développement de carrière *m*; ~ **expectations** *n pl* HRM attentes professionnelles *f pl*; ~ **goals** *n pl* HRM objectifs professionnels *m pl*; ~ **guidance** *n* HRM orienta-

tion professionnelle *f*; ~ **ladder** *n* HRM ascension professionnelle *f*; ~ **management** *n* HRM gestion de carrière *f*; ~ **path** *n* HRM plan de carrière *m*; ~ **planning** *n* HRM plan de carrière *m*; ~ **prospects** *n pl* HRM perspectives de carrière *f pl*, perspectives professionnelles *f pl*

Career: ~ **Development Loan** *n UK (CDL)* BANK, HRM, WEL prêt de développement de carrière *m*

careerist[1] *adj* HRM carriériste

careerist[2] *n* HRM arriviste *mf*

careers: ~ **adviser** *n* HRM, WEL *in schools* conseiller d'orientation *m*, conseiller d'orientation professionnelle *m*; ~ **officer** *n* HRM, WEL *in schools* conseiller d'orientation *m*, conseiller d'orientation professionnelle *m*, conseiller-orientateur *m*

carefully *adv* GEN COMM prudemment

cargo *n* TRANSP cargaison *f*, chargement *m*, marchandises *f pl*; ~ **-accounting device** *n* TRANSP bordereau de comptabilité de la cargaison *m*; ~ **aircraft** *n* TRANSP avion-cargo *m*; ~ **assembly** *n* TRANSP groupage des marchandises *m*; ~ **boat** *n* TRANSP cargo *m*; ~ **capacity** *n (cc)* TRANSP capacité de chargement *f*, capacité utile *f*; ~ **center** *n AmE*, ~ **centre** *n BrE* TRANSP centre de chargement *m*; ~ **claim** *n* TRANSP réclamation concernant les marchandises *f*; ~ **claims procedure** *n* TRANSP procédure de réclamation concernant les marchandises *f*; ~ **clearance** *n* IMP/EXP dédouanement de chargement *m*; ~ **configuration** *n* TRANSP configuration du chargement *f*; ~ **declaration** *n* TRANSP déclaration de chargement *f*; ~ **delivery terms** *n pl* TRANSP conditions de livraison des marchandises *f pl*; ~ **derrick** *n* TRANSP *shipping* mât de charge *m*; ~ **disassembly** *n* TRANSP dégroupage des marchandises *m*; ~ **dues** *n pl* TRANSP *shipping* frais de fret *m pl*; ~ **-handling charge** *n (CHC)* TRANSP frais de manutention *m pl*, frais de manutention des marchandises *m pl*; ~ **-handling equipment** *n* TRANSP *shipping* matériel de manutention *m*; ~ **homeward** *n (ANT cargo outward)* TRANSP *shipping* fret de retour *m*; ~ **in isolation** *n* TRANSP cargaison isolée *f*, marchandises isolées *f pl*; ~ **inspector** *n* HRM, TRANSP inspecteur du fret *m*; ~ **insurance** *n* INS assurance sur facultés *f*; ~ **liner** *n* TRANSP *shipping* cargo de ligne régulière *m*, cargo mixte *m*; ~ **manifest** *n* TRANSP manifeste de marchandises *m*, *shipping* manifeste de marchandises *m*; ~ **marking symbol** *n* TRANSP marquage des marchandises *m*; ~ **mix** *n* TRANSP ensemble de marchandises *m*; ~ **net** *n* TRANSP *cargo-handling equipment* filet d'élingue *m*; ~ **oil** *n (c/o)* TRANSP huile de carter *f*; ~ **outward** *n (ANT cargo homeward)* TRANSP *shipping* fret aller *m*; ~ **plan** *n* TRANSP plan d'arrimage *m*, plan de chargement *m*; ~ **plane** *n infrml* TRANSP avion-cargo *m*; ~ **ship safety construction certificate** *n* TRANSP certificat de sécurité de construction pour navire de charge *m*; ~ **ship safety equipment certificate** *n* TRANSP certificat de sécurité du matériel d'armement pour navire de charge *m*;

~ shut-out *n* TRANSP cargaison exclue *f*, marchandises exclues *f pl*; **~ stowage** *n* TRANSP arrimage de la cargaison *m*, arrimage des marchandises *m*; **~ superintendent** *n* HRM, TRANSP directeur des services du fret *m*; **~ surveyor** *n* HRM, TRANSP inspecteur du fret *m*; **~ tag** *n* TRANSP étiquette de marchandises *f*; **~ tank** *n* (*CT*) ENVIR, TRANSP citerne de cargo *f*, citerne à cargaison *f*; **~ tank center** *n AmE*, **~ tank centre** *n BrE* (*CTC*) TRANSP citerne centrale de cargaison *f*; **~ tank common** *n* (*CTX*) TRANSP *shipping* citerne standard *f*; **~ tank wing** *n* (*CTW*) TRANSP *shipping* citerne latérale *f*, citerne latérale de cargaison *f*; **~ tonnage** *n* TRANSP capacité de chargement *f*, capacité utile *f*, tonnage de cargaison *m*; **~ traffic procedures committee** *n* (*CTPC*) GEN COMM, TRANSP commission pour les procédures de mouvement de cargaisons *f*; **~ transfer** *n* TRANSP transbordement de marchandises *m*, transfert de marchandises *m*; **~ transit** *n* TRANSP transit de marchandises *m*; **~ tray** *n* TRANSP *cargo-handling equipment* plateau de cargaison *m*; **~ vessel** *n* TRANSP *shipping* cargo *m*; ◆ **~ tonne kilometers used** *AmE*, **~ tonne kilometres used** *BrE* TRANSP tonne-kilomètres fret complètes *f pl*

Cargo: **~ Accounts Settlement System** *n* (*CASS*) TRANSP système de règlement des comptes marchandises *m*; **~ IMP** *n* (*Cargo Information Message Procedures*) TRANSP procédures pour messages d'information sur le fret; **~ Information Message Procedures** *n pl* (*Cargo IMP*) TRANSP procédures pour messages d'information sur le fret

Caribbean: **~ Development Bank** *n* (*CDB*) BANK Banque de développement des Caraïbes *f*

caring: **~ capitalism** *n* ECON, POL capitalisme bénévole *m*; **~ society** *n* ECON, POL société altruiste *f*, société humanitaire *f*

carload: **~ rate** *n* TRANSP tarif charge complète *m*, tarif par wagon *m*

carnet *n* IMP/EXP autorisation d'importation temporaire *f*, passavant *m*; **~ system** IMP/EXP *EU* système à carnet *m*

carr: **~ fwd** *abbr* (*carriage forward*) GEN COMM, TRANSP p.d. (*port dû*); **~ pd** *abbr* (*carriage paid*) TRANSP p.p. (*port payé*)

carriage:[1] **~ -paid** *adj* TRANSP franco

carriage[2] *n* TRANSP factage *m*, transport *m*, voiture *f*, *rail* wagon voyageurs *m*; **~ charge** *n* IMP/EXP, TRANSP *shipping* frais de port *m pl*; **~ expenses** *n pl* IMP/EXP, TRANSP *shipping* frais de port *m pl*; **~ international** *n* (ANT *cabotage*) TRANSP transport international *m*; **~ return** *n* (*CR*) COMP retour de chariot *m*, retour de curseur *m*; ◆ **~ forward** (*CF, carr fwd*) GEN COMM, TRANSP port dû *m* (*p.d.*); **~ -free** IMP/EXP franco de port; **~ and insurance paid to** (*CIP*) IMP/EXP port et assurance payés jusqu'à, port payé assurance comprise jusqu'à; **~ paid** (*carr pd*) TRANSP port payé *m* (*p.p.*); **~ paid to** (*CPT*) IMP/EXP port payé jusqu'à

Carriage: **~ of Goods by Road Act** *n* LAW *1965*, TRANSP loi relative au transport des marchandises par route; **~ of Goods by Sea Act** *n* (*COGSA*) LAW, TRANSP *1924, 1971* loi relative au transport des marchandises par mer

carriageway *n* TRANSP piste *f*, voie *f*

carried: **~ down** *adj* (*cd*) ACC *on balance sheet* à reporter; **~ forward** *adj* (*CF*) ACC, GEN COMM *bookkeeping* à reporter

carrier *n* COMP porteuse *f*, FIN porteur *m*, émetteur *m*, TRANSP *aviation* transporteur aérien *m*, *road* camionneur *m*, entreprise de camionnage *f*, entreprise de transports routiers *f*, transporteur *m*; **~ haulage** TRANSP *shipping* acheminement par le transporteur maritime *m*; **~'s liability** INS assurance de responsabilité *f*; **~'s lien** TRANSP privilège du transporteur *m*, privilège du voiturier *m*; ◆ **~'s risk** (*CR*) TRANSP aux risques et périls du transporteur, risque du transporteur *m*

carrot: **~ and stick** *n* MGMNT *negotiations* méthode de la carotte et du bâton *f*; **~ and stick approach** *n* MGMNT méthode de la carotte et du bâton *f*; **~ and stick method** *n* MGMNT méthode de la carotte et du bâton *f*

carry:[1] **~ -back** *n* ACC, TAX application à une année antérieure *f*, report en amont *m*, report rétrospectif *m*, report sur les exercices précédents *m*, report sur une année antérieure *m*; **~ -forward** *n* ACC, TAX report en aval *m*, report prospectif *m*, report sur les exercices suivants *m*, report sur une année ultérieure *m*; **~ -over** *n* ACC, FIN report *m*; **~ -over business** *n* STOCK report sur exercice suivant *m*; **~ -over effect** *n* MEDIA *print* effet de rappel *m*, effet de rémanence *m*; **~ -over loss** *n* ACC déficit reportable sur les années suivantes *m*; **~ -over stocks** *n pl* GEN COMM stocks de report *m pl*, stocks reportés *m pl*

carry[2] *vt* FIN comptabiliser, enregistrer, STOCK *risk* comporter, TRANSP *goods* transporter; **~ back** ACC, TAX reporter en amont, reporter en arrière; **~ down** ACC, FIN reporter, reporter en avant; **~ forward** ACC, FIN reporter prospectivement, reporter sur un exercice ultérieur; **~ on** GEN COMM *business* diriger, exploiter, faire marcher; **~ out** ACC *audit* effectuer, GEN COMM *instruction, order* exécuter, *plans, policies* mettre en oeuvre, mettre en pratique, mettre à exécution, HRM *duties* remplir, PATENTS *invention* réaliser, S&M *research, survey* mener; ◆ **~ information on** GEN COMM apporter des éléments sur, contenir des renseignements sur; **~ a loss** ACC, FIN enregistrer une perte; **~ out a trial on a new product** GEN COMM mettre un nouveau produit à l'essai; **~ a report** GEN COMM *newspaper* contenir un rapport

carrying: **~ capacity** *n* TRANSP *shipping* capacité de charge *f*, charge utile *f*, jauge *f*, tonnage *m*; **~ capacity in number and length in holds** *n* (*CHo*) TRANSP *of ship* charge utile dans les cales en nombre et longueur *f*; **~ capacity in number and length on deck** *n* (*CDK*) TRANSP *shipping* charge utile sur le pont en nombre et longueur *f*;

~ **cash** n FIN coût de portage m; ~ **charge** n PROP frais de jouissance m pl, STOCK frais de couverture m pl, frais de portage m pl, frais de possession m pl, TRANSP *commodities* frais de possession m pl; ~ **cost** n STOCK frais de couverture m pl, frais de portage m pl, frais de possession m pl; ~ **-out** n PATENTS mise en oeuvre f

cart n *AmE (cf trolley BrE)* TRANSP chariot m

cartage n TRANSP camionnage m, factage m

cartel n ECON, HRM cartel m; ~ **commission** GEN COMM commission des cartels f

carton n TRANSP carton m, emballage en carton m

cartouche n TRANSP cartouche f

cartridge n TRANSP cartouche f

carve: ~ **-out rules** n pl TAX dispositions sur les biens restreints f pl

carving: ~ **note** n *UK* TRANSP *shipping* feuille autorisant l'inscription sur le navire de son nom/numéro et son jaugeage

CAS abbr *Can (Central Accounting System)* ACC SCC *(Can) (système central de comptabilité)*

case:[1] ~ **-sensitive** adj COMP qui n'utilise que les majuscules ou les minuscules

case[2] n LAW affaire f, cas m, cause f, procès m, LEIS valise f, MEDIA *print* casse f, TRANSP, TRANSP *(CS)* caisse f; ~ **file** n GEN COMM dossier m; ~ **for the defence** n *BrE* LAW la défense f; ~ **for the defense** n *AmE see case for the defence BrE*; ~ **for the prosecution** n LAW accusation f; ~ **history** n GEN COMM dossier personnel m, historique m, S&M *advertising* exemple typique m; ~ **law** n HRM jurisprudence f, LAW droit jurisprudentiel m, jurisprudence f; ~ **notes** n GEN COMM dossier m; ~ **oil** n *(clo)* TRANSP *shipping* huile de carter f; ~ **packaging** n *(Cl-)* TRANSP emballage en caisses m; ~ **papers** n pl GEN COMM pièces d'un dossier f pl; ~ **shift** n COMP inversion f; ~ **study** n GEN COMM, S&M étude de cas f; ~ **study method** n MGMNT *formulation of policy* méthode de l'étude de cas f; ◆ **in this** ~ GEN COMM dans le cas présent

CASE abbr *(computer-aided software engineering, computer-assisted software engineering)* COMP CPAO *(conception de programmes assistée par ordinateur)*

casebound[1] adj MEDIA *book* cartonné

casebound:[2] ~ **book** n MEDIA *print* livre cartonné m, livre emboîté m, livre relié en dur m

cash:[1] ~ **-poor** adj *(ANT cash-rich)* ACC, FIN pauvre en liquidité; ~ **-rich** adj *(ANT cash-poor)* ACC, FIN riche en liquidité; ~ **-settled** adj GEN COMM *delivery procedure* réglé en espèces; ~ **-strapped** adj FIN sans liquidité, à court de liquidité

cash[2] n ACC caisse f, disponibilités f pl, *funds in cash or at disposal of cashier* encaisse f, *funds available for a particular use* fonds m pl, *liquid capital of organization* trésorerie f, ADMIN trésorerie f, FIN fonds m pl, *amount available immediately* liquidités f pl, *available capital* disponibilités f pl, liquide m, *funds in cash or at disposal of cashier* encaisse f, *liquid capital of*

organization trésorerie f, *notes, coins* argent liquide m, espèces f pl, GEN COMM *currency* monnaie f, *legal tender* argent m, *money paid at time of purchase* argent comptant m, comptant m, S&M *money paid at time of purchase* argent comptant m, comptant m; ~ **account** n BANK compte au comptant m, compte d'espèces m, compte de caisse m; ~ **accounting** n *(SYN cash basis)* ACC comptabilité de caisse f; ~ **acknowledgment** n FIN reconnaissance de dépôt f, récépissé m; ~ **advance** n GEN COMM avance de trésorerie f, crédit de caisse m, débours m; ~ **against documents** n *(CAD)* IMP/EXP comptant contre documents; ~ **assets** n pl ACC actif liquide m; ~ **balance** n ACC solde de caisse m, solde de trésorerie m; ~ **bargain** n STOCK marché au comptant m, marché à prime m, opération au comptant f; ~ **basis** n *(SYN cash accounting)* ACC comptabilité de caisse f; ~ **basis of accounting** n ACC comptabilité de caisse f, comptabilité de trésorerie f; ~ **benefit** n GEN COMM avantage supplémentaire m, prestation en espèces f, INS prestation en espèces f; ~ **bonus** n STOCK *on bonds* prime en argent f; ~ **box** n GEN COMM caisse f; ~ **budget** n ACC budget de trésorerie m; ~ **budgeting** n ACC préparation des budgets de trésorerie f, ECON budget de trésorerie m; ~ **buyer** n S&M acheteur au comptant m; ~ **card** n BANK carte de crédit f, carte de retrait bancaire f; ~ **and carry arbitrage** n STOCK arbitrage cash-and-carry m, arbitrage comptant-terme m; ~ **certificate** n FIN bon de caisse m; ~ **collection** n FIN entrée de caisse f; ~ **contribution** n ACC apport en espèces m; ~ **control** n ACC contrôle de caisse m; ~ **control record** n ACC registre de contrôle de caisse m; ~ **control system** n ACC système de contrôle de la caisse m; ~ **conversion cycle** n FIN cycle de conversion de liquidités m; ~ **cow** n jarg ECON mine d'or f, vache à lait f *(jarg)*; ~ **cow product** n GEN COMM produit vache à lait m, produit à forte rentabilité m; ~ **credit** n *(ANT purchase credit)* GEN COMM crédit d'achat m, crédit de caisse m; ~ **crop** n ECON culture commerciale f, culture de rapport f, récolte de rapport f, récolte destinée à la vente f, ENVIR récolte de rapport f, récolte destinée à la vente f; ~ **deal** n ACC transaction au comptant f; ~ **and debt position** n BANK situation de la caisse et de la dette; ~ **deficit** n ACC déficit de caisse m, déficit de trésorerie m; ~ **delivery option** n STOCK option donnant lieu à un règlement en espèces f; ~ **department** n GEN COMM service de la caisse m; ~ **deposit acknowledgment** n FIN *of receipt of order* reconnaissance de dépôt f; ~ **deposits ratio** n ACC, BANK, ECON, FIN coefficient de trésorerie m, ratio de trésorerie m; ~ **desk** n BANK, GEN COMM, S&M caisse f; ~ **disbursement** n ACC, BANK, FIN débours m, décaissement m, sortie de fonds f; ~ **discount** n S&M escompte de caisse m; ~ **-dispensing machine** n BANK billetterie automatique f, distributeur automatique de billets m, distributeur de billets m; ~ **dividend** n FIN, STOCK dividende en espèces *m*; ~ **drawdown** *n* ACC *government accounting* paiement comptant *m*; ~ **earnings** *n* FIN bénéfices en espèces *m pl*; ~ **economy** *n* ECON économie du sans facture *f*; ~ **equivalence** *n* S&M équivalence de valeur *f*; ~ **equivalent** *n* FIN quasi-espèces *f pl*, équivalent de trésorerie *f pl*; ~ **exchange rate** *n* ECON cours des changes au comptant *m*; ~ **flow** *n* ACC cash-flow *m*, fonds autogénérés *m pl*, marge brute d'autofinancement *f*, MBA, flux de l'encaisse *m*, flux de trésorerie *m*, mouvements de l'encaisse *m pl*, mouvements de trésorerie *m pl*; ~ **flow accounting** *n* ACC comptabilité de caisse *f*, comptabilité de trésorerie *f*; ~ **flow forecast** *n* ACC prévision de trésorerie *f*; ~ **flow per share** *n* STOCK MBA par action, fonds autogénérés par action *m pl*, marge brute d'autofinancement par action *f*; ~ **flow problem** *n* ACC problème de liquidité *m*, problème de trésorerie *m*; ~ **flow squeeze** *n* GEN COMM coup de bélier *m* (*infrml*); ~ **forecast** *n* ACC, FIN plan de trésorerie *m*, prévision de caisse *f*, prévision de trésorerie *f*; ~ **holdings** *n pl* ACC disponibilités *f pl*; ~ **in bank** *n* BANK fonds disponibles en banque *m pl*; ~ **in hand** *n* ACC, GEN COMM argent en caisse *m*, fonds de caisse *m*; ~ **in transit** *n* ACC *government accounting* effets en transit *m pl*; ~ **-in value** *n* FIN valeur liquidative *f*; ~ **inflow** *n* (ANT *cash outflow*) ACC, BANK, ECON, FIN, GEN COMM recettes liquides *f pl*, rentrée d'argent *f*, rentrée de fonds *f*; ~ **journal** *n* ACC livre de caisse *m*; ~ **limit** *n* ECON limite de trésorerie *f*, plafond des dépenses *m*, FIN, HRM limite des disponibilités de trésorerie *f*, limite du disponible *f*; ~ **loss** *n* INS sinistre au comptant *m*; ~ **management** *n* ACC, FIN, MGMNT gestion de trésorerie *f*; ~ **management account** *n* (*CMA*) FIN compte de gestion de fonds *m*; ~ **management system** *n* BANK système de gestion de caisse *m*, système de gestion de trésorerie *m*; ~ **management techniques** *n pl* MGMNT techniques de gestion de trésorerie *f pl*; ~ **manager** *n* FIN, HRM responsable financier *m*, trésorier *m*; ~ **market** *n* STOCK marché au comptant *m*; ~ **market rates** *n pl* STOCK taux du marché au comptant *m*; ~ **messenger insurance** *n* INS assurance vol sur la personne *f*; ~ **needs** *n pl* ACC besoins de liquidités *m pl*; ~ **office** *n* ACC, ADMIN, FIN bureau de la caissière *m*, bureau du caissier *m*, caisse *f*, trésorerie *f*; ~ **on delivery** *n* (*COD*) IMP/EXP, S&M livraison contre remboursement, paiement à la livraison *m*; ~ **on shipment** *n* (*cos*) TRANSP *shipping* comptant à l'expédition *m*; ~ **operation** *n* ACC opération de caisse *f*, opération de trésorerie *f*; ~ **outflow** *n* (ANT *cash inflow*) ACC, BANK décaissement *m*, sortie d'argent *f*, sortie de fonds *f*, sortie de trésorerie *f*, ECON sortie d'argent *f*, FIN décaissement *m*, sortie d'argent *f*, sortie de fonds *f*, sortie de trésorerie *f*, GEN COMM sortie d'argent *f*; ~ **payment** *n* ACC paiement comptant *m*, BANK paiement comptant *m*, paiement en espèces *m*; ~ **payments journal** *n* ACC journal des sorties de caisse *m*; ~ **position** *n* ACC situation de

caisse *f*, situation de trésorerie *f*; ~ **purchase** *n* GEN COMM achat au comptant *m*; ~ **ratio** *n* ACC, BANK, ECON, FIN coefficient de trésorerie *m*, ratio de trésorerie *m*; ~ **receipt** *n* ACC, FIN recettes *f pl*, recettes au comptant *f pl*, recettes en espèces *f pl*, rentrées d'argent *f pl*, rentrées de fonds *f pl*; ~ **receipts journal** *n* ACC journal des recettes au comptant *m*, journal des rentrées de fonds *m*; ~ **refunding date** *n* STOCK *interest rate futures* date de remboursement en espèces *f*; ~ **register** *n* GEN COMM caisse *f*, S&M caisse *f*, caisse enregistreuse *f*; ~ **requirements** *n pl* ACC besoins de liquidités *m pl*; ~ **reserve** *n* ACC réserve de trésorerie *f*, BANK réserve en espèces *f*; ~ **resource** *n* ACC, FIN ressource de trésorerie *f*; ~ **risk** *n* STOCK risque trésorien *m*; ~ **-settled option** *n* STOCK option donnant lieu à un règlement en espèces *f*; ~ **settlement** *n* FIN, STOCK liquidation en espèces *f*, règlement en espèces *m*; ~ **short** *n* ACC différence de caisse *f*, écart de caisse *m*; ~ **statement** *n* ACC bordereau de caisse *m*, état de caisse *m*; ~ **streams** *n pl* FIN rentrées de fonds *f pl*; ~ **surplus** *n* ACC excédent de caisse *m*, excédent de trésorerie *m*; ~ **surrender value** *n* INS *life insurance* valeur de rachat *f*, valeur de rachat au comptant *f*; ~ **transaction** *n* ACC opération de caisse *f*, opération de trésorerie *f*, GEN COMM opération au comptant *f*, opération de caisse *f*; ~ **transfer** *n* ACC transfert pécuniaire *m*, BANK transfert de fonds *m*; ~ **value** *n* ACC valeur de caisse *f*; ~ **value life insurance** *n* US INS valeur de rachat d'assurance vie *f*; ~ **voucher** *n* ACC pièce de caisse *f*, pièce justificative de caisse *f*; ~ **withdrawal** *n* BANK retrait d'espèces *m*, retrait en espèces *m*; ◆ ~ **before delivery** (*CBD*) GEN COMM, S&M livraison dès réception du paiement, paiement avant la livraison *m*; **for** ~ (*flc*) GEN COMM comptant, contre espèces; **have** ~ **flow problems** ACC avoir des difficultés de trésorerie; **have** ~ **in hand** FIN avoir de l'argent disponible, avoir de l'argent en caisse; **have** ~ **on hand** FIN avoir de l'argent disponible, avoir de l'argent en caisse; ~ **in advance** ACC paiement d'avance en espèces *m*, payé comptant à l'avance; **on a** ~ **received basis** ACC *supplies only for cash* au fur et à mesure que le paiement est reçu; ~ **with order** (*CWO*) FIN, GEN COMM, S&M paiement à la commande *m*, payable à la commande; **strapped for** ~ *jarg* ECON à court d'argent

cash³ *vt* BANK *cheque* encaisser, toucher; ~ **in** STOCK *bonds* réaliser, se faire rembourser; ~ **in on** FIN *demand* exploiter, profiter de, tirer profit de

cashable *adj* BANK encaissable, payable à vue

cashbook *n* ACC livre de banque *m*, livre de caisse *m*

cashier *n* BANK, S&M caissier *m*; ~**'s check** *AmE*, ~**'s cheque** *BrE* BANK traite bancaire *f*; ~**'s error allowance** GEN COMM passe de caisse *f*

cashiering: ~ **department** *n* UK FIN service des

recettes et des dépenses *m*, service encaissement *m*

cashless: ~ **payment system** *n* BANK système de paiement sans argent *m*; ~ **society** *n* GEN COMM société sans argent *f*

casino *n* LEIS casino *m*

cask *n* *(ck)* TRANSP fût *m*, tonneau *m*

CASS *abbr* *(Cargo Accounts Settlement System)* TRANSP système de règlement des comptes marchandises *m*

cassette *n* COMMS, COMP cassette *f*; ~ **player** COMP lecteur de cassette *m*; ~ **recorder** GEN COMM magnétocassette *m*, magnétophone à cassettes *m*

cast:[1] ~ **-iron hub non-ferrous blades propeller** *n* *(CIHBB)* TRANSP *shipping* hélice à moyeu en fonte et à pales non-ferreuses *f*; ~ **-iron hub steel blades propeller** *n* *(CIHSB)* TRANSP *shipping* hélice à moyeu en fonte et à pales en acier *f*

cast:[2] ~ **off** *vt* MEDIA *advertising*, S&M *advertising* calibrer

casting: ~ **off** *n* TRANSP *shipping* largage des amarres *m*

Castries *pr n* GEN COMM Castries *n pr*

casual: ~ **labor** *n* *AmE see casual labour BrE*; ~ **laborer** *n* *AmE see casual labourer BrE*; ~ **labour** *n* *BrE* HRM *personnel, staff* main-d'oeuvre occasionnelle *f*, main-d'oeuvre temporaire *f*, personnel intérimaire *m*; ~ **labourer** *n BrE* HRM intérimaire *mf*, *on building site* ouvrier sans travail fixe *m*, *on farm* journalier *m*; ~ **show-business labor** *n AmE*, ~ **show-business labour** *n BrE* HRM intermittents du spectacle *m pl*; ~ **work** *n* HRM travail intermittent *m*, travail occasionnel *m*, travail temporaire *m*; ~ **worker** *n* HRM employé temporaire *m*, travailleur intermittent *m*, travailleur temporaire *m*

casualty: ~ **insurance** *n* INS assurance-accidents et risques divers *f*

CAT *abbr* COMP *(computer-aided teaching, computer-assisted teaching)* EAO *(enseignement assisté par ordinateur)*, COMP *(computer-aided translation, computer-assisted translation)* TAO *(traduction assistée par ordinateur)*, COMP *(computer-aided testing, computer-assisted testing)* TAO *(test assisté par ordinateur)*, WEL *(computer-aided teaching, computer-assisted teaching)* EAO *(enseignement assisté par ordinateur)*, WEL *(computer-aided testing, computer-assisted testing)* TAO *(test assisté par ordinateur)*

Catalan *n* GEN COMM *language* catalan *m*

catalog *n* *AmE see catalogue BrE*

catalogue *n* *BrE* GEN COMM *of errors* fichier *m*, liste *f*, *of products* catalogue *m*; ~ **price** GEN COMM, S&M prix catalogue *m*, prix de catalogue *m*, prix public *m*

catalyst *n* GEN COMM catalyseur *m*

catalytic: ~ **converter** *n* ENVIR *in vehicle* pot catalytique *m*

catastrophe: ~ **cover** *n* INS couverture de pointe *f*; ~ **hazard** *n* INS risque de catastrophe *m*; ~ **policy** *n*

INS police contre catastrophe *f*, police de catastrophe *f*; ~ **reserve** *n* INS réserve pour catastrophe *f*; ~ **risk** *n* INS risque de catastrophe *m*; ~ **theory** *n* MATH théorie catastrophe *f*

catastrophic: ~ **loss** *n* GEN COMM perte catastrophique *f*, perte énorme *f*

catch:[1] ~ **-all account** *n* BANK compte omnibus *m*; ~ **line** *n* S&M *advertising* slogan publicitaire *m*; ~ **-up demand** *n* ECON rattrapage de la demande *m*; ~ **-up effect** *n* HRM effet de rattrapage *m*; ~ **-up increase** *n* HRM augmentation de rattrapage *f*

catch:[2] ~ **up** *vi* GEN COMM rattraper; ◆ ~ **up for lost time** GEN COMM rattraper le temps perdu, rattraper son retard

catching: ~ **-up hypothesis** *n* ECON hypothèse du rattrapage économique *f*

catchment: ~ **area** *n* S&M zone d'appel *f*, zone d'attraction *f*, zone de chalandise *f*

categorical: ~ **grant** *n* POL subvention catégorique *f*

categorization *n* GEN COMM catégorisation *f*

categorize *vt* ADMIN classer, GEN COMM catégoriser, classer, classer par catégories

category *n* GEN COMM, PATENTS catégorie *f*; ~ **B share** STOCK action ordinaire avec droit de vote

cater: ~ **for** *vt* GEN COMM *food* s'occuper de la nourriture, *needs* pourvoir à, s'adresser à, satisfaire

catering *n* LEIS restauration *f*, TRANSP armement *m*, ravitaillement *m*; ~ **officer** HRM, TRANSP *shipping* officier d'intendance *m*; ~ **trade** LEIS restauration *f*

cathode: ~ **ray tube** *n* *(CRT)* COMP tube à rayons cathodiques *m* *(TRC)*

cathodic: ~ **protection** *n* TRANSP *shipping* protection cathodique *f*

cats: ~ **and dogs** *n pl* STOCK actions et obligations de valeur douteuse *f pl*

CATS *abbr* STOCK *(computer-assisted trading system)* système de cotation électronique *m*, STOCK US *(Certificate of Accrual on Treasury Securities)* bon du Trésor américain à coupon zéro

cattle *n* ECON bétail *m*; ~ **container** TRANSP conteneur à bestiaux *m*; ~ **float** *Aus (cf cattle truck, stock car AmE)* TRANSP bétaillère *f*; ~ **truck** *(cf cattle float Aus)* TRANSP bétaillère *f*

causa sine qua non *n frml* GEN COMM condition sine qua non *loc f*

cause:[1] *n* LAW action *f*, POL cause *f*; ~ **of action** LAW *claim* droit d'action *m*, fondement d'une action *m*; ~ **of cancellation** INS cause de résiliation *f*, motif de résiliation *m*; ~ **of loss** INS cause du sinistre *f*

cause:[2] *vt* GEN COMM causer, occasionner, provoquer; ◆ ~ **concern** GEN COMM préoccuper; ~ **undue hardship** TAX *to taxpayer* porter indûment préjudice

causes *n pl* GEN COMM causes *f pl*; ~ **of unemployment** HRM causes de chômage *f pl*

caution *n* GEN COMM circonspection *f*, mise en garde *f*, prudence *f*, LAW avertissement *m*; **~ money** GEN COMM caution *f*, dépôt de garantie *m*, LAW caution *f*, cautionnement *m*

cautionary *adj* LAW donné en garantie

cautious *adj* GEN COMM prudent, précautionneux

caveat emptor *phr* LAW aux risques de l'acheteur *loc m*, que l'acheteur prenne garde *loc m*, sans garantie du fournisseur

caveat venditor *phr* LAW aux risques du vendeur *loc m*

CAXB *abbr (composite auxiliary boiler)* TRANSP *shipping* chaudière auxiliaire mixte *f*

CAXBS *abbr (composite auxiliary boiler survey)* TRANSP *shipping* visite de la chaudière auxiliaire mixte *f*

CB *abbr BrE (container base)* TRANSP *shipping* magasin de groupage *m*

CBD *abbr* ECON *(central business district)* centre d'affaires d'une ville *m*, GEN COMM *(cash before delivery)*, S&M *(cash before delivery)* livraison dès réception du paiement *loc f*, paiement avant la livraison *m*

CBF *abbr UK (Central Bank Facility)* BANK banque centrale *f*

CBI *abbr (Confederation of British Industry)* GEN COMM, IND ≈ CNPF *(Conseil national du patronat français)*

cbm *abbr (cubic meter, cubic metre)* GEN COMM m3 *(mètre cube)*

CBM *abbr (conventional mooring buoy)* TRANSP *shipping* corps-mort traditionnel *m*

CBO *abbr US (Congressional Budget Office)* FIN Commission des finances *f*, POL Bureau du budget du Congrès *m*

CBOE *abbr (Chicago Board Options Exchange)* STOCK bourse des options de Chicago, ≈ MONEP *(Marché des options négociables de Paris)*

CBS: ~ Tendency index *n* STOCK indice des principales valeurs de la Bourse d'Amsterdam

CBT *abbr* COMP *(computer-based training)* EAO *(enseignement assisté par ordinateur)*, STOCK *US (Chicago Board of Trade)* bourse des matières premières et des contrats à terme de Chicago, ≈ MATIF *(France)*, TRANSP *(clean ballast tank)* *shipping* citerne à ballast propre *f*, WEL *(computer-based training)* EAO *(enseignement assisté par ordinateur)*

cc *abbr* ADMIN *(carbon copy)*, COMMS *(carbon copy)* copie carbone *f*, réplique *f*, COMMS *(charges collect)* prélèvement de droits *m*, GEN COMM *(cubic capacity, cubic centimeter, cubic centimetre)* cc *(cylindrée)*, cm³ *(centimètre cube)*, GEN COMM *(civil commotion)* insurrection populaire *f*, INS *(continuation clause)* clause de prolongation *f*, clause de report *f*, INS *(civil commotion)* insurrection populaire *f*, trouble intérieur *m*, POL *(civil commotion)* insurrection populaire *f*, émeute *f*, TRANSP *(canvas cover)* bâche non-imperméable *f*, gaine en toile à voile *f*,

TRANSP *(cargo capacity)* capacité de chargement *f*, capacité utile *f*, TRANSP *(container control)* contrôle des conteneurs *m*

CC *abbr* ECON *(Chamber of Commerce)* Chambre de commerce *f*, GEN COMM *UK (county council)* ≈ conseil général *m*

CCA *abbr* ACC *(current cost accounting)* comptabilité aux coûts de remplacement *f*, comptabilité de coûts courants *f*, TAX *(capital cost allowance)* DPA *(Can)* *(déduction pour amortissement)*

CCC *abbr* ECON *(Canadian Chamber of Commerce)* Chambre de commerce canadienne *f*, IMP/EXP *(Customs Cooperation Council)* conseil de la coopération douanière

CCCN *abbr (Customs Cooperation Council nomenclature)* IMP/EXP nomenclature du conseil de coopération douanière

CCL *abbr (customs clearance)* IMP/EXP dédouanement *m*

CCLN *abbr (consignment note control label number)* TRANSP numéro de l'étiquette de contrôle du bordereau d'expédition *m*

CC/O *abbr (certificate of consignment/origin)* IMP/EXP certificat d'expédition/d'origine *m*

CCS *abbr* IMP/EXP *(customs clearance status)* état de dédouanement *m*, TRANSP *(consolidate-cargo service)* service de groupage *m*

CCT *abbr* ECON *(compensating common tariff)* tarif commun compensatoire *m*, IMP/EXP *(common customs tariff)* *EU* tarif douanier commun *m*, tarif douanier communautaire *m*

cd *abbr* ACC *(carried down)* à reporter, STOCK *(cum dividend)* avec dividende *loc m*, coupon attaché *m*, dividende attaché *m*

CD *abbr* ADMIN *(consular declaration)* carte consulaire *f*, déclaration consulaire *f*, BANK *(certificate of deposit)* CD *(certificat de dépôt)*, COMP *(compact disk)* CD *(disque compact)*, ECON *(certificate of deposit)* CD *(certificat de dépôt)*, IMP/EXP *(consular declaration)* carte consulaire *f*, déclaration consulaire *f*, IMP/EXP *(customs declaration)* déclaration en douane *f*, STOCK *(certificate of deposit)* bond CD *(certificat de dépôt)*, TRANSP *(commercial dock)* bassin de commerce *m*, port de commerce *m*, TRANSP *(clutch drive)* entraînement d'embrayage *m*, transmission par engrenages réducteurs *f*, TRANSP *(customs declaration)* *shipping* déclaration en douane *f*

CDA *abbr (capital dividend account)* TAX CDC *(compte de dividende en capital)*

CDE *abbr (Canadian development expense)* ECON FAC *(frais d'aménagement au Canada)*

CD-I *abbr (compact disk interactive)* COMP CDI *(disque compact interactif)*

CDK *abbr (carrying capacity in number and length on deck)* TRANSP *shipping* charge utile sur le pont en nombre et longueur *f*

CDL *abbr UK (Career Development Loan)* BANK, HRM, WEL prêt de développement de carrière *m*

CD-ROM *abbr (compact disk read-only memory)* COMP *hardware* CD-ROM *(disque CD-ROM)*

CDV *abbr (current domestic value)* IMP/EXP valeur intérieure actuelle *f*

CE *abbr (Council of Europe)* POL CE *(Conseil de l'Europe)*

CEA *abbr* ECON *(Council of Economic Advisers)* Comité des conseillers économiques *m*, Réunion des conseillers économiques *f*, STOCK *US (Commodity Exchange Authority)* bourse de commerce

cease:[1] ~ **-trading order** *n* STOCK interdiction d'opérations *f*

cease[2] **1.** *vt* GEN COMM cesser; **2.** *vi* GEN COMM prendre fin; ♦ ~ **to be extant** TAX cesser d'exister; ~ **to have effect** LAW *contract* arriver à échéance, devenir caduc, prendre fin; ~ **trading** GEN COMM cesser ses activités

CEC *abbr UK (Clothing Export Council)* IMP/EXP conseil d'exportation de l'habillement

cedant *n* INS, LAW cédant *m*

cede *vt* INS, LAW céder

Cedel *n* STOCK *settlement of bonds* organisme de compensation des valeurs mobilières (Luxembourg - Centrale de livraison de valeurs mobilières)

cedi *n* GEN COMM cédi *m*

ceding: ~ **company** *n* INS compagnie cédante *f*

CEE *abbr (Canadian exploration expense)* TAX FEC *(frais d'exploration au Canada)*

Ceefax® *n UK* COMMS service de télétexte de la BBC

CEIC *abbr (closed-end investment company)* FIN SICAF *(société d'investissement à capital fermé ou fixe)*

ceiling *n* ECON, HRM, S&M, STOCK plafond *m*; ~ **price** ECON prix plafond *m*; ~ **rate** STOCK *interest rate futures* taux plafond *m*; ~ **tax rate** TAX taux plafond de l'impôt *m*

cell *n* COMP *case f*, cellule *f*, TRANSP *container securing* cellule *f*; ~ **guide** TRANSP *container securing* cellule de guidage *f*; ~ **organization** IND *production* organisation cellulaire *f*

cellphone *n* COMMS téléphone cellulaire *m*, téléphone portatif *m*, GEN COMM téléphone cellulaire *m*, téléphone sans fil *m*

cellular: ~ **container ship** *n* TRANSP navire porte-conteneurs spécialisé *m*, porte-conteneurs entièrement cellulaire *m*; ~ **phone** *n* COMMS téléphone cellulaire *m*, téléphone portatif *m*; ~ **radio** *n* COMMS radio cellulaire *f*

Celsius *n* GEN COMM Celsius *m*

CEMA *abbr (Customs and Excise Management Act)* IMP/EXP, LAW loi régissant l'administration des impôts indirects et des droits de douanes

cement: ~ **wagon** *n* TRANSP wagon à ciment *m*

CENE *abbr (Commission on Energy and the Environment)* ENVIR Commission sur l'énergie et l'environnement *f*

censorship *n* COMMS, MEDIA censure *f*

censure *vt* GEN COMM critiquer, réprouver

census *n* ECON recensement *m*, GEN COMM dénombrement *m*, recensement *m*, IND, MATH, S&M recensement *m*; ~ **of business** *US* ECON recensement de l'activité économique *m*; ~ **of manufactures** *US* ECON, IND recensement de fabrications *m*; ~ **of retail trade** *US* ECON, S&M recensement du commerce de détail *m*

cent *n* BANK, GEN COMM cent *m*

center *n AmE see* **centre** *BrE*

centerfold *n AmE see* **centrefold** *BrE*

centigrade *adj* GEN COMM centigrade

centiliter *n AmE*, **centilitre** *n BrE (cl)* GEN COMM centilitre *m (cl)*

centime *n (c.)* GEN COMM centime *m (c.)*

centimeter *n AmE*, **centimetre** *n BrE (cm)* GEN COMM centimètre *m (cm)*

central: ~ **bank** *n* BANK, ECON banque centrale *f*; ~ **bank transactions** *n pl* BANK, ECON transactions de la banque centrale *f pl*; ~ **branch** *n* BANK succursale centrale *f*; ~ **business district** *n (CBD)* ECON *of city* centre d'affaires d'une ville *m*, quartier central d'affaires *m*; ~ **buying** *n* S&M achat dans un centre commercial *m*, achat dans une centrale d'achats *m*; ~ **freight booking office** *n* TRANSP *aviation* bureau central de réservation de transport aérien *m*; ~ **freight bureau** *n (CFB)* TRANSP bureau central de transport *m*; ~ **government** *n* GEN COMM administration centrale *f*; ~ **government item** *n* FIN élément des administrations centrales *m*; ~ **occupation** *n* HRM emploi principal *m*; ~ **place theory** *n* ECON *population* théorie de l'implantation centrale des villes dans une région *f*; ~ **planning** *n* MGMNT planification centralisée *f*; ~ **processing unit** *n (CPU)* COMP *hardware* processeur central *m*, unité centrale *f*, unité centrale de traitement *f (UC)*; ~ **rate** *n* ECON *of DM in the EMS* taux pivot *m*; ~ **reservation office** *n* LEIS bureau central des réservations *m*; ~ **reservation system** *n* LEIS système de réservation central *m*; ~ **supplies depot** *n* GEN COMM service du matériel *m*; ~ **tendency** *n* MATH tendance centrale *f*

Central:[1] ~ **African** *adj* GEN COMM centrafricain; ~ **American** *adj* GEN COMM centraméricain

Central:[2] ~ **Accounting System** *n Canada (CAS)* ACC système central de comptabilité *m (Canada) (SCC)*; ~ **African Customs and Economics Union** *n (UDEAC)* IMP/EXP Union douanière et économique de l'Afrique centrale *f (UDEAC)*; ~ **American Common Market** *n (CACM)* ECON *set up in October 1993* Marché commun d'Amérique centrale *m (MCAC)*; ~ **Arbitration Committee** *n* HRM *UK (CAC)*, IND *UK (CAC)*, LAW *UK (CAC)* ≈ Conseil des prud'hommes *m*, STOCK *(CAC)* comité central d'arbitrage des litiges *m*, commission d'arbitrage centrale *f*; ~ **Bank Facility** *n UK (CBF)* BANK banque centrale *f*; ~ **European Time** *n (CET)* GEN COMM heure de l'Europe centrale *f*; ~ **Office of Information** *n (COI)* ADMIN Bureau central de l'information *m*; ~ **Register** *n UK* STOCK registre central des firmes autorisées; ~ **Standard Time** *n US (CST)* GEN COMM heure normale des États du centre des États-Unis *f*; ~ **Statistical Office** *n UK (CSO)* ECON ≈ Institut national de la statistique et des études économiques *m (INSEE)*

Central:[3] ~ **Africa** *pr n* GEN COMM Afrique centrale *n pr*; ~ **African Republic** *pr n* GEN COMM République centrafricaine *f*; ~ **America** *pr n* GEN COMM Amérique centrale *f*

centralization *n* GEN COMM centralisation *f*

centralize *vt* GEN COMM centraliser

centralized[1] *adj* GEN COMM centralisé

centralized:[2] ~ **institution** *n* GEN COMM institution centralisée *f*; ~ **money** *n* BANK monnaie centrale *f*, monnaie à haute puissance *f*

centrally: ~ -**financed program** *n AmE*, ~ -**financed programme** *n BrE* ACC programme financé par l'administration centrale *m*; ~ -**planned economy** *n (CPE)* ECON, POL économie planifiée *f*

centre *n BrE* COMMS, GEN COMM, IND centre *m*; ~ **girder** *BrE* TRANSP *shipping* support central *m*; ~ **of gravity** *BrE* TRANSP centre de gravité *m*; ~ **periphery system** *BrE* ECON système centre périphérie *m*; ~ **spread** *BrE* MEDIA *print* annonce occupant les deux pages centrales, double page centrale *f*, vraie double *f*

Centre: ~ **for Economic and Social Information** *n (CESI)* WEL centre d'informations économiques et sociales *m*; ~ **for Policy Studies** *n UK (CPS)* ECON Centre des études politiques *m*; ~ **for Political Studies** *n* POL ≈ IEP, ≈ Institut d'études politiques *m*

centrefold *n BrE* MEDIA occupant les deux pages centrales, double page centrale *m*, vraie double *f*

Centronics: ~ **interface**® *n* COMP interface parallèle Centronics® *f*

CEO *abbr* HRM *US (chief executive officer)*, MGMNT *US (chief executive officer, managing director)* DG *(directeur général)*, PDG *(président-directeur général)*

CERF *abbr (Council of Europe Resettlement Fund)* BANK FRCE *(Fonds de rétablissement du conseil de l'Europe)*

cert. *abbr (certificate, certification)* ADMIN acte *m*, certif. *(certificat)*, FIN certif. *(certificat)*, titre *m*, GEN COMM, PATENTS certif. *(certificat)*, WEL certif. *(certificat)*, diplôme *m*

certain *adj* GEN COMM certain, sûr

certainty *n* GEN COMM certitude *f*

certificate[1] *n (cert.)* ACC rapport *m*, ADMIN acte *m*, certificat *m (certif.)*, FIN rapport *m*, FIN certificat *m (certif.)*, titre *m*, GEN COMM, PATENTS certificat *m (certif.)*, WEL certificat *m (certif.)*, diplôme *m*; ~ **of amortized revolving debt** *UK (CARD)* FIN certificat de dette renouvelable amortie *m*; ~ **of analysis** TRANSP certificat d'analyse *m*; ~ **of competency** TRANSP *shipping* brevet d'aptitude *m*, certificat d'aptitude *m*; ~ **of conditioning** TRANSP certificat de conditionne-

ment *m*; ~ **of consignment/origin** *(CC/O)* IMP/EXP certificat d'expédition/d'origine *m*; ~ **of deposit** BANK, ECON bon de caisse *m*, certificat de dépôt *m*, FIN certificat de dépôt *m*, GEN COMM bon de caisse *m*, STOCK *bond* bon de caisse *m*, certificat de dépôt *m*; ~ **of deposit market** BANK marché des certificats de dépôt *m*; ~ **of exemption** TAX certificat d'exemption *m*, certificat d'exonération *m*; ~ **of existence** INS certificat de vie *m*; ~ **of health** WEL certificat médical de bonne santé *m*; ~ **of incorporation** LAW acte constitutif d'une personne morale *m*; ~ **of indebtedness** TAX titre de créance *m*; ~ **of independence** HRM certificat d'indépendance *m*; ~ **of inspection** TRANSP certificat de contrôle *m*; ~ **of insurance** *(CI)* INS attestation d'assurance *f*, certificat d'assurance *m*; ~ **of manufacture** IND certificat de fabrication *m*; ~ **of occupancy** PROP certificat d'occupation *m*; ~ **of origin** *(c/o)* IMP/EXP certificat d'origine *m*; ~ **of origin and consignment** *(C/OC)* IMP/EXP certificat d'origine et d'expédition *m*; ~ **of ownership** GEN COMM certificat de propriété *m*, titre de propriété *m*, LAW certificat de propriété *m*, PROP certificat de propriété *m*, titre de propriété *m*; ~ **of posting** COMMS, TRANSP récépissé d'un envoi *m*; ~ **of pratique** IMP/EXP certificat de pratique *m*; ~ **of quality** IMP/EXP, TRANSP certificat de qualité *m*; ~ **of registration** LAW *intellectual property*, PATENTS *intellectual property* certificat d'enregistrement *m*, TAX certificat d'agrément *m*; ~ **of registry** TRANSP *shipping* acte de nationalisation *m*, certificat d'immatriculation *m*; ~ **of shipment** TRANSP *shipping* certificat d'expédition *m*; ~ **of survey** TRANSP *shipping* certificat de visite *m*; ~ **of title** PROP titre de propriété *m*; ~ **of use** PROP certificat d'utilisation *m*; ~ **of value** *UK (CV)* IMP/EXP attestation de valeur *f*; ~ **of value and origin** *UK (CVO)* IMP/EXP attestation de valeur et d'origine *f*; ~ **of weight** TRANSP certificat de poids *m*

certificate[2] *vt* GEN COMM, IND, LAW, PATENTS *product*, TRANSP certifier

Certificate: ~ **of Accrual on Treasury Securities** *n US (CATS)* STOCK bon du Trésor américain à coupon zéro

certificateless: ~ **municipals** *n pl* STOCK bons de collectivités locales sans certificat *m pl*

Certificates: ~ **of Government Receipts** *n pl (COUGRs)* FIN certificats émis par le gouvernement et rémunérés par des émissions de bons de Trésor, ≈ Fonds d'État libres d'intérêt nominal *m pl*, STOCK certificats émis par le gouvernement et rémunérés par des émissions de bons du Trésor, ≈ Fonds d'État libres d'intérêt nominal *m pl (France) (FELIN)*

certification *n (cert.)* GEN COMM authentification *f*, certification *f*, IND certification *f*, homologation *f*, LAW authentification *f*, certification *f*, PATENTS *requirements for products* certification *f*, homologation *f*, TAX attestation *f*, certificat *m (certif.)*; ~ **by spouse** TAX attestation du conjoint *f*; ~ **mark**

BANK, GEN COMM *(SYN assay mark) on gold and silver* marque d'essai *f*, HRM homologation *f*, IND licence d'homologation *f*, visa de certification *m*, IND *(SYN assay mark) on gold and silver* marque d'essai *f*, LAW visa de certification *m, labour relations* licence d'homologation *f*, PATENTS marque de certification *f*

Certification: **~ Officer** *n* ADMIN *UK (CO)* agent certificateur *m*, HRM *UK* syndicaliste indépendant *m*

certified: **~ accountant** *n UK (CA)* ACC expert-comptable *m*; **~ accounts** *n pl* ACC comptes certifiés *m pl*; **~ administration manager** *n* HRM directeur administratif diplômé *m*; **~ check** *n AmE*, **~ cheque** *n BrE* ACC chèque visé *m*, BANK chèque certifié *m*; **~ copy** *n* ADMIN, LAW copie conforme *f*; **~ declaration of origin** *n* IMP/EXP déclaration d'origine certifiée *f*; **~ employee benefit specialist** *n US* HRM expert en prestations sociales; **~ financial planner** *n* FIN planificateur financier agréé *m*; **~ financial statement** *n* ACC, FIN bilan certifié *m*, état financier certifié *m*; **~ general accountant** *n* ACC comptable général agréé *m*; **~ institution** *n* TAX établissement certifié *m*; **~ invoice** *n* ACC facture certifiée *f*; **~ mail** *n AmE*, **~ post** *n BrE* COMMS courrier recommandé *m*, envoi recommandé *m*; **~ property** *n* TAX bien certifié *m*; **~ public accountant** *n US (CPA)* ACC expert-comptable *m*; **~ true copy** *n* LAW copie certifiée conforme *f*

certify *vt* GEN COMM *diploma* viser

certifying: **~ officer** *n* ADMIN agent certificateur *m*

CES[1] *abbr (Committee of European Shipowners)* TRANSP comité des armateurs européens

CES:[2] **~ production function** *n (Constant Elasticity of Substitution production function)* ECON fonction de production caractérisée par une élasticité constante de l'effet de substitution

CESI *abbr (Centre for Economic and Social Information)* WEL centre d'informations économiques et sociales *m*

cessation: **~ of interest** *n UK* BANK suspension d'intérêt *f*; **~ of payment of premiums** *n* INS cessation de paiement des primes *f*, suspension de paiement des primes *f*

cesser: **~ clause** *n* TRANSP *shipping* clause limitative de responsabilité *f*

cession *n* GEN COMM abandon *m*, LAW cession *f*; **~ of portfolio** GEN COMM, INS cession de portefeuille *f*

cestui que trust *n frml* GEN COMM bénéficiaire du trust *m*

CET *abbr* ECON *(common external tariff)* tarif extérieur commun *m*, GEN COMM *(Central European Time)* heure de l'Europe centrale *f*

CETA *abbr US (Comprehensive Employment and Training Act)* HRM accord sur l'emploi et la formation

ceteris paribus *phr frml* GEN COMM toutes choses

étant égales, toutes choses étant égales par ailleurs

CF *abbr* ACC *(carried forward)* à reporter, GEN COMM *(carriage forward)* p.d. *(port dû)*, GEN COMM *(cubic feet)* pied cube *m*, GEN COMM *(carried forward)* à reporter, TRANSP *(carriage forward)* p.d. *(port dû)*

CFA: **~ franc** *n* GEN COMM franc CFA *m*

CFB *abbr (central freight bureau)* TRANSP bureau central de transport *m*

CFBH *abbr (Corporation of Foreign Bondholders)* STOCK société des détenteurs d'obligations étrangers *f*

CFC *abbr (chlorofluorocarbon)* ENVIR CFC *(chlorofluorocarbone)*

CFE *abbr UK (college of further education)* WEL centre d'enseignement postscolaire *m*

CFF *abbr (compensatory financial facility)* FIN compensation financière *f*

CFO *abbr (chief financial officer)* FIN, HRM directeur financier *m*, responsable financier *m*

CFS *abbr AmE (container freight station)* TRANSP *shipping* magasin de groupage *m*

CFTB *abbr (cylindrical fire tube boiler)* TRANSP *shipping* chaudière cylindrique ignitubulaire *f*, chaudière cylindrique à tubes de fumée *f*

CFTC *abbr US (Commodity Futures Trading Commission)* STOCK Commission de contrôle des marchés de matières premières *f*, Commission des opérations à terme sur les marchandises *f*

CG *abbr (coastguard)* HRM *organization* gendarmerie maritime *f, person* garde-côte *m*, gendarme maritime *m*, membre de la gendarmerie maritime *m*

CGA *abbr (color/graphics adaptor, colour/graphics adaptor)* COMP CGA *(adaptateur graphique couleur)*

CGPM *abbr (General Conference of Weights and Measures)* GEN COMM conférence générale des poids et mesures *f*

CGT *abbr dat (capital gains tax)* ECON, TAX impôt sur les plus-values *m*

ch *abbr (chancery)* LAW cour de la chancellerie *f*

Chad *pr n* GEN COMM Tchad *m*

Chadian[1] *adj* GEN COMM tchadien

Chadian[2] *n* GEN COMM *person* Tchadien *m*

chain *n* GEN COMM, S&M *supermarket*, TRANSP *cargo handling* chaîne *f*; **~ bank** *US* BANK banque à succursales multiples *f*; **~ of command** GEN COMM hiérarchie *f*, HRM hiérarchie *f*, hiérarchie de commandement *f*, portée de commandement *f*, MGMNT hiérarchie *f*, portée de commandement *f*, voie hiérarchique *f*; **~ of distribution** GEN COMM, IND circuit de distribution *m*; **~ feeding** COMP alimentation continue *f*; **~ index method** ACC, ECON méthode de l'indice-chaîne *f*; **~ lashing** TRANSP *cargo handling* saisine à chaîne *f*; **~ migration** GEN COMM déménagement en chaîne *m*; **~ of**

production IND chaîne de production *f*; ~ **production** IND production à la chaîne *f*; ~ **sling** TRANSP *cargo handling* élingue en chaîne *f*; ~ **store** GEN COMM grand magasin *m*, S&M grand magasin *m*, magasin à succursales multiples *m*; ~ **superstore** *UK* S&M supermarché à succursales multiples *m*; ~ **tensioner** TRANSP tendeur de chaîne *m*

chair[1] *n* HRM président *m*; ♦ **be in the** ~ HRM, MGMNT *for meetings* diriger les débats

chair[2] *vt* HRM, MGMNT *meeting* présider

chairman *n* HRM président *m*, président du conseil d'administration *m*; ~ **of the administrative board** HRM, MGMNT président du conseil d'administration *m*; ~ **of the board** HRM président du conseil *m*; ~ **of the board of directors** HRM, MGMNT président-directeur général *m*; ~ **of the board of management** HRM, MGMNT président du directoire *m*, président-directeur général *m*; ~ **and chief executive** *US (cf chairman and managing director UK)* HRM, MGMNT président-directeur général *m*; ~ **elect** GEN COMM actuel président *m*, président élu *m*; ~ **of the executive committee** HRM président du comité exécutif *m*; ~ **and managing director** *UK (cf chairman and chief executive US)* HRM, MGMNT président-directeur général *m*; ~ **of the supervisory board** HRM président du conseil de surveillance *m*; ~**'s brief** MGMNT discours du président *m*, mot du président *m*

chairperson *n* HRM président *m*, présidente *f*

chairwoman *n* HRM présidente *f*

challenge[1] *n* GEN COMM défi *m*

challenge[2] *vt* GEN COMM défier, LAW contester

chamber *n* POL chambre *f*

Chamber: ~ **of Commerce** *n (CC)* ECON Chambre de commerce *f*; ~ **of Trade** *n* ECON, POL Chambre des métiers *f*

chambers *n pl* LAW cabinet *m*, chambre *f*

champagne: ~ **communist** *n infrml* POL milliardaire rouge *m (infrml)*; ~ **socialism** *n infrml* POL la gauche caviar *f (infrml)*

chance *adj* GEN COMM *meeting, remark, etc.* fortuit

Chancellor: ~ **of the Exchequer** *n UK* ECON le ministre des finances britannique, chancelier de l'Échiquier *m*, FIN ≈ ministre des Finances *m*, POL le ministre des finances britannique, chancelier de l'Échiquier *m*

chancery *n (ch)* LAW cour de la chancellerie *f*

change[1] *n* COMP changement *m*, modification *f*, ECON *in demand or supply* changement *m*, GEN COMM changement *m*, monnaie *f*, *in price* variation *f*, évolution *f*, STOCK *in price* variation *f*; ~ **of address** *n* COMMS changement d'adresse *m*; ~ **of beneficiary provision** *n* INS *life insurance* modification de la clause d'attribution du bénéficiaire *f*, modification de la disposition du bénéficiaire *f*; ~ **dispenser** *n* BANK distributeur de monnaie *m*; ~ **dump** *n* COMP vidage de mouvements *m*; ~ **files** *n pl* COMP fichier de mise

à jour *m*, fichier mouvements *m*; ~ **of itinerary** *n* TRANSP modification d'itinéraire *f*; ~ **management** *n* HRM, MGMNT gestion du changement *f*; ~ **request** *n (CR)* TRANSP réaménagement *m*, *aviation* requête formulée par le client *f*

change[2] **1.** *vt* GEN COMM changer, transformer; **2.** *vi* GEN COMM changer, se transformer; ♦ ~ **hands** S&M *money, goods or businesses* changer de main, changer de propriétaire; ~ **into cash** GEN COMM convertir en espèces

channel[1] *n* ADMIN voie *f*, COMMS canal *m*, voie *f*, COMP piste de bande magnétique *f*, voie *f*, GEN COMM voie *f*, MEDIA *broadcast* canal *m (Fra)*, chaîne *f (Can)*; ~ **of communication** ADMIN canal de communication *m*, liaison dans l'entreprise *f*, voie de communication *f*, GEN COMM canal de communication *m*, voie de communication *f*, HRM, MGMNT canal de communication *m*, liaison dans l'entreprise *f*, voie de communication *f*, S&M voie de communication *f*; ~ **of distribution** ADMIN, GEN COMM canal de distribution *m*, S&M canal de distribution *m*, circuit de distribution *m*; ~ **for orders** S&M circuit de commandes *m*; ~ **management** MGMNT gestion des canaux de communication *f*; ~ **of sales** S&M circuit de vente *m*; ♦ **go through the proper** ~**s** GEN COMM *company* passer par la voie hiérarchique

channel[2] *vt* GEN COMM *funds into project* canaliser; ~ **through** GEN COMM diriger

Channel: ~ **money** *n UK* TRANSP *shipping* acompte sur salaire arriéré d'un marin britannique; ~ **Tunnel** *n* TRANSP tunnel sous la Manche *m*

chaos: ~ **theory** *n (SYN butterfly effect)* STOCK théorie du chaos *f*

chapel *n UK* HRM *of trade union* section *f*

CHAPS *abbr US (Clearing House Automatic Payments System)* BANK Chambre de compensation interbancaire internationale *f*

chapter *n* GEN COMM *of organization* section *f*

character *n* COMP, GEN COMM, HRM, MEDIA *printing* caractère *m*; ~ **array** COMP jeu de caractères *m*; ~ **-at-a-time printer** COMP imprimante caractère par caractère *f*; ~ **card** COMP fichier confidentiel *m*; ~ **density** COMP densité d'enregistrement *f*, densité de caractères *f*; ~ **file** COMP fichier confidentiel *m*; ~ **pitch** COMP commande des majuscules *f*; ~ **set** COMP jeu de caractères *m*; ~ **string** COMP chaîne de caractères *f*

characteristic[1] *adj* GEN COMM caractéristique; ♦ ~ **of** GEN COMM propre à

characteristic[2] *n* S&M *of area, shop or product* caractéristique *f*

characteristics: ~ **theory** *n* ECON *of consumer demand* théorie des caractéristiques *f*

characterizing: ~ **portion** *n* PATENTS partie caractérisante *f*

charcoal *n* ENVIR, IND charbon de bois *m*

charge[1] *n* ACC débit *m*, COMMS coût d'une communication téléphonique *m*, FIN charge *f*,

GEN COMM *cost, debt* frais *m pl*, prix *m*, LAW chef d'accusation *m*, chef d'inculpation *m*; ~ **account** ACC, BANK compte d'achats à crédit *m*; ~ **-back** US BANK réimputation *f*; ~ **buyer** BrE *(cf credit buyer AmE)* S&M acheteur à crédit *m*; ~ **card** BANK carte d'achat *f*; ~ **hand** HRM chef d'équipe *m*; ~ **on land** TAX charge sur un bien-fonds *f*; ~ **ticket** GEN COMM note de débit *f*; ◆ **at no ~ property** TAX sûreté sur un bien *f*; ◆ **at no ~** GEN COMM gratis, gratuit, gratuitement; **be in ~** GEN COMM être délégué, être préposé, être responsable; **be in ~ of** GEN COMM commander, s'occuper de, être chargé de, être responsable de; **in ~** HRM en fonction; **in ~ of** GEN COMM responsable de; **without ~** *(w.c.)* GEN COMM gratis, gratuit, gratuitement, sans frais

charge[2] *vt* GEN COMM *fee* demander, faire payer, LAW inculper, S&M porter au compte de; ~ **against** GEN COMM déduire de, imputer à, porter en réduction sur; ~ **off** ACC amortir, imputer à l'exercice, passer en charges; ~ **to** GEN COMM *expenses* imputer à; ◆ ~ **an expense to an account** BANK, FIN imputer une dépense à un compte; ~ **interest** BANK prélever un intérêt; ~ **sth to sb's account** BANK faire mettre qch sur le compte de qn; ~ **to an account** GEN COMM porter au débit d'un compte

chargeable[1] *adj* GEN COMM imputable; ~ **to tax** TAX imposable, soumis à l'impôt

chargeable:[2] ~ **staff** *n pl* HRM personnel à charge *m*

charges *n pl* ACC, FIN charges *f pl*, GEN COMM charges *f pl*, frais *m pl*; ~ **collect** *(cc)* COMMS prélèvement de droits *m*; ~ **on banking transactions** BANK frais bancaires *m pl*, frais de banque *m pl*; ~ **prepaid** IMP/EXP, TRANSP frais payés d'avance *m pl*

charging: ~ **wharf** *n* TRANSP quai de chargement *m*

charitable: ~ **activity** *n* TAX, WEL activité de bienfaisance *f*; ~ **donation** *n* TAX, WEL don de charité *m*, don à une oeuvre de charité *m*; ~ **donations credit** *n* TAX, WEL crédit pour dons de charité *m*; ~ **foundation** *n* TAX, WEL fondation de charité *f*; ~ **gift** *n* TAX, WEL don de charité *m*; ~ **organization** *n* TAX, WEL oeuvre de bienfaisance *f*, oeuvre de charité *f*, organisation caritative *f*; ~ **purposes** *n pl* TAX, WEL fins charitables *f pl*; ~ **trust** *n* TAX, WEL fondation d'utilité publique *f*

charity *n* GEN COMM bienfaisance *f*, TAX, WEL oeuvre de bienfaisance *f*, organisation caritative *f*, organisme de charité *m*; ~ **fundraising** *n* WEL collecte de bienfaisance *f*; ~ **funds** *n pl* TAX, WEL caisse de secours *f*; ~ **number** *n* TAX, WEL numéro d'enregistrement de l'organisme de charité *m*; ~ **sale** *n* S&M vente de charité *f*; ~ **sponsorship** *n* WEL parrainage de bienfaisance *m*

chart[1] *n* COMP, GEN COMM diagramme *m*, graphique *m*, tableau *m*, MATH graphique *m*; ~ **of accounts** ACC code comptable *m*, plan comptable *m*, FIN plan comptable *m*; ~ **point** MATH donnée de tableau *f*

chart[2] *vt* GEN COMM *progress* tracer une courbe

charta partita *n frml* GEN COMM charte-partie *f*

charter[1] *n* LAW *lease, licence* affrètement *m, of rights* charte *f*, TRANSP *of vehicles* affrètement *m*, charter *m*; ~ **broker** TRANSP *shipping* courtier d'affrètement *m*; ~ **contract** TRANSP contrat d'affrètement *m*; ~ **flight** *(ANT scheduled flight)* TRANSP vol affrété *m*, vol charter *m*; ~ **party** *(CP)* TRANSP *shipping* charte-partie *f*; ~ **party bill of lading** *(C/P bill of lading)* IMP/EXP, TRANSP *shipping* connaissement charte-partie *m*; ~ **party fraud** LAW, TRANSP tromperie sur la charte-partie *f*; ~ **party freight** TRANSP fret de charte-partie *m*; ~ **plane** TRANSP avion charter *m*

charter[2] *vt* LAW accorder une charte à, TRANSP *vehicle* affréter, noliser

chartered: ~ **accountant** *n* UK *(CA)* ACC expert-comptable *m*; ~ **aeroplane** *n* BrE TRANSP avion affrété *m*, avion charter *m*; ~ **aircraft** *n* TRANSP avion affrété *m*, avion charter *m*; ~ **airplane** *n* AmE *see chartered aeroplane BrE*; ~ **bank** *n* US BANK banque à charte *f*; ~ **company** *n* GEN COMM compagnie à charte *f*; ~ **financial consultant** *n* US FIN consultant financier agréé *m*; ~ **flight** *n* TRANSP vol affrété *m*, vol charter *m*; ~ **life underwriter** *n* US INS a.v.a., agent d'assurance-vie agréé *m*, assureur-vie agréé *m*; ~ **plane** *n infrml* TRANSP avion affrété *m*, avion charter *m*

Chartered: ~ **Institute of Transport** *n* UK TRANSP institut privilégié des transports

charterer *n* HRM chargeur *m*, IMP/EXP, TRANSP affréteur *m*, chargeur *m*; ~**'s pay dues** *n pl (cpd)* TRANSP *shipping* rémunération de l'affréteur *f*

chartering *n* TRANSP affrètement *m*, nolisement *m*; ~ **agent** TRANSP agent d'affrètement *m*; ~ **broker** TRANSP *shipping* courtier d'affrètement *m*

chartism *n* STOCK analyse chartiste *f*

chartist *n* STOCK chartiste *mf*, conjoncturiste *mf*, opérateur sur graphique *m*

chase: ~ **eighths** *n jarg* STOCK chasseur de centimes *m (jarg)*

chattel *n* LAW, PROP bien meuble *m*; ~ **mortgage** US BANK hypothèque sur biens meubles *f*

chattels: ~ **personal** *n pl* PROP biens personnels *m pl*

CHC *abbr (cargo-handling charge)* TRANSP frais de manutention *m pl*, frais de manutention des marchandises *m pl*

cheap *n* GEN COMM bon marché, peu cher, peu onéreux, économique; ~ **execution** UK STOCK exécution bon marché *f*; ~ **money policy** BANK politique de l'argent à bon marché *f*, politique du crédit à bon marché *f*

cheaper *adj* GEN COMM meilleur marché, moins cher, moins onéreux

cheapest: ~ **to deliver** *phr (CTD)* STOCK obligation la moins chère à livrer *(OMCL)*

check[1] *n* ACC AmE *(cf tick BrE)* marque *f*, BANK AmE *see cheque BrE*, COMP contrôle *m*, test *m*, vérification *f*, GEN COMM AmE *(cf tick BrE)* marque *f*, GEN COMM *AmE (cf bill BrE) account in hotel* note *f*, *in restaurant* addition *f*; ~ **bit** *n* COMP bit de contrôle *m*; ~ **box** *n US* COMP case à cocher *f*; ~ **card** *n AmE see cheque card BrE*; ~ **character** *n* COMP caractère de contrôle *m*; ~ **clearing** *n AmE see cheque clearing BrE*; ~ **-clearing system** *n AmE see cheque-clearing system BrE*; ~ **counterfoil** *n AmE see cheque counterfoil BrE*; ~ **credit** *n AmE see cheque credit BrE*; ~ **digit** *n* COMP chiffre de contrôle *m*, clé numérique de contrôle *f*, GEN COMM *for assuring correctness of a number* chiffre de contrôle *m*; ~ **form** *n AmE see cheque form BrE*; ~ **in the amount of** *n AmE see cheque to the amount of BrE*; ~ **in favor of sb** *n AmE see cheque in favour of sb BrE*; ~ **issue** *n AmE see cheque issue BrE*; ~ **-kiting** *n AmE see cheque-kiting BrE*; ~ **list** *n* GEN COMM check-list *m*, liste de contrôle *f*, liste des points à contrôler *f*; ~ **made to cash** *n AmE see cheque made to cash BrE*; ~ **mark** *n AmE (cf tick mark BrE)* ACC marque de pointage *f*, GEN COMM marque de contrôle *f*; ~ **-off** *n* HRM prélèvement de la cotisation syndicale *m*; ~ **payment** *n AmE see cheque payment BrE*; ~ **payment system** *n AmE see cheque payment system BrE*; ~ **protector** *n AmE see cheque protector BrE*; ~ **register** *n AmE see cheque register BrE*; ~ **requisition** *n AmE see cheque requisition BrE*; ~ **signer** *n AmE see cheque signer BrE*; ~ **-signing machine** *n AmE see cheque-signing machine BrE*; ~ **stub** *n AmE see cheque stub BrE*; ~ **-up** *n* WEL visite médicale *f*; ~ **writer** *n AmE see cheque writer BrE*; ~ **-writer machine** *n AmE see cheque-writer machine BrE*; ~ **-writing machine** *n AmE see cheque-writing machine BrE*; ◆ **make a ~ payable to sb** *AmE see make a cheque payable to sb BrE*; **raise a ~** *AmE (cf make out a cheque BrE)* BANK faire un chèque; **raise a ~ to sb** *AmE (cf make out a cheque to sb BrE)* BANK établir un chèque à l'ordre de qn

check² **1.** *vt* GEN COMM cocher, contrôler, vérifier; ~ **in** LEIS, TRANSP *luggage* enregistrer, inscrire; ~ **off** GEN COMM cocher; **2.** *vi* ~ **in** LEIS, TRANSP *at airport* se présenter à l'enregistrement, *at hotel* se présenter à la réception; ~ **out** GEN COMM, LEIS *of hotel* quitter sa chambre; ◆ ~ **box** *AmE (cf tick the box BrE)*, GEN COMM cocher la case

checkbook *n AmE see chequebook BrE*

checker *n* HRM manutentionnaire *mf*, pointeur *m*, S&M *AmE (cf checkout assistant BrE)* caissier *m*

checking *n* GEN COMM vérification *f*; ~ **account** *AmE (cf C/A, current account BrE)* ACC, BANK, FIN, GEN COMM compte courant *m (c/c)*; ~ **account balance** *AmE see current account balance BrE*; ~ **account customer** *AmE see current account customer BrE*; ~ **account holder** *AmE see current account holder BrE*; ~ **account surplus** *AmE see current account surplus BrE*

checklist *n* GEN COMM fiche de suivi *f*

checkout *n* S&M caisse *f*, caisse de sortie *f*;

~ **assistant** *BrE (cf checker AmE)* S&M caissier *m*; ~ **clerk** *AmE* S&M caissier *m*; ~ **lane** S&M caisse de sortie *f*

checkpoint *n* COMP point de contrôle *m*, point de reprise *m*, TRANSP point de contrôle *m*

checksum *n* COMP *data transfer* somme de contrôle *f*, total de contrôle *m*

chemical: ~ **carrier** *n* TRANSP *shipping* chimiquier *m*; ~ **fertilizer** *n* ENVIR engrais chimique *m*; ~ **input** *n* ENVIR *agriculture* apport chimique *m*; ~ **tanker** *n* TRANSP *shipping* chimiquier *m*; ~ **works** *n* [inv pl] IND fabrique de produits chimiques *f*

chemicals *n pl* IND produits chimiques *m pl*

cheque *n BrE* BANK chèque *m*; ~ **card** *n BrE* BANK carte d'identité bancaire *f*; ~ **clearing** *n BrE* BANK compensation de chèques *f*; ~ **-clearing system** *n BrE* BANK système de compensation de chèques *m*; ~ **counterfoil** *n BrE* BANK talon de chèque *m*; ~ **credit** *n BrE* BANK accréditif *m*; ~ **form** *n BrE* BANK formule de chèque *f*; ~ **in favour of sb** *n BrE* BANK chèque payable à l'ordre de qn *m*; ~ **issue** *n BrE* ACC émission de chèques *f*; ~ **-kiting** *n BrE* BANK émission de chèque sans provision *f*; ~ **made to cash** *n BrE* BANK chèque au porteur *m*, chèque payable au porteur *m*; ~ **payment** *n BrE* BANK paiement par chèque *m*, règlement par chèque *m*; ~ **payment system** *n BrE* BANK système de règlement des chèques *m*; ~ **protector** *n BrE* BANK protecteur de chèque *m*; ~ **register** *n BrE* ACC livre des chèques *m*, registre des chèques *m*; ~ **requisition** *n BrE* ACC demande de chèque *f*; ~ **signer** *n BrE* GEN COMM machine à signer *f*; ~ **-signing machine** *n BrE* GEN COMM machine à signer *f*; ~ **stub** *n BrE* BANK talon de chèque *m*; ~ **to the amount of** *n BrE* BANK chèque d'un montant de *m*; ~ **writer** *n BrE* BANK chécographe *m*, machine à écrire les chèques *f*; ~ **-writer machine** *n BrE* BANK chécographe *m*, machine à écrire les chèques *f*; ~ **-writing machine** *n BrE* BANK chécographe *m*, machine à écrire les chèques *f*; ◆ **make a ~ payable to sb** *BrE* BANK établir un chèque à l'ordre de qn; **make out a ~** *BrE (cf raise a check AmE)* BANK faire un chèque; **make out a ~ to sb** *BrE (cf raise a check to sb AmE)* BANK établir un chèque à l'ordre de qn

Cheque: ~ **and Credit Clearing Company Ltd** *n UK* BANK opérateur londonien qui compense un grand nombre de chèques

chequebook *n BrE* BANK carnet de chèques *m*, chéquier *m*; ~ **journalism** *pej BrE* MEDIA journalisme à sensation *m*

chi: ~ **square** *n* MATH *statistics* carré chi *m*; ~ **square test** *n* MATH *statistical method* test du carré chi *m*; ~ **-squared distribution** *n* MATH *statistics* distribution en carré chi *f*

Chicago: ~ **Board Options Exchange** *n US (CBOE)* STOCK bourse des options de Chicago, ≈ Marché des options négociables de Paris *m (MONEP)*; ~ **Board of Trade** *n US (CBT)*

STOCK bourse des matières premières et des contrats à terme de Chicago, ≈ Marché à terme d'instruments financiers m *(MATIF)*; ~ **Mercantile Exchange** n *(CME)* STOCK bourse des matières premières de Chicago; ~ **Rice and Cotton Exchange** n STOCK marché du riz et du coton de Chicago; ~ **School** n ECON école de Chicago f

chief n *(*SYN *boss, head, senior)* ADMIN, HRM MGMNT chef m; ~ **accountant** n ACC chef comptable m, directeur de comptabilité m; ~ **accounting officer** n ACC chef comptable m, directeur de comptabilité m; ~ **assets** n pl STOCK actif principal m; ~ **buyer** n GEN COMM, HRM, S&M chef d'approvisionnement m, chef des achats m, chef du service achats m, directeur des achats m, responsable des achats m; ~ **clerk** n ADMIN chef de bureau m, HRM chef de bureau m, commis principal m, MGMNT chef de bureau m; ~ **economist** n ECON, GEN COMM économiste en chef m; ~ **engineer** n HRM, TRANSP *shipping* chef mécanicien m, ingénieur en chef m; ~ **executive** n HRM, MGMNT cadre sup m *(infrml)*, cadre supérieur m, directeur général m; ~ **executive officer** n US *(CEO, managing director)* HRM, MGMNT directeur général m *(DG)*, président-directeur général m *(PDG)*; ~ **financial officer** n *(CFO)* FIN, HRM directeur financier m, responsable financier m; ~ **immigration officer** n *(CIO)* HRM chef du service immigration m, officier supérieur de la police des frontières m, supérieur à la P.A.F. m; ~ **inspector** n *(CI)* HRM inspecteur en chef m, inspecteur principal m; ~ **mate** n HRM *ship* second m; ~ **officer** n HRM *shipping*, TRANSP commandant m; ~ **operating officer** n *(COO)* GEN COMM, HRM chef de service m; ~ **petty officer** n *(CPO)* HRM, TRANSP premier maître m; ~ **place of business** n ACC, GEN COMM établissement principal m; ~ **sub** n *infrml* UK MEDIA *print* secrétaire de rédaction m; ~ **sub-editor** n BrE MEDIA *print* secrétaire de rédaction m; ~ **traffic controller** n HRM *railway traffic*, TRANSP chef de la circulation m; ~ **value** n *(CV)* GEN COMM valeur principale f

child:[1] ~ **-centered** adj AmE, ~ **-centred** adj BrE WEL centré sur l'enfant

child[2] n [pl -dren] GEN COMM enfant m; ~ **benefit** UK ECON, WEL allocations familiales f pl; ~ **care expense deduction** TAX déduction pour frais de garde d'enfant f; ~ **claimed** TAX enfant déclaré à charge m, enfant visé par une déduction m; ~ **tax credit** TAX crédit d'impôt pour enfants m; ~**'s deferred assurance** INS assurance des enfants différée f; ~**'s insurance** INS assurance des enfants f

childcare: ~ **expenses** n pl TAX, WEL frais de garde d'enfants m pl

childless: ~ **couple** n PROP ménage sans enfants m

Chile pr n GEN COMM Chili m

Chilean[1] adj GEN COMM chilien

Chilean[2] n GEN COMM *person* Chilien m

chime n TRANSP *shipping* jable m

China pr n GEN COMM Chine f

Chinese[1] adj GEN COMM chinois

Chinese[2] n GEN COMM *language* chinois m, *person* Chinois m; ~ **modernization drive** n ECON, POL campagne de modernisation de la Chine f; ~ **money** n *jarg* UK STOCK monnaie de singe f *(infrml)*; ~ **wall** n pl FIN, BANK *insider trading* muraille de Chine f

chip n COMP microplaquette f, pastille f, puce f, puce électronique f; ~ **-based card** COMP carte à mémoire f, carte à puce f; ~ **card** COMP carte à mémoire f, carte à puce f

chipboard n GEN COMM agglo. *(infrml)*, aggloméré m, panneau en aggloméré m, *in EU regulations* panneau de copeaux m, *in furniture stores* panneau de particules m

CHIPS abbr US *(Clearing House Interbank Payments System)* BANK Chambre de compensation interbancaire internationale f

chisel: ~ **fork** n TRANSP lame f

chlorofluorocarbon n *(CFC)* ENVIR *pollution* chlorofluorocarbone m *(CFC)*

CHo abbr *(carrying capacity in number and length in holds)* TRANSP *shipping* charge utile dans les cales en nombre et longueur f

choice n GEN COMM choix m; ~ **of goods** GEN COMM choix de marchandises m

choose vti GEN COMM choisir

chose n LAW chose f, objet m; ~ **in action** LAW droit incorporel m

Christian: ~ **name** n BrE *(cf given name AmE)* ADMIN prénom m

Christmas: ~ **bonus** n HRM prime de fin d'année f

CHS abbr *(continuous survey cycle hull)* TRANSP *shipping* visite de la coque en vue d'une reclassification continue f

chunk: ~ **down** vt *jarg* GEN COMM fragmenter, parcelliser; ◆ ~ **a project** *jarg* FIN, GEN COMM, MGMNT découper un projet en tranches

churn vt BANK *bank, broker* faire tourner

churning n FIN, S&M escroquerie f

CI abbr HRM *(chief inspector)* inspecteur en chef m, inspecteur principal m, INS *(certificate of insurance)* attestation d'assurance f, certificat d'assurance m

CIC abbr *(committee for industrial cooperation)* IND comité de coopération industrielle

CICA abbr *(Canadian Institute of Chartered Accountants)* ACC Institut canadien des comptables agréés m

CIE abbr IMP/EXP UK *(Committee on Invisible Exports)* comité des exportations invisibles, IMP/EXP UK *(captain's imperfect entry)* entrée incomplète du capitaine f

CIF[1] abbr *(cost, insurance and freight)* IMP/EXP, TRANSP CAF *(coût, assurance, fret)*

CIF:[2] ~ **contract** n IMP/EXP contrat CAF m; ◆ ~ **landed** IMP/EXP CAF à quai

CIFAS abbr UK *(Credit Industry Fraud Avoidance*

System) FIN système anti-fraude de l'industrie du crédit *m*

CIF&C *abbr (cost, insurance, freight and commission)* IMP/EXP coût, assurance, fret et commission *loc m*

CIFC&E *abbr (cost, insurance, freight, commission and exchange)* IMP/EXP coût, assurance, fret, commission et change *loc m*

CIFC&I *abbr (cost, insurance, freight, commission and interest)* IMP/EXP coût, assurance, fret, commission et intérêt *loc m*

CIF&I *abbr (cost, insurance, freight and interest)* IMP/EXP coût, assurance, fret et intérêt *loc m*

CIFI&E *abbr (cost, insurance, freight, interest and exchange)* IMP/EXP coût, assurance, fret, intérêt et change *loc m*

CIFW *abbr (cost, insurance and freight/war)* IMP/EXP coût, assurance et fret/guerre *loc m*

CIHBB *abbr (cast-iron hub non-ferrous blades propeller)* TRANSP *shipping* hélice à moyeu en fonte et à pales non-ferreuses *f*

CIHSB *abbr (cast-iron hub steel blades propeller)* TRANSP *shipping* hélice à moyeu en fonte et à pales en acier *f*

CIM *abbr (computer-integrated manufacture, computer-integrated manufacturing)* COMP, IND FIO *(fabrication intégrée par ordinateur)*

cinema *n BrE (cf motion pictures, movie theater AmE)* LEIS, MEDIA cinéma *m*; **~ advertising** MEDIA, S&M publicité au cinéma *f*

CIO *abbr* HRM *(chief immigration officer)* officier supérieur de la police des frontières *m*, officier supérieur à la P.A.F. *m*, HRM *US (Congress of Industrial Organizations)* ≈ CGT *(Confédération générale du travail)*

CIP *abbr (carriage and insurance paid to)* IMP/EXP port et assurance payés jusqu'à *loc m*, port payé assurance comprise jusqu'à *loc m*

CIR *abbr (cage inventory record)* TRANSP inventaire de cabine *m*

circle *n* GEN COMM *political, business circle* cercle *m*, milieu *m*, LEIS *theatre* balcon *m*

circuit *n* COMP circuit *m*, LAW circonscription *f*; **~ breaker mechanism** *US* STOCK mécanisme de coupe-circuit *m*; **~ terminating equipment** COMP équipement de termination de circuit de données *m*; **~ working** TRANSP système carrousel *m*

circular *n* COMMS circulaire *f*, prospectus *m*, GEN COMM circulaire *f*; **~ calculation** TAX calcul en cercle fermé *m*; **~ flow** ECON flux circulaire *m*; **~ migration** ECON *population* migration circulaire *f*

circulate *vt* COMMS *information, news* propager

circulating: **~ capital** *n* ECON, FIN capitaux circulants *m pl*, capitaux roulants *m pl*, fonds de roulement *m*; **~ medium** *n* FIN monnaie d'échange *f*

circulation *n* BANK, ECON circulation *f*, MEDIA *of newspapers* diffusion *f*, tirage *m*; **~ breakdown** *n* GEN COMM analyse sectorielle *f*; **~ department** *n* MEDIA *print* service de la diffusion *m*, service des ventes *m*; **~ figures** *n pl* MEDIA chiffres de tirage *m pl*; **~ manager** *n* HRM *print*, MEDIA *print* directeur du service des ventes *m*, responsable du service de distribution *m*; ◆ **in ~** BANK en circulation

circumflex *n* COMP *keyboard* accent circonflexe *m*

circumstance *n* GEN COMM circonstance *f*

circumstances *n pl* GEN COMM circonstances *f pl*; ◆ **in similar ~** GEN COMM dans des circonstances semblables; **under the ~** GEN COMM dans ces circonstances

circumstantial: **~ evidence** *n* LAW preuve indirecte *f*

CIRM *abbr (International Radio-Maritime Committee)* COMMS CIRM *(Comité international radio-maritime)*

CIS *abbr (Commonwealth of Independent States)* ECON, GEN COMM, POL CEI *(Communauté des États indépendants)*

citation *n* LAW citation *f*

cite *vt* LAW citer

citizen *n* GEN COMM, LAW habitant *m*, POL citoyen *m*, habitant *m*; **~ bonds** *n pl* STOCK type de bon émis par les collectivités locales; **eldest ~** *n* GEN COMM doyen *m*; **oldest ~** *n* GEN COMM doyen *m*

Citizen's: **~ Charter** *n UK* POL initiative gouvernementale britannique de 1991 dont le but est d'offrir des services publics de meilleure qualité

Citizens: **~ Advice Bureau** *n UK (CAB)* ADMIN bureau d'aide et conseil aux citoyens

citizenship *n* POL citoyenneté *f*

city *n* GEN COMM ville *f*; **~ center** *AmE*, **~ centre** *BrE* GEN COMM centre-ville *m*; **~ planner** *AmE (cf town planner BrE)* ADMIN, POL, WEL urbaniste *mf*; **~ planning** *AmE (cf town planning BrE)* ADMIN, POL, WEL urbanisme *m*

City: **~ Grant** *n UK* GEN COMM *government aid* subvention accordée par la ville *f*; **~ and Regional Planning** *n* ADMIN ≈ Direction de l'aménagement du territoire *f*; **the ~** *n UK* FIN centre des affaires à Londres, la City *f*

civil: **~ action** *n* LAW action civile *f*; **~ assessment** *n* TAX cotisation au civil *f*; **~ aviation** *n* TRANSP aviation civile *f*; **~ commotion** *n (cc)* GEN COMM insurrection populaire *f*, INS insurrection populaire *f*, trouble intérieur *m*, POL insurrection populaire *f*, émeute *f*; **~ law** *n* LAW droit civil *m*; **~ liability** *n* LAW responsabilité civile *f*; **~ penalty** *n US* LAW peine pécuniaire civile *f*; **~ proceedings** *n pl* LAW procès civil *m*; **~ rights** *n pl* LAW droits civils *m pl*, droits civiques *m pl*, libertés publiques *f pl*; **~ rights act** *n US* LAW *1964* loi sur les droits civiques *f*; **~ servant** *n* ADMIN, HRM, WEL fonctionnaire *mf*; **~ service** *n (CS)* GEN COMM Administration *f*, fonction publique *f*; **~ status** *n* LAW état civil *m*; **~ wrong** *n* LAW atteinte aux droits d'un individu *f*

Civil: **~ Aviation Authority** *n UK (CAA)* TRANSP autorité de l'aviation civile, ≈ Direction générale de l'aviation civile *f (France)*; **~ Service Commission** *n (CSC)* ADMIN ≈ Commission de la fonction publique *f*

civilian: ~ **employment** n HRM emploi civil m

ck abbr (cask) TRANSP fût m, tonneau m

CKD abbr (completely knocked down) TRANSP complètement désassemblé, en pièces détachées loc f

cl abbr GEN COMM (centiliter, centilitre) cl (centilitre), TRANSP (continuous liner) shipping navire de ligne continue m, TRANSP (craft loss) shipping perte d'embarcation f

CL abbr (Corporation of Lloyd's) INS une association d'assureurs et d'agents d'assurance

cladding n TRANSP shipping bardage m

claim¹ n ACC, FIN créance f, GEN COMM réclamation f, HRM trade union revendication syndicale f, INS droit m, réclamation f, LAW revendication f, réclamation f, PATENTS revendication f, TAX, TRANSP réclamation f, WEL benefit demande d'indemnité f; ~ **for damages** LAW demande de dommages et intérêts f; ~ **for indemnification** INS demande d'indemnisation f, demande d'indemnité f; ~ **for personal exemption** TAX demande d'exemption personnelle f; ~ **for refund** TAX demande de remboursement f; ~ **form** INS formulaire de déclaration de sinistre m; ~ **paid** INS sinistre payé m, sinistre réglé m; ~ **payment** INS règlement de sinistre m; ~ **of recourse** INS recours m; ~ **settlement** INS règlement de sinistre m

claim² vt HRM expenses revendiquer, LAW déclarer, prétendre, revendiquer, réclamer, TAX indiquer, WEL benefit faire une demande de; ♦ ~ **an amount** TAX déclarer un montant, déduire un montant; ~ **as a dependant** TAX compter comme personne à charge, déclarer à sa charge; ~ **compensation** LAW demander réparation, réclamer un dédommagement; ~ **damages** INS, LAW demander des dommages et intérêts, réclamer des dommages et intérêts; ~ **a deduction** TAX demander une déduction; ~ **expenses** HRM faire une demande de remboursement

claimant n LAW demandeur m, partie requérante f, requérant m; **the** ~ INS assuré m, sinistré m

claims: ~ **adjuster** n INS inspecteur régleur m; ~ **adjustment** n INS règlement de sinistre m; ~ **department** n INS service des sinistres m, service régleur m; ~ **of different categories** n pl LAW revendications de différentes catégories f pl; ~ **expenses** n pl INS frais de règlement m pl; ~ **incurring fees** n pl LAW revendications donnant lieu au paiement de redevances f pl; ~ **inspector** n HRM inspecteur des plaintes m; ~ **and liabilities** n pl ACC dettes et engagements m pl; ~ **manager** n HRM, INS chef du service des réclamations m; ~ **prevention** n INS prévention de sinistre f; ~ **procedure** n INS procédure de réclamation f; ~ **reserve** n INS réserve pour sinistres f; ~ **of the same category** n pl LAW revendications de la même catégorie f pl; ~ **settlement fund** n INS caisse de règlement des sinistres m, fonds de règlement des sinistres m

clamping: ~ **force** n TRANSP cargo handling force de serrage f

clandestine adj GEN COMM clandestin

clarify vt GEN COMM clarifier, éclairer

class¹ n GEN COMM classe f, PATENTS in International Patent Classification or Nice Classification, STOCK option catégorie f, classe f, TRANSP classe f; ~ **action** LAW action collective en justice f, recours collectif en justice m; ~ **of business** TAX catégorie d'entreprise f; ~ **of construction** INS catégorie de bâtiment f, type de construction m; ~ **of employment** TAX catégorie d'emploi f; ~ **of insurance** INS branche d'assurance f, type d'assurance m; ~ **object** GEN COMM article de classification m; ~ **of options** STOCK catégorie d'options f, classe d'options f; ~ **of payments** TAX catégorie de paiements f; ~ **of property** PROP, TAX catégorie de biens f; ~ **of risk** INS catégorie de risques f; ~ **savings theory** ECON econometrics théorie sur l'épargne des classes f; ~ **of shares** STOCK classe d'actions f; ~ **struggle** ECON, POL lutte des classes f

class² vt ADMIN, GEN COMM classer

classic: ~ **example** n GEN COMM exemple bien connu m, exemple-type m, tarte à la crème f (infrml)

classical: ~ **dichotomy** n ECON dichotomie classique f; ~ **economics** n ECON 1752-82 classicisme économique m, théorie classique f, école classique f; ~ **model** n ECON modèle classique m; ~ **savings theory** n ECON econometrics théorie classique de l'épargne f

classification n GEN COMM, HRM classification f; ~ **of accounts** ACC codification des comptes f; ~ **by object** GEN COMM classification par objet f; ~ **certificate** TRANSP shipping certificat de classification m; ~ **of risks** INS classification des risques f

classified: ~ **ad** n infrml MEDIA, S&M annonce classée f, petite annonce f; ~ **advert** n infrml MEDIA, S&M annonce classée f, petite annonce f; ~ **advertisement** n MEDIA, S&M annonce classée f, petite annonce f, petite annonce classée f; ~ **return** n TAX déclaration classifiée f; ~ **stock** n STOCK action ordinaire classée f, actions réparties en catégories distinctes f pl

classify vt ADMIN restrict access to classer, classer confidentiel, classer secret, GEN COMM classer, classifier

clause n HRM clause f, disposition f, INS in policy avenant m, clause f, LAW of contract article m, clause f

claused: ~ **bill of lading** n IMP/EXP shipping, TRANSP connaissement avec réserves m, connaissement brut m, connaissement clausé m

claw n TRANSP shipping griffe f

clawback n FIN récupération f, TAX of capital gains tax relief disposition de récupération f

clay: ~ **ore** n ENVIR minerai argileux m

Clayton: ~ **Act** n US ECON 1914 loi Clayton f

Cld *abbr (cleared)* BANK compensé

clean:[1] **~ b/l** *abbr (clean bill of lading)* IMP/EXP, TRANSP connaissement net *m*, connaissement sans réserves *m*

clean[2] *adj* ACC sans dettes, ECON *international trade* libre, ENVIR *car* non-polluant, propre, GEN COMM libre de dettes; **~ -assessed** TAX *return* réglé

clean[3] *n* ACC rapport d'audit favorable *m*, rapport d'audit sans réserve *m*, STOCK transaction équilibrant achat et vente; **~ acceptance** *n (*SYN *general acceptance)* BANK acceptation sans réserve *f*; **~ ballast tank** *n (CBT)* TRANSP *shipping* citerne à ballast propre *f*; **~ bill** *n* ECON, FIN effet libre *m*; **~ bill of health** *n* GEN COMM, WEL patente de santé nette *f*; **~ bill of lading** *n (clean b/l)* IMP/EXP, TRANSP connaissement net *m*, connaissement sans réserves *m*; **~ float** *n* ECON flottement pur *m*; **~ hands** *n pl* GEN COMM en mains propres *f pl*, mains propres *f pl*, LAW obligation d'attitude irréprochable pour bénéficier de l'"equity"; **~ opinion** *n infrml* ACC opinion sans réserve *f*; **~ product** *n* ENVIR produit écologique *m*, éco-produit *m*; **~ record** *n* LAW casier judiciaire vierge *m*; **~ report of findings** *n* TRANSP conclusions nettes *f pl*; **~ signature** *n* GEN COMM signature sans réserve *f*; **~ technology** *n* ENVIR technologie non-polluante *f*, technologie propre *f*, technologie écologique *f*

clean:[4] **~ up** *vt* ENVIR assainir, décontaminer, dépolluer, nettoyer, remettre en état

cleaning: **~ -up operation** *n* ENVIR opération d'assainissement *f*, opération de nettoyage *f*

cleanup: **~ campaign** *n* ENVIR campagne d'assainissement *f*, campagne de nettoyage *f*; **~ fund** *n* INS *life insurance* fonds de liquidation *m*

clear:[1] **~ -cut** *adj* GEN COMM bien distinct, net, franc; **~ of debts** *adj* ACC sans endettement, GEN COMM libre de dettes; ◆ **make ~** GEN COMM préciser

clear:[2] **~ days** *n pl* TRANSP *shipping* jours francs *m pl*; **~ loss** *n* FIN, GEN COMM perte sèche *f*; **~ profit** *n* FIN bénéfice net *m*; **~ thinking** *n* GEN COMM perception claire *f*; **~ title** *n US* LAW titre incontestable *m*, titre irréfragable *m*, titre irréfutable *m*

clear[3] *vt* BANK *cheque, funds* compenser, COMP *wipe out, erase* effacer, vider, FIN *debt* liquider, s'acquitter de, *mortgage* purger, GEN COMM *loan* liquider, rembourser, *profit* faire un bénéfice de, rapporter, LAW disculper, innocenter, TRANSP *transhipment permit* apurer; ◆ **~ the market** *jarg* STOCK réexaminer les termes d'une transaction

clearance *n* IMP/EXP *customs* dédouanement *m*, formalités douanières *f pl*, S&M liquidation *f*, soldes *m pl*; **~ agent** IMP/EXP agent du dédouanement *m*; **~ of cargo goods** IMP/EXP dédouanement de cargaison *m*; **~ inwards** IMP/EXP déclaration d'entrée en douane *f*, manifeste d'entrée *m*, permis d'entrée *m*; **~ outward of a vessel** IMP/EXP déclaration de sortie de navire *f*; **~ outwards**

IMP/EXP déclaration de sortie de douane *f*, manifeste de sortie *m*, permis de sortie *m*; **~ sale** S&M liquidation *f*, soldes *m pl*; **~ of ship** IMP/EXP déclaration en douane de navire *f*

cleared[1] *adj (Cld)* BANK compensé; **~ without examination** *(CWE)* IMP/EXP dédouanement sans inspection *m*

cleared:[2] **~ check** *n AmE*, **~ cheque** *n BrE* BANK chèque compensé *m*; **~ reject** *n* TAX déclaration rejetée réglée *f*

clearer *n* BANK, FIN banque de dépôt *f*

clearing *n* BANK clearing *m*, compensation interbancaire *f*, *of account* liquidation *f*, *of cheque* compensation *f*, ECON compensation *f*, *international trade* clearing *m*, FIN *of debt*, GEN COMM acquittement *m*; **~ account** *n* ECON *international trade* compte de clearing *m*; **~ agent** *n* BANK agent de compensation *m*, IMP/EXP agent en douane *m*; **~ agreement** *n* ECON *international trade* accord de clearing *m*; **~ balance statement** *n* BANK relevé de solde de compensation *m*; **~ bank** *n* BANK, FIN banque de dépôt *f*; **~ center** *n AmE*, **~ centre** *n BrE* BANK centre de compensation *m*; **~ corporation** *n US* BANK chambre de compensation *f*; **~ day** *n* BANK jour de compensation *m*; **~ entry** *n* BANK écriture de compensation *f*; **~ house** *n* BANK chambre de compensation *f*, STOCK comptoir de liquidation *m*; **~ house funds** *n pl* BANK fonds compensés *m pl*; **~ market** *n* ECON marché de compensation *m*; **~ member** *n* FIN adhérent compensateur *m*, membre compensateur *m*, STOCK *currency options* membre compensateur *m*, membre d'une chambre de compensation *m*; **~ position** *n* BANK position de compensation *f*; **~ process** *n* BANK processus de compensation *m*; **~ report** *n* BANK relevé de compensation *m*; **~ system** *n* STOCK système de compensation *m*

Clearing: **~ House Automatic Payments System** *n US (CHAPS)* BANK Chambre de compensation interbancaire internationale *f*; **~ House Interbank Payments System** *n US (CHIPS)* BANK Chambre de compensation interbancaire internationale *f*

clerical: **~ error** *n* ACC erreur d'écriture *f*, ADMIN erreur d'écriture *f*, faute de copiste *f*, faute de frappe *f*; **~ personnel** *n* ADMIN personnel de bureau *m*; **~ staff** *n* ADMIN, HRM personnel de bureau *m*, personnel de secrétariat *m*; **~ work** *n* ADMIN, HRM travail de bureau *m*, travail de secrétariat *m*; **~ work measurement** *n (CWM)* ADMIN, HRM chronométrage des travaux administratifs *m*; **~ worker** *n* ADMIN, HRM emploi de bureau *m*

clerk *n* ADMIN, HRM commis *m*, emploi de bureau *m*, LAW clerc *m*, greffier *m*; **~ of works** HRM conducteur de travaux *m*

click *vt* COMP *key, mouse button* cliquer

client *n* GEN COMM, S&M *of advertising agency* client *m*; **~ account** FIN compte client *m*; **~ agreement letter** *UK* FIN lettre d'accord du client *f*;

~ base S&M base de clientèle *f*; **~ card** GEN COMM carte-client *f*; **~ department** GEN COMM service après-vente *m*, service clientèle *m*; **~ firm** S&M société cliente *f*; **~ -led marketing policy** S&M politique dictée par les besoins de la clientèle *f*

clientele *n* GEN COMM achalandage *m*, clientèle *f*

clients *n pl* GEN COMM clientèle *f*; **~' ledger** *n* ACC, BANK, FIN grand livre auxiliaire des clients *m*, grand livre des ventes *m*

client/server *n* COMP client/serveur *m*

climb *vi* ECON *price, currency* monter, *unemployment* grimper, s'accroître, GEN COMM augmenter; ♦ **~ the ladder** HRM grimper dans la hiérarchie; **~ the promotion ladder** HRM gravir les échelons de la hiérarchie

clip: **~ art** *n* COMP image clip art *f*, image graphique *f*, vignette *f*; **~ -on unit** *n* *(COU)* TRANSP *refrigeration* groupe frigorifique amovible *m*

clipboard® *n* COMP presse-papier *m*

clipping *n* *AmE (cf cutting BrE)* MEDIA *from newspaper* coupure *f*, coupure de journal *f*, coupure de presse *f*

cloakroom *n* *(cf baggage checkroom AmE)* GEN COMM, TRANSP consigne *f*

clock:[1] **~ -calendar** *n* COMP *hardware* horloge-calendrier *f*; **~ card** *n* IND carte de pointage *f*; **~ rate** *n* COMP fréquence de base *f*; **~ signal** *n* COMP signal d'horloge *m*

clock:[2] **~ in** *vi* HRM, IND pointer en arrivant; **~ off** HRM, IND pointer en sortant; **~ on** HRM, IND pointer en arrivant; **~ out** HRM, IND pointer en sortant

clocking: **~ -in** *n* HRM pointage *m*

clone[1] *n* COMP, GEN COMM clone *m*

clone[2] *vt* COMP, GEN COMM cloner

close[1] *adj* GEN COMM *cooperation, relationship* proche, étroit; ♦ **in ~ touch with** GEN COMM en rapport étroit avec

close[2] *n* GEN COMM clôture *f*, STOCK clôture *f*, cours de clôture *m*; **~ company** *BrE (cf close corporation AmE)* GEN COMM compagnie proche *f*; **~ corporation** *AmE (cf close company BrE)* GEN COMM compagnie proche *f*; **~ corporation plan** *UK* STOCK projet de société fermée à peu d'actionnaires; **~ correlation** MATH corrélation proche *f*; **~ -down** MEDIA *broadcast* fin des émissions *f*; **~ examination** GEN COMM examen approfondi *m*; **~ of the market** STOCK clôture de marché *f*; ♦ **at the ~** STOCK en clôture, à la clôture

close[3] **1.** *vt* ACC arrêter, COMP *file, session* fermer, terminer, GEN COMM fermer, *session, sale* clôturer, conclure, S&M conclure, STOCK liquider; **~ down** GEN COMM *business, factory* fermer définitivement; **~ out** GEN COMM *goods* liquider avant fermeture; **2.** *vi* **~ down** GEN COMM *of business, shop* fermer définitivement, *radio, television* terminer les émissions; ♦ **~ a deal** STOCK liquider une opération; **~ the gap** ECON, FIN combler le déficit; **~ the meeting** GEN COMM lever la séance;

~ a position FIN inverser une position, STOCK *options on currency futures* déboucler une position, liquider une position

closed[1] *adj* COMP, GEN COMM fermé; **~ -out** STOCK liquidé

closed:[2] **~ account** *n* ACC, BANK compte fermé *m*, FIN compte clos *m*, compte soldé *m*; **~ box container** *n* TRANSP *shipping* conteneur ordinaire *m*; **~ circuit** *n* COMP circuit fermé *m*; **~ company** *n* *BrE (cf closed corporation AmE)* ECON entreprise familiale *f*, société très fermée *f*, GEN COMM compagnie proche *f*; **~ container** *n* TRANSP *shipping* conteneur fermé *m*; **~ corporation** *n* *AmE (cf closed company BrE)* ECON entreprise familiale *f*, société très fermée *f*, GEN COMM compagnie proche *f*; **~ economy** *n* *(ANT open economy)* ECON, POL économie fermée *f*; **~ -end fund** *n* *(ANT open-end fund)* FIN société d'investissement à capital fermé ou fixe *f*; **~ -end investment company** *n* *(CEIC)* FIN société d'investissement à capital fermé ou fixe *f* *(SICAF)*; **~ -end investment fund** *n* FIN société d'investissement à capital fermé ou fixe *f*; **~ -end investment trust** *n* FIN société de gestion de portefeuille à capital non-variable *f*; **~ -end management company** *n* *UK* FIN société de gestion à capital fixe *f*; **~ -end mortgage** *n* BANK, PROP emprunt hypothécaire plafonné *m*; **~ -end mutual fund** *n* *US* STOCK fonds d'investissement à capital fixe *m*; **~ height** *n* TRANSP *of fork-lift truck* hauteur fermée *f*; **~ population** *n* *(ANT open population)* ECON population fermée *f*; **~ position** *n* FIN position non-dénouée *f*, STOCK position liquidée *f*, position non-dénouée *f*; **~ question** *n* *(ANT open-ended question)* GEN COMM, S&M *market research* question fermée *f*; **~ questionnaire** *n* *(ANT open-ended questionnaire)* GEN COMM questionnaire non-directif *m*, S&M *market research* questionnaire directif *m*; **~ season** *n* MEDIA *broadcast* période creuse *f*; **~ -shelter deck** *n* TRANSP *shipping* pont-abri fermé *m*, TRANSP *(CSD)* *vessel* navire à pont-abri couvert *m*; **~ shop** *n* HRM monopole syndical *m*; **~ stock** *n* S&M article sans suite *m*, stock fermé *m*; **~ union** *n* HRM syndicat exerçant un monopole de l'embauche

closely: **~ connected profession** *n* HRM profession connexe *f*; **~ held corporation** *n* ECON société fermée *f*, STOCK société à nombre d'actionnaires réduit *f*

closing *n* GEN COMM clôture *f*, PROP conclusion *f*, STOCK clôture *f*; **~ balance** *n* *(ANT opening balance)* ACC, BANK, FIN solde de clôture *m*, solde à l'arrêté des comptes *m*; **~ bid** *n* GEN COMM dernière enchère *f*, dernière offre *f*; **~ cost** *n* PROP *real estate* prix de conclusion *m*; **~ costs** *n pl* FIN coûts en fin d'exercice *m pl*, coûts à la clôture *m pl*; **~ date** *n* GEN COMM date limite *f*, dernier délai *m*, PROP *US* date de clôture *f*; **~ -down costs** *n* GEN COMM frais de liquidation *m pl*; **~ entry** *n* ACC écriture de clôture *f*; **~ inventory** *n* ACC inventaire du prix d'exercice *m*; ~ **price** *n* STOCK cours de clôture *m*, dernier cours *m*, dernière cotation *f*; ~ **purchase** *n UK* STOCK achat à la clôture *m*; ~ **purchase transaction** *n* (ANT *closing sale transaction*) STOCK achat de liquidation *m*, achat liquidatif *m*; ~ **quotation** *n* STOCK cours de clôture *m*, dernière cotation *f*; ~ **range** *n* STOCK fourchette des cours en fin de séance *f*; ~ **rate method** *n BrE* (*cf current rate method AmE*) ACC *of currency translation for consolidated accounts* système des taux de clôture *m*; ~ **sale transaction** *n* (ANT *closing purchase transaction*) STOCK vente de liquidation *f*, vente liquidative *f*; ~ **session** *n* STOCK séance de clôture *f*; ~ **statement** *n* PROP clôture de compte *f*; ~ **stock** *n* STOCK stock en fin d'exercice *m*, stock final *m*; ~ **time** *n* GEN COMM heure de fermeture *f*; ~ **trade** *n* STOCK opération de liquidation *f*, opération liquidative *f*, transaction de clôture *f*; ~ **transaction** *n* STOCK opération de liquidation *f*, opération liquidative *f*, transaction de clôture *f*; ◆ ~ **the accounts** ACC arrêt des comptes *m*; **at** ~ STOCK en clôture, à la clôture

closure *n* GEN COMM, STOCK clôture *f*

cloth: ~ **cap pensions** *n pl* HRM, WEL régime de retraite des ouvriers *m*

clothing: ~ **business** *n* IND confection *f*, industrie de la fringue *f* (*infrml*); ~ **industry** *n* IND confection *f*, industrie de la fringue *f* (*infrml*)

Clothing: ~ **Export Council** *n UK* (*CEC*) IMP/EXP conseil d'exportation de l'habillement

cloud: ~ **on title** *n US* PROP nuage sur titre *m*

CLSB *abbr* (*Committee of London and Scottish Bankers*) BANK commission des banquiers londoniens et écossais

club: ~ **class** *n* TRANSP classe affaires *f*, classe club *f*; ~ **good** *n* ECON bien collectif *m*

Club: ~ **of Rome** *n* ECON *1968 onwards* Club de Rome *m*

cluster *n* COMP *of terminals* cluster *m*, grappe *f*, secteur *m*, GEN COMM groupe *m*; ~ **analysis** S&M *market research* analyse par segments *f*, typologie *f*; ~ **controller** COMP contrôleur de grappe *m*; ~ **of countries** S&M groupe de pays partageant certaines caractéristiques; ~ **housing** PROP habitations en grappe *f pl*; ~ **sample** S&M *market research* échantillon segmental *m*; ~ **sampling** S&M *market research* sondage par grappes *m*, sondage par segments *m*

clustering *n* S&M segmentation *f*

clutch: ~ **drive** *n* (*CD*) TRANSP *shipping* entraînement d'embrayage *m*, transmission par engrenages réducteurs *f*; ~ **hook** *n* TRANSP *shipping* manille *f*

cm *abbr* GEN COMM (*centimeter AmE, centimetre BrE*) cm (*centimètre*), TRANSP (*condition monitoring*) *shipping* contrôle d'état *m*

CM *abbr* (*Common Market*) ECON, POL Marché commun *m*

CMA *abbr* (*cash management account*) FIN compte de gestion de fonds *m*

cmdty *abbr* (*commodity*) ECON, GEN COMM, IND marchandise *f*, produit *m*, *food, product* denrée *f*, *raw material* matière première *f*, produit de base *m*, STOCK marchandise *f*, matière première *f*

CME[1] *abbr* (*Chicago Mercantile Exchange*) STOCK bourse des matières premières de Chicago

CME:[2] ~ **Clearing House** *n* STOCK chambre de compensation du Chicago Mercantile Exchange

CMEA *abbr* (*Council for Mutual Economic Aid*) ECON COMECON (*Conseil de l'aide économique mutuelle*)

CMO *abbr* (*collateralized mortgage obligation*) BANK, FIN hypothèque garantie par nantissement *f*

CMS *abbr* (*Capital Markets System*) STOCK *World Bank* système des marchés financiers mondiaux *m*

CMSA *abbr US* (*Consolidated Metropolitan Statistical Area*) ADMIN regroupement de zone statistique métropolitaine *m*

CN *abbr* FIN (*credit note*), GEN COMM (*credit note*) note de crédit *f*, INS (*cover note*) lettre de couverture *f*, note de couverture *f*, police provisoire *f*, TRANSP (*consignment note*) bordereau d'expédition *m*, feuille de route *f*, lettre de voiture *f*

cnee *abbr* (*consignee*) TRANSP consignataire *mf*, destinataire *mf*

cnmt *abbr* (*consignment*) TRANSP consignation *f*, en consignation *loc f*, envoi *m*, expédition *f*

CNS *abbr UK* (*continuous net settlement*) STOCK liquidation en continu *f*, règlement en continu *m*

c/o *abbr* COMMS (*care of*), GEN COMM (*care of*) aux bons soins de, chez, IMP/EXP (*certificate of origin*) certificat d'origine *m*, TRANSP (*cargo oil, case oil*) huile de carter *f*

Co: and ~ *abbr* (*and company*) GEN COMM et Cie (*et compagnie*)

Co. *abbr* (*company*) ECON, GEN COMM Cie (*compagnie*), Sté (*société*)

CO *abbr* (*Certification Officer*) ADMIN agent certificateur *m*

co-accused *n* LAW coinculpé *m*

coach *n* TRANSP car *m*, autocar *m*, *rail* voiture *f*; ~ **company** LEIS, TRANSP compagnie de cars *f*; ~ **station** TRANSP gare routière *f*

coal *n* ENVIR, IND charbon *m*, houille *f*; ~ **berth** *n* TRANSP *shipping* quai réservé aux charbonniers *m*; ~ **carrier** *n* TRANSP *shipping* charbonnier *m*, navire charbonnier *m*; ~ **deposit** *n* IND gisement de charbon *m*, gisement de houille *m*; ~ **dust** *n* ENVIR poussière de charbon *f*; ~ **-fired power station** *n* IND usine thermique à houille *f*; ~ **industry** *n* ENVIR, IND industrie houillère *f*, industrie minière *f*; ~ **mine** *n* IND charbonnage *m*, houillère *f*, mine de charbon *f*; ~ **mining** *n* IND charbonnage *m*; ~ **propulsion** *n* TRANSP *shipping* propulsion à charbon *f*; ~ **reserves** *n pl* ENVIR, IND réserves de charbon *f pl*, réserves de houille *f pl*

coalition n GEN COMM, POL government coalition f; ~ **alliance** POL alliance de coalition f; ~ **government** POL gouvernement de coalition m

coaming n TRANSP shipping hiloire de panneau f; ~ **bridge fitting** TRANSP shipping pontet d'hiloire m; ~ **chock** TRANSP shipping taquet d'hiloire m

Coase n ECON théorie de l'entreprise f

coastal: ~ **pollution** n ENVIR pollution côtière f, pollution des côtes f, pollution du littoral f

coaster n TRANSP person caboteur m, vessel navire cargo sans ligne régulière m

coastguard n (CG) HRM organization gendarmerie maritime f, person garde-côte m, gendarme maritime m, membre de la gendarmerie maritime m

coasting n TRANSP shipping cabotage m; ~ **broker** TRANSP shipping caboteur m; ~ **trade** TRANSP shipping cabotage m, commerce de cabotage m

coaxial: ~ **cable** n COMP hardware câble coaxial m

Cobb: ~ **Douglas production function** n ECON fonction de production de Cobb-Douglas f

COBOL® abbr (Common Ordinary Business-Oriented Language) COMP COBOL® (langage COBOL)

COBRA abbr (Continent Britain and Asia) TRANSP consortium des conteneurs en Grande-Bretagne et sur l'Asie

cobweb n ECON modèle d'analyse cobweb m

C/OC abbr (certificate of origin and consignment) IMP/EXP certificat d'origine et d'expédition m

Cocom abbr (Coordinating Committee for Multilateral Export controls) IMP/EXP comité de coordination pour le contrôle multilatéral des exportations m

COD abbr (cash on delivery) IMP/EXP, S&M livraison contre remboursement loc f, paiement à la livraison m

code n COMMS dialling code m, indicatif m, post code postal m, COMP code m, GEN COMM indicatif m, LAW code m; ~ **of accounts** ACC code de comptes m; ~ **of advertising practice** S&M code de pratique publicitaire m; ~ **of arbitration** STOCK code d'arbitrage m; ~ **box** IMP/EXP case à code f; ~ **check** COMP contrôle de programmation m; ~ **of conduct** GEN COMM, TRANSP on board code de conduite m; ~ **element** COMP codet m; ~ **of ethics** GEN COMM déontologie f, éthique f, MGMNT éthique f; ~ **line** COMP ligne de code f, ligne de programmation f; ~ **name** COMP nom de code m; ~ **of practice** GEN COMM code de bonne conduite m, déontologie f, LAW UK déontologie f, règlements et usages m pl; ~ **of procedure** STOCK code de procédure m; ~ **of professional responsibility** US LAW code de responsabilité professionnelle m; ~ **set** COMP code de caractères m, jeu de caractères m; ~ **sheet** COMP feuille de programmation f; ~ **UN** IMP/EXP code ONU m

codec abbr (coder-decoder) COMP codec (codeur-décodeur)

coded: ~ **data entry** n COMP saisie codée de données f; ~ **message** n COMMS message codé m

codefendant n LAW coinculpé m

coder: ~ **-decoder** n (codec) COMP codeur-décodeur m (codec)

codetermination n HRM codétermination f, détermination conjointe f; ~ **rights** n pl STOCK droits de codétermination m pl

codicil n LAW codicille m

codification n GEN COMM codification f

coding n COMMS codage m, COMP programming language codage m, programmation f; ~ **of accounts** ACC identification attribution de codes comptables f; ~ **error** COMP erreur de programmation f; ~ **manual** ACC manuel du code des comptes m; ~ **system** ACC système d'attribution de codes comptables m

co-director n GEN COMM, HRM, MGMNT codirecteur m

co-ed[1] adj (coeducational) WEL mixte

co-ed[2] n UK WEL école mixte f

coeducational[1] adj (co-ed) WEL mixte

coeducational:[2] ~ **high school** n WEL lycée mixte m; ~ **school** n UK WEL école mixte f

coefficient n MATH coefficient m; ~ **of correlation** MATH statistics coefficient de corrélation m; ~ **of determination** MATH statistics coefficient de détermination m; ~ **of multiple correlation** MATH statistics coefficient de corrélation multiple m; ~ **of multiple determination** MATH statistics coefficient de détermination multiple m; ~ **of variation** MATH statistics coefficient d'écart m

coercive adj GEN COMM coercitif

coffee: ~ **break** n HRM pause-café f

Coffee: ~, **Sugar & Cocoa Exchange** n US STOCK bourse du café, du sucre et du cacao de New-York

cofferdam n TRANSP shipping cofferdam m, maille sèche f

cofinance vt ECON, FIN, GEN COMM cofinancer

cofinancing n ECON, FIN, GEN COMM cofinancement m, financement conjoint m

cognate: ~ **disciplines** n pl WEL disciplines affinitaires f pl, disciplines voisines f pl

cognition n MGMNT knowledge connaissance f

cognitive: ~ **behavior** n AmE, ~ **behaviour** n BrE S&M comportement informatif m; ~ **consonance** n ECON consonance cognitive f; ~ **dissonance** n ECON dissonance cognitive f; ~ **ergonomics** n pl ADMIN ergonomie cognitive f, ergonomie de l'information f

COGSA abbr (Carriage of Goods by Sea Act) LAW, TRANSP 1924, 1971 loi relative au transport des marchandises par mer

coherence n GEN COMM cohérence f

coherency n GEN COMM cohérence f

coherent adj GEN COMM cohérent

cohesion n GEN COMM cohésion f; ~ **fund** ECON EU fonds de cohésion m

COI *abbr* (*Central Office of Information*) ADMIN Bureau central de l'information *m*

coin *n* GEN COMM *piece* monnaie *f*, pièce de monnaie *f*; **~ machine insurance** INS assurance de distributeurs *f*; **~ wrapper** BANK papier à enrouler les pièces

coinage *n* BANK, ECON, FIN monnaie *f*; **~ system** ECON système monétaire *m*

coincide: 1. *vt* **~ with** GEN COMM coïncider avec 2. *vi* GEN COMM coïncider

coincident: **~ indicators** *n pl* ECON *econometrics* indicateurs simultanés *m pl*

coinsurance *n* INS coassurance *f*, participation de l'assuré à l'assurance *f*

coinsured *adj* INS coassuré

coinsurer *n* INS coassureur *mf*

col *abbr* GEN COMM (*column*) colonne *f*, MEDIA (*column*) colonne *f*, rubrique *f*, TRANSP (*collision*) abordage *m*, collision *f*

COLA *abbr US* (*cost-of-living adjustment*) ACC indexation des salaires *f*, ECON, HRM indexation des salaires *f*, indexation sur le coût de la vie *f*

Colbertism *n* POL colbertisme *m*

cold: **~ boot** *n* COMP démarrage à froid *m*; **~ call** *n* S&M *by sales representative* visite impromptue *f*; **~ calling** *n* S&M démarchage par téléphone *m*; **~ canvass** *n* GEN COMM, S&M prospection à l'improviste *f*; **~ start** *n* COMP, GEN COMM démarrage à froid *m*; **~ storage** *n* IND chambre frigorifique *f*, chambre froide *f*, TRANSP chambre frigorifique *f*, chambre froide *f*, entreposage frigorifique *m*; **~ storage plant** *n* IND entrepôt frigorifique *m*; **~ store** *n* TRANSP *shipping* entrepôt frigorifique *m*; **~ store terminal** *n* TRANSP *shipping* terminal frigo *m*; **~ type** *n* ADMIN *printing* composition sans plomb *f*, fonte froide *f*

coll *abbr* (*collision*) TRANSP abordage *m*, collision *f*

collaborate *vi* GEN COMM collaborer, coopérer

collaboration *n* GEN COMM collaboration *f*, coopération *f*

collaborative *adj* GEN COMM coopératif, *action* de collaboration *loc f*, en collaboration *loc f*, HRM coopératif

collaborator *n* HRM collaborateur *m*

collapse¹ *n* GEN COMM *in prices* chute brutale *f*, dégringolade *f* (*infrml*), effondrement *m*, STOCK effondrement *m*

collapse² *vi* GEN COMM *system*, STOCK s'effondrer

collapsed *adj* GEN COMM *companies* échoué

collapsible: **~ container** *n* (*coltainer*) TRANSP conteneur démontable *m*, conteneur pliant *m*, conteneur repliable *m*

collar *n* STOCK collar *m*, tunnel de taux *m*

collateral¹ *adj* FIN subsidiaire, GEN COMM *phenomenon* concomitant, MATH parallèle

collateral² *n* ECON, FIN gage *m*, nantissement *m*; **~ acceptance** FIN acceptation de cautionnement *f*; **~ assignment** INS allocation de garantie *f*,

allocation de nantissement *f*; **~ bill** STOCK effet de nantissement *m*; **~ loan** BANK emprunt garanti *m*, prêt garanti *m*; **~ security** ECON, FIN nantissement *m*, titre déposé en garantie *m*; **~ trust bond** STOCK obligation garantie par nantissement de titres *f*, obligation nantie *f*

collateralize *vt* BANK garantir par nantissement

collateralized: **~ mortgage obligation** *n* (*CMO*) BANK, FIN hypothèque garantie par nantissement *f*; **~ preferred share** *n* TAX action privilégiée avec garantie *f*

collating: **~ sequence** *n* COMP ordre de classement des caractères *m*, ordre lexicographique *m*, séquence de classement *f*

collation *n* COMP interclassement *m*

collator *n* COMP interclasseuse *f*; **~ code** COMP code d'interclassement *m*; **~ number** COMP numéro d'interclassement *m*

colleague *n* HRM collaborateur *m*, collègue *mf*, confrère *m*, consoeur *f*

collect:¹ **~ call** *n* AmE (*cf reverse charge call BrE*) COMMS *telephone* appel en PCV *m* (*Fra*), appel à frais virés *m* (*Can*), communication en PCV *f*

collect² *vt* COMMS lever, FIN *debt* recouvrir, *payment* encaisser, *payments in finance house* recouvrer, GEN COMM recouvrir, *statistics, information* ramasser, rassembler, recueillir, STOCK *premium* ramasser, toucher; **make a ~ call** AmE (*cf make a reverse charge call to sb BrE*) COMMS appeler en PCV, appeler à frais virés (*Can*), téléphoner en PCV (*Fra*); ♦ **~ sums due** FIN faire la recette

collected: **~ and delivered** *phr* (*C&D*) GEN COMM emporté et livré

collectible *n* GEN COMM objet de collection *m*

collecting: **~ bank** *n* BANK banque de recouvrement *f*; **~ charge** *n* GEN COMM frais de recouvrement *m pl*

collection *n* ACC encaissement *m*, encaissement des créances *m*, recouvrement *m*, recouvrement des créances *m*, BANK encaissement *m*, COMMS levée *f*, FIN encaissement *m*, encaissement des créances *m*, recouvrement *m*, recouvrement des créances *m*, GEN COMM recouvrement des créances *m*, recouvrement *m*, TAX levée *f*, perception *f*, recouvrement *m*; **~ of accounts** ACC encaissement de comptes clients *m*; **~ agent** TAX agent de recouvrement *m*; **~ agreement** TAX accord de perception *m*; **~ of a bill** ACC *bill of exchange* encaissement d'un effet *m*, encaissement d'une traite *m*; **~ charge** GEN COMM commission d'encaissement *f*, frais d'encaissement *m pl*, frais de recouvrement *m pl*, TRANSP frais d'enlèvement *m pl*; **~ cost** GEN COMM coût du recouvrement *m*, frais de recouvrement *m pl*; **~ of customs duties** TAX perception des droits de douane *f*; **~ of debts** ACC, FIN, GEN COMM recouvrement de créances *m*, recouvrement de dettes *m*; **~ -only check** AmE, **~ -only cheque** BrE BANK chèque à porter en compte *m*; **~ period** ACC *of debts* période moyenne de recouvrement *f*; ~ **of premiums** INS encaissement de primes *m*; ~ **of public money** TAX perception des deniers publics *f*; ~ **ratio** (SYN *average collection period*) ACC, BANK durée moyenne de règlement des comptes clients *f*, délai moyen de recouvrement des créances *m*, période moyenne d'encaissement *f*, ratio de recouvrement *m*; ~ **tariff** IMP/EXP tarif de recouvrement *m*; ◆ ~ **and delivery** (*C&D*) GEN COMM ramassage et livraison; **for** ~ STOCK *security* pour recouvrement *m*; **make a** ~ WEL faire une collecte; ~ **on wheels** (*COW*) TRANSP enlèvement par route *m*

collective¹ *adj* GEN COMM collectif

collective:² ~ **accident insurance** *n* INS assurance collective contre les accidents *f*, assurance-accidents collective *f* (*jarg*); ~ **agreement** *n* HRM, IND, LAW accord patronat-syndicats *m*, cc, convention collective *f*; ~ **bargaining** *n* HRM négociation collective *f*; ~ **bargaining agreement** *n* HRM, IND, LAW accord patronat-syndicats *m*, cc, convention collective *f*; ~ **conciliation** *n* UK HRM conciliation collective *f*; ~ **dismissal** *n* UK HRM licenciement collectif *m*; ~ **good** *n* ECON bien public *m*; ~ **grievance procedure** *n* UK HRM procédure prud'hommale collective *f*; ~ **insurance** *n* INS assurance collective *f*; ~ **investment undertaking** *n* FIN organisme de placement collectif *m*; ~ **mark** *n* PATENTS marque collective *f*; ~ **pay agreement** *n* HRM accord collectif sur les salaires *m*

collectively *adv* GEN COMM collectivement

collectivism *n* POL collectivisme *m*

collectivization *n* ECON, PROP collectivisation *f*

collectivize *vt* ECON, PROP collectiviser

collector *n* IMP/EXP receveur *m*; ~ **of taxes** HRM, TAX receveur des impôts *m*; ~**'s office** IMP/EXP bureau du receveur *m*

college *n* GEN COMM école supérieure *f*; ~ **of further education** UK (*CFE*) WEL centre d'enseignement postscolaire *m*

collier *n* TRANSP *shipping* cargo charbonnier *m*, charbonnier *m*

colliery *n* IND charbonnage *m*, *mine* houillère *f*, mine *f*; ~ **working days** *n pl* IND jours de travail à la mine de houille *m pl*

collision *n* (*col, coll*) TRANSP abordage *m*, collision *f*; ~ **bulkhead** TRANSP *shipping* cloison d'abordage *f*; ~ **clause** INS *marine* clause de collision *f*; ~ **coverage** INS tierce collision *f*; ~ **insurance** INS tierce collision *f*

collusion *n* ECON collusion *f*

collusive: ~ **oligopoly** *n* ECON oligopole collusif *m*

Colombia *pr n* GEN COMM Colombie *f*

Colombian¹ *adj* GEN COMM colombien

Colombian² *n* GEN COMM *person* Colombien *m*

Colombo *pr n* GEN COMM Colombo *n pr*

colon *n* GEN COMM colon *m*

colony *n* GEN COMM colonie *f*

color *n* AmE see colour BrE

color/graphics: ~ **adaptor** *n* AmE see colour/graphics adaptor BrE

colour *n* BrE COMP couleur *f*; ~ **display** BrE COMP écran couleur *m*; ~ **supplement** BrE MEDIA *print* supplément couleur *m*; ~ **of title** BrE PROP couleur du titre *f*

colour/graphics: ~ **adaptor** *n* BrE (*CGA*) COMP adaptateur graphique couleur *m* (*CGA*)

coltainer *n* (*collapsible container*) TRANSP *shipping* conteneur démontable *m*, conteneur pliant *m*, conteneur repliable *m*

column *n* (*col*) GEN COMM *table* colonne *f*, MEDIA *print* colonne *f*, rubrique *f*; ~ **heading** ACC intitulé de colonne *m*; ~ **inch** MEDIA *print* espace d'une colonne de large sur un pouce de haut; ~ **move** COMP *spreadsheet command* déplacement de colonne *m*

columnar: ~ **journal** *n* ACC livre à colonnes *m*

columnist *n* MEDIA *newspaper* chroniqueur *m*

com. *abbr* ADMIN (*commission*), BANK (*commission*) *payment*, ECON (*commission*) commission *f*, GEN COMM (*committee*) com (*commission*), GEN COMM (*commission*) *order* commande *f*, *warrant* mandat *m*, HRM (*committee*) com (*comité*), HRM (*commission*) *fee* commission *f*, pourcentage *m*, MGMNT (*committee*), POL (*committee*) com (*comité*), S&M (*commission*) commission *f*, STOCK (*commission*) courtage *m*, droit de courtage *m*, frais de courtage *m pl*

co-manager *n* GEN COMM, HRM *international banking*, MGMNT codirecteur *m*

comb *abbr* GEN COMM (*combination*) association *f*, coalition *f*, combinaison *f*, TRANSP (*combined*) *shipping* mixte

COMB *abbr* (*combination*) MATH combinaison *f*

combat *vt* GEN COMM *unemployment, drug trafficking* combattre, lutter contre

combi: ~ **carrier** *n* TRANSP *shipping* transporteur mixte *m*; ~ **ship** *n* TRANSP *shipping* cargo mixte *m*

combination *n* GEN COMM (*comb*) association *f*, coalition *f*, combinaison *f*, MATH (*COMB*) combinaison *f*; ~ **acts** UK HRM *legislation of 1799 and 1800* loi sur les coalitions *f*; ~ **carrier** TRANSP *shipping* pétrolier-minéralier *m*; ~ **charge** TRANSP tarif groupé *m*; ~ **of charges** TRANSP groupage des frais *m*; ~ **rate** TRANSP tarif groupé *m*; ~ **of rates** TRANSP groupage des tarifs *m*, tarif de soudure *m*, tarifs soudés *m pl*

combine¹ *n* LAW association *f*, cartel *m*, corporation *f*; ~ **committee** HRM comité d'entreprise du consortium *m*

combine² *vt* GEN COMM associer, combiner; ~ **with** GEN COMM combiner avec

combined¹ *adj* (*comb*) TRANSP *shipping, holds* mixte

combined:² ~ **amount** *n* TAX montant global *m*; ~ **balance sheet** *n* FIN bilan consolidé *m*; ~ **cycle power station** *n* TRANSP *shipping* centrale mixte *f*; ~ **financial statement** *n* ACC, FIN état financier consolidé *m*; ~ **issue** *n* MEDIA *print* numéro couplé *m*; ~ **mark** *n* PATENTS marque combinée *f*; ~ **premium** *n* INS prime multirisque *f*; ~ **shop insurance** *n* INS assurance combinée de magasins *f*; ~ **statement of income** *n* ACC état des résultats consolidé *m*; ~ **ticket** *n* LEIS billets combinés *m pl*; ~ **total claim** *n* TAX déduction combinée *f*; ~ **trade** *n* GEN COMM commerce intégré *m*; ~ **transport** *n* (*CT*) TRANSP transport combiné *m*, transport multimodal *m*; ~ **transport bill of lading** *n* (*CTBL*) IMP/EXP, TRANSP connaissement de transport combiné *m*; ~ **transport document** *n* (*CTD*) TRANSP document de transport combiné *m*; ~ **transport operation** *n* TRANSP opération de transport combiné *f*; ~ **transport operator** *n* (*CTO*) TRANSP commissionnaire de transport combiné *m*, entrepreneur de transport combiné *m*, organisateur de transport combiné *m* (*ETC*)

combustible: ~ **material** *n* ENVIR, IND matériau combustible *m*

combustion: ~ **plant** *n* ENVIR, IND installation de combustion *f*

come: **1.** *vt* GEN COMM arriver, venir; ~ **before** LAW *court* comparaître devant; ~ **from** GEN COMM provenir de, venir de; ~ **to** GEN COMM se chiffrer à; **2.** *vi* ~ **along** GEN COMM faire des progrès; ~ **off** GEN COMM réussir, se réaliser; ~ **out** MEDIA *print* paraître, sortir, être publié; ◆ ~ **at the top** GEN COMM venir en tête

comeback: **make a** ~ *phr* GEN COMM opérer un retour

COMECON *abbr* (*Council for Mutual Economic Aid*) ECON COMECON (*Conseil de l'aide économique mutuelle*)

COMET *abbr* (*Common Market Medium Term Model*) ECON *econometrics* modèle économique à moyen terme pour la communauté européenne *m*

COMEX *abbr US* (*Commodities Exchange*) STOCK bourse des matières premières de New-York, ≈ la COMEX *f*

comfort: ~ **letter** *n* ACC lettre de soutien *f*, FIN lettre d'accord présumé *f*

Comit: ~ **index** *n* STOCK indice Comit *m*

comma *n* COMP, MATH, MEDIA virgule *f*

command[1] *n* COMP commande *f*, instruction *f*, ordre *m*, GEN COMM commandement *m*, ordre *m*, HRM, MGMNT commandement *m*; ~ **economy** ECON, POL économie planifiée *f*; ~ **file** COMP fichier de commande *m*; ~ **key** COMP *keyboard* touche de commande *f*; ~ **line** COMP ligne de commande *f*; ~ **and control regulation** ADMIN, LAW règlement de commande et de contrôle *m*; ◆ **be in** ~ **of** GEN COMM commander

command[2] *vt* GEN COMM *order* commander, ordonner; ◆ ~ **a very high price** GEN COMM valoir très cher

commencement: ~ **of cover** *n* INS mise en couverture *f*; ~ **of coverage** *n* INS date d'effet de couverture *f*, prise d'effet du contrat d'assurance *f*; ~ **of a policy** *n* INS effet d'une police *m*

commencing: ~ **salary** *n* *frml* HRM salaire d'embauche *m*, salaire de départ *m*

commensurate[1] *adj* GEN COMM proportionné

commensurate:[2] ~ **charge** *n* GEN COMM *EU regulation* droit proportionné *m*; ~ **taxation** *n* TAX équivalence des charges fiscales *f*

comment[1] *n* GEN COMM commentaire *m*, observation *f*, remarque *f*

comment[2] *vi* GEN COMM faire des commentaires *loc m*, faire des observations *loc f*, faire des remarques *loc f*

commentary *n* GEN COMM commentaire *m*

commerce *n* GEN COMM affaires *f pl*, commerce *m*, S&M commerce *m*

commercial[1] *adj* GEN COMM commercial, marchand; ◆ **no** ~ **value** (*n.c.v.*) GEN COMM sans valeur commerciale

commercial[2] *n* GEN COMM, MEDIA, S&M *TV, radio* pub *f* (*infrml*), publicité *f*, spot *m* (*infrml*), spot publicitaire *m*; ~ **accounts** *n pl* ACC comptes commerciaux *m pl*; ~ **activity** *n* TAX activité commerciale *f*; ~ **acumen** *n* GEN COMM sens du commerce *m*; ~ **advantage** *n* GEN COMM avantage commercial *m*; ~ **agent** *n* GEN COMM agent commercial *m*; ~ **analysis** *n* FIN analyse commerciale *f*; ~ **artist** *n* HRM *advertising*, S&M *advertising* créateur publicitaire *m*, dessinateur de publicité *m*, graphiste *mf*; ~ **bank** *n* BANK, FIN banque commerciale *f*, banque de dépôt *f*; ~ **banking** *n* BANK opérations des banques commerciales *f pl*, *retail* services aux entreprises *m pl*, services bancaires commerciaux *m pl*; ~ **bill** *n* *AmE* (SYN *trade bill*) BANK, FIN titre commercial *m*; ~ **blanket bond** *n* INS *employee cover* garantie générale commerciale *f*, garantie générale de commerce *f*; ~ **break** *n* MEDIA *broadcast* coupure publicitaire *f*, interruption publicitaire *f*, page de publicité *f*, écran publicitaire *m*; ~ **broker** *n US* GEN COMM, PROP courtier en immobilier commercial *m*; ~ **cargo** *n* TRANSP cargaison commerciale *f*, marchandises commerciales *f pl*; ~ **center** *n* *AmE*, ~ **centre** *n* *BrE* S&M centre commercial *m*; ~ **code** *n* GEN COMM, LAW code de commerce *m*; ~ **computer** *n* COMP ordinateur civil *m*, ordinateur de gestion *m*; ~ **concern** *n* ECON, GEN COMM entreprise commerciale *f*; ~ **considerations** *n pl* GEN COMM contreparties commerciales *f pl*, rémunérations commerciales *f pl*; ~ **contract** *n* GEN COMM, LAW contrat commercial *m*; ~ **credit insurance** *n US* INS assurance crédit commercial *f*; ~ **designer** *n* HRM, S&M *advertising* créateur publicitaire *m*, dessinateur de publicité *m*, graphiste *mf*; ~ **developer** *n* GEN COMM, PROP promoteur commercial *m*; ~ **development** *n* GEN COMM développement commercial *m*; ~ **dock** *n* (*CD*) TRANSP *shipping* bassin de commerce *m*, port de commerce *m*; ~ **efficiency** *n* ECON rendement économique *m*; ~ **establishment** *n* GEN COMM maison de commerce *f*, établissement commercial *m*; ~ **forgery policy** *n* INS contrat contre le faux et usage de faux *m*; ~ **form** *n* INS formulaire commercial *m*, police commercielle *f*, TRANSP formulaire commercial *m*; ~ **health insurance** *n US* INS *from profit-making insurance companies* assurance commerciale maladie *f*; ~ **hedgers** *n pl* STOCK opérateurs en couverture sur les marchés des matières premières; ~ **insurance policy** *n* INS assurance commerciale *f*; ~ **interest** *n* ECON, GEN COMM intérêt commercial *m*; ~ **invoice** *n* ACC facture commerciale *f*; ~ **law** *n* GEN COMM, LAW droit commercial *m*; ~ **lease** *n* GEN COMM bail commercial *m*; ~ **lending** *n* BANK crédit aux entreprises *m*, opérations de crédit commercial *f pl*, prêts commerciaux *m pl*; ~ **lending power** *n* BANK pouvoir de crédit commercial *m*, pouvoir en matière de crédit commercial *m*; ~ **letting** *n UK* PROP location commerciale *f*; ~ **loan** *n* BANK prêt commercial *m*; ~ **manager** *n* HRM, MGMNT, S&M cadre commercial *m*, directeur commercial *m*; ~ **marine** *n dat see mercantile marine, merchant marine* ; ~ **market** *n* GEN COMM marché *m*; ~ **occupancy** *n* GEN COMM, PROP occupation commerciale *f*; ~ **paper** *n (CP)* BANK *short-term instrument* billet de trésorerie *m (BT)*, FIN papier commercial *m*, GEN COMM effet de commerce *m*, papier commercial *m*; ~ **policy** *n* ECON, GEN COMM, IMP/EXP, MGMNT, POL politique commerciale *f*; ~ **port** *n* TRANSP port de commerce *m*; ~ **premises** *n pl* PROP locaux commerciaux *m pl*; ~ **property** *n* GEN COMM, PROP immobilier commercial *m*; ~ **property policy** *n* INS, PROP assurance des biens commerciaux *f*, bail à loyer d'immeuble commercial *m*; ~ **radio** *n* GEN COMM *broadcast*, MEDIA *broadcast* radio commerciale *f*; ~ **radio station** *n* MEDIA *broadcast* station de radio commerciale *f*; ~ **representation** *n* GEN COMM, S&M représentation commerciale *f*; ~ **research** *n* GEN COMM recherche commerciale *f*; ~ **risk** *n* GEN COMM, IND, INS risque commercial *m*; ~ **risk analysis** *n UK* FIN analyse des risques commerciaux *f*; ~ **sickness insurance policy** *n* INS contrat d'assurance maladie *m*; ~ **stocks** *n pl* GEN COMM stocks marchands *m pl*; ~ **storage** *n* TRANSP stockage commercial *m*; ~ **strategy** *n* ECON, GEN COMM stratégie commerciale *f*; ~ **targets** *n pl* GEN COMM objectifs commerciaux *m pl*; ~ **television** *n* MEDIA *broadcast* télévision commerciale *f*; ~ **trade** *n* ECON, IMP/EXP, S&M échanges commerciaux *m pl*; ~ **traveler** *n AmE*, ~ **traveller** *n BrE* GEN COMM représentant de commerce *m*, voyageur de commerce *m*, voyageur représentant placier *m*, VRP, HRM voyageur de commerce *m*, S&M représentant de commerce *m*, voyageur de commerce *m*, voyageur représentant placier *m*, VRP; ~ **treaty** *n* ECON, POL accord commercial *m*; ~ **trust** *n* TAX fiducie commerciale *f*; ~ **value movement order** *n (CVMO)* GEN COMM bon de transfert de marchandise *m*; ~ **vehicle** *n* TRANSP utilitaire *m*, véhicule utilitaire *m*; ~ **venture** *n* GEN COMM entreprise commerciale risquée *f*, MGMNT entreprise *f*, entreprise commerciale *f*, entreprise commerciale risquée *f*;

~ **well** *n* ENVIR puits en exploitation *m*; ~ **world** *n* GEN COMM monde du commerce *m*

Commercial: ~ **Officer** *n UK* GEN COMM, MGMNT attaché commercial à l'ambassade de France; ~ **Relations and Exports** *n pl UK (CRE)* IMP/EXP relations commerciales et exportations *f pl*

commercialism *n* FIN *profit-making* esprit commercial *m*, GEN COMM *on large scale* affairisme *m (infrml)*

commercialization *n* GEN COMM, S&M commercialisation *f*

commercialize *vt* GEN COMM, S&M commercialiser

commercially *adv* GEN COMM, S&M commercialement

commingling *n* STOCK *securities, trust banking* mélange des titres des clients avec les titres détenus par la société; ~ **of funds** LAW fusion de capitaux *f*

commissary *n US* GEN COMM intendance *f*; ~ **goods** *n pl* IMP/EXP marchandises à faibles droits douaniers *f pl*

commission[1] *n (com.)* ADMIN *payment*, BANK *payment*, ECON commission *f*, GEN COMM *order* commande *f*, *warrant* mandat *m*, HRM *fee* commission *f*, pourcentage *m*, S&M commission *f*, STOCK courtage *m*, droit de courtage *m*, frais de courtage *m pl*; ~ **account** BANK compte de commission *m*; ~ **agent** HRM agent *m*, commissionnaire *m*, commissionnaire en marchandises *m*, courtier *m*; ~ **broker** *US* STOCK courtier à la commission *m*; ~ **for acceptance** BANK commission d'acceptation *f*; ~ **house** STOCK maison de commission *f*, maison de courtage *f*; ~ **of inquiry** HRM commission d'enquête *f*; ~ **merchant** HRM agent *m*, commissionnaire *m*, courtier *m*; ~ **rate** BANK taux de commission *m*; ~ **representative** HRM représentant au pourcentage *m*, représentant à la commission *m*; ~ **salesman** HRM agent *m*, commissionnaire *m*, courtier *m*, vendeur à commission *m*; ~ **salesperson** HRM agent *m*, commissionnaire *m*, courtier *m*, courtière *f*, vendeur à commission *m*, vendeuse à commission *f*; ~ **saleswoman** HRM agent *m*, commissionnaire *m*, courtière *f*, vendeuse à commission *f*; ~ **system** HRM système de rémunération *m*, système à la commission *m*

commission[2] *vt* ADMIN *request, empower*, BANK, GEN COMM mandater, TRANSP mettre en service

Commission: ~ **of the European Community** *n* ECON Commission des communautés européennes *f*; ~ **on Energy and the Environment** *n (CENE)* ENVIR Commission sur l'énergie et l'environnement *f*

commissionaire *n UK* HRM, LEIS *of hotel* portier *m*

commissioner *n* ADMIN, GEN COMM commissaire *m*; ~ **for the rights of trade union members** *UK (CROTUM)* HRM délégué chargé des droits des membres des syndicats

Commissioner: ~ **of Customs and Excise** *n UK* IMP/EXP ≈ commissionnaire chargé du recouvrement des droits de douane *m*, TAX ≈ agent comptable du Trésor *m*, ≈ commissionnaire chargé du recouvrement des droits de douane *m*; ~ **of Inland Revenue** *n UK* TAX ≈ Percepteur des impôts *m*, ≈ agent comptable du Trésor *m*

commissioning *n* TRANSP mise en service *f*

commit *vt* GEN COMM *money, time,* MGMNT consacrer; ◆ ~ **forgery** LAW se rendre coupable d'un faux; ~ **o.s. to** GEN COMM s'engager à

commitment *n* GEN COMM *promise, pledge* engagement *m*, promesse *f*, LAW engagement *m*, obligation *f*; ~ **authority** FIN autorisation d'engagement *f*; ~ **control** LAW contrôle des engagements *m*; ~ **document** LAW document d'engagement *m*; ~ **fee** BANK commission d'engagement *f*, commission sur le montant d'un prêt non-utilisé *f*; ~ **record** LAW registre des engagements *m*

committed: ~ **costs** *n pl* ACC coûts engagés *m pl*

committee *n (com.)* GEN COMM commission *f*, conseil *m*, HRM comité *m*, conseil *m*, MGMNT comité *m*, commission *f*, conseil *m*, POL comité *m*, commission *f*; ~ **for industrial co-operation** *(CIC)* IND comité de coopération industrielle; ~ **of inquiry** POL commission d'enquête *f*; ~ **of inspection** LAW comité d'inspection *m*, commission d'inspection *f*; ~ **meeting** GEN COMM réunion de comité *f*, réunion de commission *f*; ~ **member** ADMIN commissaire *mf*, GEN COMM commissaire *mf*, membre d'une commission *m*; ◆ **be on a** ~ GEN COMM être membre d'un comité

Committee: ~ **of European Shipowners** *n (CES)* TRANSP comité des armateurs européens; ~ **for the Simplification of International Trade Procedures** *n (SIPROCOM)* ADMIN *based in Belgium* Comité pour la simplification des procédures du commerce international *m*; ~ **of London and Scottish Bankers** *n (CLSB)* BANK *clearing banks in Britain* commission des banquiers londoniens et écossais; ~ **on Invisible Exports** *n (CIE)* IMP/EXP comité des exportations invisibles; ~ **on Scientific and Technical Research** *n (CREST)* IND comité pour la recherche scientifique et technique; ~ **on Uniform Securities Identification Procedures** *n US (CUSIP)* STOCK ≈ Agence française de codification *f*, ≈ commission de codification des titres *f*; ~ **of Public Accounts** *n UK* ACC *parliamentary committee* ≈ Cours des comptes *f (France)*; ~ **of Shipowners Associations of the European Community** *n* ADMIN comité des associations d'armateurs des communautés européennes; ~ **of Twenty** *n (C-20)* GEN COMM Comité des Vingt *m*

commodification: ~ **of money** *n* ECON transformation de la monnaie en marchandises *f*

commodities *n pl* ECON, GEN COMM marchandises *f pl*; ~ **index** *n UK* STOCK indice des marchandises *m*, indice des matières premières *m*; ~ **trading** *n* STOCK opérations sur marchandises *f pl*

Commodities: ~ **Exchange** *n US (COMEX)* STOCK bourse des matières premières de New-York, ≈ Bourse des marchandises *f*, ≈ bourse du commerce *f*, ≈ la COMEX *f*

commodity *n* ECON, GEN COMM, IND *(cmdty)* marchandise *f, consumer good* article *m*, produit *m, food, product* denrée *f, raw material* matière première *f*, produit de base *m*, S&M *consumer good* article *m*, produit *m*, STOCK matière première *f*, STOCK *(cmdty)* marchandise *f*; ~ **agreement** *n* ECON accord sur les matières premières *m*; ~ **analysis** *n UK* STOCK analyse des marchandises *f*, analyse des matières premières *f*; ~ **approach** *n* S&M approche du produit *f*; ~ **broker** *n* FIN, S&M, STOCK courtier en marchandises *m*, courtier en matières premières *m*; ~ **cartel** *n* ECON cartel des matières premières *m*; ~ **contract** *n* STOCK contrat de marchandises *m*; ~ **credit** *n* BANK crédits commerciaux *m pl*; ~ **currency** *n* STOCK monnaie marchandise *f*; ~ **exchange** *n US* STOCK bourse de marchandises *f*; ~ **fetishism** *n* ECON, S&M culte aveugle du produit *m*, fétichisme *m*; ~ **flow** *n* GEN COMM circulation des marchandises *f*; ~ **futures** *n pl* FIN contrat à terme de marchandises *m*, contrats à terme sur matières premières *m pl*, STOCK contrat à terme de marchandises *m*, contrats à terme sur matières premières *m pl*, marchandises à terme *f pl*; ~ **futures contract** *n* FIN, STOCK contrat à terme de marchandises *m*; ~ **futures market** *n* STOCK marché à terme des matières premières *m*; ~ **futures trading** *n* STOCK opération à terme sur les marchandises *f*; ~ **market** *n* STOCK bourse de commerce *f*, bourse de marchandises *f*, marché de futures et d'options de marchandises *m*, marché de matières premières *m*; ~ **mix** *n* TRANSP ensemble de marchandises *m*; ~ **paper** *n* STOCK créance nantie par des marchandises *f*; ~ **price** *n* STOCK cours des denrées *m*, prix de marchandises *m*, prix des denrées *m*; ~ **pricing** *n* STOCK fixation des prix par le jeu du marché *f*; ~ **rate** *n* TRANSP tarif préférentiel *m*; ~ **reserve currency** *n* ECON monnaie de réserve basée sur la valeur d'un panier de produits de base; ~ **stabilization schemes** *n* ECON dispositifs de stabilisation des prix des matières premières *m pl*; ~ **standard** *n* STOCK étalon marchandises *m*; ~ **tax** *n* ECON, TAX taxe sur la consommation *f*; ~ **terms of trade** *n* ECON termes de l'échange *m pl*; ~ **trade structure** *n* ECON structure du commerce extérieur par type de produit *f*; ~ **trades** *n pl* ECON matière première échangée sur les marchés internationaux *f*; ~ **trading** *n* STOCK opérations sur marchandises *f pl*

Commodity: ~ **Exchange Authority** *n US (CEA)* STOCK bourse de commerce; ~ **Futures Trading Commission** *n US (CFTC)* STOCK Commission de contrôle des marchés de matières premières *f*, Commission des opérations à terme sur les marchandises *f*

common[1] *adj* GEN COMM *frequent* courant, *shared* commun

common:[2] ~ **area** *n* PROP parties communes *f pl*;

~ **average** n INS *maritime* avarie commune f; ~ **carrier** n IND *European energy networks* entrepreneur général de transports m, entreprise de transport public f, TRANSP entrepreneur de transports m, entrepreneur général de transports m, transporteur m; ~ **code of practice** n GEN COMM déontologie commune f; ~ **cost** n ECON charge commune f; ~ **currency** n ECON, FIN monnaie commune f, monnaie unique f, GEN COMM monnaie unique f; ~ **customs tariff** n *(CCT)* IMP/EXP *European Union* tarif douanier commun m, tarif douanier communautaire m; ~ **denominator** n GEN COMM *decision making* dénominateur commun m; ~ **directive** n LAW, POL *European Union* directive commune f; ~ **disaster clause** n US INS *life insurance* clause de décès simultanés f, théorie des comourants f; ~ **distinguishing factor** n GEN COMM, HRM *votes in ballot* facteur commun de distinction m; ~ **dividend** n STOCK dividende ordinaire m, dividende sur actions ordinaires m; ~ **dollars** n pl FIN, GEN COMM, IMP/EXP dollars indexés m; ~ **element** n US PROP *in condominium* élément commun m; ~ **equity** n STOCK action ordinaire f, capital actions ordinaires m; ~ **external tariff** n *(CET)* ECON tarif extérieur commun m; ~ **labor** n AmE, ~ **labour** n BrE HRM main-d'oeuvre non-qualifiée f; ~ **language** n GEN COMM langage commun m, langue commune f; ~ **law** n LAW droit coutumier m; ~ **-law marriage** n LAW concubinage m, union de fait f; ~ **-law spouse** n LAW concubin m, conjoint de fait m; ~ **learnings** n pl WEL apprentissages communs m pl; ~ **ownership** n ECON droits de propriété collectifs m pl; ~ **policy** n GEN COMM, POL politique commune f; ~ **pricing** n GEN COMM entente illicite en matière de prix f; ~ **revenue** n ACC, ECON produit d'exploitation commun m; ~ **seal** n LAW sceau légal m; ~ **sense** n GEN COMM bon sens m; ~ **service agency** n ADMIN organisme de services communs m; ~ **service cost distribution system** n ACC système de répartition du coût des services communs m; ~ **share** n BrE *(cf common stock AmE)* ACC, ECON, STOCK action ordinaire f; ~ **share certificate** n BrE *(cf common stock certificate AmE)* STOCK certificat d'actions ordinaires m; ~ **share dividend** n BrE *(cf common stock dividend AmE)* STOCK dividende ordinaire m, dividende sur actions ordinaires m; ~ **share investment** n BrE *(cf common stock investment AmE)* STOCK investissement en actions ordinaires m, placement en actions ordinaires m; ~ **shareholder** n STOCK actionnaire ordinaire m; ~ **shares equivalent** n BrE *(cf common stock equivalent AmE)* STOCK équivalent en actions ordinaires m; ~ **shares fund** n BrE *(cf common stock fund AmE)* STOCK fonds d'actions ordinaires m, fonds de placement en actions ordinaires m; ~ **stock** n AmE *(cf common share BrE, ordinary share BrE)* ACC, ECON, STOCK action ordinaire f; ~ **stock certificate** n AmE *(cf common share certificate BrE)* STOCK certificat d'actions ordinaires m;

~ **stock dividend** n AmE *(cf common share dividend BrE)* STOCK dividende ordinaire m, dividende sur actions ordinaires m; ~ **stock equivalent** n AmE *(cf common shares equivalent BrE)* STOCK équivalent en actions ordinaires m; ~ **stock fund** n AmE *(cf common shares fund BrE)* STOCK fonds d'actions ordinaires m, fonds de placement en actions ordinaires m; ~ **stock investment** n AmE *(cf common share investment BrE)* STOCK investissement en actions ordinaires m, placement en actions ordinaires m; ~ **stockholder** n STOCK actionnaire ordinaire m; ~ **stockholders' equity** n STOCK capitaux propres m pl; ~ **user facility** n GEN COMM service multi-usagers m

Common: ~ **Agricultural Policy charges** n pl ECON frais de la PAC m pl; ~ **Market** n *(CM)* ECON Marché commun m, POL marché commun m; ~ **Market Medium Term Model** n *(COMET)* ECON *econometrics* modèle économique à moyen terme pour la communauté européenne m; ~ **Ordinary Business-Oriented Language** n *(COBOL)* COMP langage COBOL m *(COBOL)*; the ~ **Agricultural Policy** n *(CAP)* ECON, POL *EU* la politique agricole commune f *(PAC)*

commonality n IND standardisation f

Commons: the ~ n pl UK POL les Communes f pl

Commonwealth n ECON, POL Commonwealth m; ~ **of Independent States** *(CIS)* ECON, GEN COMM, POL Communauté des États indépendants f *(CEI)*; ~ **Preference** UK IMP/EXP régime préférentiel appliqué aux importations du Commonwealth au Royaume-Uni

communal¹ adj GEN COMM commun, communautaire, public

communal:² ~ **economy** n ECON économie communale f; ~ **ownership** n LAW, PROP copropriété f

commune n ECON, POL commune f

communicate vt COMMS, GEN COMM communiquer, transmettre

communication n COMMS communication f, liaison f, transmission f, *fax, letter* communication f, COMP communication f, liaison f, transmission f, GEN COMM communication f, liaison f, HRM, LAW, MGMNT, POL *European Union* communication f; ~ **barrier** n COMMS, GEN COMM obstacle à la communication m; ~ **gap** n COMMS, GEN COMM absence de communication f, manque de communication m; ~ **media** n pl COMMS moyens de communication m pl, supports de communication m pl, médias m pl, MEDIA les supports de communication m pl, moyens de communication m pl, médias m pl, S&M médias m pl; ~ **network** n COMMS réseau de transmission m; ~ **skills** n pl HRM aptitudes à la communication f pl, facilités à communiquer f pl; ~ **strategy** n COMMS stratégie de communication f; ~ **technology** n COMMS technologie de communication f

communications n pl COMMS moyen de communication m, TRANSP *roads, railways* moyens de communication *m pl*; ~ **network** *n* COMP réseau de communication *m*; ~ **satellite** *n* COMMS satellite de communication *m*; ~ **theory** *n* COMMS, HRM, MGMNT théorie de la communication *f*

communicator *n* COMMS communicateur *m*

communiqué *n* COMMS, GEN COMM, S&M communiqué *m*

communism *n* ECON, POL communisme *m*

Communist: ~ **China** *pr n* GEN COMM Chine communiste *f*

community¹ *adj* GEN COMM communautaire

community² *n* GEN COMM communauté *f*; ~ **action** *n* GEN COMM *EU* action collective *f*, action communautaire *f*; ~ **association** *n* PROP association communautaire *f*; ~ **of goods** *n* GEN COMM communauté de biens *f*; ~ **imports** *n pl* IMP/EXP importations communautaires *f pl*; ~ **of interests** *n* GEN COMM communauté d'intérêts *f*; ~ **network** *n* COMMS réseau de télévision par câble *m*; ~ **property** *n* US LAW bien en communauté *m*; ~ **spirit** *n* GEN COMM esprit communautaire *m*

Community: ~ **aid** *n* ECON *European Union* aide communautaire *f*; ~ **budget** *n* ECON, FIN, POL *European Union* Budget communautaire *m*, Budget de la Communauté *m*; ~ **Charter of Fundamental Social Rights of Workers** *n* HRM *European Union* charte communautaire des droits sociaux fondamentaux des travailleurs *f*; ~ **goods** *n pl* IMP/EXP marchandises communautaires *f pl*; ~ **Programme** *n* BrE *(CP)* ECON travaux d'utilité collective *m pl (TUC)*, HRM, POL programme communautaire *m*, programme d'utilité publique *m*, travaux d'utilité collective *m pl*, WEL travaux d'utilité collective *m pl (TUC)*; ~ **Trade Mark Office** *n* LAW office européen des marques *m*, PATENTS *European Union* Bureau de marque de fabrique *m*; ~ **transit** *n (CT)* IMP/EXP, TRANSP *European Union* transit communautaire *m*; ~ **treatment** *n* IMP/EXP traitement communautaire *m*

communization *n* PROP *of land* collectivisation *f*

communize *vt* PROP *land* collectiviser

commutability *n* GEN COMM interchangeabilité *f*, permutabilité *f*, LAW commuabilité *f*

commutable *adj* GEN COMM interchangeable, permutable, LAW commuable

commutate *vt* GEN COMM commuter

commutation *n* INS, LAW commutation *f*, TRANSP *AmE* (SYN *commuting*) migrations alternantes *f pl*, trajets journaliers *m pl*; ~ **right** INS faculté de rachat *f*; ~ **ticket** *AmE (cf season ticket BrE)* GEN COMM carte d'abonnement *f*

commutative *adj* LAW commutatif

commute 1. *vt* GEN COMM commuer, convertir, échanger, LAW commuer; **2.** *vi* GEN COMM faire la navette *loc f*

commuter *n* TRANSP banlieusard *m*, navetteur *m* *(Bel)*, *aircraft* avion de transport régional *m*; ~ **airline** TRANSP compagnie de transport régional *f*, compagnie régionale *f*; ~ **belt** *UK* GEN COMM grande banlieue *f*

commuting *n (cf commutation AmE)* TRANSP migrations alternantes *f pl*, trajets journaliers *m pl*

Comoran¹ *adj* GEN COMM comorien

Comoran² *n* GEN COMM *person* Comorien *m*

Comorian¹ *adj* GEN COMM comorien

Comorian² *n* GEN COMM *person* Comorien *m*

Comoros *pr n* [inv pl] GEN COMM Comores *f pl*

co-mortgagor *n* US LAW co-débiteur hypothécaire *m*

compact *n* GEN COMM *verbal agreement* entente *f*, *written agreement* accord *m*, contrat *m*, convention *f*, LAW convention *f*; ~ **disk** *(CD)* COMP disque compact *m (CD)*; ~ **disk interactive** *(CD-I)* COMP disque compact interactif *m (CDI)*; ~ **disk read-only memory** *(CD-ROM)* COMP disque CD-ROM *m (CD-ROM)*

companies: ~ **act** *n* UK GEN COMM, IND, LAW loi sur les sociétés *f*, loi sur les sociétés commerciales et industrielles *f*

Companies: ~ **Code** *n Australia* LAW code régissant les sociétés; ~ **Registration Office** *n (CRO)* GEN COMM, LAW ≈ Registre du commerce et des services *m (RCS)*

companionway *n* TRANSP *shipping* descente *f*

company *n (Co.)* ECON, GEN COMM compagnie *f (Cie)*, entreprise *f*, firme *f*, société *f (Sté)*, MGMNT entreprise *f*; ~ **accounts** *n pl* ACC, FIN, GEN COMM comptes sociaux *m pl*; ~ **agreement** *n* HRM accord par branche *m*; **and** ~ *n (and Co)* GEN COMM et compagnie *f (et Cie)*; ~ **apartment** *n AmE (company flat)* PROP logement de fonction *m*; ~ **attorney** *n AmE (cf company lawyer BrE)* GEN COMM, LAW conseiller juridique d'une entreprise *m*; ~ **bargaining** *n* HRM négociation par branche *f*; ~ **benefit** *n* HRM complément de salaire *m*; ~ **benefits** *n pl* HRM avantages annexes *m pl*, avantages sociaux *m pl*; ~ **car** *n* GEN COMM, TRANSP voiture d'entreprise *f*, voiture de fonction *f*, voiture de société *f*; ~ **credit card** *n* BANK, FIN carte de crédit professionnelle *f*; ~ **director** *n* GEN COMM, MGMNT chef d'entreprise *m*; ~ **executive** *n* ADMIN, GEN COMM, HRM, MGMNT cadre d'entreprise *m*, dirigeant d'entreprise *m*; ~ **failure** *n* GEN COMM échec d'une société *m*; ~ **flat** *n BrE (company apartment)* PROP logement de fonction *m*; ~ **flotation** *n* STOCK lancement d'entreprise *m*; ~ **goal** *n* GEN COMM but de l'entreprise *m*; ~ **house** *n* PROP logement de fonction *m*; ~ **law** *n* GEN COMM, IND, LAW droit des sociétés *m*; ~ **lawyer** *n* GEN COMM *BrE (cf company attorney AmE)* conseiller juridique d'une entreprise *m*, GEN COMM *UK business law expert* juriste d'entreprise *m*, HRM *UK* juriste d'entreprise *mf*, IND *UK* juriste d'entreprise *m*, LAW *BrE (cf company attorney AmE) expert* conseiller juridique d'une entreprise *m*, LAW *UK within firm* juriste d'entreprise *m*; ~ **-level agreement** *n* HRM accord au niveau d'une société *m*; **~ liquidity** *n* FIN liquidité de la société *f*; **~ logo** *n* GEN COMM, S&M logotype de la société *m*; **~ logotype** *n* GEN COMM, S&M logotype de la société *m*; **~ manager** *n* GEN COMM, MGMNT chef d'entreprise *m*; **~ meeting** *n* GEN COMM, MGMNT assemblée des actionnaires *f*, réunion des actionnaires *f*; **~ model** *n* ACC, FIN, GEN COMM modèle de l'entreprise *m*; **~ objective** *n* GEN COMM objectif de l'entreprise *m*; **~ philosophy** *n* GEN COMM philosophie de l'entreprise *f*; **~ planning** *n* GEN COMM planification de l'entreprise *f*; **~ policy** *n* GEN COMM politique de l'entreprise *f*; **~ profile** *n* GEN COMM profil de l'entreprise *m*; **~ promotion** *n* STOCK lancement d'entreprise *m*; **~ results** *n pl* FIN, GEN COMM performances de la société *f pl*, résultats de la société *m pl*; **~ seal** *n* GEN COMM, LAW sceau légal *m*; **second largest ~** *n* GEN COMM deuxième société *f*; **~ secretary** *n UK* ADMIN, HRM secrétaire général *m*; **~ sector** *n* ECON secteur des sociétés privées *m*; **~ sickness insurance scheme** *n* INS assurance maladie propre à l'entreprise *f*, caisse maladie propre à l'entreprise *f*; **~ -specific card** *n* FIN carte privative *f*; **~ strategy** *n* GEN COMM stratégie de l'entreprise *f*; **~ structure** *n* GEN COMM structure de l'entreprise *f*; **~ tax** *n* TAX impôt sur les sociétés *m*, IS; **~ technical specialist export salesman** *n* IMP/EXP spécialiste technique des ventes à l'exportation *m*; **~ town** *n* ECON ville dont l'économie dépend d'une seule entreprise; **~ union** *n* HRM syndicat maison *m*; **~'s affairs** *n pl* GEN COMM affaires de l'entreprise *loc f*

comparability *n* HRM *of pay* alignement *m*, comparabilité *f*

comparable[1] *adj* GEN COMM comparable

comparable:[2] **~ basis** *n* ACC *of reporting* base comparable *f*; **~ worth** *n Australia (CW)* HRM principe adopté en 1972 dont le but est de payer les travailleurs de façon égale. Il a introduit trois phases uniformes afin d'éviter la discrimination sexuelle; ◆ **of ~ worth** HRM de salaire égal

comparative[1] *adj* GEN COMM *value* comparatif, relatif

comparative:[2] **~ advantage** *n* ECON avantage comparatif *m*; **~ advertising** *n* S&M publicité comparative *f*; **~ financial statement** *n* ACC, FIN bilan comparable *m*, état comparatif *m*; **~ negligence** *n* LAW part de responsabilité relative *f*; **~ statement** *n* FIN état comparatif *m*; **~ statics** *n* ECON statique comparative *f*

comparatively *adv* GEN COMM relativement

compare *vt* GEN COMM comparer; **~ to** GEN COMM comparer à; **~ with** GEN COMM comparer avec

compared: **~ with** *phr* GEN COMM par rapport à *loc m*

comparison *n* GEN COMM comparaison *f*; **~ shopping** S&M achat réfléchi comparatif *m*; **~ test** GEN COMM test comparatif *m*

compartment *n* TRANSP compartiment *m*

compartmentalization *n* GEN COMM *of agricultural common market* cloisonnement *m*

compartmentalize *vt* ADMIN compartimenter, GEN COMM cloisonner, MGMNT compartimenter

compatibility *n* COMP, IND *of products* compatibilité *f*

compatible *adj* COMP compatible; ◆ **~ with** GEN COMM compatible avec

compel *vt* GEN COMM contraindre; ◆ **~ sb to do sth** GEN COMM contraindre qn à faire qch

compensate *vt* GEN COMM compenser, contrebalancer, rémunérer, HRM *pay* rémunérer, LAW dédommager, indemniser; **~ for** GEN COMM compenser; ◆ **~ for a fall in demand** GEN COMM compenser une chute de la demande; **~ sb for sth** GEN COMM dédommager qn pour qch, indemniser qn pour qch

compensated: **~ demand curve** *n* ECON courbe de demande compensée *f*

compensating[1] *adj* FIN, GEN COMM, STOCK compensatoire

compensating:[2] **~ balance** *n* BANK solde compensateur *m*; **~ common tariff** *n (CCT)* ECON tarif commun compensatoire *m*; **~ error** *n* ACC erreur de compensation *f*; **~ income** *n UK* STOCK revenu compensateur *m*, revenu compensatoire *m*; **~ loss** *n UK* STOCK perte compensatoire *f*; **~ product** *n* IMP/EXP produit compensatoire *m*; **~ wage differential** *n* HRM écart des salaires *m*, écart salarial *m*

compensation *n* ECON compensation *f*, GEN COMM indemnisation *f*, rémunération *f*, HRM indemnisation *f*, indemnité *f*, *payment* rémunération *f*, INS compensation *f*, dédommagement *m*, réparation *f*, LAW indemnisation *f*, indemnité *f*, TAX compensation *f*, dédommagement *m*; **~ agreement** *n* ECON *international trade* accord de compensation *m*; **~ claim** *n* LAW demande d'indemnité *f*; **~ fee** *n* COMMS *post* indemnité en cas de perte *f*; **~ for damage** *n* INS compensation des dommages *f*, réparation du dommage *f*; **~ for loss** *n* INS compensation des pertes *f*; **~ fund** *n UK* STOCK caisse de garantie *f*, fond de garantie *m*; **~ money** *n* HRM indemnité pécuniaire *f*; **~ principle** *n* ECON principe de compensation *m*; **~ settlement** *n* LAW accord d'indemnisation *m*; **~ stocks** *n pl UK* STOCK actions de compensation *f pl*; **~ tax** *n* TAX impôt de redressement *m*, taxe compensatrice *f*; ◆ **in ~** GEN COMM en contrepartie

compensatory[1] *adj* FIN, GEN COMM, STOCK compensatoire

compensatory:[2] **~ amount** *n* ECON montant compensatoire *m*; **~ damages** *n pl* LAW dommages-intérêts compensatoires *m pl*; **~ finance** *n* *(SYN deficit financing, pump priming)* ECON financement par le déficit *m*, mesures d'incitation économique *f pl*, recours à l'impasse budgétaire *m*; **~ financial facility** *n (CFF)* FIN compensation financière *f*; **~ fiscal policy** *n* TAX politique de déficit budgétaire *f*; **~ levy** *n* IMP/EXP prélèvement compensatoire à l'exportation *m*; ~ **stock option** *n UK* STOCK prime en options sur actions *f*, régime d'actionnariat compensatoire *m*; ~ **time** *n* HRM congé de récupération *m*, heures récupérées *f pl*

compete: 1. *vt* ~ **against** ECON, GEN COMM, S&M concurrencer, faire concurrence à, être en concurrence avec *loc f*; ~ **with** ECON, GEN COMM, S&M concurrencer, faire concurrence à, être en concurrence avec *loc f* **2.** *vi* ECON, GEN COMM, S&M concourir, être concurrents *loc m*, être en concurrence *loc f*

competence *n* ECON compétence *f*, GEN COMM aptitude *f*, capacité *f*, compétence *f*, HRM attributions *f pl*, LAW compétence *f*; ~ **of court** LAW compétence d'un tribunal *f*

competent: ~ **party** *n* LAW *contract* partie ayant capacité à contracter *f*

competing: ~ **group** *n* GEN COMM, HRM, S&M groupe concurrentiel *m*; ~ **requirements** *n pl* GEN COMM besoins concurrents *m pl*

competition *n* ECON, GEN COMM, HRM, IND, PATENTS, S&M compétition *f*, concurrence *f*; ~ **acts** *n pl* POL lois sur la concurrence *f pl*; ~ **policy** *n* POL, S&M politique vis-à-vis de la concurrence *f*; ♦ **be in** ~ ECON, GEN COMM, S&M être en concurrence; **be in** ~ **with** ECON, GEN COMM être en concurrence avec; **in close** ~ ECON, GEN COMM, S&M en concurrence étroite

competitive[1] *adj* ECON, GEN COMM, S&M compétitif, concurrentiel; ♦ **have a** ~ **advantage over sb** GEN COMM avoir un avantage concurrentiel sur qn

competitive:[2] ~ **advantage** *n* ECON avantage concurrentiel *m*; ~ **bid** *n* S&M réponse à un appel d'offre *f*, soumission *f*; ~ **bidding** *n* GEN COMM système d'appel d'offres *m*, système de soumission *m*; ~ **business** *n* GEN COMM entreprise compétitive *f*, entreprise concurrentielle *f*; ~ **demand** *n* S&M demande concurrente *f*; ~ **edge** *n* ECON, S&M avance sur les concurrents *f*, avantage concurrentiel *m*; ~ **fringe** *n* ECON entreprises marginales *f*, entreprises à la marge *f*; ~ **parity** *n UK (cf defensive budgeting, defensive spending)* S&M alignement sur la concurrence *m*; ~ **-parity method** *n* S&M méthode d'alignement sur la concurrence *f*; ~ **position** *n* ECON, GEN COMM position concurrentielle *f*; ~ **price** *n* ECON, S&M prix compétitif *m*, prix concurrentiel *m*; ~ **pricing** *n* GEN COMM, S&M fixation des prix à des niveaux compétitifs *f*; ~ **process** *n* ECON processus compétitif *m*; ~ **rate** *n* S&M tarif concurrentiel *m*; ~ **stimulus** *n* ECON, S&M stimulant compétitif *m*; ~ **strategy** *n* ECON, GEN COMM, S&M stratégie concurrentielle *f*; ~ **tactics** *n pl* ECON, MGMNT, S&M tactique concurrentielle *f*; ~ **tendering** *n* ECON, GEN COMM soumission concurrentielle *f*; ~ **thrust** *n* ECON, S&M percée commerciale *f*; ~ **trading** *n* ECON, S&M commerce concurrentiel *m*

competitiveness *n* ECON, GEN COMM, S&M compétitivité *f*

competitor *n* ECON, GEN COMM, S&M compétiteur *m*, concurrent *m*; ~ **analysis** S&M analyse des concurrents *f*

competitors: be ~ *phr* S&M être concurrents *loc m*

compilation *n* ACC établissement des états financiers *m*

compile *vt* COMP compiler, GEN COMM compiler, dresser, rassembler

compiler *n* COMP compilateur *m*

complain *vi* GEN COMM se plaindre

complaint *n* GEN COMM réclamation *f*, LAW *civil action* demande introductive d'instance *f*, *criminal law* plainte *f*

complaints: ~ **procedure** *n* GEN COMM réclamation *f*, LAW procédure de dépôt de plainte *f*

complement *n* ACC complément *m*, ECON produit lié *m*, GEN COMM complément *m*, S&M produit lié *m*

complementary[1] *adj* COMP, GEN COMM complémentaire

complementary:[2] ~ **technology** *n* GEN COMM technologie complémentaire *f*, technologie incrémentielle *f*

complete[1] *adj* GEN COMM achevé, *whole* complet, entier, total

complete:[2] ~ **audit** *n* ACC audit complet *m*

complete[3] *vt* ADMIN compléter, GEN COMM *finish* achever, finir, terminer, *make whole* compléter, remplir

completed[1] *adj* GEN COMM *finished* achevé, fini, terminé, LAW *in contracts* accompli

completed:[2] ~ **contract method** *n* ACC méthode de l'achèvement des travaux *f*, méthode de reconnaissance en fin de contrat *f*; ~ **operations insurance** *n* INS, PROP assurance responsabilité civile après travaux *f*

completely *adv* GEN COMM complètement, entièrement; ♦ ~ **knocked down** *(CKD)* TRANSP complètement désassemblé, en pièces détachées

completeness *n* ACC *of accounting data* intégralité *f*

completion *n* GEN COMM *of work* achèvement *m*; ~ **basis** ACC reconnaissance en fin de transaction *f*; ~ **bond** *US* LAW, PROP garantie de bonne exécution *f*; ~ **date** GEN COMM date d'achèvement *f*; ~ **of end use** *UK* IMP/EXP utilisation à bonne fin *f*; ~ **program** *AmE*, ~ **programme** *BrE* ENVIR programme de complétion *m*; ~ **of sale** PROP signature d'une vente *f*; ♦ **near** ~ GEN COMM en phase d'achèvement

complex[1] *adj* GEN COMM complexe

complex[2] *n* GEN COMM, PROP *of buildings* complexe *m*, ensemble *m*; ~ **capital structure** ECON structure en capital complexe *f*; ~ **economy** ECON économie complexe *f*; ~ **transaction** *UK* BANK transaction complexe *f*; ~ **trust** *US* LAW fidéicommis complexe *m*

compliance *n* GEN COMM conformité *f*, consentement *m*, LAW conformité *f*, observation *f*; ~ **audit** *n* ACC audit de conformité *m*, révision de conformité *f*; ~ **cost** *n* TAX coût d'observation *m*; ~ **costs** *n pl* ACC coûts de soumission *m pl*, frais de mise en conformité *m pl*, ADMIN frais d'adaptation *m pl*, frais d'administration *m pl*, frais de mise en conformité *m pl*; ~ **department** *n* STOCK service de contrôle interne *m*; ~ **test** *n* GEN COMM test de conformité *m*; ◆ **be in** ~ **with** GEN COMM être en conformité avec; **in** ~ **with** LAW conformément à; **in** ~ **with the law** LAW en vertu de la loi

complicate *vt* GEN COMM compliquer; ◆ ~ **matters** GEN COMM compliquer la vie; ~ **things** GEN COMM compliquer la vie

complication *n* GEN COMM complication *f*

complimentary: ~ **close** *n* COMMS formule de politesse *f*; ~ **copy** *n* GEN COMM, MEDIA spécimen gratuit *m*; ~ **subscription** *n* GEN COMM, MEDIA abonnement gratuit *m*

compliments *n pl* COMMS compliments *m pl*

comply: ~ **with** *vt* GEN COMM obéir à, *request* accéder à, LAW *rules* obéir à, respecter, se conformer à; ◆ ~ **with the law** LAW se soumettre à la loi; ~ **with the regulations** GEN COMM respecter le règlement

compo *abbr infrml (workers' compensation)* HRM indemnisation des accidents du travail *f*, indemnisation des accidentés du travail *f*, indemnisation des victimes d'accidents de travail *f*

component[1] *adj* GEN COMM composant, constituant

component[2] *n* COMP composant *m*, ECON composant *m*, élément *m*, GEN COMM composant *m*, composante *f*, élément *m*, IND composant *m*, pièce *f*; ~ **factory** IND usine de composants *f*, usine de pièces détachées *f*; ~ **part** COMP *electronic*, ECON composant *m*, GEN COMM *of system* composant *m*, composante *f*, élément constitutif *m*, IND composant *m*

composed: ~ **of** *phr* GEN COMM composé de

composite[1] *adj* GEN COMM combiné, composite

composite:[2] ~ **auxiliary boiler** *n (CAXB)* TRANSP *shipping* chaudière auxiliaire mixte *f*; ~ **auxiliary boiler survey** *n (CAXBS)* TRANSP *shipping* visite de la chaudière auxiliaire mixte *f*; ~ **commodity** *n* ECON produit composite *m*; ~ **currency** *n* BANK, ECON, FIN *European Community* monnaie composite *f*; ~ **currency unit** *n* BANK, ECON, FIN unité monétaire composite *f*; ~ **depreciation** *n* FIN amortissement par classes hétérogènes *m*; ~ **index** *n* ECON, FIN indice composite *m*, indice composé *m*; ~ **insurance** *n* INS assurance avec participation aux bénéfices *f*; ~ **insurance company** *n* INS société d'assurance toutes branches *f*; ~ **leading index** *n* STOCK *statistics* indice avancé composite *m*, indice composite principal *m*; ~ **leading indicator** *n* STOCK *statistics* indica-

teur avancé composite *m*, indicateur composite principal *m*; ~ **mark** *n* PATENTS marque combinée *f*; ~ **package** *n* S&M vente jumelée *f*; ~ **packaging** *n* TRANSP emballage composite *m*; ~ **rate** *n* GEN COMM taux composite *m*; ~ **spread** *n* BANK écart composite *m*; ~ **trailer** *n* TRANSP remorque composée *f*; ~ **yield** *n* BANK rendement composite *m*

composite:[3] ~ **a resolution** *vt* HRM, POL faire accepter une résolution au niveau fédéral *loc f*

composition *n* GEN COMM *agreement* compromis *m*, *make-up* composition *f*, LAW *with creditor* accommodement *m*, arrangement *m*, compromis *m*

compound:[1] ~ **annual growth** *n* ECON, FIN croissance annuelle globale *f*; ~ **annual rate** *n UK (CAR)* BANK *of interest* taux annuel composé *m*, taux d'intérêt composé *m*; ~ **deferment** *n* IMP/EXP différé composé *m (France)*; ~ **duty** *n* IMP/EXP, TAX *customs* droit composé *m*, droit mixte *m*; ~ **entry** *n* ACC écriture multiple *f*; ~ **expansion engine** *n (C)* TRANSP *shipping* machine à expansion mixte *f*; ~ **growth rate** *n* ECON, FIN taux de croissance global *m*; ~ **interest** *n* BANK, ECON, FIN, GEN COMM intérêt composé *m*, intérêts composés *m pl*; ~ **interest bond** *n* FIN obligation à intérêts composés *f*; ~ **journal entry** *n* ACC, FIN écriture du journal multiple *f*; ~ **yield** *n* FIN rendement global *m*

compound[2] *vt* LAW composer, transiger; ◆ ~ **a debt** BANK, FIN, LAW régler une dette à l'amiable, transiger sur une dette

comprehensive[1] *adj* GEN COMM *report, review, answer* complet, détaillé, exhaustif, INS multirisque

comprehensive:[2] ~ **agreement** *n* HRM accord d'ensemble *m*; ~ **annual financial report** *n (CAFR)* ECON, FIN, MGMNT rapport financier annuel détaillé *m*; ~ **bank guarantee** *n* BANK garantie bancaire globale *f*; ~ **budget** *n* FIN budget directeur *m*, budget général *m*; ~ **crime endorsement** *n* INS avenant à un contrat combiné pour couvrir les devises, le faux et usage des faux des déposants, les détournements des employés, la monnaie, les mandats et les titres; ~ **extended-term banker's guarantee** *n (CXBG)* BANK garantie bancaire globale de longue durée *f*; ~ **general liability insurance** *n* INS assurance responsabilité civile générale *f*; ~ **glass insurance** *n* INS assurance bris de glace globale *f*; ~ **health-care system** *n* WEL prise en charge totale des soins médicaux *f*; ~ **insurance** *n* INS assurance combinée *f*, assurance tous risques *f*; ~ **insurance policy** *n* INS police d'assurance tous risques *f*, police multirisque *f*, *automobile* police multirisque *f*; ~ **liability insurance** *n* INS assurance responsabilité civile générale *f*; ~ **personal liability insurance** *n* INS assurance responsabilité civile des particuliers *f*; ~ **policy** *n* INS assurance multirisque *f*, assurance tous risques *f*; ~ **responsibility** *n* GEN COMM responsabilité globale *f*; ~ **tax reform** *n* ECON, TAX réforme fiscale globale *f*

Comprehensive: ~ **Employment and Training Act** *n US (CETA)* HRM accord sur l'emploi et la formation

compress *vt* COMP *file, data,* HRM *salary,* TRANSP comprimer

compression *n* COMP *of data,* HRM *of salary,* TRANSP compression *f*

comprise *vt* GEN COMM comporter, comprendre, embrasser, englober, inclure

comprised: ~ **total loss** *n* INS *marine* perte totale transigée *f*; ◆ **be** ~ **of** GEN COMM être composé de

compromise[1] *n* GEN COMM accommodement *m*, compromis *m*, transaction *f*; ~ **agreement** GEN COMM accord de compromis *m*; ~ **decision** GEN COMM décision de compromis *f*; ~ **solution** GEN COMM solution de compromis *f*

compromise[2] **1.** *vt* GEN COMM *project* compromettre, mettre en danger, mettre en péril; **2.** *vi* GEN COMM accepter un compromis, transiger

comptroller *n* ACC contrôleur de gestion *m*, ADMIN intendant *m*, FIN contrôleur *m*, vérificateur *m*, économe *m*, POL *governmental* contrôleur de gestion *m*, contrôleur financier *m*

Comptroller: ~ **General** *n US* ACC, POL Président de la cour des comptes *m*; ~ **of The Currency** *n US* BANK organisme américain de contrôle des banques

compulsive: ~ **buying** *n* S&M achat impulsif *m*

compulsory[1] *adj* GEN COMM *power* coercitif, contraignant, forcé, *regulation* obligatoire

compulsory:[2] ~ **arbitration** *n UK* HRM *labour disputes* arbitrage d'office *m*, arbitrage obligatoire *m*; ~ **competitive tendering** *n UK* GEN COMM, POL soumission obligatoire en vue d'adjudication *loc f*; ~ **deduction** *n* GEN COMM franchise obligatoire *f*, prélèvement obligatoire *m*; ~ **expenditure** *n* ECON dépenses obligatoires *f pl*; ~ **insurance** *n* INS assurance obligatoire *f*, obligation d'assurance *f*; ~ **licence** *n BrE* LAW, PATENTS licence obligatoire *f*; ~ **license** *n AmE see compulsory licence BrE*; ~ **liquidation** *n* ACC, FIN, GEN COMM, LAW liquidation forcée *f*; ~ **margin** *n UK* STOCK dépôt obligatoire *m*, marge obligatoire *f*; ~ **purchase** *n* GEN COMM, LAW expropriation *f*; ~ **purchase order** *n UK* LAW, PROP ordre d'achat obligatoire *m*, ordre d'expropriation *m*; ~ **redundancy** *n* HRM licenciement sec *m*; ~ **retirement** *n BrE (cf mandatory retirement AmE)* HRM mise à la retraite d'office *f*, retraite obligatoire *f*; ~ **saving** *n UK* FIN économie obligatoire *f*, épargne obligatoire *f*; ~ **third-party insurance** *n* INS assurance RC obligatoire *f*, assurance responsabilité civile obligatoire *f*, responsabilité civile *f*

Compulsory: ~ **Purchase Act** *n UK* LAW loi relative à l'expropriation

computation *n* COMP calcul *m*, estimation *f*, évaluation *f*

computational: ~ **error** *n* COMP erreur de calcul *f*

compute *vt* COMP calculer, estimer, évaluer

computer: ~ **-aided** *adj* COMP assisté par ordinateur; ~ **-assisted** *adj* COMP assisté par ordinateur; ~ **-based** *adj* COMP informatisé; ~ **-controlled** *adj* COMP géré par ordinateur; ~ **-driven** *adj* COMP piloté par ordinateur; ~ **literate** *adj* COMP ayant des connaissances en informatique *loc f*, ayant une formation en informatique *loc f*, initié à l'informatique *m*; ~ **-operated** *adj* COMP géré par ordinateur; ~ **-oriented** *adj* COMP automatisé

computer[3] *n* COMP ordinateur *m, calculating machine* calculateur *m*; ~ **accounting** *n* ACC, COMP comptabilité informatisée *f*; ~ **age** *n* COMP l'ère de l'informatique *f*, l'ère de l'ordinateur *f*; ~ **-aided design** *n (CAD)* COMP, IND conception assistée par ordinateur *f*, création assistée par ordinateur *f (CAO)*; ~ **-aided design and computer-aided manufacturing** *n (CAD/CAM)* COMP, IND conception et fabrication assistées par ordinateur *fpl (CFAO)*; ~ **-aided design and drafting** *n* COMP, IND conception et dessin assistés par ordinateur *mpl*; ~ **-aided engineering** *n (CAE)* COMP, IND ingénierie assistée par ordinateur *f (IAO)*; ~ **-aided instruction** *n (CAI)* COMP, WEL enseignement assisté par ordinateur *m (EAO)*; ~ **-aided language learning** *n (CALL)* COMP, WEL apprentissage des langues assisté par ordinateur *m*; ~ **-aided learning** *n (CAL)* COMP, WEL enseignement assisté par ordinateur *m (EAO)*; ~ **-aided learning program** *n* COMP, WEL logiciel d'enseignement assisté par ordinateur *m*; ~ **-aided manufacture** *n (CAM)* COMP, IND fabrication assistée par ordinateur *f (FAO)*; ~ **-aided manufacturing** *n (CAM)* COMP, IND fabrication assistée par ordinateur *f (FAO)*; ~ **-aided software engineering** *n* COMP conception de programmes assistée par ordinateur *f*, IND ingénierie logicielle assistée par ordinateur *f*; ~ **-aided teaching** *n (CAT)* COMP, WEL enseignement assisté par ordinateur *m (EAO)*; ~ **-aided testing** *n (CAT)* COMP, WEL test assisté par ordinateur *m (TAO)*; ~ **-aided translation** *n (CAT)* COMP traduction assistée par ordinateur *f (TAO)*; ~ **-assisted design** *n (CAD)* COMP, IND conception assistée par ordinateur *f*, création assistée par ordinateur *f (CAO)*; ~ **-assisted design and computer-assisted manufacturing** *n (CAD/CAM)* COMP, IND conception et fabrication assistées par ordinateur *fpl (CFAO)*; ~ **-assisted design and drafting** *n (CADD)* COMP, IND conception et dessin assistés par ordinateur *mpl*; ~ **-assisted engineering** *n (CAE)* COMP, IND ingénierie assistée par ordinateur *f (IAO)*; ~ **-assisted instruction** *n (CAI)* COMP, WEL enseignement assisté par ordinateur *m (EAO)*; ~ **-assisted language learning** *n (CALL)* COMP, WEL apprentissage des langues assisté par ordinateur *m*; ~ **-assisted learning** *n (CAL)* COMP, WEL enseignement assisté par ordinateur *m (EAO)*; ~ **-assisted learning program** *n* COMP, WEL logiciel d'enseignement assisté par ordinateur *m*; ~ **-assisted manufacture** *n* *(CAM)* COMP, IND fabrication assistée par ordinateur *f* *(FAO)*; ~ **-assisted manufacturing** *n* *(CAM)* COMP, IND fabrication assistée par ordinateur *f* *(FAO)*; ~ **-assisted software engineering** *n* COMP conception de programmes assistée par ordinateur *f*, IND ingénierie logicielle assistée par ordinateur *f*; ~ **-assisted teaching** *n* *(CAT)* COMP, WEL enseignement assisté par ordinateur *m* *(EAO)*; ~ **-assisted testing** *n* *(CAT)* COMP, WEL test assisté par ordinateur *m* *(TAO)*; ~ **-assisted trading system** *n* *(CATS)* STOCK système de cotation électronique *m*; ~ **-assisted translation** *n* *(CAT)* COMP traduction assistée par ordinateur *f* *(TAO)*; ~ **bank** *n* COMP banque de données *f*, fichier central *m*; ~ **-based training** *n* *(CBT)* COMP enseignement assisté par ordinateur *m*, formation programmée *f*, WEL enseignement assisté par ordinateur *m* *(EAO)*; ~ **center** *n* *AmE*, ~ **centre** *n* *BrE* COMP centre de calcul *m*, centre informatique *m*; ~ **circles** *n* *pl* COMP *people* milieux informatiques *m* *pl*; ~ **code** *n* COMP code machine *m*; ~ **communication** *n* COMMS, COMP télématique *f*; ~ **company** *n* COMP constructeur d'ordinateurs *m*, société informatique *f*; ~ **conferencing** *n* COMMS, COMP téléconférence informatisée *f*; ~ **consultancy firm** *n* COMP société de services et de conseils en informatique *f*, SSCI; ~ **consultant** *n* COMP conseil en informatique *m*; ~ **crime insurance** *n* INS assurance contre la fraude informatique *f*; ~ **department** *n* COMP service informatique *m*; ~ **design** *n* COMP *hardware* conception de système *f*; ~ **engineer** *n* COMP informaticien *m*, ingénieur informatique *m*; ~ **engineering** *n* COMP génie informatique *m*, ingénierie informatique *f*; ~ **environment** *n* COMP configuration matérielle *f*, paysage informatique *m*; ~ **expert** *n* COMP informaticien *m*; ~ **file** *n* COMP fichier informatique *m*, fichier sur ordinateur *m*; ~ **fraud** *n* COMP, LAW fraude informatique *f*; ~ **graphics** *n* *pl* COMP infographie *f*, informatique graphique *f*; ~ **hacker** *n* COMP pirate informatique *m*; ~ **hacking** *n* COMP piratage informatique *m*; ~ **input** *n* COMP entrée de l'ordinateur *f*, input de l'ordinateur *m*; ~ **instruction** *n* COMP instruction machine *f*; ~ **-integrated manufacture** *n* *(CIM)* COMP, IND fabrication intégrée par ordinateur *f* *(FIO)*; ~ **-integrated manufacturing** *n* *(CIM)* COMP, IND fabrication intégrée par ordinateur *f*, production intégrée par ordinateur *f*; ~ **knowledge** *n* COMP connaissances en informatique *f* *pl*; ~ **language** *n* COMP langage d'ordinateur *m*, langage de programmation *m*, langage informatique *m*, langage machine *m*; ~ **law** *n* COMP, LAW droit de l'informatique *m*; ~ **-leasing business** *n* COMP, S&M activité de location d'ordinateurs *f*; ~ **-leasing firm** *n* COMP, S&M société de location d'ordinateurs *f*; ~ **line** *n* COMP gamme d'ordinateurs *f*; ~ **literacy** *n* COMP connaissances en informatique *f* *pl*, culture informatique *f*; ~ **log** *n* COMP journal de marche *m*; ~ **mail** *n* ADMIN, COMMS, COMP courrier électronique *m*; ~ **map** *n* COMP carte infographique *f*; ~ **memory** *n* COMP mémoire d'ordinateur *f*; ~ **network** *n* COMMS, COMP complexe d'ordinateurs *m*, réseau d'ordinateurs *m*, réseau informatique *m*; ~ **operation** *n* COMP opération machine *f*; ~ **operator** *n* COMP opérateur sur ordinateur *m*; ~ **output** *n* COMP sortie d'ordinateur *f*; ~ **package** *n* COMP logiciel informatique *m*; ~ **paper** *n* COMP papier informatique *m*; ~ **phobic** *n* COMP ordinophobe *mf*; ~ **print-out** *n* COMP listage *m*, listage d'ordinateur *m*, listage informatique *m*, listing *m*, listing informatique *m*, sortie imprimée *f*, sortie sur imprimante *f*, sortie sur papier *f*; ~ **processing** *n* COMP traitement informatique *m*, traitement par ordinateur *m*; ~ **program** *n* COMP programme d'ordinateur *m*, programme informatique *m*, programme machine *m*; ~ **programmer** *n* COMP programmeur *m*, programmeur sur ordinateur *m*; ~ **programming** *n* COMP programmation *f*; ~ **range** *n* COMP gamme d'ordinateurs *f*; ~ **room** *n* COMP salle des machines *f*, salle des ordinateurs *f*; ~ **run** *n* COMP passage en machine *m*, phase de traitement *f*, unité de traitement *f*; ~ **science** *n* COMP informatique *f*, informatique théorique *f*, ordinatique *f*; ~ **scientist** *n* COMP informaticien *m*; ~ **screen** *n* COMP écran d'ordinateur *m*, écran informatique *m*; ~ **security** *n* COMP sécurité informatique *f*; ~ **services** *n* *pl* COMP services en informatique *m* *pl*; ~ **services company** *n* COMP société de services d'ingénierie informatique *f*, SSII; ~ **simulation** *n* COMP simulation par ordinateur *f*, simulation sur ordinateur *f*, simulé *m*; ~ **software** *n* COMP logiciel *m*, logiciel informatique *m*; ~ **software licence** *n* *BrE* COMP licence informatique *f*; ~ **software license** *n* *AmE see* *computer software licence BrE*; ~ **strategy** *n* COMP stratégie informatique *f*; ~ **system** *n* COMP système informatique *m*; ~ **technology** *n* COMP technique informatique *f*, technologie informatique *f*; ~ **terminal** *n* COMP terminal d'ordinateur *m*, terminal informatique *m*; ~ **time** *n* COMP heures machines *f* *pl*, temps machine *m*; ~ **trading** *n* *US* COMP système de transactions automatisées *m*, ECON système de transactions automatisées *m*, transactions automatisées *f* *pl*; ~ **vendor** *n* COMP constructeur d'ordinateurs *m*, fournisseur d'ordinateurs *m*; ~ **virus** *n* COMP virus informatique *m*; ~ **whizz kid** *n* *infrml* COMP petit génie de l'informatique *m*; ~ **wizard** *n* COMP génie de l'informatique *m*, surdoué de l'informatique *m*; ~ **world** *n* COMP milieux informatiques *m* *pl*

computerate *adj* *jarg* COMP ayant des connaissances en informatique *loc f*, ayant une formation en informatique *loc f*

computerization *n* COMP *of information* mise sur ordinateur *f*, *of system, workplace* automatisation *f*, informatisation *f*, *processing* traitement par ordinateur *m*

computerize *vt* COMP *information* traiter par ordinateur, *process* mettre sur ordinateur, *system*, *workplace* automatiser, gérer par ordinateur, informatiser

computerized¹ *adj* COMP automatisé, informatisé

computerized:² ~ **accounting system** *n* ACC, COMP système de comptabilité sur ordinateur *m*; ~ **banking** *n* BANK, COMP bancatique *f*, banque électronique *f*; ~ **file** *n* COMP fichier informatisé *m*; ~ **management** *n* COMP, MGMNT, S&M gestion automatisée *f*, gestion informatisée *f*, gestion par ordinateur *f*; ~ **market timing system** *n* COMP, STOCK système d'analyse des tendances assisté par ordinateur *m*

computerphobic *adj* COMP ordinophobe

computing *n* COMP *use of computers*, GEN COMM informatique *f*; ~ **center** *AmE*, ~ **centre** *BrE* COMP centre de calcul *m*; ~ **company** COMP société informatique *f*; ~ **power** COMP puissance de calcul *f*; ~ **room** COMP salle des machines *f*; ~ **show** COMP salon informatique *m*; ~ **speed** COMP vitesse de calcul *f*

con: ~ **artist** *n infrml* GEN COMM escroc *m*; ~ **man** *n infrml* GEN COMM escroc *m*

Conakry *pr n* GEN COMM Conakry *n pr*

concatenation *n* COMP chaînage *m*, concaténation *f*, enchaînement *m*

conceal *vt* GEN COMM *information* ne pas divulguer, *object, truth* cacher, dissimuler

concealed: ~ **assets** *n pl* ACC actif latent *m*; ~ **unemployment** *n* ECON, HRM chômage caché *m*

concealment *n* LAW *of information* dissimulation *f*, non-divulgation *f*; ~ **of losses** ACC, STOCK dissimulation de pertes *f*

conceive *vt* GEN COMM concevoir

concentrate *vt* GEN COMM concentrer; ~ **on** GEN COMM s'appliquer à, se concentrer sur; ~ **upon** GEN COMM se concentrer sur; ◆ ~ **one's attention on** GEN COMM concentrer son attention sur

concentrated *adj* GEN COMM intense; ◆ **be** ~ **on** GEN COMM porter sur

concentration *n* ECON, IND concentration *f*; ~ **economy** ECON économie d'échelle liée à la concentration géographique d'une industrie; ~ **of industry** IND concentration industrielle *f*; ~ **ratio** ECON ratio de concentration *m*

concept *n* GEN COMM concept *m*; ~ **of accrual** ACC principe de rattachement à l'exercice *m*; ~ **test** S&M test de concept *m*

conceptual: ~ **framework** *n* ACC *standards* cadre conceptuel *m*, cadre conceptuel de la comptabilité *m*

concern *n* ECON *business organization* affaire *f*, entreprise *f*, firme *f*, maison *f*, FIN intérêt de subordination *m*, *share* intérêt *m*, GEN COMM intérêt de subordination *m*, *business organization* affaire *f*, entreprise *f*, firme *f*, *share* entreprise *f*, intérêt *m*, HRM *labour relations* problème préoccupant *m*, MGMNT entreprise *f*

concerned *adj* GEN COMM intéressé

concerning *prep* GEN COMM concernant, en ce qui concerne *loc*

concerted: ~ **effort** *n* GEN COMM effort concerté *m*

concession *n* ACC réduction *f*, GEN COMM remise *f*, réduction *f*, tarif réduit *m*, *distribution right* concession *f*, LAW concession *f*, PROP réduction *f*, S&M, STOCK concession *f*, TAX abattement fiscal *m*, allègement *m*

concessionaire *n* GEN COMM concessionnaire *mf*

concessional¹ *adj* GEN COMM avantageux, de concession *loc f*, de faveur, favorable

concessional:² ~ **aid** *n* ECON *development assistance*, POL assistance privilégiée *f*; ~ **export** *n* IMP/EXP, POL exportation concessionnaire *f*; ~ **terms** *n pl* GEN COMM conditions de faveur *f pl*

concessionary¹ *adj* GEN COMM concessionnaire, à prix réduit *loc m*

concessionary² *n* GEN COMM concessionnaire *mf*; ~ **rate** GEN COMM taux privilégié *m*, LEIS tarif réduit *m*

concessioner *n* GEN COMM concessionnaire *mf*

conciliate *vt* GEN COMM, HRM apaiser, concilier, LAW concilier, POL apaiser

conciliation *n* GEN COMM *labour disputes*, HRM *labour disputes*, LAW *labour disputes* conciliation *f*; ~ **board** GEN COMM commission d'arbitrage *f*, HRM, STOCK commission d'arbitrage *f*, conseil d'arbitrage *m*; ~ **officer** HRM conciliateur *m*; ~ **procedure** *UK* HRM, LAW procédure de conciliation *f*

conciliator *n* HRM *labour disputes* conciliateur *m*

conclude *vt* GEN COMM, S&M conclure, finir, terminer; ~ **from** GEN COMM déduire de, inférer de

concluded *adj* GEN COMM, S&M fini

conclusion *n* GEN COMM *of agreement* conclusion *f*, *of contract* passation *f*

conclusive¹ *adj* GEN COMM, LAW concluant, probant, péremptoire

conclusive:² ~ **evidence** *n* LAW preuve concluante *f*, preuve irréfragable *f*, preuve péremptoire *f*

concomitant *adj* GEN COMM concomitant

concrete¹ *adj* GEN COMM *data, facts* concret

concrete:² ~ **evidence** *n* LAW preuve matérielle *f*; ~ **labor** *n* *AmE*, ~ **labour** *n* *BrE* (*ANT abstract labour*) HRM travail concret *m*, *workers* main-d'oeuvre concrète *f*

concur *vi* GEN COMM *agree* s'entendre, être d'accord *loc m*, *coincide* arriver en même temps, coïncider, LAW concourir, converger, s'entendre, être d'accord *loc m*

concurrent: ~ **processing** *n* COMP traitement concurrent *m*, traitement simultané *m*; ~ **returns** *n pl* TAX déclarations simultanées *f pl*, simultanées *f pl*

condemn *vt* GEN COMM, PROP condamner

condemnation *n* GEN COMM condamnation *f*, PROP condamnation *f*, expropriation pour cause d'utilité publique *f*

condensing: ~ **turbine** *n* TRANSP *shipping* turbine à condensation *f*

condition *n* GEN COMM, LAW condition *f*;

~ **monitoring** *(cm)* TRANSP *shipping* contrôle d'état *m*; ~ **precedent** *US* LAW condition suspensive *f*; ~ **subsequent** *US* LAW condition résolutoire *f*; ◆ **on ~ that** GEN COMM à condition de, à condition que

conditional: ~ **branch** *n* COMP branchement conditionnel *m*; ~ **clause** *n* LAW clause conditionnelle *f*; ~ **contract** *n* *US* LAW contrat conditionnel *m*; ~ **endorsement** *n* FIN endossement conditionnel *m*; ~ **indorsement** *n* FIN endossement conditionnel *m*; ~ **market order** *n* *UK* STOCK *futures* ordre au mieux conditionnel *m*, ordre conditionnel *m*; ~ **protection** *n* PATENTS protection conditionnelle *f*; ~ **sale** *n* S&M vente sous condition *f*; ~ **sales agreement** *n* S&M vente sous condition *f*

conditions *n pl* ECON *market* circonstances *f pl*, conditions *f pl*, LAW *of contract* conditions *f pl*, S&M *market* circonstances *f pl*, conditions *f pl*; ~ **of carriage** TRANSP conditions de transport *f pl*; ~ **of contract** TRANSP conditions contractuelles *f pl*, conditions d'un contrat *f pl*; ~ **of employment** HRM conditions d'embauche *f pl*; ~ **of sale** ECON, GEN COMM, IMP/EXP, S&M conditions de vente *f pl*; ~ **of tender** GEN COMM conditions de l'offre *f pl*, conditions de soumission *f pl*; ~ **of use** GEN COMM conditions d'utilisation *f pl*

condominium *n* *AmE* *(cf cooperative BrE)* PROP immeuble en copropriété *m*

conducive: ~ **to** *adj* GEN COMM contribuant à, favorable à, favorisant, qui contribue à *loc*, qui engendre *loc*; ◆ **be ~ to** GEN COMM *growth* contribuer à, engendrer, favoriser

conduct[1] *n* GEN COMM conduite *f*, HRM comportement *m*, conduite *f*, tenue *f*, MGMNT comportement *m*; ~ **of law suit** LAW exercice de poursuites judiciaires *m*; ~ **money** GEN COMM dépôt de garantie *m*

conduct[2] *vt* GEN COMM *business, campaign, inquiry, meeting* conduire, mener, *manage, carry out* diriger, *poll, survey* effectuer, faire, HRM conduire; ~ **the investigation** LAW instruire; ~ **a survey** S&M enquêter

confectioner *n* *(CTN)* S&M marchand de journaux-buraliste *m*

confederation *n* POL confédération *f*

Confederation: ~ **of British Industry** *n* *(CBI)* GEN COMM, IND ≈ Conseil national du patronat français *m* *(CNPF)*

confer *vt* GEN COMM, LAW *right* accorder, conférer, WEL *degree* conférer; ◆ ~ **a privilege on sb** GEN COMM conférer un privilège à qn

conference *n* GEN COMM colloque *m*, MGMNT conférence *f*, réunion *f*, *convention* colloque *m*, congrès *m*, POL assemblée *f*, congrès *m*; ~ **call** *n* COMMS *audio* conférence téléphonique *f*, téléconférence *f*; ~ **delegate** *n* MGMNT congressiste *mf*, délégué *m*, participant *m*, POL congressiste *mf*; ~ **line** *n* TRANSP *shipping* conférence maritime *f*; ~ **member** *n* MGMNT congressiste *mf*, délégué *m*, participant *m*, POL congressiste *mf*;

~ **proceedings** *n pl* MGMNT actes de conférence *m pl*, débats de conférence *m pl*, travaux de conférence *m pl*; ~ **report** *n* S&M compte-rendu de conférence *m*; ~ **system** *n* GEN COMM conférence maritime *f*; ~ **table** *n* MGMNT table de conférence *f*; ~ **venue** *n* MGMNT lieu du congrès *m*

confession *n* GEN COMM, LAW aveu *m*

confide: ~ **sth to sb** *phr* GEN COMM confier qch à qn

confidence *n* GEN COMM, MATH confiance *f*; ~ **coefficient** MATH *statistics* coefficient de confiance *m*; ~ **game** GEN COMM abus de confiance *m*, escroquerie *f*; ~ **interval** MATH *statistics* écart de confiance *m*; ~ **level** MATH *statistics* niveau de confiance *m*; ~ **man** GEN COMM escroc *m*; ~ **trick** GEN COMM abus de confiance *m*, escroquerie *f*; ~ **trickster** GEN COMM escroc *m*

confidential[1] *adj* GEN COMM, LAW, TAX confidentiel

confidential:[2] ~ **clerk** *n* GEN COMM homme de confiance *m*; ~ **information** *n* LAW informations confidentielles *f pl*; ~ **secretary** *n* HRM secrétaire privé *m*

confidentiality *n* LAW, TAX confidentialité *f*; ~ **agreement** LAW *intellectual property*, PATENTS *intellectual property* accord de confidentialité *m*

config *abbr* *(configuration)* COMP *of file* config *(configuration)*

configuration *n* *(config)* COMP *of file* combinaison *f*, configuration *f* *(config)*; ~ **control** COMP gestion de la configuration *f*

configure *vt* COMP configurer

confirm *vt* GEN COMM confirmer, corroborer, LAW *decree* entériner, homologuer, TAX *assessment* ratifier; ◆ ~ **receipt of** COMMS, GEN COMM accuser réception de

confirmation *n* ACC demande de vérification *f*, GEN COMM *of plans* confirmation *f*, ratification *f*, LAW ratification *f*, *of decision* confirmation *f*, entérinement *m*, STOCK avis d'exécution *m*, avis d'opéré *m*; ~ **notice** GEN COMM avis d'exécution *m*, avis de confirmation *m*; ~ **of order** GEN COMM, S&M confirmation d'un ordre *f*, confirmation d'une commande *f*; ~ **of renewal** INS confirmation de renouvellement *f*

confirmed: ~ **credit** *n* BANK crédit confirmé *m*; ~ **irrevocable credit** *n* BANK crédit irrévocable confirmé *m*; ~ **letter of credit** *n* BANK lettre de crédit confirmée *f*; ◆ **be ~** GEN COMM se confirmer

confirming: ~ **bank** *n* BANK *international trade* firme spécialisée dans la mise en contact d'acheteur et d'exportateur, qui joue le rôle d'intermédiaire et conseiller et garantit la solvabilité de l'acheteur; ~ **house** *n* ECON, FIN, IMP/EXP *international trade* agence spécialisée dans la mise en contact d'exportateurs et d'acheteurs

confiscate *vt* GEN COMM confisquer

confiscation *n* GEN COMM confiscation *f*, saisie *f*

conflagration: ~ **area** *n* INS zone de conflagration *f*

conflict[1] *n* GEN COMM, HRM, POL conflit *m*; ~ **of interest** GEN COMM conflit d'intérêts *m*; ~ **of law** LAW *international* conflit de loi *m*

conflict[2] *vi* GEN COMM être en désaccord *loc m*, être incompatibles

conflicting[1] *adj* GEN COMM contraire

conflicting:[2] ~ **evidence** *n* LAW preuve contradictoire *f*, témoignage contradictoire *m*; ~ **interest** *n* GEN COMM intérêt personnel opposé et divergent *m*

confluence *n* GEN COMM *of interest* convergence *f*; ~ **analysis** *(CA)* MATH *statistics* analyse de confluence *f*

confluent *adj* GEN COMM convergent

conform: ~ **to** *vt* GEN COMM *standards* se conformer à, être en conformité avec *loc f*, LAW se conformer à

conformed: ~ **copy** *n* LAW *of legal document* copie conforme *f*

conformity *n* GEN COMM accord *m*, conformité *f*, ressemblance *f*; ~ **to accounting rules** ACC régularité *f*; ◆ **in** ~ **with** ACC, GEN COMM conformément à

confront *vt* GEN COMM affronter, confronter, faire face à

confrontation *n* GEN COMM affrontement *m*, confrontation *f*

congestion *n* COMMS *market* encombrement *m*, *telephone lines* saturation *f*, GEN COMM *market*, TRANSP *market* encombrement *m*; ~ **surcharge** TAX surtaxe d'encombrement *f*, TRANSP *shipping* surtaxe d'encombrement portuaire *f*

conglomerate *n* ECON conglomérat *m*, FIN conglomérat *m*, fusion dans un conglomérat *f*; ~ **diversification** ECON, FIN diversification de type congloméral *f*; ~ **merger** ECON, FIN fusion dans un conglomérat *f*

Congo *pr n* GEN COMM Congo *m*

Congolese[1] *adj* GEN COMM congolais

Congolese[2] *n* GEN COMM *person* Congolais *m*

congress *n* MGMNT, POL congrès *m*

Congress *n US* POL Congrès *m*; ~ **of Industrial Organizations** *US (CIO)* HRM *unions* ≈ Confédération générale du travail *f (CGT)*

Congressional[1] *adj US* POL du Congrès *loc m*

Congressional:[2] ~ **Budget and Impoundment Control Act** *n US* POL loi du Congrès sur le contrôle budgétaire et fiscal; ~ **Budget Office** *n US (CBO)* FIN Commission des finances *f*, POL Bureau du budget du Congrès *m*

congressman *n US* POL ≈ député *m*

congresswoman *n US* POL ≈ députée *f*

congruence *n* GEN COMM conformité *f*

congruent: ~ **with** *phr* GEN COMM conforme à

conjecture *vi* ECON conjecturer

conjunction *n* GEN COMM *of circumstances* concours *m*; ◆ **in** ~ **with** GEN COMM, LAW conjointement avec

connect *vt* COMMS assurer la correspondance avec, mettre en communication avec, relier, COMP, GEN COMM connecter, raccorder

connected: ~ **by blood relationship** *adj* TAX uni par les liens du sang; ◆ ~ **with** GEN COMM, TAX rattaché à

connecting: ~ **carrier** *n* TRANSP transporteur qui assure la correspondance *m*; ~ **flight** *n* TRANSP correspondance *f*, vol de correspondance *m*

connection *n* GEN COMM jonction *f*, liaison *f*, lien *m*, rapport *m*, relation *f*, TRANSP *airlines* correspondance *f*; ~ **time** COMP temps de connexion *m*

cons *abbr UK (consols)* FIN consolidés *m pl*, rente perpétuelle *f*, GEN COMM fonds consolidés *m pl*, STOCK fonds d'État *m pl*, rente d'État *f*

consciousness *n* GEN COMM conscience *f*

consecutive[1] *adj* GEN COMM consécutif, successif

consecutive:[2] ~ **days** *n pl* GEN COMM jours consécutifs *m pl*, jours successifs *m pl*, jours de suite *m pl*

consensus *n* GEN COMM accord général *m*, consensus *m*; ~ **agreement** GEN COMM accord consensuel *m*

consent[1] *n* GEN COMM assentiment *m*, consentement *m*; ~ **decree** LAW jugement entérinant un accord *m*; ~ **executed** TAX consentement souscrit *m*; ◆ **by common** ~ GEN COMM, LAW d'un commun accord

consent:[2] ~ **to** *vt* GEN COMM consentir à

consequence *n* GEN COMM conséquence *f*, contrecoup *m*, suites *f pl*; ◆ **as a** ~ GEN COMM en conséquence, par conséquent; **in** ~ GEN COMM en conséquence, par conséquent

consequences *n pl* GEN COMM, POL conséquences *f pl*

consequential: ~ **damage** *n* INS dommages consécutifs *m pl*, dommages indirects *m pl*, TRANSP dommage indirect *m*; ~ **damages** *n pl* LAW dommages-intérêts indirects *m pl*; ~ **effect** *n* LAW *of court action* conséquences indirectes *f pl*; ~ **loss** *n* INS pertes indirectes *f pl*, risque indirect *m*; ~ **-loss policy** *n* INS police pertes indirectes *f*

consequently *adv* GEN COMM en conséquence *loc f*, par conséquent

conservation *n* ENVIR conservation *f*, protection *f*, préservation *f*; ~ **camp** ENVIR camp écologique *m*; ~ **of natural resources** ENVIR conservation financièrement rentable des ressources *f*; ~ **of portfolio** GEN COMM préservation du portefeuille *f*

conservationist *n* ENVIR écolo *mf (infrml)*, écologiste *mf*

conservatism *n* GEN COMM, POL conservatisme *m*; ~ **principle** ACC principe de prudence *m*

conservative[1] *adj* GEN COMM *spending, estimate* prudent, POL conservateur

conservative[2] *n* POL conservateur *m*; ~ **accounting** ACC comptabilité prudente *f*; ~ **estimate** GEN COMM évaluation prudente *f*

Conservative: ~ **Party** *n UK* POL Parti conservateur *m*

conserve *vt* ENVIR économiser

consgt *abbr (consignation)* TRANSP consignation *f*, envoi *m*, expédition *f*

consider *vt* GEN COMM considérer

considerable *adj* ECON *debt* considérable, *demand* considérable, GEN COMM considérable, conséquent *(infrml)*, non-négligeable, relativement important, *debt* considérable

considerably *adv* GEN COMM considérablement

consideration *n* GEN COMM considération *f*, INS capital constitutif *m*, cause *f*, LAW *contract* contrepartie *f*, *money* rémunération *f*, rétribution *f*, *reflection* examen *m*, STOCK valeur d'une transaction hors frais; ~ **for sale** GEN COMM prix de vente *m*; ◆ **upon further** ~ GEN COMM à la réflexion

considered *adj* GEN COMM considéré; ◆ **be** ~ **for** HRM *position, assignment* être pressenti pour

consign *vt* TRANSP consigner, envoyer, expédier

consignation *n (consgt)* TRANSP consignation *f*, envoi *m*, expédition *f*

consignee *n (cnee)* TRANSP consignataire *mf*, destinataire *mf*

consigner *n see consignor*

consignment *n (cnmt)* TRANSP consignation *f*, envoi *m*, expédition *f*; ~ **insurance** INS assurance de consignation *f*, assurance livraison *f*, assurance sur facultés *f*; ~ **note** *(CN)* TRANSP bordereau d'expédition *m*, feuille de route *f*, lettre de voiture *f*; ~ **note control label number** *(CCLN)* TRANSP numéro de l'étiquette de contrôle du bordereau d'expédition *m*; ~ **sale** TRANSP vente en dépôt *f*; ◆ **on** ~ TRANSP en consignation, en dépôt

consignor *n* IMP/EXP, TRANSP consignateur *m*, expéditeur *m*

consistency *n* ACC *of procedures* continuité *f*, permanence *f*, GEN COMM cohérence *f*, logique *f*, MGMNT logique *f*; ~ **check** GEN COMM contrôle d'uniformité *m*, contrôle de cohérence *m*; ~ **principle** ACC *of procedures* principe de la permanence *m*

consistent *adj* GEN COMM *argument* cohérent, conséquent, logique, MGMNT *in methods* conséquent, logique; ◆ ~ **with** GEN COMM compatible avec, d'accord avec

consistently *adv* GEN COMM de façon cohérente *loc f*

consolidate:[1] ~ **-cargo container service** *n* TRANSP service de groupage conteneurs *m*; ~ **-cargo service** *n (CCS)* TRANSP service de groupage *m*

consolidate[2] *vt* ACC, BANK consolider, ECON renforcer, FIN *funds, loan* consolider, GEN COMM *companies* fusionner, *knowledge* renforcer, *position* concrétiser, consolider, raffermir, *resources* réunir, HRM consolider, TRANSP grouper

consolidated[1] *adj* ACC, BANK consolidé, ECON consolidé, renforcé, FIN consolidé, GEN COMM consolidé, raffermi, renforcé, HRM consolidé; ◆ **on a** ~ **basis** FIN sur une base consolidée

consolidated:[2] ~ **accounting** *n* UK ACC *including foreign currency* comptabilité consolidée *f*; ~ **accounts** *n pl* ACC comptes consolidés *m pl*; ~ **annuities** *n pl* UK FIN fonds consolidés *m pl*, rentes consolidées *f pl*; ~ **audited accounts** *n pl* ACC comptes vérifiés consolidés *m pl*; ~ **balance sheet** *n* ACC bilan consolidé *m*; ~ **base capital** *n* BANK, ECON, FIN, GEN COMM capital de base consolidé *m*; ~ **cash flow statement** *n* ACC tableau de financement consolidé *m*; ~ **data plate** *n* TRANSP plaque indicatrice *f*; ~ **debenture stock** *n* UK STOCK obligations non-garanties consolidées *f pl*; ~ **delivery** *n* TRANSP livraison groupée *f*; ~ **figures** *n pl* ACC chiffres consolidés *m pl*; ~ **financial statement** *n* ACC, FIN état financier consolidé *m*; ~ **fund** *n* UK ECON, FIN, TAX fonds d'amortissement de la dette publique *m*; ~ **fund standing services** *n pl* UK ECON services permanents du fond d'amortissement *m pl*; ~ **net profit** *n* ACC bénéfice net consolidé *m*; ~ **quotation system** *n* STOCK système centralisé de cotation *m*; ~ **rate** *n* TRANSP tarif groupé *m*; ~ **statement of condition** *n* US FIN bilan consolidé *m*; ~ **stock** *n* UK FIN fonds consolidés *m pl*, rentes consolidées *f pl*; ~ **tape** *n* STOCK téléscripteur *m*

Consolidated: ~ **Metropolitan Statistical Area** *n* US *(CMSA)* ADMIN regroupement de zone statistique métropolitaine *m*; ~ **Revenue Fund** *n* Canada FIN Trésor *m*

consolidation *n* ACC *of accounts* consolidation *f*, intégration *f*, BANK *of loan*, FIN *of loan* consolidation *f*, unification *f*, GEN COMM *of holdings* consolidation *f*, fusion *f*, *of knowledge* renforcement *m*, HRM consolidation *f*, TRANSP groupage *m*, groupement *m*; ~ **depot** TRANSP dépôt de groupage *m*; ~ **loan** BANK, FIN emprunt consolidé *m*; ~ **method** ACC *annual* modalités de consolidation *f pl*; ~ **of shares** FIN, STOCK regroupement d'actions *m*

consolidator *n* TRANSP groupeur *m*

consols *n pl* UK *(cons)* FIN fonds consolidés *m pl*, GEN COMM consolidés *m pl*, rente perpétuelle *f*, STOCK fonds d'État *m pl*, rente d'État *f*

consortium *n* [pl *-tia*] BANK, FIN consortium *m*, GEN COMM consortium *m*, groupe *m*, groupement d'entreprises *m*, HRM cartel *m*; ~ **bank** BANK, FIN consortium bancaire *m*; ~ **of banks** BANK, FIN pool bancaire *m*

conspectus *n* FIN rapport de synthèse *m*, GEN COMM vue d'ensemble *f*, vue générale *f*

conspicuous: ~ **consumption** *n* ECON, S&M consommation ostentatoire *f*

constant[1] *adj* GEN COMM constant; ◆ **at** ~ **prices** GEN COMM en prix constants

constant[2] *n* COMP, MATH constante *f*; ~ **capital** *n* ECON capital fixe *m*; ~ **dollar plan** *n* ECON projet en dollar constant *m*, GEN COMM plan en dollar constant *m*, projet en dollar constant *m*; ~ **dollars** *n pl* US ECON dollars constants *m pl*; ~ **-payment loan** *n* UK BANK prêt à remboursement régulier *m*; ~ **prices** *n pl* ECON, S&M prix constants *m pl*;

~ **returns to scale** *n pl* ECON, FIN, STOCK rendements d'échelle constants *m pl*; ~ **risk** *n* INS risque constant *m*

Constant: ~ **Elasticity of Substitution production function** *n (CES production function)* ECON fonction de production caractérisé par une élasticité constante de l'effet de substitution

constantly *adv* GEN COMM à tout moment *loc m*

constituent[1] *adj* GEN COMM composant, constituant

constituent[2] *n* POL électeur *m*; ~ **company** STOCK société constituante *f*

constitute *vt* ADMIN, GEN COMM *problem, threat* constituer; ◆ ~ **an infringement** LAW constituer une contrefaçon; ~ **a quorum** ADMIN, GEN COMM, MGMNT constituer un quorum

constituted *adj* GEN COMM établi, LAW *trust* constitué, institué

constitution *n* GEN COMM *establishment*, LAW constitution *f*, POL constitution *f*, statuts *m pl*, STOCK *establishment* constitution *f*

constitutional[1] *adj* LAW, POL constitutionnel

constitutional:[2] ~ **foundation** *n* ADMIN base constitutionnelle *f*; ~ **strike** *n* HRM, IND, LAW grève légale *f*

constr *abbr (construction)* GEN COMM, IND, PROP construction *f*

constrain *vt* GEN COMM contraindre; ◆ ~ **sb to do sth** GEN COMM contraindre qn à faire qch

constraining: ~ **factor** *n* ECON *restricting production or sale*, IND, S&M facteur de contrainte *m*

constraint *n* ACC contrainte *f*, entrave *f*, privation de liberté *f*, ECON *on monetary policy* contrainte *f*, GEN COMM, HRM, LAW contrainte *f*, entrave *f*, privation de liberté *f*

construct *vt* GEN COMM construire

constructed *adj* PROP construit

construction *n (constr)* GEN COMM, IND, PROP construction *f*; ~ **activities** *n pl* GEN COMM activités de construction *f pl*; ~ **cost index** *n UK* STOCK indice du coût de la construction *m*; ~ **industry** *n* IND industrie du bâtiment *f*, le bâtiment *m*; ~ **loan** *n* BANK, IND prêt à la construction *m*; ~ **rate** *n* TRANSP tarif de construction *m*; ~ **subsidy** *n* TRANSP *shipping* prime à la construction *f*; ~ **unit value** *n (CUV)* TRANSP valeur de l'unité de construction *f*; ~ **and use** *n UK* IND, LAW restrictions légales en matière de construction et utilisation des véhicules automobiles, construction et utilisation *f*; ~ **worker** *n* IND ouvrier du bâtiment *m*; ◆ **under** ~ IND en cours de construction

constructive: ~ **dismissal** *n* HRM démission forcée *f*, démission provoquée *f*; ~ **eviction** *n* PROP expulsion constructive *f*; ~ **notice** *n US* LAW connaissance présumée des faits *f*; ~ **total loss** *n (CTL)* INS *abandonment clauses* perte censée totale *f*, perte réputée totale *f*, perte totale relative *f*; ~ **total loss only** *n (CTLO)* INS *marine* perte

censée totale uniquement *f*, perte réprimée totale seulement *f*

consul *n* GEN COMM, POL consul *m*

consulage *n* IMP/EXP consulage *m*, droits consulaires *m pl*, frais consulaires *m pl*

consular: ~ **declaration** *n (CD)* ADMIN *duty-free*, IMP/EXP *duty-free* carte consulaire *f*, déclaration consulaire *f*; ~ **fees** *n pl* IMP/EXP honoraires consulaires *m pl*

consulate *n* POL consulat *m*

Consulate-General *n* GEN COMM, POL Consul général *m*, Consulat général *m*

consult *vt* GEN COMM consulter; ◆ ~ **a lawyer** LAW consulter un avocat; ~ **sb about sth** GEN COMM consulter qn sur qch

consultancy *n* ADMIN conseil *m*, GEN COMM cabinet-conseil *m*, conseil *m*, HRM conseil *m*, MGMNT cabinet-conseil *m*, conseil *m*; ~ **work** ADMIN conseil *m*, GEN COMM conseil *m*, expertise *f*, HRM conseil *m*, MGMNT conseil *m*, expertise *f*

consultant *n* ACC, COMP conseil *m*, conseiller *m*, consultant *m*, GEN COMM conseiller *m*, HRM conseil *m*, conseiller *m*, consultant *m*, MGMNT conseil *m*, conseiller *m*, consultant *m*, expert-conseil *m*; ~ **engineer** GEN COMM, IND ingénieur-conseil *m*; ~ **service** ECON assistance technique *f*, service conseil *m*

consultation *n* GEN COMM, HRM consultation *f*; ◆ **in** ~ **with** GEN COMM en consultation avec

consultative[1] *adj* GEN COMM, HRM consultatif; ~ **-democratic** MGMNT *leadership style* démocratique consultatif

consultative:[2] ~ **bodies** *n pl* GEN COMM *committees and boards* organe consultatif *m*, organisme consultatif *m*; ~ **committee** *n* ADMIN comité consultatif *m*, GEN COMM comité consultatif *m*, commission consultative *f*, HRM comité consultatif *m*, POL commission consultative *f*

Consultative: ~ **Shipping Group** *n (CSG)* TRANSP groupe maritime consultatif

consulting: ~ **engineer** *n* GEN COMM, IND ingénieur-conseil *m*; ~ **firm** *n* GEN COMM cabinet d'experts *m*, société de conseil *f*; ~ **service** *n* GEN COMM service conseil *m*

consumables *n pl* GEN COMM consommables *m pl*

consume *vt* ECON, ENVIR, GEN COMM, IND, S&M *use* consommer

consumer:[1] ~ **-orientated** *adj* COMP orienté grand public *loc*

consumer[2] *n* ECON, ENVIR, GEN COMM, IND, S&M consommateur *m*; ~ **acceptance** *n* S&M acceptation par les consommateurs *f*, réceptivité des consommateurs *f*; ~ **advertising** *n* S&M publicité grand public *f*; ~ **advisory service** *n* S&M service conseil au consommateur *m*; ~ **age group** *n* S&M tranche d'âge du consommateur *f*; ~ **banking** *n* BANK services bancaires au consommateur *m pl*; ~ **behavior** *n AmE*, ~ **behaviour** *n BrE* S&M comportement du consommateur *m*; ~ **brand** *n* S&M marque grand public *f*; ~ **brands** *n* S&M

produits de grande consommation *m pl*; ~ **choice** *n* S&M choix du consommateur *m*, préférence du consommateur *f*; ~ **credit** *n* ECON, FIN crédit à la consommation *m*; ~ **credit act** *n UK* LAW loi sur le crédit à la consommation *f*; ~ **credit market** *n* BANK, FIN marché du crédit à la consommation *m*; ~ **demand** *n* S&M *market research* demande des consommateurs *f*; ~ **durables** *n pl* ECON, IND biens de consommation durables *m pl*, S&M articles d'équipement *m pl*, biens d'équipement ménager *m pl*, biens de consommation durables *m pl*, produits de consommation durables *m pl*; ~ **equilibrium** *n* ECON équilibre des consommateurs *m*; ~ **expectations** *n pl* GEN COMM attentes du consommateur *f pl*; ~ **expenditure** *n* ECON, S&M dépenses de consommation *f pl*; ~ **expenditure survey** *n US* (SYN *consumer price index*) ACC, ECON enquête sur les dépenses de consommation *f*; ~ **goods** *n pl* ECON, ENVIR, IND, S&M biens de consommation *m pl*; ~ **goods company** *n* GEN COMM société de biens de grande consommation *f*; ~ **goods or services** *n pl* TAX marchandises de consommation ou services *f pl*; ~ **habits** *n pl* GEN COMM, S&M habitudes de consommation *f pl*; ~ **hardgoods** *n pl* GEN COMM biens de consommation durables *m pl*; ~ **installment loan** *n AmE*, ~ **instalment loan** *n BrE* BANK prêt à la consommation remboursable par versements échelonnés *m*, prêt à tempérament aux consommateurs *m*; ~ **issues** *n pl* S&M problèmes relatifs aux consommateurs *m pl*; ~ **-led marketing policy** *n* S&M politique dictée par les besoins des consommateurs *f*; ~ **lending** *n* BANK crédit à la consommation *m*, prêt à la consommation *m*, FIN prêt à la consommation *m*; ~ **leveraging** *n* BANK, FIN endettement du consommateur *m*; ~ **loan** *n* BANK, FIN prêt personnel *m*, prêt à la consommation *m*; ~ **loan institute** *n* BANK, FIN institut des prêts à la consommation *m*; ~ **loyalty** *n* S&M fidélité du consommateur *f*; ~ **magazine** *n* GEN COMM magazine de grande diffusion *m*, revue du consommateur *f*, MEDIA revue du consommateur *f*; ~ **market** *n* S&M marché de la consommation *m*, marché des produits de grande consommation *m*; ~ **marketing** *n* S&M marketing des produits de grande consommation *m*; ~ **needs** *n pl* S&M besoins des consommateurs *m pl*; ~ **organization** *n* S&M organisme de défense des consommateurs *m*; ~ **-orientated product** *n* IND, S&M produit grand public *m*; ~ **orientation** *n* S&M orientation vers le consommateur *f*; ~ **panel** *n* S&M *market research* groupe témoin *m*, panel de consommateurs *m*; ~ **patterns** *n pl* GEN COMM, S&M habitudes des consommateurs *f pl*; ~ **policy** *n* GEN COMM *European Union* politique de défense du consommateur *f*; ~ **preference** *n* GEN COMM préférence du consommateur *f*; ~ **price** *n* S&M prix à la consommation *m*; ~ **price index** *n* (*CPI, consumer expenditure survey*) ACC, ECON indice des prix à la consommation *m* (*IPC*); ~ **product** *n* ECON, IND, S&M produit de consommation *m*; ~ **products** *n pl* ECON, S&M produits de consom-

mation courante *m pl*; ~ **profile** *n* S&M profil du consommateur *m*; ~ **protection** *n* LAW, S&M défense des intérêts du consommateur *f*, protection du consommateur *f*; ~ **protection legislation** *n* POL, S&M législation relative à la protection des consommateurs *f*; ~ **protection legislation of sale** *n* LAW, S&M législation relative à la protection du consommateur en matière de vente; ~ **relations manager** *n* HRM, MGMNT chef du service consommateurs *m*, directeur clientèle *m*, directeur des relations avec la clientèle *m*, S&M chef du service consommateurs *m*, directeur clientèle *m*; ~ **requirement** *n* S&M exigence des consommateurs *f*; ~ **research** *n* S&M recherche des besoins des consommateurs *f*, étude de consommation *f*, étude de marché *f*; ~ **resistance** *n* S&M résistance des consommateurs *f*; ~ **response** *n* S&M réaction des consommateurs *f*; ~ **satisfaction** *n* S&M satisfaction du consommateur *f*; ~ **society** *n* ECON, POL société de consommation *f*; ~ **sovereignty** *n* ECON, S&M le client roi *m*, souveraineté du consommateur *f*; ~ **spending** *n* S&M consommation *f*, dépense des ménages *f*, dépenses de consommation *f pl*; ~**'s surplus** *n* (ANT *producer's surplus*) ECON surplus du consommateur *m*; ~ **survey** *n* S&M enquête auprès des consommateurs *f*, étude de consommation *f*; ~ **test** *n* S&M test de consommation *m*; ~ **trends** *n pl* S&M tendances de la consommation *f pl*; ~ **watchdog** *n* GEN COMM, S&M organisme chargé de défendre les intérêts des consommateurs; ♦ **have little ~ appeal** S&M *product* présenter peu d'attrait pour les consommateurs

Consumer: ~ **Credit Protection Act** *n US* LAW, S&M loi relative à la protection du consommateur en matière de crédit à la consommation

consumerism *n* ECON, S&M consumérisme *m*, défense des consommateurs *f*

consumerist *n* ECON, S&M consumériste *mf*, défenseur des consommateurs *m*

consumers': ~ **panel** *n* S&M groupe témoin *m*

Consumers': ~ **Advisory Council** *n AmE* (*CAC*) WEL commission consultative des consommateurs; ~**' Association** *n* (*CA*) GEN COMM ≈ Association de défense du consommateur *f*, ≈ Institut national de la consommation *m*, ≈ Organisation de défense des consommateurs *f*

consummate *vt* GEN COMM consommer, parfaire

consumption *n* ECON, ENVIR, IND, S&M consommation *f*; ~ **externality** *n* ECON effets externes dans la consommation *m pl*; ~ **function** *n* ECON fonction de consommation *f*; ~ **goods** *n pl* ECON biens de consommation *m pl*; ~ **pattern** *n* ECON modèle de consommation *m*, schéma de consommation *m*; ~ **per capita** *n* ECON consommation par tête *f*; **per capita** ~ *n* ECON consommation par tête *f*; ~ **rate of interest** *n UK* (*CRI*) FIN taux d'intérêt à la consommation *m*; ~ **tax** *n* TAX taxe de consommation *f*

contact[1] *n* GEN COMM *person* contact *m*, interlocuteur *m*, relation *f*; ~ **damage** TRANSP *shipping* avarie à la suite d'abordage *f*; ~ **report** S&M compte-rendu de contact *m*; ◆ **come into ~ with** GEN COMM entrer en contact avec, entrer en relation avec, prendre contact avec

contact[2] *vt* GEN COMM contacter; ◆ **~ sb about sth** GEN COMM contacter qn au sujet de qch

contain *vt* ECON contenir, GEN COMM *demand, inflation* contenir, maîtriser, modérer, restreindre, LAW restreindre

container *n* TRANSP *ISO unit* container *m*, conteneur *m*; ~ **base** *n* BrE *(CB, container freight station)* TRANSP *shipping* magasin de groupage *m*; ~ **berth** *n* TRANSP *shipping* poste à quai pour navires porte-conteneurs *m*, quai à conteneurs *m*; ~ **bill** *n* IMP/EXP *shipping*, TRANSP *shipping* connaissement reçu pour embarquement *m*; ~ **car** *n* US TRANSP *rail* wagon porte-conteneurs *m*; ~ **control** *n* *(cc)* TRANSP contrôle des conteneurs *m*; ~ **depot** *n* TRANSP *shipping* aire de stockage des conteneurs *f*; ~ **dock** *n* TRANSP dock pour la manutention des conteneurs *m*; ~ **dues** *n pl* TAX *shipping*, TRANSP *shipping* taxes et droits sur les conteneurs *f pl*; ~ **frame** *n* TRANSP *shipping* structure du conteneur *f*; ~ **freight station** *n* AmE *(CFS, container base)* TRANSP *shipping* magasin de groupage *m*; ~ **head** *n* TRANSP *shipping* avant du conteneur *m*; ~ **import cargo manifest** *n* IMP/EXP, TRANSP *shipping* manifeste de marchandises pour conteneurs *m*; ~ **leasing** *n* TRANSP crédit-bail de conteneurs *m*, location de conteneurs *f*; ~ **line** *n* TRANSP ligne transconteneur *f*; ~ **load** *n* TRANSP charge complète d'un conteneur *f*, chargement du conteneur *m*, conteneur complet *m*; ~ **market** *n* TRANSP marché des conteneurs *m*; ~ **on flat car** *n* AmE *(cf container on flat wagon BrE)* TRANSP conteneur sur wagon découvert à bords plats *m* *(vieilli)*, conteneur sur wagon plat *m*; ~ **on flat wagon** *n* BrE *(cf container on flat car AmE)* TRANSP conteneur sur wagon découvert à bords plats *m* *(vieilli)*, conteneur sur wagon plat *m*; ~ **operator** *n* TRANSP opérateur de conteneurs *m*; ~ **packing certificate** *n* TRANSP certificat d'empotage du conteneur *m*; ~ **park** *n* TRANSP parc de conteneurs *m*; ~ **part load** *n* TRANSP chargement partiel du conteneur *m*, conteneur de détail *m*; ~ **pool** *n* TRANSP parc de conteneurs *m*; ~ **port** *n* TRANSP port de conteneurs *m*; ~ **premium** *n* S&M prime conditionnement *f*, prime emballage *f*; ~ **safety convention** *n* *(CSC)* TRANSP accord de sécurité sur les conteneurs *m*; ~ **service** *n* TRANSP service conteneurs *m*, service transconteneurs *m*; ~ **service tariff** *n* *(CST)* TRANSP tarif du service conteneur *m*; ~ **ship** *n* TRANSP navire porte-conteneurs *m*, porte-conteneurs *m*; ~ **space allocation** *n* TRANSP réservation d'espace conteneur *f*; ~ **stack** *n* TRANSP pile de conteneurs *f*; ~ **stuffing** *n* TRANSP empotage *loc m*, garniture du conteneur *f*; ~ **terminal** *n* TRANSP *shipping* terminal maritime *m*, terminal à conteneurs *m*; ~ **transport** *n* TRANSP transport par conteneurs *m*; ~ **unstuffing** *n*

TRANSP dépotage *m*; ~ **use** *n* TRANSP utilisation des conteneurs *f*, utilisation du conteneur *f*; ~ **user analysis** *n* TRANSP analyse des utilisateurs de conteneur *f*; ~ **utilization** *n* TRANSP utilisation des conteneurs *f*, utilisation du conteneur *f*; ~ **yard** *n* *(CY)* TRANSP dépôt de conteneurs *m*

containerization *n* TRANSP *shipping freight* conteneurisation *f*, mise en conteneurs *f*

containerize *vt* TRANSP conteneuriser, mettre en conteneurs

containerized[1] *adj* TRANSP conteneurisé

containerized:[2] ~ **shipping** *n* TRANSP *shipping* expédition en conteneur *f*

containment *n* ECON *of credit* retenue *f*, POL *of Communism* politique de limitation de l'expansion *f*

contaminate *vt* ENVIR, IND contaminer, polluer, LAW vicier

contaminated[1] *adj* ENVIR, IND contaminé

contaminated:[2] ~ **site** *n* ENVIR site contaminé *m*

contamination *n* ENVIR contamination *f*, pollution *f*, IND contamination *f*; ~ **fallout** ENVIR, IND retombées de polluants *f pl*

contango *n* UK ACC, FIN, STOCK report *m*; ~ **business** UK STOCK opération de report *f*; ~ **day** UK STOCK jour des reports *m*; ~ **rate** UK STOCK intérêt de report *m*

cont'd *abbr* *(continued)* GEN COMM à suivre

contemporaneous: ~ **externality** *n* *(ANT sequential externality)* ECON externalité contemporaine *f*

contempt: ~ **of court** *n* LAW outrage à la cour *m*, outrage à magistrat *m*; ◆ **in ~ of court** LAW coupable du délit d'outrage à la cour, coupable du délit d'outrage à magistrat

content *n* GEN COMM contenu *m*, teneur *f*, LAW *of abstract* contenu *m*

contention *n* GEN COMM désaccord *m*

contents *n pl* COMP *of file, document* contenu *m*, GEN COMM contenu *m, of list* table des matières *f*

contest[1] *n* GEN COMM combat *m*, concours *m*, lutte *f*

contest[2] *vt* INS *clause* attaquer, contester, discuter, LAW *will* attaquer, contester

contestable: ~ **clause** *n* INS clause contestable *f*; ~ **markets thesis** *n* ECON théorie des marchés ouverts à la concurrence *f*

contested[1] *adj* S&M *market* disputé

contested:[2] ~ **claim** *n* FIN créance litigieuse *f*

context:[1] ~ **-sensitive** *adj* COMP contextuel

context[2] *n* GEN COMM cadre *m*; ~ **-sensitive help** COMP *software* aide contextuelle *f*

contiguous *adj* COMP, GEN COMM contigu

continent *n* GEN COMM continent *m*; ~ **of Europe** GEN COMM continent européen *m*

Continent *n* GEN COMM Europe continentale *f*; ~ **Britain and Asia** *(COBRA)* TRANSP consortium des conteneurs en Grande-Bretagne et sur l'Asie

continental[1] *adj* GEN COMM continental

continental:[2] ~ **trade** *n* ECON commerce trans-

Manche *m*, S&M commerce avec l'Europe continentale *m*, commerce trans-Manche *m*

contingencies: ~ **vote** *n pl* FIN crédit pour
éventualités *m*

contingency *n* GEN COMM imprévu *m*, éventualité
f, événement imprévu *m*, événement inattendu *m*;
~ **arrangements** *n pl* GEN COMM dispositions en
cas d'imprévu *f pl*, mesures en cas d'urgence *f pl*;
~ **fund** *n* FIN *personal budgets* caisse de prévoyance *f*, fonds de prévoyance *m*, fonds pour
éventualités *m*; ~ **management** *n* MGMNT gestion
de l'imprévu *f*, gestion de la contingence *f*,
gestion tenant compte des imprévus *f*; ~ **order** *n*
STOCK ordre sous condition *m*; ~ **payments** *n pl*
ACC *budgeting* charges imprévues *f pl*; ~ **plan** *n*
GEN COMM, MGMNT plan d'urgence *m*, plan de
secours *m*; ~ **planning** *n* GEN COMM tenir compte
de l'imprévu, MGMNT, POL programme tenant
compte des imprévus *m*; ~ **reserve** *n* FIN fonds de
réserve *m*, provision pour imprévus *f*, réserve
pour éventualités *f*, MGMNT fonds de prévoyance
m; ~ **theory** *n* MGMNT théorie de la contingence *f*

contingent[1] *adj* GEN COMM *liability* accidentel,
aléatoire, fortuit, imprévu, éventuel

contingent:[2] ~ **asset** *n* ACC actif latent *m*, actif
potentiel *m*, actif éventuel *m*; ~ **budget** *n* FIN
budget conjoncturel *m*; ~ **business interruption
insurance** *n* INS assurance contre la carence des
fournisseurs *f*; ~ **claim** *n* ACC, FIN réclamation
potentielle *f*; ~ **consideration** *n* GEN COMM
contrepartie conditionnelle *f*; ~ **expenses** *n pl*
ACC charges latentes *f pl*, dépenses imprévues *f pl*;
~ **fee** *n* GEN COMM honoraires éventuels *m pl*;
~ **liabilities** *n pl* ACC engagements éventuels *m pl*,
FIN, LAW dette éventuelle *f*, engagements éventuels *m pl*, obligation éventuelle *f*, passif éventuel
m; ~ **market** *n* INS marché conditionnel *m*;
~ **obligation** *n* TAX obligation conditionnelle *f*;
~ **order** *n* STOCK ordre lié *m*

contingently *adv* GEN COMM accidentellement, à
l'improviste

continual: ~ **professional education** *n* ACC, WEL
formation professionnelle continue *f*

continuation: ~ **clause** *n* *(cc)* INS clause de
prolongation *f*, clause de report *f*; ~ **day** *n* STOCK
jour des reports *m*

continue *vt* BANK *programme* poursuivre, GEN
COMM continuer; ◆ ~ **doing** GEN COMM continuer
à faire; ~ **to do** GEN COMM continuer à faire

continued[1] *adj* *(cont'd)* GEN COMM à suivre

continued:[2] ~ **success** *n* GEN COMM *of person,
company, product* réussite constante *f*, succès
constant *m*, succès ininterrompu *m*, succès
permanent *m*

continuing[1] *adj* GEN COMM *interest* soutenu,
investment constant, *support* incessant, sans faille

continuing:[2] ~ **appropriation authorities** *n pl* FIN
crédits permanents *m pl*; ~ **commitment** *n* GEN
COMM engagement permanent *m*; ~ **corporation** *n*
TAX corporation assurant la continuation *f*;

~ **cost** *n* ACC coût permanent *m*; ~ **education
tax** *n* TAX taxe sur la formation professionnelle *f*

continuity *n* S&M continuité *f*; ~ **of employment** *UK*
HRM continuité de l'emploi *f*; ~ **thesis** ECON thèse
de la continuité *f*

continuous[1] *adj* GEN COMM continu

continuous:[2] ~ **assessment** *n* HRM, WEL contrôle
continu *m*, contrôle continu de l'acquisition des
connaissances *m* *(frml)*; ~ **audit** *n* ACC audit en
continu *m*, contrôle continu *m*, vérification
continue *f*, vérification permanente *f*; ~ **budget**
n FIN budget perpétuel *m*; ~ **-flow production** *n*
IND production continue *f*; ~ **forms** *n pl* GEN
COMM listings pré-imprimés *m pl*; ~ **hull survey** *n*
(CS) TRANSP *shipping* visite de la coque en vue
d'une reclassification continue *f*; ~ **inventory** *n*
GEN COMM inventaire continu *m*, inventaire en
cours *m*, inventaire permanent *m*; ~ **labor** *n* *AmE*,
~ **labour** *n* *BrE* HRM travail en continu *m*; ~ **liner**
n *(cl)* TRANSP *shipping* navire de ligne continue
m; ~ **market** *n* STOCK marché en continu *m*; ~ **net
settlement** *n* *UK* *(CNS)* STOCK liquidation en
continu *f*, règlement en continu *m*; ~ **process** *n*
ECON, IND procédé de fabrication en continu *m*,
S&M inventaire permanent *m*; ~ **process
production** *n* IND production en continu *f*;
~ **production** *n* IND production en continu *f*;
~ **promotion** *n* S&M *advertising* fidélisation *f*;
~ **reinforcement** *n* HRM renforcement en cours
m; ~ **stationery** *n* ADMIN, COMP papier en continu
m; ~ **stocktaking** *n* *(CS)* ECON inventaire permanent *m*, GEN COMM inventaire permanent *m*,
inventaire en cours *m*; ~ **survey** *n* S&M enquête
permanente *f*, TRANSP *shipping* reclassification
continue *f*; ~ **survey cycle** *n* *(CSC)* GEN COMM
cycle d'enquête permanent *m*; ~ **survey cycle hull**
n *(CHS)* TRANSP *shipping* visite de la coque en
vue d'une reclassification continue *f*; ~ **survey
cycle machinery** *n* TRANSP *shipping* visite des
machines en vue d'une reclassification continue *f*;
~ **survey of the hull quoting date** *n* *(CS)* TRANSP
visite de la coque en vue d'une reclassification
continue *f*; ~ **variable** *n* MATH *statistics* variable
continue *f*

continuously: ~ **offered payment rights in Swiss
francs** *n pl* *(COPS)* STOCK créances comptables
émises continuellement en francs suisses *f pl*
(COPS)

Continuously: ~ **Offered Longer-Term Securities** *n
pl* STOCK papier à terme offert en permanence *m*,
titres à long terme offerts en continu *m pl*

contour *n* GEN COMM profil *m*

contra[1] *n* ACC contrepartie *f*, écriture de compensation *f*, FIN écriture de compensation *f*;
~ **account** ACC compte d'attente *m*, compte de
régularisation *m*; ~ **broker** STOCK courtier qui traite
la partie opposée de la transaction; ~ **entry** ACC, FIN
contre-passation *f*, écriture de compensation *f*,
écriture de contrepartie *f*

contra[2] *vt* ACC contre-passer, contrepartie *f*

contra preferentem *phr frml* GEN COMM malgré mes/tes/ses préférences *loc*

contraband *n* IMP/EXP *activity*, TAX *activity* contrebande *f*, *goods* marchandises de contrebande *f pl*

contract[1] *n* FIN, GEN COMM, LAW, S&M contrat *m*; ~ **agreement** *n* LAW accord contractuel *m*; ~ **bargaining** *n* HRM négociations salariales *f pl*; ~ **bond** *n* GEN COMM garantie de bonne fin *f*; ~ **carrier** *n* TRANSP transporteur contractuel *m*; ~ **compliance** *n* HRM, LAW conformité au contrat *f*; ~ **delivery date** *n UK* STOCK *currency futures* date d'échéance *f*, jour de livraison du contrat *m*; ~ **delivery month** *n BrE* (SYN *contract month*) STOCK *currency futures* mois d'échéance *m*, mois de livraison du contrat *m*; ~ **of employment** *n* HRM, LAW contrat d'emploi *m*; ~ **for the sale of goods** *n* LAW, S&M contrat de vente de biens *m*; ~ **for services** *n* HRM contrat de service *m*, LAW contrat de services *m*; ~ **hire** *n* GEN COMM location contractuelle *f*, location sous contrat *f*, HRM location longue durée *f*; ~ **holdback** *n* GEN COMM *refundable amount* retenue de garantie *f*; ~ **of indemnity** *n* INS *property and liability insurance* contrat d'indemnisation *m*, contrat d'indemnité *m*; ~ **joint venture** *n* GEN COMM coentreprise sans création de société *f*, joint-venture sans création de société *m*; ~ **labor** *n AmE*, ~ **labour** *n BrE* HRM main-d'oeuvre contractuelle *f*; ~ **licence** *n BrE* IMP/EXP licence contractuelle *f*; ~ **license** *n AmE see contract licence BrE*; ~ **maintenance** *n* GEN COMM entretien prévu par le contrat *m*; ~ **month** *n* GEN COMM mois de livraison *m*, STOCK *(cf contract delivery month BrE) futures* mois d'échéance *m*, mois de livraison *m*; ~ **note** *n* STOCK bordereau d'achat *m*, bordereau de vente *m*; ~ **party** *n* LAW partie contractante *f*; ~ **payment** *n* ACC paiement contractuel *m*; ~ **price** *n US* TAX *instalment sale* prix contractuel *m*, prix forfaitaire *m*; ~ **rent** *n* PROP loyer contractuel *m*; ~ **of sale** *n* BANK, LAW, S&M contrat de vente *m*; ~ **size** *n* STOCK *currency futures* quotité du contrat *f*; ~ **specifications** *n pl* LAW stipulations contractuelles *f pl*, stipulations d'un contrat *f pl*; ~ **system** *n* TRANSP *shipping* système de transport contractuel *m*; ~ **that can be upheld** *n* LAW contrat valide *m*; ~ **value** *n* STOCK *futures* montant du contrat *m*, valeur du contrat *f*; ~ **work** *n* HRM travail à forfait *m*

contract[2] **1.** *vt* GEN COMM *debt* contracter, *growth* rétrécir, ~ **in** GEN COMM *work* sous-traiter; **2.** *vi* ECON se contracter, se réduire, ~ **out** FIN *UK of state earnings-related pension scheme* se retirer de, GEN COMM se dégager, se libérer, soustraire; ◆ ~ **a loan** FIN contracter un emprunt; ~ **out of an agreement** LAW rompre un contrat; ~ **out of sth** GEN COMM cesser de cotiser à qch; ~ **to do sth** GEN COMM s'engager par contrat à faire qch

contracting *n* ECON embauche *f*; ~ **holder** FIN titulaire contractant *m*; ~ **out** GEN COMM, WEL *of services to private sector* sous-traitance *f*; ~ **-out clause** LAW clause de renonciation *f*;

~ **party** LAW cocontractant *m*, contractant *m*, partie contractante *f*, PROP contractant *m*; ~ **state** LAW état contractant *m*

contraction *n* ECON contraction *f*, rétrécissement *m*, GEN COMM rétrécissement *m*; ~ **of demand** (ANT *expansion of demand*) S&M amenuisement de la demande *m*, rétrécissement de la demande *m*

contractionary: ~ **national income gap** *n* ECON *econometrics* écart récessionniste *m*; ~ **pressure** *n* ECON poussée récessionniste *f*

contractor *n* HRM *party to contract* contractant *m*, *supplier of labour* entrepreneur *m*, IND *supplier* entrepreneur *m*, LAW *party to contract* contractant *m*, PROP *party to contract* contractant *m*, *supplier of building materials* entrepreneur *m*; ~**'s all risks insurance** INS assurance tous risques chantier *f*; ~**'s yard** PROP chantier de matériaux de construction *m*, dépôt de matériaux de construction *m*

contracts: ~ **manager** *n* ADMIN, HRM directeur chargé des contrats *m*; ~ **officer** *n* ADMIN, HRM cadre chargé des contrats *m*

contractual[1] *adj* GEN COMM, LAW conventionnel

contractual[2]: ~ **liability** *n* GEN COMM, LAW correction *f*, obligation contractuelle *f*, responsabilité contractuelle *f*; ~ **loan rate** *n* STOCK *Eurodollar futures* taux contractuel du prêt *m*, taux de prêt contractuel *m*; ~ **obligation** *n* LAW obligation contractuelle *f*; ~ **payment** *n* ACC paiement contractuel *m*; ~ **plan** *n* STOCK plan d'investissement contractuel *m*; ~ **provision** *n* LAW disposition contractuelle *f*; ~ **relationship** *n* GEN COMM lien contractuel *m*, relation contractuelle *f*; ~ **savings** *n pl* FIN économies contractuelles *f pl*, épargne contractuelle *f*

contrarian *n* STOCK investisseur à contre-courant *m*, investisseur à contre-tendance *m*

contrary *n* GEN COMM contraire *m*; ◆ **on the** ~ GEN COMM au contraire *loc m*; ~ **to** GEN COMM contraire à

contrast *n* COMP contraste *m*

contravene *vt* GEN COMM, LAW contrevenir à

contribute *vt* ECON contribuer, GEN COMM contribuer, cotiser, *article* soumettre, *ideas, experience* apporter, INS cotiser; ~ **to** MEDIA *newspaper, magazine* collaborer à

contributed: ~ **capital** *n* STOCK capital d'apport *m*

contribution *n* GEN COMM cotisation *f*, *personal, financial* apport *m*, *personal* contribution *f*, INS cotisation *f*, TAX *for political parties* contribution *f*; ~ **analysis** FIN méthode des coûts variables *f*; ~ **of capital** FIN apport de capital *m*; ~ **margin** ACC marge sur coûts variables *f*; ~ **payable on self-employed earnings** TAX *pensions* cotisations à payer sur le revenu d'un travail indépendant *f pl*; ~ **profit** ACC *cost accounting* marge sur coûts variables *f*; ~ **standard** ECON norme de répartition des revenus selon la productivité des facteurs de production; ~ **to funeral expenses** INS cotisation aux frais des obsèques *f*, cotisation aux frais funéraires *f*; ◆ **make a ~** GEN COMM *capital* faire un apport; **make a ~ to** GEN COMM apporter une contribution à

contributions: **~ through employment** *n pl* TAX *pensions* cotisations d'employé *f pl*

contributor *n* ECON *European Union* contributeur *m*, MEDIA collaborateur *m*, TAX cotisant *m*, donateur *m*; **~ of capital** GEN COMM apporteur de capitaux *m*, bailleur de fonds *m*, souscripteur *m*

contributory[1] *adj* LAW accessoire

contributory:[2] **~ earnings from employment** *n pl* TAX *pensions* gains cotisables d'un emploi *m pl*; **~ negligence** *n* LAW faute de la victime *f*, négligence dans le chef de la victime *f*, part de responsabilité imputée à la victime dans l'accident *f*; **~ pension fund** *n* (ANT *noncontributory pension fund*) FIN, HRM, WEL caisse de retraite avec cotisation salariale *f*; **~ pension plan** *n* (ANT *noncontributory pension plan*) FIN, HRM, WEL régime de retraite mixte *m*, système de retraite par répartition *m*; **~ pension scheme** *n* (ANT *noncontributory pension scheme*) FIN, HRM, WEL régime de retraite mixte *m*, système de retraite par répartition *m*; **~ self-employed earnings** *n pl* TAX *pensions* gains cotisables d'un travail indépendant *m pl*; **~ sickness fund** *n* HRM, WEL caisse d'assurance maladie contributive *f*; **~ value** *n* INS valeur contributive *f*

control[1] *n* COMP commande *f*, gestion *f*, pilotage *m*, ECON contrôle *m*, régulation *f*, GEN COMM autorité *f*, contrôle *m*, régulation *f*, IMP/EXP contrôle *m*, IND régulation *f*, POL contrôle *m*, S&M *direct marketing* témoin *m*; **~ account** ACC compte de contrôle *m*; **~ block** STOCK bloc de contrôle *m*; **~ character** COMP caractère de commande *m*; **~ command** COMP commande de contrôle *f*; **~ data** COMP données de contrôle *f*; **~ information** GEN COMM information de contrôle *f*; **~ key** (*CTRL key*) COMP *keyboard* touche de commande *f*, touche de contrôle *f* (*touche CTRL*); **~ law** LAW droit régissant le pouvoir et l'autorité *m*; **~ panel** COMP panneau de commande *m*, pupitre de commande *m*, GEN COMM tableau de bord *m*; **~ procedure** COMP procédure de commande *f*; **~ program** COMP programme de contrôle *m*; **~ stock** STOCK actions de contrôle *f pl*; **~ of substances hazardous to health** UK (*COSHH*) HRM *regulations*, IND contrôle des matières dangereuses pour la santé *m*, contrôle des substances présentant un danger pour la santé *m*; **~ ticket** TRANSP billet de contrôle *m*; ◆ **keep costs under ~** GEN COMM maîtriser les coûts

control[2] *vt* ECON *inflation* juguler, FIN *market*, GEN COMM contrôler; ◆ **~ costs** GEN COMM freiner les coûts, maîtriser les coûts; **~ the purse strings** *infrml* ECON tenir les cordons de la bourse (*infrml*)

Control-Alt-Delete *phr* (*CAD*) COMP Ctrl-Alt-Del (*CAD*)

controllable: **~ cost** *n* ACC coût contrôlable *m*, coût maîtrisable *m*, coût maîtrisé *m*

controlled: **~ atmosphere** *n* (*CA*) ENVIR environnement stabilisé *m*, milieu constant *m*; **~ commodity** *n* UK STOCK marchandise réglementée *f*, matière première contrôlée *f*; **~ company** *n* STOCK corporation contrôlée *f*; **~ corporation** *n* STOCK corporation contrôlée *f*; **~ dumping** *n* ENVIR dépôt contrôlé de déchets *m*; **~ economy** *n* ECON économie dirigée *f*, économie réglementée *f*; **~ market** *n* ECON marché officiel *m*; **~ rate** *n* ECON *currency exchange*, FIN taux de change réglementé *m*; **~ transit** *n* TRANSP transit contrôlé *m*; **~ wildcat drilling** *n* ENVIR forage d'exploration contrôlé *m*, forage sauvage sous contrôle *m*

controller *n* ACC *governmental* contrôleur de gestion *m*, contrôleur financier *m*, FIN contrôleur *m*, vérificateur *m*, POL contrôleur de gestion *m*

controlling: **~ account** *n* ACC compte collectif *m*; **~ company** *n* GEN COMM société dominante *f*; **~ corporation** *n* STOCK corporation dominante *f*; **~ interest** *n* HRM participation majoritaire *f*, STOCK bloc de contrôle *m*; **~ shareholder** *n* STOCK actionnaire majoritaire *m*

controversial *adj* GEN COMM discutable, sujet à controverse

controversy *n* GEN COMM controverse *f*, polémique *f*

conv *abbr* GEN COMM (*converted*), PROP (*converted*) conv. (*converti*), TRANSP (*conveyance*) acheminement *m*, transport *m*

convene *vt* GEN COMM, MGMNT *for a meeting* convoquer

convenience *n* GEN COMM convenance *f*; **~ bill** *n* BANK, FIN, GEN COMM traite de complaisance *f*; **~ flag** *n* TRANSP *shipping* pavillon de complaisance *m*; **~ food** *n* S&M aliment prêt à cuire *m*, aliment tout préparé *m*, plat tout préparé *m*; **~ goods** *n pl* S&M produits d'achat courant *m pl*, produits de consommation courante *m pl*, produits de grande consommation *m pl*, produits de grande diffusion *m pl*; **~ products** *n* GEN COMM produits de consommation courante *m pl*; **~ sampling** *n* MATH, S&M échantillonnage aléatoire *m*; **~ shop** *n BrE* (*cf convenience store AmE*) S&M boutique de proximité *f*, magasin de proximité *m*; **~ store** *n AmE* (*cf convenience shop BrE*) S&M boutique de proximité *f*, magasin de proximité *m*; ◆ **at sb's ~** GEN COMM à la convenance de qn

convenient: **~ speed** *n* TRANSP *shipping* vitesse appropriée *f*

convening *n* GEN COMM, MGMNT convocation *f*

convenor *n* HRM responsable de section *m*

convention *n* ACC principe *m*, GEN COMM colloque *m*, convention *f*, LAW convention *f*, MGMNT colloque *m*, congrès *m*, POL congrès *m*; **~ hotel**

GEN COMM, MGMNT, PROP hôtel de congrès *m*, hôtel recevant des congrès *m*; **~ participant** MGMNT congressiste *mf*, délégué *m*, participant *m*, POL congressiste *mf*

conventional: **~ cargo** *n* TRANSP cargaison traditionnelle *f*; **~ mooring buoy** *n (CBM)* TRANSP *shipping* corps-mort traditionnel *m*; **~ mortgage** *n* BANK prêt hypothécaire classique *m*

converge *vi* GEN COMM *ideas, activities* converger, être convergent

convergence *n (ANT divergence)* ECON, GEN COMM, POL *of opinions, results*, STOCK *of futures price* convergence *f*; **~ hypothesis** ECON hypothèse de la convergence *f*; **~ thesis** POL thèse de la convergence *f*

convergent *adj* ECON, GEN COMM, POL convergent

conversational: **~ entry** *n* COMP saisie en mode conversationnel *f*; **~ mode** *n* COMP mode conversationnel *m*, mode dialogué *m*

conversationally *adv* COMP en mode conversationnel *loc m*

conversely *adv* GEN COMM inversement, réciproquement

conversion *n* COMP conversion *f*, ECON, FIN *of currency* conversion *f*, convertissement *m*, GEN COMM conversion *f*, transformation *f*, PROP *of buildings*, STOCK conversion *f*; **~ cost** ACC coût de transformation *m*; **~ date** STOCK date de conversion *f*; **~ factor** MATH, STOCK facteur de conversion *m*; **~ factor for employee contributions** INS *defined benefit pension plan* facteur de conversion de cotisations salariales *m*; **~ issue** FIN, STOCK émission de conversion *f*; **~ loan** BANK, FIN emprunt de conversion *m*, prêt de conversion *m*; **~ parity** *UK* STOCK parité de conversion *f*; **~ premium** STOCK prime de conversion *f*; **~ price** FIN, STOCK prix de conversion *m*; **~ rate** BANK, ECON, FIN taux de conversion *m*; **~ ratio** STOCK ratio de conversion *m*; **~ right** STOCK droit de conversion *m*

convert *vt* COMP, ECON *currency*, FIN, GEN COMM convertir; ♦ **~ into capital** ECON, FIN, GEN COMM capitaliser; **~ into cash** GEN COMM convertir en espèces

converted *adj (conv)* GEN COMM, PROP converti *(conv.)*

convertibility *n* FIN, STOCK convertibilité *f*

convertible[1] *adj* FIN, STOCK convertible

convertible[2] *n* STOCK action convertible *f*, obligation convertible *f*; **~ bond** *n* FIN, STOCK obligation convertible *f*; **~ bonds** *n pl* ACC emprunts obligatoires convertibles *m pl*; **~ currency** *n* ECON *econometrics*, FIN devise convertible *f*; **~ debenture** *n* STOCK obligation convertible *f*; **~ issue** *n* FIN émission convertible *f*; **~ loan stock** *n* STOCK capitaux empruntés convertibles *m pl*; **~ preferred share** *n* STOCK action privilégiée convertible *f*; **~ preferred stock** *n* STOCK action privilégiée convertible *f*; **~ security** *n* FIN titre convertible *m*, STOCK valeur convertible *f*; **~ share**

n STOCK action convertible *f*; **~ stock** *n* STOCK action convertible *f*; **~ subordinated loan** *n* FIN emprunt subordonné convertible *m*; **~ term life insurance** *n US* INS condition de conversion d'assurance-vie *f*

convey *vt* LAW *property* céder, transférer, transmettre, TRANSP *goods, passengers* acheminer, transporter

conveyance *n* LAW *property* cession *f*, transfert *m*, transmission *f*, TRANSP *(conv)* acheminement *m*, transport *m*; **~ of goods** TRANSP transport de marchandises *m*

conveyor: **~ belt** *n* LEIS tapis roulant *m*, TRANSP tapis roulant *m*, transporteur automatique *m*, transporteur à bande *m*

convict *vt* LAW condamner

conviction *n* LAW condamnation *f*

convocation *n* GEN COMM, MGMNT convocation *f*

convoke *vt* GEN COMM, MGMNT convoquer

convoking *n* GEN COMM, MGMNT convocation *f*

COO *abbr* GEN COMM *(chief operating officer)* chef de service *m*, GEN COMM *(country of origin)* pays d'origine *m*, HRM *(chief operating officer)* chef de service *m*, IMP/EXP *(country of origin)* pays d'origine *m*

cooling: **~ -off period** *n* GEN COMM *before signing contract* délai de réflexion *m*, HRM période de détente *f*, relation patronat-syndicat au point mort *f*, STOCK période de réflexion *f*; **~ system** *n* ENVIR, IND dispositif de réfrigération *m*

coop *n* GEN COMM *(cooperative)* coop *f*, coopé *f* *(coopérative)* PROP *US* partage de commission *m*; **~ advertising** *(cooperative advertising)* S&M publicité collective *f*, publicité groupée *f*, publicité à frais partagés *f*

cooperage *n* TRANSP tonnellerie *f*

cooperate *vi* GEN COMM collaborer, coopérer

cooperation *n* GEN COMM collaboration *f*, concours *m*, coopération *f*; **~ agreement** GEN COMM *between nations* accord de coopération *m*

cooperative *n* GEN COMM *(coop)* coopérative *f*, coopérative de vente en gros *f* *(coop)* PROP *BrE* *(cf condominium AmE)* immeuble en copropriété *m*; **~ advertising** *(coop advertising)* S&M *arrangement in retailing* publicité collective *f*, publicité groupée *f*, publicité à frais partagés *f*; **~ corporation** TAX corporation coopérative *f*; **~ credit association** GEN COMM association coopérative de crédit *f*; **~ credit institution** GEN COMM institution coopérative de crédit *f*, société mutuelle de crédit *f*; **~ education** *US* WEL enseignement alterné *m*; **~ farm** ECON *agricultural*, POL coopérative agricole *f*; **~ federalism** POL fédéralisme coopératif *m*; **~ society** GEN COMM coop *f*, coopérative *f*, société coopérative *f*, société mutuelle *f*; **~ store** GEN COMM coopé *f*, coopérative de vente en gros *f*

Cooperative: **~ Wholesale Society** *n (CWS)* GEN COMM coopérative de gros *f*, société coopérative de consommation *f*

cooperator *n* GEN COMM, IND coopérateur *m*

coopt *vt* GEN COMM, HRM coopter

coordinate *vt* GEN COMM, TRANSP coordonner

coordinated *adj* GEN COMM *systems*, TRANSP coordonné

coordinating *adj* GEN COMM coordinateur

Coordinating: ~ **Committee for Multilateral Export controls** *n (Cocom)* IMP/EXP comité de coordination pour le contrôle multilatéral des exportations *m*

coordination *n* GEN COMM, MGMNT, TRANSP coordination *f*

coordinator *n* GEN COMM, HRM, MGMNT coordinateur *m*

co-owner *n* HRM, PROP, TAX copropriétaire *mf*

co-ownership *n* PROP copropriété *f*

COP *abbr (custom of port)* TRANSP usage du port *m*

COPANT *n US (Pan American Standards Commission)* GEN COMM association panaméricaine de normalisation

Copenhagen *pr n* GEN COMM Copenhague *n pr*

copier *n* ADMIN, COMMS, GEN COMM *office equipment* copieur *m*, machine à photocopier *f*, photocopieuse *f*

copper *n* ENVIR cuivre *m*; ~ **ore** ENVIR minerai de cuivre *m*

coppers *n pl* STOCK cuprifères *m pl*, valeurs cuprifères *f pl*

coprocessor *n* COMP *hardware* coprocesseur *m*

COPS *abbr* STOCK *(continuously offered payment rights in Swiss francs)* COPS *(créances comptables émises continuellement en francs suisses)*, STOCK *(covered option securities)* titre d'une option couverte *m*

copy:[1] ~ **-protected** *adj* COMP incopiable, protégé contre la copie

copy[2] *n* COMP copie *f*, reproduction *f*, GEN COMM *counterfeit article* contrefaçon *f*, copie *f*, imitation *f*, *duplicate* copie *f*, reproduction *f*, *of newspaper, magazine* exemplaire *m*, numéro *m*, *text as opposed to title* texte *m*; ~ **adapter** S&M rédacteur publicitaire *m*; ~ **appeal** S&M *advertising* attrait du message *m*, axe publicitaire du message *m*; ~ **chief** GEN COMM chef de conception *m*, chef de rédaction *m*; ~ **date** GEN COMM, S&M date limite de remise des documents *f*; ~ **deadline** GEN COMM date limite de remise des documents *f*, MEDIA date limite de la remise d'un texte *f*, tombée *f*; ~ **department** GEN COMM service de rédaction *m*; ~ **editor** MEDIA *print* préparateur de copie *m*, réviseur *m*, secrétaire de rédaction *m*; ~ **platform** GEN COMM axe de la campagne *m*, charte de création *f*; ~ **-protected disk** COMP disquette protégée *f*; ~ **protection** COMP *software* protection contre la copie *f*; ~ **strategy** S&M *advertising* stratégie de communication *f*

copy[3] *vt* COMP *software command* copier, dupliquer, reproduire, GEN COMM copier, reproduire;

~ **-protect** COMP protéger contre la copie; ◆ ~ **from the original** GEN COMM reproduire d'après l'original, s'inspirer de l'original

copying *n* GEN COMM *process* duplication *f*, reprographie *f*

copyreader *n US* MEDIA *print* correcteur-rédacteur *m*

copyright *n* LAW *data, software* copyright *m*, droits d'auteur *m pl*, PATENTS *data, software* copyright *m*, droit d'auteur *m*; ~ **material** LAW *intellectual property*, PATENTS *intellectual property* oeuvre protégée conformément à la loi sur la propriété littéraire et artistique; ◆ ~ **reserved** LAW, PATENTS tous droits réservés

Copyright: ~ **Act** *n* LAW, PATENTS Convention sur les droits d'auteur *f*

copywriter *n* S&M concepteur-rédacteur *m*, rédacteur publicitaire *m*

copywriting *n* S&M conception *f*

corr. *abbr (correspondence)* GEN COMM corresp. *(correspondance)*

cordless[1] *adj* COMMS *mechanism, periphery* sans fiche

cordless:[2] ~ **digital telecommunications** *n pl* COMMS télécommunications numériques sans fil *f pl*

cordoba *n* GEN COMM cordoba *f*

core *n* COMP *hardware* mémoire centrale *f*, noyau *m*, tore *m*, GEN COMM coeur *m*, essentiel *m*, fond *m*; ~ **business** *n* ECON métier de base *m*, GEN COMM activité principale *f*; ~ **consumer price inflation** *n* ECON inflation structurelle des prix à la consommation *f*; ~ **curriculum** *n* WEL programme de base *m*; ~ **definition** *n* GEN COMM définition de base *f*; ~ **economy** *n* ECON économie dominante *f*; ~ **firm** *n* ECON, GEN COMM entreprise dominante *f*, firme dominante *f*; ~ **funding** *n* FIN financement de base *m*; ~ **hours** *n pl* IND plages horaires fixes *f pl*; ~ **inflation** *n* ECON inflation structurelle *f*; ~ **inflation rate** *n* ECON taux de l'inflation structurelle *m*; ~ **memory** *n* COMP mémoire centrale *f*; ~ **-periphery** *n* ECON centre-périphérie *m*; ~ **product** *n* S&M produit leader *m*; ~ **region** *n* ECON région centrale *f*; ~ **size** *n* COMP capacité de mémoire *f*; ~ **storage** *n* COMP mémoire principale *f*, mémoire à tores *f*; ~ **time** *n* HRM plage fixe *f*; ~ **workforce** *n UK* HRM les employés ayant le plus d'ancienneté

corner[1] *n* GEN COMM monopole *m*; ~ **casting** TRANSP pièce de coin *f*; ~ **post** TRANSP montant d'angle *m*; ~ **shop** *BrE (cf corner store AmE)* S&M magasin de proximité *m*; ~ **store** *AmE (cf corner shop BrE)* S&M magasin de proximité *m*

corner[2] *vt* ECON, FIN, S&M *market*, STOCK *market* accaparer; ◆ ~ **sb** GEN COMM mettre qn au pied du mur

cornerer *n* FIN, S&M, STOCK accapareur *m*

cornering: ~ **the market** *n* ECON, FIN, S&M, STOCK accaparement du marché *m*

cornerstone *n* GEN COMM pierre angulaire *f*

cornucopia n ECON corne d'abondance f

corp. abbr (corporation) GEN COMM corporation f, société commerciale f

corporate: ~ **account deposit** n BANK dépôt effectué par une entreprise m; ~ **accountability** n GEN COMM, MGMNT responsabilité des sociétés f; ~ **advertising** n S&M publicité de prestige f, publicité institutionnelle f; ~ **affiliate** n ECON, GEN COMM filiale f, société affiliée f, société apparentée f; ~ **asset** n ACC, FIN élément d'actif m; ~ **banking** n BANK services bancaires aux entreprises m pl; ~ **beneficiary** n TAX corporation bénéficiaire f; ~ **bond** n US STOCK local obligation municipale f, private obligation émise par une société privée f; ~ **campaign** n S&M campagne institutionnelle f; ~ **client** n BANK entreprise cliente f, société cliente f; ~ **credit** n BANK crédit aux entreprises m, crédit aux grandes entreprises m; ~ **credit card** n BANK, FIN carte de crédit professionnelle f; ~ **credit manager** n BANK directeur du crédit aux entreprises m; ~ **culture** n GEN COMM culture d'entreprise f; ~ **customer** n BANK entreprise cliente f, société cliente f; ~ **data center** n AmE, ~ **data centre** n BrE COMP centre informatique d'entreprise m; ~ **database** n COMP base de données d'entreprise f; ~ **debenture** n STOCK obligation de société f; ~ **debt securities** n pl BANK bons de caisse m pl; ~ **earning power** n ECON rentabilité des entreprises f; ~ **earnings** n pl ACC bénéfices de l'entreprise m pl; ~ **entity** n TAX entité constituée f; ~ **executive** n MGMNT dirigeant de société m; ~ **finance** n FIN finance d'entreprise f; ~ **financing** n FIN financement de sociétés m; ~ **financing committee** n FIN comité de financement des sociétés m; ~ **financing project** n FIN projet de financement de grandes entreprises m; ~ **goal** n GEN COMM but de l'entreprise m; ~ **governance** n ADMIN, ECON, GEN COMM, MGMNT gestion d'entreprise f; ~ **growth** n GEN COMM croissance de l'entreprise f; ~ **image** n GEN COMM image de l'entreprise f, image de marque f; ~ **income tax** n TAX impôt sur le revenu des corporations m, impôts sur les sociétés m pl; ~ **insider** n GEN COMM initié membre d'une société m; ~ **investment** n FIN investissements des sociétés m pl; ~ **investor** n UK STOCK investisseur commercial m; ~ **issue** n FIN émission de titres f; ~ **law** n GEN COMM, IND, LAW droit des entreprises m, droit des sociétés m; ~ **lawyer** n GEN COMM, IND juriste d'entreprise m, LAW avocat d'entreprise m, juriste d'entreprise m; ~ **lending** n BANK, FIN prêts aux entreprises m pl; ~ **lending market** n BANK, FIN marché des prêts aux entreprises m; ~ **loan** n BANK, FIN prêt à une société m, STOCK obligation du secteur privé f; ~ **management** n MGMNT direction d'entreprise f; ~ **manager** n MGMNT dirigeant d'une corporation m; ~ **member** n STOCK société membre f; ~ **mission** n GEN COMM vocation de la société f, MGMNT mission d'entreprise f, vocation de la société f; ~ **model** n ACC, FIN, GEN COMM modèle

de l'entreprise m; ~ **morality** n GEN COMM probité de l'entreprise f; ~ **name** n GEN COMM raison sociale f; ~ **network** n COMP réseau d'entreprise m; ~ **objective** n GEN COMM objectif de l'entreprise m; ~ **plagiarism** n GEN COMM, PATENTS plagiat de brevets d'entreprise m; ~ **planning** n GEN COMM planification de l'entreprise f; ~ **policy** n GEN COMM politique de l'entreprise f; ~ **purchaser** n TAX corporation acheteuse f; ~ **raider** n FIN, STOCK prédateur m, racheteur de sociétés m; ~ **raiding** n FIN rachat d'une société m, STOCK pillage m, rachat d'une société m; ~ **savings** n pl FIN épargne des entreprises f; ~ **seal** n BANK sceau de la banque m; ~ **spending** n TAX dépenses des entreprises f pl; ~ **sponsorship** n S&M advertising, promotion mécénat d'entreprise m; ~ **state** n POL état corporatif m; ~ **status** n UK HRM statut d'entreprise m; ~ **strategic planning** n MGMNT planification stratégique d'entreprise f, stratégie de l'entreprise f; ~ **strategy** n GEN COMM stratégie de l'entreprise f; ~ **structure** n GEN COMM structure de l'entreprise f; ~ **surtax** n TAX surtaxe des corporations f; ~ **tax** n TAX impôt sur les sociétés m, IS; ~ **tax credit** n TAX crédit d'impôt des corporations m; ~ **treasurer** n HRM trésorier d'entreprise m, trésorier de société m; ~ **turnaround** n GEN COMM, MGMNT redressement d'entreprises m; ~ **veil** n jarg GEN COMM tissu d'entreprises m

corporation n (corp.) GEN COMM corporation f, société commerciale f; ~ **law** GEN COMM, IND, LAW droit des sociétés m; ~ **loan** UK FIN issued by local government prêt aux sociétés m, STOCK émission des autorités locales f; ~ **tax** BrE (cf business income tax Canada) TAX impôt sur les sociétés m, IS

Corporation: ~ **of Foreign Bondholders** n UK (CFBH) STOCK société des détenteurs d'obligations étrangers f; ~ **of Lloyd's** n (CL) INS une association d'assureurs et d'agents d'assurance

corporatism n GEN COMM, POL corporatisme m

corporeal[1] adj (ANT incorporeal) ACC, ECON, FIN, GEN COMM, LAW corporel

corporeal:[2] ~ **hereditaments** n pl (ANT incorporeal hereditaments) LAW biens corporels transmissibles par héritage m pl

corpus n LAW civil law corpus m

corr. abbr (correspondence) COMMS corresp. (correspondance)

correct[1] adj GEN COMM correct, exact, juste, LAW correct

correct[2] vt GEN COMM errors, proofs corriger, rectifier, MEDIA corriger

corrected: ~ **invoice** n FIN facture rectificative f; ~ **probability** n FIN, MATH probabilité corrigée f

correcting: ~ **entry** n ACC écriture d'extourne f, écriture d'inventaire f, écriture de correction f (Can), écriture de redressement f, écriture de régularisation f, écriture rectificative f

correction *n* GEN COMM *of price*, LAW correction *f*, rectification *f*, STOCK correction *f*; ~ **maintenance** GEN COMM dépannage *m*

corrective: ~ **action** *n* GEN COMM correction *f*; ~ **subsidy** *n* ECON subvention corrective *f*, POL impôt correctif *m*, subvention corrective *f*, TAX impôt correctif *m*; ~ **tax** *n* POL, TAX impôt correctif *m*

correctly *adv* GEN COMM correctement, exactement

correlate *vt* MATH mettre en corrélation

correlation *n* MATH *statistics* corrélation *f*; ~ **ratio** *UK* STOCK *interest rate futures* ratio corrélatif *m*, ratio de corrélation *m*

correspond: ~ **to** *vt* GEN COMM *be equivalent* correspondre à, être équivalent à; ~ **with** GEN COMM *be similar* correspondre à, être équivalent à, COMMS *by letter* correspondre, GEN COMM cadrer, correspondre à

correspondence *n (corr.)* COMMS correspondance *f (corresp.)* GEN COMM *letters* correspondance *f*, courrier *m*; ~ **school** WEL établissement d'enseignement par correspondance *m*

correspondent *n* BANK, FIN correspondant *m*, HRM journaliste *mf*, MEDIA correspondant *m*, envoyé *m*, journaliste *mf*; ~ **bank** BANK banque correspondante *f*

corresponding *adj* GEN COMM *equivalent* correspondant

corroborate *vt* GEN COMM corroborer

corrosion *n* IND corrosion *f*; ~ **damages** *n pl* INS dommages imputables à la corrosion *m pl*; ~ **-resistant material** *n* IND, TRANSP matière résistante à la corrosion *f*, matériau résistant à la corrosion *m*

corrugated: ~ **container** *n* TRANSP conteneur ondulé *m*

corrupt *vt* POL, S&M corrompre

corruption *n* GEN COMM, POL, S&M corruption *f*

corset *n infrml* BANK, ECON, FIN, POL contrôle de la masse monétaire *m*, encadrement du crédit *m*

cos *abbr* MATH *(cosine)* cos *(cosinus)*, TRANSP *(cash on shipment) shipping* comptant à l'expédition *m*

COSHH *abbr UK (control of substances hazardous to health)* HRM, IND *regulations* contrôle des matières dangereuses pour la santé *m*, contrôle des substances présentant un danger pour la santé *m*

cosign *vt* GEN COMM, LAW cosigner

cosignatory[1] *adj* GEN COMM, LAW cosignataire

cosignatory[2] *n* GEN COMM, LAW cosignataire *mf*

cosine *n (cos)* MATH cosinus *m (cos)*

cost:[1] ~ **-effective** *adj* ACC productif, rentable, GEN COMM rentable; ~ **-sensitive** *adj* ECON, GEN COMM, S&M *customer* sensible au coût, sensible au niveau des coûts

cost[2] *n* ECON, FIN, S&M coût *m*; ~ **accounting** *n* ACC comptabilité analytique *f*, comptabilité industrielle *f*, FIN, MGMNT comptabilité analytique *f*;

~ **allocation** *n* ACC affectation des charges *f*, ventilation des coûts *f*; ~ **amount** *n* TAX coût indiqué *m*; ~ **analysis** *n* ACC, FIN analyse des coûts *f*; ~ **application** *n* ECON affectation d'un coût *f*, imputation d'un coût *f*; ~ **apportionment** *n* ACC répartition des charges *f*, ventilation des coûts *f*; ~ **approach** *n* FIN, PROP approche par les coûts *f*; ~ **awareness** *n* GEN COMM, S&M connaissance des coûts *f*, sensibilité aux coûts *f*; ~ **base** *n* TAX prix de base *m*; ~ **-benefit analysis** *n* FIN analyse coûts-avantages *f*, analyse coûts-rendements *f*, rapport coûts-avantages *m*; ~ **of borrowing** *n* BANK frais d'emprunt *m pl*; ~ **of carry** *n* FIN coût de portage *m*, STOCK frais de portage *m pl*; ~ **center** *n AmE*, ~ **centre** *n BrE* ACC centre de coût *m*; ~ **of compliance** *n* ENVIR coût de mise en conformité *m*; ~ **consciousness** *n* GEN COMM conscience des coûts *f*, sensibilité aux coûts *f*; ~ **containment** *n* ECON, FIN compression du prix de revient *f*, resserrement des coûts *m*; ~ **control** *n* ACC maîtrise des coûts *f*; ~ **-effectiveness** *n* ACC rapport coût-efficacité *m*, rentabilité *f*, ECON rentabilité *f*, FIN rapport coût-efficacité *m*, rentabilité *f*, GEN COMM, PROP, S&M, STOCK rentabilité *f*; ~ **-effectiveness analysis** *n* ACC, ECON, FIN, S&M, STOCK analyse de rentabilité *f*, analyse du rapport coût-efficacité *f*; ~ **escalation cover** *n UK* INS garantie contre la hausse des prix *f*; ~ **estimate** *n* GEN COMM devis estimatif *m*, estimatif *m*, estimation *f*, estimation des coûts *f*; ~ **factor** *n* ACC facteur coût *m*, élément du coût *m*; ~ **forecast** *n* ACC prévision de coûts *f*; ~ **of freight** *n* TRANSP *shipping* coût de fret *m*; ~ **of funds** *n* BANK, FIN coût des capitaux *m*; ~ **of funds plus** *n* BANK coût majoré des fonds *m*; ~ **of goods manufactured** *n* ACC, ECON, IND coût des marchandises produites *m*; ~ **of goods sold** *n* ACC, ECON, IND coût de la production vendue *m*; ~ **leader** *n* ECON entreprise leader pour les coûts *f*; ~ **of living** *n* ECON, GEN COMM coût de la vie *m*; ~ **of a loan** *n* BANK *to lender* coût d'un prêt *m*; ~ **of meals and lodging** *n* TAX frais de repas et de logement *m pl*; ~ **method** *n* ACC *for intercorporate investments* comptabilisation à la valeur d'acquisition *f*, *inventory* méthode d'évaluation des stocks au prix coûtant *f*; ~ **objective** *n* ECON coût limite *m*; ~ **-of-living adjustment** *n US (COLA)* ACC indexation des salaires *f*, ECON, HRM indexation des salaires *f*, indexation sur le coût de la vie *f*; ~ **-of-living allowance** *n* GEN COMM, HRM, WEL indemnité de vie chère *f*; ~ **-of-living index** *n* ECON, WEL indice du coût de la vie *m*; ~ **-of-living tax allowance** *n* TAX crédit d'impôt pour le coût de la vie *m*; ~ **-of-living tax credit** *n Canada* TAX crédit d'impôt pour le coût de la vie *m*; ~ **overrun** *n* ECON dépassement des coûts *m*; ~ **per vehicle mile** *n* TRANSP prix du kilomètre-véhicule *m*; ~ **price** *n* GEN COMM prix d'achat *m*, prix de revient *m*; ~ **of proceedings** *n* GEN COMM frais de procédure *m pl*; ~ **of production** *n* ACC, FIN, IND coût de production *m*; ~ **-push inflation** *n* ECON inflation générée par augmentation de coûts *f*, inflation par les coûts *f*, inflation par les prix de revient *f*; **~ ratio** *n* ACC ratio du prix coûtant au prix de détail *m*; **~ records** *n pl UK* STOCK dossier de coût *m*, enregistrements des coûts *m pl*; **~ reduction** *n* ACC, ECON, FIN, GEN COMM réduction des coûts *f*; **~ of replacement** *n* INS frais de remplacement *m pl*; **~ of sales** *n* ACC coût de la production vendue *m*, ECON coût d'achat des marchandises vendues *m*, coût de la production vendue *m*, IND coût de la production vendue *m*, S&M coût d'achat des marchandises vendues *m*; **~ -shared program** *n AmE*, **~ -shared programme** *n BrE* POL programme à frais partagés *m*; **~ standard** *n* ACC, ECON coût standard *m*, FIN, GEN COMM coût standard *m*, norme de prix de revient *f*; **~ structure** *n* ACC, FIN, GEN COMM structure des coûts *f*; **~ of treatment** *n* INS frais de traitement *m pl*; **under ~ freight rate** *n* TRANSP *distribution* tarif fret à perte *m*; **~ variance** *n* ACC, FIN, GEN COMM, HRM, S&M, STOCK écart de prix *m*; **~ -volume-profit analysis** *n* ACC, FIN analyse coûts-volume-profits *f*; **♦ at ~** GEN COMM au prix de revient, à prix coûtant; **~ and freight** *(C&F)* IMP/EXP *to named port of destination*, TRANSP coût et fret *(C&F)*; **~ and insurance** *(C&I, c&i)* IMP/EXP coût et assurance *(C&A)*; **~, insurance and freight** *(CIF)* IMP/EXP, TRANSP coût, assurance, fret *(CAF)*; **~, insurance, freight and commission** *(CIF&C)* IMP/EXP coût, assurance, fret et commission; **~, insurance, freight, commission and exchange** *(CIFC&E)* IMP/EXP coût, assurance, fret, commission et change; **~, insurance, freight, commission and interest** *(CIFC&I)* IMP/EXP coût, assurance, fret, commission et intérêt; **~, insurance, freight and interest** *(CIF&I)* IMP/EXP coût, assurance, fret et intérêt; **~, insurance, freight, interest and exchange** *(CIFI&E)* IMP/EXP coût, assurance, fret, intérêt et change; **~, insurance, freight landed** TRANSP *cargo delivery* coût, assurance, fret à quai; **~, insurance and freight/war** *(CIFW)* IMP/EXP coût, assurance et fret/guerre

COST *abbr (European Cooperation in Science and Technology)* IND Coopération européenne en matière de science et de technologie *f*

Costa:[1] **~ Rican** *adj* GEN COMM costaricien

Costa:[2] **~ Rican** *n* GEN COMM *person* Costaricien *m*

Costa:[3] **~ Rica** *pr n* GEN COMM Costa Rica *m*

costing *n* ACC établissement des prix de revient *m*, établissement du coût de production *m*, évaluation des coûts *f*

costly *adj* GEN COMM *action* qui coûte cher *loc*, *materials* coûteux, onéreux

costs *n pl* ECON, FIN coûts *m pl*, dépens *m pl*, frais *m pl*, LAW dépens *m pl*, frais *m pl*, S&M coûts *m pl*, dépens *m pl*, frais *m pl*; **~ of clearance of debris** INS frais de déblaiement *m pl*; **~ taxable to sb** TAX frais à la charge de qn *m pl*

COT *abbr (customer's own transport)* TRANSP transport privé du client *m*

cotenancy *n* PROP colocation *f*

cotenant *n* PROP colocataire *mf*

cottage: **~ industry** *n* IND industrie artisanale *f*

cotton *n* IND, STOCK coton *m*

COU *abbr (clip-on unit)* TRANSP groupe frigorifique amovible *m*

couchette *n* TRANSP *train/boat passenger accommodation* couchette *f*

cough: **~ up** *vi infrml BrE* GEN COMM casquer (*infrml*)

COUGRs *abbr (Certificates of Government Receipts)* FIN ≈ FELIN *(Fonds d'État libres d'intérêt nominal)*, STOCK certificats émis par le gouvernement et rémunérés par des émissions de bons de Trésor, ≈ FELIN *(Fonds d'État libres d'intérêt nominal)*

council *n* ADMIN *UK* ≈ municipalité *f*, *local government* conseil municipal *m*, GEN COMM *meeting*, HRM *meeting*, MGMNT *meeting* conseil *m*, POL *local government* conseil municipal *m*, *UK* ≈ municipalité *f*; **~ block** *n UK (cf public housing unit US)* PROP, WEL habitation à loyer modéré *f*, HLM; **~ flats** *n pl UK (cf public housing unit US)* PROP, WEL habitation à loyer modéré *f*, HLM; **~ tax** *n UK* TAX, WEL ≈ impôts locaux *m pl (France)*

Council: **~ of Economic Advisers** *n (CEA)* ECON Comité des conseillers économiques *m*, Réunion des conseillers économiques *f*; **~ of Europe** *n (CE)* POL Conseil de l'Europe *m (CE)*; **~ of Europe Resettlement Fund** *n (CERF)* BANK Fonds de rétablissement du conseil de l'Europe *m (FRCE)*; **~ for Mutual Economic Aid** *n (CMEA, COMECON)* ECON Conseil de l'aide économique mutuelle *m (COMECON)*; **~ of Ministers** *n* ECON *EU* Conseil des ministres *m*; **~ of State** *n* POL Conseil d'État *m*; **~ of the Stock Exchange** *n UK* STOCK ≈ CBV, ≈ Conseil des bourses de valeurs *m*

councillor *n* ADMIN *member of a council*, POL *member of a council* conseiller *m*

counsel[1] *n* GEN COMM, HRM conseiller *m*, LAW *advice* conseil *m*, consultation *f*, *lawyer* avocat *m*; **~ for the prosecution** *UK (cf prosecuting attorney US)* LAW avocat général *m*

counsel[2] *vt* LAW conseiller, recommander, *criminal* inciter au crime

counseling *n AmE*, **counselling** *n BrE* ADMIN, GEN COMM, HRM, MGMNT, STOCK conseils *m pl*

counsellor *n* GEN COMM, HRM conseiller *m*

count:[1] **~ of indictment** *n* LAW chef d'accusation *m*, chef d'inculpation *m*

count[2] *vt* COMP, GEN COMM, MATH compter, POL *votes* décompter; **~ up** COMP, GEN COMM, MATH compter

counter[1] *n* BANK caisse *f*, comptoir *m*, guichet *m*, FIN guichet *m*, GEN COMM *shop* caisse *f*, comptoir *m*, *supermarket* caisse *f*; **~ -advertising** S&M publicité sur comptoir *f*; **~ check** *AmE see counter cheque BrE*; **~ check form** *AmE see counter cheque form BrE*; **~ cheque** *BrE* BANK chèque de guichet *m*, chèque omnibus *m*; ~ **cheque form** *BrE* BANK bordereau de chèque de guichet *m*; ~ **purchase** ECON *international* achat de compensation *m*, compensation *f*; ~ **trade** ECON commerce de compensation *m*, commerce de troc *m*

counter² *vt* GEN COMM contrer, faire opposition à *loc f*

counteract *vt* GEN COMM compenser, contrecarrer, neutraliser

counterbalance *vt* GEN COMM contrebalancer

counterclaim *n* LAW demande reconventionnelle *f*

counterfeit¹ *n* LAW contrefaçon *f*

counterfeit² *vt* ACC, BANK, GEN COMM, LAW contrefaire

counterfeiter *n* LAW contrefacteur *m*

counterfeiting *n* LAW contrefaçon *f*

countermand *vt* GEN COMM décommander

countermark *n* GEN COMM contremarque *f*

countermeasure *n* GEN COMM contre-mesure *f*, mesure de compensation *f*

counteroffer *n* S&M contre-offre *f*

counterpart *n* ECON *in foreign exchange deal* contrepartie *f*

counterparty *n* *UK* STOCK contrepartie *f*

countersign *vt* GEN COMM contresigner

countervailing: ~ **duties** *n pl* IMP/EXP droits compensatoires *m pl*; ~ **power** *n* ECON contrepoids *m*, pouvoir compensatoire *m*

counting *n* GEN COMM comptage *m*

country:¹ ~ **-damaged** *adj* IMP/EXP endommagé à l'origine; ~ **-specific** *adj* ECON *development aid* spécifique à un pays

country² *n* GEN COMM pays *m*; ~ **club at the top** *jarg* MGMNT membre d'un club ou détenteur d'une carte de crédit; ~ **code** BANK code de pays *m*; ~ **damage** IMP/EXP, INS avarie aux marchandises due au mauvais temps *f*, avarie avant embarcation *f*; ~ **of destination** IMP/EXP pays destinataire *m*; ~ **exposure** ECON risque-pays *m*; ~ **fund** *UK* STOCK fonds national *m*; ~ **of origin** *(COO)* GEN COMM provenance *f*, GEN COMM, IMP/EXP pays d'origine *m*; ~ **report** ECON rapport pays *m*; ~ **risk** FIN *provisions* risque lié au pays *m*, risque-pays *m*; ~ **of ultimate risk** GEN COMM pays à haut risque *m*; ~ **whence consigned** *(CWC)* TRANSP pays d'expédition *m*

Countryside: ~ **Commission** *n* *UK* ENVIR commission pour la campagne; ~ **Council for Wales** *n* ENVIR commission galloise de protection des espaces naturels

county *n* *UK* GEN COMM ≈ comté *m*, ≈ département *m*; ~ **council** *UK* *(CC)* GEN COMM ≈ conseil général *m*; ~ **court** LAW tribunal civil *m*, tribunal d'instance *m*; ~ **seat** *AmE*, ~ **town** *BrE* GEN COMM chef-lieu de comté *m*

County: ~ **Hall** *n* *UK* GEN COMM siège du conseil de comté

coupled: ~ **with** *adj* COMP, GEN COMM ajouté à,

apparié à, en communication directe avec *loc f*, raccordé à

coupon *n* FIN coupon *m*, GEN COMM *money-off* bon *m*, coupon *m*, S&M *advertising* bon de réduction *m*, point-cadeau *m*, timbre-épargne *m* (*vieilli*), STOCK coupon *m*; ~ **bond** FIN obligation à coupons *f*; ~ **rate** STOCK taux d'intérêt contractuel *m*, taux d'intérêt nominal *m*; ~ **registered bond** FIN obligation nominative à coupons *f*; ~ **yield** STOCK rendement coupon *m*

courier *n* COMMS coursier *m*, messager *m*; ~ **firm** COMMS entreprise de messageries *f*; ~ **service** COMMS messagerie *f*

Cournot's: ~ **duopoly model** *n* ECON modèle du duopole de Cournot *m*

course *n* GEN COMM *progress* cours *m*, WEL cours *m* (*jarg*); ~ **of action** MGMNT cours de l'action *m*, ligne de conduite *f*; ♦ **in the ~ of a business** TAX dans le cours d'une entreprise; **in the ~ of carrying on a business** TAX dans le cadre de l'exploitation d'une entreprise; **in the ~ of earning income** TAX en tirant un revenu de; **in the ~ of negotiations** GEN COMM au cours des négociations

court *n* LAW cour *f*, tribunal *m*; ~ **of arbitration** *n* LAW cour d'arbitrage *f*, juridiction d'arbitrage *f*; ~ **of competent jurisdiction** *n* LAW tribunal compétent *m*; ~ **entitled to adjudicate** *n* LAW juridiction compétente *f*; ~ **of inquiry** *n* *UK* HRM commission d'enquête *f*; ~ **of law** *n* LAW cour de justice *f*, palais de justice *m*; ~ **order** *n* LAW décision de justice *f*, décision judiciaire *f*, ordonnance *f*, ordonnance de la cour *f*, ordonnance du tribunal *f*, ordre *m*; ~ **of petty session** *n* LAW justice de paix *f*; ~ **procedure** *n* LAW procédure judiciaire *f*; ~ **proceedings** *n pl* LAW débats *m pl*, poursuites judiciaires *f pl*; ~ **of record** *n* *US* LAW tribunal dont les actes font foi jusqu'à inscription en faux; ♦ **~ is now in session** LAW le tribunal est en cours d'audience, le tribunal est en séance

Court: ~ **of Appeal** *n* *(CA)* LAW cour d'appel *f*, ≈ Cour de cassation *m* (*France*); ~ **of Auditors** *n* ACC *EC* Cour des comptes *f*; ~ **of First Instance** *n* LAW, POL *European Union* tribunal de grande instance *m*, tribunal de première instance *m*; ~ **of Justice** *n* LAW, POL *European Union* Cour de justice *f*

covariance *n* MATH *statistics* covariance *f*

covenant *n* LAW contrat *m*, convention *f*, engagement formel *m*; ~ **not to compete** LAW convention de non-concurrence *f*

covenantor *n* LAW contractant *m*, partie contractante *f*

cover¹ *n* COMP *peripheral, device* capot *m*, carter *m*, housse *f*, INS *BrE (cf coverage AmE)* couverture *f*, STOCK *(C'vr)* couverture *f*, garantie *f*; ~ **against stranding** INS garantie contre l'échouement *f*; ~ **note** *(CN)* INS lettre de couverture *f*, note de couverture *f*, police provisoire *f*; ~ **ratio** ACC, FIN taux de couverture *m*

cover[2] *vt* FIN *loss* absorber, couvrir, GEN COMM *payments* couvrir, faire face à, INS, STOCK couvrir; **~ up** GEN COMM cacher, dissimuler; ♦ **~ the cost of** GEN COMM couvrir les frais de

coverage *n* INS *AmE (cf cover BrE)* couverture *f*, LEIS *sport* retransmission *f*, MEDIA ensemble des informations *m*; **~ fees** *n pl* LEIS *sport* droits de retransmission *m pl*; ♦ **give a lot of media ~ to** MEDIA médiatiser

covered[1] *adj* INS, STOCK *call or put option* couvert; ♦ **be ~** INS avoir des garanties; **~ by insurance** INS couvert par l'assurance

covered:[2] **~ call** *n* UK (ANT *uncovered call*) STOCK option d'achat couverte *f*, option d'achat sur titres détenus *f*; **~ call option** *n* (ANT *uncovered call option*) STOCK option d'achat couverte *f*; **~ call write** *n* (ANT *covered put write*) STOCK option d'achat couverte *f*; **~ dry container** *n* TRANSP *shipping* conteneur sec fermé *m*; **~ gangway** *n* TRANSP *shipping* passerelle couverte *f*; **~ long** *n* STOCK *options* achat d'option couverte *m*; **~ option** *n* STOCK option couverte *f*; **~ option securities** *n pl* (*COPS*) STOCK titre d'une option couverte *m*; **~ option writing** *n* STOCK vente couverte *f*, vente d'options couvertes *f*; **~ position** *n* UK STOCK *options* position couverte *f*; **~ put** *n* STOCK put couvert *m*, vente d'option couverte *f*; **~ put write** *n* (ANT *covered call write*) STOCK option d'achat à découvert *f*; **~ short** *n* STOCK *options* vente d'option couverte *f*; **~ short position** *n* STOCK position vendeur couverte *f*; **~ warrant** *n* FIN warrant couvert *m*; **~ writer** *n* STOCK vendeur de call couvert *m*

covering: **~ letter** *n* ADMIN, COMMS lettre confirmative *f*, lettre d'introduction *f*, lettre de couverture *f*

COW *abbr* TRANSP *(collection on wheels)* enlèvement par route *m*, TRANSP *(crude oil washing) shipping* lavage au brut *m*

cowboy *n* *infrml* IND cow-boy *m* (*infrml*); **~ economy** *infrml* *AmE* (SYN *spaceman economy*) ECON économie du gaspillage et de l'irresponsabilité

co-worker *n* HRM collaborateur *m*, collègue *mf*

C/P: **~ bill of lading** *n* *(charter party bill of lading)* IMP/EXP, TRANSP *shipping* connaissement charte-partie *m*

CP *abbr* BANK *(commercial paper)* BT *(billet de trésorerie)*, ECON *(Community Programme)* TUC *(travaux d'utilité collective)*, FIN *(commercial paper)* papier commercial *m*, GEN COMM *(coupon)* c., coup. *(coupon)*, GEN COMM *(commercial paper)* effet de commerce *m*, papier commercial *m*, HRM *(Community Programme)*, POL *(Community Programme)* TUC *(travaux d'utilité collective)*, TRANSP *(charter party) shipping* charte-partie *f*, WEL *(Community Programme)* TUC *(travaux d'utilité collective)*

CPA *abbr* ACC *US (certified public accountant)*

expert-comptable *m*, ECON *(critical path analysis)* analyse du chemin critique *f*

cpd *abbr* *(charterer's pay dues)* TRANSP *shipping* rémunération de l'affréteur *f*

CPE *abbr* *(centrally-planned economy)* ECON, POL économie planifiée *f*

CPI *abbr* *(consumer price index)* ACC, ECON *econometrics* IPC *(indice des prix à la consommation)*

CPM *abbr* *(critical path method)* ECON, GEN COMM, MATH méthode du chemin critique *f*

CPO *abbr* *(chief petty officer)* HRM, TRANSP premier maître *m*

CPP *abbr* *(current purchasing power)* ECON pouvoir d'achat courant *m*

CPR *abbr* *(Canadian Pacific Railway)* TRANSP compagnie des chemins de fer canadienne

CPS *abbr* ECON *US (current population survey)* ≈ études comparatives de la population *f pl*, ECON *UK (Centre for Policy Studies)* Centre des études politiques *m*

CPT *abbr* *(carriage paid to)* IMP/EXP port payé jusqu'à *loc m*

CPU *abbr* *(central processing unit)* COMP UC *(unité centrale)*

Cr *abbr* ACC *(credit)* cr. *(crédit)*, ACC *(creditor)*, BANK *(creditor)* créditeur *m*, FIN *(credit)* cr. *(crédit)*, FIN *(creditor)* créditeur *m*, GEN COMM *(credit)* cr. *(crédit)*, HRM *(creditor)* créditeur *m*, TRANSP *(crane)* grue *f*

CR *abbr* COMP *(carriage return)* retour de chariot *m*, retour de curseur *m*, GEN COMM *(current rate)* taux actuel *m*, taux courant *m*, TRANSP *(change request)* RFC *(requête formulée par le client)*, TRANSP *(carrier's risk)* aux risques et périls du transporteur *loc m*, risque du transporteur *m*, TRANSP *(change request)* réaménagement *m*

craft: **~ loss** *n* *(cl)* TRANSP *shipping* perte d'embarcation *f*; **~ union** *n* HRM syndicat de métier *m*

craftsman *n* HRM artisan *m*

crane *n* *(Cr)* TRANSP grue *f*; **~ driver** TRANSP grutier *m*; **~ -jib-type fork-lift truck** TRANSP *cargo handling* chariot élévateur à grue *m*; **~ operator** TRANSP grutier *m*

crash[1] *n* COMP panne *f*, plantage *m*, écrasement *m*, STOCK krach *m*, TRANSP accident *m*, écrasement *m*

crash[2] *vi* COMP se planter *(infrml)*, tomber en panne, STOCK *prices, economic activity* s'effondrer, TRANSP avoir un accident *loc m*, s'écraser

crate *n* TRANSP caisse *f*, caisse à claire-voie *f*

crawling: **~ peg** *n* ECON parité à crémaillère *f*; **~ peg system** *n* ECON régime de parité à crémaillère *m*

CRC *abbr* *(camera-ready copy)* MEDIA *print* copie prête à filmer *f*, copie prête à la reproduction *f*, copie prête à reproduire *f*

CRE *abbr* UK *(Commercial Relations and Exports)*

IMP/EXP relations commerciales et exportations *f pl*

cream:[1] **the ~ of the crop** *n infrml* HRM la fine fleur *f*

cream:[2] **~ off** *vt* GEN COMM *money, demand* prélever, écrémer

create *vt* ECON *demand* créer, GEN COMM *agency* créer, fonder, *opportunities* créer, dégager, S&M *market* créer; ♦ **~ a charge on a property** TAX créer une sûreté sur un bien

creation *n* GEN COMM création *f*

creative: **~ accounting** *n* ACC comptabilité assouplie *f*, comptabilité créative *f*; **~ department** *n* S&M service création *m*; **~ destruction** *n* ECON destruction créatrice *f*; **~ federalism** *n* POL fédéralisme créateur *m*; **~ marketing** *n* S&M créativité commerciale *f*, marketing de création *m*; **~ strategy** *n* S&M *advertising* stratégie de création *f*; **~ thinking** *n* GEN COMM, MGMNT imagination *f*, matière grise *f*, pensée créatrice *f*

creativeness *n* GEN COMM créativité *f*

creativity *n* GEN COMM créativité *f*

credentials *n pl* HRM états de service *m pl*

credibility *n* GEN COMM crédibilité *f*

credit[1] *n (Cr)* ACC, FIN, GEN COMM *liabilities* crédit *m (cr.)*; **~ account** *n (C/A)* ACC, BANK compte d'achats à crédit *m*; **~ account voucher** *n* BANK justificatif de compte créditeur *m*; **~ adviser** *n* FIN conseiller en crédit *m*; **~ advisor** *n* FIN conseiller en crédit *m*; **~ agency** *n* ADMIN, FIN agence d'évaluation de la solvabilité *f*; **~ agreement** *n* BANK, FIN accord de crédit *m*, GEN COMM accord de crédit *m*, convention de crédit *f*; **~ analysis** *n* BANK, STOCK analyse de crédit *f*; **~ analyst** *n* BANK, STOCK analyste *mf*; **~ balance** *n* BANK, FIN solde créditeur *m*; **~ bureau** *n* FIN *credit information* agence de notation *f*, agence de rating *f*, bureau de cotation *m*; **~ buyer** *n AmE (cf charge buyer BrE)* S&M acheteur à crédit *m*; **~ card** *n* ACC, BANK carte de crédit *f*; **~ card booking** *n* LEIS location par carte de crédit *f*; **~ card call** *n* COMMS appel carte de crédit *m*; **~ -card imprinter** *n* BANK, GEN COMM imprimante à cartes *f*, presse imprimante de cartes magnétiques *f*; **~ card issuer** *n* BANK, GEN COMM organisme émetteur de cartes de crédit *m*, émetteur de cartes de crédit *m*; **~ card payment** *n* BANK paiement par carte *m*, règlement par carte *m*; **~ card transaction** *n* GEN COMM opération sur carte de crédit *f*; **~ ceiling** *n* GEN COMM découvert autorisé *m*, limite de crédit *f*, plafond de crédit *m*; **~ column** *n* ACC, FIN colonne créditrice *f*, colonne des crédits *f*; **~ conditions** *n pl* BANK, ECON, FIN, S&M conditions de crédit *f pl*; **~ control** *n* BANK, ECON, FIN, POL contrôle du crédit *m*, encadrement du crédit *m*; **~ controller** *n* BANK, FIN vérificateur des crédits *m*, HRM vérificateur des crédits *m (Can)*; **~ counsellor** *n* FIN conseiller en crédit *m*; **~ department** *n* BANK service du crédit *m*; **~ entry** *n* ACC écriture passée au crédit *f*; **~ facility** *n* BANK facilité de crédit *f*;

~ granting *n* BANK concession de crédit *f*, délivrance de crédit *f*, mise à disposition de crédit *f*, octroi de crédit *m*; **~ grantor** *n* BANK distributeur de crédit *m*, fournisseur de crédit *m*; **~ guarantee** *n* GEN COMM caution *f*; **~ history** *n* BANK antécédents en matière de crédit *m pl*; **~ information** *n* ACC renseignements sur crédit *m pl*; **~ institution** *n* BANK, FIN établissement de crédit *m*; **~ instrument** *n* STOCK *interest rate futures* titre de créance *m*; **~ insurance** *n* INS assurance crédit *f*; **~ limit** *n* GEN COMM découvert autorisé *m*, limite de crédit *f*, plafond de crédit *m*; **~ line** *n* BANK (SYN *bank line*), FIN *(cf bank line, line of credit AmE)* autorisation de crédit *f*, crédit autorisé *m*, ligne de crédit *f*, ligne de découvert *f*, marge de crédit *f (Can)*; **~ loss** *n* GEN COMM créance irrécouvrable *f*, perte sur créance *f*; **~ management** *n* ACC, FIN gestion de créances *f*; **~ market** *n* GEN COMM marché du crédit *m*; **~ memorandum** *n* FIN bulletin de versement *m*; **~ money** *n* BANK, FIN monnaie fiduciaire *f*; **~ multiplier** *n* FIN multiplicateur de crédit *m*; **~ note** *n (CN)* FIN, GEN COMM note de crédit *f*; **~ officer** *n* FIN agent de crédit *m*; **~ order** *n* S&M commande à crédit *f*; **~ outstanding** *n* ACC crédits en cours *m pl*, encours de crédit *m*; **~ policy** *n* GEN COMM politique de crédit *f*; **~ protection insurance** *n UK* INS assurance protection de crédit *f*; **~ rating** *n* FIN degré de solvabilité *m*, réputation de solvabilité *f*, standing *m*, tranche de crédit *f*, évaluation du crédit *f*, S&M réputation de solvabilité *f*; **~ rating system** *n* FIN, GEN COMM système d'évaluation de la solvabilité *m*; **~ reference agency** *n* FIN agence de notation *f*, agence de rating *f*, bureau de cotation *m*; **~ report** *n* ACC, GEN COMM rapport de solvabilité *m*; **~ requirements** *n pl* BANK, ECON, FIN, S&M conditions de crédit *f pl*; **~ reserves** *n pl* FIN provisions de crédit *f pl*; **~ restriction** *n* BANK, ECON, FIN, POL encadrement du crédit *m*; **~ risk** *n* FIN risque de contrepartie *m*, S&M risque de crédit *m*; **~ sale** *n* S&M vente à crédit *f*; **~ score** *n* FIN *calculated by finance house* notation *f*; **~ scoring** *n* FIN dépôts en devises *m pl*, multiplicateur de crédit *m*, évaluation du crédit *f*; **~ side** *n* ACC, FIN côté du crédit *m*; **~ slip** *n* GEN COMM bulletin de versement *m*; **~ squeeze** *n* BANK, ECON, FIN, POL encadrement du crédit *m*, restriction du crédit *f*; **~ standing** *n* FIN, S&M réputation de solvabilité *f*; **~ tranche** *n* FIN tranche de crédit *f*; **~ tranche facility** *n* ECON tranche de crédit *f*; **~ transfer** *n* BANK virement *m*; **~ union** *n* BANK, FIN caisse de crédit *f*, caisse populaire *f*; **~ voucher** *n* GEN COMM bon de remboursement *m*, bulletin de versement *m*

credit[2] *vt* ACC, BANK *account*, FIN créditer

Credit: **~ Industry Fraud Avoidance System** *n UK (CIFAS)* FIN système anti-fraude de l'industrie du crédit *m*; **~ suisse index** STOCK indice du Crédit Suisse *m*

creditable[1] *adj* TAX donnant droit à un crédit *loc m*

creditable:[2] ~ **input tax** *n* TAX taxe sur intrants donnant droit à un crédit *f*

credited: ~ **to** *adj* FIN porté au crédit de

creditor *n* ACC compte fournisseur *m*, ACC *(Cr)* créditeur *m*, ADMIN, BANK créancier *m*, BANK *(Cr)* créditeur *m*, FIN créancier *m*, prêteur *m*, FIN *(Cr)* HRM *(Cr)* créditeur *m*, LAW créancier *m*; ~ **department** ADMIN ministère créancier *m*; ~ **position** ACC situation des dettes dues aux fournisseurs *f*; ~ **rights life assurance** *(SYN creditor rights life insurance)* INS bénéficiaire à titre onéreux *m*, créancier bénéficiaire *m*; ~ **rights life insurance** *(SYN creditor rights life assurance)* INS bénéficiaire à titre onéreux *m*, créancier bénéficiaire *m*

creditors': ~ **committee** *n* FIN commission de créanciers *f*; ~ **ledger** *n* ACC livre des créditeurs *m*

creditworthiness *n* FIN, GEN COMM solvabilité *f*

creditworthy *adj* FIN, GEN COMM solvable

creeping: ~ **inflation** *n* ECON inflation larvée *f*, inflation rampante *f*; ~ **tender** *n* FIN, STOCK *takeovers* offre rampante *f*

cremation: ~ **expenses insurance** *n* INS assurance des frais d'incinération *f*

Creole *n* GEN COMM *language* créole *m*

CREST *abbr (Committee on Scientific and Technical Research)* IND comité pour la recherche scientifique et technique

crew *n* TRANSP équipage *m*; ~ **agreement** *UK* TRANSP *shipping* contrat d'embauche *m*; ~ **manifest** TRANSP *shipping* déclaration d'équipage *f*; ~ **manning** TRANSP *shipping* affectation de l'équipage *f*; ~ **member** TRANSP *shipping* membre d'équipage *m*

CRI *abbr (consumption rate of interest)* FIN taux d'intérêt à la consommation *m*

crime *n* LAW crime *m*, délit *m*

criminal[1] *adj* LAW criminel

criminal:[2] ~ **negligence** *n* LAW faute grave *f*; ~ **offence** *n* LAW délit *m*, infraction pénale *f*

crisis *n* BANK crise *f*, ECON crise *f*, récession *f*, FIN crise *f*, GEN COMM, HRM, POL récession *f*; ~ **management** MGMNT gestion des crises *f*

criterion *n* [pl -ria] GEN COMM critère *m*

critic *n* GEN COMM critique *m*

critical[1] *adj* COMP critique, GEN COMM *crucial* critique, décisif

critical:[2] ~ **level** *n* GEN COMM seuil critique *m*; ~ **mass** *n* ECON, GEN COMM, S&M masse critique *f*; ~ **path** *n* COMP *planning* chemin critique *m*; ~ **path analysis** *n (CPA)* ECON analyse du chemin critique *f*; ~ **path method** *n (CPM)* ECON, GEN COMM, MATH méthode du chemin critique *f*; ~ **path theory** *n* ECON, GEN COMM, MATH méthode du chemin critique *f*; ~ **region** *n* MATH *statistical testing* zone critique *f*; ~ **success** *n* LEIS *theatre* succès d'estime *m*; ~ **value** *n* MATH *statistics* valeur critique *f*

criticize *vt* GEN COMM critiquer

CRN *abbr (customs registered number)* IMP/EXP numéro d'inscription douanière *m*

CRO *abbr (Companies Registration Office)* GEN COMM, LAW ≈ RCS *(Registre du commerce et des services)*

Croat *n* GEN COMM *person* Croate *mf*

Croatia *pr n* GEN COMM Croatie *f*

Croatian *adj* GEN COMM croate

crook *n infrml* LAW escroc *m*

crooked: ~ **lawyer** *n infrml* LAW avocat marron *m*

crop[1] *n* ECON culture *f*, récolte *f*, ENVIR, GEN COMM récolte *f*; ~ **failure** ECON, ENVIR *agricultural* perte de récolte *f*; ~ **hail insurance** INS assurance contre la grêle *f*, assurance des récoltes contre la grêle *f*; ~ **rotation** ECON, ENVIR assolement *m*, rotation des cultures *f*

crop:[2] **if anything should ~ up** *phr* GEN COMM en cas d'empêchement *loc m*

cross:[1] ~ **-border** *adj* GEN COMM transnational

cross[2] *n* STOCK transaction dont l'achat et la vente sont assurés par le même courtier; ~ **assembler** *n* COMP assembleur croisé *m*; ~ **-border demergers** *n pl* ECON déconcentrations transfrontières *f pl*; ~ **-border financial transaction** *n* FIN transaction financière transfrontalière *f*; ~ **-border joint venture** *n* MGMNT entreprise internationale *f*; ~ **-border merger** *n* ECON fusion transfrontière *f*, fusion transnationale *f*, GEN COMM fusion transnationale *f*, STOCK fusion transfrontière *f*; ~ **-border trade** *n* ECON commerce transfrontalier *m*; ~ **-border trading** *n* GEN COMM commerce frontalier *m*, IMP/EXP commerce frontalier *m*, échanges aux frontières *m pl*; ~ **-border transaction** *n* ECON transaction transfrontières *f*; ~ **check** *n AmE*, ~ **cheque** *n BrE* BANK chèque barré *m*; ~ **couponing** *n* S&M *promotion* couponnage croisé *m*; ~ **-currency exposure** *n* ECON *international trade*, FIN risque des parités croisées *m*; ~ **-currency swap** *n* FIN crédit croisé *m*; ~ **default** *n* BANK, FIN défaut croisé *m*; ~ **demand** *n* TAX demande reconventionnelle *f*; ~ **elasticity of demand** *n* ECON, S&M élasticité croisée de la demande *f*; ~ **-footing** *n* MATH *spreadsheet* positions croisées *f pl*; ~ **-frontier transfer** *n* TRANSP *of hazardous waste* transfert entre frontières *m*; ~ **guarantee** *n* BANK cautionnement réciproque *m*; ~ **hedge** *n* STOCK couverture croisée *f*; ~ **hedging** *n* STOCK couverture croisée *f*; ~ **holdings between companies** *n pl* STOCK participation croisée *f*; ~ **liability** *n* INS recours entre coassurés *m*, responsabilité croisée *f*; ~ **licensing** *n* COMP *technology transfer* création de licence croisée *f*, GEN COMM, LAW concession réciproque de licences *f*; ~ **member** *n* TRANSP *of container* transverse *f*; ~ **merchandising** *n UK* S&M présentation de produits complémentaires côte à côte; ~ **price elasticity of demand** *n* ECON, S&M élasticité croisée de la demande par rapport au prix *f*; ~ **rate** *n* ECON, FIN parité croisée *f*; ~ **reference** *n* COMP référence croisée *f*; ~ **refer-**

ence listing *n* COMP liste de correspondances *f*; ~ **section** *n* GEN COMM coupe transversale *f*, profil *m*, vue en coupe *f*, *of population* portrait complet *m*, échantillon représentatif *m*; ~ **section data** *n* (*CSD*) ECON *econometrics* données croisées *f pl*; ~ **subsidization** *n* FIN dépôts en devises *m pl*, GEN COMM interfinancement *m*; ~ **subsidy** *n* FIN aide d'interfinancement *f*; ~ **tabulation** *n* MATH *statistics* résultats croisés *m pl*

cross[3] *vt* BANK *cheque* barrer, IMP/EXP *frontier*, LEIS *frontier*, TRANSP *frontier* traverser; ~ **hedge** STOCK faire une couverture croisée; ♦ ~ **a picket line** HRM traverser un cordon de grévistes; ~ **specially** BANK *cheque* barrer spécialement

cross-Channel: ~ **trade** *n* ECON commerce trans-Manche *m*, S&M *international trade* commerce avec l'Europe continentale *m*, commerce trans-Manche *m*

crossed: ~ **check** *n AmE*, ~ **cheque** *n BrE* BANK chèque barré *m*; ~ **trade** *n* STOCK transaction croisée *f*

crossover: ~ **vote** *n US* POL transfert de vote *m*

cross-ownership *n* GEN COMM, MEDIA interpro-priété *f*; ~ **test** *n* TAX critère de propriété croisée *m*; ~ **threshold** *n* TAX seuil de propriété croisée *m*

CROTUM *abbr UK* (*commissioner for the rights of trade union members*) HRM délégué chargé des droits des membres des syndicats

crowd[1] *n* STOCK groupe de négociation *m*

crowd:[2] ~ **out** *vt* ECON *borrowers, investors*, FIN évincer

crowding: ~ **hypothesis** *n* ECON hypothèse de la discrimination par l'excédent d'offre de main-d'oeuvre pour une catégorie d'emploi donnée; ~ **out** *n* ECON *of borrowing, investment*, FIN effet d'éviction *m*

crown: ~ **jewels** *n infrml* ECON joyaux de la couronne *m pl*

Crown: ~ **corporation** *n* ADMIN société d'État *f*; ~ **royalty** *n* TAX redevance à la Couronne *f*; ~ **share** *n* TAX part de la Couronne *f*

CRT *abbr* (*cathode ray tube*) COMP *hardware* TRC (*tube à rayons cathodiques*)

crude: ~ **carrier** *n* ENVIR, TRANSP navire pétrolier *m*; ~ **goods** *n pl* GEN COMM produits bruts *m pl*; ~ **oil** *n* ENVIR, IND pétrole brut *m*; ~ **oil emulsion** *n* ENVIR, TRANSP *shipping, sea water* émulsion de pétrole brut *f*; ~ **-oil refinery** *n* ENVIR, IND raffinerie de pétrole brut *f*; ~ **oil washing** *n* (*COW*) TRANSP *shipping, in tankers* lavage au brut *m*; ~ **petroleum** *n* ENVIR, IND pétrole brut *m*

cruzeiro *n* GEN COMM cruzeiro *m*

cryogenic *n* TRANSP liquide cryogénique *m*; ~ **liquid** TRANSP liquide cryogénique *m*

CS *abbr* ECON (*continuous stocktaking*) inventaire permanent *m*, GEN COMM (*civil service*) Administration *f*, fonction publique *f*, GEN COMM (*continuous stocktaking*) inventaire permanent *m*, inventaire en cours *m*, TRANSP (*case*) caisse *f*,

TRANSP (*curtain-sided trailer*) remorque à ridelles *f*, TRANSP (*continuous survey*) *shipping* reclassification continue *f*, TRANSP (*continuous hull survey, continuous survey of the hull quoting date*) *shipping* visite de la coque en vue d'une reclassification continue *f*

CSC *abbr* ADMIN (*Civil Service Commission*) ≈ Commission de la fonction publique *f*, GEN COMM (*continuous survey cycle*) cycle d'enquête permanent *m*, TRANSP (*container safety convention*) accord de sécurité sur les conteneurs *m*

CSD *abbr* ECON (*cross section data*) données croisées *f pl*, TRANSP (*closed shelter deck*) *shipping* navire à pont-abri couvert *m*, pont-abri fermé *m*

CSG *abbr* (*Consultative Shipping Group*) TRANSP groupe maritime consultatif

csl *abbr* (*counsel*) LAW avocat *m*, conseil *m*, consultation *f*

CSO *abbr UK* (*Central Statistical Office*) ECON ≈ INSEE (*Institut national de la statistique et des études économiques*)

CST *abbr* GEN COMM *US* (*Central Standard Time*) heure normale des États du centre des États-Unis *f*, TRANSP (*container service tariff*) tarif du service conteneur *m*

CT *abbr* ENVIR (*cargo tank*) citerne de cargo *f*, citerne à cargaison *f*, GEN COMM (*cubic tonnage*) tonnage cube *m*, IMP/EXP (*customs transaction code*) code de transaction des douanes *m*, IMP/EXP (*Community transit*) transit communautaire *m*, TRANSP (*cargo tank*) citerne de cargo *f*, citerne à cargaison *f*, TRANSP (*customs transaction code*) code de transaction des douanes *m*, TRANSP (*Community transit*) transit communautaire *m*, TRANSP (*combined transport*) transport combiné *m*, transport multimodal *m*

CTBL *abbr* (*combined transport bill of lading*) IMP/EXP, TRANSP connaissement de transport combiné *m*

CTC *abbr* (*cargo tank centre*) TRANSP citerne centrale de cargaison *f*

CTD *abbr* STOCK (*cheapest to deliver*) OMCL (*obligation la moins chère à livrer*), TRANSP (*combined transport document*) document de transport combiné *m*

CTL *abbr* (*constructive total loss*) INS *shipping* perte censée totale *f*, perte réputée totale *f*, perte totale relative *f*

CTLO *abbr* (*constructive total loss only*) INS *marine* perte censée totale uniquement *f*, perte réprimée totale seulement *f*

CTN *n* (*confectioner*) S&M marchand de journaux-buraliste *m*

CTO *abbr* (*combined transport operator*) TRANSP ETC (*entrepreneur de transport combiné*)

CTPC *abbr* (*cargo traffic procedures committee*) GEN COMM, TRANSP commission pour les procédures de mouvement de cargaisons *f*

ctr *abbr* (*cutter*) TRANSP *shipping* cotre *m*, vedette *f*

CTRL: ~ **key** *abbr (control key)* COMP touche CTRL *f (touche de contrôle)*

CTT *abbr (capital transfer tax)* TAX droits de mutation *m pl*

CTW *abbr (cargo tank wing)* TRANSP *shipping* citerne latérale *f*

C-20 *abbr (Committee of Twenty)* GEN COMM Comité des Vingt *m*

CTX *abbr (cargo tank common)* TRANSP *shipping* citerne standard *f*

cu *abbr (cubic)* GEN COMM cube; ~ **ft** *(cubic feet)* GEN COMM pied cube *m*; ~ **in** *(cubic inch)* GEN COMM pouce cube *m*

Cuba *pr n* GEN COMM Cuba *f*

cubage *n* TRANSP *volume* cubage *m*

Cuban[1] *adj* GEN COMM cubain

Cuban[2] *n* GEN COMM *person* Cubain *m*

cubature *n* TRANSP *volume* cubage *m*

cube:[1] ~ **-cutting** *n* TRANSP *shipping* déclaration frauduleuse de cubage *f*

cube:[2] ~ **out** *vi* TRANSP dépasser le cubage

cubic[1] *adj (cu)* GEN COMM cube

cubic:[2] ~ **capacity** *n (cc)* GEN COMM cylindrée *f (cc)*; ~ **centimeter** *n AmE*, ~ **centimetre** *n BrE (cc)* GEN COMM centimètre cube *m (cm³)*; ~ **contents** *n pl* TRANSP *volume* cubage *m*; ~ **feet** *n (CF, cu ft)* GEN COMM pied cube *m*; ~ **inch** *n (cu in)* GEN COMM pouce cube *m*; ~ **meter** *n AmE*, ~ **metre** *n BrE (cbm)* GEN COMM mètre cube *m (m³)*; ~ **tonnage** *n (CT)* GEN COMM *of a ship* tonnage cube *m*

CUKCC *abbr (Canada-United Kingdom Chamber of Commerce)* ECON chambre de commerce anglo-canadienne

cul: ~ **-de-sac** *n* PROP, TRANSP cul-de-sac *m*

culminate: ~ **in** *vt* GEN COMM aboutir à, se solder par

culpable *adj* LAW coupable

cultivated: ~ **acreage** *n* TAX superficie cultivée *f*

cultivation *n* ECON *agricultural* culture *f*

cultural[1] *adj* GEN COMM, LEIS, MEDIA culturel

cultural:[2] ~ **center** *n AmE*, ~ **centre** *n BrE* GEN COMM centre culturel *m*; ~ **revolution** *n* POL révolution culturelle *f*

culture *n* GEN COMM, LEIS, MEDIA culture *f*; ~ **shock** GEN COMM choc culturel *m*

cum:[1] ~ **and ex** *adj* STOCK avec et sans

cum[2] *prep (ANT ex)* STOCK avec; ◆ ~ **coupon** STOCK coupon attaché *m*; ~ **dividend** *(cd)* STOCK *with dividend still to be paid* avec dividende, coupon attaché *m*, dividende attaché *m*; ~ **rights** STOCK avec droits, droits attachés *m pl*; ~ **rights period** STOCK période avec droits *f*; ~ **warrant** STOCK avec droit de souscription, avec warrant

cum. *abbr (cumulative)* ACC, STOCK *dividends* cum. *(cumulatif)*

cumulative[1] *adj (cum.)* ACC, STOCK *dividends* cumulatif *(cum.)*

cumulative:[2] ~ **deduction account** *n* TAX compte des déductions cumulatives *m*; ~ **dividend** *n* STOCK dividende cumulatif *m*; ~ **eligible capital** *n* TAX montant cumulatif des immobilisations admissibles *m*; ~ **gains limit** *n* TAX plafond des gains cumulatifs *m*; ~ **imputed amount** *n* TAX montant cumulatif imputé *m*; ~ **liability** *n* INS responsabilité cumulative *f*; ~ **net capital loss** *n* TAX perte en capital nette cumulative *f*; ~ **net investment loss** *n* TAX perte nette cumulative sur placement *f*; ~ **net taxable capital gain** *n* TAX gain en capital imposable net cumulatif *m*; ~ **offset account** *n* TAX compte compensatoire cumulatif *m*; ~ **penetration** *n* S&M audience cumulée *f*; ~ **preference share** *n BrE (cf cumulative preferred stock AmE)* STOCK action de priorité cumulative *f*; ~ **preferred stock** *n AmE (cf cumulative preference share BrE)* STOCK action de priorité cumulative *f*; ~ **security** *n* STOCK valeur cumulative *f*; ~ **small business gains account** *n* TAX compte des gains cumulatifs d'une petite entreprise *m*; ~ **voting** *n* POL vote plural *m*, STOCK *of stockholders* vote cumulatif *m*

cupidity *n* GEN COMM cupidité *f*

curable: ~ **depreciation** *n* ECON dépréciation non-irrémédiable *f*

curator *n* FIN, LAW, PROP *bankruptcy* curateur *m*

curb: ~ **market** *n US* STOCK marché hors bourse *m*

Curb: **the** ~ *n infrml (SYN AMEX, American Stock Exchange)* FIN, STOCK la bourse de New York secondaire où sont listées les valeurs qui n'apparaissent pas au New York Stock Exchange

currency *n (CY)* BANK monnaie *f*, ECON, FIN devise *f*, monnaie *f*; ~ **accounts** *n pl* FIN tranche de crédit *f*; ~ **adjustment factor** *n (CAF)* TRANSP *shipping* surcharge monétaire *f*; ~ **appreciation** *n* ECON, FIN appréciation d'une devise *f*, appréciation d'une monnaie *f*, appréciation monétaire *f*; ~ **arbitrage** *n* STOCK arbitrage sur devises *m*; ~ **basket** *n* ECON, FIN panier de devises *m*; ~ **of a bill** *n* ACC échéance d'une traite *f*; ~ **and bunker adjustment factor** *n (CABAF)* TRANSP *shipping* surcharge monétaire et de soutage *f*; ~ **call option** *n (ANT currency put option)* STOCK option d'achat sur devises *f*; ~ **code** *n* BANK code de la devise *m*; ~ **contract** *n* STOCK *money market* contrat sur devise *m*; ~ **deposits** *n pl* FIN dépôts en devises *m pl*; ~ **depreciation** *n* ECON, FIN dépréciation d'une monnaie *f*, dépréciation monétaire *f*; ~ **devaluation** *n* ECON dévaluation d'une monnaie *f*, dévaluation monétaire *f*; ~ **draft** *n* BANK traite en devises *f*; ~ **futures** *n pl* FIN, STOCK contrat à termes de change *m*, contrat à termes de devises *m*; ~ **futures contract** *n* FIN, STOCK contrat à termes de change *m*, contrat à termes de devises *m*; ~ **futures market** *n* STOCK marché à terme de devises *m*; ~ **holdings** *n pl* ECON, FIN avoirs en devises *m pl*; ~ **in circulation** *n* ECON devises en circulation *f*, monnaie en circulation *f*; ~ **linked** *n* FIN option de monnaies *f*; ~ **market** *n* FIN marché des changes *m*; ~ **mix** *n* BANK composition en devises *f*; ~ **option** *n* STOCK contrat d'option sur devises *m*, option de change *f*, option sur devises *f*; ~ **options contract** *n* STOCK contrat d'option sur devises *m*, option sur devises *f*; ~ **options seller** *n* STOCK vendeur d'options sur devises *m*; ~ **options writer** *n* STOCK vendeur d'options sur devises *m*; ~ **put option** *n* (ANT *currency call option*) STOCK option de vente sur devises *f*; ~ **reform** *n* ECON réforme monétaire *f*; ~ **reordering** *n* FIN, IMP/EXP réaménagement des devises *m*; ~ **restriction** *n* ECON restriction monétaire *f*; ~ **revaluation** *n* ECON réévaluation d'une monnaie *f*, réévaluation monétaire *f*; ~ **risk** *n* ECON *macroeconomics*, FIN risque de change *m*; ~ **stabilization scheme** *n* ECON projet de stabilisation monétaire *m*; ~ **standard** *n* STOCK étalon devise *m*; ~ **swap** *n* FIN échange de devises *m*, échange à terme de devises *m*, STOCK échange à terme de devises *m*; ~ **symbol** *n* COMP symbole monétaire *m*; ~ **unit** *n* BANK, ECON, FIN unité monétaire *f*; ~ **value** *n* BANK, ECON, FIN taux de change *m*; ~ **zone** *n* GEN COMM zone monétaire *f*

Currency: ~ **School** *n* UK ECON école monétariste *f*

current¹ *adj* GEN COMM en cours, *exchange rate* actuel, courant; ◆ **at ~ prices** GEN COMM au prix actuel

current² *n* COMP, IND courant *m*, courant électrique *m*; ~ **account** *n* ACC, FIN, GEN COMM *BrE* (*C/A, checking account AmE*) compte courant *m* (*c/c*); ~ **account balance** *n* *BrE* BANK, GEN COMM solde de compte courant *m*; ~ **account customer** *n* *BrE* BANK titulaire d'un compte courant *m*; ~ **account holder** *n* *BrE* BANK titulaire d'un compte courant *m*; ~ **account surplus** *n* *BrE* BANK, ECON excédent des opérations courantes *m*, excédent du compte courant *m*; ~ **adaptor** *n* *AmE* (*cf mains adaptor BrE*) COMP, IND adaptateur secteur *m*; ~ **affairs** *n pl* MEDIA, POL l'actualité *f*; ~ **annuity** *n* INS rente en cours *f*, rente en cours de paiement *f*; ~ **assets** *n pl* (ANT *current liability*) ACC actif circulant *m*; ~ **assumption whole life insurance** *n* INS assurance-vie entière hypothèse courante *f*; ~ **blend** *n* STOCK panachage à court terme *m*; ~ **business year** *n* ACC, FIN, TAX exercice en cours *m*; ~ **cost** *n* ACC coût courant *m*, coût de remplacement *m*, ECON, INS coût de remplacement *m*; ~ **cost accounting** *n* (*CCA*) ACC comptabilité aux coûts de remplacement *f*, comptabilité de coûts courants *f*; ~ **cost basis** *n* ACC base de prix de revient actuel *f*; ~ **dollars** *n pl* ACC, ECON dollars courants *m pl*; ~ **domestic value** *n* (*CDV*) IMP/EXP valeur intérieure actuelle *f*; ~ **economic trend** *n* ECON, GEN COMM, POL conjoncture *f*, conjoncture actuelle *f*, tendance économique actuelle *f*; ~ **entry price** *n* ACC prix d'entrée actuel *m*; ~ **event** *n* GEN COMM événement d'actualité *m*; ~ **events** *n pl* GEN COMM l'actualité *f*; ~ **expenditure** *n* FIN frais d'exploitation actuels *m pl*; ~ **fiscal plan** *n* TAX plan financier de l'exercice courant *m*; ~ **fiscal year** *n* TAX exercice courant *m*; ~ **grants to persons** *n pl* ECON transferts courants vers les particuliers *m pl*;

~ **holdings** *n pl* STOCK participations actuelles *f pl*; ~ **insurance** *n* INS assurance en cours *f*, assurance en vigueur *f*; ~ **liability** *n* (ANT *current assets*) BANK dette à court terme *f*; ~ **loop** *n* COMP *for transferring data* boucle de courant *f*; ~ **market price** *n* S&M, STOCK cours du marché *m*, prix courant du marché *m*; ~ **market value** *n* S&M valeur marchande actuelle *f*, STOCK valeur au cours du marché *f*, valeur marchande actuelle *f*; ~ **operating profit** *n* ACC bénéfice d'exploitation actuel *m*; ~ **population survey** *n* US (*CPS*) ECON ≈ études comparatives de la population *f pl*; ~ **price** *n* ECON prix courant *m*, FIN prix courant *m*, tarif *m*; ~ **purchasing power** *n* (*CPP, inflation accounting*) ECON pouvoir d'achat courant *m*; ~ **rate** *n* (*CR*) GEN COMM taux actuel *m*, taux courant *m*; ~ **rate method** *n* *AmE* (*cf closing rate method BrE*) ACC *of currency translation for consolidated accounts* système des taux de clôture *m*; ~ **ratio** *n* ACC coefficient de liquidité *m*, ratio de liquidité générale *m*, ratio de solvabilité à court terme *m*, ratio du fonds de roulement *m*, BANK coefficient de liquidité *m*, ratio de liquidité générale *m*, FIN, STOCK coefficient de liquidité *m*, ratio de liquidité *m*, taux de liquidité *m*; ~ **return** *n* STOCK *annual income from an investment* rendement actuel *m*, rendement courant *m*; ~ **revenues** *n pl* ACC, FIN recettes courantes *f pl*; ~ **risk** *n* ECON risque actuel *m*; ~ **savings account** *n* BANK compte d'épargne courant *m*; ~ **spending** *n* ECON dépenses courantes *f pl*, dépenses en cours *f pl*; ~ **stock** *n* STOCK stock en cours *m*; ~ **value** *n* ACC, BANK, FIN valeur actuelle *f*; ~ **value accounting** *n* ACC comptabilité de la valeur actuelle *f*; ~ **year** *n* GEN COMM année en cours *f*, exercice en cours *m*; ~ **year disposition** *n* TAX disposition de l'année courante *f*; ~ **yield** *n* STOCK rendement actuel *m*, rendement courant *m*, taux actuariel *m*

currently *adv* BANK, GEN COMM actuellement

curriculum *n* GEN COMM programme d'études *m*, WEL programme *m*, programme d'études *m*; ~ **vitae** ADMIN (*CV*), GEN COMM (*CV*), HRM (*CV, résumé*) curriculum vitae *m* (*CV*)

cursor *n* COMP curseur *m*; ~ **control pad** COMP clavier de commande du curseur *m*

curtailment *n* GEN COMM *of programme* raccourcissement *m*

curtain: ~ **-sided trailer** *n* (*CS*) TRANSP remorque à ridelles *f*

curtesy *n* LAW, PROP usage gracieux qui confère au mari des intérêts viagers sur les propriétés qui appartenaient à sa femme durant le mariage

curtilage *n* LAW, PROP enclos avec habitation *m*, terrain entourant la maison d'habitation *m*

curve *n* ECON, MATH courbe *f*

curvilinear: ~ **relationship** *n* MATH *statistics* rapport curviligne *m*

cushion: ~ **tire** *n* *AmE*, ~ **tyre** *n* *BrE* TRANSP bandage creux *m*

CUSIP[1] *abbr US (Committee on Uniform Securities Identification Procedures)* STOCK ≈ AFC *(Agence française de codification)*

CUSIP:[2] ~ **number** *n* STOCK numéro CUSIP *m*, ≈ code de l'AFC *m*

custodian *n* LAW gardien *m*, STOCK conservateur de titres *m*, dépositaire *mf*, WEL gardien *m*; ~ **account fee** BANK droits de garde *m pl*; ~ **fee** BANK droits de garde *m pl*; ~ **of property** LAW administrateur séquestre *m*

custodianship: ~ **account** *n* BANK compte de dépôt de titres *m*

custody *n* LAW *of child* garde *f*, STOCK conservation *f*, WEL *of child* garde *f*; ~ **account** BANK compte de dépôt de titres *m*; ~ **account charge** BANK droits de garde *m pl*; ~ **charge** BANK droits de garde *m pl*; ~ **and control** LAW, WEL *of child* garde et surveillance *f*; ~ **of shares** STOCK conservation d'actions *f*

custom:[1] ~ **-made** *adj* GEN COMM fabriqué sur commande, fait sur mesure, IND fabriqué sur commande

custom[2] *n* GEN COMM usage *m, clientele* achalandage *m*, clientèle *f*, LAW coutume *f*; ~ **builder** PROP entrepreneur sur mesure *m*; ~ **fence** ECON, GEN COMM, IMP/EXP, POL barrière douanière *f*; ~ **of port** *(COP)* TRANSP usage du port *m*; ◆ ~ **and practice** HRM, IND habitudes et accords d'industrie *f pl*; ~ **and trade practices** HRM accords intersyndicaux et d'industrie en matière de politique sociale *m pl*

customary[1] *adj* LAW coutumier

customary:[2] ~ **despatch** *n* TRANSP célérité habituelle *f*, expédition ordinaire *f*; ~ **dispatch** *n see customary despatch* ; ~ **tare** *n* TAX tare d'usage *f*

customer:[1] ~ **-driven** *adj* COMP tributaire des clients; ~ **-orientated** *adj* GEN COMM axé sur la clientèle, orienté vers la clientèle *loc f*

customer[2] *n* GEN COMM, S&M client *m*; ~ **account** *n* FIN compte client *m*; ~ **awareness** *n* S&M mémorisation *f*; ~ **base** *n* S&M clientèle *f*; ~ **billing** *n* ACC facturation des clients *f*; ~ **card** *n* ACC fiche de client *f*; ~ **care** *n* S&M attention portée aux besoins de la clientèle *loc f*, souci du client *m*; ~ **confidence** *n* S&M confiance de la clientèle *f*; ~ **liaison** *n* GEN COMM, S&M liaison avec la clientèle *f*; ~ **needs** *n pl* S&M besoins de la clientèle *m pl*; ~ **orientation** *n* S&M orientation vers le client *f*; ~'**s own transport** *n (COT)* TRANSP transport privé du client *m*; ~ **profile** *n* S&M profil de la clientèle *m*; ~ **relations manager** *n* HRM directeur des relations avec la clientèle *m*; ~ **research** *n* S&M *market research* étude des besoins de la clientèle *f*; ~ **service** *n* GEN COMM service clientèle *m*, S&M service à la clientèle *m*; ~ **-service representative** *n* HRM représentant du service clientèle *m*; ~ **support** *n* S&M support client *m*

customers *n pl* GEN COMM clientèle *f*; ~' **ledger** *n* ACC, BANK, FIN grand livre auxiliaire des clients

m, grand livre des ventes *m*; ~' **net debit balance** *n* STOCK solde débiteur net des clients *m*

customize *vt* COMP *hardware, software* personnaliser, IND *production* fabriquer sur mesure, personnaliser

customized[1] *adj* COMP *solution*, GEN COMM *solution*, S&M personnalisé

customized:[2] ~ **keyboard** *n* COMP clavier personnalisé *m*; ~ **service** *n* S&M service personnalisé *m*

customs *n pl* LEIS douane *f*, TAX droits de douane *m pl*; ~ **additional code** *n (CAC)* IMP/EXP, TRANSP code supplémentaire des douanes *m*; ~ **agency** *n* IMP/EXP agence de transit en douane *f*; ~ **arrangements** *n pl* GEN COMM, IMP/EXP régime douanier *m*; ~ **barrier** *n* COM, ECON, IMP/EXP, POL barrière douanière *f*; ~ **broker** *n* HRM courtier en douane *m*, IMP/EXP courtier en douane *m, shipping* commissionnaire en douane *m*; ~ **cargo clearance** *n* IMP/EXP formalités douanières d'une cargaison *f pl*; ~ **check** *n* IMP/EXP vérification douanière *f*; ~ **clearance** *n (CCL)* IMP/EXP dédouanement *m*; ~ **clearance agent** *n* IMP/EXP agent du dédouanement *m*; ~ **clearance status** *n (CCS)* IMP/EXP état de dédouanement *m*; ~ **collector** *n* IMP/EXP receveur des douanes *m*; ~ **consignee** *n* IMP/EXP, TRANSP consignataire douanier *m*; ~ **convention on the international transit of goods** *n (ITI)* IMP/EXP convention douanière sur le transit international des marchandises *f*; ~ **court** *n US* IMP/EXP, LAW tribunal réglant les litiges douaniers *m*; ~ **declaration** *n (CD)* IMP/EXP, TRANSP *shipping* déclaration en douane *f*; ~ **duty** *n* IMP/EXP droits de douane *m pl*; ~ **entry** *n* IMP/EXP déclaration en douane *f*; ~ **examination** *n* IMP/EXP vérification douanière *f*; ~ **formalities** *n pl* IMP/EXP formalités douanières *f pl*; ~ **house report** *n* IMP/EXP rapport de bureau de douane *m*; ~ **invoice** *n* IMP/EXP facture de douane *f*; ~ **officer** *n* HRM agent en douane *m*, douanier *m*, HRM *UK* employé des douanes britanniques, receveur *m*, IMP/EXP agent en douane *m*, douanier *m*; ~ **pre-entry exports** *n pl* IMP/EXP déclaration en douane avant exportation *f*; ~ **pre-entry imports** *n pl* IMP/EXP déclaration en douane avant importation *f*; ~ **procedure** *n* IMP/EXP procédure douanière *f*; ~ **registered number** *n (CRN)* IMP/EXP numéro d'inscription douanière *m*; ~ **regulations** *n pl* IMP/EXP règlements douaniers *m pl*; ~ **service** *n* IMP/EXP service des douanes *m*; ~ **station** *n* IMP/EXP poste de douane *m*; ~ **tariff** *n* IMP/EXP tarif douanier *m*; ~ **transaction code** *n (CT)* IMP/EXP, TRANSP code de transaction des douanes *m*; ~ **union** *n* ECON, HRM, IMP/EXP union douanière *f*; ~ **valuation** *n* IMP/EXP évaluation douanière *f*; ~ **value per gross kilogram** *n AmE*, ~ **value per gross kilogramme** *n BrE (CVGK)* IMP/EXP valeur en douane par kilo brut *f*; ~ **value per gross pound** *n (CVGP)* IMP/EXP valeur en douane par livre brute *f*; ◆ **no** ~ **value** *(n.c.v.)* IMP/EXP sans valeur douanière

Customs: ~ **Co-operation Council** *n (CCC)* IMP/

EXP conseil de la coopération douanière; **~ Co-operation Council nomenclature** *n (CCCN)* IMP/EXP nomenclature du conseil de coopération douanière; **~ and Excise** *n UK (C&E)* IMP/EXP administration des douanes *f*, régie *f*; **~ and Excise department** *n UK* IMP/EXP service des douanes *m*; **~ and Excise Management Act** *n (CEMA)* IMP/EXP, LAW loi régissant l'administration des impôts indirects et des droits de douanes

cut¹ *n* ACC, ECON, FIN restriction *f*; **~ paper** COMP papier feuille à feuille *m*

cut² *vt* COMP *software* couper, ECON *prices* brader, FIN comprimer, GEN COMM casser, couper, S&M *prices* brader, TAX alléger; **~ back** HRM comprimer; **~ down** HRM comprimer; ◆ **~ one's losses** GEN COMM faire la part du feu, réduire les pertes; **~ and paste** COMP couper-coller; **~ the rates** HRM casser les prix

cutback *n* ACC, ECON, FIN, GEN COMM coupe sombre *f*, réduction des coûts *f*

cutoff: **~ bank reconciliation** *n* BANK rapprochement bancaire de contrôle *m*; **~ date** *n* BANK date butoir *f*, date du relevé périodique des chèques *f*, FIN *international* date butoir *f*; **~ period** *n* BANK bilan périodique des chèques *m*, relevé périodique des chèques *m*; **~ point** *n* ECON *capital budgeting* point butoir *m*, FIN, TAX plafond *m*; **~ procedures** *n pl* ACC procédures de clôture des comptes *f pl*, procédures de fin d'exercice *f pl*

cutter *n (ctr)* TRANSP *shipping* cotre *m*, vedette *f*

cutthroat: **~ competition** *n* ECON, GEN COMM, HRM, IND, S&M concurrence acharnée *f*, concurrence féroce *f*, concurrence sauvage *f*

cutting *n* FIN compression *f*, MEDIA *BrE (cf clipping AmE) from newspaper* article *m*, coupure *f*, coupure de journal *f*, coupure de presse *f*

CUV *abbr (construction unit value)* TRANSP valeur de l'unité de construction *f*

CV *abbr* ADMIN *(curriculum vitae)*, GEN COMM *(curriculum vitae)* CV *(curriculum vitae)*, GEN COMM *(chief value)* valeur principale *f*, HRM *(curriculum vitae)* CV *(curriculum vitae)*, IMP/EXP *UK (certificate of value)* attestation de valeur *f*

CVGK *abbr (customs value per gross kilogram, customs value per gross kilogramme)* IMP/EXP valeur en douane par kilo brut *f*

CVGP *abbr (customs value per gross pound)* IMP/EXP valeur en douane par livre brute *f*

CVMO *abbr (commercial value movement order)* GEN COMM bon de transfert de marchandise *m*

CVO *abbr UK (certificate of value and origin)* IMP/EXP attestation de valeur et d'origine *f*

C'vr *abbr (cover)* STOCK couverture *f*, garantie *f*

cw *n (call waiting)* COMMS, COMP appel en attente *m*

CW *abbr Australia (comparable worth)* HRM principe adopté en 1972 dont le but est de payer les travailleurs de façon égale. Il a introduit trois phases uniformes afin d'éviter la discrimination sexuelle

CWC *abbr (country whence consigned)* TRANSP pays d'expédition *m*

CWE *abbr (cleared without examination)* IMP/EXP dédouanement sans inspection *m*

CWM *abbr (clerical work measurement)* ADMIN, HRM chronométrage des travaux administratifs *m*

CWO *abbr (cash with order)* FIN, GEN COMM, S&M paiement à la commande *m*, payable à la commande

CWS *abbr (Cooperative Wholesale Society)* GEN COMM coopérative de gros *f*, société coopérative de consommation *f*

cwt *abbr* GEN COMM *US (hundredweight)* 45,36 kg, GEN COMM *UK (hundredweight)* 50,8 kg

CXBG *abbr (comprehensive extended-term banker's guarantee)* BANK garantie bancaire globale de longue durée *f*

CY *abbr* BANK *(currency)* monnaie *f*, ECON *(currency)*, FIN *(currency)* devise *f*, monnaie *f*, TRANSP *(cylinder)* cylindre *m*, TRANSP *(container yard)* dépôt de conteneurs *m*

cybernetics *n* COMP cybernétique *f*

CYCLD *abbr (cycloidal propeller)* TRANSP *shipping* hélice cycloïdale *f*

cycle *n* ACC, ECON, FIN, GEN COMM, IMP/EXP, IND, STOCK cycle *m*; **~ insurance** INS assurance des bicyclettes *f*; **~ stock** STOCK valeurs cycliques *f pl*

cyclic: **~ variation** *n* ECON variation conjoncturelle *f*

cyclical¹ *adj (ANT noncyclical)* ECON, FIN, GEN COMM, STOCK cyclique

cyclical:² **~ company** *n* STOCK entreprise cyclique *f*; **~ demand** *n* ECON demande cyclique *f*; **~ fluctuation** *n* STOCK *in commodity prices* valeurs cycliques *f pl*; **~ industry** *n* ECON, IND industrie cyclique *f*; **~ stock** *n* ECON, STOCK stock conjoncturel *m*; **~ trade** *n* ECON commerce cyclique *m*, commerce sensible à la conjoncture *m*, GEN COMM, S&M commerce cyclique *m*; **~ unemployment** *n* ECON, HRM chômage conjoncturel *m*, chômage cyclique *m*; **~ variations** *n pl* ECON, GEN COMM variations cycliques *f pl*

cycloidal: **~ propeller** *n (CYCLD)* TRANSP *shipping* hélice cycloïdale *f*

cylinder *n* COMP, TRANSP cylindre *m*

cylindrical: **~ fire tube boiler** *n (CFTB)* TRANSP *shipping* chaudière cylindrique ignitubulaire *f*, chaudière cylindrique à tubes de fumée *f*; **~ water tube boiler** *n* TRANSP *shipping* chaudière cylindrique aquatubulaire *f*, chaudière cylindrique à tubes d'eau *f*; **~ water tube boiler survey** *n* TRANSP *shipping* visite de la chaudière cylindrique aquatubulaire *f*, visite de la chaudière cylindrique à tubes d'eau *f*

cymogene *n* IND, TRANSP *classified cargo* cymogène *m*

Cypriot¹ *adj* GEN COMM chypriote, cypriote

Cypriot² *n* GEN COMM *person* Chypriote *mf*, Cypriote *mf*

Cyprus *pr n* GEN COMM Chypre *f*

Czech[1] *adj* GEN COMM tchèque

Czech[2] *n* GEN COMM *language* tchèque *m, person* Tchèque *mf*

Czech:[3] ~ **Republic** *pr n* GEN COMM République tchèque *f*

Czechoslovak[1] *adj obs* GEN COMM tchécoslovaque (*obs*)

Czechoslovak[2] *n* GEN COMM *person* Tchécoslovaque *mf* (*obs*)

Czechoslovakia *pr n obs* GEN COMM appelée la République tchèque depuis 1989, Tchécoslovaquie *f* (*obs*)

Czechoslovakian[1] *adj obs* GEN COMM tchécoslovaque (*obs*)

Czechoslovakian[2] *n* GEN COMM *person* Tchécoslovaque *mf* (*obs*)

D

D *abbr* COMMS *(delivery)*, GEN COMM *(delivery)* livr. *(livraison)*, HRM, MGMNT *(director)*, D *(directeur)*, STOCK *(delivery)*, TRANSP *(delivery)* livr. *(livraison)*, TRANSP *(diagonal engine)* moteur diagonal *m*, TRANSP *(dry bulk container) shipping* conteneur à pulvérulents *m*

D/A *abbr* BANK *(deposit account)* compte de dépôt *m*, compte sur livret *m*, COMP *(design automation)* CAO *(conception assistée par ordinateur)*, COMP *(digital-analog)* N/A *(numérique-analogique)*, GEN COMM *(documents against acceptance)* documents contre acceptation *m pl*, GEN COMM *(days after acceptance)* jours après acceptation *m pl*, HRM *(defence advisor, defence attaché, defense advisor, defense attaché)* conseiller en matière de défense *m*, IND *(design automation)* CAO *(conception assistée par ordinateur)*, LAW *US (district attorney)* ≈ procureur de la République *m (France)*, ≈ procureur du Roi *m (Belgique)*, TRANSP *(discharge afloat) shipping* déchargement sur rade *m*

DAC *abbr* COMP *(digital-analog converter)* CNA *(convertisseur numérique-analogique)*, ECON *(Development Aid Committee, Development Assistance Committee)* comité d'aide au développement *m*

DAF *abbr (delivered at frontier)* IMP/EXP livraison à la frontière *loc f*, TRANSP livraison à la frontière *loc f*, rendu à la frontière

DAGAS *abbr (Dangerous Goods Advisory Service)* IMP/EXP, TRANSP service consultatif pour les produits dangereux

daily[1] *adj* GEN COMM journalier, quotidien

daily[2] *adv* GEN COMM quotidiennement, tous les jours *loc m*

daily[3] *n* MEDIA quotidien *m*; **~ activity report** GEN COMM relevé quotidien des opérations *m*; **~ allowance** INS allocation journalière *f*, allocation quotidienne *f*, indemnité journalière *f*; **~ balance interest calculation** BANK méthode par paliers *f*, méthode par échelles *f*; **~ closing balance** ACC solde quotidien à la fermeture *m*; **~ compensation** INS indemnité journalière *f*, indemnité quotidienne *f*; **~ deposit** BANK dépôt quotidien *m*; **~ interest** BANK intérêt quotidien *m*; **~ interest account** BANK compte à intérêt quotidien *m*; **~ interest deposit** BANK dépôt à intérêt quotidien *m*; **~ interest savings account** BANK compte d'épargne à intérêt quotidien *m*; **~ limit** STOCK écart maximal de cours *m*; **~ loan** BANK prêt au jour le jour *m*; **~ money rate** BANK taux au jour le jour *m*, taux d'argent au jour le jour *m*; **~ newspaper** MEDIA quotidien *m*; **~ position statement** ACC relevé quotidien de la situation *m*; **~ price limit** STOCK limite de fluctuation quotidienne *f*, limite de variation quotidienne *f*, options écart maximal de cours quotidien *m*; **~ publication** MEDIA quotidien *m*; **~ settlement** STOCK liquidation fictive quotidienne *f*; **~ settlement price** STOCK cours de clôture *m*, cours de compensation *m*; **~ trading limit** STOCK limite de variation quotidienne *f*, écart maximal de cours quotidien *m*; **~ volume** STOCK volume quotidien *m*

Daily: **~ Range Factor** *n (DRF)* STOCK facteur de la fourchette quotidienne plus haut-plus bas

dairy: **~ farm** *n* ECON *agricultural* ferme laitière *f*; **~ products** *n pl* GEN COMM produits laitiers *m pl*

daisy: **~ chain** *n* STOCK activité boursière fictive *f*; **~ -chain scheme** *n jarg* GEN COMM plan en chaîne *m*

daisywheel *n* COMP, MEDIA *printing* marguerite *f*, marguerite d'impression *f*; **~ printer** COMP, MEDIA imprimante à marguerite *f*

Dakar *pr n* GEN COMM Dakar *n pr*

dalasi *n* GEN COMM dalasi *m*

damage *n* GEN COMM *to goods, property* dégâts *m pl*, INS dommage *m*, dégâts *m pl*, LAW dommage *m*, *to company, reputation* atteinte *f*, TRANSP *to ship, shipment* avarie *f*, dommage *m*; **~ caused by fire** INS dommage causé par un incendie *m*, dégâts causé par un incendie *m*; **~ limitation** GEN COMM limitation des dommages *f*, limitation des dégâts *f*; **~ report** INS rapport d'expertise *m, ship, cargo* rapport d'avaries *m*; **~ survey** INS expertise des dégâts *f, ship, cargo* expertise des avaries *f*; **~ to goods in custody** INS dommages aux marchandises en entrepôt *m pl*; **~ to property** INS dégâts matériels *m pl*; **~ to rented property** INS dommages aux biens loués *m pl*, dégâts aux biens loués *m pl*; **~ whilst loading and unloading** INS dommages lors du chargement et du déchargement *m pl*

damaged *adj* GEN COMM, INS, TRANSP avarié; ♦ **~ in transit** TRANSP avarié en cours de route, endommagé en cours de route

damages *n pl* INS, LAW dommages et intérêts *m pl*, dommages-intérêts *m pl*

Damascus *pr n* GEN COMM Damas *n pr*

dampen *vt* ECON *growth* freiner, étouffer, GEN COMM *enthusiasm* doucher *(infrml)*, refroidir

Dane *n* GEN COMM *person* Danois *m*

danger *n* GEN COMM, HRM alerte *f*, danger *m*; **~ point** GEN COMM cote d'alerte *f*; ♦ **in ~ of** GEN COMM en danger de

Danger! *n* HRM *on notice, sign* Danger! *m*

dangerous: **~ cargo** *n* TRANSP marchandises dangereuses *f pl*; **~ cargo compound** *n* TRANSP entrepôt de marchandises dangereuses *m*; **~ goods** *n pl* GEN COMM, IND, S&M, TRANSP produits dangereux *m pl*; ~ **goods authority form** *n* TRANSP autorisation de transport de marchandises dangereuses *f*; ~ **goods note** *n (DGN)* TRANSP bordereau de marchandises dangereuses *m*; ~ **goods on board** *n (DGB)* TRANSP produits dangereux à bord *m pl*; ~ **goods rate** *n* TRANSP tarif applicable aux marchandises dangereuses *m*; ~ **goods regulations** *n pl* TRANSP règlement applicable aux marchandises dangereuses *m*; ~ **substance** *n* ENVIR substance dangereuse *f*, substance toxique *f*; ~ **waste** *n* ENVIR déchets dangereux *m pl*

Dangerous: ~ **Goods Advisory Service** *n (DAGAS)* IMP/EXP, TRANSP service consultatif pour les produits dangereux

Danish¹ *adj* GEN COMM danois

Danish² *n* GEN COMM *language* danois *m*

DAP *abbr (documents against payment)* GEN COMM DP *(documents contre paiement)*

Dar es Salaam *pr n* GEN COMM Dar es Salaam *n pr*

Dari *n* GEN COMM *language* dari *m*

dash *n* MEDIA *typography* tiret *m*, tiret cadratin *m*

dashed: ~ **line** *n* COMP ligne de pointillés *f*

data *n* COMP, ECON données *f pl*, GEN COMM données *f pl*, informations *f pl*; ~ **acquisition** *n* COMP, ECON acquisition de données *f*; ~ **bank** *n* COMP banque de données *f*, fichier central *m*; ~ **bit** *n* COMP bit d'information *m*; ~ **broadcasting** *n* COMMS diffusion de données *f*; ~ **bus** *n* COMP bus de données *m*; ~ **capture** *n* COMP saisie de données *f*; ~ **card** *n* COMP carte mécanographique *f*; ~ **carrier** *n* COMP transporteur de données *m*; ~ **collection** *n (SYN data gathering)* COMP collecte de données *f*, rassemblement de données *m*, recueil de données *m*; ~ **communications** *n pl* COMMS, COMP communication de données *f*, transmission de données *f*; ~ **communications equipment** *n (DCE)* COMP équipement de termination de circuit de données *m*; ~ **compression** *n* COMP compression de données *f*; ~ **conversion** *n* COMP conversion de données *f*; ~ **entry** *n* COMP introduction de données *f*, saisie de données *f*; ~ **entry keyboarder** *n* COMP opérateur de saisie de données *m*; ~ **entry terminal** *n* COMP unité de saisie *f*; ~ **field** *n* COMP champ de données *m*; ~ **file** *n* COMP fichier de données *m*; ~ **flow** *n* COMP circulation des données *f*; ~ **flow chart** *n* MATH, MGMNT organigramme de données *m*; ~ **freight receipt** *n (DFR)* TRANSP *shipping* document fret rapide *m*, reçu de chargement *m*; ~ **gathering** *n (SYN data collection)* COMP collecte de données *f*, rassemblement de données *m*, recueil de données *m*; ~ **handling** *n* COMP manipulation de données *f*; ~ **input** *n* COMP entrée de données *f*, saisie de données *f*; ~ **integrity** *n* COMP intégrité de données *f*; ~ **link** *n* COMP liaison de données *f*; ~ **management** *n* COMP gestion de données *f*; ~ **mining** *n* ECON *econometrics* zèle excessif dans l'analyse économétrique; ~ **network** *n* COMMS réseau informatique *m*, COMP réseau de données *m*, réseau informatique *m*; ~ **output** *n* COMP sortie

de données *f*; ~ **plate** *n* TRANSP *on container* plaque indicatrice *f*; ~ **preparation** *n* ADMIN, COMP préparation des données *f*; ~ **privacy** *n* BrE *(cf data security AmE)* COMP confidentialité des données *f*; ~ **processing** *n* ADMIN informatique *f*, COMP traitement de l'information *m*, traitement des données *m, service* informatique *f*, GEN COMM informatique *f*; ~ **processing insurance** *n* INS assurance informatique *f*, assurance sur le traitement des données *f*; ~ **protection** *n* COMP protection des données *f*; ~ **protection act** *n UK* COMP, LAW loi protégeant les données *f*; ~ **rate** *n* COMP vitesse de transmission de données *f*; ~ **retrieval** *n* COMP extraction de données *f*; ~ **security** *n AmE (cf data privacy BrE)* COMP confidentialité des données *f*; ~ **set** *n* COMP ensemble de données *m*; ~ **sharing** *n* COMP partage de données *m*; ~ **storage** *n* COMP mémorisation de données *f*, stockage de données *m*; ~ **stream** *n* GEN COMM flux de données *m*; ~ **structure** *n* COMP structure de données *f*; ~ **terminal equipment** *n (DTE)* COMP *hardware* équipement terminal de traitement de données *m (ETTD)*; ~ **transfer** *n* COMP transfert de données *m*; ~ **transfer rate** *n* COMP débit de transfert des données *m*; ~ **type** *n* COMP type de données *m*

database *n* COMP base de données *f*; ~ **management** COMP gestion de données *f*; ~ **management system** *(DBMS)* COMP système de gestion de bases de données *m (SGBD)*

Datapost® *n UK* COMMS service postal britannique pour paquets urgents, courrier express *m*, ≈ Chronopost® *m (France)*

date *n* GEN COMM *of bill* échéance *f, of year* date *f*; ~ **draft** GEN COMM traite à échéance fixe *f*; ~ **of exercise** STOCK *of option* date de levée *f*; ~ **of filing** PATENTS date de dépôt *f*; ~ **fixed by proclamation** TAX date fixée par proclamation *f*; ~ **of grant** PATENTS date de délivrance *f*, STOCK *of shares for employees* date d'attribution *f*; ~ **of invoice** GEN COMM date de facture *f*; ~ **of issue** INS date d'émission *f*; ~ **marking** S&M *prepackaged goods* marquage de la date de péremption *m*; ~ **of maturity** STOCK date d'échéance *f*; ~ **of payment** GEN COMM, STOCK date de paiement *f*, date de versement *f*; ~ **of record** STOCK *dividends* date d'enregistrement *f*; ~ **of registration** PATENTS date d'enregistrement *f*; ♦ **at a later** ~ GEN COMM ultérieurement; **by** ~ COMP par date; ~ **as postmark** GEN COMM pour la date se référer au cachet de la poste; **keep up to** ~ ADMIN *filing* maintenir à jour, GEN COMM se maintenir à la page, être dans le mouvement, être dans le vent, être informé, être à la page; **months after** ~ GEN COMM mois après date, mois d'échéance *m*; ~ **new boilers fitted** *(NB)* TRANSP *for vessels* date d'installation d'une nouvelle chaudière *f*; **to** ~ GEN COMM à ce jour

dating *n* GEN COMM réaménagement *m*, rééchelonnement *m*

daughter: ~ **company** *n* GEN COMM société captive *f*

davit *n* TRANSP *shipping* bossoir *m*

dawn: ~ **raid** *n* FIN *(SYN Saturday night special)* tentative d'OPA surprise *f*, STOCK attaque à l'aube *f*, attaque à l'ouverture *f*

day *n* BANK, FIN, GEN COMM, HRM, STOCK, TRANSP *shipping, charter party term* jour *m*; ~ **loan** BANK prêt au jour le jour *m*; ~ **off** HRM jour de congé *m*; ~ **order** STOCK ordre jour *m*; ~ **release** HRM, WEL congé de formation rémunéré *m*; ~ **shift** HRM équipe de jour *f*; ~ **of shipment** TRANSP date d'expédition *f*; ~ **-to-day funding activity** FIN opération de financement quotidienne *f*; ~ **-to-day loan** BANK prêt au jour le jour *m*; ~ **-to-day money** BANK, FIN argent au jour le jour *m*; ~ **trader** STOCK scalper *m*; ~ **trading** STOCK scalpage *m*, spéculation à la journée *f*; ~**'s mail** *AmE (cf day's post BrE)* COMMS courrier du jour *m*; ~**'s post** *BrE (cf day's mail AmE)* COMMS courrier du jour *m*; ◆ **every** ~ GEN COMM tous les jours; **every other** ~ GEN COMM tous les deux jours; **from** ~ **to day** GEN COMM de jour en jour; **give the employees a** ~ **off** HRM accorder une journée de congé aux employés; **on a** ~ **-to-day basis** GEN COMM au jour le jour

daybook *n (db)* ACC, GEN COMM journal *m*, main courante *f*

daylight: ~ **saving** *n* GEN COMM heure d'été *f*

days: ~ **after acceptance** *n pl (D/A)* GEN COMM jours après acceptation *m pl*; ~ **after sight** *n pl* GEN COMM jours de vue *m pl*; ~ **of grace** *n pl* ACC jours de franchise *m pl*, jours de grâce *m pl*, GEN COMM délai *m*, LAW jours de franchise *m pl*, jours de grâce *m pl*; ~ **to delivery** *n pl* STOCK *currency futures* jours restant jusqu'à livraison *m pl*; ~ **to maturity** *n pl* STOCK jours restant jusqu'à échéance *m pl*; ◆ **ten** ~ **after sight pay** HRM paiement à dix jours de vue *m*; **under 60** ~ GEN COMM sous 60 jours

daywork *n* HRM travail de jour *m*

dayworker *n* HRM ouvrier de l'équipe de jour *m*

db *abbr* ACC *(daybook)* jl *(journal)*, GEN COMM *(decibel)* db *(décibel)*, GEN COMM *(daybook)* jl *(journal)*, STOCK *(debenture)* obl. *(obligation)*, TRANSP *(double bottom)* double fond *m*, TRANSP *(double-ended)* à double façade

DBA *abbr (do business as)* GEN COMM exercer sous le nom de *loc m*

dbb *abbr (deals, battens, boards)* IND bois blanc, tasseaux, planches *m pl*

dbc *abbr (double bottom center, double bottom centre)* TRANSP *shipping* centre double fond *m*

DBE *abbr (despatch money payable both ends, dispatch money payable both ends)* TRANSP *shipping* bonification payable au chargement et au déchargement *loc f*, prime de célérité payable au chargement et au déchargement *f*

DBEATS *abbr (despatch payable both ends all time saved, dispatch payable both ends all time saved)* TRANSP *shipping* bonification payable au chargement et au déchargement pour temps gagné *f*, prime de célérité payable au chargement et au déchargement pour temps gagné *f*

DBELTS *abbr (dispatch payable both ends on laytime saved)* TRANSP *shipping* bonification payable au chargement et au déchargement pour temps gagné *f*

Dbk *abbr (drawback)* GEN COMM, IMP/EXP remboursement des droits de douane *m*

DBMS *abbr (database management system)* COMP SGBD *(système de gestion de bases de données)*

DC *abbr* COMP *(direct current)* courant continu *m*, ECON *(developed country)* pays développé *m*, IND *(direct current)* courant continu *m*, INS *(deviation clause)* marine clause de déviation *f*, clause dérogatoire *f*, POL *(developed country)* pays développé *m*

DCA *abbr (debt collection agency)* FIN bureau de recouvrement de créances *m*

DCE *abbr* COMP *(data communications equipment) hardware* équipement de termination de circuit de données *m*, ECON *(domestic credit expansion)* développement du crédit intérieur *m*

DCF *abbr (discounted cash flow)* ACC, FIN valeur actualisée nette *f*

DCO *abbr (debt collection order)* FIN ordre de recouvrement de créances *m*

DCom *abbr (Doctor of Commerce)* HRM, WEL docteur en science commerciale *m*

DComL *abbr (Doctor of Commercial Law)* LAW, WEL docteur en droit commercial *m*

DCP *abbr dat (freight paid to)* IMP/EXP, TRANSP fret payé jusqu'à *m*, fret payé à *m*

DCS *abbr (departure control system)* TRANSP système de contrôle des départs *m*

dd *abbr* GEN COMM *(due date)* date d'échéance *f*, échéance *f*, GEN COMM *(delivered)* livré, STOCK *(due date)* date d'échéance *f*, échéance *f*, TRANSP *(delivered)* rendu

DD *abbr* BANK *(direct debit)* avis de prélèvement *m*, prélèvement automatique *m*, prélèvement autorisé *m*, GEN COMM *(demand draft)* prélèvement automatique *m*, traite à vue *f*, IMP/EXP *(delivered at docks) shipping* livraison à quai *f*, rendu à quai, TRANSP *(dry docking)* mise en cale sèche *f*, TRANSP *(delivered at docks) shipping* livraison à quai *f*, rendu à quai

DDA *abbr (duty deposit account)* IMP/EXP compte de dépôt de droits douaniers *m*

DDB *abbr (distributed database)* COMP base de données répartie *f*

DDD[1] *abbr AmE (direct distance dialing)* COMMS appel automatique longue distance *loc m*, automatique interurbain *m*, l'automatique *m*

DDD[2] *n* STOCK notation de Standard & Poor's pour une obligation à haut risque, DDD *f*

DDE *abbr (direct data entry)* COMP saisie directe *f*, saisie en ligne *f*

DDO *abbr (dispatch discharging only)* TRANSP bonification au déchargement *loc f*, prime de célérité au déchargement *f*

DDP *abbr (delivered duty paid)* IMP/EXP livraison franco de douane *loc f*, rendu droits acquittés

DDU *abbr (delivered duty unpaid)* IMP/EXP rendu droits non-acquittés

D-E *abbr (diesel-electric)* TRANSP diesel-électrique

DE *abbr obs UK (Department of Employment)* ECON a fusionné en juillet 1995 avec le Department for Education afin de former le Department of Education and Employment (DEE), ≈ ministère du Travail et de l'Emploi *m*, HRM ≈ ministère du Travail et de l'Emploi *m*

dead: ~ **account** *n* BANK compte inactif *m*; ~ **-end job** *n BrE (cf blind-alley job AmE)* ACC emploi sans avenir *m*, impasse professionnelle *f*; ~ **key** *n* ADMIN *on keyboard* touche option *f*, COMP touche morte *f*; ~ **letter** *n* COMMS lettre mise au rebut *f*, lettre retournée *f*; ~ **load** *n* GEN COMM poids mort *m*; ~ **rise** *n* GEN COMM *linked with sales* acculement *m*, hausse sans effet *f*, TRANSP *shipping, deck* relevé des varangues *m*; ~ **stock** *n* S&M invendus *m pl*; ~ **time** *n (SYN down time)* HRM chômage technique *m*; ~ **weight** *n* GEN COMM port en lourd *m*, TRANSP *(D/W)* port en lourd *m*, tonnage en lourd *m (PL)*; ~ **weight all told** *n (DWAT)* TRANSP port en lourd total *m*; ~ **weight capacity** *n (DWC)* TRANSP port en lourd *m*, tonnage en lourd *m*; ~ **weight cargo** *n* GEN COMM, TRANSP *shipping* marchandises lourdes *f pl*; ~ **weight cargo capacity** *n (DWCC)* TRANSP port en lourd *m*, tonnage en lourd *m*; ~ **weight tonnage** *n (DWT)* GEN COMM tonnage de portée en lourd *m*, TRANSP port en lourd *m*, tonnage en lourd *m*

Dead: ~ **Letter Office** *n (DLO)* ADMIN bureau des rebuts

deadbeat *n* S&M mauvais payeur *m*

deadfreight *n (DF)* TRANSP faux fret *m*, fret sur le vide *m*

deadhead[1] *n infrml* GEN COMM *AmE (cf queue jumper BrE)* resquilleur *m*, TRANSP *AmE* camion roulant à vide *m*, train roulant à vide *m*

deadhead[2] *vi AmE infrml* TRANSP déplacer à vide

deadheading *n AmE* TRANSP retour à vide *m*

deadline *n* BANK délai *m*, COM échéance *f*, ECON, FIN délai *m*, GEN COMM date limite *f*, dernier délai *m*, délai *m*, délai de rigueur *m*, HRM, MGMNT, STOCK délai *m*

deadlock *n jarg* COMP arrêt complet *m*, blocage *m*, blocage complet *m*, étreinte fatale *f*, GEN COMM impasse *f*

deadlocked *adj jarg* COMP bloqué

deal[1] *n* GEN COMM accord *m*, affaire *f*, *contract* coup *m (infrml)*, marché *m*, S&M vente *f*; ◆ **clinch a ~** GEN COMM, S&M conclure un marché, conclure une affaire; **make a good ~ by** GEN COMM *goods, products* tirer beaucoup de profit de; **the ~ is off** GEN COMM l'accord n'est pas fait, l'affaire est annulée, le marché est rompu

deal:[2] **1.** *vt* ~ **with** COMMS, GEN COMM *arrangement, crisis* traiter de **2.** *vi* S&M *customer* s'occuper de, GEN COMM être en activité, STOCK *on stock exchange* faire des opérations boursières, négocier en bourse; ◆ ~ **with the mail** COMMS ouvrir le courrier; **make a ~** GEN COMM conclure un marché, faire une affaire

dealer *n* FIN agent *mf*, GEN COMM concessionnaire *mf*, dépositaire *mf*, concessionnaire *mf*, S&M fournisseur *m*, négociant *m*, marchand *m*, STOCK contrepartiste *mf*, dealer *m*, négociant *m*, opérateur *m*; ~ **in securities** STOCK contrepartiste *mf*, dealer *m*, négociant en titres *m*; ~ **incentive** S&M prime d'encouragement pour le négociant *f*; ~ **network** STOCK réseau de contrepartistes *m*

dealing *n* S&M *drug* trafic *m*, STOCK opération *f*; ~ **floor** STOCK parquet *m*, salle des marchés *f*; ~ **restriction** ECON, GEN COMM restriction du commerce *f*, réglementation des transactions *f*, POL restriction du commerce *f*

dealings *n pl* HRM, MGMNT rapports *m pl*; ~ **for the account** FIN opérations de liquidation *f pl*, opérations à terme *f pl*

deals: ~ **and battens** *n pl* IND *timber* bois blanc et tasseaux *m pl*; ~, **battens, boards** *n pl (dbb)* IND *shipping of timber* bois blanc, tasseaux, planches *m pl*

dear *adj* GEN COMM cher, coûteux

Dear: ~ **Madam** *phr* COMMS Madame *f*, Mademoiselle *f*

death: ~ **benefit** *n* INS capital décès *m*, prestation de décès *f*; ~ **certificate** *n* GEN COMM, LAW acte de décès *m*; ~ **duties** *n pl dated BrE (cf death tax AmE)* TAX droits de succession *m pl*, impôt sur les successions *m*; ~ **rate** *n* GEN COMM taux de mortalité *m*; ~ **risk** *n* INS risque de décès *m*; ~ **tax** *n AmE (cf death duties BrE)* TAX droits de succession *m pl*, impôt sur les successions *m*

debasement *n* ECON *of currency* dépréciation *f*

debatable *adj* GEN COMM contestable

debate *vt* GEN COMM discuter, débattre

debenture *n (db)* STOCK obligation *f*, obligation non-garantie *f (obl.)*; ~ **bond** STOCK certificat d'obligation *m*; ~ **capital** STOCK capital obligations *m*; ~ **holder** STOCK détenteur de débentures *m*, porteur d'obligations non garanties *m*, porteur de débentures *m*; ~ **loan** STOCK prêt obligataire *m*; ~ **stock** STOCK obligations non-garanties *f pl*

debit[1] *n* ACC, BANK, FIN, GEN COMM, PROP débit *m*; ~ **account** ACC, BANK compte débiteur *m*; ~ **balance** ACC, BANK, FIN solde débiteur *m*; ~ **card** BANK, S&M carte bancaire *f*; ~ **column** ACC, FIN colonne des débits *f*, colonne débitrice *f*; ~ **entry** ACC écriture passée au débit *f*; ~ **float** BANK flottant *m*; ~ **interest** FIN intérêts débiteurs *m pl*; ~ **memorandum** *US* BANK note de débit *f*; ~ **note** *(D/N)* GEN COMM note de débit *f*; ~ **ratio** FIN ratio débiteur *m*; ~ **return** TAX déclaration avec solde dû *f*; ~ **side** ACC, FIN côté du débit *m*

debit[2] *vt* ACC, BANK *account*, FIN débiter

debited: be ~ to *phr* ACC *account* être débité de

debits *n pl* STOCK *options on Eurodollar futures* débits *m pl*

de bonis non administratis *phr* PROP bien non administré

debottleneck *vt* ECON désengorger

debrief *vt* ECON, MGMNT débriefer, faire le bilan *loc m*

debriefing *n* GEN COMM compte-rendu *m*, interrogation *f*, MGMNT debriefing *m*, réunion de mise au point *f*

debt *n* ACC créance *f*, ECON endettement *m*, FIN *short term* créance *f*, dette *f*, endettement *m*, GEN COMM dette *f*, *owing money* endettement *m*; **~ burden** *n* ECON, POL poids de la dette *m*; **~ charges** *n pl* ACC frais rattachés à une dette *m pl*; **~ collection** *n* ACC, FIN, GEN COMM recouvrement de créances *m*, recouvrement de dettes *m*; **~ collection agency** *n* *(DCA)* FIN bureau de recouvrement de créances *m*; **~ collection order** *n* *(DCO)* FIN ordre de recouvrement de créances *m*; **~ collector** *n* FIN, GEN COMM agent de recouvrement de créances *m*; **~ coverage ratio** *n* ACC, FIN taux de couverture de la dette *m*; **~ -equity ratio** *n* FIN rapport dettes-actions *m*; **~ -equity swap** *n* FIN transformation de créances en participation *f*, échange de créances contre actifs *m*; **~ financing** *n* FIN financement par emprunt bancaire *m*, financement par émission d'obligations *m*, remboursement des emprunts *m*; **~ forgiveness** *n* FIN remise de dette *f*; **~ instrument** *n* FIN, GEN COMM titre de créance *m*; **~ manager** *n* HRM gestionnaire de la dette *m*; **~ obligation** *n* ACC titre de créance *m*; **~ obligations** *n pl* ECON *of developing countries*, POL impératifs de la dette *m pl*; **~ ratio** *n* ACC, BANK, FIN, STOCK ratio d'endettement *m*; **~ recovery period** *n* STOCK délai de recouvrement *m*, DR; **~ relief** *n* ECON, POL allègement de la dette *m*; **~ rescheduling** *n* ACC, BANK, FIN, GEN COMM rééchelonnement de la dette *m*; **~ retirement** *n* ACC remboursement de dette *m*; **~ security** *n* GEN COMM titre d'emprunt *m*, titre de créance *m*; **~ service** *n* ACC service de la dette *m*; **~ service indicators** *n pl* ECON, POL indicateurs de service de la dette *m pl*; **~ swap** *n* FIN échange de créances *m*; ◆ **~ due by** ACC dette exigible le, dette échue le; **~ due from** ACC créance due depuis; **~ due to** ACC dette due à; **forgo a ~** FIN, GEN COMM remettre une dette; **get into ~** ACC, FIN, GEN COMM s'endetter; **~ owed to** ACC dette active *f*

debtor *n* *(Dr)* ACC, ADMIN, FIN, GEN COMM, LAW débiteur *m*; **~ department** ADMIN ministère débiteur *m*

debtors *n pl* ACC, ECON comptes clients *m pl*

debug *vt* *infrml* COMP déboguer, dépanner, mettre au point

debugger *n* *infrml* COMP débogueur *m*

debugging *n* *infrml* COMP débogage *m*, mise au point *f*

Dec. *abbr* *(December)* GEN COMM déc. *(décembre)*

decade *n* GEN COMM décade *f*, décennie *f*; ◆ **in the ~ to 1995** GEN COMM dans les dix années qui ont précédé 1995

deceased[1] *adj* LAW décédé, défunt

deceased:[2] **~ estate** *n* GEN COMM masse successorale *f*; **~ person** *n* LAW défunt *m*, personne décédée *f*

decelerate *vi* ECON, GEN COMM *growth* ralentir

deceleration *n* ECON, GEN COMM ralentissement *m*

December *n* *(Dec.)* GEN COMM décembre *m* *(déc.)*

decent *adj* GEN COMM convenable

decentralization *n* GEN COMM, IND, MGMNT, POL décentralisation *f*

decentralize *vt* GEN COMM, IND, MGMNT, POL décentraliser

decentralized: ~ management *n* MGMNT gestion décentralisée *f*; **~ market economy** *n* *(DME)* ECON économie de marché décentralisée *f*

deceptive: ~ advertising *n* S&M publicité mensongère *f*; **~ packaging** *n* S&M emballage trompeur *m*

decibel *n* *(db)* GEN COMM décibel *m* *(db)*

decide: ~ on *vt* GEN COMM convenir de; **~ to do** GEN COMM convenir de faire; **~ upon** GEN COMM convenir de

decimal: ~ currency *n* ECON décimalisation *f*; **~ digit** *n* COMP chiffre décimal *m*; **~ notation** *n* COMP numération décimale *f*; **~ number** *n* COMP nombre décimal *m*, MATH chiffre décimal *m*; **~ point** *n* COMP, MATH virgule *f*; **~ -to-binary conversion** *n* COMP conversion de décimale en binaire *f*, conversion décimale-binaire *f*

decimalization *n* ECON *currency* décimalisation *f*, MATH conversion *f*

decimalize *vt* ECON *currency* décimaliser, MATH transposer

decision *n* GEN COMM décision *f*; **~ aids** GEN COMM aides à la décision *f pl*; **~ analysis** MGMNT analyse de la décision *f*; **~ maker** GEN COMM, MGMNT décideur *m*; **~ making** MGMNT prise de décision *f*; **~ -making process** MGMNT processus de prise de décision *m*; **~ -making unit** S&M unité de prise de décision *f*; **~ model** MGMNT modèle de décision *m*; **~ package** FIN module de décision *m*, MGMNT décision globale *f*; **~ process** MGMNT processus de la décision *m*; **~ support system** *(DSS)* MGMNT système d'aide à la décision *m*; **~ table** COMP table de décision *f*; **~ theory** HRM, MGMNT théorie des décisions *f*; **~ tree** HRM, MGMNT arbre de décision *m*; **~ unit** GEN COMM unité de décision *f*; ◆ **make a ~** GEN COMM, MGMNT prendre une décision; **make a snap ~** GEN COMM se décider tout d'un coup *(infrml)*; **take a ~** GEN COMM, MGMNT prendre une décision

decisive *adj* GEN COMM concluant, décisif, déterminant, LAW concluant

deck *n* COMP *for magnetic tapes* dérouleur de

bande *m*, TRANSP *(DK) shipping* pont *m*; ~ **boy** HRM mousse *m*; ~ **cargo** TRANSP *shipping* chargement en pontée *m*, pontée *f*; ~ **cargo certificate** TRANSP *shipping* certificat de chargement en pontée *m*, certificat de pontée *m*; ~ **department** TRANSP *shipping* service pont *m*; ~ **fitting** TRANSP *shipping* élément de fixation sur le pont *m*; ~ **hand** HRM *of ship*, TRANSP matelot de pont *m*; ~ **line** TRANSP *shipping, freeboard* ligne de pont *f*; ~ **load** TRANSP *shipping* pontée *f*; **on ~ bill of lading** IMP/EXP connaissement sur le pont *m*; ~ **socket** TRANSP *container securing* socle *m*; **under ~ tank** *(UnDk)* TRANSP *shipping* citerne en cale *f*, citerne sous le pont *f*

declaration *n* GEN COMM, LAW déclaration *f*; ~ **of dividend** STOCK déclaration de dividende *f*; ~ **of origin** IMP/EXP déclaration d'origine *f*; ~ **of trust** LAW déclaration formelle de fidéicommis *f*

declare *vt* COMMS, COMP *programming language*, IMP/EXP *goods to customs officer*, STOCK, TAX *on tax return* déclarer; ♦ ~ **on oath** LAW déclarer sous serment; ~ **an option** STOCK répondre à une prime

declared: ~ **dividend** *n* STOCK dividende déclaré *m*; ~ **value for carriage** *n* TRANSP valeur déclarée pour le transport *f*; ~ **value for customs** *n* IMP/EXP, TRANSP valeur déclarée en douane *f*

decline[1] *n* ECON déclin *m*, *in employment, demand, trade* baisse *f*, GEN COMM *in output* baisse *f*, *in prices, support* baisse *f*, fléchissement *m*, IND déclin *m*

decline[2] *vi* ECON diminuer, décliner, être en baisse *loc f*, GEN COMM *price* baisser

declining: ~ **balance depreciation** *n* ACC, FIN amortissement dégressif *m*; ~ **balance method** *n* ACC système d'amortissement dégressif *m*; ~ **industrial area** *n* ECON, IND zone industrielle en déclin *f*; ~ **industry** *n* *(SYN ailing industry)* ECON, IND industrie affaiblie *f*, industrie en déclin *f*; ~ **interest rate** *n* BANK, ECON, FIN taux d'intérêt en baisse *m*; ~ **market** *n* STOCK marché en baisse *m*; ~ **share** *n* ECON, STOCK action en baisse *f*, action qui fléchit *f*, valeur en baisse *f*, valeur qui fléchit *f*

DECnet® *n* COMP *software* DECnet® *m*, architecture de réseau de DEC *f*

decoder *n* COMP *hardware* décodeur *m*

decommission *vt* ENVIR *industrial or nuclear plant*, IND déclasser

decommissioning *n* ENVIR *of industrial or nuclear plant*, IND déclassement *m*

decommitment *n* ACC désengagement *m*

decompartmentalization *n* STOCK décloisonnement *m*

DEcon *abbr* *(Doctor of Economics)* ECON, HRM docteur en sciences économiques *m*

decrease[1] *n* GEN COMM diminution *f*, *in price* baisse *f*; ~ **in value** GEN COMM diminution de valeur *f*, perte de valeur *f*; ~ **of risk** INS diminution du risque *f*

decrease[2] **1.** *vt* GEN COMM diminuer, réduire; **2.** *vi* ECON *population* diminuer, *price* baisser

decreasing: ~ **liquidity order** *n* *(ANT increasing liquidity order)* ACC ordre de liquidité décroissante *m*; ~ **order** *n* COMP ordre décroissant *m*; ~ **rate** *n* FIN taux dégressif *m*; ~ **tax** *n* *(SYN degressive tax)* TAX impôt dégressif *m*

decree[1] *n* LAW ordonnance *f*; ~ **absolute** LAW décret irrévocable *m*

decree[2] *vt* LAW, TAX édicter

decrement *vt* COMP décrémenter

decriminalize *vt* LAW décriminaliser, légaliser

decryption *n* *(ANT encryption)* COMMS, COMP *programming language* déchiffrement *m*, décodage *m*, décryptage *m*

dedicated *adj* COMP *hardware* dédié, spécialisé, GEN COMM *for specific purpose* spécialisé

dedication *n* PROP *of land* consécration *f*

de die in diem *phr* GEN COMM de jour en jour *loc m*

dedomiciling *n* GEN COMM, TAX dédomiciliation *f*

deduce *vt* GEN COMM déduire

deduct *vt* GEN COMM, MATH déduire; ♦ ~ **tax** TAX retenir l'impôt

deductibility *n* TAX déductibilité *f*

deductible[1] *adj* FIN, TAX déductible

deductible[2]: ~ **clause** *n* INS clause de franchise *f*, clause déductible *f*; ~ **farm loss** *n* TAX perte agricole déductible *f*

deduction *n* FIN, GEN COMM retenue *f*, TAX prélèvement *m*, retenue *f*; ~ **at source** FIN, TAX retenue à la source *f*; ~ **for expenses** TAX déduction pour dépenses *f*; ~ **for gifts** TAX déduction pour dons *f*; ~ **for loan losses** TAX déduction pour pertes sur prêts *f*; ~ **new for old** INS déduction du vieux au neuf *f*; ♦ **make a ~** TAX opérer une déduction, opérer une retenue, pratiquer une déduction, pratiquer une retenue

deductive: ~ **reasoning** *n* LAW, MATH, MGMNT raisonnement déductif *m*, raisonnement par déduction *m*

DEE *abbr UK* *(Department of Education and Employment)* ECON ≈ ministère du Travail et de l'Emploi *m*

deed *n* LAW acte *m*, acte authentique *m*, acte de proprieté *m*, PROP acte authentique *m*; ~ **of assignation** GEN COMM acte de cession *m*, contrat de cession *m*, LAW contrat de cession *m*; ~ **of covenant** *UK* TAX acte de donation *m*; ~ **in lieu of foreclosure** LAW, PROP acte tenant lieu de saisie d'hypothèque *m*; ~ **of partnership** LAW acte d'association *m*, contrat de société *m*; ~ **poll** LAW acte unilatéral *m*; ~ **restriction** LAW, PROP clause restrictive d'un acte *f*, clause restrictive d'un contrat *f*; ~ **of trust** LAW acte de fiducie *m*, acte de fidéicommis *m*, acte fiduciaire *m*

deem *vt* GEN COMM considérer, estimer; ♦ ~ **necessary** GEN COMM estimer nécessaire, juger nécessaire

deemed[1] *adj* GEN COMM considéré, jugé

deemed:[2] ~ **disposition** *n* TAX disposition présumée *f*, disposition réputée *f*

deep:[1] ~ **-rooted** *adj* GEN COMM profondément ancré, profondément structurel; ~ **-seated** *adj* GEN COMM *problems* profond, profondément ancré, profondément structurel; ◆ ~ **in the money** STOCK *option* très en dedans; ~ **out of the money** STOCK *option* très en dehors

deep[2] *adv* GEN COMM, STOCK profondément, très

deep:[3] ~ **discount bond** *n* STOCK obligation négociée bien en dessous du pair *f*, obligation à escompte important *f*; ~ **discounts** *n pl* TAX rabais importants *m pl*; ~ **-sea broker** *n* HRM courtier au long cours *m*, courtier de marine *m*; ~ **-sea shipping lane** *n* TRANSP route de navigation en eau profonde *f*; ~ **tank** *n (DT)* TRANSP *shipping* caisse profonde *f*, cale à eau *f*; ~ **tank aft** *n (DTa)* TRANSP *shipping* cale à eau d'arrière *f*; ~ **tank forward** *n (DTf)* TRANSP *shipping* cale à eau d'avant *f*

deeply *adv* GEN COMM, STOCK profondément

deepwater: ~ **berth** *n* TRANSP *shipping* poste en eau profonde *m*; ~ **harbor** *n* AmE, ~ **harbour** *n* BrE TRANSP *shipping* port en eau profonde *m*; ~ **route** *n* TRANSP route en eau profonde *f*

def. *abbr (deferred)* ACC à reporter, GEN COMM dif. *(différé)*, à reporter

de facto[1] *adv* LAW de facto, de fait *loc m*

de facto:[2] ~ **corporation** *n* ECON, GEN COMM société de fait *f*; ~ **manager** *n* MGMNT gestionnaire de fait *m*; ~ **population** *n* ECON population de facto *f*, population de fait *f*

defalcation *n* LAW détournement *m*

defamation *n* LAW diffamation *f*

defamatory *adj* LAW diffamatoire

defame *vt* LAW calomnier, diffamer

default[1] *adj* COMP, GEN COMM implicite, par défaut

default[2] *n* COMP *operating system* défaut *m*, FIN *on debt, fine* non-paiement *m*, GEN COMM *on loan, mortgage* non-remboursement *m*; ~ **device** COMP unité implicite *f*; ~ **directory** COMP *operating system* répertoire par défaut *m*; ~ **drive** COMP *operating system* lecteur par défaut *m*; ~ **interest** BANK arriéré d'intérêts *m*, intérêt sur arriérés *m*, intérêts en souffrance *m pl*; ~ **judgment** LAW jugement par défaut *m*; ~ **option** COMP option par défaut *f*; ~ **of payment** BANK défaut de paiement *m*; ◆ **by** ~ COMP implicite, par défaut, GEN COMM par défaut

default[3] *vi* GEN COMM faire défaut de paiement *loc m*, ne pas honorer ses échéances, être en état de cessation de paiement *loc m*

defaulting: ~ **witness** *n* LAW témoin défaillant *m*

defeasance *n* FIN, STOCK *corporate finance* désendettement *m*

defeat *vt* GEN COMM aller à l'encontre de, contrarier, déjouer, faire échouer

defect *n* GEN COMM malfaçon *f*, vice *m*, LAW vice *m*

defective[1] *adj* GEN COMM, S&M défectueux

defective:[2] ~ **services** *n pl* GEN COMM *consumer protection* service chargé des malfaçons et défauts de fabrication *m*; ~ **title** *n* LAW titre contestable *m*, titre imparfait *m*

defence *n* BrE GEN COMM, POL défense *f*; ~ **advisor** BrE *(D/A)* HRM conseiller en matière de défense *m*; ~ **attaché** BrE *(D/A)* HRM attaché militaire *m*, conseiller en matière de défense *m*; ~ **envelope** BrE FIN enveloppe de défense *f*; ~ **lawyer** UK *(cf defense attorney US)* LAW avocat de la défense *m*; ~ **production revolving fund** BrE FIN fonds renouvelable de la production de défense *m*; ~ **of suit against insured** BrE INS *liability insurance* poursuite contre assuré *f*; **the** ~ BrE LAW la défense *f*

Defence: ~ **Department** *n* UK *(cf Defense Ministry US)* POL ≈ ministère de la Défense nationale *m*; ~ **Minister** *n* UK *(cf Defense Secretary US)* POL ≈ ministre de la Défense nationale *m*

defend *vt* GEN COMM *person, interest* défendre

defendant *n* LAW accusé *m*, défendeur *m*; **the** ~ LAW l'accusé *mf*

defense *n* AmE see defence BrE

Defense: ~ **Ministry** *n* US *(cf Defence Department UK)* POL ≈ ministère de la Défense nationale *m*; ~ **Secretary** *n* US *(cf Defence Minister UK)* POL ≈ ministre de la Défense nationale *m*

defensive: ~ **budgeting** *n* UK *(cf competitive parity)* S&M alignement sur la concurrence *m*; ~ **securities** *n* STOCK valeurs défensives *f pl*; ~ **spending** *n* UK *(cf competitive parity)* S&M alignement sur la concurrence *m*; ~ **strategy** *n* GEN COMM stratégie de défense *f*, stratégie défensive *f*

defer *vt* GEN COMM *decision* ajourner, différer, proroger, reporter, retarder, LAW, MGMNT reporter; ◆ ~ **a debt** ACC, FIN reporter le remboursement d'une dette; ~ **payment** ACC, FIN reporter un paiement; ~ **tax** TAX reporter l'impôt

deferment *n* GEN COMM ajournement *m*, remise *f*, sursis *m*, LAW prorogation *f*

deferral *n* TAX report *m*; ~ **of taxes** TAX report de l'impôt *m*

deferred[1] *adj (def.)* ACC reporté, à reporter, GEN COMM reporté, à reporter, *shares* différé

deferred:[2] ~ **amount** *n* TAX montant différé *m*; ~ **annuity** *n* INS rente différée *f*, rente à paiement différé *f*; ~ **benefits and payments** *n pl* INS rentes et paiements différés *f pl*; ~ **billing** *n* S&M facturation différée *f*; ~ **charge** *n* ACC charge à répartir sur plusieurs exercices *f*, frais différés *m pl*, frais reportés *m pl*; ~ **compensation** *n* HRM *salary* indemnité différée *f*; ~ **compensation plan** *n* AmE HRM retraite à indemnités différées *f*; ~ **contribution plan** *n* HRM participation différée aux bénéfices *f*; ~ **credit** *n* ACC produits constatés d'avance *m pl*, revenu reporté *m*, TAX revenu reporté *m*; ~ **futures** *n pl* FIN, STOCK contrats à terme différés *m pl*; ~ **group annuity** *n* HRM versement différé d'annuités *m*; ~ **income** *n* ACC produits constatés d'avance *m pl*, revenu reporté *m*, TAX revenu reporté *m*; **~ income tax** *n* TAX impôt sur le revenu reporté *m*; **~ income tax reserve** *n* TAX réserve pour impôts sur le revenu reportés *f*; **~ interest bond** *n* STOCK obligation à intérêt différé *f*; **~ maintenance** *n* PROP *appraisal* entretien différé *m*; **~ payment** *n* ACC paiement par versements échelonnés *m*, GEN COMM paiement différé *m*, paiement reporté *m*; **~ payment annuity** *n* INS rente différée *f*, rente à paiement différé *f*; **~ profit-sharing** *n* HRM participation différée aux bénéfices de l'entreprise *f*; **~ profit-sharing plan** *n* TAX impôt reporté *m*; **~ rebate** *n* TRANSP *shipping* rabais différé *m*; **~ retirement** *n* HRM retraite différée *f*; **~ retirement credit** *n* HRM pension différée *f*; **~ revenue** *n* ACC, TAX revenu reporté *m*; **~ share** *n* STOCK action à dividende différé *f*, action à droit réduit *f*; **~ stock** *n* STOCK action à dividende différé *f*; **~ tax** *n* ACC, TAX impôt différé *m*, impôt latent *m*; **~ tax accounting** *n* TAX méthode de l'impôt reporté *f*; **~ tax assets** *n pl* ACC, TAX impôts latents actifs *m pl*; **~ tax liabilities** *n pl* ACC, TAX fiscalité latente passive *f*, provision pour impôts différés *f*; **~ taxation** *n* ACC, TAX impôts différés *m pl*; **~ wage increase** *n* HRM augmentation différée des salaires *f*

deficiency *n* FIN insuffisance *f*, GEN COMM défaut *m*, manque *m*, TAX déficit *m*; **~ judgment** LAW jugement compensatoire *m*; **~ letter** STOCK lettre de la Commission des opérations de Bourse demandant une révision du prospectus; **~ payment** ECON *agriculture* paiement différentiel *m*

deficient[1] *adj* GEN COMM déficient, insuffisant

deficient:[2] **~ tax installment** *n AmE*, **~ tax instalment** *n BrE* TAX acompte provisionnel insuffisant *m*

deficit *n* ACC, ECON, FIN déficit *m*; **~ balance of payments** ECON balance des paiements déficitaire *f*; **~ financing** (SYN *compensatory finance*) ECON financement par le déficit *m*, mesures d'incitation économique *f pl*, recours à l'impasse budgétaire *m*; **~ net worth** ECON valeur nette du déficit *f*; **~ spending** ECON financement par l'emprunt *m*, impasse budgétaire *f*; **~ spending policy** ACC *governmental accounting* politique de relance par le déficit budgétaire *f*; ♦ **make up the ~** ECON, FIN combler le déficit

defined: **~ -benefit pension plan** *n* FIN, HRM système de retraite à prestation définie *m*

definite: **~ laytime** *n* TRANSP *shipping, charter party term* staries définies *f pl*

definition *n* GEN COMM définition *f*; **~ of items** INS définition des articles *f*; **~ of limits** INS définition des limites *f*

deflagrating: **~ explosive** *n* TRANSP *dangerous classified transported goods* explosif déflagrant *m*, explosif à déflagration *m*

deflate *vt* ECON *economy* faire baisser, provoquer la déflation, ralentir

deflated *adj* ECON *earnings* à la baisse

deflation *n* ECON déflation *f*, désinflation *f*

deflationary: **~ gap** *n* ECON *econometrics* écart déflationniste *m*, écart récessionniste *m*; **~ pressures** *n pl* ECON pressions déflationnistes *f pl*

deflator *n* MATH facteur de déflation *m*

deforestation *n* ENVIR déboisement *m*, déforestation *f*

defraud *vt* LAW escroquer, frauder

defraudation *n* TAX détournement d'impôts *m*

defrauded: **~ tax** *n* TAX impôt éludé *m*

defray *vt* FIN, GEN COMM couvrir, rembourser; ♦ **~ the cost of** GEN COMM couvrir les frais de; **~ the expenses of** GEN COMM couvrir les frais de, payer les dépenses de

defunct[1] *adj* GEN COMM défunt

defunct:[2] **~ company** *n* ECON, GEN COMM société dissoute *f*

degradation *n* ENVIR *of cities* dégradation *f*, détérioration *f*

degree *n* GEN COMM *measure* degré *m*, HRM degré *m*, mesure *f*, WEL *education* diplôme *m*; **~ of damage** INS degré de dommage *m*; **~ of disablement** INS degré d'incapacité *m*, degré d'invalidité *m*; **~ of exposure** STOCK *to the market* degré de risque *m*; **~ of fluctuation** STOCK *in futures price* amplitude de fluctuation *f*, niveau de fluctuation *m*; **~ measure** MATH mesure de degrés *f*; **~ of risk** GEN COMM niveau de risque *m*

degrees: **~ Centigrade** *n pl* GEN COMM degrés Celsius *m pl*; **~ Fahrenheit** *n pl* GEN COMM degrés Fahrenheit *m pl*

degression *n* MATH dégression *f*

degressive: **~ tax** *n* (SYN *decreasing tax*) TAX impôt dégressif *m*

dehire *vt AmE* (SYN *dismiss*) HRM licencier

dehiring *n AmE* (SYN *dismissal*) HRM licenciement *m*

de-icing: **~ fluid** *n* TRANSP fluide de dégivrage *m*

deindustrialization *n* (ANT *industrialization*) ECON, IND, POL désindustrialisation *f*

deintensified: **~ farming** *n* ENVIR désintensification des cultures *f*

de jure[1] *adv* LAW de droit *loc m*, de jure

de jure:[2] **~ population** *n* ECON population de droit *f*, population de jure *f*

del: **~ credere** *n* GEN COMM ducroire; **~ credere agent** *n* GEN COMM, S&M commissionnaire ducroire *m*

DEL *abbr* COMP (*delete character*) caractère d'effacement *m*, GEN COMM, HRM (*delegate*) dl. (*délégué*)

delay *n* COMP délai d'attente *m*, retard *m*, GEN COMM retard *m*

delayed: **~ delivery** *n* STOCK livraison différée *f*; **~ flight** *n* TRANSP vol retardé *m*

delaying: **~ tactics** *n pl* GEN COMM manoeuvres dilatoires *f pl*

delegate[1] *n (DEL)* GEN COMM, HRM délégué *m (dl.)*

delegate[2] *vi* MGMNT *powers, responsibilities* déléguer

delegation *n* GEN COMM *of people* délégation *f*; ~ **of authority** GEN COMM délégation de pouvoir *f*; ~ **of authorization** GEN COMM délégation d'autorisation *f*; ~ **of signing authority** GEN COMM délégation de la qualité de fondé de pouvoir *f*, délégation de signature *f*

delegatus non potest delegare *phr* GEN COMM il n'appartient pas au délégué de déléguer son autorité

delete:[1] ~ **character** *n (DEL)* COMP caractère d'effacement *m*

delete[2] *vt* ACC *debt* abandonner, annuler, COMP effacer, supprimer, GEN COMM rayer, *from list* radier

deletion *n* ACC *of debt* annulation *f*, GEN COMM, LAW *of provisions* suppression *f*; ~ **of a debt** ACC abandon d'une dette *m*, radiation de dette *f*

delict *n* LAW *Scots Law* délit *m*

delinquency *n* ACC montant d'un compte douteux *m*, FIN, GEN COMM défaut de paiement *m*

delinquent[1] *adj* FIN non-payé, échu, GEN COMM délinquant, non-payé, échu

delinquent:[2] ~ **taxpayer** *n* TAX contribuable contrevenant *m*

delisting *n* STOCK radiation de la cote *f*

deliver *vt* GEN COMM *goods* livrer, *service* fournir, *speech* prononcer, POL *opinion, parliament* soumettre, STOCK *shares* livrer; ♦ ~ **a lecture** WEL faire une conférence, *at university* faire cours

deliverable[1] *adj* GEN COMM, IMP/EXP, STOCK livrable; ♦ **in a ~ state** LAW en état livrable

deliverable:[2] ~ **bills** *n pl* STOCK bons livrables *m pl*; ~ **security** *n* STOCK valeur livrable *f*

delivered *adj (dd)* GEN COMM livré, TRANSP rendu; ♦ ~ **at docks** *(DD)* IMP/EXP, TRANSP *shipping* livraison à quai *f*, rendu à quai; ~ **at frontier** *(DAF)* IMP/EXP, TRANSP *named place* livraison à la frontière, rendu à la frontière; ~ **domicile** TRANSP rendu à domicile; ~ **duty paid** *(DDP)* IMP/EXP livraison franco de douane, rendu droits acquittés; ~ **duty unpaid** *(DDU)* IMP/EXP livraison droits non payés, rendu droits non-acquittés; ~ **ex quay** *(DEQ)* IMP/EXP *duty paid* livraison franco de douane à quai, rendu à quai droits acquittés; ~ **ex ship** *(DES)* IMP/EXP *named port of destination*, TRANSP livraison au navire, rendu ex ship

delivering: ~ **carrier** *n* TRANSP transporteur livrant *m*

delivery *n (D, dely)* COMMS *of post*, GEN COMM livraison *f (livr.)* GEN COMM *passport, receipt*, STOCK *shares* délivrance *f*, STOCK, TRANSP livraison *f (livr.)*; ~ **broker** *n* STOCK courtier livreur *m*; ~ **charge** *n* TRANSP frais de livraison *m pl*, taxes de tonnage *f pl*; ~ **date** *n* STOCK date de livraison *f*; ~ **day** *n* STOCK jour de livraison *m*; ~ **man** *n* GEN COMM livreur *m*; ~ **month** *n* STOCK *futures*

mois d'échéance *m*, mois de livraison *m*; ~ **note** *n* ACC bon de livraison *m*, TRANSP bon de livraison *m*, bulletin de livraison *m*; ~ **notice** *n* TRANSP avis de livraison *m*; ~ **on wheels** *n (DOW)* TRANSP *by road* livraison par route *f*; ~ **order** *n (DO)* TRANSP bon de livraison *m*; ~ **performance** *n* TRANSP exécution de la livraison *f*; ~ **period** *n* STOCK période de livraison *f*; ~ **receipt** *n* TRANSP reçu de livraison *m*, récépissé de livraison *m*; ~ **service** *n* TRANSP service de livraison *m*; ~ **slip** *n* STOCK avis de livraison *m*; ~ **system** *n* STOCK *futures* système de livraison *m*; ~ **terms of sale** *n pl* IMP/EXP conditions de livraison de la vente *f pl*; ~ **time** *n* GEN COMM date de livraison *f*, délai de livraison *m*; ~ **turnround** *n* GEN COMM délai de livraison *m*; ~ **woman** *n* GEN COMM livreuse *f*; ♦ **make** ~ **of** STOCK *currency* faire une livraison de, livrer; ~ **and redelivery** *(dely and re-dely)* TRANSP livraison et re-livraison; ~ **versus payment** STOCK paiement contre livraison

Delphi: ~ **technique** *n* MGMNT technique de mise au courant *f*

delta:[1] ~ **-neutral** *adj* STOCK *options on Eurodollar futures* delta neutre

delta[2] *n* FIN, STOCK *options on Eurodollar futures* delta *m*; ~ **coefficient** *AmE (cf delta factor BrE)* FIN, STOCK coefficient delta *m*, facteur delta *m*; ~ **factor** *BrE (cf delta coefficient AmE)* FIN, STOCK coefficient delta *m*, facteur delta *m*; ~ **hedging** FIN couverture delta *f*, delta hedging *m*; ~ **-neutral straddles** STOCK *options* opération liée sur option à delta neutre *f*, strangle sur option à delta neutre *m*; ~ **-neutral strangle** STOCK *options* opération liée sur option à delta neutre *f*, strangle sur option à delta neutre *m*; ~ **stock** BANK compte de placement *m*, STOCK *UK* valeur delta *f*, valeur peu active *f*, valeur peu dynamique *f*

de luxe: ~ **cabin** *n* TRANSP *shipping* cabine de luxe *f*

dely *abbr (delivery)* COMMS livraison *f (livr.)* GEN COMM livraison *f (livr.)*, *passport, receipt* délivrance *f* STOCK, TRANSP livraison *f (livr.)*; ~ **and re-dely** *(delivery and redelivery)* TRANSP livraison et re-livraison *loc f*

DEM *abbr (Domestic Equities Market)* STOCK marché des actions nationales *m*

demand[1] *n* ECON, GEN COMM *request*, S&M demande *f*, TAX demande formelle *f*; ~ **account** BANK compte à vue *m*; ~ **assessment** ECON évaluation de la demande *f*; ~ **curve** ECON courbe de demande *f*; ~ **deposit** BANK dépôt à vue *m*; ~ **draft** *(DD)* GEN COMM prélèvement automatique *m*, traite à vue *f*; ~ **for goods** ECON demande de biens *f*; ~ **for money** ECON demande de monnaie *f*; ~ **forecasting** S&M prévision de la demande *f*; ~ **-led growth** ECON, GEN COMM croissance induite par la demande *f*; ~ **loan** BANK prêt à vue *m*; ~ **money** BANK, FIN argent au jour le jour *m*; ~ **note** FIN, GEN COMM *instrument* billet à ordre payable à vue *m*; **on** ~ **bond** BANK *merchant* obligation sur demande *f*; ~ **pattern**

ECON schéma de la demande *m*; ~ **price** ECON prix selon la demande *m*; ~ **-pull inflation** ECON, GEN COMM inflation par la demande *f*; ~ **schedule** ECON barème des prix selon la demande; ♦ **be in great** ~ HRM *skill shortage jobs* être très recherché; **in** ~ GEN COMM, HRM *skill, jobs* recherché; **on** ~ ACC sur demande, sur présentation, à vue

demand² *vt* GEN COMM demander, HRM revendiquer, TAX exiger

demanning *n* HRM dégraissage *m*

demarcation *n* HRM *trade unions* démarcation *f*; ~ **dispute** UK HRM conflit d'identité *m*

demarketing *n* S&M non-marketing *m*

dematerialization *n* ECON dématérialisation *f*

dematerialized *adj* (SYN *paperless*) STOCK *certificates of deposit* dématérialisé

demerge *vt* GEN COMM scinder

demerger¹ *n* ECON *of companies*, GEN COMM déconcentration *f*, scission *f*

demerger² *vt* (SYN *unbundle*) GEN COMM défusionner, dégrouper

demerit: ~ **good** *n* ECON mal tutélaire *m*

demijohn *n* TRANSP dame-jeanne *f*

de minimis *adv* LAW caractère futile de la cause *m*, de minimis

demise: ~ **charter party** *n* TRANSP charte-partie à temps *f*

demised: ~ **premises** *n pl* PROP locaux à bail *m pl*

democracy *n* GEN COMM, POL démocratie *f*

democratic¹ *adj* GEN COMM, POL démocratique

democratic:² ~ **centralism** *n* POL centralisme démocratique *m*; ~ **management** *n* HRM, MGMNT direction démocratique *f*

Democratic: ~ **People's Republic of Korea** *pr n* GEN COMM Corée du Nord *f*, République populaire de Corée *f*

democratically *adv* GEN COMM démocratiquement

demogrant *n* HRM subvention démographique *f*

demographic: ~ **accounting** *n* ECON comptabilité démographique *f*; ~ **transition** *n* ECON révolution démographique *f*, transition démographique *f*

demographics *n pl* S&M, WEL profil démographique *m*

demography *n* ECON démographie *f*

demolition *n* PROP démolition *f*; ~ **costs** *n pl* PROP coûts de démolition *m pl*, frais de démolition *m pl*

demonetization *n* ECON démonétisation *f*

demonetize *vt* ECON démonétiser

demonstrate *vt* GEN COMM *by table, graph* expliquer

demonstration *n* GEN COMM manifestation *f*

demoralize *vt* HRM démoraliser

demotion *n* HRM rétrogradation *f*

demotivate *vt* HRM démotiver

demotivation *n* HRM démotivation *f*

demountable: ~ **system** *n* TRANSP système démontable *m*

demurrage *n* TRANSP surestaries *f pl*

demurrer *n* LAW exception péremptoire *f*, fin de non-recevoir *f*

denationalization *n* (ANT *nationalization*) ECON, POL dénationalisation *f*

denationalize *vt* ECON, POL dénationaliser

denial: ~ **of opinion** *n* GEN COMM récusation *f*

Denmark *pr n* GEN COMM Danemark *m*

Dennison's: ~ **law** *n* ECON loi de Dennison *f*

denom. *abbr* (*denomination*) ECON coup. (*coupure*)

denominate *vt* ECON libeller

denomination *n* (*denom.*) ECON *coins* valeur *f*, *notes* coupure *f*

denominator *n* GEN COMM dénominateur *m*

de novo *adv* LAW de nouveau, de novo

densely:¹ ~ **-populated** *adj* ECON fortement peuplé

densely:² ~ **populated area** *n* ECON zone très fortement peuplée *f*

density *n* PROP densité *f*; ~ **zoning** US LAW, PROP plan d'urbanisation réglementant l'aménagement du territoire

dental: ~ **insurance** *n* INS assurance dentaire *f*, assurance soins dentaires *f*

deny *vt* LAW *entitlement* contester, nier

department *n* (*dept*) ADMIN *in company* service *m* (*serv.*), GEN COMM département *m*, *in company* division *f*, service *m* (*serv.*), *in store* rayon *m*, HRM *in company* service *m* (*serv.*), POL ministère *m*, S&M *in store* rayon *m*; ~ **head** HRM, MGMNT chef de service *m*, directeur de département *m*, directeur du service *m*; ~ **manager** HRM chef de rayon *m*, chef de service *m*, S&M *in department store* chef de rayon *m*; ~ **store** GEN COMM, S&M grand magasin *m*; ~ **store chain** GEN COMM, S&M chaîne de grands magasins *f*; ~ **store sale** S&M soldes des grands magasins *m pl*

Department: ~ **of Commerce** *n* US (*cf Department of Trade* UK) GEN COMM, POL ≈ ministère du Commerce *m*; ~ **of Defense** *n* US (*DOD*) POL ≈ ministère de la Défense nationale *m*; ~ **for Education** *n obs* UK (*DFE*) WEL a fusionné en juillet 1995 avec le Department of Employment afin de former le Department of Education and Employment (DEE), ≈ ministère de l'Éducation nationale *m*; ~ **of Education** *n* US WEL ≈ ministère de l'Éducation nationale *m*; ~ **of Education and Employment** *n* UK (*DEE*) ECON ≈ ministère du Travail et de l'Emploi *m*; ~ **of Employment** *n obs* UK (*DE*) ECON, HRM a fusionné en juillet 1995 avec le Department of Education and Science afin de former le Department of Education and Employment (DEE), ≈ ministère du Travail et de l'Emploi *m*; ~ **of Energy** *n* US (*DOE*) POL ≈ ministère de l'Énergie *m*; ~ **of the Environment** *n* UK (*DOE*) ENVIR, POL ≈ ministère de l'Environnement *m*; ~ **of Health** *n* UK (*DOH, Department of Health and Human Services*) POL, WEL ≈ ministère de la Santé *m*; ~ **of Health and Human Services** *n* US (*cf Department of Health* UK) POL, WEL ≈ ministère de la Santé *m*; ~ **of Health and Social**

Security *n obs UK (DHSS)* WEL consiste maintenant du Department of Health (DoH) et du Department of Social Security (DSS), ≈ ministère de la Santé et des Affaires sociales *m*; ~ **of Housing and Urban Development** *n US* POL, WEL ≈ ministère du Logement et de l'Urbanisme *m*; ~ **of Industry** *n US (DI, DOI, Department of Trade and Industry)* IND ≈ ministère de l'Industrie *m*; ~ **of Labor** *n US* ADMIN ≈ ministère du Travail *m*; ~ **of Social Security** *n UK (DSS)* POL, WEL ≈ ministère des Affaires sociales *m*; ~ **of Trade** *n UK (cf Department of Commerce US)* GEN COMM, POL ≈ ministère du Commerce *m*; ~ **of Trade and Industry** *n UK (DTI)* ECON, GEN COMM, POL ≈ ministère du Commerce et de l'Industrie *m*; ~ **of Transport** *n UK (DTp)* COMMS, IND, TRANSP ≈ ministère des Transports *m*

departmental: ~ **account** *n* ADMIN compte de ministère *m*; ~ **assets** *n pl* ACC avoirs du ministère *m pl*; ~ **bank account** *n* ADMIN, BANK *government accounting* compte bancaire de ministère *m*; ~ **corporation** *n* ADMIN établissement public *m*; ~ **head** *n* GEN COMM chef d'atelier *m*, chef de service *m*, HRM, MGMNT chef de département *m*, S&M chef de rayon *m*; ~ **line object** *n* ADMIN article d'exécution *m*, directives et objectifs ministériels *m pl*; ~ **management** *n* GEN COMM direction de service *f*, gestion de service *f*, MGMNT gestion par département *f*; ~ **manager** *n* GEN COMM chef de service *m*, HRM chef de département *m*, chef de rayon *m*, MGMNT chef de département *m*, S&M *in shop* chef de rayon *m*; ~ **minister** *n* ADMIN ministre titulaire d'un portefeuille *m*; ~ **object** *n* ADMIN article d'exécution *m*, directives et objectifs ministériels *m pl*; ~ **plan** *n* GEN COMM, MGMNT plan de divisions *m*; ~ **program** *n AmE*, ~ **programme** *n BrE* ADMIN programme ministériel *m*

Departmental: ~ **Expenditure Plan** *n* ADMIN programme des dépenses du ministère; ~ **Reporting System** *n* ADMIN système de rapports ministériels *m*

departmentalization *n* GEN COMM cloisonnement *m*, départementalisation *f*

departmentalize *vt* GEN COMM cloisonner

departure *n* GEN COMM, TRANSP départ *m*; ~ **control system** *(DCS)* TRANSP système de contrôle des départs *m*; ~ **lounge** TRANSP salle d'embarquement *f*; ~ **tax** TAX taxe d'aéroport *f*

depend: ~ **on** *vt* GEN COMM reposer essentiellement sur, GEN COMM *(SYN rely on)* compter sur

dependant *n* LAW, TAX personne à charge *f*; ~ **tax credit** TAX crédit pour personne à charge *m*

dependency: ~ **culture** *n jarg* WEL culture de dépendance *f (jarg)*, société d'assistés *f*; ~ **ratio** *n* WEL taux de dépendance *m*; ~ **theory** *n* ECON, POL théorie de la dépendance *f*

dependent¹ *adj* GEN COMM à charge, TAX dépendant; ♦ **be** ~ **on** GEN COMM dépendre de

dependent:² ~ **child** *n* TAX enfant à charge *m*; ~ **claim** *n* PATENTS revendication dépendante *f*; ~ **coverage** *n* INS couverture pour personne à charge *f*; ~ **patent** *n* PATENTS brevet dépendant *m*

de-planing *n AmE* TRANSP débarquement de l'avion *m*

depletable: ~ **externality** *n* ECON économie dépendante *f*

depletion *n* ECON *of resources* amortissement *m*, épuisement *m*, TAX épuisement *m*; ~ **allowance** TAX déduction pour épuisement *f*; ~ **base** TAX base de la déduction pour épuisement *f*; ~ **recapture** ACC récupération de la déduction pour épuisement *f*; ~ **reserve** ACC provision pour épuisement *f*

deploy *vt* GEN COMM déployer, HRM *team* affecter

deployment *n* GEN COMM déploiement *m*, HRM affectation *f*

depolluted *adj* ENVIR *water* dépollué

depolluting: ~ **ship** *n* ENVIR, TRANSP navire dépollueur *m*

depopulation *n* GEN COMM dépeuplement *m*

deport *vt* WEL *immigrant* expulser

deportation *n* WEL expulsion *f*

deposit¹ *n* ACC acompte *m*, caution *f*, BANK, FIN acompte *m*, dépôt *m*, GEN COMM dépôt *m, as security* acompte *m*, caution *f*, cautionnement *m*, consigne *f*, dépôt de garantie *m*, IND gisement *m*, LAW caution *f*, consignation *f*, dépôt *m*, PATENTS dépôt *m*, PROP acompte *m*, S&M arrhes *f pl*, TRANSP *as security* consigne *f*; ~ **account** *n UK (D/A)* BANK compte de dépôt *m*, compte sur livret *m*; ~ **agreement** *n* LAW contrat de dépôt *m*; ~ **balance** *n* BANK solde de dépôt *m*; ~ **bank** *n* BANK, FIN banque de dépôt *f*; ~ **book** *n* BANK carnet de dépôt *m*, livret de dépôt *m*; ~ **facility** *n* ADMIN service de dépôt *m*; ~ **institution** *n* ADMIN, BANK, FIN banque de dépôt *f*, dépôt légal *m*, institution de dépôts *f*; ~ **instrument** *n* BANK instrument de dépôt *m*; ~ **insurance** *n* INS garantie par l'Etat des dépôts à terme; ~ **interest** *n* BANK intérêt sur les dépôts *m*; ~ **liabilities** *n* BANK passif-dépôts *m*, élément du passif-dépôts *m*; ~ **money** *n* BANK monnaie de banque *f*, monnaie scripturale *f*; ~ **multiplier** *n* ECON *econometrics* multiplicateur des réserves bancaires *m*; ~ **note** *n* BANK billet de dépôts *m*; ~ **passbook** *n* BANK carnet de dépôt *m*, livret de dépôt *m*; ~ **premium** *n* INS prime de dépôt *f*, prime provisionnelle *f*; ~ **rate** *n* BANK taux d'intérêt créditeur *m*, taux servi sur les dépôts *m*; ~ **receipt** *n (DR)* BANK reçu de dépôt *m*, récépissé de dépôt *m*; ~ **slip** *n* BANK bordereau de dépôt *m*, bordereau de versement *m*; ~ **and trust accounts** *n pl* BANK comptes de dépôt et de fiducie *m pl*; ~ **with** *n* BANK dépôt à *m*; ♦ **take a** ~ STOCK *Eurodollar time deposit* emprunter, prendre un dépôt

deposit² *vt* BANK, FIN, GEN COMM déposer; ♦ ~ **margin** STOCK déposer une marge

depositary *n (cf depository)* ADMIN, BANK, FIN

banque de dépôt *f*, dépositaire *mf*, dépôt légal *m*, institution de dépôts *f*

Depositary: ~ **Institutions Deregulation & Monetary Control Act** *n US* BANK, ECON, LAW législation fédérale américaine prévoyant la libéralisation du système bancaire

deposition *n* LAW déclaration sous serment d'un témoin *f*, déposition sous serment *f*, témoignage en justice consigné par écrit *m*

depositor *n* BANK, FIN déposant *m*; ~'**s forgery insurance** INS assurance contre le faux en écriture du déposant *f*

depository *n* ADMIN, BANK, FIN banque de dépôt *f*, dépositaire *mf*, dépôt légal *m*, institution de dépôts *f*, GEN COMM garde-meubles *m*

Depository: ~ **Institutions Deregulation and Monetary Control Act** *n US (DIDMCA)* POL *1980* loi sur la dérégulation des institutions de dépôt et le contrôle monétaire; ~ **Trust Company** *n US (DTC)* STOCK ≈ organe de dépôt de titres *m*, ≈ société interprofessionnelle pour la compensation des valeurs mobilières *f (France) (SICOVAM)*

depot *n* TRANSP gare *f*, *storage* dépôt *m*, garage *m*; ~ **charges** *n pl* IMP/EXP frais d'entrepôt *m pl*

depreciable: ~ **amount** *n* ACC montant amortissable *m*, valeur à amortir *f*; ~ **asset** *n* ACC actif amortissable *m*; ~ **basis** *n* ACC base d'amortissement *f*; ~ **cost** *n* ACC coût amortissable *m*; ~ **life** *n* ECON, TAX durée de vie comptable *f*; ~ **property** *n* ACC biens amortissables *m pl*, immobilisations amortissables *f pl*; ~ **real estate** *n* FIN, PROP immobilier sujet à dépréciation *m*

depreciate 1. *vt* ACC amortir, *special write-down* créer une provision pour dépréciation, ECON *currency* déprécier, dévaloriser, *investment, assets* amortir; **2.** *vi* ECON se déprécier, se dévaloriser

depreciated: ~ **cost** *n* ACC coût amorti *m*

depreciation *n* ACC *investment, asset* amortissement *m*, *special write-down* dépréciation *f*, ECON amortissement *m*, *of currency* dépréciation *f*, dévalorisation *f*, FIN, PROP dépréciation *f*; ~ **adjustment** ACC ajustement de l'amortissement *m*; ~ **allowance** ACC dotation aux amortissements *f*; ~ **of fixed assets** BANK dotations aux amortissements *f pl*; ~ **recapture** ACC, TAX récupération de l'amortissement *f*; ~ **reserve** ACC, BANK, FIN provision pour dépréciation *f*; ~ **reserve fund** ACC provision pour dépréciation *f*; ~ **schedule** ACC plan d'amortissement *m*

depressed[1] *adj* ECON *prices, profits, wages* en baisse *loc f*, *regions* en déclin *loc m*, STOCK *commodity prices* déprimé

depressed:[2] ~ **area** *n* ECON zone en crise *f*, zone en déclin *f*, zone sinistrée *f*; ~ **region** *n* ECON région en crise *f*, région en déclin *f*, région sinistrée *f*

depression *n* ECON crise économique *f*, dépression *f*, récession *f*, GEN COMM, POL récession *f*

deprived *adj* LAW *of assets* privé

dept. *abbr (department)* ADMIN, GEN COMM, HRM, POL, S&M serv. *(service)*

depth: ~ **alongside** *n* TRANSP *shipping* profondeur au quai *f*; ~ **analysis** *n* MGMNT analyse en profondeur *f*; ~ **interview** *n* S&M *research technique* entretien en profondeur *m*; ~ **polling** *n* POL sondage en profondeur *m*; ~ **sounder** *n (DS)* TRANSP sondeur *m*; ◆ **in** ~ GEN COMM en profondeur

deputy: ~ **chairman** *n* HRM vice-président *m*; ~ **chief executive** *n* HRM, MGMNT directeur général adjoint *m*; ~ **director** *n* HRM, MGMNT directeur adjoint *m*, sous-directeur *m*; ~ **editor** *n* MEDIA *newspaper, magazine* rédacteur en chef adjoint *m*; ~ **leader** *n UK* POL vice-président *m*; ~ **manager** *n* HRM, MGMNT directeur adjoint *m*, sous-directeur *m*; ~ **managing director** *n* HRM, MGMNT directeur général adjoint *m*; ~ **member of the board of management** *n* HRM, MGMNT membre suppléant du directoire *m*; ~ **minister** *n* ADMIN, POL ministre délégué *m*, sous-ministre *m*

Deputy: ~ **Receiver General** *n* ADMIN sous-receveur général *m*, FIN sous-receveur général *m (Can)*; ~ **Speaker** *n UK* POL vice-président des communes *m*

DEQ *abbr (delivered ex quay)* IMP/EXP livraison franco de douane à quai *loc f*, rendu à quai droits acquittés

der *abbr (derrick)* TRANSP *shipping* mât de charge *m*

derating: ~ **certificate** *n* TRANSP *shipping* certificat de dératisation *m*

derecognition *n UK* HRM *of trade union* refus de reconnaissance *m*

deregistration *n* FIN *of pension plan* retrait d'agrément *m*

deregulate *vt* GEN COMM dérégler, *prices* libérer

deregulation *n* ECON *international trade* déréglementation *f*, GEN COMM déréglementation *f*, *of prices* libération *f*, POL déréglementation *f*, dérégulation *f*

dereliction: ~ **of duty** *n* LAW manquement au devoir *m*

Derivation: ~ **Schedule** *n* ACC Tableau de calcul *m*

derivative *n* FIN, STOCK instrument financier dérivé *m*; ~ **instrument** FIN, STOCK instrument dérivé *m*; ~ **product** IND, S&M produit dérivé *m*

derived: ~ **demand** *n* ECON demande dérivée *f*

derogation *n* LAW atteinte *f*, dérogation *f*

derogatory: ~ **stipulation** *n* LAW stipulation dérogatoire *f*

derrick *n (der)* TRANSP *shipping* mât de charge *m*; ◆ **under ship's** ~ TRANSP sous palan

DERV *abbr* ENVIR *(diesel-engined road vehicle fuel)*, IND *(diesel-engined road vehicle fuel)*, TRANSP *(diesel-engined road vehicle fuel)* gas-oil *m*, gazole *m*, TRANSP *(diesel-engined road vehicle)* véhicule routier à moteur diesel *m*

DES *abbr* IMP/EXP *(delivered ex ship)*, TRANSP *(delivered ex ship)* livraison au navire *loc f*, rendu ex ship

descending: ~ **tops** *n pl* STOCK ligne de sommets baissière *f*, ligne de tendance descendante *f*

descent *n* LAW, PROP transmission de biens par voie de succession ab intestat

describe *vt* GEN COMM décrire

description *n* GEN COMM description *f*, LAW description *f*, désignation *f*, signalement *m*, sorte *f*, PATENTS, PROP description *f*, S&M description *f*, désignation *f*, signalement *m*; ~ **of operational risk** INS caractéristiques du risque d'exploitation *f pl*, description du risque d'exploitation *f*; ~ **of risk** INS caractéristiques du risque *f pl*, description du risque *f*

descriptive[1] *adj* PATENTS descriptif

descriptive:[2] ~ **labeling** *n* AmE, ~ **labelling** *n* BrE S&M étiquetage informatif *m*; ~ **statistics** *n pl* MATH statistique descriptive *f*

deselect *vt* COMP désélectionner, supprimer, HRM réorienter, POL UK *candidate* retirer l'investiture de

deselection *n* UK POL retrait de l'investiture *m*

desertification *n* ENVIR désertification *f*

design *n* GEN COMM *sketch* conception *f*, projet *m*, PATENTS dessin *m*, modèle *m*; ~ **aids** GEN COMM aides à la conception *f pl*; ~ **automation** *(D/A)* COMP, IND conception assistée par ordinateur *f*, création assistée par ordinateur *f (CAO)*; ~ **draft** AmE, ~ **draught** BrE TRANSP tirant d'eau maximal *m*; ~ **engineer** COMP ingénieur d'études *m*; ~ **engineering** GEN COMM étude de conception *f*; ~ **and layout** S&M *of store* conception et agencement *f*; ~ **office** GEN COMM bureau d'étude *m*, bureau de design *m*, bureau de dessin *m*; ~ **right** LAW droit à la propriété industrielle *m*; ~ **weight** TRANSP poids constructeur *m*, poids de calcul *m*, poids prévu *m*

designate *vt* GEN COMM désigner, nommer

designated[1] *adj* GEN COMM désigné, nommé

designated:[2] ~ **amount** *n* TAX montant attribué *m*; ~ **beneficiary** *n* TAX bénéficiaire assimilé *m*, bénéficiaire étranger *m*; ~ **benefit** *n* TAX avantage déterminé *m*; ~ **income** *n* FIN *trust* revenu de distribution *m*; ~ **investment exchange** *n* UK STOCK marché d'investissement agréé *m*; ~ **office** *n* PATENTS office désigné *m*; ~ **property** *n* TAX bien désigné *m*; ~ **region** *n* TAX région désignée *f*; ~ **shareholder** *n* TAX actionnaire déterminé *m*; ~ **surplus** *n* TAX surplus désigné *m*

Designated: ~ **Order Turnaround** *n* US *(DOT)* STOCK ≈ Information et transmission d'ordres *loc f*

designation *n* PATENTS désignation *f*

Designs: ~ **Registry** *n* UK LAW, PATENTS *intellectual property* registre des oeuvres ou modèles créés et déposés

desire: ~ **to purchase** *n* (SYN *demand*) GEN COMM demande *f*

desk *n* ECON table de change *f*, GEN COMM bureau *m*, pupitre *m*; ~ **planner** ADMIN concepteur sur papier *m*; ~ **research** S&M *market research* recher-

che documentaire *f*; ~ **trader** STOCK négociateur aux pupitres *m*

deskilling *n* HRM *of workforce* déqualification *f*

desktop[1] *adj* COMP de bureau *loc m*

desktop:[2] ~ **computer** *n* COMP ordinateur de bureau *m*; ~ **publishing** *n (DTP)* COMP publication assistée par ordinateur *f (PAO)*; ~ **unit** *n* COMP ordinateur de bureau *m*

desktop:[3] ~ **-publish** *vt* MEDIA micro-éditer

deslopping: ~ **barge** *n* TRANSP *shipping* marie-salope *f*

despatch[1] *n see dispatch*

despatch[2] *see dispatch*

despatcher *n see dispatcher*

despatching *n see dispatching*

destination *n* COMP, TRANSP destination *f*; ~ **airport** TRANSP aéroport d'arrivée *m*; ~ **marketing** S&M marketing de destination *m*; ~ **port** TRANSP *shipping* port d'arrivée *m*

destitute: **the** ~ *n* ECON les démunis *m pl*

destruction *n* ENVIR *of rainforests* destruction *f*

destructive: ~ **competition** *n* ECON concurrence destructive *f*, concurrence sauvage *f*, GEN COMM, HRM, S&M concurrence sauvage *f*

detachable: ~ **front end** *n* TRANSP *trailer* avant amovible *m*; ~ **warrant** *n* STOCK bon de souscription d'actions détachable *m*

detail *n* GEN COMM particularité *f*, précision *f*

detailed: ~ **account** *n* GEN COMM décompte *m*, rapport détaillé *m*; ~ **tax calculation** *n* TAX calcul détaillé de l'impôt *m*

details *n pl* ACC, ECON, GEN COMM, TAX, TRANSP renseignements *m pl*; ~ **of dependant** TAX précisions sur la personne à charge *f pl*

detain *vt* GEN COMM *delay* retenir

detention *n* TRANSP *of ship, cargo* saisie *f*

deter *vt* GEN COMM dissuader, décourager, détourner

deteriorate 1. *vt* GEN COMM empirer; **2.** *vi* GEN COMM se détériorer

deterioration *n* GEN COMM détérioration *f*

determination *n* LAW *in tribunal* décision judiciaire *f*, TAX décision *f*, détermination *f*

determine *vt* ECON *price* déterminer, fixer

deterrent *n* GEN COMM effet dissuasif *m*, mesure dissuasive *f*

detonating: ~ **explosive** *n* TRANSP *dangerous classified transported goods* explosif détonant *m*

detonator *n* TRANSP détonateur *m*

detour *n* GEN COMM détour *m*

detriment: **to the** ~ **of** *phr* GEN COMM au détriment de, au préjudice de *loc m*

de-unionization *n* UK HRM désyndicalisation *f*

Deutsche: ~ **Mark** *n* GEN COMM deutsche Mark *m*

devalorization *n* ECON dévalorisation *f*

devaluate *vt* ECON *currency* dévaluer

devaluation *n* ECON dévaluation *f*

devalue *vt* ECON dévaluer

devanning n TRANSP dépotage m

develop vt COMP system, software développer, ENVIR viabiliser, GEN COMM développer, élaborer, IND développer, PROP viabiliser, TRANSP développer

developed: ~ **country** n (DC) ECON, POL pays développé m; ~ **market** n S&M marché exploité m; **the ~ world** n GEN COMM les pays développés m pl

developer n PROP promoteur m

developing: ~ **country** n ECON, GEN COMM, POL pays en voie de développement m, PVD, pays moins avancé m, PMA

development n ECON développement m, expansion f, industrialisation f, GEN COMM développement m, expansion f, IND of prototype, new model, POL développement m, expansion f, industrialisation f, S&M of product développement m; ~ **aid** ECON, POL aide au développement f; ~ **area** UK ECON zone à développer f, zone à urbaniser f; ~ **assistance** ECON, POL assistance au développement f; ~ **director** HRM administrateur chargé du développement m; ~ **economics** ECON, GEN COMM, POL économie du développement f; ~ **expenditure** ACC frais de développement m pl; ~ **management** GEN COMM, MGMNT gestion du développement f, perfectionnement des cadres m; ~ **manager** HRM, MGMNT directeur du développement m; ~ **planning** ECON, FIN, MGMNT, POL programme de développement m; ~ **policy** POL politique de développement f; ~ **potential** GEN COMM potentiel d'expansion m, potentiel de développement m; ~ **program** AmE, ~ **programme** BrE ECON, FIN, MGMNT, POL programme de développement m; ~ **project** ECON, POL projet de développement m; ~ **region** ECON, POL région à développer f; ~ **stage enterprise** ECON, POL entreprise au stade du développement f; ~ **zone** ECON UK zone à urbaniser f

Development: ~ **Aid Committee** n (DAC, Development Assistance Committee) ECON comité d'aide au développement m; ~ **Assistance Committee** n (SYN DAC, Development Aid Committee) ECON of the OECD comité d'aide au développement m

developmental[1] adj IND, PROP, WEL du développement

developmental:[2] ~ **drilling program** n AmE, ~ **drilling programme** n BrE ECON programme de mise en valeur d'anciens forages m

deviation n LAW dérogation f; ~ **clause** (DC) INS marine clause de déviation f, clause dérogatoire f; ~ **fraud** TRANSP shipping déroutement frauduleux m; ~ **policy** MGMNT politique déviationniste f

device:[1] ~ **-independent** adj COMP indépendant du type d'unité, non-titulaire du type d'unité; ~ **-specific** adj COMP propre à une unité

device[2] n COMP dispositif m, périphérique m, unité f, GEN COMM, IND mécanisme m; ~ **driver** COMP programming gestionnaire de périphérique m,

pilote de périphérique m; ~ **mark** PATENTS marque figurative f

devise[1] n LAW, PROP legs m, legs de biens immobiliers m

devise[2] vt LAW léguer

devisee n LAW, PROP héritier testamentaire m, légataire mf

devote vt GEN COMM, MGMNT consacrer

dew: ~ **point** n GEN COMM point de rosée m

DF abbr TRANSP (deadfreight) faux fret m, fret sur le vide m, TRANSP (direction finder) shipping radiogoniomètre m

DFE WEL UK (Department for Education a fusionné en juillet 1995 avec le Department of Employment afin de former le Department of Education and Employment (DEE), ≈ ministère de l'Éducation nationale m

DFR abbr (data freight receipt) TRANSP shipping document fret rapide m, reçu de chargement m

dft abbr (draft) BANK, FIN traite f

DFT abbr (direct fund transfer) BANK virement direct de fonds m

D-G abbr (director-general) HRM, MGMNT DG, PDG (directeur général)

DGB abbr (dangerous goods on board) TRANSP produits dangereux à bord m pl

DGN abbr (dangerous goods note) TRANSP bordereau de marchandises dangereuses m

Dhaka pr n GEN COMM Dacca n pr

d1/2D abbr (dispatch half demurrage) TRANSP prime de célérité payable au taux de la demi-surestarie f

DHSS abbr obs UK (Department of Health and Social Security) WEL consiste maintenant du Department of Health (DoH) et du Department of Social Security (DSS), ≈ ministère de la Santé et des Affaires sociales m

DI abbr US (Department of Industry) IND ≈ ministère de l'Industrie m

diagnosis n GEN COMM diagnostic m

diagnostic n COMP diagnostique m; ~ **message** COMP programming language message de diagnostique m; ~ **routine** GEN COMM programme de diagnostic m

diagonal: ~ **engine** n (D) TRANSP moteur diagonal m; ~ **expansion** n ECON expansion diagonale f; ~ **ply** n TRANSP pneumatic tyre carcasse diagonale f; ~ **spread** n STOCK écart diagonal m

diagram n GEN COMM schéma m

dial:[1] ~ **tone** n AmE (cf dialling tone BrE) COMMS tonalité f

dial[2] vt COMMS composer, signaler (Can)

dialing AmE, **dialling** BrE: ~ **code** n COMMS, GEN COMM telephone indicatif m; ~ **tone** n BrE (cf dial tone AmE) COMMS tonalité f

dialog n AmE see dialogue BrE

dialogue n BrE COMP, GEN COMM dialogue m; ~ **box** BrE COMP boîte de dialogue f, fenêtre de dialogue f, zone de dialogue f

diamond: ~ **investment trust** *n* STOCK *trade* fonds d'investissement diamantaire *m*

diary *n* ADMIN, GEN COMM agenda *m*

dictate *vt* ADMIN, GEN COMM dicter

dictionary *n* COMP dictionnaire *m*

dictum meum pactum *phr frml* GEN COMM dictum meum pactum (*frml*)

DIDMCA *abbr US (Depository Institutions Deregulation and Monetary Control Act)* POL loi sur la dérégulation des institutions de dépôt et le contrôle monétaire

die *vi* GEN COMM mourir; ♦ ~ **intestate** GEN COMM mourir intestat

diesel:[1] ~ **-electric** *adj (D-E)* TRANSP *machinery* diesel-électrique

diesel:[2] ~ **-electric engine** *n* TRANSP moteur diesel-électrique *m*; ~ **-engined road vehicle** *n BrE (DERV)* TRANSP véhicule routier à moteur diesel *m*; ~ **-engined road vehicle fuel** *n BrE (DERV)* ENVIR, IND, TRANSP gas-oil *m*, gazole *m*; ~ **oil** *n (DO)* ENVIR, IND, TRANSP gas-oil *m*, gazole *m*

differ *vi* GEN COMM différer

difference *n* GEN COMM différence *f*; ~ **equation** ECON *econometrics* équation de différence *f*; ~ **-in-conditions insurance** INS assurance complémentaire ou supplémentaire aux conditions *f*; ~ **-in-limits insurance** INS assurance des limites différentes *f*; ~ **-in-value insurance** INS assurance des valeurs différentes *f*; ♦ **make up the** ~ ECON, FIN combler l'écart, GEN COMM rajouter la différence

differences *n pl* STOCK soldes *m pl*

differential *n* GEN COMM, HRM *yield* différentiel *m*, écart *m*, TRANSP *road transport* différentiel *m*; ~ **advantage** ECON avantage différentiel *m*, avantage marginal *m*; ~ **analysis** MGMNT analyse différentielle *f*, analyse modulée *f*; ~ **lock** TRANSP blocage de différentiel *m*; ~ **pay** HRM salaire différentiel *m*, écart des salaires *m*; ~ **price** ECON, S&M prix différentiel *m*; ~ **pricing** ECON fixation de prix différentiels *f*, politique de prix différentiels *f*, S&M différenciation des prix *f*; ~ **theory of rent** ECON théorie différentielle de la rente *f*; ~ **wage** HRM écart des salaires *m*

differentiate *vt* GEN COMM différencier; ♦ ~ **between** GEN COMM faire la différence entre

differentiated: ~ **goods** *n pl* S&M produits différenciés *m pl*; ~ **marketing** *n* S&M marketing de différenciation *m*; ~ **products** *n pl* S&M produits différenciés *m pl*

differentiation *n* S&M différenciation *f*; ~ **strategy** UK S&M stratégie de différenciation *f*

difficult[1] *adj* GEN COMM difficile

difficult:[2] ~ **customer** *n* GEN COMM, S&M client difficile *m*

difficulty *n* GEN COMM difficulté *f*, empêchement *m*

diffusion: ~ **index** *n* ECON *econometrics* indice de diffusion *m*; ~ **rate** *n* IND *production* taux de diffusion *m*

dig: ~ **in one's heels** *phr infrml* GEN COMM se braquer

digit *n* COMP chiffre *m*

digital:[1] *adj* COMMS *communications technology* numérique, COMP digital, numérique, GEN COMM numérique; ~ **-analog** *(D/A)* COMP numérique-analogique *(N/A)*

digital:[2] ~ **-analog converter** *n (DAC)* COMP convertisseur numérique-analogique *m (CNA)*; ~ **computer** *n* COMP calculateur numérique *m*, ordinateur analogique *m*, ordinateur numérique *m*; ~ **data** *n* COMP données numériques *f pl*; ~ **keyboard** *n* COMP clavier numérique *m*; ~ **keypad** *n* COMP clavier numérique *m*; ~ **selective calling** *n (DSC)* COMMS appel sélectif numérique *m*; ~ **sort** *n* COMP tri numérique *m*

digitize *vt* GEN COMM numériser

digits: ~ **deleted** *n* STOCK chiffres manquants *m pl*

dilapidation *n* PROP délâbrement *m*

dilution *n* HRM, STOCK dilution *f*; ~ **of equity** STOCK dilution de l'avoir des actionnaires *f*, dilution du bénéfice par action *f*; ~ **of labor** *AmE*, ~ **of labour** *BrE* HRM adjonction de main-d'oeuvre non qualifiée *f*

DIM *abbr (Diploma in Industrial Management)* WEL diplôme de gestion des entreprises *m*

dime *n US* FIN pièce de dix cents *f*

diminish *vt* GEN COMM diminuer

diminishing: ~ **marginal rate of substitution** *n* ECON taux marginal de substitution décroissant *m*; ~ **marginal utility law** *n* ECON loi de l'utilité marginale décroissante *f*; ~ **returns law** *n* ECON, FIN loi des rendements décroissants *f*; ~ **returns to scale** *n pl* ECON, FIN, STOCK rendements d'échelle décroissants *m pl*

dimmed *adj* COMP *screen* estompé

dinar *n* GEN COMM dinar *m*

dining: ~ **car** *n* TRANSP wagon-restaurant *m*

dinkie *n jarg (double income no kids)* ECON couple sans enfants avec deux revenus

diode *n* COMP *hardware* diode *f*

dip *vi* GEN COMM *profits* fléchir

Dip. *abbr (diploma)* HRM, WEL diplôme *m*

DIP[1] *abbr (dual-in-line package)* COMP boîtier à double rangée de connexions *m*

DIP:[2] ~ **switch** *n (dual-in-line package switch)* COMP *hardware* commutateur DIP *m*, interrupteur à positions multiples *m*, micro-interrupteur *m*

DipCom *abbr (Diploma of Commerce)* WEL diplôme d'études commerciales *m*, diplôme d'études de commerce *m*

DipEcon *abbr (Diploma of Economics)* WEL diplôme en sciences économiques *m*

diploma *n (Dip.)* HRM, WEL diplôme *m*

Diploma: ~ **of Commerce** *n (DipCom)* WEL diplôme d'études commerciales *m*, diplôme d'études de commerce *m*; ~ **of Economics** *n (DipEcon)* WEL diplôme en sciences économiques *m*; ~ **in Industrial Management** *n* *(DIM)* WEL diplôme de gestion des entreprises *m*; ~ **in Public Administration** *n* *(DipPA)* WEL diplôme d'administration de l'état *m*, diplôme d'administration publique *m*; ~ **in Technology** *n* *(DipTech)* WEL diplôme universitaire de technologie *m* *(DUT)*

diplomacy *n* MGMNT diplomatie *f*

diplomatic: ~ **bag** *n* *BrE* *(cf diplomatic pouch AmE)* COMMS valise diplomatique *f*; ~ **mission** *n* POL mission diplomatique *f*; ~ **pouch** *n* *AmE* *(cf diplomatic bag BrE)* COMMS valise diplomatique *f*; ~ **service department** *n* GEN COMM, POL Département du service diplomatique *m*

Diplomatic: ~ **Service Post** *n* ADMIN malle diplomatique *f*; **the** ~ **Service** *n* *UK* ADMIN ≈ la diplomatie *f*

DipPA *abbr* *(Diploma in Public Administration)* WEL diplôme d'administration de l'état *m*, diplôme d'administration publique *m*

DipTech *abbr* *(Diploma in Technology)* WEL DUT *(diplôme universitaire de technologie)*

dir. *abbr* *(direct)* TRANSP direct

direct[1] *adj* *(dir.)* TRANSP *route* direct; ◆ ~ **or held covered** INS *marine* direct ou présumé couvert

direct:[2] ~ **access** *n* COMP accès direct *m*, accès sélectif *m*; ~ **action advertising** *n* S&M publicité d'embauche *f*, publicité par correspondance *f*, publicité par coupon-réponse *f*; ~ **bill of lading** *n* IMP/EXP, TRANSP *shipping* connaissement direct *m*; ~ **booking** *n* LEIS réservation directe *f*; ~ **call** *n* COMMS appel automatique *m*; ~ **charge-off method** *n* ACC *bad debt* système de radiation direct *m*; ~ **clearer** *n* BANK membre adhérent *m*; ~ **clearing member** *n* BANK membre adhérent *m*; ~ **-connect modem** *n* COMMS, COMP *hardware* modem à connexion directe *m*; ~ **cost** *n* *(ANT indirect cost)* ACC charge directe *f*, coût direct *m*, frais directs *m pl*, ECON coût direct *m*, FIN charge directe *f*, coût direct *m*, frais directs *m pl*; ~ **cost of sales** *n* GEN COMM, S&M coût variable des ventes *m*; ~ **costing** *n* ACC méthode des coûts directs *f*; ~ **current** *n* *(DC)* COMP, IND courant continu *m*; ~ **data entry** *n* *(DDE)* COMP saisie directe *f*, saisie en ligne *f*; ~ **debit** *n* *(DD)* BANK avis de prélèvement *m*, prélèvement automatique *m*, prélèvement autorisé *m*; ~ **delivery** *n* TRANSP livraison directe *f*; ~ **deposit** *n* *Can* BANK virement automatique *m*, virement automatique de fonds *m*; ~ **deposit transaction** *n* *Can* BANK mouvement de virement automatique *m*; ~ **dialing** *n* *AmE*, ~ **dialling** *n* *BrE* COMMS téléphone automatique *m*; ~ **discrimination** *n* *UK* HRM embauche préférentielle *f*; ~ **distance dialing** *n* *AmE* *(DDD, subscriber trunk dialling)* COMMS appel automatique longue distance *loc m*, automatique interurbain *m*, l'automatique *m*; ~ **equity** *n* TAX intérêt direct *m*; ~ **expense** *n* ACC charge directe *f*, coût direct *m*, frais directs *m pl*, ECON coût direct *m*, FIN charge directe *f*, coût direct *m*, frais directs *m pl*; ~ **financial leasing**

agreement *n* ECON contrat de location-financement *m*; ~ **foreign investment** *n* ECON investissement étranger direct *m*; ~ **fund transfer** *n* *(DFT)* BANK virement direct de fonds *m*; ~ **and indirect taxation** *n* ECON, TAX imposition directe et indirecte *f*; ~ **-indirect taxes ratio** *n* ECON, TAX coefficient des impôts directs-indirects *m*; ~ **insurance** *n* INS assurance directe *f*; ~ **insurer** *n* INS assureur direct *m*; ~ **investment** *n* STOCK investissement direct *m*, placement direct *m*; ~ **labor** *n* *AmE* *see direct labour BrE*; ~ **labor costs** *n pl* *AmE* *see direct labour costs BrE*; ~ **labor organization** *n* *AmE* *see direct labour organization BrE*; ~ **labour** *n* *BrE* *(ANT indirect labour)* ACC, ECON, HRM main-d'oeuvre directe *f*; ~ **labour costs** *n pl* *BrE* ACC charges de main-d'oeuvre directes *f pl*, IND *production* coûts de la main-d'oeuvre *m pl*, coûts salariaux directs *m pl*; ~ **labour organization** *n* *UK* *(DLO)* HRM organisation de la main-d'oeuvre directe, GEN COMM syndicat ouvrier; ~ **liability** *n* LAW responsabilité directe *f*; ~ **line** *n* COMMS ligne directe *f*; ~ **mail** *n* ADMIN publicité directe *f*, S&M publicité directe *f*, publicité directe par correspondance *f*, publipostage *m*; ~ **mail advertising** *n* S&M publicité directe *f*, publicité directe par correspondance *f*, publipostage *m*; ~ **mail shot** *n* S&M mailing *m*; ~ **mailing** *n* S&M publicité directe *f*, publicité directe par correspondance *f*, publipostage *m*; ~ **marketing** *n* S&M marketing direct *m*; ~ **material** *n* ECON matière première directe *f*; ~ **overhead** *n* ECON, FIN charge directe de structure *f*; ~ **participation program** *n* *AmE*, ~ **participation programme** *n* *BrE* FIN programme de participation directe *m*; ~ **payment** *n* ECON *grants* paiement direct *m*; ~ **port** *n* *(DP)* TRANSP *shipping* port direct *m*; ~ **production** *n* ECON production directe *f*; ~ **response** *n* S&M publicité directe par correspondance *f*, *telephone selling* publicité directe *f*, réponse directe *f*; ~ **response advertising** *n* S&M publicité d'embauche *f*, publicité par correspondance *f*, publicité par coupon-réponse *f*; ~ **route** *n* TRANSP itinéraire direct *m*, route directe *f*, trajet direct *m*; ~ **sale** *n* S&M vente directe *f*; ~ **selling** *n* S&M vente directe *f*; ~ **spending envelope** *n* FIN enveloppe de dépenses directes *f*; ~ **spending program** *n* *AmE*, ~ **spending programme** *n* *BrE* ACC *government* programme de dépenses directes *m*; ~ **tax** *n* ECON, TAX imposition directe *f*; ~ **taxation** *n* ECON imposition directe *f*, TAX contributions directes *f pl*, imposition directe *f*; ~ **taxes** *n pl* TAX contributions directes *f pl*; ~ **trader input** *n* *(DTI)* IMP/EXP entrée directe commerçant *f*; ~ **transhipment** *n* TRANSP *shipping* transbordement direct *m*; ~ **yield** *n* STOCK rendement direct *m*

direct[3] *vt* MEDIA réaliser, MGMNT *organization* diriger

Direct: ~ **Marketing Association** *n* *US* *(DMA)* S&M association du marketing direct

directed: ~ **interview** *n* S&M *market research* interview dirigée *f*; ~ **verdict** *n* LAW verdict recommandé au jury par le juge s'il estime les faits incontestables

direction *n* ECON *of interest rates* orientation *f*, tendance *f*, MEDIA réalisation *f*, MGMNT direction *f*; ~ **finder** *(DF)* TRANSP *shipping* radiogoniomètre *m*

directions: ~ **for use** *n pl* GEN COMM mode d'emploi *m*

directive *n* LAW, POL directive *f*

directly:[1] ~ **-transported** *adj* IMP/EXP, TRANSP *EU* acheminé directement, directement transporté

directly[2] *adv* GEN COMM *(ANT indirectly)*, MATH *(ANT inversely)* directement; ◆ ~ **related to** GEN COMM directement lié à; ~ **responsible to** GEN COMM directement responsable vis-à-vis de

directly:[3] ~ **unproductive profit-seeking activities** *n pl (DUP)* ECON activités à but lucratif non directement productives *f pl*

director *n* HRM *(D)* directeur *m*, dirigeant *m (D)*, MEDIA réalisateur *m*, MGMNT directeur *m*, dirigeant *m (D)*; ~ **-general** *(D-G)* HRM, MGMNT directeur général *m (DG)*, président-directeur général *m (PDG)*; ~ **of public relations** *(DPR)* HRM *advertising*, S&M chef du service des relations publiques *m*, directeur des relations publiques *m*, responsable des relations publiques *m*

Director: ~ **General of Fair Trading** *n UK* GEN COMM Directeur général de la Concurrence et des prix *m*; ~ **of Labor Relations** *n AmE*, ~ **of Labour Relations** *n BrE* HRM Directeur des Affaires Sociales *m*; ~ **of Public Prosecutions** *n UK (DPP, district attorney)* LAW ≈ procureur de la République *m (France)*, ≈ procureur du Roi *m (Belgique)*

directorate *n* GEN COMM, HRM, MGMNT conseil d'administration *m*, CA

Directorate: ~ **of Overseas Surveys** *n (DOS)* GEN COMM direction des enquêtes à l'étranger

directors': ~ **circular** *n* GEN COMM circulaire du conseil d'administration *f*; ~ **fees** *n pl* HRM jetons de présence *m pl*; ~ **and officers' liability insurance** *n* INS assurance responsabilité civile des administrateurs et des officiers *f*; ~ **report** *n* GEN COMM rapport annuel *m*; ~ **shares** *n* STOCK actions réservées aux membres du conseil d'administration *f*

directorship *n* HRM direction *f*

directory *n* COMP annuaire *m*, catalogue *m*, répertoire *m*, GEN COMM annuaire *m*; ~ **assistance** *n* COMMS assistance-annuaire *f (Can)*, service d'assistance annuaire *m*; ~ **enquiries** *n pl BrE (cf directory information AmE)* COMMS assistance-annuaire *f (Can)*, renseignements téléphoniques *m pl (Fra)*, service d'assistance annuaire *m*; ~ **information** *n AmE (cf directory enquiries BrE)* COMMS assistance-annuaire *f (Can)*, renseignements téléphoniques *m pl (Fra)*, service d'assistance annuaire *m*

dirham *n* GEN COMM dirham *m*

dirty: ~ **bill** *n* IMP/EXP, TRANSP *shipping* connaissement avec réserves *m*, connaissement brut *m*, connaissement clausé *m*; ~ **bill of lading** *n* IMP/EXP, TRANSP *shipping* connaissement avec réserves *m*, connaissement brut *m*, connaissement clausé *m*; ~ **float** *n* ECON flottement impur *m*; ~ **money** *n* TRANSP *shipping* indemnité de travail salissant *f*; ~ **tricks campaign** *n* POL campagne diffamatoire *f*

disability *n* HRM invalidité *f*, *of employee* handicap *m*; ~ **allowance** TAX crédit pour personnes handicapées *m*; ~ **annuity** INS, WEL garantie invalidité *f*, prestation pour incapacité *f*, rente d'invalidité *f*; ~ **benefit** WEL garantie invalidité *f*, prestation pour incapacité *f*, rente d'invalidité *f*; ~ **buy-out insurance** *US* INS assurance invalidité rachetable *f*; ~ **cover** INS assurance invalidité *f*; ~ **credit** *Can* TAX crédit pour personnes handicapées *m*; ~ **income insurance** *US* INS assurance de rente d'invalidité *f*; ~ **insurance** INS assurance incapacité *f*, assurance invalidité *f*; ~ **of partner buy and sell insurance** INS assurance achat-vente contre l'invalidité du partenaire *f*; ~ **percentage table** INS barème d'invalidité *m*, table d'invalidité *f*; ~ **tax allowance** TAX crédit d'impôt pour personnes handicapées *m*; ~ **tax credit** *Can* TAX crédit d'impôt pour personnes handicapées *m*

disabled[1] *adj* COMP hors service, non-disponible

disabled:[2] ~ **quota** *n* HRM proportion de travailleurs handicapés *f*; ~ **workers** *n pl* HRM travailleurs handicapés *m pl*

disablement *n* GEN COMM invalidité *f*; ~ **pension** FIN, WEL pension d'invalidité *f*

disadvantage *n* GEN COMM désavantage *m*, inconvénient *m*

disadvantaged *adj* ECON, POL désavantagé

disadvantageous *adj* GEN COMM désavantageux

disaffirm *vt* GEN COMM défaire, dénoncer

disagio *n* GEN COMM courtage *m*

disagree 1. *vt* ~ **with** s'opposer à **2.** *vi (ANT agree)* GEN COMM ne pas être d'accord *loc m*, être en désaccord *loc m*

disagreement *n* GEN COMM *dispute* différend *m*, désaccord *m*

disallow *vt* GEN COMM ne pas accepter, rejeter, TAX *deduction* rejeter; ◆ ~ **a deduction** TAX ne pas admettre une déduction, refuser une déduction

disappointing *adj* GEN COMM décevant

disarmament *n* WEL désarmement *m*

disaster: ~ **clause** *n* INS clause de catastrophe *f*, clause de sauvegarde *f*

disbursable *adj* ACC, FIN déboursable

disburse *vt* ACC, FIN débourser

disbursement *n* ACC, BANK, FIN débours *m*; ~ **commission** GEN COMM commission sur débours *f*; ~ **quota** TAX *charities* contingent des versements *m*

disburser *n* FIN agent payeur *m*, officier payeur *m*

disc. *abbr (discount)* GEN COMM discompte *m*, esc. *(escompte)*

DISC *abbr US (Domestic International Sales*

Corporation) GEN COMM société nationale de ventes à l'exportation

discharge[1] *n* FIN acquittement *m*, paiement *m*, règlement *m, of bankrupt* réhabilitation *f*, GEN COMM *of debt* acquittement *m*, paiement *m*, règlement *m*, LAW *of bankrupt* réhabilitation *f, of contract* accomplissement *m*, extinction *f, of prisoner* libération *f*, WEL libération *f*; **~ afloat** *(D/A)* TRANSP *shipping* déchargement sur rade *m*; **~ at sea** ENVIR, IND *pollution* rejet en mer *m*; **~ of bankruptcy** FIN, LAW réhabilitation de faillite *f*; **~ in bankruptcy** FIN, LAW réhabilitation du failli *f*; **~ of lien** LAW extinction d'un gage *f*, extinction d'un privilège *f*, purge d'un privilège *f*; **~ of mortgage** BANK libération d'hypothèque *f*; **~ port** TRANSP port de déchargement *m*; **~ of the trustee** LAW libération du fidéicommissaire *f*

discharge[2] *vt* BANK régler, GEN COMM *bill* acquitter, *debt* acquitter, régler, HRM renvoyer, LAW *obligation* accomplir, exécuter, remplir, *debt* acquitter, régler, *bankrupt* réhabiliter, *prisoner* libérer, WEL libérer

discharged *adj* LAW, WEL en liberté *loc f*

discharging: **~ berth** *n* TRANSP *shipping* poste de déchargement *m*; **~ wharf** *n* TRANSP débarcadère *m*, quai de déchargement *m*

disciplinary: **~ lay-off** *n* HRM mise à pied pour motif disciplinaire *f*; **~ measures** *n pl* LAW mesures disciplinaires *f pl*; **~ procedure** *n* HRM procédure disciplinaire *f*; **~ rule** *n* HRM règle disciplinaire *f*, règlement disciplinaire *m*

discipline[1] *n* GEN COMM, HRM discipline *f*

discipline[2] *vt* LAW discipliner, prendre des sanctions, punir

disciplined: **~ movement** *n* TRANSP mouvement planifié *m*

disclaim *vt* LAW, TAX répudier

disclaimer *n* INS démenti *m*, renonciation à un droit *f*, LAW désistement *m*, renonciation *f*, répudiation *f*, TAX répudiation *f*; **~ of opinion** ACC refus d'exprimer une opinion *m*

disclose *vt* GEN COMM divulguer, révéler

disclosed: **~ reserves** *n pl* ACC réserves déclarées *f pl*

disclosure *n* STOCK publication *f*; **~ of information** HRM divulgation d'information *f*; **~ of the invention** PATENTS exposé de l'invention *m*; **~ requirement** GEN COMM obligation d'information *f*, STOCK exigence de publication *f*

discomfort: **~ index** *n* ECON indice d'inconfort *m*

discontent: **~ in the workplace** *n* HRM mécontentement sur le lieu de travail *m*

discontinue *vt* GEN COMM *service* supprimer, IND *production* arrêter, WEL *service* supprimer; ◆ **~ an appeal** TAX se désister d'un appel

discontinued: **~ operations** *n pl* ACC secteurs d'activités abandonnés *m pl*

discount[1] *n* ACC réduction *f*, BANK *bills* escompte *m*, ECON *between currencies* déport *m*, FIN rabais *m*, remise *f*, GEN COMM discompte *m*, remise *f*, ristourne *f*, escompte *m*, réduction *f*, S&M rabais *m*, remise *f*, ristourne *f*, réduction *f*, STOCK disaggio *m*, déport *m*, escompte *m, shares* décote *f*; **~ bill** *n* ACC billet à escompte *m*; **~ bond** *n* STOCK obligation au-dessous du pair *f*, obligation à escompte *f*; **~ broker** *n* STOCK courtier exécutant *m*; **~ brokerage** *n* STOCK courtage réduit *m*; **~ center** *n AmE*, **~ centre** *n BrE* S&M magasin discompte *m*, magasin discount *m*; **~ charges** *n pl* ACC frais d'escompte *m pl*; **~ house** *n* S&M magasin discompte *m*, magasin discount *m*, magasin mini-marge *m*, STOCK opérateur principal du marché *m*, OPM; **~ market** *n* FIN marché d'escompte *m*; **~ market loan** *n* FIN fonds d'escompte *m*; **~ mechanism** *n* FIN mécanisme d'escompte *m*; **~ price** *n* FIN prix discompte *m*, prix discompté *m*; **~ rate** *n* BANK, FIN taux d'escompte *m*; **~ sale** *n* GEN COMM vente au rabais *f*; **~ selling** *n* GEN COMM vente au rabais *f*; **~ shop** *n BrE (SYN discount house, discount store)* S&M magasin discompte *m*, magasin discount *m*, magasin mini-marge *m*; **~ stockbroker** *n* STOCK courtier exécutant *m*; **~ store** *n (cf discount house, discount shop BrE)* S&M magasin discompte *m*, magasin discount *m*, magasin mini-marge *m*; **~ travel** *n* LEIS voyages à tarif réduit *m pl*; **~ window** *n AmE* FIN prises en pension *f pl*; **~ yield** *n* STOCK rendement d'une valeur vendue en dessous du pair *m*; ◆ **at a ~** *(AAD)* FIN avec un déport *m*, à escompte, STOCK avec une décote, à escompte; **at a two per cent ~** STOCK avec une décote de deux pour cent; **give sb a ~** S&M consentir une remise à qn; **no ~** *(ND)* S&M pas de rabais; **on a ~ basis** STOCK sur une base d'escompte

discount[2] *vt* BANK escompter, FIN discompter, GEN COMM faire une remise de *loc f*, MGMNT réduire, S&M *goods* solder, STOCK escompter, prendre en compte

discounted: **~ bill** *n* BANK effet escompté *m*; **~ bond** *n* STOCK obligation au-dessous du pair *f*, obligation à escompte *f*; **~ cash flow** *n (DCF)* ACC, FIN valeur actualisée nette *f*; **~ loan** *n* BANK prêt escompté *m*; **~ present value** *n* FIN valeur actualisée *f*; **~ share price** *n* STOCK prix actualisé de l'action *m*

discounter *n* FIN discompteur *m*

discounting *n* ACC, ECON, FIN actualisation *f*; **~ banker** BANK banquier en escompte *m*; **~ of bills** *BrE (cf discounting of notes AmE)* ACC escompte d'effets de commerce *m*; **~ of notes** *AmE (cf discounting of bills BrE)* ACC escompte d'effets de commerce *m*

discourage *vt* GEN COMM décourager

discouraged: **~ worker hypothesis** *n* HRM hypothèse de l'employé découragé *f*; **~ workers** *n* HRM travailleurs démotivés *m pl*

discovery *n* LAW communication de pièces *f*; **~ sampling** MATH échantillon d'exploration *m*

discrepancy *n* GEN COMM différend *m*, désaccord *m*, écart *m*

discrete: ~ **variable** n MATH *statistics* variable discrète f

discretion n GEN COMM discrétion f; ◆ **at our** ~ GEN COMM à notre discrétion; **at the** ~ **of** GEN COMM au bon vouloir de, à la discrétion de

discretionary[1] adj ECON, GEN COMM discrétionnaire

discretionary:[2] ~ **account** n FIN clientèle privée gérée f, compte discrétionnaire m; ~ **authority** n BANK pouvoir discrétionnaire m; ~ **cost** n ECON coût discrétionnaire m; ~ **deduction** n TAX déduction discrétionnaire f; ~ **fiscal policy** n ECON, TAX politique fiscale discrétionnaire f; ~ **income** n ECON revenu discrétionnaire m; ~ **limit** n BANK limite discrétionnaire f; ~ **policy** n ECON, POL politique discrétionnaire f; ~ **share** n STOCK part discrétionnaire f; ~ **spending power** n ECON *of government*, POL pouvoir d'achat discrétionnaire m; ~ **trust** n LAW fidéicommis doté de pouvoirs discrétionnaires

discriminate vt GEN COMM discriminer; ~ **against** GEN COMM établir une discrimination envers

discriminating: ~ **monopoly** n ECON monopole discriminatoire m

discrimination n ECON, GEN COMM, WEL discrimination f; **no** ~ **factor** GEN COMM facteur de non-discrimination m

discriminatory: ~ **taxation of foreigners** n TAX imposition discriminatoire des étrangers f

discuss vt GEN COMM discuter, débattre

discussion n GEN COMM discussion f, débat m; ◆ **under** ~ GEN COMM en cours de discussion, soumis à discussion

diseconomy n ECON déséconomie f; ~ **of scale** (ANT *economy of scale*) ECON, IND déséconomie d'échelle f

disembark vti TRANSP débarquer

disembarkation n TRANSP débarquement m

disequilibrium n ECON déséquilibre m; ~ **economics** ECON théorie économique du déséquilibre f; ~ **price** ECON prix de déséquilibre m

disguised: ~ **unemployment** n ECON, HRM chômage déguisé m

dishonest adj GEN COMM malhonnête

dishonor[1] n AmE see dishonour BrE

dishonor[2] AmE see dishonour BrE

dishonored: ~ **bill** n AmE see dishonoured bill BrE; ~ **bill of exchange** n AmE see dishonoured bill of exchange BrE; ~ **check** n AmE see dishonoured cheque BrE

dishonour[1] n BrE BANK défaut d'acceptation de paiement m

dishonour[2] vt BrE BANK, FIN *cheque* ne pas honorer; ◆ ~ **a cheque** BrE, BANK *said of the drawee* refuser de payer un chèque

dishonoured: ~ **bill** n BrE GEN COMM effet refusé m; ~ **bill of exchange** n BrE IMP/EXP traite impayée f; ~ **cheque** n BrE BANK chèque impayé m

disincentive n ECON désincitation f, effet décourageant m; ~ **effect** ECON effet de désincitation m, effet dissuasif m

disinflation n ECON désinflation f

disinformation n POL désinformation f

disintegration n ECON désincorporation f, GEN COMM désintégration f, POL désincorporation f

disintermediate vt ECON procéder à une désintermédiation

disintermediation n BANK, ECON désintermédiation f

disinvestment n FIN désinvestissement m

disjoint: ~ **events** n pl GEN COMM événements mutuellement alternatifs m pl, événements mutuellement exclusifs m pl

disk n ADMIN, COMP disque m, disque souple m, disquette f; ~ **drive** n COMP lecteur de disques m, unité de disque f; ~ **operating system**® n (*DOS*) COMP système d'exploitation à disques® m (*DOS*); ~ **pack** n COMP chargeur m; ~ **space** n COMP espace disque m; ~ **unit** n COMP unité de disque f

diskette n ADMIN, COMP disque souple m, disquette f; ~ **drive** ADMIN unité de disquette f, COMP lecteur de disquettes m, unité de disquette f

dismantling n ECON *of barriers* démantèlement m

dismiss vt (*cf dehire AmE*) HRM licencier, renvoyer

dismissal n (*cf dehiring AmE*) HRM exclusion f, licenciement m, renvoi m; ~ **procedure** HRM procédure de renvoi f; ~ **wage** HRM indemnité de licenciement f

disorderly: ~ **market** n STOCK marché confus et non-transparent m

disparaging: ~ **statements** n pl LAW déclarations dénigrantes f pl

disparity n GEN COMM disparité f, écart m

dispatch[1] n TRANSP expédition f, *charge* bonification f, prime de célérité f; ~ **bay** TRANSP quai de chargement m; ~ **department** TRANSP service d'expédition m; ~ **money** TRANSP *shipping* bonification f, prime de célérité f; ~ **note** TRANSP bordereau d'expédition m, bulletin d'expédition m; ◆ ~ **discharging only** (*DDO*) TRANSP bonification au déchargement, prime de célérité au déchargement f; ~ **half demurrage** (*d1/2D*) TRANSP *shipping* prime de célérité payable au taux de la demi-surestarie f; ~ **loading only** (*DLO*) TRANSP *shipping* bonification au chargement, bonification payable pour temps gagné au chargement; ~ **money payable both ends** (*DBE*) TRANSP *shipping, loading and discharge ports* bonification payable au chargement et au déchargement, prime de célérité payable au chargement et au déchargement f; ~ **money payable on time saved during loading** TRANSP *shipping* bonification payable pour temps gagné au chargement, prime de célérité payable au temps gagné au chargement f; ~ **payable both ends all time saved** (*DBEATS*) TRANSP *loading and discharging ports* bonification payable au chargement et au déchargement pour temps gagné *f,* prime de célérité payable au chargement et au déchargement pour temps gagné *f;* ~ **payable both ends on laytime saved** *(DBELTS)* TRANSP *shipping, loading and discharge ports* bonification payable au chargement et au déchargement pour temps gagné *f*

dispatch[2] *vt* COMP acheminer, expédier, TRANSP *aviation* acheminer, expédier, réguler, répartir

dispatcher *n* IMP/EXP expéditeur *m,* TRANSP expéditeur *m, aviation* régulateur *m,* répartiteur *m*

dispatching *n* COMP acheminement *m,* TRANSP acheminement *m,* expédition *f, aviation* régulation *f,* répartition *f;* ~ **charge** GEN COMM frais d'envoi *m pl,* frais d'expédition *m pl*

dispensation *n* LAW dispense *f*

displacement: ~ **loaded** *n (*SYN *displacement tonnage)* TRANSP *shipping* déplacement en charge *m;* ~ **tonnage** *n (*SYN *displacement loaded)* TRANSP *shipping* déplacement en charge *m*

display[1] *n* COMMS, COMP affichage *m,* visualisation *f,* écran *m,* GEN COMM étalage *m,* S&M panneau d'affichage *m,* étalage *m;* ~ **advertisement** MEDIA grande annonce *f;* ~ **device** COMP unité de visualisation *f,* écran de visualisation *m;* ~ **file** COMP fichier de visualisation *m,* fichier graphique *m;* ~ **monitor** COMP écran de visualisation *m;* ~ **setting** COMP réglage de l'affichage *m;* ~ **stand** MEDIA *for books, newspapers* présentoir *m;* ~ **unit** COMP unité d'affichage *f*

display[2] *vt* COMP afficher, présenter sur écran, visualiser, GEN COMM, S&M afficher

displayed: ~ **price** *n* ECON, S&M prix affiché *m*

disponent: ~ **owner** *n* TRANSP *shipping* armateur disposant *m,* utilisateur comme armateur *m;* ~ **user** *n* COMP, ECON, GEN COMM utilisateur final *m*

disposable: ~ **income** *n* ECON, TAX revenu disponible *m*

disposal *n* FIN, LAW, STOCK cession *f,* TAX disposition *f;* ~ **facility** ENVIR *waste* déchetterie *f,* installation d'élimination des déchets *f;* ~ **of securities** STOCK cession de titres *f,* cession de valeurs mobilières *f*

dispose: ~ **of** *vt* S&M *stock* écouler, TAX disposer de

disposition *n* TAX disposition *f*

dispossess:[1] ~ **proceedings** *n pl* LAW, PATENTS procédure d'expropriation *f*

dispossess[2] *vt* LAW déposséder, PROP déposséder, exproprier

dispute[1] *n* GEN COMM *boardroom* conflit *m,* désaccord *m,* HRM, POL conflit *m;* ~ **procedure** GEN COMM, HRM procédure de règlement des conflits *f,* procédure en cas de conflit *f;* ~ **resolution** HRM résolution de conflit *f;* ◆ **in** ~ HRM *with employer* en conflit

dispute[2] *vt* LAW *claim* contester, *will* attaquer, contester

disputed: ~ **tax** *n* TAX impôt contesté *m*

disputes: ~ **committee** *n* HRM commission des conflits sociaux *f*

disruption *n* GEN COMM interruption *f,* perturbation *f*

dissaving *n* ECON désépargne *f*

disseminate *vt* GEN COMM, POL propager, TRANSP *container contents* dégrouper

dissemination *n* GEN COMM *of information* diffusion *f*

dissolution *n* GEN COMM, HRM, LAW, POL *of parliament* dissolution *f*

dissolve *vt* GEN COMM *partnership, parliament* dissoudre

distance: ~ **freight** *n* TRANSP *shipping* fret de distance *m;* ~ **learning** *n* WEL apprentissage à distance *m,* télé-enseignement *m*

distancing *n* HRM sous-traitance *f*

distilling *n* GEN COMM distillation *f*

distinction *n* GEN COMM *difference* différence *f,* distinction *f, outstanding quality* distinction *f;* ◆ **make a** ~ **between** GEN COMM distinguer entre, faire la différence entre

distinctive *adj* PATENTS distinctif

distinctiveness *n* PATENTS caractère distinctif *m*

distinguished *adj* GEN COMM, HRM *career* remarquable, éminent

distort *vt* ECON, FIN *figures,* GEN COMM *facts, text* altérer

distortion *n* ECON, FIN, GEN COMM distorsion *f*

distraint *n* LAW, PROP saisie *f,* saisie-exécution *f;* ~ **of property** LAW, PROP saisie *f*

distressed: ~ **property** *n* PROP propriété saisie *f*

distributable: ~ **profit** *n* ACC résultat net de l'exercice *m*

distribute *vt* FIN répartir, ventiler, GEN COMM *information* distribuer, répartir

distributed[1] *adj* COMP décentralisé, réparti; ◆ **when** ~ STOCK comme si coté, sous réserve d'émission

distributed:[2] ~ **computing** *n* COMP informatique répartie *f,* traitement décentralisé *m;* ~ **database** *n (DDB)* COMP base de données répartie *f;* ~ **profit** *n* ACC bénéfices attribués aux actionnaires *m pl,* FIN bénéfices distribués *m;* ~ **system** *n* COMP système décentralisé *m*

distributing: ~ **syndicate** *n* STOCK syndicat de placement *m*

distribution *n* ECON répartition *f,* FIN répartition *f,* ventilation *f,* GEN COMM distribution *f,* répartition *f,* LAW *estate* distribution *f,* partage *m,* répartition *f,* S&M *by manufacturer* distribution *f,* STOCK placement *m,* TRANSP *by manufacturer* distribution *f, of load* répartition *f;* ~ **allowance** *n* S&M remise de distribution *f;* ~ **area** *n* STOCK fourchette de variation du cours *f;* ~ **of capital** *n* ECON, TAX répartition de capital *f;* ~ **center** *n* AmE, ~ **centre** *n* BrE TRANSP centre de distribution *m;* ~ **cost analysis** *n* S&M analyse des coûts de distribution *f;* ~ **costs** *n pl* ACC, TRANSP coûts de distribution *m pl,* frais de distribution *m pl;* ~ **depot** *n* TRANSP dépôt de distribution *m;*

~ **manager** n MGMNT, TRANSP chef de distribution m; ~ **of net profit** n ACC répartition du résultat net f; ~ **network** n COMP réseau de distribution m, GEN COMM circuit de commercialisation m, circuit de distribution m, réseau de distribution m, IND circuit de distribution m; ~ **office** n (DO) TRANSP bureau de distribution m; ~ **planning** n GEN COMM, TRANSP planification de distribution f, planning de distribution m; ~ **policy** n GEN COMM, TRANSP politique de distribution f; ~ **of risks** n INS dispersion des risques f, répartition des risques f; ~ **service** n TRANSP service de distribution m; ~ **of wealth** n ECON, POL répartition des richesses f

distributive: ~ **ability** n TRANSP capacité de distribution f

distributor n IMP/EXP, S&M, TRANSP distributeur m

district n ENVIR, GEN COMM in town quartier m; ~ **agreement** UK HRM accord au niveau d'une région m; ~ **attorney** US (D/A, Director of Public Prosecutions) LAW ≈ procureur de la République m (France), ≈ procureur du Roi m (Belgique); ~ **court** US LAW tribunal fédéral de première instance m; ~ **heating boiler plant** IND installation de chaudières pour le chauffage urbain f; ~ **heating power station** ENVIR, IND centrale électrique de chauffage urbain f; ~ **manager** HRM directeur régional m; ~ **officer** (DO) HRM, MGMNT responsable régional m; ~ **traffic superintendent** (DTS) HRM, TRANSP railway directeur régional de circulation m, directeur régional des transports m; ~ **training officer** (DTO) HRM directeur régional de la formation professionnelle m, responsable régional de la formation professionnelle m

District: ~ **Council** n UK ADMIN conseil de district m

disturbance: ~ **term** n MATH statistics durée de perturbation f

disutility n ECON désutilité f

div. abbr (dividend) FIN, STOCK div. (dividende)

diverge vi ECON, GEN COMM exchange rates diverger

divergence n (ANT convergence) ECON, GEN COMM, POL of opinions, results, STOCK of futures price divergence f; ~ **indicator** ECON EU indicateur de divergence m; ~ **threshold** ECON seuil de divergence m

divergent: ~ **thinking** n MGMNT avis divergent m

diverse adj GEN COMM différent, varié

diversification n ECON, HRM, MGMNT, STOCK diversification f; ~ **strategy** S&M stratégie de diversification f

diversified: ~ **company** n ECON, GEN COMM entreprise diversifiée f

diversify vt GEN COMM diversifier, varier; ◆ ~ **risk** STOCK diversifier les risques

diversity n GEN COMM, S&M diversité f

divest: ~ **o.s. of** vt TAX se défaire de

divestiture n LAW dessaisissement m, dépossession f

divestment n FIN scission d'actif f

divide vt COMP diviser; ~ **up** GEN COMM fractionner; ◆ ~ **into plots** PROP lotir

divided: ~ **by** phr MATH divisé par

dividend n (div.) FIN, STOCK dividende m (div.); ~ **addition** n INS addition de dividende f, majoration de dividende f; ~ **allowance** n TAX exemption pour dividendes f; ~ **announcement** n STOCK déclaration de dividende f; ~ **bond** n STOCK obligation participante f; ~ **coupon** n STOCK coupon de dividende m; ~ **cover** n ACC, FIN taux de couverture du dividende m; ~ **coverage** n STOCK couverture des dividendes f; ~ **coverage ratio** n STOCK ratio de couverture des dividendes m; ~ **declaration** n STOCK déclaration de dividende f; ~ **eligible for interest and dividends income deduction** n STOCK dividende donnant droit à la déduction pour revenus en intérêts et en dividendes m; ~ **fund** n STOCK fonds de dividendes m; ~ **gross-up** n STOCK majoration des dividendes f; ~ **in arrears** n STOCK dividende à terme échu m; ~ **in kind** n STOCK dividende en nature m; ~ **income** n STOCK revenu de dividende m; ~ **net** n ACC dividende net m; ~ **payable** n ACC dividende à payer m; ~ **payout ratio** n ACC pourcentage du bénéfice net distribué en dividende m; ~ **per share** n ACC balance sheet, STOCK dividende par action m, DPA; ~ **policy** n FIN, STOCK politique de dividendes f, politique de versement des dividendes f; ~ **-price ratio** n FIN rapport dividende-prix m; ~ **reinvestment** n STOCK réinvestissement des dividendes m; ~ **reinvestment plan** n STOCK plan d'épargne avec capitalisation m, plan de réinvestissement des dividendes m; ~ **requirements** n pl ACC besoins en dividende m pl; ~ **rollover plan** n STOCK achat et vente d'actions pour bénéficier du paiement du dividende; ~ **stripping** n FIN, TAX démembrement de dividendes m; ~ **tax** n TAX impôt sur les dividendes m; ~ **tax credit** n TAX avoir fiscal m, crédit d'impôt pour dividendes m; ~ **voucher** n STOCK certificat de dividende m; ~ **warrant** n FIN ordonnance de paiement f; ~ **yield** n STOCK rendement boursier m, rendement des actions m

Divisia: ~ **money index** n (SYN money supply) ECON masse monétaire f

division n GEN COMM division f, S&M of market segmentation f; ~ **head** HRM, MGMNT chef de secteur m, directeur de division m; ~ **of labor** AmE, ~ **of labour** BrE ECON division du travail f; ~ **manager** HRM, MGMNT chef de division m, chef de département m; ~ **of powers** GEN COMM, POL répartition des pouvoirs f; ~ **of thought** MGMNT divergence de points de vue f

divisional: ~ **head** n HRM, MGMNT chef de division m, chef de département m; ~ **management** n MGMNT gestion cellulaire f, gestion par département f; ~ **manager** n HRM, MGMNT chef de division m, chef de secteur m

divisionalization n HRM sectorisation f

divorced: ~ **spouse** n LAW conjoint divorcé m, époux divorcé m

DIY *abbr (do-it-yourself)* GEN COMM bricolage *m*

Djibouti *pr n* GEN COMM Djibouti *n pr*

Djibuti *n* GEN COMM *person* Djibutien *m*

Djibutian *n* GEN COMM *person* Djibutien *m*

DK *abbr* TRANSP *(deck) shipping* pont *m*, TRANSP *(duct keel) shipping* quille caisson *f*

DKY *abbr (donkey boiler)* TRANSP *shipping* chaudière auxiliaire *f*

DLO *abbr* ADMIN *(Dead Letter Office)* bureau des rebuts, HRM *(direct labour organization)* organisation de la main d'oeuvre directe, TRANSP *(dispatch loading only) shipping* bonification au chargement *loc f*, bonification payable pour temps gagné au chargement *loc f*

DMA *abbr US (Direct Marketing Association)* S&M association du marketing direct

dm/d *abbr (molded depth, moulded depth)* TRANSP *shipping* creux sur quille *m*

DME *abbr (decentralized market economy)* ECON économie de marché décentralisée *f*

D/N *abbr (debit note)* GEN COMM note de débit *f*

DO *abbr* ENVIR *(diesel oil)* gas-oil *m*, gazole *m*, HRM *(duty officer)* officier de service *m*, responsable en permanence *m*, HRM *(district officer)* responsable régional *m*, IND *(diesel oil)* gas-oil *m*, gazole *m*, MGMNT *(district officer)* responsable régional *m*, TRANSP *(delivery order)* bon de livraison *m*, TRANSP *(distribution office)* bureau de distribution *m*, TRANSP *(diesel oil)* gas-oil *m*, gazole *m*, TRANSP *(dock operations)* opérations portuaires *f pl*

DOC: ~ **credit** *n (documentary credit)* IMP/EXP crédit documentaire *m*

dock *n* LAW *UK* banc des accusés *m*, TRANSP *shipping* bassin *m*, dock *m*; ~ **charges** *n pl* TRANSP *shipping* droits de bassin *m pl*; ~ **charter** *n* TRANSP *shipping* charte-partie avec indication de quai *f*; ~ **container park** *n* TRANSP *shipping* aire de stockage des conteneurs *f*; ~ **dues** *n pl* TRANSP *shipping* droits de bassin *m pl*; ~ **leveler** *n AmE*, ~ **leveller** *n BrE* TRANSP *shipping* appareil de mise à niveau *m*; ~ **operations** *n pl (DO)* TRANSP opérations portuaires *f pl*; ~ **receipt** *n* TRANSP *shipping* reçu provisoire *m*; ~ **warrant** *n (D/W)* IMP/EXP, LAW, TRANSP *shipping* bulletin de dépôt *m*, certificat d'entrepôt *m*, récépissé d'entrepôt *m*, warrant *m*

docker *n BrE (cf longshoreman AmE)* HRM docker *m*, débardeur *m*

docking *n* TRANSP amarrage *m*; ~ **survey** TRANSP *shipping* visite à sec *f*

doctor *n* HRM, WEL médecin *m*

Doctor *n (Dr)* GEN COMM, HRM, WEL *title* docteur *m (Dr)*; ~ **of Commerce** *(DCom)* HRM, WEL docteur en science commerciale *m*; ~ **of Commercial Law** *(DComL)* LAW, WEL docteur en droit commercial *m*; ~ **of Economics** *(DEcon)* ECON, GEN COMM docteur en sciences économiques *m*; ~ **of Laws** *(LLD)* LAW, WEL docteur en droit *m*; ~ **of Philosophy** *(DPhil, PhD)* WEL doctorat *m*

doctorate *n* WEL doctorat *m*

doctrine: ~ **of substantial performance** *n* LAW doctrine de l'exécution substantielle d'un contrat *f*

document *n* ADMIN, COMP, GEN COMM document *m*; ~ **code** COMP code de document *m*; ~ **feeder** COMP dispositif d'alimentation de document *m*; ~ **holder** *(SYN binder, file, folder)* ADMIN, GEN COMM classeur *m*; ~ **mode** COMP *word processing* mode document *m*; ~ **name** COMP nom de document *m*; ~ **rate** COMP vitesse de traitement des documents *f*; ~ **reader** COMP lecteur de documents *m*; ~ **retrieval** COMP recherche documentaire *f*; ~ **retrieval system** COMP système de recherche documentaire *m*

documentary *n* MEDIA documentaire *m*; ~ **credit** FIN, IMP/EXP *(DOC credit)* crédit documentaire *m*; ~ **draft** IMP/EXP, TRANSP *shipping* traite documentaire *f*; ~ **evidence** GEN COMM preuve documentaire *f*, LAW preuve écrite *f*; ~ **fraud** GEN COMM fraude documentaire *f*

documentation *n* ADMIN, COMP, GEN COMM documentation *f*

documents: ~ **against acceptance** *n pl (D/A)* GEN COMM documents contre acceptation *m pl*; ~ **against payment** *n pl (DAP, DP)* GEN COMM documents contre paiement *m pl (DP)*; ~ **of title** *n pl* LAW documents établissant le droit de propriété *m pl*, titre de propriété *m*

DOD *abbr US (Department of Defense)* POL ≈ ministère de la Défense nationale *m*

Dodoma *pr n* GEN COMM Dodoma *n pr*

DOE *abbr* ENVIR *UK (Department of the Environment)*, POL *UK (Department of the Environment)* ≈ ministère de l'Environnement *m*, POL *US (Department of Energy)* ≈ ministère de l'Énergie *m*

dog: ~ **bone bridge** *n* TRANSP *cargo handling* pontet en os de chien *m*; ~ **hooks** *n pl* TRANSP *cargo handling equipment* pinces *f pl*

DOH *abbr UK (Department of Health)* POL, WEL ≈ ministère de la Santé *m*

Doha *pr n* GEN COMM Doha *n pr*

DOI *abbr US (Department of Industry)* IND ≈ ministère de l'Industrie *m*

do-it-yourself *n (DIY)* GEN COMM bricolage *m*

dol. *abbr (dollar)* GEN COMM dol. *(dollar)*

doldrums: **in the** ~ *phr* ECON, GEN COMM dans le marasme *loc m*

dole *n infrml BrE (cf welfare AmE)* ECON, HRM, WEL allocation chômage *f*, chômedu *m (infrml)*; ~ **office** *infrml BrE (cf welfare office AmE)* HRM bureau d'aide sociale *m*; ♦ **on the** ~ *infrml UK* WEL au chômage, au chômedu *(infrml)*

dollar *n* ECON, FIN, GEN COMM dollar *m*, GEN COMM dollar *m*; ~ **area** ECON zone dollar *f*; ~ **balance** ECON balance dollar *f*; ~ **bid** STOCK *options* offre en dollars *f*; ~ **cost averaging** STOCK investissements à valeur constante en dollars *m pl*; ~ **drain** ECON déficit en dollars du commerce extérieur des États-Unis; ~ **-for-dollar offset** STOCK compensation dollar contre dollar *f*; ~ **gap** ECON pénurie de dollars *f*; ~ **overhang** FIN, IMP/EXP offre excédentaire de dollars *f*; ~ **premium** STOCK *options* prime en dollars *f*; ~ **price** STOCK prix du dollar *m*, prix libellé en dollars *m*; ~ **rate** STOCK taux du dollar *m*; ~ **shortage** STOCK manque de dollars *m*; ~ **spot and forward** FIN dollar au comptant et à terme *m*; ~ **standard** ECON étalon dollar *m*; ~ **transaction** BANK opération en dollars *f*; ~ **value** STOCK valeur de dollar *f*; ◆ ~ **price of the ECU** STOCK valeur de l'écu exprimée en dollars *f*

dollarization *n* ECON dollarisation *f*

dolly *n jarg* TRANSP *rail* diabolo *m*, essieu simple *m*

dolphin *n* TRANSP *shipping* duc d'Albe *m*

domain *n* MATH *statistics* domaine *m*

domestic[1] *adj* ECON intérieur, national, TRANSP *network* intérieur

domestic:[2] ~ **absorption** *n* ECON utilisation sur le marché intérieur de la production nationale de biens et de services; ~ **agreement** *n UK* HRM accord interne *m*; ~ **airline** *n* (ANT *international airline*) TRANSP compagnie aérienne domestique *f*, ligne aérienne intérieure *f*; ~ **airline company** *n* TRANSP compagnie aérienne domestique *f*; ~ **asset** *n* BANK actif national *m*, élément d'actif national *m*; ~ **bank** *n* BANK, ECON banque nationale *f*; ~ **business** *n* GEN COMM affaires intérieures *f pl*; ~ **consumption** *n* ECON consommation ménagère *f*, *of country* consommation intérieure *f*, consommation nationale *f*, GEN COMM *household* consommation ménagère *f*; ~ **corporation** *n* ECON, GEN COMM entreprise nationale *f*; ~ **credit expansion** *n* (*DCE*) ECON *balance of payments* développement du crédit intérieur *m*; ~ **demand** *n* ECON demande intérieure *f*; ~ **economy** *n* ECON système économique national *m*; ~ **export financing** *n* ECON, IMP/EXP financement des exportations nationales *m*; ~ **financing** *n* GEN COMM financement intérieur *m*; ~ **flight** *n* LEIS vol domestique *m*, TRANSP vol domestique *m*, vol intérieur *m*; ~ **industry** *n* IND industrie intérieure *f*; ~ **investments** *n pl* ECON investissements nationaux *m pl*; ~ **issue** *n* STOCK émission de titres nationaux *f*; ~ **liabilities** *n pl* BANK passif national *m*; ~ **market** *n* ECON, S&M marché intérieur *m*; ~ **money market** *n* ECON, FIN marché monétaire national *m*; ~ **output** *n* ECON, IND production nationale *f*; ~ **rate** *n* TRANSP tarif intérieur *m*; ~ **risk** *n* INS risque ménager *m*; ~ **sales** *n pl* S&M ventes sur le marché intérieur *f pl*; ~ **securities market** *n* STOCK marché intérieur des valeurs mobilières *m*; ~ **subsidiary** *n* ECON filiale intérieure *f*; ~ **system** *n* ECON système économique national *m*; ~ **trade** *n* ECON, GEN COMM, IMP/EXP commerce intérieur *m*; ~ **waste** *n* ENVIR déchets ménagers *m pl*

Domestic: ~ **Equities Market** *n* (*DEM*) STOCK marché des actions nationales *m*; ~ **International Sales Corporation** *n US* (*DISC*) GEN COMM société nationale de ventes à l'exportation

domicile *n* LAW domicile *m*; ~ **taxation** TAX imposition d'après le domicile *f*

domiciled *adj* LAW domicilié

dominant[1] *adj* GEN COMM dominant

dominant:[2] ~ **firm** *n* ECON entreprise dominante *f*, firme dominante *f*, GEN COMM entreprise dominante *f*; ~ **position** *n* ECON position dominante *f*; ~ **tenement** *n* PROP fonds dominant *m*

dominate *vt* ECON *market* dominer

Dominica *pr n* GEN COMM Dominique *f*

Dominican[1] *adj* GEN COMM *from Dominican Republic* dominicain, *from Dominica* dominiquais

Dominican[2] *n* GEN COMM *person from Dominican Republic* Dominicain *m*, *person from Dominica* Dominiquais *m*

Dominican:[3] ~ **Republic** *pr n* GEN COMM République dominicaine *f*

donated: ~ **stock** *n* STOCK action rendue gracieusement à la société; ~ **surplus** *n* STOCK crédit au bénéfice de l'actionnaire provenant d'une donation d'actions

donation *n* GEN COMM, TAX don *m*; ~ **pledged** TAX don promis *m*

donee *n* TAX donataire *mf*

dong *n* GEN COMM dong *m*

dongle *n* COMP clé électronique de protection *f*, dispositif de protection électronique *m*

donkey: ~ **boiler** *n* (*DKY*) TRANSP *ship's machinery* chaudière auxiliaire *f*

donkeyman *n* TRANSP *shipping* nettoyeur *m*

Donoghue's: ~ **Money Fund average** *n US* STOCK Indice Donoghue des fonds monétaires *m*

donor *n* GEN COMM, TAX donateur *m*; ~ **agency** WEL agence donatrice *f*; ~ **aid** ECON *development assistance*, POL aide au développement *f*; ~ **country** ECON *overseas aid*, POL pays bailleur de fonds *m*, pays donateur *m*; ~ **government** POL, WEL gouvernement donateur *m*

Donovan: ~ **Commission** *n UK* HRM commission Donovan

doomwatcher *n* GEN COMM prophète de malheur *m*

door:[1] ~ **-to-door** *adj* TRANSP porte à porte, à domicile

door:[2] ~ **to door** *adv* TRANSP à domicile

door:[3] ~ **-to-door clause** *n* INS clause de porte-à-porte *f*; ~ **-to-door salesman** *n* GEN COMM, HRM démarcheur à domicile *m*; ~ **-to-door selling** *n* (SYN *house-to-house selling*) S&M démarchage *m*, porte à porte *m*, vente en porte-à-porte *f*, vente à domicile *f*; ◆ ~ **-to-depot** TRANSP porte à dépôt *f*

doors: ~ **open at** *phr* GEN COMM *for exhibition, conference* ouverture à

dormant: ~ **account** *n* BANK compte inactif *m*

dormitory: ~ **suburb** *n BrE* (*cf bedroom community AmE*) HRM ville-dortoir *f*

DOS®[1] *abbr* COMP (*disk operating system*) DOS® (*système d'exploitation à disques*), GEN COMM

(Directorate of Overseas Surveys) direction des enquêtes à l'étranger

DOS:² ~ **prompt** *n* COMP invite du DOS *m*

dossier *n* ADMIN dossier *m*

dot *n* COMP point *m*; ~ **command** COMP commande précédée d'un point *f*; ~ **-matrix printer** COMP *hardware* imprimante matricielle *f*; ~ **printer** COMP imprimante matricielle *f*

DOT *abbr US (Designated Order Turnaround)* STOCK ≈ Information et transmission d'ordres *loc f*

dots: ~ **per inch** *n pl (dpi)* COMP *typeface* points par pouce *m pl (ppp)*

dotted: ~ **line** *n* MATH *on graph* ligne pointillée *f*

double:¹ ~ **-acting** *adj* IND *machinery* à double action, à double effet; ~ **-barreled** *adj AmE*, ~ **-barrelled** *adj BrE* STOCK obligation de collectivité locale à double garantie; ~ **-ended** *adj (db)* TRANSP *boiler* à double façade; ~ **-income** *adj* ECON *family, household* à deux revenus; ~ **-precision** *adj* COMP à double précision; ~ **-sided** *adj* COMP à double face

double:² ~ **account** *n* ACC compte double *m*; ~ **bottom** *n (db)* TRANSP *ship* double fond *m*; ~ **bottom center** *n AmE*, ~ **bottom centre** *n BrE (dbc)* TRANSP *shipping* centre double fond *m*; ~ **-click** *n* COMP double-clic *m*; ~ **-click speed** *n* COMP vitesse du double-clic *f*; ~ **counting** *n* FIN calcul double *m*; ~ **damages** *n pl* LAW *award* dommages-intérêts doubles *m pl*; ~ **-decked pallet** *n* TRANSP palette à double plancher *f*; ~ **-decker** *n* TRANSP autobus à impériale *m*; ~ **declining balance** *n* ACC *depreciation* amortissement dégressif double *m*; ~ **density** *n* COMP double densité *f*; ~ **-density disk** *n* COMP disquette double densité *f*; ~ **-digit inflation** *n* ECON, FIN inflation à deux chiffres *f*; ~ **dip** *n jarg* ECON rechute *f*; ~ **-dipper** *n jarg* HRM cumulard *m*; ~ **-dipping** *n jarg* HRM cumul *m*, cumul d'emploi *m*; ~ **eagle** *n* US *(SYN twenty dollars)* FIN double aigle *m*, pièce de vingt dollars *f*; ~ **-entry accounting** *n* ACC comptabilité en partie double *f*; ~ **-entry book-keeping** *n* ACC comptabilité en partie double *f*; ~ **-entry method** *n* ACC *book-keeping* méthode à partie double *f*; ~ **-entry visa** *n* ADMIN visa accordé pour deux entrées *m*; ~ **insurance** *n* INS assurance cumulative *f*, double assurance *f*; ~ **manning** *n* HRM duplication de main d'oeuvre *f*; ~ **option** *n* STOCK double option *f*, option du double *f*, opération sur double option *f*; ~ **reduction** *n (DR)* GEN COMM deuxième démarque *f*, double réduction *f*; ~ **room** *n* LEIS *in hotel* chambre double *f*, chambre pour deux personnes *f*; ~ **-sided disk** *n* COMP *software* disque double face *m*; ~ **-sided diskette** *n* COMP *software* disquette double face *f*; ~ **space** *n* COMP double interligne *m*; ~ **spacing** *n* COMP double interligne *m*; ~ **spread** *n* MEDIA, S&M publicité sur double page *f*; ~ **spread advertising** *n* MEDIA, S&M publicité sur double page *f*; ~ **stack** *n* TRANSP empilage double *m*, gerbage double *m*; ~ **stacker**

n TRANSP *container securing* pièce de gerbage double *f*; ~ **stacking** *n* TRANSP empilage double *m*, gerbage double *m*; ~ **strike** *n* COMP double frappe *f*, frappe répétée *f*; ~ **taxation** *n (SYN duplicate taxation)* TAX double imposition *f*; ~ **taxation agreement** *n* TAX convention de double imposition *f*; ~ **taxation relief** *n (DTR)* TAX suppression de la double imposition *f*; ~ **time** *n* HRM *pay* heure comptée double *f*; ~ **width gangway** *n* TRANSP *shipping* passerelle double *f*; ~ **width passenger gangway** *n* TRANSP *shipping* passerelle double *f*

double:³ **1.** *vt* ~ **-stack** TRANSP *containers* empiler en double piles, gerber en doubles piles; **2.** *vi* ~ **-click** COMP *dtp* cliquer deux fois, double cliquer, faire un double clic *loc m*; ~ **-dip** *infrml* HRM cumuler, MATH doubler

double:⁴ ~ **income no kids** *phr jarg (dinkie)* ECON couple sans enfants avec deux revenus

doubtful: ~ **debt** *n* ACC créance douteuse *f*, BANK, ECON, FIN créance douteuse *f*, créance irrécouvrable *f*; ~ **debt provision** *n* FIN provision pour créances douteuses *f*; ~ **debtors** *n pl* ACC débiteurs douteux *m pl*

dove: ~ **-tail socket** *n* TRANSP *container securing* socle en queue d'aronde *m*

Dow: ~ **Jones** *n* US FIN Dow Jones *m*; ~ **-Jones-average** *n* STOCK indice Dow Jones *m*; ~ **-Jones index** *n* STOCK indice Dow Jones *m*; ~ **-Jones industrial average** *n* STOCK Indice Dow Jones des 30 valeurs industrielles *m*; ~ **theory** *n* STOCK théorie de Dow *f*

DOW *abbr (delivery on wheels)* TRANSP livraison par route *f*

dower *n* LAW douaire *f*

down¹ *adj* COMP *direction, position* abaissé, *system* arrêté, en panne, non-disponible; ~ **-market** *(ANT up-market)* GEN COMM, S&M bas de gamme; ~ **-the-line** GEN COMM subordonné; ♦ **be ~** ECON être en baisse; **be ~ on** GEN COMM tomber sur *(infrml)*

down:² ~ **arrow** *n* COMP *on keyboard* flèche verticale *f*; ~ **-market product** *n* S&M produit bas de gamme *m*; ~ **-market service** *n* S&M service bas de gamme *m*; ~ **payment** *n* ACC, BANK, FIN, GEN COMM, S&M acompte *m*; ~ **-the-line personnel** *n* HRM personnel subalterne *m*; ~ **time** *n* COMP durée d'immobilisation *f*, temps mort *m*, durée d'indisponibilité *f*, temps d'arrêt *m*, ECON, GEN COMM durée d'immobilisation *f*, temps mort *m*, HRM chômage technique *m*, IND durée d'immobilisation *f*, temps mort *m*

down:³ ~ **tools** *phr* HRM *break from work* arrêter de travailler, cesser le travail, *strike* se mettre en grève

downgrade *vt* HRM *job* déclasser

downgrading *n* HRM rétrogradation *f*

downhill: **go ~** *phr* GEN COMM *business* aller mal, péricliter

download *vt* COMP télécharger

downloadable: ~ **font** *n* COMP police de caractères téléchargeable *f*

downscale *vt* MGMNT déclasser

downside: ~ **break-even** *n* STOCK *options* point mort à la baisse *m*; ~ **break-even point** *n* STOCK *options* point mort à la baisse *m*; ~ **risk** *n* STOCK évaluation du risque de baisse *f*

downsize[1] *n jarg* HRM compression de personnel *f*

downsize[2] *vt* HRM *workforce* dégraisser

downsizing *n jarg* HRM dégraissage *m*, licenciement *m*, réduction d'effectifs *f*

downstream[1] *adv* (ANT *upstream*) GEN COMM en aval

downstream:[2] ~ **float** *n* (ANT *upstream float*) GEN COMM flottage en aval *m*, marge aval *f*, provision en aval *f*

downswing *n* ECON baisse *f*, fléchissement *m*, ralentissement *m*, repli *m*, GEN COMM ralentissement *m*

downtick *n* (ANT *uptick*) STOCK cours inférieur au cours précédent *m*, négociation à un cours inférieur *f*, échelon de cotation inférieur *m*

downtrend *n* (ANT *uptrend*) ECON orientation à la baisse *f*, tendance à la baisse *f*

downturn *n* (ANT *upturn*) ECON déclin *m*, GEN COMM baisse *f*, STOCK *market* repli *m*, retournement à la baisse *m*

downward[1] *adj* (ANT *upward*) COMP *on screen* descendant, vers le bas, GEN COMM *move, trend* baissier, vers le bas, à la baisse

downward:[2] ~ **communication** *n* MGMNT communication avec la base *f*; ~ **compatibility** *n* (ANT *upward compatibility*) COMP *programming* compatibilité descendante *f*; ~ **correction** *n* STOCK correction à la baisse *f*; ~ **movement** *n* (ANT *upward movement*) STOCK mouvement vers le bas *m*, mouvement à la baisse *m*, tendance baissière *f*, tendance à la baisse *f*; ~ **pressure** *n* (ANT *upward pressure*) ECON *on currency, interest rates* pression inflationniste *f*; ~ **revision** *n* (ANT *upward revision*) GEN COMM révision à la baisse *f*; ~ **spiral** *n* (ANT *upward spiral*) GEN COMM *in wages, prices* descente en spirale *f*, spirale descendante *f*; ~ **trend** *n* (ANT *upward trend*) STOCK mouvement vers le bas *m*, mouvement à la baisse *m*, tendance baissière *f*, tendance à la baisse *f*

downwards *adv* (ANT *upwards*) COMP vers le bas, GEN COMM vers le bas, à la baisse

downzoning *n* PROP rezonage *m*

dowry *n* PROP dot *f*

doz. *abbr* (*dozen*) GEN COMM douz. (*douzaine*)

dozen *n* (*doz.*) GEN COMM douzaine *f* (*douz.*)

DP *abbr* GEN COMM (*documents against payment*) DP (*documents contre paiement*), GEN COMM (*dynamic positioning*) positionnement dynamique *m*, TRANSP (*direct port*) *shipping* port direct *m*

DPhil *abbr* (*Doctor of Philosophy*) WEL doctorat *m*

dpi *abbr* (*dots per inch*) COMP ppp (*points par pouce*)

DPP *abbr* UK (*Director of Public Prosecutions*) LAW ≈ procureur de la République *m* (*France*), ≈ procureur du Roi *m* (*Belgique*)

DPR *abbr* (*director of public relations*) HRM, S&M *advertising* chef du service des relations publiques *m*, directeur des relations publiques *m*, responsable des relations publiques *m*

Dr *abbr* ACC (*debtor*), ADMIN (*debtor*), FIN (*debtor*) débiteur *m*, GEN COMM (*Doctor*) Dr (*docteur*), GEN COMM (*debtor*) débiteur *m*, HRM (*Doctor*) *title* Dr (*docteur*), LAW (*debtor*) débiteur *m*, WEL (*Doctor*) Dr (*docteur*)

DR *abbr* BANK (*deposit receipt*) reçu de dépôt *m*, récépissé de dépôt *m*, GEN COMM (*dead rise*) acculement *m*, hausse sans effet *f*, GEN COMM (*double reduction*) deuxième démarque *f*, double réduction *f*

Drachma *n* GEN COMM drachme *m*

draft[1] *n* BANK traite *m*, COMP brouillon *m*, première monture *f*, avant-projet *m*, FIN traite *m*, GEN COMM *of letter, speech* brouillon *m*, LAW projet d'acte *m*, TRANSP AmE *see draught BrE*; ~ **agreement** GEN COMM protocole d'accord *m*; ~ **amendment** LAW, POL amendement provisoire *m*; ~ **budget** ACC projet de budget *m*; ~ **clause** LAW clause provisoire *f*; ~ **contract** GEN COMM, LAW projet de contrat *m*; ~ **directive** LAW *EU*, POL avant-projet de directive *m*, directive préliminaire *f*; ~ **for collection** BANK effet en recouvrement *m*, effet à l'encaissement *m*; ~ **mode** COMP mode brouillon *m*, mode listage *m*; ~ **order** LAW *compulsory purchase* commande provisoire *f*; ~ **printing** COMP qualité brouillon *f*, qualité listing *f*; ~ **project** GEN COMM avant-projet *m*, pré-projet *m*; ~ **prospectus** STOCK projet de prospectus *m*; ~ **resolution** LAW projet de résolution *m*; ~ **stage** LAW, POL phase provisoire *f*, phase préliminaire *f*

draft[2] *vt* GEN COMM rédiger, ébaucher, LAW, POL esquisser, rédiger, ébaucher

drafted *adj* GEN COMM, LAW, POL esquissé, rédigé, ébauché

drag:[1] ~ **anchor** *n* TRANSP *shipping* ancre flottante *f*

drag:[2] ~ **her anchors** *phr* TRANSP chasser ses ancres

drain *n* ECON *of resources* hémorragie *f*

draining: ~ **reserves** *n pl* ECON ponctionnement des réserves *m*

Dram: ~ **Shop Act** *n* US LAW législation américaine réglementaire des débits de boisson

DRAM *abbr* (*dynamic random access memory*) COMP *hardware* RAM dynamique *f*

drama: ~ **critic** *n* LEIS, MEDIA critique de théâtre *m*

drastic: ~ **cut** *n* ACC, ECON, FIN, GEN COMM coupe sombre *f*; ~ **measures** *n* ECON mesures draconiennes *f pl*, mesures drastiques *f pl*

draught *n BrE* TRANSP *of ship* tirant d'eau *m*

draw[1] *n* BANK tirage au sort *m*

draw[2] *vt* BANK tirer, GEN COMM tirer, *stock* entamer, HRM *benefit, allowance* percevoir, LAW,

POL rédiger; **~ from** HRM prélever sur; **~ up** GEN COMM *plan, will* faire, *report* rédiger, établir, HRM *shortlist* dresser, LAW rédiger, POL *white paper* dresser, rédiger; ◆ **~ a check** *AmE*, **~ a cheque** *BrE*, BANK faire un chèque, émettre un chèque; **~ a distinction between** GEN COMM faire une distinction entre; **~ on one's savings** FIN puiser dans ses économies; **~ up the agenda** MGMNT dresser l'ordre du jour, établir l'ordre du jour; **~ up a statement of account** BANK faire un relevé de compte

drawback *n* GEN COMM désavantage *m*, inconvénient *m*, GEN COMM *(Dbk)*, IMP/EXP *(Dbk)* remboursement des droits de douane *m*

drawbar: **~ combination** *n* TRANSP train routier *m*; **~ trailer** *n* TRANSP remorque *f*, remorque à timon *f*

drawdown *n* BANK encaissement d'une tranche de prêt *m*, tirage *m*, versement d'une tranche de prêt *m*

drawee *n* BANK tiré *m*

drawer *n* BANK souscripteur *m*, tireur *m*

drawing *n* BANK *of cheque, draft* tirage *m*, *on loan* prélèvement *m*, GEN COMM dessin *m*; **~ account** BANK compte de retraits *m*; **~ board** MGMNT tableau *m*; **~ file** COMP fichier de dessins *m*, fichier graphique *m*; **~ officer** BANK agent tireur *m*; **~ software** COMP logiciel de dessins *m*, logiciel graphique *m*; **~ up** GEN COMM *of report* établissement *m*

drawn: **~ bill** *n* ECON effet tiré *m*; **~ bond** *n* STOCK obligation à échéance *f*

dredge *vti* TRANSP draguer

dredger *n* TRANSP *boat* dragueur *m*

dredging *n* TRANSP *shipping* dragage *m*; **~ anchor** TRANSP *shipping* ancre à draguer *f*

dressed: **~ return** *n* (SYN *edited return*) TAX déclaration mise au point *f*

DRF *abbr (Daily Range Factor)* STOCK facteur de la fourchette quotidienne plus haut-plus bas

drilling: **~ program** *n* *AmE*, **~ programme** *n* *BrE* ENVIR programme de forage *m*

drinking: **~ water** *n* ENVIR eau potable *f*, eau à boire *f*

drive[1] *n* GEN COMM *campaign, effort*, S&M campagne *f*

drive[2] *vt* GEN COMM pousser; **~ down** ECON *price* faire baisser; ◆ **~ a hard bargain** GEN COMM être dur en affaires

driven *adj* GEN COMM motivé; ◆ **~ by** GEN COMM *a certain factor* imposé par, provoqué par

driver *n* COMP *hardware* circuit de commande *m*, pilote *m*, programme *m*, *software* gestionnaire de périphérique *m*, logiciel de commande *m*, logiciel de pilotage *m*, GEN COMM conducteur *m*, HRM chauffeur *mf*; **~'s cab** TRANSP cabine de conduite *f*; **~'s licence** *BrE* TRANSP permis de conduire *m*; **~'s license** *AmE see driver's licence BrE*

Driver: **~ and Vehicle Licensing Centre** *n* UK *(DVLC)* TRANSP centre d'émission des permis de conduire et de vignettes automobiles

drivetime *n* S&M heure de pointe *f*

driving: **~ force** *n* ECON, GEN COMM moteur *m*; **~ test** *n* TRANSP permis de conduire *m*

drop[1] *n* ECON *in demand, inflation* baisse *f*, *in spending* chute *f*, GEN COMM baisse *f*, baisse de volume *f*, chute *f*, S&M *in price, orders*, STOCK chute *f*; **~ -lock stock** STOCK obligation à taux flottant qui passe à taux fixe lorsque le taux de référence chute au-delà d'un certain niveau; **~ shipping** *US* S&M *merchandizing* intermédiaire en gros *m*

drop[2] **1.** *vt* GEN COMM laisser tomber **2.** *vi* ECON, GEN COMM baisser, chuter, S&M chuter, STOCK baisser, chuter; ◆ **~ everything** HRM tout laisser en plan *(infrml)*; **~ out** GEN COMM *from project* se retirer, WEL *from university* abandonner

dropout *n* COMP perte d'information *f*

drought *n* ENVIR sécheresse *f*

drug *n* GEN COMM médicament *m*; **~ economy** ECON économie de la drogue *f*; **~ industry** IND industrie pharmaceutique *f*; **~ trade** IND, S&M commerce de produits pharmaceutiques *m*; **~ trafficking** IMP/EXP trafic de drogue *m*

drum *n* COMP tambour *m*, TRANSP bidon *m*; **~ plotter** COMP enregistreur à tambour *m*, traceur à tambour *m*; **~ printer** COMP imprimante à tambour *f*; **~ safety valve** *(DSV)* TRANSP soupape de sûreté du bidon *f*

drummer *n infrml AmE* GEN COMM voyageur de commerce *m*, HRM, S&M représentant *m*, voyageur de commerce *m*

dry: **~ barrel** *n* TRANSP baril sec *m*; **~ battery** *n* TRANSP *shipping* batterie sèche *f*; **~ bulk cargo** *n* TRANSP vrac sec *m*; **~ bulk container** *n (D)* TRANSP *shipping* conteneur à pulvérulents *m*; **~ cargo** *n* TRANSP marchandises sèches *f pl*; **~ dock** *n* TRANSP *shipping* bassin de radoub *m*, cale sèche *f*; **~ docking** *n (DD)* TRANSP *shipping* mise en cale sèche *f*; **~ freight** *n* TRANSP fret sec *m*, marchandises sèches *f pl*; **~ goods** *n pl* S&M produits d'épicerie *m pl*; **~ measure** *n* GEN COMM mesure pour produits secs *f*; **~ plate clutch** *n* TRANSP *single, double* embrayage à plaque sèche *m*, embrayage à plateau sec *m*; **~ quart** *n US* GEN COMM 1.136 litre, dry quart américain *m*, quart américain *m*; **~ weight** *n* TRANSP poids à sec *m*

DS *abbr (depth sounder)* TRANSP sondeur *m*

DSC *abbr (digital selective calling)* COMMS appel sélectif numérique *m*

DSS *abbr* MGMNT *(decision support system)* système d'aide à la décision *m*, POL *UK (Department of Social Security)*, WEL *UK (Department of Social Security)* ≈ ministère des Affaires sociales *m*

DSV *abbr (drum safety valve)* TRANSP soupape de sûreté du bidon *f*

DT *abbr (deep tank)* TRANSP caisse profonde *f*, cale à eau *f*

DTa *abbr (deep tank aft)* TRANSP *shipping* cale à eau d'arrière *f*

DTC *abbr US (Depository Trust Company)* STOCK ≈ SICOVAM, ≈ organe de dépôt de titres *m (société interprofessionnelle pour la compensation des valeurs mobilières)*

DTE *abbr (data terminal equipment)* COMP *hardware* ETTD *(équipement terminal de traitement de données)*

DTf *abbr (deep tank forward)* TRANSP *shipping* cale à eau d'avant *f*

DTI *abbr* ECON *UK (Department of Trade and Industry)*, GEN COMM *UK (Department of Trade and Industry)* ≈ ministère du Commerce et de l'Industrie *m*, IMP/EXP *(direct trader input)* entrée directe commerçant *f*, POL *UK (Department of Trade and Industry)* ≈ ministère du Commerce et de l'Industrie *m*

DTO *abbr (district training officer)* HRM directeur régional de la formation professionnelle *m*, responsable régional de la formation professionnelle *m*

DTP *abbr (desktop publishing)* MEDIA *print* PAO *(publication assistée par ordinateur)*

DTp *abbr UK (Department of Transport)* COMMS, IND, TRANSP ≈ ministère des Transports *m*

DTR *abbr (double taxation relief)* TAX suppression de la double imposition *f*

DTS *abbr (district traffic superintendent)* HRM, TRANSP directeur régional de circulation *m*, directeur régional des transports *m*

D2-MAC: **~ standard** *n* GEN COMM *satellite broadcasting* standard D2MAC *m*

dual: **~ capacity** *n* STOCK *of stockbrokers* capacité double *f*, capacité multiple *f*; **~ contract** *n* LAW contrat double *m*; **~ economy** *n* ECON, POL économie duale *f*; **~ exchange rate** *n* ECON double taux de change *m*; **~ federalism** *n* POL bifédéralisme *m*; **~ -in-line package** *n (DIP)* COMP boîtier à double rangée de connexions *m*; **~ -in-line package switch** *n (DIP switch)* COMP interrupteur à positions multiples *m*; **~ job holding** *n* HRM cumul d'emploi *m*; **~ labor market** *n AmE*, **~ labour market** *n BrE* ECON double marché du travail *m*; **~ listing** *n* STOCK cumul d'inscriptions *m*; **~ pitch** *n* ADMIN double corps de caractères *m*; **~ -purpose fund** *n* STOCK fonds d'investissement à capital fixe et à deux catégories d'actions; **~ residence** *n* TAX double résidence *f*; **~ responsibility** *n* HRM *EU regulation* cumul de responsabilités *m*; **~ skilling** *n* HRM bivalence *f*, polyvalence *f*; **~ sourcing** *n (ANT single sourcing)* GEN COMM approvisionnement auprès de deux sources *m*; **~ valuation clause** *n* INS *marine* clause de double évaluation *f*; **~ -wheel fork lift truck** *n* TRANSP chariot élévateur à roues jumelées *m*

dubious: **~ accounts** *n pl* ACC créances douteuses *f pl*

Dublin *pr n* GEN COMM Dublin *n pr*

duct: **~ keel** *n (DK)* TRANSP *shipping* quille caisson *f*

dud: **~ check** *n infrml AmE*, **~ cheque** *n infrml BrE* BANK chèque en bois *m (infrml)*, chèque sans provision *m*

due:[1] **~ and unpaid** *adj* TAX échu et impayé

due:[2] **~ bill** *n AmE (SYN I owe you, IOU)* TRANSP reconnaissance de dette *f*; **~ capital** *n* FIN capital échu *m*; **~ date** *n (dd)* GEN COMM, STOCK date d'échéance *f*, échéance *f*; **~ date of filing** *n* TAX *of return* date limite de production *f*, date prescrite de production *f*; **~ date of premium** *n* INS jour d'échéance de la prime *m*; **~ date of renewal** *n* INS jour d'échéance de renouvellement *m*; **~ diligence** *n* FIN diligence normale *f*; ♦ **at ~ date** FIN, GEN COMM, STOCK à la date d'échéance

dues *n pl* HRM cotisation *f*, cotisation syndicale *f*

duly: **~ signed** *phr* GEN COMM dûment signé

dumb: **~ barge** *n* TRANSP *shipping* allège *f*, barge *f*; **~ craft** *n* TRANSP *shipping* chaland sans moteur *m*; **~ terminal** *n (ANT intelligent terminal, smart terminal)* COMP terminal muet *m*, terminal non-autonome *m*, terminal non-intelligent *m*, terminal passif *m*

dummy *n* LAW homme de paille *m*, prête-nom *m*; **~ activity** GEN COMM activité artificielle *f*, activité écran *f*; **~ variable** ECON *econometrics* variable auxiliaire *f*

dump[1] *n* COMP *data transfer* vidage de transfert sur disque *m*; **~ bin** GEN COMM, S&M présentoir en vrac *m*; **~ site** ENVIR site de décharge *m*

dump[2] *vt* COMP copier, transférer, vider, ENVIR *waste at sea* déverser, jeter, rejeter

dumping *n* COMP dumping *m*, vidage de transfert sur disque *m*, ENVIR *of waste* décharge *f*, dépôt de déchets *m*, mise en décharge *f*, rejet *m*, GEN COMM dumping *m*, STOCK vente à perte *f*; **~ ground** *n* ENVIR décharge *f*, lieu d'immersion *m*, site de décharge *m*; **~ standards** *n pl* ENVIR normes de déversement *f pl*, normes de rejet *f pl*

dun *vt* FIN, GEN COMM, S&M relancer

dunnage *n* TRANSP bois de fardage *m*, fardage *m*

duopoly *n* ECON duopole *m*

dup. *abbr (duplicate)* COMP, GEN COMM double *m*, LAW duplicata *m*

DUP *abbr (directly unproductive profit-seeking activities)* ECON activités à but lucratif non directement productives *f pl*

duplex[1] *adj* COMP bidirectionnel, duplex, MEDIA *printing* recto-verso

duplex[2] *n* PROP *AmE (cf maisonette BrE)* apartment duplex *m*, PROP *AmE (cf semi-detached house BrE)* house maison jumelée *f*, maisonette *f*; **~ computer** COMP système duplex *m*

duplicate[1] *n (dup.)* COMP double *m*, doublon *m*, GEN COMM double *m*, LAW duplicata *m*; **~ sailing** TRANSP navire supplémentaire *m*; **~ taxation** *(SYN double taxation)* TAX double imposition *f*

duplicate[2] *vt* COMP copier, dupliquer, GEN COMM copier

duplicated: ~ **record** *n* COMP copie d'enregistrement *f*

duplication: ~ **of benefits** *n* INS double couverture *f*, reproduction des bénéfices *f*

duplicatory *adj* GEN COMM duplicateur

Du Pont: ~ **formula** *n* FIN formule Du Pont *f*

durable: ~ **household goods** *n pl* ECON, IND biens d'équipement ménager *m pl*, biens de consommation durables *m pl*

durables *n pl* S&M biens durables *m pl*

duration *n* GEN COMM durée *f*; ~ **of benefits** INS durée de la garantie *f*; ~ **of guaranty** GEN COMM durée de la garantie *f*; ♦ **for the** ~ **of** GEN COMM pour la durée de

Durbin-Watson: ~ **statistic** *n* (*DW statistic*) MATH *statistics* statistique Durbin-Watson *f*

duress *n* LAW contrainte *f*, vice du consentement *m*

Dushanbe *pr n* GEN COMM Duchambe *n pr*

dust: ~ **cover** *n* COMP housse *f*

dustbin: ~ **lorry** *n* BrE (*cf garbage truck AmE*) ENVIR benne à ordures *f*

Dutch[1] *adj* GEN COMM hollandais, néerlandais

Dutch[2] *n* GEN COMM *language* hollandais *m*, néerlandais *m*; ~ **auction** S&M enchère au rabais *f*, enchère décroissante *f*; ~ **disease** ECON la tuile de Groningue *f*, maladie hollandaise *f*

Dutchman *n* GEN COMM *person* Hollandais *m*, Néerlandais *m*

Dutchwoman *n* GEN COMM *person* Hollandaise *f*, Néerlandaise *f*

dutiable: ~ **cargo** *n* IMP/EXP, TAX, TRANSP cargaison soumise aux droits de douane *f*; ~ **cargo list** *n* IMP/EXP bordereau de cargaison soumise aux droits de douane *m*; ~ **goods** *n pl* TAX biens taxables *m pl*

duty:[1] ~ **-free** *adj* IMP/EXP détaxé, en franchise douanière *loc f*, exempt de droit de douane, hors taxes

duty[2] *n* LAW devoir *m*, TAX droit *m*, impôt *m*, taxe *f*; ~ **of assured clause** *n* INS clause traitant des droits de l'assuré *f*; ~ **deposit account** *n* (*DDA*) IMP/EXP compte de dépôt de droits douaniers *m*; ~ **-free allowance** *n* UK IMP/EXP quantités autorisées de produits hors taxe *f pl*; ~ **-free goods** *n pl* UK TAX marchandises détaxées *f pl*, marchandises hors taxes *f pl*; ~ **-free shop** *n* LEIS UK, TAX, TRANSP boutique hors taxes *f*; ~ **officer** *n* (*DO*)

HRM officier de service *m*, responsable en permanence *m*; ~ **suspension** *n* IMP/EXP suspension de droits *f*

DVLC *abbr* UK (*Driver and Vehicle Licensing Centre*) TRANSP centre d'émission des permis de conduire et de vignettes automobiles

D/W *abbr* COM (*dock warrant*) warrant *m*, IMP/EXP bulletin de dépôt *m*, récépissé d'entrepôt *m*, warrant *m*, LAW (*dock warrant*) bulletin de dépôt *m*, certificat d'entrepôt *m*, récépissé d'entrepôt *m*, warrant *m*, S&M (*dock warrant*) warrant *m*, TRANSP (*dead weight*) PL (*port en lourd*), TRANSP (*dock warrant*) bulletin de dépôt *m*, certificat d'entrepôt *m*, récépissé d'entrepôt *m*, warrant *m*

DW: ~ **statistic** *n* (*Durbin-Watson statistic*) MATH statistique Durbin-Watson *f*

DWAT *abbr* (*deadweight all told*) TRANSP port en lourd total *m*

DWC *abbr* (*deadweight capacity*) TRANSP PL (*port en lourd*)

DWCC *abbr* (*deadweight cargo capacity*) TRANSP PL (*port en lourd*)

dwelling *n* PROP logement *m*, TAX domicile *m*, logis *m*, WEL logement *m*

dwindle *vi* GEN COMM *demand* diminuer

DWT *abbr* (*deadweight tonnage*) TRANSP PL (*port en lourd*)

dynamic[1] *adj* GEN COMM *growth, personality* dynamique

dynamic:[2] ~ **economics** *n* ECON modèle économique dynamique *m*; ~ **evaluation** *n* GEN COMM analyse dynamique *f*; ~ **hedging** *n* FIN couverture delta *f*, delta hedging *m*; ~ **management model** *n* MGMNT modèle dynamique de gestion *m*; ~ **positioning** *n* (*DP*) GEN COMM positionnement dynamique *m*; ~ **programming** *n* COMP, GEN COMM, MATH programmation dynamique *f*; ~ **RAM** *n* COMP RAM dynamique *f*, mémoire vive dynamique *f*; ~ **random access memory** *n* (*DRAM*) COMP *hardware* mémoire vive dynamique *f*

dynamically: ~ **inconsistent policy** *n* POL politique dynamiquement incohérente *f*

dynamism *n* GEN COMM dynamisme *m*

dysfunction *n* HRM mauvais fonctionnement *m*

dysfunctional *adj* MGMNT dysfonctionnel

E

E *abbr* GEN COMM *(east)* est *m*, TRANSP *(East compass point)* navigation E *(quart est)*

EA *abbr UK (Employment Act)* HRM, LAW loi sur l'emploi

EAAA *abbr (European Association of Advertising Agencies)* S&M Association européenne des agences de publicité *f*

EABC *abbr (European/ASEAN Business Council)* GEN COMM Conseil d'affaires européen/ANASE *m*

EAEC *abbr (European Atomic Energy Community)* IND CEEA *(Communauté européenne de l'énergie atomique)*

eager: ~ **beaver** *n infrml* HRM *person* bête de travail *f (infrml)*, personne avide de réussite *f*, personne avide et travailleuse *f*

eagle *n US (SYN ten dollars)* FIN aigle *m*, pièce de dix dollars *f*

E&OE *abbr (errors and omissions excepted)* GEN COMM SEO *(sauf erreur ou omission)*

earlier: ~ **application** *n* PATENTS demande antérieure *f*; ~ **priority** *n* PATENTS priorité antérieure *f*

early: ~ **adapter** *n jarg* S&M consommateur précoce *m*, pionnier *m*, réceptif précoce *m*, *level of purchaser* consommateur qui s'adapte rapidement à un nouveau produit; ~ **-closing day** *n UK* GEN COMM jour de fermeture avancée *m*; ~ **edition** *n BrE (cf bulldog edition AmE)* MEDIA *of newspaper* première édition matinale *f*, édition du matin *f*; ~ **exercise** *n* STOCK *options* exercice anticipé *m*; ~ **filing** *n* TAX *of return* production hâtive *f*; ~ **fringe** *n* MEDIA *evening viewers, listeners* tranche horaire du soir *f*, *morning viewers, listeners* tranche matinale *f (jarg)*; ~ **majority** *n jarg* S&M *type of purchaser* majorité innovatrice *f*; ~ **publication** *n* MEDIA, PATENTS publication précoce *f*; ~ **redemption** *n* FIN rachat anticipé *m*; ~ **retirement** *n* HRM pension anticipée *f (Bel)*, prépension *f (Bel)*, préretraite *f*, préretraite obligatoire *f*, retraite anticipée *f*, retraite anticipée obligatoire *f*; ~ **retirement annuity** *n* HRM pension anticipée *f (Bel)*, rente anticipée *f*, retraite anticipée *f*; ~ **retirement benefits** *n pl* HRM prestations de préretraite *f pl*; ~ **retirement pension** *n* HRM préretraite *f*; ~ **retirement scheme** *n* FIN, HRM pension de retraite anticipée *f*; ~ **-withdrawal penalty** *n* FIN, STOCK pénalité pour retrait anticipé *f*

earmark *vt* ECON, FIN *funds, resources* affecter, destiner, réserver

earmarked: ~ **check** *n AmE*, ~ **cheque** *n BrE* BANK chèque réservé *m*; ~ **gold** *n* ECON or détenu par les banques de la Federal Reserve pour les comptes étrangers et internationaux; ~ **tax** *n* TAX impôt affecté à une fin spéciale *m*, impôt spécifique *m*;

◆ **be ~ for** GEN COMM *promotion* être sélectionné pour

earmarking *n* ECON *of resources* affectation *f*, allocation *f*, FIN, TAX *(SYN ring fencing) of public funds* affectation *f*

earn *vt* BANK *interest* produire, rapporter, GEN COMM *reputation* acquérir, se faire, HRM *income* gagner; ◆ ~ **a fast buck** *infrml* GEN COMM gagner de l'argent rapidement, se faire rapidement du fric *(infrml)*; ~ **a living** *(SYN make a living)* ECON gagner sa vie; ~ **one's keep** GEN COMM gagner sa vie; ~ **a salary of** HRM gagner un salaire de, toucher un salaire de; ~ **40 K** HRM gagner 40.000; ~ **40,000** HRM gagner 40.000; ~ **£100 a week** HRM gagner £100 par semaine

earned: ~ **depletion** *n* TAX épuisement gagné *m*; ~ **income** *n* TAX revenu gagné *m*; ~ **income allowance** *n* HRM déduction au titre des revenus salariaux *f*; ~ **interest** *n* ACC intérêt gagné *m*; ~ **premium** *n* INS prime absorbée *f*, prime acquise *f*; ~ **surplus** *n* ACC bénéfices non-distribués *m pl*

earnest: ~ **money** *n* PROP arrhes *f pl*, STOCK arrhes *f pl*, dépôt de garantie *m*

earning: ~ **capacity** *n* ACC capacité bénéficiaire *f*, GEN COMM capacité bénéficiaire *f*, capacité de gain *f*, HRM capacité bénéficiaire *f*; ~ **performance** *n* ECON, GEN COMM productivité *f*; ~ **power** *n* ACC capacité bénéficiaire *f*, rentabilité *f*, GEN COMM capacité bénéficiaire *f*, HRM capacité bénéficiaire *f*, rentabilité *f*; ~ **streams** *n pl* FIN rentrées d'argent *f pl*

earnings *n pl* FIN bénéfice *m*, GEN COMM rémunération *f*, HRM gains *m pl*, rémunération *f*; ~ **amount** *n* TAX montant des gains *m*; ~ **base** *n* FIN base de bénéfices *f*; ~ **ceiling** *n* HRM salaire plafond *m*; ~ **differential** *n* HRM écart de rémunération *m*; ~ **drift** *n (SYN wage drift)* HRM dérapage des salaires *m*, dérive des salaires *f*, tendance à la hausse des salaires *f*; ~ **forecast** *n* ECON, FIN, GEN COMM prévision de bénéfices *f*, résultats prévisionnels *m pl*; ~ **on assets** *n pl* ACC, STOCK rendement des actifs *m*, rendement des fonds propres *m*; ~ **per share** *n pl (EPS)* ACC, FIN, STOCK bénéfices par action *m pl (BPA)*; ~ **performance** *n* ACC, FIN *of a stock* rentabilité *f*; ~ **period** *n* TAX période de gains *f*; ~ **report** *n* FIN rapport financier *m*; ~ **test** *n* TAX examen de revenu *m*; ~ **yield** *n* FIN rendement *m*, STOCK rendement boursier *m*, rendement des actions *m*

earphones *n pl* GEN COMM écouteurs *m pl*

earth *vt BrE (cf ground AmE)* COMP, TRANSP mettre à la terre

earthing *n BrE (cf grounding AmE)* COMP, TRANSP mise à la terre *f*

earthquake: **~ insurance** *n* INS assurance contre les tremblements de terre *f*

ease[1] *n* TRANSP facilité *f*; **~ of handling** TRANSP facilité de manutention *f*

ease[2] **1.** *vt* ECON *credit controls* desserrer, *economic policy* détendre; **2.** *vi* **~ off** GEN COMM *demand* diminuer

easement *n* PROP servitude *f*

easing *n* ECON *of credit control, restrictions* détente *f*

east *n* (*E*) GEN COMM est *m*

East: **~ Caribbean Common Market** *n* (*ECCM*) ECON Marché commun des Caraïbes orientales *m*; **~ compass point** *n* (*E*) TRANSP *navigation* quart est *m* (*E*); **~ European Trade Council** *n* GEN COMM Conseil commercial d'Europe de l'Est *m*

eastbound *adj* TRANSP à destination est *loc f*

eastern *adj* GEN COMM de l'est *loc m*, oriental

Eastern: **~ Bloc** *n* POL bloc de l'Est *m*; **~ -bloc country** *n* POL pays du bloc de l'Est *m*; **~ Europe** *n* POL Europe de l'Est *f*; **~ European Time** *n* (*EET*) GEN COMM heure de l'Europe de l'Est *f*; **~ Standard Time** *n* US (*EST*) GEN COMM heure de l'Est *f*

easy[1] *adj* GEN COMM aisé, facile

easy:[2] **~ money** *n* ECON argent facile *m* (*infrml*); **~ money policy** *n* ECON politique d'argent facile *f*; **~ option** *n* MGMNT décision facile *f*; **~ payment** *n* BANK facilité de paiement *f*; **~ terms** *n* BANK facilité de paiement *f*

eat: **1.** *vt* **~ into** GEN COMM *savings, reserves* entamer; **2.** *vi* **~ out** LEIS *in restaurant* dîner dehors, sortir dîner

EAT *abbr* HRM UK (*Employment Appeal Tribunal*) autorité judiciaire compétente en matière d'emploi, LEIS (*estimated arrival time*), TRANSP (*estimated arrival time*) date probable d'arrivée *f*, heure d'arrivée prévue *f*

ebb: **~ tide** *n* TRANSP *shipping* marée descendante *f*

EBRD *abbr* (*European Bank for Reconstruction and Development*) BANK, ECON, POL BERD (*Banque européenne pour la reconstruction et le développement*)

EBU *abbr* (*European Broadcasting Union*) COMMS, MEDIA UER (*Union européenne de radiodiffusion*)

EC[1] *abbr* (*European Community*) ECON CE (*Communauté européenne*)

EC:[2] **~ -mark** *n* IND *on toys meeting EU standards of safety* conformité aux normes de la C.E *f*

ECB *abbr* (*European Central Bank*) BANK, ECON Banque centrale européenne *f*

ECCM *abbr* (*East Caribbean Common Market*) ECON Marché commun des Caraïbes orientales *m*

ECDC *abbr* (*Economic Cooperation among Developing Countries*) ECON Accord de coopération économique entre pays en voie de développement *m*

ECE *abbr* (*Economic Commission for Europe*) ECON CEE (*Commission économique européenne*)

ECG *abbr* (*European Cooperation Grouping*) LAW, POL Groupement de coopération européen *m*

ECGD *abbr* UK (*Export Credit Guarantee Department*) IMP/EXP service de garantie des crédits à l'exportation, ≈ COFACE (*Compagnie française d'assurance pour le commerce extérieur*)

echelon *n* HRM, MGMNT échelon *m*

echo: **~ sounder** *n* TRANSP *shipping* sondeur U.S. *m*, sondeur par ultrasons *m*; **~ -sounding device** *n* (*ESD*) TRANSP *shipping* sondeur par ultrasons *m* (*sondeur U.S.*)

ECI *abbr* (*export consignment identifying number*) IMP/EXP numéro identifiant des marchandises à l'exportation

Eclectic: **~ Keynesian** *n* ECON Keynésien éclectique *m*

ECMT: **~ permit** *n* European Community Motor Transport TRANSP *road haulage* permis CEMT *m* (*Communauté européenne transport automobile*)

Eco: **~ Audit and Management System** *n* ENVIR EU Audit des systèmes de management environnemental *m*

ECOCOM *abbr* (*Economic Commission for Europe for Trade and Technology Division*) ADMIN division de la commission économique européene pour le commerce et la technologie *f*

ECOFIN *abbr* (*European Community Finance Ministers*) ECON, FIN, POL ministres des finances de la communauté européenne *m pl*

ecolabeling *n* AmE, **ecolabelling** *n* BrE ENVIR application du label écologique communautaire *f*

ecological[1] *adj* ENVIR, POL écologique

ecological:[2] **~ character** *n* ENVIR, IND *of products for sale* caractère écologique *m*; **~ damage** *n* ENVIR, IND dégradation écologique *f*; **~ indicator** *n* ENVIR, IND indicateur écologique *m*; **~ recovery** *n* ENVIR, IND assainissement écologique *m*

ecologically *adj* ENVIR écologiquement; ◆ **~ sound** ENVIR non-nuisible à l'environnement

ecology *n* ENVIR écologie *f*; **~ lobby** ENVIR, POL lobby écologiste *m*; **~ lobby group** ENVIR, POL groupe de pression des écologistes *m*; **~ pressure group** ENVIR, POL groupe de pression des écologistes *m*

econometric *adj* ECON, GEN COMM économétrique

econometrician *n* ECON, GEN COMM économétricien *m*

econometrics *n* ECON, GEN COMM économétrie *f*

economic[1] *adj* ECON, FIN, GEN COMM économique

economic:[2] **~ activity** *n* ECON activité économique *f*; **~ advancement** *n* ECON, GEN COMM, POL développement économique *m*, essor économique *m*; **~ adviser** *n* ADMIN, ECON, POL *to bank, government* conseiller économique *m*; **~ agent** *n* ECON agent économique *m*; **~ analysis** *n* ECON, FIN analyse économique *f*; **~ analyst** *n* HRM, S&M, STOCK conjoncturiste *mf*; **~ austerity** *n* ECON, POL austérité économique *f*; ~ **base** *n* ECON indice de base *m*; ~ **batch quantity** *n* ECON, IND, MGMNT effectif de série économique *m*; ~ **benefit** *n* ECON avantage économique *m*, intérêt économique *m*; ~ **boom** *n* ECON, GEN COMM, POL boom économique *m*, essor économique *m*, période de prospérité économique *f*; ~ **climate** *n* ECON, GEN COMM, POL climat économique *m*, conjoncture *f*, conjoncture actuelle *f*; ~ **conditions** *n pl* ECON, GEN COMM, POL conditions économiques *f pl*, conjoncture *f*, conjoncture actuelle *f*; ~ **conservation** *n* ENVIR conservation des ressources compatible avec l'économie *f*, conservation des ressources naturelles *f*, conservation financièrement rentable des ressources *f*, préservation de l'environnement compatible avec l'économie *f*, préservation financièrement rentable de l'environnement *f*; ~ **cost** *n* ECON coût économique *m*; ~ **crime** *n* ECON, LAW, POL crime économique *m*; ~ **crisis** *n* ECON crise économique *f*; ~ **criteria** *n pl* ECON critères économiques *m pl*; ~ **cycle** *n* ECON, GEN COMM, IMP/EXP cycle économique *m*; ~ **data** *n pl* ECON données économiques *f pl*; ~ **depreciation** *n* ECON, PROP *real estate* dépréciation économique *f*; ~ **development** *n* ECON, GEN COMM, POL développement économique *m*; ~ **devolution** *n* ECON, POL décentralisation économique *f*; ~ **efficiency** *n* ECON rendement économique *m*; ~ **expansion** *n* ECON expansion économique *f*; ~ **forecasting** *n* *(SYN Treasury model)* ECON prévisions économiques *f pl*; ~ **freedom** *n* ECON, POL liberté économique *f*; ~ **geography** *n* ECON géographie économique *f*; ~ **good** *n* ECON bien économique *m*; ~ **growth** *n* ECON croissance économique *f*; ~ **growth rate** *n* ECON taux de croissance économique *m*; ~ **incentive** *n* ECON incitation économique *f*; ~ **indicator** *n* ECON indicateur économique *m*, *econometrics* clignotant économique *m*, POL indicateur économique *m*; ~ **institution** *n* ECON institution économique *f*; ~ **integration** *n* ECON intégration économique *f*; ~ **intelligence** *n* ECON information économique *f*; ~ **journal** *n* ECON, MEDIA journal économique *m*; ~ **laws** *n pl* ECON, LAW lois économiques *f pl*; ~ **life** *n* FIN, S&M durée de vie économique *f*, vie économique *f*; ~ **loss** *n* ECON perte économique *f*; ~ **man** *n* *(SYN homo economicus)* ECON homme économique *m*; ~ **manufacturing quantity** *n* ECON, IND, MGMNT quantité économique de fabrication *f*, quantité économique de production *f*, série économique de fabrication *f*; ~ **methodology** *n* ECON méthodologie économique *f*; ~ **methods** *n pl* ECON méthodes économiques *f pl*; ~ **mission** *n* ECON, MGMNT mission économique *f*; ~ **model** *n* ECON modèle économique *m*; ~ **news** *n* ECON informations économiques *f pl*; ~ **obsolescence** *n* ECON obsolescence économique *f*; ~ **order quantity** *n* *(EOQ)* ECON, IND, MATH, MGMNT quantité optimale de commande *f*, quantité optimale de réapprovisionnement *f*, quantité économique de réapprovisionnement *f*, quantité économique à

commander *f*; ~ **outlook** *n* ECON, GEN COMM, POL perspectives économiques *f pl*; ~ **paradigm** *n* ECON paradigme économique *m*; ~ **planning** *n* ECON, ENVIR, POL planification économique *f*; ~ **planning unit** *n* *(EPU)* ECON bureau de planification économique *m*; ~ **position** *n* ECON position économique *f*; ~ **profit** *n* ECON bénéfice économique *m*; ~ **programming** *n* ECON programmation économique *f*; ~ **prospects** *n pl* ECON, GEN COMM, POL perspectives économiques *f pl*; ~ **reform** *n* ECON, POL réforme économique *f*; ~ **rent** *n* ECON loyer économique *m*, rente économique *f*; ~ **report** *n* ECON rapport économique *m*; ~ **research** *n* ECON, S&M recherche en économie *f*, études économiques *f pl*; ~ **resource** *n* ECON ressource économique *f*; ~ **sanctions** *n pl* ECON, POL sanctions économiques *f pl*; ~ **section** *n* MEDIA *of newspaper* pages économiques *f pl*, rubrique économique *f*, section Économie *f*; ~ **situation** *n* ECON, GEN COMM, POL situation économique *f*; ~ **slowdown** *n* ECON, GEN COMM ralentissement économique *m*; ~ **strategy** *n* ECON, GEN COMM, POL stratégie économique *f*; ~ **summit** *n* ECON, POL sommet économique *m*; ~ **system** *n* ECON, POL système économique *m*; ~ **theory** *n* ECON théorie économique *f*; ~ **trend** *n* ECON conjoncture économique *f*, tendance économique *f*, évolution de la situation économique *f*, évolution économique *f*, GEN COMM conjoncture économique *f*; ~ **union** *n* ECON, POL *EU* union économique *f*; ~ **value** *n* ECON valeur de remplacement *f*, valeur économique *f*; ~ **viability** *n* ECON, FIN viabilité économique *f*; ~ **welfare** *n* WEL bien-être économique *m*; ~ **well-being** *n* ECON, POL bien-être économique *m*

Economic: ~ **Commission for Europe** *n* *(ECE)* ECON Commission économique européenne *f* *(CEE)*; ~ **Commission for Europe for Trade and Technology Division** *n* *(ECOCOM)* ADMIN division de la commission économique pour le commerce européen et *f*; ~ **Commission for Western Africa** *n* *(ECWA)* ECON Commission économique pour l'Afrique occidentale *f*; ~ **Community of West African States** *n* *(ECOWAS)* ECON Communauté économique de l'Afrique de l'Ouest *f* *(CEAO)*; ~ **Cooperation among Developing Countries** *n* *(ECDC)* ECON Accord de coopération économique entre pays en voie de développement *m*; ~ **and Monetary Union** *n* *(EMU)* ECON, POL Union économique et monétaire *f* *(UEM)*; ~ **Planning Agency** *n* *(EPA)* HRM ≈ Agence de planification économique *f*; ~ **and Social Committee** *n* *(ESC)* ECON *EU* Comité économique et social *m*; ~ **Trends Annual Survey** *n* UK *(ETAS)* ECON *econometrics* rapport annuel sur les tendances de l'économie

economical[1] *adj* GEN COMM économique

economical:[2] ~ **use of resources** *n* ENVIR exploitation mesurée des ressources *f*, exploitation économique des ressources *f*

economically *adv* ECON, FIN, GEN COMM, S&M

économiquement; ◆ ~ **backward** ECON, POL *area* en retard économique

economics *n pl* [+sing v] WEL sciences économiques *f pl*, économie *f*; ~ **of crime** ECON économie du crime *f*; ~ **of law** ECON, LAW économie du droit *f*; ~ **and psychology** ECON, WEL économie et psychologie *f*

economism *n* ECON économisme *m*

economist *n* ECON, POL économiste *mf*

economize: ~ **on** *vt* GEN COMM économiser

economy:[1] ~ **-wide** *adj* ECON touchant l'ensemble de l'économie

economy[2] *n* ECON, POL économie *f*; ~ **of abundance** ECON économie d'abondance *f*; ~ **class** LEIS, TRANSP *(tourist class,* ANT *first class)* classe touriste *f*, classe économique *f*; ~ **-class flight** LEIS, TRANSP vol en classe économique *m*; ~ **fare** LEIS, TRANSP tarif en classe économique *m*; ~ **flight** LEIS, TRANSP vol en classe économique *m*; ~ **pack** GEN COMM, S&M paquet économique *m*; ~ **of scale** (ANT *diseconomy of scale)* ECON, IND économie d'échelle *f*; ~ **of scope** ECON, IND polyvalence de la production *f*, économie de champ *f*; ~ **of size** ECON économie dimensionnelle *f*; ~ **size** S&M taille économique *f*; ~ **of size** IND économie dimensionnelle *f*; ~ **ticket** LEIS, TRANSP billet en classe économique *m*; ◆ **as an ~ measure** GEN COMM par mesure d'économie

ecosystem *n* ENVIR écosystème *m*

ecotoxicological *adj* ENVIR écotoxicologique

ECOWAS *abbr (Economic Community of West African States)* ECON CEAO *(Communauté économique de l'Afrique de l'Ouest)*

ECP *abbr (Eurocommercial paper)* FIN europapier commercial *m*, STOCK billet de trésorerie euro *m*, papier eurocommercial *m*

ECPD *abbr (export cargo packing declaration)* IMP/ EXP, TRANSP déclaration d'emballage de cargaison exportée *f*

ECPS *abbr (Environment and Consumer Protection Service)* ENVIR *EU* Service de protection du consommateur et de l'environnement *m*

ECSC *abbr (European Coal and Steel Community)* ECON CECA *(Communauté européenne du charbon et de l'acier)*

ECSI *abbr (export cargo shipping instruction)* IMP/ EXP, TRANSP instruction de transport de cargaison exportée *f*

ECU *abbr (European Currency Unit)* BANK, ECON, FIN ECU *(unité monétaire européenne)*

Ecuador *pr n* GEN COMM Équateur *m*

Ecuadoran *n* GEN COMM *person* Écuadorien *m*, Équatorien *m*

Ecuadorian[1] *adj* GEN COMM écuadorien, équatorien

Ecuadorian[2] *n* GEN COMM *person* Écuadorien *m*, Équatorien *m*

ECWA *abbr (Economic Commission for Western*

Africa) ECON Commission économique pour l'Afrique occidentale *f*

ed. *abbr (edition)* COMP, GEN COMM, MEDIA éd., édit. *(édition)*

ED[1] *abbr (Eurodollar)* ECON, FIN, STOCK eurodollar *m*

ED:[2] ~ **future** *n* ECON, FIN, STOCK contrat à terme sur eurodollars *m*

EDF *abbr (European Development Fund)* ECON, POL FDE *(Fonds de développement européen)*

edge:[1] *vi* ~ **ahead** ECON prendre de l'avance petit à petit; ~ **up** ECON monter lentement, progresser lentement

edge:[2] **have the ~ on sb** *phr* GEN COMM avoir l'avantage sur qn *loc m*; **have the ~ over sb** *phr* GEN COMM avoir l'avantage sur qn *loc m*

EDI *abbr* COMMS *(electronic data interchange)* EDI *(échange de données informatisées)*, COMMS *(electronic document interchange)* EDI *(échange de documents informatisés)*, COMP *(electronic data interchange)* EDI *(échange de données informatisées)*, COMP *(electronic document interchange)* EDI *(échange de documents informatisés)*

edict *n* GEN COMM décret *m*

Edinburgh *pr n* GEN COMM Édimbourg *n pr*

edit:[1] ~ **menu** *n* COMP menu édition *m*; ~ **mode** *n* COMP mode d'édition *m*

edit[2] *vt* COMP *arrange data, document* mettre en forme, modifier, éditer, *correct text, document* corriger, réviser, MEDIA mettre en forme *(jarg)*

edited: ~ **return** *n* (SYN *dressed return)* TAX déclaration mise au point *f*

editing *n* MEDIA édition *f*

edition *n (ed.)* COMP édition *f (éd.)*, GEN COMM, MEDIA rédaction *f*, édition *f (éd.)*

editor *n* COMP *software* programme d'édition *m*, HRM *publishing* correcteur *m*, rédacteur *m*, MEDIA *newspapers* rédacteur en chef *m, press, radio, TV* directeur de collection *m*, directeur de la rédaction *m, publishing* correcteur *m*, rédacteur *m, series* directeur de la publication *m*

editorial *n (cf leader BrE)* MEDIA *in newspaper, magazine* éditorial *m*; ~ **advertising** GEN COMM publicité rédactionnelle *f*; ~ **staff** MEDIA équipe de rédaction *f*; ~ **writer** MEDIA *newspapers* éditorialiste *mf*

editorialist *n* GEN COMM éditorialiste *mf*

editorship *n* GEN COMM, MEDIA rédaction *f*

EDP *abbr (electronic data processing)* COMP TEI *(traitement électronique de l'information)*

educated[1] *adj* HRM *person* instruit

educated:[2] ~ **guess** *n* HRM supposition éclairée *f*

education *n* WEL enseignement *m*, éducation *f*; ~ **credit** TAX crédit pour études *m*

educational: ~ **background** *n* WEL formation *f*; ~ **development** *n* GEN COMM, WEL développement pédagogique *m*; ~ **endowment** *n* INS assurance mixte éducation *f*; ~ **establishment** *n* (SYN *educational institution)* TAX, WEL établissement d'enseignement *m*, établissement scolaire *m*, établissement éducatif *m*; ~ **institution** *n* (SYN *educational establishment)* TAX, WEL établissement d'enseignement *m*, établissement scolaire *m*, établissement éducatif *m*; ~ **organization** *n* TAX organisation à caractère éducatif *f*

EEA *abbr* ECON *(European economic area)* zone économique européenne *f*, FIN *(Exchange Equalization Account)* fonds de stabilisation des changes *m*

EEB *abbr (European Environmental Bureau)* ENVIR Bureau européen pour l'environnement *m*

EEIG *abbr (European Economic Interest Grouping)* ECON, POL GIEE *(Groupement d'intérêt économique européen)*

EEOC *abbr US (Equal Employment Opportunity Commission)* HRM commission pour l'égalité des chances pour l'emploi

EET *abbr (Eastern European Time)* GEN COMM heure de l'Europe de l'Est *f*

EF *abbr (European Foundation)* GEN COMM Fondation européenne *f*

effect[1] *n* GEN COMM incidence *f*; ◆ **come into ~** LAW *act, regulation, rule* devenir effectif, entrer en vigueur; **in ~** GEN COMM en effet; **with ~ from** *(wef)* GEN COMM avec effet à compter du, à partir de

effect[2] *vt* GEN COMM *settlement* effectuer

effective[1] *adj* COMP effectif, GEN COMM efficace

effective:[2] ~ **control** *n* FIN contrôle de fait *m*; ~ **date** *n* GEN COMM date d'effet *f*, date d'entrée en vigueur *f*; ~ **debt** *n* BANK dette réelle *f*; ~ **demand** *n* (SYN *effectual demand)* ECON, GEN COMM, S&M demande effective *f*; ~ **exchange rate** *n* ECON, FIN taux de change effectif *m*; ~ **funding rate** *n* STOCK *interest rate futures* taux de financement effectif *m*; ~ **horsepower** *n (ehp)* IND puissance réelle *f*; ~ **interest date** *n* TAX date d'entrée en vigueur de l'intérêt *f*; ~ **management** *n* MGMNT direction efficace *f*; ~ **net worth** *n* ACC valeur nette réelle *f*; ~ **rate** *n* ACC taux réel *m*; ~ **rate of assistance** *n* ECON, IND taux d'assistance effectif *m*; ~ **rate of protection** *n* ECON, IND taux de protection effectif *m*; ~ **tax rate** *n* TAX taux d'imposition effectif *m*; ~ **yield** *n* STOCK rendement effectif *m*, rendement réel *m*; ◆ **be ~** COMP être en vigueur

effectively *adv* GEN COMM effectivement, efficacement, utilement; ◆ ~ **closed** TRANSP *packing* totalement étanche

effectiveness *n* GEN COMM efficacité *f*

effects: **no ~** *phr (NE)* GEN COMM sans effet

effectual: ~ **demand** *n* (SYN *effective demand)* ECON, GEN COMM, S&M demande effective *f*

efficiency *n* ECON compétence *f*, efficience *f*, productivité *f*, rendement *m*, GEN COMM compétence *f*, efficacité *f*, efficience *f*, productivité *f*, IND, S&M efficience *f*, rendement *m*; ~ **agreement** *UK* HRM accord de rendement *m*; ~ **audit** ACC

contrôle d'efficience *m*; ~ **drive** GEN COMM, HRM campagne d'efficacité *f*; ~ **engineer** HRM ingénieur-conseil *m*; ~ **ratio** ECON ratio d'efficience *m*; ~ **real wage** HRM salaire réel efficient *m*; ~ **variance** FIN, GEN COMM écart de rendement *m*; ~ **wage** ECON, HRM salaire efficient *m*

efficient[1] *adj* ADMIN efficace, COMP performant, ECON, GEN COMM compétent, efficace, efficient

efficient:[2] ~ **allocation** *n* ECON allocation efficiente *f*; ~ **job mobility** *n* ECON, HRM mobilité efficiente de la main d'oeuvre *f*; ~ **market** *n* ECON *theory* marché efficient *m*; ~ **portfolio** *n* STOCK portefeuille efficient *m*; ~ **real wage** *n* ECON salaire réel efficient *m*

effluence *n* ENVIR effluence *f*

effluent *n* ENVIR effluent *m*, rejet *m*; ~ **discharge** ENVIR décharge d'effluent *f*; ~ **fee** ECON, ENVIR taxe sur les effluents *f*; ~ **monitor** ENVIR système de contrôle de la radioactivité d'effluent *m*; ~ **standard** ENVIR norme de rejet d'effluent *f*

EFL *abbr* FIN *(external financing limit)* limite de financement externe *f*, WEL *(English as a Foreign Language)* anglais comme langue étrangère *m*

EFT *abbr (electronic funds transfer)* BANK, FIN transfert électronique de fonds *m*, télévirement *m*

EFTA *abbr (European Free Trade Association)* ECON AELE *(Association européenne de libre-échange)*

EFTPOS *abbr (electronic funds transfer at point of sale)* BANK transfert électronique de fonds au point de vente *m*, télévirement au point de vente *m*

EFTS *abbr (electronic funds transfer system)* BANK système de télévirement *m*

e.g. *abbr (exempli gratia, for example)* GEN COMM ex. *(par exemple)*

EGA *abbr (enhanced graphics adaptor, enhanced graphics array)* COMP AGA *(adaptateur graphique couleur)*

egalitarian *adj* POL égalitarien

egalitarianism *n* POL égalitarisme *m*

EGM *abbr (extraordinary general meeting)* MGMNT AGE *(assemblée générale extraordinaire)*

egress *n* GEN COMM sortie *f*

Egypt *pr n* GEN COMM Égypte *f*

Egyptian[1] *adj* GEN COMM égyptien

Egyptian[2] *n* GEN COMM *person* Égyptien *m*

ehp *abbr (effective horsepower)* IND puissance réelle *f*

EHS *abbr (extra high strength)* IND à très haute résistance *loc f*

EI *abbr UK (employee involvement)* HRM participation *f*

EIB *abbr (European Investment Bank)* BANK BEI *(Banque européenne d'investissement)*

EIM *abbr (European Interprofessional Market)* STOCK Marché interprofessionnel européen *m*

EIS *abbr UK (export intelligence service)* IMP/EXP service de renseignements pour l'exportation

EITZ *abbr (English Inshore Traffic Zone)* TRANSP zone de navigation côtière de l'Angleterre *f*

eject *vt* COMP *card, disk* éjecter

ejection *n* COMP *card, disk* éjection *f*

ejectment *n* LAW, PROP action en revendication de biens *f*, procédure d'éviction *f*

ejusdem generis *phr frml* GEN COMM de nature semblable *loc f*

elapsed: ~ **time** *n* COMP temps écoulé *m*

elastic[1] *adj* ECON élastique

elastic:[2] ~ **demand** *n* ECON, S&M demande élastique *f*; ~ **supply** *n* ECON, S&M offre élastique *f*

elasticity *n* ECON élasticité *f*; ~ **of anticipation** ECON élasticité d'anticipation *f*; ~ **of demand** ECON, S&M élasticité de la demande *f*; ~ **of demand and supply** ECON, S&M élasticité de la demande et de l'offre *f*; ~ **of expectations** ECON élasticité des anticipants *f*; ~ **of substitution** ECON élasticité de substitution *f*; ~ **of supply** ECON, S&M élasticité de l'offre *f*

ELB *abbr (export licensing branch)* IMP/EXP bureau des autorisations d'exportation *m*

elect *vt* GEN COMM élire, *course of action* choisir, opter, HRM choisir, POL choisir, élire; ♦ ~ **sb to the board** GEN COMM élire qn au conseil d'administration

elected: ~ **office** *n* POL office élu *m*

election *n* POL choix *m*, élection *f*, TAX choix *m*; ~ **campaign** *n* POL campagne électorale *f*; ~ **results** *n pl* POL résultats du scrutin *m pl*

elective[1] *adj (cf appointive AmE)* GEN COMM obtenu par nomination

elective:[2] ~ **income** *n* TAX revenu étalé *m*

elector *n* POL électeur *m*

electoral: ~ **register** *n* (SYN *electoral roll*) GEN COMM, POL liste électorale *f*; ~ **roll** *n* (SYN *electoral register*) GEN COMM, POL liste électorale *f*

electorate: **the** ~ *n* GEN COMM, POL les électeurs *m pl*

electric: ~ **train** *n* TRANSP train électrique *m*

electrical: ~ **appliance** *n* GEN COMM appareil électrique *m*; ~ **current** *n* COMP, IND courant *m*, courant électrique *m*; ~ **engineer** *n* GEN COMM ingénieur électricien *m*; ~ **engineering** *n* IND génie électrique *m*; ~ **exemption clause** *n* INS *property insurance* clause d'exonération pour installation électrique *f*

Electrical: ~ **Trades Union** *n* UK (ETU) GEN COMM syndicat britannique d'électriciens

electricity *n* COMP, IND courant *m*, courant électrique *m*; ~ **bill** *BrE (cf hydro bill Can)* IND facture d'électricité *f*; ~ **consumption** ENVIR, GEN COMM, IND consommation d'électricité *f*; ~ **generation** IND génération d'électricité *f*; ~ **sector** IND secteur électrique *m*

electrification *n* TRANSP *of railways* électrification *f*

electronic: ~ **accounting system** *n* ACC système comptable électronique *m*; ~ **banking** *n* BANK,

COMP bancatique *f*, banque électronique *f*; ~ **calculator** *n* COMP machine à calculer électronique *f*; ~ **component** *n* COMP *hardware* composant électronique *m*; ~ **data interchange** *n* (EDI) COMMS, COMP échange de données informatisées *m* (EDI); ~ **data processing** *n* (EDP) COMP analyse électronique des données *f*, traitement électronique de l'information *m*, traitement électronique des données *m*; ~ **document interchange** *n* (EDI) COMMS, COMP échange de documents informatisés *m* (EDI); ~ **engineer** *n* GEN COMM ingénieur électronicien *m*; ~ **funds transfer** *n* (EFT) BANK, FIN transfert électronique de fonds *m*, télévirement *m*; ~ **funds transfer at point of sale** *n* (EFTPOS) BANK transfert électronique de fonds au point de vente *m*, télévirement au point de vente *m*; ~ **funds transfer system** *n* (EFTS) BANK système de télévirement *m*; ~ **mail** *n (e-mail)* ADMIN, COMMS, COMP *network system* courrier électronique *m*, messagerie électronique *f*; ~ **news gathering** *n* COMP, MEDIA collecte électronique d'informations *f*; ~ **office** *n* ADMIN, GEN COMM bureau électronique *m*; ~ **payment** *n* FIN paiement électronique *m*; ~ **payment terminal** *n* (EPT) FIN terminal de paiement électronique *m* (TPE); ~ **point of sale** *n* (EPOS) GEN COMM point de vente électronique *m*; ~ **posting board** *n* STOCK tableau d'affichage électronique *m*; ~ **publishing** *n* COMP, MEDIA édition électronique *f*; ~ **shopping** *n* COMP télé-achat *m*; ~ **typewriter** *n* GEN COMM machine à écrire électronique *f*

electronically: ~ **programmable read only memory** *n* (EPROM) COMP *programming language* mémoire morte programmable électroniquement *f* (EPROM)

electronics *n* IND électronique *f*

electrostatic: ~ **printer** *n* COMP *hardware* imprimante électrostatique *f*

element *n* GEN COMM *factor* élément *m*; ~ **of risk** GEN COMM facteur risque *m*

elementary: ~ **loss** *n* INS perte simple *f*

elephant's: ~ **foot** *n* TRANSP *fixed lashing* pied d'éléphant *m*

elevator *n* AmE *(cf lift BrE)* GEN COMM ascenseur *m*; ~ **liability insurance** US INS assurance responsabilité civile couvrant l'ascenseur *f*

eligibility *n* GEN COMM, TAX admissibilité *f*; ~ **for tax relief** TAX droit à un allègement d'impôts *m*; ~ **requirement** GEN COMM condition d'admissibilité *f*, condition d'éligibilité *f*, HRM condition d'éligibilité *f*; ~ **rule** TAX règle d'admissibilité *f*; ~ **test** BANK test d'admissibilité *m*

eligible[1] *adj* BANK bancable, GEN COMM admissible, LAW *to vote* éligible; ~ **for** GEN COMM admissible pour, ayant droit à; ♦ **be** ~ **for sth** GEN COMM présenter les conditions requises pour *(frml)*, *subsidy, grant* avoir droit à; ~ **for retirement** HRM admis à faire valoir ses droits à la retraite

eligible:[2] ~ **asset** *n* FIN actif escomptable *m*;

~ asset cost *n* TAX coût admissible d'un bien *m*; **~ bill** *n* BANK effet escomptable *m*; **~ expense** *n* TAX frais admissibles *m pl*; **~ individual** *n* TAX particulier admissible *m*; **~ liability** *n* FIN dettes escomptables *f pl*; **~ paper** *n* BANK effet bancable *m*

eliminate *vt* GEN COMM éliminer

elite *n* GEN COMM élite *f*

El Salvador *pr n* GEN COMM Salvador *m*

elsewhere: **not ~ specified** *phr (NES)* GEN COMM non-précisé par ailleurs, non-spécifié par ailleurs

em: **~ dash** *n* MEDIA *typography* tiret cadratin *m*, tiret long *m*; **~ space** *n* MEDIA *typography* tiret cadratin *m*

EMA *abbr (European Monetary Agreement)* GEN COMM AME *(Accord monétaire européen)*

e-mail *n (electronic mail)* ADMIN, COMMS, COMP courrier électronique *m*, messagerie électronique *f*

emancipation *n* LAW, POL émancipation *f*

embargo *n* TRANSP embargo *m*

embark *vt* TRANSP embarquer; **~ on** GEN COMM *course of action* entamer, s'engager dans

embarkation *n* TRANSP *shipping* embarquement *m*; **~ card** GEN COMM carte d'embarquement *f*; **~ port** GEN COMM port d'embarquement *m*

embassy *n* GEN COMM, POL ambassade *f*

embed *vt* COMP inclure, incorporer, intercaler, intégrer

embedded[1] *adj* COMP imbriqué, inclus, incorporé, intégré

embedded:[2] **~ command** *n* COMP commande intégrée *f*; **~ option** *n* STOCK opération intégrée *f*

embezzle *vt* FIN *funds*, GEN COMM, LAW détourner

embezzlement *n* FIN *of funds*, GEN COMM, LAW détournement *m*

embezzler *n* FIN, GEN COMM, LAW escroc *m*

emblements *n pl* LAW *agriculture* fruits naturels annuels *m pl*

embodied: **~ technical progress** *n* IND progrès technique incorporé *m*, progrès technique mis en application *m*

embodiment *n* PROP incorporation *f*

EMCF *abbr (European Monetary Cooperation Fund)* ECON, POL FMEC *(Fonds monétaire européen de coopération)*

emergency *n (emy)* GEN COMM urgence *f*; **~ aid** *n* ECON, POL *development aid* aide d'urgence *f*; **~ call** *n* COMMS appel d'urgence *m*; **~ exit** *n* HRM sortie de secours *f*; **~ landing** *n* TRANSP atterrissage forcé *m*; **~ measures** *n pl* GEN COMM, POL mesures d'urgence *f pl*; **~ powers** *n pl* HRM, POL pouvoirs d'exception *m pl*; **~ service** *n* WEL service d'urgence *m*

EMF *abbr (European Monetary Fund)* ECON, POL FME *(Fonds monétaire européen)*

EMI *abbr (European Monetary Institute)* ECON, POL Institut monétaire européen *m*

eminent: **~ domain** *n* PROP domaine éminent *m*

emission *n* ENVIR *of gases* émission *f*; **~ charges** *n*

pl ENVIR *pollution* redevances d'émission *f pl*; **~ data** *n pl* GEN COMM données antérieures *f pl*; **~ fee** *n* ENVIR *pollution* droit d'émission *m*; **~ limit** *n* ENVIR *pollution* limite d'émission *f*; **~ reductions banking** *n* ENVIR *pollution* stockage de réduction des émissions *m*; **~ standard** *n* ENVIR *pollution* norme d'émission *f*

empanel *vt* LAW constituer

emphasis *n* GEN COMM accent *m*

emphatic *adj* GEN COMM emphatique

empirical[1] *adj* GEN COMM, MATH empirique

empirical:[2] **~ data** *n* ECON, MATH données empiriques *f pl*

employ *vt* GEN COMM *method* employer, utiliser, HRM *method* employer

employable *adj* HRM apte au travail

employed *adj* HRM salarié; ◆ **be ~** HRM, TAX être employé

employee *n* HRM employé *m*, salarié *m*; **~ association** *n* HRM association d'employés *f*; **~ benefit** *n* HRM complément de salaire *m*; **~ benefit plan** *n* HRM régime de prestations aux employés *m*; **~ benefits** *n pl* HRM avantages annexes *m pl*, avantages en nature *m pl*, avantages sociaux *m pl*; **~ communications** *n pl* HRM communication interne *f*; **~ contributions** *n pl* HRM contributions des salariés *f pl*; **~ counseling** *n AmE*, **~ counselling** *n BrE* HRM conseil des employés *m*; **~ involvement** *n UK (EI)* HRM participation *f*; **~ involvement and participation** *n* GEN COMM, HRM, MGMNT cogestion *f*; **~ pension plan** *n* HRM régime de pension d'employés *m*; **~ profile** *n* HRM profil du salarié *m*; **~ profit sharing** *n* HRM participation des employés aux bénéfices *f*; **~ profit sharing plan** *n* HRM, STOCK régime de participation des employés aux bénéfices *m*; **~ ratio** *n* HRM coefficient d'employés *m*; **~ relations** *n pl* HRM relations avec les employés *f pl*, relations ouvrières *f pl*; **~ retirement income security act** *n* HRM, LAW loi sur la sécurité des revenus des employés en retraite *f*; **~ share ownership plan** *n (ESOP, employee stock ownership plan)* STOCK plan d'investissement du personnel *m*, HRM système de participation *m*; **~ shareholding scheme** *n* HRM, STOCK actionnariat des salariés *m*; **~'s job history** *n* HRM étude de l'expérience professionnelle d'un candidat *f*; **~ stock option** *n* HRM, STOCK option d'achat d'actions accordée à des employés *m*; **~ stock option plan** *n* HRM, STOCK plan d'options d'achat d'actions *m*, plan de souscription à des actions *m*; **~ stock ownership plan** *n* HRM, STOCK *(ESOP, employee share ownership plan)* plan d'investissement du personnel *m*; **~ trust** *n* TAX fiducie d'employés *f*

employees': **~ committee** *n* ACC comité d'entreprise *m*

employer *n* HRM employeur *m*; **~ express term** HRM formule expressément utilisée par l'employeur *f*; **~ interference** HRM immixtion du patronat dans les affaires syndicales *f*; ~'s **contribution** ACC *to social security charges and similar*, HRM, TAX cotisation patronale *f*; ~'s **legal obligation to fund** HRM *pension* obligation légale de cotiser au système de retraite *f*; ~'s **liability coverage** INS assurance RC de l'employeur *f*, assurance responsabilité civile de l'employeur *f*; ~'s **occupational pension scheme** *UK* HRM, TAX plan de retraite professionnelle de l'employeur *m*; ~'s **return** ACC, TAX déclaration patronale *f*

employers': ~ **association** *n* HRM union patronale *f*

employment *n* ECON, HRM, POL emploi *m*; ~ **agency** *n* GEN COMM, HRM agence de placement *f*, bureau de placement *m*; ~ **bureau** *n* GEN COMM, HRM agence de placement *f*, bureau de placement *m*; ~ **contract** *n* HRM contrat d'embauche *m*, contrat de travail *m*; ~ **expense** *n* TAX frais relatifs à un emploi *m pl*; ~ **expenses** *n pl* GEN COMM frais de main d'oeuvre *m pl*; ~ **figures** *n pl* ECON, POL chiffres de l'emploi *m pl*, statistiques de l'emploi *f pl*; ~ **function** *n* ECON fonction d'emploi *f*; ~ **income** *n* TAX revenu d'emploi *m*; ~ **law** *n* HRM, LAW, POL droit du travail *m*, droit social *m*, législation du travail *f*; ~ **multiplier** *n* ECON multiplicateur de l'emploi *m*; ~ **office** *n UK* GEN COMM, HRM entreprise de travail temporaire, agence de placement *f*, bureau de placement *m*; ~ **protection law** *n* HRM, LAW loi sur la protection du travail; ~ **protection rights** *n pl UK* HRM droits des employés à la protection contre les risques professionnels; ~ **record** *n* GEN COMM, HRM emplois successifs *m pl*, expérience professionnelle *f*; ~ **relationship** *n* HRM *EU regulations* relations de travail *f pl*; ~ **search** *n* HRM recherche d'emploi *f*; ~ **situation** *n* GEN COMM situation de l'emploi *f*; ~ **tax** *n* TAX taxe sur l'emploi *f*; ~ **tax credit** *n* TAX crédit d'impôt d'emploi *m*; ~ **tax deduction** *n* TAX déduction d'impôt à l'emploi *f*; ~ **test** *n* HRM *selection* période d'essai *f*; ~ **training** *n BrE (ET)* HRM formation *f*, formation à l'emploi *f*; ♦ **on the ~ front** HRM du point de vue de l'emploi, sur le front de l'emploi

Employment: ~ **Act** *n (EA)* HRM, LAW loi sur le travail; ~ **Appeal Tribunal** *n UK (EAT)* HRM autorité judiciaire compétente en matière d'emploi; ~ **Protection Act** *n UK (EPA)* HRM, LAW loi sur la protection de l'emploi *f*; ~ **Protection Consolidation Act** *n UK (EPCA)* HRM *1978* loi sur la protection du travail; ~ **Retirement Income Security Act** *n US (ERISA)* STOCK loi de garantie des revenus des travailleurs retraités; ~ **Service** *n UK* HRM ≈ Agence nationale pour l'emploi *f* *(France)*, ≈ ANPE *(France)*, ≈ Association pour l'emploi dans l'industrie et le commerce *f* *(France)*, ≈ ASSEDIC *(France)*

emporium *n* GEN COMM, S&M grand magasin *m*

empower *vt* POL donner du pouvoir à; ♦ ~ **sb to do** GEN COMM autoriser qn à faire

empty[1] *adj* GEN COMM, TRANSP vide

empty:[2] ~ **nesters** *n pl infrml* ECON, PROP *housing market* ménage sans enfants *m*

empty[3] *vt* GEN COMM vider

EMS *abbr (European Monetary System)* ECON *EU* SME *(Système monétaire européen)*

EMU *abbr* ECON *(Economic and Monetary Union)* UEM *(Union économique et monétaire)*, ECON *(European Monetary Union)* UME *(Union monétaire européenne)*, POL *(Economic and Monetary Union)* UEM *(Union économique et monétaire)*, POL *(European Monetary Union)* UME *(Union monétaire européenne)*

emulate *vt* COMP *software, protocol*, GEN COMM émuler

emulation *n* COMP *software, protocol* émulation *f*; ~ **board** COMP carte d'émulation *f*; ~ **card** COMP carte d'émulation *f*; ~ **software** COMP logiciel d'émulation *m*

emulator *n* COMP émulateur *m*

emy *abbr (emergency)* GEN COMM urgence *f*

en:[1] ~ **route** *adv* GEN COMM en route *loc f*

en:[2] ~ **dash** *n* MEDIA *typography* tiret court *m*, tiret demi-cadratin *m*

enable *vt* COMP *hardware* valider, *software* mettre en service

enabling: ~ **clause** *n* LAW clause d'habilitation *f*

enact *vt* LAW décréter, ordonner, promulguer, édicter, POL décréter, ordonner, promulguer, TAX édicter

enacted: ~ **by** *phr* LAW édicté par, TAX pris par, édicté par

enactment *n* LAW promulgation *f*, POL décret *m*, ordonnance *f*, promulgation *f*, texte législatif *m*

enc. *abbr (enclosed)* COMMS ci-inclus, ci-joint, joint, GEN COMM ci-inclus, ci-joint, inclus, joint

encashable *adj* BANK encaissable

encashing: ~ **agent** *n* TAX agent encaisseur *m*

encashment *n* ACC, BANK, FIN encaissement *m*; ~ **schedule** ACC calendrier d'encaissement *m*

encl. *abbr (enclosed)* COMMS ci-inclus, ci-joint, joint, GEN COMM ci-inclus, ci-joint, inclus, joint

enclave: ~ **economy** *n* ECON économie enclavée *f*

enclose *vt* COMMS joindre, GEN COMM inclure

enclosed[1] *adj (enc., encl.)* COMMS, GEN COMM ci-inclus, ci-joint, joint

enclosed:[2] ~ **dock** *n* TRANSP *shipping* dock fermé *m*; ~ **port** *n* TRANSP *shipping* port fermé *m*

enclosure *n* GEN COMM p.j., pièce jointe *f*

encode *vt* COMP encoder, programmer

encoding *n* BANK codage *m*

encompass *vt* GEN COMM inclure

encounter *vt* GEN COMM *problem* rencontrer

encourage *vt* GEN COMM encourager

encouragement *n* GEN COMM encouragement *m*, incitation *f*, HRM incitation *f*

encouraging *adj* GEN COMM encourageant

encroach: ~ **on** *vt* LAW empiéter, usurper; ~ **upon** LAW empiéter, usurper

encroachment *n* LAW empiétement *m*, usurpation *f*

encryption *n* (ANT *decryption*) COMMS, COMP *programming language* chiffrement *m*, codage *m*, cryptage *m*

encumbered: ~ **by** *phr* GEN COMM encombré

encumbrance *n* LAW, POL charge *f*, servitude *f*

end¹ *n* GEN COMM fin *f*; ~ **consumer** *n* ENVIR, IND consommateur final *m*; ~ **of file** *n* *(EOF)* COMP fin de fichier *f*; ~ **-of-file mark** *n* COMP marque de fin de fichier *f*; ~ **-of-line character** *n* COMP caractère de fin de ligne *m*; ~ **-of-line goods** *n pl* S&M fin de série *f*; ~ **of financial year** *n* ACC fin de l'exercice *f*; ~ **of message** *n* *(EOM)* COMP fin de message *f*; ~ **of month** *n* ACC fin de mois *f*; ~ **-of-month account** *n* BANK liquidation de fin de mois *f*; ~ **product** *n* GEN COMM produit final *m*; ~ **result** *n* GEN COMM résultat final *m*; ~ **-of-season sale** *n* GEN COMM, S&M solde de fin de saison *m*; ~ **of the tax year** *n* TAX fin de l'année d'imposition *f*; ~ **of the taxation year** *n* TAX fin de l'année d'imposition *f*; ~ **use goods** *n pl* IMP/EXP produits d'utilisation finale *m pl*; ~ **use trader** *n* IMP/EXP marchand de produits d'utilisation finale *m*; ~ **-user** *n* COMP utilisateur final *m*; ~ **-user certificate** *n* ECON certificat pour répondre à la demande de la clientèle; ~ **-user computing** *n* COMP informatique individuelle *f*; ♦ **at the ~ of the day** GEN COMM en fin de compte, en fin de journée; **come to an ~** GEN COMM *event* prendre fin, se conclure

end² **1.** *vt* GEN COMM conclure; **2.** *vi* GEN COMM finir

endanger *vt* GEN COMM mettre en danger

endangered: ~ **species** *n* ENVIR espèce en voie d'extinction *f*, espèce menacée *f*

endeavor *n* *AmE*, **endeavour** *n* *BrE* GEN COMM tentative *f*

endemic *adj* GEN COMM endémique

ending: ~ **balance** *n* ACC (ANT *opening balance*), BANK, FIN (ANT *opening balance*) solde de clôture *m*, solde à l'arrêté des comptes *m*; ~ **inventory** *n* ACC inventaire de clôture *m*

endless: ~ **sling** *n* TRANSP *cargo handling equipment* élingue sans fin en fils d'acier *f*

endogenizing: ~ **the exogenous** *phr* ECON *econometrics* endogénisation des variables exogènes *f*

endogenous: ~ **variable** *n* ECON *econometrics* variable endogène *f*

endorse *vt* BANK, GEN COMM *warrant* endosser; ~ **back** BANK contre-passer

endorsee *n* ACC cessionnaire *mf*, BANK cessionnaire *mf*, endossataire *mf*

endorsement *n* BANK endos *m*, endossement *m*, S&M *of product* approbation *f*, sanction *f*; ~ **stamp** BANK timbre d'endos *m*

endorser *n* BANK endosseur *m*

endorsor *n* BANK endosseur *m*

endowment *n* LAW dotation *f*; ~ **assurance** INS assurance mixte *f*, assurance à capital différé *f*; ~ **insurance** INS assurance à capital différé *f*;

~ **policy** BANK, INS *mortgages* assurance à capital différé *f*

ENEA *abbr* *(European Nuclear Energy Authority)* GEN COMM ENEA *(Autorité européenne de l'énergie nucléaire)*

energy:¹ ~ **-efficient** *adj* ENVIR *machine* d'un bon rendement énergétique

energy² *n* ENVIR, IND énergie *f*; ~ **conservation** *n* ENVIR économie de l'énergie *f*; ~ **crisis** *n* ECON, IND crise de l'énergie *f*, crise énergétique *f*; ~ **efficiency** *n* ENVIR rendement économique *m*; ~ **management** *n* MGMNT gestion du travail *f*; ~ **mutual fund** *n* ENVIR fonds commun de l'énergie *m*; ~ **policy** *n* GEN COMM, POL politique de l'énergie *f*, politique énergétique *f*; ~ **recovery** *n* ENVIR *recycling* récupération de l'énergie *f*; ~ **reserves** *n pl* ENVIR, IND réserves énergétiques *f pl*; ~ **resource** *n* ENVIR, IND ressource énergétique *f*; ~ **source** *n* GEN COMM source de l'énergie *f*; ~ **supply** *n* GEN COMM alimentation en énergie *f*, alimentation énergétique *f*; ~ **system** *n* GEN COMM système énergétique *m*; ~ **technology** *n* ENVIR, IND technologie énergétique *f*

ENF *abbr* *(enforcement)* LAW exécution *f*, mise en application *f*, mise en vigueur *f*

enforce *vt* GEN COMM *one's rights* faire valoir, LAW appliquer, faire exécuter, mettre en application, mettre en vigueur

enforceable *adj* (ANT *unenforceable*) LAW applicable, exécutoire

enforced *adj* GEN COMM obligatoire

enforcement *n* *(ENF)* LAW exécution *f*, mise en application *f*, mise en vigueur *f*; ~ **action** TAX mesure d'exécution *f*; ~ **order** GEN COMM mise en demeure *f*; ~ **procedure** GEN COMM procédure coercitive *f*

enfranchise *vt* GEN COMM, POL accorder le droit de vote

ENG *abbr* *(engine)* IND, TRANSP moteur *m*

engage *vt* HRM *staff* engager

engaged¹ *adj* COMMS *BrE* *(cf busy AmE)* *telephone*, GEN COMM occupé; ♦ **be ~ in** MGMNT *activity* s'occuper de; **be ~ in doing** GEN COMM être occupé à faire

engaged:² ~ **tone** *n* *BrE* *(cf busy signal AmE)* COMMS *telephone* signal d'occupation *m*, tonalité d'occupation *f*

engagement *n* GEN COMM engagement *m*, rendez-vous *m*; ♦ **without ~** GEN COMM sans garantie

Engel: ~ **coefficient** *n* ECON coefficient d'Engel *m*; ~**'s Law** *n* ECON loi d'Engel *f*

engine *n* *(ENG)* IND, TRANSP moteur *m*; ~ **builder** IND *marine* constructeur de machines *m*, serrurier-mécanicien *m*; ~ **casing** TRANSP *shipping* encaissement des machines *m*; ~ **designer** HRM *ships machinery* concepteur de moteurs *m*; ~ **of growth** ECON moteur de croissance *m*; ~ **room** *(ER)* TRANSP *shipping* chambre des machines *f*, compartiment moteur *m*; ~ **-room boy** HRM *ship* machiniste *m*; ~ **transplant** *jarg* TRANSP échange moteur *m*

engineer *n* GEN COMM, HRM, IND ingénieur *m*

engineering *n* IND technique *f*; ~ **consultant** *n* GEN COMM, IND ingénieur-conseil *m*; ~ **department** *n* GEN COMM département d'ingénierie *m*; ~ **and design department** *n* GEN COMM bureau d'étude *m*, service technique *m*; ~ **firm** *n* GEN COMM bureau d'étude *m*; ~ **insurance** *n pl* INS assurance des ingénieurs *f*, branche technique d'assurance *f*; ~ **manager** *n* HRM directeur technique *m*; ~ **process** *n* GEN COMM procédé de fabrication *m*; ~ **works** *n pl* GEN COMM usine de construction mécanique *f*

England *pr n* GEN COMM Angleterre *f*

English[1] *adj* GEN COMM anglais

English[2] *n* GEN COMM *language* anglais *m*; ~ **as a Foreign Language** *n* (*EFL*) WEL anglais comme langue étrangère *m*; ~ **Estates** *n* PROP l'Immobilier Anglais; ~ **Heritage** *n* ENVIR organisme partiellement autonome chargé du maintien des monuments historiques; ~ **Inshore Traffic Zone** *n* (*EITZ*) TRANSP zone de navigation côtière de l'Angleterre *f*; ~ **-speaking world** *n* GEN COMM monde anglophone *m*; **the** ~ *n pl* GEN COMM les Anglais *m pl*; ~ **Tourist Board** *n* (*ETB*) LEIS office de tourisme d'Angleterre

Englishman *n* GEN COMM *person* Anglais *m*

Englishwoman *n* GEN COMM *person* Anglaise *f*

engraved: ~ **form** *n* BANK formule gravée *f*

enhance *vt* ECON *purchasing power* rehausser

enhanced[1] *adj* COMP *quality, features* amélioré, enrichi, perfectionné

enhanced:[2] ~ **graphics adaptor** *n* (*EGA*) COMP adaptateur graphique couleur *m* (*AGA*); ~ **graphics array** *n* (*EGA*) COMP adaptateur graphique couleur *m* (*AGA*)

enhancement *n* COMP *computer system* amélioration *f*, perfectionnement *m*

enjoin *vt* MGMNT imposer

enjoy *vt* GEN COMM *benefits, reputation* jouir de

enlarged: ~ **copy** *n* GEN COMM agrandissement *m*, cliché agrandi *m*; ~ **edition** *n* GEN COMM édition augmentée *f*

enlargement *n* GEN COMM agrandissement *m*

enquiries: **make** ~ *phr* GEN COMM demander des renseignements, faire une enquête *loc f*, formuler une demande de renseignements

enquiry: ~ **desk** *n* GEN COMM bureau d'information *m*, bureau de renseignements *m*; ~ **form** *n* GEN COMM formulaire de demande de renseignements *m*; ~ **office** *n* ADMIN bureau de renseignements *m*; ~ **program** *n* COMP programme d'interrogation *m*

enriched: ~ **program** *n* AmE, ~ **programme** *n* BrE GEN COMM programme élargi *m*; ~ **tax expenditure** *n* TAX dépense fiscale accrue *f*

enrichment *n* GEN COMM *of job* enrichissement *m*

enrollment *n* AmE, **enrolment** *n* BrE GEN COMM *art* engagement *m*, *number* immatriculation *f*

enter:[1] ~ **key** *n* (SYN *return key*) COMP *keyboard* touche Entrée *f*, touche Retour *f*

enter[2] *vt* COMP *data* entrer, introduire, saisir; ◆ ~ **an appeal** LAW faire appel; ~ **goods for warehousing** GEN COMM déclarer des marchandises pour l'entreposage; ~ **information onto a register** GEN COMM inscrire des informations dans un registre; ~ **into an agreement** GEN COMM passer un accord; ~ **into a contract with** GEN COMM passer un contrat avec; ~ **into force** LAW entrer en vigueur; ~ **an item in the ledger** GEN COMM passer une écriture dans le grand livre; ~ **the labor market** *AmE*, ~ **the labour market** *BrE* GEN COMM arriver sur le marché du travail; ~ **the market** ECON arriver sur le marché; ~ **a plea** LAW faire valoir une exception; ~ **recession** ECON entrer en récession; ~ **a writ** LAW signifier une assignation

entered:[1] ~ **in** *adj* IMP/EXP déclaré entré

entered:[2] ~ **ship** *n* INS *marine* déclaration d'entrée ou de sortie faite *f*

enterprise *n* ECON, GEN COMM entreprise *f*, entreprise commerciale *f*, MGMNT entreprise *f*; ~ **allowance** *UK* FIN aide à la création d'entreprise *f*; ~ **union** HRM syndicat d'entreprise *m*; ~ **zone** (*EZ*) ECON, HRM, IND, PROP parc d'affaires *m*, zone d'activité économique *f*, zone d'aménagement concerté *f* (*ZAC*), zone d'entreprise *f*

Enterprise: ~ **Investment Scheme** *n* *UK* ECON projet du gouvernement britannique, pour encourager l'investissement dans les PME, par l'octroi d'incitations fiscales., plan d'expansion économique *m*

enterpriser *n* ECON entrepreneur *m*

enterprising *adj* GEN COMM entreprenant

entertain *vt* GEN COMM *client* amuser, divertir, recevoir

entertainment *n* GEN COMM divertissement *m*; ~ **allowance** GEN COMM frais de représentation *m pl*; ~ **complex** LEIS complexe de loisirs *m*; ~ **expense** TAX frais de représentation *m pl*

entirety *n* GEN COMM totalité *f*; ◆ **in its** ~ GEN COMM dans sa totalité

entitle *vt* GEN COMM autoriser; ◆ ~ **sb to do** GEN COMM autoriser qn à faire

entitled *adj* GEN COMM autorisé; ◆ ~ **to adjudicate** LAW compétent à juger, habilité à juger

entitlement *n* LAW droit *m*

entity *n* LAW entité *f*; ~ **convention** ACC inventaire de clôture *m*

entrance *n* GEN COMM, TRANSP *to building, premises* entrée *f*; ~ **card** GEN COMM carte d'entrée *f*; ~ **examination** GEN COMM examen d'entrée *m*; ~ **fee** GEN COMM droit d'inscription *m*; ~ **ticket** GEN COMM billet d'entrée *m*; ~ **visa** ADMIN visa d'entrée *m*

entrepreneur *n* ECON, GEN COMM entrepreneur *m*

entrepreneurial[1] *adj* ECON, GEN COMM entrepreneurial

entrepreneurial:[2] **~ risk** *n* GEN COMM risque lié aux initiatives économiques *m*; **~ spirit** *n* GEN COMM, MGMNT esprit d'entreprise *m*

entrepreneurship *n* GEN COMM, MGMNT esprit d'entreprise *m*

entrust: ~ sb with sth *phr* GEN COMM confier qch à qn

entry *n* ACC écriture *f*, ADMIN *in register, diary, log* entrée *f*, FIN écriture *f*, IMP/EXP déclaration douanière *f*, STOCK *into market* entrée *f*; **~ acceptance data** COMP données d'acceptation de saisie *f pl*; **~ barrier** *(ANT exit barrier)* ECON, IMP/EXP barrière d'entrée *f*; **~ into force** LAW entrée en vigueur *f*; **~ -level job** HRM emploi de départ *m*; **~ permit** ADMIN visa d'entrée *m*, GEN COMM autorisation d'accès *f*; **~ price** *(ANT exit price)* STOCK *futures* cours de la transaction *m*; **~ processing unit** *(EPU)* IMP/EXP unité de traitement des déclarations *f*; **~ stamp** IMP/EXP *on arrival in new country* tampon d'entrée *m*; **~ visa** ADMIN visa d'entrée *m*; ◆ **~ inwards** IMP/EXP déclaration d'entrée en douane *f*; **make an ~ against sb** ACC débiter le compte de qn; **~ outwards** IMP/EXP déclaration de sortie de douane *f*

enumerate *vt* GEN COMM énumérer

enumeration *n* GEN COMM énumération *f*

envelope *n* ADMIN *stationery*, COMMS, HRM enveloppe *f*; **~ curve** *n* ECON courbe d'enveloppe *f*; **~ level** *n* GEN COMM niveau de l'enveloppe *m*; **~ procedures and rules** *n pl* GEN COMM méthodes et règles relatives aux enveloppes *f pl*

Envireg *n* ENVIR Envireg *m*

environment *n* COMP, ENVIR environnement *m*; **~ policy** ENVIR, POL politique de l'environnement *f*; **~ scan** ENVIR balayage de l'environnement *m*

Environment: ~ and Consumer Protection Service *n (ECPS)* ENVIR *EU* Service de protection du consommateur et de l'environnement *m*

environmental[1] *adj* ENVIR lié à l'environnement

environmental:[2] **~ action program** *n AmE*, **~ action programme** *n BrE* ECON programme d'action environnemental *m*; **~ analysis** *n* MGMNT analyse de l'environnement *f*; **~ compatibility** *n* ENVIR compatibilité avec l'environnement *f*; **~ conditions** *n pl* ENVIR conditions ambiantes *f pl*; **~ control** *n* ENVIR contrôle de l'environnement *m*, protection de l'environnement *f*; **~ damage** *n* GEN COMM atteinte à l'environnement *f*, détérioration de l'environnement *f*; **~ determinism** *n* ENVIR déterminisme du milieu *m*; **~ development** *n* ENVIR, GEN COMM développement écologique *m*; **~ forecasting** *n* ENVIR prévisions sur l'environnement *f pl*; **~ goods** *n pl* ENVIR biens d'environnement *m pl*; **~ hygiene** *n* ENVIR hygiène de l'environnement *f*; **~ impact** *n* ENVIR impact environnemental *m*, impact sur l'environnement *m*; **~ impact assessment** *n* ENVIR évaluation de l'impact sur l'environnement *f*; **~ impact statement** *n* ENVIR, LAW compte-rendu de l'impact environnemental *m*; **~ issue** *n*

ENVIR, POL problème écologique *m*, question écologique *f*; **~ law** *n* ENVIR, LAW droit de l'environnement *m*; **~ lobby** *n* ENVIR, POL groupe de pression écologique *m*; **~ lobby group** *n* ENVIR, POL groupe de pression écologique *m*; **~ planning** *n* ENVIR aménagement de l'environnement *m*; **~ policy** *n* ENVIR, POL politique de l'environnement *f*, politique environnementale *f*; **~ pressure group** *n* ENVIR, POL groupe de pression écologique *m*; **~ problem** *n* ENVIR, POL problème écologique *m*; **~ protection** *n* ENVIR protection de l'environnement *f*; **~ protection agency** *n (EPA)* ENVIR agence pour la protection de l'environnement *f*; **~ quality standards** *n pl* ENVIR normes de qualité de l'environnement *f pl*; **~ question** *n* ENVIR, POL question écologique *f*; **~ scanner** *n* ENVIR analyste de l'environnement *m*, spécialiste de l'environnement *m*; **~ scanning** *n* ENVIR repérage de l'environnement *m*; **~ standard** *n* ENVIR norme environnementale *f*, norme écologique *f*; **~ tax** *n* ENVIR *pollution* redevance au profit de l'environnement *f*

Environmental: ~ Health Officer *n UK* ENVIR, HRM responsable de l'hygiène du milieu *m*, responsable de la salubrité de l'environnement *m*; **~ Management System** *n* ENVIR Système de management environnemental *m*; **~ Protection Act 1990** *n UK* ENVIR loi britannique de 1990 sur la protection de l'environnement

environmentalism *n* ENVIR environnementalisme *m*, écologisme *m*

environmentalist *n* ENVIR écolo *mf (infrml)*, écologiste *mf*

environmentally:[1] **~ -aware** *adj* ENVIR respectueux de l'environnement; **~ -benign** *adj* ENVIR qui ne porte pas atteinte à l'environnement *loc f*; **~ -friendly** *adj* ENVIR *goods* respectueux de l'environnement, écophile

environmentally:[2] **~ -friendly product** *n* ENVIR produit vert *m*, produit écologique *m*; **~ -sensitive zone** *n* ENVIR zone écologiquement fragile *f*

Environmentally: ~ -Sensitive Area *n UK* ENVIR zone écologiquement fragile *f*

envisage *vt* GEN COMM envisager, prévoir

envision *vt* GEN COMM envisager

EO *abbr (executive officer)* HRM, MGMNT cadre sup *m (infrml)*, cadre supérieur *m*

EOC *abbr UK (Equal Opportunities Commission)* HRM commission pour l'égalité des chances pour l'emploi

EOE *abbr (European Options Exchange)* STOCK Bourse d'options européenne *f*

EOF *abbr (end of file)* COMP fin de fichier *f*

eohp *abbr (except otherwise herein provided)* GEN COMM sauf dispositions contraires du présent

EOM *abbr (end of message)* COMP fin de message *f*

EOP *abbr UK (Equal Opportunity Policy)* HRM politique de l'égalité de traitement *f*

EOQ *abbr (economic order quantity)* ECON, IND,

MATH, MGMNT quantité optimale de commande *f*, quantité optimale de réapprovisionnement *f*, quantité économique de réapprovisionnement *f*, quantité économique à commander *f*

EOQC *abbr (European Organization for Quality Control)* ADMIN Organisation européenne pour le contrôle de qualité *f*

EOTC *abbr (European Organization for Testing and Certification)* GEN COMM Organisme européen de contrôle et certification *m*

EP *abbr* ECON *(European Parliament)* Parlement européen *m*, IMP/EXP *(export promotion)* promotion des exportations *f*

EPA *abbr* ENVIR *(environmental protection agency)* agence pour la protection de l'environnement *f*, HRM *(Economic Planning Agency)* ≈ Agence de planification économique *f*, HRM *UK (Employment Protection Act)* loi sur la protection de l'emploi *f*, IND *(European Productivity Agency)* Agence européenne de productivité *f*, LAW *UK (Employment Protection Act)* loi sur la protection de l'emploi *f*

EPCA *abbr UK (Employment Protection Consolidation Act)* HRM loi sur la protection du travail

EPF *abbr (established programmes financing, established programs financing)* FIN financement des programmes établis *m*, financement institués de programmes *m*

ephemeralization *n jarg* ECON éphéméralisation *f* *(jarg)*

EPO *abbr (European Patent Organization)* LAW Organisation européenne de brevets *f*

EPOS *abbr (electronic point of sale)* GEN COMM point de vente électronique *m*

EPROM *abbr (electronically programmable read only memory)* COMP *programming language* EPROM *(mémoire morte programmable électroniquement)*

EPS *abbr (earnings per share)* ACC, FIN, STOCK BPA *(bénéfices par action)*

EPT *abbr (electronic payment terminal)* FIN TPE *(terminal de paiement électronique)*

EPU *abbr* ECON *(economic planning unit)* bureau de planification économique *m*, GEN COMM *(European Payments Union)* UEP *(Union européenne des paiements)*, IMP/EXP *(entry processing unit)* unité de traitement des déclarations *f*

EqPA *abbr UK (Equal Pay Act)* HRM, LAW loi sur l'égalité des salaires *f*

equal[1] *adj* MATH égal; ◆ **all else being ~** GEN COMM toutes choses étant égales par ailleurs; **all things being ~** GEN COMM toutes choses égales, toutes choses étant égales, toutes choses étant égales par ailleurs; **in ~ proportions** GEN COMM à parts égales; **on ~ terms** GEN COMM à armes égales; **~ and opposite** GEN COMM égaux et opposés

equal:[2] **~ employment opportunity** *n* HRM égalité des chances face à l'emploi *f*; **~ footing** *n* GEN COMM égalité *f*; **~ opportunities employer** *n* HRM

employeur respectant l'égalité des chance *m*; **~ opportunity** *n* HRM égalité des chances *f*; **~ pay** *n* HRM égalité des salaires *f*, égalité salariale *f*; **~ product curve** *n* ECON courbe isoquante *f*; **~ value** *n* STOCK *currency futures prices* valeur égale *f*; **~ voting rights** *n pl* GEN COMM, LAW, MGMNT *of partners* égalité des droits de vote *f*

equal[3] *vt* MATH égaler

Equal: **~ Credit Opportunity Act** *n US* LAW *antidiscrimination* loi protégeant contre toute forme de discrimination dans l'octroi de crédit; **~ Employment Opportunity Commission** *n US (EEOC)* HRM commission pour l'égalité des chances pour l'emploi; **~ Opportunities Commission** *n* HRM *UK (EOC)* commission pour l'égalité des chances pour l'emploi; **~ Opportunity Policy** *n UK (EOP)* HRM politique de l'égalité des chances *f*; **~ Pay Act** *n UK (EqPA)* HRM, LAW *1963* loi sur l'égalité des salaires *f*; **~ Pay Directive** *n* HRM *1975, issued by European Commission* Directive d'égalité des salaires *f*; **~ Protection of the Laws** *n US* LAW, POL *constitution* principe de l'égalité devant la loi *m*; **~ Value Amendment** *n UK* HRM *1983* égalité salariale entre hommes et femmes *f*

equality *n* HRM égalité *f*; **~ standard** POL standard d'égalité *m*

equalization *n* TAX péréquation *f*, péréquation fiscale *f*; **~ fund** INS fonds de compensation *m*, fonds de régularisation *m*; **~ payment** TAX paiement de péréquation *m*; **~ of revenue and expenditure** FIN équilibre des recettes et des dépenses *m*; **~ of taxes** TAX péréquation des impôts *f*

equalize *vt* GEN COMM égaliser

equation *n* GEN COMM, MATH équation *f*

Equatorial:[1] **~ Guinean** *adj* GEN COMM guinéen équatorial

Equatorial:[2] **~ Guinean** *n* GEN COMM *person* Guinéen équatorial *m*

Equatorial:[3] **~ Guinea** *pr n* GEN COMM Guinée équatoriale *f*

equilibrium *n* ECON équilibre *m*; **~ basis** STOCK *currency futures* base d'équilibre *f*; **~ GNP** ECON PIB d'équilibre *m*; **~ price** ECON prix d'équilibre *m*; **~ quantity** ECON quantité d'équilibre *f*; **~ wage rate** ECON taux de salaire d'équilibre *m*

equipment *n* COMP, GEN COMM, IND matériel *m*, équipement *m*; **~ dealers insurance** *n* INS assurance de revendeurs de matériel *f*; **~ failure** *n* GEN COMM panne d'appareil *f*, panne de machine *f*; **~ goods** *n pl* ECON biens d'équipement *m pl*; **~ handover agreement** *n* IND Accord sur la passation des équipements *m*; **~ leasing** *n* ECON location de matériel *m*, IND crédit-bail immobilier *m*, PROP crédit-bail de biens d'équipement *m*; **~ trust bond** *n* FIN titres garantis par le nantissement du matériel *m pl*; **~ trust certificate** *n* TRANSP certificat d'authenticité de l'équipement *m*

equitable[1] *adj* GEN COMM *fair* équitable, LAW juste, équitable

equitable:[2] **~ distribution** *n* GEN COMM distribution équitable *f*, répartition équitable *f*

equity *n* ACC *stockholders' equity (US), share capital and reserves (UK)* capitaux propres *m pl*, fonds propres *m pl*, BANK valeur de réalisation nette *f*, valeur de réalisation réelle *f*, valeur nette *f*, valeur nette réelle *f*, FIN fonds propres *m pl*, équité *f*, LAW, PROP équité *f*, STOCK actif net *m*, actions *f pl*; **~ accounting** *n* ACC comptabilisation des participations à la méthode de la mise en équivalence *f*; **~ base** *n* ACC base de participation *f*; **~ capital** *n* ACC, ECON capital actions *m*, FIN capital actions *m*, financement sur fonds propres *m*, STOCK avoir des propriétaires *m*, capital actions *m*, capitaux propres *m pl*, fonds propres *m pl*; **~ capital base** *n* ACC capitaux propres *m pl*; **~ dilution** *n* STOCK dilution de l'avoir des actionnaires *f*; **~ financing** *n* FIN financement sur fonds propres *m*; **~ funds** *n pl* ACC capitaux propres *m pl*, fonds propres *m pl*; **~ holder** *n* STOCK détenteur d'actions *m*, porteur d'actions *m*; **~ holdings** *n pl* STOCK avoirs en actions *m pl*, portefeuille d'actions *m*; **~ investment** *n* GEN COMM investissement en actions *m*, placement en actions *m*, STOCK titre de participation *m*; **~ investment fund** *n* STOCK fonds d'investissement en actions *m*; **~ investor** *n* STOCK investisseur en actions *m*; **~ issue** *n* STOCK émission de capital *f*; **~ joint venture** *n* GEN COMM coentreprise avec création de société commune *f*, joint-venture avec création de société commune *m*; **~ kicker** *n* STOCK obligation convertible en action *f*; **~ -linked mortgage** *n* FIN hypothèque investie en actions *f*, prêt hypothécaire investi en actions *m*; **~ -linked policy** *n* STOCK police d'assurance-vie indexée sur le cours des valeurs boursières *f*; **~ market** *n* FIN, STOCK marché des actions *m*, marché financier *m*; **~ method** *n* ACC méthode de la mise en équivalence *f*; **~ method of accounting** *n* ACC méthode de la comptabilisation de la mise en équivalence *f*; **~ option** *n* STOCK option sur action *f*, option sur valeurs mobilières *f*; **~ ownership** *n* STOCK participation *f*; **~ -related bonds** *n pl* STOCK obligations assimilables à des actions *f pl*; **~ -related futures** *n pl* FIN, STOCK contrats à terme sur actions *m pl*; **~ savings account** *n* STOCK compte d'épargne en actions *m*, CEA; **~ security** *n* STOCK titre de participation *m*; **~ share** *n* STOCK action de participation *f*, action à revenu variable *f*; **~ trading** *n* STOCK négociation d'actions *f*, opération sur actions *f*; **~ turnover** *n* STOCK ratio entre le chiffre d'affaires et la masse des actions ordinaires; **~ value** *n* BANK valeur de réalisation nette *f*, valeur de réalisation réelle *f*, valeur nette *f*, valeur nette réelle *f*; **~ warrant** *n* STOCK bon de souscription d'actions *m*; ♦ **have an ~ interest** STOCK avoir de l'intérêt sur des actions, avoir une participation en actions; **take**

an ~ stake in STOCK prendre une participation en actions dans

equivalence *n* GEN COMM, IMP/EXP équivalence *f*

equivalent *n* GEN COMM équivalent

ER *abbr (engine room)* TRANSP *shipping* chambre des machines *f*, compartiment moteur *m*

ERA *abbr (exchange rate agreement)* ECON, FIN accord sur les taux de change *m*

eradicate *vt* ADMIN mettre fin à, GEN COMM supprimer

erase *vt* COMP effacer

erasion *n* COMP effacement *m*

ERC *abbr (European Registry of Commerce)* GEN COMM Registre du commerce européen *m*

ERDF *abbr (European Regional Development Fund)* ECON FEDER *(Fonds européen de développement régional)*

erect *vt* GEN COMM *customs barriers* dresser, ériger

erection: ~ insurance *n* INS assurance montage *f*

ergonomic *adj* ADMIN, COMP, GEN COMM, HRM ergonomique

ergonomically:[1] **~ -designed** *adj* COMP *work station* de conception ergonomique *loc f*

ergonomically[2] *adv* COMP du point de vue ergonomique *loc m*

ergonomics *n pl* ADMIN *office*, COMP, GEN COMM, HRM ergonomie *f*

ergonomist *n* GEN COMM, HRM ergonome *m*

ergophobia *n* GEN COMM, HRM ergophobie *f*, hantise du travail *f*

ERISA *abbr* US *(Employment Retirement Income Security Act)* STOCK loi de garantie des revenus des travailleurs retraités

ERM *abbr (exchange rate mechanism)* ECON *EU* MTC *(mécanisme de taux de change)*

erode *vt* GEN COMM *business confidence* dégrader, miner, *power* ronger

erosion *n* ECON, ENVIR *of land*, STOCK *of an option's premium or the time value of an option* érosion *f*

err *vi* GEN COMM *in judgment* se tromper

errand *n* GEN COMM commission *f*, course *f*

erratic *adj* GEN COMM irrégulier

erratum *n* [pl -ta] GEN COMM *catalogue of errors* erratum *m*

erroneous *adj* GEN COMM erroné

error:[1] **~ -free** *adj* COMP exempt d'erreur

error[2] *n* COMP erreur *f*, GEN COMM erreur *f*, faute *f*, LAW, MATH *statistics* erreur *f*; **~ control** COMP traitement des erreurs *m*; **~ of law** LAW erreur de droit *f*; **~ message** COMP message d'erreur *m*; **~ rate** COMP taux d'erreurs *m*; **~ recovery** COMP reprise sur erreur *f*; **~ report** COMP rapport d'erreurs *m*; ♦ **make an ~** GEN COMM faire une erreur

errors: ~ and omissions *n pl* ECON erreurs et omissions *f pl*; **~ and omissions clause** *n* INS clause d'erreurs et d'omissions *f*, clause de la responsabilité civile professionnelle *f*; ♦ ~ **and omissions excepted** *(E&OE)* GEN COMM sauf erreur ou omission *(SEO)*

ersatz *n* GEN COMM succédané *m*

ES *abbr (expert system)* COMP, GEN COMM SE *(système expert)*

ESA *abbr (European Space Agency)* GEN COMM ASE *(Agence spatiale européenne)*

Esc *abbr (escape key, escape)* COMP *keyboard* Esc *(touche Esc)*

ESC *abbr* ECON *(Economic and Social Committee)* Comité économique et social *m*, GEN COMM *(escudo)* ESC *(escudo)*

escalate 1. *vt* GEN COMM faire monter **2.** *vi* GEN COMM *prices* monter en flèche

escalation: ~ **clause** *n* INS clause contre l'augmentation de prix *f*, clause de surenchère *f*

escalator *n* GEN COMM escalier roulant *m*; ~ **clause** HRM clause de sauvegarde *f*

escape *n* *(Esc)* COMP *keyboard* touche Esc *f* *(Esc)*; ~ **character** COMP caractère Esc *m*, caractère d'échappement *m*; ~ **clause** LAW clause de sauvegarde *f*, clause dérogatoire *f*; ~ **key** *(Esc)* COMP *keyboard* touche d'échappement *f*; ~ **sequence** COMP séquence Esc *f*, séquence d'échappement *f*

escheat *n* LAW, PROP déshérence *f*

escort *vt* GEN COMM *visitor* accompagner, escorter

escrow *n* FIN blocage de titres *m*, mise en main tierce *f*; ~ **account** BANK compte de mise en main tierce *m*; ~ **agent** FIN tiers responsable de titres bloqués *m*; ~ **agreement** LAW contrat de dépôt *m*; ~ **clause** TRANSP *shipping* clause de séquestre *f*; ♦ **in** ~ GEN COMM en dépôt fiduciaire

escudo *n* *(ESC)* GEN COMM escudo *m* *(ESC)*

ESD *abbr (echo-sounding device)* TRANSP *shipping* sondeur U.S. *m* *(sondeur par ultrasons)*

ESF *abbr (European Social Fund)* ECON, POL FSE *(Fonds social européen)*

ESOP *abbr (employee share ownership plan BrE, employee stock ownership plan AmE)* STOCK plan d'investissement du personnel *m*

esp. *abbr (especially)* GEN COMM spécialement, surtout

especially *adv (esp.)* GEN COMM spécialement, surtout

espionage *n* GEN COMM espionnage *m*

esprit: ~ **de corps** *n* GEN COMM esprit de corps *m*

ESRO *abbr (European Space Research Organization)* GEN COMM Organisme de recherche spatiale européenne *m*

essential: ~ **feature** *n* PATENTS caractéristique essentielle *f*; ~ **foodstuffs** *n pl* GEN COMM denrées de première nécessité *f pl*; ~ **industry** *n* ECON, IND industrie capitale *f*

essentials: **the** ~ *n pl* GEN COMM l'essentiel *m*

est. *abbr (established)* GEN COMM fondé, établi

EST *abbr US (Eastern Standard Time)* GEN COMM heure de l'Est *f*

establish *vt* GEN COMM former, *company* fonder, établir, *fact, date* établir; ♦ ~ **a direct link with** COMMS établir une liaison directe avec; ~ **quotas for** ECON, GEN COMM, IMP/EXP contingenter

established[1] *adj (est.)* GEN COMM fondé, établi

established:[2] ~ **programs financing** *n* AmE see *established programmes financing BrE*; ~ **programmes financing** *n* BrE *(EPF)* FIN financement des programmes établis *m*, financement instituée de programmes *m*

establishment *n* GEN COMM fondation *f*, établissement *m*, HRM établissement *m*, STOCK maison *f*; ~ **-level bargaining** UK HRM négociation au niveau de l'établissement *f*, négociation par établissement *f*; **the** ~ GEN COMM le groupe dirigeant *m*

Establishment: **the** ~ *n* UK POL la classe dirigeante *f*

estate *n* TAX succession *f*; ~ **agency** *n* BrE *(cf real estate agency AmE)* PROP agence immobilière *f*; ~ **agent** *n* BrE *(cf realtor AmE)* PROP *person* agent immobilier *m*, marchand de biens *m*, marchand de fonds *m*; ~ **agents** *n pl* BrE *(cf real estate agents AmE)* PROP *shop* cabinet d'immobilier *m*; ~ **of bankrupt** *n* TAX actif du failli *m*; ~ **distribution** *n* PROP répartition immobilière *f*; ~ **duty** *n* TAX droit sur la valeur globale de la succession *m*; ~ **economy** *n* ECON économie caractérisée par de grands domaines agricoles sous domination étrangère; ~ **executor** *n* LAW exécuteur *m*, exécuteur testamentaire *m*; ~ **freezing** *n* Can TAX gel successoral *m*; ~ **in abeyance** *n* GEN COMM succession vacante *f*; ~ **in reversion** *n* LAW, PROP biens grevés d'une reversion *m pl*; ~ **in severalty** *n* PROP propriété individuelle *f*; ~ **income** *n* FIN, PROP, TAX revenu d'une succession *m*, revenu immobilier *m*; ~ **manager** *n* FIN, LAW administrateur de biens *m*, régisseur *m*; ~ **planning** *n* FIN, LAW, PROP *wills* organisation réglementaire relative à une succession *f*, réglementation relative au lotissement des propriétés foncières *f*; ~ **revenue** *n* FIN, LAW revenu foncier *m*, revenu provenant d'investissements immobiliers *m*, revenu provenant du patrimoine *m*, PROP revenu foncier *m*; ~ **tax** *n* US TAX droits de succession *m pl*

estimate[1] *n* FIN, MATH, S&M *statistics* estimation *f*, TAX montant estimatif *m*; ♦ **at the highest** ~ *(ANT at the lowest estimate)* GEN COMM selon l'estimation la plus élevée; **at the lowest** ~ *(ANT at the highest estimate)* GEN COMM selon l'estimation la plus basse

estimate[2] *vt* FIN estimer, GEN COMM estimer, évaluer

estimated: ~ **amount** *n* TAX montant estimatif *m*; ~ **arrival time** *n* *(EAT)* LEIS, TRANSP date probable d'arrivée *f*, heure d'arrivée prévue *f*; ~ **charges** *n pl* ACC charges prévues *f pl*; ~ **cost** *n* ACC coût estimé *m*; ~ **costs** *n* ACC charges prévues *f pl*; ~ **deductions** *n pl* TAX déductions estimatives *f pl*; ~ **financial report** *n* FIN document financier prévisionnel *m*; **~ lapse** *n* ACC péremption prévue *f*; **~ realizable value** *n* ACC, BANK, ECON, FIN valeur réalisable estimative *f*; **~ revenue** *n* ACC revenu estimé *m*; **~ time of arrival** *n* *(ETA)* TRANSP date probable d'arrivée *f*, heure d'arrivée prévue *f*; **~ time of departure** *n* *(ETD)* GEN COMM, TRANSP heure de départ prévue *f*; **~ time of sailing** *n* *(ETS)* GEN COMM, TRANSP heure de départ prévue *f*; **~ trading account** *n* FIN compte prévisionnel d'exploitation *m*; **~ value** *n* INS valeur estimative *f*, valeur estimée *f*

estimates: ~ of expenditure *n pl* FIN Budget des dépenses *m*

estimating: ~ systems costs *n pl* ACC, FIN évaluation des coûts de systèmes *f*

estimation: ~ sampling *n* MATH *statistics* échantillon d'estimation *m*; ◆ **in my ~** GEN COMM à mon avis

estimator *n* S&M responsable de l'évaluation du prix de revient *m*

Estonia *pr n* GEN COMM Estonie *f*

Estonian[1] *adj* GEN COMM estonien

Estonian[2] *n* GEN COMM *language* estonien *m*, *person* Estonien *m*

estoppel *n* LAW interdiction faite aux parties de revenir sur une déclaration

estovers *n* LAW, PROP droit d'affouage *m*

estranged: ~ spouse *n* LAW épouse séparée *f*, époux séparé *m*

estuarial: ~ service *n* TRANSP *shipping* service portuaire fluvial *m*

estuary *n* TRANSP *shipping* estuaire *m*

ET *abbr BrE (employment training)* HRM formation *f*, formation à l'emploi *f*

ETA *abbr (estimated time of arrival)* TRANSP date probable d'arrivée *f*, heure d'arrivée prévue *f*

et alii *phr* GEN COMM et autres

ETAS *abbr UK (Economic Trends Annual Survey)* ECON *econometrics* rapport annuel sur les tendances de l'économie

ETB *abbr (English Tourist Board)* LEIS office de tourisme d'Angleterre

ETC *abbr* GEN COMM *(European Trade Committee)* Commission européenne du commerce *f*, TRANSP *(explosion of total contents)* explosion du contenu total *f*

ETD *abbr (estimated time of departure)* GEN COMM, TRANSP heure de départ prévue *f*

ethical[1] *adj* MGMNT, WEL moral

ethical:[2] **~ investment** *n* ENVIR placement éthique *m*; **~ unit trust** *n* ECON SICAV éthique *f*

ethics *n pl* GEN COMM, MGMNT *business conduct* éthique *f*

Ethiopia *pr n* GEN COMM Éthiopie *f*

Ethiopian[1] *adj* GEN COMM éthiopien

Ethiopian[2] *n* GEN COMM *person* Éthiopien *m*

ethnic: ~ minority *n* POL, WEL minorité ethnique *f*; **~ monitoring** *n* HRM surveillance des origines du personnel *f*

etiquette *n* COMP, GEN COMM protocole *m*

et non *phr frml* GEN COMM et non

ETO *abbr (European Transport Organization)* TRANSP Organisation européenne de transport *f*

ETPO *abbr (European Trade Promotion Organization)* GEN COMM Organisme européen pour la promotion du commerce *m*

ETS *abbr (estimated time of sailing)* GEN COMM, TRANSP heure de départ prévue *f*

ETSI *abbr (European Telecommunications Standards Institute)* COMMS Association de normalisation des télécommunications *f*

ETU *abbr UK (Electrical Trades Union)* GEN COMM syndicat britannique d'électriciens

ETUC *abbr (European Trade Union Confederation)* HRM Confédération syndicale européenne *f*

et ux *phr frml* LAW *old legal documents* et épouse *loc f*

EU[1] *abbr (European Union)* ECON *from Nov 1st 1993,* POL UE *(Union européenne)*

EU:[2] **~ Directive** *n* LAW, POL directive de l'Union européenne *f*, directive européenne *f*; **~ transit form** *n* TRANSP formulaire de transit CEE *m*

EUA *abbr (European unit of account)* BANK, ECON, FIN UCE *(unité de compte européenne)*

Euler's: ~ Theorem *n* ECON *theory* théorème d'Euler *m*

Euro:[1] **~ Co-op** *abbr (European Community of Consumers' Co-operatives)* GEN COMM Communauté européenne des coopératives de consommateurs *f*; **~ MP** *abbr (European Member of Parliament)* POL député du Parlement Européen *m*, membre du Parlement Européen *m*

Euro-[2] *pref* GEN COMM euro-

Eurobanking *n* BANK opérations bancaires en eurodevises *f pl*

Eurobond *n* BANK euro-emprunt *m*, STOCK euro-obligation *f*; **~ issue** STOCK émission d'euro-obligations *f*; **~ market** ECON *international stock* marché des euro-obligations *m*

Euro-Canadian: ~ dollar issue *n* STOCK émission d'euro-obligations en dollars canadiens *f*

Eurocapital: ~ market issue *n* STOCK émission sur l'euromarché des capitaux *f*

Eurocard® *n* BANK Eurocard® *f*

eurocentric *adj* GEN COMM eurocentrique

Eurocheque *n* BANK, ECON eurochèque *m*

Eurocommercial: ~ paper *n* *(ECP)* FIN europapier commercial *m*, STOCK *money market* billet de trésorerie euro *m*, papier eurocommercial *m*

Eurocontrol *n* TRANSP eurocontrol *m*

Eurocurrency *n* BANK, ECON eurodevise *f*, euro-monnaie *f*; **~ market** STOCK marché des eurodevises *m*; **~ rate** ECON cours d'une eurodevise *m*

Eurodollar *n* *(ED)* ECON, FIN, STOCK eurodollar *m*; **~ bond** ECON, FIN, STOCK obligation en eurodollars *f*; **~ future** ECON, FIN, STOCK contrat à terme sur eurodollars *m*; **~ index** ECON, FIN, STOCK indice de l'eurodollar *m*; ~ **market** ECON, FIN, STOCK marché de l'eurodollar *m*; ~ **Rate** ECON, FIN, STOCK cours de l'eurodollar *m*; ~ **spread** STOCK *LIBOR futures contract* marge eurodollar *f*, écart LIBOR-eurodollar *m*; ~ **time deposit** ECON, FIN, STOCK dépôt à terme en eurodollars *m*; ~ **time deposit funds** ECON, FIN, STOCK fonds de dépôt en eurodollars *m pl*; ~ **time deposit futures** ECON, FIN, STOCK contrat à terme sur dépôt en eurodollars *m*; ~ **time deposit futures contract** ECON, FIN, STOCK contrat à terme sur dépôt en eurodollars *m*

Euro Fer *n* *(Association of European Steel Producers)* IND association des producteurs européens d'acier

Eurofranc *n* ECON eurofranc *m*

Euromarket *n* ECON euromarché *m*

Euromoney *n* BANK, ECON eurodevise *f*, euromonnaie *f*; ~ **deposit** ECON dépôt en euromonnaie *m*

Euronet *n* COMMS Euronet *m*

Europallet *n* GEN COMM europalette *f*

Europe *n* GEN COMM Europe *f*

European[1] *adj* GEN COMM européen

European:[2] ~ **affairs** *n pl* GEN COMM, POL affaires européennes *f pl*; ~ **Agricultural Fund** *n* *(UAF)* ECON, FIN, POL Fonds agricole européen *m*; ~ **Association of Advertising Agencies** *n* *(EAAA)* S&M Association européenne des agences de publicité *f*; ~ **Atomic Energy Community** *n* *(EAEC)* IND Communauté européenne de l'énergie atomique *f* *(CEEA)*; ~ **Bank for Reconstruction and Development** *n* *(EBRD)* BANK, ECON, POL Banque européenne pour la reconstruction et le développement *f* *(BERD)*; ~ **Broadcasting Union** *n* *(EBU)* COMMS, MEDIA Union européenne de radiodiffusion *f* *(UER)*; ~ **Central Bank** *n* *(ECB)* BANK, ECON Banque centrale européenne *f*; ~ **Coal and Steel Community** *n* *(ECSC)* ECON Communauté européenne du charbon et de l'acier *f* *(CECA)*; ~ **Commission** *n* ECON Commission européenne *f*; ~ **Committee for Standardization** *n* ECON Centre européen de normalisation *m*, CEN; ~ **Committee of Legal Co-operation** *n* LAW Comité européen de coopération juridique *m*; ~ **Community** *n* *(EC)* ECON Communauté européenne *f* *(CE)*; ~ **Community Budget** *n* ECON, FIN, POL Budget communautaire *m*; ~ **Community of Consumers' Co-operatives** *n* *(Euro Co-op)* GEN COMM Communauté européenne des coopératives de consommateurs *f*; ~ **Community Finance Ministers** *n pl (ECOFIN)* ECON, FIN, POL ministres des finances de la communauté européenne *m pl*; ~ **Convention on Human Rights** *n* WEL Convention européenne des droits de l'homme *f*; ~ **Cooperation Grouping** *n* *(ECG)* LAW, POL Groupement de coopération européen *m*; ~ **Cooperation in Science and Technology** *n* *(COST)* IND Coopération européenne en matière de science et de technologie *f*; ~ **Court** *n* LAW, POL Cour européenne *f*; ~ **Court of Justice** *n* LAW, POL

Cour de justice européenne *f*; ~ **Currency Unit** *n* *(ECU)* BANK, ECON, FIN unité monétaire européenne *f* *(ECU)*; ~ **Development Fund** *n* *(EDF)* ECON, POL Fonds de développement européen *m* *(FDE)*; ~ **economic area** *n* *(EEA)* ECON zone économique européenne *f*; ~ **Economic Interest Grouping** *n* *(EEIG)* ECON, POL Groupement d'intérêt économique européen *m* *(GIEE)*; ~ **Energy Charter** *n* GEN COMM Charte européenne de l'énergie *f*; ~ **Environmental Bureau** *n* *(EEB)* ENVIR Bureau européen pour l'environnement *m*; ~ **Foundation** *n* *(EF)* GEN COMM Fondation européenne *f*; ~ **Free Trade Association** *n* *(EFTA)* ECON Association européenne de libre-échange *f* *(AELE)*; ~ **Insurance Committee** *n* INS Comité européen des assurances *m*; ~ **Interprofessional Market** *n* *(EIM)* STOCK Marché interprofessionnel européen *m*; ~ **Investment Bank** *n* *(EIB)* BANK *merchant* Banque européenne d'investissement *f* *(BEI)*; ~ **Member of Parliament** *n* *(Euro MP, European MP)* POL député du Parlement Européen *m*, membre du Parlement Européen *m*; ~ **Monetary Agreement** *n* *(EMA)* GEN COMM Accord monétaire européen *m* *(AME)*; ~ **Monetary Cooperation** *n* ECON, POL Coopération économique européenne *f*; ~ **Monetary Cooperation Fund** *n* BANK Fonds européen de coopération monétaire *m*, ECON, POL Fonds monétaire européen de coopération *m*; ~ **Monetary Fund** *n* *(EMF)* ECON, POL Fonds monétaire européen *m* *(FME)*; ~ **Monetary Institute** *n* *(EMI)* ECON, POL Institut monétaire européen *m*; ~ **Monetary System** *n* *(EMS)* ECON Système monétaire européen *m* *(SME)*; ~ **Monetary Union** *n* *(EMU)* ECON, POL Union monétaire européenne *f* *(UME)*; ~ **MP** *n* *(European Member of Parliament)* POL député du Parlement Européen *m*, membre du Parlement Européen *m*; ~ **Nuclear Energy Authority** *n* *(ENEA)* GEN COMM Autorité européenne de l'énergie nucléaire *f* *(ENEA)*; ~ **option** *n* STOCK option de type européen *f*, option européenne *f*; ~ **Options Exchange** *n* *(EOE)* STOCK Bourse d'options européenne *f*; ~ **Organization for Nuclear Research** *n* IND Centre européen pour la recherche nucléaire *m*, CERN; ~ **Organization for Quality Control** *n* *(EOQC)* ADMIN Organisation européenne pour le contrôle de qualité *f*; ~ **Organization for Testing and Certification** *n* *(EOTC)* GEN COMM Organisme européen de contrôle et certification *m*; ~ **pallet pool** *n* TRANSP parc européen de palettes *m*; ~ **Parliament** *n* *(EP)* ECON Parlement européen *m*; ~ **patent** *n* PATENTS brevet européen *m*; ~ **patent application** *n* PATENTS demande de brevet européen *f*; ~ **Patent Convention** *n* LAW, PATENTS *intellectual property* Convention européenne sur les brevets *f*; ~ **Patent Organization** *n* *(EPO)* LAW Organisation européenne de brevets *f*; ~ **Payments Union** *n* *(EPU)* GEN COMM Union européenne des paiements *f* *(UEP)*; ~ **Productivity Agency** *n* *(EPA)* IND Agence européenne de productivité *f*; ~ **Regional**

Development Fund *n* *(ERDF)* ECON Fonds européen de développement régional *m* *(FEDER)*; ~ **Registry of Commerce** *n* *(ERC)* GEN COMM Registre du commerce européen *m*; ~ **Shippers Council** *n* TRANSP Conseil des armateurs européens *m*; ~ **Single Market** *n* ECON, POL, S&M, STOCK Marché unique européen *m*; ~ **Social Charter** *n* POL Charte sociale européenne *f*; ~ **Social Fund** *n* *(ESF)* ECON, POL Fonds social européen *m* *(FSE)*; ~ **Space Agency** *n* *(ESA)* GEN COMM Agence spatiale européenne *f* *(ASE)*; ~ **Space Research Organization** *n* *(ESRO)* GEN COMM Organisme de recherche spatiale européenne *m*; ~ **-style option** *n* STOCK option de type européen *f*, option européenne *f*; ~ **Symposium on Inspection and Control** *n* IND Colloque européen des organisations de contrôle *m*; ~ **Telecommunications Standards Institute** *n* *(ETSI)* COMMS Association de normalisation des télécommunications *f*; ~ **terms** *n pl* ECON *currency trading*, POL conditions européennes *f pl*; ~ **Trade Committee** *n* *(ETC)* GEN COMM Commission européenne du commerce *f*; ~ **Trade Promotion Organization** *n* *(ETPO)* GEN COMM Organisme européen pour la promotion du commerce *m*; ~ **Trade Union Confederation** *n* *(ETUC)* HRM Confédération syndicale européenne *f*; ~ **Transport Organization** *n* *(ETO)* TRANSP Organisation européenne de transport *f*; ~ **Union** *n* *(EU)* ECON, POL Union européenne *f* *(UE)*; ~ **Union Treaty** *n* GEN COMM Traité de l'Union européenne *m*; ~ **unit of account** *n* *(EUA)* BANK, ECON, FIN unité de compte européenne *f* *(UCE)*; ~ **zone charge** *n* *(EZC)* TRANSP *haulage* zone de tarification européenne *f*

European/ASEAN: ~ **Business Council** *n* *(EABC)* GEN COMM Conseil d'affaires européen/ANASE *m*

Europhiliac *adj* GEN COMM europhile

Europhobic *adj* GEN COMM europhobe

Eurorates *n pl* BANK eurotaux *m pl*

Eurorebel *n* GEN COMM eurorebelle *m*, eurosceptique *m*

Eurosceptic *n* GEN COMM eurorebelle *m*, eurosceptique *m*

Eurosecurity *n* FIN eurovaleur mobilière *f*

Eurovision *n* MEDIA Eurovision *f*

evade *vt* TAX *tax* frauder, se soustraire à

evaluate *vt* GEN COMM évaluer

evaluation *n* GEN COMM évaluation *f*; ~ **questionnaire** GEN COMM questionnaire d'évaluation *m*

evasive *adj* GEN COMM *action* dilatoire, *reply* évasif

even[1] *adj* COMP, MATH *numbers* pair; ~ **-numbered** GEN COMM en nombre pair; ◆ **on an ~ keel** TRANSP en assiette nulle, sans différence, à égal tirant d'eau

even:[2] ~ **parity** *n* COMP parité *f*

even:[3] **1.** *vt* ~ **up** GEN COMM compenser; **2.** *vi* ~ **out** GEN COMM *prices* s'égaliser

evened: ~ **-out position** *phr* BANK position fermée *f*

evening: ~ **class** *n* GEN COMM, WEL cours du soir *m*; ~ **peak** *n* ENVIR, GEN COMM période de demande maximum de la soirée *f*; ~ **trade** *n* STOCK marché après bourse *m*

evenly: ~ **spread** *adj* GEN COMM réparti uniformément

event *n* COMP, GEN COMM événement *m*; ~ **of default** BANK cas de défaut *m*, déchéance du terme *f*, FIN déchéance du terme *f*

events: ~ **subsequent to the closing date** *phr* ACC événements postérieurs à la date de clôture *m pl*

eventuality *n* GEN COMM éventualité *f*

eventually *adv* GEN COMM finalement

eventuate *vi* GEN COMM se concrétiser

ever: ~ **-increasing** *adj* ECON *demand*, GEN COMM en croissance constante *loc f*

evergreen *n* BANK, FIN crédit permanent non-confirmé *m*; ~ **credit** BANK, FIN crédit permanent non-confirmé *m*

evict *vt* LAW, PROP expulser

eviction *n* LAW, PROP *of tenant* expulsion *f*; ~ **order** LAW, PROP arrêt d'expulsion *m*

evidence *n* LAW déposition *f*, preuve *f*, témoignage *m*; ~ **of indebtedness** TAX preuve de créance *f*; ~ **of title** LAW, PROP preuve du titre *f*; ~ **of use** PATENTS preuve de l'utilisation *f*; ◆ **be in ~** GEN COMM être fortement présent; **give ~** LAW déposer, témoigner; **give ~ on oath** LAW déposer sous la foi du serment; ~ **of** GEN COMM preuve de, évidence de

evident *adj* GEN COMM évident, LAW probant

evolution *n* GEN COMM évolution *f*

evolutionary: ~ **theory** *n* ECON *of firm* théorie évolutionniste *f*

evolve *vi* GEN COMM évoluer

ex *adv* (ANT *cum*) STOCK ex, sans

ex. *abbr* BANK *(exchange)* change *m*, ECON *(exchange)* change *m*, échange *m*, FIN *(exchange)* change *m*, GEN COMM *(examined)* examiné, GEN COMM *(excluding)* excepté, à l'exception de *loc f*, GEN COMM *(example)* exemple *m*, GEN COMM *(extra)* extra *m*, supplément *m*, GEN COMM *(exchange)* échange *m*, STOCK *(exchange)* change *m*, échange de valeurs *m*; ~ **div.** *(ex-dividend)* STOCK ex-d, ex-div. *(ex-dividende)*

exact:[1] ~ **change** *n* GEN COMM appoint *m*

exact[2] *vt* GEN COMM exiger

exacting *adj* GEN COMM exigeant

exaggerated *adj* GEN COMM exagéré, surévalué

ex allotment *n* FIN ex répartition *f*

exam: ~ **results** *n pl* GEN COMM résultats d'examen *m pl*

examination *n* HRM examen *m*, IMP/EXP *by customs* fouille *f*, visite *f*, LAW, WEL examen *m*; ~ **of proposal** INS examen de la demande d'assurance *m*, examen de proposition *m*, examen de soumission *m*; ◆ **on ~** GEN COMM après examen; **under ~** GEN COMM *matter, technique* à l'étude

examine *vt* GEN COMM *application* examiner, IMP/
EXP fouiller, visiter, inspecter

examined *adj (ex., exd)* GEN COMM examiné

examiner *n* GEN COMM examinateur *m*, HRM
examinateur *m, of candidate* évaluateur *m*, IMP/
EXP *customs* inspecteur *m*, LAW, WEL examinateur
m

example *n (ex.)* GEN COMM exemple *m*; ◆ **for ~**
(e.g.) GEN COMM par exemple *(ex.)*

ex ante[1] *adj* ECON ex ante

ex ante:[2] **~ variables** *n pl frml* ECON variables ex
ante *f pl (frml)*

exceed *vt* ECON *supply*, GEN COMM dépasser

exceeding: not ~ *phr* GEN COMM n'excédant pas

except *prep* GEN COMM excepté, sauf, à l'exception
de; ◆ **~ as otherwise provided** *(SYN unless
otherwise provided)* TAX sauf disposition
contraire; **~ otherwise herein provided** *(eohp)*
GEN COMM sauf dispositions contraires du présent

excepted *adj* TRANSP *shipping* sauf; ◆ **Fridays and
holidays ~** *(FHEx)* GEN COMM sauf vendredis et
jours fériés, sauf vendredis et périodes de congé;
Sundays and holidays ~ GEN COMM sauf dimanches et jours fériés, TRANSP *(S&H/exct, SHEX)
shipping, chartering term* dimanches et jours fériés
exceptés

exception *n* GEN COMM *special case* exception *f*,
INS exclusion *f*; ◆ **make an ~** GEN COMM faire une
exception; **with the ~ of** GEN COMM à l'exception
de

exceptional[1] *adj* GEN COMM *case, circumstances*
exceptionnel

exceptional:[2] **~ depreciation** *n* ACC, TAX amortissement dérogatoire *m*; **~ expenses** *n pl* ACC
balance sheet charges exceptionnelles *f pl*; **~ item**
n TRANSP article exceptionnel *m*; **~ write-off** *n*
ACC abandon exceptionnel *m*

exceptions: ~ clause *n* LAW *shipping*, TRANSP
shipping clause d'exonération *f*

excess[1] *adj* GEN COMM excès *m*

excess[2] *n* INS complément *m*, franchise *f*;
~ amount *n* TAX excédent *m*; **~ baggage** *n* LEIS,
TRANSP excédent de bagages *m*; **~ baggage
charge** *n* LEIS, TRANSP supplément pour excédent
de bagages *m*; **~ capacity** *n* ECON capacité
excédentaire *f*, capacité inutilisée *f*, surcapacité
f, GEN COMM surcapacité *f*, IND capacité excédentaire *f*, capacité inutilisée *f*, surcapacité *f*;
~ capacity theorem *n* ECON théorème de la
surcapacité *m*; **~ cash** *n* ACC excédent de caisse
m, excédent de trésorerie *m*; **~ contribution** *n* TAX
prime en trop *f*; **~ demand** *n* ECON, S&M demande
excédentaire *f*; **~ employment** *n* GEN COMM
suremploi *m*; **~ fare** *n* LEIS, TRANSP supplément
m; **~ insurance** *n* GEN COMM assurance complémentaire *f*; **~ liabilities** *n pl* INS *marine*
engagements excédentaires *m pl*; **~ of loss** *n* INS
excédent des sinistres *m*; **~ of loss reinsurance** *n*
INS réassurance en excédent de sinistres *f*;

~ mortality *n* INS surmortalité *f*; **~ profits tax** *n*
TAX impôt sur les bénéfices exceptionnels *m*;
~ reserve *n* BANK réserve excédentaire *f*, réserve
supplémentaire *f*; **~ shares** *n pl* STOCK actions
détenues en surnombre par un actionnaire; **~ supply**
n ECON, S&M offre excédentaire *f*; ◆ **in ~ of** GEN
COMM supérieur à

excessive[1] *adj* GEN COMM abusif, excessif

excessive:[2] **~ taxation** *n (SYN overtaxation)* TAX
fiscalité excessive *f*, impôts excessifs *m pl*,
surimposition *f*

excessively *adj* GEN COMM excessivement

exch. *abbr (exchange)* BANK change *m*, ECON
change *m*, échange *m*, FIN change *m*, GEN COMM
échange *m*, STOCK bourse *f*, change *m*, échange
de valeurs *m*

Exch. *abbr (Exchequer)* BANK Échiquier *m*

exchange[1] *n* BANK change *m*, COMMS *telephone*
central *m*, ECON *currency, money* change *m*,
échange *m*, FIN change *m*, GEN COMM échange
m, STOCK bourse *f*, change *m*; **~ arbitrage** *n*
STOCK arbitrage interplace *m*; **~ charge** *n* BANK
frais d'encaissement *m pl*; **~ contract** *n* LAW
contrat d'échange *m*; **~ of contracts** *n* GEN COMM
signature des contrats *f*, échange de contrats *m*,
LAW échange de contrats *m*; **~ control** *n* ECON
government policy, POL contrôle des changes *m*;
~ control officer *n* HRM directeur du contrôle des
changes *m*; **~ cross rate** *n* ECON, FIN parité
croisée *f*; **~ delivery settlement price** *n* STOCK
cours de liquidation *m*; **~ department** *n* STOCK
département du change *m*; **~ differences** *n pl*
ECON, FIN différences de change *f pl*; **~ discount** *n*
STOCK déport de change *m*; **~ efficiency** *n* ECON,
FIN efficience des échanges *f*; **~ fund** *n* STOCK
fonds des changes *m*; **~ of information** *n* GEN
COMM échange d'information *m*; **~ offer** *n* STOCK
offre publique d'échange *f*, OPE; **~ office** *n* BANK
bureau de change *m*; **~ rate** *n* BANK, ECON, FIN
taux de change *m*; **~ rate agreement** *n (ERA)*
ECON, FIN accord sur les taux de change *m*; **~ rate
fluctuations** *n pl* ECON, FIN fluctuations des taux
de change *f pl*; **~ rate mechanism** *n (ERM)* ECON
EU mécanisme de taux de change *m (MTC)*;
~ rate movements *n pl* ECON, FIN fluctuations des
taux de change *f pl*; **~ rate regime** *n* ECON, FIN
régime de taux de change *m*; **~ rate target zone** *n*
ECON, FIN zone cible de change *f*; **~ risk** *n* ECON,
FIN risque de change *m*; **~ screen** *n* STOCK écran
de transactions *m*; **~ of securities** *n* STOCK
échange de titres *m*; **~ traded option** *n* STOCK
option cotée en Bourse *f*, option inscrite à la cote
f, option négociable *f*; **~ value** *n* STOCK valeur
d'échange *f*; ◆ **in ~** GEN COMM en contrepartie; **in
~ for** ACC en échange de

exchange[2] *vt* COMMS *information, views* échanger;
◆ **~ contracts** GEN COMM, LAW, PROP signer les
contrats; **~ one thing for another** ECON, GEN
COMM échanger qch contre qch d'autre

Exchange: ~ Equalization Account *n (EEA)* FIN
fonds de stabilisation des changes *m*

exchanged: ~ **share** *n* STOCK action échangée *f*

Exchequer *n (Exch.)* BANK Échiquier *m*

excisable: ~ **goods** *n pl* IMP/EXP, TAX biens passibles de droits *m pl*, produits soumis à l'accise *m pl*

excise *n* TAX contributions indirectes *f pl*; ~ **bond** GEN COMM *customs* acquis à caution *m*; ~ **duty** TAX contributions indirectes *f pl*, droit d'accise *m*; ~ **tax** TAX droit d'accise *m*

exciseman *n* IMP/EXP, TAX employé des contributions indirectes *m*

exciseperson *n* IMP/EXP, TAX employé des contributions indirectes *m*, employée des contributions indirectes *f*

excisewoman *n* IMP/EXP, TAX employée des contributions indirectes *f*

excl. *abbr (excluding, exclusive of)* GEN COMM excepté, à l'exception de *loc f*

ex claim *n* LAW ex droit *m*

exclude *vt* GEN COMM exclure, *from list* écarter

excluded[1] *adj* GEN COMM exclu

excluded:[2] ~ **consideration** *n* TAX contrepartie exclue *f*; ~ **corporation** *n* TAX corporation exclue *f*; ~ **dividend** *n* TAX dividende exclu *m*; ~ **obligation** *n Can* TAX obligation exclue *f*; ~ **period** *n* TAX période d'exclusion *f*; ~ **property** *n* TAX bien exclu *m*; ~ **sector** *n* IND secteur exclu *m*

excluding *prep (ex., excl.)* GEN COMM excepté, à l'exception de *loc f*, à l'exclusion de *loc f*

exclusion *n* GEN COMM, INS *in policy*, TAX exclusion *f*; ~ **clause** GEN COMM clause d'exclusion *f*, clause d'exonération *f*, exclusion de garantie *f*, INS clause d'exclusion *f*; ~ **principle** ECON principe d'exclusion *m*; ◆ **to the ~ of** GEN COMM à l'exclusion de

exclusive[1] *adj* GEN COMM exclusif; ~ **of** *(excl.)* GEN COMM excepté, à l'exception de, à l'exclusion de; ~ **of tax** ECON, FIN, TAX hors taxes; ◆ ~ **of loading and unloading** *(xl & ul)* IMP/EXP, TRANSP chargement et déchargement exclus; ~ **of post and packing** GEN COMM frais d'emballage et d'envoi non compris *m pl*

exclusive:[2] ~ **agency agreement** *n* LAW contrat d'agence exclusive *m*, contrat de représentation exclusive *m*; ~ **agency listing** *n* PROP *property brokers* contrat d'exclusivité *m*; ~ **distribution** *n* *(exdis)* POL *of information to select group* divulgation exclusive *f*; ~ **licence** *n BrE* PATENTS licence exclusive *f*; ~ **license** *n AmE see exclusive licence BrE*; ~ **monopoly** *n* ECON monopole exclusif *m*; ~ **right** *n* LAW droit exclusif *m*; ~ **right to sell listing** *n* PROP droit exclusif de vente *m*; ~ **taxation** *n* TAX imposition exclusive *f*

exclusively *adv* GEN COMM exclusivement

ex-coupon[1] *adj (XC, ex.cp.)* GEN COMM, STOCK ex-coupon *(ex-c, ex-coup)*

ex-coupon[2] *n* GEN COMM, STOCK coupon détaché *m*

ex.cp. *abbr (ex-coupon)* GEN COMM, STOCK ex-c, ex-coup *(ex-coupon)*

exculpatory *adj* BANK, LAW qui disculpe, qui innocente

excursion: ~ **fare** *n* LEIS tarif excursion *m*

excused: **be** ~ *phr* GEN COMM se faire excuser

exd *abbr (examined)* GEN COMM examiné

ex-directory *adj BrE (XD, unlisted)* COMMS sur la liste rouge *loc f*

exdis *abbr jarg (exclusive distribution)* POL divulgation exclusive *f*

ex-div. *abbr (ex-dividend)* STOCK dividende détaché *m*

ex. div. *abbr (ex dividend)* STOCK ex-d, ex-div. *(ex-dividende)*

ex dividend *n (XD, ex. div.)* STOCK ex-dividende *m* *(ex-div.)*; ~ **date** STOCK date ex-dividende *f*

ex-dividend[1] *adj (XD, ex. div.)* STOCK ex-dividende *(ex-d)*

ex-dividend[2] *n (ex-div.)* STOCK *without dividend* dividende détaché *m*

ex docks *n pl* TRANSP franco à quai

exec. *abbr* ACC *(executive)*, ADMIN *(executive)*, HRM *(executive)* cadre *mf*, LAW *(executor)* exécuteur *m*, exécuteur testamentaire *m*

execute *vt* COMP exécuter, GEN COMM *order, piece of work* réaliser, *project, plan* mettre à exécution, *purpose, sb's wishes* accomplir, LAW *contract, document* valider, *deed* exécuter, *will* exécuter, STOCK exécuter

executed: ~ **contract** *n* LAW contrat exécuté *m*, contrat validé *m*

execution *n* LAW exécution *f*, validation *f*, MGMNT *of a policy*, STOCK exécution *f*; ~ **time** COMP durée d'exécution *f*

executive[1] *adj* HRM, MGMNT, POL exécutif

executive[2] *n* ACC *(exec.)* ADMIN *(exec.)* cadre *mf*, HRM *(exec.)* cadre *mf*, instances dirigeantes *f pl*, MGMNT directeur *m*; ~ **advancement** *n* HRM promotion des cadres *f*, MGMNT autodéveloppement *m*, promotion des cadres *f*; ~ **assistant** *n* ADMIN, HRM adjoint exécutif *m*, cadre adjoint *m*; ~ **board** *n* GEN COMM, HRM, MGMNT conseil d'administration *m*, CA; ~ **class** *n* TRANSP classe affaires *f*, classe club *f*; ~ **committee** *n* HRM comité exécutif *m, of a union* commission exécutive *f*, MGMNT *decision-making* comité de direction *m*; ~ **competence** *n* MGMNT compétence de management *f*; ~ **development** *n* GEN COMM, MGMNT perfectionnement des cadres *m*; ~ **director** *n* ADMIN, HRM directeur exécutif *m*; ~ **grade** *n* HRM niveau cadre *m*; ~ **leasing** *n* MGMNT crédit-bail pour cadre *m*, emprunt de cadres *m*; ~ **lounge** *n* TRANSP *air and ship* salle d'embarquement Classe Club *f*, salon Classe Club *m*; ~ **manager** *n* ADMIN, HRM directeur exécutif *m*; ~ **manpower strategy** *n* HRM, MGMNT stratégie des cadres *f*; ~ **officer** *n (EO)* HRM, MGMNT cadre sup *m (infrml)*, cadre supérieur *m*; ~ **option scheme** *n* STOCK plan d'investissement pour cadres *m*; ~ **perks** *n pl infrml* HRM avantages complémentaires des personnels d'encadrement *m pl*; ~ **perquisites** *n pl frml* HRM avantages complémentaires des personnels d'encadrement *m pl*; ~ **promotion** *n* HRM, MGMNT promotion des cadres *f*; ~ **remuneration** *n* HRM, MGMNT rémunération des cadres *f*; ~ **search** *n* HRM recherche de cadres *f*, MGMNT assistance au recrutement des cadres *f*; ~ **search firm** *n* HRM cabinet de recrutement des cadres *m*; ~ **secretary** *n* HRM, MGMNT assistant personnel *m*, secrétaire de direction *m*, secrétaire particulier *m*; ~ **share option scheme** *n* STOCK plan d'investissement en actions pour cadres *m*; ~ **stress** *n* HRM le stress des cadres *m*; ~ **-style housing** *n* PROP logement pour cadres *m*; ~ **suite** *n* HRM bureau de la direction *m*; ~ **training** *n* HRM, MGMNT formation des cadres *f*; ~ **vice president** *n* HRM vice-président directeur général *m*

executor *n (exec., exor)* LAW *of will* exécuteur *m*, exécuteur testamentaire *m*

executory *adj* LAW exécutoire

executrix *n* LAW *of will* exécuteur *m*, exécuteur testamentaire *m*

exempli gratia *adv frml (e.g.)* GEN COMM par exemple *loc m (ex.)*

ex-employee *n* HRM ancien employé *m*

exempt[1] *adj (ANT nonexempt)* GEN COMM, TAX exempt, exonéré

exempt:[2] ~ **corporation** *n* TAX corporation dispensée *f*; ~ **deficit** *n* TAX déficit exonéré *m*; ~ **dividend** *n* STOCK dividende exonéré d'impôt *m*; ~ **earnings** *n pl* TAX gains exonérés *m pl*; ~ **income** *n* TAX revenu exonéré *m*; ~ **interest** *n* TAX intérêt exonéré *m*; ~ **percentage** *n* TAX pourcentage d'exonération *m*; ~ **period** *n* TAX période d'exonération *f*; ~ **securities** *n pl* STOCK titres non soumis à la réglementation sur les valeurs; ~ **surplus** *n* TAX surplus exonéré *m*

exempt[3] *vt* GEN COMM, TAX exempter, exonérer

exempted: ~ **sum** *n* TAX somme exonérée *f*

exemption *n* GEN COMM, TAX exclusion *f*, exemption *f*, exonération *f*; ~ **clause** GEN COMM *contract clause* clause d'exonération *f*, exclusion de garantie *f*; ~ **for dependent children** TAX exemption pour enfants à charge *f*; ~ **from payment of premium** INS dispense de paiement de la prime *f*, exonération de paiement de la prime *f*

exercisable *adj* STOCK *options* levable

exercise[1] *n* GEN COMM exercice *m*, STOCK *option* levée *f*; ~ **date** GEN COMM *right* date d'exercice *f*, STOCK *option* date d'exercice *f*, date de levée *f*; ~ **deadline** STOCK date limite d'exercice *f*, date limite de levée *f*; ~ **limit** STOCK limite de levée *f*; ~ **notice** STOCK avis de levée *m*, notification d'exercice *f*; ~ **of an option** STOCK levée de l'option *f*; ~ **price** STOCK prix d'exercice *m*, prix de levée *m*; ~ **procedure** STOCK *options* procédure

d'exercice *f*, procédure de levée *f*; ~ **of undue authority** GEN COMM abus d'autorité *m*

exercise[2] *vt* LAW *right* exercer, S&M *franchise* gérer, STOCK *option* exercer, *rights* exercer, lever

exert *vt* GEN COMM *effect* exercer

ex factory *adv* GEN COMM départ usine *m*

ex gratia[1] *adj frml* GEN COMM à titre gracieux *loc m*

ex gratia:[2] ~ **payment** *n frml* FIN paiement à titre d'exemple *m*, prestation bénévole *f*, HRM, INS paiement à titre de faveur *m*, prestation bénévole *f*

exhaust:[1] ~ **emission** *n* ENVIR, TRANSP émission de gaz d'échappement *f*; ~ **gas** *n* ENVIR effluent gazeux *m*, gaz brûlé *m*, gaz d'échappement *m*, TRANSP gaz brûlé *m*, gaz d'échappement *m*

exhaust[2] *vt* GEN COMM *resources* épuiser

exhaustive *adj* GEN COMM exhaustif

exhibit *vt* GEN COMM *goods* exposer

exhibition *n* GEN COMM, PATENTS exposition *f*, S&M exposition *f*, *commercial* foire *f*; ~ **center** *AmE*, ~ **centre** *BrE* GEN COMM palais des expositions *m*, parc d'expositions *m*, pavillon de foire *m*; ~ **forwarding** IMP/EXP envoi de marchandises d'exposition *m*; ~ **risks insurance** INS assurance des expositions *f*, assurance tous risques expositions *f*; ~ **room** GEN COMM salle d'exposition *f*

ex hypothesi *adv frml* GEN COMM qui parle de soi-même

existing: ~ **plant** *n* ENVIR, IND usine en service *f*, usine existante *f*; ~ **SME** *n* GEN COMM PME existante *f*

exit[1] *n* TRANSP sortie *f*; ~ **barrier** *(ANT entry barrier)* ECON, IMP/EXP barrière de sortie *f*; ~ **interview** HRM entrevue de départ *f*; ~ **price** *(ANT entry price)* STOCK prix de sortie *m*; ~ **-voice** *(SYN quit rate)* ECON taux de départs *m*

exit[2] *vti* COMP sortir

ex-legal *adj* LAW hors du cadre légal

ex mill *adv* IMP/EXP, TRANSP *delivery* départ usine *m*, sortie usine *loc f*

ex nudo pacto non oritur actio *phr frml* GEN COMM, LAW *contract* d'une promesse vaine il ne sort pas d'action

ex officio[1] *adj frml* HRM de par ses fonctions *loc f*, officiellement, *member* de plein droit, ex officio *(frml)*, LAW *member* de plein droit, ex officio *(frml)*

ex officio:[2] ~ **member** *n frml* GEN COMM, HRM membre d'office *m*

exogenous: ~ **expectations** *n pl* ECON anticipations exogènes *f pl*; ~ **variable** *n* ECON variable exogène *f*

exor *abbr (executor)* LAW exécuteur *m*, exécuteur testamentaire *m*

exorbitant *adj* GEN COMM abusif, exhorbitant

exotic: ~ **currency** *n* ECON devise exotique *f*

exp. *abbr (export)* IMP/EXP exportation *f*

expand *vt* GEN COMM *activity, business, network, range* agrandir, développer, élargir, étendre

expandable *adj* COMP *hardware, software,* GEN COMM extensible, extensif, évolutif

expanded: ~ **memory** *n* COMP mémoire d'expansion *f*, mémoire étendue *f*

expansion *n* ECON financement de croissance *m, of company* développement *m*, essor *m*, expansion *f*, FIN financement de croissance *m*, GEN COMM *of company*, IND *of company*, POL développement *m*, essor *m*, expansion *f*, S&M développement *m*; ~ **board** COMP carte d'extension *f*; ~ **card** COMP carte d'extension *f*; ~ **of demand** (ANT *contraction of demand*) S&M accroissement de la demande *m*; ~ **strategy** ECON, GEN COMM stratégie d'expansion *f*, stratégie de croissance *f*

expansionary *adj* ECON *policy* expansionniste

ex parte[1] *adj* LAW ex parte, unilatéral

ex parte:[2] ~ **application** *n frml* TAX requête ex parte *f*, requête unilatérale *f*

expatriate *n* GEN COMM expatrié *m*; ~ **executive** GEN COMM, HRM cadre supérieur en mission à l'étranger *m*

expect *vt* GEN COMM s'attendre à

expectancy: ~ **theory of motivation** *n* HRM théorie de la motivation par les attentes *f*

expectation *n* ECON, GEN COMM anticipation *f*, MATH valeur attendue *f*; ◆ **in** ~ **of** GEN COMM en prévision de

expected[1] *adj* GEN COMM *result, outcome* attendu, prévu

expected:[2] ~ **actual capacity** *n* ECON capacité réelle prévue *f*; ~ **date** *n* GEN COMM date prévue *f*; ~ **mortality** *n* INS mortalité probable *f*, mortalité présumée *f*; ~ **perils** *n pl* INS risques prévus *m pl*; ~ **value** *n* (SYN *expectation*) MATH valeur attendue *f*

expediency *n* GEN COMM convenance *f*

expedite *vt* GEN COMM accélérer, diligenter, expédier

expendable[1] *adj* GEN COMM non-réutilisable, utilisable sans restrictions

expendable:[2] ~ **goods** *n pl* GEN COMM biens non-durables *m pl*; ~ **pallet** *n* TRANSP palette non-réutilisable *f*, palette perdue *f*

expendables *n pl* COMP *paper, peripherals* consommables *m pl*

expenditure *n* ECON, FIN, GEN COMM dépense *f*, dépenses *f pl*; ~ **base** TAX base de dépenses *f*, investissement de base *m*; ~ **budget** GEN COMM budget des dépenses *m*; ~ **limit** TAX limite de dépenses *f*, plafond des dépenses *m*; ~ **tax** ECON, TAX taxe sur la consommation *f*, taxe sur les dépenses du consommateur *f*

expense *n* ACC dépense *f*; ~ **account** ACC compte de charges *m*, frais de représentation *m pl*, HRM frais de représentation *m pl*, relevé de frais *m*; ~ **allowance** TAX allocation pour frais *f*; ~ **budget** ACC budget des dépenses *m*; ~ **center** *AmE*, ~ **centre** *BrE* ACC centre de coûts *m*; ~ **item** ACC dépense *f*; ~ **preference** MGMNT frais prioritaires *m pl*; ~ **ratio** ECON ratio coût-chiffre d'affaires *m*,

STOCK pourcentage de frais *m*; ~ **report** ACC note de frais *f*; ◆ **go to great** ~ GEN COMM se lancer dans de grosses dépenses; **go to the** ~ **of** GEN COMM faire la dépense de

expenses *n pl* ACC *statement of income* charges *f pl*, débit *m*, frais *m pl*, FIN, GEN COMM charges *f pl*; ~ **incurred** ACC dépenses effectuées *f pl*; ◆ **all** ~ **paid** GEN COMM tous frais payés

expensive[1] *adj* GEN COMM cher, coûteux

expensive:[2] ~ **easy money** *n* FIN crédit bon marché coûteux *m*

experience[1] *n* GEN COMM acquis *m*, expérience *f*; ~ **curve** ECON, HRM, WEL courbe d'expérience *f*; ~ **deficiency** FIN, INS déficit actuariel *m*, insuffisance actuarielle *f*; ~ **loss** FIN, INS déficit actuariel *m*, insuffisance actuarielle *f*; ~ **rating** INS tarification personnalisée *f*, tarification selon la statistique *f*; ~ **refund** INS bonification *f*, ristourne de participation *f*

experience[2] *vt* GEN COMM *growth* connaître, faire l'expérience de; ◆ ~ **rapid growth** ECON connaître une croissance rapide

experienced[1] *adj* HRM ayant de l'expérience *loc f*, ayant du métier *loc m*, ayant fait ses preuves *loc f*, expérimenté

experienced:[2] ~ **investor** *n* STOCK investisseur averti *m*, investisseur chevronné *m*; ~ **workforce** *n* HRM main-d'oeuvre expérimentée *f*

experiment *n* GEN COMM expérience *f*

expert[1] *adj* GEN COMM expert

expert[2] *n* GEN COMM expert *m*; ~ **knowledge** HRM savoir de spécialiste *m*; ~ **network** GEN COMM réseau d'experts *m*, réseau de spécialistes *m*; ~ **power** MGMNT pouvoirs donnés par l'expérience *m pl*; ~ **system** (*ES*) COMP, GEN COMM système expert *m* (*SE*); ~ **witness** LAW expert cité comme témoin *m*

expertise *n* GEN COMM compétence *f*

expiration *n AmE* (*cf expiry BrE*) GEN COMM date expiration *f*, échéance *f*, STOCK échéance *f*; ~ **cycle** STOCK cycle d'échéances *m*; ~ **date** GEN COMM, STOCK date d'expiration *f*; ~ **month** STOCK mois d'expiration *m*, mois d'échéance *m*; ~ **notice** INS *policy* avis d'expiration *m*

expire *vi* GEN COMM *lapse* arriver à échéance, expirer; ◆ ~ **in-the-money** STOCK expirer dans le cours; ~ **worthless** STOCK expirer sans valeur

expired: ~ **bill** *n* BANK effet périmé *m*

expiry *n BrE* (*cf expiration AmE*) GEN COMM expiration *f*, échéance *f*, STOCK échéance *f*; ~ **of agreement** HRM date d'expiration d'une obligation *f*; ~ **date** GEN COMM, STOCK date d'expiration *f*, date d'échéance *f*; ~ **month** STOCK mois d'expiration *m*, mois d'échéance *m*

ex-pit: ~ **transaction** *n* STOCK transaction hors corbeille *f*

explain *vti* GEN COMM expliquer

explanation *n* ACC *given in notes to accounts to explain departure from rules* justification *f*

ex plantation *adv* IMP/EXP, TRANSP *delivery* départ plantation *m*

explicit[1] *adj* GEN COMM explicite

explicit:[2] ~ **contract** *n* LAW contrat explicite *m*, contrat sans ambiguïté *m*; ~ **cost** *n* ECON coût explicite *m*

explode *vt* COMP ventiler

exploding *n* COMP ventilation *f*

exploit *vt* GEN COMM *minerals, land, talent,* HRM *workers, person's credulity,* IND *minerals, lands, talent* exploiter

exploitation *n* ECON, ENVIR *of rainforests, natural resources* exploitation *f*; ~ **in industry** IND, PATENTS application industrielle *f*

exploited: ~ **resource** *n* ENVIR ressource exploitée *f*

exploration: ~ **and development expense tax credit** *n* TAX crédit d'impôt au titre des dépenses d'exploration et d'aménagement *m*

explosion *n* GEN COMM flambée *f*; ~ **of total contents** *(ETC)* TRANSP explosion du contenu total *f*; ◆ **no ~ of the total contents** *(NETC)* TRANSP contenu indivisible *m*

explosive *n* TRANSP explosif *m*; ~ **article** TRANSP article explosif *m*; ~ **substance** TRANSP *dangerous classified transported goods* matière explosive *f*

exponent *n* MATH exposant *m*

exponential: ~ **function** *n* COMP, MATH fonction exponentielle *f*; ~ **growth** *n* MATH croissance exponentielle *f*; ~ **notation** *n* COMP, MATH notation exponentielle *f*; ~ **smoothing** *n* ECON, MATH *forecasting technique* lissage exponentiel *m*; ~ **trend** *n* GEN COMM tendance exponentielle *f*

export:[1] ~ **-orientated** *adj* IMP/EXP orienté vers l'exportation

export[2] *n (exp.)* IMP/EXP exportation *f*; ~ **agent** *n* HRM, IMP/EXP commissionnaire exportateur *m*; ~ **berth** *n* IMP/EXP, TRANSP quai réservé aux exportations *m*; ~ **cargo packing declaration** *n (ECPD)* IMP/EXP, TRANSP déclaration d'emballage de cargaison exportée *f*; ~ **cargo shipping instruction** *n (ECSI)* IMP/EXP, TRANSP instruction de transport de cargaison exportée *f*; ~ **clerk** *n* HRM, IMP/EXP employé à l'exportation *m*; ~ **club** *n* IMP/EXP club des exportateurs *m*; ~ **company** *n* IMP/EXP maison d'exportation *f*; ~ **consignment identifying number** *n (ECI)* IMP/EXP numéro identifiant des marchandises à l'exportation; ~ **control** *n* ECON, IMP/EXP contrôle des exportations *m*; ~ **coordinator** *n* HRM, IMP/EXP coordinateur des exportations *m*; ~ **credit** *n* BANK, ECON, IMP/EXP crédit à l'exportation *m*; ~ **credit insurance** *n* IMP/EXP, INS assurance crédit des exportateurs *f*, assurance du crédit à l'exportation *f*; ~ **data folder** *n UK* IMP/EXP dossier d'informations sur l'exportation; ~ **depot charges** *n pl* IMP/EXP frais d'entreposage à l'exportation *m pl*; ~ **director** *n* HRM, IMP/EXP administrateur des exportations *m*, directeur des exportations *m*, directeur export *m*; ~ **documentation** *n* IMP/EXP documentation exportation *f*; ~ **documentation**

procedure *n* IMP/EXP procédure de documentation exportation *f*; ~ **earnings** *n pl* ECON, IMP/EXP bénéfices à l'exportation *m pl*, gains à l'exportation *m pl*; ~ **facilitation organization** *n* IMP/EXP organisation d'aide aux exportations *f*; ~ **factoring** *n* IMP/EXP affacturage des exportations *m*; ~ **figures** *n pl* IMP/EXP taux des exportations *m*; ~ **finance** *n* ECON, FIN, IMP/EXP financement à l'exportation *m*; ~ **finance house** *n* FIN, IMP/EXP société de financement à l'exportation *f*; ~ **firm** *n* IMP/EXP maison d'exportation *f*; ~ **of goods order** *n* IMP/EXP commande d'exportation de marchandises *f*; ~ **house** *n* IMP/EXP maison d'exportation *f*; ~ **intelligence service** *n UK (EIS)* IMP/EXP service de renseignements pour l'exportation; ~ **invoice** *n* IMP/EXP facture d'exportation *f*; ~ **-led economic recovery** *n* ECON, IMP/EXP redressement économique lié aux exportations *m*, redressement économique tiré par les exportations *m*; ~ **-led growth** *n* ECON, IMP/EXP croissance entraînée par les exportations *f*; ~ **licence** *n BrE* IMP/EXP licence d'exportation *f*; ~ **licence application form** *n BrE* IMP/EXP formulaire de demande de licence d'exportation *m*; ~ **licence expiry date** *n BrE* IMP/EXP date d'expiration de licence d'exportation *f*; ~ **licence number** *n BrE* IMP/EXP numéro de licence d'exportation *m*; ~ **license** *n AmE see export licence BrE*; ~ **license application form** *n AmE see export licence application form BrE*; ~ **license expiry date** *n AmE see export licence expiry date BrE*; ~ **license number** *n AmE see export licence number BrE*; ~ **licensing branch** *n (ELB)* IMP/EXP bureau des autorisations d'exportation *m*; ~ **loan** *n* BANK, ECON, IMP/EXP crédit à l'exportation *m*; ~ **management company** *n* IMP/EXP, MGMNT société de gestion d'exportations *f*; ~ **manager** *n* HRM, IMP/EXP administrateur des exportations *m*, directeur des exportations *m*, directeur export *m*; ~ **market** *n* ECON, IMP/EXP marché à l'exportation *m*; ~ **market research** *n* IMP/EXP, S&M étude de marché à l'exportation *f*; ~ **marketing manager** *n* HRM, IMP/EXP directeur marketing des exportations *m*; ~ **merchant** *n* HRM, IMP/EXP négociant exportateur *m*; ~ **office** *n* IMP/EXP bureau d'exportation *m*; ~ **order check list** *n* IMP/EXP liste de contrôle des commandes d'exportation *f*; ~ **packer** *n* IMP/EXP emballeur d'exportations *m*; ~ **performance** *n* IMP/EXP performance à l'exportation *f*; ~ **permit** *n* IMP/EXP autorisation d'exporter *f*; ~ **prices** *n pl* ECON, IMP/EXP prix à l'exportation *m pl*; ~ **promotion** *n (EP)* IMP/EXP promotion des exportations *f*; ~ **regulations** *n pl* IMP/EXP réglementation des exportations *f*; ~ **reject** *n* IMP/EXP article impropre à l'exportation *m*; ~ **sales** *n pl* IMP/EXP, S&M ventes à l'exportation *f pl*; ~ **sector** *n* IMP/EXP secteur exportateur *m*; ~ **services voucher** *n* IMP/EXP quittance des services exportation *f*; ~ **shed** *n* IMP/EXP hangar des exportations *m*; ~ **subsidy** *n* IMP/EXP prime à l'exportation *f*, subvention à l'exportation *f*; ~ **surplus** *n* ECON, IMP/EXP excédent d'exportation *m*; ~ **tax** *n* IMP/EXP, TAX taxe à l'exportation *f*; ~ **turnover** *n* IMP/EXP chiffre d'affaires à l'exportation *m*

Export: ~ **Credit Guarantee Department** *n* UK *(ECGD)* IMP/EXP service de garantie des crédits à l'exportation, ≈ Compagnie française d'assurance pour le commerce extérieur *f* *(France)* *(COFACE)*; ~ **Representative Service** *n* UK IMP/EXP service de représentation à l'exportation

exportation *n* IMP/EXP exportation *f*

exported *adj* IMP/EXP exporté

exporter *n* IMP/EXP exportateur *m*

Export-Import: ~ **Bank** *n* US IMP/EXP banque d'import-export *f*

exporting *adj* IMP/EXP exportateur

EXPORTIT *abbr* UK *(Information Technology Export Organization)* IMP/EXP organisation d'exportation de la technologie de l'information

expose *vt* STOCK exposer; ~ **sth in detail** GEN COMM exposer qch en détail; ~ **to** GEN COMM *pressures* exposer à

exposed: ~ **net asset position** *n* GEN COMM position nette débitrice *f*; ~ **net liability position** *n* BANK compte-rendu de passif net *m*; ~ **sector** *n* GEN COMM secteur exposé *m*, secteur à risque *m*

exposition *n* STOCK risque *m*

ex post¹ *adj frml* ECON ex post *(frml)*; ~ **facto** *frml* LAW ex post facto *(frml)*, par après

ex post:² ~ **variables** *n pl* ECON variables ex post *f pl*

exposure *n* FIN risque *m*, S&M *advertising* contact *m*, couverture *f*; ~ **draft** ACC exposé-sondage *m*, projet de norme *m*, projet mise à l'étude *m*

express¹ *adj* GEN COMM *intent* exact, précis

express² *n* TRANSP *transportation service* express *m*; ~ **agency** *n* GEN COMM agence de messageries *f*; ~ **authority** *n* GEN COMM autorisation expresse *f*; ~ **condition** *n* GEN COMM condition expresse *f*; ~ **contract** *n* LAW contrat explicite *m*; ~ **mail service** *n* COMMS courrier express *m*, ≈ Chronopost® *m* *(France)*, GEN COMM courrier exprès *m*; ~ **telegraphic money transfer** *n* FIN transfert financier télégraphique express *m*; ~ **terms** *n pl* HRM points expressément formulés *m pl*, *of contract* termes précisés *m pl*; ~ **warranty** *n* GEN COMM garantie expresse *f*

express³ *vt* GEN COMM exprimer

expressage *n* GEN COMM transport par service rapide *m*

expression *n* COMP *programming languages*, GEN COMM expression *f*

expressway *n* Can *(cf freeway AmE, motorway BrE, superhighway AmE, throughway AmE)* TRANSP autoroute *f*

expropriation *n* LAW, PROP emprise *f*; ~ **asset** TAX contre-valeur de biens expropriés *f*

expunged *adj* TRANSP rayé

ExQ *abbr* *(ex quay)* IMP/EXP, TRANSP *shipping*

livrable à quai, à prendre à quai *loc m*, à quai *loc m*

ex quay *adv* *(ExQ)* IMP/EXP, TRANSP *shipping* livrable à quai, à prendre à quai *loc m*, à quai *loc m*

ex-rights¹ *adj* STOCK droit détaché *m*, ex-droit, sans droit

ex-rights:² ~ **date** *n* STOCK date ex-droits *f*; ~ **period** *n* STOCK période ex-droits *f*

ExS *abbr* *(ex ship)* IMP/EXP, TRANSP départ navire *m*, à enlever à bord

ex ship *adv* *(ExS)* IMP/EXP, TRANSP départ navire *m*, à enlever à bord

extend *vt* BANK *loan*, FIN *loan* accorder, consentir, GEN COMM *clientele, knowledge* élargir, *power* étendre, *research, study* approfondir, LAW *rules, time limit* proroger; ◆ ~ **the time limit for sth** GEN COMM provoquer l'échéance de qch

extended: ~ **cover** *n* INS extension à des risques annexes *f*, garantie annexe *f*; ~ **coverage** *n* INS extension à des risques annexes *f*, garantie annexe *f*; ~ **coverage endorsement** *n* US INS avenant *m*, avenant concernant les garanties annexes *m*; ~ **deferment** *n* ACC crédit des droits et taxes *m*, crédit des obligations cautionnées *m*; ~ **memory** *n* COMP mémoire d'expansion *f*, mémoire étendue *f*; ~ **payment** *n* BANK délai supplémentaire de paiement *m*; ~ **program** *n* AmE, ~ **programme** *n* BrE GEN COMM programme intensifié *m*; ~ **terms** *n pl* BANK prolongation d'échéance *f*, prorogation d'échéance *f*

extendible: ~ **bond** *n* STOCK obligation à échéance prorogeable *f*

extension *n* COMP *file name* extension *f*, LAW prorogation *f*, TAX *of time* rallonge *f*; ~ **costs** *n pl* INS coûts de couverture supplémentaire *m pl*, frais d'extension *m pl*; ~ **fee** *n* BANK commission de reconduction *f*; ~ **for returns** *n* TAX prorogation de délais pour les déclarations *f*; ~ **fork** *n* TRANSP fourche à rallonge *f*; ~ **services** *n pl* FIN, GEN COMM, MGMNT services logistiques *m pl*; ~ **of time** *n* GEN COMM délai supplémentaire *m*; ~ **of time limits** *n* LAW prorogation des délais *f*

extensive: ~ **farming** *n* ECON, ENVIR *agriculture* cultures extensives *f pl*

extent *n* GEN COMM, PATENTS *of protection* étendue *f*; ~ **of damage** INS degré des dommages *m*, étendue des dégâts *f*

extenuating: ~ **circumstances** *n pl* LAW circonstances atténuantes *f pl*

external: ~ **account** *n* BANK, ECON, POL balance des paiements *f*, compte de non-résident *m*; ~ **audit** *n* ACC, FIN audit externe *m*, contrôle externe *m*, révision externe *f*, vérification externe *f* *(Can)*; ~ **balance** *n* ECON, POL équilibre de la balance des paiements *m*; ~ **border** *n* GEN COMM frontière extérieure *f*, frontière nationale *f*; ~ **borrowings** *n pl* FIN emprunts extérieurs *m pl*; ~ **cost** *n* ACC charge externe *f*; ~ **debt** *n* ECON, POL dette extérieure *f*; ~ **debt ratio** *n* ECON, POL ratio d'endettement extérieur *m*; ~ **debtor** *n* ACC débiteur externe *m*; ~ **document** *n* GEN COMM document externe *m*; ~ **economy** *n* (ANT *internal economy*) ECON économie extérieure *f*; ~ **economy of scale** *n* ECON, IND économie d'échelle externe *f*; ~ **financing** *n* FIN financement externe *m*; ~ **financing limit** *n* (*EFL*) FIN limite de financement externe *f*; ~ **funds** *n pl* FIN fonds externes *m pl*; ~ **government policy** *n* ECON, POL politique extérieure *f*; ~ **labor market** *n* AmE, ~ **labour market** *n* BrE ECON marché du travail externe *m*; ~ **market** *n* GEN COMM marché extérieur *m*, marché étranger *m*; ~ **procedure** *n* TRANSP procédure externe *f*; ~ **relations** *n pl* GEN COMM, MGMNT relations extérieures *f pl*; ~ **report** *n* GEN COMM rapport externe *m*; ~ **shock** *n* ECON choc externe *m*; ~ **trade guarantee** *n* INS garantie de commerce extérieur *f*, garantie de solidarité professionnelle *f*; ~ **trade indicator** *n* ECON indicateur du commerce extérieur *m*; ~ **trade surplus** *n* ECON, IMP/EXP excédent commercial étranger *m*, excédent du commerce extérieur *m*

externality *n* ECON effet externe *m*, externalité *f*

externalize *vt* ECON externer

extinction *n* ENVIR disparition *f*, extinction *f*; ~ **of an action** LAW extinction d'une action *f*, extinction d'une instance *f*

extort *vt* GEN COMM extorquer

extortion: ~ **insurance** *n* INS assurance contre l'extorsion *f*, assurance contre le chantage *f*

extra[1] *adj* GEN COMM en supplément *loc m*, non-compris, supplémentaire; ~ **high strength** (*EHS*) IND à très haute résistance *loc f*

extra[2] *n* (*ex.*) GEN COMM extra *m*, supplément *m*; ~ **-billing** ACC surfacturation *f*; ~ **charge** ACC supplément *m*; ~ **dividend** STOCK dividende exceptionnel *m*; ~ **freight** GEN COMM surfret *m*; ~ **interest** GEN COMM intérêt supplémentaire *m*; ~ **pay** HRM sursalaire *m*; ~ **postage** COMMS, GEN COMM affranchissement supplémentaire *m*; ~ **-special-quality steel cable** TRANSP *ship's equipment* câble en acier de première qualité *m*; ~ **tare** GEN COMM surtare *f*

extract[1] *n* GEN COMM *from document* extrait *m*; ~ **from the register** LAW extrait du registre *m*

extract[2] *vt* ENVIR extraire, GEN COMM *information* tirer, *minerals, energy resources* extraire

extractable: ~ **reserves** *n pl* ENVIR *energy resources* réserves extractibles *f pl*

extraction *n* GEN COMM *oil, gas* extraction *f*

extractive: ~ **industries** *n pl* GEN COMM, IND *mining* industries extractives *f pl*, industries minières *f pl*

extra-EU *adj* GEN COMM hors CE

extraordinary: ~ **charge** *n* ACC *balance sheets* charge exceptionnelle *f*; ~ **dividend** *n* STOCK dividende exceptionnel *m*; ~ **expenditure** *n* ACC dépense exceptionnelle *f*; ~ **expenses** *n pl* ACC frais extraordinaires *m pl*; ~ **gain** *n* ACC profit exceptionnel *m*; ~ **general meeting** *n* (*EGM*) MGMNT assemblée générale extraordinaire *f* (*AGE*); ~ **item** *n* FIN *revenue* profit exceptionnel *m*, GEN COMM poste exceptionnel *m*, élément extraordinaire *m*, TAX élément exceptionnel *m*; ~ **items** *n pl* ACC *revenue* profits exceptionnels *m pl*; ~ **loss** *n* ACC perte exceptionnelle *f*; ~ **meeting** *n* GEN COMM assemblée extraordinaire *f*

extrapolation *n* MATH extrapolation *f*

extrapolative: ~ **expectations** *n pl* ECON anticipations par extrapolation *f pl*

extraterritorial: ~ **enforcement** *n* LAW application extraterritoriale *f*

extreme: ~ **hardship** *n* TAX situation financière extrêmement difficile *f*

extremum *n frml* ECON valeur externe *f*

extrinsic: ~ **motivation** *n* HRM motivation extrinsèque *f*; ~ **value** *n* STOCK *options* valeur extrinsèque *f*

ex turpi causa non oritur action *phr frml* GEN COMM nulle action n'est admissible si ses causes sont honteuses

EXW *abbr* (*ex works*) IMP/EXP départ usine *m*, à l'endroit des travaux *loc*

ex warehouse *adv* GEN COMM départ d'entrepôt *m*

ex-warrant *n* STOCK bon de souscription détaché *m*, ex-bon de souscription *m*

ex-wharf: ~ **price** *n* IMP/EXP prix départ quai *m*

ex works *phr* (*EXW*) IMP/EXP *named place* départ usine *m*, à l'endroit des travaux; ~ **export packing** IMP/EXP, TRANSP *cargo delivery* emballage export-départ usine *m*

eye:[1] ~ **-catching** *adj* S&M *marketing* accrocheur

eye:[2] ~ **bolt** *n* TRANSP piton à oeil *m*; ~ **contact** *n* S&M *marketing* contact visuel *m*; ~ **-hand span** *n* ADMIN empan visuo-manuel *m*; ~ **-voice span** *n* ADMIN empan visuo-vocal *m*; ~ **witness** *n* LAW témoin oculaire *m*; ◆ **with an ~ to doing** S&M en vue de faire

EZ *abbr* (*enterprise zone*) ECON, HRM, IND, PROP ZAC (*zone d'aménagement concerté*)

EZC *abbr* (*European zone charge*) TRANSP zone de tarification européenne *f*

F

F¹ *abbr* ENVIR *(fresh water)* eau douce *f*, GEN COMM *(Fahrenheit)* Fahrenheit *m*

F:² **~ statistic** *n* MATH statistique F *f*

f.a.a. *abbr (free of all average)* GEN COMM franc de toute avarie

FAA *abbr US (Federal Aviation Administration)* TRANSP administration fédérale de l'aviation

FAB *abbr (forwarder air waybill)* IMP/EXP, TRANSP lettre de transport aérien du transitaire *f*

fabric *n* GEN COMM étoffe *f*

fabricate *vt* GEN COMM *goods* fabriquer

fabricator *n* HRM fabricant *m*

fac *abbr* TRANSP *(forwarding agent's commission)* commission du transitaire *f*, TRANSP *(fast as can) cargo delivery* aussi vite que possible

facade *n* PROP *of building* façade *f*

faccop *abbr (fast as can)* TRANSP *cargo delivery* aussi vite que possible

face:¹ **~ amount** *n (SYN face of policy)* INS capital nominal *m*; **~ page** *n* MEDIA page de titre *f*; **~ of policy** *n (SYN face amount)* INS capital nominal *m*; **~ -to-face selling** *n* S&M vente directe *f*; **~ value** *n* STOCK valeur faciale *f*, valeur nominale *f*; ♦ **at ~ value** STOCK à la valeur faciale, à la valeur nominale

face² *vt* GEN COMM *criticism, attacks, future, problem* faire face à; **~ up to** GEN COMM *problem, responsibility* faire face à, *somebody* affronter; ♦ **~ the facts** GEN COMM regarder les choses en face; **~ a risk** GEN COMM, STOCK être exposé à un risque

facilitate *vt* GEN COMM faciliter

facilitation *n* TRANSP *of goods traffic* facilitation *f*, *of trade procedures* assouplissement *m*

facilities *n pl* HRM *for trade union representatives* installations *f pl*, possibilités offertes *f pl*

facility *n* COMP fonction *f*, installation *f*, produit *m*, unité *f*, GEN COMM facilité *f*, installation *f*; **~ letter** IMP/EXP lettre de complaisance *f*; **~ trip** *jarg* POL voyage d'étude *m*, voyage de fonction *m*

facing *n* S&M *merchandising, marketing* linéaire *m*, surface de présentation *f*

facsimile *n* ADMIN *(SYN fax) document* copie *f*, fac-similé *m*, télécopie *f*, ADMIN *(SYN fax machine) hardware* fax *m*, télécopieur *m*, COMMS *(SYN fax) document* copie *f*, fac-similé *m*, télécopie *f*, COMMS *(SYN fax machine) hardware* fax *m*, télécopieur *m*; **~ signature** GEN COMM signature en fac-similé *f*; **~ transaction** ADMIN, COMMS envoi par télécopie *m*; **~ transmission** ADMIN, COMMS émission d'une télécopie *f*

fact *n* GEN COMM, LAW fait *m*; **~ -finding mission** GEN COMM enquête *f*, mission d'enquête *f*, LAW enquête *f*

faction *adj* HRM faction *f*

factious *adj* HRM factieux

factoblig *abbr (facultative/obligatory)* INS *reinsurance* facultatif obligatoire

factor *n* ECON facteur de production *m*, FIN agent *mf*, facteur de production *m*, GEN COMM coefficient *m*, facteur *m*, indice *m*, moyen de production *m*; **~ analysis** MATH analyse factorielle *f*; **~ -augmenting technical progress** IND progrès technique augmentant les facteurs *m*; **~ cost** ACC, ECON, IND coût des facteurs *m*; **~ endowment** ECON, IND dotation en facteurs de production *f*; **~ income** ECON, IND revenu des facteurs de production *m*; **~ market** ECON, IND marché des facteurs de production *m*; **~ of production** ECON, IND facteur de production *m*; **~ productivity** ECON, IND productivité des facteurs de production *f*, rendement factoriel *m*; **~ tax** ECON, TAX taxe sur un facteur de production *f*; ♦ **be a ~** GEN COMM entrer en ligne de compte

factorage *n* FIN commission d'affacturage *f*

factorial¹ *adj* MATH *statistics* factoriel

factorial:² **~ terms of trade** *n pl* ECON termes factoriels de l'échange *m pl*

factoring *n* ACC *of debts*, FIN affacturage *m*, MATH affacturage *m*, factorage *m*, factoring *m*; **~ company** FIN société d'affacturage *f*

factory *n* IND usine *f*; **~ farming** *n* ECON agriculture industrielle *f*, ENVIR agriculture industrielle *f*, élevage industriel *m*, IND *agricultural* agriculture industrielle *f*; **~ floor** *n* IND atelier *m*; **~ hand** *n* HRM ouvrier d'usine *m*; **~ incentive scheme** *n (SYN plant incentive scheme)* HRM, IND système de primes d'encouragement *m*; **~ inspector** *n UK* IND, WEL inspecteur du travail *m*; **~ overheads** *n pl* ACC, ECON, FIN, IND frais généraux de fabrication *m pl*; **~ shop** *n* S&M magasin d'usine *m*, usine center *f*; **~ supplies** *n pl* ACC fournitures consommables *f pl*

Factory: **~ Inspectorate** *n UK (cf Health and Safety Inspectorate)* WEL Inspection du travail *f*

facts: **~ and figures** *n pl* GEN COMM les faits et les chiffres *m pl*

factual¹ *adj* GEN COMM basé sur des faits

factual:² **~ error** *n* GEN COMM erreur sur les faits *f*; **~ evidence** *n* LAW preuve factuelle *f*

facultative¹ *adj* GEN COMM facultatif

facultative:² **~ placing** *n* INS placement facultatif *m*

facultative/obligatory *adj (factoblig)* INS *reinsurance* facultatif obligatoire

faculty *n* WEL faculté *f*

fad *n* ECON, GEN COMM, S&M mode passagère *f*

Fahrenheit *n (F)* GEN COMM Fahrenheit *m*

fail:[1] ~ **position** n STOCK défaut m, défaut de livraison m

fail[2] vi BANK of bank faire faillite, COMP of hardware tomber en panne, échouer, GEN COMM of company faire faillite, échouer; ♦ ~ **in one's duty** GEN COMM manquer à son devoir; ~ **to agree** HRM quitter la table des négociations; ~ **to deliver** STOCK securities ne pas pouvoir livrer; ~ **to observe the law** LAW ne pas observer la loi; ~ **to receive** STOCK ne pas pouvoir recevoir

failed: ~ **delivery** n STOCK défaut m, défaut de livraison m

failure n COMP of hardware défaillance f, panne f, échec m, GEN COMM of company échec m; ~ **analysis** MGMNT analyse de l'échec f; ~ **in payment** GEN COMM défaut de paiement m; ~ **rate** GEN COMM taux d'échecs m; ~ **to accept** GEN COMM refus m; ~ **to agree** (FTA) HRM absence d'accord f; ~ **to appear** LAW défaut de comparution m, non-comparution f; ~ **to comply** LAW inobservation f, TAX défaut de se conformer m; ~ **to deliver** GEN COMM non-livraison f; ~ **to deliver a security on value date** STOCK fait de ne pas livrer un titre à la date de règlement m

fair[1] adj GEN COMM, LAW correct, honnête, juste, loyal, équitable; ♦ ~ **day's pay** UK HRM salaire moyen d'une journée m; ~ **day's work** UK HRM travail moyen d'une journée m

fair:[2] ~ **average quality** n (FAQ) GEN COMM qualité commerciale f; ~ **business practices** n pl GEN COMM pratiques commerciales honnêtes f pl, pratiques commerciales loyales f pl, pratiques commerciales respectant la libre concurrence f pl; ~ **competition** n (ANT unfair competition) ECON, GEN COMM, IND, LAW, PATENTS, S&M concurrence loyale f; ~ **dismissal** n HRM licenciement justifié m, licenciement régulier m; ~ **employment** n HRM égalité des droits des travailleurs f; ~ **market rent** n PROP loyer modéré m; ~ **market value** n GEN COMM juste valeur marchande; ~ **play** n GEN COMM fair-play m, franc-jeu m; ~ **presentation** n AmE (cf true and fair view BrE) ACC image fidèle f; ~ **rate of return** n ACC, FIN rendement équitable m, STOCK rendement raisonnable m; ~ **rent** n PROP loyer équitable m; ~ **rental value** n PROP juste valeur locative loc, loyer modéré m, rendement équitable m; ~ **return** n ACC, FIN rendement équitable m; ~ **sample** n GEN COMM échantillon représentatif m; ~ **share** n GEN COMM part équitable f; ~ **trade** n S&M pricing libre-échange réciproque m; ~ **trading** n ECON, LAW pratiques commerciales loyales f pl; ~ **value** n ACC of assets valeur équitable f, STOCK of shares juste valeur; ~ **value adjustments** n pl ACC first consolidation of a subsidiary attribution du prix d'achat d'une filiale aux éléments d'actif et de passif de la société; ~ **wear and tear** n GEN COMM usure normale f

Fair: ~ **Access To Insurance Requirements Plan** n US (FAIR plan) INS régime de libre accès aux besoins d'assurance m; ~ **Credit Reporting Act** n US LAW loi définissant le taux d'endettement admissible chez un débiteur; ~ **Employment Commission** n BrE (FEC) HRM Northern Ireland commission de contrôle de l'emploi; ~ **Labor Standards Act** n US (FLSA) LAW réglementation fédérale du droit du travail

FAIR: ~ **plan** n US (Fair Access To Insurance Requirements Plan) INS régime de libre accès aux besoins d'assurance m

fairway n TRANSP chenal m, passe f

fait accompli n GEN COMM fait accompli m

faithful adj GEN COMM exact, fidèle

faithfulness n GEN COMM fidélité f

FAK abbr (freight all kinds) TRANSP à l'unité de chargement loc f

fake vt GEN COMM document maquiller; ♦ ~ **the marks** jarg STOCK tricher sur les prix

faking n GEN COMM maquillage m

fall[1] n ECON chute f, GEN COMM in price baisse f, chute f, GEN COMM AmE (cf autumn BrE) seasons automne m, S&M, STOCK chute f; ~ **of currency** ECON baisse de la monnaie f; ~ **in the bank rate** BANK, ECON réduction du taux d'escompte f; ~ **in foreign exchange reserves** BANK, ECON, STOCK baisse des réserves en devises f; ~ **in population** ECON baisse de la population f; ~ **in supplies** ECON contraction de l'offre f; ~ **in value** STOCK baisse de valeur f

fall:[2] **1.** vt ~ **back on** vi GEN COMM, INS avoir recours à; ~ **in with** GEN COMM proposal accepter; **2.** vi ECON price, GEN COMM, S&M chuter, STOCK baisser, chuter; ~ **apart** GEN COMM plan, negotiations tomber à l'eau (infrml); ~ **away** GEN COMM numbers diminuer; ~ **behind** GEN COMM être à la traîne; ~ **down** GEN COMM plan, building s'effondrer; ~ **through** GEN COMM plan, project tomber à l'eau (infrml); ♦ ~ **behind schedule** GEN COMM prendre du retard; ~ **foul of the law** LAW agir illégalement, se mettre dans l'illégalité, tomber sous le coup de la loi; ~ **foul of** GEN COMM person s'attirer le mécontentement de, se brouiller avec; ~ **foul of the tax authorities** TAX avoir des ennuis avec le fisc; ~ **in value** STOCK baisser de valeur; ~ **into abeyance** LAW tomber en désuétude; ~ **short of** GEN COMM expectations, target être inférieur à; ~ **within the scope of** LAW entrer dans le champ d'application de, tomber dans le champ d'application de

fall-back n GEN COMM plan de secours m; ~ **option** MGMNT option de repli f; ~ **pay** GEN COMM salaire minimum garanti m; ~ **position** POL position de repli f

fallen: ~ **angel** n STOCK ange déchu m; ~ **building clause** n INS property clause d'écroulement de bâtiment f

fallibility n GEN COMM faillibilité f

fallible adj GEN COMM faillible

falling: ~ **price** n ECON cours en baisse m, cours en repli m, prix en baisse m pl; ~ **trend** n STOCK tendance baissière f

fallout *n infrml* GEN COMM, POL *consequences* conséquences *f pl*, retombées *f pl*

fallow *adj* ECON *agricultural land* en jachère

falsa demonstratio non nocet *phr frml* GEN COMM fausse démonstrtion ne nuit pas *f (frml)*

false: ~ **advertising** *n* S&M publicité mensongère *f*; ~ **advertising claim** *n* S&M annonce mensongère *f*; ~ **alarm** *n* GEN COMM fausse alerte *f*; ~ **declaration** *n* TAX *in document* faux énoncé *m*; ~ **economy** *n* ECON, GEN COMM fausse économie *f*; ~ **or deceptive entry** *n* TAX inscription fausse ou trompeuse *f*; ~ **or deceptive statement** *n* TAX déclaration fausse ou trompeuse *f*; ~ **or misleading information** *n* LAW information erronée ou trompeuse *f*; ~ **return** *n* TAX déclaration fausse *f*; ~ **statement** *n* TAX déclaration fausse *f*; ~ **witness** *n* LAW faux témoin *m*

falsification *n* ACC maquillage *m, of accounts* falsification *f*, truquage *m*, BANK maquillage *m*, GEN COMM falsification *f*, LAW falsification *f*, maquillage *m*

falsify *vt* ACC falsifier, *figures* maquiller, BANK *cheque* falsifier, maquiller, FIN altérer, GEN COMM falsifier, LAW falsifier, truquer, *evidence* maquiller

falsifying *n* ACC, BANK, LAW maquillage *m*

falter *vi* ECON chanceler

familiar *adj* GEN COMM familier; ◆ **be** ~ **with** GEN COMM bien connaître, être au fait de

family *n* GEN COMM *group of people, products* famille *f*; ~ **allowance** *n* HRM, TAX, WEL allocation familiale *f*; ~ **allowance payments** *n pl* HRM, TAX allocations familiales *f pl*; ~ **audience** *n* MEDIA écoute familiale *f*; ~ **benefit contribution** *n* TAX cotisation allocation familiale *f*; ~ **business** *n* IND commerce familial *m*; ~ **circumstances** *n pl* HRM, TAX, WEL situation de famille *f*; ~ **fare** *n* TRANSP tarif familles *m*; ~ **farm corporation** *n* TAX corporation agricole familiale *f*; ~ **of funds** *n* STOCK famille de fonds de placement *f*; ~ **hour** *n jarg* MEDIA *broadcasting* heure de grande écoute *f*; ~ **income** *n* TAX revenu familial *m*; ~ **income policy** *n* INS police revenu familial garanti *f*; ~ **income threshold** *n* TAX seuil de revenu familial *m*; ~ **life cycle** *n* S&M cycle de vie familiale *m*; ~ **-size pack** *n* S&M emballage familial *m*, paquet familial *m*; ~ **-size package** *n* S&M emballage familial *m*, paquet familial *m*; ~ **tree** *n* GEN COMM, MGMNT arbre généalogique *m*; ~ **violence** *n* WEL violence familiale *f*

Family: ~ **Expenditure Survey** *n UK (FES)* ECON *econometrics* enquête annuelle du gouvernement britannique sur les dépenses des familles et ménages

famous *adj* GEN COMM célèbre

fancy: ~ **goods** *n pl* GEN COMM nouveautés *f pl*

F&D *abbr (freight and demurrage)* INS, TRANSP fret et surestarie *m*

Fannie: ~ **Mae** *n infrml US (FNMA, Federal National Mortgage Association)* FIN, PROP association nationale fédérale hypothécaire

fanzine *n* MEDIA *magazine* fanzine *m*

FAO *abbr (Food and Agriculture Organization)* ECON Organisation pour l'alimentation et l'agriculture *f*

FAQ *abbr* GEN COMM *(fair average quality)* qualité commerciale *f*, TRANSP *(free alongside quay)* shipping FAQ *(franco à quai)*

far: ~ **-flung** *adj* GEN COMM *network* vaste; ~ **-reaching** *adj* GEN COMM *consequences* d'une portée considérable *loc f*; ~ **-seeing** *adj (*SYN *far-sighted)* GEN COMM clairvoyant, qui voit loin *loc*; ~ **-sighted** *adj (*SYN *far-seeing)* GEN COMM clairvoyant, qui voit loin *loc*

fare: ~ **pricing** *n* GEN COMM fixation des tarifs *f*; ~ **war** *n* TRANSP guerre des tarifs *f*

farm:[1] ~ **equipment** *n* ECON *agriculture* équipement agricole *m*; ~ **implements** *n pl* ECON *agriculture* matériel agricole *m*; ~ **laborer** *n AmE*, ~ **labourer** *n BrE* HRM employé de ferme *m*, ouvrier agricole *m*; ~ **loan** *n* BANK, ECON prêt agricole *m*, prêt aux agriculteurs *m*; ~ **lobby** *n* POL groupe de pression agricole *m*; ~ **lobby group** *n* POL groupe de pression agricole *m*; ~ **loss** *n* TAX perte agricole *f*; ~ **policy** *n* ECON, ENVIR, POL *agriculture* politique agricole *f*; ~ **pressure group** *n* POL groupe de pression agricole *m*; ~ **produce** *n* ECON *agriculture* produit de la ferme *m*; ~ **shop** *n UK* S&M boutique dans une exploitation agricole qui vend les produits agricoles de la ferme à des prix inférieurs à ceux des magasins habituels; ~ **subsidy** *n* ECON, POL *agriculture* subvention aux agriculteurs *f*; ~ **surplus** *n* ECON *agriculture* excédent agricole *m*; ~ **tenancy** *n* PROP location fermière *f*

farm:[2] ~ **out** *vt* GEN COMM *work* externer, sous-traiter

farmer *n* ECON, ENVIR agriculteur *m*

farmhand *n* HRM employé de ferme *m*, ouvrier agricole *m*

farming *n* ECON, ENVIR agriculture *f*, GEN COMM culture *f*; ~ **business** GEN COMM, IND entreprise agricole *f*, exploitation agricole *f*; ~ **income** ECON *agriculture*, GEN COMM revenu agricole *m*; ~ **method** ECON *agriculture* méthode d'exploitation agricole *f*

farmland *n* ECON terre agricole *f*, terres cultivées *f pl*

farther: ~ **in** *phr* STOCK *options* échéance proche *loc f*; ~ **out** *phr* STOCK *options* échéance lointaine *loc f*

FAS *abbr (free alongside ship, free alongside steamer)* TRANSP *cargo delivery* FLB *(franco le long du bord)*

FASB *abbr US (Financial Accounting Standards Board)* ACC commission de normalisation de la comptabilité financière

fascism *n* POL fascisme *m*

fashion *n* ECON mode *f*, GEN COMM, S&M mode *f*, vogue *f*; ~ **designer** *n* GEN COMM, IND couturier *m*; ~ **editor** *n* MEDIA rédacteur de mode *m*; ~ **goods** *n pl* S&M articles de mode *m pl*; ~ **house** *n* GEN COMM maison de couture *f*; ~ **magazine** *n* MEDIA journal de mode *m*, revue de mode *f*; **~ model** *n* GEN COMM mannequin *m*; **~ parade** *n* GEN COMM présentation de collections *f*; **~ show** *n* GEN COMM défilé de mode *m*; ◆ **in ~** (ANT *out of fashion*) GEN COMM en vogue, à la mode; **out of ~** (ANT *in fashion*) GEN COMM démodé, passé de mode; **set the ~ for** GEN COMM lancer la mode de

fast[1] *adj* GEN COMM rapide; **~ -growing** ECON, GEN COMM à croissance rapide; **~ -track** GEN COMM accéléré; ◆ **as ~ as the vessel can deliver** TRANSP cadence maximale de déchargement *f*; **as ~ as the vessel can receive** TRANSP cadence maximale de chargement *f*; **be on the ~ track** HRM être promis à gravir rapidement les échelons

fast[2] *adv* GEN COMM vite; ◆ **~ as can** (*fac, faccop*) TRANSP *cargo delivery* aussi vite que possible

fast[3] **~ decline** *n* STOCK *currency expectations* chute rapide *f*; **~ food** *n* S&M restauration rapide *f*; **~ lane** *n* TRANSP voie rapide *f*; **~ market** *n* STOCK marché accéléré *m*; **~ -moving article** *n* GEN COMM article à forte rotation *m*, article à grand débit *m*; **~ -moving consumer goods** *n pl* (*FMCG*) S&M biens de consommation courante *m pl*, produits de grande consommation à forte rotation *m pl*; **~ rise** *n* STOCK *currency expectation* hausse rapide *f*; **~ track** *n* GEN COMM parcours rapide *m*, voie rapide *f*; **~ tracking** *n* HRM ascension rapide *f*, plan de carrière ambitieux *m*, promotion rapide *f*

fastening *n* GEN COMM fixation *f*

FAT *abbr* (*file allocation table*) COMP table d'allocation des fichiers *f*

fatal: **~ accident** *n* WEL accident ayant entraîné la mort *m*, accident mortel *m*; **~ error** *n* COMP erreur bloquante *f*, erreur fatale *f*

fatality *n* WEL accident ayant entraîné la mort *m*, accident mortel *m*

father: **~ of the chapel** *n* UK HRM secrétaire de section *m*; **~ file** *n* COMP fichier créateur *m*, fichier de base *m*, fichier père *m*

fathom *n* GEN COMM *forestry* 216 pieds cubes, brasse *f*, GEN COMM *unit of measurement of timber* brasse *f*

fault:[1] **~ -tolerant** *adj* COMP insensible aux défaillances, insensible aux pannes, à tolérance de pannes *loc f*

fault[2] *n* COMP anomalie *f*, défaillance *f*, erreur *f*, GEN COMM malfaçon *f*, *in a system* anomalie *f*; **~ -tolerant system** COMP système insensible aux défaillances *m*, système insensible aux pannes *m*; **~ tree analysis** GEN COMM analyse de l'arborescence des défaillances *f*; ◆ **no ~** INS *damage insurance* sans égard à la responsabilité

fault[3] *vt* GEN COMM trouver des défauts à

faultless *adj* GEN COMM irréprochable

faults: **~ diagnosis clinic** *n* MGMNT détection des erreurs *f*

faulty[1] *adj* GEN COMM défectueux

faulty:[2] **~ good** *n* S&M article défectueux *m*; **~ installation** *n* INS installation défectueuse *f*

faux: **~ pas** *n* GEN COMM faux pas *m*, gaffe *f* (*infrml*)

favor[1] *n* AmE see *favour* BrE

favor[2] *vt* AmE see *favour* BrE

favorability *n* AmE see *favourability* BrE

favorable[1] *adj* AmE see *favourable* BrE

favorable:[2] **~ balance of trade** *n* AmE see *favourable balance of trade* BrE; **~ business conditions** *n pl* AmE see *favourable business conditions* BrE; **~ business outlook** *n* AmE see *favourable business outlook* BrE; **~ economic climate** *n* AmE see *favourable economic climate* BrE; **~ economic conditions** *n pl* AmE see *favourable economic conditions* BrE; **~ exchange** *n* AmE see *favourable exchange* BrE; **~ rate** *n* AmE see *favourable rate* BrE; **~ trade balance** *n* AmE see *favourable trade balance* BrE; **~ variance** *n* AmE see *favourable variance* BrE

favour[1] *n* BrE GEN COMM service *m*; ◆ **be in ~ of** BrE GEN COMM approuver; **in ~ of** BrE GEN COMM *project, suggestion* favorable à

favour[2] *vt* BrE GEN COMM *course of action* favoriser

favourability *n* BrE S&M favorabilité *f*

favourable[1] *adj* BrE (ANT *unfavourable*) ACC favorable, GEN COMM *price, conditions* propice, *rate of exchange* favorable

favourable:[2] **~ balance of trade** *n* BrE IMP/EXP balance commerciale excédentaire *f*; **~ business conditions** *n pl* BrE ECON conjoncture favorable *f*; **~ business outlook** *n* BrE ECON conjoncture favorable *f*; **~ economic climate** *n* BrE ECON climat économique favorable *m*; **~ economic conditions** *n pl* BrE ECON conditions économiques favorables *f pl*, conjoncture favorable *f*; **~ exchange** *n* BrE STOCK cours avantageux *m*; **~ rate** *n* BrE ECON taux favorable *m*; **~ trade balance** *n* BrE ECON balance des paiements excédentaire *f*; **~ variance** *n* BrE ACC écart favorable *m*

fax[1] *n* ADMIN (SYN *facsimile*) *hardware* copie *f*, fac-similé *m*, télécopie *f*, ADMIN (SYN *fax machine*) *hardware* fax *m*, télécopieur *m*, COMMS (SYN *facsimile*) *document* copie *f*, fac-similé *m*, télécopie *f*, COMMS (SYN *fax machine*) *hardware* fax *m*, télécopieur *m*, COMMS fax *m*, COMMS *hardware* télécopieur *m*; **~ machine** ADMIN *hardware* fax *m*, télécopieur *m*, COMMS fax *m*, COMMS *hardware* télécopieur *m*; **~ transmission** ADMIN, COMMS émission d'une télécopie *f*

fax[2] *vt* ADMIN, COMMS envoyer par fax, envoyer par télécopie, télécopier

FBD *abbr* (*freeboard*) TRANSP *shipping* franc-bord *m*

FBIM *abbr* (*Fellow of the British Institute of Management*) MGMNT membre de l'institut britannique de gestion

f/c *abbr* (*for cash*) GEN COMM comptant, contre espèces

FC *abbr* (*fiberglass covers, fibreglass covers*) TRANSP panneaux de cale en fibre de verre *m pl*

FC&S *abbr (free of capture and seizure)* INS franc de capture et de saisie

FCAR *abbr (free of claim for accident reported)* INS *marine* franc de réclamation pour accident signalé, franc de sinistre pour l'accident constaté

FCC *abbr* GEN COMM *(French Chamber of Commerce)* Chambre de commerce française *f*, TRANSP *(fully cellular container ship)* navire porte-conteneurs spécialisé *m*, porte-conteneurs entièrement cellulaire *m*

FCCA *abbr (Fellow of the Chartered Association of Certified Accountants)* ACC ≈ membre de l'Association des Comptables d'entreprise certifiés *m*

FCCUK *abbr (French Chamber of Commerce for the United Kingdom)* GEN COMM chambre de commerce français pour le Royaume-Uni *m*

FCGI *abbr (Fellow of the City and Guilds of London Institute)* GEN COMM membre de l'institut britannique de l'enseignement technique

FCI *abbr (Fellow of the Institute of Commerce)* GEN COMM membre de l'institut commercial

FCL *abbr (full container load)* TRANSP conteneur complet *m*

FCMA *abbr (Fellow of the Chartered Institute of Management Accountants)* ACC membre de l'institut des comptables de coûts et de gestion

fco. *abbr (franco)* TRANSP fco *(franco)*

FCO *abbr UK (Foreign and Commonwealth Office)* ADMIN ≈ ministère des Affaires étrangères et du Commonwealth *m*

FCR *abbr (forwarder's certificate of receipt)* TRANSP attestation de prise en charge du transitaire *f*

fcsrcc *abbr (free of capture, seizure, and riots and civil commotions)* INS franc de capture, de saisie et émeutes et mouvements

FCT *abbr (forwarder's certificate of transport, freight forwarder's combined transport bill of lading)* IMP/EXP, TRANSP connaissement de transport combiné du transitaire *m*

fd *abbr* TRANSP *(free domicile)* franco domicile, TRANSP *(free discharge)* franco déchargement, TRANSP *(free dispatch)* sans bonification pour temps gagné, sans prime de célérité, TRANSP *(forced draft, forced draught)* combustion control tirage forcé *m*

F/d *abbr (free dock)* TRANSP FAQ *(franco à quai)*

FD *abbr (free dock)* TRANSP FAQ *(franco à quai)*

FDA *abbr US (Food and Drug Administration)* ADMIN office des produits alimentaires et pharmaceutiques

FD&D[1] *abbr (freight, demurrage and defence, freight, demurrage and defense)* INS, TRANSP cargaison, surestaries et défense *loc f*

FD&D[2] ~ **cover** *n (freight, demurrage and defence cover, freight, demurrage and defense cover)* INS, TRANSP couverture de cargaison, surestaries et défense *f*

FDIC *abbr US (Federal Deposit Insurance Corporation)* INS *company* organisme fédéral d'assurance et des dépôts bancaires *m*

FDX *abbr (full-duplex)* COMP bidirectionnel, duplex intégral, semi-duplex, simultané

feasibility: ~ **report** *n* COMP, GEN COMM analyse préalable *f*, étude de faisabilité *f*, étude préalable *f*; ~ **study** *n* COMP, GEN COMM étude de faisabilité *f*, étude préalable *f*; ~ **survey** *n* COMP, GEN COMM étude de faisabilité *f*, étude préalable *f*

feasible *adj* GEN COMM faisable, réalisable

featherbedding *n* ECON, HRM subvention à une industrie *f*, subventionnement *m*

feature *n* COMP caractéristique *f*, fonction *f*, option *f*, GEN COMM caractéristique *f*, MEDIA *in newspaper* article de fond *m*, grand reportage *m*, PATENTS, S&M caractéristique *f*; ~ **article** MEDIA *in newspaper* article de fond *m*, article vedette *m*; ~ **film** MEDIA grand film *m*

features: ~ **desired to be protected** *n pl* PATENTS caractéristiques pour lesquelles la protection est souhaitée

Feb. *abbr (February)* GEN COMM fév. *(février)*

February *n (Feb.)* GEN COMM février *m (fév.)*

FEC *abbr UK (Fair Employment Commission)* HRM commission de contrôle de l'emploi d'Irlande du Nord

fed. *abbr (federal)* GEN COMM féd. *(fédéral)*

Fed: ~ **funds** *n pl US* BANK fonds de la Réserve Fédérale *m pl*; **the ~** *n infrml US* BANK, ECON banque centrale des États-Unis, réserve fédérale *f*, conseil d'administration de la Réserve Fédérale

federal[1] *adj (fed.)* GEN COMM fédéral *(fed.)*; ~ **-level** GEN COMM au niveau fédéral *loc m*

federal:[2] ~ **agency issue** *n US (cf federal agency security)* FIN valeur émise par une agence fédérale, fonds d'État *m*, émission d'agence fédérale *f*; ~ **agency security** *n US (cf federal agency issue)* FIN valeur émise par une agence fédérale, fonds d'État *m*, émission d'agence fédérale *f*; ~ **deficit** *n US* ECON déficit budgétaire fédéral *m*, déficit fédéral *m*; ~ **dividend tax credit** *n Can* TAX crédit d'impôt fédéral pour dividendes *m*; ~ **election** *n US* POL élection fédérale *f*; ~ **finance** *n* ECON *US* financement fédéral *m*, *government's system of handling money* finance fédérale *f*, *revenue sharing* redistribution partielle des recettes de l'État *f*, FIN *US* financement fédéral *m*, FIN *US (SYN unconditional grant)* subvention sans condition *f*; ~ **financial program** *n AmE*, ~ **financial programme** *n BrE* ECON programme financier fédéral; ~ **funds** *n pl US* BANK *public money* argent au jour le jour *m*, fonds publics *m pl*, *same-day money* fonds du jour au lendemain *m pl*, FIN argent au jour le jour *m*; ~ **funds rate** *n US* BANK taux des fonds fédéraux *m*, taux interbancaire *m*; ~ **government** *n* POL gouvernement fédéral *m*; ~ **government bond** *n US* STOCK bon du Trésor à long terme *m*, obligation du gouvernement fédéral *f*; ~ **retail sales tax** *n* TAX taxe fédérale sur les ventes au détail *f*; ~ **sales tax**

n TAX taxe de vente fédérale f; ~ **sales tax credit** n Can TAX crédit pour taxe fédérale sur les ventes m; ~ **tribunal** n HRM, LAW tribunal fédéral m

Federal: ~ **Aviation Administration** n US (FAA) TRANSP administration fédérale de l'aviation; ~ **Deposit Insurance Corporation** n US (FDIC) INS company organisme fédéral d'assurance et des dépôts bancaires m; ~ **Express** n TRANSP Federal Express m; ~ **Farm Credit System** n US ECON système de crédit agricole fédéral m; ~ **funds** n pl US BANK fonds de la Réserve Fédérale m pl; ~ **Home Loan Bank Board** n US BANK bureau fédéral bancaire de prêts hypothécaires; ~ **Home Loan Bank System** n US FIN système bancaire fédéral de prêts hypothécaires m; ~ **Home Loan Board** n US FIN bureau fédéral de prêts au logement; ~ **Home Loan Mortgage Corporation** n US (FHLMC) FIN, PROP société fédérale des prêts hypothécaires f; ~ **Housing Administration** n US (FHA) PROP administration fédérale du logement f; ~ **Insurance Contributions Act** n US (FICA) INS loi fédérale sur le financement de l'assurance sociale, acte fédéral sur les cotisations de l'assurance sociale m; ~ **Intermediate Credit Bank** n US BANK, FIN banque fédérale de crédit à moyen terme; ~ **Land Bank** n US BANK banque foncière fédérale; ~ **Maritime Board** n US (FMB) IND bureau maritime fédéral; ~ **Maritime Commission** n US (FMC) TRANSP commission fédérale maritime; ~ **National Mortgage Association** n US (FNMA, Fannie Mae) FIN, PROP association nationale fédérale hypothécaire; ~ **Open Market Committee** n US (FOMC) STOCK commission boursière fédérale du marché libre, ≈ Commission des opérations de Bourse f (France) (COB); ~ **Parliament** n POL parlement fédéral m; ~ **Power Commission** n US (FPC) IND commission fédérale de l'énergie; ~ **Reserve** n US BANK, ECON réserve fédérale f; ~ **Reserve Bank** n US BANK, ECON Banque de la réserve fédérale f, Banque fédérale américaine de réserve f; ~ **Reserve Board** n US (FRB) BANK, ECON conseil d'administration de la Réserve Fédérale; ~ **Reserve note** n US BANK billet de banque émis par la réserve fédérale des USA; ~ **Reserve Open Market Committee** n US ECON, FIN commission boursière fédérale sur le marché libre; ~ **Reserve System** n US BANK, ECON banque centrale des États-Unis; ~ **Savings and Loan Insurance Corporation** n US (FSLIC) BANK caisse nationale d'assurance de l'épargne et des prêts, ≈ société fédérale d'assurance épargne et crédit f; ~ **Trade Commission** n US (FTC) POL commission fédérale du commerce

federalism n POL fédéralisme m

federally:[1] ~ **regulated** adj TAX sous réglementation fédérale

federally:[2] ~ **-regulated exchange** n US STOCK place bourse réglementée par les autorités fédérales f, system échange réglementé par les autorités fédérales m

federated: ~ **company** n HRM société fédérée f

federation n POL fédération f

fee n BANK frais m pl, GEN COMM honoraires m pl, LAW droits m pl, honoraires m pl, redevances f pl, MEDIA for freelance writer honoraires m pl, for journalist pige f, STOCK frais m pl, royalties f pl, rémunération f, tantième m; ~ **-based service** BANK prestation de service f, service payant m; ~ **-for-service policy** ADMIN politique de la rémunération des services f; ~ **income** ACC recettes d'honoraires f pl; ~ **split** ACC of accountancy firm analyse des revenus f; ~ **system** MEDIA publishing rémunération aux honoraires f

feed[1] n COMP alimentation f, avance f; ~ **bin** COMP magasin d'alimentation m; ~ **holes** n pl COMP perforations d'entraînement f pl; ~ **rate** COMP vitesse d'alimentation f

feed[2] vt COMP paper into machine alimenter, faire avancer

feedback n COMMS retour d'information m, COMP remontée de l'information f, retour d'information m, GEN COMM feedback m, information en retour f, réaction f, rétroaction f

feeder n TRANSP caisson de compensation m, feeder m; ~ **line** TRANSP ligne affluente f; ~ **service** TRANSP service d'apport m, service feeder m; ~ **ship** (SYN mother ship) TRANSP collecteur m, navire collecteur m, navire d'apport m, navire d'éclatement m; ~ **vessel** TRANSP collecteur m, navire collecteur m, navire d'apport m, navire d'éclatement m

feedstuffs n pl ECON agricultural aliments pour bétail m pl

feel:[1] ~ **of the market** n GEN COMM idée générale du marché f

feel:[2] ~ **the pinch** phr infrml ECON être à court d'argent, être à sec (infrml)

feel-good: ~ **factor** n GEN COMM, POL sentiment de bien être m

felicific: ~ **calculus** n ECON calcul de satisfaction des utilitaristes m

fellow:~ **candidate** n BrE (cf running mate AmE) POL colistier m; ~ **traveler** n AmE, ~ **traveller** n BrE POL communisant m, compagnon de route m

Fellow: ~ **of the British Association of Accountants and Auditors** n ACC membre de l'association britannique des experts-comptables de société; ~ **of the British Institute of Management** n (FBIM) MGMNT membre de l'institut britannique de gestion; ~ **of the Chartered Association of Certified Accountants** n (FCCA) ACC ≈ membre de l'Association des Comptables d'entreprise certifiés m; ~ **of the Chartered Institute of Management Accountants** n (FCMA) ACC membre de l'institut des comptables de coûts et de gestion; ~ **of the City and Guilds of London Institute** n (FCGI) GEN COMM membre de l'institut britannique de l'enseignement technique; ~ **of the Institute of Actuaries** n (FIA) FIN membre de l'institut des actuaires; ~ **of the Institute of Bankers** n (FIB)

BANK membre de l'institut des banquiers; **~ of the Institute of Chartered Shipbrokers** *n (FICS)* HRM membre de l'institut des courtiers maritimes agréés; **~ of the Institute of Commerce** *n (FCI)* GEN COMM membre de l'institut commercial; **~ of the Institute of Company Accountants** *n UK (FICA)* ACC membre de l'institut des experts-comptables d'entreprise; **~ of the Institute of Export** *n (FIEx)* HRM membre de l'institut des exportateurs; **~ of the Institute of Marine Engineers** *n (FIME)* membre de l'institut des ingénieurs de marine; **~ of the Institute of Personnel Management** *n (FIPM)* HRM membre de l'institut des directeurs du personnel; **~ of the Royal Institute of Chartered Surveyors** *n (FRICS)* GEN COMM membre de l'institut royal d'experts immobiliers

felonious *adj* LAW criminel

fence: **sit on the ~** *phr infrml* GEN COMM ménager la chèvre et le chou *(infrml)*

fend: **~ off** *vt* GEN COMM *question* éluder

ferrous *adj* ENVIR ferreux

ferry *n* TRANSP ferry *m*; **~ berth** TRANSP poste réservé aux transbordeurs *m*; **~ boat** TRANSP ferry *m*, navire transbordeur *m*, transbordeur *m*, traversier *m (Can)*; **~ company** TRANSP compagnie maritime *f*; **~ line** TRANSP compagnie maritime *f*; **~ line manager** HRM directeur de compagnie maritime *m*; **~ ramp** TRANSP rampe de transbordeur *f*

fertilize *vt* ECON, ENVIR fertiliser

fertilizer *n* ECON, ENVIR engrais *m*

FES *abbr UK (Family Expenditure Survey)* ECON *econometrics* enquête annuelle du gouvernement britannique sur les dépenses des familles et ménages

fetch: **~ a good price** *vi* GEN COMM atteindre une jolie somme, faire une jolie somme

feudalism *n* POL féodalisme *m*, féodalité *f*

few: **a ~ francs** *phr* GEN COMM quelques francs

FF *abbr* COMP *(form feed)* changement de page *m*, présentation de feuille *f*, saut de page *m*, GEN COMM *(French franc)* FF *(franc français)*

FFA *abbr (free from alongside)* TRANSP FLB *(franco le long du bord)*

FFCR *abbr (freight forwarder's certificate of receipt)* TRANSP attestation de prise en charge du transitaire *f*

FFI *abbr (for further instructions)* GEN COMM pour toute instruction complémentaire *loc f*

FGA *abbr* GEN COMM *(free of general average)* FAC *(franc d'avaries communes)*, GEN COMM *(foreign general average)* avarie commune étrangère *f*

fh *abbr (first half)* GEN COMM *of month* première quinzaine *f*

FHA *abbr* BANK *UK (Finance House Association)*, FIN *UK (Finance House Association)* association de sociétés de crédit, PROP *US (Federal Housing Administration)* administration fédérale du logement *f*

FHBR *abbr UK (finance house base rate)* FIN taux de base d'une société de crédit

FHEx *abbr (Fridays and holidays excepted)* GEN COMM sauf vendredis et jours fériés, sauf vendredis et périodes de congé

FHLMC *abbr US (Federal Home Loan Mortgage Corporation)* FIN, PROP société fédérale des prêts hypothécaires *f*

fi *abbr (free in)* TRANSP frais de chargement en sus du fret *m pl*, franco chargement

FIA *abbr (Fellow of the Institute of Actuaries)* FIN membre de l'institut des actuaires

FIAS *abbr* STOCK *(Foreign Investment Advisory Service)* service conseil en investissements à l'étranger, TRANSP *(free in and stowed)* bord arrimé, frais de chargement et d'arrimage en sus du fret *m pl*

fiat: **~ money** *n US* BANK, FIN monnaie fiduciaire *f*, monnaie fiduciaire d'appoint *f*

FIB *abbr* BANK *(Fellow of the Institute of Bankers)* membre de l'institut des banquiers, TRANSP *(free into barge)* *shipping* franco allège, TRANSP *(free into bunkers)* *shipping* franco soutes

FIBC *abbr (flexible intermediate and bulk container)* TRANSP conteneur en vrac et intermédiaire articulé *m*

fiber: **~ optic cable** *n AmE see fibre optic cable BrE*; **~ optics** *n pl [+sing v] AmE see fibre optics BrE*

fiberboard *n AmE see fibreboard BrE*

fiberglass *n AmE see fibreglass BrE*

fibre: **~ optic cable** *n BrE* IND câble à fibre optique *m*; **~ optics** *n pl [+sing v] BrE* COMMS *technology* fibre optique *f*, COMP optique des fibres *f*, IND fibre optique *f*

fibreboard *n BrE* IND carton dur *m*; **~ can** *BrE* TRANSP boîte en carton dur *f*

fibreglass *n BrE* IND fibre de verre *f*; **~ covers** *n pl BrE (FC)* TRANSP panneaux de cale en fibre de verre *m pl*

FIBS *abbr (financial information and budgeting systems)* FIN systèmes d'information financière et budgétaire *m pl*

FIC *abbr (free insurance and carriage)* TRANSP franco assurance et transport

FICA *abbr* ACC *UK (Fellow of the Institute of Company Accountants)* membre de l'institut des experts-comptables d'entreprise, INS *US (Federal Insurance Contributions Act)* loi fédérale sur le financement de l'assurance sociale, acte fédéral sur les cotisations de l'assurance sociale *m*

FICS *abbr (Fellow of the Institute of Chartered Shipbrokers)* HRM membre de l'institut des courtiers maritimes agréés

fictitious *adj* GEN COMM fictif

fiddle *vt infrml* GEN COMM trafiquer *(infrml)*

fidelity *n* GEN COMM fidélité *f*; **~ bond** INS assurance de garantie *f*, assurance détournements et escroqueries du fait des employés *f*; **~ guarantee** INS assurance contre les détournements *f*, garantie fidélité *f*; **~ insurance** INS assurance détournement et vol *f*

fiduciarily *adv* LAW fiduciairement

fiduciary *n* LAW fiduciaire *m*, représentant *m*; **~ account** *n* BANK compte en fiducie *m*, compte fiduciaire *m*; **~ activities** *n pl* LAW activités fiduciaires *f pl*; **~ banking** *n* BANK opérations bancaires fiduciaires *f pl*, services bancaires de fiducie *m pl*; **~ bond** *n* LAW garantie fiduciaire *f*; **~ currency** *n* BANK, FIN monnaie fiduciaire *f*; **~ investment** *n* BANK, FIN investissement fiduciaire *m*; **~ issue** *n* BANK émission fiduciaire *f*; **~ operation** *n* BANK opération fiduciaire *f*

field *n* COMP champ *m*, zone *f*, IND domaine *m*, secteur *m*; **~ of activity** GEN COMM branche d'activité *f*, champ d'activité *m*; **~ audit** TAX vérification sur place *f*; **~ of endeavor** *AmE*, **~ of endeavour** *BrE* TAX domaine d'activité *m*; **~ investigator** S&M *market research* enquêteur *m*; **~ operator** GEN COMM homme de terrain *m*; **~ organization** GEN COMM antenne sur le terrain *f*, IMP/EXP *of company* organisation sur le terrain *f*; **~ research** S&M *market research* recherche sur le terrain *f*; **~ sales manager** HRM chef de terrain *m*, directeur des ventes-clientèle *m*; **~ staff** HRM personnel de terrain *m*; **~ support** GEN COMM assistance à la clientèle *f*; **~ survey** S&M *market research* enquête sur le terrain *f*; **~ of taxation** *(SYN tax field)* TAX champ d'imposition *m*, domaine d'imposition *m*, domaine fiscal *m*; **~ testing** S&M essai sur le terrain *m*; **~ theory of motivation** HRM théorie de la motivation par le terrain *f*; **~ trip** WEL *for one day* sortie éducative *f*, *for several days* voyage d'étude *m*, voyage d'étude sur le terrain *m*; **~ worker** S&M *market research* enquêteur sur le terrain *m*

fierce *adj* GEN COMM *competition* acharné

FIEx *abbr (Fellow of the Institute of Export)* HRM membre de l'institut des exportateurs

FIFO *abbr (first in, first out)* ACC *inventory method* PEPS *(premier entré, premier sorti)*

fifth: **~ -generation computer** *n* COMP ordinateur de cinquième génération *m*; **~ wheel** *n* TRANSP *of semitrailer* sellette d'attelage *f*; **~ -wheel coupling** *n* TRANSP *of semitrailer* attelage pivotant *m*, sellette d'attelage *f*

fifty: **~ odd** *phr infrml* GEN COMM cinquante et quelques *(infrml)*

fight *vt* GEN COMM combattre, lutter contre; **~ back** GEN COMM rendre les coups; **~ for** GEN COMM se bagarrer pour *(infrml)*; ♦ **~ a losing battle against** GEN COMM se battre en pure perte contre; **don't ~ the tape** *jarg* STOCK ne pas aller contre la tendance

figurative: **~ device** *n* PATENTS marque combinée *f*

figure *n* ECON, FIN *number* chiffre *m*, GEN COMM *of drawing, number* figure *f*, MATH *number*, S&M chiffre *m*

figures *n pl* GEN COMM *data* chiffres *m pl*, données *f pl*; ♦ **~ adjusted for seasonal variations** GEN COMM données corrigées en fonction des variations saisonnières; **in round ~** GEN COMM en chiffres ronds; **~ out today** GEN COMM chiffres parus aujourd'hui *m pl*

fih *abbr (free in harbor, free in harbour)* TRANSP franco à port

Fiji *pr n* GEN COMM Fidji *f*

Fijian[1] *adj* GEN COMM fidjien

Fijian[2] *n* GEN COMM *person* Fidjien *m*

FIL *abbr (financial intermediary loan)* FIN prêt d'intermédiaire financier *m*, prêt financier intermédiaire *m*

file[1] *n* ADMIN dossier *m*, fichier *m*, ADMIN *(SYN binder, document holder, folder)* classeur *m*, COMP fichier *m*, table d'allocation des fichiers *f*, GEN COMM *(SYN document holder)* classeur *m*; **~ allocation table** *(FAT)* COMP table d'allocation des fichiers *f*; **~ compression** COMP compression de fichiers *f*; **~ conversion** COMP conversion de fichiers *f*; **~ copy** ADMIN exemplaire d'archives *m*; **~ directory** COMP répertoire de fichiers *m*; **~ management** COMP gestion de fichiers *f*; **~ menu** COMP menu fichier *m*; **~ protection** COMP protection de fichiers *f*; **~ server** COMP serveur de fichiers *m*; **~ sharing** COMP partage de fichiers *m*, utilisation collective de fichier *f*; ♦ **~ not found** COMP *message on screen* fichier introuvable

file[2] *vt* ADMIN *document* archiver, classer, GEN COMM *document* soumettre, *document* classer, LAW *a claim* déposer, faire, *document* déposer; **~ away** ADMIN, GEN COMM classer; ♦ **~ an application** GEN COMM faire acte de candidature; **~ a claim** INS déposer une demande, faire une demande; **~ a claim for damages** LAW intenter un procès en dommages-intérêts, poursuivre pour dommages-intérêts; **~ for bankruptcy** ACC déposer le bilan; **~ a lawsuit** LAW engager des poursuites judiciaires, intenter un procès; **~ a return** TAX produire une déclaration; **~ a tax return** TAX envoyer une déclaration d'impôts

filer *n Can* TAX déclarant *m*

filing *n* GEN COMM *clerical duty* classement *m*, LAW *of application* dépôt *m*, TAX *Canada of a return* production *f*; **~ basket** GEN COMM corbeille de rangement *f*; **~ cabinet** ADMIN *for documents* classeur *m*, *for index cards* fichier *m*, GEN COMM classeur *m*; **~ drawer** GEN COMM tiroir classeur *m*; **~ statement** STOCK avenant au dossier d'inscription *m*; **~ system** ADMIN fichage *m*, système de classement des fiches *m*

Filipino *n* GEN COMM *person* Philippin *m*

fill:[1] **~ -or-kill** *n (FOK)* STOCK ordre immédiat *m*

fill[2] *vt* GEN COMM *order* exécuter; **~ in** ADMIN *date* compléter, GEN COMM *form*, IMP/EXP remplir; **~ -or-kill** *(FOK)* STOCK exécuter ou annuler; **~ out** ADMIN compléter, GEN COMM *form* remplir; ♦ **~ a gap** GEN COMM *market* répondre à un besoin; **~ a manpower gap** HRM correspondre à un poste inoccupé; **~ a vacancy** HRM pourvoir un poste; **~ the vacuum** GEN COMM remplir un vide

filler: ~ **advertisement** *n* MEDIA bouche-trou *m*, filler advertisement *m*, publicité bouche-trou *f*; ~ **traffic** *n* TRANSP trafic de remplissage *m*

fill-in *n* HRM remplaçant *m*

fills *n pl* MEDIA *print* ajout *m*, article bouche-trou *m*, filler *m*

film *n* (*cf motion picture AmE, movie*) LEIS, MEDIA film *m*; ~ **advertising** *n* (*cf motion picture advertising AmE*) LEIS, MEDIA publicité cinématographique *f*; ~ **festival** *n* MEDIA festival cinématographique *m*, festival du cinéma *m*, festival du film *m*; ~ **industry** *n* (*cf motion picture industry AmE*) LEIS, MEDIA industrie cinématographique *f*; ~ **-maker** *n* MEDIA cinéaste *mf*, réalisateur *m*; ~ **-making** *n* (*cf cinema BrE, movie-making AmE*) LEIS, MEDIA cinéma *m*; ~ **rights** *n pl* LAW, MEDIA droits cinématographiques *m pl*, droits d'adaptation cinématographique *m pl*; ~ **script** *n* MEDIA scénario *m*; ~ **test** *n* MEDIA bout d'essai *m*

filmsetter *n* MEDIA *typesetting machine* photocomposeuse *f*

filmsetting *n BrE* (*cf photocomposition AmE*) MEDIA *print* photocomposition *f*

filter *n* COMP filtre *m*

filtering: ~ **down** *n US* PROP paupérisation de l'habitat *f*

FIMBRA *abbr UK* (*Financial Intermediaries, Managers and Brokers Association*) FIN association des intermédiaires, gestionnaires et agents financiers

FIME *abbr* (*Fellow of the Institute of Marine Engineers*) HRM membre de l'institut des ingénieurs de marine

fin: ~ **-type stabilizer** *n* (*FIN*) TRANSP stabilisateur à ailerons *m*

FIN *abbr* (*fin-type stabilizer*) TRANSP *shipping* stabilisateur à ailerons *m*

final[1] *adj* GEN COMM final

final:[2] ~ **acceptance** *n* GEN COMM *of goods after testing, usually marking the start of guarantee period* acceptation définitive *f*; ~ **accounts** *n pl* ACC comptes de fin d'exercice *m pl*; ~ **assembly** *n* GEN COMM assemblage définitif *m*; ~ **balance** *n* ACC balance de clôture *f*; ~ **check-in** *n* TRANSP *for passengers* contrôle d'embarquement *m*; ~ **contract settlement price** *n* STOCK *futures* cours de liquidation du contrat final *m*, prix forfaitaire contractuel final *m*; ~ **Court of Appeal** *n* LAW ≈ Cour de cassation *m* (*France*); ~ **demand** *n* ECON, S&M, TAX demande finale *f*; ~ **dividend** *n* STOCK solde de dividende *m*; ~ **goods** *n pl* ECON, GEN COMM, IND produits finis *m pl*; ~ **income** *n* ECON revenu final *m*; ~ **installment** *n BrE* FIN versement libératoire *m*; ~ **instalment** *n AmE see final installment BrE*; ~ **mortgage payment** *n* BANK, FIN solde d'hypothèque *m*; ~ **offer arbitration** *n* ECON, LAW arbitrage par médiateur interposé *m*; ~ **orders** *n* GEN COMM carnet de commandes fermes *m*; ~ **products** *n pl* ECON, GEN COMM, IND produits finis *m pl*; ~ **proof** *n* GEN

COMM, MEDIA *printing, photography* bon à tirer *m*, BAT; ~ **prospectus** *n* STOCK prospectus d'émission définitif *m*; ~ **settlement price** *n* STOCK cours de liquidation *m*; ~ **trading day** *n* STOCK dernier jour de transaction *m*, dernière journée de transactions *f*; ~ **warning** *n* HRM *to employee* dernier avertissement *m*, dernière réprimande *f*

finalize *vt* GEN COMM *contract* conclure, mettre au point, S&M *contract* conclure

finally *adv* GEN COMM finalement

finance[1] *n* FIN finance *f*; ~ **act** *UK* ACC, ECON, FIN, LAW loi de finances *f*; ~ **bill** POL projet de loi des finances *m*; ~ **charge** BANK frais financiers *m pl*; ~ **company** FIN société de crédit *f*, société de financement *f*; ~ **company paper** FIN valeur de société de crédit *f*; ~ **house** *UK* FIN société de crédit *f*, société de financement *f*; ~ **house base rate** *UK* (*FHBR*) FIN taux de base d'une société de crédit; ~ **lease** ACC contrat de crédit-bail *m*; ~ **minister** FIN ministre des Finances *m*; ~ **paper** FIN effet financier *m*, papier de financement *m*, papier financier *m*

finance[2] *vt* FIN financer; ◆ ~ **the difference** ECON financer la différence; ~ **directly** FIN financer directement

Finance: ~ **House Association** *n UK* (*FHA*) BANK, FIN association de sociétés de crédit

finances *n pl* GEN COMM finances *f pl*

financial[1] *adj* FIN financier; ◆ **be in ~ straits** FIN être dans une situation financière difficile; **in ~ difficulty** BANK, ECON, FIN, GEN COMM gêné; **in ~ surplus** ECON, FIN en excédent financier

financial:[2] ~ **accounting** *n* ACC comptabilité de gestion *f*, FIN comptabilité de gestion *f*, comptabilité financière *f*, comptabilité générale *f*; ~ **administration** *n* ACC, ADMIN, FIN, GEN COMM gestion des finances *f*; ~ **administration act** *n* LAW loi de gestion financière *f*; ~ **advertising** *n* S&M publicité financière *f*; ~ **agent** *n* FIN conseiller financier *m*; ~ **aid** *n* ECON, FIN, POL aide financière *f*; ~ **analysis** *n* FIN analyse financière *f*, diagnostic financier *m*; ~ **appraisal** *n* FIN évaluation financière *f*; ~ **asset** *n* FIN actif financier *m*; ~ **assistance** *n* ECON, FIN, POL aide financière *f*, soutien financier *m*; ~ **auditing** *n* ACC vérification comptable *f*; ~ **backer** *n* FIN bailleur de fonds *m*, commanditaire *mf*, GEN COMM, MEDIA commanditaire *mf*; ~ **backing** *n* ECON, FIN, POL appui financier *m*, soutien financier *m*; ~ **balance** *n* ECON tableau économique d'ensemble *m*; ~ **burden** *n* FIN charge financière *f*; ~ **capacity** *n* ACC, BANK, ECON, FIN, GEN COMM capacité financière *f*; ~ **capital** *n* FIN capital financier *m*; ~ **center** *n AmE*, ~ **centre** *n BrE* BANK place bancaire *f*, ECON, FIN centre financier *m*, place financière *f*; ~ **circles** *n pl* FIN milieux financiers *m pl*; ~ **claim** *n* ACC créance financière *f*; ~ **climate** *n* ECON, FIN climat financier *m*; ~ **company** *n* FIN compagnie financière *f*, société financière *f*; ~ **conglomerate** *n* FIN conglomérat financier *m*;

~ **control** n FIN contrôle financier m; ~ **controller** n ACC of organization contrôleur financier m; ~ **correspondent** n MEDIA correspondant financier m; ~ **crisis** n BANK, ECON, FIN crise financière f; ~ **difficulty** n BANK, ECON, FIN, GEN COMM gêne f; ~ **director** n FIN, HRM directeur financier m, responsable financier m; ~ **disclosure** n FIN divulgation financière f; ~ **economy** n ECON, FIN économie financière f; ~ **encumbrance** n FIN charge financière f; ~ **engineering** n FIN ingénierie financière f; ~ **enterprise** n FIN entreprise financière f; ~ **field** n FIN domaine financier m; ~ **firm** n FIN société financière f; ~ **flow** n ACC, ECON, FIN flux financier m; ~ **forecasts** n pl ECON, FIN prévisions financières f pl; ~ **future** n FIN contrat à terme normalisé m, STOCK contrat financier normalisé m, contrat financier à terme m, contrat à terme normalisé m, CATIF; ~ **futures contract** n FIN contrat à terme d'instrument financier m, contrat à terme de taux d'intérêt m, contrat à terme normalisé m, STOCK accord financier à terme m, contrat financier normalisé m, contrat financier à terme m, contrat à terme d'instrument financier m, contrat à terme de taux d'intérêt m, contrat à terme normalisé m, CATIF; ~ **futures market** n STOCK marché financier à terme m, marché à terme d'instruments financiers m (France), marché à terme de titres financiers m; ~ **gearing** n BrE (cf financial leverage AmE) ACC, BANK, FIN, STOCK effet de levier m, levier financier m; ~ **highlights** n pl ACC résultats-clés m pl; ~ **history** n FIN antécédents financiers m pl; ~ **holding company** n FIN société financière de portefeuille f; ~ **holding group** n FIN groupe de portefeuille financier m; ~ **incentive** n FIN stimulation financière f; ~ **industry** n FIN secteur financier m; ~ **information and budgeting systems** n pl (FIBS) FIN systèmes d'information financière et budgétaire m pl; ~ **institution** n FIN institution financière f; ~ **instrument** n FIN instrument financier m; ~ **intermediary** n FIN intermédiaire financier m; ~ **intermediary loan** n (FIL) FIN prêt d'intermédiaire financier m, prêt financier intermédiaire m; ~ **intermediation** n FIN intermédiation financière f; ~ **investment** n ECON, FIN, IND, S&M investissement financier m; ~ **involvement** n FIN intéressement m; ~ **journalism** n FIN, MEDIA presse financière f; ~ **lease** n FIN, GEN COMM, TRANSP bail financier m; ~ **leasing** n BANK, FIN crédit-bail financier m; ~ **leverage** n AmE (cf financial gearing BrE) ACC, BANK, FIN, STOCK effet de levier m, levier financier m; ~ **leverage ratio** n FIN ratio d'endettement financier m, structure du passif financier f, taux d'endettement financier m; ~ **magnate** n FIN magnat de la finance m; ~ **management** n ACC, ADMIN, FIN, GEN COMM, MGMNT gestion des finances f; ~ **management rate of return** n (FMRR) FIN taux de rendement de la gestion financière m; ~ **management report** n FIN, MGMNT rapport de gestion financière m; ~ **management system** n FIN système de gestion

financière m, SGF; ~ **manager** n FIN, HRM directeur financier m, responsable financier m; ~ **market** n ECON place financière f, FIN, STOCK marché des capitaux m, marché financier m, place financière f; ~ **marketplace** n FIN, STOCK marché financier m; ~ **means** n pl FIN fonds m pl, moyens financiers m pl; ~ **muscle** n HRM surface financière f; ~ **news** n FIN, MEDIA informations financières f pl; ~ **officer** n ADMIN agent financier régional m; ~ **package** n FIN ensemble de produits financiers m; ~ **panic** n ECON, FIN panique financière f; ~ **paper** n FIN effet financier m, papier de financement m, papier financier m; ~ **participation scheme** n UK HRM for employees système de participation financière m; ~ **period** n ACC exercice comptable m; ~ **perspective** n ECON, FIN perspectives financières f pl; ~ **planner** n STOCK conseiller en planification financière m; ~ **planning** n FIN, MGMNT plan financier m, planning financier m; ~ **policy** n FIN politique financière f; ~ **position** n ACC situation financière f; ~ **profit or loss** n ACC annual accounts résultat financier m; ~ **pyramid** n FIN pyramide financière f; ~ **ratio** n FIN coefficient financier m; ~ **reporting** n FIN reportage financier m; ~ **requirements** n pl FIN besoins financiers m pl; ~ **responsibility clause** n US INS automobile insurance clause de responsabilité financière f; ~ **review** n FIN, GEN COMM examen financier m; ~ **reward** n FIN, STOCK qualification financière f, récompense financière f; ~ **risk** n FIN, STOCK risque financier m; ~ **sector** n ECON, FIN secteur financier m; ~ **services** n pl FIN services financiers m pl; ~ **services industry** n FIN secteur des services financiers m, services financiers m pl; ~ **signing authority** n FIN pouvoir de signer les documents financiers m; ~ **simulation software** n COMP, FIN logiciel de simulation financière m; ~ **situation** n ACC situation financière f; ~ **sophisticate** n FIN spécialiste des questions financières m; ~ **stability** n ECON, FIN stabilité financière f; ~ **standard** n FIN, GEN COMM norme financière f; ~ **standing** n FIN of company situation financière f; ~ **statement** n ACC état financier m, FIN rapport financier m, état financier m; ~ **statement analysis** n ACC évaluation de la situation d'une entreprise utilisant les états financiers; ~ **strategy** n FIN, GEN COMM stratégie financière f; ~ **strength** n FIN of bank, company force financière f; ~ **structure** n FIN, GEN COMM structure financière f; ~ **summary** n FIN, GEN COMM état financier récapitulatif m; ~ **supermarket** n FIN supermarché de produits financiers m; ~ **support** n ECON, FIN, POL soutien financier m; ~ **support staff** n FIN personnel financier de soutien m; ~ **system** n FIN, GEN COMM système financier m; ~ **verification** n ACC vérification comptable f; ~ **visibility** n FIN transparence financière f; ~ **wizard** n FIN génie de la finance m; ~ **world** n FIN monde de la finance m; ~ **year** n (FY) ACC exercice m, exercice comptable m, exercice financier m, ECON, FIN, POL, TAX starting April 6th année budgétaire f, exercice *m*, exercice financier *m*; ◆ ~ **year ended** TAX exercice clos *m*

Financial: ~ **Accounting Standards Board** *n US (FASB)* ACC commission de normalisation de la comptabilité financière; ~ **Intermediaries, Managers and Brokers Association** *n UK (FIMBRA)* FIN association des intermédiaires, gestionnaires et agents financiers; ~ **Reporting Council** *n UK* ACC Conseil d'information financière *m*; ~ **Reporting Standard** *n (FRS)* ACC norme comptable *f*; ~ **Services Act** *n UK (FSA)* FIN *1986* loi sur les services financiers; ~ **Statement and Budget Report** *n (FSBR)* FIN état financier et rapport budgétaire; ~ **Times** *n UK (FT)* MEDIA *newspaper* Financial Times *m*; ~ **Times Actuaries All Shares Index** *n UK* STOCK indice du Financial Times et de l'Institut des actuaires; ~ **Times Industrial Ordinary Share Index** *n UK (FT Index, FTO)* STOCK indice des actions industrielles ordinaires du Financial Times; ~ **Times Stock Exchange index** *n UK (FT-SE, Footsie)* STOCK indice FTSE des 100 valeurs *m (FTSE)*

financially: ~ **sound** *adj* GEN COMM financièrement solide

financier *n* BANK financier *m*

financing *n* ACC, FIN financement *m*; ~ **adjustment** FIN ajustement multiplicateur *m*; ~ **package** FIN montage financier *m*; ~ **plan** FIN plan de financement *m*; ~ **rate** STOCK *futures pricing* taux de financement *m*

find *vt* COMP rechercher, trouver; ◆ ~ **the balance** STOCK déterminer l'équilibre, établir le bilan; ~ **fault with** GEN COMM trouver à redire à; ~ **sb guilty** LAW reconnaître qn coupable, rendre un verdict de culpabilité; ~ **sb not guilty** LAW reconnaître qn non-coupable, rendre un verdict de non culpabilité

finder's: ~ **fee** *n* GEN COMM commission de démarcheur *f*, S&M *US* honoraires de recherche *m pl*

finding *n* LAW *of investigation, tribunal* conclusion *f*, décision *f*

findings *n pl* LAW *of investigation, tribunal* conclusions *f pl*

fine[1] *n* HRM, LAW amende *f*; ~ **-tuning** COMP *of program* mise au point *f*, ECON *of demand* gestion macroéconomique *f*, réglage *m*

fine:[2] ~ **sb** *phr* LAW condamner qn à une amende

fine-tune *vt* COMP *program* mettre au point, ECON *economy* ajuster en fonction de la demande globale, régler avec précision, GEN COMM mettre au point

finish 1. *vt* GEN COMM conclure, finir, terminer; **2.** *vi* GEN COMM finir, se terminer; ◆ ~ **in the money** STOCK finir par être payant, terminer dans le cours; ~ **work** GEN COMM finir le travail

finished[1] *adj* GEN COMM fini

finished:[2] ~ **goods** *n pl* ECON, GEN COMM, IND produits finis *m pl*; ~ **products** *n pl* ECON, GEN COMM, IND produits finis *m pl*

finite[1] *adj* ENVIR *resources* limité, non-renouvelable

finite:[2] ~ **life real estate investment trust** *n* FIN société d'investissement immobilier à vie *f*

Finland *pr n* GEN COMM Finlande *f*

Finn *n* GEN COMM *person* Finlandais *m*

Finnish[1] *adj* GEN COMM finlandais

Finnish[2] *n* GEN COMM *language* finnois *m*; **the ~** *n pl* GEN COMM les Finlandais *m pl*, les Finnois *m pl*

Fins: the ~ *n pl* GEN COMM les Finlandais *m pl*, les Finnois *m pl*

FIO[1] *abbr (free in and out)* IMP/EXP, TRANSP BAB *(bord à bord)*

FIO:[2] ~ **charter** *n (free-in-and-out charter)* TRANSP *charter party* charte-partie bord à bord *f*; ◆ ~ **and stowed** *(free in, out and stowed)* TRANSP *shipping* bord à bord et arrimage; ~ **and trimmed** *(free in, out and trimmed)* TRANSP *shipping* bord à bord et choulage

FIPM *abbr (Fellow of the Institute of Personnel Management)* HRM membre de l'institut des directeurs du personnel

firavv *abbr (first available vessel)* TRANSP premier navire disponible *m*

fire:[1] ~ **-resistant** *adj (SYN fire-resistive)* GEN COMM coupe-feu; ~ **-resistive** *adj (SYN fire-resistant)* GEN COMM coupe-feu

fire[2] *n* INS incendie *m*; ~ **door** *n* HRM porte coupe-feu *f*; ~ **drill** *n* HRM exercice d'évacuation *m*; ~ **escape** *n* HRM escalier de secours *m*, sortie de secours *f*; ~ **exit** *n* HRM escalier de secours *m*, sortie de secours *f*; ~ **hazard** *n* HRM, IND, INS risque d'incendie *m*; ~ **insuring agreement** *n US* INS concordat incendie risque *m*; ~ **legal liability insurance** *n US* INS *for lessor* assurance de responsabilité locative *f*; ~ **prevention** *n* HRM, IND, INS mesures de sécurité contre incendie *f pl*; ~ **regulations** *n pl* HRM, IND règlements en matière d'incendie *m pl*; ~ **-resistant construction** *n (SYN fire-resistive construction)* ENVIR, IND, INS construction ignifuge *f*, construction à l'épreuve du feu *f*; ~ **-resistive construction** *n (SYN fire-resistant construction)* ENVIR, IND, INS construction ignifuge *f*, construction à l'épreuve du feu *f*; ~ **risk on freight** *n (frof)* TRANSP risque d'incendie sur fret *m*; ~ **screen** *n* GEN COMM écran de cheminée *m*; ~ **tube boiler** *n (FTB)* TRANSP chaudière ignitubulaire *f*, chaudière à tubes de fumée *f*; ~ **-tube boiler survey** *n (FTBS)* TRANSP visite de la chaudière ignitubulaire *f*, visite de la chaudière à tubes de fumée *f*

fire[3] *vt* HRM *employee* vider *(infrml)*, *staff* licencier, lourder qn *(infrml)*, renvoyer, virer *(infrml)*

fireproof *adj* GEN COMM incombustible

firing *n infrml* HRM *of staff* licenciement *m*, renvoi *m*

firm[1] *adj* GEN COMM *order*, STOCK ferme

firm[2] *n* ECON compagnie *f*, entreprise *f*, firme *f*, société *f*, GEN COMM cabinet *m*, compagnie *f*, entreprise *f*, firme *f*, société *f*, MGMNT entreprise *f*, STOCK maison *f*; ~ **belief** GEN COMM conviction *f*;

~ **bid** STOCK demande ferme *f*; ~ **bid price** STOCK cours acheteur ferme *m*; ~ **buyer** (ANT *firm seller*) STOCK acheteur ferme *m*; ~ **commitment** STOCK *securities underwriting* engagement de prise ferme *m*, engagement ferme *m*; ~ **commitment underwriting** STOCK engagement de prise ferme *m*, garantie d'engagement ferme *f*; ~ **consumption** ECON autoconsommation par l'entreprise productrice *f*; ~ **deal** GEN COMM marché ferme *m*; ~ **offer** STOCK offre ferme *f*; ~ **offer price** STOCK cours de vente ferme *m*, cours vendeur ferme *m*; ~ **order** S&M commande ferme *f*; ~ **quotation** STOCK cours ferme *m*; ~ **quote** STOCK cotation ferme *f*, cours ferme *m*; ~ **seller** (ANT *firm buyer*) STOCK vendeur ferme *m*

firm[3] *vi* GEN COMM *currency*, S&M se raffermir

firmness *n* GEN COMM *of market, shares* fermeté *f*, solidité *f*

firmware *n* COMP micrologiciel *m*, microprogramme *m*

first[1] *adj* GEN COMM premier *m*; ~ **-generation** COMP, IND de première génération (*jarg*); ~ **-rate** GEN COMM de première classe; ◆ ~ **in, first out** (*FIFO*) ACC *inventory method* premier entré, premier sorti (*PEPS*)

first[2] ~ **-aid kit** *n* HRM, WEL trousse d'urgence *f*, trousse de premiers secours *f*; ~ **available vessel** *n* (*firavv*) TRANSP premier navire disponible *m*; ~ **best** *n* STOCK optimum de premier rang *m*; ~ **best economy** *n* ECON économie équilibrée à l'optimum de premier rang *f*; ~ **call date** *n* STOCK date de premier appel *f*, première date de remboursement *f*; ~ **carrier** *n* TRANSP premier transporteur *m*; ~ **class** *n* LEIS, TRANSP (ANT *economy class*) première classe *f*; ~ **-class mail** *n* AmE (*cf first-class post BrE*) COMMS courrier au tarif normal *m*; ~ **-class post** *n* BrE (*cf first-class mail AmE*) COMMS courrier au tarif normal *m*; ~ **dealing day** *n* STOCK premier jour des opérations *m*; ~ **economy** *n* ECON, POL économie première *f*; ~ **edition** *n* BrE (*cf bulldog edition AmE*) MEDIA *of newspaper* première édition matinale *f*, édition du matin *f*; ~ **generation** *n* COMP, IND première génération *f*; ~ **-generation computer** *n* COMP ordinateur de première génération *m*; ~ **half** *n* GEN COMM *of year* premier semestre *m*, GEN COMM (*fh*) *of month* première quinzaine *f*; ~ **lien** *n* PROP premier privilège *m*; ~ **-line management** *n* GEN COMM, HRM, MGMNT maîtrise *f*; ~ **mate** *n* HRM second *m*; ~ **mortgage** *n* BANK hypothèque de premier rang *f*, prêt hypothécaire de premier rang *m*, PROP hypothèque de premier rang *f*; ~ **mortgage loan** *n* BANK prêt hypothécaire de premier rang *m*; ~ **name** *n* ADMIN, HRM prénom *m*; ~ **notice day** *n* (ANT *last notice day*) FIN premier jour de notification *m*; ~ **occurrence penalty** *n* TAX pénalité pour première contravention *f*; ~ **owner of copyright** *n* LAW, PATENTS *intellectual property* premier détenteur des droits d'auteur *m*; ~ **preference share** *n* STOCK action privilégiée de

premier rang *f*; ~ **preferred stock** *n* STOCK action privilégiée de premier rang *f*, premières actions privilégiées *f pl*; ~ **quarter** *n* ACC, FIN, GEN COMM premier trimestre *m*; ~ **vice president** *n* HRM premier vice-président *m*

First: ~ **Development Decade** *n* POL première décennie de développement *f*; ~ **World** *n* ECON, POL (ANT *Fourth World, Second World, Third World*) grands pays industrialisés *m pl*

1Q *abbr* (*first quarter*) GEN COMM premier trimestre *m*

FIS *abbr* (*freight, insurance and shipping charges*) IMP/EXP, TRANSP *shipping* fret, assurance et frais d'expédition *m*

fiscal[1] *adj* ACC, ECON, FIN budgétaire, fiscal, GEN COMM budgétaire, POL budgétaire, fiscal

fiscal:[2] ~ **agent** *n* STOCK agent financier *m*; ~ **austerity** *n* ECON austérité budgétaire *f*; ~ **barrier** *n* ECON barrière fiscale *f*; ~ **deficit** *n* ACC déficit budgétaire *m*, déficit financier *m*, ECON, FIN, GEN COMM, POL déficit budgétaire *m*; ~ **drag** *n* TAX décalage fiscal *m*; ~ **equalization** *n* TAX péréquation *f*; ~ **federalism** *n* (SYN *top-sided federalism*) ECON, POL fédéralisme fiscal *m*; ~ **frontier** *n* ECON, POL *EU trade* frontière fiscale *f*; ~ **law** *n* (SYN *law of taxation, tax law*) TAX droit fiscal *m*; ~ **mobility** *n* (SYN *Tiebout hypothesis*) ECON mobilité fiscale *f*; ~ **month** *n* TAX mois d'exercice *m*; ~ **multiplier** *n* ECON multiplicateur fiscal *m*; ~ **offset** *n* TAX compensation financière *f*; ~ **period** *n* FIN exercice financier *m*; ~ **policy** *n* ECON, POL, TAX politique budgétaire *f*, politique fiscale *f*; ~ **projections** *n pl* TAX prévisions financières *f pl*; ~ **quarter** *n* TAX trimestre d'exercice *m*; ~ **surplus** *n* FIN, TAX excédent financier *m*; ~ **year** *n* (*FY*) ACC exercice *m*, exercice comptable *m*, exercice financier *m*, ECON, FIN, POL, TAX *starting October 1st* année budgétaire *f*, exercice *m*, exercice financier *m*; ◆ ~ **year ended** TAX exercice clos *m*; ~ **year then ended** *n* ACC, FIN exercice clos à cette date *m*

fiscalist *n* TAX fiscaliste *mf*

fish: ~ **dock** *n* TRANSP quai réservé aux bateaux de pêche *m*; ~ **farm** *n* ECON, IND élevage piscicole *m*; ~ **farming** *n* ECON, IND pisciculture *f*

Fisher: ~ **effect** *n* ECON effet Fisher *m*; ~ **theorem** *n* ECON hypothèse de Fisher *f*

fishery *n* ECON, GEN COMM, IND pêcherie *f*

fishing *n* ECON, IND pêche *f*; ~ **grounds** *n pl* ECON lieux de pêche *m pl*; ~ **port** *n* ECON, IND port de pêche *m*

fit:[1] ~ **and proper** *adj* LAW ad hoc, adapté, convenable

fit[2] *n* STOCK investissement adapté *m*; ~ **investment** STOCK investissement adapté *m*, investissement sain *m*

fit[3] *vt* GEN COMM *requirements* remplir; ~ **out** GEN COMM *office* équiper, TRANSP *office* armer

fit:[4] **must** ~ *phr* (SYN *must match*) PATENTS

intellectual property doit s'adapter *loc*, obligation d'adaptation *f*

fitment *n* GEN COMM élément encastré *m*

fitness *n* WEL *of staff* adaptation *f*

fitting: ~ **out** *n* TRANSP *of ship* armement *m*; ~ **room** *n* GEN COMM *in shop* salon d'essayage *m*

fittings: ~ **and fixtures** *n pl* GEN COMM installations et agencements *f pl*

five: ~ **-for-one split** *n* STOCK *of shares in capital restructuring* division cinq pour une *f*, partage d'actions cinq pour une *m*; ~ **hundred dollar rule** *n* STOCK règle des cinq cents dollars *f*; ~ **per cent rule** *n* STOCK pratique des cinq pour cent *f*, règle des cinq pour cent *f*; ~ **-pound note** *n* UK *(cf fiver)* FIN billet de cinq livres *m*; ~ **-year formula** *n* BANK formule quinquennale *f*; ~ **-year plan** *n* ACC plan quinquennal *m*

fiver *n infrml* UK *(cf five-pound note)* FIN billet de cinq livres *m*

fiw *abbr (free into wagon)* TRANSP *rail* franco wagon

fix *vt* FIN fixer; ◆ ~ **the price of** S&M fixer le prix de; ~ **quotas** IMP/EXP *for an import* établir des quotas; ~ **up an interview** HRM convenir d'une entrevue

fixation *n* STOCK détermination *f*, fixage *m*

fixed[1] *adj* GEN COMM fixe

fixed:[2] ~ **advance** *n* ACC avance fixe *f*; ~ **annuity** *n* INS rente fixe *f*; ~ **asset assessment** *n* ACC, FIN évaluation des immobilisations *f*; ~ **asset management** *n* ACC, FIN gestion des immobilisations *f*; ~ **asset policy** *n pl* ACC politique d'immobilisation *f*; ~ **assets** *n pl* ACC actif immobilisé *m*, immobilisations *f pl*, valeurs immobilisées *f pl*, FIN, GEN COMM *land, properties, buildings* immobilisations *f pl*; ~ **benefits** *n pl* GEN COMM indemnité fixe *f*; ~ **capital** *n* FIN capital fixe *m*, capital immobilisé *m*; ~ **charge** *n* ACC, ECON, GEN COMM charge fixe *f*, frais fixes *m pl*; ~ **-charge coverage** *n* ACC, FIN taux de couverture des frais financiers fixes *m*; ~ **charges** *n pl* ACC, ECON, GEN COMM frais fixes *m pl*; ~ **cost** *n* ACC, ECON charge fixe *f*, coût fixe *m*, GEN COMM charge fixe *f*; ~ **costs** *n pl* (SYN *indirect costs, overheads*) FIN frais fixes *m pl*; ~ **crane** *n* TRANSP grue fixe *f*; ~ **deposit** *n* BANK dépôt à terme *m*; ~ **disk** *n* COMP *hardware* disque dur *m*, disque fixe *m*; ~ **duty** *n* TAX taxe fixe *f*; ~ **exchange rate** *n* ECON taux de change fixe *m*; ~ **expense** *n* ACC, ECON, GEN COMM charge fixe *f*, frais fixes *m pl*; ~ **expiration date** *n* STOCK *options* date d'échéance fixe *f*; ~ **fee** *n* GEN COMM redevance fixe *f*; ~ **head** *n* TRANSP tête fixe *f*; ~ **hedge** *n* STOCK couverture fixe *f*; ~ **income** *n* STOCK revenu fixe *m*, valeur à revenu fixe *f*; ~ **income investment** *n* STOCK investissement à revenu fixe *m*; ~ **income investment company** *n* FIN compagnie d'investissement à revenu fixe *f*; ~ **income securities market** *n* STOCK marché des valeurs à revenu fixe *m*; ~ **income security** *n* STOCK valeur à revenu fixe *f*; ~ **installment** *n* *AmE*, ~ **instalment** *n* *BrE* FIN

versement fixe *m*; ~ **-interest loan** *n* FIN prêt à intérêt fixe *m*; ~ **-interest security** *n* STOCK valeur à taux fixe *f*; ~ **lashing plate** *n* TRANSP point d'ancrage soudé *m*; ~ **liabilities** *n pl* FIN passif exigible à terme *m*; ~ **link** *n* TRANSP tunnel sous la Manche *m*; ~ **-link span** *n* TRANSP *at ramp berth* rampe d'appontement fixe *f*; ~ **loan** *n* BANK prêt fixe *m*; ~ **maturity** *n* BANK échéance fixée *f*; ~ **overheads** *n pl* ACC, FIN frais généraux fixes *m pl*; ~ **-period deposit** *n* BANK dépôt à période fixée *m*; ~ **place of business** *n* LAW, TAX établissement fixe *m*, établissement fixe d'affaires *m*; ~ **plant** *n* (ANT *flexible plant*) ECON, IND installation fixe *f*; ~ **-point number** *n* MATH nombre à précision déterminée *m*; ~ **premium** *n* INS prime fixe *f*, prime forfaitaire *f*; ~ **price** *n* ACC forfait *m*, S&M prix fixe *m*, STOCK forfait *m*, *put options* prix fixe *m*; ~ **-price contract** *n* S&M contrat prix fixe *m*; ~ **-price offering** *n* STOCK offre forfaitaire *f*; ~ **-rate bond** *n* STOCK bon à taux fixe *m*, obligation à taux fixe *f*, BTF; ~ **-rate loan** *n* BANK emprunt à taux fixe *m*, prêt à taux fixe *m*; ~ **-rate mortgage** *n* BANK hypothèque à taux fixe *f*; ~ **-rate security** *n* STOCK valeur à taux fixe *f*; ~ **route** *n* TRANSP trajet fixe *m*; ~ **salary** *n* HRM salaire fixe *m*; ~ **supply** *n* ECON offre fixe *f*; ~ **tax rate** *n* TAX taux fixe de l'impôt *m*; ~ **-term agreement** *n* HRM accord à durée déterminée *m*, accord à terme fixe *m*; ~ **-term contract** *n* HRM contrat à durée déterminée *m*, CDD; ~ **-term deal** *n* HRM contrat à durée déterminée *m*, CDD; ~ **-term deposit** *n* BANK dépôt à échéance fixe *m*; ~ **-term loan** *n* BANK prêt à durée fixe *m*, prêt à échéance fixée *m*

fixing *n* STOCK *of prices* fixage *m*, fixing *m*, établissement *m*; ~ **of costs** STOCK établissement des frais *m*, établissement des prix *m*; ~ **-up expense** *infrml* PROP *of residence* frais de remise en état *m pl*

fixture *n* PROP agencement *m*; ~ **rate** TRANSP tarif forfaitaire *m*

fixtures: ~ **and fittings** *n pl* ACC reprise *f*

F-key *n* *(function key)* COMP *computer keyboard* touche F *f* *(touche de fonction)*

F/L® *abbr* BrE *(freightliner)* TRANSP *rail* train-bloc de conteneurs *m*

flag[1] *n* COMP drapeau *m*, indicateur *m*, TRANSP pavillon *m*; ~ **of convenience** TRANSP pavillon de complaisance *m*; ~ **discrimination** TRANSP privilège de pavillon *m*

flag[2] *vt* COMP indiquer, signaler

flagging[1] *adj* ECON *demand, economy* en baisse *loc f*

flagging:[2] ~ **out** *n* TRANSP sortie de pavillon *f*

flagship: ~ **site** *n* GEN COMM, S&M site vedette *m*; ~ **store** *n* S&M magasin de prestige *m*

flare: ~ **up** *vi* GEN COMM *anger, trouble* éclater

flash: ~ **of inspiration** *n* GEN COMM éclair de génie *m*; ~ **point in degrees centigrade** *n* *(FP-oC)* GEN COMM point de combustion en degrés Celsius *m*; ~ **point in degrees fahrenheit** *n* *(FP-oF)* GEN

COMM point de combustion en degrés fahrenheit *m*

flat[1] *adj* GEN COMM *dull* plat, terne, *unchanged* fixe, fixé, STOCK *market* calme, stable; ~ **-rate** ECON forfaitaire, inclusive, GEN COMM, INS, S&M forfaitaire

flat[2] *n BrE (cf apartment AmE)* PROP appartement *m*, logement *m*; ~ **-bed** TRANSP véhicule articulé à plate-forme *m*; ~ **bond** STOCK obligation sans intérêt *f*; ~ **car** *US* TRANSP *railway wagon* plate-forme *f*, wagon découvert à bords plats *m* (*vieilli*), wagon plat *m*; ~ **container** TRANSP *container* conteneur plate-forme *m*; ~ **fee** BANK commission fixe *f*, FIN commission forfaitaire *f*; ~ **grant** WEL aide pécuniaire uniforme *f*; ~ **organization** MGMNT organisation uniforme *f*; ~ **quotation** STOCK cotation sans intérêt *f*; ~ **rack** TRANSP *container* conteneur plate-forme *m*; ~ **rate** S&M tarif fixe *m*, tarif non-dégressif *m*, TAX taux uniforme *m*; ~ **-rate bonus** HRM prime forfaitaire *f*, prime non hiérarchisée *f*, prime à taux fixe *f*; ~ **-rate fee** GEN COMM droits à taux fixe *m pl*, redevance forfaitaire *f*, taxe forfaitaire *f*; ~ **rate of pay** HRM taux uniforme de salaire *m*; ~ **-rate price** GEN COMM, S&M prix forfaitaire *m*; ~ **-rate subscription** FIN abonnement à forfait *m*; ~ **-rate tax** TAX impôt forfaitaire *m*; ~ **-rate withholding** TAX prélèvement forfaitaire *m*; ~ **scale** HRM uniformisation des salaires *f*; ~ **sum** STOCK forfait *m*; ~ **tax** TAX impôt uniforme *m*; ◆ **at a ~ price** STOCK à forfait, à solde nul; **at a ~ rate** STOCK *buy, sell* à taux fixe

flatly *adv* GEN COMM *deny* catégoriquement

flatten *vi* MATH *curve* s'aplatir; ~ **out** GEN COMM se stabiliser

flaunt *vt* GEN COMM étaler

flavoring *AmE*, **flavouring** *BrE*: **no** ~ *phr* GEN COMM sans arôme artificiel

flaw *n* GEN COMM défaut *m*, imperfection *f*

flawed *adj* GEN COMM imparfait

fleet *n* TRANSP *of ships, aircraft* flotte *f*; ~ **of cars** TRANSP parc automobile *m*; ~ **manager** HRM *of cars* directeur du parc *m*, directeur du parc automobile *m, of ships, aircraft* directeur de la flotte *m, of trains* directeur du train *m*; ~ **planning** TRANSP *for ships, aircraft* gestion de la flotte *f, for cars* gestion du parc *f*; ~ **policy** INS *for cars* assurance des parcs automobiles *f, for ships, aircraft* police flotte *f*, TRANSP *for cars* assurance des parcs automobiles *f*; ~ **rationalization** TRANSP *of cars* rationalisation du parc *f*, rationalisation du parc automobile *f, of ships, aircraft* rationalisation de la flotte *f*; ~ **utilization** TRANSP utilisation du parc *f*, utilisation du parc automobile *f, of ships, aircraft* utilisation de la flotte *f*

Flemish *n* GEN COMM *language* flamand *m*

flexibility *n* GEN COMM flexibilité *f*, souplesse *f*; ~ **of time** HRM flexibilité des horaires *f*

flexible[1] *adj* GEN COMM flexible, souple

flexible:[2] ~ **accelerator** *n* ECON accélérateur flexible

m; ~ **budget** *n* ECON budget variable *m*; ~ **exchange rate** *n* ECON taux de change flexible *m*; ~ **firm** *n* ECON entreprise flexible *f*, GEN COMM firme souple et mobile *f*; ~ **intermediate and bulk container** *n (FIBC)* TRANSP conteneur en vrac et intermédiaire articulé *m*; ~ **-payment mortgage** *n (FPM)* PROP hypothèque à règlements variables *f*; ~ **plant** *n (ANT fixed plant)* ECON, IND installation flexible *f*; ~ **-rate term deposit** *n* BANK dépôt à terme à intérêt flexible *m*, dépôt à terme à intérêt variable *m*; ~ **schedule** *n* HRM horaire flexible *m*; ~ **steel wire rope** *n* TRANSP *cargo handling equipment* câble souple en fils d'acier *m*; ~ **time** *n* HRM flexibilité des horaires *f*; ~ **working hours** *n pl* HRM flexibilité des horaires *f*, horaires aménagés *m pl*, horaires de travail à la carte *m pl*, horaires à la carte *m pl*

flexitime *n* HRM flexibilité des horaires *f*, horaires aménagés *m pl*, horaires de travail à la carte *m pl*, horaires à la carte *m pl*

flexprice *n* ECON, GEN COMM prix flexible *m*

flextime *n* HRM flexibilité des horaires *f*, horaires aménagés *m pl*, horaires de travail à la carte *m pl*, horaires à la carte *m pl*

flick *vt* COMP *screen* scintiller

flicker:[1] ~ **-free** *adj* COMP *screen* sans scintillement

flicker[2] *n* COMP *of screen* scintillement *m*

flier *n see flyer*

flight *n* TRANSP vol *m*; ~ **attendant** TRANSP *(SYN air hostess) female* hôtesse de l'air *f*, TRANSP *(SYN steward) male* steward *m*; ~ **of capital** ECON fuite de capitaux *f*; ~ **coupon** *jarg* TRANSP coupon de vol *m*; ~ **from money** ECON fuite devant la monnaie *f*; ~ **information** TRANSP informations de vol *f pl*; ~ **number** TRANSP numéro de vol *m*; ~ **scheduler** TRANSP programmateur de vol *m*; ~ **stage** TRANSP tronçon de vol *m*, étape de vol *f*; ~ **strategy** TRANSP stratégie de vol *f*; ~ **ticket** TRANSP coupon de vol *m*; ~ **time** TRANSP temps de vol *m*; ~ **time information** TRANSP horaires des vols *m pl*; ~ **to quality** STOCK fuite vers la qualité *f*

flip: ~ **chart** *n* GEN COMM, S&M chevalet à feuilles mobiles *m*, flip-chart *f*, tableau à feuilles mobiles *m*

flip-flop *n* COMP *hardware* bascule *f*, bascule électronique *f*, TRANSP *containers* bascule *f*; ~ **arbitration** HRM arbitrage par compensations successives *m*, changements d'avis successifs *m pl*, virages à 180 degrés *m pl*

float:[1] ~ **time** *n* BANK, IMP/EXP jours de valeur *m pl*

float[2] **1.** *vt* GEN COMM créer, STOCK *currency* laisser flotter, *new issue* introduire en bourse, lancer; **2.** *vi* BANK *rate* fluctuer; ◆ ~ **a loan** BANK émettre un emprunt

floater *n* INS *US* contrat d'abonnement *m*, garantie à tous endroits *f*, STOCK *US* obligation à taux variable *f*

floating[1] *adj* BANK *interest rate, exchange rate* flottant

floating[2] *n* STOCK *of bond issues, stock* émission *f*;

~ berth *n* TRANSP poste flottant *m*; **~ cargo policy** *n* INS, TRANSP police flottante *f*, police maritime flottante *f*; **~ crane** *n* TRANSP ponton-grue *m*; **~ currency** *n* ECON, FIN devise flottante *f*; **~ currency exchange rate** *n* ECON taux de change flottant *m*; **~ debt** *n* FIN dette flottante *f*; **~ dock** *n* TRANSP dock flottant *m*; **~ exchange rate** *n* ECON taux de change flottant *m*; **~ interest rate** *n* BANK, ECON *of exchange* taux d'intérêt flottant *m*, taux d'intérêt variable *m*, taux flottant *m*, taux variable *m*; **~ marine policy** *n* (*FP*) INS, TRANSP *shipping* police flottante *f*, police maritime flottante *f*; **~ -point number** *n* MATH nombre en virgule flottante *m*; **~ policy** *n* INS contrat d'abonnement *m*, police d'abonnement *f*; **~ production, storage and off-loading vessel** *n* (*FPSO*) TRANSP *ship* navire de production, stockage et déchargement au large *m*; **~ production system** *n* (*FPS*) TRANSP système de production au large *m*; **~ production vessel** *n* (*FPV*) TRANSP *ship* navire de production au large *m*; **~ rate** *n* BANK, ECON *of interest, exchange* taux flottant *m*, taux variable *m*; **~ rate bond** *n* STOCK BTV, bon à taux variable *m*; **~ -rate debenture** *n* STOCK obligation à taux flottant *f*, obligation à taux variable *f*; **~ -rate deposit** *n* STOCK *interest-rate futures* dépôt à taux flottant *m*, dépôt à taux variable *m*; **~ -rate investment** *n* STOCK *interest-rate futures* investissement à taux flottant *m*, investissement à taux variable *m*; **~ -rate loan** *n* BANK emprunt à taux flottant *m*, emprunt à taux variable *m*; **~ -rate note** *n* (*FRN*) STOCK obligation à taux flottant *f*, obligation à taux variable *f*; **~ -rate preferred share** *n* STOCK action privilégiée à taux flottant *f*, valeur privilégiée à taux variable *f*; **~ -rate security** *n* STOCK valeur à taux flottant *f*, valeur à taux variable *f*; **~ securities** *n pl* STOCK titres non achetés *m pl*, valeurs de spéculation *f pl*, valeurs variables *f pl*; **~ stock** *n* STOCK flottant *m*, offre flottante *f*; **~ supply** *n* STOCK flottant *m*, offre flottante *f*; **~ voter** *n* POL électeur girouette *m* (*infrml*)

flog *vt infrml BrE* GEN COMM fourguer (*infrml*)

flood: **~ insurance** *n* INS assurance contre les inondations *f*; **~ plain** *n* PROP terres inondables *f*

floodable: **~ length** *n* TRANSP longueur envahissable *f*

floor *n* ECON, FIN *lowest price* garantie de taux plancher *f*, plancher *m*, GEN COMM, IND *of room* plancher *m*, STOCK *lowest price* garantie de taux plancher *f*, plancher *m*, *of stock exchange* parquet *m*, TRANSP *of ship* varangue *f*; **~ -area ratio** MATH *property* rapport sol-terrain *m*; **~ bearing** TRANSP *of ship* portée du plancher *f*; **~ broker** STOCK courtier membre du parquet *m*; **~ loading** TRANSP *of ship* charge sur le plancher *f*; **~ loan** FIN prêt minimum *m*; **~ official** STOCK autorité du parquet *f*, fonctionnaire boursier *m*; **~ plan** PROP *of rooms* plan d'étage *m*; **~ plan insurance** INS assurance de plan d'étage *f*; **~ planning** BANK planification de base *f*; **~ price** ECON, FIN prix plancher *m*, GEN COMM, S&M mise à prix *f*, STOCK prix plancher *m*; **~ rate** STOCK *interest-rate futures* taux plancher *m*; **~ return** STOCK *interest-rate futures* rapport plancher *m*; **~ space** PROP espace habitable *m*, surface au sol *f*; **~ trader** STOCK *exchange trading* négociant courtier de parquet *m*, négociant du parquet *m*, négociateur individuel de parquet *m*, NIP

flooring *n* BANK planification de base *f*

flop *n infrml* LEIS *theatre, film* navet *m* (*infrml*); ◆ **be a ~** LEIS faire un bide

floppy *n* ADMIN, COMP disque souple *m*, disquette *f*; **~ disk** ADMIN COMP disque souple *m*, disquette *f*; **~ disk drive** ADMIN, COMP lecteur de disques souples *m*, lecteur de disquettes *m*, unité de disque souple *f*, unité de disquette *f*

florin *n* GEN COMM florin *m*, gulden *m*

flotation *n* STOCK lancement *m*, émission *f*; **~ cost** STOCK frais d'émission *m pl*, frais de lancement *m pl*

flotsam *n* TRANSP épave flottante *f*

flourish *vi* GEN COMM *business, competition* prospérer, être florissant

flourishing *adj* GEN COMM florissant

flow[1] *n* ACC *of funds* flux *m*, variation *f*, COMP *of data* circulation *f*, flot *m*, *of operations* déroulement *m*, ECON, FIN *of money* flux *m*, GEN COMM flux *m*, *of orders* afflux *m*, TRANSP *of goods or passenger traffic* flux *m*; **~ chart** COMP ordinogramme *m*, organigramme *m*, GEN COMM organigramme *m*, MATH graphique d'acheminement *m*, graphique d'évolution *m*, graphique de circulation *m*, MGMNT diagramme *m*, graphique d'acheminement *m*, graphique d'évolution *m*, graphique de circulation *m*; **~ concept** STOCK concept d'écoulement *m*; **~ control** COMP commande de flux *f*, contrôle de flux *m*; **~ diagram** MATH diagramme de circulation *m*, organigramme *m*, MGMNT diagramme de circulation *m*; **~ of funds** ACC *balance* flux de trésorerie *m*, flux financier *m*, mouvements de fonds *m pl*, ECON, FIN flux de capitaux *m*, flux de trésorerie *m*, flux financier *m*, STOCK *municipal bonds* mouvements de fonds *m pl*, utilisation des fonds *f*; **~ line** GEN COMM, MATH ligne de production *f*, TRANSP *of pallets* ligne de liaison *f*; **~ of money** ECON, FIN flux monétaire *m*; **~ -of-funds account** ECON, FIN compte des flux financiers *m*; **~ -of-funds table** FIN *national accounts* tableau des opérations financières *m*, TOF; **~ of orders** GEN COMM afflux de commandes *m*; **~ process chart** MATH, MGMNT diagramme de circulation *m*, graphique d'acheminement *m*, graphique d'évolution *m*, graphique de circulation *m*; **~ production** IND fabrication à la chaîne *f*; **~ -through** *US* TAX *method of accounting* transfert *m*; **~ -through basis** TAX méthode de l'impôt exigible *f*; **~ -through share** STOCK action accréditive *f*; ◆ **go with the ~** HRM suivre le mouvement

flow^2 *vi* FIN *capital, money* affluer; ~ **out** ECON *money* sortir; ◆ ~ **out of the country** ECON *money* sortir du pays

flower: ~ **bond** *n* STOCK obligation à fleur

fl.oz *abbr (fluid ounce)* GEN COMM once liquide *f*

FLSA *abbr US (Fair Labor Standards Act)* LAW réglementation fédérale du droit du travail

FLT *abbr (fork-lift truck)* TRANSP chariot élévateur à fourche *m*

fluctuate *vi* GEN COMM fluctuer, varier, STOCK *price of shares, rate of exchange* fluctuer

fluctuating: ~ **currency** *n* ECON, FIN devise flottante *f*

fluctuation *n* ECON *of economy* fluctuation *f*, GEN COMM *of prices, interest rates* fluctuation *f*, variation *f*, STOCK *of prices, interest rates* variation *f*; ~ **band** ECON *ERM* marge de flottement *f*, marge de fluctuation *f*; ~ **limit** STOCK limite de fluctuation *f*, limite de variation *f*, limite de variation des cours *f*, écart maximal de cours *m*

fluid: ~ **ounce** *n (fl.oz)* GEN COMM once liquide *f*

flurry: ~ **of activity** *n* STOCK agitation *f*

flush:^{1} ~ **left** *adj* (ANT *flush right*) COMMS, COMP *document, printing*, MEDIA aligné à gauche, au fer à gauche, justifié à gauche; ~ **right** *adj* (ANT *flush left*) COMMS, COMP *document, printing*, MEDIA aligné à droite, au fer à droite, justifié à droite

flush:^{2} ~ **deck** *n* TRANSP pont ras *m*; ~ **deck socket** *n* TRANSP socle à plat pont *m*

flutter: **have a** ~ *phr infrml UK* GEN COMM *gamble* parier, STOCK *on stock market* boursicoter

flux *n* GEN COMM flux *m*

fly:^{1} ~ **-cruise** *n* LEIS forfait vol-croisière *m*; ~ **posting** *n* S&M affichage sauvage *m*; ~ **tipping** *n* ENVIR décharge illégale *f*

fly^2 *vi* TRANSP voler

flyer *n* MEDIA *advertisement* prospectus *m*, tract *m*, STOCK *speculative transaction* spéculation au hasard

flying: ~ **bridge** *n* TRANSP *of ship* passerelle haute *f*; ~ **doctor** *n* *Australia* WEL médecin long-courrier *m*, médecin volant *m*; ~ **pickets** *n pl* HRM piquets de grève *m pl*; ~ **visit** *n* GEN COMM visite éclair *f*

flyleaf *n* MEDIA *print* page de garde *f*

fm *abbr (fathom)* GEN COMM *unit of measurement of timber* brasse *f*

FM *abbr (frequency modulation)* COMMS FM *(modulation de fréquence)*

FMB *abbr US (Federal Maritime Board)* IND bureau maritime fédéral

FMC *abbr US (Federal Maritime Commission)* TRANSP commission fédérale maritime

FMCG *abbr (fast-moving consumer goods)* S&M biens de consommation courante *m pl*, produits de grande consommation à forte rotation *m pl*

FMRR *abbr (financial management rate of return)* FIN taux de rendement de la gestion financière *m*

FNMA *abbr US (Fannie Mae, Federal National Mortgage Association)* FIN, PROP association nationale fédérale hypothécaire

fo *abbr* GEN COMM *(for orders)* pour instructions *loc f*, TRANSP *(free out terms)* frais de déchargement en sus du fret *m pl*, TRANSP *(free overboard, free overside)* franco sous palan

FOA *abbr* GEN COMM *US (Foreign Operations Administration)* administration des opérations à l'étranger, TRANSP *(free on aircraft)* FAB aéroport *(franco à bord aéroport)*

FOB^1 *abbr (free on board)* TRANSP *cargo delivery* FAB *(franco à bord)*; ~ **& T** *(free on board and trimmed)* TRANSP franco à bord et arrimé

FOB:^{2} ~ **airport** *n (free on board airport)* TRANSP FAB aéroport *(franco à bord aéroport)*

FOC *abbr (free of charge)* GEN COMM franco, gratis, gratuit, gratuitement

focal: ~ **point** *n* GEN COMM *of discussion* point central *m*

focus^1 *n* GEN COMM point focal *m*; ~ **group** POL, S&M *market research* groupe cible *m*, point central *m*

focus^2 *vt* GEN COMM concentrer, focaliser; ~ **on** GEN COMM se concentrer sur; ~ **upon** GEN COMM se concentrer sur; ◆ ~ **one's attention on** GEN COMM concentrer son attention sur

FOD *abbr (free of damage)* GEN COMM intact, INS sans avaries

FOE *abbr (Friends of the Earth)* ENVIR ≈ Amis de la Terre *m pl*

FOIA *abbr US (Freedom of Information Act)* LAW loi sur la liberté de l'information

FOK^1 *n (fill-or-kill)* STOCK ordre immédiat *m*

FOK^2 *vt (fill-or-kill)* STOCK exécuter ou annuler

folder *n* ADMIN (SYN *binder, document holder, file*), GEN COMM (SYN *document holder*) classeur *m*

folding: ~ **lashing plate** *n* TRANSP *lashing equipment* plaque d'accrochage de saisine rabattable *f*

follow:^{1} ~ **-up** *n* GEN COMM rappel *m*, relance *f*, suivi *m*; ~ **-up letter** *n* COMMS lettre de rappel *f*, lettre de relance *f*, S&M lettre de relance *f*

follow^2 *vt* GEN COMM, MATH *curve* suivre; ~ **up** GEN COMM *request, suggestion, wish* donner suite à, GEN COMM assurer le suivi, poursuivre, suivre, MGMNT poursuivre; ◆ ~ **the fortunes** INS *re-insurance* suivre les fortunes; ~ **the path of** GEN COMM suivre la voie de; ~ **a similar pattern** GEN COMM *of demand* suivre un modèle similaire; ~ **suit** GEN COMM faire de même; ~ **sth through** GEN COMM *project, scheme* aller jusqu'au bout de qch, mener qch à terme, poursuivre jusqu'au bout

follower *n* GEN COMM disciple *m*

following: ~ **day** *n* GEN COMM lendemain *m*

follows: **as** ~ *phr* COMMS, GEN COMM comme suite *loc f*

FOMC *abbr US (Federal Open Market Committee)* STOCK commission boursière fédérale du marché libre, ≈ COB (*France*) (*Commission des opérations de Bourse*)

font *n* COMP *typography*, MEDIA *print* fonte *f*, jeu de caractères *m*, police *f*, police de caractères *f*; ~ **family** COMP *typography*, MEDIA *print* famille de caractères *f*; ~ **file** COMP fichier de caractères *m*

food: ~ **aid** *n* ECON, POL *development assistance* aide alimentaire *f*; ~ **chain** *n* ECON, ENVIR chaîne alimentaire *f*; ~ **law** *n* LAW législation relative à l'alimentation *f*; ~ **processing** *n* IND traitement des denrées alimentaires *m*; ~ **-processing industry** *n* ECON, ENVIR agroalimentaire *m*, IND agroalimentaire *m*, industrie alimentaire *f*; ~ **retailing** *n* S&M commerce alimentaire de détail *m*; ~ **store** *n* S&M magasin d'alimentation *m*; ~ **surplus** *n* [pl -ses] ECON excédent alimentaire *m*

Food: ~ **and Agriculture Organization** *n* (*FAO*) ECON Organisation pour l'alimentation et l'agriculture *f*; ~ **and Drug Administration** *n* US (*FDA*) ADMIN office des produits alimentaires et pharmaceutiques

foodstuffs *n pl* ECON, GEN COMM, IND aliments *m pl*, produits alimentaires *m pl*

foot *n* [pl feet] (*ft*) GEN COMM pied *m*

football: ~ **pools** *n* LEIS loto sportif sur les résultats des matchs de football

footer *n* COMP *of document* bas de page *m*, pied de page *m*, titre de bas de page *m*

footing *n* US MATH addition *f*; ◆ **on the same** ~ GEN COMM sur le même pied

footloose: ~ **industry** *n* (ANT *locked-in industry*) IND industrie libre *f*, industrie sans entraves *f*

footnote *n* COMP *document* note en bas de page *f*, GEN COMM renvoi *m*; ~ **disclosure** ACC divulgation notée en bas de page *f*

Footsie *abbr* UK (*FT-SE 100 Share index, Financial Times Stock Exchange index*) STOCK indice Footsie *m* (*indice FTSE des 100 valeurs*)

FOQ *abbr* (*free on quay*) TRANSP *shipping* FAQ (*franco à quai*)

FOQ-FOQ *abbr* (*free on quay to free on quay*) TRANSP franco à quai - franco à quai

f.o.r. *abbr* (*free on rail*) TRANSP franco gare, franco sur rail, franco wagon

Forbes: ~ **500** *n* GEN COMM *annual listings by Forbes magazine of the largest US publicly-owned corporations ranked four ways: by sales, assets, profits and market value* les 500 de Forbes

forbid *vt* GEN COMM défendre

force:[1] ~ **majeure** *n* GEN COMM, LAW force majeure *f*; ◆ **come into** ~ GEN COMM entrer en vigueur, être applicable, LAW *act, regulation, rule* entrer en vigueur

force[2] *vt* GEN COMM contraindre, forcer; ~ **down** ECON *interest rates* faire baisser; ◆ **be in** ~ GEN COMM être en vigueur; ~ **into early retirement** HRM mettre en préretraite obligatoire; ~ **the issue** GEN COMM brusquer la question; ~ **sb to do sth** GEN COMM contraindre qn à faire qch, forcer qn à faire qch, obliger qn à faire qch

forced: ~ **currency** *n* ECON, FIN, STOCK cours forcé *m*; ~ **draft** *n* AmE, ~ **draught** *n* BrE (*fd*) TRANSP *combustion control* tirage forcé *m*; ~ **landing** *n* TRANSP *of aircraft* atterrissage forcé *m*; ~ **sale of stock** *n* GEN COMM, LAW *in reserves*, S&M vente forcée de marchandises *f*; ~ **savings** *n pl* ECON, FIN épargne forcée *f*

forceful *adj* GEN COMM *argument* de poids *loc m*

forcible: ~ **entry** *n* LAW *by police* perquisition *f*, *by thief* effraction *f*

Fordism *n* ECON fordisme *m*

fore:[1] ~ **-and-aft** *adj* TRANSP de l'avant à l'arrière *loc m*

fore:[2] ~ **peak tank** *n* (*FPT*) TRANSP *of ship* coqueron avant *m*; ◆ **come to the** ~ GEN COMM se mettre en évidence

forecast *n* ACC, ECON, FIN, GEN COMM prévision *f*, étude prévisionnelle *f*, LEIS *sport* pronostic *m*, MATH, S&M *marketing* prévision *f*, étude prévisionnelle *f*

forecaster *n* GEN COMM prévisionniste *mf*

forecasting *n* ACC prévision *f*, ECON prévision *f*, *long term* prospective *f*, FIN, MATH, S&M *marketing* prévision *f*

forecastle *n* TRANSP *of ship* gaillard *m*, plage avant *f*

foreclose *vt* FIN, LAW saisir; ◆ ~ **a mortgage** FIN saisir un bien hypothéqué

foreclosure *n* LAW *action* forclusion *f*, saisie *f*, saisie d'un bien hypothéqué *f*; ~ **sale** S&M vente sur saisie *f*

forefront: **at the** ~ *phr* IND *of research and development* à l'avant-garde *loc f*, à la pointe *loc f*

forego *vt* GEN COMM renoncer à; ◆ ~ **a debt** FIN, GEN COMM remettre une dette

foreground[1] *adj* COMP d'avant-plan *loc m*, de premier plan

foreground[2] *n* COMP avant-plan *m*, premier plan *m*; ~ **program** COMP programme prioritaire *m*

foreign[1] *adj* GEN COMM étranger; ~ **-controlled** GEN COMM sous contrôle étranger; ~ **-going** TRANSP *vessel* long-courrier; ~ **-owned** GEN COMM sous contrôle étranger

foreign:[2] ~ **account** *n* BANK compte étranger *m*, compte à l'étranger *m*; ~ **accrual tax** *n* TAX impôt étranger accumulé *m*; ~ **affairs** *n pl* POL affaires étrangères *f pl*; ~ **affiliate** *n* STOCK filiale étrangère *f*; ~ **agent** *n* GEN COMM agent à l'étranger *m*; ~ **aid** *n* ECON, POL aide étrangère *f*, aide à l'étranger *f*; ~ **assets** *n pl* STOCK avoirs extérieurs *m pl*, avoirs étrangers *m pl*, créances sur l'étranger *f pl*, dépôts étrangers *m pl*; ~ **bank** *n* BANK banque étrangère *f*; ~ **banking** *n* BANK banque à l'étranger *f*, commerce de banque à l'étranger *m*, opérations bancaires étrangères *f pl*; ~ **bill** *n* BANK facture de l'étranger *f*; ~ **bond** *n* ECON, FIN, STOCK obligation étrangère *f*; ~ **borrowing** *n* BANK emprunts étrangers *m pl*; ~ **branch** *n* BANK filiale étrangère *f*; ~ **buying house** *n* IMP/EXP maison d'achat étrangère *f*; ~ **check issue** *n* AmE, ~ **cheque**

issue n BrE BANK émission de chèque sur l'étranger f; ~ **company** n GEN COMM, LAW société étrangère f; ~ **competitor** n ECON, GEN COMM, S&M concurrent étranger m; ~ **-controlled bank** n BANK banque sous contrôle étranger f; ~ **-controlled enterprise** n GEN COMM entreprise sous contrôle étranger f; ~ **corporation** n GEN COMM, LAW société de droit étranger f, société étrangère f; ~ **correspondent** n MEDIA correspondant à l'étranger m, envoyé permanent à l'étranger m; ~ **currency** n ECON monnaie étrangère f, FIN, GEN COMM devise f, devise étrangère f, monnaie étrangère f; ~ **currency allowance** n FIN allocation de devises f; ~ **currency loan** n ECON, FIN prêt en devises étrangères m; ~ **currency outflow** n ECON sortie de devises étrangères f; ~ **currency transaction** n BANK, ECON, FIN transaction en devises f; ~ **currency translation** n ECON conversion de devises f; ~ **currency translation reserve** n ACC annual accounts écart de conversion m; ~ **currency unit** n BANK, ECON, FIN unité de compte étrangère f; ~ **demand** n ECON, S&M demande étrangère f; ~ **dividends** n pl STOCK dividendes étrangers m pl; ~ **editor** n MEDIA chef du service étranger m; ~ **emission** n ENVIR, IND pollution émission étrangère f; ~ **exchange** n (forex) BANK currency devises f pl, BANK, ECON, FIN change m, opération de change f, STOCK change m, devises f pl; ~ **exchange account** n BANK, FIN compte d'opérations de change m, compte en devises m; ~ **exchange advisory service** n BANK, FIN, STOCK service de conseil des devises m; ~ **exchange broker** n BANK, FIN, STOCK cambiste mf, courtier en devises m; ~ **exchange deal** n STOCK opération de change f, opération sur des devises f; ~ **exchange dealer** n BANK, FIN, STOCK cambiste mf, courtier en devises m; ~ **exchange department** n BANK, FIN, STOCK service du change m; ~ **exchange earner** n GEN COMM personne rémunérée en devises étrangères; ~ **exchange hedge** n ACC couverture de change f; ~ **exchange holdings** n pl BANK avoirs en devises m pl; ~ **exchange market** n FIN marché des changes m; ~ **exchange office** n BANK bureau de change m; ~ **exchange reserves** n pl ECON réserves de change f pl, réserves en devises f pl; ~ **exchange risk** n ECON, FIN risque de change m; ~ **exchange trader** n BANK, FIN, STOCK cambiste mf; ~ **firm** n GEN COMM entreprise étrangère f, firme étrangère f, société étrangère f, LAW société étrangère f; ~ **flag** n TRANSP pavillon étranger m; ~ **general average** n (FGA) GEN COMM avarie commune étrangère f; ~ **-going passenger ship** n TRANSP long-courrier à passagers m; ~ **-going passenger vessel** n TRANSP long-courrier à passagers m; ~ **-going ship** n TRANSP long-courrier m; ~ **-going vessel** n TRANSP long-courrier m; ~ **government** n POL gouvernement étranger m; ~ **income** n TAX revenu de source étranger m; ~ **investment** n FIN investissement à l'étranger m, GEN COMM investissement étranger m, investissement à

l'étranger m, placement étranger m, STOCK investissement à l'étranger m; ~ **investment income** n FIN, TAX revenu de placements étrangers m; ~ **investment limit** n FIN plafond des investissements à l'étranger m; ~ **investor** n FIN investisseur étranger m; ~ **language** n GEN COMM langue étrangère f; ~ **market** n ECON marché étranger m, S&M marché extérieur m, marché étranger m; ~ **merger** n GEN COMM, STOCK fusion avec une entreprise étrangère f, unification étrangère f; ~ **minister** n POL ministre des Affaires étrangères m; ~ **money order** n BANK mandat de l'étranger m; ~ **national** n ADMIN, HRM ressortissant étranger m; ~ **-owned bank** n BANK banque étrangère f; ~ **-owned company** n GEN COMM une firme sous contrôle étranger f; ~ **-owned container** n TRANSP conteneur sous contrôle étranger m; ~ **property** n TAX bien étranger m; ~ **sales** n pl S&M vente à l'étranger f; ~ **section** n STOCK marché étranger m, section étrangère f; ~ **security** n STOCK valeur de société étrangère f, valeur étrangère f; ~ **share** n STOCK action de société étrangère f, action étrangère f; ~ **stock** n STOCK action de société étrangère f, action étrangère f; ~ **student** n HRM, WEL étudiant étranger m; ~ **tax** n TAX impôt étranger m; ~ **tax carry-over** n TAX report d'impôt étranger m; ~ **tax credit** n TAX crédit pour impôt étranger m; ~ **trade** n ECON, GEN COMM, IMP/EXP commerce extérieur m; ~ **trade multiplier** n ECON multiplicateur du commerce extérieur m; ~ **trade surplus** n ECON, IMP/EXP excédent commercial étranger m, excédent du commerce extérieur m; ~ **venture** n GEN COMM implantation à l'étranger f; ~ **worker** n HRM, WEL travailleur étranger m

Foreign: ~ **and Commonwealth Office** n UK (FCO) ADMIN ≈ ministère des Affaires étrangères et du Commonwealth m; ~ **Investment Advisory Service** n (FIAS) STOCK service conseil en investissements à l'étranger; ~ **Operations Administration** n US (FOA) GEN COMM administration des opérations à l'étranger; ~ **Secretary** n UK POL ≈ ministre des Affaires étrangères m

foreigner n GEN COMM étranger m

foreman n [pl -men] HRM chef d'équipe m, contremaître m

forename n ADMIN, HRM prénom m

forepeak n TRANSP of ship coqueron avant m, peak avant m

foresee vt GEN COMM prédire

foreseeable[1] adj GEN COMM prévisible; ◆ **in the ~ future** GEN COMM dans un avenir prévisible

foreseeable:[2] ~ **risk** n STOCK risque envisageable m, risque prévisible m

foreshore n LAW laisse de mer f

forest n ECON, ENVIR, IND bois m, forêt f

forestry n ENVIR, IND sylviculture f

Forestry: ~ **Commission** n UK ENVIR, IND ≈ les Eaux et Forêts f pl

forewoman n [pl -men] HRM contremaîtresse f

forex *n (foreign exchange)* BANK *currency* devises *f pl*; ~ **option** *(FX option)* STOCK option de change *f*, option sur devises *f*; ~ **trading** BANK *merchant* opérations en devises *f pl*

forfaiting *n* ECON, FIN *international trade* affacturage à forfait *m*, IMP/EXP vente à forfait *f*

forfeit *vt* GEN COMM perdre par confiscation

forfeited: ~ **security** *n* INS cautionnement perdu *m*

forfeiture *n* LAW perte d'un bien par confiscation *f*, perte d'un droit pour inexécution d'une obligation *f*

forge 1. *vt* ACC, BANK, GEN COMM, LAW *counterfeit* contrefaire, falsifier; **2.** *vi* ~ **ahead** GEN COMM prendre de l'avance; ◆ ~ **a link with** GEN COMM établir un lien avec

forged[1] *adj* GEN COMM faux

forged:[2] ~ **check** *n AmE*, ~ **cheque** *n BrE* BANK chèque falsifié *m*, faux chèque *m*

forger *n* BANK contrefacteur *m*

forgery *n* ACC falsification *f*, BANK contrefaçon *f*, fausse signature *f*, GEN COMM falsification *f*, LAW contrefaçon *f*, falsification *f*, faux *m*

forgivable: ~ **loan** *n* FIN subvention remboursable sous condition *f*

forgive: ~ **sb sth** *vt* GEN COMM pardonner qch à qn

forgiveness: ~ **of tax** *n* TAX remise d'impôt *f*, remise gracieuse d'impôt *f*

forgo: ~ **collection of a debt** *phr* ACC abandonner une créance

forint *n* GEN COMM forint *m*

fork: ~ -**lift truck** *n (FLT)* TRANSP chariot élévateur à fourche *m*; ~ **pocket** *n* TRANSP *in container* passage de fourche *m*

form[1] *n* COMP formulaire *m*, imprimé *m*, masque *m*, papier *m*, GEN COMM *of abstract* forme *f*, PATENTS *printed* formulaire *m*; ~ **feed** *(FF)* COMP changement de page *m*, présentation de feuille *f*, saut de page *m*; ~ **8K** STOCK formulaire 8K *m*; ~ **4** STOCK formulaire 4 *m*; ~ **10K** STOCK formulaire 10K *m*; ~ **10Q** STOCK formulaire 10Q *m*; ◆ **in the** ~ **of** GEN COMM sous la forme de

form[2] *vt* GEN COMM *committee, alliance* former, établir, *new business* créer, former, *subsidiary* créer; ◆ ~ **a partnership** GEN COMM s'associer

formal[1] *adj* GEN COMM officiel

formal:[2] ~ **agreement** *n* GEN COMM accord officiel *m*; ~ **arrangement** *n* GEN COMM accord officiel *m*; ~ **communication** *n* COMMS communication hiérarchique *f*, transmission de l'information par voie hiérarchique *f*; ~ **dinner** *n* GEN COMM dîner officiel *m*; ~ **economy** *n* ECON économie officiellement répertoriée *f*; ~ **indexation** *n* TAX indexation légale *f*; ~ **management development** *n* MGMNT développement d'une gestion officielle *m*; ~ **notice** *n* GEN COMM préavis en règle *m*; ~ **receipt** *n* GEN COMM reçu en bonne et due forme *m*; ~ **submission date** *n* FIN date de la présentation officielle *f*; ~ **trade links** *n pl* ECON, GEN COMM relations commerciales officielles *f pl*

formality *n* GEN COMM formalité *f*

formalization *n* HRM mise en forme juridique *f*

formalize *vt* GEN COMM formaliser, officialiser, préciser

format[1] *n* ADMIN formatage *m*, COMP format *m*

format[2] *vt* COMP *disk* formater, mettre en forme

Format: ~ **1** *n BrE (cf Format 2)* ACC Format 1 *m*; ~ **2** *n BrE (cf Format 1)* ACC Format 2 *m*

formation *n* GEN COMM, STOCK *of corporation* constitution *f*; ~ **expense** ACC frais de premier établissement *m pl*

formative *adj* GEN COMM formateur

formatting *n* COMP *of disk* formatage *m*, mise en forme *f*

former: ~ **customer** *n* S&M ancien client *m*; ~ **spouse** *n* LAW ex-conjoint *m*, ex-épouse *f*, ex-époux *m*

forms: ~ **design sheet** *n* ADMIN modèle de présentation de formulaires nouveaux *m*

formula *n* [pl -lae] MATH formule *f*; ~ **funding** FIN méthode de financement préétablie *f*; ~ **investing** STOCK méthode d'investissement préétablie *f*

formulate *vt* GEN COMM *policy* formuler, mettre au point

formulation *n* GEN COMM, MGMNT *of policy* formulation *f*, mise au point *f*

forthcoming *adj* GEN COMM prochain, à venir

fortieth *adj* GEN COMM quarantième; ◆ **in the** ~ **place** GEN COMM quarantième

fortnight: ~ **tomorrow** *n* GEN COMM dans deux semaines *loc f*

fortnightly *adj* GEN COMM bimensuel

fortress: ~ **Europe** *n jarg* POL *EU* forteresse Europe *f (jarg)*

fortuitous: ~ **loss** *n* INS perte fortuite *f*

fortune *n* GEN COMM fortune *f*

Fortune: ~ **Service 500** *n US* GEN COMM les 500 sociétés des services de Fortune

forty: ~ - **to fifty-year-olds** *n* ECON les quarante à cinquante ans *m pl*; **the** ~ **to fifty age group** *n* ECON les quarante à cinquante ans *m pl*

forum *n* POL forum *m*

forward:[1] ~ -**forward** *adj* ECON, STOCK terme à terme; ~ -**looking** *adj* GEN COMM *person, project* tourné vers l'avenir; ~ -**thinking** *adj* GEN COMM *person* qui regarde vers l'avenir *loc f*

forward[2] *adv* TRANSP à l'avant *loc m*

forward:[3] ~ **averaging** *n (ANT backward averaging)* TAX *of income* étalement *m*; ~ **borrowing rate** *n* STOCK *currency futures* taux d'emprunt à terme *m*, taux des emprunts à terme *m*; ~ **buying** *n* FIN, STOCK achat à terme *m*; ~ **contract** *n* FIN contrat à terme *m*, contrat à terme gré à gré *m*, STOCK contrat à livraison différé *m*, contrat à terme *m*, contrat à terme gré à gré *m*; ~ **cover** *n* STOCK couverture à terme *f*; ~ **delivery** *n* STOCK livraison à terme *f*; ~ **exchange** *n* ECON change à terme *m*; ~ **exchange contract** *n* BANK opération de change à terme *f*; ~ **exchange market** *n* STOCK marché des opérations de change à terme *m*, marché à terme de devises *m*; ~ **exchange rate** *n* ECON taux de change à terme *m*, STOCK cours du change à terme *m*, taux de change à terme *m*; ~ **-forward contract** *n* FIN, STOCK contrat terme-terme *m*, contrat à terme reporté *m*; ~ **-forward currency deal** *n* ECON opération d'achat et de vente sur le marché des changes à terme *f*; ~ **integration** *n* (ANT *backward integration*) ECON, IND, MGMNT intégration en aval *f*, intégration en avant *f*; ~ **investment return** *n* STOCK *interest-rate futures* intérêt d'investissement à terme *m*, rendement sur investissement à terme *m*; ~ **linkage** *n* (ANT *backward linkage*) ECON, IND enchaînement avant *m*, liens en aval *m pl*; ~ **margin** *n* ECON *international trade* marge à terme *f*; ~ **market** *n* STOCK marché à terme *m*; ~ **operation** *n* STOCK opération à terme *f*; ~ **perpendicular** *n* (FP) TRANSP perpendiculaire avant *f* (PPAV); ~ **planning** *n* FIN planification à terme *f*, GEN COMM plan à longue échéance *m*; ~ **position** *n* STOCK position à terme *f*, situation à terme *f*; ~ **pricing** *n* STOCK établissement des prix à terme *m*; ~ **purchase contract** *n* GEN COMM contrat d'achat à terme *m*; ~ **rate** *n* ECON cours à terme *m*, taux pour les opérations à terme *m*, FIN taux à terme *m*, STOCK cours à terme *m*, taux à terme *m*; ~ **rate agreement** *n* (FRA) FIN, STOCK *interest-rate instruments* accord de taux futur *m*, accord de taux à terme *m*; ~ **rate spread** *n* GEN COMM écart entre les cours du terme *m*; ~ **sales contract** *n* GEN COMM contrat de vente à terme *m*; ~ **scheduling** *n* (ANT *backward scheduling*) MGMNT programmation progressive *f*; ~ **security** *n* STOCK valeur à terme *f*; ~ **spread agreement** *n* (FSA) STOCK accord de répartition à terme *m*, accord sur étalement à terme *m*; ~ **stock** *n* S&M articles en vente dans les locaux d'un magasin de détail mais qui ne sont pas accessibles aux patrons; ~ **swap** *n* FIN, STOCK échange financier à terme *m*, échange à terme *m*; ~ **transaction** *n* STOCK transaction à terme *f*; ~ **vertical integration** *n* (ANT *backward vertical integration*) ECON, IND, MGMNT intégration verticale en aval *f*, intégration verticale en avant *f*

forward[4] **1.** *vt* COMMS *parcel, document sent to former address* expédier, faire suivre; **2.** *vi* ~ **-average** TAX étaler son revenu

forwarder *n* (*fwdr*) COMMS *sender of parcel, carrier to new address* expéditeur *m*, IMP/EXP *carrier* expéditeur *m*, transitaire *mf*, TRANSP *sender of parcel, carrier to new address* r expéditeur *m*; ~ **air waybill** (*FAB*) IMP/EXP, TRANSP lettre de transport aérien du transitaire *f*; ~'s **bill of lading** IMP/EXP, TRANSP connaissement de l'expéditeur *m*; ~'s **certificate of receipt** (*FCR*) TRANSP attestation de prise en charge du transitaire *f*; ~'s **certificate of transport** (*FCT*) IMP/EXP, TRANSP connaissement de transport combiné du transitaire *m*

forwarding *n* STOCK expédition *f*, TRANSP factage *m*; ~ **address** *n* COMMS, GEN COMM adresse de

réexpédition *f*; ~ **agency** *n* TRANSP bureau de transitaires *m*; ~ **agent** *n* S&M agent expéditeur *m*, transitaire *mf*, TRANSP commissionnaire de transport *m*, groupeur *m*, transitaire *mf*; ~ **agent's bill of lading** *n* IMP/EXP, TRANSP connaissement du transitaire *m*; ~ **agent's commission** *n* (*fac*) TRANSP commission du transitaire *f*; ~ **agent's receipt** *n* TRANSP récépissé du transitaire *m*; ~ **clerk** *n* HRM, TRANSP employé d'expédition *m*; ~ **company** *n* TRANSP *road* commissionnaire de transport *m*, transitaire *mf*, transporteur *m*, transporteur routier *m*; ~ **in bulk** *n* TRANSP expédition groupée *f*; ~ **instructions** *n pl* COMMS, TRANSP instructions d'expédition *f pl*, ordre de réexpédition *m*; ~ **station** *n* TRANSP *rail* gare d'expédition *f*

FOS *abbr* (*free on ship, free on steamer*) TRANSP FAB (*franco à bord*)

fossil: ~ **fuel** *n* ENVIR, IND combustible fossile *m*

foster *vt* GEN COMM *environment, relationship* favoriser

f.o.t. *abbr* (*free on truck*) TRANSP *rail* franco wagon

foul: ~ **bill of health** *n* WEL patente de santé brute *f*; ~ **bill of lading** *n* IMP/EXP, TRANSP connaissement avec réserves *m*, connaissement brut *m*, connaissement clausé *m*

foundation *n* GEN COMM, TRANSP fondation *f*

founder: ~ **member** *n* GEN COMM membre fondateur *m*

founding: ~ **company** *n* GEN COMM société fondatrice *f*

fountain: ~ **pen** *n* GEN COMM stylo à plume *m*

four: ~ **-berth cabin** *n* TRANSP *on ship* cabine à quatre personnes *f*; ~ **freedoms** *n pl* ECON *EU* les quatre libertés *f pl*; ~ **-star petrol** *n BrE* ENVIR super *m* (*infrml*), supercarburant *m*; ~ **-track band** *n* TRANSP bande à quatre pistes *f*; ~ **-way entry pallet** *n* TRANSP palette à quatre entrées *f*; ~ **-way pallet** *n* TRANSP palette à quatre entrées *f*

fours: **on all** ~ *phr jarg* LAW analogie entre deux cas *f*, similitude de cas *f* (*jarg*)

fourth: ~ **cover** *n* MEDIA, S&M *advertising of book, brochure* quatrième de couverture *f*; ~ **-generation computer** *n* COMP ordinateur de quatrième génération *m*; ~ **market** *n* STOCK quatrième marché *m*; ~ **quarter** *n* (4Q) GEN COMM quatrième trimestre *m*

Fourth: ~ **Company Law Directive** *n pl* LAW quatrième directive sur le droit des sociétés *f*; ~ **Company Law Directives** *n pl* GEN COMM quatrième directive sur le droit des sociétés *f*; ~ **European Community Directive** *n* ACC, POL quatrième directive de la Communauté Européenne *f*; ~ **European Directive** *n* ACC, POL quatrième directive européenne *f*; ~ **World** *n* ECON, POL (ANT *First World, Second World, Third World*) quart-monde *m*

4Q *abbr* (*fourth quarter*) GEN COMM quatrième trimestre *m*

FP *abbr* GEN COMM *(fully paid)* lib., payé intégralement, INS *(floating marine policy)* shipping police flottante *f*, police maritime flottante *f*, TRANSP *(forward perpendicular)* shipping PPAV *(perpendiculaire avant)*, TRANSP *(floating marine policy)* shipping police flottante *f*, police maritime flottante *f*

FPA[1] *abbr (free of particular average)* INS FAP *(franc d'avarie particulière)*

FPA:[2] **~ unless** *phr* INS *marine insurance* FAP sauf

FPC *abbr US (Federal Power Commission)* IND commission fédérale de l'énergie

FPM *abbr (flexible-payment mortgage)* PROP hypothèque à règlements variables *f*

FP-oC *abbr (flash point in degrees centigrade)* GEN COMM point de combustion en degrés Celsius *m*

FP-oF *abbr (flash point in degrees fahrenheit)* GEN COMM point de combustion en degrés fahrenheit *m*

FPS *abbr (floating production system)* TRANSP *shipping* système de production au large *m*

FPSO *abbr (floating production, storage and offloading vessel)* TRANSP navire de production, stockage et déchargement au large *m*

FPT *abbr (fore peak tank)* TRANSP *of ship* coqueron avant *m*

FPV *abbr (floating production vessel)* TRANSP *ship* navire de production au large *m*

FPZ *abbr (free port zone)* TRANSP *shipping* zone portuaire franche *f*

F/R *abbr (freight release)* TRANSP BAD *(bon à délivrer)*

FRA *abbr (forward rate agreement, future rate agreement)* FIN, STOCK accord de taux à terme *m*, ATF *(accord de taux futur)*

fraction *n* MATH fraction *f*

fractional: ~ cash reserve *n* BANK couverture fractionnaire *f*, encaisse fractionnaire *f*, réserve fractionnaire *f*; **~ discretion order** *n* STOCK ordre "environ"; **~ lot** *n* GEN COMM lot fractionnaire *m*; **~ reserve** *n* BANK couverture fractionnaire *f*, encaisse fractionnaire *f*, réserve fractionnaire *f*; **~ reserve banking** *n* BANK opérations de banque sur la réserve fractionnaire *f pl*; **~ share** *n* STOCK fraction d'action *f*, parts fractionnaires *f pl*

fractionalize *vt* MATH fractionner

fragile *adj* TRANSP *goods* fragile

fragmentation *n* COMP *of disk*, ECON, GEN COMM *of market* fragmentation *f*

fragmented: ~ bargaining *n* HRM négociation par tranches *f*; **~ market** *n* ECON, GEN COMM marché fragmenté *m*, marché non-homogène *m*

frame *n* COMP cadre *m*, image *f*, page *f*, trame *f*, TRANSP *part of ship's hull* couple *m*, membrures *f pl*; **~ height** TRANSP hauteur du châssis *f*; **~ of mind** GEN COMM, HRM humeur *f*

framework *n* GEN COMM *of institution* cadre *m*; ◆ **in the ~ of** GEN COMM dans le cadre de

framing *n (FRMG)* TRANSP *part of ship's hull* membrures *f pl*

franc *n* GEN COMM franc *m*

France *pr n* GEN COMM France *f*

franchise *n* GEN COMM contrat de franchisage *m*, franchise *f*, S&M franchise *f*, *media* exclusivité *f*; **~ agreement** COMMS accord de franchise *m*; **~ financing** FIN financement de franchise *m*; **~ tax** *US* TAX patente *f*

franchised: ~ dealer *n UK* GEN COMM concessionnaire titulaire d'une franchise

franchisee *n* S&M franchisé *m*

franchising *n* GEN COMM franchisage *m*, franchise *f*

franchisor *n* S&M franchiseur *m*

franco *adv (fco.)* TRANSP franco *(fco)*

Franco-English *adj* GEN COMM franco-anglais, franco-britannique

fr & cc *abbr (free of riots and civil commotions)* TRANSP sans émeutes ou troubles civils

frank:[1] **~ discussions** *n pl jarg* GEN COMM, POL discussions franches *f pl*

frank[2] *vt* COMMS *letter, parcel* affranchir

franking: ~ machine *n BrE (cf postage meter AmE, postal meter AmE)* COMMS machine à affranchir *f*

fraud *n* LAW dol *m*, fraude *f*; **~ prevention** LAW prévention des fraudes *f*, répression des fraudes *f*

Fraud: ~ Squad *n UK* GEN COMM brigade de la répression des fraudes

fraudulence *n* LAW caractère frauduleux *m*

fraudulent: ~ bankruptcy *n* GEN COMM, LAW banqueroute frauduleuse *f*, faillite frauduleuse *f*; **~ entry** *n* ACC, LAW fausse écriture *f*; **~ misrepresentation** *n* INS escroquerie à l'assurance *f*, fausse déclaration intentionnelle *f*

fraudulently *adv* LAW avec une intention frauduleuse *loc f*, frauduleusement

FRB *abbr US (Federal Reserve Board)* BANK, ECON conseil d'administration des banques centrales

FRC *abbr (free carrier)* TRANSP franco transporteur

Freddie: ~ Mac *n infrml US* FIN, PROP société fédérale des prêts hypothécaires *f*

free[1] *adj* COMP *available* disponible, libre, GEN COMM *available* disponible, libre, *not requiring payment* gratis, gratuit, TRANSP gratuit, sans péage; **~ -format** *adj* COMP à structure non-imposée; ◆ **~ of address** TRANSP sans adresse; **~ of all additives** ENVIR, GEN COMM sans additifs; **~ of all average** *(f.a.a.)* GEN COMM franc de toute avarie; **~ of all taxation** TAX exempt de tout impôt; **~ alongside quay** *(FAQ)* TRANSP franco le long du quai, franco à quai *(FAQ)*; **~ alongside ship** *(FAS)* TRANSP *cargo delivery* franco le long du bord *(FLB)*, franco le long du vapeur *(vieilli)*, franco sous palan; **~ alongside steamer** *dat see free alongside ship* ; **~ of capture and seizure** *(FC&S)* INS franc de capture et de saisie; **~ of capture, seizure, and riots and civil commotions** *(fcsrcc)* INS franc de capture, de saisie et émeutes et mouvements; ~ **of charge** *(FOC, foc)* GEN COMM franco, gratis, gratuit, gratuitement; ~ **of claim for accident reported** *(FCAR)* INS *marine* franc de réclamation pour accident signalé, franc de sinistre pour l'accident constaté; ~ **and clear** *US* LAW, PROP *title* franc de toute charge, non-grevé; ~ **of damage** *(FOD)* GEN COMM intact, INS sans avaries; ~ **dock** *(Fld, FD)* TRANSP franco à quai *(FAQ)*; ~ **domicile** *(fd)* TRANSP franco domicile; ~ **from alongside** *(FFA)* TRANSP franco le long du bord *(FLB)*; ~ **of general average** *(FGA)* GEN COMM franc d'avarie grosse, franc d'avaries communes; ~ **in** *(fi)* TRANSP frais de chargement en sus du fret *m pl*, franco chargement; ~ **in harbor** *AmE*, ~ **in harbour** *BrE (fih)* TRANSP franco à port; ~ **in and out** *(FIO)* IMP/EXP, TRANSP bord à bord *(BAB)*; ~ **in, out and stowed** *(FIO and stowed)* TRANSP bord à bord et arrimage, frais de chargement, de déchargement et d'arrimage en sus du fret *m pl*; ~ **in, out, stowed and trimmed** TRANSP bord à bord arrimage et choulage, frais de chargement, de déchargement et d'arrimage en sus du fret *m pl*; ~ **in, out and trimmed** *(FIO and trimmed)* TRANSP bord à bord et choulage, frais de chargement, de déchargement et d'arrimage en sus du fret *m pl*; ~ **in and stowed** *(FIAS)* TRANSP bord arrimé, frais de chargement et d'arrimage en sus du fret *m pl*; ~ **insurance and carriage** *(FIC)* TRANSP franco assurance et transport; ~ **into barge** *(FIB)* TRANSP franco allège; ~ **into bunkers** *(FIB)* TRANSP franco soutes; ~ **into wagon** *(fiw)* TRANSP *rail* franco wagon; ~ **on aircraft** *(FOA)* TRANSP franco à bord aéroport *(FAB aéroport)*; ~ **on board** *(FOB)* TRANSP franco à bord *(FAB)*; ~ **on board airport** *(FOB airport)* TRANSP franco à bord aéroport *(FAB aéroport)*; ~ **on board and trimmed** *(FOB & T)* TRANSP franco à bord et arrimé; ~ **on quay** *(FOQ)* TRANSP franco à quai *(FAQ)*; ~ **on quay to free on quay** *(FOQ-FOQ)* TRANSP franco à quai - franco à quai; ~ **on rail** *(f.o.r.)* TRANSP franco gare, franco sur rail, franco wagon; ~ **on ship** *(FOS)* TRANSP franco à bord *(FAB)*; ~ **on steamer** *dat (FOS)* TRANSP franco à bord *(FAB)*; ~ **on truck** *(f.o.t.)* TRANSP *rail* franco wagon; ~ **on wharf** *(f.o.t.)* TRANSP franco à quai; ~ **overboard** *(fo)* TRANSP franco sous palan; ~ **overside** *(fo)* TRANSP franco sous palan; ~ **of particular average** *(FPA)* INS franc d'avarie particulière *(FAP)*; ~ **of riots and civil commotions** *(fr & cc)* TRANSP sans émeutes ou troubles civils; ~ **of term** TRANSP sans terme particulier

free[2] *adv* GEN COMM gratis, gratuitement

free:[3] ~ **access and choice** *n* GEN COMM libre-service *m*; ~ **allowance** *n* GEN COMM, TRANSP *of luggage* franchise *f*; ~ **baggage allowance** *n BrE (cf free luggage allowance AmE)* TRANSP franchise pour bagages *f*; ~ **banking** *n* BANK franchise bancaire *f*; ~ **carrier** *n (FRC)* TRANSP *named*

place franco transporteur; ~ **circulation** *n* ENVIR libre circulation *f*; ~ **competition** *n* ECON, GEN COMM, S&M concurrence libre *f*; ~ **delivery** *n* TRANSP livraison gratuite *f*; ~ **depreciation** *n* FIN amortissement économique franc *m*; ~ **discharge** *n (fd)* TRANSP franco déchargement; ~ **dispatch** *n (fd)* TRANSP sans bonification pour temps gagné, sans prime de célérité; ~ **economy** *n* ECON, POL économie libérale *f*; ~ **enterprise** *n* ECON, POL libre entreprise *f*; ~ **enterprise economy** *n* ECON, POL économie de libre entreprise *f*; ~ **enterprise market** *n* ECON, POL, S&M marché de libre entreprise *m*; ~ **enterprise system** *n* ECON, POL système de libre entreprise *m*; ~ **-for-all** *n infrml* GEN COMM, S&M foire d'empoigne *f*; ~ **house** *n* TRANSP franco domicile; ~ **-in-and-out charter** *n (FIO charter)* TRANSP *charter party* charte-partie bord à bord *f*; ~ **-in clause** *n* TRANSP clause de fret bord *f*; ~ **lodging** *n* TAX logement gratuit *m*; ~ **luggage allowance** *n AmE (cf free baggage allowance BrE)* TRANSP franchise pour bagages *f*; ~ **market** *n* ECON, GEN COMM, POL, S&M marché libre *m*; ~ **medical treatment** *n* WEL soins gratuits *m pl*; ~ **movement** *n* ECON *of goods and services* libre circulation *f*; ~ **movement of labor** *n AmE*, ~ **movement of labour** *n BrE* ECON, LAW libre circulation de la main d'oeuvre *f*; ~ **newspaper** *n (SYN freesheet)* MEDIA *print* journal gratuit *m*; ~ **and open market** *n* ECON, S&M marché libre et ouvert *m*; ~ **out terms** *n pl (fo)* TRANSP frais de déchargement en sus du fret *m pl*; ~ **paper** *n* MEDIA journal gratuit *m*; ~ **port** *n* IMP/EXP port entrepôt *m*, port franc *m*; ~ **port zone** *n (FPZ)* TRANSP zone portuaire franche *f*; ~ **-rein leadership** *n* HRM autorité qui s'exerce en douceur *f*; ~ **ride** *n infrml* STOCK opération aux frais de la princesse *f (jarg)*, opération sans bourse délier *f*, voyage gratuit *m*; ~ **rider** *n infrml* HRM profiteur de grève *m*, travailleur non-syndiqué *m*, TRANSP passager clandestin *m*; ~ **-riding** *n* STOCK opération aux frais de la princesse *f (jarg)*, opération sans bourse délier *f*, voyage gratuit *m*; ~ **right of exchange** *n* STOCK droit d'échange gratuit *m*, droit d'échange libre *m*; ~ **sale agreement** *n* TRANSP accord de libre vente *m*; ~ **sample** *n* GEN COMM échantillon gratuit *m*; ~ **sea carrier** *n* TRANSP franco transporteur maritime *f*; ~ **trade** *n* ECON, POL libre-échange *m*; ~ **-trade agreement** *n (FTA)* ECON, POL accord de libre-échange *m*; ~ **-trade area** *n (SYN free zone)* ECON, GEN COMM, IMP/EXP, POL zone de libre-échange *f*, zone franche *f*; ~ **-trade zone** *n (FTZ)* ECON, GEN COMM, IMP/EXP, POL zone de libre-échange *f*, zone franche *f*; ~ **zone** *n (SYN free-trade area)* ECON, GEN COMM, IMP/EXP, POL zone de libre-échange *f*, zone franche *f*

free:[4] ~ **-ride** *vi infrml* HRM opérer en dehors de son lieu de travail

Free: ~ **Banking School** *n UK* BANK école de la franchise bancaire

freeboard *n (FBD)* TRANSP franc-bord *m*

freed: ~ **up** *adj* STOCK *security* libéré

freedom *n* GEN COMM *immunity* exemption *f*, *liberty* liberté *f*, LAW *liberty* liberté *f*; ~ **of action** GEN COMM liberté d'action *f*; ~ **of association** GEN COMM, POL liberté d'association *f*; ~ **of choice** POL liberté de choix *f*; ~ **of competition** ECON, POL liberté de concurrence *f*; ~ **of establishment** POL *in EU* liberté d'établissement *f*; ~ **of movement** POL liberté de circulation *f*

Freedom: ~ **of Information Act** *n* US *(FOIA)* LAW loi sur la liberté de l'information

Freefone®[1] *adj* BrE *(cf toll-free AmE)* COMMS *telephone* gratuit

Freefone:[2] ~ **call**® *n* BrE *(cf toll-free call AmE)* COMMS appel gratuit *m*, appel interurbain gratuit *m*, appel sans frais *m (Can)*; ~ **number** *n* BrE *(cf toll-free number AmE)* COMMS numéro gratuit *m*, service d'appel gratuit *m*, ≈ numéro vert *m*

freehold *n* PROP pleine propriété *f*, propriété foncière libre *f*; ~ **owner** PROP plein propriétaire *m*; ~ **property** ACC *annual accounts* terrains *m pl*, PROP pleine propriété *f*, propriété foncière libre *f*

freeholder *n* PROP foncier à perpétuité *m*, plein propriétaire *m*

freelance[1] *adj* HRM, MEDIA free-lance, indépendant

freelance[2] *n* HRM, MEDIA *worker* free-lance *mf*, travailleur indépendant *m*; ~ **contract** HRM contrat de travail indépendant *m*; ~ **correspondent** HRM, MEDIA journaliste indépendant *m*, journaliste payée à la pige *m*, pigiste *mf*; ~ **journalist** HRM, MEDIA journaliste indépendant *m*, journaliste payée à la pige *m*, pigiste *mf*; ~ **worker** HRM, MEDIA travailleur indépendant *m*; ~ **writer** HRM, MEDIA pigiste *mf*, écrivain indépendant *m*, écrivain payé à la pige *m*

freelancer *n* HRM, MEDIA travailleur indépendant *m*

freely: ~ **negotiable credit** *n* ECON, FIN *international trade* crédit librement négociable *m*

Freepost® *n* BrE *(cf Business Reply Mail AmE)* COMMS p.p., port payé *m*

freesheet *n* (SYN *free newspaper*) MEDIA *print* journal gratuit *m*

freestanding *adj* COMP autonome

Freetown *pr n* GEN COMM Freetown *n pr*

freeway *n* AmE *(cf expressway Can, motorway BrE, superhighway, throughway)* TRANSP autoroute *f*

freeze[1] *n* BANK gel *m*, ECON *of credit, wages, prices* blocage *m*, gel *m*, FIN, GEN COMM, TAX gel *m*

freeze[2] *vt* BANK geler, ECON *rents, prices* bloquer, geler, FIN, GEN COMM, TAX geler; ◆ ~ **an account** BANK bloquer un compte

freezing *n* BANK, ECON gel *m*, FIN *of credit, wages, prices* blocage *m*, gel *m*, GEN COMM, TAX gel *m*

freight *n* *(frt)* TRANSP cargaison *f*, fret *m*, marchandises *f pl*; ~ **car** *n* AmE *(cf goods wagon BrE)* TRANSP fourgon *m*; ~ **container** *n* TRANSP conteneur de fret *m*; ~, **demurrage and defence**

cover *n* BrE *(FD&D cover)* INS, TRANSP couverture de cargaison, surestaries et défense *f*; ~, **demurrage and defense cover** *n* AmE *see freight, demurrage and defence cover BrE*; ~ **forwarder** *n* TRANSP commissionnaire de transport *m*, transitaire *mf*, transporteur routier *m*; ~ **forwarder's certificate of receipt** *n (FFCR)* TRANSP attestation de prise en charge du transitaire *f*; ~ **forwarder's combined transport bill of lading** *n (FCT)* IMP/EXP, TRANSP connaissement de transport combiné du transitaire *m*; ~ **futures contract** *n* FIN, STOCK contrat à terme de fret *m*; ~ **futures market** *n* STOCK marché du fret à terme *m*, marché à terme sur les valeurs de transport *m*; ~ **insurance** *n* INS assurance des marchandises transportées *f*, assurance du fret *f*; ~, **insurance and shipping charges** *n pl (FIS)* IMP/EXP, TRANSP fret, assurance et frais d'expédition *m*; ~ **manifest** *n* TRANSP manifeste de fret *m*; ~ **market** *n* STOCK marché des valeurs de transport *m*, marché du fret *m*; ~ **policy** *n* INS *marine* police de fret *f*; ~ **release** *n (F/R)* TRANSP bon à délivrer *m (BAD)*; ~ **sales representative** *n* UK GEN COMM représentant en fret *m*; ~ **strategy** *n* TRANSP stratégie de fret *f*; ~ **tariff** *n* TRANSP tarif marchandises *m*; ~ **terminal** *n* TRANSP terminal de fret *m*; ~ **ton** *n (frt ton, ft)* GEN COMM tonne kilométrique *f*; ~ **traffic** *n* TRANSP trafic marchandises *m*; ~ **train** *n* AmE *(cf goods train BrE)* TRANSP train de marchandises *m*; ~ **transport** *n* TRANSP transport de marchandises *m*; ◆ ~ **all kinds** *(FAK)* TRANSP à l'unité de chargement; ~ **and demurrage** *(F&D)* INS, TRANSP fret et surestarie *m*; ~, **demurrage and defence** BrE *(FD&D)* INS, TRANSP cargaison, surestaries et défense; ~, **demurrage and defense** AmE *see freight, demurrage and defence BrE*; ~ **forward** *(frt fwd)* GEN COMM, TRANSP fret payable à destination *m*, port dû *m (p.d.)*; ~ **and insurance paid** INS, TRANSP *to a named place* fret et assurance payé à; ~ **paid to** *(DCP)* IMP/EXP, TRANSP fret payé jusqu'à *m*, fret payé à *m*; ~ **prepaid** *(frt ppd)* TRANSP fret payé d'avance *m*, fret payé à l'expédition *m*, port payé *m*

Freight: ~ **Transport Association** *n* UK *(FTA)* GEN COMM association du transport de fret

freighter *n* TRANSP *aircraft* avion-cargo *m*, *ship* cargo *m*, navire de charge *m*, navire de transport *m*, paquebot *m*

freightliner® *n* BrE *(F/L)* TRANSP *rail* train-bloc de conteneurs *m*

French[1] *adj* GEN COMM français; ~ **-made** GEN COMM de fabrication française

French[2] *n* GEN COMM *language* français *m*; ~ **Chamber of Commerce** *n (FCC)* GEN COMM Chambre de commerce française *f*; ~ **Chamber of Commerce for the United Kingdom** *n (FCCUK)* GEN COMM chambre de commerce français pour le Royaume-Uni *m*; ~ **Chamber of Commerce in Great Britain** *n* GEN COMM Chambre de commerce française en Grande-Bretagne *f*; ~ **franc** *n (FF)*

GEN COMM franc français *m (FF)*; ~ **gold franc** *n* GEN COMM franc or *m*; ~ **government bond** *n* STOCK obligation assimilable du Trésor *f*, OAT; ~ **Shippers' Council** *n (FSC)* IMP/EXP Conseil des affréteurs français *m*; ~ **-speaking world** *n* GEN COMM monde francophone *m*; **the** ~ *n pl* GEN COMM les Français *m pl*; ~ **treasury bond** *n* STOCK obligation assimilable du Trésor *f*, OAT

Frenchman *n* GEN COMM *person* Français *m*

Frenchwoman *n* GEN COMM *person* Française *f*

frequency *n* MATH, MEDIA *radio*, S&M *advertising* fréquence *f*; ~ **curve** MATH *statistics* courbe de fréquence *f*; ~ **distribution** MATH *statistics* distribution des fréquences *f*, répartition de fréquence *f*; ~ **modulation** *(FM)* COMMS modulation de fréquence *f (FM)*; ~ **polygon** MATH *statistics* polygone de fréquence *m*; ~ **table** MATH *statistics* table de fréquence *f*

fresh: ~ **food** *n* S&M produits frais *m pl*; ~ **goods** *n pl* S&M produits frais *m pl*; ~ **money** *n* FIN, GEN COMM argent frais *m*; ~ **water** *n (F, FW)* ENVIR eau douce *f*; ~ **water allowance** *n (FWA)* TRANSP correction pour eau douce *f*; ~ **water damage** *n (FWD)* TRANSP avarie par l'eau douce *f*

Fri. *abbr (Friday)* GEN COMM vendredi *m*

FRICS *abbr (Fellow of the Royal Institute of Chartered Surveyors)* GEN COMM membre de l'institut royal d'experts immobiliers

friction *n* GEN COMM *between parties* désaccord *m*; ~ **feed** COMP *hardware* entraînement par friction *m*; ~ **-feed printer** COMP *hardware* imprimante à entraînement par friction *f*

frictional: ~ **unemployment** *n* ECON, HRM chômage frictionnel *m*

Friday *n (Fri.)* GEN COMM vendredi *m*

Friedman *n* ECON mécanisme de transmission *m*

friendly[1] *adj* COMP, S&M convivial

friendly:[2] ~ **agreement** *n* GEN COMM, LAW accord à l'amiable *m*; ~ **society** *n* BrE *(cf benefit society AmE)* FIN association de secours mutuel *f*, société de prévoyance *f*, société de secours mutuel *f*; ~ **suit** *n* LAW procès à l'amiable *m*; ~ **takeover** *n* STOCK prise de contrôle amicale *f*

Friends: ~ **of the Earth** *n pl (FOE)* ENVIR ≈ Amis de la Terre *m pl*

fringe: ~ **bank** *n* BANK banque secondaire *f*; ~ **banking crisis** *n* BANK crise des opérations bancaires secondaires *f*; ~ **benefit** *n* HRM complément de salaire *m*; ~ **benefits** *n pl* HRM *for employee* avantages annexes *m pl*, avantages divers *m pl*, avantages en nature *m pl*, avantages sociaux *m pl*; ~ **market** *n* S&M, STOCK marché marginal *m*; ~ **meeting** *n* POL réunion en marge *f*

frisk *vt infrml* IMP/EXP fouiller

FRMG *abbr (framing)* TRANSP *part of ship's hull* membrures *f pl*

FRN *abbr (floating-rate note)* STOCK OTV *(obligation à taux variable)*

frof *abbr (fire risk on freight)* TRANSP risque d'incendie sur fret *m*

from *prep* TRANSP en provenance de *loc f*

front:[1] ~ **-end** *adj* COMP frontal; ~ **-running** *adj* GEN COMM de premier plan

front[2] *n* MEDIA couverture *f*, *person* animateur *m*; ~ **desk** *n* ADMIN réception *f*; ~ **-end computer** *n* COMP frontal *m*, ordinateur frontal *m*; ~ **-end costs** *n pl* ECON *international trade* coûts de commercialisation *m pl*, frais de commercialisation *m pl*; ~ **-end finance** *n* FIN finance d'ouverture *f*; ~ **-end financing** *n* FIN financement initial *m*; ~ **-end load** *n* STOCK charge au départ *f*, commission payable d'avance *f*; ~ **-end loading** *n* FIN méthode de prélèvement des frais d'achat sur les premiers versements *f*; ~ **-end loan** *n* FIN prêt initial *m*; ~ **-end money** *n* FIN liquidité d'ouverture *f*; ~ **-end payment** *n* HRM versement initial *m*; ~ **foot** *n* US PROP *measured along front of a lot* pied de façade *m*; ~ **line** *n jarg* MEDIA *reporting*, POL point chaud *m*; ~ **-line employees** *n pl* HRM personnel sur le terrain *m*; ~ **man** *n* MEDIA *broadcast* présentateur *m*; ~ **money** *n* FIN liquidité d'ouverture *f*; ~ **-of-house jobs** *n pl (ANT back-of-house jobs)* ADMIN postes d'accueil *m pl*, service d'accueil *m*; ~ **office** *n* ADMIN *administrative office* bureau central *m*, maison mère *f*, *reception area* réception *f*, STOCK salle des marchés *f*; ~ **-office personnel** *n* ADMIN personnel de réception *m*; ◆ **be** ~ **-page news** MEDIA *print* être à la une

frontage *n* PROP façade *f*

frontier *n* ECON, GEN COMM, IMP/EXP frontière *f*; ~ **control** ECON, IMP/EXP *of goods* contrôle aux frontières *m*, contrôle frontalier *m*; ~ **customs post** IMP/EXP poste douanier frontalier *m*; ~ **worker** HRM travailleur frontalier *m*

fronting *n* INS *marine* façade *f*; ~ **loan** FIN prêt de façade *m*

frontrunning *n* STOCK non-respect de la règle de priorité *m*, utilisation abusive d'informations privilégiées *f*

frozen[1] *adj* BANK gelé, ECON, FIN bloqué, gelé, GEN COMM gelé, TAX *assets, credits* bloqué, gelé

frozen:[2] ~ **account** *n* BANK compte gelé *m*; ~ **assets** *n pl* FIN actif gelé *m*, fonds gelés *m pl*; ~ **credits** *n pl* FIN crédits bloqués *m pl*, crédits gelés *m pl*; ~ **receivables** *n pl* FIN *balance sheet* créances gelées *f pl*, créances immobilisées *f pl*

FRS *abbr (Financial Reporting Standard)* ACC norme comptable *f*

frt *abbr (freight)* TRANSP cargaison *f*, fret *m*, marchandises *f pl*; ~ **fwd** *(freight forward)* GEN COMM, TRANSP fret payable à destination *m*, p.d. *(port dû)*; ~ **ppd** *(freight prepaid)* TRANSP fret payé d'avance *m*, fret payé à l'expédition *m*, p.p. *(port payé)*; ~ **ton** *(freight ton)* GEN COMM tonne kilométrique *f*

fruit: ~ **carrier** *n* TRANSP *ship* cargo fruitier *m*; ~ **farmer** *n* ECON, IND *agriculture* producteur de fruits *m*; ~ **farming** *n* ECON, IND *agriculture* arboriculture fruitière *f*; ~ **terminal** *n* TRANSP entrepôt de fruits *m*

fruition: come to ~ *phr* GEN COMM se réaliser

fruitless *adj* GEN COMM stérile

frustration: ~ of contract *n* LAW impossibilité d'exécuter un contrat *f*, résolution de contrat *f*

FSA *abbr* FIN *UK (Financial Services Act)* loi sur les services financiers, STOCK *(forward spread agreement)* accord de répartition à terme *m*, accord sur étalement à terme *m*

FSBR *abbr (Financial Statement and Budget Report)* FIN état financier et rapport budgétaire

FSC *abbr (French Shippers' Council)* IMP/EXP Conseil des affréteurs français *m*

FSLIC *abbr US (Federal Savings and Loan Insurance Corporation)* BANK caisse nationale d'assurance de l'épargne et des prêts, ≈ société fédérale d'assurance épargne et crédit *f*

ft *abbr* GEN COMM *(foot)* pied *m*, GEN COMM *(freight ton)* tonne kilométrique *f*, TRANSP *(fuel terms)* conditions de carburant *f pl*

FT[1] *abbr* UK *(Financial Times)* MEDIA *newspaper* Financial Times *m*

FT:[2] ~ **Index** *n* UK *(Financial Times Industrial Ordinary Share Index)* STOCK indice des actions industrielles ordinaires du Financial Times

FTA *abbr* ECON *(free-trade agreement)* accord de libre-échange *m*, GEN COMM *UK (Freight Transport Association)* association du transport de fret, HRM *(failure to agree)* absence d'accord *f*, POL *(free-trade agreement)* accord de libre-échange *m*

FTB *abbr (fire tube boiler)* TRANSP *shipping* chaudière ignitubulaire *f*, chaudière à tubes de fumée *f*

FTBS *abbr (fire-tube boiler survey)* TRANSP *shipping* visite de la chaudière ignitubulaire *f*, visite de la chaudière à tubes de fumée *f*

FTC *abbr US (Federal Trade Commission)* POL commission fédérale du commerce

FTO *abbr* HRM *UK (full-time official)* permanent *m*, STOCK *UK (Financial Times Industrial Ordinary Share Index)* indice des actions industrielles ordinaires du Financial Times

FT-SE[1] *abbr UK (Financial Times Stock Exchange index)* STOCK Indice de la Bourse de Londres *m*, FTSE, ≈ L'indice CAC40 *m (indice FTSE des 100 valeurs)*

FT-SE:[2] ~ **Eurotrack 100 index** *n UK* STOCK indice FTSE eurotrack des 100 valeurs européennes; ~ **Eurotrack 200 index** *n UK* STOCK moyenne quotidienne des principales valeurs boursières britannique, indice FTSE des 200 valeurs *m*; ~ **100 Share index** *n UK (Footsie)* STOCK indice FTSE 100 *m*, indice FTSE des 100 valeurs *m*

FTZ *abbr (free-trade zone)* ECON, GEN COMM, IMP/EXP, POL zone de libre-échange *f*, zone franche *f*

fuel:[1] ~ **efficiency** *n* ENVIR rendement du combustible *m*; ~ **oil** *n* TRANSP fioul *m*, mazout *m*; ~ **oil tank farm** *n* TRANSP dépôt de mazout *m*; ~ **surcharge** *n* TRANSP surtaxe pour combustibles

f; ~ **tax** *n* TAX taxe sur les carburants *f*; ~ **terms** *n pl (ft)* TRANSP conditions de carburant *f pl*

fuel[2] *vt* ECON *inflation* alimenter, entretenir

fulcrum *n* GEN COMM point d'appui *m*

fulfil *vt BrE* GEN COMM *commitment, obligation* s'acquitter de, *obligations* honorer

fulfill *AmE see* **fulfil** *BrE*

fulfillment *n AmE*, **fulfilment** *n BrE* S&M *subscriptions, book club memberships* exécution *f*

full[1] *adj* GEN COMM plein; ~ **-duplex** *adj (FDX)* COMP bidirectionnel, duplex intégral, semi-duplex, simultané; ~ **-screen** *adj* COMP plein écran *m*, pleine page *f*; ~ **-time** *adj* HRM à temps complet, à temps plein; ♦ **at ~ capacity** GEN COMM à plein rendement, à plein régime; **be in ~ swing** POL battre son plein; ~ **and down** TRANSP chargé en poids et en cubage, plein et chargé à ses marques; ~ **faith and credit** *US* STOCK pleine confiance et crédit *f*; **in ~ settlement** ACC pour solde de tout compte; ~ **loaded weight and capacity** *(FWC)* TRANSP *of container* poids et capacité à charge complète

full:[2] **in ~** *adv* GEN COMM intégralement

full:[3] ~ **adder** *n* COMP *hardware* additionneur complet *m*; ~ **air brakes** *n pl* TRANSP freins à air comprimé *m pl*; ~ **basis** *n* ACC *on road vehicle* régime plein *m*; ~ **board** *n* LEIS pension complète *f*; ~ **container load** *n (FCL)* TRANSP *container movement term* conteneur complet *m*; ~ **-cost method** *n* ACC méthode du coût complet *f*, méthode du coût de revient complet *f*, FIN méthode des coûts complets *f*; ~ **-cost pricing** *n* ECON, S&M méthode du prix de revient complet *f*; ~ **costing** *n* ACC *cost accounting* valorisation à leur coût total *f*; ~ **coupon bond** *n* STOCK obligation à intérêt élevé *f*, obligation à prime complète *f*; ~ **cover** *n* INS couverture complète *f*, couverture totale *f*, pleine garantie *f*, MEDIA *of event* couverture complète *f*; ~ **coverage** *n* INS couverture complète *f*, couverture totale *f*, pleine garantie *f*, MEDIA *of event* couverture complète *f*, MEDIA *of news* bonne couverture *f*; ~ **disclosure** *n* INS, LAW divulgation complète *f*; ~ **employment** *n* ECON, POL plein emploi *m*; ~ **-employment budget** *n* ACC, ECON, POL budget de plein emploi *m*; ~ **employment economy** *n* ECON économie de plein emploi *f*; ~ **exemption** *n* TAX dégrèvement total *m*; ~ **fare** *n* TRANSP plein tarif *m*; ~ **free forklift truck** *n* TRANSP *cargo handling* chariot élévateur totalement libre *m*; ~ **liability** *n* GEN COMM, INS, LAW responsabilité pleine et entière *f*; ~ **lot** *n jarg AmE* ACC lot régulier *m (Fra)*, quotité *f (Can)*; ~ **member** *n* GEN COMM membre à part entière *m*; ~ **name** *n* GEN COMM nom et prénoms *m*; ~ **-page advertisement** *n* MEDIA *in newspaper, magazine*, S&M placard publicitaire *m*; ~ **particulars** *n pl* GEN COMM tous les détails *m pl*; ~ **protection** *n* PATENTS protection pleine et entière *f*; ~ **quotation** *n* STOCK cotation complète *f*; ~ **rate** *n* HRM tarif complet *m*; ~ **-scale investigation** *n* TAX enquête exhaustive *f*;

~ -screen editor *n* COMP *word processing* éditeur plein écran *m*, éditeur pleine page *m*; **~ -screen terminal** *n* COMP *hardware* terminal plein écran *m*; **~ -service agency** *n* MEDIA, S&M *advertising* agence de publicité globale *f*; **~ -service broker** *n* STOCK courtier tous services *m*, courtier à service complet *m*; **~ session** *n* GEN COMM, POL assemblée plénière *f*; **~ share** *n* STOCK action entière *f*; **~ taxation year** *n* TAX année complète d'imposition *f*; **~ -time attendance** *n* TAX fréquentation à plein temps *f*; **~ -time attendant** *n* TAX préposé à plein temps *m*; **~ -time employment** *n* HRM emploi à plein temps *m*; **~ -time official** *n* *BrE (FTO)* HRM *of union* permanent *m*; **~ -timer** *n* GEN COMM, HRM employé à plein temps *m*; **~ weight** *n* GEN COMM poids juste *m*

fully:[1] **~ booked** *adj* GEN COMM complet; **~ comp** *adj infrml (fully comprehensive)* INS tous risques; **~ comprehensive** *adj (fully comp)* INS tous risques; **~ distributed** *adj* STOCK entièrement distribué, totalement souscrit *loc m*; **~ paid** *adj (FP)* GEN COMM libéré, payé intégralement *(lib.)*; **~ valued** *adj* STOCK entièrement expertisé, à sa pleine valeur *loc f*

fully:[2] **~ cellular container ship** *n (FCC)* TRANSP navire porte-conteneurs spécialisé *m*, porte-conteneurs entièrement cellulaire *m*; **~ comprehensive insurance policy** *n* INS police d'assurance tous risques *f*; **~ diluted earnings per share** *n pl* STOCK bénéfice dilué par action *m*; **~ -paid policy** *n* INS *life policy* police payée intégralement *f*; **~ -paid share** *n* STOCK action entièrement libérée *f*, action payée entièrement *f*, action totalement libérée *f*; **~ performing loan** *n* BANK prêt entièrement productif *m*; **~ quoted company** *n* STOCK société entièrement cotée *f*; **~ registered bond** *n* STOCK obligation essentiellement nominative *f*; **~ registered security** *n* STOCK titre essentiellement nominatif *m*

fumes *n pl* ENVIR fumées *f pl*

function[1] *n* COMP fonction *f*, GEN COMM *party* réception officielle *f*, *role* fonction *f*, rôle *m*, HRM rôle *m*, MATH fonction *f*, MGMNT réception officielle *f*; **~ key** *(F-key)* COMP *keyboard* touche de fonction *f (touche F)*; ◆ **as a ~ of** GEN COMM en fonction de

function[2] *vi* GEN COMM fonctionner

functional[1] *adj* GEN COMM fonctionnel

functional:[2] **~ analysis** *n* COMP, GEN COMM analyse fonctionnelle *f*; **~ analysis of costs** *n pl* ACC *annual accounts* répartition fonctionnelle des charges d'exploitation *f*; **~ approach** *n* GEN COMM, IND démarche fonctionnelle *f*; **~ authority** *n* HRM autorité fonctionnelle *f*; **~ costing** *n* ACC attribution des charges par fonction *f*; **~ currency** *n* ECON devise d'exploitation *f*; **~ financing** *n* FIN financement fonctionnel *m*; **~ flexibility** *n* HRM polyvalence *f*; **~ income distribution** *n* ECON répartition du revenu national entre les facteurs de production *f*; **~ layout** *n*

GEN COMM implantation fonctionnelle *f*; **~ management** *n (SYN horizontal specialization)* MGMNT gestion par fonctions *f*; **~ obsolescence** *n* S&M obsolescence fonctionnelle *f*; **~ organization** *n* GEN COMM organisation fonctionnelle *f*, organisation horizontale *f*, organisation par secteurs d'activité *f*, HRM, MGMNT organisation fonctionnelle *f*, organisation horizontale *f*; **~ relations** *n pl* GEN COMM, MGMNT liaisons fonctionnelles *f pl*; **~ responsibility** *n* GEN COMM, MGMNT responsabilité fonctionnelle *f*

functioning *n* ADMIN, GEN COMM fonctionnement *m*

fund[1] *n* GEN COMM caisse *f*, fonds *m pl*; **~ accounting** ACC comptabilité par fonds *f*; **~ appropriation** ACC *governmental* crédit créant un fond *m*; **~ management** BANK *investment banking* gestion de fonds *f*; **~ manager** FIN *pensions* gestionnaire de fonds *m*; **~ -raising** FIN appel de fonds *m*, collecte de fonds *f*; **~ -raising project** WEL collecte de fonds *f*

fund[2] *vt* FIN *debt* consolider, *project* financer; ◆ **~ a loan** BANK, FIN consolider un emprunt

fundamental[1] *adj* GEN COMM fondamental

fundamental:[2] **~ analysis** *n* FIN *of financial statements, investments* analyse fondamentale *f*; **~ equilibrium** *n* ECON équilibre fondamental *m*

funded: **~ debt** *n* ECON, FIN dette consolidée *f*, STOCK dette consolidée *f*, dette remboursée par un fonds *f*; **~ pension plan** *n* US *(cf funded retirement plan)* HRM *pensions* système de retraite *m*, système de retraite par accumulation *m*; **~ property** *n* PROP biens en rente *m pl*; **~ retirement plan** *n* US *(cf funded pension plan)* HRM système de retraite par accumulation *m*

funding *n* FIN consolidation *f*, financement *m*; **~ agency** FIN société de financement *f*; **~ gap** FIN déficit financier *m*; **~ source** FIN source de financement *f*

funds *n pl* FIN fonds *m pl*, GEN COMM caisse *f*, fonds *m pl*; **~ abroad** *n pl* BANK fonds à l'étranger *m pl*; **~ from operations** *n pl* ACC fonds venant d'opérations *m pl*; **~ statement** *n* ACC tableau des variations de fonds *m*; **~ transfer** *n* BANK, FIN transfert de fonds *m*; ◆ **no ~** *(NF)* GEN COMM défaut de provision *m*

fungible[1] *adj* HRM *person*, LAW *goods* interchangeable

fungible:[2] **~ asset** *n* FIN actif fongible *m*

fungibles *n pl* ECON fongibles *m pl*

funnel[1] *n* TRANSP *of ship* cheminée *f*

funnel[2] *vt* GEN COMM canaliser, diriger, orienter

furlough *n* AmE HRM *laying off of staff* mise en chômage temporaire *f*, *leave of absence* autorisation de congé *f*

furniture *n* GEN COMM mobilier *m*, *book trade* livres de fond *m pl (infrml)*; **~ depot** GEN COMM *warehouse* garde-meubles *m*

further[1] *adv* COMMS de plus, en outre; ◆ **~ to your letter** COMMS en réponse à votre lettre, suite à votre lettre; ~ **to your telephone call** COMMS en réponse à votre appel, suite à votre appel

further:[2] ~ **education** *n* WEL formation permanente *f*; ~ **information** *n* GEN COMM plus amples renseignements *m pl*

further[3] *vt* GEN COMM, HRM, S&M promouvoir

furtherance: in ~ **of this goal** *phr* GEN COMM pour servir cet objectif

fuse *vt* FIN fondre

fuselage *n* TRANSP coque intérieure *f*

fusion *n* FIN fonte *f*

future[1] *adj* GEN COMM *contract* à terme; ♦ **at some** ~ **date** GEN COMM à une date ultérieure

future[2] *n* GEN COMM avenir *m*; ~ **development zone** *n* ECON, HRM, PROP zone d'aménagement différé *f*, ZAD; ~ **goods** *n pl* GEN COMM marchandises livrables à terme *f pl*; ~ **orders** *n pl* GEN COMM, S&M commandes futures *f pl*; ~ **price** *n* STOCK cours à terme *m*, prix à terme *m*; ~ **prospect** *n* HRM perspectives d'avenir *f pl*; ~ **rate agreement** *n (FRA)* FIN, STOCK accord de taux futur *m (ATF)*, accord de taux à terme *m*; ~ **tax credits** *n pl* ACC crédits d'impôts à venir *m pl*; ~ **trends** *n pl* GEN COMM tendances futures *f pl*; ♦ **in** ~ GEN COMM à l'avenir; **in the** ~ GEN COMM à l'avenir; **in the near** ~ GEN COMM dans un proche avenir

futures *n pl* STOCK opérations à terme *f pl, yen* devises *f pl*; ~ **contract** *n* FIN, STOCK contrat à terme *m*, contrat à terme d'instrument financier *m*; ~ **exchange council** *n* STOCK Conseil des marchés à terme *m*, CMT; ~ **expiration date** *n AmE (cf futures expiry date BrE)* STOCK expiration du contrat à terme *f*, échéance de contrat à terme *f*; ~ **expiry date** *n BrE (cf futures expiration date AmE)* STOCK expiration du contrat à terme *f*, échéance de contrat à terme *f*; ~ **liquidation rate** *n* STOCK taux de liquidation d'opération à terme

m, taux de liquidation du contrat à terme *m*; ~ **market** *n* STOCK marché à terme *m*; ~ **option contract** *n* STOCK contrat d'option sur contrat à terme *m*, contrat d'option à terme *m*; ~ **position** *n* STOCK position à terme *f*; ~ **price change** *n* STOCK changement de cours à terme *m*, changement de prix à terme *m*; ~ **-registered broker** *n* STOCK courtier sur contrats à terme agréé *m*; ~ **sales** *n pl* GEN COMM ventes à découvert *f pl*; ~ **trading** *n* STOCK commerce à terme *m*, transactions sur contrats à terme *f pl*; ~ **transaction** *n* STOCK commerce à terme *m*, transaction sur contrat à terme *f*

fuzzy: ~ **loan** *n* BANK prêt aux termes mal définis *m*

FW *abbr (fresh water)* ENVIR eau douce *f*

FWA *abbr (fresh water allowance)* TRANSP *shipping* correction pour eau douce *f*

FWC *abbr (full loaded weight and capacity)* TRANSP *of container* poids et capacité à charge complète *loc m*

FWD *abbr (fresh water damage)* TRANSP *shipping* avarie par l'eau douce *f*

fwdr *abbr (forwarder)* COMMS expéditeur *m*, IMP/EXP *carrier* expéditeur *m*, transitaire *mf*, TRANSP expéditeur *m*

FX[1] *abbr (foreign exchange)* BANK, ECON, FIN change *m*, STOCK change *m*, devises *f pl*

FX:[2] ~ **option** *n (forex option)* STOCK option de change *f*, option sur devises *f*

FY *abbr (financial year, fiscal year)* ACC exercice *m*, exercice comptable *m*, exercice financier *m*, ECON, FIN, POL, TAX année budgétaire *f*, exercice *m*, exercice financier *m*

FYI *abbr (for your information)* GEN COMM à titre d'information *loc m*, à titre de renseignement *loc m*, à titre indicatif *loc m*, STOCK pour information *loc f*

G

g *abbr* GEN COMM *see gross weight* poids brut *m*, GEN COMM *(gram, gramme)* g *(gramme)*, TRANSP *(general purpose freight container)* conteneur pour usage général *m*, TRANSP *(galliot) shipping* galiote *f*

GA *abbr* GEN COMM *(General Assembly)* AG *(assemblée générale)* GEN COMM *(general authorization)* autorisation générale *f*, INS *(general average)* a.c. *(avarie commune)* MATH *(general average) statistics* moyenne générale *f*; ~ **con** *(general average contribution)* INS contribution pour avarie commune; ~ **dep** *(general average deposit)* GEN COMM cautionnement pour avarie commune *m*

GAAP *abbr* US *(Generally Accepted Accounting Principles)* ACC PCGA *(Principes comptables généralement admis)*

GAAS *abbr* US *(Generally Accepted Auditing Standards)* ACC normes d'audit généralement acceptées *f pl*

GAB *abbr (general arrangements to borrow)* FIN AGE *(accords généraux d'emprunt)*

Gabon *pr n* GEN COMM Gabon *m*

Gabonese¹ *adj* GEN COMM gabonais

Gabonese² *n* GEN COMM *person* Gabonais *m*

Gaborone *pr n* GEN COMM Gabrone *n pr*

GAC *abbr (general average certificate)* INS certificat d'avarie commune *m*

gadget *n* GEN COMM gadget *m*

gag: ~ **order** *n* US *jarg* LAW interdiction de publier les débats *f*, MEDIA *(cf reporting restrictions UK)* embargo *m*, interdiction de rapporter les débats *f*; ~ **rule** *n* US POL règle du baillon *f*

gage¹ *n AmE see gauge BrE*

gage² *vt AmE see gauge BrE*

gagging: ~ **order** *n jarg* UK LAW interdiction de publier les débats *f*

gain¹ *n* ACC gain *m*, ECON, FIN gain *m*, profit *m*, GEN COMM profit *m*, STOCK *on position values*, TAX gain *m*; ~ **contingency** ACC, ECON, FIN gain aléatoire *m*; ◆ **make ~s** ACC, FIN, STOCK faire des gains, réaliser des gains

gain² *vi* GEN COMM gagner, STOCK *increase value* se valoriser; ◆ ~ **entry to** FIN enregistrer des gains sur; ~ **experience** HRM acquérir de l'expérience; ~ **formal approval from** GEN COMM obtenir l'accord officiel de; ~ **ground** GEN COMM gagner du terrain; ~ **in value** STOCK gagner de la valeur, gagner en valeur; ~ **momentum** GEN COMM *trend* s'accélérer; ~ **a toehold in the market** GEN COMM s'introduire dans le marché; ~ **value** STOCK gagner de la valeur, gagner en valeur

gainful¹ *adj* GEN COMM rémunérateur, *business* rentable, *occupation* lucratif

gainful:² ~ **employment** *n* FIN activité lucrative *f*

gal *abbr* GEN COMM US *(gallon)* 3.7854 litres, gallon *m*, GEN COMM UK *(gallon)* 4.546 litres, gallon *m*

gallery *n* GEN COMM, S&M galerie *f*

galley *n* MEDIA *print* galée *f*, placard *m*, épreuve en placard *f*, TRANSP *ship's kitchen* cuisine *f*, *ship* galère *f*; ~ **proof** MEDIA *print* galée *f*, placard *m*

galliot *n (g)* TRANSP galiote *f*

gallon *n* GEN COMM US *(gal)* 3.7854 litres, gallon *m*, GEN COMM UK *(gal)* 4.546 litres, gallon *m*

galloping: ~ **inflation** *n* ECON spirale inflationniste *f*

Gallup: ~ **poll** *n* POL, S&M *market research* sondage Gallup *m*

Gambia *pr n* GEN COMM Gambie *f*

Gambian¹ *adj* GEN COMM gambien

Gambian² *n* GEN COMM *person* Gambien *m*

gamble¹ *n* GEN COMM *risk* pari *m*; ◆ **take a ~** GEN COMM prendre des risques

gamble² **1.** *vt* FIN miser; **2.** *vi* GEN COMM miser, parier; ◆ ~ **on the stock exchange** STOCK jouer à la bourse

game *n* ECON, GEN COMM, MGMNT, POL jeu *m*; ~ **plan** GEN COMM plan d'action *m*, stratégie *f*; ~ **theory** ECON, HRM, MGMNT théorie des jeux *f*

gamesmanship *n* GEN COMM art de gagner par des astuces *m*

gaming *n* GEN COMM combat *m*

gamma *n* STOCK gamma *m*; ~ **coefficient** *AmE (cf gamma factor BrE)* FIN, STOCK coefficient gamma *m*, facteur gamma *m*; ~ **factor** *BrE (cf gamma coefficient AmE)* FIN, STOCK coefficient gamma *m*, facteur gamma *m*; ~ **stock** *UK* STOCK action gamma *f*, action peu active *f*

gang: ~ **piecework** *n* HRM travail d'équipe à la pièce *m*

Gang: ~ **of Four** *n* ECON Bande des Quatre *f*

ganger *n* HRM chef d'équipe *m*

gangway *n* TRANSP passerelle de débarquement *f*

gantry *n* TRANSP *cargo handling* grue portique *f*, portique *m*; ~ **crane** TRANSP *cargo handling* grue portique *f*, portique *m*

Gantt: ~ **chart** *n* COMP diagramme de Gantt *m*

GAO *abbr* US *(General Accounting Office)* ACC Bureau de comptabilité générale *m*

gap *n* FIN *deficit* découvert *m*, *disparity* écart *m*, GEN COMM, STOCK écart *m*; ~ **analysis** BANK analyse d'écarts *f*; ~ **filer** *Canada* TAX déclarant irrégulier *m*; ~ **financing** FIN financement du déficit *m*; ~ **loan** BANK, FIN prêt-relais *m*; ~ **sheet** *jarg* HRM liste des points à perfectionner *f*; ~ **study** GEN COMM, S&M étude des écarts *f*

garage n STOCK nom donné à l'étage ajouté au niveau de la "corbeille" de la Bourse de New York, garage m

garbage n COMP informations parasites f pl, informations éparses f pl, rebut m, ENVIR AmE (cf rubbish BrE) déchets m pl, détritus m, ordures f pl, rebut m; ~ **chute** AmE (cf rubbish chute BrE) ENVIR vide-ordures m; ~ **collection** AmE (cf refuse collection BrE) GEN COMM ramassage des ordures ménagères m; ~ **in, garbage out** (GIGO) COMP rebut à l'entrée et à la sortie m, telle entrée, telle sortie loc; ~ **truck** AmE (cf dustbin lorry BrE) ENVIR benne à ordures f

garboard: ~ **strake** n TRANSP virure de galbord f

garden: ~ **apartment** n AmE (cf garden flat BrE) PROP appartement en rez-de-jardin m; ~ **flat** n BrE (cf garden apartment AmE) PROP appartement en rez-de-jardin m

Garn: ~ **St Germain Depository Institutions Act** n US BANK 1982 loi instituant les entrepôts Garn St Germain

garnish vt LAW opérer une saisie-arrêt, pratiquer une saisie-arrêt

garnishee n LAW tiers saisi m

garnishment n LAW saisie-arrêt f

gas[1] abbr ENVIR AmE (gasoline), IND, TRANSP carburant m, essence f

gas[2] n ENVIR, GEN COMM gaz m; ~ **company** ENVIR compagnie du gaz f; ~ **exploration licence** BrE IND autorisation de prospection de gaz f, licence de prospection de gaz f; ~ **exploration license** AmE see gas exploration licence BrE; ~ **industry** ENVIR, IND industrie du gaz f, industrie gazière f, secteur du gaz m; ~ **and natural gas liquids tax** TAX taxe sur le gaz naturel et les liquides extraits du gaz f; ~ **oil** ENVIR, IND, TRANSP gas-oil m, gazole m; ~ **pipeline** IND for gas gazoduc m; ~ **recovery** ENVIR production de gaz naturel f; ~ **station** AmE (cf petrol station BrE) TRANSP station-service f; ~ **turbine** TRANSP turbine à gaz f; ~ **turbine ship** (GT) TRANSP navire à turbines à gaz m

gaseous: ~ **waste** n ENVIR déchet sous forme gazeuse m

gasoline n AmE (cf gas, petrol BrE) ENVIR, IND, TRANSP carburant m, essence f; ~ **engine vehicle** n AmE (cf petrol engine vehicle BrE) ENVIR, TRANSP véhicule à moteur à essence m; ~ **expenses** n pl AmE TAX frais d'essence m pl

gasworks n pl IND usine à gaz f

gate n LEIS attendance nombre de spectateurs m, takings entrée f; ~ **number** TRANSP aviation numéro de porte m; ~ **pass** GEN COMM autorisation de sortie de marchandises f

gatefold n MEDIA book, magazine encart dépliant m, encart à volets m

gateway n COMMS wide-area networks centre de transit international m, passerelle f, système de communication interréseau m, TRANSP centre de transit international m, aviation point d'accès m, porte d'entrée f

gather vt GEN COMM recueillir; ◆ ~ **in the stops** STOCK regrouper aux arrêts; ~ **information** GEN COMM recueillir des informations, recueillir des renseignements; ~ **intelligence** GEN COMM recueillir des informations, recueillir des renseignements; ~ **speed** GEN COMM prendre de la vitesse

gathering n GEN COMM meeting assemblée f

GATT abbr (General Agreement on Tariffs and Trade) ECON, POL GATT (Accord général sur les tarifs et le commerce)

gauge[1] n BrE GEN COMM trends indicateur m; ◆ **out of** ~ BrE (OOG) TRANSP engagement du gabarit m

gauge[2] vt BrE GEN COMM calculer, mesurer

gavel n GEN COMM auctioneer marteau m

GAW abbr US (guaranteed annual wage) HRM salaire annuel garanti m, salaire minimum interprofessionnel garanti m, SMIG

gazump vt UK LAW, PROP augmenter le prix après acceptation de l'offre initiale

gazumping n UK LAW fait de rompre une promesse de vente pour une offre plus élevée, acceptation d'une suroffre f, PROP augmentation du prix après acceptation de l'offre initiale, suroffre f

Gb abbr (gigabyte) COMP Go (gigaoctet)

GB abbr (Great Britain) GEN COMM Grande-Bretagne f

GBL abbr IMP/EXP (groupage bill of lading) connaissement de groupage m, IMP/EXP (government bill of lading) connaissement public m, TRANSP (groupage bill of lading) connaissement de groupage m, TRANSP (government bill of lading) connaissement public m

GC abbr TRANSP (general cargo) cargaison mixte f, divers m pl, marchandises diverses f pl, TRANSP (grain capacity, grain cubic) shipping capacité volumétrique en céréales f, volume grain m, TRANSP (gyrocompass) shipping compas gyroscopique m, gyrocompas m

GCA abbr (gold clause agreement) TRANSP accord de la clause or m

GCM abbr (general clearing member) STOCK ACG (adhérent compensateur général)

GCR abbr (general commodity rate) STOCK taux général des matières premières m

GCSE abbr UK (General Certificate of Secondary Education) WEL ≈ B.d.C. (Brevet des Collèges)

GCW abbr (gross combination weight) TRANSP articulated vehicle poids maximal d'un véhicule articulé m

GDH abbr (goods on hand) TRANSP stocks existants m pl

GDP[1] abbr (gross domestic product) ECON PIB (produit intérieur brut)

GDP[2] ~ **per capita** n ECON PIB par habitant m; ~ **per head** n ECON PIB par habitant m

gds abbr (goods) ECON biens m pl, GEN COMM, IND

articles *m pl*, produits *m pl*, PATENTS biens *m pl*, S&M articles *m pl*, produits *m pl*

GE *abbr (general equilibrium)* ECON équilibre général *m*

gear: ~ **manufacturer** *n (GR)* TRANSP fabricant d'engrenages *m*

gearbox *n* TRANSP boîte de vitesses *f*

geared: **be** ~ **towards** *phr* MGMNT être orienté vers

gearing *n BrE (cf leverage AmE)* ACC, BANK, FIN, STOCK effet d'endettement *m*, effet de levier *m*, levier financier *m*; ~ **adjustment** *BrE (cf leverage adjustment AmE)* FIN redressement du taux d'endettement *m*, redressement financier *m*; ~ **ratio** *BrE (cf leverage ratio AmE)* ACC, BANK, FIN, STOCK ratio d'endettement *m*, ratio de levier *m*, taux d'endettement *m*

gears *n pl (GRS)* TRANSP engrenage *m*

GEB *abbr (Group Executive Board)* HRM bureau exécutif du consortium *m*, bureau exécutif du groupe *m*

GEM *abbr US (growing-equity mortgage)* BANK hypothèque à capital croissant *f*, hypothèque à paiements croissants *f*

GEMMS *abbr (gilt-edged market makers)* STOCK SVT *(spécialistes en valeurs du Trésor)*

gender: ~ **discrimination** *n* HRM, LAW discrimination entre hommes et femmes *f*, discrimination sexuelle *f*, sexisme *m*

general[1] *adj* GEN COMM, MGMNT général; ~ **purpose** *(GP)* GEN COMM à usage général *loc m*, à vocation générale *loc f*

general:[2] ~ **acceptance** *n* BANK *(SYN clean acceptance)*, GEN COMM *document* acceptation sans réserve *f*; ~ **administrative expenses** *n pl* HRM charges générales d'exploitation *f pl*; ~ **administrator** *n* HRM gérant général *m*; ~ **agent** *n* LAW agent général *m*, représentant général *m*; ~ **arrangements to borrow** *n (GAB)* FIN accords généraux d'emprunt *m pl (AGE)*; ~ **authorization** *n (GA)* GEN COMM autorisation générale *f*; ~ **average** *n (GA)* INS *marine* avarie commune *f (a.c.)*, MATH *statistics* moyenne générale *f*; ~ **average act** *n* INS *marine* loi relative à l'avarie commune *f*, loi relative à l'avarie grosse *f*; ~ **average certificate** *n (GAC)* INS certificat d'avarie commune *m*; ~ **average contribution** *n (GA con)* INS contribution pour avarie commune; ~ **average deposit** *n (GA dep)* INS cautionnement pour avarie commune *m*; ~ **average guarantee** *n* INS *marine* garantie d'avarie commune *f*; ~ **average in full** *n* INS *cargo insurance* avarie commune intégrale *f*, avarie grosse *f*; ~ **averaging** *n* TAX *of income* établissement de la moyenne générale *m*; ~ **cargo** *n (GC)* TRANSP cargaison mixte *f*, divers *m pl*, marchandises diverses *f pl*; ~ **cargo berth** *n* TRANSP poste à marchandises diverses *m*; ~ **cargo and container berth** *n* TRANSP poste à marchandises diverses et conteneurs *m*; ~ **cargo rate** *n* TRANSP tarif marchandises diverses *m*; ~ **cargo ship** *n* TRANSP cargo de divers *m*, cargo de

marchandises diverses *m*; ~ **clearing member** *n (GCM)* STOCK adhérent compensateur général *m (ACG)*; ~ **commodity rate** *n (GCR)* STOCK taux général des matières premières *m*; ~ **contractor** *n* GEN COMM entrepreneur *m*; ~ **counsel** *n (SYN head of the legal department)* HRM chef du département juridique *m*; ~ **creditor** *n* ACC créancier non-garanti *m*; ~ **election** *n* POL élections législatives *f pl*; ~ **equilibrium** *n (GE)* ECON équilibre général *m*; ~ **equilibrium analysis** *n* ECON *theoretical model* analyse d'équilibre général *f*; ~ **exclusion clause** *n* GEN COMM, INS *marine* clause d'exclusion générale *f*; ~ **expense** *n* ACC, GEN COMM frais généraux *m pl*; ~ **expenses** *n pl* GEN COMM frais généraux *m pl*; ~ **fund** *n* FIN fonds courants *m pl*; ~ **government net worth** *n* POL situation nette du gouvernement *f*; ~ **government services** *n pl* ECON *balance of trade* services des administrations publiques *m pl*; ~ **governmental expenditure** *n (GGE)* ECON, FIN, POL dépenses des administrations publiques *f pl*, dépenses publiques *f pl*; ~ **holiday** *n* HRM fête publique *f*; ~ **income tax** *n* TAX impôt général sur le revenu *m*; ~ **journal** *n* ACC livre-journal général *m*; ~ **ledger** *n* ACC grand livre *m*; ~ **liability insurance** *n* INS garantie générale d'assurance de responsabilité civile *f*; ~ **lien** *n* PROP privilège général *m*; ~ **loan and collateral agreement** *n* STOCK accord général d'emprunt et de nantissement *m*, accord général de prêt et nantissement *m*; ~ **management** *n* ADMIN, MGMNT direction générale *f*; ~ **manager** *n (GM)* HRM, MGMNT directeur général *m (DG)*; ~ **market equilibrium** *n* ECON équilibre général du marché *m*; ~ **meeting** *n (GM)* GEN COMM assemblée générale *f (AG)*; ~ **meeting of shareholders** *n* STOCK assemblée générale des actionnaires *f*; ~ **merchandise** *n* TRANSP marchandises mixtes *f pl*; ~ **mortgage** *n* BANK hypothèque générale *f*; ~ **mortgage bond** *n* STOCK obligation hypothèque générale *f*; ~ **obligation bond** *n US (G-O bond)* STOCK *municipal bond* engagement d'hypothèque générale *m*, obligation des collectivités locales garantie *f*; ~ **partner** *n* ACC associé général *m*, HRM commandite *m*, STOCK associé général *m*, associé à responsabilité illimitée *m*; ~ **policy committee** *n* GEN COMM commission de politique générale *f*; ~ **price level accounting** *n (GPLA)* ACC comptabilité indexée sur le niveau général des prix *f*; ~ **provisions** *n pl* ACC *provisions for bad debts against no particular debtor* provisions générales pour risques *f pl*; ~ **purpose berth** *n* TRANSP poste polyvalent *m*; ~ **purpose freight container** *n (g)* TRANSP conteneur pour usage général *m*; ~ **reserves** *n pl* ECON réserve générale *f*, réserve légale *f*; ~ **secretary** *n* HRM *of union* secrétaire général *m*; ~ **service contract** *n UK* TRANSP contrat de service général *m*; ~ **service partner** *n* ACC, STOCK associé général de service *m*; ~ **statement** *n* ACC, GEN COMM relevé général *m*; ~ **strike** *n* HRM grève générale *f*; **the** ~ **public** *n* GEN COMM le grand public *m*; ~ **trader** *n* TRANSP navire de divers *m*; ~ **training** *n* HRM formation générale *f*; ~ **transire** *n* IMP/EXP laissez général *m*, passavant général *m*; ~ **union** *n* HRM syndicat général *m*; ~ **warranty deed** *n US* PROP acte notarié de garantie générale *m*

General: ~ **Accounting Office** *n US (GAO)* ACC Bureau de comptabilité générale *m*; ~ **Accounting Officer** *n US* ACC directeur de comptabilité générale *m*; ~ **Agreement on Tariffs and Trade** *n (GATT)* ECON, POL Accord général sur les tarifs et le commerce *m (GATT)*; ~ **Agreement to Borrow** *n* ECON Accord général d'emprunt *m*; ~ **Assembly** *n (GA)* GEN COMM *UN* assemblée générale *f (AG)*; ~ **Certificate of Secondary Education** *n UK (GCSE)* WEL ≈ Brevet des Collèges *m (B.d.C.)*; ~ **Conference of Weights and Measures** *n (CGPM)* GEN COMM conférence générale des poids et mesures; ~ **Executive Manager** *n* HRM Secrétaire général *m*; ~ **Household Survey** *n (GHS)* ECON *econometrics* enquête générale sur les ménages; ~ **Theory** *n* ECON Théorie générale *f*

generalist *n* GEN COMM, HRM *person* généraliste *mf*

generalize *vi* GEN COMM généraliser

generalized[1] *adj* GEN COMM généralisé

generalized:[2] ~ **least squares** *n pl (GLS)* MATH moindres carrés généralisés *m pl*; ~ **medium** *n* ECON, FIN moyen d'échange généralisé *m*; ~ **system of preferences** *n* ECON système de préférences généralisé *m*; ~ **system of tariffs and preferences** *n (GSTP)* IMP/EXP système généralisé des tarifs et préférences *m (SGTP)*

generally: ~ **quoted market interest rate** *n* ECON taux d'intérêt généralement coté du marché *m*

Generally: ~ **Accepted Accounting Principles** *n pl US (GAAP)* ACC Principes comptables généralement admis *m pl (PCGA)*; ~ **Accepted Auditing Standards** *n pl US (GAAS)* ACC normes d'audit généralement acceptées *f pl*

generate *vt* COMP créer, générer, émettre, ECON *income, profits* générer, produire, GEN COMM *ideas* produire, *waste, power, profit* générer, STOCK *profits* générer; ◆ ~ **income** STOCK produire un revenu

generating: ~ **station** *n* ENVIR, IND centrale électrique *f*

generation *n* COMP *model*, FIN *of profits*, GEN COMM *of profit, income, data*, IND *in product development* génération *f*; ~ **gap** WEL conflit des générations *m*; ~ **-skipping transfer** GEN COMM *of financial assets or property* transfert qui saute une génération

generative: ~ **city** *n* ECON ville moteur *f*

generic[1] *adj* GEN COMM, S&M *marketing* générique

generic:[2] ~ **appeal** *n* S&M appel publicitaire générique *m*; ~ **brand** *n* S&M marque générique *f*; ~ **business plan** *n* GEN COMM plan d'entreprise générique *m*; ~ **job title** *n* HRM définition de poste *f*, intitulé de l'emploi *m*; ~ **market** *n* S&M marché générique *m*

genius *n* GEN COMM génie *m*

gentleman's: ~ **agreement** *n* GEN COMM accord reposant sur l'honneur *m*, accord à l'amiable *m*, LAW accord à l'amiable *m*

gentlemen *n pl* GEN COMM *form of address* Messieurs *m pl*

gentrification *n UK* ECON, WEL embourgeoisement *m*

genuine: ~ **article** *n* GEN COMM article authentique *m*; ~ **occupational qualification** *n BrE (GOQ, bona fide occupational qualification)* HRM qualification professionnelle véritable *f*

geodemography *n* S&M *market research* géodémographie *f*

geographic *adj* GEN COMM géographique

geographical[1] *adj* GEN COMM géographique

geographical:[2] ~ **area** *n* GEN COMM zone géographique *f*; ~ **trade structure** *n* ECON structure géographique du commerce extérieur *f*

geography *n* GEN COMM géographie *f*

geometric: ~ **mean** *n (GM)* MATH moyenne géométrique *f*; ~ **progression** *n* ECON, MATH progression géométrique *f*

geopolitical *adj* POL géopolitique

Georgetown *pr n* GEN COMM Georgetown *n pr*

Georgia *pr n* GEN COMM Géorgie *f*

Georgian[1] *adj* GEN COMM géorgien

Georgian[2] *n* GEN COMM *person* Géorgien *m*

German[1] *adj* GEN COMM allemand

German[2] *n* GEN COMM *language* allemand *m*, *person* Allemand *m*; **the ~ economic miracle** ECON le miracle économique allemand *m*

Germany *pr n* GEN COMM Allemagne *f*

gerrymander *vi* POL pratiquer le charcutage électoral, truquer *(infrml)*

gerrymandering *n* POL charcutage électoral *m*

gestation: ~ **period** *n* ECON période de gestation *f*

get *vt* GEN COMM obtenir; ◆ ~ **ahead** GEN COMM réussir dans la vie; ~ **in touch with** GEN COMM contacter; ~ **in touch with sb about sth** GEN COMM contacter qn au sujet de qch; ~ **into sb's good books** GEN COMM s'attirer les bonnes grâces de qn; ~ **through to sb** COMMS obtenir la communication avec qn; ~ **worse** GEN COMM empirer

GGE *abbr (general governmental expenditure)* ECON, FIN, POL dépenses des administrations publiques *f pl*, dépenses publiques *f pl*

Ghana *pr n* GEN COMM Ghana *m*

Ghanaian[1] *adj* GEN COMM ghanéen

Ghanaian[2] *n* GEN COMM *person* Ghanéen *m*

GHS *abbr (General Household Survey)* ECON *econometrics* enquête générale sur les ménages

Gibraltar *pr n* GEN COMM Gibraltar *n pr*

GIC *abbr* GEN COMM *UK (guaranteed investment contract)* contrat de placement garanti *m*, INS *(guaranteed income contract)* contrat de revenus garantis *m*

Giffen: ~ **good** n ECON, S&M bien de Giffen m; ~ **paradox** n ECON paradoxe de Giffen m

gift n TAX don m; ~ **by will** TAX don par testament m; ~ **causa mortis** LAW donation faite dans la perspective d'un décès imminent f, donation à cause de mort f; ~ **deed** LAW acte de donation m; ~ **inter vivos** LAW donation entre vifs f; ~ **promotion** S&M advertising promotion-cadeau f; ~ **of property** TAX don de biens m; ~ **tax return** TAX déclaration d'impôt sur les dons f; ~ **token** GEN COMM, S&M chèque-cadeau m; ~ **voucher** GEN COMM, S&M chèque-cadeau m; ~**s tax** TAX impôt sur les dons m

gifted adj WEL child doué

gigabyte n (Gb) COMP gigaoctet m (Go)

GIGO abbr (garbage in, garbage out) COMP rebut à l'entrée et à la sortie m, telle entrée, telle sortie loc

gilt n UK STOCK fonds d'État m, obligation d'état f, valeur de premier ordre f; ~ **-edged bill of exchange** n STOCK lettre de change de premier ordre f; ~ **-edged market** n STOCK government securities marché des gilts m, marché des valeurs de premier ordre m; ~ **-edged market makers** n pl (GEMMS) STOCK spécialistes en valeurs du Trésor m pl (SVT); ~ **-edged security** n FIN, STOCK valeur de premier choix f, valeur de premier ordre f; ~ **-edged stock** n STOCK bénéfices par action m pl, valeur de grande qualité f, valeur de premier ordre f; ~ **-edged stocks** n pl UK STOCK placements sûrs du Royaume-Uni m pl

gilts n UK STOCK obligations d'état f pl, valeurs de premier choix f pl; ~ **market** STOCK marché des valeurs de premier ordre m

gimmick n S&M trouvaille f, truc m, TAX subterfuge m

gin: ~ **out** vt infrml GEN COMM débroussailler (infrml)

Gini: ~ **coefficient** n ECON econometrics coefficient de Gini m

Ginnie: ~ **Mae** n infrml US (GNMA) BANK, FIN, PROP société de prêt hypothécaire immobilier f; ~ **Mae pass-through** n STOCK passé par l'association générale nationale des hypothèques

girder n TRANSP hiloire renversée f, hiloire sous barrots f, shipping carlingue f, support m

giro n BANK virement m

Girobank n UK BANK ≈ service des chèques postaux m

gist n GEN COMM essentiel m

give 1. vt GEN COMM consacrer, donner, MGMNT consacrer; ~ **up** STOCK points céder; **2.** vi ~ **back** jarg HRM industrial relations revenir sur les avantages acquis; ~ **in** GEN COMM céder; ♦ ~ **bribes** (ANT take bribes), GEN COMM corrompre

give-away: ~ **magazine** n MEDIA print magazine gratuit m, revue gratuite f

giveback n jarg HRM industrial relations retour sur les avantages acquis m

given: ~ **the circumstances** phr GEN COMM étant donné les circonstances; ~ **name** phr AmE (cf Christian name BrE) ADMIN prénom m

giver n STOCK acheteur m; ~ **for a call** STOCK acheteur d'une option d'achat m, donneur d'option d'achat m; ~ **for a call of more** STOCK donneur d'achat d'encore à prime m; ~ **for a put** STOCK donneur d'une option de vente m; ~ **for a put and call** STOCK donneur de double option m; ~ **on stock** STOCK donneur en valeurs m; ~ **of option money** STOCK donneur de primes m

GLAM abbr infrml (Gray, Leisured, Affluent, Married AmE, Grey, Leisured, Affluent, Married BrE) ECON econometrics le beau monde de 45 à 60 ans, oisif, grisonnant, marié et riche

glamor: ~ **issue** n jarg AmE see glamour issue BrE; ~ **stock** n AmE see glamour stock BrE

glamour: ~ **issue** n jarg BrE STOCK émission d'une valeur vedette f; ~ **stock** n BrE STOCK valeur vedette f

glare: ~ **-free** adj COMP screen antiréfléchissant

glasnost n POL glasnost f, la transparence f

glass: ~ **insurance** n INS assurance bris de glace f; ~ **-reinforced cladding** n TRANSP gainage chargé de verre m; ~ **wool** n IND laine de verre f

Glass: ~ **Steagall Act** n US BANK loi bancaire Glass Steagall

gliding: ~ **rate** n STOCK taux glissant m, taux mobile m; ~ **shift** n jarg HRM horaires variables m pl, équipe à horaires adaptables f; ~ **time** n jarg HRM équipe à horaires adaptables f

glitch n COMP problème technique m, operating system signal transitoire m

global[1] adj GEN COMM comprehensive global, worldwide mondial

global:[2] ~ **balance** n ENVIR équilibre planétaire m; ~ **bank** n BANK banque universelle f; ~ **custody** n FIN conservation globale f, conservation internationale f; ~ **deregulation** n ECON déréglementation mondiale f; ~ **emission** n ENVIR, IND pollution émission globale f; ~ **financial center** n AmE, ~ **financial centre** n BrE ECON, FIN centre financier international m, place financière internationale f; ~ **financial market** n ECON, FIN marché financier international m; ~ **harmonization** n ACC, ECON, FIN harmonisation au niveau mondial f, harmonisation globale f; ~ **image** n S&M image globale f; ~ **marketing** n S&M marketing global m; ~ **memory** n COMP mémoire commune f; ~ **monetarism** n ECON, POL monétarisme global m; ~ **network** n COMP réseau mondial m; ~ **search** n COMP of document, data recherche globale f; ~ **strategy** n GEN COMM stratégie d'ensemble f; ~ **variable** n COMP programming variable globale f; ~ **warming** n ENVIR réchauffement de l'atmosphère m

Global: ~ **Environment Monitoring System** n ENVIR Système mondial de surveillance continue de l'environnement m; ~ **Maritime Distress and Safety System** n (GMDSS) TRANSP shipping

Système mondial de détresse et de sécurité en mer *m*; **~ Positioning System** *n US (GPS)* TRANSP *shipping* système américain de localisation à couverture mondiale

globalization *n* ECON, GEN COMM globalisation *f*, mondialisation *f*

globalize *vt* ECON, GEN COMM globaliser, mondialiser

globally *adv* GEN COMM *universally* globalement, *worldwide* mondialement, à l'échelle mondiale *loc f*

GLOBEX *n* STOCK GLOBEX *m*

gloom *n* STOCK pessimisme *m*

glory *n* GEN COMM gloire *f*

glossary *n* GEN COMM glossaire *m*

glossy: **~ mag** *n infrml (glossy magazine)* MEDIA magazine de luxe *m*; **~ magazine** *n (glossy mag)* MEDIA magazine de luxe *m*; **~ paper** *n* COMMS, GEN COMM, MEDIA papier brillant *m*, papier glacé *m*

GLS *abbr (generalized least squares)* MATH *statistics* moindres carrés généralisés *m pl*

glut[1] *n* ECON, GEN COMM surabondance *f*; **~ on the market** ECON, GEN COMM encombrement du marché *m*

glut[2] *vt* ECON *economy, market*, GEN COMM *economy, market* inonder, saturer, S&M saturer

GM *abbr* ACC, ECON, FIN *(gross margin)* marge brute *f*, EBE *(excédent brut d'exploitation)*, GEN COMM *(general meeting)* AG *(assemblée générale)*, HRM *(general manager)* DG *(directeur général)*, MATH *(geometric mean)* moyenne géométrique *f*, MGMNT *(general manager)* DG *(directeur général)*

GMB *abbr (good merchantable brand)* IND marque loyale et marchande *f*

GMDSS *abbr (Global Maritime Distress and Safety System)* TRANSP *shipping* Système mondial de détresse et de sécurité en mer *m*

GMT *abbr (Greenwich Mean Time)* GEN COMM GMT *(heure de Greenwich)*

GNI *abbr (gross national income)* ECON revenu national brut *m*

GNMA *abbr US (Government National Mortgage Association, Ginnie Mae)* BANK, FIN, PROP société de prêt hypothécaire immobilier *f*

GNP[1] *abbr (gross national product)* ECON PIB *(produit intérieur brut)*, PNB *(produit national brut)*

GNP:[2] **~ -based own resource** *n* ECON ressource propre calculée en fonction du PIB *f*

go: **1.** *vt* **~ against** STOCK aller contre, être défavorable à; **~ round** IND, PROP visiter; **~ through** GEN COMM *examine* dépouiller; **2.** *vi* GEN COMM aller; **~ down** *(ANT go up)* ECON *price* diminuer, être en baisse; **~ under** GEN COMM *company* couler *(infrml)*, faire faillite; **~ up** *(ANT go down)* ECON *price* augmenter, être en hausse; ◆ **~ back to square one** GEN COMM retourner à la

case départ; **~ bankrupt** ACC faire faillite, GEN COMM *company* couler *(infrml)*; **~ bust** *infrml* GEN COMM faire faillite; **~ a bear** *(ANT go a bull)* STOCK spéculer à la baisse; **make a ~ of sth** GEN COMM réussir qch; **~ negative** *jarg* POL, S&M chercher les défauts de l'adversaire, mener une campagne négative; **~ under the rule** *jarg* STOCK être assujetti à la règle; **~ well** GEN COMM marcher

G-O: **~ bond** *abbr US (general obligation bond)* STOCK *municipal bond* engagement d'hypothèque générale *m*, obligation des collectivités locales garantie *f*

goal *n* GEN COMM objectif *m*; **~ congruence** MGMNT réalité des objectifs *f*; **~ programming** MGMNT organisation des objectifs *f*; **~ -seeking** GEN COMM, MGMNT recherche d'objectifs *f*, recherche des buts *f*; **~ setting** GEN COMM fixation d'objectifs *f*, établissement d'objectifs *m*, MGMNT mise au point des objectifs *f*; **~ system** *(SYN tax farming)* ECON, TAX collecte des impôts par fermage *f*; **~ variable** POL variable du but *f*

go-between *n* GEN COMM intermédiaire *mf*

godown *n infrml* TRANSP *Far East* entrepôt *m*

gods *n pl* LEIS *in theatre* poulailler *m*

go-go: **~ fund** *n jarg* FIN fonds hautement spéculatif *m*

GOH *abbr (goods on hand)* TRANSP stocks existants *m pl*

going:[1] **~ short** *adj* STOCK *sale* à découvert *loc m*

going:[2] **~ concern** *n* ACC *principle* continuité d'exploitation *f*, GEN COMM entreprise prospère *f*; **~ -concern concept** *n* ACC principe de la continuité de l'exploitation *m*; **~ -concern principle** *n* ACC principe de la continuité de l'exploitation *m*; **~ -concern value** *n* ACC valeur d'une entreprise prospère *f*, valeur de l'entreprise en continuité d'exploitation *f*; **the ~ rate** *n* FIN, GEN COMM, HRM taux en vigueur *m*

gold *n* FIN or *m*; **~ bullion** FIN or monétaire *m*, GEN COMM lingots d'or *m pl*; **~ bullion standard** ECON, FIN, GEN COMM étalon de lingots d'or *m*; **~ card** BANK carte or *f*; **~ clause agreement** *(GCA)* TRANSP accord de la clause or *m*; **~ coin** BANK pièce en or *f*; **~ cover** ECON couverture or *f*; **~ credit** STOCK crédit en or *m*; **~ currency** BANK monnaie en or *f*; **~ demonetization** ECON démonétisation de l'or *f*; **~ disc** BrE, LEIS *recording industry* disque d'or *m*; **~ disk** AmE see **gold disc** BrE; **~ exchange standard** ECON, FIN, GEN COMM étalon de change or *m*, étalon-or de change *m*; **~ fixing** BANK fixing *m*; **~ franc** ECON franc or *m*; **~ market** ECON, FIN marché de l'or *m*; **~ mine** GEN COMM mine d'or *f*; **~ -mining company** ENVIR, IND société d'extraction de l'or *f*; **~ mutual fund** STOCK SICAV en mines d'or *f*, fonds d'investissement en valeurs aurifères *m*; **~ ore** ENVIR minerai d'or *m*; **~ point** IMP/EXP point d'or *m*; **~ price** STOCK prix de l'or *m*; **~ producer** IND producteur d'or *m*; **~ reserves** ECON réserves d'or *f pl*; **~ rush** GEN COMM ruée vers l'or *f*; **~ shortage**

ECON pénurie d'or *f;* ~ **standard** BANK, ECON, FIN étalon-or *m*

goldbrick *vi infrml US* HRM flémarder, tirer au flanc

goldbug *n* ECON partisan d'un retour à l'étalon or *m*

golden: ~ **age** *n* GEN COMM âge d'or *m;* ~ **formula** *n UK* HRM formule magique *f;* ~ **handcuffs** *n pl* GEN COMM contrat très favorable auquel on consent pour garder un cadre, contrat très avantageux *m;* ~ **handshake** *n* HRM prime d'adieu *f,* prime de départ *f,* prime pour bons et loyaux services *f;* ~ **hello** *n* HRM prime de recrutement *f;* ~ **parachute** *n infrml* FIN indemnité de départ *f;* ~ **rate** *n* HRM tarif promotionnel *m;* ~ **rule** *n* ECON, GEN COMM règle d'or *f;* ~ **share** *n* STOCK action préférentielle *f,* action spécifique *f;* ~ **triangle** *n* ECON le triangle d'or *m*

goldsmith: ~ **banking system** *n* BANK système bancaire de l'orfèvrerie *m*

gondola *n* S&M *shop fitting* gondole *f,* TRANSP *rail* wagon découvert *m,* wagon découvert à bords plats *m* (*vieilli*), wagon plat *m;* ~ **flat** TRANSP *type of container* conteneur plat *m*

good[1] *adj* BANK *debt* bon, certain, FIN *debt* bon, certain, *investment, securities* sûr, STOCK *investment, securities* sûr; ~ **sound merchantable** (*gsm*) GEN COMM qualité loyale et marchande; ♦ **in** ~ **faith** INS de bonne foi; **not in** ~ **delivery** STOCK *unmatched trade* pas de bonne livraison

good:[2] ~ **bargain** *n* GEN COMM bonne affaire *f;* ~ **business background** *n* GEN COMM bonne expérience des affaires *f;* ~ **credit risk** *n* BANK bon risque de crédit *m;* ~ **delivery** *n* STOCK bonne délivrance *f,* livraison correcte *f;* ~ **faith** *n* GEN COMM bonne foi *f;* ~ **-faith bargaining** *n* (*ANT blue-sky bargaining*) HRM, IND négociation sérieuse *f;* ~ **-faith deposit** *n* STOCK dépôt de bonne foi *m, commodities, securities* dépôt initial *m;* ~ **food guide** *n* IND, LEIS guide gastronomique *m;* ~ **housekeeping** *n* MGMNT bonne gestion *f;* ~ **luck** *n* GEN COMM veine *f;* ~ **merchantable brand** *n* (*GMB*) IND marque loyale et marchande *f;* ~ **money** *n* BANK *US* bon argent *m,* ECON *Gresham's Law* bonne monnaie *f;* ~ **news** *n pl* GEN COMM bonnes nouvelles *f pl;* ~ **return** *n* ACC *on investment* bon rendement *m;* ~ **risk** *n* INS bon risque *m;* ~ **-till-canceled order** *n AmE,* ~ **-till-cancelled order** *n BrE* (*GTC order*) STOCK ordre valable jusqu'à annulation *m,* ordre à révocation *m;* ~ **-till-date order** *n* (*GTD order*) STOCK ordre qui est valable seulement jusqu'à la date précisée; ~ **title** *n* LAW, PROP bon titre *m,* bon titre de propriété *m;* ♦ **in** ~ **working order** GEN COMM en bon état fonctionnement; **make** ~ *infrml* GEN COMM *damage* réparer, *succeed* faire de l'argent

Good: ~ **Housekeeping Seal** *n US* S&M *consumer protection* le label de qualité du magazine Good Housekeeping

Goodhart's: ~ **law** *n* ECON loi de Goodhart *f*

goodness: ~ **-of-fit test** *n* MATH *statistical procedure* test de bonne répartition *m*

goods *n pl* ECON marchandises *f pl, property* biens *m pl,* GEN COMM marchandises *f pl,* GEN COMM, IND articles *m pl,* produits *m pl,* LAW biens *m pl,* S&M articles *m pl,* produits *m pl,* TRANSP fret *m,* marchandises *f pl;* ~ **and chattels** *n pl* TAX biens meubles *m pl;* ~ **covered by warrant** *n pl* GEN COMM marchandises couvertes par un certificat *f pl;* ~ **department** *n* GEN COMM service des marchandises *m;* ~ **depot** *n* GEN COMM, TRANSP entrepôt des marchandises *m;* ~ **for re-export** *n pl* IMP/EXP marchandises à réexporter *f pl;* ~ **of foreign origin** *n pl* GEN COMM marchandises de provenance étrangère *f pl;* ~ **on approval** *n pl* GEN COMM marchandises à l'essai *f pl;* ~ **on hand** *n pl* (*GDH, GOH*) TRANSP stocks existants *m pl;* ~ **received note** *n* ACC bon de réception *m,* IMP/EXP, TRANSP bulletin de quittance des marchandises *m;* ~ **and services** *n pl* ECON biens et services *m pl;* ~ **and services tax** *n Canada* (*GST*) TAX taxe de prestation de service *f* (*TPS*); ~ **and services tax credit** *n Canada* (*GST credit*) TAX crédit pour taxe sur les produits et services *m* (*crédit pour TPS*); ~ **train** *n BrE* (*cf freight train AmE*) TRANSP train de marchandises *m;* ~ **truck** *n BrE* (*cf boxcar AmE*) TRANSP wagon de marchandises couvert *m;* ~ **wagon** *n BrE* (*cf freight car AmE*) TRANSP fourgon *m*

goodwill *n* ACC achalandage *m* (*Can*), fonds commercial *m,* survaleur *m,* écart d'acquisition positif *m,* GEN COMM clientèle *f,* droit à la clientèle *m,* fonds commercial *m;* ~ **amortization** ACC amortissement de l'écart de première consolidation *m,* amortissement du fonds de commerce *m;* ~ **money** ACC fonds de commerce *m,* GEN COMM fonds commercial *m;* ~ **on consolidation** ACC écart de première consolidation *m*

goon: ~ **squad** *n jarg US* HRM milice anti-grèves *f,* milice patronale *f,* vigiles *m pl*

goose *vt jarg* HRM pratiquer un électrochoc (*jarg*)

GOP *abbr infrml US* (*Grand Old Party*) POL parti républicain

GOQ *abbr BrE* (*genuine occupational qualification*) HRM qualification professionnelle véritable *f*

gorilla *n infrml UK* GEN COMM personne occupant une position influente; ~ **scale** *jarg* HRM nomination des cadres

go-slow *n BrE* (*cf slowdown AmE*) HRM grève perlée *f*

gourde *n* GEN COMM gourde *f*

govern *vt* LAW régir, POL gouverner, régir

governing: ~ **board** *n* ACC, ADMIN, GEN COMM, HRM, MGMNT conseil d'administration *m,* CA; ~ **body** *n* ACC, ADMIN, GEN COMM, HRM, MGMNT conseil de direction *m;* ~ **principle** *n* GEN COMM idée directrice *f,* idée dominante *f*

government:[1] ~ **-backed** *adj* FIN, POL bénéficiant d'une aide publique *loc f,* soutenu par l'État; ~ **-financed** *adj* ECON, FIN, POL financé par l'État, subventionné par les pouvoirs publics; ~ -funded *adj* ECON, FIN, POL financé par l'État, subventionné par les pouvoirs publics; ~ -owned *adj* GEN COMM, POL *company* public; ~ -regulated *adj* POL réglementé par l'État; ~ -sponsored *adj* FIN, POL *project* patronné par l'État; ~ -supported *adj* FIN, POL *project* soutenu financièrement par les pouvoirs publics, soutenu par l'État; ~ -to-government *adj* POL d'État à État *loc m*

government[2] *n (govt)* POL administration *f*, gouvernement *m*; ~ accounting *n* ACC, POL *principles and procedures* comptabilité publique *f*; ~ agency *n* ADMIN agence gouvernementale *f*, organisme public *m*; ~ annuity *n* FIN rente sur l'État *f*; ~ assistance *n* TAX aide gouvernementale *f*; ~ bill of lading *n (GBL)* IMP/EXP, TRANSP connaissement public *m*; ~ bond *n* ECON *(cf yearling BrE)* obligation à un an *f*, STOCK bon du Trésor *m*, obligation d'état *f*, titre d'État *m*; ~ broker *n* STOCK agent du trésor *m*, courtier du gouvernement *m*; ~ contract *n* GEN COMM, LAW contrat d'État *m*, contrat public *m*, contrat-adjudication de l'État *m*; ~ -controlled corporation *n* ADMIN société contrôlée par l'État *f*; ~ defence appropriations *n* BrE POL budget de la défense *m*; ~ defense appropriations *n* AmE *see government defence appropriations BrE*; ~ department *n* ADMIN département gouvernemental *m*, ministère *m*; ~ enterprise *n* ECON activité financée sur fonds publics *f*; ~ finance *n* FIN finances publiques *f pl*; ~ grant *n* ECON subvention de l'État *f*; ~ intervention *n* ADMIN, ECON, POL intervention de l'État *f*; ~ investment *n* FIN investissements de l'État *m pl*; ~ loan *n* FIN emprunt d'État *m*, prêt d'État *m*; ~ obligations *n pl US (cf Treasury bill bonds)* BANK, ECON, STOCK bons du Trésor *m pl*, valeurs du Trésor *f pl*; ~ relations *n pl* POL relations gouvernementales *f pl*; ~ report *n* GEN COMM, POL rapport parlementaire *m*; ~ research grant *n* FIN subvention publique pour la recherche *f*; ~ role *n* POL rôle du gouvernement *m*; ~ securities *n pl* BANK *US* bons du Trésor *m pl*, ECON, POL titres d'État *m pl*; ~ -sponsored enterprise *n (GSE)* FIN entreprise soutenue par l'État *f*; ~ stock *n* STOCK titre d'État *m*, valeur d'État *f*; ~ tap stocks *n pl UK* STOCK valeurs d'État émises en robinet continu *f pl*

Government: ~ National Mortgage Association *n US (GNMA)* FIN société de prêt hypothécaire immobilier *f*; ~ State Secretariat *n* POL Secrétariat d'État du gouvernement *m*

governmental[1] *adj* POL gouvernemental

governmental:[2] ~ accounting *n* ACC, POL comptabilité publique *f*

governments *n pl infrml US* ECON titres émis par l'État *m pl*

governor *n* ADMIN gouverneur *m*; ~ general ADMIN, POL gouverneur général *m*

govt *abbr (government)* POL administration *f*, gouvernement *m*

GP *abbr (general purpose)* GEN COMM à usage général *loc m*, à vocation générale *loc f*

GPLA *abbr (general price level accounting)* ACC comptabilité indexée sur le niveau général des prix *f*

GPS *abbr US (Global Positioning System)* TRANSP *shipping* système américain de localisation à couverture mondiale

GR *abbr (gear manufacturer)* TRANSP fabricant d'engrenages *m*

grab[1] *n* TRANSP *cargo handling equipment* grappin *m*

grab[2] *vt* GEN COMM *attention* attirer, *opportunity* saisir

grace: ~ days *n pl* ACC, LAW jours de franchise *m pl*, jours de grâce *m pl*; ~ period *n* ACC, LAW délai de franchise *m*, délai de grâce *m*

grade[1] *n* HRM catégorie *f*, *on salary scale* indice *m*, échelon *m*, MGMNT échelon *m*, S&M *quality of product* catégorie *f*, qualité *f*, *size of product* calibre *m*; ~ creep *jarg* HRM augmentation rampante *f*; ~ crossing TRANSP traverse *f*; ~ drift HRM dérapage catégoriel *m*

grade[2] *vt* ADMIN classer, GEN COMM *by quality* classer, *by size* calibrer, classer

graded: ~ by size *phr* GEN COMM *produce* classé par catégorie

gradual *adj* GEN COMM graduel, progressif

gradualism *n* POL politique des petits pas *f (infrml)*, réformisme *m*

gradualist: ~ monetarism *n* ECON monétarisme gradualiste *m*

gradually *adv* GEN COMM graduellement

graduate[1] *n* GEN COMM licencié *m*, HRM diplômé *m*, licencié *m*, WEL bachelier *m*, diplômé *m*, licencié *m*; ~ school of business WEL école supérieure de commerce *f*

graduate[2] *vi* WEL *US from school* obtenir le baccalauréat, WEL *UK from university* obtenir sa licence, obtenir son diplôme

graduated[1] *adj* GEN COMM *container* gradué, TAX progressif; ◆ in ~ stages GEN COMM graduellement, progressivement

graduated:[2] ~ income tax *n* TAX impôt progressif sur le revenu *m*; ~ interest *n* FIN intérêts échelonnés *m pl*; ~ lease *n* PROP loyer progressif *m*; ~ -payment mortgage *n* BANK hypothèque à paiements échelonnés *f*; ~ payments *n pl* FIN payements échelonnés *m pl*; ~ pension scheme *n* HRM régime de retraite proportionnel *m*; ~ tax *n* TAX impôt progressif *m*; ~ wage *n* HRM salaire modulé *m*

graft[1] *n infrml* FIN magouille *f*, HRM dur travail *m*, LAW fait d'obtenir frauduleusement une somme d'argent de l'État en corrompant un agent public, corruption de fonctionnaire *f*, concussion *f*, POL magouille *f (infrml)*, pot-de-vin *m*, tripotage *m pl*

graft[2] 1. *vt* LAW obtenir frauduleusement une somme d'argent de l'État en corrompant un agent public, corrompre; 2. *vi* HRM travailler dur

Graham: **~ and Dodd method of investing** *n* STOCK méthode d'investissement de Graham et Dodd *f*

grain: **~ capacity** *n (GC)* TRANSP capacité volumétrique en céréales *f*, volume grain *m*; **~ charter party** *n* TRANSP contrat d'affrètement de céréales *m*; **~ crop** *n* ECON, ENVIR récolte de céréales *f*; **~ cubic** *n (GC)* TRANSP capacité volumétrique en céréales *f*, volume grain *m*; **~ elevator** *n* TRANSP *cargo handling equipment* élévateur de grain *m*; **~ exchange** *n* STOCK bourse aux grains *f*; **~ terminal** *n* TRANSP centre céréalier *m*

gram *n see gramme*

Gramm: **~ Rudman Hollings Act** *n* US LAW, POL loi du Congrès sur le contrôle budgétaire et fiscal

gramme *n (g)* GEN COMM gramme *m (g)*

Grammy *n* US MEDIA *award* distinction récompensant les meilleures oeuvres musicales américaines de l'année

granary *n* TRANSP *storage* entrepôt de céréales *m*

grand: **~ jury** *n* US LAW jury d'accusation *m*; **~ larceny** *n* US LAW vol qualifié *m*; **~ total** *n* BANK, GEN COMM somme totale *f*, total général *m*

Grand: **~ Old Party** *n infrml US (GOP)* POL parti républicain

grandfather: **~ clause** *n* LAW clause d'antériorité *f*, clause de droits acquis *f*

grandfathering *n* TAX droits acquis *m pl*

granny: **~ bonds** *n pl infrml UK* STOCK bons de grand-mères *m pl*

grant:[1] **~ -aided** *adj* ECON, POL subventionné par l'État; **~ -maintained** *adj* ECON, POL subventionné par l'État

grant[2] *n* ECON, FIN subvention *f*, GEN COMM aide *f*, LAW concession *f*, PATENTS attribution *f*, délivrance *f*, PROP *property conveyance* octroi *m*, WEL aide *f*, *student* bourse *f*; **~ -in-aid** POL subvention de l'État *f*, subvention financière *f*, subvention proportionnelle *f*; ♦ **in ~ form** FIN sous forme de subvention

grant[3] *vt* BANK, FIN *credit* accorder, allouer, *loan, overdraft* consentir, GEN COMM *concessions* accorder, octroyer, *request* accéder à, LAW *will* homologuer, valider, PATENTS *licence* attribuer, délivrer, PROP *tenancy* accorder, STOCK *option* consentir; ♦ **~ credit** FIN accorder un crédit; **~ extended credit** FIN accorder un crédit de longue durée; **~ interim supply** ACC accorder des fournitures intérimaires, ouvrir des crédits provisoires; **~ a licence** *BrE* ADMIN, GEN COMM *premises, trade* accorder une licence; **~ a license** *AmE, see* grant a licence *BrE*; **~ a loan to sb** BANK, FIN accorder un prêt à qn, consentir un prêt à qn

grantee *n* LAW, PROP bénéficiaire *mf*

granting *n* LAW attribution *f*, concession *f*, validation *f*; **~ of credit** BANK concession de crédit *f*, délivrance de crédit *f*, mise à disposition de crédit *f*, octroi de crédit *m*

grantor *n* LAW concédant *m*, PROP concédant *m*,

STOCK vendeur *m*; **~ trust** LAW, PROP fidéicommis de concédant *m*

grants: **~ economics** *n* ECON économie des transferts *f*; **~ expenditures** *n pl* FIN dépenses en subventions *f pl*

grapevine: **the ~** *n* GEN COMM téléphone arabe *m*

graph *n* COMP, MATH graphe *m*, graphique *m*; **~ plotter** COMP, MATH traceur de courbes *m*

graphic[1] *adj* COMP, MATH graphique

graphic:[2] **~ character** *n* COMP caractère graphique *m*; **~ data processing** *n* COMP infographie *f*; **~ database** *n* COMP base de données graphiques *f*; **~ design** *n* S&M *advertising* conception graphique *f*; **~ designer** *n* HRM, S&M graphiste *mf*; **~ display terminal** *n* COMP terminal graphique *m*; **~ software** *n* COMP graphiciel *m*, logiciel graphique *m*, progiciel logique *m*

graphical: **~ editing** *n* MEDIA *print, computer* édition graphique *f*

graphically: **~ illustrated** *adj* GEN COMM, MEDIA illustré à grand renfort de détails

graphics *n pl* COMP graphique *f*, graphiques *m pl*, graphisme *m*, infographie *f*, MEDIA graphique *f*, graphiques *m pl*, graphisme *m*, images *f pl*, représentations graphiques *f pl*; **~ board** *n* COMP carte graphique *f*; **~ card** *n* COMP *graphics* carte graphique *f*; **~ file** *n* COMP fichier graphique *m*; **~ mode** *n* COMP mode graphique *m*; **~ printer** *n* COMP imprimante graphique *f*

grapple: **~ with** *vt* GEN COMM *difficulty* se colleter avec; ♦ **~ with a problem** GEN COMM être aux prises avec un problème

grasping *adj* GEN COMM âpre au gain

grass: **~ -roots movement** *n* GEN COMM, POL mouvement populaire *m*, mouvement qui part de la base *m*; **~ -roots support** *n* POL appui populaire *m*; **the ~ -roots** *n pl* POL la base *f*

gratify *vt* GEN COMM *desire* satisfaire à

gratis[1] *adj* GEN COMM gratis, gratuit

gratis[2] *adv* GEN COMM gratis, gratuitement

gratuitous[1] *adj* GEN COMM gratuit

gratuitous:[2] **~ loan** *n* FIN prêt à titre gratuit *m*

gratuity *n* GEN COMM pourboire *m*, tuyau *m* *(infrml)*, TAX gratification *f*

graveyard: **~ market** *n* STOCK marché baissier sans issue *m*, marché mort *m*; **~ shift** *n* AmE *(SYN night shift)* HRM équipe de nuit *f*

graving: **~ dock** *n* TRANSP cale sèche *f*, forme de radoub *f*

gray: **~ belt** *n jarg AmE see* grey belt *BrE*; **~ market** *n AmE see* grey market *BrE*; **~ society** *n AmE see* grey society *BrE*

Gray: **~ , Leisured, Affluent, Married** *infrml AmE see* Grey, Leisured, Affluent, Married *BrE*

grayscale *n AmE see* greyscale *BrE*

grazing *n jarg* GEN COMM chapardage *m*

grease *vt* IND graisser; ♦ **~ sb's palm** *infrml* GEN COMM graisser la patte à qn *(infrml)*

Great:[1] **~ Depression** *n* ECON grande crise économique de la fin du XIXème en G.B. et des années 30 aux Etats-Unis

Great:[2] ~ **Britain** *pr n (GB)* GEN COMM Grande-Bretagne *f*

greater *adj* GEN COMM plus grand

Greece *pr n* GEN COMM Grèce *f*

greed *n* GEN COMM cupidité *f*

greedy *adj* GEN COMM âpre au gain

Greek[1] *adj* GEN COMM grec

Greek[2] *n* GEN COMM *language* grec *m, person* Grec *m*

green[1] *adj* ENVIR vert, écologique, écologiste, POL vert, écologique; ~ **-conscious** ENVIR *consumers* soucieux de la protection de l'environnement *loc f*, vert, écologiste

green:[2] ~ **ban** *n Australia* HRM boycott vert *m*; ~ **belt** *n* ENVIR *around towns* ceinture verte *f*; ~ **card** *n* ADMIN *US* carte de séjour *f*, HRM carte verte *f*, HRM *US* carte de séjour *f*, INS *US*, TRANSP, WEL carte verte *f*, WEL *US* carte de séjour *f*; ~ **conditionality** *n* ENVIR conditionnalité écologique; ~ **currency** *n* ECON monnaie verte *f*; ~ **energy** *n* ENVIR, IND énergie verte *f*; ~ **issue** *n* ENVIR, POL problème concernant la protection de l'environnement *m*, problème écologique *m*; ~ **labeling scheme** *n AmE*, ~ **labelling scheme** *n BrE* ENVIR, S&M *of products on sale* programme d'étiquetage des produits écologiques *m*; ~ **light** *n* GEN COMM *authorization* feu vert *m*; ~ **lobby** *n* ENVIR, POL groupe de pression des écologistes *m*, lobby écologiste *m*; ~ **petrol** *n* ENVIR essence verte *f*, gasohol *m*, IND, TRANSP gasohol *m*; ~ **pound** *n* ECON livre verte *f*; ~ **revolution** *n* ECON, ENVIR *agriculture* révolution verte *f*; ~ **sea** *n* TRANSP baleine *f*, paquet de mer *m*; ~ **stripe price** *n* STOCK prix pour petits ordres *m*, prix à raie verte *m*

Green: ~ **Discussion Paper** *n* LAW, POL *EU* publication exposant les principes généraux d'un projet; ~ **Paper** *n UK* LAW, POL *parliament* avant-projet de loi; **the** ~ **Party** *n* ENVIR, POL le parti écologiste *m*, les Verts *m pl*

greenback *n infrml US* ECON, FIN billet vert *m (infrml)*, dollar *m*, GEN COMM dollar *m*

greenfield: ~ **site** *n* GEN COMM, IND, PROP zone industrielle nouvelle *f*; ~ **site company** *n UK* HRM société au vert *f*, société à la campagne *f*

greenhouse: ~ **effect** *n* ENVIR effet de serre *m*; ~ **effect gas** *n* ENVIR gaz à effet de serre *m*; ~ **gas** *n* ENVIR gaz à effet de serre *m*

greening *n* ENVIR écologisation *f, of public opinion* prise de conscience écologiste *f*

greenlining *n jarg* ENVIR, WEL réhabilitation des quartiers défavorisés *f*, rénovation de vieux quartiers *f*

greenmail *n US* STOCK chantage financier *m*

Greenpeace *n* ENVIR Greenpeace *m*

Greens: the ~ *n pl* ENVIR, POL les Verts *m pl*

Greenwich: ~ **Mean Time** *n (GMT)* GEN COMM heure de Greenwich *f (GMT)*

greetings *n pl* COMMS compliments *m pl*, salutations *f pl*

Grenada *pr n* GEN COMM Grenade *f*

Grenadian[1] *adj* GEN COMM grenadin

Grenadian[2] *n* GEN COMM *person* Grenadin *m*

Gresham's: ~ **law** *n* ECON loi de Gresham *f*

grey:[1] ~ **belt** *n jarg BrE* ECON zone troisième âge *f*; ~ **market** *n BrE* STOCK marché gris *m*, marché grisâtre *m*, marché parallèle *m*; ~ **society** *n BrE* ECON société vieillissante *f*

grey:[2] ~ **-hair** *vt jarg UK* GEN COMM profiter de l'expérience d'un aîné

Grey: ~, Leisured, Affluent, Married *phr infrml BrE (GLAM)* ECON *econometrics* le beau monde de 45 à 60 ans, oisif, grisonnant, marié et riche

greyscale *n BrE* COMP échelle de gris *f*

grid *n* COMP, MATH grille *f*; ~ **structure** FIN, GEN COMM structure en grille *f*

grievance *n* GEN COMM grief *m*, HRM litige *m*, revendication *f*; ~ **arbitration** HRM conciliation prud'homale *f*; ~ **and disciplinary procedure** GEN COMM, HRM procédure de règlement des conflits *f*; ~ **procedure** HRM procédure pour résoudre des griefs *f*, procédure prud'hommale *f*; ♦ **have a** ~ **against sb** GEN COMM avoir un grief contre qn

GRM *abbr (gross rent multiplier)* PROP multiplicateur de loyer brut *m*

gross[1] *adj* ACC brut

gross[2] *n* GEN COMM, MATH grosse *f*; ~ **amount** *n* ACC montant brut *m*; ~ **assets** *n pl* FIN actif brut *m*; ~ **billing** *n US* S&M facturation globale *f*; ~ **book value** *n* ACC valeur comptable brute *f*; ~ **cash flow** *n* ACC, ECON résultat brut d'exploitation *m*, FIN produit brut *m*, résultat brut d'exploitation *m*, GEN COMM résultat brut d'exploitation *m*; ~ **combination weight** *n (GCW)* TRANSP *articulated vehicle* poids maximal d'un véhicule articulé *m*; ~ **cost** *n* TAX *of property* coût brut *m*; ~ **debt** *n* FIN dette brute *f*; ~ **dividend** *n* ACC dividende brut *m*; ~ **dividend yield** *n (Y'ld-Gr's)* ECON, STOCK rendement boursier brut *m*, rendement de dividende brut *m*, rendement des actions brut *m*; ~ **domestic product** *n (GDP)* ECON produit intérieur brut *m (PIB)*; ~ **domestic product at factor cost** *n* ECON produit intérieur brut au coût des facteurs *m*; ~ **domestic product at market prices** *n* ECON produit intérieur brut aux prix du marché *m*; ~ **earnings** *n pl* ACC, GEN COMM, HRM revenu brut *m*; ~ **excess reinsurance policy** *n* INS réassurance en excédent brut de sinistre *f*; ~ **federal debt** *n US* ECON dette nationale brute de l'État fédéral; ~ **fixed capital formation** *n* ECON, GEN COMM formation brute de capital fixe *f*; ~ **income** *n* ACC chiffre d'affaires *m*, revenu brut *m*, GEN COMM, HRM revenu brut *m*; ~ **investment** *n* ACC investissement brut *m*; ~ **investment revenue** *n* FIN, TAX revenu brut de placements *m*; ~ **leasable area** *n AmE* PROP surface brute louable *f*; ~ **lease** *n AmE* PROP bail brut *m*; ~ **margin** *n (GM)* ACC, ECON, FIN excédent brut d'exploitation *m (EBE)*, marge brute *f*; ~ **mass** *n (g)* GEN COMM masse brute *f*; ~ **miscarriage of justice** *n* LAW atteinte flagrante aux droits d'une partie *f*, déni de justice flagrant *m*, erreur judiciaire flagrante *f*; ~ **misconduct** *n* HRM faute grave *f*, manquement grave à la discipline *m*; ~ **national debt** *n* ECON dette nationale brute *f*; ~ **national expenditure** *n* ECON dépenses nationales brutes *f pl*; ~ **national income** *n (GNI)* ECON revenu national brut *m*; ~ **national product** *n (GNP)* ECON produit national brut *m (PNB)*; ~ **negligence** *n* LAW faute lourde *f*; ~ **operating income** *n* ACC *profit and loss accounts* revenu brut d'exploitation *m*; ~ **pay** *n* HRM salaire brut *m*; ~ **profit** *n* ACC, FIN bénéfice brut *m*; ~ **profit margin** *n* ACC marge bénéficiaire brute *f*; ~ **profit method** *n* ACC méthode du bénéfice brut *f*; ~ **profit ratio** *n* ACC coefficient de bénéfice brut *m*; ~ **rate** *n* TRANSP taux brut *m*; ~ **register ton** *n (GRT)* GEN COMM tonne de jauge brute *f*, tonneau de jauge brut *m*; ~ **registered tonnage** *n* TRANSP jauge brute *f*; ~ **rent** *n* TAX loyer brut *m*; ~ **rent multiplier** *n (GRM)* PROP multiplicateur de loyer brut *m*; ~ **revenue** *n* ACC, GEN COMM, HRM revenu brut *m*; ~ **revenue requirement** *n* TAX critère de recettes brutes *m*; ~ **sales** *n* ACC, GEN COMM, HRM revenu brut *m*; ~ **savings** *n pl* FIN épargne brute *f*; ~ **social product** *n* ECON produit social brut *m*; ~ **spread** *n* STOCK marge brute *f*, échelonnement brut *m*; ~ **state product** *n* ECON produit intérieur brut de l'État *m*; ~ **tare weight** *n* TRANSP tare brute *f*; ~ **ton** *n* GEN COMM *maritime* tonne forte *f*; ~ **tonnage** *n (GT)* GEN COMM tonnage brut *m*; ~ **train weight** *n (GTW)* TRANSP *road vehicle* poids maximal d'un train routier *m, train* tonnage brut complet *m*; ~ **-up** *n* TAX majoration *f*; ~ **vehicle weight** *n (GVW)* TRANSP poids total en charge *m (PTC)*; ~ **wage** *n* HRM salaire brut *m*; ~ **weight** *n (gr.wt.)* GEN COMM poids brut *m*; ~ **yield** *n* ACC, ECON, FIN, GEN COMM, TAX rendement brut *m*

grossed: ~ **-up dividend** *n* FIN, STOCK dividende majoré *m*

grossing: ~ **up** *vt* ACC majoration *f*

ground:[1] ~ **control** *n* TRANSP *aviation* contrôle au sol *m*; ~ **crew** *n* TRANSP *aviation* équipe au sol *f*; ~ **handling** *n* TRANSP *aviation* assistance en escale *f*, service d'escale *m*; ~ **handling agent** *n* TRANSP *aviation* société d'assistance en escale *f*, société de service d'escale *f*; ~ **lease** *n* PROP bail à terrain *m*; ~ **level** *n* PROP rez-de-chaussée *m*; ~ **plan** *n* GEN COMM plan de base *m*; ~ **rent** *n* PROP loyer de la terre *m*; ~ **rules** *n pl* GEN COMM règles de base *f pl*; ~ **transportation** *n* TRANSP navette *f*, transport terrestre *m*; ~ **zero** *n* GEN COMM point d'impact *m*; ◆ **get off the ~** GEN COMM *business, project* démarrer; **make solid ~** STOCK faire des progrès

ground[2] *vt* AmE *(cf earth BrE)* COMP *electrical equipment*, TRANSP mettre à la terre

grounding *n* AmE *(cf earthing BrE)* COMP *physics*, TRANSP mise à la terre *f*

groundless *adj* GEN COMM non-fondé, non-justifié

grounds *n pl* GEN COMM, INS motif *m*, LAW motif *m, for opposition, revocation* motifs *m pl*; ~ **for dismissal** HRM motifs de renvoi *m pl*; ◆ **on ~ of expediency** GEN COMM pour des raisons d'opportunité; **on the ~ of ill health** HRM *retirement or leave* pour raisons de santé

groundwork *n* GEN COMM travail préparatoire *m*; ◆ **do the ~ on** GEN COMM débroussailler

group[1] *n* ACC groupe *m*, GEN COMM groupe *m*, groupement *m*; ~ **accounts** *n pl* ACC comptes consolidés *m pl*, comptes de groupe *m pl*; ~ **of assets** *n* ACC, FIN groupe d'éléments d'actif *m*; ~ **banking** *n* BANK consortium de banques *m*, syndicat de banques *m*; ~ **of banks** *n* BANK groupement bancaire *m*; ~ **bonus** *n* HRM prime collective *f*, prime d'équipe *f*; ~ **chief accountant** *n* ACC chef comptable *m*, directeur de comptabilité *m*; ~ **of companies** *n* GEN COMM groupe de sociétés *m*, groupement d'entreprises *m*; ~ **of connected clients** *n* FIN groupe de clients liés *m*; ~ **contract** *n* GEN COMM contrat collectif *m*; ~ **credit insurance** *n* US INS assurance crédit collective *f*; ~ **disability insurance** *n* US INS assurance invalidité de groupe *f*, assurance invalidité groupe *f*; ~ **dynamics** *n pl* HRM dynamique de groupe *f*; ~ **health insurance** *n* US INS assurance collective contre la maladie *f*, assurance de groupe contre la maladie *f*; ~ **incentive** *n* HRM prime collective *f*, prime d'équipe *f*; ~ **incentive scheme** *n* UK HRM prime collective d'incitation au rendement *f*; ~ **interview** *n* GEN COMM interview collective *f*; ~ **leader** *n* HRM accompagnateur *m*, animateur de groupe *m*; ~ **life insurance** *n* US INS assurance-vie de groupe *f*; ~ **piecework** *n* HRM travail d'équipe à la pièce *m*; ~ **profit** *n* ACC bénéfice consolidé *m*; ~ **structure** *n* GEN COMM structure de groupe *f*; ~ **training** *n* HRM action collective de formation *f*; ~ **travel** *n* LEIS voyages de groupe *m pl*; ~ **working** *n* HRM travail de groupe *m*

group[2] *vt* MATH, TRANSP grouper

Group: ~ **Executive Board** *n (GEB)* HRM bureau exécutif du consortium *m*, bureau exécutif du groupe *m*; ~ **of Seven** *n (G7)* ECON *international trade* Groupe des Sept *m (G7)*

groupage *n* TRANSP groupage *m*; ~ **agent** TRANSP groupeur *m*; ~ **bill of lading** *(GBL)* IMP/EXP, TRANSP connaissement de groupage *m*; ~ **depot** TRANSP centre de groupage *m*, dépôt de groupage *m*; ~ **operator** IMP/EXP, TRANSP commissionnaire de groupage *m*, commissionnaire groupeur *m*; ~ **rate** TRANSP tarif de groupage *m*

grouping *n* MATH *statistics* groupage *m*

grow 1. *vt* IND produire; **2.** *vi* ECON, GEN COMM croître; ◆ ~ **old** GEN COMM vieillir

growing[1] *adj* GEN COMM croissant

growing:[2] ~ **demand** *n* ECON demande en augmentation *f*, demande en hausse *f*; ~ **-equity mortgage**

n US (GEM) BANK hypothèque à capital croissant *f*, hypothèque à paiements croissants *f*

growth *n* COMP croissance *f*, évolution *f*, ECON *of market, industry* croissance *f*, expansion *f*, *of profits, income* progression *f*, GEN COMM, S&M *of market* croissance *f*; ~ **accounting** ACC, ECON comptabilité de croissance *f*; ~ **fund** STOCK fonds de croissance *m*; ~ **in value** STOCK *type of shares legislation* valeur croissante *f*; ~ **index** ECON indice de croissance *m*; ~ **industry** ECON, IND industrie en croissance rapide *f*; ~ **path** GEN COMM sentier de croissance *m*; ~ **pole** ECON, IND pôle de croissance *m*; ~ **potential** ECON, GEN COMM potentiel de croissance *m*; ~ **rate** COMP, ECON, GEN COMM, STOCK taux de croissance *m*; ~ **savings certificate** BANK certificat d'épargne cumulative *m*; ~ **stock** STOCK taux de croissance *m*, valeur de croissance *f*; ~ **strategy** ECON, GEN COMM stratégie de croissance *f*; ~ **theory of the firm** ECON théorie de croissance de l'entreprise *f*

GRS *abbr (gears)* TRANSP engrenage *m*

GRT *abbr (gross register ton)* GEN COMM tonne de jauge *f*, tonneau de jauge brute *m*

gr.wt. *abbr (gross weight)* GEN COMM poids brut *m*

GSE *abbr (government-sponsored enterprise)* FIN entreprise soutenue par l'État *f*

G7 *abbr (Group of Seven)* ECON G7 *(Groupe des Sept)*

gsm *abbr (good sound merchantable)* GEN COMM qualité loyale et marchande

G-spool *n jarg* S&M *advertising* génération *f*

GST *abbr (goods and services tax)* TAX TPS *(taxe de prestation de service)*; ~ **credit** *(goods and services tax credit)* TAX crédit pour TPS *m (crédit pour taxe sur les produits et services)*

GSTP *abbr (generalized system of tariffs and preferences)* IMP/EXP SGTP *(système généralisé des tarifs et préférences)*

GT *abbr* GEN COMM *(gross tonnage)* tonnage brut *m*, TRANSP *(gas turbine ship) shipping* navire à turbines à gaz *m*

GTC: ~ **order** *n (good-till-canceled order, good-till-cancelled order)* STOCK ordre valable jusqu'à annulation *m*, ordre à révocation *m*

GTD: ~ **order** *n (good-till-date order)* STOCK ordre qui est valable seulement jusqu'à la date précisée

GTW *abbr (gross train weight)* TRANSP *road vehicle* poids maximal d'un train routier *m, train* tonnage brut complet *m*

guarantee[1] *n* BANK caution *f*, garantie *f*, GEN COMM *for goods*, INS garantie *f*, LAW *pledge* caution *f*, garantie *f*; ~ **agreement** *n* BANK accord de garantie *m*, engagement de garantie *m*, STOCK engagement de garantie *m*; ~ **deed** *n* BANK acte de cautionnement *m*; ~ **letter** *n* STOCK lettre d'aval *f*, lettre d'engagement *f*; ~ **liability** *n* ACC obligation de garantie *f*; ~ **pay** *n* HRM salaire de garantie *m*; ~ **payments** *n pl* HRM versements de garantie *m pl*; ~ **of signature** *n* BANK certification

de signature *f*; ◆ **under** ~ GEN COMM sous garantie

guarantee[2] *vt* BANK avaliser, *loan, cheque* cautionner, garantir, GEN COMM *assure* assurer, certifier, *goods* garantir, IND, LAW certifier

guaranteed[1] *adj (guar)* GEN COMM garanti

guaranteed:[2] ~ **annual wage** *n US (GAW)* HRM salaire minimum interprofessionnel garanti *m (SMIG)*, salaire annuel garanti *m*; ~ **bill** *n* STOCK billet garanti *m*, effet avalisé *m*; ~ **bond** *n* FIN, STOCK obligation garantie *f*; ~ **delivery** *n* GEN COMM, STOCK livraison garantie *f*; ~ **facility** *n* FIN crédit garanti *m*; ~ **income** *n* FIN revenu garanti *m*; ~ **income contract** *n (GIC)* INS contrat de revenus garantis *m*; ~ **income supplement** *n* TAX supplément de revenu garanti *m*; ~ **insurability** *n AmE* INS *life insurance* garantie d'assurabilité *f*; ~ **investment** *n* GEN COMM placement garanti *m*; ~ **investment certificate** *n* BANK, FIN certificat de placement garanti *m*; ~ **investment contract** *n UK (GIC)* GEN COMM contrat de placement garanti *m*; ~ **issue** *n* STOCK émission garantie *f*; ~ **letter of credit** *n* BANK lettre de crédit garantie *f*; ~ **minimum agricultural wage** *n* ECON salaire minimum agricole garanti *m*, SMAG; ~ **minimum wage** *n* HRM salaire minimum garanti *m*, salaire minimum interprofessionnel garanti *m*, SMIG; ~ **mortgage** *n* BANK hypothèque garantie *f*; ~ **price** *n* FIN prix garanti *m*; ~ **security** *n* STOCK titre garanti *m*, valeur garantie *f*; ~ **share** *n* STOCK action garantie *f*; ~ **stock** *n* STOCK actions à dividende garanti *f pl*; ~ **term** *n* BANK durée garantie *f*; ~ **wage** *n* HRM salaire garanti *m*; ~ **week** *n* HRM semaine garantie *f*

guarantor *n* BANK avaliseur *m*, GEN COMM garant *m*, répondant *m*, LAW fidéjusseur *m*; ~ **underwritten note** *(GUN)* STOCK note de garantie d'avaliste *f*

guaranty *n* BANK *debt* caution *f*, garantie *f*, GEN COMM *to undertake obligation*, INS garantie *f*, LAW caution *f*, garantie *f*; ~ **bond** STOCK bon de cautionnement *m*; ~ **fund** BANK fonds de cautionnement *m*; ~ **savings bank** BANK caisse d'épargne *f*

guard *n* HRM gardien *m*

guardian *n* LAW tuteur *m*; ~ **deed** PROP acte de tutelle *m*

Guatemala *pr n* GEN COMM Guatemala *m*; ~ **City** GEN COMM Guatemala *n pr*

Guatemalan[1] *adj* GEN COMM guatémaltèque

Guatemalan[2] *n* GEN COMM *person* Guatémaltèque *mf*

gudgeon *n* TRANSP fémelot *m*

guesstimate[1] *n infrml* GEN COMM estimation approximative *f*, estimation au jugé *f*, estimation au pifomètre *f (infrml)*

guesstimate[2] *vt* GEN COMM estimer au pifomètre *(infrml)*, faire une estimation au jugé *loc f*

guestworker *n* HRM travailleur immigré *m*

guidance *n* ADMIN conseils *m pl*, GEN COMM

conseils *m pl*, orientation *f*, HRM, MGMNT, STOCK conseils *m pl*

guide *n* GEN COMM *manual* guide *m*, manuel *m*, HRM accompagnateur *m*, LEIS guide *m*; **~ price** GEN COMM cours directeur *m*

guideline *n* ADMIN, GEN COMM, HRM, MGMNT, STOCK directive *f*; **~ lives** *n pl US* PROP barèmes de durées de vie du matériel *m pl*; ◆ **ten percent ~** TAX directive des dix pour cent *f*

guiding: **~ principle** *n* GEN COMM principe directeur *m*

guild *n* HRM corporation *f*, corps de métier *m*; **~ socialism** *UK* HRM corporatisme *m*

guilder *n* GEN COMM florin *m*, gulden *m*

guilty[1] *adj* LAW coupable

guilty:[2] **~ party** *n* LAW coupable *mf*

Guinea *pr n* GEN COMM Guinée *f*

Guinea-Bissau *pr n* GEN COMM Guinée-Bissau *f*

Guinean[1] *adj* GEN COMM guinéen

Guinean[2] *n* GEN COMM *language* guinéen *m*, *person* Guinéen *m*

Gulf: **~ Plus** *n* ECON prix au départ du Golfe *m*; **~ War** *n* ECON, GEN COMM, POL guerre du Golfe *f*

gun:[1] **~ jumping** *n* STOCK opération sur information confidentielle

gun[2] *vt* GEN COMM, STOCK provoquer une cession forcée, c'est-à-dire forcer un rival à vendre un certain nombre d'actions que l'on souhaite acheter

GUN *abbr* (*guarantor underwritten note*) STOCK note de garantie d'avaliste *f*

gunslinger *n* FIN spéculateur *m*

gunwale *n* TRANSP lisse de plat-bord *f*

gutter *n* MEDIA *print* blanc de couture *m*, petits fonds *m pl*

gutterpress: **the ~** *n* MEDIA presse à scandale *f*, presse à sensation *f*

guttersnipe *n jarg* S&M *advertising* affichette de rue *f*

guy *n* TRANSP *rope* retenue *f*

Guyana *pr n* GEN COMM Guyane *f*

Guyanese[1] *adj* GEN COMM guyanais

Guyanese[2] *n* GEN COMM *person* Guyanais *m*

GVW *abbr* (*gross vehicle weight*) TRANSP *road vehicle* PTC (*poids total en charge*)

gypsy *n* TRANSP *loading* poupée *f*

gyrocompass *n* (*GC*) TRANSP compas gyroscopique *m*, gyrocompas *m*

H

h *abbr* GEN COMM *(hour)*, TRANSP *(hour)* h *(heure)*, TRANSP *(hoy) shipping* bugalet *m*

H: **~ of C** *abbr* UK *(House of Commons)* POL Chambre des communes; **~ of L** *abbr* UK *(House of Lords)* POL Chambre des lords

ha *abbr* GEN COMM *(hectare)* ha *(hectare)*, TRANSP *(hatchway) of ship* panneau *m*, écoutille *f*

habeas corpus *n* LAW habeas corpus *m*

habendum *n frml* LAW, PROP habendum *m*

habitat *n* ENVIR *wildlife* habitat *m*

hack *vt* COMP *break into system, computer* pirater; **~ into** COMP *system* pirater

hacker:[1] **~ -proof** *adj infrml* COMP *system, computer* protégé contre les pirates

hacker[2] *n* COMP *illegal* pirate informatique *m*, *legal* passionné d'informatique *m*

hacking *n* COMP effraction informatique *f*, piratage informatique *m*

haggle: 1. *vt* **~ about** GEN COMM, S&M *price* chicaner sur, discuter du, marchander sur; **~ over** GEN COMM, S&M *price* chicaner sur, discuter du, marchander sur; **2.** *vi* GEN COMM, S&M marchander; **~ with sb** GEN COMM marchander avec qn

haggling *n* GEN COMM, S&M marchandage *m*

Hague:[1] **~ Rules** *n pl* TRANSP *shipping* règles de La Haye *f pl*; **The ~ Rules** *n pl* TRANSP Conventions de La Haye *f pl*; **~ Visby Rules** *n pl* TRANSP *shipping* règles de La Haye et de Visby *f pl*

Hague:[2] **The ~** *pr n* GEN COMM La Haye *n pr*

Haiti *pr n* GEN COMM Haïti *m*

Haitian[1] *adj* GEN COMM haïtien

Haitian[2] *n* GEN COMM *person* Haïtien *m*

half:[1] **~ -duplex** *adj (HDX)* COMP semi-duplex; **~ -monthly** *adj* GEN COMM bimensuel; **~ -yearly** *adj* GEN COMM, STOCK *dividend, bond* semestriel

half:[2] **~ -yearly** *adv* GEN COMM *pay* semestriellement

half[3] *n* GEN COMM, MATH moitié *f*; **~ adder** COMP *hardware* demi-additionneur *m*; **~ board** LEIS *accommodation* demi-pension *f*; **~ a dozen** GEN COMM demi-douzaine *f*; **~ fare** TRANSP demi-tarif *m*; **~ height** *(H/H)* TRANSP *container* conteneur demi-hauteur *m*; **~ -life** *infrml* STOCK *of mortgage bond* demi-purge *f*, moitié de vie *f*; **~ a strike price interval** STOCK *Eurodollar options* intervalle d'un demi-point *m*; **~ -tilt container** *(HT)* TRANSP conteneur semi-bâché *m*; **~ -time survey** *(HT)* TRANSP visite à la mi-période *f*; **~ year** GEN COMM semestre *m*; **~ -year rule** TAX règle de la demi-année *f*; **~ -yearly dividend** STOCK dividende semestriel *m*; ◆ **be on ~ -time** GEN COMM, HRM travailler à mi-temps

halftone *n* MEDIA *print* demi-teinte *f*

hall: **~ test** *n* S&M *market research* test dans un édifice public *m*

halo *n* S&M *advertising* halo *m*; **~ effect** GEN COMM effet de halo *m*

Halsey: **~ Premium Plan** *n* US HRM système de primes Halsey *m*

halt *n* STOCK *of trading* arrêt *m*; **~ of trading** STOCK arrêt des opérations *m*, suspension des transactions *f*

halve *vt* GEN COMM réduire de moitié

Hamburg: **~ Rules** *n pl* TRANSP *shipping* règles de Hambourg *f pl*

Hamilton *pr n* GEN COMM Hamilton *n pr*

hammer:[1] **~ price** *n jarg* STOCK prix bradé après faillite *m*

hammer[2] *vt* GEN COMM *criticize* critiquer, STOCK *person* déclarer insolvable; ◆ **~ home** GEN COMM *point* bien insister sur; **~ the market** STOCK pousser à la vente

hammered *adj jarg* STOCK *person* déclaré insolvable

hamper *vt* GEN COMM *growth* empêcher, gêner

hand:[1] **~ -held** *adj* COMP portatif; **~ -woven** *adj* IND tissé à la main

hand:[2] **~ calculator** *n* GEN COMM, MATH calculette *f*; **~ pallet-transporter** *n* TRANSP *cargo handling equipment* transpalette *m*; ◆ **at ~** GEN COMM *in question* en question; **come to ~** GEN COMM arriver à destination; **go ~ in hand with** GEN COMM aller de pair avec; **in ~** GEN COMM *being dealt with* en main

handbarrow *n* TRANSP diable *m*

handbill *n* COMMS prospectus *m*

handbook *n* GEN COMM manuel *m*

handicapped: **~ person** *n* HRM handicapé *m*

handle[1] *n* COMP poignée *f*

handle[2] *vt* GEN COMM *objects* manier, *situation* gérer; ◆ **~ with care** GEN COMM *notice on parcels* à manier avec précaution, fragile; **~ large sums of money** FIN gérer de grosses sommes d'argent

handling *n* *(hdlg)* GEN COMM, TRANSP *of goods* manutention *f*; **~ allowance** STOCK indemnité de manutention *f*, remise pour manutention *f*; **~ charge** ADMIN, GEN COMM, S&M *for processing order* frais de gestion *m pl*, frais de manutention *m pl*

handmade *adj* IND fait à la main

hands:[1] **~ -off** *adj* GEN COMM non interventionniste; **~ -on** *adj* HRM *experience, training* direct, pratique, sur le tas

hands:[2] **~ -off policy** *n* ECON, GEN COMM politique de non-intervention *f*; **~ -on experience** *n* HRM expérience de terrain *f*; **~ -on session** *n* POL discussion en prise directe *f*; ~ **-on training** *n* HRM apprentissage pratique *m*, formation pratique *f*; ◆ **in the ~ of** GEN COMM *under the ownership of* entre les mains de; **in the ~ of a third party** GEN COMM en main tierce; **our ~ are tied** GEN COMM nous avons les mains liées

handwriting *n* COMMS *document* manuscrit *m*

handwritten *adj* COMMS *document* manuscrit

handyman *n* HRM factotum *m*, homme à tout faire *m*, homme de peine *m*

hang:¹ ~ **-out** *n infrml* PROP solde d'amortissement *m*

hang:² ~ **up** *vi* COMMS *on phone* raccrocher

hang:³ ~ **on, please!** *phr infrml* COMMS *on phone* ne quittez pas, s'il vous plaît !

Hang: ~ **Seng index** *n* STOCK indice Hang Seng *m*, indice Hongkong *m*

Hanoi *pr n* GEN COMM Hanoi *n pr*

Harare *pr n* GEN COMM Harare *n pr*

harbor *n AmE see* **harbour** *BrE*

harbour *n BrE* TRANSP port *m*; ~ **authority** *n BrE* TRANSP autorité portuaire *f*; ~ **dues** *n pl BrE* TAX droits de port *m pl*; ~ **facilities** *n pl BrE* IMP/EXP, TRANSP installations portuaires *f pl*; ~ **master** *n BrE* HRM capitaine de port *m*

hard¹ *adj* GEN COMM *data, facts* concret, *difficult* difficile, *rigid* solide; ~ **-hit** GEN COMM *seriously affected* durement touché; ◆ **make things ~ for sb** GEN COMM mener la vie dure à qn

hard:² ~ **bargaining** *n* GEN COMM négociations serrées *f pl*; ~ **card** *n* COMP carte disque dur *f*; ~ **cash** *n* ECON, FIN espèces *f pl*; ~ **commodity** *n* ECON, IND minerai lourd *m*; ~ **copy** *n* ADMIN, COMMS copie imprimée *f*, COMP copie imprimée *f*, sortie papier *f*, tirage *m*, trace écrite *f*, épreuve *f*; ~ **core** *n* GEN COMM *group of people* noyau dur *m*; ~ **-core unemployed** *n AmE (cf* long-term unemployed *BrE)* ECON chômeur de longue durée *m*, demandeur d'emploi de longue durée *m*, HRM chômeur de longue durée *m*; ~ **cost** *n* FIN *construction, real estate* coût de base *m*; ~ **costs** *n pl* FIN coûts essentiels *m pl*; ~ **currency** *n* ECON devise forte *f*; ~ **discount** *n* FIN grosse remise *f*, maxi-discompte *m*; ~ **discounter** *n* FIN maxi-discompteur *m*; ~ **disk** *n* COMP *hardware* disque dur *m*; ~ **disk drive** *n (HDD)* COMP unité de disque dur *f*; ~ **disk management** *n* COMP *operating system* gestion de disque dur *f*; ~ **disk unit** *n* COMP unité de disque dur *f*; ~ **error** *n* COMP erreur matérielle *f*, erreur récurrente *f*; ~ **and fast rules** *n pl* GEN COMM règles absolues *f pl*; ~ **goods** *n pl* GEN COMM biens d'équipement *m pl*; ~ **hat** *n* HRM, IND casque de chantier *m*; ~ **landing** *n (ANT* soft landing*)* ECON, GEN COMM atterrissage brutal *m*; ~ **loan** *n* BANK prêt aux conditions commerciales *m*, prêt aux conditions du marché *m*, prêt remboursable en monnaie forte *m*; ~ **money** *n jarg* ECON argent solide *m*, monnaie forte *f*, POL fonds soutenu *m*, subvention de l'État à l'éducation *f pl*, WEL subvention de l'État à l'éducation *f*

pl; ~ **page break** *n* COMP *word-processed document* changement de page obligatoire *m*; ~ **return** *n* COMP retour à la ligne obligatoire *m*; ~ **sell** *n (ANT* soft sell*)* S&M vente agressive *f*, vente forcée *f*; ~ **sell tactics** *n pl* S&M politique de promotion agressive *f*; ~ **selling** *n* S&M vente agressive *f*; ~ **-top container** *n* TRANSP conteneur à toit amovible *m*

hardback¹ *adj (SYN* hardcover*)* MEDIA *book* cartonné, emboîté, relié en dur

hardback² *n (SYN* hardcover*)* MEDIA *book* livre cartonné *m*, livre emboîté *m*, livre relié en dur *m*; ~ **book** MEDIA livre cartonné *m*, livre emboîté *m*, livre relié en dur *m*

hardbound: ~ **book** *n* MEDIA livre cartonné *m*, livre emboîté *m*, livre relié en dur *m*

hardcover¹ *adj (SYN* hardback*)* MEDIA *book* cartonné, emboîté, relié en dur

hardcover² *n (SYN* hardback*)* MEDIA *book* livre cartonné *m*, livre emboîté *m*, livre relié en dur *m*; ~ **book** MEDIA livre cartonné *m*, livre emboîté *m*, livre relié en dur *m*

harden *vi* GEN COMM, S&M *of market* se raffermir

hardening: ~ **market** *n* GEN COMM, S&M marché qui se raffermit *m*

hardline *adj* POL pur et dur

hardliner *n* POL pur et dur *m*

hardship *n* WEL pauvreté *f*, privation *f*; ~ **categories** *n pl* WEL catégories sociales défavorisées *f pl*, les classes sociales défavorisées *m pl* (*infrml*)

hardtop *n* TRANSP voiture à toit de tôle amovible *f*

hardware *n* COMP hardware *m*, matériel *m*, équipement *m*; ~ **compatibility** *n* COMP compatibilité du matériel *f*; ~ **configuration** *n* COMP configuration matérielle *f*; ~ **device** *n* COMP dispositif câblé *m*; ~ **failure** *n* COMP défaillance matérielle *f*, incident machine *m*, panne machine *f*; ~ **firm** *n* COMP constructeur d'ordinateurs *m*; ~ **interrupt** *n* COMP interruption matérielle *f*; ~ **requirements** *n pl* COMP configuration matérielle *f*; ~ **security** *n* COMP sécurité du matériel *f*; ~ **specialist** *n* COMP spécialiste du matériel *m*, technicien de hardware *m*; ~ **upgrade** *n* COMP amélioration matérielle *f*, extension matérielle *f*, évolution matérielle *f*

harmful: ~ **effect** *n* ENVIR *pollution* effet nocif *m*, effet nuisible *m*

harmonic: ~ **mean** *n* MATH *statistics* moyenne harmonique *f*

harmonization *n* ACC, ECON *of trade barriers*, IMP/EXP *EU*, LAW, POL harmonisation *f*; ~ **conference** TRANSP conférence de harmonisation *f*; ~ **process** ECON, GEN COMM, IMP/EXP *EU*, LAW, POL processus d'harmonisation *m*

harmonize *vt* ECON, GEN COMM *laws, taxes*, IMP/EXP *EU*, LAW, POL harmoniser

harsh *adj* ECON, GEN COMM *competition* dur, sévère, âpre

hasten *vt* GEN COMM diligenter

hatch *n* TRANSP *of ship* panneau *m*, écoutille *f*; **~ coaming** TRANSP *of ship* hiloire d'écoutille *f*, hiloire de cale *f*; **~ covering** TRANSP *of ship* panneau d'écoutille *m*

hatchman *n* [pl -men] HRM *of ship* responsable de la mise en cale *m*

hatchway *n* (*ha*) TRANSP *of ship* panneau *m*, écoutille *f*

haulage *n* TRANSP camionnage *m*, roulage *m*, transport routier *m*; **~ company** TRANSP entreprise de camionnage *f*, entreprise de transport *f*, entreprise de transports routiers *f*; **~ contractor** (*SYN trucking contractor*) TRANSP camionneur *m*, entrepreneur de transports *m*, entrepreneur de transports routiers *m*, transporteur *m*; **~ depot** TRANSP gare routière *f*

hauler *n* AmE (*cf haulier BrE*) TRANSP camionneur *m*, entrepreneur de transports *m*, entrepreneur de transports routiers *m*, transporteur *m*

haulier *n* TRANSP *BrE* (*cf trucking company AmE*) *company* camionneur *m*, entreprise de camionnage *f*, entreprise de transport *f*, entreprise de transports routiers *f*, transporteur *m*, TRANSP *BrE* (*cf hauler AmE*) *person* camionneur *m*, entrepreneur de transports *m*, entrepreneur de transports routiers *m*, transporteur *m*

Havana:[1] **~ Charter** *n* ECON Charte de la Havane *f*

Havana[2] *pr n* GEN COMM La Havane *n pr*

have *vt* GEN COMM avoir; ◆ **~ it out for good with sb** *infrml* GEN COMM s'expliquer une bonne fois pour toutes avec qn

haven *n* GEN COMM havre *m*, refuge *m*

HAWB *abbr* (*house air waybill*) IMP/EXP, TRANSP *aviation* lettre de groupage aérien *f*

hawk *vt* GEN COMM colporter

hawker *n* GEN COMM colporteur *m*, marchand ambulant *m*

hazard *n* GEN COMM danger *m*, risque *m*; **~ insurance** *US* INS assurance hasard *f*, assurance risque *f*

hazardous: **~ cargo** *n* TRANSP marchandises dangereuses *f pl*; **~ chemicals** *n pl* (*hazchem*) IMP/EXP, IND produit chimique dangereux *m*, TRANSP produits chimiques dangereux *m pl*; **~ polluting substance** *n* (*HPS*) TRANSP substance polluante dangereuse *f*; **~ substance** *n* ENVIR substance dangereuse *f*, substance nocive *f*

hazchem *abbr* (*hazardous chemicals*) IMP/EXP, IND produit chimique dangereux *m*, TRANSP produits chimiques dangereux *m pl*

h.b. *abbr* (*hours of business*) GEN COMM heures d'ouverture *f pl*, heures de bureau *f pl*, heures de réception de clientèle *f pl*, heures ouvrables *f pl*

HC *abbr* TRANSP (*high cube*) *container* conteneur hors-normes *m*, HC (*conteneur hors-cotes*), TRANSP (*hydraulic coupling*) *of ship* accouplement hydraulique *m*, TRANSP (*heating coil*) *of ship* bobine thermique *f*, serpentin de réchauffage *m*

HD *abbr* (*high density*) COMP HD (*haute densité*)

HDD *abbr* COMP (*high-density disk*) disquette à haute densité *f*, COMP (*hard disk drive*) unité de disque dur *f*

hdlg *abbr* (*handling*) GEN COMM, TRANSP *of goods* manutention *f*

HDX *abbr* (*half-duplex*) COMP semi-duplex

HE *abbr* HRM (*Her Excellency*) *ambassadress* Son Excellence Madame l'Ambassadrice *f*, HRM (*His Excellency*) *ambassador* Son Excellence Monsieur l'Ambassadeur *f*, HRM (*Her Excellency, His Excellency*) *high-ranking official* Son Excellence *f*; **~ Cls B** (*heating coil in bunkers*) TRANSP *in bunkers* serpentin de réchauffage dans les soutes *m*

head *n* ADMIN (*SYN boss, chief, senior*) chef *m*, GEN COMM tête *f*, HRM (*SYN boss, chief, senior*) chef *mf*, MEDIA *in newspaper* blanc de tête *m*, gros titre *m*, manchette *f*, titre *m*, MGMNT (*SYN boss, chief, senior*) chef *m*; **~ accountant** *n* ACC chef comptable *m*; **~ buyer** *n* GEN COMM, HRM, S&M chef d'approvisionnement *m*, chef des achats *m*, chef du service achats *m*, directeur des achats *m*, responsable des achats *m*; **~ clerk** *n* ADMIN chef de bureau *m*, HRM chef de bureau *m*, premier commis *m*, LAW premier clerc *m*, principal *m*, MGMNT chef de bureau *m*; **~ count** *n* GEN COMM *of people present* comptage du nombre de personnes présentes *m*; **~ crash** *n jarg* COMP écrasement de la tête *m*; **~ foreman** *n* [pl -men] HRM chef d'atelier *m*; **~ lease** *n* LAW bail initial *m*; **~ of the legal department** *n* (*SYN general counsel*) HRM chef du département juridique *m*; **~ office** *n* (*HO*) ACC *registered address of company*, BANK siège social *m*, GEN COMM agence centrale *f*, siège social *m*, MGMNT administration centrale *f*, siège social *m*; **~ of the personnel department** *n* (*SYN personnel director*) HRM, MGMNT chef du personnel *m*, chef du service personnel *m*, directeur des ressources humaines *m*, directeur du personnel *m*, DRH; **~ and shoulders** *n* ECON *curve* courbe en profil de buste *f*; **~ of state** *n* POL chef d'état *m*; **~ waiter** *n* HRM maître d'hôtel *m*; ◆ **have a ~ start** GEN COMM être avantagé dès le départ

header *n* ADMIN *of document*, COMP (*SYN header-block*) en-tête *m*, marge en-tête *f*, marge supérieure *f*, MEDIA marge en-tête *f*, *of TV broadcast* bande-annonce *f*, en-tête *m*, marge supérieure *f*; **~ bar** TRANSP *of container* coiffe d'extrémité *f*; **~ -block** (*SYN header*) COMP en-tête *m*, marge en-tête *f*, marge supérieure *f*

headhunt 1. *vt* HRM *recruit* rechercher, recruter; **2.** *vi* HRM chasser les têtes, recruter des cadres

headhunted: **be ~** *phr* HRM être recherché par les chasseurs de têtes

headhunter *n* HRM *person* chasseur de têtes *m*

heading *n* ACC *of balance sheet* chapitre *m*, rubrique *f*, titre *m*, ADMIN, COMP, MEDIA en-tête *m*

headline n MEDIA in newspaper blanc de tête m, gros titre m, manchette f, titre m; ~ **rate** (ANT underlying inflation rate, underlying rate) ECON taux d'inflation apparent m

headphones n pl GEN COMM écouteurs m pl

headquarter vt AmE ADMIN company installer le siège de

headquarters n pl ADMIN (HQ), HRM (HQ) direction centrale f, quartier général m, siège social m, TAX of tax office administration centrale f

heads n pl MEDIA in newspaper gros titres m pl, manchette f, titres m pl; ~ **of agreement** GEN COMM principes fondamentaux m pl

headway: **make ~** phr GEN COMM faire des progrès loc m

health n GEN COMM santé f; ~ **benefits** n pl WEL prestations maladie f pl; ~ **care** n GEN COMM services de santé m pl; ~ **care industry** n IND, WEL secteur de la santé m, secteur sanitaire m; ~ **center** n AmE, ~ **centre** n BrE WEL centre médico-social m; ~ **club** n LEIS centre de remise en forme m; ~ **economics** n ECON, WEL économie de la santé f, évaluation des coûts de la santé publique f; ~ **education** n WEL enseignement de l'hygiène m; ~ **farm** n WEL établissement de cure m; ~ **foods** n pl WEL aliments macrobiotiques m pl, aliments naturels m pl; ~ **hazard** n WEL risque pour la santé m, risque sanitaire m; ~ **insurance** n INS assurance maladie f; ~ **insurance contribution** n TAX cotisation assurance maladie f; ~ **insurance scheme** n HRM système d'assurance maladie m; ~ **maintenance organization** n US (HMO) INS organisation de médecine préventive et curative f; ~ **officer** n HRM, WEL inspecteur des services de santé m; ~ **record** n WEL dossier médical m; ~ **regulations** n pl HRM, LAW, WEL réglementation relative à la santé publique f, règlements sanitaires m pl; ~ **risk** n WEL risque pour la santé m; ~ **and safety** n HRM hygiène et sécurité du travail f; ~ **sector** n IND, WEL secteur de la santé m, secteur sanitaire m; ~ **services plan** n INS assurance maladie f

Health: ~ **Authority** n UK ADMIN, WEL administration régionale de la santé publique f; ~ **and Safety at Work Act** n UK (HSWA) HRM, LAW 1974 loi sur la santé et la sécurité au travail; ~ **and Safety Commission** n UK WEL comité pour la sécurité et la protection de la santé sur le lieu de travail; ~ **and Safety Executive** n UK (HSE) WEL bureau de la sécurité et de la protection de la santé (agence nationale qui assure la santé et la sécurité du personnel aux locaux du travail); ~ **and Safety Inspectorate** n UK (cf Factory Inspectorate) WEL Inspection du travail f

healthy adj GEN COMM competition, market en bonne santé, sain

hear: ~ **a case in chambers** phr LAW juger en chambre du conseil, juger en référé; ~ **sth through the grapevine** phr GEN COMM apprendre qch de manière indirecte

hearing n LAW audience f, audition f, interrogatoire m

hearsay n GEN COMM on-dit m, ouï-dire m, rumeur f, LAW déposition sur la foi d'autrui f

heated: ~ **container** n TRANSP conteneur calorifique m

heater n (htr) GEN COMM appareil de chauffage m

heating: ~ **coil** n (HC) TRANSP on ship bobine thermique f, serpentin de réchauffage m; ~ **coil in bunkers** n (HE Cls B) TRANSP serpentin de réchauffage dans les soutes f

heavily[1] adv GEN COMM taxed lourdement; ♦ ~ **traded** STOCK activement négocié, négocié massivement

heavily:[2] ~ **indebted middle-income country** n (HIC) FIN pays à revenu moyen et à fort endettement m

heavy[1] adj ECON demand considérable, fort, GEN COMM demand considérable, fort, goods, weight lourd, STOCK lourd

heavy:[2] ~ **advertising** n S&M publicité intensive f; ~ **demand** n ECON demande considérable f, forte demande f; ~ **engineering** n (ANT light engineering) IND industrie lourde f; ~ **fuel** n ENVIR combustible lourd m; ~ **goods traffic** n TRANSP trafic de poids lourds m; ~ **goods vehicle** n (HGV) TRANSP poids lourd m; ~ **industrial plant** n IND entreprise industrielle lourde f; ~ **industry** n (ANT light industry) IND industrie lourde f; ~ **jet** n TRANSP gros-porteur m; ~ **lift** n (H/L) TRANSP cargo handling colis lourd m; ~ **lift mast crane** n TRANSP bigue f, mât de charge pour colis lourds m; ~ **lift ship** n TRANSP transporteur de colis lourds m; ~ **lifting beam** n TRANSP portique pour colis lourds m; ~ **metal** n ENVIR pollution métal lourd m; ~ **metal concentration** n ENVIR concentration de métaux lourds f; ~ **share** n STOCK action lourde f, action à prix élevé f; ~ **user** n COMP gros utilisateur m; ~ **viewer** n S&M téléspectateur assidu m

hectare n (ha) GEN COMM hectare m (ha)

hedge[1] n STOCK arbitrage m, couverture f, opération de couverture à terme f; ~ **against inflation** FIN, INS couverture contre l'inflation f; ~ **clause** STOCK clause de couverture f, clause de sauvegarde f; ~ **cost** STOCK coût de couverture m, frais de couverture m pl; ~ **fund** jarg STOCK fonds d'arbitrage m, fonds de sauvegarde m; ~ **management** STOCK gestion de couverture f; ~ **manager** STOCK gestionnaire de couverture m; ~ **period** STOCK période de couverture f; ~ **ratio** STOCK ratio de couverture m; ~ **trading** STOCK négoce de titres sauvegardés m, opérations de couverture f pl

hedge[2] **1.** vt FIN risk, STOCK risk couvrir; **2.** vi FIN, STOCK se couvrir; ♦ ~ **one's bets** GEN COMM se couvrir

hedged: ~ **asset** n ACC élément d'actif couvert m; ~ **liability** n ACC élément de passif couvert m; ~ **short sale** n STOCK vente à découvert protégée f;

~ tender *n* STOCK cours légal couvert *m*, offre d'achat *f*

hedger *n* STOCK opérateur en couverture *m*

hedging *n* FIN, STOCK couverture *f*, opération de couverture *f*, opération de couverture à terme *f*, opération de protection *f*, protection des placements *f*; **~ goal** *n* FIN, STOCK objectif d'arbitrage *m*, objectif de couverture *m*, visée de couverture *f*; **~ operations** *n pl* FIN, STOCK arbitrage en couverture de risques *m*, compensations des risques de change *f pl*, opérations de couverture à terme *f pl*; **~ strategy** *n* FIN, STOCK stratégie de couverture *f*

hefty *adj* *infrml* ECON *price, debt,* GEN COMM *price, debt* considérable

hegemony *n* POL hégémonie *f*

height *n* *(hgt)* GEN COMM hauteur *f*

heighten *vt* GEN COMM *tension, fear* intensifier

heir *n* LAW, PROP héritier *m*

heiress *n* LAW, PROP héritière *f*

heirs: ~ and assigns *n pl* LAW, PROP *deeds, wills* héritiers et ayants droit *m pl*

held: not ~ *adj* STOCK non-détenu, non-valable; ◆ **~ or direct covered** INS *marine* couverture directe *f*

helicopter *n* TRANSP hélicoptère *m*; **~ money** *jarg* ECON augmentation rapide de la masse monétaire *f*, hyperinflation de la monnaie *f*

heliport *n* TRANSP héliport *m*

helistop *n* TRANSP hélistation *f*

helm *n* TRANSP *ship* barre *f*

help *n* COMP aide *f*; **~ key** COMP touche d'aide *f*; **~ mode** COMP mode aide *m*; **~ screen** COMP aide en ligne *f*, aide à l'écran *f*, écran d'aide *m*; **~ -wanted advertising** HRM avis d'offres d'emplois *m pl*

Helsinki *pr n* GEN COMM Helsinki *n pr*

hemline: ~ theory *n* STOCK théorie des mini et maxi-jupes *f*

Her: ~ Excellency *n* *(HE)* HRM *ambassadress* Son Excellence Madame l'Ambassadrice *f, high-ranking official* Son Excellence *f*; **~ Majesty's Customs** *n* UK *(HMC)* IMP/EXP douanes de Sa Majesté; **~ Majesty's Customs and Excise** *n* UK *(HMC&E)* IMP/EXP administration britannique des contributions indirectes, la Régie de Sa Majesté *f*; **~ Majesty's Government** *n* UK *(HMG)* GEN COMM le gouvernement de sa majesté; **~ Majesty's Ship** *n* UK *(HMS)* TRANSP vaisseau de Sa Majesté; **~ Majesty's Stationery Office** *n* UK *(HMSO)* ADMIN, GEN COMM ≈ Imprimerie nationale *f*

hereby: I the undersigned ~ testify that *phr* LAW j'atteste par la présente que, je soussigné certifie que

herein *adv* COMMS, GEN COMM, LAW ci-inclus, ci-joint

hereto *adv* COMMS, GEN COMM, LAW à ceci, à cela

heretofore *adv* COMMS, GEN COMM, LAW jusqu'ici

hereunder *adv* COMMS, GEN COMM, LAW ci-dessous

herewith *adv* COMMS, GEN COMM ci-inclus, ci-joint

Hermes: ~ model *n* ECON modèle Hermès *m*

hesiflation *n jarg* ECON *macroeconomics* croissance hésitante dans un contexte d'inflation élevée

hesitant[1] *adj* GEN COMM, STOCK hésitant

hesitant:[2] **~ market** *n* STOCK marché hésitant *m*

heterogeneous[1] *adj* *(*ANT *homogeneous)* GEN COMM hétérogène

heterogeneous:[2] **~ cargo** *n* TRANSP marchandises non-homogènes *f pl*

heteroscedasticity *n* *(*ANT *homoscedasticity)* MATH *statistics* hétéroscédasticité *f*

heuristic *adj* COMP, GEN COMM, MGMNT *problem solving* heuristique

heuristics *n pl* [+sing v] COMP, GEN COMM, MGMNT heuristique *f*

hgt *abbr* *(height)* GEN COMM hauteur *f*

HGV *abbr* *(heavy goods vehicle)* TRANSP poids lourd *m*

H/H *abbr* *(half height)* TRANSP *container* conteneur demi-hauteur *m*

hhd *abbr* *(hogshead)* TRANSP *barrel, unit of measurement* barrique *f*

hi:[1] **~ -tech** *adj see high-tech*

hi:[2] **~ tech** *n* COMP, IND technologie de pointe *f*

HIC *abbr* *(heavily indebted middle-income country)* FIN pays à revenu moyen et à fort endettement *m*

Hicks: ~ Charts *n pl* ECON graphiques de Hicks *m pl*

hidden: ~ agenda *n* GEN COMM intentions cachées *f pl*, MGMNT, POL programme secret *m*; **~ asset** *n* ACC actif latent *m*, actif sous-évalué *m*; **~ damage** *n* INS *maritime* gros dommages *m pl*; **~ decision** *n* GEN COMM décision cachée *f*; **~ file** *n* COMP fichier caché *m*; **~ inflation** *n* ECON inflation cachée *f*, inflation déguisée *f*; **~ reserves** *n pl* BANK réserves occultes *f pl*, réserves secrètes *f pl*; **~ tax** *n* TAX impôt déguisé *m*; **~ unemployment** *n* ECON, HRM chômage caché *m*, chômage déguisé *m*

hide *vt* COMP *window, tree* masquer

hierarchical: ~ menu *n* COMP menu hiérarchique *m*

hierarchy *n* GEN COMM, HRM, MGMNT hiérarchie *f*; **~ of effects** S&M *marketing model* hiérarchie des effets *f*; **~ of needs** HRM hiérarchie des besoins *f*; **~ of objectives** GEN COMM hiérarchie des objectifs *f*

high[1] *adj* GEN COMM *price, wage* élevé, STOCK *futures price* plafond, élevé, *price, wage* élevé; **~ -caliber** *AmE*, **~ -calibre** *BrE* HRM *staff, graduate* gros calibre; **~ -class** GEN COMM *hotel* de catégorie supérieure *loc f*; **~ -end** COMP *equipment, system* de haute gamme *loc f*, haut de gamme, GEN COMM, S&M haut de gamme; **~ -level** COMP, MGMNT, POL évolué; **~ -powered** GEN COMM *person* important; **~ -profile** GEN COMM *company* à haut profil, GEN COMM *job* bien en vue, très en vue *loc f*, à haut profil, S&M *product* à forte image de marque *loc f*, à haut profil;

~ **-resolution** COMP *graphics, scanner VDU* haute résolution, à haute résolution; ~ **-return** FIN, STOCK *shares, investment* à rendement élevé *loc m*; ~ **-risk** STOCK *market* haut risque, à risque élevé *loc m*; ~ **-stream** *jarg* (ANT *low-stream industry*) IND hautement perfectionné, technologiquement avancé; ~ **-street** *UK* S&M *fashion* de la rue *loc f*; ~ **-tech** (ANT *low-tech*) COMP, IND à haute technologie; ~ **-technology** COMP, IND à haute technologie; **too** ~ (ANT *too low*) GEN COMM *price, wage* trop haut, trop élevé; ~ **-volume** STOCK à volume élevé *loc m*; ~ **-yield** FIN, STOCK à rendement élevé *loc m*; ~ **-yielding** FIN, STOCK à rendement élevé *loc m*

high:[2] ~ **achiever** *n* (ANT *low achiever*) GEN COMM *person* sujet doué *m*; ~ **added-value product** *n* ECON, IND, S&M produit à forte valeur ajoutée *m*; ~ **commission** *n* GEN COMM haut commissariat *m*; ~ **-cost labor** *n AmE*, ~ **-cost labour** *n BrE* HRM main-d'oeuvre à coût élevé *f*; ~ **credit** *n* BANK, FIN crédit maximum *m*; ~ **cube** *n* TRANSP (HC, ANT *low cube*) *cargo* marchandises à densité élevée *f pl*, *container* conteneur hors-cotes *m* (HC), conteneur hors-normes *m*; ~ **density** *n* (HD) COMP haute densité *f* (HD); ~ **-density cargo** *n* (ANT *low-density cargo*) TRANSP marchandises à densité élevée *f pl*; ~ **-density disk** *n* (HDD) COMP disquette à haute densité *f*; ~ **-density freight** *n* (ANT *low-density freight*) TRANSP marchandises à densité élevée *f pl*; ~ **earner** *n* GEN COMM personne à gros revenus *loc m*; ~ **employment surplus** *n* ECON, HRM surplus du plein emploi *m*; ~ **-end computing** *n* COMP grande informatique *f*; ~ **finance** *n* FIN haute finance *f*; ~ **-flier** *n* GEN COMM *person* cadre de haut vol *m*, cadre à haut potentiel *m*, personne ambitieuse *f*, star *f* (*infrml*), HRM *civil service* grand commis de l'État *m*, haut fonctionnaire *m*, STOCK valeur en vogue *f*, valeur volatile *f*; ~ **-flyer** *n see* high-flier; ~ **-flying stock** *n* STOCK valeur en vogue *f*, valeur volatile *f*; ~ **frequency radiotelephone** *n* (RTh) TRANSP *shipping* radiotéléphone haute fréquence *m*; ~ **frequency radiotelephony** *n* (RTh) TRANSP *shipping* radiotéléphonie haute fréquence *f*; ~ **-geared takeover** *n BrE* GEN COMM, STOCK rachat d'entreprise financé par un fort endettement *m*, reprise à fort effet de levier *f*; ~ **gearing** *n BrE* ACC, BANK, FIN, STOCK effet de levier élevé *m*, taux d'endettement élevé *m*; ~ **gearing ratio** *n BrE* ACC, BANK, FIN, STOCK ratio d'endettement élevé *m*; ~ **-grade bond** *n* STOCK obligation de premier ordre *f*, obligation de première qualité *f*; ~ **-impact case** *n* TAX cas qui a une incidence considérable *m*; ~ **-income taxpayer** *n* (ANT *low-income taxpayer, middle-income taxpayer*) TAX contribuable à revenu élevé *m*; ~ **-level decision** *n* GEN COMM décision prise à haut niveau *f*; ~ **-level language** *n* (HLL) COMP langage de haut niveau *m*, langage évolué *m*; ~ **-level waste** *n* ENVIR déchets de forte activité *m pl*; ~ **leverage** *n AmE see* high gearing

BrE; ~ **leverage ratio** *n AmE see* high gearing ratio *BrE*; ~ **-leveraged takeover** *n AmE see* high-geared takeover *BrE*; ~ **loader** *n* TRANSP *vehicle* gros transporteur *m*; ~ **and low prices** *n pl* STOCK cours extrêmes *m pl*; ~ **office** *n* HRM fonction élevée *f*; ~ **-order language** *n* COMP langage de haut niveau *m*, langage évolué *m*; ~ **-powered money** *n* ECON monnaie à haute puissance *f*; ~ **-premium convertible debenture** *n* STOCK obligation convertible à haut rendement *f*, obligation convertible à prime élevée *f*; ~ **-pressure selling** *n* S&M vente agressive *f*; ~ **-pressure turbine** *n* (HPTB) TRANSP *of ship* turbine haute pression *f*; ~ **price** *n* GEN COMM, STOCK *currency futures* prix élevé *m*; ~ **-quality product** *n* S&M produit d'excellente qualité *m*; ~ **rate of investment** *n* ECON, FIN taux d'investissement élevé *m*; ~ **return** *n* STOCK revenu élevé *m*; ~ **rise** *n* PROP *building* tour d'habitation *f*; ~ **-risk venture** *n* GEN COMM entreprise à haut risque *f*; ~ **-speed memory** *n* COMP mémoire ultra-rapide *f*; ~ **-speed printer** *n* COMP imprimante rapide *f*; ~ **-speed train** *n* (HST) TRANSP ≈ train à grande vitesse *m* (TGV); ~ **standard of living** *n* (ANT *low standard of living*) WEL niveau de vie élevé *m*; ~ **standards** *n pl* GEN COMM niveau élevé *m*; ~ **stowage factor** *n* (ANT *low stowage factor*) TRANSP coefficient d'arrimage élevé *m*, coefficient d'encombrement élevé *m*, fort coefficient d'arrimage; ~ **-stream industry** *n jarg* (ANT *low-stream industry*) IND industrie artisanale *f*; ~ **street** *n BrE* (*cf* main street *AmE*) GEN COMM *main street in a town*, PROP, S&M grand-rue *f*; ~ **-street bank** *n UK* BANK grande banque de dépôt *f*; ~ **-street prices** *n pl UK* GEN COMM prix du commerce *m pl*; ~ **-street share shop** *n UK* STOCK courtier ayant pignon sur rue *m*, courtier de quartier *m*; ~ **-street spending** *n UK* ECON dépenses de grande consommation *f pl*, dépenses du grand public *f pl*; ~ **-tech stock** *n* STOCK valeurs des industries de haute technologie *f pl*, valeurs haute-tech *f pl*; ~ **technology** *n* COMP, IND technologie de pointe *f*; ~ **-technology industry** *n* IND industrie à haute technologie *f*; ~ **-value clearings** *n pl* BANK compensations de valeurs élevées *f pl*; ~ **value to low weight ratio** *n* (ANT *low value to high weight ratio*) TRANSP rapport valeur élevée-poids faible *m*; **very** ~ **frequency** *n* (VHF) GEN COMM *radio frequency* hyperfréquence *f*, très haute fréquence *f*; **very** ~ **frequency radiotelephony** *n* (RTv) TRANSP *shipping* radiotéléphonie très haute fréquence *f*; **very** ~ **frequency telephone** *n* (RTv) TRANSP *shipping* radiotéléphone très haute fréquence *m*; ~ **volume** *n* STOCK volume important *m*; ~ **-water mark** *n* (HWM) TRANSP *maritime* laisse de haute mer *f*; ~ **-water ordinary spring tide** *n* (HWOST) TRANSP *maritime* pleine mer de vive-eau *f*; ~ **-yield financing** *n* FIN financement à rendement élevé *m*

High: **the** ~ **Court** *n UK* LAW *England and Wales* Cour suprême *f*

higher: ~ **education** *n* WEL enseignement supérieur *m*; ~ **income bracket** *n* ECON tranche supérieure de revenus *f*

Higher: ~ **National Certificate** *n UK (HNC)* WEL certificat national d'études techniques supérieures; ~ **National Diploma** *n UK (HND)* WEL diplôme national d'études techniques supérieures, diplôme national supérieur *m*

highest: ~ **and best use** *n AmE* PROP *of building* utilisation la plus rentable *f*; ~ **bid** *n* STOCK offre la plus élevée *f*; ~ **bidder** *n* GEN COMM *at auction* plus offrant *m, in submitting tender* mieux disant *m*, STOCK plus offrant *m*; ~ **price** *n* GEN COMM, STOCK cours le plus haut *m*, prix le plus élevé *m*; ~ **tender** *n* GEN COMM mieux disant *m*; ~ **tenderer** *n* GEN COMM mieux disant *m*

highlight *vt* COMP *word-processed document* contraster, mettre en évidence, GEN COMM *differences* souligner

highlighted *adj* COMP contrasté, mis en évidence

highlighting *n* COMP mise en évidence *f*

highlights *n pl* GEN COMM *outstanding moments* temps forts *m pl*

highly: ~ **competitive** *adj* ECON, GEN COMM, S&M *market* très compétitif, très concurrentiel; ~ **-geared** *adj* STOCK *shares* à ratio d'endettement élevé *loc m*; ~ **skilled** *adj* HRM *person* hautement qualifié

highs *n pl* STOCK valeurs au plus haut *f pl*, valeurs en hausse *f pl*

highway: ~ **order** *n* LAW, PROP *compulsory purchase* arrêté d'expropriation pour cause d'utilité publique

hike¹ *n* ACC, ECON hausse *f*, FIN augmentation *f*, GEN COMM *in price* augmentation *f*, hausse *f*

hike² *vt* GEN COMM *price* augmenter, majorer

hinder *vt* GEN COMM gêner

Hindi¹ *adj* GEN COMM hindi, hindoustani

Hindi² *n* GEN COMM hindoustani *m, language* hindi *m*

hindrance *n* ADMIN entrave *f*

hindsight *n* TAX évaluation a posteriori *f*

hinge: ~ **on** *vt* GEN COMM dépendre de

hint *n* GEN COMM conseil *m*, tuyau *m* (*infrml*)

hinterland *n* TRANSP arrière-pays *m*, hinterland *m*

hints: ~ **to exporters** *n pl* IMP/EXP conseils aux exportateurs *m pl*

hire¹ *n* GEN COMM *of tool*, TRANSP *of car* location *f*; ~ **purchase** *BrE (HP)* FIN location-vente *f*, vente à crédit *f*, vente à tempérament *f*, PROP vente à tempérament *f*, S&M location-vente *f*, vente à crédit *f*, vente à tempérament *f*; ~ **-purchase agreement** FIN accord d'achat à crédit *m*, S&M accord d'achat à crédit *m*, contrat de crédit à la consommation *m*; ◆ **off** ~ TRANSP suspension d'affrètement *f*; **on** ~ **purchase** FIN *buy* à crédit

hire² *vt* GEN COMM *staff* embaucher, engager, *tool* louer, HRM *staff* embaucher, engager, TRANSP *car* louer; ◆ ~ **and fire** HRM embaucher et renvoyer; ~ **money** *jarg* FIN emprunter de l'argent

hirer *n* PROP loueur *m*

hiring *n* GEN COMM *of staff* embauchage *m*, embauche *f, of tool* louage *m*, HRM *of tool, boat staff* embauchage *m*, embauche *f*, TRANSP *of car* location *f*; ~ **and firing** HRM embauchage et renvoi *m*

His: ~ **Excellency** *n (HE)* HRM *ambassador* Son Excellence Monsieur l'Ambassadeur *f, high-ranking official* Son Excellence *f*; ~ **Majesty's Customs** *n UK* IMP/EXP douanes de Sa Majesté; ~ **Majesty's Customs and Excise** *n UK (HMC&E)* IMP/EXP administration britannique des contributions indirectes; ~ **Majesty's Government** *n UK (HMG)* GEN COMM Gouvernement de Sa Majesté; ~ **Majesty's Ship** *n UK (HMS)* TRANSP vaisseau de Sa Majesté; ~ **Majesty's Stationery Office** *n UK (HMSO)* ADMIN, GEN COMM ≈ Imprimerie nationale *f*

histogram *n* MATH histogramme *m*

historical¹ *adj* ACC, ECON, GEN COMM *accounts, records* historique

historical:² ~ **cost** *n* ACC coût historique *m*; ~ **cost principles** *n pl* ACC principes du coût historique *m pl*; ~ **data** *n pl* GEN COMM, MATH données antérieures *f pl*; ~ **exchange rate** *n* ECON cours de change d'origine *m*, cours de change historique *m*; ~ **loss** *n* ACC perte primitive d'acquisition *f*, perte à l'origine *f*; ~ **trade** *n* TRANSP commerce historique *m*; ~ **volatility** *n* STOCK volatilité historique *f*; ~ **yield** *n* STOCK rendement historique *m*

historically *adv* GEN COMM du point de vue historique *loc m, in the past* par le passé

hit:¹ ~ **-or-miss** *adj infrml* GEN COMM *method* empirique

hit:² ~ **-and-run strike** *n* HRM grève éclair *f*; ~ **list** *n infrml* GEN COMM, POL liste des priorités *f*, S&M liste-cible *f*; ~ **order** *n* STOCK ordre immédiat ou annuler *m*, ordre immédiat *m*

hit³ *vt* COMP frapper, ECON *affect* affecter, toucher; ◆ ~ **the bid** STOCK enchérir, toucher le cours offert; ~ **the bricks** *AmE* HRM faire grève; ~ **the headlines** GEN COMM faire les gros titres des journaux; ~ **the jackpot** GEN COMM gagner le gros lot; ~ **the market** GEN COMM *product* arriver sur le marché

hive: ~ **off** *vt* GEN COMM *company* essaimer, rendre indépendant, revendre

H/L *abbr (heavy lift)* TRANSP *cargo handling* colis lourd *m*

HL *abbr UK (House of Lords)* POL Chambre des lords

HLL *abbr (high-level language)* COMP langage de haut niveau *m*, langage évolué *m*

HLT *abbr (high-leveraged takeover)* GEN COMM, STOCK rachat d'entreprise financé par un fort endettement *m*, reprise à fort effet de levier *f*

HMC *abbr UK (Her Majesty's Customs)* IMP/EXP douanes britanniques

HMC&E *abbr UK (Her Majesty's Customs and*

Excise, His Majesty's Customs and Excise) IMP/ EXP la Régie de Sa Majesté

HMG *abbr* UK *(Her Majesty's Government, His Majesty's Government)* GEN COMM Gouvernement de Sa Majesté

HMO *abbr* US *(health maintenance organization)* INS organisation de médecine préventive et curative *f*

HMS *abbr* UK *(Her Majesty's Ship, His Majesty's Ship)* TRANSP vaisseau de Sa Majesté

HMSO *abbr* UK *(Her Majesty's Stationery Office, His Majesty's Stationery Office)* ADMIN, GEN COMM ≈ Imprimerie nationale *f*

HNC *abbr* UK *(Higher National Certificate)* WEL certificat national d'études techniques supérieures

HND *abbr* UK *(Higher National Diploma)* WEL diplôme national d'études techniques supérieures, diplôme national supérieur *m*

ho *abbr (hold)* TRANSP *of aircraft, ship* cale *f*

HO *abbr (head office)* ACC *registered address of company*, BANK siège social *m*, GEN COMM agence centrale *f*, siège social *m*, MGMNT administration centrale *f*, siège social *m*

hoard *vti* STOCK *money* thésauriser

hogging *n* TRANSP arc *m*

hogshead *n (hhd)* TRANSP *barrel, unit of measurement* barrique *f*

hoist *n* TRANSP *cargo handling* palan *m*

hold[1] *n (ho)* TRANSP *of aircraft, ship* cale *f*; ~ -harmless agreements *n pl* LAW présomption contractuelle de responsabilité de l'une des parties; ~ -harmless clause *n* LAW clause par laquelle une partie accepte de protéger une autre partie; ~ -harmless provision *n jarg* POL prévoyance inoffensive *f*

hold[2] *vt* ECON, FIN *margins* maintenir, GEN COMM *contain* contenir, *inquiry* faire, *margins* maintenir, *referendum* organiser, STOCK *bonds, shares* détenir, *market* détenir, soutenir, TRANSP contenir; ~ off GEN COMM *postpone* remettre à plus tard; ◆ ~ as security INS détenir en garantie; ~ funds for a check *AmE*, ~ funds for a cheque *BrE* BANK bloquer les fonds pour un chèque; ~ in check ECON *prices* contenir, maîtriser; ~ an in-service training *jarg* HRM monter un stage de formation, organiser un stage de formation; ~ the line COMMS *on phone* rester en ligne; ~ one's ground GEN COMM tenir bon; ~ a position STOCK avoir une situation; ~ power POL être au pouvoir; ~ the purse strings *infrml* ECON tenir les cordons de la bourse *(infrml)*; ~ sb responsible for sth GEN COMM tenir qn responsable de qch; ~ the stage GEN COMM avoir la vedette, occuper le devant de la scène; ~ two jobs HRM cumuler

holdback *n* HRM *deduction* prélèvement *m*, PROP retenue *f*; ~ pay HRM *delay in payment* prélèvement temporaire *m*

holder *n* STOCK acheteur *m*, détenteur *m*, titulaire *mf*; ~ for value BANK *of bill of exchange* détenteur contre valeur *m*; ~ in due course LAW porteur de

bonne foi *m*; ~ of record STOCK *of securities, shares* porteur *m*

holding *n* LAW tenure *f*, STOCK *of securities, shares* détention *f*, tenure *f*; ~ company ACC société mère holding *f*, GEN COMM holding *m*, société de holding *f*, société de portefeuilles *f*, LAW, PROP, TAX société de portefeuilles *f*; ~ corporation GEN COMM, LAW, PROP, TAX corporation de portefeuille *f*; ~ gain ACC plus-value *f*; ~ in a bank BANK participation dans une banque *f*; ~ pattern *jarg* FIN, GEN COMM, STOCK actionnariat à tendance normale *m*; ~ period STOCK durée d'actionnariat *f*, période de détention *f*

holdings *n pl* STOCK avoirs *m pl*, participations *f pl*; ◆ have ~ in a company GEN COMM, S&M avoir des participations dans une entreprise

holdover: ~ effect *n* GEN COMM effet de rémanence *m*; ~ tenant *n AmE (cf sitting tenant BrE)* PROP locataire débordant *m*

hole *n* COMP *in punched paper* perforation *f*

holiday *n BrE (cf vacation AmE)* GEN COMM, HRM, LEIS congé *m*, vacances *f pl*; ~ accommodation *n* LEIS, PROP logement de vacances *m*; ~ entitlement *n* HRM droit à congé *m*; ~ leave *n* HRM congé annuel *m*; ~ and leisure insurance *n* INS assurance loisirs *f*, assurance vacances *f*; ~ -maker *n BrE (cf vacationer AmE, vacationist AmE)* GEN COMM, LEIS vacancier *m*; ~ pay *n BrE (cf vacation pay AmE)* HRM congés payés *m pl*; ~ period *n* LEIS période de vacances *f*; ◆ do ~ work *BrE* GEN COMM travailler pendant ses vacances; go on ~ *BrE (cf take a holiday, take a vacation AmE)* HRM, LEIS prendre des vacances; take a ~ *BrE (cf go on holiday, take a vacation AmE)* HRM, LEIS prendre des vacances

holidays *n pl BrE* GEN COMM, HRM, LEIS vacances *f pl*; ~ with pay *BrE (cf vacation with pay AmE)* HRM congés payés *m pl*

home:[1] ~ -grown *adj* GEN COMM *not produced abroad* du pays *loc m*, local

home[2] *n* ADMIN foyer *m*; ~ address *n* GEN COMM adresse du domicile *f*, adresse personnelle *f*; ~ affairs *n pl* POL affaires intérieures *f pl*; ~ automation *n* S&M domotique *f*; ~ banking *n* BANK opérations bancaires sur le marché intérieur *f pl*; ~ computer *n* COMP ordinateur domestique *m*; ~ country *n* GEN COMM, IMP/EXP pays d'origine *m*; ~ -country control *n* FIN contrôle national *m*; ~ equity loan *n* BANK prêt sur la valeur nette d'une maison *m*; ~ improvement *n* PROP amélioration de l'habitat *f*; ~ improvement loan *n* BANK, WEL prêt d'amélioration résidentielle *m*, prêt destiné à l'amélioration de l'habitat *m*; ~ loan *n* BANK prêt immobilier *m*; ~ loss payment *n* PROP paiement de perte d'habitat *m*; ~ market *n* ECON marché intérieur *m*; ~ mortgage *n* BANK prêt hypothécaire résidentiel *m*, prêt hypothécaire à l'habitation *m*; ~ mortgage loan *n* BANK prêt hypothécaire résidentiel *m*, prêt hypothécaire à l'habitation *m*; ~ office expenses *n pl* TAX frais de bureau à domicile *m pl*; **~ ownership** *n* PROP propriété d'habitat *f*; **~ production** *n* ECON, IND production à domicile *f*; **~ products** *n pl* ECON, GEN COMM produits nationaux *m pl*; **~ purchase loan** *n* BANK prêt consenti pour l'achat d'une maison *m*, prêt immobilier *m*; **~ sales** *n pl* S&M ventes sur le marché intérieur *f pl*; **~ trade** *n* ECON, GEN COMM, IMP/EXP commerce intérieur *m*; **~ trade passenger ship** *n* TRANSP navire à passagers de grand cabotage *m*; **~ trade ship** *n* TRANSP navire de grand cabotage *m*; **~ use entry** *n* ADMIN entrée de l'entrepôt des douanes *f*

homeless: **~ person** *n* WEL sans-abri *mf*, sans-logis *m*; **the ~** *n pl* WEL les sans-abri *m pl*, les sans-logis *m pl*

homeowner *n* INS, PROP, TAX propriétaire *mf*; **~ warranty program** *US* INS aux États-Unis, programme d'assurance privée protégeant les acheteurs contre les défauts mécaniques et de construction

homeowners': **~ association** *n* PROP association des propriétaires d'habitat *f*; **~ equity account** *n* BANK compte en fonds propres de propriétaires de maisons *m*; **~ policy** *n* INS assurance habitation *f*

homestead *n* *US* PROP propriété *f*

homeward: **~ voyage** *n* *(ANT outward voyage)* TRANSP voyage de retour *m*

homework *n* ECON, HRM travail en réseau *m*, travail à domicile *m*

homeworker *n* HRM travailleur à domicile *m*

homo economicus *n frml* (SYN *economic man*) ECON homo economicus *m (frml)*

homogeneous[1] *adj* *(ANT heterogeneous)* GEN COMM homogène

homogeneous:[2] **~ cargo** *n* TRANSP marchandises homogènes *f pl*; **~ goods** *n pl* ECON, IND produit banal *m*; **~ market** *n* S&M marché homogène *m*; **~ oligopoly** *n* ECON oligopole homogène *m*

homologation *n* IMP/EXP homologation *f*

homoscedasticity *n* *(ANT heteroscedasticity)* MATH *statistics* homoscédasticité *f*

homo sovieticus *n frml* ECON homo sovieticus *m (frml)*

Honduran[1] *adj* GEN COMM hondurien

Honduran[2] *n* GEN COMM *person* Hondurien *m*

Honduras *pr n* GEN COMM Honduras *m*

honest[1] *adj* GEN COMM honnête, loyal

honest:[2] **~ broker** *n* IND, POL *in negotiations* médiateur *m*

honesty *n* GEN COMM honnêteté *f*, loyauté *f*

honeycomb: **~ slip indorsement** *n see honeycomb slip endorsement* ; **~ slip** *n* FIN, STOCK *underwriting* bon nid d'abeilles *m*; **~ slip endorsement** *n* FIN, INS, STOCK *underwriting* endossement de bon nid d'abeilles *m*

Hong Kong *pr n* GEN COMM Hongkong *n pr*

honor[1] *n* *AmE see honour BrE*

honor[2] *vt* *AmE see honour BrE*

honorarium *n frml* GEN COMM *fee* honoraires *m pl*

honorary[1] *adj* HRM *member* honoraire, sur la base du bénévolat, *rank* honorifique; ◆ **in an ~ capacity** HRM à titre honoraire

honorary:[2] **~ chairman** *n* HRM président d'honneur *m*; **~ membership** *n* HRM *official* activité bénévole *f*, activité non rétribuée *f*, honorariat *m*; **~ president** *n* HRM président d'honneur *m*

honour[1] *n BrE* GEN COMM honneur *m*; **~ policy** *BrE* LAW police sans effet légal *f*

honour[2] *vt BrE* BANK *cheque*, GEN COMM *signature* honorer

hood *n* COMP *cover for computer* capot *m*

hook:[1] **~ damage** *n* TRANSP *cargo handling* avarie due aux crocs *f*

hook[2] *vt* COMP *hardware*, GEN COMM connecter, raccorder; **~ up** COMP *hardware*, GEN COMM connecter, raccorder

hopper *n* TRANSP *receptacle* trémie *f*; **~ side tank (HSDT)** TRANSP trémie latérale *f*; **~ tank** TRANSP trémie *f*

hoppertainer *n* TRANSP *container* conteneur-trémie *m*

horizon: **~ analysis** *n* FIN analyse de la situation *f*; ◆ **on the ~** GEN COMM prévu

horizontal[1] *adj* *(ANT vertical)* ECON, GEN COMM, IND, MEDIA, STOCK, TAX horizontal

horizontal:[2] **~ amalgamation** *n* *(ANT vertical amalgamation)* GEN COMM fusion horizontale *f*; **~ analysis** *n* ACC analyse à travers plusieurs exercices *f*; **~ balance sheet** *n* ACC *continental Europe* bilan en forme de compte *m*; **~ business combination** *n* *(ANT vertical business combination)* ECON, GEN COMM concentration horizontale *f*; **~ communication** *n* *(ANT vertical communication)* GEN COMM communication horizontale *f*; **~ discrimination** *n* *(ANT vertical discrimination)* ECON discrimination horizontale *f*; **~ divestiture** *n jarg* IND cession horizontale *f*; **~ equity** *n* *(ANT vertical equity)* ECON, TAX avoir horizontal *m*, équité horizontale *f*; **~ expansion** *n* *(ANT vertical expansion)* ECON croissance horizontale *f*, développement horizontal *m*, GEN COMM expansion horizontale *f*; **~ integration** *n* *(ANT vertical integration)* ECON, GEN COMM, IND intégration horizontale *f*, intégration latérale *f*; **~ merger** *n* *(ANT vertical merger)* ECON fusion horizontale *f*; **~ publication** *n jarg* MEDIA *print* publication horizontale *f (jarg)*; **~ specialization** *n* (SYN *functional management*) MGMNT gestion par fonctions *f*; **~ spread** *n* *(ANT vertical spread)* STOCK opération mixte horizontale *f*, spread calendaire *m*, spread horizontal *m*; **~ union** *n* *(ANT vertical union)* HRM syndicat professionnel *m*, syndicat regroupant les adhérents par niveau *m*; **~ -vertical amalgamation** *n* ECON intégration horizontale-verticale *f*

horse: **~ trading** *n* IND, POL maquignonnage *m*

horsepower *n* *(HP)* TRANSP cheval *m*, cheval-vapeur *m*, puissance en chevaux *f*

hospital: **~ care insurance plan** *n* INS, WEL assurance des frais d'hospitalisation *f*, assurance hospitalisation *f*, régime d'assurance-hospitalisation *m*; ~ **expenses** *n pl* INS, TAX frais d'hospitalisation *m pl*; ~ **revenue bond** *n* FIN obligation à long terme émise par une collectivité *f*

hospitalization: ~ **plan** *n* INS plan d'hospitalisation *m*

host:[1] ~ **-driven** *adj* COMP géré par le système central

host[2] *n* COMP hôte *m*, ordinateur principal *m*; ~ **city** GEN COMM ville d'accueil *f*; ~ **country** GEN COMM pays d'accueil *m*, LEIS pays hôte *m*

hostile: ~ **fire** *n* INS foyer à caractère d'incendie *m*, incendie *m*; ~ **takeover bid** *n* STOCK OPA hostile *f*, offre publique d'achat hostile *f*, tentative de prise de contrôle inamicale *f*, tentative de prise de contrôle sauvage *f*

hot[1] *adj jarg* GEN COMM *newly issued* neuf, tout chaud, *stolen* piqué *(infrml)*, HRM *industrial relations* perturbé, tendu; ♦ **in the ~ seat** HRM *put a candidate* sur la sellette

hot:[2] ~ **bills** *n pl* BANK, FIN, GEN COMM billets neufs *m pl*; ~ **card list** *n* BANK liste d'oppositions *f*; ~ **cargo** *n* TRANSP *dangerous cargo* cargaison névralgique *f*; ~ **cargo clause** *n* TRANSP clause de non-déchargement *f*; ~ **issue** *n jarg US* STOCK émission brûlante *f*, émission très attendue *f*; ~ **key** *n* COMP touche d'activation *f*, touche rapide *f*; ~ **line** *n* COMMS *between heads of government* téléphone rouge *m, phone* ligne ouverte vingt-quatre heures sur vingt-quatre *f*, COMP assistance téléphonique *f*, ligne directe *f*, permanence téléphonique *f*; ~ **list** *n* BANK liste d'oppositions *f*; ~ **money** *n* ECON, FIN capitaux flottants *m pl*, capitaux fébriles *m pl*; ~ **shop** *n jarg* S&M *advertising, esp. 1960s* studio de création *m*; ~ **stock** *n infrml* GEN COMM *stolen* stock volé *m*, STOCK *new issue* action nouvellement émise très demandée *f*, valeurs brûlantes *f pl (jarg)*; ~ **water boiler** *n (HWB)* TRANSP *of ship* chaudière à eau chaude *f*

hot:[3] ~ **-key** *vt* COMP *quickly access* accéder directement à

hotel *n* GEN COMM, LEIS hôtel *m*; ~ **accommodation** GEN COMM logement à l'hôtel *m*; ~ **manager** HRM gérant d'hôtel *m*, responsable d'hôtel *m*; ~ **proprietor** HRM, PROP propriétaire d'hôtel *m*; ~ **register** GEN COMM, LEIS registre de l'hôtel *m*

hour *n (h, hr)* GEN COMM, TRANSP heure *f (h)*

hourly[1] *adj* GEN COMM horaire

hourly:[2] ~ **rate** *n* HRM taux horaire *m*; ~ **wage** *n* HRM salaire horaire *m*; ~ **worker** *n (ANT wage worker)* HRM ouvrier payé à l'heure *m*, travailleur payé à l'heure *m*

hours: ~ **of business** *n pl (h.b.)* GEN COMM heures d'ouverture *f pl*, heures de bureau *f pl*, heures de réception de clientèle *f pl*, heures ouvrables *f pl*

house:[1] **out-~** *adj* GEN COMM externe

house[2] *n* PROP *building* maison *f*, STOCK maison *f*, maison de titres *f*; ~ **account** *n* STOCK compte maison *m*; ~ **air waybill** *n (HAWB)* IMP/EXP, TRANSP *aviation* lettre de groupage aérien *f*; ~ **bill** *n* IMP/EXP, TRANSP *of lading* connaissement de groupage *m*; ~ **bill of lading** *n* IMP/EXP, TRANSP connaissement de groupage *m*; ~ **-building loan** *n* BANK prêt à la construction de logement *m*; ~ **journal** *n* GEN COMM revue d'entreprise *f*, MEDIA journal d'entreprise *m*, publication d'entreprise *f*, revue d'entreprise *f*; ~ **magazine** *n* GEN COMM revue d'entreprise *f*, MEDIA journal d'entreprise *m*, publication d'entreprise *f*, revue d'entreprise *f*; ~ **maintenance requirement** *n* STOCK solde minimum de titres exigé *m*; ~ **mortgage** *n* BANK, PROP hypothèque immobilière *f*; ~ **prices** *n pl* PROP, S&M prix immobiliers *m pl*; ~ **purchase** *n* PROP, S&M achat de maison *m*; ~ **search** *n* LAW perquisition à domicile *f*, visite domiciliaire *f*; ~ **style** *n* GEN COMM style de l'entreprise *m*, style maison *m*, MEDIA *publishing, television* charte graphique *f*, graphisme maison *m*; ~ **-to-house sampling** *n* S&M distribution d'échantillons gratuits en porte à porte *f*; ~ **-to-house selling** *n (SYN door-to-door selling)* S&M démarchage *m*; ~ **/depot** *n* TRANSP domicile/dépôt; ♦ ~ **-to-house** TRANSP domicile à domicile; ~ **to house** IMP/EXP domicile à domicile

House: ~ **of Commons** *n UK (H of C)* POL Chambre des communes; ~ **of Lords** *n UK (H of L, HL)* POL Chambre des lords; ~ **of Representatives** *n US* POL Chambre des représentants *f*; **the ~** *n infrml* POL *UK* Chambre des communes, le Parlement britannique, STOCK la bourse de Londres, ≈ le Palais *m*

house/depot *n* IMP/EXP domicile/dépôt *loc m*

household *n* GEN COMM ménage *m*; ~ **appliance** *n* GEN COMM, S&M appareil ménager *m*; ~ **behavior** *n AmE*, ~ **behaviour** *n BrE* ECON comportement des ménages *m*; ~ **commodity** *n* GEN COMM article de ménage *m*; ~ **consumption** *n* ECON consommation des ménages *f*; ~ **decision-making** *n* ECON processus de décision des ménages *m*; ~ **durables** *n pl* S&M biens ménagers durables *m pl*; ~ **effects** *n pl* TRANSP mobilier domestique *m*; ~ **name** *n* S&M nom de marque *m*; ~ **waste** *n* ENVIR ordures ménagères *f pl*

Houses: **the ~ of Parliament** *n pl UK* POL le Parlement britannique

housewife *n* [pl -ives] S&M *consumer, not having a career* ménagère *f*

housing *n* PROP, WEL logement *m*; ~ **accommodation** PROP, WEL logement *m*; ~ **allowance** GEN COMM, HRM, WEL indemnité de logement *f*; ~ **benefit** *UK* WEL aide au logement *f*, allocation logement *f*; ~ **bond** PROP emprunt-logement *m*; ~ **code** LAW, PROP code du logement *m*; ~ **complex** PROP complexe immobilier *m*, grand ensemble *m*, lotissement *m*; ~ **construction tax** TAX taxe sur la construction de logements *f*; ~ **corporation** TAX corporation de logement *f*; ~ **development** *AmE* (SYN *housing estate*) PROP, WEL cité ouvrière *f*, complexe immobilier *m*, groupe HLM *m*, lotissement *m*; ~ **estate** *(cf housing development AmE, housing project AmE)* PROP, WEL cité ouvrière *f*, complexe immobilier *m*, groupe HLM *m*, lotissement *m*; ~ **industry** IND le bâtiment *m*; ~ **loan** BANK prêt à l'habitation *m*; ~ **market** PROP, S&M marché du logement *m*; ~ **project** PROP *planned* projet de lotissement *m*, PROP *AmE* (SYN *housing estate*) cité ouvrière *f*, complexe immobilier *m*, groupe HLM *m*, lotissement *m*, WEL *planned* projet de lotissement *m*, WEL *AmE* (SYN *housing estate*) cité ouvrière *f*, complexe immobilier *m*, groupe HLM *m*, lotissement *m*; ~ **scheme** PROP, WEL *plan* plan d'accession au logement *m*; ~ **shortage** WEL pénurie de logements *f*; ~ **stock** PROP parc immobilier *m*; ~ **subsidy** WEL aide au logement *f*, allocation logement *f*

Housing: ~ **and Urban Development Department** *n* US *(HUD Department)* PROP département logement et urbanisation

hover: ~ **around** *vi* GEN COMM *prices* osciller autour de

hovercraft *n* TRANSP aéroglisseur *m*, hydroglisseur *m*, hydrofoil *m*, hydroptère *m*

hoverport *n* TRANSP gare aéroglisseur *f*, port d'aéroglisseurs *m*, terminal d'aéroglisseurs *m*

HOW *abbr* US *(homeowner warranty program)* INS garantie d'exécution de contrat de construction de résidence

hoy *n (h)* TRANSP bugalet *m*

HP *abbr* FIN *BrE (hire purchase)* location-vente *f*, vente à crédit *f*, vente à tempérament *f*, PROP *BrE (hire purchase)* vente à tempérament *f*, S&M *BrE (hire purchase)* location-vente *f*, vente à crédit *f*, vente à tempérament *f*, TRANSP *(horsepower)* CV *(cheval-vapeur)*

HPS *abbr (hazardous polluting substance)* TRANSP substance polluante dangereuse *f*

HPTB *abbr (high-pressure turbine)* TRANSP *of ship* turbine haute pression *f*

HQ *abbr (headquarters)* ADMIN, HRM direction centrale *f*, quartier général *m*, siège social *m*

hr *abbr (hour)* GEN COMM, TRANSP h *(heure)*

HRD *abbr (human resource development)* HRM développement des ressources humaines *m*

HRM *abbr (human resource management)* HRM GRH *(gestion des ressources humaines)*

HRP *abbr (human resource planning)* HRM gestion prévisionnelle de l'emploi *f*, planification de l'emploi *f*, planification des effectifs *f*, planification des ressources humaines *f*, recrutement et gestion des effectifs *loc m*

HSDT *abbr (hopper side tank)* TRANSP trémie latérale *f*

HSE *abbr* UK *(Health and Safety Executive)* WEL bureau de la sécurité et de la protection de la santé

HST *abbr (high-speed train)* TRANSP ≈ TGV *(train à grande vitesse)*

HSWA *abbr* UK *(Health and Safety at Work Act)* HRM, LAW loi de 1974 sur la santé et la sécurité au travail

HT *abbr* TRANSP *(half-tilt container)* conteneur semi-bâché *m*, TRANSP *(half-time survey)* visite à la mi-période *f*

htr *abbr (heater)* GEN COMM appareil de chauffage *m*

hub *n* TRANSP *aviation, rail, road haulage* centre *m*, moyeu *m*, pivot *m*; ~ **of activity** GEN COMM centre d'activité *m*; ~ **branch** BANK succursale centrale *f*; ~ **reduction** TRANSP *road haulage* réduction du point central *f*

huckster *n* S&M vendeur baratineur *m*, S&M *AmE advertising* publicitaire *mf*

HUD: ~ **Department** *n* US *(Housing and Urban Development Department)* PROP département logement et urbanisation

huge *adj* GEN COMM *redundancies*, HRM massif

Hulbert: ~ **rating** *n* FIN cotation Hulbert *f*

hulk *n* TRANSP *of ship* carcasse de navire *f*, ponton *m*

hull *n* TRANSP *of ship* coque *f*, corps de navire *m*; ~ **insurance** INS *marine* assurance sur corps *f*; ~ **underwriter** INS *marine* assureur sur corps *m*

human: ~ **asset accounting** *n* ECON, FIN, HRM, IND, S&M évaluation du capital humain *f*; ~ **capital** *n* ECON, FIN, HRM, IND, S&M capital humain *m*; ~ **consumption** *n* ENVIR *of water*, GEN COMM, S&M consommation humaine *f*; ~ **engineering** *n* ADMIN, COMP, GEN COMM ergonomie *f*, HRM adaptation du travail à l'homme *f*, ergonomie *f*; ~ **factor** *n* HRM facteur humain *m*; ~ **relations** *n pl* GEN COMM relations humaines *f pl*, HRM *management theory* théorie des relations humaines *f*, *relationships* relations humaines *f pl*; ~ **resource** *n* HRM ressource humaine *f*; ~ **resource accounting** *n* HRM évaluation des ressources humaines *f*; ~ **resource administration** *n* HRM administration des ressources humaines *f*; ~ **resource development** *n (HRD)* HRM développement des ressources humaines *m*; ~ **resource management** *n (HRM)* HRM gestion des ressources humaines *f (GRH)*; ~ **resource planning** *n (HRP, manpower planning)* HRM gestion prévisionnelle de l'emploi *f*, planification de l'emploi *f*, planification des effectifs *f*, planification des ressources humaines *f*, recrutement et gestion des effectifs *loc m*; ~ **resources** *n pl* HRM personnel *m*, ressources humaines *f pl*; ~ **rights** *n pl* LAW droits de l'homme *m pl*, libertés publiques *f pl*; ~ **-scale economics** *n* ECON économie à l'échelle humaine *f*

Humphrey-Hawkins: ~ **Act** *n* US LAW loi Humphrey-Hawkins

hundred *n* MATH cent *m*

hundredweight *n* GEN COMM US *(cwt)* 45,36 kg, GEN COMM UK *(cwt)* 50,8 kg

Hungarian[1] *adj* GEN COMM hongrois

Hungarian[2] *n* GEN COMM *language* hongrois *m*, *person* Hongrois *m*

Hungary *pr n* GEN COMM Hongrie *f*

Hunt: ~ **Commission** *n* US STOCK Commission Hunt

hurdle *n* GEN COMM obstacle *m*; ~ **rate** ECON *expenditure* taux de rendement minimal *m*; ~ **rate of return** FIN taux d'actualisation *m*

husband *n* LAW époux *m*

hush: ~ **money** *n* infrml GEN COMM bribe pot-de-vin *m*

hustle:[1] ~ **and bustle** *n* GEN COMM tourbillon d'activité *m*

hustle[2] *vt* GEN COMM *bump into* bousculer, *sell* fourguer (*infrml*)

HWB *abbr (hot water boiler)* TRANSP *of ship* chaudière à eau chaude *f*

HWM *abbr (high-water mark)* TRANSP *shipping* laisse de haute mer *f*

HWOST *abbr (high-water ordinary spring tide)* TRANSP *shipping* pleine mer de vive-eau *f*

hybrid[1] *adj* COMP, GEN COMM hybride

hybrid:[2] ~ **auction** *n* STOCK adjudication hybride *f*, enchère hybride *f*; ~ **computer** *n* COMP ordinateur hybride *m*

HYC *abbr (hydraulic coupling)* TRANSP *of ship* accouplement hydraulique *m*

HYD: ~ **PRO UN** *abbr (hydraulic propulsion unit)* TRANSP *of ship* propulseur hydraulique *m*

hydraulic: ~ **coupling** *n (HC, HYC)* TRANSP *of ship* accouplement hydraulique *m*; ~ **propulsion unit** *n (HYD PRO UN)* TRANSP *of ship* propulseur hydraulique *m*

hydraulically: ~ **operated gangway** *n* TRANSP *onto ship* passerelle hydraulique *f*

hydro[1] *abbr (hydroelectric)* ENVIR *electricity supply, power* hydroélectrique

hydro[2] *n* ENVIR centrale hydro-électrique *f*, IND *Can (hydroelectric) electricity supply, power* éner-

gie hydro-électrique *f*; ~ **bill** *Can (cf electricity bill BrE)* IND facture d'électricité *f*; ~ **-electricity plant** IND centrale hydro-électrique *f*

hydrocarbon *n* ENVIR, IND hydrocarbure *m*; ~ **slick** ENVIR, IND nappe d'hydrocarbures *f*

hydroelectric[1] *adj (hydro)* ENVIR, IND *energy, power, scheme* hydroélectrique

hydroelectric:[2] ~ **power** *n* ENVIR, IND énergie hydro-électrique *f*; ~ **power station** *n* ENVIR, IND centrale hydro-électrique *f*, centrale usine hydro-électrique *f*

hydrofoil *n* TRANSP *vessel* hydrofoil *m*, hydroglisseur *m*, hydroptère *m*

hydrometer *n* ENVIR hydromètre *m*

hygroscopic[1] *adj* ENVIR hygroscopique

hygroscopic:[2] ~ **substance** *n* ENVIR *capable of absorbing water vapour from atmosphere* substance hygroscopique *f*

hype *n* MEDIA, S&M *publicity* battage publicitaire *m* (*jarg*), *publicity campaign* campagne publicitaire agressive *f*

hyperinflation *n* ECON hyperinflation *f*

hypermarket *n* GEN COMM hypermarché *m*, S&M grande surface *f*, hypermarché *m*

hyphenation *n* COMP, MEDIA césure *f*

hypothecate *vt* LAW hypothéquer, nantir

hypothecation *n* ECON *expenditure* engagement de dépenses *m*

hypothesis *n* ECON, GEN COMM hypothèse *f*; ~ **testing** MATH *statistics* essai d'hypothèse *m*

hypothetical[1] *adj* GEN COMM hypothétique

hypothetical:[2] ~ **circumstances** *n pl* GEN COMM circonstances hypothétiques *f pl*; ~ **conditions** *n pl* GEN COMM conditions hypothétiques *f pl*; ~ **question** *n* GEN COMM question hypothétique *f*; ~ **situation** *n* GEN COMM situation hypothétique *f*

hysteresis *n* ECON *lag* hystérésis *f*, hystérèse *f*

I

i *abbr (interest)* BANK, ECON, FIN intérêt *m*

IA *abbr (interest accrued)* ACC, BANK, FIN, GEN COMM, STOCK IC *(intérêts courus)*

IACS *abbr UK (International Association of Classification Societies)* GEN COMM association internationale des sociétés de classification

IADB *abbr (Inter-American Development Bank)* BANK BIAD *(Banque inter-américaine de développement)*

IAEC *abbr (International Association of Environmental Co-ordinators)* ENVIR association internationale des coordinateurs de l'environnement

IAM *abbr UK (Institute of Administrative Management)* MGMNT ≈ Institut de la gestion administrative *m*

IAPH *abbr (International Association of Ports and Harbours)* IMP/EXP Association internationale des ports *f*

IAPIP *abbr (International Association for the Protection of Industrial Property)* LAW association internationale pour la protection de la propriété industrielle

IARA *abbr (International Agricultural Research Institute)* IND Institut international de recherche agricole

IASC *abbr (International Accounting Standards Committee)* ACC Comité international des normes de comptabilité *m*

IATA[1] *abbr (International Air Transport Association)* TRANSP IATA *(Association internationale des transports aériens)*

IATA:[2] **~ air waybill** *n* IMP/EXP, TRANSP lettre de transport aérien IATA *f*; **~ cargo agent** *n* TRANSP agent de fret IATA *m*; **~ member** *n* TRANSP membre de l'IATA *m*

IB *abbr (in bond)* IMP/EXP, TAX en entrepôt sous douane *loc m*

IBC *abbr (intermediate bulk container)* TRANSP conteneur de vrac intermédiaire *m*

IBEC *abbr (International Bank for Economic Cooperation)* BANK *COMECON* Banque internationale pour la coopération économique *f*

IBELS *abbr UK (interest-bearing eligible liabilities)* BANK dettes admissibles portant intérêts *f pl*, obligations produisant des intérêts *f pl*

IBF *abbr (international banking facility)* BANK facilité bancaire internationale *f*, opérations bancaires internationales *f pl*

ibid. *abbr (ibidem)* GEN COMM ibid. *(ibidem)*

ibidem *adv (ibid.)* GEN COMM ibidem *(ibid.)*

IBM®[1] *abbr (International Business Machines®)* COMP IBM®

IBM:[2] **~ -compatible** *adj* COMP compatible IBM

IBOR *abbr (interbank offered rate)* BANK, ECON, STOCK taux interbancaire offert *m*, taux interbancaire proposé *m*

IBRC *abbr UK (Insurance Brokers' Registration Council)* INS conseil d'immatriculation des courtiers d'assurance *m*

IBRD *abbr (International Bank of Reconstruction and Development)* BANK BIRD *(Banque internationale pour la reconstruction et le développement)*

IC *abbr* COMP *(integrated circuit)* CI *(circuit intégré)*, FIN *UK (Investment Committee) of the Association of British Insurers and National Association of Pension Funds* commission des investissements *f*, TRANSP *(inland container)* conteneur pour le transport intérieur *m*

ICA *abbr* ACC *UK (Institute of Chartered Accountants)* association professionnelle des experts-comptables, GEN COMM *UK (International Cooperation Administration)* administration internationale de la coopération

ICAC *abbr (International Cotton Advisory Committee)* IND Comité consultatif international du coton

ICAEW *abbr UK (Institute of Chartered Accountants in England and Wales)* ACC institut des experts-comptables d'Angleterre et du pays de Galles

ICAI *abbr (Institute of Chartered Accountants in Ireland)* ACC institut des experts-comptables d'Irlande

ICAO *abbr (International Civil Aviation Organization)* TRANSP OACI *(Organisation de l'aviation civile internationale)*

ICA's *abbr (International Commodity Agreements)* STOCK accords internationaux sur les matières premières *m pl*, accords internationaux sur les produits de base *m pl*

ICAS *abbr UK (Institute of Chartered Accountants of Scotland)* ACC institut des experts-comptables d'Écosse

ICC *abbr* ECON *(income-consumption curve)* courbe de demande par rapport aux revenus du consommateur *f*, ECON *(industrial and commercial company)* société industrielle et commerciale *f*, GEN COMM *(International Control Centre)* Centre international de contrôle du crédit *m*, GEN COMM *(industrial and commercial company)* société industrielle et commerciale *f*

ICCH *abbr UK (International Commodities Clearing House)* STOCK chambre internationale de compensation pour les produits de base *f*

ICD *abbr (inland clearance depot)* IMP/EXP bureau de dédouanement de l'intérieur *m*

iceberg: ~ **company** n jarg GEN COMM société iceberg f

icebreaker n TRANSP ship brise-glace m

Iceland pr n GEN COMM Islande f

Icelander n GEN COMM person Islandais m

Icelandic[1] adj GEN COMM islandais

Icelandic[2] n GEN COMM language islandais m

ICEM abbr (Intergovernmental Committee for European Migration) WEL Commission intergouvernementale des migrations européennes f

ICETT abbr UK (Industrial Council for Educational & Training Technology) WEL Conseil industriel pour la technologie en matière d'éducation et de formation m

ICFTU abbr (International Confederation of Free Trade Unions) HRM confédération internationale des syndicats de libre-échange

ICHCA abbr (International Cargo Handling Coordination Association) IND association de coordination de la manipulation des chargements

ICIE abbr (International Centre for Industry and the Environment) IND centre international pour l'industrie et l'environnement

ICITO abbr UK (Interim Commission of the International Trade Organization) GEN COMM commission intérimaire de l'organisation internationale du commerce

ICJ abbr (International Court of Justice) LAW, POL Cour internationale de justice f

ICMA abbr UK (Institute of Cost and Management Accountants) ACC association professionnelle des comptables en management

icon n COMP, GEN COMM icône f; ◆ **by** ~ COMP par icône

ICON abbr (indexed currency option note) STOCK billet d'option de change indexé m

ICOR abbr (incremental capital-output ratio) FIN taux de rendement du capital différentiel m, taux incrémental de dépenses en capital m

ICS abbr (International Chamber of Shipping) TRANSP chambre internationale maritime

ICTB abbr (International Customs Tariffs Bureau) IMP/EXP BITD (Bureau international des tarifs douaniers)

ICU abbr (International Clearing Union) ECON Union de clearing internationale f

id. abbr (idem) GEN COMM id. (idem)

ID[1] abbr GEN COMM (identification) ID (identification), IMP/EXP (import duty) tax droit d'entrée m, taxe à l'importation f, S&M, TAX (identification) ID (identification)

ID[2] n (identity card) ADMIN carte d'identité f; ~ **number** COMP numéro d'identification m

IDA abbr ECON (International Development Association) Association internationale pour le développement f, ECON (Industrial Development Authority) administration du développement industriel f, IMP/EXP (import duty act) loi sur les taxes à l'importation f, IND (Industrial Develop-

ment Authority) administration du développement industriel f

IDB abbr BrE (interdealer broker) BANK courtier internégociants m, intermédiaire entre courtiers m

IDBS abbr (interdealer broker system) STOCK SIAM (système des intermédiaires entre courtiers)

IDD abbr (international direct dialing, international direct dialling) COMMS appel international automatique m, l'automatique international m

ideal: ~ **capacity** n ECON capacité maximale f, capacité théorique f; ~ **limit** n ECON limite d'une zone de chalandise f

ideas: ~ **man** n [pl -men] GEN COMM, S&M concepteur m; ~ **woman** n [pl -men] GEN COMM, S&M conceptrice f

idem adj (id.) GEN COMM idem (id.)

identification n (ID) GEN COMM, S&M identification f (ID) TAX of returns désignation f, identification f (ID); ~ **number** COMP numéro d'identification m; ~ **problem** ECON econometrics problème d'identification m

identifier n COMP identificateur m

identity: ~ **card** n (ID) ADMIN carte d'identité f

id est phr (i.e., that is to say) GEN COMM c'est-à-dire (c-à-d)

IDF abbr (interdepartmental flexibility) HRM flexibilité entre services f

idle[1] adj COMP hardware, GEN COMM inactif, HRM worker au chômage loc m, IND factory, machinery, plant arrêté, TRANSP ship désarmé, inemployé

idle:[2] ~ **balance** n FIN solde non-mouvement m; ~ **capacity** n ECON, IND capacité inutilisée f, potentiel sous-utilisé m; ~ **cash** n STOCK argent oisif m (jarg); ~ **money** n ECON, FIN argent improductif m (jarg), argent qui dort m (jarg); ~ **shipping** n TRANSP navires désarmés m pl, navires inemployés m pl; ~ **time** n COMP temps d'inactivité m, HRM heures inemployées f pl; ~ **tonnage** n TRANSP tonnage désarmé m, tonnage inemployé m

IDRC abbr UK (International Development Research Centre) GEN COMM centre de recherche international de développement

i.e. abbr (id est, that is to say) GEN COMM c-à-d (c'est-à-dire)

IEA abbr ECON UK (Institute of Economic Affairs) institut des affaires économiques m, ENVIR (International Energy Agency) agence internationale de l'énergie

IEM abbr (International Equities Market) STOCK marché international des actions m, marché international des capitaux m

if: ~, **as and when** phr STOCK sous les réserves d'usage

IFAP abbr (International Federation of Agricultural Producers) IND FIPA (Fédération internationale des producteurs agricoles)

IFC *abbr (international finance corporation)* FIN SFI *(société financière internationale)*

IFD *abbr (International Federation for Documentation)* GEN COMM FID *(Fédération internationale de documentation)*

IFSE *abbr (International Federation of Stock Exchanges)* STOCK FIBV *(Fédération internationale des bourses de valeurs)*

IFTU *abbr (International Federation of Trade Unions)* HRM IFTU *(Fédération syndicale internationale)* Fédération internationale des syndicats *f*

igloo *n* TRANSP *aviation* igloo *m*

IGLU *abbr (index growth linked units)* STOCK *index-linked Swiss franc instruments* unités indexées liées à la croissance *f pl*

igniter *n* TRANSP *hazardous cargo* détonateur *m*

ignorance: ~ **of the law is no excuse** *phr* LAW nul n'est censé ignorer la loi

ignorantia juris neminem excusat *phr frml* LAW nul n'est censé ignorer la loi

ignore *vt* LAW *claim* rejeter

ihp *abbr (indicated horsepower)* GEN COMM cheval-vapeur indiqué *m*

IIB *abbr (international investment bank)* BANK Banque internationale d'investissement *f*

IIF *abbr (Institute for International Finance)* FIN Institut de finances internationales *m*, Institut international de finance *m*

I/L *abbr (import licence BrE, import license AmE)* IMP/EXP licence d'importation *f*

ILA *abbr US (International Longshoremen's Association)* TRANSP association internationale des débardeurs

ill: ~ **will** *n* GEN COMM, HRM mauvaise volonté *f*

illegal[1] *adj* GEN COMM clandestin, LAW illicite, illégal

illegal:[2] ~ **alien** *n* LAW étranger en situation irrégulière *m*; ~ **character** *n* COMP, MEDIA caractère interdit *m*; ~ **dividend** *n US* LAW dividende illicite *m*; ~ **immigrant** *n* LAW immigré clandestin *m*; ~ **immigration** *n* LAW immigration clandestine *f*; ~ **operation** *n* COMP opération interdite *f*, opération non valide *f*; ~ **payoff** *n* LAW, POL versement illégal *m*; ~ **practices** *n pl* LAW actes illicites *m pl*, manoeuvres frauduleuses *f pl*, pratiques illégales *f pl*; ~ **strike** *n* HRM, IND, LAW grève illicite *f*

illegally *adv* LAW illégalement

illiquid[1] *adj* ACC en brèche de trésorerie *loc f*, non-liquide

illiquid:[2] ~ **assets** *n pl* ACC actif non-disponible *m*

illth *n* ECON mal tutélaire *m*

illusory: ~ **profit** *n* ACC, FIN profit fictif *m*, profit illusoire *m*

illustrate *vt* GEN COMM, MEDIA *book* illustrer

illustrated[1] *adj* GEN COMM, MEDIA illustré

illustrated:[2] ~ **magazine** *n* MEDIA illustré *m*, magazine illustré *m*, revue illustrée *f*

illustration *n* GEN COMM *example, picture*, MEDIA *example, picture* illustration *f*

ILO[1] *abbr* HRM *(International Labour Office)* BIT *(Bureau international du travail)*, HRM *(International Labour Organization)* OIT *(Organisation internationale du travail)*

ILO:[2] ~ **Conventions** *n pl* HRM accords BIT *m pl*

ILOC *abbr (irrevocable letter of credit)* BANK lettre de crédit irrévocable *f*

ILWU *abbr US (International Longshoremen's and Warehousemen's Union)* IND syndicat international des débardeurs et des magasiniers

image *n* COMP, GEN COMM, MEDIA, S&M image *f*; ~ **advertising** S&M publicité institutionnelle *f*; ~ **file** COMP fichier vidéo *m*; ~ **projection** S&M projection d'image de marque *f*

imaging *n* COMP prise d'images *f*, S&M élaboration de l'image *f*

IMB *abbr (International Maritime Bureau)* TRANSP Bureau maritime international *m*

imbalance *n* ACC déséquilibre *m*; ~ **of orders** STOCK déséquilibre des commandes *m*, déséquilibre des ordres *m*; ~ **of trade** ECON *between countries* déséquilibre commercial *m*

imbalanced: ~ **working** *n* TRANSP exploitation déséquilibrée *f*

IMC *abbr (International Maritime Committee)* TRANSP Comité maritime international *m*

IMDGC *abbr (International Maritime Dangerous Goods Code)* TRANSP *shipping* Code maritime international des marchandises dangereuses *m*

IMF *abbr (International Monetary Fund)* BANK, ECON, FIN FMI *(Fonds monétaire international)*

IMM[1] *abbr (International Monetary Market)* ECON, STOCK MMI *(Marché monétaire international)*

IMM:[2] ~ **CD index** *n (International Monetary Market Certificate of Deposit index)* STOCK indice des certificats de dépôt du MMI *m (indice des certificats de dépôt du Marché monétaire international)*; ~ **T-bill index** *n (International Monetary Market Treasury-bill index)* STOCK indice des bons du trésor du MMI *m (indice des bons du trésor du Marché monétaire international)*; ~ **Three-Month Add-On Index** *n (International Money Market Three-Month Add-On Index)* STOCK rajout trimestriel à l'indice du marché monétaire international; ~ **Three-Month Discount Index** *n (International Monetary Market Three-Month Discount Index)* STOCK indice de décompte trimestriel du MMI *m (indice de décompte trimestriel du Marché monétaire international)*

immediate[1] *adj* GEN COMM immédiat; ◆ **for** ~ **attention** GEN COMM urgent; **for** ~ **release** MEDIA *print* pour diffusion immédiate, pour publication immédiate, prière d'insérer immédiatement

immediate:[2] ~ **access** *n* COMP accès immédiat *m*; ~ **aim** *n* GEN COMM objectif immédiat *m*; ~ **capital gain** *n* ACC, ECON, FIN, TAX gain en capital immédiat *m*; ~ **delivery** *n* GEN COMM livraison immédiate *f*; ~ **family** *n* STOCK famille immédiate *f*, parents proches *m pl*; ~ **money transfer** *n* *(IMT)* BANK transfert d'argent immédiat *m*; ~ **occupancy** *n* PROP possession immédiate *f*, *apartment* appartement occupé *m*; ~ **-or-cancel order** *n* *(IOC order)* STOCK ordre immédiat *m*, ordre immédiat ou annuler *m* *(ordre IOC)*; ~ **possession** *n* PROP, WEL jouissance immédiate *f*; ~ **rebate** *n* TRANSP rabais immédiat *m*

immigrant *n* ADMIN immigré *m*; ~ **worker** HRM travailleur immigré *m*

immigration *n* ADMIN, ECON, LAW immigration *f*; ~ **control** ADMIN contrôle de l'immigration *m*; ~ **officer** *(IO)* ADMIN, HRM agent du service de l'immigration *m*, fonctionnaire de l'immigration *m*, officier de police du service de l'immigration *m*, ≈ agent de la P.A.F. *m* *(Fra)*, ≈ agent de la Police de l'air et des frontières *m* *(Fra)*; ~ **policy** LAW, POL politique d'immigration *f*

imminent: ~ **peril** *n* INS risque imminent *m*

immiseration *n* ECON paupérisation *f*

immiserizing: ~ **growth** *n* ECON croissance paupérisante *f*

immovable: ~ **estate** *n* PROP bien immobilier *m*; ~ **property** *n* PROP propriété immobilière *f*

immunity *n* LAW exemption *f*, exonération *f*, immunité *f*

immunization *n* FIN immunisation *f*

IMO *abbr* IND *(International Miners' Organization)* Organisation internationale des mineurs, TRANSP *(International Maritime Organization)* Organisation maritime internationale

imp. *abbr* *(import, importation)* IMP/EXP imp. *(importation)*

IMPA *abbr* *(International Maritime Pilots' Association)* TRANSP association internationale des pilotes maritimes

impact *n* ACC, BANK effet *m*, ENVIR impact *m*, FIN effet *m*, GEN COMM *on someone or something* impact *m*, influence *f*, INS, LAW, TAX *of loss* effet *m*; ~ **effect** ECON effet d'impact *m*; ~ **multiplier** ECON multiplicateur d'impact *m*; ~ **printer** COMP imprimante à impact *f*; ~ **study** S&M étude de l'impact *f*; ♦ **have an ~ on** GEN COMM influer sur

impacted: ~ **area** *n* TAX quartier surpeuplé *m*

impair *vt* ECON *purchasing power* affaiblir, diminuer, FIN *capital* diminuer

impaired: ~ **capital** *n* FIN capital diminué *m*

impairment *n* TAX déficience *f*; ~ **of value** BANK *of security*, STOCK baisse de valeur *f*, réduction de valeur *f*

impartial *adj* GEN COMM impartial, objectif

impasse *n* GEN COMM impasse *f*

imperfect: ~ **competition** *n* *(ANT perfect competition)* ECON, S&M concurrence imparfaite *f*; ~ **market** *n* ECON, S&M marché imparfait *m*; ~ **obligation** *n* LAW obligation morale *f*

imperial: ~ **gallon** *n* GEN COMM *measure* 4,546 litres, gallon impérial *m*

imperialism *n* POL impérialisme *m*

impetus *n* GEN COMM impulsion *f*, incitation *f*, HRM incitation *f*

impinge: ~ **on** *vt* LAW *rights* empiéter sur

implement *vt* COMP *system* implémenter, mettre en application, mettre en oeuvre, GEN COMM *article, plan* réaliser, *contract* exécuter, mettre en oeuvre

implementation *n* COMP mise en application *f*, mise en oeuvre *f*, *of system* implémentation *f*, GEN COMM *of article, plan* mise en oeuvre *f*, *of contract* exécution *f*, mise en oeuvre *f*; ~ **lag** ECON délai de mise en oeuvre *m*

implications *n pl* GEN COMM, POL conséquences *f pl*, répercussions *f pl*

implicit: ~ **contract theory** *n* ECON théorie du contrat implicite *f*; ~ **cost** *n* ECON coût implicite *m*; ~ **marginal income** *n* ECON revenu marginal implicite *m*

implied[1] *adj* FIN, GEN COMM, LAW, STOCK implicite, tacite

implied:[2] ~ **condition** *n* GEN COMM condition tacite *f*; ~ **consent** *n* LAW consentement implicite *m*; ~ **contract** *n* LAW contrat tacite *m*, quasi-contrat *m*; ~ **easement** *n* LAW servitude implicite *f*; ~ **in fact contract** *n* LAW contrat tacite *m*; ~ **obligation** *n* GEN COMM obligation implicite *f*; ~ **repo rate** *n* *infrml* US FIN taux de rendement implicite *m*; ~ **term** *n* LAW *of contract* condition tacite *f*; ~ **terms** *n pl* HRM conditions implicites *f pl*; ~ **volatility** *n* STOCK volatilité implicite *f*; ~ **warranty** *n* LAW garantie implicite *f*

imply *vt* GEN COMM sous-entendre

import[1] *n* *(imp.)* IMP/EXP importation *f* *(imp.)*; ~ **allowance** *n* ECON, IMP/EXP tolérance à l'importation *f*; ~ **berth** *n* IMP/EXP, TRANSP *at dock* quai réservé aux importations *m*; ~ **clerk** *n* HRM, IMP/EXP employé chargé des importations *m*; ~ **credit** *n* IMP/EXP lettre de créance à l'importation *f*, lettre de crédit pour l'importation *f*; ~ **depot charges** *n pl* IMP/EXP frais d'entreposage à l'importation *m pl*; ~ **documentation supervisor** *n* HRM, IMP/EXP inspecteur des documents d'importation *m*; ~ **duty** *n* *(ID)* IMP/EXP *tax* droit d'entrée *m*, taxe à l'importation *f*; ~ **duty act** *n* *(IDA)* IMP/EXP loi sur les taxes à l'importation *f*; ~ **earnings** *n pl* ECON, IMP/EXP gains à l'importation *m pl*; ~ **-export** *n* COMP transférabilité *f*, IMP/EXP import-export *m*; ~ **gold** *n* IMP/EXP or d'importation *m*; ~ **groupage operator** *n* HRM opérateur des groupages import *m*; ~ **letter of credit** *n* IMP/EXP lettre de créance à l'importation *f*, lettre de crédit pour l'importation *f*; ~ **licence** *n* BrE *(I/L)* IMP/EXP licence d'importation *f*; ~ **license** *n* AmE *see import licence* BrE; ~ **licensing** *n* IMP/EXP autorisation d'importation *f*; ~ **manager** *n* HRM, IMP/EXP directeur des importations *m*; ~ **penetration ratio** *n* IMP/EXP taux de pénétration des importations *m*;

~ permit *n* IMP/EXP autorisation d'importer *f*;
~ price *n* ECON, IMP/EXP prix à l'importation *m*;
~ quota *n* ECON, IMP/EXP contingent d'importation *m*, quota à l'importation *m*; **~ regulations** *n pl* IMP/EXP réglementation des importations *f*;
~ release note *n (IRN)* IMP/EXP décharge d'importation *f*; **~ sales executive** *n* HRM responsable des ventes d'importation *m*; **~ shed** *n* IMP/EXP hangar des importations *m*; **~ substitution** *n* IMP/EXP substitution d'importation *f*; **~ surplus** *n* ECON, IMP/EXP excédent d'importation *m*; **~ tariff** *n* ECON, IMP/EXP tarif des importations *m*; **~ trade** *n* ECON, IMP/EXP commerce d'importation *m*

import[2] *vt* COMP *data*, IMP/EXP *goods* importer

important: **~ office** *n* HRM fonction élevée *f*; **very ~ cargo** *n (VIC)* TRANSP cargaison très importante *f*; **very ~ object** *n (VIO)* TRANSP objet très important *m*; **very ~ person** *n (VIP)* GEN COMM personnage de marque *m*

importation *n (imp.)* IMP/EXP importation *f (imp.)*

imported[1] *adj* ECON, IMP/EXP importé

imported:[2] **~ goods** *n pl* IMP/EXP marchandises importées *f pl*; **~ inflation** *n* ECON inflation importée *f*

importer *n* IMP/EXP importateur *m*

importing *adj* IMP/EXP importateur

impose *vt* GEN COMM *burden, restriction* imposer, *fine, penalty* infliger, LAW *limit, restriction, law* imposer; ◆ **~ extreme hardship on sb** TAX, WEL placer qn dans une situation financière extrêmement difficile; **~ a fine on sb** LAW condamner qn à une amende, imposer une amende à qn; **~ a tax on** TAX mettre un impôt sur, mettre une taxe sur, taxer

imposition *n* GEN COMM, LAW *of burden, law, limit, restriction* imposition *f*, TAX impôt *m*, taxe *f*

impound:[1] **~ account** *n* FIN fonds mis de côté *m pl*

impound[2] *vt* LAW confisquer, saisir, *illegally parked car* mettre en fourrière, TRANSP *ship* mettre en eau

impounding *n* LAW confiscation *f*, *of illegally parked car* mise en fourrière *f*, TRANSP *of ship* mise en eau *f*

impoverished *adj* FIN appauvri

impress *vt* GEN COMM impressionner

impression *n* COMP caractère spécial *m*, GEN COMM impression *f*, MEDIA caractère spécial *m*, *of book, newspaper* impression *f*, tirage *m*; ◆ **make an ~ on** GEN COMM impressionner

impressive *adj* GEN COMM *growth, increase* impressionnant

imprest *n* FIN avance temporaire *f*; **~ account** ACC compte d'avances à montant fixe *m*; **~ fund** ACC avance de fonds à plafond *f*; **~ system** ACC système d'avance de fonds à plafond *m*

imprinter *n* GEN COMM *machine* imprimante à cartes *f*, presse imprimante de cartes magnétiques *f*

imprisonment *n* LAW emprisonnement *m*, incarcération *f*, réclusion *f*

improper *adj* GEN COMM abusif

improve *vt* ENVIR *site* viabiliser, GEN COMM *situation, translation* améliorer, PROP *site* viabiliser

improved: **~ land** *n* PROP terre améliorée *f*

improvement *n* ECON *of capital goods* amélioration *f*, GEN COMM *in balance of trade, in trading position* amélioration *f*, *in system* perfectionnement *m*; **~ patent** PATENTS brevet de perfectionnement *m*

improvements *n pl* PROP améliorations *f pl*; **~ and betterments insurance** *n* INS assurance d'améliorations locatives *f*

impulse: **~ buy** *n* S&M achat impulsif *m*, achat spontané *m*; **~ buyer** *n* S&M acheteur impulsif *m*; **~ buying** *n* S&M achat d'impulsion *m*, achat impulsif *m*; **~ goods** *n pl* S&M produits d'appel *m pl*, produits de choc *m pl*; **~ purchase** *n* S&M achat impulsif *m*, achat spontané *m*; **~ sale** *n* S&M vente d'appel *f*, vente de choc *f*

impure: **~ public good** *n* ECON bien public impur *m*

imputed: **~ cost** *n* ACC frais imputés *m pl*, ECON coût supplétif *m*; **~ income** *n* ACC, ECON, TAX revenu implicite *m*, revenu imputé *m*; **~ interest** *n* TAX *tax law* intérêts imputés *m pl*; **~ value** *n* ACC valeur imputée *f*

IMRO *abbr* UK *(Investment Managers' Regulatory Organization)* STOCK organisation de surveillance des gestionnaires d'investissement *f*

IMRS *abbr (Industrial Market Research Services)* S&M Services d'études de marché industriel *m pl*

IMS *abbr (Institute of Manpower Studies)* HRM Institut d'études sur la main d'oeuvre *m*

IMT *abbr (immediate money transfer)* BANK transfert d'argent immédiat *m*

in *prep* GEN COMM dans

inability: **~ to work** *n* TAX, WEL incapacité de travailler *f*

inaccuracy *n* GEN COMM, MATH *of figures, calculation* inexactitude *f*

inactive[1] *adj* COMP déconnecté, désactivé, inactif, FIN *bill* dormant, inactif, peu actif, STOCK *asset* dormant, inactif, peu actif, *market* calme

inactive:[2] **~ account** *n* BANK compte inactif *m*; **~ asset** *n* STOCK actif dormant *m*, avoir inactif *m*; **~ bond** *n* STOCK obligation inactive *f*, obligation peu active *f*; **~ post** *n* STOCK groupe de négociation peu actif *m*, poste inactif *m*; **~ stock** *n* STOCK action dormante *f*, action inactive *f*, action peu active *f*

inadvertently *adv* GEN COMM par inadvertance

inalienable *adj* LAW *right* inaliénable

inaugural: **~ flight** *n* TRANSP vol d'inauguration *m*; **~ sailing** *n* TRANSP *of ship* voyage inaugural *m*; **~ schedule** *n* TRANSP desserte inaugurale *f*; **~ transit** *n* TRANSP transit inaugural *m*

in-basket: **~ situation** *phr jarg (SYN in-tray exercise)* ADMIN en suspens, à régler

in-bond: ~ **manufacturing** n IMP/EXP fabrication en entrepôt sous douane f

inbound: ~ **flight** n LEIS vol de retour m, TRANSP vol d'arrivée m, vol de retour m; ~ **investor** n ECON *into a country* investisseur étranger m; ~ **passengers** n pl TRANSP passagers au retour m pl, passagers à l'arrivée m pl

Inc. abbr US *(incorporated company)* GEN COMM *in company name* SARL *(société à responsabilité limitée)*

incapacity n GEN COMM, LAW, TAX, WEL incapacité f

incendiarism n INS, LAW incendie volontaire m

incentive n ECON gratification f, FIN clause attrayante f, incitation f, GEN COMM incitation f, stimulant m, HRM gratification f, incitation f, stimulant m, S&M *sales* incitation f, stimulant m, TAX encouragement m, incitation f; ~ **bonus** HRM prime d'encouragement f; ~ **commission** S&M prime d'encouragement f; ~ **contract** GEN COMM contrat avec primes de rendement m; ~ **contracting** GEN COMM contrats avec primes de rendement m pl; ~ **effect** ECON effet d'incitation m; ~ **fee** S&M honoraires d'encouragement m pl; ~ **pay** HRM prime de rentabilité f; ~ **payment system** HRM système de primes d'encouragement m; ~ **plan** HRM plan d'encouragement m; ~ **rate** AmE TRANSP *freight rate* tarif d'abonnement m; ~ **scheme** HRM participation aux bénéfices f, programme de stimulants salariaux m, système de primes d'encouragement m; ~ **stock option** *(ISO)* STOCK *US tax* intéressement par option de souscription d'actions m, option d'action à prime f; ~ **wage** HRM salaire au rendement m; ~ **wage plan** HRM programme de salaires au rendement m, programme de stimulants salariaux m

incestuous: ~ **share dealing** n STOCK commerce incestueux d'actions m

Inchmaree: ~ **clause** n INS *in hull policy* clause de négligence f

inchoate adj LAW *document* incomplet

incidence n ECON incidence f

incidental[1] adj GEN COMM *outlay* accessoire

incidental:[2] ~ **allowances** n pl ACC, GEN COMM *expenses* faux frais m pl, frais accessoires m pl; ~ **charges** n pl ACC frais accessoires m pl; ~ **damages** n pl LAW dommages-intérêts accessoires m pl; ~ **expenses** n pl ACC faux accessoires m pl, faux frais m pl, GEN COMM *of salesman* faux frais m pl

incidentals: ~ **allowance** n pl ACC faux accessoires m pl, indemnité de frais accessoires f, GEN COMM indemnité de frais accessoires f

incineration n ENVIR, IND *of waste* incinération f; ~ **plant** ENVIR, IND usine d'incinération f

incinerator n ENVIR, IND incinérateur m

incitative: ~ **planning** n jarg POL *in socialist country* planification avec intéressement

incl. abbr GEN COMM *(included, inclusive)* compris, inclus, GEN COMM *(including)* compris, y compris

include vt GEN COMM comporter, comprendre, inclure

included[1] adj *(incl.)* GEN COMM compris, inclus; ♦ **companies** ~ **within consolidation** ACC *annual accounts* perimètre de consolidation m; **Fridays and holidays** ~ TRANSP *shipping, chartering term* vendredis et jours fériés compris; **Sundays and holidays** ~ *(SHINC)* TRANSP *shipping, chartering term* dimanches et jours fériés compris

included:[2] ~ **angle** n TRANSP *cargo handling* angle de dégagement m

including prep *(incl.)* GEN COMM y compris

inclusion n GEN COMM inclusion f; ~ **rate** TAX *for capital gains and losses* taux d'inclusion m

inclusive[1] adj GEN COMM *price* compris, inclus, tout compris, GEN COMM compris, inclus; ♦ **both dates** ~ *(bdi)* GEN COMM inclusivement

inclusive:[2] ~ **terms** n pl GEN COMM prix tout compris m; ~ **tour** n *(IT)* LEIS, TRANSP voyage tout compris m

income:[1] ~ **-elastic** adj ECON élastique par rapport au revenu; ~ **-tested** adj TAX en fonction du revenu loc f

income[2] n ACC *of company* bénéfice m, bénéfice brut m, *of person* revenu m, ECON *of company, country* recettes f pl, *of person* revenu m, FIN bénéfice brut m, revenu m, TAX *of company, country* recettes f pl, *of person* revenu m; ~ **accounts** n pl ACC comptes de recettes et dépenses m pl; ~ **amounts** n pl TAX sommes déclarées comme revenu f pl; ~ **approach** n PROP approche de rendement f; ~ **attribution rules** n pl Can TAX règles d'attribution de revenu f pl; ~ **available for fixed charges** n ACC, TAX revenu disponible pour charges fixes m; ~ **averaging** n FIN évaluation d'une moyenne de revenus f, TAX établissement de la moyenne du revenu m; ~ **band** n TAX tranche de revenu f; ~ **bond** n STOCK obligation à revenu variable f; ~ **bracket** n TAX tranche de revenu f; ~ **budget** n ACC budget de recettes m; ~ **-consumption curve** n *(ICC)* ECON courbe de demande par rapport aux revenus du consommateur f; ~ **debenture** n STOCK obligation à revenu variable f; ~ **differential** n ECON différentiel de revenu m; ~ **distribution** n ECON, TAX répartition du revenu f; ~ **effect** n ECON effet de revenu m; ~ **-elasticity of demand** n ECON, S&M élasticité de la demande par rapport au revenu f, élasticité-revenu de la demande f; ~ **for the year** n TAX revenu pour l'année m; ~ **from discounting** n BANK revenu d'escompte m; ~ **from interest** n ACC produits financiers m pl; ~ **from participations** n ACC produits de participations m pl; ~ **from securities** n ACC, STOCK produits des immobilisations financières m pl, revenu de portefeuille m; ~ **from services** n ACC prestations de services f pl; ~ **gain** n ACC bénéfices de revenus m pl; ~ **group** n S&M *market research* tranche de revenu f; ~ **investment company** n FIN société d'investissement de revenus *f*; ~ **limited partnership** *n* ACC association limitée au résultat *f*; ~ **measure** *n* ECON mesure du revenu *f*; ~ **per head** *n* ECON revenu par habitant *m*; ~ **property** *n* AmE PROP immobilier de rapport *m*; ~ **range** *n* TAX palier de revenu *m*; ~ **redistribution** *n* ECON redistribution des revenus *f*; ~ **replacement** *n* INS *disability income insurance* remplacement du revenu *m*, rente d'invalidité en remplacement de revenu *f*; ~ **splitting** *n* TAX fractionnement du revenu *m*; ~ **spread** *n* FIN étalement des revenus *m*; ~ **statement** *n* ACC compte de pertes et profits *m*, compte de résultat *m*; ~ **stream** *n* ECON flux des revenus *m*; ~ **subject to tax** *n* TAX revenu assujetti à l'impôt *m*; ~ **and substitution effects** *n pl* ECON effets de revenu et de substitution *m pl*; ~ **support** *n* WEL *UK (cf supplementary benefit)* indemnité complémentaire *f*, WEL *UK* soutien au revenu *m*; ~ **tax** *n* ECON, TAX impôt sur le revenu *m*; ~ **tax act** *n* TAX loi de l'impôt sur le revenu *f*; ~ **tax deferral** *n* TAX report de l'impôt sur le revenu *m*; ~ **tax package** *n* TAX dossier de la déclaration *m*; ~ **tax rate** *n* TAX taux de l'impôt sur le revenu *m*; ~ **tax refund** *n* TAX remboursement de l'impôt sur le revenu *m*; ~ **tax regulations** *n pl* TAX règlements de l'impôt sur le revenu *m pl*; ~ **tax return** *n* ACC déclaration fiscale *f*, liasse fiscale *f*, TAX déclaration de revenus *f*; ~ **taxed at a lower rate** *n* TAX revenu imposé à un taux inférieur *m*; ~ **terms of trade** *n pl* ECON termes de l'échange par rapport aux revenus des exploitations *m pl*; ~ **test** *n* TAX évaluation de l'état des revenus *f*; ~ **-tested supplement** *n* WEL complément proportionnel aux ressources *m*; ~ **threshold** *n* TAX seuil de revenu *m*; ~ **velocity of money** *n* ECON vitesse de circulation revenu de la monnaie *f*, vitesse de transformation de la monnaie en revenu *f*

incomes: ~ **policy** *n* ECON, FIN politique des revenus *f*, HRM politique salariale *f*, politique des revenus *f*, POL politique salariale *f*

incoming: ~ **call** *n* COMMS *phone* appel de l'extérieur *m*; ~ **data** *n pl* COMP données en entrée *f pl*; ~ **flight** *n* LEIS vol de retour *m*, TRANSP vol d'arrivée *m*, vol de retour *m*; ~ **goods** *n pl* GEN COMM marchandises à l'arrivée *f pl*, marchandises à la réception *f pl*; ~ **mail** *n* AmE (cf incoming post BrE) COMMS courrier du jour *m*, courrier à l'arrivée *m*; ~ **order** *n* S&M commande reçue *f*; ~ **post** *n* BrE (cf incoming mail AmE) COMMS courrier du jour *m*, courrier à l'arrivée *m*

in-company *adj* GEN COMM maison

incompatible *adj* GEN COMM incompatible

incompetence *n* ECON, GEN COMM, HRM, IND incompétence *f*

incompetent *adj* ECON, GEN COMM, HRM, IND incapable, incompétent, LAW incapable

incomplete *adj* GEN COMM inachevé, incomplet

incompleted *adj* GEN COMM inachevé

incontestable: ~ **clause** *n* INS *life insurance* clause d'incontestabilité *f*, clause incontestable *f*

inconvertible: ~ **money** *n* ECON argent inconvertible *m*, argent non-convertible *m*, monnaie inconvertible *f*

incorporate *vt* GEN COMM *company* constituer, *include* incorporer, *merge* fusionner

incorporated[1] *adj* GEN COMM *included* incorporé, LAW *UK institution, company* constitué

incorporated:[2] ~ **company** *n* US *(Inc.)* GEN COMM association constituée en société commerciale *f*, société constituée *f*, société enregistrée *f*, société à responsabilité limitée *f* *(SARL)*

incorporation *n* GEN COMM *of company* constitution *f*, constitution en société *f*, constitution en société par actions *f*, LAW *of company* constitution *f*, constitution en société *f*, STOCK constitution *f*, enregistrement *m*, enregistrement de société *m*

incorporeal[1] *adj* (ANT *corporeal*) ACC, ECON, FIN, GEN COMM, LAW incorporel

incorporeal:[2] ~ **hereditaments** *n pl* (ANT *corporeal hereditaments*) LAW biens incorporels transmissibles par héritage *m pl*; ~ **property** *n* LAW, PROP bien incorporel *m*

INCOTERM *abbr* (*international commercial term*) ECON *international trade* INCOTERME (*terme commercial international*)

increase[1] *n* ACC, ECON hausse *f*, GEN COMM *in price* augmentation *f*, hausse *f*, HRM *in wages* augmentation *f*, S&M majoration *f*; ~ **in prices** ACC hausse des prix *f*, majoration de prix *f*, ECON augmentation des prix *f*, hausse des prix *f*, majoration de prix *f*, renchérissement *m*, FIN hausse des prix *f*, majoration de prix *f*, GEN COMM augmentation des prix *f*, hausse des prix *f*, majoration de prix *f*, renchérissement *m*, S&M hausse des prix *f*, majoration de prix *f*; ~ **in value** FIN plus-value *f*

increase[2] **1.** *vt* GEN COMM augmenter, majorer, S&M majorer; **2.** *vi* ECON croître, GEN COMM augmenter, croître, progresser; ♦ ~ **in value** GEN COMM, PROP se valoriser; ~ **the supply** ECON accroître l'offre, augmenter l'offre; ~ **tenfold** GEN COMM décupler; ~ **twofold** GEN COMM doubler

increased: ~ **value** *n* (*iv*) FIN plus-value *f*

increasing[1] *adj* GEN COMM croissant

increasing:[2] ~ **liquidity order** *n* (ANT *decreasing liquidity order*) ACC ordre de liquidité croissante *m*; ~ **opportunity costs law** *n* ECON, FIN loi des coûts d'opportunité croissants *f*; ~ **returns to scale** *n pl* ECON, FIN, STOCK rendements d'échelle croissants *m pl*

increasingly *adv* GEN COMM de plus en plus

incremental[1] *adj* COMP incrémentiel, marginal, par augmentation *loc f*, ECON *cost* marginal

incremental:[2] ~ **analysis** *n* ACC, GEN COMM, MGMNT, TAX analyse marginale *f*; ~ **capital-output ratio** *n* (*ICOR*) FIN taux de rendement du capital différentiel *m*, taux incrémental de dépenses en capital *m*; ~ **cash flow** *n* ACC, FIN cash marginal *m*, marge brute d'autofinancement marginale *f*; ~ **cost of capital** *n* FIN coût différentiel du capital *m*; ~ **oil revenue tax** *n* *(IORT)* TAX impôt sur les revenus pétroliers supplémentaires *m*; ~ **payment** *n* HRM salaire de croissance *m*; ~ **scale** *n* HRM échelle de croissance des salaires *f*; ~ **spending** *n* S&M augmentation des dépenses *f*; ~ **tax** *n* TAX impôt supplémentaire *m*; ~ **technology** *n* GEN COMM technologie complémentaire *f*, technologie incrémentielle *f*

incumbent[1] *adj* ADMIN *officer, official* titulaire, POL *minister* en exercice *loc m*

incumbent[2] *n* ADMIN, POL titulaire *mf*

incur *vt* GEN COMM *debts* contracter, encourir, *expenses* encourir, engager; ◆ ~ **cost** ACC, FIN, GEN COMM, TAX encourir des dépenses, engager des dépenses, engager des frais; ~ **debts** ACC, FIN contracter des dettes, encourir des dettes; ~ **expenses** ACC, FIN, GEN COMM, TAX encourir des dépenses, engager des dépenses, engager des frais

incurable: ~ **depreciation** *n* PROP *appraisal* dépréciation irrémédiable *f*

incurred: ~ **costs** *n pl* ACC frais engagés *m pl*; ~ **expenses** *n pl* ACC, GEN COMM, TAX dépenses encourues *f pl*, dépenses engagées *f pl*, frais engagés *m pl*

indebted *adj* ECON, FIN, GEN COMM endetté; ◆ ~ **to** ECON, FIN, GEN COMM endetté envers

indebtedness *n* FIN dette *f*, titre de créance *m*, GEN COMM *money owed* dette *f*

indecomposability *n* ECON indécomposabilité *f*

indefinite[1] *adj* GEN COMM indéterminé

indefinite:[2] ~ **laytime** *n* TRANSP staries non-définies *f pl*

indemnify *vt* INS indemniser

indemnity *n* FIN indemnisation *f*, INS dédommagement *m*, indemnisation *f*, indemnité *f*, LAW compensation *f*, dédommagement *m*, indemnité *f*; ~ **fund** HRM caisse de solidarité patronale *f*

indent *n* ADMIN alinéa *m*; ~ **house** GEN COMM société d'exportation *f*

indentation *n* COMP *word-processing*, MEDIA *print* décalage *m*, mise en retrait *f*

indenture *n* STOCK accord *m*

independence *n* ACC, FIN, GEN COMM indépendance *f*

independent[1] *adj* GEN COMM indépendant, HRM autonome; ◆ ~ **of** GEN COMM indépendant de

independent:[2] ~ **adjuster** *n* INS expert d'assurance *m*, expert indépendant *m*; ~ **audit** *n* ACC, FIN audit externe *m*, contrôle externe *m*, révision externe *f*, vérification externe *f* *(Can)*; ~ **auditor** *n* ACC auditeur indépendant *m* *(Fra)*, commissaire aux comptes indépendant *m* *(Fra)*, reviseur indépendant *m* *(Bel)*, réviseur indépendant *m* *(Fra)*, vérificateur indépendant *m* *(Can)*; ~ **broker** *n* STOCK courtier indépendant *m*; ~ **claim** *n* PATENTS revendication indépendante *f*; ~ **expert** *n* HRM expert indépendant *m*; ~ **inquiry** *n* LAW enquête autonome *f*, enquête indépendante *f*; ~ **local radio** *n* GEN COMM, MEDIA radio locale

indépendante *f*; ~ **review committee** *n* UK HRM commission indépendante de révision des salaires et des conventions *f*; ~ **school** *n* GEN COMM, WEL école libre *f*; ~ **spherical aluminium tank** *n* *BrE* *(IS)* TRANSP cuve sphérique indépendante en aluminium *f*; ~ **spherical aluminum tank** *n* *AmE see independent spherical aluminium tank BrE*; ~ **store** *n* S&M magasin indépendant *m*; ~ **tank** *n* *(IT)* TRANSP cuve autoporteuse *f*, cuve indépendante *f*; ~ **tank common** *n* *(ITX)* TRANSP cuve autoporteuse standard *f*, cuve indépendante standard *f*; ~ **tank wing** *n* *(ITW)* TRANSP cuve autoporteuse latérale *f*, cuve indépendante latérale *f*; ~ **trade union** *n* HRM syndicat indépendant *m*; ~ **union** *n* HRM syndicat indépendant *m*; ~ **variable** *n* MATH variable indépendante *f*

Independent *n* POL non-inscrit *m*; ~ **Television** UK *(ITV)* S&M chaîne de télévision britannique indépendante, diffusant des programmes régionaux

in-depth[1] *adj* GEN COMM approfondi

in-depth:[2] ~ **analysis** *n* GEN COMM analyse approfondie *f*; ~ **business plan** *n* GEN COMM plan d'entreprise détaillé *m*; ~ **discussion** *n* GEN COMM discussion approfondie *f*; ~ **interview** *n* HRM, S&M, WEL interview en profondeur *f*; ~ **study** *n* GEN COMM étude détaillée *f*

indeterminate: ~ **-premium life insurance** *n* INS assurance-vie à prime indéterminée *f*; ~ **waste** *n* ENVIR déchets de faible et moyenne activité *m pl*

index:[1] ~ **-linked** *adj* BANK, ECON, FIN, HRM, STOCK indexé

index[2] *n* [pl -dices] ADMIN contenu *m*, index *m*, table des matières *f*, COMP index *m*, ECON, FIN index *m*, indice *m*, GEN COMM index *m*, STOCK *average* indice *m*, indice boursier *m*; ~ **basis** *n* MATH *comparative calculation* indice de base *m*; ~ **card** *n* GEN COMM fiche *f*; ~ **-card file** *n* HRM fichier *m*; ~ **of coincident indicators** *n* FIN indice des indicateurs simultanés *m*; ~ **file** *n* COMP fichier d'index *m*, GEN COMM fichier *m*; ~ **fund** *n* STOCK fonds indice *m*, fonds indiciel *m*; ~ **futures** *n pl* FIN, STOCK contrats à terme indexés *m pl*; ~ **growth linked units** *n pl* *(IGLU)* STOCK *index-linked Swiss franc instruments* unités indexées liées à la croissance *f pl*; ~ **of lagging indicators** *n* FIN indice des indicateurs retardés d'activité *m*; ~ **of leading indicators** *n* FIN indice des indicateurs de tête *m*, STOCK indice des grandes valeurs *m*, indice des indicateurs de tête *m*; ~ **lease** *n* PROP loyer indexé *m*; ~ **-linked gilt** *n* STOCK obligation d'État indexée *f*, valeur indexée de premier choix *f*; ~ **-linked guaranteed minimum wage** *n* HRM salaire minimum interprofessionnel de croissance *m*, SMIC; ~ **-linked stock** *n* UK FIN, STOCK actions indexées *f pl*; ~ **linking** *n* HRM indexation sur le coût de la vie *f*; ~ **of longer leading indicators** *n* FIN indice des indicateurs à longue durée *m*; ~ **number** *n* ECON *econometrics* indice *m*, nombre indice *m*, MATH indice *m*; ~ **option** *n* STOCK option d'indexation *f*, option de mise sur indice *f*; ~ **options** *n pl* STOCK options sur indice *f* pl; **~ point** n STOCK point d'indice m; **~ price** n STOCK prix de l'indice m; **~ of shorter leading indicators** n FIN indice des indicateurs à courte durée m; **~ -tied loan** n ACC emprunt indexé m, prêt indexé m, ECON, FIN emprunt indexé m; **~ -tracking fund** n FIN fonds de placement suivant un indice m

Index: **~ and Option Market division** n US *(IOM division)* STOCK *of the Chicago Mercantile Exchange* département de l'indice et du marché à option

indexation n BANK, ECON, FIN, HRM, STOCK indexation f

indexed[1] adj BANK, ECON, FIN, HRM, MATH indexé

indexed:[2] **~ bond** n BANK, FIN, STOCK obligation indexée f; **~ currency option note** n *(ICON)* STOCK billet d'option de change indexé m; **~ life insurance** n INS assurance-vie indexée f; **~ loan** n BANK, ECON, FIN emprunt indexé m, prêt indexé m; **~ security** n BANK, FIN, STOCK titre indexé m

Indexed: **~ Security Investment Plan** n STOCK plan d'investissement en titres indexés m

indexing n BANK, ECON, FIN, HRM indexation f, STOCK *of portfolio* indexation f, pondération f

India pr n GEN COMM Inde f

Indian[1] adj GEN COMM indien

Indian[2] n GEN COMM *person* Indien m

indicated: **~ horsepower** n *(ihp)* GEN COMM cheval-vapeur indiqué m; **~ yield** n STOCK rapport indiqué m, rendement indiqué m

indication: **~ of interest** n STOCK indice d'intérêt m, manifestation d'intérêt f; **~ of source** n PATENTS indication de provenance f

indicative[1] adj GEN COMM indicatif; ◆ **~ of** GEN COMM indicatif de

indicative:[2] **~ planning** n *jarg* ECON planification indicative f

indicator n ECON indicateur m, *econometrics* clignotant m, POL, S&M, STOCK indicateur m; **~ variable** ECON *econometrics* variable indicateur f

indictment n LAW mise en accusation f

indifference: **~ curve** n ECON courbe d'indifférence f

indirect: **~ authorization** n BANK autorisation indirecte f; **~ cost** n *(ANT direct cost)* ACC, ECON, FIN charge indirecte f, coût indirect m, frais indirects m pl; **~ costs** n pl *(SYN fixed costs)* FIN frais indirects m pl; **~ discrimination** n HRM discrimination indirecte f, discrimination masquée f; **~ expense** n ACC, ECON, FIN charge indirecte f, coût indirect m, frais indirects m pl; **~ export trading** n IMP/EXP *sales abroad* commerce des exportations indirectes m; **~ labor** n AmE *see indirect labour BrE*; **~ labor costs** n pl AmE *see indirect labour costs BrE*; **~ labour** n BrE *(ANT direct labour)* ACC, ECON, HRM main-d'oeuvre indirecte f; **~ labour costs** n pl BrE ACC, ECON, HRM coûts indirects de main-d'oeuvre m pl; **~ route** n TRANSP itinéraire détourné m; **~ tax** n

ECON, TAX imposition indirecte f; **~ taxation** n ECON imposition indirecte f, TAX contributions indirectes f pl, imposition indirecte f; **~ taxes** n pl TAX contributions indirectes f pl; **~ workers** n pl HRM personnel de service et de remplacement m

indirectly adv *(ANT directly)* GEN COMM indirectement; ◆ **~ related to** GEN COMM en rapport indirect avec

indiscountable adj BANK inescomptable

indiscriminate: **~ dumping** n ENVIR décharge non contrôlée f

indispensable: **~ labor** n AmE, **~ labour** n BrE *(cf necessary labour)* HRM *Marxist theory* travail nécessaire m

individual[1] adj GEN COMM individuel

individual[2] n GEN COMM *person* individu m; **~ annuity policy** n INS police de rente individuelle f; **~ bargaining** n HRM négociation individuelle f; **~ clearing member** n STOCK adhérent compensateur individuel m; **~ company accounts** n pl ACC comptes d'entreprise individuelle m pl, comptes sociaux m pl, FIN, GEN COMM comptes sociaux m pl; **~ company audited accounts** n pl ACC comptes sociaux audités m pl, comptes vérifiés d'entreprise individuelle m pl; **~ conciliation** n HRM conciliation privée f; **~ consumer** n GEN COMM, S&M consommateur individuel m; **~ firm** n GEN COMM entreprise individuelle f; **~ grievance procedure** n HRM procédure prud'hommale privée f; **~ import licence** n BrE IMP/EXP licence d'importation individuelle f; **~ import license** n AmE *see individual import licence BrE*; **~ income tax** n TAX impôt sur le revenu des particuliers m; **~ income tax return** n TAX déclaration d'impôt sur le revenu des particuliers f; **~ investor** n STOCK investisseur individuel m; **~ licence** n BrE IMP/EXP licence individuelle f; **~ license** n AmE *see individual licence BrE*; **~ life insurance** n US INS assurance-vie individuelle f; **~ rights** n pl HRM droits individuels m pl

individualism n HRM *of employee, manager* individualisme m

individualization n WEL personnalisation f

individually adv GEN COMM individuellement

indivisibility n ECON, MATH indivisibilité f

indivisible: **~ export** n IMP/EXP exportation indivisible f; **~ load** n TRANSP masse indivisible f

Indonesia pr n GEN COMM Indonésie f

Indonesian[1] adj GEN COMM indonésien

Indonesian[2] n GEN COMM *language* indonésien m, *person* Indonésien m

indoor: **~ sales manager** n HRM directeur des ventes intérieures m, directeur des ventes sédentaires m

indorse vt *see endorse*

indorsee n *see endorsee*

indorsement n *see endorsement*

indorser n *see endorser*

indorsor n *see endorsor*

induced: ~ **draft** *n* FIN traite induite *f*; ~ **technical progress** *n* ECON progrès technique induit *m*

inducement *n* GEN COMM *bribe* pot-de-vin *m*, LAW incitation *f*; ~ **good** ECON bien d'incitation *m*; ~ **mechanism** ECON mécanisme des retombées technologiques par incitation *m*; ~ **payment** TAX paiement incitatif *m*

induction *n* GEN COMM *of new employee* accueil *m*, intégration *f*, HRM *of new employee* accueil *m*, mise au courant *f*; ~ **course** GEN COMM, HRM stage d'accueil *m*

industrial[1] *adj* ECON, IND *nation, production, conditions, chemical*, STOCK *stock market classification* industriel

industrial:[2] ~ **accident** *n* HRM, IND, WEL accident du travail *m*; ~ **action** *n* HRM, IND action revendicative *f*, grève *f*, mouvements sociaux *m pl*; ~ **activity** *n* IND activité industrielle *f*; ~ **advertising** *n* S&M publicité industrielle *f*; ~ **application** *n* IND *of machine*, PATENTS application industrielle *f*; ~ **arbitration** *n* HRM arbitrage en matière de conflits du travail *m*; ~ **base** *n* IND base industrielle *f*; ~ **boilers** *n pl* IND grosse chaudronnerie *f*; ~ **capacity utilization** *n* ECON, IND utilisation du potentiel industriel *f*; ~ **capitalism** *n* ECON, IND capitalisme industriel *m*; ~ **carrier** *n* TRANSP transporteur pour compte propre *m*; ~ **center** *n* AmE, ~ **centre** *n* BrE IND centre industriel *m*; ~ **circles** *n pl* GEN COMM milieux industriels *m pl*; ~ **and commercial company** *n pl (ICC)* ECON, GEN COMM société industrielle et commerciale *f*; ~ **complex** *n* IND, PROP, S&M complexe industriel *m*; ~ **concentration** *n* IND concentration industrielle *f*; ~ **conflict** *n* ECON, HRM conflit du travail *m*, conflit social *m*; ~ **cooperation** *n* IND coopération industrielle *f*; ~ **country** *n* ECON, IND, POL pays industrialisé *m*; ~ **court** *n* UK HRM, IND, LAW ≈ Conseil des prud'hommes *m*; ~ **demand** *n* IND demande industrielle *f*; ~ **democracy** *n* GEN COMM démocratie industrielle *f*, HRM *workers' participation* démocratie d'entreprise *f*, propriété publique *f*, POL autogestion *f*; ~ **development bond** *n* STOCK *US* bon de développement industriel *m*, obligation de développement industriel *f*; ~ **discharge** *n* ENVIR, IND *into river* rejet industriel *m*; ~ **disease** *n* HRM maladie de travail *f*, maladie professionnelle *f*; ~ **dispute** *n* ECON, HRM conflit du travail *m*, conflit social *m*; ~ **dynamics** *n pl* [+sing v] IND dynamique industrielle *f*; ~ **economics**, *n pl* [+sing v] ECON, IND économie industrielle *f*; ~ **engineering** *n* IND génie industriel *m*; ~ **equipment** *n* ACC *annual accounts* matériel *m*, outillage industriel *m*; ~ **espionage** *n* GEN COMM espionnage industriel *m*, HRM contre-espionnage industriel *m*, IND contre-espionnage industriel *m*, espionnage industriel *m*; ~ **estate** *n* BrE *(cf industrial park AmE)* GEN COMM zone industrielle *f*, IND, PROP, S&M complexe industriel *m*, site industriel *m*, zone industrielle *f*; ~ **fatigue** *n* HRM surmenage *m*; ~ **finance** *n* FIN finance

industrielle *f*, financement industriel *m*; ~ **goods** *n pl* ECON, IND biens industriels *m pl*; ~ **health** *n* HRM, WEL santé sur le lieu de travail *f*; ~ **hygiene** *n* HRM, WEL hygiène du travail *f*; ~ **incident** *n* HRM incident au travail *m*; ~ **inertia** *n* IND inertie industrielle *f*; ~ **injury insurance** *n* INS assurance-accidents du travail *f*; ~ **loan** *n* STOCK emprunt industriel *m*; ~ **marketing** *n* S&M marketing des produits industriels *m*; ~ **muscle** *n* HRM surface industrielle *f*; ~ **nation** *n* ECON, POL nation industrialisée *f*; ~ **occupancy** *n* IND, PROP occupation industrielle *f*; ~ **organization** *n (IO)* IND organisation industrielle *f*; ~ **park** *n* AmE *(cf industrial estate BrE)* GEN COMM zone industrielle *f*, IND, PROP, S&M complexe industriel *m*, site industriel *m*, zone industrielle *f*; ~ **plant** *n* IND établissement industriel *m*; ~ **policy** *n* ECON, IND politique industrielle *f*; ~ **process** *n* ENVIR, IND processus industriel *m*, procédé industriel *m*; ~ **production** *n* ECON, IND production industrielle *f*; ~ **products** *n pl* IND produits industriels *m pl*; ~ **property** *n* IND, PATENTS, PROP propriété industrielle *f*; ~ **property protection** *n* IND, PATENTS, PROP protection de la propriété industrielle *f*; ~ **psychology** *n* HRM psychologie du travail *f*, IND psychologie du travail *f*, psychologie industrielle *f*, MGMNT psychologie industrielle *f*; ~ **refuse** *n* ECON, ENVIR, IND déchets industriels *m pl*; ~ **relations** *n pl* HRM *between management and union* relations syndicales *f pl*, HRM *between management and workers* relations du travail *f pl*, relations humaines dans l'entreprise *f pl*, relations industrielles *f pl*, relations professionnelles *f pl*; ~ **relations director** *n* HRM *in charge of negotiations between management and union* directeur des relations syndicales *m*, *in charge of relations between management and workers* directeur des relations humaines *m*, directeur des relations industrielles *m*, directeur des relations professionnelles *m*; ~ **relations manager** *n* HRM *in charge of relations between management and workers* directeur des relations humaines *m*, directeur des relations industrielles *m*, directeur des relations professionnelles *m*, *in charge of negotiations between management and union* directeur des relations syndicales *m*; ~ **rent** *n* IND, PROP loyer industriel *m*; ~ **research** *n* S&M *market research* enquête sur des produits industriels *f*, recherche appliquée *f*; ~ **revolution** *n* ECON, IND révolution industrielle *f*; ~ **safety** *n* HRM, WEL sécurité industrielle *f*; ~ **sector** *n* IND secteur industriel *m*; ~ **security** *n* FIN *asset* valeur industrielle *f*, HRM, IND *counterespionage* contre-espionnage industriel *m*; ~ **services** *n pl* IND services industriels *m pl*; ~ **share** *n* STOCK valeur industrielle *f*; ~ **site** *n* IND site industriel *m*; ~ **source** *n* ENVIR *of pollution* source industrielle *f*; ~ **spirit** *n* IND essence industrielle *f*; ~ **strife** *n* HRM conflit social *m*; ~ **system** *n* IND système industriel *m*; ~ **trade** *n* GEN COMM échanges industriels *m pl*; ~ **and trade policy adjustment loan** *n (ITPAL)* FIN prêt d'ajustement de politique industrielle et commerciale *m*; ~ **training** *n* HRM formation professionnelle *f*; ~ **training grant** *n* FIN subvention à la formation dans l'industrie *f*; ~ **tribunal** *n* UK (IT) HRM, IND, LAW ≈ Conseil des prud'hommes *m*; ~ **union** *n* HRM, WEL syndicat d'industrie *m*; ~ **unrest** *n* HRM malaise social *m*; ~ **vehicle** *n* TRANSP véhicule industriel *m*; ~ **waste** *n* ECON, ENVIR, IND déchets industriels *m pl*, effluent industriel *m*; ~ **wastewater** *n* ENVIR eau résiduaire *f*

Industrial: ~ **Council for Educational & Training Technology** *n* UK (ICETT) WEL Conseil industriel pour la technologie en matière d'éducation et de formation *m*; ~ **Development Authority** *n* (IDA) ECON, IND administration du développement industriel *f*; ~ **Market Research Services** *n* (IMRS) S&M Services d'études de marché industriel *m pl*; ~ **Planning Department** *n* US IND ≈ ministère de la Planification industrielle *m*; ~ **Relations Policy Committee** *n* (IRPC) HRM commission sur la politique des relations industrielles

industrialist *n* ECON, IND industriel *m*

industrialization *n* (ANT *deindustrialization*) ECON, IND, POL industrialisation *f*

industrialized[1] *adj* ECON, IND, POL industrialisé

industrialized:[2] ~ **countries of the West** *n pl* ECON pays industrialisés occidentaux *m pl*; ~ **country** *n* ECON, IND, POL pays industrialisé *m*

industry *n* ECON, IND industrie *f*; ~ **minister** GEN COMM ministre de l'Industrie *m*; ~ **standard** ECON, IND norme industrielle *f*; ~ **-wide agreement** HRM, IND convention généralisée à tout le secteur *f*

inefficiency *n* ECON, GEN COMM, HRM, IND *of person, machine* incompétence *f*, inefficacité *f*, inefficience *f*; ~ **in the market** STOCK inefficacité sur le marché *f*, non-efficience du marché *f*

inelastic: ~ **demand** *n* ECON demande inélastique *f*; ~ **supply** *n* ECON offre inélastique *f*

inelasticity *n* ECON inélasticité *f*; ~ **of demand** ECON inélasticité de la demande *f*; ~ **of supply** ECON inélasticité de l'offre *f*

ineligible: ~ **paper** *n* BANK effet non-acceptable *m*

inequality *n* ECON, HRM, LAW, POL inégalité *f*

inertia: ~ **salesman** *n* S&M vendeur par correspondance *m*; ~ **selling** *n* S&M vente forcée *f*, vente par correspondance *f*

inertial: ~ **effect** *n* POL effet d'inertie *m*; ~ **inflation** *n* ECON inflation sous-jacente *f*

inevitable *adj* GEN COMM inévitable

inevitably *adv* GEN COMM inévitablement

inexhaustible *adj* ENVIR inépuisable

inexpensive *adj* GEN COMM peu cher

inf. *abbr* (*information*) ACC, ECON renseignements *m pl*, GEN COMM informations *f pl*, renseignements *m pl*, TAX, TRANSP renseignements *m pl*

infant: ~ **industry** *n* IND industrie naissante *f*; ~ **industry argument** *n* IND raison propre à une industrie naissante *f*; ~ **mortality** *n* WEL mortalité infantile *f*

infected: ~ **ship** *n* TRANSP navire en quarantaine *m*

inferential: ~ **statistics** *n pl* [+sing v] MATH statistique déductive *f*

inferior: ~ **good** *n* ECON, IND bien inférieur *m*; ~ **goods** *n pl* GEN COMM produits de qualité inférieure *m pl*

infession *n jarg* (SYN *stagflation*) ECON récession provoquée par l'inflation *f*

infinite *adj* ENVIR illimité, inépuisable

infirm *adj* TAX atteint d'incapacité

inflatable: ~ **dunnage** *n* TRANSP fardage gonflable *m*, sacs gonflables *m pl*; ~ **life raft** *n* TRANSP *boat* radeau de sauvetage pneumatique *m*; ~ **raft** *n* TRANSP *boat* radeau pneumatique *m*

inflate *vt* ECON *economy* relancer, GEN COMM *price* faire monter, gonfler

inflation *n* ECON inflation *f*; ~ **accounting** ACC comptabilité aux coûts de remplacement *f*, comptabilité de coûts courants *f*, ECON comptabilité d'inflation *f*; ~ **-adjusted deficit** ECON déficit corrigé pour tenir compte de l'inflation *m*; ~ **-adjusted income** ACC bénéfices en monnaie constante *m pl*, revenu ajusté compte tenu de l'inflation *m*; ~ **endorsement** INS *property insurance* avenant couvrant l'inflation *m*; ~ **illusion** ECON illusion inflationniste *f*; ~ **rate** ECON taux d'inflation *m*

inflationary[1] *adj* ECON inflationniste

inflationary:[2] ~ **expectations** *n pl* ECON anticipations inflationnistes *f pl*; ~ **gap** *n* ECON écart inflationniste *m*; ~ **pressure** *n* ECON pression inflationniste *f*; ~ **spiral** *n* ECON spirale inflationniste *f*; ~ **trend** *n* ECON tendance inflationniste *f*

inflationist *n* ECON partisan de l'inflation *m*

in-flight: ~ **catering** *n* TRANSP restauration en vol *f*; ~ **entertainment** *n* TRANSP distractions en vol *f pl*; ~ **facilities** *n pl* TRANSP facilités en vol *f pl*; ~ **film** *n* TRANSP film en vol *m*; ~ **information** *n* TRANSP renseignements en vol *m pl*; ~ **magazine** *n* TRANSP revue de la compagnie aérienne *f*; ~ **meal** *n* TRANSP repas en vol *m*; ~ **music** *n* TRANSP musique en vol *f*; ~ **service** *n* TRANSP service en vol *m*

inflow *n* (ANT *outflow*) ACC, BANK, ECON, FIN, GEN COMM entrée *f*; ~ **of funds** (ANT *outflow of funds*) ACC, BANK, ECON, FIN, GEN COMM rentrée de fonds *f*

influence[1] *n* GEN COMM ascendant *m*, influence *f*; ◆ **have ~ over** GEN COMM avoir de l'ascendant sur, exercer une influence sur

influence[2] *vt* GEN COMM *costs* influer sur

influential *adj* GEN COMM influent; ◆ **be ~** GEN COMM avoir de l'influence

info *abbr* (*information*) ACC, ECON renseignements *m pl*, GEN COMM informations *f pl*, renseignements *m pl*, TAX, TRANSP renseignements *m pl*

inform *vt* COMMS avertir, aviser, informer, GEN COMM informer

informal[1] *adj* GEN COMM *visit* informel

informal:[2] ~ **agreement** *n* GEN COMM accord officieux *m*; ~ **arrangement** *n* GEN COMM accord officieux *m*; ~ **economy** *n* ECON économie informelle *f*; ~ **interview** *n* HRM, MEDIA entretien informel *m*; ~ **leader** *n* HRM autorité naturelle *f*, leader naturel *m*, leader spontané *m*; ~ **meeting** *n* GEN COMM réunion informelle *f*; ~ **organization** *n* GEN COMM *club, society* organisation non-officielle *f*, *method of management* organisation informelle *f*

informality *n* HRM caractère non formalisé *m*

informant *n* TAX dénonciateur *m*

informatics *n pl* [+sing v] COMP informatique *f*

information *n* ACC *(inf., info)* ECON *(inf., info)* renseignements *m pl*, GEN COMM *(inf., info)* informations *f pl*, TAX *giving details of somebody's activities* dénonciation *f*, TAX *(inf., info)* TRANSP *(inf., info)* renseignements *m pl*; ~ **agreement** GEN COMM accord d'information *m*; ~ **bit** COMP bit d'information *m*; ~ **broadcast** MEDIA diffusion de l'information *f*, les moyens de communication *m pl*, les supports de communication *m pl*, massmédia *m pl*; ~ **bureau** GEN COMM bureau de renseignements *m*; ~ **desk** GEN COMM bureau de renseignements *m*; ~ **flow** COMP, GEN COMM flux de l'information *m*; ~ **handling** COMP manipulation de l'information *f*, traitement de l'information *m*, GEN COMM traitement de l'information *m*, traitement des informations *m*; ~ **highway** COMP autoroute d'informations *f*; ~ **network** COMMS réseau informatique *m*, COMP réseau d'information *m*, réseau informatique *m*; ~ **officer** HRM cadre à l'information *m*, chef du service des renseignements *m*; ~ **processing** COMP informatique *f*, traitement de l'information *m*; ~ **retrieval** COMP extraction de l'information *f*, recherche d'informations *f*, recherche documentaire *f*, récupération de l'information *f*; ~ **retrieval system** COMP système de recherche documentaire *m*; ~ **return** TAX déclaration de renseignements *f*; ~ **storage** COMP stockage d'informations *m*; ~ **storage capacity** COMP capacité de stockage des données *f*; ~ **system** COMP système d'information *m*, système informatique *m*; ~ **technology** *(IT)* COMP informatique *f*, technologie de l'information *f*; ~ **theory** COMP, MATH *statistics*, MGMNT théorie de l'information *f*; ~ **transfer** COMP transfert d'information *m*; ◆ **for your** ~ *(FYI)* GEN COMM à titre d'information, à titre de renseignement, à titre indicatif, STOCK pour information

Information: ~ **Technology Export Organization** *n* UK *(EXPORTIT)* IMP/EXP organisation d'exportation de la technologie de l'information

informative: ~ **advertising** *n* S&M publicité informative *f*; ~ **labeling** *n* AmE, ~ **labelling** *n* BrE S&M étiquetage informatif *m*

informed[1] *adj* GEN COMM *decision, argument* bien informé, *person* informé; ◆ ~ **about** GEN COMM au courant de; **keep sb** ~ COMMS, GEN COMM tenir qn au courant

informed:[2] ~ **public** *n* GEN COMM public bien informé *m*

infra *adv* *(* ANT *supra)* GEN COMM infra

infrastructural *adj* ECON, GEN COMM d'infrastructure *loc f*

infrastructure *n* ECON, GEN COMM infrastructure *f*

infringe *vt* GEN COMM contrevenir à, LAW contrevenir à, enfreindre, violer, PATENTS enfreindre, violer; ◆ ~ **the law** LAW contrevenir à la loi, enfreindre la loi, violer la loi

infringement *n* GEN COMM contravention *f*, LAW contravention *f*, infraction *f*, violation *f*, PATENTS contrefaçon *f*, violation *f*; ~ **of the law** LAW contravention à la loi *f*, infraction à la loi *f*, violation d'un droit *f*

infringer *n* PATENTS contrefacteur *m*

ingenuity *n* GEN COMM ingéniosité *f*

ingot *n* GEN COMM *of metal* lingot *m*

ingress *n* GEN COMM entrée *f*

inhabitant *n* GEN COMM, LAW, POL habitant *m*

inherent: ~ **explosion clause** *n* INS *property insurance* assurance explosion due à la nature même du risque *f*; ~ **risk** *n* STOCK risque inhérent *m*; ~ **vice** *n* GEN COMM, TRANSP vice propre *m*

inherit *vt* LAW *money, property* hériter; ◆ ~ **sth from sb** LAW *money, property* hériter qch de qn

inheritance *n* LAW *act, right, property* héritage *m*, succession *f*; ~ **duty** TAX droit sur les biens transmis par décès *m*; ~ **tax** UK TAX droits de mutation *m pl*, droits de succession *m pl*

inherited: ~ **audience** *n jarg* MEDIA *broadcast* audience héritée de l'émission précédente *f*; ~ **property** *n* LAW bien reçu en héritage *m*

inhibit *vt* COMP bloquer, empêcher, interdire

in-home: ~ **banking** *n* BANK opérations bancaires intérieures *f pl*

inhospitable *adj* GEN COMM inhospitalier

in-house[1] *adj* COMP *service, worker* interne, *system* maison, GEN COMM *translator* maison, HRM en interne, sur site *loc m*, à l'interne

in-house:[2] ~ **operation** *n* STOCK opération interne *f*; ~ **software** *n* COMP logiciel maison *m*; ~ **system** *n* COMP système interne *m*, système maison *m*; ~ **training** *n* HRM formation sur site *f*, formation dans l'entreprise *f*; ~ **valuation** *n* PROP estimation interne *f*

initial[1] *adj* ACC *interest*, FIN *interest*, GEN COMM *cost*, STOCK *investment*, TAX initial

initial[2] *n* GEN COMM *letter of the alphabet* initiale *f*; ~ **assessment** TAX *of a return* cotisation initiale *f*; ~ **boiling point** GEN COMM point d'ébullition initial *m*; ~ **capital** FIN capital d'apport *m*, capital initial *m*, mise de fonds initiale *f*, STOCK capital de départ *m*, capital initial *m*; ~ **expenditure** FIN dépense initiale *f*; ~ **funding** FIN consolidation initiale *f*; ~ **inventory** ACC stock au début de l'exercice *m*, stock d'ouverture *m*, stock initial *m*,

stock à l'ouverture de l'exercice *m*; **~ margin**
STOCK *cash or collateral deposited with a futures
broker* dépôt de garantie *m*, dépôt initial *m*,
marge initiale *f*; **~ margin level** STOCK niveau de
marge initiale *m*, niveau du dépôt initial *m*;
~ margin requirement STOCK demande de marge
initiale *f*, exigence de dépôt initial *f*; **~ outlay** ACC
mise de fonds initiale *f*, *on purchase* coût d'entrée
m, mise initiale *f*, première mise de fonds *f*, ECON,
FIN, GEN COMM, IND mise de fonds initiale *f*;
~ public offering *AmE (IPO)* STOCK offre
publique initiale *f*, première émission publique
f; **~ year** TAX année initiale *f*

initialization *n* COMP initialisation *f*

initialize *vt* COMP *operating system, printer* initialiser

initiate *vt* COMP *software* lancer

initiating: **~ explosive** *n* TRANSP *dangerous classified transported goods* explosif d'amorçage *m*

initiation: **~ dues** *n pl* (SYN *initiation fees*) TAX
droits d'adhésion *m pl*; **~ fees** *n pl* (SYN *initiation
dues*) TAX droits d'adhésion *m pl*

initiative *n* MGMNT initiative *f*; ◆ **take the ~**
MGMNT prendre l'initiative

initiator *n* POL initiateur *m*

injection *n* ECON, FIN *of funds* injection *f*

injunction *n* LAW injonction *f*; **~ bond** LAW mise en
demeure avec garantie *f*

injured: **~ party** *n* LAW partie lésée *f*

injuria sine damno *phr* LAW atteinte à un droit
n'entraînant aucun dommage

injurious: **~ affection** *n* LAW affectation hypothécaire malveillante *f*, mise en gage préjudiciable *f*

injury *n* HRM *of employee* blessure *f*; **~ independent
of all other means** INS *health insurance* blessure
indépendante *f*

ink: **~ -jet printer** *n* COMP imprimante à jet d'encre *f*

in-kind: **~ transfer** *n* WEL virement en nature *m*

inland: **~ carrier** *n* IMP/EXP, TRANSP transporteur
intérieur *m*; **~ clearance depot** *n (ICD)* IMP/EXP
bureau de dédouanement de l'intérieur *m*;
~ container *n (IC)* TRANSP conteneur pour le
transport intérieur *m*; **~ haulage** *n* IMP/EXP,
TRANSP acheminement intérieur *m*; **~ marine
insurance** *n* INS assurance de navigation intérieure *f*, assurance fluviale *f*; **~ rail depot** *n (IRD)*
IMP/EXP, TRANSP bureau de dédouanement ferroviaire intérieur *m*; **~ waterway** *n* TRANSP voie
fluviale *f*, voie navigable *f*; **~ waterway vessel** *n*
TRANSP *boat* bateau fluvial *m*

Inland: **~ Revenue stamp** *n UK* TAX timbre fiscal
m; **the ~ Revenue** *n* TAX *UK (IR) organization,
system* service des impôts britannique, le Fisc *m*
(*infrml*), TAX *UK payments* les contributions
directes *f pl*

INMARSAT *abbr (International Maritime Satellite
Organization)* COMMS Organisation internationale de satellites maritimes *f*

inner: **~ city** *n* ENVIR, WEL centre-ville *m*; **~ -city
areas** *n pl* ENVIR, WEL quartiers déshérités *m pl*;

~ harbor *n AmE*, **~ harbour** *n BrE* TRANSP port
intérieur *m*

innovate *vti* GEN COMM innover

innovation *n* GEN COMM, IND *introducing something
new* innovation *f*, *something new* nouveauté *f*;
~ center *AmE*, **~ centre** *BrE* IND centre d'innovation *m*

innovative *adj* GEN COMM innovateur, novateur

innovator *n* GEN COMM innovateur *m*, novateur *m*,
S&M *marketing* innovateur *m*

inoculate *vt* IMP/EXP vacciner

inoculation *n* IMP/EXP vaccination *f*

inoperative: **~ clause** *n* LAW clause inopérante *f*

in pari delicto *phr* LAW in pari delicto

in personam *phr* LAW contre une personne
déterminée, in personam, relatif à une personne
déterminée

in-plant: **~ training** *n* HRM, IND formation dans
l'entreprise *f*

input[1] *n* COMP *data* données d'entrée *f pl*, *putting in
data* entrée *f*, ECON facteur de production *m*, GEN
COMM *putting in data* entrée *f*, input *m*, IND
facteur de production *m*, input *m*; **~ cost** ACC
coût d'entrée *m*; **~ data** COMP données d'entrée *f
pl*; **~ device** COMP périphérique d'entrée *m*, unité
d'entrée *f*; **~ factor** FIN facteur d'entrée *m*;
~ keyboard COMP clavier de saisie *m*; **~ message**
COMP message d'entrée *m*; **~ tax credit** *Can (ITC)*
TAX crédit de taxe sur intrants *m (CTI)*

input[2] *vt* COMP *data* entrer, introduire, saisir

input/output *n (I/O)* COMP entrée/sortie *f (E/S)*;
~ analysis COMP, ECON, FIN, IND, MATH analyse
d'entrée/sortie *f*, analyse des intrants et des
extrants *f*, analyse intrants-extrants *f*; **~ error
message** COMP message d'erreur d'entrée/sortie
m; **~ processor** COMP processeur d'entrée/sortie
m; **~ table** COMP tableau d'entrées/sorties *m*,
ECON, FIN, IND tableau d'entrées/sorties *m*,
tableau d'échanges inter-industriels *m*, MATH
tableau d'échanges inter-industriels *m*

inputs *n pl* ECON, IND input *m*, moyens de
production *m pl*

inquire: **~ at the office** *phr* GEN COMM adressez-
vous au bureau

inquiry *n* COMP consultation *f*, interrogation *f*, LAW,
TAX enquête *f*; **~ desk** GEN COMM bureau
d'information *m*, bureau de renseignements *m*;
~ form GEN COMM formulaire de demande de
renseignements *m*; **~ office** ADMIN bureau de
renseignements *m*; **~ program** COMP programme
d'interrogation *m*

in rem *phr* LAW in rem, relatif à l'exercice du droit
de propriété

inroads: **make ~** *phr* GEN COMM pénétrer

ins. *abbr* INS (*insurance*) asse. (*assurance*), TRANSP
(*insulated*) isotherme

INSA *abbr (International Shipowners' Association)*
TRANSP association internationale des armateurs

insert[1] *n* MEDIA encart *m*

insert[2] *vt* COMP, GEN COMM, MEDIA, S&M *advertising* insérer

in-service: ~ **training** *n* HRM stage de formation dans l'entreprise *m*, stage de formation sur le lieu de travail *m*, stage de formation sur site *m*

inset *n* MEDIA encart *m*

inshore: ~ **traffic zone** *n* TRANSP zone de navigation côtière *f*

inside: ~ **back cover** *n* MEDIA *of book, magazine* troisième de couverture *f*; ~ **front** *n* MEDIA *of book, magazine* deuxième de couverture *f*; ~ **front cover** *n* MEDIA *of book, magazine* deuxième de couverture *f*; ~ **information** *n* FIN, STOCK information d'initié *f*; ~ **lot** *n* PROP lotissement interne *m*

insider *n* FIN initié *m*, GEN COMM *of corporation* dirigeant *m*, STOCK initié *m*; ~ **dealing** FIN, STOCK délit d'initié *m*, opérations d'initiés *f pl*, transaction d'initié *f*; ~ **report** FIN, STOCK déclaration d'initié *f*; ~ **trading** FIN, STOCK opérations d'initiés *f pl*, transaction d'initié *f*; ~ **wage setting** (ANT *outsider wage setting*) ECON, HRM détermination des salaires entre initiés *f*

insofar: ~ **as** *phr AmE*, **in so far as** *phr BrE* GEN COMM dans la mesure où *loc f*

insoluble *adj* GEN COMM insoluble

insolvency *n* ACC, GEN COMM, IND, LAW *having insufficient assets* carence *f*, insolvabilité *f*, insuffisance de capital *f*; ~ **clause** INS *reinsurance contract* clause d'insolvabilité *f*; ~ **legislation** GEN COMM, IND, LAW législation relative à la liquidation judiciaire *f*, législation sur la faillite *f*

insolvent *adj* ACC, GEN COMM, IND, LAW insolvable

inspect *vt* HRM inspecter, IMP/EXP visiter

inspection *n* GEN COMM contrôle *m*, examen *m*, inspection *f*, *visit* visite d'inspection *f*, IND *of product* contrôle *m*, examen *m*, inspection *f*; ~ **of files** PATENTS *of application* inspection du dossier *f*

inspector *n* GEN COMM contrôleur *m*, HRM inspecteur *m*, IMP/EXP visiteur *m*, TAX contrôleur *m*; ~ **general of banks** BANK inspecteur général des banques *m*; ~ **of taxes** UK TAX inspecteur des contributions directes *m*

inspectorate *n* ENVIR *inspectors* inspection *f*, IND, WEL *function* inspectorat *m*

inst. *abbr* COMP (*installed*) installé, GEN COMM (*institute*) institut *m*

instal *see* install

install *vt* COMP *network* mettre en place, *software, peripherals, systems* installer, GEN COMM mettre en place

installation *n* COMP, GEN COMM installation *f*; ~ **diskette** COMP disquette d'installation *f*

installed *adj* (*inst.*) COMP installé

installment *n* AmE *see* instalment BrE

installments: **in** ~ *phr AmE see* in instalments BrE

instalment *n* BrE ACC acompte *m*, mensualité *f*, BANK, FIN acompte *m*, versement *m*, *monthly* mensualité *f*, GEN COMM acompte *m*, fascicule *m*;

~ **base** *n BrE* ACC base de crédit *f*; ~ **contract** *n BrE* BANK contrat de crédit *m*, LAW contrat de vente à tempérament *m*, contrat à exécution échelonnée *m*, contrat à tempérament *m*; ~ **credit** *n BrE* BANK, FIN crédit remboursable à terme *m*; ~ **loan** *n BrE* BANK, FIN prêt remboursable par versements *m*, prêt à tempérament *m*; ~ **payments** *n pl BrE* BANK, FIN paiements d'achat à crédit *m pl*, versements échelonnés *m pl*; ~ **purchase** *n BrE* GEN COMM achat à tempérament *m*; ~ **repayment schedule** *n BrE* BANK, FIN calendrier de remboursement d'achat à crédit *m*, calendrier de remboursement par versements *m*; ~ **sale** *n BrE* FIN, PROP, S&M vente à tempérament *f*

instalments: **in** ~ *phr BrE* BANK par versements, à tempérament, FIN par versements

instance: **in the first** ~ *phr* GEN COMM en premier lieu; **in this** ~ *phr* GEN COMM dans le cas présent *loc m*

instant: ~ **monetarism** *n* ECON monétarisme instantané *m*

instead: ~ **of** *phr* GEN COMM au lieu de *loc m*

institute[1] *n* (*inst.*) GEN COMM institut *m*; ~ **clause** INS marine clause de l'institut *f*

institute:[2] ~ **an appeal** *phr* TAX interjeter appel

Institute: ~ **of Administrative Management** *n UK* (*IAM*) MGMNT ≈ Institut de la gestion administrative *m*; ~ **of Bankers** *n* (*IOB*) BANK Institut des banquiers *m*; ~ **of Chartered Accountants** *n UK* (*ICA*) ACC association professionnelle des experts-comptables; ~ **of Chartered Accountants in England and Wales** *n UK* (*ICAEW*) ACC institut des experts-comptables d'Angleterre et du pays de Galles; ~ **of Chartered Accountants in Ireland** *n* (*ICAI*) ACC institut des experts-comptables d'Irlande; ~ **of Chartered Accountants of Scotland** *n UK* (*ICAS*) ACC institut des experts-comptables d'Écosse; ~ **of Cost and Management Accountants** *n UK* (*ICMA*) ACC association professionnelle des comptables; ~ **of Economic Affairs** *n UK* (*IEA*) ECON institut des affaires économiques *m*; ~ **for International Finance** *n* (*IIF*) FIN Institut de finances internationales *m*, Institut international de finance *m*; ~ **of London Underwriters** *n* INS institut des souscripteurs de Londres; ~ **of Manpower Studies** *n* (*IMS*) HRM Institut d'études sur la main d'oeuvre *m*; ~ **of Office Management** *n* (*IOM*) MGMNT institut de la gestion de bureaux; ~ **of Personnel Management** *n UK* (*IPM*) MGMNT Institut de gestion du personnel *m*; ~ **of Practitioners in Advertising** *n UK* (*IPA*) S&M institut des publicitaires; ~ **of Public Relations** *n UK* (*IPR*) S&M institut des relations publiques; ~ **of Shipping and Forwarding Agents** *n* (*ISFA*) TRANSP institut d'agents maritimes et de transitaires; ~ **of stockbrokers** *n* FIN Compagnie des agents de change *f*, CAC; ~ **of Transport Administration** *n UK* TRANSP institut de gestion des transports; ~ **of Travel Agents** *n UK* LEIS, TRANSP institut des agents de voyages

institution n BANK, ECON, FIN institution f, GEN COMM of change introduction f, organization institution f, établissement m, STOCK institution f, TAX of appeal introduction f

institutional: ~ **advertising** n S&M publicité institutionnelle f; ~ **economics** n US ECON l'école économique américaine de Velben à Galbraith, institutionnalisme m; ~ **investor** n STOCK investisseur institutionnel m; ~ **lender** n FIN prêteur institutionnel m

instruction n COMP program instruction f; ~ **book** GEN COMM guide d'utilisation m, guide de l'utilisateur m, manuel d'utilisation m; ~ **leaflet** MEDIA print mode d'emploi m, notice explicative f; ~ **manual** GEN COMM guide d'utilisation m, guide de l'utilisateur m, manuel d'utilisation m

instructions n pl COMMS instructions f pl, GEN COMM book guide de l'utilisateur m, manuel d'utilisation m, on how to use something guide d'utilisation m, mode d'emploi m, notice explicative f, orders instructions f pl, TRANSP instructions f pl; ◆ **for further ~** (FFI) GEN COMM pour toute instruction complémentaire

instructive adj HRM formateur

instrument n ACC effet m, BANK, FIN effet m, instrument m, GEN COMM instrument m, INS effet m, LAW acte juridique m, effet m, instrument m, titre m, STOCK instrument m, TAX effet m

instrumental adj GEN COMM capital productif

instrumentalities: ~ **of transportation** n pl INS assurance d'intermédiaires de transport f

instrumentality n US FIN instrumentalité f

insufficient adj BANK, FIN insuffisant; ◆ ~ **funds** BANK défaut de provision m, sans couverture suffisante, FIN fonds insuffisants m pl

insufficiently: ~ **stamped** phr COMMS letter, envelope pas suffisamment affranchi

insulate vt STOCK couvrir, isoler, protéger

insulated[1] adj (ins.) TRANSP isotherme

insulated:[2] ~ **capacity** n TRANSP of container capacité frigorifique f, capacité isotherme f; ~ **container** n TRANSP conteneur isotherme m; ~ **tank container** n (IT) TRANSP conteneur-citerne isotherme m; ~ **tanktainer** n TRANSP conteneur-citerne isotherme m; ~ **van** n TRANSP fourgon isotherme m

insurable: ~ **interest** n INS intérêt assurable m, intérêt d'assurance m; ~ **risk** n INS risque assurable m; ~ **title** n INS titre assurable m

insurance n (ins.) INS assurance f (asse.); ~ **agency** n INS cabinet d'assurances m; ~ **agent** n INS agent d'assurance m; ~ **annuity** n INS annuité d'assurance f; ~ **broker** n INS agent d'assurances m, assureur mf, courtier d'assurance m; ~ **broking** n INS courtage d'assurance m; ~ **business** n INS entreprise d'assurance f; ~ **certificate** n INS attestation d'assurance f; ~ **charge** n INS frais d'assurance m pl; ~ **claim** n INS déclaration de sinistre f, sinistre d'assurance m; ~ **company** n INS compagnie d'assurances f,

société d'assurances f; ~ **contract** n INS contrat d'assurance m; ~ **corporation** n INS compagnie d'assurances f, société d'assurances f; ~ **cost** n INS coût d'assurance m, frais d'assurance m pl; ~ **cover** n BrE (cf insurance coverage AmE) INS couverture d'assurance f, garantie d'assurance f; ~ **coverage** n AmE (cf insurance cover BrE) INS couverture d'assurance f, garantie d'assurance f; ~ **factoring** n INS affacturage d'assurance m, factoring d'assurance m; ~ **firm** n INS cabinet d'assurances m; ~ **in force** n INS assurance en cours f, assurance en vigueur f; ~ **industry** n INS industrie des assurances f; ~ **market** n INS marché de l'assurance m, marché des assurances m; ~ **plan** n INS plan d'assurance m, régime d'assurance m; ~ **policy** n INS police d'assurance f; ~ **premium** n INS prime d'assurance f; ~ **proceeds** n pl INS produits d'assurance m pl; ~ **property** n INS bien d'assurance m; ~ **scheme** n INS plan d'assurance m, régime d'assurance m; ~ **settlement** n INS règlement d'assurance m

Insurance: ~ **Brokers' Registration Council** n UK (IBRC) INS conseil d'immatriculation des courtiers d'assurance m; ~ **Ombudsman Bureau** n UK (IOB) INS bureau de médiateur en matière d'assurance m

insure:[1] **not-to-~ clause** n INS avis de résiliation à l'échéance m, clause d'assurance refusée f

insure[2] vt INS assurer; ◆ ~ **o.s. against fire** INS s'assurer contre l'incendie; ~ **o.s. against risk** INS s'assurer contre un risque

insured: ~ **account** n INS at a financial institution compte assuré m; ~ **loss caused deliberately** n INS dommage causé avec intention loc m; ~ **peril** n INS risque assuré m; **the ~** n INS assuré m, l'assuré m

insurer n INS assureur mf, compagnie d'assurances f; **~'s claim** INS réclamation de l'assureur f

insurgent adj GEN COMM insurgé

int. abbr ACC, BANK, ECON, FIN, GEN COMM (interest) in property intérêts m pl, participation f, on borrowings int. (intérêt), INS (intermediate survey) expertise intermédiaire f, STOCK (interest) on borrowings int. (intérêt)

intake n GEN COMM of new employees admission f, of new orders arrivée f, TAX of returns arrivages m pl

intangible[1] adj (ANT tangible) ACC, ECON, FIN, GEN COMM, LAW incorporel

intangible:[2] ~ **asset** n (ANT tangible asset) ACC actif incorporel m, immobilisation incorporelle f, valeur incorporelle f, FIN, GEN COMM actif immatériel m, immobilisation incorporelle f, valeur incorporelle f; ~ **asset worth** n ACC valeur des immobilisations incorporelles f; ~ **contribution** n GEN COMM contribution incorporelle f; ~ **drilling and development cost** n ACC frais incorporels de forage et développement m pl; ~ **fixed asset** n (ANT tangible fixed asset) ACC, FIN, GEN COMM immobilisation incorporelle f; ~ **property** n ACC actif incorporel m; ~ **reward** n

HRM avantage impalpable *m*; ~ **value** *n* ACC *goodwill* valeur incorporelle *f*; ~ **wealth** *n* (ANT *tangible wealth*) ECON biens intangibles *m pl*, richesse incorporelle *f*

integral *n* TRANSP *container* conteneur intégral *m*; ~ **part** GEN COMM partie intégrante *f*

integrate *vt* COMP, ECON, FIN, GEN COMM, HRM, IND, MGMNT, TRANSP incorporer, intégrer

integrated[1] *adj* COMP, ECON, FIN, GEN COMM, HRM, IND, MGMNT, TRANSP intégré; ♦ ~ **into** GEN COMM intégré à

integrated:[2] ~ **circuit** *n* (IC) COMP circuit intégré *m* (CI); ~ **company** *n* GEN COMM société intégrée *f*; ~ **management system** *n* MGMNT système intégré de gestion *m*; ~ **pollution control** *n* (IPC) ENVIR lutte antipollution intégrée *f*; ~ **project management** *n* (IPM) FIN, MGMNT gestion intégrée de projet *f*; ~ **services digital network** *n pl* (ISDN) COMMS réseau numérique à intégration de services *m* (RNIS); ~ **software** *n* COMP logiciel intégré *m*; ~ **tug-barge** *n* (ITB) TRANSP pousseur-barge intégré *m*

integration *n* COMP, ECON, FIN, GEN COMM, HRM, IND, MGMNT, TRANSP intégration *f*; ~ **with social security** HRM *of pension* intégration à la sécurité sociale *f*

integrator *n* IMP/EXP, TRANSP intégrateur *m*, transporteur intégral *m*

integrity *n* GEN COMM intégrité *f*

intellectual: ~ **property** *n* LAW, MEDIA, PATENTS propriété intellectuelle *f*; ~ **property rights** *n pl* LAW, MEDIA, PATENTS droits de propriété intellectuelle *m pl*

intelligent[1] *adj* COMP *function*, GEN COMM *person, analysis* intelligent

intelligent:[2] ~ **document** *n* COMP *information retrieval* document expert *m*, document intelligent *m*; ~ **information retrieval** *n* COMP recherche documentaire intelligente *f*; ~ **terminal** *n* (ANT *dumb terminal*) COMP terminal intelligent *m*

Intelpost® *n* COMMS *international message transmission by fax* ≈ Postclair® *m* (Fra)

intensification *n* ECON *of farming techniques* amplification *f*, extension *f*, intensification *f*

intensify 1. *vt* GEN COMM *effort* intensifier; **2.** *vi* GEN COMM *slowdown, competition* s'intensifier

intensive[1] *adj* GEN COMM intensif

intensive:[2] ~ **farming** *n* ECON, ENVIR agriculture intensive *f*; ~ **livestock farming** *n* ECON, ENVIR élevage de bétail intensif *m*; ~ **production** *n* ECON, IND exploitation intensive *f*

intent: ~ **on** *phr* GEN COMM décidé à, résolu à

intention *n* GEN COMM intention *f*

intentional: ~ **discharge** *n* ENVIR, IND *pollution* rejet intentionnel *m*

interactive[1] *adj* COMP conversationnel, interactif, GEN COMM interactif

interactive:[2] ~ **computing** *n* COMP informatique interactive *f*; ~ **mode** *n* COMP mode interactif *m*;

~ **processing** *n* COMP traitement interactif *m*; ~ **system** *n* COMP système interactif *m*

inter alia *adv frml* GEN COMM entre autres

Inter-American: ~ **Development Bank** *n* (IADB) BANK Banque inter-américaine de développement *f* (BIAD)

interavailability *n* TRANSP possibilité de changer d'itinéraire, utilisant éventuellement les services d'une autre compagnie

interbank: ~ **business** *n* BANK opérations interbancaires *f pl*; ~ **deposit** *n* BANK dépôt de banque à banque *m*, dépôt interbancaire *m*; ~ **exchange rate** *n* BANK, ECON taux interbancaire *m*; ~ **market** *n* ECON marché interbancaire *m*; ~ **offered rate** *n* (IBOR) BANK, ECON, STOCK taux interbancaire offert *m*, taux interbancaire proposé *m*; ~ **rate** *n* BANK, ECON taux interbancaire *m*; ~ **transactions** *n pl* BANK opérations interbancaires *f pl*; ~ **transfer** *n* BANK virement interbancaire *m*

interchange: ~ **container** *n* TRANSP conteneur interchangeable *m*; ~ **flight** *n* TRANSP vol interligne *m*; ~ **of letters** *n* COMMS échange de lettres *m*

InterCity *n* UK TRANSP *train* rapide *m*

intercoastal[1] *adj* TRANSP de cabotage *loc m*

intercoastal:[2] ~ **tanker** *n* TRANSP *ship* bateau-citerne caboteur *m*

intercom *n* COMMS interphone *m*

intercommodity: ~ **spread** *n* STOCK marge des produits de base *f*, stratégie d'écart sur matières premières *f*

intercommunity: ~ **trade** *n* ECON, S&M *EU* commerce intercommunautaire *m*

intercompany: ~ **comparison** *n* GEN COMM comparaison inter-entreprises *f*; ~ **market** *n* STOCK marché des intermédiaires *m*; ~ **profits** *n pl* FIN bénéfices inter-sociétés *m pl*

interconnection *n* GEN COMM interconnexion *f*

intercontinental *adj* TRANSP intercontinental

intercooler *n* TRANSP *heat exchanger* refroidisseur intermédiaire *m*, échangeur thermique intermédiaire *m*, ETI

interdealer: ~ **broker** *n* BrE (IDB) BANK courtier internégociants *m*, intermédiaire entre courtiers *m*; ~ **broker system** *n* (IDBS) STOCK système des intermédiaires entre courtiers *m* (SIAM)

interdelivery: ~ **spread** *n* STOCK *currency futures* stratégie d'écart sur livraisons *f*, étalement inter-livraison *m*

interdepartmental[1] *adj* ADMIN, GEN COMM, HRM interdépartemental

interdepartmental:[2] ~ **flexibility** *n* (IDF) HRM flexibilité entre services *f*; ~ **settlement** *n* LAW, POL règlement interministériel *m*; ~ **settlement advice** *n* FIN, POL avis de règlement interministériel *m*

interdependence *n* ECON, GEN COMM, POL interdépendance *f*

interdependent[1] *adj* ECON, GEN COMM, POL inter-dépendant

interdependent:[2] **~ economy** *n* ECON, POL économie interdépendante *f*

interdepot: **~ transfer** *n* TRANSP transfert entre dépôts *m*

interest:[1] **~ -bearing** *adj* ACC portant intérêt, BANK portant intérêt, productif d'intérêts, rémunéré; **~ -free** *adj* FIN *credit* sans intérêt

interest[2] *n* ACC, BANK *(i, int.)* intérêts *m pl*, BANK *on borrowings* intérêt *m (int.)*, ECON *(i, int.)* intérêt *m (int.)*, FIN *(i, int.)* intérêt *m (int.)*, *in property* intérêts *m pl*, participation *f*; **~ accrued** *n (IA)* ACC, BANK, FIN, GEN COMM, STOCK intérêts courus *m pl*, intérêts cumulés *m pl (IC)*; **~ arrearage** *n* BANK arriéré d'intérêts *m*, intérêt sur arriérés *m*, intérêts en souffrance *m pl*; **~ -bearing deposits** *n pl* BANK dépôts portant intérêts *m pl*; **~ -bearing eligible liabilities** *n pl UK (IBELS)* BANK dettes admissibles portant intérêts *f pl*, obligations produisant des intérêts *f pl*; **~ -bearing instrument** *n* FIN instrument financier à intérêt *m*, STOCK instrument financier à intérêt *m*, instrument portant intérêt *m*; **~ -bearing liabilities** *n pl* BANK emprunts portant intérêts *m pl*; **~ -bearing security** *n* STOCK titre portant intérêt *m*; **~ -bearing trading portfolio** *n* STOCK portefeuille d'affaires portant intérêt *m*, portefeuille de valeurs portant intérêt *m*; **~ -bearing yield** *n* STOCK rendement portant intérêt *m*; **~ charge** *n* ACC, BANK *on loan* charges d'intérêts *f pl*, FIN charge financière *f*; **~ charges** *n pl* ACC, BANK *on loan* charges d'intérêts *f pl*; **~ check** *n AmE*, **~ cheque** *n BrE* BANK chèque d'intérêt *m*; **~ coupon** *n* FIN coupon d'intérêt *m*; **~ earned** *n* ACC *profit and loss account* produits financiers *m pl*; **~ elasticity of savings** *n* ECON élasticité-intérêts de l'épargne *f*; **~ formula** *n* BANK, FIN formule de calcul d'intérêt *f*; **~ -free deposit** *n* BANK dépôt sans intérêt *m*; **~ -free loan** *n* BANK, FIN emprunt sans intérêt *m*, emprunt à taux nul *m*, prêt sans intérêt *m*, prêt à taux nul *m*; **~ group** *n* GEN COMM association *f*, groupe d'intérêt *m*, groupement d'intérêt *m*; **~ in real property** *n* STOCK intérêt dans des biens immeubles *m*; **~ income** *n* BANK produit d'intérêts *m*; **~ margin** *n* BANK marge d'intérêt *f*; **~ on arrears** *n* BANK arriéré d'intérêts *m*, intérêt sur arriérés *m*, intérêts en souffrance *m pl*; **~ on bonds** *n* STOCK intérêt d'obligation *m*, intérêt obligataire *m*, intérêt sur obligation *m*; **~ -only loan** *n* BANK prêt capitalisé à l'échéance *m*; **~ operations** *n pl* ACC *profit and loss account* calculs d'intérêts *m pl*; **~ paid** *n* ACC *profit and loss account* intérêts versés *m pl*; **~ payment** *n* BANK, FIN versement d'intérêt *m*; **~ penalty** *n* BANK pénalité d'intérêt *f*; **~, profit and dividends** *n pl (IPD)* ECON revenu en provenance de l'étranger *m*; **~ rate adjustment** *n* BANK, ECON, FIN rajustement de taux d'intérêt *m*; **~ rate capping** *n* BANK garantie de taux plafond *f*; **~ rate cartel** *n* BANK cartel des taux d'intérêt *m*;

~ rate ceiling *n* BANK, ECON plafond sur les taux d'intérêt *m*; **~ rate contract** *n* FIN, STOCK *interest rate futures* contrat de taux d'intérêt *m*, contrat à terme sur taux d'intérêt *m*; **~ rate differential** *n* BANK, ECON différentiel de taux d'intérêt *m*, écart entre les taux d'intérêt *m*; **~ rate exposure** *n* BANK risque de taux d'intérêt *m*, risque lié au taux d'intérêt *m*, STOCK *interest rate futures* exposition de taux d'intérêt *f*, risque de taux d'intérêt *m*, risque lié au taux d'intérêt *m*; **~ -rate future** *n* FIN, STOCK contrat à terme sur taux d'intérêt *m*; **~ -rate futures contract** *n* FIN, STOCK contrat de taux d'intérêt à terme *m*, contrat à terme sur taux d'intérêt *m*; **~ -rate futures prices** *n pl* FIN, STOCK prix de taux d'intérêt à terme *m pl*, prix des contrats à terme sur taux d'intérêt *m*; **~ rate instrument** *n* FIN, STOCK instrument de taux d'intérêt *m*; **~ rate movement** *n* BANK, ECON mouvement des taux d'intérêt *m*; **~ rate net of all charges** *n* FIN taux d'intérêt net de toutes charges *m*; **~ rate option** *n* STOCK option à taux d'intérêt *f*; **~ rate quotation** *n* BANK, ECON cotation d'un taux d'intérêt *f*; **~ rate rebate** *n* BANK, ECON, TAX bonification du taux d'intérêt *f*, diminution du taux d'intérêt *f*; **~ rate risk** *n* BANK, STOCK risque de taux d'intérêt *m*, risque lié au taux d'intérêt *m*; **~ rate sensitivity** *n (SYN interest sensitivity)* ECON sensibilité aux taux d'intérêt *f*; **~ rate subsidy** *n* FIN prime sur taux d'intérêt *f*; **~ rate swap** *n* FIN échange de taux d'intérêt *m*, STOCK contrat d'échange de taux d'intérêts *m*, échange de taux d'intérêt *m*, CETI; **~ rebate** *n* BANK, ECON, TAX bonification d'intérêt *f*, diminution d'intérêt *f*; **~ received** *n* BANK intérêt perçu *m*; **~ relief** *n* ECON, TAX abattement fiscal sur les intérêts versés *m*; **~ risk** *n* FIN risque lié à l'intérêt *m*; **~ roll-over date** *n* BANK date d'écoulement de l'intérêt *f*, date de révision du taux d'intérêt *f*; **~ -sensitive expenditure** *n* FIN dépense sensible au loyer de l'argent *f*; **~ sensitivity** *n (SYN interest rate sensitivity)* ECON sensibilité aux taux d'intérêt *f*; **~ spread** *n* BANK marge d'intérêt *f*; ◆ **and ~** STOCK avec intérêt

interested[1] *adj* GEN COMM intéressé

interested:[2] **~ party** *n* GEN COMM partie intéressée *f*, LAW ayant droit *m*, partie intéressée *f*

interface[1] *n* COMP interface *f*, jonction *f*, liaison *f*, GEN COMM interface *f*

interface[2] **1.** *vt* COMP *two or more devices*, GEN COMM *two or more departments* connecter, inter-facer; **~ with** COMP être connecté à, être relié à; **2.** *vi* GEN COMM être connecté à, COMP *two or more devices* être connecté, être relié, GEN COMM *two or more departments* être connecté

interfere: **~ in** *vt* GEN COMM intervenir dans, s'immiscer dans, s'ingérer dans; **~ with** LAW *contract* contrecarrer, entraver

interference *n* COMP *electronic* parasites *f pl*, GEN COMM ingérence *f*, intervention *f*, LAW *intruding* ingérence *f*, intrusion *f*; **~ with contract** *UK* HRM interférence avec le contrat *f*

interfirm: ~ **comparison** n GEN COMM comparaison inter-entreprises f

intergenerational: ~ **distribution of income** n ECON distribution des revenus entre les générations f; ~ **equity** n ECON justice fiscale entre générations f

intergovernmental[1] adj GEN COMM organization, summit intergouvernemental

intergovernmental:[2] ~ **organization** n ADMIN organisme intergouvernemental m

Intergovernmental: ~ **Committee for European Migration** n (ICEM) WEL Commission intergouvernementale des migrations européennes f; ~ **Oceanographic Commission** n (IOC) TRANSP based in Paris Commission océanographique intergouvernementale f

intergroup[1] adj HRM intergroupal

intergroup:[2] ~ **relations** n pl HRM rapports entre groupes m pl, relations entre groupes f pl

interim[1] adj GEN COMM intérimaire, report, job provisoire, temporaire

interim[2] n GEN COMM intérim m; ~ **accounts** n pl ACC comptes de mi-année m pl, comptes semestriels m pl; ~ **agreement** n GEN COMM accord provisoire m; ~ **audit** n ACC audit de mi-année m, audit intérim m; ~ **certificate** n STOCK temporary certificate for a new issue, which is exchanged for a permanent certificate at a later date certificat provisoire m; ~ **dividend** n ACC acompte sur dividende m, STOCK dividende de mi-année m, dividende intérimaire m; ~ **financing** n FIN financement intérimaire m, financement provisoire m; ~ **injunction** n LAW, PATENTS injonction provisoire f; ~ **loan** n BANK, FIN crédit de relais m, crédit-relais m, prêt-relais m; ~ **relief** n HRM dégrèvement pour l'emploi précaire m; ~ **report** n ACC rapport périodique m; ~ **statements** n pl ACC, FIN bilan de mi-année m, état financier semestriel m; ◆ **in the** ~ GEN COMM entre-temps, pendant l'intérim

Interim: ~ **Commission of the International Trade Organization** n UK (ICITO) GEN COMM commission intérimaire de l'organisation internationale du commerce

interindustry: ~ **competition** n ECON, IND concurrence entre le secteur primaire et secondaire f, concurrence inter-industries f; ~ **trade** n IND échanges entre industries m pl

interior: ~ **robbery policy** n INS police contre le vol intérieur f

interline: ~ **agreement** n TRANSP aviation accord interligne m; ~ **carrier** n TRANSP aviation transporteur interligne m

interliner n jarg TRANSP aviation passager transféré d'une compagnie aérienne à une autre m

interlinked: ~ **transaction** n (SYN package deal) ECON contrat global m

interlocking: ~ **directorate** n GEN COMM direction intriquée f, LAW conseil d'administration indépendant m, directoire interdépendant m, MGMNT

direction intriquée f; ~ **directorship** n GEN COMM administration de liaison f

interlocutory n LAW, PATENTS injonction provisoire f; ~ **decree** LAW décision interlocutoire f, jugement avant dire m

Intermarket: ~ **Trading System** n US (ITS) STOCK système commercial inter-marché m, système de transaction inter-marchés m

intermediary n FIN, GEN COMM intermédiaire mf; ~ **company** n GEN COMM société auxiliaire f; ~ **corporation** n GEN COMM société intermédiaire f; ~ **goods** n pl GEN COMM demi-produits m pl

intermediate[1] adj GEN COMM intermédiaire

intermediate:[2] ~ **broker** n STOCK remisier m; ~ **bulk container** n (IBC) TRANSP conteneur de vrac intermédiaire m; ~ **container** n TRANSP conteneur intermédiaire m; ~ **credit** n BANK, FIN crédit à moyen terme m; ~ **financing** n BANK financement intermédiaire m; ~ **good** n ECON, IND bien intermédiaire m; ~ **loan** n BANK, FIN prêt à moyen terme m; ~ **stage** n FIN phase intermédiaire f; ~ **survey** n (int.) INS expertise intermédiaire f; ~ **target** n POL cible intermédiaire f; ~ **technology** n IND production technologie intermédiaire f; ~ **term** n BANK, FIN, GEN COMM moyen terme m; ~ **-term credit** n BANK, FIN crédit à moyen terme m

intermediation n FIN intermédiation f

intermittent adj GEN COMM, IND intermittent

intermodal[1] adj TRANSP intermodal

intermodal:[2] ~ **container** n TRANSP conteneur intermodal m, conteneur multimodal m; ~ **packaging** n TRANSP emballage intermodal m; ~ **transport** n TRANSP transport combiné m; ~ **transport law** n TRANSP règlement du transport combiné m; ~ **transport system** n TRANSP système de transport combiné m

internal[1] adj GEN COMM within organization, country interne

internal:[2] ~ **assessment** n GEN COMM, WEL évaluation interne f; ~ **audit** n ACC, FIN audit interne m, vérification interne f (Can); ~ **balance** n ECON, POL équilibre interne m; ~ **check** n GEN COMM contrôle interne m; ~ **communication** n COMMS, GEN COMM, HRM, MGMNT communication interne f; ~ **consumption** n ENVIR consommation intérieure f; ~ **control** n ACC, FIN, GEN COMM contrôle interne m; ~ **debt** n ECON dette publique f; ~ **economy** n (ANT external economy) ECON économie intérieure f; ~ **economy of scale** n ECON, IND économie d'échelle interne f; ~ **expansion** n ECON of capital accroissement interne m, croissance interne f, croissance par autofinancement f; ~ **fare** n TRANSP aviation tarif pour vol domestique m, tarif pour vol intérieur m; ~ **financing** n FIN autofinancement m, financement interne m; ~ **flight** n LEIS vol domestique m, TRANSP vol domestique m, vol intérieur m; ~ **funding** n ACC, FIN consolidation interne f; ~ **labor market** n AmE see internal labour market

BrE; ~ **labor market contracting** *n AmE see internal labour market contracting BrE*; ~ **labour market** *n BrE* ECON *within company*, POL marché interne du travail *m*; ~ **labour market contracting** *n BrE* ECON pratique d'embauche sur le marché interne du travail *f*; ~ **market** *n* ECON marché intérieur *m*; ~ **policy** *n* ECON, POL politique intérieure *f*; ~ **procedure** *n* TRANSP procédure interne *f*; ~ **rate of discount** *n* ACC taux d'escompte interne *m*; ~ **rate of return** *n (IRR)* ACC, FIN taux de rentabilité interne *m*, taux de rentabilité intérieur *m*, taux interne de rentabilité *m*; ~ **search** *n* HRM *for staff* recrutement interne *m*; ~ **storage** *n* COMP mémoire interne *f*; ~ **transactions** *n pl* ACC opérations internes *f pl*

Internal: ~ **Revenue code** *n US* TAX code des impôts *m*; **the ~ Revenue** *n US* TAX *organization, system* service des impôts américain, le Fisc *m* (*infrml*), *payments* les contributions directes *f pl*; **the ~ Revenue Service** *n US (IRS)* TAX *organization, system* service des impôts américain, le Fisc *m* (*infrml*)

internalization *n* STOCK intérieurisation *f*, transfert interne *m*

internalize *vt* GEN COMM *skill* assimiler à fond

internalizing *n* ECON *of externality* internalisation *f*

internally: ~ **funded pension** *n* HRM retraite constituée dans l'entreprise *f*; ~ **generated funds** *n pl* ACC autofinancement *m*

inter-nation: ~ **equity** *n* ECON justice fiscale inter-pays *f*

international[1] *adj (intl)* COMMS, ECON, GEN COMM, POL international *(intl)*; ◆ **at ~ level** GEN COMM au niveau international, sur le plan international, à l'échelon international; **on an ~ scale** GEN COMM à l'échelle internationale

international:[2] ~ **affairs** *n pl* POL affaires internationales *f pl*; ~ **agency** *n* GEN COMM agence internationale *f*; ~ **agreement** *n* LAW, POL accord international *m*, convention internationale *f*; ~ **airline** *n (ANT domestic airline)* TRANSP compagnie aérienne internationale *f*, ligne aérienne internationale *f*; ~ **airline company** *n* TRANSP compagnie aérienne internationale *f*; ~ **airport** *n* TRANSP aéroport international *m*; ~ **application** *n* PATENTS demande internationale *f*; ~ **auditing standards** *n pl* ACC normes internationales de comptabilité *f pl*; ~ **banking** *n* BANK opérations bancaires internationales *f pl*; ~ **banking act** *n* BANK loi sur les opérations bancaires internationales *f*; ~ **banking facility** *n (IBF)* BANK facilité bancaire internationale *f*, opérations bancaires internationales *f pl*; ~ **call** *n* COMMS *telephone* appel international *m*; ~ **carriage** *n* TRANSP transport international *m*; ~ **cartel** *n* ECON cartel international *m*; ~ **clearing house** *n* BANK chambre de compensation internationale *f*; ~ **commercial term** *n (INCOTERM)* ECON terme commercial international *m (INCOTERME)*; ~ **comparisons** *n pl* ECON comparaisons internationales *f pl*; ~ **competitiveness** *n* ECON, IND,

S&M compétitivité internationale *f*; ~ **convention center** *n AmE*, ~ **convention centre** *n BrE* S&M centre des congrès internationaux *m*; ~ **credit** *n* BANK crédit international *m*; ~ **customs transit document** *n* TRANSP carnet TIR *m*, carnet de transport international routier *m*; ~ **direct dialing** *n AmE*, ~ **direct dialling** *n BrE (IDD)* COMMS appel international automatique *m*, l'automatique international *m*; ~ **driver's licence** *n BrE* ADMIN, TRANSP permis de conduire international *m*; ~ **driver's license** *n AmE see international driver's licence BrE*; ~ **driving permit** *n* ADMIN, TRANSP permis de conduire international *m*; ~ **economic cooperation** *n* ECON, POL coopération économique internationale *f*; ~ **finance corporation** *n (IFC)* FIN société financière internationale *f (SFI)*; ~ **financial management** *n* ECON gestion de capitaux internationaux *f*, FIN gestion de capitaux internationaux *f*, gestion financière internationale *f*; ~ **freight forwarder** *n* TRANSP commissionnaire de transport international *m*; ~ **gateway** *n* TRANSP *airport* point d'accès international *m*, porte d'entrée internationale *f*; ~ **investment bank** *n (IIB)* BANK Banque internationale d'investissement *f*; ~ **law** *n* LAW, POL droit international *m*; ~ **liquidity** *n* BANK, ECON, FIN liquidité internationale *f*; ~ **liquidity ratios** *n pl* BANK, ECON, FIN taux internationaux de liquidité *m pl*; ~ **load line certificate** *n* TRANSP certificat international de franc-bord *m*; ~ **monetary system** *n* ECON système monétaire international *m*; ~ **money draft** *n* BANK mandat de paiement international *m*; ~ **money flow** *n* ECON flux monétaires internationaux *m pl*; ~ **money order** *n* BANK mandat international *m*; ~ **organization** *n* GEN COMM organisation internationale *f*; ~ **payment** *n* ECON paiement international *m*; ~ **payment order** *n (IPO)* BANK ordre de paiement international *m*; ~ **preliminary examining authority** *n* PATENTS administration chargée de l'examen préliminaire *f*; ~ **registration** *n* PATENTS enregistrement international *m*; ~ **representation** *n* GEN COMM représentation internationale *f*; ~ **reserve** *n* ECON réserve internationale *f*; ~ **road haulage permit** *n* ADMIN, TRANSP permis de conduire international pour transports routiers *m*, permis international de conduite d'un véhicule de transport *m*; ~ **searching authority** *n* PATENTS administration chargée de la recherche internationale *f*; ~ **-standard hotel** *n* LEIS hôtel international *m*; ~ **standards** *n pl* ENVIR normes internationales *f pl*; ~ **subscriber dialing** *n AmE*, ~ **subscriber dialling** *n BrE (ISD)* COMMS téléphone automatique international *m*; ~ **syndication** *n* BANK syndicalisme international *m*; ~ **trade** *n* ECON, GEN COMM, IMP/EXP, IND, S&M commerce international *m*; ~ **trade law** *n* ECON, LAW, POL, S&M droit international commercial *m*; ~ **trade theory** *n* ECON théorie du commerce international *f*; ~ **trading certificate** *n (ITC)* ECON certificat de commerce international *m*; ~ **traffic** *n* TRANSP

trafic international *m*, transport international *m*;
~ **travel** *n* GEN COMM, TRANSP déplacements
internationaux *m pl*; ~ **union** *n* ECON, HRM
syndicat international *m*; ~ **wage levels** *n pl*
ECON, HRM niveaux internationaux des salaires
m pl

International: ~ **Accounting Standards Committee**
n (IASC) ACC Comité international des normes
de comptabilité *m*; ~ **Agricultural Research
Institute** *n (IARA)* IND Institut international de
recherche agricole; ~ **Aid and Loan Bulletin** *n* BANK
Bulletin international d'assistance et prêts *m*;
~ **Air Transport Association** *n (IATA)* TRANSP
Association internationale des transports aériens
f (IATA); ~ **Association of Classification
Societies** *n* UK *(IACS)* GEN COMM association
internationale des sociétés de classification; ~ **Association of Environmental Co-ordinators** *n (IAEC)*
ENVIR association internationale des coordinateurs
de l'environnement; ~ **Association for the Distribution of Food Products** *n* S&M, TRANSP Association
internationale de la distribution des produits
alimentaires *f*; ~ **Association for the Protection of
Industrial Property** *n (IAPIP)* LAW Association
internationale pour la protection de la propriété
industrielle; ~ **Association of Ports and Harbours**
n (IAPH) IMP/EXP Association internationale des
ports *f*; ~ **Bank for Economic Cooperation** *n
(IBEC)* BANK *COMECON* Banque internationale pour la coopération économique *f*; ~ **Bank of
Reconstruction and Development** *n (IBRD)*
BANK Banque internationale pour la reconstruction et le développement *f (BIRD)*; ~ **Business
Machines**® *n pl (IBM*®*)* COMP IBM®; ~ **Cargo
Handling Coordination Association** *n (ICHCA)*
IND association de coordination de la manipulation
des chargements; ~ **Centre for Industry and the
Environment** *n (ICIE)* IND centre international
pour l'industrie et l'environnement; ~ **Chamber of
Shipping** *n (ICS)* TRANSP chambre internationale
maritime; ~ **Civil Aviation Organization** *n (ICAO)*
TRANSP Organisation de l'aviation civile internationale *f (OACI)*; ~ **Clearing Union** *n (ICU)*
ECON Union de clearing internationale *f*; ~ **Commodities Clearing House** *n* UK *(ICCH)* STOCK
chambre internationale de compensation pour les
produits de base *f*; ~ **Commodity Agreements** *n pl
(ICA's)* STOCK accords internationaux sur les
matières premières *m pl*, accords internationaux
sur les produits de base *m pl*; ~ **Confederation of
Free Trade Unions** *n (ICFTU)* HRM Confédération
internationale des syndicats de libre-échange;
~ **Control Centre** *n (ICC)* GEN COMM Centre
international de contrôle du crédit *m*; ~ **Convention on Carriage of Goods by Rail** *n* UK GEN
COMM convention internationale sur le transport
ferroviaire des marchandises; ~ **Cooperation
Administration** *n* UK *(ICA)* GEN COMM administration internationale de la coopération; ~ **Cotton
Advisory Committee** *n (ICAC)* IND Comité
consultatif international du coton; ~ **Court of**

Justice *n (ICJ)* LAW, POL Cour internationale
de justice *f*; ~ **Customs Tariffs Bureau** *n (ICTB)*
IMP/EXP Bureau international des tarifs douaniers
m (BITD); ~ **Development Association** *n (IDA)*
ECON Association internationale pour le développement *f*; ~ **Development Research Centre** *n*
UK *(IDRC)* GEN COMM centre de recherche
international de développement; ~ **Energy Agency**
n (IEA) ENVIR agence internationale de l'énergie;
~ **Equities Market** *n (IEM)* STOCK marché international des actions *m*, marché international des
capitaux *m*; ~ **Federation of Agricultural
Producers** *n (IFAP)* IND Fédération internatio-
nale des producteurs agricoles *f (FIPA)*;
~ **Federation for Documentation** *n (IFD)* GEN
COMM Fédération internationale de documenta-
tion *f (FID)*; ~ **Federation of Forwarding Agents'
Associations** *n* TRANSP Fédération internationale
des associations de transitaires et assimilés *f*,
FIATA; ~ **Federation of Freight Forwarders'
Associations** *n* TRANSP Fédération internationale
des associations de transitaires et assimilés *f*,
FIATA; ~ **Federation of Stock Exchanges** *n
(IFSE)* STOCK Fédération internationale des
bourses de valeurs *f (FIBV)*; ~ **Federation of
Trade Unions** *n (IFTU)* HRM Fédération syndi-
cale internationale *f (FSI)*, Fédération
internationale des syndicats *f*; ~ **Hotel
Association** *n* LEIS ≈ Association internationale
de l'hôtellerie *f*; ~ **Institute for Unification of
Private Law** *n* LAW ≈ Institut international pour
l'unification du droit privé *m*; ~ **Labour
Organization** *n* UK *(ILO)* HRM *United Nations*
Organisation internationale du travail *f (OIT)*;
~ **Longshoremen's Association** *n* US *(ILA)*
TRANSP association internationale des débardeurs;
~ **Longshoremen's and Warehousemen's Union** *n*
US *(ILWU)* IND syndicat international des débar-
deurs et des magasiniers; ~ **Maritime Bureau** *n
(IMB)* TRANSP Bureau maritime international *m*;
~ **Maritime Committee** *n (IMC)* TRANSP Comité
maritime international *m*; ~ **Maritime Dangerous
Goods Code** *n (IMDGC)* TRANSP *shipping* Code
maritime international des marchandises dange-
reuses *m*; ~ **Maritime Organization** *n (IMO)*
TRANSP organisation maritime internationale; ~ **Mar-
itime Pilots' Association** *n (IMPA)* TRANSP
association internationale des pilotes maritimes;
~ **Maritime Satellite Organization** *n
(INMARSAT)* COMMS Organisation internationale de satellites maritimes *f*; ~ **Miners'
Organization** *n (IMO)* IND Organisation internationale des mineurs; ~ **Monetary Fund** *n (IMF)*
BANK, ECON, FIN Fonds monétaire international
m (FMI); ~ **Monetary Market** *n (IMM)* ECON,
STOCK Marché monétaire international *m
(MMI)*; ~ **Monetary Market Certificate of Deposit index** *n (IMM CD index)* STOCK indice des
certificats de dépôt du Marché monétaire international *m (indice des certificats de dépôt du
MMI)*; ~ **Monetary Market Three-Month Discount Index** *n (IMM Three-Month Discount*

Index) STOCK indice de décompte trimestriel du Marché monétaire international *m (indice de décompte trimestriel du MMI)*; ~ **Monetary Market Treasury-bill index** *n (IMM T-bill index)* STOCK indice des bons du trésor du Marché monétaire international *m (indice des bons du trésor du MMI)*; ~ **Money Market Three-Month Add-On Index** *n (IMM Three-Month Add-On Index)* STOCK rajout trimestriel à l'indice du Marché monétaire international; ~ **Office of Epizootics** *n (IOE)* TRANSP Office international des épizooties *m (OIE)*; ~ **Oil Tanker and Terminal Safety Group** *n (IOTTSG)* TRANSP groupe international sur la sécurité des pétroliers et des terminaux; ~ **Options Market** *n (IOM)* STOCK marché international des options *m*, marché à options international *m*, marché à primes international *m*; ~ **Organization of Employers** *n (IOE)* HRM organisation internationale des employeurs; ~ **Organization for Legal Metrology** *n* LAW Organisation internationale de métrologie légale *f*, OIML; ~ **Organization of Securities Commission** *n (IOSCO)* STOCK commission de l'organisation internationale des valeurs *f*; ~ **Petroleum Exchange** *n UK (IPE)* STOCK bourse internationale des produits pétroliers *f*, marché international du pétrole *m*; ~ **Press Institute** *n (IPI)* MEDIA Institut international de la presse; ~ **Primary Market Association** *n (IPMA)* STOCK Association internationale du marché primaire *f*; ~ **Radio-Maritime Committee** *n (CIRM)* COMMS Comité international radio-maritime *m (CIRM)*; ~ **Recruitment Unit** *n (IRU)* HRM Unité internationale de recrutement *f*; ~ **Register of Potentially Toxic Chemicals** *n (IRPTC)* ENVIR, IND Registre international des substances chimiques potentiellement toxiques *m (RISCPT)*; ~ **Road Transport Union** *n (IRU)* TRANSP Syndicat international des transporteurs routiers *m*; ~ **SAR** *n* WEL ≈ Recherches et secours internationaux *m pl*; ~ **Search & Rescue** *n* WEL ≈ Recherches et secours internationaux *m pl*; ~ **Securities Market Association** *n (ISMA)* STOCK Association internationale des bourses de valeurs *f*, Association internationale du marché des valeurs *f*; ~ **Securities Regulatory Organization** *n (ISRO)* STOCK Organisation de surveillance pour les valeurs internationales *f*, Organisme régulateur des titres internationaux *m*; ~ **Shipowners' Association** *n (INSA)* TRANSP Association internationale des armateurs; ~ **Shipping Federation** *n (ISF)* TRANSP Fédération internationale de la navigation *f*; ~ **Social Service** *n (ISS)* WEL ≈ Service social international *m*; ~ **Standard Book Number** *n (ISBN)* MEDIA *print* International Standard Book Number *m (ISBN)*; ~ **Standard Serial Number** *n (ISSN)* MEDIA *print* International Standard Serial Number *m (ISSN)*; ~ **Standards Organization** *n (ISO)* GEN COMM Organisation internationale de normalisation *f*; ~ **Standards Organization/Open Systems Interconnection** *n (ISO/OSI)* COMP interconnexion de systèmes ouverts de l'organisation internationale des standards; ~ **Statistical Institute** *n UK (ISI)* GEN COMM Institut international des statistiques; ~ **Stock Exchange** *n (ISE)* STOCK *of the UK and Republic of Ireland* ≈ Société des bourses françaises *f (France) (SBF)*; ~ **Sugar Agreement** *n (ISA)* ECON ≈ Accord international sur le sucre *m (AIS)*; ~ **Sugar Council** *n (ISC)* IND Conseil international du sucre *m*; ~ **Sugar Organization** *n (ISO)* IND Organisation internationale du sucre *f*; ~ **Swap Dealers' Association** *n (ISDA)* STOCK Association internationale des opérateurs de swaps *f*; ~ **Telecommunications Union** *n (ITU)* COMMS Union internationale des télécommunications *f (UIT)*; ~ **Tin Council** *n (ITC)* IND conseil international de l'étain; ~ **Trade Organization** *n (ITO)* GEN COMM Organisation internationale du commerce; ~ **Transport Workers' Federation** *n (ITF)* TRANSP Fédération internationale des ouvriers du transport *f (FIOT)*; ~ **Union of Official Travel Organizations** *n (IUOTO)* TRANSP Syndicat international des organisations officielles de voyages *m*; ~ **Union of Railways** *n (IUR)* ADMIN Union internationale des chemins de fer *f (UICF)*, TRANSP Syndicat international des cheminots *m*; ~ **Wheat Agreement** *n (IWA)* ECON Accord international sur le blé *m (AIB)*; ~ **Wheat Council** *n (IWC)* GEN COMM Conseil international du blé *m (CIB)*

internationalism *n* POL internationalisme *m*

internationalization *n* ECON, GEN COMM internationalisation *f*

internationalize *vt* ECON, GEN COMM internationaliser

Internet *n* COMMS Internet *m*

interoperability *n* COMP interfonctionnement *m*, FIN, IND *of production equipment* interopérabilité *f*

Inter-Parliamentary: ~ **Union** *n (IPU)* POL Union interparlementaire *f (UIP)*

interpersonal: ~ **skills** *n pl* HRM aptitudes interpersonnelles *f pl*

interplay *n* GEN COMM interaction *f*

interpleader *n* LAW action pétitoire incidente *f*

interpolation *n* GEN COMM, MATH interpolation *f*

inter praesentes *adv frml* GEN COMM entre les personnes présentes

interpret *vt* COMMS *language, speech*, GEN COMM *behaviour, thoughts* interpréter

interpretation *n* COMMS, GEN COMM interprétation *f*; ♦ **give a loose ~ of sth** GEN COMM donner une interprétation peu rigoureuse de qch

interpreter *n* COMMS interprète *mf*, COMP *program* interpréteur *m*

interpreting *n* COMMS *of foreign language* interprétation *f*

interrelation *n* MATH *statistics* corrélation *f*

interrogatories *n pl* LAW questions écrites échangées entre parties ou adressées aux témoins, interrogatoire écrit *m*

interrupt *vt* COMP, GEN COMM interrompre

interruption *n* COMP, GEN COMM interruption *f*

inter se *adv frml* GEN COMM entre eux

interstate *adj US* GEN COMM *commerce, road* entre états *phr, law* inter-état

Interstate: ~ **Land Sales Act** *n US* PROP loi inter-état sur les ventes de terrains

interunion: ~ **dispute** *n* HRM conflit intersyndical *m*

interval: ~ **estimate** *n* MATH *statistics* estimation d'écart *f*; ~ **scale** *n* GEN COMM échelle d'intervalle *f*; ~ **service** *n* LEIS, TRANSP service régulier *m*

intervene *vi* GEN COMM intervenir

intervention *n* ECON, GEN COMM, POL *EU* intervention *f*; ~ **currency** ECON, FIN *EU* devise d'intervention *f*; ~ **price** ECON, FIN *EU* prix d'intervention *m*

interventionist[1] *adj* ECON, POL *EU* interventionniste

interventionist[2] *n* ECON, POL *EU* interventionniste *mf*

interview[1] *n* GEN COMM interview *f*, HRM entretien *m*, entrevue *f*, interview *f*, MEDIA, S&M interview *f*; ~ **guide** HRM guide d'entrevue *m*

interview[2] *vt* HRM *sb for a job* faire passer un entretien à *loc m*

interviewee *n* HRM candidat *m*, interviewé *m*, personne reçue *f*, MEDIA interviewé *m*

interviewer *n* MEDIA intervieweur *m*, S&M *market research* enquêteur *m*; ~ **bias** MEDIA, S&M *market research* partialité de l'enquêteur *f*

inter vivos *adv* LAW entre vifs; ~ **trust** *n* LAW fidéicommis entre vifs *m*

intervote: ~ **transfer** *n* FIN virement entre crédits *m*

intestacy *n* LAW succession ab intestat *f*

intestate *adj* LAW ab intestat, intestat

in-the-money[1] *adj* (*ITM,* ANT *out-of-the-money*) STOCK argenté, dans le cours *loc m*, en jeu *loc m*

in-the-money:[2] ~ **call** *n* STOCK appel argenté *m*, option d'achat dans l'argent *f*, option d'achat dans le cours *f*; ~ **call option** *n* STOCK option d'achat argenté *f*, option d'achat dans l'argent *f*, option d'achat dans le cours *f*, option d'achat en dedans *f*; ~ **option** *n* (ANT *out-of-the-money option*) STOCK option dans la monnaie *f*, option dans le cours *f*, option in-the-money *f*; ~ **put** *n* STOCK option de vente dans le cours *f*, vente d'argenté *f*; ~ **put option** *n* STOCK option de vente d'argenté *f*, option de vente dans l'argent *f*, option de vente dans le cours *f*, option de vente en dedans *f*

intimidation *n* HRM intimidation *f*

intl *abbr* (*international*) COMMS, ECON, GEN COMM, POL intl (*international*)

in-town: ~ **store** *n* S&M magasin au centre-ville *m*

intra: ~ **number** *n* ADMIN numéro intra *m*

intra-commodity: ~ **spread** *n* STOCK marge entre produits *f*, stratégie d'écart sur matières premières *f*

intra-Community: ~ **trade** *n* ECON, POL *within EU* commerce intracommunautaire *m*

intradepartmental *adj* ADMIN intraministériel

intra-EU: ~ **trade** *n* ECON, POL commerce intracommunautaire *m*

intragroup: ~ **relations** *n pl* HRM rapports au sein du groupe *m pl*, relations intergroupales *f pl*

intra-period: ~ **tax allocation** *n* ACC répartition des impôts de l'exercice *f*

intrastate *adj US* GEN COMM à l'intérieur de l'état

intra vires *adj* LAW statutaire

in-tray: ~ **exercise** *phr* (SYN *in-basket situation*) ADMIN en suspens, à régler

intrinsic: ~ **motivation** *n* HRM motivation intrinsèque *f*; ~ **value** *n* ECON, STOCK valeur intrinsèque *f*

introduce *vt* GEN COMM, LAW *changes* introduire; ◆ ~ **legislation** LAW faire passer une législation, légiférer

introduction *n* GEN COMM *to book, speech* introduction *f*, STOCK *of new shares* introduction *f*, introduction à la cote *f*

introductory: ~ **course** *n* WEL phase d'introduction *f*; ~ **offer** *n* S&M offre de lancement *f*; ~ **price** *n* S&M prix de lancement *m*; ~ **stage** *n* S&M *marketing* phase de lancement *f*

intrusive *adj* S&M *radio* importun

intuitive: ~ **management** *n* MGMNT management intuitif *m*

inure *vt* PROP habituer

inv. *abbr* (*invoice*) ACC, BANK, FIN, GEN COMM fre (*facture*)

invalidate *vt* GEN COMM *ballot* annuler, invalider, LAW *contract* annuler, *deed* vicier, *judgement* casser, infirmer, *will, election* invalider

invalidation *n* GEN COMM *of ballot* annulation *f*, invalidation *f*, LAW *of contract* annulation *f, of judgement* cassation *f*, infirmation *f, of will, election* invalidation *f*

invaluable *adj* GEN COMM inestimable

invent *vt* GEN COMM, IND, PATENTS inventer

invention *n* GEN COMM, IND, PATENTS invention *f*

inventive[1] *adj* GEN COMM *approach, mind, person* inventif

inventive:[2] ~ **step** *n* PATENTS activité inventive *f*

inventor *n* GEN COMM, IND, PATENTS inventeur *m*

inventory *n* ACC (SYN *stocks*) inventaire *m*, stocks *m pl*, GEN COMM *of property* inventaire *m*, IND (SYN *stocks*) inventaire *m*, stocks *m pl*, INS *list* inventaire *m*; ~ **allowance** FIN déduction pour inventaire *f*; ~ **book** ACC livre d'inventaire *m*; ~ **certificate** ACC attestation d'inventaire *f*; ~ **computation** GEN COMM calcul de la valeur des stocks *m*; ~ **control** *AmE* (*cf stock control BrE*) ACC, ECON, FIN, STOCK contrôle des stocks *m*, gestion des stocks *f*; ~ **controller** GEN COMM, HRM responsable des stocks *m*; ~ **costing** ACC inventaire *m*; ~ **cycle** STOCK cycle court lié aux fluctuations des stocks *m*; ~ **evaluation** ACC inventaire m; ~ **file** GEN COMM fichier de stock m; ~ **financing** ACC financement de stocks m; ~ **item** GEN COMM unité en stock f; ~ **management** ACC, ECON, FIN, IND, MGMNT gestion des stocks f; ~ **planning** ACC gestion prévisionnelle des stocks f, ECON gestion prévisionnelle des stocks f, organisation des inventaires f, FIN gestion prévisionnelle des stocks f, STOCK gestion prévisionnelle des stocks f, organisation des inventaires f; ~ **pricing** ACC valorisation des stocks f; ~ **shortage** ECON, GEN COMM freinte de stock f, écart sur stock m; ~ **shrinkage** ECON, GEN COMM freinte de stock f, écart sur stock m; ~ **turnover** ACC, ECON, FIN rotation des stocks f; ~ **valuation** ACC inventaire m, GEN COMM valorisation des stocks f; ~ **valuation adjustment** ACC réajustement après inventaire m

inverse[1] *adj* MATH inverse

inverse[2] *n* MATH contraire m, inverse m; ~ **condemnation** LAW action en réparation du préjudice matériel subi suite à une expropriation pour cause d'utilité publique, PROP action en réparation d'un préjudice matériel intentée contre les pouvoirs

inversely *adv* (ANT *directly*) MATH inversement

inversion *n* ECON inversion f

invert *vt* COMP inverser, GEN COMM intervertir

inverted: ~ **commas** *n pl* COMP *word-processing*, MEDIA *print* guillemets m pl; ~ **market** *n jarg* STOCK marché en déport m; ~ **scale** *n* STOCK échelle inversée f; ~ **yield curve** *n* (SYN *negative yield curve*) BANK, ECON, STOCK courbe de rapport inversée f, courbe des taux inversée f

invest 1. *vt* ACC *money* investir, placer, BANK, ECON investir, FIN *money* investir, placer, IND, S&M, STOCK investir; **2.** *vi* ACC, BANK, ECON investir, FIN faire des placements, investir, IND, S&M investir, STOCK faire des placements, investir; ♦ ~ **in an annuity** INS placer de l'argent en viager; ~ **in bonds** FIN, STOCK investir en obligations; ~ **in property** FIN, PROP faire un placement immobilier; ~ **in shares** FIN, STOCK investir en actions, investir en valeurs

investee *n* FIN, STOCK entreprise dans laquelle on investit

investible *adj* FIN, STOCK susceptible d'investissement *loc m*

investigate *vt* GEN COMM *situation* enquêter, examiner, étudier, LAW *crime* enquêter, enquêter sur

investigating: ~ **committee** *n* LAW commission d'enquête f

investigation *n* GEN COMM *of situation* enquête f, examen m, étude f, LAW *of crime* enquête f; ~ **officer** HRM agent d'enquête m, enquêteur m; ♦ **make ~s into** GEN COMM enquêter sur

investigative: ~ **approach** *n* TAX *to field audits* approche par l'enquête f

investigatory: ~ **powers** *n pl* LAW *of court* pouvoirs d'enquête m pl, pouvoirs d'instruction m pl

investment:[1] ~ **-grade** *adj* US STOCK de premier ordre, de qualité supérieure *loc f*

investment[2] *n* ACC, BANK investissement m, ECON, FIN investissement m, placement m, IND, S&M investissement m, STOCK investissement m, placement m; ~ **abroad** *n* FIN, GEN COMM, STOCK investissement à l'étranger m; ~ **account** *n* BANK compte de placement m; ~ **account security** *n* BANK titre de placement m, titre du compte de placement m, valeur de placement f, valeur du compte de placement f; ~ **activity** *n* ECON activité d'investissement f; ~ **advice** *n* FIN, STOCK conseils en investissements m pl; ~ **adviser** *n* STOCK conseiller en placements m; ~ **advisers' act** *n* FIN loi sur les conseillers en investissements f, loi sur les consultants en placements f; ~ **advisor** *n* see *investment adviser* ; ~ **advisors' act** *n* see *investment advisers' act* ; ~ **allowance** *n* FIN déduction pour placements f; ~ **analysis** *n* ACC, ECON, FIN, S&M, STOCK analyse d'investissements f, étude de rentabilité f; ~ **analyst** *n* FIN, STOCK analyste d'investissements m, analyste de placements m; ~ **appraisal** *n* ACC, ECON, FIN, STOCK appréciation des investissements f, évaluation d'investissement f; ~ **bank** *n* US BANK, FIN banque d'affaires f, banque d'investissement f; ~ **banker** *n* US (cf *merchant banker* UK) BANK banquier d'affaires m, banquier d'investissement m, spécialiste des services de banque d'affaires m, spécialiste des services de banque d'investissement m; ~ **banking** *n* US (cf *merchant banking* UK) BANK opérations sur valeurs de placement f; ~ **base** *n* BANK base de placement f; ~ **bond** *n* INS obligation f; ~ **budget** *n* ACC, ECON, FIN budget d'investissement m; ~ **business** *n* FIN, STOCK secteur des investissements m; ~ **center** *n* AmE, ~ **centre** *n* BrE FIN, STOCK centre d'investissement m, centre de rentabilité m; ~ **certificate** *n* BANK certificat de dépôt m, certificat de placement m, ECON certificat de dépôt m, FIN certificat de dépôt m, certificat de placement m, STOCK certificat d'investissement m, certificat de dépôt m, CI; ~ **climate** *n* ECON climat d'investissement m; ~ **club** *n* FIN groupe d'investissement en commun m, STOCK club d'investissement m, groupe d'investissement en commun m; ~ **company** *n* FIN, STOCK société d'investissement f, société de placement f, société de portefeuilles f; ~ **company act** *n* FIN, LAW, STOCK loi sur les sociétés d'investissement f; ~ **company act of 1940** *n* FIN, LAW, STOCK loi de 1940 sur les sociétés d'investissement f; ~ **consultant** *n* STOCK conseiller en placements m, consultant en investissement m; ~ **contract** *n* STOCK contrat d'investissement m; ~ **corporation** *n* FIN, STOCK corporation de placement f, société d'investissement f; ~ **counsel** *n* STOCK conseiller en placements m, consultant en investissement m; ~ **counseling** *n* AmE, ~ **counselling** *n* BrE FIN, STOCK conseil en placements m, conseils en investissements m pl; ~ **criteria** *n pl* FIN critères d'investissement m pl;

~ dealer *n* FIN, STOCK courtier en valeurs mobilières *m*, négociant en valeurs mobilières *m*; **~ expense** *n* TAX frais de placement *m pl*; **~ firm** *n* FIN, STOCK entreprise d'investissement *f*, société d'investissement *f*, société de placement *f*, société de portefeuilles *f*; **~ fund** *n* FIN, STOCK société d'investissement *f*; **~ fund for shares** *n* STOCK fonds de placement en actions *m*; **~ gold coin** *n* FIN pièce d'or d'investissement *f*; **~ goods** *n pl* FIN biens d'investissement *m pl*, S&M biens d'équipement *m pl*; **~ grade** *n* STOCK classe d'investissement *f*; **~ grant** *n* ACC subvention d'investissement *f*; **~ hedger** *n* STOCK *insurance* couverture d'investissement *f*, *person* arbitragiste d'investissement *mf*; **~ history** *n* FIN, STOCK historique d'un investissement *m*, évolution d'un investissement *f*; **~ incentive** *n* BANK encouragement à l'investissement *m*; **~ income** *n* FIN revenu d'investissements *m*, revenu de placements *m*, INS revenu de placements *m*, STOCK revenu d'investissements *m*, revenu de placements *m*; **~ income tax** *n* TAX impôt sur le revenu de placements *m*; **~ life cycle** *n* STOCK cycle de vie d'un investissement *m*; **~ loss** *n* STOCK perte sur investissement *f*; **~ management** *n* FIN, STOCK gestion d'investissements *f*; **~ mix** *n* FIN, STOCK stratégie des investissements *f*; **~ multiplier** *n* ECON *econometrics* multiplicateur d'investissement *m*; **~ objective** *n* FIN objectif de placement *m*; **~ opportunity** *n* BANK occasion d'investissement *f*; **~ plan** *n* FIN plan d'investissement *m*; **~ policy** *n* ECON, FIN, POL, STOCK politique d'investissement *f*; **~ portfolio** *n* BANK, FIN, STOCK portefeuille d'investissement *m*; **~ program** *n* *AmE*, **~ programme** *n* *BrE* FIN, STOCK programme d'investissement *m*; **~ project** *n* FIN, STOCK projet de placement *m*; **~ property** *n* PROP immobilier de placement *m*; **~ reserve system** *n* FIN méthode de réserve d'investissement *f*; **~ restriction** *n* ECON freins à l'investissement *m pl*, restriction à l'investissement *f*; **~ revenue** *n* FIN, INS, STOCK revenu de placements *m*; **~ review** *n* FIN, STOCK étude d'investissement *f*; **~ savings account** *n* BANK compte d'épargne-placement *m*; **~ service** *n* FIN, STOCK service d'investissement *m*; **~ software** *n* COMP, FIN, STOCK logiciel de gestion des investissements *m*; **~ spending** *n* FIN, GEN COMM, STOCK dépense d'investissement *f*; **~ strategy** *n* FIN, STOCK stratégie d'investissement *f*; **~ strategy committee** *n* FIN, STOCK comité de stratégie d'investissement *m*; **~ tax credit** *n* *(ITC)* TAX crédit d'impôt à l'investissement *m* *(CII)*; **~ trust** *n* FIN, STOCK fonds commun de placement *m*, fonds de placement *m*; **~ yield** *n* BANK, FIN, STOCK rendement de placement *m*

Investment: **~ Advisory Service** *n* *US* STOCK service conseil en investissements *m*, service conseil en placements *m*; **~ Committee** *n* *UK* *(IC)* FIN *of the Association of British Insurers and National Association of Pension Funds* commission des investissements *f*; **~ Managers'**

Regulatory Organization *n* *UK* *(IMRO)* STOCK organisation de surveillance des gestionnaires d'investissement *f*

investor *n* ECON investisseur *m*, FIN investisseur *m*, épargnant *m*, *in shares* actionnaire *mf*, IND investisseur *m*, STOCK investisseur *m*, *in shares* actionnaire *mf*; **~ group** FIN, STOCK groupe d'investisseurs *m*; **~ protection** STOCK protection de l'investisseur *f*; **~ relations department** FIN, STOCK *of major public company* département de relations actionnaires *m*, service des relations avec les investisseurs *m*

investors: **~ service bureau** *n* FIN, STOCK bureau de relations actionnaires *m*, bureau de service actionnaires *m*, bureau des relations avec les investisseurs *m*

investors': **~ indemnity account** *n* BANK compte d'indemnisation d'acheteurs de titres de placement *m*

Investors': **~ Compensation Scheme** *n* *UK* STOCK *organized by the SIB* fonds de garantie des investisseurs *m*, système de compensation des actionnaires *m*

invisible[1] *adj* ECON, FIN *asset* invisible

invisible:[2] **~ balance** *n* FIN balance des invisibles *f*; **~ earnings** *n pl* ECON, FIN gains invisibles *m pl*; **~ export** *n* ECON, IMP/EXP exportation invisible *f*; **~ foot** *n* ECON fait d'aller s'implanter là où les infrastructures sont les meilleures et les impôts les moins élevés pour éviter d'être trop touché par la redistribution des revenus; **~ hand** *n* *jarg* ECON *coined by Adam Smith* main invisible *f*; **~ handshake** *n* GEN COMM accord implicite *m*, accord secret *m*, sous-entendu *m*; **~ import** *n* ECON, IMP/EXP importation invisible *f*; **~ supply** *n* GEN COMM approvisionnement invisible *m*; **~ trade** *n* ECON commerce d'invisibles *m*; **~ trade balance** *n* ECON balance commerciale des invisibles *f*

invisibles *n pl* ECON, GEN COMM, IMP/EXP invisibles *m pl*

invitation *n* GEN COMM invitation *f*; **~ to tender** LAW appel d'offres *m*

invite *vt* GEN COMM *comments, suggestions* solliciter; ◆ **~ subscriptions for** GEN COMM ouvrir une souscription pour

invoice[1] *n* ACC *(inv.)*, BANK *(inv.)*, FIN *(inv.)* facture *f*, GEN COMM bordereau *m*, *(inv.)* facture *f*; **~ amount** FIN, GEN COMM montant dû *m*; **~ book** GEN COMM facturier *m*; **~ clerk** GEN COMM facturier *m*; **~ cost** ACC coût de facture *m*; **~ in the currency of the overseas buyer** ACC, IMP/EXP facture établie dans la devise de l'acheteur étranger *f*; **~ in the currency of the overseas seller** ACC, IMP/EXP facture établie dans la devise du vendeur étranger *f*; **~ in a third currency** ACC facture établie en devise indépendante *f*, facture établie en devise tierce *f*; **~ price** STOCK *of a deliverable CD* prix de facture *m*; **~ value** *(iv)* FIN, GEN COMM valeur de la facture *f*

invoice[2] *vt* ACC, FIN, GEN COMM *company, person, goods* facturer; ♦ **~ cost and charges** ACC facturer les coûts et charges; **~ sb for sth** GEN COMM facturer qch à qn

invoicing *n* ACC facturation *f*; **~ amount** FIN, GEN COMM montant dû *m*; **~ department** ACC, GEN COMM service facturation *m*

invoke *vt* GEN COMM *law, penalty* invoquer

involuntary: **~ bankruptcy** *n* ACC, FIN, GEN COMM, LAW faillite forcée *f*, faillite prononcée à la demande des créanciers *f*; **~ conversion** *n* INS destruction involontaire *f*, PROP conversion involontaire *f*; **~ employment** *n* ECON, HRM emploi involontaire *m*; **~ investment** *n* FIN investissement involontaire *m*; **~ lien** *n* LAW privilège obligatoire *m*; **~ liquidation** *n* ACC, FIN, GEN COMM, LAW liquidation involontaire *f*, liquidation judiciaire *f*; **~ trust** *n US* LAW fidéicommis institué sans document formel *m*; **~ unemployment** *n* ECON, HRM chômage involontaire *m*

involve *vt* GEN COMM *expenses* entraîner, impliquer, PATENTS *inventive step* impliquer

involvement *n* GEN COMM *in activity* participation *f*; **~ of employees** HRM implication du personnel *f*

inward: **~ bill of lading** *n* IMP/EXP, TRANSP connaissement d'entrée *m*; **~ cargo** *n* IMP/EXP, TRANSP chargement de retour *m*; **~ charges** *n pl* IMP/EXP, TRANSP frais à l'entrée *m pl*; **~ clearing bill** *n* IMP/EXP, TRANSP déclaration de dédouanement d'entrée *f*; **~ freight department** *n* IMP/EXP, TRANSP service du fret à l'arrivée *m*; **~ investment** *n* FIN *from overseas* investissement étranger *m*; **~ investor** *n* FIN *from overseas* investisseur étranger *m*; **~ payment** *n* (ANT *outward payment*) ACC, BANK, FIN encaissement *m*, paiement reçu *m*; **~ process relief** *n* (*IPR*) IMP/EXP, TRANSP dégrèvement du traitement des entrées; **~ processing** *n* IMP/EXP, TRANSP traitement des entrées *m*

inwards: **~ mission** *n* S&M marketing visant à faciliter à un exportateur la promotion de son produit ou son service; **~ processing relief** *n* (*IPR*) IMP/EXP, TRANSP dégrèvement du traitement des entrées

Inwood: **~ Annuity Factor** *n* INS facteur Inwood d'annuité *m*

I/O[1] *abbr* (*input/output*) COMP E/S (*entrée/sortie*)

I/O:[2] **~ error message** *n* COMP message d'erreur d'entrée/sortie *m*

IO *abbr* ADMIN (*immigration officer*), HRM (*immigration officer*) agent du service de l'immigration *m*, fonctionnaire de l'immigration *m*, officier de police du service de l'immigration *m*, ≈ agent de la P.A.F. *m* (*Fra*), ≈ agent de la Police de l'air et des frontières *m* (*Fra*), IND (*industrial organization*) organisation industrielle *f*

IOB *abbr* BANK (*Institute of Bankers*) Institut des banquiers *m*, INS *UK* (*Insurance Ombudsman Bureau*) bureau de médiateur en matière d'assurance *m*

IOC[1] *abbr* (*Intergovernmental Oceanographic Commission*) COMMS Commission océanographique intergouvernementale *f*

IOC:[2] **~ order** *n* (*immediate-or-cancel order*) STOCK ordre IOC *m* (*ordre immédiat ou annuler*)

IOE *abbr* HRM (*International Organization of Employers*) Organisation internationale des employeurs, TRANSP (*International Office of Epizootics*) OIE (*Office international des épizooties*)

IOM[1] *abbr* MGMNT (*Institute of Office Management*) institut de la gestion de bureaux, STOCK (*International Options Market*) marché international des options *m*, marché à options international *m*, marché à primes international *m*

IOM:[2] **~ division** *n US* (*Index and Option Market division*) STOCK *of the Chicage Mercantile Exchange* département de l'indice et du marché à option

IORT *abbr* (*incremental oil revenue tax*) TAX impôt sur les revenus pétroliers supplémentaires *m*

IOSCO *abbr* (*International Organization of Securities Commission*) STOCK commission de l'organisation internationale des valeurs *f*

iota *n* GEN COMM iota *m*

IOTTSG *abbr* (*International Oil Tanker and Terminal Safety Group*) TRANSP groupe international sur la sécurité des pétroliers et des terminaux

IOU[1] *abbr* (*I owe you*) BANK, FIN, GEN COMM, TRANSP reconnaissance de dette *f*

IOU:[2] **~ money** *n* FIN, STOCK lettre de change *f*

IPA *abbr UK* (*Institute of Practitioners in Advertising*) S&M institut des publicitaires

IPC *abbr* (*integrated pollution control*) ENVIR lutte antipollution intégrée *f*

IPD *abbr* (*interest, profit and dividends*) ECON revenu en provenance de l'étranger *m*

IPE *abbr UK* (*International Petroleum Exchange*) STOCK bourse internationale des produits pétroliers *f*, marché international du pétrole *m*

IPI *abbr* (*International Press Institute*) MEDIA institut international de la presse

IPM *abbr* FIN (*integrated project management*), MGMNT (*integrated project management*) gestion intégrée de projet *f*, MGMNT *UK* (*Institute of Personnel Management*) Institut de gestion du personnel *m*

IPMA *abbr* (*International Primary Market Association*) STOCK Association internationale du marché primaire *f*

IPO *abbr* BANK (*international payment order*) ordre de paiement international *m*, STOCK *AmE* (*initial public offering*) offre publique initiale *f*, première émission publique *f*

IPR *abbr* IMP/EXP (*inward process relief, inwards processing relief*) dégrèvement du traitement des entrées, LAW (*property rights*), PROP (*property rights*) droits de propriété *m pl*, S&M *UK* (*Institute of Public Relations*) institut des relations publiques, TRANSP (*inward process relief, inwards* *processing relief*) dégrèvement du traitement des entrées

ipso facto *adv frml* GEN COMM ipso facto (*frml*)

IPU *abbr (Inter-Parliamentary Union)* POL UIP (*Union interparlementaire*)

IR *abbr* HRM (*industrial relations*) relations humaines dans l'entreprise *f pl*, relations industrielles *f pl*, relations professionnelles *f pl*, relations syndicales *f pl*, TAX *UK (the Inland Revenue) organization, system* le Fisc *m* (*infrml*)

Irak *pr n see Iraq*

Iraki[1] *adj see Iraqi*

Iraki[2] *n see Iraqi*

Iran *pr n* GEN COMM Iran *m*

Iranian[1] *adj* GEN COMM iranien

Iranian[2] *n* GEN COMM *language* iranien *m, person* Iranien *m*

Iraq *pr n* GEN COMM Irak *m*, Iraq *m*

Iraqi[1] *adj* GEN COMM irakien, iraquien

Iraqi[2] *n* GEN COMM *language* irakien *m*, iraquien *m, person* Irakien *m*, Iraquien *m*

IRD *abbr (inland rail depot)* IMP/EXP, TRANSP bureau de dédouanement ferroviaire intérieur *m*

Ireland *pr n* GEN COMM Irlande *f*

Irish[1] *adj* GEN COMM irlandais

Irish:[2] **the ~** *n pl* GEN COMM *person* les Irlandais *m pl*

Irish:[3] **~ Republic** *pr n* GEN COMM République d'Irlande *f*

Irishman *n* GEN COMM *person* Irlandais *m*

Irishwoman *n* GEN COMM *person* Irlandaise *f*

IRN *abbr* ENVIR (*iron*) fer *m*, IMP/EXP (*import release note*) décharge d'importation *f*, IND (*iron*) fer *m*

iron[1] *n (IRN)* ENVIR, IND fer *m*; **~ law of wages** ECON loi d'airain des salaires *f*; **~ ore** IND minerai de fer *m*; **~ -ore carrier** TRANSP *ship* minéralier *m*

iron:[2] **~ out** *vt* GEN COMM *difficulty, problem* aplanir

ironworks *n pl* IND usine sidérurgique *f*

IRPC *abbr (Industrial Relations Policy Committee)* HRM commission sur la politique des relations industrielles

IRPTC *abbr (International Register of Potentially Toxic Chemicals)* ENVIR, IND RISCPT (*Registre international des substances chimiques potentiellement toxiques*)

IRR *abbr (internal rate of return)* ACC, FIN taux de rentabilité interne *m*, taux de rentabilité intérieur *m*, taux interne de rentabilité *m*

irrecoverable: ~ debt *n* BANK, ECON, FIN, GEN COMM créance irrécouvrable *f*

irreducible *adj* GEN COMM *minimum* irréductible

irrefutable *adj* GEN COMM irréfutable, LAW *assumption, claim, evidence* irréfragable

irregular: ~ market *n* STOCK marché irrégulier *m*

irregularity *n* GEN COMM anomalie *f*, irrégularité *f*, LAW vice de forme *m*; **~ report** TRANSP rapport d'irrégularité *m*

irrelevant *adj* PATENTS étranger au sujet

irreparable[1] *adj* GEN COMM *disaster, wrong, mistake* irréparable

irreparable:[2] **~ damage** *n* LAW dommage irréparable *m*; **~ harm** *n* LAW préjudice irréparable *m*

irreplaceable *adj* GEN COMM irremplaçable

irrespective: ~ of *prep* GEN COMM sans tenir compte de

irreversible *adj* GEN COMM *decision, verdict* irrévocable, *process* irréversible

irrevocable[1] *adj* LAW irrévocable

irrevocable:[2] **~ credit** *n* BANK crédit irrévocable *m*; **~ credit line** *n* BANK autorisation de crédit irrévocable *f*; **~ letter of credit** *n (ILOC)* BANK lettre de crédit irrévocable *f*; **~ trust** *n* LAW fidéicommis irrévocable *m*

IRS *abbr US (the Internal Revenue Service)* TAX le Fisc *m* (*infrml*)

IRU *abbr* HRM (*International Recruitment Unit*) Unité internationale de recrutement *f*, TRANSP (*International Road Transport Union*) Syndicat international des transporteurs routiers *m*

is: as ~ *adj* GEN COMM en l'état *loc m*

IS *abbr (independent spherical aluminium tank, independent spherical aluminum tank)* TRANSP *shipping, liquefied natural gas carrier* cuve sphérique indépendante en aluminium *f*

ISA *abbr (International Sugar Agreement)* ECON ≈ AIS (*Accord international sur le sucre*)

ISBN *abbr (International Standard Book Number)* MEDIA *print* ISBN (*International Standard Book Number*)

ISC *abbr (International Sugar Council)* IND Conseil international du sucre *m*

ISD *abbr (international subscriber dialing, international subscriber dialling)* COMMS téléphone automatique international *m*

ISDA *abbr (International Swap Dealers' Association)* STOCK Association internationale des opérateurs de swaps *f*

ISDN *abbr (integrated services digital network)* COMMS RNIS (*réseau numérique à intégration de services*)

ISE *abbr (International Stock Exchange)* STOCK ≈ SBF (*France*) (*Société des bourses françaises*)

ISF *abbr (International Shipping Federation)* TRANSP Fédération internationale de la navigation *f*

ISFA *abbr (Institute of Shipping and Forwarding Agents)* TRANSP institut d'agents maritimes et de transitaires

ISI *abbr UK (International Statistical Institute)* GEN COMM Institut international des statistiques

Islamabad *pr n* GEN COMM Islamabad *n pr*

Islamic: ~ banking *n* BANK opérations bancaires islamiques *f pl*

island *n* S&M *in shop* îlot *m*; **~ display** S&M *in shop* position isolée *f*; **~ site** *jarg* S&M *in shop* emplacement isolé *m*

ISMA *abbr* *(International Securities Market Association)* STOCK Association internationale des bourses de valeurs *f*, Association internationale du marché des valeurs *f*

ISO *abbr* GEN COMM *(International Standards Organization)* Organisation internationale de normalisation *f*, IND *(International Sugar Organization)* Organisation internationale du sucre *f*, STOCK *(incentive stock option) tax* intéressement par option de souscription d'actions *m*, option d'action à prime *f*

isocost *n* ECON isocoût *m*

isolate *vt* GEN COMM isoler

isolated[1] *adj* GEN COMM isolé

isolated:[2] ~ **state** *n* ECON, POL *of closed economy* état isolé *m*

isolationist[1] *adj* POL isolationniste

isolationist[2] *n* POL isolationniste *mf*

ISO/OSI *abbr* *(International Standards Organization/Open Systems Interconnection)* COMP interconnexion de systèmes ouverts de l'organisation internationale des standards

isoproduct: ~ **curve** *n* ECON courbe isoquante *f*

isoquant *n* ECON isoquant *m*

Israel *pr n* GEN COMM Israël *m*

Israeli[1] *adj* GEN COMM israélien

Israeli[2] *n* GEN COMM *person* Israélien *m*

ISRO *abbr* *(International Securities Regulatory Organization)* STOCK Organisation de surveillance pour les valeurs internationales *f*, Organisme régulateur des titres internationaux *m*

ISS *abbr* *(International Social Service)* WEL ≈ Service social international *m*

ISSN *abbr* *(International Standard Serial Number)* MEDIA *print* ISSN *(International Standard Serial Number)*

issuance *n* TAX délivrance *f*; ~ **facility** FIN facilité d'émission garantie *f*

issue[1] *n* GEN COMM *topic of discussion* question *f*, LAW *descendants* descendance en ligne directe *f*, *topic of discussion* point en litige *m*, problème *m*, question *f*, sujet *m*, STOCK *action of issuing, shares issued* émission *f*; ~ **card** IND carte de sortie de stock *f*; ~ **date** STOCK date d'émission *f*; ~ **management** *jarg* UK S&M *public relations* préparation du public à l'introduction d'un sujet important; ~ **market** STOCK marché des émissions *m*; ~ **premium** STOCK prime d'émission *f*; ~ **price** STOCK prix d'émission *m*; ~ **voucher** IND bon de sortie de stock *m*; ◆ **at** ~ GEN COMM dont il s'agit, en question

issue[2] *vt* COMP, FIN *cheque, shares, bond, banknote* émettre, MEDIA *magazine, newspaper* faire paraître, livrer, publier, *prospectus* lancer, STOCK émettre; ◆ ~ **by tender** FIN émettre par adjudication; ~ **a letter of credit** STOCK émettre une lettre de crédit; ~ **shares at a discount** STOCK émettre des actions à l'escompte; ~ **a warrant** LAW lancer un mandat; ~ **a writ against sb** LAW assigner qn en justice, signifier un acte judiciaire à qn

issued[1] *adj* FIN, STOCK émis; ~ **and outstanding** STOCK émis et en circulation

issued:[2] ~ **capital** *n* STOCK capital souscrit *m*, capital émis *m*; ~ **share capital** *n* ACC capital souscrit *m*, FIN capital social souscrit *m*

issuer *n* FIN, STOCK émetteur *m*

issues: ~ **with currency options** *n pl* STOCK émissions assorties d'options de change *f pl*

issuing[1] *adj* BANK, FIN, STOCK émetteur

issuing:[2] ~ **authority** *n* ADMIN *of passport* autorité compétente pour délivrer *f*; ~ **bank** *n* BANK banque émettrice *f*; ~ **banker** *n* BANK banquier émetteur *m*; ~ **carrier** *n* TRANSP *aviation* transporteur émetteur *m*; ~ **company** *n* STOCK société émettrice *f*; ~ **house** *n* STOCK banque de placement *f*, établissement responsable de l'émission *m*

IT *abbr* COMP *(information technology)* informatique *f*, technologie de l'information *f*, HRM *UK (industrial tribunal)*, IND *UK (industrial tribunal)*, LAW *UK (industrial tribunal)* ≈ Conseil des prud'hommes *m*, LEIS *(inclusive tour)* voyage tout compris *m*, TRANSP *(insulated tank container)* conteneur-citerne isotherme *m*, TRANSP *(inclusive tour)* voyage tout compris *m*, TRANSP *(independent tank) shipping, liquefied natural gas carrier* cuve autoporteuse *f*, cuve indépendante *f*

Italian[1] *adj* GEN COMM italien

Italian[2] *n* GEN COMM *language* italien *m*, *person* Italien *m*

italic *adj* COMP, MEDIA *typography* italique

italics *n pl* COMP, MEDIA *typography* italique *m*; ◆ **in** ~ COMP, MEDIA en italique

Italy *pr n* GEN COMM Italie *f*

ITB *abbr* *(integrated tug-barge)* TRANSP *shipping* pousseur-barge intégré *m*

ITC *abbr* ECON *(international trading certificate)* certificat de commerce international *m*, IND *(International Tin Council)* conseil international de l'étain, TAX *(investment tax credit)* CII *(crédit d'impôt à l'investissement)*, TAX *Can (input tax credit)* CTI *(crédit de taxe sur intrants)*

item *n* ACC *entry* article *m*, poste *m*, écriture *f*, COMP élément *m*, FIN écriture *f*, GEN COMM *for sale* article *m*, *on agenda* point *m*, question *f*; ~ **analysis** MATH *statistics* analyse d'article *f*; ◆ ~ **approved for inclusion** GEN COMM question dont l'inclusion a été approuvée *f*

itemization *n* GEN COMM *of bill, invoice* détail *m*

itemized[1] *adj* ACC *bill, billing, invoice* détaillé

itemized:[2] ~ **deductions** *n pl* TAX déduction des frais réels *f*; ~ **pay statement** *n* HRM bulletin de salaire analytique *m*

items: ~ **in the estimates** *n pl* FIN postes du budget des dépenses *m pl*; ~ **on the agenda** *n pl* GEN COMM questions à l'ordre du jour *f pl*

iteration *n* COMP itération *f*

iterative: ~ **warnings** *n pl* (SYN *repeated warnings*) COMP avertissements répétés *m pl*

ITF *abbr* *(International Transport Workers' Federation)* TRANSP FIOT *(Fédération internationale des ouvriers du transport)*

ITI *abbr* *(customs convention on the international transit of goods)* IMP/EXP convention douanière sur le transit international des marchandises *f*

itinerary *n* LEIS itinéraire *m*, route *f*, TRANSP itinéraire *m*

ITM *abbr* *(in-the-money)* STOCK argenté, dans le cours *loc m*, en jeu *loc m*

ITO *abbr* *(International Trade Organization)* GEN COMM organisation internationale du commerce

ITPAL *abbr* *(industrial and trade policy adjustment loan)* FIN prêt d'ajustement de politique industrielle et commerciale *m*

ITS *abbr* US *(Intermarket Trading System)* STOCK système commercial inter-marché *m*, système de transaction inter-marchés *m*

ITU *abbr* *(International Telecommunications Union)* COMMS UIT *(Union internationale des télécommunications)*

ITV *abbr* UK *(Independent Television)* S&M chaîne de télévision britannique indépendante, diffusant des programmes régionaux

ITW *abbr* *(independent tank wing)* TRANSP *shipping, liquefied natural gas carrier* cuve autoporteuse latérale *f*, cuve indépendante latérale *f*

ITX *abbr* *(independent tank common)* TRANSP *shipping, liquefied natural gas carrier* cuve autoporteuse standard *f*, cuve indépendante standard *f*

IUOTO *abbr* *(International Union of Official Travel Organizations)* TRANSP Syndicat international des organisations officielles de voyages *m*

IUR *abbr* *(International Union of Railways)* ADMIN UICF *(Union internationale des chemins de fer)*, TRANSP Syndicat international des cheminots *m*

iv *abbr* FIN *(increased value)* plus-value *f*, FIN *(invoice value)*, GEN COMM *(invoice value)* valeur de la facture *f*

Ivorian[1] *adj* GEN COMM ivoirien

Ivorian[2] *n* GEN COMM *person* Ivoirien *m*

Ivory: **~ Coast** *pr n* GEN COMM Côte-d'Ivoire *f*

IWA *abbr* *(International Wheat Agreement)* ECON AIB *(Accord international sur le blé)*

IWC *abbr* *(International Wheat Council)* GEN COMM CIB *(Conseil international du blé)*

J

J[1] *abbr* LAW *(judge)* juge *m*, LAW *(justice)* justice *f*

J:[2] ~ **curve** *n* ECON courbe en J *f*; ~ **-shaped frequency curve** *n* MATH *statistics* courbe de fréquence en forme de J *f*

J/A *abbr (joint account)* BANK compte bancaire en commun *m*, compte conjoint *m*, compte en commun *m*, compte joint *m*

jack: ~ **up** *vt infrml* GEN COMM *price*, S&M augmenter, majorer

jacket *n* COMP *of disk* jaquette *f*, pochette *f*

Jakarta *pr n* GEN COMM Djakarta *n pr*

jam[1] *n* COMP *of printer* bourrage *m*, GEN COMM *infrml* pétrin *m* *(infrml)*; ◆ **in a** ~ *infrml* GEN COMM dans le pétrin *(infrml)*

jam[2] *vi* IND se coincer

Jamaica:[1] ~ **Agreement** *n* ECON Accord de la Jamaïque *m*

Jamaica[2] *pr n* GEN COMM Jamaïque *f*

Jamaican[1] *adj* GEN COMM jamaïcain, jamaïquain

Jamaican[2] *n* GEN COMM *person* Jamaïcain *m*, Jamaïquain *m*

Jan. *abbr (January)* GEN COMM janv. *(janvier)*

J&WO *abbr (jettisoning and washing overboard)* INS *marine* jet à la mer et enlèvement par une lame *m*

Jane: ~ **Doe** *n* US LAW toute femme non-identifiée, demanderesse fictive *f*, ≈ Madame Dupont *f*

January *n* *(Jan.)* GEN COMM janvier *m (janv.)*; ~ **sales** *n pl* S&M soldes de janvier *m pl*

Japan:[1] ~ **External Trade Organization** *n UK* GEN COMM office japonais du commerce extérieur; ~ **Trade Advisory Group** *n (JTAG)* GEN COMM comité consultatif japonais des échanges commerciaux

Japan[2] *pr n* GEN COMM Japon *m*

Japanese[1] *adj* GEN COMM japonais

Japanese[2] *n* GEN COMM *language* japonais *m*, *person* Japonais *m*; ~ **External Trade Organization** *(JETRO)* GEN COMM office du commerce extérieur japonais; **the** ~ GEN COMM *person* les Japonais *m pl*

japanization *n* ECON *international trade* japanisation *f*

jargon *n* GEN COMM jargon *m*

jawbone *vt US* POL faire pression sur *loc f*

jawboning *n US* POL pressions gouvernementales *f pl*

JCCC *abbr UK (Joint Customs Consultative Committee)* IMP/EXP comité paritaire consultatif des douanes

JCS *abbr (joint container service)* TRANSP service conteneur commun *m*

JDI *abbr (joint declaration of interest)* BANK déclaration conjointe d'intérêts *f*, déclaration d'intérêts en commun *f*

JEC *abbr (Joint Economic Committee of Congress)* ECON *between House and Senate* commission mixte économique du Congrès américaine

jeopardize *vt* GEN COMM *job* mettre en danger, mettre en péril, *situation* compromettre

jeopardy: ~ **assessment** *n* TAX cotisation de protection *f*; ~ **collection procedures** *n pl* TAX procédures de recouvrement de protection *f pl*

jerque: ~ **note** *n* IMP/EXP certificat de dédouanement d'entrée *m*

Jerusalem *pr n* GEN COMM Jérusalem *n pr*

jetfoil *n* TRANSP hydrofoil *m*, hydroptère *m*, hydroglisseur *m*

jetlagged: **be** ~ *phr* GEN COMM, TRANSP souffrir du décalage horaire *loc m*

JETRO *abbr (Japanese External Trade Organization)* GEN COMM office du commerce extérieur japonais

jetsam *n* TRANSP épave rejetée *f*

jettison[1] *n* TRANSP jet à la mer *m*

jettison[2] *vt* TRANSP *shipping* jeter par-dessus bord

jettisoning: ~ **and washing overboard** *n (J&WO)* INS *marine* jet à la mer et enlèvement par une lame *m*

jetway *n* TRANSP *aviation* passerelle télescopique *f*

jiffy: ~ **bag**® *n* COMMS enveloppe rembourrée *f*

jingle *n* S&M *advertising* jingle *m*

JIT *abbr* HRM *(just-in-time)* juste à temps, à flux tendus *loc m*, HRM *(just-in-time production)* production dans les délais impartis *f*, production à flux tendus *f*, IND *(just-in-time)* juste à temps, à flux tendus *loc m*, IND *(just-in-time production)* production dans les délais impartis *f*, production à flux tendus *f*, MEDIA *(just-in-time) delivery* juste à temps, à flux tendus *loc m*

JJ *abbr* LAW *(judges)* juges *m pl*, LAW *(justices)* justices *f pl*

JMC *abbr (Joint Maritime Commission)* HRM, TRANSP commission maritime conjointe

jnr *abbr (junior)* GEN COMM *employee, post* subalterne *mf*, *son* fils *m*, *young* jeune

job *n* COMP travail *m*, GEN COMM *specific project* tâche *f*, *work* travail *m*, HRM emploi *m*, travail *m*, métier *m*; ~ **action** *n jarg* HRM, IND action revendicative *f*, grève *f*; ~ **advertisement** *n* HRM offre d'emploi *f*; ~ **analysis** *n* HRM analyse de poste *f*, analyse des tâches *f*, analyse par poste de travail *f*; ~ **application** *n* ADMIN, GEN COMM candidature *f*, HRM candidature *f*, demande d'emploi *f*; ~ **appraisal** *n* HRM évaluation de l'emploi *f*, évaluation des postes *f*, évaluation des tâches *f*; ~ **assignment** *n* GEN COMM, HRM affectation des tâches *f*, répartition des tâches *f*; ~ **bank** *n* HRM répertoire opérationnel des métiers et des emplois *m*, ROME; ~ **breakdown** *n* HRM décomposition des tâches *f*; ~ **card** *n* HRM fiche de poste *f*; ~ **challenge** *n* HRM, MGMNT exigences de poste *f pl*; ~ **classification** *n* HRM classification des emplois *f*, classification des fonctions *f*; ~ **cluster** *n* ECON, HRM groupe d'emplois *m*; ~ **competence** *n* HRM compétence dans le travail *f*; ~ **content** *n* HRM contenu du travail *m*; ~ **control** *n* COMP gestion des travaux *f*; ~ **cost sheet** *n* ECON fiche de prix de revient *f*; ~ **cost system** *n* ACC méthode de détermination des coûts de fabrication par lot *f*; ~ **costing** *n* HRM évaluation du coût d'un poste *f*; ~ **creation** *n* HRM création de poste *f*; ~ **depth** *n* HRM rayonnement *m*; ~ **description** *n* HRM description de poste *f*, définition de fonction *f*; ~ **design** *n* HRM conception de tâche *f*; ~ **enlargement** *n* HRM extension des tâches *f*, élargissement du travail *m*; ~ **enrichment** *n* HRM aménagement de poste *m*, enrichissement des emplois *m*; ~ **entry** *n* COMP soumission de travaux *f*; ~ **evaluation** *n* HRM qualification du travail *f*, évaluation de l'emploi *f*, évaluation des postes *f*; ~ **evaluation scale** *n* HRM échelle de cotation des emplois *f*; ~ **evaluation scheme** *n* HRM système de classification des emplois *m*; ~ **expectations** *n pl* HRM perspectives de carrière *f pl*; ~ **flexibility** *n* HRM flexibilité des emplois *f*; ~ **freeze** *n* ECON, HRM gel de l'emploi *m*; ~ **hopper** *n* HRM personne professionnellement instable *f*, personne qui change fréquemment d'emplois *f*; ~ **hopping** *n* HRM changement fréquent d'emplois *m*; ~ **hunter** *n* HRM demandeur d'emploi *m*, personne à la recherche d'un emploi *f*; ~ **hunting** *n* HRM recherche d'emploi *f*; ~ **improvement** *n* HRM amélioration des tâches *f*; ~ **interest** *n* HRM intérêt des tâches *m*; ~ **jumper** *n* HRM personne professionnellement instable *f*, personne qui change fréquemment d'emplois *f*; ~ **legislation** *n* HRM, LAW législation du travail *f*; ~ **lot** *n* GEN COMM lot d'articles divers *m*; ~ **market** *n* ECON, HRM marché du travail *m*; ~ **mobility** *n* HRM mobilité professionnelle *f*; ~ **offer** *n* HRM offre d'emploi *f*; ~ **opportunity** *n* HRM débouché *m*, possibilités d'emploi *f pl*, poste qui se libère *m*; ~ **order** *n* IND ordre de fabrication *m*; ~ **order costing** *n* IND estimation du prix de revient par commande *f*; ~ **performance** *n* HRM rendement au travail *m*; ~ **profile** *n* HRM description de fonction *f*, description de poste *f*, profil de l'emploi *m*; ~ **prospects** *n pl* HRM perspectives de carrière *f pl*; ~ **queue** *n* COMP file d'attente de travaux *f*, HRM ≈ file d'attente à l'ANPE *f* (*Fra*) ≈ file d'attente à l'Agence nationale pour l'emploi *f* (*Fra*); ~ **regulation** *n* HRM redéfinition du contenu d'un poste *f*; ~ **-related accommodation** *n* BrE HRM logement de fonction *m*; ~ **-related accommodations** *n pl* AmE see *job-related accommodation* BrE; ~ **-related injury** *n* HRM blessure liée à l'exercice d'une profession *f*; ~ **requirements** *n pl* HRM, MGMNT exigences de poste *f pl*; ~ **retraining course** *n* HRM cours de recyclage professionnel *m*; ~ **review** *n* HRM évaluation de l'emploi *f*, évaluation des postes *f*, évaluation des tâches *f*; ~ **rotation** *n* HRM rotation des postes *f*, roulement *m*; ~ **satisfaction** *n* HRM satisfaction au travail *f*; ~ **search** *n* HRM recherche d'emploi *f*; ~ **security** *n* HRM sécurité de l'emploi *f*; ~ **security agreement** *n* HRM accord sur la sécurité de l'emploi *m*; ~ **seeker** *n* GEN COMM demandeur d'emploi *m*, D.E.; ~ **segregation** *n* HRM discrimination sexuelle à l'embauche *f*; ~ **share** *n* HRM partage de l'emploi *m*, partage du travail *m*; ~ **share scheme** *n* HRM système de partage du travail *m*; ~ **sharing** *n* HRM partage de l'emploi *m*, partage du travail *m*; ~ **shop** *n* HRM entreprise de travaux sur commandes *f*; ~ **simplification** *n* HRM, MGMNT simplification des tâches *f*, SDT; ~ **skills** *n pl* HRM aptitudes pour le poste *f pl*; ~ **spec** *n* infrml *see job specification* ; ~ **specialization** *n* HRM spécialisation du poste *f*; ~ **specification** *n* HRM caractéristiques du poste *f pl*, fixation des tâches *f*, profil du poste *m*; ~ **splitting** *n* HRM partage de poste *m*; ~ **study** *n* HRM analyse de poste *f*; ~ **ticket** *n* HRM bon de travail *m*; ~ **title** *n* HRM description de poste *f*, désignation de l'emploi *f*, qualification *f*, titre de fonction *m*; ~ **training** *n* HRM formation professionnelle *f*; ~ **vacancy** *n* HRM poste à pourvoir *m*, vacance de poste *f*; ~ **wastage** *n* HRM gâchis d'emploi *m*; ◆ **have two ~s** HRM cumuler; **out of a ~** HRM au chômage

job:³ ~ **backwards** *vi jarg* STOCK recalculer a posteriori, travailler à reculons

jobber *n dat UK* (SYN *market maker*) STOCK titre remplacé depuis le Big Bang de 1986 par market maker, contrepartiste *mf*, courtier en valeurs *m*, jobber *m*, négociant en titres *m*, négociateur en valeurs mobilières *m*; ~ **in contangos** STOCK contrepartiste reporteur *m*; ~**'s spread** STOCK *difference in price* fourchette de prix du jobber *f*, *margin* marge d'un contrepartiste *f*; ~**'s turn** STOCK marge d'un contrepartiste *f*

jobbing *n* GEN COMM vente en gros *f*, HRM courtage *m*, IND fabrication sur commande *f*, STOCK courtage *m*

Jobcentre *n UK* HRM bureau des services nationaux de l'emploi *m*, bureau local pour l'emploi *m*, service de l'emploi *m*, ≈ Agence nationale pour l'emploi *f* (*Fra*), ≈ ANPE (*Fra*)

jobless¹ *adj* ECON, HRM sans emploi

jobless:² ~ **person** *n* GEN COMM chômeur *m*; ~ **rate** *n* HRM taux de chômage *m*; **the ~** *n pl* ECON, HRM les chômeurs *m pl*, les sans-emplois *m pl*

jobs: get ~ for the boys *phr infrml* HRM placer ses petits copains (*infrml*)

jockey *n jarg* FIN responsable de la gestion d'un investissement *m*

jogging *n jarg* BANK *storing information* enregistrement d'un fonds d'information *m*

John: ~ **Doe** n US LAW toute personne non-identifiée, demandeur fictif m, ≈ Monsieur Dupont m

join 1. vt GEN COMM unir, HRM *union* adhérer à; **2.** vi ~ **together** GEN COMM *companies* s'associer; ♦ ~ **the dole queue** BrE, HRM être mis au chômage

joinder n HRM réunion f, union f; ~ **of appeals** TAX jonction des appels f

joined adj AmE (SYN *subjoined*) COMMS *document* en annexe *loc f*

joint¹ adj GEN COMM *communiqué* commun, LAW, TAX conjoint

joint:² ~ **account** n (J/A) BANK compte bancaire en commun m, compte conjoint m, compte en commun m, compte joint m; ~ **account agreement** n BANK accord de compte en commun m; ~ **action** n LAW action collective f; ~ **applicant** n PATENTS codéposant m; ~ **assignment** n GEN COMM mission commune f; ~ **auditor** n ACC co-commissaire mf, commissaire aux comptes coresponsable m, commissaire aux comptes en double mandat m; ~ **authorization** n BANK autorisation conjoint f; ~ **bank account** n BANK compte bancaire en commun m, compte conjoint m, compte en commun m, compte joint m; ~ **bond** n STOCK obligation co-émise f, obligation conjointe f; ~ **charge** n TRANSP tarif commun m; ~ **committee** n HRM commission mixte f, commission paritaire f; ~ **consultation** n GEN COMM consultation bilatérale f, MGMNT consultation paritaire f; ~ **consultative committee** n HRM comité d'entreprise m, commission paritaire consultative f, CE; ~ **container service** n (JCS) TRANSP service conteneur commun m; ~ **costs** n pl ECON coûts conjoints m pl; ~ **custody** n BANK, LAW *of child* garde conjointe f; ~ **debtor** n FIN co-débiteur m; ~ **declaration of interest** n (JDI) BANK déclaration conjointe d'intérêts f, déclaration d'intérêts en commun f; ~ **demand** n ECON demande conjointe f; ~ **designation** n PATENTS désignation conjointe f; ~ **director** n GEN COMM, HRM, MGMNT codirecteur m; ~ **equity venture company** n (SYN *JV, joint venture*) GEN COMM joint-venture m, société en participation f, société mixte f; ~ **estate** n LAW biens communs m pl, communauté de biens f; ~ **fare** n TRANSP tarif commun m; ~ **guarantee** n FIN caution solidaire f; ~ **heir** n LAW cohéritier m; ~ **holder** n STOCK codétenteur m, cotitulaire mf; ~ **insurance** n INS assurance conjointe f; ~ **liability** n BANK responsabilité collective f, responsabilité conjointe f, LAW coresponsabilité f, responsabilité collective f, responsabilité conjointe f, TAX obligation solidaire f, responsabilité collective f, responsabilité conjointe f; ~ **loan** n BANK prêt conjoint m; ~ **management** n GEN COMM, HRM, MGMNT cogestion f, cogérance f; ~ **manager** n GEN COMM, HRM, MGMNT codirecteur m, cogérant m; ~ **negotiation** n GEN COMM, HRM, MGMNT, STOCK négociation paritaire f; ~ **occupancy** n TAX cohabitation f; ~ **operator** n GEN COMM, IND coopérateur m; ~ **owner** n HRM, PROP, TAX

copropriétaire mf; ~ **ownership** n BANK propriété conjointe f, LAW copropriété f, PROP propriété conjointe f; ~ **partnership** n GEN COMM coassociation f; ~ **product cost** n ACC coût de produits liés m; ~ **production committee** n HRM comité d'entreprise m; ~ **products** n pl ECON produits liés m pl; ~ **promissory note** n FIN billet solidaire m; ~ **rate** n TRANSP tarif commun m; ~ **regulation** n HRM co-régulation f; ~ **representation** n GEN COMM démarche collective f, HRM démarche collective f, représentation paritaire f, MGMNT démarche collective f; ~ **service** n TRANSP service commun m; ~ **and several liability** n LAW responsabilité conjointe et solidaire f; ~ **and several obligation** n LAW obligation conjointe et solidaire f; ~ **signature** n BANK signature collective f, GEN COMM, LAW cosignature f; ~ **statement** n GEN COMM déclaration commune f; ~ **-stock bank** n BANK, FIN banque de dépôt f; ~ **-stock company** n STOCK société par actions f; ~ **and survivor annuity** n US INS rente conjointe au dernier survivant f, rente réversible f; ~ **tenancy** n PROP indivision f, propriété indivise f; ~ **tenants** n pl STOCK cotitulaires avec droit de survivance m pl, locataires en commun m pl; ~ **venture** n (JV) ACC coentreprise f, ECON coentreprise f, joint-venture m, GEN COMM joint-venture m, société en participation f, société mixte f, *action* coentreprise f, opération conjointe f, MGMNT *action* action concertée f, coentreprise f, *company* entreprise conjointe f, société d'exploitation en commun f, STOCK *action* coentreprise f, *company* entreprise en participation f; ~ **-venture bank** n pl BANK banque en participation f; ~ **-venture company** n ACC, ECON coentreprise f, GEN COMM coentreprise f, joint-venture m, opération conjointe f, société en participation f, société mixte f, MGMNT coentreprise f, entreprise conjointe f, société d'exploitation en commun f, STOCK coentreprise f, entreprise en participation f; ~ **-venture investment bank** n BANK banque d'affaires en participation f, banque d'investissement en participation f; ~ **-venture merchant bank** n BANK banque d'affaires en participation f, banque d'investissement en participation f; ~ **working party** n (JWP) HRM groupe de travail paritaire m

Joint: ~ **Cargo Committee** n UK TRANSP ≈ Commission de groupage f; ~ **Customs Consultative Committee** n UK (JCCC) IMP/EXP comité paritaire consultatif des douanes; ~ **Economic Committee of Congress** n (JEC) ECON *between House and Senate* commission mixte économique du Congrès américain; ~ **Hull Understandings** n INS *marine* accords communs de l'assurance corps m pl; ~ **Maritime Commission** n (JMC) HRM, TRANSP commission maritime conjointe; ~ **Research Centre** n IND EURATOM centre de recherche commun

jointly adv TAX conjointement, ensemble, solidairement; ~ **and severally** GEN COMM *liable*, LAW *liable* conjointement et solidairement; ♦ ~ **and severally liable for** GEN COMM, LAW conjointement et solidairement responsable de

joker *n US* LAW clause ambiguë *f*, échappatoire *f*

Jordan *pr n* GEN COMM Jordanie *f*

Jordanian[1] *adj* GEN COMM jordanien

Jordanian[2] *n* GEN COMM *person* Jordanien *m*

jot: ~ **down** *vt* GEN COMM prendre note de

journal *n* ACC jl, journal *m*, GEN COMM revue *f*, MEDIA journal *m*, revue *f*; ~ **entry** ACC, FIN écriture comptable *f*

journalism *n* MEDIA journalisme *m*

journalist *n* HRM, MEDIA journaliste *mf*

journalize *vt* ACC comptabiliser au journal

journey: ~ **planner** *n* TRANSP information voyageurs *f*; ~ **planning** *n* TRANSP organisation des déplacements *f*

journeyman *n* [pl -men] HRM ouvrier à part entière *m*

joystick *n* COMP manche à balai *m*, manette de jeux *f*

JP *abbr* (*justice of the peace*) HRM juge d'instance *m*, juge de paix *m*

jr *abbr* (*junior*) GEN COMM *employee, post* subalterne *mf*, son fils *m*, *young* jeune

JTAG *abbr UK* (*Japan Trade Advisory Group*) GEN COMM comité consultatif japonais des échanges commerciaux

judge[1] *n* (*J*) LAW juge *m*

judge[2] *vt* LAW juger

judges *n pl* (*JJ*) LAW juges *m pl*; ~' **rules** *UK* LAW interrogatoire pendant la garde à vue *m*

judgment *n* GEN COMM jugement *m*, LAW arrêt *m*, décision *f*, jugement *m*, PROP indemnisation *f*, jugement *m*; ~ **creditor** *US* FIN, LAW créancier titulaire d'un jugement exécutoire pour le montant d'un crédit; ~ **debtor** *US* FIN débiteur dont les biens peuvent être saisis par suite d'un jugement, LAW débiteur contre lequel un jugement a été obtenu; ~ **lien** *US* LAW privilège judiciaire *m*; ~ **proof** LAW débiteur à qui on ne peut opposer un titre de créance même avec un acte judiciaire; ~ **sample** LAW enquête par échantillonnage *f*; ♦ **go against one's** ~ GEN COMM aller à l'encontre de sa propre conscience; **sit in** ~ **over** LAW juger, se faire juge des actes d'autrui

judicial[1] *adj* LAW judiciaire

judicial:[2] ~ **affairs** *n pl* LAW affaires judiciaires *f pl*; ~ **arbitrator** *n* LAW juge-arbitre *m*; ~ **bond** *n* LAW caution judiciaire *f*, cautionnement judiciaire *m*; ~ **foreclosure** *n* LAW vente judiciaire *f*, vente par autorité de justice *f*; ~ **notice** *n* LAW connaissance d'office *f*; ~ **proceedings** *n pl* LAW poursuites judiciaires *f pl*; ~ **sale** *n* LAW vente judiciaire *f*, vente par autorité de justice *f*; ~ **separation** *n* LAW séparation de corps *f*, séparation judiciaire *f*

judiciary *n* LAW pouvoir judiciaire *m*, système judiciaire *m*

juggernaut *n* TRANSP *truck* poids lourd avec remorque ou semi-remorque, mastodonte *m*

Jul. *abbr* (*July*) GEN COMM juil. (*juillet*)

July *n* (*Jul.*) GEN COMM juillet *m* (*juil.*)

jumble: ~ **sale** *n BrE* (*cf rummage sale AmE*) S&M braderie d'objets usagés *f*, vente de charité *f*

jumbo *n* TRANSP gros-porteur *m*, jumbo-jet *m*; ~ **certificate of deposit** STOCK certificat de très grand dépôt; ~ **derrick** TRANSP *cargo handling* bigue *f*; ~ **jet** *infrml* TRANSP gros-porteur *m*, jumbo-jet *m*; ~ **loan** BANK prêt d'une très grande somme *m*

jumboization *n* TRANSP allongement *m*, jumboïsation *f* (*infrml*)

jump *n* GEN COMM *in prices* flambée *f*, montée en flèche *f*

jumpy *adj* ECON *market* nerveux

Jun. *abbr* (*June*) GEN COMM juin *m*

June *n* (*Jun.*) GEN COMM juin *m*; ~ **call** (*ANT June put*) STOCK *or any month* option d'achat de juin *f*; ~ **put** (*ANT June call*) STOCK *or any month* option de vente de juin *f*

jungle *n infrml* GEN COMM embrouillamini *m* (*infrml*)

junior[1] *adj* (*jnr, jr*) GEN COMM *son* fils *m*, *young* jeune

junior[2] *n* (*jnr, jr*) GEN COMM *employee, post* subalterne *mf*, subordonné *m*; ~ **counsel** *UK* LAW avocat subordonné à l'avocat principal *m*; ~ **creditor** BANK créancier non-prioritaire *m*; ~ **debt** FIN dette de deuxième rang *f*; ~ **issue** *US* STOCK émission secondaire *f*; ~ **lien** LAW gage de second rang *m*, privilège de second rang *m*; ~ **manager** HRM jeune cadre *m*, sous-directeur *m*; ~ **mortgage** *US* BANK, PROP hypothèque de deuxième rang *f*; ~ **motorman** HRM *ship* machiniste *m*; ~ **partner** GEN COMM associé minoritaire *m*; ~ **position** HRM poste de débutant *m*; ~ **refunding** FIN, STOCK remboursement de second rang *m*; ~ **security** *US* STOCK valeur de second rang *f*, valeur de seconde catégorie *f*; ~ **share** STOCK action de dividende *f*, action de seconde catégorie *f*

junk: ~ **bond** *n* STOCK obligation de pacotille *f*, obligation pourrie *f* (*infrml*), obligation sans valeur *f*, obligation spéculative à haut risque *f*; ~ **food** *n* WEL nourriture peu diététique *f*; ~ **mail** *n* COMMS imprimés publicitaires *m pl*

junket[1] *n infrml AmE* TRANSP voyage aux frais de la princesse *m* (*infrml*)

junket[2] *vi AmE* TRANSP voyager aux frais de la princesse (*infrml*)

juridical: ~ **person** *n* LAW personne morale *f*; ~ **position** *n* LAW situation juridique *f*

juridification *n* HRM excès de réglementation légale *m*, juridisme *m*

jurisdiction *n* LAW circonscription judiciaire *f*, compétence *f*, juridiction *f*, POL circonscription judiciaire *f*, domaine d'attributions *m*, juridiction *f*, zone de responsabilité *f*, compétence *f*;

~ dispute HRM conflit de compétence *m*; ♦ **come under the ~ of** ADMIN, LAW relever de la compétence de, relever de la juridiction de

jurisdictional: **~ strike** *n* HRM grève provoquée par un conflit d'attributions syndicales

jurisprudence *n* LAW droit *m*, jurisprudence *f*

jury *n* LAW jury *m*, LEIS *theatre* public de la première *m*; **~ of executive opinion** MATH *statistics* jury d'opinion exécutive *m*; **~ trial** LAW procès avec jury *m*; ♦ **have a ~ trial** LAW passer en assises, être jugé par un jury

jus disponendi *n frml* GEN COMM loi de disposition *f*

just:[1] **~ -in-time** *adj (JIT)* HRM, IND, MEDIA *delivery* juste à temps, à flux tendus *loc m*

just:[2] **~ compensation** *n* LAW, PROP indemnité juste *f*, indemnité équitable *f*; **~ -in-time production** *n (JIT)* HRM, IND production dans les délais impartis *f*, production à flux tendus *f*; **~ noticeable difference** *n* ADMIN différence à peine sensible *f*; **~ price** *n* ECON juste prix *m*; **~ wage** *n* ECON, HRM juste salaire *m*

justice *n (J)* LAW justice *f*; **~ ministry** LAW ≈ ministère de la Justice *m*; **~ of the peace** *(JP)* HRM juge d'instance *m*, juge de paix *m*; ♦ **get ~** LAW obtenir gain de cause

justices *n pl (JJ)* LAW justices *f pl*

justifiable *adj* GEN COMM justifiable, LAW légitime

justification *n* COMP, GEN COMM justification *f*

justified[1] *adj* COMMS, COMP justifié, GEN COMM *reason* fondé, justifié; ♦ **be ~ in doing** LAW être en droit de faire, être fondé à faire

justified:[2] **~ price** *n* STOCK cours justifié *m*, prix justifié *m*

justify *vt* COMMS, COMP *text* justifier

JV *abbr (joint venture)* ACC coentreprise *f*, ECON coentreprise *f*, joint-venture *m*, GEN COMM joint-venture *m*, société en participation *f*, société mixte *f*, *action* coentreprise *f*, opération conjointe *f*, MGMNT *action* action concertée *f*, coentreprise *f*, *company* entreprise conjointe *f*, société d'exploitation en commun *f*, STOCK *action* coentreprise *f*, *company* entreprise en participation *f*

JWP *abbr (joint working party)* HRM groupe de travail paritaire *m*

K

K *abbr* ECON *BrE (knighthood)*, POL *(knighthood)* titre de chevalier *m*

Kabul *pr n* GEN COMM Kaboul *n pr*

kaffir: **~ circus** *n jarg* STOCK courtiers spécialisés en valeurs d'Afrique du Sud

Kaldor-Hicks': **~ compensation principle** *n* ECON principe de compensation de Kaldor-Hicks *m*

Kampala *pr n* GEN COMM Kampala *n pr*

kangaroo: **~ crane** *n* TRANSP *cargo handling equipment* grue kangourou *f*; **~ ticket** *n infrml US* POL liste kangourou *f*

Kansas: **~ city board of trade** *n (KCBT)* STOCK marché boursier de Kansas City *m*

Kathmandu *pr n* GEN COMM Katmandu *n pr*

Kazak¹ *adj* GEN COMM kazakh

Kazak² *n* GEN COMM *person* Kazakh *mf*

Kazakh¹ *adj* GEN COMM kazakh

Kazakh² *n* GEN COMM *person* Kazakh *mf*

Kazakhstan *pr n* GEN COMM Kazakhstan *m*

kb *abbr (kilobyte)* COMP ko *(kilo-octet)*

KBS *abbr (knowledge-based system)* COMP système expert *m*

KC *abbr* GEN COMM *(kilogram per square centimeter AmE, kilogramme per square centimetre BrE)* kilogramme au centimètre carré *m*, HRM, LAW *UK (King's Counsel)* avocat de la Couronne, ≈ bâtonnier de l'ordre *m*

KCBT *abbr (Kansas city board of trade)* STOCK marché boursier de Kansas City *m*

keep *vt* COMP *file* conserver, GEN COMM garder; **~ down** ECON *inflation* contenir; **~ up with** GEN COMM *competitor* se maintenir au même niveau que, *developments* se tenir au courant de, *payments* être à jour de *loc m, standards* maintenir

keeping: **in ~ with** *phr* GEN COMM en accord avec *loc m*

keg *n* TRANSP barillet *m*, tonnelet *m*

keiretsu *n* GEN COMM *diagram, chart of company hierarchy* keiretsu *f*

Kenya *pr n* GEN COMM Kenya *m*

Kenyan¹ *adj* GEN COMM kényen

Kenyan² *n* GEN COMM *person* Kényen *m*

kerb: **~ market** *n (SYN unlisted market)* STOCK marché hors bourse *m*, second marché *m*; **~ weight** *n* TRANSP *of motor vehicle* poids en ordre de marche *m*

ketch *n* TRANSP *sailing vessel* ketch *m*

key¹ *n* COMP clé *f*, clé d'accès *f*, *on keyboard* touche *f*; **~ currency** *n* ECON, FIN devise clé *f*, monnaie clé *f*; **~ data** *n pl* GEN COMM données clés *f pl*; **~ feature** *n* GEN COMM caractéristique clé *f*; **~ industry** *n* IND industrie clé *f*, industrie princi-

pale *f*; **~ issue** *n* GEN COMM question clé *f*; **~ money** *n* PROP *for rented apartment* pas de porte *m*, reprise *f*; **~ person life and health insurance** *n US* INS assurance société de vie et de maladie *f*; **~ point** *n* GEN COMM point essentiel *m*; **~ rate** *n* ECON, FIN *interest rates* taux directeur *m, wage* taux de salaire de référence *m*; **~ sequence** *n* COMP séquence de touches *f*; **~ stage** *n* GEN COMM *in process* phase clé *f*; **~ telephone set** *n* COMMS téléphone à poussoirs *m (Can)*, téléphone à touches *m*; **~ word** *n* COMP, GEN COMM mot clé *m*

key² *vt* COMP *data, text* entrer, saisir; **~ in** COMP *data, text* entrer, saisir

keyboard:¹ **~ -operated** *adj* COMP commandé par clavier

keyboard² *n* COMP clavier *m*; **~ equivalent** COMP équivalent clavier *m*; **~ operator** COMP claviste *mf*; **~ shortcut** COMP raccourci clavier *m*

keyboarder *n* COMP claviste *mf*

keyhole: **~ socket** *n* TRANSP *container securing* insert de pont *m*

keylock *n* COMP verrou de sécurité *m*

Keynes': **~ effect** *n* ECON effet Keynes *m*; **~ expectations** *n pl* ECON anticipations keynésiennes *f pl*; **~ General Theory** *n* ECON théorie générale de Keynes *f*; **~ Plan** *n* ECON plan de Keynes *m*

Keynesian¹ *adj* ECON keynésien

Keynesian:² **~ cross diagram** *n* ECON diagramme croisé de Keynes *m*; **~ economics** *n* ECON, POL keynésianisme *m*; **~ equilibrium** *n* ECON équilibre keynésien *m*; **~ multiplier** *n* ECON *econometrics* multiplicateur de Keynes *m*; **~ policy** *n* ECON, POL politique keynésienne *f*

Keynesianism *n* ECON, POL keynésianisme *m*

keypad *n* COMP clavier *m*, pavé de touches *m*, pavé numérique *m*

keypunch *n* COMP perforatrice à clavier *f*

keypuncher *n* COMP perforatrice *f*

keystone *n* ECON *of economy* clé de voûte *f*, pilier *m*

keystroke *n* COMP frappe d'une touche *f*; **~ rate** ADMIN, COMP cadence de frappe *f*

keyword: **~ search** *n* COMP recherche par mot clé *f*

kg *abbr (kilogram, kilogramme)* GEN COMM kg *(kilogramme)*

Khartoum *pr n* GEN COMM Khartoum *n pr*

Khmer *n* GEN COMM *language* khmer *m*

kickback *n* FIN dessous-de-table *m*, pot-de-vin *m*, ristourne *f*, GEN COMM dessous-de-table *m*, HRM commission clandestine *f*, dessous-de-table *m*, pot-de-vin *m*, LAW dessous-de-table *m*, pot-de-vin *m*, POL commission clandestine *f*, dessous-de-table *m*, pot-de-vin *m*, S&M dessous-de-table *m*

kicker *n infrml US* FIN incitant *m*

kidnap: ~ **insurance** *n* INS assurance contre l'enlèvement *f*

Kiev *pr n* GEN COMM Kiev *n pr*

Kigali *pr n* GEN COMM Kigali *n pr*

kill *vt* S&M tuer

killer: ~ **bees** *n pl* FIN abeilles à gros rapport *f pl*; ~ **bond** *n* STOCK obligation rapportant gros *f*

killing *n infrml* STOCK bénéfice énorme *m*, gros bénéfice *m*; ◆ **make a** ~ *infrml* FIN faire un bénéfice énorme, faire un gros bénéfice, GEN COMM s'en mettre plein les poches (*infrml*), se remplir les poches

kilo *n* (*kilogram, kilogramme*) GEN COMM kilo *m* (*kilogramme*)

kilobyte *n* (*kb*) COMP kilo-octet *m* (*ko*)

kilogram *n AmE see* kilogramme *BrE*

kilogramme *n BrE* (*kg, kilo*) GEN COMM kilogramme *m* (*kg*); ~ **per square centimetre** *BrE* (*KC*) GEN COMM kilogramme au centimètre carré *m*

kiloliter *n AmE*, **kilolitre** *n BrE* (*kl*) GEN COMM kilolitre *m* (*kl*)

kilometer *n AmE see* kilometre *BrE*

kilometers: ~ **per hour** *n pl AmE see* kilometres per hour *BrE*

kilometre *n BrE* (*km*) GEN COMM kilomètre *m* (*km*)

kilometres: ~ **per hour** *n pl BrE* (*km/h*) GEN COMM kilomètre/heure *m* (*km/h*)

kiloton *n* (*kt*) GEN COMM kilotonne *f* (*kt*)

kilowatt *n* (*kW*) GEN COMM kilowatt *m* (*kW*); ~ **-hour** (*kWh*) GEN COMM kilowatt-heure *m* (*kWh*)

kina *n* GEN COMM kina *m*

kind: **in** ~ *phr* GEN COMM *benefit, payment* en nature *loc f*

king: ~ **post** *n* TRANSP mâtereau *m*

King's: ~ **Counsel** *n UK* (*KC*) HRM, LAW avocat de la Couronne, ≈ bâtonnier de l'ordre *m*; ~ **enemies** *n pl UK* LAW ennemis de la Couronne *m pl*, ennemis du Roi *m pl*; ~ **warehouse** *n* IMP/EXP entrepôt des domaines *m*

Kingston *pr n* GEN COMM Kingston *n pr*

Kingstown *pr n* GEN COMM Kingstown *n pr*

kinked: ~ **demand curve** *n* ECON courbe de demande coudée *f*

Kinshasa *pr n* GEN COMM Kinshasa *n pr*

kip *n* GEN COMM kip *m*

Kishinev *pr n* GEN COMM Kichinev *n pr*

kite[1] *n infrml* LAW avocat commis d'office *m*, STOCK billet de complaisance *m*, cerf-volant *m*, traite en l'air *f* (*infrml*)

kite[2] *vi* STOCK faire monter les taux artificiellement *loc m*, manipuler les cours à la hausse

kiting *n* BANK tirage en l'air *m*, tirage à découvert *m*

kl *abbr* (*kiloliter, kilolitre*) GEN COMM kl (*kilolitre*)

km *abbr* (*kilometer, kilometre*) GEN COMM km (*kilomètre*)

km/h *abbr* (*kilometers per hour, kilometres per hour*) GEN COMM km/h (*kilomètre/heure*)

kneeling *n* TRANSP *road vehicle* agenouillement *m*, baraquage *m*

knighthood *n BrE* (*K*) ECON, POL titre de chevalier *m*

knob *n* COMP bouton *m*

knock:[1] ~ **-for-knock** *adj* INS mutuel, à torts partagés

knock[2] *n* GEN COMM *low price* prix défiant toute concurrence *m, misfortune* coup *m*; ~ **-for-knock agreement** INS *following an accident* exonération mutuelle *f*; ~ **-on effect** GEN COMM réaction en chaîne *f*

knock:[3] **1.** *vt* ~ **down** GEN COMM *goods at auction* adjuger, *price* baisser; **2.** *vi* ~ **off** *infrml* GEN COMM *stop work* finir le travail, HRM cesser le travail

knockdown: ~ **price** *n* GEN COMM prix réduit *m*

knocker *n infrml* S&M *sales* démarcheur *m*

knockoffs *n pl infrml* IND *fashion industry* articles démarqués *m pl*

knockout *n* FIN, S&M entente illicite entre enchérisseurs *f*; ~ **agreement** FIN, S&M entente illicite entre enchérisseurs *f*; ~ **axle** TRANSP *of road trailer* axe d'éjection *m*; ~ **competition** GEN COMM compétition avec épreuves éliminatoires *f*

knot *n* GEN COMM noeud *m*

know:[1] ~ **-how** *n infrml* GEN COMM, PATENTS savoir-faire *m*; ~ **-how agreement** *n* LAW accord de savoir-faire *m*, contrat de savoir-faire *m*, PATENTS *intellectual property* contrat de savoir-faire *m*; ◆ **in the** ~ **about** *infrml* GEN COMM au courant de

know[2] *vt* GEN COMM *knowledge generally* savoir, *person, fact, information* connaître, savoir; ◆ ~ **your customer** STOCK bien connaître son client

knowledge:[1] ~ **-intensive** *adj* GEN COMM à forte intensité de connaissances *loc f*

knowledge[2] *n* GEN COMM acquis *m*, connaissance *f*; ~ **base** WEL *social work* base de connaissance *f*; ~ **-based industry** IND industrie basée sur la connaissance *f*, industrie basée sur le savoir *f*; ~ **-based system** (*KBS*) COMP système expert *m*; ◆ **have a working** ~ **of** WEL avoir de bonnes connaissances de

knowledgeable *adj* GEN COMM bien informé

known[1] *adj* GEN COMM connu; **not** ~ GEN COMM inconnu; ◆ ~ **by name** GEN COMM connu de nom

known:[2] ~ **loss** *n* INS dommages connus *m pl*

Korean[1] *adj* GEN COMM coréen

Korean[2] *n* GEN COMM *language* coréen *m, person* Coréen *m*

koruna *n* GEN COMM koruna *f*

krona *n* GEN COMM krona *f*

krone *n* GEN COMM krone *f*

Krugerrand *n* ECON krugerrand *m*

kt *abbr (kiloton)* GEN COMM kt *(kilotonne)*

Kuala: ~ **Lumpur** *pr n* GEN COMM Kuala Lumpur *n pr*

kudos *n* GEN COMM gloire *f*

kuna *n* GEN COMM kuna *m*

kurtosis *n* MATH *statistics* kurtose *m*

Kuwait *pr n* GEN COMM Koweït *m*; ~ **City** GEN COMM Koweït City *n pr*

Kuwaiti[1] *adj* GEN COMM koweïtien

Kuwaiti[2] *n* GEN COMM *person* Koweïtien *m*

kW *abbr (kilowatt)* GEN COMM kW *(kilowatt)*

kwacha *n* GEN COMM kwancha *m*

kwanza *n* GEN COMM kwanza *m*

kWh *abbr (kilowatt-hour)* GEN COMM kWh *(kilowatt-heure)*

kyat *n* GEN COMM kyat *m*

Kyrgyzstan *pr n* GEN COMM Kyrghyzstan *m*

L

l *abbr (liter, litre)* GEN COMM l *(litre)*

L/A *abbr* GEN COMM *(letter of authority)* lettre d'autorité *f*, TRANSP *(Lloyd's Agent) shipping* agent de la Lloyds *m*, TRANSP *(landing account) shipping* frais de débarquement *m pl*, frais de mise à terre *m pl*

lab *n* IND laboratoire *m*

LAB *abbr* STOCK *(local authority bill, local authority bond)* loi sur les administrations locales *f*, obligation d'administration locale ou régionale *f*, TRANSP *(live animals on board)* animaux vivants à bord

label *n* COMP label *m*, référence *f*, étiquette *f*, GEN COMM vignette *f*, étiquette *f*, MEDIA label *m*, maison de disque *f*, S&M label *m*, marque *f*, étiquette *f, of designer* griffe *f*, TRANSP *on luggage* étiquette *f*; **~ clause** *(lc)* GEN COMM préambule *m*

labeled: ~ file *n AmE see* labelled file *BrE*

labeling *n AmE see* labelling *BrE*

labelled: ~ file *n BrE* COMP fichier avec labels *m*

labelling *n BrE* S&M étiquetage *m*; **~ laws** *n pl BrE* LAW lois relatives à l'étiquetage *f pl*

labor:[1] **~ -intensive** *adj AmE see* labour-intensive *BrE*; **~ -saving** *adj AmE see* labour-saving *BrE*

labor[2] *n AmE see* labour *BrE*

labor[3] *vi AmE see* labour *BrE*

Labor: ~ Management Relations Act *n US* LAW *1947* loi sur les rapports patrons-ouvriers *f*; **~ Management Reporting and Disclosure Act** *n US* HRM *1959* loi sur la publicité de l'information en matière de rapports patronaux

laboratory *n* IND laboratoire *m*; **~ techniques** *n pl jarg* S&M *marketing* techniques de laboratoire *f pl*

laborer *n AmE see* labourer *BrE*

laboring: the ~ class *n AmE see* the labouring class *BrE*

labour:[1] **~ -intensive** *adj BrE* ECON *sector*, HRM, IND *sector* travaillistique, à fort coefficient de main-d'oeuvre, à forte intensité de main-d'oeuvre *loc f*; **~ -saving** *adj BrE* HRM qui allège le travail, qui facilite le travail *loc m*

labour[2] *n BrE* ECON main-d'oeuvre *f*, HRM, IND *workers* main-d'oeuvre *f, work* travail *m*; **~ administration** *n BrE* ADMIN direction du travail et de l'emploi *f*; **~ agreement** *n BrE* HRM, IND, LAW accord patronat-syndicats *m*, cc, convention collective *f*; **~ -augmenting technical progress** *n BrE* ECON progrès technique facteur d'accroissement de la main d'oeuvre *m*; **~ clause** *n BrE* HRM clause concernant les salariés *f*; **~ contract** *n BrE* GEN COMM contrat de travail *m*; **~ cost** *n BrE* ECON, HRM, TAX coût de main-d'oeuvre *m*, coût salarial *m*; **~ court** *n BrE* HRM cour du travail *f*, tribunal du travail *m*, ≈ Conseil des prud'hommes *m*, IND ≈ Conseil des prud'hommes *m*, LAW cour du travail *f*, tribunal du travail *m*, ≈ Conseil des prud'hommes *m*; **~ demand** *n BrE* ECON, HRM demande de main-d'oeuvre *f*; **~ dispute** *n BrE* ECON, HRM conflit du travail *m*; **~ disutility theory** *n BrE* ECON théorie de la désutilité de la main-d'oeuvre *f*; **~ exchange** *n* GEN COMM, HRM bourse du travail *f*; **~ force** *n BrE* ECON population active *f, within a firm* effectif *m*, main-d'oeuvre *f*, HRM *within a firm* effectif *m*, main-d'oeuvre *f*, IND main-d'oeuvre *f*, population active *f*; **~ force participation rate** *n BrE (LFPR)* HRM intéressement du personnel *m*, participation de la main d'oeuvre *f*; **~ force recruitment** *n BrE* ECON, HRM zone de recrutement de la main-d'oeuvre *f*; **~ inspector** *n BrE* IND inspecteur du travail *m*; **~ intensive** *n BrE* ECON, HRM consommateur de main-d'oeuvre non-capitalistique *m*; **~ -intensive economy** *n BrE* ECON économie de main-d'oeuvre *f*; **~ -intensive industry** *n BrE* HRM, IND secteur à fort coût de main-d'oeuvre *m*; **~ law** *n BrE* HRM, LAW, POL droit du travail *m*, droit social *m*; **~ laws** *n pl BrE* HRM législation du travail *f*; **~ market** *n BrE* ECON, HRM marché de l'emploi *m*, marché du travail *m*; **~ market policy** *n BrE* POL politique de l'emploi *f*; **~ market rigidities** *n pl BrE* ECON, HRM rigidité des salaires *f*; **~ mobility** *n BrE* ECON, HRM mobilité de la main-d'oeuvre *f*; **~ movement** *n BrE* HRM mouvement ouvrier *m*; **~ -only subcontracting** *n BrE* HRM limitations de sous-traitance aux salariés *f pl*; **~ piracy** *n BrE* HRM détournement de main-d'oeuvre *m*; **~ pool** *n BrE* ECON, HRM bassin d'emploi *m*, réserve de main-d'oeuvre *f*; **~ power** *n BrE* HRM capital humain *m*, matériel humain *m*; **~ process theory** *n BrE* HRM théorie de l'analyse préalable de la main-d'oeuvre *f*; **~ relations** *n pl BrE* HRM relations ouvrières *f pl*, relations sociales *f pl*; **~ shed** *n jarg BrE* ECON, HRM bassin d'emploi *m*, zone de recrutement de la main-d'oeuvre *f*; **~ shedding** *n BrE* HRM dégraissage de main-d'oeuvre *m*; **~ shortage** *n BrE* HRM pénurie de main-d'oeuvre *f*; **~ supply** *n BrE* ECON offre de main-d'oeuvre *f*; **~ theory of value** *n BrE* ECON théorie de la valeur travail *f*; **~ troubles** *n pl BrE* HRM problèmes sociaux *m pl*; **~ turnover** *n BrE* ECON, HRM mutation de personnel *f*, rotation du personnel *f*; **~ unrest** *n BrE* HRM malaise social *m*; **~'s share of national income** *n BrE* ECON part du revenu national qui revient à la main d'oeuvre *f*

labour[3] *vi BrE* HRM oeuvrer, travailler dur

Labour: ~ Party *n UK* POL Parti travailliste *m*; **~ Relations Agency** *n UK (LRA)* HRM, IND, LAW ≈ Conseil des prud'hommes *m*; **~ Representa-**

tion Committee n (*LRC*) HRM caisse de financement des députés du monde ouvrier *f*

labourer n *BrE* HRM manoeuvre *m*

labouring: the ~ class n *BrE* (SYN *the working class*) ECON, POL la classe ouvrière *f*

LAC *abbr* (*Lights Advisory Committee*) GEN COMM comité consultatif des phares et balises

laches n pl LAW négligence *f*, négligence coupable *f*

lack:[1] **~ of raw material** n ENVIR pénurie de matières premières *f*

lack[2] vi GEN COMM *confidence, support* manquer de; ◆ **~ consistency** GEN COMM manquer de cohérence; **~ experience** HRM manquer d'expérience

lacking: be ~ in *phr* GEN COMM manquer de; **be ~ in consistency** *phr* GEN COMM manquer de cohérence

ladder: ~ of participation n *jarg* POL échelle de participation *f*

lade vt TRANSP charger

laden: ~ in bulk *phr* TRANSP chargé en vrac

ladies n pl *frml* GEN COMM Mesdames *f pl*, Mesdemoiselles *f pl*; **~ and gentlemen** *frml* GEN COMM *form of address* Mesdames et Messieurs *m pl*

lading n TRANSP chargement *m*, mise à bord *f*; **~ port** TRANSP port d'embarquement *m*, port de chargement *m*

Laffer: ~ curve n ECON courbe de Laffer *f*

lag[1] n ECON, GEN COMM décalage *m*, délai de réaction *m*, temps de réponse *m*; **~ response** ECON, GEN COMM décalage *m*, délai de réaction *m*, temps de réponse *m*; **~ risk** BANK risque de retard *m*

lag:[2] **1.** vt GEN COMM traîner derrière, être en retard sur *loc m*, S&M *competitor* être en retard sur *loc m*; **2.** vi **~ behind** GEN COMM être à la traîne

lagan n TRANSP épave marquée par une bouée *f*

laggard n S&M *marketing* conservateur *m*, STOCK trainard *f* (*infrml*)

lagged: ~ variable n MATH variable décalée *f*

lagging: ~ indicator n (ANT *leading indicator*) ECON *econometrics* indicateur retardé d'activité *m*

Lagos pr n GEN COMM Lagos *n pr*

LAIA *abbr* (*Latin American Integration Association*) ECON zone de libre-échange latino-américaine *f*

laid:[1] **~ -up** *adj* GEN COMM *ship, car* mis en réserve, TRANSP *shipping* désarmé

laid:[2] **~ -up tonnage** n TRANSP navires désarmés *m pl*

laissez: ~ -faire n ECON, POL laisser-faire *m*; **~ -faire economy** n ECON, POL libéralisme économique *m*, économie de laissez-faire *f*

lambs n pl *infrml* STOCK boursiers néophytes *m pl*, moutons *m pl*

lame: ~ duck n GEN COMM *company*, STOCK canard boiteux *m* (*infrml*)

LAN *abbr* (*local area network*) COMP RLE (*réseau local d'entreprise*)

LANBY *abbr* (*large automatic navigational buoy*) TRANSP *shipping* balise automatique LANBY *f*

land n ECON, ENVIR, PROP terre *f*; **~ act** LAW loi relative à l'évaluation des indemnités d'expropriation; **~ bank** BANK, FIN, PROP crédit foncier *m*; **~ banking** BANK, FIN, PROP opération bancaire de terre *f*; **~ carriage** TRANSP transport par terre *m*, transport terrestre *m*; **~ certificate** GEN COMM, LAW, PROP certificat de propriété *m*; **~ compensation code** PROP code de compensation foncière *m*; **~ contract** LAW, PROP contrat foncier *m*; **~ degradation** ENVIR dégradation des sols *f*; **~ developer** ENVIR, GEN COMM, PROP promoteur *m*; **~ development** ENVIR, PROP viabilisation foncière *f*; **~ economy** ECON économie de l'occupation des sols *f*; **~ improvement** ENVIR, PROP viabilisation *f*, viabilisation de terrain *f*; **~ in abeyance** LAW terres en jachère *f pl*, PROP biens jacents *m pl*; **~ lease** PROP location foncière *f*; **~ office** ADMIN administration des domaines *f*; **~ ownership** ECON, ENVIR propriété foncière *f*; **~ reform** ECON, ENVIR *agricultural* réforme agraire *f*; **~ register** *BrE* (*cf cadastre, real estate register AmE*) TAX cadastre *m*; **~ registration** LAW, PROP inscription au cadastre *f*, inscription au registre foncier *f*; **~ registry** LAW, PROP bureau du cadastre *m*, registre foncier *m*, TAX *BrE* (*cf real estate registry AmE*) cadastre *m*; **~ rent** FIN, LAW, PROP revenu foncier *m*; **~ trust** LAW, PROP acte foncier en matière de propriété foncière; **~ use** ENVIR *local level* occupation des sols *f*; **~ -use intensity** ENVIR intensité de l'utilisation des sols *f*; **~ -use planning** ECON, ENVIR, WEL aménagement du territoire *m*, plan d'occupation des sols *m*; **~ -use regulation** LAW, PROP réglementation foncière *f*; **~ -use succession** PROP succession d'utilisation des sols *f*; **~ -value tax** TAX impôt sur la valeur cadastrale *m*; ◆ **~, tenements, and hereditaments** LAW, PROP propriété foncière, habitations et biens immobiliers hérités

landbridge n TRANSP pont terrestre *m*; **~ rate** TRANSP tarif pont terrestre *m*

landed: ~ cost n IMP/EXP, TRANSP prix à quai *m*; **~ property** n PROP bien-fonds *m*; **~ terms** n pl IMP/EXP, TRANSP franco déchargement

landfill n ENVIR site de décharge *m*; **~ site** ENVIR décharge contrôlée *f*, site de décharge contrôlée *m*

landing n TRANSP atterrissage *m*, mise à terre *f*; **~ account** (*L/A*) TRANSP frais de débarquement *m pl*, frais de mise à terre *m pl*; **~ card** TRANSP carte de débarquement *f*; **~ certificate** TRANSP certificat de débarquement *m*; **~ charge** TRANSP frais de débarquement *m pl*, frais de mise à terre *m pl*; **~ and delivering** TRANSP *of cargo* déchargement et livraison *f*; **~ gear** TRANSP *on trailer* béquille *f*; **~ officer** *UK* HRM, TRANSP *shipping* employé de débarquement *m*; **~ order** TRANSP autorisation de déchargement *f*; **~ permit** TRANSP permis de débarquement *m*; **~ stage** TRANSP débarcadère *m*, quai de déchargement *m*; ◆ ~ **storage delivery** *(LSD)* IMP/EXP, TRANSP mise à terre, magasinage et livraison

landlocked *adj* ENVIR enfermé dans les terres, sans accès à la mer, PROP enclavé, sans littoral

landlord *n* PROP, WEL propriétaire *mf*

landmark *n* GEN COMM point de repère *m*, repère *m*, LAW *case* borne *f*, point de repère *m*, repère *m*

landowner *n* PROP propriétaire terrien *m*

landscape[1] *adj* COMP, GEN COMM, MEDIA *document layout* à l'italienne

landscape:[2] ~ **format** *n* COMP, GEN COMM, MEDIA format horizontal *m*, format à l'italienne *m*, présentation à l'italienne *f*; ~ **mode** *n* COMP, MEDIA format horizontal *m*, format à l'italienne *m*, présentation à l'italienne *f*; ~ **page** *n* MEDIA page à l'italienne *f*

landscape[3] *vt* ENVIR *wasteland*, PROP *office* aménager

lane *n* TRANSP voie *f*

language *n* COMP, S&M *advertising* langage *m*; ~ **arts** *n pl jarg* WEL arts du langage *m pl*; ◆ **in plain** ~ GEN COMM en clair

Lao *n* GEN COMM *language* laotien *m*

Laos *pr n* GEN COMM Laos *m*

Laotian[1] *adj* GEN COMM laotien

Laotian[2] *n* GEN COMM *person* Laotien *m*

La Paz *pr n* GEN COMM La Paz *n pr*

lapse *n* INS *policy termination* abandon *m*, déchéance *f*, LAW *of contract* expiration *f*, *of legal right* déchéance *f*; ~ **of time** GEN COMM laps de temps *m*

lapsed: ~ **funds** *n pl* ACC fonds périmés *m pl*; ~ **option** *n* STOCK option expirée *f*, option à échéance dépassée *f*

lapsing *n* ACC péremption prévue *f*; ~ **appropriation** ACC annulation de crédits *f*; ~ **resources** ACC *governmental accounting* expiration d'affectation *f*; ~ **schedule** ACC *balance sheets* calendrier d'expirations *m*

laptop[1] *adj* COMP portable

laptop[2] *n* COMP portable *m*; ~ **computer** COMP ordinateur portable *m*

larceny *n* LAW vol *m*

large[1] *adj* ECON, GEN COMM *purchase* grand, gros, important; **in** ~ **quantities** GEN COMM en grandes quantités; ~ **-scale** ECON, GEN COMM *project* grand, gros, important, à grande échelle; ◆ **on a** ~ **scale** GEN COMM sur une grande échelle; **to a** ~ **extent** GEN COMM en grande partie; **very** ~ **-scale** *(VLS)* ECON, GEN COMM à très grande échelle

large:[2] ~ **automatic navigational buoy** *n (LANBY)* TRANSP balise automatique LANBY *f*; ~ **display advertisement** *n* MEDIA, S&M placard publicitaire *m*; ~ **employer** *n* HRM gros employeur *m*; ~ **exposure** *n* FIN grand risque *m*; ~ **order** *n* GEN COMM, S&M commande importante *f*; ~ **producer** *n* ECON, IND gros producteur *m*; ~ **quantity** *n* GEN COMM grosse quantité *f*; ~ **risk** *n* INS risque considérable *m*, risque important *m*; ~ **-scale exporter** *n* ECON, IMP/EXP, S&M gros exportateur *m*; ~ **-scale farming** *n* ECON, IND *agricultural* exploitation à grande échelle *f*; ~ **-scale importer** *n* ECON, IMP/EXP, S&M gros importateur *m*; ~ **-scale industry** *n* IND grande industrie *f*; ~ **-scale model** *n* ECON *econometrics* macromodèle économique *m*; ~ **-scale production** *n* IND production à grande échelle *f*; **very** ~ **crude carrier** *n (VLCC)* TRANSP *shipping* très gros transporteur de brut *m*

largely *adv* GEN COMM en grande partie

larger *adj* GEN COMM plus grand

largest: **the** ~ **investors** *n pl* STOCK les investisseurs les plus importants *m pl*, les plus gros investisseurs *m pl*

laser: ~ **banking** *n* BANK opérations bancaires laser *f pl*; ~ **beam** *n* IND rayon laser *m*; ~ **printer** *n* ADMIN *office equipment*, COMP imprimante à laser *f*; ~ **scanner** *n* COMP, MEDIA *print* lecteur laser *m*

LASH *abbr (lighter aboard ship)* TRANSP *shipping* navire porte-barges *m*, porte-barges *m*

lasher *n* HRM, TRANSP employé du lamanage *m*, gréeur *m*, lamaneur *m*, saisisseur *m*

lashing *n* TRANSP saisissage *m*; ~ **cage** TRANSP boîtier d'amarrage *m*; ~ **eye** TRANSP anneau de saisissage *m*; ~ **plate** TRANSP plaque d'accrochage de saisine *f*; ~ **point** TRANSP point fixe du saisissage *m*; ~ **pot** TRANSP crapaudine pour saisissage *f*

Laspeyres: ~ **index** *n* ECON *econometrics, retail price index* indice de Laspeyre *m*

last[1] *adj* GEN COMM dernier; ~ **-minute** GEN COMM de dernière minute; ◆ **as a** ~ **resort** GEN COMM en dernier ressort; ~ **in, first out** *(LIFO)* ACC *evaluation of stock*, HRM dernier entré, premier sorti *(DEPS)*; **in** ~ **position** GEN COMM à la dernière place

last:[2] ~ **carrier** *n* TRANSP dernier transporteur *m*; ~ **-day hours** *n pl* STOCK heures du dernier jour *f pl*; ~ **day of trading** *n* STOCK dernier jour de transaction *m*; ~ **half** *n (lh)* GEN COMM *of month* dernière quinzaine *f*; ~ **in, first out price** *n* STOCK *portfolio theory* dernier prix en premier *m*, prix dernier entré, premier sorti *m*; ~ **-minute decision** *n* GEN COMM décision de dernière minute *f*; ~ **notice day** *n (ANT first notice day)* FIN dernier jour de notification *m*; ~ **-offer arbitration** *n* HRM arbitrage de la dernière chance *m*; ~ **resort** *n* GEN COMM dernier ressort *m*; ~ **sale** *n* STOCK dernière mise en vente *f*; ~ **trading day** *n* STOCK dernier jour de cotation *m*, dernier jour de transaction *m*; ~ **will and testament** *n* LAW dernières volontés *f pl*

last[3] *vi* GEN COMM durer, perdurer, tenir

lat. *abbr (latitude)* GEN COMM lat. *(latitude)*

LATAG *abbr (Latin American Trade Advisory Group)* GEN COMM Comité consultatif latino-américain des échanges commerciaux *m*

late: ~ **capitalism** *n* ECON néo-capitalisme *m*; ~ **delivery** *n* GEN COMM livraison tardive *f*; ~ **filer** *n* TAX déclarant retardataire *m*; ~ **filing** *n* TAX *of returns* production tardive *f*; ~ **fringe** *n* *jarg US* MEDIA *broadcast* créneau après les heures de grande écoute *m*, tranche horaire de fin de soirée *f*; ~ **majority** *n jarg* S&M *marketing* majorité tardive *f*; ~ **night** *n* MEDIA *broadcast* créneau après les heures de grande écoute *m*, tranche de la nuit *f*; ~ -**night opening** *n* GEN COMM ouverture en nocturne *f*; ~ **payment** *n* FIN paiement tardif *m*; ~ **tape** *n* STOCK bande tardive *f*, téléscripteur en retard *m*

lateness *n* HRM arrivée tardive *f*

latent: ~ **defect** *n* LAW, PROP défaut caché *m*, vice caché *m*

later *adj* GEN COMM ultérieur

lateral[1] *adj* GEN COMM *movement* latéral

lateral:[2] ~ **integration** *n* ECON, GEN COMM, IND intégration horizontale *f*, intégration latérale *f*; ~ **thinking** *n* COMMS, GEN COMM, MGMNT pensée latérale *f*

latest[1] *adj* S&M *developments* dernier; ◆ **at the** ~ GEN COMM au plus tard, dernier délai *m*

latest:[2] ~ **addition** *n* GEN COMM *to product range* dernier-né *m*; ~ **date** *n* GEN COMM date limite *f*; ~ **estimate** *n* (*L/E*) GEN COMM devis le plus récent *m*; **the** ~ **fashion** *n* GEN COMM la dernière mode *f*

latex *n* IND latex *m*

Latin: ~ **American Free Trade Association** *n obs* ECON maintenant Latin American Integration Association, zone de libre-échange latino-américaine *f*; ~ **American Integration Association** *n* (*LAIA*) ECON zone de libre-échange latino-américaine *f*; ~ **American Trade Advisory Group** *n* (*LATAG*) GEN COMM Comité consultatif latino-américain des échanges commerciaux *m*

latitude *n* (*lat.*) GEN COMM latitude *f* (*lat.*)

latter *adj* GEN COMM dernier *m*

lattice: ~ -**sided container** *n* TRANSP conteneur en treillis *m*, conteneur à claire-voie *m*

Latvia *pr n* GEN COMM Lettonie *f*

Latvian[1] *adj* GEN COMM letton

Latvian[2] *n* GEN COMM *language* letton *m*, *person* Letton *m*

launch[1] *n* MEDIA, S&M, TRANSP lancement *m*; ~ **party** MEDIA *for book* pot de lancement *m* (*infrml*), réception organisée pour le lancement d'un livre *f*

launch[2] *vt* FIN *shares* émettre, GEN COMM créer, S&M *product* lancer, lancer sur le marché, STOCK *shares* émettre, TRANSP *shipping* lancer, mettre à l'eau; ◆ ~ **an appeal** GEN COMM *to public* lancer un appel; ~ **a bond issue** STOCK émettre des obligations; ~ **a national campaign** S&M *advertising* lancer une campagne nationale; ~ **on the market** S&M lancer sur le marché; ~ **a takeover bid for a company** GEN COMM lancer une OPA contre une société

launching *n* MEDIA, S&M lancement *m*

launder *vt* FIN, GEN COMM *money* blanchir

laundering *n* GEN COMM *of money* blanchiment *m*, blanchissement *m*; ~ **money** BANK blanchissement de l'argent *m*

laundry: ~ **list** *n jarg US* POL liste détaillée des priorités

Lautro *n* UK (*Life Assurance and Unit Trust Regulatory Organization*) FIN organisme régulateur des assurances-vie et des SICAV *m*

lavatory *n* BrE (*cf rest room AmE, toilet, washroom AmE*) GEN COMM toilettes *f pl*

law:[1] **by** ~ *adv* LAW conformément à la loi

law[2] *n* LAW *legal system* droit *m*, loi *f*; ~ **of comparative advantage** ECON *international trade* loi de l'avantage comparatif *f*; ~ **of diminishing marginal utility** ECON loi de l'utilité marginale décroissante *f*; ~ **firm** LAW bureau d'avocats *m*, cabinet d'avocats *m*, cabinet juridique *m*, société de conseil juridique *f*, étude d'avocats *f*; ~ **of the flag** GEN COMM, LAW loi du pavillon *f*; ~ **of increasing costs** ECON, FIN loi des coûts croissants *f*; ~ **of large numbers** MATH loi des grands nombres *f*; ~ **practice** LAW bureau d'avocats *m*, cabinet d'avocats *m*, cabinet juridique *m*; ~ **of reciprocal demand** ECON loi de la demande réciproque *f*; ~ **of reflux** (*cf Banking School UK*) ECON loi du reflux *f*; ~ **school** WEL faculté de droit *f*; ~ **suit** LAW poursuites judiciaires *f pl*, procès *m*; ~ **of supply and demand** ECON, S&M loi de l'offre et de la demande *f*; ~ **of taxation** (*SYN fiscal law*) TAX droit fiscal *m*; ~ **of value** ECON loi de la valeur *f*; ~ **of variable proportions** ECON loi des proportions variables *f*; ~ **29** *jarg* GEN COMM loi du bon sens *f*; ◆ **as the** ~ **stands at present** LAW en l'état actuel de la législation; **in the eyes of the** ~ LAW au regard de la loi, en vertu de la loi; **keep within the** ~ LAW rester dans la légalité

lawful[1] *adj* LAW légal

lawful:[2] ~ **means** *n pl* LAW moyens légaux *m pl*

lawfully *adv* LAW légalement

lawfulness *n* LAW légalité *f*

lawyer[1] *n* LAW avocat *m*

lay[1] *adj* GEN COMM *magistrate* laïque

lay:[2] ~ **members** *n pl* HRM assesseurs non juristes *m pl*; ~ -**off** *n* HRM chômage technique *m*, licenciement *m*, mise en chômage temporaire *f*, mise à pied *f*; ~ -**off pay** *n* HRM prime de licenciement *f*; ~ **official** *n* HRM *industrial relations* délégué syndical *m*; ~ -**up berth** *n* TRANSP poste de désarmement *m*; ~ -**up return** *n* INS *marine* ristourne de mise en rade *f*

lay[3] *vt* LAW *charge, accusation* porter, POL *put forward* soumettre; ~ **down** LAW *laws* imposer, stipuler, établir; ~ **off** HRM licencier, mettre en chômage technique; ◆ ~ **the basis for** GEN COMM jeter les bases de; ~ **claim to** LAW avoir des prétentions à, prétendre à, revendiquer; ~ **down the rules** ADMIN arrêter des dispositions, imposer des règles; ~ **an embargo on** GEN COMM mettre un embargo sur; ~ **the emphasis on** GEN COMM insister sur; ~ **the ground for sth** GEN COMM préparer le terrain pour qch; ~ **a proposal before a committee** GEN COMM soumettre une proposition à une commission; ~ **sth on for sb** GEN COMM préparer qch pour qn

layday *n* TRANSP jour de planche *m*, starie *f*

layer *n* COMP *network, circuitry* couche *f*

laying: ~ **off** *n* HRM licenciement *m*, mise en chômage temporaire *f*, mise à pied *f*

layout *n* ACC présentation *f*, ADMIN disposition *f*, mise en page *f*, COMP *wordprocessed document* mise en page *f*; ~ **character** COMP caractère de mise en page *m*, caractère de présentation *m*; ~ **chart** ADMIN schéma de présentation typographique d'une lettre *m*

laytime *n* TRANSP temps de planche *m*; ~ **saved** TRANSP staries gagnées *f pl*, temps de planche gagné *m*; ◆ **all ~ saved** TRANSP *shipping* estaries gagnées *f pl*

lazaretto *n* IMP/EXP lazaret *m*

lb *abbr (pound)* GEN COMM lb *(livre)*

LBO *abbr (leveraged buyout)* FIN désintéressement pour endettement *m*, GEN COMM rachat d'entreprise financé par l'endettement *m*, STOCK achat adossé *m*, achat avec effet de levier *m*, achat d'endettement *m*, prise de contrôle adossée *f*, rachat par levier *m*, rachat d'entreprise financé par l'endettement *m*

LBP *abbr (length between perpendiculars)* TRANSP *shipping* LPP *(longueur entre perpendiculaires)*

lc *abbr* FIN *(local currency)* monnaie locale *f*, GEN COMM *(label clause)* préambule *m*, IMP/EXP *(local currency)* monnaie locale *f*

l.c. *abbr (lower case)* ADMIN, COMP, MEDIA bas de casse *m*, lettre de bas de casse *f*, lettre minuscule *f*, minuscule *f (majuscule)*

L/C *abbr (letter of credit)* BANK, FIN L/C *(lettre de crédit)*

LC *abbr* GEN COMM *US (Library of Congress)* bibliothèque du Congrès, ≈ BN *(Bibliothèque Nationale)*, HRM *UK (Lord Chancellor)* ≈ ministre de la Justice *m*

LCA *abbr (life cycle assessment)* ENVIR évaluation du cycle de vie *f*

LCCI *abbr (London Chamber of Commerce & Industry)* GEN COMM Chambre de commerce et d'industrie de Londres *f*

LCD *abbr (lowest common denominator)* GEN COMM plus petit dénominateur commun *m*

LCE *abbr obs (London Commodity Exchange)* STOCK depuis 1987, the London Futures and Options Exchange, Bourse de matières premières de Londres *f*

LCH *abbr* ECON *(life-cycle hypothesis)* hypothèse du cycle de vie *f*, STOCK *(London Clearing House)* Caisse/Chambre de compensation de Londres

LCJ *abbr UK (Lord Chief Justice)* HRM ≈ président de la Haute Cour de Justice *m (France)*

LCL[1] *abbr (less than carload, less than container load)* TRANSP conteneur de groupage *m*, envoi de détail *m*

LCL:[2] ~ **depot** *n* TRANSP dépôt LCL *m*; ~ **door** *n* TRANSP porte LCL *f*

ld *abbr (load)* TRANSP charge *f*

LDC *abbr (less developed country)* ECON, GEN COMM, POL international PMA *(pays moins avancé)*, PVD *(pays en voie de développement)*

ldg *abbr (loading)* COMP, TRANSP chargement *m*; ~ **& dly** *(loading and delivery)* TRANSP chargement et livraison *loc m*

LDMA *abbr (London Discount Market Association)* BANK, FIN Association du marché de l'escompte de Londres *f*

L/E *abbr (latest estimate)* GEN COMM devis le plus récent *m*

LEA *abbr (Local Entreprise Agency)* WEL bureau des entreprises locales

lead:[1] ~ **-free** *adj* ENVIR sans plomb; ◆ ~ **-free fuel** ENVIR combustible sans plomb *m*

lead[2] *n* MEDIA *BrE main news story* article de tête *m*, *paragraph of news story* drapeau de tête *m*, paragraphe de tête *m*, PROP meneur *m*; ~ **bank** BANK banque chef de file *f*; ~ **-free petrol** *BrE (cf unleaded gas AmE, unleaded petrol)* ENVIR essence sans plomb *f*; ~ **management** MGMNT, S&M management directif *m*; ~ **ore** ENVIR minerai de plomb *m*; ~ **story** MEDIA *in newspaper* article de fond *m*, article qui fait la une *m*, leader *m*; ~ **time** GEN COMM délai de mise en oeuvre *m*, *of stock* délai de réapprovisionnement *m*, IND *in delivery* délai de livraison *m*, *in production* délai de fabrication *m*, *of plan* délai de réalisation *m*, délai de suite *m*, temps de latence *m*, S&M *of new product* délai de démarrage *m*, délai de mise en production *m*, *of stock* délai de livraison *m*, *plan* délai de réalisation *m*, délai de suite *m*, TRANSP *in delivery* délai de livraison *m*, délai de suite *m*; ~ **-time delay** GEN COMM retard d'introduction *m*; ◆ **take the ~** MGMNT prendre les devants; **take the ~ in doing sth** GEN COMM être le premier à faire qch

lead[3] *vt* HRM, MGMNT diriger, mener; ~ **with** MEDIA *story, headline, picture* mettre à la une; ◆ ~ **for the defence** *UK*, LAW être l'avocat principal de la défense; ~ **for the defense** *US see lead for the defence UK*; ~ **with a story** MEDIA mettre une histoire à la une

leader *n* GEN COMM dirigeant *m*, meneur *m*, HRM *person* leader *m*, IND meneur *m*, INS apériteur *m*, assureur principal *m*, LAW *UK* avocat principal *m*, MEDIA *BrE (SYN editorial) leading editorial in newspaper, magazine* leader *m*, POL meneur *m*, S&M *in market* leader *m*, S&M *US* produit d'appel bon marché *m*, STOCK *share* valeur vedette *f*; ~ **merchandising** S&M vente forcée d'articles plus chers que ceux en promotion; ~ **pricing** S&M *sales* vente à perte *f*, vente à prix sacrifié *f*; ~ **writer** MEDIA *newspapers* éditorialiste *mf*

leaders: ~ **and laggards** *n pl* STOCK valeurs vedettes et titres à la traîne *f pl*

leadership *n* GEN COMM *of company* autorité *f*, commandement *m*, style de direction *m*, HRM, MGMNT commandement *m*, direction *f*; ~ **qualities** *n pl* GEN COMM qualités de chef *f pl*

leading: ~ **article** *n UK* MEDIA article-réclame *m*, leader *m*, *in newspaper* article qui fait la une *m*, leader *m*; ~ **edge** *n* S&M avant-garde *f*; ~ **firms ratio** *n* ECON ratio de concentration *m*; ~ **indicator** *n* ECON *(ANT lagging indicator)* econometrics indicateur avancé de tendance *m*, indicateur de tendance *m*, MATH indicateur principal *m*; ~ **industries** *n pl* IND industries de pointe *f pl*; ~ **line** *n* PATENTS *for reference sign* ligne directrice *f*, S&M articles en réclame *m pl*; ~ **seaman** *n* HRM, TRANSP matelot de première classe *m*; ~ **stock** *n* *(SYN blue chip)* STOCK valeur vedette *f*; ~ **underwriter** *n* FIN apériteur *mf*; ~ **underwriter agreement** *n* INS *marine* convention de souscripteur principal *f*; ~ **underwriters' agreement for marine cargo business** *n (LUAMC)* INS *marine* convention de souscripteurs principaux pour assurance transport marin; ~ **underwriters' agreement for marine hull business** *n (LUAMH)* INS *marine* convention de souscripteurs principaux pour assurance sur corps de navire

leads: ~ **and lags** *n pl* STOCK meneurs et traînards *m pl*

leaf *n* BANK *of cheque book*, GEN COMM volant *m*, MEDIA, S&M *advertising* feuille *f*

league *n* GEN COMM catégorie *f*, classe *f*

League: ~ **International for Creditors** *n (LIC)* BANK ligue internationale des créditeurs

leak[1] *n* GEN COMM fuite *f*, *of information* fuite *f*

leak[2] *vt* GEN COMM, MEDIA *information* divulguer

leakage *n* ECON, GEN COMM fuite *f*, TRANSP coulage *m*; ◆ ~ **and breakage** *(lkg & bkg)* TRANSP coulage et casse

leaky *adj infrml* POL *bucket* percé, qui fuit

lean: ~ **year** *n* ECON année de vaches maigres *f*, année difficile *f*

leaning: ~ **towards** *n* HRM tendance à *f*

leap: ~ **year** *n* GEN COMM année bissextile *f*

leapfrog *vi jarg* GEN COMM *prices* faire l'objet d'une surenchère *loc f*, HRM enfoncer, faire un bond par rapport à, surenchérir

leapfrogging *n* HRM course-poursuite *f*, surenchère *f*, surenchère salariale *f*

LEAPS *abbr (long-term equity anticipation securities)* STOCK options de longue durée *f pl*

learn *vt* GEN COMM, HRM, WEL *facts, language* apprendre, *skill* acquérir; ◆ ~ **the ropes** HRM acquérir de l'expérience

learning: ~ **-by-doing** *n* ECON apprentissage sur le tas *m*; ~ **curve** *n* ECON, HRM, WEL courbe d'accoutumance *f*, courbe d'apprentissage *f*, courbe d'expérience *f*

lease[1] *n* LAW, PROP bail *m*, contrat de bail *m*; ~ **acquisition cost** FIN coût d'une reprise d'un

bien à bail *m*; ~ **agreement** BANK, PROP contrat de location *m*; ~ **company** GEN COMM société de leasing *f*; ~ **financing** BANK financement de baux financiers *m*; ~ **-lend** PROP prêt-bail *m*; ~ **option** PROP bail avec option d'achat *m*, convention de bail avec option d'achat *f*; ~ **with option to purchase** PROP bail avec option d'achat *m*

lease[2] *vt* PROP louer à bail

leaseback *n* LAW, PROP cession-bail *f*

leased[1] *adj* GEN COMM loué à bail

leased:[2] ~ **line** *n* COMP ligne louée *f*

leasehold *n* ACC droit de bail *m*, PROP tenure à bail *f*; ~ **estate** GEN COMM bien pris à bail *m*; ~ **improvement** FIN, PROP amélioration locative *f*; ~ **insurance** INS assurance locative *f*; ~ **interest** PROP bien-fonds loué à bail *m*, droit de tenure à bail *m*, tenure à bail *f*; ~ **mortgage** PROP hypothèque sur bien loué *f*; ~ **property** PROP propriété louée *f*, propriété à bail *f*; ~ **value** FIN, PROP valeur locative *f*

leasing *n* BANK crédit-bail *m*, PROP crédit-bail *m*, leasing *m*; ~ **agreement** FIN contrat de crédit-bail *m*; ~ **company** PROP société de crédit-bail *f*; ~ **corporation** FIN société de crédit-bail *f*

least: ~ **-cost** *n* ACC moindre coût *m*; ~ **-favored regions** *n pl AmE*, ~ **-favoured regions** *n pl BrE* ECON régions les plus défavorisées *f pl*; ~ **squares method** *n* MATH *statistics* méthode des moindres carrés *f*

leather: ~ **goods** *n pl* ENVIR, S&M articles en cuir *m pl*

leave[1] *n* GEN COMM, HRM, LEIS congé *m*; ~ **of absence** GEN COMM congé spécial *m*, HRM autorisation d'absence *f*, congé spécial *m*

leave[2] *vt* GEN COMM, HRM *job* quitter, LAW *money, property* laisser, léguer; ~ **behind** GEN COMM distancer; ◆ ~ **in the lurch** *infrml* HRM tout laisser en plan *(infrml)*; ~ **the matter open** GEN COMM laisser la question en suspens; ~ **port** TRANSP appareiller; ~ **a space** COMP laisser un espace

Lebanese[1] *adj* GEN COMM libanais

Lebanese[2] *n* GEN COMM *person* Libanais *m*

Lebanon *pr n* GEN COMM Liban *m*

LEC *abbr UK (Local Export Control)* IMP/EXP conseil local de l'exportation

lecture *n* WEL cours *m*

lecturer *n* GEN COMM conférencier *m*, HRM, WEL chargé de cours *mf*

LED *abbr (light-emitting diode)* COMP DEL *(diode électroluminescente)*

lede *n AmE see* **lead** *BrE*

ledger *n* ACC *bookkeeping* grand livre *m*, livre *m*; ~ **account** ACC compte de grand livre *m*; ~ **balance** ACC solde d'un compte du grand livre *m*; ~ **posting** ACC écriture au grand livre *f*

Leeward: ~ **Islands** *n pl* GEN COMM Iles Sous-le-Vent *f pl*

left:[1] ~ **-justified** *adj (ANT right-justified)* COMMS, COMP, MEDIA aligné à gauche, au fer à gauche *loc*

m, justifié à gauche; ~ **-of-center** *adj AmE*, ~ **-of-centre** *adj BrE* POL de centre gauche *loc m*; ~ **-wing** *adj* (ANT *right-wing*) POL de gauche

left:[2] ~ **column** *n* (ANT *right column*) ACC colonne de gauche *f*; ~ **-hand column** *n* (ANT *right-hand column*) GEN COMM colonne de gauche *f*; ~ **-hand drive** automobile *n AmE* (ANT *right-hand drive automobile*) TRANSP voiture avec la conduite à gauche *f*; ~ **-hand drive car** *n BrE* (ANT *right-hand drive car*) TRANSP voiture avec la conduite à gauche *f*; ~ **-luggage locker** *n BrE* (*cf baggage locker AmE*) GEN COMM consigne automatique *f*; ~ **-luggage office** *n BrE* (*cf baggage checkroom AmE*) GEN COMM, TRANSP consigne *f*; ~ **shift** *n* (ANT *right shift*) COMP décalage à gauche *m*

left:[3] ~ **-justify** *vt* (ANT *right-justify*) COMMS, COMP, MEDIA aligner à gauche, justifier à gauche

leftism *n* (ANT *rightism*) POL gauchisme *m*

leg *n* STOCK *of spread* base *f*, jambe *f*

legacy *n* LAW héritage *m*, legs *m*; ~ **duty** *BrE* (*cf legacy tax AmE*) TAX droits de succession *m pl*, impôt sur les successions *m*; ~ **tax** *AmE* (*cf legacy duty BrE*) TAX droits de succession *m pl*, impôt sur les successions *m*

legal[1] *adj* LAW *error, investigation, power* judiciaire, *owner, claim* légitime, *recognized by law* légal, *relating to law* juridique

legal:[2] ~ **action** *n* LAW action en justice *f*, voies de droit *f pl*; ~ **advice** *n* LAW conseil juridique *m*; ~ **adviser** *n* LAW avocat-conseil *m*, conseiller juridique *m*; ~ **advisor** *n* LAW avocat-conseil *m*, conseiller juridique *m*; ~ **aid** *n* LAW, WEL aide juridique *f*; ~ **charges** *n pl* LAW frais de contentieux *m pl*, frais de justice *m pl*, frais judiciaires *m pl*; ~ **claim** *n* LAW créance légitime *f*, revendication légitime *f*; ~ **costs** *n pl* LAW *awarded by the court* frais et dépens *m pl*; ~ **department** *n* LAW contentieux *m*, service du contentieux *m*, service juridique *m*; ~ **description** *n* LAW description juridique *f*, description légale *f*; ~ **document** *n* LAW acte authentique *m*, document authentique *m*; ~ **effect** *n* TAX effet juridique *m*; ~ **enactment** *n* LAW texte législatif *m*, texte promulgué *m*; ~ **enforceability** *n* HRM caractère exécutoire d'une convention collective *m*; ~ **entity** *n* LAW, PATENTS entité juridique *f*, personne morale *f*; ~ **expense insurance** *n* INS *personal* assurance de la protection juridique *f*, assurance défense et recours *f*; ~ **expenses** *n pl* LAW frais de justice *m pl*, frais judiciaires *m pl*, honoraires d'avocat *m pl*; ~ **fees** *n pl* LAW honoraires d'avocat *m pl*; ~ **force** *n* LAW force de loi *f*; ~ **formalities** *n pl* LAW formalités juridiques *f pl*, formalités légales *f pl*; ~ **framework** *n* LAW cadre juridique *m*; ~ **harmonization** *n* LAW, POL *EU* harmonisation du droit *f*, harmonisation juridique *f*; ~ **holiday** *n AmE* GEN COMM jour de fête légale *m*, jour férié *m*, IND, TAX jour férié *m*; ~ **immunity** *n* LAW immunité légale *f*; ~ **investment** *n* STOCK investissement de qualité *m*, investissement licite *m*; ~ **liability** *n* LAW responsabilité légale *f*; ~ **list** *n US*

STOCK liste des investissements authentiques *f*; ~ **monopoly** *n* ECON monopole légal *m*; ~ **name** *n* ADMIN, LAW nom légal *m*; ~ **notice** *n* LAW notification requise par la loi *f*, préavis légal *m*; ~ **obligation** *n* (SYN *perfect obligation*) LAW obligation juridique *f*, obligation légale *f*; ~ **officer** *n* LAW conseiller juridique *m*, fonctionnaire de l'ordre judiciaire *m*; ~ **opinion** *n* LAW avis de droit *m*, avis motivé d'un avocat *m*, avis juridique *m*; ~ **person** *n* LAW, PATENTS personne morale *f*; ~ **practitioner** *n* LAW homme de loi *m*; ~ **predecessor** *n* LAW, PATENTS prédécesseur en droit *m*; ~ **proceedings** *n pl* LAW action en justice *f*, poursuites judiciaires *f pl*, procès *m*; ~ **recognition** *n* LAW reconnaissance légale *f*; ~ **redress** *n* LAW réparation en justice *f*, réparation légale *f*; ~ **representative** *n* LAW représentant légal *m*; ~ **requirement** *n* LAW condition légale requise *f*, exigence juridique *f*, obligation légale *f*; ~ **reserve** *n* ACC réserve légale *f*; ~ **reserve life insurance company** *n* INS compagnie d'assurance-vie réserve légale *f*; ~ **reserves** *n pl* LAW réserves légales *f pl*; ~ **residence** *n* LAW domicile légal *m*, résidence légale *f*; ~ **revaluation** *n* ACC, LAW réévaluation légale *f*; ~ **right** *n* LAW droit légal *m*, droit reconnu légalement *m*, droit résultant d'un contrat *m*, droit résultant de la loi *m*; ~ **section** *n* LAW partie juridique *f*, section juridique *f*, service juridique *m*; ~ **separation** *n* LAW séparation légale *f*; ~ **services** *n pl* LAW services juridiques *m pl*; ~ **settlement** *n* LAW concordat *m*, concordat judiciaire *m*, règlement judiciaire *m*; ~ **standing** *n* LAW situation juridique *f*; ~ **status** *n* LAW statut légal *m*; ~ **strike** *n* HRM, IND, LAW grève légale *f*; ~ **system** *n* LAW système juridique *m*; ~ **tender** *n* FIN cours légal *m*, monnaie légale *f*, pouvoir libératoire *m*; ~ **transfer** *n* STOCK *of shares* transfert d'actions *m*, transfert légal *m*; ~ **wrong** *n* LAW violation d'un droit *f*

Legal: ~ **Exchange Information Service** *n* (*LEXIS*) LAW base de données juridiques *f*

legalistic *adj* LAW légaliste

legality *n* LAW légalité *f*

legalization *n* LAW légalisation *f*

legalize *vt* LAW légaliser

legally:[1] ~ **binding** *adj* LAW juridiquement tenu, lié juridiquement, légalement contraignant; ~ **bound** *adj* LAW tenu de par la loi, tenu par la loi

legally[2] *adv* LAW juridiquement, légalement

legally:[3] ~ **bind** *vt* LAW lier juridiquement, être juridiquement contraignant

legatee *n* LAW, PROP héritier *m*, légataire *mf*

leggy *adj jarg* MEDIA *film* qui tient l'affiche longtemps *loc f*, à succès *loc m*

Legion: the ~ **of Honour** *n* POL la Légion d'honneur *f*

legislate *vi* LAW légiférer

legislation *n* [inv sg] LAW loi *f*, législation *f*

legislative[1] *adj* LAW législatif

legislative:[2] ~ **body** n LAW corps législatif m; ~ **power** n LAW pouvoir législatif m

legislator n LAW, POL législateur m

legislature n LAW corps législatif m

legless: be ~ phr jarg LEIS film faire un bide

Lehman: ~ **Investment Opportunity Notes** n (LIONs) STOCK Lettre Lehman sur les investissements m, Lettre de Lehman sur les Opportunités d'Investissement m, titres de l'établissement Lehman Brothers m pl

leisure n GEN COMM convenance f, loisir m, LEIS loisir m; ~ **center** AmE, ~ **centre** BrE LEIS centre de loisirs m; ~ **facility** GEN COMM, LEIS installation de loisirs f; ~ **industry** IND, LEIS industrie des loisirs f; ~ **time** GEN COMM, LEIS temps de loisirs m; ♦ **at sb's ~** GEN COMM à la convenance de qn

lek n GEN COMM lek m

lemonade: ~ **-stand capitalism** n jarg ECON capitalisme de boutiquier m (infrml)

lempira n GEN COMM lempira m

len. abbr (lengthened) GEN COMM prolongé, rallongé

lend vt BANK, FIN prêter, STOCK Eurodollar time deposit placer en report, prêter; ♦ ~ **against security** STOCK prêter contre titre, prêter sur nantissement; ~ **on security** STOCK prêter sur gage, prêter sur nantissement; ~ **weight to** GEN COMM argument, assumption donner du poids à

lendable:[1] adj BANK prêtable

lendable:[2] ~ **funds** n pl BANK fonds prêtables m pl

lender n BANK prêteur m; ~ **of last resort** BANK prêteur de dernier ressort m

lending n FIN prêt m; ~ **at a premium** n FIN prêt au-dessus du pair m, prêt à prime m; ~ **banker** n BANK banquier prêteur m; ~ **business** n BANK opérations de prêt f pl; ~ **ceiling** n GEN COMM plafond d'un prêt m; ~ **institution** n BANK, FIN institution de crédit f, institution de prêt f, établissement de crédit m; ~ **officer** n BANK agent de prêts m, chargé de prêts mf, préposé aux prêts m; ~ **policy** n BANK politique de prêt f; ~ **power** n BANK opération de prêt f, pouvoir de prêt m; ~ **rate** n BANK taux de prêt m; ~ **securities** n pl FIN nantissement de prêt m pl

length n GEN COMM, TRANSP longueur f; ~ **between perpendiculars** (LBP) TRANSP ship's hull longueur entre perpendiculaires f (LPP); ~ **overall** (LOA) TRANSP longueur hors tout f, longueur totale f; ~ **of service** HRM durée de service f

lengthen vt (ANT shorten) STOCK allonger

lengthened adj (len.) GEN COMM prolongé, rallongé

leone n GEN COMM leone m

leptokurtic n MATH statistics leptokurtique m

Lesotho pr n GEN COMM Lesotho m

less:[1] ~ **-than-perfect** adj GEN COMM loin d'être parfait

less[2] adv ACC, GEN COMM moins

less:[3] ~ **developed country** n (LDC) ECON, GEN COMM, POL pays en voie de développement m (PVD), pays moins avancé m (PMA); ~ **favored area** n AmE, ~ **favoured area** n BrE ECON agricultural zone défavorisée f; ~ **than carload** n (LCL) TRANSP envoi de détail m; ~ **than container load** n (LCL) TRANSP conteneur de groupage m

less[4] prep FIN, MATH moins

lessee n LAW, PROP locataire mf, locataire à bail m, preneur m, preneur à bail m

lesser: to a ~ extent phr GEN COMM à un moindre degré loc m

lessor n LAW, PROP bailleur m, donneur à bail m

let[1] n UK PROP location f; ~ **property** PROP location immobilière f

let[2] vt UK PROP accommodation louer; ♦ ~ **out a contract to** GEN COMM passer un contrat avec; **to ~** BrE PROP à louer

lethal: ~ **dose** n ENVIR pollution dose fatale f

letter n ADMIN, COMMS lettre f, PROP of accommodation loueur m; ~ **of advice** n COMMS, GEN COMM lettre d'avis f; ~ **of allotment** n COMMS stock exchange avis d'attribution d'actions m; ~ **of apology** n COMMS lettre d'excuse f; ~ **of application** n FIN from investor lettre de souscription f, HRM candidate lettre de candidature f; ~ **of appointment** n COMMS, HRM lettre de nomination f; ~ **of assignment** n GEN COMM avis de cession m; ~ **of attorney** n LAW procuration f; ~ **of authority** n (L/A) GEN COMM lettre d'autorité f; ~ **of comfort** n GEN COMM lettre d'accord f; ~ **of commitment** n GEN COMM lettre d'engagement f; ~ **of consent** n COMMS, GEN COMM lettre de consentement f; ~ **of cooperation** n GEN COMM lettre de coopération f; ~ **of credit** n (L/C) BANK, FIN lettre de crédit f (L/C); ~ **dated the sixth** n COMMS lettre datée du six f; ~ **of direction** n GEN COMM lettre d'instruction f; ~ **of hypothecation** n BANK lettre hypothécaire f; ~ **of indemnity** n (L/I) BANK, GEN COMM caution f, lettre de garantie f; ~ **of inquiry** n COMMS lettre de demande de renseignements f; ~ **of intent** n GEN COMM lettre de déclaration d'intention f, STOCK lettre d'intention f; ~ **of introduction** n COMMS lettre d'introduction f, lettre de recommandation f; ~ **quality** n (LQ) COMP qualité courrier f; ~ **-quality font** n COMP police de caractères qualité courrier f; ~ **-quality printer** n COMP imprimante qualité courrier f; ~ **of recommendation** n HRM lettre de recommandation f; ~ **of renunciation** n STOCK rights issue lettre de renoncement f, lettre de renonciation f; ~ **of resignation** n COMMS, GEN COMM lettre de démission f; ~ **stock** n STOCK action non-échangeable en bourse f, lettre d'attribution f; ~ **of subordination** n COMMS lettre de subordination f; ~ **of subrogation** n COMMS lettre de créance f, lettre subrogatoire f; ~ **of transmittal** n ADMIN lettre de transmission f; ♦ **to the ~** GEN COMM à la lettre

letterfoot n COMMS emplacement de la signature m

lettering n MEDIA *printing* gravure f, lettrage m

lettertype n ADMIN modèle de lettre m

letting n PROP *by owner of an apartment* location f; **~ out** PROP *by owner of an apartment* location f

leu n GEN COMM leu m

lev n GEN COMM lev m

level:[1] **~ -headed** adj GEN COMM *analysis* calme

level[2] n COMP niveau m, seuil m, ECON, GEN COMM *amount* niveau m, *percentage* taux m, HRM, MGMNT *rank* niveau m, échelon m; **~ crossing** TRANSP traverse f; **~ debt service** US TAX *municipal charter* service d'endettement stabilisé m; **~ of expenditure** ECON niveau de dépenses m; **~ of investment** GEN COMM niveau d'investissement m; **~ money** jarg GEN COMM *second-hand car trade* chiffre rond m; **~ of orders** S&M niveau de commandes m; **~ payment** BANK remboursement en tranches égales m; **~ -payment mortgage** US FIN crédit hypothécaire remboursable par mensualités fixes m, hypothèque à remboursements fixes f; **~ premium** INS prime constante f, prime nivelée f; **~ repayment** BANK remboursement en tranches égales m; **~ of significance** MATH *statistics* niveau de signification m; **~ of support** ECON *subsidies* niveau de soutien m

level:[3] **~ off** vi ECON se stabiliser; **~ out** ECON, HRM *of number, quantity, amount* se stabiliser; ◆ **~ criticism at** GEN COMM critiquer

leveling n AmE see *levelling* BrE

levelling n BrE FIN, GEN COMM nivellement m; **~ -off** BrE ECON stabilisation f; **~ -out** BrE FIN, GEN COMM nivellement m; **~ pedestal** BrE TRANSP *container securing* palier de mise à niveau m

lever n GEN COMM levier financier m; **~ tensioner** TRANSP tendeur de levier m

leverage[1] n ACC, BANK, FIN AmE (*cf gearing* BrE) effet d'endettement m, effet de levier m, levier financier m, POL force d'appui f, pression indirecte f, STOCK AmE (*cf gearing* BrE) effet d'endettement m, effet de levier m, levier financier m; **~ adjustment** AmE (*cf gearing adjustment* BrE) FIN redressement du taux d'endettement m, redressement financier m; **~ lease** FIN location indexée f; **~ ratio** AmE (*cf gearing ratio* BrE) ACC, BANK, FIN, STOCK ratio d'endettement m, ratio de levier m, taux d'endettement m

leverage:[2] **~ up** vi FIN augmenter le ratio d'endettement

leveraged: **~ bid** n STOCK offre indexée f; **~ buyout** n (*LBO*) FIN désintéressement pour endettement m, GEN COMM rachat d'entreprise financé par l'endettement m, STOCK achat adossé m, achat avec effet de levier m, achat d'endettement m, désintéressement pour endettement m, prise de contrôle adossée f, rachat par levier m, rachat d'entreprise financé par l'endettement m; **~ company** n ACC entreprise fortement endettée f; **~ lease** n PROP location endettée f; **~ management buy-in** n (*LMBI*) FIN, GEN COMM, MGMNT, STOCK rachat d'une entreprise par des investisseurs m (*REI*); **~ management buyout** n (*LMBO*) FIN, GEN COMM, MGMNT, STOCK rachat d'une entreprise par ses salariés m (*RES*), rachat de parts de gestionnaires endettés m; **~ stock** n FIN actions achetées à crédit f pl, valeur de croissance f

levy[1] n FIN imposition f, perception f, taxation f, IMP/EXP impôt m, prélèvement m, taxe f, TAX impôt m, levée f, taxe f; **~ of taxes** TAX levée d'impôts f

levy[2] vt LAW réquisitionner, saisir, TAX lever, percevoir, prélever, *fine* imposer

levying n TAX levée f; **~ of taxes** TAX levée d'impôts f

LEXIS abbr (*Legal Exchange Information Service*) LAW base de données juridiques f

lex scripta n frml GEN COMM droit statutaire m

lf abbr (*line feed*) COMP changement de ligne m, passage à la ligne m, saut de page m

LFPR abbr (*labor force participation rate, labour force participation rate*) HRM intéressement du personnel m, participation de la main d'oeuvre f

LGS abbr (*liquid assets and government securities*) FIN liquidités et titres d'État f pl

lh abbr (*last half*) GEN COMM dernière quinzaine f

L/I abbr (*letter of indemnity*) BANK, GEN COMM lettre de garantie f

liabilities n pl ACC, FIN passif m

liability n FIN charge f, INS, LAW, TAX responsabilité f; **~ cost** STOCK *interest rate futures* coût d'obligation m, frais d'engagement m pl; **~ dividend** ACC dividende sur obligations m; **~ for tax** TAX assujettissement à l'impôt m; **~ insurance** INS assurance de responsabilité f, assurance responsabilité civile f; **~ insuring agreement** INS contrat d'assurance responsabilité civile m; **~ issuer** STOCK émetteur d'engagement m, émetteur de dette m; **~ item** ACC poste de passif m; **~ ledger** FIN registre des créances m; **~ management** ACC, BANK, FIN, MGMNT, STOCK gestion du passif f; **~ manager** ACC, BANK, FIN, MGMNT gestionnaire du passif m, STOCK gestionnaire de la dette m, gestionnaire du passif m; **~ method** ACC *deferred tax computation*, FIN méthode comptable du passif f; **~ no-fault automobile insurance** US INS *personal* assurance responsabilité civile automobile sans égard au responsable f; **~ rate** STOCK *interest rate futures* taux d'obligation m; ◆ **without any ~ on our part** GEN COMM sans engagement de notre part

liable adj LAW responsable; **~ for** GEN COMM, TAX assujetti à; **~ to** GEN COMM sujet à; ◆ **~ for damages** LAW tenu de payer des dommages et intérêts; **~ for tax** TAX assujetti à l'impôt; **~ to a fine** LAW passible d'amende; **~ to a penalty** LAW passible d'une pénalité; **~ to prosecution** LAW passible de prosécution

liaison n COMMS *work in liaison with* liaison f; ◆ **in ~ with** COMMS en liaison avec

LIARS *abbr (Lloyd's Instantaneous Accounting Record System)* INS système Lloyd's de comptabilité instantanée

libel[1] *n* LAW diffamation *f*, *publishing* diffamation *f*, *publication* écrit diffamatoire *m*, MEDIA *publishing* diffamation *f*; ~ **laws** *n pl* LAW lois contre la diffamation *f pl*; ~ **proceedings** *n pl* LAW poursuites en diffamation *f pl*, procès en diffamation *m*

libel[2] *vt* LAW diffamer

libeling *n AmE*, **libelling** *n BrE* TRANSP détention *f*

libellous *adj BrE* LAW calomnieux, diffamatoire

libelous *adj AmE see libellous BrE*

liberal[1] *adj* GEN COMM libéral, POL de centre gauche *loc m*, libéral

liberal:[2] ~ **collectivism** *n* POL collectivisme libéral *m*

Liberal *n* POL libéral *m*

liberalism *n* ECON libéralisme *m*

liberalization *n* ECON, GEN COMM, LAW libéralisation *f*; ~ **of trade** ECON *international* libéralisation du commerce *f*

liberalize *vt* ECON, GEN COMM, LAW libéraliser

Liberia *pr n* GEN COMM Libéria *m*

Liberian[1] *adj* GEN COMM libérien

Liberian[2] *n* GEN COMM *person* Libérien *m*

libertarian: ~ **economics** *n* ECON libéralisme économique *m*, théorie libertaire de l'économie *f*

liberty *n* GEN COMM, LAW liberté *f*; ~ **ship** TRANSP liberty ship *m*; ◆ **at** ~ LAW en liberté

LIBID *abbr (London Interbank Bid Rate)* STOCK taux d'emprunt interbancaire de Londres *m*, taux de l'offre interbancaire de Londres *m*

LIBOR[1] *abbr (London Interbank Offered Rate)* BANK, STOCK TIOL *(taux interbancaire offert à Londres)*

LIBOR:[2] **average** ~ *n* STOCK TIOL moyen *m*; ~ **futures contract** *n* FIN, STOCK contrat à terme sur TIOL *m*

library *n* COMP, GEN COMM bibliothèque *f*; ~ **rate** *US* COMMS tarif bibliothèque *m*; ~ **service** GEN COMM bibliothèque *f*

Library: ~ **of Congress** *n US (LC)* GEN COMM bibliothèque du Congrès, ≈ Bibliothèque Nationale *f (France) (BN)*

Libreville *pr n* GEN COMM Libreville *n pr*

Libya *pr n* GEN COMM Libye *f*

Libyan[1] *adj* GEN COMM libyen

Libyan[2] *n* GEN COMM *person* Libyen *m*

LIC *abbr UK (League International for Creditors)* BANK ligue internationale des créditeurs

licence *n BrE* BANK *of bank* permis *m*, LAW droit d'utilisation *m, for activity* autorisation *f*, concession *f*, licence *f*, permis *m*, MEDIA *for TV* redevance *f*, PATENTS licence *f*, PROP droit d'utilisation *m*, privilège *m*, TRANSP *for driver* permis *m*; ~ **bond** *n BrE* LAW engagement de se conformer aux lois locales nécessaires pour certains permis; ~ **holder** *n BrE* GEN COMM détenteur d'une licence *m*; ~ **laws** *n pl BrE* LAW droits

régissant l'octroi de permis, de licences; ◆ **under** ~ *BrE* LAW, PATENTS sous licence

licensable *adj* IMP/EXP nécessitant une licence

license[1] *n AmE see licence BrE*

license[2] *vt* ADMIN, GEN COMM *authorize* autoriser, *register* faire immatriculer; ◆ ~ **sb to do** GEN COMM autoriser qn à faire

licensed *adj* ADMIN, GEN COMM autorisé, LAW, PATENTS *intellectual property* breveté, patenté, sous licence

licensee *n* LAW, PATENTS *intellectual property* concessionnaire d'une licence *m*, titulaire d'une licence *m*

licensing *n* ADMIN autorisation *f*, ECON *international trade* octroi de licence *m*, pratique de fabrication sous licence *f*, GEN COMM autorisation *f*, IMP/EXP *international trade* octroi de licence *m*, pratique de fabrication sous licence *f*; ~ **agreement** *n* LAW accord de cession de licence *m*; ~ **examination** *n* GEN COMM, LAW enquête d'autorisation *f*; ~ **laws** *n pl* LAW lois relatives à l'octroi de licences *f pl*, législation relative au contrat de licence *f*; ~ **requirement** *n* IMP/EXP condition d'obtention d'une licence *f*; ~ **standards** *n pl* ENVIR normes d'exploitation *f pl*

licensor *n* PATENTS donneur d'une licence *m*

LICOM *abbr (London Interbank Currency Options Market)* STOCK marché interbancaire des options sur devises de Londres *m*

lie: ~ **with** *vt* LAW incomber à

Liechtenstein *pr n* GEN COMM Liechtenstein *m*

Liechtensteiner *adj* GEN COMM du Liechtenstein

lien *n* LAW droit de gage *m*, nantissement *m*, privilège *m*; ~ **-theory states** *n pl* LAW états qui connaissent la théorie du privilège

liens: ~ **for taxes** *n pl* TAX créances privilégiées du fisc *f pl*; ~ **tax** *n* TAX privilèges en garantie d'impôt *m pl*, privilèges fiscaux *m pl*, privilèges sur biens imposés *m pl*

lieu:[1] ~ **days** *n pl* HRM journées de remplacement *f pl*; ~ **rate** *n* HRM taux applicable aux journées de remplacement *m*

lieu:[2] **in** ~ **of** *phr* GEN COMM au lieu de *loc m*, à la place de *loc f*

life *n* GEN COMM, INS vie *f*, STOCK *of option* durée *f*, durée de vie *f*; ~ **annuitant** *n* PROP rentier viager *m*; ~ **assurance** *n BrE* INS *personal* assurance-vie *f*; ~ **assurance policy** *n BrE* INS police d'assurance-vie *f*; ~ **cycle** *n* S&M *of firm or product* courbe de vie *f*, cycle de vie *m*; ~ **-cycle analysis** *n* S&M *marketing* analyse du cycle de vie *f*; ~ **cycle assessment** *n (LCA)* ENVIR évaluation du cycle de vie *f*; ~ **-cycle hypothesis** *n (LCH)* ECON hypothèse du cycle de vie *f*; ~ **estate** *n* PROP immobilier en viager *m*; ~ **expectancy** *n* GEN COMM *of machine* durée probable *f, of person* espérance de vie *f*; ~ **insurance** *n* INS assurance-vie *f*; ~ **insurance business** *n* INS opérations d'assurance sur la vie *f pl*; ~ **insurance company** *n* INS compagnie d'assurance-vie *f*; ~ **insurance**

corporation *n* INS compagnie d'assurance-vie *f*; ~ **insurance policy** *n* INS police d'assurance sur la vie *f*; ~ **insurance premium** *n* INS prime d'assurance-vie *f*; ~ **insurer** *n* INS assureur de la vie *m*; ~ **interest** *n* LAW usufruit *m*; ~ **-saving apparatus** *n (LSA)* TRANSP engin de sauvetage *m*, matériel de sauvetage *m*; ~ **savings** *n pl* BANK épargne d'une vie *f*; ~ **tenancy** *n* PROP bail à vie *m*; ~ **tenant** *n* LAW usufruitier *m*, PROP locataire à vie *m*

Life: ~ **Assurance and Unit Trust Regulatory Organization** *n* UK *(Lautro)* FIN organisme régulateur des assurances-vie et des SICAV *m*

lifeboat *n* TRANSP canot de sauvetage *m*, embarcation de sauvetage *f*; ~ **ethics** *n pl infrml* POL opportunisme *m*; ~ **operation** *n* infrml BANK opération de renflouement *f*

lifeless *adj* STOCK inanimé

lifestyle *n* GEN COMM style de vie *m*; ~ **concept** S&M *marketing* concept des styles de vie *m*; ~ **merchandising** UK S&M point de vente dont les rayons sont disposés conformément au style de vie des consommateurs; ~ **segmentation** S&M *marketing* segmentation des styles de vie *f*

lifetime *n* STOCK durée de vie *f*; ~ **averaging** ECON, TAX imposition moyenne à long terme *f*; ~ **employment** HRM emploi à vie *m*

LIFFE *abbr (London International Financial Futures Exchange)* STOCK bourse des options de Londres, ≈ MONEP *(Marché des options négociables de Paris)*, ≈ MATIF *(Marché à terme d'instruments financiers) (Fra)*

LIFO *abbr (last in, first out)* ACC, HRM DEPS *(dernier entré, premier sorti)*

lift[1] *n* BrE *(cf elevator AmE)* GEN COMM ascenseur *m*; ~ **on/lift off** *(lo/lo)* TRANSP *type of ship* navire à manutention verticale *m*

lift[2] *vt* GEN COMM *ban, sanctions* lever, LAW *ban, sanctions* lever, *control, restriction* abolir, supprimer, PROP *AmE mortgage* purger; ♦ ~ **a leg** *jarg* STOCK fermer une position de stellage

Lift: ~ **on/Lift off** *n (Lo/Lo)* TRANSP *system* manutention verticale *f*

LIFT *abbr* UK *(London International Freight Terminal)* TRANSP terminal de fret international de Londres *m*

lifting *n* GEN COMM *of ban, sanction*, LAW *of ban, sanction* levée *f*, *of control, restriction* suppression *f*, TRANSP *car* remodelage *m*, restylage *m*

light[1] *adj* GEN COMM *interest, trading* faible

light[2] *n* COMP *indicator* voyant lumineux *m*; ~ **cargo** *n* TRANSP marchandises légères *f pl*; ~ **displacement** *n* TRANSP déplacement léger *m*; ~ **dues** *n pl* TRANSP droits de phare *m pl*; ~ **-emitting diode** *n (LED)* COMP diode électroluminescente *f (DEL)*; ~ **engineering** *n (ANT heavy engineering)* IND industrie mécanique légère *f*; ~ **industry** *n (ANT heavy industry)* IND industrie légère *f*; ~ **pen** *n* COMP photostyle *m*; ~ **vessel** *n (LTV)* TRANSP bateau-feu *m*

lighter *n* TRANSP allège *f*, barge *f*; ~ **aboard ship** *(LASH)* TRANSP navire porte-barges *m*, porte-barges *m*; ~ **carrier** TRANSP navire porte-barges *m*, porte-barges *m*

lighterage *n* TRANSP frais d'allège *m pl*; ~ **berth** TRANSP poste d'acconage *m*, poste de chalandage *m*; ~ **charge** TRANSP droit d'acconage *m*

lightning: ~ **strike** *n* HRM grève surprise *f*, grève éclair *f*

Lights: ~ **Advisory Committee** *n (LAC)* GEN COMM *of GCBS* comité consultatif des phares et balises

like: ~ **-kind property** *n* US TAX propriété de même type *f*

likelihood *n* GEN COMM probabilité *f*, quasi-certitude *f*

likely[1] *adj* GEN COMM probable

likely:[2] ~ **outcome** *n* GEN COMM *of negotiations* issue probable *f*, résultat probable *m*

Lilongwe *pr n* GEN COMM Lilongwe *n pr*

Lima *pr n* GEN COMM Lima *n pr*

limdis *abbr jarg (limited distribution)* POL divulgation restreinte *f*

LIMEAN *abbr (London Interbank Mean Rate)* STOCK taux interbancaire moyen de Londres *m*, taux moyen interbancaire de Londres *m*, taux moyen interbancaire des eurobanques de Londres *m*

limit[1] *n* GEN COMM *costs, prices* limite *f*, LAW *restriction* limitation *f*, STOCK limite *f*, ordre à cours limité *m*; ~ **order** STOCK ordre limité *m*, ordre à cours limité *m*; ~ **price** ECON prix plafond *m*; ~ **up** STOCK hausse maximum *f*

limit[2] *vt* GEN COMM, LAW limiter, restreindre, STOCK *risk* limiter; ♦ ~ **the number of** GEN COMM limiter le nombre de

limitation *n* GEN COMM limitation *f*, limite *f*

limited[1] *adj* GEN COMM limité

limited:[2] ~ **annual statements** *n pl* ACC comptes annuels abrégés *m pl*; ~ **audit** *n* ACC *auditing* audit d'une étendue limitée *m*, audit restreint *m*; ~ **authorization** *n* IMP/EXP autorisation limitée *f*; ~ **check** *n* LAW contrôle limité *m*, contrôle partiel *m*; ~ **company** *n* UK GEN COMM compagnie limitée *f*, société anonyme *f*; ~ **discretion** *n* STOCK appréciation limitée *f*, appréciation restreinte *f*; ~ **distribution** *n* POL *(limdis)* divulgation restreinte *f*, TRANSP distribution restreinte *f*; ~ **edition** *n* MEDIA édition à tirage limité *f*; ~ **liability company** *n* BrE *(Ltd)* GEN COMM société à responsabilité limitée *f (SARL)*; ~ **market** *n* ECON, S&M marché étroit *m*; ~ **occupancy agreement** *n* LAW, PROP contrat d'occupation partielle *m*; ~ **order** *n* STOCK ordre à cours limité *m*; ~ **owner** *n* LAW, PROP propriétaire usufruitier *m*; ~ **partner** *n* GEN COMM, HRM, LAW associé commanditaire *m*, commanditaire *mf*; ~ **partnership** *n* GEN COMM associé en participation *m*, STOCK société en commandite *f*; ~ **payment life insurance** *n* US INS *personal* vie entière à primes temporaires *f*; ~ **policy** *n* INS

police limitée *f*; ~ **postponed accounting** *n* IMP/
EXP comptabilité différée limitée *f*; ~ **recourse
debt** *n* BANK créances assorties de recours limités
f pl; ~ **recourse finance** *n* BANK, FIN financement
à recours limité *m*; ~ **recourse financing** *n* BANK,
FIN financement à recours limité *m*; ~ **term** *n* INS
durée limitée *f*; ~ **trading authorization** *n* STOCK
autorisation restreinte de négoce

limousine: ~ **liberals** *n pl infrml* POL la gauche
caviar *f* (*infrml*)

linage *n see lineage*

line *n* COMMS, COMP ligne *f*, GEN COMM bénéfice
net *m*, gamme *f*, GEN COMM *AmE* (*cf queue BrE*)
file d'attente *f*, queue *f*, HRM opérationnels *m pl*,
MEDIA ligne *f*, S&M gamme *f*, ligne *f*, *advertising*
ligne *f*, STOCK file *f*, ligne *f*, TRANSP ligne *f*, voie *f*;
~ **assistant** *n* HRM attaché opérationnel *m*; ~ **of
attack** *n* GEN COMM angle d'attaque *m*;
~ **authority** *n* HRM, MGMNT autorité hiérarchique
f; ~ **of command** *n* MGMNT voie hiérarchique *f*;
~ **of credit** *n* BANK, FIN *AmE* (*SYN bank line,
credit line*) autorisation de crédit *f*, crédit autorisé *m*, ligne de crédit *f*, ligne de découvert *f*,
marge de crédit *f* (*Can*); ~ **editor** *n* COMP éditeur
de ligne *m*, éditeur ligne à ligne *m*; ~ **executive** *n*
HRM dirigeant opérationnel *m*; ~ **extension** *n* S&M
élargissement de la gamme *m*; ~ **feed** *n* (*lf*) COMP
changement de ligne *m*, passage à la ligne *m*, saut
de page *m*; ~ **function** *n* GEN COMM structure
fonctionnelle *f*; ~ **of least resistance** *n* GEN COMM
ligne de moindre résistance *f*; ~ **management** *n*
MGMNT *managers* responsables opérationnels *m
pl, system* direction hiérarchique *f*; ~ **manager** *n*
HRM, MGMNT agent de maîtrise *m*, chef d'atelier
m, contremaître *m*, surveillant de premier niveau
m, cadre hiérarchique *m*, chef direct *m*, chef
hiérarchique *m*, directeur hiérarchique *m*, responsable opérationnel *m*; ~ **object** *n* ADMIN
article d'exécution *m*, directives et objectifs
ministériels *m pl*; ~ **organization** *n* GEN COMM
structure hiérarchique *f*, HRM organisation hiérarchique *f*, MGMNT organisation hiérarchique *f*,
organisation opérationnelle *f*, organisation verticale *f*; ~ **position** *n* HRM poste opérationnel *m*;
~ **printer** *n* COMP imprimante ligne par ligne *f*;
~ **production** *n* IND production à la chaîne *f*;
~ **relations** *n pl* GEN COMM liaisons hiérarchiques
f pl; ~ **responsibility** *n* GEN COMM responsabilité
hiérarchique *f*; ~ **slip** *n* INS faculté de souscription
à aliments *f*; ~ **space** *n* MEDIA *printing* interligne
m; ~ **and staff management** *n* HRM, MGMNT
direction en structure mixte *f*; ~ **and staff
organization** *n* HRM, MGMNT organisation mixte
f, structure mixte *f*; ~ **stamp** *n UK* INS tampon *m*;
~ **supervisor** *n* HRM, MGMNT agent de maîtrise *m*,
contremaître *m*, superviseur de premier niveau *m*;
◆ **in ~ with** GEN COMM *inflation, expectations*
conforme à

lineage *n* MEDIA *print* lignage *m* (*jarg*), nombre de
lignes d'une petite annonce *m*, tarif à la ligne *m*

linear: ~ **measure** *n* GEN COMM mesure linéaire *f*;

~ **program** *n AmE see linear programme BrE*;
~ **programme** *n BrE* ECON *econometrics*, MATH
programme linéaire *m*; ~ **programming** *n* COMP,
ECON *econometrics*, MATH programmation
linéaire *f*; ~ **regression** *n* ACC, MATH *statistics*
régression linéaire *f*; ~ **relationship** *n* HRM relation linéaire *f*; ~ **responsibility** *n* MATH, MGMNT
responsabilité hiérarchique *f*

liner *n* TRANSP liner *m*, navire de ligne *m*, navire
régulier *m*; ~ **broker** *n* TRANSP courtier d'affrètement à la cueillette *m*, courtier à la cueillette *m*;
~ **conference** *n* TRANSP conférence maritime *f*;
~ **conference code** *n* TRANSP code de conduite
des conférences maritimes *m*; ~ **consortium** *n*
TRANSP consortium de compagnies de ligne *m*;
~ **rate** *n* TRANSP fret à l'unité payante *m*; ~ **terms**
n pl TRANSP conditions des lignes régulières *f pl*;
~ **voyage simulation** *n* TRANSP simulation de
voyage en navire de ligne *f*; ◆ **no ~** (*NL*) TRANSP
hors conférence

lingua: ~ **franca** *n* [pl -s] GEN COMM lingua franca *f*

link¹ *n* COMP liaison *f*, ECON *trade*, FIN *trade*
relation *f*, GEN COMM liaison *f*, lien *m*, rapport *m*,
relation *f*, MEDIA *TV, radio*, TRANSP liaison *f*;
~ **span** TRANSP rampe d'appontement *f*

link² *vt* COMP *peripherals, connections* chaîner,
connecter, relier, GEN COMM connecter, lier, unir,
MEDIA *TV, radio* établir une liaison entre, STOCK
lier

linkage *n* ECON *international relations* association *f*,
GEN COMM liaison *f*; ~ **models** *n pl* ECON
econometrics modèles macro-économiques
comparatifs *m pl*

linked *adj* STOCK indexé, lié

lion's: **the ~ share** *n* GEN COMM la part du lion *loc f*

LIONs *abbr* (*Lehman Investment Opportunity
Notes*) STOCK Lettre Lehman sur les investissements *m*, Lettre de Lehman sur les Opportunités
d'Investissement *m*, titres de l'établissement
Lehman Brothers *m pl*

liquefied: ~ **natural gas** *n* (*LNG*) ENVIR, IND,
TRANSP gaz naturel liquéfié *m* (*GNL*); ~ **natural
gas carrier** *n* TRANSP transporteur de GNL *m*,
transporteur de gaz naturel liquéfié *m*

liquid¹ *adj* BANK *funds*, FIN liquide

liquid² *n* IND, TRANSP liquide *m*; ~ **assets** *n pl* ACC
actif disponible *m*, disponibilités *f pl*, liquidités *f
pl*, FIN actif disponible *m*, actif négociable *m*,
actif réalisable *m*, liquidités *f pl*, valeurs disponibles *f pl*; ~ **assets and government securities** *n pl*
(*LGS*) FIN liquidités et titres d'État *f pl*; ~ **assets
ratio** *n* ACC, BANK, FIN, STOCK ratio de liquidités
m, taux de liquidités *m*; ~ **bulk cargo** *n* TRANSP
chargement liquide *m*; ~ **capital** *n* STOCK capital
liquide *m*; ~ **debt** *n* FIN dette liquide *f*; ~ **funds** *n
pl* ACC disponibilités *f pl*, fonds disponibles *m pl*;
~ **market** *n* STOCK marché des disponibilités *m*,
marché liquide *m*; ~ **measure** *n* GEN COMM
mesure de capacité liquide *f*; ~ **petroleum gas** *n*
(*LPG*) ENVIR, IND, TRANSP gaz de pétrole

liquéfié *m* *(GPL)*; ~ **petroleum gas carrier** *n* TRANSP transporteur de GPL *m*, transporteur de gaz de pétrole liquéfié *m*; ~ **quart** *n* *US* GEN COMM 0.946 litre, quart liquide *m*; ~ **ratio** *n* ACC taux de liquidité *m*, taux des disponibilités *m*, taux disponible *m*, BANK, FIN, STOCK taux de liquidité *m*; ~ **savings** *n pl* FIN épargne liquide *f*; ~ **waste** *n* ENVIR effluent liquide *m*; ~ **yield option note** *n* *(LYON)* STOCK billet d'option de rendement en liquide *m*, note d'option sur rendement disponible *f*

liquidate 1. *vt* ACC amortir, FIN *capital* mobiliser, *debt* liquider, régler, GEN COMM liquider, régler, LAW *assets, stock, company* liquider, *capital* mobiliser, *debt* régler, STOCK liquider; **2.** *vi* FIN, LAW entrer en liquidation; ◆ ~ **a position** FIN inverser une position, STOCK déboucler une position, liquider une position

liquidated[1] *adj* STOCK *options* liquidé

liquidated:[2] ~ **damages** *n pl* LAW dommages-intérêts liquidés *m pl*; ~ **debt** *n* ACC dette satisfaite *f*

liquidating: ~ **dividend** *n* FIN dividende de liquidation *m*, solde de dividende *m*; ~ **value** *n* ACC, FIN *of asset of company* valeur de liquidation *f*

liquidation *n* ACC liquidation *f*, FIN *of company, stock* liquidation *f*, *of capital* mobilisation *f*, *of debt* remboursement *m*, GEN COMM *of debt* remboursement *m*, LAW *of company, stock* liquidation *f*, *of capital, debt* mobilisation *f*, STOCK convertissement *m*; ~ **dividend** ACC dividende de liquidation *m*; ◆ **go into voluntary** ~ GEN COMM déposer son bilan

liquidator *n* ACC, FIN, LAW liquidateur *m*

liquidities *n pl* ACC liquidités *f pl*

liquidity *n* ACC, BANK, FIN, STOCK liquidité *f*; ~ **adequacy** *n* ACC liquidités *f pl*; ~ **crisis** *n* BANK, GEN COMM manque de liquidités *m*; ~ **diversification** *n* STOCK diversification des liquidités *f*, diversification en fonction de la liquidité *f*; ~ **famine** *n* FIN pénurie de moyens de paiement *f*; ~ **preference** *n* ECON préférence pour la liquidité *f*; ~ **problems** *n pl* ACC problèmes de liquidité *m pl*; ~ **ratio** *n* ACC, BANK, FIN, STOCK coefficient de liquidité *m*, ratio de liquidité *m*, taux de liquidité *m*; ~ **squeeze** *n* FIN compression des liquidités *f*; ~ **trap** *n* ECON piège de la liquidité *m*

liquidization *n* STOCK liquidation *f*

liquor: ~ **store** *n* *Can* *(cf off-licence BrE)* S&M magasin de vins et de spiritueux qu'il est interdit de consommer sur place

lira *n* GEN COMM lire *f*

Lisbon *pr n* GEN COMM Lisbonne *n pr*

lis pendens *n* LAW affaire en instance *f*, litispendance *f*

list[1] *n* COMP, GEN COMM liste *f*, PROP *US* liste *f*, liste immobilière *f*; ~ **broker** GEN COMM courtier en fichiers *m*; ~ **of candidates** POL liste des candidats *f*; ~ **of deliverable bonds** STOCK gisement *m*;

~ **price** GEN COMM, S&M *sales, retail* prix catalogue *m*, prix de catalogue *m*; ~ **of priorities** GEN COMM, POL liste des priorités *f*; ◆ **make a** ~ GEN COMM faire une liste

list[2] *vt* GEN COMM lister, STOCK coter, inscrire à la cote

listed[1] *adj* STOCK *on stock exchange* coté, coté en bourse, inscrit, inscrit à la cote; ◆ ~ **at** STOCK coté à

listed:[2] ~ **bank** *n* BANK, FIN banque de dépôt *f*; ~ **building** *n* *UK* PROP monument classé *m*; ~ **company** *n* FIN, STOCK société cotée *f*, société cotée en bourse *f*; ~ **option** *n* STOCK option cotée *f*, option cotée en bourse *f*, option inscrite à la cote *f*, option négociable *f*; ~ **securities** *n pl* STOCK titres cotés *m pl*, valeurs cotées *f pl*; ~ **security** *n* STOCK valeur cotée en bourse *f*, valeur inscrite à la cote *f*; ~ **share** *n* *(ANT unlisted share)* STOCK action cotée *f*, action inscrite à la cote officielle *f*

listeners': ~ **habits** *n pl* MEDIA *broadcast* habitudes d'écoute *f pl*, habitudes des téléspectateurs *f pl*

listening: ~ **time** *n* MEDIA heure d'écoute *f*

listing *n* COMP listage *m*, listing *m*, FIN inscription *f*, GEN COMM listage *m*, listing *m*, LAW *stock exchange* cotation *f*, PROP liste *f*, liste immobilière *f*, STOCK cotation *f*, liste *f*; ~ **agent** *n* *US* PROP agent de listage *m*; ~ **application** *n* STOCK demande d'inscription à la cote *f*; ~ **particulars** *n pl* STOCK informations nécessaires à l'admission à la cote *f pl*, renseignements de listage *m pl*; ~ **requirements** *n pl* STOCK conditions requises au listage *f pl*, exigences pour la cotation *f pl*

listless *adj* GEN COMM *market, trading* sans ressort

liter *n* *AmE see litre BrE*

literal *n* MEDIA *printing* coquille *f*, faute d'impression *f*; ~ **error** MEDIA *printing* coquille *f*, faute d'impression *f*

literary: ~ **critic** *n* GEN COMM, MEDIA critique littéraire *m*

Lithuania *pr n* GEN COMM Lituanie *f*

Lithuanian[1] *adj* GEN COMM lituanien

Lithuanian[2] *n* GEN COMM *person* Lituanien *m*

litigant *n* LAW partie en litige *f*, plaideur *m*

litigate 1. *vt* LAW contester; **2.** *vi* LAW plaider

litigation *n* LAW contentieux *m*, litige *m*; ~ **risk** ACC *provisions* risque de litige *m*

litre *n* *BrE* *(l)* GEN COMM litre *m* *(l)*

little: ~ **dragons** *n pl* *infrml* ECON, POL *Asian countries* petits dragons *m pl* *(infrml)*

live[1] *adj* LEIS *sport*, MEDIA *broadcast* en direct; ◆ ~ **animals on board** *(LAB)* TRANSP *aviation* animaux vivants à bord

live:[2] ~ **broadcast** *n* MEDIA émission en direct *f*; ~ **food** *n* IND *health food trade* produits frais *m pl*; ~ **program** *n* *AmE*, ~ **programme** *n* *BrE* MEDIA *broadcast* programme en direct *m*, émission en direct *f*

live³ *vi* GEN COMM vivre; ◆ ~ **beyond one's means** GEN COMM vivre au-dessus de ses moyens

livestock *n* GEN COMM bétail *m*

living: ~ **benefits of life insurance** *n pl* INS indemnités de subsistance sur assurance vie *f pl*; ~ **conditions** *n pl* WEL conditions de vie *f pl*; ~ **dead** *n jarg* STOCK morts vivants *m pl*, situation de blocage *f*; ~ **expenses** *n pl* GEN COMM frais de séjour *m pl*, indemnités de subsistance *f pl*, TAX frais de subsistance *m pl*; ~ **space** *n* WEL espace vital *m*; ~ **wage** *n* WEL minimum vital *m*; ◆ **make a** ~ *(SYN earn a living)* ECON gagner sa vie

Ljubljana *pr n* GEN COMM Ljubljana *n pr*

lkg: ~ **& bkg** *abbr (leakage and breakage)* TRANSP coulage et casse *loc m*

LL *abbr (load line)* TRANSP *shipping* ligne de charge *f*

LLB *abbr (Bachelor of Laws)* WEL *degree* ≈ licence de droit *f*, *person* ≈ licencié en droit *m*

LLD *abbr (Doctor of Laws)* LAW, WEL docteur en droit *m*

Lloyd's: ~ **Agent** *n (L/A)* TRANSP *shipping* agent de la Lloyds *m*; ~ **Corporation** *n UK* INS *marine* syndicat de la Lloyd *m*; ~ **Instantaneous Accounting Record System** *n (LIARS)* INS système Lloyd's de comptabilité instantanée; ~ **List** *n* TRANSP *shipping* publication quotidienne du Lloyd's indiquant les mouvements de navire; ~ **Loading List** *n* TRANSP *shipping* guide hebdomadaire de l'exportateur maritime; ~ **of London** *n* INS Lloyd's de Londres; ~ **Machinery Certificate** *n (LMC)* TRANSP *shipping* attestation du Lloyd's indiquant le bon état des machines; ~ **member** *n* INS assureur Lloyd's *m*; ~ **Register** *n* INS *marine* registre du Lloyd's *m*; ~ **Register of Shipping** *n* INS registre de navigation du Lloyd's *m*; ~ **Underwriting Agents' Association** *n (LUAA)* INS association des agents souscripteurs du Lloyd's

LM: ~ **curve** *n* ECON courbe LM *f*

LMBI *abbr (leveraged management buy-in)* FIN, GEN COMM, MGMNT, STOCK REI *(rachat d'une entreprise par des investisseurs)*

LMBO *abbr (leveraged management buyout)* FIN, GEN COMM, MGMNT, STOCK RES *(rachat d'une entreprise par ses salariés)*

LMC *abbr (Lloyd's Machinery Certificate)* TRANSP *shipping* attestation du Lloyd's indiquant le bon état des machines

LME *abbr (London Metal Exchange)* STOCK Bourse des métaux de Londres *f*

LNG *abbr (liquefied natural gas)* ENVIR, IND, TRANSP *shipping* GNL *(gaz naturel liquéfié)*

lo *abbr (low loader)* TRANSP remorque surbaissée *f*, remorque à plate-forme surbaissée *f*, wagon à plate-forme surbaissée *m*

LOA *abbr (length overall)* TRANSP *shipping* LHT *(longueur hors tout)*

load¹ *n* STOCK droit d'acquisition *m*, frais de commission *m pl*, TRANSP *(ld)* charge *f*, chargement *m*; ~ **factor** ECON *manufacturing* facteur de charge *m*, indice de charge *m*, taux de charge *m*, GEN COMM coefficient d'utilisation de la capacité *m*, facteur de charge *m*, indice de charge *m*, taux de charge *m*, IMP/EXP facteur de charge *m*, IND facteur de charge *m*, indice de charge *m*, taux de charge *m*, MATH coefficient d'utilisation de la capacité *m*, facteur de charge *m*, indice de charge *m*, taux de charge *m*, TRANSP coefficient de remplissage *m*, taux d'occupation *m*, facteur de charge *m*, *airline* taux de remplissage *m*; ~ **fund** FIN, STOCK *which charges handling fee* fonds de placement *m*; ~ **line** *(LL)* TRANSP ligne de charge *f*; ~ **line certificate** TRANSP *ship's document* certificat de franc-bord *m*; ~ **line convention** TRANSP convention sur les lignes de charge *f*; ~ **line zone** TRANSP zone de ligne de charge *f*; ~ **-on-top system** TRANSP *oil tanker* système de chargement sur résidus *m*; ~ **plan** TRANSP plan de charge *m*; ~ **port** TRANSP port de chargement *m*; ~ **sheet** TRANSP bordereau de charge *m*; ◆ **under** ~ TRANSP en charge

load² *vt* COMP *software* charger, INS *premium* majorer, TRANSP charger, embarquer

loading *n* COMP *(ldg)* chargement *m*, HRM impact *m*, TRANSP *(ldg)* chargement *m*; ~ **agent** HRM, IMP/EXP, TRANSP chargeur *m*; ~ **allocation** TRANSP affectation de chargement *f*; ~ **broker** HRM chargeur *m*, courtier maritime *m*, IMP/EXP chargeur *m*, TRANSP *shipping* chargeur *m*, courtier maritime *m*; ~ **date** TRANSP jour de chargement *m*; ~ **dock** TRANSP quai de chargement *m*; ~ **overside** TRANSP chargement par allèges *m*, chargement sous palan *m*; ~ **platform** TRANSP *vehicles* trottoir de chargement *m*; ~ **space** GEN COMM surface de charge *f*; ◆ ~ **and delivery** *(ldg & dly)* TRANSP chargement et livraison

loadmate *n* TRANSP système informatique embarqué *m*

loan *n* ACC emprunt *m*, BANK *money borrowed* emprunt *m*, *money lent* prêt *m*, ECON, FIN, GEN COMM, STOCK emprunt *m*; ~ **account** BANK compte d'avances *m*, compte de prêts *m*; ~ **agreement** BANK contrat de prêt *m*; ~ **application** BANK demande de prêt *f*; ~ **authorization** BANK autorisation de prêt *f*; ~ **capital** ACC, FIN capital d'emprunt *m*, capital obligations *m*, financement par l'emprunt *m*, STOCK capital obligations *m*; ~ **certificate** FIN certificat d'emprunt *m*, certificat de prêt *m*, titre de prêt *m*; ~ **commitment** BANK engagement de prêt *m*; ~ **company** FIN société de crédit *f*; ~ **crowd** STOCK la bande du crédit; ~ **default** BANK défaut de paiement de prêt *m*; ~ **demand** BANK demande de crédit *f*; ~ **department** FIN service du crédit *m*; ~ **exposure** FIN risque du crédit *m*; ~ **fee** BANK commission de montage *f*, frais de montage *m pl*; ~ **guarantee** FIN garantie de prêt *f*; ~ **guarantee scheme** FIN *for rural development* plan de garantie de prêts *m*; ~ **holder** FIN détenteur d'un prêt *m*; ~ **insurance** FIN assurance de crédit *f*; ~ **investment** FIN investissement en prêt *m*; ~ **loss**

BANK emprunt irrécouvrable *m*, perte sur prêts *f*; ~ **loss provision** BANK, FIN provision pour perte sur prêt *f*; ~ **market** FIN marché du crédit *m*; ~ **officer** BANK agent de prêts *m*, chargé de prêts *mf*, préposé aux prêts *m*; ~ **on trust** BANK prêt d'honneur *m*; ~ **origination fee** BANK commission de montage *f*, frais de montage *m pl*; ~ **portfolio** BANK portefeuille des prêts *m*; ~ **-pricing date** STOCK date de mise à prix d'emprunt *f*; ~ **recipient** BANK bénéficiaire d'un prêt *m*; ~ **recovery** BANK prêt recouvré *m*, recouvrement de prêt *m*; ~ **repayment** ACC, BANK, FIN, GEN COMM remboursement de prêt *m*; ~ **repayment schedule** BANK, FIN calendrier de remboursement d'emprunt *m*; ~ **shark** *infrml* FIN prêt à taux usuraires *m*, usurier *m*; ~ **stock** ACC, FIN, STOCK capital obligations *m*, obligations *f pl*; ~ **swap** FIN, STOCK échange à terme de types d'emprunts *m*; ~ **-to-value ratio** *(LTV)* BANK, FIN rapport emprunt-valeur *m*, rapport prêt-valeur *m*, ratio prêt sur valeur *m*; ~ **value** BANK rapport prêt-garantie *m*, INS valeur d'emprunt *f*; ~ **write-off** BANK perte sèche sur prêt *f*; ~ **yield** BANK, STOCK rapport de prêt *m*, rendement d'un prêt *m*; ♦ **make a ~ to sb** BANK, FIN accorder un prêt à qn, consentir un prêt à qn

loanable: ~ **funds theory** *n* FIN théorie des fonds prêtables *f*

loans: ~, **investments and advances** *n pl* ACC prêts, participations et avances *loc*; ~, **investments and advances to international organizations** *n pl* ACC prêts, dotations en capital et avances aux organismes internationaux *loc*; ~ **to related companies** *n pl* ACC créances rattachées à des participations *f pl*

lobby[1] *n* POL lobby *m*; ~ **group** POL groupe de pression *m*, lobby *m*; ♦ **on ~ terms** *jarg BrE (cf not for attribution AmE)* MEDIA *print*, POL de source confidentielle, de source officieuse, non-divulgable

lobby[2] *vt* POL exercer une pression sur

lobbying *n* POL activité en faveur de groupes de pression, lobbying *m*, sollicitations *f pl* (*jarg*)

lobbyist *n* LAW lobbyiste *mf*

local[1] *adj* ADMIN local, municipal, COMP, GEN COMM local

local[2] *n* HRM section syndicale *f*, unité locale *f*, STOCK local *m*, négociateur individuel de parquet *m*, NIP; ~ **agreement** *n* HRM accord local *m*; ~ **area network** *n (LAN)* COMP réseau local *m*, réseau local d'entreprise *m (RLE)*; ~ **authority** *n* ADMIN administration locale *f*, autorités locales *f pl*, ADMIN *UK* ≈ municipalité *f*, POL administration locale *f*, autorités locales *f pl*, POL *UK* ≈ municipalité *f*; ~ **authority bill** *n (LAB)* POL loi sur les administrations locales *f*, obligation d'administration locale ou régionale *f*; ~ **authority bond** *n (LAB)* STOCK bon d'administration locale *m*, obligation d'administration locale ou régionale *f*; ~ **call** *n* COMMS appel local *m*; ~ **charge** *n* TRANSP tarif local *m*, taxe locale *f*;

~ **charge rate call** *n* COMMS appel à prix partagé *m*; ~ **charge rate trunk call** *n* COMMS appel à prix partagé *m*; ~ **council** *n* ADMIN, POL ≈ municipalité *f*; ~ **currency** *n (lc)* FIN, IMP/EXP monnaie locale *f*; ~ **custody** *n* FIN conservation locale *f*; ~ **election** *n* GEN COMM élection locale *f*; ~ **emission** *n* ENVIR, IND *pollution* émission locale *f*; ~ **export control** *n* IMP/EXP *UK* contrôle local des exportations *m*; ~ **firm** *n* FIN, GEN COMM entreprise locale *f*; ~ **government** *n* ADMIN, POL autorités locales *f pl*, ≈ municipalité *f*; ~ **government finance** *n* POL finances des collectivités locales *f pl*; ~ **handicraft** *n* HRM artisanat local *m*; ~ **import control** *n* IMP/EXP contrôle local des importations *m*; ~ **industry** *n* IND industrie locale *f*; ~ **labor** *n AmE see local labour BrE*; ~ **labor market** *n AmE see local labour market BrE*; ~ **labour** *n BrE* HRM main-d'oeuvre locale *f*; ~ **labour market** *n BrE* ECON marché du travail régional *m*; ~ **monopoly** *n* ECON monopole régional *m*; ~ **newspaper** *n* MEDIA journal local *m*; ~ **paper** *n* MEDIA *press* journal local *m*; ~ **public good** *n* ECON bien public local *m*; ~ **shop** *n BrE (cf local store AmE)* S&M commerce de proximité *m*, magasin de proximité *m*; ~ **skills** *n pl* HRM capacités locales *f pl*; ~ **store** *n AmE (cf local shop BrE)* S&M commerce de proximité *m*, magasin de proximité *m*; ~ **tax** *n* TAX impôt municipal *m*, taxe locale *f*; ~ **time** *n* GEN COMM, MEDIA heure locale *f*; ~ **union** *n* HRM syndicat local *m*; ~ **variable** *n* COMP variable locale *f*

Local: ~ **Entreprise Agency** *n (LEA)* WEL bureau des entreprises locales; ~ **Export Control** *n UK (LEC)* IMP/EXP conseil local de l'exportation

locality *n* PROP *of a property* lieudit *m*

localization *n* COMP *software* adaptation *f*, localisation *f*

locate *vt* GEN COMM localiser

located *adj* GEN COMM sis, situé

location *n* GEN COMM localisation *f*, situation *f*; ~ **theory** ECON théorie de la concentration géographique *f*; ♦ **any one ~** *(AOLOC)* INS, TRANSP marine en un seul lieu

locator *n* TRANSP cône *m*

LOCH *abbr UK (London Options Clearing House)* FIN ≈ SCMC *(Société de compensation des marchés conditionnels)*

lock:[1] ~ **-chamber** *n* TRANSP sas *m*; ~ **-up option** *n* FIN, STOCK *of corporate takeovers* option d'immobilisation *f*

lock[2] *vt* COMP *file* verrouiller; ~ **in** GEN COMM renfermer, STOCK arrêter, verrouiller, renfermer, s'assurer de; ~ **out** STOCK empêcher, écarter; ♦ ~ **in a rate** STOCK *interest rate futures* bloquer un cours

lockaway *n jarg* STOCK valeur à long terme *f*

locked:[1] ~ **-in** *adj US* GEN COMM renfermé, STOCK *situation* bloqué, renfermé

locked:[2] ~ **canal** *n* TRANSP canal éclusé *m*; ~ **-in**

industry *n* (ANT *footloose industry*) IND industrie figée *f*; ~ -**in knowledge** *n* ECON connaissances techniques non-transférables *f pl*, connaissances techniques non-transposables *f pl*, IND connaissance figée *f*, savoir figé *m*; ~ -**in value** *n* STOCK *of shares allocated to employees* valeur fixe *f*, valeur renfermée *f*; ~ **market** *n* STOCK marché bloqué *m*, marché figé *m*

locking *n* TRANSP *of containers* blocage *m*, verrouillage *m*

lockout *n* GEN COMM fermeture d'usine *f*, lock-out *m*, HRM fermeture des ateliers *f*, lock-out *m*, grève *f*, IND grève *f*

loco *adj* IMP/EXP, TRANSP prix sur place *m*

lodge *vti* WEL loger; ♦ ~ **an appeal** LAW interjeter appel, TAX interjeter appel, se pourvoir en appel; ~ **a complaint** GEN COMM déposer une plainte

log[1] *n* ADMIN *record* journal *m*, registre *m*, COMP, TAX journal *m*, TRANSP journal *m, of plane* carnet de vol *m, of ship* livre de bord *m*; ~ **book** ADMIN *record* journal *m*, registre *m*, TAX journal *m*, TRANSP journal *m, of plane* carnet de vol *m, of ship* livre de bord *m*; ~ **file** COMP fichier de consignation *m*

log:[2] ~ **in** *vi* COMP ouvrir une session, se connecter; ~ **off** COMP mettre fin à une session, se déconnecter, sortir du système; ~ **on** COMP ouvrir une session, se connecter; ~ **out** COMP mettre fin à une session, se déconnecter, sortir du système, terminer une session

logging *n* GEN COMM exploitation forestière *f*

logic *n* COMP, GEN COMM, MGMNT logique *f*

logical *adj* GEN COMM, MGMNT logique; ♦ **it's** ~ GEN COMM c'est logique

logistic: ~ **cycle** *n* ECON cycle logistique *m*, mouvement de longue durée *m*; ~ **process** *n* IND, MATH processus logistique *m*

logistical *adj* COMMS, COMP, GEN COMM, MATH, TRANSP logistique

logistically *adv* COMP, GEN COMM, MATH, TRANSP logistiquement

logistics *n pl* [+sing v] COMP, GEN COMM, MATH, TRANSP logistique *f*

logo *n* GEN COMM, S&M logo *m*, logotype *m*

logoptics *n* GEN COMM pictogramme *m*

logotype *n* GEN COMM, S&M logotype *m*

logroll *vt US* POL renvoyer l'ascenseur

logrolling *n US* POL entreaide entre politiciens *f*, roulage de bûches *m* (*infrml*)

lo/lo *abbr* (*lift on/lift off*) TRANSP *ship, vessel* navire à manutention verticale *m*

Lo/Lo *abbr* (*Lift on/Lift off*) TRANSP *system* manutention verticale *f*

Lombard: ~ **rate** *n* BANK taux Lombard *m*

Lomé:[1] ~ **Convention** *n* ECON *trade*, POL Convention de Lomé *f*, les accords de Lomé *m pl*

Lomé[2] *pr n* GEN COMM Lomé *n pr*

London:[1] ~ **Clearing House** *n* (*LCH*) STOCK Caisse/Chambre de compensation de Londres;

~ **Commodity Exchange** *n obs* (*LCE*) STOCK depuis 1987, the London Futures and Options Exchange, Bourse de matières premières de Londres *f*; ~ **Discount Market Association** *n* (*LDMA*) BANK, FIN Association du marché de l'escompte de Londres *f*; ~ **FOX** *n* (*London Futures and Options Exchange*) STOCK bourse des marchés à terme et options de Londres, ≈ Palais Grognard *m*; ~ **Futures and Options Exchange** *n* (*London FOX*) STOCK bourse des marchés à terme et options de Londres, ≈ Palais Grognard *m*; ~ **gold fixing** *n* BANK fixation du prix de l'or à Londres *f*; ~ **Interbank Bid Rate** *n* (*LIBID*) STOCK taux d'emprunt interbancaire de Londres *m*, taux de l'offre interbancaire de Londres *m*; ~ **Interbank Currency Options Market** *n* (*LICOM*) STOCK marché interbancaire des options sur devises de Londres *m*; ~ **Interbank Mean Rate** *n* (*LIMEAN*) STOCK taux interbancaire moyen de Londres *m*, taux moyen interbancaire de Londres *m*, taux moyen interbancaire des eurobanques de Londres *m*; ~ **Interbank Offered Rate** *n* (*LIBOR*) BANK, STOCK taux interbancaire offert à Londres *m* (*TIOL*); ~ **International Financial Futures Exchange** *n UK* (*LIFFE*) STOCK bourse des options de Londres, ≈ Marché des options négociables de Paris *m* (*MONEP*), ≈ Marché à terme d'instruments financiers *m* (*MATIF*); ~ **International Freight Terminal** *n* (*LIFT*) TRANSP terminal de fret international de Londres *m*; ~ **Metal Exchange** *n* (*LME*) STOCK Bourse des métaux de Londres *f*; ~ **Options Clearing House** *n UK* (*LOCH*) STOCK ≈ Société de compensation des marchés conditionnels *f* (*Fra*) (*SCMC*); ~ **Regional Transport** *n UK* (*LRT*) TRANSP autorité londonienne de transports publics; ~ **School of Economics** *n UK* (*LSE*) ECON École Supérieure d'Économie de Londres *f*; ~ **Stock Exchange** *n* (*the LSE*) STOCK la bourse de Londres, ≈ Bourse de commerce de Paris *f*, ≈ la Bourse de Paris *f*, ≈ le Palais Brongniart *m*; ~ **Stock Exchange Board** *n* STOCK ≈ Conseil de la bourse de Londres *m*, ≈ commission de la bourse de Londres *f*; ~ **Tourist Board** *n* (*LTB*) LEIS office de tourisme de Londres; ~ **Traded Options Market** *n* (*LTOM*) STOCK Marché des options négociants de Londres *m*, marché commercial à options de Londres *m*, marché des options négociables de Londres *m*, marché des options négociées de Londres *m*; ~ **Trader Options Market** *n* (*LTOM*) STOCK *created in 1978* Bourse des options négociables de Londres *f*, Marché des options négociants de Londres *m*, marché commercial à options de Londres *m*, marché des options négociables de Londres *m*, marché des options négociées de Londres *m*; ~ **weighting** *n UK* GEN COMM, HRM, WEL indemnité de résidence Londres *f*; ~ **Chamber of Commerce & Industry** *n* (*LCCI*) GEN COMM Chambre de commerce et d'industrie de Londres *f*

London[2] *pr n* GEN COMM Londres *n pr*

long[1] *adj* GEN COMM long; ~ **-dated** (ANT *medium-dated, short-dated*) STOCK à long terme; ~ **-distance** COMMS interurbain, à longue distance; ~ **-established** GEN COMM établi depuis longtemps; ~ **-haul** TRANSP long-courrier; ~ **-range** TRANSP long-courrier; ~ **-standing** GEN COMM durable; ~ **-term** (ANT *medium-term, short-term*) ACC, BANK, FIN, GEN COMM *placement, contract*, STOCK à long terme; ♦ **be ~ in futures** STOCK avoir une position longue sur contrat à terme, faire des marchés à long terme; **go ~** STOCK aller loin, prendre une position longue; ~ **in a currency** ECON *international trade* excédentaire dans une devise donnée; **in the ~ term** (ANT *in the medium term, in the short term*) GEN COMM à long terme

long[2] *n* MEDIA *radio signal* longue *f*, STOCK *sb who has sold less than they have bought* compte en compte *m* (*jarg*), personne en position longue *f* (*jarg*); ~ **bond** *n* STOCK bon à longue échéance *m*, obligation à long terme *f*; ~ **butterfly** *n* STOCK *of options* achat d'un écart papillon *m*, papillon long *m*; ~ **butterfly call** *n* STOCK *of options* achat d'un écart papillon sur option d'achat *m*, option d'achat de papillon long *f*; ~ **butterfly put** *n* STOCK *of options* achat d'un écart papillon sur option de vente *m*, option de vente de papillon long *f*; ~ **call** *n* STOCK long call *m*, position acheteur sur options d'achat *f*; ~ **call position** *n* STOCK position de longue option d'achat *f*; ~ **coupon** *n* STOCK long coupon *m*, premier coupon *m*, obligation à long terme *f*; ~ **-distance call** *n* COMMS appel interurbain *m*, appel longue distance *m*, communication interurbaine *f*, communication à longue distance *f*; ~ **exercise price** *n* STOCK cote longue *f*; ~ **form** *n* (ANT *short form*) IMP/EXP, TRANSP connaissement intégral *m*; ~ **fraud** *n* GEN COMM fraude étendue *f*; ~ **futures position** *n* (ANT *short futures position*) STOCK *options* position longue sur contrat à terme *f*, position à terme long *f*; ~ **-haul aircraft** *n* TRANSP long-courrier *m*; ~ **-haul passenger aircraft** *n* TRANSP long-courrier à passagers *m*; ~ **hedge** *n* STOCK couverture longue *f*, long hedge *m*, longue couverture *f*; ~ **lease** *n* FIN bail à long terme *m*; ~ **leg** *n* STOCK position compensée *f*; ~ **period** *n* ECON période longue *f*; ~ **position** *n* (ANT *short position*) FIN position longue *f*, STOCK position acheteur *f*, position en compte *f*, position longue *f*; ~ **put** *n* STOCK long put *m*, position acheteur sur options de vente *f*; ~ **put position** *n* STOCK position de longue option de vente *f*; ~ **-range aircraft** *n* TRANSP long-courrier *m*; ~ **-range forecast** *n* GEN COMM prévision à long terme *f*; ~ **-range passenger aircraft** *n* TRANSP long-courrier à passagers *m*; ~ **-range planning** *n* FIN, GEN COMM planification à long terme *f*; ~ **-range transport** *n* ENVIR transport à grande distance *m*, TGD; ~ **-range transport of air pollutants** *n* ENVIR transport à grande distance

des polluants aéroportés *m*, TGDPA; ~ **room** *n* UK IMP/EXP longue salle *f*; ~ **straddle** *n* STOCK achat d'un straddle *m*, long califourchon *m*; ~ **straddle position** *n* STOCK position de long califourchon *f*, position longue d'un straddle *f*; ~ **strangle** *n* STOCK *options* achat d'un strangle *m*, long étranglement *m*; ~ **strike price** *n* STOCK cote longue *f*; ~ **tail** *n* INS répercussion éventuelle et tardive *f*; ~ **term** *n* INS *marine* longue durée *f*; ~ **-term blended cost rate** *n* (*LTB*) FIN taux des coûts à long terme tous frais mélangés *m*; ~ **-term bond** *n* STOCK obligation à long terme *f*; ~ **-term bond option** *n* STOCK option d'obligation à long terme *f*; ~ **-term budget** *n* FIN budget à long terme *m*; ~ **-term credit bank** *n* BANK banque de crédits à long terme *f*; ~ **-term debt** *n* FIN dette à long terme *f*, emprunt à plus d'un an *m*; ~ **-term equity anticipation securities** *n pl* (*LEAPS*) STOCK avoir en valeurs d'anticipation à long terme *m*, options de longue durée *f pl*; ~ **-term financial investments** *n pl* ACC immobilisations financières *f pl*; ~ **-term financing** *n* FIN financement à long terme *m*; ~ **-term gain** *n* TAX plus-value à long-terme *f*; ~ **-term government bond** *n* STOCK bon du Trésor à long terme *m*; ~ **-term liability** *n* ACC, FIN dette à long terme *f*; ~ **-term loan** *n* (ANT *short-term loan*) BANK prêt à long terme *m*; ~ **-term loss** *n* TAX perte à long-terme *f*; ~ **-term objective** *n* GEN COMM objectif à long terme *m*; ~ **-term planning** *n* FIN, GEN COMM planification à long terme *f*; ~ **-term prime rate** *n* (*LTPR*) FIN taux de base à long terme *m*; ~ **-term security** *n* (ANT *short-term security*) STOCK valeur à long terme *f*; ~ **-term team** *n* WEL équipe de travail à long terme *f*; ~ **-term trend** *n* GEN COMM tendance à long terme *f*; ~ **-term unemployed** *n* BrE (*LTU, cf hard-core unemployed AmE*) ECON chômeur de longue durée *m*, demandeur d'emploi de longue durée *m*; ~ **-term unemployment** *n* ECON, HRM chômage de longue durée *m*; ~ **ton** *n* GEN COMM tonne forte *f*; ~ **value position** *n* STOCK position de compensation en compte *f*; ~ **wave** *n* ECON cycle long *m*, mouvement de longue durée *m*; ~ **-wave cycle** *n* ECON cycle de longue durée *m*; ~ **weekend** *n* GEN COMM long week-end *m*, un week-end prolongé *m*

Long: ~ **Boom** *n* ECON les trente glorieuses *f pl*

longer: ~ **-term asset** *n* STOCK avoir à échéance plus longue *m*; ~ **-term option** *n* STOCK option à plus long terme *f*, option à échéance plus courte *f*, option à échéance plus longue *f*

longevity: ~ **pay** *n* HRM salaire selon l'ancienneté dans le poste *m*

longform *n jarg US* MEDIA *broadcast* émission de reportages *f*

longitudinal[1] *adj* GEN COMM longitudinal

longitudinal:[2] ~ **data** *n* MATH *statistics* données longitudinales *f pl*; ~ **framing** *n* TRANSP couples longitudinaux *m pl*, membrures longitudinales *f pl*, système longitudinal *m*

longs *n pl* STOCK longs *m pl*, obligations à plus de 15 ans *f pl*

longshoreman *n AmE (cf docker BrE)* HRM docker *m*, débardeur *m*

look: **1.** *vt* ~ **at** GEN COMM regarder; ~ **for** GEN COMM chercher; ~ **into** GEN COMM examiner, étudier; ~ **round** PROP visiter; **2.** *vi* ~ **ahead** GEN COMM regarder vers l'avenir; ◆ ~ **at the figures** GEN COMM examiner les chiffres; ~ **for a job** HRM chercher un emploi; ~ **for a property to rent** PROP chercher une location; ~ **promising** GEN COMM *prospects* sembler intéressant; ~ **to sb for sth** GEN COMM se tourner vers qn pour qch

lookout:[1] ~ **book** *n jarg* ADMIN liste d'indésirables *f*

lookout:[2] **be on the** ~ **for** *phr* GEN COMM guetter, être à l'affût de

lookup *n* COMP consultation *f*; ~ **table** COMP table de référence *f*

loop *n obs US* POL *of top-level advisers* cercle des intimes *m* (*obs*)

loophole *n* LAW faille *f*; ~ **in the law** LAW faille dans la législation *f*, lacune *f*

loose:[1] ~ **-leaf** *adj* GEN COMM à feuilles mobiles *loc f*

loose:[2] ~ **cargo** *n* TRANSP chargement en vrac *m*, marchandises en vrac *f pl*; ~ **change** *n* GEN COMM monnaie *f*

loosen: ~ **one's purse strings** *phr* FIN dénouer les cordons de sa bourse *loc f*

Lord: ~ **Chancellor** *n UK (LC)* HRM ≈ ministre de la Justice *m*; ~ **Chief Justice** *n UK (LCJ)* HRM ≈ président de la Haute Cour de Justice *m (Fra)*

Lorenz: ~ **curve** *n* ECON courbe de Lorenz *f*

lorry *n BrE (cf truck AmE)* TRANSP camion *m*; ~ **driver** *BrE (cf teamster AmE, truck driver AmE, trucker AmE)* TRANSP camionneur *m*, chauffeur de camion *m*, conducteur de camion *m*, routier *m*; ~ **loading reception area** *BrE (cf truck loading reception area AmE)* TRANSP zone de chargement des camions *f*; ~ **-mounted crane** *BrE (cf truck-mounted crane AmE)* TRANSP camion-grue *m*, grue sur camion *f*; ~ **reception area** *BrE (cf truck reception area AmE)* TRANSP zone de chargement des camions *f*

lorryload *n BrE (cf truckload AmE)* TRANSP cargaison *f*

lose *vt* GEN COMM, LAW *case*, POL *elections* perdre; ◆ ~ **ground** GEN COMM *in competition* perdre du terrain; ~ **one's job** HRM perdre son emploi, perdre son travail

loss *n* BANK, FIN *capital* perte *f*, INS perte *f*, sinistre *m*; ~ **adjuster** HRM, INS régleur d'avaries communes *m*; ~ **adjustment expense** INS frais d'expertise *m pl*; ~ **carry-back** ACC *taxation*, FIN report d'une perte en amont *m*, report rétrospectif d'une perte *m*; ~ **carry-forward** ACC report d'une perte sur une année ultérieure *m*, *balance sheets* report de perte *m*; ~ **of claim** LAW perte d'un droit pour inexécution d'une obligation *f*, perte du droit à l'indemnité *f*, perte du droit à revendication *f*;

~ **contingency** FIN *balance sheets* prévoyance pour pertes *f*; ~ **of custom** GEN COMM baisse de clientèle *f*; ~ **function** MATH *statistics* fonction de déperdition *f*; ~ **in transit** TRANSP déchet de route *m*, freinte de route *f*; ~ **in value of assets** ACC dépréciation de l'actif *f*; ~ **leader** S&M article vendu à perte *m, marketing* article d'appel *m*, produit d'appel *m*; ~ **leader pricing** S&M *sales* vente à perte *f*, vente à prix sacrifié *f*; ~ **limitation** FIN limitation des pertes *f*; ~ **-maker** S&M article générateur de pertes *m*; ~ **of market** GEN COMM perte de marché *f*; ~ **-of-income insurance** INS *personal* assurance perte de revenu *f*; ~ **on depreciable property** ACC perte sur des biens amortissables *f*; ~ **of pay** HRM perte de salaire *f*; ~ **pricing** *jarg* S&M *marketing* technique du prix d'appel *f*; ~ **of priority** PATENTS perte de la priorité *f*; ~ **provision** ACC, ECON provision pour risques et changes *f*; ~ **ratio** BANK coefficient de perte *m*, INS rapport sinistres-primes *m*; ◆ **take a** ~ STOCK subir une perte, vendre à perte

losses: ~ **carried forward** *phr* ACC pertes reportées *f pl*, report des pertes *m*; ~ **suffered** *phr* LAW pertes subies *f pl*, préjudice subi *m*

lot *n* GEN COMM, IND lot *m*; ~ **and block** *US* PROP lotissement et pâté *m*; ~ **line** PROP ligne délimitant un lot selon le relevé d'une propriété

Lotharingian: ~ **axis** *n* ECON axe lotharingien *m*

lottery *n* GEN COMM, LEIS loterie *f*; ~ **winnings** *n pl* FIN, TAX gains de loterie *m pl*

Louvre: ~ **Accord** *n* ECON, POL Accord du Louvre *m*

low[1] *adj* GEN COMM *income, rate* faible, *price, wage* bas, faible, STOCK *futures price* bas; ~ **-cost** GEN COMM à prix réduit; ~ **-grade** S&M *quality* inférieur; ~ **-key** GEN COMM discret; ~ **-paid** HRM *job* mal payé; ~ **-polluting** ENVIR *technology* peu polluant; ~ **-priced** GEN COMM, STOCK à bas prix; ~ **-profile** (*ANT high-profile*) GEN COMM discret, à profil bas, S&M *product* à profil bas; ~ **-stream industry** *jarg* (*ANT high-stream, high-stream industry*) IND technologiquement rétrogradé; ~ **-tech** (*ANT high-tech*) COMP, IND peu élaboré; **too** ~ (*ANT too high*) GEN COMM *price, estimate* trop bas; ~ **-yielding** STOCK à faible rendement; ◆ **be** ~ **in** GEN COMM être pauvre en; ~ **in** GEN COMM juste en (*frml*), à court en (*infrml*); ~ **on** GEN COMM manquer de, à court de

low[2] *n* ECON, GEN COMM, STOCK niveau bas *m*, point bas *m*; ~ **abstraction** *n jarg* HRM faible aptitude à l'abstraction *f*; ~ **achiever** *n* (*ANT high achiever*) GEN COMM *person* sujet peu doué *m*; ~ **-cost loan** *n* BANK prêt à faible taux *m*; ~ **cube** *n* (*ANT high cube*) TRANSP marchandises à faible densité *f pl*; ~ **-density cargo** *n* (*ANT high-density cargo*) TRANSP marchandises à faible densité *f pl*; ~ **-density freight** *n* (*ANT high-density freight*) TRANSP marchandises à faible densité *f pl*; ~ **end of the market** *n* (*ANT top end of the market*) S&M bas de gamme du marché *m*; ~ **end of the range** *n* STOCK bas de gamme *m*; ~ **-flier** *n* MGMNT cadre à

moindre potentiel *m*; ~ **-flyer** *n see low-flier*;
~ **-geared capital** *n* FIN capital à faible taux
d'endettement *m*; ~ **gearing ratio** *n BrE (cf low
leverage ratio AmE)* ACC, BANK, FIN, STOCK ratio
d'endettement bas *m*; ~ **-income household** *n*
S&M *market research* foyer à faible revenu *m*;
~ **-income taxpayer** *n (ANT high-income taxpayer,
middle-income taxpayer)* TAX contribuable à
faible revenu *m*; ~ **-interest loan** *n* BANK emprunt
à faible intérêt *m*, prêt à faible intérêt *m*; ~ **-level
waste** *n* ENVIR déchets de faible activité *m pl*;
~ **leverage ratio** *n AmE (cf low gearing ratio BrE)*
ACC, BANK, FIN, STOCK ratio d'endettement bas
m; ~ **loader** *n (lo)* TRANSP remorque surbaissée *f*,
remorque à plate-forme surbaissée *f*, wagon à
plate-forme surbaissée *m*; ~ **-margin high-space
good** *n* S&M article volumineux et à faible marge
m; ~ **memory** *n* COMP mémoire basse *f*, partie
inférieure de la mémoire *f*; ~ **pay** *n* HRM bas
salaire *m*; ~ **pressure** *n (LP)* GEN COMM basse
pression *f*, dépression *f*; ~ **-pressure turbine** *n
(LPTB)* TRANSP turbine BP *f*, turbine basse
pression *f*; ~ **price** *n* STOCK *currency futures* bas
prix *m*, cours bas *m*; ~ **-profile coaster** *n* TRANSP
chaland de mer *m*; ~ **season** *n* GEN COMM basse
saison *f*; ~ **standard of living** *n (ANT high standard
of living)* WEL faible niveau de vie *m*, niveau de
vie bas *m*; ~ **stowage factor** *n (ANT high stowage
factor)* TRANSP coefficient d'arrimage bas *m*,
coefficient d'encombrement bas *m*, faible coefficient d'arrimage *m*; **the ~ -paid** *n pl* HRM, WEL
les petits salaires *m pl*; ~ **tide** *n* TRANSP marée
basse *f*; ~ **value to high weight ratio** *n (ANT high
value to low weight ratio)* TRANSP rapport valeur
faible-poids élevé *m*; ~ **water** *n (lw)* TRANSP basse
mer *f*, marée basse *f*; ~ **water ordinary spring tide**
n (LWOST) TRANSP basse mer de vive-eau *f*
lowball *n jarg* S&M *sales* devis de participation *m*
lowballer *n jarg* STOCK rapetisseur *m (jarg)*
lower:[1] ~ **case** *n (l.c.)* ADMIN, COMP, MEDIA bas de
casse *m*, lettre de bas de casse *f*, lettre minuscule *f*,
minuscule *f*; ~ **-case letter** *n (ANT upper-case
letter)* ADMIN, COMP, MEDIA bas de casse *m*, lettre
de bas de casse *f*, lettre minuscule *f*, minuscule *f*;
~ **of cost or market** *n* ACC *balance sheets* la plus
basse entre le coût d'entrée et la valeur actuelle
loc; ~ **deck** *n* TRANSP *aircraft, ship* pont inférieur
m; ~ **deck container** *n* TRANSP conteneur LD-3 *m*,
conteneur pour pont inférieur *m*; ~ **hold** *n (Lw)*
TRANSP cale *f*; ~ **income bracket** *n* ECON tranche
inférieure de revenus *f*; ~ **limit** *n* ECON, FIN, GEN
COMM, IND, STOCK plancher *m*; ~ **price** *n* STOCK
prix plus bas *m*, prix réduit *m*; ~ **quartile** *n* MATH
statistics 1er quartile *m*, quartile inférieur *m*; **the
~ -paid** *n pl* HRM les bas salaires *loc m*
lower[2] *vt* GEN COMM *price, standard* baisser,
diminuer
lowering: ~ **of taxation** *n* TAX diminution des
impôts *f*
lowest: ~ **bidder** *n* GEN COMM moins-disant *m*,
STOCK soumissionnaire le moins disant *m*;

~ **common denominator** *n (LCD)* GEN COMM
plus petit dénominateur commun *m*; ~ **price** *n*
GEN COMM cours le plus bas *m*, STOCK cours le
plus bas *m*, prix le plus bas *m*; ~ **tender** *n* GEN
COMM moins-disant *m*; ~ **tenderer** *n* GEN COMM
moins-disant *m*
loyalty *n* GEN COMM *of customer, employee* fidélité
f; ~ **bonus** STOCK prime de fidélité *f*
LP *abbr (low pressure)* GEN COMM basse pression *f*,
dépression *f*
LPG *abbr (liquid petroleum gas)* ENVIR, IND,
TRANSP *shipping* GPL *(gaz de pétrole liquéfié)*
LPTB *abbr (low-pressure turbine)* TRANSP *shipping*
turbine BP *f*, turbine basse pression *f*
LQ *abbr (letter quality)* COMP qualité courrier *f*
Lr *abbr (lugger)* TRANSP *shipping* chasse-marée *m*,
lougre *m*
LRA *abbr UK (Labour Relations Agency)* HRM,
IND, LAW ≈ Conseil des prud'hommes *m*
LRC *abbr (Labour Representation Committee)*
HRM caisse de financement des députés du monde
ouvrier *f*
LRT *abbr UK (London Regional Transport)*
TRANSP autorité londonienne de transports publics
ls *abbr (lump sum)* TRANSP *freight* forfait *m*,
somme forfaitaire *f*
LSA *abbr (life-saving apparatus)* TRANSP *shipping*
engin de sauvetage *m*, matériel de sauvetage *m*
LSD *abbr (landing storage delivery)* IMP/EXP,
TRANSP mise à terre, magasinage et livraison *loc f*
LSE *abbr UK (London School of Economics)* ECON
École Supérieure d'Économie de Londres *f*; **the ~**
(London Stock Exchange) STOCK la bourse de
Londres, ≈ Bourse de commerce de Paris *f*, ≈ la
Bourse de Paris *f*, ≈ le Palais Brongniart *m*
LTB *abbr* FIN *(long-term blended cost rate)* taux des
coûts à long terme tous frais mélangés *m*, LEIS
(London Tourist Board) office de tourisme de
Londres
Ltd *abbr UK (limited liability company)* GEN COMM
SA *(société anonyme)*, SARL *(société à respons-
abilité limitée)*
LTOM *abbr (London Traded Options Market,
London Trader Options Market)* STOCK Bourse
des options négociables de Londres *f*, Marché des
options négociants de Londres *m*, marché des
options négociables de Londres *m*, marché des
options négociées de Londres *m*
LTPR *abbr (long-term prime rate)* FIN taux de base
à long terme *m*
LTU *abbr (long-term unemployed)* ECON, HRM
chômeur de longue durée *m*, DELD *(demandeur
d'emploi de longue durée)*
LTV *abbr* BANK *(loan-to-value ratio)*, FIN *(loan-to-
value ratio)* rapport emprunt-valeur *m*, rapport
prêt-valeur *m*, ratio prêt sur valeur *m*, TRANSP
(light vessel) shipping bateau-feu *m*
LUAA *abbr (Lloyd's Underwriting Agents'*

Association) INS association des agents souscripteurs du Lloyd's

LUAMC *abbr (leading underwriters' agreement for marine cargo business)* INS *marine* convention de souscripteurs principaux pour assurance transport marin

LUAMH *abbr (leading underwriters' agreement for marine hull business)* INS *marine* convention de souscripteurs principaux pour assurance sur corps de navire

Luanda *pr n* GEN COMM Luanda *m*

Lucas: ~ **supply function** *n* ECON fonction de l'offre de Lucas *f*

luck *n* GEN COMM veine *f*

lucky: ~ **break** *n* GEN COMM coup de bol *m* (*infrml*), coup de chance *m*, coup de pot *m* (*infrml*)

lucrative *adj* GEN COMM lucratif

Luddism *n* UK HRM luddisme *m*

luddite *n* HRM luddite *mf*

luffing: ~ **crane** *n* TRANSP *cargo handling* grue à portée variable *f*

luggage *n* LEIS, TRANSP bagages *m pl*; ~ **label** LEIS, TRANSP étiquette à bagages *f*; ~ **trolley** *BrE* (*cf baggage cart AmE*) TRANSP chariot à bagages *m*

lugger *n* (*Lr*) TRANSP chasse-marée *m*, lougre *m*

lull *n* GEN COMM accalmie *f*

lulu *n* US POL indemnité parlementaire *f*

lumber *n* AmE IND *sawn, split timber* bois d'oeuvre *m*

lump *n* HRM forfait de sous-traitance *m*; ~ **of labor fallacy** *AmE*, ~ **of labour fallacy** *BrE* HRM sophisme de la main d'oeuvre au forfait *m*; ~ **sum** FIN somme globale *f*, HRM montant global *m*, prix forfaitaire *m*, INS *life insurance* somme forfaitaire *f*, somme globale *f*, TRANSP *freight* forfait *m*, somme forfaitaire *f*; ~ **-sum charter** TRANSP affrètement en bloc *m*, charte-partie en travers *f*; ~ **-sum contract** HRM contrat au forfait

m; ~ **-sum distribution** STOCK distribution de montant global *f*, distribution en une fois *f*; ~ **-sum freight** TRANSP fret à forfait *m*; ~ **-sum price** GEN COMM prix forfaitaire *m*; ~ **-sum purchase** FIN achat à montant global *m*

Lump: the ~ *n* UK HRM *building trade*, TAX les ouvriers indépendants *m pl*

lunch: there's no such thing as a free ~ *phr* GEN COMM on n'a rien pour rien

luncheon: ~ **voucher** *n* BrE (*LV*) HRM chèque-déjeuner *m*, chèque-repas *m*, ticket-repas *m*, ticket-restaurant *m*

Lusaka *pr n* GEN COMM Lusaka *n pr*

Luxembourg *pr n* GEN COMM Luxembourg *m*, *capital* Luxembourg *n pr*

Luxemburger *n* GEN COMM *person* Luxembourgeois *m*

Luxemburgian *adj* GEN COMM luxembourgeois

luxury[1] *adj* S&M *goods* de luxe *loc m*

luxury[2] *n* S&M *goods* luxe *m*; ~ **goods** *n pl* ECON biens de luxe *m pl*, GEN COMM articles de luxe *m pl*, IND biens de luxe *m pl*, S&M articles de luxe *m pl*; ~ **tax** *n* TAX taxe sur les articles de luxe *f*

LV *abbr BrE (luncheon voucher)* HRM chèque-déjeuner *m*, chèque-repas *m*, ticket-repas *m*, ticket-restaurant *m*

lw[1] *abbr (low water)* TRANSP *shipping* marée basse *f*, BM (*basse mer*)

lw:[2] **mean** ~ *n* TRANSP BM moyenne *f*

Lw *abbr (lower hold)* TRANSP *shipping* cale *f*

LWOST *abbr (low water ordinary spring tide)* TRANSP *shipping* basse mer de vive-eau *f*

lying: ~ **idle** *phr* BANK *money* inutilisé; ~ **off** *phr* TRANSP amarré au large

LYON *abbr (liquid yield option note)* STOCK billet d'option de rendement en liquide *m*, note d'option sur rendement disponible *f*

M

m *abbr* GEN COMM *(meter AmE, metre BrE)* m *(mètre)*, GEN COMM *(month)* mois *m*, TRANSP *(midship) shipping* centre du navire *m*, milieu du navire *m*, TRANSP *(motorship) shipping* navire à moteur *m*

M *abbr (monetary aggregates)* ECON M *(agrégats monétaires)*

m/a *abbr (my account)* GEN COMM mon compte *m*

Maastricht: **~ Summit** *n* GEN COMM *EU* Sommet de Maastricht *m*

MABEETA *abbr* GEN COMM Association mixte d'économie, d'échanges et de commerce Malaisie Grande-Bretagne *f*

Macedonia *pr n* GEN COMM Macédonie *f*

Macedonian[1] *adj* GEN COMM macédonien

Macedonian[2] *n* GEN COMM *person* Macédonien *m*

MACH *abbr (modular automated container handling)* TRANSP manutention modulaire et automatisée de conteneurs *f*

machine:[1] **~ -based** *adj* COMP automatisé, mécanisé, IND automatisé; **~ -made** *adj* GEN COMM fait en série, produit en série, IND *production* automatisé; **~ -readable** *adj* COMP *bar codes* compréhensible par la machine, directement exploitable, exploitable par la machine, lisible par la machine

machine[2] *n* COMP, GEN COMM, IND machine *f*; **~ accounting** *n* ACC comptabilité mécanographique *f*; **~ address** *n* COMP adresse absolue *f*, adresse réelle *f*; **~ -aided translation** *n (MAT)* COMP traduction assistée par ordinateur *f (TAO)*; **~ -assisted translation** *n (MAT)* COMP traduction assistée par ordinateur *f (TAO)*; **~ code** *n* COMP code machine *m*; **~ dynamics** *pl* ADMIN dynamique des machines *f*; **~ operator** *n* HRM, IND mécanicien *m*, opérateur de machine *m*; **~ run** *n* COMP, TRANSP passage en machine *m*; **~ safety** *n* IND, WEL sécurité machine *f*; **~ tool** *n* IND machine-outil *f*; **~ translation** *n (MT)* COMP traduction automatique *f*

machinery *n* ADMIN rouages administratifs *m pl*, COMP machines *f pl*, ECON mécanisme *m*, rouages *m pl*, rouages administratifs *m pl*, GEN COMM, IND *in factory* machines *f pl*, LAW fonctionnement *m*, rouages *m pl*, TRANSP *shipping* machines *f pl*; **~ aft** *(mchy aft)* TRANSP machines d'arrière *f pl*; **~ damage co-insurance clause** INS *hull* assurance machines *f*; **~ forward** *(mchy fwd)* TRANSP machines d'avant *f pl*; **~ survey** *(MS)* TRANSP visite des machines *f*

machtpolitik *n jarg* POL politique de la force *f*

Macmillan: **~ gap** *n* FIN écart Macmillan *m*

macro[1] *n* COMP *instruction* macro *f*

macro-[2] *pref* GEN COMM macro-

macrocomputing *n (ANT microcomputing)* COMP grande informatique *f*, macroinformatique *f*

macroeconomic[1] *adj (ANT microeconomic)* ECON macroéconomique

macroeconomic:[2] **~ demand schedule** *n* ECON tableau macroéconomique de la demande *m*; **~ policy** *n* ECON, POL politique macroéconomique *f*

macroeconomics *n (ANT microeconomics)* ECON *econometrics* macroéconomie *f*

macroenvironment *n* GEN COMM macroenvironnement *m*

macromarketing *n* S&M macromarketing *m*

macrowaste *n* ENVIR macrodéchet *m*

Madagascan[1] *adj* GEN COMM malgache

Madagascan[2] *n* GEN COMM *person* Malgache *mf*

Madagascar *pr n* GEN COMM Madagascar *f*

made[1] *adj* GEN COMM, IND confectionné, fabriqué, fait, produit; **~ up** GEN COMM, IND confectionné; ◆ **~ in France** GEN COMM, IND fabriqué en France, produit en France; **~ to last** GEN COMM, IND fait pour durer; **~ to measure** IND *tailoring* fait sur mesure

made:[2] **~ bill** *n jarg* ECON effet tiré à l'étranger *m*

Madrid *pr n* GEN COMM Madrid *n pr*

MAFF *abbr UK (Ministry of Agriculture, Fisheries and Food)* ADMIN ≈ ministère de l'Agriculture, de la Pêche et de l'Alimentation *m*

mag *n infrml (magazine)* MEDIA jl *(journal)*

magazine *n* GEN COMM, MEDIA journal *m*, magazine *m*, publication *f*, périodique *m*, revue *f*

magic: **~ quadrilateral** *n* ECON carré magique *m*

magistrate *n* LAW juge *m*, magistrat *m*

magistrates': **~ court** *n* LAW tribunal d'instance *m*; **~ entitled to adjudicate** *n pl* LAW juges compétents *m pl*, magistrats compétents *m pl*

magnate *n* GEN COMM magnat *m*

magnetic: **~ card** *n* BANK, COMP carte magnétique *f*; **~ core** *n* COMP mémoire à tores *f*, tore magnétique *m*; **~ disk** *n* COMP disque magnétique *m*; **~ storage** *n* COMP, IND mémoire magnétique *f*; **~ tape** *n* COMP, IND bande magnétique *f*; **~ tape recorder** *n* GEN COMM magnétophone *m*

magnitude *n* MATH grandeur *f*; **~ of a right** LAW importance d'un droit *f*

maiden: **~ voyage** *n* TRANSP premier voyage *m*, voyage inaugural *m*

mail[1] *n* COMMS *letters* correspondance *f*, courrier *m*, *service* envoyer par la poste, poste *f*; **~ carrier** *n* AmE *(cf postman BrE)* COMMS facteur *m*; **~ clerk** *n* ADMIN chargé de courrier *m*, COMMS chargé de courrier *mf*; **~ fraud** *n* COMMS, S&M *advertising* publipostage frauduleux *m*; **~ merge** *n* ADMIN,

COMMS publipostage *m*, COMP courrier person-nalisé *m*, fusion avec un fichier d'adresses *f*, publipostage *m*; ~ **order** *n (MO)* ADMIN, COMMS, COMP vente par correspondance *f (VPC)*, S&M commande par correspondance *f*, vente par correspondance *f (VPC)*, vente sur catalogue *f*; ~ **-order business** *n* S&M achat et vente par correspondance *m*, entreprise de vente par correspondance *f*, vente par correspondance *f*, vente sur catalogue *f*, *firm* maison de vente par correspondance *f*; ~ **-order catalog** *n AmE*, ~ **-order catalogue** *n BrE* S&M catalogue de vente par correspondance *m*; ~ **-order company** *n* S&M maison de vente par correspondance *f*; ~ **-order firm** *n* S&M maison de vente par correspondance *f*; ~ **-order selling** *n* S&M vente par correspondance *f*, vente sur catalogue *f*; ~ **transfer** *n (MT)* BANK transfert par courrier *m*; ~ **van** *n BrE* COMMS fourgon postal *m*, wagon postal *m*; ◆ **through the** ~ *AmE (cf through the post BrE)* COMMS par la poste

mail² *vt AmE (cf post BrE)* COMMS *letter* envoyer, expédier, mettre à la poste, poster

mailbox *n* ADMIN, COMMS *AmE (cf postbox BrE)*, COMP boîte aux lettres *f*

mailcar *n AmE (cf mailcoach BrE)* COMMS fourgon postal *m*, wagon postal *m*

mailcoach *n BrE (cf mailcar AmE)* COMMS fourgon postal *m*, wagon postal *m*

mailing *n* ADMIN publipostage *m*, COMMS mailing *m*, publipostage *m*, COMP mailing *m*, *advertising, promotional* publipostage *m*, *dispatch* envoi par la poste *m*, S&M envoi par la poste *m*, envoi publicitaire par la poste *m*, mailing *m*, publipostage *m*, *advertising* publipostage *m*; ~ **address** COMMS adresse d'envoi *f*, adresse de publipostage *f*, adresse postale *f*; ~ **card** COMMS, GEN COMM carte-réponse *f*; ~ **list** COMMS fichier *m*, liste d'adresses *f*, S&M liste d'adresses *f*, liste de diffusion *f*; ~ **shot** COMMS envoi de prospectus *m*, envoi publicitaire par la poste *m*, envoi publicitaire par le mailing *m*, mailing *m*, publi-postage *m*, S&M *advertising* mailing *m*, publipostage *m*

mailman *n AmE (cf postman BrE)* COMMS facteur *m*

mailshot *n* COMMS, S&M mailing *m*, publipostage *m*; ◆ **do a** ~ COMMS faire un mailing, faire un publipostage

main¹ *adj* GEN COMM essentiel, premier, principal

main:² ~ **branch** *n* BANK succursale principale *f*, GEN COMM maison mère *f*; ~ **engine** *n (ME)* TRANSP moteur principal *m*; ~ **file** *n* COMP fichier maître *m*, fichier principal *m*, GEN COMM fichier principal *m*; ~ **hatch** *n (MH)* TRANSP grand panneau *m*; ~ **line** *n* TRANSP *rail* grande ligne *f*, ligne principale *f*, GL; ~ **menu** *n* COMP menu principal *m*; ~ **office** *n* GEN COMM direction générale *f*, siège social *m*; ~ **residence** *n* PROP, TAX résidence principale *f*; ~ **screen** *n* COMP écran principal *m*; ~ **street** *n AmE (cf high street BrE)*

GEN COMM, PROP, S&M grand-rue *f*; ~ **trading partners** *n pl* ECON, POL principaux partenaires commerciaux *m pl*

mainframe *n* COMP gros ordinateur *m*, gros système *m*, ordinateur central *m*, processeur central *m*, unité centrale de traitement *f*

mainline *adj* TRANSP *railway station* de grandes lignes *loc f*

mains *n pl BrE (cf supply network AmE)* COMP, IND alimentation secteur *f*; ~ **adaptor** *n BrE (cf current adaptor AmE)* COMP, IND adaptateur secteur *m*

mainstream: ~ **economics** *n pl* ECON théorie économique dominante *f*

mainstreaming *n* WEL système de classe unique *m*

mainstreeting *n Canada* POL bain de foule *m*

maintain *vt* ADMIN *office* assurer, entretenir, COMMS *good relations* entretenir, maintenir

maintenance *n* COMP maintenance *f*, GEN COMM, IND conservation *f*, entretien *m*, maintenance *f*, LAW *of spouse, child* aide pécuniaire *f*, aliments *m pl*, entretien *m*; ~ **allowance** *n* LAW allocation d'entretien *f*; ~ **bond** *n* GEN COMM, LAW garantie *f*; ~ **charges** *n pl (SYN maintenance expenses)* GEN COMM frais d'entretien *m pl*, frais de maintenance *m pl*; ~ **crew** *n* HRM, IND équipe d'entretien *f*; ~ **department** *n* IND service d'en-tretien *m*; ~ **engineer** *n* HRM, IND ingénieur d'entretien *m*, technicien d'entretien *m*; ~ **equipment** *n* GEN COMM, IND matériel d'en-tretien *m*; ~ **expenditures** *n pl* TAX impenses *f pl*; ~ **expenses** *n pl (SYN maintenance charges)* GEN COMM frais d'entretien *m pl*, frais de maintenance *m pl*; ~ **fee** *n* BANK *for account* frais de tenue de compte *m pl*, PROP prestation d'entretien *f*; ~ **margin** *n* STOCK couverture de maintien *f*, marge de maintenance *f*, *futures* marge d'entre-tien *f*; ~ **of membership** *n* HRM adhésion jusqu'à expiration de la convention collective *f*; ~ **payments** *n pl* LAW allocation d'entretien *f*; ~ **personnel** *n pl (SYN maintenance staff)* HRM, IND personnel d'entretien *m*; ~ **schedule** *n* GEN COMM programme d'entretien *m*, programme de mise à jour *m*; ~ **staff** *n pl (SYN maintenance personnel)* HRM, IND personnel d'entretien *m*; ◆ ~, **repair and overhaul** *(MRO)* TRANSP entretien, réparation et révision

major¹ *adj* GEN COMM principal

major:² ~ **account** *n* ACC, BANK, GEN COMM grand compte *m*; ~ **currency** *n* BANK, ECON, FIN monnaie dominante *f*, monnaie principale *f*; ~ **foreign exchange market** *n* ECON marché des devises principales *m*, FIN marché des devises principales *m*, principal marché des changes *m*; ~ **producer** *n* ECON, IND *of commodity* gros producteur *m*, principal producteur *m*; ~ **road** *n* TRANSP route principale *f*; ~ **trend** *n* GEN COMM tendance dominante *f*

Major: ~ **Market index** *n (MMI)* STOCK important indice du marché *f*, indice MMI *m*, indice du marché principal *m*, le Major Market Index *m* (*I*)

majority *n* GEN COMM, LAW *age*, POL majorité *f*; ~ **decision** GEN COMM décision prise à la majorité *f*; ~ **holding** (ANT *minority holding*) STOCK participation majoritaire *f*, propriétaire majoritaire *m*; ~ **interest** (ANT *minority interest*) STOCK participation majoritaire *f*, propriétaire majoritaire *m*; ~ **interest partner** STOCK associé majoritaire *m*; ~ **ownership** STOCK propriétaire majoritaire *m*; ~ **rule** POL démocratie *f*, système majoritaire *m*, règle majoritaire *f*; ~ **rule voting** STOCK vote à la majorité *m*; ~ **shareholder** STOCK actionnaire majoritaire *m*; ~ **shareholding** (ANT *minority shareholding*) STOCK actionnariat majoritaire *m*, participation majoritaire *f*; ~ **stake** (ANT *minority stake*) STOCK participation majoritaire *f*; ~ **stockholder** STOCK actionnaire majoritaire *m*; ~ **verdict** LAW verdict rendu à la majorité *m*; ~ **vote** GEN COMM vote majoritaire *m*

make[1] *n* GEN COMM fabrication *f*, forme *f*, marque *f*, marque de contrôle *f*, S&M marque *f*; ~ **-or-buy decision** GEN COMM option produire ou acheter *f*; ~ **-up** *jarg* FIN solde des comptes *m*; ~ **-up pay** HRM rattrapage de salaire *m*

make[2] *vt* GEN COMM confectionner, construire, fabriquer, faire, *sale* conclure, IND confectionner, PATENTS *invention* réaliser, S&M *sale* conclure; ~ **out** FIN *cheque* libeller, GEN COMM *invoice* établir, *list* dresser, faire, établir; ~ **up** BANK *of accounts* arrêter, établir, ECON combler, compenser, FIN *deficit* combler, GEN COMM *garment* confectionner, *list* dresser, établir, *sum* faire l'appoint, IND *garment* confectionner; ~ **up for** GEN COMM *compensate* compenser; ◆ ~ **an advance payment** BANK, FIN verser un acompte; ~ **an approach to sb** S&M *to sell sth* faire une proposition à qn; ~ **a bid** STOCK faire une enchère; ~ **a deal** S&M conclure un marché; ~ **forecasts** FIN, GEN COMM, LEIS faire des pronostics; ~ **a freephone call to sb** *BrE* (*cf call sb toll-free AmE*) COMMS appeler qn par numéro vert; ~ **money** GEN COMM faire de l'argent; ~ **a sale** GEN COMM faire une vente; ~ **up for lost time** GEN COMM rattraper le temps perdu, rattraper son retard; ~ **up one's accounts** ACC arrêter ses comptes; ~ **£100 a week** GEN COMM se faire £100 par semaine, HRM gagner £100 par semaine

maker *n* HRM constructeur *m*, IND constructeur *m*, fabricant *m*, LAW *of note* rédigeur *m*, tireur *m*

makeshift: ~ **solution** *n* GEN COMM solution de fortune *f*

making *n* ACC, FIN *of profit* réalisation *f*, GEN COMM *of position* construction *f*, création *f*, IND *of clothes* confection *f*, façon *f*, *of machine* construction *f*, fabrication *f*; ~ **up** ACC *for losses* compensation *f*, *of balance sheet* préparation *f*; ~ **-up price** (*M/U*) GEN COMM ajustement des prix *m*, cours de compensation *m*, cours de liquidation *m*; ◆ **have the ~s of** GEN COMM avoir l'étoffe de

makuta *n* GEN COMM makuta *m pl*

MAL *abbr* (*Malaysian ringgit*) GEN COMM ringgit *m*

Malabo *pr n* GEN COMM Malabo *n pr*

mala fide *adj* LAW de mauvaise foi *loc f*

Malagasy *n* GEN COMM *language* malgache *m*

Malawi *pr n* GEN COMM Malawi *m*

Malawian[1] *adj* GEN COMM malawien

Malawian[2] *n* GEN COMM *person* Malawien *m*

Malay *n* GEN COMM *language* malais *m*

Malaysia *pr n* GEN COMM Malaisie *f*

Malaysian[1] *adj* GEN COMM malais

Malaysian[2] *n* GEN COMM *person* Malaisien *m*; ~ **ringgit** (*MAL*) GEN COMM ringgit *m*

Maldives *pr n* [inv pl] GEN COMM Maldives *f pl*

Maldivian *adj* GEN COMM des Maldives *n pr*

Malé *pr n* GEN COMM Malé *n pr*

malfunction *n* GEN COMM défaillance *f*, mauvais fonctionnement *m*, IND défaillance *f*

malfunctioning *n* GEN COMM mauvais fonctionnement *m*

Mali *pr n* GEN COMM Mali *m*

Malian[1] *adj* GEN COMM malien

Malian[2] *n* GEN COMM *person* Malien *m*

malicious: ~ **acts clause** *n* INS *hull policy* clause d'actes malveillants *f*; ~ **damage** *n* LAW dommage causé avec intention *loc m*; ~ **damage clause** *n* INS *marine, cargo policy* clause de dommages par acte malveillant *f*; ~ **mischief** *n* LAW méfait prémédité *m*

maliciously *adv* LAW avec intention de nuire *loc f*, avec préméditation *loc*

malingerer *n* HRM tire-au-flanc *m*

malingering *n* HRM absentéisme injustifié *m*, panne d'oreiller *f* (*infrml*), simulation de maladie *f*

mall *n* GEN COMM, S&M galerie marchande *f*

malleable: ~ **capital** *n* ECON capitaux malléables *m pl*

Maloney: ~ **Act** *n* LAW, STOCK loi Maloney relative à la Commission des Opérations de Bourse

malpractice *n* LAW faute professionnelle *f*, négligence professionnelle *f*

Malta *pr n* GEN COMM Malte *f*

Maltese[1] *adj* GEN COMM maltais

Maltese[2] *n* GEN COMM *language* maltais *m*, *person* Maltais *m*; ~ **pound** (*MTA*) GEN COMM livre maltaise *f*

Malthusian: ~ **law of population** *n* ECON, POL loi de Malthus sur la population *f*

mammoth[1] *adj* GEN COMM énorme; ◆ **on a ~ scale** GEN COMM sur une échelle gigantesque

mammoth:[2] ~ **reduction** *n* S&M *sales* prix sacrifié *m*; ~ **size** *n* S&M mégadimension *f*

man:[1] ~ **-made** *adj* IND artificiel, synthétique

man:[2] ~ **-machine system** *n* ADMIN système homme-machine *m*; ~ **-made fiber** *n* *AmE*, ~ **-made fibre** *n* *BrE* ENVIR fibre synthétique *f*

man[3] *vt* HRM fournir du personnel à, pourvoir en

personnel, *machine* assurer la manoeuvre de, *stand* assurer l'accueil de, assurer la permanence de, garder, tenir; ◆ ~ **a shift** HRM composer une équipe

man:[4] **the ~ in the street** *phr* GEN COMM l'homme de la rue *loc m*, monsieur tout-le-monde *m*

manage *vt* GEN COMM conduire, gérer, *company, hotel* gérer, MGMNT gérer; ~ **to** GEN COMM réussir à

manageable *adj* GEN COMM faisable

managed: ~ **account** *n* ACC comptabilité de gestion *f*, compte géré *m*, FIN comptabilité de gestion *f*; ~ **bond** *n* ECON, STOCK obligation contrôlée *f*; ~ **cost** *n* ACC coût maîtrisable *m*, coût maîtrisé *m*, ECON, FIN coût contrôlé *m*; ~ **costs** *n pl* FIN coûts maîtrisés *m pl*; ~ **currency** *n* ECON, FIN devise contrôlée *f*, devise à haute puissance *f*; ~ **currency fund** *n* ECON, FIN fonds géré en devises *m*; ~ **economy** *n* ECON, POL économie planifiée *f*; ~ **floating system** *n* ECON système unique de changes flottants *m*; ~ **loan** *n* BANK prêt géré *m*; ~ **news** *n* POL censure *f*, information contrôlée *f*; ~ **trade** *n* ECON, GEN COMM, IND commerce planifié *m*

management *n* ADMIN management *m, concept* gestion *f, people* administration *f*, direction *f*, ECON management *m*, GEN COMM *concept* gestion *f*, gérance *f*, management *m*, organisation *f*, *people* cadres *m pl*, conduite *f*, direction *f*, encadrement *m*, HRM cadres *m pl*, encadrement *m*, personnel d'encadrement *m*, MGMNT encadrement *m*, management *m, concept* gestion *f, people* cadres *m pl*; ~ **accountancy** *n* ACC, FIN, MGMNT comptabilité analytique *f*, comptabilité de gestion *f*; ~ **accountant** *n* ACC, FIN, MGMNT contrôleur de gestion *m*, responsable de comptabilité analytique *m*; ~ **accounting** *n* ACC, FIN, MGMNT comptabilité analytique *f*, comptabilité de gestion *f*; ~ **accounts** *n pl* ACC, FIN, MGMNT comptes analytiques *m pl*, tableau de bord *m*; ~ **audit** *n* ACC, FIN contrôle de gestion *m*, HRM audit de direction *m*, audit de management *m*, MGMNT audit de direction *m*, audit de management *m*, contrôle de gestion *m*; ~ **board** *n* ACC, ADMIN conseil de direction *m*, GEN COMM conseil de direction *m*, directoire *m*, HRM conseil de direction *m*, MGMNT conseil de direction *m*, directoire *m*; ~ **buy-in** *n* FIN, MGMNT apport de gestion *m*; ~ **buyout** *n (MBO)* FIN, GEN COMM, STOCK rachat d'une entreprise par ses salariés *m*, rachat de direction endettée *m*, rachat de parts de gestionnaires *m (RES)*; ~ **by exception** *n* MGMNT gestion par exception *f*; ~ **by objectives** *n (MBO)* MGMNT direction par objectifs *f (DPO)*; ~ **by responsibility center** *n AmE*, ~ **by responsibility centre** *n BrE* ACC, MGMNT centre de gestion par responsabilité *m*; ~ **by walking around** *(MBWA)* MGMNT management baladeur *m*; ~ **chart** *n* ADMIN, MATH, MGMNT tableau de bord *m*; ~ **committee** *n* GEN COMM comité directeur *m*, MGMNT comité de direction *m*, POL *European*

Commission comité directeur *m*; ~ **competence** *n* MGMNT compétence de management *f*; ~ **consultancy** *n* MGMNT cabinet de conseil en gestion *m*; ~ **consultant** *n* COMP conseil en gestion d'entreprise *m*, conseiller en gestion d'entreprise *m*, conseiller en organisation *m*, MGMNT conseil en direction *m*, conseil en gestion *m*, conseil en gestion d'entreprise *m*, conseiller en gestion d'entreprise *m*, ingénieur-conseil *m*; ~ **contract** *n* MGMNT contrat du management *m*; ~ **control** *n* ACC, FIN *auditing* contrôle de gestion *m*, MGMNT contrôle de direction *m*, contrôle de gestion *m*; ~ **development** *n* GEN COMM, MGMNT formation au management *f*, perfectionnement des cadres *m*; ~ **expenses** *n* ACC, MGMNT frais de gestion *m pl*; ~ **fee** *n* BANK commission de chef de file *f*, frais de gestion *m pl*, PROP *real estate* honoraires de gestion *m pl*, STOCK *for managing portfolio* frais de gestion *m pl*, prestation de gestion *f*; ~ **game** *n* MGMNT jeu d'entreprise *m*, simulation de gestion *f*; ~ **information** *n* COMP, MGMNT information d'organisation de la gestion *f*; ~ **information system** *n (MIS)* COMP, MGMNT informatique de gestion *f*, système d'information de management *m*, système de gestion informatisé *m*, système intégré de gestion *m (SIG)*; ~ **organization** *n* HRM type d'organisation interne *m*; ~ **and personnel office** *n (MPO)* ADMIN, MGMNT bureau de la direction et du personnel *m*; ~ **potential** *n* GEN COMM, MGMNT potentiel des cadres *m*; ~ **practices** *n pl* MGMNT procédures de gestion *f pl*; ~ **ratio** *n* FIN ratio de gestion *m*, HRM taux d'encadrement *m*, MGMNT ratio de gestion *m*; ~ **reshuffle** *n* MGMNT remaniement de l'équipe dirigeante *m*; ~ **science** *n* MATH, MGMNT science de la gestion *f*; ~ **services** *n pl* FIN services de conseil *m pl*, services de direction *m pl*, services fonctionnels *m pl*, MGMNT services d'état-major *m pl*, services de conseil interne *m pl*, services fonctionnels *m pl*; ~ **of shares** *n* STOCK gestion d'actions *f*; ~ **skills** *n pl* MGMNT compétence de gestion *f*; ~ **staff** *n* HRM, MGMNT personnel d'encadrement *m*, personnel dirigeant *m*; ~ **structure** *n* MGMNT structure de gestion *f*; ~ **style** *n* GEN COMM, MGMNT style de gestion *m*, style directorial *m*, style managérial *m*; ~ **succession planning** *n* MGMNT plans de remplacement *m pl*, plans de succession *m pl*; ~ **support** *n* HRM, MGMNT soutien au management *m*, soutien à l'encadrement *m*; ~ **system** *n* MGMNT système de gestion *m*, système de direction *m*; ~ **team** *n* HRM, MGMNT équipe de direction *f*; ~ **technique** *n* MGMNT technique de gestion *f*; ~ **theory** *n* MGMNT théorie de la gestion de l'entreprise *f*; ~ **training** *n* HRM stage de direction d'entreprise *m*, MGMNT formation des cadres *f*

Management: ~ **Consultants Association** *n UK (MCA)* MGMNT association des consultants de gestion

manager *n (mgr)* HRM, MGMNT chef *mf*, dirigeant *m*, gestionnaire *mf*, gérant *m*, manager *m*, responsable *mf*, directeur *m*; ~'s office ADMIN, MGMNT bureau du directeur *m*, direction *f*

manageress *n* HRM, MGMNT directrice *f*, gérante *f*

managerial[1] *adj* GEN COMM, MGMNT de direction *loc f*, de gestion *loc f*, directorial

managerial:[2] ~ **accounting** *n* ACC, FIN, MGMNT comptabilité analytique *f*, comptabilité de gestion *f*, comptabilité de gestion stratégique *f*; ~ **effectiveness** *n* MGMNT efficacité de la direction *f*; ~ **function** *n* MGMNT fonction de direction *f*; ~ **grid** *n* MGMNT *leadership behaviour* grille de gestion *f*; ~ **position** *n* HRM, MGMNT poste de direction *m*; ~ **prerogative** *n* HRM prérogatives de la direction *f pl*; ~ **revolution** *n* ADMIN révolution technocratique *f*, MGMNT, POL révolution managériale *f*; ~ **staff** *n pl* GEN COMM cadres *m pl*, HRM, MGMNT cadres *m pl*, personnel de direction *m*; ~ **structure** *n* GEN COMM hiérarchie *f*, HRM, MGMNT hiérarchie *f*, structure hiérarchique *f*; ~ **style** *n* MGMNT style de direction *m*

managers: ~ **and workers** *n pl* HRM, MGMNT patronat et travailleurs *loc*

managing[1] *adj* ADMIN, HRM, MGMNT dirigeant

managing[2] *n* GEN COMM conduite *f*; ~ **director** ACC *(MD)* directeur général *m*, gérant de société *m* *(DG)*, HRM, MGMNT *UK (MD)* directeur général *m* *(DG)*, président-directeur général *m* *(PDG)*; ~ **owner** TRANSP armateur-gérant *m*; ~ **partner** HRM associé gérant *m*; ~ **underwriter** BANK apériteur *m*

Managua *pr n* GEN COMM Managua *n pr*

Manama *pr n* GEN COMM Manama *n pr*

manat *n* GEN COMM manat *m*

Manchester: ~ **International Freight Terminal** *n* *(MIFT)* TRANSP terminal de fret international de Manchester *m*; ~ **School** *n* UK ECON école de Manchester *f*

M&A *abbr (mergers and acquisitions)* ECON, STOCK F&A *(fusions et acquisitions)*

mandarin *n* POL *government* mandarin politique *m*

Mandarin *n* GEN COMM *language* mandarin *m*

mandate *n* GEN COMM, LAW mandat *m*

mandated: ~ **programme** *n* UK MEDIA *instructed by independent broadcasting authority* programme imposé aux télévisions par l'IBA *m*

mandatory[1] *adj* LAW impératif, obligatoire

mandatory:[2] ~ **accounting plans** *n pl* ACC plans comptables obligatoires *m pl*; ~ **copy** *n* S&M *advertising* texte publicitaire obligatoire *m*; ~ **injunction** *n* LAW injonction donnée par un tribunal *f*; ~ **provision** *n* INS disposition obligatoire *f*, provision réglementaire *f*; ~ **quote period** *n* STOCK période de cotation obligatoire *f*, période obligatoire d'affichage des prix *f*; ~ **retirement** *n* AmE *(cf compulsory retirement BrE)* HRM mise à la retraite d'office *f*, retraite obligatoire *f*

maneuver *n* AmE *see* manoeuvre *BrE*

maneuvring: ~ **basin** *n* AmE *see* manoeuvring basin *BrE*

manifest *n* IMP/EXP, TRANSP manifeste *m*; ~ **of cargo** IMP/EXP, TRANSP manifeste de marchandises *m*; ~ **clerk** HRM, IMP/EXP, TRANSP employé aux déclarations en douane *m*; ~ **crisis** POL *European Council* crise manifeste *f*

manifold *n* GEN COMM papier à polycopier *m*, polycopie *f*

Manila *pr n* GEN COMM Manille *n pr*

manipulate *vt* ACC, GEN COMM manipuler; ♦ ~ **the figures** ACC, FIN manipuler les chiffres; ~ **the market** STOCK agir sur le marché

manipulation *n* GEN COMM, MGMNT manipulation *f*, STOCK *market* tripotages *m pl*

manipulator *n* GEN COMM manipulateur *m*, STOCK *of market* agioteur *mf*, manipulateur *m*

manned: ~ **service** *n* ADMIN permanence *f*, service assuré *m*

manning *n* HRM effectif *m*, personnel *m*; ~ **level** HRM niveau des effectifs *m*; ~ **scale** TRANSP échelle des effectifs *f*

manoeuvre *n* BrE GEN COMM manoeuvre *f*

manoeuvring: ~ **basin** *n* BrE TRANSP bassin d'évitage *m*

manpower *n* ECON main-d'oeuvre *f*, HRM effectif *m*, main-d'oeuvre *f*, IND main-d'oeuvre *f*; ~ **aid** *n* HRM, POL *for developing countries* mise à disposition de main-d'oeuvre *f*; ~ **audit** *n* ACC, HRM inventaire des effectifs *m*; ~ **costs** *n pl* ACC frais de personnel *m pl*; ~ **forecast** *n* GEN COMM, HRM prévision de l'emploi *f*; ~ **forecasting** *n* GEN COMM, HRM prévision de l'emploi *f*, prévision de main-d'oeuvre *f*; ~ **management** *n* HRM, MGMNT gestion des effectifs *f*; ~ **planning** *n* *(SYN human resource planning)* HRM gestion prévisionnelle de l'emploi *f*, planification de l'emploi *f*, planification des effectifs *f*, planification des ressources humaines *f*, recrutement et gestion des effectifs *loc m*; ~ **policy** *n* HRM politique de la main d'oeuvre *f*

Manpower: ~ **Services Commission** *n obs* UK *(MSC)* HRM commission des services de main d'oeuvre, maintenant Training Agency

manual[1] *adj* GEN COMM, HRM, IND manuel

manual[2] *n* GEN COMM *for reference* manuel *m*; ~ **feed** COMP chargement manuel *m*; ~ **labor** AmE, ~ **labour** BrE HRM, IND travailleurs manuels *m pl*; ~ **mode** MATH *of calculation* méthode manuelle *f*; ~ **skill** HRM, IND aptitude manuelle *f*; ~ **system** *(MS)* TRANSP système manuel *m*; ~ **union** UK HRM syndicat de travailleurs manuels *m*; ~ **work** HRM, IND travail manuel *m*; ~ **worker** HRM, IND ouvrier *m*, travailleur manuel *m*

manually *adv* COMP, GEN COMM manuellement, à la main *loc f*

manufacture *vt* IND fabriquer; ♦ ~ **under licence** BrE, ~ **under license** AmE IND *production* fabriquer qch sous licence

manufactured[1] *adj (mfd)* GEN COMM, IND fabriqué, manufacturé

manufactured:[2] ~ **goods** n pl ECON, IND produits manufacturés m pl

manufacturer n GEN COMM fabricant m, HRM constructeur m, IND constructeur m, fabricant m; ~'s **brand** S&M marque du fabricant f; ~'s **and contractor's liability insurance** US INS *company* assurance responsabilité civile des fabricants et des entreprises f; ~'s **export agent** IMP/EXP commissionnaire exportateur du fabricant m; ~'s **output insurance** INS *company* assurance de rendement industriel f, assurance tous risques de biens industriels f; ~'s **price** S&M prix de fabrique m; ~'s **recommended price** *(MRP)* S&M prix public m, prix recommandé par le fabriquant m

manufacturers n pl *(mfrs)* GEN COMM, IND fabricants m pl

manufactures n pl ECON, IND produits manufacturés m pl

manufacturing n IND fabrication f; ~ **activity** n IND activité manufacturière f; ~ **base** n IND base industrielle f; ~**-based economy** n ECON économie manufacturière f; ~ **capacity** n IND capacité de production f, potentiel de production m; ~ **company** n ECON, IND société industrielle f; ~ **control** n IND contrôle de fabrication m; ~ **costs** n pl ACC *profit and loss account*, ECON, IND coûts de fabrication m pl; ~ **expenses** n pl ACC frais de fabrication m pl; ~ **industry** n IND industrie de transformation f, industrie manufacturière f; ~ **inventory** n IND stock fabrication m; ~ **order** n S&M *sales* bon de commande m; ~ **overheads** n pl ACC, ECON, FIN, IND coûts fixes de fabrication m pl, frais généraux de fabrication m pl; ~ **process** n IND *production* processus de fabrication m; ~ **and processing profits** n pl IND, TAX bénéfices de fabrication et de transformation m pl; ~ **profits** n pl ECON bénéfices de fabrication m pl; ~ **rights** n pl IND, LAW, PATENTS droits de fabrication m pl; ~ **sector** n ECON, IND secteur de production m; ~ **system** n IND système de fabrication m; ~ **under licence** n BrE IND fabrication sous licence f; ~ **under license** n AmE *see manufacturing under licence BrE*; ~ **workforce** n HRM personnel de fabrication m, personnel de production m, personnel de production m, IND personnel de fabrication m, personnel de production m

manuscript n *(MS)* TAX manuscrit m *(MS)*

map n COMP topogramme m, topographie f

Maputo pr n GEN COMM Maputo n pr

Mar. abbr *(March)* GEN COMM mars m

MAR: ~ **policy** n INS *cargo* assurance sur facultés f

MARAD abbr US *(Maritime Administration)* TRANSP administration maritime

March n *(Mar.)* GEN COMM mars m

margin n ACC, ADMIN, BANK marge f, ECON marge f, *between rates of interest* écart m, MEDIA *on page*, PATENTS marge f, S&M marge bénéficiaire f, STOCK appel de marge m, marge de sécurité f, couverture f, dépôt m, marge f, *paid by client* couverture f; ~ **account** STOCK compte de couverture m, compte à marge m; ~ **buying** STOCK achat marginal m, achat à découvert m; ~ **call** STOCK appel de marge m; ~ **call-replenish to initial level** STOCK *currency trading* appel de marge pour reconstituer l'apport initial m, appel de marge-réapprovisionner au niveau initial m; ~ **department** STOCK service des garanties m, service des opérations sur marge m; ~ **deposit** STOCK *currency futures* dépôt de couverture m, dépôt de marge m; ~ **of error** ACC, GEN COMM marge d'erreur f; ~ **gearing** BrE *(cf margin leverage AmE)* STOCK *futures* effet de levier de la marge m; ~ **leverage** AmE *(cf margin gearing BrE)* STOCK *futures* effet de levier de la marge m; ~ **maintenance** STOCK appel de marge m, marge de sécurité f; ~ **of profit** ACC, ECON, FIN, S&M marge bénéficiaire f; ~ **purchase** STOCK achat marginal m, achat à découvert m; ~ **requirement** STOCK dépôt obligatoire m; ~ **requirements** BANK nécessité de couverture f; ~ **of safety** ACC, FIN, HRM, IND marge de sécurité f; ~ **security** STOCK marge de sécurité f, titre acquis sur marge m; ~ **shrinkage** ACC diminution de marge f; ~ **stop** ADMIN margeur m; ~ **trading** STOCK négoce marginal m, transactions sur marge f pl; ♦ **on** ~ FIN sur marge, à découvert

marginal[1] adj GEN COMM de marge loc f, marginal

marginal:[2] ~ **account** n BANK compte marginal m; ~ **analysis** n ACC, ECON, FIN analyse marginale f; ~ **cost** n ACC, ECON, FIN coût marginal m; ~ **cost curve** n ECON courbe des coûts marginaux f; ~ **cost pricing** n ECON fixation des prix en fonction du coût marginal f; ~ **costing** n ACC, ECON, FIN comptabilité marginale f, méthode des coûts marginaux f, évaluation marginale des prix de revient f; ~ **efficiency of capital** n *(MEC)* ECON efficacité marginale du capital f; ~ **efficiency of investment** n ECON efficacité marginale des investissements f; ~ **firm** n ECON entreprise marginale f; ~ **note** n ADMIN note en marge f, note marginale f; ~ **physical product** n *(MPP)* ECON produit marginal physique m; ~ **pricing** n ACC, ECON, FIN, S&M fixation marginale du prix f; ~ **principle of allocation** n *(MPA)* ECON principe marginal d'attribution m; ~ **private cost** n ECON coût privé marginal m; ~ **producer** n ECON, IND producteur marginal m; ~ **product** n IND, S&M produit marginal m; ~ **product of labor** n AmE, ~ **product of labour** n BrE ECON produit marginal de la main-d'oeuvre m, produit marginal du travail m; ~ **productivity** n ECON, IND productivité marginale f; ~ **productivity theory** n ECON théorie de la productivité marginale f; ~ **profit** n ECON bénéfice marginal m; ~ **propensity to consume** n *(MPC)* ECON propension marginale à consommer f; ~ **propensity to import** n *(MPI)* ECON, IMP/EXP tendance marginale à importer f *(TMI)*; ~ **propensity to invest** n BANK, ECON, FIN propension marginale à investir f; ~ **propensity to save** n *(MPS)* BANK, ECON, FIN propension marginale à épargner f; ~ **property** n PROP propriété marginale *f*; ~ **rate** *n* TAX taux marginal *m*; ~ **rate of substitution** *n (MRS)* ECON taux marginal de substitution *m*; ~ **rate of transformation** *n* ECON taux marginal de transformation *m*; ~ **return on capital** *n* FIN, STOCK rendement marginal sur le capital *m*; ~ **revenue** *n* ECON, FIN recette marginale *f*; ~ **significance** *n* ECON utilité marginale *f*; ~ **social cost** *n* ECON coût social marginal *m*; ~ **tax rate** *n* TAX taux marginal d'impôt *m*; ~ **utility** *n* ECON utilité marginale *f*; ~ **worker** *n* HRM travailleur marginal *m*

marginalism *n* ECON marginalisme *m*

marginalists *n pl* ECON marginalistes *m pl*

marginalize *vt* ACC, ECON, FIN, GEN COMM marginaliser

marginally *adv* GEN COMM marginalement

marine¹ *adj* TRANSP maritime

marine:² ~ **diesel oil** *n* TRANSP diesel marin *m*; ~ **engineer** *n* HRM, TRANSP *shipping* ingénieur maritime *m*; ~ **insurance** *n* INS, TRANSP assurance maritime *f*; ~ **insurance fraud** *n* INS dol d'assurance maritime *m*, fraude d'assurance maritime *f*; ~ **insurance policy** *n (MIP)* INS, TRANSP police d'assurance maritime *f*; ~ **insurance policy certificate** *n* INS attestation d'assurance maritime *f*; ~ **oil berth** *n* TRANSP quai réservé à la manutention du diesel marin *m*; ~ **piracy** *n* TRANSP piraterie *f*; ~ **pollution** *n* ENVIR pollution marine *f*; ~ **risk analyst** *n* HRM analyste des risques maritimes *m*; ~ **superintendent** *n* HRM, TRANSP *shipping* inspecteur maritime *m*

marital: ~ **status** *n* LAW situation de famille *f*, état civil *m*, état matrimonial *m*

maritime¹ *adj* TRANSP maritime

maritime:² ~ **canal** *n* TRANSP canal maritime *m*; ~ **fraud** *n* LAW, TRANSP fraude maritime *f*; ~ **fraud prevention** *n* LAW, TRANSP prévention des fraudes maritimes *f*, répression des fraudes maritimes *f*; ~ **industrial development area** *n (MIDA)* IND zone de développement maritime industriel; ~ **law** *n* LAW, TRANSP droit de la mer *m*, droit maritime *m*; ~ **lien** *n* LAW, TRANSP privilège maritime *m*; ~ **loan** *n* FIN prêt maritime *m*; ~ **peril** *n* INS fortune de mer *f*, péril de la mer *m*; ~ **risk** *n* INS *marine* risque maritime *m*; ~ **service** *n* TRANSP service maritime *m*; ~ **shipping** *n* TRANSP trafic maritime *m*; ~ **terminal** *n* TRANSP terminal maritime *m*; ~ **trade** *n* ECON, GEN COMM, IMP/EXP, TRANSP commerce maritime *m*

Maritime: ~ **Administration** *n US (MARAD)* TRANSP administration maritime; ~ **Pollution** *n (MARPOL)* ENVIR *convention* Pollution maritime *f (MARPOL)*; ~ **Transport Committee** *n (MTC)* TRANSP *OECD* commission des Transports Maritimes

mark¹ *n* FIN *Deutschmark* mark allemand *m*, LAW, PATENTS marque *f*, STOCK cours de référence *m*; ~ **with high reputation** PATENTS marque de haute renommée *f*; ~ **to mark** *jarg* STOCK compensation *f*; ~ **to market** STOCK appel de marge du jour *m*; ~ **-to-the-market** STOCK fluctuations journalières *f pl*; ~ **-up** GEN COMM augmentation d'un prix de vente *f*, MEDIA *print* préparation de copie *f*, S&M *of prices* augmentation *f*, hausse *f*, majoration *f*, marge *f*, *of sales, margin* marge bénéficiaire *f*; ~ **-up inflation** ECON inflation administrée *f*

mark² *vt* GEN COMM *merchandise* marquer; ~ **down** S&M *price* baisser; ~ **off** ACC *a sum against something* marquer un prix; ~ **up** GEN COMM, S&M *price* majorer; ◆ ~ **stock** ACC coter le stock

Mark *n* GEN COMM mark *m*

markdown *n* GEN COMM démarque *f*, S&M *in price* rabais *m*, remise *f*, réduction *f*

marked¹ *adj* GEN COMM *decline, difference* marqué

marked:² ~ **check** *n AmE*, ~ **cheque** *n BrE* BANK chèque marqué *m*; ~ **price** *n* S&M prix marqué *m*

marker *n* ADMIN, GEN COMM marqueur *m*; ~ **pen** ADMIN, GEN COMM marqueur *m*

market:¹ **at** ~ *adj* STOCK *price* au cours du marché *loc m*; ~ **-driven** *adj* GEN COMM mercatis; ~ **-orientated** *adj* ECON, S&M orienté par le marché; ~ **-sensitive** *adj* S&M sensible au marché

market² *n* ECON, GEN COMM, S&M, STOCK marché *m*; ~ **acceptance** *n* S&M acceptation du produit par le marché *f*; ~ **adjustment** *n* ECON ajustement du marché *m*; ~ **aim** *n* S&M objectif de marché *m*; ~ **analysis** *n* S&M étude de marché *f*, STOCK analyse de marché *f*; ~ **analyst** *n* HRM, S&M, STOCK analyste-marché *m*, conjoncturiste *mf*; ~ **appraisal** *n* GEN COMM, S&M évaluation du marché *f*; ~ **area** *n* S&M segment du marché *m*, zone de chalandise *f*; ~ **awareness** *n* S&M conscience du marché *f*; ~ **base** *n* S&M définition de marché *f*; ~ **behavior** *n AmE*, ~ **behaviour** *n BrE* S&M comportement du marché *m*; ~ **capitalization** *n* STOCK capitalisation boursière *f*; ~ **clearing price** *n* ECON prix de compensation du marché *m*; ~ **close** *n* STOCK clôture de marché *f*; ~ **comparison approach** *n* GEN COMM, PROP, S&M *real estate* alignement sur les prix du marché *m*; ~ **concentration** *n* ECON concentration du marché *f*; ~ **conditions** *n pl* GEN COMM, S&M conjoncture du marché *f*; ~ **confidence** *n* S&M confiance du marché *f*; ~ **correction** *n* STOCK correction *f*, rectification *f*; ~ **creation** *n* S&M création de marché *f*; ~ **cycle** *n* ECON, GEN COMM cycle du marché *m*; ~ **day** *n* STOCK jour de bourse *m*; ~ **dealing** *n* FIN activités sur un marché *f pl*; ~ **demand** *n* ECON demande du marché *f*; ~ **development** *n* S&M évolution du marché *f*; ~ **disclosure** *n* STOCK divulgation sur le marché *f*; ~ **discrimination coefficient** *n* ECON coefficient de discrimination du marché *m*; ~ **distortion** *n* ECON distorsion du marché *f*; ~ **dynamics** *n pl* S&M dynamique de marché *f*; ~ **economy** *n* ECON, POL économie de marché *f*; ~ **entry** *n* S&M mise sur le marché *f*; ~ **entry guarantee scheme** *n* S&M plan de garantie de pénétration de marché *m*; ~ **entry option** *n* IMP/EXP option d'entrée sur le marché *f*; ~ **environment** *n* S&M environnement du marché *m*; **~ equilibrium** *n* ECON équilibre du marché *m*; **~ evaluation** *n* GEN COMM, S&M évaluation du marché *f*; **~ expansion** *n* S&M développement du marché *m*; **~ exploration** *n* S&M prospection des marchés *f*; **~ failure** *n* ECON distorsion du marché *f*; **~ forces** *n pl* ECON, POL, S&M forces du marché *f pl*, tendances du marché *f pl*; **~ forecast** *n* GEN COMM, S&M pronostic relatif au marché *m*, prévisions du marché *f pl*; **~ form** *n* ECON structure du marché *f*; **~ fragmentation** *n* ECON, GEN COMM fragmentation *f*; **~ gap** *n* (SYN *market opening, market opportunity*) S&M créneau *m*; **~ gardener** *n* BrE (*cf truck farmer AmE*) ECON maraîcher *m*; **~ gardening** *n* BrE (*cf truck farming AmE*) ECON *agricultural* maraîchage *m*; **~ hours** *n pl* STOCK heures de bourse *f pl*, heures de négociation *f pl*; **~ -if-touched order** *n* (*MIT order*) STOCK ordre au cours exact *m*; **~ index** *n* STOCK indice boursier *m*; **~ indicator** *n* GEN COMM, S&M indicateur de marché *m*; **~ intelligence** *n* S&M information commerciale *f*; **~ leader** *n* GEN COMM entreprise leader *f*, S&M innovateur *m*, leader du marché *m*; **~ leadership** *n* S&M position de numéro 1 *f*; **~ letter** *n* US STOCK lettre d'information aux investisseurs *f*; **~ line** *n* GEN COMM courbe du marché *f*; **~ maker** *n* STOCK (*cf jobber UK, stockjobber UK*) contrepartiste *mf*, courtier en valeurs *m*, jobber *m*, négociant en titres *m*, négociateur en valeurs mobilières *m*, STOCK *UK* adhérent mainteneur de marché *m*, AMM, créateur de marchés *m*, mainteneur de marché *m*, market maker *m*, teneur de marché *m*; **~ management** *n* MGMNT, S&M gestion commerciale *f*; **~ mechanism** *n* ECON mécanisme du marché *m*; **~ niche** *n* S&M créneau commercial *m*, niche *f*; **~ objective** *n* S&M cible *f*; **~ opening** *n* (SYN *market gap, market opportunity*) S&M créneau *m*; **~ operations** *n pl* STOCK opérations de marché *f pl*; **~ opportunity** *n* (SYN *market gap, market opening*) S&M créneau *m*, créneau commercial *m*; **~ order** *n* STOCK *to buy or sell a security* ordre au cours du marché *m*, ordre au mieux *m*; **~ order on the close** *n* (*MOC*) STOCK ordre au mieux à la clôture *m*, ordre au prix du marché en fin de séance *m*; **~ outperformer** *n* STOCK qui fait mieux que le marché; **~ participant** *n* STOCK *futures* participant du marché *m*; **~ penetration** *n* S&M pénétration du marché *f*; **~ plan** *n* S&M plan de marché *m*; **~ planning** *n* S&M plan de marché *m*; **~ position** *n* STOCK *on currency* position de marché *f*; **~ potential** *n* S&M marché tendanciel *m*, potentiel du marché *m*; **~ power** *n* ECON pouvoir d'un acheteur sur le marché *m*; **~ presence** *n* S&M présence sur un marché *f*; **~ price** *n* ECON, GEN COMM prix du marché *m*, S&M prix du marché *m*, prix marchand *m*, STOCK cours de la Bourse *m, last price* cours du marché *m*, prix du marché *m*; **~ pricing** *n* FIN, S&M tarification en fonction du marché *f*; **~ profile** *n* S&M profil d'un marché *m*; **~ prospects** *n pl* S&M perspectives commerciales *f pl*, perspectives du marché *f pl*; **~ prospects service** *n* S&M service

des perspectives du marché *m*; **~ psychology** *n* GEN COMM, S&M psychologie de marché *f*; **~ rate** *n* STOCK taux du marché *m*; **~ rate of discount** *n* GEN COMM taux d'escompte du marché *m*; **~ rate of interest** *n* ECON, FIN taux d'intérêt du marché *m*; **~ rating** *n* S&M cours de la Bourse *m*; **~ receptiveness** *n* STOCK réceptivité du marché *f*; **~ recovery** *n* GEN COMM redressement du marché *m*, STOCK reprise boursière *f*; **~ rent** *n* ECON, POL, PROP loyer du marché *m*; **~ report** *n* S&M étude de marché *f*; **~ research** *n* S&M analyse des marchés *f*, étude de marché *f*; **~ resistance** *n* S&M résistance du marché *f*; **~ review** *n* FIN bulletin financier *m*; **~ rigger** *n* STOCK contrepartiste occulte *m*; **~ rigging** *n* STOCK manipulation de marchés *f*; **~ risk** *n* STOCK risque du marché *m*; **~ risk premium** *n* STOCK prime de risque de marché *f*; **~ saturation** *n* GEN COMM, S&M saturation du marché *f*; **~ sector** *n* S&M secteur de marché *m*; **~ segment** *n* S&M segment du marché *m*, strate de marché *f*; **~ segmentation** *n* S&M segmentation du marché *f*; **~ selection overseas** *n* ECON *international trade* prospection d'un marché étranger potentiel *f*; **~ sensitivity** *n* GEN COMM instabilité du marché *f*; **~ share** *n* ECON, S&M part de marché *f*; **~ skimming** *n* S&M *pricing* écrémage du marché *m*; **~ slump** *n* STOCK dégringolade du marché *f*; **~ socialism** *n* ECON, POL troisième voie *f*; **~ structure** *n* ECON, S&M structure du marché *f*; **~ study** *n* GEN COMM examen des débouchés *m*, S&M examen des débouchés *m*, étude de marché *f*; **~ support** *n* S&M soutien du marché *m*; **~ survey** *n* S&M étude de marché *f*, étude des débouchés *f*; **~ system** *n* ECON système de marché *m*; **~ test** *n* S&M marché-test *m*, test de vente *m*, vente expérimentale *f*; **~ testing** *n* ECON, POL simulation de privatisation *f*, S&M essai de marché *m*, essai de vente *m*; **~ timing** *n* STOCK période porteuse pour le marché *f*; **~ tone** *n* STOCK ambiance du marché *f*; **~ transparency** *n* GEN COMM transparence du marché *f*; **~ trend** *n* ECON, GEN COMM, S&M orientation du marché *f*, tendance du marché *f*; **~ valuation** *n* STOCK évaluation boursière *f*; **~ value** *n* ACC *balance sheets* valeur actuelle *f*, FIN valeur marchande *f*, GEN COMM valeur vénale *f*, INS, PROP valeur du marché *f*, S&M valeur marchande *f*, STOCK prix du marché *m*, valeur marchande *f*; **~ value clause** *n* INS, PROP clause de la valeur vénale *f*, valeur du marché *f*; **~ value versus actual cash value** *n* PROP valeur marchande contre valeur comptant réelle *f*; **~ value-weighted index** *n* STOCK indice pondéré de valeur marchande *m*, indice pondéré par la capitalisation boursière *m*; **~ view** *n* STOCK aperçu du marché *m*, vue du marché *f*; ◆ **at the ~** STOCK au mieux; **at the ~ call** STOCK à l'appel du marché; **at the ~ price** STOCK au cours de la Bourse; **away from the ~** STOCK hors marché, loin du marché; **come onto the ~** S&M arriver sur le marché; **make a ~** STOCK conclure une affaire, maintenir le marché, se porter contrepartiste, tenir le marché;

no ~ STOCK *broker's term* marché hors cote *m*, pas de marché; **on the ~** GEN COMM, PROP en vente

market³ *vt* GEN COMM commercialiser, S&M commercialiser, distribuer, trouver un débouché pour

Market: **~ Eye** *n* STOCK *London Stock Exchange* information sur le marché en temps réel; **~ Research Corporation of America** *n (MRCA)* S&M société américaine des études de marché

marketability *n* STOCK commerciabilité *f*, négociabilité *f*

marketable¹ *adj* GEN COMM commercialisable, de qualité marchande *loc f*, négociable, vendable, S&M commercialisable, marchand, STOCK *shares* négociable

marketable:² **~ bond** *n* STOCK obligation négociable *f*, titre de placement *m*; **~ discharge permit** *n* (SYN *transferable discharge permit*) GEN COMM autorisation de décharge négociable *f*; **~ instrument** *n* (ANT *nonmarketable instrument*) BANK instrument négociable *m*; **~ securities** *n pl* STOCK titres de placement *m pl*, valeurs de placement *f pl*; **~ title** *n (cf merchantable title AmE)* PROP titre négociable *m*; **~ value** *n* S&M valeur marchande *f*

marketeer *n* HRM, S&M expert en marketing *m*, mercateur *m*, spécialiste en marketing *m*

marketing *n* GEN COMM commercialisation *f*, S&M commercialisation *f*, marketing *m*, stratégie commerciale *f*, mercatique *f (frml)*; **~ agreement** S&M accord marketing *m*; **~ appropriation** S&M dotations budgétaires affectées au marketing *f pl*; **~ authorization** S&M *for pharmaceuticals* autorisation de mise sur le marché *f*, AMM; **~ board** S&M agence de commercialisation *f*, office de régularisation *m*; **~ budget** ACC, S&M budget de marketing *m*; **~ channel** ADMIN, GEN COMM canal de distribution *m*, S&M canal de distribution *m*, circuit commercial *m*, circuit de distribution *m*; **~ concept** S&M concept marketing *m*, démarche marketing *f*; **~ conference** S&M réunion marketing *f*; **~ cost** S&M coûts marketing *m pl*; **~ cost variance** S&M écart des coûts marketing *m*; **~ department** ADMIN, S&M service marketing *m*; **~ director** HRM, MGMNT, S&M directeur commercial *m*, directeur du marketing *m*; **~ information system** *(MIS)* S&M système d'information de marketing *m (SIM)*; **~ manager** HRM, MGMNT, S&M directeur commercial *m*, directeur du marketing *m*; **~ mix** S&M formule de marketing *f*, marketing-mix *m*; **~ officer** HRM, S&M chargé de la mercatique *mf*, chargé du marketing *mf*; **~ plan** S&M plan marketing *m*; **~ policy** S&M politique de marketing *f*; **~ profile** S&M profil marketing *m*; **~ research** S&M recherche commerciale *f*, recherche marketing *f*, *market research* étude de marché *f*; **~ and sales plan** S&M plan marketing et ventes *m*; **~ strategy** S&M stratégie commerciale *f*, stratégie de marché *f*, stratégie marketing *f*

marketplace *n* GEN COMM, S&M place du marché *f*

marking *n* FIN cotation *f*, S&M marquage *m*; **~ -to-market** STOCK fluctuations journalières *f pl*

markka *n* GEN COMM markka *m*

MARPOL *abbr (Maritime Pollution)* ENVIR *Convention 1978* MARPOL *(Pollution maritime)*

marriage: **~ breakdown** *n* LAW rupture du lien conjugal *f*, rupture du mariage *f*, échec du mariage *m*; **~ contract** *n* LAW contrat de mariage *m*

married: **~ couples' allowance** *n UK* TAX abattement pour couples mariés *m*; **~ exemption** *n* TAX exemption de marié *f*; **~ man** *n* ADMIN, LAW, TAX homme marié *m*; **~ woman** *f* ADMIN, LAW, TAX femme mariée

marry *vt* STOCK faire des opérations symétriques *loc f*; **~ up** S&M *sales, auction* marier

Marshall: **~ Plan** *n* ECON Plan Marshall *m*

mart *n* GEN COMM, PROP, S&M centre de commerce *m*

martingale *n* MATH martingale *f*

Marxian: **~ economics** *n* ECON, POL économie marxiste *f*

Marxism *n* POL marxisme *m*

Marxist¹ *adj* POL marxiste

Marxist² *n* POL marxiste *mf*

Maseru *pr n* GEN COMM Maseru *n pr*

mask *vt* S&M *advertising* cacher

mass: **~ appeal** *n* S&M appel publicitaire de masse *m*; **~ communication** *n* MEDIA communication de masse *f*; **~ mailing** *n* COMMS, COMP mailing *m*, publipostage *m*, S&M mailing *m*; **~ marketing** *n* S&M marketing de masse *m*; **~ media** *n* COMMS mass-média *m pl*, moyens de communication *m pl*, supports de communication *m pl*, MEDIA moyens de communication *m pl*, médias *m pl*, S&M médias *m pl*; **~ memory** *n* COMP mémoire de grande capacité *f*, mémoire de masse *f*; **~ production** *n* IND fabrication en grandes séries *f*, fabrication en série *f*, production en masse *f*; **~ rapid transit** *n (MRT)* TRANSP *Singapore* transport collectif rapide *m*; **~ redundancy** *n* HRM licenciement collectif *m*; **~ risk** *n* INS risque de masse *m*; **~ storage** *n* COMP mémoire de grande capacité *f*, mémoire de masse *f*; **~ storage device** *n* COMP mémoire de grande capacité *f*, mémoire de masse *f*; **~ transit railroad** *n AmE (MTR, mass transit railway)* TRANSP réseau ferroviaire de transport collectif *m*; **~ transit railway** *n BrE (MTR, mass transit railroad)* TRANSP réseau ferroviaire de transport collectif *m*; **~ transit system** *n AmE (cf public transport system BrE)* TRANSP transports en commun *m pl*; **~ unemployment** *n* ECON, HRM chômage de masse *m*, chômage à grande échelle *m*

massage: **~ the figures** *phr* ACC, FIN habiller le bilan, manipuler les chiffres, STOCK habiller le bilan

masses: **the ~** *n pl* POL les masses *f pl*

massive *adj* GEN COMM important, massif, HRM massif

mass-produce *vt* IND *production* produire en grandes séries

mass-produced *adj* IND fabriqué en grandes séries, produit en grandes séries

mast *n* TRANSP mât *m*; ~ **step** TRANSP emplanture *f*

master *n* HRM *shipping* capitaine *mf*, commandant *m*, MEDIA *broadcast* copie antenne *f*, TRANSP *shipping* capitaine *mf*, commandant *m*, patron *m*; ~ **air waybill** *(MAWB)* IMP/EXP, TRANSP lettre de transport aérien groupé *f*; ~ **-at-arms** HRM, TRANSP capitaine d'armes *m*; ~ **budget** ACC budget principal *m*; ~ **card** COMP carte maîtresse *f*; ~ **change** *(MC)* TRANSP *aviation* spécification de changement notifié *f (SCN)*; ~ **copy** ADMIN, COMP, GEN COMM original *m*; ~ **document** ADMIN, COMP document de base *m*, document maître *m*; ~ **file** COMP fichier de base *m*, fichier principal *m*, fichier père *m*, GEN COMM fichier principal *m*; ~ **key** COMP clé principale *f*; ~ **lease** PROP bail maître *m*; ~ **limited partnership** GEN COMM société en commandite *f*; ~ **owner** HRM armateur *m*, patron *m*; ~ **pallet** TRANSP palette principale *f*; ~ **plan** ECON plan directeur *m*, MGMNT plan d'ensemble *m*; ~ **policy** US INS *company* police de base *f*; ~ **-servant rule** GEN COMM, HRM régulation employeur-employé *f*, LAW clause par laquelle une partie accepte de protéger une autre partie; ~**'s certificate** TRANSP brevet de capitaine *m*

Master: ~ **of Business Administration** *n (MBA)* WEL ≈ maîtrise de gestion des entreprises *f*, ≈ titulaire d'une maîtrise de gestion *m*; ~ **of Commerce** *n (MCom)* GEN COMM ≈ maîtrise en sciences économiques *f*, ≈ titulaire d'une maîtrise en sciences économiques *m*; ~ **of Economics** *n (MEcon)* GEN COMM ≈ maîtrise en sciences économiques *f*, ≈ titulaire d'une maîtrise en sciences économiques *m*; ~ **of Science** *n (MSc)* GEN COMM ≈ maîtrise de sciences *f*, ≈ titulaire d'une maîtrise de sciences *m*

Mastercard® *n* BANK carte de crédit

masthead *n* MEDIA *in newspaper or magazine* générique *m*, nom d'ours *m*, ours *m*

masts *n pl* TRANSP mâture *f*

MAT *abbr* COMP *(machine-aided translation, machine-assisted translation)* TAO *(traduction assistée par ordinateur)*, GEN COMM *(material)* documentation *f*, informations *f pl*, MATH *(moving annual total) statistics* total annuel mobile *m*

match[1] *vt* GEN COMM *results* correspondre à, S&M *success* égaler; ~ **up to** GEN COMM être l'égal de

match:[2] **must** ~ *phr* (SYN *must fit*) PATENTS *intellectual property* doit s'adapter, obligation d'adaptation *f*

matched:[1] ~ **book** *n* STOCK compte à solde nul *m*, option couplée *f*; ~ **order** *n* STOCK ordre lié *m*; ~ **orders** *n pl* STOCK ordres similaires *m pl*; ~ **sale-purchase transaction** *n* STOCK opération d'achat-vente compensée *f*; ~ **securities** *n pl* STOCK ordres couplés *m pl*; ~ **trade** *n* STOCK opérations commerciales compensées *f pl*

matched:[2] ~ **and lost** *phr* STOCK couplé et perdu

matching: ~ **grant** *n* FIN subvention de contrepartie *f*; ~ **principle** *n* US ACC *costs with revenues* rattachement des charges et des produits *m*

mate: ~**'s receipt** *n (MR)* IMP/EXP, TRANSP bon de chargement *m*, certificat de bord *m*, reçu de bord *m*

material[1] *adj* GEN COMM *significant* important, significatif

material[2] *n* ECON matière *f*, matériau *m*, GEN COMM matériaux *m pl*, matériel *m*, *fabric* étoffe *f*, GEN COMM *information* documentation *f*, informations *f pl*, IND matière *f*, matériaux *m pl*; ~ **balance** ECON balance matières *f*; ~ **barrier** ECON, POL *EU* barrière matérielle *f*; ~ **circumstance** INS *marine* circonstances matérielles *f pl*; ~ **fact** GEN COMM fait pertinent *m*; ~ **good** ECON, IND bien matériel *m*; ~ **interest** STOCK *in company* intérêt matériel *m*, relations d'affaires *f pl*; ~ **man** IND fournisseur de matériaux *m*; ~ **representation** INS *marine* assertion déterminante *f*

materialism *n* ECON, POL matérialisme *m*

materiality *n* ACC *reports* importance relative *f*; ~ **level** ACC seuil d'importance relative *m*

materialize *vi* GEN COMM matérialiser, se concrétiser

materialized: ~ **labor** *n AmE*, ~ **labour** *n BrE* HRM travail matérialisé *m*

materials *n pl* ECON, GEN COMM, IND matériaux *m pl*; ~ **accounting** *n* ACC comptabilité des matières premières *f*, inventaire matériel *m*; ~ **handling** *n* GEN COMM, TRANSP manutention *f*; ~ **transfer note** *n* GEN COMM bon de transfert de matériel *m*

maternity: ~ **allowance** *n* HRM, WEL allocation de maternité *f*; ~ **benefit** *n* HRM, WEL allocation de maternité *f*; ~ **leave** *n* HRM, WEL congé de maternité *m*; ~ **pay** *n* HRM, WEL indemnité de maternité *f*; ~ **protection** *n* INS assurance maternité *f*

mathematical: ~ **economics** *n* ECON, MATH économie analytique *f*; ~ **programming** *n* MATH programmation mathématique *f*

matinée *n* LEIS *theatre* matinée *f*

matrix *n* COMP, MATH matrice *f*; ~ **analysis** ECON analyse matricielle *f*; ~ **management** MATH, MGMNT organisation en matrices *f*; ~ **organization** MATH, MGMNT structure matricielle *f*; ~ **printer** COMP imprimante matricielle *f*; ~ **trading** STOCK arbitrage entre obligations à taux différents *m*; ♦ **go** ~ *jarg* GEN COMM adopter une organisation matricielle

matter *n* GEN COMM affaire *f*, cas *m*, matière *f*, sujet *m*; ~ **of opinion** GEN COMM question d'opinion *f*; ~ **of urgency** GEN COMM quelque chose d'urgent; ♦ **as a** ~ **of routine** GEN COMM automatiquement

matters: ~ **to be followed up** *phr* GEN COMM points sur lesquels il convient de revenir, à suivre

mature[1] *adj* FIN échu, GEN COMM, HRM *person* mature

mature:[2] ~ **economy** *n* ECON économie mature *f*; ~ **market** *n* S&M marché arrivé à la maturité *m*, STOCK marché en pleine maturité *m*

mature[3] *vi* STOCK maturer, échoir, venir à échéance

matured[1] *adj* STOCK arrivé à maturité, arrivé à échéance, échu

matured:[2] ~ **bonds** *n pl* STOCK obligations échues *f pl*, obligations à échéance *f pl*; ~ **coupon** *n* STOCK coupon échu *m*; ~ **endowment** *n* INS *personal* capital échu *m*

maturing: ~ **security** *n* STOCK valeur arrivant à échéance *f*, valeur venant à échéance *f*; ~ **value** *n* STOCK valeur arrivant à échéance *f*, valeur venant à échéance *f*

maturity *n* FIN échéance *f*, HRM *of person* maturité *f*; ~ **bands** *n pl* BANK, ECON, FIN, STOCK périodes d'échéance *f pl*; ~ **date** *n* BANK date d'échéance *f*, ECON date d'échéance *f*, date échéance *f*, FIN, STOCK date d'échéance *f*; ~ **mismatch** *n* BANK, ECON, FIN, STOCK erreur de date d'échéance *f*; ~ **structure of debt** *n* BANK, ECON, FIN, STOCK échéancier de dette *m*; ~ **transformation** *n* BANK, ECON, FIN, STOCK changement de date d'échéance *m*; ~ **value** *n* BANK, ECON, FIN, STOCK valeur à échéance *f*; ♦ **at** ~ STOCK à l'échéance, à maturité; **come to** ~ GEN COMM arriver à échéance, venir à échéance

Mauritania *pr n* GEN COMM Mauritanie *f*

Mauritanian[1] *adj* GEN COMM mauritanien

Mauritanian[2] *n* GEN COMM *person* Mauritanien *m*

Mauritian[1] *adj* GEN COMM mauricien

Mauritian[2] *n* GEN COMM *person* Mauricien *m*

Mauritius *pr n* GEN COMM Île Maurice *f*

MAWB *abbr (master air waybill)* IMP/EXP, TRANSP lettre de transport aérien groupé *f*

max. *abbr (maximal, maximum)* GEN COMM, MATH max. *(maximal)*

maximal[1] *adj (max., ANT minimal)* GEN COMM, MATH maximal *(max.)*

maximal:[2] ~ **market spread** *n* STOCK écart maximal hauts-bas *m*

maximation *n* ACC maximalisation *f*

maximin *n* ECON maximin *m*

maximization *n* ACC maximalisation *f*, GEN COMM optimisation *f*

maximize *vt* ACC, FIN, GEN COMM maximaliser, maximiser, STOCK maximaliser

maximum[1] *adj (max.)* GEN COMM maximal, maximum *(max.)*, MATH maximum *(max.)*

maximum[2] *n* GEN COMM, MATH maximum *m*; ~ **allowable deduction** TAX déduction maximale admissible *f*; ~ **capacity** IND capacité maximale *f*; ~ **capital gains mutual fund** STOCK SICAV à plus-value maximum *f*, fonds de placement à plus-values maximales *m*; ~ **claim** TAX déduction maximale *f*; ~ **coverage** STOCK couverture maximale *f*; ~ **efficiency** ECON, IND efficacité maximale *f*, efficacité maximum *f*, rendement maximal *m*, rendement maximum *m*; ~ **likelihood estimator** *(MLE)* MATH *statistics* estimateur de probabilité maximale *m*; ~ **load** TRANSP charge limite *f*, charge maximale *f*; ~ **market spread** STOCK écart maximal hauts-bas *m*; ~ **output** ECON, IND rendement maximum *m*; ~ **practical capacity** ECON capacité maximale de production *f*; ~ **price** IND, S&M prix maximum *m*; ~ **price change** STOCK variation maximale des cours autorisée *f*, écart maximal de cours *m*; ~ **price fluctuation** STOCK variation maximale des cours autorisée *f*, écart maximal de cours *m*; ~ **rate** BANK taux plafond *m*; ~ **return** STOCK *options* rapport maximum *m*, rendement maximum *m*; ~ **risk** STOCK *options* risque maximum *m*; ♦ **up to a** ~ **of** GEN COMM jusqu'à concurrence de, à concurrence d'un plafond de

may: **it** ~ **reasonably be considered** *phr* GEN COMM il est raisonnable de considérer

May *n* GEN COMM mai *m*

Mayday *n* STOCK signal de détresse

Mb *abbr (megabyte)* COMP Mo *(méga-octet)*

MBA *abbr (Master of Business Administration)* WEL ≈ maîtrise de gestion des entreprises *f*, ≈ titulaire d'une maîtrise de gestion *m*

Mbabane *pr n* GEN COMM Mbabane *n pr*

MBE *abbr UK (Member of the Order of the British Empire)* GEN COMM, POL membre de l'ordre de l'empire britannique

MBIM *abbr (Member of the British Institute of Management)* MGMNT adhérent de l'institut britannique de gestion

MBO *abbr* FIN, GEN COMM *(management buyout)* RES *(rachat d'une entreprise par ses salariés)*, MGMNT *(management by objectives)* DPO *(direction par objectifs)*, MGMNT, STOCK *(management buyout)* RES *(rachat d'une entreprise par ses salariés)*

MBS *abbr (mortgage-backed security)* STOCK titre de créance hypothécaire *m*, valeur garantie par hypothèque *f*

MBWA *abbr (management by walking around)* MGMNT management baladeur *m*

MC *abbr* INS *(metaling clause, metalling clause)* clause de doublage *f*, TRANSP *(master change)* SCN *(spécification de changement notifié)*, TRANSP *(mobile crane)* grue mobile *f*, grue roulante *f*

MCA *abbr* ECON , FIN *(monetary compensation amount, monetary compensatory amount)* montant compensatoire monétaire *m*, MGMNT *UK (Management Consultants Association)* association des consultants de gestion

M-CATS *abbr (municipal certificate of accrual on treasury securities)* STOCK certificat municipal d'accumulation de bons du Trésor

McFadden: ~ **Act** *n US* BANK, LAW loi MacFadden *f*

mcht *abbr (merchant)* HRM marchand *m*

mchy *abbr* (*machinery*) TRANSP machines *f pl*; **~ aft** (*machinery aft*) TRANSP machines d'arrière *f pl*; **~ fwd** (*machinery forward*) TRANSP machines d'avant *f pl*

mCi *abbr* (*millicurie*) GEN COMM millicurie *m*

MCO *abbr* (*miscellaneous charges order*) TRANSP *aviation* bon pour services divers *m*

MCom *abbr* (*Master of Commerce*) GEN COMM ≈ maîtrise en sciences économiques *f*, ≈ titulaire d'une maîtrise en sciences économiques *m*

MCT *abbr* TRANSP (*moment to change trim*) moment nécessaire pour faire varier l'assiette *m*, TRANSP (*minimum connecting time*) temps minimum de correspondance *m*

MD *abbr* ACC (*managing director*) DG (*directeur général*), HRM, MGMNT *UK* (*managing director*) DG (*directeur général*), PDG (*président-directeur général*)

MDW *abbr* (*measured daywork*) HRM travail compté *m*, travail à la journée *m*

me: **~ -too firm** *n* S&M société plagiaire *f*

ME *abbr* (*main engine*) TRANSP moteur principal *m*

meal: **~ allowance** *n* HRM indemnité de repas *f*; **~ ticket** *n* *AmE* (*cf luncheon voucher BrE*) HRM chèque-déjeuner *m*, chèque-repas *m*, ticket-repas *m*, ticket-restaurant *m*

meals: **~ on wheels** *n pl* WEL repas livré à domicile

mean[1] *n* ACC, GEN COMM, MATH *statistics* moyenne *f*; **~ amount on deposit** INS montant moyen en dépôt *m*; **~ cost** ACC cm, coût moyen *m*; **~ deviation** FIN, MATH *statistics* écart moyen *m*, écart type *m*; **~ effective pressure** (*mep*) GEN COMM pression effective moyenne *f*; **~ high water at springs** (*MHWS*) TRANSP pleine mer de viveeau moyenne *f* (*PM de VE moyenne*); **~ price** ECON, S&M prix moyen *m*; **~ return** STOCK *security analysis* rapport moyen *m*, rendement moyen *m*; **~ sea level** (*MSL*) TRANSP niveau moyen de la mer *m*; **~ tidal level** (*MTL*) TRANSP niveau moyen de la marée *m*; **~ time** (*MT*) GEN COMM temps moyen *m*; **~ time between failures** (*MTBF*) TRANSP temps moyen de bon fonctionnement *m*; **~ value** MATH *statistics* valeur moyenne *f*

mean[2] *vt* GEN COMM vouloir dire

means *n* [inv pl] ECON, FIN, GEN COMM moyen *m*, moyens *m pl*; **~ of communication** COMMS moyen de communication *m*; **~ of conveyance** TRANSP moyen de transport *m*; **~ of payment** BANK, ECON, FIN, GEN COMM moyens de paiement *m pl*; **~ test** TAX examen des ressources *m*; **~ of transport** TRANSP moyen de transport *m*; ♦ **as a ~ of** GEN COMM en tant que moyen de; **have the ~ to** GEN COMM avoir les moyens de

measure[1] *n* GEN COMM *step* mesure *f*, TRANSP *volume* cubage *m*; **~ of control** ECON *of prices* mesure de contrôle *f*; **~ of economic welfare** (*MEW*) ECON, HRM, WEL mesure de bien-être économique *f*; **~ of indemnity** INS étendue de l'indemnité *f*

measure[2] *vt* ECON, GEN COMM, HRM mesurer; ♦ **~ sb's performance** HRM mesurer le rendement de qn

measured: **~ daywork** *n* (*MDW*) HRM travail compté *m*, travail à la journée *m*

measurement *n* MATH dimension *f*, TRANSP *nautical* jaugeage *m*, *volume* cubage *m*; **~ freight** *n* TRANSP marchandises légères *f pl*; **~ goods** *n pl* TRANSP marchandises au cubage *f pl*, marchandises d'encombrement *f pl*; **~ ton** *n* TRANSP tonne d'encombrement *f*; **~ tonne** *n* GEN COMM tonne d'arrimage *f*

measuring: **~ tape** *n* GEN COMM mètre à ruban *m*

meat: **~ mountain** *n* ECON *EU* montagne de viande *f*; **~ packing** *n* IND conserverie de viande *f*

MEC *abbr* (*marginal efficiency of capital*) ECON efficacité marginale du capital *f*

mechanic *n* HRM, IND mécanicien *m*; **~'s lien** IND, PROP privilège du constructeur *m*

mechanical: **~ engineering** *n* IND mécanique *f*; **~ handling equipment** *n* (*MHE*) TRANSP *cargo* matériel de manutention mécanique *m*

mechanically: **~ ventilated container** *n* TRANSP conteneur ventilé *m*

mechanism *n* ECON, GEN COMM, IND mécanisme *m*

mechanization *n* IND mécanisation *f*; **~ of cargo handling** TRANSP mécanisation de la manutention *f*

mechanize *vt* GEN COMM, IND mécaniser

mechanized *adj* GEN COMM mécanisé

MEcon *abbr* (*Master of Economics*) GEN COMM ≈ maîtrise en sciences économiques *f*, ≈ titulaire d'une maîtrise en sciences économiques *m*

media[1] *adj* MEDIA médiatique

media[2] *n* COMMS, MEDIA médias *m pl*, S&M médias *m pl*, supports *m pl*; **~ analysis** *n* MEDIA, S&M analyse des médias *f*; **~ budget** *n* ACC, MEDIA budget d'achat d'espaces *m*; **~ buyer** *n* (*ANT media seller*) HRM, MEDIA, S&M acheteur de médias *m*; **~ buying** *n* (*ANT media selling*) MEDIA, S&M *advertising* achat de médias *m*; **~ event** *n* MEDIA événement médiatique *m*; **~ fragmentation** *n* MEDIA, S&M *advertising* segmentation des médias *f*; **~ options** *n pl* MEDIA, S&M *advertising* option-médias *f*; **~ plan** *n* MEDIA, S&M *advertising* plan média *m*; **~ planner** *n* MEDIA, S&M *advertising* chargé d'études média *mf*, médiaplanneur *m*; **~ planning** *n* MEDIA, S&M *advertising* média planning *m*, plan média *m*; **~ schedule** *n* MEDIA calendrier de campagne *m*, plan média *m*, S&M plan média *m*; **~ selection** *n* MEDIA, S&M *advertising* choix des médias *m*, choix des supports *m*, sélection des médias *f*; **~ seller** *n* (*ANT media buyer*) HRM, MEDIA, S&M vendeur de médias *m*; **~ selling** *n* (*ANT media buying*) MEDIA, S&M *advertising* vente de médias *f*; **the ~** *n* COMMS les médias *m pl*, MEDIA les moyens de communication *m pl*, les médias *m pl*, les supports de communication *m pl*, S&M les médias *m pl*; ~ **weight** *n* MEDIA, S&M *advertising* poids-média *m*

median[1] *adj* MATH *statistics* médian

median[2] *n* MATH médiane *f*; ~ **amount** TAX médiane *f*; ~ **rule** GEN COMM, MATH règle de la médiane *f*

mediate: ~ **between** *vt* GEN COMM arbitrer entre, GEN COMM, HRM agir en médiateur, arbitrer

mediation *n* GEN COMM, HRM arbitrage *m*, médiation *f*, IND arbitrage *m*, LAW arbitrage *m*, médiation *f*, POL médiation *f*

mediator *n* GEN COMM arbitre *m*, médiateur *m*, HRM médiateur *m*

medical[1] *adj* GEN COMM, WEL médical

medical:[2] ~ **assistance** *n* GEN COMM, WEL assistance médicale *f*; ~ **care insurance plan** *n* INS, WEL régime d'assurance maladie *m*; ~ **costs** *n pl* GEN COMM, INS frais médicaux *m pl*; ~ **engineering** *n* IND ingénierie médicale *f*; ~ **examination** *n* WEL examen médical *m*, visite médicale *f*; ~ **expense credit** *n* TAX crédit pour frais médicaux *m*; ~ **expenses** *n pl* TAX frais médicaux *m pl*; ~ **grounds** *n pl* HRM, WEL raisons médicales *f pl*; ~ **insurance** *n* INS assurance maladie *f*, assurance médicale *f*; ~ **officer** *n* (*MO*) HRM, WEL médecin *m*; ~ **officer of health** *n* (*MOH*) HRM, WEL directeur de la santé publique *m*, médecin départemental *m*, officier de santé *m*

medicament *n* GEN COMM médicament *m*

medicine *n* GEN COMM médicament *m*

Mediterranean: ~ **basin** *n* ECON, GEN COMM, POL bassin méditerranéen *m*; ~ **bloc** *n* ECON, GEN COMM, POL pays méditerranéens *m pl*

medium:[1] ~ **-dated** *adj* (ANT *long-dated, short-dated*) STOCK à moyen terme, à terme moyen; ~ **-term** *adj* (ANT *long-term, short-term*) ACC, BANK, FIN, GEN COMM, STOCK à moyen terme; ◆ **in the ~ term** (ANT *in the long term, in the short term*) GEN COMM à moyen terme

medium[2] *n* [pl -dia] COMMS moyen de communication *m*, média *m*, ECON, FIN moyens *m pl*, GEN COMM, MEDIA média *m*, S&M *radio, television* support *m*; ~ **of account** ACC moyenne d'un compte *f*; ~ **of exchange** ECON, FIN intermédiaire des échanges *m*, moyen d'échange *m*, moyen de paiement *m*; ~ **frequency radiotelephone** (*RTm*) TRANSP *shipping* radiotéléphone moyenne fréquence *m*; ~ **frequency radiotelephony** (*RTm*) TRANSP *shipping* radiotéléphonie moyenne fréquence *f*; ~ **of redemption** ECON, FIN moyen de rachat *m*; ~ **term** BANK, FIN, GEN COMM moyen terme *m*; ~ **-term bond** STOCK bon à moyen terme *m*, obligation à moyen terme *f*; ~ **-term Euronote** STOCK *money market* euro-obligation à moyen terme *f*, eurodevise à moyen terme *f*; ~ **-term financial strategy** ECON stratégie financière à moyen terme *f*; ~ **-term instrument** STOCK instrument à moyen terme *m*; ~ **-term loan** (*MTL*) BANK prêt à moyen terme *m*; ~ **-term note** BANK

billet à moyen terme *m*, FIN (*MTN*) billet à moyen terme *m*, bon à moyen terme négociable *m* (*BMTN*)

Medspa *n* ENVIR Medspa *m*

meet *vt* GEN COMM rencontrer, *conditions* remplir, *requirements* répondre à, *targets* honorer, satisfaire; ◆ ~ **costs** ACC, FIN, GEN COMM faire face à des frais; ~ **the demands** MGMNT *of union* faire face aux demandes; ~ **a goal** MGMNT répondre à un objectif; ~ **the needs** GEN COMM répondre aux besoins de; ~ **one's obligations** GEN COMM remplir ses obligations

meeting *n* ADMIN réunion *f*, GEN COMM assemblée *f*, réunion *f*, HRM, MGMNT réunion *f*; ~ **of the minds** GEN COMM, LAW accord de volonté *m*; ◆ **the ~ broke up** GEN COMM la session fut levée

mega: ~ **electron volt** *n* (*MeV*) GEN COMM méga-électron-volt *m*

megabit *n* COMP mégabit *m*

megabucks *n pl infrml* GEN COMM millions de dollars *m pl*

megabyte *n* (*Mb*) COMP méga-octet *m* (*Mo*)

megacorp *n jarg* (*megacorporation*) GEN COMM grande entreprise *f*

megacorporation *n* (*megacorp*) GEN COMM grande entreprise *f*

megalomania *n* HRM mégalomanie *f*

megalomaniac *n* HRM mégalomane *mf*

megawatt *n* (*MW*) GEN COMM mégawatt *m* (*MW*)

member *n* GEN COMM membre *mf*, HRM associé *m*, *of company* membre *mf*, *of union* adhérent *m*, syndiqué *m*; ~ **bank** *AmE* (ANT *nonmember bank*) BANK banque affiliée *f*; ~ **of the board** HRM administrateur *m*; ~ **of the board of management** HRM membre du directoire *m*; ~ **of a commission** GEN COMM membre d'une commission *m*; ~ **of a committee** GEN COMM membre d'une commission *m*, membre d'un comité *m*; ~ **corporation** STOCK société affiliée *f*, établissement membre d'une bourse *m*; ~ **firm** STOCK firme affiliée *f*, société membre *f*, société affiliée *f*, société de bourse *f*; ~ **of the public** GEN COMM membre du public *m*; ~ **short sale ratio** STOCK coefficient de vente à découvert d'un affilié; ~ **of staff** HRM membre du personnel *m*; ~ **state** (*MS*) POL *EU* état-membre *m*; ~ **of the supervisory board** HRM membre du conseil de surveillance *m*; ~ **of a syndicate** HRM syndicataire *m*; ~ **of a trade union** HRM syndiqué *m*; ~ **of a union** HRM membre d'un syndicat *m*

Member: ~ **of the British Institute of Management** *n* (*MBIM*) MGMNT adhérent de l'institut britannique de gestion; ~ **of the European Parliament** *n* (*MEP*) POL député du Parlement Européen *m*, membre du Parlement Européen *m*; ~ **of the Institute of Chartered Accountants** *n* *UK* (*MICA*) GEN COMM membre de l'ordre des experts-comptables de Grande Bretagne; ~ **of the Order of the British Empire** *n* *UK* (*MBE*) GEN

COMM, POL membre de l'ordre de l'empire britannique; ~ **of Parliament** *n UK (MP)* POL ≈ député *m*, ≈ femme député *f*

members: ~ **rank and file** *n pl* HRM *as opposed to the leaders* membres *m pl*, ouvriers *m pl*

membership *n* GEN COMM adhésion *f*, qualité de membre *f*; ~ **card** *n* GEN COMM carte de membre *f*; ~ **dues** *n pl* TAX cotisations de membre *f pl*

memo *n* ADMIN circulaire *f*, mémorandum *m*, note de service *f*, COMMS mémorandum *m*; ~ **account** ACC compte hors bilan *m*, compte pour mémoire *m*; ~ **item** ACC poste hors bilan *m*, poste pour mémoire *m*, écriture pour mémoire *f*

memorandum *n* [pl -da] ADMIN note *f*, ADMIN circulaire *f*, mémorandum *m*, note de service *f*, COMMS mémorandum *m*, LAW mémoire *m*, mémorandum *m*; ~ **account** *n* ACC compte hors bilan *m*, compte pour mémoire *m*; ~ **of agreement** *n* LAW protocole d'accord *m*; ~ **allocation** *n* GEN COMM affectation pour mémoire *f*; ~ **and articles** *n pl* LAW statuts *m pl*; ~ **of association** *n* LAW acte constitutif de société *m*, charte constitutive *f*, statuts *m pl*; ~ **of intent** *n* GEN COMM déclaration d'intention *f*; ~ **item** *n* ACC poste hors bilan *m*, poste pour mémoire *m*, écriture pour mémoire *f*

memorize *vt* GEN COMM mémoriser

memory:[1] ~ -**hungry** *adj infrml* COMP gourmand en mémoire

memory[2] *n* COMP, GEN COMM mémoire *f*; ~ **bank** COMP banc de mémoire *m*, bloc de mémoire *m*; ~ **capacity** COMP capacité de mémoire *f*; ~ **card** COMP carte mémoire *f*; ~ **chip** COMP puce mémoire *f*; ~ **dump** COMP vidage de mémoire *m*; ~ **expansion board** COMP carte d'extension mémoire *f*; ~ **extension** COMP extension mémoire *f*; ~ **print-out** COMP impression du contenu de la mémoire *f*, vidage de mémoire sur imprimante *m*; ~ **resident** COMP résident en mémoire *m*; ~ **typewriter** GEN COMM *office equipment* machine à écrire à mémoire *f*; ~ **upgrade** COMP extension mémoire *f*

men: **the ~ at the top** *n pl infrml* HRM les dirigeants *m pl*; ~**'s department** *n* GEN COMM, S&M rayon hommes *m*

menial: ~ **job** *n* HRM petit boulot *m*

mens rea *n* LAW sentiment de culpabilité *m*

mental: ~ **or physical impairment** *n* TAX déficience mentale ou physique *f*

mention *vt* GEN COMM indiquer en passant, indiquer pour mention, mentionner

mentioned: **as ~ above** *phr* (ANT *as mentioned below*) COM mentionné ci-dessus, COMMS mentionné ci-dessus, mentionné plus haut, précité, susmentionné; **as ~ below** *phr* (ANT *above-mentioned, as mentioned above*) COMMS mentionné ci-dessous, mentionné plus bas, sous-mentionné

menu:[1] ~ -**driven** *adj* COMP piloté par menus

menu[2] *n* COMP, LEIS menu *m*; ~ **bar** COMP barre des menus *f*

mep *abbr* (*mean effective pressure*) GEN COMM pression effective moyenne *f*

MEP *abbr* (*Member of the European Parliament*) POL député du Parlement Européen *m*, membre du Parlement Européen *m*

mercantile[1] *adj* GEN COMM mercantile

mercantile:[2] ~ **affairs** *n pl* GEN COMM affaires commerciales *f pl*; ~ **agency** *n* FIN, S&M agence commerciale *f*; ~ **bank** *n* BANK banque de commerce *f*; ~ **exchange** *n* STOCK bourse de commerce *f*, bourse de marchandises *f*; ~ **law** *n* GEN COMM, LAW droit commercial *m*; ~ **marine** *n* TRANSP marine marchande *f*; ~ **open-stock burglary insurance** *n* INS *company* assurance commerciale contre le vol du stock initial *f*; ~ **robbery insurance** *n* INS *company* assurance commerciale contre le vol *f*; ~ **safe burglary insurance** *n* INS *company* assurance commerciale contre le vol par effraction de coffres-forts *f*

Mercantile: ~ **Marine Services Association** *n (MMSA)* GEN COMM, TRANSP association de la marine marchande

mercantilism *n* ECON mercantilisme *m*

mercantilist[1] *adj* ECON mercantiliste

mercantilist[2] *n* ECON mercantiliste *mf*

merchandise *n* S&M marchandises *f pl*; ~ **allowance** S&M rabais sur marchandise *m*; ~ **balance of trade** ECON balance des marchandises *f*; ~ **broker** FIN, S&M courtier en marchandises *m*; ~ **control** S&M gestion des marchandises *f*; ~ **inventory** ACC *balance sheets*, GEN COMM, S&M inventaire des produits frais *m*, stock de marchandises *m*

merchandiser *n* HRM merchandiser *m*, présentoir-géant *m*, responsable des techniques marchandes *m*

merchandising *n* GEN COMM commercialisation *f*, S&M commercialisation *f*, marchandisage *m*, merchandising *m*, techniques marchandes *f pl*; ~ **director** HRM, MGMNT, S&M directeur commercial *m*, directeur de merchandising *m*; ~ **service** S&M service de merchandising *m*

merchant *n (mcht)* HRM marchand *m*; ~ **bank** *UK* BANK, FIN *retail* banque commerciale *f*, banque d'affaires *f*; ~ **banker** *UK (cf investment banker US)* BANK banquier d'affaires *m*, banquier d'investissement *m*, spécialiste des services de banque d'affaires *m*, spécialiste des services de banque d'investissement *m*; ~ **banking** BANK banque d'affaires *f*, opérations de banque d'affaires *f pl*, services bancaires d'investissement *m pl*, services de banque d'affaires *m pl*, services de banque d'investissement *m pl*, BANK *UK (cf investment banking US)* opérations sur valeurs de placement *f*, FIN banque d'affaires *f*, opérations de banque d'affaires *f pl*, services bancaires d'investissement *m pl*, services de banque d'affaires *m pl*, services de banque d'investissement *m pl*; ~ **capitalism** ECON, POL capitalisme d'affaires *m*; ~ **haulage** *(MH)* IMP/EXP *shipping*, TRANSP acheminement par le négociant *m*; ~ **marine** TRANSP marine marchande *f*; ~ **navy** TRANSP marine marchande *f*; ~ **service** TRANSP marine marchande *f*; ~ **ship** TRANSP navire de commerce *m*, navire marchand *m*; ~ **shipping** TRANSP navires de commerce *m pl*; ~ **shipping Act** UK (*MSA*) LAW, TRANSP loi sur la marine marchande *f*; ~ **trading** ECON négoce *m*; ~ **vessel** TRANSP navire de commerce *m*, navire marchand *m*

Merchant: ~ **Navy and Airline Officers Association** *n* UK (*MNAOA*) TRANSP association des officiers de la marine marchande et des lignes aériennes; ~ **Navy Discipline Organisation** *n* UK (*MNDO*) TRANSP service de discipline de la marine marchande; ~ **Navy Establishment** *n* UK (*MNE*) TRANSP établissement de la marine marchande; ~ **Navy Establishment Administration** *n* UK (*MNEA*) TRANSP direction d'établissements de la marine marchande; ~ **Navy Officers Pension Fund** *n* UK (*MNOPF*) TRANSP *shipping*, WEL *shipping* caisse de retraite des officiers de la marine marchande; ~ **Navy Training Board** *n* UK (*MNTB*) TRANSP comité de formation de la marine marchande; ~ **Shipping Dangerous Goods Amendment Rules** *n pl* LAW, TRANSP règlement relatif à la transportation des marchandises dangereuses par mer; ~ **Shipping Regulations** *n pl* LAW, TRANSP règlement de la marine marchande

merchantable[1] *adj* GEN COMM, S&M commercialisable, vendable

merchantable:[2] ~ **quality** *n* LAW, S&M qualité marchande *f*; ~ **title** *n* AmE (*cf marketable title*, ANT *nonmerchantable title*) PROP titre négociable *m*

Mercosur *n* ECON *international trade* Marché commun du cône sud *m*, le Mercosur *m*

merge[1] *n* COMP *of document, computer file* fusion *f*; ~ **and purge** *jarg* ADMIN, COMMS *advertising*, S&M *advertising* déduplication *f*

merge[2] *vt* ADMIN, COMMS, COMP fusionner, POL unifier, STOCK amalgamer, fusionner; ~ **into** GEN COMM fusionner en, ADMIN *files*, GEN COMM *companies* fusionner

merger *n* ECON contre-offre publique d'achat *f*, fusion *f*, rachat *m*, FIN contre-OPA *f*, contre-offre publique d'achat *f*, rachat *m*, GEN COMM, STOCK fusion *f*, rachat *m*; ~ **accounting** BrE (*cf pooling of interests AmE*) ACC absorption *f*, fusion *f*; ~ **arbitrage** STOCK arbitrage de fusion *m*; ~ **company** FIN société née d'une fusion *loc f*

mergers: ~ **and acquisitions** *n pl* (*M&A*) ECON, STOCK fusions et acquisitions *f pl* (*F&A*)

meridian *n* GEN COMM méridien *m*

merino: ~ **wool** *n* ENVIR laine mérinos *f*

merit: ~ **bad** *n* ECON mal tutélaire *m*; ~ **good** *n* ECON bien tutélaire *m*; ~ **increase** *n* (SYN *merit pay*) HRM *in pay* augmentation au mérite *f*; ~ **pay** *n* (SYN *merit increase*) HRM augmentation au mérite *f*; ~ **raise** *n* AmE *see merit rise BrE*;

~ **rating** *n* GEN COMM appréciation du mérite *f*, HRM appréciation du mérite *f*, classement au mérite *m*; ~ **rise** *n* BrE HRM augmentation au mérite *f*; ~ **wants** *n pl* ECON besoins en biens tutélaires *m pl*

meritocracy *n* HRM méritocratie *f*, promotion au mérite *f*

merits: **on its** ~ *phr* LAW de façon objective *loc f*, en toute objectivité *loc*, sur le fond *loc m*

MES *abbr* (*minimum efficient scale*) ECON échelle minimale d'efficience *f*

mesoeconomy *n* ECON mésoéconomie *f*

mesokurtic *n* MATH *statistics* mesokurtique *m*

message *n* COMMS, COMP, S&M message *m*; ~ **handling** COMMS, COMP traitement de messages *m*; ~ **switching** COMMS commutation de messages *f*

messenger *n* COMMS *in office* commissionnaire *mf*, coursier *m*, messager *m*, LAW commissionnaire *mf*; ~ **boy** COMMS, HRM garçon de courses *m*; ~ **robbery insurance** INS *company* assurance vol sur la personne *f*

met *abbr* (*measurement*) MATH dimension *f*

metacentric: ~ **height** *n* GEN COMM hauteur métacentrique *f*

metal *n* ENVIR, IND métal *m*; ~ **can** TRANSP boîte métallique *f*; ~ **market** STOCK marché des métaux *m*; ~ **packaging** ENVIR conditionnement en métal *m*, emballage métallique *m*, S&M conditionnement en métal *m*

metaling *n* AmE *see metalling BrE*

metalliferous: ~ **ore** *n* ENVIR minerai métallique *m*

metalling *n* BrE LAW clause de doublage *f*; ~ **clause** BrE (*MC*) INS clause de doublage *f*

metallist *n* ECON métalliste *mf*

metallurgist *n* HRM, IND métallurgiste *mf*

metalworker *n* HRM métallo *m* (*infrml*), ouvrier métallurgiste *m*, IND métallo *m* (*infrml*), métallurgiste *mf*

meter[1] *n* GEN COMM *device* compteur

meter[2] *n* AmE *see metre BrE*

meterage *n* AmE GEN COMM comptage *m*

metered: ~ **mail** *n* US COMMS courrier affranchi à la machine *m*

metering *n* GEN COMM comptage *m*, mesurage au compteur *m*

meters: ~ **per second** *phr* AmE *see metres per second BrE*

metes: ~ **and bounds** *n pl* PROP mesures et limites *f pl*

methetics *n* GEN COMM, MATH dynamique des groupes *f*

method *n* GEN COMM modalité *f*, mode *m*, méthode *f*, MGMNT méthode *f*; ~ **of depreciation** (SYN *straight-line method of amortization*) TAX méthode de l'amortissement linéaire *m*; ~ **of payment** ACC, FIN, GEN COMM, S&M modalité de paiement *f*, mode de paiement *m*, méthode de paiement *f*; ~ **of preparation** ACC méthode de préparation *f*; ~ **of taxation** TAX mode d'imposition *m*

methodology *n* ECON, MGMNT, S&M méthodologie *f*

methods: ~ **engineering** *n* GEN COMM étude des méthodes *f*; ~ **study** *n* GEN COMM étude des méthodes *f*

methyl: ~ **bromide** *n* TRANSP bromure de méthyle *m*

metical *n* GEN COMM metical *m*

meticulous *adj* GEN COMM méticuleux

meticulously *adv* GEN COMM méticuleusement

metre *n* (*m*) *BrE* GEN COMM mètre *m* (*m*)

metres: ~ **per second** *n pl BrE* (*m/s*) GEN COMM mètres par seconde *m pl* (*m/s*)

metric: ~ **system** *n* GEN COMM, MATH système métrique *m*, SM; ~ **ton** *n* (*mton*) GEN COMM tonne métrique *f*; ♦ **go** ~ GEN COMM adopter le système métrique

metrication *n* GEN COMM, MATH introduction du système métrique *f*

metro *n* TRANSP métro *m*

metropolis *n* GEN COMM métropole *f*

metropolitan¹ *adj* (ANT *nonmetropolitan*) GEN COMM métropolitain

metropolitan:² ~ **area** *n* ECON agglomération *f*, zone métropolitaine *f*; ~ **town** *n* GEN COMM métropole *f*

MeV *abbr* (*mega electron volt*) GEN COMM méga-électron-volt *m*

MEW *abbr* (*measure of economic welfare*) ECON, HRM, WEL mesure de bien-être économique *f*

Mexican¹ *adj* GEN COMM mexicain

Mexican² *n* GEN COMM *person* Mexicain *m*

Mexico *pr n* GEN COMM Mexique *m*; ~ **City** GEN COMM Mexico *n pr*

mezzanine: ~ **bracket** *n* STOCK souscripteurs de second rang *m pl*, tranche mezzanine *f*; ~ **debt** *n* STOCK dette mezzanine *f*; ~ **finance** *n* FIN financement mezzanine *m*; ~ **funding** *n* FIN financement mezzanine *m*; ~ **level** *n* FIN *venture capital* niveau mezzanine *m*

MFA *abbr* ECON (*Multi-Fibre Arrangement*) AMF (*accord multi-fibres*), POL (*Ministry of Foreign Affairs*) ≈ ministère des Affaires étrangères *m*

mfd *abbr* (*manufactured*) GEN COMM, IND fabriqué, manufacturé

MFN *abbr* (*most-favored nation, most-favoured nation*) ECON nation la plus favorisée *f*

M-form *phr* ECON en forme de M *loc f*

mfrs *abbr* (*manufacturers*) GEN COMM, IND fabricants *m pl*

mg *abbr* (*milligram*) GEN COMM milligramme *m*

mgr *abbr* (*manager*) HRM, MGMNT chef *mf*, dirigeant *m*, gestionnaire *mf*, gérant *m*, manager *m*, responsable *mf*, directeur *m*

MH *abbr* IMP/EXP, TRANSP (*merchant haulage*) *shipping* acheminement par le négociant *m*, TRANSP (*main hatch*) *shipping* grand panneau *m*

MHE *abbr* (*mechanical handling equipment*) TRANSP *cargo* matériel de manutention mécanique *m*

MHWS *abbr* (*mean high water at springs*) TRANSP *shipping* PM de VE moyenne (*pleine mer de vive-eau moyenne*)

MICA *abbr UK* (*Member of the Institute of Chartered Accountants*) GEN COMM membre de l'ordre des experts-comptables de Grande Bretagne

micro *n* COMP micro *m*

microchip *n* COMP microplaquette *f*, puce *f*

microcomputer *n* COMP micro-ordinateur *m*

microcomputing *n* (ANT *macrocomputing*) COMP micro-informatique *f*

microdisk *n* ADMIN disque souple *m*, disquette *f*, COMP disque souple *m*, disquette *f*, microdisquette *f*

microeconomic *adj* (ANT *macroeconomic*) ECON microéconomique

microeconomics *n* (ANT *macroeconomics*) ECON microéconomie *f*

microelectronic *adj* IND micro-électronique

microelectronics *n* IND micro-électronique *f*

microfiche *n* ADMIN, COMMS, COMP, GEN COMM microfiche *f*; ~ **reader** ADMIN, COMMS, COMP, GEN COMM microlecteur *m*

microfilm *n* ADMIN, COMMS, COMP, GEN COMM microfilm *m*

micromarketing *n* S&M micromarketing *m*

microphone *n* COMMS micro *m*, microphone *m*

microprocessor *n* COMP microprocesseur *m*

microproduction: ~ **function** *n* ECON fonction de micro-production *f*

microprogram *n* COMP microprogramme *m*

microsecond *n* GEN COMM microseconde *f*

Microsoft: ~ **Disk Operating System**® *n* (*MS-DOS*) COMP MS-DOS® *m*

mid: ~ **price** *n* STOCK cours moyen *m*, prix moyen *m*

MIDA *abbr* (*maritime industrial development area*) IND zone de développement maritime industriel

Mid-America: ~ **Commodity Exchange** *n* STOCK Bourse des marchandises Mid-America de Chicago *f*

mid-Atlantic: ~ **rates** *n* TRANSP *aviation* taux mi-Atlantique *m pl*

mid-career: ~ **plateau** *n* HRM palier en milieu de carrière *m*

middle: ~ **class** *n* ECON bourgeoisie *f*; ~ **income bracket** *n* ECON tranche moyenne de revenus *f*; ~ -**income taxpayer** *n* (ANT *high-income taxpayer, low-income taxpayer*) TAX contribuable à revenu moyen *m*; ~ **management** *n* HRM, MGMNT cadres moyens *m pl*, maîtrise *f*; ~ **manager** *n* HRM, MGMNT cadre moyen *m*; ~ **office** *n* FIN suivi de marché *m*; ~ **price** *n* STOCK cours moyen *m*; ~ **range of the market** *n* S&M tranche moyenne du marché *f*; ~ **strike option** *n* STOCK option à cours moyen *f*; ~ **strike price** *n* STOCK *options* cours d'exercice moyen *m*

Middle: ~ **Seven** *n* ACC les Sept Moyens *m pl*

midnight: ~ **deadline** *n* GEN COMM clôture à minuit *f*

midrange *adj* COMP de milieu de gamme *loc m*, intermédiaire

midship *n (m)* TRANSP centre du navire *m*, milieu du navire *m*

midships *adv* TRANSP au milieu du navire *loc m*

Midwest: ~ **Stock Exchange** *n US* STOCK Bourse du Midwest *f*, le Midwest Stock Exchange *m*

midyear *adv* GEN COMM vers le milieu de l'année

MIFT *abbr UK (Manchester International Freight Terminal)* TRANSP terminal de fret international de Manchester *m*

migrant: ~ **labor** *n AmE*, ~ **labour** *n BrE* ECON *foreign* main-d'œuvre immigrée *f*, *mobile within country* main-d'œuvre migrante *f*; ~ **status** *n* LAW statut des immigrés *m*; ~ **worker** *n* HRM travailleur migrant *m*

migration *n* COMP *data* transfert *m*, ECON migration *f*; ~ **-fed unemployment** ECON chômage entraîné par l'immigration *m*

migratory: ~ **worker** *n* HRM travailleur migrant *m*

mile *n* GEN COMM 1609 mètres, mile *m*

mileage *n* TRANSP kilométrage *m*; ~ **allowance** TAX indemnité kilométrique *f*

miles: ~ **per gallon** *n pl (mpg)* GEN COMM miles par gallon, $\approx$ kilomètres au cent *m pl*; ~ **per hour** *n pl (mph)* GEN COMM miles/heure *m pl*

milestone: ~ **chart** *n* MATH graphique des étapes critiques *m*

militant *n* POL militant *m*

military: ~ **industrial complex** *n* IND, POL complexe militaro-industriel *m*; ~ **Keynesianism** *n* ECON, POL keynésianisme militaire *m*

milk:[1] ~ **products** *n pl* GEN COMM produits laitiers *m pl*; ~ **round** *n UK* WEL recrutement annuel des étudiants universitaires

milk[2] *vt* GEN COMM *opportunity, situation* exploiter

milking: ~ **strategy** *n* S&M stratégie de milking *f*

mill *n US* TAX millième d'un dollar *m*

millage: ~ **rate** *n US* TAX millième *m*

miller *n* HRM, IND meunier *m*

milliard *n* BANK, GEN COMM milliard *m*

millicurie *n (mCi)* GEN COMM millicurie *m*

milligram *n (mg)* GEN COMM milligramme *m (mg)*

milliliter *n AmE*, **millilitre** *n BrE (ml)* GEN COMM millilitre *m (ml)*

millimeter *n AmE*, **millimetre** *n BrE (mm)* GEN COMM millimètre *m (mm)*

million *n* MATH million *m*

millionaire *n* GEN COMM millionnaire *mf*; ~ **on paper** GEN COMM millionnaire en actions *m*

millirem: ~ **per hour** *n (mrem/h)* GEN COMM millirem par heure *m (mrem/h)*

milliroentgen: ~ **per hour** *n (mr/h)* GEN COMM

milliröntgen par heure *m*, milliröntgen/heure *m (mr/h)*

millisecond *n* GEN COMM milliseconde *f*

MIMIC *abbr (moderately indebted middle-income country)* ECON, FIN, POL pays à revenu intermédiaire modérément endetté *m*

min. *abbr (minimum)* GEN COMM min. *(minimum)*; ~ **B/L** *(minimum bill of lading)* IMP/EXP, TRANSP connaissement minimum *m*

mine *n* IND mine *f*

miner *n* IND mineur *m*

mineral: ~ **-based economy** *n* ECON, IND économie fondée sur l'exploitation de minerais *f*, économie minéralière *f*; ~ **industry** *n* ENVIR, IND industrie minière *f*; ~ **oil products** *n pl* IND, TAX produits pétroliers *m pl*; ~ **resource** *n* ENVIR, IND matière minérale *f*, ressource minérale *f*, ressource minière *f*; ~ **rights** *n pl* IND, LAW, PROP droits miniers *m pl*

mini *adj* GEN COMM mini

miniaturized *adj* GEN COMM miniaturisé

minibus *n* TRANSP minibus *m*

minicomputer *n* COMP mini-ordinateur *m*

minimal[1] *adj (ANT maximal)* GEN COMM, MATH minimal

minimal:[2] ~ **state intervention** *n* ADMIN, ECON, POL intervention minimale de l'État *f*

minimax *n* ECON *games theory* minimax *m*; ~ **strategy** ECON stratégie-minimax *f*

minimize *vt* FIN *risks* minimiser

minimum[1] *adj (min.)* GEN COMM minimum *(min.)*

minimum:[2] ~ **amount** *n* TAX minimum *m*; ~ **balance** *n* BANK solde créditeur minimum *m*, solde minimal *m*; ~ **bill of lading** *n (min. B/L)* IMP/EXP, TRANSP connaissement minimum *m*; ~ **charge** *n* TRANSP tarif minimum *m*; ~ **connecting time** *n (MCT)* TRANSP temps minimum de correspondance *m*; ~ **credit balance** *n* BANK solde créditeur minimum *m*, solde minimal *m*; ~ **efficient scale** *n (MES)* ECON échelle minimale d'efficience *f*; ~ **grade** *n* HRM, WEL *required in exam* note la plus basse *f*; ~ **income tax** *n* TAX impôt minimum *m*; ~ **lease payments** *n pl* PROP *capital lease* paiements de loyer minimum *m pl*; ~ **lending rate** *n UK (MLR)* BANK *central banking*, ECON taux officiel d'escompte *m*; ~ **list heading** *n UK (MLH)* IND tête de liste minimale *f*; ~ **living wage** *n* HRM minimum vital *m*; ~ **lot area** *n US (cf minimum lot size)* PROP zone de lotissement minimum *f*; ~ **lot size** *n US (cf minimum lot area)* PROP zone de lotissement minimum *f*; ~ **maintenance** *n* STOCK couverture minimum *f*, solde de titres minimum en compte *m*; ~ **margin** *n* STOCK *options* marge minimale *f*, marge minimum *f*; ~ **margin requirement** *n* STOCK couverture minimale obligatoire *f*; ~ **pension liability** *n* FIN encours de pension minimum *m*; ~ **personal income tax** *n* TAX impôt minimum sur le revenu des particuliers *m*; ~ **price change** *n* STOCK variation de cours minimale *f*, échelon de négociation minimal *m*; ~ **price fluctuation** *n* STOCK variation de cours minimale *f*, variation minimale des cours *f*, écart minimum de fluctuation *m*; ~ **quality standards** *n pl* S&M critères de qualité minima *m pl*; ~ **quote size** *n UK (MQS)* STOCK cours minimal *m*, quotité minimale *f*; ~ **reserve requirements** *n pl (MRR)* ECON réserves légales minimales *f pl*, réserves légales minimum *f pl*; ~ **supply price of labor** *n AmE*, ~ **supply price of labour** *n BrE* ECON, HRM prix le plus bas de l'offre de main-d'oeuvre *m*, prix minimal de l'offre de main-d'oeuvre *m*; ~ **tax** *n* TAX impôt minimum *m*; ~ **tax allowance** *n* TAX crédit d'impôt minimum *m*; ~ **tax carry-over** *n* TAX report d'impôt minimum *m*; ~ **tax credit** *n Canada* TAX crédit d'impôt minimum *m*; ~ **temperature** *n (MT)* GEN COMM température minimale *f*; ~ **transfer** *n (MT)* GEN COMM transfert minimum *m*, virement minimum *m*; ~ **wage** *n* ECON, HRM, LAW, WEL salaire minimum *m*

mining *n* IND déhouillement *m*; ~ **company** *n* IND compagnie minière *f*; ~ **industry** *n* ENVIR, IND industrie minière *f*; ~ **shares** *n pl* IND, STOCK valeurs minières *f pl*; ~ **tax** *n* IND, TAX impôt minier *m*, impôt sur l'exploitation minière *m*, impôt sur les mines *m*

minipage *n* MEDIA, S&M *advertising* minipage *f*

miniseries *n* MEDIA *broadcast* mini-feuilleton *m*

minister *n* ADMIN, POL ministre *mf*, secrétaire d'État *m*; ~ **for foreign affairs** POL ministre des Affaires étrangères *m*; ~ **of foreign affairs** POL ministre des Affaires étrangères *m*

Minister: ~ **of the Environment** *n* GEN COMM, POL ministre de l'Environnement *m*; ~ **of Finance** *n* FIN ministre des Finances *m*; ~ **for the Environment** *n* GEN COMM, POL ministre de l'Environnement *m*; ~ **of Transport** *n* POL, TRANSP ministre des Transports *m*

ministerial: ~ **order** *n* LAW arrêté ministériel *m*, ordonnance émanant du pouvoir exécutif *f*

minister's: *n pl* ~ **advisers** POL cabinet ministériel *m*

ministry *n* POL ministère *m*

Ministry: ~ **of Agriculture, Fisheries and Food** *n UK (MAFF)* ADMIN ≈ ministère de l'Agriculture, de la Pêche et de l'Alimentation *m*; ~ **of Defence** *n UK (MOD)* ADMIN ≈ ministère de la Défense *m*, POL ≈ ministère de la Défense nationale *m*; ~ **of Employment** *n* ADMIN ≈ ministère du Travail *m*; ~ **of Finance** *n* ECON ≈ ministère des Finances *m*; ~ **of Foreign Affairs** *n (MFA)* POL ≈ ministère des Affaires étrangères *m*; ~ **of International Trade and Industry** *n (MITI)* IND *Japan* ≈ ministère du Commerce et de l'Industrie international *m*; ~ **of Justice** *n* LAW ≈ ministère de la Justice *m*; ~ **of Overseas Development** *n (ODM)* ECON, POL ministère du Développement Outre-mer *m*; ~ **of Tourism** *n UK (MOT)* LEIS ≈ ministère du Tourisme *m*; ~ **of**

Transport *n UK (MOT)* COMMS, IND, TRANSP ≈ ministère des Transports *m*

minivan *n* TRANSP monospace *m*

Minneapolis: ~ **Grain Exchange** *n US* STOCK Bourse aux céréales de Minnéapolis *f*, Bourse des grains de Minnéapolis *f*

minor[1] *adj* GEN COMM, LAW mineur

minor[2] *n* LAW mineur *m*; ~ **balance status** ACC statut de solde minime *m*

minority: ~ **holding** *n* GEN COMM, STOCK *(ANT majority holding)* participation minoritaire *f*; ~ **interest** *n* GEN COMM participation minoritaire *f*, STOCK intérêt minoritaire *m*, investissement minoritaire *m*, participation minoritaire *f*; ~ **interests in profit** *n* ACC part du résultat revenant aux intérêts minoritaires *f*; ~ **investment** *n* STOCK investissement minoritaire *m*; ~ **participation** *n* ACC participation minoritaire *f*; ~ **share** *n* STOCK action minoritaire *f*; ~ **shareholder** *n* STOCK actionnaire minoritaire *m*; ~ **shareholding** *n (ANT majority shareholding)* STOCK action minoritaire *f*, participation minoritaire *f*; ~ **stake** *n (ANT majority stake)* STOCK intérêt minoritaire *m*, participation minoritaire *f*; ~ **stock** *n* STOCK action minoritaire *f*; ~ **stockholder** *n* STOCK actionnaire minoritaire *m*

Minsk *pr n* GEN COMM Minsk *n pr*

mint[1] *n* BANK Monnaie *f*; ~ **par** ECON, FIN pair métallique *m*; ~ **par of exchange** ECON, FIN pair du change *m*, pair intrinsèque *m*, pair métallique *m*

mint[2] *vt* ECON *coins* battre

mintage *n* ECON *of coins* frappe *f*

minus[1] *n* MATH *symbol* moins *m*; ~ **advantage** *jarg* GEN COMM opération ratée *f*; ~ **sign** MATH moins *m*, signe moins *m*; ~ **tick** *(ANT plus tick)* STOCK cours inférieur au cours précédent *m*, négociation à un cours inférieur *f*, échelon de cotation inférieur *m*

minus[2] *prep* ACC, FIN, MATH moins

minute: ~ **book** *n* GEN COMM, LAW registre des délibérations *m*

minutes *n pl* ADMIN *of meeting* procès-verbal *m*, LAW compte-rendu *m*, compte-rendu de séance *m*

minutiae *n pl* GEN COMM minuties *f pl*

MIP *abbr (marine insurance policy)* INS, TRANSP marine police d'assurance maritime *f*

miracle *n* GEN COMM miracle *m*

MIS *abbr* COMP, MGMNT *(management information system)* SIG *(système intégré de gestion)*, SIM *(système d'information de management)*, S&M *(marketing information system)* SIM *(système d'information de marketing)*

misaligned: ~ **rate of exchange** *n* ECON taux de change mal aligné *m*

misalignment *n* GEN COMM mauvais alignement *m*

misapply *vt* LAW mal appliquer

misapprehension *n* GEN COMM malentendu *m*

misappropriate *vt* FIN détourner

misappropriation *n* ACC, FIN, GEN COMM *of money, funds* détournement *m*, LAW concussion *f*

misc. *abbr (miscellaneous)* ACC, GEN COMM divers

miscalculate *vt* ACC, ECON, FIN, GEN COMM, MATH, S&M mal calculer

miscalculation *n* ACC, ECON, FIN, GEN COMM, MATH, S&M mauvais calcul *m*

miscarriage: ~ **of justice** *n* LAW erreur judiciaire *f*

miscellaneous[1] *adj (misc.)* ACC, GEN COMM divers

miscellaneous:[2] ~ **charges order** *n* (*MCO*) TRANSP bon pour services divers *m*; ~ **expenses** *n pl* ACC frais divers *m pl*

miscoding *n* COMP erreur de programmation *f*

misconduct *n* HRM faute grave *f*, manquement à la discipline *m*

misconnection *n* LEIS absence de correspondance *f*

misdeed *n* LAW faute *f*

misdemeanor *n* US LAW délit mineur *m*, infraction mineure *f*

misdemeanour *n* UK LAW méfait *m*, délit grave *m*

misfeasance *n* LAW méfait *m*

misfile *vt* GEN COMM mal classer

mishandling *n* GEN COMM mauvaise approche *f*

misintermediation *n* FIN intermédiation ratée *f*

mislead *vt* LAW abuser, induire en erreur, tromper

misleading[1] *adj* GEN COMM, PATENTS trompeur

misleading:[2] ~ **advertising** *n* GEN COMM, S&M *advertising* publicité mensongère *f*

mismanage *vt* FIN, MGMNT mal administrer, mal gérer

mismanagement *n* MGMNT mauvaise administration *f*, mauvaise gestion *f*

mismatch *n* ACC décalage *m*, non-concordance *f*; ~ **case** TAX cas de discordance *m*

mismatched: ~ **maturity** *n* BANK échéance décalée *f*

mispricing *n* FIN évaluation erronée du prix *f*

misprint *n* MEDIA faute d'impression *f*

misrepresent *vt* GEN COMM, TAX mal représenter

misrepresentation *n* GEN COMM, TAX présentation erronée des faits *f*

miss *vt* GEN COMM manquer

Miss *n* GEN COMM Mademoiselle *f*, Mlle

missile *n* IND projectile *m*

missing[1] *adj* GEN COMM manquant

missing:[2] ~ **bill of lading** *n* (*mslb*) IMP/EXP *shipping*, TRANSP connaissement manquant *m*; ~ **cargo** *n* (*msca*) TRANSP marchandises manquantes *f pl*; ~ **market** *n* ECON marché manquant *m*; ~ **vessel** *n* TRANSP navire disparu *m*

mission *n* GEN COMM mission *f*; ~ **statement** MGMNT définition de la mission *f*

missionary: ~ **salesperson** *n* S&M prospecteur *m*; ~ **work** *n* S&M travail de prospection *m*

misstatement: ~ **of age** *n* INS *personal* déclaration erronée d'âge *f*

mistake *n* GEN COMM erreur *f*, LAW erreur *f*, faute non-intentionnelle *f*, méprise non-intentionnelle *f*; ~ **of law** LAW erreur de droit *f*

mistaken *adj* GEN COMM erroné

Mister *n* (*Mr*) GEN COMM Monsieur *m* (*M.*)

mistype *n* ADMIN faute de frappe *f*

misunderstanding *n* GEN COMM malentendu *m*

misuse *n* ENVIR *of chemicals* mauvais usage *m*, usage abusif *m*

MIT: ~ **order** *n* (*market-if-touched order*) STOCK ordre au cours exact *m*

MITI *n* (*Ministry of International Trade and Industry*) IND *Japan* ≈ ministère du Commerce et de l'Industrie international *m*

mitigating: ~ **circumstances** *n pl* LAW circonstances atténuantes *f pl*

mitigation *n* LAW allègement *m*, atténuation *f*, réduction *f*; ~ **of damages** LAW demande en réduction de dommages-intérêts *f*, obligation de limiter le dommage *f*; ~ **of taxes** TAX atténuation d'impôts *f*

mix *n* GEN COMM mélange *m*, MEDIA *recording* mixage *m*, S&M mix *m*, mix de produits *m*, mélange *m*

mixed: ~ **account** *n* STOCK compte mixte *m*; ~ **-activity holding company** *n* FIN compagnie mixte *f*, STOCK holding à activité mixte *m*, société de portefeuilles à activité mixte *f*; ~ **bundling** *n* S&M groupage *m*, lot de marchandises pures *m*, routage *m*; ~ **consignment** *n* TRANSP envoi mixte *m*; ~ **cost** *n* ACC coût semi-variable *m*, coûts mixtes *m pl*; ~ **credit** *n* FIN crédit mixte *m*; ~ **economic system** *n* ECON, POL système d'économie mixte *m*; ~ **economy** *n* ECON, POL économie mixte *f*; ~ **farming** *n* ECON *agricultural* polyculture *f*; ~ **funds** *n pl* STOCK fonds mixtes *m pl*; ~ **good** *n* ECON bien semi-privé *m*, bien semi-public *m*; ~ **peril** *n* INS risque diver *m*; ~ **policy** *n* INS police d'assurance mixte *f*; ~ **results** *n pl* GEN COMM résultats mitigés *m pl*; ~ **signals** *n pl* GEN COMM messages contradictoires *m pl*

mixing *n* MEDIA mixage *m*

ml *abbr* GEN COMM (*milliliter AmE, millilitre BrE*) ml (*millilitre*), TRANSP (*motor launch*) *shipping* canot à moteur *m*, vedette *f*

MLE *abbr* (*maximum likelihood estimator*) MATH *statistics* estimateur de probabilité maximale *m*

MLH *abbr* (*minimum list heading*) GEN COMM tête de liste minimale *f*

MLM *abbr* (*multilevel marketing*) S&M marketing multiniveau *m*, marketing à niveaux multiples *m*, vente par réseau coopté *f*

MLR *abbr* UK (*minimum lending rate*) BANK, ECON taux officiel d'escompte *m*

MLS *abbr* US (*Multiple Listing Service*) PROP service de listage multiple *m*

mm *abbr* (*millimeter AmE, millimetre BrE*) GEN COMM mm (*millimètre*)

MMC *abbr* (*money-market certificate*) ECON, FIN, STOCK certificat de marché monétaire *m*, instrument du marché monétaire *m*

MMDA *abbr US (money-market deposit account)* FIN compte de dépôt du marché monétaire *m*

MMF *abbr US (money-market fund)* ECON, FIN, STOCK fonds investi au marché monétaire *m*, fonds monétaire *m*

MMI *abbr (Major Market Index)* STOCK indice MMI *m*, I *(indice du marché principal)*

MMMF *abbr US (money-market mutual fund)* FIN fonds commun de placement du marché monétaire *m*

MMSA *abbr (Mercantile Marine Services Association)* GEN COMM, TRANSP association de la marine marchande

mm²/s *abbr (square millimeter per second AmE, square millimetre per second BrE)* GEN COMM mm²/s *(millimètre carré par seconde)*

MNAOA *abbr UK (Merchant Navy and Airline Officers Association)* TRANSP association des officiers de la marine marchande et des lignes aériennes

MNC *abbr (multinational corporation)* ECON, GEN COMM, IND multinationale *f*, société multinationale *f*

MNDO *abbr UK (Merchant Navy Discipline Organisation)* TRANSP service de discipline de la marine marchande

MNE *abbr* ECON, GEN COMM *(multinational enterprise)*, IND *(multinational enterprise)* entreprise multinationale *f*, société multinationale *f*, TRANSP *UK (Merchant Navy Establishment)* établissement de la marine marchande

MNEA *abbr UK (Merchant Navy Establishment Administration)* TRANSP direction d'établissements de la marine marchande

MNOPF *abbr UK (Merchant Navy Officers Pension Fund)* TRANSP, WEL *shipping* caisse de retraite des officiers de la marine marchande

MNTB *abbr UK (Merchant Navy Training Board)* TRANSP comité de formation de la marine marchande

m/o *abbr (my order)* GEN COMM m/o *(mon ordre)*

MO *abbr* ADMIN *(mail order)* VPC *(vente par correspondance)*, BANK *AmE (money order)* MP *(mandat postal)*, COMMS, COMP *(mail order)* VPC *(vente par correspondance)*, FIN *AmE (money order)* MP *(mandat postal)*, GEN COMM *(modus operandi)* mode opératoire *m*, HRM *(medical officer)* médecin *m*, S&M *(mail order)* VPC *(vente par correspondance)*, WEL *(medical officer)* médecin *m*

mobile: ~ **crane** *n (MC)* TRANSP grue mobile *f*, grue roulante *f*; ~ **home** *n* PROP maison mobile *f*; ~ **home certificate** *n US* BANK, STOCK *mortgage-backed security* certificat hypothécaire de résidence mobile *m*; ~ **home park** *n* PROP parc de stationnement de maisons mobiles; ~ **lift frame** *n* TRANSP *containers* châssis des molettes mobile *m*; ~ **offshore drilling unit** *n (MODU)* IND unité mobile de drainage pétrolier offshore *f*; ~ **phone** *n* ADMIN, COMMS, GEN COMM téléphone mobile *m*,

téléphone portable *m*; ~ **telephone** *n* ADMIN, COMMS, GEN COMM téléphone mobile *m*, téléphone portable *m*; ~ **worker** *n* HRM travailleur itinérant *m*, travailleur mobile *m*

mobility *n* ECON mobilité *f*; ~ **clause** *UK* HRM clause de mobilité *f*; ~ **of labor** *AmE*, ~ **of labour** *BrE* ECON, HRM mobilité de la main-d'oeuvre *f*; ~ **status** ECON *of individuals within a country* mesure de mobilité géographique *f*; ~ **trap** ECON piège de la mobilité *m*

mobilize *vt* FIN mobiliser

MOC *abbr (market order on the close)* STOCK ordre au mieux à la clôture *m*, ordre au prix du marché en fin de séance *m*

MOD *abbr UK (Ministry of Defence)* ADMIN ≈ ministère de la Défense *m*, POL ≈ ministère de la Défense nationale *m*

mode *n* COMP mode *m*, GEN COMM modalité *f*, MATH *statistics* mode *m*; ~ **of transport** TRANSP mode de transport *m*

model[1] *n* GEN COMM mannequin *m*, modèle *m*, MATH modèle *m*, S&M maquette *f*; ~ **profile** GEN COMM profil type *m*; ~ **worker** GEN COMM employé modèle *m*

model[2] *vt* MATH modéliser, MEDIA façonner

modeling *n AmE*, **modelling** *n BrE* MATH modélisation *f*

modem *n (modulator-demodulator)* COMMS, COMP modem *m (modulateur-démodulateur)*; ~ **link** COMP liaison par modem *f*

moderate[1] *adj* ECON modéré

moderate:[2] ~ **income** *n* FIN revenu intermédiaire *m*, revenu modeste *m*

moderate[3] *vt* GEN COMM modérer

moderately[1] *adv* GEN COMM modérément

moderately:[2] ~ **indebted low-income country** *n* FIN pays à faible revenu modérément endetté *m*; ~ **indebted middle-income country** *n (MIMIC)* ECON, FIN, POL pays à revenu intermédiaire modérément endetté *m*

moderates *n pl* POL modérés *m pl*

modern: ~ **economy** *n* ECON, POL économie moderne *f*; ~ **portfolio theory** *n (MPT)* STOCK modern portfolio theory *m*, théorie de gestion moderne de portefeuille *f*

modernization *n* ECON, GEN COMM, IND, POL modernisation *f*

modernize *vt* ECON, GEN COMM, IND, POL moderniser

modest[1] *adj* ECON modeste, modéré, GEN COMM *increase* modeste

modest:[2] ~ **cyclical recovery** *n* ECON redressement modéré de la conjoncture *m*

modestly *adv* GEN COMM *slightly* modérément

modification *n* GEN COMM *of data*, PROP *of buildings* modification *f*

modified[1] *adj* GEN COMM modifié

modified:[2] ~ **accrual** *n* ACC échéance modifiée *f*; ~ **life insurance** *n* INS *personal* police vie modifiée *f*; **~ net premium** *n* INS prime nette modifiée *f*; **~ rebuy** *n jarg* S&M rachat modifié *m*; **~ union shop** *n US* HRM section nouveaux syndicats de métiers *f*

modify *vt* GEN COMM modifier

MODU *abbr (mobile offshore drilling unit)* IND unité mobile de drainage pétrolier offshore *f*

modular¹ *adj* GEN COMM, MATH modulaire

modular:² **~ automated container handling** *n (MACH)* TRANSP manutention modulaire et automatisée de conteneurs *f*; **~ housing** *n US* PROP logement modulaire *m*; **~ production** *n* IND, MATH fabrication modulaire *f*

modularity *n* GEN COMM, MATH modularité *f*

modulate *vt* COMMS moduler

modulation *n* COMMS modulation *f*

modulator: **~ -demodulator** *n (modem)* COMMS, COMP modulateur-démodulateur *m (modem)*

module *n* GEN COMM, MATH module *m*

modus operandi *n frml (MO)* GEN COMM manière d'opérer *f*, mode opératoire *m*

MOF *abbr (multioption facility)* STOCK facilité multi-options *f*, facilité à options multiples *f*

MOFF *abbr (multioption financing facility)* STOCK facilité de financement multi-options *f*, facilité de financement à options multiples *f*

Mogadischu *pr n* GEN COMM Mogadiscio *n pr*

MOH *abbr (medical officer of health)* HRM, WEL directeur de la santé publique *m*, médecin départemental *m*, officier de santé *m*

moisture: **~ -proof** *adj* TRANSP étanche

mold *AmE see mould BrE*

molded: **~ depth** *n AmE see moulded depth BrE*

Moldova *pr n* GEN COMM Moldavie *f*

Moldovan¹ *adj* GEN COMM moldave

Moldovan² *n* GEN COMM *person* Moldave *mf*

mole *n* TRANSP môle *m*

mom: **~ -and-pop store** *n AmE* S&M commerce familial *m*

moment *n* GEN COMM moment *m*; **~ to change trim** *(MCT)* TRANSP moment nécessaire pour faire varier l'assiette *m*; ♦ **at a given ~** GEN COMM à un moment donné; **at a given ~ in the future** GEN COMM dans l'avenir, à un moment donné dans le futur

moments *n pl* MATH *statistics* moments *m pl*

momentum *n* ECON, MATH élan *m*

Mon. *abbr (Monday)* GEN COMM lundi *m*

Monaco *pr n* GEN COMM Monaco *n pr*

Monday *n (Mon.)* GEN COMM lundi *m*

Monegasque¹ *adj* GEN COMM monégasque

Monegasque² *n* GEN COMM *person* Monégasque *mf*

monetarism *n* ECON, POL monétarisme *m*

monetarist¹ *adj* ECON, POL monétariste

monetarist² *n* ECON *econometrics*, POL monétariste *mf*; **~ approach** ECON approche monétariste *f*

monetary¹ *adj* ECON, GEN COMM monétaire

monetary:² **~ accommodation** *n* ECON ajustement monétaire *m*; **~ aggregates** *n pl UK (M)* ECON agrégats monétaires *m pl (M)*; **~ authorities** *n pl* BANK les autorités monétaires *f pl*; **~ base** *n* ECON base monétaire *f*; **~ bloc** *n* ECON bloc monétaire *m*; **~ compensation amount** *n (MCA)* ECON, FIN *EU* montant compensatoire monétaire *m*; **~ compensatory amount** *n (MCA)* ECON, FIN *EU* montant compensatoire monétaire *m*; **~ economics** *n pl* ECON économie monétaire *f*; **~ inducement** *n* FIN incitation monétaire *f*; **~ inflation** *n* ECON inflation monétaire *f*; **~ item** *n* ACC *balance sheets* actif monétaire *m*; **~ overhang** *n* ECON accumulation d'épargne non productive *f*; **~ policy** *n* ECON, FIN, POL politique monétaire *f*; **~ reserve** *n* BANK réserve monétaire *f*, ECON coussin de devises *m*, réserve monétaire *f*; **~ restriction** *n* ECON restriction monétaire *f*; **~ standard** *n* ECON étalon monétaire *m*; **~ union** *n* FIN, POL union monétaire *f*; **~ unit** *n* BANK, ECON, FIN unité monétaire *f*

monetization *n* ECON monétisation *f*

monetize *vt* ECON monétiser

money *n* BANK, ECON, FIN monnaie *f*, GEN COMM argent *m*, monnaie *f*; **~ at call** *n* ECON ayant au jour le jour *m*; **~ broker** *n* BANK courtier monétaire *m*; **~ desk** *n* BANK antenne financière *f*; **~ illusion** *n* ECON illusion monétaire *f*; **~ income** *n* ECON, FIN, TAX revenu nominal *m*; **~ laundering** *n* FIN blanchiment de capitaux *m*; **~ lender** *n* FIN prêteur sur gages *m*; **~ market** *n* ECON, FIN, STOCK *short-term investments* marché monétaire *m*; **~ -market certificate** *n (MMC)* ECON, FIN, STOCK certificat de marché monétaire *m*, instrument du marché monétaire *m*; **~ -market department** *n* STOCK service du marché monétaire *m*; **~ -market deposit account** *n US (MMDA)* FIN compte de dépôt du marché monétaire *m*; **~ -market fund** *n US (MMF)* ECON, FIN, STOCK fonds investi au marché monétaire *m*, fonds monétaire *m*; **~ -market institution** *n* ECON, FIN, STOCK institution du marché monétaire *f*; **~ -market instrument** *n* ECON, FIN, STOCK instrument du marché monétaire *m*; **~ -market mutual fund** *n US (MMMF)* FIN fonds commun de placement du marché monétaire *m*; **~ -market paper** *n* ECON, FIN, STOCK instrument du marché monétaire *m*, papier monétaire *m*; **~ -market rate** *n* ECON, FIN, STOCK taux du marché monétaire *m*, TMM; **~ -market returns** *n pl* ECON, FIN, STOCK rendements du marché monétaire *m pl*, revenu du marché de l'argent *m*; **~ -market savings account** *n US* BANK compte de dépôts monétaires *m*; **~ -market trader** *n* ECON, FIN, STOCK opérateur sur le marché monétaire *m*; **~ mart** *n* ECON, FIN, STOCK marché monétaire *m*; **~ matters** *n pl* GEN COMM affaires d'argent *f pl*; **~ measurement** *n* FIN estimation monétaire *f*; **~ multiplier** *n* ECON multiplicateur monétaire *m*; **~ order** *n AmE (MO, postal note, postal order)* BANK, FIN mandat *m*, mandat postal *m (MP)*; **~ reserve** *n*

BANK, ECON réserve monétaire *f*; ~ **restraint** *n* ECON restriction monétaire *f*; ~ **and securities broad-form policy** *n* INS *company* police tous riques d'argent et des valeurs *f*; ~ **-spinner** *n* *infrml* FIN activité lucrative *f*, GEN COMM mine d'or *f*; ~ **spread** *n* FIN, STOCK opération mixte verticale *f*, écart monétaire *m*; ~ **supply** *n* (SYN *Divisia money index*) ECON masse monétaire *f*; ~ **transfer order** *n* BANK, FIN ordre de transfert monétaire *m*; ~ **transmission** *n* BANK transfert d'argent *m*; ~ **up front** *n* FIN, GEN COMM argent devant soi *m*; ◆ **at-the-~** STOCK au jeu, au milieu (*jarg*), à parité; **have ~ to burn** *infrml* GEN COMM avoir de l'argent à ne plus savoir qu'en faire (*infrml*); **make up the odd ~** GEN COMM faire l'appoint

moneymaker *n* GEN COMM brasseur de capitaux *m*

Mongolia *pr n* GEN COMM Mongolie *f*

Mongolian[1] *adj* GEN COMM mongol

Mongolian[2] *n* GEN COMM *person* Mongol *m*

monies: ~ **paid in** *n pl* ACC, FIN recettes effectuées *f pl*, sommes versées *f pl*; ~ **paid out** *n pl* ACC, FIN versements effectués *m pl*

monitor[1] *n* COMP moniteur *m*, écran *m*, *security* appareil de surveillance *m*, GEN COMM moniteur *m*, écran *m*

monitor[2] *vt* GEN COMM surveiller, *performance* contrôler, HRM, MGMNT *performance* contrôler, S&M *market*, TRANSP *rates* surveiller

monitoring *n* FIN, GEN COMM surveillance *f*

monkey *n* *infrml US* FIN monkey *m*

Monnet's: ~ **law** *n* ECON loi de Monnet *f*

monochrome *adj* COMP, MEDIA *screen, peripherals* monochrome

monoeconomics *n* ECON monoéconomie *f*

monogram *n* GEN COMM monogramme *m*

monometallic *adj* ECON monométalliste

monometallism *n* ECON monométallisme *m*

monometallist *n* ECON monométalliste *mf*

monopolist *n* ECON, S&M monopoliste *mf*

monopolistic[1] *adj* ECON, S&M monopoliste

monopolistic:[2] ~ **competition** *n* ECON concurrence monopolistique *f*

monopolization *n* ECON, GEN COMM, S&M monopolisation *f*

monopolize *vt* ECON, GEN COMM, S&M monopoliser

monopoly *n* ECON, GEN COMM, S&M monopole *m*; ~ **capitalism** ECON, POL capitalisme de monopole *m*, capitalisme monopolistique *m*; ~ **power** ECON pouvoir de monopole *m*; ~ **price** ECON, S&M prix de monopole *m*; ~ **profit** ECON bénéfices monopolistiques *m pl*, bénéfices élevés découlant d'un monopole *m pl*; ~ **rent** ECON, PROP loyer monopolisé *m*, rente de monopole *f*

monopsony *n* ECON monopsone *m*

monorail *n* TRANSP monorail *m*

monotonous *adj* GEN COMM monotone

Monrovia *pr n* GEN COMM Monrovia *n pr*

Montenegrin[1] *adj* GEN COMM monténégrin

Montenegrin[2] *n* GEN COMM *person* Monténégrin *m*

Montenegro *pr n* GEN COMM Monténégro *m*

Montevideo *pr n* GEN COMM Montevideo *n pr*

month *n* (*MTH, m*) GEN COMM mois *m*; ~ **order** STOCK ordre valable tout le mois *m*; ~ **-to-month tenancy** LAW bail mensuel renouvelable *m*, PROP bail mensuel renouvelable *m*, location au mois *f*; ◆ **a ~ in advance** GEN COMM un mois à l'avance

monthly[1] *adj* ACC, FIN, GEN COMM, MEDIA mensuel; ◆ **in ~ installments** *AmE*, **in ~ instalments** *BrE* ACC, FIN par mensualités

monthly[2] *adv* ACC, FIN, GEN COMM mensuellement

monthly[3] *n* MEDIA mensuel *m*; ~ **compounding of interest** *n* BANK intérêt composé mensuellement *m*; ~ **expenses** *n pl* ACC, FIN, GEN COMM frais mensuels *m pl*; ~ **installment** *n AmE*, ~ **instalment** *n BrE* ACC mensualité *f*, BANK mensualité *f*, règlement mensuel *m*, FIN mensualité *f*; ~ **investment plan** *n* STOCK plan d'investissement mensuel *m*; ~ **magazine** *n* MEDIA mensuel *m*; ~ **rate note** *n* STOCK BTM, bon à taux mensuel *m*; ~ **rent** *n* PROP loyer au mois *m*, loyer mensuel *m*; ~ **return** *n* ACC état mensuel *m*; ~ **salary** *n* HRM salaire mensuel *m*; ~ **sales** *n pl* S&M ventes mensuelles *f pl*; ~ **savings** *n* HRM *of employee* épargne mensuelle *f*; ~ **statement** *n* BANK, FIN *credit card* relevé de compte mensuel *m*; ~ **tenancy** *n* PROP location au mois *f*; ~ **wage** *n* HRM salaire mensuel *m*

months: ~ **traded** *phr* STOCK mois de transaction

Montserrat *pr n* GEN COMM Montserrat *n pr*

monument *n* *US* PROP monument *m*

moonlight:[1] ~ **economy** *n* ECON, FIN économie souterraine *f*

moonlight[2] *vt* HRM travailler au noir

moonlighter *n* HRM travailleur au noir *m*

moonlighting *n* HRM cumul d'emploi *m*, travail au noir *m*, travail clandestin *m*

mooring *n* TRANSP amarrage *m*; ~ **basin** TRANSP bassin d'amarrage *m*; ~ **buoy** TRANSP coffre d'amarrage *m*

moral[1] *adj* MGMNT, WEL moral

moral:[2] ~ **hazard** *n* INS risque moral *m*, risque subjectif *m*; ~ **law** *n* LAW droit moral *m*; ~ **obligation bond** *n* STOCK engagement obligataire moral *m*, obligation de collectivité locale garantie *f*; ~ **persuasion** *n* BANK pression morale *f*

morale *n* HRM moral *m*

moratorium *n frml* FIN, GEN COMM, LAW moratoire *m*, moratorium *m* (*frml*)

more: ~ **or less** *adv* GEN COMM plus ou moins

Morgan: ~ **Stanley Capital International World index** *n* STOCK indice boursier mondial Morgan Stanley *m*

morgue *n infrml* MEDIA *print* département des périodiques *m*, frigo *m* (*infrml*), morgue *f* (*jarg*)

Moroccan[1] *adj* GEN COMM marocain

Moroccan[2] *n* GEN COMM *person* Marocain *m*

Morocco *pr n* GEN COMM Maroc *m*

Moroni *pr n* GEN COMM Moroni *n pr*

morphological: ~ **analysis** *n* FIN, MATH analyse morphologique *f*

mortality *n* INS, WEL mortalité *f*; ~ **gain** TAX gain de mortalité *m*; ~ **loss** TAX perte de mortalité *f*; ~ **table** INS table de mortalité *f*

mortg. *abbr (mortgage)* BANK, FIN, PROP hyp. *(hypothèque)*

mortgage[1] *n (mortg.)* BANK, FIN, PROP hypothèque *f (hyp.)*; ~ **account** *n* BANK compte de prêt hypothécaire *m*; ~ **arrears** *n pl* PROP arriérés de crédit-logement *m pl*; ~ **assumption** *n* BANK acceptation d'une hypothèque *f*; ~ **-backed certificate** *n* FIN certificat garanti par hypothèque *m*; ~ **-backed security** *n (MBS)* STOCK titre de créance hypothécaire *m*, valeur garantie par hypothèque *f*; ~ **banker** *n US* BANK, FIN banquier hypothécaire *m*; ~ **bond** *n* FIN obligation hypothécaire *f*; ~ **broker** *n US* BANK, FIN courtier hypothécaire *m*; ~ **ceiling** *n* BANK, PROP plafond d'hypothèque *m*; ~ **commitment** *n* BANK, FIN engagement hypothécaire *m*; ~ **company** *n* BANK société de prêt hypothécaire *f*; ~ **correspondent** *n* BANK, FIN correspondant hypothécaire *m*; ~ **credit association** *n* FIN association de crédit hypothécaire *f*; ~ **debt** *n* BANK dette hypothécaire *f*; ~ **discount** *n* BANK, FIN remise hypothécaire *f*; ~ **insurance** *n* BANK, INS *personal* assurance d'hypothèque *f*; ~ **insurance policy** *n* INS *personal* police d'assurance hypothèque *f*; ~ **lender** *n* BANK prêteur hypothécaire *m*; ~ **lien** *n* BANK, LAW, PROP nantissement hypothécaire *m*, privilège hypothécaire *m*; ~ **life insurance** *n US* BANK, INS *personal* assurance-vie liée à l'hypothèque *f*; ~ **loan** *n* BANK crédit hypothécaire *m*, emprunt hypothécaire *m*, prêt hypothécaire *m*, prêt sur hypothèque *m*, PROP emprunt hypothécaire *m*; ~ **loan company** *n* BANK société de prêt hypothécaire *f*; ~ **loan corporation** *n* BANK société de prêt hypothécaire *f*; ~ **loans outstanding** *n pl* BANK encours des prêts hypothécaires *m*, prêts hypothécaires en cours *m pl*; ~ **market** *n* GEN COMM marché hypothécaire *m*; ~ **payment** *n* BANK, FIN versement hypothécaire *m*; ~ **portfolio** *n* BANK portefeuille des prêts hypothécaires *m*, portefeuille hypothécaire *m*; ~ **rate** *n* BANK taux de prêt hypothécaire *m*; ~ **relief** *n* BANK, FIN, TAX allègement d'un prêt hypothécaire *m*; ~ **repayment** *n* BANK remboursement d'un prêt hypothécaire *m*; ~ **rescue scheme** *n UK* BANK, PROP plan de sauvetage d'hypothèque *m*; ~ **servicing** *n* BANK, FIN remboursement d'un hypothèque *m*; ~ **statement** *n* BANK état de compte de prêt hypothécaire *m*; ~ **strip** *n* FIN démembrement hypothécaire *m*; ~ **table** *n* BANK table de paiements hypothécaires *f*

mortgage[2] **1.** *vt* BANK grever d'une hypothèque *loc*, hypothéquer; **2.** *vi* ~ **out** FIN hypothéquer

mortgagee *n* BANK créancier hypothécaire *m*, créancier sur hypothèque *m*

mortgager *n* BANK débiteur hypothécaire *m*, débiteur sur hypothèque *m*

Moscow *pr n* GEN COMM Moscou *n pr*

most:[1] ~ **active list** *n* STOCK *on a given day* liste des valeurs les plus actives *f*; ~ **-favored nation** *n AmE see most-favoured nation BrE*; ~ **-favored nation clause** *n AmE see most-favoured nation clause BrE*; ~ **-favored nation treatment** *n AmE see most-favoured nation treatment BrE*; ~ **-favoured nation** *n BrE (MFN)* ECON nation la plus favorisée *f*; ~ **-favoured nation clause** *n BrE* ECON, LAW, POL clause de la nation la plus favorisée *f*; ~ **-favoured nation treatment** *n BrE* ECON, POL *international trade* traitement de la nation la plus favorisée *m*; ~ **senior member** *n* GEN COMM doyen *m*

most:[2] **the** ~ **you can lose** *phr* STOCK le maximum que vous puissiez perdre *loc m*, le plus que vous puissiez perdre *loc*

MOT *abbr* COMMS *UK (Ministry of Transport)* ≈ ministère des Transports *m*, IND *(motor)* moteur *m*, IND *UK (Ministry of Transport)* ≈ ministère des Transports *m*, LEIS *UK (Ministry of Tourism)* ≈ ministère du Tourisme *m*, TRANSP *(motor)* moteur *m*, TRANSP *UK (Ministry of Transport)* ≈ ministère des Transports *m*

mother: ~ **ship** *n (SYN feeder ship)* TRANSP collecteur *m*, navire collecteur *m*, navire d'apport *m*, navire d'éclatement *m*

motherboard *n* COMP carte mère *f*, fond de panier *m*

mothercard *n* COMP carte mère *f*, fond de panier *m*

motif *n* GEN COMM logo *m*

motion *n* POL motion *f*; ~ **of censure** *n* POL motion de censure *f*; ~ **economy** *n* ECON économie des mouvements *f*; ~ **picture** *n AmE (SYN film, movie)* LEIS, MEDIA film *m*; ~ **picture advertising** *n AmE (SYN film advertising)* LEIS, MEDIA publicité cinématographique *f*; ~ **picture industry** *n AmE (SYN film industry)* LEIS, MEDIA industrie cinématographique *f*; ~ **pictures** *n pl AmE (cf cinema BrE, pictures BrE)* LEIS, MEDIA *art* cinéma *m*; ~ **study** *n* ECON, GEN COMM, MATH étude des mouvements *f*

motivate *vt* GEN COMM, HRM, MGMNT animer, motiver

motivated *adj* HRM motivé

motivation *n* GEN COMM, HRM, MGMNT motivation *f*

motivational[1] *adj* GEN COMM, HRM, MGMNT motivant

motivational:[2] ~ **analysis** *n* HRM analyse des motivations *f*, S&M analyse de motivation *f*; ~ **research** *n* S&M enquête de motivations *f*, recherche de motivations *f*, étude de motivations *f*

motivator *n* GEN COMM, HRM, MGMNT mobile *m*, motivateur *m*

motive *n* GEN COMM mobile *m*, motif *m*, HRM mobile *m*, INS, LAW motif *m*, MGMNT mobile *m*

motor n *(MOT)* IND, TRANSP moteur m; ~ **freight** TRANSP transport routier m; ~ **insurance** INS, TRANSP assurance automobile f; ~ **launch** *(ml)* TRANSP canot à moteur m, vedette f; ~ **merchant vessel** *(MV)* TRANSP navire marchand à moteur m; ~ **mileage allowance** UK TAX indemnité kilométrique f; ~ **premium** INS prime automobile f, TRANSP prime automobile f, prime d'assurance automobile f; ~ **ship** *(MS)* TRANSP navire à moteur m; ~ **spirit** TRANSP *fuel* essence pour moteurs f; ~ **tanker** *(MT)* TRANSP bateau-citerne à moteur m, navire-citerne à moteur m; ~ **transport officer** *(MTO)* HRM, TRANSP agent de transportation routière m, responsable des transports motorisés m; ~ **truck cargo insurance** US INS, TRANSP assurance de marchandise acheminée par les transports routiers f; ~ **vehicle** TRANSP véhicule automobile m, véhicule à moteur m; ~ **vehicle insurance** INS, TRANSP assurance automobile f; ~ **vessel** *(MV)* TRANSP navire à moteur m

motorcar n BrE *(cf automobile AmE, car)* TRANSP voiture f

motorist: ~ **inclusive tour** n LEIS voyage par voiture tout compris m

Motorman: ~ **Grade I** n TRANSP *shipping* officier mécanicien adjoint 1ère classe m; ~ **Grade II** n TRANSP *shipping* officier mécanicien adjoint 2ème classe m

motorship n *(m)* TRANSP navire à moteur m

motorway n BrE *(cf expressway Can, freeway AmE, superhighway AmE, throughway AmE)* TRANSP autoroute f

mould vt BrE MEDIA *public opinion* façonner, former

moulded: ~ **depth** n BrE *(dm/d)* TRANSP *naval architecture* creux sur quille m

mount vt S&M monter; ♦ ~ **a takeover bid for a company** GEN COMM lancer une OPA contre une société

mountain n ECON montagne f; ~ **resort** LEIS station de montagne f

mounting adj GEN COMM *increasing* croissant

mouse:[1] ~ **-driven** adj COMP commandé par souris, contrôlé par souris, piloté par souris

mouse[2] n COMP souris f; ~ **driver** COMP pilote de souris m; ~ **key** COMP touche souris f; ~ **mat** COMP tapis de souris m

movable: ~ **-link span** n TRANSP *at ramp berth* rampe d'appontement amovible f; ~ **property** n PROP biens meubles m pl, biens mobiliers m pl

move[1] n ECON *in currency* fluctuation f, STOCK mouvement m; ♦ **make the first** ~ GEN COMM faire le premier pas

move:[2] ~ **ahead** vi STOCK *of shares* progresser; ~ **in** GEN COMM emménager; ~ **out** PROP déménager; ~ **together** ECON *currencies* fluctuer, varier simultanément; ♦ ~ **house** PROP changer de logement; ~ **in tandem** STOCK évoluer en parallèle; ~ **into the money** STOCK *short calls, short puts* entrer dans le

cours; ~ **to larger premises** ADMIN emménager dans des locaux plus grands

movement n GEN COMM mouvement m, *in prices* fluctuation f, POL, STOCK mouvement m; ~ **certificate** IMP/EXP certificat de circulation m; ~ **of freight** TRANSP mouvement des marchandises m, transport de marchandises m; ~ **of labor** AmE, ~ **of labour** BrE ECON, HRM circulation de la main-d'oeuvre f

movements: ~ **on shareholders' equity** n pl ACC *annual* tableau de variation des capitaux propres m

mover: ~ **and shaker** n infrml MGMNT animateur m

movie n *(cf film, motion picture AmE)* LEIS, MEDIA film m; ~ **-making** AmE *(cf cinema BrE, film-making)* LEIS, MEDIA cinéma m; ~ **theater** AmE *(cf cinema BrE)* LEIS, MEDIA cinéma m

moving: ~ **annual total** n *(MAT)* MATH *statistics* total annuel mobile m; ~ **average** n MATH moyenne mobile f; ~ **pavement** n BrE *(cf travolator AmE)* GEN COMM, LEIS tapis roulant m, trottoir roulant m; ~ **van** n TRANSP camion de déménagement m

Mozambican[1] adj GEN COMM mozambicain

Mozambican[2] n GEN COMM *person* Mozambicain m

Mozambique pr n GEN COMM Mozambique m

MP abbr *(multipurpose)* GEN COMM multi-fonction

MPA abbr *(marginal principle of allocation)* ECON principe marginal d'attribution m

MPC abbr *(marginal propensity to consume)* ECON propension marginale à consommer f

mpg abbr *(miles per gallon)* GEN COMM miles par gallon, ≈ km au cent *(kilomètres au cent)*

mph abbr *(miles per hour)* GEN COMM miles/heure m pl

MPI abbr *(marginal propensity to import)* ECON, IMP/EXP TMI *(tendance marginale à importer)*

MPO abbr *(management and personnel office)* ADMIN, MGMNT bureau de la direction et du personnel m

MPP abbr *(marginal physical product)* ECON produit marginal physique m

MPS abbr *(marginal propensity to save)* BANK, ECON, FIN propension marginale à épargner f

MPT abbr *(modern portfolio theory)* STOCK modern portfolio theory m, théorie de gestion moderne de portefeuille f

MQS abbr UK *(minimum quote size)* STOCK cours minimal m, quotité minimale f

Mr n GEN COMM M. *(Monsieur)*

MR abbr *(mate's receipt)* IMP/EXP, TRANSP *shipping* bon de chargement m, certificat de bord m, reçu de bord m

MRA abbr *(multiple regression analysis)* ECON, FIN, MATH analyse de régression multiple f

MRCA abbr *(Market Research Corporation of America)* S&M société américaine des études de marché

mrem/h *abbr (millirem per hour)* GEN COMM millirem/h *m*, mrem/h *(millirem par heure)*

mr/h *abbr (milliroentgen per hour)* GEN COMM mr/h *(milliröntgen/heure)*

MRO *abbr (maintenance, repair and overhaul)* TRANSP entretien, réparation et révision *loc m*

MRP *abbr (manufacturer's recommended price)* S&M prix public *m*, prix recommandé par le fabriquant *m*

MRR *abbr (minimum reserve requirements)* ECON réserves légales minimales *f pl*, réserves légales minimum *f pl*

Mrs *n* GEN COMM Madame *f*, Mme

MRS *abbr (marginal rate of substitution)* ECON taux marginal de substitution *m*

MRT *abbr (mass rapid transit)* TRANSP transport collectif rapide *m*

m/s *abbr* BANK *(months after sight)* mois à vue *loc*, GEN COMM *(meters per second, metres per second)* m/s *(mètres par seconde)*

Ms *n* GEN COMM titre employé pour une femme, qui n'indique pas son statut marital

MS *abbr* POL *(member state)* EU état-membre *m*, TAX *(manuscript)* MS *(manuscrit)*, TRANSP *(manual system)* système manuel *m*, TRANSP *(machinery survey)* visite des machines *f*, TRANSP *(motor ship)* shipping navire à moteur *m*

MSA *abbr* ADMIN US *(Mutual Security Agency)* agence de caution mutuelle, LAW, TRANSP UK *(merchant shipping Act)* loi sur la marine marchande *f*

MSC *abbr obs* UK *(Manpower Services Commission)* HRM commission des services de main d'oeuvre, maintenant Training Agency

MSc *abbr (Master of Science)* WEL ≈ maîtrise de sciences *f*, ≈ titulaire d'une maîtrise de sciences *m*

msca *abbr (missing cargo)* TRANSP marchandises manquantes *f pl*

MS-DOS® *abbr (Microsoft Disk Operating System)* COMP MS-DOS® *m*

MSL *abbr (mean sea level)* TRANSP shipping niveau moyen de la mer *m*

mslb *abbr (missing bill of lading)* IMP/EXP, TRANSP connaissement manquant *m*

MT *abbr* COMP *(machine translation)* traduction automatique *f*, ECON *(mail transfer)* international trade transfert par courrier *m*, GEN COMM *(mean time)* temps moyen *m*, GEN COMM *(minimum temperature)* température minimale *f*, GEN COMM *(minimum transfer)* transfert minimum *m*, virement minimum *m*, TRANSP *(motor tanker)* shipping bateau-citerne à moteur *m*, navire-citerne à moteur *m*

MTA *abbr (Maltese pound)* GEN COMM livre maltaise *f*

MTBF *abbr (mean time between failures)* TRANSP temps moyen de bon fonctionnement *m*

MTC *abbr (Maritime Transport Committee)* TRANSP commission des Transports Maritimes

MTH *abbr (month)* GEN COMM mois *m*

MTL *abbr* BANK *(medium-term loan)* prêt à moyen terme *m*, TRANSP *(mean tidal level)* shipping niveau moyen de la marée *m*

MTN *abbr* ECON *(multilateral trade negotiation)* négociation commerciale multilatérale *f*, FIN *(medium-term note)* BMTN *(bon à moyen terme négociable)*, POL *(multilateral trade negotiation)* négociation commerciale multilatérale *f*

MTO *abbr* HRM, TRANSP *(motor transport officer)* agent de transportation routière *m*, responsable des transports motorisés *m*, TRANSP *(multimodal transport operator)* opérateur multi-transports *m*, transporteur multimodal *m*

mton *abbr (metric ton)* GEN COMM tonne métrique *f*

MTR *abbr (mass transit railroad, mass transit railway)* TRANSP réseau ferroviaire de transport collectif *m*

M/U *adj (making-up price)* GEN COMM ajustement des prix *m*, cours de compensation *m*, cours de liquidation *m*

muckraker *n* GEN COMM journaliste à sensation *m*, MEDIA journaliste à sensation *m*

multiaccess *n* COMP, GEN COMM accès multiple *m*

multiaccident *n* TRANSP accident multiple *m*

multicollinearity *n* ECON multicorrélation *f*, MATH *statistics* multicolinéarité *f*

multicurrency *n* BANK, ECON, FIN multidevise *f*; **~ loan** BANK emprunt en plusieurs monnaies *m*, prêt multidevises *m*, emprunt en plusieurs monnaies *m*

multidelivery *n* TRANSP livraison multiple *f*

multiemployer: **~ bargaining** *n (SYN association bargaining)* HRM négociation avec association patronale *f*, négociation collective *f*, négociation à plusieurs employeurs *f*

multientry: **~ visa** *n* ADMIN visa multi-transit *m*, visa permanent *m*

multifamily: **~ housing** *n* PROP, WEL logement plurifamilial *m*

Multi-Fibre: **~ Arrangement** *n (MFA)* ECON *international trade* accord multi-fibres *m (AMF)*

multijobbing *n* COMP traitement multitravail *m*

multijurisdictional *adj* LAW multijuridictionnel

multilateral[1] *adj* ECON, POL multilatéral

multilateral:[2] **~ agency** *n* ECON, POL *development assistance* agence multilatérale *f*; **~ agreement** *n* ECON, POL *international trade* accord multilatéral *m*; **~ aid** *n (SYN bilateral aid, tied aid)* ECON, POL aide multilatérale *f*; **~ development bank** *n* BANK, ECON, FIN, POL banque multilatérale de développement *f*; **~ disbursement** *n* ECON *of development aid* paiement multilatéral *m*; **~ donors** *n pl* ECON, POL *of development assistance* donateurs multilatéraux *m pl*; **~ permit** *n* TRANSP EU permis multilatéral *m*; **~ trade agreement** *n* ECON *inter-*

national trade, POL accord commercial multilatéral *m*; ~ **trade negotiation** *n (MTN)* ECON, POL négociation commerciale multilatérale *f*

Multilateral: ~ **Trade Organization** *n* ECON, POL organisation mondiale du commerce *f*

multilateralism *n* ECON *international trade*, POL multilatéralisme *m*

multilegged: ~ **sling** *n* TRANSP *cargo handling equipment* élingue araignée *f*

multilevel: ~ **marketing** *n (MLM)* S&M marketing multiniveau *m*, marketing à niveaux multiples *m*, vente par réseau coopté *f*

multilingual *adj* GEN COMM polyglotte

multimedia[1] *adj* COMP, MEDIA, S&M *advertising* multimédia

multimedia:[2] ~ **training** *n* COMP, HRM, MEDIA, WEL formation plurimédiatique *f*

multimillion: ~ **pound deal** *n* FIN transaction de plusieurs millions libellés en livres sterling *f*

multimillionaire *n* GEN COMM milliardaire *mf*

multimodal[1] *adj* TRANSP multimodal

multimodal:[2] ~ **distribution** *n* MATH *statistics* distribution multinomiale *f*; ~ **frequency curve** *n* MATH *statistics* courbe à fréquence multinomiale *f*; ~ **transport** *n* TRANSP transport multimodal *m*; ~ **transport law** *n* LAW, TRANSP loi relative au transport multimodal *f*, législation relative au transport multimodal *f*; ~ **transport operator** *n (MTO)* TRANSP opérateur multi-transports *m*, transporteur multimodal *m*; ~ **transport service** *n* TRANSP service de transport multimodal *m*

multinational[1] *adj* ECON, GEN COMM, IND multinational

multinational[2] *n* ECON, GEN COMM, IND multinationale *f*; ~ **bank** BANK banque multinationale *f*; ~ **company** ECON, GEN COMM, IND multinationale *f*, société multinationale *f*; ~ **corporation** *(MNC)* ECON, GEN COMM, IND multinationale *f*, société multinationale *f*; ~ **crew** TRANSP équipage multinational *m*; ~ **enterprise** *(MNE)* ECON, GEN COMM, IND entreprise multinationale *f*, société multinationale *f*; ~ **export credit** ECON, FIN, IMP/EXP crédit multinational à l'exportation *m*; ~ **trading** ECON, IMP/EXP commerce multinational *m*

multinationally *adv* GEN COMM de façon multinationale *loc f*

multioption: ~ **facility** *n* STOCK montage financier à options multiples *m*, STOCK facilité multi-options *f*, facilité à options multiples *f*, montage financier multi-options *m*; ~ **financing facility** *n (MOFF)* STOCK facilité de financement multi-options *f*, facilité de financement à options multiples *f*, montage financier multi-options *m*, montage financier à options multiples *m*

multiperil: ~ **insurance** *n* INS assurance combinée *f*, assurance tous risques *f*

multiplant: ~ **bargaining** *n* HRM négociation à plusieurs usines *f*

multiple[1] *adj* GEN COMM, MATH multiple

multiple[2] *n* MATH multiple *m*; ~ **accident** *n* TRANSP accident multiple *m*; ~ **-activity chart** *n* COMP tableau d'activités multiples *m*; ~ **buyer** *n* S&M *sales* acheteur multiple *m*; ~ **-contract-finance projected line of credit** *n* FIN prévision de ligne de crédit financée par plusieurs contrats *f*; ~ **correlation** *n* MATH *statistics* corrélation multiple *f*; ~ **drop** *n* TRANSP *road haulage* trajet à escales multiples *m*; ~ **-entry visa** *n* ADMIN visa multi-transit *m*, visa permanent *m*; ~ **exchange rate** *n* ECON taux de change multiple *m*; ~ **listing** *n* US PROP listage multiple *m*; ~ **management** *n* MGMNT direction multiple *f*; ~ **-management plan** *n* HRM, MGMNT management participatif *m*; ~ **regression** *n* ECON, FIN, MATH *statistics* régression multiple *f*; ~ **regression analysis** *n (MRA)* ECON, FIN, MATH analyse de régression multiple *f*; ~ **retirement ages** *n pl* HRM âge de retraite variable *m*; ~ **shop** *n* HRM unité interstatutaire de négociation; ~ **taxation** *n* TAX imposition multiple *f*; ~ **-track plan** *n jarg* WEL fonctionnement par ateliers *m*; ~ **-unit residential building** *n* ADMIN, PROP immeuble résidentiel à logements multiples *m*

Multiple: ~ **Listing Service** *n US (MLS)* PROP service de listage multiple *m*

multiplication *n* GEN COMM, MATH multiplication *f*

multiplier *n* ECON multiplicateur *m*; ~ **effect** ECON *econometrics* effet multiplicateur *m*; ~ **principle** ECON *econometrics* principe multiplicateur *m*

multiply 1. *vt* MATH multiplier; **2.** *vi* MATH se multiplier

multiport: ~ **itinerary** *n* TRANSP itinéraire à escales multiples *m*; ~ **operation** *n* TRANSP opération à escales multiples *f*

multiprocessing *n* COMP multitraitement *m*

multiprocessor *n* COMP multiprocesseur *m*

multiproduct: ~ **berth** *n* TRANSP quai polyvalent *m*

multiprogramming *n* COMP multiprogrammation *f*

multipurpose[1] *adj* COMP *peripheral, software* à usages multiples, GEN COMM multi-fonction, à usages multiples

multipurpose:[2] ~ **vessel** *n* TRANSP navire polyvalent *m*

multiquote *n* TRANSP tarifs différents *m pl*

multiracial *adj* GEN COMM multiracial

multirisk: ~ **insurance** *n* INS assurance combinée *f*, assurance multirisque *f*

multiroute *adj* TRANSP multi-route

multiskilling *n* HRM polyvalence *f*

multistage: ~ **sampling** *n* MATH *statistics* échantillonnage multiphase *m*

multistorey *adj* PROP à plusieurs étages

multitasking *n* COMP traitement multitâche *m*

multiunion: ~ **bargaining** *n UK* HRM négociation plurisyndicale *f*; ~ **plant** *n* HRM usine à syndicats multiples *f*

multiunionism *n* HRM représentation plurisyndicale *f*

multiuser *n* COMP multiutilisateur *m*; ~ **berth** TRANSP quai polyvalent *m*; ~ **document** COMP document multiutilisateur *m*; ~ **route** TRANSP route à utilisateurs multiples *f*; ~ **system** COMP système multiutilisateur *m*

multivariate: ~ **analysis** *n* MATH analyse à variantes multiples *f*

multivariety: ~ **store** *n* GEN COMM, S&M grand magasin *m*

multiyear[1] *adj* GEN COMM pluri-annuel

multiyear:[2] ~ **operational plan** *n* *(MYOP)* FIN plan de développement pluriannuel *m*, plan opérationnel pluriannuel *m*, projet d'exploitation pluriannuel *m*; ~ **rescheduling agreement** *n* *(MYRA)* FIN accord de rééchelonnement pluriannuel *m*; ~ **resource envelope** *n* FIN enveloppe budgétaire pluriannuelle *f*; ~ **restructuring agreement** *n* *(MYRA)* FIN accord de restructuration pluriannuel *m*; ~ **spending envelope** *n* FIN enveloppe pluriannuelle de dépenses *f*

Mundell-Fleming: ~ **model** *n* ECON modèle de Mundell et Fleming *m*

municipal[1] *adj* GEN COMM, POL municipal

municipal:[2] ~ **body** *n* TAX organisme municipal *m*; ~ **bond** *n* US STOCK emprunt municipal *m*, obligation émise par une collectivité locale *f*, titre hors marché *m*, obligation de collectivité locale *f*, obligation municipale *f*; ~ **bond insurance** *n* INS assurance d'obligations municipales *f*; ~ **bond insurance association** *n* INS association pour l'assurance des obligations municipales *f*; ~ **bond offering** *n* BANK offre d'obligations municipales *f*; ~ **bonds** *n pl* US BANK obligations municipales *f pl*, émissions des villes *f pl*; ~ **borough** *n* ADMIN, POL ≈ municipalité *f*; ~ **certificate of accrual on treasury securities** *n* *(M-CATS)* STOCK certificat municipal d'accumulation de bons du Trésor; ~ **dump** *n* ENVIR décharge municipale *f*; ~ **government** *n* ADMIN, POL ≈ municipalité *f*; ~ **notes** *n pl* BANK emprunts des municipalités locales *m pl*; ~ **revenue bond** *n* US STOCK obligation municipale à revenu *f*

municipality *n* ADMIN, GEN COMM, POL ≈ municipalité *f*

muniments *n pl* LAW, PROP titres de propriété *m pl*; ~ **of title** LAW, PROP titres de propriété *m pl*

murder: ~ **one** *n* *infrml* LAW homicide au premier degré *m*, meurtre au premier degré *m*, meurtre avec préméditation *m*

Murphy's: ~ **law** *n* *infrml* (SYN *Sod's law*) GEN COMM loi des séries *f*

Muscat *pr n* GEN COMM Mascate *n pr*

mutatis mutandis *phr* LAW mutatis mutandis

mutilated: ~ **note** *n* BANK billet mutilé *m*;

~ **security** *n* STOCK titre mutilé *m*, valeur à certificat endommagé *f*

mutual[1] *adj* GEN COMM commun; ♦ **by** ~ **agreement** GEN COMM, LAW avec l'accord des parties, d'un commun accord, de gré à gré; **by** ~ **consent** GEN COMM *private* de gré à gré, à l'amiable, LAW de gré à gré, à l'amiable, *general agreement* d'un commun accord, par consentement mutuel

mutual:[2] ~ **aid pact** *n* ECON, POL *international trade* pacte d'aide mutuelle *m*; ~ **benefit** *n* GEN COMM avantage réciproque *m*; ~ **benefit society** *n* INS, WEL société de secours mutuel *f*, société mutuelle *f*; ~ **border** *n* IMP/EXP, POL frontière commune *f*; ~ **corporation** *n* INS corporation mutuelle *f*, société mutualiste *f*; ~ **fund** *n* AmE *(cf unit trust BrE)* FIN, STOCK fonds commun de placement *m*, société d'investissement ouverte *f*, société d'investissement à capital variable *f*; ~ **-fund custodian** *n* BANK réserve de fonds commun de placement *f*; ~ **improvement certificate** *n* FIN certificat d'amélioration réciproque *m*; ~ **insurance company** *n* INS compagnie mutuelle *f*, compagnie mutuelle d'assurance *f*, mutuelle *f*; ~ **insurer** *n* INS assureur mutuel *m*; ~ **recognition** *n* LAW, POL EU reconnaissance mutuelle *f*; ~ **savings bank** *n* US BANK caisse de crédit mutuelle *f*; ♦ **by** ~ **consent** GEN COMM *general agreement* d'un commun accord, par consentement mutuel

Mutual: ~ **Offset System** *n* STOCK *Eurodollar futures* système de compensation mutuelle *m*; ~ **Security Agency** *n* US *(MSA)* ADMIN agence de caution mutuelle

mutuality *n* HRM accord d'information mutuelle *m*; ~ **of contract** LAW principe de la réciprocité contractuelle *m*

mutually: ~ **exclusive** *adj* GEN COMM incompatible

MV *abbr* TRANSP *(motor merchant vessel) shipping* navire marchand à moteur *m*, TRANSP *(motor vessel) shipping* navire à moteur *m*

MVT *abbr* *(aircraft movement message)* TRANSP *aviation* message concernant le mouvement des aéronefs *m*

MW *abbr (megawatt)* GEN COMM MW *(mégawatt)*

Myanmar *pr n* GEN COMM Myanmar *m*

MYOP *abbr (multiyear operational plan)* FIN plan de développement pluriannuel *m*, plan opérationnel pluriannuel *m*, projet d'exploitation pluriannuel *m*

MYRA *abbr (multiyear rescheduling agreement, multiyear restructuring agreement)* FIN accord de restructuration pluriannuel *m*

mystery: ~ **shopper** *n jarg* GEN COMM, S&M *advertising* client mystère *m*

mystique *n* GEN COMM mystique *f*

N

n. *abbr (nominal)* GEN COMM en titre *loc m*, n *(nominal)*

N *abbr* GEN COMM *(north)* N *(nord)*, GEN COMM *(new)* neuf, nouveau, TRANSP *(North compass point)* navigation N *(quart nord)*

n/a *abbr* BANK *(no-account)* pas de compte *loc*, GEN COMM *(not applicable)* ne s'applique pas *loc*, non-applicable, sans objet, GEN COMM *(no advice)* sans préavis

NAA *abbr (not always afloat)* TRANSP *shipping* pas toujours à flot *loc*

NAC *abbr (North Atlantic Conference)* TRANSP *shipping* conférence nord-atlantique *f*

NAEGA *abbr (North American Export Grain Association)* GEN COMM Association des exportateurs de céréales d'Amérique du Nord *f*

NAFA *abbr (net acquisition of financial assets)* FIN acquisition nette d'actifs financiers *f*

NAFTA *abbr (North American Free Trade Area)* ECON ALENA *(Accord de libre-échange nord-américain)*

NAHB *abbr US (National Association of Home Builders)* PROP Association nationale des entrepreneurs de logements *f*

naira *n (NR)* GEN COMM naira *m (NR)*

Nairobi *pr n* GEN COMM Nairobi *n pr*

naked: **~ call** *n (SYN uncovered call option)* STOCK option d'achat sans garantie *f*, option d'achat à découvert *f*, vente d'un call à découvert *f*; **~ call option** *n (ANT naked put option)* STOCK option d'achat découverte *f*, option d'achat à découvert *f*; **~ option** *n* STOCK option sans garantie *f*, option à découvert *f*; **~ position** *n* STOCK position à découvert *f*; **~ put** *n* STOCK option de vente sans garantie *f*, option de vente à découvert *f*; **~ put option** *n (ANT naked call option)* STOCK option de vente découverte *f*, option de vente à découvert *f*; **~ short call** *n* STOCK appel de fonds à découvert sans garantie; **~ short option position** *n* STOCK position d'option à découvert sans garantie; **~ short puts** *n pl* STOCK option de vente à découvert sans garantie; **~ writer** *n* STOCK auteur sans garantie *m*, vendeur d'option à découvert *m*

NALGO *abbr UK (National and Local Government Officers Association)* HRM, WEL syndicat des fonctionnaires des collectivités locales

Namas *abbr (National Measurement Accreditation Service)* GEN COMM ≈ Service national des poids et mesures *m*

name *n* BANK *of bank* dénomination *f*, GEN COMM *of person* nom *m*; **~ of an account** ACC, BANK intitulé de compte *m*, nom d'un compte *m*, titre du compte *m*; **~ and address** COMMS nom et adresse *loc m*; **~ badge** GEN COMM badge d'identification *m*; **~ brand** S&M marque du fabricant *f*, marque réputée *f*; **~ day** *(cf ticket day UK)* STOCK deuxième jour de liquidation *m*, veille de la liquidation *f*

named: **~ client** *n* LAW client nommément désigné *m*; **~ peril policy** *n* INS police aux risques désignés *f*, police risque énuméré *f*; **~ person** *n* LAW personne nommément désignée *f*

nameplate *n* GEN COMM plaque *f*

names *n pl* BANK, FIN, STOCK *control of interbank money market* dénominations *f pl*

Namibia *pr n* GEN COMM Namibie *f*

Namibian[1] *adj* GEN COMM namibien

Namibian[2] *n* GEN COMM *person* Namibien *m*

nanny: **~ state** *n infrml* ECON, POL État-hyperprotecteur *m*, État-providence *m*

NAR *abbr US (National Association of Realtors)* PROP Association nationale des agents immobiliers *f*

narcodollars *n pl* ECON narcodollars *m pl*

narrow[1] *adj* STOCK *spread* étroit

narrow:[2] **~ fluctuation band** *n* ECON *of Exchange Rate Mechanism* marge de fluctuation étroite *f*; **~ margin** *n* ACC marge étroite *f*; **~ market** *n (SYN thin market)* STOCK marché étroit *m*

narrow[3] *vt* GEN COMM *gap* réduire

narrowing: **~ inflation gap** *n* ECON écart d'inflation en diminution *m*

narrows *n pl* TRANSP détroit *m*, goulet *m*, passe *f*

NASA *abbr* TRANSP *(North Atlantic Shippers Association)* association des affréteurs de l'Atlantique nord, TRANSP *US (National Aeronautics and Space Administration)* NASA *f*

NASDAQ *abbr US (National Association of Securities Dealers Automated Quotations)* STOCK *OTC market* cotation automatisée de la société nationale des opérateurs en Bourse

Nassau *pr n* GEN COMM Nassau *n pr*

nat. *abbr (national)* GEN COMM nat. *(national)*

NATFHE *abbr UK (National Association of Teachers in Further Education)* HRM, WEL association nationale des enseignants de formation continue

national[1] *adj (nat.)* GEN COMM national *(nat.)*

national[2] *n* ADMIN ressortissant *m*; **~ accounting** *n* ACC comptabilité nationale *f*; **~ accounts manager** *n* ACC, FIN, HRM responsable national du budget *m*; **~ agency** *n* GEN COMM agence nationale *f*; **~ airline** *n* LEIS, TRANSP compagnie aérienne nationale *f*; **~ average** *n* ECON moyenne nationale *f*; **~ bank** *n US* BANK *retail* banque nationale *f*; **~ border** *n* GEN COMM, IMP/EXP, POL frontière nationale *f*; **~ boundary** *n* GEN COMM, IMP/EXP, POL frontière nationale *f*; **~ consumption** *n* ECON consommation nationale *f*; **~ contingency**

fund *n* FIN fonds national de prévoyance *m*; ~ **currency** *n* FIN monnaie nationale *f*; ~ **debt** *n* ECON, POL dette publique *f*; ~ **economy** *n* ECON, POL économie nationale *f*; ~ **flag tonnage** *n* TRANSP tonnage sous pavillon national *m*; ~ **flagship** *n* TRANSP navire sous pavillon national *m*; ~ **grid** *n* UK IND réseau d'interconnexion *m*; ~ **identity card** *n* ADMIN carte nationale d'identité *f*; ~ **income** *n* ECON *econometrics* produit social *m*; ~ **interest** *n* POL intérêt national *m*; ~ **law** *n* LAW droit d'un pays *m*, droit national *m*; ~ **legislation** *n* LAW législation nationale *f*; ~ **lottery** *n* ECON, LEIS loterie nationale *f*; ~ **market advisory board** *n* STOCK bureau consultatif sur le marché national *m*, comité consultatif du marché national *m*; ~ **nature reserve** *n* ENVIR réserve naturelle nationale *f*; ~ **newspaper** *n* MEDIA journal national *m*; ~ **noise standards** *n pl* ENVIR normes acoustiques nationales *f pl*; ~ **patent** *n* PATENTS brevet national *m*; ~ **press** *n* MEDIA *print* grande presse *f*, presse nationale *f*; ~ **quota** *n* ECON *international trade* quota national *m*; ~ **salary guarantee fund** *n* TAX fonds de garantie des salaires *m*; ~ **sales tax** *n* US TAX taxe de vente nationale *f*; ~ **standard shipping note** *n* (*NSSN*) IMP/EXP, TRANSP note de chargement nationale standard *f*; ~ **subsidiary structure** *n* GEN COMM structure nationale des filiales *f*; ~ **tax** *n* TAX taxe nationale *f*; ~ **trade union council** *n* UK (*NTUC*) HRM Congrès national des syndicats *m*; ~ **trend** *n* GEN COMM tendance nationale *f*; ~ **union** *n* HRM syndicat national *m*; ~ **wage award** *n* HRM décision salariale nationale; ~ **wealth** *n* ECON richesse nationale *f*

National: ~ **Aeronautics and Space Administration** *n* US (*NASA*) TRANSP Administration nationale de l'aéronautique et de l'espace; ~ **Association of Home Builders** *n* US (*NAHB*) PROP Association nationale des entrepreneurs de logements *f*; ~ **Association of Realtors** *n* US (*NAR*) PROP Association nationale des agents immobiliers *f*; ~ **Association of Securities Dealers** *n* US STOCK organisme responsable de la gestion du marché américain de gré à gré; ~ **Association of Securities Dealers Automated Quotations** *n* US (*NASDAQ*) STOCK *OTC market* cotation automatisée de la société nationale des opérateurs en Bourse; ~ **Association of Teachers in Further Education** *n* UK (*NATFHE*) HRM, WEL association nationale des enseignants de formation continue; ~ **Bank for Foreign Trade** *n* BANK *Laos* Banque nationale du commerce extérieur *f*; ~ **Banking Act** *n* US BANK *1863*, LAW *1863* loi sur les banques nationales *f*; ~ **Bureau of Standards** *n* US GEN COMM, IND, LAW association américaine de normalisation, ≈ AFNOR, ≈ Association française de normalisation *f*; ~ **Contingency Fund** *n* ECON Fonds national de prévoyance *m*; ~ **Council on International Trade Documentation** *n* (*NCITD*) GEN COMM conseil national de documentation sur les échanges internationaux;

~ **Council of Voluntary Organizations** *n* UK (*NCVO*) ADMIN conseil national des organisations bénévoles; ~ **Curriculum** *n* UK WEL *education* cursus national *m*; ~ **Data Processing Service** *n* UK (*NDPS*) COMMS *subsidiary of British Telecom* service national de traitement des informations; ~ **Dock Labour Board** *n* UK (*NDLB*) HRM conseil national de la main-d'oeuvre portuaire; ~ **Environment Board** *n* (*NEB*) ENVIR bureau du conseil national de l'environnement; ~ **Executive Committee** *n* UK (*NEC*) POL comité exclusif national; ~ **Federation of American Shipping** *n* (*NFAS*) TRANSP fédération nationale de la navigation américaine; ~ **Freight Corporation** *n* (*NFC*) TRANSP société internationale de fret; ~ **Front** *n* UK (*NF*) POL ≈ Front National *m* (*FN*); ~ **Futures Association** *n* US (*NFA*) STOCK société nationale des opérations à terme; ~ **Health Service** *n* UK (*NHS*) HRM, WEL ≈ Sécurité sociale *f* (*Sécu, SS*); ~ **Income and Product Accounts** *n* (*NIPA*) ECON *econometrics* comptes de revenu et de produits nationaux *m pl*; ~ **Industrial Recovery Act** *n* US IND, LAW loi de Redressement Industriel National *f*; ~ **Insurance** *n* UK (*NI*) HRM, WEL sécurité sociale britannique, ≈ Assurance sociale *f* (*France*); ~ **Joint Committee** *n* UK (*NJC*) HRM commission paritaire nationale; ~ **Joint Industrial Council** *n* UK (*NJIC*) HRM conseil national paritaire industriel; ~ **Labor Relations Act** *n* US POL *1935* loi nationale sur les rapports sociaux; ~ **and Local Government Officers Association** *n* UK (*NALGO*) HRM, WEL syndicat des fonctionnaires des collectivités locales; ~ **Maritime Board** *n* (*NMB*) TRANSP commission maritime nationale; ~ **Market System** *n* (*NMS*) STOCK système de marché national *m*, système national du marché *m*; ~ **Measurement Accreditation Service** *n* (*Namas*) GEN COMM ≈ Service national des poids et mesures *m*; ~ **Organization for Women** *n* US (*NOW*) FIN Organisation nationale des femmes *f*; ~ **Plan** *n* UK POL *1965* Plan national *m*; ~ **Savings** *n pl* UK STOCK épargne nationale *f*, ≈ Caisse d'épargne *f*; ~ **Savings Bank** *n* UK (*NSB*) BANK ≈ Caisse nationale d'épargne *f* (*CNE*); ~ **Savings Certificate** *n* UK BANK bon d'épargne *m*; ~ **Savings Income** *n* UK BANK revenu national de l'épargne *m*; ~ **Savings investment account** *n* UK BANK compte d'investissement de la Caisse d'épargne *m*, compte d'investissement national d'épargne *m*; ~ **Savings Register** *n* UK STOCK registre des Caisses Nationales d'Épargne *m*, registre des titres de la Caisse d'épargne *m*; ~ **Securities Clearing Corporation** *n* US STOCK société nationale de compensation de titres *f*, société nationale de compensation des valeurs *f*; ~ **Shipping Authority** *n* US TRANSP autorité maritime nationale; ~ **Trust** *n* UK ENVIR organisation britannique pour le patrimoine national; ~ **Union of Journalists** *n* UK (*NUJ*) MEDIA ≈ Syndicat national des journalistes *m* (*SNJ*); ~ **Union of Mineworkers** *n* UK (*NUM*) HRM, IND syndicat national des mineurs *m*; ~ **Union of Public Employees** *n UK (NUPE)* HRM syndicat national des employés de l'État; ~ **Union of Seamen** *n UK (NUS)* HRM, TRANSP syndicat national des marins; ~ **Wages Council** *n (NWC)* HRM conseil national des salaires

nationalism *n* POL nationalisme *m*

Nationalist: ~ **China** *pr n* GEN COMM Chine nationaliste *f*

nationalization *n (ANT denationalization)* ECON, POL nationalisation *f*

nationalize *vt* GEN COMM nationaliser

nationalized: ~ **industry** *n (SYN public interest company)* ECON, IND industrie nationalisée *f*, société d'intérêt public *f*; ~ **sector** *n* IND secteur nationalisé *m*

nationhood *n* GEN COMM, POL nationalité *f*

nationless *adj* ADMIN, POL apatride

nationwide *adj* GEN COMM national

native *n* GEN COMM natif *m*; ~ **industry** IND industrie locale *f*

NATO *abbr (North Atlantic Treaty Organization)* POL OTAN *(Organisation du Traité de l'Atlantique Nord)*

natural: ~ **business year** *n* GEN COMM année fiscale *f*; ~ **environment** *n* ENVIR milieu naturel *m*; ~ **gas** *n* ENVIR, IND gaz naturel *m*; ~ **heritage** *n* ENVIR patrimoine naturel *m*; ~ **increase** *n* ECON accroissement naturel *m*; ~ **leader** *n* HRM leader naturel *m*; ~ **monopoly** *n* ECON monopole naturel *m*; ~ **number** *n* COMP, MATH entier naturel *m*, nombre entier *m*; ~ **person** *n* PATENTS personne morale *f*, personne physique *f*; ~ **price** *n* ECON prix naturel *m*; ~ **rate of employment** *n* ECON taux naturel d'emploi *m*; ~ **rate of growth** *n* ECON taux de croissance naturel *m*; ~ **rate of interest** *n* ECON taux naturel d'intérêt *m*; ~ **rate of unemployment** *n* ECON taux naturel de chômage *m*; ~ **resource** *n* ECON, ENVIR, IND, POL ressource naturelle *f*; ~ **rights** *n pl* LAW droits fondamentaux *m pl*, droits naturels *m pl*; ~ **wastage** *n* ECON non-remplacement des départs *m*, ENVIR déperdition naturelle *f*, HRM, IND non-remplacement des départs *m*

nature *n* GEN COMM *character* caractère *m*, nature *f*, HRM caractère *m*; ~ **conservation** ENVIR défense de l'environnement *f*, protection de la nature *f*; ~ **of the invention** PATENTS nature de l'invention *f*

nautical: ~ **mile** *n* GEN COMM mile marin *m*, mile nautique *m*; ~ **registration** *n* TRANSP immatriculation maritime *f*

NAV *abbr (net asset value)* ACC, FIN valeur de l'actif net *f*, valeur patrimoniale nette *f*

naval: ~ **anchorage** *n* TRANSP mouillage réservé à la marine *m*; ~ **architect** *n* TRANSP architecte naval *m*, ingénieur des constructions navales *m*, ingénieur du génie maritime *m*; ~ **construction** *n* IND construction navale *f*; ~ **constructor** *n* IND constructeur de navires *m*; ~ **superintendent** *n* HRM, TRANSP *shipping* préfet maritime *m*

navigation *n* TRANSP navigation *f*; ~ **laws** *n pl* LAW, TRANSP Code maritime *m*, droit maritime *m*

NAWFA *abbr (North Atlantic Westbound Freight Association)* TRANSP association des transporteurs de fret à destination de l'ouest de l'Atlantique du Nord

NB *abbr* GEN COMM *(nota bene)* NB *(nota bene)*, TRANSP *(northbound)* nord, à destination nord *loc f*, *(date new boilers fitted) shipping* date d'installation d'une nouvelle chaudière *f*

NBCC *abbr (Nigerian British Chamber of Commerce)* GEN COMM Chambre de commerce britannique au Nigéria *f*

NC *abbr* ECON *(new crop) agricultural* nouvelle récolte *f*, TRANSP *(noncontinuous liner) shipping* navire de ligne à escales *m*, navire régulier à escales *m*

NCAD *abbr (notice of cancellation at anniversary date)* INS avis de résiliation à l'échéance *m*

NCD *abbr (negotiable CD, negotiable certificate of deposit)* BANK, STOCK CDN *(certificat de dépôt négociable)*

NCITD *abbr (National Council on International Trade Documentation)* GEN COMM conseil national de documentation sur les échanges internationaux

NCR *abbr (net cash requirements)* ECON, FIN, STOCK besoins en capital net *m pl*, besoins nets de trésorerie *m pl*

NCS *abbr (noncallable securities)* STOCK titres non-remboursables *m pl*

n.c.v. *abbr* GEN COMM *(no commercial value)* sans valeur commerciale, IMP/EXP *(no customs value)* sans valeur douanière

NCVO *abbr UK (National Council of Voluntary Organizations)* ADMIN conseil national des organisations bénévoles

ND *abbr* S&M *(no discount)* pas de rabais *loc*, TRANSP *(new deck) shipping* nouveau pont *m*

N'Djamena *pr n* GEN COMM N'Djamena *n pr*

NDLB *abbr UK (National Dock Labour Board)* HRM conseil national de la main-d'oeuvre portuaire

NDPS *abbr UK (National Data Processing Service)* COMMS service national de traitement des informations

NE *abbr* GEN COMM *(north east)* NE *(nord-est)*, GEN COMM *(no effects)* sans effet

neap: ~ **tide** *n* TRANSP marée de ME *f*, marée de morte-eau *f*

near[1] *adj* GEN COMM proche

near:[2] ~ **cash** *n jarg* STOCK quasi-monnaie *f (jarg)*, titres très liquides *m pl*; ~ **future** *n* GEN COMM proche avenir *m*; ~ **letter-quality printer** *n* ADMIN, COMP imprimante qualité pseudo-courrier *f*; ~ **money** *n* ECON quasi-monnaie *f*

nearby *adj* GEN COMM proche

nearbys *n pl jarg* STOCK *futures market* échéances rapprochées

nearest: ~ **month** *n* STOCK mois d'échéance le plus proche *m*, mois prochain *m*

nearly: ~ **contract** n STOCK contrat à échéance la plus courte m

NEB abbr UK (National Environment Board) ENVIR bureau du conseil national de l'environnement

NEC abbr UK (National Executive Committee) POL comité exclusif national

necessary[1] adj GEN COMM nécessaire; ♦ **the ~ changes having been made** LAW mutatis mutandis

necessary:[2] ~ **labor** n AmE, ~ **labour** n BrE (cf indispensable labour) HRM travail nécessaire m

necessitate vt GEN COMM nécessiter

necessity n S&M good indispensable m

need: **on a ~ -to-know basis** phr GEN COMM, MGMNT en fonction des informations à connaître

needle: ~ **time** n MEDIA broadcast temps de lecture m

needs n pl GEN COMM of client besoins m pl; ~ **analysis** n S&M analyse des besoins f; ~ **standard** n ECON principe de répartition égalitaire m; ~ **test** n TAX, WEL examen des besoins m; ~ **of trade** n BANK besoins de transaction m pl

needy: **the ~** n pl WEL les nécessiteux m pl

negative: ~ **amortization** n FIN loan repayment amortissement négatif m; ~ **carry** n ACC, FIN report négatif m; ~ **cash flow** n (ANT positive cash flow) ACC, FIN cash-flow négatif m, marge brute d'autofinancement négative f, variation négative de trésorerie f; ~ **correlation** n MATH corrélation négative f; ~ **elasticity** n ECON élasticité négative f; ~ **feedback** n (ANT positive feedback) ECON, GEN COMM réaction négative f; ~ **file** n BANK fichier des oppositions m; ~ **financing** n BANK, FIN financement négatif m; ~ **goodwill** n ACC sous-valeur f, écart d'acquisition négatif m; ~ **income tax** n (NIT, SYN social dividend scheme) TAX impôt négatif sur le revenu m; ~ **interest** n BANK intérêt négatif m; ~ **interest rate gap** n STOCK futures décalage négatif de taux d'intérêt m, écart entre taux d'intérêt négatif m; ~ **investment** n ECON, FIN investissement négatif m; ~ **monetary compensatory amount** n (ANT positive monetary compensatory amount) ECON, FIN montant compensatoire monétaire négatif m; ~ **net worth** n ECON valeur nette déficitaire f, valeur nette négative f; ~ **option** n jarg GEN COMM choix tacite m; ~ **pledge** n BANK clause de nantissement négative f; ~ **pledge clause** n BANK clause de nantissement négative f; ~ **reserve** n ACC réserve négative f; ~ **saving** n FIN épargne négative f; ~ **sum game** n ECON jeu à somme négative m; ~ **targeting** n jarg POL ciblage négatif m; ~ **tax expenditure** n ACC, TAX dépense fiscale négative f; ~ **working capital** n ACC balance sheets fonds de roulement négatif m; ~ **yield curve** n (SYN inverted yield curve) BANK, ECON, STOCK courbe de rapport inversée f, courbe des taux inversée f

negatively adv (ANT positively) GEN COMM négativement

neglect: ~ **clause** n INS clause de négligence f

negligence n INS omission coupable f, LAW négligence f, omission coupable f; ~ **clause** INS marine, LAW shipping, TRANSP clause de négligence f

negligently adv LAW négligemment, par négligence loc f

negotiability n STOCK commerciabilité f, négociabilité f

negotiable[1] adj BANK négociable, GEN COMM cessible, négociable, STOCK négociable; **not ~** INS non-bancable, non-négociable

negotiable:[2] ~ **bill** n BANK, FIN, STOCK lettre de change négociable f, lettre négociable f; ~ **bill of exchange** n BANK, FIN, STOCK lettre de change f, lettre de change négociable f; ~ **bill of lading** n IMP/EXP, TRANSP connaissement négociable m; ~ **CD** n (NCD) BANK, STOCK certificat de dépôt négociable m (CDN); ~ **certificate of deposit** n (NCD) BANK, STOCK certificat de dépôt négociable m (CDN); ~ **instrument** n (ANT nonnegotiable instrument) BANK effet négociable m, instrument négociable m; ~ **issue** n HRM problème relevant des conventions collectives m; ~ **order of withdrawal** n (NOW) BANK, STOCK compte-chèques rémunéré m, ordre de retrait de fonds négociable m, ordre de retrait négociable m; ~ **securities** n pl STOCK titres négociables m pl, valeurs mobilières cessibles f pl, valeurs mobilières négociables f pl

negotiate 1. vt BANK loan, STOCK négocier; **2.** vi GEN COMM, HRM négocier; ♦ **~ from strength** GEN COMM négocier en position de force

negotiated: ~ **coordination** n ECON coordination négociée f; ~ **market price** n ECON, S&M prix de marché négocié m; ~ **price** n ECON, S&M prix négocié m; ~ **underwriting** n STOCK garantie d'émission négociée f, souscription négociée f

negotiating: ~ **bank** n BANK underwriting securities banque chargée des négociations f; ~ **machinery** n HRM industrial relations mécanisme de négociation m; ~ **position** n FIN position de négociation f; ~ **procedure** n HRM procédure de négociation f; ~ **table** n HRM, MGMNT, POL réunion de négociation f

negotiation n GEN COMM, HRM négociation f; ~ **fee** BANK frais de négociation m pl; ~ **strategy** GEN COMM, HRM, STOCK stratégie de négociation f

negotiations n pl MGMNT pourparlers m pl; ♦ **during the ~** GEN COMM au cours des négociations

negotiator n MGMNT négociateur m

neighborhood n AmE see neighbourhood BrE

neighboring: ~ **country** n AmE see neighbouring country BrE

neighbourhood n BrE GEN COMM voisinage m; ~ **effect** BrE ECON externalité spatiale f; ~ **shop** BrE S&M commerce de proximité m, magasin de proximité m

neighbouring: ~ **country** n BrE GEN COMM pays limitrophe m

Neikei: ~ **average** *n* ECON indice *m*

nemo dat quod non habet *phr frml* GEN COMM personne ne peut transférer la propriété d'une chose qui ne lui appartient pas

neo: ~ -**corporatism** *n* ECON, POL néo-corporatisme *m*; ~ -**mercantilism** *n* ECON néo-mercantilisme *m*, néo-protectionnisme *m*

neoclassical: ~ **economics** *n* ECON théorie néo-classique de l'économie *f*

neo-Keynesian *n* ECON, POL néo-keynésien *m*

neo-Malthusian *n* ECON, POL néo-malthusien *m*

neo-Marxist *n* ECON, POL néo-marxiste *mf*

neon: ~ **sign** *n* GEN COMM, S&M enseigne lumineuse *f*

neo-Ricardian *n* ECON néo-ricardien *m*; ~ **theory** ECON théorie néo-ricardienne *f*

NEP *abbr (New Economic Policy)* ECON *Soviet Union* NPE *(nouvelle politique économique)*

Nepal *pr n* GEN COMM Népal *m*

Nepalese[1] *adj* GEN COMM népalais

Nepalese[2] *n* GEN COMM *person* Népalais *m*

Nepali *n* GEN COMM *language* népalais *m*

nepotism *n* HRM favoritisme *m*, népotisme *m*, piston *m* (*infrml*)

nerve: ~ **center** *n AmE*, ~ **centre** *n BrE* MGMNT hub d'éclatement *m*

NES *abbr (not elsewhere specified)* GEN COMM non-précisé par ailleurs, non-spécifié par ailleurs

nest:[1] ~ **egg** *n* BANK, GEN COMM bas de laine *m*

nest[2] *vt* COMP emboîter, imbriquer

nested *adj* COMP *data* imbriqué

nesting *n* COMP *data* imbrication *f*, TRANSP *cargo handling* emboîtage *m*

net:[1] ~ **acquisition of financial assets** *n (NAFA)* FIN acquisition nette d'actifs financiers *f*; ~ **acquisitions** *n pl* ECON, FIN acquisitions nettes *f pl*; ~ **asset amount** *n* ACC, FIN montant net de l'actif *m*; ~ -**asset-based values** *n pl* ACC, FIN valeurs basées sur l'actif net *f pl*; ~ **asset value** *n (NAV)* ACC, FIN valeur de l'actif net *f*, valeur patrimoniale nette *f*; ~ **assets** *n pl* ACC, FIN actif net *m*, valeurs nettes *f pl*; ~ **barter terms of trade** *n* ECON, IMP/EXP conditions commerciales d'échanges compensés nets *f pl*; ~ **base capital** *n* ACC, BANK, ECON, FIN, GEN COMM capital de base net *m*; ~ **book value** *n* ACC, FIN valeur comptable nette *f*; ~ **borrowing** *n* ECON, FIN montant net des emprunts *m*; ~ **capital expenditure** *n* ECON, FIN, STOCK dépenses nettes d'investissement *f pl*, mise de fonds nette *f*; ~ **capital gain** *n* ACC, ECON, FIN, TAX gain en capital après impôt *m*, gain en capital net *m*; ~ **capital loss** *n* ACC, ECON, FIN, GEN COMM, TAX moins nette *f*; ~ **capital requirements** *n pl* ECON, FIN, STOCK besoins en capital net *m pl*, capital net requis *m*; ~ **capital spending** *n* ECON, FIN, STOCK dépenses nettes d'investissement *f pl*, mise de fonds nette *f*; ~ **cash flow** *n* ACC gain net de trésorerie *m*; ~ **cash requirements** *n pl (NCR)* ECON, FIN,

STOCK besoins en capital net *m pl*, besoins nets de trésorerie *m pl*; ~ **change** *n* STOCK *of security* variation nette *f*, écart net *m*; ~ **commission income** *n* ACC, TAX revenu net sur commissions *m*; ~ **contribution** *n* ACC marge sur coûts variables *f*; ~ **cost** *n* ACC coût net *m*; ~ **credit** *n* STOCK *options* crédit net *m*; ~ **current assets** *n pl* ACC *balance sheets*, FIN actif circulant net *m*, fonds de roulement net *m*; ~ **daily loss** *n* TRANSP perte nette quotidienne *f*; ~ **daily surplus** *n* TRANSP excédent net quotidien *m*; ~ **debit** *n* STOCK *options* débit net *m*; ~ **disbursement** *n* ECON *development aid* débours nets *m pl*; ~ **dividend** *n* STOCK dividende net *m*; ~ **domestic investment** *n* ACC, ECON investissement intérieur net *m*; ~ **donator** *n (ANT net receiver)* ENVIR *of waste* exportateur net *m*; ~ **earnings** *n pl* ACC, FIN, GEN COMM, TAX bénéfices nets *m pl*; ~ **earnings per share** *n* STOCK bénéfice net par action *m*; ~ **eligible taxable capital gain** *n* ACC, ECON, FIN, TAX gain en capital imposable admissible net *m*; ~ **employment earnings** *n* TAX revenu net d'emploi *m*; ~ **equity** *n* ACC capitaux propres *m pl*, patrimoine *m*; ~ **estate** *n US* TAX valeur nette du bien *f*; ~ **federal tax** *n* TAX impôt fédéral net *m*; ~ **foreign assets** *n pl* BANK, ECON avoir extérieur net *m*; ~ **foreign income** *n* TAX revenu étranger net *m*; ~ **foreign investment** *n* ACC, ECON investissement extérieur net *m*; ~ -**form charter** *n* TRANSP charte-partie nette *f*; ~ **forward position** *n* BANK position nette à terme *f*; ~ **gain** *n* ACC, ECON, FIN, TAX gain net *m*; ~ **gainer** *n* ACC, ECON, TAX bénéficiaire net *m*; ~ **income** *n* ACC, FIN, GEN COMM, TAX bénéfice net *m*, revenu net *m*, résultat net *m*; ~ **income per share of common stock** *n* ACC, STOCK bénéfice net par action ordinaire *m*; ~ **income to net worth ratio** *n* ACC ratio du résultat aux capitaux propres *m*; ~ **interest income** *n* BANK revenu net des intérêts *m*; ~ **interest margin** *n* ACC marge nette sur les intérêts *f*; ~ **interest yield** *n* BANK, FIN *investment* rendement net des intérêts *m*; ~ **investment position** *n* BANK montant net des placements *m*; ~ **leasable area** *n* PROP surface totale des sols *f*; ~ **lending** *n* BANK montant net des prêts *m*; ~ **lending by the public sector** *n* ECON, POL crédits nets du secteur public *m pl*; ~ **line** *n* INS part nette *f*; ~ **liquid funds** *n pl* BANK, FIN fonds nets disponibles *m pl*; ~ **listing** *n* PROP liste nette *f*; ~ **loss** *n* ACC, ECON, TAX perte nette *f*; ~ **margin** *n* ACC, ECON, FIN marge nette *f*; ~ **national product** *n (n.n.p.)* ECON produit national net *m (PNN)*; ~ **operating income** *n* ACC bénéfice net d'exploitation *m*, résultat net d'exploitation *m*; ~ **operating loss** *n* ACC, GEN COMM, IND déficit net d'exploitation *m*, perte courante *f*, perte nette d'exploitation *f*; ~ **operating profit** *n* ACC, ECON, FIN, TAX résultat courant *m*; ~ **output** *n* ECON, IND, POL production nette *f*; ~ **pay** *n* HRM salaire net *m*; ~ **position** *n* FIN situation nette *f*, STOCK *securities* position nette *f*; ~ **position report** *n* STOCK relevé de la position nette *m*; ~ **premium** *n* STOCK *options* prime nette *f*; ~ **present value** *n (NPV)* ACC, ECON, FIN valeur actuelle nette *f (VAN)*; ~ **proceeds** *n pl (np)* GEN COMM, PROP produit net *m*; ~ **profit** *n* ACC, FIN, GEN COMM, S&M bénéfice net *m*; ~ **profit for the current year** *n* ACC, FIN, GEN COMM, TAX bénéfice de l'exercice *m*, résultat net *m*; ~ **profit margin** *n* ACC, GEN COMM marge bénéficiaire nette *f*; ~ **property income from abroad** *n* FIN, PROP revenu net de biens immobiliers à l'étranger *m*; ~ **purchases** *n pl* ACC, GEN COMM achats nets *m pl*; ~ **quick assets** *n pl* ACC actif net réalisable *m*; ~ **rate** *n* BANK *of interest* taux net *m*; ~ **realizable value** *n (NRV)* ACC, ECON, FIN, S&M *advertising* valeur réalisable nette *f*; ~ **realized capital gains per share** *n* STOCK plus-value nette réalisée par action *f*, revenu net par action *m*; ~ **receipts** *n pl* ACC recettes nettes *f pl*; ~ **receipts pool** *n* TRANSP recettes nettes en commun *f pl*; ~ **receiver** *n (ANT net donator)* ENVIR *of waste* importateur net *m*; ~ **recorded assets** *n pl* FIN, GEN COMM actif comptabilisé net *m*; ~ **register** *n* FIN enregistrement net *m*; ~ **register ton** *n (NRT)* GEN COMM tonne de jauge nette *f*, tonneau de jauge nette *m*; ~ **registered tonnage** *n (NRT)* GEN COMM tonnage de jauge net *m*; ~ **remittance** *n* TAX versement net *m*; ~ **rental income** *n* PROP, TAX revenu de location net *m*; ~ **reserve adjustment amount** *n* ACC montant de redressement pour provision nette *m*, montant net de l'ajustement de la réserve *m*; ~ **reserve inclusion amount** *n* ACC montant net de l'inclusion de la réserve *m*, montant pour provision nette *m*; ~ **resource income** *n* ACC, GEN COMM, TAX *of corporation* revenu net relatif à des ressources *m*; ~ **sales** *n pl* ACC, GEN COMM ventes nettes *f pl*; ~ **surplus** *n* FIN, GEN COMM *of corporation* surplus net *m*; ~ **tangible assets per share** *n pl* STOCK actif corporel net par action *m*, actif réel net par action *m*; ~ **tare weight** *n* GEN COMM tare nette *f*; ~ **taxable capital gain** *n* ACC, ECON, FIN, TAX gain en capital imposable net *m*; ~ **terms** *n pl (Nt)* IMP/EXP *shipping*, TRANSP bord à bord; ~ **tonnage** *n* GEN COMM tonnage net *m*; ~ **trading surplus** *n* ACC, ECON, FIN, GEN COMM résultat brut d'exploitation *m*; ~ **transaction** *n* STOCK opérations nettes *f pl*, transaction nette de frais *f*; ~ **value** *n* ACC, FIN valeur nette *f*; ~ **voting** *n* FIN méthode du crédit net *f*; ~ **weight** *n* GEN COMM poids net *m*; ~ **working capital** *n* ACC, FIN fonds de roulement net *m*; ~ **worth** *n* ACC, FIN valeur nette *f*, valeur patrimoniale *f*; ~ **worth assessment** *n* ACC estimation de la valeur patrimoniale *f*; ~ **yield** *n* ACC, ECON, FIN, STOCK, TAX rendement net *m*; ♦ ~ **of** FIN déduction faite de; ~ **of taxes** ACC, GEN COMM *income tax* hors impôts, IMP/EXP hors taxes, TAX *income tax* hors impôts

net[2] *vt* FIN établir la valeur nette de; ~ **against** BANK débiter de

Net: ~ **Abs** *n* INS prime nette *f*

NETC *abbr (no explosion of the total contents)* TRANSP contenu indivisible *m*

Netherlander *n* GEN COMM *person* Hollandais *m*, Néerlandais *m*, Néerlandaise *f*

Netherlandish *adj* GEN COMM hollandais

Netherlands:[1] **of The** ~ *phr* GEN COMM hollandais

Netherlands:[2] **The** ~ *pr n* GEN COMM Les Pays-Bas *m pl*

network[1] *n* BANK, COMMS, COMP, GEN COMM, MGMNT, S&M, STOCK, TRANSP réseau *m*; ~ **analysis** COMP, MGMNT analyse de réseau *f*; ~ **architecture** COMP architecture de réseau *f*; ~ **building** GEN COMM création de réseaux *f*; ~ **of sales outlets** S&M réseau de points de vente *m*

network[2] *vt* COMP interconnecter

networked *vi* COMP, GEN COMM faire partie des réseaux *loc m*

networker *n* ECON télétravailleur *m*

networking *n* BANK mise en réseau *f*, établissement de réseaux *m*, COMP interconnexion *f*, ECON travail en réseau *m*, travail à domicile *m*, GEN COMM exploitation des contacts d'affaires *f*, fonctionnement en réseau *m*, HRM travail en réseau *m*, travail à domicile *m*, MEDIA *broadcasting* gestion de réseau *f*; ~ **economy** ECON économie de télétravail *f*, économie à base de réseaux informatiques *f*; ~ **software** COMP logiciel de gestion de réseau *m*

neutral:[1] ~ **to bearish** *adj (ANT neutral to bullish)* STOCK de neutre à baissier; ~ **to bullish** *adj (ANT neutral to bearish)* STOCK de neutre à haussier

neutral:[2] ~ **budget** *n* ECON, POL budget neutre *m*; ~ **covered long** *n* STOCK *options* titre long neutre garanti *m*; ~ **covered short** *n* STOCK *options* titre court neutre garanti *m*; ~ **technical progress** *n* ECON progrès technique neutre *m*

neutralism *n* GEN COMM neutralisme *m*

neutrality *n* POL neutralité *f*; ~ **of money** ECON neutralité monétaire *f*

new[1] *adj (N)* GEN COMM neuf, nouveau; ♦ ~ **for old** INS du vieux au neuf, sans déduction pour dépréciation; **under** ~ **management** MGMNT changement de propriétaire; **under** ~ **ownership** ECON changement de propriétaire

new:[2] ~ **-account report** *n* STOCK rapport d'ouverture de compte *m*, rapport de compte nouveau *m*; ~ **business** *n* GEN COMM nouveaux clients *m pl*, nouvelles activités *f pl*; ~ **Cambridge economics** *n* UK ECON nouvelle école économique de Cambridge; ~ **charter** *n* TRANSP nouvel affrètement *m*, nouvelle charte-partie *f*; ~ **classical economics** *n* ECON nouvelle économie classique *f*, économie néo-classique *f*; ~ **crop** *n (NC)* ECON *agricultural* nouvelle récolte *f*; ~ **deck** *n (ND)* TRANSP nouveau pont *m*; ~ **economics** *n* ECON néo-keynésianisme *m*; ~ **edition** *n* MEDIA *print* nouveau tirage *m*, nouvelle édition *f*; ~ **federalism** *n* US POL néo-fédéralisme *m*; ~ **industrial state** *n* ECON le nouvel état industriel *m*; ~ **international division of labor** *n AmE*, ~ **international division of labour** *n BrE (NIDL)* ECON nouvelle division internationale du travail *f*; ~ **issue** *n* STOCK nouvelle émission *f*; ~ **Keynesian** *n* ECON, POL néo-keynésien *m*; ~ **law** *n* LAW nouvelle loi *f*; ~ **microeconomics** *n* ECON nouvelle microéconomie *f*; ~ **money** *n* BANK *restructuring of loans*, STOCK crédit de restructuration *m*; ~ **product development** *n* S&M développement de produits nouveaux *m*; ~ **protectionism** *n* ECON néo-mercantilisme *m*, néo-protectionnisme *m*; ~ **realism** *n* UK HRM nouveau réalisme *m*; ~ **share** *n* STOCK action nouvelle *f*; ~ **technology** *n* IND nouvelles technologies *f pl*; ~ **technology agreement** *n* UK HRM convention sur les nouvelles technologies *f*; ~ **town** *n* UK ECON ville nouvelle *f*; ~ **wave** *n* MEDIA, POL nouvelle vague *f*; ~ **world order** *n* POL nouvel ordre mondial *m*; ~ **year** *n* GEN COMM nouvel an *m*; ♦ ~ **money preferred** STOCK actions privilégiées de crédit de restructuration

New:[1] ~ **Commonwealth** *n* POL Nouveau Commonwealth *m*; ~ **Deal** *n* US POL New Deal *m*; ~ **Earnings Survey** *n* ECON *econometrics* nouvelle étude sur les revenus; ~ **Economic Mechanism** *n* ECON nouveau mécanisme économique *m*; ~ **Economic Policy** *n* *(NEP)* ECON *Soviet Union* nouvelle politique économique *f (NPE)*; ~ **International Economic Order** *n* *(NIEO)* ECON nouvel ordre économique international *m*; ~ **Investment Authority** *n* *(NIA)* STOCK nouvelle autorité de placement *f*; ~ **Jason clause** *n* *(NJ)* TRANSP *shipping, charter party* clause New Jason *f*; ~ **Left** *n* ECON, POL nouvelle gauche radicale *f*; ~ **Right** *n* ECON, POL nouvelle droite *f*; ~ **York Cotton Exchange** *n* US STOCK Bourse du coton de New York *f*, Marché du coton de New-York *m*; ~ **York Curb Exchange** *n* US STOCK American Stock Exchange *m*, Marché hors cote de New York *m*; ~ **York Futures Exchange** *n* US *(NYFE)* STOCK Marché des transactions à terme de New York *m*, Marché à terme de New-York *m*; ~ **York Mercantile Exchange** *n* US *(NYME, NYMEX)* STOCK marché à terme de produits pétroliers et de platine de New York; ~ **York prime loan rate** *n* *(NYPLR)* BANK taux de prêt préférentiel de New York *m*, taux préférentiel de New York *m*; ~ **York Shipping Association** *n* *(NYSA)* TRANSP association maritime de New York; ~ **York Stock Exchange** *n* *(NYSE)* STOCK la bourse de New York; ~ **York Stock Exchange composite index** *n* STOCK indice composite du New York Stock Exchange *m*, indice composé de la bourse de New York *m*; ~ **Zealander** *n* GEN COMM *person* Néo-Zélandais *m*

New:[2] ~ **Delhi** *pr n* GEN COMM New Delhi *n pr*; ~ **Zealand** *pr n* GEN COMM Nouvelle-Zélande *f*

newly:[1] ~ **-elected** *adj* GEN COMM nouvellement élu; ~ **-privatized** *adj* ECON privatisé de fraîche date

newly:[2] ~ **industrialized country** *n* *(NIC)* ECON, IND nouveau pays industrialisé *m*, pays nouvellement industrialisé *m*; ~ **-industrializing economies** *n pl* *(NIEs)* ECON, IND économies

de pays à industrialisation récente *f pl*, économies nouvellement industrialisées *f pl*

news *n* GEN COMM informations *f pl*, MEDIA actualités *f pl*, informations *f pl*, journal *m*; ~ **advisory** *n jarg* MEDIA *public relations* communiqué *m*; ~ **agency** *n* BrE *(cf wire service AmE)* COMMS, MEDIA *press* agence de presse *f*; ~ **bulletin** *n* COMMS, MEDIA bulletin d'informations *m*, flash info *m*, jl, journal *m*; ~ **conference** *n* MEDIA conférence de presse *f*; ~ **coverage** *n* MEDIA couverture d'un événement *f*, couverture médiatique *f*; ~ **editor** *n* COMMS, MEDIA rédacteur *m*; ~ **flash** *n* COMMS, MEDIA flash d'information *m*, flash info *m*; ~ **headline** *n* COMMS, MEDIA *print* titres de l'actualité *m pl*; ~ **item** *n* COMMS, MEDIA information *f*; ~ **pictures** *n pl* MEDIA reportage photographique *m*; ~ **release** *n* COMMS, MEDIA communiqué de presse *m*; ~ **report** *n* MEDIA émission de reportages *f*; ~ **roundup** *n* MEDIA informations en bref *f pl*, point *m*, résumé des informations *m*; ~ **vendor** *n* S&M marchand de journaux *m*; ♦ **be the first one to hear the** ~ MEDIA avoir la primeur de l'information

newsagent *n* S&M marchand de journaux *m*; ~ **and tobacconist** S&M marchand de journaux-buraliste *m*

newscaster *n* MEDIA journaliste de télévision *m*, journaliste radio *m*

newsletter *n* COMMS, GEN COMM bulletin *m*, circulaire *f*

newspaper *n* MEDIA jl, journal *m*; ~ **advertising** MEDIA, S&M publicité-presse *f*; ~ **publisher** MEDIA *print* directeur de journal *m*, directeur de la publication *m*; ~ **syndicate** US MEDIA *print* agence de vente de reportages pour la presse

newsroom *n* MEDIA *print* salle de rédaction *f*

next[1] *adj* GEN COMM prochain; ~ **-day** TRANSP *delivery* du jour au lendemain *loc m*

next:[2] ~ **day** *n* GEN COMM lendemain *m*; ~ **month** *n* GEN COMM mois prochain *m*; ~ **size down** *n* GEN COMM dimension immédiatement inférieure *f*, taille au-dessous *f*

NF *abbr* GEN COMM *(no funds)* défaut de provision *m*, POL UK *(National Front)* ≈ FN *(Front National)*

NFA *abbr* US *(National Futures Association)* STOCK société nationale des opérations à terme

NFAS *abbr* *(National Federation of American Shipping)* TRANSP fédération nationale de la navigation américaine

NFC *abbr* *(National Freight Corporation)* TRANSP société internationale de fret

n-firm: ~ **concentration ratio** *n* ECON ratio de concentration à n entreprises *m*

NFTZ *abbr* *(Non Free Trade Zone)* ECON, GEN COMM, IMP/EXP, POL zone de non libre-échange *f*

NGO *abbr* *(nongovernmental organization)* GEN COMM ONG *(organisation non-gouvernementale)*

NHP *abbr* *(nominal horsepower)* GEN COMM puissance nominale *f*

NHS *abbr UK (National Health Service)* HRM, WEL ≈ SS *(France)*, ≈ Sécu *(France, infrml) (Sécurité sociale)*

NI *abbr UK (National Insurance)* HRM, WEL sécurité sociale britannique, ≈ Assurance sociale *f (France)*

NIA *abbr (New Investment Authority)* STOCK nouvelle autorité de placement *f*

Niamey *pr n* GEN COMM Niamey *n pr*

NIB *abbr (Nordic Investment Bank)* BANK BNI *(Banque nordique d'investissement)*

NIBM1 *abbr (non-interest-bearing M1)* ECON M1 non porteur d'intérêts *m*

NIC *abbr (newly industrialized country)* ECON, IND NPI *(nouveau pays industrialisé)*

Nicaragua *pr n* GEN COMM Nicaragua *m*

Nicaraguan[1] *adj* GEN COMM nicaraguayen

Nicaraguan[2] *n* GEN COMM *person* Nicaraguayen *m*

niche *n* GEN COMM créneau *m*, HRM spécialisation réussie *f*, S&M créneau *m*, créneau porteur *m*, niche *f*; **~ bank** BANK banque créneau *f*; **~ marketing** S&M *advertising* marketing du créneau *m*; **~ trading** GEN COMM, S&M commerce spécialisé *m*

Nicosia *pr n* GEN COMM Nicosie *n pr*

NIDL *abbr (new international division of labor AmE, new international division of labour BrE)* ECON nouvelle division internationale du travail *f*

NIEO *abbr (New International Economic Order)* ECON nouvel ordre économique international *m*

NIEs *abbr (newly-industrializing economies)* ECON, IND économies de pays à industrialisation récente *f pl*, économies nouvellement industrialisées *f pl*

NIF *abbr (note issuance facility)* FIN facilité de soutien de programme d'émission d'effets *f*, facilité renouvelable à prise ferme *f*, ligne de crédit ouverte par l'émission de titres à court *f*

Niger *pr n* GEN COMM Niger *m*; **~ Republic** GEN COMM République du Niger *f*

Nigeria *pr n* GEN COMM Nigéria *m*

Nigerian[1] *adj* GEN COMM nigérien

Nigerian[2] *n* GEN COMM *person* Nigérien *m*; **~ British Chamber of Commerce** *(NBCC)* GEN COMM Chambre de commerce britannique au Nigéria *f*

night: **~ depository** *n* BANK trésor de nuit *m*, trésor permanent *m*; **~ letter** *n US* COMMS lettre de nuit *f*, télégramme *m*; **~ safe** *n* BANK coffre de nuit *m*; **~ shift** *n (cf graveyard shift AmE)* HRM équipe de nuit *f*; **~ trunk** *n (Nt)* TRANSP transport de nuit *m*; **~ watchman** *n* HRM gardien de nuit *m*, veilleur *m*; **~ work** *n* HRM travail de nuit *m*

Nikkei: **~ average** *n* STOCK Indice Nikkei *m*; **~ index** *n* STOCK Indice Nikkei *m*

nil: **~ paid** *phr* STOCK capital non-appelé *m*, non-payé

NIMBY[1] *abbr (not in my backyard)* ENVIR attitude de celui qui est un faveur d'un projet à condition que celui-ci ne soit pas effectué près de chez lui

NIMBY:[2] **~ syndrome** *n* ENVIR syndrome de rejet *m*

nine: **~ bond rule** *n* STOCK règle des neuf obligations *f*, règlement de neuf garanties *m*

ninety: **~ -nine-year lease** *n* BANK bail emphytéotique *m*

NIPA *abbr (National Income and Product Accounts)* ECON *econometrics* comptes de revenu et de produits nationaux *m pl*

NIT *abbr (negative income tax)* TAX impôt négatif sur le revenu *m*

nitrogen: **~ fertilizer** *n* ENVIR engrais azoté *m*

NJ *abbr (New Jason clause)* TRANSP *shipping* clause New Jason *f*

NJC *abbr UK (National Joint Committee)* HRM commission paritaire nationale

NJIC *abbr UK (National Joint Industrial Council)* HRM conseil national paritaire industriel

NL *abbr (no liner)* TRANSP *shipping* hors conférence

NMB *abbr (National Maritime Board)* TRANSP commission maritime nationale

NMS *abbr* STOCK *(National Market System)* système de marché national *m*, système national du marché *m*, STOCK *UK (normal market size)* quotité normale *f*, taille normale du marché *f*

n.n.p. *abbr (net national product)* ECON PNN *(produit national net)*

NNRF *abbr (non-negotiable report of findings)* GEN COMM compte-rendu non-négociable *m*

no. *abbr (number)* GEN COMM n° *(numéro)*, MATH nombre *m*

nos. *abbr (numbers)* MATH nos *(numéros)*

no-account *adj (n/a)* BANK pas de compte

Nobel: **~ Prize for Economics** *n* ECON Prix Nobel d'économie *m*

no-claims: **~ bonus** *n UK* INS bonus pour non sinistre *m*, ristourne *f*

no-cure-no-pay *phr* INS *marine* pas de remède pas d'honoraires

node *n* COMP noeud *m*

no-growth *adj* ECON de croissance nulle *loc f*, de croissance zéro *loc f*

noise *n* COMP bruit *m*, parasite *m*, ECON *econometrics* bruit blanc *m*, parasite *m*; **~ emission** ENVIR émission sonore *f*; **~ insulation** ENVIR, GEN COMM isolation phonique *f*; **~ level** ENVIR niveau sonore *m*; **~ pollution** ENVIR nuisances acoustiques *f pl*

no-lien: **~ affidavit** *n* LAW attestation sous serment d'absence de privilège *f*

no-load: **~ fund** *n US* STOCK fonds sans frais *m*

nolo contendere *n frml* LAW je ne souhaite pas contester *loc*

nominal[1] *adj (n.)* GEN COMM *in name only* en titre *loc m*, nominal, nominatif

nominal:[2] **~ assets** *n pl* ACC actif fictif *m*; **~ capital** *n* ACC capital pourvu dans les statuts *m*; **~ damages** *n pl* LAW dommages-intérêts symboliques *m pl*; **~ GDP** *n* ECON PIB nominal *m*; **~ growth** *n* ECON croissance nominale *f*; **~ horsepower** *n (NHP)* GEN COMM puissance nominale *f*; ~ **income** *n* ECON, FIN, TAX revenu nominal *m*; ~ **interest** *n* FIN, STOCK intérêt nominal *m*; ~ **interest rate** *n* FIN, STOCK taux d'intérêt nominal *m*; ~ **ledger** *n* ACC grand livre *m*; ~ **loan rate** *n* FIN taux nominal d'emprunt *m*; ~ **paid-up capital** *n* STOCK capital versé nominal *m*; ~ **pay** *n* GEN COMM, HRM salaire nominal *m*; ~ **price** *n* ACC prix théorique *m*; ~ **quotation** *n* STOCK cotation nominale *f*, cours estimé *m*; ~ **scale** *n* GEN COMM échelle nominale *f*; ~ **value** *n* ACC, FIN, STOCK valeur nominale *f*; ~ **wage** *n* GEN COMM, HRM salaire nominal *m*; ~ **wages** *n pl* GEN COMM, HRM salaire nominal *m*; ~ **yield** *n* STOCK *of fixed-income security* coupon *m*, taux nominal *m*

nominate *vt* GEN COMM désigner

nomination *n* GEN COMM nomination *f*

nominee *n* BANK propriétaire pour compte *m*, GEN COMM personne désignée *f*; ~ **account** STOCK compte d'intermédiaire *m*, compte prête-nom *m*; ~ **company** BANK, GEN COMM, STOCK société intermédiaire *f*, société prête-nom *f*; ~ **name** STOCK nom d'emprunt *m*, nom de l'intermédiaire *m*; ~ **shareholder** STOCK actionnaire intermédiaire *m*, actionnaire-paravent *m*

non: ~ **return valve** *n* TRANSP clapet non-retour *m*

Non: ~ **Free Trade Zone** *n* *(NFTZ)* ECON, GEN COMM, IMP/EXP, POL zone de non libre-échange *f*

nonaccelerating: ~ **inflation rate of unemployment** *n* ECON taux naturel de chômage *m*

nonacceptance *n* BANK *of bill, note* défaut d'acceptation *m*, GEN COMM non-acceptation *f*

nonaccrual *adj* BANK à intérêt non-comptabilisé *loc m*

nonaccruing: ~ **loan** *n* BANK emprunt à risques *m*

nonadjustable: ~ **rate** *n* BANK taux non-rajustable *m*

nonaffiliated *adj* HRM autonome

nonagricultural: ~ **use** *n* ENVIR, PROP utilisation non-agricole *f*

no-name *adj* STOCK pas de nom

nonappearance *n* LAW non-comparution *f*

nonapproved[1] *adj* STOCK *options* non-approuvé

nonapproved:[2] ~ **pension scheme** *n* FIN régime de retraite non-agréé *m*

non-arm's-length *adj* BANK, TAX avec lien de dépendance *loc m*

nonaudit *n* ACC, TAX non-vérification *f*

nonbank: ~ **bank** *n* BANK, STOCK entreprise non-bancaire admise au marché monétaire *f*, institution financière para-bancaire *f*, établissement non-bancaire admis au marché monétaire *m*, ENBAMM; ~ **financial institution** *n* BANK, STOCK entreprise non-bancaire admise au marché monétaire *f*, établissement non-bancaire admis au marché monétaire *m*, ENBAMM; ~ **sector** *n* FIN secteur non-bancaire *m*

nonbasic: ~ **commodity** *n* ECON marchandise non-essentielle *f*, produit non-essentiel *m*, produit

secondaire *m*; ~ **industry** *n* ECON, IND industrie secondaire *f*

non-biodegradable *adj* GEN COMM non-biodégradable

nonbudgetary *adj* ACC *governmental* extra-budgétaire, non-budgétaire

non-business: ~ **income** *n* TAX bénéfices non-commerciaux *m pl*, BNC; ~ **income tax** *n* TAX impôt sur le revenu ne provenant pas d'une entreprise *m*

noncallable[1] *adj* STOCK *bond* non-rachetable, non-remboursable

noncallable:[2] ~ **bond** *n* STOCK obligation non-remboursable *f*; ~ **feature** *n* STOCK non-rachet *m*; ~ **securities** *n pl* *(NCS)* STOCK titres non-remboursables *m pl*

noncash: ~ **payment system** *n* BANK système de paiement non-financier *m*; ~ **rewards** *n pl* *(SYN nonmonetary rewards)* HRM paiement en nature *m*, rétribution en nature *f*

noncheckable: *AmE*, **nonchequable** *BrE*: ~ **account** *n* BANK compte sans privilège de chèques *m*, compte sans tirage de chèques *m*; ~ **deposit** *n* BANK dépôt non-transférable par chèque *m*, dépôt sans tirage de chèques *m*

nonclearing: ~ **item** *n* BANK effet non-admis à la compensation *m*, instrument non-compensable *m*; ~ **member** *n* STOCK membre de non-compensation *m*, membre non-compensant *m*

noncommercial: ~ **cargo** *n* TRANSP cargaison non-commerciale *f*

non-Communist *adj* POL non-communiste

noncompeting: ~ **group** *n* GEN COMM, HRM, S&M groupe non-concurrentiel *m*

noncompetitive: ~ **bid** *n* STOCK *to buy Treasury Bills* offre non-concurrentielle *f*

noncompliance *n* LAW *with law* inobservation *f*, *with order* refus d'obtempérer *m*

noncompulsory[1] *adj* GEN COMM facultatif

noncompulsory:[2] ~ **expenditure** *n* ECON dépenses non-obligatoires *f pl*

noncondensing *adj* TRANSP sans condensation

nonconference: ~ **line vessel** *n* TRANSP navire hors-conférence *m*

nonconforming: ~ **use** *n* LAW, PROP usage non-conforme *m*

nonconformity *n* LAW non-conformité *f*

nonconsolidated *adj* ACC non-consolidé

noncontestability: ~ **clause** *n* INS clause de non-contestabilité *f*

noncontinuous: ~ **liner** *n* *(NC)* TRANSP navire de ligne à escales *m*, navire régulier à escales *m*

noncontribution: ~ **clause** *n* INS clause de non-contribution *f*

noncontributory: ~ **pension fund** *n* *(ANT contributory pension fund)* FIN, HRM, WEL caisse de retraite sans cotisation salariale *f*; ~ **pension plan** *n* *(ANT contributory pension plan)* FIN, HRM, WEL pension non-contributive *f*, régime de retraite entièrement financé par l'employeur *m*; **~ pension scheme** *n* (ANT *contributory pension scheme*) FIN, HRM, WEL pension non-contributive *f*, régime de retraite entièrement financé par l'employeur *m*

nonconvertible *adj* STOCK *bond* non-convertible

noncumulative[1] *adj* STOCK non-cumulatif

noncumulative:[2] **~ preferred stock** *n* STOCK action à dividende prioritaire non-cumulative *f*; **~ tax** *n* TAX impôt non-cumulatif *m*

noncurrent: ~ asset *n* ACC actif à long terme *m*; **~ loan** *n* BANK prêt en souffrance *m*

noncyclical *adj* (ANT *cyclical*) ECON, FIN, GEN COMM, STOCK non-cyclique

nondebugged *adj* COMP non-débogué

nondeductibility *n* HRM, TAX *of employer contributions* non-déductibilité *f*

nondemise: ~ charter party *n* TRANSP charte-partie à temps *f*

nondestructive: ~ testing *n* IND essai non-destructif *m*

nondisclosure *n* INS non-divulgation *f*, réticence *f*

nondiscretionary: ~ trust *n* STOCK holding sans mandat de gestion

nondiscrimination: ~ notice *n* UK HRM avis de non-discrimination *m*

nondisturbance: ~ clause *n* US BANK *mortgage contract*, IND, PROP *mineral rights, mortgage contract* clause de non-incommodement *f*

nondurable: ~ goods *n pl* ECON, IND, S&M biens de consommation non-durables *m pl*, denrées périssables *f pl*, marchandises périssables *f pl*

nonemployment *n* ECON, HRM, WEL chômage *m*

nonencashable: ~ deposit *n* BANK dépôt non-encaissable *m*

non est factum *phr frml* GEN COMM ce n'est pas de mon fait *loc m*

non-EU: ~ national *n* GEN COMM, POL non-ressortissant de l'UE *m*

nonexecution *n* LAW inexécution *f*, non-exécution *f*

nonexecutive[1] *adj* HRM, MGMNT non-dirigeant

nonexecutive:[2] **~ director** *n* HRM, MGMNT administrateur externe *m*, administrateur non-dirigeant *m*

nonexempt *adj* (ANT *exempt*) GEN COMM, TAX non-exempté

nonfeasance *n* LAW délit d'abstention *m*

nonfiler *n* TAX *taxpayer* personne non-déclarante *f*

nonfiling *n* TAX *of return, form* non-production *f*

nonfinancial: ~ reward *n* ECON, HRM satisfaction non-financière *f* (*jarg*)

nonforfeiture *n* LAW absence de renoncement *f*, non-résiliation *f*

nonfulfillment *n* AmE *see* nonfulfilment BrE

nonfulfilment *n* BrE LAW non-exécution *f*; **~ of contract** BrE LAW inexécution du contrat *f*, non-exécution du contrat *f*, non-respect du contrat *m*

nonfungible: ~ goods *n pl* GEN COMM, LAW biens non-fongibles *m pl*

nongoal: ~ equilibrium *n* ECON équilibre des seules forces économiques

nongovernmental: ~ organization *n* (*NGO*) GEN COMM organisation non-gouvernementale *f* (*ONG*)

non-interest-bearing: ~ deposit *n* BANK dépôt non-productif d'intérêt *m*, dépôt non-rémunéré *m*; **~ M1** *n* (*NIBM1*) ECON M1 non porteur d'intérêts *m*; **~ securities** *n pl* STOCK titres non rémunérés *m pl*, valeurs ne portant pas intérêt *f pl*

non-interest-earning: ~ deposit *n* BANK dépôt sans intérêt *m*

nonintervention *n* ECON, POL non-intervention *f*

nonliability *n* LAW absence de responsabilité *f*, non-responsabilité *f*; **~ company** GEN COMM société non-responsabilité *f*

nonlife: ~ insurance *n* INS assurance I.A.R.D. *f*, non-assurance-vie *f*

nonlinear: ~ correlation *n* MATH *statistics* corrélation non-linéaire *f*; **~ pricing** *n* ECON tarification non-linéaire *f*; **~ programming** *n* COMP, ECON, MATH programmation non-linéaire *f*

nonmandatory *adj* LAW *guidelines* facultatif, n'ayant pas un caractère obligatoire, non-obligatoire

nonmanual: ~ union *n* HRM syndicat d'employés *m*

nonmanufacturing: ~ sector *n* IND secteur non-manufacturier *m*

nonmarket: ~ sector *n* ECON secteur non-marchand *m*

nonmarketable: ~ instrument *n* (ANT *marketable instrument*) BANK instrument non-négociable *m*

nonmember *n* GEN COMM non-membre *mf*, personne étrangère *f*; **~ bank** *AmE* (ANT *member bank*) BANK banque non-affiliée *f*, banque non-membre *f*; **~ firm** STOCK firme non-affiliée *f*, établissement non-membre *m*

nonmembership *n* HRM *of union* non-adhésion *f*

nonmerchantable: ~ title *n* *AmE* (ANT *merchantable title*) PROP titre non-négociable *m*

nonmetropolitan *adj* (ANT *metropolitan*) GEN COMM non-métropolitain

nonmonetary: ~ investment *n* ACC, ECON, FIN achat public d'objets d'art *m*, achat public d'objets précieux *m*; **~ rewards** *n pl* (SYN *noncash rewards*) HRM rétribution en nature *f*

non-negotiable: ~ bill of lading *n* IMP/EXP, TRANSP colis confié *m*, connaissement non-négociable *m*; **~ instrument** *n* (ANT *negotiable instrument*) BANK effet non-négociable *m*, instrument non-négociable *m*; **~ report of findings** *n* (*NNRF*) GEN COMM compte-rendu non-négociable *m*

nonobservance: ~ of conditions *n* GEN COMM inobservation des conditions *f*, non-respect des conditions *m*

nonobvious *adj* GEN COMM ambigu

nonoccupying: ~ **owner** *n* LAW, PROP propriétaire non-occupant *m*

nonofficial: ~ **trade organization** *n* *(NOTO)* HRM organisation professionnelle non-répertoriée *f*, organisation professionnelle sans existence officielle *f*, syndicat non-officiel *m*

non-oil: ~ **balance** *n* ECON balance hors produits pétroliers *f*; ~ **country** *n* ENVIR pays non-producteur de pétrole *m*

nonoperating: ~ **expense** *n* ACC, GEN COMM, IND frais de fonctionnement auxiliaire *m pl*; ~ **revenue** *n* ACC, GEN COMM, IND autres produits de gestion courante *m pl*, produits divers de gestion courante *m pl*

nonparametric: ~ **statistics** *n pl* MATH statistiques non-paramétriques *f pl*

nonparticipating: ~ **preferred stock** *n* STOCK action de priorité sans participation *f*, action sans participation *f*; ~ **share** *n* STOCK action non-participante *f*, action non-participative *f*

nonpatrial *adj dat UK* (ANT *patrial*) ADMIN interdit de séjour

nonpayment *n* BANK *of bill, note* défaut de paiement *m*

nonpecuniary: ~ **returns** *n pl* HRM revenu non-pécunier *m*

nonpenalized: ~ **adjustment** *n* TAX rajustement sans pénalité *m*; ~ **taxable income** *n* TAX revenu imposable non-pénalisé *m*

nonperformance *n* LAW non-exécution *f*

nonperforming: ~ **assets** *n* STOCK avoirs non-productifs *m pl*; ~ **credit** *n* BANK avoir non-productif *m*; ~ **loan** *n* BANK prêt non-productif *m*

nonproductive[1] *adj* GEN COMM, IND, MGMNT, STOCK non-productif

nonproductive:[2] ~ **loan** *n* BANK *retail* prêt non-productif *m*

nonprofessional: ~ **behavior** *n* *AmE*, ~ **behaviour** *n* *BrE* HRM comportement non-conforme aux règles de la profession *m*

nonprofit[1] *adj AmE* (*cf non-profit-making BrE*) ACC, FIN, TAX déficitaire, sans but lucratif, à but non-lucrative *loc m*

nonprofit:[2] ~ **organization** *n* *AmE* (*cf non-profit-making organization BrE*) GEN COMM entreprise sans but lucratif *f*; ~ **accounting** *n* ACC comptabilité d'une entreprise sans but lucratif *f*; ~ **enterprise** *n* *(NPE)* ECON entreprise à but non-lucratif *f*

non-profit-making[1] *adj BrE* (*cf nonprofit AmE*) ACC, FIN, TAX déficitaire, sans but lucratif, à but non-lucrative *loc m*

non-profit-making:[2] ~ **accounting** *n* ACC comptabilité d'une entreprise sans but lucratif *f*; ~ **enterprise** *n* *(NPE)* ECON entreprise à but non-lucratif *f*; ~ **organization** *n* *BrE* GEN COMM entreprise sans but lucratif *f*

nonproject: ~ **aid** *n* POL *development* aide non-affectée *f*

nonpublic: ~ **information** *n* *US* COMMS, GEN COMM informations non-communiquées au public *f pl*

nonpurpose: ~ **loan** *n* STOCK prêt à affectation non-déterminée

nonqualifying: ~ **annuity** *n* FIN annuité non-statutaire *f*; ~ **business** *n* GEN COMM, TAX entreprise non-admissible *f*; ~ **share** *n* STOCK action non-admissible *f*; ~ **stock option** *n* STOCK option de titres non-statutaire

nonrecourse *n* FIN sans recours; ~ **finance** BANK, FIN financement sans recours *m*, financement à forfait *m*; ~ **financing** BANK, FIN financement sans recours *m*, financement à forfait *m*; ~ **loan** BANK, FIN prêt sans recours *m*, prêt à forfait *m*

nonrecurring: ~ **appropriation** *n* FIN crédit extraordinaire *m*; ~ **charge** *n* ACC *annual* charge non-courante *f*

nonrecyclable *adj* (ANT *recyclable*) ENVIR non-recyclable

nonrefundable[1] *adj* STOCK non-remboursable

nonrefundable:[2] ~ **deposit** *n* S&M acompte non-remboursable *m*; ~ **fee** *n* S&M honoraires non-remboursables *m pl*

nonrenewable: ~ **natural resource** *n* ECON, ENVIR ressource naturelle non-renouvelable *f*; ~ **resource** *n* (ANT *renewable resource*) ECON, ENVIR ressource non-renouvelable *f*

nonresident[1] *adj* TAX non-résident

nonresident[2] *n* GEN COMM non-résident *m*; ~ **bank** BANK banque étrangère *f*; ~ **company** GEN COMM, LAW, TAX société non-résidente *f*, société étrangère *f*; ~ **tax** TAX impôt des non-résidents *m*; ~ **tax deduction** *Canada* TAX retenue d'impôt des non-résidents *f*

nonresidential: ~ **mortgage** *n* BANK prêt hypothécaire autre qu'à l'habitation *m*, prêt hypothécaire sur un immeuble non résidentiel *m*

nonreusable *adj* ENVIR perdu

nonreversible: ~ **laytime** *n* TRANSP staries non-réversibles *f pl*, temps de planche non-réversible *m*

nonroutine: ~ **decisions** *n pl* GEN COMM, MGMNT décisions exceptionnelles *f pl*

nonscheduled *adj* HRM non-planifié

nonsegregated: ~ **account** *n* STOCK compte sans ségrégation *m*, compte à titulaire non-désigné *m*

nonsmoking: ~ **lounge** *n* LEIS, TRANSP salon non-fumeur *m*

nonstandard: ~ **mail** *n* *UK* COMMS courrier non-standard *m*

nonstatutory *adj* LAW non-statutaire, qui n'est pas prévu par un texte de loi

nonsterling: ~ **area** *n* *(NSA)* ECON zone non-sterling *f*

nonstop: ~ **flight** *n* TRANSP vol sans escale *m*

nonstore: ~ **retailing** *n* S&M vente hors magasin *f*

nontariff: ~ **barrier** *n* *(NTB)* ECON, GEN COMM, IMP/EXP, POL barrière non-douanière *f*, barrière non-tarifaire *f*; ~ **trade barrier** *n* ECON, GEN

COMM, IMP/EXP barrière non-tarifaire au commerce *f*

nontax: ~ **revenue** *n* FIN, TAX recettes non-fiscales *f pl*

nontaxable[1] *adj* TAX non-assujetti à l'impôt, non-imposable

nontaxable:[2] ~ **beneficiary** *n* TAX bénéficiaire non-imposable *m*; ~ **obligation** *n* TAX obligation non-imposable *f*; ~ **profitable firm** *n* GEN COMM, TAX entreprise rentable non-imposable *f*; ~ **year** *n* TAX année non-imposable *f*, année sans revenu imposable *f*

nontaxpaying *adj* TAX non-contribuable *mf*

nontradeables *n* ECON biens non-marchands *m pl*

nontransferable: ~ **debentures** *n pl* BANK obligations nominatives *f pl*

nonunion[1] *adj* HRM à personnel non-syndiqué *loc m*

nonunion:[2] ~ **firm** *n* HRM *industrial relations* société sans représentation syndicale *f*; ~ **labor** *n* AmE, ~ **labour** *n* BrE HRM main-d'oeuvre non-syndiquée *f*, personnel non-syndiqué *m*; ~ **worker** *n* HRM ouvrier non-syndiqué *m*

nonutilized *adj* GEN COMM *line of credit* non-utilisé

nonvariable *adj* BANK non-variable

nonverbal: ~ **communication** *n* GEN COMM, HRM, MGMNT communication non-verbale *f*

non-vessel-operating: ~ **carrier** *n* *(NVOC)* TRANSP service de ligne maritime sans navire *m*; ~ **common carrier** *n* *(NVOCC)* TRANSP service de ligne maritime sans navire *m*

non-vessel-owning: ~ **carrier** *n* *(NVOC)* TRANSP service de ligne maritime sans navire *m*; ~ **common carrier** *n* *(NVOCC)* TRANSP service de ligne maritime sans navire *m*

nonvoting: ~ **share** *n* STOCK action sans droit de vote *f*; ~ **stock** *n* STOCK action sans droit de vote *f*

nonworking: ~ **spouse** *n* HRM, WEL conjoint au foyer *m*

non-zero-sum: ~ **game** *n* ECON jeu à somme non nulle *m*

nop *abbr* *(not otherwise provided)* GEN COMM non-fourni par ailleurs, non-prévu par ailleurs

no-par: ~ **stock** *n* STOCK action non-pair *f*

no-par-value[1] *adj* *(NPV)* STOCK sans valeur nominale *(SVN)*

no-par-value:[2] ~ **share** *n* STOCK action sans valeur nominale *f*

Nordic: ~ **countries** *n pl* GEN COMM, POL pays scandinaves *m pl*; ~ **Investment Bank** *n* *(NIB)* BANK Banque nordique d'investissement *f* *(BNI)*

norm *n* GEN COMM norme *f*

normal: ~ **capacity** *n* ECON, IND capacité de production normale *f*; ~ **conditions** *n pl* GEN COMM conditions normales *f pl*; ~ **course of business** *n* GEN COMM affaires courantes *f pl*, cours habituel de l'entreprise *m*, cours normal de l'entreprise *m*, cours normal des affaires *m*; ~ **distribution** *n* MATH *statistics* distribution nor-

male *f*; ~ **good** *n* ECON bien normal *m*; ~ **investment practice** *n* FIN pratique d'investissement normale *f*; ~ **laytime** *n* TRANSP staries habituelles *f pl*; ~ **market size** *n* BrE *(NMS)* STOCK quotité normale *f*, taille normale du marché *f*; ~ **price** *n* ECON, GEN COMM, S&M prix normal *m*; ~ **profit** *n* ECON, GEN COMM, S&M profit normal *m*; ~ **rate** *n* TRANSP tarif normal *m*; ~ **relationship** *n* STOCK *in currency futures prices* relation normale *f*, relations normales *f pl*; ~ **retirement** *n* HRM départ en retraite à l'âge normal *m*, âge de la retraite *m*; ~ **retirement age** *n* HRM âge normal de départ à la retraite *m*; ~ **tax** *n* TAX impôt uniforme *m*; ~ **trading unit** *n* STOCK quotité normale de transaction *f*, unité commerciale normale *f*; ~ **wear and tear** *n* ACC, PROP, TAX *depreciation* usure normale *f*

normalcy *n* AmE, **normality** *n* BrE GEN COMM normalité *f*

normative[1] *adj* MGMNT selon les normes

normative:[2] ~ **economics** *n* ECON économie normative *f*; ~ **forecasting** *n* GEN COMM prévisions normatives *f pl*

Norris-La Guardia: ~ **Act** *n* US HRM *1932* loi Norris-La Guardia

north *n* *(N)* GEN COMM nord *m* *(N)*; ~ **east** *(NE)* GEN COMM nord-est *m* *(NE)*; ~ **west** *(NW)* GEN COMM nord-ouest *m* *(NO)*

North:[1] ~ **African** *adj* GEN COMM d'Afrique du Nord, nord-africain; ~ **American** *adj* GEN COMM d'Amérique du Nord, nord-américain; ~ **Korean** *adj* GEN COMM nord-coréen

North:[2] ~ **African** *n* GEN COMM *person* Nord-Africain *m*; ~ **American** *n* GEN COMM *person* Nord-Américain *m*; ~ **American Export Grain Association** *n* *(NAEGA)* GEN COMM Association des exportateurs de céréales d'Amérique du Nord *f*; ~ **American Free Trade Area** *n* *(NAFTA)* ECON Accord de libre-échange nord-américain *m* *(ALENA)*; ~ **Atlantic Conference** *n* *(NAC)* TRANSP *shipping* conférence nord-atlantique *f*; ~ **Atlantic rates** *n pl* TRANSP taux nord-atlantique *m pl*; ~ **Atlantic Shippers Association** *n* *(NASA)* TRANSP association des affréteurs de l'Atlantique nord; ~ **Atlantic Treaty Organization** *n* *(NATO)* POL Organisation du Traité de l'Atlantique Nord *f* *(OTAN)*; ~ **Atlantic Westbound Freight Association** *n* *(NAWFA)* TRANSP association des transporteurs de fret à destination de l'ouest de l'Atlantique du Nord; ~ **compass point** *n* *(N)* TRANSP *navigation* quart nord *m* *(N)*; ~ **Korean** *n* GEN COMM *person* Nord-Coréen *m*; ~ **Sea gas** *n* IND gaz de la mer du Nord *m*

North:[3] ~ **Africa** *pr n* GEN COMM Afrique du Nord *f*; ~ **America** GEN COMM Amérique du Nord *f*; ~ **Korea** *pr n* GEN COMM Corée du Nord *f*, République populaire de Corée *f*

northbound *adj* *(NB)* TRANSP nord, à destination nord *loc f*

northern *adj* GEN COMM du nord *loc m*

Northern:[1] ~ **Irish** *adj* GEN COMM de l'Irlande du Nord

Northern:[2] **the** ~ **Irish** *n pl* GEN COMM *person* les Irlandais du Nord *m pl*

Northern:[3] ~ **Ireland** *pr n* GEN COMM Irlande du Nord *f*

Norway *pr n* GEN COMM Norvège *f*

Norwegian[1] *adj* GEN COMM norvégien

Norwegian[2] *n* GEN COMM *person* Norvégien *m*

no-show *n* LEIS non-présentation *f*

no-smoking: ~ **area** *n* ENVIR, GEN COMM, HRM zone anti-fumée *f*

no-strike: ~ **agreement** *n* HRM accord de non-recours à la grève *m*, contrat de non-recours à la grève *m*; ~ **clause** *n* HRM *union* clause de non-recours à la grève *f*; ~ **deal** *n* HRM contrat de non-recours à la grève *m*

nostro: ~ **account** *n* BANK compte nostro *m*

nota bene *phr (NB)* GEN COMM nota bene *(NB)*, note *f*, remarque *f*

notarize *vt* LAW authentifier, certifier conforme, légaliser

notary: ~ **public** *n* LAW notaire *m*

notational *adj* GEN COMM porteur d'une notation

note[1] *n* ACC, BANK, FIN effet *m*, GEN COMM bordereau *m*, INS, LAW, TAX effet *m*; ~ **disclosure** GEN COMM présentation d'informations par voie de notes *f*; ~ **issuance facility** *(NIF)* FIN facilité de soutien de programme d'émission d'effets *f*, facilité renouvelable à prise ferme *f*, ligne de crédit ouverte par l'émission de titres à court *f*; ~ **issue** BANK émission fiduciaire *f*; ~ **payable** ACC, FIN e. à p, effet à payer *m*; ~ **purchased under resale agreement** ACC, FIN *asset* valeur reçue en pension *f*; ~ **receivable** ACC, FIN e. à r, effet à recevoir *m*, traite à recevoir *f*; ◆ **keep a** ~ **of** GEN COMM garder une trace écrite de; **make a** ~ **of sth** GEN COMM prendre note de qch; **make a promissory** ~ FIN souscrire un billet à ordre

note[2] *vt* GEN COMM *point* constater, remarquer

notebook *n* COMP notebook *m*

notes: ~ **to the accounts** *n pl* ACC annexe à porter sur les comptes *f*; ~ **to the financial statements** *n pl* ACC annexe *f*; ~ **under repurchase agreement** *n pl* ACC, FIN *liabilities* valeurs données en pension *f pl*

notice *n* COMMS, GEN COMM avis *m*, notification *f*, préavis *m*, LAW avis *m*, mise en demeure *f*, notification *f*, préavis *m*; ~ **of abandonment** INS *marine* avis de délaissement *m*; ~ **account** BANK compte à préavis *m*; ~ **of appeal** PATENTS acte de recours *m*, TAX avis d'appel *m*; ~ **of application** TAX avis de requête *m*; ~ **of assessment** TAX avis de cotisation *m*; ~ **of assignment** STOCK *currency options* avis d'assignation *m*, avis d'assignation de levée *m*, avis de transfert *m*; ~ **board** *BrE (cf bulletin board AmE)* COMMS, COMP, GEN COMM, HRM panneau d'affichage *m*, tableau d'affichage *m*; ~ **of call** STOCK avis de rachat *m*; ~ **of**

cancellation STOCK avis de résolution *m*; ~ **of cancellation at anniversary date** *(NCAD)* INS avis de résiliation à l'échéance *m*; ~ **of cancellation clause** INS préavis de clause de résiliation *m*; ~ **of default** FIN relevé d'erreurs *m*; ~ **deposit** BANK dépôt à préavis *m*; ~ **of dishonor** *AmE*, ~ **of dishonour** *BrE* BANK avis de refus *m*; ~ **of intention** LAW avertissement préalable *m*, préavis *m*; ~ **of objection** TAX avis d'opposition *m*; ~ **of opposition** PATENTS acte d'opposition *m*; ~ **of original assessment** TAX avis de cotisation originale *m*; ~ **period** HRM délai de préavis *m*; ~ **of readiness** TRANSP avis de mise à disposition *m*, lettre d'avis navire prêt à charger *f*; ~ **of reassessment** TAX avis de nouvelle cotisation *m*; ~ **of revocation** STOCK *of an option* avis de révocation *m*; ~ **of shipment** TRANSP avis d'expédition *m*; ~ **to quit** PROP avis de congé *m*; ◆ **escape** ~ GEN COMM échapper à l'attention; **give 5 days'** ~ HRM donner 5 jours de préavis; **give** ~ **to quit** PROP *to landlord, tenant* donner congé, donner congé à un locataire; **without prior** ~ GEN COMM sans préavis

notification *n* PATENTS signification *f*, TAX notification *f*

notify:[1] ~ **address** *n* IMP/EXP, TRANSP adresse à notifier *f*

notify[2] *vt* LAW *of decision* notifier, signifier; ◆ ~ **sb of sth** GEN COMM avertir qn de qch, aviser qn de qch

noting: ~ **protest** *n* TRANSP rapport de mer *m*

notional[1] *adj* FIN *saving, charge, profit, loan* fictif

notional:[2] ~ **rent** *n* PROP loyer notionnel *m*

NOTO *abbr (nonofficial trade organization)* HRM organisation professionnelle non-répertoriée *f*, organisation professionnelle sans existence officielle *f*, syndicat non-officiel *m*

no-trade: ~ **equilibrium** *n* ECON équilibre autarcique *m*

notwithstanding *adv* GEN COMM nonobstant, par dérogation; ◆ ~ **any other provision** GEN COMM nonobstant les autres dispositions; ~ **the provisions of** LAW par dérogation aux clauses de, par dérogation aux dispositions de

Nouakchott *pr n* GEN COMM Nouakchott *n pr*

nought *n* ACC, FIN, GEN COMM, MATH zéro *m*

Nov. *abbr (November)* GEN COMM nov. *(novembre)*

novation *n* GEN COMM, LAW novation *f*

novelty *n* PATENTS, S&M nouveauté *f*; ~ **value** S&M valeur de nouveauté *f*

November *n (Nov.)* GEN COMM novembre *m (nov.)*

novus actus interveniens *n frml* GEN COMM intervention d'un tiers *f*

NOW[1] *abbr* BANK *(negotiable order of withdrawal)* compte-chèques rémunéré *m*, ordre de retrait de fonds négociable *m*, ordre de retrait négociable *m*, FIN *US (National Organization for Women)* Organisation nationale des femmes *f*, STOCK *(negotiable order of withdrawal)* compte-chèques rémunéré *m*, ordre de retrait de fonds négociable *m*, ordre de retrait négociable *m*

NOW:[2] ~ **Account** *n* *US* BANK, STOCK compte-chèques rémunéré *m*

noxious: ~ **gas** *n* ENVIR, IND gaz toxique *m*

np *abbr* (*net proceeds*) GEN COMM, PROP produit net *m*

NPE *abbr* (*nonprofit enterprise*) ECON entreprise à but non-lucratif *f*

NPV *abbr* ACC (*net present value*), ECON (*net present value*), FIN (*net present value*) VAN (*valeur actuelle nette*), STOCK (*no-par value*) SVN (*sans valeur nominale*)

NR *abbr* ENVIR (*nuclear reactor*) réacteur nucléaire *m*, GEN COMM (*naira*) NR (*naira*), IND (*nuclear reactor*) réacteur nucléaire *m*, INS (*no risk until confirmed*) pas de risque avant confirmation *loc*

NRAD *abbr* (*no risk after discharge*) INS acquit libératoire *m*

NRT *abbr* GEN COMM (*net registered tonnage*) tonnage de jauge net *m*, GEN COMM (*net register ton*) tonne de jauge nette *f*, tonneau de jauge nette *m*

NRV *abbr* (*net realizable value*) ACC, ECON, FIN, S&M valeur réalisable nette *f*

NSA *abbr* (*non-sterling area*) ECON zone non-sterling *f*

NSB *abbr* *UK* (*National Savings Bank*) BANK ≈ CNE (*Caisse nationale d'épargne*)

n.s.f. *abbr* (*not sufficient funds*) BANK, GEN COMM fonds insuffisants *m pl*, insuffisance de provision *f*

NSF: ~ **check** *n* *AmE*, ~ **cheque** *n* *BrE* (*not-sufficient-funds cheque*) BANK chèque sans provision *m*

nspf *abbr* (*not specially provided for*) GEN COMM non-expressément prévu *loc*

NSSN *abbr* (*national standard shipping note*) IMP/EXP, TRANSP *shipping* note de chargement nationale standard *f*

Nt *abbr* IMP/EXP (*net terms*) bord à bord, TRANSP (*night trunk*) transport de nuit *m*, TRANSP (*net terms*) *shipping* bord à bord

NTB *abbr* (*nontariff barrier*) ECON, GEN COMM, IMP/EXP, POL barrière non-douanière *f*, barrière non-tarifaire *f*

NTUC *abbr* *UK* (*national trade union council*) HRM Congrès national des syndicats *m*

nuance *vt* GEN COMM, POL nuancer

nuclear[1] *adj* IND *energy* nucléaire

nuclear:[2] ~ **energy** *n* ENVIR, IND énergie nucléaire *f*; ~ **industry** *n* ENVIR, IND industrie nucléaire *f*; ~ **physicist** *n* HRM, IND physicien atomiste *m*, physicien nucléaire *m*; ~ **plant** *n* ENVIR, IND centrale nucléaire *f*; ~ **power station** *n* ENVIR, IND centrale nucléaire *f*; ~ **reactor** *n* (*NR*) ENVIR, IND réacteur nucléaire *m*; ~ **waste** *n* ENVIR déchets nucléaires *m pl*

nudum pactum *n* LAW contrat sans effet juridique *m*

nugatory: ~ **payment** *n* FIN paiement sans contre-partie *m*

nuisance *n* GEN COMM nuisance *f*, LAW acte dommageable *m*, dommage *m*, nuisance *f*, tort causé à autrui *m*

NUJ *abbr* *UK* (*National Union of Journalists*) MEDIA ≈ SNJ (*Syndicat national des journalistes*)

null[1] *adj* LAW, MATH nul; ~ **and void** LAW nul et non avenu

null:[2] ~ **hypothesis** *n* MATH *statistics* hypothèse nulle *f*

NUM *abbr* *UK* (*National Union of Mineworkers*) HRM, IND syndicat national des mineurs *m*

number[1] *n* (*no.*) GEN COMM numéro *m* (*n°*) MATH chiffre *m*, nombre *m*; ~ **cruncher** *n* COMP *machine* ordinateur de calcul *m*, ordinateur principal *m*, GEN COMM *machine* machine à calculer *f*, *person* comptable *mf*; ~ **crunching** *n* ACC calcul comptable *m*, COMP calcul *m*, calcul comptable *m*, FIN calcul comptable *m*; ~ **of employees** *n* ACC, HRM *balance sheet* nombre de salariés *m*; ~ **facts** *n pl* WEL numération *f*; ~ **one priority** *n* GEN COMM priorité absolue *f*; ~ **plate** *n* *BrE* (*cf license plate AmE*) TRANSP numéro d'immatriculation *m*; ~ **of shares issued** *n* STOCK nombre d'actions émises *m*; ◆ **it's a cushy ~!** *infrml* GEN COMM c'est la planque! (*infrml*)

number[2] *vt* GEN COMM, MATH, PATENTS numéroter; ◆ ~ **consecutively** PATENTS numéroter consécutivement, numéroter de façon continue

numbered: ~ **account** *n* BANK compte anonyme *m*, compte numérique *m*

numbering *n* GEN COMM, MATH, PATENTS numérotation *f*

numbers *n pl* (*nos.*) MATH numéros *m pl* (*nos*)

numeric[1] *adj* COMP, ECON, MATH numérique; ~ **alphabetic** MATH alphanumérique

numeric:[2] ~ **character** *n* COMP, MATH caractère numérique *m*; ~ **keypad** *n* COMP *on keyboard* bloc de touches numériques *m*, pavé numérique *m*

numerical: ~ **control** *n* FIN, MATH commande numérique *f*; ~ **filing** *n* ADMIN, GEN COMM classement numérique *m*; ~ **flexibility** *n* *UK* HRM à horaire variable *loc m*

NUPE *abbr* *UK* (*National Union of Public Employees*) HRM syndicat national des employés de l'État

nursing: ~ **home** *n* WEL maison de santé *f*

NUS *abbr* *UK* (*National Union of Seamen*) HRM, TRANSP syndicat national des marins *m*

NVD *abbr* (*no value declared*) IMP/EXP sans valeur déclarée

NVOC *abbr* (*non-vessel-operating carrier*, *non-vessel-owning carrier*) TRANSP *shipping* service de ligne maritime sans navire *m*

NVOCC *abbr* (*non-vessel-operating common carrier*, *non-vessel-owning common carrier*) TRANSP service de ligne maritime sans navire *m*

NW *abbr (north west)* GEN COMM **NO** *(nord-ouest)*

NWC *abbr (National Wages Council)* HRM conseil national des salaires

NYFE *abbr US (New York Futures Exchange)* STOCK Marché des transactions à terme de New York *m*, Marché à terme de New-York *m*

NYME *abbr US (New York Mercantile Exchange)* STOCK marché à terme de produits pétroliers et de platine de New York

NYMEX *abbr US (New York Mercantile Exchange)* STOCK marché à terme de produits pétroliers et de platine de New York

NYPLR *abbr US (New York prime loan rate)* BANK taux de prêt préférentiel de New York *m*, taux préférentiel de New York *m*

NYSA *abbr US (New York Shipping Association)* TRANSP association maritime de New York

NYSE *abbr US (New York Stock Exchange)* STOCK la bourse de New York

O

O *abbr* *(outboard)* TRANSP *shipping, motor* hors-bord

o/a *abbr* GEN COMM *(on account of)* en raison de *loc f*, à cause de *f*, GEN COMM *(overall)* total

OA *abbr* *(office automation)* ADMIN, COMP, IND bureautique *f*

OAG *abbr* *(official airline guide)* TRANSP *aviation* consignes officielles d'une compagnie d'aviation *f pl*

O&M *abbr* *(organization and methods)* GEN COMM, HRM, MGMNT organisation scientifique du travail *f*, OM *(organisation et méthodes)*

OAP *abbr* *BrE* *(old age pensioner)* GEN COMM, HRM, WEL retraité *m*

OARS *abbr* *(Opening Automated Report System)* STOCK système de rapport automatisé d'ouverture

OAS *abbr* *(Organization of American States)* ECON, WEL Organisation des états américains *f*

OASDHI *abbr* *US* *(old age, survivors, disability and health insurance)* INS ≈ ASIRGD *(Assurance santé-invalidité-retraite et garantie-décès)*

oath *n* LAW serment *m*; ♦ **under ~** LAW sous serment

OAU *abbr* *(Organization of African Unity)* ECON OUA *(Organisation de l'unité africaine)*

OBE *abbr* *(Officer of the Order of the British Empire)* GEN COMM officier de l'ordre de l'empire britannique

obey *vt* GEN COMM obéir à, LAW obéir à, respecter, se conformer à

obiter dictum *n frml* [pl -ta] GEN COMM, LAW avis en aparté *m*

object[1] *n* GEN COMM *aim* objet *m, of debate, meeting* objectif *m*

object:[2] **~ to** *vt* GEN COMM *proposal* s'opposer à, GEN COMM objecter; ♦ **~ to an assessment** TAX s'opposer à une cotisation, s'opposer à une évaluation

objection *n* GEN COMM objection *f*, TAX *to assessment* opposition *f*; ♦ **make an ~** GEN COMM faire une objection, émettre une objection; **~ overruled** LAW objection rejetée; **~ sustained** LAW objection admise

objective[1] *adj* GEN COMM objectif

objective[2] *n* ECON *of firm*, GEN COMM, MGMNT, S&M finalité *f*, objectif *m*; **~ function** *n* MATH fonction objective *f*; **~ indicators** *n pl* GEN COMM, MGMNT, S&M indicateurs d'objectif *m pl*; **~ setting** *n* GEN COMM, MGMNT, S&M définition des objectifs *f*; **~ value** *n* ECON valeur objective *f*

obligate *vt* GEN COMM contraindre; ♦ **to be obliged to do sth** LAW être dans l'obligation de faire qch, être obligé de faire qch

obligated: to be ~ to do sth *phr* GEN COMM être

dans l'obligation de faire qch *loc f*, être obligé de faire qch

obligation *n* GEN COMM, LAW obligation *f*; **~ bond** FIN *mortgage bond* titre d'obligataire *m*; ♦ **be under a legal ~ to** LAW être dans l'obligation légale de, être légalement obligé de; **be under an ~ to do** GEN COMM être tenu de faire; **no ~ to buy** S&M entrée libre; **without ~** S&M sans engagement de votre part

obligatory *adj* GEN COMM obligatoire

oblige:[1] **~ line** *n* INS *marine* ligne d'obligeance *f*

oblige[2] *vt* GEN COMM *do favour* contraindre, obliger, rendre service à; **~ so** GEN COMM faire une faveur à qn; ♦ **~ sb to do sth** GEN COMM contraindre qn à faire qch, forcer qn à faire qch, obliger qn à faire qch

obliged: be ~ to *phr* GEN COMM être tenu de; **I should be much ~** *phr frml* GEN COMM je vous saurais gré *(frml)*

obligee *n* LAW créancier *m*, obligataire *mf*

obligor *n* LAW obligé *m*

OBO *abbr* *(order book official)* STOCK spécialiste de certains marchés d'options

OBS *abbr* *(off-balance-sheet)* ACC, FIN hors bilan

observance *n* GEN COMM, LAW *of rule* respect *m*

observation *n* GEN COMM observation *f*, remarque *f*; **~ test** ACC, FIN *auditing* test d'observation *m*

observatory *n* GEN COMM observatoire *m*

observe *vt* LAW observer, respecter

observer *n* GEN COMM, POL observateur *m*

obsolescence *n* GEN COMM, S&M désuétude *f*, obsolescence *f*, vieillissement *m*; **~ clause** INS clause de vétusté *f*

obsolete *adj* GEN COMM dépassé, obsolète, périmé

obstacle *n* GEN COMM empêchement *m*, obstacle *m*

obstruct *vt* GEN COMM bloquer, entraver, gêner

obtain 1. *vt* FIN *funds*, GEN COMM obtenir, procurer, LAW *permission*, PATENTS *consent* obtenir; **2.** *vi* GEN COMM avoir cours, prévaloir; ♦ **~ by fraud** LAW obtenir frauduleusement; **~ permission in writing** COMMS obtenir la permission par écrit; **~ security** STOCK prendre des garanties

obtainable *adj* GEN COMM disponible

obtainment *n* GEN COMM obtention *f*

OBU *abbr* *(offshore banking unit)* BANK, FIN, TAX *investment* succursale extraterritoriale *f*, succursale offshore *f*

obvious *adj* GEN COMM manifeste, évident

OC *abbr* GEN COMM *(overcharge)* majoration *f*, surcharge *f*, IND *(oil-bearing continuous liner)* pétrolier de ligne sans escales *m*, INS *(open cover)* police ouverte *f*, S&M *(overcharge)* majoration *f*, surcharge *f*, TRANSP *(open charter)* affrètement ouvert *m*, charter ouvert *m*, TRANSP *(old charter)* ancien affrètement *m*, vieux charter *m*, TRANSP *(oil-bearing continuous liner)* pétrolier de ligne sans escales *m*

OCAS *abbr (Organization of Central American States)* ECON, POL Organisation des États de l'Amérique Centrale

OCC *abbr (options clearing corporation)* STOCK société de compensation d'actions *f*, société de compensation des options *f*

occasion *n* GEN COMM *circumstance* circonstance *f*, occasion *f*, MGMNT occasion *f*; ◆ **on a similar ~** GEN COMM dans des circonstances semblables; **should the ~ arise** GEN COMM le cas échéant, si l'occasion se présente

occasional[1] *adj* GEN COMM occasionnel

occasional:[2] **~ worker** *n* HRM travailleur occasionnel *m*

occupancy *n* LAW, PROP occupation *f*; **~ cost** PROP, TAX coût d'habitation *m*, coût d'occupation *m*; **~ level** PROP niveau d'occupation *m*

occupant *n* HRM *of post* titulaire *mf*, LAW occupant *m*, PROP, TAX occupant *m*

occupation *n* HRM métier *m*, *post* profession *f*, *protest action* occupation des locaux *f*, LAW occupation *f*, possession effective de terres *f*, prise de possession *f*, PROP possession effective de terres *f*, prise de possession *f*, profession *f*

occupational[1] *adj* HRM professionnel

occupational:[2] **~ accident** *n* HRM, IND, WEL accident du travail *m*; **~ analysis** *n* HRM analyse de poste professionnel *f*; **~ disease** *n* HRM maladie de travail *f*, maladie professionnelle *f*; **~ hazard** *n* GEN COMM, HRM, INS risque du métier *m*, risque professionnel *m*; **~ health** *n* HRM, WEL hygiène du travail *f*; **~ illness** *n* HRM maladie de travail *f*, maladie professionnelle *f*; **~ MAC** *n* *(occupational maximum allowable concentration)* ENVIR concentration maximale admissible *f*; **~ maximum allowable concentration** *n* *(occupational MAC)* ENVIR concentration maximale admissible *f*; **~ mobility** *n* ECON mobilité du travail *f*, mobilité professionnelle *f*; **~ pension** *n* HRM, WEL retraite professionnelle *f*; **~ pension plan** *n* *UK* FIN, HRM, WEL régime de retraite professionnel *m*; **~ pension scheme** *n* *UK* FIN, HRM, WEL système de retraite professionnelle *m*; **~ segregation** *n* ECON, HRM ségrégation au travail *f*, ségrégation professionnelle *f*; **~ threshold limit value** *n* *(occupational TLV)* ENVIR *at place of work* concentration maximale admissible *f*; **~ TLV** *n* *(occupational threshold limit value)* ENVIR *at place of work* concentration maximale admissible *f*; **~ union** *n* *UK* HRM syndicat professionnel *m*

occupier *n* PROP occupant *m*

occupy *vt* HRM *position*, PROP occuper

OCD *abbr (other checkable deposits)* BANK autres dépôts vérifiables *m pl*

ocean:[1] **~ -going** *adj* TRANSP *vessel* au long cours, long-courrier

ocean:[2] **~ bill of lading** *n* IMP/EXP, TRANSP connaissement à ordre *m*; **~ freight** *n* TRANSP fret au long cours *m*; **~ -going passenger ship** *n* TRANSP long-courrier à passagers *m*; **~ -going passenger vessel** *n* TRANSP long-courrier à passagers *m*; **~ -going ship** *n* TRANSP long-courrier *m*; **~ -going vessel** *n* TRANSP long-courrier *m*, navire au long cours *m*; **~ liner** *n* TRANSP paquebot *m*, paquebot de ligne *m*; **~ marine protection and indemnity insurance** *n* INS, TRANSP *marine* assurance maritime de protection et de l'indemnité *f*; **~ vessel** *n* TRANSP long-courrier *m*, navire long-courrier *m*

OCR *abbr (optical character recognition)* COMP ROC *(reconnaissance optique des caractères)*

Oct. *abbr (October)* GEN COMM oct. *(octobre)*

October *n* *(Oct.)* GEN COMM octobre *m* *(oct.)*

O/D *abbr* BANK *(overdraft)* découvert *m*, découvert bancaire *m*, BANK *(overdrawn)* à découvert *loc m*

ODA *abbr* *UK* *(Overseas Development Administration)* ECON, POL ≈ Organisme du développement outre-mer *m*

odd[1] *adj* COMP impair, GEN COMM disparate, *number* impair, *one of pair* dépareillé

odd:[2] **~ change** *n* GEN COMM monnaie *f*; **~ -job man** *n* HRM factotum *m*, homme de peine *m*, homme à tout faire *m*; **~ jobs** *n pl* HRM petits boulots *m pl*, travaux menus *m pl*; **~ lot** *n* STOCK quotité inférieure *f* *(jarg)*, transaction sur rompu *f*, rompu de titres *m*; **~ -lot dealer** *n* STOCK négociateur sur rompus de titres *m*; **~ -lot short-sale ratio** *n* STOCK coefficient rompus-ventes à découvert *m*; **~ -lot theory** *n* STOCK théorie des rompus de titres *f*; **~ one** *n* GEN COMM *of pair* demi-paire *f*; **~ size** *n* IND *production* taille peu courante *f*; **the ~ one out** *n* HRM l'exception dans le groupe *f*, l'intrus *m*; **~ -value pricing** *n* S&M pratique des prix magiques *f*

oddment *n* GEN COMM article en solde *m*, S&M article dépareillé *m*, article en solde *m*

oddments *n pl* S&M fins de série *f pl*

ODI *abbr* *UK* *(Overseas Development Institute)* ECON, POL ≈ Institut du développement outre-mer *m*

ODM *abbr (Ministry of Overseas Development)* ECON ministère du Développement Outre-mer, POL ministère du développement outre-mer

odor *n* *AmE see odour BrE*

odour *n* *BrE* ENVIR odeur *f*; **~ control** *BrE* ENVIR lutte contre les odeurs *f*

OEC *abbr (overpaid entry certificate)* IMP/EXP certificat d'entrée trop perçue *m*

OECD *abbr (Organization for Economic Cooperation and Development)* ECON OCDE *(Organisation de coopération et de développement économique)*

OECF *abbr (Overseas Economic Cooperation Fund)* ECON fonds de coopération économique outre-mer

OEEC *abbr (Organization for European Economic*

Cooperation) ECON OECE *(Organisation europé-enne de coopération économique)*

OEIC *abbr (open-end investment company)* FIN, STOCK FCP *(fonds commun de placement)*, SICAV *(société d'investissement à capital variable)*

OF *abbr (open full)* TRANSP plein ouvert

off *adj* COMP éteint

off-balance-sheet[1] *adj (OBS)* ACC, FIN hors bilan

off-balance-sheet:[2] ~ **commitments** *n pl* ACC, FIN engagements hors bilan *m pl*; ~ **finance** *n* ACC, FIN financement hors bilan *m*; ~ **financing** *n* ACC, FIN financement hors bilan *m*

offence *n* LAW délit *m*, infraction *f*, violation *f*, violation d'un droit *f*

offer[1] *n* GEN COMM, S&M, STOCK offre *f*; ~ **and acceptance** GEN COMM, LAW offre et acceptation *f*; ~ **for sale** STOCK offre publique de vente *f*, OPV; ~ **price** BANK, ECON, FIN, GEN COMM cours vendeur *m*, STOCK cours vendeur *m*, prix offert *m*; ~ **wanted** STOCK offre demandée *f*; ◆ **make an** ~ GEN COMM faire une offre; **on** ~ S&M en vente; **or nearest** ~ *(ono)* MEDIA, S&M à débattre

offer[2] *vt* GEN COMM offrir, proposer, HRM *job* proposer; ◆ ~ **considerable scope** GEN COMM offrir beaucoup de possibilités; ~ **one's services** GEN COMM proposer ses services

offered *adj* STOCK offert, vendeur

offeree *n* FIN, GEN COMM, LAW destinataire d'une offre *m*

offerer *n* GEN COMM offrant *m*

offering *n* STOCK *of new shares* nouvelle émission *f*, offre *f*; ~ **date** STOCK *new issue* date de mise sur le marché *f*; ~ **price** STOCK prix d'offre *m*; ~ **scale** STOCK échelle d'offre *f*

off-exchange: ~ **instrument** *n* FIN instrument hors change *m*

office *n* ACC, ADMIN, BANK, GEN COMM, LAW *building, room* bureau *m*; ~ **accommodation** *n* ADMIN, GEN COMM espace bureau *m*; ~ **aid** *n* ADMIN, GEN COMM matériel de bureau *m*; ~ **automation** *n (OA)* ADMIN, COMP, IND bureautique *f*; ~ **block** *n* GEN COMM, PROP immeuble de bureaux *m*; ~ **boy** *n* GEN COMM garçon de bureau *m*, HRM commis *m*, garçon de bureau *m*; ~ **building** *n* GEN COMM, PROP immeuble de bureaux *m*; ~ **equipment** *n* ADMIN, GEN COMM matériel de bureau *m*, équipement de bureau *m*; ~ **expenses** *n pl* ACC, GEN COMM frais d'adminis-tration *m pl*; ~ **hours** *n pl* GEN COMM heures de bureau *f pl*; ~ **job** *n* ADMIN, HRM travail de bureau *m*; ~ **management** *n* ADMIN, MGMNT organisation des bureaux *f*; ~ **manager** *n* ADMIN, HRM, MGMNT chef de bureau *m*, directeur de bureau *m*; ~ **planning** *n* ADMIN, GEN COMM planification des bureaux *f*; ~ **premises** *n pl* GEN COMM locaux de bureaux *m pl*, PROP locaux commerciaux *m pl*, locaux de bureaux *m pl*; ~ **requisites** *n pl* ADMIN, GEN COMM fournitures de bureau *f pl*; ~ **routine** *n* ADMIN, GEN COMM travail courant de bureau *m*;

~ **space** *n* GEN COMM locaux de bureaux *m pl*, PROP locaux commerciaux *m pl*, locaux de bureaux *m pl*; ~ **staff** *n pl* ADMIN, HRM personnel de bureau *m*; ~ **stationery** *n* ADMIN fournitures de bureau *f pl*; ~ **supplies** *n pl* ADMIN, GEN COMM fournitures de bureau *f pl*; ~ **technology** *n* ADMIN bureautique *f*, technologie de bureau *f*; ~ **work** *n* ADMIN, HRM travail de bureau *m*; ~ **worker** *n* HRM employé *m*; ◆ **for** ~ **use only** ADMIN réservé au personnel, réservé à l'administration; **in** ~ HRM en fonction

Office: ~ **of Fair Trading** *n UK (OFT)* ECON ≈ Direction de la concurrence, de la consomma-tion et de la répression de fraudes *f (Fra)*; ~ **of Gas Supply** *n UK (Ofgas)* ADMIN service du Gaz; ~ **of International Trade** *n (OIT)* GEN COMM Bureau de commerce international *m*; ~ **of Inter-state Land Sales Registration** *n US (OILSR)* PROP bureau d'inscription cadastre des ventes immobilières interétat *m*; ~ **of Management and Budget** *n US (OMB)* MGMNT service du gouver-nement américain en charge de la préparation du budget; ~ **of Population Censuses and Surveys** *n UK (OPCS)* WEL bureau des recensements et enquêtes de population; ~ **of Telecommunications** *n UK (Oftel)* COMMS Bureau des télécommuni-cations *m*

officer *n* BANK dirigeant *m*, HRM agent *m*; ~ **with statutory authority** HRM Fondé de pouvoir supérieur *m*

Officer: ~ **of the Order of the British Empire** *n (OBE)* GEN COMM officier de l'ordre de l'empire britannique

offices: ~ **for sale** *n pl* PROP bureaux à vendre *m pl*

official[1] *adj* GEN COMM officiel

official[2] *n* ADMIN agent *mf*, fonctionnaire *mf*, HRM *of union* permanent *m*; ~ **action** *n UK* HRM, IND action revendicative *f*, grève officielle *f*, LAW *strike* grève officielle *f*; ~ **airline guide** *n (OAG)* TRANSP consignes officielles d'une compagnie d'aviation *f pl*; ~ **check** *n AmE*, ~ **cheque** *n BrE* BANK chèque officiel *m*; ~ **depository** *n* MEDIA *print* dépositaire officiel *m*; ~ **development assistance** *n* ECON, POL aide officielle au déve-loppement *f*, aide publique au développement *f*; ~ **document** *n* ADMIN document officiel *m*; ~ **exchange rate** *n* BANK, ECON, FIN taux de change officiel *m*; ~ **figures** *n pl* BANK, ECON, FIN, GEN COMM, POL chiffres officiels *m pl*; ~ **financing** *n* ECON, FIN financement officiel *m*; ~ **list** *n* STOCK cote boursière *f*, cote officielle *f*; ~ **log** *n* TRANSP journal réglementaire *m*, livre de bord *m*; ~ **logbook** *n (OLB)* TRANSP journal réglemen-taire *m*, livre de bord *m*; ~ **market** *n* ECON marché officiel *m*; ~ **no.** *n (official number, on)* TRANSP numéro d'immatriculation *m*, numéro officiel *m*; ~ **notice of sale** *n* FIN déclaration officielle de vente *f*; ~ **number** *n (official no., on)* TRANSP numéro d'immatriculation *m*, numéro officiel *m*; ~ **quotation** *n* GEN COMM, INS cotation officielle *f*; ~ **rate** *n* BANK, ECON, FIN taux officiel d'escompte *m*; ~ **receipt** *n* TAX reçu officiel *m*; ~ **receiver** *n* FIN, GEN COMM, LAW administrateur judiciaire *m*; ~ **statement** *n* GEN COMM communiqué officiel *m*; ~ **strike** *n* HRM grève approuvée par le syndicat *f*, grève avec préavis *f*, grève officielle *f*, IND, LAW *labour* grève approuvée par le syndicat *f*, grève officielle *f*; ~ **supported export credit** *n* FIN, IMP/EXP crédit à l'exportation bénéficiant d'un soutien public *m*; ~ **valuer** *n* INS, LAW expert *m*, expert désigné par les tribunaux *m*

Official: ~ **Journal** *n* (*OJ*) ECON *EU* Journal officiel *m* (*JO*)

officialese *n* ADMIN, COMMS jargon administratif *m*

officially *adv* GEN COMM officiellement

off-licence *n* LAW *BrE permit* licence permettant la vente de boissons alcoolisées à emporter, S&M *BrE* (*cf liquor store Can, package store AmE*) magasin de vins et de spiritueux qu'il est interdit de consommer sur place

off-limits: ~ **area** *n* GEN COMM zone interdite *f*

off-line *adj* (ANT *on-line*) COMP autonome, différé, en différé, hors ligne, non-connecté, GEN COMM non-connecté

off-load *vt* GEN COMM *responsibility, work* décharger, TRANSP débarquer, décharger

off-loading *n* TRANSP déchargement *m*

off-peak[1] *adj* GEN COMM, TRANSP en période de creux *loc f*; ~ **day** GEN COMM jour creux *m*

off-peak:[2] ~ **charges** *n pl* GEN COMM tarif réduit aux heures creuses *m*; ~ **day** *n* GEN COMM journée à tarif réduit *f*; ~ **fare** *n* LEIS, TRANSP tarif réduit *m*; ~ **season** *n* LEIS, TRANSP basse saison *f*

off-prime *adj* ECON inférieur au taux de base (*Fra*), inférieur au taux préférentiel (*Can*)

off-profile: ~ **return** *n* TAX déclaration non standard *f*

off-sale: ~ **date** *n* (ANT *on-sale date AmE*) MEDIA date de retour *f*

off-season *adj* GEN COMM hors-saison

offset[1] *n* ACC, FIN contrepartie *f*, STOCK compensation *f*, compensation de couverture *f*, position de couverture *f*, contrepartie *f*, position inverse *f*

offset[2] *vt* ACC, FIN, STOCK compenser; ◆ ~ **a debit against a credit** ACC compenser un débit par un crédit; ~ **a loss** STOCK compenser les pertes

offsetting: ~ **entry** *n* ACC, FIN écriture de compensation *f*; ~ **transaction** *n* STOCK opération compensatrice *f*, opération de compensation *f*

offshore[1] *adj* BANK extraterritorial, ENVIR offshore, FIN extraterritorial, GEN COMM en mer *loc f*, extraterritorial, offshore

offshore[2] *adv* GEN COMM en mer *loc f*, offshore

offshore:[3] ~ **banking** *n* BANK, TAX banque offshore *f*; ~ **banking unit** *n* (*OBU*) BANK, FIN, TAX *investment* succursale extraterritoriale *f*, succursale offshore *f*; ~ **center** *n AmE*, ~ **centre** *n BrE* BANK centre offshore *m*, place extraterritoriale *f*, FIN place extraterritoriale *f*; ~ **dollars** *n pl* BANK

dollars offshore *m pl*; ~ **funds** *n pl* FIN fonds offshore *m pl*, TAX fonds de l'étranger *m pl*; ~ **installation** *n* TRANSP installation en mer *f*, installation offshore *f*; ~ **investment** *n* FIN investissement extraterritorial *m*; ~ **oilfield** *n* IND champ pétrolifère en mer *m*; ~ **place** *n* BANK, FIN place extraterritoriale *f*; ~ **reprise** *n* FIN reprise offshore *f*; ~ **technology** *n* IND technologie en mer *f*; ~ **trust** *n* FIN, LAW acte fiduciaire établi outre-mer *m*, fiducie offshore *f*; ~ **well** *n* ENVIR, IND puits en mer *m*

off-site: ~ **cost** *n* PROP *construction* frais hors-site *m pl*

off-the-board *adj* STOCK hors cote

off-the-job: ~ **training** *n* (ANT *on-the-job training*) HRM formation en dehors de l'entreprise *f*, formation extérieure *f*, formation hors de l'entreprise *f*

off-the-peg *adj* GEN COMM, S&M *fashion* prêt-à-porter

off-the-record *adj* GEN COMM officieux

off-the-shelf: ~ **company** *n* GEN COMM société tiroir *f*

Ofgas *abbr UK* (*Office of Gas Supply*) ADMIN service du Gaz

OFT *abbr UK* (*Office of Fair Trading*) ECON ≈ Direction de la concurrence, de la consommation et de la répression de fraudes *f* (*Fra*)

Oftel *n UK* (*Office of Telecommunications*) COMMS Bureau des télécommunications *m*

OGIL *abbr* (*open general import licence BrE, open general import license AmE*) IMP/EXP licence ouverte d'importation générale *f*

OGM *abbr* (*ordinary general meeting*) GEN COMM, MGMNT, STOCK AGO (*assemblée générale ordinaire*)

OHMS *abbr* (*On Her Majesty's Service*) COMMS, GEN COMM au service de sa Majesté *loc m*

OID[1] *abbr* (*original issue discount*) FIN, STOCK escompte de première émission *m*, prime d'émission *f*; ~ **bond** (*original issue discount bond*) STOCK obligation vendue au-dessous du pair à l'émission *f*

OID:[2] ~ **bond** *n* (*original issue discount bond*) FIN obligation vendue au-dessous du pair à l'émission *f*

oil:[1] ~ **-bearing** *adj* IND pétrolifère; ~ **-rich** *adj* ECON *country* riche en pétrole

oil[2] *n* ENVIR huile *f*, pétrole *m*, IND pétrole *m*, TRANSP huile *f*; ~ **analyst** *n* IND analyste pétrolier *m*; ~ **-bearing continuous liner** *n* (*OC*) IND, TRANSP navire pétrolier à long cours continu *m*, pétrolier de ligne sans escales *m*; ~ **carrier** *n* IND, TRANSP pétrolier *m*; ~ **clearance vessel** *n* ENVIR, TRANSP navire dépollueur *m*; ~ **company** *n* ENVIR société pétrolière *f*, IND compagnie pétrolière *f*, société pétrolière *f*; ~ **crisis** *n* ECON choc pétrolier *m*; ~ **deposit** *n* IND gisement de pétrole *m*, gisement pétrolifère *m*; ~ **exploration licence** *n BrE* IND autorisation de prospection pétrolière *f*, licence de prospection pétrolière *f*; ~ **exploration license** *n AmE see oil exploration licence BrE*; ~ **-exporting countries** *n pl* GEN COMM, IND, POL pays exportateurs de pétrole *m pl*; ~ **field** *n* IND terrain pétrolifère *m*; ~ **gage** *n AmE see oil gauge BrE*; ~ **and gas lease** *n* IND, LAW concession gazière et pétrolière *f*; ~ **and gas limited partnership** *n* GEN COMM société limitée en matière de pétrole et gas *f*; ~ **and gas lottery** *n* ENVIR loterie du gaz et du pétrole *f*, zonage du gaz et du pétrole *m*; ~ **gauge** *n BrE* ENVIR, TRANSP indicateur du niveau d'huile *m*; ~ **glut** *n* ECON, ENVIR, IND surabondance de pétrole *f*; ~ **industry** *n* IND industrie pétrolière *f*; ~ **pipeline** *n* ENVIR, IND oléoduc *m*; ~ **platform** *n* ENVIR, IND plate-forme de forage *f*, plate-forme pétrolière *f*; ~ **pollution** *n* ENVIR, IND pollution par le pétrole *f*, pollution par les hydrocarbures *f*; ~ **price increase** *n* ECON augmentation du prix du pétrole *f*, hausse du prix du pétrole *f*; ~ **price rise** *n* ECON augmentation du prix du pétrole *f*, hausse du prix du pétrole *f*; ~ **-producing country** *n* ECON, ENVIR, POL pays producteur de pétrole *m*; ~ **recovery skimmer** *n* ENVIR, IND récupérateur de pétrole *m*; ~ **recovery vessel** *n* ENVIR, TRANSP navire dépollueur *m*; ~ **refinery** *n* ENVIR, IND raffinerie de pétrole *f*; ~ **regeneration plant** *n* ENVIR usine de régénération des huiles usées *f*; ~ **revenue tax** *n* TAX impôt sur les revenus pétroliers *m*; ~ **rig** *n* ENVIR, IND derrick *m*, installation de forage *f*, plate-forme de forage *f*; ~ **sector** *n* ECON secteur pétrolier *m*; ~ **shares** *n pl* STOCK valeurs pétrolières *f pl*; ~ **shortage** *n* ECON, IND pénurie de pétrole *f*; ~ **slick** *n* ENVIR, IND nappe de pétrole *f*; ~ **slick sinking** *n* ENVIR coulage des nappes *m*; ~ **spill** *n* ENVIR, IND déversement de pétrole *m*, marée noire *f*; ~ **spillage** *n* ENVIR, IND déversement de pétrole *m*, marée noire *f*; ~ **tanker** *n* IND, TRANSP pétrolier *m*; ~ **terminal** *n* ENVIR, IND terminal pétrolier *m*; ~ **waste** *n* ENVIR déchets huileux *m pl*

oil³ *vt* IND graisser; ◆ ~ **sb's palm** *infrml* GEN COMM graisser la patte à qn (*infrml*)

OILSR *abbr US (Office of Interstate Land Sales Registration)* PROP bureau d'inscription cadastre des ventes immobilières interétat *m*

oiltight *adj (OT)* TRANSP étanche au pétrole, étanche aux hydrocarbures

OIT *abbr (Office of International Trade)* GEN COMM Bureau de commerce international *m*

OJ *abbr (Official Journal)* ECON *EU* JO (*Journal officiel*)

OJT *abbr (on-the-job training)* HRM formation dans l'entreprise *f*, formation en entreprise *f*, formation sur le tas *f*, formation sur le terrain *f*, formation sur site *f*, stage en centre de formation *m*

Okun's: ~ **law** *n US* ECON loi d'Okun *f*

OLB *abbr (official logbook)* TRANSP *shipping* journal réglementaire *m*, livre de bord *m*

old¹ *adj* GEN COMM *former* ancien; ~ **-fashioned** GEN COMM démodé

old:² ~ **age pension** *n* FIN assurance vieillesse *f*, pension de retraite *f*, INS, WEL pension de retraite *f*, pension vieillesse *f*; ~ **-age pension plan** *n* FIN régime de retraite vieillesse *m*; ~ **-age pension scheme** *n* FIN régime de retraite vieillesse *m*; ~ **age pensioner** *n BrE (OAP)* GEN COMM, HRM, WEL retraité *m*; ~ **age, survivors, disability and health insurance** *n US (OASDHI)* INS ≈ Assurance santé-invalidité-retraite et garantie-décès *f* (*ASIRGD*); ~ **charter** *n (OC)* TRANSP ancien affrètement *m*, vieux charter *m*; ~ **law** *n* LAW ancien droit *m*, ancienne loi *f*, droit ancien *m*

Old: ~ **Lady of Threadneedle Street** *n UK* BANK rue dans la City de Londres reconnue pour ses banques dont la Banque d'Angleterre, Old Lady of Threadneedle Street *f*

OLG *abbr (overlapping generations model)* ECON théorème d'équivalence de Ricardo *m*

oligopolistic *adj* ECON, POL oligopolistique

oligopoly *n* ECON, IND, POL monopole partagé *m*, oligopole *m*

oligopsony *n* ECON oligopsone *f*

OM *abbr (options market)* STOCK marché à options *m*

OMA *abbr (orderly market agreement)* ECON, STOCK accord de régulation du marché *m*

Oman *pr n* GEN COMM Oman *m*

Omani¹ *adj* GEN COMM omanais

Omani² *n* GEN COMM *person* Omanais *m*

OMB *abbr US (Office of Management and Budget)* MGMNT service du gouvernement américain en charge de la préparation du budget

ombudsman *n* [*pl* -men] POL médiateur *m*, STOCK arbitre *m*

omission *n* GEN COMM omission *f*

omit *vt* GEN COMM omettre; ◆ ~ **to do sth** GEN COMM négliger de faire qch

omitted: ~ **dividend** *n* ACC dividende omis *m*, dividende passé *m*

omnibus: ~ **survey** *n* S&M *market research* étude multiclients *f*

omnicarrier *n* TRANSP cargo polyvalent *m*

on¹ *abbr (official no., official number)* TRANSP numéro d'immatriculation *m*, numéro officiel *m*

on² *adj* COMP allumé, connecté

On: ~ **Her Majesty's Service** *phr (OHMS)* COMMS, GEN COMM au service de sa Majesté *loc m*

on-board¹ *adj* COMP embarqué, interne, TRANSP à bord

on-board:² ~ **entertainment** *n* LEIS, TRANSP animation à bord *f*

on-carriage *n* TRANSP postacheminement *m*

once: ~ **more** *adv* LAW de nouveau, de novo

oncosts *n* IND dépenses indivises *f pl*, frais généraux *m pl*

on-deck: ~ **bill of lading** *n* TRANSP connaissement sur le pont *m*

one:[1] ~ -for-one *adj* STOCK un pour un; ~ -off *adj* GEN COMM hors-série, spécial; ~ -way *adj* COMP unidirectionnel

one:[2] ~ -cent sale *n* US S&M deux pour le prix d'un *loc m*; ~ class *n* LEIS, TRANSP classe unique *f*; ~ country, two systems *n* ECON *Hong Kong after 1997* un pays, deux systèmes économiques *loc m*; ~ -crop economy *n* ECON, IND économie de monoculture *f*; ~ -eighth *n* (1/8) GEN COMM, MATH un huitième *m* (1/8); ~ -family home *n* PROP logement pour une famille *m*, WEL logement d'une famille *m*, logement pour une famille *m*; ~ -fifth *n* (1/5) GEN COMM, MATH un cinquième *m* (1/5); ~ for the shelf *n jarg* STOCK valeur de père de famille *f* (*jarg*); ~ -half *n* (1/2) GEN COMM, MATH un demi *m* (1/2); ~ -house veto *n* US POL règle de veto d'une des deux chambres; ~ -hundred per cent location *n* S&M emplacement où un commerce devrait faire un volume de vente optimum par rapport à d'autres emplacements du marché local; ~ -minute manager *n* MGMNT manager peu efficace; ~ -ninth *n* (1/9) GEN COMM, MATH un neuvième *m* (1/9); ~ -off cash gifts *n pl* TAX dons spéciaux en argent *m pl*; ~ per cent spread *n* STOCK écart d'un pour cent *m*; ~ -piece box *n* TRANSP caisse à un compartiment *f*; ~ -price law *n* ECON, LAW loi du prix unique *f*; ~ -program-to-one-vote convention *n* AmE, ~ -programme-to-one-vote convention *n* BrE FIN convention un programme-un crédit *f*; ~ -quarter *n* (1/4) GEN COMM, MATH un quart *m* (1/4); ~ -seventh *n* (1/7) GEN COMM, MATH un septième *m* (1/7); ~ -sixth *n* (1/6) GEN COMM, MATH un sixième *m* (1/6); ~ -stop shopping center *n* AmE, ~ -stop shopping centre *n* BrE GEN COMM centre commercial *m*, commerce intégré *m*, grande surface *f*; ~ -tailed test *n* MATH *statistics* test à une issue *m*; ~ -tenth *n* (1/10) GEN COMM, MATH un dixième *m* (1/10); ~ -third *n* (1/3) GEN COMM, MATH un tiers *m* (1/3); ~ thousand dollars *n pl* GEN COMM mille dollars *m pl*; ~ -time buyer *n* S&M acheteur occasionnel *m*; ~ -time rate *n* S&M *advertising* tarif maximum ne donnant pas droit à un tarif dégressif; ~ -to-one straddle *n* STOCK *options* ordre lié un contre un *m*; ~ -trial learning *n* WEL apprentissage à une épreuve *m*; ~ -trip sling *n* TRANSP *cargo* élingue perdue *f*; ~ -way lease *n* TRANSP bail d'expédition *m*; ~ -way protection *n* STOCK ordre lié un pour un *m*, protection perdue *f*; ~ -way ticket *n* AmE (*cf single BrE, single ticket BrE*) TRANSP aller simple *m*; ◆ ~ after the other GEN COMM au fur et à mesure

1/8 *n* (*one-eighth*) GEN COMM, MATH 1/8 (*un huitième*)

1/5 *n* (*one-fifth*) GEN COMM, MATH 1/5 (*un cinquième*)

1/2 *n* (*one-half*) GEN COMM, MATH 1/2 (*un demi*)

1/9 *n* (*one-ninth*) GEN COMM 1/9 (*un neuvième*), MATH 1/9 (*un neuvième*)

1/4 *n* (*one-quarter*) GEN COMM, MATH 1/4 (*un quart*)

1/7 *n* (*one-seventh*) GEN COMM, MATH 1/7 (*un septième*)

1/6 *n* (*one-sixth*) GEN COMM, MATH 1/6 (*un sixième*)

1/10 *n* (*one-tenth*) GEN COMM, MATH 1/10 (*un dixième*)

1/3 *n* (*one-third*) GEN COMM, MATH 1/3 (*un tiers*)

ongoing[1] *adj* GEN COMM en cours *loc m*, *concern* constant, continu, permanent

ongoing:[2] ~ management system *n* MGMNT système de direction continu *m*

on-lending *n* FIN prêt de l'argent emprunté *m*, rétrocession de fonds empruntés *f*

on-line[1] *adj* (*ANT off-line*) COMP, GEN COMM connecté, en ligne *loc f*, interactif

on-line:[2] ~ banking *n* BANK traitement en direct des opérations bancaires *m*; ~ data service *n* COMP serveur télématique *m*; ~ database *n* COMP base de données connectée *f*, base de données en ligne *f*; ~ help *n* COMP aide à l'écran *f*; ~ rate *n* TRANSP *air freight rate* tarif sur réseau *m*; ~ system *n* COMP système connecté *m*, système en ligne *m*, système interactif *m*

ono *abbr* (*or nearest offer*) MEDIA, S&M à débattre

on-sale: ~ date *n* AmE (*ANT off-sale date*) MEDIA *of magazine, periodical* date de mise en vente *f*, date de parution *f*

onset *n* GEN COMM origine *f*

onshore[1] *adj* (*ANT offshore*) GEN COMM à terre

onshore:[2] ~ banking *n* BANK opérations bancaires effectuées à partir du territoire national *f pl*; ~ terminal *n* ENVIR, IND terminal intérieur *m*

on-the-job: ~ training *n* (*OJT*, *ANT off-the-job training*) HRM formation dans l'entreprise *f*, formation en entreprise *f*, formation sur le tas *f*, formation sur le terrain *f*, formation sur site *f*, stage en centre de formation *m*

on-the-spot: ~ reporter *n* MEDIA envoyé spécial *m*

onward: ~ clearing *n* BANK compensation-aller *f*, remise en compensation *f*; ~ flight *n* TRANSP vol de correspondance *m*

O/o *abbr* GEN COMM (*order of*) commande de *loc f*, l'ordre de *loc*, TRANSP (*ore-oil ship*) pétrolier-minéralier *m*

OOG *abbr* (*out of gage AmE, out of gauge BrE*) TRANSP engagement du gabarit *m*

OP *abbr* INS (*open policy*) police d'abonnement *f*, police flottante *f*, police maritime flottante *f*, MEDIA (*out of print*) épuisé, TRANSP (*open policy*) police d'abonnement *f*, police flottante *f*, police maritime flottante *f*

OPCS *abbr* UK (*Office of Population Censuses and Surveys*) WEL bureau des recensements et enquêtes de population

OPEC *abbr* (*Organization of Petroleum Exporting Countries*) ECON, ENVIR, POL OPEP (*Organisation des pays exportateurs de pétrole*)

open[1] *adj* COMP *file, document* ouvert, *system, network* extensible, GEN COMM extensible, STOCK *futures price* ouvert; ~ **-end** ADMIN *envelope* s'ouvrant à l'extrémité; ~ **-ended** COMP, GEN COMM extensible, ouvert, évolutif; ~ **full** *(OF)* TRANSP *side door container* plein ouvert; ~ **-plan** GEN COMM *office* non-cloisonné; ◆ ~ **-to-buy** S&M ouvert à l'achat; ~ **to debate** GEN COMM sujet à discussion; ~ **to several interpretations** GEN COMM susceptible d'interprétations diverses

open:[2] ~ **account** *n* GEN COMM compte ouvert *m*; ~ **-account business** *n* GEN COMM opérations en compte courant *f pl*; ~ **admissions** *n pl* WEL libre accès *m*; ~ **balance** *n* GEN COMM balance impayé *f*; ~ **bid** *n* MGMNT offre ouverte *f*; ~ **-cargo insurance policy** *n* INS, TRANSP police d'abonnement *f*, police flottante *f*, police maritime flottante *f*; ~ **charter** *n (OC)* TRANSP affrètement ouvert *m*, charter ouvert *m*; ~ **check** *n AmE*, ~ **cheque** *n BrE* BANK chèque non-barré *m*, chèque ouvert *m*; ~ **container** *n* TRANSP conteneur découvert *m*, conteneur ouvert *m*; ~ **contract** *n* FIN, STOCK position ouverte *f*; ~ **cover** *n (OC)* INS police ouverte *f*; ~ **credit** *n* GEN COMM compte ouvert *m*; ~ **day** *n BrE (cf open house AmE)* PROP portes ouvertes *f pl*; ~ **deck** *n* TRANSP pont découvert *m*, pont ouvert *m*; ~ **distribution** *n* TRANSP distribution de masse *f*, distribution ouverte *f*; ~ **dock** *n* TRANSP bassin de marée *m*; ~ **-door policy** *n* GEN COMM, MGMNT, POL politique de la porte ouverte *f*; ~ **dump** *n* ENVIR décharge brute *f*; ~ **economy** *n (ANT closed economy)* ECON, POL économie ouverte *f*; ~ **-end** *n* S&M *advertising* espace libre, réservé à la fin d'un programme de télévision; ~ **-end contract** *n* LAW, S&M contrat de vente mentionnant les parties, les biens vendus et le prix; ~ **-end fund** *n* FIN, STOCK société d'investissement à capital variable *f*, société de placement à capital variable *f*, société à capital variable *f*; ~ **-end investment company** *n (OEIC)* FIN, STOCK fonds commun de placement *m (FCP)*, société d'investissement ouverte *f*, société d'investissement à capital variable *f (SICAV)*, société de placement à capital variable *f*, société de portefeuilles à capital variable *f*; ~ **-end investment trust** *n* FIN, STOCK société d'investissement à capital variable *f*, société de placement à capital variable *f*, société de portefeuilles à capital variable *f*; ~ **-end mortgage** *n* FIN créance hypothécaire à taux d'intérêt variable *f*; ~ **-ended agreement** *n* HRM convention à finalité variable *f*; ~ **-ended contract** *n* LAW contrat de vente mentionnant les parties, les biens vendus et le prix; ~ **-ended flight reservation** *n* LEIS, TRANSP réservation de vol ouverte *f*; ~ **-ended mortgage** *n* BANK hypothèque sans date limite *f*; ~ **-ended position** *n* FIN, STOCK position ouverte *f*; ~ **-ended question** *n (ANT closed question)* GEN COMM, S&M *market research* question ouverte *f*; ~ **-ended questionnaire** *n (ANT closed questionnaire)* GEN COMM questionnaire directif *m*, S&M *market research* questionnaire non-directif *m*; ~ **-ended risk** *n*

STOCK *options* risque ouvert *m*; ~ **general import licence** *n BrE (OGIL)* IMP/EXP licence ouverte d'importation générale *f*; ~ **general import license** *n AmE see open general import licence BrE*; ~ **house** *n AmE (cf open day BrE)* PROP portes ouvertes *f pl*; ~ **housing** *n US* WEL accès au logement sans discrimination *m*; ~ **individual licence** *n BrE* IMP/EXP licence individuelle ouverte *f*; ~ **individual license** *n AmE see open individual licence BrE*; ~ **interest** *n* FIN, STOCK position de place *f*, position ouverte *f*; ~ **listing** *n* PROP liste ouverte *f*; ~ **long position** *n* STOCK position acheteur initiale *f*; ~ **market** *n* ECON marché libre *m*, marché monétaire *m*, GEN COMM marché libre *m*, POL marché libre *m*, marché monétaire *m*, S&M marché libre *m*; ~ **-market committee** *n* ECON commission du marché monétaire; ~ **-market operations** *n pl* ECON opérations sur le marché monétaire *f pl*; ~ **-market rate** *n* BANK taux hors banque *m*; ~ **-market trading** *n* ECON *international* opérations sur le marché monétaire *f pl*; ~ **mortgage** *n* BANK, FIN créance hypothécaire à taux variable *f*; ~ **network** *n* COMP réseau ouvert *m*; ~ **order** *n* STOCK ordre good-till-cancelled *m*, ordre ouvert *m*, ordre à révocation *m*; ~ **outcry** *n* STOCK à la criée *loc f*; ~ **-outcry action** *n* STOCK opération à la criée *f*; ~ **-outcry auction market** *n* STOCK enchère à la criée *f*; ~ **-outcry system** *n* STOCK système à la criée *m*; ~ **-plan office** *n* ADMIN bureau paysager *m*; ~ **policy** *n (OP)* INS, TRANSP *marine* police d'abonnement *f*, police flottante *f*, police maritime flottante *f*; ~ **population** *n (ANT closed population)* ECON population ouverte *f*; ~ **port** *n* TRANSP port à marée *m*; ~ **position** *n* FIN position ouverte *f*, STOCK marché libre *m*, position ouverte *f*; ~ **price** *n* STOCK prix ouvert *m*; ~ **registry** *n (OR)* TRANSP libre immatriculation *f*; ~ **-shelf filing** *n* ADMIN classement en rayonnages *m*; ~ **-shelter deck** *n (OSD)* TRANSP *vessel* navire à pont-abri ouvert *m*; ~ **shop** *n* GEN COMM chantier qui admet les ouvriers non-syndiqués *m*, HRM *company* chantier qui admet les ouvriers non-syndiqués *m*, *policy* appartenance non obligatoire à un syndicat *f*; ~ **short position** *n* STOCK position vendeur initiale *f*; ~ **-sided container** *n* TRANSP conteneur à paroi latérale ouvrante *m*; ~ **space** *n* PROP *within a developed area* aire ouverte *f*; ~ **stock** *n* S&M article faisant partie d'un tout que l'on peut acheter à la pièce; ~ **storage** *n* TRANSP terre-plein *m*; ~ **-systems interconnection** *n (OSI)* COMP interconnexion de systèmes ouverts *f (ISO)*; ~ **tax** *n* TAX taxe directe *f*, taxe franche *f*; ~ **tendering** *n* GEN COMM soumission ouverte *f*; ~ **ticket** *n* LEIS billet open *m*; ~ **-top container** *n (OT)* TRANSP conteneur à toit ouvert *m*; ~ **-top reefer** *n* TRANSP conteneur frigorifique à toit ouvert *m*; ~ **-topped container** *n (OT)* TRANSP conteneur à toit ouvert *m*; ~ **-topped reefer** *n* TRANSP *container* conteneur frigorifique à toit ouvert *m*; ~ **union** *n* HRM syndicat ouvert *m*;

~ -**wall container** *n* TRANSP conteneur à paroi latérale ouvrante *m*

open³ **1.** *vt* BANK, COMP *file, document* ouvrir; **2.** *vi* ~ **up** GEN COMM *companies, branches etc* ouvrir; ◆ ~ **an account** BANK ouvrir un compte; ~ **a bank account with** BANK ouvrir un compte bancaire avec; ~ **a file** ADMIN ouvrir un dossier; ~ **the door** GEN COMM *on opportunities* ouvrir la porte; ~ **the door to** GEN COMM *opportunity* ouvrir la porte à; ~ **here** COMMS ouvrir ici; ~ **a long position** STOCK ouvrir une position longue, ouvrir à la hausse; ~ **the mail** COMMS dépouiller le courrier, ouvrir le courrier; ~ **the market up to competition** GEN COMM ouvrir le marché à la concurrence; ~ **a position** (ANT *close a position, liquidate a position*) STOCK *options on currency futures* ouvrir une position; ~ **a short position** STOCK ouvrir une position courte, ouvrir à la baisse; ~ **trading** STOCK ouvrir les transactions

opencast: ~ **method** *n* IND *of mining* exploitation à ciel ouvert *f*, ouvrage à ciel ouvert *m*; ~ **mining** *n* BrE *(cf strip mining AmE)* IND exploitation à ciel ouvert *f*, ouvrage à ciel ouvert *m*

opening¹ *adj* STOCK *trade* initial

opening² *n* GEN COMM *of meeting* débouché *m*, début de séance *m*, ouverture de séance *f*; ~ **balance** *n* (ANT *closing balance, ending balance*) ACC, BANK, FIN solde d'ouverture *m*, solde initial *m*; ~ **bank** *n* BANK banque de placement *f*; ~ **bid** *n* S&M enchère initiale *f*, première offre *f*; ~ **hours** *n pl* GEN COMM heures d'ouverture *f pl*; ~ **inventory** *n* ADMIN stock au début de l'exercice *m*, stock d'ouverture *m*, stock initial *m*, stock à l'ouverture de l'exercice *m*; ~ **position** *n* STOCK position initiale *f*, position à l'ouverture *f*; ~ **price** *n* STOCK cours d'ouverture *m*, premier cours *m*; ~ **quotation** *n* STOCK cotation à l'ouverture *f*, premier cours *m*; ~ **of tenders** *n* GEN COMM lancement d'un appel d'offres *m*; ~ **up** *n* STOCK décloisonnement *m*; ◆ **at the** ~ STOCK à l'ouverture; **late** ~ **Friday** GEN COMM nocturne le vendredi *f*

Opening: ~ **Automated Report System** *n* *(OARS)* STOCK système de rapport automatisé d'ouverture

openness *n* POL la transparence *f*

operand *n* MATH opérateur *m*

operate 1. *vt* GEN COMM *business* exploiter; **2.** *vi* GEN COMM fonctionner; ~ **in tandem** MGMNT fonctionner en tandem

operating: ~ **account** *n* ACC, BANK compte d'exploitation *m*; ~ **budget** *n* ACC, FIN budget d'exploitation *m*; ~ **capacity** *n* ECON, IND capacité de fonctionnement *f*; ~ **capital requirements** *n pl* ECON, GEN COMM besoins financiers d'exploitation *m pl*; ~ **costs** *n pl* ACC charges d'exploitation *f pl*, frais d'exploitation *m pl*; ~ **cycle** *n* ACC cycle d'exploitation *m*; ~ **division** *n* GEN COMM division opérationnelle *f*; ~ **efficiency** *n* TRANSP efficacité d'exploitation *f*; ~ **expenditure** *n* ACC, IND dépenses d'exploitation *f pl*; ~ **expenditure vote** *n* ACC *government* crédit pour dépenses de fonctionne-

ment *m*; ~ **expenses** *n pl* ACC charges d'exploitation *f pl*, frais d'exploitation *m pl*, TRANSP *of ship* coûts d'exploitation *m pl*, frais d'exploitation *m pl*; ~ **gearing** *n* BrE *(cf operating leverage AmE)* ACC effet de levier de l'exploitation *m*; ~ **grant** *n* ACC subvention d'exploitation *f*; ~ **income** *n* ACC bénéfice d'exploitation *m*; ~ **instructions** *n pl* GEN COMM mode de fonctionnement *m*; ~ **interest** *n* GEN COMM droit d'exploitation *m*; ~ **lease** *n* ACC bail d'exploitation à court terme *m*; ~ **leverage** *n* AmE *(cf operating gearing BrE)* ACC effet de levier de l'exploitation *m*; ~ **loss** *n* ACC *balance sheets* perte d'exploitation *f*; ~ **management** *n* MGMNT direction opérationnelle *f*; ~ **plan** *n* TRANSP plan d'exploitation *m*; ~ **profit** *n* ACC bénéfice d'exploitation *m*, résultat des opérations *m*; ~ **schedule** *n* TRANSP horaire *m*, programme d'exploitation *m*; ~ **statement** *n* ACC compte de résultat *m*; ~ **strategy** *n* TRANSP stratégie d'exploitation *f*; ~ **subsidy** *n* TRANSP subvention d'exploitation *f*

operation *n* GEN COMM, MGMNT opération *f*; ~ **lease** FIN bail d'exploitation *m*, TRANSP bail d'exploitation *m*, concession d'exploitation *f*; ~ **system** *(o.s.)* COMP système d'exploitation *m*; ~ **time** GEN COMM durée de fonctionnement *f*, durée de réalisation *f*; ◆ **come into** ~ LAW *act, regulation, rule* entrer en vigueur

operational¹ *adj* GEN COMM, MGMNT opérationnel

operational:² ~ **analysis** *n* HRM, IND analyse d'opérations *f*; ~ **audit** *n* ACC, FIN, MGMNT audit opérationel *m*; ~ **balance** *n* BANK solde d'exploitation *m*; ~ **budget** *n* ACC, FIN budget d'exploitation *m*; ~ **control** *n* GEN COMM contrôle des opérations *m*; ~ **environment** *n* COMP *software* cadre d'exploitation *m*, cadre d'utilisation *m*; ~ **investment** *n* ACC *in buildings and equipment* investissement d'exploitation *m*; ~ **manager** *n* GEN COMM, HRM, MGMNT chef d'exploitation *m*, directeur des opérations *m*; ~ **plan framework** *n* FIN cadre du plan opérationnel *m*; ~ **planning** *n* GEN COMM planification des opérations *f*; ~ **research** *n* *(OR)* GEN COMM, MGMNT, S&M recherche opérationnelle *f* *(RO)*; ~ **staff** *n* GEN COMM équipe opérationnelle *f*

operations *n pl* GEN COMM activités *f pl*, opérations *f pl*; ~ **analysis** *n* HRM analyse des tâches *f*, analyse du travail *f*; ~ **audit** *n* ACC, FIN *auditing* audit d'exploitation *m*, audit des opérations *m*; ~ **breakdown** *n* GEN COMM, HRM, IND, MGMNT décomposition des tâches *f*; ~ **department** *n* ADMIN, STOCK *back office of brokerage firm* post-marché *m*, service des opérations *m*; ~ **management** *n* GEN COMM, MGMNT gestion des opérations *f*; ~ **manager** *n* GEN COMM, HRM, MGMNT chef d'exploitation *m*, directeur des opérations *m*; ~ **research** *n* GEN COMM, MGMNT, S&M recherche opérationnelle *f*

operative *n* HRM, IND, MGMNT opérationnel *m*, personnel de production *m*

operator *n* GEN COMM exploitant *m*, opérateur *m*; ~ **system** COMMS système de positions automatisées de téléphonistes *m*

opinion *n* GEN COMM, LAW avis *m*, opinion *f*; ~ **leader** S&M *market research* leader d'opinion *m*; ~ **poll** S&M *market research* sondage d'opinion *m*; ~ **polling** S&M *market research* sondage d'opinion *m*; ~ **shopping** ACC *auditing* chalandage d'opinion *m*; ~ **survey** S&M enquête d'opinion *f*; ~ **of title** LAW *property*, PROP certificat de validité d'un titre *m*; ◆ **in my** ~ GEN COMM à mon avis

OPM *abbr (other peoples' money)* FIN vente fictive d'obligations *f*, STOCK fonds empruntés *m pl*

opportunism *n* POL *Marxism* opportunisme *m*

opportunistic: ~ **behavior** *n AmE*, ~ **behaviour** *n BrE* ECON comportement opportuniste *m*

opportunities: ~ **to hear** *phr jarg (OTH)* MEDIA, S&M *advertising, radio* occasions d'entendre *f pl*; ~ **to see** *phr jarg (OTS)* MEDIA, S&M *advertising, television* occasions de voir *f pl*

opportunity *n* GEN COMM, MGMNT occasion *f*; ~ **cost** ACC, ECON coût d'opportunité *m*, coût de substitution *m*, FIN coût d'opportunité *m*, coût d'option *m*, produit de l'emploi alternatif *m*; ◆ **give sb the** ~ **to** GEN COMM donner à qn l'occasion de; **have the** ~ **to** GEN COMM avoir l'occasion de

oppose *vt* GEN COMM s'opposer à

opposing: ~ **vote** *n* POL voix contre *f*

opposite¹ *adj* GEN COMM contraire

opposite² *n* GEN COMM contraire *m*; ~ **number** HRM *in another organization* homologue *m*; ~ **transaction** GEN COMM transaction inverse *f*

opposition *n* GEN COMM, PATENTS, POL opposition *f*; ~ **proceedings** *n pl* PATENTS procédure d'opposition *f*

opt:¹ ~ **-out** *n* MEDIA *broadcast* décrochage local *m*

opt:² **1.** *vt* ~ **for** GEN COMM opter pour, MGMNT se décider; **2.** *vi* ~ **out** WEL *schools* se retirer

optical: ~ **character recognition** *n (OCR)* COMP reconnaissance optique des caractères *f (ROC)*; ~ **scanner** *n* COMP, IND, S&M lecteur optique *m*; ~ **wand** *n* COMP, IND, S&M crayon-lecteur optique *m*

optimal: ~ **control** *n* ECON contrôle optimal *m*; ~ **peg** *n* ECON, FIN parité indexée optimale *f*; ~ **rate of pollution** *n* ECON, ENVIR taux optimal de pollution *m*; ~ **tariff** *n* ECON, IMP/EXP tarif optimal *m*; ~ **taxation** *n* TAX imposition optimale *f*; ~ **work effort** *n* ECON, HRM, IND effort de travail optimal *m*

optimality *n* ECON optimalité *f*

optimistic *adj (ANT pessimistic)* GEN COMM optimiste

optimization *n* ECON, GEN COMM, IND optimisation *f*; ~ **problem** MATH problème d'optimisation *m*

optimize *vt* ECON, FIN, GEN COMM, IND optimiser; ◆ ~ **the objective function** GEN COMM optimiser la fonction objective

optimum¹ *adj* GEN COMM optimal

optimum:² ~ **capacity** *n* ECON, IND capacité optimale *f*, capacité optimum *f*; ~ **city** *n* ECON ville de taille optimale pour la rationalisation des investissements; ~ **currency area** *n* ECON, FIN zone monétaire optimale *f*; ~ **firm** *n* ECON entreprise ayant atteint l'échelle minimale d'efficience, entreprise optimum *f*; ~ **population** *n* ECON, WEL population optimale *f*

option *n* COMP, FIN option *f*, GEN COMM choix *m*, option *f*, STOCK option *f*; ~ **account** *n* FIN *credit card* compte d'options *m*; ~ **bargain** *n* STOCK marché au comptant *m*, marché à prime *m*; ~ **bargains** *n pl* STOCK opérations sur le marché à options *f pl*; ~ **buyer** *n (ANT option seller)* STOCK acheteur *m*, acheteur d'option *m*, détenteur *m*, titulaire *mf*; ~ **-buying hedge** *n* STOCK couverture par achat d'option *f*; ~ **class** *n* STOCK catégorie d'options *f*, classe d'options *f*; ~ **contract** *n* STOCK contrat d'option *m*, option *f*; ~ **coverage** *n* STOCK couverture d'une option *f*, garantie d'option *f*; ~ **demand** *n* ECON demande d'option *f*, demande de commanditaire *f*; ~ **eligible security** *n* STOCK titre pouvant faire l'objet d'options *m*; ~ **exercise** *n* STOCK levée de l'option *f*; ~ **fee** *n* FIN *hire purchase* frais d'option *m pl*; ~ **forward contract** *n* IMP/EXP, S&M option de contrat à terme *f*; ~ **holder** *n* STOCK acheteur d'option *m*, détenteur d'options *m*, titulaire *mf*; ~ **mutual fund** *n* STOCK fonds d'investissement en options *m*, placement de fonds commun d'options *m*; ~ **period** *n* STOCK durée d'option *f*, période de l'option *f*; ~ **premium** *n* STOCK prime *f*, prix d'option *m*; ~ **price** *n* STOCK prime *f*, prix d'option *m*; ~ **-pricing formula** *n* STOCK formule d'évaluation des options *f*, formule de l'établissement du prix de l'option *f*; ~ **-pricing parameter** *n* STOCK *Delta* paramètre d'évaluation d'option *m*; ~ **-pricing theory** *n* STOCK théorie d'évaluation des options *f*, théorie de l'établissement du prix de l'option *f*; ~ **seller** *n (ANT option buyer)* STOCK vendeur *m*, vendeur d'option *m*; ~ **-selling hedge** *n* STOCK couverture par vente d'option *f*; ~ **series** *n* STOCK série d'options *f*; ~ **spread** *n* STOCK stratégie d'option *f*, écart *m*, écart d'option *m*; ~ **strike price** *n (ANT put strike price)* STOCK prix d'exercice d'une option de vente *m*; ~ **theorist** *n* STOCK théoricien d'option *m*, théoricien des options *m*; ~ **writer** *n* STOCK vendeur d'option *m*

Option: ~ **Clearing Corporation** *n US* STOCK Organisme de compensation des options pour tous les marchés *m*

optional¹ *adj* GEN COMM facultatif

optional:² ~ **character** *n* COMP, MEDIA caractère spécial *m*; ~ **feature** *n* STOCK caractéristique optionnelle *f*, élément au choix *m*; ~ **item** *n* FIN poste facultatif *m*; ~ **modes of settlement** *n* INS *life insurance* modes facultatifs de règlement *m pl*; ~ **payment bond** *n* STOCK obligation à mode de paiement optionnel *f*

options: ~ **clearing corporation** *n (OCC)* STOCK

société de compensation d'actions *f*, société de compensation des options *f*; **~ exchanges** *n* STOCK marchés d'options *m pl*, échanges d'options *m pl*; **~ market** *n* (*OM*) STOCK marché à options *m*; **~ on currency futures** *n pl* STOCK options sur contrat à terme sur devises *f pl*, options sur contrats à terme *f pl*; **~ writer** *n* STOCK vendeur *m*

OR *abbr* GEN COMM (*operational research*) RO (*recherche opérationnelle*), INS (*owner's risk*) aux risques et périls du freteur *loc m*, MGMNT, S&M (*operational research*) RO (*recherche opérationnelle*), TRANSP (*owner's risk*) *shipping* aux risques et périls du freteur *loc m*, TRANSP (*open registry*) *shipping* libre immatriculation *f*

oral: **~ contract** *n* LAW contrat verbal *m*, convention verbale *f*; **~ note** *n* POL communication officieuse *f*; **~ proceedings** *n pl* PATENTS procédure orale *f*

orange: **~ goods** *n pl* S&M produits à durée de vie moyenne *m pl*

ord. *abbr* (*order, order of the court*) LAW arrêt *m*, commande *f*, injonction *f*, jugement *m*, ordonnance *f*, ordre *m*

order[1] *n* FIN ordonnance *f*, GEN COMM commande *f*, LAW *from courts* arrêt *m*, commande *f*, injonction *f*, jugement *m*, ordonnance *f*, ordre *m*, S&M *for goods and services* commande *f*, STOCK ordre d'achat *m*, ordre de vente *m*; **~ bill of lading** IMP/EXP, TRANSP connaissement à ordre *m*; **~ book** GEN COMM carnet de commandes *m*; **~ book official** (*OBO*) STOCK spécialiste de certains marchés d'options; **~ by post** COMMS, GEN COMM commande par correspondance *f*; **~ card** S&M carte-réponse *f*; **~ of the court** (*ord.*) LAW arrêt *m*, injonction *f*, jugement *m*, ordonnance *f*, ordre *m*; **~ of discharge** TAX ordonnance de libération *f*, ordonnance libératoire *f*; **~ entry** S&M enregistrement de commande *m*; **~ flow pattern** S&M *direct mail* tendance du flux des commandes *f*; **~ form** S&M *direct marketing* bon de commande *m*; **~ of magnitude** MATH ordre de grandeur *m*; **~ number** S&M *fulfilment* numéro de commande *m*; **~ paper** BANK papier ordre *m*; **~ point system** TRANSP système de point de réapprovisionnement *m*, système de seuil de réapprovisionnement *m*; **~ regulation** TRANSP réglementation des commandes *f*; **~ to pay** ACC mandat *m*, ordre de paiement *m*; ◆ **be out of ~** GEN COMM *machine* être en panne, être hors d'usage; **by ~** GEN COMM p.o., par ordre *m*; **in ~ of importance** GEN COMM par ordre d'importance; **in ~ of priority** GEN COMM par ordre de priorité; **in the ~ specified** PATENTS suivant l'ordre indiqué, suivant l'ordre prévu; **my ~** (*m/o*) GEN COMM mon ordre *m* (*m/o*); **~ of** (*O/o*) GEN COMM commande de, l'ordre de; **on ~** S&M en commande; **to the ~ of** BANK à l'ordre de, GEN COMM au compte de, LAW à l'ordre de

order[2] *vt* GEN COMM commander, demander, TRANSP *taxi* demander

orderly: **~ market** *n* ECON, STOCK marché ordonné *m* (*jarg*), ordre sur le marché *m*; **~ market agreement** *n* (*OMA*) ECON, STOCK accord de régulation du marché *m*

orders: **for ~** *phr* (*fo*) GEN COMM pour instructions *loc f*; **~ on hand** *phr* GEN COMM, S&M commandes en cours *f pl*

ordinal: **~ data entry** *n* COMP saisie de données ordinales *f*; **~ scale** *n* MATH succession ordinale *f*; **~ utility** *n* ECON utilité ordinale *f*

ordinalist: **~ revolution** *n* ECON révolution ordinaliste *f*

ordinance *n* US LAW arrêté municipal *m*, ordonnance *f*

ordinarily: **~ resident** *adj* LAW habituellement domicilié, résidant habituellement

ordinary[1] *adj* STOCK ordinaire

ordinary:[2] **~ account** *n* BANK compte ordinaire *m*; **~ annuity** *n* INS rente ordinaire *f*; **~ business** *n* TAX activités habituelles *f pl*, entreprise habituelle *f*; **~ engineer assistant** *n* HRM, IND assistant machiniste *m*; **~ gain** *n* TAX gain normal *m*; **~ general meeting** *n* (*OGM*) GEN COMM, MGMNT, STOCK *of shareholders* assemblée générale ordinaire *f* (*AGO*); **~ income** *n* TAX revenu normal *m*; **~ interest** *n* FIN intérêt ordinaire *m*, intérêt simple *m*; **~ loss** *n* TAX perte normale *f*; **~ and necessary business expenses** *n pl* TAX frais commerciaux ordinaires et nécessaires *m pl*; **~ payroll exclusion endorsement** *n* GEN COMM, INS avenant d'exclusion de la masse salariale *m*; **~ profit before taxation** *n* ACC, ECON, FIN, TAX *annual* résultat courant *m*; **~ seaman** *n* HRM, TRANSP *shipping* matelot de troisième classe *m*; **~ share** *n* BrE (*cf common stock AmE*) ACC, ECON, STOCK action ordinaire *f*; **~ shareholder** *n* STOCK actionnaire ordinaire *m*; **~ spring tide** *n* (*OST*) TRANSP marée de vive-eau *f* (*marée de VE*); **~ stockholder** *n* STOCK actionnaire ordinaire *m*; **~ ticket** *n* LEIS, TRANSP billet plein-tarif *m*

ore *n* IND minerai *m*; **~ carrier** TRANSP minéralier *m*; **~ -oil ship** (*O/o*) TRANSP pétrolier-minéralier *m*

org. *abbr* (*organization*) ADMIN, GEN COMM ordonnance *f*, organisme *m*, LEIS organisme *m*

organic: **~ composition of capital** *n* ECON composition organique du capital *f*; **~ farming** *n* ECON, ENVIR agriculture biologique *f*; **~ foodstuffs** *n pl* ENVIR, GEN COMM aliments biologiques *m pl*; **~ growth** *n* ECON, GEN COMM croissance organique *f*; **~ material** *n* ENVIR produit biologique *m*; **~ premium** *n* ECON *agricultural* prime organique *f*

organicity *n* *jarg* GEN COMM participation des employés *f*

organization *n* (*org.*) ADMIN, GEN COMM ordonnance *f*, organisme *m*, LEIS *company* organisme *m*; **~ behavior** *n* AmE, **~ behaviour** *n* BrE GEN COMM, HRM système d'organisation *m*; **~ chart** *n* GEN COMM, MGMNT organigramme *m*; **~ cost** *n* FIN frais de premier établissement *m pl*; **~ culture**

n MGMNT culture de l'organisation *f*; ~ **development** *n* MGMNT développement organisationnel *m*; ~ **man** *n* MGMNT dévoué *m*; ~ **and methods** *n pl* (*O&M*) GEN COMM organisation et méthodes *f*, organisation scientifique du travail *f*, HRM, MGMNT organisation et méthodes *f*, organisation scientifique du travail *f* (*OM*); ~ **planning** *n* GEN COMM, MGMNT planification d'entreprise *f*, planification de l'organisation *f*; ~ **structure** *n* GEN COMM, MGMNT structure d'organisation *f*; ~ **theory** *n* ECON théorie de l'organisation *f*, théorie organisationnelle *f*, GEN COMM théorie organisationnelle *f*, MGMNT théorie de l'organisation *f*, théorie organisationnelle *f*; ~ **woman** *n* MGMNT dévouée *f*

Organization: ~ **of African Unity** *n* (*OAU*) ECON Organisation de l'unité africaine *f* (*OUA*); ~ **of American States** *n* (*OAS*) ECON, WEL Organisation des états américains *f*; ~ **of Central American States** *n* (*OCAS*) ECON, POL Organisation des États de l'Amérique Centrale; ~ **for Economic Cooperation and Development** *n* (*OECD*) ECON Organisation de coopération et de développement économique *f* (*OCDE*); ~ **for European Economic Cooperation** *n* (*OEEC*) ECON Organisation européenne de coopération économique *f* (*OECE*); ~ **for International Exhibitions** *n* ADMIN Bureau international des expositions *m*; ~ **for Trade Cooperation** *n* (*OTC*) ECON *international* Organisation pour la coopération commerciale *f*; ~ **of Petroleum Exporting Countries** *n* (*OPEC*) ECON, ENVIR, POL Organisation des pays exportateurs de pétrole *f* (*OPEP*)

organizational: ~ **behavior** *n AmE*, ~ **behaviour** *n BrE* HRM, MGMNT, S&M comportement de l'homme dans l'organisation *m*; ~ **change** *n* MGMNT mutation des structures *f*; ~ **chart** *n* MGMNT organigramme *m*; ~ **convenience** *n* GEN COMM facilité d'organisation *f*; ~ **development** *n* MGMNT développement organisationnel *m*; ~ **economics** *n* ECON économie organisationnelle *f*; ~ **effectiveness** *n* MGMNT efficacité organisatrice *f*; ~ **pathology** *n* HRM, MGMNT mal des organisations *m*; ~ **politics** *n pl* POL politique des organisations *f*; ~ **psychology** *n* MGMNT psychologie d'organisation *f*; ~ **shape** *n* GEN COMM forme organisationnelle *f*; ~ **size** *n* GEN COMM taille d'une organisation *f*; ~ **symbol** *n* GEN COMM logo *m*; ~ **theory** *n* ECON, GEN COMM, MGMNT théorie organisationnelle *f*; ~ **unit** *n* ADMIN, MGMNT division administrative *f*

organize *vt* GEN COMM organiser, HRM *workers* syndiquer

organized: ~ **crime** *n* LAW crime organisé *m*; ~ **labor** *n AmE*, ~ **labour** *n BrE* HRM main-d'oeuvre syndiquée *f*; ~ **markets** *n pl* ECON, GEN COMM, S&M marchés organisés *m pl*

orientation *n* GEN COMM *for newcomer* période d'accueil *f*, POL orientation *f*

origin *n* IND, S&M provenance *f*; ~ **and destination study** S&M *market research* étude de la provenance et de la destination *f*

original[1] *adj* COMP, GEN COMM original

original[2] *n* ADMIN, COMP, GEN COMM original *m*; ~ **address** COMMS adresse d'origine *f*; ~ **assessment** TAX cotisation originale *f*, évaluation d'origine *f*; ~ **bid** GEN COMM offre originale *f*; ~ **capital** FIN capital d'origine *m*; ~ **cost** ACC *public utilities* frais d'achat *m pl*, prix initial *m*; ~ **device** GEN COMM procédé original *m*; ~ **document** ADMIN, COMP, GEN COMM original *m*; ~ **entry** ACC *bookkeeping* écriture originale *f*; ~ **invoice** ACC, GEN COMM facture originale *f*; ~ **issue discount** (*OID*) FIN, STOCK escompte de première émission *m*, prime d'émission *f*; ~ **issue discount bond** (*OID bond*) FIN, STOCK obligation vendue au-dessous du pair à l'émission *f*; ~ **margin** STOCK marge de départ *f*, marge initiale *f*; ~ **maturity** STOCK durée de crédit initiale *f*; ~ **order** S&M première commande *f*; ~ **owner** GEN COMM propriétaire d'origine *m*, propriétaire obligé *m*, TAX *of car* propriétaire d'origine *m*, propriétaire initial *m*, propriétaire obligé *m*; ~ **slip** INS fiche initiale de souscription *f*

originate: ~ **from** *vt* GEN COMM venir de

originating: ~ **document** *n* TAX acte introductif d'instance *m*, document originaire *m*

originator *n* BANK initiateur *m*

orlop *n* TRANSP faux-pont *m*

orphan *n* MEDIA *printing* isolation en bas de page *f*, orphelin *m*

o.s. *abbr* COMP (*operation system*) système d'exploitation *m*, ECON (*out of stock*) épuisé, GEN COMM (*out of stock*) en rupture de stock *loc f*, épuisé, S&M (*out of stock*) en rupture de stock *loc f*, manque en magasin *m*, épuisé

OSD *abbr* (*open-shelter deck*) TRANSP *shipping* navire à pont-abri ouvert *m*

OSI *abbr* (*open-systems interconnection*) COMP ISO (*interconnexion de systèmes ouverts*)

Oslo *pr n* GEN COMM Oslo *n pr*

ost *abbr* (*ordinary spring tide*) TRANSP marée de VE *f* (*marée de vive-eau*)

ot *abbr* (*on track*) TRANSP en voie *loc f*

OT *abbr* HRM (*overtime*) heures supp' *f pl* (*infrml*), HS (*heures supplémentaires*), TRANSP (*open-top container, open-topped container*) conteneur à toit ouvert *m*, TRANSP (*oiltight*) *shipping* étanche au pétrole, étanche aux hydrocarbures

OTAR *abbr* (*overseas tariff and regulations*) IMP/EXP tarif et réglementations extérieurs *loc m*

OTC[1] *abbr* ECON (*Organization for Trade Cooperation*) *international* Organisation pour la coopération commerciale *f*, STOCK *US* (*over-the-counter*) hors cote, titre de hors-cote *m*, WEL (*over-the-counter*) *medication* sans ordonnance

OTC[2] ~ **market** *n US* ECON, STOCK marché de gré à gré *m*, marché hors cote *m*; ~ **option** *n US* STOCK option négociée de gré à gré *f*, option négociée hors Bourse *f*, option négociée hors cote *f*

OTCM *abbr US (over-the-counter market)* ECON, STOCK marché de gré à gré *m*, marché hors cote *m*

OTH *abbr (opportunities to hear)* MEDIA, S&M *advertising, radio* occasions d'entendre *f pl*

other[1] *adj* GEN COMM autre; ◆ **in ~ respects** GEN COMM à d'autres égards; **~ things being equal** ECON toutes choses étant égales par ailleurs, GEN COMM toutes choses égales, toutes choses étant égales

other:[2] **~ assets** *n pl* ACC, BANK, FIN autres éléments d'actif *m pl*; **~ beneficiary** *n* FIN *profit sharing plan* autre bénéficiaire *m*; **~ checkable deposits** *n (OCD)* BANK autres dépôts vérifiables *m pl*; **~ income** *n* ACC, TAX, WEL autre revenu *m*, autres produits *m pl*, produits divers *m pl*; **~ insurance clause** *n* INS clause de pluralité d'assurance *f*; **~ liabilities** *n pl* ACC, BANK, FIN autres dettes *f pl*; **~ peoples' money** *n (OPM)* FIN vente fictive d'obligations *f*, STOCK fonds empruntés *m pl*; **~ receivables** *n pl* ACC, BANK, FIN *assets* autres comptes financiers *m pl*

otherwise *adv* GEN COMM par ailleurs; ◆ **not ~ provided** *(nop)* GEN COMM non-fourni par ailleurs, non-prévu par ailleurs; **not ~ specified** GEN COMM non-spécifié par ailleurs; **unless ~ agreed** GEN COMM sauf avis contraire, sauf stipulation contraire; **unless ~ provided** *(SYN except as otherwise provided)* TAX sauf disposition contraire; **unless ~ required** GEN COMM sauf indication contraire; **unless ~ specified** GEN COMM sauf stipulation contraire

OTM *abbr (out-of-the-money)* STOCK en dehors, hors du cours, hors-jeu

OTS *abbr* ECON UK *(Overseas Trade Statistics)* Statistiques du commerce extérieur *f pl*, MEDIA *(opportunities to see) advertising, television* occasions de voir *f pl*, POL UK *(Overseas Trade Statistics)* Statistiques du commerce extérieur *f pl*, S&M *(opportunities to see) advertising, television* occasions de voir *f pl*

Ottawa *pr n* GEN COMM Ottawa *n pr*

Ouagadougou *pr n* GEN COMM Ouagadougou *n pr*

Ouguiya *n* GEN COMM ouguiya *m*

ounce *n (oz)* GEN COMM once *f*

our:[1] **~ ref.** *abbr (our reference)* GEN COMM n/réf *(notre référence)*, nos rf. *(nos référence)*

our:[2] **~ own make** *n* S&M notre propre marque *f*; **~ reference** *n (our ref.)* GEN COMM nos références *f pl*, notre référence *f (n/réf)*

oust *vt* HRM *from job* évincer

out: **~ of** *prep* GEN COMM hors de

outbid *vt* FIN, GEN COMM enchérir sur, S&M *auction* enchérir sur, surenchérir

outboard[1] *adj (O)* TRANSP hors-bord

outboard[2] *n* TRANSP hors-bord *m*

outcome *n* GEN COMM résultat *m*

outcry *n* GEN COMM protestation *f*; **~ market** STOCK marché de vente à la criée *m*

outdated *adj* S&M *idea, product* démodé

outfall: **~ pipe** *n* ENVIR déversoir d'égout *m*; **~ sewer** *n* ENVIR déversoir d'égout *m*

outflow *n (ANT inflow)* ACC, BANK, ECON, FIN, GEN COMM sortie *f*; **~ of funds** *(ANT inflow of funds)* ACC, BANK, ECON, FIN, GEN COMM sortie de fonds *f*

outgoing: **~ call** *n* COMMS appel de départ *m*; **~ mail** *n* COMMS courrier au départ *m*, courrier en partance *m*, courrier à expédier *m*

outgoings *n pl* ACC, BANK, FIN débours *m*

outlaw *vt* LAW déclarer illégal, interdire, proscrire

outlay *n* ACC, ECON dépenses d'investissement *f pl*, mise de fonds initiale *f*, FIN dépenses d'investissement *f pl*, mise de fonds initiale *f*, mise *f*, GEN COMM, IND dépenses d'investissement *f pl*, mise de fonds initiale *f*; **~ creep** *jarg* ACC, ADMIN, FIN dérapage *m*

outlays: **~ or expenses** *n pl* ACC débours ou dépenses *m pl*

outlet *n* ENVIR *for dangerous waste* débouché *m*, S&M débouché *m*, point de vente *m*; **~ store** S&M point de vente *m*

outlier *n* MATH *statistics* marginal *m*

outline[1] *n* GEN COMM aperçu *m*, profil *m*, schéma *m*

outline[2] *vt* GEN COMM mettre en relief, souligner

outlook *n* ECON, GEN COMM perspective *f*; **~ of the world** GEN COMM vision du monde *f*

out-of-charge: **~ note** *n* IMP/EXP bordereau de sortie de frais *m*

out-of-court: **~ settlement** *n* LAW règlement à l'amiable *m*

out-of-favor *AmE*, **out-of-favour** *BrE*: **~ stock** *n* FIN, IND, STOCK titre boudé *m*

out-of-state: **~ corporation** *n* GEN COMM, LAW société non-résidente *f*, société étrangère *f*

out-of-the-money[1] *adj (OTM, ANT in-the-money)* STOCK en dehors, hors du cours, hors-jeu

out-of-the-money:[2] **~ call** *n (ANT out-of-the-money put)* STOCK option d'achat en dehors *f*, option d'achat hors du cours *f*; **~ option** *n (ANT in-the-money option)* STOCK option en dehors *f*, option hors du cours *f*, option hors la monnaie *f*, option out-of-the-money *f*; **~ put** *n (ANT out-of-the-money call)* STOCK option de vente en dehors *f*, option de vente hors du cours *f*

out-of-town: **~ center** *n AmE*, **~ centre** *n BrE* GEN COMM, S&M centre commercial suburbain *m*; **~ store** *n* S&M magasin en dehors de la ville *m*

outpace *vt* ECON, GEN COMM, IND dépasser

outperform *vt* ECON l'emporter sur; ◆ **~ the market** STOCK faire mieux que le marché

outperformance *n* STOCK performance supérieure *f*

outplacement *n* GEN COMM, HRM décrutement *m*, essaimage *m*, outplacement *m*, reclassement *m*; **~ agency** HRM cabinet de placement *m*, cabinet de placement en dehors de l'entreprise *m*

output[1] *n* ACC production *f*, COMP résultat *m*, sortie *f*, ECON chiffre d'affaires *m (CA)*, output *m*, production *f*, productivité *f*, rendement *m*, résultat de sortie *m*, GEN COMM productivité *f*, HRM rendement *m*, IND production *f*, productivité *f*, rendement *m*; **~ bonus** *n* HRM, IND prime de rendement *f*; **~ budgeting** *n* ACC *governmental*, FIN, HRM, MGMNT rationalisation des choix budgétaires *f*; **~ data** *n pl* COMP données de sortie *f pl*; **~ device** *n* COMP périphérique de sortie *m*; **~ file** *n* COMP fichier de sortie *m*, fichier résultant *m*; **~ per head** *n* HRM, IND rendement par ouvrier *m*; **~ per hour** *n* HRM, IND rendement horaire *m*; **~ tax** *n* TAX impôt de sortie *m*; **~ variance** *n* MATH *statistics* variance des sorties *f*; **~ volume** *n* GEN COMM, IND volume de production *m*

output[2] *vt* COMP *data, text* sortir

outright: **~ forward purchase** *n* ECON *international trade* achat à terme *m*; **~ gift** *n* TAX don net *m*; **~ loss** *n* FIN, GEN COMM perte sèche *f*; **~ ownership** *n* PROP propriété absolue *f*

outset: **at the ~** *phr* GEN COMM dès le départ *loc m*

outside: **~ director** *n* HRM, MGMNT administrateur externe *m*; **~ finance** *n* ECON, FIN finance globale *f*; **~ lag** *n* POL retard extérieur *m*; **~ money** *n* ECON, FIN monnaie externe *f*; ◆ **it is ~ my remit** GEN COMM ce n'est pas dans mes attributions; **~ the reference of** GEN COMM, LAW hors de la compétence de

outsider *n* GEN COMM personne extérieure *f*; **~ broker** STOCK courtier non membre *m*; **~ wage setting** (ANT *insider wage setting*) ECON, HRM fixation des salaires par une personne extérieure *f*

outsourcing *n* MGMNT approvisionnement à l'extérieur *m*

outstanding[1] *adj* ACC *debt, amount, obligation* arriéré, impayé, à rembourser, GEN COMM arriéré, en cours *loc m*, *objection, appeal* en instance, HRM *objection, appeal* en instance, STOCK en circulation *loc f*, en cours *loc m*

outstanding[2] *n* ACC, BANK encours *m*; **~ advance** *n* ACC avance en cours *f*; **~ balance** *n* ACC solde impayé *m*; **~ capital stock** *n* STOCK nombre d'actions émises *m*; **~ check** *n* *AmE*, **~ cheque** *n* *BrE* BANK chèque en circulation *m*; **~ commitment** *n* (SYN *undischarged commitment*) ACC engagement en cours *m*; **~ credit** *n* ACC crédits en cours *m pl*, encours de crédit *m*; **~ debt** *n* ACC créance à recouvrer *f*, dette active *f*, encours de la dette *m*; **~ entry** *n* ACC écriture non-réglée *f*; **~ item** *n* ACC effet en circulation *m*; **~ loan** *n* BANK prêt impayé *m*, prêt non-remboursé *m*; **~ loans** *n pl* BANK encours de prêts *m pl*, prêts en cours *m pl*; **~ matters** *n pl* GEN COMM questions en suspens *f pl*; **~ mortgage loans** *n pl* BANK encours des prêts hypothécaires *m*, prêts hypothécaires en cours *m pl*; **~ order** *n* GEN COMM, S&M commande en attente *f*; **~ principal balance** *n* ACC solde à payer du principal *m*; **~ shares** *n pl* STOCK actions en circulation *f pl*; **the ~ amount** *n* GEN COMM le restant de la somme *m*

outvote *vt* GEN COMM obtenir une majorité sur

outvoted: **be ~** *phr* GEN COMM être mis en minorité

outward:[1] **~ -looking** *adj* GEN COMM *approach* ouvert sur l'extérieur

outward:[2] **~ cargo** *n* IMP/EXP, TRANSP cargaison d'aller *f*, chargement d'aller *m*; **~ freight department** *n* IMP/EXP, TRANSP service du fret de sortie *m*; **~ mission** *n* IMP/EXP, TRANSP mission à l'étranger *f*, visite à l'étranger *f*; **~ payment** *n* (ANT *inward payment*) ACC, BANK, FIN décaissement *m*; **~ voyage** *n* (SYN *homeward voyage*) TRANSP voyage d'aller *m*

outweigh *vt* GEN COMM prévaloir sur

outwork *n* ECON, HRM travail à domicile *m*

over[1] *abbr* FIN en excès *loc m*

over:[2] **~ age 55 home sale exemption** *phr* US TAX exonération sur vente de domiciles aux plus de 55 ans; **~ the last decade** *phr* GEN COMM depuis les dix dernières années; **~ the last year or so** *phr* GEN COMM depuis un an environ; **~ one year** *phr* GEN COMM sur un an; **~ a period of time** *phr* GEN COMM au cours d'une certaine période; **~ the telephone** *phr* COMMS *talks, negotiations* au téléphone

overaccumulation *n* ECON suraccumulation *f*

overachiever *n* (ANT *underachiever*) WEL surdoué *m*

overage *n* GEN COMM surplus *m*, PROP excédent *m*

overall[1] *adj* (*ola*) GEN COMM global, total

overall[2] *adv* GEN COMM globalement

overall:[3] **~ company objectives** *n pl* GEN COMM objectifs globaux de l'entreprise *m pl*; **~ expenses method** *n* ACC méthode des coûts moyens *f*, méthode des coûts moyens annuels *f*, méthode des dépenses globales *f*; **~ length** *n* TRANSP longueur hors tout *f*, longueur totale *f*; **~ market price coverage** *n* STOCK cours du marché *m*, couverture générale du prix du marché *f*; **~ rate of return** *n* ACC taux de rentabilité *m*; **~ width** *n* TRANSP largeur totale *f*

overaward: **~ payment** *n* *Australia* HRM paiement sur décision de justice *m*

overbooked *adj* LEIS *hotels*, TRANSP *flights* surbooké

overbooking *n* LEIS *of hotel*, TRANSP *of flight* surréservation *f*

overbought *adj* STOCK suracheté

overcapacity *n* (ANT *undercapacity*) ECON, GEN COMM, IND surcapacité *f*

overcapitalized *adj* (ANT *undercapitalized*) GEN COMM, IND sur-capitalisé

overcentre: **~ tensioner** *n* TRANSP *lashing* tendeur à détente brusque *m*

overcharge *n* (*OC*) GEN COMM, S&M majoration *f*, surcharge *f*

overcommitment *n* FIN engagement excédentaire *m*

overcompensation *n* HRM excès d'indemnisation *m*

overdependence *n* GEN COMM surdépendance *f*

overdiversification n STOCK diversification excessive f

overdraft n BANK découvert m, découvert bancaire m, FIN découvert m; ~ **facility** ACC facilité de caisse f, BANK autorisation de découvert f, facilité de caisse f, facilité de paiement f, FIN facilité de caisse f; ~ **lending** BANK prêts par découvert m pl; ~ **protection** BANK autorisation de découvert f

overdraw vt BANK tirer à découvert; ♦ ~ **an account** BANK mettre un compte à découvert

overdrawn adj (O/D) BANK account à découvert loc m

overdrive n TRANSP surmultiplication f

overdue[1] adj ACC arriéré, en souffrance, échu, GEN COMM arriéré

overdue:[2] ~ **payment** n FIN arriéré m

overemployment n (ANT underemployment) ECON, GEN COMM, HRM suremploi m

overestimate vt FIN surestimer

overexploitation n ENVIR, IND surexploitation f

overextended adj ECON, GEN COMM ayant pris des engagements au-dessus de ses moyens

overfunding n ECON surconsolidation f

overgrazing n ENVIR surpâturage m

overhang n STOCK excédent m, reliquat m

overhaul[1] n IND, MGMNT of system, TRANSP remise en état f, révision f

overhaul[2] vt IND, TRANSP revoir

overhead: ~ **charge** n FIN, GEN COMM frais généraux m pl; ~ **charges** n pl ACC frais généraux m pl, FG; ~ **projector** n GEN COMM, MGMNT rétroprojecteur m; ~ **transparency** n GEN COMM transparent m, MGMNT overhead projector acétat m, transparent m

overheads n pl ACC frais généraux m pl, FG, FIN, GEN COMM frais généraux m pl; ~ **recovery** n ACC, FIN couverture des frais généraux f

overheated:[1] ~ **economy** n ECON économie en surchauffe f

overheated:[2] **be** ~ vi ECON être surchauffé

overheating n ECON surchauffe f

overheight: ~ **cargo** n TRANSP in open-top container chargement trop élevé m

overimprovement n PROP suramélioration f

overindebtedness n BANK surendettement m

overinsured adj INS surassuré m

overissue n BANK surémission f, émission excédentaire f

overland: ~ **transport** n TRANSP transport terrestre m

overlapping: ~ **generations model** n (OLG) ECON théorème d'équivalence de Ricardo m

overlay n ADMIN guide transparent m

overlearning n WEL surapprentissage m

overman vt HRM suréquiper en personnel

overmanned adj HRM ayant un excédent de main-d'oeuvre loc m

overmanning n HRM excédent de main-d'oeuvre m,

sureffectif m, surplus de main-d'oeuvre m, staff surplus de personnel m

overnight[1] adj GEN COMM d'une nuit, de nuit

overnight[2] adv GEN COMM de nuit

overnight:[3] ~ **deposit** n BANK dépôt de nuit m; ~ **funds** n pl BANK same-day money fonds du jour au lendemain m pl; ~ **money** n BANK, FIN argent au jour le jour m; ~ **repurchase** n STOCK faculté de rachat au jour le jour f, mise en pension du jour au lendemain f; ~ **security** n STOCK titre du jour au lendemain m, valeur en solde en fin de journée f; ~ **travel** n LEIS, TRANSP voyages de nuit m pl

overpaid[1] adj HRM trop bien payé

overpaid:[2] ~ **entry certificate** n (OEC) IMP/EXP certificat d'entrée trop perçue m

overpayment n ACC, FIN paiement en trop m, surpaiement m

overpivot: ~ **area** n TRANSP aviation tarif au kilo excédant le poids pivot m; ~ **weight** n TRANSP aviation excédent au poids pivot m

overplacing n BANK placement excessif m

overprice vt (ANT underprice) S&M mettre un prix trop élevé à

overpriced adj (ANT underpriced) GEN COMM trop cher, S&M surtarifé

overproduce vt (ANT underproduce) ECON, IND surproduire

overproduction n (ANT underproduction) ECON, IND surproduction f

overprovision n ECON surfourniture f

overrepresent vt (ANT underrepresent) S&M sur-représenter

overrepresentation n (ANT underrepresentation) S&M sur-représentation f

override[1] n HRM honoraires dérogatoires m pl

override[2] vt GEN COMM annuler, outrepasser, passer outre, POL passer outre

overriding[1] adj GEN COMM trend, factor, consideration dérogatoire

overriding:[2] ~ **commission** n INS underwriting supercommission f, surcommission f; ~ **interest** n GEN COMM droit dérogatoire m

overrule vt MGMNT, POL decision annuler, rejeter

overruling n MGMNT, POL annulation f

overrun n ECON dépassement m, IND production excédent de production m

overseas[1] adj GEN COMM étranger, à l'étranger loc m

overseas:[2] ~ **agent** n GEN COMM agent à l'étranger m, représentant à l'étranger m; ~ **aid** n ECON, POL aide extérieure f; ~ **assets** n pl ECON, POL actif détenu à l'étranger m, avoirs extérieurs m pl; ~ **branch** n IMP/EXP direct trading succursale à l'étranger f; ~ **customer** n IMP/EXP, S&M client d'outre-mer m, client étranger m; ~ **department** n GEN COMM of France département d'Outre-Mer m, DOM; ~ **employment tax credit** n TAX crédit d'impôt de travail à l'étranger m, crédit d'impôt pour emploi à l'étranger *m*; **~ government** *n* POL gouvernement étranger *m*; **~ investment cover** *n* INS couverture des investissements extérieurs *f*; **~ investor** *n* FIN investisseur étranger *m*; **~ market** *n* ECON, S&M marché extérieur *m*, marché étranger *m*; **~ project fund** *n* ECON *international trade* Fonds d'aide aux projets à l'exportation *m*; **~ status report** *n* IMP/EXP rapport sur l'état des marchés étrangers *m*; **~ tariff and regulations** *n* *(OTAR)* IMP/EXP tarif et réglementations extérieurs *loc m*; **~ tariff regulations** *n pl* IMP/EXP réglementation du tarif extérieur *f*; **~ tourism** *n* GEN COMM, LEIS tourisme étranger *m*; **~ tourist** *n* GEN COMM, LEIS touriste étranger *m*; **~ trade fairs and seminars** *n pl* IMP/EXP salons professionnels et séminaires à l'étranger *m pl*; **~ visitor** *n* ADMIN, GEN COMM visiteur étranger *m*

Overseas: ~ Development Administration *n* *UK (ODA)* ECON, POL ≈ Organisme du développement outre-mer *m*; **~ Development Institute** *n* *UK (ODI)* ECON, POL *international* ≈ Institut du développement outre-mer *m*; **~ Economic Cooperation Fund** *n* *(OECF)* ECON fonds de coopération économique avec l'étranger; **~ Trade Statistics** *n pl* *UK (OTS)* ECON, POL Statistiques du commerce extérieur *f pl*

oversee *vt* GEN COMM contrôler

overseer *n* HRM chef d'équipe *m*, contremaître *m*

overshoot *vt* GEN COMM dépasser

overshooting: ~ price *n* ECON prix excessif *m*

overside: ~ discharge *n* TRANSP déchargement sous palan *m*, déchargement sur allèges *m*; **~ loading** *n* TRANSP *shipping* chargement par allèges *m*, chargement sous palan *m*

oversold *adj* STOCK survendu

overspend *n* ACC dépense en trop *f*, dépense excessive *f*

overspending *n* FIN dépassement de budget *m*

overspill: ~ town *n* GEN COMM ville satellite *f*

overstaff *vt* HRM suréquiper en personnel

overstaffed *adj* HRM en sureffectifs, qui souffre d'un surplus de personnel *loc m*, à effectif pléthorique *loc m*

overstaffing *n* HRM personnel pléthorique *m*, personnel trop nombreux *m*, surabondance de personnel *f*, sureffectif *m*

overstep *vt* GEN COMM *difficulty* franchir

overstimulated: be ~ *vi* ECON être suractivé, être surchauffé

overstretch *vt* MGMNT donner un surcroît de travail à *loc m*

overstuffing *n* TRANSP surremplissage *m*

oversubscribed *adj* STOCK sursouscrit

oversubscription *n* STOCK *of shares* dépassement de souscription *m*, souscription excédentaire *f*, souscription surpassée *f*

oversupply *n* ECON pléthore de l'offre *f*, surabondance de l'offre *f*

overtax *n* TAX impôt excessif *m*, surcharge *f*, surimposition *f*, surtaxe *f*

overtaxation *n* *(*SYN *excessive taxation)* TAX fiscalité excessive *f*

over-the-counter[1] *adj* *(OTC)* STOCK *US* hors cote, titre de hors-cote *m*, WEL *medication* sans ordonnance

over-the-counter:[2] **~ derivative instrument** *n* *US* FIN, STOCK instrument dérivé hors bourse *m*; **~ market** *n* *US (OTCM)* ECON, STOCK marché de gré à gré *m*, marché hors cote *m*; **~ medicine** *n* S&M médicament grand-public *m*, médicament sans ordonnance *m*; **~ option** *n* *US* STOCK option négociée de gré à gré *f*, option négociée hors Bourse *f*, option négociée hors cote *f*; **~ retailing** *n* S&M commerce traditionnel *m*; **~ trading** *n* *US* FIN opérations sur le marché hors cote *f pl*

overtime *n* *(OT)* HRM heures supplémentaires *f pl (heures supp')*; **~ ban** *n* HRM refus d'effectuer des heures supplémentaires *m (frml)*, refus des heures supplémentaires *m*; **~ hours** *n pl* HRM heures supplémentaires *f pl*; **~ pay** *n* HRM rémunération des heures supplémentaires *f*; **~ premium** *n* HRM prime d'heures supplémentaires *f*

overtonnaging *n* TRANSP *shipping* surcapacité de cales *f*

overtrading *n* ECON mauvaise maîtrise de son activité commerciale, STOCK dépassement d'opérations financières *m*, transactions excessives *f pl*

overturn *vi* TRANSP chavirer

overurbanization *n* ECON excès d'urbanisation *m*, urbanisation excessive *f*

overuse *n* ENVIR *of chemicals* abus *m*, utilisation excessive *f*, GEN COMM utilisation excessive *f*

overvaluation *n* ACC, ECON, STOCK surévaluation *f*

overvalue *vt* ACC, ECON, STOCK surévaluer

overvalued[1] *adj* ACC, ECON, STOCK surévalué

overvalued:[2] **~ currency** *n* ECON devise surévaluée *f*, monnaie surévaluée *f*

overview *n* GEN COMM aperçu *m*, généralités *f pl*

overwhelm *vt* GEN COMM accabler

overwriting *n* STOCK sous-estimation *f*

owe *vt* GEN COMM devoir; ♦ **I ~ you** BANK, FIN, GEN COMM, TRANSP *(IOU)* reconnaissance de dette *f*; **~ sth to sb** GEN COMM devoir qch à qn

own[1] *adj* GEN COMM propre

own:[2] **~ brand** *n* S&M marque de distributeur *f*; **~ rate of interest** *n* ECON taux d'intérêt propre *m*; **~ resource** *n* ECON, ENVIR, POL ressource propre *f*; **~ shares** *n pl* *BrE (cf treasury stock AmE)* ACC actions rachetées par la société *f pl*

owner *n* GEN COMM propriétaire *mf*, PATENTS titulaire *mf*, PROP propriétaire *mf*, TRANSP *shipping, P&I club membership terms* armateur *m*; **~ -manager** HRM, MGMNT propriétaire-gérant *m*; **~ occupation** PROP occupation par le propriétaire *f*; **~ -occupied farmland** PROP terre agricole occupée par le propriétaire *f*; **~ -occupied home** TAX logement de type propriétaire-occupant *m*, logement occupé par le propriétaire *m*; ~ -**occupier** PROP propriétaire-occupant *m*; ~ -**operator** GEN COMM propriétaire-exploitant *m*; ~'**s broker** TRANSP *shipping* courtier de l'armateur *m*; ◆ **at** ~'**s risk** GEN COMM aux risques et périls du propriétaire, INS aux risques du propriétaire; ~'**s risk** *(OR)* INS, TRANSP *shipping* aux risques et périls du freteur

owners': ~ **and contractors' protective liability insurance** *n* INS assurance responsabilité civile indirecte des propriétaires et entrepreneurs *f*; ~ **landlords' and tenants' liability policy** *n* INS

company police de la responsabilité civile des propriétaires et des locataires *f*

ownership *n* GEN COMM possession *f*, PROP propriété *f*; ~ **form** *n US* LAW, PROP forme de propriété *f*; ~ **rights under life insurance** *n pl* INS *personal* droits de propriété garantis par assurance vie *m pl*; ◆ **come under public** ~ ECON être nationalisé

oz *abbr (ounce)* GEN COMM once *f*

ozone: ~ **depletion** *n* ENVIR diminution de l'ozone *f*, raréfaction de l'ozone *f*; ~ **layer** *n* ENVIR couche d'ozone *f*

P

p *abbr (pence)* GEN COMM pence *m*; **~ to p** *(port to port)* IMP/EXP, TRANSP *shipping* port à port *loc m*

p.a. *abbr* GEN COMM *(per annum)* p.a. *(par an)*, INS *(particular average)* marine avarie particulière *f*, avarie partielle *f*

PA[1] *abbr* ADMIN *(power of attorney)* procuration *f*, HRM *(personal assistant)* assistant personnel *m*, secrétaire de direction *m*, secrétaire particulier *m*, LAW *(power of attorney)* procuration *f*, MGMNT *(personal assistant)* assistant personnel *m*, secrétaire de direction *m*, secrétaire particulier *m*

PA:[2] **~ system** *n (public address system)* COMMS système de sonorisation *m*

pa'anga *n* GEN COMM pa'anga *m*

Paasche: ~ index *n* ECON *econometrics* indice de Paasche *m*

PABX *abbr UK (private automatic branch exchange)* COMMS *telephone* autocommutateur privé *m*

pace *n* GEN COMM *of trend* rythme *m*; **~ of change** GEN COMM rapidité de changement *f*; ◆ **keep ~ with** GEN COMM se maintenir au même niveau que; **set the ~** GEN COMM donner le pas

pacesetter *n* GEN COMM *company* société leader *f*

pacify *vt* GEN COMM, HRM, POL apaiser

pack[1] *n* GEN COMM paquet *m*; **~ shot** S&M *advertising* plan-paquet *m*

pack[2] *vt* COMP *data* comprimer; **~ up** GEN COMM, S&M, TRANSP emballer

package *n (pkg)* COMMS colis *m*, paquet *m*, COMP progiciel *m*, FIN *of grants, incentives*, MGMNT *of deals, proposals*, POL *of reforms* ensemble *m*, S&M *advertising, direct mail* paquet promotionnel *m*; **~ code** *n* S&M code emballage *m*; **~ deal** *n* ECON, GEN COMM, HRM contrat global *m*, LEIS contrat global *m*, forfait *m*, panier *m*, TRANSP contrat global *m*; **~ design** *n* S&M *advertising, direct mail* conception d'un paquet promotionnel *f*, conception de l'emballage *f*; **~ goods** *n pl* TRANSP marchandises emballées *f pl*; **~ holiday** *n BrE (cf package tour, package vacation AmE)* LEIS forfait *m*, voyage organisé *m*; **~ mortgage** *n* FIN prêt global *m*; **~ operator** *n* LEIS, TRANSP organisateur de voyages *m*; **~ store** *n AmE (cf off-licence BrE)* S&M magasin de vins et de spiritueux qu'il est interdit de consommer sur place; **~ tour** *n BrE (cf package holiday, package vacation AmE)* LEIS forfait *m*, voyage organisé *m*; **~ tour operator** *n* LEIS, TRANSP organisateur de voyages *m*; **~ vacation** *n AmE (cf package holiday BrE, package tour BrE)* LEIS forfait *m*, voyage organisé *m*

packaged: ~ goods *n pl* S&M produits conditionnés

m pl; **~ software** *n* COMP logiciel prêt à l'emploi *m*; **~ timber** *n* TRANSP bois en lots *m*

packaging *n (pkg.)* GEN COMM emballage *m*, S&M conditionnement *m*, *set of items sold as one* lot *m*, TRANSP conditionnement *m*, emballage *m*; **~ certificate** *n* TRANSP *containers* certificat d'empotage *m*; **~ cost** *n* IND coût d'emballage *m*; **~ credit** *n* BANK crédit global *m*; **~ laws** *n pl* GEN COMM lois de l'arrivage *f pl*, LAW lois relatives à l'arrivage *f pl*; **~ list** *n* IMP/EXP, TRANSP bordereau de colisage *m*, liste de colisage *f*; **~ materials** *n pl* S&M *marketing* composants de conditionnement *m pl*

packer *n* GEN COMM emballeur *m*

packet *n* COMP groupe de bits *m*, paquet *m*, GEN COMM paquet *m*; **~ switching telephone network** GEN COMM réseau téléphonique de transmission de donnés par paquets *f*; **weekly pay ~** GEN COMM paie hebdomadaire *f*

packing *n* COMP compression *f*, GEN COMM emballage *m*, S&M, TRANSP conditionnement *m*, emballage *m*; **~ case** TRANSP caisse *f*; **~ density** COMP *of data* densité d'enregistrement *f*; **~ instruction** TRANSP instruction relative à l'emballage *f*, notice d'emballage *f*; **~ list** IMP/EXP, TRANSP bordereau de colisage *m*, liste de colisage *f*

Pac-Man: ~ defense *n US* STOCK *corporate mergers and acquisitions* contre-OPA *f*, contre-offre publique d'achat *f*, défense du Pac Man *f*; **~ strategy** *n US* FIN stratégie Pac-Man *f*

pad *n* COMP bloc *m*; **~ eye** TRANSP *lashing* piton à oeil *m*

padding *n* GEN COMM gonflement *m*

paddle *n* TRANSP *shipping* aube *f*, pale *f*; **~ steamer** *(PS)* TRANSP bateau à aubes *m*, propulseur de babord et de tribord *m*

page[1] *n (pg.)* COMP, GEN COMM page *f (p.)*; **~ break** COMP changement de page *m*; **~ depth** COMP hauteur de page *f*; **~ layout** MEDIA mise en page *f*; **~ length** COMP nombre de lignes par page *m*; **~ number** GEN COMM numéro de page *m*; **~ setting** MEDIA mise en page *f*; **~ traffic** *jarg UK* S&M *advertising* estimation du nombre de lecteurs d'une publication; **~ -turner** MEDIA best-seller *m*, succès de librairie *m*

page[2] *vt* COMMS *telecom* demander

paginate *vt* ADMIN, COMP paginer

pagination *n* ADMIN, COMP pagination *f*

paging *n* COMMS appel de personnes *m*; **~ device** COMMS dispositif de recherche de personne *m*

PAI *abbr (performance appraisal interview)* HRM entretien d'évaluation *m*, interview d'évaluation des performances *f*

paid[1] *adj (pd)* FIN *amount, dividend* acquitté, payé, versé, GEN COMM, HRM *person, work* payé, rémunéré; ♦ be ~ a rate of HRM percevoir un salaire horaire de; ~ by agent *(PBA)* TRANSP *shipping* réglé par l'agent; ~ by the hour HRM payé à l'heure; ~ by the piece HRM payé à la pièce; ~ hourly HRM payé à l'heure; ~ in advance GEN COMM payé d'avance, à valoir; ~ on delivery *(POD)* TRANSP paiement à la livraison, payé à la livraison; ~ piece rate HRM payé à la pièce; poorly ~ HRM mal payé

paid[2] ~ holiday *n BrE (cf paid leave, paid vacation AmE)* HRM congés payés *m pl*; ~ -in capital *n* STOCK capital d'apport *m*, capital versé *m*; ~ -in surplus *n AmE (cf share premium BrE)* ACC *balance sheets*, FIN, STOCK prime d'émission *f*; ~ instrument *n* FIN acquit *m*; ~ leave *n (cf paid holiday BrE, paid vacation AmE)* HRM congés payés *m pl*; ~ -out capital *n* FIN capital remboursé *m*; ~ -up addition *n* INS bonification d'assurance libérée *f*; ~ -up capital *n* FIN capital libéré *m*; ~ -up common share *n* STOCK action ordinaire entièrement libérée *f*; ~ -up member *n UK* HRM syndiqué à jour avec ses cotisations; ~ vacation *n AmE (cf paid holiday BrE, paid leave)* HRM congés payés *m pl*

pail *n* TRANSP seau *m*

painstaking *adj* GEN COMM méticuleux

painstakingly *adv* GEN COMM méticuleusement

paint: ~ the tape *phr jarg* STOCK multiplier les transactions fictives

paired: ~ comparisons *n pl* GEN COMM comparaisons croisées *f pl*; ~ shares *n pl* STOCK actions appariées *f pl*, actions en paire *f pl*

Pakistan *pr n* GEN COMM Pakistan *m*

Pakistani[1] *adj* GEN COMM pakistanais

Pakistani[2] *n* GEN COMM *person* Pakistanais *m*

PAL *abbr* FIN *(program adjustment loan AmE, programme adjustment loan BrE)* prêt-programme d'ajustement *m*, MEDIA *(phase alternation line) TV* PAL *m*

pallet *n* TRANSP palette *f*; ~ fork TRANSP *cargo handling* fourche à palettes *f*; ~ net TRANSP filet à palettes *m*; ~ truck TRANSP *cargo handling* chariot élévateur pour palettes *m*, transpalette *m*

palletizable *adj* TRANSP palettisable

palletization *n* TRANSP palettisation *f*

palletize *vt* TRANSP palettiser

palletized: ~ stowage *n* TRANSP arrimage sur palettes *m*

pamphlet *n* GEN COMM dépliant *m*

Pan: ~ American Standards Commission *n US (COPANT)* GEN COMM association panaméricaine de normalisation

Panama *pr n* GEN COMM Panama *m*; ~ City GEN COMM Panama City *n pr*

Panamanian[1] *adj* GEN COMM panaméen

Panamanian[2] *n* GEN COMM *person* Panaméen *m*

Panamax: ~ vessel *n* TRANSP *shipping* panamax *m*

Pan-American[1] *adj* GEN COMM panaméricain

Pan-American:[2] ~ Tracing and Reservations System *n (PANTRAC)* TRANSP *aviation* système pan-américain de tracement et des réservations *m*

P&I: ~ club *n (protection and indemnity club)* TRANSP club de protection et d'indemnisation mutuelle

P&L[1] *abbr (profit and loss)* ACC *annual accounts* P et P *(pertes et profits)*

P&L:[2] ~ account *n* ACC compte de pertes et profits *m*, comptes de résultats *m pl*

p&p *abbr (postage and packing)* COMMS frais de port et d'emballage *m pl*, port et emballage *m pl*

P&R *abbr (park and ride)* TRANSP P.R. *(parc relais)*

P&S *abbr (purchase and sale statement)* STOCK état des achats et des ventes *m*

panel *n* COMP panneau *m*, tableau *m*; ~ envelope ADMIN, COMMS, GEN COMM enveloppe à fenêtre *f*; ~ testing S&M *market research* test sur un panel *m*

Pan-European *adj* GEN COMM paneuropéen

panic:[1] ~ -stricken *adj* GEN COMM frappé de panique

panic:[2] ~ buying *n* GEN COMM achats de précaution *m pl*

panic[3] *vi* GEN COMM paniquer

PANTRAC *abbr (Pan-American Tracing and Reservations System)* TRANSP *aviation* système pan-américain de tracement et des réservations *m*

paper *n* ADMIN document *m*, papier *m*, FIN titre *m*, debt papier *m*, MEDIA *newspaper* jl, journal *m*, POL *government publication* livre *m*; ~ feed *n* COMP alimentation du papier *f*; ~ gold *n* BANK or-papier *m*; ~ industry *n* ENVIR, IND industrie du papier *f*, papeterie *f*; ~ loss *n* STOCK moins non réalisé sur titres *m*, moins sur titres *m*; ~ mill *n* ENVIR, IND fabrique de papier *f*, papeterie *f*, usine de papeterie *f*, usine à papier *f*; ~ millionaire *n* GEN COMM millionnaire en actions *m*; ~ money *n* BANK, FIN monnaie fiduciaire *f*; ~ profit *n* ACC profit non matérialisé *m*, FIN bénéfice non-réalisé *m*, bénéfice théorique *m*, profit non matérialisé *m*; ~ profit or loss *n* STOCK gain ou perte sur titres *loc m*, produit fictif ou moins-value *loc m*; ~ pulp *n* ENVIR pâte à papier *f*; ~ punch *n* GEN COMM perforation *f*; ~ qualifications *n pl* WEL titres *m pl*; ~ shredder *n* ADMIN *office equipment*, COMP déchiqueteuse *f*; ~ stacker *n* COMP récepteur de papier *m*; ~ tape *n* COMP bande de papier *f*, bande perforée *f*; ~ throw *n* COMP saut de papier *m*; ~ track *n* COMP chemin de papier *m*; ~ weight *n* COMP grammage *m*

paperback *n* MEDIA livre de poche *m*; ~ book MEDIA livre de poche *m*

paperless[1] *adj (SYN dematerialized)* STOCK *certificates of deposit* dématérialisé, sans papier

paperless:[2] ~ entry *n* BANK, COMP écriture informatique *f*; ~ trading *n* COMP transactions automatisées *f pl*, transactions informatisées *f pl*

paperwork *n* ADMIN paperasserie *f* (*infrml*), travail administratif *m*

Papua: **~ New Guinea** *pr n* GEN COMM Papouasie-Nouvelle-Guinée *f*

par *n* GEN COMM, STOCK pair *m*; **~ bond** STOCK obligation remboursable au pair *f*; **~ delivery** STOCK cession au pair *f*, livraison au pair *f*; **~ stock** STOCK action à valeur nominale *f*; **~ trading** STOCK opérations boursières au pair *f pl*, transaction au pair *f*; **~ value** (*p.v.*) STOCK parité *f*, valeur au pair *f*, valeur nominale *f*; **~ value of currency** STOCK valeur au pair d'une devise *f*; **~ value share** STOCK action à valeur nominale *f*; **~ value stock** STOCK action à valeur nominale *f*; ♦ **above ~** (ANT *below par*) ACC, GEN COMM, STOCK *price of bonds* au-dessus du pair; **at ~** BANK, GEN COMM au pair, à la valeur nominale; **below ~** (ANT *above par*) ACC, GEN COMM, STOCK au-dessous du pair

PAR *abbr* (*prescribed aggregate reserve*) BANK réserve globale visée par règlement *f*, RTP

paradox: **~ of thrift** *n* ECON paradoxe de l'épargne *m*; **~ of value** *n* ECON paradoxe de la valeur *m*; **~ of voting** *n* ECON paradoxe du vote *m*

paraffin: **~ wax** *n* IND cire de paraffine *f*, paraffine dure *f*

paragraph *n* ADMIN alinéa *m*, paragraphe *m*, LAW paragraphe *m*

Paraguay *pr n* GEN COMM Paraguay *m*

Paraguayan[1] *adj* GEN COMM paraguayen

Paraguayan[2] *n* GEN COMM *person* Paraguayen *m*

paralegal[1] *adj* LAW paralégal

paralegal[2] *n* LAW juriste *mf*

parallel[1] *adj* GEN COMM parallèle

parallel:[2] **~ access** *n* COMP accès en parallèle *m*; **~ currency** *n* ECON monnaie parallèle *f*; **~ currency strategy** *n* ECON stratégie de la monnaie parallèle *f*; **~ import** *n* IMP/EXP importation parallèle *f*; **~ interface** *n* COMP interface parallèle *f*; **~ loan** *n* BANK, ECON, FIN emprunt parallèle *m*, prêt parallèle *m*; **~ market economy** *n* ECON, POL économie de marché parallèle *f*; **~ plants** *n pl* IND usines parallèles *f pl*; **~ pricing** *n* ECON tarification parallèle *f*; **~ processing** *n* COMP *of tasks* traitement en parallèle *m*, traitement en simultanéité *m*; **~ standard** *n* GEN COMM double étalon *m*; **~ trading** *n* GEN COMM commerce parallèle *m*; ♦ **in ~** GEN COMM en parallèle; **in ~ with** GEN COMM en parallèle avec, parallèlement à

Paramaribo *pr n* GEN COMM Paramaribo *n pr*

parameter *n* COMP, GEN COMM, MATH *statistics* paramètre *m*; **~ -driven software** COMP logiciel paramétrable *m*, logiciel piloté par paramètres *m*

parameters: **set ~** *phr* MATH fixer les paramètres

parametric[1] *adj* COMP, MATH paramétrique

parametric:[2] **~ programming** *n* COMP, MATH programmation paramétrique *f*; **~ statistics** *n pl* MATH statistique paramétrique *f*

parasitic: **~ city** *n* ECON ville parasite *f*

parcel[1] *n* COMMS colis *m*, paquet *m*, PROP *of land* parcelle *f*, STOCK *of shares* paquet *m*; **~ post** COMMS service de colis postaux *m*, service de messageries *m*; **~ post insurance** COMMS, INS assurance des colis postaux *f*

parcel:[2] **~ out** *vt* LAW morceler, PROP morceler, parcelliser; **~ up** LAW, PROP morceler

parceling: **~ out** *n* AmE *see parcelling out BrE*; **~ up** *n* AmE *see parcelling up BrE*

parcelling: **~ out** *n* BrE PROP *of land* morcellement de terrain *m*; **~ up** *n* BrE PROP *of land* morcellement de terrain *m*

parcels: **~ awaiting delivery** *n pl* GEN COMM colis en instance de livraison *m pl*; **~ market** *n* COMMS, TRANSP marché des messageries *m*; **~ van** *n* TRANSP camion de messageries *m*

pardon: **I beg your ~** *phr* GEN COMM je vous demande pardon

parent *n* COMP père *m*, LAW parent *m*; **~ bank** *n* FIN banque mère *f*; **~ company** *n* GEN COMM société de holding *f*, société mère *f*; **~ company dividend** *n* ACC dividende de la société mère *m*; **~ corporation** *n* STOCK corporation mère *f*; **~ Crown corporation** *n* GEN COMM société d'État mère *f*; **~ dividends** *n pl* STOCK dividendes de la société mère *m pl*; **~ sailing** *n* TRANSP *shipping* départ principal *m*; **~ service** *n* TRANSP *shipping* service principal *m*

parental[1] *adj* GEN COMM parental

parental:[2] **~ leave** *n* HRM, WEL congé parental *m*

parenthesis *n* ADMIN parenthèse *f*

Pareto: **~ analysis** *n* GEN COMM analyse de Pareto *f*; **~ efficiency** *n* ECON efficience au sens de Pareto *f*, rendement de Pareto *m*; **~ improvement** *n* ECON optimum de Pareto *m*; **~ optimality** *n* ECON ophélimité *f*, optimalité de Pareto *f*; **~ optimum** *n* ECON optimum de Pareto *m*; **~'s law** *n* ECON *income distribution* loi de Pareto *f*

pari passu *phr frml* GEN COMM de pair avec *loc m*

Paris:[1] **~ financial futures market** *n* STOCK marché à terme d'instruments financiers de Paris *m*; **~ Interbank Offered Rate** *n* (*PIBOR*) BANK taux interbancaire offert à Paris *m* (*TIOP*); **the ~ Stock Exchange** STOCK la Bourse de Paris *f*

Paris[2] *pr n* GEN COMM Paris *n pr*

parity *n* COMP, ECON, FIN parité *f*, HRM parité *f*, égalité *f*, MATH parité *f*, STOCK pair *m*, WEL parité *f*; **~ bit** COMP bit de parité *m*; **~ bond** STOCK obligation émise au pair *f*; **~ check** COMP contrôle de parité *m*; **~ clause** INS clause de parité *f*; **~ of exchange** BANK parité de change *f*; **~ on rates** TRANSP parité des taux *f*; **~ price** GEN COMM *of commodity, service* prix au pair *m*; **~ pricing** ECON détermination des prix à parité *f*; **~ ratio** STOCK rapport de parité *m*

park: **~ and ride** *n* (*P&R*) TRANSP parc de dissuasion *m*, parc relais *m* (*P.R.*)

parking *n* STOCK mise en attente *f*, parking *m*; **~ lot** AmE (*cf car park BrE*) GEN COMM parc de stationnement *m*, parking *m*; **no ~ area** TRANSP zone de stationnement interdit *f*; **no ~ zone** TRANSP zone de stationnement interdit *f*

parliament *n* GEN COMM, POL parlement *m*

parliamentary[1] *adj* POL parlementaire

parliamentary:[2] **~ appropriation** *n* ACC, FIN crédit parlementaire *m*; **~ private secretary** *n* UK *(PPS)* POL parlementaire attaché à un ministre; **~ procedure** *n* MGMNT procédure parlementaire *f*; **~ vote** *n* ACC, FIN crédit parlementaire *m*

part *n* ADMIN partie *f*, GEN COMM proportion *f*; **~ -analysis training** GEN COMM, HRM formation par étapes *f*; **~ -cancellation** GEN COMM, LAW, PATENTS annulation partielle *f*; **~ exchange** GEN COMM reprise *f*; **~ load** TRANSP charge incomplète *f*, chargement partiel *m*, envoi de détail *m*; **~ ownership** PROP copropriété *f*; **~ payment** FIN paiement partiel *m*; **~ shipment** IMP/EXP, TRANSP expédition partielle *f*; ◆ **be ~ and parcel of sth** GEN COMM faire partie intégrante de qch; **for my ~** GEN COMM pour ma part; **in ~ payment** HRM en règlement partiel

partial[1] *adj* GEN COMM *biased* partial, *incomplete* partiel

partial:[2] **~ basis** *n* FIN base partielle *f*, *of bill* acceptation partielle *f*; **~ bulkhead** *n* *(PBH)* TRANSP *shipping* cloison partielle *f*; **~ consideration** *n* ACC paiement partiel *m*; **~ delivery** *n* STOCK livraison partielle *f*; **~ equilibrium** *n* ECON équilibre partiel *m*; **~ equilibrium analysis** *n* ECON *econometrics* analyse d'équilibre partiel *f*; **~ eviction** *n* PROP expulsion partielle *f*; **~ loss** *n* *(PL)* INS dommages partiels *m pl*, perte partielle *f*, sinistre partiel *m*; **~ provision basis** *n* ACC *for calculating deferred taxation* base de provision partielle *f*; **~ release** *n* LAW *property*, PROP décharge partielle *f*, libération partielle *f*; **~ taking** *n* LAW, PROP acquisition partielle *f*; **~ unemployment** *n* ECON, HRM chômage partiel *m*; **~ withdrawal** *n* STOCK retrait partiel *m*; **~ write-off** *n* ACC radiation partielle *f*

partially[1] *adv* GEN COMM partiellement; ◆ **~ knocked down** *(PKD)* TRANSP *consignment* partiellement déchargé

partially:[2] **~ -privatized company** *n* ECON société à économie mixte *f*, SEM

partial/total: **~ loss** *n* *(PTL)* INS perte partielle ou totale *f*

participant *n* STOCK *in a market* intervenant *m*, participant *m*

participate *vi* GEN COMM participer

participating[1] *adj* GEN COMM participant

participating:[2] **~ bond** *n* STOCK obligation participante *f*; **~ carrier** *n* TRANSP transporteur participant *m*; **~ insurance** *n* INS *personal* assurance avec participation aux bénéfices *f*; **~ interest** *n* STOCK intérêt de participation *m*, participation *f*; **~ policy** *n* INS police avec participation aux bénéfices *f*; **~ preference share** *n* STOCK action préférentielle *f*; **~ preferred stock** *n*

AmE STOCK action préférentielle *f*; **~ security** *n* STOCK titre de participation *m*, titre participatif *m*

participation *n* ACC, GEN COMM participation *f*; **~ agreement** LAW accord de participation *m*; **~ certificate** STOCK *dividends* certificat de participation *m*, titre de participation *m*; **~ fee** BANK commission de participation *f*; **~ loan** BANK, FIN crédit syndical *m*, prêt participant *m*; **~ rate** HRM taux de participation *m*

participative[1] *adj* MGMNT participatif

participative:[2] **~ management** *n* MGMNT direction participative *f*

particular[1] *adj* INS particulier; ◆ **with ~ average** *(WPA)* INS avec avaries particulières, avec avaries simples

particular:[2] **~ average** *n* *(p.a.)* INS *marine* avarie particulière *f*, avarie partielle *f*; **~ charge** *n* INS frais particuliers *m pl*

particulars: **~ of sale** *n pl* PROP description de la propriété à vendre *f*

partition *n* ADMIN *office equipment* cloison *f*, COMP partition *f*, LAW, PROP morcellement de terrain *m*, partage *m*

partly[1] *adv* GEN COMM partiellement; ◆ **~ paid** STOCK *shares* partiellement libéré

partly:[2] **~ -finished goods** *n pl* ECON, IND biens semi-finis *m pl*; **~ paid up shares** *n pl* STOCK actions non-entièrement libérées *f pl*, titres partiellement payés *m pl*

partner *n* ECON, GEN COMM associé *m*, partenaire *mf*

partnership *n* FIN société en nom collectif *f*, GEN COMM association *f*, société en nom collectif *f*, POL *between countries* partenariat *m*; **~ income** TAX revenu de société *m*; **~ life and health insurance** INS *company* assurance-vie et maladie appliquée aux affaires *f*

parts: **~ per million** *n pl* *(ppm)* GEN COMM partie par million *f* *(p.p.m.)*

part-time[1] *adj* GEN COMM, HRM à mi-temps, à temps partiel *loc adj*

part-time:[2] **~ employee** *n* GEN COMM, HRM employé à mi-temps *m*, employé à temps partiel *m*; **~ employment** *n* GEN COMM, HRM emploi à mi-temps *m*, emploi à temps partiel *m*, travail à mi-temps *m*, travail à temps partiel *m*; **~ job** *n* GEN COMM, HRM poste à temps partiel *m*; **~ work** *n* GEN COMM, HRM travail à mi-temps *m*, travail à temps partiel *m*; **~ worker** *n* GEN COMM, HRM travailleur à mi-temps *m*, travailleur à temps partiel *m*

part-timer *n* GEN COMM, HRM travailleur à mi-temps *m*, travailleur à temps partiel *m*

party *n* LAW *in contract* partie *f*; **~ line** COMMS ligne commune *f*, ligne multipoint *f*, ligne partagée *f*, ligne à postes groupés *f*, POL ligne du parti *f*, politique du parti *f*; **~ ticket** LEIS *for group* billet collectif *m*; **~ to an agreement** HRM partie prenante dans une convention *f*; **~ to a contract**

LAW partie contractante *f*; ~ **to an estate** LAW cohéritier *m*; ~ **wall** LAW, PROP mur mitoyen *m*

pass[1] *n* GEN COMM laissez-passer *m*; ~ **-along** *jarg* ECON, S&M répercussion *f*; ~ **-along readership** *jarg* S&M *advertising* lectorat secondaire *m*; ~ **-through charge** *AmE (cf throughput charge BrE)* ADMIN frais de passage *m pl*, frais de traitement *m pl*; ~ **-through loan** FIN prêt intermédiaire *m*; ~ **-through security** FIN titre avec rétrocession immédiate *m*

pass[2] *vt* ACC *an entry* passer, ECON *budget* faire adopter, faire voter, FIN *dividend* omettre le paiement, LAW faire passer, *judgement* prononcer, rendre, *resolution* adopter, prendre, POL approuver; ~ **off** GEN COMM *goods* faire passer; ~ **on** ECON *cost*, GEN COMM répercuter; ~ **sth for press** MEDIA *print* donner qch à tirer; ◆ ~ **inspection** LAW recevoir un agrément après contrôle technique, recevoir un visa d'inspection favorable, satisfaire au contrôle; ~ **sentence** LAW prononcer une condamnation; ~ **sth over in silence** GEN COMM passer qch sous silence

passbook *n* BANK livret de banque *m*, livret de compte *m*

passed[1] *adj* GEN COMM passé

passed:[2] ~ **dividend** *n* ACC dividende non-déclaré *m*, dividende omis *m*

passenger *n* TRANSP passager *m*, voyageur *m*; ~ **aircraft** *n* TRANSP avion passagers *m*, aéronef de passagers *m (frml)*; ~ **analysis** *n* TRANSP analyse des données passagers *f*; ~ **care** *n* TRANSP, WEL accueil des passagers *m*; ~ **certificate** *n (PC)* TRANSP certificat de transport de passagers *m*; ~ **control** *n* LEIS limitation du nombre de passagers *f*; ~ **coupon** *n* LEIS souche *f*; ~ **dues** *n pl* LEIS taxe passager *f*; ~ **fare** *n* TRANSP prix du billet *m*, tarif voyageurs *m*; ~ **ferry** *n* TRANSP ferry *m*, transbordeur *m*; ~ **lift** *n* GEN COMM ascenseur *m*; ~ **list** *n* TRANSP liste des passagers *f*; ~ **lounge** *n* TRANSP salon d'attente *m*, salon passagers *m*; ~ **manifest** *n* TRANSP liste des passagers *f*, manifeste des passagers *m*; ~ **market** *n* TRANSP marché voyageurs *m*; ~ **mile** *n* TRANSP kilomètre-passager *m*, kilomètre-voyageur *m*; ~ **miles per vehicle hour** *n pl* TRANSP kilomètres-passagers par heure de circulation du véhicule *m pl*, kilomètres-voyageurs par heure de circulation du véhicule *m pl*; ~ **number certificate** *n* TRANSP certificat de nombre de passagers *m*; ~ **-rated traffic** *n* TRANSP trafic à tarif passagers *m*, trafic à tarif voyageurs *m*; ~ **safety certificate** *n* TRANSP, WEL certificat de sécurité pour navire à passagers *m*; ~ **service** *n* TRANSP service voyageurs *m*; ~ **ship** *n* TRANSP paquebot *m*; ~ **strategy** *n* TRANSP stratégie passagers *f*, stratégie voyageurs *f*; ~ **tariff** *n* TRANSP tarif passagers *m*, tarif voyageurs *m*; ~ **terminal** *n* TRANSP aérogare *f*, terminal *m*; ~ **throughput** *n* TRANSP capacité de traitement des passagers *f*; ~ **toll** *n* TRANSP taxe passager *f*; ~ **tonnage** *n* TRANSP navire à passagers *m*; ~ **train** *n* TRANSP train de voyageurs *m*,

train voyageurs *m*; ~ **vehicle** *n* TRANSP véhicule de tourisme *m*, véhicule passager *m*; ~ **vehicle ferry** *n* TRANSP car-ferry *m*, transbordeur de passagers et véhicules *m*

passer-by *n* GEN COMM passant *m*

passing[1] *adj* TAX *property* dévolu, transmis

passing:[2] ~ **of risk** *n* INS dépassement de risques *m*

passive[1] *adj* S&M *advertising* passif

passive:[2] ~ **activities** *n pl* TAX activités passives *f pl*; ~ **bond** *n* STOCK obligation ne portant pas d'intérêt *f*, obligation sans intérêt *f*; ~ **income** *n* TAX revenu de placements *m*; ~ **investor** *n* FIN investisseur passif *m*

passport *n* ADMIN passeport *m*; ~ **check** ADMIN contrôle des passeports *m*; ~ **control** ADMIN contrôle des passeports *m*; ~ **holder** ADMIN titulaire d'un passeport *m*

password *n* COMP mot de passe *m*

past:[1] ~ **-due** *adj* ACC arriéré, en souffrance, nonréglé à l'échéance, échu, GEN COMM arriéré

past:[2] ~ **-due claim** *n* ACC créance en retard *f*; ~ **service benefit** *n* US FIN *private pension plan* prestation d'attribution de droits de retraite *f*; ~ **year** *n* GEN COMM exercice écoulé *m*

paste:[1] ~ **-up** *n* GEN COMM disposition *f*, MEDIA, S&M *advertising* collage *m*, montage *m*

paste[2] *vt* COMP *wordprocessed document* insérer

pasteboard *n* IND *type of fibreboard* carton contrecollé *m*

pasting: ~ **sides** *n pl* MEDIA encollage du dos des livres *m*

pat. *abbr (patent)* GEN COMM brevet *m*, LAW *property*, PATENTS brevet *m*, brevet d'invention *m*

patent *n (pat.)* GEN COMM brevet *m*, LAW *property*, PATENTS brevet *m*, brevet d'invention *m*; ~ **agent** *n* LAW, PATENTS *intellectual property* agent en brevet d'invention *m*; ~ **application** *n* PATENTS demande de brevet *f*; ~ **certificate** *n* PATENTS certificat de brevet *m*; ~ **information network** *n* UK LAW, PATENTS *intellectual property* réseau d'information relatif aux brevets d'invention *m*; ~ **of invention** *n* LAW, PATENTS brevet d'invention *m*; ~ **life** *n* LAW, PATENTS durée d'un brevet *f*, durée de validité d'un brevet *f*; ~ **monopoly** *n* IND *from government to inventor/producer* monopole en matière de brevets *m*; ~ **proprietor** *n* PATENTS titulaire du brevet *m*; ~ **protection** *n* LAW, PATENTS protection conférée par un brevet *f*; ~ **renewal fees** *n pl* GEN COMM droits annuels de maintien d'un brevet *m pl*; ~ **rights** *n pl* LAW, PATENTS droits exclusifs d'exploitation *m pl*, propriété industrielle *f*; ~ **royalties** *n pl* FIN royalties dues par le concessionnaire d'un brevet *f pl*; ~ **specifications** *n pl* LAW demande de dépôt de brevet *f*, demande de dépôt de brevet *f*, mémoire descriptif de brevet *m, printed* description de brevet *f*; ~ **trading** *n* GEN COMM, PATENTS échange de brevets *m*; ◆ ~ **pending** *(pat. pend.)* LAW brevet dont l'homologation est en cours *m*, brevet déposé *m*, PATENTS brevet déposé *m*, demande de brevet déposée *f*

Patent: ~ **Cooperation Treaty** *n* *(PCT)* LAW, PATENTS *intellectual property* traité de coopération relatif aux brevets d'invention *m*; ~ **Office** *n* UK *(Pat. Off.)* PATENTS Office des Brevets du Royaume-Uni

patentability *n* PATENTS brevetabilité *f*

patentable[1] *adj* LAW, PATENTS brevetable, qui peut être breveté

patentable:[2] ~ **invention** *n* PATENTS invention brevetable *f*

Patents: ~ **Advisory Committee** *n* ACC bureau des brevets

paternalism *n* MGMNT paternalisme *m*

paternity: ~ **leave** *n* HRM, WEL *childcare* congé parental *m*

path *n* COMP branche *f*, chemin *m*, voie d'accès *f*

pathway *n* COMP chemin d'accès *m*

pat.: ~ **pend.** *abbr (patent pending)* LAW brevet dont l'homologation est en cours *m*, brevet déposé *m*, PATENTS brevet déposé *m*, demande de brevet déposée *f*

Pat.: ~ **Off.** *abbr* UK *(Patent Office)* PATENTS Office des Brevets du Royaume-Uni

patrial *adj dat* UK *(*ANT *nonpatrial)* ADMIN d'ici, du pays *loc m*

patrimonial[1] *adj* POL territorial

patrimonial:[2] ~ **industry** *n* IND industrie patrimoniale *f*

patronage *n* GEN COMM apport commercial *m*

pattern *n* COMP configuration *f*, motif *m*, GEN COMM *of consumption* tendance *f*; ~ **bargaining** *jarg* HRM négociation modèle *f*; ~ **of economic activity** ECON schéma d'activité économique *m*, type d'activité économique *m*; ~ **settlement** ECON accord type *m*, HRM règlement-type *m*

pauper *n* GEN COMM indigent *m*

pave: ~ **the way for sth** *phr* GEN COMM frayer le chemin à qch, préparer le terrain pour qch

pawn *n* GEN COMM gage *m*

pawnbroker *n* FIN prêteur sur gages *m*

pawned: ~ **stock** *n* STOCK titres en pension *m pl*

pawnshop *n* FIN bureau de prêteur sur gages *m*

pay[1] *n* GEN COMM gages *m pl*, rémunération *f*, HRM rémunération *f*, salaire *m*; ~ **as cargo** *n* INS police pertes indirectes *f*, police pertes indirectes sur facultés *f*; ~ **-as-you-go** *n* HRM *AmE* système de retenue à la source *m*, S&M paiement au fur et à mesure *m*; ~ **bill** *n* *AmE (cf payslip BrE)* HRM bulletin de paie *m*, bulletin de salaire *m*, fiche de paie *f*; ~ **check** *n AmE*, ~ **cheque** *n BrE* BANK chèque de règlement de salaire *m*, HRM chèque de salaire *m*; ~ **comparability** *n* HRM comparabilité des salaires *f*; ~ **and conditions** *n pl* HRM salaire et conditions de travail *m pl*; ~ **differential** *n* HRM hiérarchie salariale *f*, écart des salaires *m*, écart salarial *m*; ~ **freeze** *n* ECON, HRM gel des salaires *m*; ~ **in lieu of notice** *n* HRM paie tenant lieu de

préavis *f*; ~ **-in slip** *n* *AmE (cf paying-in slip BrE)* BANK bordereau de dépôt *m*, bordereau de versement *m*; ~ **packet** *n* *BrE (cf pay check AmE)* HRM chèque de salaire *m*, enveloppe *f*, salaire payé en espèces *m (frml)*; ~ **pause** *n* HRM blocage des salaires *m*; ~ **period** *n* TAX période de paie *f*; ~ **phone** *n BrE (cf pay station AmE)* COMMS téléphone public *m*; ~ **policy** *n* ECON, FIN politique des revenus *f*, HRM politique des revenus *f*, politique salariale *f*, POL politique salariale *f*; ~ **review** *n* HRM révision des salaires *f*; ~ **round** *n* HRM série de négociations salariales *f*; ~ **sheet** *n* HRM bulletin de paie *m*, bulletin de salaire *m*, fiche de paie *f*; ~ **statement** *n* HRM état des rémunérations versées *m*; ~ **station** *n* *AmE (cf pay phone BrE)* COMMS téléphone public *m*; ~ **talks** *n pl* HRM négociations salariales *f pl*; ♦ ~ **for work at time rates** HRM *EU regulations* rémunération accordée pour un travail payé au temps; **get a ~ rise** HRM obtenir une augmentation de salaire

pay[2] **1.** *vt* BANK verser, FIN verser, *instalment* effectuer, GEN COMM payer, rémunérer, *make financial settlement* régler, payer, HRM rémunérer, PATENTS *fee* acquitter, régler; ~ **in** BANK payer en, verser, FIN verser; ~ **off** BANK *debt* rembourser, régler, éteindre, *mortgage* purger, ECON *debt of a developing country* rembourser, FIN liquider, GEN COMM *debt* acquitter, congédier, liquider, renvoyer, régler, *employee* licencier, PROP *mortgage* purger; ~ **off creditors** BANK désintéresser, rembourser; ~ **out** ACC débourser, décaisser; **2.** *vi* ~ **back** FIN être rentable; ♦ ~ **as you earn** UK *(PAYE)*, ACC, HRM, TAX retenue de l'impôt sur le revenu à la source *f*; ~ **a bill** GEN COMM payer la facture, payer la note, régler la facture, régler la note; ~ **by giro** BANK payer par virement bancaire; ~ **by the quarter** GEN COMM payer par trimestre, payer trimestriellement; ~ **by the week** HRM payer à la semaine; ~ **by the year** GEN COMM payer à l'année; ~ **a call on sb** GEN COMM rendre visite à qn; ~ **cash** FIN, GEN COMM payer au comptant, payer cash, payer en espèces, payer en liquide; ~ **a debt in full** FIN acquitter une dette intégralement; ~ **a deposit** BANK verser des arrhes, verser un acompte; ~ **expenses by money order** BANK, FIN mandater des frais; ~ **and file** TAX *corporation tax compliance system* payer et classer; ~ **for cargo by measurement** TRANSP payer le fret au cubage, payer le fret au volume; ~ **for the expenses of** GEN COMM supporter les frais de; ~ **in cash** FIN, GEN COMM payer au comptant, payer cash, payer en espèces, payer en liquide; ~ **in kind** FIN payer en nature; ~ **in specie** FIN, GEN COMM payer en espèces; ~ **money down** BANK verser des arrhes; ~ **money into** BANK *account* approvisionner; ~ **on account** BANK verser un acompte; ~ **on the line** *jarg* GEN COMM payer rubis sur l'ongle; ~ **over the odds for sth** GEN COMM payer qch au prix fort; ~ **sb a flat rate** TRANSP payer qn au forfait; ~ **sb a fortune** HRM faire un pont d'or à qn; ~ **to the order of** BANK payer à l'ordre de; ~ **top dollar for sth** *AmE* GEN COMM payer qch au prix fort; ~ **a visit to sb** GEN COMM rendre visite à qn

payable *adj* GEN COMM payable; ◆ ~ **after notice** FIN payable à préavis; ~ **at maturity** FIN, GEN COMM payable à échéance; ~ **at sight** FIN payable sur demande, payable à vue; ~ **in advance** GEN COMM exigible d'avance, payable à l'avance; ~ **monthly in arrears** FIN payable mensuellement à terme échu; ~ **on** FIN *date* avec jouissance au; ~ **on demand** FIN payable sur demande, payable à vue; ~ **on presentation** FIN payable sur demande, payable à vue

payables: ~ **at year-end** *n pl AmE (PAYE)* ACC comptes à payer à la fin de l'exercice *m pl (CAPAFE)*

payback *n* HRM payback *m*, récupération *f*, S&M *marketing* versement *m*; ~ **method** *n* ACC, FIN méthode d'amortissement *f*; ~ **period** *n* ACC période de remboursement *f*, HRM délai de récupération *m*, période de remboursement *f*, période de récupération *f*; ~ **provisions** *n pl* FIN provisions d'amortissement *f pl*

payday *n* HRM jour de paie *m*

paydown *n* STOCK *bonds, lending* paiement comptant *m*, remboursement d'une obligation par une nouvelle émission *m*, remboursement d'une partie du principal *m*

PAYE[1] *abbr* ACC *AmE (Payables at Year-End)* CAPAFE *(comptes à payer à la fin de l'exercice)*, ACC *UK (pay as you earn)*, HRM *UK (pay as you earn)*, TAX *UK (pay as you earn)* retenue de l'impôt sur le revenu à la source *f*

PAYE[2] ~ **Audit** *n UK* TAX *specialist section of the Inland Revenue* vérification de la retenue de l'impôt sur le revenu à la source; ~ **remittances** *n pl UK* TAX règlements de l'impôt sur le revenu à la source *m pl*

payee *n* ACC bénéficiaire *mf*, preneur *m*

payer *n* GEN COMM payeur *m*, tireur *m*

paying *n* BANK, GEN COMM versement *m*; ~ **agent** TAX agent payeur *m*; ~ **bank** BANK banque payeuse *f*; ~ **banker** BANK banquier payeur *m*; ~ **guest** *(PG)* GEN COMM hôte payant *m*, pensionnaire *m*; ~ **in** BANK versement *m*; ~ **-in book** BANK carnet de versement *m*; ~ **-in slip** *BrE (cf pay-in slip AmE)* BANK bordereau de dépôt *m*, bordereau de versement *m*

payload *n (PL)* TRANSP charge utile *f (CU)*

paymaster *n* ACC, FIN agent comptable *m (Fra)*, comptable public *m (Bel)*, *of wages* agent payeur *m*

payment *n (PYT)* BANK, FIN, GEN COMM versement *m*; ~ **of annuity** TAX service de la rente *m*; ~ **authorization** GEN COMM autorisation de prélèvement *f*; ~ **bond** GEN COMM, LAW garantie de paiement *f*; ~ **by results** *(PBR)* HRM paiement en fonction des résultats *m*, salaire au rendement *m*, salaire basé sur le rendement *m*, salaire en

fonction des résultats *m*; ~ **commitment** BANK, FIN *loans* obligation de paiement *f*; ~ **date** GEN COMM, STOCK date de paiement *f*; ~ **device** FIN moyen de paiement *m*; ~ **guarantee** ACC garantie de paiement *f*; ~ **in advance** ACC paiement anticipé *m*, paiement en avance *m*; ~ **in arrears** ACC paiement en arriérés *m*; ~ **in due course** STOCK paiement en temps voulu *m*, paiement à date due *m*; ~ **in full on allotment** FIN libération à la participation *f*; ~ **in kind** GEN COMM paiement en nature *m*; ~ **-in-kind bond** *(PIK bond)* FIN caution garantissant le paiement en nature de la main-d'oeuvre *f*; ~ **method** FIN méthode de paiement *f*, S&M méthode de paiement *f*, type de paiement *m*; ~ **on account** BANK provision *f*; ~ **on behalf of others** ACC paiement pour le compte d'autrui *m*; ~ **order** ACC mandat *m*, ordre de paiement *m*; ~ **requisition** ACC demande de paiement *f*; ~ **stopped** BANK *on cheque or draft* opposition au paiement *f*, opposition du débiteur *f*; ~ **system** ECON système de paiement *m*; ~ **transfer** BANK transfert social *m*; ~ **type** FIN, S&M méthode de paiement *f*; ~ **under protest** GEN COMM, LAW paiement contre son gré *m*; ~ **under reserve** FIN paiement sous réserve *m*; ◆ **keep up** ~ **on one's mortgage** FIN poursuivre ses remboursements hypothécaires; ~ **made to** GEN COMM paiement fait à; **make a** ~ GEN COMM effectuer un paiement, effectuer un versement, faire un versement; **make a down** ~ BANK, FIN verser des arrhes, verser un acompte

payoff *n* ECON rapport *m*, GEN COMM bénéfice *m*, HRM gains *m pl*, rentabilité *f*, résultats *m pl*, paie de départ *f*

payola *n infrml US* S&M *advertising* pot-de-vin *m (infrml)*

payout *n* BANK remboursement final *m*, remise totale *f*, GEN COMM reversement *m*, S&M *marketing* versement *m*; ~ **period** GEN COMM période de récupération *f*; ~ **ratio** S&M *marketing* ratio de versement *m*

payroll *n* ACC traitement du personnel *m*, HRM liste du personnel *f*, livre de paie *m*, registre du personnel *m*, masse salariale *f*; ~ **cost** *n* ECON, HRM, TAX coût salarial *m*; ~ **deduction** *n* HRM *from gross earnings* prélèvement sur le salaire *m*; ~ **deduction scheme** *n* FIN, HRM *for payments to charities* système de déductions sociales *m*; ~ **deductions account** *n* FIN, HRM compte de retenues sur la paie *m*; ~ **distribution** *n* FIN, HRM ventilation de la paie *f*; ~ **savings plan** *n* HRM plan d'économies sur la masse salariale *m*; ~ **taxes** *n pl* TAX charges sociales *f pl*, cotisations de Sécurité sociale *f pl*, cotisations sociales *f pl*; ◆ **be on the** ~ HRM faire partie du personnel

payslip *n BrE (cf pay bill AmE)* HRM bulletin de paie *m*, bulletin de salaire *m*, fiche de paie *f*

PB *abbr* TRANSP *(poop and bridge) shipping* château-dunette *m*, dunette et passerelle *f pl*, TRANSP *(permanent ballast) shipping* lest fixe *m*,

lest permanent *m*, TRANSP *(permanent bunker)*
shipping soute fixe *f*, soute permanente *f*

PBA *abbr (paid by agent)* TRANSP *shipping* réglé
par l'agent

PBDS *abbr UK (Publishers and Booksellers Delivery Service)* MEDIA ≈ Service de messagerie des éditeurs et libraires *m*

PBF *abbr (poop, bridge and forecastle)* TRANSP *shipping* gaillard-château-dunette *m*

PBH *abbr (partial bulkhead)* TRANSP *shipping* cloison partielle *f*

PBR *abbr (payment by results)* HRM paiement en fonction des résultats *m*, salaire au rendement *m*, salaire basé sur le rendement *m*, salaire en fonction des résultats *m*

PBS *abbr US (Public Broadcasting System)* MEDIA services de radio-télévision publics

PBX *abbr UK (private branch exchange)* COMMS *telephone* autocommutateur privé *m*

pc *abbr* ACC *(petty cash)*, FIN *(petty cash)* menue monnaie *f*, petite caisse *f*, GEN COMM *(piece)* pièce *f*, HRM *(petty cash)* menue monnaie *f*, petite caisse *f*, MATH *(per cent)* p., p. cent *(pour cent)*, TRANSP *(platform crane)* grue plate-forme *f*

PC[1] *abbr* COMP *(personal computer)* OP *(ordinateur personnel)*, LAW *UK (Privy Council)* conseil privé, TRANSP *(passenger certificate)* certificat de transport de passagers *m*

PC:[2] ~ **-based** *adj* COMP *software, hardware, service* pour PC

PC:[3] ~ **-compatibility** *n* COMP compatibilité PC *f*

PCC *abbr* ECON *(price consumption curve)* courbe de consommation déterminée par le prix *f*, TRANSP *(pure car carrier)* *shipping* transporteur d'automobiles *m*

PCT *abbr (Patent Cooperation Treaty)* LAW, PATENTS *intellectual property* traité de coopération relatif aux brevets d'invention *m*

PCTC *abbr (pure car and truck carrier)* TRANSP *shipping* transporteur d'automobiles et de camions *m*

pd *abbr* COMMS *(postdated)* postdaté, FIN *(paid)* *amount, dividend* acquitté, payé, versé, HRM *(paid)* *person, work* payé, rémunéré, IMP/EXP *(port dues)*, TRANSP *(port dues)* *shipping* droits de port *m pl*

PDI *abbr* ECON *(personal disposable income)* revenu disponible des particuliers *m*, revenu personnel disponible *m*, TRANSP *(predelivery inspection)* contrôle avant livraison *m*

PDM *abbr (physical distribution management)* MGMNT, TRANSP gestion de la distribution physique *f*

PDZ *abbr (priority development zone)* ECON, HRM, PROP ZUP *(zone à urbaniser en priorité)*

peace: ~ **dividend** *n* POL dividendes de la paix *m pl*

peaceful: ~ **picketing** *n* HRM *industrial action* piquets de grève pacifiques *m pl*

peak[1] *n* ECON niveau maximum *m*, niveau record

m; ~ **hour** MEDIA *broadcast* heure d'écoute maximale *f*, heure de grande écoute *f*, TRANSP *traffic* heure de pointe *f*; ~ **importing season** IMP/EXP haute saison des importations *f*; ~ **level** STOCK niveau maximum *m*, niveau record *m*; ~ **-load pricing** ECON tarification de pointe *f*, tarification en charge maximum *f*, tarification en pointe de consommation *f*; ~ **period** ENVIR période de pointe *f*, TRANSP heures d'affluence *f pl*, heures de pointe *f pl*; ~ **price** STOCK prix maximum *m*, prix record *m*; ~ **rate** GEN COMM *for telephone calls* plus haut niveau *m*; ~ **season** ECON haute saison *f*; ~ **time** S&M *television viewing* heure de grande écoute *f*

peak[2] *vi* ECON atteindre son maximum, atteindre son niveau record

peculation *n* FIN, GEN COMM, LAW détournement *m*

pecuniary[1] *adj* FIN, GEN COMM, LAW pécuniaire

pecuniary:[2] ~ **economy of scale** *n* ECON, FIN, IND économie d'échelle financière *f*; ~ **external economy** *n* ECON, FIN économie externe financière *f*; ~ **return** *n* ECON, FIN rapport financier *m*, revenu financier *m*

peddle *vt* GEN COMM *goods* colporter

pedestal *n* TRANSP *container securing equipment* palier de mise à niveau *m*

pedestrian *n* GEN COMM piéton *m*

pedestrianization *n* S&M *of shopping street* création d'une zone piétonnière *f*

pedlar *n* GEN COMM colporteur *m*, marchand ambulant *m*

peg *vt* ECON, FIN *currency* indexer, stabiliser, STOCK *price* fixer

pegged: ~ **exchange rate** *n* ECON, FIN taux de change de soutien *m*, taux de change indexé *m*; ~ **price** *n* ECON prix contrôlé *m*, prix indexé *m*, GEN COMM prix indexé *m*; ~ **rate of exchange** *n* ECON, FIN taux de change de soutien *m*, taux de change indexé *m*

pegging *n* STOCK blocage *m*, fixation *f*, soutien des prix *m*, stabilisation *f*; ~ **device** ECON mécanisme d'indexation *m*; ~ **system** ECON système d'indexation *m*

Peking *pr n* GEN COMM Pékin *n pr*

pelican: ~ **hook** *n* TRANSP *cargo securing equipment* croc à échappement *m*

pen: ~ **-based computer** *n* COMP ordinateur sans clavier *m*

penalize *vt* LAW infliger une sanction à, pénaliser, sanctionner

penalty *n* BANK pénalité *f*, surcharge *f*, LAW amende *f*, peine *f*, pénalité *f*, sanction *f*; ~ **clause** INS clause pénale *f*, LAW clause pénale *f*, peine contractuelle *f*; ~ **for breach of contract** LAW dédit de rupture de contrat *m*; ~ **for late tax payment** TAX majoration de retard *f*; ~ **for noncompliance** LAW pénalité pour infraction *f*; ~ **rate** LAW taux de pénalisation *m*; ~ **return** TAX déclaration comportant une pénalité *f*

pence *n* UK *(p)* GEN COMM pence *m*

pendency *n* LAW *of case* litispendance *f*

pending:[1] *adj* GEN COMM en attente *loc f*, en instance *loc*, HRM en instance *loc*

pending:[2] ~ **business** *n* GEN COMM affaires en cours *f pl*; ~ **tray** *n* GEN COMM corbeille des affaires en cours *f*

pendulum: ~ **arbitration** *n* HRM arbitrage par compensation *m*

penetrate *vti* GEN COMM pénétrer; ◆ ~ **the market** S&M pénétrer le marché

penetration *n* S&M pénétration *f*; ~ **pricing** GEN COMM fixation du prix d'appel *f*, S&M politique de prix de pénétration par la base *f*, *marketing* stratégie de bas prix *f*; ~ **rate** S&M *marketing* taux de pénétration *m*

peniche *n* TRANSP *canal boat* péniche *f*

pennant *n* STOCK *chart pattern resembling a pointed flag* figure en flamme *f*

penny *n* GEN COMM penny *m*; ~ **share** STOCK action peu chère *f*, action à deux sous *f* (*infrml*); ~ **stock** *AmE* (ANT *blue chip*) STOCK action valant moins d'un dollar, action peu chère *f*, action à deux sous *f* (*infrml*)

pension:[1] *n* FIN pension *f*, retraite de vieillesse *f*, retraite *f*, HRM, WEL retraite *f*; ~ **adjustment** *n* FIN, INS facteur d'équivalence *m*, TAX facteur d'équivalence *m*, réajustement de pension *m*; ~ **charges** *n pl* ACC primes de retraite *f pl*; ~ **contributions** *n pl* FIN, HRM, TAX cotisations à régime de retraite *f pl*; ~ **corporation** *n* INS société de gestion de retraite *f*; ~ **costs** *n pl* ACC primes de retraite *f pl*; ~ **earnings cap** *n* TAX plafond des bénéfices retraite *m*; ~ **fund** *n* ACC, FIN, HRM, INS caisse de retraite *f*, fonds de retraite *m*; ~ **-holder** *n* FIN, HRM, WEL pensionné *m*; ~ **income** *n* TAX revenu de pension *m*; ~ **income credit** *n* TAX crédit d'impôt pour pension *m*, crédit de l'impôt sur les pensions *m*, crédit pour revenu de pension *m*; ~ **liabilities** *n pl* ACC engagements de retraite *m pl*; ~ **payment** *n* TAX service de la rente *m*; ~ **plan** *n* FIN, HRM, INS, WEL régime de retraite *m*; ~ **plan funding** *n* FIN financement d'un plan de retraite *m*; ~ **plan liability reserve** *n* FIN réserve obligatoire des régimes de retraite *f*

pension:[2] ~ **off** *vt* FIN, HRM *employee* mettre à la retraite

pensionable[1] *adj* FIN, HRM ouvrant droit à pension

pensionable:[2] ~ **age** *n* HRM âge d'effet de la retraite *m*, âge de la mise à la retraite *m*; ~ **earnings** *n pl* HRM, INS, TAX salaire cotisable *m*; ~ **employment** *n* HRM, INS emploi donnant droit à la retraite *m*

pent: ~ **-up demand** *n* ECON, S&M demande accumulée *f*; ~ **-up energy** *n* GEN COMM force contenue *f*

penthouse *n* PROP appartement de grand luxe bâti sur le toit d'un immeuble

pentiolite *n* TRANSP pentiolite *m*

peon *n jarg* HRM larbin *m* (*infrml*)

people:[1] ~ **-intensive** *adj* HRM exigeant beaucoup de personnes

people:[2] ~ **mover** *n* TRANSP système de transfert *m*, système de transport urbain automatique *m*, système hectométrique *m*; ~ **-related problems** *n pl* GEN COMM, HRM problèmes humains *m pl*; ~'s **democracy** *n* POL démocratie populaire *f*

People's: ~ **Republic of China** *pr n* GEN COMM République populaire de Chine *f*

PEP *abbr UK* (*personal equity plan*) FIN, STOCK plan d'épargne en actions *m*, plan personnel de capitalisation *m*

per:[1] ~ **pro.** *abbr frml* (*per procurationem*) GEN COMM p.p. (*par procuration*)

per:[2] ~ **capita debt** *n* ECON dette par habitant *f*; ~ **capita GDP** *n* ECON PIB par habitant *m*; ~ **capita income** *n* ECON revenu par habitant *m*; ~ **contract basis** *n* STOCK *brokerage commission* base du contrat *f*, contrat par contrat *m*; ~ **kilometer rate** *n AmE*, ~ **kilometre rate** *n BrE* TRANSP *taxis* taux kilométrique *m*; ~ **share earnings** *n pl* STOCK bénéfices par action *m pl*; ~ **unit tax** *n* TAX impôt par unité *m*

per[3] *prep* GEN COMM par; ◆ ~ **annum** (*p.a.*) GEN COMM par an (*p.a.*); **as** ~ **statement** BANK suivant relevé; ~ **capita** GEN COMM par habitant; ~ **cent** (*pc*) MATH pour cent (*p., p. cent*); ~ **day** IND *output* journalier; ~ **diem** GEN COMM par jour; ~ **hatch per day** TRANSP par panneau et par jour; **on a** ~ **call basis** COMP sur appel; ~ **procuration** (*p.p.*) GEN COMM par ordre de, par procuration (*p.p.*); ~ **procurationem** *frml* (*per pro.*) GEN COMM par ordre de, par procuration (*p.p.*); ~ **se** GEN COMM en soi *loc*; ~ **share** STOCK par action; ~ **square foot** (*psf*) PROP *rent* ≈ le mètre carré *m*; ~ **stirpes** LAW *distribution of an estate* par ligne familiale, par souche; ~ **workable hatch per day** TRANSP *shipping* par panneau utilisable et par jour; ~ **working hatch per day** TRANSP *shipping* par panneau utilisable et par jour

PER *abbr* (*price-earnings ratio*) ACC, FIN, STOCK CCR (*coefficient de capitalisation des résultats*)

percentage *n* GEN COMM, MATH pourcentage *m*; ~ **analysis** MATH *statistics* analyse pourcentuelle *f*; ~ **of capital held** ACC *balance sheet* quote-part du capital détenu *f*; ~ **change** FIN pourcentage de variation *m*; ~ **-of-completion basis** ACC base de pourcentage d'achèvement *f*; ~ **-of-completion method** ACC méthode de pourcentage d'achèvement *f*; ~ **of depreciation** TRANSP *shipping* pourcentage de dépréciation *m*; ~ **distribution** MATH *statistics* ventilation en pourcentage *f*; ~ **grant** WEL aide au pourcentage *f*; ~ **interest** TAX *in income or property of a trust* pourcentage d'intérêt *m*, quote-part *f*; ~ **lease** PROP *retail* bail en pourcentage *m*; ~ **point** FIN point de pourcentage *m*; ~ **of product price spent on promotion** S&M *advertising* budget-promotion *m*; ~ **-of-sales method** S&M *advertising, budgets* méthode basée sur le pourcentage des ventes *f*; ◆ **as a** ~ **of** GEN

COMM, MATH comme pourcentage de; **in ~ terms** GEN COMM en termes de pourcentage

percentagewise *adv* MATH en guise de pourcentage *loc m*

percentile *n* MATH centile *m*; **~ ranking** MATH *statistics* classement par pourcentage *m*

perception *n* GEN COMM perception *f*

perestroika *n* POL perestroïka *f*

perfect: **~ competition** *n* (*ANT imperfect competition*) ECON, S&M concurrence parfaite *f*; **~ hedge** *n* STOCK couverture parfaite *f*; **~ market** *n* ECON marché parfait *m*; **~ monopoly** *n* ECON monopole absolu *m*, monopole parfait *m*; **~ obligation** *n* (*SYN legal obligation*) LAW obligation juridique *f*; **~ price discrimination** *n* ECON discrimination parfaite par les prix *f*; **~ substitute** *n* ECON succédané parfait *m*

perfected[1] *adj* GEN COMM mis au point

perfected:[2] **~ security** *n* BANK nantissement de crédit *m*

perform *vt* GEN COMM *entertainment* jouer, *job* exécuter; ◆ **~ the office of** HRM avoir une fonction de

performance *n* ACC *of company* résultats *m pl*, GEN COMM *of work* exécution *f*, GEN COMM *of services* exécution de services *f*, prestation de services *f*, HRM *at work* performance *f*, prestation *f*, LAW *of contractual duty* exécution *f*, S&M *marketing* performance *f*, STOCK *of shares, options* performance *f*, rendement *m*; **~ against objectives** HRM, MGMNT réalisations comparées aux projets *f pl*; **~ appraisal** GEN COMM, HRM, IND, MGMNT évaluation des performances *f*, évaluation des résultats *f*; **~ appraisal interview** (*PAI*) HRM entretien d'évaluation *m*, interview d'évaluation des performances *f*; **~ bond** GEN COMM garantie de bonne fin *f*; **~ budget** FIN budget fonctionnel *m*; **~ budgeting** ACC, FIN, HRM, MGMNT rationalisation des choix budgétaires *f*; **~ evaluation** GEN COMM, HRM, IND, MGMNT évaluation des performances *f*, évaluation des résultats *f*; **~ fund** STOCK fonds spéculatifs *m pl*; **~ guarantee** S&M, STOCK garantie de bonne exécution *f*, garantie en bonne fin *f*; **~ indicator** GEN COMM, HRM, IND, MGMNT clignotant *m*, indicateur de performance *m*, PROP indicateur de performance *m*; **~ marketing** S&M marketing de comportement *m*; **~ measurement** GEN COMM, HRM, IND, MGMNT mesure de performances *f*, mesure du rendement *f*; **~ monitoring** GEN COMM, HRM, IND, MGMNT contrôle de la performance *m*; **~ rating** FIN *investment* jugement d'allure *m*, notation des résultats *f*, HRM jugement d'allure *m*; **~ -related indicator** GEN COMM, HRM, IND, MGMNT, PROP indicateur de performance *m*; **~ -related pay** (*PRP*) HRM salaire au rendement *m*, salaire lié aux résultats *m*; **~ review** GEN COMM, HRM, IND, MGMNT évaluation des performances *f*, évaluation des résultats *f*; **~ of services** (*SYN service delivery*) GEN COMM prestation de services *f*; **~ standard** ACC, HRM norme de rendement *f*;

~ stock STOCK valeur de croissance *f*; **~ target** GEN COMM, HRM, IND, MGMNT objectif de performance *m*; **~ testing** GEN COMM, HRM, IND *packaging*, MGMNT essai de vérification des performances *m*

performing: **~ rights** *n pl* LAW, MEDIA droit d'exécution *m*, droits d'auteur *m pl*, droits de représentation *m pl*, TAX droits d'auteur *m pl*

peril *n* INS *marine* péril *m*, risque *m*; **~ point** ECON, IMP/EXP point critique *m*

perils: **~ of the sea** *n pl* INS *marine insurance*, TRANSP *shipping* fortune de mer *f*

period *n* ECON délai *m*, période *f*, époque *f*, GEN COMM *of time* période *f*, époque *f*; **~ cost** GEN COMM frais encourus pendant une période donnée *m pl*; **~ of digestion** STOCK délai de placement *m*; **~ entry scheme** *UK* IMP/EXP système d'entrée en douane pour une période donnée *m*; **~ expense** GEN COMM frais encourus pendant une période donnée *m pl*; **~ of grace** LAW délai de grâce *m*, PATENTS délai supplémentaire *m*; **~ of payment** BANK délai de paiement *m*, terme d'échéance *m*; ◆ **for the ~** ACC pour la période considérée; **within a ~ of** GEN COMM dans un délai de

periodic[1] *adj* GEN COMM périodique

periodic:[2] **~ amounts** *n pl* TAX sommes périodiques *f pl*; **~ inventory method** *n* ACC méthode d'inventaire périodique *f*; **~ payment plan** *n* FIN plan de remboursement périodique *m*; **~ purchase deferred contract** *n* FIN bordereau d'achat différé périodique *m*

periodical[1] *adj* GEN COMM périodique

periodical[2] *n* MEDIA périodique *m*; **~ survey** TRANSP *shipping* visite périodique *f*

peripheral[1] *adj* COMP, GEN COMM périphérique

peripheral[2] *n* COMP périphérique *m*; **~ capitalism** *n* ECON, POL capitalisme périphérique *m*; **~ computer** *n* COMP ordinateur satellite *m*; **~ device** *n* COMP unité périphérique *f*; **~ equipment** *n* COMP matériel périphérique *m*, IND unités périphériques *f pl*; **~ workers** *n pl* HRM travailleurs périphériques *m pl*

peripherals *n pl* GEN COMM périphériques *m pl*, MEDIA, S&M *public relations* marginaux *m pl*

periphery: **~ firm** *n* ECON entreprise périphérique *f*

perishable[1] *adj* S&M *food* périssable

perishable:[2] **~ goods** *n pl* S&M denrées périssables *f pl*

perishables *n pl* S&M denrées périssables *f pl*

perjury *n* LAW faux serment *m*, parjure *m*

perk *n infrml* (*SYN perquisite*) HRM avantage *m*; ◆ **be a ~ of the job** HRM faire partie des avantages du métier

PERL *abbr* (*public enterprise rationalization loan, public enterprise reform loan, public enterprise rehabilitation loan*) FIN PREP (*prêt à la rationalisation des entreprises publiques*)

permanent[1] *adj* GEN COMM permanent

permanent:[2] ~ **account** *n* ACC comptes de bilan *m pl*; ~ **address** *n* COMMS adresse habituelle *f*; ~ **appointment** *n* HRM titularisation *f*; ~ **arms economy** *n* ECON, POL économie d'armement permanente *f*; ~ **ballast** *n* (*PB*) TRANSP *shipping* lest fixe *m*, lest permanent *m*; ~ **bunker** *n* (*PB*) TRANSP soute fixe *f*, soute permanente *f*; ~ **contract** *n* HRM contrat à durée indéterminée *m*, CDI; ~ **employment** *n* HRM emploi permanent *m*; ~ **financing** *n* FIN financement permanent *m*; ~ **income-bearing share** *n* (*PIBs*) STOCK obligation non-amortissable des building sociétés *f*; ~ **income hypothesis** *n* ECON hypothèse de la permanence du revenu *f*; ~ **participation** *n* ACC *balance sheet* participation permanente *f*; ~ **residence** *n* GEN COMM, LAW résidence habituelle *f*; ~ **resident** *n* GEN COMM, LAW résident permanent *m*; ~ **water ballast** *n* (*PWB*) TRANSP *shipping* lest d'eau fixe *m*, lest liquide permanent *m*

permissible[1] *adj* GEN COMM, LAW acceptable, tolérable

permissible:[2] ~ **error** *n* GEN COMM erreur acceptable *f*

permission *n* COMP, GEN COMM autorisation *f*

permit[1] *n* LAW autorisation *f*, permis *m*; ~ **bond** LAW garantie de permis *f*

permit[2] *vt* GEN COMM, LAW autoriser; ◆ ~ **sb to do** GEN COMM autoriser qn à faire

permit-free *adj* LAW qui n'est pas soumis à autorisation *loc f*, qui ne nécessite pas un permis *loc m*

permitted *adj* GEN COMM, LAW autorisé

permutation *n* MATH permutation *f*

perpendicular: ~ **spread** *n* STOCK écart perpendiculaire *m*

perpetual[1] *adj* GEN COMM, STOCK perpétuel

perpetual:[2] ~ **bond** *n* STOCK obligation perpétuelle *f*; ~ **inventory** *n* ACC *balance sheet* inventaire permanent *m*, inventaire perpétuel *m*, FIN inventaire tournant *m*; ~ **lease** *n* PROP bail perpétuel *m*, bail à vie *m*; ~ **preferred share** *n* STOCK action de priorité perpétuelle *f*, action privilégiée perpétuelle *f*

perpetuity *n* STOCK perpétuité *f*, rente perpétuelle *f*; ◆ **in** ~ GEN COMM à perpétuité

perquisite *n frml* (SYN *perk*) HRM avantage *m*

person *n* ADMIN, GEN COMM, LAW personne *f*; ~ **of independent means** GEN COMM rentier *m*; ~ **-job fit** HRM ajustement de la personne à son poste *m*; ~ **liable to tax** TAX personne imposable *f*; ~ **skilled in the art** PATENTS homme du métier *m*; ~ **-to-person call** *AmE* COMMS communication avec préavis *f*

persona *n* GEN COMM, HRM personne physique *f*

personal: ~ **allowance** *n* BANK *UK* (*cf personal credit Canada, personal exemption US*) crédit personnel *m*, exemption personnelle *f*, indemnité individuelle *f*, TAX *UK* abattement fiscal personnel *m*, TAX *UK* (*cf personal credit Canada,*

personal exemption US) crédit personnel *m*, exemption personnelle *f*, indemnité individuelle *f*; ~ **assistant** *n* (*PA*) HRM, MGMNT assistant personnel *m*, secrétaire de direction *m*, secrétaire particulier *m*; ~ **baggage** *n* LEIS, TRANSP bagages personnels *m pl*; ~ **bank** *n* BANK banque aux particuliers *f*; ~ **banking services** *n pl* BANK services bancaires aux particuliers *m pl*; ~ **benefit** *n* TAX avantage personnel *m*, profit personnel *m*; ~ **call** *n* COMMS appel avec préavis *m*; ~ **capitalism** *n* IND capitalisme individuel *m*; ~ **computer** *n* (*PC*) COMP ordinateur individuel *m*, ordinateur personnel *m* (*OP*); ~ **credit** *n* Canada (*cf personal allowance UK, personal exemption US*) BANK, TAX crédit personnel *m*, exemption personnelle *f*, indemnité individuelle *f*; ~ **details** *n pl* ADMIN coordonnées *f pl*; ~ **disposable income** *n* (*PDI*) ECON revenu disponible des particuliers *m*, revenu personnel disponible *m*; ~ **effects** *n pl* GEN COMM effets personnels *m pl*; ~ **equity plan** *n UK* (*PEP*) FIN, STOCK plan d'épargne en actions *m*, plan personnel de capitalisation *m*; ~ **estate** *n* PROP, TAX bien immobilier personnel *m*; ~ **exemption** *n US* (*cf personal allowance UK, personal credit Canada*) BANK, TAX crédit personnel *m*, exemption personnelle *f*, indemnité individuelle *f*; ~ **expenses** *n pl* TAX frais personnels *m pl*; ~ **export scheme** *n UK* IMP/EXP régime d'exportation privé *m*; ~ **financial planning software** *n* COMP, FIN logiciel personnel de planification financière *m*; ~ **growth** *n* GEN COMM, HRM autodéveloppement *m*, développement personnel *m*; ~ **guarantee** *n* BANK *of loan*, FIN caution personnelle *f*; ~ **holding company** *n US* (*PHC*) TAX société individuelle de portefeuille *f*; ~ **identification number** *n* (*PIN*) BANK code personnel *m*, numéro d'identification personnel *m*; ~ **income** *n* ECON, TAX revenu des personnes physiques *m*, revenu personnel *m*; ~ **income distribution** *n* ECON distribution du revenu des particuliers *f*, répartition du revenu des particuliers *f*; ~ **income tax** *n* TAX impôt individuel sur le revenu *m*; ~ **income tax allowance** *n* TAX crédit d'impôt individuel sur le revenu *m*, crédit d'impôt personnel *m*; ~ **income tax credit** *n* Canada TAX crédit d'impôt individuel sur le revenu *m*, crédit d'impôt personnel *m*; ~ **influence** *n* GEN COMM influence personnelle *f*; ~ **injury** *n* LAW lésion corporelle *f*; ~ **liability** *n* GEN COMM, LAW responsabilité personnelle *f*; ~ **living expenses** *n pl* GEN COMM frais de subsistance *m pl*; ~ **loan** *n* BANK, FIN prêt personnel *m*, prêt à la consommation *m*; ~ **money** *n* FIN argent personnel *m*; ~ **particulars** *n pl* ADMIN coordonnées *f pl*; ~ **pension plan** *n* INS régime de retraite indépendant *m*; ~ **pension scheme** *n UK* FIN, TAX régime de retraite personnelle *m*; ~ **profit** *n* TAX profit personnel *m*; ~ **property** *n* GEN COMM, INS propriété mobilière *f*, PROP bien immobilier personnel *m*, biens personnels *m pl*, propriété mobilière *f*, TAX bien immobilier personnel *m*, bien meuble *m*; ~ **property floater** *n* INS assurance

expressément consentie *f*; ~ **savings** *n pl* BANK épargne des particuliers *f*; ~ **secretary** *n* (*P*/*Sec, PS*) HRM, MGMNT assistant personnel *m*, secrétaire de direction *m*, secrétaire particulier *m*; ~ **sector** *n* ECON secteur des particuliers *m*, secteur individuel *m*; ~ **sector liquid assets** *n* FIN actif disponible personnel *m*; ~ **selling** *n* S&M *marketing* vente personnelle *f*; ~ **services business** *n* FIN commerce personnel de services *m*, entreprise de prestation de services personnels *f*; ~ **share** *n* STOCK action nominative *f*; ~ **statute** *n* HRM statut personnel *m*; ~ **tax allowance** *n* TAX crédit d'impôt personnel *m*; ~ **tax credit** *n Canada* TAX crédit d'impôt personnel *m*

personality *n* HRM caractère *m*

personalization *n* S&M *advertising* personnalisation *f*

personalized: ~ **check** *n AmE*, ~ **cheque** *n BrE* BANK chèque personnalisé *m*

personally: ~ **liable** *adj* LAW personnellement responsable; ~ **responsible** *adj* LAW *for liabilities* personnellement responsable

personalty *n* (SYN *personal property*) TAX bien immobilier personnel *m*, bien meuble *m*

personnel:[1] ~ **-intensive** *adj* HRM *industry* nécessitant beaucoup de personnel

personnel[2] *n* HRM personnel *m*, ressources humaines *f pl*; ~ **department** *n* HRM direction des ressources humaines *f*, direction du personnel *f*, service du personnel *m*, DRH; ~ **director** *n* (SYN *head of the personnel department*) HRM, MGMNT chef du personnel *m*, chef du service personnel *m*, directeur des ressources humaines *m*, directeur du personnel *m*, DRH; ~ **expenses** *n pl* ACC frais de personnel *m pl*; ~ **management** *n* (SYN *staff management*) HRM, MGMNT administration du personnel *f*, direction du personnel *f*, gestion du personnel *f*; ~ **manager** *n* HRM, MGMNT chef du personnel *m*, chef du service personnel *m*; ~ **overheads** *n pl* HRM frais de personnel *m pl*; ~ **policy** *n* HRM politique du personnel *f*; ~ **psychology** *n* HRM, MGMNT psychologie d'entreprise *f*; ~ **rating** *n* HRM appréciation du personnel *f*, notation de la main-d'oeuvre *f*; ~ **specification** *n* HRM caractéristiques du personnel *f pl*, profil de compétences *m*

persons: ~ **concerned** *n pl* GEN COMM intéressés *m pl*

persuasion *n* GEN COMM *influence* persuasion *f*

PERT *n* (*program evaluation and review technique, programme evaluation and review technique*) MGMNT méthode PERT *f* (*méthode de programmation optimale*)

pertain: ~ **to** *vi* GEN COMM se rapporter à

pertaining: ~ **to** *prep* GEN COMM se rapportant à *loc*

pertinence: ~ **tree** *n* MGMNT arbre de pertinence *m*

Peru *pr n* GEN COMM Pérou *m*

Peruvian[1] *adj* GEN COMM péruvien

Peruvian[2] *n* GEN COMM *person* Péruvien *m*

perverse: ~ **price** *n* ECON effet pervers du prix *m*, prix pervers *m*

peseta *n* (*pta.*) GEN COMM peseta *f* (*pta.*)

peso *n* GEN COMM peso *m*

pessimistic *adj* (ANT *optimistic*) GEN COMM pessimiste

pesticide *n* ENVIR, IND pesticide *m*

petition[1] *n* GEN COMM pétition *f*, LAW demande *f*, requête *f*

petition[2] *vt* GEN COMM solliciter

petrobond *n* STOCK pétro-obligation *f*

petrochemical: ~ **currency** *n* FIN, IMP/EXP pétrodevise *f*, pétrodollar *m*

petrocurrency *n* ECON pétrodevise *f*

petrodollar *n* ECON pétrodollar *m*

petrol *n BrE* (*cf gas AmE, gasoline AmE*) ENVIR, IND, TRANSP carburant *m*, essence *f*; ~ **engine vehicle** *BrE* (*cf gasoline engine vehicle AmE*) ENVIR, TRANSP véhicule à moteur à essence *m*; ~ **station** *BrE* (*cf gas station AmE*) TRANSP station-service *f*

petroleum: ~ **compensation** *n* FIN indemnisation pétrolière *f*; ~ **compensation revolving fund** *n* FIN fonds renouvelable d'indemnisation pétrolière *m*; ~ **industry** *n* IND industrie pétrolière *f*; ~ **product** *n* ENVIR produit pétrolier *m*; ~ **revenue tax** *n* (*PRT*) TAX impôt sur les revenus pétroliers *m*; ~ **sector** *n* ECON secteur pétrolier *m*

PETs *n pl UK* (*potentially exempt transfers*) TAX transferts potentiellement exonérés *m pl*

petty: ~ **cash** *n* (*pc*) ACC, FIN, HRM menue monnaie *f*, petite caisse *f*; ~ **cash book** *n* ACC livre de caisse *m*; ~ **cash fund** *n* ACC *bookkeeping*, GEN COMM fonds de caisse *m*; ~ **cash voucher** *n* ACC *bookkeeping* justificatif de caisse *m*; ~ **expenses** *n pl* ACC, FIN dépenses mineures *f pl*; ~ **officer** *n* HRM contremaître *m*, sous-officier *m, motorman* mécanicien *m*, officier mécanicien *m*, IND *motorman* mécanicien *m*, officier mécanicien *m*, TRANSP *shipping* contremaître *m*, sous-officier *m*; ~ **officers** *n pl* HRM, TRANSP *shipping* maistrance *f*; ~ **official** *n* HRM petit fonctionnaire *m*; ~ **regulations** *n pl* FIN, GEN COMM règlements tracassiers *m pl*

PEWP *abbr UK* (*Public Expenditure White Paper*) ECON livre blanc sur les dépenses publiques

PF *abbr* (*poop and forecastle*) TRANSP *shipping* gaillard-dunette *m*

pfennig *n* GEN COMM pfennig *m*

PFI *abbr* (*position-finding instrument*) TRANSP *shipping* radiogoniomètre *m*

PFP *abbr* (*policy framework paper*) ECON, STOCK DCPE (*document-cadre de politique économique*)

pg. *abbr* (*page*) COMP, GEN COMM p. (*page*)

PG *abbr* (*paying guest*) GEN COMM hôte payant *m*, pensionnaire *m*

PGCE *abbr UK* (*Postgraduate Certificate of Education*) WEL ≈ CAPES (*Certificat d'aptitude au professorat d'enseignement du second degré*)

PHA *abbr* *(port health authority)* TRANSP, WEL autorité portuaire de la santé *f*

phantom: ~ **capital** *n* STOCK capital fictif *m*; ~ **income** *n* TAX revenu fantôme *m*; ~ **share** *n* STOCK action fictive *f*, titre fictif *m*; ~ **share option** *n* STOCK option de souscription à des actions fictives *f*, option de titre fictif *f*; ~ **stock plan** *n* STOCK option de souscription à des actions fictives *f*, plan sur titre fictif *m*; ~ **tax** *n* TAX impôt fictif *m*

pharmaceutical[1] *adj* IND pharmaceutique

pharmaceutical:[2] ~ **industry** *n* IND industrie pharmaceutique *f*

pharmaceuticals *n pl* IND produits pharmaceutiques *m pl*

phase[1] *n* GEN COMM *of project* phase *f*; ~ **alternation line** *(PAL)* MEDIA *TV* PAL *m*; ~ **zero** *jarg* ADMIN phase initiale *f*

phase:[2] ~ **in** *vt* COMP *technology, service, system* adopter progressivement, mettre en place progressivement, GEN COMM *new technique, way of working* adopter progressivement, introduire progressivement; ~ **out** COMP *technology, service, system*, GEN COMM *old technique, way of working* abandonner progressivement, retirer progressivement, supprimer progressivement, éliminer progressivement

phasing: ~ **in** *n* *(ANT phasing out)* COMP *of technology, service, system*, GEN COMM *of new technique, way of working* adoption progressive *f*, introduction progressive *f*, mise en place progressive *f*; ~ **out** *n* *(ANT phasing in)* COMP *of technology, service, system*, GEN COMM *of old technique, way of working* abandon progressif *m*, suppression progressive *f*, élimination progressive *f*

PHC *abbr* US *(personal holding company)* TAX société individuelle de portefeuille *f*

PhD *abbr* *(Doctor of Philosophy)* WEL doctorat *m*

Philadelphia: ~ **Stock Exchange** *n* US *(PHLX)* STOCK Bourse de Philadelphie

Philippine *adj* GEN COMM philippin

Philippines *pr n* [inv pl] GEN COMM Philippines *f pl*

Phillips: ~ **curve** *n* ECON courbe de Phillips *f*

philosophy *n* GEN COMM philosophie *f*

PHLX *abbr* US *(Philadelphia Stock Exchange)* STOCK Bourse de Philadelphie

Phnom Penh *pr n* GEN COMM Phnom Penh *n pr*

phone[1] *n* COMMS appareil *m*, téléphone *m*; ~ **book** COMMS Bottin® *m* *(France)*, annuaire téléphonique *m*; ~ **call** COMMS appel téléphonique *m*, communication téléphonique *f*, coup de fil *m* *(infrml)*, coup de téléphone *m*; ~ **card** COMMS Télécarte® *f*, carte de téléphone *f*; ~ **desk** STOCK boxe téléphonique *m*; ~ **-in** COMMS, MEDIA *radio, TV* émission à ligne ouverte *f*; ~ **-in poll** COMMS sondage par téléphone *m*; ~ **-in program** *AmE*, ~ **-in programme** *BrE* COMMS, MEDIA *radio, TV* émission à ligne ouverte *f*; ~ **marketing** S&M mercaphonie *f*, mercatique téléphonique *f*;

~ **number** *(tel. no.)* COMMS numéro de téléphone *m* *(n° tél.)*; ◆ **on the** ~ COMMS au téléphone

phone[2] **1.** *vt* COMMS appeler, passer un coup de fil à *(infrml)*, téléphoner à; **2.** *vi* COMMS téléphoner; ~ **back** COMMS rappeler

phoning *n* FIN démarchage téléphonique *m*

phosphate: ~ **berth** *n* TRANSP *shipping* quai réservé aux phosphatiers *m*

photocomposition *n* *AmE* *(cf filmsetting BrE)* MEDIA photocomposition *f*

photocopier *n* ADMIN, COMMS, GEN COMM *machine* copieur *m*, machine à photocopier *f*, photocopieuse *f*, *person* photocopieur *m*

photocopy[1] *n* ADMIN, COMMS, GEN COMM photocopie *f*

photocopy[2] *vt* ADMIN, COMMS, GEN COMM faire une photocopie de *loc f*, photocopier

photocopying: ~ **machine** *n* ADMIN, COMMS, GEN COMM copieur *m*, machine à photocopier *f*, photocopieuse *f*

Photostat® *n* ADMIN, COMMS, GEN COMM Photostat® *m*, photocopie *f*

physical: ~ **assets** *n pl* ACC, ECON, FIN actif corporel *m*, biens corporels *m pl*; ~ **collateral** *n* BANK garantie matérielle *f*; ~ **commodity** *n* STOCK denrée *f*, matière première *f*; ~ **delivery** *n* STOCK livraison matérielle *f*, livraison physique *f*; ~ **depreciation** *n* ACC *annual accounts* dépréciation matérielle *f*, dépérissement *m*; ~ **deterioration** *n* ACC *annual accounts* dépérissement *m*, détérioration matérielle *f*; ~ **distribution management** *n* *(PDM)* MGMNT, TRANSP gestion de la distribution physique *f*; ~ **examination** *n* GEN COMM *of object* contrôle physique *m*, WEL *of person* visite médicale *f*; ~ **injury** *n* WEL dommages corporels *m pl*, dommages d'ordre physique *m pl*; ~ **inventory** *n* ACC inventaire physique *m*; ~ **market** *n* STOCK marché au comptant *m*; ~ **or mental handicap** *n* WEL handicap physique ou mental *m*; ~ **quality of life index** *n* *(PQLI)* ECON *econometrics* qualité physique de l'indice de vie *f*

physically *adv* GEN COMM physiquement

physiocrat *n* ECON physiocrate *mf*

piastre *n* GEN COMM piastre *f*

PIBOR *abbr* *(Paris Interbank Offered Rate)* BANK TIOP *(taux interbancaire offert à Paris)*

PIBs *abbr* *(permanent income-bearing share)* STOCK obligation non-amortissable des building sociétés *f*

pick:[1] ~ **-up** *n jarg* MEDIA communiqué *m*; ~ **-up bond** *n* STOCK obligation qui reprend; ~ **-up cost** *n* TRANSP frais de ramassage *m pl*; ~ **-up service** *n* TRANSP service de ramassage *m*

pick[2] **1.** *vt* GEN COMM *fruit* cueillir, *select* choisir; **2.** *vi* ~ **up** ECON *economy* repartir, reprendre, MEDIA *TV and radio* capter, TRANSP *cargo* prendre; ◆ ~ **up the tab** *infrml* GEN COMM régler la note; ~ **-your-own** *(PYO)* GEN COMM *farm produce* cueillette à la ferme *f*

picked: ~ **ports** *n pl (pp)* TRANSP *shipping* ports de cueillette *m pl*

picket[1] *n* HRM, IND *group* piquet de grève *m, individual* gréviste *mf*; ~ **line** HRM, IND piquet de grève *m*

picket[2] **1.** *vt* HRM, IND *factory* mettre un piquet de grève devant; **2.** *vi* HRM, IND disposer des piquets de grève

picketing *n* HRM, IND mise en place de piquets de grève *f*

pickings *n pl* TRANSP *cotton* époutiage *m*

pictogram *n* MATH *statistics* pictogramme *m*

picture *n* GEN COMM *outlook, prospects* image *f*, tableau *m*, MEDIA image *f*; ◆ **in the ~ about** GEN COMM au courant de

pictures *n BrE (cf cinema, motion pictures AmE)* LEIS, MEDIA *art, place* cinéma *m*

pie: ~ **chart** *n* COMP, GEN COMM, MATH *statistics* camembert *m*, diagramme circulaire *m*, graphique camembert *m*, graphique circulaire *m*

piece *n (pc)* GEN COMM pièce *f*; ~ **of advice** GEN COMM conseil *m*; ~ **of information** GEN COMM information *f*; ~ **of legislation** LAW loi *f*, type de législation particulier *m*, élément de la loi *m*; ~ **rate** HRM salaire aux pièces *m*, salaire à la pièce *m*; ~ **-rate typographer** HRM, MEDIA pigiste *mf*; ~ **wage** HRM salaire aux pièces *m*, salaire à la pièce *m*; ◆ **at ~ rate** HRM à la tâche

piecework *n* HRM travail aux pièces *m*, travail à la pièce *m*; ~ **system** HRM système de travail aux pièces *m*, système de travail à la pièce *m*

pier *n* TRANSP *breakwater* digue *f, landing stage* embarcadère *m*; ◆ ~ **to house** IMP/EXP, TRANSP quai à domicile; ~ **to pier** IMP/EXP, TRANSP quai à quai

PIF *abbr (purchase issue facility)* STOCK facilité d'émission d'achat *f*

piggyback:[1] ~ **legislation** *n* LAW, POL législation secondaire *f*; ~ **loan** *n* FIN emprunt gigogne *m*, prêt-logement gigogne *m*; ~ **registration** *n* STOCK inscription gigogne *f*; ~ **traffic** *n jarg AmE (cf road-rail transport BrE)* TRANSP ferroutage *m*

piggyback[2] *vt* TRANSP *vehicle* ferrouter

Pigou: ~ **effect** *n* ECON effet Pigou *m*, effet de bien-être *m*

Pigouvian: ~ **subsidy** *n* ECON subvention selon Pigou *f*; ~ **tax** *n* ECON, TAX impôt selon Pigou *m*

PIK: ~ **bond** *n (payment-in-kind bond)* FIN caution garantissant le paiement en nature de la main-d'oeuvre *f*

piker *n jarg* STOCK boursicoteur *m*, petit joueur *m* (*jarg*)

pile: ~ **-up** *n infrml* TRANSP accident multiple *m*

pilot[1] *adj* GEN COMM pilote

pilot[2] *n* MEDIA *broadcast* pilote *m (jarg)*, TRANSP *aviation* pilote *m*, pilote de ligne *m, shipping* pilote *m*; ~ **boat** TRANSP bateau-pilote *m*; ~ **-in-command** HRM, TRANSP *aviation* commandant de bord *m*; ~ **launch** S&M *marketing* lancement-test

m; ~ **plan** GEN COMM, IND *production* plan pilote *m*; ~ **production** GEN COMM, IND fabrication pilote *f*, présérie *f*; ~ **project** GEN COMM, MGMNT projet d'essai *m*; ~ **run** GEN COMM présérie *f*; ~ **scheme** GEN COMM projet pilote *m*; ~ **study** GEN COMM étude pilote *f*

pilotage *n* TRANSP *fee* droits de pilotage *m pl, handling of aircraft, ship* pilotage *m*; ~ **tug** TRANSP remorqueur pilote *m*

pin *n* COMP *of paper feeder* picot d'entraînement *m*; ~ **money** GEN COMM salaire d'appoint *m*

PIN *abbr (personal identification number)* BANK NIP (*numéro d'identification personnel*)

pinch: ~ **bar** *n* TRANSP *cargo handling equipment* pince à levier *f*

pinion *n* TRANSP pignon *m*

pink: ~ **button** *n UK jarg* STOCK commis aux communications *m*; ~ **economy** *n* ECON secteur d'affaires profitable aux homosexuels et souvent dirigé par eux-mêmes; ~ **sheet** *n US* GEN COMM *OTC stocks* feuille rose *f*; ~ **slip** *n infrml AmE (cf redundancy letter BrE)* COMMS, HRM lettre de licenciement *f*, lettre de renvoi *f*

Pink: ~ **Book** *n UK* ECON *balance of payments accounts* Livre Rose; ~ **Paper** *n UK* POL papier rose *m*

pinlock *n* TRANSP *container securing* cône d'empilage *m*

pint *n (pt)* GEN COMM chopine *f (Can)*, pint *m*, pinte *f*

pintle *n* TRANSP *shipping* aiguillot *m*

pioneer[1] *n* IND pionnier *m*; ~ **product** S&M innovation *f*

pioneer[2] *vt* GEN COMM innover

PIOPIC *abbr (Protection & Indemnity of Oil Pollution Indemnity Clause)* ENVIR protection et indemnité de la clause d'indemnité de la pollution par les hydrocarbures

pipe: ~ **-laying ship** *n* TRANSP navire poseur d'oléoducs *m*

pipeline *n* COMMS, ENVIR pipeline *m*, IND pipeline *m, for oil* oléoduc *m*; ◆ **in the ~** COMMS *order* en cours de traitement, GEN COMM *project* en cours de réalisation

piracy *n* COMP piratage *m*, GEN COMM pillage *m*, MEDIA piratage *m*

pirate:[1] ~ **radio** *n* MEDIA radio pirate *f*

pirate[2] *vt* COMP, MEDIA pirater

pit *n* STOCK *traders* corbeille *f (jarg)*, groupe de cotation *m*, pit *m*

pitch *n* COMP espacement *m*, STOCK *UK area on the Stock Exchange floor* territoire *m, traders* groupe de cotation *m*

pitfall *n* GEN COMM inconvénient *m*

Pittsburgh: ~ **-plus** *n US* ECON prix de l'acier au départ de Pittsburgh

pivot: ~ **weight** *n* TRANSP *aviation* poids pivot *m*

pixel *n* COMP pixel *m*

PKD *abbr (partially knocked down)* TRANSP *consignment* partiellement déchargé

pkg *abbr (package)* COMMS colis *m*, paquet *m*, COMP progiciel *m*, train *m*, FIN *of grants, incentives,* MGMNT *of deals, proposals,* POL *of reforms* ensemble *m*, S&M *advertising, direct mail* paquet promotionnel *m*

pkg. *abbr (packaging)* GEN COMM emballage *m*, S&M conditionnement *m*, emballage *m, set of items sold as one* lot *m*, TRANSP conditionnement *m*, emballage *m*; ~ **instr.** *(packing instruction)* TRANSP instruction relative à l'emballage *f*

pkt. *abbr (packet)* GEN COMM paquet *m*

PL *abbr* INS *(partial loss)* dommages partiels *m pl*, perte partielle *f*, sinistre partiel *m*, TRANSP *(payload)* CU *(charge utile),* TRANSP *(protective location) of oil tanker* localisation défensive *f*

PLA *abbr (Port of London Authority)* GEN COMM port autonome de Londres

place[1] *n* GEN COMM lieu *m*; ~ **of abode** LAW domicile *m*, résidence *f*; ~ **of acceptance** *(POA)* TRANSP lieu de réception *m*; ~ **of business** GEN COMM établissement commercial *m*; ~ **of delivery** *(POD)* TRANSP lieu de livraison *m*, réception *f*; ~ **of destination** TRANSP lieu de destination *m*; ~ **of employment** HRM lieu d'emploi *m*; ~ **of origin** TRANSP lieu d'origine *m*; ~ **of payment** BANK lieu de paiement *m*; ~ **of residence** TAX lieu de résidence *m*; ~ **utility** ECON utilité de lieu *f*; ~ **of work** HRM lieu de travail *m*

place[2] *vt* GEN COMM *article, item, person* mettre, *order* passer; ♦ ~ **a deposit** STOCK placer un dépôt; ~ **an embargo on** GEN COMM mettre un embargo sur; ~ **emphasis on** GEN COMM mettre l'accent sur; ~ **a hold on an account** BANK bloquer un compte; ~ **in custody** LAW placer sous garde; ~ **in trust** LAW confier, mettre en fidéicommis; ~ **a question on the agenda** GEN COMM, MGMNT mettre une question à l'ordre du jour; ~ **under guardianship** WEL mettre en tutelle

placement *n* HRM stage *m*, STOCK vente *f, of bonds* placement *m*; ~ **ratio** BANK, FIN ratio de placement *m*; ~ **test** HRM contrat d'emploi à l'essai *m*

placing *n* STOCK vente directe *f*

plain: ~ **vanilla swap** *n* FIN swap simple *m*

plaintiff *n* LAW demandeur *m*, plaignant *m*

plan[1] *n* ECON, GEN COMM, MGMNT, PROP plan *m*, projet *m*; ~ **B** GEN COMM, MGMNT plan de réserve *m*

plan[2] *vt* GEN COMM planifier, projeter, préparer; ♦ ~ **ahead for sth** GEN COMM préparer qch

planchette *n* BANK *on banknote* planchette *f*

plane *n infrml* TRANSP avion *m*

planetary: ~ **gear** *n* TRANSP *shipping* engrenage planétaire *m*, engrenage épicycloïdal *m*

plank *n* POL *of campaign, programme* point *m*, thème *m*

planned: ~ **capacity** *n* ECON, IND capacité de production pour une année donnée *f*; ~ **economy** *n* ECON, POL économie planifiée *f*;

~ **environment** *n* ENVIR milieu aménagé *m*; ~ **obsolescence** *n* (SYN *built-in obsolescence*) ECON, GEN COMM, IND, S&M désuétude calculée *f*, obsolescence programmée *f*, vieillissement programmé *m*; ~ **unit development** *n (PUD)* PROP aménagement d'unité planifiée *m*

planning *n* GEN COMM plan *m*, planification *f*, planning *m*, établissement des plannings *m*; ~ **approval** *n (cf building permit AmE, planning permission BrE)* ADMIN, ENVIR, PROP permis de construire *m*; ~ **authority** *n* ADMIN, ENVIR responsables de l'aménagement du territoire *m pl*; ~ **commission** *n* PROP commission de la planification d'urbanisme *f*; ~ **department** *n* GEN COMM, MGMNT direction de planning *f*, service de planification *m*, service planning *m*, PROP commission de la planification d'urbanisme *f*; ~ **element memorandum** *n* FIN exposé de l'élément de planification *m*; ~ **horizon** *n* ECON *in socialist countries* années limites du plan *f pl*; ~ **maintenance** *n* ADMIN entretien systématique *m*; ~ **permission** *n BrE (cf building permit AmE, planning approval)* ADMIN, ENVIR, PROP permis de construire *m*; ~, **programming, budgeting** *n US (PPB)* POL planification, programmation, budgétisation *f pl*; ~, **programming, budgeting system** *n (PPBS)* ACC, FIN, HRM, MGMNT rationalisation des choix budgétaires *f (RCB),* système de planning, de budget et de programmation *m*; ~ **restrictions** *n pl* ADMIN, ENVIR, LAW, PROP limitations à la planification *f pl*

Planning: ~ **and Compensation Act** *n UK* LAW loi relative à l'aménagement du territoire et à l'indemnisation des personnes expropriées

plant *n* ACC *fixed assets* installations industrielles *f pl*, installations techniques *f pl*, IND *equipment* matériel *m*, équipement *m, factory* unité de production *f*, usine *f*, usine de production *f, fixed assets* installations industrielles *f pl*, installations techniques *f pl*; ~ **agreement** *n* HRM, IND accord au niveau d'usine *m*; ~ **bargaining** *n* GEN COMM, HRM, IND négociation au niveau de l'usine *f*, négociation au niveau local *f*; ~ **capacity** *n* GEN COMM, IND capacité de l'usine *f*; ~ **hire** *n* GEN COMM, IND location d'équipement *f*; ~ **incentive scheme** *n* (SYN *factory incentive scheme*) HRM, IND système de primes d'encouragement *m*; ~ **interruption** *n* GEN COMM, IND fermeture d'usine *f*; ~ **layout study** *n* GEN COMM, IND étude des implantations *f*; ~ **location** *n* GEN COMM, IND implantation d'usine *f*, localisation de l'usine *f*; ~ **and machinery** *n pl* GEN COMM, IND usine et matériels *f*; ~ **maintenance** *n* GEN COMM, IND entretien de l'équipement *m*; ~ **management** *n* GEN COMM, IND, MGMNT gestion d'usine *f*; ~ **manager** *n* GEN COMM, HRM, IND chef d'établissement *m*, directeur d'usine *m*; ~ **manufacturing** *n* IND production d'usine *f*; ~ **operator** *n* IND opérateur d'usine *m*

plantation *n* ECON, IND plantation *f*

plastic[1] *adj* ENVIR, IND plastique

plastic[2] *n* ENVIR, IND matière plastique *f*, plastique *m*; ~ **money** BANK carte bancaire *f*; ~ **waste** ENVIR, IND déchets plastiques *m pl*

plastics *n* IND matières plastiques *f pl*; ~ **industries** IND industrie plastique *f*

plat: ~ **book** *n* US LAW, PROP registre foncier *m*

platform *n* COMP *software, hardware,* IND *for oil drilling* plate-forme *f*; ~ **crane** *(pc)* TRANSP grue plate-forme *f*; ~ **vehicle** TRANSP véhicule-plate-forme *m*

platinum: ~ **disc** *n* MEDIA *recording industry* disque de platine *m*

platykurtic *n* MATH *statistics* platykurtique *m*

play[1] *n* STOCK jeu *m*; ◆ **come into** ~ GEN COMM *factor* entrer en jeu

play[2] *vt* GEN COMM jouer; ◆ ~ **it by ear** GEN COMM improviser, y aller au pifomètre *(infrml)*; ~ **the market** STOCK jouer le marché; ~ **a part in** GEN COMM jouer un rôle dans, participer à; ~ **a role in** GEN COMM jouer un rôle dans, participer à; ~ **safe** GEN COMM ne pas prendre de risques

playbook *n jarg US* GEN COMM programme *m*

player *n* GEN COMM, MGMNT *in negotiations* intervenant *m*

plc *abbr UK (public limited company)* GEN COMM société à responsabilité limitée *f (SARL)*, GEN COMM société anonyme *(SA)*

PLC *abbr (product life cycle)* ECON, IND, S&M *marketing* CVP *(cycle de vie d'un produit)*

plea: ~ **-bargaining** *n* LAW négociation entre accusation et défense, l'accusé plaidant coupable

plead *vti* GEN COMM, LAW plaider; ◆ ~ **guilty** LAW plaider coupable; ~ **ignorance** GEN COMM invoquer son ignorance, prétexter l'ignorance

pleading *n* LAW plaidoirie *f*, plaidoyer *m*

pleasant: ~ **working environment** *n* HRM environnement professionnel agréable *m*

please *adv* COMMS s'il vous plaît; ◆ ~ **accept our apologies** COMMS veuillez accepter nos excuses; ~ **add our name to your mailing list** COMMS veuillez nous inscrire sur votre liste de diffusion; ~ **excuse me** GEN COMM veuillez m'excuser; ~ **forward** COMMS faire suivre SVP, prière de faire suivre; ~ **let us have your prices** GEN COMM veuillez nous indiquer vos prix; ~ **let us know which date suits you** COMMS veuillez nous indiquer la date qui vous convient; ~ **reply** *(RSVP)* COMMS répondez s'il vous plaît, veuillez répondre s'il vous plaît; ~ **submit your quotations** GEN COMM veuillez nous indiquer vos prix; ~ **telex your confirmation** COMMS confirmez par télex SVP; ~ **turn over** *(PTO)* COMMS tournez s'il vous plaît *(TSVP)*

pledge *n* BANK bien transporté en gage *m*, bien transporté en nantissement *m*, gage *m*, nantissement *m*; ~ **security** BANK titre transporté en gage *m*, titre transporté en nantissement *m*, valeur mobilière transportée en gage *f*, valeur mobilière transportée en nantissement *f*

pledged: ~ **security** *n* BANK valeur nantie *f*

pledging *n* BANK mise en gage *f*, nantissement *m*

plenary *adj* POL *parliamentary session* plénier

plimsoll: ~ **line** *n* TRANSP *shipping* disque de franc-bord *m*, marque de franc-bord *f*

plot[1] *n* GEN COMM *secret plan* complot *m*, PROP *of land* lot *m*; ~ **plan** *US* PROP plan de lot *m*

plot[2] *vt* MATH *graph,* PROP tracer

plottage: ~ **value** *n US* PROP valeur de rapportage *f*

plotter *n* COMP, MATH traceur de courbes *m*

plotting: ~ **board** *n* COMP table traçante *f*; ~ **pen** *n* COMP traceur *m*; ~ **table** *n* GEN COMM table traçante *f*

plough: ~ **back** *vt BrE* GEN COMM, STOCK *profits in business* réinvestir

ploughback *n BrE* ACC autofinance *f*, bénéfice réinvesti *m*, FIN autofinancement *m*, bénéfice réinvesti *m*

plow: ~ **back** *vt AmE see* plough back *BrE*

plowback *n AmE see* ploughback *BrE*

PLR *abbr (public lending right)* MEDIA droits compensant un auteur sur le prêt de ses ouvrages en bibliothèque

PLTC *abbr (port liner terms charge)* TRANSP *shipping* frais de manutention à la charge de la marchandise *m pl*

plug[1] *n infrml* COMP connexion *f*, fiche *f*, prise *f*, prise de courant *f*, S&M *advertising* coup de pouce publicitaire *m*, TRANSP *shipping* prise *f*

plug[2] *vt* MEDIA *promote* faire de la pub pour *loc f* *(infrml)*; ~ **in** COMP brancher, connecter, enficher, GEN COMM brancher, connecter

plum: ~ **book** *n jarg US* ADMIN, POL liste des postes à pourvoir par la Présidence

plunge[1] *n* GEN COMM dégringolade *f*

plunge[2] *vi* GEN COMM dégringoler

pluralism *n* HRM *industrial relations* pluralisme *m*

plus[1] *adj* GEN COMM positif

plus[2] *adv* GEN COMM *advantage* plus

plus[3]: ~ **sign** *n* GEN COMM, MATH signe plus *m*; ~ **tick** *n (ANT minus tick)* STOCK cours supérieur au cours précédent *m*, négociation à un cours supérieur *f*, échelon de cotation supérieur *m*

plus[4] *prep* GEN COMM, MATH plus

plussage *n infrml UK* HRM avantages accordés *m pl*

plying: ~ **limit** *n* TRANSP *shipping* secteur géographique desservi *m*

plywood *n* IND *material* contre-plaqué *m*; ~ **drum** TRANSP tambour en contreplaqué *m*

pm *abbr (post meridiem)* GEN COMM après-midi

PM *abbr (prime minister)* POL Premier ministre *m*

PMSA *abbr US (primary metropolitan statistical area)* GEN COMM zone primaire de statistique métropolitaine *f*

PMTS *abbr (predetermined motion time system)* ECON, FIN, MGMNT PMTS *(méthode des temps prédéterminés)*

PN *abbr (promissory note)* BANK, FIN B/. *(billet à ordre)*

pneumatic: ~ **tensioner** *n* TRANSP tendeur pneumatique *m*

PNQ *abbr UK (private notice question)* POL question posée au Premier ministre dans la Chambre des Communes

PO *abbr* BANK *BrE (postal order)* MP *(mandat postal)*, COMMS *(post office)* b. de p. *(bureau de poste)*, FIN *BrE (postal order)* MP *(mandat postal)*

POA *abbr (place of acceptance)* TRANSP lieu de réception *m*

poaching *n* HRM débauchage *m*

POB *abbr (post office box)* COMMS BP *(boîte postale)*

pocket *n* ECON *of consumer* poche *f*, porte-monnaie *m*; ~ **calculator** GEN COMM calculatrice à poche *f*, calculette *f*, MATH calculatrice de poche *f*, calculette *f*; ~ **computer** COMP ordinateur de poche *m*; ~ **money** GEN COMM argent de poche *m*; ◆ **be out of** ~ GEN COMM en être de sa poche, en être pour ses frais

pocketbook: ~ **issue** *n infrml US* POL, WEL question touchant au portefeuille *f*

POD *abbr* FIN *(proof of debt)* justification de dette *f*, titre de créances *m*, GEN COMM *(proof of delivery)*, TRANSP *(proof of delivery)* justification de livraison *f*, TRANSP *(place of delivery)* lieu de livraison *m*, réception *f*, TRANSP *(paid on delivery)* paiement à la livraison *loc m*

point[1] *n* COMP virgule *f*, FIN *US real estate, commercial lending*, GEN COMM *for discussion* point *m*, MATH point *m*, virgule *f*, POL *US* candidat présidentiel favori *m*, STOCK *on index of share prices* point *m*; ~ **of departure** IMP/EXP point de départ *m*; ~ **elasticity** ECON élasticité ponctuelle *f*; ~ **of entry** GEN COMM *into a country* lieu d'entrée *m*; ~ **estimate** MATH évaluation du point *f*; ~ **of export** IMP/EXP point d'exportation *m*; ~ **and figure chart** STOCK graphique des chiffres et des points *m*, graphique en point et figure *m*; ~ **of law** LAW point de droit *m*; ~ **of origin** TRANSP lieu d'origine *m*; ~ **price** STOCK *options* prix du point *m*; ~ **of sale** *(POS)* S&M lieu de vente *m (LV)*, point de vente *m (PV)*; ~ **-of-sale advertising** MEDIA, S&M publicité sur le lieu de vente *f*, PLV; ~ **-of-sale material** S&M matériel de publicité sur le lieu de vente *m*; ~ **-of-sale promotion** MEDIA publicité sur le lieu de vente *f*, PLV, S&M promotion sur le lieu de vente *f*, PLV; ~ **-of-sale terminal** *(POST)* S&M terminal point de vente *m (TPV)*; ~ **of view** GEN COMM point de vue *m*; ◆ **make a** ~ **of** GEN COMM prendre soin de

point:[2] ~ **to** *vt* GEN COMM *indicate* souligner

pointer *n* COMP curseur *m*, pointeur *m*, GEN COMM *indication* indicateur *m*, MGMNT *presentation aid* tuyau *m*

points: ~ **rating** *n* HRM barème par points *m*;

~ **-rating method** *n* GEN COMM, MATH, MGMNT méthode de qualification par points *f*; ~ **of suspension** *n pl* ADMIN, MEDIA *typography* pointillés *m pl*, points de suspension *m pl*

poison: ~ **pill** *n jarg* FIN pilule empoisonnée *f (jarg)*

Poland *pr n* GEN COMM Pologne *f*

polarization *n* COMMS, FIN polarisation *f*

Pole *n* GEN COMM *person* Polonais *m*

police *n* LAW gendarmerie *f*, police *f*; ~ **force** LAW gendarmerie *f*, police *f*; ~ **intelligence** LAW service de renseignements de la police *m*; ~ **power** LAW, POL pouvoir policier *m*; ~ **record** LAW casier judiciaire *m*

policy *n* ECON, GEN COMM, MGMNT, POL politique *f*; ~ **of the big stick** POL politique du gros bâton *f*; ~ **decision** GEN COMM, MGMNT, POL décision de principe *f*; ~ **dividend** INS bonification de police *f*, participation de police *f*; ~ **execution** GEN COMM, MGMNT, POL exécution de la politique *f*, mise en oeuvre de la politique *f*; ~ **formulation** GEN COMM, MGMNT, POL expression de la politique *f*; ~ **framework paper** *(PFP)* ECON, STOCK document-cadre de politique économique *m (DCPE)*; ~ **harmonization** ECON harmonisation de la politique *f*; ~ **lag** POL formulation de la politique *f*, mise en oeuvre de la politique *f*; ~ **loan** INS *personal* avance sur contrat *f*, avance sur police *f*; ~ **mix** MGMNT mélange de politiques *m*; ~ **proof of interest** *(PPI)* INS *marine* police de justification d'intérêt *f*, police preuve de l'intérêt assuré *f*; ~ **reserve** INS provision mathématique *f*; ~ **and resource management** MGMNT gestion des ressources *f*; ~ **statement** GEN COMM, MGMNT, POL déclaration d'objectifs *f*; ~ **to bearer** TAX police au porteur *f*

Policy: ~ **and Expenditure Management System** *n* FIN système de gestion des secteurs de dépenses *m*

policyholder *n* INS assuré *m*, souscripteur *m*

policymaker *n* GEN COMM, MGMNT, POL décideur *m*, décideur de politique *m*

policymaking *n* GEN COMM, MGMNT, POL définition de politique *f*

Polish[1] *adj* GEN COMM polonais

Polish[2] *n* GEN COMM *language* polonais *m*; ~ **notation** MATH notation polonaise *f*

polite *adj* GEN COMM aimable, poli

political[1] *adj* GEN COMM, POL politique

political:[2] ~ **affairs** *n pl* POL affaires politiques *f pl*; ~ **business cycle** *n* GEN COMM, POL conjoncture politique *f*; ~ **change** *n* GEN COMM, POL changement politique *m*; ~ **climate** *n* GEN COMM, POL climat politique *m*, conjoncture politique *f*; ~ **contribution** *n* POL contribution politique *f*, cotisation politique *f*; ~ **contribution tax** *n* TAX crédit d'impôt pour contributions politiques *m*; ~ **cooperation** *n* ADMIN, POL coopération politique *f*; ~ **donation** *n* HRM don en soutien aux activités politiques *m*; ~ **economy** *n* ECON, POL, WEL économie politique *f*; ~ **editor** *n* MEDIA chef du service politique *m*; ~ **fund** *n* HRM *of trade* *union* caisse politique *f*, fonds servant aux activités politiques *m*; ~ **group** *n* POL groupe politique *m*; ~ **institution** *n* POL institution politique *f*; ~ **issue** *n* GEN COMM, POL question politique *f*; ~ **levy** *n* UK HRM *from trade union member* prélèvement d'une contribution au Labour Party; ~ **party** *n* GEN COMM, POL parti politique *m*; ~ **practice** *n* POL pratique politique *f*; ~ **question** *n* GEN COMM, POL question politique *f*; ~ **refugee** *n* POL réfugié politique *m*; ~ **risk** *n* GEN COMM, POL risque lié à la politique *m*; ~ **situation** *n* GEN COMM, POL situation politique *f*; ~ **stability** *n* GEN COMM, POL stabilité politique *f*; ~ **strike** *n* HRM, POL grève politique *f*; ~ **system** *n* GEN COMM, POL système politique *m*; ~ **thinking** *n* POL pensée politique *f*; ~ **union** *n* POL *EU* union politique *f*

politically *adv* GEN COMM, POL politiquement

politician *n* GEN COMM, POL homme politique *m*

politicize *vt* POL politiser

poll *n* GEN COMM *in election* scrutin *m*, élection *f*, *survey* sondage *m*; ~ **tax** *obs* UK TAX, WEL remplacé par council tax en 1993, ≈ impôts locaux *m pl* (*France*)

polling *n* COMP *network, modem* appel *m*, interrogation *f*; ~ **booth** POL isoloir *m*; ~ **day** POL jour des élections *m*; ~ **station** POL bureau de vote *m*

pollutant *n* ENVIR polluant *m*

pollute *vt* ENVIR, IND contaminer

polluted[1] *adj* ENVIR, IND contaminé, pollué

polluted:[2] ~ **air** *n* ENVIR air pollué *m*

polluter *n* ENVIR pollueur *m*; ~ **pays principle** ENVIR, LAW, WEL principe pollueur-payeur *m*

pollution *n* ENVIR contamination *f*, pollution *f*, IND *of product* contamination *f*, dépérissement *m*; ~ **charge** ENVIR redevance de pollution *f*; ~ **control** ENVIR contrôle de l'environnement *m*, lutte antipollution *f*; ~ **emitter** ENVIR, IND source de pollution *f*; ~ **source** ENVIR, IND source de pollution *f*; ~ **tax** ENVIR redevance de pollution *f*

polycentrism *n* POL polycentrisme *m*

polymerizable: ~ **material** *n* TRANSP *dangerous cargo* matière polymérisable *f*

polytechnic *n* UK *obs* GEN COMM école supérieure *f*

pon *abbr* (*pontoon*) TRANSP *shipping* ponton *m*

P-1 *abbr* (*prime paper*) FIN, STOCK papier commercial de premier ordre *m*

pontoon *n* (*pon*) TRANSP *shipping* ponton *m*

pony *n* US MEDIA *print* communiqué d'agence *m*

POO *abbr* (*port operations officer*) HRM, TRANSP responsable des opérations portuaires *m*

pool[1] *n* ADMIN *typists* pool *m*, ECON consortium *m*, pool *m*, FIN groupement *m*, pool *m*, mise en commun *f*, GEN COMM *resources* groupement *m*, INS mise en commun *f*, pool *m*, STOCK pool *m*, tour de table *m*; ~ **of vehicles** TRANSP parc de véhicules *m*

pool[2] *vt* ECON *resources* mettre en commun, GEN COMM *resources, abilities* coordonner, grouper

pooling *n* FIN, INS mise en commun *f*; ~ **arrangements** *n pl* GEN COMM dispositifs de mise en commun des ressources *m pl*; ~ **of interests** *n* AmE (*cf merger accounting BrE*) ACC *balance sheet* absorption *f*, fusion *f*; ~ **system** *n* TRANSP système de mise en commun *m*

pools *n pl* UK LEIS *football* ≈ loto sportif *m* (*France*)

poop *n* TRANSP *shipping* dunette *f*; ~ **and bridge** *n pl* (*PB*) TRANSP *shipping* château-dunette *m*, dunette et passerelle *f pl*; ~, **bridge and forecastle** *n pl* (*PBF*) TRANSP *shipping* gaillard-château-dunette *m*; ~ **and forecastle** *n pl* (*PF*) TRANSP *shipping* gaillard-dunette *m*

poor[1] *adj* ECON *country* pauvre, *demand* faible, WEL *family, person* pauvre

poor:[2] ~ **service** *n* S&M service médiocre *m*

Poor: ~ **Laws** *n pl* UK WEL *1597, 1601* lois sur l'assistance publique

pop: ~ **-down menu** *n* COMP menu déroulant *m*; ~ **-up** *n jarg* S&M *advertising* pop-up *m* (*jarg*); ~ **-up menu** *n* COMP menu surgissant *m*

POP *abbr* (*post office preferred*) COMMS formats postaux normalisés *m pl*

popular[1] *adj* GEN COMM du public, populaire, MEDIA grand public; ♦ **by ~ request** GEN COMM à la demande générale

popular:[2] ~ **capitalism** *n* ECON, POL capitalisme populaire *m*

popularism *n* POL politique de providence *f*

popularist *n* POL providentiel *m*

popularity: ~ **rating** *n* GEN COMM, POL cote de popularité *f*

population *n* ECON, S&M population *f*; ~ **census** *n* ECON, MATH *statistics* recensement de la population *m*; ~ **density** *n* ECON, POL densité de la population *f*, densité de peuplement *f*; ~ **explosion** *n* ECON, POL explosion démographique *f*; ~ **policy** *n* ECON, POL politique démographique *f*; ~ **statistics** *n pl* MATH, POL statistique démographique *f*

porcupine: ~ **provisions** *n pl* (*SYN shark repellents*) FIN *takeovers* antirequins *m pl*

pork *infrml* US POL pot-de-vin *m*; ~ **barrel** *infrml* US POL magouille *f* (*infrml*); ~ **chop** US HRM pistonné *m*

port *n* COMP point d'accès *m*, port d'accès *m*, TRANSP port *m*; ~ **access** *n* IMP/EXP, TRANSP entrée du port *f*; ~ **agent** *n* IMP/EXP, TRANSP agent portuaire *m*; ~ **of arrival** *n* IMP/EXP, TRANSP *harbour, airport* port d'arrivée *m*; ~ **charge** *n* IMP/EXP, TRANSP frais de port *m pl*; ~ **control** *n* TRANSP contrôle portuaire *m*; ~ **of destination** *n* IMP/EXP, TRANSP port de destination *m*; ~ **director** *n* HRM, TRANSP administrateur du port *m*, directeur du port *m*; ~ **disbursements** *n pl* IMP/EXP, TRANSP débours de port *m pl*; ~ **of discharge** *n* IMP/EXP, TRANSP port de déchargement *m*; ~ **dues** *n pl* (*pd*) IMP/EXP, TRANSP droits de port *m pl*; ~ **of entry** *n* IMP/EXP, TRANSP port d'arrivée *m*; ~ **facilities** *n pl* IMP/EXP, TRANSP installations portuaires *f pl*; ~ **health authority** *n (PHA)* TRANSP, WEL autorité portuaire de la santé *f*; ~ **interchange** *n* IMP/EXP, TRANSP *shipping* interconnexion portuaire *f*; ~ **layout** *n* IMP/EXP, TRANSP aménagement portuaire *m*; ~ **liner terms charge** *n (PLTC)* TRANSP *shipping* frais de manutention à la charge de la marchandise *m pl*; ~ **of loading** *n* IMP/EXP, TRANSP port de chargement *m*; ~ **management** *n* HRM, TRANSP gestion portuaire *f*; ~ **manager** *n* HRM, TRANSP administrateur du port *m*, directeur du port *m*; ~ **of necessity** *n* IMP/EXP, TRANSP port de refuge *m*; ~ **operation** *n* TRANSP exploitation portuaire *f*; ~ **operations officer** *n (POO)* HRM, TRANSP responsable des opérations portuaires *m*; ~ **of registry** *n* TRANSP *shipping* port d'armement *m*, port d'attache *m*; ~ **of shipment** *n* TRANSP port de charge *m*; ~ **and starboard thruster** *n* TRANSP propulseur de babord et de tribord *m*; ~ **statistics** *n pl* IMP/EXP, TRANSP statistiques portuaires *f pl*; ~ **surcharge** *n* IMP/EXP, TRANSP droits de port supplémentaires *m pl*; ~ **tariff** *n* IMP/EXP, TRANSP tarif portuaire *m*; ~ **tax** *n* IMP/EXP, TRANSP taxe de débarquement *f*; ~ **throughput** *n* IMP/EXP, TRANSP trafic portuaire *m*; ~ **traffic** *n* IMP/EXP, TRANSP trafic portuaire *m*; ~ **traffic control** *n* TRANSP *shipping* contrôle du trafic portuaire *m*; ~ **turnaround time** *n AmE*, ~ **turnround time** *n BrE* TRANSP *shipping* tour de rôle *m*; ~ **users' committee** *n* IMP/EXP, TRANSP comité d'usagers du port *m*; ◆ **make** ~ TRANSP arriver au port; ~ **to port** *(p to p)* IMP/EXP, TRANSP *shipping* port à port

Port:[1] ~ **of London Authority** *n (PLA)* GEN COMM port autonome de Londres

Port:[2] ~ **-au-Prince** *pr n* GEN COMM Port-au-Prince *n pr*; ~ **Louis** *pr n* GEN COMM Port Louis *n pr*; ~ **Moresby** *pr n* GEN COMM Port Moresby *n pr*; ~ **of Spain** *pr n* GEN COMM Port of Spain *n pr*

portability *n* COMP portabilité *f*

portable[1] *adj* ADMIN *typewriter* portatif, COMP *software, hardware which can be transferred* portable, HRM *industrial relations* transférable

portable[2] *n* COMP portable *m*; ~ **computer** COMP ordinateur portable *m*, portable *m*; ~ **gangway** TRANSP *shipping* passerelle de débarquement *f*

portainer: ~ **crane** *n* TRANSP *cargo handling* portique à conteneurs *m*

portal: ~ **berth** *n* TRANSP *shipping* quai à manutention horizontale *m*; ~ **crane** *n* TRANSP *cargo handling* grue portique *f*, portique *m*; ~ **-to-portal pay** *n* HRM indemnité de porte à porte *f*

porter *n* HRM maître d'hôtel *m*

portfolio *n* GEN COMM, POL *of government activity*, STOCK portefeuille *m*; ~ **balance** FIN équilibre de portefeuille *m*; ~ **beta score** STOCK *volatility of portfolio* mesure du coefficient bêta d'un portefeuille *f*, score bêta de portefeuille *m*; ~ **dividend** STOCK dividende de portefeuille *m*; ~ **income** FIN, INS, STOCK revenu de placements *m*; ~ **insurance**

INS, STOCK assurance de portefeuille *f*; ~ **investment** FIN, STOCK investissement de portefeuille *m*; ~ **management** BANK, FIN, GEN COMM, MGMNT, STOCK gestion de portefeuille *f*; ~ **management service** BANK, FIN, MGMNT, STOCK service de gestion de portefeuille *m*; ~ **management theory** BANK, FIN, STOCK *investment decision approach* théorie de gestion de portefeuille *f*; ~ **manager** BANK, FIN, GEN COMM, MGMNT, STOCK gestionnaire de portefeuille *m*; ~ **reinsurance** INS réassurance de portefeuille *f*; ~ **selection** FIN, STOCK sélection de portefeuille *f*; ~ **split** FIN, STOCK fractionnement de portefeuille *m*; ~ **switching** FIN, STOCK arbitrage de portefeuille *m*; ~ **theory** BANK, FIN, STOCK *investment decision approach* théorie de portefeuille *f*; ~ **trade** BANK, FIN, STOCK transactions de portefeuille *f pl*; ~ **transfer** GEN COMM, INS cession de portefeuille *f*, transfert de portefeuille *m*

porting *n* COMP *software* portage *m*

portion *n* FIN *of dividend, amount* fraction *f*, partie *f*

Porto Novo *pr n* GEN COMM Porto Novo *n pr*

portrait[1] *adj* COMP, GEN COMM, MEDIA à la française

portrait[2] *n* COMP, MEDIA portrait *m*; ~ **format** COMP *document layout*, MEDIA format en hauteur *m*, format portrait *m*, format vertical *m*, format à la française *m*

Portugal *pr n* GEN COMM Portugal *m*

Portuguese[1] *adj* GEN COMM portugais

Portuguese[2] *n* GEN COMM *language* portugais *m*, *person* Portugais *m*

POS[1] *abbr (point of sale)* S&M LV *(lieu de vente)*, PV *(point de vente)*

POS:[2] ~ **advertising** *n* S&M publicité PLV *f*; ~ **machine** *n* S&M terminal point de vente *m*; ~ **terminal** *n* S&M terminal point de vente *m*

pose *vt* GEN COMM *problem, threat* constituer

position[1] *n* ACC, BANK situation *f*, GEN COMM *point of view* point de vue *m*, *situation* position *f*, HRM poste *m*, STOCK position *f*; ~ **account** STOCK compte de position *m*; ~ **of authority** HRM poste de commandement *m*; ~ **-finding instrument** *(PFI)* TRANSP *shipping* radiogoniomètre *m*; ~ **limit** STOCK limite d'emprise *f*; ~ **net credit** STOCK *options* crédit net de position *m*; ~ **net delta** STOCK *options* delta net de position *m*; ~ **paper** *jarg* POL compte-rendu *m*, rapport *m*; ~ **-risk capital** STOCK capital soumis au risque de position *m*; ~ **trader** STOCK négociateur de positions à long terme *m*; ~ **trading** STOCK négociation sur positions à long terme *f*, position trading *f*; ◆ **be in a** ~ **to do** GEN COMM être en mesure de faire, être à même de faire; ~ **closed** BANK, GEN COMM guichet fermé *m*; **in an exposed** ~ GEN COMM position exposée *f*; **take a** ~ STOCK *on currency* se placer; **take a long** ~ STOCK aller loin, prendre une position longue; **take a straddle** ~ STOCK prendre une position de straddle, se placer à cheval

position[2] *vt* GEN COMM, S&M, STOCK *client in contract* positionner; **~ oneself** GEN COMM se positionner

positioning *n* GEN COMM, S&M, STOCK positionnement *m*

positive[1] *adj* GEN COMM *favourable* favorable, *yield* positif

positive:[2] **~ action** *n* HRM *BrE (cf affirmative action AmE) in recruiting* discrimination positive *f*, mesures anti-discriminatoires *f pl*, politique anti-discriminatoire *f*, LAW acte manifeste *m*, acte positif *m*, POL, WEL *BrE (cf affirmative action AmE) in recruiting* discrimination positive *f*, mesures anti-discriminatoires *f pl*, politique anti-discriminatoire *f*; **~ cash flow** *n* (ANT *negative cash flow*) ACC, FIN cash-flow positif *m*, marge brute d'autofinancement positive *f*, variation positive de trésorerie *f*; **~ confirmation** *n* ACC *auditing* confirmation positive *f*; **~ correlation** *n* MATH *between two variables* corrélation positive *f*; **~ discrimination** *n* *BrE (cf affirmative action AmE)* HRM, POL, WEL discrimination positive *f*, mesures anti-discriminatoires *f pl*, politique anti-discriminatoire *f*; **~ economics** *n* ECON *econometrics* économie positive *f*; **~ feedback** *n* (ANT *negative feedback*) ECON, GEN COMM réaction positive *f*, rétroaction positive *f*; **~ file** *n* BANK fichier de contrôle positif *m*; **~ gearing** *n BrE (cf positive leverage AmE)* ACC, FIN effet de levier positif *m*; **~ interest-rate gap** *n* ECON écart positif entre les taux d'intérêt *m*; **~ labor relations** *n pl AmE*, **~ labour relations** *n pl BrE* HRM relations directes patronat-employés *f pl*; **~ leverage** *n AmE (cf positive gearing BrE)* ACC, FIN effet de levier positif *m*; **~ monetary compensatory amount** *n* (ANT *negative monetary compensatory amount*) ECON, FIN montant compensatoire monétaire positif *m*; **~ neutrality** *n* POL neutralité positive *f*; **~ response** *n* GEN COMM réponse affirmative *f*; **~ -sum game** *n* ECON jeu à somme positive *m*; **~ yield curve** *n* BANK, ECON, STOCK courbe des taux positive *f*

positively *adv* (ANT *negatively*) GEN COMM positivement

possession *n* LAW, PROP possession *f*

possibilism *n* POL politique du possible *f*

possibility *n* GEN COMM possibilité *f*

post[1] *n* COMMS *BrE letters* courrier *m*, envoyer par la poste, *service* correspondance *f*, poste *f*, HRM *job* poste *m*; **~ -bankruptcy** *n* FIN après faillite; **~ -closing trial balance** *n* ACC balance après clôture *f*; **~ -entry closed shop** *n* HRM monopole syndical après l'embauche *m*; **~ -entry discrimination** *n* ECON discrimination après l'accès au marché du travail *f*; **~ -flight information** *n* TRANSP information après-vol *f*; **~ -industrial society** *n* ECON, POL société post-industrielle *f*; **~ office** *n* ADMIN bureau de poste *m*, COMMS bureau de poste *m*; **~ office box** *n (POB)* COMMS boîte postale *f (BP)*; **~ office savings bank** *n* BANK caisse d'épargne de la poste *f*; **~ pallet** *n*

TRANSP palette à montants *f*, palette à ridelles *f*; **~ -purchase remorse** *n jarg* S&M dépression post-achat *f*; **~ -shipment inspection** *n* TRANSP contrôle après expédition *m*; ◆ **~ office preferred** *(POP)* COMMS formats postaux normalisés *m pl*; **through the ~** *BrE (cf through the mail AmE)* COMMS par la poste

post[2] *vt* ACC comptabiliser, porter, porter sur un compte, COMMS *BrE (cf mail AmE) letter* envoyer, expédier, mettre à la poste, poster, GEN COMM *notice* afficher, HRM *employee* affecter, *team* affecter, muter, STOCK *margin deposit* afficher; ◆ **~ an entry** ACC porter une écriture; **~ margin** STOCK afficher une marge; **~ up an account** BANK mettre un compte à jour

Post: ~ Office Giro account *n* BANK *UK* ≈ compte chèques postal *m*, BANK *UK (cf postal checking account US)* compte courant postal *m*

POST *abbr (point-of-sale terminal)* S&M TPV *(terminal point de vente)*

postage *n* COMMS *charges, rates* tarifs postaux *m pl, cost* tarif d'affranchissement *m*; **~ due** *n* COMMS taxe postale *f*; **~ -due stamp** *n* COMMS timbre-taxe *m*; **~ meter** *n AmE (cf franking machine BrE)* COMMS machine à affranchir *f*; **~ and packing** *n pl (p&p)* COMMS frais de port et d'emballage *m pl*, port et emballage *m pl*; **~ -paid impression** *n (PPI)* COMMS, GEN COMM, IMP/EXP pré-impression *f*; **~ rates** *n pl* COMMS tarifs postaux *m pl*; **~ stamp** *n* COMMS timbre *m*, timbre-poste *m*; **~ stamp remittance** *n* GEN COMM *method of payment* paiement en timbres-poste *m*; ◆ **~ paid** *(p.p.)* COMMS, GEN COMM port payé *m (p.p.)*

postal: ~ address *n* COMMS adresse postale *f*; **~ assistant** *n* HRM auxiliaire des postes *m*, employé des postes *m*; **~ ballot** *n BrE (cf absentee ballot AmE)* HRM vote par correspondance *m*; **~ checking account** *n US (cf Post Office Giro account UK)* BANK compte courant postal *m*; **~ code** *n BrE (cf zip code AmE)* COMMS code postal *m*; **~ export** *n* IMP/EXP exportation envoyée par la poste *f*; **~ meter** *n AmE (cf franking machine BrE)* COMMS machine à affranchir *f*; **~ note** *n Aus (cf money order AmE, postal order BrE)* BANK, FIN mandat *m*, mandat postal *m*; **~ order** *n BrE (PO, cf money order AmE, postal note Aus)* BANK, FIN mandat *m*, mandat postal *m*; **~ remittance** *n* ACC versement postal *m*; **~ service** *n* COMMS service postal *m*; **~ vote** *n* HRM, POL vote par correspondance *m*; **~ worker** *n* HRM employé des postes *m*

postassessing *n* TAX mesure de postcotisation *f*, postévaluation *f*

postaudit *n* TAX vérification a posteriori *f*

postbox *n* ADMIN *BrE (cf mailbox AmE)*, COMMS *BrE (cf mailbox AmE)*, COMP *(SYN mailbox)* boîte aux lettres *f*

postcode *n BrE (cf zip code AmE)* COMMS code postal *m*

post-Communist *adj* GEN COMM post-communiste

postdate *vt* COMMS postdater

postdated[1] *adj (pd)* COMMS postdaté

postdated:[2] ~ **check** *n AmE*, ~ **cheque** *n BrE* BANK chèque postdaté *m*

posted:[1] ~ **price** *n jarg* ECON, TAX *of oil* prix de vente hors taxe de mise à disposition du pétrole

posted:[2] **be** ~ *phr* HRM être en poste *loc m*

post-election *adj* GEN COMM post-électoral

postentry *n* IMP/EXP, TRANSP *shipping* déclaration supplémentaire *f*

poster *n* MEDIA, S&M affiche *f*; ~ **advertising** S&M publicité par affichage *f*; ~ **display** S&M *advertising* affichage *m*; ~ **site** S&M *advertising* panneau d'affichage portatif *m*

postgraduate *n* WEL diplômé de l'université *m*

Postgraduate: ~ **Certificate of Education** *n UK (PGCE)* WEL ≈ Certificat d'aptitude au professorat d'enseignement du second degré *m (CAPES)*

postimplementation: ~ **audit** *n* GEN COMM vérification a posteriori *f*

posting *n* ACC comptabilisation *f*, ADMIN, GEN COMM *of notice* affichage *m*, HRM affectation *f*, nomination *f, of team* affectation *f*, LAW *civil procedure* affichage *m, commercial* transaction *f*; ~ **error** ACC erreur d'écriture *f*, erreur de comptabilisation *f*

post-Keynesians *n pl* ECON post-keynésiens *m pl*

postman *n BrE (cf mail carrier AmE, mailman AmE)* COMMS facteur *m*, postier *m*

postmark *n* COMMS cachet de la poste *m*

postmaturity: ~ **interest** *n* BANK intérêts de retard *m pl*, intérêts moratoires *m pl*

post meridiem *adv (pm)* GEN COMM après-midi

post-paid *phr (p.p.)* COMMS, GEN COMM port payé *m (p.p.)*

postpone *vt* GEN COMM remettre, remettre à plus tard, retarder; ◆ ~ **tax** TAX différer le paiement de l'impôt

postponement *n* GEN COMM remise *f*, remise à plus tard *f*

postscript *n (PS)* COMMS post-scriptum *m (PS)*

PostScript: ~ **printer**® *n* COMP *page description language* imprimante PostScript® *f*

postwar[1] *adj* ECON d'après-guerre

postwar:[2] ~ **boom** *n* ECON prospérité d'après-guerre *f*; ~ **period** *n* ECON période d'après-guerre *f*

pot *n* TRANSP *shipping* crapaudine *f*; ◆ ~ **is clean** *jarg* STOCK émission totalement écoulée *f*

potential[1] *adj* GEN COMM potentiel

potential[2] *n* GEN COMM potentiel *m*; ~ **buyer** PROP, S&M acheteur potentiel *m*; ~ **commitment** GEN COMM engagement potentiel *m*; ~ **income** ECON revenu potentiel *m*; ~ **investor** STOCK investisseur potentiel *m*, investisseur éventuel *m*; ~ **output** ECON, IND potentiel de croissance de production *m*, produit potentiel *m*; ~ **profit** STOCK plus-value

éventuelle *f*, profit potentiel *m*; ◆ **have** ~ GEN COMM avoir du potentiel, être prometteur

potentially[1] *adv* GEN COMM potentiellement

potentially:[2] ~ **exempt transfers** *n pl UK (PETs)* TAX transferts potentiellement exonérés *m pl*

poultry: ~ **farm** *n* ECON élevage de volailles *m*

pound *n* ECON *currency* livre *f*, GEN COMM *(lb)* livre *f (lb)*; ~ **"spot" and "forward"** ECON cours de la livre au comptant et à terme; ~ **sterling** GEN COMM livre sterling *f*

pounds: ~ **per square inch** *n pl (PSI)* TRANSP livres par pouce carré *f pl*

pour: ~ **autre vie** *phr* LAW pour autre vie

poverty *n* WEL pauvreté *f*; ~ **line** WEL seuil de pauvreté *m*; ~ **trap** ECON, WEL appauvrissement paradoxal *m*, cercle vicieux de la pauvreté *m*

power[1] *n* COMP *electrical* alimentation *f*, courant *m*, courant électrique *m*, ENVIR énergie *f*, GEN COMM *capability* autorité *f, political entity* pouvoir *m*, IND courant *m*, courant électrique *m*, puissance *f*, énergie *f*; ~ **of appointment** *n* LAW faculté de distribution des biens conférée à un légataire *f*; ~ **of attorney** *n (PA)* ADMIN, LAW procuration *f*; ~ **fail** *n* COMP coupure d'alimentation *f*, panne d'électricité *f*, panne de courant *f*, panne de secteur *f*; ~ **failure** *n* COMP coupure d'alimentation *f*, panne d'électricité *f*, panne de courant *f*, panne de secteur *f*; ~ **pack** *n* TRANSP *shipping* bloc d'alimentation *m*, groupe électrogène portable *m*; ~ **politics** *n pl* POL politique d'intimidation *f*, politique du coup de force *f*; ~ **of recourse** *n* LAW droit de recours *m*, faculté de recours *f*, voies de recours *f pl*; ~ **of sale** *n* LAW pouvoir de vendre *m*, pouvoir de vente *m*, PROP pouvoir de vente *m*; ~ **station** *n* ENVIR, IND centrale électrique *f*; ~ **steering** *n* TRANSP direction assistée *f*; ~ **struggle** *n* POL lutte pour le pouvoir *f*; ~ **surge** *n* COMP, IND pointe de puissance *f*, surtension *f*; ~ **takeoff** *n* TRANSP prise de force *f*, prise de mouvement *f*; ~ **-to-weight ratio** *n* TRANSP rapport puissance-poids *m*; ◆ **have the** ~ **to** GEN COMM avoir le pouvoir de; **in** ~ POL *government* au pouvoir; ~ **of media** MEDIA puissance des médias *f*

power[2] *vt* COMP *electrically* alimenter; ~ **off** COMP mettre hors tension; ~ **on** COMP mettre sous tension; ~ **up** COMP mettre sous tension

powerful *adj* GEN COMM puissant

powering: ~ **off** *n* COMP mise hors tension *f*; ~ **on** *n* COMP mise sous tension *f*; ~ **up** *n* COMP mise sous tension *f*

p.p. *abbr* COMMS *(post-paid, postage paid)* p.p. *(port payé)*, GEN COMM *(per procuration)* p.p. *(par procuration)*, GEN COMM *(post-paid, postage paid)* p.p. *(port payé)*

pp *abbr (picked ports)* TRANSP *shipping* ports de cueillette *m pl*

pp. *abbr (prepaid)* GEN COMM payé d'avance, prépayé

PPB *abbr (planning, programming, budgeting)* POL planification, programmation, budgétisation *f pl*

PPBS *abbr (planning, programming, budgeting system)* ACC, FIN, HRM, MGMNT RCB *(rationalisation des choix budgétaires)*

PPI[1] *abbr* ACC *(producer price index)* indice des prix à la production *m*, COMMS *(postage-paid impression)* pré-impression *f*, ECON *(producer price index) econometrics* indice des prix à la production *m*, GEN COMM *(postage-paid impression)*, IMP/EXP *(postage-paid impression)* pré-impression *f*, INS *(policy proof of interest) marine* police de justification d'intérêt *f*, police preuve de l'intérêt assuré *f*

PPI:[2] ~ **policy** *n* INS police de justification d'intérêt *f*, police preuve de l'intérêt assuré *f*

ppm *abbr (parts per million)* GEN COMM p.p.m. *(partie par million)*

PPP *abbr* ECON *(purchasing power parity)* PPA *(parité du pouvoir d'achat)*, FIN *(profit and performance planning)*, MGMNT *(profit and performance planning)* prévision de bénéfices et de performances *f*, WEL *(Private Patients Plan)* programme hospitalier de clientèle privée

PPS *abbr* POL *UK (parliamentary private secretary)* parlementaire attaché à un ministre, TRANSP *(precise positioning service) shipping, satellite navigation* service de positionnement précis *m*

PQLI *abbr (physical quality of life index)* ECON *econometrics* qualité physique de l'indice de vie *f*

pr. *abbr (price)* ECON px *(prix)*, valeur *f*, GEN COMM px *(prix)*, STOCK cours *m*

PR[1] *abbr* POL *(proportional representation)* RP *(représentation proportionnelle)*, S&M *(public relations) advertising* RP *(relations publiques)*

PR:[2] ~ **agency** *n* S&M agence de RP *f*

PRA *abbr (purchase and resale agreement)* STOCK accord de prise en pension *m*, faculté d'achat et de revente *f*, prise en pension *f*

practicability *n* FIN, GEN COMM viabilité *f*

practicable *adj* FIN, GEN COMM viable

practical: ~ **politics** *n pl* POL politique d'expédients *f*; ~ **use** *n* HRM *application of skills* usage pratique *m*

practice[1] *n* GEN COMM *of professional person* cabinet *m*, LAW *use* coutume *f*, exercice *m*, pratique *f*, procédure *f*, usage *m*; ◆ **in** ~ GEN COMM en pratique

practice[2] *AmE*, **practise** *vt BrE* GEN COMM, LAW pratiquer

practising *adj* GEN COMM, LAW en exercice *loc m*

pragmatic *adj* GEN COMM pragmatique

pragmatically *adv* GEN COMM de façon pragmatique *loc f*

Prague *pr n* GEN COMM Prague *n pr*

praxeology *n* ECON praxéologie *f*

preamble *n* GEN COMM *to agreement, contract*, PATENTS préambule *m*

prearrange *vt* GEN COMM prédéterminer

prearranged *adj* GEN COMM prédéterminé

preassessing *n* TAX mesure de précotisation *f*, préévaluation *f*

preaudit *n* TAX vérification préalable *f*

preauthorized: ~ **check** *n AmE*, ~ **cheque** *n BrE* BANK chèque par procuration *m*, chèque préautorisé *m*; ~ **payment** *n* BANK paiement de prélèvement *m*, paiement par avis de prélèvement *m*, règlement par avis de prélèvement *m*

prebankruptcy *n* TAX avant-faillite *f*

prebill *n* S&M facturation anticipée *f*

pre-budget *adj* ECON pré-budgétaire

precautionary[1] *adj* GEN COMM préventif; ◆ **as a** ~ **measure** GEN COMM par mesure de précaution, par mesure préventive

precautionary:[2] ~ **demand for money** *n* ECON demande de monnaie à titre de précaution *f*; ~ **measure** *n* GEN COMM mesure de précaution *f*, mesure préventive *f*; ~ **motive** *n* GEN COMM motif de prévention *m*; ~ **principle** *n* ENVIR principe de précaution *m*; ~ **saving** *n* ECON épargne de précaution *f*

precede *vt* GEN COMM précéder

precedence *n* GEN COMM préséance *f*; ◆ **take** ~ **over** GEN COMM avoir la priorité sur, avoir la préséance sur

preceding[1] *adj* GEN COMM précédent

preceding:[2] ~ **taxation year** *n* TAX année d'imposition antérieure *f*; ~ **year** *n* GEN COMM année précédente *f*

precharacterizing: ~ **portion** *n* PATENTS préambule *m*

precinct *n* GEN COMM, S&M galerie marchande *f*

precious: ~ **metal** *n* ENVIR métal précieux *m*

precise: ~ **positioning service** *n (PPS)* TRANSP *shipping, satellite navigation* service de positionnement précis *m*

precision: ~ **engineering** *n* IND mécanique de précision *f*

preclude *vt* GEN COMM exclure d'avance

precompute *vt* FIN *interest in instalment loans* préétablir

precondition *n* GEN COMM préambule *m*

predate *vt* GEN COMM antidater

predated *adj* GEN COMM antidaté

predating *n* GEN COMM antidatation *f*

predator *n* GEN COMM, S&M prédateur *m*

predatory: ~ **competition** *n* ECON, GEN COMM, HRM, IND, S&M concurrence acharnée *f*, concurrence féroce *f*, concurrence sauvage *f*; ~ **pricing** *n* ECON pratique de prix sauvage *f*, tarification sauvage *f*

predecessor *n* GEN COMM prédécesseur *m*; ~ **in title** PATENTS prédécesseur en droit *m*

predelivery: ~ **inspection** *n (PDI)* TRANSP contrôle avant livraison *m*

predetermine *vt* GEN COMM prédéterminer

predetermined[1] *adj* GEN COMM prédéterminé

predetermined:[2] ~ **motion time system** n *(PMTS)* ECON, FIN, MGMNT méthode des temps prédéterminés *f (PMTS)*; ~ **price** n STOCK cours prédéterminé *m*, prix prédéterminé *m*

predict vt GEN COMM prévoir

predictable[1] *adj* GEN COMM prévisible

predictable:[2] ~ **life** n ACC *of business assets* durée de vie prévue *f*

predicted *adj* GEN COMM prévu

prediction n GEN COMM prévision *f*

pre-eminent *adj* GEN COMM, HRM prééminent, remarquable

pre-emption: ~ **right** n STOCK droit de préemption *m*, droit préférentiel de souscription *m*

pre-emptive: ~ **bid** n STOCK ouverture préventive *f*; ~ **right** n STOCK droit de préemption *m*, droit préférentiel de souscription *m*

pre-emptor n LAW acquéreur *m*

pre-entry n IMP/EXP déclaration préalable *f*; ~ **closed shop** HRM monopole syndical préalable à l'embauche *m*; ~ **discrimination** ECON discrimination qui bloque l'accès au marché du travail *f*

pre-existing: ~ **use** n PROP utilisation préexistante *f*

pref. *abbr (preference)* GEN COMM préf. *(préférence)*

prefabricated[1] *adj* PROP préfabriqué

prefabricated:[2] ~ **housing** n PROP logement préfabriqué *m*

preference n *(pref.)* GEN COMM préférence *f (préf.)*; ~ **dividend** *BrE (cf preferred dividend AmE)* ACC dividende sur actions privilégiées *m*; ~ **share** *BrE (cf preferred stock AmE)* ACC, FIN, STOCK action de priorité *f*, action de préférence *f*, action privilégiée *f*, action à dividende prioritaire *f*, ADP

preferential: ~ **creditor** n GEN COMM créancier privilégié *m*; ~ **form** n STOCK formule préférentielle *f*, partie réservée d'une émission *f*; ~ **interest rate** n BANK taux bonifié *m*; ~ **rate** n BANK *of interest on loan* taux préférentiel *m*; ~ **shop** n GEN COMM entreprise à préférence syndicale *f*, HRM *industrial relations*, IND entreprise à monopole syndical *f*; ~ **treatment** n GEN COMM traitement de faveur *m*

preferred: ~ **beneficiary** n TAX bénéficiaire privilégié *m*; ~ **creditor** n GEN COMM créancier privilégié *m*; ~ **dividend** n *AmE (cf preference dividend BrE)* ACC dividende sur actions privilégiées *m*; ~ **dividend coverage** n ACC couverture du dividende privilégié par le bénéfice *f*; ~ **habitat theory** n FIN théorie du lieu préféré *f*; ~ **investment certificate** n STOCK certificat d'investissement prioritaire *m*, CIP; ~ **rate** n GEN COMM taux privilégié *m*; ~ **risk** n INS risque privilégié *m*; ~ **stock** n *AmE (cf preference share BrE)* ACC, FIN, STOCK action de priorité *f*, action de préférence *f*, action privilégiée *f*, action à dividende prioritaire *f*, ADP; ~ **stock ratio** n STOCK pourcentage d'actions de priorité *m*, taux d'action préférentiel *m*

prefinancing: ~ **credit** n BANK crédit de préfinancement *m*

preinspection: ~ **requirement** n BANK exigence préalable à l'inspection *f*

prejudice n GEN COMM *damage* préjudice *m*; ◆ **without** ~ *(WP)* GEN COMM sans préjudice, INS sans constituer de précédent, sous toutes réserves

prejudicial *adj* GEN COMM préjudiciable

prelease n PROP bail préalable *m*

preliminary: ~ **day** n STOCK jour des reports *m*; ~ **estimate** n GEN COMM devis estimatif *m*; ~ **examination** n PATENTS examen préliminaire *m*; ~ **expenses** n pl ACC frais d'établissement *m pl*; ~ **investigation** n LAW enquête préliminaire *f*, instruction *f*; ~ **prospectus** n STOCK prospectus préliminaire *m*

preloading: ~ **inspection** n TRANSP contrôle avant chargement *m*

premature *adj* GEN COMM prématuré

premier: ~ **borrower** n *BrE (cf prime borrower AmE)* BANK, FIN emprunteur de premier ordre *m*, emprunteur très solvable *m*

premise n GEN COMM prémisse *f*; ◆ **on the** ~ **that** GEN COMM dans l'hypothèse où

premises n pl GEN COMM, IND locaux *m pl*, PROP lieux *m pl*

premium n BANK *for loan*, FIN, HRM *industrial relations*, INS prime *f*, LAW prime *f*, reprise *f*, S&M *advertising* prime *f*, STOCK prime *f*, prix d'option *m*, prix au-dessus du pair *m*, *futures market* excédent de prix *m*, prime *f*, *of option* prix *m*; ~ **bond** n STOCK obligation à primes *f*; ~ **bonus** n HRM, STOCK salaire à prime de rendement *m*; ~ **and discount on exchange** n pl FIN pertes et bénéfices de change *f pl*; ~ **grade** n GEN COMM première qualité *f*; ~ **-grade gasoline** n *AmE (cf premium-grade petrol BrE)* ENVIR super *m (infrml)*, supercarburant *m*; ~ **-grade petrol** n *BrE (cf premium-grade gasoline AmE)* ENVIR super *m (infrml)*, supercarburant *m*; ~ **income** n INS recette de primes *f*, revenu des primes *m*; ~ **loan** n BANK emprunt à prime *m*; ~ **offer** n GEN COMM offre spéciale *f*, S&M *marketing* offre autopayante *f*, offre spéciale *f*; ~ **over bond value** n STOCK prime sur valeur de l'obligation *f*; ~ **over conversion value** n STOCK prime sur valeur de conversion *f*; ~ **pay** n HRM salaire bonifié *m*; ~ **price** n S&M prix fort *m*, prix majoré *m*, prix élevé *m*; ~ **pricing** n S&M fixation d'un prix fort *f*, fixation d'un prix majoré *f*, fixation d'un prix élevé *f*; ~ **quotation** n STOCK cotation au-dessus de la valeur nominale *f*, cotation au-dessus du pair *f*; ~ **raid** n STOCK attaque avec offre supérieure au cours du marché; ~ **rate** n INS, STOCK taux de prime *m*; ~ **reserve** n FIN, STOCK réserve prime d'émission *f*; ~ **savings account** n BANK compte d'épargne à taux bonifié *m*; ~ **statement** n FIN décompte de prime *m*; ~ **transfer** n INS transfert de prime *m*; ◆ **at a** ~ FIN, GEN COMM à prime, STOCK *bond, share* au-dessus du pair

Premium: ~ **Bonds** *n pl UK* FIN, STOCK obligations à lots *f pl*, obligations à terme *f pl*; ~ **Savings Bonds** *n pl UK* FIN, STOCK obligations à lots *f pl*, obligations à terme *f pl*

premiums: ~ **reducing** *phr* INS *marine* prime dégressive *f*

prenuptial: ~ **agreement** *n* LAW contrat prénuptial *m*; ~ **contract** *n* LAW contrat prénuptial *m*

pre-owned: ~ **car** *n* TRANSP voiture d'occasion *f*

prepackaged *adj* S&M *goods* préemballé

prepaid[1] *adj* COMMS port payé *m*, GEN COMM payé d'avance, port payé *m*, prépayé

prepaid:[2] ~ **charges** *n pl* TRANSP frais payés d'avance *m pl*; ~ **expense** *n* ACC dépense payée d'avance *f*; ~ **expenses** *n pl* ACC charges payées d'avance *f pl*; ~ **interest** *n* FIN intérêt payé d'avance *m*; ~ **letter of credit** *n* BANK lettre de crédit payée d'avance *f*; ~ **ticket advice** *n (PTA)* TRANSP avis de billet prépayé *m*

preparation *n* GEN COMM préparation *f*

prepare *vt* GEN COMM préparer; ♦ ~ **the financial statements** FIN dresser les états financiers; ~ **a return** TAX remplir une déclaration

preparer *n* ADMIN rédacteur *m*

prepayment *n* ACC charge payée d'avance *f*; ~ **clause** FIN, INS clause de paiement par anticipation *f*; ~ **penalty** BANK pénalité de remboursement anticipé *f*; ~ **privilege** FIN option de paiement par anticipation *f*

preplanning *n* GEN COMM planification préliminaire *f*

preproduction: ~ **expenditure** *n* FIN dépense avant fabrication *f*

prerecorded[1] *adj* MEDIA en différé, enregistré à l'avance, pré-enregistré

prerecorded:[2] ~ **broadcast** *n* MEDIA *TV and radio* émission en différé *f*, émission enregistrée à l'avance *f*, émission pré-enregistrée *f*

prerequisite *n* GEN COMM condition préalable *f*

preretiree *n* HRM prépensionné *m* (*Bel*), préretraité *m*

prerogative *n* LAW prérogative *f*

Pres. *abbr* (*President*) POL président *m*

presale *n* PROP vente sur plans *f*; ~ **order** STOCK ordre d'achat préalable *m*, ordre préalable à la vente *m*

preschool: ~ **center** *n AmE*, ~ **centre** *n BrE* WEL centre de préscolarisation *m*

prescribe *vt* LAW ordonner, prescrire

prescribed[1] *adj* GEN COMM déterminé par règlement, prescrit, prévu par règlement, réglementaire, visé par règlement; ♦ **within** ~ **limits** LAW dans les délais prescrits; **within the** ~ **time** GEN COMM dans les délais prescrits

prescribed:[2] ~ **aggregate reserve** *n (PAR)* BANK réserve globale visée par règlement *f*, réserve totale prescrite *f*; ~ **contract** *n* GEN COMM contrat prescrit *m*; ~ **form** *n* TAX formulaire prescrit *m*, formulaire réglementaire *m*; ~ **information** *n* TAX renseignements prescrits *m pl*, renseignements réglementaires *m pl*; ~ **price** *n* GEN COMM prix imposé *m*; ~ **rate** *n* TAX taux prescrit *m*; ~ **share** *n* STOCK action visée par règlement *f*; ~ **time** *n* GEN COMM délai prescrit *m*; ~ **venture capital corporation** *n* FIN corporation à capital de risque visée par règlement *f*

prescription *n* MGMNT remède *m*, PROP *US* (SYN *prescriptive right*) droit consacré par l'usage *m*, droit consacré par la prescription *m*, WEL *for medicine* ordonnance *f*

prescriptive: ~ **right** *n (cf prescription US)* PROP droit consacré par l'usage *m*, droit consacré par la prescription *m*

present[1] *adj* ECON, GEN COMM actuel; ♦ **at the** ~ **time** GEN COMM actuellement; **in the** ~ **state of affairs** GEN COMM les choses étant ce qu'elles sont, étant donné les circonstances

present:[2] ~ **value factor** *n* FIN facteur d'actualisation *m*; ~ **value method** *n* ACC, ECON, FIN méthode d'actualisation *f*

present[3] *vt* GEN COMM *report* présenter; ♦ ~ **a bill for discount** (ANT *present a bill for reception*), BANK présenter un effet à l'escompte, présenter une facture pour remise; ~ **a bill for reception** (ANT *present a bill for discount*) BANK présenter une facture pour réception; ~ **a check for payment** *AmE*, ~ **a cheque for payment** *BrE* BANK présenter un chèque au paiement; ~ **a draft for acceptance** BANK présenter une traite à l'acceptation; ~ **sth fairly** ACC *auditing* donner une image fidèle de qch

presentation *n* MGMNT, S&M présentation *f*; ~ **copy** MEDIA *print* exemplaire en service de presse *m*, spécimen *m*; ~ **of documents** IMP/EXP présentation de documents *f*

presenter *n* MEDIA présentateur *m*

presentment *n* BANK *of bill of exchange* présentation *f*

preservation *n* ENVIR *of habitat* protection *f*, préservation *f*

preservative *n* IND *food processing* conservateur *m*

preservatives: **no** ~ *phr* IND sans conservateur; **no** ~ **or additives** *phr* IND sans conservateur ni additif

preserve *vt* ENVIR protéger, préserver, GEN COMM *opportunity* préserver, IND *food* conserver

preserved: ~ **foods** *n pl* GEN COMM conserves *f pl*

preset *adj* COMP pré-défini

preshipment: ~ **inspection** *n* TRANSP contrôle avant expédition *m*

preside: ~ **over** *vt* GEN COMM *meeting* présider

presidency *n* GEN COMM, POL présidence *f*

president *n* GEN COMM *of meeting* président *m*, HRM, MGMNT président-directeur général *m*

President *n* (*Pres.*) POL *of state* président *m*; ~ **of the Group Executive Board** *US* HRM président du bureau exécutif *m*; ~ **of the Treasury Board** *US* FIN président du Conseil du Trésor *m*

presidential: ~ **election** n POL élections présidentielles f pl; ~ **election cycle theory** n STOCK théorie du cycle des élections présidentielles f

presiding: ~ **judge** n LAW président de tribunal m

presidium n HRM présidium m

presling n TRANSP *cargo handling* chargement préélingué m

preslinging n TRANSP *cargo handling* pré-élingage m

press[1] n MEDIA presse f; ~ **advertisement** n S&M annonce par voie de presse f; ~ **advertising** n S&M publicité-presse f; ~ **agency** n MEDIA agence de presse f; ~ **agent** n MEDIA attaché de presse m; ~ **availability** n jarg MEDIA, POL séance de réponses aux questions de la presse; ~ **campaign** n MEDIA campagne de presse f; ~ **clipping** n AmE (cf press cutting BrE) MEDIA coupure de journal f, coupure de presse f; ~ **conference** n MEDIA conférence de presse f; ~ **copy** n MEDIA exemplaire de presse m, exemplaire en service de presse m, spécimen m; ~ **coverage** n MEDIA couverture de presse f; ~ **cutting** n BrE (cf press clipping AmE) MEDIA coupure de journal f, coupure de presse f; ~ **flesh** n jarg POL bain de foule m; ~ **kit** n MEDIA dossier de presse m; ~ **launch** n MEDIA lancement dans la presse m; ~ **officer** n HRM, MEDIA, POL, S&M responsable du service de presse m; ~ **photographer** n MEDIA photographe de presse mf; ~ **relations** n pl MEDIA *relationship* relations avec la presse f pl, *service* service de presse m; ~ **release** n COMMS, MEDIA communiqué de presse m; ♦ **go to** ~ MEDIA passer sous presse

press[2] vt COMP *button* appuyer sur

pressure n GEN COMM pression f; ~ **group** POL groupe de pression m; ♦ **come under** ~ **from** GEN COMM se trouver contraint de, subir la pression de

Prestel® n UK COMMS service de vidéotexte de British Telecom, ≈ Télétel® m (France)

prestige: ~ **advertising** n S&M publicité de prestige f; ~ **pricing** n S&M politique de prix d'écrémage f, tarification de prestige f

prestigious adj GEN COMM prestigieux

presumption n GEN COMM, PATENTS présomption f

presumptive: ~ **tax** n TAX imposition présomptive f

pretax: ~ **earnings** n pl ECON, FIN, GEN COMM, TAX gains avant imposition m pl; ~ **rate of return** n ECON, FIN, GEN COMM, TAX taux de rendement avant imposition m; ~ **yield** n ACC, ECON, FIN, GEN COMM, TAX rendement brut m

Pretoria pr n GEN COMM Pretoria n pr

pretreatment n ENVIR *of waste before dumping* traitement préliminaire m

prevail vi GEN COMM *hold good* prédominer, régner, POL régner

prevailing[1] adj GEN COMM prédominant

prevailing:[2] ~ **market price** n STOCK cours du marché m, prix courant du marché m; ~ **party** n LAW partie gagnante f

prevent vt GEN COMM empêcher

preventative: ~ **maintenance** n ADMIN, GEN COMM, IND, MGMNT entretien préventif m, maintenance préventive f

prevention n ENVIR *of atmospheric, water, noise pollution* lutte f

Prevention: ~ **of Fraud Act** n UK FIN, LAW *investment* loi relative à la prévention des fraudes

preventive: ~ **maintenance** n ADMIN, GEN COMM, IND, MGMNT entretien préventif m, maintenance préventive f

preview vt COMP *wordprocessed document* prévisualiser

previous: ~ **engagement** n GEN COMM engagement antérieur m; ~ **history** n GEN COMM, HRM, WEL antécédents m pl; ~ **year** n GEN COMM année précédente f

prexy n jarg US MGMNT président

price:[1] ~ -**sensitive** adj S&M sensible au prix

price[2] n (pr.) ECON prix m (px), valeur f, GEN COMM prix m (px) STOCK *of a security* cours m; ~ **advantage** STOCK avantage de prix m, avantage tarifaire m; ~ **after hours** STOCK cours après clôture m, cours après l'heure de fermeture m, cours hors Bourse m; ~ **behavior** AmE, ~ **behaviour** BrE STOCK *shares, options* comportement des cours m, comportement du prix m; ~ **bid** STOCK offre de prix f; ~ **bunching** (SYN *price staggering*) ECON fixation des prix étalée f, fixation synchronisée des prix f; ~ **ceiling** ECON plafond de prix m; ~ **change** STOCK *futures* changement de prix m, variation de prix f; ~ **competitiveness** GEN COMM, S&M, STOCK compétitivité des prix f; ~ **consumption curve** (PCC) ECON courbe de consommation déterminée par le prix f; ~ **control** (SYN *public pricing*) ECON, FIN, S&M contrôle des prix m, politique des prix f; ~ **cut** ECON, FIN, GEN COMM, S&M baisse de prix f, rabais m, réduction des prix f; ~ **cutting** ECON, FIN, GEN COMM rabais des prix m, réduction des prix f, S&M rabais des prix m, réduction des prix f, *underselling* gâchage des prix m; ~ **deregulation** GEN COMM libération des prix f; ~ **deterioration** ECON détérioration des prix f; ~ **determination** ECON, GEN COMM, S&M détermination des prix f, fixation des prix f, établissement des prix m; ~ **differential** ACC, FIN écart de prix m, GEN COMM, HRM, S&M différence de prix f, écart de prix m, STOCK écart de prix m; ~ **discrimination** GEN COMM, S&M discrimination de prix f, prix discriminatoires m pl, tarif discriminatoire m; ~ -**earnings multiple** ACC, FIN, STOCK coefficient de capitalisation des résultats m, rapport cours-bénéfice m, ratio cours-bénéfice m; ~ -**earnings ratio** (PER) ACC, FIN, STOCK *share* coefficient de capitalisation des résultats m (CCR), rapport cours-bénéfice m, ratio cours-bénéfice m; ~ **effect** ECON effet de prix m;

~ **elasticity** ECON, GEN COMM, S&M élasticité-prix *f*; ~ **escalation** ECON flambée des prix *f*; ~ **ex-works** GEN COMM, S&M prix départ usine *m*; ~ **factor** STOCK coefficient de conversion *m*; ~ **-fixing** ECON *by government* contrôle des prix *m*, FIN contrôle des prix *m*, entente illicite sur les prix *f*, fixation des prix *f*, LAW accord sur les prix *m*, entente illicite sur les prix *f*, S&M entente illicite sur les prix *f*, *by shopkeeper* fixation des prix *f*; ~ **flexibility** ECON, GEN COMM, S&M flexibilité des prix *f*, élasticité-prix *f*; ~ **floor** ECON plancher des prix *m*; ~ **fluctuation** STOCK variation de prix *f*; ~ **fluctuation limit** STOCK limite de fluctuation *f*, limite de variation *f*; ~ **for the account** BANK cours à terme *m*; ~ **freeze** ECON, GEN COMM blocage des prix *m*, gel des prix *m*; ~ **gap** ACC, FIN, GEN COMM, HRM, S&M écart de prix *m*, STOCK gap *m*, écart vide *m*, écart de prix *m*; ~ **in the streets** STOCK cours hors Bourse *m*; ~ **incentive** ECON, S&M motivation par les prix *f*; ~ **increase** ACC, ECON, FIN, GEN COMM, S&M augmentation des prix *f*, hausse des prix *f*, majoration de prix *f*, renchérissement *m*; ~ **index** ACC, ECON, FIN indice des prix *m*; ~ **index level** STOCK niveau de l'indice des cours *m*, niveau de l'indice des prix *m*; ~ **inelasticity** ECON inélasticité des prix *f*, non-élasticité des prix *f*; ~ **inflation** ECON inflation par les prix *f*; ~ **label** S&M étiquette *f*; ~ **leader** ECON entreprise leader en matière de prix, S&M leader au niveau des prix *m*, prix directeur *m*; ~ **leadership** ECON, S&M fixation des prix par une entreprise leader *f*, rôle dominant en matière de prix *m*; ~ **level** ECON niveau de prix *m*; ~ **level accounting** ACC comptabilité indexée *f*, comptabilité indexée sur le niveau général des prix *f*; ~ **level change** GEN COMM fluctuation du niveau des prix *f*; ~ **limit** STOCK cours limite *m*, limite de prix *f*; ~ **-lining** S&M ajustement des prix *m*; ~ **list** GEN COMM, S&M liste des prix *f*, tarif *m*, STOCK cote *f*, liste des cours *f*; ~ **loss** STOCK baisse de cours *f*; ~ **maintenance** GEN COMM, S&M maintien des prix *m*, vente à prix imposé *f*; ~ **maker** ECON faiseur de prix *m*, fixeur de prix *m*; ~ **marker** GEN COMM *on shelf* porte-étiquettes *m*; ~ **mechanism** ECON mécanisme des prix *m*; ~ **move** STOCK fluctuation des cours *f*, mouvement du cours *m*; ~ **offered** GEN COMM prix offert *m*, STOCK cours vendeur *m*, prix offert *m*; ~ **on rail** TRANSP prix sur wagon *m*; ~ **perception** ECON illusion monétaire *f*, perception du prix *f*; ~ **-performance ratio** GEN COMM rapport prix-performance *m*; ~ **pressure** ECON pression sur les prix *f*; ~ **protection** STOCK *futures* protection du cours *f*; ~ **quotation list** GEN COMM, STOCK liste des cours *f*; ~ **range** ECON, S&M fourchette de prix *f*, gamme de prix *f*, échelle des prix *f*, éventail des prix *m*, STOCK fourchette de prix *f*; ~ **rate** *(SYN time rate)* ECON, HRM salaire horaire *m*; ~ **regulation** ECON, POL réglementation des prix *f*; ~ **rigidity** ECON rigidité des prix *f*; ~ **rise** ACC, ECON, FIN, GEN COMM, S&M augmentation des

prix *f*, hausse des prix *f*, majoration de prix *f*, renchérissement *m*; ~ **scanner** S&M scanneur de prix *m*; ~ **schedule** S&M barème des prix *m*, tarif *m*; ~ **-sensitive information** ECON renseignements d'initié *m pl*; ~ **sensitivity** ECON, GEN COMM, S&M élasticité-prix *f*; ~ **spread** STOCK opération mixte verticale *f*, spread vertical *m*; ~ **stability** ECON stabilité des prix *f*; ~ **stabilization** ECON stabilisation des prix *f*; ~ **staggering** *(SYN price bunching)* ECON fixation des prix étalée *f*, fixation synchronisée des prix *f*; ~ **sticker** S&M étiquette de prix *f*; ~ **structure** ECON, FIN, S&M structure de prix *f*; ~ **supervision** ECON, FIN, S&M contrôle des prix *m*, politique des prix *f*; ~ **supervisor** ECON contrôleur des prix *m*; ~ **support** FIN *agricultural subsidy* soutien des prix *m*; ~ **swing** STOCK variation de prix *f*; ~ **system** ECON système de prix *m*; ~ **tag** S&M étiquette de prix *f*; ~ **taker** ECON preneur de prix *m*; ~ **taking** ECON fait de suivre en matière de fixation des prix; ~ **tick** STOCK *currency market* fluctuation de prix *f*, échelon de cotation *m*; ~ **ticket** S&M étiquette de prix *f*; ~ **trend** FIN tendance du cours *f*; ~ **twist** ECON opération twist *f*; ~ **variance** GEN COMM écart sur les prix *m*; ~ **variation** STOCK variation de prix *f*; ~ **variation clause** S&M clause de variation des prix *f*; ~ **volatility** STOCK *shares* degré de volatilité du cours *m*; ~ **war** ECON, GEN COMM, S&M guerre des prix *f*; ~ **-weighted index** STOCK indice pondéré des cours *m*, indice pondéré par les prix *m*; ◆ **at ~** GEN COMM *price* à prix

price[3] *vt* ECON, FIN, GEN COMM, S&M déterminer le prix de, fixer le prix de

pricer *n* FIN priseur *m*

prices: ~ and incomes agreement *n* HRM accord sur les prix et les revenus *m*; ~ **and incomes policy** *n* ECON, POL politique des prix et des revenus *f*; ~ **on application** *n pl* GEN COMM prix sur demande *m pl*; ~ **policy** *n* ECON, FIN, S&M politique des prix *f*; ◆ **at ~ ranging from** GEN COMM à des prix allant de; ~ **can go down as well as up** STOCK les cours peuvent aussi bien baisser que monter, les cours peuvent aussi bien descendre que monter; ~ **have been marked down** STOCK les prix ont été réduits, les prix se sont inscrits en baisse

pricey *adj infrml* FIN, GEN COMM, STOCK chérot *(infrml)*, coûteux

pricing *n* ECON établissement des prix *m*, GEN COMM, S&M fixation des prix *f*, tarification *f*, établissement des prix *m*, évaluation *f*; ~ **arrangement** ECON entente sur les prix *f*; ~ **down** S&M baisse des prix *f*; ~ **model** STOCK modèle d'évaluation d'un prix *m*; ~ **policy** S&M politique des prix *f*; ~ **review** S&M révision des prix *f*; ~ **strategy** S&M politique des prix *f*; ~ **up** S&M augmentation du prix *f*, hausse du prix *f*

pricy *adj infrml see pricey*

prima facie *phr frml* GEN COMM à première vue

prima facie evidence *n* LAW commencement de preuve *m*, preuve prima facie *f*

primage n FIN, TAX, TRANSP chapeau du capitaine m, indemnité sur fret f, primage m

primarily adv GEN COMM essentiellement

primary[1] adj GEN COMM premier, primaire

primary:[2] ~ **action** n HRM *strike action* action syndicale f, revendication f; ~ **activities** n pl (ANT *secondary activities, tertiary activities*) ECON, GEN COMM, IND activités du secteur primaire f pl, services primaires m pl; ~ **boycott** n HRM boycott primaire m; ~ **capital** n ECON, FIN capital bancaire m, valeur de premier choix f; ~ **commodity** n ECON, IND, STOCK produit de base m; ~ **commodity prices** n pl STOCK cours des produits de base m pl, prix des produits de base m pl; ~ **dealer** n ECON spécialiste en valeurs du Trésor m, SVT; ~ **deficit** n ECON déficit effectif m; ~ **distribution** n STOCK *of new issue* placement initial m; ~ **earnings per share** n STOCK bénéfices premiers par action m pl, revenu net par action après impôt et dividende prioritaire m; ~ **explosive** n TRANSP *dangerous goods* explosif primaire m; ~ **industry** n ECON, GEN COMM, IND industrie du secteur primaire f, industrie primaire f; ~ **instrument of indebtedness** n BANK, FIN titre de créance principale m; ~ **issue** n STOCK émission initiale f; ~ **labor market** n AmE, ~ **labour market** n BrE ECON marché du travail constitué par les salariés des grandes entreprises, marché du travail primaire m; ~ **market** n ECON, STOCK *futures market* marché primaire m; ~ **market area** n ECON marché primaire m, STOCK marché primaire m, zone du marché primaire f; ~ **market dealer** n STOCK courtier du marché primaire m, négociateur sur le marché primaire m; ~ **metropolitan statistical area** n US (PMSA) GEN COMM zone primaire de statistique métropolitaine f; ~ **offering** n STOCK *of new issue* placement initial m; ~ **package** n GEN COMM emballage primaire m; ~ **product** n ECON produit de base m; ~ **ratio** n ECON ratio des bénéfices d'exploitation sur le capital employé m; ~ **recovery** n TAX récupération primaire f; ~ **reserve** n BANK, FIN réserve primaire f; ~ **resource** n ENVIR, IND ressource primaire f; ~ **sector** n (ANT *secondary sector*) ECON, IND secteur primaire m

prime: ~ **age worker** n HRM novice m; ~ **borrower** n AmE (*cf premier borrower BrE*) BANK, FIN emprunteur de premier ordre m, emprunteur très solvable m; ~ **contract** n LAW contrat premier m, contrat principal m; ~ **contractor** n GEN COMM maître d'oeuvre m; ~ **cost** n ECON charge supplémentaire f, prix coûtant m, prix de revient initial m; ~ **entry** n ACC première écriture f, IMP/EXP déclaration principale f; ~ **lending rate** n US (*cf base lending rate UK*) ECON, FIN, STOCK taux de base m (*France*), taux préférentiel m (*Canada*); ~ **listening time** n MEDIA *broadcast* heure d'écoute maximale f, heure de grande écoute f, prime-time m (*jarg*), période de pointe f; ~ **location** n PROP emplacement de premier choix m; ~ **minister** n (*PM*) POL Premier ministre m; ~ **paper** n (*P-1*)

FIN, STOCK papier commercial de premier ordre m; ~ **position** n S&M *in the market* position de choix f; ~ **range audit** n ACC vérification de premier palier f (*Can*); ~ **range file** n TAX dossier de premier palier m, dossier de premier rang m; ~ **rate** n US (*cf base rate UK*) ECON, FIN, STOCK taux de base m (*France*), taux préférentiel m (*Canada*); ~ **rate of interest** n BANK taux d'intérêt de base m (*France*), taux d'intérêt préférentiel m (*Canada*); ~ **rate loan** n BANK prêt accordé au taux de base m (*France*), prêt accordé au taux préférentiel m (*Canada*), prêt à taux de base m (*France*), prêt à taux préférentiel m (*Canada*); ~ **responsibility center** n AmE, ~ **responsibility centre** n BrE ACC, FIN, MGMNT centre de responsabilité principale m; ~ **site** n PROP *retail* site de premier choix m; ~ **time** n MEDIA *broadcast* heure d'écoute maximale f, heure de grande écoute f, période de pointe f; ~ **unit** n PROP unité principale f; ~ **viewing time** n MEDIA *broadcast* heure d'écoute maximale f, heure de grande écoute f, prime-time m (*jarg*), période de pointe f

Prime: ~ **1** n FIN, STOCK qualité supérieure f

primitive: ~ **economy** n ECON économie primitive f

principal[1] adj STOCK principal

principal[2] n BANK donneur d'ordres m; ~ **accounting system** n ACC système comptable principal m; ~ **of accrual** n ACC principe de rattachement à l'exercice m; ~ **amount** n FIN montant en capital m, principal m; ~ **assets** n pl ACC actif principal m; ~ **business** n GEN COMM activité principale f, entreprise principale f; ~ **carrier** n TRANSP transporteur principal m; ~ **customer** n GEN COMM, S&M client principal m; ~ **debtor** n FIN, S&M débiteur principal m; ~ **executive committee** n HRM *of trade union* commission exécutive principale f; ~ **file** n TAX *of taxpayer* dossier principal m; ~ **place of business** n ACC, GEN COMM siège social m, établissement principal m; ~ **residence** n TAX résidence principale f; ~ **stockholder** n STOCK actionnaire principal m; ~ **sum** n FIN, INS somme en capital f; ~ **value** n STOCK valeur principale f; ◆ **on a ~ -to-principal basis** STOCK *interbank money market* sur une base de principal à principal

principally adv GEN COMM principalement

principle n GEN COMM, MATH principe m; ~ **of conservatism** ACC principe de prudence m; ~ **of equalization** TAX principe de la péréquation m; ~ **of voluntary compliance** TAX principe de l'observation volontaire m; ◆ **on ~** GEN COMM par principe

print:[1] **in ~** adj MEDIA disponible; **out of ~** adj (*OP*) MEDIA épuisé

print:[2] ~ **driver** n COMP pilote d'impression m; ~ **line** n COMP ligne à imprimer f; ~ **media** n MEDIA médias de presse écrite m pl; ~ **-out** n ADMIN lisitng m, listage m, sortie d'imprimante f, sortie imprimée f, COMP listage m, listing m, sortie d'imprimante f, sortie imprimée f; ~ **preview** n

COMP aperçu avant impression *m*; **~ run** *n* MEDIA tirage *m*

print[3] **1.** *vt* ADMIN, COMP, MEDIA imprimer; **~ out** ADMIN, COMP *document* sortir sur imprimante; **2.** *vti* **~ in landscape** MEDIA imprimer à l'italienne; **~ in portrait** MEDIA imprimer à la française

printed[1] *adj* ADMIN, COMP, MEDIA imprimé; ◆ **~ in bold type** COMP, MEDIA imprimé en caractères gras

printed:[2] **~ form** *n* GEN COMM imprimé *m*; **~ matter** *n* GEN COMM *BrE (cf third-class matter AmE) postage* imprimés *m pl*, MEDIA imprimé *m*; **~ return** *n* TAX déclaration imprimée *f*; **the ~ word** *n* COMMS l'écrit *m*; **~ writing paper** *n* COMMS papier à en-tête *m*

printer *n* COMP, GEN COMM imprimante *f*, imprimeur *m*, MEDIA *device* imprimante *f, person* imprimeur *m*; **~ font** COMP police imprimante *f*; **~ port** COMP porte d'imprimante *f*

printing *n* COMP, MEDIA impression *f*; **~ press** MEDIA presse à imprimer *f*; **~ speed** COMP vitesse d'impression *f*; **~ unit** COMP, GEN COMM, MEDIA imprimante *f*; **~ works** IND, MEDIA imprimerie *f*

prior[1] *adj* GEN COMM préalable

prior:[2] **~ art** *n* PATENTS état de la technique *m*; **~ judicial authorization** *n* LAW autorisation judiciaire préalable *f*; **~ -lien bond** *n* STOCK obligation prioritaire *f*, titre préférentiel *m*; **~ patent** *n* PATENTS brevet antérieur *m*; **~ period** *n* ACC exercice antérieur *m*; **~ period adjustment** *n* ACC redressement affecté aux exercices antérieurs *m*; **~ -preferred stock** *n* STOCK action préférentielle *f*, action superprivilégiée *f*; **~ use** *n* GEN COMM, PATENTS usage antérieur *m*; **~ year adjustment** *n* ACC redressement affecté aux exercices antérieurs *m*

prior:[3] **~ to** *prep* GEN COMM avant

Priorities: **~ and Planning Committee** *n* ADMIN Comité des priorités et de la planification *m*

prioritize *vt* ADMIN, GEN COMM, MGMNT faire passer en premier, mettre en priorité, prioritiser

priority[1] *adj* GEN COMM prioritaire

priority[2] *n* GEN COMM, PATENTS priorité *f*; **~ allocation** STOCK *of shares* adjudication prioritaire *f*, affectation de priorité *f*; **~ date** LAW, PATENTS *intellectual property* date de priorité *f*; **~ development zone** *(PDZ)* ECON, HRM, PROP zone à urbaniser en priorité *f (ZUP)*; **~ mail** *US* COMMS courrier urgent *m*; **~ payment instrument** BANK instrument de paiement privilégié *m*; **~ right** LAW, PATENTS droit de priorité *m*; **~ share** FIN, STOCK action prioritaire *f*; ◆ **give ~ to** GEN COMM accorder la priorité à; **take ~ over** GEN COMM avoir la priorité sur, avoir la préséance sur

prisoners': **~ dilemma** *n* ECON *game theory* dilemme des deux prisonniers *m*

privacy *n* LAW vie privée *f*; **~ laws** *n pl* LAW lois relatives aux atteintes à la vie privée

private[1] *adj* GEN COMM privé; **~ -sector** ECON, GEN COMM du secteur privé, privé; ◆ **by ~ contract** GEN COMM, LAW de gré à gré, à l'amiable; **go ~** *infrml* ECON passer de l'épargne publique à l'épargne privée, WEL *medicine* passer au secteur privé

private:[2] **~ account** *n* ACC, BANK, FIN compte particulier *m*; **~ agency** *n* GEN COMM agence privée *f*; **~ arrangement** *n* GEN COMM, LAW accord à l'amiable *m*; **~ attorney** *n* LAW fondé de pouvoir *m*; **~ automatic branch exchange** *n* UK *(PABX)* COMMS *telephone* autocommutateur privé *m*; **~ bank** *n* BANK banque privée *f*; **~ banking** *n* BANK services bancaires aux particuliers *m pl*; **~ branch exchange** *n* UK *(PBX)* COMMS *telephone* autocommutateur privé *m*, commutateur privé *m*; **~ brand** *n* S&M marque de distributeur *f*; **~ company** *n* GEN COMM société fermée *f*, société privée *f*, société à responsabilité limitée *f*; **~ consumption** *n* ECON, GEN COMM consommation des ménages *f*; **~ contract** *n* GEN COMM, LAW contrat sous seing privé *m*, marché privé *m*; **~ contribution** *n* ECON *aid, pension fund*, FIN contribution privée *f*; **~ cost** *n* ECON coût privé *m*, coût social *m*; **~ cost of unemployment** *n* ECON, HRM, WEL coût personnel du chômage *m*; **~ enterprise** *n* ECON entreprise privée *f*, libre entreprise *f*, POL libre entreprise *f*; **~ enterprise system** *n* ECON système de l'entreprise privée *m*; **~ foundation** *n* TAX fondation privée *f*; **~ fuel** *n* ENVIR *used by employee* carburant privé *m*; **~ good** *n (ANT public good)* ECON bien privé *m*; **~ health fund** *n* HRM, WEL caisse privée d'assurance maladie *f*; **~ health scheme** *n* UK HRM, WEL système privé d'assurance maladie *m*; **~ health services plan** *n* INS, WEL régime privé d'assurance maladie *m*; **~ hearing** *n* LAW audience à huis clos *f*; **~ holding corporation** *n* STOCK société de portefeuilles privée *f*; **~ hospital** *n* WEL clinique privée *f*; **~ hospital treatment** *n* WEL soins en clinique *m pl*; **~ household** *n* GEN COMM ménage *m*; **~ income** *n* ECON, GEN COMM, TAX revenu personnel *m*; **~ individual** *n* GEN COMM particulier *m*; **~ institution** *n* GEN COMM institution privée *f*; **~ investment** *n* FIN, STOCK investissement du secteur privé *m*; **~ investor** *n* FIN, STOCK investisseur privé *m*, petit actionnaire *m*; **~ issue** *n* STOCK émission à diffusion restreinte *f*; **~ law** *n* LAW droit privé *m*; **~ ledger** *n* ACC grand livre *m*; **~ lender** *n* FIN prêteur privé *m*; **~ lesson** *n* WEL cours particulier *m*; **~ limited company** *n* UK GEN COMM, STOCK société à responsabilité limitée *f (SARL)*; **~ marginal benefit** *n* ECON utilité marginale privée *f*; **~ means** *n pl* FIN moyens privés *m pl*; **~ mortgage insurance** *n* INS assurance hypothèque privée *f*; **~ notice question** *n* UK *(PNQ)* POL question posée au Premier ministre dans la Chambre des Communes; **~ office** *n* ADMIN bureau privé *m*; **~ patient** *n* WEL patient privé *m*, patient titre privé *m*; **~ placement** *n* BANK, FIN placement privé *m*; **~ placing** *n* BANK, FIN placement privé *m*; **~ property** *n* PROP propriété privée *f*; **~ purpose bond** *n* STOCK obligation pour le secteur privé; **~ rate of discount** *n* BANK, ECON taux hors banque *m*, taux privé de l'escompte *m*; **~ road** *n* TRANSP voie privée *f*; **~ ruling** *n* TAX réglementation privée *f*; **~ school** *n* US (*cf public school UK*) GEN COMM, WEL école libre *f*, école privée *f*; **~ secretary** *n* HRM secrétaire particulier *m*, secrétaire privé *m*; **~ sector awards** *n pl* ECON arrêts du secteur public *m*, HRM arrêts du secteur privé *m pl*; **~ sector borrower** *n* BANK emprunteur du secteur privé *m*; **~ sector company** *n* ECON société du secteur privé *f*, GEN COMM société du secteur privé *f*, société à responsabilité limitée *f*; **~ sector enterprise** *n* ECON, GEN COMM entreprise du secteur privé *f*; **~ sector investment** *n* ECON investissement du secteur privé *m*; **~ sector liquidity** *n* (*PSL*) ECON liquidité du secteur privé *f*; **~ terms** *n pl* GEN COMM accords privés *m pl*, conditions convenues *f pl*; **the ~ sector** *n* ECON le secteur privé *m*; **~ treaty** *n* PROP acte sous seing privé *m*; **~ tuition** *n* WEL cours particulier *m*

Private: **~ Patients Plan** *n* (*PPP*) WEL programme hospitalier de clientèle privée

privately: **~ owned company** *n* ECON société privée *f*

privatization *n* ECON, GEN COMM privatisation *f*; **~ proceeds** *n pl* ECON, GEN COMM produit de privatisation *m*, recettes de privatisation *f pl*; **~ program** *n AmE*, **~ programme** *n BrE* ECON, GEN COMM programme de privatisations *m*

privatize *vt* ECON, GEN COMM privatiser

privatized *adj* ECON, GEN COMM privatisé

privilege *n US* STOCK option *f*

privileged *adj* FIN protégé, LAW privilégié

privileges: **without ~** *phr* (*x pri*) GEN COMM sans privilège

privity *n* LAW rapport contractuel *m*

Privy: **~ Council** *n UK* (*PC*) LAW conseil privé

prize *n* FIN, GEN COMM prix *m*; **~ bond** FIN obligation à lots *f*

pro *n* GEN COMM pro *m* (*infrml*), LEIS *sport* pro *m* (*infrml*), professionnel *m*; **~ -strike ballot** HRM *for motion* vote pour la grève *m*; **~ -strike vote** HRM vote favorable à la grève *m*

PRO *abbr* (*public relations officer*) HRM, S&M chef du service des relations publiques *m*, directeur des relations publiques *m*, responsable des relations publiques *m*

proactive[1] *adj* GEN COMM, MGMNT, POL proactif

proactive:[2] **~ strategy** *n* GEN COMM, MGMNT, POL stratégie proactive *f*

pro-American *adj* POL proaméricain

probability *n* GEN COMM, MATH *statistics*, MGMNT probabilité *f*; **~ sample** MATH *statistics* échantillon probabiliste *m*; **~ theory** MATH *statistics*, MGMNT théorie des probabilités *f*

probable[1] *adj* GEN COMM probable

probable:[2] **~ error** *n* MATH *statistics* erreur probable *f*

probate[1] *n* LAW validation *f*; **~ court** LAW tribunal des successions *m*, tribunal des successions et des tutelles *m*; **~ duty** LAW droit de timbre *m*, droit de timbre sur les successions *m*, droits de succession *m pl*; **~ price** STOCK prix homologué *m*

probate[2] *vt* LAW valider

probation: **~ period** *n* (SYN *probationary period*) HRM période d'essai *f*

probationary: **~ employee** *n* HRM employé à l'essai *m*; **~ period** *n* (SYN *probation period*) HRM période d'essai *f*

problem *n* GEN COMM problème *m*; **~ analysis** MATH, MGMNT analyse de problèmes *f*; **~ area** GEN COMM, MGMNT domaine problématique *m*, zone critique *f*; **~ assessment** GEN COMM, MGMNT évaluation des problèmes *f*; **~ customer** GEN COMM, S&M client difficile *m*; **~ determination** COMP identification d'incident *f*; **~ loan** FIN emprunt à risque *m*; **~ solver** COMP analyste *mf*; **~ solving** COMP, GEN COMM, MATH, MGMNT résolution de problèmes *f*

problematic *adj* GEN COMM problématique

PROBO *abbr* (*product/oil/bulk/ore carrier*) TRANSP *shipping* pétrolier-vraquier-minéralier-transporteur de produits *m*

procedural[1] *adj* ADMIN, GEN COMM, HRM, LAW, MGMNT procédural, procédurier

procedural:[2] **~ agreement** *n* HRM *collective bargaining* accord de procédure *m*; **~ issue** *n* ADMIN, GEN COMM question de procédure *f*

procedure *n* ADMIN, GEN COMM, HRM, LAW procédure *f*

proceed: **~ with** *vt* GEN COMM réaliser, GEN COMM procéder

proceedings *n pl* LAW acte de procédure *m*, poursuites *f pl*, poursuites judiciaires *f pl*, procédure *f*, *debate* débats *m pl*, délibérations *f pl*, PATENTS *before the European Patent Organization* procédure *f*

proceeds *n pl* FIN, GEN COMM produit *m*; **~ from resale** GEN COMM, PROP produit de la revente *m*; **~ of sales** GEN COMM produit de la vente *m*

process[1] *n* COMP opération *f*, processus *m*, traitement *m*, GEN COMM processus *m*, IND *production* procédé *m*; **~ analysis** GEN COMM analyse des méthodes *f*; **~ chart** COMP organigramme *m*; **~ control** GEN COMM, IND automatisme industriel *m*, gestion de processus industriel *f*, régulation de processus *f*; **~ costing** ACC, IND comptabilisation par processus *f*, comptabilité par fabrication *f*; **~ engineering** IND processus de fabrication en continu *m*; **~ equipment layout** IND production groupée *f*; **~ worker** HRM photograveur *m*; ◆ **in ~** GEN COMM en cours

process[2] *vt* BANK *cheque* traiter, COMP *data* exécuter, traiter, GEN COMM traiter, IND *food* traiter, *goods for re-exportation* transformer

processed: **~ food** *n* IND produit alimentaire industriel *m*

processing n BANK of cheque traitement m, COMP of data exécution f, traitement m, IND of food traitement m, steel transformation f, PATENTS of application, TAX traitement m; ~ **fee** n ADMIN, FIN droit d'administration m; ~ **industry** n IND industrie de transformation f, industrie manufacturière f; ~ **plant** n IND usine de traitement f; ~ **profits** n pl ECON bénéfices de transformation m pl; ~ **stage** n IND phase de production f

processor n COMP processeur m, unité centrale f

pro-communist adj POL procommuniste

procuration: ~ **fee** n FIN, GEN COMM commission sur prêt f

procuratory: ~ **letter** n LAW lettre d'accréditation f, lettre de procuration f

procurement n GEN COMM approvisionnement m, S&M obtention f; ~ **agent** GEN COMM acheteur m; ~ **cost** FIN, GEN COMM coût de passation de commande m; ~ **department** GEN COMM achats m pl, service des achats m; ~ **manager** GEN COMM, HRM, S&M chef d'approvisionnement m; ~ **officer** GEN COMM responsable des achats m

procuring: ~ **cause** n LAW cause déterminante f, diligence des intermédiaires f

produce[1] n ECON denrées alimentaires f pl, GEN COMM denrées alimentaires f pl, produits m pl, IND produit m, produits m pl

produce[2] vt ECON, GEN COMM, IND produire

producer n ECON of produce, food producteur m, IND of machinery, goods fabricant m; ~ **advertising** n S&M publicité du fabricant f; ~ **buyer** n IND acheteur industriel m; ~ **price** n ECON, ENVIR prix à la production m; ~ **price index** n (PPI) ACC, ECON indice des prix à la production m; ~ **subsidy** n ECON subvention à la production f; ~'**s brand** n S&M marque du fabricant f; ~'**s goods** n pl ECON biens d'équipement m pl, biens de production m pl; ~'**s profits** n pl LEIS bénéfices du producteur m pl; ~'**s surplus** n (ANT consumer's surplus) ECON surplus du producteur m

product n ECON, GEN COMM, IND, S&M produit m; ~ **acceptance** n S&M acceptation d'un produit f; ~ **adaptation** n GEN COMM adaptation du produit f; ~ **advertising** n S&M publicité de produit f; ~ **analysis** n S&M analyse de produit f; ~ **awareness** n S&M notoriété d'un produit f; ~ **classification** n GEN COMM classification de produit f; ~ **compatibility** n ECON, IND compatibilité-produit f; ~ **conception** n S&M conception de produit f; ~ **cost** n S&M coût du produit m; ~ **costing** n ACC comptabilité de coûts par produit f, S&M estimation du prix de revient d'un produit f; ~ **creation** n S&M création de produit f; ~ **cycle** n ECON, IND, S&M cycle de développement d'un produit m, cycle de vie d'un produit m; ~ **design** n S&M conception de produit f, dessin de produit m; ~ **development** n S&M mise au point du produit f; ~ **differentiation** n S&M différenciation de produits f; ~ **diversification** n S&M diversification de

produits f; ~ **dynamics** n pl S&M dynamique des produits f; ~ **engineer** n HRM, IND ingénieur de produit m; ~ **engineering** n S&M étude de produit f; ~ **evaluation** n S&M évaluation de produit f; ~ **generation** n S&M création de produit f; ~ **group** n S&M grille de produits f, groupe de produits m; ~ **image** n S&M image de marque f; ~ **improvement** n S&M amélioration de produit f; ~ **initiation** n S&M apprentissage de produit m; ~ **introduction** n S&M lancement de produit m; ~ **knowledge** n S&M connaissance du produit f; ~ **launch** n S&M lancement de produit m; ~ **leader** n S&M produit d'appel bon marché m; ~ **liability** n S&M responsabilité du fabricant f; ~ **life** n S&M vie d'un produit f; ~ **life cycle** n (PLC) ECON, IND, S&M marketing cycle de vie d'un produit m (CVP); ~ **life expectancy** n S&M espérance de vie d'un produit f; ~ **line** n GEN COMM, IND, S&M collection de produits f, gamme de produits f, ligne de produits f, série de produits f; ~ **management** n MGMNT, S&M gestion de produit f; ~ **manager** n GEN COMM, HRM, MGMNT chef de produit m, directeur de produit m, S&M chef de produit m; ~ **marketing** n GEN COMM commercialisation f, S&M commercialisation f, marketing de produit m; ~ **mix** n S&M ensemble de produits m, mix de produits m, produit-mix m, éventail des produits en vente m; ~ **moment formula** n MATH statistics formule de moment de produit f; ~ **organization** n GEN COMM organisation à base de produits f; ~ **performance** n S&M caractéristiques du produit f pl, comportement du produit m; ~ **planning** n S&M planification de produit f; ~ **portfolio** n FIN, S&M, STOCK portefeuille de produits m; ~ **profile** n S&M profil du produit m; ~ **profitability** n ACC, FIN, S&M rentabilité de produit f; ~ **range** n GEN COMM, IND, S&M gamme de produits f, éventail des produits m; ~ **reliability** n S&M fiabilité du produit f; ~ **research** n S&M recherche de produit f, étude de produit f; ~ **standard** n S&M norme d'un produit f; ~ **standards** n pl IND, LAW normes de produit f pl; ~ **strategy** n GEN COMM, S&M stratégie de produit f; ~ **tanker** n TRANSP shipping transporteur de produits m; ~ **testing** n S&M test de produit m; ~/**oil/bulk/ore carrier** n (PROBO) TRANSP shipping pétrolier-vraquier-minéralier-transporteur de produits m

production n ECON production f, IND department, place where goods are made unité de production f, making production f, S&M motor industry série f; ~ **asymmetry** n ECON asymétrie de production f; ~ **bonus** n IND prime de production f, prime de rendement f; ~ **brigade** n jarg ECON, POL socialist countries brigade de production agricole f (jarg); ~ **capacity** n IND capacité de production f, potentiel de production m; ~ **chain** n IND chaîne de production f; ~ **complex** n IND complexe de production m; ~ **control** n GEN COMM, IND, MGMNT gestion de la production f, régulation de production f, surveillance de la production f;

~ **cost** *n* ACC, FIN, IND coût de production *m*;
~ **department** *n* IND service de la production *m*;
~ **director** *n* HRM, IND, MEDIA *publishing, press*
chef de fabrication *m*, chef de production *m*,
directeur de fabrication *m*, directeur de la
production *m*, directeur technique *m*; ~ **ecology**
n ENVIR étude du rendement écologique *f*;
~ **engineering** *n* GEN COMM, IND, MGMNT organisation de la production *f*, techniques de la
production *f pl*; ~ **function** *n* ECON fonction de
production *f*; ~ **goods** *n pl* IND biens de production *m pl*, installations techniques *f pl*;
~ **implement** *n* IND outil de production *m*;
~ **incentive** *n* HRM, IND encouragement à la
production *m*, incitation au rendement *f*; ~ **line**
n IND chaîne de production *f*; ~ **loan** *n* BANK, FIN
prêt de production *m*; ~ **management** *n* GEN
COMM, IND, MGMNT gestion de la production *f*,
organisation de la production *f*; ~ **manager** *n*
HRM, IND, MEDIA *publishing, press* chef de
fabrication *m*, chef de production *m*, directeur
de fabrication *m*, directeur de la production *m*,
directeur technique *m*; ~ **planning** *n* GEN COMM,
IND, MGMNT planning de la production *m*,
programmation de la production *f*; ~ **planning
and control** *n* GEN COMM, IND, MGMNT projet et
contrôle de la production *m*, surveillance de la
production *f*; ~ **plant** *n* IND unité de production *f*,
usine de production *f*; ~ **possibility frontier** *n*
ECON frontière des possibilités de production *f*,
FPP; ~ **process** *n* IND processus de production *m*,
procédé de fabrication *m*; ~ **rate** *n* IND, STOCK
taux de production *m*; ~ **revenue** *n* FIN, IND
revenu de production *m*; ~ **revenue tax** *n* TAX
impôt sur le revenu de production *m*; ~ **run** *n* IND
passage de production *m*; ~ **schedule** *n* GEN
COMM, IND, MGMNT ordonnancement de la
production *m*, programme de fabrication *m*;
~ **scheduling** *n* GEN COMM, IND, MGMNT programmation de la production *f*; ~ **standard** *n* GEN
COMM, IND norme de production *f*; ~ **target** *n*
GEN COMM, IND objectif de production *m*;
~ **technique** *n* GEN COMM, IND technique de
production *f*; ~ **unit** *n* IND unité de production *f*;
~ **volume** *n* GEN COMM, IND volume de production *m*; ~ **worker** *n* HRM, IND employé de
production *m*, ouvrier de la production *m, on
production line* travailleur à la chaîne *m*
productive[1] *adj* HRM *workforce* productif
productive:[2] ~ **capital** *n* ECON, FIN capitaux productifs *m pl*; ~ **labor** *n* *AmE*, ~ **labour** *n* *BrE*
ECON, HRM main-d'oeuvre productive *f*;
~ **maintenance** *n* ADMIN, IND entretien productif
m; ~ **potential** *n* ECON, IND potentiel de croissance
de production *m*, potentiel de production *m*
productivity *n* ECON, GEN COMM, IND efficience *f*,
rendement *m, output* productivité *f*; ~ **agreement**
n HRM, IND, LAW accord de productivité *m*,
accord de rendement *m*; ~ **bargaining** *n* ECON
discussions sur l'intéressement à la productivité *f*
pl, HRM, IND négociation des contrats de pro-

ductivité *f*, LAW négociation de la productivité *f*,
négociation des contrats de productivité *f*;
~ **campaign** *n* GEN COMM, IND, S&M campagne
de productivité *f*; ~ **drive** *n* GEN COMM, IND, S&M
campagne de productivité *f*; ~ **gains** *n pl* GEN
COMM, IND gains de productivité *m pl*;
~ **measurement** *n* GEN COMM, IND mesure de la
productivité *f*; ~ **shock** *n* ECON coup porté à la
productivité *m*
products: ~ **and completed operations insurance** *n*
INS assurance de produits et des opérations termi-
nées
Prof *abbr* (*Professor*) HRM prof (*professeur*)
profession *n* HRM profession *f*, profession libérale
f
professional[1] *adj* HRM libéral, professionnel
professional[2] *n* GEN COMM professionnel *m*, LEIS
sport professionnel *m*; ~ **achievements** *n pl* GEN
COMM *on CV*, HRM expérience professionnelle *f*;
~ **body** *n* GEN COMM groupement professionnel
m; ~ **code of ethics** *n* GEN COMM déontologie *f*;
~ **ethics** *n pl* GEN COMM déontologie *f*; ~ **income**
n TAX revenu de profession libérale *m*;
~ **indemnity** *n* GEN COMM, IND, LAW responsabilité
professionnelle *f*; ~ **liability** *n* GEN COMM, INS,
LAW responsabilité professionnelle *f*; ~ **liability
insurance** *n* INS assurance de responsabilité
professionelle *f*; ~ **qualifications** *n pl* HRM compétences professionnelles *f pl*, qualifications
professionnelles *f pl*; ~ **secrecy** *n* GEN COMM
secret professionnel *m*; ~ **services** *n pl* GEN COMM
services professionnels *m pl*; ~ **status** *n* HRM
statut professionnel *m*; ~ **trader** *n* ECON opérateur
professionnel *m*
professionalism *n* GEN COMM professionnalisme *m*
professionalization *n* HRM professionnalisation *f*
Professor *n* (*Prof*) HRM professeur *m* (*prof*)
profile *n* GEN COMM *of business, competitor, market*
profil *m*, TRANSP *shipping* élévation du plan des
formes *f*; ~ **risk** FIN profil de risque *m*; ♦ **keep a
low** ~ GEN COMM adopter un profil bas, se
montrer discret, maintenir un profil bas
profit:[1] ~ **-motivated** *adj* ECON motivé par le profit;
not-for-~ *adj* *AmE* GEN COMM à but non-lucratif
loc m
profit[2] *n* ECON, FIN, S&M bénéfice commercial *m*,
bénéfices *m pl*, profit *m*; ~ **before tax** ACC, FIN
bénéfices avant impôts *m pl*; ~ **carried forward**
ACC, FIN report à nouveau *m*; ~ **ceiling** ECON, FIN
plafonnement des bénéfices *m*; ~ **center** *AmE see
profit centre* *BrE*; ~ **center accounting** *AmE see
profit centre accounting* *BrE*; ~ **centre** *BrE* ACC,
ECON, FIN, GEN COMM centre de profit *m*;
~ **centre accounting** *BrE* ACC, FIN comptabilité
par centres de profits *f*; ~ **-factor analysis** FIN,
GEN COMM analyse des facteurs de profit *f*; ~ **for
the financial year** ACC, FIN, GEN COMM, TAX
bénéfice de l'exercice *m*; ~ **for the year after
taxes** ACC, FIN bénéfice de l'exercice après impôts
m; ~ **goal** ACC, FIN objectif de profit *m*; ~ **graph**

ACC, FIN courbe de rentabilité *f*, courbe des bénéfices *f*; ~ **impact** FIN, GEN COMM incidence sur le profit *f*; ~ **implication** FIN, GEN COMM répercussion sur les bénéfices *f*; ~ **improvement** FIN, GEN COMM amélioration de la rentabilité *f*; ~ **and loss** *(P&L)* ACC *annual accounts* pertes et profits *f pl (P et P)*; ~ **and loss account** *(*SYN *profit and loss statement)* ACC compte de pertes et profits *m*, compte de résultat *m*; ~ **and loss statement** *(*SYN *profit and loss account)* ACC compte de pertes et profits *m*, compte de résultat *m*; ~ **-making enterprise** GEN COMM compagnie rentable *f*; ~ **margin** ACC, ECON, FIN, S&M marge bénéficiaire *f*; ~ **maximization** ECON maximalisation des profits *f*, FIN maximisation des bénéfices *f*, maximisation du profit *f*, GEN COMM maximisation du profit *f*, S&M maximalisation des profits *f*; ~ **motive** ECON, FIN, S&M motivation par le profit *f*, recherche du profit *f*; ~ **optimization** ECON, FIN optimisation du profit *f*; ~ **outlook** ECON, FIN perspective de profit *f*; ~ **performance** FIN rendement *m*; ~ **and performance planning** *(PPP)* FIN, MGMNT prévision de bénéfices et de performances *f*; ~ **planning** FIN, MGMNT planification des bénéfices *f*, prévision des bénéfices *f*; ~ **potential** FIN potentiel de bénéfice *m*; ~ **profile** FIN profil de profit *m*; ~ **projection** ECON, FIN, GEN COMM projection des profits *f*; ~ **-related pay** ACC *(PRP)*, HRM salaire lié aux bénéfices *m*; ~ **requirement** FIN critère de rentabilité *m*, exigence de rentabilité *f*; ~ **sensitivity analysis** ACC *project assessment* analyse de la sensibilité du résultat *f*; ~ **-sharing** ACC, FIN intéressement aux bénéfices *m*, participation aux bénéfices *f*, HRM intéressement du personnel aux bénéfices *m*, participation aux bénéfices de l'entreprise *f*; ~ **-sharing bond** STOCK obligation participante *f*; ~ **-sharing plan** *US (cf profit-sharing scheme UK)* FIN plan d'intéressement aux bénéfices *m*, plan de participation aux bénéfices *m*, système de partage des bénéfices *m*; ~ **-sharing scheme** *UK (cf profit-sharing plan US)* FIN plan d'intéressement aux bénéfices *m*, plan de participation aux bénéfices *m*, système de partage des bénéfices *m*; ~ **squeeze** ECON, FIN contraction des bénéfices *f*, politique des prix *f*, resserrement des bénéfices *m*; ~ **strategy** FIN, MGMNT stratégie de profit *f*; ~ **taking** ECON, FIN, MGMNT prise de bénéfices *f*; ~ **-taking strategy** ECON, FIN, MGMNT stratégie de participation *f*, stratégie de prise de bénéfices *f*; ~ **target** ACC, FIN objectif de profit *m*; ~ **test** ACC, FIN test de rentabilité *m*; ◆ **at a ~ of** GEN COMM pour un bénéfice de; **make a ~** ACC, FIN, GEN COMM, STOCK réaliser un bénéfice; **take a ~** ACC, FIN, GEN COMM, STOCK réaliser un bénéfice

profitability *n* ACC, ECON, FIN, GEN COMM rentabilité *f*; ~ **analysis** ACC, ECON, FIN, S&M, STOCK analyse de rentabilité *f*, étude de rentabilité *f*; ~ **ratio** ECON, FIN ratio de rentabilité *m*; ~ **requirement** FIN critère de rentabilité *m*, exigence de rentabilité *f*

profitable *adj* ACC, ECON, FIN, GEN COMM rentable

profitably *adv* ACC, ECON, FIN, GEN COMM utilement

profiteer *n* FIN profiteur *m*

profits: ~ **policy** *n* INS police d'assurance contre le manque à gagner *f*; ~ **tax** *n* ACC, TAX impôt sur les bénéfices *m*; **with-~ endowment assurance** *n* INS assurance mixte avec participation aux bénéfices *f*; ◆ ~ **surpassed forecasts in the first quarter** FIN les bénéfices du premier trimestre ont dépassé les prévisions

profit / volume: ~ **ratio** *n (P/V)* ACC, FIN rapport profit et changement de quantités vendues *m*, rapport profit sur ventes *m*, ratio de volume de bénéfices *m*

pro forma[1] *adj* GEN COMM pour la forme *loc f*, pro forma

pro forma:[2] ~ **billing** *n* ACC facturation par anticipation *f*; ~ **invoice** *n* FIN, GEN COMM, IMP/EXP facture pro forma *f*; ~ **return** *n* FIN, TAX déclaration pro forma *f*

profound *adj* GEN COMM, STOCK profond

profoundly *adv* GEN COMM, STOCK profondément

profusion *n* GEN COMM profusion *f*

prognosis *n* [pl -ses] GEN COMM pronostic *m*

prognosticate *vi* GEN COMM prognostiquer

prognostication *n* GEN COMM pronostic *m*

program[1] *n AmE see programme BrE*

program[2] *AmE see programme BrE*

programmable: ~ **function** *n* COMP fonction programmable *f*

programmatic *adj* COMP par programme *loc m*

programme[1] *n BrE* ECON, GEN COMM programme *m*, MEDIA *broadcast* programme *m*, émission *f*, MGMNT programme *m*; ~ **adjustment loan** *BrE (PAL)* FIN prêt-programme d'ajustement *m*; ~ **aid** *BrE* ECON *development* aide-programme *f*; ~ **budgeting** *BrE* ACC, FIN, HRM, MGMNT budgétisation de programmes *f*, rationalisation des choix budgétaires *f*; ~ **deal** *BrE* ECON contrat de programme *m*; ~ **evaluation plan** *BrE* GEN COMM plan d'évaluation de programme *m*; ~ **evaluation and review technique** *BrE (PERT)* MGMNT méthode de programmation optimale *f (méthode PERT)*; ~ **file** *BrE* ADMIN fichier de programme *m*; ~ **forecast** *BrE* GEN COMM prévision de programme *f*; ~ **package** *BrE* COMP progiciel *m*; ~ **structure** *BrE* GEN COMM structure de programme *f*; ~ **trade** *BrE* GEN COMM transaction programmée par ordinateur *f*; ~ **trading** *BrE* STOCK négociation assistée par ordinateur *f*, système de protection par programme informatique *m*

programme[2] *vt BrE* GEN COMM programmer

programmed: ~ **instruction** *n* WEL enseignement programmé *m*; ~ **learning** *n* WEL enseignement programmé *m*; ~ **management** *n* MGMNT direction par programmes *f*, gestion programmée *f*

programmer *n* COMP, HRM analyste *mf*

programming *n* COMP, GEN COMM programmation *f*, élaboration de programmes *f*; ~ **aid** COMP, GEN COMM outils de programmation *m pl*; ~ **language** *(APL)* COMP langage de programmation *m*

progress *n* GEN COMM, IND progrès *m*; ~ **control** *n* GEN COMM, IND, MGMNT contrôle de la production *m*, suivi de la production *m*, surveillance de la production *f*; ~ **payments** *n pl* FIN paiements en cours *m pl*; ~ **report** *n* GEN COMM compte-rendu sur l'état d'avancement des travaux *m*; ◆ **in** ~ GEN COMM en cours; **make** ~ GEN COMM progresser; **make quick** ~ GEN COMM avancer à pas de géant

progressive[1] *adj* GEN COMM progressif

progressive:[2] ~ **income tax system** *n* TAX système d'impôt progressif *m*, système de l'impôt progressif sur le revenu *m*; ~ **scale** *n* TAX barème progressif *m*, échelle progressive *f*; ~ **tax** *n* TAX impôt progressif *m*; ~ **tax system** *n* TAX système d'impôt progressif *m*

progressively *adv* GEN COMM progressivement

prohibit *vt* COMP empêcher, interdire, GEN COMM interdire, proscrire, IMP/EXP, LAW interdire

prohibited: ~ **goods** *n pl* GEN COMM, IMP/EXP, LAW marchandises prohibées *f pl*

prohibition *n* GEN COMM, IMP/EXP, LAW interdiction *f*; ~ **notice** HRM *health and safety* avis d'interdiction *m*; ~ **right** PATENTS droit d'interdire *m*

prohibitive *adj* GEN COMM abusif, prohibitif

project[1] *n* GEN COMM projet *m*; ~ **agent** HRM agent de projet *m*, assistant au chef de projet *m*; ~ **aid** ECON *development* aide-projet *f*; ~ **analysis** ECON, FIN, GEN COMM, MGMNT étude de projet *f*, évaluation de projet *f*; ~ **appraisal** ECON, FIN, GEN COMM, MGMNT étude de projet *f*, évaluation de projet *f*; ~ **approval** GEN COMM approbation de projet *f*; ~ **assessment** ECON, FIN, GEN COMM, MGMNT étude de projet *f*, évaluation de projet *f*; ~ **engineer** GEN COMM, IND, MGMNT ingénieur projet *m*; ~ **financing** FIN financement de projets *m*; ~ **forwarding** TRANSP projet d'expédition *m*; ~ **leader** HRM chef de projet *m*; ~ **management** FIN, HRM, MGMNT gestion du projet *f*, projet management *m*; ~ **manager** HRM chef de projet *m*, directeur de projet *m*; ~ **note** STOCK avis de projet *m*, bon du Trésor pour la construction immobilière *m*; ~ **participants' insolvency cover** INS couverture de l'insolvabilité des participants au projet *f*; ~ **planning** FIN, GEN COMM, MGMNT plan de projet *m*; ~ **sponsor** FIN, GEN COMM promoteur de projet *m*

project[2] *vt* GEN COMM projeter

projected[1] *adj* GEN COMM *figures, sales* projeté

projected:[2] ~ **benefit obligation** *n* HRM obligation anticipée de nouvelles mesures sociales *f*

projectile *n* TRANSP *dangerous classified cargo* projectile *m*

projection *n* ECON, GEN COMM, MATH projection *f*

projector *n* GEN COMM *slide, film* projecteur *m*

proletarian: ~ **internationalism** *n* ECON, POL internationalisme prolétarien *m*

proletarianization *n* ECON, POL prolétarisation *f*

proletariat *n* ECON, POL prolétariat *m*

prolonged *adj* GEN COMM prolongé

prom: ~ **dk** *abbr (promenade deck)* TRANSP *shipping* pont promenade *m*

promenade: ~ **deck** *n (prom dk)* TRANSP *shipping* pont promenade *m*

prominent *adj* GEN COMM important

promise[1] *n* GEN COMM promesse *f*

promise[2] *vt* GEN COMM promettre; ◆ ~ **to pay** GEN COMM s'engager à payer; ~ **to sell** S&M faire une promesse de vente

promissory: ~ **note** *n (PN)* BANK, FIN billet à note *m*, billet à ordre *m*

promo *n* *infrml (promotion)* S&M *advertising* promo *(infrml) (promotion)*

promotary: ~ **company** *n* US FIN société de financement *f*

promote *vt* GEN COMM *encourage* encourager, promouvoir, *foster* favoriser, HRM *move up in rank* accorder une promotion à, promouvoir, S&M *publicize* faire de la publicité pour, promouvoir; ◆ ~ **efficiency** GEN COMM favoriser l'efficacité

promoted: **be** ~ *phr* HRM avoir une promotion *loc f*, être promu *loc*

promoter *n* GEN COMM *of plans* promoteur *m*, TAX promoteur *m*, promoteur d'abris fiscaux *m*

promotion *n* HRM *of personnel* avancement *m*, promotion *f*, S&M *of product, service* promo *f* *(infrml)*, promotion *f*, STOCK *of company* lancement *m*; ~ **cost** FIN frais de premier établissement *m pl*; ~ **ladder** HRM échelle des promotions *f*; ~ **leaflet** S&M argumentaire *m*; ~ **mix** S&M *advertising* moyens d'action promotionnelle *m pl*

promotional[1] *adj* GEN COMM, S&M promotionnel

promotional:[2] ~ **allowance** *n* FIN, S&M *advertising* budget de la publicité *m*; ~ **budget** *n* FIN, S&M *advertising* budget de la publicité *m*; ~ **exercise** *n* S&M *marketing* campagne promotionnelle *f*; ~ **mix** *n* S&M *advertising* moyens d'action promotionnelle *m pl*; ~ **policy** *n* GEN COMM, S&M politique de promotion *f*; ~ **sale** *n* GEN COMM vente promotionnelle *f*

prompt[1] *adj* GEN COMM, TRANSP ponctuel

prompt[2] *n* COMP message guide-opérateur *m*; ~ **note** FIN demande de paiement *f*, mémoire de vente *m*; ~ **payment** FIN paiement rapide *m*

prompt[3] *vt* GEN COMM *give rise to* pousser, provoquer

proof: ~ **of debt** *n (POD)* FIN justification de dette *f*, titre de créances *m*; ~ **of delivery** *n (POD)* GEN COMM, TRANSP justification de livraison *f*; ~ **of loss** *n* INS justification de perte *f* LAW preuve *f*, MEDIA *printing, photography* épreuve *f*; ~ **of ownership** *n* STOCK *of shares* titre de propriété *m*; ~ **of title** *n* LAW, PROP justification de titre *f*, titre de propriété *m*; ◆ **at ~ stage** MEDIA à l'essai, *printing* au stade des épreuves

proofread *vi* MEDIA *print* corriger des épreuves

proofreader *n* MEDIA correcteur *m*, lecteur *m*

prop[1] *n* TRANSP *shipping* épontille *f*

prop:[2] **~ up** *vt* ECON *currency* soutenir

propagate *vt* GEN COMM, POL propager

propane *n* GEN COMM, TRANSP *dangerous classified cargo* propane *m*

propeller *n* TRANSP *of aircraft, ship* hélice *f*

propensity *n* ECON, GEN COMM propension *f*; **~ to consume** ECON propension à consommer *f*; **~ to invest** BANK, ECON, FIN propension à investir *f*; **~ to save** ECON propension moyenne à économiser *f*, propension à épargner *f*; **~ to work** ECON propension à travailler *f*

propertied: **~ class** *n* PROP les possédants *m pl*

property *n* GEN COMM immobilier *m*, propriété *f*, PROP immobilier *m*, propriété *f*, *land* terrain *m*, S&M *belongings* biens *m pl*, propriété *f*; **~ acquired** *n* PROP immobilier acquis *m*; **~ bond** *n* FIN, PROP obligation immobilière *f*; **~ and casualty policy insuring agreement** *n* INS police d'assurance incendie accidents risques divers *f*; **~ company** *n* GEN COMM, PROP société immobilière *f*; **~ damage** *n* PROP dommage matériel *m*; **~ depreciation insurance** *n* INS assurance de la dépréciation des biens *f*; **~ developer** *n* PROP promoteur immobilier *m*; **~ development** *n* PROP promotion immobilière *f*; **~ development project** *n* PROP projet de promotion immobilière *m*; **~ held in joint names** *n* PROP propriété indivise *f*; **~ income** *n* FIN, PROP, TAX revenu de biens *m*, revenu immobilier *m*; **~ insurer** *n* INS assureur de biens *m*, assureur immobilier *m*; **~ investment company** *n* FIN, PROP société d'investissement immobilière *f*; **~ line** *n* PROP *boundary* limites de propriété *f pl*; **~ management** *n* MGMNT, PROP gestion immobilière *f*; **~ market** *n* PROP marché de l'immobilier *m*; **~ owner** *n* PROP propriétaire immobilier *m*; **~ rights** *n pl* LAW, PROP droits de propriété *m pl*; **~ speculator** *n* PROP spéculateur immobilier *m*; **~ tax** *n* TAX taxe immobilière *f*; **~ tax allowance** *n* TAX crédit d'impôts fonciers *m* (*Can*), déduction de taxe immobilière *f*; **~ tax credit** *n Can* TAX crédit d'impôts fonciers *m* (*Can*), déduction de taxe immobilière *f*; **~ valuation** *n BrE* (*cf real estate appraisal AmE*) PROP évaluation de biens immobiliers *f*, évaluation immobilière *f*

proportion *n* GEN COMM, MATH proportion *f*; ◆ **as a ~ of** GEN COMM, MATH comme pourcentage de, comme proportion de; **in ~ to** GEN COMM par rapport à

proportional[1] *adj* GEN COMM proportionnel

proportional:[2] **~ income tax** *n* TAX impôt proportionnel sur le revenu *m*; **~ rate** *n* FIN tarif proportionnel *m*; **~ representation** *n* (*PR*) POL représentation proportionnelle *f* (*RP*); **~ tax** *n* TAX impôt proportionnel *m*

proportionality *n* GEN COMM proportionalité *f*

proportionally *adv* GEN COMM proportionnellement

proportionate[1] *adj* GEN COMM en proportion *loc f*

proportionate:[2] **~ grant** *n* ECON subvention d'aide *f*, subvention financière *f*, subvention proportionnelle *f*

proportionately *adv* GEN COMM proportionnellement

proposal *n* GEN COMM projet *m*, proposition *f*, MGMNT proposition *f*; ◆ **our ~ still stands** GEN COMM notre proposition reste valable *f*

propose *vt* GEN COMM proposer, *toast* porter, POL *motion* présenter, soumettre

proposed *adj* GEN COMM, TAX proposé, éventuel

proposer *n* GEN COMM auteur de proposition *m*, parrain *m*, INS contractant *m*, souscripteur *m*

proposition *n* GEN COMM proposition *f*

proprietary[1] *adj* GEN COMM *having a trade name* de marque *loc f*, de marque déposée *loc f*, *privately owned* privé

proprietary:[2] **~ brand** *n* GEN COMM marque déposée *f*; **~ company** *n* GEN COMM société de holding *f*, société mère *f*; **~ drug** *n* GEN COMM, WEL médicament vendu sous marque *m*; **~ goods** *n pl* GEN COMM articles de marque *m pl*; **~ insurance** *n* INS assurance à primes fixes *f*; **~ rights** *n pl* STOCK droits de propriété *m pl*; **~ software** *n* COMP logiciel maison *m*, logiciel propre à un constructeur *m*, logiciel propriétaire *m*

proprietor *n* GEN COMM *of business*, HRM, MGMNT propriétaire *mf*, propriétaire exploitant *m*, PATENTS titulaire *mf*, *of intellectual property* propriétaire *mf*

proprietorship *n* GEN COMM, PROP droit de propriété *m*, entreprise individuelle *f*, entreprise à propriétaire unique *f*

pro rata[1] *adj frml* GEN COMM, HRM proportionnel

pro rata[2] *adv* GEN COMM au prorata; ◆ **on a ~ basis** GEN COMM au prorata

pro rata:[3] **~ freight** *n* TRANSP frais de transport au prorata *m pl*

prorate *vt* GEN COMM partager proportionnellement, répartir au prorata

proration *n* GEN COMM répartition au prorata *f*, TRANSP système des quotes-parts *m*; **~ mileage** TRANSP ≈ kilométrage réparti au prorata *m*; **~ rate** TRANSP taux de répartition au prorata *m*

pros: **~ and cons** *phr* GEN COMM le pour et le contre *loc m*

prosecute *vt* LAW poursuivre; ◆ **~ for forgery** LAW poursuivre en contrefaçon, poursuivre pour faux

prosecuting: **~ attorney** *n US* (*cf counsel for the prosecution UK*) LAW avocat général *m*

prosecution *n* LAW *act* action publique *f*, poursuites *f pl*, *lawyers acting for the state* ministère public *m*, partie plaignante *f*

prospect[1] *n* GEN COMM, S&M *potential buyer* client potentiel *m*, client éventuel *m*, prospect *m*

prospect² *vt* ENVIR *region*, S&M *market* prospecter

prospecting *n* ENVIR, S&M prospection *f*

prospective¹ *adj* GEN COMM, S&M *customer* potentiel, éventuel

prospective:² ~ **buyer** *n* PROP acheteur potentiel *m*; ~ **customer** *n* GEN COMM, S&M client potentiel *m*, client éventuel *m*, prospect *m*; ~ **rating** *n* INS tarification envisagée *f*

prospector *n* ENVIR, S&M prospecteur *m*

prospectus *n* FIN prospectus *m*, STOCK prospectus *m*, prospectus d'admission *m*

prosperity *n* ECON prospérité *f*; ~ **indicator** ECON indicateur de prospérité *m*

prosperous *adj* ECON prospère

pro tanto *phr frml* GEN COMM dans cette mesure *loc f*

protean: ~ **economy** *n* ECON économie protéenne *f*

protect 1. *vt* ECON, ENVIR, GEN COMM, LAW, PATENTS protéger; **2.** *v refl* ~ **oneself** COM se protéger; ◆ ~ **the interests of** GEN COMM *country, producers, consumers* protéger les intérêts de; ~ **oneself against** GEN COMM *risk* se protéger contre; ~ **o.s. from sth** GEN COMM se protéger de qch

protection *n* ECON, ENVIR, GEN COMM, LAW, PATENTS protection *f*

Protection: ~ **and Indemnity Association** *n* INS *marine* Association de la protection et de l'indemnité; ~ **and Indemnity Club** *(P&I club)* TRANSP club de protection et d'indemnisation mutuelle; ~ **& Indemnity of Oil Pollution Indemnity Clause** *n (PIOPIC)* ENVIR protection et indemnité de la clause d'indemnité de la pollution par les hydrocarbures

protectionism *n* ECON protectionnisme *m*

protective: ~ **award** *n* HRM sentence arbitrale de protection *f*; ~ **covenant** *n* FIN convention de protection *f*; ~ **duties** *n pl* TAX droits protecteurs *m pl*; ~ **location** *n (PL)* TRANSP *of oil tanker* localisation défensive *f*; ~ **safety screen** *n* GEN COMM écran de sécurité *m*

protest¹ *n* TRANSP *shipping* déclaration d'avaries *f*; ~ **charges** *n pl* LAW frais de protêt *m pl*; ~ **strike** *n* HRM grève revendicative *f*; ~ **vote** *n* POL vote de protestation *m*; ◆ **make a** ~ GEN COMM protester

protest² *vi* GEN COMM protester

protocol *n* COMP, GEN COMM *diplomacy, etiquette* protocole *m*

protoindustrialization *n* HRM débuts de l'industrialisation *m pl*

protoproletariat *n* ECON protoprolétariat *m*

prototype *n* GEN COMM, S&M prototype *m*

prove 1. *vt* GEN COMM prouver, LAW valider; **2.** *vi* ~ **right** GEN COMM s'avérer vrai, se révéler vrai; ~ **to be** GEN COMM se révéler; ~ **wrong** GEN COMM s'avérer faux, se révéler faux; ◆ ~ **a debt** ACC établir une créance; ~ **one's identity** LAW justifier de son identité, prouver son identité

proven: ~ **track record** *n* GEN COMM, HRM réputation bien établie *f*

provide *vt* FIN *funds, goods, services* accorder, consentir, fournir, GEN COMM fournir; ~ **against** GEN COMM se prémunir contre; ◆ ~ **against a risk** INS s'assurer contre un risque; ~ **a loan** FIN consentir un prêt; ~ **a market for** STOCK *trading shares* fournir un marché pour; ~ **sb with a loan** BANK, FIN accorder un prêt à qn, consentir un prêt à qn; ~ **technical assistance** GEN COMM fournir un soutien technique, fournir une assistance technique

provided: **not** ~ **for** *phr* BANK pas prévu; ~ **that** *phr* GEN COMM pourvu que, sous réserve que, à condition que *loc f*

provident: ~ **fund** *n* FIN caisse de prévoyance *f*

provider *n* GEN COMM fournisseur *m*

providing: ~ **that** *phr* GEN COMM à condition de *loc f*, à condition que *loc f*

provincial¹ *adj* GEN COMM provincial

provincial:² ~ **Crown corporation** *n* ADMIN société d'État provinciale *f*

proving *n* LAW validation *f*

provision *n* GEN COMM, LAW *of an act* clause *f*, disposition *f*, fourniture *f*, stipulation *f*, S&M fourniture *f*, TAX disposition *f*; ~ **for bad debts** ACC, BANK *(SYN allowance for bad debts)* provision pour créances douteuses *f*; ~ **for contingency** ACC provision pour risques *f*; ~ **for depreciation** ACC dotation aux amortissements *f*, provision pour dépréciation *f*, BANK, FIN provision pour dépréciation *f*; ~ **for loan loss** BANK provision pour créances douteuses *f*; ~ **of services** GEN COMM prestation de services *f*; ◆ **make** ~ **for** GEN COMM faire provision pour

provisional: ~ **acceptance** *n* GEN COMM *of goods, on delivery, before testing* acceptation provisoire *f*; ~ **bond** *n* STOCK obligation provisoire *f*; ~ **collection of taxes act** *n* TAX loi sur le recouvrement provisoire de l'impôt *f*; ~ **invoice** *n* GEN COMM facture provisoire *f*; ~ **policy** *n* INS police provisoire *f*; ~ **protection** *n* PATENTS protection provisoire *f*

provisionally *adv* GEN COMM provisoirement, temporairement

provisions *n pl* LAW *of an act* dispositions *f pl*, stipulations *f pl*; ~ **and bunkering** TRANSP *shipping* avitaillement et soutage *m pl*; ◆ **the** ~ **hereof** COMMS les dispositions des présentes *f pl*

proxy *n* ECON délégation de pouvoir *f*, procuration *f*, LAW mandataire *mf*; ~ **fight** STOCK bataille de procurations; ~ **statement** LAW déclaration de procuration *f*, procuration *f*; ~ **vote** POL vote par procuration *m*

proxyholder *n* LAW *civil law* fondé de pouvoir *m*

PRP *abbr* ACC *(profit-related pay)* salaire lié aux bénéfices *m*, HRM *(performance-related pay)* salaire au rendement *m*

PRT *abbr (petroleum revenue tax)* TAX impôt sur les revenus pétroliers *m*

prudent¹ *adj* GEN COMM prudent

prudent:² ~ **-man rule** *n* US GEN COMM règle de modération *f*, STOCK gestion de bon père de famille *f*, règle de l'homme prudent *f*, règles de prudence *f pl*; ~ **policy** *n* BANK politique de prudence *f*

prudential¹ *adj* GEN COMM de prudence *loc f*, prudent, GEN COMM US *local administration* administratif

prudential:² ~ **committee** *n* US GEN COMM, MGMNT comité de gestion *m*; ~ **consideration** *n* BANK considération de prudence *f*

prudently *adv* GEN COMM avec prudence *loc f*, prudemment

pruning *n* ACC, GEN COMM diminution *f*, réduction *f*

PS *abbr* COMMS *(postscript)* PS *(post-scriptum)*, HRM *(personal secretary)*, MGMNT *(personal secretary)* assistant personnel *m*, secrétaire de direction *m*, secrétaire particulier *m*, TRANSP *(paddle steamer)* bateau à aubes *m*, propulseur de babord et de tribord *m*

PSBR *abbr* UK *(public sector borrowing requirement)* ECON, FIN besoins de financement du secteur public *m pl*

PSDR *abbr* UK *(public sector debt repayment)* ECON remboursement de la dette de l'État *m*, remboursement de la dette publique *m*

PSE *abbr* *(public service employment)* HRM emploi dans la fonction publique *m*

P/Sec *abbr* *(personal secretary)* HRM, MGMNT assistant personnel *m*, secrétaire de direction *m*, secrétaire particulier *m*

pseudo: ~ **production function** *n* ECON fonction de pseudo-production *f*, pseudo fonction de production *f*

psf *abbr* *(per square foot)* PROP ≈ le mètre carré *m*

PSI *abbr* *(pounds per square inch)* TRANSP livres par pouce carré *f pl*

PSL *abbr* *(private sector liquidity)* ECON liquidité du secteur privé *f*

PSV *abbr* *(public service vehicle)* TRANSP véhicule de transport public *m*

psychic: ~ **income** *n jarg* ECON, HRM gratification psychologique *f*, revenu psychique *m (jarg)*, satisfaction psychologique apportée par le travail *f (jarg)*

psychographics *n pl* S&M *market research* segmentation du marché en fonction de critères psychologiques

psychological: ~ **economy** *n* ECON économie psychologique *f*; ~ **price** *n* S&M *marketing* prix psychologique *m*; ~ **pricing** *n* S&M *marketing* prix psychologique *m*; ~ **test** *n* HRM test psychologique *m*

psychology *n* ECON, HRM, S&M psychologie *f*

psychometric: ~ **test** *n* HRM, MATH, S&M test psychométrique *m*

psychometrics *n* [+sing v] HRM psychométrie *f*

pt *abbr* *(pint)* GEN COMM chopine *f (Can)*, pint *m*, pinte *f*

pta. *abbr* *(peseta)* GEN COMM pta. *(peseta)*

PTA *abbr* *(prepaid ticket advice)* TRANSP avis de billet prépayé *m*

PTL *abbr* *(partial/total loss)* INS perte partielle ou totale *f*

PTO *abbr* *(please turn over)* COMMS TSVP *(tournez s'il vous plaît)*

public¹ *adj* GEN COMM, POL public; ◆ **go** ~ STOCK faire appel public à l'épargne, s'introduire en bourse, se transformer en société ouverte, émettre dans le public, être introduit en bourse; **in the** ~ **sphere** GEN COMM dans le domaine public, POL dans la vie politique

public:² ~ **access** *n* GEN COMM *to information* accès du public *m*; ~ **accounts** *n pl* ACC comptes de l'état *m pl*, comptes publics *m pl*; ~ **address system** *n (PA system)* COMMS système de sonorisation *m*; ~ **administration** *n* GEN COMM administration publique *f*; ~ **amenities** *n pl* WEL équipements collectifs *m pl*; ~ **authority** *n* GEN COMM corps constitués *m pl*, TAX administration *f*, organisme public *m*; ~ **body** *n* ADMIN, GEN COMM corporation *f*, organisme public *m*, établissement public *m*; ~ **choice theory** *n* ECON théorie du choix politique des gouvernants *f*; ~ **company** *n* GEN COMM société anonyme *f*; ~ **consumption** *n* ECON consommation des services publics *f*; ~ **contract** *n* ECON, GEN COMM *industry, engineering,* LAW marché public *m*; ~ **corporation** *n* UK GEN COMM corporation publique *f*, établissement public *m*, TAX corporation publique *f*, régie d'État *f*, société nationale *f*, société publique *f*, établissement public *m*; ~ **debt** *n* ECON dette publique *f*; ~ **debt envelope** *n* FIN enveloppe de la dette publique *f*; ~ **debt service** *n* FIN service de la dette publique *m*; ~ **development** *n* PROP *of land* mise en oeuvre du domaine public *f*; ~ **distribution** *n* STOCK *of securities* émission publique *f*; ~ **domain** *n* MEDIA domaine public *m*; ~ **domain software** *n* COMP logiciel du domaine public *m*; ~ **economics** *n* [+sing v] ECON étude des décisions économiques de l'État; ~ **education** *n* GEN COMM, WEL US école publique *f*; ~ **engagement** *n* GEN COMM obligation officielle *f*; ~ **enterprise** *n* ECON entreprise publique *f*, GEN COMM secteur public *m*; ~ **enterprise rationalization loan** *n (PERL)* FIN prêt à la rationalisation des entreprises publiques *m (PREP)*; ~ **enterprise reform loan** *n (PERL)* FIN prêt à la réforme des entreprises publiques *m (PREP)*; ~ **enterprise rehabilitation loan** *n (PERL)* FIN prêt au redressement des entreprises publiques *m (PREP)*; ~ **examination** *n* GEN COMM examen public *m*; ~ **expenditure** *n* ECON, FIN, POL dépenses publiques *f pl*; ~ **expenditure control** *n* ECON contrôle des dépenses publiques *m*; ~ **expenditure survey** *n* ECON enquête sur les dépenses publiques *f*; ~ **finance** *n* FIN finances publiques *f pl*; ~ **foundation** *n* TAX fondation publique *f*; ~ **good** *n* (ANT *private good*) ECON bien public *m*, bien social *m*; ~ **health** *n* GEN COMM santé publique *f*; ~ **highway** *n* ADMIN, TRANSP voie publique *f*; ~ **holiday** *n* GEN COMM fête légale *f*, jour férié *m*, HRM fête publique *f*; ~ **hospital** *n* WEL hôpital public *m*; ~ **housing unit** *n* US (*cf council block UK, council flats UK*) PROP, WEL habitation à loyer modéré *f*, HLM; ~ **interest company** *n* (SYN *nationalized industry*) ECON, IND industrie nationalisée *f*, société d'intérêt public *f*; ~ **investor** *n* FIN investisseur public *m*; ~ **invitation to bid** *n* GEN COMM offre publique d'enchère *f*; ~ **issue** *n* STOCK appel public à l'épargne *m*, émission publique *f*; ~ **law** *n* LAW droit public *m*; ~ **lending right** *n* (*PLR*) MEDIA droits compensant un auteur sur le prêt de ses ouvrages en bibliothèque; ~ **limited company** *n* BrE (*UK*) GEN COMM société anonyme *f* (*SA*), société à responsabilité limitée *f* (*SARL*); ~ **limited partnership** *n* STOCK société en commandite *f*, société en commandite par actions *f*; ~ **loan** *n* FIN emprunt d'État *m*, emprunt public *m*; ~ **offering** *n* STOCK offre publique de vente *f*, OPV; ~ **opinion,** *n* [inv sg] GEN COMM opinion publique *f*; ~ **order act** *n* UK HRM, LAW *1986* loi sur l'ordre public *f*; ~ **outcry** *n* GEN COMM tollé général *m*; ~ **ownership** *n* ECON, FIN propriété publique *f*; ~ **pricing** *n* (SYN *price control*) ECON, FIN, S&M contrôle des prix *m*, politique des prix *f*; ~ **procurement** *n* GEN COMM achats publics *m pl*, fourniture publique *f*, marchés publics *m pl*; ~ **procurement contract** *n* ECON, GEN COMM, LAW marché public *m*; ~ **prosecutor** *n* LAW *department* ministère public *m*, *person* procureur général *m*; ~ **purse** *n* ECON le Trésor Public *m*, les deniers de l'État *m pl*; ~ **records** *n pl* GEN COMM archives de l'État *f pl*; ~ **relations** *n pl* (*PR*) S&M relations publiques *f pl* (*RP*); ~ **relations agency** *n* S&M agence de relations publiques *f*; ~ **relations department** *n* S&M service des relations publiques *m*; ~ **relations officer** *n* (*PRO*) HRM, S&M chef du service des relations publiques *m*, directeur des relations publiques *m*, responsable des relations publiques *m*; ~ **resource** *n* GEN COMM ressource publique *f*; ~ **revenue** *n* ECON revenus de l'État *m pl*, revenus publics *m pl*; ~ **sale** *n* GEN COMM, S&M vente aux enchères *f*, vente publique *f*, vente à la criée *f*; ~ **school** *n* GEN COMM *UK* (*cf private school US*) *fee-paying* école libre *f*, école privée *f*, GEN COMM *US non fee-paying* école publique *f*, WEL *UK* (*cf private school US*) *fee-paying* école libre *f*, école privée *f*, WEL *US non fee-paying* école publique *f*; ~ **sector** *n* ECON secteur public *m*; ~ **sector balance sheet** *n* ECON bilan du secteur public *m*; ~ **sector body** *n* ECON, TAX organisme du secteur public *m*; ~ **sector borrowing requirement** *n* UK (*PSBR*) ECON, FIN besoins de financement du secteur public *m pl*; ~ **sector debt repayment** *n* UK (*PSDR*) ECON remboursement de la dette de l'État *m*, remboursement de la dette publique *m*; ~ **sector deficit** *n* ECON, FIN déficit du secteur public *m*; ~ **sector enterprise** *n*

ECON entreprise du secteur public *f*; ~ **sector pay** *n* ECON salaire du secteur public *m*; ~ **service** *n* GEN COMM fonction publique *f*, services publics *m pl*; ~ **service body** *n* GEN COMM organisme de services publics *m*; ~ **service contract** *n* GEN COMM marché des services publics *m*; ~ **service corporation** *n* US ADMIN service public non-étatisé *m*; ~ **service employment** *n* (*PSE*) HRM emploi dans la fonction publique *m*; ~ **service minibus** *n* TRANSP minibus de transport en commun *m*; ~ **service vehicle** *n* (*PSV*) TRANSP véhicule de transport public *m*; ~ **spending** *n* ECON, FIN, POL dépenses publiques *f pl*; ~ **spending plans** *n pl* ECON, FIN, POL prévisions de dépenses publiques *f pl*; ~ **spending ratio** *n* ECON, FIN ratio des dépenses publiques sur le produit intérieur brut *m*; **the** ~ *n* GEN COMM, S&M *public relations* le public *m*; ~ **transport** *n* TRANSP transports en commun *m pl*; ~ **transport system** *n* BrE (*cf mass transit system AmE*) TRANSP transports en commun *m pl*; ~ **transportation** *n* TRANSP transports en commun *m pl*; ~ **use** *n* PATENTS usage public *m*; ~ **utility** *n* ADMIN, ECON, GEN COMM, TAX service public *m*; ~ **warning** *n* GEN COMM avertissement public *m*; ~ **welfare** *n* WEL assistance publique *f*; ~ **works** *n pl* ECON travaux publics *m pl*; ~ **works program** *n* AmE, ~ **works programme** *n* BrE GEN COMM programme de travaux publics *m*; ♦ **the ~ at large** GEN COMM le grand public *m*

Public: ~ **Broadcasting System** *n* US (*PBS*) MEDIA services de radio-télévision publics; ~ **Expenditure White Paper** *n* UK (*PEWP*) ECON livre blanc sur les dépenses publiques

publication *n* MEDIA *publishing of book* parution *f*, publication *f*; ~ **date** MEDIA *print* date de parution *f*, date de publication *f*; ♦ ~ **of sale of property** PROP publicité foncière *f*

publicity *n* S&M pub *f*, publicité *f*; ~ **department** *n* S&M service de publicité *m*; ~ **expenses** *n pl* S&M dépenses publicitaires *f pl*; ~ **man** *n* HRM publicitaire *m*; ~ **manager** *n* HRM, MEDIA, S&M chef de publicité *m*, chef du service publicité *m*, directeur de la publicité *m*; ~ **material** *n* S&M matériel publicitaire *m*; ~ **stunt** *n* S&M astuce publicitaire *f*, truc publicitaire *m* (*infrml*)

publicly:[1] ~ **-funded** *adj* GEN COMM à fonds publics *loc m*

publicly:[2] ~ **listed company** *n* FIN, STOCK société cotée en bourse *f*, société dont les actions sont cotées en bourse *f*; ~ **owned company** *n* ECON entreprise publique *f*; ~ **traded company** *n* FIN, STOCK société cotée en bourse *f*, société dont les actions sont cotées en bourse *f*; ~ **traded share** *n* STOCK action cotée en bourse *f*, action émise dans le public *f*

publish *vt* MEDIA *book, article* publier *newspaper, magazine* éditer, PATENTS publier

published[1] *adj* MEDIA *magazine* écrit; ♦ ~ **monthly** MEDIA *magazine* mensuel, qui paraît tous les mois

published:[2] ~ **accounts** *n pl* ACC comptes publics *m* *pl*, plaquettes *f pl*, états financiers *m pl*; ~ **charge** *n* FIN tarif publié *m*; ~ **fare** *n* TRANSP prix publié *m*; ~ **information** *n* GEN COMM publications *f pl*; ~ **price** *n* GEN COMM, S&M prix public *m*; ~ **rate** *n* FIN tarif publié *m*, taux publié *m*; ~ **research** *n* MEDIA recherches éditées *f pl*

publisher *n* HRM, MEDIA éditeur *m*

Publishers: ~ **and Booksellers Delivery Service** *n* UK *(PBDS)* MEDIA ≈ Service de messagerie des éditeurs et libraires *m*

publishing *n* MEDIA *business, profession* édition *f, publication of book* publication *f*; ~ **company** MEDIA maison d'édition *f*; ~ **firm** MEDIA maison d'édition *f*; ~ **house** MEDIA maison d'édition *f*

PUD *abbr (planned unit development)* PROP aménagement d'unité planifiée *m*

Puerto:[1] ~ **Rican** *adj* GEN COMM portoricain

Puerto:[2] ~ **Rican** *n* GEN COMM *person* Portoricain *m*

Puerto:[3] ~ **Rico** *pr n* GEN COMM Porto Rico *f*

PUF *abbr (purchase underwriting facility)* FIN, INS mécanisme de garantie d'achat *m*

pula *n* GEN COMM pula *m*

pull[1] *n* MEDIA *proof* première épreuve *f*; ~ **-down menu** COMP menu déroulant *m*

pull:[2] **1.** *vt* ~ **in** *jarg* FIN rapporter; ~ **off** FIN *deal* conclure, mener à bien; **2.** *vi* ~ **out** GEN COMM *withdraw* se retirer; ◆ ~ **off a deal** GEN COMM conclure un marché, mener une affaire à bien, S&M conclure un marché; ~ **the plug** *infrml* STOCK cesser de soutenir un cours *(jarg)*, se retirer; ~ **the rug out from under sb** GEN COMM couper l'herbe sous le pied de qn; ~ **strings for sb** *infrml (cf pull wires for sb AmE)* GEN COMM pistonner qn *(infrml)*, tirer les ficelles pour qn *(infrml)*; ~ **wires for sb** *infrml AmE* (SYN *pull strings for sb*) GEN COMM pistonner qn *(infrml)*, tirer les ficelles pour qn *(infrml)*

pulse *n* COMP impulsion *f*

pump:[1] ~ **priming** *n* ECON amorçage de pompe *m*, politique de soutien *f*, ECON financement par le déficit *m*, mesures d'incitation économique *f pl*, recours à l'impasse budgétaire *m*

pump:[2] ~ **funds into** *phr* FIN injecter des fonds dans *loc m*

punch[1] *n* COMP *device* perforateur *m*, perforatrice *f*; ~ **card** COMP carte perforée *f*; ~ **card operator** ADMIN mécanographe *m*; ~ **code** COMP code de perforation *m*; ~ **list** COMP liste de modifications *f*; ~ **operator** ADMIN mécanographe *m*

punch:[2] ~ **in** *vt* COMP *data* introduire; ◆ ~ **the time clock** HRM, IND pointer

punched: ~ **card** *n* COMP carte perforée *f*; ~ **paper** *n* US LEIS *theatre* invitation *f*

punctuality *n* GEN COMM, TRANSP ponctualité *f*, régularité *f*; ~ **analysis** TRANSP analyse de régularité *f*; ~ **performance** TRANSP résultats de régularité *m pl*

puncturing *n* TRANSP perforage *m*

punitive: ~ **damages** *n pl* INS dommages-intérêts

punitifs *m pl*, dommages-intérêts à titre exemplaire *m pl*

punt *n* GEN COMM livre irlandaise *f*, STOCK boursicotage *m*

punter *n* GEN COMM *better* parieur *m, customer* client *m*, STOCK boursicoteur *m*

pupil *n* WEL élève *mf*

purchase *n* GEN COMM, S&M *object* achat *m*, TRANSP *hoist* moufle *mf*, palan *m*; ~ **acquisition** *n* FIN reprise *f*; ~ **of assets** *n* GEN COMM achat de valeurs *m*; ~ **book** *n* S&M journal des achats *m*, livre des achats *m*; ~ **cost** *n* ACC *of assets* coût d'achat *m*; ~ **credit** *n (ANT cash credit)* GEN COMM achat à crédit *m*, crédit d'achat *m*; ~ **decision** *n* GEN COMM décision d'achat *f*; ~ **for settlement** *n* STOCK achat pour liquidation *m*, achat à terme *m*; ~ **fund** *n* GEN COMM fonds de rachat *m*; ~ **group** *n* FIN syndicat de garantie *m*; ~ **group agreement** *n* FIN accord de syndicat de garantie *m*; ~ **invoice** *n* GEN COMM facture d'achat *f*; ~ **issue facility** *n (PIF)* STOCK facilité d'émission d'achat *f*; ~ **method** *n* ACC *of accounting for an acquisition* méthode d'achat au prix coûtant *f*, méthode de consolidation par intégration globale *f*; ~ **money mortgage** *n* BANK, FIN, PROP prix achat garanti hypothécairement *m*; ~ **order** *n* ACC bon de commande *m*, commande *f*; ~ **price** *n* FIN, S&M, STOCK prix d'achat *m*; ~ **price method** *n* STOCK *of valuation of interest-bearing investment positions* méthode du prix d'achat *f*; ~ **and resale agreement** *n (PRA)* STOCK accord de prise en pension *m*, faculté d'achat et de revente *f*, prise en pension *f*; ~ **returns and allowances** *n pl* S&M retours et réfactions sur achats *m pl*; ~ **and sale statement** *n (P&S)* STOCK déclaration d'achat et de vente *f (jarg)*, relevé de compte *m*, état des achats et des ventes *m*; ~ **tax** *n* TAX taxe sur les achats *f*; ~ **underwriting facility** *n (PUF)* FIN, INS mécanisme de garantie d'achat *m*; ◆ **make a** ~ GEN COMM faire un achat

purchased: ~ **company** *n* GEN COMM société acquise *f*; ~ **good** *n* GEN COMM bien acquis *m*

purchases: ~ **journal** *n* ACC journal des achats *m*; ~ **ledger** *n* ACC journal des achats *m*

purchasing *n* GEN COMM, S&M achat *m*, approvisionnement *m*; ~ **company** *n* GEN COMM société preneuse *f*; ~ **costs** *n pl* GEN COMM frais d'achat *m pl*; ~ **department** *n* GEN COMM achats *m pl*, service des achats *m*; ~ **hedge** *n* STOCK couverture longue *f*, long hedge *m*; ~ **manager** *n* GEN COMM, HRM, S&M chef des achats *m*, directeur des achats *m*; ~ **motivator** *n* S&M mobile d'achat *m*; ~ **officer** *n* HRM, S&M responsable des achats *m*; ~ **power** *n* ECON, GEN COMM pouvoir d'achat *m*; ~ **power parity** *n (PPP)* ECON parité du pouvoir d'achat *f (PPA)*

pure: ~ **bundling** *n* ECON lot de marchandises composites *m*, lot de marchandises pures *m*, vente par ensembles *f*, vente par lots *f*; ~ **capitalism** *n* ECON, POL capitalisme pur *m*;

~ car carrier *n (PCC)* TRANSP *shipping* transporteur d'automobiles *m*; **~ car and truck carrier** *n (PCTC)* TRANSP *shipping* transporteur d'automobiles et de camions *m*; **~ competition** *n* ECON concurrence pure *f*; **~ credit economy** *n* ECON pure économie de crédit *f*, économie totalement fondée sur le crédit *f*; **~ economic rent** *n* ECON rente économique pure *f*; **~ holding company** *n* FIN société holding bancaire *f*; **~ inflation** *n* ECON inflation pure *f*; **~ interest rate** *n* ECON, FIN taux d'intérêt brut *m*; **~ market economy** *n* ECON, POL économie de marché intégrale *f*; **~ monopoly** *n* ECON monopole intégral *m*, monopole pur *m*; **~ play** *n jarg* STOCK société à activité unique *f*; **~ profit** *n* ECON, FIN, S&M bénéfice net *m*

purification *n* ENVIR, IND purification *f*, épuration *f*; **~ plant** ENVIR station d'épuration *f*

purpose *n* GEN COMM *aim* but *m*, objet *m, use* usage *m*; **~ loan** STOCK prêt pour achat de titres *m*

purpose-built[1] *adj* PROP, TRANSP construit sur mesure, fabriqué sur demande

purpose-built:[2] **~ block** *n* PROP *of flats* immeuble construit pour une fonction *m*; **~ tonnage** *n* TRANSP navire spécial *m*; **~ vehicle** *n* TRANSP véhicule construit sur commande *m*

purser *n* HRM, TRANSP *on ship, aircraft* commissaire de bord *m*

pursuant: **~ to article 120** *phr* LAW conformément à l'article 120, en vertu de l'article 120

pursue *vt* GEN COMM *policy* poursuivre

purveyor *n* GEN COMM fournisseur *m*; ◆ **~ of fine foods** GEN COMM fournisseur d'alimentation fine *m*

push:[1] **~ -button telephone** *n* COMMS téléphone à clavier *m*, téléphone à touches *m*; **~ incentive** *n* S&M *sales* prime à la vente *f*; **~ money** *n* HRM, S&M *sales* excédent d'argent *m*, indemnité de licenciement *f*, prime au vendeur *f*; **~ -tow barge** *n* TRANSP pousseur-barge *m*

push[2] *vt* GEN COMM pousser; **~ back** TRANSP *aircraft* refouler; ◆ **~ sb to the limit** GEN COMM pousser qn à bout; **~ sb to the wall** GEN COMM mettre qn au pied du mur; ◆ **~ sb into bankruptcy** COM acculer qn

pushback *n* TRANSP *aircraft* refoulement *m*

Pushtu *n* GEN COMM *language* pushtu *m*

put[1] *n (ANT call)* STOCK option de vente *f*, put *m*; **~ bond** STOCK obligation remboursable à périodes déterminées *f*; **~ broker** STOCK courtier en options non-agréé *m*; **~ buyer** *(ANT put seller)* STOCK acheteur d'option de vente *m*; **~ buying hedge** STOCK couverture par achat d'options de vente *f*; **~ and call** STOCK double option *f (jarg)*, options de vente et d'achat *f pl*, stellage *m (jarg)*; **~ delta** *(ANT call delta)* STOCK delta d'une option de vente *m*; **~ exercise price** *(ANT call exercise price)* STOCK prix de levée de l'option de vente *m*; **~ -in-use rule** TAX règle de mise en service *f*; **~ option** *(ANT call option)* STOCK contrat d'option de vente *m*, option de vente *f*; **~ option**

exercise price *(ANT call option exercise price)* STOCK prix de levée de l'option de vente *m*; **~ option premium** *(ANT call option premium)* STOCK cours de l'option de vente *m*, premium de l'option de vente *m*, prix d'option de vente *m*; **~ option price** *(ANT call option price)* STOCK prime de vente *f*; **~ option writer** *(ANT call option writer)* STOCK vendeur d'options de vente *m*; **~ premium** *(ANT call premium)* STOCK prime de vente *f*, prix d'option de vente *m*, prix de l'option de vente *m*; **~ price** *(ANT call price)* STOCK prix de revente *m*; **~ provision** *(ANT call provision)* STOCK provision pour le prix d'une revente; **~ purchase** STOCK long put *m*, position acheteur sur options de vente *f*; **~ rate** *(ANT call rate)* STOCK *of stocks, shares* taux de l'option de vente *m*; **~ ratio backspread** *(ANT call ratio backspread)* STOCK *options* écart inverse sur ratio d'options de vente *m*; **~ seller** *(ANT put buyer)* STOCK acheteur d'option d'achat *m*; **~ spread** *(ANT call spread)* STOCK opération mixte sur options de vente *m*; **~ strike** STOCK *options* prix d'exercice d'une option de vente *m*; **~ strike price** *(ANT call strike price, option strike price)* STOCK prix de levée de l'option de vente *m*; **~ through** STOCK application des cours cotés hors de la séance précédente *f*; **~ warrant** *(ANT call warrant)* STOCK warrant à la vente *m*; **~ writer** *(ANT call writer)* STOCK *on currency futures* acheteur d'option de vente *m*; **~ writing** *(ANT call writing)* STOCK achat d'options de vente *m*; ◆ **~ of more option** STOCK option du double pour livrer *f*

put[2] *vt* GEN COMM mettre; **~ away** BANK *money in a bank* mettre de côté; **~ back** GEN COMM proroger, retarder; **~ forward** GEN COMM *proposal* avancer, proposer; **~ in** GEN COMM *report* remettre; **~ in order** BANK *account* régulariser; **~ off** GEN COMM proroger, retarder; **~ up** ECON *capital*, FIN *capital* relever; ◆ **~ the address on** GEN COMM, MEDIA, S&M mettre l'adresse sur; **~ an advert in the paper** S&M mettre une annonce dans le journal; **~ a check in the box** *AmE (cf put a tick in the box BrE)* GEN COMM cocher la case; **~ a damper on** GEN COMM jeter un froid sur; **~ a deposit** FIN verser des arrhes; **~ an embargo on** GEN COMM mettre un embargo sur; **~ the final touches to** GEN COMM mettre la dernière main à; **~ the finishing touches to** GEN COMM mettre la dernière main à; **~ forward a proposal** GEN COMM avancer une proposition; **~ a guard on** GEN COMM *somebody* surveiller; **~ in an application** HRM faire acte de candidature, faire une demande, proposer sa candidature; **~ in an application for a job** HRM faire une demande d'emploi, poser sa candidature pour un emploi; **~ in a bid** GEN COMM mettre une enchère; **~ in a claim** LAW déposer une réclamation, faire une réclamation, faire valoir ses droits; **~ in danger** GEN COMM mettre en danger; **~ in a good word for sb** GEN COMM glisser un mot en faveur de qn; **~ in order** GEN COMM mettre en ordre; **~ in place** GEN COMM mettre en place; ~ **in a plea** LAW plaider; ~ **in position** GEN COMM mettre en place; ~ **in touch** COMMS mettre en contact, mettre en relation; ~ **in a word for sb** GEN COMM glisser un mot en faveur de qn; ~ **into cold storage** *infrml* GEN COMM remettre à plus tard; ~ **into effect** GEN COMM *policy* mettre en vigueur; ~ **into execution** GEN COMM mettre à exécution; ~ **into force** LAW mettre en vigueur; ~ **into order** GEN COMM mettre en ordre; ~ **into port** TRANSP relâcher; ~ **into practice** GEN COMM mettre en pratique; ~ **into receivership** LAW mettre en liquidation, placer sous administration judiciaire; ~ **it another way** GEN COMM autrement dit; ~ **money down** FIN verser des arrhes, verser un acompte; ~ **on the back burner** GEN COMM laisser de côté; ~ **on a bold front** GEN COMM faire bonne contenance; ~ **on the market** PROP mettre en vente; ~ **on short allowance** ECON, FIN rationner, réduire à la portion congrue, GEN COMM *individual* réduire à la portion congrue, *supplier* rationner; ~ **on a spurt** GEN COMM *hurry* accélérer, mettre les gaz (*infrml*), *work harder* se retrousser les manches; ~ **one's affairs in order** GEN COMM mettre de l'ordre dans ses affaires; ~ **one's back into it** GEN COMM donner un coup de collier; ~ **one's seal to sth** GEN COMM apposer son sceau sur qch; ~ **out for tender** GEN COMM lancer un appel d'offres; ~ **out a statement** GEN COMM publier une déclaration; ~ **pressure on sb** GEN COMM mettre la pression sur qn; ~ **a question on the agenda** GEN COMM, MGMNT mettre une question à l'ordre du jour; ~ **sb forward for a job** HRM proposer qn pour un poste; ~ **sb in the picture** GEN COMM mettre qn au courant; ~ **sb up for a job** HRM proposer qn pour un poste; ~ **sth down in writing** GEN COMM consigner qch par écrit; ~ **sth in the window** GEN COMM présenter qch sous un jour favorable; ~ **sth into production** IND entreprendre la production de qch; ~ **sth on record** GEN COMM consigner qch par écrit; ~ **a suggestion before a committee** GEN COMM soumettre une proposition à un comité; ~ **a tax on** TAX mettre un impôt sur, mettre une taxe sur; ~ **through to** COMMS mettre en communication avec; ~ **a tick in the box** *BrE* (*cf put a check in the box AmE*) GEN COMM cocher la case; ~ **to the test** GEN COMM mettre à l'épreuve; ~ **to the vote** POL mettre aux voix; ~ **up for sale** PROP mettre en vente; ~ **up for tender** GEN COMM faire une soumission; ~ **a veto on** GEN COMM mettre son veto à

put's: ~ **strike** *n* (ANT *call's strike*) STOCK cours d'exercice de l'option de vente *m*, prix d'exercice d'une option de vente *m*

p.v. *abbr* (*par value*) STOCK parité *f*, valeur au pair *f*, valeur nominale *f*

P/V *abbr* ACC, FIN (*profit/volume ratio*) rapport profit et changement de quantités vendues *m*, rapport profit sur ventes *m*, ratio de volume de bénéfices *m*

PWB *abbr* (*permanent water ballast*) TRANSP *shipping* lest d'eau fixe *m*, lest liquide permanent *m*

PYO *abbr* (*pick-your-own*) GEN COMM *farm produce* cueillette à la ferme *f*

Pyongyang *pr n* GEN COMM Pyongyang *n pr*

pyramid:[1] ~ **selling** *n* S&M vente pyramidale *f*, vente à la boule de neige *f*

pyramid[2] *vi* GEN COMM structurer en holdings, PROP, STOCK acheter des titres sur gains précédents

pyramidal *adj* GEN COMM pyramidal

pyramiding *n* GEN COMM structure en pyramide *f*

pyrometer *n* GEN COMM pyromètre *m*

pyrophoric: ~ **liquid** *n* TRANSP *dangerous classified cargo* liquide pyrophorique *m*

pyrotechnic: ~ **substance** *n* TRANSP *dangerous classified cargo* matière pyrotechnique *f*

PYT *abbr* (*payment*) BANK, FIN, GEN COMM versement *m*

Q

Q *abbr* *(quadruple expansion engine)* TRANSP *shipping* machine à quadruple expansion *f*

QA *abbr* *(quality assurance)* IND, MGMNT, S&M assurance de la qualité *f*, contrôle de la qualité *m*

Qatar *pr n* GEN COMM Qatar *m*

Qatari[1] *adj* GEN COMM qatarien

Qatari[2] *n* GEN COMM *person* Qatarien *m*

QC *abbr* HRM *UK (Queen's Counsel)* avocat de la Couronne, ≈ bâtonnier de l'ordre *m*, IND *(quality control)* contrôle de la qualité *m*, LAW *UK (Queen's Counsel)* avocat de la Couronne, ≈ bâtonnier de l'ordre *m*, MGMNT *(quality control)*, S&M *(quality control)* contrôle de la qualité *m*

Qco *abbr* *(quantity at captain's option)* TRANSP *shipping* quantité à l'avantage du navire *f*

QL *abbr* *(query language)* COMP langage d'interrogation *m*, langage de requête *m*

qnty *abbr* *(quantity)* GEN COMM, MATH qté *(quantité)*

QPC *abbr* *(quasi-propulsive coefficient)* TRANSP *of engine* rendement propulsif *m*

QR *abbr* *(quantitative restriction)* ECON, IND restriction quantitative *f*

Q-sailing *n* TRANSP départ non-publié *m*

QST *abbr* *(Quebec sales tax)* TAX TVQ *(taxe de vente de Quebec)*

qt. *abbr* GEN COMM *(quantity)* qté *(quantité)*, GEN COMM *(quart)* quart *m*, MATH *(quantity)* qté *(quantité)*

qtr *abbr* *(quarter)* GEN COMM quart *m*

quadrennial: **~ survey** *n* TAX *of vessels* expertise quadriennale *f*, visite quadriennale *f*

quadriad *n* *US* ECON quadriade *f*

quadripartite: **~ agreement** *n* GEN COMM accord quadripartite *m*

quadruple: **~ expansion engine** *n* *(Q)* TRANSP *shipping* machine à quadruple expansion *f*; **~ stacker** *n* TRANSP pièce de gerbage quadruple *f*

quadruplicate: **in ~** *phr* GEN COMM en quatre exemplaires *loc m*

qualification *n* ACC avis réservé sur la qualité des comptes *m*, qualification des comptes *f*, GEN COMM *academic* qualification *f*, *modifying condition* condition *f*, réserve *f*, *suitability* capacité *f*, compétence *f*, HRM *for job* qualification *f*, WEL *for benefit* admissibilité *f*; **~ of opinion** *n* ACC réserve apportée à un rapport d'audit *f*; **~ period** *n* WEL *for benefit* période d'admissibilité *f*; **~ shares** *n pl* STOCK actions statutaires *f pl*; ◆ **have the right ~s for the job** HRM avoir le profil de l'emploi, avoir les qualifications nécessaires pour le poste

qualified[1] *adj* GEN COMM *suitable* compétent,

qualifié, *trained* diplômé, qualifié; ◆ **~ to do sth** GEN COMM qualifié pour faire qch

qualified:[2] **~ acceptance** *n* BANK acceptation conditionnelle *f*, acceptation restreinte *f*; **~ accountant** *n* ACC commissaire aux comptes *m* *(Fra)*, expert-comptable *m*; **~ activities** *n* TAX *manufacturing and processing* activités admissibles *f pl*, activités qualifiées *f pl*; **~ approval** *n* GEN COMM approbation modérée *f*; **~ borrowing** *n* BANK emprunts de référence *m pl*; **~ endorsement** *n* BANK endos conditionnel *m*; **~ expenditure** *n* TAX dépense acceptable *f*, dépense admissible *f*; **~ indorsement** *n see qualified endorsement* ; **~ insurance corporation** *n* INS assurance contre les intempéries *f*, compagnie agréée d'assurance *f*; **~ investment** *n* STOCK placement admissible *m*; **~ majority** *n* GEN COMM, POL majorité qualifiée *f*; **~ majority vote** *n* GEN COMM, POL vote à la majorité qualifiée *m*; **~ opinion** *n* GEN COMM opinion avec réserve *f*; **~ pension income** *n* TAX revenu de pension admissible *m*, revenu de pension designée *m*; **~ relation** *n* TAX proche admissible *m*, relation qualifiée *f*; **~ report** *n* ACC rapport réservé *m*; **~ transportation equipment** *n* TRANSP matériel de transport admissible *m*

qualify 1. *vt* GEN COMM *statement* préciser; **~ for** GEN COMM, HRM *holiday pay*, LAW *aid*, WEL *benefit* avoir droit à; **2.** *vi* GEN COMM obtenir son diplôme, qualifier, HRM qualifier; **~ for** ADMIN remplir les conditions; ◆ **~ sb to do sth** HRM autoriser qn à faire qch, donner à qn le droit de faire qch, donner à qn les compétences pour faire qch

qualifying[1] *adj* GEN COMM permettant

qualifying:[2] **~ annuity** *n* FIN annuité conditionnelle *f*; **~ debt obligation** *n* TAX créance admissible *f*, engagement de dette qualifiée *m*; **~ distribution** *n* ACC *made by a company* répartition conditionnelle *f*; **~ farmer** *n* TAX agriculteur admissible *m*, agriculteur qualifiable *m*; **~ holding** *n* FIN participation qualifiée *f*; **~ item** *n* FIN élément éligible *m*; **~ period** *n* TAX période admissible *f*, période de qualification *f*; **~ share** *n* STOCK action admissible *f*, action à droit d'entrée au conseil d'administration *f*; **~ shares** *n pl* STOCK actions statutaires *f pl*; **~ small business corporation** *n* TAX corporation exploitant une petite entreprise admissible *f*, petite entreprise commerciale qualifiable *f*; **~ stock option** *n* STOCK option de souscripteurs d'actions sans impôt *f*, option de vente garantie *f*; **~ taxable dividends** *n pl* TAX dividendes imposables admissibles *m pl*; **~ utility** *n* STOCK valeur des services publics à avantages fiscaux *f*

qualitative[1] *adj* GEN COMM qualitatif

qualitative:[2] ~ **analysis** *n* IND, MATH, MGMNT, S&M *market research* analyse qualitative *f*; ~ **approach** *n* STOCK approche qualitative *f*; ~ **controls** *n pl* BANK *on lending or deposits* contrôles qualitatifs *m pl*; ~ **methodology** *n* S&M *market research* méthodologie qualitative *f*; ~ **research** *n* S&M *market research* recherche qualitative *f*

qualitatively *adv* GEN COMM qualitativement

quality *n* S&M qualité *f*; ~ **assessment** *n* GEN COMM, IND, MGMNT évaluation de la qualité *f*; ~ **asset** *n* FIN avoir de qualité *m*; ~ **of assets** *n* FIN qualité des immobilisations *f*; ~ **assurance** *n* *(QA)* IND, MGMNT, S&M assurance de la qualité *f*, contrôle de la qualité *m*; ~ **brand** *n* GEN COMM, S&M marque de qualité *f*; ~ **certificate** *n* IMP/EXP, TRANSP certificat de qualité *m*; ~ **circle** *n* HRM, IND, MGMNT cercle de qualité *m*; ~ **control** *n* *(QC)* IND, MGMNT, S&M contrôle de la qualité *m*; ~ **of earnings** *n* FIN qualité des bénéfices *f*; ~ **goods** *n pl* GEN COMM marchandises de qualité *f pl*; ~ **label** *n* GEN COMM, S&M label de qualité *m*; ~ **of the labor force** *n AmE* ~ **of the labour force** *n BrE* ECON, HRM qualité de la main-d'oeuvre *f*; ~ **of life** *n* ECON, HRM, WEL qualité de vie *f*; ~ **loan** *n* BANK prêt de qualité *m*; ~ **management** *n* IND, MGMNT, S&M gestion de la qualité *f*; ~ **market** *n* S&M *marketing* marché de qualité *m*; ~ **newspaper** *n* MEDIA *print* journal de qualité *m*, journal sérieux *m*; ~ **paper** *n* MEDIA journal de qualité *m*, journal sérieux *m*; ~ **-price ratio** *n* GEN COMM, S&M *marketing* rapport qualité-prix *m*; ~ **standards** *n pl* GEN COMM critères de qualité *m pl*, normes de qualité *f pl*; ~ **of water** *n* ENVIR, WEL qualité de l'eau *f*; ~ **of working life** *n* *(QWL)* HRM qualité de la vie active *f*, qualité de la vie au travail *f*, qualité de la vie professionnelle *f*

quantification *n* ADMIN approche quantitative *f*

quantify *vt* MATH quantifier

quantitative[1] *adj* GEN COMM quantitatif

quantitative:[2] ~ **analysis** *n* IND, MATH, MGMNT, S&M *market research* analyse quantitative *f*; ~ **controls** *n pl* BANK *on lending or deposits* contrôles quantitatifs *m pl*; ~ **methodology** *n* S&M *market research* méthodologie quantitative *f*; ~ **research** *n* S&M *market research* recherche quantitative *f*; ~ **restriction** *n* *(QR)* ECON, IND restriction quantitative *f*; ~ **rules** *n pl* STOCK règles quantitatives *f pl*

quantity *n* *(qnty, qt.)* GEN COMM, MATH quantité *f* *(qté)*; ~ **at captain's option** *(Qco)* TRANSP *shipping* quantité à l'avantage du navire *f*; ~ **buyer** GEN COMM centrale d'achat *f*; ~ **discount** ACC, GEN COMM, S&M remise sur la quantité *f*, remise sur volume *f*; ~ **permitted** IMP/EXP quantité autorisée *f*, tolérance *f*; ~ **surveying** IND mesure de la quantité *f*; ~ **surveyor** IND *person* calculateur de quantité *m*; ~ **theory of money** ECON monétarisme *m*, théorie quantitative de la monnaie *f*

quantum *n* GEN COMM, MATH quantum *m*; ♦ ~ **meruit** GEN COMM dans la mesure de ses mérites

quarantine *n* GEN COMM, IMP/EXP quarantaine *f*; ~ **dues** *n pl* IMP/EXP frais de quarantaine *m pl*

quart *n* *(qt.)* GEN COMM quart *m*

quarter *n* GEN COMM *of year* trimestre *m*, GEN COMM *(qtr)* one-fourth quart *m*; ~ **end** ACC fin de trimestre *f*; ~ **-page advertisement** MEDIA, S&M publicité quart de page *f*; ~ **of a pound** GEN COMM quart de livre *m*; ~ **-up price** *jarg* STOCK hausse de prix de 0,25% *f*; ♦ **every** ~ GEN COMM *of year* chaque trimestre, tous les trimestres

quarterdeck *n* TRANSP *shipping* gaillard d'arrière *m*

quartering *n jarg* HRM *industrial relations* pénalisation pour manque de ponctualité *f*

quarterly[1] *adj* GEN COMM, MEDIA *magazine* trimestriel

quarterly[2] *adv* GEN COMM, MEDIA trimestriellement

quarterly[3] *n* MEDIA *print* publication trimestrielle *f*; ~ **dividend** STOCK dividende trimestriel *m*; ~ **installment** *AmE*, ~ **instalment** *BrE* ACC remboursement trimestriel *m*, trimestrialité *f*, versement trimestriel *m*, TAX acompte trimestriel *m*; ~ **rate bond** STOCK BTT, bon à taux trimestriel *m*

quartile: ~ **deviation** *n* ECON déviation quartile *f*

quash *vt* GEN COMM *decision, proposal* rejeter, LAW *order, verdict* annuler, casser

quashing *n* GEN COMM *of decision, proposal* rejet *m*, LAW *of order* annulation *f*, *of verdict* annulation *f*, cassation *f*

quasi:[1] ~ **-contract** *n* LAW quasi-contrat *m*; ~ **-fixed factor** *n* ECON facteur quasi-fixe *m*; ~ **-independence** *n* GEN COMM quasi-indépendance *f*; ~ **-manufacturer** *n* IND *retail chains* quasi-fabricant *m*; ~ **-money** *n* GEN COMM monnaie de singe *f*; ~ **-performing loan** *n* BANK prêt quasi-productif *m*; ~ **-propulsive coefficient** *n* *(QPC)* TRANSP *of engine* rendement propulsif *m*; ~ **-rent** *n* ECON quasi-rente *f*; ~ **-statutory allocation** *n* LAW affectation quasi-législative *f*

quasi-[2] *pref* GEN COMM quasi-

quay *n* TRANSP *in port* quai *m*; ~ **fitting** TRANSP *shipping* aménagement au quai *m*; ♦ ~ **to quay** IMP/EXP, TRANSP *shipping* quai à quai

quayage *n* IMP/EXP, TRANSP droits de quai *m pl*, quaiage *m*

Quebec: ~ **sales tax** *n* *(QST)* TAX taxe de vente de Quebec *f* *(TVQ)*

Queen's: ~ **Counsel** *n UK* *(QC)* HRM, LAW avocat de la Couronne, ≈ bâtonnier de l'ordre *m*; ~ **enemies** *n pl UK* LAW ennemis de la Couronne *m pl*, ennemis de la Reine *m pl*

query[1] *n* COMP consultation *f*, interrogation *f*, GEN COMM demande *f*, question *f*; ~ **language** *(QL)* COMP langage d'interrogation *m*, langage de requête *m*

query[2] *vt* GEN COMM mettre en doute

Quesnay *n* ECON tableau économique *m*

question[1] *n* GEN COMM question *f*; ~ **of jurisdiction**

LAW question de compétence *f*; **~ time** *UK* POL *parliament* séance des questions *f*; ◆ **in ~** GEN COMM en question

question[2] *vt* GEN COMM questionner, LAW contester

questionnaire *n* GEN COMM, S&M questionnaire *m*

quetzal *n* GEN COMM quetzal *m*

queue[1] *n* COMP file d'attente *f*, GEN COMM *BrE (cf line AmE)* file d'attente *f*, queue *f*; **~ jumper** *BrE (cf deadhead AmE)* GEN COMM resquilleur *m*

queue[2] **1.** *vt* COMP mettre en file d'attente; **2.** *vi* **~ up** *BrE (cf wait in line AmE)* GEN COMM faire la queue *loc f*

queueing *n* COMP mise en file d'attente *f*; **~ system** ECON file d'attente *f*, rationnement *m*; **~ theory** COMP, ECON, MATH théorie des files d'attente *f*

quick[1] *adj* GEN COMM rapide

quick:[2] **~ assets** *n pl* ACC, FIN actif disponible *m*, actif négociable *m*, actif réalisable *m*; **~ assets ratio** *n* FIN ratio d'actifs disponibles *m*; **~ -disbursing loan** *n* BANK prêt à décaissement rapide *m*; **~ fix** *n* GEN COMM bouclage rapide *m*; **~ flip** *n* TAX opération vente-rachat *f (jarg)*, petit gain rapide *m*, vente-rachat de titres *f*; **~ ratio** *n (SYN acid-test ratio)* ACC, BANK, FIN ratio d'actifs et passifs monétaires à court terme *m*, ratio de liquidité immédiate *m*, taux de liquidité immédiate *m*; **~ -release tensioner** *n* TRANSP tendeur à déclenchement rapide *m*; **~ returns** *n pl* FIN rentrées de fonds rapides *f pl*; **~ sale** *n* GEN COMM, S&M vente facile *f*; **~ succession** *n* TAX succession consécutive *f*, suite rapide *f*; **~ tite**® *n* TRANSP *containers* quick-tite® *m*

quickly: **as ~ as possible** *phr* GEN COMM aussi vite que possible

quid *n* *UK* GEN COMM *pound sterling* livre *f*

quid pro quo *n frml* GEN COMM compensation *f*

quiet[1] *adj* GEN COMM *market, business* calme

quiet:[2] **~ enjoyment** *n* PROP jouissance tranquille *f*; **~ title suit** *n* LAW, PROP action possessoire *f*

qui facit per alium facit ipse *phr frml* GEN COMM, LAW quand on fait faire qch par un tiers on le fait soi-même

qui facit per alium facit per se *phr frml* GEN COMM, LAW quand on fait faire qch par un tiers on le fait soi-même

quintal *n* GEN COMM quintal *m*

quit:[1] **~ rate** *n* ECON, HRM taux de départs *m*

quit[2] *vi* COMP sortir, HRM *resign* démissionner

quitclaim *n* LAW renonciation à un droit *f*; **~ deed** LAW, PROP acte de garantie de tranquillité *m*

Quito *pr n* GEN COMM Quito *n pr*

quod vide *phr frml (qv)* GEN COMM, MEDIA voir

quoin *n* TRANSP cale *f*, coin *m*

quondam *adj frml* GEN COMM ancien, d'autrefois

quorum *n* GEN COMM quorum *m*; ◆ **form a ~** ADMIN, GEN COMM, MGMNT constituer un quorum; **have a ~** ADMIN, GEN COMM, MGMNT constituer un quorum

quota *n* ECON contingent *m*, quota *m*, GEN COMM contingent *m*, quota *m*, quotité *f*, IMP/EXP contingent *m*, quota *m*; **~ fixing** ECON, GEN COMM, IMP/EXP contingentement *m*; **~ sample** S&M *market research* échantillon par quota *m*; **~ sampling** S&M *market research* sondage par quota *m*; **~ system** ECON contingentement *m*, GEN COMM, IMP/EXP contingentement *m*, système de quotas *m*

quotable *adj* STOCK cotable

quotation *n* FIN cote *f*, cours *m*, GEN COMM *estimate* devis *m*, INS cotation *f*, STOCK cotation *f*, cote *f*, cours *m*; **~ board** STOCK tableau de cotation *m*; **~ spread** STOCK écart de cours *m*

quote[1] *n* FIN cote *f*, cours *m*, GEN COMM *estimate* devis *m*, STOCK cote *f*, cours *m*; **~ value** STOCK valeur à la cote *f*

quote[2] *vt* GEN COMM *price, cost* indiquer, STOCK *at par* coter; ◆ **~ a reference number** COMMS rappeler un numéro de référence

quoted[1] *adj* STOCK coté, coté en bourse; ◆ **~ at** STOCK coté à

quoted:[2] **~ company** *n* FIN, STOCK société cotée en bourse *f*; **~ price** *n* STOCK cours inscrit à la cote officielle *m*, prix coté *m*; **~ securities** *n pl* STOCK titres admis à la cote officielle *m pl*, valeurs cotées *f pl*; **~ security** *n* STOCK valeur cotée en bourse *f*, valeur inscrite à la cote *f*; **~ share** *n (ANT unquoted share)* STOCK action cotée *f*, action inscrite à la cote officielle *f*

quotient *n* MATH quotient *m*

quo warranto *phr* LAW quo warranto

qv *abbr (quod vide)* GEN COMM, MEDIA *print* voir

QWERTY: **~ keyboard** *n* COMP clavier QWERTY *m*

QWL *abbr (quality of working life)* HRM qualité de la vie active *f*, qualité de la vie au travail *f*, qualité de la vie professionnelle *f*

R

R *abbr* GEN COMM *(riveted)* fixé, riveté, GEN COMM *(reconditioned)* remis à neuf *loc*, rénové, GEN COMM *(refrigerated)* réfrigéré, PROP *(reconditioned)* rénové, TRANSP *(refrigerated container)* conteneur frigorifique *m*, TRANSP *(refrigeration)* réfrigération *f*, TRANSP *(refrigerated)* réfrigéré, TRANSP *(reduce class rate)* air freight classification tarif de classification avec réduction *m*

R/A *abbr (refer to acceptor)* GEN COMM voir le tiré

Rabat *pr n* GEN COMM Rabat *n pr*

rabbi *n jarg US* POL parrain politique *m*

Race: **~ Relations Act** *n UK (RRA)* LAW loi protégeant l'égalité des droits pour chaque race

racial: **~ discrimination** *n* HRM discrimination raciale *f*

rack *n* COMP armoire *f*, râtelier *m*; **~ jobber** *jarg* GEN COMM, S&M grossiste qui approvisionne les rayons des grandes surfaces; ◆ **go to ~ and ruin** GEN COMM *economy* aller à vau-l'eau

racketeering *n* POL affairisme *m*

racking *n* TRANSP gauchissement oblique *m*

RAD *abbr (raised afterdeck)* TRANSP *shipping* pont arrière surélevé *m*

radar *n* TRANSP *shipping* radar *m*; **~ alert** STOCK surveillance étroite des formes commerciales dans l'éventualité d'un rachat, surveillance maximale *f*

radiation *n* ENVIR, IND rayonnement *m*; **~ dose** ENVIR dose de rayonnement *f*; **~ pollution** ENVIR pollution par les rayonnements *f*; **~ protection** ENVIR protection contre les rayonnements *f*

radical[1] *adj* GEN COMM, POL radical

radical:[2] **~ economics** *n* ECON radicalisme économique *m*

radio *n* COMMS, GEN COMM, MEDIA radio *f*; **~ advertising** MEDIA, S&M publicité radiophonique *f*; **~ announcement** MEDIA *broadcast* annonce radiophonique *f*; **~ audience** MEDIA *broadcast* audience radiophonique *f*, auditeurs *m pl*; **~ broadcast** MEDIA *programme* émission de radio *f*, émission radiophonique *f*; **~ broadcasting** MEDIA diffusion radiophonique *f*; **~ commercial** S&M message publicitaire à la radio *m*; **~ direction finder** *(RDF)* TRANSP radiogoniomètre *m*; **~ journalist** MEDIA journaliste radio *m*; **~ log** COMMS journal radio *m*; **~ officer** COMMS, HRM *shipping* officier radio *m*; **~ program** *AmE*, **~ programme** *BrE* MEDIA *broadcast* émission de radio *f*, émission radiophonique *f*; **~ set** COMMS, MEDIA *broadcast* poste de radio *m*; **~ station** MEDIA *broadcast* station de radio *f*

radioactive: **~ fallout** *n* ENVIR, IND retombées radioactives *f pl*; **~ pollution** *n* ENVIR pollution radioactive *f*; **~ substance** *n* ENVIR substance radioactive *f*

radiophone *n (RP)* COMMS radiotéléphone *m*

radiotelegram *n* COMMS radiotélégramme *m*

radiotelegraphy *n (RT)* COMMS radiotélégraphie *f*

radiotelephone *n (RT)* COMMS radiotéléphone *m*

radiotelephony *n (RT)* COMMS radiotéléphonie *f*

RAFT *abbr (revolving acceptance facility by tender)* FIN acceptation renouvelable par offre

rag *n infrml* MEDIA *newspaper* canard *m* (*infrml*), feuille de chou *f* (*infrml*), torchon *m* (*infrml*); **~ content** ENVIR, IND *of paper* proportion de chiffon *f*; **~ trade** *infrml* IND confection *f*, industrie de la fringue *f*, industrie textile *f*

raid[1] *n* GEN COMM incursion *f*, raid *m*, STOCK attaque *f*

raid[2] *vt* FIN entamer, STOCK puiser dans; ◆ **~ a company** FIN, GEN COMM, STOCK attaquer une société, lancer une OPA contre une société; **~ the market** STOCK attaquer le marché, exercer de la pression à la baisse sur le marché

raidable *adj* STOCK opéable

raider *n* STOCK attaquant *m*, lanceur d'OPA *m*, prédateur *m*, raider *m*

rail *n* TRANSP *means of transport* ch. de f., chemin de fer *m*, *track* rail *m*; **~ -air link** *n* TRANSP liaison train-avion *f*; **~ freight** *n* TRANSP transport par chemin de fer *m*; **~ guided tour** *n* LEIS excursion en train avec guide *f*; **~ link** *n* TRANSP liaison ferroviaire *f*; **~ network** *n* TRANSP réseau de chemin de fer *m*, réseau ferroviaire *m*; **~ shares** *n pl* STOCK actions de chemin de fer *f pl*, valeurs de chemin de fer *f pl*; **~ shipment** *n* TRANSP expédition par chemin de fer *f*; **~ strike** *n* HRM, TRANSP grève des cheminots *f*, grève des chemins de fer *f*; **~ terminal** *n* TRANSP gare *f*; **~ tour** *n* LEIS excursion en train *f*; **~ traffic** *n* TRANSP trafic ferroviaire *m*; **~ transport** *n* TRANSP transport ferroviaire *m*; **~ traveler** *n AmE*, **~ traveller** *n BrE* TRANSP usager des chemins de fer *m*; **~ user** *n* TRANSP usager des chemins de fer *m*

Rail: **~ Europe Senior Card** *n UK* TRANSP Carte Vermeil permettant jusqu'à 50% de réduction sur les billets de chemin de fer en Europe

railcar *n* TRANSP *railway* automotrice *f*

railcard *n UK* TRANSP en Grande-Bretagne, une carte de voyage permettant les jeunes, les retraités ou les familles nombreuses d'acheter des billets de chemin de fer à prix réduit

railhead *n* TRANSP tête de ligne *f*

railroad *n AmE (cf railway BrE)* TRANSP ch. de f., chemin de fer *m*, voie ferrée *f*; **~ bill** *n AmE (cf railway bill BrE)* TRANSP lettre de voiture ferroviaire *f*; **~ consignment note** *n AmE (cf railway consignment note BrE)* TRANSP lettre de voiture ferroviaire *f*; **~ line** *n AmE (cf railway line*

BrE) TRANSP voie ferrée *f*; ~ **retirement act** *n US* HRM loi sur les retraites des cheminots; ~ **securities** *n pl AmE (cf railway securities BrE)* STOCK titres de chemin de fer *m pl*; ~ **service** *n AmE (cf railway service BrE)* TRANSP service ferroviaire *m*; ~ **station** *n AmE (cf railway station BrE, train station BrE)* TRANSP gare *f*; ~ **system** *n AmE (cf railway system BrE)* TRANSP réseau de chemin de fer *m*, réseau ferroviaire *m*; ~ **timetable** *n AmE (cf railway timetable BrE)* TRANSP horaire des trains *m*; ~ **track** *n AmE (cf railway track BrE)* TRANSP voie ferrée *f*; ~ **worker** *n AmE (cf railway worker BrE, railwayman BrE)* HRM, TRANSP cheminot *m*

railroader *n AmE (cf railway worker BrE, railwayman BrE)* HRM, TRANSP cheminot *m*

Railrover® *n UK* TRANSP billet d'une durée déterminée avec kilométrage illimité

railway *n BrE (cf railroad AmE)* TRANSP ch. de f., chemin de fer *m*, voie ferrée *f*; ~ **bill** *n BrE (cf railroad bill AmE)* TRANSP lettre de voiture ferroviaire *f*; ~ **consignment note** *n BrE (cf railroad consignment note AmE)* TRANSP lettre de voiture ferroviaire *f*; ~ **line** *n BrE (cf railroad line AmE)* TRANSP voie ferrée *f*; ~ **securities** *n pl BrE (cf railroad securities AmE)* STOCK titres de chemin de fer *m pl*; ~ **service** *n BrE (cf railroad service AmE)* TRANSP service ferroviaire *m*; ~ **station** *n BrE (cf railroad station AmE, train station)* TRANSP gare *f*; ~ **system** *n BrE (cf railroad system AmE)* TRANSP réseau de chemin de fer *m*, réseau ferroviaire *m*; ~ **timetable** *n BrE (cf railroad timetable AmE)* TRANSP horaire des trains *m*; ~ **track** *n BrE (cf railroad track AmE)* TRANSP voie ferrée *f*; ~ **worker** *n BrE (cf railroad worker AmE, railroader AmE)* HRM, TRANSP cheminot *m*; ~ **yard** *n BrE (cf railyard AmE)* TRANSP dépôt *m*

railwayman *n [pl -men] BrE (cf railroad worker AmE, railroader AmE)* HRM, TRANSP cheminot *m*

railyard *n AmE (cf railway yard BrE)* TRANSP dépôt *m*

rain: ~ **insurance** *n* INS assurance contre les intempéries *f*

rainbow: ~ **book** *n UK* ADMIN registre gouvernemental listant les salaires des fonctionnaires en les différenciant par un système de couleurs selon leur rang et leur occupation

rainforest *n* ENVIR forêt ombrophile *f*

raise[1] *n AmE see rise BrE*

raise[2] *vt* FIN *capital* mobiliser, GEN COMM *embargo* lever, *price, value* augmenter, LAW, TAX lever; ♦ ~ **the alarm** GEN COMM donner l'alarme; ~ **awareness of** ENVIR faire prendre conscience de; ~ **capital** STOCK lever des capitaux, mobiliser des capitaux, se procurer des capitaux; ~ **a check** *AmE (cf make out a cheque BrE)* BANK faire un chèque; ~ **external funds** GEN COMM mobiliser des fonds extérieurs; ~ **finance** FIN, GEN COMM réunir des fonds; ~ **funds** FIN, GEN COMM réunir des fonds, se procurer de l'argent, se

procurer des capitaux; ~ **in line with inflation** ECON *price, benefit* relever conformément à l'inflation; ~ **a loan** BANK émettre un emprunt; ~ **money** FIN, GEN COMM réunir des fonds, se procurer de l'argent, se procurer des capitaux; ~ **money on sth** GEN COMM emprunter de l'argent sur qch; ~ **an objection** GEN COMM émettre une objection; ~ **a tax** TAX imposer une taxe, lever une taxe

raised: ~ **afterdeck** *n (RAD)* TRANSP *shipping* pont arrière surélevé *m*; ~ **bridge** *n (RB)* TRANSP *shipping* passerelle surélevée *f*; ~ **deck** *n (Rdk)* TRANSP *shipping* pont surélevé *m*; ~ **deck socket** *n* TRANSP *shipping* socle en saillie *m*; ~ **foredeck** *n (RFD)* TRANSP *shipping* demi-gaillard *m*; ~ **quarterdeck** *n (RQD)* TRANSP *shipping* demi-dunette *f*; ~ **shelter deck** *n (RSD)* TRANSP *shipping* pont-abri surélevé *m*

raising *n* FIN *of capital* mobilisation *f*, GEN COMM *of embargo* levée *f*, *of price, value* augmentation *f*, LAW, TAX levée *f*; ~ **of capital** FIN mobilisation de fonds *f*; ~ **of funds** FIN mobilisation de fonds *f*

rake[1] *n* TRANSP *shipping* quête *f*, élancement *m*; ~ **of wagons** TRANSP rame de wagons *f*

rake:[2] ~ **in** *vt* GEN COMM ramasser

rally[1] *n* ECON, STOCK *of market, shares* redressement *m*, reprise *f*

rally[2] *vi* ECON, STOCK *of market, shares* reprendre, se redresser

rallying *n* ECON, STOCK *of market, shares* redressement *m*, reprise *f*; ~ **point** GEN COMM, TRANSP point de ralliement *m*

RAM[1] *abbr (random access memory)* COMP mémoire RAM *f*, mémoire vive *f*

RAM:[2] ~ **disk** *n (random access memory disk)* COMP disque virtuel *m*

rambler *n* PROP flâneuse *f*

ramp[1] *n infrml* GEN COMM *UK swindle* majoration exorbitante des prix *f*, TRANSP rampe *f*; ~ **stillage** TRANSP chevalet de rampe *m*

ramp:[2] ~ **up** *vt infrml* GEN COMM *production* augmenter

ramped: ~ **cargo berth** *n* TRANSP *shipping* quai de roulage *m*

Ramsey: ~ **prices** *n pl* ECON prix Ramsey *m pl*; ~ **saving rule** *n* ECON règle de l'épargne selon Ramsey *f*; ~ **savings model** *n* ECON modèle de l'épargne selon Ramsey *m*

RAN *abbr (revenue anticipation note)* STOCK avis fiscal anticipé *m*

rancher *n* PROP *manager* propriétaire de ranch *m*, PROP *jarg ranch-style suburban property* ranch *m*

rand *n* GEN COMM rand *m*

R&CC *abbr (riots and civil commotions)* WEL émeutes et troubles de l'ordre public *m pl*

R&D[1] *abbr (research and development)* IND R&D *(recherche et développement)*

R&D:[2] ~ **expenditures** *n pl* TAX dépenses de R&D *f pl*

random: ~ **access** *n* COMP accès direct *m*; ~ **access memory** *n* *(RAM)* COMP mémoire RAM *f*, mémoire vive *f*; ~ **access memory disk** *n* *(RAM disk)* COMP disque virtuel *m*; ~ **check** *n* MATH *statistics* contrôle par sondage *m*, contrôle par sélection aléatoire *m*; ~ **error** *n* MATH *statistics* erreur aléatoire *f*; ~ **factor** *n* ECON, GEN COMM facteur aléatoire *m*; ~ **number** *n* COMP, MATH nombre aléatoire *m*; ~ **-number generator** *n* MATH *statistics* générateur de nombres aléatoires *m*; ~ **observation method** *n* MATH, MGMNT, S&M méthode des observations instantanées *f*; ~ **sample** *n* MATH échantillon aléatoire *m*; ~ **sampling** *n* MATH *statistics*, S&M sondage aléatoire *m*, échantillonnage aléatoire *m*; ~ **selection** *n* MATH sélection aléatoire *f*; ~ **sizes** *n pl* GEN COMM tailles tout-venant *f pl*; ~ **variable** *n* MATH *statistics* variable aléatoire *f*; ~ **variation** *n* ECON variation aléatoire *f*; ~ **walk** *n* ECON, STOCK marche erratique *f*, variation aléatoire *f*; ~ **walk theory** *n* ECON, STOCK théorie des variations aléatoires *f*; ◆ **at ~** COMP, GEN COMM, MATH au hasard

randomization *n* MATH *statistics* génération de nombres aléatoires *f*, procédé de répartition aléatoire *m*

randomly *adv* COMP, GEN COMM, MATH de façon aléatoire *loc f*

range *n* GEN COMM gamme *f*, MATH échelle *f*, S&M gamme *f*, STOCK *futures market* fourchette *f* *(jarg)*, écart maximal hauts-bas *m*, TAX palier de revenu *m*, tranche de revenu *f*; ~ **of options** GEN COMM panoplie d'options *f*; ~ **of products** GEN COMM, IND, S&M gamme de produits *f*; ◆ **be out of ~** GEN COMM être hors de portée

Rangoon *pr n* GEN COMM Rangoon *n pr*

rank[1] *n* GEN COMM rang *m*; ~ **correlation** MATH *statistics* corrélation de rang *f*; ~ **order** MATH ordre de rang *m*; **the ~ and file** POL la base *f*

rank:[2] **1.** *vt* ~ **above** *(ANT rank below)* GEN COMM être supérieur à; ~ **after** GEN COMM, STOCK être primé par; ~ **below** *(ANT rank above)* GEN COMM être le subordonné de **2.** *vi* ECON, GEN COMM se classer

ranking *n* GEN COMM, HRM classement *m*

rapid[1] *adj* GEN COMM rapide

rapid:[2] ~ **growth** *n* ECON, IND croissance rapide *f*; ~ **premium decay** *n* STOCK *options* déclin rapide de la prime *m*, dépréciation rapide de prime *f*; ~ **technological progress** *n* ECON, IND progrès technologique rapide *m*; ~ **transit system** *n* TRANSP réseau express régional *m*

rapprochement *n* POL rapprochement *m*

raster *n* COMP trame *f*

rat: ~ **race** *n* GEN COMM foire d'empoigne *f*

RAT *abbr* *(ready assets trusts)* STOCK trusts d'actifs disponibles *m pl*

ratable *adj* GEN COMM *value* imposable

ratchet: ~ **effect** *n* ECON effet de cliquet *m*

rate *n* COMMS coût d'une communication télépho-

nique *m*, COMP taux *m*, ECON *price* cours *m*, tarif *m*, *speed* cadence *f*, vitesse *f*, FIN *price* cours *m*, tarif *m*, GEN COMM *price* cours *m*, tarif *m*, *speed* cadence *f*, vitesse *f*, HRM *of work*, IND *of production* cadence *f*; ~ **asked** STOCK taux demandé *m*; ~ **below cost** TRANSP tarif à perte *m*; ~ **bill** *UK* TAX projet de loi sur les impôts locaux; ~ **ceiling** BANK, ECON, FIN *interest rates* plafond des taux *m*; ~ **class** TRANSP catégorie de tarif *f*; ~ **cutting** GEN COMM, TRANSP réduction des tarifs *f*; ~ **of decay** STOCK *options* taux de déclin *m*, taux de dépréciation *m*; ~ **of depreciation** ACC taux d'amortissement *m*; ~ **differential** STOCK *interest rate futures* différentiel de taux *m*, écart de taux *m*; ~ **dilution** TRANSP dilution des tarifs *f*; ~ **of discount** BANK, FIN taux d'escompte *m*; ~ **of exchange** BANK, ECON, FIN taux de change *m*; ~ **of exploitation** ECON taux d'exploitation *m*, valeur d'excédent *f*; ~ **fixing** HRM calcul du temps passé *m*; ~ **flexibility** ECON, TRANSP flexibilité des tarifs *f*; ~ **floor** BANK, ECON, FIN *interest rates* plancher des taux *m*; ~ **for the job** HRM salaire proposé pour l'emploi *m*; ~ **of increase** ECON taux *m*, taux d'accroissement *m*, taux d'augmentation *m*; ~ **of interest** BANK, ECON, FIN intérêt *m*; ~ **not reported** *(RNR)* TRANSP tarif non-répertorié *m*; ~ **of relief** TAX taux de dégrèvement *m*; ~ **resetter** *(RR)* STOCK rétablisseur de taux *m*; ~ **resetting** *(RR)* STOCK refixation de taux *f*; ~ **of return** ACC, BANK, FIN rentabilité *f*, taux de rendement *m*; ~ **of return on capital employed** *(RORCE)* ECON, FIN taux de rendement des capitaux investis *m*, taux de rendement sur le capital employé *m*; ~ **risk** BANK risque de taux *m*; ~ **of rolling** STOCK taux de roulement *m*; ~ **support grant** *UK* *(RSG)* ECON subvention de l'État aux collectivités locales *f*, subvention de soutien de taux *f*; ~ **of surplus value** BANK taux de la valeur excédentaire *m*; ~ **of tax** TAX taux d'imposition *m*, taux d'impôt *m*; ~ **of taxation** TAX taux d'imposition *m*, taux d'impôt *m*; ~ **trend** TRANSP tendance tarifaire *f*; ~ **war** TRANSP guerre des tarifs *f*; ◆ **at a ~ of** GEN COMM à raison de; **take the ~** STOCK prendre le taux, reporter; ~ **to be agreed** *(RTBA)* TRANSP tarif à déterminer *m*

rated:[1] **not ~** *adj* FIN *securities rating services, mercantile agencies* pas coté

rated:[2] ~ **policy** *n* INS police tarifée *f*

ratepayer *n* TAX contribuable *mf*

rates *n pl* *UK* TAX, WEL remplacé par council tax en 1993, ≈ impôts locaux *m pl* *(France)*; ~ **and classifications** *n pl* *US* COMMS tarifs et classifications *m pl*; ~ **clerk** *n* HRM *shipping*, TRANSP *shipping* employé aux droits de port *m*; ~ **formulation** *n* TRANSP élaboration des tarifs *f*; ~ **officer** *n* HRM, TRANSP *shipping* percepteur des droits de port *m*; ~ **review** *n* GEN COMM révision des tarifs *f*; ~ **strategy** *n* TRANSP stratégie tarifaire *f*; ~ **structure** *n* TRANSP structure tarifaire *f*

ratification *n* GEN COMM *of treaty* ratification *f*,

validation *f*, LAW validation *f*, *of treaty* ratification *f*

ratified *adj* LAW ratifié

ratify *vt* GEN COMM *treaty* ratifier, LAW valider

rating *n* FIN notation *f*, STOCK notation *f*, émission *f*; ~ **agency** FIN agence d'évaluation financière *f*, agence de notation *f*, ADEF; ~ **scale** GEN COMM échelle d'évaluation *f*

ratio *n* ACC coefficient *m*, ratio *m*, rapport *m*, BANK, ECON ratio *m*, FIN rapport *m*, ratio *m*, MATH rapport *m*, STOCK ratio *m*, TRANSP rapport *m*; ~ **analysis** MATH *statistics* analyse de rapport *f*; ~ **call spread** (ANT *ratio put spread*) STOCK *options* écart vertical sur ratio d'options de vente *m*; ~ **decidendi** *frml* GEN COMM facteur décisif *m*; ~ **of external debt to exports** ECON, IMP/EXP ratio de la dette extérieure sur les exportations *m*; ~ **put spread** (ANT *ratio call spread*) STOCK *options* écart vertical sur ratio d'options d'achat *m*; ~ **scale** MATH échelle de grandeur *f*; ~ **writer** STOCK vendeur d'options d'achat partiellement à découvert *m*; ◆ **the ~ of x to y** ACC le ratio de x à y

ration *vt* ECON, FIN, GEN COMM rationner

rational[1] *adj* GEN COMM *reasonable* raisonnable

rational:[2] ~ **decision** *n* GEN COMM *game theory* décision raisonnable *f*; ~ **expectations** *n pl* (*RE*) ECON anticipations rationnelles *f pl*, prévisions rationnelles *f pl*; ~ **management** *n* MGMNT gestion rationnelle *f*

rationale *n* GEN COMM raisonnement *m*

rationalization *n* ECON, FIN, GEN COMM, IND, MGMNT, TRANSP rationalisation *f*; ~ **program** *AmE*, ~ **programme** *BrE* ECON, GEN COMM programme de rationalisation *m*

rationalize *vt* ECON, FIN, GEN COMM, IND, MGMNT, TRANSP rationaliser

rationing *n* ECON file d'attente *f*, rationnement *m*, système des files d'attente *m*

RATS *abbr* (*Restricted Articles Terminal System*) TRANSP *IATA* système de terminal pour articles réglementés *m*

ratten *vt* *US* HRM *industrial relations* forcer une grève des travailleurs en leur retirant outils et matériel

raw[1] *adj* COMP, MATH brut, non-traité

raw:[2] ~ **data** *n* COMP, MATH données brutes *f pl*, données non traitées *f pl*, données à traiter *f pl*; ~ **land** *n* PROP terre vierge *f*; ~ **material** *n* IND matière brute *f*, matière première *f*

Rawlsian: ~ **difference principle** *n* ECON principe de différence de Rawls *m*; ~ **justice** *n* ECON justice rawlsienne *f*

RB *abbr* TRANSP (*rubber bearing*) roulement en caoutchouc *m*, TRANSP (*raised bridge*) *shipping* passerelle surélevée *f*

RBT *abbr* (*rebuilt*) GEN COMM reconstruit

RC *abbr* TRANSP (*return cargo*) cargaison de retour *f*, TRANSP (*reversing gear clutch*) embrayage de renversement de marche *m*

RCC *abbr* *UK* (*Rural Community Council*) POL conseil intercommunal en zone rurale

RCCA *abbr* (*route capacity control airline*) TRANSP transporteur aérien pour le contrôle de la capacité des routes *m*

RCC&S (*riots, civil commotions and strikes*) WEL émeutes, troubles de l'ordre public et grèves *m pl*

rcvd *abbr* (*received*) GEN COMM pour acquit *loc m*, reçu

Rd *abbr* (*running day*) TRANSP jour courant *m*, jours consécutifs *m pl*

Rd. *abbr* (*road*) TRANSP route *f* (*r.*)

RD *abbr* BANK (*refer to drawer*) retour au tiroir *loc m*, voir le tireur, ECON (*reserve deposit*) dépôt de couverture bancaire *m*, réserve obligatoire *f*

RDA *abbr* *UK* (*rural development area*) ECON zone d'aménagement rural *f*, zone de développement rural *f*

RDB *abbr* (*relational database*) COMP BDR (*base de données relationnelles*)

RDBTN *abbr* (*round bottom*) TRANSP *of ship* fond rond *m*

RDC *abbr* (*running down clause*) INS *marine* clause d'abordage *f*

RDF *abbr* (*radio direction finder*) TRANSP radio-goniomètre *m*

Rdk *abbr* (*raised deck*) TRANSP *shipping* pont surélevé *m*

RDS *abbr* *US* (*rural delivery service*) COMMS service de livraisons gratuites en zone rurale *m*

re *prep* GEN COMM au sujet de, concernant, en ce qui concerne, quant à, relativement à, à propos *loc m*

RE *abbr* ECON (*rational expectations*) anticipations rationnelles *f pl*, prévisions rationnelles *f pl*, STOCK *UK* (*Royal Exchange*) bourse de commerce de Londres

reach[1] *n* S&M audience cumulée *f*; ~ **and frequency** *n* S&M *advertising* portée et fréquence *f*; ◆ **be within ~** GEN COMM être à portée de main; **without a ~** GEN COMM sans accroc

reach[2] *vt* GEN COMM *deal*, S&M *settlement* conclure; ◆ ~ **an accommodation with sb** GEN COMM arriver à un compromis avec qn; ~ **the age limit** GEN COMM être touché par la limite d'âge; ~ **an agreement** GEN COMM parvenir à un accord; ~ **a compromise** GEN COMM aboutir à un compromis; ~ **a deal** GEN COMM, S&M conclure un marché, conclure une affaire; ~ **saturation point** GEN COMM arriver à saturation; ~ **a total of** GEN COMM atteindre un total de

reachable: ~ **on arrival** *phr* (SYN *always accessible*) TRANSP *shipping* à disposition à l'arrivée *loc f*

reachback *n* TAX arriéré *m*

react *vi* GEN COMM réagir; ◆ ~ **well under stress** HRM bien réagir dans des circonstances difficiles

reaction *n* GEN COMM réaction *f*; ~ **function** ECON fonction de réaction *f*; ~ **time** ADMIN temps de latence *m*, temps de réaction *m*

reactionary¹ *adj* POL réactionnaire

reactionary² *n* POL réactionnaire *mf*

reactivate *vt* COMP *software* relancer, remettre en activité

reactive¹ *adj* GEN COMM réactif

reactive:² ~ **strategy** *n* GEN COMM stratégie réactive *f*

read¹ *n* COMP lecture *f*; ~ **head** COMP tête de lecture *f*; ~ **only memory** *(ROM)* COMP mémoire ROM *f*, mémoire fixe *f*, mémoire morte *f*

read² *vt* COMP lire, GEN COMM corriger, lire; ♦ ~ **law** WEL faire son droit; ~ **the tape** STOCK lire le téléscripteur

reader *n* COMP lecteur *m*, MEDIA *newspaper editorial-style advertisement* publi-reportage *m*, publicité rédactionnelle *f*, *print* lecteur *m*, S&M *advertising* annonce d'apparence rédactionnelle *f*

readership *n* MEDIA *of newspaper, book* audience *f*, circulation *f*, diffusion *f*, lectorat *m*; ~ **profile** S&M *market research* profil du lectorat *m*; ~ **survey** S&M *market research* enquête auprès des lecteurs *f*

readies *n pl infrml* FIN liquide *m*

reading *n* COMP, GEN COMM lecture *f*; ~ **notice** *jarg* MEDIA *advertising* publi-reportage *m*, publicité rédactionnelle *f* *(jarg)*

ReadMe: ~ **document** *n* COMP Ouvrez-moi *m*; ~ **file** *n* COMP fichier Lisez-Moi *m*

read/write *n* COMP lecture/écriture *f*; ~ **head** COMP tête de lecture/écriture *f*

ready¹ *adj* GEN COMM prêt; ~ **-to-wear** GEN COMM, S&M prêt-à-porter; ♦ ~ **for shipment** TRANSP prêt pour l'expédition; ~ **to hand** GEN COMM sous la main; ~, **willing and able** GEN COMM *brokerage* prêt, volontaire et capable

ready:² ~ **assets trusts** *n pl (RAT)* STOCK trusts d'actifs disponibles *m pl*; ~ **berth** *n* TRANSP *shipping* quai mis à disposition *m*; ~ **cash** *n* FIN argent liquide *m*, liquide *m*, liquidités *f pl*; ~ **-made meal** *n* S&M repas tout prêt *m*; ~ **money** *n* FIN argent liquide *m*, liquide *m*, liquidités *f pl*; ~ **reckoner** *n* GEN COMM barème de calculs *m*

reaffirm *vt* GEN COMM réaffirmer

reafforestation *n* ENVIR reboisement *m*

Reaganomics *n* ECON, POL la reaganomie *f*

real¹ *adj* ACC, ECON, FIN, GEN COMM réel; ~ **-time** COMP en temps réel; ♦ **in** ~ **terms** ECON en termes réels

real:² ~ **address** *n* COMP adresse réelle *f*; ~ **agreement** *n* LAW bail *m*; ~ **bills doctrine** *n* *(cf Banking School UK)* ECON théorie des effets commerciaux d'Adam Smith *f*; ~ **cost** *n* *(SYN actual cost)* ACC coût réel *m*, coût réellement engagé *m*, TAX coût effectif *m*, coût réel *m*; ~ **earnings** *n pl* ACC, ECON, HRM revenu réel *m*; ~ **economy of scale** *n* ECON, IND économie d'échelle effective *f*; ~ **estate** *n* PROP bien immobilier *m*, biens immobiliers *m pl*; ~ **estate agency** *n* *AmE (cf estate agency BrE)* PROP agence immobilière *f*; ~ **estate agents** *n pl* *AmE (cf estate agents BrE)* PROP cabinet d'immobilier *m*;

~ **estate appraisal** *n* *AmE (cf property valuation BrE)* PROP évaluation de biens immobiliers *f*, évaluation immobilière *f*; ~ **estate closing** *n* *AmE* PROP conclusion de vente immobilière *f*; ~ **estate commission** *n* PROP commission sur vente immobilière *f*; ~ **estate company** *n* PROP société immobilière *f*; ~ **estate fund** *n* *US* ACC fonds de placement en biens immobiliers *m*; ~ **estate gain** *n* PROP gain immobilier *m*; ~ **estate investment trust** *n* *US (REIT)* BANK fonds de placements immobiliers *m*, STOCK société civile de placement immobilier *f (SCPI)*; ~ **estate market** *n* PROP marché de l'immobilier *m*; ~ **estate register** *n* *AmE (cf cadastre, land register BrE)* TAX cadastre *m*; ~ **estate registry** *n* *AmE (cf land registry BrE)* TAX cadastre *m*; ~ **exchange rate** *n* STOCK taux de change réel *m*; ~ **GDP growth** *n* ECON croissance effective du PIB *f*, croissance réelle du PIB *f*; ~ **growth** *n* ECON croissance effective *f*, croissance réelle *f*; ~ **income** *n* ACC, ECON, HRM revenu réel *m*; ~ **interest rate** *n* FIN taux d'intérêt réel *m*; ~ **investment** *n* BANK *for hospitals, schools* investissement collectif *m*; ~ **money** *n* *jarg* ECON valeur réelle de l'argent *f*; ~ **number** *n* COMP, MATH nombre réel *m*; ~ **pay** *n* ACC, ECON, HRM salaire réel *m*; ~ **property** *n* STOCK biens immeubles *m pl*; ~ **rate of return** *n* *(RRR)* BANK taux de rendement réel *m*; ~ **storage** *n* COMP mémoire réelle *f*; ~ **time** *n* ACC, COMP, ECON temps réel *m*; ~ **volume** *n* IND *of production* volume réel *m*; ~ **wage** *n* ACC, ECON, HRM salaire réel *m*; ~ **-wage hypothesis** *n* ECON hypothèse des salaires réels *f*

realism *n* GEN COMM réalisme *m*, LAW doctrine du pragmatisme juridique *f*, réalisme *m*, POL réalisme *m*

realistic *adj* GEN COMM réaliste

realizable¹ *adj* ACC, FIN, GEN COMM, STOCK réalisable

realizable:² ~ **assets** *n pl* ACC, STOCK actif réalisable *m*

realization: ~ **of assets** *n* ACC, STOCK cession d'éléments d'actif *f*, réalisation d'éléments d'actif *f*

realize *vt* ACC, FIN *goal* réaliser, GEN COMM *become aware of* prendre conscience de, se rendre compte de, *goal* réaliser, STOCK *profit* réaliser; ♦ ~ **assets** ACC, STOCK réaliser des actifs, réaliser des éléments d'actif

realized: ~ **gains** *n pl* ACC, FIN, TAX gains réalisés *m pl*; ~ **losses** *n pl* FIN pertes réalisées *f pl*; ~ **minimum return** *n* STOCK *interest rate futures* rendement minimum réalisé *m*, rentrées minimales réalisées *f pl*

reallocate *vt* ACC, COMP, FIN réaffecter

reallocation *n* ACC, COMP, FIN réaffectation *f*

reallowance *n* STOCK réattribution *f*

realpolitik *n* POL realpolitik *f*

realtor *n* *AmE (cf estate agent BrE)* PROP agent

immobilier *m*, marchand de biens *m*, marchand de fonds *m*

reap *vt* FIN *profits*, GEN COMM récolter; ◆ **~ the benefits** FIN, STOCK récolter les bénéfices; **~ the rewards** FIN, STOCK récolter les récompenses, récolter les rémunérations

reapply: **~ for a job** *phr* HRM reposer sa canditature à un emploi

rear: **~ -ramp-loading trailer** *n* TRANSP remorque de chargement par rampe arrière *f*

REART *abbr* *(restricted articles)* TRANSP *aviation* article réglementé *m*

reason *n* GEN COMM raison *f*; ◆ **for any ~** GEN COMM pour quelque raison que ce soit

reasonable[1] *adj* GEN COMM raisonnable

reasonable:[2] **~ expense** *n* GEN COMM frais raisonnables *m pl*; **~ output** *n* HRM, IND rendement raisonnable *m*; **~ person** *n* GEN COMM personne qui suit la règle de modération *loc f*, personne raisonnable *f*; **~ price** *n* GEN COMM prix raisonnable *m*

reasoned: **~ amendment** *n* POL amendement raisonné *m*

reasoning *n* GEN COMM raisonnement *m*

reassess *vt* TAX fixer une nouvelle cotisation pour, réévaluer

reassessment *n* TAX nouvelle cotisation *f*, réévaluation *f*; **~ of tax, interest or penalties** *n pl* TAX nouvelle cotisation à l'égard de l'impôt, des intérêts ou des pénalités *f*, réévaluation d'impôt, d'intérêts ou de pénalisations *f*

reassign *vt* ACC, COMP, FIN réaffecter

reassignment *n* ACC, COMP, FIN réaffectation *f*

rebagging *n* TRANSP remise en sac *f*

rebate *n* BANK, ECON *of interest* bonification *f*, diminution *f*, FIN *of interest* bonification *f*, diminution *f*, *of money paid* rabais *m*, remise *f*, ristourne *f*, GEN COMM *on goods* remise *f*

rebateable *adj* GEN COMM soumis à un rabais

reboot *vt* COMP réamorcer, réinitialiser

rebooting *n* COMP relance *f*, réamorçage *m*, réinitialisation *f*

rebuild *vt* COMP *hardware* reconstruire, *software* reconstituer, GEN COMM reconstruire

rebuilt *adj* *(RBT)* GEN COMM reconstruit

rebuy *vt* S&M faire un achat répété *loc m*

recalculate *vt* MATH recalculer

recall[1] *n* GEN COMM *of faulty goods* rappel *m*, STOCK *of option* rachetée *f*, rappel *m*; **~ study** GEN COMM étude de rappel *f*

recall[2] *vt* GEN COMM *faulty goods* rappeler, STOCK *option* racheter, rappeler

recapitalization *n* ECON, FIN, STOCK restructuration du capital *f*

recapturable: **~ depreciation** *n* ACC amortissement récupérable *m*

recast *vt* FIN *debt* refondre

recede *vi* GEN COMM *volume* décliner, reculer

receipt[1] *n* *(recpt, rept)* BANK, FIN reçu *m*, GEN COMM quittance *f*, reçu *m*, récépissé *m*, S&M reçu *m*, récépissé *m*, STOCK reçu *m*, TRANSP reçu *m*, récépissé *m*; **~ book** GEN COMM carnet de quittances *m*; **~ for documents** PATENTS récépissé de documents *m*; **~ for payment** GEN COMM quittance *f*; **~ of goods** *(ROG)* TRANSP *cargo* réception des marchandises *f*; **~ slip** GEN COMM quittance *f*; **~ stamp** COMMS timbre de quittance *m*; ◆ **be in ~ of** GEN COMM *letter, payment* recevoir; **on ~** GEN COMM *of goods, document* sur réception; **on ~ of** GEN COMM dès réception de

receipt[2] *vt* GEN COMM *invoice* acquitter

receipts *n pl* ACC, FIN rentrées *f pl*, STOCK *futures* recettes *f pl*, rentrées *f pl*; **~ credited to the fund** ACC, FIN recettes à valoir sur le crédit *f pl*

receivable *n* ACC, FIN créance *f*; **~ basis** ACC *of accounting* comptabilité client *f*, comptabilité de trésorerie *f*, méthode de la comptabilité de trésorerie *f*; **~ method** ACC comptabilité client *f*, comptabilité de trésorerie *f*, méthode de la comptabilité de trésorerie *f*

receivables *n pl* ACC, ECON clients *m pl*, comptes clients *m pl*, créances *f pl*, débiteurs *m pl*; **~ turnover** *n* FIN volume d'effets à recevoir *m*

receive *vt* GEN COMM recevoir; ◆ **~ benefit** UK, HRM, WEL toucher des allocations, toucher des prestations sociales, vivre de l'aide sociale; **~ financial help** GEN COMM bénéficier d'une aide financière; **~ notice of** GEN COMM apprendre que; **~ versus payment** FIN recevoir contre paiement

received[1] *adj* *(rcvd)* GEN COMM pour acquit *loc m*, reçu

received:[2] **~ -for-shipment bill of lading** *n* IMP/EXP, TRANSP *shipping* connaissement reçu pour embarquement *m*

receiver *n* ACC liquidateur *m*, FIN administrateur judiciaire *m*, liquidateur *m*, GEN COMM administrateur judiciaire *m*, HRM destinataire *mf*, LAW administrateur judiciaire *m*, liquidateur *m*; **~ and manager** FIN, GEN COMM, LAW *bankruptcy* administrateur judiciaire *m*, syndic de faillite *m*; **~ of wrecks** HRM, TRANSP *senior customs officer* receveur des épaves *m*; ◆ **be in the hands of the ~** GEN COMM, IND, LAW être en règlement judiciaire

Receiver: **~ General for Canada** *n* ADMIN, FIN receveur général du Canada *m*

receiver's: **~ agent** *n* HRM agent du receveur *m*; **~ certificate** *n* FIN certificat du receveur général *m*; ◆ **at ~ risk** GEN COMM aux risques du destinataire

receivership *n* ACC mise en administration judiciaire *f*, mise en liquidation *f*, FIN, GEN COMM mise en administration judiciaire *f*, LAW administration judiciaire *f*, mise en administration judiciaire *f*; ◆ **go into ~** FIN, GEN COMM, IND être mis en règlement judiciaire, LAW être placé sous administration judiciaire

receiving:[1] ~ **benefit** *adj BrE (cf on welfare AmE)* HRM assisté

receiving:[2] ~ **carrier** *n* TRANSP *shipping* transporteur destinataire *m*; ~ **date** *n* TRANSP *shipping* date de réception des marchandises *f*; ~ **department** *n* GEN COMM, TRANSP service de réception *m*; ~ **and loading cargo** *n* TRANSP *shipping* réception et chargement des marchandises *f*; ~ **office** *n (RO)* GEN COMM bureau de messageries *m*, bureau de réception *m*, PATENTS office récepteur *m*; ~ **order** *n (RO)* TRANSP ordonnance de mise sous séquestre *f*; ~ **station** *n* TRANSP *rail* gare de destination *f*

recent *adj* GEN COMM récent; ♦ **in ~ years** GEN COMM au cours des dernières années

reception *n* ADMIN accueil *m*, réception *f*, GEN COMM réception *f*; ~ **area** ADMIN foyer *m*, zone d'accueil *f*, LEIS, TRANSP zone d'enregistrement *f*; ~ **depot** TRANSP entrepôt de réception *m*; ~ **point** LEIS bureau d'enregistrement *m*

receptionist *n* ADMIN, GEN COMM, HRM réceptionnaire *mf*, réceptionniste *mf*

receptiveness *n* GEN COMM réceptivité *f*

receptor *n* ENVIR, GEN COMM récepteur *m*

recess *n* UK LAW, POL *of Parliament* vacation *f*

recession *n* ECON crise économique *f*, récession *f*, GEN COMM, HRM, POL récession *f*

recessionary[1] *adj* ECON, POL récessionniste

recessionary:[2] ~ **gap** *n* ECON écart déflationniste *m*, écart récessionniste *m*; ~ **phase** *n* ECON phase de récession *f*, phase récessionniste *f*

recipient *n* FIN, GEN COMM bénéficiaire *mf*, HRM *of allowance* allocataire *mf*, prestataire *m*, TAX acquéreur *m*, récipiendaire *m*; ~ **bank** BANK banque bénéficiaire *f*

reciprocal[1] *adj* GEN COMM réciproque

reciprocal[2] *n* MATH réciproque *f*; ~ **agreement** *n* LAW, PATENTS *intellectual property* accord bilatéral *m*, contrat bilatéral *m*; ~ **buying** *n* S&M compensation *f*; ~ **ratio** *n* MATH rapport réciproque *m*; ~ **taxation agreement** *n* TAX accord de réciprocité fiscale *m*; ~ **trading** *n* GEN COMM commerce réciproque *m*; ~ **trading agreements** *n pl* ECON *international trade* accords commerciaux de réciprocité *m pl*

reciprocally *adv* GEN COMM réciproquement

reciprocity *n* ECON, GEN COMM réciprocité *f*

reckon *vt* COMP, GEN COMM, MATH compter; ~ **up** COMP, GEN COMM, MATH compter

reckoning *n* ACC calcul *m*, compte *m*; ♦ ~ **by** ACC à compter de

reclaim *vt* ENVIR *land* mettre en valeur, remettre en valeur, régénérer

reclaimed: ~ **area** *n* ENVIR, PROP terrain remis en valeur *m*

reclaiming *n* ENVIR *of land* mise en valeur *f*, remise en valeur *f*, régénération *f*, TRANSP *of cargo, luggage* récupération *f*

reclassification *n* GEN COMM, HRM reclassement *m*, reclassification *f*

reclassify *vt* GEN COMM reclasser

recmd *abbr (recommissioned)* GEN COMM réintégré

recognition *n* HRM *of trade union* reconnaissance *f*, LAW confirmation *f*, reconnaissance *f*, MGMNT *of trade union* reconnaissance *f*; ~ **lag** ECON délai d'identification *m*, délai de mise en oeuvre *m*, retard d'identification *m*; ~ **of loss** ACC constatation d'une perte *f*, reconnaissance d'une perte *f*; ~ **-only clause** UK HRM clause de simple reconnaissance de la représentation *f*; ~ **-only practice** UK HRM usage de simple reconnaissance de la représentation *m*

recognize *vt* ACC *transaction* constater, GEN COMM, HRM *trade union* reconnaître; ♦ ~ **a loss** ACC constater une perte

recognized[1] *adj* GEN COMM reconnu

recognized:[2] ~ **gain** *n* TAX gain reconnu *m*; ~ **investment exchange** *n (RIE)* STOCK marché d'investissement agréé *m*; ~ **political party** *n* POL, TAX parti politique reconnu *m*; ~ **professional body** *n* UK *(RPB)* FIN corps professionnel reconnu *m*, organisme professionnel *m*, organisme spécialisé accrédité *m*; ~ **third-world investment firm** *n* FIN entreprise d'investissement reconnues de pays tiers *f*; ~ **trade union** *n* UK HRM syndicat reconnu *m*

recommend *vt* GEN COMM recommander

recommendation *n* GEN COMM recommandation *f*

recommended: ~ **retail price** *n (RRP)* S&M *sales* prix conseillé *m*

recommissioned *adj (recmd)* GEN COMM réintégré

recompile *vt* COMP recompiler

reconcile *vt* ACC, BANK *accounting statements* rapprocher, GEN COMM réconcilier; ♦ ~ **an account** ACC faire le point d'un compte

reconciliation *n* ACC *of accounting statements* concordance *f*, rapprochement *m*, BANK rapprochement *m*; ~ **account** BANK, STOCK compte collectif *m*; ~ **of accounts** ACC concordance *f*, rapprochement de comptes *m*; ~ **bill** US ACC, ECON, FIN, LAW loi de finances *f*, projet de loi de finances *m*; ~ **statement** ACC état de concordance *m*, état de rapprochement *m*; ~ **table** ACC tableau de concordance *m*

recondition *vt* GEN COMM remettre en bon état, remettre à neuf, rénover, PROP rénover

reconditioned *adj (R)* GEN COMM remis à neuf, rénové, PROP rénové

reconditioning *n* GEN COMM remise à neuf *f*, rénovation *f*, PROP rénovation *f*

reconfiguration *n* GEN COMM reconfiguration *f*

reconsider *vt* GEN COMM reconsidérer, TAX examiner de nouveau, réexaminer; ♦ ~ **an assessment** TAX réexaminer une évaluation

reconsideration: ~ **of an assessment** *n* TAX nouvel examen d'une cotisation *m*, reconsidération d'une évaluation *f*

reconsign *vt* TRANSP reconsigner

reconstruct *vt* ECON, GEN COMM, STOCK reconstituer, reconstruire

reconstruction *n* ECON, GEN COMM, STOCK *of company* reconstitution *f*, reconstruction *f*

recontract *n* ECON contrat définitif *m*

reconversion *n* COMP, ECON, IND *of factory* reconversion *f*

reconvert *vt* COMP, ECON, IND *factory* reconvertir

reconveyance *n* PROP retransmission *f*

record:¹ ~ **-high** *adj* ECON *profits, unemployment* à un niveau record *loc m*

record² *n* COMP enregistrement *m*, GEN COMM *best result* record *m*, *written* archive *f*, dossier *m*; ~ **company** *n* MEDIA maison de disque *f*; ~ **date** *n* GEN COMM date d'enregistrement *f*; ~ **format** *n* COMP format d'enregistrement *m*; ~ **keeper** *n* ADMIN archiviste *mf*; ~ **key** *n* COMP clé d'enregistrement *f*; ~ **locking** *n* COMP verrouillage d'enregistrement *m*; ~ **results** *n pl* GEN COMM résultats record *m pl*; ~ **sales** *n pl* S&M ventes record *f pl*

record³ *vt* COMMS enregistrer, GEN COMM *transaction* consigner, enregistrer, écrire, STOCK *a low* toucher, *highest or lowest level, price* atteindre; ◆ ~ **in the register** PATENTS inscrire au registre; ~ **a meeting** GEN COMM établir le procès-verbal d'une réunion

recorded¹ *adj* MEDIA *broadcast* en différé

recorded:² ~ **delivery** *n* COMMS envoi avec avis de réception *m*; ~ **market information** *n* STOCK information de marché enregistrée *f*

recording *n* COMMS, GEN COMM enregistrement *m*

records *n pl* ACC registres *m pl*, registres et pièces comptables *m pl*, ADMIN archives *f pl*, dossier *m*, registres *m pl*, GEN COMM registres *m pl*, registres et pièces comptables *m pl*; ~ **management** *n* MGMNT administration des archives *f*

recoup 1. *vt* GEN COMM *money* récupérer, *somebody* indemniser; **2.** *v refl* ~ **oneself** GEN COMM se dédommager

recourse *n* GEN COMM recours *m*; ~ **loan** FIN emprunt de recours *m*; ◆ **have** ~ **to** GEN COMM, INS *company* avoir recours à; **with** ~ INS *company* avec recours; **without** ~ BANK, GEN COMM, INS *company* sans recours

recover 1. *vt* ACC *debt* recouvrir, COMP *lost file, data*, ENVIR *material* récupérer, FIN *debt* recouvrir, GEN COMM *assets* recouvrir, récupérer; **2.** *vi* ECON, GEN COMM repartir, reprendre, se redresser

recoverable: ~ **debt** *n* ACC dette recouvrable *f*; ~ **material** *n* ENVIR *recycling* matière récupérable *f*, matériau récupérable *m*; ~ **reserve** *n* ECON, ENVIR *of minerals* ressource récupérable *f*, ressource réutilisable *f*

recovery *n* ACC *of assets* recouvrement *m*, récupération *f*, COMP *of lost file, data* récupération *f*, *return to normal* reprise *f*, ECON redressement économique *m*, reprise *f*, reprise économique *f*, FIN *of assets* recouvrement *m*, récupération *f*, GEN

COMM *of market, of assets* recouvrement *m*, redressement *m*, reprise *f*, récupération *f*, TAX *of assets* recouvrement *m*; ~ **of basis** TAX recouvrement de base *m*; ~ **of expenses** ACC, FIN, GEN COMM recouvrement des dépenses *m*, récupération des frais *f*; ~ **plan** ECON plan de redressement *m*; ~ **scheme** GEN COMM plan de relance *m*; ~ **vehicle** *BrE (cf towtruck AmE)* TRANSP dépanneuse *f*

recpt *abbr (receipt)* BANK, FIN reçu *m*, GEN COMM quittance *f*, reçu *m*, récépissé *m*, S&M reçu *m*, récépissé *m*, STOCK reçu *m*, TRANSP reçu *m*, récépissé *m*

recreational: ~ **facility** *n* LEIS aire de détente *f*

recruit *vt* HRM recruter

recruiting: ~ **area** *n* ECON, HRM zone de recrutement de la main-d'oeuvre *f*; ~ **office** *n* HRM bureau de recrutement *m*; ~ **officer** *n* HRM officier de recrutement *m*, recruteur *m*

recruitment *n* HRM embauche *f*, recrutement *m*; ~ **agency** *n* HRM cabinet de recrutement des cadres *m*; ~ **bonus** *n* HRM prime de recrutement *f*; ~ **consultant** *n* HRM conseil en recrutement *m*; ~ **manager** *n* HRM directeur du recrutement *m*; ~ **and selection** *n* HRM sélection et recrutement *m*

rectification *n* GEN COMM *of situation*, POL rectification *f*

rectify *vt* GEN COMM *situation*, POL rectifier

recto *n (ANT verso)* GEN COMM, MEDIA recto *m*

recurrent: ~ **disability** *n* HRM invalidité répétée *f*; ~ **spot contracting** *n* HRM contrat sur place renouvelé *m*

recursive: ~ **system** *n* ECON *econometrics* système récursif *m*

recyclable *adj (ANT nonrecyclable)* ENVIR recyclable

recycle *vt* ENVIR recycler

recycled: ~ **paper** *n* ENVIR, GEN COMM papier recyclé *m*

recycling *n* ENVIR recyclage *m*; ~ **method** GEN COMM méthode de recyclage *f*; ~ **of waste** ENVIR recyclage des déchets *m*

red¹ *adj* GEN COMM rouge

red:² ~ **button** *n jarg* UK STOCK *clerk* bouton rouge *m (jarg)*, commis à la compensation *m*; ~ **circling** *n* UK HRM *reformation of pay structure* refait de la grille salariale; ~ **clause** *n* BANK *international trade*, TRANSP *shipping* clause rouge *f*; ~ **clause credit** *n* BANK, TRANSP *shipping* crédit accordé avec clause rouge *m*; ~ **goods** *n pl jarg* S&M *advertising* produits de grande consommation *m pl*; ~ **and green system** *n* IMP/EXP *customs declaration system* système rouge et vert *m*; ~ **herring** *n* STOCK prospectus provisoire *m*, prospectus provisoire avant une nouvelle émission d'actions *m*; ~ **-herring prospectus** *n* STOCK prospectus provisoire *m*, prospectus provisoire avant une nouvelle émission d'actions *m*; ~ **-line clause** *n* BANK *international trade*, TRANSP *shipping* clause rouge *f*; ~ **tape** *n* ADMIN excès de formalités administratives *m*; ◆ **in the ~** BANK, FIN *in debt* à découvert

red. *abbr (redeemable)* ACC, STOCK amortissable, rachetable, remb. *(remboursable)*

Red:[1] **~ Book** *n infrml US* FIN annuaire par profession ou par entreprise; **~ Star**® *n UK* TRANSP service de messageries du chemin de fer britannique

Red:[2] **~ China** *pr n* GEN COMM Chine rouge *f*

redeem *vt* ACC rembourser, ECON, FIN racheter, GEN COMM amortir, encaisser, racheter, rembourser, PROP *mortgage* purger, STOCK amortir, encaisser, racheter, rembourser

redeemable[1] *adj (red.)* ACC *before maturity, in advance*, STOCK *stock, share, bond* amortissable, rachetable, remboursable *(remb.)*

redeemable:[2] **~ bond** *n* STOCK obligation amortie *f*, obligation amortissable *f*, obligation rachetable *f*, obligation remboursable *f*; **~ preference share** *n* STOCK action de priorité amortissable *f*, action privilégiée amortissable *f*; **~ retractable preferred share** *n* STOCK action privilégiée rachetable au gré de l'acheteur et de l'entrepreneur *f*; **~ stock** *n* STOCK actions rachetables *f pl*, actions remboursables *f pl*, capital actions remboursable *m*

redeemed[1] *adj* ACC, STOCK *bond* amorti, remboursé, *share* racheté

redeemed:[2] **~ debenture** *n* STOCK obligation amortie *f*, obligation amortissable *f*, obligation rachetable *f*, obligation remboursable *f*

redelivery *n* TRANSP délivraison *f*

redemption *n* ACC rachat *m*, remboursement *m*, FIN remboursement *m*, GEN COMM, STOCK amortissement *m*; **~ amount** STOCK rachat *m*; **~ before due date** FIN remboursement anticipé *m*, remboursement avant la date d'échéance *m*; **~ bond** STOCK obligation de conversion *f*, prime de remboursement *f*; **~ call** STOCK appel au rachat *m*; **~ date** STOCK date de remboursement *f*, date de règlement *f*; **~ fee** STOCK frais de rachat *m pl*; **~ premium** ACC prime de remboursement *f*; **~ price** STOCK prix de rachat *m*; **~ table** ACC plan de remboursement *m*, tableau de remboursement *m*; **~ value** STOCK valeur de rachat *f*; **~ yield** STOCK rendement sur remboursement *m*, taux actuariel *m*

redeploy *vt* GEN COMM, HRM reclasser, redéployer, réorganiser, réorienter

redeployment *n* GEN COMM, HRM reclassement *m*, redéploiement *m*, réorganisation *f*, réorientation *f*; **~ premium** HRM prime de réorientation *f*

redeposit *vt* BANK *of bank* déposer de nouveau, redéposer

redevelop *vt* ECON, PROP réaménager

redevelopment *n* ECON, PROP réaménagement *m*

rediscount *n* ACC, FIN réescompte *m*; **~ rate** ACC taux de réescompte *m*

rediscountable *adj* ACC, FIN réescomptable

rediscounter *n* ACC, FIN réescompteur *m*

rediscounting *n* ACC, FIN réescompte *m*

redlining *n* BANK, FIN refus d'accorder des prêts hypothécaires, GEN COMM zone interdite

redress[1] *n* LAW réparation *f*, réparation légale *f*

redress[2] *vt* GEN COMM, LAW *errors* réparer; ◆ **~ the balance** ACC, GEN COMM redresser l'équilibre

REDS *abbr UK (Registered Excise Dealers and Shippers)* IMP/EXP ≈ commissionnaires en douane et transitaires *m pl*

reduce:[1] **~ class rate** *n (R)* TRANSP *air freight classification* tarif de classification avec réduction *m*

reduce[2] *vt* ECON *price, investment* diminuer, freiner, ralentir, réduire, FIN réduire, GEN COMM *expenses* diminuer, réduire, *price* baisser, réduire, HRM comprimer, TAX alléger

reduced[1] *adj* GEN COMM diminué, réduit

reduced:[2] **~ fare** *n* TRANSP tarif réduit *m*; **~ form equation** *n* ECON équation de forme réduite *f*; **~ lead time** *n* IND diminution du temps de réalisation *f*; **~ price** *n* S&M prix réduit *m*; **~ rate** *n* GEN COMM, TAX taux réduit *m*; **~ tax** *n* TAX impôt réduit *m*

reducing: ~ balance *n* ACC, FIN amortissement dégressif *m*; **~ balance method** *n* ACC système d'amortissement dégressif *m*

reduction *n* ACC restriction *f*, réduction *f*, ECON, FIN restriction *f*, GEN COMM réduction *f*, HRM *of salary* compression *f*, TAX allègement *m*; **~ for senior citizen** TAX réduction pour personne âgée *f*; **~ in capital** STOCK réduction de capital *f*; **~ in force (RIF)** HRM réduction d'emplois secondaires *f*, suppression d'emplois *f*

redundancy *n* COMP redondance *f*, HRM *cutting back of workforce* dégraissage *m*, *dismissal of employee* licenciement *m*; **~ benefit** HRM indemnité de licenciement *f*; **~ check** COMP contrôle par redondance *m*; **~ consultation** HRM consultation en vue de reconversion *f*, entretien de reconversion *m*, entretien de réorientation de carrière *m*; **~ letter** *BrE (cf pink slip AmE)* COMMS, HRM lettre de licenciement *f*, lettre de renvoi *f*; **~ pay** HRM indemnité de licenciement *f*, prime de licenciement *f*, prime de reconversion *f*; **~ payment** HRM indemnité de licenciement *f*, prime de licenciement *f*, prime de reconversion *f*; **~ procedure** HRM procédure de licenciement *f*; **~ severance pay** HRM indemnité de licenciement *f*; **~ severance payment** HRM indemnité de licenciement *f*

Redundancy: ~ Payments Act *n UK (RPA)* HRM *1965* loi sur les primes de reconversions

redundant[1] *adj* GEN COMM *building, machinery* inutilisé, HRM *personnel* en surnombre, licencié; ◆ **be made ~** HRM être licencié, être mis au chômage; **make ~** HRM licencier

redundant:[2] **~ farmland** *n* ECON *agriculture* terres en jachère *f pl*

re-educate *vt* GEN COMM, HRM réhabiliter

reefer *n* TRANSP *container* conteneur frigorifique *m*, frigo *m (infrml)*; **~ carrier** *(ref., reefer ship)*

TRANSP *shipping* cargo frigorifique *m*, navire polytherme *m*; **~ container** TRANSP conteneur frigorifique *m*; **~ ship** *(ref., reefer carrier)* TRANSP *shipping* cargo frigorifique *m*, navire polytherme *m*; **~ trade** ECON *international* négoce du frigorifique *m*

reel *n* COMP bobine *f*

re-election *n* GEN COMM, POL réélection *f*

re-embark *vti* GEN COMM, TRANSP rembarquer

re-emphasize *vt* GEN COMM remettre l'accent sur

re-employ *vt* GEN COMM, HRM remployer, réembaucher, réengager, *method, product* réemployer, *of employee* rengager, réintégrer, *hostilities* reprendre

re-employment *n* HRM remploi *m*, rengagement *m*, reprise *f*, réembauche *f*, réemploi *m*, *of employee* réengagement *m*, réincorporation *f*, réintégration *f*

re-endorsement *n* BANK nouvel aval *m*

re-engage *vt* HRM rembaucher, remployer, rengager, reprendre, réembaucher, réemployer, réengager, réincorporer, réintégrer

re-engagement *n* HRM remploi *m*, rengagement *m*, reprise *f*, réembauche *f*, réemploi *m*, réengagement *m*, réincorporation *f*, réintégration *f*

re-enter *vt* COMP *data, program* refrapper, relancer

re-establish *vt* GEN COMM rétablir

re-establishment *n* GEN COMM rétablissement *m*

re-examination *n* GEN COMM nouvel examen *m*, réexamen *m*

re-examine *vt* GEN COMM examiner de nouveau, réexaminer

re-export *n* IMP/EXP réexportation *f*

re-exportation *n* IMP/EXP réexportation *f*

re-exporter *n* IMP/EXP réexportateur *m*

ref. *abbr* GEN COMM *(reference)* rf. *(référence)*, TRANSP *(reefer carrier, reefer ship) shipping* cargo frigorifique *m*, navire polytherme *m*

refer: **~ to** *vt* GEN COMM *document, letter* se référer à, LAW *to another court* renvoyer devant, soumettre à; ♦ **~ to acceptor** *(R/A)*, GEN COMM voir le tiré; **~ to drawer** *(RD)* BANK retour au tiroir, voir le tireur

referee: **~ in case of need** *n* BANK recommandataire *m*

reference[1] *n* GEN COMM *(ref.)* référence *f (rf.)* HRM *of employee* référence *f*; **~ bank** BANK banque de référence *f*; **~ currency** ECON devise de référence *f*; **~ cycle** ECON cycle de référence *m*; **~ group** GEN COMM groupe de référence *m*; **~ level** FIN niveau de référence *m*; **~ line** PATENTS ligne directrice *f*; **~ material** ADMIN documentation *f*; **~ number** COMMS, MEDIA numéro de référence *m*; **~ point** GEN COMM point de repère *m*; **~ sign** PATENTS signe de référence *m*; ♦ **by ~ to** GEN COMM par rapport à; **have excellent ~s** HRM avoir d'excellentes références; **take up sb's ~s** HRM *for job application* prendre des renseignements sur qn; **~ to** PATENTS référence à; **with ~ to** COMMS en

nous référant à, en référence à, GEN COMM au sujet de, concernant, en ce qui concerne, quant à, relativement à, en référence à; **with ~ to your enquiry** COMMS comme suite à votre demande, en nous référant à votre demande; **with ~ to your letter** COMMS en ce qui concerne votre lettre, suite à votre lettre; **your ~** *(yr ref.)* COMMS votre référence *(V/réf.)*

reference[2] *prep* GEN COMM au sujet de, concernant, en ce qui concerne, en référence à, quant à, relativement à; ♦ **~ our telex** *(ROT)* COMMS référence notre télex

referendum *n* GEN COMM, POL référendum *m*

referral: **by ~ to** *phr* GEN COMM par référence à *loc f*

referred: **~ to in paragraph 1** *phr* GEN COMM décrit au paragraphe 1 *loc m*, visé à l'alinéa 1 *loc*

referring: **~ to** *phr* GEN COMM par référence à *loc f*

refinance:[1] **~ credit** *n* BANK crédit de refinancement *m*

refinance[2] *vt* BANK, FIN refinancer

refinancing *n* BANK, FIN refinancement *m*; **~ risk** BANK risque de refinancement *m*

refined[1] *adj* IND *metal* affiné, *oil* raffiné

refined:[2] **~ metal** *n* IND métal affiné *m*

refinement *n* COM raffinement *m*

refiner *n* IND raffineur *m*

refinery *n* IND raffinerie *f*

refining *n* IND raffinage *m*

reflate *vt* ECON *economy* faire repartir, relancer

reflation *n* ECON relance *f*

reflect *vt* GEN COMM *sb's opinion* refléter

reflected: **be ~ in** *phr* GEN COMM se traduire par

refloat *vt* ECON renflouer; ♦ **~ a loan** BANK émettre un nouvel emprunt

refloating *n* ECON renflouement *m*

refocusing *n* GEN COMM recentrage *m*

reform[1] *n* ECON, GEN COMM, POL réforme *f*; **~ package** POL projet de réforme *m*; **~ program** *AmE*, **~ programme** *BrE* ECON, POL programme de réformes *m*

reform[2] *vt* ECON, GEN COMM, POL réformer

reformat *vt* COMP *disk* reformater, remettre en forme

reformism *n* POL *Marxism* réformisme *m*

reforward *vt* TRANSP réexpédier

reforwarded *adj* TRANSP réexpédié

reforwarding *n* TRANSP réexpédition *f*

refrain: **~ from** *vt* GEN COMM s'abstenir de

refresh *vt* COMP *computer screen* rafraîchir, *update memory* régénérer

refresher *n* UK LAW honoraires supplémentaires *m pl*

refrigerated[1] *adj* *(R)* GEN COMM, TRANSP réfrigéré

refrigerated:[2] **~ box van** *n* TRANSP fourgon frigorifique *m*; **~ capacity** *n* TRANSP *of container* capacité frigorifique *f*, capacité isotherme *f*; **~ container** *n* *(R)* TRANSP conteneur frigorifique *m*; **~ lorry** *n* *BrE* *(cf refrigerated truck AmE)*

TRANSP camion frigorifique *m*, camion isotherme *m*; ~ **ship** *n* TRANSP cargo frigorifique *m*, navire frigorifique *m*, navire polytherme *m*; ~ **truck** *n* *AmE (cf refrigerated lorry BrE)* TRANSP camion frigorifique *m*, camion isotherme *m*; ~ **vessel** *n* TRANSP *shipping* cargo frigorifique *m*, navire frigorifique *m*, navire polytherme *m*; ~ **warehouse** *n* GEN COMM entrepôt frigorifique *m*

refrigeration *n (R)* GEN COMM, TRANSP réfrigération *f*

refuel 1. *vt* ECON *vehicle* ravitailler, ravitailler en carburant, *inflation* relancer; **2.** *vi* TRANSP se ravitailler, se ravitailler en carburant

refueling *n AmE*, **refuelling** *n BrE* TRANSP ravitaillement *m*

refugee *n* GEN COMM réfugié *m*; ~ **capital** FIN capitaux spéculatifs *m pl*

refund¹ *n* GEN COMM remboursement *m*, STOCK remboursement *m*, remboursement d'une émission obligataire par une autre *m*, TAX dégrèvement *m*, remboursement *m*, remboursement d'un paiement en trop *m*; ~ **return** TAX déclaration avec remboursement *f*, remboursement en retour *m*; ~ **slip** GEN COMM bulletin de versement *m*

refund² *vt* ACC, BANK, ECON, GEN COMM, TAX rembourser

refundable¹ *adj* ACC, BANK, ECON, GEN COMM, TAX remboursable

refundable:² ~ **deposit** *n* GEN COMM acompte remboursable *m*; ~ **prepaid credit** *n* TAX crédit remboursable payé d'avance *m*; ~ **tax credit** *n* TAX crédit d'impôt remboursable *m*

refurbish *vt* GEN COMM remettre en bon état, remettre à neuf, rénover, PROP rénover

refurbishment *n* GEN COMM remise à neuf *f*, rénovation *f*, PROP rénovation *f*

refusal *n* GEN COMM refus *m*, PATENTS refus *m*, rejet *m*

refuse¹ *n BrE* ENVIR déchets *m pl*, ordures *f pl*, ordures ménagères *f pl*; ~ **collection** *BrE (cf garbage collection AmE)* GEN COMM ramassage des ordures ménagères *m*; ~ **collection vehicle** ENVIR benne à ordures *f*; ~ **disposal** ENVIR élimination des ordures ménagères *f*; ~ **dump** ENVIR dépôt de résidus *m*

refuse² *vt* GEN COMM refuser; ◆ ~ **acceptance of a draft** BANK refuser d'accepter une traite; ~ **sb bail** LAW refuser de mettre qn en liberté sous caution

regard: have a high ~ for sb *phr* GEN COMM avoir beaucoup d'estime pour qn; **with ~ to** *phr* GEN COMM concernant, en ce qui concerne

regarding *prep* GEN COMM au sujet de, concernant, en ce qui concerne, quant à, relativement à, à propos

regd. *abbr (registered)* COMMS mail r. *(recommandér)*

regime *n* GEN COMM régime *m*

region *n* COMP, GEN COMM, POL région *f*; ◆ **in the ~ of** GEN COMM *approximately* environ, à peu près

regional¹ *adj* GEN COMM régional

regional:² ~ **agreement** *n* ECON *international trade* accord régional *m*; ~ **airline** *n* TRANSP compagnie de transport régional *f*, compagnie régionale *f*; ~ **airline company** *n* TRANSP compagnie de transport régional *f*, compagnie régionale *f*; ~ **bank** *n* BANK banque régionale *f*; ~ **banking pacts** *n pl* BANK accords entre banques régionales *m pl*; ~ **center** *n AmE*, ~ **centre** *n BrE* GEN COMM centre régional *m*; ~ **development** *n* ECON développement régional *m*; ~ **economics** *n* ECON économie régionale *f*; ~ **employment premium** *n (REP)* HRM indemnité d'emploi régional *f*, prime à l'emploi régional *f*; ~ **grouping** *n* ECON *North American Free Trade Agreement* regroupement régional *m*; ~ **manager** *n* HRM, MGMNT chef de région *m*, responsable régional *m*, S&M chef de région *m*; ~ **market** *n* S&M marché régional *m*; ~ **multiplier** *n* ECON multiplicateur régional *m*; ~ **office** *n* GEN COMM bureau régional *m*; ~ **organization** *n* MGMNT organisation par région *f*; ~ **patent** *n* PATENTS brevet régional *m*; ~ **policy** *n* ECON politique régionale *f*, égalisation interrégionale *f*, IND politique régionale *f*; ~ **quota** *n* ECON *international trade* quota régional *m*; ~ **representation** *n* S&M *of store chain* représentation régionale *f*; ~ **selective assistance** *n UK (RSA)* ECON assistance régionale sélective *f*; ~ **stock exchange** *n* STOCK bourse régionale *f*; ~ **tax effects** *n pl* ACC effets fiscaux régionaux *m pl*; ~ **trend** *n* S&M tendance régionale *f*; ~ **wage bargaining** *n* HRM négociation salariale au plan régional *f*

regionally *adv* GEN COMM au niveau régional *loc m*

register¹ *n* ADMIN, COMP, GEN COMM, INS, LAW *of business name*, PATENTS registre *m*; ~ **of companies** ADMIN *office* enregistrement *m*, registre des sociétés *m*, *record* registre du commerce *m*, GEN COMM registre du commerce *m*; ~ **of members** GEN COMM, LAW registre des actionnaires *m*; ~ **office** ADMIN bureau de l'état civil *m*; ~ **tonnage** GEN COMM *maritime* tonnage de jauge *m*

register² *vt* ADMIN agréer, GEN COMM faire enregistrer, immatriculer, *letter* recommander, *pension scheme* agréer, LAW *business name* enregistrer, TAX, TRANSP immatriculer; ◆ ~ **a high** GEN COMM *on stock market* enregistrer une hausse

Register: ~ **Book** *n* TRANSP *shipping* registre du Lloyd's *m*

registered¹ *adj* ADMIN agréé, COMMS *(regd.)* mail, post par envoi recommandé, recommandé *(r.)*, TAX, TRANSP immatriculé; ◆ ~ **in Canada** LAW, TAX *vessel*, TRANSP *vehicle* immatriculé au Canada

registered:² ~ **address** *n* COMMS, GEN COMM *of company* adresse du siège social *f*; ~ **applicant for work** *n* GEN COMM demandeur d'emploi *m*, D.E.;

~ baggage *n* (SYN *baggage checked*) TRANSP *luggage* bagages enregistrés *m pl*; **~ bond** *n* STOCK obligation immatriculée *f*, obligation nominative *f*; **~ charity** *n* TAX oeuvre caritative reconnue *f*, organisme de charité enregistré *m*; **~ company** *n* ADMIN société immatriculée *f*, société inscrite au registre du commerce *f*; **~ competitive market maker** *n* STOCK teneur de marché agréé *m*; **~ competitive trader** *n* STOCK négociateur agréé *m*; **~ design** *n* LAW, PATENTS modèle déposé *m*; **~ equity market maker** *n* STOCK teneur de marché agréé pour les actions *m*, teneur de marché d'actions nominatives *m*; **~ life insurance policy** *n* INS police d'assurance-vie agréée *f*; **~ mail** *n* COMMS courrier recommandé *m*, envoi recommandé *m*; **~ manager** *n* HRM, TRANSP *shipping* responsable de conformité aux règlements *m*, responsable des permis de transport maritime *m*; **~ mark** *n* LAW, PATENTS marque déposée *f*; **~ office** *n* GEN COMM, LAW *of company* siège social *m*; **~ offices** *n pl* GEN COMM, LAW *of company* filiales *f pl*; **~ options broker** *n* STOCK courtier d'options agréé *m*; **~ options trader** *n* STOCK négociateur d'options agréé *m*; **~ owner** *n* STOCK *of bond* propriétaire immatriculé *m*; **~ pension plan** *n* INS régime de retraite agréé *m*; **~ political party** *n* TAX parti politique reconnu *m*; **~ post** *n* COMMS courrier recommandé *m*, envoi recommandé *m*; **~ proprietor** *n* LAW, PROP propriétaire inscrit au registre du cadastre *m*; **~ representative** *n* STOCK représentant agréé *m*; **~ retirement income fund** *n* (*RRIF*) INS caisse de retraite agréée *f*; **~ retirement savings plan** *n* (*RRSP*) INS régime enregistré d'épargne-retraite *m*; **~ secondary offering** *n* STOCK offre secondaire enregistrée; **~ security** *n* STOCK titre nominatif *m*, valeur nominative *f*; **~ share** *n* ACC, STOCK action nominative *f*; **~ shareholder** *n* STOCK actionnaire inscrit *m*; **the ~ unemployed** *n pl* UK HRM, WEL les chômeurs inscrits à l'Agence nationale pour l'emploi *m*; **~ title** *n* ADMIN titre de propriété inscrit au registre du cadastre *m*; **~ ton** *n* GEN COMM tonne de jauge *f*; **~ trademark** *n* GEN COMM, LAW, PATENTS marque déposée *f*; **~ unemployment** *n* ECON, HRM chômage déclaré *m*; **~ user** *n* COMP, LAW, PATENTS usager inscrit sur le registre *m*, utilisateur inscrit au registre *m*

Registered: **~ Excise Dealers and Shippers** *n pl* UK (*REDS*) IMP/EXP ≈ commissionnaires en douane et transitaires *m pl*; **~ International Exchange** *n* UK (*RIE*) STOCK échanges internationaux autorisés *m pl*

registrant *n* STOCK *securities* courtier attitré *m*

registrar *n* **~ of deeds** *n* ADMIN, LAW receveur de l'enregistrement *m*; **~ fee** *n* TAX droit d'inscription *m*, honoraires de registraire *m pl*; **~ of mortgages** *n* PROP conservateur des hypothèques *m*; **~ of transfers** *n* FIN agent comptable des transferts *m*; **~'s office** *n* ADMIN bureau de l'état civil *m*

registration *n* ADMIN agrément *m*, enregistrement

m, inscription *f*, GEN COMM *of company name* inscription *f*, INS *of pension plan* agrément *m*, LAW *of business name*, PATENTS enregistrement *m*, inscription *f*, PROP inscription *f*, TAX, TRANSP *of vehicle* immatriculation *f*; **~ as French** TRANSP *shipping* francisation *f*; **~ fee** FIN, GEN COMM, STOCK frais d'inscription *m pl*; **~ number** GEN COMM numéro d'enregistrement *m*, numéro d'immatriculation *m*; **~ office** ADMIN bureau d'enregistrement *m*; **~ statement** STOCK état des enregistrements *m*, état des émissions publiques de titres *m*; **~ threshold** TAX *for VAT* seuil d'enregistrement *m*

registry *n* ADMIN *action* inscription *f*, *office* bureau de l'enregistrement *m*, enregistrement *m*; **~ of deeds** ADMIN, LAW, PROP bureau d'enregistrement des actes *m*; **~ office** UK ADMIN bureau de l'enregistrement *m*, l'administration de l'enregistrement *f*, l'enregistrement *m*, *for civil ceremonies, records* bureau de l'état civil *m*; **~ of shipping** TRANSP immatriculation des navires *f*

regression *n* MATH *statistics* régression *f*; **~ analysis** MATH *statistics* analyse de régression *f*; **~ curve** MATH *statistics* courbe de régression *f*

regressive[1] *adj* GEN COMM, MATH régressif

regressive:[2] **~ expectations** *n pl* MATH *statistics* attentes régressives *f pl*; **~ supply** *n* ECON offre régressive *f*; **~ tax** *n* TAX impôt régressif *m*; **~ taxation** *n* TAX imposition régressive *f*

regret *n* GEN COMM regret *m*, STOCK retour de souscription; ♦ **~ to inform sb that** GEN COMM avoir le regret d'informer qn que

regretfully *adv* GEN COMM malheureusement

regroup *vt* GEN COMM regrouper

regular[1] *adj* GEN COMM régulier

regular:[2] **~ and continuous basis** *n* TAX base régulière et continue *f*; **~ expenditure** *n* FIN dépense régulière *f*; **~ hours** *n pl* GEN COMM heures normales *f pl*; **~ meeting** *n* GEN COMM, MGMNT réunion normale *f*; **~ payments** *n pl* GEN COMM paiements réguliers *m pl*; **~ service** *n* LEIS, TRANSP service régulier *m*; **~ statements** *n pl* GEN COMM relevés réguliers *m pl*; **~ way delivery** *n* GEN COMM livraison par voie ordinaire *f*, STOCK livraison ordinaire *f*, livraison à 5+5 *f*, transmission de titres au porteur ordinaire *f*

regulate *vt* ECON *flow* régler, *industry, market* réglementer, *money supply* contrôler, GEN COMM réglementer, régler, IND *machine* régler, LAW contrôler, réglementer, régler

regulated: **~ agreement** *n* UK FIN accord réglementé *m*; **~ commodity** *n* STOCK marchandise réglementée *f*, matière première réglementée *f*; **~ firm** *n* ECON entreprise réglementée *f*; **~ industry** *n* IND industrie réglementée *f*; **~ investment company** *n* FIN société d'investissement réglementée *f*; **~ market** *n* FIN marché réglementé *m*

regulation *n* ECON *of flow* règlement *m*, *of industry, market* réglementation *f*, *of money supply* contrôle *m*, GEN COMM réglementation *f*, règlement *m*,

LAW contrôle *m*, réglementation *f*, règlement *m*, TAX règlement *m*; ~ **authority** GEN COMM, LAW autorité de régulation *f*

Regulation: ~ **D** *n US* FIN *Federal Reserve Board* réglementation D *f*; ~ **K** *n US* FIN réglementation K *f*; ~ **Q** *n US* FIN réglementation Q *f*; ~ **School** *n* ECON école de la régulation *f*; ~ **T** *n US* FIN réglementation T *f*; ~ **Z** *n US* FIN réglementation Z *f*

regulations *n pl* GEN COMM, LAW, TAX règlements *m pl*; ◆ **make** ~ GEN COMM, LAW, TAX établir des règlements

regulator *n* LAW organisme de réglementation *m*, TAX régulateur *m*

regulatory[1] *adj* LAW régulateur

regulatory:[2] ~ **agency** *n* GEN COMM agence de tutelle *f*; ~ **authority** *n* GEN COMM, LAW autorité de régulation *f*, autorité réglementaire *f*, organisme de réglementation *m*, organisme de tutelle *m*; ~ **body** *n* GEN COMM, LAW autorité de régulation *f*, autorité réglementaire *f*, organisme de réglementation *m*, organisme de tutelle *m*; ~ **capture** *n* ECON détournement des objectifs d'une réglementation *m*; ~ **committee** *n* POL *European Commission* comité régulateur *m*; ~ **measures** *n pl* LAW mesures de réglementation *f pl*, mesures réglementaires *f pl*; ~ **system** *n* LAW système réglementaire *m*

Regulatory: ~ **News Service** *n UK (RNS)* STOCK service d'information relative à la réglementation, ≈ chronoval *m*

rehabilitate *vt* ENVIR *abandoned waste dumping site* remettre en état, réhabiliter, GEN COMM *reputation, company*, LAW réhabiliter

rehabilitation *n* ENVIR *of abandoned waste dumping site* remise en état *f*, réhabilitation *f*, GEN COMM *of reputation, company* réhabilitation *f*; ~ **import credit** *(RIC)* ECON, FIN crédit à l'importation pour le redressement économique *m*; ~ **import loan** *(RIL)* FIN emprunt de redressement *m*, prêt de l'importation pour le redressement économique *m*

rehypothecation *n* STOCK nantissement d'un prêt par titres *m*, nouvelle inscription hypothécaire *f*

reign[1] *n* GEN COMM, POL règne *m*

reign[2] *vi* GEN COMM, POL régner

reimage *vt* S&M changer l'image de

reimburse *vt* GEN COMM rembourser

reimbursement *n* GEN COMM remboursement *m*

reimpose *vt* GEN COMM réimposer

rein: **give free** ~ **to** *phr* GEN COMM *anger, emotion* donner libre cours à

reinforce *vt* GEN COMM *effect, impact* renforcer

reinforcement *n* GEN COMM *of effect, impact* renforcement *m*

reinfusion *n* FIN réinjection *f*

reins: **slacken the** ~ *phr* ECON relâcher la bride, relâcher les rênes

reinstate *vt* GEN COMM *employee* réintégrer

reinstated *adj* GEN COMM réintégré

reinstatement *n* GEN COMM *of employee* réintégration *f*

reinsurance *n* INS réassurance *f*; ~ **company** INS compagnie de réassurance *f*, société de réassurance *f*

reinvent: ~ **the wheel** *phr* GEN COMM inventer le fil à couper le beurre *(infrml)*

reinvest *vt* GEN COMM, STOCK replacer, réinvestir

reinvestment *n* GEN COMM, STOCK nouveau placement *m*, replacement *m*, réinvestissement *m*; ~ **of dividends** STOCK réinvestissement des dividendes *m*; ~ **loss** GEN COMM perte de réinvestissement *f*; ~ **privilege** STOCK droit de réinvestissement automatique *m*, privilège de réinvestissement *m*; ~ **rate** GEN COMM, STOCK *interest rate futures* taux de réinvestissement *m*

reissue[1] *n* BANK *of bill of exchange* renouvellement *m*, STOCK nouvelle émission *f*

reissue[2] *vt* BANK *bill of exchange* renouveler, STOCK réémettre, émettre de nouveau

REIT *abbr US (real estate investment trust)* BANK fonds de placements immobiliers *m*, STOCK SCPI *(société civile de placement immobilier)*

reiterate *vi* GEN COMM réitérer

reject:[1] ~ **bin** *n* GEN COMM panier de rebut *m*

reject[2] *vt* GEN COMM rejeter

rejection *n* GEN COMM, LAW, PATENTS rejet *m*

rejuvenate *vt* ECON *economy* moderniser, rajeunir

rejuvenation *n* ECON *of economy* modernisation *f*, rajeunissement *m*

related: ~ **business** *n* TAX *in relation to a charity* activité commerciale complémentaire *f*, commerce affilié *m*; ~ **group** *n* TAX groupe lié *m*; ~ **party** *n* GEN COMM partie associée *f*; ~ **persons** *n pl* TAX personnes apparentées *f pl*, personnes liées *f pl*

relation *n* GEN COMM rapport *m*, relation *f*; ◆ **in** ~ **to** GEN COMM par rapport à

relational: ~ **database** *n (RDB)* COMP base de données relationnelles *f (BDR)*

relations *n pl* ECON, GEN COMM *between parties* relations *f pl*, HRM, MGMNT rapports *m pl*, relations *f pl*; ~ **analysis** *n* HRM analyse relationnelle *f*

relationship *n* ECON, FIN, GEN COMM relation *f*, TAX lien de parenté *m*

relative[1] *adj* GEN COMM relatif; ◆ **in** ~ **terms** GEN COMM en termes relatifs; ~ **to** GEN COMM relatif à

relative:[2] ~ **concentration** *n* MATH *statistics* concentration relative *f*; ~ **error** *n* COMP erreur relative *f*; ~ **income hypothesis** *n* ECON hypothèse du revenu relatif *f*; ~ **price** *n* ECON prix relatif *m*; ~ **price level** *n* ECON niveau de prix relatifs *m*; ~ **surplus value** *n* ECON plus-value relative *f*

relatively *adv* GEN COMM relativement

relativities *n pl* HRM relativités *f pl*

relaunch[1] *n* GEN COMM *of programme, product*, S&M relancement *m*

relaunch[2] *vt* GEN COMM *programme, product,* S&M relancer

relax *vt* GEN COMM *rule* relâcher, MGMNT *policy* assouplir

relaxation *n* GEN COMM *of rule* relâchement *m*, MGMNT *of law, policy* assouplissement *m*

release[1] *n* BANK *of cheque* libération *f*, COMP *version of software, product* lancement *m*, mise sur le marché *f*, GEN COMM *of new product* lancement *m*, sortie *f*, LAW, WEL *from prison* libération *f*; **~ date** STOCK *for shares allocated to employees* date de distribution *f*, date de libération *f*; **~ for shipment** TRANSP autorisation de sortie *f*; **~ note** *(RN)* TRANSP *cargo* bordereau de livraison *m*; **~ or surrender** TAX abandon *m*, libération ou rachat *m*; **~ of recognizance** LAW libération sous caution *f*

release[2] *vt* COMP *version of software, product* lancer, mettre sur le marché, GEN COMM *information* communiquer, LAW, WEL *from prison* libérer; ♦ **~ on bail** LAW libérer sous caution, mettre en liberté provisoire sous caution

released *adj* LAW en liberté *loc f*

relevance *n* GEN COMM à propos *loc m*

relevant: **~ act** *n UK* HRM, IND, LAW *trade unions* acte d'incitation *m*, action syndicale appropriée *f*; **~ authority** *n* INS autorité compétente *f*; **~ cost base** *n* TAX *of property* coût utile de base *m*, prix de base approprié *m*; **~ period** *n* TAX période applicable *f*, période utile *f*; **~ test** GEN COMM essai de fiabilité *m*

reliability *n* GEN COMM, S&M fiabilité *f*; **~ test** GEN COMM essai de fiabilité *m*

reliable *adj* GEN COMM fiable

reliance *n* GEN COMM confiance *f*

relief *n* ACC dérogation *f*, TAX dégrèvement *m*; **~ goods** *n pl* IMP/EXP biens d'assistance *m pl*; **~ on business assets** *n* TAX dégrèvement sur biens commerciaux *m*; **~ sailing** *n* TRANSP navire supplémentaire *m*; **~ shift** *n (SYN swing shift)* HRM poste de relève *m*, équipe suppléante *f*, équipe tournante *f*

relieve *vt* HRM *take over from* relever, TAX dégrever

religious: **~ discrimination** *n* HRM discrimination pour motifs religieux *f*; **~ monitoring** *n* HRM contrôle des appartenances religieuses du personnel *m*; **~ organization** *n* TAX organisme religieux *m*

relinquish *vt* GEN COMM *power, freedom* abandonner, LAW *responsibility* délaisser; ♦ **~ an inheritance** LAW renoncer à une succession

reload *vt* COMP *software* recharger, relancer, TRANSP *vehicle, ship, cargo* recharger

reloading *n* COMP relance *f*

relocatable[1] *adj* COMP *area of memory* réadressable, translatable

relocatable:[2] **~ address** *n* COMP adresse translatable *f*

relocate *vt* GEN COMM *company, employee* déplacer, replacer, transférer

relocation *n* COMP réadressage *m*, translation *f*, GEN COMM *of company, employee* déplacement *m*, replacement *m*, transfert *m*

reluctant: **~ to do sth** *phr* GEN COMM peu disposé à faire qch

rely: **~ on** *vt (SYN depend on)* GEN COMM compter sur

remain *vi* GEN COMM rester; ♦ **~ in suspense** GEN COMM *in abeyance* rester en suspens; **~ on board** *(ROB)* TRANSP *cargo* reste à bord; **~ undecided** GEN COMM *question, issue, matter* ne toujours pas être réglé; **~ undelivered** GEN COMM *goods* ne toujours pas être livré

remainder *n* MATH reste *m*

remainderman *n* [pl -men] FIN soldeur *m*

remake *n* LEIS *film* remake *m*

remand[1] *n* LAW ajournement *m*, renvoi *m*; ♦ **on ~** LAW *criminal* en détention préventive

remand[2] *vt* LAW *case* ajourner, renvoyer; ♦ **~ in custody** LAW mettre en détention préventive

remapping *n* COMP reconfiguration *f*, redéfinition *f*

remargining *n* FIN renantissement *m*

remark[1] *n* GEN COMM remarque *f*

remark[2] *vt* GEN COMM observer, remarquer

remarketing *n* S&M marketing de relance *m*

remedy[1] *n* GEN COMM *legal, financial* remède *m*, solution *f*

remedy[2] *vt* GEN COMM *situation* remédier à; ♦ **~ abuses** GEN COMM remédier aux abus

reminder: **~ call** *n* COMMS appel de rendez-vous *m*

remise *n* LAW suspension *f*

remission *n* TAX remise *f*; **~ of charges** TAX détaxe *f*, remise de charges *f*; **~ of tax** TAX remise d'impôt *f*

remit[1] *n* GEN COMM attributions *f pl*; **~ rate** MEDIA *print* part éditeur *f*

remit[2] *vt* HRM *industrial relations* enterrer, remettre aux calendes grecques, LAW *sentence, debt* remettre, renvoyer

remittal *n* LAW *of sentence, debt* remise *f*, renvoi *m*

remittance *n* BANK envoi de fonds *m*, versement *m*; **~ account** BANK compte de remise non soldé *m*; **~ account number** TAX numéro de compte de versements *m*, numéro de compte pour le règlement *m*; **~ advice** BANK avis de remise à l'encaissement *m*; **~ for collection** BANK remise en recouvrement *f*, remise à l'encaissement *f*; **~ policy** GEN COMM politique à l'égard des remises de dettes *f*; **~ return** TAX déclaration avec versement *f*, formulaire de versement *m*; **~ seal** BANK cachet de numéraire *m*, cachet pour colis de titres *m*; **~ slip** GEN COMM bordereau de paiement *m*; **~ of tax** TAX versement d'impôt *m*

remnants *n pl* GEN COMM *remains* vestiges *m pl*

remote[1] *adj* COMP distant, par satellite *loc m*, éloigné, à distance; **~ -controlled** COMP commandé, télécommandé, à distance

remote:[2] **~ access** *n* COMP accès à distance *m*, téléconsultation *f*; **~ batch processing** *n* COMP télétraitement par lots *m*; ~ **control** *n* COMMS commande à distance *f*, télécommande *f*; ~ **maintenance** *n* COMP télémaintenance *f*; ~ **possibility** *n* GEN COMM éventualité peu probable *f*; ~ **printing** *n* COMP télé-impression *f*; ~ **processing** *n* COMP télétraitement *m*; ~ **support** *n* COMP télé-assistance *f*

removal *n* ENVIR *of oil by separators* épuration *f*, GEN COMM *of goods, restriction* enlèvement *m*, *of tariff barrier* suppression *f*, *to new premises* déménagement *m*, IND *of oil by separators* épuration *f*; ~ **allowance** HRM indemnité de déménagement *f*; ~ **bond** FIN garantie sur déménagement *f*; ~ **note** IMP/EXP bordereau d'enlèvement *m*; ~ **of tax distortions** TAX suppression des déformations d'imposition *f*; ~ **van** TRANSP camion de déménagement *m*

remove *vt* COMP extraire, supprimer, GEN COMM *goods, restriction* enlever, *tariff barrier* supprimer; ◆ **do not** ~ GEN COMM à consulter sur place

remuneration *n* GEN COMM, HRM rémunération *f*; ~ **package** HRM salaire et avantages complémentaires *m pl*

remunerative *adj* GEN COMM rémunérateur

rename *vt* COMP renommer

render *vt* GEN COMM *cause to become* rendre; ◆ ~ **an accounting for sth** ACC établir une comptabilité de qch; ~ **null and void** LAW invalider, rendre nul et non avenu; ~ **obsolete** GEN COMM rendre désuet, rendre périmé

rendering: ~ **of services** *n* GEN COMM prestation de services *f*, services rendus *m pl*

renegotiate *vti* GEN COMM renégocier

renegotiated: ~ **rate mortgage** *n* BANK, PROP hypothèque à taux renégocié *f*

renegotiation *n* GEN COMM renégociation *f*

renew *vt* FIN *credit* renouveler, GEN COMM reconduire, renouveler, PATENTS renouveler, PROP *option* reconduire; ◆ ~ **one's subscription** MEDIA se réabonner

renewable: ~ **resource** *n* (ANT *nonrenewable resource*) ECON, ENVIR ressource renouvelable *f*

renewal *n* FIN *of credit* renouvellement *m*, GEN COMM reconduction *f*, renouvellement *m*, PATENTS renouvellement *m*, POL *of government*, WEL *of system* rénovation *f*; ~ **fee** PATENTS taxe annuelle *f*; ~ **of mortgage** BANK renouvellement d'hypothèque *m*; ~ **option** PROP option de reconduction *f*; ~ **of a subscription** MEDIA réabonnement *m*

renewed *adj* GEN COMM redoublé, renouvelé

renounce *vt* GEN COMM renoncer à

renovate *vt* GEN COMM remettre en bon état, remettre à neuf, rénover, PROP rénover

renovated *adj* GEN COMM remis à neuf, rénové, PROP rénové

renovation *n* GEN COMM remise à neuf *f*, rénovation *f*

renown *n* GEN COMM célébrité *f*, renommée *f*

renowned *adj* GEN COMM célèbre, de renom

rent:[1] ~ **-free** *adj* TAX exempt de loyer

rent[2] *n* GEN COMM *machine* prix de location *m*, PROP *of apartment, office* loyer *m*, *of car* location *f*; ~ **allowance** *n* WEL aide locative *f*; ~ **charge** *n* PROP, WEL redevance foncière *f*; ~ **collector** *n* PROP encaisseur de loyers *m*, receveur des loyers *m*; ~ **-free period** *n* PROP période gratuite *f*; ~ **freeze** *n* PROP gel des loyers *m*; ~ **pcm** *n BrE* (*rent per calendar month*) PROP loyer au mois *m*, loyer mensuel *m*; ~ **per calendar month** *n BrE* (*rent pcm*) PROP loyer au mois *m*, loyer mensuel *m*; ~ **rebate** *n* WEL diminution de loyer *f*, remboursement de loyer *m*, réduction sur le loyer *f*; ~ **receipt** *n* PROP quittance de loyer *f*; ~ **-up period** *n* PROP temps pour tout louer *m*; ◆ **for** ~ *AmE* PROP à louer

rent[3] *vt* PROP louer; ~ **out** PROP louer; ◆ **to** ~ PROP à louer

Rent: ~ **-a-Container** *n* (*Rentcon*) TRANSP société de location de conteneurs

rentable: ~ **area** *n* PROP quartier locatif *m*

rental *n* PROP *of apartment, office* loyer *m*, *of car* location *f*, *of machine* prix de location *m*; ~ **agreement** GEN COMM, PROP contrat de location *m*; ~ **cost** TAX *of property* coût de location *m*, montant locatif *m*; ~ **income** PROP, TAX revenu de location *m*, revenu locatif *m*; ~ **level** PROP niveau locatif *m*; ~ **payment** PROP paiement locatif *m*; ~ **period** TAX période de location *f*; ~ **rate** PROP taux locatif *m*; ~ **right** LAW, PATENTS *intellectual property* droit d'exploitation *m*, loyer *m*, redevance *f*; ~ **term** PROP terme locatif *m*; ~ **value** TAX valeur locative *f*

rentals *n pl* TAX biens de location *m pl*, locations *f pl*, loyers *m pl*

rental/turnover: ~ **ratio** *n* ACC taux locatif *m*

Rentcon *abbr* (*Rent-a-Container*) TRANSP société de location de conteneurs

renter *n* PROP *hirer, tenant* locataire *mf*, *owner* loueur *m*; ~ **'s tax credit** *Canada* TAX crédit d'impôt aux locataires *m* (*Can*)

rentier *n* PROP rentier *m*

renting *n* PROP *of apartment, office* loyer *m*, *of car* location *f*; ~ **out** PROP location *f*

reopener: ~ **clause** *n* HRM clause de réexamen avant terme *f*, clause de réouverture de la négociation *f*

reorder: ~ **form** *n* GEN COMM bon de commande de réassortiment *m*; ~ **point** *n* ACC seuil de commande *m*, seuil de réapprovisionnement *m*

reorganization *n* ECON restructuration *f*, FIN, GEN COMM, HRM, IND, MGMNT, STOCK restructuration *f*, réorganisation *f*; ~ **of capital** FIN remaniement de capital *m*

reorganize *vt* ECON, FIN, GEN COMM, HRM, IND, MGMNT, STOCK restructurer, réorganiser

rep *n* GEN COMM représentant *m*, LEIS troupe de théâtre de province *f*

Rep. *abbr US (Representative)* POL député *mf*, représentant *m*

REP *abbr (regional employment premium)* HRM indemnité d'emploi régional *f*, prime à l'emploi régional *f*

repack *vt* GEN COMM, IMP/EXP remballer, rempaqueter

repackage *vt* S&M *marketing* reconditionner

repackaging *n* S&M *marketing* reconditionnement *m*

repacking *n* GEN COMM, IMP/EXP remballage *m*, rempaquetage *m*

repair¹ *n* PROP réparation *f*; **~ kit** GEN COMM trousse de réparation *f*; **~ shop** GEN COMM atelier de réparation *m*; ◆ **in good ~** GEN COMM en bon état

repair² *vt* GEN COMM réparer

repairman *n* [pl -men] GEN COMM réparateur *m*

repairwoman *n* [pl -men] GEN COMM réparatrice *f*

reparation: **~ for damage** *n* INS indemnisation des dommages *f*

repatriate *vt* ECON *profits* rapatrier

repatriation *n* ECON *of profits* rapatriement *m*; **~ of capital** FIN, MGMNT remise de capital à la société mère *f*; **~ of funds** ECON rapatriement de capitaux *m*, rapatriement de fonds *m*; **~ of overseas funds** ECON rapatriement de capitaux détenus à l'étranger *m*, rapatriement de fonds étrangers *m*; **~ of profits** ECON rapatriement de bénéfices *m*

repay *vt* BANK, ECON *loan*, GEN COMM rembourser

repayable *adj* ACC, BANK, ECON, GEN COMM, TAX remboursable; **~ on demand** GEN COMM remboursable sur demande

repayment *n* BANK, ECON, GEN COMM remboursement *m*; **~ by acceleration** LAW remboursement par déchéance du terme *m*; **~ claim** TAX réclamation de remboursement *f*; **~ over 2 years** BANK remboursement échelonné sur 2 ans *m*; **~ schedule** BANK calendrier d'amortissement *m*, calendrier de remboursement *m*, FIN calendrier de remboursement *m*; **~ term** FIN délai de remboursement *m*

repeal *vt* LAW abroger, annuler; ◆ **~ a tax** TAX abroger un impôt

repeat:¹ **~ business** *n* GEN COMM commande renouvelée *f*; **~ buying** *n jarg* S&M *marketing* achats répétés *m pl*; **~ demand** *n* GEN COMM demande renouvelée *f*; **~ purchase** *n* GEN COMM achat renouvelé *m*; **~ rate** *n* S&M *marketing* taux de rachat *m*; **~ sales** *n pl* S&M ventes de renouvellement *f pl*, ventes répétées *f pl*

repeat² *vt* GEN COMM répéter

repeated: **~ warnings** *n pl* (SYN *iterative warnings*) GEN COMM avertissements répétés *m pl*

repercussions *n pl* GEN COMM contrecoup *m*, répercussions *f pl*

repertoire *n* COMP *instructions* répertoire *m*

repertory *n* LEIS troupe de théâtre de province *f*; **~ company** LEIS troupe de théâtre de province *f*

repetitive: **~ strain injury** *n (RSI)* ADMIN atteinte due à des tensions répétées *f*

replace *vt* GEN COMM remplacer; ◆ **~ the receiver** COMMS *telephone* raccrocher

replacement *n* GEN COMM remplacement *m*, échange standard *m*; **~ bond** STOCK obligation de remplacement *f*; **~ capital** FIN financement de remplacement *m*; **~ clause** INS *marine* clause de remplacement *f*; **~ cost** ACC coût de remplacement *m*, coût à l'origine *m*, ECON, INS coût de remplacement *m*; **~ cost accounting** (SYN *replacement costing*) ACC comptabilité au prix de remplacement *f*; **~ costing** (SYN *replacement cost accounting*) ACC comptabilité au prix de remplacement *f*; **~ engine** GEN COMM moteur de rechange *m*; **~ investment** ACC provision pour dépréciation *f*; **~ labor force** *AmE*, **~ labour force** *BrE* HRM main-d'oeuvre de remplacement *f*; **~ market** GEN COMM marché de remplacement *m*; **~ part** (SYN *spare part*) GEN COMM pièce de rechange *f*; **~ planning** ACC planification du remplacement *f*; **~ price** GEN COMM prix de remplacement *m*; **~ property** TAX bien de remplacement *m*; **~ ratio** WEL taux de remplacement *m*; **~ tax** TAX impôt de remplacement *m*; **~ technology** GEN COMM technologie de remplacement *f*; **~ value** ACC valeur de remplacement *f*

replay *vt* COMP relire, réécouter

replenish *vt* BANK *account*, FIN réapprovisionner, S&M restocker; ◆ **~ one's stocks** GEN COMM se réapprovisionner

replevin *n* LAW action possessoire *f*, mainlevée de saisie *f*

reply¹ *n* GEN COMM réponse *f*, LAW réplique *f*, réponse du demandeur *f*; **~ coupon** S&M coupon-réponse *m*; **~ device** S&M *mail order merchandising* coupon-réponse *m*; **~ paid** COMMS réponse payée *f*; **~ -paid card** COMMS carte avec réponse payée *f*, carte-réponse payée *f*; **~ vehicle** S&M *mail order merchandising* carte-réponse *f*

reply² *vi* GEN COMM répondre; ◆ **~ by return** COMMS répondre par retour du courrier

REPO *abbr AmE (repurchase agreement)* FIN contrat de vente à réméré *m*, STOCK contrat de vente à réméré *m*, mise en pension *f*, pension livrée *f*, prise en pension *f*

report¹ *n* ACC, ECON, FIN rapport *m*, GEN COMM compte-rendu *m*, rapport *m*, mémoire *m*, MEDIA reportage *m*; **~ card** *AmE (cf appraisal BrE)* HRM évaluation *f*; **~ file** COMP fichier d'édition *m*; **~ generation** COMP génération d'états *f*, génération de programmes d'édition *f*; **~ terminal** COMP terminal d'édition *m*, terminal éloigné *m*

report:² **~ a loss** *vi* (ANT *report a profit*) ACC constater une perte, déclarer une perte; **~ a profit** (ANT *report a loss*) ACC constater un profit, déclarer un profit; ◆ **~ one's conclusions** GEN COMM rapporter ses conclusions; **~ one's findings** GEN COMM rendre compte des résultats

reported: **as ~** *phr* MEDIA comme annoncé

reporter *n* MEDIA reporter *m*

reporting *n* ACC information comptable *f*, information financière *f*, S&M mercatique téléphonique *f*; ~ **corporation** *n* GEN COMM société déclarante *f*; ~ **currency** *n* FIN devise comptable *f*; ~ **day** *n* TRANSP *shipping* jour de déclaration *m*; ~ **dealer** *n* STOCK correspondant en valeurs du Trésor *m*, CVT; ~ **of income** *n* TAX déclaration de revenu *f*; ~ **object** *n* GEN COMM article de rapport *m*; ~ **object code** *n* ACC code d'article de rapport *m*; ~ **period** *n* TAX période de déclaration *f*; ~ **policy** *n* FIN convention de présentation *f*; ~ **requirements** *n pl* TAX conditions de déclaration *f pl*, exigences de déclaration *f pl*, exigences relatives aux déclarations *f pl*; ~ **restrictions** *n pl* UK *(cf gag order US)* MEDIA embargo *m*, interdiction de rapporter les débats *f*; ~ **standards** *n pl* GEN COMM normes de présentation de l'information *f pl*; ~ **system** *n* FIN système d'information comptable *m*; ~ **treatment** *n* ACC présentation des comptes annuels *f*

repositioning *n* S&M *marketing* repositionnement *m*

repository *n* ADMIN dépôt *m*

represent *vt* GEN COMM représenter, LAW attester, déclarer

representation *n* GEN COMM représentation *f*, LAW attestation *f*, déclaration *f*

representative *n* GEN COMM représentant *m*, visiteur *m*, LAW, PATENTS mandataire *mf*; ~ **firm** ECON entreprise représentative de son secteur d'activité; ~ **sample** MATH *statistics* échantillon type *m*

Representative *n* US *(Rep.)* POL député *mf*, représentant *m*

repressive: ~ **tax** *n* TAX impôt répressif *m*

reprocess *vt* ENVIR retraiter

reprocessing *n* ENVIR retraitement *m*; ~ **plant** ENVIR usine de retraitement *f*

reproduction *n* ECON reproduction *f*, GEN COMM copie *f*; ~ **cost** ACC valeur de reconstruction *f*; ~ **rate** ECON taux de reproduction *m*

reprogram *vt* COMP reprogrammer

reprography *n* MEDIA *print* reprographie *f*

rept *abbr (receipt)* BANK, FIN reçu *m*, GEN COMM quittance *f*, reçu *m*, récépissé *m*, S&M reçu *m*, récépissé *m*, STOCK reçu *m*, TRANSP reçu *m*, récépissé *m*

Republic: ~ **of Ireland** *pr n* GEN COMM République d'Irlande *f*

republish *vt* MEDIA *print* republier, rééditer

repudiate *vt* HRM *industrial action* contester, nier, refuser de prendre part à

repurchase *n* ECON *of debt* prise de contrôle *f*; ~ **agreement** FIN *AmE (REPO, RP)* contrat de vente à réméré *m*, STOCK *(REPO, RP)* contrat de vente à réméré *m*, mise en pension *f*, pension livrée *f*, prise en pension *f*; ~ **rate** BANK taux des prises en pension *m*

repurchased: ~ **share** *n* STOCK action autodétenue *f*

reputable: ~ **brand** *n* GEN COMM marque réputée *f*

reputation *n* GEN COMM réputation *f*

request[1] *n* GEN COMM demande *f*, requête *f*; ~ **for change** *(RFC)* TRANSP réaménagement *m*, *aviation* requête formulée par le client *f (RFC)*; ~ **for payment** FIN demande de paiement *f*; ~ **for proposals** FIN demande de propositions *f*; ~ **to off-load** TRANSP demande de décharger *f*; ◆ **at the ~ of** GEN COMM à la demande de; **make a ~** GEN COMM faire une demande; **make a ~ to the appropriate authority** GEN COMM faire une demande auprès des autorités compétentes

request[2] *vt* GEN COMM demander

require *vt* GEN COMM nécessiter, *action* exiger; ~ **sth of sb** GEN COMM exiger qch de qn

required: ~ **action** *n* GEN COMM action nécessaire *f*; ~ **freight rate** *n (RFR)* TRANSP tarif marchandises demandé *m*; ~ **rate of return** *n* FIN taux de rendement requis *m*; ~ **rental on capital** *n* ECON, FIN revenu minimal attendu du capital *m*; ~ **reserve ratio** *n* BANK coefficient de réserves obligatoires *m*; ~ **reserves** *n pl* BANK réserves obligatoires *f pl*

requirement *n* GEN COMM exigence *f*, TAX demande péremptoire *f*, exigence *f*

requirements *n pl* GEN COMM besoins *m pl*

requisition: ~ **for payment** *n* ACC demande de paiement *f*

rerouting *n* TRANSP détournement d'itinéraire *m*, modification d'itinéraire *f*

rerun[1] *n* COMP reprise *f*, réexécution *f*, GEN COMM reprise *f*

rerun[2] *vt* COMP, GEN COMM repasser, réexécuter

resale *n* GEN COMM, S&M revente *f*; ~ **market** S&M marché de la revente *m*; ~ **price** S&M prix de revente *m*; ~ **price maintenance** *(RPM)* ECON, FIN maintien du prix de revente *m*, prix de vente imposé *m*; ~ **value** S&M valeur de revente *f*

reschedule *vt* BANK *debt*, FIN, GEN COMM réaménager, rééchelonner

rescheduling *n* BANK *of debt*, FIN, GEN COMM réaménagement *m*, rééchelonnement *m*

rescind *vt* LAW annuler, rescinder

rescission *n* LAW annulation *f*, rescision *f*

res communis *phr* LAW, PROP copropriété *f*

rescription *n* STOCK *bills and money market paper* bon de marché monétaire *m*, bon du Trésor *m*, rescription *f (dat)*

rescue: **come to the ~ of** *phr* GEN COMM venir en aide à, venir à la rescousse de

research:[1] ~ -**intensive** *adj* IND *production* à fort coefficient de recherche; ~ -**orientated** *adj* IND orienté vers la recherche

research[2] *n* GEN COMM, HRM, IND, MGMNT recherche *f*, S&M *market research* enquête *f*, étude *f*; ~ **budget** ACC budget de recherche *m*; ~ **department** GEN COMM bureau d'étude *m*, service de recherche *m*; ~ **and development** *(R&D)* IND recherche et développement *f* *(R&D)*; ~ **and development limited partnership** FIN société en commandite de recherche et de développement *f*; ~ **and development product** IND, S&M produit recherche et développement *m*; ~ **director** HRM directeur de la recherche *m*; ~ **grant** TAX subvention de recherches *f*, subvention pour la recherche *f*; ~ **laboratory** IND laboratoire de recherche *m*; ~ **objective** GEN COMM objectif de recherche *m*; ~ **program** *AmE*, ~ **programme** *BrE* IND, WEL programme de recherche *m*; ~ **student** GEN COMM, WEL étudiant-chercheur *m*; ~ **survey** S&M *market research* suivi d'enquêtes *m*, suivi d'études de marché *m*; ~ **team** S&M *market research* équipe de chercheurs *f*; ~ **worker** GEN COMM, S&M, WEL chercheur *m*

researcher *n* GEN COMM *at university* chercheur *m*, MEDIA *newspaper, TV* documentaliste *mf*, S&M *market research*, WEL *at university* chercheur *m*

reseller: ~ **market** *n* S&M marché de la revente *m*

reservable[1] *adj* BANK soumis aux réserves

reservable:[2] ~ **day** *n* BANK jour des opérations au compte de réserve *m*

reservation *n* GEN COMM *of company name*, LEIS *of hotel room, theatre ticket*, S&M, TRANSP *of ticket, seat* réservation *f*; ~ **of cargo** TRANSP réservation de cargaison *f*; ~ **counter** GEN COMM, LEIS, TRANSP service des réservations *m*; ~ **form** GEN COMM, TRANSP confirmation de réservation *f*; ~ **price** S&M *auction sale* mise à prix *f*, prix de départ *m*, prix de réserve *m*, prix demandé *m*, prix minimum *m*, réserve *f*; ~ **system** GEN COMM, TRANSP système de réservation *m*; ~ **wage** *(SYN supply price)* HRM salaire d'offre minimum *m*; ◆ **make a ~** GEN COMM, LEIS *at hotel* réserver une chambre, TRANSP *for flight, train or bus journey* prendre une réservation, retenir une place; **off the ~** *jarg AmE (*ANT *on the reservation)* POL en congé du parti; **on the ~** *jarg AmE (*ANT *off the reservation)* POL dans la ligne du parti, fidèle à son parti

reserve[1] *n* ACC, BANK, ECON, ENVIR, FIN réserve *f*, S&M *auction sale* mise à prix *f*, prix de départ *m*, prix de réserve *m*, prix demandé *m*, prix minimum *m*, réserve *f*, TAX réserve *f*; ~ **account** *n* BANK compte de réserve *m*; ~ **army of labor** *n* *AmE*, ~ **army of labour** *n* *BrE* ECON, HRM réserve de main-d'oeuvre *f*; ~ **assets** *n pl* BANK actif de réserve *m*; ~ **-assets ratio** *n* ACC, FIN rapport passif-réserves *m*; ~ **bank** *n* BANK banque de réserve *f*; ~ **base** *n* BANK base de réserve *f*; ~ **burden** *n* BANK réserves *f pl*; ~ **currency** *n* GEN COMM monnaie de réserve *f*; ~ **deposit** *n (RD)* ECON dépôt de couverture bancaire *m*, réserve obligatoire *f*; ~ **entry** *n* ACC écriture de contrepassement *f*; ~ **for credit risk losses** *n* BANK provision pour pertes sur risques de crédit *f*; ~ **for statutory overruns** *n* ACC réserve pour dépassement des crédits législatifs *f*; ~ **for unpaid claims** *n* INS provisions pour sinistre à payer *f pl*,

réserve pour indemnités à liquider *f*, réserve pour réclamations non réglées *f*; ~ **fund** *n* FIN caisse de prévoyance *f*; ~ **liability** *n* INS passif de réserve *m*; ~ **price** *n* *BrE (cf upset price AmE)* GEN COMM, S&M *auction sale* mise à prix *f*, prix de départ *m*, prix de réserve *m*, prix demandé *m*, prix minimum *m*, réserve *f*; ~ **rate** *n* BANK coefficient de réserve *m*; ~ **ratio** *n* BANK coefficient de réserve *m*; ~ **requirements** *n pl* BANK réserves obligatoires *f pl*; ~ **-stock control** *n* GEN COMM contrôle du stock *m*; ◆ **keep in ~** GEN COMM garder en réserve

reserve[2] *vt* ADMIN, GEN COMM, LEIS, S&M, TRANSP réserver; ◆ ~ **judgment** LAW prononcer un jugement sous toutes réserves, réserver un jugement; ~ **the right to do** BANK, GEN COMM se réserver le droit de faire

Reserve: ~ **Bank of Australia** *n* BANK banque de réserve d'Australie *f*

reserved *adj* GEN COMM réservé

reserves *n pl* ACC, BANK, ECON, FIN réserves *f pl*

reset[1] *n* COMP remise à l'état initial *f*, remise à zéro *f*, restauration *f*, réinitialisation *f*; ~ **button** COMP bouton de remise à zéro *m*, touche de remise à zéro *f*

reset[2] *vt* COMP *clock, counter* remettre à zéro, *data* restaurer, réinitialiser

resettle *vt* GEN COMM *company* réimplanter

resettlement *n* GEN COMM *of company* réimplantation *f*

res gestae *phr frml* LAW faits matériels d'une affaire *m pl*, res gestae *(frml)*

reship *vt* TRANSP réexpédier

reshipped *adj* TRANSP réexpédié

reshipping *n* TRANSP réexpédition *f*

reside *vi* LAW, PROP, TAX résider; ◆ ~ **and work** LAW, PROP, TAX avoir domicile et travail, résider et travailler

residence *n* GEN COMM, PROP, TAX résidence *f*; ~ **permit** ADMIN carte de séjour *f*, permis de résidence *m*, permis de séjour *m*, HRM, WEL carte de séjour *f*; ~ **status** TAX condition de résidence *f*, détermination de la résidence *f*, détermination du lieu de résidence *f*; ~ **visa** ADMIN carte de séjour *f*, permis de résidence *m*, permis de séjour *m*, HRM, WEL carte de séjour *f*

residency *n* BANK *of depositor* statut résidentiel *m*, GEN COMM adresse *f*

resident[1] *adj* ADMIN, COMP, GEN COMM, TAX résidant

resident[2] *n* ADMIN, GEN COMM, TAX résident *m*; ~ **alien** ADMIN résident étranger *m*; ~ **bank** BANK banque résidente *f*; ~ **manager** PROP directeur résident *m*; ~ **population** ECON population résidente *f*; ~ **taxpayer** TAX résident contribuable *m*; ~ **trust** *UK* LAW acte fidéicommis établi au Royaume-Uni

residential[1] *adj* PROP *construction* résidentiel

residential:[2] ~ **accommodation** *n* PROP *having no commercial use* immeubles à usage d'habitation *m pl*; ~ **amount** *n* HRM revenu résiduel *m*; ~ **course** *n*

HRM stage à temps complet *m*; ~ **energy credit** *n* ENVIR crédit énergétique résidentiel; ~ **mortgage** *n* BANK prêt hypothécaire résidentiel *m*, prêt hypothécaire à l'habitation *m*; ~ **mortgage loan** *n* BANK prêt hypothécaire résidentiel *m*, prêt hypothécaire à l'habitation *m*; ~ **occupancy** *n* PROP immeuble d'habitation *m*; ~ **service contract** *n* INS *property* marché des services *m*; ~ **tax rate** *n* TAX taux de l'impôt foncier *m*

residual: ~ **error** *n* ECON erreur résiduelle *f*; ~ **family** *n* WEL foyer récalcitrant *m*; ~ **financial instrument** *n* FIN instrument financier résiduel *m*; ~ **lender** *n* FIN prêteur résiduel *m*; ~ **value** *n* TAX valeur résiduelle *f*

residuary: ~ **estate** *n* LAW, PROP, TAX propriété résiduaire *f*, propriété résiduelle *f*; ~ **legatee** *n* LAW légataire à qui échoit le reste d'une succession

residue *n* ENVIR *from industrial production* débris *m*, résidu *m*, FIN actif net *m*, reliquat *m*

residuum *n* LAW reste *m*, résidu *m*

resignation *n* ADMIN démission *f*, HRM démission *f*, résignation *f*; ~ **letter** COMMS, GEN COMM lettre de démission *f*; ◆ **hand in one's** ~ ADMIN, HRM démissionner, remettre sa démission

resigning: ~ **addendum** *n* INS *marine* addendum de renonciation *m*

resilience *n* ECON *of economy* ressort *m*, résistance *f*, HRM *of character* résistance *f*

res integra *phr frml* LAW res integra (*frml*)

res ipsa loquitur *phr frml* GEN COMM, LAW cela se passe de commentaires, la chose parle d'elle-même, res ipsa loquitur (*frml*)

resistance *n* GEN COMM résistance *f*; ~ **level** STOCK niveau de résistance *m*, palier de résistance *m*

res judicata *phr frml* LAW affaire jugée *f*, res judicata (*frml*)

res nullius *phr frml* LAW, PROP chose qui n'appartient à personne, res nullius (*frml*)

resolution *n* COMP *of screen* définition *f*, GEN COMM, MGMNT *decision, determination* décision *f*, résolution *f*; ◆ **make a composite** ~ HRM *on federal level*, POL faire accepter une résolution au niveau fédéral

resolutive: ~ **clause** *n* LAW clause résolutoire *f*

resolutory: ~ **condition** *n* LAW condition résolutoire *f*

resolve[1] *n* GEN COMM, MGMNT décision *f*, résolution *f*

resolve[2] *vt* GEN COMM *differences* régler, *problem* résoudre, MGMNT *problem* résoudre

resource *n* ACC, BANK, ECON, ENVIR, FIN, GEN COMM, HRM, IND, TAX *mineral* ressource *f*; ~ **aggregation** GEN COMM agrégation des ressources *loc f*; ~ **allocation** COMP, ECON prêt indexé *m*, FIN allocation des ressources *f*, répartition des ressources *f*; ~ **appraisal** ECON examen des ressources *m*, évaluation des ressources *f*, MGMNT examen des ressources *m*; ~ **availability** FIN disponibilité des ressources *f*; ~ **economics** ECON politique économique des ressources et de l'envi-

ronnement *f*; ~ **income** ACC, TAX *natural resources* revenu relatif à des ressources *m*, source de revenus *f*; ~ **industry** IND industrie extractive *f*; ~ **profile** GEN COMM profil des ressources *m*; ~ **time** GEN COMM durée d'utilisation de ressources *f*

resources *n pl* BANK, ECON, FIN, GEN COMM, HRM ressources *f pl*; ~ **management** *n* ENVIR, IND, MGMNT gestion des ressources *f*

respect:[1] **in this** ~ *phr* GEN COMM dans ce domaine, à ce propos; **in** ~ **of** *phr* GEN COMM quant à; **with** ~ **to** *phr* GEN COMM concernant, en ce qui concerne

respect[2] *vt* LAW respecter

respectable *adj* GEN COMM convenable

respectful *adj* GEN COMM respectueux

respectively *adv* GEN COMM respectivement

res perit domino *phr frml* LAW doctrine selon laquelle la perte d'une chose retombe sur son maître

respite: **without** ~ *phr* COMMS *from work* sans cesse, sans relâche, sans répit

respondeat superior *phr frml* GEN COMM doctrine selon laquelle le commettant répond des actes de son mandataire; que le supérieur soit tenu pour responsable, LAW doctrine selon laquelle le supérieur soit tenu pour responsable

respondent *n* LAW défendeur *m*, S&M *to market research survey* personne interrogée *f*

response *n* GEN COMM réponse *f*; ~ **projection** S&M *advertising* prévision des réponses *f*; ~ **rate** S&M *marketing* taux de réponse *m*; ◆ **give sb a dusty** ~ *infrml* GEN COMM envoyer promener qn (*infrml*), envoyer qn sur les roses (*infrml*); **in** ~ **to** GEN COMM *your advertisement* en réponse à, suite à

responsibility *n* ECON charge *f*, GEN COMM charge *f*, responsabilité *f*; ~ **accounting** FIN comptabilité des sections *f*; ~ **budgeting** ACC *by area of management responsibility* budgétisation en fonction de la gestion *f*; ~ **center** *AmE see* responsibility centre *BrE*; ~ **-center manager** *AmE see* responsibility centre manager *BrE*; ~ **centre** *BrE* ACC, FIN, MGMNT centre de responsabilité *m*; ~ **-centre manager** *BrE* ACC gestionnaire de centre de responsabilité *m*, responsable d'un centre de gestion *m*; ~ **classification** ACC classification par responsabilité *f*; ◆ **take** ~ **for sth** GEN COMM prendre la responsabilité de qch

responsible *adj* GEN COMM responsable; ◆ ~ **in law** LAW responsable en droit, responsable légalement

responsive *adj* ECON, GEN COMM qui réagit rapidement, sensible

rest:[1] ~ **account** *n* (*SYN rest fund*) STOCK fonds de réserve *m*; ~ **fund** *n* (*SYN rest account*) STOCK fonds de réserve *m*; ~ **room** *n AmE* (*cf lavatory BrE, toilet BrE, washroom*) GEN COMM toilettes *f pl*; **the** ~ **of the world** *n* (*ROW*) ECON le reste du monde *m*

rest:[2] ~ **heavily on** *phr* GEN COMM peser lourdement sur; ~ **one's case** *phr* LAW conclure sa plaidoirie, conclure son plaidoyer

restart[1] *n* COMP *of system, hardware* redémarrage *m*, relance *f*, ECON *of economy* redémarrage *m*; ~ **program** COMP programme de relance *m*

restart[2] *vt* COMP *system, hardware* redémarrer, relancer, ECON *economy* redémarrer

restaurant *n* GEN COMM restaurant *m*; ~ **car** TRANSP wagon-restaurant *m*; ~ **proprietor** HRM propriétaire de restaurant *m*

restaurateur *n* GEN COMM, HRM restaurateur *m*

resting: ~ **order** *n* STOCK ordre de vente *m*, ordre en attente *m*

restitutio in integrum *phr frml* HRM, LAW réintégration de qn dans sa position

restock *vt* S&M réapprovisionner

restore *vt* COMP *file, directory* remettre en bon état, restaurer, GEN COMM rétablir; ◆ ~ **law and order** LAW rétablir l'ordre public

restowage *n* TRANSP réarrimage *m*

restraint: ~ **of alienation** *n* LAW interdiction d'aliénation *f*, restriction au pouvoir d'aliéner un bien *f*; ~ **of trade** *n* ECON entrave à la liberté du commerce *f*, restriction à la liberté du commerce *f*

restrict *vt* GEN COMM *numbers*, LAW *rights* limiter, restreindre

restricted[1] *adj* LAW *rights* limité, POL secret

restricted:[2] ~ **account** *n* STOCK compte de marge en débit *m*, compte limité *m*; ~ **area** *n* TRANSP *aviation* zone réglementée *f*, *on road* zone limitée *f*; ~ **articles** *n* (*REART*) TRANSP *aviation* article réglementé *m*; ~ **credit** *n* BANK crédit restreint *m*; ~ **letter of credit** *n* BANK lettre de crédit limitée *f*; ~ **market** *n* ECON marché restreint *m*; ~ **speed area** *n* TRANSP *on road* zone à vitesse limitée *f*; ~ **surplus** *n* *AmE* (*cf undistributable reserves BrE*) ACC réserves indisponibles *f pl*

Restricted: ~ **Articles Terminal System** *n* (*RATS*) TRANSP *IATA* système de terminal pour articles réglementés *m*

restricting *adj* GEN COMM contraignant

restriction *n* GEN COMM, LAW, TRANSP restriction *f*; ~ **of credit** FIN limitation du crédit *f*

restrictive[1] *adj* ECON, GEN COMM, IND restrictif

restrictive:[2] ~ **monetary policy** *n* ECON politique monétaire restrictive *f*; ~ **practice** *n* ECON atteinte à la libre concurrence *f*, IND pratique restrictive *f*, LAW atteinte à la libre concurrence *f*; ~ **practices** *n pl* IND *by trade unions* pratiques restrictives *f pl*, LAW ententes *f pl*, entraves au commerce *f pl*, pratiques restrictives *f pl*

Restrictive: ~ **Practices Court** *n* UK (*R.P.Ct.*) GEN COMM, LAW tribunal chargé de l'application des lois antitrusts, tribunal statuant sur toute atteinte à la libre concurrence *m*

restructure *vt* ECON, FIN, GEN COMM, HRM, IND, MGMNT, STOCK restructurer

restructured[1] *adj* ECON, FIN, GEN COMM, HRM, IND, MGMNT, STOCK restructuré

restructured:[2] ~ **loan** *n* BANK prêt restructuré *m*

restructuring *n* ECON, FIN, GEN COMM, HRM, IND, MGMNT, STOCK restructuration *f*; ~ **of industry** IND restructuration industrielle *f*

result[1] *n* GEN COMM résultat *m*, suite *f*; ◆ **as a ~** GEN COMM en conséquence, par conséquent; **with the ~ that** GEN COMM de sorte que

result:[2] ~ **in** *vt* GEN COMM aboutir à, entraîner

results *n pl* FIN, GEN COMM *trading figures* résultats *m pl*; ◆ **get ~** HRM obtenir de bons résultats

resume *vi* GEN COMM *start again* repartir, reprendre

résumé *n* GEN COMM *summary* résumé *m*, HRM *AmE* (SYN *curriculum vitae*) curriculum vitae *m*

resurgence: ~ **in prices** *n* GEN COMM nouvelle flambée des prix *f*

resyndication: ~ **limited partnership** *n* PROP société resyndicataire en commandite *f*

retail[1] *adj* S&M au détail *loc m*, de détail *loc m*

retail:[2] ~ **audit** *n* S&M *marketing* contrôle des points de vente *m*; ~ **bank** *n* BANK, FIN banque commerciale *f*, banque de réseau *f*; ~ **banking** *n* BANK banque de détail *f*, services bancaires de détail *m pl*; ~ **broker** *n* STOCK courtier de détail *m*; ~ **business** *n* S&M commerce de détail *m*; ~ **center** *n* *AmE*, ~ **centre** *n* *BrE* GEN COMM, PROP, S&M centre de commerce *m*; ~ **coop** *n* S&M coopérative de détaillants *f*; ~ **cooperative** *n* S&M coopérative de détaillants *f*; ~ **deposit** *n* STOCK dépôt de détail *m*; ~ **deposits** *n pl* BANK dépôts bancaires *m pl*; ~ **-display allowance** *n* S&M remise au détaillant pour mise en avant des produits *f*; ~ **floorspace** *n* S&M surface consacrée à la vente au détail *f*; ~ **food business** *n* S&M commerce alimentaire de détail *m*; ~ **food trade** *n* S&M commerce alimentaire de détail *m*; ~ **house** *n* FIN société de courtage *f*; ~ **investor** *n* FIN épargnant *m*; ~ **management** *n* S&M gestion de la vente au détail *f*; ~ **margin** *n* S&M marge de détail *f*; ~ **network** *n* S&M réseau de détaillants *m*; ~ **offer** *n* STOCK offre au détail *f*; ~ **outlet** *n* S&M point de vente de services de détail *m*; ~ **park** *n* GEN COMM, S&M zone commerciale *f*; ~ **price index** *n* (*RPI*) ECON, GEN COMM indice des prix de détail *m*; ~ **price maintenance** *n* (*RPM*) S&M *sales* maintien du prix de revente *m*, prix de vente imposé *m*; ~ **property** *n* PROP immobilier détaillé *m*; ~ **sale** *n* S&M vente au détail *f*; ~ **sales analysis** *n* S&M analyse des ventes au détail *f*; ~ **trade** *n* S&M commerce de détail *m*; ~ **trader** *n* S&M détaillant *m*; ~ **warehouse** *n* S&M entrepôt de vente au détail *m*

retail[3] **1.** *vt* S&M détailler, vendre au détail; **2.** *vi* S&M se détailler, se vendre au détail

retailer *n* S&M détaillant *m*, fournisseur *m*

retailing *n* S&M vente au détail *f*

retain *vt* STOCK *shares* garder, retenir; ◆ ~ **sb's services** GEN COMM s'attacher les services de qn

retainage *n* PROP retenue *f*

retained: ~ **earnings** *n pl* ACC, FIN bénéfices non-distribués *m pl*, bénéfices non-répartis *m pl*; ~ **income** *n* ACC, FIN bénéfices non-distribués *m pl*, bénéfices non-répartis *m pl*; ~ **profits** *n pl* ACC, FIN bénéfices non-distribués *m pl*, bénéfices non-répartis *m pl*

retainer *n* FIN somme versée à l'avance *f*, PROP loyer réduit *m*; ◆ **be on a** ~ GEN COMM être sous contrat

retaliation: in ~ *phr* GEN COMM en représailles *loc f*

retaliatory: ~ **eviction** *n* PROP expulsion de représailles *f*; ~ **measures** *n pl* GEN COMM mesures de représailles *f pl*

retendering *n* STOCK nouvelle offre *f*

retention *n* INS rétention *f*; ~ **bond** ECON, STOCK *international trade* obligation de garantie *f*; ~ **date** GEN COMM date d'expiration *f*; ~ **money** GEN COMM dépôt de garantie *m*; ~ **on wages** HRM retenue sur salaire *f*; ~ **period** STOCK *for shares allocated to employees* période de maintien *f*; ~ **requirement** TAX demande de retenue *f*

rethink *vt* GEN COMM repenser

retire 1. *vt* ECON racheter, FIN mettre à la retraite, racheter, GEN COMM racheter, HRM mettre à la retraite, STOCK racheter, rembourser; **2.** *vi* HRM prendre sa retraite; ◆ ~ **from business** GEN COMM se retirer des affaires; ~ **on a pension** HRM toucher une retraite

retired: ~ **person** *n (cf retiree AmE)* GEN COMM, HRM, WEL retraité *m*

retiree *n AmE (cf retired person)* GEN COMM, HRM, WEL retraité *m*

retirement *n* FIN retraite *f*, GEN COMM cessation d'activité *f*, HRM, WEL retraite *f*; ~ **age** *n* HRM âge de la retraite *m*; ~ **annuity policy** *n UK* FIN, TAX police d'assurance qui fournit une rente viagère à l'âge de la retraite; ~ **contribution** *n* TAX cotisation retraite *f*; ~ **of debt** *n* FIN retraite de dette *f*; ~ **fund** *n* ACC, FIN, HRM, INS caisse de retraite *f*; ~ **income** *n* HRM, TAX revenu de retraite *m*; ~ **income security act** *n* HRM, LAW loi sur la sécurité des revenus des personnes retraitées *f*; ~ **issue certificate** *n UK* STOCK bon du Trésor indexé *m*, emprunt d'État indexé *m*; ~ **pay** *n* FIN, INS, WEL pension de retraite *f*; ~ **payments** *n pl* FIN *EU* indemnités de cessation *f pl*; ~ **pension** *n* FIN, INS, WEL pension de retraite *f*; ~ **pension rights** *n pl* FIN *EU* droit à pension d'ancienneté *m*; ~ **plan** *n* FIN, HRM, INS, WEL régime de retraite *m*; ~ **relief** *n UK* TAX allègement de retraite *m*; ~ **savings plan** *n* BANK, FIN, HRM plan d'épargne-retraite *m*; ~ **savings program** *n AmE*, ~ **savings programme** *n BrE* BANK, FIN, HRM plan d'épargne-retraite *m*; ~ **scheme** *n* FIN, HRM, INS, WEL régime de retraite *m*; ◆ **go into** ~ HRM partir en retraite; **take early** ~ HRM prendre une retraite anticipée

retiring: ~ **allowance** *n* FIN, INS, WEL pension de retraite *f*

retracement *n* GEN COMM renversement de la tendance *m*

retractable[1] *adj* STOCK *share, bond* encaissable par anticipation, rachetable au gré du porteur

retractable:[2] ~ **bond** *n* STOCK obligation encaissable par anticipation *f*; ~ **share** *n* STOCK action rachetable au gré du porteur *f*

retraction *n* STOCK encaissement par anticipation *m*, rachat par anticipation *m*

retraining *n* HRM recyclage *m*; ~ **course** HRM stage de recyclage *m*

retranslation *n* ECON *of foreign currency* reconversion *f*

retrench *vt* ECON, FIN, HRM *costs* réduire

retrenchment *n* ECON, FIN, HRM *of costs* réduction *f*

retrieval *n* COMP extraction *f*, récupération *f*; ~ **time** COMP temps d'accès à l'information *m*

retrieve *vt* COMP *data, file* extraire, rapatrier, retrouver, récupérer

retroactive[1] *adj* GEN COMM rétroactif

retroactive:[2] ~ **adjustment** *n* ECON ajustement rétroactif *m*; ~ **classification** *n* POL classement rétroactif *m*

retrogress *vi* ECON régresser

retrogression *n* ECON régression *f*

retrospective: ~ **claim** *n* INS demande rétroactive de déduction *f*; ~ **pay** *n* HRM arriéré de salaire *m*; ~ **rebate** *n* TRANSP *shipping* remise consentie avec effet rétroactif *f*

return[1] *n* ACC rendement *m*, COMMS, COMP retour *m*, FIN rendement *m*, GEN COMM rendement *m*, retour *m*, S&M retour *m*, STOCK taux de rendement *m*; ~ **address** COMMS adresse de l'expéditeur *f*; ~ **of amount overpaid** GEN COMM *by tax-collection services* restitution d'un trop-perçu *f*; ~ **cargo** *(RC)* TRANSP cargaison de retour *f*; ~ **fare** *BrE (cf round-trip fare AmE)* TRANSP prix d'un aller-retour *m*; ~ **flight** LEIS, TRANSP vol de retour *m*; ~ **freight** TRANSP fret de retour *m*; ~ **of guarantee** GEN COMM restitution de la garantie *f*; ~ **of income** TAX déclaration de revenus *f*; ~ **load** TRANSP chargement de retour *m*; ~ **on assets** ACC, FIN rendement de l'actif *m*, taux de rentabilité des actifs utilisés *m*, FIN rendement des fonds propres *m*, STOCK rendement de l'actif *m*, taux de rentabilité des actifs utilisés *m*; ~ **on capital** *(ROC)* ACC, ECON, FIN rendement du capital *m*; ~ **on capital employed** *(ROCE)* ACC, ECON, FIN rentabilité des capitaux investis *f (RCI)*; ~ **on equity** *(ROE)* ACC, FIN, STOCK rendement de l'action *m*, rendement des capitaux propres *m*, rendement des fonds propres *m*; ~ **on invested capital** *(ROIC)* ACC, ECON, FIN rendement du capital investi *m*; ~ **on investment** *(ROI)* ACC, FIN rendement des actifs *m*, rendement des investissements *m*, rentabilité d'investissements *f*, rentabilité des actifs *f*, taux de rentabilité d'un investissement *m*; ~ **on net assets** ACC, FIN, STOCK rendement de l'actif net *m*; ~ **on net assets employed** ACC, FIN, STOCK rendement de l'actif net employé *m*, taux de rentabilité des actifs nets utilisés *m*; ~ **on real estate** PROP revenu immobilier *m*; ~ **on sales** ACC taux de bénéfice au chiffre d'affaires *m*, FIN rentabilité des ventes *f*, S&M marge commerciale *f*, rentabilité des ventes *f*, taux de marge brute *m*; ~ **ticket** BrE *(cf round-trip ticket AmE)* TRANSP aller-retour *m*, billet aller-retour *m*; ~ **to sender** COMMS retour à l'envoyeur; ~ **to work** HRM retour à l'emploi *m*; ◆ **by** ~ **of post** COMMS par retour du courrier; **in** ~ **for** GEN COMM en échange de

return² *vt* COMMS *package sent to invalid address*, GEN COMM, S&M *goods sold* renvoyer, retourner; ◆ ~ **to port for orders** *(RP)*, TRANSP *shipping* retour au port en attendant des instructions; ~ **to sender** COMMS retourner à l'envoyeur

returnable¹ *adj* ENVIR *bottle* consigné

returnable:² ~ **goods** *n pl* GEN COMM marchandises consignées *f pl*

returned: ~ **book** *n* MEDIA invendu *m*; ~ **check** *n* AmE, ~ **cheque** *n* BrE BANK chèque refusé *m*, chèque retourné *m*; ~ **goods** *n pl* GEN COMM marchandises reprises *f pl*, marchandises retournées *f pl*

returns: ~ **to scale** *n pl* ECON, FIN, STOCK rendements d'échelle *m pl*

retype *vt* COMP refrapper

reunification *n* GEN COMM *of Germany* réunification *f*

Reunion: ~ **Island** *pr n* GEN COMM Ile de la Réunion *f*, Réunion *f*

reuse¹ *n* ENVIR remploi *m*

reuse² *vt* ENVIR remployer, réutiliser

REV *abbr (reversing)* GEN COMM renversement *m*

revalorization *n* ECON revalorisation *f*

revaluation *n* ACC, ECON, FIN réévaluation *f*; ~ **of assets** ACC, FIN réévaluation des actifs *f*; ~ **of exchange rate** ECON réévaluation du taux de change *f*; ~ **reserves** ACC réserves de réévaluation *f pl*

revalue *vt* ACC *assets*, ECON, FIN réévaluer

revamp *vt* GEN COMM moderniser, rénover, transformer, S&M *product image, shop design* rafraîchir

revamping *n* GEN COMM modernisation *f*, rénovation *f*, transformation *f*, S&M *of product image, shop design* rafraîchissement *m*

revealed: ~ **preference** *n* ECON indice d'utilité *m*, préférence révélée *f*, util *m*

revenue *n* ACC revenu *m*, ECON, FIN, TAX *Inland Revenue* impôts *m pl, company, individual* recettes *f pl*, revenu *m*; ~ **allocation** *n* GEN COMM répartition des recettes *f*, TAX attribution des recettes *f*, TRANSP *obtained from transport service* répartition des recettes *f*; ~ **anticipation note** *n (RAN)* STOCK avis fiscal anticipé *m*; ~ **budget** *n* ACC budget de recettes *m*, budget de ventes *m*; ~ **center** *n* AmE, ~ **centre** *n* BrE GEN COMM services fiscaux *m pl*; ~ **curve** *n* ECON courbe de recettes *f*; ~ **department** *n* TAX service des contributions *m*; ~ **dependency** *n* FIN abattement pour personne à charge *m*; ~ **dilution** *n* GEN COMM dilution des revenus *f*; ~ **earner** *n* ECON générateur de recettes *m*; ~ **economy** *n* ECON économie collectiviste *f*; ~ **and expenses** *n pl* ACC produits et charges *m pl*; ~ **guarantee** *n* TAX garantie de revenu *f*, garantie des recettes *f*; ~ **loss** *n* ACC perte courante *f*, perte d'exploitation *f*; ~ **maximization** *n* ECON, S&M maximisation des recettes *f*, optimisation des revenus *f*, optimisation des ventes *f*; ~ **neutral** *n* TAX contribution neutre *f*; ~ **office** *n* TAX bureau des contributions *m*; ~ **officer** *n* HRM, TAX inspecteur des impôts *m*; ~ **production** *n* ECON, GEN COMM production de revenus *f*; ~ **project** *n* GEN COMM projet d'accroissement des revenus *m*; ~ **ruling** *n* TAX code des impôts *m*; ~ **sharing** *n* US ECON finance fédérale *f*, redistribution partielle des recettes de l'État *f*; ~ **test** *n* ACC critère de recettes *m*; ~ **trust account** *n* FIN compte de recettes en fiducie *m*

reversal *n* ACC *bookkeeping* contre-passation *f*, passation *f*, FIN contre-passation *f*

reverse:¹ ~ **causation hypothesis** *n* ECON hypothèse du renversement de la relation de cause à effet *f*; ~ **channel** *n* COMP canal de retour *m*, voie de retour *f*; ~ **charge call** *n* BrE *(cf collect call AmE)* COMMS appel en PCV *m (Fra)*, appel à frais virés *m (Can)*, communication en PCV *f*; ~ **conversion** *n* STOCK conversion inverse *f*, stratégie d'arbitrage inversée *f*; ~ **discrimination** *n* WEL discrimination inverse *f*, racisme à l'envers *m*; ~ **engineering** *n* GEN COMM démontage *m*; ~ **gearing** *n* BrE *(cf reverse leverage AmE)* ACC, FIN effet de levier négatif *m*; ~ **income tax** *n* TAX impôt sur le revenu inversé *m*; ~ **J-shaped frequency curve** *n* MATH courbe de fréquence en J renversé *f*; ~ **leverage** *n* AmE *(cf reverse gearing BrE)* ACC, FIN effet de levier négatif *m*; ~ **printing** *n* COMP impression de droite à gauche *f*; ~ **repurchase** *n* FIN mise en pension inverse *f*; ~ **repurchase agreement** *n* FIN contrat de vente à réméré *m*, STOCK contrat de vente à réméré *m*, prise en pension *f*; ~ **split** *n* FIN, STOCK regroupement d'actions *m*; ~ **takeover** *n* ECON, FIN OPA à rebours *f*, contre-OPA *f*, contre-offre publique d'achat *f*, prise de contrôle *f*; ~ **triangular merger** *n* ECON, GEN COMM fusion triangulaire inversée *f*; ~ **video** *n* COMP vidéo inverse *f*; ~ **yield gap** *n* BANK, ECON, STOCK courbe des taux inversée *f*, écart de rendement inverse *m*

reverse² *vt* ACC contre-passer, ECON *trend*, GEN COMM inverser; ◆ ~ **the charges** BrE *(cf call collect AmE)*, COMMS téléphoner en PCV *(Fra)*, appeler à frais virés *(Can)*; ~ **an entry** ACC contre-passer une écriture; **make a** ~ **charge call to sb** BrE *(cf call collect AmE, call sb collect AmE, make a collect call AmE)* COMMS appeler en PCV, appeler à frais virés *(Can)*, téléphoner en PCV *(Fra)*; ~ **a mortgage** BANK contre-passer une hypothèque; ~ **a swap** STOCK contre-passer un crédit croisé, inverser un swap

reversed: ~ **takeover** *n* ECON, FIN OPA à rebours *f*, contre-OPA *f*, contre-offre publique d'achat *f*, prise de contrôle *f*

reversible[1] *adj* TRANSP *shipping, charter party* réversible

reversible:[2] ~ **kingpin** *n* TRANSP *on trailer* pivot d'attelage réversible *m*; ~ **lay days** *n pl* TRANSP *shipping, charter party* jours de planche réversibles *m pl*, staries réversibles *f pl*; ~ **laytime** *n* TRANSP *shipping, charter party* temps de planche réversible *m*; ~ **pallet** *n* TRANSP palette réversible *f*; ~ **stacking cone** *n* TRANSP cône d'empilage réversible *m*

reversing *n* ACC, FIN contre-passation *f*, GEN COMM renversement *m*; ~ **entry** ACC écriture d'annulation *f*, écriture de contrepassation *f*; ~ **gear clutch** *(RC)* TRANSP embrayage de renversement de marche *m*

reversionary: ~ **annuity** *n* INS rente de survie *f*, rente réversible *f*; ~ **bonus** *n* ECON, FIN, INS bonus réversible *m*, prime de fin de contrat *f*; ~ **factor** *n* MATH *statistics* facteur de réversion *m*; ~ **value** *n* PROP valeur de réversion *f*

reversioner *n* HRM bénéficiaire d'une rente réversible *m*

review[1] *n* HRM révision *f*, MGMNT révision *f*, *examination* examen *m*; ~ **body** HRM organisme de révision salariale; ◆ **under** ~ GEN COMM en cours de révision

review[2] *vt* GEN COMM, HRM, LAW, MGMNT revoir, réviser

revise *vt* GEN COMM réviser, LAW modifier, réviser; ◆ ~ **downward** GEN COMM revoir à la baisse; ~ **upward** GEN COMM revoir à la hausse

revised: ~ **edition** *n* MEDIA *print, publishing* édition corrigée et augmentée *f*, édition revue et corrigée *f*; ~ **figures** *n pl* GEN COMM chiffres corrigés *m pl*; ~ **net income** *n* TAX revenu net révisé *m*; ~ **version** *n* MEDIA *print, publishing* version actualisée *f*, version révisée *f*

revision *n* GEN COMM révision *f*, LAW modification *f*, révision *f*

revitalization *n* GEN COMM revitalisation *f*

revival *n* LEIS *of show* reprise *f*

revive *vt* GEN COMM ranimer

revocable[1] *adj* GEN COMM révocable

revocable:[2] ~ **credit** *n* BANK crédit révocable *m*; ~ **trust** *n* FIN société d'investissement révocable *f*

revocation *n* FIN *of pension plan* annulation *f*, PATENTS nullité *f*

revoke *vt* FIN *pension plan* annuler, PATENTS déclarer nul

revolution *n* ECON, POL révolution *f*

revolving: ~ **acceptance facility by tender** *n* *(RAFT)* FIN acceptation renouvelable par offre; ~ **bank line** *n* FIN ligne de crédit renouvelable *f*; ~ **charge account** *n* BANK accord de paiement différé renouvelable *m*; ~ **credit** *n* BANK, FIN crédit permanent *m*, crédit renouvelable *m*, crédit revolving *m*; ~ **credit line** *n* FIN ligne de crédit renouvelable *f*; ~ **fund** *n* FIN fonds renouvelable

m; ~ **line of credit** *n* FIN ligne de crédit renouvelable *f*; ~ **underwriting facility** *n* *(RUF)* INS *investment banking* garantie d'émission renouvelable *f*, moyen de souscription renouvelable *m*

reward *n* GEN COMM rétribution *f*; ◆ **as a** ~ **for** GEN COMM en récompense de

rewarding *adj* GEN COMM, HRM *job* gratifiant

rewind *vt* COMP, MEDIA *cassette, tape* rembobiner

rewrite *vt* COMP *software* récrire, réécrire, écrire de nouveau, GEN COMM remanier, récrire, réécrire, MEDIA *print* mettre en forme (*jarg*), remanier, récrire, réécrire

Reykjavik *pr n* GEN COMM Reykjavik *n pr*

rf *abbr* (*rise of floor*) TRANSP acculement *m*, relevé des varangues *m*

RFC *abbr* (*request for change*) TRANSP réaménagement *m*, aviation RFC (*requêt formulée par le client*)

RFD *abbr* (*raised foredeck*) TRANSP *shipping* demi-gaillard *m*

RFR *abbr* (*required freight rate*) TRANSP tarif marchandises demandé *m*

RHA *abbr* UK (*Road Haulage Association*) TRANSP association britannique des transports routiers

rhetoric *n* ECON, GEN COMM rhétorique *f*

Rhinelands: ~ **hourglass** *n* ECON axe lotharingien *m*

RHV *abbr* (*road haulage vehicle*) TRANSP poids lourd *m*

rial *n* GEN COMM rial *m*

ribbed: ~ **furnace** *n* TRANSP *shipping* foyer à parois ondulés *m*

ribbon *n* MEDIA *print* bandeau *m*; ~ **cartridge** COMP cartouche de ruban *f*

RIC *abbr* (*rehabilitation import credit*) ECON, FIN crédit à l'importation pour le redressement économique *m*

Ricardian: ~ **equivalence theorem** *n* (SYN *Ricardo invariance principle*) ECON principe d'invariance de Ricardo *m*, théorème d'équivalence de Ricardo *m*; ~ **theory of value** *n* ECON loi de la valeur de Ricardo *f*

Ricardo: ~ **effect** *n* ECON effet Ricardo *m*; ~ **invariance principle** *n* (SYN *Ricardian equivalence theorem*) ECON principe d'invariance de Ricardo *m*, théorème d'équivalence de Ricardo *m*

rich[1] *adj* GEN COMM riche; ◆ **get** ~ GEN COMM s'enrichir

rich:[2] **the** ~ *n* GEN COMM les riches *m pl*

rid: **get** ~ **of** *phr* GEN COMM se débarrasser de

RIE *abbr* STOCK (*recognized investment exchange*) marché d'investissement agréé *m*, STOCK UK (*Registered International Exchange*) échanges internationaux autorisés *m pl*

riel *n* GEN COMM riel *m*

RIF *abbr* (*reduction in force*) HRM réduction d'emplois secondaires *f*, suppression d'emplois *f*

rig: ~ **the market** *phr* STOCK manipuler le marché, provoquer une hausse fictive du marché

Riga *pr n* GEN COMM Riga *n pr*

rigged: ~ **market** *n* STOCK marché manipulé *m*, marché trafiqué à la hausse *m*

rigger *n* HRM, TRANSP *shipping* employé du lamanage *m*, gréeur *m*, lamaneur *m*, saisisseur *m*

rigging *n jarg* HRM *industrial relations* coup *m*, STOCK *of market* manipulation *f*

right:[1] ~ -**justified** *adj (*ANT *left-justified)* COMMS, COMP, MEDIA aligné à droite, au fer à droite, justifié à droite; ~ -**wing** *adj (*ANT *left-wing)* POL de droite; ◆ **be on the ~ track** GEN COMM être sur la bonne voie

right[2] *n* LAW droit *m*; ~ **of appeal** LAW droit d'appel *m*, droit de recours *m*; ~ **column** *(*ANT *left column)* ACC colonne de droite *f*; ~ **of combination** LAW droit syndical *m*; ~ **of entry** LAW droit de prendre possession *m*; ~ **of establishment** LAW droit d'établissement *m*; ~ -**hand column** *(*ANT *left-hand column)* GEN COMM colonne de droite *f*; ~ -**hand drive automobile** *AmE (*ANT *left-hand drive automobile)* TRANSP voiture avec la conduite à droite *f*; ~ -**hand drive car** *BrE (*ANT *left-hand drive car)* TRANSP voiture avec la conduite à droite *f*; ~ **of interest in a share** STOCK droit afférent à une action *m*; ~ **of offset** BANK droit de compensation *m*; ~ **on share issue** STOCK droit de souscription *m*; ~ **of recovery** LAW droit d'indemnisation *m*, droit à des dommages-intérêts *m*, droit à réparation *m*; ~ **of redemption** FIN droit de remboursement *m*; ~ **of redress** LAW droit à réparation *m*; ~ **of reply** LAW droit de réponse *m*; ~ **of rescission** LAW droit de rescision *m*; ~ **of residence** ADMIN droit de résidence *m*, droit de séjour *m*; ~ **of resumption** LAW droit de reprise *m*; ~ **of return** GEN COMM droit de retour *m*; ~ **shift** *(*ANT *left shift)* COMP décalage à droite *m*; ~ **of survivorship** LAW droit du survivant *m*; ~ **time** TRANSP *of departure, arrival* heure précise *f*; ~ **to associate** POL liberté d'association *f*; ~ **to convert** STOCK droit de conversion *m*; ~ **to dissociate** *UK* HRM liberté de dissociation *f*; ~ **to know** POL droit à l'information *m*; ~ **to manage** HRM liberté de direction *f*; ~ **to organize** HRM liberté syndicale *f*; ~ **to a patent** LAW, PATENTS droit au brevet *m*; ~ **to strike** HRM droit de grève *m*; ~ **to vote** POL droit de vote *m*; ~ **to work** HRM, LAW droit au travail *m*; ~ **to work state** *US* LAW État du droit au travail *m*; ~ **of way** LAW droit de passage *m*; ◆ **give the ~** GEN COMM *to do sth* accorder le droit; **give sb the ~ to do** GEN COMM accorder à qn le droit de faire, autoriser qn à faire; **with no ~ of appeal** LAW sans appel

right[3] *vt* ACC *balance*, GEN COMM *balance* redresser; ~ -**justify** *(*ANT *left-justify)* COMMS, COMP, MEDIA *print* aligner à droite, justifier à droite

Right: ~ **Honourable** *adj (Rt Hon)* POL très honorable

rightful: ~ **heir** *n* LAW, PROP héritier légitime *m*; ~ **owner** *n* LAW propriétaire légitime *m*

rightism *n (*ANT *leftism)* POL *Communist countries* droitisme *m*

rights *n pl* LAW, PATENTS *intellectual property* droits *m pl*; ~ **and actions** *n pl* LAW, PATENTS *intellectual property* droits et actions *m pl*; ~ **afforded by sb** *n pl* PATENTS droits conférés par qn *m pl*; ~ **of conversion** *n pl* STOCK droits de conversion *m pl*; ~ **of exchange** *n pl* STOCK droits d'échange *m pl*; ~ **holder** *n* STOCK porteur de droits de souscription *m*; ~ **issue** *n* ACC émission d'actions aux ayants-droit *f*, LAW droit préférentiel de souscription *m*, STOCK émission de droits préférentiels de souscription *f*; ◆ **all ~ reserved** LAW, PATENTS tous droits réservés

rigid: ~ **vehicle** *n* TRANSP véhicule rigide *m*, véhicule simple *m*

RIL *abbr (rehabilitation import loan)* FIN emprunt de redressement *m*, prêt de l'importation pour le redressement économique *m*

RIN *abbr UK (Royal Institute of Navigation)* TRANSP institut britannique de la navigation

ring[1] *n* STOCK corbeille *f (jarg)*; ~ **fence** *jarg* ECON, FIN, TAX mesure protectionniste de certains secteurs industriels afin de conserver les employeurs (uniquement en temps de guerre); ~ **fencing** ECON, FIN, TAX *(*SYN *earmarking)* affectation spéciale de fonds publics *f*; ~ **road** TRANSP périphérique *m*, rocade *f*

ring:[2] **1.** *vt* ~ -**fence** ECON, FIN, TAX *fund, grant* réserver; **2.** *vi* ~ **off** COMMS raccrocher

ringgit *n* GEN COMM ringgit *m*

ringing: ~ **out** *n jarg* STOCK *futures market* liquidation d'un contrat à terme avant maturité *f*, règlement anticipé *m*

riots: ~ **and civil commotions** *n pl (R&CC)* WEL émeutes et troubles de l'ordre public *m pl*; ~, **civil commotions and strikes** *n pl (RCC & S)* WEL émeutes, troubles de l'ordre public et grèves *m pl*

riparian[1] *adj* LAW riverain

riparian[2] *n* LAW riverain *m*; ~ **rights** *n pl* LAW droits des riverains *m pl*, riveraineté *f*

ripper: ~ **bill** *n jarg US* POL projet de loi éventreur *m*

ripple: ~ **effect** *n* ECON effet en cascade *m*

rise[1] *n (*ANT *drop)* ACC, ECON hausse *f*, FIN augmentation *f*, GEN COMM augmentation *f*, *in prices, rent* hausse *f*, montée *f*, HRM *BrE in wages* augmentation *f*; ~ **of floor** *(rf)* TRANSP acculement *m*, relevé des varangues *m*; ~ **in prices** ACC, ECON, FIN, GEN COMM, S&M augmentation des prix *f*, majoration de prix *f*, renchérissement *m*, hausse des prix *f*; ◆ **give ~ to** GEN COMM *interest, suspicions* susciter

rise:[2] **1.** *vt* ~ **to** GEN COMM *position* accéder à; **2.** *vi* ECON monter, GEN COMM monter, progresser, POL *parliament* lever la séance; **2.** *vi* ~ **again** ECON, GEN COMM monter à nouveau, remonter

rising[1] *adj* ECON en hausse *loc f*, GEN COMM croissant, en hausse *loc f*

rising:[2] ~ **bottoms** *n pl jarg* STOCK actions de base en hausse *f pl*, ligne de creux haussière *f*; ~ **cost** *n*

ECON coût en augmentation *m*, coût en hausse *m*; ~ **interest rate** *n* BANK, ECON, FIN taux d'intérêt en hausse *m*, taux en augmentation *m*; ~ **tendency** *n* STOCK *of market* tendance à la hausse *f*; ~ **trend** *n* GEN COMM tendance à la hausse *f*; ~ **unemployment** *n* ECON, WEL chômage en augmentation *m*, chômage en hausse *m*

risk:[1] **at** ~ *adj* STOCK menacé, à vos risques *loc m*; ~ **averse** *adj* ECON, GEN COMM *game theory* opposé au risque; ~ **-free** *adj* STOCK sans risque; ~ **-minimizing** *adj* STOCK peu risqué; ~ **-orientated** *adj* GEN COMM qui tient compte du risque *loc m*

risk[2] *n* ACC, BANK, ECON, FIN, GEN COMM, INS, MATH *statistics*, STOCK risque *m*; ~ **-adjusted discount rate** *n* FIN risque corrigé selon le taux d'escompte *m*; ~ **analysis** *n* FIN analyse des risques *f*; ~ **arbitrage** *n* STOCK arbitrage des risques *m*; ~ **assessment** *n* FIN appréciation des risques *f*; ~ **asset system** *n* BANK système d'évaluation des risques *m*; ~ **aversion** *n* ECON, GEN COMM aversion pour le risque *f*; ~ **-avoiding capital** *n* FIN financement par capital sans risque *m*; ~ **-based banking standards** *n pl* BANK système d'évaluation des risques *m*; ~ **-based premium** *n* INS assurance à la prime de risque *f*; ~ **-bearing capital** *n* FIN financement par capital risque *m*; ~ **capital** *n* BANK, FIN, GEN COMM capital risque *m*, capital à risque *m*; ~ **exposure** *n* ACC exposition aux risques *f*, risque encouru *m*; ~ **-free debt instrument** *n* STOCK *Treasury bills* effet sans risque *m*, instrument obligatoire sans risque *m*; ~ **in the goods** *n* LAW, TRANSP risque portant sur les marchandises *m*; ~ **lover** *n* GEN COMM amateur de risques *m*; ~ **management** *n* FIN, INS gestion des risques *f*, STOCK gestion du risque *f*; ~ **manager** *n* INS gestionnaire des risques *m*, responsable de la gestion des risques *m*; ~ **minimizing** *n* GEN COMM réduction du risque *f*; ~ **monitoring** *n* MGMNT contrôle de risques *m*; ~ **of nonrepayment** *n* BANK risque de non-remboursement *m*; ~ **package** *n* FIN ensemble des risques *m*; ~ **pooling** *n* INS mise en commun des risques *f*; ~ **position** *n* STOCK position à risque *f*, état des risques *m*; ~ **premium** *n* INS prime de risque *f*; ~ **profile** *n* INS profil de risque *m*; ~ **-related premium** *n* INS prime de risque *f*; ~ **reward** *n* ACC rapport risque-bénéfit *m*; ~ **-reward ratio** *n* ACC rapport risque-bénéfice *m*; ~ **sharing** *n* INS partage de risque *m*, partage des risques *m*; ~ **weighting** *n* FIN pondération du risque *f*; ◆ **at one's own** ~ GEN COMM à ses risques et périls; **no** ~ **after discharge** *(NRAD)* INS acquit libératoire *m*; **no** ~ **until confirmed** *(NR)* INS pas de risque avant confirmation; **spread the** ~ INS répartir le risque; **take a** ~ GEN COMM prendre un risque

riskless[1] *adj* GEN COMM sans risque, sûr

riskless:[2] ~ **transaction** *n* STOCK transaction sans risque *f*

risks: **all** ~ *n pl (AR)* INS tous risques *loc*; **all**

~ **cover** *n* INS couverture tous risques *f*; **all** ~ **insurance** *n* INS assurance tous risques *f*

risky[1] *adj* GEN COMM hasardeux, risqué

risky:[2] ~ **asset** *n* BANK valeur risquée *f*

rival: ~ **good** *n* GEN COMM bien de la concurrence *m*

river: ~ **bus** *n* TRANSP bus fluvial *m*; ~ **navigation** *n* TRANSP *shipping* navigation fluviale *f*; ~ **pollution** *n* ENVIR pollution des cours d'eau *f*

riverside: ~ **resident** *n* LAW riverain *m*

riveted *adj (R)* GEN COMM fixé, riveté; ◆ ~ **and welded** *(RW)* TRANSP *shipping* riveté et soudé

Riyadh *pr n* GEN COMM Riad *n pr*, Riyad *n pr*

riyal *n* GEN COMM riyal *m*

RK *abbr (rubbing keel)* TRANSP *shipping* fausse quille *f*

Rmb *n* GEN COMM *currency of the People's Republic of China* yuan *m*

RN *abbr (release note)* TRANSP *cargo* bordereau de livraison *m*

RNR *abbr (rate not reported)* TRANSP tarif non-répertorié *m*

RNS *abbr UK (Regulatory News Service)* STOCK service d'information relative à la réglementation, ≈ chronoval *m*

RO *abbr* GEN COMM *(receiving office)* bureau de messageries *m*, bureau de réception *m*, PATENTS *(receiving office)* office récepteur *m*, TRANSP *(receiving order)* ordonnance de mise sous séquestre *f*, TRANSP *(routing order) cargo* bordereau d'acheminement *m*

ROA *abbr (return on assets)* FIN rendement des fonds propres *m*

road *n (Rd.)* TRANSP route *f*, rue *f (r.)*; ~ **building** *n* ECON construction de routes *f*; ~ **fatalities** *n pl* TRANSP accidents mortels de la route *m pl*; ~ **-fund licence** *n BrE* TRANSP vignette *f*; ~ **-fund license** *n AmE see road-fund licence BrE*; ~ **haulage** *n* TRANSP transports routiers *m pl*; ~ **haulage vehicle** *n (RHV)* TRANSP poids lourd *m*; ~ **network** *n* TRANSP réseau routier *m*, système routier *m*; ~ **-rail transport** *n BrE (cf piggyback traffic AmE)* TRANSP ferroutage *m*; ~ **safety** *n* TRANSP sécurité routière *f*; ~ **show** *n* FIN tournée de présentation *f*, MEDIA *cinema* prolongation *f*; ~ **tax** *n* TAX péage sur voies *m*; ~ **toll** *n* TRANSP péage *m*; ~ **traffic** *n* TRANSP circulation routière *f*; ~ **train** *n Australia* TRANSP *haulage* train routier *m*; ~ **transport** *n* TRANSP transport routier *m*; ~ **works** *n pl* TRANSP travaux *m pl*

Road: ~ **Haulage Association** *n UK (RHA)* TRANSP association britannique des transports routiers

roads *n pl* TRANSP *shipping lane* rade *f*

roadside: ~ **site** *n* S&M *for advertising poster* emplacement le long d'une route *m*

rob *vt* LAW voler; ◆ ~ **sb of sth** GEN COMM, LAW voler qch à qn; ~ **the till** GEN COMM, LAW voler de l'argent dans la caisse

ROB *abbr (remain on board)* TRANSP *cargo* reste à bord *loc m*

robber *n* LAW voleur *m*

robbery *n* LAW vol *m*

Robertsonian: ~ **lag** *n* ECON écart de Robertson *m*

robot *n* IND robot *m*

robotics *n* IND robotique *f*

robotize *vt* IND robotiser

robust *adj* GEN COMM robuste, solide

ROC *abbr (return on capital)* ACC, ECON, FIN rendement du capital *m*

ROCE *abbr (return on capital employed)* ACC, ECON, FIN RCI *(rentabilité des capitaux investis)*

rock:¹ ~ **-bottom price** *n* GEN COMM prix plancher *m*

rock:² ~ **the boat** *phr* GEN COMM semer la pagaille

rocket:¹ ~ **scientist** *n jarg* STOCK société d'investissement innovatrice *f*

rocket² *vi* GEN COMM grimper en flèche *(infrml)*

rocks: **be on the** ~ *phr* GEN COMM être en faillite *loc f*

rod *n* TRANSP *lashing equipment* barre de saisissage *f*

rodent: ~ **control certificate** *n* TRANSP *of ship* certificat de dératisation *m*

ROE *abbr (return on equity)* ACC, FIN, STOCK rendement de l'action *m*, rendement des capitaux propres *m*, rendement des fonds propres *m*

ROG *abbr (receipt of goods)* TRANSP *cargo* réception des marchandises *f*

ROI *abbr (return on investment)* ACC, FIN TRI *(taux de rentabilité d'un investissement)*, rendement des actifs *m*, rendement des investissements *m*, rentabilité d'investissements *f*, rentabilité des actifs *f*

ROIC *abbr (return on invested capital)* ACC, ECON, FIN rendement du capital investi *m*

role *n* GEN COMM, HRM rôle *m*; ~ **-playing** MGMNT jeu de rôles *m*; ~ **set** MGMNT ensemble des attributions *m*

roll:¹ ~ **on/roll off** *adj (ro/ro)* TRANSP *shipping* transbordeur

roll:² ~ **-back** *n jarg* ECON baisse des prix *f (jarg)*; ~ **center diameter** *n AmE*, ~ **centre diameter** *n BrE* ADMIN *fax paper* diamètre du mandrin *m*; ~ **-down** *n* STOCK baisse des prix imposée *f*, report de position à la baisse *m*; ~ **-on container** *n* TRANSP conteneur roll-on *m*; ~ **on/roll off** *n (rol ro)* TRANSP *system* manutention horizontale *f*; ~ **on/roll off-lift on/lift off** *n (rollo)* TRANSP *system* manutention horizontale et verticale *f*; ~ **on/roll off-lift on/lift off ship** *n (rollo)* TRANSP navire à manutention horizontale et verticale *m (rollo)*; ~ **on/roll off ship** *n (rol/ro ship)* TRANSP navire à manutention horizontale *m*, roulier *m*; ~ **-out** *n* TRANSP *of vehicle* première sortie *f*, présentation *f*; ~ **-over** *n* BANK, FIN reconduction *f*, roll-over *m*, STOCK reconduction *f*, report de position *m*, TAX roulement *m*, transfert libre d'impôt *m*; ~ **-over**

credit *n* BANK crédit à taux révisable *m*, prêt à taux révisable *m*; ~ **-over credit facility** *n* BANK crédit à taux variable *m*, prêt à taux variable *m*; ~ **-over date** *n* BANK date de révision du taux *f*, date de révision du taux d'intérêt *f*, date de règlement variable *f*; ~ **-over loan** *n* BANK crédit à taux révisable *m*, fractionnement d'actions *m*, prêt à taux révisable *m*, emprunt à taux variable *m*; ~ **-over mortgage** *n* BANK prêt hypothécaire à court terme à taux d'intérêt renégociable *m*; ~ **-over order** *n* STOCK *loan, debt securities* ordre de reconduction *m*, ordre de report de position *m*; ~ **-over ratio** *n* BANK, ECON taux variable *m*; ~ **-over relief** *n* TAX dégrèvement roll-over *m*; ~ **-up** *n* GEN COMM cumul *m*

roll:³ ~ **out** *vt* S&M *marketing* introduire une marque sur un marché-test avant de la lancer à l'échelon, introduire globalement; ~ **over** BANK reconduire, *interest rates* renouveler, STOCK reconduire

rolled: ~ **-up income** *n* TAX revenu enveloppé *m*

roller: ~ **swap** *n* FIN échange renouvelable *m*

rolling: ~ **down** *n* STOCK *options* report de position à la baisse *m*, roulement à la baisse *m*; ~ **in** *n* STOCK *options* report de position *m*, roulement en arrière *m*; ~ **options positions** *n pl* STOCK *on Eurodollar futures* positions de roulement variable *f pl*; ~ **out** *n* STOCK *options* roulement en avant *m*; ~ **plan** *n* GEN COMM projet cahotique *m*; ~ **program** *n AmE*, ~ **programme** *n BrE* FIN *fleet management* programme de matériel roulant *m*; ~ **rate** *n* FIN obligation à taux glissant *f*, obligation à taux variable *f*, STOCK obligation à taux glissant *f*; ~ **-rate note** *n* FIN, STOCK obligation à taux glissant *f*, obligation à taux variable *f*; ~ **settlement** *n* STOCK règlement graduel *m*, règlement livraison en continu *m*; ~ **stock** *n* TRANSP matériel roulant *m*; ~ **strikes** *n pl jarg* HRM *industrial relations* grèves tournantes *loc f*; ~ **up** *n* STOCK *options* report de position à la hausse *m*, roulement à la hausse *m*

ro/lo *n* TRANSP *(roll on/roll off-lift on/lift off ship)* ro/lo *m (navire à manutention horizontale et verticale)*, TRANSP *(roll on/roll off-lift on/lift off)* *system* manutention horizontale et verticale *f*

ROM *abbr (read only memory)* COMP mémoire ROM *f*, mémoire fixe *f*, mémoire morte *f*

Romania *pr n* GEN COMM Roumanie *f*

Romanian¹ *adj* GEN COMM roumain

Romanian² *n* GEN COMM *language* roumain *m*, *person* Roumain *m*

Rome *pr n* GEN COMM Rome *n pr*

roof: ~ **load** *n* TRANSP *of container* charge sur le toit *f*; ~ **rail** *n* TRANSP *of container* longeron de toit *m*; ~ **tax** *n* TAX taxe d'habitation *f*

room *n* LEIS *in hotel* chambre *f*; ~ **service** LEIS *in hotel* service des chambres *m*; ~ **temperature** GEN COMM température ambiante *f*

root *n* COMP racine *f*; ~ **directory** COMP répertoire de base *m*, répertoire racine *m*; ~ **segment** COMP segment de base *m*

ROP *abbr (run of paper)* MEDIA *print* emplacement indéterminé *m*, importance d'un tirage moyen *f*, insertion sauvage *f*, S&M emplacement indéterminé *m*

RORCE *abbr (rate of return on capital employed)* ECON, FIN taux de rendement des capitaux investis *m*, taux de rendement sur le capital employé *m*

ro/ro[1] *abbr (roll on/roll off)* TRANSP manutention horizontale *f*

ro/ro[2] *adj (roll on/roll off)* TRANSP *shipping* transbordeur

ro/ro:[3] **~ berth** *n* TRANSP *shipping* quai ro/ro *m*; **~ drivers' restaurant** *n* TRANSP *shipping* restaurant réservé aux chauffeurs de véhicules ro/ro *m*; **~ rates** *n pl* TRANSP *ship rates* tarifs ro/ro *m pl*; **~ ship** *n (roll on/roll off ship)* TRANSP ro/ro *m (navire à manutention horizontale)*; **~ vessel** *n* TRANSP *ship* navire à manutention horizontale *m*, roulier *m*

Roseau *pr n* GEN COMM Roseau *n pr*

roster *n* HRM *personnel duty* tableau de service *m*

rosy *adj* GEN COMM *prospects* souriant

ROT *abbr (reference our telex)* COMMS référence notre télex *loc f*

rotating: **~ shift** *n* HRM équipe de travail posté *f*

rotation: **~ clause** *n* BANK *underwriting* clause de rotation *f*; ♦ **in ~** GEN COMM à tour de rôle

rouble *n* GEN COMM rouble *m*

rough *n* S&M *advertising* montage préalable *m*; **~ draft** LAW brouillon *m*, premier projet *m*; **~ estimate** GEN COMM devis approximatif *m*; **~ guide** GEN COMM approximation *f*; ♦ **make things ~ for sb** *infrml* GEN COMM mener la vie dure à qn

roughly: **~ equivalent** *phr* GEN COMM à peu près équivalent

round:[1] **~-the-clock** *adj* (SYN *around-the-clock*) GEN COMM 24 heures sur 24

round[2] *n* ECON négociations commerciales *f pl*, round *m*; **~ bottom** *n (RDBTN)* TRANSP *of ship* fond rond *m*; **~ brackets** *n pl* COMP, MEDIA *typography* parenthèses *f pl*; **~ C/P** *n (round charter party)* TRANSP contrat d'affrètement aller-retour *m*; **~ charter party** *n (round C/P)* TRANSP contrat d'affrètement aller-retour *m*; **~ figure** *n* GEN COMM chiffre rond *m*; **~ file** *n jarg* GEN COMM *wastepaper bin* poubelle *f*; **~ lot** *n jarg US* GEN COMM lot régulier *m*, STOCK lot régulier *m*, quotité *f*; **~ number** *n* GEN COMM chiffre rond *m*; **~ robin** *n* COMMS *letter* pétition *f*; **~ sum** *n* GEN COMM montant arrondi *m*, somme en chiffres ronds *f*; **~ sum allowances** *n pl* TAX indemnités sommes rondes *f pl*; **~ table** *n* GEN COMM table ronde *f*; **~-the-clock service** *n (cf around-the-clock service AmE)* GEN COMM service 24 heures sur 24 *m*; **~ trip** *n* STOCK aller-retour *m*; **~-trip cost** *n* TRANSP coût aller-retour *m*; **~-trip fare** *n AmE (cf return fare BrE)* TRANSP prix d'un aller-retour *m*; **~-trip rate** *n* TRANSP *tariff* tarif

aller-retour *m*; **~-trip ticket** *n AmE (cf return ticket BrE)* TRANSP aller-retour *m*, billet aller-retour *m*; **~-trip time** *n* TRANSP durée aller-retour *f*; **~ turn** *n* STOCK commission d'aller-retour *f*; **~ the world service** *n (Rws)* TRANSP *shipping* service tour-du-monde *m*

round:[3] **~ off** *vt* ACC *number*, FIN *figure* arrondir, GEN COMM *meeting* compléter; **~ up** MATH arrondir

roundabout *n BrE (cf traffic circle AmE)* GEN COMM, TRANSP rond-point *m*

roundhouse *n* PROP rotonde *f*

rounding: **~ error** *n* MATH erreur d'arrondi *f*

roundtripping *n jarg* BANK, FIN, STOCK retrait *m*

roundturn *n* STOCK commission d'entrée et de sortie du marché *f*

route[1] *n* TRANSP route *f*; **~ analysis** TRANSP analyse de route *f*; **~ capacity** TRANSP capacité de route *f*; **~ capacity control airline** *(RCCA)* TRANSP transporteur aérien pour le contrôle de la capacité des routes *m*; **~ diversion** TRANSP déroutement *m*; **~ option** TRANSP option de route *f*; **~ order** TRANSP acheminement de l'envoi *m*; **~ planning** TRANSP programmation d'itinéraires *f*

route[2] *vt* COMP acheminer, GEN COMM acheminer, router, TRANSP acheminer, organiser le trafic, router

router *n* COMP routeur *m*

routes: **~ section** *n* TRANSP service de routage *m*

routine[1] *adj* GEN COMM courant

routine[2] *n* COMP sous-programme *m*, GEN COMM programme *m*, routine *f*; **~ check** *n* GEN COMM contrôle de routine *m*; **~ control** *n* TRANSP vérification de routine *f*; **~ duties** *n pl* GEN COMM affaires courantes *f pl*; **~ maintenance** *n* GEN COMM entretien de routine *m*

routing *n* COMP *of data*, GEN COMM acheminement *m*, routage *m*, TRANSP acheminement *m*, routage *m*, organisation du trafic *f*; **~ certificate** TRANSP certificat d'acheminement *m*; **~ order** *(RO)* TRANSP *cargo* bordereau d'acheminement *m*

row *n* GEN COMM *of figures* ligne *f*, TRANSP pile *f*

ROW *abbr (the rest of the world)* ECON le reste du monde *m*

Royal: **~ Economic Society** *n* ECON société royale d'économie; **~ Exchange** *n UK (RE)* STOCK bourse de commerce de Londres; **~ Institute of Naval Architects** *n UK* TRANSP institut royal des architectes navals; **~ Institute of Navigation** *n UK (RIN)* TRANSP institut britannique de la navigation; **~ Mint** *n UK* ECON institut royal d'émission de la monnaie, ≈ Hôtel de la Monnaie *m*; **~ Society of Arts** *n UK (RSA)* WEL Académie royale des arts *f*

royalties *n pl* LAW droits d'auteur *m pl*, MEDIA *print* droits d'auteur *m pl*, royalties *f pl*, TAX droits d'auteur *m pl*

royalty *n* GEN COMM *to author, composer* droits d'auteur *m pl*, *to landowner, patentee* redevance *f*, MEDIA *to author* droits d'auteur *m pl*, pourcentage *m*, redevance *f*, TAX droits d'auteur *m pl*, redevance *f*; **~ exemption limit** TAX exemption maximale pour redevances *f*, limite d'exonération de droits d'auteur *f*; **~ holder** TAX bénéficiaire de redevances *m*, détenteur de droits d'auteur *m*, détenteur de redevances *m*; **~ system** TAX régime de redevances *m*, système des droits d'auteur *m*; **~ trust** ENVIR société de gestion des redevances *f*

RP *abbr* COMMS *(radiophone)* radiotéléphone *m*, FIN *(repurchase agreement)* contrat de vente à réméré *m*, STOCK *(repurchase agreement)* contrat de vente à réméré *m*, mise en pension *f*, pension livrée *f*, prise en pension *f*, TRANSP *(return to port for orders)* shipping retour au port en attendant des instructions *loc m*

RPA *abbr UK (Redundancy Payments Act)* HRM 1965 loi sur les primes de reconversions

RPB *abbr UK (recognized professional body)* FIN corps professionnel reconnu *m*, organisme professionnel *m*, organisme spécialisé accrédité *m*

R.P.Ct. *abbr UK (Restrictive Practices Court)* GEN COMM, LAW tribunal chargé de l'application des lois antitrusts, tribunal statuant sur toute atteinte à la libre concurrence *m*

RPI *abbr (retail price index)* ECON, GEN COMM indice des prix de détail *m*

RPM *abbr* ECON *(resale price maintenance)*, FIN *(resale price maintenance)*, S&M *(retail price maintenance)* sales maintien du prix de revente *m*, prix de vente imposé *m*

RQD *abbr (raised quarterdeck)* TRANSP shipping demi-dunette *f*

RR *abbr* STOCK *(rate resetting)* refixation de taux *f*, STOCK *(rate resetter)* rétablisseur de taux *m*

RRA *abbr UK (Race Relations Act)* LAW loi protégeant l'égalité des droits pour chaque race

RRIF *abbr (registered retirement income fund)* INS caisse de retraite agréée *f*

RRP *abbr (recommended retail price)* S&M sales prix conseillé *m*

RRR *abbr (real rate of return)* BANK taux de rendement réel *m*

RRSP *abbr (registered retirement savings plan)* INS régime enregistré d'épargne-retraite *m*

RSA *abbr* ECON *UK (regional selective assistance)* assistance régionale sélective *f*, WEL *UK (Royal Society of Arts)* Académie royale des arts *f*

RSD *abbr (raised shelter deck)* TRANSP shipping pont-abri surélevé *m*

RSG *abbr UK (rate support grant)* ECON subvention de l'État aux collectivités locales *f*, subvention de soutien de taux *f*

RSI *abbr (repetitive strain injury)* ADMIN atteinte due à des tensions répétées *f*

RSVP *abbr (please reply)* COMMS RSVP *(répondez s'il vous plaît)*

Rt: ~ Hon *abbr UK (Right Honourable)* POL très honorable

RT *abbr* COMMS *(radiotelegraphy)* radiotélégraphie *f*, COMMS *(radiotelephony)* radiotéléphonie *f*, COMMS *(radiotelephone)* radiotéléphone *m*

RTBA *abbr (rate to be agreed)* TRANSP tarif à déterminer *m*

RTh *abbr* TRANSP *(high frequency radiotelephony)* radiotéléphonie haute fréquence *f*, TRANSP *(high frequency radiotelephone)* shipping radiotéléphone haute fréquence *m*

RTm *abbr* TRANSP *(medium frequency radiotelephony)* radiotéléphonie moyenne fréquence *f*, TRANSP *(medium frequency radiotelephone)* shipping radiotéléphone moyenne fréquence *m*

RTv *abbr* TRANSP *(very high frequency radiotelephony)* radiotéléphonie très haute fréquence *f*, TRANSP *(very high frequency telephone)* shipping radiotéléphone très haute fréquence *m*

rubber: ~ band *n* GEN COMM élastique *m*; **~ bearing** *n (RB)* TRANSP roulement en caoutchouc *m*; **~ check** *n infrml AmE*, **~ cheque** *n infrml BrE* BANK chèque en bois *m (infrml)*, chèque sans provision *m*; **~ stamp** *n* GEN COMM tampon *m*; **~ -tired traffic** *n AmE*, **~ -tyred traffic** *n BrE* TRANSP trafic sur pneus *m*

rubbing: ~ keel *n (RK)* TRANSP shipping fausse quille *f*

rubbish *n BrE (cf garbage AmE)* ENVIR déchets *m pl*, détritus *m*, ordures *f pl*, rebut *m*; **~ chute** *BrE (cf garbage chute AmE)* ENVIR vide-ordures *m*

ruble *n see* **rouble**

RUF *abbr (revolving underwriting facility)* INS *investment banking* garantie d'émission renouvelable *f*, moyen de souscription renouvelable *m*

ruin *vt* GEN COMM *company* couler

rule[1] *n* ECON, FIN, GEN COMM, LAW, MGMNT, PATENTS, STOCK, TAX règle *f*; **~ book** GEN COMM règlement *m*, HRM règlement intérieur *m*; **~ of law** LAW suprématie du droit *f*, état de droit *m*; **~ of thumb** GEN COMM méthode empirique *f*; **~ 405** *US* FIN loi 405 *f*, règle 405 *f*; **~ of the 78s** FIN règle des 78 *f*; **~ of 72** FIN règle du 72 *f*; ♦ **under the ~** *jarg US* STOCK d'après les règles

rule[2]: **~ out** *vt* GEN COMM exclure, écarter

ruled: ~ paper *n* GEN COMM papier réglé *m*

ruler *n* GEN COMM règle *f*

rules: ~ of fair practice *n pl* STOCK code des usages *m*, règles de pratique équitable *f pl*; **~ and regulations** *n pl* LAW statuts et règlements *m pl*; **~ versus discretion** *n pl* ECON règles anti-discrétionnaires *f pl*

ruling *n* LAW décision *f*, jugement *m*, ordonnance *f*; **~ class** *n* POL classe dirigeante *f*; **~ price** *n* S&M cours en vigueur *m*, cours pratiqué *m*; ♦ **at ~ prices** GEN COMM aux tarifs en vigueur; **give a ~ in favor of sb** *AmE*, **give a ~ in favour of sb** *BrE* GEN COMM rendre un jugement en faveur de qn

Rumania *pr n see* **Romania**

Rumanian[1] *adj see* **Romanian**

Rumanian[2] *n see* **Romanian**

rummage: ~ **sale** *n* *AmE (cf jumble sale BrE)* S&M braderie d'objets usagés *f*, vente de charité *f*

rumor *n* *AmE*, **rumour** *n* *BrE* GEN COMM rumeur *f*

run:[1] ~ **-of-the-mill** *adj* GEN COMM banal, quelconque

run:[2] ~ **-around** *n* MEDIA *print* habillage *m* (*jarg*); ~ **-in** *n* TRANSP *of ship* fesses *f pl*; ~ **on the banks** *n* BANK, STOCK panique bancaire *f*, ruée sur les banques *f*; ~ **on the dollar** *n* (SYN *rush on the dollar*) BANK, STOCK ruée sur le dollar *f*; ~ **of paper** *n* (*ROP*) MEDIA *print* emplacement indéterminé *m*, importance d'un tirage moyen *f*, insertion sauvage *f*, S&M emplacement indéterminé *m*; ~ **of schedule** *n* LAW tenue des barèmes d'imposition *f*; ~ **of the ship** *n* TRANSP coulée du navire *f*; ~ **time** *n* COMP *of program* durée de l'exécution *f*, GEN COMM délai d'exécution *m*; ~ **-up** *n* STOCK hausse *f*; ◆ **in the ~ -up to** GEN COMM *event, elections* pendant la période précédant

run[3] **1.** *vt* COMP *program* exécuter, GEN COMM s'occuper de, *manage* conduire, gérer, MGMNT *company, hotel* gérer, s'occuper de; ~ **down** ECON *liquid assets* diminuer, réduire, FIN réduire; ~ **into** GEN COMM *amount to* s'élever à; **2.** *vi* BANK *interest* courir, GEN COMM, LAW *durer*; ~ **back** STOCK aller à contre-courant; ~ **on** FIN continuer à courir; ~ **out** FIN être épuisé, GEN COMM *stocks* s'épuiser; ◆ ~ **an ad in the paper** S&M insérer une annonce dans le journal, mettre une annonce dans le journal; ~ **aground** TRANSP *ship* échouer; ~ **a concession** GEN COMM *in store* être concessionnaire; ~ **a deficit** (ANT *run a surplus*) ECON avoir un déficit, présenter un déficit; ~ **an errand** GEN COMM faire une commission, faire une course; ~ **foul of the tax authorities** TAX avoir des ennuis avec l'administration fiscale; ~ **low** GEN COMM *stocks* s'épuiser, STOCK avoir un cours faible; ~ **the risk of** GEN COMM courir le risque de; ~ **short of** GEN COMM se trouver à court de; ~ **the show** GEN COMM faire marcher l'affaire; ~ **smoothly** GEN COMM bien fonctionner; ~ **a surplus** (ANT *run a deficit*) ECON avoir un excédent, présenter un excédent; ~ **up a debt** BANK laisser grossir une dette; ~ **up a deficit** FIN accumuler un déficit

runaway: ~ **industry** *n* IND industrie diversifiée *f*; ~ **inflation** *n* ECON hyperinflation *f*, spirale inflationniste *f*; ~ **shop** *n jarg* HRM, IND atelier fugitif *m*

runner *n* GEN COMM messager *m*, HRM courrier *m*, encaisseur *m*, STOCK coursier *m*, runner *m*, grouillot *m*

running *n* GEN COMM conduite *f*; ~ **ahead** *n* STOCK *stockbroking* hausse *f*, non-respect de la règle de priorité *m*, utilisation abusive d'informations privilégiées *f*; ~ **broker** *n* STOCK courtier en exercice *m*; ~ **cost** *n* TRANSP *shipping, chartering* coût d'exploitation *m*, frais d'exploitation *m pl*; ~ **costs** *n pl* ADMIN *of civil service* dépenses courantes *f pl*, dépenses de fonctionnement *f pl*, GEN COMM charges courantes *f pl*, dépenses

courantes *f pl*, frais de fonctionnement *m pl*; ~ **day** *n* (*Rd*) TRANSP jour courant *m*, jours consécutifs *m pl*; ~ **down clause** *n* (*RDC*) INS *marine* clause d'abordage *f*; ~ **expenses** *n pl* ACC charges d'exploitation *f pl*, dépenses de fonctionnement *f pl*, FIN dépenses de fonctionnement *f pl*, GEN COMM dépenses courantes *f pl*, frais de fonctionnement *m pl*; ~ **hour** *n* TRANSP *shipping, charter party term* heure courante *f*; ~ **in period** *n* GEN COMM période de rodage *f*; ~ **interest** *n* BANK intérêts en cours *m pl*; ~ **mate** *n* *AmE (cf fellow candidate BrE)* POL colistier *m*; ~ **number** *n* GEN COMM numéro d'ordre *m*; ~ **total** *n* GEN COMM cumul *m*; ~ **working day** *n* TRANSP *shipping, charter party term* jour courant de travail *m*; ◆ **be out of the ~** GEN COMM ne plus être dans la course; **in the ~ for** GEN COMM *promotion* sur les rangs pour

runoff *n* INS queue de portefeuille *f*, *insurance, reinsurance* liquidation de sinistres *f*, POL *US* éliminatoire *f*; ~ **election** *US* POL élection éliminatoire *f*

runway *n* TRANSP piste *f*

rupee *n* GEN COMM roupie *f*

rupiah *n* GEN COMM rupiah *f*

rural: ~ **area** *n* ECON zone rurale *f*; ~ **community** *n* ECON communauté rurale *f*; ~ **delivery service** *n* *US (RDS)* COMMS service de livraisons gratuites en zone rurale *m*; ~ **development area** *n* *UK (RDA)* ECON zone d'aménagement rural *f*, zone de développement rural *f*; ~ **economy** *n* ECON économie rurale *f*; ~ **land** *n* PROP terre rurale *f*; ~ **sector** *n* ECON, IND secteur agricole *m*

Rural: ~ **Community Council** *n* *UK (RCC)* POL conseil intercommunal en zone rurale

rush: ~ **hour** *n* GEN COMM heure de pointe *f*; ~ **job** *n* GEN COMM travail d'urgence *m*; ~ **on the dollar** *n* (SYN *run on the dollar*) BANK, STOCK ruée sur le dollar *f*; ~ **order** *n* GEN COMM, S&M commande urgente *f*

Russia *pr n* GEN COMM Russie *f*

Russian[1] *adj* GEN COMM russe

Russian[2] *n* GEN COMM *language* russe *m*, *person* Russe *mf*

Russian:[3] ~ **Federation** *pr n* GEN COMM Fédération russe *f*

rust: ~ **bucket** *n* *infrml* TRANSP *ship* rafiot *m* (*infrml*)

rustbelt *n* *US* IND région des industries en déclin *f*

rusty *adj* GEN COMM rouillé

RW *abbr (riveted and welded)* TRANSP *shipping* riveté et soudé

Rwanda[1] *n* GEN COMM Ruanda *n pr*

Rwanda[2] *pr n* GEN COMM Rwanda *m*

Rwandan[1] *adj* GEN COMM ruandais, rwandais

Rwandan[2] *n* GEN COMM Rwandais *m*, *person* Ruandais *m*

Rws *abbr (round the world service)* TRANSP *shipping* service tour-du-monde *m*

ryal *n* GEN COMM rial *m*

S

S¹ *abbr* TRANSP *(station)* gare *f*, TRANSP *(South compass point) navigation* S *(quart sud)*, TRANSP *(single expansion engine) shipping* machine à expansion simple *f*, TRANSP *(starboard side) shipping* tribord *m*

S:² ~ **curve** *n* ECON courbe en S *f*

s/a *abbr* TRANSP *(safe arrival)* heureuse arrivée *f*, TRANSP *(single-acting) machinery* à simple effet

s.a.a.r. *abbr (seasonally adjusted annual rate)* ECON taux annuel corrigé des variations saisonnières *m*

sack *vt infrml BrE* HRM *employee* licencier, lourder *(infrml)*, renvoyer, vider *(infrml)*, virer *(infrml)*; ◆ **get the ~** *infrml* HRM être renvoyé, être viré *(infrml)*; **give sb the ~** *infrml* HRM flanquer qn à la porte *(infrml)*, lourder qn *(infrml)*

sacking *n infrml* HRM *of worker* licenciement *m*

sacrifice *vt* INS sacrifier

SAD *abbr (single administrative document)* ADMIN, IMP/EXP, TRANSP *EU* DAU *(document administratif unique)*

saddle: ~ **tank** *n* TRANSP *shipping* citerne transversale en hauteur *f*

s.a.e *abbr UK (stamped addressed envelope, cf s.a.s.e.)* COMMS, GEN COMM enveloppe affranchie *f*, enveloppe timbrée à vos nom et adresse *f*

SAEF *abbr UK (SEAQ Automated Execution Facility)* STOCK système international de cotation automatisé *m*

SAF *abbr (structural adjustment facility)* FIN facilité d'ajustement structurel *f*

SAFCON: ~ **certificate** *n* TRANSP *shipping* certificat de sécurité de construction pour navire de charge *m*

safe *n* BANK coffre-fort *m*; ~ **arrival** *(s/a)* TRANSP heureuse arrivée *f*; ~ **asset** FIN actif sûr *m*; ~ **berth** TRANSP *shipping* poste d'amarrage sûr *m*; ~ **custody department** BANK service des coffres *m*; ~ **deposit** BANK coffre *m*, dépôt en coffre *m*, dépôt en coffre-fort *m*; ~ **-deposit box** *(SYN safety-deposit box)* BANK coffre *m*, dépôt en coffre *m*, dépôt en coffre-fort *m*; ~ **-deposit vault** BANK salle des coffres *f*, salle des coffres-forts *f*; ~ **estimate** GEN COMM estimation prudente *f*; ~ **harbor rule** *AmE*, ~ **harbour rule** *BrE* TAX règle de l'abri sûr *f*; ~ **hedge** STOCK couverture sûre *f*, opération de couverture sûre *f*; ~ **investment** BANK placement sûr *m*; ~ **port** TRANSP *shipping* port sûr *m*; ~ **working load** IND charge admissible de fonctionnement *f*, charge de travail de sécurité *f*; ◆ **to be on the ~ side** GEN COMM par précaution, pour plus de sûreté

safeguard¹ *n* LAW *clause* sauvegarde *f*

safeguard² *vt* GEN COMM *assets* sauvegarder, *secret* garder; ◆ ~ **against inflation** ECON se protéger contre l'inflation

safekeeping *n* BANK garde des valeurs *f*, services de garde *m pl*; ~ **of assets** BANK garde des valeurs actives *f*

safety *n* WEL sécurité *f*; ~ **bank** *n* GEN COMM stock de dépannage *m*; ~ **belt** *n* TRANSP ceinture de sécurité *f*; ~ **-deposit box** *n (SYN safe-deposit box)* BANK coffre *m*, dépôt en coffre *m*, dépôt en coffre-fort *m*; ~ **-deposit box charges** *n pl* BANK frais de case de coffre-fort *m pl*; ~ **equipment certificate** *n* TRANSP *shipping* certificat de sécurité du matériel d'armement *m*; ~ **hazard** *n* GEN COMM risque pour la sécurité *m*; ~ **management** *n* HRM, MGMNT gestion de la sécurité *f*; ~ **margin** *n* ACC, FIN, GEN COMM marge de sécurité *f*; ~ **measure** *n* GEN COMM mesure de sécurité *f*; ~ **officer** *n* GEN COMM, HRM responsable de la sécurité *m*; ~ **precaution** *n* GEN COMM mesure de sécurité *f*; ~ **regulations** *n pl* GEN COMM, HRM, IND règles de sécurité *f pl*; ~ **representative** *n* HRM *of trade union* délégué aux questions de sécurité *m*; ~ **requirements** *n pl* IND *for products* exigences de sécurité *f pl*; ~ **standards** *n pl* GEN COMM, IND normes de sécurité *f pl*; ~ **stock** *n* ECON, GEN COMM, IND, STOCK stock de précaution *m*, stock de sécurité *m*, stock tampon *m*; ~ **vault** *n* BANK salle des coffres *f*, salle des coffres-forts *f*; ~ **violation** *n* LAW infraction aux règles de sécurité *f*

Safety: ~ **Commission** *n US (cf Safety Committee)* WEL Commission de sécurité *f*; ~ **Committee** *n US (cf Safety Commission)* WEL *private sector* Commission de sécurité *f*

sag¹ *n* STOCK fléchissement *m*

sag² *vi* STOCK fléchir

sagging¹ *adj* GEN COMM en baisse *loc f*

sagging² *n* TRANSP *shipping* contre-arc *m*

sail TRANSP voyager en bateau; ~ **through** GEN COMM gagner facilement; ◆ ~ **close to the wind** GEN COMM friser l'illégalité

sailing *n* TRANSP navigation *f*, *departure* départ *m*; ~ **card** TRANSP liste des navires en partance *f*; ~ **date** *(S/D)* TRANSP date de départ *f*, jour de départ *m*; ~ **schedule** TRANSP liste de départs *f*; ~ **vessel** *(SV)* TRANSP navire à voiles *m*

sailor *n* TRANSP matelot *m*

Saint-Denis *pr n* GEN COMM Saint-Denis *n pr*

salable *adj AmE see* saleable *BrE*

salariat *n* HRM salariat *m*

salaried: ~ **agent** *n* HRM agent commercial salarié *m*, agent rémunéré au fixe *m*; ~ **employee** *n* HRM salarié *m*; ~ **staff** *n* HRM personnel salarié *m*

salaries: ~ **and wages** *n pl* GEN COMM rémunération *f*, HRM rémunération *f*, traitements et salaires *loc*; ~, **wages and fringe benefits** *n pl* HRM *paid by employer* rémunérations et charges sociales *f pl*, salaires et charges sociales *m pl*

salary *n* HRM salaire *m*; ~ **adjustment reserve allotment** *(SARA)* HRM affectation de réserve pour le rajustement des salaires *f*, répartition de la réserve d'ajustement des salaires *f*; ~ **base** HRM base salariale *f*; ~ **check** *AmE*, ~ **cheque** *BrE* BANK chèque de règlement de salaire *m*, HRM chèque de salaire *m*; ~ **deduction** HRM prélèvement à la source *m*, retenue à la source *f*; ~ **deferral arrangement** HRM entente d'échelonnement du traitement *f*; ~ **earner** HRM salarié *m*; ~ **grade** HRM indice de traitement *m*; ~ **harmonization** HRM *of salaries, wages* harmonisation salariale *f*; ~ **increase** HRM augmentation de salaire *f*; ~ **progression curve** HRM courbe d'augmentation de salaire *f*; ~ **rate** HRM taux de rémunération *m*; ~ **reduction plan** HRM plan de réduction des salaires *m*; ~ **review** HRM révision des salaires *f*, révision des traitements *f*, réévaluation des salaires *f*, réévaluation des traitements *f*; ~ **sacrifice scheme** *UK* TAX système du sacrifice salarial *m*; ~ **scale** HRM grille des salaires *f*; ~ **scheme** HRM système de rémunération *m*; ~ **structure** ECON, HRM structure des salaires *f*; ◆ ~ **to be negotiated** HRM salaire à débattre

sale *n* GEN COMM, S&M *act of selling* vente *f*, *at reduced prices* solde *m*, vente-réclame *f*, STOCK *of securities* vente *f*; ~ **agreement** *n* BANK accord de vente *m*, contrat de vente *m*, LAW, S&M contrat de vente *m*; ~ **by auction** *n* GEN COMM, S&M vente aux enchères *f*, vente à la criée *f*; ~ **by tender** *n* S&M vente par soumission *f*, vente par voie d'adjudication *f*; ~ **charges** *n pl* S&M frais commerciaux *m pl*; ~ **commission** *n* S&M commission de vente *f*; ~ **for the account** *n* BANK vente à terme *f*; ~ **for delivery** *n* STOCK vente pour livraison *f*, vente à couvert *f*; ~ **goods** *n pl* GEN COMM soldes *m pl*; ~ **item** *n* GEN COMM, S&M article en réclame *m*, article en solde *m*; ~ **and leaseback** *n* ACC vente et location d'une immobilisation *f*, LAW, PROP cession-bail *f*; ~ **on approval** *n* S&M vente à l'essai *f*; ~ **price** *n* GEN COMM prix de solde *m*, prix de vente *m*; ~ **proceeds** *n pl* GEN COMM produit de la vente *m*; ~ **and purchase broker** *n* HRM, LAW, TRANSP intermédiaire en cession de navires *m*; ~ **value** *n* S&M valeur marchande *f*; ~ **of vessel clause** *n* INS *hull clause*, TRANSP clause de vente de navire *f*; ◆ **for** ~ GEN COMM, PROP en vente; **make a** ~ STOCK effectuer une vente, faire une vente; **on** ~ GEN COMM, PROP, S&M en vente; **on** ~ **or return** GEN COMM vendu avec possibilité de retour, S&M vendu ou repris; ~ **or exchange** GEN COMM vente avec possibilité d'échanger la marchandise; ~ **subject to safe arrival** S&M vente sous réserve d'arrivée en bon état *f*

saleable *adj BrE* GEN COMM vendable

sales *n pl* ACC chiffre d'affaires *m*, ventes *f pl*, CA, FIN chiffre d'affaires *m*, CA, GEN COMM *proceeds* chiffre d'affaires *m*, chiffre de ventes *m*, ventes *f pl*, CA, S&M chiffre de ventes *m*, ventes *f pl*; ~ **account** *n* S&M compte de ventes *m*; ~ **activity** *n* GEN COMM, S&M ventes *f pl*; ~ **agency** *n* S&M agence commerciale *f*; ~ **analysis** *n* S&M analyse des ventes *f*; ~ **analyst** *n* HRM analyste commercial *m*, analyste des ventes *m*; ~ **appeal** *n* S&M attraction commerciale *f*, attrait commercial *m*; ~ **area** *n* S&M *in store* surface de vente *f*, *territory* secteur de vente *m*, territoire de vente *m*; ~ **assistant** *n* GEN COMM, HRM employé de magasin *m*; ~ **book** *n* S&M journal des ventes *m*, livre des ventes *m*; ~ **budget** *n* S&M budget commercial *m*; ~ **call** *n* S&M visite de représentant *f*; ~ **campaign** *n* S&M campagne de vente *f*; ~ **charge** *n* STOCK commission d'achat *f*, frais de vente *m pl*; ~ **clerk** *n AmE (cf shop assistant BrE)* GEN COMM, HRM commis de magasin *m*, employé de magasin *m*, vendeur *m*; ~ **conference** *n* S&M réunion de vendeurs *f*; ~ **contract** *n* BANK, LAW, S&M contrat de vente *m*; ~ **coverage** *n* S&M couverture du marché *f*; ~ **department** *n* S&M direction des ventes *f*, département commercial *m*, service commercial *m*, service des ventes *m*; ~ **director** *n* HRM administrateur commercial *m*; ~ **discount** *n* S&M escompte sur ventes *m*; ~ **drive** *n* S&M animation des ventes *f*, campagne de vente *f*; ~ **effectiveness test** *n* S&M vérification de l'efficacité des ventes *loc f*; ~ **engineer** *n* HRM ingénieur commercial *m*, technico-commercial *m*; ~ **enquiry** *n* S&M demande de renseignements *f*; ~ **estimate** *n* S&M estimation des ventes *f*; ~ **executive** *n* HRM, MGMNT, S&M cadre commercial *m*; ~ **figures** *n pl* GEN COMM chiffre de ventes *m*, S&M chiffre d'affaires *m*, chiffre de ventes *m*, CA; ~ **force** *n* S&M force de vente *f*, équipe de vente *f*; ~ **forecast** *n* ECON, S&M prévision de ventes *f*; ~ **goal** *n* S&M objectif de vente *m*; ~ **of goods law** *n* LAW, S&M loi sur les ventes de marchandises *f*; ~ **incentive** *n* S&M *for salesperson* incitation à la vente *f, for the buyer* offre promotionnelle *f*; ~ **journal** *n* S&M journal des ventes *m*; ~ **leaflet** *n* S&M prospectus de vente *m*; ~ **ledger** *n* ACC, BANK, FIN grand livre des clients *m*, grand livre des ventes *m*, grand livre des comptes clients *m*; ~ **letter** *n* S&M lettre publicitaire *f*; ~ **literature** *n* S&M brochure commerciale *f*, documentation publicitaire *f*; ~ **management** *n* MGMNT, S&M administration des ventes *f*, direction commerciale *f*, direction des ventes *f*, gestion des ventes *f*, organisation des ventes *f*; ~ **manager** *n* HRM, MGMNT, S&M chef du service des ventes *m*, directeur commercial *m*, directeur des ventes *m*, responsable des ventes *m*; ~ **maximization** *n* S&M maximisation des recettes *f*, optimisation des revenus *f*; ~ **mix** *n* S&M mix des produits en vente *m*, éventail des produits en vente *m*; ~ **network** *n* S&M réseau de vente *m*; ~ **objective** *n* S&M objectif commercial *m*; ~ **offensive** *n* S&M offensive commerciale *f*; ~ **office** *n* S&M agence commerciale *f*; ~ **opportunity** *n* S&M créneau commercial *m*; ~ **personnel** *n* S&M personnel de vente *m*; ~ **pitch** *n* S&M baratin commercial *m* (*infrml*); ~ **planning** *n* S&M planification des ventes *f*; ~ **policy** *n* GEN COMM, S&M politique de vente *f*; ~ **portfolio** *n* S&M argumentaire *m*; ~ **potential** *n* S&M potentiel de vente *m*; ~ **presentation** *n* S&M argumentaire de vente *m*; ~ **projection** *n* ECON, S&M prévision de ventes *f*; ~ **promotion** *n* S&M promotion des ventes *f*; ~ **quota** *n* S&M quota de ventes *m*; ~ **ratio** *n* S&M ratio des ventes *m*; ~ **receipt** *n* S&M reçu *m*; ~ **record** *n* S&M registre des ventes *m*; ~ **rep** *n* infrml (*sales representative*) GEN COMM voyageur de commerce *m*, HRM, S&M agent commercial *m*, représentant *m*, voyageur de commerce *m*; ~ **representative** *n* (*sales rep*) GEN COMM voyageur de commerce *m*, HRM, S&M agent commercial *m*, représentant *m*, voyageur de commerce *m*; ~ **returns** *n pl* S&M *revenues* recettes *f pl, statistics* statistiques sur les ventes *f pl, unsold items* invendus *m pl*; ~ **revenue** *n* S&M chiffre d'affaires *m*, recettes de ventes *f pl*, CA; ~ **slip** *n* GEN COMM *from cash register* ticket de caisse *m*; ~ **slump** *n* S&M mévente *f*; ~ **talk** *n* S&M argumentaire de vente *m*; ~ **target** *n* S&M objectif de vente *m*; ~ **tax** *n* S&M, TAX taxe sur les ventes *f*; ~ **tax credit** *n US* TAX crédit de taxe sur les ventes *m*; ~ **technique** *n* S&M technique de vente *f*; ~ **territory** *n* S&M territoire de vente *m*; ~ **test** *n* S&M vente expérimentale *f*; ~ **type lease** *n* FIN location-vente *f*; ~ **volume** *n* ACC volume de ventes *m*, S&M chiffre d'affaires *m*, volume de ventes *m*, CA

salesagent *n* GEN COMM agent commercial *m*, HRM, S&M vendeur *m*

salesman *n* GEN COMM vendeur *m*, HRM commercial *m, door-to-door* représentant *m, in shop* vendeur *m*, S&M commercial *m*, représentant *m*

salesmanship *n* S&M art de la vente *m*

salesperson *n* HRM commercial *m*, commerciale *f, door-to-door* représentant *m*, représentante *f, in shop* vendeur *m*, vendeuse *f*, S&M commercial *m*, commerciale *f*, representant *m*, représentante *f*

saleswoman *n* GEN COMM vendeuse *f*, HRM commerciale *f, door-to-door* représentante *f, in shop* vendeuse *f*, S&M commerciale *f* représentante *f*

Sallie: ~ **Mae** *abbr US* (*Student Loan Marketing Association*) FIN, WEL Association de gestion des prêts étudiants *f*

salt:[1] ~ **water** *n* TRANSP eau salée *f*

salt:[2] ~ **a memo** *phr jarg US* ADMIN truquer une circulaire

Salvadoran[1] *adj* GEN COMM salvadorien

Salvadoran[2] *n* GEN COMM *person* Salvadorien *m*

Salvadorean[1] *adj* GEN COMM salvadorien

Salvadorean[2] *n* GEN COMM *person* Salvadorien *m*

Salvadorian[1] *adj* GEN COMM salvadorien

Salvadorian[2] *n* GEN COMM *person* Salvadorien *m*

salvage *n* TRANSP *shipping* sauvetage *m*;

~ **agreement** *n* TRANSP *shipping* contrat de sauvetage *m*; ~ **bond** *n* ECON, STOCK obligation de garantie *f*; ~ **charges** *n pl* TRANSP *shipping* frais de sauvetage *m pl*; ~ **loss** *n* INS perte de sauvetage *f*; ~ **value** *n* ECON valeur résiduelle de liquidation *f*; ◆ **without benefit of** ~ (*wbs*) INS *marine* sans bénéfice du sauvetage

salvaged: ~ **return** *n* TAX déclaration réchappée *f*, déclaration sauvée *f*

salvor *n* TRANSP *shipping* sauveteur *m*

SAMA *abbr* (*Saudi Arabian Monetary Agency*) FIN Agence monétaire d'Arabie Saoudite *f*

same: ~ **language** *n* GEN COMM même langue *f*; ◆ **do the** ~ *phr* GEN COMM faire de même; **in the** ~ **terms** GEN COMM de la même façon; **in the** ~ **way** GEN COMM de la même façon; **on the** ~ **wavelength** GEN COMM *in agreement* sur la même longueur d'onde; ~ **job, same pay** *phr* HRM à travail égal, salaire égal *loc m*

same-day[1] *adj* TRANSP le jour même *loc m*

same-day:[2] ~ **delivery** *n* GEN COMM livraison dans la journée *f*; ~ **value** *n* BANK valeur jour *f*

sample *n* COMP exemple *m*, échantillon *m*, GEN COMM, MATH *statistics* échantillon *m*; ~ **audit** ACC, GEN COMM vérification par sondages *f*; ~ **card** GEN COMM carte d'échantillons *f*; ~ **data** COMP données type *f pl*; ~ **drawing** MATH *statistics* prise d'échantillon *f*; ~ **licence** *BrE* IMP/EXP licence temporaire d'exportation *f*; ~ **license** *AmE see sample licence BrE*; ~ **mailing** COMMS envoi d'échantillons *m*; ~ **mean** MATH *statistics* moyenne de l'échantillon *f*, échantillon type *m*; ~ **rate** GEN COMM tarif des échantillons *m*; ~ **study** S&M *market research* étude témoin *f*; ~ **survey** S&M *market research* enquête par sondage *f*; ◆ **take a** ~ MATH *statistics* prendre un échantillon

sampling *n* GEN COMM, MATH échantillonnage *m*; ~ **deviation** MATH *statistics* écart type de l'échantillon *m*; ~ **error** MATH *statistics* erreur d'échantillon *f*, erreur d'échantillonnage *f*; ~ **frame** MATH *statistics* cadre d'échantillonnage *m*; ~ **grid** MATH *statistics* grille d'échantillonnage *f*; ~ **offer** GEN COMM offre d'essai *f*; ~ **variance** MATH *statistics* variance de l'échantillon *f*

Samson: ~ **post** *n* TRANSP *shipping* mâtereau *m*

samurai: ~ **bond** *n* STOCK *Japan* obligation samouraï *f*

San: ~ **José** *pr n* GEN COMM San José *n pr*; ~ **Juan** *pr n* GEN COMM San Juan *n pr*; ~ **Salvador** *pr n* GEN COMM San Salvador *n pr*

Sanaa *pr n* GEN COMM Sanaa *n pr*

sanction[1] *n* GEN COMM sanction *f*

sanction[2] *vt* LAW sanctionner

s&c *abbr* (*shipper and carrier*) TRANSP chargeur et transporteur *loc m*, courtier d'affrètement maritime *m*

S&FA *abbr* (*shipping and forwarding agent*) HRM, IMP/EXP, TRANSP agent maritime-transitaire *m*, chargeur transitaire *m*

S&H/exct *abbr* *(Sundays and holidays excepted)*
TRANSP *shipping* dimanches et jours fériés exceptés *loc m*

sandwich: ~ **course** *n* WEL formation par alternance *f*; ~ **lease** *n* *infrml* PROP bail sandwich *m*
(infrml)

SANR *abbr* *(subject approval no risk)* INS risque
couvert sous réserve d'acceptation *m*, sans risque
sous réserve d'acceptation des conditions

sans: ~ **serif** *n* COMP, MEDIA *typography* caractère
sans empattement *m*

Santiago *pr n* GEN COMM Santiago *n pr*

Santo Domingo *pr n* GEN COMM Santo Domingo *n
pr*

SARA *abbr* *(salary adjustment reserve allotment)*
HRM ARRT *(affectation de réserve pour le
rajustement des salaires)*

Sarajevo *pr n* GEN COMM Sarajevo *n pr*

s.a.s.e. *abbr US* *(self-addressed stamped envelope,
cf s.a.e)* COMMS, GEN COMM enveloppe affranchie
f, enveloppe timbrée à vos nom et adresse *f*

Sat. *abbr* *(Saturday)* GEN COMM samedi *m*

satellite *n* COMMS, MEDIA satellite *m*;
~ **broadcasting** MEDIA radiodiffusion par satellite
f; ~ **communication** COMMS communication par
satellite *f*; ~ **computer** COMP ordinateur satellite
m; ~ **television** MEDIA *broadcast* télévision par
satellite *f*; ~ **town** GEN COMM ville satellite *f*

satisfaction *n* FIN *of debt* liquidation *f*, GEN COMM
satisfaction *f*; ~ **note** *jarg* INS attestation de
satisfaction *f*; ~ **piece** *jarg* PROP bon d'acquittement *m*; ◆ **in** ~ **of** ACC en paiement de, en
règlement de

satisfactory *adj* GEN COMM convenable, satisfaisant

satisfied: **be** ~ **with** *phr* GEN COMM se contenter de,
être satisfait de; ~ **with** *phr* GEN COMM satisfait de

satisfy *vt* FIN liquider, GEN COMM *debt* liquider,
demand répondre à, *requirement* satisfaire

saturate *vt* ECON, GEN COMM, S&M *market* saturer

saturation *n* COMP, S&M *of market* saturation *f*;
~ **campaign** S&M *advertising* campagne de saturation *f*; ~ **point** GEN COMM, S&M point de
saturation *m*

Saturday *n* *(Sat.)* GEN COMM samedi *m*; ~ **night
special** *jarg* *(SYN dawn raid)* FIN tentative d'OPA
surprise *f*

saucer *n* MATH *statistics* soucoupe *f*

Saudi[1] *adj* GEN COMM saoudien; ~ **Arabian** GEN
COMM saoudien

Saudi[2] *n* GEN COMM *person* Saoudien *m*; ~ **Arabian**
GEN COMM *person* Saoudien *m*; ~ **Arabian Monetary Agency** *(SAMA)* FIN Agence monétaire
d'Arabie Saoudite *f*

Saudi:[3] ~ **Arabia** *pr n* GEN COMM Arabie Saoudite *f*

save *vt* BANK faire une économie de, mettre de
côté, économiser, épargner, COMP *storage data*
sauvegarder, stocker, FIN, GEN COMM économiser;
◆ ~ **as you earn** *UK* *(SAYE)*, ECON, HRM plan

d'épargne national par prélèvements mensuels;
~ **energy** GEN COMM faire des économies d'énergie; ~ **for a rainy day** GEN COMM garder une poire
pour la soif

saver *n* FIN épargnant *m*

savings:[1] ~ **-linked** *adj* GEN COMM lié à l'épargne

savings[2] *n pl* ACC, BANK économies *f pl*, épargne *f*;
~ **account** *n* BANK compte d'épargne *m*, dépôt à
terme *m*; ~ **account passbook** *n* BANK livret de
compte d'épargne *m*, LEP; ~ **bank** *n* BANK
banque d'épargne *f*, caisse d'épargne *f*, STOCK
caisse d'épargne *f*; ~ **bankbook** *n* BANK livret
d'épargne populaire *m*, LEP; ~ **bond** *n US* BANK
bon d'épargne *m*; ~ **book** *n* BANK livret d'épargne
populaire *m*, livret de compte d'épargne *m*, LEP;
~ **certificate** *n* STOCK bon d'épargne *m*, certificat
d'épargne *m*; ~ **deposit** *n* BANK compte d'épargne
m; ~ **function** *n* ECON *of country* fonction
d'épargne *f*; ~ **passbook** *n* BANK livret d'épargne
populaire *m*, LEP; ~ **plan** *n* BANK régime
d'épargne *m*; ~ **ratio** *n* ECON possibilités d'épargne *f pl*, propension moyenne à économiser *f*,
propension moyenne à épargner *f*, taux d'épargne
des ménages *m*; ~ **-to-income ratio** *n* BANK, FIN
ratio épargne-revenus *m*

say: ~ **a few words of welcome** *phr* GEN COMM
prononcer quelques mots de bienvenue; **have a
~ in sth** *phr* GEN COMM avoir son mot à dire dans
qch *loc m*; **that is to** ~ *phr* *(SYN i.e., id est)* GEN
COMM c'est-à-dire

SAYE *abbr UK* *(save as you earn)* ECON, HRM plan
d'épargne national par prélèvements mensuels

Say's: ~ **law** *n* ECON loi de Say *f*

SB *abbr* *(short bill)* TRANSP traite à courte
échéance *f*

SBA *abbr* *(small business administration)* GEN
COMM administration des petites entreprises *f*,
gestion d'une petite entreprise *f*

SBAC *abbr* *(Society of British Aerospace
Companies)* TRANSP société des entreprises aérospatiales britanniques

SBDB *abbr* *(small business development bond)* GEN
COMM ODPE *(obligation pour le développement
de la petite entreprise)*

SBM *abbr* *(single-buoy mooring)* TRANSP *shipping*
amarrage sur un seul coffre *m*

SBP *abbr* *(solid non-ferrous propeller)* TRANSP
shipping hélice monobloc nonferreuse *f*

SBT *abbr* *(segregated ballast tank)* TRANSP *shipping* ballast séparé *m*

SC *abbr* LEIS *(Sports Council)* organisme autonome
d'encouragement aux activités sportives, TRANSP
(slip coupling) couplage extensible *m*, TRANSP
(steel covers) couvercle d'acier *m*, panneaux de
cale en acier *m pl*

scab *n pej* HRM *strikebreaker* briseur de grève *m*,
who takes over striker's job jaune *f* *(péj)*; ~ **unions**
n pl pej HRM *industrial relations* syndicats
patronaux *m pl*

scalar: ~ **principle** *n* HRM principe de l'échelle des salaires *m*

scale[1] *n* GEN COMM échelle *f, of problem* grille *f,* échelle *f*; ~ **charge** TAX frais du barème *m pl*; ~ **of charges** GEN COMM tableau des tarifs *m*; ~ **of commission** STOCK barème de commission *m,* échelle de commission *f*; ~ **of points value** HRM échelle de notation du personnel *f*; ~ **-up** GEN COMM extension d'échelle *f*

scale:[2] ~ **down** *vt* STOCK ralentir, réduire; ◆ ~ **the ladder** HRM grimper dans la hiérarchie

scaler *n* HRM *industrial relations* échelle des salaires *f*

scalp[1] *n infrml US* STOCK *profits* petit profit *m, securities* opération de scalpage *f*

scalp[2] *vt* STOCK *tickets* vendre au-dessous du prix normal, STOCK *US securities* boursicoter *(jarg)*

scalper *n US* STOCK scalper *m,* spéculateur sur la journée *m,* trafiqueur *m, securities* conseiller en investissement, ≈ boursicoteur *m (jarg)*

scalping *n infrml US* STOCK scalpage *m,* scalping *m*

scamp *n jarg* S&M *advertising* ébauche *f*

scan:[1] ~ **area** *n* COMP zone de numérisation *f*

scan[2] *vt* COMP *electronic* faire un balayage *loc m,* lire, numériser, scanner

scandal *n* GEN COMM scandale *m*

Scandinavia *n* GEN COMM Scandinavie *f*

scanner *n* COMP numériseur *m,* scanneur *m*

scanning *n* COMP *electronic* analyse *f,* lecture *f,* numérisation *f,* GEN COMM scrutation *f*

scant: ~ **coverage** *n (*ANT *full coverage)* MEDIA couverture médiocre *f*

scantling *n* TRANSP *shipping* échantillon *m,* échantillonnage *m*; ~ **draft** *AmE,* ~ **draught** *BrE* TRANSP *shipping* tirant d'eau maximal *m*

scarce *adj* ECON peu abonné, *resources* peu abondant, rare, GEN COMM rare

scarcely: ~ **scheduled** *adj* GEN COMM pas prévu *(infrml)*

scarcity: ~ **value** *n* ECON valeur de rareté *f*

scatter: ~ **diagram** *n* MATH *statistics* diagramme de dispersion *m,* schéma de dispersion *m,* MGMNT diagramme de dispersion *m*

scattered: ~ **site housing** *n jarg BrE (cf scattersite housing AmE)* WEL dispersion des logements *f*

scattergram *n* MATH *statistics* schéma de dispersion *m*

scattersite: ~ **housing** *n jarg AmE (cf scattered site housing BrE)* WEL dispersion des logements *f*

scavenger: ~ **sale** *n infrml* PROP vente nécrophage *f*

scenario *n* ECON hypothèse *f,* GEN COMM hypothèse *f,* scénario *m*

scenic: ~ **easement** *n* PROP servitude touristique *f*

scepticism *n BrE* GEN COMM scepticisme *m*

schedular: ~ **tax** *n* TAX impôt programmé *m*

schedule[1] *n* FIN calendrier *m,* horaire *m,* plan de travail *m,* programme *m,* GEN COMM horaire *m, list* programme *m, timetable* emploi du temps *m,* MGMNT calendrier *m,* horaire *m,* plan de travail *m,* programme *m*; ~ **of repayments** BANK programme de remboursements *m*; ◆ **be on** ~ GEN COMM être dans les temps, être à l'heure; **on** ~ GEN COMM *train, etc* à l'heure, HRM sans retard sur l'horaire

schedule[2] *vt* GEN COMM dresser, programmer, MGMNT programmer

scheduled[1] *adj* TRANSP régulier; ◆ **as** ~ ADMIN, GEN COMM comme prévu, conformément au programme *(frml),* selon le planning; **be** ~ **for** GEN COMM être programmé pour, être prévu pour; **be** ~ **to begin in** GEN COMM devoir commencer en, être prévu pour

scheduled:[2] ~ **flight** *n* LEIS, TRANSP vol régulier *m*; ~ **prices** *n pl* GEN COMM prix selon le tarif *m pl*; ~ **service** *n* LEIS, TRANSP ligne régulière *f,* service régulier *m*

scheduling *n* IND *production,* MGMNT ordonnancement *m,* programmation *f*

scheme *n* ADMIN programme *m,* système *m,* TAX *tax evasion* manoeuvre frauduleuse *f,* stratagème frauduleux *m*

schilling *n* GEN COMM schilling *m*

scholarship *n* TAX bourse d'études *f*

school *n* GEN COMM, WEL école *f*; ~ **-leaver** *UK* HRM jeune à la fin de ses études secondaires; ~ **report** GEN COMM bulletin scolaire *m*

School: ~ **of Public Management** *n* WEL École Nationale d'Administration *f,* ENA

schooner *n (Sr)* TRANSP *shipping* goélette *f*

science: ~ **park** *n* IND parc scientifique *m*; ~ **and technology for environmental protection programme** *n (STEP)* ENVIR *EU* science et technologie pour la protection de l'environnement *f*

scientific: ~ **management** *n* IND gestion scientifique *f,* MATH, MGMNT gestion scientifique *f,* organisation scientifique *f,* organisation scientifique du travail *f,* OST; ~ **programming** *n* MATH programmation mathématique *f*; ~ **research** *n* IND recherche scientifique *f*; ~ **research expenditure** *n UK* TAX *capital allowances* frais de recherche scientifique *m pl*; ~ **research and experimental development expenditure** *n* TAX dépenses de recherche scientifique et de développement expérimental *f pl*

scientist *n* HRM savant *m*

SCIP *abbr (solid cast-iron propeller)* TRANSP *shipping* hélice monobloc en fonte de fer *f*

scissor: ~ **lift** *n* TRANSP monte-charge à ciseaux *m*

SCN *abbr (specification change notice)* TRANSP *aviation* SCN *(spécification de changement notifié)*

scoop *n* MEDIA *print* exclusivité *f,* scoop *m (jarg)*; ◆ **make a** ~ *infrml* GEN COMM réussir un grand coup

scope *n* GEN COMM étendue *f,* étendue de la

vérification *f*, PATENTS *of claims* portée *f*, étendue *f*; **~ of agreement** HRM extension de convention *f*; **~ of bargaining** HRM extension de négociation *f*; **~ of coverage** INS champ d'application de la couverture *m*, étendue de la garantie *f*; **~ of employment** HRM activités relevant d'emploi désigné *f pl*; ◆ **there is ~ for improvement** GEN COMM cela laisse à désirer

scorched: ~ -earth policy *n* FIN politique consistant pour une société devenue la cible d'une offre publique d'achat à se rendre moins attrayante aux yeux de l'acquéreur

score[1] *n* GEN COMM score *m*; ◆ **on that ~** GEN COMM à cet égard

score[2] *vt* GEN COMM *point* marquer; ◆ **~ a good viewership** MEDIA avoir une bonne audience; **~ a hit** GEN COMM remporter un grand succès

Scot *n* GEN COMM *person* Écossais *m*

scotch: ~ derrick *n* TRANSP mât de charge à rotation de 270° *m*

Scotland *pr n* GEN COMM Écosse *f*

Scotsman *n* GEN COMM *person* Écossais *m*

Scotswoman *n* GEN COMM *person* Écossaise *f*

Scottish *adj* GEN COMM écossais

SCP *abbr* ECON *(structure-conduct-performance model)* modèle structure-conduite-performance *m*, IMP/EXP *(simplified clearance procedure)* procédure de dédouanement simplifiée *f*, STOCK *(sterling commercial paper)* papier commercial en livres sterling *m*

scrambled: ~ message *n* COMMS *satellite communication* message brouillé *m*

scrap:[1] **~ -and-build regulation** *n* TRANSP *shipping* réglementation vieux pour neuf *f*; **~ dealer** *n* GEN COMM, HRM ferrailleur *m*; **~ metal** *n* ENVIR, GEN COMM ferraille *f*; **~ paper** *n* GEN COMM brouillon *m*; **~ yard** *n* GEN COMM chantier de ferraille *m*

scrap[2] *vt* GEN COMM *idea, project* abandonner, laisser tomber, écarter

scrape: ~ along *vi infrml* GEN COMM se débrouiller; **~ through** GEN COMM s'en tirer de justesse

scratch[1] *n* COMP brouillon *m*; **~ area** COMP zone de travail *f*; **~ disk** COMP disque de travail *m*; **~ file** COMP fichier de travail *m*; **~ pad** COMP mémoire de travail *f*, zone de travail *f*; ◆ **come up to ~** *infrml* GEN COMM se montrer à la hauteur

scratch:[2] **~ out** *vt* GEN COMM rayer

scratching *n* GEN COMM *initialling an agreement* griffonnage *m*

screamline *vt jarg* MEDIA *print* titrer en gros caractères

screen[1] *n* COMP écran *m*, GEN COMM écran *m, in room* paravent *m*; **~ advertising** S&M publicité cinématographique *f*; **~ capture** COMP saisie d'écran *f*; **~ copy** COMP recopie d'écran *f*; **~ driver** COMP pilote d'écran *m*; **~ dump** COMP vidage d'écran *m*; **~ editor** COMP éditeur d'écran *m*; **~ test** MEDIA bout d'essai *m*, essai filmé *m*

screen[2] *vt* GEN COMM, HRM *candidate, application*

passer au crible, sélectionner; **~ out** HRM éliminer à la présélection; ◆ **~ sb for a job** HRM passer au crible la candidature de qn

screening *n* GEN COMM, HRM *of candidates* présélection *f*; **~ board** HRM jury de présélection *m*; **~ process** HRM présélection *f*

screw *n* TRANSP ridoir *m*; **~ -down non return valve** TRANSP clapet de non-retour blocable *m*; **~ propulsion** TRANSP *shipping* propulsion par hélice *f*; **~ steamer** TRANSP *shipping* vapeur à hélices *m*

scrimp: ~ and save *phr* GEN COMM lésiner

scrip: ~ dividend *n* FIN dividende différé *m*; **~ issue** *n* FIN, STOCK attribution d'actions gratuites *f*, émission d'actions gratuites *f*

scripophily *n* STOCK scripophilie *f*

scroll:[1] **~ arrow** *n* COMP flèche de défilement *f*

scroll[2] *vt* COMP *image, text* faire défiler; **~ down** *(ANT scroll up)* COMP faire défiler vers le bas; **~ up** *(ANT scroll down)* COMP faire défiler vers le haut

scrolling *n* COMP défilement *m*; **~ down** COMP défilement vers le bas; **~ up** COMP défilement vers le haut *m*

scrutiny: come under ~ *phr* GEN COMM être examiné, POL *Parliament* venir en lecture

SCSP *abbr (solid cast-steel propeller)* TRANSP *shipping* hélice monobloc en fonte d'acier *f*

scuttle *vt* TRANSP *shipping* saborder

scuttling *n* TRANSP *shipping* sabordage *m*

S/D *abbr (sailing date)* TRANSP *shipping* date de départ *f*, jour de départ *m*

SD *abbr* BANK *(sight draft)*, GEN COMM *(sight draft)* traite à vue *f*, IND *(standard design)* de série, INS *(sea damage)*, TRANSP *(sea damage)* *shipping* fortune de mer *f*

SDA *abbr UK (Sex Discrimination Act)* HRM loi relative à la discrimination sexuelle

S d/k *abbr (shelter deck)* TRANSP *shipping* pont-abri *m*

SDR *abbr (special drawing rights)* BANK droits particuliers de retrait *m pl*, LAW DTS *(droits de tirage spéciaux)*

SDRIBOR *abbr UK (six month SDRs interbank offered rate)* BANK taux interbancaire offert pour droits de tirage spéciaux sur six mois

SDT *abbr (side tank)* TRANSP *shipping* citerne latérale *f*

SDW *abbr (side wheel)* TRANSP roue latérale *f*

SE *abbr (southeast)* GEN COMM, TRANSP *shipping* sud-est *m*

sea:[1] **~ -damaged** *adj* TRANSP *shipping, grain trade* avarié par eau de mer

sea[2] *n* TRANSP *mode of transport* mer *f*; **~ anchor** TRANSP *shipping* ancre flottante *f*; **~ carrier** TRANSP transporteur maritime *m*; **~ damage** *(SD)* INS, TRANSP fortune de mer *f*; **~ insurance** INS assurance maritime *f*; **~ law** LAW, TRANSP droit de la mer *m*, droit maritime *m*; **~ letter**

TRANSP congé *m*, congé de navigation *m*, passeport *m*; ~ **port** TRANSP port de mer *m*, port maritime *m*; ~ **risk** TRANSP risque de mer *m*; ~ **route** TRANSP route maritime *f*; ~ **transport** ECON transport maritime *m*; ~ **waybill** IMP/EXP, TRANSP *shipping* lettre de transport maritime *f*

SEA *abbr (Single European Act)* LAW, POL AUE *(Acte unique européen)*

seaborne *adj* TRANSP *freight* transporté par mer

seafarming *n* ECON *agricultural* aquaculture *f*

seagoing: ~ **barge** *n* TRANSP *shipping* chaland de mer *m*; ~ **trade** *n* ECON, GEN COMM, IMP/EXP, TRANSP commerce maritime *m*

seal[1] *n* GEN COMM *of company* cachet *m*; ~ **of approval** GEN COMM homologation *f*, sceau d'approbation *m*; ~ **of quality** GEN COMM marque de qualité *f*

seal:[2] ~ **off** *vt* GEN COMM fermer

sealed[1] *adj* GEN COMM scellé

sealed:[2] ~ **tender** *n* COMMS soumission cachetée *f*; ◆ **in a** ~ **envelope** GEN COMM sous pli cacheté

sealing: ~ **wax** *n* COMMS cire à cacheter *f*

seaman *n* TRANSP matelot *m*; ~ **grade I** HRM, TRANSP matelot de première classe *m*; ~ **grade II** HRM, TRANSP matelot de seconde classe *m*

seaport *n* TRANSP port de mer *m*, port maritime *m*

SEAQ[1] *abbr (Stock Exchange Automated Quotation)* STOCK système de cotation automatisé *m*

SEAQ:[2] ~ **Automated Execution Facility** *n UK (SAEF)* STOCK système international de cotation automatisé *m*; ~ **International** *n UK* STOCK système international de cotation des valeurs étrangères automatisé

SEAQI *abbr (Stock Exchange Automated Quotation International)* STOCK système international de cotation des valeurs étrangères automatisé

search[1] *n* COMP, GEN COMM, HRM, IND, MGMNT recherche *f*, PATENTS recherche *f*, visite *f*, TAX fouille et perquisition *f pl*; ~ **key** COMP clé de recherche *f*; ~ **report** PATENTS rapport de recherche *m*; ~ **and seizure** GEN COMM perquisition et saisie *f*; ~ **warrant** LAW mandat de perquisition *m*; ◆ **be in** ~ **of** GEN COMM être à la recherche de

search[2] *vt* COMP *file, document* chercher, faire une recherche de, IMP/EXP fouiller, visiter, LAW visiter; ~ **for** GEN COMM chercher, fouiller; ~ **out** HRM *job* rechercher; ◆ ~ **a file for sth** GEN COMM rechercher qch dans un fichier; ~ **and replace** COMP *on word processor* fonction de recherche et remplacement *f*

Search: ~ **and Advisory Service** *n UK* LAW, PATENTS service de recherche et de conseil de l'office britannique des brevets

seaside: ~ **resort** *n* GEN COMM station balnéaire *f*

season *n* LEIS saison *f*; **off** ~ GEN COMM hors saison *f*, morte saison *f*; ~ **ticket** *BrE (cf commutation ticket AmE)* GEN COMM carte d'abonnement *f*; ~ **ticket holder** *BrE* GEN COMM abonné *m*

seasonal[1] *adj* GEN COMM saisonnier

seasonal:[2] ~ **adjustments** *n pl* ECON, MATH, POL *statistics* variations saisonnières *f pl*; ~ **factor** *n* ECON facteur saisonnier *m*; ~ **fluctuations** *n pl* ECON, MATH, POL variations saisonnières *f pl*; ~ **swing** *n* GEN COMM fluctuation saisonnière *f*; ~ **swings** *n pl* ECON, MATH, POL variations saisonnières *f pl*; ~ **unemployment** *n* ECON, HRM chômage saisonnier *m*; ~ **variations** *n pl* ECON série chronologique *f*, variations saisonnières *f pl*, MATH, POL variations saisonnières *f pl*; ~ **worker** *n* HRM saisonnier *m*

seasonality: ~ **of demand** *n* ECON saisonnalité de la demande *f*

seasonally:[1] ~ **adjusted** *adj* ECON, GEN COMM corrigé en fonction des variations saisonnières, désaisonnalisé

seasonally:[2] ~ **adjusted annual rate** *n (s.a.a.r.)* ECON taux annuel corrigé des variations saisonnières *m*; ~ **adjusted figures** *n pl* FIN données corrigées des variations saisonnières *f pl*, données désaisonnalisées *f pl*; ~ **unadjusted employment figures** *n pl* HRM nombre de chômeurs en données non corrigées des variations saisonnières *m*

seasoned[1] *adj* GEN COMM assaisonné

seasoned:[2] ~ **certificate of deposit** *n* STOCK certificat de dépôt négociable sur le marché secondaire *m*, coupon émis depuis plus de trois mois *m*; ~ **loan** *n* BANK obligation émise depuis plus de trois mois *f*

seat *n* LEIS place *f*, POL *in Parliament* siège *m*; ~ **belt** *n* TRANSP ceinture de sécurité *f*; ~ **mile** *n* LEIS place-mille *f*; ~ **pitch** *n* TRANSP pas de siège *m*; ~ **reservation system** *n* LEIS système de réservation des places *m*; ◆ ~ **kilometers used** *AmE*, ~ **kilometres used** *BrE* LEIS place-kilomètre utilisée *f*; ~ **miles per engine hour** LEIS place-milles par heure-moteur *f*

SEAT *abbr UK (Stock Exchange Alternative Trading Service)* STOCK tableau électronique de cotations *m*

SEATAG *abbr (South East Asia Trade Advisory Group)* ECON, IMP/EXP groupe consultatif commercial d'Asie du Sud-Est

seaworthiness *n* TRANSP *shipping* navigabilité *f*, état de navigabilité *m*

SEB *abbr* STOCK *US (Specialist Electronic Book)* annuaire électronique spécialisé *m*, carnet électronique spécialisé *m*, TRANSP *(single-ended boiler) shipping* chaudière ordinaire *f*

sec. *abbr* ADMIN *(secretary)* secrétaire *mf*, GEN COMM *(second)* s. *(seconde)*, HRM *(secretary)*, MGMNT *(secretary)* secrétaire *mf*

SEC *abbr (Securities and Exchange Commission)* STOCK ≈ COB *(France) (Commission des opérations de Bourse)*

SECAL *abbr (sector adjustment loan)* FIN emprunt de redressement sectoriel *m*

second:[1] ~ **-grade** *adj* GEN COMM inférieur; ~ **to none** *adj* GEN COMM sans pareil

second[2] *n (sec.)* GEN COMM seconde *f (s.)*; ~ **best** ECON *Pareto optimum* deuxième rang *m*; ~ **carrier** TRANSP deuxième transporteur *m*; ~ **-class citizen** GEN COMM citoyen de seconde classe *m*; ~ **-class mail** COMMS courrier à tarif réduit *m*; ~ **-class paper** FIN titre de deuxième ordre *m*; ~ **-class post** COMMS courrier à tarif réduit *m*; ~ **debenture** FIN obligation de deuxième rang *f*; ~ **-degree price discrimination** GEN COMM tarif discriminatoire de second ordre *m*; ~ **economy** ECON part d'économie de marché en pays socialiste; ~ **generation** MEDIA deuxième génération *f*; ~ **-generation product** S&M produit de deuxième génération *m*; ~ **-generation type** PROP *of warehouse* type deuxième génération *m*; ~ **half of the year** GEN COMM deuxième semestre *m*; ~ **-hand car** TRANSP voiture d'occasion *f*; ~ **-hand market** GEN COMM brocante *f*, friperie *f*, *trade in used goods* marché de l'occasion *m*; ~ **-hand shop** *BrE (cf thrift shop AmE)* S&M magasin de brocante *m*; ~ **-hand vehicle** TRANSP véhicule d'occasion *m*; ~ **home** PROP, TAX résidence secondaire *f*; ~ **installment base** *AmE*, ~ **instalment base** *BrE* TAX *deuxième base des acomptes provisionnels f*; ~ **market** ECON *second marché m*; ~ **mortgage** BANK, PROP *hypothèque de deuxième rang f*; ~ **mortgage lending** FIN *prêt hypothécaire de deuxième rang m*; ~ **offence** *BrE* LAW *récidive f*; ~ **offense** *AmE see second offence BrE*; ~ **or further occurrence penalty** TAX *pénalisation pour récidive f, pénalité pour récidive f*; ~ **quarter** *(2Q)* GEN COMM *deuxième trimestre m*; ~ **-rank consultant** HRM *consultant de deuxième ordre m, consultant junior m*; ~ **reading** LAW, POL *of bill, directive deuxième lecture f, seconde lecture f*; ~ **residence** PROP, TAX *résidence secondaire f*; ~ **-tier company** GEN COMM *société de deuxième ordre f*

second:[3] ~ **-guess** *vt infrml* GEN COMM anticiper l'action de, décider contre l'avis de

Second: ~ **World** *n* ECON, POL *(ANT First World, Fourth World, Third World) centrally planned economies* les pays socialistes *m pl*; ~ **World War** *n* GEN COMM deuxième guerre mondiale *f*

secondary: ~ **action** *n* HRM revendication complémentaire *f*; ~ **activities** *n pl (ANT primary activities, tertiary activities)* ECON, GEN COMM, IND activités du secteur secondaire *f pl*, services secondaires *m pl*; ~ **bank** *n* BANK, FIN banque d'affaires *f*; ~ **banking crisis** *n* BANK crise des banques d'affaires *f*; ~ **boycott** *n* HRM boycott complémentaire *m*; ~ **claim** *n* ACC créance de deuxième rang *f*; ~ **distribution** *n* STOCK revente de titres *f*; ~ **education** *n* WEL enseignement secondaire *m*, second degré *m*; ~ **employment** *n* HRM travail non-déclaré *m*; ~ **explosive** *n* TRANSP *classified goods* explosif secondaire *m*; ~ **income** *n* FIN revenu accessoire *m*; ~ **labor market** *n AmE*, ~ **labour market** *n BrE* HRM marché des emplois non-déclarés *m*; ~ **legislation** *n* LAW *EU*, POL *EU* législation secondaire *f*, textes d'application *m pl*;

~ **market** *n* ECON, STOCK marché secondaire *m*; ~ **offering** *n* STOCK deuxième mise sur le marché *f*, offres sur deuxième marché *f pl*; ~ **picketing** *n* HRM piquet de grève devant une autre entreprise *m*; ~ **-primary distribution** *n* STOCK placement d'un bloc de contrôle *m*; ~ **sector** *n (ANT primary sector)* ECON, IND secteur secondaire *m*; ~ **standard** *n* ENVIR *for pollution levels to protect vegetation* norme de pureté de l'air *f*

Secondary: ~ **Market Association** *n (SMA)* STOCK Association du marché secondaire *f*

secondly *adv* GEN COMM deuxièmement

secondment *n* HRM *army* détachement *m*, mise en disponibilité *f*

2Q *abbr (second quarter)* GEN COMM deuxième trimestre *m*

secrecy *n* GEN COMM secret *m*

secret[1] *adj* GEN COMM clandestin, secret

secret:[2] ~ **ballot** *n* HRM *before industrial action* vote à bulletin secret *m*; ~ **payment** *n* HRM rémunération occulte *f*; ~ **reserve** *n* FIN fonds occultes *m pl*; ~ **reserves** *n pl* ACC réserves cachées *f pl*, réserves latentes *f pl*

secretarial: ~ **skills** *n pl* HRM compétences en matière de secrétariat *f pl*; ~ **staff** *n* ADMIN, HRM personnel de secrétariat *m*

secretariat *n* HRM, POL *government* secrétariat *m*

secretary *n* ADMIN *(sec.)* secrétaire *mf*, ADMIN *US* ministre *mf*, HRM *(sec.)*, MGMNT *(sec.)* secrétaire *mf*, POL *US* ministre *mf*; ~ **s office** *n* ADMIN secrétariat *m*

Secretary: ~ **of State** *n* ADMIN *UK* ministre *mf*, ministre d'État *m*, secrétaire d'État *m*, POL *US* ≈ ministre des Affaires étrangères *m*, POL *UK* ministre *mf*, ministre d'État *m*, secrétaire d'État *m*, ≈ ministre des Affaires étrangères *m*; ~ **of State for Transport** *n UK* TRANSP ≈ ministre des Transports *m*; ~ **of the Treasury** *n US* FIN ≈ ministre des Finances *m*

section *n* GEN COMM rayon *m*, *in CICA Handbook* chapitre *m*, rubrique *f*, LAW *of act* article *m*, section *f*, MEDIA rubrique *f*, POL *of act* article *m*, section *f*, S&M rayon *m*

sectional: ~ **rate** *n* TRANSP *aviation* chapitre du tarif *m*

sector[1] *n* COMP *of disk*, GEN COMM *of economy* secteur *m*; ~ **adjustment lending** ECON prêt à taux bonifié pour aider un secteur particulier de l'économie; ~ **adjustment loan** *(SECAL)* FIN emprunt de redressement sectoriel *m*; ~ **analysis** GEN COMM analyse sectorielle *f*; ~ **investment and maintenance loan** *(SIM)* FIN prêt d'investissement et d'entretien sectoriel *m (IES)*; ~ **-specific aid** ECON, POL *development* aide spécifique à un secteur *f*

sector[2] *vt* COMP *disk* sectoriser

sectoral[1] *adj* ECON *interests* sectoriel

sectoral:[2] ~ **accounting plan** *n* ACC plan professionnel *m*; ~ **strategy** *n* MGMNT stratégie sectorielle *f*

secular: ~ **trend** *n* ECON tendance à long terme *f*

secure[1] *adj* ECON *financially* de tout repos, sûr

secure:[2] ~ **job** *n* HRM emploi assuré *m*

secure[3] *vt* BANK *loan* garantir, STOCK *price in futures contract* garantir, s'assurer de; ◆ ~ **a debt by mortgage** BANK garantir une dette par hypothèque; ~ **an investment** BANK garantir un placement; ~ **new orders** GEN COMM obtenir de nouvelles commandes

secured: ~ **advance** *n* BANK avance garantie *f*, avance sur garantie *f*; ~ **bond** *n* FIN, STOCK obligation garantie *f*; ~ **credit** *n* BANK crédit garanti *m*; ~ **creditor** *n* ACC créancier garanti *m*; ~ **debenture** *n* FIN, STOCK obligation garantie *f*; ~ **debt** *n* BANK créance garantie *f*, dette garantie *f*; ~ **fixed-term loan** *n* BANK prêt garanti à terme fixe *m*; ~ **loan** *n* BANK emprunt garanti *m*, prêt garanti *m*; ~ **personal loan** *n* BANK prêt personnel garanti *m*

securing: ~ **pad** *n* TRANSP *lashing equipment* dispositif d'accrochage *m*

securities *n pl* STOCK titres *m pl*, valeurs *f pl*; ~ **account** *n* BANK compte de dépôt de titres *m*; ~ **act** *n* LAW loi relative aux titres et valeurs mobilières *f*, loi relative aux valeurs mobilières *f*; ~ **act of 1933** *n* FIN loi de 1933 relative aux titres et valeurs mobilières; ~ **acts amendments of 1975** *n pl* STOCK amendements de 1975 à la loi sur les valeurs mobilières; ~ **administrator** *n* GEN COMM administrateur des valeurs mobilières *m*; ~ **analysis** *n* FIN analyse financière *f*; ~ **borrowing** *n* BANK emprunt boursier *m*; ~ **business** *n* STOCK activités boursières *f pl*, opérations boursières *f pl*; ~ **cancellation** *n* STOCK annulation de titres *f*; ~ **company** *n* STOCK maison de titres *f*; ~ **dealing** *n* STOCK opération sur titres *f*, opération sur valeurs mobilières *f*; ~ **department** *n* STOCK service des titres *m*; ~ **exchange** *n* STOCK Bourse *f*, marché boursier *m*; ~ **firm** *n* STOCK maison de titres *f*; ~ **held in trust** *n pl* STOCK *SGAT* titres détenus en fiducie *m pl*; ~ **house** *n* STOCK bourse *f*, maison de titres *f*; ~ **in portfolio** *n pl* STOCK valeurs en portefeuille *f pl*; ~ **lending** *n* BANK prêt boursier *m*; ~ **listing** *n* STOCK cote boursière *f*, cote officielle *f*; ~ **loan** *n* STOCK prêt boursier *m*, prêt de titres *m*; ~ **long** *n pl* STOCK titres en compte *m pl*, valeurs en compte *f pl*; ~ **market** *n* FIN marché de valeurs mobilières *m*; ~ **portfolio** *n* STOCK portefeuille de titres *m*; ~ **short** *n pl* STOCK titres à découvert *m pl*, valeurs à découvert *f pl*; ~ **sold under repurchase agreement** *n* STOCK titres vendus en pension livrée *m pl*, titres vendus à réméré *m pl*; ~ **tax** *n* TAX impôt sur le revenu des valeurs mobilières *m*, impôt sur les valeurs *m*; ~ **transaction** *n* STOCK opération sur titres *f*, opération sur valeurs mobilières *f*; ~ **wanted** *n pl* STOCK titres demandés *m pl*, valeurs demandées *f pl*

Securities: ~ **Association** *n* STOCK association des opérations boursières; ~ **Exchange Act 1934** *n* US STOCK loi sur les bourses de valeurs de 1934; ~ **and Exchange Commission** *n* US (*SEC*) STOCK ≈ Commission des opérations de Bourse *f* (*France*) (*COB*); ~ **and Futures Authority** *n* UK (*SFA*) STOCK organisme de surveillance des bourses de valeurs et des marchés à terme; ~ **and Investments Board** *n* UK (*SIB*) STOCK ≈ Commission des opérations de Bourse *f* (*France*) (*COB*); **The** ~ **Association** *n pl* UK (*TSA*) STOCK ≈ Conseil des bourses de valeurs *m* (*CBV*)

securitization *n* BANK valeurisation *f*, FIN, STOCK titrisation *f*

securitize *vt* FIN, STOCK titriser

security *n* ADMIN sécurité *f*, BANK gage *m*, garantie *f*, COMP sécurité *f*, FIN cautionnement *m*, GEN COMM *pledge* cautionnement *m*, garantie *f*, sûreté *f*, *safety* caution *f*, sécurité *f*, INS cautionnement *m*, STOCK t., titre *m*, titre d'investissement *m*, val., valeur *f*, valeur mobilière *f*; ~ **backup** *n* COMP copie de sauvegarde *f*, copie de secours *f*; ~ **bond for down payment** *n* STOCK nantissement pour acompte *m*, obligation garantie pour acompte *f*; ~ **borrowing** *n* (*ANT security lending*) FIN emprunt de titres *m*; ~ **check** *n* GEN COMM contrôle de sécurité *m*; ~ **copy** *n* COMP copie de sauvegarde *f*, copie de secours *f*; ~ **dealer** *n* STOCK garant *m*, négociant en titres *m*; ~ **disposal** *n* STOCK aliénation de titres *f*, aliénation de valeurs mobilières *f*, cession de titres *f*, cession de valeurs mobilières *f*; ~ **holder** *n* STOCK porteur de titres *m*, porteur de valeurs *m*; ~ **holding** *n* STOCK titre détenu *m*, valeur détenue *f*; ~ **interest** *n* STOCK sûreté *f*; ~ **leak** *n* GEN COMM fuite *f*; ~ **lending** *n* (*ANT security borrowing*) FIN prêt de titres *m*; ~ **margin** *n* GEN COMM marge de sécurité *f*; ~ **market line** *n* STOCK relation rendement d'une valeur *f*, spécialité boursière *f*; ~ **measure** *n* GEN COMM mesure de sécurité *f*; ~ **rating** *n* STOCK cotation boursière *f*, cote en Bourse *f*, notation d'une valeur *f*; ~ **risk** *n* INS personne susceptible de compromettre la sécurité d'une société; ~ **services** *n pl* ADMIN services de sécurité *m pl*; ~ **of tenure** *n* PROP bail assuré *m*; ◆ **have** ~ **of tenure** HRM *employee* être titularisé

secus *adv* GEN COMM au contraire *loc m*, autrement

SEDOL *abbr* UK (*Stock Exchange Daily Official List*) STOCK ≈ BOCB (*France*) (*Bulletin officiel des cours de la Bourse*)

see *vti* GEN COMM voir; ~ **over** MEDIA voir au dos, voir au verso; ~ **overleaf** MEDIA *print* voir au dos, voir au verso

seed: ~ **capital** *n* FIN capitaux d'amorçage *m pl*, financement d'amorçage *m*; ~ **money** *n* FIN capital d'apport *m*, capital de départ *m*, capitaux d'amorçage *m pl*, capitaux de lancement *m pl*, investissement initial *m*

seek *vt* GEN COMM *advice* demander, *approval* chercher, quêter, *employment* chercher, *help* rechercher, HRM rechercher; ◆ ~ **a job** HRM chercher un emploi; ~ **legal advice** LAW consulter un conseiller juridique, demander un conseil juridique; **~ a market** STOCK chercher la contre-partie, rechercher un marché; **~ redress** LAW demander réparation

seepage *n* GEN COMM *water* fuite *f*, infiltration *f*

segment[1] *n* COMP *of file, program* segment *m*, MATH *in pie chart* tranche *f*, S&M *of market* segment *m*; **~ information** GEN COMM informations segmentaires *f pl*; **~ margin** ACC bénéfice sectoriel *m*; **~ of the market** S&M segment du marché *m*; **~ profit** ACC profit sectoriel *m*

segment[2] *vt* GEN COMM, MGMNT *of policy*, S&M *of market* segmenter

segmental: **~ reporting** *n* ACC analyse par secteur d'activité *f*

segmentation *n* S&M segmentation *f*; **~ strategy** *UK* S&M stratégie de segmentation *f*

segmented: **~ labor market theory** *n* AmE, **~ labour market theory** *n* BrE ECON théorie de la segmentation du marché de la main-d'oeuvre *f*; **~ return** *n* TAX déclaration segmentée *f*

segregated[1] *adj* GEN COMM isolé, séparé

segregated:[2] **~ ballast tank** *n* *(SBT)* TRANSP *shipping* ballast séparé *m*; **~ ballast tank-protective location** *n* TRANSP *oil tanker* ballast séparé-localisation défensive *m*; **~ free position** *n* STOCK position de titres en garde *f*

segregation *n* COMMS *separating* ségrégation *f*

seigniorage *n* GEN COMM seigneuriage *m*

select:[1] **~ committee** *n* *UK* POL commission d'enquête *f*

select[2] *vt* GEN COMM choisir, sélectionner

selected[1] *adj* GEN COMM sélectionné

selected:[2] **~ dealer agreement** *n* STOCK contrat de courtier sélectionné *m*, contrat de souscription et de mise sur le marché *m*

selection *n* COMP *of data, information*, HRM sélection *f*; **~ bias** MATH *statistics* biais de sélection *m*; **~ board** HRM jury de sélection *m*

selective: **~ distribution** *n* GEN COMM distribution sélective *f*; **~ hedge** *n* STOCK couverture sélective *f*

Selective: **~ Employment Tax** *n* TAX impôt sur le travail sélectif *m*; **~ Financial Assistance** *n* *UK* ECON *regional development* Aide financière sélective *f*

self:[1] **~ -catering** *adj* PROP en location; **~ -contained** *adj* GEN COMM indépendant; **~ -financing** *adj* ACC, FIN autofinancé; **~ -generated** *adj* ACC *increase in capital and reserves* autogénéré; **~ -governing** *adj* ADMIN, POL, TRANSP *shipping* autonome; **~ -liquidating** *adj* FIN auto-amortissable; **~ -sufficient** *adj* ECON, GEN COMM autosuffisant, indépendant; **~ -supporting** *adj* GEN COMM indépendant; **~ -taught** *adj* WEL autodidacte; ◆ **be ~ -sufficient** GEN COMM se suffire à soi-même

self:[2] **~ -actualization** *n* HRM autoréalisation *f*; **~ -addressed envelope** *n* COMMS enveloppe à vos nom et adresse *f*; **~ -addressed stamped envelope** *n* *AmE* *(s.a.s.e.)* COMMS, GEN COMM enveloppe affranchie *f*, enveloppe timbrée à vos nom et adresse *f*; **~ -amortizing mortgage** *n* BANK, PROP hypothèque auto-amortissable *f*; **~ -appraisal** *n* HRM autocritique *f*; **~ -assessing system** *n* TAX système d'autocotisation *m*, système d'autoévaluation *m*; **~ -assessment** *n* TAX auto-évaluation *f*, autocotisation *f*; **~ -dealing** *n* STOCK opérations d'initié *f pl*; **~ -demounting pallet** *n* TRANSP palette à démontage automatique *f*; **~ -drive hire vehicle** *n* TRANSP véhicule de location sans chauffeur *m*; **~ -drive rental vehicle** *n* TRANSP véhicule de location sans chauffeur *m*; **~ -employed person** *n* HRM, TAX travailleur indépendant *m*; **~ -employed worker** *n* HRM, TAX travailleur indépendant *m*; **~ -employment** *n* TAX profession libérale *f*, travail indépendant *m*; **~ -employment income** *n* TAX revenu d'un travail indépendant *m*, revenu de profession libérale *m*; **~ -financing** *n* ACC auto-financement *m*, FIN autofinancement *m*, financement interne *m*; **~ -fulfilling prophecy** *n* GEN COMM prédiction auto-réalisée *f*; **~ -generated funds** *n pl* FIN fonds autogénérés *m pl*; **~ -governing nation** *n* POL pays autonome *m*; **~ -governing port** *n* TRANSP *shipping* port autonome *m*; **~ -government** *n* POL autonomie *f*; **~ -help** *n* GEN COMM auto-assistance *f*; **~ -help passenger luggage trolley** *n* TRANSP chariot à bagages *m*; **~ -insurance** *n* INS auto-assurance *f*, propre assurance *f*; **~ -liquidator** *n* S&M *advertising* offre auto-payante *f*; **~ -loading** *n* IND chargement automatique *m*; **~ -loading trailer** *n* TRANSP remorque autochargeable *f*; **~ -management** *n* HRM, MGMNT autogestion *f*; **~ -motivation** *n* GEN COMM, HRM automotivation *f*; **~ -polishing copolymer** *n* *(SPC)* TRANSP copolymère autolisseur *m*; **~ -propelled barge** *n* TRANSP *shipping* automoteur *m*, chaland auto-moteur *m*; **~ -propelled hyperbaric lifeboat** *n* *(SPHL)* TRANSP *shipping* canot de sauvetage hyperbare autopropulsé *m*; **~ -regulating organization** *n* *UK* *(SRO)* STOCK organisation autonome *f*, organisme auto-réglementé *m*; **~ -regulation** *n* BANK, ECON autoréglementation *f*; **~ -regulatory organization** *n* *UK* *(SRO)* GEN COMM organisation de centrales des intermédiaires financiers *f*, organisation indépendante *f*, organisme autorégulateur *m*; **~ -restraint** *n* FIN, GEN COMM retenue *f*; **~ -service** *n* GEN COMM, LEIS libre-service *m*, self *m* *(infrml)*, self-service *m*; **~ -service banking** *n* BANK libre-service bancaire *m*; **~ -sufficiency** *n* ECON autosuffisance *f*; **~ -sufficient economy** *n* ECON économie autarcique *f*, économie autosuffisante *f*; **~ -supporting debt** *n* FIN dette indépendante *f*; **~ -trimming hatch** *n* TRANSP *shipping* panneau auto-arrimeur *m*, panneau à arrimage automatique *m*

sell:[1] **~ -by date** *n* S&M *of food* date limite de vente *f*; **~ -off** *n* STOCK dégagement *m*; **~ -stop order** *n* STOCK ordre de cession de vente *m*, ordre de vente

stop *m*; ~ **up** *n jarg* S&M produit d'appel *m*; ~ **up**
product *n* S&M produit d'appel *m*

sell[2] **1.** *vt* GEN COMM céder, vendre; ~ **back** *(*ANT
buy back) STOCK revendre; ~ **forward** STOCK
vendre à terme; ~ **off** FIN liquider, GEN COMM
liquider, *stock* solder, STOCK liquider; ~ **out** FIN
réaliser, vendre, S&M *goods*, STOCK *futures market*
réaliser; ~ **up** FIN liquider, GEN COMM faire saisir,
liquider, STOCK liquider; **2.** *vi* ~ **out** GEN COMM,
STOCK liquider; ♦ ~ **at auction** GEN COMM, S&M
vendre aux enchères, vendre à la criée; ~ **at**
market STOCK vendre au cours du marché; ~ **a**
bear *(*ANT *buy a bull)* STOCK vendre à découvert;
~ **by auction** GEN COMM, S&M vendre aux
enchères, vendre à la criée; ~ **by private treaty**
GEN COMM vendre de gré à gré; ~ **for the account**
STOCK vendre à terme; ~ **for delivery** STOCK
vendre à couvert; ~ **for the settlement** STOCK
vendre à terme; ~ **in bulk** S&M vendre en gros;
~ **on close** *jarg* STOCK *futures market* vendre à la
clôture; ~ **on commission** S&M vendre à la
commission; ~ **on credit** S&M vendre à crédit,
vendre à terme; ~ **on trust** S&M fournir des
marchandises à crédit; ~ **sb an idea** S&M vendre
une idée à qn; ~ **short** STOCK vendre à découvert;
~ **short against the box** STOCK vendre des titres
empruntés alors que le vendeur en est détenteur;
~ **spot** STOCK vendre au comptant; ~ **sth for scrap**
GEN COMM vendre qch à la casse

seller *n* GEN COMM vendeur *m*, STOCK *(*ANT *buyer)*
vendeur *m*, vendeur d'option *m*; ~**'s market** *(*ANT
buyer's market) ECON marché favorable aux
vendeurs *m*, marché vendeur *m*, marché à la
hausse *m*, PROP, S&M marché vendeur *m*, marché
à la hausse *m*, STOCK marché haussier *m*, marché
orienté à la hausse *m*, marché vendeur *m*, marché
à la hausse *m*; ~**'s option** *(s.o.,* ANT *buyer's*
option) ECON prime vendeur *f*, GEN COMM au
choix du vendeur *loc m*, livraison au gré du
vendeur *f*, option de vente *f*, prime vendeur *f*,
STOCK au choix du vendeur *loc m*, livraison au gré
du vendeur *f*, option de vente *f*, prime vendeur *f*;
~**'s rate** *(*ANT *buyer's rate)* ACC taux vendeur *m*,
BANK, ECON, FIN, GEN COMM, STOCK cours
vendeur *m*; ♦ **at** ~ **'s risk** *(*ANT *at buyer's risk)*
STOCK aux risques du vendeur

selling *n* GEN COMM, S&M vente *f*; ~ **agent** *n* STOCK
agent de placement *m*; ~ **climax** *n* S&M, STOCK
record de vente *m*, vente au plus haut *f*;
~ **concession** *n* STOCK commission de mise sur
le marché *f*, concession de vente *f*; ~ **expenses** *n*
pl ACC frais de commercialisation *m pl*, frais de
vente *m pl*; ~ **hedge** *n* STOCK couverture de vente
f, short hedge *m*; ~ **point** *n* GEN COMM, S&M *of*
product, service argument de vente *m*; ~ **policy** *n*
GEN COMM, S&M politique de vente *f*; ~ **price** *n*
S&M prix de vente *m*; ~ **short** *n* STOCK vente à
découvert *f*; ~ **space** *n* S&M espace de vente *m*

sellout *n infrml* FIN liquidation *f*; ♦ **be a** ~ *infrml*
LEIS *theatre* jouer à guichets fermés

SEM *abbr (special employment measures)* HRM
mesures particulières pour l'emploi *f pl*

semiannual[1] *adj* GEN COMM semestriel

semiannual:[2] ~ **dividend** *n* STOCK dividende semestriel *m*

semiblack: ~ **market** *n* ECON marché à moitié au
noir *m*

semicolon *n* GEN COMM point-virgule *m*

semiconductor *n* COMP, IND semi-conducteur *m*

semi-detached: ~ **house** *n* BrE *(cf duplex AmE)*
PROP maison jumelée *f*, maisonnette *f*

semidurable *adj* GEN COMM *goods* semi-durable

semielliptic: ~ **spring** *n* GEN COMM ressort semi-
elliptique *m*

semifinished[1] *adj* GEN COMM, IND *goods* semi-fini

semifinished:[2] ~ **goods** *n pl* ACC produits intermédiaires *m pl*; ~ **product** *n* IND produit semi-fini
m

semifixed: ~ **cost** *n* ACC coût semi-fixe *m*

semi-industrialized *adj* ECON, POL *countries* semi-
industrialisé

semi-interquartile: ~ **range** *n* MATH *statistics* écart
interquartile *m*

semiknocked: ~ **down** *adj (SKD)* TRANSP *packag-*
ing partiellement démonté

seminar *n* MGMNT séminaire *m*

semi portal: ~ **crane** *n* TRANSP *shipping* grue semi-
portique *f*, semi-portique *m*

semiprivate: ~ **bank** *n* BANK banque semi-privée *f*

semiprocessed: ~ **products** *n pl* GEN COMM, IND
demi-produits *m pl*

semi public: ~ **company** *n* ECON société à économie mixte *f*, SEM

semi rigid: ~ **receptacle** *n* TRANSP conteneur semi-
rigide *m*, récipient semi-rigide *m*

semiskilled[1] *adj* HRM spécialisé

semiskilled:[2] ~ **labor** *n AmE*, ~ **labour** *n BrE* ECON
main-d'oeuvre spécialisée *f*, ouvriers spécialisés *m*
pl

semitrailer *n* TRANSP semi-remorque *f*

semivariable: ~ **costs** *n pl* ACC charges semi-
variables *f pl*, frais semi-variables *m pl*, ECON,
FIN charges semi-variables *f pl*; ~ **expense** *n* ACC
coût semi-variable *m*

senate *n US* POL sénat *m*

send *vt* COMP *data, information* envoyer, transmettre, GEN COMM *letter, document* faire parvenir;
~ **in** GEN COMM *order* envoyer avant la date limite,
envoyer à temps, *request* faire; ♦ ~ **away for sth**
COMMS commander qch par correspondance, se
faire envoyer qch; ~ **by fax** ADMIN, COMMS
envoyer par fax, envoyer par télécopie; ~ **by**
mail *(cf send by post)* COMMS envoyer par la
poste, expédier par la poste; ~ **by post** *(cf send by*
mail) COMMS envoyer par la poste, expédier par
la poste; ~ **off for sth** COMMS commander qch par
correspondance, se faire envoyer qch; ~ **an order**
by wire COMMS passer une commande par
télégramme; ~ **sb for sth** GEN COMM envoyer qn

chercher qch; ~ **sth by certified mail** *AmE (cf send sth by registered post BrE)* COMMS envoyer qch en recommandé; ~ **sth by parcel post** COMMS envoyer qch par colis postal; ~ **sth by registered post** *BrE (cf send sth by certified mail AmE)* COMMS envoyer qch en recommandé; ~ **sth via an agent** GEN COMM envoyer qch par l'intermédiaire d'un agent; ~ **under plain cover** COMMS envoyer sous pli discret; ~ **a written request** GEN COMM faire une demande par écrit

Senegal *pr n* GEN COMM Sénégal *m*

Senegalese[1] *adj* GEN COMM sénégalais

Senegalese[2] *n* GEN COMM *person* Sénégalais *m*

senior[1] *adj* BANK de premier rang, père, GEN COMM *(Snr) in age* aîné, *in rank* principal, supérieur, HRM *(Snr)* principal; ◆ **be ~** HRM *longest-serving* avoir de l'ancienneté

senior[2] *n (SYN boss, chief, head)* ADMIN chef *m*, HRM chef *mf*, MGMNT chef *m*; ~ **citizen** TAX, WEL personne âgée *f*; ~ **senior citizen's rail pass** carte vermeil® *f*; ~ **civil servant** ADMIN, HRM fonctionnaire titulaire *m*; ~ **clerk** ADMIN chef de bureau *m*, HRM chef de bureau *m*, commis principal *m*, LAW premier clerc *m*, principal *m*, MGMNT chef de bureau *m*; ~ **debt** BANK créance prioritaire *f*; ~ **executive** HRM, MGMNT cadre sup *m (infrml)*, cadre supérieur *m*; ~ **export clerk** HRM chef du bureau des exportations *m*; ~ **financial auditor** ACC vérificateur financier supérieur *m*; ~ **financial officer** ACC agent financier supérieur *m*; ~ **import clerk** HRM chef du bureau des importations *m*; ~ **loan** BANK prêt principal *m*; ~ **management** HRM, MGMNT cadres sup *m pl (infrml)*, cadres supérieurs *m pl*; ~ **manager** HRM, MGMNT cadre sup *m (infrml)*, cadre supérieur *m*; ~ **officer *(SO)*** HRM officier supérieur *m*; ~ **partner** GEN COMM associé majoritaire *m*; ~ **refunding** FIN, STOCK remboursement prioritaire *m*; ~ **security** STOCK titre prioritaire *m*, titre privilégié *m*; ~ **systems analyst** COMP analyste système confirmé *m*; **the ~ officer** HRM le doyen des officiers *m*; ~ **vice president** *US* HRM, MGMNT responsable supérieur *m*

seniority *n* HRM ancienneté *f*; ~ **bonus** HRM prime d'ancienneté *f*; ~ **premium** HRM bonification d'ancienneté *f*; ~ **principle** HRM principe d'ancienneté *m*; ~ **system** HRM ancienneté *f*

sense: ~ **of responsibility** *n* GEN COMM sens des responsabilités *m*; ◆ **it makes ~** GEN COMM c'est logique, ça se tient *(infrml)*

sensitive[1] *adj* STOCK *market* instable, sensible

sensitive:[2] ~ **form** *n* TAX formulaire sensible *m*, formule à usage restreint *f*; ~ **market** *n* STOCK marché instable *m*, marché sensible *m*; ~ **zone** *n* ENVIR zone vulnérable *f*

sensitivity: ~ **analysis** *n* FIN *measuring effect of change in a variable*, MATH *statistics* analyse de sensibilité *f*; ~ **training** *n* GEN COMM, HRM éducation de la sensibilité *f*

sensitize *vt* GEN COMM sensibiliser

sensory: ~ **deprivation** *n* MGMNT privation sensorielle *f*; ~ **overload** *n* MGMNT surcharge sensorielle *f*

sentence[1] *n* LAW *in court* condamnation *f*

sentence[2] *vt* LAW *in court* condamner

Seoul *n* GEN COMM Séoul *n pr*

separate:[1] ~ **customer** *n* STOCK concept du client séparé *m*, déposant distinct *m*; ~ **residence** *n* TAX résidence distincte *f*, résidence indépendante *f*; ~ **tax return** *n* TAX déclaration d'impôt séparée *f*, déclaration de revenus distincts *f*

separate:[2] **under ~ cover** *phr* COMMS sous pli séparé

Separate: ~ **Trading of Registered Interest and Principal Securities** *n (STRIPS)* STOCK démembrement *m*

separation: ~ **agreement** *n* LAW accord de séparation *m*

separator *n* COMP séparateur *m*

SEPON *abbr* UK *(Stock Exchange Pool Nominees)* STOCK société intermédiaire pour la compensation des titres *f*

Sept. *abbr (September)* GEN COMM sept. *(septembre)*

September *n (Sept.)* GEN COMM septembre *m (sept.)*

sequence *n* COMP ordre *m*, séquence *f*, GEN COMM séquence *f*; ~ **error** COMP erreur de classement *f*; ~ **number** COMP, MATH numéro d'ordre *m*

sequential[1] *adj* COMP, GEN COMM séquentiel

sequential:[2] ~ **access** *n* COMP accès séquentiel *m*; ~ **analysis** *n* FIN, MATH *statistics*, S&M analyse séquentielle *f*; ~ **externality** *n (ANT contemporaneous externality)* ECON externalité séquentielle *f*; ~ **number** *n* MATH numéro d'ordre *m*; ~ **sampling** *n* MATH *statistics* échantillonnage successif *m*, échantillonnage séquentiel *m*

sequestration *n* FIN séquestration *f*

sequestrator *n* FIN administrateur séquestre *m*

Serb[1] *adj* GEN COMM serbe

Serb[2] *n* GEN COMM *language* serbe *m*, *person* Serbe *mf*

Serbia *pr n* GEN COMM Serbie *f*

Serbian[1] *adj* GEN COMM serbe

Serbian[2] *n* GEN COMM *language* serbe *m*, *person* Serbe *mf*

Serbo-Croat[1] *adj* GEN COMM serbo-croate

Serbo-Croat[2] *n* GEN COMM *language* serbo-croate *m*, *person* Serbo-croate *mf*

Serbo-Croatian[1] *adj* GEN COMM serbo-croate

Serbo-Croatian[2] *n* GEN COMM *person* Serbo-croate *mf*

serial[1] *adj* COMP en série, sériel; ~ **-parallel** COMP série-parallèle

serial:[2] ~ **access** *n* COMP accès séquentiel *m*; ~ **adaptor** *n* COMP adaptateur série *m*; ~ **bond** *n* STOCK obligation échéant en série *f*, obligation échéant par tranches *f*; ~ **computer** *n* COMP calculateur sériel *m*, ordinateur sériel *m*;

~ **correlation** n MATH *statistics* corrélation sérielle f; ~ **number** n COMP, GEN COMM, PATENTS numéro de série m; ~ **operation** n COMP opération en série f; ~ **port** n COMP port série m; ~ **printer** n COMP imprimante série f; ~ **processing** n COMP traitement série m; ~ **reader** n COMP lecteur série m

seriatim adv frml GEN COMM au fur et à mesure loc, successivement

series:[1] **in a** ~ adv GEN COMM au fur et à mesure loc

series:[2] ~ **of options** n STOCK série d'options f

serif n COMP empattement m

serious[1] adj COMP, GEN COMM, STOCK, TAX grave

serious:[2] ~ **misdeclaration penalty** n UK TAX pénalisation importante pour fausse déclaration f

Serious: ~ **Fraud Office** n UK (SFO) STOCK bureau d'investigation des fraudes graves m

SERPS abbr UK (State Earnings Related Pension Scheme) ECON régime de retraite étatique basé sur le salaire

servant n HRM domestique mf

serve vt GEN COMM *community* servir, LAW *notice* notifier, signifier, S&M *market* servir; ◆ ~ **the company** HRM être au service de la société; ~ **counternotice** LAW *land compensation* signifier un avis contraire; ~ **on a committee** GEN COMM être membre d'un comité; ~ **the purpose** GEN COMM faire l'affaire; ~ **sb with a warrant** GEN COMM délivrer un mandat à qn

server n COMP serveur m

service[1] n COMP contrôle m, maintenance f, service m, GEN COMM maintenance f, service m, IND maintenance f, LAW *of writ, demand, notice* signification f, TRANSP ligne f; ~ **abuse** n GEN COMM *of machine, tool* utilisation anormale f; ~ **agreement** n COMP, GEN COMM contrat de maintenance m; ~ **boat** n TRANSP *shipping* embarcation de service f; ~ **bureau** n COMP centre de traitement à façon m; ~ **card** n COMP carte à bande magnétique f; ~ **charge** n BANK frais d'administration m pl, frais de gestion de comptes m pl, frais de service m pl; ~ **company** n COMP *manufacturer* société de service f; ~ **contract** n COMP contrat de maintenance m, GEN COMM contrat de maintenance m, contrat de travail m, HRM contrat de service m, LAW contrat de services m; ~ **delivery** n (SYN *performance, performance of services*) GEN COMM prestation de services f; ~ **engineer** n HRM technicien de maintenance m; ~ **enterprise** n GEN COMM entreprise de services f, prestataire de services m; ~ **fee** n GEN COMM, HRM rémunération de service f; ~ **handbook** n GEN COMM guide d'entretien m; ~ **hours** n pl GEN COMM heures d'utilisation f pl; ~ **in employment** n HRM états de service m pl; ~ **industry** n ECON, IND *company* industrie de service f, *sector* secteur tertiaire m; ~ **jobs** n pl HRM emplois des services m pl, emplois du secteur tertiaire m pl; ~ **manual** n GEN COMM guide d'entretien m, notice d'entretien f; ~ **mark** n LAW visa de signification m, PATENTS marque de

service f; ~ **pick up** n TRANSP service de ramassage m; ~ **provider** n GEN COMM société de commercialisation des services f; ~ **qualification** n HRM *continuity of employment* compétence dans le service f; ~ **sector** n ECON, IND secteur des services m; ~ **station** n TRANSP station-service f; ◆ ~ **not included** GEN COMM service non-compris m

service[2] vt ENVIR viabiliser, GEN COMM *market* servir, PROP viabiliser; ◆ ~ **a loan** FIN servir les intérêts

services n pl ECON secteur tertiaire m, services m pl, GEN COMM prestations f pl, PATENTS services m pl; ~ **-to-government envelope** ADMIN enveloppe des services de l'État f; ◆ **for** ~ **rendered** GEN COMM pour services rendus

servicing n COMP entretien m, intervention f, FIN *debt* service m

session n COMP session f, POL *of Parliament* session f, séance f

set[1] n COMP *of data, values* ensemble m, jeu m, série f, MATH ensemble m, TRANSP *shipping* direction du courant f; ~ **of accounts** n ACC ensemble d'états financiers m; ~ **of chattels** n TAX ensemble de biens mobiliers m; ~ **of claims** n PATENTS jeu de revendications m; ~ **of measures** n GEN COMM série de mesures f; ~ **-off** n BANK compensation f; ~ **of options** n STOCK groupe d'options m; ~ **of rules** n GEN COMM règlement m; ~ **-up** n COMP montage m, GEN COMM organisation f, système m; ~ **-up costs** n pl ACC, FIN frais d'établissement m pl; ~ **-up fee** n BANK commission de montage f, frais de montage m pl

set[2] vt COMP donner une valeur à, instaurer, *preset value* attribuer 1 à la valeur du bit, mettre à 1, ECON *value* fixer, GEN COMM *record* établir; ~ **against** ACC déduire; ~ **aside** ECON *agricultural* mettre de côté, mettre en jachère; ~ **forth** GEN COMM exposer, présenter; ~ **off** ACC, FIN, STOCK *loss* compenser; ~ **out** GEN COMM *conditions* formuler, indiquer; ~ **up** COMP *install* installer, *start* configurer, initialiser, mettre en route, GEN COMM installer, monter, *business* créer, HRM *committee* constituer, LAW *claim* déposer une réclamation, faire une réclamation; ◆ ~ **about doing** GEN COMM commencer à faire; **be** ~ **on doing sth** GEN COMM être résolu à faire qch; ~ **a date** GEN COMM fixer une date; ~ **a new high** ECON établir un nouveau record à la hausse; ~ **off a debit against a credit** ACC compenser un débit par un crédit; ~ **a price-point** ECON fixer un prix forfaitaire, pratiquer un prix d'appel; ~ **rules** GEN COMM définir des règles; ~ **sail** TRANSP *person* partir en bateau, *vessel* prendre la mer; ~ **sth in motion** GEN COMM amorcer un mouvement; ~ **a term to** ADMIN, GEN COMM mettre fin à; ~ **up in business** GEN COMM se lancer dans les affaires, monter en affaires; ~ **up in business on one's own** GEN COMM se mettre à son compte; ~ **up on one's own account** GEN COMM *in business* se mettre à son compte

setback *n* GEN COMM échec *m*

sets: in ~ of *phr* GEN COMM par jeux de, par séries de

setting: ~ -up costs *n pl* ACC frais d'établissement *m pl*

settings *n pl* COMP options *m pl*, paramètres *m pl*

settle 1. *vt* BANK *transactions*, GEN COMM *question* régler; **2.** *vi* GEN COMM *in job, residence, country* s'installer, s'établir; ♦ **~ an account** BANK, FIN, IND régler un compte; **~ amicably** HRM, LAW régler à l'amiable; **~ the bill** GEN COMM payer la facture, payer la note, régler la facture, régler la note; **~ a dispute** GEN COMM, HRM, IND, LAW régler un conflit; **~ a dispute by arbitration** GEN COMM, HRM, IND, LAW régler un conflit par arbitrage; **~ the figure** LAW *of compensation* décider du montant, fixer le montant; **~ in cash** FIN, STOCK régler au comptant, régler en espèces; **~ old scores** GEN COMM régler des comptes

settlement *n* BANK, FIN *of debt*, GEN COMM *of debt*, LAW règlement *m*, STOCK *futures price* règlement *m*, règlement à terme *m*; **~ account** BANK compte arrêté *m*; **~ of account** BANK compte arrêté de compte *m*; **~ bargain** STOCK marché à terme *m*; **~ date** STOCK *security* date de règlement *f*, jour de règlement *m*; **~ day** STOCK jour de règlement *m*; **~ of debts** BANK *with other banks or the government* règlement de dettes *m*; **~ discount** FIN conditions de règlement *f pl*; **~ draft** BANK effet de règlement *m*; **~ market** STOCK marché à terme *m*; **~ per contra** BANK compensation *f*; **~ price** STOCK cours de compensation *m*; **~ to the market** STOCK liquidation fictive quotidienne *f*; **~ transaction** STOCK transaction à terme *f*; ♦ **come to an amicable ~** LAW s'arranger à l'amiable; **in ~** GEN COMM *of a debt* en règlement; **make a ~ on sb** GEN COMM faire une donation en faveur de qn

settlements: ~ department *n* BANK *merchant bank* service des règlements *m*

settling: ~ of an annuity *n* LAW constitution d'une rente *f*

settlor *n UK* LAW constituant *m*, donateur *m*, fondateur *m*

Seventh: ~ Company Law Directive *n* GEN COMM, LAW, POL *EU* Septième directive relative au droit de sociétés *f*; **~ EU Directive** *n* ACC Septième directive de l'UE *f*

sever: ~ links with *phr* ECON couper les liens avec, rompre les liens avec

severally: ~ liable *adj* LAW solidairement responsable, solidairement tenu; ♦ **~ but not jointly** STOCK individuellement mais non-conjointement

severance *n* PROP *from land* séparation *f*; **~ pay** HRM indemnité de cessation d'emploi *f*, indemnité de licenciement *f*; **~ wage** HRM indemnité de cessation d'emploi *f*, indemnité de licenciement *f*

severe: ~ reduction *n* ACC, ECON, FIN, GEN COMM coupe sombre *f*

severely: ~ indebted low-income country *n (SILIC)* FIN pays au revenu bas sévèrement

endetté *m*; **~ indebted middle-income country** *n (SIMIC)* FIN pays au revenu moyen sévèrement endetté *m*

sewage *n* ENVIR eaux usées *f pl*; **~ disposal** *n* ENVIR vidange des eaux usées *f*; **~ treatment** *n* ENVIR traitement des eaux usées *m*; **~ treatment plant** *n* ENVIR station d'épuration des eaux usées *f*; **~ treatment works** *n pl* ENVIR station d'épuration des eaux d'égout *f*

sex: ~ discrimination *n* HRM, LAW discrimination entre hommes et femmes *f*, discrimination sexuelle *f*, sexisme *m*; **~ stereotyping** *n* HRM préjugés sexistes *m pl*, MEDIA préjugés liés au sexe des employés *m pl*

Sex: ~ Discrimination Act *n UK (SDA)* HRM loi relative à la discrimination sexuelle

sexual: ~ discrimination *n* HRM, LAW discrimination entre hommes et femmes *f*, discrimination sexuelle *f*, sexisme *m*; **~ division of labor** *n AmE*, **~ division of labour** *n BrE* HRM division du travail entre hommes et femmes *f*; **~ harassment** *n* HRM harcèlement sexuel *m*

Seychelles *pr n* GEN COMM Seychelles *f pl*

SF *abbr (sparring fitting)* TRANSP *shipping* vaigrage *m*

SFA *abbr UK (Securities and Futures Authority)* STOCK organisme de surveillance des bourses de valeurs et des marchés à terme

SFO *abbr UK (Serious Fraud Office)* STOCK bureau d'investigation des fraudes graves *m*

SFTC *abbr (standard freight trade classification)* TRANSP classement standard du commerce de marchandises *m*

SG *abbr (specific gravity)* GEN COMM poids spécifique *m*

sgd *abbr (signed)* COMMS s. *(signé)*

SH *abbr (superheater)* TRANSP surchauffeur *m*

shackle *n* TRANSP *cargo handling* manille *f*

shade *vt* GEN COMM *amount, quantity* diminuer progressivement

shading *n* COMP *illustration* ombrage *m*

shadow[1] *n* GEN COMM ombre *f*; **~ cabinet** *UK* POL cabinet fantôme *m*; **~ chancellor** *UK* POL chancelier de l'Échiquier fantôme *m*; **~ economy** ECON, FIN économie souterraine *f*; **~ price** ACC prix virtuel *m*

shadow[2] *vt* STOCK *currency* s'aligner sur

shady *adj* GEN COMM douteux

shaft: ~ horsepower *n (shp)* TRANSP *of turbine* puissance sur l'arbre *f*; **~ tunnel** *n* TRANSP *shipping* tunnel de l'arbre *m*

shake:[1] **~ -out** *n* ECON resserrement du marché intervenant après une période d'inflation, HRM réduction du nombre d'employés, dégraissage *m*, STOCK *industry* resserrement du marché intervenant après une période d'inflation

shake:[2] **~ off** *vt* GEN COMM se défaire de; **~ out** GEN COMM *staff* réduire; **~ up** GEN COMM secouer

shakedown *n infrml* GEN COMM *US* swindle

chantage *m*, racket *m* (*infrml*), HRM réduction du personnel *f*, TRANSP voyage d'essai *m*

shaky *adj* GEN COMM *company* branlant

shallow: ~ **market** *n* ECON, STOCK marché atone *m*, marché peu actif *m*

sham: ~ **trading** *n* STOCK transaction fictive *f*, vente fictive *f*

shape[1] *n* ECON *of economy*, MATH *of curve* forme *f*; ~ **of the world economy** ECON conjoncture mondiale *f*, forme de l'économie mondiale *f*

shape[2] **1.** *vt* GEN COMM façonner, STOCK *options price* déterminer; **2.** *vi* ~ **up** GEN COMM promettre, se développer

Shapley: ~ **value** *n* ECON valeur de Shapley *f*

share[1] *n* ACC action *f*, part sociale *f*, *profits* quote-part dans les résultats *f*, FIN action *f*, GEN COMM *fraction* part *f*, STOCK *publicly-held* action *f*, titre *m*; ~ **allotment** *n* STOCK distribution d'actions *f*; ~ **borrowing** *n* STOCK emprunt d'actions *m*; ~ **capital** *n* ACC, ECON, FIN, STOCK capital actions *m*, capital social *m*; ~ **certificate** *n* BrE (*cf stock certificate AmE*) STOCK certificat d'action *m*, certificat d'investissement *m*, CI, titre d'action *m*; ~ **class** *n* STOCK classe d'actions *f*; ~ **dividend** *n* STOCK dividende d'actions *m*; ~ **economy** *n* ECON, STOCK économie d'actionnariat *f*; ~ **index** *n* STOCK indice boursier *m*, indice des actions *m*, indice des cours des actions *m*; ~ **investments in other companies** *n pl* ACC *annual* participations *f pl*; ~ **issue for cash** *n* STOCK émission d'actions de numéraire *f*; ~ **issued for cash** *n* STOCK action de numéraire *f*; ~ **of market** *n* ECON, S&M part de marché *f*; ~ **option** *n* STOCK option d'achat d'actions *f*; ~ **option scheme** *n* HRM, TAX, WEL *employee benefits* système d'option sur les bénéfices *m*; ~ **ownership** *n* STOCK actionnariat *m*; ~ **participation scheme** *n* HRM, STOCK, WEL *for employees* plan d'intéressement des employés *m*, programme de participation boursière *m*; ~ **premium** *n* BrE (*cf paid-in surplus AmE*) ACC, FIN, STOCK prime d'émission *f*; ~ **price performance** *n* FIN, STOCK performance du prix des actions *f*; ~ **of production plan** *n* GEN COMM, IND intéressement *m*; ~ **redemption** *n* STOCK rachat d'actions *m*; ~ **register** *n* STOCK registre des actions *m*; ~ **repurchase plan** *n* STOCK plan de rachat des actions *m*, programme de rachat d'actions *m*; ~ **scheme** *n* HRM, STOCK, WEL *for employees* offre d'achat d'actions *f*, plan d'intéressement des employés *m*; ~ **split** *n* STOCK division d'actions *f*; ~ **support operation** *n* STOCK opération de soutien du cours de l'action *f*; ~ **transfer** *n* STOCK transfert d'actions *m*; ◆ **have a ~ in a business** GEN COMM avoir des intérêts dans une affaire; **take a ~ in sth** GEN COMM participer à qch

share[2] *vt* COMP *software, peripherals*, GEN COMM partager; ~ **out** GEN COMM distribuer, partager

sharecropper *n US* ECON *agriculture* métayer *m*

sharecropping *n US* ECON système de métayage *m*

shared: ~ **accommodation** *n* TAX cohabitation *f*, logement partagé *m*; ~ **-appreciation mortgage** *n* BANK hypothèque à évaluation partagée *f*, prêt hypothécaire avec participation à la plus-value *m*, PROP hypothèque à évaluation partagée *f*; ~ **-cost program** *n* AmE, ~ **-cost programme** *n* BrE POL programme à frais partagés *m*; ~ **database** *n* COMP base commune de données *f*, base partagée de données *f*; ~ **monopoly** *n* ECON monopole partagé *m*, oligopole *m*

shareholder *n* HRM associé *m*, STOCK *public* actionnaire *mf*

shareholders': ~ **equity** *n* STOCK avoir des actionnaires *m*, capitaux propres *m pl*, fonds propres *m pl*, situation nette *f*; ~ **meeting** *n* HRM assemblée des actionnaires *f*, assemblée générale des actionnaires *f*

shareholding *n* STOCK actionnariat *m*, possession d'actions *f*, valeur mobilière de participation *f*

shares *n pl* STOCK actions *f pl*; ~ **authorized** STOCK actions déclarées *f pl*, capital nominal *m*; ~ **outstanding** STOCK actions en circulation *f pl*, actions émises *f pl*; ◆ **go ~ with** GEN COMM partager les frais avec

shareware *n* COMP logiciel contributif *m*, logiciel à contribution *m*, shareware *m*

shark: ~ **repellents** *n pl* (SYN *porcupine provisions*) FIN *takeovers* antirequins *m pl*; ~ **watcher** *n* STOCK détecteur de requin *m*

sharp[1] *adj* GEN COMM *rally* vigoureux; ◆ **at 7 o'clock ~** GEN COMM à 7 heures précises

sharp[2]: ~ **drop** *n* ECON forte baisse *f*; ~ **movement** *n* STOCK *of option price* mouvement brusque *m*, mouvement soudain *m*; ~ **practice** *n* IND, POL maquignonnage *m*; ~ **rise** *n* ECON *price* forte augmentation *f*, forte hausse *f*

sharply *adv* ACC brutalement, de manière prononcée *loc f*, GEN COMM *fall* brusquement

SHC *abbr* (*super high cube*) TRANSP SHC (*conteneur spécial hors-cotes*)

shed *vt* GEN COMM *workers, stock* réduire, se défaire de, STOCK céder; ◆ ~ **light on** GEN COMM *point, issue* clarifier

sheet *n jarg* PATENTS *of drawing* feuille *f*, S&M *UK advertising* taille standard d'une affiche *f*; ~ **feeder** COMP chargeur feuille à feuille *m*; ~ **feeding** COMP alimentation feuille à feuille *f*

shekel *n* GEN COMM shekel *m*

shelf *n* GEN COMM, S&M rayon *m*; ~ **display** S&M présentoir de gondole *m*; ~ **filler** S&M *in store* réassortisseur *m*; ~ **life** S&M *of product* durée de vie *f*; ~ **price** S&M *of product* prix sur linéaire *m*; ~ **registration** *US* STOCK enregistrement d'émissions de titres à date indéterminée *m*; ~ **space** GEN COMM, S&M linéaire *m*, rayonnage *m*; ~ **-talker** *jarg* S&M *advertising* étiquette promotionnelle *f*

shell[1]: ~ **company** *n jarg* GEN COMM société écran *f*, TAX société fictive *f*; ~ **corporation** *n* GEN COMM société écran *f*; ~ **operation** *n* STOCK opération fictive *f*, société coquille *f*; ~ **plating** *n* TRANSP *shipping* bordé de coque *loc f*, bordé extérieur *m*

shell:[2] ~ **out** *vi infrml* GEN COMM casquer *(infrml)*

shelter *n* TAX *from tax* abri *m*; ~ **deck** *(S d/k)* TRANSP *shipping* pont-abri *m*

sheltered: ~ **employment** *n* HRM emploi protégé *m*; ~ **industries** *n pl* IND industries protégées de la concurrence étrangère *f pl*

shelve *vt* GEN COMM remettre

shelving *n* GEN COMM, S&M rayonnage *m*

Sherman: ~ **anti-trust act of 1890** *n* FIN, GEN COMM, LAW loi Sherman de 1890 destinée à lutter contre les trusts

SHEX *abbr (Sundays and holidays excepted)* TRANSP *shipping* dimanches et jours fériés exceptés *loc m*

shield *vt* GEN COMM protéger

shift *n* COMP *on keyboard* décalage *m*, shift *m*, ECON *in demand or supply curve* modification *f*, GEN COMM *in emphasis* déplacement *m*; ~ **differential** HRM écart entre équipes *m*; ~ **in consumption** S&M modification de la consommation *f*; ~ **key** COMP touche majuscule *f*; ~ **work** HRM travail par équipes *m*, travail posté *m*, travail par relais *m*, IND travail par équipes *m*, travail posté *m*; ~ **worker** HRM, IND travailleur posté *m*

shifting: ~ **berth** *n* TRANSP *shipping* agent maritime *m*, déhalage du navire d'un poste à l'autre *loc*; ~ **board** *n* TRANSP bardis *m*; ~ **of the tax burden** *n* TAX décalage du poids de l'impôt *m*, répercussion de la charge de l'impôt *f*; ~ **of taxes** *n* TAX décalage d'impôts *m*

shilling *n* GEN COMM shilling *m*

SHINC *abbr (Sundays and holidays included)* TRANSP *shipping* dimanches et jours fériés compris *loc m*

ship[1] *n* TRANSP vaisseau *m*; ~ **-broker** *n* HRM, TRANSP courtier maritime *m*; ~ **conversion** *n* TRANSP réarmement *m*; ~ **design strategy** *n* TRANSP stratégie de conception *f*; ~ **management** *n* TRANSP gestion du déplacement des navires *f*; ~ **plan** *n* TRANSP plan du navire *m*; ~ **planning** *n* TRANSP *design* plan d'arrimage *m*; ~ **specification** *n* TRANSP spécification du navire *f*; ~ **subsidy** *n* TRANSP prime à la construction ou à l'exploitation d'un navire *f*, subvention à la construction ou à l'exploitation d'un navire *f*; ~ **survey** *n* TRANSP visite du navire *f*; ~ **turn-around time** *n AmE*, ~ **turnround time** *n BrE* TRANSP temps de rotation du navire *m*; ~**'s agent** *n* IMP/EXP, TRANSP consignataire de navires *m*; ~**'s articles** *n pl* TRANSP rôle d'équipage *m*; ~**'s chandler** *n* TRANSP *purchasing* approvisionneur de la marine *m*, fournisseur de navires *m*, ship-chandler *m*; ~**'s clerk** *n* TRANSP *port* chef des pointeurs *m*; ~**'s cubic capacity** *n* TRANSP capacité volumétrique du navire *f*; ~**'s delivery order** *n* TRANSP bon d'enlèvement du navire *m*; ~**'s husband** *n* TRANSP armateur-gérant *m*; ~**'s inward report** *n* IMP/EXP, TRANSP rapport d'entrée de

navire *m*; ~**'s log** *n* TRANSP journal de bord *m*; ~**'s manifest** *n* TRANSP manifeste *m*; ~**'s option** *n* TRANSP option *f*; ~**'s papers** *n pl* LAW, TRANSP documents de bord *m pl*; ~**'s protest** *n* LAW, TRANSP rapport de mer *m*; ~**'s rail** *n* TRANSP bastingage *m*; ~**'s special survey** *n (SS)* TRANSP visite spéciale *f*; ◆ ~ **lost or not lost** *(SL/NL)* INS *marine* navire perdu ou non-perdu

ship[2] *vt* TRANSP *freight* charger, expédier; ◆ ~ **by rail** TRANSP expédier par le train

shipboard: ~ **conveyor belt and elevator system** *n* TRANSP *cargo-handling* système de convoyeur et d'élévateur à bord *m*; ~ **facility** *n* LEIS, TRANSP installation à bord *f*; ~ **management** *n* TRANSP gestion à bord *f*

shipborne: ~ **barge** *n* TRANSP barge *f*, bargette *f*

shipbuilder *n* IND constructeur de navires *m*

Shipbuilders: ~ **and Repairers National Association** *n UK (SRNA)* TRANSP association nationale des constructeurs et réparateurs de navires

shipbuilding *n* IND construction navale *f*

shipment *n* TRANSP envoi *m*, expédition *f*

shipowner *n* IMP/EXP, TRANSP armateur *m*; ~**'s liability** *(SOL)* INS, LAW, TRANSP responsabilité de l'armateur *f*

shipped:[1] ~ **aboard** *adj* IMP/EXP, TRANSP embarqué à bord; ~ **on board** *adj* IMP/EXP, TRANSP embarqué

shipped:[2] ~ **bill** *n* IMP/EXP, TRANSP connaissement embarqué *m*; ~ **bill of lading** *n* IMP/EXP, TRANSP connaissement embarqué *m*

shipper *n* HRM chargeur *m*, IMP/EXP, TRANSP affréteur *m*, chargeur *m*, consignateur *m*, expéditeur *m*; ~ **and carrier** *(s&c)* TRANSP chargeur et transporteur *loc m*, courtier d'affrètement maritime *m*; ~ **weight** *(SW)* TRANSP poids transitaire *m*; ~**'s letter of instruction** IMP/EXP, TRANSP lettre d'instruction du chargeur *f*; ~**'s letter of instruction for issuing air waybills** IMP/EXP, TRANSP bordereau d'instruction de l'expéditeur pour l'émission d'une lettre de transport aérien *m*

shipping *n* TRANSP expédition *f*; ~ **address** *n* TRANSP adresse du destinataire *f*; ~ **agency** *n* TRANSP agence maritime *f*; ~ **agent** *n* GEN COMM agent maritime *m*; ~ **business** *n* GEN COMM affaires maritimes *f pl*; ~ **clerk** *n* TRANSP expéditionnaire *mf*; ~ **company** *n* TRANSP compagnie de navigation *f*; ~ **documents** *n pl* IMP/EXP documents d'expédition *m pl*, pièces d'embarquement *f pl*, TRANSP documents de transport maritime *m pl*; ~ **and forwarding agent** *n (S&FA)* HRM, IMP/EXP, TRANSP agent maritime-transitaire *m*, chargeur transitaire *m*; ~ **instructions** *n pl* TRANSP instructions d'expédition *f pl*; ~ **invoice** *n* IMP/EXP, TRANSP facture d'expédition *f*, facture de transport *f*; ~ **lane** *n* TRANSP voie de navigation *f*; ~ **line** *n* TRANSP compagnie de navigation *f*, ligne maritime *f*; ~ **loan** *n* BANK prêt à la navigation *m*; ~ **note** *n (S/N)* TRANSP note de chargement *f*; ~ **office** *n* TRANSP agence maritime *f*; ~ **officer** *n* IMP/EXP, TRANSP *customs* douanier affecté aux opérations d'import/export *m*; ~ **overcapacity** *n* TRANSP surcapacité de cales *f*; ~ **port** *n* TRANSP port de chargement *m*; ~ **register** *n* TRANSP registre d'immatriculation *m*; ~ **ton** *n* TRANSP tonneau d'affrètement *m*; ~ **trade** *n* TRANSP armement *m*

Shiprepairers: ~ **and Shipbuilders Independent Association** *n* UK (*SSIA*) TRANSP association indépendante des réparateurs et constructeurs de navire

shipyard: ~ **subsidy** *n* TRANSP *government* subvention à un chantier naval *f*

shirker *n* *infrml* GEN COMM tire-au-flanc *m*

shock *n* ECON, FIN, GEN COMM choc *m*; ~ **inflation** ECON inflation induite par les chocs externes *f*

shoe: ~ **trade** *n* GEN COMM commerce de la chaussure *m*

shoot¹ *n* S&M *advertising, photo session* séance *f*, *advertising, film* tournage *m*

shoot:² ~ **up** *vi* GEN COMM monter en flèche

shop¹ *n* GEN COMM *BrE* (*cf store AmE*) boutique *f*, commerce *m*, magasin *m*, S&M *advertising agency* boîte *f* (*jarg*), S&M *BrE* (*cf store AmE*) commerce *m*, magasin *m*; ~ **assistant** *n* *BrE* (*cf sales clerk AmE*) GEN COMM, HRM commis de magasin *m*, employé de magasin *m*, vendeur *m*; ~ **floor** *n* HRM, IND *place* atelier *m*, *workers* ouvriers *m pl*; ~ **-floor agreement** *n* UK HRM accord avec la base *m*; ~ **-floor bargaining** *n* UK HRM négociation avec la base *f*; ~ **-floor participation** *n* HRM participation ouvrière *f*; ~ **front** *n* GEN COMM devanture de magasin *f*; ~ **steward** *n* HRM, IND délégué d'atelier *m*, délégué syndical *m*; ~ **window** *n* GEN COMM vitrine *f*; ~**'s articles** *n pl* HRM contrat d'embauche *m*

shop:² ~ **around** *vi* GEN COMM, S&M *for the best price* comparer les prix

shopkeeper *n* *BrE* (*cf storekeeper AmE*) GEN COMM, S&M commerçant *m*, petit commerçant *m*

shopkeepers': ~ **liability insurance** *n* UK INS assurance responsabilité civile des commerçants *f*

shoplifting *n* LAW, S&M vol à l'étalage *m*

shopper *n* S&M client *m*

shopping *n* GEN COMM le shopping *m*, les courses *f pl*; ~ **bag** GEN COMM sac à provisions *m*; ~ **basket** ECON, GEN COMM panier de la ménagère *m*; ~ **center** *AmE*, ~ **centre** *BrE* GEN COMM centre commercial *m*; ~ **good** GEN COMM achat réfléchi *m*; ~ **list** GEN COMM liste de commissions *f*; ~ **mall** *AmE* (*cf shopping precinct BrE*) GEN COMM centre commercial *m*, galerie marchande *f*, zone commerçante *f*, zone piétonnière *f*, S&M galerie marchande *f*, zone commerçante *f*; ~ **precinct** *BrE* (*cf shopping mall AmE*) GEN COMM galerie marchande *f*, zone commerçante *f*, zone piétonnière *f*, S&M galerie marchande *f*, zone commerçante *f*; ◆ **do out-of-town** ~ S&M faire ses achats à l'extérieur; **go** ~ GEN COMM faire des achats

shore *n* TRANSP *of sea* côte *f*, rivage *m*, *prop* accore

mf; ~ **-based gantry crane** TRANSP *port* portique sur quai *m*

short¹ *adj* GEN COMM court; ~ **-dated** (*ANT long-dated, medium-dated*) STOCK à court terme, à échéance proche; ~ **-handed** HRM à court de main d'oeuvre, à court de personnel; ~ **-haul** TRANSP à courte distance; ~ **-landed** TRANSP *cargo* débarqué en moins; ~ **-lived** GEN COMM de courte durée, éphémère; ~ **-range** ACC, BANK, FIN, GEN COMM *forecast* à court terme; ~ **-run** GEN COMM de courte durée; ~ **-shipped** TRANSP *shipping* manquant à l'embarquement; ~ **-sighted** GEN COMM *approach, plan* imprévoyant; ~ **-staffed** HRM à court de main d'oeuvre, à court de personnel; ~ **-term** ACC, BANK, FIN à court terme, GEN COMM de courte durée, GEN COMM à court terme, STOCK *bond, debt* à court terme, à courte échéance; ◆ **be on** ~ **time** HRM travailler à horaire réduit; **be** ~ **in futures** STOCK faire des marchés à court terme, être à découvert sur contrat à terme; **be** ~ **-staffed** HRM manquer de personnel; **go** ~ STOCK vendre à découvert; **in** ~ **supply** GEN COMM à court de; **in the** ~ **term** (*ANT in the long term, in the medium term*) GEN COMM dans l'immédiat; ~ **in a currency** BANK à court d'une devise; ~ **of** GEN COMM à court de; ~ **of money** BANK gêné, ECON gêné, à court d'argent, FIN, GEN COMM gêné

short² *n* STOCK bourse à découvert *f*, short *f*, *government stock* bon d'État à court terme *m* (*jarg*), *futures market* marché à court terme *m*; ~ **account** *n* STOCK compte à découvert *m*; ~ **account position** *n* STOCK position d'un compte à découvert *f*; ~ **against the box** *n* STOCK vente de titres empruntés dont le vendeur est détenteur; ~ **bill** *n* (*SB*) TRANSP traite à courte échéance *f*; ~ **butterfly** *n* STOCK *options* vente d'un écart papillon *f*; ~ **call** *n* STOCK *options* position vendeur sur option d'achat *f*, short call *m*; ~ **call position** *n* STOCK position vendeur sur option d'achat *f*; ~ **circuit** *n* IND court-circuit *m*; ~ **closing** *n* INS, STOCK clôture à découvert *f*; ~ **coupon** *n* STOCK coupon à court terme *m*, obligation à maturité courte *f*; ~ **covering** *n* STOCK couverture de position *f*, rachat *m*, rachat des vendeurs à découvert *m*; ~ **date financing rate** *n* STOCK *futures pricing* taux de financement à court terme *m*; ~ **delivery** *n* GEN COMM livraison partielle *f*; ~ **form** *n* (*ANT long form*) IMP/EXP, TRANSP *bill of lading* connaissement abrégé *m*, connaissement shortform *m*; ~ **form bill of lading** *n* IMP/EXP, TRANSP connaissement abrégé *m*, connaissement shortform *m*; ~ **futures position** *n* (*ANT long futures position*) STOCK cours à court terme *m*, position courte sur contrat à terme *f*; ~ **hedge** *n* STOCK couverture courte *f*, couverture à court terme *f*, couverture de vente *f*, short hedge *m*; ~ **interest** *n* BANK solde provisoire; ~ **interest theory** *n* STOCK théorie de la position de place vendeur *f*; ~ **international voyage** *n* TRANSP *shipping* voyage international de courte distance *m*; ~ **market** *n* STOCK marché à court terme *m*, marché à découvert *m*; **~ option position** *n* STOCK cours à court terme *m*, position courte sur option *f*; **~ position** *n* (ANT *long position*) FIN position courte *f*, STOCK position courte *f*, position vendeur *f*, position à découvert *f*; **~ put** *n* STOCK option de vente vendue *f*, vente d'une option de vente *f*, position vendeur sur option de vente *f*, short put *m*; **~ put position** *n* STOCK position vendeur sur option de vente *f*; **~ -range maturity date** *n* STOCK *Eurodollar time deposits* date d'échéance à court terme *f*; **~ -range planning** *n* FIN, GEN COMM, MGMNT planification à court terme *f*; **~ run** *n* (*SR*) IND *production period* petite série *f*; **~ sale** *n* STOCK vente à découvert *f*; **~ -sale rule** *n* STOCK règle de la vente à découvert *f*, règlement des ventes à terme *m*; **~ sea shipping** *n* TRANSP cabotage *m*; **~ sea trade** *n* TRANSP commerce maritime trans-manche *m*; **~ seller** *n* STOCK vendeur à découvert *m*; **~ selling** *n* STOCK vente à découvert *f*; **~ shipment** *n* TRANSP *shipping* marchandises manquantes *f pl*; **~ squeeze** *n jarg* STOCK resserrement du crédit à découvert *m*, étranglement des vendeurs à découvert *m*; **~ straddle** *n* STOCK *options* marché à double prime à court terme *m*, vente de straddle *f*; **~ straddle position** *n* STOCK position de vente de straddle *f*, état du marché à double prime à court terme *m*; **~ strangle** *n* STOCK *options* main mise à court terme *f*, vente de strangle *f*; **~ take-off and landing** *n* (*STOL*) TRANSP *aircraft* avion à décollage et atterrissage courts *m* (*ADAC*); **~ taxation year** *n* TAX année privilégiée à court terme *f*, année à imposition restreinte *f*; **~ -term advance** *n* BANK concours à court terme *m*; **~ -term bond** *n* STOCK obligation à court terme *f*; **~ -term contract** *n* HRM contrat à court terme *m*; **~ -term credit** *n* BANK crédit à court terme *m*; **~ -term debt** *n* BANK dette à court terme *f*, passif exigible *m*, passif à court terme *m*; **~ -term deposit** *n* BANK dépôt à court terme *m*; **~ -term fluctuations** *n pl* ECON variations à court terme *f pl*; **~ -term gain or loss** *n* STOCK gain ou perte à court terme *loc m*; **~ -term interest rate** *n* ECON taux d'intérêt à court terme *m*; **~ -term interest rate futures contract** *n* FIN contrat à terme sur taux d'intérêt à court terme *m*, STOCK contrat sur les taux d'intérêt des opérations à court terme *m*, contrat à terme sur taux d'intérêt à court terme *m*; **~ -term interest-rate risk** *n* STOCK *financial futures* risque lié au taux d'intérêt à court terme *m*, risque sur les taux d'intérêt à court terme *m*; **~ -term investment assets** *n pl* STOCK actif investi à court terme *m*, investissement à court terme *m*; **~ -term investment portfolio** *n* STOCK portefeuille d'investissement à court terme *m*; **~ -term liabilities** *n pl* ACC, FIN créditeurs à court terme *m pl*, emprunts et dettes à courte terme *m pl*; **~ -term loan** *n* (ANT *long-term loan*) BANK emprunt à court terme *m*; **~ -term market** *n* STOCK marché monétaire *m*; **~ -term money market** *n* STOCK marché monétaire à court terme *m*; **~ -term money-market instrument** *n* STOCK

balance sheet, assets instrument du marché monétaire à court terme *m*, valeurs du marché monétaire à court terme *f pl*; **~ -term note issuance facility** *n* (*SNIF*) STOCK facilité de soutien de programme d'émission d'effets *f*, émission d'une obligation à court terme *f*; **~ -term objective** *n* GEN COMM objectif à court-terme *m*; **~ -term planning** *n* FIN, GEN COMM, MGMNT planification à court terme *f*; **~ -term prepayments** *n pl* ACC charges payées d'avance *f pl*; **~ -term security** *n* (ANT *long-term security*) STOCK valeur à court terme *f*, valeur à terme *f*; **~ -term vehicle park** *n* (*STVP*) TRANSP parking courte durée *m*; **~ -term workers** *n pl* HRM travailleurs sous contrat à court terme *m pl*; **~ -termism** *n* STOCK vue à court terme *f*, établissement à court terme *m*; **~ -time working** *n* ECON chômage partiel *m*, HRM chômage partiel *m*, mise en chômage temporaire *f*

short:[3] **~ -change** *vt* GEN COMM *give too little money* ne pas rendre assez de monnaie à, *swindle* escroquer, rouler; **~ -circuit** IND court-circuiter; ♦ **be ~ of** GEN COMM manquer de; **~ a contract** STOCK vendre un contrat

shortage *n* ECON pénurie *f*, GEN COMM insuffisance *f*, HRM *of manpower* manque *m*; **~ economy** ECON économie de pénurie *f*, économie de type soviétique *f*; **~ of staff** GEN COMM manque de personnel *m*

shortages *n pl* ACC, GEN COMM *of cash, stock entries in accounts* manquants *m pl*

shorten *vt* GEN COMM, STOCK raccourcir

shorter: **~ -term liability** *n* STOCK dette à plus court terme *f*, obligation à plus court terme *f*; **~ -term option** *n* STOCK option à plus court terme *f*

shortfall *n* ACC, GEN COMM, TRANSP déficit *m*, insuffisance *f*, manque *m*; **~ in earnings** GEN COMM manque à gagner *m*

shorthand *n* ADMIN sténo, sténographie *f*; **~ typist** ADMIN sténodactylo *mf*; **~ writer** ADMIN sténo (*infrml*), sténographe *mf*

shortlist[1] *n* GEN COMM, HRM liste restreinte *f*

shortlist[2] *vt* GEN COMM, HRM sélectionner, établir une liste restreinte

shortlisted: **be ~** *phr* HRM être retenu

shorts *n pl* UK STOCK bons du Trésor à court terme *m pl*, découvert *m*

shot: **~ in the dark** *n* GEN COMM gros risque *m*

shoulder:[1] **~ period** *n* GEN COMM intersaison *f*

shoulder[2] *vt* GEN COMM *burden* assumer, endosser

show[1] *n* S&M salon *m*; **~ business** GEN COMM monde du spectacle *m*; **~ card** GEN COMM pancarte *f*; **~ flat** PROP appartement-témoin *m*; **~ house** PROP maison témoin *f*

show[2] *vt* GEN COMM *demonstrate* montrer, signaler; **~ in** GEN COMM *visitor* faire entrer; **~ out** GEN COMM reconduire; ♦ **~ a balance of** ACC présenter un solde de; **~ a loss of** ACC, FIN enregistrer une perte de; **~ one's hand** GEN COMM dévoiler ses intentions; **~ a rise in exports** GEN COMM, IMP/

EXP montrer une hausse des exportations; **~ sb around the factory** *AmE*, **~ sb round the factory** *BrE* GEN COMM *visitor* faire visiter l'usine à qn; **~ a surplus** ACC enregistrer un bénéfice

showcase *n* GEN COMM *in shop* présentoir *m*

showdown *n* GEN COMM épreuve de force *f*

showpiece *n* GEN COMM *article* joyau *m*

shp *abbr (shaft horsepower)* TRANSP *of turbine* puissance sur l'arbre *f*

shr. *abbr (share)* STOCK act. *(action)*

shredder *n* ADMIN *equipment* broyeur *m*, déchiqueteuse *f*

shrink:[1] **~ -packaging** *n* GEN COMM, TRANSP emballage sous film rétractable *m*; **~ -wrapping** *n* GEN COMM, TRANSP emballage sous film rétractable *m*

shrink[2] *vi* ECON, GEN COMM diminuer

shrinkage *n* S&M vol à l'étalage *m*

shrinking: **~ market** *n* GEN COMM marché qui se rétrécit *m*

SHSV *abbr (superheater safety valve)* TRANSP soupape de sûreté du surchauffeur *f*

shunter *n* STOCK arbitragiste de place en place *mf*

shunto *n* HRM shunto *m*

shut:[1] **~ -out** *n* TRANSP marchandises exclues *f pl*; **~ -out cargo** *n* TRANSP marchandises exclues *f pl*

shut:[2] **~ down** *vt* GEN COMM fermer définitivement, fermer; **~ off** GEN COMM *area, zone* interdire l'accès à; ◆ **~ up shop** GEN COMM se retirer des affaires

shutdown *n* COMP arrêt *m*, fermeture *f*, ECON fermeture *f*, immobilisation *f*, FIN immobilisation *f*, GEN COMM *of machine, factory* arrêt *m*, fermeture *f*, IND fermeture *f*, immobilisation *f*; **~ price** GEN COMM prix de clôture *m*

shuttle *n* TRANSP *flight* navette *f*; **~ service** TRANSP service de navette *m*

shyster *n* *infrml* LAW avocat marron *m*, avocat véreux *m* *(infrml)*

SIB *abbr* STOCK *UK (Securities and Investments Board)* ≈ COB *(France) (Commission des opérations de Bourse)*

SIBOR *abbr (Singapore Interbank Offered Rate)* BANK TIOS *(taux interbancaire offert à Singapour)*

SIC *abbr (standard industrial classification)* IND classification industrielle standard *f*

sick: **~ allowance** *n* HRM allocation maladie *f*; **~ building syndrome** *n* ADMIN syndrome des bâtiments insalubres *m*; **~ leave** *n* HRM, WEL congé de maladie *m*; **~ -pay scheme** *n* UK HRM, WEL système d'indemnité de maladie *m*; ◆ **be off ~** *infrml* HRM être absent pour cause de maladie

sickness: **~ benefit** *n* GEN COMM indemnité de maladie *f*, HRM allocation maladie *f*, indemnité de maladie *f*, prestation en cas de maladie *f*, WEL indemnité de maladie *f*; **~ insurance** *n* HRM assurance maladie *f*; **~ insurance premium** *n* HRM, INS, WEL prime d'assurance maladie *f*;

~ pay *n* GEN COMM, HRM, WEL indemnisation de maladie *f*, indemnité de maladie *f*

side: **~ -by-side trading** *n* STOCK transaction simultanée sur une valeur et sur une option sur la valeur; **~ effect** *n* GEN COMM effet secondaire *m*; **~ frame handling** *n* TRANSP *loading* manutention par chariot latéral *f*; **~ issue** *n* GEN COMM question d'intérêt secondaire *f*; **~ note** *n* GEN COMM *on document, in margin* note marginale *f*; **~ tank** *n* *(SDT, ST)* TRANSP *shipping* citerne latérale *f*; **~ wheel** *n* *(SDW)* TRANSP roue latérale *f*; ◆ **on the ~** GEN COMM au noir

sideline: **~ job** *n* HRM emploi annexe *m*, emploi secondaire *m*

sidestep *vt* GEN COMM *question, problem* esquiver

sidetrack *n* *AmE* TRANSP voie de garage *f*, voie de triage *f*

sidetracked: **get ~** *phr* GEN COMM s'écarter de son sujet

sideways: **~ market** *n* STOCK *period in which prices trade within a narrow range, showing only small changes up or down* marché calme *m*, marché indécis *m*

siding *n* TRANSP raccordement privé *m* *(Bel)*, voie de raccordement *f*, TRANSP *BrE rail* embranchement particulier *m*, voie de chargement *f*, voie de garage *f*, voie de triage *f*

siege: **~ economy** *n* ECON économie de blocus *f*, économie de siège *f*

Sierra:[1] **~ Leonean** *adj* GEN COMM sierra-leonien

Sierra:[2] **~ Leonean** *n* GEN COMM *person* Sierra-Leonien *m*

Sierra:[3] **~ Leone** *pr n* GEN COMM Sierra Leone *f*

siftproof: **~ packaging** *n* TRANSP emballage imperméable *m*; **~ receptacle** *n* TRANSP récipient non-poreux *m*

sight *n* FIN *treaty* vue *f*; **~ bill** *n* FIN traite à vue *f*; **~ deposit** *n* BANK dépôt à vue *m*; **~ draft** *n* *(SD)* BANK, GEN COMM traite à vue *f*; ◆ **at ~** *(A/S)* BANK, FIN, GEN COMM, STOCK sur présentation, à vue; **at ~ draft** *AmE* BANK traite à vue *f*; **months after ~** *(m/s)* BANK mois à vue

sighting: **~ bills of lading** *phr* TRANSP *cargo* inspection des connaissements *f*

sign[1] *n* GEN COMM *indication*, MATH *plus or minus* signe *m*

sign[2] **1.** *vt* GEN COMM *contract, document* apposer sa signature, signer; **2.** *vi* **~ in** HRM *at factory, office* pointer en arrivant; **~ off** HRM, IND *at factory, office* pointer en sortant; **~ on** WEL s'inscrire au chômage; **~ up** GEN COMM s'inscrire; ◆ **~ a legal agreement** LAW s'engager par contrat, signer un contrat légal; **~ on the dotted line** ADMIN signer sur les pointillés

signal *n* GEN COMM *indication* signe *m*; **~ jamming** COMMS brouillage *m*; **~ light** COMP voyant lumineux *m*

signaling *n* *AmE*, **signalling** *n* *BrE* ECON clignotement des indicateurs économiques *m*

signatory n LAW *of contract, treaty* signataire *mf*;
♦ **be a ~ to** ENVIR *an agreement* être signataire de

signature n COMP signature *f*; **~ card** BANK carte
de signature *f*, carte spécimen *f*, fiche de spécimen
de signature *f*, fiche-signature *f*; **~ tune** MEDIA
broadcast indicatif musical *m*, jingle *m*, sonal *m*;
♦ **for ~** GEN COMM pour signature, à signer

signed adj *(sgd)* COMMS signé *(s.)*

significance: **~ test** n MATH *statistics* test de
signification *m*

significant adj GEN COMM significatif

significantly adv GEN COMM considérablement

signify vt GEN COMM *indicate* signifier

signing: **~ and accounting** n ACC signature pour
acceptation *loc f*; **~ authority** n BANK dépôt des
signatures *m*; **~ officer** n BANK signataire autorisé
m; **~ -on** n HRM, WEL inscription aux ASSEDIC *f*,
inscription à l'Association pour l'emploi dans
l'industrie et le commerce *f*; **~ slip** n ACC
bordereau de signature *m*

signpost n TRANSP poteau indicateur *m*

SIL abbr FIN *(specific investment loan)* prêt spécial
à l'investissement *m*, IMP/EXP, TRANSP *(specific
individual licence BrE, specific individual license
AmE)* permis spécifique individuel *m*

silent: **~ majority** n POL majorité silencieuse *f*;
~ partner n AmE *(cf sleeping partner BrE)* FIN
associé commanditaire *m*, commanditaire *mf*,
GEN COMM associé commanditaire *m*, bailleur
de fonds *m*, commanditaire *mf*, HRM, LAW associé
commanditaire *m*, commanditaire *mf*

SILIC abbr *(severely indebted low-income country)*
FIN pays au revenu bas sévèrement endetté *m*

silicon: **~ chip** n COMP, IND puce de silicon *f*, puce
électronique *f*

sill n TRANSP *of lock* radier *m*

silver n ENVIR, GEN COMM *metal*, IND argent *m*;
~ ore ENVIR minerai argentifère *m*; **~ ring** *jarg*
FIN, LEIS enceinte des bookmakers *f (jarg)*;
~ standard FIN étalon argent *m*; **~ Thursday**
STOCK le Jeudi d'argent *m*

SIM abbr *(sector investment and maintenance loan)*
FIN IES *(prêt d'investissement et d'entretien
sectoriel)*

SIMEX abbr *(Singapore International Monetary
Exchange)* STOCK bourse d'échange internationale
de Singapour

SIMIC abbr *(severely indebted middle-income
country)* FIN pays au revenu moyen sévèrement
endetté *m*

similar adj GEN COMM semblable

similarity n PATENTS similitude *f*

SIMO: **~ chart** n ADMIN diagramme SIMO *m*

simple[1] adj GEN COMM facile, simple

simple:[2] **~ contract** n GEN COMM convention
verbale *f*; **~ deferment** n ACC *system* crédit
d'enlèvement *m*, FIN *system* sursis simple *m*;
~ fraction n MATH fraction simple *f*; **~ interest** n
BANK, GEN COMM intérêt simple *m*; **~ labor** n

AmE, **~ labour** n *BrE* HRM *Marxism* manoeuvres
m pl; **~ linear regression** n ACC, MATH régression
simple linéaire *f*; **~ majority** n POL majorité simple
f; **~ yield** n STOCK rendement simple *m*

simplex n COMP *transmission* simplex *m*, transmission unidirectionnelle *f*

Simplification: **~ of International Trade Procedures
Committee** n UK ADMIN Commission de simplification des procédures du commerce international

simplified[1] adj GEN COMM simplifié

simplified:[2] **~ clearance procedure** n *(SCP)* IMP/
EXP *customs* procédure de dédouanement simplifiée *f*; **~ employee pension plan** n HRM, WEL
système simplifié de retraite des employés *m*;
~ procedure for goods carried by rail n *(SPGER)*
TRANSP procédure simplifiée pour marchandises
transportées par chemin de fer *f*

simplify vt GEN COMM alléger, simplifier; ♦
~ matters GEN COMM simplifier les choses

simulate vt COMP, GEN COMM simuler

simulation n COMP, GEN COMM simulation *f*;
~ model ECON modèle de simulation *m*;
~ modeling *AmE*, **~ modelling** *BrE* ECON modélisation de simulation *f*

simulcast n *(simultaneous broadcast)* MEDIA
diffusion simultanée *f (jarg)*, simultané *m*, transmission simultanée *f*

simultaneous[1] adj GEN COMM simultané

simultaneous:[2] **~ broadcast** n *(simulcast)* MEDIA
diffusion simultanée *f (jarg)*, simultané *m*, transmission simultanée *f*; **~ payments clause** n FIN
reinsurance, INS *reinsurance* clause de paiements
équivalents *f*; **~ translation** n GEN COMM traduction simultanée *f*

SIN abbr *(social insurance number)* TAX, WEL NAS
(numéro d'assurance sociale)

Sincerely: **~ yours** phr *AmE (cf Yours sincerely
BrE)* COMMS *letter ending* je vous prie d'agréer,
Madame/Monsieur, l'expression de mes senti-
ments les meilleurs, veuillez agréer, Madame/
Monsieur, l'expression de mes sentiments les plus
distingués

sinecure n HRM sinécure *f*

sine die phr *frml* LAW sine die *(frml)*

Singapore:[1] **~ dollar invoice** n FIN *trade* facture
libellée en dollar malaysien; **~ Interbank Offered
Rate** n *(SIBOR)* BANK taux interbancaire offert
à Singapour *m (TIOS)*; **~ International Monetary
Exchange** n *(SIMEX)* STOCK bourse d'échange
internationale de Singapour

Singapore[2] pr n GEN COMM Singapour *m*

Singaporean[1] adj GEN COMM singapourien

Singaporean[2] n GEN COMM *person* Singapourien *m*

single[1] adj ADMIN, FIN, LAW célibataire, LEIS *room*
individuel; **~ -acting** *(sla)* TRANSP *machinery* à
simple effet; **~ -deck** TRANSP *ship* à pont unique
m; **~ -density** COMP simple densité; **~ -sided**
COMP *diskette* simple face

single[2] n LEIS *theatre* place isolée *f*, place séparée *f*,

TRANSP *sleeping car* simple *m*, TRANSP *BrE (cf one-way ticket AmE, single ticket) fare* aller simple *m*; ~ **administrative document** *n (SAD)* ADMIN, IMP/EXP, TRANSP *EU* document administratif unique *m (DAU)*; ~ **arbitrator** *n UK* HRM conciliateur unique *m*; ~ **back** *n* TRANSP *road* remorque vide rentrant de la livraison *f*; ~ **-berth cabin** *n* TRANSP cabine pour une personne *f*; ~ **-buoy mooring** *n (SBM)* TRANSP *shipping* amarrage sur un seul coffre *m*; ~ **capacity** *n* STOCK capacité simple *f*, capacité unique *f*; ~ **-capacity trading** *n* STOCK activité réservée *f*, transactions en capacité unique *f pl*; ~ **channel** *n UK* HRM canal unique d'information *m*; ~ **commission** *n* STOCK commission unique *f*; ~ **-contract finance** *n* FIN financement contractuel unique *m*; ~ **-country data capture** *n* ADMIN saisie unique des données concernant le pays d'origine *f*; ~ **currency** *n* ECON, FIN, GEN COMM monnaie unique *f*; ~ **-employer bargaining** *n UK* HRM négociation avec employeur unique *f*; ~ **-ended boiler** *n (SEB)* TRANSP *ship* chaudière ordinaire *f*; ~ **-entry book-keeping** *n* ACC comptabilité en partie simple *f*; ~ **-entry visa** *n* ADMIN visa accordé pour une entrée *m*; ~ **European currency** *n* ECON monnaie unique européenne *f*; ~ **expansion engine** *n (S)* TRANSP *shipping* machine à expansion simple *f*; ~ **factorial terms of trade** *n pl* ECON termes de l'échange *m pl*; ~ **-family dwelling** *n* PROP logement d'une famille *m*, logement pour une famille *m*, WEL logement pour une famille *m*; ~ **-family home** *n AmE (cf single-family house BrE)* GEN COMM maison individuelle *f (Can)*, maison unifamiliale *f (Fra)*; ~ **-family house** *n BrE (cf single-family home AmE)* GEN COMM maison individuelle *f (Can)*, maison unifamiliale *f (Fra)*; ~ **-family housing** *n* PROP logement d'une famille *m*, logement pour une famille *m*, WEL logement pour une famille *m*; ~ **income** *n* HRM salaire unique *m*; ~ **labor market** *n AmE*, ~ **labour market** *n BrE (SLM)* HRM marché unique du travail *m*; ~ **man** *n* ADMIN, LAW, TAX célibataire *m*; ~ **manning** *n* TRANSP conduite à un seul agent *f*; ~ **parent** *n* TAX parent unique *m*; ~ **-parent family** *n* TAX, WEL famille monoparentale *f*; ~ **payment** *n* FIN paiement unique *m*; ~ **-person household** *n* S&M célibataire *mf*; ~ **person's allowance** *n* TAX abattement pour personnes seules *m*; ~ **-point mooring** *n (SPM)* TRANSP *oil tanker* méthode d'amarrage sur un seul point fixe *f*; ~ **precision** *n* COMP simple précision *f*; ~ **premium** *n* HRM prime unique *f*; ~ **-premium deferred annuity** *n* FIN annuité différée à prime unique *f*; ~ **-premium life insurance** *n* INS assurance-vie à prime unique *f*; ~ **-reduction gearing** *n (Sr)* TRANSP *shipping* réducteur simple *m*; ~ **room** *n* LEIS chambre individuelle *f*, chambre pour une personne *f*; ~ **-room supplement** *n* LEIS pension complète *f*; ~ **-sheet feeder** *n* COMP introducteur feuille à feuille *m*; ~ **-sided disk** *n (SSD)* COMP disque monoface *m*, disque simple face *m*; ~ **-sided**

double density *n (SSDD)* COMP simple face-double densité; ~ **-sided single density** *n (SSSD)* COMP simple face-simple densité; ~ **sourcing** *n (ANT dual sourcing)* GEN COMM approvisionnement auprès d'une source unique *m*; ~ **spacing** *n* COMP interligne simple *m*; ~ **-state municipal bond fund** *n* FIN fonds obligataire municipal *m*; ~ **status** *n* HRM statut unique *m*; ~ **table bargaining** *n UK* HRM négociation à un seul niveau *f*; ~ **tax credit** *n Canada* TAX crédit de personne vivant seule *m*, déduction fiscale unique *f*; ~ **tax movement** *n* TAX mouvement d'imposition unique *m*; ~ **ticket** *n BrE (cf one-way ticket AmE, single)* TRANSP aller simple *m*; ~ **-union agreement** *n UK* HRM accord syndical unique *m*, contrat de syndicat unique *m*, convention à syndicat unique *f*; ~ **-union deal** *n UK* HRM accord syndical unique *m*, contrat de syndicat unique *m*, convention à syndicat unique *f*; ~ **-width gangway** *n* TRANSP *shipping* passerelle simple *f*; ~ **woman** *n* ADMIN, LAW, TAX célibataire *f*

single:[3] ~ **out** *vt* GEN COMM distinguer, désigner

Single: ~ **European Act** *n (SEA)* LAW, POL Acte unique européen *m (AUE)*; ~ **European Market** *n* ECON, POL, S&M, STOCK Marché unique européen *m*; ~ **Market** *n* ECON, POL, S&M, STOCK marché unique *m*

singly *adv* GEN COMM séparément

Sinhalese *n* GEN COMM *language* cingalais *m*

sinking: ~ **fund** *n* ACC, FIN, STOCK fonds d'amortissement *m*; ~ **fund loan** *n* ACC prêt au fonds d'amortissement *m*

siphon: ~ **off** *vt* GEN COMM *money* détourner

SIPROCOM *abbr (Committee for the Simplification of International Trade Procedures)* ADMIN Comité pour la simplification des procédures du commerce international *m*

SIS *abbr (special intermediate survey)* TRANSP visite spéciale intermédiaire *f*

sister: ~ **company** *n* GEN COMM société-soeur *f*; ~ **ship** *n* TRANSP navire du même type *m*, sistership *m*

sit:[1] ~ **-down strike** *n* HRM grève avec occupation des locaux *f*, grève sur le tas *f*; ~ **-in** *n* HRM *industrial action* grève avec occupation des locaux *f*; ~ **-in strike** *n* HRM grève sur le tas *f*

sit[2] *vi* POL *Parliament* siéger; ♦ ~ **tight** GEN COMM ne pas bouger

sit. *abbr (situation)* HRM carrière *f*, emploi *m*

SITC *abbr (Standard International Trade Classification)* ECON, GEN COMM classification des normes du commerce international *f*

site *n* COMP emplacement *m*, site *m*, GEN COMM emplacement *m*, IND *for work* chantier *m*; ~ **audit** GEN COMM audit sur site *m*; ~ **development** ENVIR *dumping* implantation *f*; ~ **engineer** HRM, IND ingénieur de chantier *m*; ~ **foreman** HRM chef de chantier *m*; ~ **licence** *BrE* COMP licence sur site *f*; ~ **license** *AmE see site licence BrE*; ~ **manager**

HRM, IND directeur de chantier *m*; ~ **operation** ENVIR *dumping* exploitation d'un site *f*; ~ **planning** COMP étude d'aménagement des locaux *f*; ~ **selection** ENVIR *for dumping* sélection d'un site *f*

Site: ~ **of Special Scientific Interest** *n (SSSI)* ENVIR Site d'intérêt scientifique spécial *m*

siting *n* IND implantation *f*

sitrep *abbr (situation report)* GEN COMM rapport de situation *m*

sits.: ~ **vac.** *abbr BrE (situations vacant)* HRM offres d'emploi *f pl*, postes à pourvoir *m pl*

sitting: ~ **tenant** *n BrE (cf holdover tenant AmE)* PROP locataire débordant *m*

situation *n (sit.)* HRM carrière *f*, emploi *m*; ~ **report** *(sitrep)* GEN COMM rapport de situation *m*; ◆ **have the ~ well in hand** GEN COMM avoir la situation bien en main

situations: ~ **vacant** *n pl BrE (sits. vac.)* HRM offres d'emploi *f pl*, postes à pourvoir *m pl*

six: ~ **month SDRs interbank offered rate** *n UK (SDRIBOR)* BANK taux interbancaire offert pour droits de tirage spéciaux sur six mois; ~ **-monthly periods** *n pl* GEN COMM semestres *m pl*

sixties: **in the ~** *phr* GEN COMM pendant les années soixante

sizable *adj see sizeable*

size[1] *n* COMP capacité *f*, format *m*, longueur *f*, volume *m*, ECON *of economy, population* envergure *f*, taille *f*, GEN COMM grandeur *f*; ~ **distribution** MATH *statistics* distribution par grandeur *f*

size:[2] ~ **up** *vt* GEN COMM juger, évaluer

sizeable[1] *adj* ECON *demand, debt* assez important, GEN COMM conséquent *(infrml)*

sizeable:[2] ~ **budget** *n* ECON gros budget *m*

SKD *abbr (semiknocked down)* TRANSP partiellement démonté

skeletal: ~ **trailer** *n* TRANSP remorque nue *f*

skeleton: ~ **contract** *n* GEN COMM contrat type *m*; ~ **service** *n* TRANSP service de permanence *m*; ~ **staff** *n* HRM personnel réduit *m*

sketch *n* GEN COMM esquisse *f*

skewed: ~ **frequency curve** *n* MATH *statistics* courbe de fréquence embrochée *f*

skewness *n* MATH *statistics* embrochage *m*

skid *n* TRANSP *cargo handling* patin *m*

skill *n* GEN COMM, HRM habileté *f*; ~ **differential** HRM différentiel de qualifications *m*

skilled[1] *adj* HRM qualifié

skilled:[2] ~ **labor** *n AmE*, ~ **labour** *n BrE* ECON main-d'oeuvre professionnelle *f*, HRM main-d'oeuvre spécialisée *f*, ouvriers spécialisés *m pl*, main-d'oeuvre professionnelle *f*, main-d'oeuvre qualifiée *f*; ~ **union** *n UK* HRM syndicat d'ouvriers qualifiés *m*; ~ **worker** *n* HRM ouvrier professionnel *m*, ouvrier qualifié *m*, ouvrier spécialisé *m*, O.S.

skill-intensive *adj* HRM exigeant une grande qualification

skills *n pl* GEN COMM capacités *f pl*; ~ **analysis** *n* HRM analyse de qualification *f*, analyse des aptitudes *f*

skimming *n* GEN COMM fraude fiscale *f*; ~ **policy** S&M politique d'écrémage *f*

skimp: ~ **on** *vt infrml* GEN COMM *food, material* lésiner sur, être radin sur *(infrml)*

skin *n* TRANSP *shipping* coque intérieure *f*

skip[1] *n* BANK débiteur sans adresse *m*, COMP saut *m*; ~ **-payment privilege** FIN privilège d'exemption de paiement *m*

skip[2] *vt* COMP omettre, passer, sauter; ◆ ~ **the details** GEN COMM omettre les détails, sauter les détails; ~ **a payment** BANK sauter un paiement

Skopje *pr n* GEN COMM Skopje *n pr*

sky: ~ **marshal** *n* HRM, TRANSP agent de sécurité en vol *m*

skyrocket *vi infrml* GEN COMM grimper en flèche *(infrml)*

sky's: **the ~ the limit** *phr* GEN COMM tout est possible, tout va

SL *abbr (surveillance licence BrE, surveillance license AmE)* IMP/EXP licence de surveillance *f*

slack[1] *adj* GEN COMM *control* relâché, *demand* calme, *season* creuse, *worker* négligeant, *work* négligé, STOCK lourd; ◆ **be ~** HRM se relâcher

slack[2] *n* ECON *business* marasme *m*, GEN COMM *sales* ralentissement *m*; ~ **fill** *jarg* S&M remplissage truqué *m*; ~ **period** GEN COMM morte saison *f*, période creuse *f*; ~ **water** TRANSP *shipping* étale de courant *m*, étale du flot *m*; ◆ **take up the ~** *infrml* ECON *in economy* relancer un secteur affaibli

slack:[3] ~ **off** *vi* GEN COMM ralentir

slacken **1.** *vt* GEN COMM relâcher; **2.** *vi* ECON *recovery* ralentir

slackening *n* ACC réduction *f*, GEN COMM *of demand* affaiblissement *m*, réduction *f*

slander:[1] ~ **action** *n* LAW procès en diffamation *m*

slander[2] *vt* LAW diffamer

slanderous *adj* LAW diffamatoire

slant *vt* GEN COMM *information, facts* présenter avec parti pris

slapdash *adj* GEN COMM *work* bâclé *(infrml)*

slash *n* COMP, MEDIA *typography* barre oblique *f*

slate *n US* POL liste des candidats *f*

S/LC *abbr (sue and labor clause AmE, sue and labour clause BrE)* INS clause de recours et de conservation *f*

sleeper *n* HRM bailleur de fonds *m*, TRANSP voiture-lit *f*, VL, wagon-lit *m*, WL

sleeping: ~ **beauty** *n* STOCK société opéable *f*; ~ **car** *n* TRANSP voiture-lit *f*, VL, wagon-lit *m*, WL; ~ **economy** *n* ECON avoirs dormants *m pl*; ~ **partner** *n BrE (cf silent partner AmE)* FIN associé commanditaire *m*, commanditaire *mf*, GEN COMM associé commanditaire *m*, bailleur de fonds *m*, commanditaire *mf*, HRM, LAW associé commanditaire *m*, commanditaire *mf*

slice: ~ **of market** *n* ECON, S&M part de marché *f*

slick[1] *adj* GEN COMM *glib* rusé

slick[2] *n* ENVIR, IND *oil* nappe *f*

slide:[1] ~ **projector** *n* MEDIA projecteur de diapositives *m*; ~ **rule** *n* GEN COMM, MATH règle à calcul *f*; ~ **ruler** *n* GEN COMM, MATH règle à calcul *f*

slide[2] *vi* ECON, GEN COMM *price* glisser

sliding: ~ **fifth wheel** *n* TRANSP *semitrailer* attelage pivotant coulissant *m*, sellette coulissante *f*; ~ **parity** *n* STOCK parité en légère baisse *f*, parité glissante *f*; ~ **scale** *n* ACC, GEN COMM échelle mobile *f*; ~ **wage scale** *n* HRM échelle mobile des salaires *f*

slight *adj* GEN COMM léger

slightly: ~ **less than** *phr* GEN COMM légèrement inférieur à

slim: ~ **down** *vt* ECON *workforce*, GEN COMM alléger, dégraisser

slim-line *adj* COMP *hardware design* extra-plat, mini, surbaissé

sling *n* TRANSP *cargo handling* élingue *f*

slip[1] *n* GEN COMM bordereau *m*; ~ **coupling** *(SC)* TRANSP couplage extensible *m*; ~ **sheet** TRANSP bâche *f*

slip[2] *vi* ECON, GEN COMM *price* glisser, STOCK baisser, déraper; ~ **back** GEN COMM *prices, profits* reculer

slippage *n* GEN COMM dérapage *m*

slipway *n* TRANSP *shipping* cale de construction *f*, cale de lancement *f*

SLM *abbr* *(single labor market, single labour market)* HRM marché unique du travail *m*

SLMA *abbr* US *(Student Loan Marketing Association)* STOCK organisme de garantie des prêts étudiants *m*

SL/NL *abbr* *(ship lost or not lost)* INS *marine* navire perdu ou non-perdu *loc m*

slog *n* HRM travail pénible *m*

slogan *n* MEDIA accroche *f*, S&M *advertising* slogan *m*

sloop *n* *(Sp)* TRANSP *shipping* sloop *m*

slope *n* GEN COMM pente *f*

slot[1] *n* COMP *for expansion card* fente *f*, ouverture *f*, GEN COMM créneau *m*, TRANSP *shipping* tranche horizontale de cellule *f*

slot:[2] ~ **in** *vt* COMP insérer

Slovak[1] *adj* GEN COMM slovaque

Slovak[2] *n* GEN COMM *person* Slovaque *mf*

Slovak:[3] ~ **Republic** *pr n* GEN COMM *post 1989* Slovaquie *f*

Slovakia *pr n* GEN COMM Slovaquie *f*

Slovakian[1] *adj* GEN COMM slovaque

Slovakian[2] *n* GEN COMM *person* Slovaque *mf*

Slovene[1] *adj* GEN COMM slovène

Slovene[2] *n* GEN COMM *language* slovène *m, person* Slovène *mf*

Slovenia *pr n* GEN COMM Slovénie *f*

Slovenian[1] *adj* GEN COMM slovène

Slovenian[2] *n* GEN COMM *person* Slovène *mf*

slow[1] *adj* ECON *recovery*, GEN COMM lent; ~ **to reply** GEN COMM lent à répondre

slow:[2] ~ **decline** *n* STOCK *currency expectations* baisse lente *f*, lent déclin *m*; ~ **rise** *n* STOCK *currency expectations* hausse lente *f*, lente remontée *f*; ~ **steaming** *n* TRANSP *shipping* ralentissement *m*; ~ **train** *n* AmE *(cf accommodation train)* TRANSP omnibus *m*

slow:[3] ~ **down** *vi* ECON se ralentir

slowdown *n* ECON, GEN COMM ralentissement *m*, HRM *AmE (cf go-slow BrE) industrial action* grève perlée *f*

sluggish *adj* GEN COMM morose, STOCK faible, morose, *market* lourd, stagnant

sluggishness *n* GEN COMM *of demand* apathie *f*, inertie *f*, morosité *f*, STOCK morosité *f*

sluice: ~ **-gate price** *n jarg* ECON *EU* prix minimum à l'importation pour les produits agricoles non-communautaires

slump *n* BANK crise *f*, ECON crise *f*, récession *f*, marasme *m*, FIN crise *f*, GEN COMM *in oil prices, world trade*, HRM, POL récession *f*, STOCK affaissement *m*; ~ **in sales** GEN COMM mévente *f*

slumpflation *n jarg* ECON récession conjuguée à l'inflation *f*

slush: ~ **fund** *n* POL caisse noire *f*

Slutsky: ~ **effect** *n* ECON effet Slutsky *m*; ~ **equation** *n* ECON équation de Slutsky *f*

SMA *abbr* STOCK *(Secondary Market Association)* Association du marché secondaire *f*, STOCK *(special miscellaneous account)* compte de divers *m*

smack *n* TRANSP *ship* barque de pêche *f*, semaque *m (vieilli)*, smack *m*

small[1] *adj* GEN COMM *purchase* faible, peu important; ~ **-scale** ECON *company, business* de petite taille; ◆ **on a** ~ **scale** GEN COMM sur une petite échelle

small:[2] ~ **ads** *n pl* MEDIA, S&M petite annonce *f*; ~ **business** *n* GEN COMM, TAX petite entreprise *f*; ~ **business administration** *n (SBA)* GEN COMM administration des petites entreprises *f*, gestion d'une petite entreprise *f*; ~ **business bond** *n* GEN COMM obligation pour petite entreprise *f*; ~ **business deduction** *n* TAX déduction accordée aux petites entreprises *f*, déduction aux petites entreprises *f*; ~ **business development bond** *n (SBDB)* GEN COMM obligation pour le développement de la petite entreprise *f (ODPE)*; ~ **business investment amount** *n* TAX montant d'investissement de petite entreprise *m*, montant d'un placement dans des petites entreprises *m*; ~ **business property** *n* TAX bien de petite entreprise *m*, propriété de petite entreprise *f*; ~ **business venture capital tax credit** *n* TAX crédit d'impôt aux petites entreprises pour capital de risque *m*, crédit d'impôt sur le capital risque des petites entreprises *m*; ~ **change**

n infrml GEN COMM, POL concessions mineures *f pl*; ~ **claims** *n pl* LAW litiges de moindre intérêt *m pl*; ~ **claims court** *n* LAW tribunal d'instance *m*; ~ **damage** *n* INS dommages peu importants *m pl*; ~ **denomination** *n* BANK petite coupure *f*; ~ **employer** *n* HRM petit employeur *m*; ~ **firm** *n* GEN COMM petite entreprise *f*; ~ **investors** *n pl* (ANT *big investors*) FIN, STOCK petit capital *m*; ~ **and medium-sized companies** *n pl* GEN COMM petites et moyennes entreprises *f pl*; ~ **and medium-sized enterprises** *n pl (SME)* GEN COMM petites et moyennes entreprises *f pl (PME)*; ~ **and medium-sized manufacturing companies** *n pl (SMME)* GEN COMM petites et moyennes industries *f pl (PMI)*; ~ **print** *n* LAW *in contract* passage imprimé en petits caractères *m*, petits caractères *m pl*; ~ **producer's tax credit** *n Canada* TAX crédit d'impôt pour petits producteurs *m*, déductions fiscales aux petits producteurs *f*; ~ **savings** *n pl* BANK, FIN la petite épargne *f*; ~ **speculator** *n* STOCK boursicoteur *m*

smallholder *n* ECON *agricultural* petit cultivateur *m*

smalls *n pl jarg* MEDIA, S&M *advertising* petite annonce *f*

smart: ~ **card** *n* BANK carte magnétique *f*, carte à mémoire *f*, carte à puce *f*, COMP carte magnétique *f*, carte à microprocesseur *f*, carte à mémoire *f*, carte à puce *f*, GEN COMM carte à mémoire *f*, carte à puce *f*, IMP/EXP, TRANSP smart card *m*; ~ **money** *n* FIN réserve d'argent *f*; ~ **terminal** *n* (ANT *dumb terminal*) COMP terminal autonome *m*, terminal intelligent *m*

SME *abbr (small and medium-sized enterprises)* GEN COMM PME *(petites et moyennes entreprises)*

smelt *vt* IND fondre

smelting: ~ **works** *n pl* IND fonderie *f*

SMME *abbr (small and medium-sized manufacturing companies)* GEN COMM PMI *(petites et moyennes industries)*

SMMT *abbr UK (Society of Motor Manufacturers and Traders)* TRANSP société des constructeurs et négociants automobiles

smoke: ~ **room** *n* GEN COMM fumoir *m*

smokeless: ~ **fuel** *n* ENVIR, IND *pollution* combustible non-fumigène *m*; ~ **powder** *n* TRANSP *classified cargo* poudre sans fumée *f*; ~ **zone** *n* ENVIR, IND zone où les foyers ouverts sont interdits

smokestack *n* IND cheminée d'usine *f*, TRANSP cheminée *f*; ~ **American stocks** *n pl* STOCK valeurs des industries lourdes; ~ **industry** *n* GEN COMM industrie traditionnelle *f*

smoking:[1] ~ **room** *n* GEN COMM fumoir *m*; ◆ ~ **is not permitted** GEN COMM défense de fumer, il est interdit de fumer; ~ **is prohibited** GEN COMM défense de fumer, il est interdit de fumer; **no** ~ GEN COMM défense de fumer, il est interdit de fumer

smooth:[1] ~ **running** *n* GEN COMM *of machine, business* bon fonctionnement *m*

smooth[2] *vt* MATH lisser; ~ **out** GEN COMM *difficulty, surface* aplanir

smoothing *n* MATH lissage *m*

SMP *abbr (special multiperil insurance)* INS assurance combinée spécifique *f*, police multirisque spéciale *f*

SMSA *abbr (standard metropolitan statistical area)* MATH *statistics* zone standard de statistique métropolitaine *f*

smuggle *vt* IMP/EXP faire du trafic de, faire passer clandestinement; ◆ ~ **through customs** IMP/EXP, LAW, TAX passer en contrebande à la douane, passer en fraude à la douane

smuggling *n* IMP/EXP, TAX contrebande *f*

S/N *abbr (shipping note)* TRANSP note de chargement *f*

SNA *abbr (System of National Accounts)* ACC système de comptabilité nationale *m*

snag *n infrml* GEN COMM *problem, hitch* inconvénient *m*, problème *m*

snake *n* ECON *EU* serpent *m*, serpent monétaire *m*; ~ **check** *infrml* POL contrôle anti-serpent *m*; ~ **in the tunnel** ECON *1973* serpent dans le tunnel *m*

snap:[1] ~ **strike** *n* HRM grève surprise *f*

snap:[2] ~ **up** *vt* GEN COMM saisir

snatch *vt* GEN COMM s'emparer de

sneak: ~ **preview** *n* MEDIA *cinema, television* avant-première surprise *f*, banc d'essai *m*

sneezed: **not to be** ~ **at** *phr infrml* GEN COMM à ne pas dédaigner

SNIF *abbr (short-term note issuance facility)* STOCK facilité de soutien de programme d'émission d'effets *f*, émission d'une obligation à court terme *f*

SNIG *abbr (sustained non-inflationary growth)* ECON croissance non-inflationniste soutenue *f*

snipe *n jarg US* POL affichage sauvage *m*

snood *n* TRANSP *on pallets* gaine *f*, housse *f*

snowball *vi* GEN COMM faire boule de neige *loc f*

snowbelt *n US* ECON régions neigeuses *f pl*

Snr *abbr (senior)* GEN COMM *in age* aîné, *in rank* principal, supérieur, HRM principal

snugging *n* ECON, FIN, POL resserrement de la politique monétaire *m*

s.o. *abbr* BANK *UK (standing order)* ordre de paiement permanent *m*, ordre de transfert permanent *m*, ordre permanent *m*, GEN COMM *(seller's option)*, STOCK *(seller's option)* livraison au gré du vendeur *f*

SO *abbr (senior officer)* HRM officier supérieur *m*

soar *vi* ECON monter en flèche, GEN COMM *profits, prices* grimper en flèche *(infrml)*, monter en flèche

soaring *adj* GEN COMM *price, popularity* qui monte en flèche

social[1] *adj* GEN COMM social

social:[2] ~ **accounting** *n* ACC comptabilité des charges sociales ou comptes publics *f*; ~ **adjustment cost** *n* HRM coût d'adaptation sociale *m*; ~ **analysis** *n* S&M, WEL analyse sociale *f*; ~ **assis-**

tance payment *n* TAX, WEL *Can (cf social security payment BrE)* paiement d'assistance sociale *m*, prestation d'assistance sociale *f*; ~ **benefits** *n pl* WEL avantages sociaux *m pl*; ~ **capital** *n* ECON capital social *m*; ~ **category** *n* S&M *market research* catégorie sociale *f*; ~ **charter** *n* GEN COMM *EU* charte sociale *f*; ~ **choice theory** *n* ECON théorie du choix social *f*; ~ **class** *n* POL catégorie sociale *f*, classe *f*; ~ **compact** *n* HRM, POL contrat social *m*; ~ **conscience fund** *n* ECON fonds pour le développement de la conscience sociale *m*; ~ **consciousness mutual fund** *n* FIN fonds mutuel d'entraide sociale *m*; ~ **contract** *n* HRM, POL contrat social *m*; ~ **contributions tax** *n* TAX contribution sociale de solidarité *f*; ~ **cost** *n* ECON coût social *m*; ~ **cost of monopoly** *n* ECON coût social d'un monopole *m*; ~ **cost of unemployment** *n* HRM, WEL coût social du chômage *m*; ~ **democracy** *n* ECON, POL social-démocratie *f*; ~ **development envelope** *n* POL enveloppe de développement social *f*; ~ **development tax** *n* *Canada* TAX impôt de progrès social *m*; ~ **dividend scheme** *n* ECON système de dividende social *m*, TAX impôt négatif sur le revenu *m*; ~ **good** *n* ECON bien public *m*, bien social *m*; ~ **insurance** *n* HRM, WEL assurance sociale *f*; ~ **insurance number** *n (SIN)* TAX, WEL numéro d'assurance sociale *m*, numéro d'immatriculation sécurité sociale *m*; ~ **liberalism** *n* ECON, POL libéralisme social *m*; ~ **market economy** *n* ECON économie sociale de marché *f*; ~ **outcasts** *n pl* WEL les exclus *m pl*; ~ **overhead capital** *n* FIN capital social *m*; ~ **ownership** *n* HRM démocratie d'entreprise *f*, propriété publique *f*; ~ **policy** *n* GEN COMM politique sociale *f*; ~ **product** *n* ECON produit social *m*, revenu national *m*; ~ **profit** *n* ECON analyse coût-rendement *f*, profit social *m*; ~ **rate of discount** *n* FIN taux d'escompte social *m*; ~ **secretary** *n* HRM secrétaire social *m*; ~ **security** *n* HRM aide sociale *f*; ~ **security act** *n* LAW loi sur la sécurité sociale *f*; ~ **security contributions** *n pl* HRM contributions de sécurité sociale *f pl*, TAX cotisations sociales *f pl*; ~ **security creditor** *n* ACC dettes sociales *f pl*; ~ **security payment** *n* BrE *(cf social assistance payment Can)* WEL paiement d'assistance sociale *m*, prestation d'assistance sociale *f*; ~ **spending** *n* FIN dépenses sociales *f pl*; ~ **standing** *n* WEL position sociale *f*; ~ **status** *n* WEL standing *m*; ~ **strata** *n pl* WEL couches sociales *f pl*; ~ **stratification** *n* WEL couches sociales *f pl*, stratification sociale *f*; ~ **studies** *n pl* WEL étude des sciences humaines *f*, étude des sciences sociales *f*; ~ **system** *n* WEL système social *m*; ~ **wants** *n pl* WEL besoins sociaux *m pl*; ~ **welfare** *n* WEL avantages sociaux *m pl*; ~ **welfare function** *n* ECON, WEL fonction de bien-être social *f*; ~ **work** *n* HRM, WEL assistance sociale *f*; ~ **worker** *n* HRM, WEL assistant social *m*, travailleur social *m*

Social: ~ **Contract** *n* *UK* HRM politique contractuelle *f*; ~ **Development Committee** *n* POL *short title* comité de développement social *m*; ~ **Security benefits** *n pl* HRM allocations de la Sécurité Sociale *f pl*, prestations de la Sécurité Sociale *f pl*, prestations sociales *f pl*

socialism *n* ECON, POL socialisme *m*

socialist *n* ECON, POL socialiste *mf*; ~ **economy** ECON, POL économie socialiste *f*

Socialist: ~ **Labor Party** *n* *US* POL Parti travailliste socialiste *m*

socialite *n* POL membre de la haute société *m*

socialization *n* WEL socialisation *f*

socially: ~ **necessary labor time** *n* *AmE*, ~ **necessary labour time** *n* *BrE* HRM heure de travail socialement nécessaire *f*

Society: ~ **of British Aerospace Companies** *n* *(SBAC)* TRANSP société des entreprises aérospatiales britanniques; ~ **for Worldwide Interbank Financial Telecommunications** *n* *(SWIFT)* BANK, COMMS Société internationale de télécommunications financières interbanques *f*; ~ **of Motor Manufacturers and Traders** *n* *UK* *(SMMT)* TRANSP société des constructeurs et négociants automobiles

sociocultural *adj* S&M socioculturel

socioeconomic[1] *adj* ECON, S&M socio-économique

socioeconomic:[2] ~ **climate** *n* ECON climat socio-économique *m*; ~ **status** *n* ECON statut socio-économique *m*

sociometric *adj* MATH, S&M sociométrique

socioprofessional: ~ **group** *n* GEN COMM catégorie socio-professionnelle *f*, CSP

sociotechnical: ~ **system** *n* ADMIN système socio-technique *m*

Sod's: ~ **law** *n* *infrml* (SYN *Murphy's law*) GEN COMM loi des séries *f*

SOFFEX *abbr (Swiss Options and Financial Futures Exchange)* STOCK bourse d'échange des options et valeurs à terme Suisse

Sofia *pr n* GEN COMM Sofia *n pr*

soft:[1] ~ **budget** *n* FIN budget en baisse *m*; ~ **commission** *n* STOCK commission en nature *f*, commission faible *f*; ~ **commodity** *n* STOCK matière première agricole *f*, produit en baisse *m*; ~ **copy** *n* COMP affichage sur écran *m*, présentation visuelle *f*, texte d'écran *m*, visualisation *f*; ~ **cost** *n* GEN COMM coût accessoire *m*, coût périphérique *m*; ~ **-cover** *n* MEDIA livre de poche *m*, livre à couverture souple *m*; ~ **-cover book** *n* MEDIA livre de poche *m*, livre à couverture souple *m*; ~ **currency** *n* ECON, GEN COMM devise faible *f*; ~ **drink** *n* GEN COMM boisson non-alcoolisée *f*; ~ **error** *n* COMP erreur intermittente *f*, erreur temporaire *f*; ~ **funding** *n* *jarg* ADMIN financement non-durable *m*, fonds publics à taux favorable *m pl*; ~ **goods** *n pl* GEN COMM biens de consommation non-durables *m pl*; ~ **keyboard** *n* COMP clavier programmable *m*, clavier à touches programmables *m*; ~ **landing** *n* *(ANT hard landing)* ECON, GEN COMM atterrissage en douceur *m*; ~ **loan** *n* ECON prêt bonifié *m*, prêt à conditions particulièrement favorables *m*, FIN crédit à taux privilégié *m*; **~ market** *n* ECON *unstable and declining* marché en baisse *m*, marché morose *m*, marché peu actif *m*, STOCK marché morose *m*, marché peu actif *m, unstable and declining* marché en baisse *m*; **~ modeling** *n AmE*, **~ modelling** *n BrE* ECON modélisation discrète *f*; **~ money** *n* WEL contribution déductible *f, education* fonds de provenance inconnue *m pl*; **~ offer** *n* GEN COMM offre variable *f*; **~ sectoring** *n* COMP sectorisation logicielle *f*; **~ sell** *n* (ANT *hard sell)* S&M promotion discrète *f*, vente par des méthodes de persuasion *f*; **~ spot** *n* GEN COMM faible *m*; **~ technology** *n* ECON, ENVIR, IND technologie douce *f*; **~ -top container** *n* TRANSP conteneur bâché *m*

soft:[2] **~ -pedal** *vt infrml* GEN COMM, POL minimiser

soften: **~ up** *vt* GEN COMM *client* baratiner *(infrml)*

software:[1] **~ -driven** *adj* COMP piloté par logiciel

software[2] *n* COMP logiciel *m*, logiciel informatique *m*, progiciel *m*; **~ application** COMP application logicielle *f*; **~ broker** STOCK courtier en logiciel *m*, courtier en valeurs de sociétés de logiciel *m*; **~ company** COMP société en logiciel *f*; **~ and computer services company** COMP société de services et de conseils en informatique *f*; **~ engineer** COMP ingénieur logiciel *m*, ingénieur programmeur *m*; **~ engineering** COMP génie logiciel *m*; **~ house** COMP société en logiciel *f*; **~ language** COMP langage de programmation *m*; **~ package** COMP progiciel *m*; **~ piracy** COMP piratage de logiciel *m*; **~ release** COMP version de logiciel *f*; **~ rot** COMP dégradation des performances *f*

Sohyo *n* HRM *Japan* sohyo *m*

soil: **~ bank** *n US* ECON *agricultural* banque du sol *f*; **~ degradation** *n* ENVIR détérioration du sol *f*; **~ erosion** *n* ENVIR érosion du sol *f*

soiled *adj* GEN COMM *goods* défraîchi

sol *n* GEN COMM sol *m*

SOL *abbr (shipowner's liability)* INS, LAW, TRANSP *shipping* responsabilité de l'armateur *f*

solar: **~ power** *n* ENVIR, IND énergie solaire *f*

sold: **~ daybook** *n* GEN COMM journal des ventes *m*; **~ ledger** *n* GEN COMM livre d'achats *m*, livre des ventes *m*; **~ message** *n* TRANSP message de vente *m*; **~ -out market** *n* FIN contrat à terme non-disponible *m*, STOCK contrat à terme non-disponible *m*, marché épuisé *m*

sole[1] *adj* BANK exclusif

sole:[2] **~ agency** *n* GEN COMM, PROP contrat d'exclusivité *m*; **~ agent** *n* ECON agent commercial exclusif *m*, GEN COMM agent exclusif *m*, concessionnaire exclusif *m*, seul dépositaire *m*, S&M agent commercial exclusif *m*; **~ arbitrator** *n* INS arbitre unique *m*; **~ bargaining agent** *n UK* HRM négociateur unique *m*; **~ bargaining rights** *n pl UK* HRM droits à position de négociateur unique *m pl*; **~ of exchange** *n* BANK seule de change *f*; **~ inventor** *n* PATENTS seul inventeur *m*, unique

inventeur *m*; **~ legatee** *n* LAW légataire universel *m*; **~ owner** *n* PROP seul propriétaire *m*; **~ proprietor** *n* GEN COMM entreprise individuelle *f*, entreprise unipersonnelle *f*, MGMNT propriétaire *mf*; **~ proprietorship** *n* GEN COMM, PROP droit de propriété *m*, entreprise individuelle *f*, entreprise à propriétaire unique *f*; **~ trader** *n* ACC exploitant individuel *m*, GEN COMM entreprise individuelle *f*, entreprise unipersonnelle *f*; ◆ **with the ~ object of doing** GEN COMM avec pour objectif de faire, à seule fin de faire

solicit *vt* GEN COMM solliciter

solicitation *n* S&M démarchage *m*

solicitor *n UK* LAW conseiller juridique *m*

solid:[1] **~ -state** *adj* GEN COMM transistorisé *(vieilli)*

solid:[2] **~ cast-iron propeller** *n (SCIP)* TRANSP *shipping* hélice monobloc en fonte de fer *f*; **~ cast-steel propeller** *n (SCSP)* TRANSP *shipping* hélice monobloc en fonte d'acier *f*; **~ -frame securing system** *n* TRANSP *containers* système d'arrimage au cadre fixe *m*; **~ gold** *n* ENVIR or massif *m*; **~ line** *n* MATH *on graph* ligne continue *f*; **~ non-ferrous propeller** *n (SBP)* TRANSP *shipping* hélice monobloc nonferreuse *f*; **~ waste** *n* ENVIR déchets solides *m pl*; ◆ **on ~ ground** GEN COMM en terrain sûr

solidarity *n* ECON, HRM, POL solidarité *f*; **~ action** HRM *industrial action* mouvement de solidarité *m*

Solow: **~ residual** *n* ECON résidu de Solow *m*

solus: **~ position** *n* MEDIA, S&M emplacement isolé *m*

solution *n* GEN COMM, MGMNT résolution *f*, PATENTS *of problem* solution *f*

solve *vt* GEN COMM, MGMNT *problem* résoudre

solvency *n* ACC solvabilité *f*; **~ margin** FIN marge de solvabilité *f*; **~ ratio** ACC taux de solvabilité *m*, FIN *credit institution* ratio de solvabilité *m*

solvent[1] *adj* FIN, GEN COMM solvable

solvent:[2] **~ debt** *n* BANK dette solvable *f*

Somali[1] *adj* GEN COMM somalien

Somali[2] *n* GEN COMM *language* somali *m, person* Somalien *m*

Somalia *pr n* GEN COMM Somalie *f*

Somalian[1] *adj* GEN COMM somalien

Somalian[2] *n* GEN COMM *person* Somalien *m*

son *n* GEN COMM fils *m*

soon: **as ~ as possible** *phr (a.s.a.p.)* COMMS, GEN COMM aussitôt que possible *loc*, dans les meilleurs délais *loc m*, dès que possible *loc*, le plus tôt possible *loc*

s.o.p. *abbr (standard operating procedure)* GEN COMM mode d'exploitation normal *m*, procédure normale à suivre *f*

sophisticated[1] *adj* GEN COMM sophistiqué

sophisticated:[2] **~ market** *n* STOCK marché falsifié *m*, marché sophistiqué *m*

sophistication *n* ECON complexité *f*, GEN COMM sophistication *f*, S&M *of market* complexité *f*

sor *abbr (starboard)* TRANSP *shipping* tribord *m*

sorry *adj* COMMS désolé; ♦ **I'm ~** GEN COMM veuillez m'excuser; **~ to have kept you waiting** COMMS désolé de vous avoir fait attendre; **~ to keep you waiting** COMMS désolé de vous avoir fait attendre

sort[1] *n* COMP tri *m*; **~ file** COMP fichier de tri *m*; **~ key** COMP critère de tri *m*

sort:[2] **~ out** *vt* GEN COMM faire le tri de *loc m*

sorter *n* GEN COMM trieur *m*

sought: **~ -after** *adj* GEN COMM, HRM recherché

sound[1] *adj* GEN COMM solide, sûr; ♦ **on a ~ footing** GEN COMM sur des bases saines

sound[2] *n* COMP son *m*; **~ check** *n* COMMS contrôle du son *m*; **~ currency** *n* GEN COMM devise saine *f*; **~ effects** *n pl* MEDIA bruitage *m*, effets sonores *m pl*, trucages sonores *m pl*; **~ insulation** *n* COMMS, ENVIR isolation acoustique *f*, isolation phonique *f*; **~ projector** *n* GEN COMM projecteur sonore *m*

sound:[3] **~ out** *vt* GEN COMM questionner discrète-ment

soundtrack *n* COMMS *of broadcast* piste sonore *f*

source *n* COMP source *f*; **~ address** COMP adresse émettrice *f*; **~ and application of funds** ACC tableau des emplois et des ressources de finance *m*, état de flux de trésorerie *m*, état de variations de trésorerie *m*; **~ and applications of funds statement** FIN tableau de financement *m*; **~ of capital** FIN base du capital *f*; **~ code** COMP code source *m*; **~ computer** COMP machine de compila-tion *f*, ordinateur de compilation *m*; **~ credibility** S&M crédibilité de la source *f*; **~ data** COMP données de base *f pl*; **~ disk** COMP disque source *m*; **~ document** ACC document de base *m*; **~ file** COMP fichier source *m*; **~ of funds** ACC, FIN ressource de financements *f*; **~ of income** ACC, TAX source de revenus *f*; **~ language** COMP, GEN COMM langage source *m*; **~ object** ACC article d'origine *m pl*; **~ program** COMP programme d'origine *m*, programme source *m*, programme symbolique *m*; **~ tax** TAX impôt retenu à la source *m*, impôt à la source *m*; ♦ **at ~** TAX *tax relief* à la source; **~ and disposition of funds** ACC, FIN ressources et emplois de capitaux *f pl*

sources: **~ of funds** *n pl* ACC provenance des fonds *f*

sourcing *n* GEN COMM approvisionnement *m*, S&M sourçage *m*; **~ expert** S&M sourceur *m*

south *n* GEN COMM sud *m*

South:[1] **~ African** *adj* GEN COMM d'Afrique du Sud, sud-africain; **~ American** *adj* GEN COMM d'Amé-rique du Sud, sud-américain; **~ Korean** *adj* GEN COMM sud-coréen

South:[2] **~ African** *n* GEN COMM *person* Sud-Africain *m*; **~ African gold shares** *n pl* STOCK valeurs or sud-africaines *f pl*; **~ America** *n* GEN COMM Amérique du Sud *f*; **~ American** *n* GEN COMM *person* Sud-Américain *m*; **~ Atlantic rates** *n pl* TRANSP taux d'Atlantique sud *m pl*; **~ compass point** *n (S)* TRANSP *navigation* quart sud *m (S)*; **~ East Asia Trade Advisory Group** *n (SEATAG)*

ECON, IMP/EXP groupe consultatif commercial d'Asie du Sud-Est; **~ Korean** *n* GEN COMM *person* Sud-Coréen *m*

South:[3] **~ Africa** *pr n* GEN COMM Afrique du Sud *f*; **~ Korea** *pr n* GEN COMM Corée du Sud *f*

southbound *adj* TRANSP sud, à destination sud *loc f*

southeast[1] *adj* TRANSP *shipping* sud-est

southeast[2] *n (SE)* COM, TRANSP *shipping* sud-est *m*

Southeast: **~ Asia** *n* GEN COMM Asie du Sud-Est *f*

southeastern *adj* TRANSP *shipping* sud-est

southern *adj* GEN COMM du sud *loc m*

southwest[1] *adj (SW)* GEN COMM sud-ouest

southwest[2] *n (SW)* TRANSP sud-ouest *m*

sovereign *n* GEN COMM *coin*, POL souverain *m*; **~ borrower** BANK emprunteur public *m*; **~ loan** FIN prêt garanti par l'État *m*; **~ risk** FIN risque d'insolvabilité de l'État emprunteur *m*, risque souverain *m*; **~ risk loan** BANK prêt à risque souverain *m*

Soviet: **~ -type economy** *n* ECON économie de pénurie *f*, économie de type soviétique *f*; **~ Union** *n* GEN COMM Union soviétique *f*

Sp *abbr (sloop)* TRANSP *shipping* sloop *m*

SPA *abbr (subject to particular average)* INS assujetti à l'avarie particulière

space *n* COMMS, COMP *in text*, MEDIA espace *m*; **~ arbitrage** *n* GEN COMM arbitrage de place à place *m*; **~ bar** *n* COMP barre d'espacement *f*; **~ broker** *n* S&M *advertising* courtier en publicité *m*; **~ buyer** *n (ANT space seller)* S&M *advertising* acheteur d'espace *m*; **~ buying** *n (ANT space selling)* S&M *advertising* achat d'espace *m*; **~ rates** *n pl* S&M *advertising* tarifs d'espace *m pl*, tarifs d'insertion *m pl*; **~ seller** *n (ANT space buyer)* S&M *advertising* vendeur d'espace *m*; **~ selling** *n (ANT space buying)* S&M *advertising* vente d'espace *f*; **~ shuttle** *n* TRANSP navette spatiale *f*; **~ writer** *n* HRM, MEDIA *print* pigiste *mf*

spaceman: **~ economy** *n (cf cowboy economy AmE)* ECON économie du gaspillage et de l'irres-ponsabilité

spacer *n* TRANSP entretoise *f*

Spain *pr n* GEN COMM Espagne *f*

span: **~ of control** *n* GEN COMM étendue des responsabilités *f*, étendue du contrôle *f*, éventail de contrôle *m*

Spaniard *n* GEN COMM *person* Espagnol *m*

Spanish[1] *adj* GEN COMM espagnol

Spanish[2] *n* GEN COMM *language* espagnol *m*; **the ~** *n pl* GEN COMM *person* les Espagnols *m pl*

SPAR *abbr (Standard Portfolio Analysis of Risk)* FIN analyse des risques liés au portefeuille *f*

spare: **~ capacity** *n* ECON, IND capacité inutilisée *f*, potentiel inemployé *m*, TRANSP surcroît de capacité *m*; **~ cash** *n* GEN COMM argent en trop *m*; **~ part** *n (SYN replacement part)* GEN COMM pièce de rechange *f*; **~ time** *n* GEN COMM temps libre *m*

spares *n pl* IND pièces détachées *f pl*

spark: **~ off** *vt* GEN COMM *criticism, discussion, debate* déclencher, provoquer

sparring: **~ fitting** *n (SF)* TRANSP *shipping* vaigrage *m*

sparsely:[1] **~ populated** *adj* ECON *area, region* faiblement peuplé

sparsely:[2] **~ populated area** *n* ECON zone peu peuplée *f*, zone à faible population *f*

spate *n* GEN COMM vague *f*

spatial: **~ benefit limitation** *n* ECON limites spatiales à l'utilisation des biens sociaux locaux *f pl*; **~ distribution** *n* GEN COMM, MATH distribution spatiale *f*; **~ duopoly** *n* ECON duopole local *m*; **~ equalization** *n* ECON, IND politique régionale *f*; **~ monopoly** *n* ECON monopole local *m*; **~ oligopoly** *n* ECON oligopole local *m*

SPC *abbr* PATENTS *(supplementary protection certificate)* certificat de protection renforcée *m*, certificat de protection supplémentaire *m*, TRANSP *(self-polishing copolymer)* copolymère autolisseur *m*

speaker *n* GEN COMM *in meeting* conférencier *m*, orateur *m*

spearhead *n* GEN COMM *of campaign* fer de lance *m*

Spearman's: **~ rank correlation formula** *n* MATH *statistics* théorie du facteur général de Spearman *f*

spec: **~ house** *n* PROP immobilier de spéculation *m*; ◆ **on ~** *infrml* GEN COMM sur descriptif *loc m*, HRM *job application* spontané

special: **~ accounts** *n pl* ACC comptes spéciaux *m pl*; **~ arbitrage account** *n* STOCK compte spécial d'arbitrage *m*; **~ arrangements** *n pl* GEN COMM dispositions particulières *f pl*; **~ assessment** *n* TAX évaluation spéciale *f*; **~ -bracket firm** *n* BANK établissement de catégorie particulière *m*; **~ case** *n* LAW jugement gracieux *m*, jugement gracieux sur requête *m*; **~ circumstances** *n pl* GEN COMM circonstances particulières *f pl*; **~ clearing** *n* UK BANK compensation particulière *f*; **~ commercial exchange rate** *n* ECON *Russia* taux de change spécial appliqué au commerce *m*; **~ commissioner** *n* UK TAX *tax appeals* commissaire spécial *m*; **~ correspondent** *n* MEDIA envoyé spécial *m*; **~ credit facility** *n* BANK ligne de crédit spéciale *f*; **~ deposit** *n* BANK dépôt exceptionnel *m*; **~ district bond** *n* STOCK obligation des collectivités locales financée par impôt *f*; **~ drawing rights** *n pl (SDR)* BANK droits particuliers de retrait *m pl*, LAW droits de tirage spéciaux *m pl (DTS)*; **~ economic zone** *n* ECON *China* zone économique spéciale *f*; **~ employment measures** *n pl (SEM)* HRM mesures particulières pour l'emploi *f pl*; **~ endorsement** *n* BANK endossement spécial *m*; **~ fourth-class mail** *n* COMMS tarif postal réduit spécial *m*; **~ indorsement** *n see*

special endorsement ; **~ intermediate survey** *n (SIS)* TRANSP visite spéciale intermédiaire *f*; **~ journal** *n* ACC journal auxiliaire *m*; **~ jury** *n* LAW jury ad hoc *m*, jury spécial *m*; **~ meeting** *n* GEN COMM assemblée extraordinaire *f*, réunion extraordinaire *f*, séance extraordinaire *f*; **~ miscellaneous account** *n (SMA)* STOCK compte de divers *m*; **~ multiperil insurance** *n (SMP)* INS assurance combinée spécifique *f*, police multi-risque spéciale *f*; **~ non-marketable bonds** *n* STOCK *issued by the government of Canada* obligations particulières non-négociables *f pl*, obligations spéciales non-négociables *f pl*; **~ offer** *n* GEN COMM offre spéciale *f*, promotion *f*, S&M *advertising* offre spéciale *f*, promo *f (infrml)*, promotion *f*; **~ partner** *n* GEN COMM associé commanditaire *m*, associé en participation *m*, LAW associé en participation *m*; **~ provisions** *n pl* TAX *National Insurance contributions* réserves spéciales *f pl*; **~ purchase** *n* S&M *advertising* offre promotionnelle *f*; **~ -purpose allotment** *n* GEN COMM affectation à but spécial *f*; **~ reserve** *n* ACC réserve spéciale *f*; **~ situation** *n* GEN COMM situation particulière *f*; **~ survey** *n (SS)* TRANSP visite spéciale *f*; **~ survey of the hull** *n (SSH)* TRANSP *shipping* visite spéciale de la coque *f*; **~ survey of the machinery** *n (SSM)* TRANSP *shipping* visite spéciale des machines *f*; **~ tax bond** *n* STOCK obligation imposable spéciale *f*; **~ tax rate** *n* TAX taux d'imposition spécial *m*; **~ terms** *n pl* GEN COMM conditions spéciales *f pl*; **~ terms for the trade** *n pl* GEN COMM tarif spécial pour les membres de la profession *m*; **~ traffic notice** *n (STN)* TRANSP affiche spéciale circulation *f*; **~ type** *n* TRANSP type spécial *m*; **~ warrant** *n* POL mandat spécial *m*; ◆ **on ~ offer** S&M promotionnel; **~ provision for losses on transborder claims** BANK provision spéciale pour pertes sur créances hors frontières *f*

Special: **~ Branch** *n* UK LAW service de contre-espionnage et de lutte contre la subversion interne; **~ Recovery Capital Projects Program** *n Canada (SRCPP)* GEN COMM programme spécial de relance des projets d'investissement *m*

specialist *n* GEN COMM expert *m*, spécialiste *mf*, STOCK spécialiste de la valeur *m*; **~ block purchase and sale** STOCK achat et vente de blocs de titres par un spécialiste *m*; **~ information** GEN COMM informations spécialisées *f pl*; **~ knowledge** HRM savoir de spécialiste *m*; **~'s short-sale ratio** STOCK coefficient des ventes à découvert des spécialistes *m*, taux à court terme de spécialiste *m*

Specialist: **~ Electronic Book** *n* US *(SEB)* STOCK annuaire électronique spécialisé *m*, carnet électronique spécialisé *m*

speciality *n* GEN COMM spécialité *f*; **~ advertising** S&M publicité par cadeaux-primes *f*; **~ selling** S&M vente à domicile *f*

specialization *n* GEN COMM, HRM spécialisation *f*

specialize: **~ in** *vt* GEN COMM se spécialiser dans

specialized *adj* IND spécialisé

specially: **not ~ provided for** *phr (nspf)* GEN COMM non expressément prévu, pas spécialement prévu

specialty: **~ retailer** *n AmE* S&M détaillant spécialisé *m*

specie *n* GEN COMM espèces *f pl*; **~ flow mechanism** BANK mécanisme de mouvement en numéraire *m*; **~ point** GEN COMM point d'or *m*; ◆ **in ~** GEN COMM *payment* en espèces

specific[1] *adj* GEN COMM spécifique

specific:[2] **~ amount** *n* GEN COMM montant déterminé *m*; **~ commitment** *n* GEN COMM engagement spécifique *m*; **~ commodity rates** *n pl* IMP/EXP, TRANSP *air freight* tarifs préférentiels *m pl*; **~ duty** *n* IMP/EXP, TAX droit spécifique *m*; **~ egalitarianism** *n* ECON égalitarisme spécifique *m*; **~ gravity** *n (SG)* GEN COMM poids spécifique *m*; **~ individual licence** *n BrE (SIL)* IMP/EXP, TRANSP permis spécifique individuel *m*; **~ individual license** *n AmE see specific individual licence BrE*; **~ investment loan** *n (SIL)* FIN prêt spécial à l'investissement *m*; **~ payment** *n* GEN COMM paiement déterminé *m*; **~ performance** *n* LAW exécution intégrale du contrat par décision de justice *f*, exécution pure et simple *f*; **~ provisions** *n* BANK provisions spécifiques *f pl*; **~ tax** *n* IMP/EXP droit spécifique *m*; **~ training** *n* HRM formation spécifique *f*

specification *n* MATH *statistics* spécification *f*; **~ change notice** *(SCN)* TRANSP *aviation* spécification de changement notifié *f (SCN)*; **~ of goods** PATENTS liste des produits *f*; **~ of services** PATENTS liste des services *f*

specifications *n pl* PATENTS *printed* descriptif *m*, mémoire descriptif *m*

specifics *n pl* BANK provisions spécifiques *f pl*; ◆ **get down to ~** GEN COMM entrer dans les détails

specified[1] *adj* GEN COMM précisé, spécifié; ◆ **at the ~ tenor** GEN COMM à l'échéance prescrite

specified:[2] **~ employer** *n* TAX employeur désigné *m*; **~ financial institution** *n* FIN, TAX institution financière désignée *f*; **~ gift** *n* TAX don désigné *m*; **~ member** *n* TAX associé déterminé *m*, membre spécifié *m*; **~ percentage** *n* TAX pourcentage déterminé *m*; **~ person** *n* TAX personne apparentée *f*, personne spécifiée *f*; **~ property** *n* TAX bien désigné *m*; **~ purpose** *n* TAX fin admise *f*, raison spécifiée *f*; **~ -purpose accounts** *n pl Canada* ACC, POL comptes à fins déterminées *m pl (Canada)*; **~ rate** *n* TRANSP tarif spécifié *m*; **~ right** *n* TAX droit particulier *m*, droit prescrit *m*; **~ shareholder** *n* TAX *of corporation* actionnaire désigné *m*

specimen: **~ copy** *n* GEN COMM copie type *f*, spécimen *m*; **~ invoice** *n* GEN COMM modèle de facture *m*; **~ signature** *n* BANK signature témoin *f*, spécimen de signature *m*; **~ signature card** *n* BANK carte de spécimen de signature *f*

spectacular *n jarg* S&M *mail-order* panneau géant animé *m*

spectail *n* STOCK courtier spéculateur *m*

speculate *vi* ECON conjecturer, GEN COMM spéculer

speculation *n* GEN COMM, STOCK spéculation *f*; ◆ **on ~** GEN COMM sur descriptif, HRM *job application* spontané

speculative[1] *adj* STOCK spéculatif

speculative:[2] **~ demand** *n* ECON *for money* demande spéculative *f*; **~ fund** *n* STOCK fonds spéculatifs *m pl*; **~ stock** *n (ANT blue chip)* STOCK valeur spéculative *f*; **~ trading** *n* STOCK opérations spéculatives *f pl*, transactions spéculatives *f pl*

speculator *n* STOCK spéculateur *m*

speech: **~ processing** *n* COMP traitement de la parole *m*, traitement vocal *m*; **~ recognition** *n* COMP reconnaissance de la parole *f*, reconnaissance vocale *f*; **~ recognition software** *n* COMP logiciel de reconnaissance de la parole *m*, logiciel de reconnaissance vocale *m*; ◆ **make a ~** MGMNT faire un discours

speed[1] *n* COMP débit *m*, vitesse *f*, ECON vitesse *f*

speed:[2] **~ up** *vti* GEN COMM accélérer

speeding: **~ -up** *n* GEN COMM, HRM accélération *f*

speedy *adj* GEN COMM rapide

spell: **~ out** *vt* GEN COMM expliquer point par point

spellcheck *n* COMP *program* correcteur d'orthographe *m*, correcteur orthographique *m*, vérificateur d'orthographe *m*

spellchecker *n* COMP *program* correcteur d'orthographe *m*, correcteur orthographique *m*, vérificateur d'orthographe *m*

spending: **~ authority** *n* ECON, POL autorisation de dépenser *f*; **~ level** *n* GEN COMM niveau de dépenses *m*; **~ money** *n* GEN COMM argent de poche *m*; **~ patterns** *n pl* GEN COMM, S&M habitudes d'achat *f pl*; **~ power** *n* GEN COMM pouvoir d'achat *m*; **~ spree** *n* GEN COMM de folles dépenses *loc f*; **~ surge** *n* ECON, GEN COMM montée soudaine des dépenses *f*

spendthrift *n* GEN COMM dépensier *m*

SPGER *abbr (simplified procedure for goods carried by rail)* TRANSP procédure simplifiée pour marchandises transportées par chemin de fer *f*

sphere: **~ of activity** *n* GEN COMM champ d'activité *m*, sphère *f*

SPHL *abbr (self-propelled hyperbaric lifeboat)* TRANSP *shipping* canot de sauvetage hyperbare autopropulsé *m*

spike[1] *n jarg* STOCK *futures market* hausse brutale *f*, pointe *f*

spike[2] *vt* MEDIA *print* mettre à la corbeille, rejeter *(jarg)*

spill:[1] **~ -off effect** *n* GEN COMM retombée *f*

spill:[2] **~ over** *vi* GEN COMM *effect* se répandre

spillage *n* ENVIR, IND déversement accidentel *m*

spillover *n* ECON retombées *f pl*; **~ effect** ECON effet d'entraînement *m*, effet de retombées *m*, GEN COMM retombée *f*

spin:[1] **~ -off** *n* ECON, FIN, GEN COMM essaimage *m*, IND *secondary product* sous-produit *m*; **~ -off effect** *n* S&M retombées économiques *f pl*

spin:[2] **~ off** *vt* GEN COMM essaimer; ◆ **~ red tape** *jarg* ADMIN compliquer la vie en formalités

spiral *n* ECON *of prices* spirale *f*; **~ bevel axle** TRANSP essieu à denture hélicoïdale *m*

spiralling: **~ inflation** *n* ECON spirale inflationniste *f*

splash[1] *n* MEDIA *print* manchette *f*

splash[2] **1.** *vt* MEDIA *print* mettre en manchette (*jarg*); **2.** *vi* **~ out** *infrml* GEN COMM claquer du fric (*infrml*), faire des folies

splinter: **~ group** *n* POL groupe séparatiste *m*; **~ union** *n* HRM syndicat dissident *m*

splintered: **~ authority** *n* MGMNT autorité fragmentée *f*

split:[1] **~ charter** *n* TRANSP *air freight* affrètement partagé *m*; **~ commission** *n* POL commission partagée *f*; **~ offering** *n* STOCK offre de répartition *f*; **~ rating** *n* FIN classement divergent *m*; **~ screen** *n* COMP écran divisé *m*, écran fractionné *m*; **~ -second timing** *n* GEN COMM précision à la seconde près *f*; **~ shift** *n* HRM équipe dédoublée *f*; **~ ticket** *n* US POL liste partagée *f*

split[2] **1.** *vt* BANK répartir, ventiler; **2.** *vi* **~ up** GEN COMM *party, meeting* se disperser; ◆ **~ the difference** GEN COMM couper la poire en deux, partager la différence

splitting *n* BANK ventilation *f*; **~ spreads** *n pl* STOCK *options on Eurodollar futures* écarts de répartition *m pl*

SPM *abbr (single-point mooring)* TRANSP *shipping* méthode d'amarrage sur un seul point fixe *f*

spoilage *n* GEN COMM déchet *m*

spoiled: **~ voting paper** *n* GEN COMM bulletin blanc *m*, bulletin de vote blanc *m*

spoiler *n jarg* POL gâcheur *m*

spoils: **~ system** *n* US POL système des dépouilles *m*

spoilt: **~ ballot paper** *n* POL bulletin de vote nul *m*

spokesperson *n* MEDIA porte-parole *m*

sponsor[1] *n* FIN promoteur *m*, GEN COMM sponsor *m*, *person* parrain *m*, LEIS sponsor *m*, MEDIA *of programme* commanditaire *mf*, sponsor *m*, WEL *person* donateur *m*; **~ demand** ECON demande d'option *f*

sponsor[2] *vt* GEN COMM *commercially*, LEIS *sport* sponsoriser, MEDIA parrainer, sponsoriser

sponsorship *n* FIN, LEIS *sport* sponsoring *m*, S&M mécénat *m*, parrainage *m*, sponsorisation *f*

spontaneous: **~ combustion** *n* TRANSP combustion spontanée *f*; **~ ignition temperature** *n* GEN COMM point de combustion spontanée *m*

spool:[1] **~ file** *n* COMP fichier à traitement différé *m*

spool[2] *vt* COMP faire un spooling *loc m*

spooling *n* COMP désynchronisation des entrées/sorties *f*, spooling *m*, spouling *m*, traitement différé des entrées/sorties *m*

spoon: **~ -feed** *vt* GEN COMM *information* donner à la petite cuillère, mâcher le travail à *loc*

sporadic[1] *adj* GEN COMM sporadique

sporadic:[2] **~ maintenance** *n* GEN COMM entretien

sporadique *m*; **~ service** *n* TRANSP service sporadique *m*

sport *n* GEN COMM sport *m*

sports: **~ editor** *n* MEDIA chef du service des sports *m*; **~ event** *n* GEN COMM, LEIS événement sportif *m*

Sports: **~ Council** *n (SC)* LEIS organisme autonome d'encouragement aux activités sportives

spot[1] *adj* STOCK au comptant *loc m*

spot:[2] **~ business** *n* GEN COMM opération au comptant *f*; **~ cash** *n* FIN argent liquide *m*; **~ charter** *n* TRANSP affrètement spot *m*; **~ check** *n* GEN COMM *quality* contrôle-surprise *m*, IMP/EXP *customs* fouille au hasard *f*; **~ commodity** *n* STOCK marchandise disponible *f*, matière première au comptant *f*; **~ cotton** *n* IND coton disponible immédiatement *m*; **~ coverage** *n* MEDIA *television* direct *m*, reportage sur place *m*, émission en direct *f*; **~ credit** *n* BANK, FIN crédit ponctuel *m*; **~ currency market** *n* ECON, FIN marché des devises au comptant *m*; **~ delivery** *n* STOCK *currency futures* livraison au comptant *f*, livraison immédiate *f*; **~ delivery month** *n* STOCK mois de livraison immédiate *m*, prochain mois de livraison *m*; **~ exchange rate** *n* ECON cours des changes au comptant *m*; **~ market** *n* STOCK marché au comptant *m*; **~ month** *n* STOCK mois de livraison *m*, mois de livraison immédiate *m*; **~ position** *n* STOCK disponibilité *f*, position au comptant *f*; **~ price** *n* STOCK cours au comptant *m*, prix au comptant *m*; **~ quotation** *n* STOCK cotation du disponible *f*; **~ rate** *n* STOCK cours au comptant *m*, taux de comptant *m*; **~ rate spread** *n* STOCK écart entre les cours du comptant *m*; **~ transaction** *n* STOCK transaction au comptant *f*; **~ zoning** *n* PROP zonage de lieu *m*; ◆ **on the ~** GEN COMM sur place

spot:[3] **~ -check** *vt* GEN COMM contrôler au hasard, IND *for quality* sonder; ◆ **~ the winner** GEN COMM *in lottery* tirer le bon numéro

spotlight *n* GEN COMM lumière des projecteurs *f*

spousal ira *n frml* BANK compte de retraite individuel au nom de l'épouse *m*

spouse *n* LAW conjoint *m*, conjointe *f*, épouse *f*, époux *m*, TAX conjoint *m*, conjointe *f*; **~ fare** LEIS, TRANSP tarifs conjoint *m pl*; **~'s allowance** TAX allocation au conjoint *f*

spout *n* TRANSP bec *m*

spread[1] *n* BANK marge *f*, GEN COMM, S&M *of stores in a particular area* prolifération *f*, STOCK marge *f*, *of options* opération mixte *f*, spread *m*; **~ effect** ECON effet d'osmose *m*, effet de contagion *m*; **~ order** STOCK ordre d'écart *m*, ordre mixte *m*; **~ position** STOCK position mixte *f*; **~ risk** STOCK risque lié à la marge *m*; **~ sheet** STOCK tableau de ventilation *m*; **~ trading** STOCK *currency market* étalement *m*

spread[2] *vt* FIN *repayments* échelonner, GEN COMM étaler, INS *risks* répartir

spreader *n* TRANSP palonnier *m*, palonnier rectangulaire *m*, spreader *m*

spreading *n* FIN *of costs* ventilation *f*, STOCK opération de spread *f*, opération mixte *f*; ~ **agreement** STOCK accord d'échelonnement *m*

spreadover *n jarg* HRM *industrial relations* étalement *m*

spreadsheet *n* ACC, ADMIN, COMP, FIN feuille de calcul électronique *f*, tableur *m*; ~ **program** COMP tableau électronique *m*, tableur *m*

spree: **go on a spending** ~ *phr* GEN COMM claquer du fric *(infrml)*, faire des folies

spring *n* GEN COMM *season* printemps *m*; ~ **multi-year operational plan submission** POL présentation du plan opérationnel pluriannuel de printemps *f*; ~ **tide** TRANSP *shipping* marée de vive-eau *f*

sq *abbr (square)* GEN COMM c *(carré)*

SQC *abbr (statistical quality control)* MATH contrôle statistique de qualité *m*

squander *vt* GEN COMM *money, resources, time* gaspiller

squandering *n* GEN COMM gaspillage *m*

square[1] *adj (sq)* GEN COMM carré *(c)*; ◆ ~ **millimeter per second** *AmE*, ~ **millimetre per second** *BrE (mm²/s)* GEN COMM millimètre carré par seconde *(mm²/s)*

square[2] *n* GEN COMM, MATH carré *m*, STOCK solde *m*, square *m*; ~ **brackets** *n pl* COMP, MEDIA *typography* crochets *m pl*; ~ **foot** *n* GEN COMM pied carré *m*; ~ **footage** *n* PROP *of building* métrage carré *m*; ~ **of the hatch** *n* TRANSP *shipping* carré de panneau *m*; ~ **kilometer** *n* *AmE*, ~ **kilometre** *n* *BrE (km²)* GEN COMM kilomètre carré *m (km²)*; ~ **measures** *n pl* GEN COMM *for surface area* mesures de superficie *f pl*, mesures de surface *f pl*; ~ **mile** *n* GEN COMM mile carré *m*

squat *n* TRANSP *shipping* accroupissement *m*

squatter's: ~ **rights** *n pl* LAW, PROP droits de l'occupant de fait *m pl*, droits de l'occupant sans titre *m pl*

squeegee: ~ **agreement** *n jarg* STOCK accord de rachat de titre à perte et à une date prédéterminée

squeeze:[1] ~ **clamp** *n* TRANSP *cargo-handling* dispositif de serrage *m*; ~ **and freeze** *n jarg* ECON gel des salaires et des prix *m*

squeeze[2] *vt* ECON *prices* bloquer; ◆ ~ **the bears** *jarg* STOCK faire la chasse au découvert *(jarg)*, étrangler les baissiers à découvert *(jarg)*; ~ **the shorts** *jarg* STOCK faire la chasse au découvert *(jarg)*, étrangler les baissiers à découvert *(jarg)*

Sr *abbr* TRANSP *(schooner)* goélette *f*, TRANSP *(single-reduction gearing)* *shipping* réducteur simple *m*

SR *abbr (short run)* IND petite série *f*

SR&CC *abbr (strikes, riots and civil commotions)* LAW grèves, émeutes et insurrections civiles *loc f*

SRCPP *abbr Canada (Special Recovery Capital Projects Program)* GEN COMM programme spécial de relance des projets d'investissement *m*

Sri:[1] ~ **Lankan** *adj* GEN COMM sri-lankais

Sri:[2] ~ **Lankan** *n* GEN COMM *person* Sri-Lankais *m*

Sri:[3] ~ **Lanka** *pr n* GEN COMM Sri Lanka *m*

SRNA *abbr UK (Shipbuilders and Repairers National Association)* TRANSP association nationale des constructeurs et réparateurs de navires

SRO *abbr* GEN COMM *UK (self-regulatory organization)* organisation de centrales des intermédiaires financiers *f*, organisation indépendante *f*, organisme autorégulateur *m*, STOCK *UK (self-regulating organization)* organisation autonome *f*, organisme auto-réglementé *m*

SS *abbr* TRANSP *(steamship)* vap. *(vapeur)*, TRANSP *(ship's special survey, special survey)* visite spéciale *f*

SSA *abbr (standard spending assessment)* ECON évaluation standard des dépenses *f*

SSAP *abbr UK (Statement of Standard Accounting Practice)* ACC norme comptable *f*

SSC *abbr (Swiss Shippers Council)* TRANSP Conseil des affréteurs suisses *m*

SSD *abbr (single-sided disk)* COMP disque monoface *m*, disque simple face *m*

SSDD *abbr (single-sided double density)* COMP simple face-double densité

SSH *abbr (special survey of the hull)* TRANSP *shipping* visite spéciale de la coque *f*

SSIA *abbr UK (Shiprepairers and Shipbuilders Independent Association)* TRANSP association indépendante des réparateurs et constructeurs de navire

SSM *abbr (special survey of the machinery)* TRANSP *shipping* visite spéciale des machines *f*

SSP *abbr* INS *UK (statutory sick pay)* prestation maladie réglementaire *f*, TRANSP *(stainless-steel propeller)* *shipping* hélice en acier inoxydable *f*

SSSD *abbr (single-sided single density)* COMP simple face-simple densité

SSSI *abbr (Site of Special Scientific Interest)* ENVIR Site d'intérêt scientifique spécial *m*

SST *abbr (supplementary service tariff)* TRANSP tarif de services supplémentaires *m*

St:[1] ~ **Petersburg paradox** *n* ECON paradoxe de Saint-Pétersbourg *m*

St:[2] ~ **George's** *pr n* GEN COMM Saint-George's *n pr*; ~ **John's** *pr n* GEN COMM Saint-Jean *n pr*, Saint-John's *n pr*; ~ **Lucia** *pr n* GEN COMM *Windward Islands* Sainte-Lucie *f*; ~ **Vincent** *pr n* GEN COMM *Windward Islands* Saint-Vincent *m*

ST *abbr (side tank)* TRANSP *shipping* citerne latérale *f*

stabex: ~ **system** *n* ECON *agricultural* système stabex *m*

stability *n* ECON, POL, TRANSP *shipping* stabilité *f*; ~ **zone** WEL zone de stabilité *f*

stabilization *n* ECON *of exchange rates* stabilisation *f*; ~ **fund** TAX fonds de stabilisation *m*; ~ **policy** ECON politique conjoncturelle *f*

stabilize 1. *vt* ECON stabiliser; **2.** *vi* ECON se stabiliser

stabilized: ~ **price** *n* ECON prix stabilisé *m*

stabilizer *n* ECON, TRANSP *shipping* stabilisateur *m*

stable[1] *adj* GEN COMM stable

stable:[2] ~ **equilibrium** *n* ECON équilibre stable *m*; ~ **rate** *n* TRANSP tarif stable *m*

stack[1] *n* COMP *data* pile *f*, TRANSP empilage *m*

stack[2] *vt* TRANSP empiler

Stackelberg: ~ **duopoly model** *n* ECON modèle duopolistique de Stackelberg *m*

stacker *n* TRANSP *container securing* pièce de gerbage *f*

stacking *n* TRANSP *cargo handling* gerbage *m*; ~ **of cargo** TRANSP gerbage des marchandises *m*, gerbage du chargement *m*; ~ **fitting** TRANSP *container handling* pièce biconique de saisissage *f*

staff[1] *n* HRM personnel *m*; ~ **appraisal** *n* HRM, MGMNT appréciation du personnel *f*, évaluation du personnel *f*; ~ **assistant** *n* HRM attaché fonctionnel *m*; ~ **association** *n* HRM association d'employés *f*, association du personnel *f*; ~ **audit** *n* ACC, HRM inventaire des effectifs *m*; ~ **canteen** *n* HRM restaurant d'entreprise *m*; ~ **captain** *n* HRM, TRANSP *shipping* officier chargé des passagers *m*; ~ **commitment** *n* HRM engagement du personnel *m*; ~ **cost** *n* HRM charges de personnel *f*; ~ **cutback** *n* HRM compression de personnel *f*, réduction du personnel *f*; ~ **department** *n* HRM service du personnel *m*; ~ **forecasting** *n* HRM prévision des effectifs *f*; ~ **incentive** *n* HRM encouragement du personnel *m*, stimulants *m pl*; ~ **inspection** *n* HRM inspection du personnel *f*; ~ **levy** *n* HRM, TAX contribution du personnel *f*; ~ **management** *n* (SYN *personnel management*) HRM, MGMNT administration du personnel *f*, direction du personnel *f*, gestion du personnel *f*; ~ **manager** *n* HRM, MGMNT chef du personnel *m*, chef du service personnel *m*; ~ **mobility** *n* HRM mobilité du personnel *f*; ~ **organization** *n* GEN COMM, HRM, MGMNT organisation fonctionnelle *f*, organisation horizontale *f*; ~ **planning** *n* HRM, MGMNT planification des effectifs *f*; ~ **provident fund** *n* HRM caisse de prévoyance du personnel *f*; ~ **reduction** *n* HRM compression de personnel *f*, réduction du personnel *f*; ~ **relations** *n pl* HRM relations du travail *f pl*; ~ **representative** *n* HRM délégué du personnel *m*, représentant du personnel *m*, représentant du personnel *m*; ~ **resourcing** *n* HRM recrutement et gestion des effectifs; ~ **shortage** *n* GEN COMM manque de personnel *m*; ~ **status** *n* HRM statut de cadre *m*; ~ **strategy** *n* HRM stratégie du potentiel humain *f*; ~ **training** *n* HRM formation du personnel *f*; ~ **transfer** *n* ECON, HRM mutation de personnel *f*, transfert de personnel *m*; ~ **turnover** *n* ECON rotation du personnel *f*, HRM mouvement du personnel *m*, mutation du personnel *f*, rotation

du personnel *f*; ~ **welfare fund** *n* HRM, WEL caisse de solidarité du personnel *f*; ◆ ~ **and line** HRM structure staff and line *f*

staff[2] **1.** *vt* HRM *office* pourvoir en personnel; **2.** *vi* ~ **up** HRM recruter du personnel

staffed *adj* HRM pourvu en personnel

staffer *n* HRM membre du personnel *m*

staffing *n* HRM dotation en personnel *f*, recrutement du personnel *m*; ~ **level** HRM niveau des effectifs *m*

stag *n* GEN COMM, STOCK loup *m*

stage[1] *n* GEN COMM *of negotiations* phase *f*, stade *m*, étape *f*; ~ **payment** FIN paiement par étape *m*; ~ **of transition** ECON *towards Western-style market economies* étape de transition *f*; ◆ **at some** ~ GEN COMM à un moment donné

stage[2] *vt* MGMNT *conference* organiser; ◆ ~ **a go-slow** HRM organiser une grève perlée; ~ **a strike** HRM organiser une grève; ~ **a walkout** HRM faire une grève surprise

staged: ~ **agreement** *n* UK HRM accord progressif *m*

stages: ~ **theory** *n* ECON théorie des étapes *f*; ◆ **in** ~ GEN COMM par étapes

stagflation *n* (SYN *infession*) ECON stagflation *f*

stagger[1] *n* GEN COMM décalage *m*

stagger[2] *vt* GEN COMM *costs* décaler

staggered: ~ **board of directors** *n* ADMIN, GEN COMM, HRM, MGMNT CA tournant *m*, conseil d'administration tournant *m*; ~ **election** *n* POL élection échelonnée *f*; ~ **holidays** *n pl* BrE (*cf staggering of vacations AmE*) HRM étalement des vacances *m*

staggering[1] *adj* FIN *amount, difference* stupéfiant, GEN COMM incroyable

staggering:[2] ~ **maturities** *n pl* STOCK échelonnement des échéances *m*; ~ **of vacations** *n* AmE (*cf staggered holidays BrE*) HRM étalement des vacances *m*

staggism *n* STOCK spéculation *f*

staging *n* HRM organisation par paliers *f*

stagnant *adj* ECON stagnant, stationnaire

stagnate *vi* ECON stagner

stagnation *n* ECON marasme *m*, stagnation *f*

STAGs *abbr* UK (*sterling transferable accruing government securities*) STOCK obligation à coupon zéro basée sur des bons du Trésor

stainless: ~ **steel** *n* IND acier inoxydable *m*; ~ **-steel propeller** *n* (*SSP*) TRANSP *shipping* hélice en acier inoxydable *f*

stake[1] *n* FIN, GEN COMM *in company* enjeu *m*, STOCK participation *f*; ◆ **at** ~ GEN COMM *matter* en jeu; **the** ~ **s are high** GEN COMM l'enjeu est très important *loc m*

stake[2] *vt* FIN miser

stakeholder *n* GEN COMM dépositaire d'enjeux *m*

stakrak: ~ **cargo unit** *n* TRANSP unité de chargement stakrak *f*

stale[1] *adj* STOCK *market* lourd

stale:² ~ **bill of lading** n IMP/EXP, TRANSP connaissement périmé m; ~ **bull** n jarg STOCK titre détenu sans profit m; ~ **check** n AmE, ~ **cheque** n BrE BANK chèque périmé m; ~ **-dated check** n AmE, ~ **-dated cheque** n BrE BANK chèque périmé m

stalemate n GEN COMM impasse f; ◆ **have reached a** ~ GEN COMM être dans une impasse loc f

stalemated adj GEN COMM discussions, negotiations dans l'impasse loc f

stalls n pl LEIS theatre orchestre m

stamp¹ n GEN COMM vignette f; ~ **duty** (SYN stamp tax) TAX droit de timbre m; ~ **pad** GEN COMM tampon encreur m; ~ **tax** (SYN stamp duty) TAX droit de timbre m

stamp² vt GEN COMM affranchir; ~ **out** ECON abuse, inflation enrayer, juguler; ◆ ~ **the date** ADMIN on form apposer la date au tampon

stamped: ~ **addressed envelope** n BrE (s.a.e) COMMS, GEN COMM enveloppe affranchie f, enveloppe timbrée à vos nom et adresse f

stampede n GEN COMM of investors débandade f

stamping: ~ **machine** n COMMS machine à affranchir f

stance n GEN COMM on issue position f

stanchion n TRANSP shipping chandelier m, support m, épontille f

stand:¹ ~ **-alone** adj COMP computer, system autonome, individuel, indépendant

stand² n S&M advertising panneau d'affichage m, at exhibition stand m; ~ **-alone system** COMP système autonome m; ~ **-in** HRM remplacement m; ◆ **make a** ~ **against a decision** GEN COMM s'opposer résolument à une décision

stand:³ **1.** vt ~ **at** GEN COMM amount, balance, total s'élever à, se situer à; ~ **for** GEN COMM initials signifier, vouloir dire; ~ **in for** HRM remplacer; ~ **off** HRM employees mettre en chômage partiel; ~ **out for** GEN COMM pay, conditions revendiquer; ~ **up for** GEN COMM person, interest défendre; **2.** vi ~ **down** POL of candidate se désister; ~ **over** GEN COMM of subject, item on agenda rester en suspens; ◆ ~ **as guarantor for sb** FIN se porter aval pour qn, GEN COMM se porter garant de qn; ~ **at a discount** STOCK être au-dessous de sa valeur nominale; ~ **at a premium** STOCK être au-dessus de sa valeur nominale; ~ **the cost of** GEN COMM supporter le coût de; ~ **firm** GEN COMM ne pas bouger, rester ferme, tenir bon; ~ **firm in the belief that** GEN COMM tenir bon en sachant que; ~ **for election** POL poser sa candidature à une élection, se présenter aux élections; ~ **a good chance of** GEN COMM avoir une bonne chance de; ~ **in line** COMP, GEN COMM faire la queue; ~ **a loss** GEN COMM supporter une perte; **not** ~ **a chance** HRM ne pas avoir la moindre chance; ~ **one's ground** GEN COMM ne pas bouger, tenir bon; ~ **surety for sb** BANK cautionner qn, répondre de qn, répondre pour qn, se porter caution pour qn, se porter garant de qn; ~ **up to wear** GEN COMM material, fabric faire beaucoup d'usage

standage: ~ **area** n TRANSP terre-plein m

standard¹ adj GEN COMM model standard, quality ordinaire; ~ **design** (SD) IND de série; ~ **-rated** TAX aux taux standard; ◆ **it is** ~ **practice** GEN COMM c'est la manière habituelle de procéder; **it is** ~ **practice to do so** GEN COMM c'est la manière habituelle de procéder

standard² n COMP norme f, GEN COMM quality standard m, GEN COMM étalon m, LAW norme f, standard m; ~ **agreement** n GEN COMM contrat standard m, contrat type m; ~ **allotment** n POL affectation courante f; ~ **code** n GEN COMM code uniforme m; ~ **commodity** n STOCK bien étalon m; ~ **contract** n GEN COMM contrat standard m; ~ **cost** n ACC, ECON, FIN coût standard m, GEN COMM coût de revient standard m, coût standard m, prix de revient standard m; ~ **cost accounting** n ACC comptabilité analytique standardisée f, méthode du coût de revient standard f, FIN comptabilité analytique standardisée f, GEN COMM comptabilité analytique standardisée f, méthode du coût de revient standard f; ~ **cost system** n ACC comptabilité analytique standardisée f, méthode du coût de revient standard f, FIN comptabilité analytique standardisée f, GEN COMM comptabilité analytique standardisée f, méthode du coût de revient standard f; ~ **costing** n ACC comptabilisation en coûts standards f, FIN méthode des coûts standards f, GEN COMM comptabilisation en coûts standards f; ~ **costs** n pl FIN coûts standards m pl; ~ **deduction** n TAX déduction forfaitaire f, prélèvement forfaitaire m; ~ **deviation** n FIN, MATH statistics écart type m; ~ **directory of advertisers** n S&M annuaire général des annonceurs m; ~ **of equalization** n GEN COMM norme de péréquation f; ~ **error** n MATH statistics erreur type f; ~ **error of estimate** n MATH statistics erreur type d'estimation f; ~ **error of the mean** n MATH statistics erreur type de moyenne f; ~ **export levy** n IMP/EXP, TAX perception standard à l'exportation f; ~ **fire policy** n US INS police incendie normalisée f, police incendie type f; ~ **freight trade classification** n (SFTC) TRANSP of Council for Mutual Economic Assistance classement standard du commerce de marchandises m; ~ **grade** n GEN COMM niveau de référence m; ~ **of hygiene** n WEL norme d'hygiène f; ~ **individual income tax** n TAX impôt normal sur le revenu des particuliers m, impôt standard sur le revenu des particuliers m; ~ **industrial classification** n (SIC) IND classification industrielle standard f; ~ **industrial classification system** n IND système de classification industrielle standard m; ~ **of living** n ECON niveau de vie m, standard de vie m, standing m; ~ **metropolitan statistical area** n (SMSA) MATH statistics zone standard de statistique métropolitaine f; ~ **object** n POL article courant m; ~ **object code** n POL code d'article courant m; ~ **object of expenditure** n POL article courant de dépense m; ~ **object of revenue** n POL article courant de recette m; ~ **operating**

procedure *n (s.o.p.)* GEN COMM mode d'exploitation normal *m*, procédure normale à suivre *f*; ~ **performance** *n* GEN COMM rendement standard *m*, HRM rendement moyen *m*, rendement standard *m*, IND rendement standard *m*; ~ **price** *n* ECON, GEN COMM, S&M prix standard *m*; ~ **rate** *n* UK TAX *National Insurance contributions* taux standard *m*; ~ **-rate tax** *n* TAX impôt forfaitaire *m*, impôt à taux standard *m*; ~ **return** *n* LEIS, TRANSP *ticket* aller-retour plein-tarif *m*; ~ **shipping note** *n* IMP/EXP, TRANSP note de chargement normalisée *f*; ~ **single** *n* LEIS, TRANSP *ticket* aller plein-tarif *m*, aller simple plein-tarif *m*; ~ **size** *n* COMP, GEN COMM format standard *m*; ~ **slip** *n* TRANSP *shipping* bon normalisé *m*; ~ **specimen signature card** *n* BANK carte normalisée de spécimen de signature *f*; ~ **spending assessment** *n (SSA)* ECON évaluation standard des dépenses *f*; ~ **tax** *n* TAX impôt normal *m*, impôt ordinaire *m*, impôt régulier *m*, impôt standard *m*; ~ **time** *n* GEN COMM temps de référence *m*, temps standard *m*, HRM durée forfaitaire *f*, délai fixe *m*

Standard: ~ **Interchange Facilities** *n pl* TRANSP moyens d'échange standard *m pl*; ~ **International Trade Classification** *n (SITC)* ECON, GEN COMM classification des normes du commerce international *f*; ~ **and Poor** *n* US STOCK agence de notation Standard and Poor; ~ **Portfolio Analysis of Risk** *n (SPAR)* FIN analyse des risques liés au portefeuille *f*

standardization *n* ACC normalisation *f*, standardisation *f*, GEN COMM normalisation *f*, standardisation *f*, unification *f*, uniformisation *f*, LAW, S&M normalisation *f*, standardisation *f*, uniformisation *f*; ~ **agreement** GEN COMM accord de normalisation *m*; ~ **of salaries** HRM uniformisation des salaires *f*

standardize *vt* GEN COMM unifier, uniformiser, LAW, S&M normaliser, standardiser, uniformiser

standardized[1] *adj* GEN COMM normalisé

standardized:[2] ~ **production** *n* IND fabrication standardisée *f*

standards: ~ **and practices** *n pl* US LAW, MEDIA normes et pratiques *f pl*, service veillant au respect de la déontologie *m*; ♦ **by the company's** ~ GEN COMM selon les normes de la compagnie; **set the** ~ MGMNT donner le la

standby[1] *adj* GEN COMM *equipment* de réserve *loc f*, de secours, TRANSP *passenger* en attente *loc f*

standby[2] *n* HRM astreinte *f*; ~ **agreement** *n* GEN COMM accord stand-by *m*; ~ **charges** *n pl* BANK frais pour droit d'accès *m pl*, frais pour droit d'usage *m pl*; ~ **credit** *n* BANK crédit de soutien *m*, crédit standby *m*; ~ **duty** *n* HRM service d'astreinte *m*; ~ **facility** *n* BANK crédit de soutien *m*; ~ **line of credit** *n* BANK crédit de soutien *m*; ~ **loan** *n* FIN prêt de soutien *m*; ~ **power plant** *n* IND groupe électrogène de secours *m*; ~ **rate** *n* HRM salaire du personnel d'astreinte *m*; ~ **ticket** *n* TRANSP billet stand-by *m*; ~ **underwriter** *n* FIN *securities, lending* souscripteur de soutien *m*; ♦ **be on** ~ GEN COMM

être d'astreinte, TRANSP *plane* être sur liste d'attente

standfirst *n jarg* MEDIA *print* amorce *f*

standing: ~ **advance** *n* BANK avance permanente *f*; ~ **authorization** *n* IMP/EXP autorisation permanente *f*; ~ **committee** *n* POL *European Parliament* commission permanente *f*; ~ **deposit** *n* UK IMP/EXP acompte permanent *m*; ~ **down** *n* HRM mise à pied *f*; ~ **order** *n* UK *(s.o.)* BANK ordre de paiement permanent *m*, ordre de transfert permanent *m*, ordre permanent *m*; ~ **procedure** *n* GEN COMM procédure courante *f*; ~ **travel advance** *n* GEN COMM avance de déplacement permanente *f*

Standing: ~ **Committee on Miscellaneous Estimates** *n* POL Commission permanente d'estimations diverses *f*, Commission permanente des prévisions budgétaires en général *f*; ~ **Committee on Public Accounts** *n* POL Commission permanente des comptes publics *f*

standoff *n* GEN COMM *deadlock* impasse *f*, *inconclusive encounter* affrontement indécis *m*, HRM situation de blocage *f*, temps d'arrêt *m*

stands *n pl jarg* STOCK stands *m pl (jarg)*

standstill: ~ **agreement** *n* FIN, GEN COMM, LAW accord moratoire *m*, moratorium *m (frml)*

staple: ~ **commodity** *n* ECON, S&M produit tertiaire *m*; ~ **export** *n* IMP/EXP exportation principale *f*; ~ **stock** *n* GEN COMM stock principal *m*

stapler *n* GEN COMM agrafeuse *f*

star *n* MEDIA star du moment *f*, vedette *f*; ~ **fitting** TRANSP *shipping* crapaudine pour pied d'éléphant *f*; ~ **network** COMP réseau en étoile *m*; ~ **product** S&M produit locomotive *m*, produit vedette *m*

starboard *n (sor)* TRANSP *shipping* tribord *m*; ~ **side** *(S)* TRANSP *shipping* tribord *m*

start:[1] ~ **-up** *adj* GEN COMM *costs* de démarrage *loc m*, STOCK *venture capital* de départ *loc m*

start[2] *n* COMP *of file* début *m*, *of machine, peripheral* démarrage *m*, mise en route *f*, GEN COMM départ *m*; ~ **bit** *n* COMP bit de début *m*, bit de départ *m*; ~ **-up** *n* ECON démarrage *m*, GEN COMM démarrage *m*, phase de démarrage *f*; ~ **-up capital** *n* FIN capital d'apport *m*, capital initial *m*, mise de fonds initiale *f*, financement de démarrage *m*, STOCK capital initial *m*; ~ **-up costs** *n pl* ACC, FIN frais d'établissement *m pl*, frais de démarrage *m pl*; ~ **-up financing** *n* FIN financement de lancement *m*; ~ **-up loan** *n* FIN prêt initial *m*; ♦ **get off to a flying** ~ GEN COMM *business, project* prendre un bon départ

start[3] **1.** *vt* GEN COMM se mettre à, *firm, company* créer; ~ **up** GEN COMM créer **2.** *vi* GEN COMM commencer; ~ **up** ECON démarrer, GEN COMM commencer, débuter, démarrer; ♦ ~ **doing** GEN COMM commencer à faire; ~ **an entry** ACC ouvrir une écriture; ~ **a fashion** GEN COMM lancer une mode; ~ **a fashion for** GEN COMM lancer la mode de; ~ **from scratch** GEN COMM partir de zéro; ~ **in business** GEN COMM se lancer dans les affaires, se monter en affaires; ~ **sb off as** HRM faire démarrer qn en qualité de; ~ **to do** GEN COMM commencer à faire; ~ **up in business** GEN COMM se lancer dans les affaires; ~ **work** GEN COMM se mettre au travail

starter: ~ **home** n PROP maison de début f

starting:[1] ~ **point** n GEN COMM point de départ m; ~ **price** n STOCK cours initial m; ~ **salary** n HRM salaire d'embauche m, salaire de départ m; ~ **wage** n HRM salaire d'embauche m, salaire de départ m

starting:[2] ~ **from** phr GEN COMM à partir de

state:[1] ~ **-aided** adj ECON, POL subventionné par l'État; ~ **-of-the-art** adj COMP avancé, de pointe, GEN COMM à la pointe du progrès, état de l'art loc f, IND technology, S&M equipment dernier cri

state[2] n COMP, POL état m, GEN COMM US ≈ état m; ~ **of affairs** GEN COMM situation f; ~ **of the art** GEN COMM état de l'art m, PATENTS état de la technique m; ~ **bond** STOCK obligation d'état f; ~ **capitalism** ECON, POL Marxism capitalisme d'état m; ~ **control** ECON, POL contrôle d'État m, contrôle étatique m; ~ **of the economy** ECON situation de l'économie f, état de l'économie m; ~ **education** GEN COMM, WEL UK école publique f; ~ **enterprise** ECON entreprise d'État f, entreprise publique f; ~ **government tribunal** HRM tribunal du gouvernement d'état m; ~ **help** WEL aide de l'État f; ~ **intervention** ADMIN, ECON, POL intervention de l'État f; ~ **-owned plantation** IND Indonesia plantation nationale f; ~ **ownership** ECON, POL propriété d'État f; ~ **pension** UK WEL retraite de l'État f; ~ **of registry** TRANSP État d'immatriculation m; ~ **school** GEN COMM école d'État f, établissement national m, GEN COMM, WEL UK école publique f; ~ **subsidy** ECON subvention de l'État f; ~ **tax** TAX impôt de l'État m; ◆ **in a** ~ GEN COMM à l'abandon; **in a bad** ~ GEN COMM en mauvais état; **in a bad** ~ **of repair** GEN COMM en mauvais état

state[3] vt GEN COMM account spécifier; ◆ ~ **categorically** GEN COMM déclarer catégoriquement; ~ **the obvious** GEN COMM enfoncer une porte ouverte

State: ~ **Earnings Related Pension Scheme** n UK (SERPS) ECON régime de retraite étatique basé sur le salaire; ~ **Secretariat** n POL secrétariat d'État m

stated: ~ **capital** n ACC capital social m; ~ **value** n ACC (SYN book value) valeur comptable f, ACC, FIN Canada valeur attribuée f

stateless[1] adj ADMIN, POL apatride

stateless:[2] ~ **currency** n ECON devise apatride f (jarg)

statement n ACC état m, COMMS communiqué m, COMP instruction f, GEN COMM bordereau m, communiqué m, énoncé m, LAW déclaration f, exposé m, rapport m, mémoire m, S&M communiqué m; ~ **of affairs** BANK in bankruptcy, GEN COMM bilan de liquidation m, bilan de réalisation éventuelle m; ~ **analysis** ACC analyse d'une

situation comptable f; ~ **of assets and liabilities** ACC, FIN bilan m; ~ **of claim** LAW acte introductif d'instance m, citation f; ~ **of condition** FIN banking, finance relevé de modalités d'émission m; ~ **of earnings** US ACC état des résultats m; ~ **of financial position** ACC, FIN bilan m; ~ **in lieu of prospectus** UK STOCK rapport financier utilisé comme prospectus; ~ **of income** US ACC comptes de résultats m pl; ~ **of income and expenses** ACC état de produits et de charges m; ~ **of instruments issued** BANK relevé des effets émis m; ~ **of objectives** MGMNT énoncé des objectifs m; ~ **of prosecution** LAW réquisitoire m; ~ **of terms and conditions** HRM énoncé des clauses et conditions m; ~ **of witness** LAW déposition du témoin f, témoignage m; ◆ **make a** ~ LAW faire une déclaration

Statement: ~ **of Revenue and Expenditure** n ACC État des recettes et dépenses m; ~ **of Standard Accounting Practice** n UK (SSAP) ACC norme comptable f

static[1] adj ECON output, price stationnaire, statique

static:[2] ~ **method** n ACC pensions méthode statique f; ~ **model** n ECON modèle statique m

station n COMP poste m, terminal m, TRANSP gare f; ~ **break** MEDIA advertising, radio page de publicité f; ~ **manager** TRANSP chef de gare m; ~ **time** US MEDIA for broadcasting heure locale f, temps d'antenne m, temps réservé aux émissions du network m, temps émission m; ◆ **at** ~ **price** GEN COMM, TRANSP prix en gare de départ

stationary: ~ **state economy** n ECON économie d'un pays à la population fictivement figée, état de non-croissance m, état stationnaire m

stationer n GEN COMM papetier m

stationery n ADMIN, GEN COMM papeterie f

stationmaster n TRANSP chef de gare m

statistical[1] adj MATH statistique

statistical:[2] ~ **control** n MATH contrôle statistique m; ~ **inference** n MATH déduction statistique f; ~ **modeling** n AmE, ~ **modelling** n BrE MATH modelage statistique m; ~ **population** n MATH échantillon de population m; ~ **process control** n MATH contrôle statistique de l'outil de production m; ~ **quality control** n (SQC) MATH contrôle statistique de qualité m; ~ **returns** n pl MATH résultats statistiques m pl, statistiques officielles f pl; ~ **risk** n MATH risque statistique m; ~ **sampling** n MATH échantillon statistique m, échantillonnage aléatoire m, échantillonnage statistique m, S&M échantillonnage aléatoire m; ~ **significance** n MATH signification statistique f; ~ **software** n COMP, MATH logiciel statistique m; ~ **spread** n MATH portée statistique f, étalement statistique m

Statistical: ~ **Return** n UK TAX value-added bilan statistique m

statistically: ~ **significant** adj MATH statistiquement significatif

statistician n MATH statisticien m

statistics n pl [+sing v] MATH statistique f

status *n* COMP statut *m*, état *m*, GEN COMM position *f*, statut *m*, état *m*; **~ bar** COMP barre d'état *f*; **~ information** GEN COMM renseignements commerciaux *m pl*; **~ line** COMP ligne d'état *f*; **~ message** COMP message d'état *m*; **~ offender** *US* LAW mineur délinquant placé en foyer d'accueil; **~ report** GEN COMM, MGMNT rapport sur la solvabilité *m*, état d'avancement *m*; **~ seeker** GEN COMM personne qui a soif d'être socialement reconnue; **~ symbol** GEN COMM marque de prestige *f*

statute *n* LAW loi *f*, statut *m*; **~ book** *UK* LAW code *m*, recueil des lois *m*; **~ of frauds** LAW loi subordonnant la possibilité d'introduire une action en matière contractuelle à la rédaction d'une note par la partie poursuivie; **~ law** LAW droit écrit *m*, PATENTS loi *f*; **~ of limitations** LAW prescription *f*; ◆ **by ~** LAW selon la loi

statutes: **~ of limitation of action** *n pl* LAW lois fixant la prescription d'une action en justice *f pl*

statutory[1] *adj* LAW légal, prévu par la loi, réglementaire, statutaire; ◆ **have ~ effect** LAW avoir force de loi, avoir force réglementaire

statutory:[2] **~ account** *n pl* GEN COMM comptes sociaux *m pl*; **~ accounts** *n pl* ACC comptes légales *m pl*, comptes sociaux *m pl*, comptes statutaires *m pl*, FIN comptes sociaux *m pl*; **~ allocation** *n* POL affectation réglementaire *f*; **~ appropriation** *n* POL crédit réglementaire *m*; **~ appropriations** *n pl* LAW affectations statutaires de crédit *f pl*, donations statutaires *f pl*; **~ audit** *n* ACC audit légal *m*; **~ authority** *n* POL autorité réglementaire *f*; **~ body** *n* LAW organisme assurant un service public *m*, organisme officiel *m*; **~ books** *n pl* LAW registres statutaires *m pl*; **~ company** *n* GEN COMM société concessionnaire *f*; **~ exclusion** *n* INS *marine* exclusion statutaire *f*; **~ exemption** *n* LAW exemption statutaire *f*, exonération statutaire *f*; **~ expenditure** *n* ECON, FIN, POL dépense réglementaire *f*; **~ foreclosure** *n* LAW forclusion légale *f*, saisie légale d'une hypothèque *f*; **~ holiday** *n* GEN COMM jour férié *m*; **~ immunities** *n pl* HRM, LAW *trade union* immunités légales *f pl*, immunités syndicales *f pl*; **~ immunity** *n* LAW exemption statutaire *f*, exonération statutaire *f*, immunité légale *f*, immunité statutaire *f*; **~ incidence** *n* TAX incidence statutaire *f*; **~ instrument** *n* LAW décret d'application *m*; **~ investment** *n* FIN investissement légal *m*; **~ item** *n* POL article réglementaire *m*; **~ meeting** *n* LAW assemblée statutaire *f*; **~ merger** *n* LAW fusion conforme aux statuts *f*, fusion légale *f*; **~ minimum wage** *n* HRM salaire minimum garanti *m*, salaire minimum interprofessionnel de croissance *m*, SMIC; **~ notice** *n* LAW délai de préavis *m*, délai de préavis légal *m*; **~ obligation** *n* LAW obligation légale *f*, obligation prévue par la loi *f*, obligation statutaire *f*; **~ policy** *n* *UK* HRM politique règlementaire *f*; **~ program** *n* *AmE*, **~ programme** *n* *BrE* POL programme réglementaire *m*; **~ report** *n* GEN COMM rapport présenté lors de la création d'une société;

~ requirement *n* POL demande réglementaire *f*; **~ right** *n* *UK* LAW droit prévu par la loi *m*, droit statutaire *m*; **~ sick pay** *n* *UK* (*SSP*) INS prestation maladie réglementaire *f*; **~ tax rate** *n* TAX taux d'imposition prévu par la loi *m*, taux statutaire d'imposition *m*; **~ vote** *n* POL vote réglementaire *m*; **~ voting** *n* LAW vote statutaire *m*

stave: **~ off** *vt* GEN COMM écarter

stay:[1] **~ of appeal** *n* LAW suspension d'appel *f*; **~ -in strike** *n* HRM grève avec occupation des locaux *f*, grève sur le tas *f*; **~ -out strike** *n* HRM grève sans occupation des locaux *f*

stay[2] *vi* GEN COMM rester; ◆ **~ in-the-money** STOCK rester dans le cours; **~ informed** COMMS rester informé; **~ out** HRM rester en grève

staying: **~ power** *n* FIN endurance *f*

Std *abbr* (*standard*) GEN COMM étalon *m*

STD *abbr* *BrE* (*subscriber trunk dialling*) COMMS appel automatique longue distance *loc m*, automatique interurbain *m*, l'automatique *m*

steadily *adv* GEN COMM régulièrement, solidement

steady[1] *adj* GEN COMM *growth, rate* uniforme

steady:[2] **~ -growth method** *n* GEN COMM *subscription source evaluation technique* méthode de croissance régulière *f*; **~ -state economy** *n* ECON économie d'un pays à la population fictivement figée, état de non-croissance *m*, état stationnaire *m*; **~ -state equilibrium** *n* ECON équilibre permanent *m*

steadying: **~ factor** *n* ECON facteur de stabilisation *m*

steal *vi* LAW voler; ◆ **~ sth from sb** LAW voler qch à qn

steam *n* TRANSP vapeur *f*; **~ emission** ENVIR, IND évaporation *f*; **~ -heated generator** TRANSP *shipping* générateur à vapeur *m*; **~ turbine** TRANSP turbine à vapeur *f*; ◆ **go full ~** IND tourner à plein régime

steamboat *n* TRANSP bateau à vapeur *m*, vapeur *m*

steamer *n* TRANSP bateau à vapeur *m*, navire à vapeur *m*, vapeur *m*; ◆ **any one ~** (*AOS*) INS, TRANSP *marine* par bateau à vapeur

steamroller[1] *n* IND rouleau compresseur *m*

steamroller[2] *vt* GEN COMM *project* imposer son influence pour faire passer un projet

steamship *n* (*SS*) TRANSP navire à vapeur *m*, vapeur *m* (*vap.*)

steel:[1] **~ -intensive** *adj* IND *production* à forte utilisation d'acier *loc f*

steel[2] *n* ENVIR acier *m*; **~ -collar worker** *n* HRM robot *m*; **~ covers** *n pl* (*SC*) TRANSP couvercle d'acier *m*, panneaux de cale en acier *m pl*; **~ securities** *n pl* STOCK valeurs des industries sidérurgiques *f pl*; **~ terminal** *n* TRANSP terminal acier *m*; **~ wire rope** *n* (*SWR*) TRANSP câble en fils d'acier *m*

steelworker *n* HRM métallo *m* (*infrml*), IND métallo *m* (*infrml*), métallurgiste *mf*, ouvrier sidérurgiste *m*

steelworks *n pl* IND aciérie *f*

steep *adj* ECON fort

steepen *vi* MATH *curve* s'abaisser

steeply *adv* GEN COMM verticalement

steering *n* LAW, PROP direction *f*; ~ **committee** BANK, FIN, GEN COMM *rescheduling of debt* comité de restructuration *m*, commission d'organisation *f*; ~ **system** TRANSP direction *f*, système de direction *m*

stellage: ~ **straddle option** *n* STOCK option à risques limités *f*

stem[1] *n* TRANSP *shipping* étrave *f*

stem[2] *vt* GEN COMM arrêter; ~ **from** GEN COMM découler de, provenir de, résulter de

stencil *vt* ADMIN *with carbon paper* polycopier

stenographer *n* ADMIN sténo (*infrml*), sténographe *mf*

stenography *n* ADMIN sténo, sténographie *f*

step:[1] ~ **-by-step** *adj* COMP *program, operation, routine* pas à pas

step[2] *n* GEN COMM *action taken* démarche *f*, pas *m*; ~ **cost** FIN frais progressifs *m pl*; ~ **transaction** TAX opération en série *f*; ~ **-up lease** FIN bail accéléré *m*; ~ **-up loan** BANK prêt progressif *m*; ◆ **keep in ~ with one's competitors** GEN COMM rester dans la course

step:[3] **1.** *vt* ~ **up** GEN COMM *increase* accélérer; **2.** *vi* ~ **back** GEN COMM reculer; ~ **in** GEN COMM *intervene* intervenir

STEP *abbr* (*science and technology for environmental protection programme*) ENVIR *EU* science et technologie pour la protection de l'environnement programme *f*

stepback *n* GEN COMM recul *m*

stepped:[1] ~ **-up** *adj* GEN COMM *activity* intensifié, *output* accru, augmenté

stepped:[2] ~ **bond** *n* STOCK série d'obligations à intérêt identique mais progressif *f*; ~ **-up basis** *n* TAX base augmentée *f*

steps: ~ **method** *n* COMP méthode progressive *f*; ◆ **take such ~ as are considered necessary** LAW faire les démarches nécessaires et appropriées, prendre les mesures qui sont jugées nécessaires, prendre toutes les mesures nécessaires

sterilization *n* FIN stérilisation *f*

sterling *n* (*stg*) GEN COMM sterling *m* (*ster.*); ~ **area** ECON, FIN, GEN COMM, IMP/EXP zone sterling *f*; ~ **balance** FIN balance sterling *f*; ~ **commercial paper** (*SCP*) STOCK billet de trésorerie en livres sterling *m*, papier commercial en livres sterling *m*; ~ **M3** FIN sterling M3 *m*; ~ **transferable accruing government securities UK** (*STAGs*) STOCK obligation à coupon zéro basée sur des bons du Trésor; ~ **warrant into gilt edged stock UK** (*SWING*) STOCK bon de souscription d'obligations d'État *m*; ~ **zone** ECON, FIN, GEN COMM, IMP/EXP zone sterling *f*

stern *n* TRANSP *shipping* arrière *m*; ~ **thruster** TRANSP *shipping* propulseur latéral arrière *m*; ~ **wheel** TRANSP *shipping* roue arrière *f*

stevedore *n* (*stvdr*) HRM docker *m*, TRANSP arrimeur *m*, docker *m*

stevedoring: ~ **department** *n* TRANSP service d'arrimage *m*; ~ **gang** *n* HRM, TRANSP équipe de dockers *f*, équipe de débardeurs *f*

steward *n* ADMIN économe *m*, TRANSP steward *m*

stewardship *n* ADMIN intendance *f*, économat *m*

stg *abbr* (*sterling*) GEN COMM ster. (*sterling*)

stick:[1] ~ **-on label** *n* ADMIN, COMMS étiquette adhésive *f*

stick[2] **1.** *vt* COMMS, GEN COMM coller; ~ **to** GEN COMM se montrer irréductible sur; ~ **up for** *infrml* GEN COMM *workers, rights* défendre; **2.** *vi* IND se coincer; ◆ ~ **no bills** S&M *advertising* défense d'afficher

sticker *n* GEN COMM vignette *f*

sticking: ~ **point** *n* GEN COMM point d'arrêt *m*

sticky: ~ **deal** *n* STOCK émission hasardeuse *f*; ~ **price** *n* ECON prix peu flexible *m*; ~ **situation** *n* *infrml* GEN COMM situation épineuse *f*

stiff[1] *adj* ECON *competition* fort, serré, sévère

stiff:[2] ~ **vessel** *n* TRANSP navire de forte stabilité *m*, navire qui rappelle dur *m*, navire qui se redresse doucement *m*

stiffen *vt* GEN COMM *law, rule* durcir, renforcer

stillage *n* TRANSP *rack* *m*

stimulate *vt* ECON *demand* encourager, stimuler, GEN COMM *confidence, support, demand* activer, encourager, stimuler

stimulating *adj* HRM *competition, discussion* stimulant

stimulative: ~ **measure** *n* ECON mesure de relance *f*

stimulus *n* GEN COMM stimulant *m*; ◆ **be a ~ for exports** IMP/EXP stimuler les exportations

stint: **do one's ~** *phr* HRM faire sa part de travail *loc f*

stipulate *vt* GEN COMM stipuler

stipulation: **on the ~ that** *phr* GEN COMM à la condition expresse que *loc f*

STN *abbr* (*special traffic notice*) TRANSP affiche spéciale circulation *f*

stochastic: ~ **term** *n* MATH *statistics* durée stochastique *f*

stock[1] *n* FIN actions *f pl*, titre *m*, valeur *f*, GEN COMM parc *m*, S&M *in shop* réserve *f*, stock *m*, STOCK action *f*, obligation à long terme *f*, titre *m*, val., valeur *f*, valeurs *f pl*; ~ **arbitrage** *n* STOCK arbitrage de portefeuille *m*, arbitrage sur actions *m*; ~ **borrowing** *n* STOCK emprunt d'actions *m*; ~ **brokerage firm** *n* STOCK firme de courtiers *f*, maison de courtage *f*; ~ **of bullion** *n* BANK, GEN COMM réserve métallique *f*; ~ **car** *n* AmE (*cf cattle float Aus*) TRANSP bétaillère *f*; ~ **certificate** *n* AmE (*cf share certificate BrE*) STOCK certificat d'action *m*, certificat d'investissement *m*, CI, titre d'action *m*; ~ **check** *n* AmE, ~ **cheque** *n* BrE BANK traite à vue *f*; ~ **contract** *n* STOCK contrat d'option *m*, option *f*; ~ **control** *n BrE (cf inventory control AmE)* ACC, ECON, FIN, STOCK contrôle des stocks *m*, gestion des stocks *f*; ~ **controller** *n* GEN COMM, HRM responsable des stocks *m*; ~ **dividend** *n US* ACC, STOCK dividende en actions *m*, dividende-actions *m*; ~ **draft** *n* STOCK traite nantie par des titres *f*; ~ **exchange** *n* STOCK bourse de valeurs mobilières *f*; ~ **exchange committee** *n* STOCK chambre syndicale des agents de change *f*; ~ **exchange hours** *n pl* STOCK heures de bourse *f pl*, heures de négociation *f pl*; ~ **exchange list** *n* STOCK cote boursière *f*, cote officielle *f*; ~ **exchange price index** *n* STOCK indice boursier *m*, indice des actions *m*, indice des cours des actions *m*; ~ **exchange quotation** *n* STOCK cours en Bourse *m*; ~ **exchange transaction** *n* STOCK opération boursière *f*, opération de Bourse *f*; ~ **in hand** *n* GEN COMM stock disponible *m*; ~ **index arbitrage** *n* STOCK arbitrage d'indice *m*; ~ **index contract** *n* STOCK contrat sur l'indice des cours *m*; ~ **index future** *n* FIN, STOCK contrat à terme sur indice *m*, contrat à terme sur indice boursier *m*; ~ **index futures** *n pl* FIN, STOCK contrats à terme indexés *m pl*; ~ **index futures market** *n* STOCK marché des contrats à terme sur indice *m*; ~ **index option** *n* STOCK option d'indexation *f*, option de mise sur indice *f*; ~ **indexes and averages** *n pl* STOCK indices boursiers *m pl*; ~ **insurance company** *n* STOCK compagnie d'assurance des valeurs *f*; ~ **inventory** *n* ENVIR inventaire des réserves *m*, évaluation des réserves *f*; ~ **issue** *n* STOCK émission d'actions *f*; ~ **issue bonus** *n* ACC prime d'émission *f*; ~ **jobbery** *n UK* STOCK agiotage *m*, manipulation des prix *f*; ~ **line** *n* S&M article référencé *m*, article suivi *m*; ~ **list** *n* STOCK cours de la Bourse *m*; ~ **management** *n* S&M gestion des stocks *f*; ~ **market** *n* STOCK Bourse *f*, marché boursier *m*; ~ **market capitalization** *n* STOCK capitalisation boursière *f*; ~ **market collapse** *n* STOCK effondrement du marché *m*; ~ **market cycle** *n* STOCK cycle du marché *m*; ~ **market index** *n* STOCK indice boursier *m*; ~ **market price index** *n* STOCK indice boursier *m*; ~ **on the ~ exchange** *n* STOCK à la corbeille *f* (*jarg*); ~ **option** *n* STOCK option d'achat d'actions *f*, option sur actions *f*; ~ **option plan** *n* HRM, STOCK plan d'options d'achat d'actions *m*, plan de souscription à des actions *m*; ~ **ownership** *n* STOCK actionnariat *m*; ~ **portfolio** *n* FIN, STOCK portefeuille d'actions *m*; ~ **power** *n* STOCK procuration autorisant le transfert d'actions *f*; ~ **price index** *n* STOCK indice boursier *m*; ~ **purchase plan** *n* STOCK plan d'achat d'actions *m*; ~ **purchase warrant** *n* STOCK bon de souscription *m*, bon de souscription d'actions *m*; ~ **quotation** *n* STOCK cours des actions *m*; ~ **quoted officially** *n* GEN COMM action à la cote officielle *f*; ~ **receipt** *n* STOCK reçu d'action *m*; ~ **record** *n* STOCK service d'enregistrement des valeurs *m*; ~ **register** *n* STOCK registre des actions *m*; ~ **right** *n* STOCK droit de souscription *m*; ~ **rotation** *n* S&M rotation

des stocks *f*; ~ **sheet** *n* GEN COMM fiche d'inventaire *f*; ~ **shortage** *n* GEN COMM, S&M rupture de stock *f*; ~ **split** *n AmE* STOCK division d'actions *f*, fractionnement d'actions *m*; ~ **split-down** *n* STOCK réduction du nombre d'actions *f*; ~ **with subscription rights** *n* STOCK titre avec bons de souscription *m*; ~ **symbol** *n* STOCK code des valeurs *m*; ~ **tips** *n pl* STOCK tuyaux boursiers *m pl*; ~ **transfer agent** *n* HRM, STOCK responsable des transferts de titres *m*; ~ **transfer form** *n* STOCK formulaire de transport d'actions *m*; ~ **turn** *n* GEN COMM rotation des stocks *f*; ~ **turnover** *n* ACC, ECON mouvement des stocks *m*, rotation des stocks *f*, FIN rotation des stocks *f*, IND, STOCK mouvement des stocks *m*, rotation des stocks *f*; ~ **valuation** *n* ACC inventaire *m*, évaluation des stocks *f*, GEN COMM valorisation des stocks *f*; ~ **watcher** *n* STOCK service de surveillance des titres *m*; ~ **yield** *n* STOCK rendement d'une action *m*; ◆ **in ~** ECON, GEN COMM, S&M en magasin, en stock; **on the ~ exchange** STOCK en bourse, sur le parquet; **out of ~** (*o.s.*) ECON épuisé, GEN COMM en rupture de stock, épuisé, S&M en rupture de stock, manque en magasin *m*, épuisé

stock[2] *vt* GEN COMM *goods* avoir en stock, *supply* approvisionner; ~ **up on** GEN COMM s'approvisionner en

Stock: ~ **Exchange Alternative Trading Service** *n UK (SEAT)* STOCK tableau électronique de cotations *m*; ~ **Exchange Automated Quotation** *n (SEAQ)* STOCK système de cotation automatisé *m*; ~ **Exchange Automated Quotation International** *n (SEAQI)* STOCK système international de cotation des valeurs étrangères automatisé; ~ **Exchange Daily Official List** *n UK (SEDOL)* STOCK ≈ Bulletin officiel des cours de la Bourse *m* (*France*) (*BOCB*); ~ **Exchange Pool Nominees** *n pl UK (SEPON)* STOCK société intermédiaire pour la compensation des titres *f*; **the ~ Exchange** *n* STOCK ≈ le Palais *m*, ≈ le Palais Brongniart *m*; **the ~ Market** *n* STOCK ≈ le Palais *m*, ≈ le Palais Brongniart *m*

stockbreeder *n* GEN COMM éleveur *m*

stockbroker *n* STOCK agent de change *m*, courtier *m*, courtier de Bourse *m*, courtier en valeurs *m*, courtier en valeurs mobilières *m*

stockbroking *n* STOCK profession de courtier en bourse *f*

stockholder *n* STOCK actionnaire *mf*, détenteur de titres *m*

stockholders': ~ **equity** *n* ACC capitaux propres *m pl*, patrimoine *m*, STOCK capitaux propres *m pl*

stockholding *n* STOCK possession d'actions *f*

Stockholm *pr n* GEN COMM Stockholm *n pr*

stockist *n UK* S&M fournisseur *m*, STOCK stockiste *mf*

stockjobber *n dat UK* (*SYN market maker*) STOCK titre remplacé depuis le Big Bang de 1986 par market maker, contrepartiste *mf*, courtier en valeurs *m*, jobber *m*, négociant en titres *m*, négociateur en valeurs mobilières *m*

stockkeeping: ~ **unit** *n* GEN COMM unité d'élevage *f*

stockman *n* AmE (cf warehouseman) HRM magasinier *m*

stockout: ~ **cost** *n* GEN COMM coût de rupture de stock *m*

stockperson *n* GEN COMM animals gardeur de bestiaux *m*, éleveur de bestiaux *m*

stockpile[1] *n* GEN COMM réserve *f*, stock *m*

stockpile[2] *vt* GEN COMM stocker

stockpiling *n* GEN COMM stockage *m*

stocks *n pl* ACC titres *m pl*, ACC, IND inventaire *m*, stocks *m pl*; ◆ **while ~ last** S&M pendant la durée des stocks

stocktaking *n* ECON inventaire des stocks *m*, ENVIR inventaire des réserves *m*, évaluation des réserves *f*, GEN COMM, S&M inventaire des stocks *m*; ~ **sale** GEN COMM vente pour cause d'inventaire *f*; ~ **value** ACC valeur d'inventaire *f*

stockyard *n* GEN COMM parc à bestiaux *m*

STOL *abbr* (short take-off and landing) TRANSP aircraft ADAC (avion à décollage et atterrissage courts)

stop:[1] ~ **bit** *n* COMP bit d'arrêt *m*, élément d'arrêt *m*; ~ **-go cycle of inflation** *n* ECON cycle d'inflation en sinusoïde *m*; ~ **-go policy** *n* UK ECON politique de l'escarpolette *f*, politique des coups d'accordéon *f*; ~ **-limit order** *n* STOCK ordre stop *m*; ~ **loss** *n* STOCK ordre stop *m*; ~ **-loss order** *n* STOCK *futures market* ordre limité inversé *m*, ordre stop *m*; ~ **-loss reinsurance** *n* INS réassurance en excédent de pertes *f*, traité de réassurance *m*; ~ **-loss rules** *n pl* BANK *investment* mécanisme pour minimiser les pertes *m*; ~ **order** *n* STOCK ordre stop *m*; ~ **-out price** *n* US STOCK prix plancher accepté pour une adjudication de bons du Trésor *m*; ~ **payment** *n* BANK contre-ordre *m*, opposition *f*; ~ **-payment order** *n* BANK ordre de suspendre les paiements *m*; ~ **signal** *n* COMP signal d'arrêt *m*; ~ **time** *n* COMP temps d'arrêt *m*; ◆ ~ **-and-go** ECON à coups d'accordéon *loc m*

stop[2] **1.** *vt* COMP arrêter, interrompre, GEN COMM *payment, work, proceedings* suspendre; **2.** *vi* ~ **over** TRANSP faire une escale; ◆ ~ **bidding** GEN COMM *at auction sale* se retirer des enchères; ~ **a check** *AmE*, ~ **a cheque** *BrE* BANK bloquer un chèque, faire opposition à un chèque, suspendre le paiement d'un chèque; ~ **payment of a check** *AmE*, ~ **payment of a cheque** *BrE* BANK faire opposition à un chèque; ~ **payment on a check** *AmE*, ~ **payment on a cheque** *BrE* BANK faire opposition à un chèque; ~ **sb's allowance** GEN COMM couper les vivres à qn; ~ **a stock** STOCK accepter de remettre une transaction dont on a garanti le prix; ~ **work** HRM arrêter de travailler, cesser le travail; ~ **working** HRM cesser le travail

stopover *n* TRANSP escale *f*

stoppage *n* GEN COMM cessation *f*, HRM retenue *f*,

strike arrêt de travail *m*; ~ **in transit** LAW, S&M droit de poursuite *m*; ~ **of trade** GEN COMM embargo commercial *m*

stopped: ~ **bonds** *n pl* FIN titres frappés d'opposition *m pl*; ~ **check** *n* AmE, ~ **cheque** *n* BrE BANK chèque frappé d'opposition *m*; ~ **stock** *n* STOCK transaction à prix garanti remise à plus tard *f*

stopping *n* GEN COMM cessation *f*

stopwatch: ~ **studies** *n pl* MGMNT études chronométriques *f pl*

storage *n* COMP *action* mémorisation *f*, stockage *m*, *place* mémoire *f*, GEN COMM, IND emmagasinage *m*, entreposage *m*, magasinage *m*, TRANSP emmagasinage *m*, entreposage *m*, magasinage *m*, stockage *m*; ~ **allocation** *n* COMP affectation de la mémoire *f*; ~ **area** *n* COMP zone de mémoire *f*, GEN COMM aire de stockage *f*, surface de stockage *f*; ~ **capacity** *n* GEN COMM capacité de stockage *f*; ~ **charges** *n pl* GEN COMM frais de magasinage *m pl*; ~ **device** *n* COMP périphérique de stockage *m*; ~ **dump** *n* COMP vidage de mémoire *m*; ~ **facility** *n* ENVIR *for toxic waste* installation de stockage *f*, GEN COMM, IND unité de stockage *f*; ~ **map** *n* COMP topogramme de mémoire *m*, topographie de mémoire *f*; ~ **medium** *n* COMP support de stockage *m*; ~ **requirements** *n pl* COMP encombrement *m*; ~ **tank** *n* ENVIR, TRANSP citerne de stockage *f*

store[1] *n* COMP mémoire *f*, GEN COMM *warehouse* magasin *m*, GEN COMM *AmE* (cf shop BrE) S&M *AmE* (cf shop BrE) commerce *m*, magasin *m*; ~ **accounting** ACC comptabilité de magasin *f*, comptabilité des matières *f*, comptabilité des stocks *f*, inventaire matériel *m*; ~ **audit** ACC gestion des stocks *f*; ~ **brand** S&M marque de distributeur *f*; ~ **group** S&M groupe de distribution *m*; ~ **promotion** S&M ventes promotionnelles *f pl*; ~ **of value** ECON réserve de valeur *f*

store[2] *vt* COMP mémoriser, *data* stocker, TRANSP *goods* emmagasiner, entreposer, stocker

storehouse *n* GEN COMM entrepôt *m*, magasin *m*

storekeeper *n* AmE (cf shopkeeper BrE) GEN COMM, S&M commerçant *m*, petit commerçant *m*

storekeepers': ~ **liability insurance** *n* US INS assurance responsabilité civile des commerçants *f*

storeman *n* HRM magasinier *m*

storeroom *n* GEN COMM magasin *m*, salle de stockage *f*

storming *n* HRM algarade *f*, emportements *m pl*

storyboard *n* S&M *advertising* scénario de message publicitaire *m*

stow *vt* TRANSP *cargo* arrimer

stowage *n* TRANSP arrimage *m*; ~ **area** TRANSP zone d'arrimage *f*; ~ **factor** GEN COMM capacité de transport *f*; ~ **order** TRANSP ordre d'arrimage *m*; ~ **plan** TRANSP plan d'arrimage *m*, plan de chargement *m*

straddle *n* STOCK opération liée *f*, ordre lié *m*, straddle *m*; ~ **buyer** (ANT straddle seller) STOCK acheteur d'un straddle *m*, acheteur de double option *m*; **~ carrier** TRANSP chariot cavalier *m*; **~ combination** STOCK combinaison de straddle *f*; **~ seller** *(*ANT *straddle buyer)* STOCK vendeur d'un straddle *m*, vendeur de double option *m*; **~ writer** STOCK vendeur d'un straddle *m*, vendeur de double option *m*

straight:[1] **~ bill of lading** *n* IMP/EXP, TRANSP *shipping* connaissement nominatif *m*, connaissement à personne désignée *m*; **~ bond** *n* STOCK obligation non-convertible *f*; **~ investment** *n* BANK investissement à rendement fixe *m*; **~ life insurance policy** *n* *(*SYN *whole life insurance policy)* INS police d'assurance-vie entière *f*; **~ lift** *n* TRANSP *cargo-handling* appareil de levage droit *m*; **~ -line amortization** *n* ACC amortissement constant *m*, amortissement linéaire *m*; **~ -line depreciation** *n* ACC amortissement constant *m*, amortissement linéaire *m*; **~ -line method** *n* ACC *depreciation* méthode linéaire *f*; **~ -line method of amortization** *n* *(*SYN *method of depreciation)* TAX méthode de l'amortissement linéaire *m*; **~ -line method of depreciation** *n* ACC, FIN méthode d'amortissement linéaire *f*; **~ loan** *n* BANK prêt simple *m*

straight:[2] **get sth ~** *phr* GEN COMM mettre les choses au point

straighten: ~ out *vi* GEN COMM se redresser

straightforward *adj* GEN COMM clair

straightforwardly *adv* GEN COMM franchement

straightforwardness *n* GEN COMM franchise *f*

straights: ~ market *n* FIN marché des obligations à taux fixe *m*

strained *adj* GEN COMM *relationship* tendu

straits *n pl* TRANSP détroit *m*

strake *n* TRANSP virure *f*

stranded: ~ goods *n pl* INS épaves *f pl*

strangle *n* STOCK *options position* strangle *m*

stranglehold: have a ~ on the market *phr* ECON, S&M avoir le quasi-monopole du marché *loc m*

strap *n* STOCK strap *m*; **~ option** STOCK strap *m*

strapping *n* TRANSP courroies *f pl*

strategic[1] *adj* MGMNT stratégique

strategic:[2] **~ alliance** *n* GEN COMM, MGMNT alliance stratégique *f*; **~ business unit** *n* ECON, GEN COMM, MGMNT domaine d'activité stratégique *m*; **~ interdependence** *n* GEN COMM, MGMNT interdépendance des stratégies *f*; **~ issue** *n* MGMNT question de stratégie *f*; **~ management accounting** *n* ACC, FIN, MGMNT comptabilité de gestion stratégique *f*; **~ overview** *n* POL aperçu stratégique *m*; **~ plan** *n* GEN COMM plan stratégique *m*; **~ planning** *n* GEN COMM plan stratégique *m*, MGMNT planification stratégique d'entreprise *f*, stratégie d'entreprise *f*; **~ tax planning** *n* TAX planification stratégique de l'impôt *f*

strategy *n* GEN COMM stratégie *f*; **~ formulation** ECON, GEN COMM élaboration des stratégies *f*; **~ implementation** GEN COMM, MGMNT application des stratégies *f*

stratified: ~ random sampling *n* MATH, S&M *sta-*

tistics échantillonnage aléatoire par tranche *m*; **~ sampling** *n* MATH, S&M *statistics* échantillonnage par couches *m*, échantillonnage par tranche *m*

stratum *n* WEL couche *f*

straw: ~ boss *n* *infrml* PROP patron de paille *m*; **~ poll** *n* S&M *market research* sondage d'opinion *m*; **~ vote** *n* S&M *market research* sondage d'opinion *m*

strawboard *n* IND carton paille *m*

stream:[1] **on ~** *adj* GEN COMM prédominant, en régime de croisière *loc m*

stream:[2] **come on ~** *phr* IND *oil industry* commencer la production, entrer en service; **go against the ~** *phr* GEN COMM aller à contre-courant

streamer *n* MEDIA *print* manchette *f*, titre flamboyant *m*

streamline *vt* ECON, FIN, IND rationaliser

streamlining *n* ECON, FIN, IND rationalisation *f*

street *n* GEN COMM rue *f*; **~ book** *n jarg* STOCK *futures market* enregistrement quotidien des transactions *m*; **~ dealings** *n pl* STOCK transactions hors bourse *f pl*; **~ money** *n jarg AmE* POL argent du porte-à-porte *m*; **~ name** *n* STOCK titres détenus par un courtier pour un client *m pl*; **~ price** *n* STOCK cours après bourse *m*; **~ trader** *n BrE (cf street vendor AmE)* GEN COMM colporteur *m*, marchand ambulant *m*; **~ vendor** *n AmE (cf street trader BrE)* GEN COMM colporteur *m*, marchand ambulant *m*

strength *n* GEN COMM force *f*, *of market* vigueur *f*, STOCK *of currency* force *f*; **~ of materials** IND résistance des matériaux *f*; ♦ **be on the ~** HRM faire partie du personnel

strengthen *vt* ECON, GEN COMM consolider

strengthened *adj* ECON, GEN COMM renforcé

strengthening *n* ECON *of currency* consolidation *f*, renforcement *m*, GEN COMM consolidation *f*

strengths: ~, weaknesses, opportunities and threats analysis *n* *(SWOT)* GEN COMM, S&M analyse des forces, des faiblesses, des opportunités et des menaces *f*

stress[1] *n* HRM tension nerveuse *f*; **~ factor** HRM facteur stress *m*; **~ interview** HRM entretien de gestion du stress *m*

stress[2] *vt* GEN COMM insister sur

strict: ~ cost price *n* ACC prix de revient calculé au plus juste *m*; **~ foreclosure** *n* LAW saisie d'hypothèque sans faculté de rachat *f*; **~ time limit** *n* GEN COMM terme de rigueur *m*; ♦ **~ adherence to the contract** LAW respect strict du contrat *m*

strike[1] *n* HRM, IND grève *f*; **~ action** *n* HRM grève revendicative *f*; **~ benefits** *n pl* HRM allocations-grévistes *f pl*; **~ call** *n* HRM mot d'ordre de grève *m*; **~ clause** *n* HRM fermeture en cas de grève *f*; **~ committee** *n* HRM comité de grève *m*; **~ -free agreement** *n* HRM accord de non-recours à la grève *m*; **~ -free deal** *n* HRM accord de non-recours à la grève *m*; **~ fund** *n* HRM caisse syndicale de grève *f*; **~ pay** *n* HRM allocation aux grévistes *f*; ~ **picket** *n* HRM, IND piquet de grève *m*; ~ **price** *n* STOCK prix de levée *m, on Eurodollar futures* prix d'exercice *m*; ~ **rate** *n jarg* S&M taux de réussite *m*; ~ **threat** *n* HRM menace de grève *f*; ~ **yield** *n* STOCK *interest rate futures* rendement à la levée *m*; ◆ **come out on** ~ *UK* HRM se mettre en grève; **go on** ~ HRM cesser le travail, se mettre en grève; **on** ~ HRM en grève

strike² **1.** *vt* GEN COMM *cord, key* frapper, LAW *jury* constituer; **2.** *vi* HRM cesser le travail, faire grève; ◆ ~ **a balance** GEN COMM trouver le juste milieu; ~ **a bargain** GEN COMM, S&M conclure un marché, conclure une affaire; ~ **a deal** GEN COMM, S&M conclure un marché, conclure une affaire; ~ **in sympathy** HRM se mettre en grève de solidarité; ~ **it rich** *infrml* GEN COMM faire fortune, tenir le filon *(infrml)*; ~ **sb off the list** GEN COMM rayer qn de la liste

strikebound *adj* HRM paralysé par une grève

strikebreaker *n* HRM briseur de grève *m*

strikebreaking *n* HRM refus de faire grève *m*

strikeover *n* COMP *on word processor* surfrappe *f*

striker *n* HRM, IND gréviste *mf*

strikes: ~, **riots and civil commotions** *n pl (SR&CC)* LAW grèves, émeutes et insurrections civiles *loc f*

striking: ~ **price** *n* STOCK prix d'exercice *m*

string *n* COMP chaîne *f*

stringent *adj* FIN *market* tendu, GEN COMM *measures, programme* rigoureux

stringently *adv* GEN COMM rigoureusement

stringer *n jarg* HRM, MEDIA correspondant local *m*, journaliste indépendant *m*, pigiste *mf*, journaliste payé à la pige *m*

strings: **no** ~ **attached** *phr* GEN COMM sans conditions, sans conditions restrictives

strip¹ *n* STOCK obligation démembrée *f*, obligation à coupon zéro *f*, obligation à coupons détachés *f*, strip *m*; ~ **bond** STOCK félin *m*, obligation démembrée *f*, obligation à coupon zéro *f*, obligation à coupons détachés *f*; ~ **development** GEN COMM développement en bande *m*; ~ **mining** *AmE (cf opencast mining BrE)* IND exploitation à ciel ouvert *f*, ouvrage à ciel ouvert *m*

strip² *vt* TRANSP dépoter

stripped: ~ **bond** *n* STOCK félin *m*, obligation démembrée *f*, obligation à coupon zéro *f*, obligation à coupons détachés *f*; ~ **security** *n* STOCK titre démembré *m*

stripping *n* IMP/EXP, TRANSP *container* dépotage *m*

STRIPS *abbr (Separate Trading of Registered Interest and Principal Securities)* STOCK démembrement *m*

strong¹ *adj* ECON *currency* fort, GEN COMM *indication* manifeste, GEN COMM *reputation* solide

strong:² ~ **bearish play** *n jarg (ANT strong bullish play)* STOCK *options* jeu à la baisse *m*; ~ **bullish play** *n jarg (ANT strong bearish play)* STOCK *options* jeu à la hausse *m*; ~ **equilibrium** *n* ECON

équilibre à toute épreuve *m*; ~ **supporter of** *n* POL partisan convaincu de *m*

strongroom *n* BANK chambre forte *f*

strop *n* TRANSP *cargo-slinging equipment* estrope *f*

structural: ~ **adjustment** *n* MGMNT réorganisation de structure *f*; ~ **adjustment facility** *n (SAF)* ECON facilité d'ajustement structurel *f*; ~ **adjustment loan** *n* ECON crédit d'ajustement structurel *m*, prêt d'ajustement structurel *m*; ~ **adjustment policy** *n* ECON politique d'ajustement structurel *f*; ~ **change** *n* MGMNT change de structure *m*; ~ **crisis** *n* ADMIN *EU* crise structurelle *f*; ~ **deficit** *n* ECON déficit structurel *m*; ~ **engineering** *n* GEN COMM, IND ponts et chaussées *m pl*; ~ **funds** *n pl* ECON *EU* fonds structurels *m pl*; ~ **inflation** *n* ECON inflation structurelle *f*; ~ **model** *n* ECON modèle structurel *m*; ~ **unemployment** *n* ECON, HRM chômage structurel *m*

structure¹ *n* GEN COMM *of company* structure *f*; ~ **-conduct-performance model** *(SCP)* ECON modèle structure-conduite-performance *m*; ~ **of the market** GEN COMM structure du marché *f*

structure² *vt* GEN COMM structurer

structured¹ *adj* GEN COMM structuré

structured:² ~ **interview** *n* HRM entrevue structurée *f*; ~ **programming** *n* COMP programmation structurée *f*

structuring *n* GEN COMM structuration *f*

stub *n* BANK *of cheque* souche *f*, talon *m*; ~ **equity** STOCK valeur spéculative d'une société surendettée *f*

stuck *adj* GEN COMM coincé

student *n* WEL élève *mf*, étudiant *m*; ~ **loan** BANK prêt étudiant *m*

Student: ~ **Loan Marketing Association** *n* FIN *US (Sallie Mae)* Association de gestion des prêts étudiants *f*, STOCK *US (SLMA)* organisme de garantie des prêts étudiants *m*, WEL *US (Sallie Mae)* Association de gestion des prêts étudiants *f*; ~ **'s t-distribution** *n* MATH *statistics* variable t de Student-Fisher *f*

studies *n pl* WEL études *f pl*

studio *n* GEN COMM studio *m*

study¹ *n* GEN COMM étude *f*; ~ **day** WEL journée d'étude *f*; ~ **group** GEN COMM, POL groupe de travail *m*; ~ **trip** WEL voyage d'étude *m*

study² *vt* WEL étudier; ◆ ~ **accountancy** ACC faire des études de comptabilité *loc f*; ~ **engineering** GEN COMM faire des études d'ingénieur *loc f*

stuff *vt* BrE TRANSP *container* empoter

stuffing *n* IMP/EXP, TRANSP *container* empotage *m*; ◆ ~ **and stripping** IMP/EXP, TRANSP *of container* empotage et dépotage

stumbling: ~ **block** *n* GEN COMM pierre d'achoppement *f*

stump: ~ **up** *vi infrml BrE* GEN COMM casquer *(infrml)*

stunt: ~ **advertising** *n* S&M publicité tapageuse *f*

stvdr *abbr (stevedore)* HRM docker *m*, TRANSP arrimeur *m*, docker *m*

STVP *abbr (short-term vehicle park)* TRANSP parking courte durée *m*

style *n* COMP, MGMNT *of management* style *m*; **~ sheet** COMP feuille de style *f*

stylist *n* GEN COMM styliste *mf*

stylize *vt* GEN COMM styliser

stylized: **~ fact** *n* ECON fait schématisé pour les besoins de l'abstraction *m*

stylus *n* COMP lecteur *m*, photostyle *m*, *pen-based device* crayon optique *m*, S&M *pen-based device* crayon optique *m*

stymied *adj* GEN COMM *thwarted* coincé, dans une impasse *loc f*

sub[1] *n* GEN COMM *BrE (subvention)* avance *f*, MEDIA *(subeditor) newspaper* secrétaire de rédaction *m*, *print* préparateur de copie *m*

sub[2] *vt (subedit)* MEDIA *print* corriger, mettre au point

subactivity *n* ECON, GEN COMM sous-activité *f*

subagent *n* GEN COMM sous-agent *m*

suballotment *n* POL sous-affectation *f*

subchapter: **~ m** *n* TAX sous-chapitre m *m*; **~ s** *n* TAX sous-chapitre s *m*

subcharter *vt* TRANSP sous-affréter

subcompact *adj* GEN COMM miniaturisé

subcontract[1] *n* GEN COMM contrat de sous-traitance *m*, sous-traitance *f*, IND contrat de sous-traitance *m*

subcontract[2] *vt* GEN COMM, HRM, LAW sous-traiter

subcontracting *n* GEN COMM, HRM sous-traitance *f*

subcontractor *n* GEN COMM, HRM sous-traitant *m*

subcustody *n* FIN conservation locale *f*

subdirectory *n* COMP sous-répertoire *m*

subdivided *adj* GEN COMM sous-divisé, subdivisé

subdivision *n* GEN COMM subdivision *f*

subedit *vt (sub)* MEDIA *print* corriger, mettre au point

subeditor *n (sub)* MEDIA *newspaper* secrétaire de rédaction *m*, *print* préparateur de copie *m*

subemployment *n* ECON sous-emploi *m*

subentry *n* COMP sous-rubrique *f*

subfile *n* ADMIN sous-fichier *m*

subgroup *n* GEN COMM sous-groupe *m*

subject[1] *n* GEN COMM matière *f*, *of agreement, speech* objet *m*, sujet *m*; **~ filing** GEN COMM classement par matières *m*; **~ matter** GEN COMM contenu *m*, matière *f*, PATENTS objet *m*

subject:[2] **~ to** *prep* GEN COMM sujet à, *change, approval* sous réserve de, *constrained* assujetti à, TAX assujetti à; ◆ **~ approval no risk** *(SANR)* INS risque couvert sous réserve d'acceptation *m*, sans risque sous réserve d'acceptation des conditions; **~ to approval** GEN COMM, S&M sous réserve d'approbation; **~ to breakage** INS sujet à la casse; **~ to change** GEN COMM sous réserve de change-ment; **~ to mortgage** PROP assujetti à hypothèque; **~ to particular average** *(SPA)* INS assujetti à l'avarie particulière; **~ to price controls** ECON *products* soumis à des contrôles de prix; **~ to quota** ECON, GEN COMM, IMP/EXP contingenté; **~ to taxation** TAX imposable; **~ unsold** GEN COMM sauf vente

subjected: **be ~ to** *phr* GEN COMM être soumis à

subjective *adj* GEN COMM subjectif

subjoined *adj (cf joined AmE)* COMMS *document* en annexe *loc f*

sub judice *adj* LAW *case, matter* devant les tribunaux

sublease *n* GEN COMM, LAW, PROP sous-location *f*

subleasing *n* GEN COMM, LAW, PROP sous-location *f*

sublessee *n* GEN COMM, LAW, PROP sous-locataire *mf*

sublet *n* GEN COMM, LAW, PROP sous-location *f*

subletting *n* GEN COMM, LAW, PROP sous-location *f*

sublicence *n BrE* GEN COMM, PATENTS sous-licence *f*

sublicense *n AmE see* sublicence *BrE*

subliminal: **~ advertising** *n* MEDIA, S&M publicité subliminale *f*

submanager *n* HRM, MGMNT sous-directeur *m*

submission *n* POL soumission *f*; **~ of bids** GEN COMM soumission des offres *f*; **~ for deletion of debts** BANK demande de radiation de dettes *f*

submit *vt* GEN COMM *bid* faire, *claim, application* faire, présenter, soumettre, PATENTS soumettre; ◆ **~ a dispute to arbitration** IND, LAW soumettre un différend à arbitrage; **~ an application for a job** HRM faire une demande d'emploi; **~ for approval** GEN COMM soumettre à l'approbation; **~ a proposal** GEN COMM, MGMNT présenter une proposition; **~ a statement of one's affairs** FIN déposer son bilan

submortgage *n* BANK sous-hypothèque *f*

suboffice *n* GEN COMM filiale *f*, succursale *f*

suboptimization *n* ECON, FIN, GEN COMM sous-optimisation *f*

subordinate[1] *n* GEN COMM subordonné *m*; **~ debt** ACC, FIN dette de second rang *f*, dette subordonnée *f*, dette à court terme *f*

subordinate[2] *vt* GEN COMM subordonner

subordinated: **~ assets** *n pl* ACC, FIN actif subordonné *m*; **~ bond issue** *n* STOCK émission d'une obligation subordonnée *f*; **~ convertible bond issue** *n* STOCK émission d'une obligation subordonnée convertible *f*; **~ debenture** *n* STOCK obligation subordonnée *f*; **~ debt** *n* STOCK dette de rang inférieur *f*, dette subordonnée *f*; **~ interest** *n* ACC, FIN intérêt de deuxième rang *m*; **~ liabilities** *n pl* ACC, FIN emprunts et dettes subordonnés *m pl*, passif subordonné *m*; **~ loan** *n* FIN emprunt subordonné *m*; **~ perpetual bond** *n* STOCK titre subordonné à durée indéterminée *m*, TSDI; **~ redeemable bond** *n* STOCK titre subordonné remboursable *m*, TSR; **~ warrant issue** *n*

STOCK émission de bon de souscription subordonné *f*

subordination: ~ **agreement** *n* ACC, FIN accord de subordination *m*; ~ **interest** *n* ACC, BANK, ECON, FIN, STOCK intérêt de subordination *m*

subpoena[1] *n* LAW *to witness* assignation à comparaître *f*, citation à comparaître *f*

subpoena[2] *vt* LAW citer, citer à comparaître

subpost: ~ **office** *n* COMMS bureau de poste annexe *m*, bureau de poste auxiliaire *m*, poste annexe *m*, poste auxiliaire *m*

subprogram *n* COMP sous-programme *m*

subrogation: ~ **clause** *n* LAW clause subrogatoire *f*

subroutine *n* COMP sous-programme *m*

subscribe 1. *vt* LAW *to confidentiality agreement* signer, souscrire à; ~ **to** GEN COMM, MEDIA s'abonner à; **2.** *vi* GEN COMM cotiser, *sign a formal document* apposer sa signature, STOCK *for shares* souscrire, souscrire à; ◆ ~ **for a loan** BANK, GEN COMM souscrire à un emprunt; ~ **to an issue** FIN souscrire à une émission

subscribed: ~ **capital** *n* STOCK capital souscrit *m*

subscriber *n* COMP abonné *m*, GEN COMM abonné *m*, souscripteur *m*, MEDIA abonné *m*; ~ **trunk dialling** *BrE* (*STD, direct distance dialing AmE*) COMMS appel automatique longue distance *loc m*, automatique interurbain *m*, l'automatique *m*

subscript *n* COMP indice *m*

subscription *n* ACC *magazine, newspaper* abonnement *m*, GEN COMM abonnement *m*, cotisation *f*, MEDIA *print* abonnement *m*, souscription *f*, POL, STOCK souscription *f*; ~ **club** STOCK *of stockbrokers* club d'actionnaires *m*, club de souscripteurs *m*; ~ **for shares** STOCK souscription d'actions *f*, souscription à des actions *f*; ~ **form** GEN COMM bulletin de souscription *m*; ~ **price** GEN COMM, STOCK prix de souscription *m*; ~ **privilege** STOCK droit de souscription prioritaire *m*, souscription privilégiée *f*; ~ **ratio** STOCK taux de souscription *m*; ~ **receivable** STOCK capital non-souscrit *m*; ~ **right** STOCK droit de souscription *m*; ~ **warrant** STOCK bon de souscription *m*

subsea: ~ **well** *n* ENVIR, IND puits sous-marin *m*

subsector *n* IND sous-secteur *m*

subsequent[1] *adj* GEN COMM consécutif, ultérieur; ~ **to** GEN COMM résultant de; ◆ **at a ~ date** GEN COMM à une date ultérieure *loc f*

subsequent[2]: ~ **event** *n* ACC événement postérieur à la date du bilan *m*

subset *n* GEN COMM sous-ensemble *m*

subshare *n* STOCK coup., coupure *f*, fraction d'une action *f*

subsidiarity *n* ECON, GEN COMM, POL subsidiarité *f*

subsidiary[1] *adj* GEN COMM auxiliaire, subsidiaire

subsidiary[2] *n* GEN COMM *company* filiale *f*; ~ **account** *n* ACC sous-compte *m*; ~ **accounting record** *n* ACC registre comptable auxiliaire *m*; ~ **accounting system** *n* ACC système comptable auxiliaire *m*; ~ **company** *n* ACC filiale *f*, société

annexe *f*, GEN COMM, HRM filiale *f*; ~ **dividends** *n pl* STOCK dividende de filiale *m*, subsides *m pl*; ~ **firm** *n* GEN COMM filiale *f*; ~ **ledger** *n* ACC, BANK, FIN grand livre auxiliaire *m*

subsidization *n* FIN, GEN COMM octroi de subventions *m*

subsidized[1] *adj* FIN *prices, funds*, GEN COMM subventionné

subsidized[2]: ~ **export** *n* ECON, IMP/EXP exportation subventionnée *f*; ~ **travel** *n* LEIS voyages tous frais payés *m pl*

subsidy *n* FIN subvention *f*, GEN COMM, WEL aide *f*

subsistence *n* HRM, WEL subsistance *f*; ~ **allowance** *n* HRM, WEL indemnité de subsistance *f*; ~ **crops** *n pl* ECON *agricultural* cultures vivrières de base *f pl*; ~ **economy** *n* ECON économie de subsistance *f*; ~ **farming** *n* ECON, ENVIR agriculture de subsistance *f*, autoconsommation *f*; ~ **theory of wages** *n* ECON loi d'airain des salaires *f*, théorie du taux de salaire de subsistance *f*; ~ **wage** *n* HRM, WEL indemnité de subsistance *f*

substance *n* IND substance *f*; **in ~ defeasance** ACC désendettement de fait *m*

substandard[1] *adj* GEN COMM de qualité inférieure *loc f*

substandard[2]: ~ **ship** *n* TRANSP navire inférieur aux normes *m*, navire sous normes *m*

substantial[1] *adj* ECON, GEN COMM considérable, important

substantial[2]: ~ **interest** *n* BANK intérêt important *m*; ~ **risk** *n* STOCK risque substantiel *m*

substantially *adv* GEN COMM considérablement, nettement, substantiellement

substantiate *vt* GEN COMM *allegation, statement* justifier, prouver; ◆ ~ **a claim** LAW fournir des preuves à l'appui d'une demande, établir le bien-fondé d'une demande, établir le bien-fondé d'une réclamation

substantive: ~ **agreement** *n* HRM accord de base *m*, accord de fond *m*; ~ **law** *n* LAW droit positif *m*

substitute[1]: ~ **product** *n* ECON, IND produit de remplacement *m*, produit de substitution *m*, service de remplacement *m*, service de substitution *m*, substitut *m*, succédané *m*

substitute[2] *vt* GEN COMM remplacer, substituer, LEIS *sport* remplacer; ◆ ~ **one thing for another** GEN COMM substituer une chose à une autre

substituted: ~ **expenses** *n pl* INS dépenses de substitution *f pl*; ~ **property** *n* TAX bien substitué *m*; ~ **share** *n* STOCK action de remplacement *f*

substitution *n* ECON substitution *f*, HRM *of job* remplacement *m*; ~ **effect** ECON effet de substitution *m*; ~ **law** LAW droit relatif à la novation de créance *m*, loi de substitution *f*, loi relative à la novation de créance *f*, loi relative à la subrogation *f*, loi relative à la substitution *f*; ~ **slope** ECON pente de substitution *f*

substructure *n* ECON, GEN COMM infrastructure *f*

subtenancy *n* GEN COMM, LAW, PROP sous-location *f*

subtenant *n* GEN COMM, LAW, PROP sous-locataire *mf*

subtotal *n* ACC total partiel *m*, MATH sous-total *m*

subtract *vt* MATH soustraire

suburb *n* GEN COMM banlieue *f*

suburbs *n pl* GEN COMM banlieue *f*; ♦ **in the outer ~** GEN COMM en grande banlieue, en lointaine banlieue

subvention *n frml BrE (sub)* GEN COMM avance *f*

subway *n* TRANSP métro *m*

succeed *vi* GEN COMM réussir

succeeding[1] *adj* GEN COMM *following* suivant

succeeding:[2] **~ account** *n* FIN liquidation suivante *f*

success *n* GEN COMM réussite *f*; **~ stories** *n pl jarg* S&M *advertising, public relations* histoires rapportées par les médias au sujet d'un produit; ♦ **be a ~** *n jarg* LEIS faire recette *loc f*

successful[1] *adj* GEN COMM *attempt, effort* qui réussit *loc, mission, partnership* réussi

successful:[2] **~ outcome** *n* GEN COMM *to negotiations* issue positive *f*, résultat heureux *m*

succession: **~ duty** *n BrE (cf succession tax AmE)* TAX droits de succession *m pl*, impôt sur les successions *m*; **~ law** *n* LAW droit des successions *m*, droit successoral *m*; **~ tax** *n AmE (cf succession duty BrE)* TAX droits de succession *m pl*, impôt sur les successions *m*

successive *adj* GEN COMM *following* consécutif à, successif

successor *n* GEN COMM successeur *m*; **~ in title** *n* PATENTS ayant cause *m*; **~ rules** *n pl* TAX règles applicables aux successeurs *f pl*, règles concernant les corporations remplaçantes *f pl*

sucre *n* GEN COMM sucre *m*

Sudan *pr n* GEN COMM Soudan *m*

Sudanese[1] *adj* GEN COMM soudanais

Sudanese[2] *n* GEN COMM *language* soudanais *m*, *person* Soudanais *m*

sue:[1] **~ and labor charges** *n pl AmE see sue and labour charges BrE*; **~ and labour clause** *n AmE see sue and labour clause BrE*; **~ and labour charges** *n pl BrE* INS frais de conservation *m pl*, frais de recours et de conservation *m pl*; **~ and labour clause** *n BrE (S/LC)* INS clause de recours et de conservation *f*; ♦ **~ and labor** *AmE*, **~ and labour** *BrE* INS mesure de conservation *f*, recours et conservation

sue[2] *vt* LAW intenter un procès à, poursuivre devant les tribunaux, poursuivre en justice; ♦ **~ for damages** LAW poursuivre pour dommages-intérêts; **~ for infringement of patent** LAW assigner en justice pour contrefaçon, assigner pour contrefaçon; **~ for libel** LAW intenter un procès en diffamation, poursuivre pour diffamation

suffer 1. *vt* ECON, PATENTS *damage* subir; **2.** *vi* ECON souffrir; ♦ **~ the consequences** GEN COMM

supporter les conséquences; **~ loss** LAW subir un préjudice, subir une perte; **~ a setback** GEN COMM essuyer un revers

sufferance: **~ wharf** *n* TRANSP quai de la douane *m*

sufficient[1] *adj* GEN COMM assez de, suffisant; ♦ **not ~ funds** *(n.s.f.)* BANK, GEN COMM fonds insuffisants *m pl*, insuffisance de provision *f*

sufficient:[2] **not-~ -funds check** *n AmE*, **not-~ -funds cheque** *n BrE (NSF cheque)* BANK chèque en bois *m (infrml)*, chèque sans provision *m*

suffrage *n* POL suffrage *m*

sugar: **~ production** *n* IND production de sucre *f*; **~ ship** *n* TRANSP *shipping* navire sucrier *m*

suggest *vt* HRM proposer

suggested: **~ retail price** *n* S&M prix au détail conseillé *m*

suggestion *n* GEN COMM propos *m*, suggestion *f*; **~ box** GEN COMM boîte à idées *f*; **~ scheme** GEN COMM système de suggestion *m*, MGMNT système d'accueil des idées *m*; ♦ **make a ~** GEN COMM faire une suggestion

suit[1] *n* LAW action *f*, procès *m*

suit[2] *vt* GEN COMM convenir à

suitability: **~ rules** *n pl* FIN règles adaptées *f pl*

suitable[1] *adj* GEN COMM *moment, conditions* propice

suitable:[2] **be ~ for** *phr* GEN COMM convenir à

suitcase *n BrE* LEIS valise *f*

sulfur: **~ dioxide** *n AmE see sulphur dioxide BrE*; **~ emission** *n AmE see sulphur emission BrE*

sulfuryl: **~ fluoride** *n AmE see sulphuryl fluoride BrE*

sulphur: **~ dioxide** *n BrE* ENVIR *acid rain* dioxyde de soufre *m*; **~ emission** *n BrE* ENVIR émission sulfureuse *f*

sulphuryl: **~ fluoride** *n BrE* TRANSP *container fumigation* fluorure de sulfuryle *m*

sum *n* BANK, GEN COMM somme *f*; **advanced ~** GEN COMM avance *f*; **assured ~** BANK capital assuré *m*; **~ at length** GEN COMM somme en toutes lettres *f*; ♦ **have the ~ wrong** GEN COMM se tromper dans les calculs

summarize *vt* GEN COMM abréger, récapituler, résumer

summary *n* ECON, FIN abrégé *m*, GEN COMM abrégé *m*, résumé *m*, sommaire *m*, PATENTS abrégé *m*; **~ application** LAW requête sommaire *f*; **~ conviction** LAW déclaration sommaire de culpabilité *f*; **~ dismissal** GEN COMM licenciement sommaire *m*, HRM licenciement sommaire *m*, renvoi pur et simple *m*; **~ judge** LAW juge des référés *m*; **~ possession** LAW possession sommaire *f*; **~ of the proceedings** GEN COMM, LAW résumé de la séance *m*; **~ report** GEN COMM rapport sommaire *m*; **~ statement** GEN COMM, LAW déclaration sommaire *f*

Summary: **~ of Input Factors** *n* ECON *PEMS form* Sommaire des facteurs d'intrant *m*

summer *n* GEN COMM été *m*; **~ recess** *UK* GEN

COMM, POL *Parliament* session parlementaire de l'été *f*

summit *n* POL sommet *m*; **~ conference** GEN COMM, POL conférence au sommet *f*

summons[1] *n* LAW assignation à comparaître *f*, commandement *m*

summons[2] *vt* LAW citer, citer à comparaître

sumptuary: **~ law** *n* LAW loi somptuaire *f*

sun: **~ protection required** *phr* GEN COMM, LEIS, TRANSP *for cargo containers* protection requise contre le soleil *loc f*

Sun. *abbr (Sunday)* GEN COMM dim. *(dimanche)*

sunbelt *n* US IND les États du sud des États-Unis *m pl*

Sunday *n (Sun.)* GEN COMM dimanche *m (dim.)*; **~ trading** GEN COMM commerce dominical *m*, ouverture des magasins le dimanche *loc*

sundries *n pl* ACC articles divers *m pl*, divers *m pl*, frais divers *m pl*

sundry: **~ accounts** *n pl* ACC comptes de divers *m pl*; **~ articles** *n pl* ACC articles divers *m pl*; **~ expenses** *n pl* ACC frais divers *m pl*

sunk: **~ cost** *n* FIN coût irrécupérable *m*, frais amortis *m pl*; **~ cost fallacy** *n* FIN illusion du coût engagé indifférent *f*; **~ costs** *n pl* FIN coûts irrécupérables *m pl*

sunrise: **~ industry** *n (ANT sunset industry)* ECON, IND industrie en croissance rapide *f*

sunset: **~ act** *n* LAW, POL loi de temporalisation *f*; **~ industry** *n (ANT sunrise industry)* ECON industrie en déclin *f*, IND industrie du passé *f*, industrie en déclin *f*, industrie obsolescente *f*; **~ law** *n jarg* US LAW législation américaine obligeant tout organisme public à se soumettre régulièrement à une réévaluation; **~ provision** *n* LAW clause-couperet *f*, disposition légale stipulant une date d'expiration *f*, disposition réglementaire stipulant une date d'expiration *f*; **~ report** *n* POL rapport de réexamen *m*

sunshine: **~ law** *n jarg* US LAW législation américaine imposant aux organismes publics de tenir régulièrement des débats en public

sunspot: **~ theory** *n* ECON théorie des taches solaires *f*

super: **~ high cube** *n (SHC)* TRANSP conteneur spécial hors-cotes *m (SHC)*; **~ multiplier** *n* ECON super multiplicateur *m*; **~ now account** *n* BANK compte de dépôt à intérêts supérieurs *m*; **~ saver** *n jarg* S&M l'affaire de la semaine *f*; **~ sinker bond** *n* STOCK obligation à coupon à long terme et à échéance courte *f*

superannuate *vt* FIN, HRM mettre à la retraite

superannuated *adj* FIN, HRM retraité

superannuation: **~ accounts** *n pl* ACC, FIN, INS comptes de pension de retraite *m pl*; **~ contribution** *n* HRM cotisations pour la retraite *f pl*; **~ fund** *n* ACC, FIN, HRM, INS caisse de retraite *f*

supercomputer *n* COMP super-ordinateur *m*

superficial: **~ loss** *n* FIN, GEN COMM perte apparente *f*

Superfund *n* US FIN fonds exceptionnels *m pl*

superheater *n (SH)* TRANSP surchauffeur *m*; **~ safety valve** *(SHSV)* TRANSP soupape de sûreté du surchauffeur *f*

superhighway *n AmE (cf expressway Can, freeway AmE, motorway BrE, throughway AmE)* TRANSP autoroute *f*

superimposed: **~ tax** *n* TAX impôt de superposition *m*, impôt superposé *m*, taxe superposée *f*

Superintendent: **~ of Bankruptcy** *n* GEN COMM, LAW commissaire aux faillites *m*, surintendant des faillites *m*; **~ of Insurance** *n* INS directeur des assurances *m*, surintendant des assurances *m*

supermarket *n* S&M supermarché *m*

superneutrality *n* ECON, POL *policies* extrême neutralité *f*

supernormal: **~ profit** *n* FIN bénéfice au-dessus de la normale *m*

supernumerary *adj* HRM surnuméraire

superpower *n* GEN COMM, POL superpuissance *f*

superscript *n* COMP, MEDIA *typography* exposant *m*

supersede *vt* GEN COMM remplacer, supplanter

superstore *n* GEN COMM, S&M hypermarché *m*

superstructure *n* GEN COMM superstructure *f*

supertanker *n* TRANSP superpétrolier *m*

supervise *vt* GEN COMM contrôler, inspecter, surveiller, HRM inspecter, surveiller, MGMNT surveiller

supervision *n* GEN COMM conduite *f*, surveillance *f*, HRM, MGMNT maîtrise *f*; **~ of credit institutions** FIN surveillance des établissements de crédit *f*

supervisor *n* COMP superviseur *m*, HRM agent de maîtrise *m*, surveillant *m*, *among blue collars* chef d'atelier *m*, chef d'équipe *m*, *among white collars* chef de service *m*, HRM *AmE FBI official, local councillor* inspecteur *m*, MGMNT agent de maîtrise *m*, surveillant *m*, *among blue collars* chef d'atelier *m*, *among white collars* chef de service *m*

supervisory[1] *adj* COMP, GEN COMM, HRM, MGMNT de contrôle *loc m*, de surveillance *loc f*

supervisory:[2] **~ board** *n* ACC, GEN COMM, HRM, MGMNT conseil de surveillance *m*; **~ management** *n* HRM, MGMNT maîtrise *f*; **~ personnel** *n* HRM personnel de maîtrise *m*, personnel de surveillance *m*

supplement[1] *n* COMP, GEN COMM, PATENTS complément *m*

supplement[2] *vt* GEN COMM augmenter

supplemental: **~ agreement** *n* GEN COMM accord supplémentaire *m*; **~ budget** *n* FIN additif budgétaire *m*; **~ technology** *n* GEN COMM technologie complémentaire *f*, technologie incrémentielle *f*

Supplementaries *n pl* FIN, POL budget des dépenses supplémentaires *m*

supplementary[1] *adj* ACC, GEN COMM, PATENTS complémentaire

supplementary:[2] **~ accounting system** *n* ACC système de comptabilité supplémentaire *m*; ~ **assistance** *n* FIN aide complémentaire *f*, prestation supplémentaire *f*; ~ **benefit** *n obs UK (cf income support)* WEL assurance sociale *f*; ~ **company pension scheme** *n* FIN, HRM régime complémentaire professionnel de prévoyance *m*; ~ **cost** *n* FIN prix coûtant *m*, prix de revient initial *m*; ~ **entry** *n* ACC, FIN écriture complémentaire *f*; ~ **estimate** *n* FIN, POL estimation supplémentaire *f*; ~ **estimates** *n pl* FIN crédits supplémentaires *m pl*; ~ **intercompany pension scheme** *n* FIN, HRM régime complémentaire interprofessionnel de prévoyance *m*; ~ **pension scheme** *n* FIN retraite complémentaire de prévoyance *f*; ~ **period** *n* TAX période complémentaire *f*; ~ **protection certificate** *n (SPC)* PATENTS certificat de protection renforcée *m*, certificat de protection supplémentaire *m*; ~ **reserve** *n* BANK réserve excédentaire *f*, réserve supplémentaire *f*; ~ **service tariff** *n (SST)* TRANSP tarif de services supplémentaires *m*; ~ **special deposits scheme** *n* BANK, FIN système de dépôts spécial complémentaire *m*; ~ **stocks guarantee** *n* IMP/EXP garantie de stocks supplémentaires *f*

Supplementary: ~ **Financing Facility** *n* FIN disposition financière complémentaire *f*

supplemented *adj* GEN COMM augmenté

supplier *n* GEN COMM fournisseur *m*; ~ **credit** IMP/EXP crédit fournisseur *m*

supplies *n pl* ECON, GEN COMM, S&M approvisionnements *m pl*, fournitures *f pl*

supply[1] *n* COMP *power, mains* alimentation *f*, GEN COMM fourniture *f*, offre *f*, POL crédits *m pl*, S&M fourniture *f*; ~ **bill** POL projet de loi des finances *m*; ~ **committee** POL commission des voies et moyens *f (Bel)*; ~ **control** ECON contrôle de l'offre *m*; ~ **function** ECON fonction d'offre *f*; ~ **of goods** ECON offre de biens *f*; ~ **network** *AmE (cf mains BrE)* COMP, IND alimentation secteur *f*; ~ **price** ECON prix de l'offre *m*, HRM salaire d'offre minimum *m*; ~ **revolving fund** ECON fonds renouvelable des approvisionnements *m*; ~ **of services** ECON offre de services *f*; ~ **shock** ECON choc d'offre *m*, choc sur l'offre *m*; ~ **-side economics** ECON économie de l'offre *f*; ~ **-side shock** ECON choc d'offre *m*, choc sur l'offre *m*, secousse sur l'offre *f*; ~ **vehicle** TRANSP véhicule rigide *m*; ◆ ~ **and demand** GEN COMM l'offre et la demande

supply[2] *vt* GEN COMM *information* fournir, S&M approvisionner; ◆ ~ **collateral** BANK donner un bien en nantissement; ~ **goods on credit** GEN COMM fournir des marchandises à crédit; ~ **goods on trust** GEN COMM fournir des marchandises à crédit

support[1] *n* COMP aide *f*, assistance *f*, soutien *m*, FIN appui *m*, GEN COMM *financial, moral* appui *m*, concours *m*, soutien *m*, TAX *of dependant* soutien *m*, subsistance *f*; ~ **activities** *n pl* COMP, GEN COMM, MGMNT fonctions complémentaires *f pl*; ~ **hotline** *n* COMP service d'assistance technique par téléphone *m*; ~ **level** *n* ECON seuil d'interven-

tion *m*; ~ **price** *n* ECON *agricultural, EU* prix de soutien *m*; ~ **service** *n* GEN COMM, HRM service logistique *m*

support[2] *vt* ECON *currency* soutenir, TAX *dependant* assurer la subsistance de, subvenir aux besoins de

supporter *n* GEN COMM partisan *m*

supporting: ~ **data** *n* MATH document justificatif *m*, données justificatives *f pl*; ~ **document** *n* LAW pièce justificative *f*; ~ **film** *n* LEIS film supplémentaire *m*; ~ **person** *n* TAX personne fournissant le soutien *f*; ~ **purchases** *n pl* GEN COMM, S&M achats de soutien *m pl*; ~ **receipt** *n* GEN COMM, S&M reçu à l'appui *m*

suppress *vt* COMP *remove* supprimer, éliminer, MEDIA *publication, newspaper etc* supprimer

suppressed: ~ **inflation** *n* ECON inflation contenue *f*

supra *adv (ANT infra)* GEN COMM supra

supranational *adj* GEN COMM supranational

Supreme: ~ **Court** *n* LAW Cour suprême *f*

surcharge *n* GEN COMM surcharge *f*; ~ **value** IMP/EXP, TRANSP valeur de surtaxe *f*

surety *n* FIN cautionnement *m*, sûreté *f*, GEN COMM cautionnement *m*, INS cautionnement *m*, fidéjusseur *m*, garantie de dépôt *f*; ~ **in cash** LAW caution en numéraire *f*; ~ **liability** BANK responsabilité du garant *f*

surface *n* PATENTS *usable, used* surface *f*; ~ **area** ECON, GEN COMM, MATH superficie *f*; ~ **mail** COMMS voie de terre *f*; ◆ **by ~ mail** COMMS par courrier ordinaire, par voie de terre

surge *n* GEN COMM flambée *f*

Suriname *pr n* GEN COMM Surinam *m*

Surinamese[1] *adj* GEN COMM surinamais

Surinamese[2] *n* GEN COMM *person* Surinamais *m*

surname *n* ADMIN nom patronymique *m*

surpass *vt* GEN COMM dépasser, surpasser

surplus[1] *n* ACC plus-value *f*, ECON surplus *m*; ~ **approach** *n* ECON approche des excédents *f*, valeur d'excédent *f*; ~ **of assets over liabilities** *n* ACC, ECON, FIN excédent de l'actif sur le passif *m*; ~ **capacity** *n* ECON, IND potentiel inemployé *m*, potentiel sous-utilisé *m*; ~ **dividend** *n* FIN superdividende *f*; ~ **reserves** *n pl* FIN réserves à des fins spécifiques *f pl*; ~ **stripping** *n* TAX dépouillement des surplus *m*, enlèvement de l'excédent *m*; ~ **value** *n* ACC approche des excédents *f*, valeur d'excédent *f*, ECON plus-value relative *f*; ◆ **in ~** ECON, GEN COMM en excédent, excédentaire; **to be in ~** ADMIN être en surplus

surplus[2] *vt* ADMIN *dismiss, fire* mettre en surnombre

surprise: ~ **function** *n* ECON fonction de surprise *f*

surrender:[1] **for ~** *adj* STOCK *said of a security* pour remise *loc f*

surrender[2] *n* GEN COMM *of document* remise *f*, INS *of policy* rachat *m*, TAX abandon *m*; ~ **charge** INS frais de rachat *m pl*; ~ **of a patent** LAW, PATENTS abandon d'un brevet *m*, abandon des droits conférés par un brevet *m*, renonciation aux droits conférés par un brevet *f*; **~ value** ACC valeur de rachat *f*; ◆ **on ~ of the bill of lading** IMP/EXP, TRANSP contre remise du connaissement

surrogates *n pl jarg US* POL subrogateurs des vedettes qui soutiennent un candidat

surroundings *n pl* GEN COMM environs *m pl*

surtax *n* TAX surtaxe *f*

surveillance *n* LAW surveillance *f*; **~ department of exchanges** STOCK service de surveillance des opérations de bourse *m*, surveillance de la bourse *f*; **~ licence** *BrE*, **~ license** *AmE (SL)* IMP/EXP licence de surveillance *f*

survey[1] *n* GEN COMM enquête de marché *f*, sondage *m*, PROP enquête *f*, S&M enquête *f*, enquête de marché *f*, étude *f*, TAX, TRANSP *vessels* visite *f*; **~ certificate** GEN COMM certificat d'expertise *m*; **~ fee** FIN, GEN COMM, WEL honoraires d'expertise *m pl*; **~ report** INS rapport d'expertise *m*

survey[2] *vt* GEN COMM faire une étude de, PROP examiner, inspecter, TRANSP visiter; ◆ **~ the situation** GEN COMM faire un tour d'horizon de la situation

surveyor *n* HRM *marine engineer* expert maritime *m*, ingénieur expert *m*, PROP géomètre *m*, géomètre expert *m*

survival: **~ process** *n* ECON *of firms* processus de survie *m*; **~ strategy** *n* GEN COMM stratégie de survie *f*

survive *vi* GEN COMM survivre

surviving: **~ spouse** *n* TAX conjoint survivant *m*

survivor: **~ policy** *n* INS assurance-vie sur deux têtes *f*

survivorship *n* LAW, PROP survie *f*; **~ account** BANK compte de survie *m*; **~ annuity** PROP rente viagère avec réversion *f*; **~ clause** *US* INS clause de survie *f*; **~ insurance** INS assurance de survie *f*

susceptible: **~ of industrial application** *phr* PATENTS susceptible d'application industrielle

susie *n jarg* TRANSP tuyau de couplage de l'amenée d'air *m*

suspected: **~ bill of health** *n* WEL patente de santé suspecte *f*

suspend *vt* GEN COMM *trading, authorization* interrompre, suspendre; ◆ **~ trading** STOCK suspendre les cotations, suspendre les transactions

suspended: **~ sentence** *n* LAW sursis *m*; **~ solid** *n* IND solide en suspension *m*; **~ trading** *n* STOCK cotation suspendue *f*, transactions suspendues *f pl*

suspense: **~ account** *n* ACC compte d'attente *m*; **~ balance** *n* BANK solde de compte d'attente *m*; **~ collator** *n* GEN COMM code d'interclassement provisoire *m*; **~ entry** *n* ACC écriture d'attente *f*; **~ return** *n* TAX déclaration en suspens *f*

suspension *n* GEN COMM cessation *f*, HRM suspension *f*; **~ seat** TRANSP siège à suspension *m*

suspensive: **~ condition** *n* LAW condition suspensive *f*

sustain *vt* ECON *growth* appuyer, soutenir, GEN COMM *confidence* entretenir, LAW *loss, injury* subir; ◆ **~ a claim** LAW admettre le bien-fondé d'une réclamation, faire droit à une demande; **~ losses** ACC supporter des pertes, supporter une perte

sustainability *n* ECON, ENVIR durabilité *f*, pérennité *f*, viabilité *f*

sustainable[1] *adj* ENVIR viable

sustainable:[2] **~ development** *n* ECON, ENVIR, POL croissance à un rythme soutenable *f*, développement maintenable *m*; **~ economic growth rate** *n* ECON, POL taux de croissance économique soutenable *m*; **~ growth** *n* ECON, POL croissance à un rythme soutenable *f*; **~ level** *n* ECON *of demand* niveau de croissance à un rythme soutenable *m*

sustained: **~ non-inflationary growth** *n (SNIG)* ECON croissance non-inflationniste soutenue *f*; **~ resurgence** *n* ECON *of growth* redémarrage soutenu *m*

sustaining: **~ grant** *n* POL subvention de soutien *f*

Suva *pr n* GEN COMM Suva *n pr*

SV *abbr (sailing vessel)* TRANSP navire à voiles *m*

SW *abbr* GEN COMM *(southwest)* sud-ouest *m*, TRANSP *(shipper weight)* poids transitaire *m*, TRANSP *(southwest)* sud-ouest *m*

Swahili *n* GEN COMM *language* swahili *m*

swamp *vt* GEN COMM envahir

swap *n* FIN échange financier *m*, STOCK swap *m*, échange financier *m, interest rate instrument* crédit croisé *m*; **~ bank line** FIN ligne de crédits croisés *f*; **~ credit line** FIN ligne de crédits croisés *f*; **~ line of credit** FIN ligne de crédits croisés *f*; **~ market** STOCK marché d'échanges croisés *m*, marché des swaps *m*; **~ network** STOCK réseau d'échanges croisés *m*, réseau de swap *m*; **~ option** FIN option d'échange *f*, STOCK option sur swap *f*

swatch *n* GEN COMM échantillon *m*

sway *vt* GEN COMM *outcome* influencer

Swazi *n* GEN COMM *person* Swazi *m*

Swaziland *pr n* GEN COMM Swaziland *m*

swear *vt* LAW jurer; ◆ **~ on affidavit** LAW déclarer par écrit, déclarer sous serment; **~ sb to secrecy** GEN COMM faire prêter serment avec devoir de réserve à qn

sweated: **~ goods** *n pl* GEN COMM marchandises produites par une main-d'oeuvre exploitée; **~ labor** *n AmE*, **~ labour** *n BrE* HRM main-d'oeuvre exploitée *f*; **~ trade** *n* GEN COMM, HRM exploitation *f*

sweatshop *n* HRM bagne *m (infrml)*

Swede *n* GEN COMM *person* Suédois *m*

Sweden *pr n* GEN COMM Suède *f*

Swedish[1] *adj* GEN COMM suédois

Swedish[2] *n* GEN COMM *language* suédois *m*

sweeping *adj* GEN COMM *changes* radical

sweetener *n infrml* FIN clause attrayante *f*, incitation *f*, pot-de-vin *m*

sweetheart: **~ agreement** *n* HRM *industrial relations* contrat de complaisance *m*, contrat de non-recours à la grève *m*, contrat-bidon *m*, IND contrat de complaisance *m*, contrat-bidon *m*; **~ contract** *n* HRM *industrial relations* contrat de complaisance *m*, contrat de non-recours à la grève *m*, contrat-bidon *m*, IND contrat de complaisance *m*, contrat-bidon *m*

swell *vt* GEN COMM *accounts, coffers, figures* gonfler

SWIFT *abbr (Society for Worldwide Interbank Financial Telecommunications)* BANK, COMMS Société internationale de télécommunications financières interbanques *f*

swim: be in the ~ *phr infrml* GEN COMM être dans le mouvement *loc m*

swimming: ~ market *n* ECON, STOCK marché actif *m*

swindle[1] *n* GEN COMM escroquerie *f*

swindle[2] *vt* GEN COMM escroquer

swindler *n* GEN COMM escroc *m*

swing[1] *n* GEN COMM oscillation *f*, *of market* fluctuation *f*, variation *f*, POL *to the left/right* revirement *m*, STOCK *of market* variation *f*; **~ credits** *n pl jarg* ECON crédit-relais entre partenaires commerciaux *m*; **~ line** *n* FIN crédit de sécurité *m*; **~ loan** *n* BANK prêt soumis à fluctuations *m*; **~ producer** *n* IND producteur de réserve *m*; **~ shift** *n* (SYN *relief shift*) HRM poste de relève *m*, équipe tournante *f*; **~ voter** *n jarg* POL électeur girouette *m* (*infrml*)

swing[2] **1.** *vt* GEN COMM balancer; **2.** *vi* GEN COMM osciller, virer, POL *to the left/right* virer; ◆ **~ a deal** *infrml* GEN COMM emporter le morceau (*infrml*), mener une affaire à bien

SWING *abbr UK (sterling warrant into gilt edged stock)* STOCK bon de souscription d'obligations d'État *m*

swinging: ~ tariff *n* IMP/EXP tarif variable *m*

swings *n pl* GEN COMM mouvements des cours *m pl*, oscillations des cours *f pl*

swipe: ~ card *n* COMMS carte à mémoire *f*

Swiss[1] *adj* GEN COMM suisse

Swiss[2] *n* GEN COMM *person* Suisse *mf*; **~ French** *n* GEN COMM *language* suisse français *m*; **~ German** *n* GEN COMM *language* suisse allemand *m*; **~ Options and Financial Futures Exchange** *n* (*SOFFEX*) STOCK bourse d'échange des options et valeurs à terme Suisse; **~ Shippers Council** *n* (*SSC*) TRANSP Conseil des affréteurs suisses *m*; **the ~** *n pl* GEN COMM les Suisses *m pl*

switch[1] *n* COMMS *device* commutateur *m*, COMP *device* commutateur *m*, interrupteur *m*, *program* aiguillage *m*; **~ dealing** ECON opération de contre-achats *f*; **~ selling** *UK* S&M vente forcée d'articles plus chers que ceux en promotion; **~ trading** GEN COMM switch *m* (*jarg*), STOCK report d'une position d'une échéance sur une autre *m*

switch[2] **1.** *vt* GEN COMM commuter, IND *production* réorienter; **~ off** COMP éteindre; **~ on** COMP mettre en marche; **~ over** GEN COMM changer, commuter,

2. *vi* GEN COMM *from one thing to another* basculer

switchboard *n* COMMS standard téléphonique *m*; **~ operator** HRM standardiste *mf*

switcher *n* GEN COMM, S&M consommateur qui change de marque *m*

switching *n* COMMS, COMP commutation *f*, STOCK arbitrage de portefeuille *m*; **~ -in rate** GEN COMM taux de clientèle *m*, taux de gain *m*; **~ -out rate** GEN COMM taux de perte de clientèle *m*

switchover *n* GEN COMM passage *m*

Switzerland *pr n* GEN COMM Suisse *f*

swop *n* GEN COMM troc *m*

SWOT *abbr (strengths, weaknesses, opportunities and threats analysis)* GEN COMM, S&M analyse des forces, des faiblesses, des opportunités et des menaces *f*

SWR *abbr (steel wire rope)* TRANSP câble en fils d'acier *m*

Syli *n* GEN COMM syli *m*

syllabus *n* WEL programme *m*, programme d'études *m*

symbiotic: ~ marketing *n* S&M marketing symbiotique *m*

symbol *n* GEN COMM symbole *m*

symbolic *adj* COMP, GEN COMM symbolique

symmetallism *n* GEN COMM symmétallisme *m*

symmetric *adj* MATH, STOCK symétrique

symmetrical: ~ frequency curve *n* MATH *statistics* courbe de fréquence symétrique *f*

symmetry *n* MATH symétrie *f*

sympathetic: ~ action *n* HRM *industrial relations* action de soutien *f*; **~ damage** *n* TRANSP dommage indirect *m*; **~ strike** *n* HRM grève de solidarité *f*, grève de soutien *f*

sympathy: ~ action *n* HRM mouvement de solidarité *m*; **~ strike** *n* HRM grève de solidarité *f*, grève de soutien *f*; ◆ **go out in ~ with** HRM *strikers* se mettre en grève par solidarité avec *m*

symposium *n* GEN COMM, MGMNT colloque *m*

sync *n infrml (synchronization)* GEN COMM sync (*infrml*) (*synchronisation*); ◆ **out of ~** ECON déphasé

synchronization *n (sync)* GEN COMM synchronisation *f (sync)*

synchronous[1] *adj* COMP synchrone

synchronous:[2] **~ system** *n* TRANSP *on ship* système synchrone *m*

syndicalism *n* HRM reconnaissance du fait syndical *f*

syndicate[1] *n* BANK consortium *m*, syndicat *m*, syndicat financier *m*, FIN consortium *m*, GEN COMM consortium *m*, syndicat *m*, MEDIA *AmE* syndicat de distribution *m*, STOCK syndicat *m*, syndicat d'émission *m*, syndicat de placement *m*, syndicat de prise ferme *m*, *of investors* consortium *m*, syndicat *m*; **~ manager** BANK *corporate financing* président de syndicat financier *m*

syndicate[2] *vt* HRM syndiquer; ◆ **~ a loan** BANK

consortialiser d'habitation, prêter en participation, FIN consortialiser un prêt, prêter en participation

syndicated: ~ **column** n MEDIA *print* article vendu à plusieurs journaux *m*, éditorial vendu à plusieurs journaux *m*; ~ **loan** n BANK, FIN crédit syndical *m*, prêt en participation *m*; ~ **swap** n FIN échange syndiqué *m*

syndication n BANK, FIN syndication *f*; ~ **capacity** S&M capacité de vente *f*; ~ **official** BANK responsable de la création d'un consortium bancaire *m*

synergism n ECON, GEN COMM synergie *f*

synergy n ECON, GEN COMM synergie *f*

synopsis n GEN COMM résumé *m*, sommaire *m*

syntax n COMP syntaxe *f*; ~ **error** COMP, MEDIA faute de syntaxe *f*; ~ **error message** COMP message de faute de syntaxe *m*

synthesis n GEN COMM synthèse *f*

synthetic[1] *adj* GEN COMM, STOCK synthétique

synthetic:[2] ~ **bond** n STOCK obligation synthétique *f*; ~ **incentive** n ECON *socialist economies* gratification collective *f* (*jarg*), prime collective *f*, HRM gratification collective *f* (*jarg*); ~ **long call** n STOCK *options* achat d'un call synthétique *m*, achat d'une option d'achat *m*; ~ **long put** n STOCK *options* achat d'un put synthétique *m*, achat d'une option de vente *m*

Syria *pr n* GEN COMM Syrie *f*

Syrian[1] *adj* GEN COMM syrien

Syrian[2] *n* GEN COMM *person* Syrien *m*

system n ADMIN *of administration* système *m*, COMP ordinateur *m*, système *m*, GEN COMM méthode *f*, *hi-fi*, *computer* système *m*, MGMNT méthode *f*; ~ **of accounts** n ACC système comptable *m*; ~ **administrator** n COMP administrateur système *m*; ~ **design** n COMP conception de système *f*; ~ **development** n COMP développement de système *m*; ~ **disk** n COMP disque système *m*; ~ **failure** n COMP *hardware* panne système *f*; ~ **file** n COMP fichier système *m*; ~ **of financial administration** n FIN système d'administration financière *m*; ~ **-managed company** n GEN COMM, MGMNT entreprise dirigée de façon systématisée *f*; ~ **-provider** n FIN fournisseur de système *m*; ~ **requirements** n pl COMP configuration nécessaire *f*; ~ **software** n COMP logiciel système *m*

System: ~ **of National Accounts** n *(SNA)* ACC système de comptabilité nationale *m*

systematic[1] *adj* GEN COMM systématique

systematic:[2] ~ **cost basis** n ACC base de coût systématique *f*; ~ **risk** n STOCK risque systématique *m*; ~ **sampling** n MATH *statistics* échantillonnage systématique *m*; ~ **withdrawal plan** n STOCK plan de retrait systématique *m*

systematize *vt* GEN COMM systématiser

systems: ~ **analysis** n COMP, GEN COMM analyse des systèmes *f*, analyse fonctionnelle *f*; ~ **analyst** n COMP analyste de systèmes *m*; ~ **approach** n COMP approche par la théorie des systèmes *f*, étude globale *f*; ~ **-based audit** n ACC audit analytique *m*, contrôle des comptes analytique *m*, révision analytique *f*, vérification analytique *f* (*Can*); ~ **-based auditing** n ACC audit analytique *m*, contrôle des comptes analytique *m*, révision analytique *f*, vérification analytique *f* (*Can*); ~ **design** n COMP analyse organique *f*; ~ **engineer** n COMP ingénieur système *m*; ~ **engineering** n COMP assistance technico-commerciale *f*; ~ **management** n ADMIN gestion fonctionnelle *f*, gestion systématisée *f*, COMP, MGMNT direction systématisée *f*, gestion par les systèmes *f*, gestion systématisée *f*; ~ **planning** n COMP, GEN COMM planification des systèmes *f*; ~ **and procedures** n pl ADMIN, COMP, GEN COMM méthodes administratives *f pl*; ~ **programmer** n COMP programmeur système *m*; ~ **programming** n COMP programmation systèmes *f*; ~ **software** n COMP logiciel de base *m*, logiciel système *m*; ~ **theory** n MGMNT théorie des systèmes *f*

T

t. *abbr* GEN COMM *(tare)* t. *(tare)*, GEN COMM *(ton, tonne)* t. *(tonne)*

T[1] *abbr* GEN COMM *(tropical)* tropique, TRANSP *(triple expansion engine)* moteur à triple expansion *m*, TRANSP *(tug)* remorqueur *m*, TRANSP *(twin-screw)* à deux hélices

T:[2] **~ form** *n* IMP/EXP formulaire T *m, customs* formulaire T *m*

TA *abbr* ACC *(transactional analysis)*, BANK *(transactional analysis)* analyse transactionnelle *f*, COMMS *(telegraphic address)* adr. tél. *(adresse télégraphique)*, ECON *(transactional analysis)*, FIN *(transactional analysis)*, GEN COMM *(transactional analysis)* analyse transactionnelle *f*, HRM UK *(Training Agency)* ≈ AFPA *(Association pour la formation professionnelle des adultes)*, MGMNT *(transactional analysis)* analyse transactionnelle *f*

TAA *abbr (transferable account area)* TRANSP zone de comptes négociables *f*

tab[1] *n* COMP tabulation *f*; **~ operator** ADMIN mécanographe *m*; **~ setting** COMP pose de tabulations *f*

tab[2] *vt* COMP faire une tabulation *loc f*

TAB *abbr US (tax anticipation bill)* TAX obligation d'impôts anticipés *f*

table[1] *n* COMP, GEN COMM *in document* table *f*, tableau *m*; **~ of contents** GEN COMM table des matières *f*; **~ of par values** STOCK table de parités *f*; **~ top** *jarg UK* S&M *advertising* photographie d'un produit seul sans aucun personnage; ♦ **on the ~** GEN COMM *proposal* sur la table des négociations

table[2] *vt* GEN COMM déposer, *postpone* remettre, LAW *amendment* déposer, POL *motion* soumettre

tabling *n* GEN COMM dépôt *m*

tabloid[1] *adj* MEDIA *print* demi-format, tabloïd *(jarg)*

tabloid[2] *n* MEDIA *newspaper* journal petit format *m*; **~ newspaper** MEDIA journal petit format *m*; **~ paper** MEDIA journal petit format *m*; **~ press** MEDIA *print* la presse populaire *f*

tabular[1] *adj* ADMIN, GEN COMM tabulaire

tabular:[2] **~ report** *n* ADMIN, GEN COMM état sous forme de tableau *m*

tabulate *vt* ADMIN, GEN COMM mettre sous forme de tableau

tabulated: in ~ form *phr* ADMIN, COM, GEN COMM sous forme de tableau

tabulating: ~ department *n* ADMIN service mécanographique *m*; **~ machine** *n* ADMIN tabulatrice *f*

tabulation *n* ADMIN, COMP tabulation *f*; **~ character** ADMIN, COMP caractère de tabulation *m*

tabulator: ~ operator *n* ADMIN mécanographe *m*

T-account *n* ACC *book-keeping*, BANK compte en T *m*

tachograph *n* TRANSP tachygraphe *m*

tacit[1] *adj* GEN COMM implicite, tacite

tacit:[2] **~ knowledge** *n* ECON connaissances techniques non-transférables *f pl*, connaissances techniques non-transposables *f pl*; **~ renewal** *n* GEN COMM reconduction tacite *f*; ♦ **by ~ agreement** GEN COMM par accord tacite

tackle[1] *n* TRANSP *equipment* palan *m*

tackle[2] *vt* GEN COMM *problem* aborder

TACs *abbr (total allowable catches)* ENVIR prises totales autorisées *f pl*

tactical: ~ plan *n* GEN COMM plan tactique *m*; **~ planning** *n* GEN COMM plan tactique *m*

tactile: ~ keyboard *n* COMP clavier tactile *m*

tag *n* COMP, TRANSP *on cargo* étiquette *f*; **~ reader** COMP lecteur d'étiquettes *m*

tagboard *n* AmE *(cf cardboard BrE)* GEN COMM carton *m*

tagline *n* S&M *advertisements* slogan *m*

tail[1] *n* GEN COMM *of list* dernière entrée *f*, INS, STOCK *treasury auctions, underwriting* suivi *m*; **~ end** GEN COMM *final part* fin *f*; **~ lift** TRANSP plate-forme de chargement *f*; **~ shaft** TRANSP *of propeller* arbre porte-hélice *m*

tail:[2] **~ away** *vi* GEN COMM diminuer, décroître

tailgating *n* STOCK suivisme *m*

tailor:[1] **~-made** *adj* GEN COMM *package* fait sur mesure, personnalisé, S&M *advertising* fait sur mesure

tailor:[2] **~-made contract** *n* LAW contrat sur mesure *m*

tailor[3] *vt* GEN COMM *clothing* façonner

tailorable *adj* GEN COMM *personalized, customized product* personnalisable

tailored *adj* GEN COMM, S&M adapté

tailoring *n* GEN COMM *of product*, S&M personnalisation *f*

tailspin *n infrml* ECON, GEN COMM chute verticale *f*; ♦ **get into a ~** GEN COMM *of market* paniquer

taint *vt* TRANSP vicier

Taipei *pr n* GEN COMM Taipeh *n pr*, Taipei *n pr*

Taiwan *pr n* GEN COMM Taiwan *m*

Taiwanese[1] *adj* GEN COMM taiwanais

Taiwanese[2] *n* GEN COMM *person* Taiwanais *m*

Tajikistan *pr n* GEN COMM Tadjikistan *m*

taka *n* GEN COMM takka *m*

take:[1] **~-home pay** *n* HRM salaire net *m*; **~-or-pay contract** *n* STOCK contrat à acompte obligatoire *m*, engagement d'acheter *m*; **~-out** *n jarg US* MEDIA *broadcast* panorama *m*, reportage *m*; **~-out loan** *n* BANK obtenir un prêt; **~-up** *n* WEL *social work* perception *f*; ~ **-up rate** *n* GEN COMM taux de souscription *m*, WEL taux de réclamation *m*; ~ **-up reel** *n* COMP bobine réceptrice *f*; ~ **-up of Treasury bills** *n* FIN remboursement des bons du Trésor *m*; ◆ **be on the** ~ *infrml* GEN COMM toucher des pots-de-vin; ~ **up legal residence** ADMIN se faire domicilier

take² **1.** *vt* GEN COMM contenir, *partner* prendre, HRM *job*, STOCK *profit* prendre, TRANSP contenir; ~ **away** GEN COMM *deduct* retrancher; ~ **back** GEN COMM *employee, goods* reprendre; ~ **down** GEN COMM *make note of* prendre en note; ~ **in** GEN COMM *cheat* rouler (*infrml*), STOCK *stock* reporter; ~ **on** GEN COMM *responsibility* assumer, prendre, HRM *staff* embaucher, engager; ~ **out** GEN COMM *subscription, patent* prendre, INS *insurance policy* souscrire; ~ **over** ECON, FIN racheter, GEN COMM racheter, *company* prendre le contrôle de, *debts* reprendre à sa charge, STOCK *issue* absorber; ~ **over from** GEN COMM prendre la succession de, remplacer, succéder à; ~ **up** BANK *loan*, FIN *bill* honorer, GEN COMM *challenge* relever, *offer, invitation* accepter, STOCK *option* lever, *shares* prendre livraison, WEL toucher; **2.** *vi* ~ **off** TRANSP décoller; ~ **place** GEN COMM avoir lieu; ◆ ~ **aboard** GEN COMM *cargo, passengers* embarquer; ~ **action** GEN COMM, MGMNT faire des démarches; ~ **administrative control** GEN COMM *of company* prendre le contrôle administratif; ~ **a bath** *jarg* STOCK boire la tasse (*infrml*), vendre à perte; ~ **bribes** (ANT *give bribes*) GEN COMM accepter un pot-de-vin, se laisser corrompre; ~ **control** GEN COMM prendre le contrôle; ~ **delivery** STOCK prendre livraison; ~ **effect** LAW entrer en vigueur, prendre effet; ~ **effect from** GEN COMM *date* entrer en vigueur à partir de, prendre effet le...; ~ **expert advice** GEN COMM demander l'avis d'un expert; ~ **an extra day off** GEN COMM *between a national holiday and a weekend* faire le pont; ~ **French leave** *infrml* GEN COMM filer à l'anglaise; ~ **industrial action** HRM faire grève, se mettre en grève; ~ **into consideration** (*TIC*) GEN COMM considérer, tenir compte de; ~ **leave** HRM prendre congé; ~ **legal advice** LAW consulter un avocat; ~ **measures** HRM, LAW *against employee* prendre des mesures, prendre des sanctions; ~ **off the market** GEN COMM, S&M retirer du marché; ~ **the offensive** GEN COMM prendre l'offensive; ~ **on extra work** HRM accepter du travail supplémentaire; ~ **one's pick** GEN COMM choisir, faire son choix; ~ **orders** GEN COMM prendre des commandes; ~ **out a loan** FIN contracter un crédit, contracter un emprunt, faire un prêt; ~ **out a policy** INS contracter une police d'assurance, souscrire à une police d'assurance; ~ **out a summons against** HRM faire assigner; ~ **over liabilities** ACC prendre le passif à sa charge; ~ **part in** GEN COMM prendre part à; ~ **possession** PROP prendre possession; ~ **public** FIN, STOCK *company* s'introduire en bourse; ~ **a reading** GEN COMM relever les indications d'un compteur; ~ **sb to**

court LAW faire un procès à qn, traîner en justice; ~ **sb's word for it** GEN COMM croire qn sur parole; ~ **7 away from 49** GEN COMM ôter 7 de 49; ~ **shape** GEN COMM *idea* prendre forme, se concrétiser; ~ **sides with sb** GEN COMM prendre parti pour qn; ~ **steps** GEN COMM effectuer des démarches, prendre des mesures; ~ **steps to do** GEN COMM prendre des mesures pour faire; ~ **sth down in shorthand** GEN COMM prendre qch en sténo; ~ **stock** ACC, ADMIN, GEN COMM, S&M dresser l'inventaire; ~ **up legal residence** LAW se faire domicilier; ~ **up a position** GEN COMM adopter une position, prendre une position; ~ **up rate** WEL taux de reclamation *m*, taux de souscription *f*; ~ **up stocks** STOCK prendre livraison des titres

takeback: ~ **bargaining** *n* HRM négociation qui revient sur les acquis, régression *f*

taken: **be** ~ **in** *phr* GEN COMM se faire avoir (*infrml*)

takeoff *n* ECON, GEN COMM, TRANSP décollage *m*

takeover *n* ECON contre-offre publique d'achat *f*, prise de contrôle *f*, rachat *m*, FIN contre-OPA *f*, contre-offre publique d'achat *f*, fusion *f*, rachat *m*, GEN COMM prise de contrôle *f*, rachat *m*, STOCK prise de contrôle *f*; ~ **attempt** FIN, GEN COMM, STOCK tentative d'OPA *f*, tentative d'offre publique d'achat *f*; ~ **bid** (*TOB*) ACC, GEN COMM, STOCK offre publique d'achat *f* (*OPA*)

taker: ~ **for a put and call** *n* STOCK donneur de stellage *m*; ~ **of a rate** *n* STOCK receveur de la prime *m*

takers: ~ **-in** *n pl* STOCK preneurs d'offre *m pl*

takeup *n* STOCK levée d'une nouvelle émission *f*; ~ **of shares** STOCK émission d'actions souscrites *f*

taking: ~ **delivery** *n* STOCK *of commodities, securities* prise de livraison *f*; ~ **up office** *n* GEN COMM entrée en fonction *f*

takings *n pl* GEN COMM recette *f*

TAL *abbr* (*technical assistance loan*) FIN prêt d'assistance technique *m*

Talisman *n* STOCK talisman *m*

talk *vi* GEN COMM parler; ◆ ~ **business** GEN COMM parler affaires; ~ **shop** *infrml* GEN COMM parler métier

talking: ~ **head** *n jarg* MEDIA *broadcast* plan d'un personnage en conversation, présentateur *m*

Tallinn *pr n* GEN COMM Tallinn *n pr*

tally:¹ ~ **clerk** *n* HRM, TRANSP *shipping* employé au pointage *m*, pointeur *m*, vérificateur *m*; ~ **register** *n* GEN COMM registre de comptage *m*; ~ **roll** *n* GEN COMM bande de contrôle *f*; ~ **sheet** *n* HRM feuille de pointage *f*; ~ **trade** *n* GEN COMM, HRM commerce à tempérament *m*

tally² **1.** *vt* TRANSP *shipping* pointer; **2.** *vi* GEN COMM cadrer; ◆ **keep** ~ **of** GEN COMM tenir compte de

talon *n* STOCK talon *m*

Tamil *n* GEN COMM *language* tamoul *m*

tamper: ~ **-proof** *adj* GEN COMM impossible à trafiquer *loc* (*infrml*)

TAMS *abbr* *(thruster-assisted mooring system)* TRANSP *shipping* système d'amarrage à propulsion *m*

TAN *abbr* *(tax anticipation note)* TAX obligation d'impôts anticipés *f*

tandem *n* TRANSP tandem *m*; ~ **account** BANK compte en tandem *m*; ~ **axle** TRANSP essieux en tandem *m pl*

T&G *abbr* *(tongued and grooved)* TRANSP affourché

tangible[1] *adj* (ANT *intangible*) ACC, ECON, FIN, GEN COMM corporel, réel, LAW corporel

tangible:[2] ~ **asset** *n* ACC, FIN immobilisation corporelle *f*, valeur corporelle *f*, valeur matérielle *f*, valeur tangible *f*, élément d'actif corporel *m*, GEN COMM immobilisation corporelle *f*, GEN COMM valeur corporelle *f*, valeur matérielle *f*, valeur tangible *f*, élément d'actif corporel *m*; ~ **capital property** *n* ACC, PROP bien en immobilisation corporel *m*; ~ **fixed asset** *n* (ANT *intangible fixed asset*) ACC, FIN, GEN COMM immobilisation corporelle *f*; ~ **net worth** *n* FIN, STOCK valeur réelle nette *f*; ~ **personal property** *n* PROP bien matériel personnel *m*; ~ **wealth** *n* (ANT *intangible wealth*) ECON biens tangibles *m pl*, richesse corporelle *f*

tank *n* TRANSP citerne *f*; ~ **car** *AmE* (*cf tank wagon BrE*) TRANSP wagon-citerne *m*; ~ **cleaning** TRANSP nettoyage des citernes *m*; ~ **container** TRANSP conteneur-citerne *m*; ~ **farm** TRANSP dépôt pétrolier *m*, parc à réservoirs de stockage *m*; ~ **pressure** TRANSP pression de citerne *f*; ~ **top** *(TT)* TRANSP plafond de ballast *m*; ~ **truck** *AmE* (*cf tanker lorry BrE*) TRANSP camion-citerne *m*; ~ **-type stabilizer** TRANSP stabilisateur à réservoir *m*; ~ **wagon** *BrE* (*cf tank car AmE*) TRANSP wagon-citerne *m*

Tankan *n* BANK, ECON, FIN prévisions économiques de la Banque du Japon

tanker *n* TRANSP *shipping* bateau-citerne *m*, navire-citerne *m*; ~ **broker** STOCK, TRANSP courtier en transports pétroliers *m*; ~ **lorry** *BrE* (*cf tank truck AmE*) TRANSP camion-citerne *m*; ~ **motor vessel** TRANSP *shipping* bateau-citerne à moteur *m*, navire-citerne à moteur *m*; ~ **owners' voluntary agreement concerning liability for oil pollution** *(TOVALOP)* ENVIR, INS, TRANSP engagement volontaire des propriétaires de pétroliers en cas de pollution pétrolière

tanktainer *n* TRANSP *shipping* conteneur-citerne *m*

Tanzania *pr n* GEN COMM Tanzanie *f*

Tanzanian[1] *adj* GEN COMM tanzanien

Tanzanian[2] *n* GEN COMM *person* Tanzanien *m*

tap[1] *n* STOCK valeur de gré à gré *f*, valeur émise en robinet continu *f* (*jarg*); ~ **bill** *n* STOCK bon émis en robinet continu *m*, effet placé de gré à gré *m*; ~ **issue** *n* STOCK émission de valeurs d'État *f*; ~ **stock tender** *n* ECON, STOCK adjudication de bons du Trésor *f*, soumission à un appel d'offres *f*; ~ **stocks** *n pl UK* STOCK valeurs d'État *f pl*

tap[2] *vt* ENVIR *oil resources*, GEN COMM *resources*, *market* exploiter; ~ **in** COMP *key in* introduire, saisir; ~ **into** GEN COMM *telephone call* capter; ◆ ~ **the market** STOCK attaquer le marché; ~ **the market for** STOCK faire appel au marché pour

tape[1] *n* COMMS, COMP, MEDIA bande *f*; ~ **cartridge** COMMS, COMP cartouche *f*, cartouche de bande *f*; ~ **drive** COMP dérouleur de bande *m*, lecteur de bande *m*, lecteur de cartouche *m*; ~ **feed** COMP mécanisme d'entraînement de bande *m*; ~ **file** COMP fichier sur bande *m*; ~ **library** GEN COMM magnétothèque *f*; ~ **machine** *BrE* (*cf ticker AmE*) ADMIN, COMP téléimprimeur *m*, téléscripteur *m*; ~ **measure** GEN COMM mètre *m*, mètre de couturière *m*; ~ **punch** COMP perforateur de bande *m*; ~ **recorder** GEN COMM magnétophone *m*; ~ **recording** COMMS enregistrement *m*; ~ **unit** GEN COMM unité de bande magnétique *f*; ◆ **on** ~ GEN COMM *recorded* enregistré

tape:[2] ~ **-record** *vt* COMMS enregistrer

taper:[1] ~ **relief** *n UK* TAX *inheritance tax, lifetime gifts* dégrèvement par effilage *m*

taper[2] **1.** *vt* TAX *tax relief* effiler; **2.** *vi* ~ **off** ECON décroître, se réduire

tapering *n* HRM système dégressif *m*

TAPS *abbr* *(turret anchored production system)* TRANSP système de production à tourelle d'ancrage *m*

tare *n* GEN COMM tare *f*, TRANSP *packaging* tare *f*; ~ **weight** GEN COMM poids à vide *m*, TRANSP poids à vide *m*, tare *f*

target[1] *n* COMP cible *f*, destinataire *mf*, GEN COMM cible *f*, objectif *m*, MEDIA cible *f*, S&M cible *f*, objectif *m*; ~ **audience** MEDIA, S&M cible *f*; ~ **buyer** S&M acheteur-cible *m*; ~ **company** GEN COMM, S&M entreprise cible *f*; ~ **computer** COMP ordinateur cible *m*; ~ **date** GEN COMM date prévue *f*; ~ **field** COMP zone destinataire *f*; ~ **language** COMP *linguistics* langage objet *m*, langue d'arrivée *f*; ~ **market** S&M marché cible *m*; ~ **price** ECON, GEN COMM, S&M prix cible *m*; ~ **pricing** GEN COMM, S&M ciblage des prix *m*; ~ **range** ECON fourchette visée *f*; ~ **rate** STOCK *interest rate futures* taux cible *m*, taux de référence *m*; ~ **risk** INS risque à cotisation et à prestations déterminées *m*; ~ **segment** S&M segment ciblé *m*; ~ **setting** GEN COMM, S&M fixation des objectifs *f*, établissement d'objectifs *m*; ~ **variable** ECON objectif visé *m*; ~ **zone** ECON *exchange rates*, FIN zone cible *f*

target[2] *vt* GEN COMM, MEDIA cibler, S&M *campaign, consumer base* cibler, viser

targeting *n* ECON, GEN COMM ciblage *m*, fixation des objectifs *f*, MEDIA ciblage *m*, S&M ciblage *m*, fixation des objectifs *f*

tariff:[1] ~ **-free** *adj* IMP/EXP sans tarif

tariff[2] *n* GEN COMM *price list*, IMP/EXP, TAX tarif *m*; ~ **barrier** ECON, GEN COMM, IMP/EXP, POL barrière douanière *f*, barrière tarifaire *f*; ~ **expenditure** ACC dépense tarifaire *f*; ~ **legislation** IMP/EXP, LAW, TAX législation douanière *f*; ~ **level** ECON,

IMP/EXP, TAX niveau tarifaire m; ~ **protection** ECON, IMP/EXP protection douanière f, protection tarifaire f; ~ **quota** ECON, GEN COMM, IMP/EXP contingent tarifaire m; ~ **rate** IMP/EXP taux tarifaire m; ~ **reform** GEN COMM, IMP/EXP réforme des tarifs douaniers f; ~ **schedule** GEN COMM, IMP/EXP barème des tarifs m; ~ **wall** ECON, GEN COMM, IMP/EXP barrière tarifaire f; ~ **war** ECON, GEN COMM guerre des tarifs f

tarification n FIN, TAX EU tarification f

taring n GEN COMM tarage m

Tashkent pr n GEN COMM Tachkent n pr

task n COMP, GEN COMM, POL tâche f; ~ **closure** jarg GEN COMM achèvement de tâche m; ~ **flexibility** HRM adaptabilité fonctionnelle f; ~ **force** HRM, POL groupe d'intervention m, groupe de réflexion m, groupe de travail m; ~ **initiation** COMP lancement de tâche m; ~ **management** COMP, MGMNT gestion des tâches f; ~ **scheduling** GEN COMM programmation des tâches f; ~ **setting** GEN COMM fixation d'objectifs de travail f; ~ **work** GEN COMM travail aux pièces m

taste n ECON, S&M préférence f

TAT abbr (transitional automated ticket) TRANSP billet automatisé de transition m

TAURUS abbr UK (Transfer & Automated Registration of Uncertified Stock) ECON, STOCK transfert et enregistrement automatisé de titres noncertifiés

TAWB abbr (through air waybill) IMP/EXP, TRANSP lettre de transport aérien de bout en bout f

tax:[1] ~ **-deductible** adj TAX déductible d'impôts, déductible fiscalement; ~ **-exempt** adj TAX exempt d'impôts, exonéré d'impôts; ~ **-free** adj ECON, FIN hors taxes, TAX exempt d'impôts, exonéré d'impôts, hors taxes

tax[2] n ACC, ECON, FIN impôt m, taxe f, TAX contribution f, impôt m, taxe f; ~ **abatement** n ECON, FIN, TAX abattement d'impôt m; ~ **adjustment** n ECON, FIN, TAX ajustement d'impôt m, redressement fiscal m; ~ **administration** n ADMIN, TAX administration fiscale f; ~ **advantage** n ECON, IND avantage fiscal m, TAX avantage fiscal m, bénéfice fiscal m; ~ **advisor** n MGMNT, TAX conseiller en fiscalité m, conseiller en matière fiscale m, conseiller fiscal m; ~ **agreement** n TAX with another country convention fiscale f; ~ **allowance** n TAX abattement fiscal m, déduction d'impôt f, déduction fiscale f, impôt déduit m, impôt retenu m, retenue d'impôt f; ~ **anticipation bill** n US (TAB) TAX obligation d'impôts anticipés f; ~ **anticipation note** n (TAN) TAX obligation d'impôts anticipés f; ~ **appeal** n TAX appel d'impôts m; ~ **arrears** n pl FIN, TAX arriéré d'impôt m; ~ **-assessed accounts** n pl ACC, TAX comptes frappés d'imposition m pl; ~ **assessment** n TAX imposition f, évaluation d'impôts f; ~ **assistance** n TAX aide fiscale f; ~ **audit** n FIN, TAX vérification fiscale f;

~ **avoidance** n ECON, FIN, TAX exemption d'impôts f, évasion fiscale f; ~ **band** n TAX tranche d'imposition f; ~ **barrier** n TAX barrière fiscale f; ~ **base** n ECON assiette d'imposition f, assiette de l'impôt f, assiette fiscale f, base d'imposition f, capacité d'imposition f, faculté contributive f, TAX assiette de l'impôt f, assiette fiscale f, base d'imposition f, capacité d'imposition f, faculté contributive f; ~ **base broadening** n ECON, TAX élargissement de l'assiette de l'impôt m, élargissement de l'assiette fiscale m; ~ **-based depreciation** n ACC, TAX amortissement dérogatoire m; ~ **-based incomes policy** n (TIP) ECON, FIN, TAX politique d'imposition des sociétés basée sur les salaires versés; ~ **basis** n ECON, TAX assiette de l'impôt f, assiette fiscale f, base d'imposition f; ~ **benefit** n (SYN tax advantage) TAX bénéfice fiscal m; ~ **bracket** n TAX tranche d'imposition f; ~ **-bracket creep** n ECON, TAX glissement d'une tranche d'imposition à l'autre m, passage d'une tranche d'imposition à une autre m; ~ **break** n ECON, IND, TAX allègement fiscal m, avantage fiscal m, dégrèvement fiscal m, réduction d'impôt f; ~ **buoyancy** n (SYN tax elasticity) ECON, TAX élasticité fiscale f; ~ **burden** n ECON, TAX charge fiscale f, fardeau fiscal m, poids de l'impôt m, pression fiscale f, taux de prélèvement fiscal m; ~ **capacity** n TAX capacité fiscale f; ~ **capitalization** n ECON capitalisation fiscale f; ~ **category** n TAX catégorie d'imposition f; ~ **charge** n ECON, TAX charge fiscale f; ~ **claims** n pl TAX créances fiscales f pl, réclamations fiscales f pl; ~ **code** n TAX code des impôts m; ~ **collection** n TAX perception de l'impôt f, recouvrement de l'impôt m; ~ **collector** n HRM, TAX percepteur m; ~ **compliance** n TAX observation fiscale f; ~ **component** n TAX composant de l'impôt m, élément constitutif de l'impôt m; ~ **concession** n TAX avoir fiscal m; ~ **consultant** n MGMNT, TAX conseil fiscal m, conseiller fiscal m; ~ **cost** n TAX coût aux fins de l'impôt m, coût de l'impôt m; ~ **court** n TAX tribunal m; ~ **credit** n ECON crédit d'impôt m, TAX avoir fiscal m, crédit d'impôt m; ~ **credit system** n TAX système de crédits d'impôt m; ~ **creditor** n ACC, TAX dettes fiscales f pl; ~ **cut** n ECON, IND, TAX réduction d'impôt f; ~ **debtor** n TAX débiteur fiscal m; ~ **deduction** n TAX abattement fiscal m, déduction d'impôt f, déduction fiscale f, impôt déduit m, impôt retenu m, retenue d'impôt f; ~ **deferral** n TAX report de l'impôt m; ~ **disc** n BrE TAX vignette f; ~ **discounting** n TAX diminution d'impôt f; ~ **disk** n AmE see tax disc BrE; ~ **district** n UK TAX division du trésor public f; ~ **dodger** n ECON fraudeur de l'impôt m, fraudeur du fisc m, TAX fraudeur de l'impôt m, fraudeur du fisc m, fraudeur fiscal m; ~ **dodging** n TAX fraude fiscale f; ~ **domicile** n TAX domicile d'imposition m; ~ **drain** n TAX drainage de l'impôt m; ~ **-efficient investments** n pl UK FIN, TAX investissements à capacité fiscale m pl; ~ **effort** n ECON, TAX effort fiscal m; ~ **elasticity** *n* (SYN *tax buoyancy*) ECON, TAX élasticité fiscale *f*; ~ **environment** *n* TAX climat fiscal *m*, environnement fiscal *m*; ~ **equalization** *n* TAX péréquation des impôts *f*; ~ **equalization account** *n* TAX compte de péréquation des impôts *m*; ~ **equalization scheme** *n* TAX *maintained by foreign employers* système de péréquation des impôts *m*; ~ **equity and fiscal responsibility act of 1982** *n* (*TEFRA*) TAX loi de 1982 sur l'équité des impôts et de la responsabilité fiscale; ~ **erosion** *n* ECON, TAX érosion fiscale *f*; ~ **evader** *n* ECON, TAX fraudeur de l'impôt *m*, fraudeur du fisc *m*, fraudeur fiscal *m*; ~ **evasion** *n* ECON, FIN, TAX fraude fiscale *f*, évasion fiscale *f*; ~ **-exempt corporation** *n* GEN COMM, TAX corporation exonérée d'impôt *f*, société exonérée d'impôts *f*; ~ **-exempt securities** *n* TAX titres exemptés d'impôts *m pl*, titres exonérés d'impôts *m pl*; ~ **-exempt special savings account** *n* UK (*TESSA*) BANK, ECON, TAX compte spécial d'épargne exonéré d'impôts *m*; ~ **exemption** *n* TAX exonération d'impôts *f*; ~ **exile** *n* TAX exil fiscal *m*, personne fuyant le fisc *f*; ~ **expenditure** *n* ECON, TAX dépenses fiscales *f pl*; ~ **expert** *n* TAX expert en fiscalité *m*, fiscaliste *mf*; ~ **fairness** *n* TAX équité fiscale *f*; ~ **farming** *n* (SYN *goal system*) ECON, TAX collecte des impôts par fermage *f*; ~ **field** *n* (SYN *field of taxation*) TAX domaine fiscal *m*; ~ **foreclosure** *n* TAX forclusion fiscale *f*; ~ **form** *n* TAX déclaration d'impôts *f*, formule fiscale *f*; ~ **fraud** *n* TAX fraude fiscale *f*; ~ **-free allowance** *n* TAX indemnité non-imposable *f*; ~ **-free shop** *n* LEIS, TAX, TRANSP boutique hors taxes *f*; ~ **gimmick** *n* TAX subterfuge fiscal *m*; ~ **guidelines** *n pl* TAX directives financières *f pl*; ~ **harmonization** *n* ECON, TAX harmonisation fiscale *f*; ~ **haven** *n* ECON, TAX paradis fiscal *m*, refuge fiscal *m*; ~ **holiday** *n* ECON, IND, LAW jour férié *m*, TAX période d'exonération fiscale *f*; ~ **immunity** *n* ECON exonération d'impôts fiscale *f*, immunité fiscale *f*, TAX exonération d'impôts *f*, immunité fiscale *f*; ~ **incentive** *n* ECON, IND avantage fiscal *m*, TAX avantage fiscal *m*, incitation fiscale *f*, mesure fiscale d'incitation *f*; ~ **incidence** *n* TAX conséquence fiscale *f*, incidence fiscale *f*; ~ **influence** *n* ACC, TAX *EU* influence fiscale *f*; ~ **inspector** *n* HRM, TAX contrôleur des droits et taxes *m*, inspecteur des impôts *m*, percepteur *m*; ~ **installment** *n* AmE, ~ **instalment** *n* BrE TAX acompte provisionnel *m*; ~ **jurisdiction** *n* LAW, TAX compétence fiscale *f*, division du trésor public *f*, juridiction fiscale *f*; ~ **law** *n* (SYN *fiscal law*) TAX droit fiscal *m*; ~ **liability** *n* TAX dette fiscale *f*, impôt à payer *m*, obligation fiscale *f*, responsabilité fiscale *f*; ~ **lien** *n* TAX privilège fiscal *m*; ~ **load** *n* TAX poids de l'impôt *m*; ~ **loophole** *n* TAX échappatoire fiscale *f*; ~ **loss carry-back** *n* TAX report à nouveau de perte fiscale *m*; ~ **measure** *n* TAX mesure fiscale *f*; ~ **offence** *n* LAW, TAX infraction fiscale *f*; ~ **offset** *n* TAX compensation fiscale *f*; ~ **on company cars** *n* TAX taxe sur les véhicules de société *f*; ~ **on**

income *n* TAX fraude fiscale *f*; ~ **otherwise payable** *n* TAX impôt payable par ailleurs *m*, impôt sinon exigible *m*; ~ **-paid guaranteed growth bond** *n* UK STOCK obligation à croissance garantie après paiement des taxes; ~ **-paid income** *n* TAX revenu libéré d'impôt *m*; ~ **payable** *n* TAX impôt exigible *m*, impôt à payer *m*; ~ **payable basis** *n* TAX méthode de l'impôt exigible *f*; ~ **penalty** *n* TAX pénalisation fiscale *f*, pénalité fiscale *f*; ~ **planning** *n* TAX planification fiscale *f*; ~ **policy** *n* ECON, POL, TAX politique fiscale *f*; ~ **position** *n* TAX position fiscale *f*; ~ **preference item** *n* TAX article fiscal privilégié *m*; ~ **privilege** *n* TAX privilège fiscal *m*; ~ **proceeds** *n pl* TAX produit de l'impôt *m*; ~ **proposal** *n* ECON, TAX proposition fiscale *f*; ~ **provision** *n* TAX disposition fiscale *f*; ~ **provisions** *n pl* ACC, TAX provisions pour impôts *f pl*; ~ **purposes** *n pl* ACC, TAX fins d'imposition *f pl*, fins fiscales *f pl*; ~ **rate** *n* TAX taux d'imposition *m*, taux d'impôt *m*; ~ **rate schedule** *n* (SYN *tax rate structure*) TAX barème d'imposition *m*, liste officielle des taux d'imposition *f*; ~ **rate structure** *n* (SYN *tax rate schedule*) TAX barème d'imposition *m*, liste officielle des taux d'imposition *f*; ~ **ratio** *n* TAX coefficient d'imposition *m*; ~ **rebate** *n* TAX dégrèvement d'impôt *m*, remboursement de taxe *m*; ~ **receipts** *n pl* ECON, TAX recettes fiscales *f pl*; ~ **record** *n* TAX dossier d'impôt *m*; ~ **reduction** *n* ECON, IND, TAX réduction d'impôt *f*; ~ **reform** *n* ECON, TAX réforme de fiscalité *f*; ~ **reform act** *n* ECON, LAW, TAX loi de réforme fiscale *f*; ~ **refund** *n* TAX remboursement d'impôt *m*, remboursement sur impôt *m*; ~ **relief** *n* ECON, IND allègement fiscal *m*, avantage fiscal *m*, dégrèvement fiscal *m*, réduction d'impôt *f*, TAX allègement fiscal *m*, avantage fiscal *m*, dégrèvement d'impôt *m*, dégrèvement fiscal *m*, réduction d'impôt *f*; ~ **relief for business vehicles** *n* TAX dégrèvement d'impôt sur les véhicules commerciaux *m*; ~ **remission** *n* TAX remise d'impôt *f*; ~ **restriction** *n* TAX limitation d'impôt *f*; ~ **return** *n* TAX déclaration d'impôt sur le revenu *f*; ~ **revenue** *n* ECON, TAX recettes fiscales *f pl*; ~ **rules** *n pl* TAX règles fiscales *f pl*; ~ **sale** *n* PROP, TAX vente après imposition *f*; ~ **schedule** *n* TAX barème d'imposition *m*; ~ **selling** *n* PROP, TAX vente avant imposition *f*; ~ **shelter** *n* TAX abri fiscal *m*; ~ **-sheltered account** *n* BANK, TAX compte dont les intérêts ne sont pas imposables; ~ **shield** *n* TAX protection fiscale *f*; ~ **software** *n* COMP, TAX logiciel de calcul fiscal *m*; ~ **status** *n* ADMIN, TAX situation fiscale *f*, statut fiscal *m*; ~ **stimuli** *n pl* TAX stimuli fiscaux *m pl*; ~ **straddle** *n* TAX enfourchement d'impôt *m*; ~ **strategy** *n* TAX stratégie fiscale *f*; ~ **structure** *n* ECON, TAX coefficient des impôts directs-indirects *m*, structure fiscale *f*; ~ **system** *n* ECON, TAX fiscalité *f*, régime fiscal *m*, système fiscal *m*; ~ **take** *n* TAX ponction fiscale *f*; ~ **threshold** *n* ECON, FIN, TAX minimum imposable *m*, seuil d'imposition minimum *m*; ~ **transparency** *n* TAX transparence fiscale *f*; ~ **treatment** *n* TAX traitement fiscal *m*; ~ **treaty** *n* TAX convention fiscale *f*; ~ **umbrella** *n* TAX ombrelle fiscale *f*; ~ **unit** *n* ECON, TAX foyer fiscal *m*; ~ **voucher** *n* STOCK, TAX attestation de paiement d'impôt sur dividendes *loc f*, pièce fiscale *f*; ~ **withholding** *n* ACC, TAX imputation de 50% du crédit d'impôt auprès du Trésor, retenue fiscale *f*, retenue d'impôt *f*; ~ **write-off** *n* TAX dépense déductible de l'impôt sur les sociétés *f*, perte sèche de l'impôt *f*; ~ **year** *n* COM année fiscale *f*, TAX exercice *m*, exercice fiscal *m*; ~ **yield** *n* TAX rendement de l'impôt *m*

taxable[1] *adj* ACC, FIN imposable, TAX imposable, soumis à l'impôt; ~ **in the hands of** TAX imposable comme revenu de

taxable:[2] ~ **allowance** *n* TAX allocation imposable *f*; ~ **allowances and benefits** *n pl* TAX allocations et avantages imposables *m pl*, allocations et prestations imposables *f pl*; ~ **article** *n* TAX article imposable *m*, matière imposable *f*; ~ **beneficiary** *n* TAX bénéficiaire imposable *m*; ~ **benefit** *n* TAX avantage imposable *m*, bénéfice imposable *m*; ~ **capacity** *n* ECON, TAX capacité d'imposition *f*, faculté contributive *f*; ~ **capital** *n* TAX capital imposable *m*; ~ **capital gain** *n* ACC, ECON, FIN gain en capital imposable *m*, TAX gain en capital imposable *m*, plus-value imposable *f*; ~ **corporation** *n* GEN COMM, TAX corporation imposable *f*, société imposable *f*; ~ **dividend** *n* TAX dividende imposable *m*; ~ **income** *n* ACC, ECON, FIN, TAX revenu imposable *m*; ~ **municipal bond** *n* TAX bon municipal imposable *m*; ~ **net gain** *n* ACC, ECON, FIN, TAX gain net imposable *m*; ~ **obligation** *n* TAX obligation imposable *f*; ~ **preferred share** *n* STOCK, TAX action privilégiée imposable *f*; ~ **profit** *n* ACC, TAX bénéfice imposable *m*; ~ **quota** *n* TAX quota imposable *m*, quotité imposable *f*; ~ **sales** *n pl* S&M, TAX ventes imposables *f pl*, ventes taxables *f pl*; ~ **social security benefits** *n pl* TAX, WEL prestations sociales imposables *f pl*; ~ **value** *n* TAX valeur imposable *f*; ~ **year** *n* TAX année d'imposition *f*

taxation *n* ECON fiscalité *f*, imposition *f*, taxation *f*, impôts *m pl*, FIN fiscalité *f*, imposition *f*, impôts *m pl*, taxation *f*, TAX fiscalité *f*, imposition *f*, taxation *f*, impôts *m pl*, *goods* imposition *f*, taxation *f*; ~ **authorities** *n pl* TAX administration fiscale *f*; ~ **capacity** *n* ECON capacité d'imposition *f*, faculté contributive *f*, TAX capacité d'imposition *f*; ~ **creditor** *n* ACC dettes fiscales *f pl*; ~ **employer number** *n* Canada TAX immatriculation fiscale d'employeur *f*, numéro de l'employeur aux fins de l'impôt *m*; ~ **office** *n* TAX bureau d'imposition *m*; ~ **officer** *n* HRM, TAX agent de l'impôt *m*, inspecteur des impôts *m*; ~ **period** *n* TAX période d'imposition *f*; ~ **system** *n* ECON, TAX fiscalité *f*, régime fiscal *m*, système fiscal *m*; ~ **year** *n* TAX année d'imposition *f*

taxed[1] *adj* TAX assujetti à l'impôt, frappé d'impôt *loc m*, imposé; ~ **at source** TAX imposé à la source

taxed:[2] ~ **capital gain** *n* ACC, ECON, FIN, TAX gain en capital imposé *m*, plus-value imposée *f*

taxes: ~ **actually paid** *n pl* ACC, TAX impôt réellement versé *m*, impôt versé *m*; ~ **due** *n pl* ACC, TAX impôt sur les sociétés *m*

taxfiler *n* Canada TAX déclarant *m*

taxflation *n* ECON, TAX inflation fiscale *f*

taxi *n* TRANSP taxi *m*; ~ **charge** TRANSP frais de taxi *m pl*; ~ **rank** BrE, ~ **stand** AmE TRANSP station de taxis *f*

taxing: ~ **capacity** *n* ECON, TAX capacité d'imposition *f*, faculté contributive *f*

taxiplane *n* US TRANSP avion-taxi *m*

taxiway *n* TRANSP piste de roulement *f*, taxiway *m*

taxman *n* [pl -men] HRM, TAX contrôleur des droits et taxes *m*, inspecteur des impôts *m*, percepteur *m*

taxmanship *n* TAX connaissance de la fiscalité *f*

taxpayer *n* TAX contribuable *mf*, déclarant *m*

Taylorism *n* ECON UK, HRM taylorisme *m*

Tbilisi *pr n* GEN COMM Tbilissi *n pr*

T-bill *n* BANK bon du Trésor à court terme *m*, bons du Trésor *m pl*, valeurs du Trésor *f pl*, ECON US *(Treasury bill)* bon du Trésor à court terme *m*, ECON US *(Treasury bill bonds)* STOCK US *(Treasury bill bonds)* bons du Trésor *m pl*, valeurs du Trésor *f pl*; ~ **futures** FIN, STOCK contrat à terme de bons du Trésor *m*; ~ **futures contract** FIN, STOCK contrat à terme de bons du Trésor *m*

TBN *abbr (total base number)* ENVIR indice de base total *m*

T-bond *n (Treasury bond)* ECON, STOCK bon du Trésor à long terme *m*, obligation du Trésor *f*

TBR *abbr (Treasury bill rate)* ECON, STOCK taux de bons du Trésor *m*

T/C *abbr* GEN COMM *(until countermanded)* jusqu'à nouvel ordre *loc*, TRANSP *(time charter)* affrètement à temps *m*

TCDC *abbr (technical cooperation amongst developing countries)* ECON, POL coopération technique entre pays en voie de développement *f*

TDA *abbr (transport distribution analysis)* TRANSP analyse de la distribution de transport *f*

TDB *abbr (Trade Development Board)* ECON *international* conseil du développement commercial *m*

TDC *abbr (top dead center AmE, top dead centre BrE)* TRANSP PMH *(point mort haut)*

TDED *abbr (Trade Data Elements Directory)* ECON *international* annuaire de données commerciales de base *m*

TDI *abbr (Trade Data Interchange)* ECON *international* échange d'informations commerciales *m*

TDP *abbr* ECON *(tradable discharge permit)*, ENVIR *(tradable discharge permit)* autorisation de décharge négociable *f*, autorisation négociable de décharge de polluants *f*

TDW *abbr (tons deadweight)* TRANSP TPL *(Tonne Port en Lourd)*

TE *abbr (triple-expansion)* TRANSP à triple expansion

tea: ~ **-importing company** *n* IMP/EXP compagnie importatrice de thé *f*

teach: ~ **-in** *n* HRM mise au courant *f*

teaching: ~ **company** *n* WEL organisme privé de formation *m*; ~ **machine** *n* WEL machine à enseigner *f*

teak: ~ **-sheathed deck** *n* TRANSP *shipping* pont doublé de teck *m*

team *n* HRM, MGMNT équipe *f*; ~ **briefing** ECON, MGMNT briefing d'équipe *m*; ~ **building** COMP, HRM, MGMNT développement d'équipe *m*, motivation d'équipe *f*; ~ **leader** HRM, MGMNT chef d'équipe *m*; ~ **player** HRM, MGMNT équipier *m*; ~ **spirit** HRM, MGMNT esprit d'équipe *m*; ~ **theory** ECON théorie des équipes *f*

teamster *n AmE (cf lorry driver BrE, truck driver, trucker)* TRANSP camionneur *m*, chauffeur de camion *m*, conducteur de camion *m*, routier *m*

Teamsters: **the** ~ *n pl US* HRM *union* les routiers *m pl*

teamwork *n* HRM, MGMNT travail d'équipe *m*

tear:[1] ~ **-proof** *adj* TRANSP indéchirable

tear:[2] ~ **-off calendar** *n* GEN COMM calendrier détachable *m*; ~ **-off coupon** *n* GEN COMM bulletin de commande détachable *m*; ~ **-off portion** *n* BANK *of cheque book,* GEN COMM volant *m*; ~ **strip** *n* GEN COMM bande à arracher *f*

teaser: ~ **ad** *n* S&M annonce à énigme *f*, publicité mystère *f*; ~ **campaign** *n* S&M *advertising* campagne teasing *f*; ~ **rate** *n* FIN taux mystère *m*

TEC *abbr UK (Training and Enterprise Council)* HRM programmes de formation en entreprises

TECH: ~ **cargo** *n (toxic, explosive, corrosive, hazardous cargo)* TRANSP *dangerous classified cargo* cargaison TECH *f (cargaison toxique, explosive, corrosive, hasardeuse)*

technical[1] *adj* GEN COMM, IND technique

technical:[2] ~ **analysis** *n* STOCK analyse technique *f*; ~ **assistance** *n* ECON, POL assistance technique *f*; ~ **assistance loan** *n (TAL)* FIN prêt d'assistance technique *m*; ~ **assistant** *n* HRM tech., technicien *m*; ~ **barrier to trade** *n* ECON entrave technique au commerce *f*; ~ **cooperation** *n* ECON, GEN COMM, POL collaboration technique *f*; ~ **cooperation amongst developing countries** *n (TCDC)* ECON, POL coopération technique entre pays en voie de développement *f*; ~ **data** *n pl* GEN COMM données techniques *f pl*; ~ **director** *n* COMP, HRM, MGMNT directeur technique *m*; ~ **efficiency** *n* ECON, IND efficacité technique *f*; ~ **field** *n* PATENTS domaine technique *m*; ~ **help to exporters** *n (THE)* IMP/EXP assistance technique aux exportateurs *f*; ~ **hitch** *n* GEN COMM incident technique *m*; ~ **manager** *n* COMP, HRM, MGMNT directeur technique *m*; ~ **market** *n* STOCK marché artificiellement soutenu *m*, marché technique *m*; ~ **mastery** *n* GEN COMM maîtrise technique *f*; ~ **point** *n* LAW question de procédure *f*, vice de

forme *m*; ~ **policy** *n* ECON politique d'entreprise *f*, politique en matière de technique *f*; ~ **profile** *n* GEN COMM profil technique *m*; ~ **progress** *n* ECON, IND progrès technique *m*; ~ **rally** *n* STOCK reprise technique *f*; ~ **salesman** *n* [pl -men] MGMNT technico-commercial *m*; ~ **saleswoman** *n* [pl -men] MGMNT technico-commerciale *f*; ~ **sign** *n* STOCK indication technique *f*, signal technique *m*; ~ **standards** *n pl* IND *of product safety* normes techniques *f pl*; ~ **support** *n* COMP, IND *for developing countries* assistance technique *f*, support technique *m*; ~ **trespass** *n jarg US* POL violation technique *f*

technicality *n* GEN COMM détail technique *m*, LAW question de procédure *f*, vice de forme *m*

technocratic *adj* GEN COMM, POL technocratique

technological: ~ **change** *n* GEN COMM, IND changement technologique *m*; ~ **edge** *n* GEN COMM, IND avance technologique *f*; ~ **forecast** *n* GEN COMM, IND prévision technologique *f*; ~ **forecasting** *n* GEN COMM, IND prévision technologique *f*; ~ **gap** *n* GEN COMM, IND retard technologique *m*; ~ **innovation** *n* GEN COMM, IND innovation technologique *f*; ~ **obsolescence** *n* GEN COMM, IND *production* vieillissement technologique *m*; ~ **rent** *n* ECON rente technologique *f*; ~ **transfer** *n* GEN COMM, IND transfert technologique *m*

technologically: ~ **advanced** *adj* GEN COMM, IND à l'avant-garde technologique *loc f*

technology *n* COMP, ECON, GEN COMM, IND technologie *f*; ~ **-and-market interface** GEN COMM, S&M interface technologie-marché *f*; ~ **-based industry** IND industrie technologique *f*; ~ **cooperation** GEN COMM, IND coopération technologique *f*; ~ **park** IND parc technologique *m*, péripole technologique *m*; ~ **transfer** COMMS, COMP, ECON, GEN COMM, IND transfert de technologie *m*, transfert technologique *m*

TED: ~ **spread** *n* STOCK *futures* spread achat de contrats à terme sur bons de Trésor et vente de contrats à terme sur Eurodollars, spread TED *m*

teenage: ~ **market** *n* S&M marché ciblé sur les jeunes *m*

TEFRA *abbr (tax equity and fiscal responsibility act of 1982)* TAX loi de 1982 sur l'équité des impôts et de la responsabilité fiscale

Tegucigalpa *pr n* GEN COMM Tegucigalpa *n pr*

Teheran *n (SYN Tehran)* GEN COMM Téhéran *n pr*

Tehran *n (SYN Teheran)* GEN COMM Téhéran *n pr*

tel. *abbr (telephone)* COMMS tél. *(téléphone)*; ~ **add.** *(telephone address)* COMMS adresse téléphonique *f*; ~ **no.** *abbr (phone number, telephone number)* COMMS n° tél. *(numéro de téléphone)*

telco *n infrml AmE (telephone company)* COMMS compagnie de téléphone *f*

telebanking *n* BANK opérations bancaires à distance *f pl*

telecommunicate *vt* COMMS télécommuniquer

telecommunication: ~ **network** *n* COMMS réseau de télécommunications *m*

telecommunications *n pl* COMMS télécommunications *f pl*

telecommuting *n* ECON travail à domicile par réseau informatique *m*, télétravail *m*

teleconference *n* COMP, S&M téléconférence *f*

telegraph: ~ **money order** *n* (*TMO*) BANK mandat postal télégraphique *m*, FIN mandat postal télégraphe *m*, mandat postal télégraphique *m*; ~ **pole** *n* COMMS poteau télégraphique *m*

telegraphic: ~ **address** *n* (*TA*) COMMS adresse télégraphique *f* (*adr. tél.*); ~ **money order** *n* (*TMO*) BANK mandat postal télégraphique *m*, FIN mandat postal télégraphe *m*, mandat postal télégraphique *m*; ~ **office** *n* (*TO*) COMMS bureau télégraphique *m*, service télégraphique *m*; ~ **transfer** *n* (*TT*) BANK, COMMS transfert télégraphique *m*, virement télégraphique *m*

telemarket *n* FIN, S&M télémarché *m*

telemarketing *n* FIN, S&M marketing téléphonique *m*, télémarketing *m*

telematics *n* [+sing v] COMMS, COMP, GEN COMM télématique *f*

telemessage *n* (*TMESS*) COMMS télémessage *m*

teleordering *n* COMP, S&M système de réapprovisionnement géré par ordinateur

telephone¹ *n* (*tel.*) COMMS appareil *m*, téléphone *m*; ~ **address** (*tel. add.*) COMMS adresse téléphonique *f*; ~ **bill** COMMS note de téléphone *f*; ~ **book** COMMS Bottin® *m* (*France*), annuaire téléphonique *m*; ~ **booking** LEIS *theatre* location par téléphone *f*; ~ **booth** *AmE* (*cf call box BrE*) COMMS cabine téléphonique *f*; ~ **call** COMMS appel téléphonique *m*, communication téléphonique *f*; ~ **company** (*telco*) COMMS compagnie de téléphone *f*; ~ **directory** COMMS Bottin® *m* (*France*), annuaire téléphonique *m*; ~ **exchange** COMMS centrale téléphonique *f*; ~ **extension** (*X*) COMMS poste *m*; ~ **interviewing** S&M *research* interview par téléphone *f*; ~ **message** COMMS message téléphonique *m*; ~ **number** (*tel. no.*) COMMS numéro de téléphone *m* (*n° tél.*); ~ **operator** COMMS opérateur *m*; ~ **receiver** COMMS récepteur téléphonique *m*; ~ **sales** FIN, S&M vente par téléphone *f*; ~ **selling** FIN, S&M vente par téléphone *f*; ~ **subscriber** COMMS abonné au téléphone *m*; ~ **tapping** COMMS mise sur écoute téléphonique *f*

telephone² *vt* COMMS téléphoner à

telephonic *adj* COMMS téléphonique

telephony *n* COMMS téléphonie *f*

teleprinter *n BrE* (*cf teletypewriter AmE*) ADMIN, COMP téléimprimeur *m*, téléscripteur *m*

teleprocessing *n* COMP télétraitement *m*

telerecording *n* COMMS téléenregistrement *m*

telesales *n pl* FIN, S&M télévente *f*, vente par téléphone *f*; ~ **person** *n* FIN, S&M télévendeur *m*

teleselling *n* FIN, S&M télévente *f*, vente par téléphone *f*

teleshopping *n* FIN, S&M téléachat *m*

telesoftware *n* (*tsw*) COMP logiciel de télétexte *m*, télélogiciel *m*

teletex® *n* COMMS Télétex® *m*, vidéographie diffusée *f*

Teletex: ~ **Output of Price Information by Computer** *n UK* (*TOPIC*) STOCK ≈ informations boursières par MINITEL *f pl*

teletext® *n UK* COMP, MEDIA télétexte *m*, vidéographie interactive *f*, vidéotex diffusé *m*, vidéotex® *m*, vidéotext diffusé *m*

Teletype® *n* COMP Télétype® *m*

teletypewriter *n AmE* (*cf teleprinter BrE*) ADMIN, COMP téléimprimeur *m*, téléscripteur *m*

televiewer *n* MEDIA téléspectateur *m*

televise *vt* COMMS, MEDIA téléviser

television *n* (*TV, telly*) COMMS, GEN COMM, MEDIA télévision *f* (*télé*); ~ **advertising** COMMS, MEDIA, S&M publicité télévisée *f*; ~ **broadcast** MEDIA émission de télévision *f*; ~ **channel** MEDIA *broadcast* chaîne de télévision *f*; ~ **commercial** MEDIA, S&M message publicitaire télévisé *m*; ~ **consumer audit** MEDIA, S&M sondage auprès d'un échantillon de téléspectateurs; ~ **journalist** MEDIA journaliste de télévision *m*; ~ **licence** *UK* LAW, MEDIA redevance de télévision *f*; ~ **network** COMMS réseau de télévision *m*; ~ **program** *AmE*, ~ **programme** *BrE* MEDIA émission de télévision *f*; ~ **screen** MEDIA écran de télévision *m*; ~ **support** COMMS, MEDIA support TV *m*

televisual *adj* COMMS, MEDIA télévisuel

telework *n* ECON, HRM télétravail *m*

teleworker *n* ECON, HRM télétravailleur *m*

teleworking *n* ECON, HRM télétravail *m*

telewriting *n* ADMIN téléautographie *f*

telex *n* (*tx.*) COMMS télex *m*

tell: ~ **sb sth in confidence** *phr* GEN COMM confier qch à qn

teller *n* BANK caissier *m*, guichetier *m*; ~'**s shortage** BANK déficit de caisse *m*

telly *n infrml BrE* (*television*) COMMS, GEN COMM, MEDIA télé (*infrml*) (*télévision*)

temp *n infrml* (*temporary*) HRM intérimaire *mf*

temperature *n* ENVIR, TRANSP température *f*; ~ **-controlled transport** IMP/EXP, TRANSP transport thermorégulé *m*, transport à température contrôlée *m*

temping *n* HRM intérim *m* (*infrml*); ~ **agency** HRM société d'intérim *f*

template *n* COMP, GEN COMM, IND *design* calibre *m*, gabarit *m*, gabarit de surface *m*

temporal: ~ **method** *n* ACC *of currency translation* méthode temporelle *f*

temporarily *adv* GEN COMM temporairement

temporary¹ *adj* GEN COMM provisoire, temporaire

temporary² *n* (*temp*) HRM intérimaire *mf*; ~ **employment** HRM emploi intérimaire *m*, emploi temporaire *m*; ~ **equilibrium** ECON équilibre temporaire *m*; ~ **importation** IMP/EXP importation temporaire *f*; ~ **job** HRM emploi intérimaire *m*, emploi temporaire *m*; ~ **residence** ADMIN, LAW, TAX résidence temporaire *f*; ~ **residence permit** ADMIN, LAW, TAX permis de séjour limité *m*; ~ **residence visa** ADMIN, LAW, TAX permis de séjour limité *m*; ~ **resident** ADMIN, LAW, TAX résident temporaire *m*; ~ **secretary** HRM dactylo intérimaire *f*, secrétaire par intérim *m*; ~ **status** LAW statut temporaire *m*; ~ **work** HRM travail temporaire *m*; ~ **worker** HRM intérimaire *mf*

ten: ~ **-dollar bill** *n* US FIN billet de dix dollars *m*; ~ **dollars** *n (cf eagle US)* FIN aigle *m*, pièce de dix dollars *f*; ~ **-pound note** *n* UK *(cf tenner)* FIN billet de dix livres *m*

tenancy *n* PROP *apartment, flat* location *f*; ~ **at will** LAW, PROP bail implicite *m*, location à durée indéterminée *f*; ~ **by the entirety** LAW, PROP location intégrale *f*; ~ **in common** LAW, PROP location en commun *f*; ~ **in severalty** LAW, PROP copropriété non-solidaire *f*, propriété indivise *f*; ~ **period** FIN, PROP période de location *f*

tenant *n* PROP locataire *mf*; ~ **farmer** ECON métayer *m*; ~'s **repair** WEL réparation locative *f*; ~'s **right** UK LAW, PROP *land compensation* droit du locataire *m*, droit du tenancier *m*

tend 1. *vt* GEN COMM servir; **2.** *vi* GEN COMM *in direction* tendre; ~ **to** GEN COMM avoir tendance à *loc f*, tendre à, tendre vers; ~ **towards** GEN COMM tendre vers, tendre à

tendency *n* GEN COMM disposition *f*, tendance *f*

tender[1] *n* ECON offre d'achat *f*, GEN COMM *buying* livraison à terme *f*, offre *f*, présentation *f*, soumission *f*, STOCK offre d'achat *f*, TRANSP *supply boat* ravitailleur *m*; ~ **bond** *n* FIN, STOCK obligation prouvant les bonnes intentions de l'acheteur; ~ **documents** *n pl* FIN, STOCK enchère *f*; ~ **offer** *n* STOCK offre d'achat *f*; ~ **panel** *n* FIN syndicat d'enchères *m*; ~ **price** *n* GEN COMM montant de l'adjudication *m*; ~ **to contract** *n* *(TTC)* GEN COMM soumission d'offre *f*; ~ **to contract cover** *n* INS *company* soumission de couverture de contrat *f*; ~ **vehicle** *n* TRANSP *supply, auxiliary* véhicule ravitailleur *m*; ♦ ~ **by private contract** LAW adjudication de gré à gré *f*

tender[2] **1.** *vt* GEN COMM faire une soumission, soumissionner, STOCK livrer, livrer à terme; **2.** *vi* ~ **for** GEN COMM soumissionner, MGMNT *contract* faire une offre pour; ~ **notice** STOCK lever une option; ♦ ~ **money in discharge of debt** LAW faire une offre d'argent pour régler une dette

tendering *n* ECON, GEN COMM, MGMNT offre *f*

tenement *n* PROP immeuble *m*

Ten-Forty *n* US ECON déclaration d'impôt sur le revenu *f*

10K: ~ **report** *n* US ACC formulaire officiel annuel que les compagnies américaines doivent remplir pour la Commission des opérations de Bourse

tenner *n* *infrml* UK *(cf ten-pound note)* FIN billet de dix livres *m*

Tennessee: ~ **Valley Authority** *n (TVA)* ECON agence fédérale de la vallée du Tennessee

tenor *n* FIN échéance *f*, LAW *words of deed* teneur *f*; ~ **bill** FIN effet à usance *m*

tentative: ~ **agenda** *n* GEN COMM ordre du jour provisoire *m*; ~ **estimate** *n* GEN COMM estimation approximative *f*, estimation au jugé *f*, estimation au pifomètre *f* *(infrml)*; ~ **plan** *n* GEN COMM avant-projet *m*

tenure *n* HRM *position* occupation *f*, LAW bail *m*, POL *position* occupation *f*, PROP bail *m*; ~ **in land** LAW, PROP période de jouissance foncière *f*

tenured: ~ **staff** *n* HRM personnel titulaire *m*

term *n* BANK *of loan* période *f*, terme *m*, *time* délai *m*, terme *m*, échéance *f*, COMMS terme *m*, LAW *stipulation* condition *f*, POL *of treaty, government, office* durée *f*; ~ **certificate** FIN certificat pour une période déterminée *m*; ~ **day** FIN, GEN COMM jour du terme *m*; ~ **deposit** BANK dépôt à terme *m*, dépôt à terme fixe *m*, dépôt à échéance fixe *m*; ~ **draft** BANK, FIN, STOCK lettre de change *f*; ~ **insurance** INS assurance temporaire *f*; ~ **insurance policy** INS police d'assurance temporaire *f*; ~ **life insurance** INS assurance-vie temporaire *f*; ~ **of limitation** GEN COMM délai de prescription *m*; ~ **loan** BANK prêt à terme *m*; ~ **of office** GEN COMM période pendant laquelle on exerce une fonction; ~ **of patent** PATENTS durée du brevet *f*; ~ **of payment** BANK délai de paiement *m*, terme d'échéance *m*; ~ **policy** BANK, INS police à terme *f*; ~ **premium** ECON prime de terme *f*; ~ **purchase** GEN COMM achat à crédit *m*; ~ **sale** GEN COMM vente à crédit *f*; ~ **structure of interest rates** ECON structure temporelle des taux d'intérêts *f*; ~ **to maturity** STOCK durée *f*, durée d'échéance *f*

terminable *adj* GEN COMM résiliable, *annuity* résiliable, INS résiliable

terminal *n* COMP poste de travail *m*, terminal *m*, TRANSP terminal *m*; ~ **bonus** *n* ECON, FIN, INS bonus réversible *m*, prime de fin de contrat *f*; ~ **charges** *n pl* FIN taxes terminales *f pl*; ~ **computer** *n* COMP ordinateur satellite *m*; ~ **emulator** *n* COMP émulateur de terminal *m*; ~ **loss** *n* ACC perte finale *f*; ~ **manager** *n* MGMNT, TRANSP directeur de terminal *m*; ~ **market** *n* STOCK marché à terme *m*; ~ **operator** *n* COMP opérateur de terminal *m*; ~ **price** *n* STOCK cours du livrable *m*, prix à terme *m*; ~ **screen** *n* COMP écran de terminal *m*; ~ **throughput** *n* TRANSP débit du terminal *m*; ~ **traffic** *n* TRANSP trafic de terminal *m*

terminate *vt* FIN *fund* discontinuer, GEN COMM, HRM, INS, LAW *contract* résilier; ♦ ~ **one's appointment** HRM donner sa démission, quitter son travail; ~ **sb's appointment** HRM licencier qn; ~ **sb's employment** HRM licencier qn

termination *n* GEN COMM cessation *f*, HRM *of employment* cessation *f*, licenciement *m*, résiliation *f*, INS *policy*, LAW *of contract* résiliation *f*; ~ **benefits** *n pl* HRM indemnités de départ *f pl*; ~ **of business** *n* GEN COMM cessation d'activité *f*;

~ clause *n* LAW clause de résiliation *f*, clause résolutoire *f*; **~ of employment with notice** *n* HRM cessation de fonctions avec préavis *f*; **~ papers** *n pl* HRM avis de licenciement *m*; **~ payments** *n pl* HRM, TAX, WEL *on retirement* paiements de terminaison *m pl*; **~ of tenancy** *n* PROP expiration du bail *f*, résiliation d'un contrat de location *f*

terminology *n* COMMS, COMP, GEN COMM terminologie *f*

terms *n pl* BANK modalités *f pl*, GEN COMM libellé *m*, termes *m pl*, LAW *of agreement* termes *m pl*, *of contract* conditions *f pl*; **~ and conditions** FIN *of payment* modalités de paiement *f pl*, GEN COMM *of arrangement* modalités *f pl*, INS *of policy* termes et conditions *m pl*, STOCK *of issue* modalités *f pl*; **~ and conditions of employment** HRM clauses et conditions d'emploi *f pl*; **~ of credit** BANK, ECON, FIN, S&M conditions de crédit *f pl*; **~ of export sale** IMP/EXP conditions de vente à l'exportation *f pl*; **~ of payment** BANK conditions de paiement *f pl*, modalités de paiement *f pl*; **~ of reference** GEN COMM *of committee* mandat *m*; **~ of sale** ECON, GEN COMM, IMP/EXP, S&M conditions de vente *f pl*; **~ of shipment** IMP/EXP, TRANSP conditions d'envoi *f pl*; **~ of tender** GEN COMM conditions de l'offre *f pl*, conditions de soumission *f pl*; **~ of trade** ECON termes de l'échange *m pl*; ◆ **come to ~** GEN COMM arriver à un accord, parvenir à un accord; **in ~ of** GEN COMM en fonction de, sous l'angle de; **not on any ~** GEN COMM sous aucune condition; **under the ~ of the contract** LAW aux termes du contrat, selon les termes du contrat

terrestrial *adj* COMMS *broadcasting* terrestre

territorial: **~ waters** *n pl* LAW, POL, TRANSP eaux territoriales *f pl*

territory *n* GEN COMM, POL, S&M *of salesperson* territoire *m*; **~ manager** HRM, MGMNT, S&M chef de région *m*

terrorism *n* POL terrorisme *m*

tertiary: **~ activities** *n pl* (ANT *primary activities, secondary activities*) ECON, GEN COMM, IND activités du secteur tertiaire *f pl*, services tertiaires *m pl*; **~ education** *n* WEL enseignement supérieur *m*; **~ product** *n* ECON produit tertiaire *m*, IND produit de base *m*, produit tertiaire *m*, S&M produit tertiaire *m*; **~ products** *n pl* ECON produits de services *m pl*; **~ sector** *n* ECON secteur tertiaire *m*

TESSA *abbr* UK (*tax-exempt special savings account*) BANK, ECON, TAX compte spécial d'épargne exonéré d'impôts *m*

test[1] *n* COMP essai *m*, test *m*, GEN COMM essai *m*, HRM *eyes, ears* examen *m*, IND *of quality* contrôle *m*, *of system, machine* essai *m*, S&M essai *m*, test *m*, WEL *eyes, ears* examen *m*; **~ area** S&M zone test *f*; **~ audit** ACC, GEN COMM contrôle par sondages *m*, vérification par sondages *f*; **~ bench** GEN COMM banc d'essai *m*; **~ card** COMMS, MEDIA *television* mire *f*; **~ drive** TRANSP course d'essai *f*, marche d'essai *f*, trajet d'essai *m*, TRANSP (SYN *test run, trial run*) essai sur route *m*; **~ equipment** COMP équipement pour tests *m*; **~ mailing** S&M *advertising* publipostage-test *m*; **~ marketing** S&M test de marché *m*, tests de marché *m pl*; **~ problem** GEN COMM problème test *m*; **~ rate of discount** ECON taux d'escompte attendu *m*; **~ run** IND *of system, machine* essai *m*, TRANSP essai sur route *m*; **~ statistic** ECON statistique-test *m*, MATH test statistique *m*; **~ town** GEN COMM ville test *f*; **~ transit** TRANSP *distribution* essai de transport *m*

test[2] *vt* COMP, GEN COMM essayer, tester, S&M essayer; **~ drive** TRANSP *car* essayer; **~ out** GEN COMM mettre à l'essai

testamentary[1] *adj* LAW testamentaire

testamentary:[2] **~ debt** *n* LAW, TAX dette testamentaire *f*; **~ trust** *n* LAW fidéicommis institué par testament *m*

testate *adj* LAW testé

testbed *n* GEN COMM banc d'essai *m*

testdeck *n* COMP jeu d'essai *m*

testee *n* GEN COMM personne ou objet qui subit un test

testify *vi* LAW témoigner

testimonial *n* HRM référence *f*; **~ advertisement** S&M testimonial *m*; ◆ **have excellent ~s** HRM avoir d'excellentes références

testimony *n* LAW témoignage *m*

testing *n* GEN COMM essai *m*, HRM *skills* évaluation *f*, IND, S&M *product, machine* essai *m*; **~ plant** IND usine d'essai *f*; **~ procedure** IND procédure d'essai *f*

Tetra Pack® *n* S&M Tetra Pack® *m*

TEU *abbr* (*twenty foot equivalent unit*) TRANSP équivalent d'un conteneur de vingt pieds, EVP (*équivalent vingt pieds*)

text *n* MEDIA texte *m*; **~ editing** COMP, MEDIA édition de texte *f*; **~ editor** COMP, MEDIA éditeur de texte *m*; **~ in full** GEN COMM texte intégral *m*; **~ mode** COMP mode texte *m*; **~ processing** ADMIN, COMP traitement de texte *m*

textbook *n* MEDIA manuel *m*; **~ case** GEN COMM exemple modèle *m*, exemple typique *m*; **~ operation** GEN COMM opération menée dans les règles de l'art *f*

textile: **~ bag** *n* TRANSP sac textile *m*; **~ bag-paper lined** *n* TRANSP sac textile doublé kraft *m*; **~ industry** *n* IND industrie textile *f*; **~ waste-wet** *n* TRANSP *dangerous cargo* déchets textiles liquides *m pl*

textiles *n pl* IND textiles *m pl*

TF *abbr* (*tropical fresh water load line*) TRANSP TD (*ligne de charge tropicale en eau douce*)

TFR *abbr* ECON (*total fertility rate*) taux global de fertilité *m*, TRANSP (*transfer*) TFR (*transfert*)

T-group: **~ training** *n* HRM *T=training* groupe de diagnostic *m*

TGWU *abbr* UK (*Transport and General Workers' Union*) HRM, IND syndicat des transports et des travailleurs confédérés *m*

Thai[1] *adj* GEN COMM thaïlandais

Thai[2] *n* GEN COMM *language* thaï *m, person* Thaïlandais *m*

Thailand *pr n* GEN COMM Thaïlande *f*

Thamphu *pr n* GEN COMM Thimbu *n pr*

thank: ~ -**you letter** *n* COMMS, GEN COMM lettre de remerciement *f*; ◆ ~ **you for your letter** COMMS merci de votre lettre

thanking: ~ **you in advance** *phr* COMMS en vous remerciant d'avance, en vous remerciant par avance; ~ **you in anticipation** *phr* COMMS en vous remerciant d'avance, en vous remerciant par avance

thanks: ~ **for your letter** *phr infrml* COMMS merci de votre lettre

Thatcherism *n UK* ECON, POL Thatchérisme *m*

THE *abbr (technical help to exporters)* IMP/EXP assistance technique aux exportateurs *f*

theater *n AmE see* theatre *BrE*

theatre *n BrE* LEIS, MEDIA théâtre *m*; ~ **critic** *BrE* LEIS, MEDIA critique de théâtre *m*

theft:[1] ~ -**proof** *adj* GEN COMM inviolable

theft[2] *n* LAW vol *m*; ~ **risk** INS risque de vol *m*

theme: ~ **park** *n* LEIS parc d'attractions *m*, parc à thème *m*; ~ **tune** *n* MEDIA *broadcast* indicatif musical *m*, refrain *m*, thème musical *m*

theonomy *n* ECON théonomie *f*

theoretical[1] *adj* GEN COMM théorique

theoretical:[2] ~ **capacity** *n* GEN COMM, IND capacité théorique *f*; ~ **income** *n* ECON revenu théorique *m*

theory *n* GEN COMM théorie *f*; ~ **of clubs** ECON théorie des clubs *f*; ~ **of comparative costs** ECON théorie des coûts comparatifs *f*; ~ **of the firm** ECON théorie de l'entreprise *f*; ~ **X** *jarg* HRM théorie X *f*; ~ **Y** *jarg* HRM théorie Y *f*; ~ **Z** *jarg* HRM théorie Z *f*; ◆ **in** ~ GEN COMM en principe

thermal: ~ **container** *n* TRANSP conteneur thermique *m*; ~ **energy** *n* ENVIR, IND énergie thermique *f*; ~ **power station** *n* ENVIR centrale thermique *f*, IND centrale thermique *f*, usine thermique *f*; ~ **reactor** *n* IND réacteur thermique *m*

thermostatic: ~ **fan** *n* IND ventilateur thermostatique *m*

thief *n* LAW voleur *m*

thin: ~ **capitalization** *n* ACC, TAX capitalisation minimale *f*; ~ **market** *n (SYN narrow market)* STOCK marché étroit *m*

think:[1] ~ -**tank** *n* GEN COMM cellule de réflexion *f*, groupe de réflexion *m*

think[2] *vt* GEN COMM penser; ◆ ~ **the unthinkable** GEN COMM concevoir l'inconcevable

thinking *n* GEN COMM *reasoning* façon de penser *f*

third:[1] ~ -**class** *adj* TRANSP *accommodation* de troisième classe; ~ -**rate** *adj* GEN COMM de troisième ordre

third:[2] ~ **age** *n* ECON troisième âge *m*; ~ **carrier** *n* TRANSP *air distribution* troisième transporteur *m*; ~ -**class** *n* TRANSP troisième classe *f*; ~ -**class degree** *n UK* WEL *education* licence sans mention *f*; ~ -**class mail** *n US* COMMS courrier à tarif très

réduit, tarif lent *m*; ~ -**class matter** *n AmE (cf printed matter BrE)* GEN COMM *postal service* imprimés *m pl*; ~ **country** *n* ECON *international trade* pays tiers *m*; ~ **country cooperation** *n* ECON *international trade* coopération avec un pays tiers *f*; ~ **currency** *n* GEN COMM troisième devise *f*, troisième monnaie *f*; ~ -**degree price discrimination** *n* GEN COMM discrimination par les prix *f*, pratique de discrimination par les prix *f*, prix discriminatoires *m pl*; ~ **flag carrier** *n* TRANSP *shipping* navire sous pavillon tiers *m*; ~ **force** *n jarg* POL troisième bloc *m*; ~ -**generation computer** *n* COMP ordinateur de troisième génération *m*; ~ **party** *n (TP)* INS, LAW, PATENTS tierce personne *f*, tiers *m*; ~ -**party check** *n US* BANK vérification par un tiers *f*; ~ -**party claim** *n* INS, LAW recours des tiers *m*, revendication d'un tiers *f*, réclamation d'un tiers *f*, réclamation faite par un tiers *f*; ~ -**party credibility** *n jarg* S&M *public relations* crédibilité au tiers *f*; ~ -**party currency** *n* IMP/EXP devise de pays tiers *f*; ~ -**party effect** *n (SYN spillover effect)* ECON effet d'entraînement *m*, effet de retombées *m*; ~ -**party fire and theft** *n* INS assurance responsabilité civile contre l'incendie et le vol *f*, incendie et vol au tiers *m*; ~ -**party insurance** *n* INS, TRANSP assurance aux tiers *f*; ~ -**party insurance cover** *n BrE (cf third-party insurance coverage AmE)* INS couverture d'assurance tiers *f*; ~ -**party insurance coverage** *n AmE (cf third-party insurance cover BrE)* INS couverture d'assurance tiers *f*; ~ -**party insurance policy** *n* INS police d'assurance tiers *f*; ~ -**party intervention** *n* HRM intervention d'un tiers *f*; ~ -**party liability** *n* LAW responsabilité au tiers *f*; ~ -**party risk** *n* INS risque au tiers *m*, risque de recours au tiers *m*; ~ -**party sale** *n* S&M vente à un tiers *f*; ~ **person** *n* GEN COMM tierce personne *f*, tiers *m*; ~ **quarter** *n (3Q)* GEN COMM troisième trimestre *m*; ~ **way** *n* ECON socialisme autogestionnaire *m*, troisième voie *f*

Third: ~ **Market** *n obs UK* FIN, STOCK aboli en 1990, réorganisé maintenant avec un marché de valeurs non-cotées, Marché en coulisse *m*, troisième marché *m*; **the** ~ **World** *n* GEN COMM le Tiers Monde *m*; ~ **World** *n* ECON, POL *(ANT First World, Fourth World, Second World)* tiers monde *m*; ~ **World country** *n* ECON pays du tiers monde *m*

thirdly *adv* GEN COMM troisièmement

3Q *abbr (third quarter)* GEN COMM troisième trimestre *m*

thirty: ~ -**day visible supply** *n* STOCK transparence à trente jours *f*, émissions prévues à trente jours *f pl*; ~ -**day wash rule** *n US* TAX règle du lessivage à trente jours *f*

Thirty: ~ **Share index** *n* IND, STOCK indice des principales valeurs industrielles *m*

thought: **give serious** ~ **to** *phr* GEN COMM *an issue* bien réfléchir à; **have second** ~**s** *phr* GEN COMM changer d'avis

thousand: ~ **million** *n* BANK, GEN COMM milliard *m*

thrash: ~ **out** *vt* GEN COMM *discuss thoroughly* discuter à fond

threat: ~ **effect** *n* ECON effet menace *m*

three:[1] ~ **-month** *adj* GEN COMM, STOCK à trois mois

three:[2] ~ **-axle vehicle** *n* TRANSP véhicule à trois essieux *m*; ~ **-course rotation** *n* ECON, ENVIR *agricultural* assolement triennal *m*; ~ **-digit industry** *n* ECON industrie à trois chiffres *f*; ~ **-island ship** *n* TRANSP navire type trois îles *m*, navire à trois superstructures *m*; ~ **-martini lunch** *n infrml AmE* TAX repas d'affaires bien arrosé *m*; ~ **-month add-on yield** *n* STOCK rendement positif à trois mois *m*; ~ **-month bond equivalent yield** *n* STOCK rendement équivalent à l'obligation à trois mois *m*; ~ **-month call** *n* STOCK *money repayable* option d'achat à trois mois *f*; ~ **-month discount yield** *n* STOCK rendement négatif à trois mois *m*; ~ **-month Eurodollar time deposit** *n* STOCK dépôt à terme en eurodollars à trois mois *m*; ~ **-month US Treasury bill** *n* STOCK bon du Trésor américain à trois mois; ~ **-months' rate** *n* FIN taux de trois mois *m*; ~ **-piece box** *n* TRANSP caisse à trois compartiments *f*; ~ **-ply organization** *n jarg* GEN COMM organisation tripartite *f*; ~ **quarters** *n pl* MATH trois-quarts *m pl*; ~ **-stage least squares** *n pl* ECON méthode des moindres carrés en trois phases *f*; ~ **-star hotel** *n* GEN COMM, LEIS hôtel trois-étoiles *m*; ~ **-way call** *n* COMMS conférence téléphonique *f*, téléconférence *f*, COMMS *AmE* appel à trois *m*; ~ **-way split** *n* GEN COMM division en trois *f*

threshold *n* COMP, ENVIR seuil *m*, HRM *industrial relations* indexation *f*, TAX seuil *m*; ~ **agreement** HRM accord sur le salaire initial *m*; ~ **amount** TAX montant déterminant *m*; ~ **level** GEN COMM niveau seuil *m*; ~ **point** STOCK seuil *m*; ~ **population** ECON population-seuil *f*; ~ **price** GEN COMM prix de seuil *m*; ~ **rate** *AmE* HRM salaire de départ *m*, salaire initial *m*; ~ **value** COMP valeur de seuil *f*; ~ **worker** *jarg US* HRM travailleur au salaire initial *m*

thrift *n US* ACC, BANK épargne *f*; ~ **institution** *US* BANK banque d'épargne *f*, caisse d'épargne *f*; ~ **shop** *AmE* (*cf second-hand shop BrE*) S&M friperie *f*, magasin de brocante *m*

Thrifts: **the** ~ *n pl infrml US* BANK caisses *f pl*

thrifty *adj* GEN COMM économe

thrive *vi* GEN COMM prospérer, être florissant

thriving *adj* GEN COMM florissant

through:[1] ~ **air waybill** *n* (*TAWB*) IMP/EXP, TRANSP lettre de transport aérien de bout en bout *f*; ~ **bill of lading** *n* IMP/EXP, TRANSP *shipping* connaissement direct *m*; ~ **charge** *n* IMP/EXP, TRANSP tarif de bout en bout *m*, tarif direct *m*, tarif forfaitaire *m*; ~ **fare** *n* TRANSP prix de bout en bout *m*, prix forfaitaire *m*; ~ **rate** *n* IMP/EXP, TRANSP tarif direct *m*, tarif forfaitaire *m*; ~ **route** *n* TRANSP itinéraire direct *m*; ~ **shipment** *n* TRANSP transport de bout à bout *m*; ~ **train** *n* TRANSP train direct *m*;

~ **transport operator** *n* TRANSP transporteur direct *m*; ~ **transport system** *n* TRANSP système de transport direct *m*

through:[2] **be** ~ **to** *phr* COMMS être en communication avec *loc f*, être en ligne avec *loc f*

throughput *n* COMP *processing capacity* capacité de traitement *f*, FIN débit *m*, rendement *m*, IND rythme de production *m*; ~ **charge** *BrE* (*cf pass-through charge AmE*) ADMIN frais de passage *m pl*, frais de traitement *m pl*

throughway *n AmE* (*cf expressway Can, freeway, motorway BrE, superhighway*) TRANSP autoroute *f*

throw: ~ **light on** *vi* GEN COMM *clarify, illuminate* éclairer; ◆ ~ **the book at sb** GEN COMM accabler qn d'accusations, opposer le règlement à qn; ~ **one's money about** *infrml* GEN COMM jeter son argent par les fenêtres (*infrml*); ~ **sb out** *infrml* HRM flanquer qn à la porte (*infrml*); ~ **a wrench into the economy** *infrml* ECON porter un coup très dur à l'économie

thrust: ~ **block** *n* TRANSP *shipping* bloc de butée *m*; ◆ **give an upward** ~ **to interest rates** FIN faire grimper les taux d'intérêts

thruster *n dat* HRM arriviste *mf*, TRANSP propulseur *m*; ~ **-assisted mooring system** (*TAMS*) TRANSP *shipping* système d'amarrage à propulsion *m*

THS: ~ **transaction** *n* STOCK transaction hors séance *f*, THS

thumb: ~ **index** *n* GEN COMM, MEDIA *on reference book* répertoire à onglets *m*

Thurs. *n* (*Thursday*) GEN COMM jeudi *m*

Thursday *n* (*Thurs.*) GEN COMM jeudi *m*

thwartship *adv* TRANSP d'un bord à l'autre du navire *loc m*, en travers de barque

TIBOR *abbr* (*Tokyo Interbank Offered Rate*) ECON TIOT (*taux interbancaire offert à Tokyo*)

TIC *abbr* (*take into consideration*) GEN COMM tenir compte de

tick[1] *n* ACC *BrE* (*cf check AmE*) GEN COMM *BrE* (*cf check AmE*) marque *f*, STOCK tick *m*, écart maximum des cours du marché *m*; ~ **box** *n* COMP case à cocher *f*; ~ **mark** *n BrE* (*cf check mark AmE*) ACC marque de pointage *f*, GEN COMM marque de contrôle *f*; ~ **size** *n infrml* STOCK valeur de pointage *f*, échelon minimal de cotation *m*; ~ **-up** *n* BANK recherche d'erreurs *f*; ◆ **on** ~ *UK* FIN à crédit

tick[2] *vt* GEN COMM *on list* cocher; ~ **off** GEN COMM *on list* cocher; ◆ ~ **the box** *BrE* (*cf check box AmE*), GEN COMM cocher la case

ticker *n* ADMIN *AmE* (*cf tape machine BrE*) COMP *AmE* (*cf tape machine BrE*) téléimprimeur *m*, téléscripteur *m*, STOCK zone de cours *f*; ~ **symbol** STOCK code des valeurs sur téléscripteur *m*, symbole de pointage *m*; ~ **tape** STOCK bande de téléscripteur *f*

ticket *n* LEIS *theatre* billet *m*, POL *US* liste *f*, STOCK fiche *f*, TRANSP billet *m*; ~ **agency** LEIS agence de voyages *f, for theatre, concert* agence de spectacles *f*, TRANSP agence de voyages *f*; ~ **analysis** TRANSP analyse des billets *f*; ~ **collector** TRANSP contrôleur *m*; ~ **day** *UK* (SYN *name day*) STOCK deuxième jour de liquidation *m*, veille de la liquidation *f*; ~ **holder** GEN COMM, LEIS, TRANSP personne munie d'un billet *f*; ~ **office** LEIS guichet des billets *m, theatre* billetterie *f*, guichet *m*, guichet de vente des billets *m*, TRANSP billetterie *f*, guichet *m*, guichet de vente des billets *m*, guichet des billets *m*; ~ **tout** LEIS revendeur de billets *m*

tickler: ~ **file** *n* BANK échéancier *m*

tidal: ~ **dock** *n* TRANSP bassin d'échouage *m*, bassin de marée *m*; ~ **fall** *n* TRANSP marnage *m*; ~ **power** *n* ENVIR, IND énergie marémotrice *f*; ~ **range** *n* TRANSP marnage *m*; ~ **river estuary** *n* TRANSP estuaire à marée *m*; ~ **river navigation** *n* TRANSP navigation en fleuve à marée *f*

tide: ~ **sb over** *phr* BANK *help out* dépanner qn

tie¹ *n* GEN COMM *bond* lien *m*; ~ **-down** TRANSP *shipping* saisissage *m*; ~ **-in advertising** *US* S&M publicité de liaison *f*; ~ **-in display** *US* S&M *advertising* promotion jumelée *f*; ~ **-in promotion** *US* S&M *manufacturer and retailer* promotion concertée *f, two products* promotion jumelée *f*; ~ **-in sale** *US* GEN COMM vente couplée *f*; ~ **-on label** GEN COMM, LEIS étiquette à oeillet *f*

tie² *vt* GEN COMM lier

Tiebout: ~ **hypothesis** *n* (SYN *fiscal mobility*) ECON hypothèse de Tiebout *f*

tied: ~ **aid** *n* (SYN *bilateral aid, multilateral aid*) ECON, POL aide liée *f*; ~ **cottage** *n* *UK* PROP logement de fonction *m*; ~ **house** *n* *UK* ECON débit de boissons lié à une brasserie *m*, PROP logement de fonction *m*; ~ **loan** *n* BANK, ECON *from one country to another* emprunt lié *m*, prêt lié *m*; ~ **-up capital** *n* ACC capital immobilisé *m*; ◆ **to be ~ to doing sth** GEN COMM, LAW être dans l'obligation de faire qch

tier *n* LEIS *theatre* gradin *m*

Tier: ~ **One assets** *n pl* STOCK *sterling assets* classe d'actifs plus liquides *f*; ~ **Two assets** *n pl* STOCK *sterling assets* classe d'actifs moins liquides *f*

tiger: ~ **team** *n jarg* *US* POL équipe d'experts *f*

tight: ~ **budget** *n* FIN budget serré *m*; ~ **controls** *n pl* LAW contrôles stricts *m pl*, contrôles sévères *m pl*, inspections renforcées *f pl*, réglementation stricte *f*; ~ **fiscal policy** *n* ECON politique de resserrement des dépenses *f*, TAX politique de resserrement budgétaire *f*, politique fiscale serrée *f*, politique fiscale restrictive *f*; ~ **market** *n* STOCK marché serré *m*, marché étroit *m*; ~ **monetary policy** *n* ECON politique d'encadrement du crédit *f*, politique de l'argent cher *f*, politique monétaire restrictive *f*; ~ **ship** *n infrml* GEN COMM, MGMNT organisation serrée *f*

tighten *vt* ECON *credit controls*, GEN COMM resserrer; ~ **up** LAW renforcer, resserrer; ◆ ~ **the monetary reins** ECON tenir la bride serrée de la

politique monétaire; ~ **the purse strings** FIN resserrer les cordons de la bourse

TIGR *abbr* (*Treasury Investment Growth Receipt*) STOCK certificat de croissance des investissements du Trésor *m*

till *n* GEN COMM, S&M caisse *f*; ~ **money** BANK, ECON encaisse *f*; ~ **receipt** BANK reçu de caisse *m*

tilt¹ *n* TRANSP bâche *f*; ~ **trailer** TRANSP *road* remorque à benne basculante *f*

tilt:² ~ **the balance** *phr* GEN COMM faire pencher la balance *loc f*

timber: ~ **ship** *n* TRANSP grumier *m*

time:¹ ~ **-barred** *adj* LAW prescrit; ~ **-consuming** *adj* GEN COMM, MGMNT qui prend beaucoup de temps *loc m*; ~ **-saving** *adj* COMP, GEN COMM *device, procedure* qui fait gagner du temps; ~ **-served** *adj* HRM rendu au terme de son temps d'apprentissage

time² *n* GEN COMM h, heure *f*, temps *m*, LAW temps *m*, TRANSP heure *f*; ~ **after sight** *n* GEN COMM délai de vue *m*; ~ **agreement** *n* TRANSP *shipping* contrat à durée déterminée *m*, CDD; ~ **arbitrage** *n* GEN COMM arbitrage dans le temps *m*; ~ **band** *n* MEDIA, TRANSP plage horaire *f*, tranche horaire *f*; ~ **bar** *n* LAW prescription *f*; ~ **bargain** *n* STOCK marché à terme *m*; ~ **bill** *n* BANK échéance à terme *f*; ~ **book** *n* HRM registre de pointage *m*; ~ **budget survey** *n* ECON, HRM enquête sur les occupations journalières *f*; ~ **buyer** *n* (ANT *time seller*) MEDIA, S&M *advertising, radio, TV* acheteur de temps *m*; ~ **C/P** *n* (*time charter party*) TRANSP *shipping* charte-partie à temps *f*; ~ **card** *n* HRM feuille de pointage *f*; ~ **chart** *n* ADMIN chronogramme *m*; ~ **charter** *n* (*T/C*) TRANSP affrètement à temps *m*; ~ **charter party** *n* (*time C/P*) TRANSP *shipping* charte-partie à temps *f*; ~ **clock** *n* HRM, IND horloge pointeuse *f*; ~ **component** *n* GEN COMM paramètre temps *m*; ~ **constraint** *n* HRM contrainte horaire *f*; ~ **deposit** *n* BANK dépôt à terme *m*; ~ **discount** *n* S&M *advertising* dégressif sur le temps acheté *loc*; ~ **for payment** *n* BANK délai de paiement *m*, terme d'échéance *m*; ~ **frame** *n* GEN COMM délai *m*, période *f*, MGMNT délai *m*; ~ **freight** *n* TRANSP fret à temps *m*; ~ **and a half** *n* HRM une fois et demie *f*; ~ **horizon** *n* MGMNT échéance *f*; ~ **lag** *n* ECON décalage *m*, retard *m*, TRANSP *between time zones* décalage horaire *m*; ~ **limit** *n* GEN COMM délai *m*; ~ **loan** *n* BANK emprunt à terme *m*; ~ **management** *n* HRM, MGMNT gestion du temps de travail *f*, organisation du temps *f*; ~ **and methods study** *n* ECON, GEN COMM, HRM étude des temps et des méthodes *f*; ~ **and motion study** *n* ECON, GEN COMM, HRM, IND étude des périodes *f*, étude des temps et des mouvements *f*; ~ **off** *n* HRM absence *f*, absence ponctuelle *f*; ~ **off the cuff** *n jarg* HRM *industrial relations* récupérer du temps sur un autre travail; ~ **-off rights** *n pl* *UK* HRM droit à du temps libre pour activités syndicales *m*; ~ **off work** *n* HRM absence ponctuelle *f*; ~ **on risk** *n* INS période de couverture *f*; ~ **policy** *n* INS police à temps *f*;

~ premium *n* STOCK prime au temps *f*; **~ rate** *n* (SYN *price rate*) ECON, HRM salaire horaire *m*; **~ risk** *n* INS risque à terme *m*; **~ segment** *n* S&M *advertising* période de programmation *f*; **~ seller** *n* (ANT *time buyer*) MEDIA, S&M *advertising, radio, television* vendeur de temps *m*; **~ series** *n pl* ECON variations saisonnières *f pl*, MATH variations saisonnières *f pl, statistics* série chronologique *f*, POL variations saisonnières *f pl*; **~ series analysis** *n* ECON analyse chronologique *f*; **~ share** *n* (SYN *unitization*) PROP multipropriété *f*; **~ -share developer** *n* HRM, PROP promoteur de programmes en multipropriété *m*; **~ -share property** *n* PROP multipropriété *f*; **~ sharing** *n* COMP partage de temps *m*, temps partagé *m*, HRM temps partagé *m*, travail en simultanéité *m*, PROP multipropriété *f*; **~ sheet** *n* HRM feuille de présence *f*; **~ slot** *n* MEDIA *advertising, radio, TV* créneau horaire *m*; **~ span** *n* ECON *of plan, project* horizon temporel *m*, GEN COMM durée *f*; **~ span of discretion** *n* GEN COMM délai de réflexion *m*; **~ spread** *n* STOCK opération mixte sur options avec dates d'échéance différentes *f*, opération mixte horizontale *f*, spread calendaire *m*, spread horizontal *m*; **~ study** *n* GEN COMM, MATH *statistics* chronométrage *m*, étude des temps *f*; **~ to market** *n* GEN COMM, S&M, STOCK délai *m*, délai de mise sur le marché *m*; **~ value** *n* STOCK *options* valeur temporelle *f*, valeur-temps *f*; **~ work** *n* HRM travail à l'heure *m*; **~ zone** *n* GEN COMM fuseau horaire *m*; ♦ **all ~ saved** TRANSP *shipping* temps gagné *m*; **at a given ~** GEN COMM à une heure déterminée; **at some ~ in the future** GEN COMM dans l'avenir, à un moment donné dans le futur; **be under ~ pressure** GEN COMM travailler sous pression, être pressé par le temps; **for the ~ being** GEN COMM pour le moment, provisoirement; **~ is of the essence** LAW le jour et l'heure sont essentiels; **on a ~ sharing basis** PROP en tant que multipropriété; **this ~ last year** GEN COMM l'année dernière à la même époque; **within the allotted ~ frame** GEN COMM dans le laps de temps imparti

timekeeper *n* GEN COMM, HRM contrôleur de présence *m*

timeliness *n* FIN opportunité *f*

timely *adj* GEN COMM en temps opportun *loc m*

timeout *n* COMP délai d'attente *m*, sortie de session *f*

timer *n* COMP chronomètre *m*

times *n pl* MATH *multiplication* fois *f pl*; **~ fixed charges** *n pl* ACC charges fixes à terme *f pl*; **~ uncovered** *n* FIN dividende à découvert *m*; ♦ **at all ~** GEN COMM à tout moment

timescale *n* ECON, FIN, GEN COMM, HRM, MGMNT délai *m*

timetable *n* FIN indicateur *m*, GEN COMM horaire *m*, indicateur *m*, HRM, MGMNT *work, project* emploi du temps *m*, TRANSP horaire *m*; **~ analysis** TRANSP analyse horaire *f*; **~ planning** TRANSP programmation horaire *f*

timing *n* COMP durée *f*, synchronisation *f*, GEN COMM *of project* calendrier *m, precise* minutage *m*; **~ differences** *n pl* ACC, TAX différences de calendrier *f pl*

tin *n* IND étain *m*; **~ ore** *n* IND minerai d'étain *m*; **~ plate** *n* IND feuille de tôle *f*; **~ shares** *n pl* STOCK valeurs stannifères *f pl*

TINA *abbr* (*there is no alternative*) GEN COMM aucune alternative n'est possible *loc f*, il n'y a pas d'alternative *loc f*

tinware *n* GEN COMM ferblanterie *f*

tip¹ *n* ENVIR site de décharge *m*, GEN COMM pourboire *m, advice* conseil *m*, tuyau *m* (*infrml*), LEIS *gratuity* pourboire *m*; **~ of the iceberg** GEN COMM sommet de l'iceberg *m*; **~ -in** MEDIA *print* encart broché *m*, hors-texte *m*; **~ -off** GEN COMM tuyau *m* (*infrml*)

tip² *vt* GEN COMM, LEIS donner un pourboire à; ♦ **~ the scales** GEN COMM faire pencher la balance

TIP *abbr* (*tax-based incomes policy*) ECON, FIN, TAX politique d'imposition des sociétés basée sur les salaires versés

tipper *n* TRANSP *vehicle* camion à benne basculante *m*, camion-benne *m*; **~ lorry** BrE (*cf tipper truck AmE*) TRANSP camion à benne basculante *m*, camion-benne *m*; **~ truck** AmE (*cf tipper lorry BrE*) TRANSP camion à benne basculante *m*, camion-benne *m*

tipping *n* ENVIR dépôt de déchets *m*, TRANSP basculage *m*

Tirana *pr n* GEN COMM Tirana *n pr*

tire *n* AmE *see* tyre BrE

tit: **~ -for-tat** *adj* GEN COMM de représailles *loc f*

title *n* ACC, GEN COMM intitulé *m*, LAW *right to own* droit *m*, MEDIA *magazines*, PATENTS *of invention* titre *m*; **~ of an account** ACC, BANK intitulé de compte *m*, nom d'un compte *m*, titre du compte *m*; **~ deed** LAW, PROP titre de propriété *m*; **~ insurance** INS garantie d'assurance *f*; **~ page** MEDIA *book* première page *f*; **~ protection insurance** INS assurance protection de garantie *f*; **~ theory state** LAW état appliquant la théorie du titre; **~ to the goods** GEN COMM, LAW, PROP titre constitutif de propriété sur la marchandise *m*, titre de propriété sur la marchandise *m*

Titograd *pr n* GEN COMM Titograd *n pr*

titular: **~ head** *n* HRM *of organization* responsable en titre *m*

T/L *abbr* (*total loss*) INS perte totale *f*

TLC *abbr* (*transferable loan certificate*) FIN certificat d'emprunt cessible *m*

TLF *abbr* (*transferable loan facility*) FIN facilité d'emprunt cessible *f*, facilité de prêt transférable *f*

TLI *abbr* (*transferable loan instrument*) FIN instrument d'emprunt cessible *m*

TLO *abbr* (*total loss only*) INS perte totale uniquement *f*

TM *abbr* HRM (*traffic manager*) chef de la circulation *m, railway traffic* directeur de la circulation ferroviaire *m*, directeur des transports *m*, TRANSP *(ton mile, tonne mile)* ≈ tk *(tonne-kilomètre)*, TRANSP *(traffic manager)* chef de la circulation *m*, directeur des transports *m*, *railway traffic* directeur de la circulation ferroviaire *m*

TMESS *abbr (telemessage)* COMMS télémessage *m*

TMO *abbr (telegraph money order, telegraphic money order)* BANK mandat postal télégraphique *m*, FIN mandat postal télégraphe *m*, mandat postal télégraphique *m*

TNC *abbr (transnational corporation)* ECON, GEN COMM, POL entreprise transnationale *f*, société transnationale *f*

TO *abbr (telegraphic office)* COMMS service télégraphique *m*

TOB *abbr (takeover bid)* ACC, GEN COMM, STOCK OPA *(offre publique d'achat)*

tobacco *n* GEN COMM tabac *m*; ~ **products** *n pl* IND, TAX produits du tabac *m pl*

Tobin: ~ **tax** *n* ECON, TAX taxe de Tobin *f*

Tobit: ~ **model** *n* ECON modèle de Tobit *m*

toehold: ~ **purchase** *n* STOCK achat précaire *m*; ♦ **get a ~ in the market** GEN COMM, S&M réaliser une première pénétration du marché

toes: **go ~ up** *phr infrml* FIN, GEN COMM faire faillite *loc f*

toggle[1] *n* COMP bascule *f*; ~ **switch** COMP interrupteur à bascule *m*

toggle[2] **1.** *vt* COMP basculer; **2.** *vi* COMP *key, switch* basculer

Togo *pr n* GEN COMM Togo *m*

Togolese[1] *adj* GEN COMM togolais

Togolese[2] *n* GEN COMM *person* Togolais *m*

toilet *n BrE (cf lavatory, rest room AmE, washroom AmE)* GEN COMM toilettes *f pl*

token *n* COMP, GEN COMM jeton *m*; ~ **money** BANK, FIN monnaie fiduciaire *f*; ~ **payment** FIN, GEN COMM paiement symbolique *m*; ~ **stoppage** HRM arrêt de travail symbolique *m*; ~ **strike** HRM grève d'avertissement *f*, grève symbolique *f*

tokenism *n* LAW en signe de reconnaissance *loc m*

Tokyo:[1] ~ **Interbank Offered Rate** *n (TIBOR)* ECON taux interbancaire offert à Tokyo *m (TIOT)*

Tokyo[2] *pr n* GEN COMM Tokyo *n pr*

told: **all ~** *phr* GEN COMM tout compris

tolerance *n* GEN COMM, IND tolérance *f*; ~ **level** FIN marge de manoeuvre *f*

toll:[1] ~ **-free**® *adj AmE (cf Freefone BrE)* COMMS *telephone* gratuit

toll[2] *n* COMMS *US* coût d'une communication téléphonique *m*, TRANSP péage d'autoroute *m*; ~ **bridge** TRANSP pont à péage *m*; ~ **call** *US* COMMS appel interurbain *m*, appel longue distance *m*, communication interurbaine *f*, communication à longue distance *f*; ~ **-free call** *AmE (cf Freefone call BrE)* COMMS appel gratuit *m*, appel interurbain gratuit *m*, appel sans frais *m* *(Can)*; ~ **-free number** *AmE (cf Freefone number BrE)* COMMS numéro gratuit *m*, service d'appel gratuit *m*, ≈ numéro vert *m*; ~ **motorway** *BrE (cf*

turnpike AmE) TRANSP autoroute à péage *f*; ♦ **take a heavy ~ of bankruptcies** FIN, HRM provoquer un lourd bilan de faillites

tollbooth *n* TRANSP poste de péage *m*

tombstone *n jarg* MEDIA, S&M avis d'émission publié dans la presse *m*; ~ **ad** *jarg* MEDIA, S&M plaquette publicitaire *f*

tom/next *adj (from tomorrow to the next business day)* STOCK *transactions* à 24h valeur lendemain

tomorrow: ~ **week** *n* GEN COMM demain en huit *m*; ♦ **from ~ to the next business day** *(tom/next)* STOCK à 24h valeur lendemain

ton *n (t.)* GEN COMM tonne *f (t.)*; ~ **kilometer** *AmE see tonne kilometre BrE*; ~ **mile** *(TM)* TRANSP tonne milliaire *f*, tonne par mile *f*, ≈ tonne-kilomètre *f (tk)*; ~ **of oil-equivalent** ENVIR tonne d'équivalent pétrole *f*

toner *n* ADMIN, COMP *for fax machine, photocopier* encre *f*, toner *m*

tongs *n pl* TRANSP *cargo lifting equipment* pinces *f pl*

tongued: ~ **and grooved** *adj (T&G)* TRANSP *timber* affourché

tonnage *n* TRANSP jauge *f*, tonnage *m*; ~ **calculation** *n* TRANSP *shipping, chartering* calcul de la jauge *m*; ~ **deck** *n* TRANSP *shipping* pont de tonnage *m*; ~ **dues** *n pl* TRANSP taxes de tonnage *f pl*; ~ **dues slip** *n* IMP/EXP, TAX, TRANSP *shipping* relevé des taxes de tonnage *m*; ~ **mark** *n* TRANSP *shipping* marque de jauge *f*; ~ **measurement** *n* TRANSP jaugeage *m*; ~ **opening** *n* TRANSP *shipping* ouverture de tonnage *f*; ~ **slip** *n* IMP/EXP, TAX, TRANSP *document* relevé des taxes de tonnage *m*

tonne *n (t.)* GEN COMM tonne *f (t.)*; ~ **kilometre** *n BrE* GEN COMM tonne kilométrique *f*; ~ **mile** *n (TM)* TRANSP tonne milliaire *f*, tonne par mile *f*, ≈ tonne-kilomètre *f*; ~ **miles per vehicle hour** *n pl* TRANSP ≈ tonnes-kilomètres par heure de circulation du véhicule *f pl*

tonnes: ~ **per centimeter** *n pl AmE*, ~ **per centimetre** *n pl BrE (TPC)* GEN COMM tonnes au centimètre *f pl*

tons: ~ **deadweight** *n pl (TDW)* TRANSP Tonne Port en Lourd *f (TPL)*

tontine *n* ECON tontine *f*

tool[1] *n* COMP outil *m*, GEN COMM instrument *m*, outil *m*; ~ **bar** COMP barre d'outils *f*

tool:[2] ~ **up** *vt* IND *factory, workshop* outiller

toolmaker *n* GEN COMM, IND outilleur *m*

toolroom *n* IND atelier d'outillage *m*

tools: ~ **of the trade** *n pl* GEN COMM outils du métier *m pl*

top:[1] ~ **-down** *adj* GEN COMM de haut en bas *adj phr*, MGMNT du sommet à la base *loc m*; ~ **-flight** *adj* GEN COMM de premier ordre, de rang supérieur *loc m*; ~ **-heavy** *adj* GEN COMM *business, company, capital structure* trop lourd du haut; ~ **-of-the-range** *adj* COMP, GEN COMM, GEN COMM, S&M, S&M *product* haut de gamme; ~ **-quality** *adj* GEN COMM de qualité supérieure

loc *f*; ~ -**ranking** *adj* GEN COMM haut placé; ~ -**rated** *adj* BANK de premier ordre; ~ -**secret** *adj* GEN COMM ultra-secret

top[2] *n* HRM *of organization* sommet *m*; ~ **brass** *n* infrml GEN COMM gros bonnets *m pl* (*infrml*); ~ **dead center** *n* AmE, ~ **dead centre** *n* BrE (*TDC*) TRANSP point mort haut *m* (*PMH*); ~ -**down approach to investing** *n* FIN démarche descendante pour investir *f*; ~ -**down linkage model** *n* ECON modèle de liaison descendante *m*; ~ **executive** *n* HRM, MGMNT cadre sup *m* (*infrml*), cadre supérieur *m*; ~ **hand** *n* jarg GEN COMM collaborateur de premier plan *m*; ~ -**hat pension** *n* infrml FIN, HRM, MGMNT, WEL retraite complémentaire des cadres supérieurs *f*; ~ **of the league** *n* GEN COMM, S&M leader *m*; ~ -**level efficiency** *n* ECON efficience maximale *f*; ~ -**level talks** *n pl* MGMNT, POL discussions au plus haut niveau *f pl*; ~ -**loader container** *n* TRANSP conteneur bâché *m*; ~ **management** *n* HRM cadres sup *m pl* (*infrml*), cadres supérieurs *m pl*, MGMNT cadres sup *m pl* (*infrml*), cadres supérieurs *m pl*, haute direction *f*; ~ **management approach** *n* MGMNT optique de la direction générale *f*; ~ **margin** *n* ADMIN, COMP marge supérieure *f*; ~ **price** *n* GEN COMM, STOCK cours le plus haut *m*; ~ **prices** *n pl* GEN COMM prix maximums *m pl*; ~ **quality** *n* GEN COMM qualité la meilleure *f*, qualité supérieure *f*; ~ -**rank product** *n* GEN COMM produit de première catégorie *m*, produit de première qualité *m*; ~ -**ranking official** *n* ADMIN haut fonctionnaire *m*; ~ **rate of tax** *n* TAX taux plafond d'imposition *m*; ~ **salaries review body** *n* UK HRM, MGMNT organisme de révision des salaires élevés *m*; ~ -**sided federalism** *n* (SYN *fiscal federalism*) ECON, POL fédéralisme fiscal *m*; ~ -**up deduction** *n* TAX déduction complémentaire *f*; ~ **wages** *n pl* HRM *high rate of pay* salaire élevé *m*; ◆ **at the ~ end** GEN COMM *of a scale* en haut; **be on ~ of one's job** HRM dominer son travail; ~ **end of the market** (ANT *low end of the market*) S&M haut de gamme du marché *m*; ~ **end of the range** S&M haut de gamme dans la série *m*; **one ~ and three copies** GEN COMM un original et trois copies; **the ~ of the line** GEN COMM le haut de la gamme *m*; ~ **of the tree** infrml GEN COMM *status* le plus élevé

top[3] **1.** *vt* GEN COMM *surpass* franchir, venir en tête de; ~ **up** UK GEN COMM compléter, *savings* faire l'appoint à; **2.** *vi* ~ **out** (ANT *bottom out*), GEN COMM *reach highest level* plafonner; ◆ ~ **the list** GEN COMM venir en tête, être à la tête

TOPIC *abbr* UK (*Teletex Output of Price Information by Computer*) STOCK ≈ informations boursières par MINITEL *f pl*

topping: ~ **out** *n* STOCK fléchissement de la hausse *m*; ~ -**up clause** *n* BANK condition au plus haut *f*

Toronto: ~ **Composite** *n* STOCK indice composite de la bourse de Toronto; **the ~ Stock Exchange** *n* Canada (*TSE*) STOCK la Bourse de Toronto *f* (*Canada*)

tort *n* LAW délit *m*; ~ **feasor** GEN COMM, LAW auteur

d'un tort *m*; ~ **liability** LAW responsabilité délictuelle *f*, responsabilité extracontractuelle *f*

tot: ~ **up** *vt* GEN COMM *numbers, amounts*, MATH additionner; ~ **up to** infrml GEN COMM s'élever à

total *n* ACC, ECON, FIN, GEN COMM, MATH total *m*; ~ **allowable catches** *n pl* (*TACs*) ENVIR *fishing* prises totales autorisées *f pl*; ~ **amount** *n* GEN COMM *of bill* montant *m*; ~ **assets** *n pl* ACC, FIN total de l'actif *m*; ~ **base number** *n* (*TBN*) ENVIR indice de base total *m*; ~ **budgetary** *n* FIN total du budgétaire *m*; ~ **capitalization** *n* FIN capitalisation globale *f*; ~ **cost** *n* ACC, ECON, GEN COMM coût total *m*; ~ **cost of the credit to the consumer** *n* FIN, GEN COMM, S&M coût total du crédit au consommateur *m*; ~ **effective exposure** *n* S&M *advertising* exposition réelle totale *f*; ~ **estimates** *n pl* FIN total des prévisions *m*; ~ **fertility rate** *n* (*TRF*) ECON taux global de fertilité *m*; ~ **field of a survey** *n* S&M l'univers d'une enquête *m*; ~ **funds applied** *n pl* FIN total des fonds imputés *m*; ~ **funds provided** *n pl* FIN total des fonds fournis *m*; ~ **income** *n* ACC, ECON, FIN, TAX revenu total *m*; ~ **liabilities** *n pl* ACC, BANK total des créditeurs *m*, total des emprunts et dettes *m*; ~ **loss** *n* GEN COMM, INS (*T/L*) perte totale *f*; ~ **loss only** *n* (*TLO*) INS perte totale uniquement *f*; ~ **net flow** *n* ECON flux net total *m*; ~ **net redemption** *n* BANK *investment* remboursement total net *m*; ~ **nonbudgetary** *n* FIN total du non-budgétaire *m*; ~ **payroll** *n* HRM *of employer* ensemble des salaires versés *m*, total des feuilles de paie *m*; ~ **plant maintenance** *n* GEN COMM, IND entretien total de l'équipement *m*; ~ **public debt** *n* ECON dette publique globale *f*, dette publique totale *f*, total de la dette publique *m*; ~ **public spending** *n* ECON dépenses publiques globales *f pl*, totalité des dépenses publiques *f*; ~ **quality control** *n* (*TQC*) GEN COMM, IND, MGMNT, S&M contrôle de la qualité globale *m* (*QG*); ~ **quality management** *n* (*TQM*) IND, MGMNT, S&M gestion de la qualité absolue *f*, gestion de la qualité globale *f* (*gestion de la QG*); ~ **revenue** *n* ACC, ECON, FIN, TAX recette totale *f*, revenu total *m*; ~ **social charges** *n pl* ACC, WEL *annual* montant des sommes versées à la sécurité sociale *m*; ~ **sum** *n* BANK, GEN COMM somme totale *f*; ~ **to date** *n* ACC, FIN cumul jusqu'à ce jour *m*, total cumulé *m*; ~ **votes cast** *n pl* GEN COMM *in ballot, election* total de suffrages exprimés *m*; ~ **wages and salaries** *n* ACC *balance sheet* montant de la masse salariale *m*, rémunération total du personnel *f*, HRM rémunération total du personnel *f*

totalizator *n* GEN COMM *machine* machine totalisatrice *f*

totalize *vt* GEN COMM *numbers, amount* totaliser

totalizer *n* GEN COMM machine totalisatrice *f*

totalling *n* GEN COMM totalisation *f*

tote: ~ **bin** *n* TRANSP caisse de manutention *f*

toto: **in ~** *phr* GEN COMM *completely* en totalité

touch:[1] ~ -**activated** *adj* COMP à commande par effleurement *loc f*; ~ **and go** *adj* GEN COMM *risky* hasardeux, très risqué; ~ **-sensitive** *adj* COMP *controls* tactile, à effleurement

touch[2] *n* STOCK touche *f*; ~ **key** COMP touche à effleurement *f*; ~ **-sensitive screen** COMP écran tactile *m*; ~ **-tone phone** COMMS téléphone à clavier *m*, téléphone à touches *m*; ◆ **keep in** ~ **with** GEN COMM rester en relation avec

touch:[3] **1.** *vt* ~ **off** GEN COMM *argument, disturbance* déclencher; **2.** *vi* ~ **-type** ADMIN, COMMS, COMP, GEN COMM taper au toucher, taper sans regarder le clavier

touched: ~ **bill of health** *n* GEN COMM, TRANSP *maritime* patente de santé suspecte *f*

touchline: **on the** ~ *phr* COMP *not taking an active part* sur la touche *f*

tough[1] *adj* GEN COMM *conditions* dur

tough:[2] ~ **competition** *n* GEN COMM forte concurrence *f*; ~ **competitor** *n* ECON, GEN COMM, S&M concurrent dangereux *m*; ~ **stance** *n* GEN COMM position inflexible *f*

tour *n* LEIS excursion *f*, tour *m*, visite *f*; ~ **company** LEIS *theatre* troupe itinérante *f*; ~ **de forage** *frml* ENVIR *structure* appareil de forage *m*; ~ **operator** LEIS, TRANSP compagnie de cars *f*, organisateur de voyages *m*; ~ **organizer** LEIS, TRANSP compagnie de cars *f*, organisateur de voyages *m*; ◆ **on** ~ LEIS *theatre* en tournée

tourism *n* LEIS tourisme *m*

tourist *n* LEIS touriste *mf*; ~ **attraction** LEIS site touristique *m*; ~ **class** LEIS, TRANSP *(SYN economy class)* classe touriste *f*; ~ **exchange rate** ECON, FIN, LEIS *formerly in Russia* taux de change réservé aux touristes *m*; ~ **fare** LEIS, TRANSP tarif touriste *m*; ~ **information bureau** LEIS syndicat d'initiative *m*; ~ **information office** LEIS syndicat d'initiative *m*; ~ **office** LEIS syndicat d'initiative *m*; ~ **season** ECON, LEIS saison touristique *f*; ~ **tax** LEIS, TAX taxe de séjour *f*; ~ **trade** LEIS tourisme *m*; ~ **visa** ADMIN visa de tourisme *m*, visa touristique *m*

Tourist: ~ **Board** *n* UK LEIS office du tourisme *m*

tout[1] *n* LEIS *for hotel* rabatteur *m*

tout[2] *vt* GEN COMM *for custom* accoster des clients, racoler; ◆ ~ **for trade** GEN COMM accoster des clients

TOVALOP *abbr (tanker owners' voluntary agreement concerning liability for oil pollution)* ENVIR, INS, TRANSP *shipping* engagement volontaire des propriétaires de pétroliers en cas de pollution pétrolière

tow[1] *n* TRANSP *pulling vehicle* remorquage *m*

tow[2] *vt* TRANSP remorquer

towage: ~ **charges** *n pl* TRANSP droit de remorquage *m*, frais de remorquage *m pl*; ~ **contractor** *n* TRANSP entrepreneur de remorquage *m*; ~ **dues** *n pl* TRANSP frais de remorquage *m pl, shipping* droit de remorquage *m*

towards: ~ **the middle of the year** *phr* GEN COMM vers le milieu de l'année

towaway: ~ **area** *n BrE (cf towaway zone AmE)*

TRANSP zone de stationnement interdit *f*; ~ **zone** *n AmE (cf towaway area BrE)* TRANSP zone de stationnement interdit *f*

towboat *n* TRANSP remorqueur *m*

tower: ~ **block** *n* PROP tour d'habitation *f*

towing *n* TRANSP remorquage *m*, tractage *m*; ~ **dolly** *jarg* TRANSP essieu de remorquage *m*

town *n* GEN COMM ville *f*; ~ **center** *AmE*, ~ **centre** *BrE* GEN COMM centre de la ville *m*, centre-ville *m*; ~ **clearing** BANK, ECON compensation sur place *f*; ~ **councillor** ADMIN, POL conseiller municipal *m*; ~ **and country planning** UK ECON, ENVIR, WEL aménagement du territoire *m*; ~ **hall** ADMIN, POL mairie *f*; ~ **house** PROP villa style village *f*; ~ **planner** *BrE (cf city planner AmE)* ADMIN, POL, WEL urbaniste *mf*; ~ **planning** *BrE (cf city planning AmE)* ADMIN, POL, WEL urbanisme *m*; ◆ **out of** ~ S&M *shop, restaurant* en dehors de la ville

Town: ~ **and Country Planning Act** *n* UK ENVIR, LAW loi relative à l'urbanisme et à l'aménagement du territoire

towtruck *n AmE (cf recovery vehicle BrE)* TRANSP dépanneuse *f*

toxic[1] *adj* ENVIR toxique

toxic:[2] ~ **effect** *n* ENVIR *pollution* effet toxique *m*; ~ **effluent** *n* ENVIR effluent toxique *m*; ~**, explosive, corrosive, hazardous cargo** *n (TECH cargo)* TRANSP *dangerous classified cargo* cargaison toxique, explosive, corrosive, hasardeuse *f (cargaison TECH)*; ~ **waste** *n* ENVIR déchet toxique *m*

toxicity *n* ENVIR toxicité *f*

toxicological *adj* ENVIR toxicologique

TP *abbr (third party)* INS, LAW, PATENTS tierce personne *f*, tiers *m*

TPC *abbr (tonnes per centimeter AmE, tonnes per centimetre BrE)* GEN COMM tonnes au centimètre *f pl*

TPI *abbr (Tropical Products Institute)* ECON Institut des produits tropicaux *m*

TQC *abbr (total quality control)* GEN COMM, IND, MGMNT, S&M QG *(contrôle de la qualité globale)*

TQM *abbr (total quality management)* IND, MGMNT, S&M gestion de la QG *f (gestion de la qualité globale)*

tr. *abbr (transfer)* ACC virt *(virement)*, BANK transfert *m*, transfert de fonds *m*, FIN virt *(virement)*

TR *abbr (triple reduction)* GEN COMM triple réduction

trabaccolo *n* TRANSP *shipping* trabac *m*

trace *vt* GEN COMM *follow trail* suivre la trace de, *locate* retrouver, TRANSP localiser; ~ **back** GEN COMM remonter jusqu'à l'origine de; ◆ ~ **a call** COMMS *telephone* déterminer l'origine d'un appel, déterminer l'origine d'une communication; ~ **a payment** BANK trouver une trace du paiement

tracer *n* GEN COMM *document* fiche de recherche *f*

track:[1] **on ~** *adj (ot)* TRANSP *rail* en voie *loc f*

track[2] *n* TRANSP voie *f*; **~ price** TRANSP prix avant chargement sur wagon *m*; **~ record** ADMIN, GEN COMM, HRM, WEL *of employee* antécédents *m pl*, parcours professionnel *m*

track[3] *vt* GEN COMM *earnings, expenditure, outlay* faire le suivi de; ◆ **keep ~ of sth** GEN COMM suivre le développement de quelque chose

trackball *n* COMP *pointer device* boule de commande *f*, boule de pointeur *f*, boule roulante *f*, trackball *m* (*jarg*)

tracking *n* GEN COMM *of sales, costs, expenses* suivi *m*; **~ study** S&M *market research* étude de bandes *f*, étude de marché *f*; **~ system** GEN COMM système de repérage *m*

tractive: ~ unit *n* TRANSP engin moteur *m*, tracteur *m*

tractor:[1] **~ -fed** *adj* COMP entraîné par ergots, entraîné par picots

tractor:[2] **~ feed** *n* COMP entraînement par ergots *m*, entraînement par picots *m*

tradable[1] *adj* ECON, GEN COMM *product* marchand

tradable:[2] **~ discharge permit** *n (TDP)* ECON autorisation de décharge négociable *f*, ENVIR autorisation de décharge négociable *f*, autorisation négociable de décharge de polluants *f*; **~ emission permit** *n* ENVIR, GEN COMM autorisation de décharge négociable *f*, autorisation négociable d'émission de polluants *f*; **~ promissory note** *n* STOCK bon à ordre négociable *m*, BON; **~ treasury bond** *n* STOCK bon du Trésor négociable *m*, BTN

trade:[1] **~ -related** *adj* ECON relatif au commerce

trade[2] *n* ECON commerce *m*, échange *m*, échanges commerciaux *m pl*, GEN COMM commerce *m*, négoce *m*, HRM *job* métier *m*, IMP/EXP, S&M *international* commerce *m*, échange *m*, échanges commerciaux *m pl*; **~ acceptance** *n* ECON, GEN COMM acceptation commerciale *f*; **~ account** *n* ECON, GEN COMM solde commercial *m*; **~ accounts payable** *n pl AmE (cf trade creditors BrE)* ACC, COM, ECON comptes fournisseurs *m pl*, poste fournisseurs *m*; **~ accounts receivable** *n pl* ACC, ECON clients *m pl*, comptes clients *m pl*, comptes débiteurs *m pl*, créances *f pl*, débiteurs *m pl*; **~ agreement** *n* ECON accord commercial *m*, traité commercial *m*, GEN COMM accord commercial *m*, POL accord commercial *m*, traité commercial *m*; **~ allowance** *n* GEN COMM remise à la profession *f*; **~ association** *n* GEN COMM, HRM association professionnelle *f*, corps de métier *m*; **~ balance** *n* ECON, IMP/EXP, POL balance commerciale *f*, balance du commerce extérieur *f*, excédent commercial *m*, solde extérieur *m*; **~ barrier** *n* ECON, GEN COMM, IMP/EXP, POL barrière commerciale *f*, barrière douanière *f*; **~ bill** *n (cf commercial bill AmE)* BANK, FIN titre commercial *m*; **~ book** *n* MEDIA *print* ouvrage d'intérêt général *m*; **~ brief** *n* ECON *international* dossier commercial *m*; **~ chamber** *n* GEN COMM chambre des métiers *f*; **~ channel** *n* GEN COMM circuit commercial *m*; **~ creation** *n* ECON, HRM, IMP/EXP création commerciale *f*; **~ credit** *n* ACC, BANK, ECON, GEN COMM crédit commercial *m*; **~ creditor** *n* ACC, ECON, GEN COMM fournisseur *m*; **~ creditors** *n pl BrE (cf trade accounts payable AmE)* ACC, COM, ECON comptes clients *m pl*, poste clients *m*; **~ custom** *n* GEN COMM habitudes du métier *f pl*; **~ cycle** *n* ECON, GEN COMM, IMP/EXP cycle économique *m*; **~ date** *n* STOCK date de l'opération *f*; **~ debtors** *n pl* COM compte créance *m*, débiteurs *m pl*, FIN compte créance *m*, ACC, ECON, GEN COMM compte créance *m*, débiteurs *m pl*; **~ deficit** *n* ACC, ECON, GEN COMM déficit de la balance commerciale *m*, déficit extérieur *m*; **~ description** *n* S&M *advertising* descriptif des marchandises à vendre *m*; **~ directory** *n* GEN COMM, S&M annuaire du commerce *m*; **~ discount** *n* ACC, GEN COMM rabais de gros *m*, S&M rabais de gros *m*, remise *f*; **~ dispute** *n* ECON, HRM conflit du travail *m*; **~ distortion** *n* ECON distorsion commerciale *f*; **~ diversion** *n* ECON, HRM, IMP/EXP diversion commerciale *f*, détour commercial dû à une union douanière *m*; **~ entrance** *n* GEN COMM entrée des fournisseurs *f*; **~ exhibition** *n* S&M *for professionals* salon professionnel *m*, *public* foire commerciale *f*; **~ facilitation** *n* ECON *international* facilité commerciale *f*; **~ fair** *n* S&M *for professionals* salon professionnel *m*, *public* foire commerciale *f*; **~ figures** *n pl* ECON chiffre d'affaires *m*, CA, chiffres de commerce *m pl*, GEN COMM *for domestic, overseas trade* chiffres de commerce *m pl*, *of company* chiffre d'affaires *m*, CA; **~ finance** *n* BANK, FIN financement des opérations commerciales *m*, financement du commerce extérieur *m*, fonds *m pl*; **~ financing** *n* BANK, FIN financement des opérations commerciales *m*, financement du commerce extérieur *m*, fonds *m pl*; **~ fixture** *n* GEN COMM, PROP aménagement du commerce *m*; **~ flow** *n* ECON, IMP/EXP *international* flux commercial *m*, volume d'échanges *m*; **~ gap** *n* ECON, GEN COMM, IMP/EXP déséquilibre commercial *m*; **~ imbalance** *n* ECON, GEN COMM, IMP/EXP déséquilibre commercial *m*; **~ -in allowance** *n* GEN COMM valeur de reprise *f*; **~ -in industrial goods** *n* IMP/EXP, IND échanges industriels *m pl*; **~ investments** *n pl* ECON investissement commercial *m*; **~ journal** *n* GEN COMM, MEDIA journal professionnel *m*, revue professionnelle *f*; **~ liberalization** *n* ECON libéralisation du commerce *f*; **~ magazine** *n* GEN COMM, MEDIA revue professionnelle *f*; **~ mart** *n* GEN COMM, S&M expomarché *m*; **~ name** *n* GEN COMM, S&M raison sociale *f*; **~ -off** *n* ECON *between two things* compromis *m*, *unemployment, inflation* échange *m*, concessions mutuelles *f pl*, GEN COMM compromis *m*, concessions mutuelles *f pl*, HRM change *m*, compromis *m*, concessions mutuelles *f pl*; **~ organization** *n* GEN COMM, HRM organisation professionnelle *f*; **~ paper** *n* GEN COMM papier d'affaires *m*; **~ paperback** *n jarg* MEDIA *print* livre broché de qualité supérieure au livre de poche; ~ **policy** *n* ECON, GEN COMM, IMP/EXP, MGMNT, POL politique commerciale *f*; ~ **practices** *n pl* ADMIN, GEN COMM, MGMNT pratiques commerciales *f pl*, pratiques et conventions du secteur *f pl*; ~ **press** *n* MEDIA *print* presse spécialisée *f*; ~ **price** *n* GEN COMM, S&M, STOCK prix d'achat *m*, prix de la transaction *m*; ~ **promotion** *n* S&M *advertising* promotion auprès des détaillants *f*, promotion-réseau *f*; ~ **protectionism** *n* ECON, IMP/EXP *international* protectionnisme commercial *m*; ~ **receivables** *n pl* ACC, ECON clients *m pl*, comptes clients *m pl*, comptes débiteurs *m pl*, créances *f pl*, débiteurs *m pl*; ~ **regime** *n* ECON régime commercial *m*; ~ **register** *n* ADMIN, GEN COMM registre du commerce *m*; ~ **regulations** *n pl* ECON, GEN COMM, LAW réglementation commerciale *f*; ~ **report** *n* STOCK avis d'opéré *m*, rapport d'opération *m*; ~ **representative** *n* HRM délégué commercial *m*; ~ **restriction** *n* ECON *international*, GEN COMM *imposed by government*, POL *international* restriction commerciale *f*, restriction du commerce *f*; ~ **returns** *n pl* GEN COMM statistiques commerciales *f pl*; ~ **route** *n* ECON, IMP/EXP, TRANSP *international* route commerciale *f*; ~ **sanctions** *n pl* ECON, IMP/EXP, POL sanctions commerciales *f pl*; ~ **secret** *n* GEN COMM secret commercial *m*; ~ **show** *n* S&M exposition *f*, foire commerciale *f*, salon interprofessionnel *m*; ~ **sign** *n* GEN COMM, S&M enseigne *f*; ~ **strategy** *n* ECON, GEN COMM, S&M stratégie commerciale *f*; ~ **surplus** *n* ECON, IMP/EXP, POL excédent commercial *m*; ~ **talks** *n pl* ECON, POL négociations commerciales *f pl*; ~ **terms** *n pl* ECON, GEN COMM, IMP/EXP, S&M conditions de vente *f pl*; ~ **ticket** *n* STOCK fiche d'ordre *f*; ~ **union** *n UK (TU, labor union US)* HRM syndicat *m*; ~ **union act** *n UK (TUA)* ECON, HRM, IND, LAW, POL *1984* loi sur les syndicats *f*; ~ **union contribution** *n UK* HRM cotisation syndicale *f*; ~ **union council** *n* HRM conseil syndical *m*; ~ **union dues** *n pl UK* HRM cotisation syndicale *f*; ~ **union immunities** *n pl UK* HRM, LAW immunités syndicales *f pl*; ~ **union and labour relations act** *n UK* ECON, HRM, IND, LAW loi sur les syndicats et les relations de travail; ~ **union liability** *n UK* HRM responsabilité syndicale *f*; ~ **union membership** *n* HRM *industrial relations* adhésion à un syndicat *f*; ~ **union movement** *n UK (cf labor union movement US)* HRM mouvement syndical *m*; ~ **union recognition** *n UK* HRM reconnaissance des syndicats *f*; ~ **union representative** *n* HRM délégué syndical *m*; ~ **union subscription** *n UK* HRM cotisation syndicale *f*; ~ **unionism** *n* HRM syndicalisme *m*; ~ **volume** *n* ECON volume des échanges commerciaux *m*; ~ **war** *n* ECON, GEN COMM, S&M guerre commerciale *f*; ~ **week** *n* GEN COMM, S&M semaine commerciale *f*; ~ **-weighted exchange rate** *n* ECON taux de change en données corrigées des changes *m*, taux de change pondéré en fonction des échanges commerciaux *m*; ~ **-weighted external value** *n* ECON *of currency* valeur externe pondérée en fonction des échanges commerciaux *f*; ~ **within the Commonwealth** *n* GEN COMM échanges à l'intérieur du Commonwealth *m pl*

trade:[3] **1.** *vt* ~ **at** STOCK s'échanger à, se négocier à; ~ **down** GEN COMM *buy cheaper house, car* racheter qch de moins cher; ~ **in** ECON *goods* faire le commerce de, GEN COMM *old model for new* vendre en reprise, STOCK négocier, transiger, ECON commercer, *with other countries* avoir des relations commerciales, GEN COMM, S&M commercer; **2.** *vi* ~ **off** ECON, GEN COMM faire un compromis, faire un échange; ◆ ~ **as a baker** GEN COMM tenir une boulangerie, être boulanger; ~ **for one's account** STOCK intervenir en Bourse pour son propre compte; ~ **in stocks and bonds** STOCK être opérateur en Bourse; ~ **one thing against another** ECON, GEN COMM commercer une chose contre une autre, troquer une chose contre une autre, échanger une chose contre une autre; ~ **one thing for another** ECON, GEN COMM commercer une chose contre une autre, troquer une chose contre une autre, échanger une chose contre une autre; ~ **under the name of** GEN COMM négocier pour le compte de; ~ **within the Commonwealth** GEN COMM entretenir des relations commerciales à l'intérieur du Commonwealth

Trade: ~ **Act 1974** *n* ECON, LAW loi sur le commerce de 1974; ~ **Data Elements Directory** *n (TDED)* ECON *international* annuaire de données commerciales de base *m*; ~ **Data Interchange** *n (TDI)* ECON *international* échange d'informations commerciales *m*; ~ **Descriptions Act** *n UK* LAW, S&M loi protégeant les consommateurs contre la publicité mensongères; ~ **Development Board** *n (TDB)* ECON *international* conseil du développement commercial *m*; ~ **Unions and Labour Relations Act** *n UK (TULRA)* HRM, IND, LAW loi sur les syndicats et les relations de travail; ~**s Union Congress** *n UK (TUC)* HRM confédération des syndicats britanniques

tradeability *n* ECON, GEN COMM aptitude à la commercialisation *f*

traded: ~ **option** *n* STOCK option négociable *f*

trademark *n* ACC, GEN COMM brevet *m*, marque *f*, marque de contrôle *f*, marque de fabrique *f*, LAW *intellectual property*, PATENTS, S&M marque *f*, marque de fabrique *f*; ~ **agent** LAW *intellectual property*, PATENTS agent de marques *m*, représentant d'une marque de fabrique *m*

trader *n* GEN COMM *shopkeeper* commerçant *m*, petit commerçant *m*, S&M *consumer goods* marchand *m, large-scale* négociant *m, shopkeeper* commerçant *m*, petit commerçant *m*, STOCK action entièrement libérée *f*, délégué en bourse *m*, négociateur *m*, spéculateur habituel *m*, opérateur *m*; ~ **in securities** STOCK négociant en valeurs *m*

tradesman's: ~ **entrance** *n* GEN COMM *on signpost* entrée de service *f*

tradesmen *n pl* GEN COMM, S&M commerçants *m pl*

tradespeople *n pl* GEN COMM, S&M commerçants *m pl*

tradeswomen *n pl* GEN COMM, S&M commerçantes *f pl*

trading *n* ECON commerce *m*, GEN COMM *business* activité commerciale *f*, commerce *m*, IMP/EXP, S&M commerce *m*; ~ **account** *n* ACC, BANK compte d'exploitation *m*; ~ **activity** *n* STOCK activité du marché *f*; ~ **area** *n* GEN COMM secteur de vente *m*, territoire de vente *m*, S&M territoire de vente *m*, *shop* zone de chalandise *f*; ~ **authorization** *n* GEN COMM, S&M autorisation d'exercer un commerce *f*, autorisation d'exercer un métier *f*; ~ **bloc** *n* ECON, POL bloc commercial *m*; ~ **book** *n* FIN *of institution* portefeuille de négociation *m*; ~ **company** *n* ECON, GEN COMM entreprise commerciale *f*, société commerciale *f*, société de commerce *f*, IMP/EXP société d'import-export *f*, société d'importation *f*, MGMNT entreprise commerciale *f*, S&M entreprise commerciale *f*, société commerciale *f*, société de commerce *f*; ~ **currencies** *n pl* ECON *international* devises *f pl*; ~ **debts** *n pl* ACC créances *f pl*, créances commerciales *f pl*; ~ **desk** *n* STOCK pupitre de négociation *m*; ~ **dividends** *n pl* STOCK dividendes négociés *m pl*, opérations de dividendes *f pl*; ~ **estate** *n* GEN COMM immeuble commercial *m*, zone industrielle *f*, IND zone industrielle *f*, PROP immeuble commercial *m*, zone industrielle *f*, S&M zone industrielle *f*; ~ **floor** *n* STOCK corbeille *f* (*jarg*), parquet *m*; ~ **halt** *n* STOCK arrêt des opérations *m*, suspension des transactions *f*; ~ **hours** *n pl* STOCK heures de bourse *f pl*, heures de négociation *f pl*; ~ **income** *n* ACC, GEN COMM, HRM revenu brut *m*; ~ **life** *n* STOCK *of currency futures* durée de vie *f*; ~ **limit** *n* TRANSP *shipping* zone de navigation *f*; ~ **losses** *n pl* ACC, GEN COMM pertes d'exploitation *f pl*; ~ **member** *n* STOCK *of exchange* membre de la Bourse des valeurs *m*, membre opérateur *m*; ~ **name** *n* GEN COMM, PATENTS nom commercial *m*; ~ **operations** *n pl* BANK, STOCK opérations en Bourse *f pl*; ~ **partner** *n* ECON, POL, S&M partenaire commercial *m*; ~ **party** *n* STOCK *money market* groupement *m*; ~ **pattern** *n* STOCK tendance du marché *f*; ~ **pit** *n jarg* STOCK corbeille *f* (*jarg*), poste de négociation *f*; ~ **port** *n* TRANSP port de commerce *m*; ~ **portfolio** *n* BANK, STOCK *investment* portefeuille d'actions *m*; ~ **post** *n jarg* STOCK corbeille *f* (*jarg*), poste de négociation *f*; ~ **program** *n AmE*, ~ **programme** *n BrE* FIN, GEN COMM programme de négoce *m*; ~ **range** *n* STOCK *commodities, securities* fourchette des prix limites de transaction *f*, éventail des négociations *m*; ~ **results** *n pl* GEN COMM *of company* chiffre d'affaires *m*, CA; ~ **right** *n* STOCK droit de traiter les options du marché donné *m*; ~ **room** *n* BANK salle de marché *f*; ~ **security** *n* STOCK valeur boursière *f*, valeur négociée *f*; ~ **session** *n* STOCK séance de bourse *f*, séance de négociation *f*; ~ **stamp** *n* GEN COMM timbre-prime *m*;

~ **standards** *n pl* GEN COMM normes commerciales *f pl*; ~ **unit** *n* STOCK *Eurodollar options* quotité *f*, unité boursière *f*, unité de transaction *f*; ~ **variation** *n* STOCK variation boursière *f*, variation minimale des cours *f*; ~ **vessel** *n* TRANSP navire de commerce *m*, navire marchand *m*; ~ **volume** *n* GEN COMM volume des opérations *m*, volume des transactions *m*; ~ **year** *n* ACC, ECON, FIN, GEN COMM exercice *m*, exercice social *m*; ◆ **be ~ at** STOCK se négocier à; **in and out ~** *jarg* STOCK faire des aller-retour, négoce d'entrée et sortie *m*; ~ **in wine** GEN COMM négoce du vin *m*; ~ **on the equity** ECON *company capital structure*, FIN pratique d'un ratio d'endettement élevé *f*

Trading: ~ **Standards Office** *n US* ECON ≈ Direction de la concurrence, de la consommation et de la répression des fraudes *f* (*Fra*)

tradition *n* GEN COMM tradition *f*

traditional *adj* GEN COMM traditionnel

traffic[1] *n* S&M, TRANSP trafic *m*; ~ **analysis** *n* TRANSP analyse du trafic *f*; ~ **builder** *n jarg* S&M *advertising* article d'appel *m* (*jarg*), cadeau de bienvenue *m*, cadeau de création de trafic *m*; ~ **circle** *n AmE* (*cf roundabout BrE*) GEN COMM, TRANSP rond-point *m*; ~ **congestion** *n* TRANSP embouteillage *m*, encombrement *m*; ~ **control** *n* TRANSP régulation de la circulation *f*, régulation du trafic *f*; ~ **control tower** *n* TRANSP *airport, seaport* tour de contrôle *f*; ~ **controller** *n* TRANSP contrôleur de la circulation *m*; ~ **counts** *n pl* S&M *advertising*, TRANSP comptage de la circulation *m*; ~ **density** *n* TRANSP densité de la circulation *f*, densité du trafic *f*; ~ **executive** *n* HRM, TRANSP responsable du trafic *m*; ~ **flow** *n* TRANSP intensité de la circulation *f*, intensité du trafic *f*; ~ **forecast** *n* TRANSP prévision de trafic *f*; ~ **jam** *n* TRANSP embouteillage *m*, encombrement *m*; ~ **lane** *n* TRANSP voie de circulation *f*; ~ **manager** *n* HRM directeur des transports *m*, HRM *(TM)* chef de la circulation *m*, *railway traffic* directeur de la circulation ferroviaire *m*, TRANSP directeur des transports *m*, TRANSP *(TM)* chef de la circulation *m*, *railway traffic* directeur de la circulation ferroviaire *m*; ~ **mixture** *n* TRANSP composition du trafic *f*; ~ **planning** *n* S&M *advertising* gestion des flux de travail *f*; ~ **potential** *n* TRANSP potentiel de trafic *m*; ~ **rights** *n pl* TRANSP droits de trafic *m pl*; ~ **separation scheme** *n* TRANSP dispositif de séparation du trafic *m*, système de séparation des sens de circulation *m*; ~ **sign** *n* TRANSP panneau de signalisation *m*; ~ **superintendent** *n (TS)* HRM, TRANSP chef de la circulation *m*, responsable des transports *m*, surveillant de circulation *m*; ~ **supervisor** *n* HRM, TRANSP inspecteur de la circulation *m*; ~ **time** *n* S&M *advertising* heure de grande écoute *f*; ~ **trend** *n* TRANSP tendance *f*; ~ **yield** *n* TRANSP rendement du trafic *m*

traffic:[2] ~ **in** *vt* GEN COMM *arms, explosives, drugs* faire le commerce de *loc m*

trafficker *n* GEN COMM trafiquant *m*

trail *vt* MEDIA *broadcast* annoncer

trailblazing *adj* GEN COMM *firm, industry, etc* innovateur

trailer *n* MEDIA *television, cinema* bande-annonce *f*, TRANSP remorque *f*; ~ **on flat car** TRANSP *rail* remorque sur wagon plat *f*; ~ **park** TRANSP aire de stationnement pour les remorques *f*; ~ **unladen weight** GEN COMM poids à vide de la remorque *m*; ~ **utilization** TRANSP utilisation des remorques *f*

train:[1] ~ **fare** *n* TRANSP prix du billet *m*; ~ **ferry** *n* TRANSP ferry *m*, navire transbordeur *m*, train-ferry *m*, transbordeur *m*; ~ **ferry deck** *n* TRANSP *shipping* pont wagons *m*; ~ **number** *n* TRANSP numéro de train *m*; ~ **station** *n* BrE *(cf railroad station AmE, railway station)* TRANSP gare *f*

train[2] **1.** *vt* HRM former; **2.** *vi* HRM faire de la formation *loc f*, être formateur

trainee *n* ADMIN, HRM stagiaire *mf*; ~ **manager** HRM, MGMNT cadre en formation *m*; ~ **programmer** COMP apprenti-programmeur *m*, élève-programmeur *m*; ~ **solicitor** *UK* LAW avocat stagiaire *m*; ~ **turnover** HRM rotation des stagiaires *f*; ~ **typist** ADMIN secrétaire-stagiaire *m*

traineeship *n* HRM stage en entreprise *m*

trainer *n* HRM formateur *m*

training *n* GEN COMM, HRM formation *f*, perfectionnement *m*; ~ **center** *n* AmE, ~ **centre** *n* BrE HRM centre de formation *m*; ~ **course** *n* HRM cours de formation professionnelle *m*; ~ **needs** *n pl* GEN COMM, HRM, S&M besoins en formation *m pl*; ~ **needs analysis** *n* GEN COMM, HRM, S&M analyse des besoins en formation *f*; ~ **officer** *n* GEN COMM, HRM cadre chargé de la formation *m*, directeur de formation *m*, responsable de la formation professionnelle *m*; ~ **pack** *n* HRM, MGMNT dossier de formation *m*; ~ **program** *n* AmE, ~ **programme** *n* BrE GEN COMM, HRM programme de formation *m*; ~ **scheme** *n* HRM plan de formation *m*; ~ **tax** *n* TAX taxe d'apprentissage *f*; ~ **of trainers** *n* HRM formation de formateurs *f*; ~ **within industry** *n* (*TWI*) HRM, IND formation dans l'entreprise *f*

Training: ~ **Agency** *n UK* (*TA*) HRM ≈ Association pour la formation professionnelle des adultes *f* (*AFPA*); ~ **and Enterprise Council** *n UK* (*TEC*) HRM programmes de formation en entreprises

trainload *n* TRANSP cargaison *f*

trait *n* GEN COMM caractéristique *f*

tramp *n* TRANSP *vessel* navire cargo sans ligne régulière *m*, tramp *m* (*vieilli*), vapeur en cueillette *m*; ~ **steamer** TRANSP vapeur en cueillette *m*

tramping *n* TRANSP *sea* tramping *m* (*vieilli*), transport maritime à la demande *m*

TRANS *abbr* (*transverse*) GEN COMM transversal

transact *vt* GEN COMM opérer une transaction, traiter

transaction *n* ACC, BANK, COMP, ECON, FIN, GEN COMM, STOCK opération *f*, transaction *f*; ~ **balance report** ACC relevé des opérations avec solde

m; ~ **cost** BANK frais par opération *m pl*; ~ **cost economics** ECON économie transactionnelle *f*; ~ **costs** GEN COMM frais de transaction *m pl*; ~ **data** COMP données de mouvement *f pl*; ~ **date** BANK, GEN COMM, STOCK date de l'opération *f*; ~ **exposure** STOCK dénonciation d'opération *f*, risque lié à la transaction *m*; ~ **fee** ACC, BANK, GEN COMM, STOCK frais de transaction *m pl*; ~ **file** COMP fichier de mise à jour *m*, fichier de transactions *m*, fichier mouvements *m*; ~ **loss** ECON *international trade* perte sur transactions *f*; ~ **management** COMP gestion transactionnelle *f*; ~ **management software** COMP logiciel de gestion transactionnelle *m*; ~ **processing** COMP traitement de mouvements *m*, traitement transactionnel *m*; ~ **profit** ECON *international trade* bénéfice sur transactions *m*; ~ **risk** STOCK risque d'opération en Bourse *m*, risque lié à la transaction *m*; ~ **status** GEN COMM, IND, S&M état d'avancement des opérations *m*; ~ **tax** STOCK, TAX impôt de Bourse *m*; ◆ **make a** ~ GEN COMM faire une opération, faire une transaction

transactional[1] *adj* ACC, BANK, COMP, ECON, FIN, GEN COMM, STOCK transactionnel

transactional:[2] ~ **analysis** *n* (*TA*) ACC, BANK, ECON, FIN, GEN COMM, MGMNT analyse transactionnelle *f*

transactions: ~ **costs** *n pl* ACC, BANK, STOCK coûts d'opération *m pl*, frais de transaction *m pl*; ~ **with customers** *n pl* BANK opérations clientèles *f pl*

transcode *vt* COMMS transcoder

transcoder *n* COMMS transcodeur *m*

transcribe *vt* COMP transcrire

transcriber *n* COMMS transcripteur *m*

transcription *n* COMP transcription *f*, GEN COMM copie conforme *f*, transcription *f*

transducer *n* COMMS transducteur *m*

transeuropean[1] *adj* GEN COMM, TRANSP transeuropéen

transeuropean:[2] ~ **network** *n* COMMS, COMP, GEN COMM, TRANSP réseau transeuropéen *m*

transfer[1] *n* ACC *of funds* virement *m*, BANK transfert *m*, transfert de fonds *m*, COMP *data* transfert *m*, FIN *of funds* virement *m*, GEN COMM *of responsibilities* transfert *m*, HRM, LAW mutation *f*, PATENTS transfert *m*, PROP mutation *f*, STOCK autorisation de virement *f*, formulaire de transfert *m*, TRANSP transfert *m*; ~ **account** *n* BANK compte de virement *m*; ~ **address** *n* COMP adresse de transfert *f*; ~ **of assets** *n* ACC transfert d'actif *m*; ~ **charge call** *n* COMMS appel en PCV *m* (*Fra*), appel à frais virés *m* (*Can*); ~ **development rights** *n pl* LAW, PROP droits de développement de cession *m pl*; ~ **earnings** *n pl* ECON gains d'opportunité *m pl*; ~ **of engagement** *n* HRM dévolution de responsabilité syndicale *f*; ~ **fee** *n* GEN COMM, LEIS *sport* montant du transfert *m*; ~ **of funds voucher** *n* BANK pièce de virement de fonds *f*, pièce justificative de virement de fonds *f*; ~ **income** *n* ECON revenu de transfert *m*;

~ manifest *n* TRANSP manifeste de transfert *m*; **~ order** *n* BANK, FIN ordre de transfert *m*, ordre de virement *m*; **~ payment** *n* BANK, FIN paiement de transfert *m*; **~ price** *n* GEN COMM prix de cession *m*, prix de cession interne *m*; **~ pricing** *n* ACC prix de transfert *m*, ECON fixation des prix de transfert *f*, FIN établissement des prix de cession *m*, GEN COMM tarification des transferts *f*, S&M *multinational companies* fixation des prix de transfert *f*; **~ problem** *n* ECON problème de transfert de capitaux *m*; **~ rate** *n* COMP vitesse de transfert *f*; **~ register** *n* STOCK registre des transferts *m*; **~ tax** *n* LAW, PROP droit de mutation *m*, TAX taxe de succession *f*; **~ of technology** *n* ECON transfert de technologie *m*; **~ of technology method** *n* ECON méthode de transfert de technologie *f*; **~ to business** *n* GEN COMM transfert aux entreprises *m*

transfer² **1.** *vt* ACC *debt* transporter, BANK transférer, virer, ECON *funds* transférer, FIN virer, HRM *to another branch of bank* déplacer, muter; **2.** *vi* TRANSP *change aircraft* changer d'avion, *change train* changer de train; ◆ **~ by endorsement** BANK transférer par endossement; **~ by wire** BANK télévirer; **~ the charges** COMMS *telephone* téléphoner en PCV (*Fra*); **~ ownership** PROP céder la propriété

Transfer: **~ & Automated Registration of Uncertified Stock** *n* ECON, STOCK *UK (TAURUS)* transfert et enregistrement automatisé de titres non-certifiés

transferability *n* STOCK *of registered shares* capacité à être transféré *f*, possibilité de virement *f*

transferable¹ *adj* GEN COMM cessible, STOCK *options* transférable, transmissible (*Can*); **not ~** STOCK non-transférable, non-transmissible

transferable²: **~ account area** *n (TAA)* TRANSP zone de comptes négociables *f*; **~ credit** *n* BANK crédit transférable *m*; **~ discharge permit** *n (SYN marketable discharge permit)* GEN COMM autorisation de décharge négociable *f*; **~ loan certificate** *n (TLC)* FIN certificat d'emprunt cessible *m*, certificat de prêt transférable *m*; **~ loan facility** *n (TLF)* FIN facilité d'emprunt cessible *f*, facilité de prêt transférable *f*; **~ loan instrument** *n (TLI)* FIN instrument d'emprunt cessible *m*, instrument de prêt transférable *m*; **~ revolving underwriting security** *n* STOCK facilité renouvelable à prise ferme transférable *f*; **~ securities** *n pl* FIN, STOCK valeurs mobilières *f pl*, valeurs transférables *f pl*

transferee *n* ACC, BANK, PATENTS cessionnaire *mf*; **~ company** GEN COMM société cessionnaire *f*

transferor *n* LAW *(cf transferrer)* cédant *m*, STOCK vendeur *m*; **~ company** GEN COMM société cédante *f*

transferred: **~ share** *n* STOCK action transférée *f*

transferrer *n (cf transferor)* LAW cédant *m*

transform *vt* ECON, GEN COMM transformer

transformation: **~ industry** *n* IND industrie de

transformation *f*; **~ problem** *n* ECON problème de transformation *m*

transfrontier *adj* GEN COMM, IMP/EXP transfrontalier

tranship *see transship*

transhipment *n see transshipment*

transient¹ *adj* GEN COMM temporaire

transient²: **~ medium** *n* S&M média éphémère *m*; **~ workers** *n pl* HRM travailleurs migrants *m pl*

transire *n* IMP/EXP laissez-passer *m*, passavant *m*

transit *n* IMP/EXP, LEIS, TRANSP transit *m*; **~ bond note** *n* IMP/EXP, TRANSP acquit de transit *m*; **~ card** *n* TRANSP *airline travel* carte de transit *f*; **~ clause** *n* INS, TRANSP *cargo policy* clause de transport *f*; **~ credit** *n* BANK crédit transitaire *m*; **~ document** *n* IMP/EXP, TRANSP document de transit *m*; **~ market** *n* ECON, FIN marché de transit *m*; **~ passenger** *n* LEIS, TRANSP voyageur en transit *m*; **~ rights** *n pl* IMP/EXP, TRANSP droits de transit *m pl*; **~ shed** *n* IMP/EXP, TRANSP hangar de transit *m*; **~ time** *n* TRANSP durée de transport *f*; **~ trade** *n* IMP/EXP, TRANSP commerce transitaire *m*; **~ traffic** *n* TRANSP trafic de transit *m*; ◆ **in ~** BANK en circulation, en cours, GEN COMM en transit

transition: **~ period** *n* GEN COMM période transitoire *f*

transitional¹ *adj* GEN COMM transitionnel

transitional²: **~ automated ticket** *n (TAT)* TRANSP billet automatisé de transition *m*; **~ period** *n* GEN COMM période de transition *f*; **~ provisions** *n pl* TAX provision transitoire *f*; **~ relief** *n* TAX allègement transitoire *m*

transitory: **~ income** *n* ECON revenu transitoire *m*

translate *vt* COMMS traduire, ECON *currency*, FIN convertir

translation *n* COMMS traduction *f*, ECON, FIN *of currency* conversion *f*, convertissement *m*; **~ difference** ACC *from consolidation of foreign subsidiaries* différence de conversion *f*; **~ differential** GEN COMM écart de conversion *m*; **~ loss** ECON, FIN perte de conversion *f*; **~ profit** ECON, FIN bénéfice de conversion *m*; **~ rate** BANK, ECON, FIN taux de conversion *m*; **~ risk** FIN risque de conversion *m*

translator *n* COMP *of language* programme de traduction *m*, *person* traducteur *m*, *software program* programme compilateur *m*, programme d'interprétation *m*, GEN COMM traducteur *m*

transmission *n* COMMS, COMP *of data* transmission *f*, MEDIA émission *f*; **~ expenses** *n pl* ACC *profit and loss* frais de transmission *m pl*; **~ mechanism** *n* ECON mécanisme de transmission *m*

transmit *vt* COMMS, MEDIA transmettre, émettre

transmittal: **~ letter** *n* ADMIN lettre de transmission *f*, COMMS lettre d'accompagnement *f*

transmitter *n* COMMS, GEN COMM, MEDIA *radio, television* émetteur *m*

transmitting *adj* COMMS, GEN COMM, MEDIA transmetteur, émetteur

transnational[1] *adj* ECON, GEN COMM, IND, POL transnational

transnational:[2] ~ **corporation** *n (TNC)* ECON, GEN COMM, POL entreprise transnationale *f*, société transnationale *f*

Transpacific: ~ **Westbound Rate Agreement** *n (TWRA)* TRANSP Accord tarifaire transpacifique en direction de l'ouest *m*

transparency *n* ACC, GEN COMM transparence *f*; ~ **of information** *jarg* POL transparence de l'information *f*

transparent *adj* COMP *device, network*, GEN COMM *of person, plans* transparent

transplant: ~ **factory** *n* IND usine transplantée *f*

transport[1] *n* TRANSP acheminement *m*, transport *m*; ~ **advertising** *n* S&M, TRANSP publicité dans les moyens de transport *f*; ~ **agent** *n* TRANSP transitaire *mf*; ~ **company** *n* TRANSP entreprise de transport *f*; ~ **controller** *n* HRM, TRANSP contrôleur des transports *m*; ~ **distribution analysis** *n (TDA)* TRANSP analyse de la distribution de transport *f*; ~ **document** *n* TRANSP *shipping* document de transport *m*; ~ **economics** *n* ECON, TRANSP économie des transports *f*; ~ **emergency card** *n (trem card)* TRANSP *road* carte d'urgence de transport *f*; ~ **facilitation** *n* TRANSP facilitation *f*; ~ **facilities** *n pl* TRANSP moyens de transport *m pl*; ~ **instruction** *n* TRANSP bordereau d'instruction *m*, fiche d'instructions de transport *f*; ~ **instruction form** *n* TRANSP bordereau d'instruction *m*, fiche d'instructions de transport *f*; ~ **insurance** *n* INS, TRANSP assurance contre les risques de transport *f*; ~ **mode** *n* TRANSP mode de transport *m*, moyen de transport *m*; ~ **quota** *n* TRANSP contingent de transport *m*; ~ **secretary** *n* POL, TRANSP ministre des Transports *m*; ~ **tax** *n* TAX taxe de transport *f*; ~ **unit** *n* TRANSP unité de transport *f*

transport[2] *vt* TRANSP acheminer, transporter; ◆ ~ **by air** TRANSP transporter par avion

Transport: ~ **Act** *n* UK LAW, TRANSP loi sur les transports *f*; ~ **and General Workers' Union** *n* UK *(TGWU)* HRM, IND syndicat des transports et des travailleurs confédérés *m*

transportable[1] *adj* TRANSP transportable

transportable:[2] ~ **moisture limit** *n* TRANSP limite d'humidité transportable *f*

transportation *n* TRANSP transport *m*; ~ **advertising** *n* S&M, TRANSP publicité dans les moyens de transport *f*; ~ **document** *n* TRANSP document de transport *m*; ~ **equipment** *n* TRANSP matériel de transport *m*; ~ **expenses** *n pl* TRANSP frais de transport *m pl*; ~ **system** *n* TRANSP système de transport *m*; ◆ ~ **charges not allowed for** TRANSP frais de transport non compris *m pl*; ~ **charges not included** GEN COMM frais de transport non compris *m pl*

Transportation: ~ **Secretary** *n* US TRANSP ≈ ministre des Transports *m*

transporting *n* TRANSP acheminement *m*

transposal *n* LAW, POL *EU* transposition *f*

transposition: ~ **error** *n* GEN COMM erreur d'inversion *f*

transship *vt* TRANSP transborder

transshipment *n* TRANSP transbordement *m*; ~ **bill of lading** IMP/EXP, TRANSP *shipping* connaissement de transbordement *m*; ~ **bond** IMP/EXP, TRANSP acquit de transit *m*; ~ **delivery order** IMP/EXP, TRANSP permis de transbordement *m*; ~ **entry** IMP/EXP, TRANSP déclaration de transbordement *f*; ~ **freight** IMP/EXP, TRANSP fret de transbordement *m*

Trans-Siberian: ~ **Railway** *n (TSR)* TRANSP Transsibérien *m*

transversal: ~ **lashing system** *n* TRANSP dispositif d'arrimage transversal *m*

transverse[1] *adj (TRANS)* GEN COMM transversal

transverse:[2] ~ **member** *n* TRANSP *fitting* transverse *f*; ~ **propulsion unit** *n* TRANSP *shipping* propulseur latéral *m*

trashy: ~ **goods** *n pl infrml* GEN COMM, S&M camelote *f*

travel: ~ **advance** *n* ECON avance sur déplacement *f*; ~ **agency** *n* LEIS, TRANSP agence de voyages *f*; ~ **agent** *n* HRM, LEIS, TRANSP agent de voyage *m*; ~ **bureau** *n* HRM, LEIS, TRANSP agence de voyages *f*; ~ **claim** *n* GEN COMM demande de remboursement de frais de déplacement *f*, demande de remboursement de frais de voyage *f*, réclamation de frais de déplacement *f*, réclamation de frais de voyage *f*; ~ **document** *n* LEIS document de voyage *m*; ~ **expense claim** *n* GEN COMM demande de remboursement de frais de déplacement *f*, demande de remboursement de frais de voyage *f*, réclamation de frais de déplacement *f*, réclamation de frais de voyage *f*; ~ **expenses** *n pl* GEN COMM, HRM, TAX frais de déplacement *m pl*, frais de voyage *m pl*; ~ **incentive** *n* UK S&M *advertising* incitation à voyager *f*; ~ **insurance** *n* INS, LEIS, TRANSP assurance voyage *f*; ~ **restriction** *n* TRANSP restriction de voyage *f*; ~ **services** *n pl* ECON, TRANSP services de transports *m pl*; ~ **-to-work area** *n* GEN COMM trajet à la zone de travail *m*; ~ **voucher** *n* TRANSP bon de voyage *m*

traveler *n AmE see* **traveller** *BrE*

travelift *n* TRANSP *cargo handling* portique sur pneus *m*, portique sur rails *m*

traveling: ~ **allowance** *n AmE see* **travelling allowance** *BrE*; ~ **expenses** *n pl AmE see* **travelling expenses** *BrE*; ~ **fair** *n AmE see* **travelling fair** *BrE*; ~ **salesman** *n AmE see* **travelling salesman** *BrE*; ~ **salesperson** *n AmE see* **travelling salesperson** *BrE*; ~ **saleswoman** *n AmE see* **travelling saleswoman** *BrE*

traveller *n BrE* LEIS voyageur *m*; ~**'s cheque** *BrE* BANK, LEIS chèque de voyage *m*

travelling: ~ **allowance** *n BrE* GEN COMM indemnité de déplacement *f*; ~ **expenses** *n pl BrE* GEN COMM, HRM, TAX frais de déplacement *m pl*, frais de voyage *m pl*; ~ **fair** *n BrE* TRANSP *going from* *place to place* exposition itinérante *f*; ~ **salesman** *n BrE* GEN COMM voyageur de commerce *m*, HRM, S&M représentant *m*, voyageur de commerce *m*; ~ **salesperson** *n BrE* COM, HRM voyageur de commerce *m*, S&M voyageur de commerce *m*, voyageuse de commerce *f*; ~ **saleswoman** *n BrE* HRM représentante *f*, voyageuse de commerce *f*, S&M voyageuse de commerce *f*

travelscator *n* S&M rampe mécanique *f*

traversable *adj* LAW contestable

traverse[1] *n* LAW contestation *f*, dénégation *f*

traverse[2] *vt* LAW, PROP violer

travolator *n AmE (cf moving pavement BrE)* GEN COMM, LEIS tapis roulant *m*, trottoir roulant *m*

trawler *n* TRANSP *ship* chalutier *m*

tray: **out-~** *n* ADMIN courrier départ *m*

treasurer *n* FIN, HRM trésorier *m*; ~ **check** *AmE*, ~ **cheque** *BrE* BANK chèque bancaire *m*; ~**'s report** FIN rapport financier *m*

treasury: ~ **note** *n* STOCK billet de trésorerie *m*, BT; ~ **stock** *n AmE (cf own shares BrE)* ACC actions rachetées par la société *f pl*; ~ **swap** *n* FIN échange cambiste *m*

Treasury *n UK* ECON ≈ ministère des Finances *m*; ~ **bill** *n US (T-bill)* ECON, STOCK bon du Trésor à court terme *m*; ~ **bill bonds** *n pl US (T-bill, cf government obligations)* BANK, ECON, STOCK bons du Trésor *m pl*, bon du Trésor à court terme *m*, valeurs du Trésor *f pl*; ~ **bill futures** *n* FIN, STOCK contrat à terme de bons du Trésor *m*; ~ **bill futures contract** *n* FIN, STOCK contrat à terme de bons du Trésor *m*; ~ **bill rate** *n (TBR)* ECON, STOCK taux de bons du Trésor *m*; ~ **bill tender** *n UK* ECON, STOCK adjudication de bons du Trésor *f*; ~ **Board** *n* POL Conseil du trésor *m*; ~ **Board contingencies vote** *n* POL crédit pour éventualités du Conseil du Trésor *m*; ~ **Board minute** *n* POL délibération du Conseil du Trésor *f*; ~ **Board Secretariat** *n* POL Secrétariat du conseil du trésor *m*; ~ **bond** *n (T-bond)* ECON, STOCK bon du Trésor à long terme *m*, obligation du Trésor *f*; ~ **Department** *n US* ECON ≈ ministère des Finances *m*; ~ **and interbank operations** *n pl* BANK *balance sheet* comptes de trésorerie et opérations interbancaires *m pl*; ~ **Investment Growth Receipt** *n (TIGR)* STOCK certificat de croissance des investissements du Trésor *m*; ~ **investments** *n pl UK* ACC *annual* valeurs mobilières de placement *f pl*; ~ **model** *n (SYN economic forecasting)* ECON prévisions économiques *f pl*; ~ **stock** *n UK* STOCK actions rachetées par la société *f pl*; ~**'s purse** *n UK* TAX Bourse du Trésor *f*

treat *vt* ENVIR, GEN COMM traiter; ◆ ~ **oneself to a meal out** *infrml* ECON s'offrir le restaurant

treaty *n* GEN COMM, POL traité *m*; ~ **port** *dat* TRANSP port ouvert au commerce international *m*; ~ **reinsurance** INS réassurance générale *f*; ~ **shopping** TAX chalandage fiscal *m*

Treaty: ~ **of Rome** *n* ECON, POL Traité de Rome *m*

treble *adj* GEN COMM triple

tree: ~ **structure** *n* COMP structure arborescente *f*, structure en arbre *f*

trem: ~ **card** *abbr (transport emergency card)* TRANSP carte d'urgence de transport *f*

tremendous *adj infrml* GEN COMM formidable

trend *n* ECON évolution *f*, GEN COMM *upward* tendance *f*; ~ **analysis** ECON analyse de tendance *f*; ~ **of events** GEN COMM cours des choses *m*, tournure des événements *f*; ~ **reversal** GEN COMM renversement de la tendance *m*; ◆ **set a** ~ GEN COMM lancer une mode; ~ **towards smaller families** GEN COMM tendance en faveur des familles moins nombreuses

trendsetter *n* GEN COMM qui crée la mode *loc f*

trendsetting *n* GEN COMM création d'une mode *f*, lancement d'une mode *m*

trendy *adj infrml UK* GEN COMM branché *(infrml)*, dernier cri

trespass: ~ **on private property** *vi* LAW entrer sans autorisation dans une propriété privée, violer une propriété privée

trespasser *n* LAW intrus *m*

trespassers: ~ **will be prosecuted** *phr* LAW défense d'entrer sous peine de poursuites *loc f*

trespassing *n* LAW violation de propriété *f*; ◆ **no** ~ GEN COMM, LAW défense d'entrer, entrée interdite, propriété privée *f*

triad *n* GEN COMM *group of three* triade *f*

trial *n* GEN COMM, IND essai *m*, LAW procès *m*, S&M essai *m*; ~ **attorney** *US* LAW avocat *m*; ~ **balance** ACC balance de vérification *f*; ~ **and error method** ECON, MATH méthode des essais et des erreurs *f*; ~ **examiner** LAW juge médiateur *m*; ~ **jury** *US* LAW jury *m*, jury populaire *m*; ~ **lawyer** *US* LAW avocat *m*; ~ **offer** GEN COMM offre essai *f*; ~ **period** ECON, HRM, S&M période d'essai *f*; ~ **run** *(SYN test drive, test run)* TRANSP essai sur route *m*; ~ **subscriber** MEDIA abonné à l'essai *m*; ~ **subscription** *(TS)* MEDIA abonnement à l'essai *m*; ◆ **give sb a** ~ GEN COMM mettre qn à l'essai

triangle: ~ **service** *n* TRANSP service triangulaire *m*

triangular[1] *adj* GEN COMM *involving three parties* triangulaire

triangular:[2] ~ **compensation** *n* ECON *with financial switch* compensation triangulaire *f*; ~ **merger** *n* ECON, GEN COMM fusion triangulaire *f*; ~ **operation** *n* ECON opération triangulaire *f*

triangulation *n* IMP/EXP triangulation *f*

trib. *n (tribunal)* LAW tribunal *m*

triback *n* TRANSP *road* train routier *m*

tribunal *n (trib.)* LAW tribunal *m*; ~ **of enquiry** *n* LAW commission d'enquête *f*; ~**s entitled to adjudicate** *n pl* LAW juridictions compétentes *f pl*, tribunaux compétents *m pl*

trickle:[1] ~ **diversions** *n pl jarg* GEN COMM maigres diversions *f pl*

trickle:[2] ~ **in** *vi* GEN COMM *in small quantities* arriver au compte-gouttes

tricks: ~ **of the trade** *phr* GEN COMM ficelles du métier *f pl*

trifling *adj* GEN COMM insignifiant

trigger:[1] ~ **mechanism** *n* GEN COMM dispositif de déclenchement *m*; ~ **point** *n* GEN COMM point de déclenchement *m*; ~ **price** *n* IMP/EXP prix minimum à l'importation *m*; ~ **pricing** *n* GEN COMM, IND fixation d'un prix de déclenchement *f*

trigger[2] *vt* GEN COMM *cost increases* déclencher

trim[1] *n* TRANSP *shipping* assiette *f*; ◆ **be in** ~ TRANSP *of ship* avoir son assiette, être équilibré; **in good** ~ *infrml* GEN COMM en bon état

trim[2] *vt* ECON, FIN *reduce* réduire; ◆ ~ **the workforce** HRM dégraisser le personnel, faire des compressions de personnel, réduire le personnel

trimmed: ~ **by the head** *phr* TRANSP *shipping* en différence négative *loc f*, en différence positive *loc f*, sur le nez *loc*; ~ **by the stern** *phr* TRANSP *shipping* en différence négative *loc f*, en différence positive *loc f*, sur le cul *loc*

trimming: ~ **tank** *n* TRANSP *shipping* caisse d'assiette *f*

trimmings *n pl* GEN COMM *add* garnitures *f pl*; ◆ **with no** ~ GEN COMM sans fioriture

Trinidad: ~ **and Tobago** *pr n* GEN COMM Trinité-et-Tobago *f*

Trinidadian[1] *adj* GEN COMM trinidadien

Trinidadian[2] *n* GEN COMM *person* Trinidadien *m*

trip: ~ **advance** *n* ECON avance sur déplacement *f*; ~ **analysis** *n* TRANSP analyse des trajets *f*; ~ **charter** *n* TRANSP *shipping* affrètement au voyage *m*; ~ **travel advance** *n* ECON avance sur déplacement *f*

tripack *n* GEN COMM *pack of three items*, S&M pack de trois *m*, paquet de trois *m*

tripartism *n* HRM concentration tripartite *f*

triple:[1] ~ **-expansion** *adj (TE)* TRANSP à triple expansion; ~ **-screw** *adj* TRANSP à trois hélices

triple:[2] ~ **-A rating** *n* GEN COMM, STOCK classification AAA *f*; ~ **expansion engine** *n (T)* TRANSP moteur à triple expansion *m*; ~ **reduction** *n (TR)* GEN COMM triple réduction; ~ **tax exempt** *n* TAX triple exemption d'impôt; ~ **witching hour** *n* US STOCK *last trading hour on the third Friday of March, June, September, and December* heure des trois sorcières *f*, heure du triple sabbat *f*

triple[3] *vt* MATH tripler

triple-A: ~ **bond** *n (SYN AAA bond)* STOCK obligation notée AAA *f*

triple-A-rated *adj* STOCK *customer*, STOCK classé AAA

triplicate: **in** ~ *adj phr* GEN COMM *document* en triple exemplaire, GEN COMM en trois exemplaires *loc m*

Tripoli *pr n* GEN COMM Tripoli *n pr*

troika *n jarg* POL troïka *f*

trolley *n BrE (cf cart AmE)* TRANSP chariot *m*

tropical[1] *adj (T)* GEN COMM tropique

tropical:[2] ~ **fresh water load line** *n (TF)* TRANSP ligne de charge tropicale en eau douce *f (TD)*; ~ **rainforest** *n* ENVIR forêt tropicale ombrophile *f*

Tropical: ~ **Products Institute** *n (TPI)* ECON Institut des produits tropicaux *m*

trouble:[1] ~ **-free** *adj* GEN COMM *vehicle, device* sans problèmes

trouble[2] *n* COMP *problem* anomalie *f*, incident *m*, panne *f*, GEN COMM difficulté *f*, ennui *m*, problème *m*; ~ **spot** GEN COMM point noir *m*; ◆ **be in** ~ GEN COMM avoir des difficultés, avoir des ennuis, avoir des problèmes; **get out of** ~ GEN COMM se tirer d'affaire; **go to a lot of** ~ GEN COMM se donner beaucoup de mal; **have a lot of** ~ GEN COMM avoir beaucoup de problèmes, en voir de toutes les couleurs *(infrml)*, en voir des vertes et des pas mûres *(infrml)*

troubleshoot *vi* COMP *locate a fault* localiser, GEN COMM régler des problèmes

troubleshooter *n* COMP *debugging* expert *m*, spécialiste en débogage *m*, technicien informatique *m*, GEN COMM dépanneur *m*

troubleshooting *n* COMP, GEN COMM dépannage *m*

trough *n* ECON *of graph, curve* creux *m*, point bas *m*

troy: ~ **ounce** *n* ECON *of gold* once troy *f*; ~ **weight** *n* GEN COMM poids troy *m*

truck *n AmE (cf lorry BrE)* TRANSP camion *m*; ~ **acts** *jarg* HRM, LAW lois sur les règlements de salaires ouvriers en nature; ~ **driver** *AmE (cf lorry driver BrE, teamster, trucker)* TRANSP camionneur *m*, chauffeur de camion *m*, conducteur de camion *m*, routier *m*; ~ **farmer** *AmE (cf market gardener BrE)* ECON maraîcher *m*; ~ **farming** *AmE (cf market gardening BrE)* ECON maraîchage *m*; ~ **loading reception area** *AmE (cf lorry loading reception area BrE)* TRANSP zone de chargement des camions *f*; ~ **-mounted crane** *AmE (cf lorry-mounted crane BrE)* TRANSP camion-grue *m*, grue sur camion *f*; ~ **reception area** *AmE (cf lorry reception area BrE)* TRANSP zone de chargement des camions *f*; ~ **service** *(cf trucking AmE)* TRANSP vol camionné *m*

truckage *n* TRANSP camionnage *m*

trucker *n AmE (cf lorry driver BrE, teamster, truck driver)* TRANSP camionneur *m*, chauffeur de camion *m*, conducteur de camion *m*, routier *m*

trucking *n AmE (SYN truck service)* TRANSP vol camionné *m*; ~ **bill of lading** *n* IMP/EXP lettre de voiture *f*; ~ **charges** *n pl* TRANSP frais de camionnage *m pl*; ~ **company** *n AmE (cf haulier BrE)* TRANSP camionneur *m*, entreprise de camionnage *f*, entreprise de transport *f*, entreprise de transports routiers *f*; ~ **contractor** *n (SYN haulage contractor)* TRANSP camionneur *m*, entrepreneur de transports *m*, entrepreneur de transports routiers *m*, transporteur *m*

truckload *n AmE (cf lorryload BrE)* TRANSP cargaison *f*

true:[1] ~ **and fair** *adj* ACC *audit, view* fidèle; ~ **to sample** *adj* GEN COMM conforme à l'échantillon

true:[2] ~ **copy** *n* ADMIN, LAW *of document* copie

conforme *f*; **~ and fair view** *n BrE (cf fair presentation AmE)* ACC image fidèle *f*; **~ lease** *n* FIN bail conforme *m*; **~ owner** *n* LAW, PROP propriétaire légitime *m*

trump: **~ card** *n* GEN COMM atout *m*

truncate *vt* COMP, GEN COMM tronquer

truncation *n* BANK dématérialisation des transferts de fonds *f*

trunk *n AmE (cf boot BrE)* TRANSP coffre *m*; **~ call** *UK* COMMS communication interurbaine *f*, communication à longue distance *f*; **~ line** COMMS ligne interurbaine *f*; **~ road** TRANSP route principale *f*

trust *n* BANK fiducie *f*, ECON trust *m*, GEN COMM confiance *f*; **~ account** BANK compte en fiducie *m*; **~ agreement** GEN COMM, LAW convention de fiducie *f*; **~ bank** BANK banque d'investissement *f*; **~ company** FIN compagnie fiduciaire *f*, société de fiducie *f*; **~ deed** LAW acte de fidéicommis *m*; **~ fund** ECON, FIN, LAW fonds d'affectation spéciale *m*, fonds en fidéicommis *m pl*; **~ instrument** LAW *document* instrument créateur d'un fidéicommis *m*; **~ mortgage** BANK hypothèque fiduciaire *f*; **~ share** MGMNT participation partielle *f*; **~ unit** STOCK part de fiducie *f*

trustbusting *n infrml US* GEN COMM action antitrust *f*

trustee *n* ADMIN administrateur *m*, BANK syndic *m*, FIN curateur *m*, LAW curateur *m*, fiduciaire *m*, PROP curateur *m*; **~ in bankruptcy** BANK syndic de faillite *m*; **~ status** STOCK fiducie *f*, statut fiduciaire *m*

trusteeship *n* LAW fidéicommis *m*

trustify *vt* GEN COMM, MGMNT réunir en trust

trustworthiness *n* GEN COMM honnêteté *f*, loyauté *f*

trustworthy *adj* GEN COMM *company* fidèle, *person* digne de confiance, loyal

truth: **~ in lending** *n jarg* BANK prêt certifié *m*, transparence bancaire en matière de prêts *f*, transparence en matière de crédits *f*, FIN, GEN COMM, LAW transparence bancaire en matière de prêts *f*, transparence en matière de crédits *f*; **~ in lending act** *n* ECON, LAW *1968* loi sur les taux réels de prêt *f*; **~ in lending law** *n* BANK, FIN, GEN COMM, LAW loi sur la transparence du crédit *f*; **~ squad** *n infrml* POL équipe de vérité *f*

truthfulness *n* ACC sincérité *f*

try: **~ out** *vt* GEN COMM, S&M essayer

TS *abbr* HRM *(traffic superintendent)* chef de la circulation *m*, responsable des transports *m*, surveillant de circulation *m*, MEDIA *(trial subscription)* abonnement à l'essai *m*, TRANSP *(traffic superintendent)* chef de la circulation *m*, responsable des transports *m*, surveillant de circulation *m*

TSA *abbr UK (The Securities Association)* STOCK ≈ CBV *(Conseil des bourses de valeurs)*

TSE *abbr Canada (the Toronto Stock Exchange)* STOCK la Bourse de Toronto *f (Canada)*

TSR *abbr (Trans-Siberian Railway)* TRANSP *rail* Transsibérien *m*

tsw *abbr (telesoftware)* COMP logiciel de télétexte *m*, télélogiciel *m*

TT *abbr* BANK *(telegraphic transfer)*, COMMS *(telegraphic transfer)* TT *(transfert télégraphique)*, TRANSP *(timetable)* horaire *m*, TRANSP *(tank top)* plafond de ballast *m*

TTC *abbr (tender to contract)* GEN COMM soumission d'offre *f*

T-test *n* MATH *statistics* test t *m*

TU *abbr UK (trade union)* HRM syndicat *m*

TUA *abbr UK (trade union act)* ECON, HRM, IND, LAW, POL loi sur les syndicats *f*

tubeshaft *n* TRANSP arbre de transmission tubulaire *m*

TUC *abbr UK (Trades Union Congress)* HRM confédération des syndicats britanniques, ≈ CGT *(Confédération générale du travail)*

Tues. *abbr (Tuesday)* GEN COMM mardi *m*

Tuesday *n (Tues.)* GEN COMM mardi *m*

tug *n (T)* TRANSP *shipping* remorqueur *m*; **~ -of-war** GEN COMM *between companies, rivals* épreuve de force *f*

tugmaster *n* TRANSP *shipping, port* tracteur de terminal *m*

tugrik *n* GEN COMM tugrik *m*

tuition: **~ fees** *n pl* WEL *of student* droits d'inscription *m pl*

TULRA *abbr UK (Trade Unions and Labour Relations Act)* HRM, IND, LAW loi sur les syndicats et les relations de travail

tumble *vi* ECON chuter, GEN COMM *cost, price* chuter, tomber, S&M, STOCK chuter

tuning *n* GEN COMM *of business procedures* réglage *m*

Tunis *pr n* GEN COMM Tunis *n pr*

Tunisia *pr n* GEN COMM Tunisie *f*

Tunisian[1] *adj* GEN COMM tunisien

Tunisian[2] *n* GEN COMM *person* Tunisien *m*

tunnel *n jarg* ECON tunnel *m (jarg)*; **~ toll** TRANSP *tariffs* péage du tunnel *m*

turbine *n* TRANSP turbine *f*; **~ steamship** TRANSP *shipping* vapeur à turbine *m*

turbo: **~ -electric** *adj* TRANSP turbo-électrique

turf: **~ accountant** *n frml* LEIS *sport* bookmaker *m*

Turk *n* GEN COMM *person* Turc *m*

Turkey *pr n* GEN COMM Turquie *f*

Turkish[1] *adj* GEN COMM turc

Turkish[2] *n* GEN COMM *language* turc *m*

Turkmenistan *pr n* GEN COMM Turkménistan *m*

turn[1] *n* STOCK différence offert-demandé *f*, écart *m*; **~ for the better** *(ANT turn for the worse)* GEN COMM amélioration *f*; **~ for the worse** *(ANT turn for the better)* GEN COMM aggravation *f*; **~ time** TRANSP *shipping port* tour de mise à quai *m*, tour de rôle *m*; ◆ **take a ~** GEN COMM *for better, worse* prendre un tournant; **take a ~ for the better** *(ANT* *take a turn for the worse)* GEN COMM aller mieux, s'améliorer, tourner bien; **take a ~ for the worse** *(*ANT *take a turn for the better)* GEN COMM empirer, tourner mal

turn:[2] **1.** *vt* **~ around** ECON, FIN redresser; **~ away** GEN COMM rejeter; **~ off** COMP mettre hors tension, éteindre; **~ on** COMP mettre en marche, mettre sous tension; **2.** *vi* **~ around** GEN COMM *business, company* se redresser; **~ over** HRM *of workforce, employees* se renouveler, TRANSP chavirer; ◆ **~ into cash** GEN COMM convertir en espèces; **~ one's attention to** GEN COMM porter son attention à; **~ out to vote** POL aller voter; **~ turtle** TRANSP *shipping* chavirer

turnabout *n* GEN COMM *charge* revirement *m*

turnaround *n AmE see turnround BrE*

turnbuckle *n (*SYN *bottlescrew)* TRANSP ridoir *m*

turning: **~ basin** *n* TRANSP *shipping, port* bassin d'évitage *m*; **~ circle** *n* TRANSP rayon de braquage *m*; **~ off** *n* COMP mise hors tension *f*; **~ on** *n* COMP mise sous tension *f*; **~ point** *n* GEN COMM point décisif *m*

turnkey *n* COMP *system, project*, GEN COMM, IND, PROP clés en main *f pl*; **~ contract** GEN COMM, PROP contrat clé en main *m*

turnout *n* GEN COMM *in election* participation *f*, IMP/EXP vidage *m*

turnover *n* ACC chiffre d'affaires *m*, CA, *accounts receivable* rotation *f*, ECON rotation *f*, FIN chiffre d'affaires *m*, CA, *accounts receivable* rotation *f*, GEN COMM chiffre d'affaires *m*, CA, rotation *f*, HRM, IND rotation *f*, S&M chiffre d'affaires *m*, CA; **~ rate** GEN COMM vitesse de rotation *f*; **~ ratio** ACC, GEN COMM rapport chiffre d'affaires-immobilisations *m*; **~ tax** TAX impôt sur le chiffre d'affaires *m*

turnpike *n AmE (cf toll motorway BrE)* TRANSP autoroute à péage *f*; **~ theorem** ECON théorème du péage *m*

turnround *n* FIN financement de redressement *m*, GEN COMM *in a trend* volte-face *f*, TRANSP *BrE of ship* rotation *f*; **~ period** GEN COMM délai aller-retour *m*; **~ time** *BrE* TRANSP *loading, unloading* durée de rotation *f*

turret: **~ anchored production system** *n (TAPS)* TRANSP système de production à tourelle d'ancrage *m*

TV[1] *abbr (television)* COMMS, GEN COMM, MEDIA télé *(infrml) (télévision)*

TV:[2] **~ commercial** *n* MEDIA, S&M message publicitaire télévisé *m*; **~ network** *n* COMMS réseau de télévision *m*

TVA *abbr (Tennessee Valley Authority)* ECON agence fédérale de la vallée du Tennessee

TWD *abbr ('tween deck, 'tween deck space)* TRANSP *shipping* entrepont *m*

tweak *vt* COMP améliorer, mettre au point, peaufiner, régler

'tween: **~ deck** *n (TWD)* TRANSP *shipping* entrepont *m*; **~ deck space** *n (TWD)* TRANSP *shipping*

entrepont *m*; **~ deck tank** *n* TRANSP citerne d'entrepont *f*

twenty: **~ dollars** *n pl (cf double eagle US)* FIN double aigle *m*, pièce de vingt dollars *f*; **~ -five cents** *n pl infrml US (cf two-bits)* FIN vingt-cinq cents *m pl*; **~ foot equivalent unit** *n (TEU)* TRANSP *containers* équivalent d'un conteneur de vingt pieds *m*, équivalent vingt pieds *m (EVP)*; **~ -four hour trading** *n* STOCK marché ouvert 24 heures sur 24 *m*, négociation 24 heures sur 24 *f*, opérations 24 heures sur 24 *f pl*, session ininterrompue *f*, transactions 24h/24 *f pl*, transactions en continu *f pl*

TWI *abbr (training within industry)* HRM, IND formation dans l'entreprise *f*

twilight: **~ shift** *n BrE* HRM équipe de nuit *f*

twin:[1] **~ -screw** *adj (T)* TRANSP *shipping* à deux hélices

twin:[2] **~ room** *n* LEIS chambre à deux lits *f*; **~ -screw steamer** *n* TRANSP *shipping* vapeur à deux hélices *m*

twisting *n jarg* FIN escroquerie *f*

twistlock *n* TRANSP *container securing* verrou tournant *m*

two:[1] **~ -sided** *adj* COMP double face; **~ -tier** *adj* HRM *structure, system* à deux niveaux

two:[2] **~ -axle vehicle** *n* TRANSP véhicule à deux essieux *m*; **~ -berth cabin** *n* TRANSP cabine à deux personnes *f*; **~ -bits** *n pl infrml US (cf twenty-five cents)* FIN vingt-cinq cents *m pl*; **~ -class vessel** *n* TRANSP *shipping* navire à deux classes *m*; **~ -digit inflation** *n* ECON, FIN inflation à deux chiffres *f*; **~ -lane deck** *n* TRANSP *shipping* garage à deux voies *m*; **~ -part tariff** *n* ECON tarif séparant coûts variables et coûts fixes *m*; **~ -rate system** *n* TAX système à deux taux *m*; **~ -sided market** *n* STOCK *interbank money* marché à double tendance *m*; **~ -tailed test** *n* MATH *statistics* test à deux issues *m*; **~ -tier bargaining** *n* HRM convention salariale applicable localement et; **~ -tier system** *n* GEN COMM système à deux niveaux *m*; **~ -way scheme** *n* TRANSP *shipping, port* zone à deux voies de navigation *f*; **~ -way split** *n* GEN COMM division en deux *f*; **~ -way street** *n* TRANSP rue à double sens *f*; **~ -way variance analysis** *n* MATH *statistics* analyse de variance à deux sens *f*

TWRA *abbr (Transpacific Westbound Rate Agreement)* TRANSP Accord tarifaire transpacifique en direction de l'ouest *m*

tx. *abbr (telex)* COMMS télex *m*

tycoon *n* HRM magnat *m*

tying: **~ contract** *n* ECON, LAW contrat exécutoire *m*

type[1] *n* COMP *typography* caractère *m*; **~ of costs** FIN catégorie de coûts *f*; **~ font** COMP police de caractères *f*; **~ -I error** *n* ECON, MATH *statistics* erreur de type I *f*; **~ -II error** *n* ECON, MATH *statistics* erreur de type II *f*

type[2] *vt* COMP taper à la machine

typebar *n* ADMIN barre porte-caractères *f*, tige à caractères *f*, COMP barre d'impression *f*

typeface *n* ADMIN, COMP, MEDIA police de caractères *f*

typesetting *n* COMP, GEN COMM composition *f*

typewrite *vi* ADMIN dactylographier, taper à la machine

typewriter *n* GEN COMM machine à écrire *f*; **~ ball** ADMIN boule IBM® *f*, sphère d'impression *f*

typewritten *adj* ADMIN, PATENTS dactylographié (*frml*), tapé à la machine (*infrml*)

typically *adv* GEN COMM typiquement

typify *vt* GEN COMM être caractéristique de

typing: **~ contract** *n* ECON contrat de frappe *m*; **~ error** *n* (*typo*) COMP, GEN COMM, MEDIA faute de frappe *f*; **~ speed** *n* GEN COMM vitesse de frappe *f*

typist *n* ADMIN secrétaire *mf*

typo[1] *abbr* (*typing error*) COMP, GEN COMM, MEDIA faute de frappe *f*

typo[2] *n* COMP, MEDIA *print* coquille *f*

typographer *n* GEN COMM, MEDIA typographe *mf*

typographical: **~ error** *n* COMP, MEDIA coquille *f*

typology *n* GEN COMM typologie *f*

tyre *n* *BrE* TRANSP pneu *m*; **~ gauge** *BrE* TRANSP contrôleur de pression des pneus *m*, manomètre pour pneus *m*

U

U *abbr* TRANSP *(universal container)* conteneur pour usage général *m*, TRANSP *(unit load) distribution* unité de charge *f*, unité de chargement *f*

U/a *abbr (underwriting account)* INS compte de souscripteur *m*

UAE *abbr (United Arab Emirates)* GEN COMM Émirats Arabes Unis *m pl*

UAF *abbr (European Agricultural Fund)* ECON, FIN, POL Fonds agricole européen *m*

UAW *abbr* US *(United Automobile Workers)* HRM TUA *(travailleurs unifié de l'automobile)*

UAWB *abbr (universal air waybill)* IMP/EXP, TRANSP LTAU *(lettre de transport aérien universelle)*

uberrimae fides *n frml* GEN COMM, LAW franchise la plus parfaite *f*

ubi remedium ibi jus *phr* LAW là où il y a un remède, il y a un droit

UBR *abbr (Uniform Business Rate)* FIN ≈ taux d'activité constant *m*, ≈ taux normalisé d'activités *m*

u.c. *abbr (upper case)* ADMIN, COMP, MEDIA capitale *f*, haut de casse *m*, lettre capitale *f*, lettre de haut de casse *f*, lettre majuscule *f*, majuscule *f*

UCITS *abbr (undertakings for collective investment in transferables)* FIN *EU* OPCVM *(organisme de placements collectifs en valeurs mobilières)*

UC&P *abbr (Uniform Customs and Practice for Documentary Credits)* ECON *international trade* unification des pratiques et coutumes pour les crédits documentaire *f*

UDEAC *abbr (Central African Customs and Economics Union)* IMP/EXP UDEAC *(Union douanière et économique de l'Afrique centrale)*

Udk *abbr (upper deck)* TRANSP pont supérieur *m*

Uganda:[1] **~ shilling invoice** *n* BANK facture établie en shillings ougandais *f*

Uganda[2] *pr n* GEN COMM Ouganda *m*

Ugandan[1] *adj* GEN COMM ougandais

Ugandan[2] *n* GEN COMM *person* Ougandais *m*

U-hypothesis *n* ECON hypothèse en U *f*

UI *abbr (unemployment insurance)* HRM AC *(assurance-chômage)*

UK *abbr (United Kingdom)* GEN COMM Royaume-Uni *m*

UKAEA *abbr (United Kingdom Atomic Energy Authority)* IND agence de l'énergie atomique du Royaume-Uni

UK/Cont *abbr (United Kingdom or Continent)* TRANSP Royaume-Uni ou Continent *n pr*

Ukraine *pr n* GEN COMM Ukraine *f*

Ukrainian[1] *adj* GEN COMM d'Ukraine, ukrainien

Ukrainian[2] *n* GEN COMM *person* Ukrainien *m*

UKREP *abbr (United Kingdom Permanent Representative to the European Community)* ECON, POL représentant permanent du Royaume-Uni à la Communauté Européenne *m*

Ulan Bator *pr n* GEN COMM Oulan Bator *n pr*

ULD *abbr (unit load device)* TRANSP *aviation* unité de chargement aérienne *f*

ullage *n* FIN, IMP/EXP manquant *m*, TRANSP *shipping* vide *m*

ult. *abbr (ultimo)* GEN COMM du mois dernier *loc m*, ultimo *(frml)*, écoulé

ultimate: ~ risk *n* BANK risque assumé en dernier ressort *m*, risque ultime *m*

ultimatum *n* GEN COMM ultimatum *m*; ◆ **give sb an ~** GEN COMM donner un ultimatum à qn

ultimo *adv frml (ult.)* GEN COMM du mois dernier *loc m*, ultimo *(frml)*, écoulé

ultra: ~ large crude carrier *n* TRANSP *shipping* transporteur de brut géant *m*

ultra vires[1]: *adj* LAW en dehors des pouvoirs, hors de compétence

ultra vires[2]: **~ vires activities** *n pl* LAW actes effectués en dehors des statuts *m pl*; **~ vires borrowing** *n* BANK emprunt hors compétences *m*

UMA *abbr (union membership agreement)* HRM accord d'appartenance syndicale *m*

umbrella: ~ agent *n* TRANSP agent coordinateur *m*; **~ committee** *n* GEN COMM comité de coordination *m*; **~ fund** *n* FIN fonds cadre *m*, fonds de consolidation *m*, fonds de coordination *m*; **~ liability insurance** *n* INS assurance responsabilité civile umbrella *f*, assurance responsabilité civile complémentaire et excédentaire *f*; **~ project** *n* GEN COMM projet cadre *m*; ◆ **under the ~ of** GEN COMM sous les auspices de

UN[1] *abbr (United Nations)* ECON, POL ONU *(Organisation des Nations Unies)*

UN:[2] **~ number** *n* TRANSP numéro UN *m*; **~ Security Council** *n* POL Conseil de sécurité de l'ONU *m*

UNA *abbr (United Nations Association)* ADMIN ANU *(Association des Nations Unies)*

unabridged *adj* GEN COMM *in full* intégral

unaccepted *adj* GEN COMM non-accepté

unaccompanied: ~ baggage *n* *(ANT accompanied baggage)* TRANSP *distribution* bagages non-accompagnés *m pl*

unaccounted:[1] **~ -for** *adj* GEN COMM inexpliqué

unaccounted:[2] **be ~ for** *phr* GEN COMM *be missing* manquer; **be ~ for in the balance sheet** *phr* ACC *amount, item* ne pas apparaître dans le bilan *loc m*

unacknowledged *adj* GEN COMM *letter, communication* sans réponse

unadjusted: in ~ figures *phr* GEN COMM en données brutes non corrigées *loc f*

unadvertised *adj* GEN COMM *not disclosed* sans publicité

unadvisable *adj* GEN COMM déconseillé

unaffiliated *adj* GEN COMM, HRM *union* non-affilié

unallocated *adj* COMP disponible, non-affecté

unallotted *adj* STOCK *shares* non-attribué

unaltered *adj* GEN COMM *share prices* inchangé

unamortized[1] *adj* ACC *debt* non-amorti

unamortized:[2] ~ **bond discount** *n* STOCK escompte d'obligation non-amorti *m*; ~ **discount on Treasury bills** *n* STOCK escompte non-amorti des bons du Trésor *m*; ~ **portion of actuarial deficiencies** *n* ACC, FIN fraction non-amortie des insuffisances actuarielles *f*; ~ **premiums on investments** *n pl* STOCK prime non-amortie des investissements *f*, primes non-amorties sur investissements *f pl*

unanimity *n* GEN COMM unanimité *f*

unanimous *adj* GEN COMM *decision* unanime

unanimously:[1] ~ **accepted** *adj* GEN COMM *motion, proposal*, HRM voté à l'unanimité

unanimously[2] *adv* GEN COMM unanimement, à l'unanimité *loc f*, HRM à l'unanimité *loc f*

unanswered: ~ **call** *n* COMMS appel resté sans réponse *m*, appel sans réponse *m*

unanticipated *adj* GEN COMM imprévu

unappropriated[1] *adj* GEN COMM non-affecté

unappropriated:[2] ~ **retained earnings** *n pl* FIN bénéfices non-distribués disponibles *m pl*; ~ **surplus** *n* GEN COMM surplus disponible *m*

unapproved: ~ **funds** *n pl* FIN fonds non-agréés *m pl*

unassailable *adj* GEN COMM *conclusion, hypothesis* irréfutable

unassessed *adj* TAX *revenue* non-imposé

unassignable *adj* LAW *property, right* inaliénable, incessible

unassured *adj* INS inassuré, non-assuré

unattainable *adj* GEN COMM inaccessible

unattended: ~ **machinery spaces** *n pl* IND *production* salle des machines sans surveillance *f*

unaudited *adj* ACC *accounts* non-audité, non-contrôlé, non-vérifié

unauthenticated[1] *adj* LAW *document* non-authentifié, non-légalisé

unauthenticated:[2] ~ **signature** *n* LAW signature non-authentifiée *f*

unauthorized: ~ **shares** *n pl* STOCK actions non-autorisées *f pl*

unavailability *n* GEN COMM indisponibilité *f*

unavailable *adj* COMP, GEN COMM indisponible

unavoidable *adj* GEN COMM inévitable

unavoidably: be ~ **detained at the last minute** *phr* GEN COMM avoir un empêchement de dernière minute *loc m*

unbacked *adj* BANK non-soldé

unbalanced: ~ **growth** *n* ECON, FIN croissance mal équilibrée *f*

unblock *vt* GEN COMM débloquer, dégager

unbounded: ~ **risk** *n* STOCK *of futures* risque illimité *m*

unbranded: ~ **goods** *n pl* GEN COMM produits libres *m pl*

unbundle *vt* COMP, GEN COMM (SYN *demerger*) défusionner, dégrouper

unbundling *n* GEN COMM dégroupage *m*

unbusinesslike *adj* GEN COMM *person* peu commerçant

uncallable[1] *adj* FIN non-appelable

uncallable:[2] ~ **loan** *n* BANK prêt irrévocable *m*

uncalled: ~ **capital** *n* FIN capital non-appelé *m*

uncashed[1] *adj* GEN COMM *cheque* non-encaissé

uncashed:[2] ~ **check** *n AmE*, ~ **cheque** *n BrE* BANK chèque non-encaissé *m*, chèque à encaisser *m*

UNCED *abbr* (*United Nations Conference on Environment and Development*) ENVIR, GEN COMM CNUED (*Conférence des Nations Unies sur l'environnement et le développement*)

uncertainty *n* ECON, GEN COMM, S&M, STOCK incertitude *f*

unchanged *adj* GEN COMM *forecast* inchangé

unchecked[1] *adj* GEN COMM *figures* non-vérifié

unchecked:[2] ~ **baggage** *n* TRANSP bagages non-enregistrés *m pl*; ~ **inflationary economy** *n* ECON économie inflationniste non-contrôlée *f*

UNCITRAL *abbr* (*United Nations Commission of International Trade Law*) LAW Commission des Nations Unies pour le droit commercial international

unclaimed: ~ **balance** *n* BANK solde non-réclamé *m*; ~ **deposit** *n* BANK dépôt non-réclamé *m*; ~ **letter** *n* COMMS lettre en souffrance *f*; ~ **right** *n* LAW droit non revendiqué *m*

uncleared *adj* BANK *cheque* non-compensé

uncollectable[1] *adj* TAX non-recouvrable

uncollectable:[2] ~ **account** *n* ACC créance irrécouvrable *f*, mauvaise créance *f*; ~ **taxes** *n pl* TAX impôts irrécouvrables *m pl*

uncollected: ~ **funds** *n pl* BANK fonds non-collectés *m pl*

uncommitted: ~ **funds** *n* FIN fonds non-engagés *m pl*

uncompromising *adj* GEN COMM intransigeant

UNCON *abbr* (*uncontainerable goods*) TRANSP marchandises non-conteneurisables *f pl*

unconditional[1] *adj* COMP inconditionnel, LAW inconditionnel, sans condition, sans réserve

unconditional:[2] ~ **acceptance** *n* GEN COMM acceptation inconditionnelle *f*; ~ **grant** *n* (*cf federal finance US*) FIN subvention sans condition *f*; ~ **remission** *n* FIN *of debt* remise absolue *f*

unconfirmed: ~ **credit** *n* BANK crédit révocable *m*

unconscionable: ~ **bargain** *n* LAW contrat léonin *m*

unconstitutional: ~ **strike** *n* HRM, IND, LAW grève illicite *f*

uncontainerable: ~ **goods** *n pl* (*UNCON*) TRANSP marchandises non-conteneurisables *f pl*

uncontested: ~ **physical search** *n jarg* (*UPS*) POL fouille incontestée *f*

uncontrollable[1] *adj* GEN COMM *inflation* irrésistible, qui ne peut pas être contenu *loc m*

uncontrollable:[2] ~ **expenditures** *n pl* FIN dépenses incompressibles *f pl*

uncontrolled: ~ **dump site** *n* ENVIR décharge sauvage *f*

unconverted[1] *adj* BANK non-converti

unconverted:[2] ~ **share** *n* STOCK action non-convertie *f*

uncorrected *adj* GEN COMM non-redressé

uncovered: ~ **advance** *n* STOCK avance à découvert *f*; ~ **amount** *n* BANK montant à découvert *m*; ~ **balance** *n* FIN découvert *m*; ~ **bear** *n* STOCK baissier à découvert *m*; ~ **call** *n* (ANT *covered call UK*) STOCK option d'achat découverte *f*, option d'achat à découvert *f*, vente d'un call à découvert *f*; ~ **call option** *n* (*naked call*, ANT *covered call option*) STOCK option d'achat découverte *f*, option d'achat à découvert *f*, vente d'un call à découvert *f*; ~ **call writer** *n* STOCK souscripteur d'action à découvert *m*, vendeur d'option d'achat à découvert *m*; ~ **hedge loss** *n* STOCK perte à découvert *f*; ~ **option** *n* STOCK option à découvert *f*; ~ **put** *n* STOCK option de vente découverte *f*, option de vente à découvert *f*; ~ **writer** *n* STOCK souscripteur d'action à découvert *m*, vendeur d'option à découvert *m*

uncrossed[1] *adj* BANK *cheque* non-barré

uncrossed:[2] ~ **check** *n* *AmE*, ~ **cheque** *n* *BrE* BANK chèque non-barré *m*

UNCTAD[1] *abbr* (*United Nations Conference on Trade and Development*) ECON CNUCED (*Conférence des Nations Unies sur le commerce et le développement*)

UNCTAD:[2] ~ **multi modal-transport convention** *n* (*UNCTAD MMO*) ECON *international trade* convention de transport multimodal de la CNUCED *f*, convention sur le transport modal de la CNUCED *f*

UNCTAD MMO *abbr* (*UNCTAD multi modal-transport convention*) ECON *international trade* convention de transport multimodal de la CNUCED *f*, convention sur le transport modal de la CNUCED *f*

uncurbed *adj* GEN COMM *rivalry, competitiveness* effréné

uncurtailed *adj* GEN COMM *competition, rights* sans restriction

uncustomed *adj* IMP/EXP libre à l'entrée

undamaged *adj* GEN COMM non-endommagé

undamped *adj* ECON *demand* soutenu

undated *adj* GEN COMM sans date

undecided *adj* GEN COMM indécis

undelete *vt* COMP restaurer

undeliverable: ~ **check** *n* *AmE*, ~ **cheque** *n* *BrE* BANK chèque non-livrable *m*

undelivered: **if** ~ **please return to sender** *phr* COMMS en cas de non-distribution prière de renvoyer à l'expéditeur *loc m*

undepletable: ~ **externality** *n* ENVIR effet irréductible *m*

undepreciated[1] *adj* ACC non-amorti, non-déprécié

undepreciated:[2] ~ **capital cost** *n* FIN fraction non amortie du coût en capital *f*; ~ **cost** *n* ACC fraction non amortie du coût *f*, fraction non amortie du coût en capital *f*, FIN fraction non amortie du coût *f*

undepressed *adj* STOCK non-déprimé

under:[1] ~ **proof** *adj* GEN COMM *spirits* teneur en alcool insuffisante *f*

under[2] *prep* GEN COMM *less than* inférieur à, moins de, GEN COMM *beneath* sous; ♦ **a little** ~ GEN COMM légèrement inférieur à, un peu moins de

underabsorb *vt* ACC sous-absorber, sous-imputer

underabsorption *n* ACC *of costs* sous-absorption *f*, sous-imputation *f*

underachiever *n* (ANT *overachiever*) WEL personne qui n'a pas le niveau *loc m*

underapplied: ~ **overheads** *n pl* ACC, FIN frais généraux sous-imputés *m pl*

underassess *vt* ACC sous-évaluer

underassessment *n* TAX sous-imposition *f*, sous-évaluation *f*

underbid *vi* (SYN *underquote*) GEN COMM offrir des conditions plus avantageuses

undercapacity *n* (ANT *overcapacity*) ECON, GEN COMM, IND sous-capacité *f*

undercapitalized *adj* (ANT *overcapitalized*) GEN COMM, IND sous-capitalisé; ♦ **be** ~ FIN ne pas disposer de fonds suffisants

undercharged: ~ **account** *n* BANK compte insuffisamment débité *m*, compte sous-débité *m*

underclass *n* ECON les démunis *m pl*

underconsumption *n* ECON sous-consommation *f*

undercover: ~ **audit** *n* ACC audit à l'insu *m*, vérification anonyme *f*, vérification cachée *f*, vérification dissimulée *f*, vérification à l'insu *f*; ~ **payment** *n* FIN, GEN COMM, HRM, LAW, POL, S&M dessous-de-table *m*

undercut *vt* ECON *competitor* vendre moins cher que, GEN COMM casser, *competitor* vendre moins cher que

undercutting *n* GEN COMM vente à des prix qui défient la concurrence *f*, vente à prix *f*

under-deck: ~ **tonnage** *n* TRANSP *shipping* jauge sous le pont *f*

underdeclaration *n* TAX *VAT* sous-déclaration *f*

underdeclared: ~ **tax** *n* TAX impôt sous-déclaré *m*

underdeveloped: ~ **country** *n* ECON, GEN COMM, POL pays en voie de développement *m*, pays sous-développé *m*, PVD

underdevelopment *n* ECON sous-développement *m*

underemployed *adj* HRM sous-employé

underemployment *n* (ANT *overemployment*) ECON, GEN COMM, HRM sous-emploi *m*

underestimate *vt* GEN COMM sous-estimer

underestimation *n* GEN COMM sous-estimation *f*, S&M devis de participation *m*

underfunded *adj* FIN insuffisamment financé; ◆ **be ~** FIN ne pas être doté de moyens de financement suffisants

undergo *vt* GEN COMM subir

undergraduate *n* WEL étudiant *m*

underground *n* TRANSP métro *m*; **~ economy** ECON économie informelle *f*, économie souterraine *f*, FIN économie souterraine *f*

underinvestment *n* BANK sous-investissement *m*

underlessee *n* GEN COMM, LAW, PROP sous-locataire *mf*

underline¹ *n* COMP *text* soulignement *m*

underline² *vt* COMP *text* souligner

underling *n* HRM subalterne *m*

underlying¹ *adj* STOCK *currency* faisant l'objet de l'option, sous-jacent

underlying:² **~ asset** *n* STOCK actif sous-jacent *m*, sous-jacent *m*; **~ bond** *n* STOCK obligation sous option *f*, obligation sous-jacente *f*; **~ debt** *n* FIN *real estate, securities* dette sous-jacente *f*; **~ futures** *n pl* FIN contrat à terme sous option *m*, contrat à terme sous-jacent *m*, STOCK contrat à terme sous option *m*, contrat à terme sous-jacent *m*, valeurs à terme sous options *f pl*; **~ futures contract** *n* FIN, STOCK contrat à terme sous option *m*, contrat à terme sous-jacent *m*; **~ inflation** *n* ECON inflation sous-jacente *f*; **~ inflation rate** *n* (ANT *headline rate*) ECON taux d'inflation sous-jacente *m*; **~ mortgage** *n* BANK, PROP hypothèque sous-jacente *f*; **~ net assets** *n pl* FIN actif net sous-jacent *m*; **~ rate** *n* (ANT *headline rate*) ECON taux sous-jacent *m*; **~ security** *n* STOCK valeur sous-jacente *f*, valeur sous-option *f*; **~ tendency** *n* GEN COMM tendance profonde *f*; **~ trend** *n* GEN COMM tendance sous-jacente *f*

undermanned *adj* HRM à court de main-d'oeuvre, TRANSP *shipping* sous-armé; ◆ **be ~** HRM manquer de personnel

undermanning *n* HRM *labour force* insuffisance d'effectifs *f*, manque de main-d'oeuvre *m*, *staff* manque de personnel *m*, sous-effectif *m*

undermargined: **~ account** *n* STOCK compte à marge *m*, compte à marge insuffisante *m*

undermentioned *adj* GEN COMM mentionné ci-dessous

undermine *vt* GEN COMM *sb's authority, a principle* saper

underpay *vt* GEN COMM *employee* sous-payer, sous-rémunérer

underperform *vi* ECON, STOCK faire une contre-performance *loc f*

underperforming *adj* GEN COMM *department, company*, IND peu rentable

underpin *vt* ECON *currency* étayer

underpopulated *adj* GEN COMM *area, region* sous-peuplé

underprice *vt* (ANT *overprice*) S&M mettre un prix trop bas à

underpriced *adj* (ANT *overpriced*) GEN COMM au-dessous de la valeur, S&M pas assez cher; ◆ **this product is ~** GEN COMM ce produit est en vente à un prix inférieur à sa vraie valeur

underprivileged *adj* GEN COMM *person, country* déshérité

underproduce *vt* (ANT *overproduce*) ECON, IND sous-produire

underproduction *n* (ANT *overproduction*) ECON, IND sous-production *f*

under-proportionately *adv* GEN COMM sous-proportionnellement

underquote *vt* (SYN *underbid*) GEN COMM faire un prix plus avantageux que ceux des autres

underrecovery: **~ of overhead costs** *n* ACC sous-imputation des frais généraux *f*

underreport *vt* GEN COMM, TAX *revenue* minorer

underreporting *n* GEN COMM, TAX *of revenue* minoration *f*

underrepresent *vt* (ANT *overrepresent*) S&M sous-représenter

underrepresentation *n* (ANT *overrepresentation*) S&M sous-représentation *f*

underrun *n* FIN *appropriation* sous-utilisation *f*

underscore¹ *n* COMP soulignement *m*

underscore² *vt* COMP *text*, GEN COMM *text* souligner

under-secretary *n* HRM sous-secrétaire *mf*

undersell *vi* GEN COMM *goods* se vendre mal; **~ o.s.** GEN COMM ne pas savoir se vendre; ◆ **~ one's competitors** S&M vendre meilleur marché que ses concurrents

underselling *n* S&M *selling at lower prices* cassage des prix *m*

undershoot: **~ a target** *phr* ECON *equation, exchange rates* tomber en deça d'un objectif

undersigned: **I the ~ declare that** *phr* INS, LAW je soussigné déclare que

underspend *vt* ACC *budget* sous-employer, GEN COMM *money, funds* ne pas dépenser totalement

underspending *n* ECON, FIN dépenses inférieures aux fonds disponibles

understaffed *adj* HRM qui manque de personnel; ◆ **be ~** HRM manquer de personnel

understaffing *n* HRM manque de personnel *m*

understand *vt* GEN COMM comprendre, entendre, reconnaître; ◆ **give sb to ~ that** GEN COMM laisser entendre à qn que

understanding *n* GEN COMM *mutual arrangement* entente *f*, *of subject* compréhension; ◆ **come to an ~** GEN COMM arriver à un accord, parvenir à un accord; **have an ~ with sb** GEN COMM s'entendre avec qn; **on the ~ that** GEN COMM étant entendu que

understatement: ~ **of income** n TAX revenu déclaré en moins m, revenu sous-déclaré m

undersubscribed adj FIN share, issue non-souscrit, STOCK issue non-couvert

undertake vt GEN COMM entreprendre; ♦ ~ **to do sth** GEN COMM task s'engager à faire qch

undertaking n ECON entreprise f, GEN COMM entreprise f, agreement promesse f, venture entreprise f, MGMNT entreprise f

undertakings: ~ **for collective investment in transferables** n pl (UCITS) FIN EU organisme de placements collectifs en valeurs mobilières m (OPCVM)

undertax vt TAX sous-imposer

under-the-counter adj GEN COMM clandestin

underuse vt GEN COMM sous-employer

underutilize vt GEN COMM sous-utiliser

undervaluation n ECON of exchange rate, GEN COMM sous-évaluation f

undervalue n STOCK of shares acquired by company employees décote f, valeur moindre f

undervalued[1] adj FIN goods sous-évalué

undervalued:[2] ~ **currency** n ECON devise sous-évaluée f

underwrite vti STOCK issue prendre ferme

underwriter n (U/W) INS marine souscripteur m

underwriting n STOCK prise ferme f; ~ **account** (U/a) INS compte de souscripteur m; ~ **agreement** STOCK contrat de garantie m, contrat de prise ferme m; ~ **commission** FIN commission de garantie f; ~ **fee** BANK, FIN commission de garantie f, commission de placement f; ~ **spread** STOCK étendue de garantie f; ~ **syndicate** INS syndicat d'émission m

underwritten adj STOCK garanti, souscrit m

undischarged[1] adj GEN COMM maritime law, debt non-déchargé

undischarged:[2] ~ **commitment** n (SYN outstanding commitment) ACC engagement actuel m, engagement en cours m

undisclosed adj FIN amount, quantity non-révélé

undiscovered: ~ **loss clause** n FIN, LAW cargo insurance clause de pertes inconnues f

undisposed: ~ **of** adj GEN COMM stock, goods non-écoulé

undistributable: ~ **capital** n FIN capital non-distribuable m; ~ **reserves** n pl BrE (cf restricted surplus AmE) ACC réserves indisponibles f pl

undistributed: ~ **allotment** n GEN COMM affectation non-répartie f; ~ **balance** n ACC solde non-réparti m; ~ **income** n ECON bénéfices non-répartis m pl; ~ **profit** n FIN bénéfices non-distribués m pl, bénéfices non-répartis m pl; ~ **profits** n pl ACC bénéfices non-distribués m pl; ~ **-profits tax** n TAX impôt sur les bénéfices non distribués m

undivided: ~ **interest** n FIN intérêt non-réparti m; ~ **profits** n pl BANK, GEN COMM bénéfices non-distribués m pl; ~ **property** n PROP biens indivisibles m pl

UnDk abbr (under deck tank) TRANSP shipping citerne en cale f, citerne sous le pont f

undocumented: ~ **worker** n HRM, LAW having no national insurance, work permit travailleur clandestin m, travailleur sans papiers m

undue: ~ **hardship** n TAX difficultés indues f pl, préjudice indu m; ~ **influence** n GEN COMM abus d'influence m

unduly adv GEN COMM à tort

unearned: ~ **dividend** n STOCK dividende fictif m; ~ **income** n FIN accounting, taxes rentes f pl; ~ **increment** n FIN property, land plus-value f; ~ **increment of land** n FIN, PROP plus-value foncière f; ~ **interest** n BANK intérêt non-gagné m, intérêt à courir m; ~ **premium** n FIN, LAW plus-value f, prime payée d'avance f, TAX plus-value de prime f

uneconomic adj ECON, GEN COMM, IND, S&M inéconomique

unemployability n HRM inaptitude au travail f

unemployable adj HRM inapte à travailler

unemployed[1] adj HRM au chômage loc m

unemployed:[2] ~ **labor force** n AmE, ~ **labour force** n BrE HRM main-d'œuvre sans emploi f; ~ **person** n GEN COMM chômeur m; **the** ~ n pl ECON, HRM les chômeurs m pl, les sans-emplois m pl

unemployment n ECON, HRM, WEL chômage m; ~ **benefit** n BrE (cf unemployment compensation AmE) ECON, HRM, WEL allocation chômage f, indemnité de chômage f; ~ **compensation** n AmE (cf unemployment benefit BrE) ECON, HRM, WEL allocation chômage f, indemnité de chômage f, indemnité-chômage f; ~ **figures** n pl ECON, POL chiffres du chômage m pl; ~ **insurance** n (UI) HRM assurance-chômage f (AC); ~ **insurance account** n HRM compte d'assurance-chômage m; ~ **insurance premium** n INS cotisation d'assurance contre le chômage f; ~ **pay** n ECON, HRM, WEL indemnité de chômage f, indemnité-chômage f; ~ **rate** n ECON, WEL taux de chômage m; ~ **spell** n HRM période de chômage f; ~ **statistics** n HRM statistiques du chômage f pl; ~ **trap** n ECON, WEL cercle vicieux du chômage m

Unemployment: ~ **Benefit Office** n UK ECON, HRM, WEL ≈ UNEDIC (France), ≈ Union nationale pour l'emploi dans l'industrie et le commerce f

unencumbered[1] adj PROP non-grevé d'hypothèque

unencumbered:[2] ~ **balance** n ACC government solde non-grevé m; ~ **estate** n PROP propriété non-grevée f

unendorsed adj BANK cheque non-endossé

unenforceable[1] adj (ANT enforceable) LAW inapplicable, non-exécutoire

unenforceable:[2] ~ **contract** n LAW contrat non-exécutoire m

unequal: ~ **exchange** n GEN COMM change inégal m; ~ **trade** n ECON international marché inégal m

unequivocal adj GEN COMM franc

uneven[1] adj GEN COMM trend irrégulier

uneven:[2] ~ **lot** *n* GEN COMM lot fractionnaire *m*

unexchangeable *adj* GEN COMM, S&M inéchangeable

unexecuted *adj* GEN COMM non-satisfait

unexpended[1] *adj* FIN *money* non-dépensé

unexpended:[2] ~ **balance** *n* FIN *of appropriation* solde inemployé *m*

unexpired[1] *adj* LAW *contract* non-expiré, toujours en vigueur

unexpired:[2] ~ **cost** *n* ECON frais qui court toujours, coût toujours valide *m*

unexplained: ~ **absence** *n* HRM absentéisme injustifié *m*

unfailing *adj* GEN COMM *remedy* infaillible

unfair: ~ **competition** *n* (ANT *fair competition*) ECON, GEN COMM, IND, LAW, PATENTS, S&M concurrence déloyale *f*; ~ **contract** *n* LAW contrat léonin *m*; ~ **dismissal** *n* HRM licenciement abusif *m*; ~ **house** *n jarg* HRM entreprise proposant des salaires inéquitables; ~ **labor practice** *n AmE*, ~ **labour practice** *n BrE* HRM pratique déloyale en matière de relations *f*; ~ **shop** *n jarg* HRM entreprise proposant des salaires inéquitables; ~ **trade** *n* GEN COMM, LAW commerce illicite *m*; ~ **trading** *n* GEN COMM, LAW commerce illicite *m*; ~ **trading practices** *n pl* GEN COMM pratiques commerciales déloyales *f pl*

unfavorable[1] *adj AmE see* unfavourable *BrE*

unfavorable:[2] ~ **balance of trade** *n AmE see* unfavourable balance of trade *BrE*; ~ **trading conditions** *n pl AmE see* unfavourable trading conditions *BrE*

unfavorably: **be** ~ **impressed** *phr AmE see* be unfavourably impressed *BrE*

unfavourable[1] *adj BrE* (ANT *favourable*) ACC défavorable, GEN COMM *price, conditions* défavorable, *rate of exchange* défavorable

unfavourable:[2] ~ **balance of trade** *n BrE* IMP/EXP balance commerciale défavorable *f*, balance commerciale déficitaire *f*, balance commerciale passive *f*; ~ **trading conditions** *n pl BrE* ECON conditions défavorables pour le commerce *f pl*

unfavourably: **be** ~ **impressed** *phr BrE* GEN COMM avoir une impression défavorable *loc f*

unfeasible *adj* GEN COMM *plan* irréalisable

unfilled: ~ **orders** *n pl* GEN COMM, S&M commandes non-satisfaites *f pl*; ~ **vacancies** *n pl* HRM offres d'emploi non-satisfaites *f pl*, postes vacants non-pourvus *m pl*

unfit *adj* GEN COMM inadéquat, inapte; ◆ ~ **for consumption** GEN COMM impropre à la consommation; ~ **to do** GEN COMM *person* impropre à faire

unfledged *adj* GEN COMM *person, company* sans expérience; ◆ **be** ~ HRM manquer d'expérience

unforeseeable *adj* GEN COMM imprévisible

unforeseen[1] *adj* GEN COMM imprévu, inattendu

unforeseen:[2] ~ **circumstances** *n pl* GEN COMM circonstances imprévues *f pl*

unformatted *adj* COMP *disk, storage* non-formaté, non-structuré

unfortunately *adv* GEN COMM malheureusement

unfounded *adj* GEN COMM *rumour, suspicion, accusation, criticism etc* sans fondement

unfriendly *adj* FIN *bid, takeover* hostile

unfulfilled *adj* GEN COMM *condition, promise* non-rempli

unfunded: ~ **debt** *n* FIN dette flottante *f*; ~ **pension scheme** *n* HRM régime de retraite sans capitalisation *m*; ~ **pensions** *n pl UK* HRM retraites sans capitaux suffisants *f pl*

ungeared: ~ **balance sheet** *n* ACC bilan bien équilibré *m*, bilan sans emprunts *m*, bilan à faible endettement *m*

ungraded *adj* GEN COMM hors série, hors-série

unhedged *adj* STOCK non-couvert

unification *n* GEN COMM *of Germany, of political party* unification *f*

unified: ~ **credit** *n* TAX crédit unifié *m*

uniform[1] *adj* GEN COMM uniforme

uniform[2] *n* GEN COMM uniforme *m*; ~ **accounting** *n* ACC comptabilité uniforme *f*; ~ **commercial code** *n* LAW code de commerce uniforme *m*; ~ **gifts to minors act** *n* LAW loi américaine réglementant la gestion d'actifs au nom d'enfants mineurs; ~ **practice code** *n US* STOCK code des usages *m*; ~ **price** *n* ECON, GEN COMM, S&M prix unique *m*; ~ **rules for collections** *n pl* BANK règles d'encaissement normalisées *f pl*; ~ **securities agent state law examination** *n* LAW examen de l'État fédéral pour les représentants en matière de valeurs mobilières uniformes

Uniform: ~ **Business Rate** *n* (*UBR*) FIN ≈ taux d'activité constant *m*, ≈ taux normalisé d'activités *m*; ~ **Customs and Practice for Documentary Credits** *n* (*UC&P*) ECON *international trade* unification des pratiques et coutumes pour les crédits documentaire *f*

uniformity *n* GEN COMM uniformité *f*; ~ **assumption** ECON hypothèse d'uniformité *f*

unify *vt* GEN COMM unifier

unilateral[1] *adj* ECON, GEN COMM, POL unilatéral

unilateral:[2] ~ **agreement** *n* ECON accord unilatéral *m*; ~ **measure** *n* ENVIR mesure unilatérale *f*; ~ **reference** *n* HRM décision unilatérale d'en référer aux prud'hommes *f*; ~ **regulation** *n* HRM réglementation unilatérale *f*

unilaterally *adv* ECON, GEN COMM, POL unilatéralement

unimodal: ~ **distribution** *n* MATH *statistics* distribution normale *f*

unimpeachable *adj* GEN COMM *contract, evidence* inattaquable, incontestable

unimpressive *adj* GEN COMM *performance etc* peu impressionnant

unimproved *adj* GEN COMM *situation, work* non-amélioré

unincorporated: ~ **business** *n* GEN COMM entreprise non-constituée en société *f*

uninfected *adj* COMP sain

uninsurable[1] *adj* INS inassurable, non-assurable

uninsurable:[2] ~ **title** *n* INS garantie inassurable *f*, garantie non-assurable *f*

uninsured *adj* INS inassuré, non-assuré

unintended: ~ **investment** *n* BANK investissement involontaire *m*

uninterruptible: ~ **power supply** *n* (*UPS*) COMP alimentation non-interruptible *f*

uninvested *adj* BANK *money* non-investi, non-placé

union *n* GEN COMM union *f*, HRM syndicat *m*, union *f*, IND, LAW, POL, WEL union *f*; ~ **affiliation** *n* HRM adhésion à un syndicat *f*; ~ **agreement** *n* HRM accord syndical *m*; ~ **-bashing** *n* *infrml* HRM antisyndicalisme *m*, persécution des syndicats *f* (*infrml*); ~ **certification** *n* HRM syndicalisation *f*; ~ **contract** *n* HRM, IND, LAW accord patronat-syndicats *m*, cc, contrat syndical *m*, convention collective *f*; ~ **density** *n* HRM taux de syndicalisation *m*; ~ **fees** *n pl* HRM cotisation syndicale *f*; ~ **government** *n* HRM direction d'un syndicat *f*; ~ **label** *n* HRM label syndical *m*; ~ **leave** *n* HRM congé pour fonctions syndicales *m*; ~ **man** *n* HRM syndicaliste *m*; ~ **member** *n* HRM membre d'un syndicat *m*; ~ **membership agreement** *n* (*UMA*) HRM accord d'appartenance syndicale *m*, accord sur l'adhérence syndicale *m*; ~ **movement** *n* HRM mouvement syndical *m*; ~ **officer** *n* HRM permanent *m*; ~ **official** *n* HRM permanent *m*; ~ **-only clause** *n* UK HRM *in contracts* clause dans un contract qui ne s'adresse qu'aux membres du syndicat *f*; ~ **-only practice** *n* UK HRM *in contracts* pratique qui ne s'adresse qu'aux membres du syndicat dans une entreprise; ~ **purchase** *n* TRANSP *cargo handling* dispositif de gréement pour utilisation en colis volant *m*, travail en colis volant *m*; ~ **rate** *n* HRM salaire proposé par les syndicats *m*; ~ **recruitment** *n* HRM recrutement syndical *m*; ~ **representative** *n* HRM délégué syndical *m*; ~ **rights** *n pl* HRM droits syndicaux *m pl*; ~ **rule book** *n* HRM règlement intérieur du syndicat *m*; ~ **rules** *n pl* HRM règlement syndical *m*; ~ **shop** *n* HRM monopole syndical de l'embauche *m*; ~ **structure** *n* HRM structure syndicale *f*; ~ **wage effect** *n* FIN effet des primes syndicales *m*; ~ **wage policy** *n* HRM politique salariale des syndicats *f*; ◆ ~ **and management** IND partenaires sociaux *m pl*

Union:[1] ~ **Membership Agreements** *n pl* UK HRM accords d'appartenance syndicale *m pl*; ~ **of Shop, Distributive & Allied Workers** *n* UK (*USDAW*) HRM Syndicat des employés de la distribution et assimilés *m*

Union:[2] ~ **of Soviet Socialist Republics** *pr n obs* (*USSR*) GEN COMM appelé maintenant la Communauté des États Indépendants, Union des Républiques Socialistes Soviétiques *f* (*obs*)

unionization *n* HRM syndicalisation *f*

unionized *adj* HRM syndicalisé

unions: ~ **and management** *phr* HRM les syndicats et le patronat *loc m*

unique[1] *adj* GEN COMM unique

unique:[2] ~ **impairment** *n* INS aggravation unique *f*; ~ **reference number** *n* (*URN*) ADMIN numéro de référence unique *m*; ~ **selling point** *n* (*USP*) S&M promesse unique de vente *f*; ~ **selling proposition** *n* (*USP*) S&M promesse unique de vente *f*

unissuable: ~ **note** *n* BANK billet impropre à la circulation *m*

unissued[1] *adj* STOCK *capital* non-émis

unissued:[2] ~ **capital stock** *n* STOCK capital non-émis *m*; ~ **stock** *n* STOCK action non-émise *f*, capital non-émis *m*; ~ **treasury share** *n* STOCK action de capital non-émise *f*

unit *n* COMP périphérique *m*, unité *f*, ECON *of currency*, GEN COMM unité *f*, STOCK combinaison de valeurs *f*, unité *f*; ~ **of account** ACC moyenne d'un compte *f*, unité de compte *f*; ~ **banking** BANK succursale de banque *f*; ~ **of a collective investment undertaking** FIN part d'un organisme de placement collectif *f*; ~ **cost** ACC prix de revient unitaire *m*; ~ **holder** STOCK détenteur d'unité *m*; ~ **labor cost** *AmE*, ~ **labour cost** *BrE* ACC coût unitaire du personnel *m*, ECON coût unitaire de la main-d'oeuvre *m*, HRM coût de main d'oeuvre par unité *m*, coût unitaire du personnel *m*, coût unitaire de la main-d'oeuvre *m*, IND coût unitaire de la main-d'oeuvre *m*; ~ **load** (*U*) TRANSP *distribution* unité de charge *f*, unité de chargement *f*; ~ **load device** (*ULD*) TRANSP unité de chargement aérienne *f*; ~ **price** GEN COMM prix unitaire *m*; ~ **pricing** GEN COMM, S&M prix à l'unité *m*, tarification à l'unité *f*; ~ **tax** TAX impôt unitaire *m*; ~ **of trading** STOCK quotité *f*, unité minimale de transaction *f*; ~ **trust** *BrE* (*cf mutual fund AmE*) FIN, STOCK fonds commun de placement *m*, société d'investissement ouverte *f*, société d'investissement à capital variable *f*; ~ **trust management** UK STOCK société d'investissement à taux variable; ~ **value** GEN COMM valeur unitaire *f*; ~ **value index** (*UVI*) ECON indice des valeurs unitaires *m*

UNITAR *abbr* (*United Nations Institute for Training and Research*) HRM Institut des Nations Unies pour la formation et la recherche *m*

unitary:[1] ~ **elastic** *adj* ECON à l'élasticité égale à 1 *loc f*

unitary:[2] ~ **approach** *n* WEL *social work* conception globale *f*; ~ **elasticity** *n* ECON élasticité unitaire *f*; ~ **model** *n* WEL *social work* modèle global *m*

Unitas: ~ **all share index** *n* STOCK indice boursier de la Bourse d'Helsinki

unite *vt* GEN COMM allier, unir

united *adj* GEN COMM uni

United:[1] ~ **Automobile Workers** *n pl* US (*UAW*) HRM travailleurs unifié de l'automobile *m pl* (*TUA*); ~ **Kingdom Atomic Energy Authority** *n* (*UKAEA*) IND agence de l'énergie atomique du

Royaume-Uni; **~ Kingdom or Continent** *(UK/ Cont)* TRANSP Royaume-Uni ou Continent *n*; **~ Kingdom Permanent Representative to the European Community** *n (UKREP)* ECON, POL représentant permanent du Royaume-Uni à la Communauté Européenne *m*; **~ Nations** *n (UN)* ECON, POL Nations Unies *f pl*, Organisation des Nations Unies *f (ONU)*; **~ Nations Association** *n (UNA)* ADMIN Association des Nations Unies *f (ANU)*; **~ Nations Commission of International Trade Law** *n (UNCITRAL)* LAW Commission des Nations Unies pour le droit commercial international; **~ Nations Conference on Environment and Development** *n (UNCED)* ENVIR, GEN COMM Conférence des Nations Unies sur l'environnement et le développement *f (CNUED)*; **~ Nations Conference on Trade and Development** *n (UNCTAD)* ECON Conférence des Nations Unies sur le commerce et le développement *f (CNUCED)*; **~ Nations Institute for Training and Research** *n (UNITAR)* HRM Institut des Nations Unies pour la formation et la recherche *m*; **~ Nations Organization** *n (UNO)* ECON, POL Organisation des Nations Unies *f (ONU)*; **~ Nations Relief and World Agency** *n (UNRWA)* ECON, POL Office de secours et de travaux des Nations Unies pour les réfugiés *m*; **~ Nations Research Institute for Social Development** *n (UNRISD)* WEL Institut de Recherche des Nations Unies pour le développement social *m (IRNUDS)*; **~ States Environmental Protection Agency** *n* ENVIR Agence des États-Unis pour la protection de l'environnement *f*; **~ States Information Agency** *n (USIA)* COMMS agence d'informations des États-Unis; **~ States Maritime Commission** *n (USMC)* TRANSP commission maritime des États-Unis; **~ States Postal Service** *n (USPS)* COMMS Poste des États-Unis *f*

United:[2] **~ Arab Emirates** *pr n (UAE)* GEN COMM Émirats Arabes Unis *m pl*; **~ Kingdom** *pr n (UK)* GEN COMM Royaume-Uni *m*; **~ States** *pr n* [inv pl] *(US)* GEN COMM États-Unis *m pl*; **~ States of America** *pr n* [inv pl] *(USA)* GEN COMM États-Unis d'Amérique *m pl*

unitization *n (*SYN *time share)* PROP multipropriété *f*

units: **~ -of-production method** *n* ACC méthode des unités de production *f*

unity: **~ of European patent** *n* PATENTS unicité du brevet européen *f*; **~ of invention** *n* PATENTS unité d'invention *f*

universal[1] *adj* GEN COMM universel

universal:[2] **~ agent** *n* LAW agent général *m*, représentant général *m*; **~ air waybill** *n (UAWB)* IMP/EXP, TRANSP lettre de transport aérien universelle *f (LTAU)*; **~ bank** *n* BANK banque universelle *f*; **~ container** *n (U)* TRANSP conteneur pour usage général *m*; **~ life insurance** *n* INS assurance-vie universelle *f*; **~ -life policy** *n* INS assurance vie-entière *f*; **~ suffrage** *n* POL suffrage universel *m*; **~ time coordinated** *n (UTC)* GEN

COMM temps universel *m*, heure universelle *f (TU)*

Universal: **~ Postal Union** *n (UPU)* ACC, COMMS Union postale universelle *f (UPU)*

universalism *n* WEL *social work* universalisme *m*

universe *n* S&M *marketing* univers *m*

university[1] *adj* GEN COMM *course, town* universitaire

university[2] *n* GEN COMM, WEL université *f*; **~ lecturer** HRM, WEL chargé de cours *mf*

unjust *adj* GEN COMM injuste

unjustified[1] *adj* COMP au kilomètre *loc m*, noncadré, non-justifié, GEN COMM, LAW injustifié

unjustified:[2] **~ absence** *n* HRM absentéisme injustifié *m*; **~ threat** *n* LAW intimidation injustifiée *f*, menace injustifiée *f*

unknown: **~ at this address** *phr* COMMS inconnu à cette adresse

unladen: **~ weight** *n* GEN COMM poids à vide *m*, TRANSP poids à vide *m*, tare *f*

unlawful[1] *adj* LAW contraire à la loi, illicite, illégal

unlawful:[2] **~ act** *n* LAW acte illicite *m*, acte illégal *m*; **~ picketing** *n* HRM installation illégale de piquets de grève *f*; **~ trespass** *n* LAW intrusion illicite sur la propriété d'autrui *f*, violation de propriété *f*

unlawfully *adv* LAW illégalement

unleaded[1] *adj* ENVIR *petrol* sans plomb

unleaded:[2] **~ gas** *n AmE (cf* lead-free petrol *BrE,* unleaded petrol *BrE)* ENVIR essence sans plomb *f*; **~ petrol** *n BrE (cf* lead-free petrol, unleaded gas *AmE)* ENVIR essence sans plomb *f*

unless: **~ caused by** *phr* INS *marine* sauf causé par; **~ general** *phr* INS sauf avarie commune, sauf disposition contraire; **~ I'm mistaken** *phr* GEN COMM sauf erreur; **~ used** *phr* TRANSP *shipping* sauf s'ils ont été utilisés

unleveraged: **~ program** *n AmE,* **~ programme** *n BrE* FIN programme sans endettement *m*

unlicensed: **~ broker** *n* STOCK courtier non-agréé *m*

unlimited[1] *adj* STOCK illimité, non-limité; **~ on the upside** STOCK illimité vers le haut, illimité à la hausse

unlimited:[2] **~ checking** *n* BANK vérification illimitée *f*; **~ company** *n* GEN COMM entreprise illimitée *f*; **~ fine** *n* GEN COMM, LAW amende illimitée *f*, amende non-limitée *f*; **~ liability** *n* GEN COMM, LAW responsabilité illimitée *f*; **~ mileage** *n* TRANSP *car-hire* kilométrage illimité *m*; **~ securities** *n pl* STOCK valeurs à cours non-limité *f pl*; **~ tax bond** *n* STOCK obligation à cours non-limité *f*

unliquidated *adj* FIN non-acquitté

unlisted[1] *adj* COMMS *AmE (cf* XD, ex-directory *BrE)* sur la liste rouge *loc f*, STOCK non-admis, non-coté, non-inscrit à la cote

unlisted:[2] **~ company** *n* GEN COMM, STOCK société non-inscrite à la cote *f*; **~ market** *n (*SYN *kerb market)* STOCK second marché *m*; **~ security** *n (*SYN *unquoted security)* STOCK valeur non-cotée *f*; **~ share** *n* (ANT *listed share*) STOCK action non-cotée *f*; **~ trader** *n* STOCK négociateur sur le marché hors cote *m*; **~ trading** *n* STOCK négociation des valeurs non cotées *f*, transactions sur valeurs non cotées *f pl*; **~ warrant** *n* STOCK bon de souscription non coté en bourse *m*

Unlisted: **~ Securities Market** *n* UK (USM) STOCK marché des valeurs non-cotées *m*, second marché *m*

unload: **~ stocks on the market** *phr* STOCK se décharger d'un paquet d'actions

unloader: **~ crane** *n* TRANSP grue de déchargement *f*

unloading *n* TRANSP déchargement *m*; **~ platform** TRANSP *rail* quai de déchargement *m*; **~ risk** GEN COMM, TRANSP risque de déchargement *m*

unlock *vt* COMP *keyboard* débloquer, déverrouiller (*jarg*), FIN *funds* débloquer, déverrouiller

unmanageable *adj* GEN COMM *business, staff* ingérable

unmanifested: **~ cargo** *n* TRANSP cargaison non-déclarée *f*, marchandises non-déclarées *f pl*

unmanned: **~ machinery spaces** *n pl* IND *production* salle des machines sans surveillance *f*

unmanufactured: **~ material** *n* IND matière première *f*

unmarketable *adj* GEN COMM, S&M invendable

unmarried *adj* ADMIN, FIN, LAW célibataire

unmatched *adj* STOCK dépareillé

unmatured *adj* STOCK *coupon, debt* non-échu

unmoor *vti* TRANSP *shipping* larguer les amarres

unmooring *n* TRANSP *shipping* largage des amarres *m*

unmortgaged *adj* BANK, PROP libre d'hypothèque

unnamed *adj* COMP *disk, file* sans nom

unnegotiable *adj* GEN COMM non-négociable

UNO *abbr* (*United Nations Organization*) ECON, POL ONU (*Organisation des Nations Unies*)

unofficial[1] *adj* GEN COMM *appointment* non-officiel, *report* non-officiel, officieux; ◆ **in an ~ capacity** GEN COMM à titre non-officiel

unofficial:[2] **~ strike** *n* HRM grève sans préavis *f*, grève sauvage *f*

unpack *vt* GEN COMM déballer

unpacked *adj* GEN COMM *not wrapped* sans emballage

unpaid[1] *adj* STOCK *dividend* non-versé

unpaid:[2] **~ bill** *n* ACC impayé *m*; **~ claim reserve** *n* INS provision pour sinistres à payer *f*; **~ dividend** *n* FIN dividende impayé *m*; **~ tax** *n* TAX impôt non-payé *m*

unpalatable *adj* GEN COMM *decision, facts* désagréable

unparalleled *adj* GEN COMM incomparable

unpatented *adj* GEN COMM, PATENTS non-breveté

unplug *vt* GEN COMM *from electrical supply* déconnecter

unpolluted *adj* ENVIR non-polluant

unpopular *adj* GEN COMM impopulaire

unpostable *adj* ACC non-comptabilisable

unprecedented *adj* GEN COMM sans précédent

unpredictable *adj* GEN COMM imprévisible

unpresented: **~ check** *n* AmE, **~ cheque** *n* BrE BANK chèque non-présenté *m*

unpriced *adj* GEN COMM dont le prix n'est pas marqué *loc m*, sans indication de prix

unprocessable *adj* COMP *data* inexploitable

unprocessed *adj* COMP, MATH *data* non-traité

unproductive[1] *adj* GEN COMM, IND, MGMNT, STOCK non-productif

unproductive:[2] **~ labor** *n* AmE, **~ labour** *n* BrE ECON, HRM main-d'oeuvre improductive *f*

unprofessional: **~ conduct** *n* GEN COMM conduite contraire au code professionnel *f*

unprofitable *adj* ACC, ECON, FIN peu rentable, GEN COMM peu rentable, peu rémunérateur

unprogrammed *adj* GEN COMM non-programmé

unprotested *adj* FIN *bill* non-protesté

unpublished *adj* GEN COMM, MEDIA inédit

unqualified[1] *adj* HRM non-qualifié

unqualified:[2] **~ acceptance** *n* FIN acceptation inconditionnelle *f*; **~ opinion** *n* ACC opinion sans réserve *f*

unquestionable *adj* GEN COMM incontestable

unquoted[1] *adj* STOCK non-admis, non-coté, non-inscrit à la cote

unquoted:[2] **~ security** *n* (SYN *unlisted security*) STOCK valeur non-cotée *f*; **~ share** *n* (ANT *quoted share*) STOCK action non-cotée *f*; **~ trading company** *n* ECON, GEN COMM, S&M société commerciale non-cotée *f*

unrealized: **~ gains** *n pl* ACC, FIN, TAX gains non-réalisés *m pl*; **~ loss** *n* (ANT *unrealized profit*) ACC perte non-réalisée *f*; **~ profit** *n* ACC bénéfice non-réalisé *m*, profit non-réalisé *m*, FIN profit non-réalisé *m*

unreasonable *adj* GEN COMM *request, price* excessif

unreceipted *adj* GEN COMM *bill, account* non-acquitté, sans la mention "pour acquit"

unrecognized *adj* GEN COMM méconnu

unrecorded[1] *adj* GEN COMM *not written down or recorded on tape* non-enregistré

unrecorded:[2] **~ deed** *n* GEN COMM instrument non-enregistré *m*

unrecoverable *adj* COMP *data, file* irrémédiable, TAX non-recouvrable

unredeemable *adj* BANK, STOCK non-amortissable, non-remboursable

unregistered[1] *adj* GEN COMM clandestin, LAW, PATENTS non-déposé

unregistered:[2] **~ labor** *n* AmE, **~ labour** *n* BrE HRM main-d'oeuvre non-déclarée *f*; **~ mark** *n* PATENTS marque non-déposée *f*; **~ person** *n* TAX non-inscrit *m*, personne non-déclarée *f*; **~ stock** *n* STOCK action non-enregistrée *f*, action non-nominative *f*; ~ **trademark** *n* GEN COMM marque non-déposée *f*

unreliable *adj* GEN COMM peu fiable, peu sûr

unremunerative *adj* GEN COMM peu rémunérateur

unrepealed *adj* GEN COMM *law* non-abrogé

unrequired: ~ **dividend** *n* ACC dividende non-réclamé *m*

unresolved *adj* GEN COMM, MGMNT *problem, question* irrésolu

unresponsive *adj* GEN COMM *market*, STOCK insensible

unrest *n* GEN COMM *amongst workforce* troubles *m pl, of person* inquiétude *f*, HRM, POL agitation *f*

unrestricted: ~ **access** *n* GEN COMM accès libre *m*; ~ **labor** *n* *AmE*, ~ **labour** *n* *BrE* HRM main-d'oeuvre non-réduite *f*; ~ **letter of credit** *n* BANK lettre de crédit illimité *f*; ~ **quota** *n* GEN COMM contingent libre *m*

unrewarding *adj* GEN COMM infructueux

UNRISD *abbr (United Nations Research Institute for Social Development)* WEL IRNUDS *(Institut de Recherche des Nations Unies pour le développement social)*

unrivalled *adj* GEN COMM sans rival

UNRWA *abbr (United Nations Relief and World Agency)* ECON, POL Office de secours et de travaux des Nations Unies pour les réfugiés *m*

unsafe: ~ **paper** *n* FIN effet douteux *m*

unsalable *adj* *AmE*, **unsaleable** *adj* *BrE* GEN COMM, S&M invendable

unscheduled *adj* GEN COMM non-planifié

unscramble *vt* GEN COMM débrouiller

unscreened *adj* GEN COMM non-trié

unscrupulous *adj* GEN COMM sans scrupules

unseasonable *adj* GEN COMM *coming at the wrong time* inopportun

unseat: ~ **the board** *phr* MGMNT remplacer les membres du conseil d'administration

unseaworthiness *n* TRANSP *of ship* mauvais état de navigabilité *m*

unsecured[1] *adj* BANK chirographaire, non-garanti

unsecured:[2] ~ **advance** *n* BANK avance non-garantie *f*, avance à découvert *f*; ~ **bond** *n* STOCK obligation non-garantie *f*; ~ **creditor** *n* ACC créancier non-garanti *m*, créancier ordinaire *m*; ~ **debt** *n* FIN dette non-garantie *f*; ~ **fixed-term loan** *n* BANK prêt à terme fixe non-garanti *m*; ~ **loan** *n* ACC emprunt non-garanti *m*, prêt non-garanti *m*, BANK emprunt non-garanti *m*; ~ **overdraft** *n* BANK découvert en blanc *m*

unsettle *vt* GEN COMM perturber

unsettled: ~ **market** *n* STOCK marché instable *m*

unsettling *adj* GEN COMM *influence* inquiétant

unshipment *n* TRANSP *unloading* débarquement *m*, déchargement *m*

unsigned *adj* GEN COMM non-signé

unskilled[1] *adj* HRM non-qualifié, non-spécialisé

unskilled:[2] ~ **labor** *n* *AmE*, ~ **labour** *n* *BrE* ECON main-d'oeuvre non-qualifiée *f*, main-d'oeuvre non-spécialisée *f*, HRM main-d'oeuvre non-qualifiée *f*, main-d'oeuvre non-spécialisée *f*, ouvriers non-qualifiés *m pl*, ouvriers non-spécialisés *m pl*; ~ **worker** *n* HRM manoeuvre *m*

unsocial: ~ **hours** *n pl* HRM heures indues *f pl*

unsold[1] *adj* GEN COMM, S&M invendu

unsold:[2] ~ **goods** *n pl* GEN COMM invendus *m pl*

unsolicited[1] *adj* GEN COMM non-sollicité

unsolicited:[2] ~ **application** *n* HRM candidature spontanée *f*; ~ **testimony** *n* LAW déposition volontaire *f*, témoignage spontané *m*

unsorted *adj* *(u/s)* GEN COMM *timber trade* non-trié

unsound: ~ **risk** *n* GEN COMM mauvais risque *m*

unspent[1] *adj* GEN COMM *money* non-dépensé

unspent:[2] ~ **cash balance** *n* ACC *governmental accounting* solde de caisse non-dépensé *m*

unspoilt: ~ **land** *n* ENVIR, IND sol naturel *m*, sol sans perturbation artificielle *m*

unstable *adj* POL *government* instable

unstamped: ~ **debentures** *n pl* STOCK obligations non-estampillées *f pl*

unsteady *adj* GEN COMM *supply, output* irrégulier

unstocked *adj* GEN COMM, S&M *store, warehouse* en rupture de stock *loc f*

unstructured[1] *adj* GEN COMM non-structuré

unstructured:[2] ~ **interview** *n* HRM, MEDIA entretien informel *m*

unstuck: **come** ~ *phr* GEN COMM *fail* tomber à l'eau

unsubsidized *adj* GEN COMM *in industry* non-subventionné

unsubstantiated *adj* GEN COMM *accusation, rumour, claim* non-fondé

unsuccessful: ~ **job application** *n* HRM demande d'emploi non-satisfaite *f*

unsuitable *adj* GEN COMM inconvenable

unsuited *adj* GEN COMM inadapté; ♦ **be** ~ **to the job** HRM *of candidate, applicant* ne pas avoir le profil voulu pour le poste

unsupported *adj* GEN COMM *statement* non-confirmé, sans preuves

unsystematic: ~ **risk** *n* GEN COMM risque aléatoire *m*

untapped *adj* GEN COMM *resources* inexploité

untargeted *adj* S&M *consumer base* insuffisamment ciblé

untenanted *adj* PROP *building* inoccupé, sans locataire

untested *adj* GEN COMM *invention, drug, product* non-testé

untied *adj* ECON, POL *development aid* non-lié

until: ~ **countermanded** *phr (T/C)* GEN COMM jusqu'à nouvel avis, jusqu'à nouvel ordre; ~ **further notice** *phr* GEN COMM jusqu'à nouvel avis, jusqu'à nouvel ordre

untimely *adj* GEN COMM inopportun

untitled *adj* COMP *disk, file* sans titre

untrained adj WEL person non-formé

untransferable adj LAW, STOCK incessible

untried adj GEN COMM non-testé, qui n'a pas été vérifié

unused[1] adj GEN COMM inutilisé, non-utilisé

unused:[2] ~ **credit** n Canada TAX crédit inutilisé m, crédit non-utilisé m; ~ **part** n TAX fraction inutilisée f, partie non-utilisée f; ~ **relief** n TAX dégrèvement non-utilisé m

unusual: ~ **item** n TRANSP article exceptionnel m; ~ **items** n pl GEN COMM écritures extraordinaires f pl

unvalued: ~ **policy** n INS police non-évaluée f

unveil vt GEN COMM proposals, plans dévoiler; ~ **a policy** POL dévoiler une politique

unverified adj GEN COMM non-testé, non-vérifié, qui n'a pas été vérifié

unvouched: ~ **for** adj GEN COMM reliability non-garanti

unwaged: **the** ~ n ECON, HRM les chômeurs m pl, les sans-emplois m pl

unwanted adj GEN COMM superfluous superflu

unwarranted adj GEN COMM injustifié

unweighted adj GEN COMM index, figures non-pondéré

unwind: ~ **a tape** phr STOCK dégager; ~ **a trade** phr STOCK déboucher une position loc f (jarg), inverser une transaction par compensation, vendre en masse

unworkable adj GEN COMM irréalisable, plan, solution impraticable

unwrap vt GEN COMM défaire

unwritten: ~ **agreement** n GEN COMM accord verbal m

up[1] adj infrml COMP functioning allumé, en marche, sous tension; ◆ ~ **14%** STOCK en hausse de 14%

up[2] vt GEN COMM bid, offer augmenter

up:[3] ~ **to** prep GEN COMM jusqu'à loc; ◆ **be** ~ **to date** GEN COMM être dans le vent; **be** ~ **to date with** GEN COMM être à jour de loc m; **be** ~ **to one's neck in work** infrml HRM être dans le travail jusqu'au cou (infrml); **be** ~ **to scratch** infrml GEN COMM se montrer à la hauteur, être à la hauteur; **be** ~ **to standard** HRM être au niveau; ~ **the line** GEN COMM, MGMNT en remontant la hiérarchie; ~ **to date on** GEN COMM au courant de

up-and-coming adj GEN COMM person plein d'avenir

upbeat adj GEN COMM attitude, forecast optimiste

upcoming: ~ **fiscal year** n GEN COMM prochain exercice fiscal m, TAX exercice suivant m, prochain exercice fiscal m

update[1] n COMP action, GEN COMM actualisation f, mise à jour f

update[2] vt COMP mettre à jour, GEN COMM actualiser, mettre à jour, mettre au courant; ~ **sb on** GEN COMM mettre qn au courant de; ~ **sb on sth** GEN COMM mettre qn au courant de qch

updating n COMP mise à jour f, GEN COMM actualisation f, mise à jour f

upfront[1] adj GEN COMM payé d'avance

upfront:[2] ~ **cost** n GEN COMM charge payable d'avance f

upgrade[1] n COMP mise à niveau f (jarg), S&M amélioration f

upgrade[2] vt COMP memory augmenter, software, hardware, system améliorer, optimiser, GEN COMM in quality améliorer, HRM post, job requalifier, revaloriser, LEIS aviation placer dans un compartiment de première classe des voyageurs munis de billets d'une classe inférieure

upgradeable adj COMP extensible, évolutif, GEN COMM extensible, évolutif, qui peut évoluer

upgraded adj S&M amélioré

upgrading n COMP augmentation de puissance f, extension f, mise à niveau f (jarg), GEN COMM promotion, HRM reclassement m; ~ **of a loan** BANK reclassement en amont d'un prêt m

upheaval n GEN COMM bouleversement m

uphold vt LAW confirmer, maintenir, soutenir

upkeep n TAX of property impenses f pl, maintien m

upload vt COMP data télécharger

up-market[1] adj COMP, GEN COMM, GEN COMM, S&M, S&M haut de gamme

up-market:[2] ~ **product** n S&M produit haut de gamme m; ~ **service** n S&M service haut de gamme m

upper:[1] ~ **cap** n BrE TAX on basic rate of relief plafond m; ~ **case** n (u.c.) ADMIN, COMP, MEDIA capitale f, haut de casse m, lettre capitale f, lettre de haut de casse f, lettre majuscule f, majuscule f; ~ **-case letter** n (ANT lower-case letter) ADMIN, COMP, MEDIA capitale f, haut de casse m, lettre capitale f, lettre de haut de casse f, lettre majuscule f, majuscule f; ~ **deck** n (Udk) TRANSP shipping pont supérieur m; ~ **income** n TAX gros revenus m pl, palier supérieur de revenu m; ~ **limit** n GEN COMM plafond m, STOCK limite supérieure f, plafond m; ~ **quartile** n MATH statistics quartile supérieur m

upper:[2] **have the** ~ **hand** phr GEN COMM avoir l'avantage loc m, avoir le dessus

ups: ~ **and downs** n pl STOCK market hauts et bas m pl, oscillations du marché f pl

UPS abbr jarg COMP (uninterruptible power supply) alimentation non-interruptible f, POL (uncontested physical search) by members of intelligence services fouille incontestée f

upset: ~ **price** n AmE (cf reserve price BrE) GEN COMM auction sale, S&M mise à prix f, prix de départ m, prix de réserve m, prix demandé m, prix minimum m, réserve f

upside: ~ **break-even** n STOCK options point mort vers le haut m, rentabilité à la hausse f; ~ **break-even point** n STOCK point mort vers le haut m, seuil de rentabilité à la hausse m; ~ **potential** n FIN potentiel à la hausse m; ~ **profit potential** n

STOCK *options* potentiel de bénéfices à la hausse *m*, potentiel de profit à la hausse *m*; **~ risk** *n* STOCK *options* risque à la hausse *m*

upskilling *n* HRM *retraining* recyclage *m*

upstairs: **~ market** *n* STOCK négociation à un cours supérieur *f*, transaction hors parquet *f*

upstream[1] *adv* (ANT *downstream*) GEN COMM en amont *loc*

upstream:[2] **~ float** *n* GEN COMM flottage en amont *m*, GEN COMM marge amont *f*; **~ loans** *n pl jarg* FIN prêts en amont *m pl*

upsurge *n* GEN COMM *in activity* poussée *f*

upswing *n* (ANT *downswing*) ECON amélioration sensible *f*, redressement *m*, reprise *f*

uptick *n* (ANT *downtick*) STOCK cours supérieur au cours précédent *m*, négociation à un cours supérieur *f*, échelon de cotation supérieur *m*

up-to-date[1] *adj* GEN COMM *information* à jour; ◆ **be ~** GEN COMM être dans le mouvement

up-to-date:[2] **~ information** *n* GEN COMM information à jour *f*

up-to-sample *adj* GEN COMM conforme à l'échantillon

up-to-the-minute *adj* GEN COMM *information* de dernier moment

uptrend *n* (ANT *downtrend*) ECON orientation à la hausse *f*, tendance à la hausse *f*

upturn *n* (ANT *downturn*) ECON amélioration *f*, amélioration sensible *f*, reprise *f*, GEN COMM, STOCK reprise *f*

UPU *abbr* (*Universal Postal Union*) ACC, COMMS UPU (*Union postale universelle*)

upvaluation *n* GEN COMM *higher valuation* révision à la hausse *f*

upward[1] *adj* (ANT *downward*) COMP ascendant, vers le haut, GEN COMM *move, trend* haussier, vers le haut, à la hausse

upward:[2] **~ compatibility** *n* (ANT *downward compatibility*) COMP *programs* compatibilité ascendante *f*; **~ movement** *n* (ANT *downward movement*) STOCK mouvement vers le haut *m*, mouvement à la hausse *m*, tendance haussière *f*, tendance à la hausse *f*; **~ pressure** *n* (ANT *downward pressure*) ECON *on budget* pression inflationniste *f*, pression à la hausse *f*; **~ revision** *n* (ANT *downward revision*) GEN COMM révision à la hausse *f*; **~ spiral** *n* ECON montée en spirale *f*, GEN COMM *in wages, prices* montée en spirale *f*, spirale ascendante *f*; **~ trend** *n* (ANT *downward trend*) STOCK *stock market* mouvement vers le haut *m*, mouvement à la hausse *m*, tendance haussière *f*, tendance à la hausse *f*

upwardly: **~ mobile** *adj* GEN COMM dynamique, qui monte, HRM dynamique

upwards *adv* (ANT *downwards*) COMP vers le haut, GEN COMM *move* vers le haut, à la hausse

urban[1] *adj* ECON urbain

urban:[2] **~ area** *n* WEL agglomération urbaine *f*; **~ development area** *n* GEN COMM zone d'aména-

gement urbain *f*; **~ development zone** *n* ECON, HRM, PROP zone à urbaniser en priorité *f*; **~ economics** *n* ECON urbanisme *m*, économie urbaine *f*; **~ planner** *n* ADMIN, POL, WEL urbaniste *mf*; **~ planning** *n* ADMIN urbanisme *m*; **~ renewal** *n* GEN COMM rénovation urbaine *f*

Urban: **~ Development Corporation** *n UK* ECON Société pour le développement urbain *f*; **~ Programme Area** *n UK* GEN COMM zone d'aménagement urbain *f*

urbanization *n* ECON urbanisation *f*

urbanize *vt* ECON urbaniser

Urdu *n* GEN COMM *language* ourdou *m*, urdu *m*

urge: **~ sb to do** *phr* GEN COMM inciter qn à faire

urgent[1] *adj* GEN COMM urgent; ◆ **be in ~ need of** GEN COMM avoir besoin de qch de toute urgence, avoir un besoin urgent de

urgent:[2] **~ mail** *n* (*cf urgent post*) COMMS courrier urgent *m*; **~ matter** *n* GEN COMM affaire sérieuse *f*; **~ order** *n* GEN COMM, S&M commande urgente *f*; **~ post** *n* (*cf urgent mail*) COMMS courrier urgent *m*

URN *abbr* (*unique reference number*) ADMIN numéro de référence unique *m*

Uruguay:[1] **~ Round** *n* ECON *initiated on Dec 15th 1993* cycle de l'Uruguay *m*, l'Uruguay Round *m*, négociations d'Uruguay *f pl*

Uruguay[2] *pr n* GEN COMM Uruguay *m*

Uruguayan[1] *adj* GEN COMM uruguayen

Uruguayan[2] *n* GEN COMM *person* Uruguayen *m*

u/s *abbr* (*unsorted*) GEN COMM non-trié

US[1] *abbr* (*United States*) GEN COMM États-Unis *m pl*

US:[2] **~ dollar financial assets** *n pl* FIN avoirs financiers libellés en dollars américains *m pl*; **~ Treasury bond** *n* STOCK bon du Trésor américain à long terme *m*, obligation du Trésor américain *f*; **~ Treasury bond market** *n* STOCK Marché des bons du Trésor américain *m*, Marché des obligation du Trésor américain *m*; **~ Treasury market** *n* FIN Marché du Trésor américain *m*

USA *abbr* (*United States of America*) GEN COMM États-Unis d'Amérique *m pl*

usable *adj* ENVIR *by-products, waste products*, GEN COMM, IND *by-products, waste products* utilisable

usance *n* FIN usance *f*, FIN échéance *f*; **~ bill** BANK traite à échéance *f*, FIN effet à usance *m*; **~ credit** BANK crédit à usance *m*; ◆ **at thirty days' ~** FIN à usance de trente jours

USDAW *abbr UK* (*Union of Shop, Distributive & Allied Workers*) HRM Syndicat des employés de la distribution et assimilés *m*

use[1] *n* GEN COMM usage *m*, PATENTS *of mark* exploitation *f*; **~ -by date** S&M date limite de consommation *f*; **~ of funds** ACC emploi de fonds *m*; **~ value** ECON valeur d'usage *f*; ◆ **have the ~ of sth** GEN COMM pouvoir se servir de qch; **make full ~ of** GEN COMM tirer parti de; **make ~ of** GEN COMM utiliser

use[2] *vt* GEN COMM *method, opportunity* utiliser; ◆ ~ **strong-arm tactics** GEN COMM employer la manière forte

used[1] *adj* ENVIR *oil* usagé

used:[2] ~ **assets** *n pl* TAX actif utilisé *m*; ~ **car** *n* TRANSP voiture d'occasion *f*; ~ **vehicle** *n* TRANSP véhicule d'occasion *m*

useful[1] *adj* GEN COMM utile; ◆ ~ **for understanding the invention** PATENTS utile pour la compréhension de l'invention; ~ **to sb** GEN COMM utile à qn

useful:[2] ~ **economic life** *n* ACC durée de vie économique *f*; ~ **life** *n* ACC *of asset* durée de vie utile *f*, GEN COMM *of device, machine, tool* durée de vie *f*

usefully *adv* GEN COMM utilement

user:[1] ~ **-friendly** *adj* (ANT *user-unfriendly*) COMP convivial, d'utilisation facile *loc f*, facile à utiliser, S&M convivial, facile à utiliser; ~ **-hostile** *adj* COMP, S&M non-convivial; ~ **-orientated** *adj* COMP personnalisé, S&M *marketing* conçu en pensant à l'utilisateur *loc m*; ~ **-unfriendly** *adj* (ANT *user-friendly*) COMP, S&M non-convivial

user[2] *n* COMP, GEN COMM usager *m*, utilisateur *m*; ~ **attitude** S&M attitude des utilisateurs *f*; ~ **charge** ACC charge de servitude *f*; ~ **cost** FIN coût utilisateur *m*; ~ **fee** BANK droits d'utilisation *m pl*, frais d'utilisation *m pl*; ~ **-friendliness** COMP, S&M convivialité *f*; ~ **group** COMP groupe d'utilisateurs *m*; ~ **interface** COMP interface utilisateur *f*; ~ **manual** COMP guide de l'utilisateur *m*; ~ **profile** S&M *marketing* profil de l'utilisateur *m*; ~ **strategy** GEN COMM, S&M stratégie de l'utilisateur *f*

USIA *abbr* (*United States Information Agency*) COMMS agence d'informations des États-Unis

USM *abbr* UK (*Unlisted Securities Market*) STOCK marché des valeurs non-cotées *m*, second marché *m*

USMC *abbr* (*United States Maritime Commission*) TRANSP commission maritime des États-Unis

USP *abbr* (*unique selling point, unique selling proposition*) S&M promesse unique de vente *f*

USPS *abbr* (*United States Postal Service*) COMMS Poste des États-Unis *f*

USSR *abbr obs* (*Union of Soviet Socialist Republics*) GEN COMM appelé maintenant la Communauté des États Indépendants, URSS (*obs*) (*Union des Républiques Socialistes Soviétiques*)

usual[1] *adj* GEN COMM habituel; ◆ **on the ~ terms** GEN COMM aux conditions habituelles; **with the ~ proviso** LAW sous les réserves d'usage

usual:[2] ~ **first name** *n* LAW prénom usuel *m*

usufruct *n* LAW usufruit *m*

usufructuary *n* LAW usufruitier *m*

usurer *n* FIN usurier *m*

usurious *adj* BANK, FIN usuraire

usury *n* BANK usure *f*

UTC *abbr* (*universal time coordinated*) GEN COMM heure universelle *f*, TU (*temps universel*)

util *n* ECON indice d'utilité *m*, util *m*

utilitarian *adj* GEN COMM utilitaire

utilitarianism *n* ECON justice rawlsienne *f*, utilitarisme *m*, utilité primordiale *f*

utilities: ~ **sector** *n* IND secteur exclu *m*, secteur public *m*

utility[1] *adj* COMP, GEN COMM utilitaire

utility[2] *n* COMP programme utilitaire *m*, utilitaire *m*, ECON utilité *f*; ~ **average** STOCK indice moyen des services publics *m*; ~ **certificate** PATENTS certificat d'utilité *m*; ~ **function** ECON fonction d'utilité *f*; ~ **model** PATENTS modèle d'utilité *m*; ~ **possibility frontier** ECON limite de l'utilité possible *f*; ~ **program** COMP programme utilitaire *m*; ~ **revenue bond** FIN obligation à long terme émise par une collectivité *f*

utilization *n* ENVIR *of natural resources* utilisation *f*; ~ **percent** GEN COMM taux de rendement *m*

utilize *vt* GEN COMM utiliser

utilized: ~ **capacity** *n* IND potentiel de production utilisé *m*

utmost: ~ **good faith** *n* INS bonne foi absolue *f*

UVI *abbr* (*unit value index*) ECON indice des valeurs unitaires *m*

U/W *abbr* (*underwriter*) INS souscripteur *m*

Uzbek[1] *adj* GEN COMM ouzbek

Uzbek[2] *n* GEN COMM *language* ouzbek *m*, *person* Ouzbek *m*

Uzbekistan *pr n* GEN COMM Ouzbékistan *m*

V

V *abbr (volt)* GEN COMM V *(volt)*

VA *abbr (value analysis)* ACC, FIN, S&M *marketing* analyse de valeur *f*

vacancy *n* HRM poste libre *m*

vacant: **~ land** *n* PROP foncier non bâti *m*; **~ lot** *n* AmE PROP *not built on* terrain non bâti *m*; **~ possession** *n* LAW jouissance immédiate *f*, libre possession *f*, PROP jouissance immédiate *f*

vacation *n AmE (cf holiday BrE)* GEN COMM, HRM, LEIS congé *m*, vacances *f pl*; **~ pay** *n AmE (cf holiday pay BrE)* HRM congés payés *m pl*; **~ with pay** *n AmE (cf holidays with pay BrE)* HRM congés payés *m pl*; ◆ **do ~ work** *AmE see do holiday work BrE*; **take a ~** *AmE (cf go on holiday BrE, take a holiday BrE)* HRM, LEIS prendre des vacances

vacationer *n AmE (cf holiday-maker BrE)* GEN COMM, LEIS vacancier *m*

vacationist *n AmE (cf holiday-maker BrE)* GEN COMM, LEIS vacancier *m*

vacations *n pl* LAW, POL vacation *f*

vaccinate *vt* IMP/EXP vacciner

vaccination *n* IMP/EXP vaccination *f*

vacuum: **~ packaging** *n* S&M conditionnement sous vide *m*; **~ relief valve** *n* TRANSP clapet de dépression *m*

Vaduz *pr n* GEN COMM Vaduz *n pr*

valid[1] *adj* ADMIN *passport* en cours de validité, non-périmé, valable, GEN COMM *argument, excuse* valable, valide; ◆ **no longer ~** GEN COMM dépassé

valid:[2] **~ invoice** *n* GEN COMM facture valide *f*; **~ passport** *n* ADMIN passeport valable *m*

validate *vt* COMP, GEN COMM *certificate, claim*, LAW, TAX valider

validation *n* COMP, GEN COMM, LAW, TAX validation *f*

validity *n* GEN COMM, LAW, PATENTS validité *f*; **~ check** *n* TAX contrôle de validité *m*; **~ period** *n* GEN COMM période de validité *f*

valise *n* GEN COMM sac de voyage *m*, LEIS *AmE* valise *f*

Valletta *pr n* GEN COMM La Valette *n pr*

valorization *n* ECON valorisation *f*, GEN COMM *of commodity* maintien artificiel *m*

valorize *vt* ECON valoriser, GEN COMM *commodity* maintenir artificiellement le prix de

valuable[1] *adj* GEN COMM de valeur; ◆ **for good and ~ consideration** LAW moyennant contrepartie valable

valuable:[2] **~ consideration** *n* GEN COMM pour une contrepartie valable *loc f*, à titre onéreux *loc m*; **~ papers insurance** *n* INS assurance des documents de valeur *f*

valuables *n pl* GEN COMM objets de valeur *m pl*

valuation *n* PROP estimation *f*, évaluation *f*, STOCK *of shares* évaluation *f*; **~ adjustment** *n* ACC ajustement d'évaluation *m*; **~ allowance** *n* ACC provision pour moins-value *f*, provision pour évaluation d'actifs *f*; **~ charge** *n* TRANSP taxation à la valeur *f*; **~ clause** *n (VC)* INS *marine* clause d'évaluation *f*; **~ criteria** *n pl* ACC critères d'évaluation *m pl*; **~ day** *n* TAX jour de l'évaluation *m*; **~ price** *n* STOCK cours estimatif *m*, prix estimatif *m*; **~ principles** *n pl* ACC principes d'évaluation *m pl*; **~ report** *n* GEN COMM rapport d'évaluation *m*; **~ restrictions** *n pl* ECON *of currency* limitations aux valorisations *f pl*; ◆ **make a ~ of sth** GEN COMM expertiser qch

value[1] *n* ECON, GEN COMM valeur *f*; **~ added** ACC, ECON *corporate*, TAX valeur ajoutée *f*; **~ -added network** *(VAN)* COMP réseau à valeur ajoutée *m*; **~ -added network service** ECON service de réseau à valeur ajoutée *m*; **~ -added reseller** *(VAR)* COMP revendeur de systèmes à valeur ajoutée *m*; **~ -added statement** ACC état de la valeur ajoutée *m*; **~ -added tax** *UK (VAT)* TAX taxe sur la valeur ajoutée *f (TVA)*; **~ analysis** *(VA)* ACC, FIN, S&M *marketing* analyse de valeur *f*; **~ at cost** ACC valeur au prix coûtant *f*; **~ broker** STOCK courtier payé au pourcentage *m*; **~ chain** FIN chaîne de valeur *f*; **~ concept** FIN concept de valeur *m*; **~ date** STOCK date de règlement *f*, jour de règlement *m*; **~ discrepancy hypothesis** ECON hypothèse de l'écart de valeur *f*; **~ engineering** ACC, FIN analyse de valeur *f*, analyse des coûts *f*; **~ for collection** ACC valeur à l'encaissement *f*; **~ in cash** BANK valeur en espèces *f*; **~ in exchange** ECON contre-valeur *f*, valeur d'échange *f*; **~ in use** ECON valeur d'usage *f*, valeur intrinsèque *f*; **~ judgment** GEN COMM jugement de valeur *m*; **~ of money** ECON valeur de l'argent *f*; **~ of one point** STOCK valeur d'un point *f*; **~ position** STOCK *short* position de compensation *f*; **~ proposal** ACC, FIN offre de valeur *f*; **~ share** STOCK action *f*; **~ subtractor** ECON soustracteur de valeur *m*; **~ surcharge** TRANSP taxe à la valeur *f*; **~ test** TAX critère de valeur *m*; **~ to the market** STOCK appel de marge du jour *m*, mark-to-the-market *m*; **~ -to-weight ratio** TRANSP *of conveyed goods* rapport valeur-poids *m*; ◆ **~ as in original policy** *(VOP)* INS valeur de la police d'origine *f*, valeur originale de la police *f*; **~ for money** GEN COMM avantageux; **get good ~ for money** ECON en avoir pour son argent; **go down in ~** STOCK perdre de la valeur; **no ~ declared** *(NVD)* IMP/EXP sans valeur déclarée

value[2] *vt* GEN COMM expertiser, PROP estimer, évaluer; ◆ **~ as marine policy** *(VMP)*, INS *marine*

évaluer en police maritime; **~ for probate** LAW
évaluer pour l'homologation d'un testament

Value: **~ Line Composite index** n US STOCK indice
composite "value line" m; **~ Line Investment
Survey** n FIN service "value line" d'évaluation
des investissements m; **~ Line Stock index** n
STOCK indice boursier "value line" m

valued[1] adj GEN COMM estimé; ◆ **~ at** STOCK coté
à, évalué à

valued:[2] **~ policy** n INS police en valeur agréé f,
police évaluée f; **~ position** n BANK position de
compensation f

valueless adj GEN COMM sans valeur

van vt AmE TRANSP empoter

VAN abbr (value-added network) COMP réseau à
valeur ajoutée m

vandalism: **~ and malicious mischief insurance** n
INS assurance contre les actes de vandalisme et de
malveillance f

vanguard: **in the ~ of progress** phr GEN COMM à la
pointe du progrès loc f

vaporizing AmE, **vapourizing** BrE: **~ oil** n IND
pétrole carburant pour tracteurs m

VAR abbr COMP (value-added reseller) revendeur
de systèmes à valeur ajoutée m, MATH (vector
autoregression) statistics autorégression de vecteur f

variability n GEN COMM, MATH variabilité f

variable[1] adj GEN COMM variable

variable[2] n COMP, MATH variable f; **~ budget** n
ECON budget flexible m, budget variable m;
~ capital n FIN capital variable m; **~ charge** n
(VC) GEN COMM charge variable f, prix variable
m; **~ cost** n ACC, ECON, FIN, TRANSP coût variable
m; **~ expenses** n pl ACC, ECON, FIN frais variables
m pl; **~ interest rate** n BANK, ECON taux d'intérêt
flottant m, taux d'intérêt variable m; **~ lending
rate** n (VLR) FIN taux de crédit variable m; **~ life
insurance** n INS assurance-vie à prestations
variables f; **~ overhead cost** n ACC, FIN frais
généraux variables m pl; **~ rate** n BANK, ECON
taux flottant m, taux variable m; **~ -rate demand
note** n BANK billet à ordre à taux variable m;
~ -rate mortgage n BANK prêt sur hypothèque à
taux variable m; **~ -size font** n COMP, MEDIA
typography police à taille variable f

variables: **~ sampling** n MATH statistics échantillonnage de variables m

variance n ACC écart m, GEN COMM, MATH
statistics variance f, écart m; **~ analysis** ACC
analyse de variance f, analyse des écarts f, MATH
analyse de variance f; ◆ **be at ~** GEN COMM of two
statements ne pas concorder; **be at ~ with sb
about sth** GEN COMM avoir des divergences
d'opinion avec qn, avoir des divergences de vue
sur qch avec qn, être en désaccord avec qn sur qch

variation n ECON revenue, expenditure variation f,
GEN COMM modification f, variation f, STOCK
variation f; **~ margin** STOCK BIFFEX term marge
de variation f

varied adj GEN COMM varié

variety n GEN COMM, S&M variété f; **~ reduction**
ECON, GEN COMM normalisation quantitative f

variometer n IND variomètre m

vary vt GEN COMM modifier, varier

varying adj GEN COMM varié; ◆ **with ~ degrees of**
GEN COMM avec plus ou moins de

vast: **~ sum** n FIN of money somme considérable f

VAT[1] abbr UK (value-added tax) TAX TVA (taxe
sur la valeur ajoutée)

VAT:[2] **~ payments** n pl UK TAX paiements de TVA
m pl; **~ registered trader** n UK TAX commerçant
inscrit à la TVA m; **~ registration number** n UK
TAX numéro d'inscription à la TVA m; **~ return** n
UK TAX déclaration de TVA f

vault n BANK salle forte f; **~ cash** BANK réserve en
espèces f; **~ reserve** US BANK réserves en
chambre forte f pl

VBLT abbr US (vee built) TRANSP shipping à fond
en V loc m

VC abbr GEN COMM (variable charge) charge
variable f, INS (valuation clause) clause d'évaluation f

VDT abbr (visual display terminal) COMP terminal
m, terminal à écran de visualisation m, visuel m

VDU abbr (visual display unit) COMP terminal m,
terminal à écran de visualisation m, unité de
visualisation f, visuel m

Veblen: **~ good** n ECON, S&M bien de Veblen m

vector n GEN COMM, MATH vecteur m;
~ autoregression (VAR) MATH statistics autorégression de vecteur f

vee:[1] **~ built** adj US (VBLT) TRANSP shipping à
fond en V loc m

vee:[2] **~ bottom** n (VEE BTM) TRANSP shipping à
fond en V m

VEE: **~ BTM** abbr (vee bottom) TRANSP shipping à
fond en V m

veep n infrml AmE (vice-president) HRM V-P (vice-
président)

veer vi GEN COMM changer de direction, tourner

vega n STOCK véga m; **~ coefficient** AmE (cf vega
factor BrE) FIN, STOCK coefficient véga m,
facteur véga m; **~ factor** BrE (cf vega coefficient
AmE) FIN, STOCK coefficient véga m, facteur
véga m

vegetable: **~ oil tank farm** n TRANSP shipping dépôt
d'huile végétale m

vegetative: **~ control** n ECON contrôle végétatif m

vehicle n GEN COMM, TRANSP véhicule m;
~ exhaust emissions n pl ENVIR, TRANSP gaz
d'échappement m; **~ leasing** n TRANSP location de
véhicules f; **~ sling** n TRANSP cargo handling
equipment élingue à véhicules f; **~ transhipment**
n IMP/EXP transbordement de véhicule m; **~ turnaround time** n AmE, **~ turnround time** n BrE
TRANSP durée de rotation du véhicule f; **~ unladen weight** n TRANSP poids du véhicule à vide m,
tare du véhicule f

vehicular: ~ **ferry** n TRANSP shipping car-ferry m, transbordeur m

velocity n COMP vitesse f, ECON vitesse f, vélocité f, FIN vitesse f, GEN COMM vélocité f; ~ **of circulation** FIN vitesse de circulation f; ~ **of circulation of money** ECON vitesse de circulation de la monnaie f; ~ **of money** FIN vitesse de circulation monétaire f

velvet n FIN rentes f pl

vendee n GEN COMM acheteur m

vendible adj GEN COMM vendable

vending n GEN COMM distribution automatique f; ~ **machine** GEN COMM, S&M distributeur automatique m, distributeur automatique de produits m, DAP

vendor n COMP fournisseur m, GEN COMM, S&M vendeur m; ~ **company** GEN COMM société apporteuse f; ~ **finance** FIN financement d'apport m; ~ **rating** GEN COMM valuation de l'apporteur f, évaluation de l'apporteur f

vendue n US GEN COMM, S&M auction vente aux enchères f, vente à la criée f

Venezuela pr n GEN COMM Venezuela m

Venezuelan[1] adj GEN COMM vénézuélien

Venezuelan[2] n GEN COMM person Vénézuélien m

vent: ~ **for surplus** n ECON possibilité d'écoulement des excédents f

ventilate vt GEN COMM concern, issue, question ventiler

ventilated: ~ **container** n TRANSP conteneur aéré m

ventilation n GEN COMM ventilation f

venture[1] n ECON, GEN COMM entreprise f, INS shipping aventure f, MGMNT entreprise f; ~ **capital** BANK, FIN, GEN COMM capital risque m, capital à risque m; ~ **capital company** FIN société de capital-risque f, société de capitaux à risque f; ~ **capital corporation** FIN société de capital-risque f, société de capitaux à risque f; ~ **capital limited partnership** FIN société en commandite de capital à risque f; ~ **capitalist** FIN, GEN COMM person financier à risque m; ~ **management** GEN COMM, MGMNT gestion des risques f; ~ **team** S&M marketing équipe chargée d'un nouveau produit loc f

venture[2] ~ **on** vt GEN COMM project entreprendre

venturer n GEN COMM créateur d'entreprises m

venturesome adj GEN COMM risky risqué

venue n GEN COMM for meeting, conference lieu m, lieu de réunion m

VER abbr (voluntary export restraint) IMP/EXP RVE (restriction volontaire des exportations)

verbal[1] adj GEN COMM verbal

verbal:[2] ~ **agreement** n GEN COMM accord verbal m, convention verbale f; ~ **communication** n GEN COMM, HRM, MGMNT communication verbale f; ~ **offer** n GEN COMM offre verbale f; ~ **warning** n HRM premier avertissement m

verbatim adv GEN COMM repeat sth textuellement

verdict n LAW verdict m

Verdoorn's: ~ **law** n LAW loi Verdoorn f

verge: **be on the** ~ **of** phr GEN COMM bankruptcy être au bord de

verifiable adj GEN COMM vérifiable

verification n ACC vérification comptable f, GEN COMM vérification f; ~ **of accounts** ACC vérification comptable f, vérification des comptes f (Can); ~ **phase** GEN COMM phase de vérification f, étape de la vérification f

verify vt GEN COMM contrôler, vérifier

versatility n COMP hardware, system polyvalence f

version n COMP version f, GEN COMM version f, type, model modèle m, MEDIA version f

verso n (vo, ANT recto) GEN COMM, MEDIA verso m (vo)

vert. abbr (vertical) ECON, GEN COMM, IND, MEDIA, STOCK, TAX vertical

vertical[1] adj (vert., ANT horizontal) ECON, GEN COMM, IND, MEDIA, STOCK, TAX vertical

vertical:[2] ~ **access** n TRANSP shipping accès vertical m; ~ **amalgamation** n (ANT horizontal amalgamation) GEN COMM fusion verticale f; ~ **analysis** n ACC analyse verticale f; ~ **balance sheet** n ACC bilan en liste m, bilan vertical m; ~ **business combination** n (ANT horizontal business combination) ECON, GEN COMM concentration verticale f; ~ **combination** n ECON intégration verticale f; ~ **communication** n (ANT horizontal communication) GEN COMM communication verticale f; ~ **discrimination** n (ANT horizontal discrimination) ECON discrimination verticale f; ~ **equity** n (ANT horizontal equity) ECON, TAX avoir vertical m, équité verticale f; ~ **expansion** n (ANT horizontal expansion) ECON croissance verticale f, développement vertical m, GEN COMM expansion verticale f; ~ **formation** n GEN COMM formation verticale f; ~ **integration** n (ANT horizontal integration) ECON, GEN COMM, IND intégration verticale f; ~ **line charting** n STOCK présentation graphique en disposition verticale f; ~ **main boiler** n TRANSP shipping chaudière principale verticale f; ~ **merger** n ECON (ANT horizontal merger) fusion verticale f, GEN COMM intégration verticale f; ~ **mobility** n HRM mobilité verticale f; ~ **organization** n MGMNT organisation verticale f; ~ **planning** n GEN COMM planification verticale f; ~ **profit and loss account format** n ACC compte de résultats en liste m, présentation verticale du compte de résultat f; ~ **promotion** n HRM avancement m; ~ **publication** n jarg MEDIA print production ciblée pour audience spécialisée f, publication verticale f (jarg), édition spécialisée f; ~ **spar** n TRANSP shipping espar vertical m; ~ **specialization** n GEN COMM spécialisation verticale f; ~ **spread** n (ANT horizontal spread) STOCK opération mixte sur options avec dates d'échéance différentes f, opération mixte verticale f, spread vertical m; ~ **takeoff and landing** n (VTOL) TRANSP avion à décollage et atterrisage vertical m (ADAV);

~ union n (ANT *horizontal union*) HRM syndicat professionnel m, syndicat regroupant les adhérents par métier m, syndicat vertical m

verticalized: **~ cargo space** n TRANSP *shipping* volume vertical réservé à la cargaison m

vertically adv GEN COMM verticalement

vessel n TRANSP *shipping* bâtiment m, navire m, vaisseau m; **~ broker** n HRM, TRANSP *maritime* courtier maritime m; **~ crossing** n TRANSP traversée d'un navire f; **~ traffic management system** n TRANSP système de gestion de trafic maritime m; **~ traffic services** n pl TRANSP services de trafic des navires m pl; ♦ **any one ~** (*AOV*) INS marine, TRANSP par navire

vest vt STOCK conférer à; ♦ **~ sb with sth** GEN COMM, LAW investir qn de qch; **~ sth in sb** GEN COMM assigner qch à qn

vested[1] adj TAX *in trustee, beneficiary* dévolu; ♦ **have a ~ interest in** GEN COMM être directement intéressé par, être intéressé dans

vested:[2] **~ benefits** n pl INS avantages acquis m pl; **~ interest** n GEN COMM droit acquis m

vestibule: **~ period** n GEN COMM période d'attente f

vet vt GEN COMM faire une enquête au sujet de loc f

Veterans: **~ Administration mortgage** n US BANK prêts hypothécaires aux vétérans m pl; **~' Land Act Fund advances** n pl POL Avances sur la caisse de la loi sur les terres destinées aux anciens f pl

veterinary: **~ certificate** n IMP/EXP certificat vétérinaire m; **~ controls** n pl IMP/EXP contrôles vétérinaires m pl

veto[1] n GEN COMM, POL veto m

veto[2] vt GEN COMM mettre son veto à

vetting n GEN COMM contrôle de sécurité m, examen m

vexed: **~ question** phr GEN COMM question controversée f, question très débattue f

VGA[1] abbr (*video graphics adaptor card, video graphics array card*) COMP carte VGA f

VGA:[2] **~ card** n COMP carte VGA f, carte vidéographique f

VHF abbr (*very high frequency*) GEN COMM VHF (*très haute fréquence*)

via prep COMMS par, via, TRANSP par, par la voie de loc f, via

viability n FIN, GEN COMM *of project*, MATH *statistics* viabilité f

viable adj FIN, GEN COMM viable

VIC abbr (*very important cargo*) TRANSP cargaison très importante f

vicarious: **~ liability** n LAW responsabilité civile f

vice: **~ -chairman** n HRM vice-président m; **~ -president** n HRM (*VP, veep*) président adjoint m, vice-président m (*V-P*), POL sous-directeur m, vice-président m

vice versa adv GEN COMM vice versa

vicious: **~ circle** n ECON cercle vicieux m

victimization n HRM représailles f pl

Victoria pr n GEN COMM Victoria n pr

victualing n AmE see **victualling** BrE

victualling n BrE TRANSP *shipping* avitaillement m; **~ bill** BrE TRANSP *shipping* facture d'avitaillement f

video n MEDIA vidéo f; **~ camera** n COMMS, MEDIA caméra vidéo f; **~ card** n COMP carte vidéo f; **~ cassette** n COMMS cassette vidéo f, MEDIA vidéocassette f; **~ conference** n COMMS, COMP vidéoconférence f; **~ conferencing** n COMMS, COMP vidéoconférence f; **~ disk** n COMP vidéodisque f; **~ display** n COMMS écran vidéo m; **~ display unit** n COMP terminal à écran de visualisation m; **~ graphics** n pl MEDIA vidéographie f; **~ graphics adaptor card** n (*VGA*) COMP carte VGA f; **~ graphics array card** n (*VGA*) COMP carte VGA f, écran VGA m; **~ library** n MEDIA vidéothèque f; **~ monitor** n COMP moniteur vidéo m; **~ piracy** n LAW, MEDIA piratage de films vidéo m; **~ recorder** n GEN COMM magnétoscope m; **~ terminal** n COMP terminal vidéo m

videocassette: **~ recorder** n GEN COMM magnétoscope m

videophone n COMMS vidéophone m, visiophone m

videoshopping n S&M vidéoachat m

videotape[1] n COMMS bande vidéo f; **~ recorder** GEN COMM magnétoscope m

videotape[2] vt COMMS *interview* enregistrer sur bande vidéo

Videotex® n COMP, MEDIA vidéographie interactive f, vidéotex® m

videotext n COMP vidéotexte m

vie: **~ with** vt GEN COMM *competitor* rivaliser avec

Vienna pr n GEN COMM Vienne n pr

Vientiane pr n GEN COMM Vientiane n pr

Vietnam pr n GEN COMM Viêt Nam m

Vietnamese[1] adj GEN COMM vietnamien

Vietnamese[2] n GEN COMM *language* vietnamien m, *person* Vietnamien m

view[1] n GEN COMM opinion f; **~ screen** COMP écran de visualisation m; **~ of the world** GEN COMM vision du monde f; ♦ **take a different ~** GEN COMM voir autrement; **take a gloomy ~ of the situation** GEN COMM envisager la situation sous un jour pessimiste; **with a ~ to** GEN COMM en vue de; **with a ~ to doing** GEN COMM dans l'intention de faire; **with this in ~** GEN COMM à cette fin

view[2] vt COMP *wordprocessed document* visualiser, PROP visiter

Viewdata® n COMP, MEDIA vidéographie interactive f

viewer n MEDIA téléspectateur m

viewing: **~ room** n MEDIA salle de projection f; **~ time** n MEDIA *broadcast* heure d'écoute f, temps d'antenne m; ♦ **by appointment only** PROP visites seulement sur rendez-vous

viewpoint n GEN COMM point de vue m

vigilance: **~ men** n pl jarg HRM comité de surveillance m

vignette *n jarg* S&M *advertising* photographie en dégradé *f*

vigorous *adj* GEN COMM vigoureux

Vikane *n* IND Vikane *m*

villa: ~ **economy** *n* ECON, POL, WEL villa-économie *f*, économie politique *f*

village: ~ **shop** *n BrE (cf village store AmE)* S&M commerce de proximité *m*, commerce rural *m*; ~ **store** *n AmE (cf village shop BrE)* S&M commerce de proximité *m*, commerce rural *m*

Vilnius *pr n* GEN COMM Vilnius *n pr*

vindicate *vt* GEN COMM *person, behaviour* justifier

vindictive: ~ **damages** *n pl* LAW dommages-intérêts en réparation d'un préjudice moral *m pl*, dommages-intérêts infligés à titre de pénalité *m pl*

vine: ~ **grower** *n* ECON, GEN COMM, IND viticulteur *m*; ~ **growing** *n* ECON *agricultural* culture de la vigne *f*, viticulture *f*, GEN COMM, IND viticulture *f*; ~ **-growing district** *n* GEN COMM, IND région viticole *f*; ~ **harvest** *n* GEN COMM vendange *f*

vineyard *n* GEN COMM vignoble *m*

vintage *n* ECON *harvest* récolte *f*, vendange *f*, *year* millésime *m*, ENVIR, GEN COMM récolte *f*; ~ **effect** ECON effet sur la productivité du vieillissement des moyens de production

vintner *n* GEN COMM, HRM négociant en vins *m*

vinyl: ~ **chloride monomer** *n* IND monomère chloruré vinylique *m*

VIO *abbr (very important object)* TRANSP objet très important *m*

violate *vt* LAW, PATENTS enfreindre, violer; ◆ ~ **the law** LAW enfreindre la loi, violer la loi; ~ **a rule** GEN COMM manquer à une règle

violation *n* LAW contravention *f*, violation *f*; ~ **of the law** LAW violation d'un droit *f*; ◆ **in** ~ **of** GEN COMM, LAW en violation de

violence *n* HRM violence *f*

VIP *abbr (very important person)* GEN COMM personnage de marque *m*

virgin *adj* PROP vierge

Virgin: ~ **Islands** *pr n* GEN COMM Iles Vierges *f pl*

virtual *adj* COMP virtuel

virtue: **by** ~ **of** *phr* GEN COMM en raison de *loc f*, en vertu de *loc*; **by** ~ **of one's position** *phr* HRM de par ses fonctions *loc f*

virtute officii *phr frml* GEN COMM en vertu de

virus:[1] ~ **-free** *adj* COMP non-contaminé

virus[2] *n* COMP virus *m*

visa *n* ADMIN visa *m*, visa de transit *m*

vis-à-vis *prep* GEN COMM vis-à-vis

viscosity *n* GEN COMM viscosité *f*

viscous: ~ **demand** *n* ECON viscosité de la demande *f*; ~ **supply** *n* ECON viscosité de l'offre *f*

visibility *n* FIN transparence *f*, GEN COMM, S&M visibilité *f*

visible[1] *adj* ECON visible

visible:[2] ~ **export** *n* ECON, IMP/EXP exportation visible *f*; ~ **hand** *n* ECON main visible *f*; ~ **import**
n IMP/EXP importation visible *f*; ~ **trade balance** *n* ECON balance commerciale des visibles *f*

visibles *n pl* ECON visibles *m pl*

vision *n* GEN COMM, MGMNT vision *f*

visit *vt* GEN COMM visiter

visitation *n* GEN COMM visite d'inspection *f*

visiting[1] *adj* GEN COMM de l'extérieur, en visite *loc f*

visiting:[2] ~ **card** *n* GEN COMM carte de visite *f*

visitor *n* GEN COMM visiteur *m*; ~ **with student authorization** ADMIN, TAX visiteur avec permis de séjour d'étudiant *m*, visiteur détenant un permis de séjour d'étudiant *m*; ~**s' book** GEN COMM livre d'or *m*; ~**'s tax** TAX taxe de séjour *f*

visual[1] *adj* COMP, GEN COMM visuel

visual[2] *n* POL visuel *m*, S&M *advertising* maquette *f*; ~ **appeal** *n* S&M attrait visuel *m*, intérêt visuel *m*; ~ **arts** *n pl* MEDIA arts plastiques *m pl*, arts visuels *m pl*; ~ **display** *n* COMP visualisation *f*; ~ **display terminal** *n (VDT)* COMP terminal *m*, terminal à écran de visualisation *m*, visuel *m*; ~ **display unit** *n (VDU)* COMP terminal *m*, terminal à écran de visualisation *m*, unité de visualisation *f*, visuel *m*; ~ **impact** *n* GEN COMM impact visuel *m*; ~ **telephone** *n* COMMS vidéophone *m*, visiophone *m*

visuals *n pl* GEN COMM *for presentation* supports visuels *m pl*

vital[1] *adj* GEN COMM *essential* indispensable

vital:[2] ~ **records management** *n* MGMNT gestion des documents essentiels *f*; ~ **revolution** *n* ECON révolution démographique *f*, révolution vitale *f*

vitiate *vt* LAW vicier

VLCC *abbr (very large crude carrier)* TRANSP *shipping* très gros transporteur de brut *m*

VLR *abbr (variable lending rate)* FIN taux de crédit variable *m*

VLS *abbr (very large-scale)* ECON, GEN COMM à très grande échelle *loc f*

VMP *abbr (value as marine policy)* INS marine évaluer en police maritime

vo *abbr (verso)* GEN COMM, MEDIA vo *(verso)*

vocation *n* HRM métier *m*, vocation *f*

vocational: ~ **guidance** *n* HRM orientation professionnelle *f*; ~ **guide** *n* HRM, WEL *person* conseiller d'orientation *m*, conseiller d'orientation professionnelle *m*; ~ **rehabilitation** *n* HRM recyclage professionnel *m*; ~ **school** *n* WEL école professionnelle *f*; ~ **training** *n* HRM formation professionnelle *f*, WEL stage *m*

vogue *n* GEN COMM, S&M vogue *f*; ◆ **in** ~ GEN COMM en vogue

voice:[1] ~ **-activated** *adj* COMP à commande vocale *loc f*; ~ **-actuated** *adj* COMP à commande vocale *loc f*

voice:[2] ~ **mail** *n* COMP messagerie vocale *f*; ~ **-over** *n* S&M commentaire sur image *m*; ~ **recognition** *n* COMP reconnaissance de la parole *f*, reconnaissance vocale *f*

void:[1] ~ **of** *adj* GEN COMM *resources etc* dépourvu de; ◆ **make** ~ GEN COMM rendre nul

void:[2] ~ **policy** *n* INS police nulle *f*

void[3] *vt* GEN COMM annuler

voidable[1] *adj* LAW annulable, résiliable

voidable:[2] ~ **policy** *n* INS police annulable *f*

voidance *n* GEN COMM *dismissal, annulment* annulation *f*, expulsion *f*

vol. *abbr (volume)* GEN COMM vol *(volume)*

volatile *adj* COMP non-rémanent, volatile, ECON, GEN COMM, STOCK volatile

volatility *n* COMP, ECON, GEN COMM, STOCK volatilité *f*

Volcoa *abbr (volume contract of affreightment)* TRANSP Volcoa *m*

volt *n (V)* GEN COMM volt *m (V)*

voltage: ~ **regulator** *n* ENVIR régulateur de tension *m*

volume *n* ACC, COMP, ECON, GEN COMM volume *m*, TRANSP cubage *m*; ~ **of business** GEN COMM volume d'affaires *m*; ~ **charge** TRANSP *tariff* taxation au volume *f*; ~ **contract of affreightment** *(Volcoa)* TRANSP contrat d'affrètement par volume *m*; ~ **deleted** STOCK volume des transactions effacé *m*, volume non indiqué *m*; ~ **discount** GEN COMM, S&M ristourne *f*; ~ **of exports** ECON volume des exportations *m*; ~ **index** GEN COMM indice du volume *m*; ~ **merchandise allowance** S&M remise quantitative *f*; ~ **of orders** GEN COMM volume des commandes *m*; ~ **ratio** ECON ratio du volume des heures travaillées par rapport aux heures budgétées; ~ **rebate** TRANSP *cargo* ristourne sur quantité *f*; ~ **of retail sales** ECON volume des ventes au détail *m*; ~ **shipping** IMP/EXP, TRANSP expédition en volume *f*; ~ **trading** STOCK négociations de blocs d'actions *f pl*, opérations sur blocs d'actions *f pl*; ~ **of trading** GEN COMM volume des opérations *m*, volume des transactions *m*

voluminous *adj* COMMS, GEN COMM, TRANSP volumineux

voluntarism *n jarg* HRM politique contractuelle *f*

voluntary: ~ **accumulation plan** *n* FIN plan d'accroissement de capital volontaire *m*; ~ **agency** *n* WEL agence bénévole *f*; ~ **arbitration** *n* HRM conciliation volontaire *f*; ~ **bankruptcy** *n* FIN dépôt de bilan *m*; ~ **body** *n* WEL organisme volontaire *m*; ~ **chain** *n* GEN COMM chaîne volontaire de distribution *f*; ~ **compliance** *n* TAX observation volontaire *f*; ~ **contributions** *n pl* UK TAX *National Insurance* contributions volontaires *f pl*; ~ **export restraint** *n (VER)* IMP/EXP restriction volontaire des exportations *f (RVE)*; ~ **insurance** *n* INS assurance facultative *f*, assurance volontaire *f*; ~ **liquidation** *n* GEN COMM liquidation volontaire *f*; ~ **policy** *n* HRM politique volontariste en matière de revenus *f*; ~ **redundancy** *n* HRM départ volontaire *m*; ~ **retirement** *n* HRM départ volontaire à la retraite *m*; ~ **unemployment** *n* HRM chômage volontaire

m; ~ **winding up** *n* GEN COMM *of business* liquidation volontaire *f*; ~ **work** *n* HRM travail volontaire *m*

volunteer[1] *n* HRM volontaire *mf*; ~ **development worker** GEN COMM travailleur volontaire pour le développement *m*

volunteer[2] *vt* GEN COMM *information* donner spontanément

VOP *abbr (value as in original policy)* INS valeur de la police d'origine *f*

vostro: ~ **account** *n* BANK compte vostro *m*

vote[1] *n* GEN COMM vote *m*, HRM suffrage *m*, vote *m*, MGMNT vote *m*, POL voix *f*, vote *m*; ~ **against** POL voix contre *f*; ~ **by proxy** POL vote par procuration *m*; ~ **by show of hands** GEN COMM, HRM vote à mains levées *m*; ~ **-netted revenue** ACC, FIN recettes nettes en vertu d'un crédit *f pl*; ~ **netting** FIN méthode du crédit net *f*; ~ **-netting revenue** ACC, FIN recettes à valoir sur le crédit *f pl*; ~ **structure** ACC, POL *government* structure des crédits *f*; ~ **wording** POL libellé d'un crédit *m*; ◆ **take a** ~ **on** POL mettre aux voix

vote[2] **1.** *vt* GEN COMM, HRM, POL voter; ~ **for** GEN COMM, HRM, POL voter; ~ **on** POL mettre aux voix; **2.** GEN COMM, HRM, MGMNT, POL voter; ◆ ~ **by ballot** HRM voter au scrutin; ~ **full supply** POL voter la dotation totale, voter la totalité des crédits; ~ **in favour of** GEN COMM, HRM, POL voter; ~ **interim supply** POL voter des crédits provisoires

voter *n* HRM votant *m*, POL votant *m*, électeur *m*; ~ **turnout** POL *at election* participation électorale *f*

voting *n* GEN COMM, HRM, MGMNT *at board meetings*, POL vote *m*; ~ **booth** *n* POL isoloir *m*; ~ **paper** *n* HRM *in union ballot* bulletin de vote *m*; ~ **power** *n* TAX pouvoir électoral *m*; ~ **procedure** *n* POL procédure électorale *f*; ~ **right** *n* POL droit de vote *m*; ~ **rights** *n pl* STOCK droits de vote *m pl*; ~ **security** *n* STOCK titre avec droit de vote *m*; ~ **share** *n* STOCK action avec droit de vote *f*; ~ **stock** *n* STOCK action avec droit de vote *f*; ~ **trust certificate** *n* STOCK certificat de vote fiduciaire *m*, certificat de vote groupé *m*

vouch:[1] ~ **mark** *n* ACC marque de pointage *f*

vouch:[2] ~ **for** *vt* GEN COMM se porter garant de

voucher *n* ACC, BANK justificatif *m*, pièce comptable *f*, pièce justificative *f*, GEN COMM pièce justificative *f*, S&M *advertising* justificatif *m*, TAX *benefits* pièce justificative *f*; ~ **system** S&M système de bons *m*

voyage *n* TRANSP voyage *m*; ~ **C/P** *n (voyage charter party)* TRANSP *shipping* charte-partie au voyage *f*; ~ **charter** *n* TRANSP affrètement au voyage *m*; ~ **charter party** *n (voyage C/P)* TRANSP *shipping* charte-partie au voyage *f*; ~ **estimate** *n* TRANSP *shipping* cotation *f*; ~ **expenses** *n pl* ACC, TRANSP *shipping, accounting* coût du voyage *m*; ~ **fixture** *n* TRANSP *shipping* affrètement au voyage *m*; ~ **policy** *n* INS *marine* police au voyage *f*; ~ **report** *n* TRANSP *shipping* rapport de mer *m*

VP *abbr (vice-president)* HRM V-P *(vice-président)*

VTOL *abbr (vertical takeoff and landing)* TRANSP ADAV *(avion à décollage et atterrisage vertical)*

vulgar: **~ economist** *n* ECON économiste vulgaire *m*

vulgarize *vt* GEN COMM banaliser

vulnerable *adj* GEN COMM vulnérable

vulture: **~ fund** *n* FIN fonds prédateur *m*

W

w *abbr* (*wood*) TRANSP bois *m*
W[1] *abbr* (*West compass point*) TRANSP *navigation* O (*quart ouest*)
W:[2] ~ **formation** *n* STOCK formation en W
W.A.[1] *abbr* (*with average*) INS avec avaries *loc*
WACCC *abbr* (*Worldwide Air Cargo Commodity Classification*) TRANSP classification mondiale de marchandises de fret aérien *f*
W.A.:[2] ~ **cover** *n* INS *marine* couverture avaries comprises *f*
wad *n infrml* BANK *of notes* liasse *f*
wage[1] *n* ECON, GEN COMM, HRM salaire *m*; ~ **agreement** *n* HRM accord salarial *m*, accord sur les salaires *m*, convention salariale *f*; ~ **-and-price guidelines** *n pl* HRM directives en matière de salaires et de prix *f pl*; ~ **arbitration** *n* HRM arbitrage en matière de salaires *m*; ~ **assignment** *n* HRM affectation des salaires *f*; ~ **bill** *n* HRM masse salariale *f*; ~ **bonus** *n* HRM prime salariale *f*; ~ **bracket** *n* HRM tranche de salaires *f*; ~ **ceiling** *n* HRM plafond *m*, plafonnement des salaires *m*; ~ **claim** *n* HRM revendication de salaire *f*, revendication salariale *f*; ~ **contour** *n* HRM profil des salaires *m*; ~ **control** *n* ECON, HRM contrôle des salaires *m*; ~ **differential** *n* HRM écart des salaires *m*, écart salarial *m*; ~ **differentials** *n* ECON différentiels de salaires *m*; ~ **diffusion** *n* ECON diffusion des augmentations de salaires dans une économie *f*; ~ **drift** *n* (SYN *earnings drift*) HRM dérapage des salaires *m*, dérive des salaires *f*, tendance à la hausse des salaires *f*; ~ **explosion** *n* HRM explosion des salaires *f*; ~ **flexibility** *n* ECON, HRM flexibilité des salaires *f*; ~ **floor** *n* HRM plancher des salaires *m*; ~ **freeze** *n* HRM blocage des salaires *m*; ~ **gap** *n* HRM fossé entre les salaires *loc*; ~ **incentive** *n* HRM stimulant salarial *m*; ~ **increase** *n* HRM augmentation de salaire *f*; ~ **indexation** *n* HRM indexation des salaires *f*; ~ **inflation** *n* ECON inflation des salaires *f*; ~ **lag** *n* HRM décalage des salaires *m*; ~ **level** *n* HRM niveau des salaires *m*; ~ **negotiations** *n pl* HRM négociations salariales *f pl*; ~ **policy** *n* ECON, FIN politique des revenus *f*, HRM politique des revenus *f*, politique salariale *f*, POL politique salariale *f*; ~ **-price inflation spiral** *n* ECON spirale inflationniste prix-salaires *f*; ~ **-price spiral** *n* ECON spirale des salaires et des prix *f*, spirale prix-salaires *f*; ~ **-push inflation** *n* ECON inflation par les salaires *f*; ~ **restraint** *n* HRM limitation des salaires *f*; ~ **rigidity** *n* ECON, HRM rigidité des salaires *f*; ~ **round** *n* ECON, HRM négociation sur le salaire *f*, série de négociations salariales *f*; ~ **and salary administration** *n* HRM direction des salaires et des traitements *f*; ~ **and salary survey** *n* HRM étude des salaires et des traitements *f*; ~ **scale** *n* HRM

échelle des salaires *f*; ~ **settlement** *n* HRM accord sur les salaires *m*; ~ **spread** *n* HRM éventail des salaires *m*; ~ **stabilization** *n* HRM stabilisation des salaires *f*; ~ **standstill** *n* HRM immobilité en matière salariale *f*; ~ **stop** *n* HRM blocage des salaires *m*; ~ **structure** *n* HRM structure des salaires *f*; ~ **subsidy** *n* ECON subvention des salaires *f*; ~ **system** *n* HRM mode de rémunération *m*, système des salaires *m*; ~ **talks** *n pl* HRM négociations salariales *f pl*; ~ **-tax spiral** *n* ECON montée de l'impôt sur les salaires *f*, spirale prix-impôts *f*, TAX montée de l'impôt sur les salaires *f*; ~ **theory** *n* ECON théorie des salaires *f*; ~ **unit** *n* HRM unité salariale *f*; ~ **withholding** *n* HRM saisie-arrêt sur salaire *f*; ~ **worker** *n* (ANT *hourly worker*) HRM travailleur payé à l'heure *m*; ~ **zone** *n* HRM zone de salaire *f*
wage[2] *vt* GEN COMM *campaign* mener; ♦ ~ **a campaign** POL, S&M mener une campagne; ~ **a negative campaign** POL, S&M mener une campagne négative
wages *n pl* GEN COMM gages *m pl*, HRM salaire *m*; ~ **act** *n* LAW loi sur les salaires *f*; ~ **fund theory** *n* ECON théorie du fonds salarial *f*; ~ **policy** *n* ECON, FIN politique des revenus *f*, HRM politique des revenus *f*, politique salariale *f*, POL politique salariale *f*
Wages: ~ **Act 1986** *n* HRM loi de 1986 sur les salaires *f*; ~ **Council** *n UK* HRM conseil des salaires
Wagner: ~ **Act 1935** *n* ECON loi Wagner 1935 *f*; ~ **'s law** *n* ECON hypothèse de Wagner *f*
wait:[1] ~ **-and-see policy** *n* ECON attentisme *m*, politique attentiste *f*; ~ **days** *n pl* GEN COMM jours d'attente *m pl*; ~ **list** *n* LEIS *aviation* billet sans garantie *m*, TRANSP liste d'attente *f*
wait[2] *vi* GEN COMM attendre; ♦ ~ **in line** GEN COMM *AmE* (*cf queue up BrE*) faire la queue
waiter *n jarg* STOCK commis *m*, coursier *m*
waiting:[1] ~ **-line theory** *n* GEN COMM théorie des files d'attente *f*; ~ **list** *n* GEN COMM liste d'attente *f*; ~ **period** *n* STOCK délai d'attente *m*, période de latence *f*; ~ **time** *n* GEN COMM période d'attente *f*
waiting:[2] ~ **a berth** *phr* TRANSP *shipping* en attente d'un poste d'amarrage *loc f*; ~ **for the other shoe to drop** *phr infrml* GEN COMM en attendant la suite des événements *loc m*
waive *vt* LAW, TAX renoncer à
waiver *n* LAW, TAX renonciation *f*; ~ **clause** INS clause d'abandon *f*, clause d'exonération *f*
waiving *n* PATENTS renonciation *f*
wake: in the ~ of *phr* GEN COMM à la suite de *loc f*
Wales *pr n* GEN COMM Pays de Galles *m*
walk:[1] ~ **-up** *adj infrml US* PROP sans ascenseur

walk:[2] **~ -through assessment** n TAX cotisation express f

walk:[3] **~ out** vi HRM cesser le travail

walkabout n POL bain de foule m

walkaway: ~ victory n GEN COMM victoire dans un fauteuil f, victoire facile f

walkie-talkie n COMMS talkie-walkie m

walkout n HRM, IND grève f, grève surprise f

walkover n infrml GEN COMM victoire dans un fauteuil f, victoire facile f

wall:[1] vt **~ out** AmE GEN COMM competition, foreign trade dresser des barrières contre

wall:[2] **go to the ~** phr GEN COMM company couler (infrml), faire faillite loc f, person perdre la partie

Wall:[1] **~ Street Journal** n GEN COMM le journal de la Bourse de New-York; **the ~ Street crash** n STOCK le krach de Wall Street loc m

Wall:[2] **~ Street** pr n US FIN Wall Street n pr

wallflower n jarg STOCK action boudée f (jarg), titre déprécié m

Wall-Streeter n STOCK boursier new-yorkais m

Walras': ~ law n ECON loi de Walras f

Walrasian: ~ stability n ECON stabilité walrassienne f

Walsh: ~ Healey Act 1935 n ECON loi Walsh Healey de 1935

wampum n infrml US FIN pognon m (infrml)

WAN abbr (wide area network) COMP grand réseau m, réseau longue distance m, réseau étendu m, MGMNT grand réseau m

wane vi GEN COMM décliner

wanted: ~ for cash phr STOCK bloc demandé au comptant loc m, demandé en espèces loc

wanting adj GEN COMM not up to required standard qui n'est pas à la hauteur; ◆ **be ~** FIN be lacking manquer

war n ECON, GEN COMM, POL, S&M guerre f; **~ babies** n pl jarg STOCK valeurs des industries de défense f pl; **~ chest** n US GEN COMM trésor de guerre m; **~ clause** n INS marine clause de guerre f; **~ fever** n GEN COMM psychose de guerre f; **~ games** n pl GEN COMM exercices militaires m pl; **~ loan** n FIN emprunt de la défense nationale m; **~ risk** n INS marine risque de guerre m; **~ tax** n TAX impôt de guerre m; **~ veteran's allowance** n TAX allocation d'ancien combattant f; ◆ **go to ~** GEN COMM entrer en guerre, se mettre en guerre; **~ risk only** (wro) INS risque de guerre exclusivement m, risque de guerre uniquement m

ward n LAW minor under control of guardian garde f, tutelle f

warehouse n GEN COMM magasin m, IMP/EXP entrepôt m, TRANSP stock dépôt m, entrepôt m; **~ book** n IMP/EXP, TRANSP stock control livre d'entrepôt m; **~ charges** n pl IMP/EXP, TRANSP frais d'entrepôt m pl, frais de magasinage m pl; **~ economy** n ECON économie d'entreposage f; **~ entry** n IMP/EXP, TRANSP customs déclaration de marchandises entreposées f; **~ keeper** n GEN

COMM surveillant d'entrepôt m, TRANSP stock control garde-magasin m, magasinier m; **~ officer** n IMP/EXP, TRANSP stock control douanier responsable d'un entrepôt sous douane m; **~ receipt** n (WR) GEN COMM, IMP/EXP, LAW, S&M, TRANSP récépissé d'entrepôt m, récépissé-warrant m; **~ supervisor** n GEN COMM, IND chef magasinier m; **~ warrant** n (WW) GEN COMM, IMP/EXP, LAW, S&M, TRANSP bulletin de consigne m, certificat d'entrepôt m, récépissé d'entrepôt m, récépissé-warrant m, warrant m

warehouseman n GEN COMM garde-magasin m, HRM AmE (cf stockman) magasinier m

warehousing n GEN COMM, IND, TRANSP emmagasinage m, entreposage m, magasinage m

wares n pl ECON, GEN COMM marchandises f pl

warm: ~ restart n COMP redémarrage automatique m; **~ -up session** n MGMNT phase de mise en train f

warn vt GEN COMM avertir, prévenir, inform avertir, aviser, instruire; ◆ **~ sb against doing sth** GEN COMM déconseiller à qn de faire qch

warning n GEN COMM, HRM avertissement m; **~ device** GEN COMM dispositif d'alarme m; **~ indicator** GEN COMM signal d'alarme m; **~ list** BANK liste d'oppositions f; **~ sign** GEN COMM panneau avertisseur m; ◆ **without ~** GEN COMM à l'improviste; **without previous ~** GEN COMM sans préavis

warrant[1] n COM, FIN, IMP/EXP warrant m, INS certificat d'option m, LAW warrant m, POL mandat m, S&M warrant m, STOCK bon de souscription m, TRANSP warrant m; **~ of attorney** LAW pouvoir m, procuration f; **~ discounting** FIN warrantage m; **~ for payment** GEN COMM ordonnance de paiement f; **~ holder** STOCK détenteur de bon de souscription m; **~ into government securities** (WINGS) STOCK bon de souscription à des titres d'État m, valeurs garanties par le gouvernement f pl; **~ issue** FIN émission de warrants f

warrant[2] vt BANK garantir

warranted[1] adj (Wld) INS garanti

warranted:[2] **~ rate of growth** n ECON taux de croissance garantie m, taux naturel de croissance m

warrantee n GEN COMM, TRANSP receveur m

warranter n see warrantor

warrantless: ~ investigation n jarg POL enquête sans mandat f

warrantor n LAW garant m

warranty n FIN autorisation f, garantie f, justification f, GEN COMM, INS, LAW garantie f; **~ bond** FIN, STOCK obligation garantie f; **~ card** BANK carte de garantie f; **~ of merchantability** GEN COMM garantie de la qualité marchande f; **~ of title** GEN COMM attestation de titre f

Warsaw:[1] **~ Convention** n TRANSP Convention de Varsovie f

Warsaw[2] pr n GEN COMM Varsovie n pr

wash: ~ **sale** n STOCK opération fictive par achat et vente simultanés f, opération à un cours fictif f, achat-vente d'une valeur m, opération rapide f

washed: ~ **overboard** phr (wob) TRANSP shipping enlevé par la mer

Washington: ~ **D.C.** pr n GEN COMM Washington D.C. n pr

washroom n AmE (cf lavatory BrE, rest room, toilet BrE) GEN COMM toilettes f pl

wastage n GEN COMM gaspillage m

waste[1] n ENVIR déchets m pl, ordures f pl, gaspillage m, GEN COMM gaspillage m, gâchis m; ~ **cube** n TRANSP shipping, packing volume perdu m; ~ **disposal** n ENVIR élimination des déchets f, évacuation des déchets f; ~ **dump** n ENVIR décharge de déchets f, dépôt de déchets m; ~ **dumping** n ENVIR mise en décharge de déchets f; ~ **gas** n ENVIR effluent gazeux m; ~ **heat boiler** n (WHB) TRANSP shipping chaudière de récupération f; ~ **heat fire tube boiler** n TRANSP shipping chaudière de récupération ignitubulaire f, chaudière de récupération à tubes de fumée f; ~ **heat water tube boiler** n (WHWTB) TRANSP shipping chaudière de récupération aquatubulaire f, chaudière de récupération à tubes d'eau f; ~ **management** n ENVIR, GEN COMM gestion de déchets f; ~ **oils** n pl ENVIR huile résiduaire f; ~ **prevention** n ENVIR prévention du gaspillage f; ~ **processing** n ENVIR transformation des déchets f; ~ **product** n ENVIR made from waste déchet m, produit de récupération m, of manufacturing process déchet de fabrication m; ~ **recycling** n ENVIR recyclage des déchets m; ~ **sorting** n ENVIR tri des déchets m; ~ **the** ~ **society** n GEN COMM la société de gaspillage f; ~ **treatment** n ENVIR traitement des déchets m; ~ **treatment plant** n ENVIR station de traitement des déchets f, usine de traitement des déchets f

waste[2] vt ENVIR, GEN COMM gaspiller

wasteful[1] adj ENVIR, IND energy énergivore

wasteful:[2] ~ **expenditure** n FIN dépenses inutiles f pl

wasteland n PROP having no buildings terrain vague m

wastepaper n ADMIN, ENVIR vieux papiers m pl

wastewater n ENVIR eau résiduaire f, eau usée f; ~ **disposal** n ENVIR vidange des eaux usées f; ~ **treatment** n ENVIR traitement des eaux usées m; ~ **treatment plant** n ENVIR station d'épuration des eaux usées f; ~ **treatment works** n pl ENVIR station d'épuration des eaux d'égout f

wasting: ~ **asset** n ENVIR déperdition d'actif f, STOCK actif défective m; ~ **assets** n pl ACC actif défective m, immobilisations défectives f pl, ECON actif consommable m, immobilisations défectibles f pl

watch:[1] ~ **list** n BANK liste de surveillance f, STOCK liste de valeurs sous surveillance f; ~ **trade** n IND commerce horloger m, industrie horlogère f

watch[2] vt STOCK value surveiller; ◆ **keep a close**

~ **on** GEN COMM surveiller de près; ~ **one's back** GEN COMM surveiller ses arrières

watchdog n GEN COMM organisme de défense des intérêts m, security chien de garde m, POL organisme de défense des intérêts m; ~ **committee** GEN COMM, POL comité de surveillance m

watching: be ~ **out for** phr GEN COMM guetter, être à l'affût de

watchman n HRM gardien m, homme de garde m, veilleur m

watchword n GEN COMM mot d'ordre m

water:[1] ~ **-generated** adj ENVIR electricity d'origine hydrique f

water:[2] ~ **ballast** n TRANSP shipping lest d'eau m, lest liquide m; ~ **company** n IND compagnie hydraulique f; ~ **damage** n GEN COMM dégâts des eaux m pl; ~ **and diamonds paradox** n ECON paradoxe de la valeur m; ~ **monitor** n TRANSP ship moniteur d'eau m; ~ **pollutant** n ENVIR polluant des eaux m; ~ **pollution** n ENVIR pollution des eaux f; ~ **supplier** n ENVIR, IND distributeur d'eau m; ~ **supply** n ENVIR alimentation en eau f; ~ **system** n GEN COMM in city réseau d'eau m; ~ **transportation** n TRANSP transport de l'eau m, transport par voie d'eau m; ~ **treatment** n ENVIR traitement des eaux m; ~ **tube auxiliary boiler** n TRANSP shipping chaudière auxiliaire aquatubulaire f, chaudière auxiliaire à tubes d'eau f; ~ **tube domestic boiler** n (wtdb) TRANSP shipping chaudière domestique aquatubulaire f, chaudière domestique à tubes d'eau f

water:[3] ~ **down** vt GEN COMM idea, policy, statement diluer

waterborne: ~ **agreement** n INS marine convention d'assurance du risque de guerre des facultés maritimes f

watered: ~ **capital** n FIN capital dilué m; ~ **stock** n STOCK action diluée f, actions surveillées f pl, surévaluation d'actif f

Waterguard: ~ **Service** n UK IMP/EXP organisme des douanes britanniques m

watermark n BANK bank note filigrane m

watermarked adj BANK bank note filigrané

waterproof[1] adj GEN COMM imperméable

waterproof:[2] ~ **paper** n IND papier bitumé m

watershed n GEN COMM tournant m, MEDIA UK television l'heure à laquelle les émissions déconseillées aux enfants peuvent être diffusées

watertight adj GEN COMM hermétique, argument, regulations indiscutable, container étanche, TRANSP étanche

wave n GEN COMM vague f; ~ **power** ENVIR, IND énergie des vagues f; ~ **theory** GEN COMM théorie de la vague f, théorie des vagues f

wax n GEN COMM cire f

way n GEN COMM façon f; **each** ~ STOCK double commission f; ~ **of life** GEN COMM mode de vie m; ◆ **be under** ~ ECON être en bonne voie, GEN

COMM faire route; **under ~** BANK en cours, GEN COMM en marche

waybill *n* IMP/EXP, TRANSP *detailing route, cost* feuille de route *f*, lettre de transport aérien *f*, lettre de voiture *f*

ways: **~ and means** *n pl* ECON voies et moyens *f pl*; **~ and means committee** *n* US POL *of the House of Representatives* commission des voies et moyens *f* (*Bel*); **~ and means committee** *n* US FIN commission des finances

wbs *abbr* (*without benefit of salvage*) INS *marine* sans bénéfice du sauvetage

w.c. *abbr* (*without charge*) GEN COMM gratis, gratuitement, sans frais, gratis, gratuit

wccon *abbr* (*whether cleared customs or not*) IMP/EXP dédouané ou non *loc*

W/d *abbr* (*warranted*) INS garanti

weak[1] *adj* ECON (*ANT strong*) *currency*, LAW *protection* faible

weak:[2] **~ market** *n* STOCK marché en baisse *m*; **~ point** *n* GEN COMM faible *m*

weaken *vt* ECON *currency value* affaiblir, diminuer

weakest: **~ link theory** *n* GEN COMM théorie du plus faible chaînon *f*

weakness: **~ investigation** *n* ACC analyse des lacunes *f*

wealth *n* ECON abondance *f*, richesse *f*, GEN COMM, HRM, IND, WEL richesse *f*; **~ distribution** ECON distribution de la richesse *f*; **~ effect** ECON effet richesse *m*; **~ of opportunities** GEN COMM beaucoup d'occasions *f*; **~ tax** TAX impôt sur la fortune *m*

Wealth: **~ of Nations** *n* ECON Richesse des nations *f*

wealthy: **the ~** *n pl* ECON, GEN COMM, WEL les riches *m pl*

wear *n* GEN COMM usure *f*; **~ and tear** GEN COMM dégradation *f*, usure *f*

wearout: **~ factor** *n* S&M *advertising* facteur d'usure *m*

weather[1] *n* GEN COMM, TRANSP temps *m*; **~ deck** TRANSP *shipping* pont découvert *m*, pont exposé *m*; **~ report** GEN COMM bulletin météorologique *m*; **~ working day** TRANSP *shipping, unloading* jour ouvrable temps permettant *m*; ◆ **~ working days, Fridays and holidays excluded** TRANSP *shipping, chartering, unloading* jours ouvrables temps permettant, vendredis et jours fériés exceptés *m pl*; **~ working days, Sundays and holidays excluded** TRANSP *shipping, chartering, unloading* jours ouvrables temps permettant, dimanches et jours fériés exceptés *m pl*

weather[2] *vt* ECON *recession* surmonter

weaving: **~ loom** *n* IND métier à tisser *m*; **~ mill** *n* IND atelier de tissage *m*; **~ trade** *n* IND industrie du tissage *f*

webs: **the ~** *n pl jarg* US MEDIA les grands réseaux américains

Wed. *abbr* (*Wednesday*) GEN COMM mercredi *m*

wedge *n* TRANSP cale *f*

Wednesday *n* (*Wed.*) GEN COMM mercredi *m*

weed: **~ out** *vt* GEN COMM *unwanted items or people* éliminer

week *n* (*wk.*) GEN COMM semaine *f*; **at a ~'s notice** GEN COMM dans un délai de sept jours; **~ order** STOCK ordre semaine *m*; ◆ **a ~ in advance** GEN COMM une semaine à l'avance; **a ~ today** GEN COMM aujourd'hui en huit; **within a ~** GEN COMM dans un délai de sept jours, dans une semaine

weekdays: **on ~** *adv* GEN COMM en semaine *loc f*

weekend: **~ freight tariff** *n* TRANSP tarif fret spécial weekend *m*; **~ return** *n* TRANSP *tariff* aller-retour de fin de semaine *m*; ◆ **take a long ~** GEN COMM prendre un weekend prolongé

weekly[1] *adj* GEN COMM hebdomadaire

weekly:[2] **~ pay packet** *n* (SYN *weekly wage packet*) HRM paie hebdomadaire *f*, salaire hebdomadaire *m*; **~ rent** *n* PROP loyer hebdomadaire *m*; **~ return** *n* BANK situation hebdomadaire *f*; **~ wage** *n* HRM paie hebdomadaire *f*, salaire hebdomadaire *m*; **~ wage packet** *n* (SYN *weekly pay packet*) HRM paie hebdomadaire *f*, salaire hebdomadaire *m*

wef *abbr* (*with effect from*) GEN COMM avec effet à compter du *loc m*, à partir de

weigh *vt* GEN COMM *arguments, options* peser, *consequences* évaluer; **~ up** GEN COMM mettre en balance, évaluer; ◆ **~ the pros and cons** GEN COMM peser le pour et le contre; **~ up the pros and cons** GEN COMM peser le pour et le contre; **~ up whether to say yes or no** GEN COMM peser la situation pour savoir s'il faut dire oui ou non

weighbridge *n* TRANSP *cargo* pont-bascule *m*

weight[1] *n* COMP poids *m*, GEN COMM poids *m*, MATH *statistics*, TRANSP poids *m*; **~ allowed free** GEN COMM franchise de poids *f*; **~ ascertained** GEN COMM poids constaté *m*; **~ of cargo** TRANSP poids de cargaison *m*, poids des marchandises *m*; **~ charge** TRANSP *tariff* tarif par poids *m*; **~ limit** GEN COMM limitation de poids *f*; **~ note** GEN COMM bulletin de pesage *m*; **~ ton** GEN COMM tonne *f*; **~ when empty** GEN COMM poids à vide *m*; ◆ **~ and/or measurements at ship's option** (*W/M*) TRANSP *shipping* poids et/ou cubage à l'avantage du navire; **~ guaranteed** (*wg*) TRANSP *stock control* poids garanti *m*

weight[2] *vt* STOCK *option positions* pondérer

weighted[1] *adj* STOCK, TAX alourdi

weighted:[2] **~ average** *n* ECON, GEN COMM, MATH moyenne pondérée *f*; **~ average cost** *n* ACC coût moyen pondéré *m*; **~ index** *n* GEN COMM, STOCK indice pondéré *m*; **~ noise level indicator** *n* ENVIR, WEL indice d'évaluation du bruit *m*

weighting *n* FIN indemnité *f*, pondération *f*, GEN COMM, HRM indemnité de vie chère *f*, MATH, S&M *marketing* pondération *f*, WEL UK indemnité de vie chère *f*

weight/measurement *n* TRANSP *tariff* poids ou cubage *loc m*

weights: **~ and measures** *phr* GEN COMM poids et mesures *m pl*

welcome:[1] ~ **message** *n* COMP message de bienvenue *m*

welcome[2] *vt* GEN COMM accueillir; ◆ GEN COMM inviter; ~ **sb's opinion on** GEN COMM être heureux d'avoir l'opinion de qn sur

welcoming: ~ **party** *n* GEN COMM comité d'accueil *m*

welfare:[1] **on** ~ *adj AmE (cf receiving benefit BrE)* HRM assisté

welfare[2] *n* ECON *AmE (cf dole BrE)* allocation chômage *f*, chômedu *m (infrml)*, GEN COMM bien-être *m*, HRM *AmE (cf dole BrE)* WEL *AmE (cf dole BrE)* allocation chômage *f*, chômedu *m (infrml)*; ~ **benefits** *n pl* HRM allocations de la Sécurité Sociale *f pl*, avantages annexes *m pl*, avantages sociaux *m pl*, prestations de la Sécurité Sociale *f pl*, prestations sociales *f pl*; ~ **department** *n* HRM service social *m*, services d'assistance sociale *m pl*; ~ **economics** *n* ECON économie du bien-être *f*; ~ **fund** *n* FIN caisse de prévoyance *f*; ~ **legislation** *n* HRM loi d'assistance sociale *f*, législation sociale *f*; ~ **office** *n AmE (cf dole office BrE)* HRM bureau d'aide sociale *m*; ~ **payment** *n* TAX prestation d'assistance *f*, prestation de bien-être social *f*; ~ **payments** *n pl* HRM, WEL allocations *f pl*; ~ **recipient** *n AmE* HRM allocataire *mf*, assisté social *m*, prestataire *m*; ~ **services** *n pl* HRM législation sociale *f*; ~ **state** *n* ECON, POL État-providence *m*; ~ **trap** *n* WEL contradiction de l'État-providence *f*; ~ **worker** *n* WEL travailleur social *m*; ◆ **be on** ~ *AmE (cf be on benefit BrE)* HRM, WEL toucher des allocations, toucher des prestations sociales, vivre de l'aide sociale; **go on** ~ *US* HRM demander de l'aide sociale

welfarist *n* POL partisan de l'État-providence *m*

well:[1] ~ **-balanced** *adj* GEN COMM *person, mind* bien équilibré, équilibré; ~ **-educated** *adj* HRM *person* instruit; ~ **-established** *adj* GEN COMM bien établi; ~ **-grounded** *adj* GEN COMM *belief* bien fondé; ~ **-informed** *adj* GEN COMM bien renseigné; ~ **-known** *adj* GEN COMM célèbre; ~ **-meaning** *adj* GEN COMM bien intentionné; ~ **-motivated** *adj* HRM motivé; ~ **-off** *adj* GEN COMM bien placé, riche; ~ **-packaged** *adj* TRANSP bien ficelé; ~ **-paid** *adj* HRM *person, job* bien rémunéré; ~ **-placed** *adj* GEN COMM bien placé; ~ **-positioned** *adj* GEN COMM bien placé; ~ **-stocked** *adj* GEN COMM bien approvisionné; ~ **-to-do** *adj* GEN COMM fortuné; ~ **-tried** *adj* GEN COMM prouvé

well[2] *adv* GEN COMM bien; ◆ **be** ~ **advised to** GEN COMM faire bien de, être bien avisé de

well[3] *n* TRANSP *shipping* puisard *m*, puits *m*; ~ **deck** TRANSP *shipping* coffre *m*

wellhead: ~ **cost** *n* IND coût brut d'extraction de gaz *m*, coût brut d'extraction pétrolière *m*; ~ **prices** *n pl* GEN COMM prix à la source *m*

Wellington *pr n* GEN COMM Wellington *n pr*

well-known: ~ **mark** *n* PATENTS marque notoire *f*

Welsh[1] *adj* GEN COMM gallois

Welsh[2] *n* GEN COMM *language* gallois *m*; **the** ~ *n pl* GEN COMM *person* les Gallois *m pl*

Welshman *n* GEN COMM *person* Gallois *m*

Welshwoman *n* GEN COMM *person* Galloise *f*

west *n* GEN COMM ouest *m*

West: ~ **compass point** *n (W)* TRANSP *navigation* quart ouest *m (O)*; **the** ~ **End** *n UK* LEIS *theatre* le West-End

westbound *adj* TRANSP ouest, à destination ouest *loc f*

western: ~ **-style** *adj* ECON de style occidental *loc m*

Western: ~ **Europe** *n* GEN COMM Europe de l'Ouest *f*, Europe occidentale *f*; ~ **European Union** *n (WEU)* POL *defence* Union de l'Europe occidentale *f (UEO)*; **the** ~ **World** *n* GEN COMM les pays occidentaux *m pl*

wet[1] *adj* TRANSP liquide; ◆ **be** ~ **behind the ears** *infrml* HRM manquer d'expérience, être un gamin *(infrml)*, être un novice, être un peu jeunot *(infrml)*

wet:[2] ~ **blanket** *n infrml* GEN COMM trouble-fête *m*; ~ **bulk cargo** *n* TRANSP *cargo* vrac liquide *m*; ~ **dock** *n* GEN COMM *maritime*, TRANSP *port* bassin à flot *m*; ~ **goods** *n pl* STOCK marchandises liquides *f pl*; ~ **sell** *n jarg* GEN COMM vente bien arrosée *f*; ~ **stock** *n* GEN COMM *spirits* les spiritueux *m pl*

wetback *n infrml AmE* GEN COMM *illegal Mexican immigrant* ouvrier mexicain entré illégalement aux États-Unis

wets *n pl infrml UK* POL *Conservative Party* modérés *m pl*

WEU *abbr (Western European Union)* POL *defence* UEO *(Union de l'Europe occidentale)*

WFP *abbr (World Food Program, World Food Programme)* ECON programme alimentaire mondial *m*

WFSE *abbr (World Federation of Stock Exchanges)* STOCK FIBV *(Fédération internationale des bourses de valeurs)*

WFTU *abbr (World Federation of Trade Unions)* HRM FSM *(fédération syndicale mondiale)*

WFUNA *abbr (World Federation of United Nations Associations)* ADMIN Fédération mondiale des associations des Nations Unies *f*

wg *abbr (weight guaranteed)* TRANSP poids garanti *m*

wgt *abbr (weight)* TRANSP poids *m*

WH *abbr (workable hatch)* TRANSP panneau utilisable *m*

wharf *n* TRANSP *port* quai *m*; ~ **charter** *n* TRANSP contrat d'affrètement au quai *m*; ~ **dues** *n pl* TRANSP *tariffs* droits de quai *m pl*; ~ **-owner's liability** *n (WOL)* LAW responsabilité du propriétaire du quai *f*

wharfage *n* TRANSP *tariff* frais de mise à quai *m pl*; ~ **charges** *n pl* TRANSP *tariff* frais de mise à quai *m pl*; ~ **dues** *n pl* TRANSP *tariff* droits de quai *m pl*

wharfinger *n* GEN COMM, HRM responsable de bassin *m*

what:[1] ~ -**if games** *n pl jarg* GEN COMM jeux d'hypothèses *m pl*

what:[2] ~ **you see is what you get** *phr (WYSIWYG)* COMP tel écran, tel écrit

WHB *abbr (waste heat boiler)* TRANSP *shipping* chaudière de récupération *f*

wheel:[1] *vi* ~ **and deal** GEN COMM être toujours en train de chercher des combines

wheel:[2] **the** ~ **has come full circle** *phr* GEN COMM la boucle est bouclée *loc f*

wheeler: ~ -**dealer** *n infrml* GEN COMM affairiste *mf* (*infrml*), brasseur d'affaires *m*, chevalier d'industrie *m*

wheelhouse *n* TRANSP *of ship* timonerie *f*

wheeling: ~ **and dealing** *n infrml* GEN COMM, STOCK affairisme *m* (*infrml*), brassage d'affaires louches *m*, combines *f pl*

wheels: the ~ **of government** *n pl* POL les rouages du gouvernement *m pl*

when: ~ **due** *adj* STOCK à l'échéance *loc f*

whereas: the ~ **clauses** *n pl* LAW les attendus *m pl*, les considérants *m pl*

wherefore: ~ **clauses** *n pl* LAW conclusions *f pl*

whether: ~ **cleared customs or not** *phr (wccon)* IMP/EXP dédouané ou non; ~ **in berth or not** *phr* TRANSP *charter party term* qu'il soit à quai ou non, à quai ou non *loc m*

whichever: ~ **is the later** *phr (*ANT *whichever is the sooner)* GEN COMM la date la moins rapprochée étant prise en considération *loc f*; ~ **is the sooner** *phr (*ANT *whichever is the later)* GEN COMM la date la plus rapprochée étant prise en considération *loc f*

whipsaw *n jarg* HRM *AmE* arme à double tranchant *f*, HRM *US union bargaining process* négociation à perte *f*, POL *US* magouille *f* (*infrml*)

whipsawed *adj jarg* STOCK cisaillé par le marché *phr*, manipulé

whiskey: ~ **seats** *n pl infrml US* LEIS *theatre* strapontins *m pl*

whistle: ~ -**blower** *n infrml* GEN COMM dénonciateur *m*; ~ -**blowing** *n infrml* LAW fait de dénoncer *loc m*, tirer la sonnette d'alarme (*infrml*)

whistlestop:[1] ~ **campaign** *n* POL campagne arrêt buffet *f*, tournée électorale *f*

whistlestop[2] *vi* POL faire une campagne arrêt buffet *loc f*, faire une tournée électorale *loc f*

white: ~ **coal** *n* ENVIR houille blanche *f*, méta *m*, métaldéhyde *m*, IND houille blanche *f*; ~ **coat rule** *n jarg* S&M *advertising* règle de la blouse blanche *f*; ~ -**collar crime** *n* LAW criminalité d'affaires *f*, criminalité en col blanc *f*; ~ -**collar union** *n* HRM syndicat d'employés *m*; ~ -**collar worker** *n* HRM col blanc *m*, employé de bureau *m*; ~ **good** *n* GEN COMM *domestic appliance cooker* appareil ménager *m*, produit blanc *m*; ~ **goods** *n pl* S&M produits blancs *m pl*; ~ **knight** *n* FIN, STOCK

takeovers chevalier blanc *m*; ~ **land** *n jarg* PROP terre blanche *f*; ~ **market** *n* ECON marché blanc *m*; ~ **noise** *n* MATH *statistics* bruit blanc *m*, parasite *m*; ~ **paper** *n* POL livre blanc *m*; ~ **revolution** *n* ECON *agriculture* révolution blanche *f*; ~ **spirit** *n* ENVIR essence blanche *f*, white-spirit *m*

White's: ~ **rating** *n* STOCK service de notation des obligations des collectivités locales de White

whitewash *vt infrml* GEN COMM blanchir

Whitleyism *n* HRM Whitleyisme *m*

whittle: ~ **down** *vt* ECON *amount, capital* rogner sur, GEN COMM *reduce* réduire peu à peu

whizz: ~ **kid** *n infrml* GEN COMM jeune prodige *m*, jeune turc *m*, petit prodige *m*

WHO *abbr (World Health Organization)* ADMIN, WEL OMS *(Organisation mondiale de la santé)*

whole: ~ **cargo charter** *n* TRANSP affrètement total *m*; ~ -**child concept** *n jarg* WEL conception de l'enfant total *f*; ~ -**life insurance** *n* INS assurance vie-entière *f*; ~ -**life insurance policy** *n (*SYN *straight life insurance policy)* INS police d'assurance-vie entière *f*; ~ **loan** *n* FIN *property* prêt global *m*; ~ **years** *n pl* TAX années accomplies *f pl*, années complètes *f pl*; ◆ **in the** ~ **world** GEN COMM dans le monde entier

wholesale[1] *adj* HRM *huge* massif

wholesale[2] *adv* GEN COMM en gros

wholesale:[3] ~ **bank** *n* BANK, FIN banque commerciale *f*, banque de réseau *f*; ~ **banking** *n* BANK banque de gros *f*, services bancaires de gros *m pl*; ~ **business** *n* GEN COMM maison de gros *f*; ~ **company** *n* GEN COMM maison de gros *f*; ~ **coop** *n* GEN COMM coopérative de gros *f*, coopérative de vente en gros *f*; ~ **cooperative** *n* GEN COMM coopérative de gros *f*, coopérative de vente en gros *f*; ~ **dealer** *n (*SYN *wholesale merchant, wholesale trader)* GEN COMM grossiste *mf*, S&M grossiste *m*; ~ **delivery** *n* GEN COMM livraison en gros *f*; ~ **deposits** *n pl* BANK dépôts de gros *m pl*; ~ **firm** *n* GEN COMM maison de gros *f*; ~ **goods** *n pl* GEN COMM marchandises de gros *f pl*, marchandises en gros *f pl*; ~ **manufacture** *n* IND fabrication en série *f*; ~ **market** *n* GEN COMM marché de gros *m*; ~ **merchant** *n (*SYN *wholesale dealer)* GEN COMM grossiste *mf*, S&M grossiste *m*; ~ **money market** *n* FIN marché monétaire de gros *m*; ~ **price** *n* GEN COMM, S&M prix de gros *m*; ~ **price index** *n* MATH *statistics* indice des prix de gros *m*; ~ **price inflation** *n* ECON inflation des prix de gros *f*; ~ **trade** *n* S&M commerce de gros *m*; ~ **trader** *n (*SYN *wholesale dealer)* GEN COMM grossiste *mf*, S&M grossiste *m*; ◆ **by** ~ GEN COMM en gros

wholesaler *n* ECON, GEN COMM *securities*, S&M, STOCK grossiste *mf*

wholesaling *n* S&M vente en gros *f*

wholly:[1] ~ **dependent** *adj* TAX entièrement à charge

wholly:[2] ~ **and exclusively** *adv* LAW entièrement et exclusivement; ◆ ~ **or in substantial part** GEN COMM en totalité, ou presque, tout ou partie

wholly:[3] ~ **-owned subsidiary** n STOCK filiale en propriété exclusive f, filiale à cent pour cent f, société filiale à cent pour cent f

whoops n FIN système public de fourniture d'électricité de Washington

whse abbr (warehouse) IMP/EXP, TRANSP entrepôt m

WHWTB abbr (waste heat water tube boiler) TRANSP shipping chaudière de récupération aquatubulaire f, chaudière de récupération à tubes d'eau f

wicket n LEIS AmE theatre guichet m, guichet de vente des billets m, guichet des billets m

wide:[1] ~ **-ranging** adj GEN COMM de grande envergure, vaste gamme; ♦ ~ **of the mark** infrml GEN COMM loin du but

wide:[2] ~ **area network** n (WAN) COMP grand réseau m, réseau longue distance m, réseau étendu m, MGMNT grand réseau m; ~ **-body aircraft** n TRANSP gros-porteur m, jumbo-jet m; ~ **-cut gas** n AmE (cf wide-cut gasoline, wide-cut petrol BrE) TRANSP carburant de large coupe m, carburant à coupe longue m, coupe de carburant f; ~ **-cut gasoline** n AmE (cf wide-cut gas, wide-cut petrol BrE) TRANSP aircraft carburant de large coupe m, carburant à coupe longue m, coupe de carburant f; ~ **-cut petrol** n BrE (cf wide-cut gas AmE, wide-cut gasoline AmE) TRANSP aircraft carburant de large coupe m, carburant à coupe longue m, coupe de carburant f; ~ **monetary base** n FIN base monétaire étendue f; ~ **opening** n STOCK écart important à l'ouverture m; ~ **range** n GEN COMM, S&M of goods gamme étendue f

widely: ~ **recognized** adj GEN COMM largement reconnu

widen vt GEN COMM gap, TAX tax base élargir

widening n GEN COMM élargissement m

wider: ~ **share ownership** n ECON économie de partenariat f

widespread adj GEN COMM répandu, étendu

widow n MEDIA printing isolation en haut de page f, veuve f; ~ **-and-orphan stock** STOCK action sans risque f; ~'s **bereavement allowance** TAX allocation de deuil de veuve f

width n COMP largeur f

wife n LAW épouse f

wild: ~ **card** n COMP joker m

wildcat: ~ **drilling** n ENVIR forage d'exploration m, forage en terrain vierge m, forage sauvage m; ~ **strike** n HRM grève sauvage f, grève surprise f; ~ **venture** n GEN COMM entreprise risquée f

wilful: ~ **default** n TAX omission volontaire f; ~ **misrepresentation of facts** n LAW fausse déclaration délibérée f, présentation volontairement déformée des faits f

Williams: ~ **act** n LAW loi Williams

win vt ENVIR coal abattre, GEN COMM customers, sb's confidence gagner; ~ **over** GEN COMM persuade convaincre; ♦ ~ **the jackpot** GEN COMM gagner le gros lot; ~ **one's spurs** GEN COMM prove oneself to be competent faire ses preuves; ~ **sb over to one's point of view** GEN COMM gagner qn à son point de vue; ~ **sb's favor** AmE, ~ **sb's favour** BrE GEN COMM person s'attirer les bonnes grâces de qn

winch n TRANSP cargo handling treuil m

Winchester: ~ **disk** n COMP hardware disque Winchester m

wind:[1] ~ **-assisted ship propulsion** n TRANSP shipping propulsion au vent f; ~ **power** n ENVIR, IND énergie éolienne f

wind:[2] **1.** vt ~ **down** FIN company démanteler, GEN COMM operations, campaign démanteler, démanteler progressivement; ~ **up** GEN COMM meeting clôturer, LAW liquider **2.** vi GEN COMM meeting, speech se terminer

wind:[3] **get a second** ~ phr GEN COMM trouver un second souffle; **take the** ~ **out of sb's sails** phr GEN COMM couper l'herbe sous le pied de qn

windfall: ~ **gain** n ECON gain exceptionnel m; ~ **loss** n ECON perte exceptionnelle f; ~ **profit** n GEN COMM bénéfice inattendu m; ~ **-profit tax** n TAX impôt sur les bénéfices exceptionnels m; ~ **-profits tax** n TAX allègements fiscaux m pl; ~ **tax** n TAX impôt sur les gains exceptionnels m

Windhoek pr n GEN COMM Windhoek n pr

winding: ~ **-up** n ACC of corporation liquidation f, GEN COMM cessation de commerce f, MGMNT of meeting liquidation f; ~ **-up arrangements** n pl LAW concordat m; ~ **-up order** n LAW ordonnance de mise en liquidation f; ~ **-up sale** n GEN COMM vente pour cessation de commerce f; ~ **-up value** n ACC valeur résiduelle de liquidation f

window n COMP fenêtre f, GEN COMM, S&M of shop vitrine f; ~ **bill** GEN COMM affichette pour vitrine f; ~ **display** GEN COMM, S&M étalage m; ~ **-dressing** ACC, BANK, FIN, GEN COMM habillage de bilan m, maquillage du bilan m, truquage du bilan m, STOCK of accounts habillage de bilan m, maquillage des comptes m, truquage du bilan m; ~ **envelope** ADMIN stationery, COMMS, GEN COMM enveloppe à fenêtre f; ~ **-guidance** TRANSP navigation à vue f; ~ **of opportunity** GEN COMM créneau m, créneau favorable m, ouverture f, possibilité f, S&M créneau favorable m; ~ **-shopping** GEN COMM lèche-vitrines m; ~ **sticker** GEN COMM affichette pour vitrine f; ♦ **be** ~ **-shopping** GEN COMM faire du lèche-vitrines; **go** ~ **-shopping** GEN COMM faire du lèche-vitrines

winds: **the** ~ **of change** n pl GEN COMM un vent de changement m

windward adv TRANSP ship au large; ♦ **to** ~ TRANSP maritime au large

Windward: ~ **Islands** pr n GEN COMM Iles du Vent n pr

wine: ~ **-bottling** n GEN COMM mise en bouteille du vin f; ~ **grower** n ECON, GEN COMM, IND viticulteur m; ~ **growing** n ECON, GEN COMM, IND viticulture f; ~ **harvest** n GEN COMM vendange *f*; ~ **industry** *n* GEN COMM, IND industrie viticole *f*, région viticole *f*; ~ **merchant** *n* GEN COMM *wholesaler* négociant en vins *m*, HRM *shopkeeper* marchand de vins *m, wholesaler* négociant en vins *m*; ~ **-producing area** *n* GEN COMM, IND région viticole *f*; ~ **waiter** *n* HRM sommelier *m*; ~ **warehouse** *n* IMP/EXP *stock control* entrepôt à vin *m*

wing *n* TRANSP paroi de cale *f*; ~ **tank** TRANSP *shipping* citerne latérale *f*

winged: ~ **pallet** *n* TRANSP palette à ailes *f*

WINGS *abbr (warrant into government securities)* STOCK valeurs garanties par le gouvernement *f pl*

winner *n* GEN COMM gagnant *m*, STOCK *bullish stock* valeur en hausse *f*; ◆ **be a one point ~** STOCK avoir gagné un point; ~ **takes all** GEN COMM vainqueur ramasse tout

winning *adj* GEN COMM *number, team* gagnant; ◆ **be on a ~ streak** GEN COMM avoir trouvé le bon filon *(infrml)*

winter *n* GEN COMM *seasons*, S&M, TRANSP hiver *m*

WIP *abbr (work in progress)* GEN COMM travail en cours *loc m*

wipe *vt* COMP, GEN COMM *tape* effacer; ~ **off** FIN apurer; ◆ ~ **the slate clean** GEN COMM passer l'éponge

WIPO *abbr (World Intellectual Property Organization)* LAW Organisation mondiale pour la propriété intellectuelle *f*

wire: ~ **lashing** *n* TRANSP câble de saisissage *m*; ~ **service** *n* COMMS service téléphonique *m*, COMMS *AmE (cf news agency BrE)*, MEDIA *AmE (cf news agency BrE)* press agence de presse *f*; ~ **transfer** *n* BANK virement télégraphique *m*

wireless: ~ **certificate** *n* TRANSP certificat radio *m*; ~ **logbook** *n* COMMS journal radio *m*

wiretapping *n* COMMS mise sur écoute téléphonique *f*

with *prep* GEN COMM avec

withdraw 1. *vt* BANK *funds* prélever, retirer, GEN COMM *offer, suggestion, remark, application* retirer; **2.** *vi* ECON *from business activity* se désengager, GEN COMM *back out of a meeting* se retirer

withdrawal *n* BANK *banking*, GEN COMM *of capital* retrait *m*, STOCK *shares* désengagement *m*; ~ **of an appeal** TAX désistement d'un appel *m*, désistement d'une plainte *m*; ~ **of capital** BANK retrait de fonds *m*; ~ **from stocks** GEN COMM prélèvement sur stocks *m*; ~ **of an objection** TAX retrait d'une opposition *m*; ~ **plan** STOCK plan de désengagement *m*; ~ **slip** BANK bordereau de retrait *m*; ~ **warrant** BANK autorisation de remboursement *f*

withhold *vt* LAW *information* dissimuler, taire

withholding *n* STOCK *securities, taxes* détention *f*, retenue *f*; ~ **tax** TAX retenue à la source *f*

within *prep* GEN COMM dans

without *prep* GEN COMM sans

witness[1] *n* LAW témoin *m*; ~ **for the defence** *BrE* LAW témoin de la défense *m*, témoin à décharge *m*; ~ **for the defense** *AmE see* witness for the defence *BrE*; ~ **for the prosecution** LAW témoin à charge *m*; ◆ **give ~ on behalf of** LAW témoigner en faveur de; **in ~ whereof** LAW en foi de quoi, en témoignage de quoi

witness[2] *vt* GEN COMM attester, témoigner, LAW certifier; ◆ ~ **sb's signature** GEN COMM contresigner

witnessing *n* LAW certification *f*

wizard *n* GEN COMM génie *m*; ◆ **be a ~ at** *infrml* GEN COMM avoir le génie de

wk. *abbr (week)* GEN COMM semaine *f*

W/M *abbr (weight and/or measurements at ship's option)* TRANSP *shipping* poids et/ou cubage à l'avantage du navire *loc m*

WMARC *abbr (World Maritime Administrative Radio Conference)* TRANSP *shipping* Conférence mondiale administrative radio-maritime *f*

WMO *abbr (World Meteorological Organization)* TRANSP Organisation météorologique mondiale *f*

wob *abbr (washed overboard)* TRANSP *shipping* enlevé par la mer *loc*

wobbly *adj* GEN COMM *recovery* hésitant

WOL *abbr* LAW *(wharf-owner's liability)* responsabilité du propriétaire du quai *f*

wolf *n jarg* STOCK spéculateur expérimenté *m*

woman: ~ **MP** *n UK* POL ≈ femme député *f*

women's: ~ **magazine** *n* MEDIA revue féminine *f*

won *n* GEN COMM won *m*

wood:[1] ~ **-sheathed** *adj (WS)* TRANSP *shipping, deck* doublé, doublé en bois

wood[2] *n (w)* TRANSP bois *m*; ~ **covers** *n pl* TRANSP panneaux de cale en bois *m pl*

wooden: ~ **pallet** *n* TRANSP *distribution* palette de bois *f*

woodlands *n pl* GEN COMM bois *m*

woods: **be out of the ~** *phr* GEN COMM sortir de l'auberge, sortir du tunnel

wool *n* GEN COMM, IND laine *f*; ~ **merchant** GEN COMM négociant en laine *m*; ~ **trade** GEN COMM commerce de la laine *m*

woolen: ~ **manufacturer** *n AmE see* woollen manufacturer *BrE*

woollen: ~ **manufacturer** *n BrE* IND fabricant de lainages *m*

word *n* COMP, GEN COMM mot *m*; ~ **of advice** GEN COMM conseil *m*; ~ **count** COMP comptage de mots *m*; ~ **and device mark** PATENTS marque combinée *f*; ~ **engineering** POL censure *f*; ~ **length** COMP longueur de mot *f*; ~ **-of-mouth advertising** S&M publicité de bouche à oreille *f*; ~ **-of-mouth marketing** S&M *marketing* marketing de bouche à oreille *m*; ~ **processing** ADMIN, COMP traitement de texte *m*; ~ **-processing center** *AmE*, ~ **-processing centre** *BrE* COMP centre de traitement de texte *m*; ~ **-processing software** COMP logiciel de traitement de texte *m*; ~ **-processing**

system COMP système de traitement de texte *m*; **~ processor** *(WP)* ADMIN *office equipment*, COMP machine à traitement de texte *f*, traitement de texte *m*; **~ speller** COMP correcteur d'orthographe *m*, correcteur orthographique *m*, vérificateur d'orthographe *m*; **~ of warning** GEN COMM avertissement *m*; **~ wrap** COMP changement de ligne automatique *m*, passage automatique à la ligne *m*, retour à la ligne automatique *m*; ◆ **have a ~ with sb about sth** GEN COMM toucher un mot à qn au sujet de qch; **take sb's ~ at face value** GEN COMM prendre les paroles de qn pour argent comptant

wording *n* BANK *of vote* libellé *m*, GEN COMM *of contract* choix des termes *m*, libellé *m*

words: **~ per minute** *phr (wpm)* ADMIN mots à la minute

work[1] *n* GEN COMM travail *m*; **~ backlog** *n* GEN COMM arriéré de travail *m*, IND arriéré de travail *m*, travail en retard *m*; **~ by contract** *n* HRM travail à forfait *m*; **~ classification** *n* HRM classification des tâches *f*; **~ content** *n* GEN COMM contenu du travail *m*; **~ contract** *n* GEN COMM louage de services *m*; **~ cycle** *n* GEN COMM, HRM cycle de travail *m*; **~ design** *n* GEN COMM schéma *m*; **~ ethic** *n* HRM éthique du travail *f*; **~ experience** *n* GEN COMM, HRM expérience professionnelle *f*; **~ flow** *n* COMP déroulement des opérations *m*, GEN COMM flux de travail *m*; **~ history** *n* HRM emplois précédents *m pl*; **~ -in** *n* HRM *in EU regulations* grève par le travail *f*; **~ -in-process** *n* AmE *see* work-in-progress *BrE*; **~ in progress** *n (WIP)* GEN COMM travail en cours; **~ -in-progress** *n BrE* ACC, ECON travaux en cours *m pl*, GEN COMM produits en cours *m pl*; **~ location** *n* HRM lieu de travail *m*; **~ mark** *n* PATENTS marque dénominative *f*, marque verbale *f*; **~ measurement** *n* GEN COMM, HRM analyse quantitative du travail *f*, IND, MGMNT mesure du travail *f*; **~ order** *n* HRM ordre d'exécution *m*, ordre de fabrication *m*; **~ organization** *n* GEN COMM organisation du travail *f*; **~ permit** *n* HRM permis de travail *m*; **~ prospects** *n pl* GEN COMM, HRM perspectives de travail *f pl*; **~ restructuring** *n* GEN COMM, HRM restructuration du travail *f*; **~ sampling** *n* HRM échantillonnage *m*; **~ schedule** *n* ADMIN calendrier des travaux *m*, feuille de présence *f*, programme de travail *m*, MGMNT programme de travail *m*; **~ sharing** *n* HRM partage du travail *m*; **~ sheet** *n* ACC chiffrier *m*, tableau *m*, COMP feuille de programmation *f*; **~ simplification** *n* HRM, MGMNT simplification des tâches *f*, SDT; **~ stoppage** *n* HRM arrêt de travail *m*; **~ stress** *n* HRM, MGMNT tension due au travail *f*; **~ study** *n* GEN COMM étude des méthodes de travail *f*, étude du travail *f*, HRM, MGMNT étude du travail *f*; **~ -to-rule** *n* HRM grève du zèle *f*; ◆ **at ~** GEN COMM *process, machine* en fonctionnement; **get down to ~** GEN COMM se mettre au travail; **out of ~** HRM au chômage, sans emploi

work[2] **1.** *vt* PATENTS mettre en oeuvre; **~ down** GEN COMM *inventories* couler; **~ on** GEN COMM travailler sur; **~ out** GEN COMM *terms, details* définir; **~ out to** GEN COMM *amount to* s'élever à; **~ through** HRM *social work* mettre tout sur la table, GEN COMM, HRM travailler; **2.** *vi* **~ together** GEN COMM travailler de concert, travailler ensemble; ◆ **~ alongside sb** HRM travailler côte à côte avec, être voisin de travail de qn; **~ alternate weekends** GEN COMM devoir travailler un weekend sur deux; **~ as part of a team** HRM participer à un travail d'équipe; **~ closely with** GEN COMM travailler en étroite collaboration avec; **~ flat out** GEN COMM travailler d'arrache-pied; **~ for abeyance** GEN COMM travail en souffrance; **~ for a living** WEL travailler pour gagner sa vie; **~ freelance** MEDIA travailler en free-lance, travailler en indépendant; **~ full-time** HRM travailler à plein temps; **~ in partnership with** MGMNT travailler en association avec; **~ in shifts** HRM travailler par équipes; **~ like a beaver** *infrml* HRM travailler comme une brute *(infrml)*, travailler d'arrache-pied; **~ out the accrued interest** BANK calculer les intérêts courus; **~ out the interest** FIN *calculate* calculer les intérêts; **~ overtime** HRM faire des heures supplémentaires; **~ part-time** GEN COMM, HRM travailler à mi-temps, travailler a temps partiel; **to ~ in tandem with** GEN COMM travailler en collaboration avec; **~ to a very tight schedule** GEN COMM travailler selon un horaire strictement minuté; **~ unsocial hours** HRM travailler aux heures où les autres se reposent

workable: **~ competition** *n* ECON niveau de concurrence réalisable *m*; **~ hatch** *n (WH)* TRANSP *charter party term* panneau utilisable *m*

workaholic *n* GEN COMM, HRM bourreau de travail *m*

workday *n* AmE *(cf working day BrE)* GEN COMM, HRM, IND jour de travail *m*, jour ouvrable *m*

worker *n* HRM travailleur *m*; **~ buyout** FIN, HRM rachat d'une entreprise par ses employés *m*; **~ compensation and employers liability insuring agreement** *US* INS assurance contre les accidents du travail et de la responsabilité civile *f*, assurance pour la garantie des rémunérations des travailleurs *f*; **~ compensation insurance** INS assurance contre les accidents du travail *f*, assurance-accidents du travail *f*; **~ control** HRM autogestion *f*; **~ director** HRM, MGMNT employé membre du conseil d'administration *m*, ouvrier membre du conseil d'administration *m*; **~ participation** HRM participation des travailleurs à la gestion *f*, participation ouvrière *f*; **~ representation** HRM représentation du personnel *f*

workers': **~ collective** *n* HRM collectif de travailleurs *m*; **~ compensation** *n (compo)* HRM indemnisation des accidents du travail *f*, indemnisation des accidentés du travail *f*, indemnisation des victimes d'accidents de travail *f*; **~ compensation act** *n* HRM, LAW loi sur l'indemnisation des travailleurs *f*; **~ control** *n*

HRM contrôle ouvrier *m*; ~ **cooperative** *n* HRM coopérative ouvrière *f*; ~ **involvement** *n* HRM implication des ouvriers *f*; ~ **participation** *n* HRM participation ouvrière *f*

workfare *n* ECON aide à la réinsertion *f*

workforce *n* ECON, HRM, IND main-d'oeuvre *f*; ~ **rating** HRM notation de la main-d'oeuvre *f*

working *n* PATENTS exploitation *f*; ~ **account** *n* ACC, BANK compte d'exploitation *m*; ~ **area** *n* COMP zone de travail *f*, HRM *for each worker* espace de travail *m*; ~ **capital** *n* FIN, GEN COMM fonds de roulement *m*; ~ **-capital advance** *n* FIN, POL avance de fonds de roulement *f*; ~ **-capital ratio** *n* FIN ratio du fonds de roulement *m*; ~ **conditions** *n pl* HRM conditions de travail *f pl*; ~ **control** *n* GEN COMM contrôle effectif *m*, participation déterminante *f*; ~ **copy** *n* TAX *return* brouillon *m*, copie de travail *f*; ~ **day** *n* BrE *(cf workday AmE)* GEN COMM, HRM, IND jour de travail *m*, jour ouvrable *m*; ~ **environment** *n* HRM environnement professionnel *m*; ~ **group** *n* GEN COMM groupe de réflexion *m*, HRM, POL groupe de travail *m*; ~ **hours** *n pl* HRM heures de travail *f pl*, horaire *m*; ~ **hypothesis** *n* GEN COMM hypothèse de travail *f*; ~ **interest** *n* FIN participation directe *f*; ~ **life** *n* GEN COMM vie active *f*; ~ **load** *n* HRM, IND, MGMNT charge de travail *f*; ~ **man** *n* HRM homme actif *m*; ~ **meeting** *n* ACC session de travail *f*, séance de travail *f*; ~ **paper** *n* POL document de travail *m*; ~ **papers** *n pl* ACC, FIN feuille de travail *f*; ~ **party** *n* GEN COMM groupe de réflexion *m*, HRM, POL groupe de travail *m*; ~ **patterns** *n pl* HRM modèles d'exploitation *m pl*; ~ **population** *n* HRM population ouvrière *f*; ~ **practice** *n* GEN COMM pratique professionnelle *f*; ~ **pressure** *n (WP)* TRANSP pression de service *f*; ~ **ratio** *n* ACC coefficient d'exploitation *m*; ~ **session** *n* ACC session de travail *f*, séance de travail *f*; ~ **storage** *n* COMP mémoire de travail *f*; **the** ~ **class** *(cf the laboring class AmE, the labouring class BrE)* ECON, POL la classe ouvrière *f*; **the** ~ **masses** *n pl* POL les masses laborieuses *f pl*; ~ **time** *n* GEN COMM heures de travail *f pl*; ~ **timetable** *n* TRANSP fascicule horaire *m*, livret de marche *m*; ~ **visa** *n* ADMIN visa en cours de validité *m*; ~ **week** *n* BrE *(cf workweek AmE)* HRM semaine de travail *f*; ~ **woman** *n* HRM femme active *f*; ◆ **all** ~ **time saved** TRANSP *shipping* estaries gagnées *f pl*, jours de planche gagnés *m pl*, staries gagnées *f pl*, temps de planche gagné *m*; ~ **time saved** TRANSP *charter* estaries gagnées *f pl*, jours de planche gagnés *m pl*, staries gagnées *f pl*, temps de planche gagné *m*

workless *adj* HRM sans travail

workload *n* HRM, IND, MGMNT charge de travail *f*

workman *n* HRM, IND ouvrier *m*

workmanship *n* GEN COMM c'est du beau travail *loc m*

workmate *n* GEN COMM, HRM camarade de travail *mf*

workplace *n* ADMIN, IIRM lieu de travail *m*;

~ **bargaining** HRM négociation collective sur le lieu de travail *f*

works *n pl* IND usine *f*, établissement *m*; ~ **canteen** *n* HRM restaurant d'usine *m*; ~ **committee** *n* UK *(cf works council)* HRM comité d'entreprise *m*, CE; ~ **contract** *n* GEN COMM contrat de travail *m*; ~ **council** *n* UK *(cf works committee)* HRM comité d'entreprise *m*, CE; ~ **manager** *n* GEN COMM chef d'établissement *m*, HRM, IND chef d'établissement *m*, directeur d'usine *m*; ~ **regulations** *n pl* HRM règlement intérieur *m*; ~ **rules** *n pl* UK HRM règlement intérieur de l'usine *m*

workshop *n* GEN COMM *training*, IND atelier *m*; ~ **bargaining** HRM négociation au niveau d'un atelier *f*

workspace *n* HRM espace de travail *m*

workstation *n* ADMIN poste de travail *m*, COMP poste de travail *m*, station de travail *f*

workweek *n* AmE *(cf working week BrE)* HRM semaine de travail *f*

world[1] *adj* GEN COMM mondial; ~ **-class** GEN COMM de classe mondiale *loc f*

world[2] *n* GEN COMM monde *m*; ~ **consumption** ECON consommation mondiale *f*; ~ **debt problem** ECON, POL problème de la dette mondiale *m*; ~ **economic grouping** ECON regroupement économique mondial *m*; ~ **economy** ECON, POL économie mondiale *f*; ~ **export** IMP/EXP exportation mondiale *f*; ~ **of finance** FIN monde de la finance *m*; ~ **inflation** ECON inflation mondiale *f*; ~ **leader** IND meneur mondial *m*, numéro un mondial *m*; ~ **market** ECON, POL marché mondial *m*; ~ **monetary reserve assets** FIN actifs des réserves monétaires mondiales *m pl*; ~ **monetary system** FIN système monétaire mondial *m*; ~ **money order** BANK mandat international *m*; ~ **price** ECON prix mondial *m*; ~ **systems perspective** ECON approche systématique du développement *f*; ~ **trade** ECON, POL commerce mondial *m*; ~ **trade center** AmE, ~ **trade centre** BrE ECON, S&M centre d'affaires international *m*; ~ **trade route** TRANSP *shipping* route commerciale transocéanique *f*; ~ **welfare** ECON, POL bien-être mondial *m*; ◆ **all over the** ~ GEN COMM dans le monde entier

World: ~ **Bank** *n* BANK Banque Mondiale *f*; ~ **Bank Group** *n* BANK, ECON, FIN Groupe de la Banque mondiale *m*; ~ **Federation of Stock Exchanges** *n (WFSE)* STOCK Fédération internationale des bourses de valeurs *f (FIBV)*; ~ **Federation of Trade Unions** *n (WFTU)* HRM Fédération syndicale mondiale *f (FSM)*; ~ **Federation of United Nations Associations** *n (WFUNA)* ADMIN Fédération mondiale des associations des Nations Unies *f*; ~ **Food Program** *n* AmE, ~ **Food Programme** *n* BrE *(WFP)* ECON programme alimentaire mondial *m*; ~ **Health Organization** *n (WHO)* ADMIN, WEL Organisation mondiale de la santé *f (OMS)*; ~ **Intellectual Property Organization** *n (WIPO)* LAW Organisation mondiale pour la propriété intellectuelle *f*; ~ **Maritime**

Administrative Radio Conference *n* *(WMARC)* TRANSP *shipping* Conférence mondiale administrative radio-maritime *f*; **~ Meteorological Organization** *n* *(WMO)* TRANSP Organisation météorologique mondiale *f*; **~ Power Conference** *n* ENVIR Conférence mondiale sur l'énergie *f*; **~ Wide Fund** *n* *(WWF)* ENVIR Fonds mondial pour la nature *m*

worldscale *n* TRANSP *shipping* échelle nominale mondiale d'affrètement *f*

worldwide[1] *adj* GEN COMM mondial; ◆ **on a ~ scale** GEN COMM à l'échelle mondiale

worldwide[2] *adv* GEN COMM mondialement, partout dans le monde

Worldwide: ~ Air Cargo Commodity Classification *n* *(WACCC)* TRANSP classification mondiale de marchandises de fret aérien *f*

worsen *vi* GEN COMM s'aggraver

worst: ~ -case projection *n* ECON cas de figure le plus pessimiste *m*, projection catastrophe *f*, GEN COMM projection catastrophe *f*; **~ -case scenario** *n* *(ANT best-case scenario)* ECON, GEN COMM, POL hypothèse pessimiste *f*, le pire des cas *m*

worth[1] *adj* GEN COMM valant; ◆ **be ~** ECON, GEN COMM, STOCK valoir; **~ £10** FIN valant 10 livres

worth[2] *n* GEN COMM valeur *f*

worthless *adj* GEN COMM qui ne vaut rien

worthwhile *adj* GEN COMM qui en vaut la peine; ◆ **be ~** GEN COMM valoir la peine, valoir le coup *(infrml)*

wove: ~ paper *n* ADMIN, IND vélin *m*

WP *abbr* ADMIN *(word processor)*, COMP *(word processor)* machine à traitement de texte *f*, traitement de texte *m*, GEN COMM *(working party)* groupe de réflexion *m*, GEN COMM *(without prejudice)* sans préjudice, INS *(without prejudice)* sans constituer de précédent, sous toutes réserves, TRANSP *(working pressure)* pression de service *f*

WPA *abbr* *(with particular average)* INS avec avaries particulières *loc*, avec avaries simples *loc*

wpm *abbr* *(words per minute)* ADMIN mots à la minute *loc*

WR *abbr* *(warehouse receipt)* GEN COMM, IMP/EXP, LAW, S&M, TRANSP récépissé d'entrepôt *m*, récépissé-warrant *m*

wrap:[1] **~ -up** *n jarg US* POL discours de clôture *m*

wrap:[2] **~ up** *vt* GEN COMM, S&M emballer, *deal* conclure, TRANSP emballer

wraparound *n* COMP *memory* bouclage *m*, *text* retour à la ligne automatique *m*; **~ annuity** FIN annuité complémentaire *f*; **~ mortgage** BANK hypothèque intégrante *f*

wrapped *adj* GEN COMM, S&M emballé

wrapper *n* GEN COMM papier d'emballage *m*

wraps: keep under ~ *phr* GEN COMM garder secret

wreck *n* TRANSP épave *f*

wring: ~ information out of sb *phr infrml* GEN

COMM soutirer des renseignements de qn, tirer les vers du nez à qn *(infrml)*

wrinkle *n infrml* STOCK tuyau *m*

writ *n* LAW commandement *m*; **~ of attachment** LAW commandement de saisie *m*, ordonnance de saisie-arrêt *f*; **~ of error** LAW renvoi en révision *m*; **~ of sequestration** LAW séquestre judiciaire *m*; **~ of subpoena** LAW assignation *f*, citation à comparaître *f*

write:[1] **~ -protected** *adj* COMP protégé en écriture

write:[2] **~ -down** *n* ACC dépréciation *f*, moins-value *f*, réduction *f*, ECON, FIN moins-value *f*, GEN COMM, STOCK dépréciation *f*, moins-value *f*, réduction *f*; **~ -in candidate** *n US* POL candidat à inscrire *m*; **~ -in vote** *n US* POL vote à inscrire *m*; **~ -off** *n* ACC radiation *f*, *of debt* annulation *f*, FIN perte sèche *f*, GEN COMM annulation *f*, perte sèche *f*; **~ -up** *n* GEN COMM description *f*; ◆ **be a ~ -off** *infrml* GEN COMM être bon pour la casse *(infrml)*, passer par pertes et profits, être irréparable

write[3] **1.** *vt* GEN COMM écrire; **~ against** STOCK vendre une option en face de; **~ back** ACC contre-passer; **~ down** ACC créer une provision pour dépréciation, réduire la valeur; **~ off** ACC *debt, loss* annuler, enregistrer une provision contre, passer aux comptes de résultat, radier, s'amortir, BANK *debt* passer par pertes et profits, FIN passer aux profits et pertes, GEN COMM annuler, TRANSP *vehicle, cargo* détruire; **~ -protect** COMP protéger; **~ up** ACC augmenter la valeur, GEN COMM *report* rédiger; **2.** *vi* **~ back** GEN COMM répondre; ◆ **~ business** INS souscrire; **~ a check** *AmE*, **~ a cheque** *BrE* BANK faire un chèque, libeller un chèque, émettre un chèque; **~ a fair copy of** GEN COMM mettre au propre; **~ a naked option** STOCK vendre une option à découvert; **~ off over ten years** ACC s'amortir sur dix ans; **~ an option against** STOCK vendre une option pour compenser une position inverse; **~ out a check** *AmE*, **~ out a cheque** *BrE* BANK faire un chèque, libeller un chèque; **~ puts to acquire stock** STOCK vendre des options de vente pour acquérir des actions; **~ sth in the margin of** ADMIN annoter; **~ a stock option** STOCK vendre une option

writer *n* STOCK vendeur *m*

writing: ~ back *n* ACC contre-passation *f*, passation *f*, reprise sur provisions *f*, FIN contre-passation *f*; **~ cash-secured put** *n* STOCK option de vente garantie par un dépôt en liquide *f*; **~ -down allowance** *n* TAX abattement fiscal *m*; **~ off** *n* ACC radiation *f*, *of debt* annulation *f*; **~ pad** *n* ADMIN bloc de papier *m*, bloc-notes *m*; ◆ **in ~** COMMS, GEN COMM par écrit; **set down in ~** GEN COMM mettre par écrit

written: ~ agreement *n* GEN COMM contrat écrit *m*, convention *f*, LAW accord écrit *m*, contrat écrit *m*, convention *f*; **~ call** *n* *(ANT written put)* STOCK option d'achat vendue *f*, option écrite *f*; **~ declaration** *n* LAW déclaration par écrit *f*, déclaration écrite *f*; **~ -down value** *n* ACC valeur amortie *f*; **~ evidence** *n* LAW preuve écrite *f*; **~ line**

n INS part souscrite *f*, partie souscrite *f*; ~ **notice** *n* HRM *of repudiation of industrial action* déclaration écrite *f*; ~ **offer** *n* GEN COMM offre écrite *f*; ~ **option** *n* STOCK option vendue *f*, option écrite *f*; ~ **order to pay** *n* ACC mandat *m*, ordre de paiement *m*; ~ **put** *n* (ANT *written call*) STOCK option de vente vendue *f*, option écrite *f*; ~ **warning** *n* HRM avertissement écrit *m*

wro *abbr (war risk only)* INS risque de guerre exclusivement *m*, risque de guerre uniquement *m*

wrong[1] *adj* GEN COMM *answer* erroné, faux; ◆ **be on the ~ track** GEN COMM faire fausse route; **get the figures ~** GEN COMM se tromper dans les chiffres

wrong:[2] ~ **connection** *n* COMMS *telephone* faux appel *m*, faux numéro *m*; ~ **number** *n* COMMS faux numéro *m*

wrong:[3] ~ **-foot** *vt* GEN COMM prendre à contrepied

wrongdoing *n* LAW faute professionnelle *f*, injustice *f*

wrongful: ~ **dismissal** *n* HRM licenciement arbitraire *m*

wrongly *adv* GEN COMM *assemble* incorrectement

wrongshipped *adj* GEN COMM reu non-conforme

wrought: ~ **-iron cable** *n* TRANSP *ship's equipment* câble de fer forgé *m*

WS *abbr (wood-sheathed)* TRANSP *shipping* doublé, doublé en bois

wt *abbr (weight)* GEN COMM p. *(poids)*

wtdb *abbr (water tube domestic boiler)* TRANSP *shipping* chaudière domestique aquatubulaire *f*, chaudière domestique à tubes d'eau *f*

WW *abbr (warehouse warrant)* GEN COMM, IMP/EXP, LAW, S&M, TRANSP bulletin de consigne *m*, récépissé d'entrepôt *m*, récépissé-warrant *m*, warrant *m*

WWF *abbr (World Wide Fund)* ENVIR Fonds mondial pour la nature *m*

WYSIWYG *abbr (what you see is what you get)* COMP tel écran, tel écrit

X

X[1] *abbr (telephone extension)* COMMS poste *m*

X:[2] ~ **efficiency** *n* ECON efficience X *f*

XC *abbr (ex-coupon)* GEN COMM, STOCK ex-c, ex-coup *(ex-coupon)*

XD *abbr* COMMS *(ex-directory, unlisted)* sur la liste rouge *loc f*, STOCK *(ex-dividend)*, STOCK *(ex dividend)* ex-d, ex-div. *(ex-dividende)*

xenophobe *n* GEN COMM xénophobe *mf*

xenophobia *n* GEN COMM xénophobie *f*

xerographic *adj* ADMIN xérographique

xenography *n* ADMIN xénographie *f*

Xerox[®1] *n* ADMIN, COMMS, GEN COMM *document* photocopie *f, machine* photocopieuse *f*

Xerox[®2] *vt* ADMIN, COMMS, GEN COMM faire une photocopie de *loc f*, photocopier

x-interest *n* FIN sans intérêt

xl: ~ **& ul** *abbr (exclusive of loading and unloading)* IMP/EXP, TRANSP chargement et déchargement exclus *loc m*

x-mill *n* IMP/EXP, TRANSP départ usine *m*, sortie usine *loc f*

x pri *abbr (without privileges)* GEN COMM sans privilège

x-quay *n* IMP/EXP, TRANSP livrable à quai, à prendre à quai *loc m*, à quai *loc m*

x-ship *n* IMP/EXP, TRANSP *shipping* ex navire *m*, à enlever à bord

x-warehouse *n* GEN COMM départ d'entrepôt *m*, à prendre en entrepôt *loc m*

x-wharf *n* IMP/EXP, TRANSP livrable à quai, à prendre à quai *loc m*, à quai *loc m*

X-Y: ~ **plotter** *n* ADMIN traceur de courbes *m*

Y

yacht: ~ **broker** n HRM, TRANSP *shipping* vendeur de bateaux m

Yamoussoukro pr n GEN COMM Yamoussoukro n pr

Yangon pr n GEN COMM Yangon n pr

Yankee: ~ **bond** n US STOCK obligation Yankee f; ~ **bond market** n US STOCK marché des obligations Yankee m, marché des obligations nationales m

Yankees n pl STOCK obligations Yankee f pl

Yaoundé pr n GEN COMM Yaoundé n pr

YAR abbr (*York Antwerp Rules*) INS règles d'York et d'Anvers

yard n GEN COMM yard m, PROP *construction* chantier m, dépôt m; ~ **dolly** TRANSP chariot de manutention m

yardage n GEN COMM longueur en yards, ≈ métrage m

yardstick n GEN COMM *of economy's progress* critère m, *to measure performance* critère d'appréciation m, critère d'évaluation m, moyen d'évaluation m, étalon m

y/c abbr (*your cable*) TRANSP votre câble m

yd abbr (*yard*) GEN COMM yard m

year:[1] ~ **-end** adj ACC, ECON, GEN COMM de fin d'année loc f; ~ **-to-year** adj GEN COMM d'une année sur l'autre loc f, d'une année à l'autre loc f

year[2] n (*yr*) GEN COMM an m, année f; ~ **of acquisition** n ACC année d'acquisition f; ~ **of assessment** n TAX année d'évaluation f; ~ **of averaging** n TAX année d'étalement f; ~ **end** n ACC clôture de l'exercice f, fin de l'exercice f, GEN COMM fin d'exercice f; ~ **-end adjustment** n ACC travaux de fin d'exercice m pl; ~ **-end adjustments for accrued expenses** n pl FIN corrections de fin d'exercice des dépenses constatées d'avance f pl; ~ **-end audit** n ACC audit de fin d'exercice m; ~ **-end closing** n ACC clôture de l'exercice f; ~ **-end dividend** n ACC dividende de fin d'exercice m; ~ **-end procedures** n pl GEN COMM procédures d'inventaire f pl; ~ **of grace survey** n (*YGS*) TRANSP *shipping* visite annuelle f; ~ **of issue** n STOCK *bonds* année d'émission f; **the** ~ **under review** n GEN COMM l'année considérée f; ~ **to date** n ACC, TAX cumul annuel jusqu'à ce jour m, cumul de l'année m, cumulé sur l'exercice en cours, total cumulé de l'année m; ◆ **each** ~ GEN COMM chaque année; ~ **ended** TAX exercice clos m; **every** ~ GEN COMM chaque année; **in the** ~ **to** GEN COMM dans l'année précédent; **one** ~ **completed** GEN COMM une année accomplie; ~ **then ended** TAX exercice clos à cette date m

yearbook n MEDIA almanach m, annuaire m

yearling n BrE (SYN *government bond*) ECON obligation à un an f

yearly[1] adj GEN COMM annuel

yearly[2] adv ACC, BANK, FIN, GEN COMM annuellement

yearly:[3] ~ **allowance** n TAX déduction annuelle f; ~ **dividend** n GEN COMM dividende annuel m; ~ **settlement** n ACC liquidation de fin d'année f

yellow: ~ **books** n pl jarg POL livres jaunes m pl France; ~ **-dog contract** n US HRM, LAW contrat de travail contenant une clause interdisant au travailleur d'adhérer à un syndicat; ~ **-dog fund** n US HRM caisse noire f; ~ **goods** n pl jarg GEN COMM produits jaunes m pl; ~ **metal** n ENVIR métal jaune m; ~ **sheets** n pl STOCK pages jaunes f pl; ~ **strip** n STOCK bande jaune f; ~ **union** n HRM syndicat bidon m (*infrml*), syndicat maison m (*infrml*)

Yellow: ~ **Book** n UK STOCK code de bonne conduite de la Bourse de Londres; ~ **Pages**® n pl UK COMMS, GEN COMM *telephone directory* Pages Jaunes® f pl

Yemen pr n GEN COMM Yémen m

Yemeni[1] adj GEN COMM yéménite

Yemeni[2] n GEN COMM *person* Yéménite mf

yen n GEN COMM yen m

Yerevan n GEN COMM Erevan n pr

YGS abbr (*year of grace survey*) TRANSP *shipping* visite annuelle f

yield[1] n ACC production f, rendement m, ECON productivité f, *agriculture* production f, rendement m, récolte f, ENVIR récolte f, FIN production f, rendement m, GEN COMM récolte f, *output* productivité f, IND production f, STOCK taux de rendement m, TAX *of tax* rendement m; ~ **adjustment** ACC ajustement de rendement m; ~ **advantage** STOCK avantage de rendement m; ~ **book** GEN COMM livre de rendement m; ~ **comparison** STOCK *Treasury bills and Eurodollar contracts* comparaison de rendement f; ~ **curve** BANK, ECON, STOCK courbe de rendement f, courbe des taux d'intérêt f; ~ **-curve inversion** ECON inversion de la courbe des taux f, inversion des courbes de taux f; ~ **equivalence** STOCK équivalence de rendement f; ~ **gap** STOCK courbe des taux f; ~ **load** TRANSP pression de fluage f; ~ **maintenance** STOCK ajustement du taux de rendement m; ~ **per acre** ECON *agriculture* rendement à l'hectare m; ~ **to average life** STOCK taux de rendement pour une durée de vie moyenne m; ~ **to call** GEN COMM rendement minimum m; ~ **to maturity** BANK (*YTM*) rendement actualisé m, rendement à l'échéance m, taux actuariel m, ECON, FIN (*YTM*) rendement à l'échéance m,

STOCK *(YTM)* rendement actualisé *m*, rendement à l'échéance *m*, taux actuariel *m*; ~ **to worst** GEN COMM rendement minimum *m*; ~ **variance** FIN, GEN COMM écart de rendement *m*

yield[2] *vt* BANK *interests* produire, GEN COMM *rendre*, STOCK *profit, loss* produire, rapporter

Y'ld-Gr's *abbr (gross dividend yield)* ECON, STOCK rendement boursier brut *m*, rendement de dividende brut *m*, rendement des actions brut *m*

York: ~ **Antwerp Rules** *n pl (YAR)* INS règles d'York et d'Anvers

young[1] *adj* GEN COMM jeune

young:[2] ~ **people** *n pl* GEN COMM les jeunes *m pl*; ~ **upwardly mobile professional** *n (yuppie)* GEN COMM bon chic, bon genre *(infrml)*, bcbg, yuppie *m*; ~ **workers** *n pl* HRM jeunes travailleurs *m pl*

your[1] *adj (yr)* COMMS votre

your:[2] ~ **letter of 5th instant** *phr* COMMS votre courrier du 5 du mois courant *(frml)*

Yours: ~ **faithfully** *phr* COMMS *letter ending* je vous prie d'agréer, Madame/Monsieur, l'expression de mes sentiments les meilleurs, veuillez agréer, Madame/Monsieur, l'expression de mes sentiments les plus distingués; ~ **sincerely** *phr BrE (cf Sincerely yours AmE)* COMMS *letter ending* je vous prie d'agréer, Madame/Monsieur, l'expression de mes sentiments les meilleurs, veuillez agréer, Madame/Monsieur, l'expression de mes sentiments les plus distingués; ~ **truly** *phr* COMMS *letter ending* je vous prie d'agréer, Madame/Monsieur, l'expression de mes sentiments les meilleurs, veuillez agréer, Madame/Monsieur, l'expression de mes sentiments les plus distingués

youth: ~ **training** *n UK (YT)* HRM formation des jeunes *f*

Youth: ~ **Training Scheme** *n UK (YTS)* ECON ≈ travaux d'utilité collective *m pl (TUC)*, HRM ≈ contrat d'emploi-solidarité *m (France)*, ≈ travaux d'utilité collective *m pl (TUC)*, POL, WEL ≈ travaux d'utilité collective *m pl (TUC)*

yo-yo:[1] ~ **stock** *n* STOCK action fluctuante *f*, valeur yo-yo *f*

yo-yo[2] *vi* GEN COMM faire le yoyo, fluctuer

yr *abbr* COMMS *(your)* votre, GEN COMM *(year)* an *m*, année *f*; ~ **ref.** *(your reference)* COMMS V/réf. *(votre référence)*

YT *abbr UK (youth training)* HRM formation des jeunes *f*

YTM *abbr (yield to maturity)* BANK rendement actualisé *m*, rendement à l'échéance *m*, taux actuariel *m*, ECON, FIN rendement à l'échéance *m*, STOCK rendement actualisé *m*, rendement à l'échéance *m*, taux actuariel *m*

YTS *abbr UK (Youth Training Scheme)* ECON ≈ TUC *(travaux d'utilité collective)*, HRM ≈ TUC *(travaux d'utilité collective)*, ≈ CES *(France) (contrat d'emploi-solidarité)*, POL, WEL ≈ TUC *(travaux d'utilité collective)*

yuan *n* GEN COMM yuan *m*

Yugoslav[1] *adj* GEN COMM yougoslave

Yugoslav[2] *n* GEN COMM *person* Yougoslave *mf*

Yugoslavia *pr n* GEN COMM Yougoslavie *f*

Yugoslavian[1] *adj* GEN COMM yougoslave

Yugoslavian[2] *n* GEN COMM *person* Yougoslave *mf*

yuppie *n (young upwardly mobile professional)* GEN COMM bon chic, bon genre *(infrml)*, bcbg, yuppie *m*

Z

Z: **~ chart** *n* MATH diagramme en Z *m*, graphique en dents de scie *m*; **~ score** *n* MATH *statistics* indice Z *m*

Zagreb *pr n* GEN COMM Zagreb *n pr*

zai: **~ -teku** *n* FIN *Japan* zai teku *m*

zaibatsu *n* ECON, IND *Japan* conglomérat industriel japonais *m*

zaïre *n* GEN COMM zaïre *m*, zaòre *m*

Zaïre *pr n* GEN COMM Zaïre *m*

Zaïrian[1] *adj* GEN COMM zaïrois

Zaïrian[2] *n* GEN COMM *person* Zaïrois *m*

Zambia:[1] **~ Airways** *n* TRANSP compagnie aérienne de Zambie

Zambia[2] *pr n* GEN COMM Zambie *f*

Zambian[1] *adj* GEN COMM zambien

Zambian[2] *n* GEN COMM *person* Zambien *m*

ZBB *abbr (zero-base budgeting)* ACC, FIN budget base zéro *m*, budgétisation base zéro *f*, technique du budget base zéro *f*

zeal *n* GEN COMM zèle *m*

ZEBRAs *abbr (zero-coupon Eurosterling bearer-registered accruing securities)* STOCK obligations en Eurosterling à coupon zéro *f pl*, valeurs ZEBRA *f pl*

zero:[1] **~ -priced** *adj* GEN COMM prix sur la base zéro *m*; **~ -rated** *adj* TAX *for VAT* non-assujetti à la TVA, taux zéro; ◆ **be ~ -rated for VAT** TAX ne pas être assujetti à la TVA

zero[2] *n* ACC, FIN, GEN COMM, MATH zéro *m*; **~ -balance account** *n* BANK compte à solde nul *m*; **~ -base budget** *n* ACC, FIN budget base zéro *m*; **~ -base budgeting** *n (ZBB)* ACC, FIN budget base zéro *m*, budgétisation base zéro *f*, technique du budget base zéro *f*; **~ -coupon bond** *n* STOCK obligation à coupon différé *f*, obligation à coupon zéro *f*, obligation à coupons détachés *f*; **~ -coupon convertible security** *n* STOCK valeur convertible à coupon zéro *f*; **~ -coupon Eurosterling bearer-registered accruing securities** *n (ZEBRAs)* STOCK obligations en Eurosterling à coupon zéro *f pl*, valeurs ZEBRA *f pl*; **~ -coupon security** *n* STOCK action coupon zéro *f*, valeur à coupon zéro *f*; **~ growth** *n* ECON croissance zéro *f*; **~ lot line** *n* PROP ligne de lotissement zéro *f*; **~ -minus tick** *n* STOCK transaction à l'échelon de cotation inférieur *f*, écart inférieur à zéro *m*; **~ -plus tick** *n* STOCK transaction à l'échelon de cotation supérieur *f*, écart supérieur à zéro *m*; **~ population growth** *n (ZPG)* ECON, POL crois-

sance démographique nulle *f*, croissance démographique zéro *f*; **~ profit** *n* FIN bénéfice nul *m*; **~ rate** *n* TAX taux zéro *m*; **~ rate of tax** *n* TAX taux nul d'imposition *m*, taux nul de taxe *m*; **~ rate taxation** *n* TAX fiscalité à taux zéro *f*; **~ -rated good** *n* TAX denrée au taux zéro *f*; **~ -rated supplies** *n pl UK* TAX *VAT* fournitures au taux zéro *f pl*; **~ rating** *n* ACC, IMP/EXP taux zéro *m*, TAX *VAT* exemption de la TVA *f*, taxation zéro *f*; **~ real interest** *n* FIN intérêt réel nul *m*; **~ state** *n* COMP état zéro *m*; **~ sum** *n* ECON somme nulle *f*; **~ -sum game** *n* ECON, MGMNT, POL jeu à somme nulle *m*; ◆ **~ defect** ACC, FIN, GEN COMM, MATH zéro défaut *m*

zero[3] *vt* COMP mettre à zéro, remettre à zéro

Zimbabwe *pr n* GEN COMM Zimbabwe *m*

Zimbabwean[1] *adj* GEN COMM zimbabwéen

Zimbabwean[2] *n* GEN COMM Zimbabwéen *m*

zinc *n* ENVIR zinc *m*; **~ ore** *n* ENVIR minerai de zinc *m*

zip: **~ code** *n* *AmE (cf postal code BrE, postcode BrE)* COMMS code postal *m*

ZIP *abbr US (zone improvement plan)* GEN COMM plan d'aménagement d'une zone *m*

zloty *n* GEN COMM zloty *m*

zone *n* COMP *computer screen* zone *f*, GEN COMM secteur *m*, zone *f*; **~ A** *(ANT zone B)* FIN zone A *f*; **~ B** *(ANT zone A)* FIN zone B *f*; **~ of employment** ECON, HRM bassin d'emploi *m*; **~ franc** IMP/EXP zone franc *f*; **~ of freedom** TRANSP zone de liberté *f*; **~ improvement plan** *US (ZIP)* GEN COMM plan d'aménagement d'une zone *m*

Zone: **~ A credit institution** *n* FIN établissement de crédit de la zone A *m*; **~ B credit institution** *n* FIN établissement de crédit de la zone B *m*

zoned: **~ advertising** *n* S&M publicité centrée sur une zone *f*; **~ campaign** *n* S&M *advertising* campagne centrée sur un secteur *f*, campagne centrée sur une zone *f*, campagne régionale *f*; **~ decimal** *n* COMP décimal non condensé *m*

zoning *n* PROP zonage *m*; **~ ordinance** PROP ordonnance de zonage *f*

zoom[1] *n* COMP zoom *m*

zoom:[2] **~ in** *vi* COMP, LEIS faire un zoom avant *loc m*; **~ out** COMP, LEIS faire un zoom arrière *loc m*

zooming *n* COMP zoom *m*

ZPG *abbr (zero population growth)* ECON, POL croissance démographique nulle *f*, croissance démographique zéro *f*

Abbreviations/Abréviations

a *abbr (alloy container)* TRANSP *shipping* conteneur en alliage *m*

A: **~ Inst M** *abbr (Associate of the Institute of Marketing)* HRM, S&M membre associé de l'institut de marketing

AA *abbr* INS *(average adjuster)* marine, TRANSP *(average adjuster)* marine dispacheur *m*, répartiteur d'avaries *m*, TRANSP *UK (Automobile Association)* association automobile britannique

AAA *abbr* INS *(Association of Average Adjusters)* association des répartiteurs d'avaries, TRANSP *(American Automobile Association)* association automobile américaine

AAAA *abbr (American Association of Advertising Agencies)* S&M association nationale américaine des agences de publicité

AACC *abbr (Airport Associations Co-ordinating Council)* TRANSP ≈ CCAA *(Conseil de coordination des associations aéroportuaires)*

AACCA *abbr (Associate of the Association of Certified and Corporate Accountants)* ACC membre associé de l'association des comptables agréés

AAD *abbr (at a discount)* FIN *forward markets* avec un déport *loc m*, à escompte *loc m*, STOCK avec une décote *loc f*, à escompte *loc m*

AAG *abbr (Area Advisory Group)* IMP/EXP groupe consultatif de zone qui s'occupe de développer les marchés étrangers vers lesquels les sociétés anglaises veulent exporter

AAR *abbr (against all risks)* INS contre tous les risques, tous risques *loc*

AAS *abbr (annual automated controls survey)* TRANSP *of ship* visite annuelle de la centrale de navigation *f*

AASMM *abbr (Associated African States, Madagascar and Mauritius)* GEN COMM OCAMM *(Organisation commune africaine, malgache et mauricienne)*

AASO *abbr (Association of American Shipowners)* TRANSP association des armateurs américains

AB *abbr (above bridges)* TRANSP sur palan *loc m*

ABAA *abbr UK (Associate of the British Association of Accountants and Auditors)* ACC membre associé de l'association britannique des comptables et des commissaires aux comptes

ABC *abbr (Australian Broadcasting Corporation)* MEDIA organisme de Radio-Télévision australien

ABCC *abbr* IND *(Association of British Chambers of Commerce)* association des chambres de commerce britanniques, IND *(Arab-British Chamber of Commerce)* chambre de commerce arabo-britannique

ABP *abbr (Associated British Ports)* TRANSP ports britanniques associés

ABS *abbr* HRM *(able-bodied seaman)* matelot de seconde classe *m*, TRANSP *(American Bureau of Shipping)* registre américain d'immatriculation (société de classification), TRANSP *(able-bodied seaman)* matelot breveté *m*, matelot qualifié *m*

ABT *abbr (American Board of Trade)* GEN COMM bureau américain du commerce

ABTA *abbr (Association of British Travel Agents)* LEIS association des agents de voyage britanniques

a/c *abbr* ACC *(account)* compte *m*, ACC *(account current)* compte de mandataire *m*, BANK *(account)*, FIN *(account)*, GEN COMM *(account)* compte *m*

AC *abbr* COMP *(alternating current)* ca *(courant alternatif)*, ECON *(advanced country)* pays industrialisé *m*, pays technologiquement avancé *m*, GEN COMM *(authorization under consideration)* autorisation en cours d'examen *f*, HRM *(assistant controller)* contrôleur adjoint *m*, IND *(advanced country)*, POL *(advanced country)* pays industrialisé *m*, pays technologiquement avancé *m*, TRANSP *(air freight container)* conteneur pour fret aérien *m*

ACAS *abbr UK (Advisory, Conciliation and Arbitration Service)* HRM service consultatif d'arbitrage et de conciliation

ACB *abbr Canada (adjusted cost base)* ACC PBR *(prix de base rajusté)*

ACC *abbr* IND *(American Chamber of Commerce)* chambre américaine de commerce, TRANSP *(automatic control certified)* commande automatique certifiée *f*, TRANSP *(acceptable container condition)* *shipping* état acceptable d'un conteneur *m*

ACCA *abbr* ACC *(Associate of the Chartered Association of Certified Accountants)* membre associé de l'association des comptables agréés, TAX *(accelerated capital cost allowance)* déduction pour amortissement accéléré *f*

acce. *abbr (acceptance)* ACC, BANK acc.

(acceptation), GEN COMM acc., *(acceptation)*, consentement *m*, LAW acc., *(acceptation)* agrément *m*, consentement *m*, PROP acc., *(acceptation)* agrément *m*, consentement *m*

acct *abbr (account)* ACC, BANK, FIN, GEN COMM compte *m*

accy *abbr (accountancy)* ACC comptabilité *f*, expertise comptable *f*

ACD *abbr (automated cash dispenser, automatic cash dispenser)* BANK DAB *(distributeur automatique de billets)*

ACE *abbr (Amex Commodities Exchange)* STOCK Bourse de commerce de l'Amex *f*

ACH *abbr (Automated Clearing House)* BANK, FIN chambre de compensation automatisée

ACIS *abbr (Associate of the Chartered Institute of Secretaries)* ADMIN membre de l'institut des secrétaires qualifiées

ACK *abbr (acknowledgement)* GEN COMM confirmation *f*

ACM *abbr (Andean Common Market)* ECON Marché Commun Andin *m*

ACMA *abbr UK (Associate of the Chartered Institute of Management Accountants)* ACC, MGMNT membre associé de l'institut des comptables de prix de revient et de gestion

ACOP *abbr (approved code of practice)* GEN COMM déontologie *f*

ACPs *abbr (African, Caribbean and Pacific countries)* ECON, POL pays de l'ACP *m pl*

ACRA *abbr UK (Associate of the Corporation of Registered Accountants)* ACC membre associé de la corporation des comptables agréés

ACRS *abbr (accelerated cost recovery system)* ACC, FIN amortissement accéléré *m*, amortissement dégressif *m*

ACS *abbr (Australian Container Service)* TRANSP *shipping* service transconteneur australien

ACSS *abbr (Automated Clearing Settlement System)* BANK SCRA *(système de compensation et de règlement automatisé)*

ACTU *abbr (Australian Council of Trade Unions)* HRM confédération des syndicats australiens

ACU *abbr (administration of the customs union)* IMP/EXP *EU* AUD *(administration de l'union des douanes)*

ACV *abbr* FIN *(actual cash value)*, STOCK *(actual cash value)* valeur de remplacement *f*, valeur effective au comptant *f*, TRANSP *(air cushion vehicle)* aéroglisseur *m*, véhicule sur coussin d'air *m*

A/D *abbr* COMP *(analog-digital)* analogique-numérique, GEN COMM *(after date)* à/c *(à compter de)*, TRANSP *(above deck) shipping* en pontée *loc f*, sur le pont *loc m*

AD-AS *abbr (aggregate demand-aggregate supply)* ECON, FIN demande et offre globale *f*, demande globale-offre globale *f*

ADB *abbr Asian Development Bank* BANK Banque asiatique de développement *f*

ADC *abbr* COMP *(analog-digital converter)* hardware CAN *(convertisseur analogique-numérique)*, GEN COMM *(advice of duration and/or charge)* IDP *(indication de durée et de prix)*

Add. *abbr (address)* COMMS adresse *f*

ADG *abbr (assistant director general)* HRM, MGMNT DGA *(directeur général adjoint)*

Adk *abbr (awning deck)* TRANSP *shipping* pont-tente *m*

admin *abbr* ADMIN gestion *f*, LAW application *f*, exécution *f*, MGMNT gestion *f*, POL administration *f*, PROP curatelle *f*, gestion *f*

ADP *abbr (automatic data processing)* COMP traitement automatique de l'information *m*, traitement automatique des données *m*

ADR *abbr* ACC *(asset depreciation range)* gamme d'amortissement d'actif *f*, plafond maximal de la période d'amortissement *m*, période d'amortissement de l'actif *f*, BANK *(American depositary receipt)*, FIN *(American depositary receipt)* certificat américain d'actions étrangers, FIN *(asset depreciation range)* GEN COMM *(American depositary receipt)* certificat américain d'actions étrangers, PROP *(asset depreciation range)* gamme d'amortissement d'actif*f*, plafond maximal de la période d'amortissement *m*, période d'amortissement de l'actif *f*, STOCK *(American depositary receipt)* certificat américain d'actions étrangers

ADV *abbr (advice enclosed)* COMMS, GEN COMM avis inclus *m*, avis joint *m*

ad val. *abbr (ad valorem)* GEN COMM, TAX ad val. *(ad valorem)*

AERE *abbr (Atomic Energy Research Establishment)* ENVIR ≈ CEA *(Commissariat à l'énergie atomique)*

AF *abbr (advance freight)* TRANSP avance sur le fret *f*, fret payé d'avance *m*

AFBD *abbr (Association of Futures Brokers and Dealers)* STOCK association des courtiers et négociants de marchandises à terme

AFDC *abbr US (Aid to Families with Dependent Children)* WEL aide aux familles ayant des enfants à charge

AFFM *abbr (Australian Financial Futures Market)* STOCK ≈ MATIF *(France) (Marché à terme d'instruments financiers)*

AFL-CIO *abbr (American Federation of Labor - Congress of Industrial Organizations)* HRM confédération générale américaine du travail

AFT *abbr (automatic funds transfer)* ACC, BANK, FIN virement automatique *m*, virement automatique de fonds *m*

AG *abbr* ACC *(Accountant General)* chef comptable *m*, directeur de comptabilité *m*, HRM *UK (Agent General)* représentant général *m*

agcy *abbr (agency)* ADMIN, GEN COMM ag. *(agence)*

AGM abbr (annual general meeting) ACC, FIN, GEN COMM, MGMNT assemblée générale annuelle f

AGNP abbr (augmented GNP) ECON, POL PNBA (PNB augmenté)

agt abbr (agent) GEN COMM, LAW agent mf, commissionnaire mf, représentant m

ah abbr (after hatch) TRANSP shipping écoutille arrière f

AHC abbr (Airport Handling Committee) TRANSP comité de manutention aux aéroports

AHM abbr (Airport Handling Manual) TRANSP manuel de la manutention aux aéroports

AHS abbr (annual hull survey) TRANSP shipping visite annuelle de la coque f

AHST abbr (anchor-handling salvage tug) TRANSP remorqueur de sauvetage m

AHT abbr (anchor-handling tug) TRANSP remorqueur m

AHTS abbr (anchor-handling tug supply, anchor-handling tug supply vessel) TRANSP remorqueur spécialisé dans la recherche et l'exploitation du pétrole

AI abbr ACC (accrued interest), BANK (accrued interest) IC (intérêts courus), COMP (artificial intelligence) IA (intelligence artificielle), FIN (accrued interest), GEN COMM (accrued interest), STOCK (accrued interest) IC (intérêts courus)

AIA abbr UK (Associate of the Institute of Actuaries) INS membre associé de l'institut des actuaires

AIB abbr (American Institute of Bankers) BANK association professionnelle américaine des banquiers

AIBD abbr (Association of International Bond Dealers) STOCK association des négociants d'obligations internationales

AIBOR abbr (Amsterdam interbank offered rate) BANK taux interbancaire offert par Amsterdam

AICPA abbr (American Institute of Certified Public Accountants) ACC association professionnelle américaine des experts-comptables

AICS abbr (Associate Institute of Chartered Shipbrokers) HRM association des courtiers maritimes agréés

AIDA abbr (attention, interest, desire, action) GEN COMM, S&M AIDA (attention, intérêt, désir, action)

AIFTA abbr ECON (Anglo-Irish Free Trade Area Agreement) accord anglo-irlandais de zone de libre-échange, HRM (Associate Institute Freight Trades Association), TRANSP (Associate Institute Freight Trades Association) association professionnelle des transporteurs

AIGSS abbr (annual inert gas system survey) ENVIR enquête annuelle sur les systèmes de gaz inertes

AIMS abbr (American Institute of Merchant Shipping) TRANSP institut américain des navires de commerce

AIWM abbr (American Institute of Weights and Measures) GEN COMM institut américain des poids et mesures

a.k.a. abbr (also known as) COMMS alias, dit, également appelé, GEN COMM alias, aussi connu sous le nom de

ALM abbr (assets and liabilities management) ACC, BANK, FIN, MGMNT GAP (gestion actif-passif) gestion du bilan f

alt. abbr (altered) GEN COMM changé, modifié

alum. abbr (aluminium BrE, aluminum AmE) ENVIR, IND aluminium m

am abbr (ante meridiem) GEN COMM avant midi, du matin

AMA abbr (Asset Management Account) FIN compte de gestion des actifs

AMEX abbr (American Stock Exchange, the Curb) FIN, STOCK la bourse de New York secondaire où sont listées les valeurs qui n'apparaissent pas au New York Stock Exchange, AMEX f

AMI: ~ Ex abbr (Associate Member of the Institute of Export) HRM, IMP/EXP membre associé du groupement des exportateurs

AMIME abbr (Associate Member of the Institute of Marine Engineers) HRM, IND membre associé du groupement des mécaniciens de marine

AML abbr (adjustable mortgage loan) BANK, FIN, PROP prêt hypothécaire variable m

AMMI abbr (American Merchant Marine Institute) TRANSP institut américain de la marine marchande

AMS abbr (annual machinery survey) TRANSP shipping visite annuelle des machines f

AMT abbr ACC (amount) of goods quantité f, of people nombre m, BANK (airmail transfer) virement interbancaire m, virement par avion m, FIN (amount) chiffre m, nombre m, GEN COMM (amount) chiffre m, nombre m, total chiffre m, montant m

AMU abbr (Arab Maghreb Union) ECON, POL Union du Maghreb arabe f

A/N abbr (alphanumeric) COMP, GEN COMM alphanumérique

ANF abbr (arrival notification form) TRANSP shipping avis d'arrivée m

ANPA abbr (American Newspaper Publishers' Association) MEDIA association américaine des Editeurs de Quotidiens

ANSI abbr (American National Standards Institute) GEN COMM, IND, LAW association américaine de normalisation, ≈ AFNOR (Association française de normalisation)

AO abbr ACC (accounting officer) comptable mf, comptable adjoint m, ACC (account of), BANK (account of), FIN (account of), GEN COMM (account of) pour le compte de loc m, HRM (accounting officer) comptable mf, comptable adjoint m

AOB abbr GEN COMM (any other business) points

divers *m pl*, INS *(any one bottom)*, TRANSP *(any one bottom) marine* par navire *loc m*

AOCB *abbr (any other competent business)* GEN COMM autres questions à l'ordre du jour *f pl*, questions diverses *f pl*

AOCTs *abbr (associated overseas countries and territories)* ECON, POL *international trade* pays et territoires d'outre-mer associés *m pl*

AOLOC *abbr (any one location)* INS, TRANSP *marine* en un seul lieu *loc m*

AOS *abbr (any one steamer)* INS, TRANSP *marine* par bateau à vapeur *loc m*

AOV *abbr (any one vessel)* INS, TRANSP *marine* par navire *loc m*

AP *abbr* COMP *(array processor)* processeur vectoriel *m*, INS *(additional premium)* prime additionnelle *f*, MEDIA US *(Associated Press)* les presses associées, STOCK UK *(associated person)* associé *m*, TRANSP *(aft perpendicular) of ship* PPAR *(perpendiculaire arrière)*

APACS *abbr UK (Association for Payment Clearing Services)* ECON Association de services de compensation des paiements *f*

APB *abbr US (Accounting Principles Board)* ACC bureau des principes en comptabilité

APBH *abbr (afterpeak bulkhead)* TRANSP *shipping* cloison du peak arrière *f*, cloison du presse-étoupe *f*

APC *abbr (average propensity to consume)* ECON propension moyenne à consommer *f*, tendance moyenne de la consommation *f*

APEC *abbr (Asia-Pacific Economic Co-operation)* ECON, POL Coopération économique en Asie-Pacifique *f*

API *abbr UK (alternative participation instrument)* STOCK instrument de participation différent *m*

APL *abbr (programming language)* COMP langage de programmation *m*

approx. *abbr (approximately)* GEN COMM approximativement, environ

Apr. *abbr (April)* GEN COMM avril *m*

APR *abbr (annual percentage rate, annualized percentage rate)* BANK, FIN, GEN COMM taux annualisé *m*, taux d'intérêt annuel *m*, taux effectif global *m*

APS *abbr (average propensity to save)* ACC, ECON tendance moyenne à économiser *f*

APT *abbr* STOCK *(arbitrage pricing theory)* théorie de l'évaluation d'arbitrage *f*, TRANSP *(aft peak tank) of ship* coqueron arrière *m*, tank de peak arrière *m*

APV *abbr (administrative point of view)* ADMIN détails administratifs *m pl*, point de vue administratif *m*, MGMNT détails administratifs *m pl*

AR *abbr* INS *(all risks)* tous risques *loc*, LEIS *(Average Revenue)* revenu moyen *m*

arb *abbr (arbitrageur)* HRM, STOCK arbitragiste *mf*

ARI *abbr (accounting rate of interest)* ACC, BANK, FIN TIC *(taux d'intérêt comptable)*

Ariel *abbr (Automated Real-time Investments Exchange)* STOCK réseau informatique pour transactions de blocs d'actions, Ariel *m*

ARM *abbr (adjustable-rate mortgage)* BANK, FIN hypothèque à taux réglable *f*, PROP prêt hypothécaire à taux réglable *m*

ARP *abbr (adjustable-rate preferred stock)* STOCK action de priorité à taux variable *f*, titre privilégié à taux variable *m*

A/S *abbr* ACC *(account sales)* compte-rendu des opérations de consignation *m*, BANK *(at sight)* sur présentation *loc f*, à vue *loc f*, FIN *(after sight)* de vue *loc f*, FIN *(at sight)* sur présentation *loc f*, à vue *loc f*, GEN COMM *(after sight)* de vue *loc f*, GEN COMM *(at sight)*, STOCK *(at sight)* sur présentation *loc f*, à vue *loc f*, TRANSP *(alongside) of quay* bord à, le long de

ASA *abbr* GEN COMM *(American Standards Association)*, IND *(American Standards Association)*, LAW *(American Standards Association)* association américaine de normalisation, ≈ AFNOR, MATH *(American Statistical Association)* association américaine de la statistique, MEDIA UK *(Advertising Standards Authority)*, S&M UK *(Advertising Standards Authority)* ≈ BVP *(Bureau de vérification de la publicité)*

a.s.a.p. *abbr (as soon as possible)* COMMS, GEN COMM aussitôt que possible *loc*, dans les meilleurs délais *loc m*, dès que possible *loc*, le plus tôt possible *loc*

ASCII *abbr (American Standard Code for Information Interchange)* COMP ASCII *m*

ASE *abbr (American Stock Exchange)* FIN, STOCK la bourse de New York secondaire où sont listées les valeurs qui n'apparaissent pas au New York Stock Exchange, AMEX *f*

ASEAN *abbr (Association of South-East Asian Nations)* ECON ANSEA *(Association des nations du Sud-Est asiatique)*

ASOA *abbr (Australian Steamship Owners Association)* TRANSP association australienne des armateurs de paquebots

asst *abbr (assistant)* GEN COMM, HRM adjoint *m*, assistant *m*, auxiliaire *mf*, MGMNT assistant *m*

ASTMS *abbr (Association of Scientific, Technical and Managerial Staff)* HRM association des personnels scientifique, technique, et d'encadrement

ATA *abbr US (Air Transport Association)* TRANSP association de transport aérien des États-Unis, ≈ DGAC *(France) (Direction générale de l'aviation civile)*

ATC *abbr (air traffic control)* TRANSP *activity* contrôle de la circulation aérienne *m*, contrôle du trafic aérien *m*, *building* tour de contrôle *f*

ATS *abbr* BANK UK *(automatic transfer service)* service de virement automatique *m*, HRM *(assistant traffic supervisor)*, TRANSP *(assistant traffic supervisor)* adjoint au contrôleur de circulation *m*, inspecteur adjoint chargé de la circulation *m*,

TRANSP *(apparent time at ship) shipping* TVL *(temps vrai local)*

ATT *abbr (air transportation tax)* TAX TTA *(taxe sur le transport aérien)*

Aug. *abbr (August)* GEN COMM août *m*

aux. *abbr (auxiliary)* TRANSP *shipping* auxiliaire *mf*, vaisseau auxiliaire *m*; **~ B** *(auxiliary boiler)* TRANSP *shipping* chaudière auxiliaire *f*

av. *abbr (average)* ACC, GEN COMM, MATH moyenne *f*

avdp. *abbr (avoirdupois)* GEN COMM poids du commerce *m*

AVR *abbr (agent's vehicle record)* TRANSP registre des véhicules du commissionnaire de transport *m*

AWB *abbr (air waybill)* IMP/EXP, TRANSP LTA *(lettre de transport aérien)*

AWD *abbr (awning deck)* TRANSP *shipping* pont-tente *m*

AWY *abbr (airway)* TRANSP voie aérienne *f*

AXB *abbr (auxiliary boiler)* TRANSP *shipping* chaudière auxiliaire *f*

B *abbr (bale capacity)* TRANSP capacité en balles *f*; **~ of E** *(Bank of England)* BANK, ECON, FIN banque d'Angleterre, ≈ BF *(Banque de France)*

BA *abbr (Bachelor of Arts)* WEL *degree* ≈ licence de lettres *f*, *person* ≈ licencié ès lettres *m*

BAA *abbr (British Airports Authority)* TRANSP administration des aéroports britanniques

BACC *abbr (British-American Chamber of Commerce)* GEN COMM chambre de commerce anglo-américaine

BAEC *abbr (British Agricultural Export Council)* IMP/EXP conseil britannique des exportations agricoles

BAF *abbr (bunker adjustment factor, bunkering adjustment factor)* TRANSP *shipping* surcharge de soutage *f*

bal. *abbr (balance)* ACC, BANK, ECON, FIN bce. *(balance)*, solde *m*

BAM *abbr (bulk air mail)* COMMS envoi en nombre par avion *m*, lettres en nombre par avion *f pl*

BAN *abbr (bond anticipation note)* STOCK bon de financement anticipé *m*, papier anticipant une obligation *m*

B&D *abbr (bad and doubtful debts)* BANK créances douteuses *f pl*

bar *abbr (barrel)* IND, TRANSP baril *m*, fût *m*, tonneau *m*

BASIC *abbr (Beginner's All-Purpose Symbolic Instruction Code)* COMP BASIC *m*

b&b *abbr (bed and breakfast)* LEIS chambre d'hôte *f*

BB *abbr* COMMS, COMP, GEN COMM, HRM *(bulletin board)* panneau d'affichage *m*, tableau d'affichage *m*, TRANSP *(below bridges)* sous palan *loc m (sur palan)*, TRANSP *(bulbous bow) shipping* bulbe d'étrave *m*, étrave à bulbe *f*

BBA *abbr (British Bankers' Association)* BANK association britannique des banquiers

BBC *abbr (British Broadcasting Corporation)* MEDIA compagnie de télévision et de radio nationale britannique, BBC *f*

BBS *abbr* COMMS *(bulletin board system)* messagerie *f*, tableau d'affichage électronique *m*, COMP *(bulletin board service) hardware* serveur télématique *m*

BC *abbr* ACC *(budget control, budgetary control)*, ECON *(budget control, budgetary control)*, FIN *(budget control, budgetary control)* contrôle budgétaire *m*, GEN COMM *(bale cubic meters, bale cubic metres)* bale *m*

BCC *abbr (British Chamber of Commerce)* GEN COMM chambre de commerce britannique

BCom *abbr (Bachelor of Commerce)* HRM, WEL *degree* ≈ licence en études commerciales *f*, *person* ≈ licencié en études commerciales *m*

BCV *abbr (barge-carrying vessel)* TRANSP *shipping* porte-barges *m*

b/d *abbr* ACC *(balance brought down)*, FIN *(balance brought down)* report à nouveau *m*, solde reporté *m*, solde à nouveau *m*, solde à reporter *m*, IND *(barrels per day)* barils par jour *m pl*, STOCK *(balance brought down)* report à nouveau *m*, solde reporté *m*, solde à nouveau *m*, solde à reporter *m*, TRANSP *(barrels per day)* barils par jour *m pl*, TRANSP *(below deck) shipping* sous le pont *(sur le pont)*

B/Dft *abbr (bank draft)* BANK chèque bancaire *m*, traite bancaire *f*

bdi *abbr (both dates inclusive)* GEN COMM inclusivement

bdl *abbr (bundle)* TRANSP ballot *m*, paquet *m*

BDO *abbr (bottom dropped out)* STOCK effondrement du cours plancher *m*, effondrement du prix plancher *m*, marché effondré *loc m*

B/E *abbr* BANK, FIN *(bill of exchange)* l/c *(lettre de change)*, IMP/EXP *(bill of entry)* déclaration d'entrée en douane *f*, IMP/EXP *(bill of exchange)*, STOCK *(bill of exchange)* l/c *(lettre de change)*

BE *abbr (Bank of England)* BANK, ECON, FIN banque d'Angleterre, ≈ BF *(Banque de France)*

BEA *abbr (Bureau of Economic Analysis)* ECON Bureau d'analyse économique *m*

BEcon *abbr (Bachelor of Economics)* HRM, WEL ≈ licencié en sciences économiques *m*

BEd *abbr (Bachelor of Education)* HRM ≈ licence d'enseignement *f*, WEL *degree* ≈ licence d'enseignement *f*, *person* ≈ licencié d'enseignement *m*

BEHA *abbr (British Export Houses' Association)* IMP/EXP association des maisons d'exportation britanniques

BES *abbr obs UK (Business Expansion Scheme)* STOCK remplacé par Enterprise Investment Scheme en 1993, plan d'expansion économique *m*

BF *abbr (bridge-forecastle)* TRANSP *shipping* château-gaillard *m*

BFE *abbr UK (Baltic Futures Exchange)* STOCK marché à terme baltique

BFO *abbr (bunker fuel oil)* TRANSP *shipping* mazout de soute *m*

BFOQ *abbr (bona fide occupational qualification, see GOQ)* HRM qualification professionelle veritable *f*

b/g *abbr dat* GEN COMM *(bonded goods)*, IMP/EXP *(bonded goods)*, IND *(bonded goods)*, TAX *(bonded goods)*, TRANSP *(bonded goods)* marchandises entreposées sous douane *f pl*, marchandises sous douane *f pl*, produits entreposés en douanes *m pl*, TRANSP *(brig) shipping* brick *m (vieilli)*

BH *abbr* TRANSP *(bulkhead) shipping* cloison *f*, WEL *(bill of health)* patente *f*, patente de santé *f (frml)*

BHC *abbr (British High Commission)* ADMIN haut-comité britannique *m*

BHCEC *abbr (British Health-Care Export Council)* IMP/EXP conseil britannique des exportations de produits sanitaires

BHEC *abbr obs (British Hospitals Export Council)* IMP/EXP conseil britannique des exportations hospitalières

bhp *abbr (brake horsepower)* TRANSP puissance au frein *f*

BHRA *abbr (British Hotels and Restaurants Association)* LEIS association britannique d'hôtels et de restaurants *f*

BIC *abbr (British Importers' Confederation)* IMP/EXP confédération des importateurs britanniques

BID *abbr (Bachelor of Industrial Design)* HRM, WEL *degree* ≈ licence en dessin industriel *f*, *person* ≈ licencié en dessin industriel *m*

BIDS *abbr (British Institute of Dealers in Securities)* STOCK institut britannique des courtiers de valeurs

BIF *abbr (British Industries Fair)* IND foire des industries britanniques

BIFFEX *abbr UK (Baltic International Freight Futures Exchange)* TRANSP bourse internationale balte des instruments financiers à terme concernant le fret

BIL *abbr (business investment loss)* TAX PTPE *(perte au titre d'un placement d'entreprise)*

BIM *abbr (British Institute of Management)* MGMNT institut britannique de gestion

BIOS *abbr (basic input/output operating system)* COMP *software* système BIOS *m*, système d'exploitation des entrées/sorties *m (système BIOS)*

BIP *abbr (baggage improvement program, baggage improvement programme)* TRANSP programme d'amélioration de la manutention des bagages *m*

BIS *abbr (Bank for International Settlements)* BANK BRI *(Banque des Règlements Internationaux)*

BISRA *abbr (British Iron & Steel Research*

Association) IND association britannique de recherche sur le fer et l'acier

bk *abbr* BANK *(bank)* banque *f*, TRANSP *(bulktainer) shipping* conteneur de vrac *m*, TRANSP *(bar keel) shipping* quille massive *f*

bkcy *abbr (bankruptcy)* ACC, BANK, FIN, GEN COMM faillite *f*

bkg *abbr (banking)* BANK opérations bancaires *f pl*, opérations de banque *f pl*

bkpt *abbr (bankrupt)* BANK, FIN, HRM failli *m*, fauché *m (infrml)*

B/L *abbr (bill of lading)* IMP/EXP, TRANSP connt *(connaissement)*

BLCC *abbr (Belgo-Luxembourg Chamber of Commerce)* GEN COMM chambre de commerce belgo-luxembourgeoise

BLEU *abbr (Belgium-Luxembourg Economic Union)* ECON, POL UEBL *(Union économique Belgique-Luxembourg)*

BLK: ~ CAR *abbr (bulk carrier)* TRANSP *shipping* transporteur en vrac *m*, vraquier *m*

BLR *abbr (boiler)* IND, TRANSP *shipping* chaudière *f*

BM *abbr* IND *(board measure)* mesure par pieds-planches *f*, métrage de planche *m*, TRANSP *(boom) shipping* bout-dehors *m*, bôme *f*, gui *m*

BMEG *abbr UK (Building Materials Export Group)* IMP/EXP groupe d'exportation de matériaux de construction

bmep *abbr (brake mean effective pressure)* TRANSP pression effective moyenne de frein *f*

BMLA *abbr (British Maritime Law Association)* LAW association britannique de droit maritime

BN *abbr (billion)* BANK, GEN COMM milliard *m*

BNC/ICC *abbr (British National Committee of the International Chamber of Commerce)* GEN COMM conseil national britannique de la chambre de commerce international

BNOC *abbr (British National Oil Corporation)* IND société nationale des pétroles britanniques

BO *abbr* ADMIN *(branch office)* agence de quartier *f*, agence locale *f*, succursale *f*, GEN COMM *(branch office)* agence *f*, bureau régional *m*, succursale *f*

BOAG *abbr (British Overseas Aid Group)* WEL groupe pour l'aide britannique outre-mer

BOF *abbr (Balance for Official Financing)* ACC, ECON balance des financements officiels *f*

BOI *abbr (Board of Investment)* GEN COMM *Philippines* commission d'investissements *f*

BOP *abbr (balance of payments)* ECON, POL balance des paiements *f*

BORO *abbr (bulk-oil and roll-on/roll-off vessel)* TRANSP *shipping* pétrolier-vraquier-roulier *m*

BOT *abbr UK (Board of Trade)* ECON Chambre de commerce *f*, ECON, GEN COMM, POL ≈ ministère du Commerce et de l'Industrie *m*

b.p. *abbr* ACC *(bill payable)*, FIN *(bill payable)* b. à p. *(billet à payer)*, TRANSP *(bollard pull) shipping* force de tirage *f*

BPA *abbr (British Ports Association)* TRANSP association des ports britanniques

bpi *abbr (bits per inch)* COMP bits par pouce *m pl*, nombre de bits par pouce *m*

bpm *abbr (best practical means)* GEN COMM meilleur moyen pratique

bps *abbr (bits per second)* COMP *programs* bps *(bits par seconde)*

BPSS *abbr (barge-mounted production and storage system)* TRANSP *shipping* système de production et d'entreposage sur allège *m*

BR *abbr* ACC *(bill receivable)* b. à r. *(billet à recevoir)*, TRANSP *UK (British Rail)* chemins de fer britanniques, ≈ SNCF *(Société nationale des chemins de fer français)*

BRAS *abbr (Building Research Advisory Service)* IND, PROP service de conseil en matière de recherche sur le bâtiment *m*

BRC *abbr (business reply card)* COMMS, GEN COMM carte-réponse *f*

BRE *abbr (business reply envelope)* COMMS, GEN COMM enveloppe-réponse *f*

Brit *abbr infrml* GEN COMM *(Britain)* Grande-Bretagne *f*, GEN COMM *(British)* britannique, GEN COMM *(Briton) person* Britannique *mf*

BRM *abbr US (Business Reply Mail)* COMMS, GEN COMM carte-réponse *f*, port payé *f*, postréponse *f*

B/S *abbr (balance sheet)* ACC, FIN bilan *m*, bilan d'inventaire *m*

BSBA *abbr (Bachelor of Science in Business Administration)* WEL *degree* ≈ licence en études d'administration des entreprises *f*, *person* ≈ licencié en études d'administration des entreprises *m*

BSC *abbr (British Shippers Council)* TRANSP conseil des affréteurs britanniques

BSc *abbr (Bachelor of Science)* HRM, WEL *degree* ≈ licence de sciences *f*, *person* ≈ licencié ès Sciences *m*

BSCP *abbr (British Standard Code of Practice)* IND, LAW code référentiel des standards de qualité en Grande-Bretagne

BSF *abbr (British Shipping Federation)* TRANSP fédération britannique des compagnies maritimes

BSI *abbr UK (British Standards Institution)* GEN COMM, LAW association britannique de normalisation, ≈ AFNOR *(Association française de normalisation)*

BSIR *abbr (Bachelor of Science in Industrial Relations)* WEL *degree* ≈ licence en sciences des relations humaines *f*, *person* ≈ licencié en sciences des relations humaines *m*

BSS *abbr (British Standards Specification)* IND, LAW ≈ norme AFNOR *f (norme de l'Association française de normalisation)*

BST *abbr* GEN COMM *(British Standard Time)* heure légale britannique, *(British Summer Time)* heure d'été en Grande-Bretagne

BTA *abbr* LEIS *(British Travel Association)* asso-ciation britannique des voyages *f*, LEIS *(British Tourist Authority)* office de tourisme de Grande-Bretagne *m*, TRANSP *(British Travel Association)* association britannique des voyages *f*

BTEC *abbr (British Technical Education Certificate)* WEL ≈ L.E.P. *(lycée d'enseignement professionnel)*

btm *abbr (bottom)* TRANSP *shipping* fond *m*

BUPA *abbr (British United Provident Association)* INS régime privé britannique d'assurance maladie

BVM *abbr (business visitors' memorandum)* GEN COMM livre d'or *m*, registre des visiteurs *m*

BWB *abbr (British Waterways Board)* TRANSP administration des voies navigables britanniques

bx *abbr (box container)* TRANSP *shipping* conteneur sec *m*

c. *abbr* GEN COMM *(centime)* c. *(centime)*, GEN COMM *(coupon)* c., coup. *(coupon)*

C *abbr* ECON *(consumption)* consommation *f*, TRANSP *(compound expansion engine) shipping* machine à expansion mixte *f*

C/- *abbr (case packaging)* TRANSP emballage en caisses *m*

C/A *abbr* ACC *(capital account)* compte de capital *m*, ACC *(checking account, credit account, current account)* balance of payments, BANK *(checking account, credit account, current account)* c/c *(compte courant)*, ECON *(capital account)* balance of payments compte de capital *m*, FIN *(checking account, current account)* c/c *(compte courant)*, FIN *(capital account)* balance of payments compte de capital *m*, GEN COMM *(checking account, current account)* c/c *(compte courant)*

CA *abbr* ACC *UK (certified accountant, chartered accountant)* expert-comptable *m*, ENVIR *(controlled atmosphere)* environnement stabilisé *m*, milieu constant *m*, GEN COMM *(Consumers' Association)* ≈ INC *(Institut national de la consommation)*, ≈ Association de défense du consommateur *f*, ≈ Organisation de défense des consommateurs *f*, LAW *(Court of Appeal)* cour d'appel *f*, ≈ Cour de cassation *m (France)*, MATH *(confluence analysis)* analyse de confluence *f*

CAA *abbr UK (Civil Aviation Authority)* TRANSP *aviation* ≈ DGAC *(France) (Direction générale de l'aviation civile)*

CAB *abbr UK (Citizens Advice Bureau)* ADMIN bureau d'aide et de conseil aux citoyens

CABAF *abbr (currency and bunker adjustment factor)* TRANSP *shipping* surcharge monétaire et de soutage *f*

CAC *abbr* HRM *UK (Central Arbitration Committee)* ≈ Conseil des prud'hommes *m*, IMP/EXP *(customs additional code)* code supplé-mentaire des douanes *m*, IND *UK (Central Arbitration Committee)*, LAW *UK (Central Arbi-tration Committee)* ≈ Conseil des prud'hommes *m*, STOCK *(Central Arbitration Committee)* comité central d'arbitrage des litiges *m*, commission d'arbitrage centrale *f*, TRANSP *(customs additional code)* code supplémentaire des douanes *m*, WEL *US (Consumers' Advisory Council)* Institut National de la Consommation

CACM *abbr (Central American Common Market)* ECON MCAC *(Marché commun d'Amérique centrale)*

CAD *abbr* COMP *(Control-Alt-Delete)* CAD *(Ctrl-Alt-Del)*, COMP *(computer-aided design, computer-assisted design) graphics* CAO *(conception assistée par ordinateur)*, IMP/EXP *(cash against documents)* comptant contre documents *loc m*, IND *(computer-aided design, computer-assisted design) graphics* CAO *(conception assistée par ordinateur)*

CAD/CAM *abbr (computer-aided design and computer-aided manufacturing, computer-assisted design and computer-assisted manufacturing)* COMP, IND *graphics* CFAO *(conception et fabrication assistées par ordinateur)*

CADD *abbr (computer-assisted design and drafting)* COMP, IND conception et dessin assistés par ordinateur *f*

CAE *abbr (computer-aided engineering, computer-assisted engineering)* COMP, IND IAO *(ingénierie assistée par ordinateur)*

CAF *abbr (currency adjustment factor)* TRANSP *shipping* surcharge monétaire *f*

CAFR *abbr (comprehensive annual financial report)* ECON, FIN, MGMNT rapport financier annuel détaillé *m*

CAI *abbr (computer-aided instruction, computer-assisted instruction)* COMP, WEL EAO *(enseignement assisté par ordinateur)*

CAL *abbr (computer-aided learning, computer-assisted learning)* COMP, WEL EAO *(enseignement assisté par ordinateur)*

CALL *abbr (computer-aided language learning, computer-assisted language learning)* COMP, WEL apprentissage des langues assisté par ordinateur *m*

CAM *abbr (computer-aided manufacture, computer-aided manufacturing, computer-assisted manufacture, computer-assisted manufacturing)* COMP, IND FAO *(fabrication assistée par ordinateur)*

CAMEL *abbr UK (capital, assets, management, earnings, liquidity)* FIN capital, actif, gestion, bénéfices et liquidité

C&D *abbr (collected and delivered, collection and delivery)* GEN COMM emporté et livré, ramassage et livraison *loc m*

C&E *abbr UK (Customs & Excise)* IMP/EXP régie *f*

C&F *abbr (cost and freight)* IMP/EXP, TRANSP C&F *(coût et fret)*

C&I *abbr (cost and insurance)* IMP/EXP C&A *(coût et assurance)*

cap *abbr* ACC *(capital)* capital *m*, ADMIN, COMP *(capital letter)* capitale *f*, lettre capitale *f*, lettre de haut de casse *f*, lettre majuscule *f*, ECON, FIN *(capital)* capital *m*, MEDIA *(capital letter)*

capitale *f*, lettre capitale *f*, lettre de haut de casse *f*, lettre majuscule *f*

CAP *abbr (the Common Agricultural Policy)* ECON, POL *European Union* PAC *(la politique agricole commune)*

capex *abbr (capital expenditure)* ECON, FIN dépenses en capital *f pl*, mise de fonds *f*, GEN COMM dépenses en capital *f pl*, immobilisations *f pl*, investissements *m pl*

CAPM *abbr (capital asset pricing model)* ECON, FIN, STOCK MEDAF *(modèle d'équilibre des actifs financiers)*

CAR *abbr UK (compound annual rate)* BANK *interest* taux annuel composé *m*, taux d'intérêt composé *m*; **~ DI SYS** *(carbon dioxide system)* TRANSP *shipping* dispositif de CO^2 *m*

CARD *abbr UK (certificate of amortized revolving debt)* FIN certificat de dette renouvelable amortie *m*

carr: **~ fwd** *abbr (carriage forward)* GEN COMM, TRANSP p.d. *(port dû)*; **~ pd** *abbr (carriage paid)* TRANSP p.p. *(port payé)*

CAS *abbr Can (Central Accounting System)* ACC SCC *(Can) (système central de comptabilité)*

CASE *abbr (computer-aided software engineering, computer-assisted software engineering)* COMP CPAO *(conception de programmes assistée par ordinateur)*

CASS *abbr (Cargo Accounts Settlement System)* TRANSP système de règlement des comptes marchandises *m*

CAT *abbr* COMP *(computer-aided teaching, computer-assisted teaching)* EAO *(enseignement assisté par ordinateur)*, COMP *(computer-aided translation, computer-assisted translation)* TAO *(traduction assistée par ordinateur)*, COMP *(computer-aided testing, computer-assisted testing)* TAO *(test assisté par ordinateur)*, WEL *(computer-aided teaching, computer-assisted teaching)* EAO *(enseignement assisté par ordinateur)*, WEL *(computer-aided testing, computer-assisted testing)* TAO *(test assisté par ordinateur)*

CATS *abbr* STOCK *(computer-assisted trading system)* système de cotation électronique *m*, STOCK *US (Certificate of Accrual on Treasury Securities)* bon du Trésor américain à coupon zéro

CAXB *abbr (composite auxiliary boiler)* TRANSP *shipping* chaudière auxiliaire mixte *f*

CAXBS *abbr (composite auxiliary boiler survey)* TRANSP *shipping* visite de la chaudière auxiliaire mixte *f*

CB *abbr BrE (container base)* TRANSP *shipping* magasin de groupage *m*

CBD *abbr* ECON *(central business district)* centre d'affaires d'une ville *m*, GEN COMM *(cash before delivery)*, S&M *(cash before delivery)* livraison dès réception du paiement *loc f*, paiement avant la livraison *m*

CBF *abbr UK (Central Bank Facility)* BANK banque centrale *f*

CBI *abbr (Confederation of British Industry)* GEN COMM, IND ≈ CNPF *(Conseil national du patronat français)*

cbm *abbr (cubic meter, cubic metre)* GEN COMM m3 *(mètre cube)*

CBM *abbr (conventional mooring buoy)* TRANSP *shipping* corps-mort traditionnel *m*

CBO *abbr US (Congressional Budget Office)* FIN Commission des finances *f*, POL Bureau du budget du Congrès *m*

CBOE *abbr (Chicago Board Options Exchange)* STOCK bourse des options de Chicago, ≈ MONEP *(Marché des options négociables de Paris)*

CBT *abbr* COMP *(computer-based training)* EAO *(enseignement assisté par ordinateur)*, STOCK *US (Chicago Board of Trade)* bourse des matières premières et des contrats à terme de Chicago, ≈ MATIF *(France)*, TRANSP *(clean ballast tank) shipping* citerne à ballast propre *f*, WEL *(computer-based training)* EAO *(enseignement assisté par ordinateur)*

cc *abbr* ADMIN *(carbon copy)*, COMMS *(carbon copy)* copie carbone *f*, réplique *f*, COMMS *(charges collect)* prélèvement de droits *m*, GEN COMM *(cubic capacity, cubic centimeter, cubic centimetre)* cc *(cylindrée)*, cm³ *(centimètre cube)*, GEN COMM *(civil commotion)* insurrection populaire *f*, INS *(continuation clause)* clause de prolongation *f*, clause de report *f*, INS *(civil commotion)* insurrection populaire *f*, trouble intérieur *m*, POL *(civil commotion)* insurrection populaire *f*, émeute *f*, TRANSP *(canvas cover)* bâche non-imperméable *f*, gaine en toile à voile *f*, TRANSP *(cargo capacity)* capacité de chargement *f*, capacité utile *f*, TRANSP *(container control)* contrôle des conteneurs *m*

CC *abbr* ECON *(Chamber of Commerce)* Chambre de commerce *f*, GEN COMM *UK (county council)* ≈ conseil général *m*

CCA *abbr* ACC *(current cost accounting)* comptabilité aux coûts de remplacement *f*, comptabilité de coûts courants *f*, TAX *(capital cost allowance)* DPA *(Can) (déduction pour amortissement)*

CCC *abbr* ECON *(Canadian Chamber of Commerce)* Chambre de commerce canadienne *f*, IMP/EXP *(Customs Cooperation Council)* conseil de la coopération douanière

CCCN *abbr (Customs Cooperation Council nomenclature)* IMP/EXP nomenclature du conseil de coopération douanière

CCL *abbr (customs clearance)* IMP/EXP dédouanement *m*

CCLN *abbr (consignment note control label number)* TRANSP numéro de l'étiquette de contrôle du bordereau d'expédition *m*

CC/O *abbr (certificate of consignment/origin)* IMP/EXP certificat d'expédition/d'origine *m*

CCS *abbr* IMP/EXP *(customs clearance status)* état de dédouanement *m*, TRANSP *(consolidate-cargo service)* service de groupage *m*

CCT *abbr* ECON *(compensating common tariff)* tarif commun compensatoire *m*, IMP/EXP *(common customs tariff)* EU tarif douanier commun *m*, tarif douanier communautaire *m*

cd *abbr* ACC *(carried down)* à reporter, STOCK *(cum dividend)* avec dividende *loc m*, coupon attaché *m*, dividende attaché *m*

CD *abbr* ADMIN *(consular declaration)* carte consulaire *f*, déclaration consulaire *f*, BANK *(certificate of deposit)* CD *(certificat de dépôt)*, COMP *(compact disk)* CD *(disque compact)*, ECON *(certificate of deposit)* CD *(certificat de dépôt)*, IMP/EXP *(consular declaration)* carte consulaire *f*, déclaration consulaire *f*, IMP/EXP *(customs declaration)* déclaration en douane *f*, STOCK *(certificate of deposit)* bond CD *(certificat de dépôt)*, TRANSP *(commercial dock)* bassin de commerce *m*, port de commerce *m*, TRANSP *(clutch drive)* entraînement d'embrayage *m*, transmission par engrenages réducteurs *f*, TRANSP *(customs declaration) shipping* déclaration en douane *f*

CDA *abbr (capital dividend account)* TAX CDC *(compte de dividende en capital)*

CDE *abbr (Canadian development expense)* ECON FAC *(frais d'aménagement au Canada)*

CD-I *abbr (compact disk interactive)* COMP CDI *(disque compact interactif)*

CDK *abbr (carrying capacity in number and length on deck)* TRANSP *shipping* charge utile sur le pont en nombre et longueur *f*

CDL *abbr UK (Career Development Loan)* BANK, HRM, WEL prêt de développement de carrière *m*

CD-ROM *abbr (compact disk read-only memory)* COMP *hardware* CD-ROM *(disque CD-ROM)*

CDV *abbr (current domestic value)* IMP/EXP valeur intérieure actuelle *f*

CE *abbr (Council of Europe)* POL CE *(Conseil de l'Europe)*

CEA *abbr* ECON *(Council of Economic Advisers)* Comité des conseillers économiques *m*, Réunion des conseillers économiques *f*, STOCK *US (Commodity Exchange Authority)* bourse de commerce

CEC *abbr UK (Clothing Export Council)* IMP/EXP conseil d'exportation de l'habillement

CEE *abbr (Canadian exploration expense)* TAX FEC *(frais d'exploration au Canada)*

CEIC *abbr (closed-end investment company)* FIN SICAF *(société d'investissement à capital fermé ou fixe)*

CEMA *abbr (Customs and Excise Management Act)* IMP/EXP, LAW loi régissant l'administration des impôts indirects et des droits de douanes

CENE *abbr (Commission on Energy and the Environment)* ENVIR Commission sur l'énergie et l'environnement *f*

CEO *abbr* HRM *US (chief executive officer)*, MGMNT *US (chief executive officer, managing director)* DG *(directeur général)*, PDG *(président-directeur général)*

CERF *abbr (Council of Europe Resettlement Fund)* BANK FRCE *(Fonds de rétablissement du conseil de l'Europe)*

cert. *abbr (certificate, certification)* ADMIN acte *m*, certif. *(certificat)*, FIN certif. *(certificat)*, titre *m*, GEN COMM, PATENTS certif. *(certificat)*, WEL certif. *(certificat)*, diplôme *m*

CES *abbr (Committee of European Shipowners)* TRANSP comité des armateurs européens

CESI *abbr (Centre for Economic and Social Information)* WEL centre d'informations économiques et sociales *m*

CET *abbr* ECON *(common external tariff)* tarif extérieur commun *m*, GEN COMM *(Central European Time)* heure de l'Europe centrale *f*

CETA *abbr US (Comprehensive Employment and Training Act)* HRM accord sur l'emploi et la formation

CF *abbr* ACC *(carried forward)* à reporter, GEN COMM *(carriage forward)* p.d. *(port dû)*, GEN COMM *(cubic feet)* pied cube *m*, GEN COMM *(carried forward)* à reporter, TRANSP *(carriage forward)* p.d. *(port dû)*

CFB *abbr (central freight bureau)* TRANSP bureau central de transport *m*

CFBH *abbr (Corporation of Foreign Bondholders)* STOCK société des détenteurs d'obligations étrangers *f*

CFC *abbr (chlorofluorocarbon)* ENVIR CFC *(chlorofluorocarbone)*

CFE *abbr UK (college of further education)* WEL centre d'enseignement postscolaire *m*

CFF *abbr (compensatory financial facility)* FIN compensation financière *f*

CFO *abbr (chief financial officer)* FIN, HRM directeur financier *m*, responsable financier *m*

CFS *abbr AmE (container freight station)* TRANSP *shipping* magasin de groupage *m*

CFTB *abbr (cylindrical fire tube boiler)* TRANSP *shipping* chaudière cylindrique ignitubulaire *f*, chaudière cylindrique à tubes de fumée *f*

CFTC *abbr US (Commodity Futures Trading Commission)* STOCK Commission de contrôle des marchés de matières premières *f*, Commission des opérations à terme sur les marchandises *f*

CG *abbr (coastguard)* HRM *organization* gendarmerie maritime *f, person* garde-côte *m*, gendarme maritime *m*, membre de la gendarmerie maritime *m*

CGA *abbr (color/graphics adaptor, colour/graphics adaptor)* COMP CGA *(adaptateur graphique couleur)*

CGPM *abbr (General Conference of Weights and Measures)* GEN COMM conférence générale des poids et mesures

CGT *abbr dat (capital gains tax)* ECON, TAX impôt sur les plus-values *m*

ch *abbr (chancery)* LAW cour de la chancellerie *f*

CHAPS *abbr US (Clearing House Automatic Payments System)* BANK Chambre de compensation interbancaire internationale *f*

CHC *abbr (cargo-handling charge)* TRANSP frais de manutention *m pl*, frais de manutention des marchandises *m pl*

CHIPS *abbr US (Clearing House Interbank Payments System)* BANK Chambre de compensation interbancaire internationale *f*

CHo *abbr (carrying capacity in number and length in holds)* TRANSP *shipping* charge utile dans les cales en nombre et longueur *f*

CHS *abbr (continuous survey cycle hull)* TRANSP *shipping* visite de la coque en vue d'une reclassification continue *f*

CI *abbr* HRM *(chief inspector)* inspecteur en chef *m*, inspecteur principal *m*, INS *(certificate of insurance)* attestation d'assurance *f*, certificat d'assurance *m*

CIC *abbr (committee for industrial cooperation)* IND comité de coopération industrielle

CICA *abbr (Canadian Institute of Chartered Accountants)* ACC Institut canadien des comptables agréés *m*

CIE *abbr* IMP/EXP *UK (Committee on Invisible Exports)* comité des exportations invisibles, IMP/EXP *UK (captain's imperfect entry)* entrée incomplète du capitaine

CIF *abbr (cost, insurance and freight)* IMP/EXP, TRANSP CAF *(coût, assurance, fret)*

CIFAS *abbr UK (Credit Industry Fraud Avoidance System)* FIN système anti-fraude de l'industrie du crédit *m*

CIF&C *abbr (cost, insurance, freight and commission)* IMP/EXP coût, assurance, fret et commission *loc m*

CIFC&E *abbr (cost, insurance, freight, commission and exchange)* IMP/EXP coût, assurance, fret, commission et change *loc m*

CIFC&I *abbr (cost, insurance, freight, commission and interest)* IMP/EXP coût, assurance, fret, commission et intérêt *loc m*

CIF&I *abbr (cost, insurance, freight and interest)* IMP/EXP coût, assurance, fret et intérêt *loc m*

CIFI&E *abbr (cost, insurance, freight, interest and exchange)* IMP/EXP coût, assurance, fret, intérêt et change *loc m*

CIFW *abbr (cost, insurance and freight/war)* IMP/EXP coût, assurance et fret/guerre *loc m*

CIHBB *abbr (cast-iron hub non-ferrous blades propeller)* TRANSP *shipping* hélice à moyeu en fonte et à pales non-ferreuses *f*

CIHSB *abbr (cast-iron hub steel blades propeller)* TRANSP *shipping* hélice à moyeu en fonte et à pales en acier *f*

CIM *abbr (computer-integrated manufacture, computer-integrated manufacturing)* COMP, IND FIO *(fabrication intégrée par ordinateur)*

CIO *abbr* HRM *(chief immigration officer)* officier supérieur de la police des frontières *m*, officier supérieur à la P.A.F. *m*, HRM *US (Congress of Industrial Organizations)* ≈ CGT *(Confédération générale du travail)*

CIP *abbr (carriage and insurance paid to)* IMP/EXP port et assurance payés jusqu'à *loc m*, port payé assurance comprise jusqu'à *loc m*

CIR *abbr (cage inventory record)* TRANSP inventaire de cabine *m*

CIRM *abbr (International Radio-Maritime Committee)* COMMS CIRM *(Comité international radio-maritime)*

CIS *abbr (Commonwealth of Independent States)* ECON, GEN COMM, POL CEI *(Communauté des États indépendants)*

ck *abbr (cask)* TRANSP fût *m*, tonneau *m*

CKD *abbr (completely knocked down)* TRANSP complètement désassemblé, en pièces détachées *loc f*

cl *abbr* GEN COMM *(centiliter, centilitre)* cl *(centilitre)*, TRANSP *(continuous liner)* shipping navire de ligne continue *m*, TRANSP *(craft loss)* shipping perte d'embarcation *f*

CL *abbr (Corporation of Lloyd's)* INS une association d'assureurs et d'agents d'assurance

Cld *abbr (cleared)* BANK compensé

clean: ~ **b/l** *abbr (clean bill of lading)* IMP/EXP, TRANSP connaissement net *m*, connaissement sans réserves *m*

CLSB *abbr (Committee of London and Scottish Bankers)* BANK commission des banquiers londoniens et écossais

cm *abbr* GEN COMM *(centimeter AmE, centimetre BrE)* cm *(centimètre)*, TRANSP *(condition monitoring)* shipping contrôle d'état *m*

CM *abbr (Common Market)* ECON, POL Marché commun *m*

CMA *abbr (cash management account)* FIN compte de gestion de fonds *m*

cmdty *abbr (commodity)* ECON, GEN COMM, IND marchandise *f*, produit *m*, *food, product* denrée *f*, *raw material* matière première *f*, produit de base *m*, STOCK marchandise *f*, matière première *f*

CME *abbr (Chicago Mercantile Exchange)* STOCK bourse des matières premières de Chicago

CMEA *abbr (Council for Mutual Economic Aid)* ECON COMECON *(Conseil de l'aide économique mutuelle)*

CMO *abbr (collateralized mortgage obligation)* BANK, FIN hypothèque garantie par nantissement *f*

CMS *abbr (Capital Markets System)* STOCK *World Bank* système des marchés financiers mondiaux *m*

CMSA *abbr US (Consolidated Metropolitan Statistical Area)* ADMIN regroupement de zone statistique métropolitaine *m*

CN *abbr* FIN *(credit note)*, GEN COMM *(credit note)* note de crédit *f*, INS *(cover note)* lettre de couverture *f*, note de couverture *f*, police

provisoire *f*, TRANSP *(consignment note)* bordereau d'expédition *m*, feuille de route *f*, lettre de voiture *f*

cnee *abbr (consignee)* TRANSP consignataire *mf*, destinataire *mf*

cnmt *abbr (consignment)* TRANSP consignation *f*, en consignation *loc f*, envoi *m*, expédition *f*

CNS *abbr UK (continuous net settlement)* STOCK liquidation en continu *f*, règlement en continu *m*

c/o *abbr* COMMS *(care of)*, GEN COMM *(care of)* aux bons soins de, chez, IMP/EXP *(certificate of origin)* certificat d'origine *m*, TRANSP *(cargo oil, case oil)* huile de carter *f*

Co: and ~ *abbr (and company)* GEN COMM et Cie *(et compagnie)*

Co. *abbr (company)* ECON, GEN COMM Cie *(compagnie)*, Sté *(société)*

CO *abbr (Certification Officer)* ADMIN agent certificateur *m*

COBOL® *abbr (Common Ordinary Business-Oriented Language)* COMP COBOL® *(langage COBOL)*

COBRA *abbr (Continent Britain and Asia)* TRANSP consortium des conteneurs en Grande-Bretagne et sur l'Asie

C/OC *abbr (certificate of origin and consignment)* IMP/EXP certificat d'origine et d'expédition *m*

Cocom *abbr (Coordinating Committee for Multilateral Export controls)* IMP/EXP comité de coordination pour le contrôle multilatéral des exportations *m*

COD *abbr (cash on delivery)* IMP/EXP, S&M livraison contre remboursement *loc f*, paiement à la livraison *m*

codec *abbr (coder-decoder)* COMP codec *(codeur-décodeur)*

COGSA *abbr (Carriage of Goods by Sea Act)* LAW, TRANSP *1924, 1971* loi relative au transport des marchandises par mer

COI *abbr (Central Office of Information)* ADMIN Bureau central de l'information *m*

col *abbr* GEN COMM *(column)* colonne *f*, MEDIA *(column)* colonne *f*, rubrique *f*, TRANSP *(collision)* abordage *m*, collision *f*

COLA *abbr US (cost-of-living adjustment)* ACC indexation des salaires *f*, ECON, HRM indexation des salaires *f*, indexation sur le coût de la vie *f*

coll *abbr (collision)* TRANSP abordage *m*, collision *f*

com. *abbr* ADMIN *(commission)*, BANK *(commission) payment*, ECON *(commission)* commission *f*, GEN COMM *(committee)* com *(commission)*, GEN COMM *(commission) order* commande *f*, *warrant* mandat *m*, HRM *(committee)* com *(comité)*, HRM *(commission) fee* commission *f*, pourcentage *m*, MGMNT *(committee)*, POL *(committee)* com *(comité)*, S&M *(commission)* commission *f*, STOCK *(commission)* courtage *m*, droit de courtage *m*, frais de courtage *m pl*

comb *abbr* GEN COMM *(combination)* association *f*, coalition *f*, combinaison *f*, TRANSP *(combined) shipping* mixte

COMB *abbr (combination)* MATH combinaison *f*

COMECON *abbr (Council for Mutual Economic Aid)* ECON COMECON *(Conseil de l'aide économique mutuelle)*

COMET *abbr (Common Market Medium Term Model)* ECON *econometrics* modèle économique à moyen terme pour la communauté européenne *m*

COMEX *abbr US (Commodities Exchange)* STOCK bourse des matières premières de New-York, ≈ la COMEX *f*

compo *abbr infrml (workers' compensation)* HRM indemnisation des accidents du travail *f*, indemnisation des accidentés du travail *f*, indemnisation des victimes d'accidents de travail *f*

config *abbr (configuration)* COMP *of file* config *(configuration)*

cons *abbr UK (consols)* FIN consolidés *m pl*, rente perpétuelle *f*, GEN COMM fonds consolidés *m pl*, STOCK fonds d'État *m pl*, rente d'État *f*

consgt *abbr (consignation)* TRANSP consignation *f*, envoi *m*, expédition *f*

constr *abbr (construction)* GEN COMM, IND, PROP construction *f*

cont'd *abbr (continued)* GEN COMM à suivre

conv *abbr* GEN COMM *(converted)*, PROP *(converted)* conv. *(converti)*, TRANSP *(conveyance)* acheminement *m*, transport *m*

COO *abbr* GEN COMM *(chief operating officer)* chef de service *m*, GEN COMM *(country of origin)* pays d'origine *m*, HRM *(chief operating officer)* chef de service *m*, IMP/EXP *(country of origin)* pays d'origine *m*

COP *abbr (custom of port)* TRANSP usage du port *m*

COPS *abbr* STOCK *(continuously offered payment rights in Swiss francs)* COPS *(créances comptables émises continuellement en francs suisses)*, STOCK *(covered option securities)* titre d'une option couverte *m*

corp. *abbr (corporation)* GEN COMM corporation *f*, société commerciale *f*

corr. *abbr (correspondence)* GEN COMM corresp. *(correspondance)*

cos *abbr* MATH *(cosine)* cos *(cosinus)*, TRANSP *(cash on shipment) shipping* comptant à l'expédition *m*

COSHH *abbr UK (control of substances hazardous to health)* HRM, IND *regulations* contrôle des matières dangereuses pour la santé *m*, contrôle des substances présentant un danger pour la santé *m*

COST *abbr (European Cooperation in Science and Technology)* IND Coopération européenne en matière de science et de technologie *f*

COT *abbr (customer's own transport)* TRANSP transport privé du client *m*

COU *abbr (clip-on unit)* TRANSP groupe frigorifique amovible *m*

COUGRs *abbr (Certificates of Government Receipts)* FIN ≈ FELIN *(Fonds d'État libres d'intérêt nominal)*, STOCK certificats émis par le gouvernement et rémunérés par des émissions de bons de Trésor, ≈ FELIN *(Fonds d'État libres d'intérêt nominal)*

COW *abbr* TRANSP *(collection on wheels)* enlèvement par route *m*, TRANSP *(crude oil washing) shipping* lavage au brut *m*

CP *abbr* BANK *(commercial paper)* BT *(billet de trésorerie)*, ECON *(Community Programme)* TUC *(travaux d'utilité collective)*, FIN *(commercial paper)* papier commercial *m*, GEN COMM *(coupon)* c., coup. *(coupon)*, GEN COMM *(commercial paper)* effet de commerce *m*, papier commercial *m*, HRM *(Community Programme)*, POL *(Community Programme)* TUC *(travaux d'utilité collective)*, TRANSP *(charter party) shipping* charte-partie *f*, WEL *(Community Programme)* TUC *(travaux d'utilité collective)*

CPA *abbr* ACC *US (certified public accountant)* expert-comptable *m*, ECON *(critical path analysis)* analyse du chemin critique *f*

cpd *abbr (charterer's pay dues)* TRANSP *shipping* rémunération de l'affréteur *f*

CPE *abbr (centrally-planned economy)* ECON, POL économie planifiée *f*

CPI *abbr (consumer price index)* ACC, ECON *econometrics* IPC *(indice des prix à la consommation)*

CPM *abbr (critical path method)* ECON, GEN COMM, MATH méthode du chemin critique *f*

CPO *abbr (chief petty officer)* HRM, TRANSP premier maître *m*

CPP *abbr (current purchasing power)* ECON pouvoir d'achat courant *m*

CPR *abbr (Canadian Pacific Railway)* TRANSP compagnie des chemins de fer canadienne

CPS *abbr* ECON *US (current population survey)* ≈ études comparatives de la population *f pl*, ECON *UK (Centre for Policy Studies)* Centre des études politiques *m*

CPT *abbr (carriage paid to)* IMP/EXP port payé jusqu'à *loc m*

CPU *abbr (central processing unit)* COMP UC *(unité centrale)*

Cr *abbr* ACC *(credit)* cr. *(crédit)*, ACC *(creditor)*, BANK *(creditor)* créditeur *m*, FIN *(credit)* cr. *(crédit)*, FIN *(creditor)* créditeur *m*, GEN COMM *(credit)* cr. *(crédit)*, HRM *(creditor)* créditeur *m*, TRANSP *(crane)* grue *f*

CR *abbr* COMP *(carriage return)* retour de chariot *m*, retour de curseur *m*, GEN COMM *(current rate)* taux actuel *m*, taux courant *m*, TRANSP *(change request)* RFC *(requête formulée par le client)*, TRANSP *(carrier's risk)* aux risques et périls du transporteur *loc m*, risque du transporteur *m*, TRANSP *(change request)* réaménagement *m*

CRC *abbr (camera-ready copy)* MEDIA *print* copie prête à filmer *f*, copie prête à la reproduction *f*, copie prête à reproduire *f*

CRE *abbr UK (Commercial Relations and Exports)* IMP/EXP relations commerciales et exportations *f pl*

CREST *abbr (Committee on Scientific and Technical Research)* IND comité pour la recherche scientifique et technique

CRI *abbr (consumption rate of interest)* FIN taux d'intérêt à la consommation *m*

CRN *abbr (customs registered number)* IMP/EXP numéro d'inscription douanière *m*

CRO *abbr (Companies Registration Office)* GEN COMM, LAW ≈ RCS *(Registre du commerce et des services)*

CROTUM *abbr UK (commissioner for the rights of trade union members)* HRM délégué chargé des droits des membres des syndicats

CRT *abbr (cathode ray tube)* COMP *hardware* TRC *(tube à rayons cathodiques)*

CS *abbr* ECON *(continuous stocktaking)* inventaire permanent *m*, GEN COMM *(civil service)* Administration *f*, fonction publique *f*, GEN COMM *(continuous stocktaking)* inventaire permanent *m*, inventaire en cours *m*, TRANSP *(case)* caisse *f*, TRANSP *(curtain-sided trailer)* remorque à ridelles *f*, TRANSP *(continuous survey)* shipping reclassification continue *f*, TRANSP *(continuous hull survey, continuous survey of the hull quoting date)* shipping visite de la coque en vue d'une reclassification continue *f*

CSC *abbr* ADMIN *(Civil Service Commission)* ≈ Commission de la fonction publique *f*, GEN COMM *(continuous survey cycle)* cycle d'enquête permanent *m*, TRANSP *(container safety convention)* accord de sécurité sur les conteneurs *m*

CSD *abbr* ECON *(cross section data)* données croisées *f pl*, TRANSP *(closed shelter deck)* shipping navire à pont-abri couvert *m*, pont-abri fermé *m*

CSG *abbr (Consultative Shipping Group)* TRANSP groupe maritime consultatif

csl *abbr (counsel)* LAW avocat *m*, conseil *m*, consultation *f*

CSO *abbr UK (Central Statistical Office)* ECON ≈ INSEE *(Institut national de la statistique et des études économiques)*

CST *abbr* GEN COMM *US (Central Standard Time)* heure normale des États du centre des États-Unis *f*, TRANSP *(container service tariff)* tarif du service conteneur *m*

CT *abbr* ENVIR *(cargo tank)* citerne de cargo *f*, citerne à cargaison *f*, GEN COMM *(cubic tonnage)* tonnage cube *m*, IMP/EXP *(customs transaction code)* code de transaction des douanes *m*, IMP/EXP *(Community transit)* transit communautaire *m*, TRANSP *(cargo tank)* citerne de cargo *f*, citerne

à cargaison *f*, TRANSP *(customs transaction code)* code de transaction des douanes *m*, TRANSP *(Community transit)* transit communautaire *m*, TRANSP *(combined transport)* transport combiné *m*, transport multimodal *m*

CTBL *abbr (combined transport bill of lading)* IMP/EXP, TRANSP connaissement de transport combiné *m*

CTC *abbr (cargo tank centre)* TRANSP citerne centrale de cargaison *f*

CTD *abbr* STOCK *(cheapest to deliver)* OMCL *(obligation la moins chère à livrer)*, TRANSP *(combined transport document)* document de transport combiné *m*

CTL *abbr (constructive total loss)* INS *shipping* perte censée totale *f*, perte réputée totale *f*, perte totale relative *f*

CTLO *abbr (constructive total loss only)* INS *marine* perte censée totale uniquement *f*, perte réprimée totale seulement *f*

CTO *abbr (combined transport operator)* TRANSP ETC *(entrepreneur de transport combiné)*

CTPC *abbr (cargo traffic procedures committee)* GEN COMM, TRANSP commission pour les procédures de mouvement de cargaisons *f*

ctr *abbr (cutter)* TRANSP *shipping* cotre *m*, vedette *f*

CTRL: ~ **key** *abbr (control key)* COMP touche CTRL *f (touche de contrôle)*

CTT *abbr (capital transfer tax)* TAX droits de mutation *m pl*

CTW *abbr (cargo tank wing)* TRANSP *shipping* citerne latérale *f*

C-20 *abbr (Committee of Twenty)* GEN COMM Comité des Vingt *m*

CTX *abbr (cargo tank common)* TRANSP *shipping* citerne standard *f*

cu *abbr (cubic)* GEN COMM cube *m*; ~ **ft** *(cubic feet)* GEN COMM pied cube *m*; ~ **in** *(cubic inch)* GEN COMM pouce cube *m*

CUKCC *abbr (Canada-United Kingdom Chamber of Commerce)* ECON chambre de commerce anglo-canadienne

cum. *abbr (cumulative)* ACC, STOCK *dividends* cum. *(cumulatif)*

CUSIP *abbr US (Committee on Uniform Securities Identification Procedures)* STOCK ≈ AFC *(Agence française de codification)*

CUV *abbr (construction unit value)* TRANSP valeur de l'unité de construction *f*

CV *abbr* ADMIN *(curriculum vitae)*, GEN COMM *(curriculum vitae)* CV *(curriculum vitae)*, GEN COMM *(chief value)* valeur principale *f*, HRM *(curriculum vitae)* CV *(curriculum vitae)*, IMP/EXP *UK (certificate of value)* attestation de valeur *f*

CVGK *abbr (customs value per gross kilogram, customs value per gross kilogramme)* IMP/EXP valeur en douane par kilo brut *f*

CVGP *abbr (customs value per gross pound)* IMP/EXP valeur en douane par livre brute *f*

CVMO *abbr (commercial value movement order)* GEN COMM bon de transfert de marchandise *m*

CVO *abbr UK (certificate of value and origin)* IMP/EXP attestation de valeur et d'origine *f*

C'vr *abbr (cover)* STOCK couverture *f*, garantie *f*

CW *abbr Australia (comparable worth)* HRM principe adopté en 1972 dont le but est de payer les travailleurs de façon égale. Il a introduit trois phases uniformes afin d'éviter la discrimination sexuelle

CWC *abbr (country whence consigned)* TRANSP pays d'expédition *m*

CWE *abbr (cleared without examination)* IMP/EXP dédouanement sans inspection *m*

CWM *abbr (clerical work measurement)* ADMIN, HRM chronométrage des travaux administratifs *m*

CWO *abbr (cash with order)* FIN, GEN COMM, S&M paiement à la commande *m*, payable à la commande

CWS *abbr (Cooperative Wholesale Society)* GEN COMM coopérative de gros *f*, société coopérative de consommation *f*

cwt *abbr* GEN COMM *US (hundredweight)* 45,36 kg, GEN COMM *UK (hundredweight)* 50,8 kg

CXBG *abbr (comprehensive extended-term banker's guarantee)* BANK garantie bancaire globale de longue durée *f*

CY *abbr* BANK *(currency)* monnaie *f*, ECON *(currency)*, FIN *(currency)* devise *f*, monnaie *f*, TRANSP *(cylinder)* cylindre *m*, TRANSP *(container yard)* dépôt de conteneurs *m*

CYCLD *abbr (cycloidal propeller)* TRANSP *shipping* hélice cycloïdale *f*

D *abbr* COMMS *(delivery)*, GEN COMM *(delivery)* livr. *(livraison)*, HRM, MGMNT *(director)*, D *(directeur)*, STOCK *(delivery)*, TRANSP *(delivery)* livr. *(livraison)*, TRANSP *(diagonal engine)* moteur diagonal *m*, TRANSP *(dry bulk container) shipping* conteneur à pulvérulents *m*

D/A *abbr* BANK *(deposit account)* compte de dépôt *m*, compte sur livret *m*, COMP *(design automation)* CAO *(conception assistée par ordinateur)*, COMP *(digital-analog)* N/A *(numérique-analogique)*, GEN COMM *(documents against acceptance)* documents contre acceptation *m pl*, GEN COMM *(days after acceptance)* jours après acceptation *m pl*, HRM *(defence advisor, defence attaché, defense advisor, defense attaché)* conseiller en matière de défense *m*, IND *(design automation)* CAO *(conception assistée par ordinateur)*, LAW *US (district attorney)* ≈ procureur de la République *m (France)*, ≈ procureur du Roi *m (Belgique)*, TRANSP *(discharge afloat) shipping* déchargement sur rade *m*

DAC *abbr* COMP *(digital-analog converter)* CNA *(convertisseur numérique-analogique)*, ECON *(Development Aid Committee, Development Assistance Committee)* comité d'aide au développement *m*

DAF *abbr (delivered at frontier)* IMP/EXP livraison à la frontière *loc f*, TRANSP livraison à la frontière *loc f*, rendu à la frontière

DAGAS *abbr (Dangerous Goods Advisory Service)* IMP/EXP, TRANSP service consultatif pour les produits dangereux

DAP *abbr (documents against payment)* GEN COMM DP *(documents contre paiement)*

db *abbr* ACC *(daybook)* jl *(journal)*, GEN COMM *(decibel)* db *(décibel)*, GEN COMM *(daybook)* jl *(journal)*, STOCK *(debenture)* obl. *(obligation)*, TRANSP *(double bottom)* double fond *m*, TRANSP *(double-ended)* à double façade

DBA *abbr (do business as)* GEN COMM exercer sous le nom de *loc m*

dbb *abbr (deals, battens, boards)* IND bois blanc, tasseaux, planches *m pl*

dbc *abbr (double bottom center, double bottom centre)* TRANSP *shipping* centre double fond *m*

DBE *abbr (despatch money payable both ends, dispatch money payable both ends)* TRANSP *shipping* bonification payable au chargement et au déchargement *loc f*, prime de célérité payable au chargement et au déchargement *f*

DBEATS *abbr (despatch payable both ends all time saved, dispatch payable both ends all time saved)* TRANSP *shipping* bonification payable au chargement et au déchargement pour temps gagné *f*, prime de célérité payable au chargement et au déchargement pour temps gagné *f*

DBELTS *abbr (dispatch payable both ends on laytime saved)* TRANSP *shipping* bonification payable au chargement et au déchargement pour temps gagné *f*

Dbk *abbr (drawback)* GEN COMM, IMP/EXP remboursement des droits de douane *m*

DBMS *abbr (database management system)* COMP SGBD *(système de gestion de bases de données)*

DC *abbr* COMP *(direct current)* courant continu *m*, ECON *(developed country)* pays développé *m*, IND *(direct current)* courant continu *m*, INS *(deviation clause) marine* clause de déviation *f*, clause dérogatoire *f*, POL *(developed country)* pays développé *m*

DCA *abbr (debt collection agency)* FIN bureau de recouvrement de créances *m*

DCE *abbr* COMP *(data communications equipment) hardware* équipement de termination de circuit de données *m*, ECON *(domestic credit expansion)* développement du crédit intérieur *m*

DCF *abbr (discounted cash flow)* ACC, FIN valeur actualisée nette *f*

DCO *abbr (debt collection order)* FIN ordre de recouvrement de créances *m*

DCom *abbr (Doctor of Commerce)* HRM, WEL docteur en science commerciale *m*

DComL *abbr (Doctor of Commercial Law)* LAW, WEL docteur en droit commercial *m*

DCP *abbr dat (freight paid to)* IMP/EXP, TRANSP fret payé jusqu'à *m*, fret payé à *m*

DCS *abbr (departure control system)* TRANSP système de contrôle des départs *m*

dd *abbr* GEN COMM *(due date)* date d'échéance *f*, échéance *f*, GEN COMM *(delivered)* livré, STOCK *(due date)* date d'échéance *f*, échéance *f*, TRANSP *(delivered)* rendu

DD *abbr* BANK *(direct debit)* avis de prélèvement *m*, prélèvement automatique *m*, prélèvement autorisé *m*, GEN COMM *(demand draft)* prélèvement automatique *m*, traite à vue *f*, IMP/EXP *(delivered at docks) shipping* livraison à quai *f*, rendu à quai, TRANSP *(dry docking)* mise en cale sèche *f*, TRANSP *(delivered at docks) shipping* livraison à quai *f*, rendu à quai

DDA *abbr (duty deposit account)* IMP/EXP compte de dépôt de droits douaniers *m*

DDB *abbr (distributed database)* COMP base de données répartie *f*

DDD *abbr AmE (direct distance dialing)* COMMS appel automatique longue distance *loc m*, automatique interurbain *m*, l'automatique *m*

DDE *abbr (direct data entry)* COMP saisie directe *f*, saisie en ligne *f*

DDO *abbr (dispatch discharging only)* TRANSP bonification au déchargement *loc f*, prime de célérité au déchargement *f*

DDP *abbr (delivered duty paid)* IMP/EXP livraison franco de douane *loc f*, rendu droits acquittés

DDU *abbr (delivered duty unpaid)* IMP/EXP rendu droits non-acquittés

D-E *abbr (diesel-electric)* TRANSP diesel-électrique

DE *abbr obs UK (Department of Employment)* ECON a fusionné en juillet 1995 avec le Department for Education afin de former le Department of Education and Employment (DEE), ≈ ministère du Travail et de l'Emploi *m*, HRM ≈ ministère du Travail et de l'Emploi *m*

Dec. *abbr (December)* GEN COMM déc. *(décembre)*

DEcon *abbr (Doctor of Economics)* ECON, HRM docteur en sciences économiques *m*

DEE *abbr UK (Department of Education and Employment)* ECON ≈ ministère du Travail et de l'Emploi *m*

def. *abbr (deferred)* ACC à reporter, GEN COMM dif. *(différé)*, à reporter

DEL *abbr* COMP *(delete character)* caractère d'effacement *m*, GEN COMM, HRM *(delegate)* dl. *(délégué)*

dely *abbr (delivery)* COMMS livraison *f (livr.)* GEN COMM livraison *f (livr.)*, *passport, receipt* délivrance *f* STOCK, TRANSP livraison *f (livr.)*; **~ and re-dely** *(delivery and redelivery)* TRANSP livraison et re-livraison *loc f*

DEM *abbr (Domestic Equities Market)* STOCK marché des actions nationales *m*

denom. *abbr (denomination)* ECON coup. *(coupure)*

dept. *abbr (department)* ADMIN, GEN COMM, HRM, POL, S&M serv. *(service)*

DEQ *abbr (delivered ex quay)* IMP/EXP livraison franco de douane à quai *loc f*, rendu à quai droits acquittés

der *abbr (derrick)* TRANSP *shipping* mât de charge *m*

DERV *abbr* ENVIR *(diesel-engined road vehicle fuel)*, IND *(diesel-engined road vehicle fuel)*, TRANSP *(diesel-engined road vehicle fuel)* gas-oil *m*, gazole *m*, TRANSP *(diesel-engined road vehicle)* véhicule routier à moteur diesel *m*

DES *abbr* IMP/EXP *(delivered ex ship)*, TRANSP *(delivered ex ship)* livraison au navire *loc f*, rendu ex ship

DF *abbr* TRANSP *(deadfreight)* faux fret *m*, fret sur le vide *m*, TRANSP *(direction finder) shipping* radiogoniomètre *m*

DFE WEL *UK (Department for Education and Science)* a fusionné en juillet 1995 avec le Department of Employment afin de former le Department of Education and Employment (DEE), ≈ ministère de l'Éducation nationale *m*

DFR *abbr (data freight receipt)* TRANSP *shipping* document fret rapide *m*, reçu de chargement *m*

dft *abbr (draft)* BANK, FIN traite *f*

DFT *abbr (direct fund transfer)* BANK virement direct de fonds *m*

D-G *abbr (director-general)* HRM, MGMNT DG, PDG *(directeur général)*

DGB *abbr (dangerous goods on board)* TRANSP produits dangereux à bord *m pl*

DGN *abbr (dangerous goods note)* TRANSP bordereau de marchandises dangereuses *m*

d1/2D *abbr (dispatch half demurrage)* TRANSP prime de célérité payable au taux de la demi-surestarie *f*

DHSS *abbr obs UK (Department of Health and Social Security)* WEL consiste maintenant du Department of Health (DoH) et du Department of Social Security (DSS), ≈ ministère de la Santé et des Affaires sociales *m*

DI *abbr US (Department of Industry)* IND ≈ ministère de l'Industrie *m*

DIDMCA *abbr US (Depository Institutions Deregulation and Monetary Control Act)* POL loi sur la dérégulation des institutions de dépôt et le contrôle monétaire

DIM *abbr (Diploma in Industrial Management)* WEL diplôme de gestion des entreprises *m*

Dip. *abbr (diploma)* HRM, WEL diplôme *m*

DIP *abbr (dual-in-line package)* COMP boîtier à double rangée de connexions *m*

DipCom *abbr (Diploma of Commerce)* WEL diplôme d'études commerciales *m*, diplôme d'études de commerce *m*

DipEcon *abbr (Diploma of Economics)* WEL diplôme en sciences économiques *m*

DipPA *abbr (Diploma in Public Administration)*

WEL diplôme d'administration de l'état *m*, diplôme d'administration publique *m*

DipTech *abbr (Diploma in Technology)* WEL DUT *(diplôme universitaire de technologie)*

dir. *abbr (direct)* TRANSP direct

disc. *abbr (discount)* GEN COMM discompte *m*, esc. *(escompte)*

DISC *abbr US (Domestic International Sales Corporation)* GEN COMM société nationale de ventes à l'exportation

div. *abbr (dividend)* FIN, STOCK div. *(dividende)*

DIY *abbr (do-it-yourself)* GEN COMM bricolage *m*

DK *abbr* TRANSP *(deck) shipping* pont *m*, TRANSP *(duct keel) shipping* quille caisson *f*

DKY *abbr (donkey boiler)* TRANSP *shipping* chaudière auxiliaire *f*

DLO *abbr* ADMIN *(Dead Letter Office)* bureau des rebuts, HRM *(direct labour organization)* organisation de la main d'oeuvre directe, TRANSP *(dispatch loading only) shipping* bonification au chargement *loc f*, bonification payable pour temps gagné au chargement *loc f*

DMA *abbr US (Direct Marketing Association)* S&M association du marketing direct

dm/d *abbr (molded depth, moulded depth)* TRANSP *shipping* creux sur quille *m*

DME *abbr (decentralized market economy)* ECON économie de marché décentralisée *f*

D/N *abbr (debit note)* GEN COMM note de débit *f*

DO *abbr* ENVIR *(diesel oil)* gas-oil *m*, gazole *m*, HRM *(duty officer)* officier de service *m*, responsable en permanence *m*, HRM *(district officer)* responsable régional *m*, IND *(diesel oil)* gas-oil *m*, gazole *m*, MGMNT *(district officer)* responsable régional *m*, TRANSP *(delivery order)* bon de livraison *m*, TRANSP *(distribution office)* bureau de distribution *m*, TRANSP *(diesel oil)* gas-oil *m*, gazole *m*, TRANSP *(dock operations)* opérations portuaires *f pl*

DOD *abbr US (Department of Defense)* POL ≈ ministère de la Défense nationale *m*

DOE *abbr* ENVIR *UK (Department of the Environment)*, POL *UK (Department of the Environment)* ≈ ministère de l'Environnement *m*, POL *US (Department of Energy)* ≈ ministère de l'Énergie *m*

DOH *abbr UK (Department of Health)* POL, WEL ≈ ministère de la Santé *m*

DOI *abbr US (Department of Industry)* IND ≈ ministère de l'Industrie *m*

dol. *abbr (dollar)* GEN COMM dol. *(dollar)*

DOS® *abbr* COMP *(disk operating system)* DOS® *(système d'exploitation à disques)*, GEN COMM *(Directorate of Overseas Surveys)* direction des enquêtes à l'étranger

DOT *abbr US (Designated Order Turnaround)* STOCK ≈ Information et transmission d'ordres *loc f*

DOW *abbr (delivery on wheels)* TRANSP livraison par route *f*

doz. *abbr (dozen)* GEN COMM douz. *(douzaine)*

DP *abbr* GEN COMM *(documents against payment)* DP *(documents contre paiement)*, GEN COMM *(dynamic positioning)* positionnement dynamique *m*, TRANSP *(direct port) shipping* port direct *m*

DPhil *abbr (Doctor of Philosophy)* WEL doctorat *m*

dpi *abbr (dots per inch)* COMP ppp *(points par pouce)*

DPP *abbr UK (Director of Public Prosecutions)* LAW ≈ procureur de la République *m (France)*, ≈ procureur du Roi *m (Belgique)*

DPR *abbr (director of public relations)* HRM, S&M *advertising* chef du service des relations publiques *m*, directeur des relations publiques *m*, responsable des relations publiques *m*

Dr *abbr* ACC *(debtor)*, ADMIN *(debtor)*, FIN *(debtor)* débiteur *m*, GEN COMM *(Doctor)* Dr *(docteur)*, GEN COMM *(debtor)* débiteur *m*, HRM *(Doctor) title* Dr *(docteur)*, LAW *(debtor)* débiteur *m*, WEL *(Doctor)* Dr *(docteur)*

DR *abbr* BANK *(deposit receipt)* reçu de dépôt *m*, récépissé de dépôt *m*, GEN COMM *(dead rise)* acculement *m*, hausse sans effet *f*, GEN COMM *(double reduction)* deuxième démarque *f*, double réduction *f*

DRAM *abbr (dynamic random access memory)* COMP *hardware* RAM dynamique *f*

DRF *abbr (Daily Range Factor)* STOCK facteur de la fourchette quotidienne plus haut-plus bas

DS *abbr (depth sounder)* TRANSP sondeur *m*

DSC *abbr (digital selective calling)* COMMS appel sélectif numérique *m*

DSS *abbr* MGMNT *(decision support system)* système d'aide à la décision *m*, POL *UK (Department of Social Security)*, WEL *UK (Department of Social Security)* ≈ ministère des Affaires sociales *m*

DSV *abbr (drum safety valve)* TRANSP soupape de sûreté du bidon *f*

DT *abbr (deep tank)* TRANSP caisse profonde *f*, cale à eau *f*

DTa *abbr (deep tank aft)* TRANSP *shipping* cale à eau d'arrière *f*

DTC *abbr US (Depository Trust Company)* STOCK ≈ SICOVAM, ≈ organe de dépôt de titres *m (société interprofessionnelle pour la compensation des valeurs mobilières)*

DTE *abbr (data terminal equipment)* COMP *hardware* ETTD *(équipement terminal de traitement de données)*

DTf *abbr (deep tank forward)* TRANSP *shipping* cale à eau d'avant *f*

DTI *abbr* ECON *UK (Department of Trade and Industry)*, GEN COMM *UK (Department of Trade and Industry)* ≈ ministère du Commerce et de l'Industrie *m*, IMP/EXP *(direct trader input)* entrée directe commerçant *f*, POL *UK (Department of Trade and Industry)* ≈ ministère du Commerce et de l'Industrie *m*

DTO *abbr (district training officer)* HRM directeur régional de la formation professionnelle *m*, responsable régional de la formation professionnelle *m*

DTP *abbr (desktop publishing)* MEDIA *print* PAO *(publication assistée par ordinateur)*

DTp *abbr UK (Department of Transport)* COMMS, IND, TRANSP ≈ ministère des Transports *m*

DTR *abbr (double taxation relief)* TAX suppression de la double imposition *f*

DTS *abbr (district traffic superintendent)* HRM, TRANSP directeur régional de circulation *m*, directeur régional des transports *m*

dup. *abbr (duplicate)* COMP, GEN COMM double *m*, LAW duplicata *m*

DUP *abbr (directly unproductive profit-seeking activities)* ECON activités à but lucratif non directement productives *f pl*

DVLC *abbr UK (Driver and Vehicle Licensing Centre)* TRANSP centre d'émission des permis de conduire et de vignettes automobiles

D/W *abbr* COM *(dock warrant)* warrant *m*, IMP/EXP bulletin de dépôt *m*, récépissé d'entrepôt *m*, warrant *m*, LAW *(dock warrant)* bulletin de dépôt *m*, certificat d'entrepôt *m*, récépissé d'entrepôt *m*, warrant *m*, S&M *(dock warrant)* warrant *m*, TRANSP *(dead weight)* PL *(port en lourd)*, TRANSP *(dock warrant)* bulletin de dépôt *m*, certificat d'entrepôt *m*, récépissé d'entrepôt *m*, warrant *m*

DWAT *abbr (deadweight all told)* TRANSP port en lourd total *m*

DWC *abbr (deadweight capacity)* TRANSP PL *(port en lourd)*

DWCC *abbr (deadweight cargo capacity)* TRANSP PL *(port en lourd)*

DWT *abbr (deadweight tonnage)* TRANSP PL *(port en lourd)*

E *abbr* GEN COMM *(east)* est *m*, TRANSP *(East compass point)* navigation E *(quart est)*

EA *abbr UK (Employment Act)* HRM, LAW loi sur l'emploi

EAAA *abbr (European Association of Advertising Agencies)* S&M Association européenne des agences de publicité *f*

EABC *abbr (European/ASEAN Business Council)* GEN COMM Conseil d'affaires européen/ANASE *m*

EAEC *abbr (European Atomic Energy Community)* IND CEEA *(Communauté européenne de l'énergie atomique)*

E&OE *abbr (errors and omissions excepted)* GEN COMM SEO *(sauf erreur ou omission)*

EAT *abbr* HRM *UK (Employment Appeal Tribunal)* autorité judiciaire compétente en matière d'emploi,

LEIS *(estimated arrival time)*, TRANSP *(estimated arrival time)* date probable d'arrivée *f*, heure d'arrivée prévue *f*

EBRD *abbr (European Bank for Reconstruction and Development)* BANK, ECON, POL BERD *(Banque européenne pour la reconstruction et le développement)*

EBU *abbr (European Broadcasting Union)* COMMS, MEDIA UER *(Union européenne de radiodiffusion)*

EC *abbr (European Community)* ECON CE *(Communauté européenne)*

ECB *abbr (European Central Bank)* BANK, ECON Banque centrale européenne *f*

ECCM *abbr (East Caribbean Common Market)* ECON Marché commun des Caraïbes orientales *m*

ECDC *abbr (Economic Cooperation among Developing Countries)* ECON Accord de coopération économique entre pays en voie de développement *m*

ECE *abbr (Economic Commission for Europe)* ECON CEE *(Commission économique européenne)*

ECG *abbr (European Cooperation Grouping)* LAW, POL Groupement de coopération européen *m*

ECGD *abbr UK (Export Credit Guarantee Department)* IMP/EXP service de garantie des crédits à l'exportation, ≈ COFACE *(Compagnie française d'assurance pour le commerce extérieur)*

ECI *abbr (export consignment identifying number)* IMP/EXP numéro identifiant des marchandises à l'exportation

ECOCOM *abbr (Economic Commission for Europe for Trade and Technology Division)* ADMIN division de la commission économique européenne pour le commerce et la technologie *f*

ECOFIN *abbr (European Community Finance Ministers)* ECON, FIN, POL ministres des finances de la communauté européenne *m pl*

ECOWAS *abbr (Economic Community of West African States)* ECON CEAO *(Communauté économique de l'Afrique de l'Ouest)*

ECP *abbr (Eurocommercial paper)* FIN europapier commercial *m*, STOCK billet de trésorerie euro *m*, papier eurocommercial *m*

ECPD *abbr (export cargo packing declaration)* IMP/EXP, TRANSP déclaration d'emballage de cargaison exportée *f*

ECPS *abbr (Environment and Consumer Protection Service)* ENVIR *EU* Service de protection du consommateur et de l'environnement *m*

ECSC *abbr (European Coal and Steel Community)* ECON CECA *(Communauté européenne du charbon et de l'acier)*

ECSI *abbr (export cargo shipping instruction)* IMP/EXP, TRANSP instruction de transport de cargaison exportée *f*

ECU *abbr (European Currency Unit)* BANK, ECON, FIN ECU *(unité monétaire européenne)*

ECWA *abbr (Economic Commission for Western*

Africa) ECON Commission économique pour l'Afrique occidentale *f*

ed. *abbr (edition)* COMP, GEN COMM, MEDIA éd., édit. *(édition)*

ED *abbr (Eurodollar)* ECON, FIN, STOCK eurodollar *m*

EDF *abbr (European Development Fund)* ECON, POL FDE *(Fonds de développement européen)*

EDI *abbr* COMMS *(electronic data interchange)* EDI *(échange de données informatisées)*, COMMS *(electronic document interchange)* EDI *(échange de documents informatisés)*, COMP *(electronic data interchange)* EDI *(échange de données informatisées)*, COMP *(electronic document interchange)* EDI *(échange de documents informatisés)*

EDP *abbr (electronic data processing)* COMP TEI *(traitement électronique de l'information)*

EEA *abbr* ECON *(European economic area)* zone économique européenne *f*, FIN *(Exchange Equalization Account)* fonds de stabilisation des changes *m*

EEB *abbr (European Environmental Bureau)* ENVIR Bureau européen pour l'environnement *m*

EEIG *abbr (European Economic Interest Grouping)* ECON, POL GIEE *(Groupement d'intérêt économique européen)*

EEOC *abbr US (Equal Employment Opportunity Commission)* HRM commission pour l'égalité des chances pour l'emploi

EET *abbr (Eastern European Time)* GEN COMM heure de l'Europe de l'Est *f*

EF *abbr (European Foundation)* GEN COMM Fondation européenne *f*

EFL *abbr* FIN *(external financing limit)* limite de financement externe *f*, WEL *(English as a Foreign Language)* anglais comme langue étrangère *m*

EFT *abbr (electronic funds transfer)* BANK, FIN transfert électronique de fonds *m*, télévirement *m*

EFTA *abbr (European Free Trade Association)* ECON AELE *(Association européenne de libre-échange)*

EFTPOS *abbr (electronic funds transfer at point of sale)* BANK transfert électronique de fonds au point de vente *m*, télévirement au point de vente *m*

EFTS *abbr (electronic funds transfer system)* BANK système de télévirement *m*

e.g. *abbr (exempli gratia, for example)* GEN COMM ex. *(par exemple)*

EGA *abbr (enhanced graphics adaptor, enhanced graphics array)* COMP AGA *(adaptateur graphique couleur)*

EGM *abbr (extraordinary general meeting)* MGMNT AGE *(assemblée générale extraordinaire)*

ehp *abbr (effective horsepower)* IND puissance réelle *f*

EHS *abbr (extra high strength)* IND à très haute résistance *loc f*

EI *abbr UK (employee involvement)* HRM participation *f*

EIB *abbr (European Investment Bank)* BANK BEI *(Banque européenne d'investissement)*

EIM *abbr (European Interprofessional Market)* STOCK Marché interprofessionnel européen *m*

EIS *abbr UK (export intelligence service)* IMP/EXP service de renseignements pour l'exportation

EITZ *abbr (English Inshore Traffic Zone)* TRANSP zone de navigation côtière de l'Angleterre *f*

ELB *abbr (export licensing branch)* IMP/EXP bureau des autorisations d'exportation *m*

EMA *abbr (European Monetary Agreement)* GEN COMM AME *(Accord monétaire européen)*

EMCF *abbr (European Monetary Cooperation Fund)* ECON, POL FMEC *(Fonds monétaire européen de coopération)*

EMF *abbr (European Monetary Fund)* ECON, POL FME *(Fonds monétaire européen)*

EMI *abbr (European Monetary Institute)* ECON, POL Institut monétaire européen *m*

EMS *abbr (European Monetary System)* ECON *EU* SME *(Système monétaire européen)*

EMU *abbr* ECON *(Economic and Monetary Union)* UEM *(Union économique et monétaire)*, ECON *(European Monetary Union)* UME *(Union monétaire européenne)*, POL *(Economic and Monetary Union)* UEM *(Union économique et monétaire)*, POL *(European Monetary Union)* UME *(Union monétaire européenne)*

emy *abbr (emergency)* GEN COMM urgence *f*

enc. *abbr (enclosed)* COMMS ci-inclus, ci-joint, joint, GEN COMM ci-inclus, ci-joint, inclus, joint

encl. *abbr (enclosed)* COMMS ci-inclus, ci-joint, joint, GEN COMM ci-inclus, ci-joint, inclus, joint

ENEA *abbr (European Nuclear Energy Authority)* GEN COMM ENEA *(Autorité européenne de l'énergie nucléaire)*

ENF *abbr (enforcement)* LAW exécution *f*, mise en application *f*, mise en vigueur *f*

ENG *abbr (engine)* IND, TRANSP moteur *m*

EO *abbr (executive officer)* HRM, MGMNT cadre sup *m (infrml)*, cadre supérieur *m*

EOC *abbr UK (Equal Opportunities Commission)* HRM commission pour l'égalité des chances pour l'emploi

EOE *abbr (European Options Exchange)* STOCK Bourse d'options européenne *f*

EOF *abbr (end of file)* COMP fin de fichier *f*

eohp *abbr (except otherwise herein provided)* GEN COMM sauf dispositions contraires du présent

EOM *abbr (end of message)* COMP fin de message *f*

EOP *abbr UK (Equal Opportunity Policy)* HRM politique de l'égalité de traitement *f*

EOQ *abbr (economic order quantity)* ECON, IND, MATH, MGMNT quantité optimale de commande *f*, quantité optimale de réapprovisionnement *f*, quantité économique de réapprovisionnement *f*, quantité économique à commander *f*

EOQC *abbr (European Organization for Quality Control)* ADMIN Organisation européenne pour le contrôle de qualité *f*

EOTC *abbr (European Organization for Testing and Certification)* GEN COMM Organisme européen de contrôle et certification *m*

EP *abbr* ECON *(European Parliament)* Parlement européen *m*, IMP/EXP *(export promotion)* promotion des exportations *f*

EPA *abbr* ENVIR *(environmental protection agency)* agence pour la protection de l'environnement *f*, HRM *(Economic Planning Agency)* ≈ Agence de planification économique *f*, HRM UK *(Employment Protection Act)* loi sur la protection de l'emploi *f*, IND *(European Productivity Agency)* Agence européenne de productivité *f*, LAW UK *(Employment Protection Act)* loi sur la protection de l'emploi *f*

EPCA *abbr UK (Employment Protection Consolidation Act)* HRM loi sur la protection du travail

EPF *abbr (established programmes financing, established programs financing)* FIN financement des programmes établis *m*, financement institués de programmes *m*

EPO *abbr (European Patent Organization)* LAW Organisation européenne de brevets *f*

EPOS *abbr (electronic point of sale)* GEN COMM point de vente électronique *m*

EPROM *abbr (electronically programmable read only memory)* COMP *programming language* EPROM *(mémoire morte programmable électroniquement)*

EPS *abbr (earnings per share)* ACC, FIN, STOCK BPA *(bénéfices par action)*

EPT *abbr (electronic payment terminal)* FIN TPE *(terminal de paiement électronique)*

EPU *abbr* ECON *(economic planning unit)* bureau de planification économique *m*, GEN COMM *(European Payments Union)* UEP *(Union européenne des paiements)*, IMP/EXP *(entry processing unit)* unité de traitement des déclarations *f*

EqPA *abbr UK (Equal Pay Act)* HRM, LAW loi sur l'égalité des salaires *f*

ER *abbr (engine room)* TRANSP *shipping* chambre des machines *f*, compartiment moteur *m*

ERA *abbr (exchange rate agreement)* ECON, FIN accord sur les taux de change *m*

ERC *abbr (European Registry of Commerce)* GEN COMM Registre du commerce européen *m*

ERDF *abbr (European Regional Development Fund)* ECON FEDER *(Fonds européen de développement régional)*

ERISA *abbr US (Employment Retirement Income Security Act)* STOCK loi de garantie des revenus des travailleurs retraités

ERM *abbr (exchange rate mechanism)* ECON *EU* MTC *(mécanisme de taux de change)*

ES *abbr (expert system)* COMP, GEN COMM SE *(système expert)*

ESA *abbr (European Space Agency)* GEN COMM ASE *(Agence spatiale européenne)*

Esc *abbr (escape key, escape)* COMP *keyboard* Esc *(touche Esc)*

ESC *abbr* ECON *(Economic and Social Committee)* Comité économique et social *m*, GEN COMM *(escudo)* ESC *(escudo)*

ESD *abbr (echo-sounding device)* TRANSP *shipping* sondeur U.S. *m (sondeur par ultrasons)*

ESF *abbr (European Social Fund)* ECON, POL FSE *(Fonds social européen)*

ESOP *abbr (employee share ownership plan BrE, employee stock ownership plan AmE)* STOCK plan d'investissement du personnel *m*

esp. *abbr (especially)* GEN COMM spécialement, surtout

ESRO *abbr (European Space Research Organization)* GEN COMM Organisme de recherche spatiale européenne *m*

est. *abbr (established)* GEN COMM fondé, établi

EST *abbr US (Eastern Standard Time)* GEN COMM heure de l'Est *f*

ET *abbr BrE (employment training)* HRM formation *f*, formation à l'emploi *f*

ETA *abbr (estimated time of arrival)* TRANSP date probable d'arrivée *f*, heure d'arrivée prévue *f*

ETAS *abbr UK (Economic Trends Annual Survey)* ECON *econometrics* rapport annuel sur les tendances de l'économie

ETB *abbr (English Tourist Board)* LEIS office de tourisme d'Angleterre

ETC *abbr* GEN COMM *(European Trade Committee)* Commission européenne du commerce *f*, TRANSP *(explosion of total contents)* explosion du contenu total *f*

ETD *abbr (estimated time of departure)* GEN COMM, TRANSP heure de départ prévue *f*

ETO *abbr (European Transport Organization)* TRANSP Organisation européenne de transport *f*

ETPO *abbr (European Trade Promotion Organization)* GEN COMM Organisme européen pour la promotion du commerce *m*

ETS *abbr (estimated time of sailing)* GEN COMM, TRANSP heure de départ prévue *f*

ETSI *abbr (European Telecommunications Standards Institute)* COMMS Association de normalisation des télécommunications *f*

ETU *abbr UK (Electrical Trades Union)* GEN COMM syndicat britannique d'électriciens

ETUC *abbr (European Trade Union Confederation)* HRM Confédération syndicale européenne *f*

EU *abbr (European Union)* ECON *from Nov 1st 1993*, POL UE *(Union européenne)*

EUA *abbr (European unit of account)* BANK, ECON, FIN UCE *(unité de compte européenne)*

Euro: **~ Co-op** *abbr (European Community of Consumers' Co-operatives)* GEN COMM Communauté européenne des coopératives de consommateurs *f*; **~ MP** *abbr (European Member*

of Parliament) POL député du Parlement Européen *m*, membre du Parlement Européen *m*

ex. *abbr* BANK *(exchange)* change *m*, ECON *(exchange)* change *m*, échange *m*, FIN *(exchange)* change *m*, GEN COMM *(examined)* examiné, GEN COMM *(excluding)* excepté, à l'exception de *loc f*, GEN COMM *(example)* exemple *m*, GEN COMM *(extra)* extra *m*, supplément *m*, GEN COMM *(exchange)* échange *m*, STOCK *(exchange)* change *m*, échange de valeurs *m*; **~ div.** *(ex-dividend)* STOCK ex-d, ex-div. *(ex-dividende)*

exch. *abbr (exchange)* BANK change *m*, ECON change *m*, échange *m*, FIN change *m*, GEN COMM échange *m*, STOCK bourse *f*, change *m*, échange de valeurs *m*

Exch. *abbr (Exchequer)* BANK Échiquier *m*

excl. *abbr (excluding, exclusive of)* GEN COMM excepté, à l'exception de *loc f*

ex.cp. *abbr (ex-coupon)* GEN COMM, STOCK ex-c, ex-coup *(ex-coupon)*

exd *abbr (examined)* GEN COMM examiné

exdis *abbr jarg (exclusive distribution)* POL divulgation exclusive *f*

ex-div. *abbr (ex-dividend)* STOCK dividende détaché *m*

ex. div. *abbr (ex dividend)* STOCK ex-d, ex-div. *(ex-dividende)*

exec. *abbr* ACC *(executive)*, ADMIN *(executive)*, HRM *(executive)* cadre *mf*, LAW *(executor)* exécuteur *m*, exécuteur testamentaire *m*

exor *abbr (executor)* LAW exécuteur *m*, exécuteur testamentaire *m*

exp. *abbr (export)* IMP/EXP exportation *f*

EXPORTIT *abbr UK (Information Technology Export Organization)* IMP/EXP organisation d'exportation de la technologie de l'information

ExQ *abbr (ex quay)* IMP/EXP, TRANSP *shipping* livrable à quai, à prendre à quai *loc m*, à quai *loc m*

ExS *abbr (ex ship)* IMP/EXP, TRANSP départ navire *m*, à enlever à bord

EXW *abbr (ex works)* IMP/EXP départ usine *m*, à l'endroit des travaux *loc*

EZ *abbr (enterprise zone)* ECON, HRM, IND, PROP ZAC *(zone d'aménagement concerté)*

EZC *abbr (European zone charge)* TRANSP zone de tarification européenne *f*

F *abbr* ENVIR *(fresh water)* eau douce *f*, GEN COMM *(Fahrenheit)* Fahrenheit *m*

f.a.a. *abbr (free of all average)* GEN COMM franc de toute avarie

FAA *abbr US (Federal Aviation Administration)* TRANSP administration fédérale de l'aviation

FAB *abbr (forwarder air waybill)* IMP/EXP, TRANSP lettre de transport aérien du transitaire *f*

fac *abbr* TRANSP *(forwarding agent's commission)* commission du transitaire *f*, TRANSP *(fast as can) cargo delivery* aussi vite que possible

faccop *abbr (fast as can)* TRANSP *cargo delivery* aussi vite que possible

factoblig *abbr (facultative/obligatory)* INS *reinsurance* facultatif obligatoire

FAK *abbr (freight all kinds)* TRANSP à l'unité de chargement *loc f*

F&D *abbr (freight and demurrage)* INS, TRANSP fret et surestarie *m*

FAO *abbr (Food and Agriculture Organization)* ECON Organisation pour l'alimentation et l'agriculture *f*

FAQ *abbr* GEN COMM *(fair average quality)* qualité commerciale *f*, TRANSP *(free alongside quay) shipping* FAQ *(franco à quai)*

FAS *abbr (free alongside ship, free alongside steamer)* TRANSP *cargo delivery* FLB *(franco le long du bord)*

FASB *abbr US (Financial Accounting Standards Board)* ACC commission de normalisation de la comptabilité financière

FAT *abbr (file allocation table)* COMP table d'allocation des fichiers *f*

FBD *abbr (freeboard)* TRANSP *shipping* franc-bord *m*

FBIM *abbr (Fellow of the British Institute of Management)* MGMNT membre de l'institut britannique de gestion

f/c *abbr (for cash)* GEN COMM comptant, contre espèces

FC *abbr (fiberglass covers, fibreglass covers)* TRANSP panneaux de cale en fibre de verre *m pl*

FC&S *abbr (free of capture and seizure)* INS franc de capture et de saisie

FCAR *abbr (free of claim for accident reported)* INS *marine* franc de réclamation pour accident signalé, franc de sinistre pour l'accident constaté

FCC *abbr* GEN COMM *(French Chamber of Commerce)* Chambre de commerce française *f*, TRANSP *(fully cellular container ship)* navire porte-conteneurs spécialisé *m*, porte-conteneurs entièrement cellulaire *m*

FCCA *abbr (Fellow of the Chartered Association of Certified Accountants)* ACC ≈ membre de l'Association des Comptables d'entreprise certifiés *m*

FCCUK *abbr (French Chamber of Commerce for the United Kingdom)* GEN COMM chambre de commerce français pour le Royaume-Uni *m*

FCGI *abbr (Fellow of the City and Guilds of London Institute)* GEN COMM membre de l'institut britannique de l'enseignement technique

FCI *abbr (Fellow of the Institute of Commerce)* GEN COMM membre de l'institut commercial

FCL *abbr (full container load)* TRANSP conteneur complet *m*

FCMA *abbr (Fellow of the Chartered Institute of Management Accountants)* ACC membre de l'institut des comptables de coûts et de gestion

fco. *abbr (franco)* TRANSP fco *(franco)*

FCO *abbr UK (Foreign and Commonwealth Office)*

ADMIN ≈ ministère des Affaires étrangères et du Commonwealth *m*

FCR *abbr (forwarder's certificate of receipt)* TRANSP attestation de prise en charge du transitaire *f*

fcsrcc *abbr (free of capture, seizure, and riots and civil commotions)* INS franc de capture, de saisie et émeutes et mouvements

FCT *abbr (forwarder's certificate of transport, freight forwarder's combined transport bill of lading)* IMP/EXP, TRANSP connaissement de transport combiné du transitaire *m*

fd *abbr* TRANSP *(free domicile)* franco domicile, TRANSP *(free discharge)* franco déchargement, TRANSP *(free dispatch)* sans bonification pour temps gagné, sans prime de célérité, TRANSP *(forced draft, forced draught)* combustion control tirage forcé *m*

F/d *abbr (free dock)* TRANSP FAQ *(franco à quai)*

FD *abbr (free dock)* TRANSP FAQ *(franco à quai)*

FDA *abbr US (Food and Drug Administration)* ADMIN office des produits alimentaires et pharmaceutiques

FD&D *abbr (freight, demurrage and defence, freight, demurrage and defense)* INS, TRANSP cargaison, surestaries et défense *loc f*

FDIC *abbr US (Federal Deposit Insurance Corporation)* INS *company* organisme fédéral d'assurance et des dépôts bancaires *m*

FDX *abbr (full-duplex)* COMP bidirectionnel, duplex intégral, semi-duplex, simultané

Feb. *abbr (February)* GEN COMM fév. *(février)*

FEC *abbr UK (Fair Employment Commission)* HRM commission de contrôle de l'emploi d'Irlande du Nord

fed. *abbr (federal)* GEN COMM féd. *(fédéral)*

FES *abbr UK (Family Expenditure Survey)* ECON *econometrics* enquête annuelle du gouvernement britannique sur les dépenses des familles et ménages

FF *abbr* COMP *(form feed)* changement de page *m*, présentation de feuille *f*, saut de page *m*, GEN COMM *(French franc)* FF *(franc français)*

FFA *abbr (free from alongside)* TRANSP FLB *(franco le long du bord)*

FFCR *abbr (freight forwarder's certificate of receipt)* TRANSP attestation de prise en charge du transitaire *f*

FFI *abbr (for further instructions)* GEN COMM pour toute instruction complémentaire *loc f*

FGA *abbr* GEN COMM *(free of general average)* FAC *(franc d'avaries communes)*, GEN COMM *(foreign general average)* avarie commune étrangère *f*

fh *abbr (first half)* GEN COMM *of month* première quinzaine *f*

FHA *abbr* BANK *UK (Finance House Association)*, FIN *UK (Finance House Association)* association de sociétés de crédit, PROP *US (Federal Housing Administration)* administration fédérale du logement *f*

FHBR *abbr UK (finance house base rate)* FIN taux de base d'une société de crédit

FHEx *abbr (Fridays and holidays excepted)* GEN COMM sauf vendredis et jours fériés, sauf vendredis et périodes de congé

FHLMC *abbr US (Federal Home Loan Mortgage Corporation)* FIN, PROP société fédérale des prêts hypothécaires *f*

fi *abbr (free in)* TRANSP frais de chargement en sus du fret *m pl*, franco chargement

FIA *abbr (Fellow of the Institute of Actuaries)* FIN membre de l'institut des actuaires

FIAS *abbr* STOCK *(Foreign Investment Advisory Service)* service conseil en investissements à l'étranger, TRANSP *(free in and stowed)* bord arrimé, frais de chargement et d'arrimage en sus du fret *m pl*

FIB *abbr* BANK *(Fellow of the Institute of Bankers)* membre de l'institut des banquiers, TRANSP *(free into barge)* shipping franco allège, TRANSP *(free into bunkers)* shipping franco soutes

FIBC *abbr (flexible intermediate and bulk container)* TRANSP conteneur en vrac et intermédiaire articulé *m*

FIBS *abbr (financial information and budgeting systems)* FIN systèmes d'information financière et budgétaire *m pl*

FIC *abbr (free insurance and carriage)* TRANSP franco assurance et transport

FICA *abbr* ACC *UK (Fellow of the Institute of Company Accountants)* membre de l'institut des experts-comptables d'entreprise, INS *US (Federal Insurance Contributions Act)* loi fédérale sur le financement de l'assurance sociale, acte fédéral sur les cotisations de l'assurance sociale *m*

FICS *abbr (Fellow of the Institute of Chartered Shipbrokers)* HRM membre de l'institut des courtiers maritimes agréés

FIEx *abbr (Fellow of the Institute of Export)* HRM membre de l'institut des exportateurs

FIFO *abbr (first in, first out)* ACC *inventory method* PEPS *(premier entré, premier sorti)*

fih *abbr (free in harbor, free in harbour)* TRANSP franco à port

FIL *abbr (financial intermediary loan)* FIN prêt d'intermédiaire financier *m*, prêt financier intermédiaire *m*

FIMBRA *abbr UK (Financial Intermediaries, Managers and Brokers Association)* FIN association des intermédiaires, gestionnaires et agents financiers

FIME *abbr (Fellow of the Institute of Marine Engineers)* HRM membre de l'institut des ingénieurs de marine

FIN *abbr (fin-type stabilizer)* TRANSP *shipping* stabilisateur à ailerons *m*

FIO *abbr (free in and out)* IMP/EXP, TRANSP BAB *(bord à bord)*

FIPM *abbr (Fellow of the Institute of Personnel*

Management) HRM membre de l'institut des directeurs du personnel

firavv *abbr (first available vessel)* TRANSP premier navire disponible *m*

1Q *abbr (first quarter)* GEN COMM premier trimestre *m*

FIS *abbr (freight, insurance and shipping charges)* IMP/EXP, TRANSP *shipping* fret, assurance et frais d'expédition *m*

fiw *abbr (free into wagon)* TRANSP *rail* franco wagon

F/L® *abbr BrE (freightliner)* TRANSP *rail* train-bloc de conteneurs *m*

fl.oz *abbr (fluid ounce)* GEN COMM once liquide *f*

FLSA *abbr US (Fair Labor Standards Act)* LAW réglementation fédérale du droit du travail

FLT *abbr (fork-lift truck)* TRANSP chariot élévateur à fourche *m*

fm *abbr (fathom)* GEN COMM *unit of measurement of timber* brasse *f*

FM *abbr (frequency modulation)* COMMS FM *(modulation de fréquence)*

FMB *abbr US (Federal Maritime Board)* IND bureau maritime fédéral

FMC *abbr US (Federal Maritime Commission)* TRANSP commission fédérale maritime

FMCG *abbr (fast-moving consumer goods)* S&M biens de consommation courante *m pl*, produits de grande consommation à forte rotation *m pl*

FMRR *abbr (financial management rate of return)* FIN taux de rendement de la gestion financière *m*

FNMA *abbr US (Fannie Mae, Federal National Mortgage Association)* FIN, PROP association nationale fédérale hypothécaire

fo *abbr* GEN COMM *(for orders)* pour instructions *loc f*, TRANSP *(free out terms)* frais de déchargement en sus du fret *m pl*, TRANSP *(free overboard, free overside)* franco sous palan

FOA *abbr* GEN COMM *US (Foreign Operations Administration)* administration des opérations à l'étranger, TRANSP *(free on aircraft)* FAB aéroport *(franco à bord aéroport)*

FOB *abbr (free on board)* TRANSP *cargo delivery* FAB *(franco à bord)*; **~ & T** *(free on board and trimmed)* TRANSP franco à bord et arrimé

foc *abbr (free of charge)* GEN COMM franco, gratis, gratuit, gratuitement

FOC *abbr (free of charge)* GEN COMM franco, gratis, gratuit, gratuitement

FOD *abbr (free of damage)* GEN COMM intact, INS sans avaries

FOE *abbr (Friends of the Earth)* ENVIR ≈ Amis de la Terre *m pl*

FOIA *abbr US (Freedom of Information Act)* LAW loi sur la liberté de l'information

FOMC *abbr US (Federal Open Market Committee)* STOCK commission boursière fédérale du marché libre, ≈ COB *(France) (Commission des opérations de Bourse)*

Footsie *abbr UK (FT-SE 100 Share index, Financial Times Stock Exchange index)* STOCK indice Footsie *m (indice FTSE des 100 valeurs)*

FOQ *abbr (free on quay)* TRANSP *shipping* FAQ *(franco à quai)*

FOQ-FOQ *abbr (free on quay to free on quay)* TRANSP franco à quai - franco à quai

f.o.r. *abbr (free on rail)* TRANSP franco gare, franco sur rail, franco wagon

FOS *abbr (free on ship, free on steamer)* TRANSP FAB *(franco à bord)*

f.o.t. *abbr (free on truck)* TRANSP *rail* franco wagon

4Q *abbr (fourth quarter)* GEN COMM quatrième trimestre *m*

FP *abbr* GEN COMM *(fully paid)* lib., payé intégralement, INS *(floating marine policy) shipping* police flottante *f*, police maritime flottante *f*, TRANSP *(forward perpendicular) shipping* PPAV *(perpendiculaire avant)*, TRANSP *(floating marine policy) shipping* police flottante *f*, police maritime flottante *f*

FPA *abbr (free of particular average)* INS FAP *(franc d'avarie particulière)*

FPC *abbr US (Federal Power Commission)* IND commission fédérale de l'énergie

FPM *abbr (flexible-payment mortgage)* PROP hypothèque à règlements variables *f*

FP-⁰C *abbr (flash point in degrees centigrade)* GEN COMM point de combustion en degrés Celsius *m*

FP-°F *abbr (flash point in degrees fahrenheit)* GEN COMM point de combustion en degrés fahrenheit *m*

FPS *abbr (floating production system)* TRANSP *shipping* système de production au large *m*

FPSO *abbr (floating production, storage and offloading vessel)* TRANSP navire de production, stockage et déchargement au large *m*

FPT *abbr (fore peak tank)* TRANSP *of ship* coqueron avant *m*

FPV *abbr (floating production vessel)* TRANSP *ship* navire de production au large *m*

FPZ *abbr (free port zone)* TRANSP *shipping* zone portuaire franche *f*

F/R *abbr (freight release)* TRANSP BAD *(bon à délivrer)*

FRA *abbr (forward rate agreement, future rate agreement)* FIN, STOCK accord de taux à terme *m*, ATF *(accord de taux futur)*

fr & cc *abbr (free of riots and civil commotions)* TRANSP sans émeutes ou troubles civils

FRB *abbr US (Federal Reserve Board)* BANK, ECON conseil d'administration des banques centrales

FRC *abbr (free carrier)* TRANSP franco transporteur

Fri. *abbr (Friday)* GEN COMM vendredi *m*

FRICS *abbr (Fellow of the Royal Institute of Chartered Surveyors)* GEN COMM membre de l'institut royal d'experts immobiliers

FRMG *abbr (framing)* TRANSP *part of ship's hull* membrures *f pl*

FRN *abbr (floating-rate note)* STOCK OTV *(obligation à taux variable)*

frof *abbr (fire risk on freight)* TRANSP risque d'incendie sur fret *m*

FRS *abbr (Financial Reporting Standard)* ACC norme comptable *f*

frt *abbr (freight)* TRANSP cargaison *f*, fret *m*, marchandises *f pl*; **~ fwd** *(freight forward)* GEN COMM, TRANSP fret payable à destination *m*, p.d. *(port dû)*; **~ ppd** *(freight prepaid)* TRANSP fret payé d'avance *m*, fret payé à l'expédition *m*, p.p. *(port payé)*

FSA *abbr* FIN UK *(Financial Services Act)* loi sur les services financiers, STOCK *(forward spread agreement)* accord de répartition à terme *m*, accord sur étalement à terme *m*

FSBR *abbr (Financial Statement and Budget Report)* FIN état financier et rapport budgétaire

FSC *abbr (French Shippers' Council)* IMP/EXP Conseil des affréteurs français *m*

FSLIC *abbr* US *(Federal Savings and Loan Insurance Corporation)* BANK caisse nationale d'assurance de l'épargne et des prêts, ≈ société fédérale d'assurance épargne et crédit *f*

ft *abbr* GEN COMM *(foot)* pied *m*, GEN COMM *(freight ton)* tonne kilométrique *f*, TRANSP *(fuel terms)* conditions de carburant *f pl*

FT *abbr* UK *(Financial Times)* MEDIA *newspaper* Financial Times *m*

FTA *abbr* ECON *(free-trade agreement)* accord de libre-échange *m*, GEN COMM UK *(Freight Transport Association)* association du transport de fret, HRM *(failure to agree)* absence d'accord *f*, POL *(free-trade agreement)* accord de libre-échange *m*

FTB *abbr (fire tube boiler)* TRANSP *shipping* chaudière ignitubulaire *f*, chaudière à tubes de fumée *f*

FTBS *abbr (fire-tube boiler survey)* TRANSP *shipping* visite de la chaudière ignitubulaire *f*, visite de la chaudière à tubes de fumée *f*

FTC *abbr* US *(Federal Trade Commission)* POL commission fédérale du commerce

FTO *abbr* HRM UK *(full-time official)* permanent *m*, STOCK UK *(Financial Times Industrial Ordinary Share Index)* indice des actions industrielles ordinaires du Financial Times

FT-SE *abbr* UK *(Financial Times Stock Exchange index)* STOCK Indice de la Bourse de Londres *m*, FTSE, ≈ L'indice CAC40 *m (indice FTSE des 100 valeurs)*

FTZ *abbr (free-trade zone)* ECON, GEN COMM, IMP/EXP, POL zone de libre-échange *f*, zone franche *f*

FW *abbr (fresh water)* ENVIR eau douce *f*

FWA *abbr (fresh water allowance)* TRANSP *shipping* correction pour eau douce *f*

FWC *abbr (full loaded weight and capacity)*

TRANSP *of container* poids et capacité à charge complète *loc m*

FWD *abbr (fresh water damage)* TRANSP *shipping* avarie par l'eau douce *f*

fwdr *abbr (forwarder)* COMMS expéditeur *m*, IMP/EXP *carrier* expéditeur *m*, transitaire *mf*, TRANSP expéditeur *m*

FX *abbr (foreign exchange)* BANK, ECON, FIN change *m*, STOCK change *m*, devises *f pl*

FY *abbr (financial year, fiscal year)* ACC exercice *m*, exercice comptable *m*, exercice financier *m*, ECON, FIN, POL, TAX année budgétaire *f*, exercice *m*, exercice financier *m*

FYI *abbr (for your information)* GEN COMM à titre d'information *loc m*, à titre de renseignement *loc m*, à titre indicatif *loc m*, STOCK pour information *loc f*

g *abbr* GEN COMM *see gross weight* poids brut *m*, GEN COMM *(gram)* g *(gramme)*, TRANSP *(general purpose freight container)* conteneur pour usage général *m*, TRANSP *(galliot)* shipping galiote *f*

GA *abbr* GEN COMM *(General Assembly)* AG *(assemblée générale)* GEN COMM *(general authorization)* autorisation générale *f*, INS *(general average)* a.c. *(avarie commune)* MATH *(general average)* statistics moyenne générale *f*; **~ con** *(general average contribution)* INS contribution pour avarie commune; **~ dep** *(general average deposit)* GEN COMM cautionnement pour avarie commune *m*

GAAP *abbr* US *(Generally Accepted Accounting Principles)* ACC PCGA *(Principes comptables généralement admis)*

GAAS *abbr* US *(Generally Accepted Auditing Standards)* ACC normes d'audit généralement acceptées *f pl*

GAB *abbr (general arrangements to borrow)* FIN AGE *(accords généraux d'emprunt)*

GAC *abbr (general average certificate)* INS certificat d'avarie commune *m*

gal *abbr* GEN COMM US *(gallon)* 3.7854 litres, gallon *m*, GEN COMM UK *(gallon)* 4.546 litres, gallon *m*

GAO *abbr* US *(General Accounting Office)* ACC Bureau de comptabilité générale *m*

gas *abbr* ENVIR AmE *(gasoline)*, IND, TRANSP carburant *m*, essence *f*

GATT *abbr (General Agreement on Tariffs and Trade)* ECON, POL GATT *(Accord général sur les tarifs et le commerce)*

GAW *abbr* US *(guaranteed annual wage)* HRM salaire annuel garanti *m*, salaire minimum interprofessionnel garanti *m*, SMIG

Gb *abbr (gigabyte)* COMP Go *(gigaoctet)*

GB *abbr (Great Britain)* GEN COMM Grande-Bretagne *f*

GBL *abbr* IMP/EXP *(groupage bill of lading)* connaissement de groupage *m*, IMP/EXP *(govern-*

ment bill of lading) connaissement public *m*, TRANSP (groupage bill of lading) connaissement de groupage *m*, TRANSP (government bill of lading) connaissement public *m*

GC *abbr* TRANSP (general cargo) cargaison mixte *f*, divers *m pl*, marchandises diverses *f pl*, TRANSP (grain capacity, grain cubic) shipping capacité volumétrique en céréales *f*, volume grain *m*, TRANSP (gyrocompass) shipping compas gyroscopique *m*, gyrocompas *m*

GCA *abbr* (gold clause agreement) TRANSP accord de la clause or *m*

GCM *abbr* (general clearing member) STOCK ACG (adhérent compensateur général)

GCR *abbr* (general commodity rate) STOCK taux général des matières premières *m*

GCSE *abbr* UK (General Certificate of Secondary Education) WEL ≈ B.d.C. (Brevet des Collèges)

GCW *abbr* (gross combination weight) TRANSP articulated vehicle poids maximal d'un véhicule articulé *m*

GDH *abbr* (goods on hand) TRANSP stocks existants *m pl*

GDP *abbr* (gross domestic product) ECON PIB (produit intérieur brut)

gds *abbr* (goods) ECON biens *m pl*, GEN COMM, IND articles *m pl*, produits *m pl*, PATENTS biens *m pl*, S&M articles *m pl*, produits *m pl*

GE *abbr* (general equilibrium) ECON équilibre général *m*

GEB *abbr* (Group Executive Board) HRM bureau exécutif du consortium *m*, bureau exécutif du groupe *m*

GEM *abbr* US (growing-equity mortgage) BANK hypothèque à capital croissant *f*, hypothèque à paiements croissants *f*

GEMMS *abbr* (gilt-edged market makers) STOCK SVT (spécialistes en valeurs du Trésor)

GGE *abbr* (general governmental expenditure) ECON, FIN, POL dépenses des administrations publiques *f pl*, dépenses publiques *f pl*

GHS *abbr* (General Household Survey) ECON econometrics enquête générale sur les ménages

GIC *abbr* GEN COMM UK (guaranteed investment contract) contrat de placement garanti *m*, INS (guaranteed income contract) contrat de revenus garantis *m*

GIGO *abbr* (garbage in, garbage out) COMP rebut à l'entrée et à la sortie *m*, telle entrée, telle sortie *loc*

GLAM *abbr* infrml (Gray, Leisured, Affluent, Married AmE, Grey, Leisured, Affluent, Married BrE) ECON econometrics le beau monde de 45 à 60 ans, oisif, grisonnant, marié et riche

GLS *abbr* (generalized least squares) MATH statistics moindres carrés généralisés *m pl*

GM *abbr* ACC, ECON, FIN (gross margin) marge brute *f*, EBE (excédent brut d'exploitation), GEN COMM (general meeting) AG (assemblée générale), HRM (general manager) DG (directeur

général), MATH (geometric mean) moyenne géométrique *f*, MGMNT (general manager) DG (directeur général)

GMB *abbr* (good merchantable brand) IND marque loyale et marchande *f*

GMDSS *abbr* (Global Maritime Distress and Safety System) TRANSP shipping Système mondial de détresse et de sécurité en mer *m*

GMT *abbr* (Greenwich Mean Time) GEN COMM GMT (heure de Greenwich)

GNI *abbr* (gross national income) ECON revenu national brut *m*

GNMA *abbr* US (Government National Mortgage Association, Ginnie Mae) BANK, FIN, PROP société de prêt hypothécaire immobilier *f*

GNP *abbr* (gross national product) ECON PIB (produit intérieur brut), PNB (produit national brut)

G-O: ~ **bond** *abbr* US (general obligation bond) STOCK municipal bond engagement d'hypothèque générale *m*, obligation des collectivités locales garantie *f*

GOH *abbr* (goods on hand) TRANSP stocks existants *m pl*

GOP *abbr* infrml US (Grand Old Party) POL parti républicain

GOQ *abbr* BrE (genuine occupational qualification) HRM qualification professionnelle véritable *f*

govt *abbr* (government) POL administration *f*, gouvernement *m*

GP *abbr* (general purpose) GEN COMM à usage général *loc m*, à vocation générale *loc f*

GPLA *abbr* (general price level accounting) ACC comptabilité indexée sur le niveau général des prix *f*

GPS *abbr* US (Global Positioning System) TRANSP shipping système américain de localisation à couverture mondiale

GR *abbr* (gear manufacturer) TRANSP fabricant d'engrenages *m*

GRM *abbr* (gross rent multiplier) PROP multiplicateur de loyer brut *m*

GRS *abbr* (gears) TRANSP engrenage *m*

GRT *abbr* (gross register ton) GEN COMM tonne de jauge *f*, tonneau de jauge brute *m*

gr.wt. *abbr* (gross weight) GEN COMM poids brut *m*

GSE *abbr* (government-sponsored enterprise) FIN entreprise soutenue par l'État *f*

G7 *abbr* (Group of Seven) ECON G7 (Groupe des Sept)

gsm *abbr* (good sound merchantable) GEN COMM qualité loyale et marchande

GST *abbr* (goods and services tax) TAX TPS (taxe de prestation de service)

GSTP *abbr* (generalized system of tariffs and preferences) IMP/EXP SGTP (système généralisé des tarifs et préférences)

GT *abbr* GEN COMM (gross tonnage) tonnage brut

m, TRANSP *(gas turbine ship) shipping* navire à turbines à gaz *m*

GTW *abbr (gross train weight)* TRANSP *road vehicle* poids maximal d'un train routier *m, train* tonnage brut complet *m*

GUN *abbr (guarantor underwritten note)* STOCK note de garantie d'avaliste *f*

GVW *abbr (gross vehicle weight)* TRANSP *road vehicle* PTC *(poids total en charge)*

h *abbr* GEN COMM *(hour)*, TRANSP *(hour)* h *(heure)*, TRANSP *(hoy) shipping* bugalet *m*

H: **~ of C** *abbr UK (House of Commons)* POL Chambre des communes; **~ of L** *abbr UK (House of Lords)* POL Chambre des lords

ha *abbr* GEN COMM *(hectare)* ha *(hectare)*, TRANSP *(hatchway) of ship* panneau *m*, écoutille *f*

HAWB *abbr (house air waybill)* IMP/EXP, TRANSP *aviation* lettre de groupage aérien *f*

hazchem *abbr (hazardous chemicals)* IMP/EXP, IND produit chimique dangereux *m*, TRANSP produits chimiques dangereux *m pl*

h.b. *abbr (hours of business)* GEN COMM heures d'ouverture *f pl*, heures de bureau *f pl*, heures de réception de clientèle *f pl*, heures ouvrables *f pl*

HC *abbr* TRANSP *(high cube) container* conteneur hors-normes *m*, HC *(conteneur hors-cotes)*, TRANSP *(hydraulic coupling) of ship* accouplement hydraulique *m*, TRANSP *(heating coil) of ship* bobine thermique *f*, serpentin de réchauffage *m*

HD *abbr (high density)* COMP HD *(haute densité)*

HDD *abbr* COMP *(high-density disk)* disquette à haute densité *f*, COMP *(hard disk drive)* unité de disque dur *f*

hdlg *abbr (handling)* GEN COMM, TRANSP *of goods* manutention *f*

HDX *abbr (half-duplex)* COMP semi-duplex

HE *abbr* HRM *(Her Excellency) ambassadress* Son Excellence Madame l'Ambassadrice *f*, HRM *(His Excellency) ambassador* Son Excellence Monsieur l'Ambassadeur *f*, HRM *(Her Excellency, His Excellency) high-ranking official* Son Excellence *f*; **~ Cls B** *(heating coil in bunkers)* TRANSP *in bunkers* serpentin de réchauffage dans les soutes *m*

hgt *abbr (height)* GEN COMM hauteur *f*

HGV *abbr (heavy goods vehicle)* TRANSP poids lourd *m*

H/H *abbr (half height)* TRANSP *container* conteneur demi-hauteur *m*

hhd *abbr (hogshead)* TRANSP *barrel, unit of measurement* barrique *f*

HIC *abbr (heavily indebted middle-income country)* FIN pays à revenu moyen et à fort endettement *m*

H/L *abbr (heavy lift)* TRANSP *cargo handling* colis lourd *m*

HL *abbr UK (House of Lords)* POL Chambre des lords

HLL *abbr (high-level language)* COMP langage de haut niveau *m*, langage évolué *m*

HLT *abbr (high-leveraged takeover)* GEN COMM, STOCK rachat d'entreprise financé par un fort endettement *m*, reprise à fort effet de levier *f*

HMC *abbr UK (Her Majesty's Customs)* IMP/EXP douanes britanniques

HMC&E *abbr UK (Her Majesty's Customs and Excise, His Majesty's Customs and Excise)* IMP/EXP la Régie de Sa Majesté

HMG *abbr UK (Her Majesty's Government, His Majesty's Government)* GEN COMM Gouvernement de Sa Majesté

HMO *abbr US (health maintenance organization)* INS organisation de médecine préventive et curative *f*

HMS *abbr UK (Her Majesty's Ship, His Majesty's Ship)* TRANSP vaisseau de Sa Majesté

HMSO *abbr UK (Her Majesty's Stationery Office, His Majesty's Stationery Office)* ADMIN, GEN COMM ≈ Imprimerie nationale *f*

HNC *abbr UK (Higher National Certificate)* WEL certificat national d'études techniques supérieures

HND *abbr UK (Higher National Diploma)* WEL diplôme national d'études techniques supérieures, diplôme national supérieur *m*

ho *abbr (hold)* TRANSP *of aircraft, ship* cale *f*

HO *abbr (head office)* ACC *registered address of company*, BANK siège social *m*, GEN COMM agence centrale *f*, siège social *m*, MGMNT administration centrale *f*, siège social *m*

HOW *abbr US (homeowner warranty program)* INS garantie d'exécution de contrat de construction de résidence

HP *abbr* FIN *BrE (hire purchase)* location-vente *f*, vente à crédit *f*, vente à tempérament *f*, PROP *BrE (hire purchase)* vente à tempérament *f*, S&M *BrE (hire purchase)* location-vente *f*, vente à crédit *f*, vente à tempérament *f*, TRANSP *(horsepower)* CV *(cheval-vapeur)*

HPS *abbr (hazardous polluting substance)* TRANSP substance polluante dangereuse *f*

HPTB *abbr (high-pressure turbine)* TRANSP *of ship* turbine haute pression *f*

HQ *abbr (headquarters)* ADMIN, HRM direction centrale *f*, quartier général *m*, siège social *m*

hr *abbr (hour)* GEN COMM, TRANSP h *(heure)*

HRD *abbr (human resource development)* HRM développement des ressources humaines *m*

HRM *abbr (human resource management)* HRM GRH *(gestion des ressources humaines)*

HRP *abbr (human resource planning)* HRM gestion prévisionnelle de l'emploi *f*, planification de l'emploi *f*, planification des effectifs *f*, planification des ressources humaines *f*, recrutement et gestion des effectifs *loc m*

HSDT *abbr (hopper side tank)* TRANSP trémie latérale *f*

HSE *abbr UK (Health and Safety Executive)* WEL bureau de la sécurité et de la protection de la santé

HST *abbr (high-speed train)* TRANSP ≈ TGV *(train à grande vitesse)*

HSWA *abbr UK (Health and Safety at Work Act)* HRM, LAW loi de 1974 sur la santé et la sécurité au travail

HT *abbr* TRANSP *(half-tilt container)* conteneur semi-bâché *m*, TRANSP *(half-time survey)* visite à la mi-période *f*

htr *abbr (heater)* GEN COMM appareil de chauffage *m*

HWB *abbr (hot water boiler)* TRANSP *of ship* chaudière à eau chaude *f*

HWM *abbr (high-water mark)* TRANSP *shipping* laisse de haute mer *f*

HWOST *abbr (high-water ordinary spring tide)* TRANSP *shipping* pleine mer de vive-eau *f*

HYC *abbr (hydraulic coupling)* TRANSP *of ship* accouplement hydraulique *m*

HYD: ~ **PRO UN** *abbr (hydraulic propulsion unit)* TRANSP *of ship* propulseur hydraulique *m*

hydro *abbr (hydroelectric)* ENVIR *electricity supply, power* hydroélectrique

i *abbr (interest)* BANK, ECON, FIN intérêt *m*

IA *abbr (interest accrued)* ACC, BANK, FIN, GEN COMM, STOCK IC *(intérêts courus)*

IACS *abbr UK (International Association of Classification Societies)* GEN COMM association internationale des sociétés de classification

IADB *abbr (Inter-American Development Bank)* BANK BIAD *(Banque inter-américaine de développement)*

IAEC *abbr (International Association of Environmental Co-ordinators)* ENVIR association internationale des coordinateurs de l'environnement

IAM *abbr UK (Institute of Administrative Management)* MGMNT ≈ Institut de la gestion administrative *m*

IAPH *abbr (International Association of Ports and Harbours)* IMP/EXP Association internationale des ports *f*

IAPIP *abbr (International Association for the Protection of Industrial Property)* LAW association internationale pour la protection de la propriété industrielle

IARA *abbr (International Agricultural Research Institute)* IND Institut international de recherche agricole

IASC *abbr (International Accounting Standards Committee)* ACC Comité international des normes de comptabilité *m*

IATA *abbr (International Air Transport Association)* TRANSP IATA *(Association internationale des transports aériens)*

IB *abbr (in bond)* IMP/EXP, TAX en entrepôt sous douane *loc m*

IBC *abbr (intermediate bulk container)* TRANSP conteneur de vrac intermédiaire *m*

IBEC *abbr (International Bank for Economic Cooperation)* BANK COMECON Banque internationale pour la coopération économique *f*

IBELS *abbr UK (interest-bearing eligible liabilities)* BANK dettes admissibles portant intérêts *f pl*, obligations produisant des intérêts *f pl*

IBF *abbr (international banking facility)* BANK facilité bancaire internationale *f*, opérations bancaires internationales *f pl*

ibid. *abbr (ibidem)* GEN COMM ibid. *(ibidem)*

IBM® *abbr (International Business Machines*®*)* COMP IBM®

IBOR *abbr (interbank offered rate)* BANK, ECON, STOCK taux interbancaire offert *m*, taux interbancaire proposé *m*

IBRC *abbr UK (Insurance Brokers' Registration Council)* INS conseil d'immatriculation des courtiers d'assurance *m*

IBRD *abbr (International Bank of Reconstruction and Development)* BANK BIRD *(Banque internationale pour la reconstruction et le développement)*

IC *abbr* COMP *(integrated circuit)* CI *(circuit intégré)*, FIN *UK (Investment Committee) of the Association of British Insurers and National Association of Pension Funds* commission des investissements *f*, TRANSP *(inland container)* conteneur pour le transport intérieur *m*

ICA *abbr* ACC *UK (Institute of Chartered Accountants)* association professionnelle des experts-comptables, GEN COMM *UK (International Cooperation Administration)* administration internationale de la coopération

ICAC *abbr (International Cotton Advisory Committee)* IND Comité consultatif international du coton

ICAEW *abbr UK (Institute of Chartered Accountants in England and Wales)* ACC institut des experts-comptables d'Angleterre et du pays de Galles

ICAI *abbr (Institute of Chartered Accountants in Ireland)* ACC institut des experts-comptables d'Irlande

ICAO *abbr (International Civil Aviation Organization)* TRANSP OACI *(Organisation de l'aviation civile internationale)*

ICA's *abbr (International Commodity Agreements)* STOCK accords internationaux sur les matières premières *m pl*, accords internationaux sur les produits de base *m pl*

ICAS *abbr UK (Institute of Chartered Accountants of Scotland)* ACC institut des experts-comptables d'Écosse

ICC *abbr* ECON *(income-consumption curve)* courbe de demande par rapport aux revenus du consommateur *f*, ECON *(industrial and commercial company)* société industrielle et commerciale *f*, GEN COMM *(International Control Centre)* Centre international de contrôle du crédit *m*, GEN COMM *(industrial and commercial company)* société industrielle et commerciale *f*

ICCH *abbr UK (International Commodities Clearing House)* STOCK chambre internationale de compensation pour les produits de base *f*

ICD *abbr (inland clearance depot)* IMP/EXP bureau de dédouanement de l'intérieur *m*

ICEM *abbr (Intergovernmental Committee for European Migration)* WEL Commission intergouvernementale des migrations européennes *f*

ICETT *abbr UK (Industrial Council for Educational & Training Technology)* WEL Conseil industriel pour la technologie en matière d'éducation et de formation *m*

ICFTU *abbr (International Confederation of Free Trade Unions)* HRM confédération internationale des syndicats de libre-échange

ICHCA *abbr (International Cargo Handling Coordination Association)* IND association de coordination de la manipulation des chargements

ICIE *abbr (International Centre for Industry and the Environment)* IND centre international pour l'industrie et l'environnement

ICITO *abbr UK (Interim Commission of the International Trade Organization)* GEN COMM commission intérimaire de l'organisation internationale du commerce

ICJ *abbr (International Court of Justice)* LAW, POL Cour internationale de justice *f*

ICMA *abbr UK (Institute of Cost and Management Accountants)* ACC association professionnelle des comptables en management

ICON *abbr (indexed currency option note)* STOCK billet d'option de change indexé *m*

ICOR *abbr (incremental capital-output ratio)* FIN taux de rendement du capital différentiel *m*, taux incrémental de dépenses en capital *m*

ICS *abbr (International Chamber of Shipping)* TRANSP chambre internationale maritime

ICTB *abbr (International Customs Tariffs Bureau)* IMP/EXP BITD *(Bureau international des tarifs douaniers)*

ICU *abbr (International Clearing Union)* ECON Union de clearing internationale *f*

id. *abbr (idem)* GEN COMM id. *(idem)*

ID *abbr* GEN COMM *(identification)* ID *(identification)*, IMP/EXP *(import duty)* tax droit d'entrée *m*, taxe à l'importation *f*, S&M, TAX *(identification)* ID *(identification)*

IDA *abbr* ECON *(International Development Association)* Association internationale pour le développement *f*, ECON *(Industrial Development Authority)* administration du développement industriel *f*, IMP/EXP *(import duty act)* loi sur les taxes à l'importation *f*, IND *(Industrial Development Authority)* administration du développement industriel *f*

IDB *abbr BrE (interdealer broker)* BANK courtier

internégociants *m*, intermédiaire entre courtiers *m*

IDBS *abbr (interdealer broker system)* STOCK SIAM *(système des intermédiaires entre courtiers)*

IDD *abbr (international direct dialing, international direct dialling)* COMMS appel international automatique *m*, l'automatique international *m*

IDF *abbr (interdepartmental flexibility)* HRM flexibilité entre services *f*

IDRC *abbr UK (International Development Research Centre)* GEN COMM centre de recherche international de développement

i.e. *abbr (id est, that is to say)* GEN COMM c-à-d *(c'est-à-dire)*

IEA *abbr* ECON UK *(Institute of Economic Affairs)* institut des affaires économiques *m*, ENVIR *(International Energy Agency)* agence internationale de l'énergie

IEM *abbr (International Equities Market)* STOCK marché international des actions *m*, marché international des capitaux *m*

IFAP *abbr (International Federation of Agricultural Producers)* IND FIPA *(Fédération internationale des producteurs agricoles)*

IFC *abbr (international finance corporation)* FIN SFI *(société financière internationale)*

IFD *abbr (International Federation for Documentation)* GEN COMM FID *(Fédération internationale de documentation)*

IFSE *abbr (International Federation of Stock Exchanges)* STOCK FIBV *(Fédération internationale des bourses de valeurs)*

IFTU *abbr (International Federation of Trade Unions)* HRM IFTU *(Fédération syndicale internationale)* f, Fédération internationale des syndicats *f*

IGLU *abbr (index growth linked units)* STOCK *index-linked Swiss franc instruments* unités indexées liées à la croissance *f pl*

ihp *abbr (indicated horsepower)* GEN COMM cheval-vapeur indiqué *m*

IIB *abbr (international investment bank)* BANK Banque internationale d'investissement *f*

IIF *abbr (Institute for International Finance)* FIN Institut de finances internationales *m*, Institut international de finance *m*

I/L *abbr (import licence BrE, import license AmE)* IMP/EXP licence d'importation *f*

ILA *abbr US (International Longshoremen's Association)* TRANSP association internationale des débardeurs

ILO *abbr* HRM *(International Labour Office)* BIT *(Bureau international du travail)*, HRM *(International Labour Organization)* OIT *(Organisation internationale du travail)*

ILOC *abbr (irrevocable letter of credit)* BANK lettre de crédit irrévocable *f*

ILWU *abbr US (International Longshoremen's and*

Warehousemen's Union) IND syndicat international des débardeurs et des magasiniers

IMB *abbr (International Maritime Bureau)* TRANSP Bureau maritime international *m*

IMC *abbr (International Maritime Committee)* TRANSP Comité maritime international *m*

IMDGC *abbr (International Maritime Dangerous Goods Code)* TRANSP *shipping* Code maritime international des marchandises dangereuses *m*

IMF *abbr (International Monetary Fund)* BANK, ECON, FIN FMI *(Fonds monétaire international)*

IMM *abbr (International Monetary Market)* ECON, STOCK MMI *(Marché monétaire international)*

IMO *abbr* IND *(International Miners' Organization)* Organisation internationale des mineurs, TRANSP *(International Maritime Organization)* Organisation maritime internationale

imp. *abbr (import, importation)* IMP/EXP imp. *(importation)*

IMPA *abbr (International Maritime Pilots' Association)* TRANSP association internationale des pilotes maritimes

IMRO *abbr UK (Investment Managers' Regulatory Organization)* STOCK organisation de surveillance des gestionnaires d'investissement *f*

IMRS *abbr (Industrial Market Research Services)* S&M Services d'études de marché industriel *m pl*

IMS *abbr (Institute of Manpower Studies)* HRM Institut d'études sur la main d'oeuvre *m*

IMT *abbr (immediate money transfer)* BANK transfert d'argent immédiat *m*

Inc. *abbr US (incorporated company)* GEN COMM *in company name* SARL *(société à responsabilité limitée)*

incl. *abbr* GEN COMM *(included, inclusive)* compris, inclus, GEN COMM *(including)* compris, y compris

INCOTERM *abbr (international commercial term)* ECON *international trade* INCOTERME *(terme commercial international)*

inf. *abbr (information)* ACC, ECON renseignements *m pl*, GEN COMM informations *f pl*, renseignements *m pl*, TAX, TRANSP renseignements *m pl*

info *abbr (information)* ACC, ECON renseignements *m pl*, GEN COMM informations *f pl*, renseignements *m pl*, TAX, TRANSP renseignements *m pl*

INMARSAT *abbr (International Maritime Satellite Organization)* COMMS Organisation internationale de satellites maritimes *f*

ins. *abbr* INS *(insurance)* asse. *(assurance)*, TRANSP *(insulated)* isotherme

INSA *abbr (International Shipowners' Association)* TRANSP association internationale des armateurs

inst. *abbr* COMP *(installed)* installé, GEN COMM *(institute)* institut *m*

int. *abbr* ACC, BANK, ECON, FIN, GEN COMM *(interest) in property* intérêts *m pl*, participation *f, on borrowings* int. *(intérêt)*, INS *(intermediate survey)* expertise intermédiaire *f*, STOCK *(interest) on borrowings* int. *(intérêt)*

intl *abbr (international)* COMMS, ECON, GEN COMM, POL intl *(international)*

inv. *abbr (invoice)* ACC, BANK, FIN, GEN COMM fre *(facture)*

I/O *abbr (input/output)* COMP E/S *(entrée/sortie)*

IO *abbr* ADMIN *(immigration officer)*, HRM *(immigration officer)* agent du service de l'immigration *m*, fonctionnaire de l'immigration *m*, officier de police du service de l'immigration *m*, ≈ agent de la P.A.F. *m (Fra)*, ≈ agent de la Police de l'air et des frontières *m (Fra)*, IND *(industrial organization)* organisation industrielle *f*

IOB *abbr* BANK *(Institute of Bankers)* Institut des banquiers *m*, INS *UK (Insurance Ombudsman Bureau)* bureau de médiateur en matière d'assurance *m*

IOC *abbr (Intergovernmental Oceanographic Commission)* COMMS Commission océanographique intergouvernementale *f*

IOE *abbr* HRM *(International Organization of Employers)* Organisation internationale des employeurs, TRANSP *(International Office of Epizootics)* OIE *(Office international des épizooties)*

IOM *abbr* MGMNT *(Institute of Office Management)* institut de la gestion de bureaux, STOCK *(International Options Market)* marché international des options *m*, marché à options international *m*, marché à primes international *m*

IORT *abbr (incremental oil revenue tax)* TAX impôt sur les revenus pétroliers supplémentaires *m*

IOSCO *abbr (International Organization of Securities Commission)* STOCK commission de l'organisation internationale des valeurs *f*

IOTTSG *abbr (International Oil Tanker and Terminal Safety Group)* TRANSP groupe international sur la sécurité des pétroliers et des terminaux

IOU *abbr (I owe you)* BANK, FIN, GEN COMM, TRANSP reconnaissance de dette *f*

IPA *abbr UK (Institute of Practitioners in Advertising)* S&M institut des publicitaires

IPC *abbr (integrated pollution control)* ENVIR lutte antipollution intégrée *f*

IPD *abbr (interest, profit and dividends)* ECON revenu en provenance de l'étranger *m*

IPE *abbr UK (International Petroleum Exchange)* STOCK bourse internationale des produits pétroliers *f*, marché international du pétrole *m*

IPI *abbr (International Press Institute)* MEDIA institut international de la presse

IPM *abbr* FIN *(integrated project management)*, MGMNT *(integrated project management)* gestion intégrée de projet *f*, MGMNT *UK (Institute of Personnel Management)* Institut de gestion du personnel *m*

IPMA *abbr (International Primary Market Association)* STOCK Association internationale du marché primaire *f*

IPO *abbr* BANK *(international payment order)* ordre de paiement international *m*, STOCK *AmE (initial*

public offering) offre publique initiale *f*, première émission publique *f*

IPR *abbr* IMP/EXP *(inward process relief, inwards processing relief)* dégrèvement du traitement des entrées, LAW *(property rights)*, PROP *(property rights)* droits de propriété *m pl*, S&M *UK (Institute of Public Relations)* institut des relations publiques, TRANSP *(inward process relief, inwards processing relief)* dégrèvement du traitement des entrées

IPU *abbr (Inter-Parliamentary Union)* POL UIP *(Union interparlementaire)*

IR *abbr* HRM *(industrial relations)* relations humaines dans l'entreprise *f pl*, relations industrielles *f pl*, relations professionnelles *f pl*, relations syndicales *f pl*, TAX *UK (the Inland Revenue) organization, system* le Fisc *m (infrml)*

IRD *abbr (inland rail depot)* IMP/EXP, TRANSP bureau de dédouanement ferroviaire intérieur *m*

IRN *abbr* ENVIR *(iron)* fer *m*, IMP/EXP *(import release note)* décharge d'importation *f*, IND *(iron)* fer *m*

IRPC *abbr (Industrial Relations Policy Committee)* HRM commission sur la politique des relations industrielles

IRPTC *abbr (International Register of Potentially Toxic Chemicals)* ENVIR, IND RISCPT *(Registre international des substances chimiques potentiellement toxiques)*

IRR *abbr (internal rate of return)* ACC, FIN taux de rentabilité interne *m*, taux de rentabilité intérieur *m*, taux interne de rentabilité *m*

IRS *abbr* US *(the Internal Revenue Service)* TAX le Fisc *m (infrml)*

IRU *abbr* HRM *(International Recruitment Unit)* Unité internationale de recrutement *f*, TRANSP *(International Road Transport Union)* Syndicat international des transporteurs routiers *m*

IS *abbr (independent spherical aluminium tank, independent spherical aluminum tank)* TRANSP *shipping, liquefied natural gas carrier* cuve sphérique indépendante en aluminium *f*

ISA *abbr (International Sugar Agreement)* ECON ≈ AIS *(Accord international sur le sucre)*

ISBN *abbr (International Standard Book Number)* MEDIA *print* ISBN *(International Standard Book Number)*

ISC *abbr (International Sugar Council)* IND Conseil international du sucre *m*

ISD *abbr (international subscriber dialing, international subscriber dialling)* COMMS téléphone automatique international *m*

ISDA *abbr (International Swap Dealers' Association)* STOCK Association internationale des opérateurs de swaps *f*

ISDN *abbr (integrated services digital network)* COMMS RNIS *(réseau numérique à intégration de services)*

ISE *abbr (International Stock Exchange)* STOCK ≈ SBF *(France) (Société des bourses françaises)*

ISF *abbr (International Shipping Federation)* TRANSP Fédération internationale de la navigation *f*

ISFA *abbr (Institute of Shipping and Forwarding Agents)* TRANSP institut d'agents maritimes et de transitaires

ISI *abbr* UK *(International Statistical Institute)* GEN COMM Institut international des statistiques

ISMA *abbr (International Securities Market Association)* STOCK Association internationale des bourses de valeurs *f*, Association internationale du marché des valeurs *f*

ISO *abbr* GEN COMM *(International Standards Organization)* Organisation internationale de normalisation *f*, IND *(International Sugar Organization)* Organisation internationale du sucre *f*, STOCK *(incentive stock option) tax* intéressement par option de souscription d'actions *m*, option d'action à prime *f*

ISO/OSI *abbr (International Standards Organization/Open Systems Interconnection)* COMP interconnexion de systèmes ouverts de l'organisation internationale des standards

ISRO *abbr (International Securities Regulatory Organization)* STOCK Organisation de surveillance pour les valeurs internationales *f*, Organisme régulateur des titres internationaux *m*

ISS *abbr (International Social Service)* WEL ≈ Service social international *m*

ISSN *abbr (International Standard Serial Number)* MEDIA *print* ISSN *(International Standard Serial Number)*

IT *abbr* COMP *(information technology)* informatique *f*, technologie de l'information *f*, HRM *UK (industrial tribunal)*, IND *UK (industrial tribunal)*, LAW *UK (industrial tribunal)* ≈ Conseil des prud'hommes *m*, LEIS *(inclusive tour)* voyage tout compris *m*, TRANSP *(insulated tank container)* conteneur-citerne isotherme *m*, TRANSP *(inclusive tour)* voyage tout compris *m*, TRANSP *(independent tank) shipping, liquefied natural gas carrier* cuve autoporteuse *f*, cuve indépendante *f*

ITB *abbr (integrated tug-barge)* TRANSP *shipping* pousseur-barge intégré *m*

ITC *abbr* ECON *(international trading certificate)* certificat de commerce international *m*, IND *(International Tin Council)* conseil international de l'étain, TAX *(investment tax credit)* CII *(crédit d'impôt à l'investissement)*, TAX *Can (input tax credit)* CTI *(crédit de taxe sur intrants)*

ITF *abbr (International Transport Workers' Federation)* TRANSP FIOT *(Fédération internationale des ouvriers du transport)*

ITI *abbr (customs convention on the international transit of goods)* IMP/EXP convention douanière sur le transit international des marchandises *f*

ITM *abbr (in-the-money)* STOCK argenté, dans le cours *loc m*, en jeu *loc m*

ITO *abbr (International Trade Organization)* GEN COMM organisation internationale du commerce

ITPAL *abbr (industrial and trade policy adjustment loan)* FIN prêt d'ajustement de politique industrielle et commerciale *m*

ITS *abbr US (Intermarket Trading System)* STOCK système commercial inter-marché *m*, système de transaction inter-marchés *m*

ITU *abbr (International Telecommunications Union)* COMMS UIT *(Union internationale des télécommunications)*

ITV *abbr UK (Independent Television)* S&M chaîne de télévision britannique indépendante, diffusant des programmes régionaux

ITW *abbr (independent tank wing)* TRANSP *shipping, liquefied natural gas carrier* cuve autoporteuse latérale *f*, cuve indépendante latérale *f*

ITX *abbr (independent tank common)* TRANSP *shipping, liquefied natural gas carrier* cuve autoporteuse standard *f*, cuve indépendante standard *f*

IUOTO *abbr (International Union of Official Travel Organizations)* TRANSP Syndicat international des organisations officielles de voyages *m*

IUR *abbr (International Union of Railways)* ADMIN UICF *(Union internationale des chemins de fer)*, TRANSP Syndicat international des cheminots *m*

iv *abbr* FIN *(increased value)* plus-value *f*, FIN *(invoice value)*, GEN COMM *(invoice value)* valeur de la facture *f*

IWA *abbr (International Wheat Agreement)* ECON AIB *(Accord international sur le blé)*

IWC *abbr (International Wheat Council)* GEN COMM CIB *(Conseil international du blé)*

J *abbr* LAW *(judge)* juge *m*, LAW *(justice)* justice *f*

J/A *abbr (joint account)* BANK compte bancaire en commun *m*, compte conjoint *m*, compte en commun *m*, compte joint *m*

Jan. *abbr (January)* GEN COMM janv. *(janvier)*

J&WO *abbr (jettisoning and washing overboard)* INS *marine* jet à la mer et enlèvement par une lame *m*

JCCC *abbr UK (Joint Customs Consultative Committee)* IMP/EXP comité paritaire consultatif des douanes

JCS *abbr (joint container service)* TRANSP service conteneur commun *m*

JDI *abbr (joint declaration of interest)* BANK déclaration conjointe d'intérêts *f*, déclaration d'intérêts en commun *f*

JEC *abbr (Joint Economic Committee of Congress)* ECON *between House and Senate* commission mixte économique du Congrès américaine

JETRO *abbr (Japanese External Trade Organization)* GEN COMM office du commerce extérieur japonais

JIT *abbr* HRM *(just-in-time)* juste à temps, à flux tendus *loc m*, HRM *(just-in-time production)* production dans les délais impartis *f*, production

à flux tendus *f*, IND *(just-in-time)* juste à temps, à flux tendus *loc m*, IND *(just-in-time production)* production dans les délais impartis *f*, production à flux tendus *f*, MEDIA *(just-in-time) delivery* juste à temps, à flux tendus *loc m*

JJ *abbr* LAW *(judges)* juges *m pl*, LAW *(justices)* justices *f pl*

JMC *abbr (Joint Maritime Commission)* HRM, TRANSP commission maritime conjointe

jnr *abbr (junior)* GEN COMM *employee, post* subalterne *mf, son* fils *m, young* jeune

JP *abbr (justice of the peace)* HRM juge d'instance *m*, juge de paix *m*

jr *abbr (junior)* GEN COMM *employee, post* subalterne *mf, son* fils *m, young* jeune

JTAG *abbr UK (Japan Trade Advisory Group)* GEN COMM comité consultatif japonais des échanges commerciaux

Jul. *abbr (July)* GEN COMM juil. *(juillet)*

Jun. *abbr (June)* GEN COMM juin *m*

JV *abbr (joint venture)* ACC coentreprise *f*, ECON, coentreprise *f*, joint-venture *m* GEN COMM joint-venture *m* société en participation *f*, société mixte *f*, *action* coentreprise *f*, opération conjointe *f*, MGMNT *action* action concertée *f*, coentreprise *f*, *company* entreprise conjointe *f*, société d'exploitation en commun *f*, STOCK *action* coentreprise *f*, *company* entreprise en participation *f*

JWP *abbr (joint working party)* HRM groupe de travail paritaire *m*

K *abbr* ECON *BrE (knighthood)*, POL *(knighthood)* titre de chevalier *m*

kb *abbr (kilobyte)* COMP ko *(kilo-octet)*

KBS *abbr (knowledge-based system)* COMP système expert *m*

KC *abbr* GEN COMM *(kilogram per square centimeter AmE, kilogramme per square centimetre BrE)* kilogramme au centimètre carré *m*, HRM, LAW *UK (King's Counsel)* avocat de la Couronne, ≈ bâtonnier de l'ordre *m*

KCBT *abbr (Kansas city board of trade)* STOCK marché boursier de Kansas City *m*

kg *abbr (kilogram)* GEN COMM kg *(kilogramme)*

kl *abbr (kiloliter, kilolitre)* GEN COMM kl *(kilolitre)*

km *abbr (kilometer, kilometre)* GEN COMM km *(kilomètre)*

km/h *abbr (kilometers per hour, kilometres per hour)* GEN COMM km/h *(kilomètre/heure)*

kt *abbr (kiloton)* GEN COMM kt *(kilotonne)*

kW *abbr (kilowatt)* GEN COMM kW *(kilowatt)*

kWh *abbr (kilowatt-hour)* GEN COMM kWh *(kilowatt-heure)*

l *abbr (liter, litre)* GEN COMM l *(litre)*

L/A *abbr* GEN COMM *(letter of authority)* lettre d'autorité *f*, TRANSP *(Lloyd's Agent) shipping* agent de la Lloyds *m*, TRANSP *(landing account)* *shipping* frais de débarquement *m pl*, frais de mise à terre *m pl*

LAB *abbr* STOCK *(local authority bill, local authority bond)* loi sur les administrations locales *f*, obligation d'administration locale ou régionale *f*, TRANSP *(live animals on board)* animaux vivants à bord

LAC *abbr (Lights Advisory Committee)* GEN COMM comité consultatif des phares et balises

LAIA *abbr (Latin American Integration Association)* ECON zone de libre-échange latino-américaine *f*

LAN *abbr (local area network)* COMP RLE *(réseau local d'entreprise)*

LANBY *abbr (large automatic navigational buoy)* TRANSP *shipping* balise automatique LANBY *f*

LASH *abbr (lighter aboard ship)* TRANSP *shipping* navire porte-barges *m*, porte-barges *m*

lat. *abbr (latitude)* GEN COMM lat. *(latitude)*

LATAG *abbr (Latin American Trade Advisory Group)* GEN COMM Comité consultatif latino-américain des échanges commerciaux *m*

lb *abbr (pound)* GEN COMM lb *(livre)*

LBO *abbr (leveraged buyout)* FIN désintéressement pour endettement *m*, GEN COMM rachat d'entreprise financé par l'endettement *m*, STOCK achat adossé *m*, achat avec effet de levier *m*, achat d'endettement *m*, prise de contrôle adossée *f*, rachat par levier *m*, rachat d'entreprise financé par l'endettement *m*

LBP *abbr (length between perpendiculars)* TRANSP *shipping* LPP *(longueur entre perpendiculaires)*

lc *abbr* FIN *(local currency)* monnaie locale *f*, GEN COMM *(label clause)* préambule *m*, IMP/EXP *(local currency)* monnaie locale *f*

l.c. *abbr (lower case)* ADMIN, COMP, MEDIA bas de casse *m*, lettre de bas de casse *f*, lettre minuscule *f*, minuscule *f (majuscule)*

L/C *abbr (letter of credit)* BANK, FIN L/C *(lettre de crédit)*

LC *abbr* GEN COMM US *(Library of Congress)* bibliothèque du Congrès, ≈ BN *(Bibliothèque Nationale)*, HRM UK *(Lord Chancellor)* ≈ ministre de la Justice *m*

LCA *abbr (life cycle assessment)* ENVIR évaluation du cycle de vie *f*

LCCI *abbr (London Chamber of Commerce & Industry)* GEN COMM Chambre de commerce et d'industrie de Londres *f*

LCD *abbr (lowest common denominator)* GEN COMM plus petit dénominateur commun *m*

LCE *abbr obs (London Commodity Exchange)* STOCK depuis 1987, the London Futures and Options Exchange, Bourse de matières premières de Londres *f*

LCH *abbr* ECON *(life-cycle hypothesis)* hypothèse du cycle de vie *f*, STOCK *(London Clearing House)* Caisse/Chambre de compensation de Londres

LCJ *abbr UK (Lord Chief Justice)* HRM ≈ président de la Haute Cour de Justice *m (France)*

LCL *abbr (less than carload, less than container load)* TRANSP conteneur de groupage *m*, envoi de détail *m*

ld *abbr (load)* TRANSP charge *f*

LDC *abbr (less developed country)* ECON, GEN COMM, POL *international* PMA *(pays moins avancé)*, PVD *(pays en voie de développement)*

ldg *abbr (loading)* COMP, TRANSP chargement *m*; **~ & dly** *(loading and delivery)* TRANSP chargement et livraison *loc m*

LDMA *abbr (London Discount Market Association)* BANK, FIN Association du marché de l'escompte de Londres *f*

L/E *abbr (latest estimate)* GEN COMM devis le plus récent *m*

LEA *abbr (Local Entreprise Agency)* WEL bureau des entreprises locales

LEAPS *abbr (long-term equity anticipation securities)* STOCK options de longue durée *f pl*

LEC *abbr UK (Local Export Control)* IMP/EXP conseil local de l'exportation

LED *abbr (light-emitting diode)* COMP DEL *(diode électroluminescente)*

len. *abbr (lengthened)* GEN COMM prolongé, rallongé

LEXIS *abbr (Legal Exchange Information Service)* LAW base de données juridiques *f*

lf *abbr (line feed)* COMP changement de ligne *m*, passage à la ligne *m*, saut de page *m*

LFPR *abbr (labor force participation rate, labour force participation rate)* HRM intéressement du personnel *m*, participation de la main d'oeuvre *f*

LGS *abbr (liquid assets and government securities)* FIN liquidités et titres d'État *f pl*

lh *abbr (last half)* GEN COMM dernière quinzaine *f*

L/I *abbr (letter of indemnity)* BANK, GEN COMM lettre de garantie *f*

LIARS *abbr (Lloyd's Instantaneous Accounting Record System)* INS système Lloyd's de comptabilité instantanée

LIBID *abbr (London Interbank Bid Rate)* STOCK taux d'emprunt interbancaire de Londres *m*, taux de l'offre interbancaire de Londres *m*

LIBOR *abbr (London Interbank Offered Rate)* BANK, STOCK TIOL *(taux interbancaire offert à Londres)*

LIC *abbr UK (League International for Creditors)* BANK ligue internationale des créditeurs

LICOM *abbr (London Interbank Currency Options Market)* STOCK marché interbancaire des options sur devises de Londres *m*

LIFFE *abbr (London International Financial Futures Exchange)* STOCK bourse des options de Londres, ≈ MONEP *(Marché des options négociables de Paris)*, ≈ MATIF *(Marché à terme d'instruments financiers) (Fra)*

LIFO *abbr (last in, first out)* ACC, HRM DEPS *(dernier entré, premier sorti)*

LIFT *abbr UK (London International Freight Terminal)* TRANSP terminal de fret international de Londres *m*

limdis *abbr jarg (limited distribution)* POL divulgation restreinte *f*

LIMEAN *abbr (London Interbank Mean Rate)* STOCK taux interbancaire moyen de Londres *m*, taux moyen interbancaire de Londres *m*, taux moyen interbancaire des eurobanques de Londres *m*

LIONs *abbr (Lehman Investment Opportunity Notes)* STOCK Lettre Lehman sur les investissements *m*, Lettre de Lehman sur les Opportunités d'Investissement *m*, titres de l'établissement Lehman Brothers *m pl*

lkg: ~ **& bkg** *abbr (leakage and breakage)* TRANSP coulage et casse *loc m*

LL *abbr (load line)* TRANSP *shipping* ligne de charge *f*

LLB *abbr (Bachelor of Laws)* WEL *degree* ≈ licence de droit *f*, *person* ≈ licencié en droit *m*

LLD *abbr (Doctor of Laws)* LAW, WEL docteur en droit *m*

LMBI *abbr (leveraged management buy-in)* FIN, GEN COMM, MGMNT, STOCK REI *(rachat d'une entreprise par des investisseurs)*

LMBO *abbr (leveraged management buyout)* FIN, GEN COMM, MGMNT, STOCK RES *(rachat d'une entreprise par ses salariés)*

LMC *abbr (Lloyd's Machinery Certificate)* TRANSP *shipping* attestation du Lloyd's indiquant le bon état des machines

LME *abbr (London Metal Exchange)* STOCK Bourse des métaux de Londres *f*

LNG *abbr (liquefied natural gas)* ENVIR, IND, TRANSP *shipping* GNL *(gaz naturel liquéfié)*

lo *abbr (low loader)* TRANSP remorque surbaissée *f*, remorque à plate-forme surbaissée *f*, wagon à plate-forme surbaissée *m*

LOA *abbr (length overall)* TRANSP *shipping* LHT *(longueur hors tout)*

LOCH *abbr UK (London Options Clearing House)* FIN ≈ SCMC *(Société de compensation des marchés conditionnels)*

lo/lo *abbr (lift on/lift off)* TRANSP *ship, vessel* navire à manutention verticale *m*

Lo/Lo *abbr (Lift on/Lift off)* TRANSP *system* manutention verticale *f*

LP *abbr (low pressure)* GEN COMM basse pression *f*, dépression *f*

LPG *abbr (liquid petroleum gas)* ENVIR, IND, TRANSP *shipping* GPL *(gaz de pétrole liquéfié)*

LPTB *abbr (low-pressure turbine)* TRANSP *shipping* turbine BP *f*, turbine basse pression *f*

LQ *abbr (letter quality)* COMP qualité courrier *f*

Lr *abbr (lugger)* TRANSP *shipping* chasse-marée *m*, lougre *m*

LRA *abbr UK (Labour Relations Agency)* HRM, IND, LAW ≈ Conseil des prud'hommes *m*

LRC *abbr (Labour Representation Committee)* HRM caisse de financement des députés du monde ouvrier *f*

LRT *abbr UK (London Regional Transport)* TRANSP autorité londonienne de transports publics

ls *abbr (lump sum)* TRANSP *freight* forfait *m*, somme forfaitaire *f*

LSA *abbr (life-saving apparatus)* TRANSP *shipping* engin de sauvetage *m*, matériel de sauvetage *m*

LSD *abbr (landing storage delivery)* IMP/EXP, TRANSP mise à terre, magasinage et livraison *loc f*

LSE *abbr UK (London School of Economics)* ECON École Supérieure d'Économie de Londres *f*; **the ~** *(London Stock Exchange)* STOCK la bourse de Londres, ≈ Bourse de commerce de Paris *f*, ≈ la Bourse de Paris *f*, ≈ le Palais Brongniart *m*

LTB *abbr* FIN *(long-term blended cost rate)* taux des coûts à long terme tous frais mélangés *m*, LEIS *(London Tourist Board)* office de tourisme de Londres

Ltd *abbr UK (limited liability company)* GEN COMM SA *(société anonyme)*, SARL *(société à responsabilité limitée)*

LTOM *abbr (London Traded Options Market, London Trader Options Market)* STOCK Bourse des options négociables de Londres *f*, Marché des options négociants de Londres *m*, marché des options négociables de Londres *m*, marché des options négociées de Londres *m*

LTPR *abbr (long-term prime rate)* FIN taux de base à long terme *m*

LTU *abbr (long-term unemployed)* ECON, HRM chômeur de longue durée *m*, DELD *(demandeur d'emploi de longue durée)*

LTV *abbr* BANK *(loan-to-value ratio)*, FIN *(loan-to-value ratio)* rapport emprunt-valeur *m*, rapport prêt-valeur *m*, ratio prêt sur valeur *m*, TRANSP *(light vessel)* *shipping* bateau-feu *m*

LUAA *abbr (Lloyd's Underwriting Agents' Association)* INS association des agents souscripteurs du Lloyd's

LUAMC *abbr (leading underwriters' agreement for marine cargo business)* INS *marine* convention de souscripteurs principaux pour assurance transport marin

LUAMH *abbr (leading underwriters' agreement for marine hull business)* INS *marine* convention de souscripteurs principaux pour assurance sur corps de navire

LV *abbr BrE (luncheon voucher)* HRM chèque-déjeuner *m*, chèque-repas *m*, ticket-repas *m*, ticket-restaurant *m*

lw *abbr (low water)* TRANSP *shipping* marée basse *f*, BM *(basse mer)*

Lw *abbr (lower hold)* TRANSP *shipping* cale *f*

LWOST *abbr (low water ordinary spring tide)* TRANSP *shipping* basse mer de vive-eau *f*

Lw *abbr (lower hold)* TRANSP *shipping* cale *f*

LWOST *abbr (low water ordinary spring tide)* TRANSP *shipping* basse mer de vive-eau *f*

LYON *abbr (liquid yield option note)* STOCK billet d'option de rendement en liquide *m*, note d'option sur rendement disponible *f*

m *abbr* GEN COMM *(meter AmE, metre BrE)* m *(mètre)*, GEN COMM *(month)* mois *m*, TRANSP *(midship) shipping* centre du navire *m*, milieu du navire *m*, TRANSP *(motorship) shipping* navire à moteur *m*

M *abbr (monetary aggregates)* ECON M *(agrégats monétaires)*

m/a *abbr (my account)* GEN COMM mon compte *m*

MABEETA *abbr* GEN COMM Association mixte d'économie, d'échanges et de commerce Malaisie Grande-Bretagne *f*

MACH *abbr (modular automated container handling)* TRANSP manutention modulaire et automatisée de conteneurs *f*

MAFF *abbr UK (Ministry of Agriculture, Fisheries and Food)* ADMIN ≈ ministère de l'Agriculture, de la Pêche et de l'Alimentation *m*

MAL *abbr (Malaysian ringgit)* GEN COMM ringgit *m*

M&A *abbr (mergers and acquisitions)* ECON, STOCK F&A *(fusions et acquisitions)*

Mar. *abbr (March)* GEN COMM mars *m*

MARAD *abbr US (Maritime Administration)* TRANSP administration maritime

MARPOL *abbr (Maritime Pollution)* ENVIR *Convention 1978* MARPOL *(Pollution maritime)*

MAT *abbr* COMP *(machine-aided translation, machine-assisted translation)* TAO *(traduction assistée par ordinateur)*, GEN COMM *(material)* documentation *f*, informations *f pl*, MATH *(moving annual total) statistics* total annuel mobile *m*

MAWB *abbr (master air waybill)* IMP/EXP, TRANSP lettre de transport aérien groupé *f*

max. *abbr (maximal, maximum)* GEN COMM, MATH max. *(maximal)*

Mb *abbr (megabyte)* COMP Mo *(méga-octet)*

MBA *abbr (Master of Business Administration)* WEL ≈ maîtrise de gestion des entreprises *f*, ≈ titulaire d'une maîtrise de gestion *m*

MBE *abbr UK (Member of the Order of the British Empire)* GEN COMM, POL membre de l'ordre de l'empire britannique

MBIM *abbr (Member of the British Institute of Management)* MGMNT adhérent de l'institut britannique de gestion

MBO *abbr* FIN, GEN COMM *(management buyout)* RES *(rachat d'une entreprise par ses salariés)*, MGMNT *(management by objectives)* DPO *(direction par objectifs)*, MGMNT, STOCK *(management buyout)* RES *(rachat d'une entreprise par ses salariés)*

MBS *abbr (mortgage-backed security)* STOCK titre

de créance hypothécaire *m*, valeur garantie par hypothèque *f*

MBWA *abbr (management by walking around)* MGMNT management baladeur *m*

MC *abbr* INS *(metaling clause, metalling clause)* clause de doublage *f*, TRANSP *(master change)* SCN *(spécification de changement notifié)*, TRANSP *(mobile crane)* grue mobile *f*, grue roulante *f*

MCA *abbr* ECON , FIN *(monetary compensation amount, monetary compensatory amount)* montant compensatoire monétaire *m*, MGMNT *UK (Management Consultants Association)* association des consultants de gestion

M-CATS *abbr (municipal certificate of accrual on treasury securities)* STOCK certificat municipal d'accumulation de bons du Trésor

mcht *abbr (merchant)* HRM marchand *m*

mchy *abbr (machinery)* TRANSP machines *f pl*; **~ aft** *(machinery aft)* TRANSP machines d'arrière *f pl*; **~ fwd** *(machinery forward)* TRANSP machines d'avant *f pl*

mCi *abbr (millicurie)* GEN COMM millicurie *m*

MCO *abbr (miscellaneous charges order)* TRANSP *aviation* bon pour services divers *m*

MCom *abbr (Master of Commerce)* GEN COMM ≈ maîtrise en sciences économiques *f*, ≈ titulaire d'une maîtrise en sciences économiques *m*

MCT *abbr* TRANSP *(moment to change trim)* moment nécessaire pour faire varier l'assiette *m*, TRANSP *(minimum connecting time)* temps minimum de correspondance *m*

MD *abbr* ACC *(managing director)* DG *(directeur général)*, HRM, MGMNT *UK (managing director)* DG *(directeur général)*, PDG *(président-directeur général)*

MDW *abbr (measured daywork)* HRM travail compté *m*, travail à la journée *m*

ME *abbr (main engine)* TRANSP moteur principal *m*

MEC *abbr (marginal efficiency of capital)* ECON efficacité marginale du capital *f*

MEcon *abbr (Master of Economics)* GEN COMM ≈ maîtrise en sciences économiques *f*, ≈ titulaire d'une maîtrise en sciences économiques *m*

mep *abbr (mean effective pressure)* GEN COMM pression effective moyenne *f*

MEP *abbr (Member of the European Parliament)* POL député du Parlement Européen *m*, membre du Parlement Européen *m*

MES *abbr (minimum efficient scale)* ECON échelle minimale d'efficience *f*

met *abbr (measurement)* MATH dimension *f*

MeV *abbr (mega electron volt)* GEN COMM méga-électron-volt *m*

MEW *abbr (measure of economic welfare)* ECON, HRM, WEL mesure de bien-être économique *f*

MFA *abbr* ECON *(Multi-Fiber Arrangement, Multi-Fibre Arrangement)* AMF *(accord multi-fibres)*,

POL *(Ministry of Foreign Affairs)* ≈ ministère des Affaires étrangères *m*

mfd *abbr (manufactured)* GEN COMM, IND fabriqué, manufacturé

MFN *abbr (most-favored nation, most-favoured nation)* ECON nation la plus favorisée *f*

mfrs *abbr (manufacturers)* GEN COMM, IND fabricants *m pl*

mg *abbr (milligram)* GEN COMM milligramme *m*

mgr *abbr (manager)* HRM, MGMNT chef *mf*, dirigeant *m*, gestionnaire *mf*, gérant *m*, manager *m*, responsable *mf*, directeur *m*

MH *abbr* IMP/EXP, TRANSP *(merchant haulage) shipping* acheminement par le négociant *m*, TRANSP *(main hatch) shipping* grand panneau *m*

MHE *abbr (mechanical handling equipment)* TRANSP *cargo* matériel de manutention mécanique *m*

MHWS *abbr (mean high water at springs)* TRANSP *shipping* PM de VE moyenne *(pleine mer de vive-eau moyenne)*

MICA *abbr UK (Member of the Institute of Chartered Accountants)* GEN COMM membre de l'ordre des experts-comptables de Grande Bretagne

MIDA *abbr (maritime industrial development area)* IND zone de développement maritime industriel

MIFT *abbr UK (Manchester International Freight Terminal)* TRANSP terminal de fret international de Manchester *m*

MIMIC *abbr (moderately indebted middle-income country)* ECON, FIN, POL pays à revenu intermédiaire modérément endetté *m*

min. *abbr (minimum)* GEN COMM min. *(minimum)*; **~ B/L** *(minimum bill of lading)* IMP/EXP, TRANSP connaissement minimum *m*

MIP *abbr (marine insurance policy)* INS, TRANSP *marine* police d'assurance maritime *f*

MIS *abbr* COMP, MGMNT *(management information system)* SIG *(système intégré de gestion)*, SIM *(système d'information de management)*, S&M *(marketing information system)* SIM *(système d'information de marketing)*

misc. *abbr (miscellaneous)* ACC, GEN COMM divers *m*

ml *abbr* GEN COMM *(milliliter AmE, millilitre BrE)* ml *(millilitre)*, TRANSP *(motor launch) shipping* canot à moteur *m*, vedette *f*

MLE *abbr (maximum likelihood estimator)* MATH *statistics* estimateur de probabilité maximale *m*

MLH *abbr (minimum list heading)* GEN COMM tête de liste minimale *f*

MLM *abbr (multilevel marketing)* S&M marketing multiniveau *m*, marketing à niveaux multiples *m*, vente par réseau coopté *f*

MLR *abbr UK (minimum lending rate)* BANK, ECON taux officiel d'escompte *m*

MLS *abbr US (Multiple Listing Service)* PROP service de listage multiple *m*

mm *abbr (millimeter AmE, millimetre BrE)* GEN COMM mm *(millimètre)*

MMC *abbr (money-market certificate)* ECON, FIN, STOCK certificat de marché monétaire *m*, instrument du marché monétaire *m*

MMDA *abbr US (money-market deposit account)* FIN compte de dépôt du marché monétaire *m*

MMF *abbr US (money-market fund)* ECON, FIN, STOCK fonds investi au marché monétaire *m*, fonds monétaire *m*

MMI *abbr (Major Market Index)* STOCK indice MMI *m*, I *(indice du marché principal)*

MMMF *abbr US (money-market mutual fund)* FIN fonds commun de placement du marché monétaire *m*

MMSA *abbr (Mercantile Marine Services Association)* GEN COMM, TRANSP association de la marine marchande

mm²/s *abbr (square millimeter per second, square millimetre per second)* GEN COMM mm²/s *(millimètre carré par seconde)*

MNAOA *abbr UK (Merchant Navy and Airline Officers Association)* TRANSP association des officiers de la marine marchande et des lignes aériennes

MNC *abbr (multinational corporation)* ECON, GEN COMM, IND multinationale *f*, société multinationale *f*

MNDO *abbr UK (Merchant Navy Discipline Organisation)* TRANSP service de discipline de la marine marchande

MNE *abbr* ECON, GEN COMM *(multinational enterprise)*, IND *(multinational enterprise)* entreprise multinationale *f*, société multinationale *f*, TRANSP *UK (Merchant Navy Establishment)* établissement de la marine marchande

MNEA *abbr UK (Merchant Navy Establishment Administration)* TRANSP direction d'établissements de la marine marchande

MNOPF *abbr UK (Merchant Navy Officers Pension Fund)* TRANSP, WEL *shipping* caisse de retraite des officiers de la marine marchande

MNTB *abbr UK (Merchant Navy Training Board)* TRANSP comité de formation de la marine marchande

m/o *abbr (my order)* GEN COMM m/o *(mon ordre)*

MO *abbr* ADMIN *(mail order)* VPC *(vente par correspondance)*, BANK *AmE (money order)* MP *(mandat postal)*, COMMS, COMP *(mail order)* VPC *(vente par correspondance)*, FIN *AmE (money order)* MP *(mandat postal)*, GEN COMM *(modus operandi)* mode opératoire *m*, HRM *(medical officer)* médecin *m*, S&M *(mail order)* VPC *(vente par correspondance)*, WEL *(medical officer)* médecin *m*

MOC *abbr (market order on the close)* STOCK ordre au mieux à la clôture *m*, ordre au prix du marché en fin de séance *m*

MOD *abbr UK (Ministry of Defence)* ADMIN ≈ ministère de la Défense *m*, POL ≈ ministère de la Défense nationale *m*

MODU *abbr (mobile offshore drilling unit)* IND unité mobile de drainage pétrolier offshore *f*

MOF *abbr (multioption facility)* STOCK facilité multi-options *f*, facilité à options multiples *f*

MOFF *abbr (multioption financing facility)* STOCK facilité de financement multi-options *f*, facilité de financement à options multiples *f*

MOH *abbr (medical officer of health)* HRM, WEL directeur de la santé publique *m*, médecin départemental *m*, officier de santé *m*

Mon. *abbr (Monday)* GEN COMM lundi *m*

mortg. *abbr (mortgage)* BANK, FIN, PROP hyp. *(hypothèque)*

MOT *abbr* COMMS *UK (Ministry of Transport)* ≈ ministère des Transports *m*, IND *(motor)* moteur *m*, IND *UK (Ministry of Transport)* ≈ ministère des Transports *m*, LEIS *UK (Ministry of Tourism)* ≈ ministère du Tourisme *m*, TRANSP *(motor)* moteur *m*, TRANSP *UK (Ministry of Transport)* ≈ ministère des Transports *m*

MP *abbr (multipurpose)* GEN COMM multi-fonction

MPA *abbr (marginal principle of allocation)* ECON principe marginal d'attribution *m*

MPC *abbr (marginal propensity to consume)* ECON propension marginale à consommer *f*

mpg *abbr (miles per gallon)* GEN COMM miles par gallon, ≈ km au cent *(kilomètres au cent)*

mph *abbr (miles per hour)* GEN COMM miles/heure *m pl*

MPI *abbr (marginal propensity to import)* ECON, IMP/EXP TMI *(tendance marginale à importer)*

MPO *abbr (management and personnel office)* ADMIN, MGMNT bureau de la direction et du personnel *m*

MPP *abbr (marginal physical product)* ECON produit marginal physique *m*

MPS *abbr (marginal propensity to save)* BANK, ECON, FIN propension marginale à épargner *f*

MPT *abbr (modern portfolio theory)* STOCK modern portfolio theory *m*, théorie de gestion moderne de portefeuille *f*

MQS *abbr UK (minimum quote size)* STOCK cours minimal *m*, quotité minimale *f*

MR *abbr (mate's receipt)* IMP/EXP, TRANSP *shipping* bon de chargement *m*, certificat de bord *m*, reçu de bord *m*

MRA *abbr (multiple regression analysis)* ECON, FIN, MATH analyse de régression multiple *f*

MRCA *abbr (Market Research Corporation of America)* S&M société américaine des études de marché

mrem/h *abbr (millirem per hour)* GEN COMM millirem/h *m*, mrem/h *(millirem par heure)*

mr/h *abbr (milliroentgen per hour)* GEN COMM mr/h *(milliröntgen/heure)*

MRO *abbr (maintenance, repair and overhaul)* TRANSP entretien, réparation et révision *loc m*

MRP *abbr (manufacturer's recommended price)* S&M prix public *m*, prix recommandé par le fabriquant *m*

MRR *abbr (minimum reserve requirements)* ECON réserves légales minimales *f pl*, réserves légales minimum *f pl*

MRS *abbr (marginal rate of substitution)* ECON taux marginal de substitution *m*

MRT *abbr (mass rapid transit)* TRANSP transport collectif rapide *m*

m/s *abbr* BANK *(months after sight)* mois à vue *loc*, GEN COMM *(meters per second, metres per second)* m/s *(mètres par seconde)*

MS *abbr* POL *(member state)* EU état-membre *m*, TAX *(manuscript)* MS *(manuscrit)*, TRANSP *(manual system)* système manuel *m*, TRANSP *(machinery survey)* visite des machines *f*, TRANSP *(motor ship)* *shipping* navire à moteur *m*

MSA *abbr* ADMIN *US (Mutual Security Agency)* agence de caution mutuelle, LAW, TRANSP *UK (merchant shipping Act)* loi sur la marine marchande *f*

MSC *abbr* obs *UK (Manpower Services Commission)* HRM commission des services de main d'oeuvre, maintenant Training Agency

MSc *abbr (Master of Science)* WEL ≈ maîtrise de sciences *f*, ≈ titulaire d'une maîtrise de sciences *m*

msca *abbr (missing cargo)* TRANSP marchandises manquantes *f pl*

MS-DOS® *abbr (Microsoft Disk Operating System)* COMP MS-DOS® *m*

MSL *abbr (mean sea level)* TRANSP *shipping* niveau moyen de la mer *m*

mslb *abbr (missing bill of lading)* IMP/EXP, TRANSP connaissement manquant *m*

MT *abbr* COMP *(machine translation)* traduction automatique *f*, ECON *(mail transfer)* international trade transfert par courrier *m*, GEN COMM *(mean time)* temps moyen *m*, GEN COMM *(minimum temperature)* température minimale *f*, GEN COMM *(minimum transfer)* transfert minimum *m*, virement minimum *m*, TRANSP *(motor tanker)* *shipping* bateau-citerne à moteur *m*, navire-citerne à moteur *m*

MTA *abbr (Maltese pound)* GEN COMM livre maltaise *f*

MTBF *abbr (mean time between failures)* TRANSP temps moyen de bon fonctionnement *m*

MTC *abbr (Maritime Transport Committee)* TRANSP commission des Transports Maritimes

MTH *abbr (month)* GEN COMM mois *m*

MTL *abbr* BANK *(medium-term loan)* prêt à moyen terme *m*, TRANSP *(mean tidal level)* *shipping* niveau moyen de la marée *m*

MTN *abbr* ECON *(multilateral trade negotiation)* négociation commerciale multilatérale *f*, FIN *(medium-term note)* BMTN *(bon à moyen terme négociable)*, POL *(multilateral trade negotiation)* négociation commerciale multilatérale *f*

MTO *abbr* HRM, TRANSP *(motor transport officer)* agent de transportation routière *m*, responsable des transports motorisés *m*, TRANSP *(multimodal transport operator)* opérateur multi-transports *m*, transporteur multimodal *m*

mton *abbr (metric ton)* GEN COMM tonne métrique *f*

MTR *abbr (mass transit railroad, mass transit railway)* TRANSP réseau ferroviaire de transport collectif *m*

MV *abbr* TRANSP *(motor merchant vessel)* shipping navire marchand à moteur *m*, TRANSP *(motor vessel)* shipping navire à moteur *m*

MVT *abbr (aircraft movement message)* TRANSP *aviation* message concernant le mouvement des aéronefs *m*

MW *abbr (megawatt)* GEN COMM MW *(mégawatt)*

MYOP *abbr (multiyear operational plan)* FIN plan de développement pluriannuel *m*, plan opérationnel pluriannuel *m*, projet d'exploitation pluriannuel *m*

MYRA *abbr (multiyear rescheduling agreement, multiyear restructuring agreement)* FIN accord de restructuration pluriannuel *m*

n. *abbr (nominal)* GEN COMM en titre *loc m*, n *(nominal)*

N *abbr* GEN COMM *(north)* N *(nord)*, GEN COMM *(new)* neuf, nouveau, TRANSP *(North compass point)* navigation N *(quart nord)*

n/a *abbr* BANK *(no-account)* pas de compte *loc*, GEN COMM *(not applicable)* ne s'applique pas *loc*, non-applicable, sans objet, GEN COMM *(no advice)* sans préavis

NAA *abbr (not always afloat)* TRANSP *shipping* pas toujours à flot *loc*

NAC *abbr (North Atlantic Conference)* TRANSP *shipping* conférence nord-atlantique *f*

NAEGA *abbr (North American Export Grain Association)* GEN COMM Association des exportateurs de céréales d'Amérique du Nord *f*

NAFA *abbr (net acquisition of financial assets)* FIN acquisition nette d'actifs financiers *f*

NAFTA *abbr (North American Free Trade Area)* ECON ALENA *(Accord de libre-échange nord-américain)*

NAHB *abbr* US *(National Association of Home Builders)* PROP Association nationale des entrepreneurs de logements *f*

NALGO *abbr* UK *(National and Local Government Officers Association)* HRM, WEL syndicat des fonctionnaires des collectivités locales

Namas *abbr (National Measurement Accreditation Service)* GEN COMM ≈ Service national des poids et mesures *m*

NAR *abbr* US *(National Association of Realtors)* PROP Association nationale des agents immobiliers *f*

NASA *abbr* TRANSP *(North Atlantic Shippers Association)* association des affréteurs de l'Atlantique nord, TRANSP US *(National Aeronautics and Space Administration)* NASA *f*

NASDAQ *abbr* US *(National Association of Securities Dealers Automated Quotations)* STOCK OTC market cotation automatisée de la société nationale des opérateurs en Bourse

nat. *abbr (national)* GEN COMM nat. *(national)*

NATFHE *abbr* UK *(National Association of Teachers in Further Education)* HRM, WEL association nationale des enseignants de formation continue

NATO *abbr (North Atlantic Treaty Organization)* POL OTAN *(Organisation du Traité de l'Atlantique Nord)*

NAV *abbr (net asset value)* ACC, FIN valeur de l'actif net *f*, valeur patrimoniale nette *f*

NAWFA *abbr (North Atlantic Westbound Freight Association)* TRANSP association des transporteurs de fret à destination de l'ouest de l'Atlantique du Nord

NB *abbr* GEN COMM *(nota bene)* NB *(nota bene)*, TRANSP *(northbound)* nord, à destination nord *loc f*, *(date new boilers fitted)* shipping date d'installation d'une nouvelle chaudière *f*

NBCC *abbr (Nigerian British Chamber of Commerce)* GEN COMM Chambre de commerce britannique au Nigéria *f*

NC *abbr* ECON *(new crop)* agricultural nouvelle récolte *f*, TRANSP *(noncontinuous liner)* shipping navire de ligne à escales *m*, navire régulier à escales *m*

NCAD *abbr (notice of cancellation at anniversary date)* INS avis de résiliation à l'échéance *m*

NCD *abbr (negotiable CD, negotiable certificate of deposit)* BANK, STOCK CDN *(certificat de dépôt négociable)*

NCITD *abbr (National Council on International Trade Documentation)* GEN COMM conseil national de documentation sur les échanges internationaux

NCR *abbr (net cash requirements)* ECON, FIN, STOCK besoins en capital net *m pl*, besoins nets de trésorerie *m pl*

NCS *abbr (noncallable securities)* STOCK titres non-remboursables *m pl*

n.c.v. *abbr* GEN COMM *(no commercial value)* sans valeur commerciale, IMP/EXP *(no customs value)* sans valeur douanière

NCVO *abbr* UK *(National Council of Voluntary Organizations)* ADMIN conseil national des organisations bénévoles

ND *abbr* S&M *(no discount)* pas de rabais *loc*, TRANSP *(new deck)* shipping nouveau pont *m*

NDLB *abbr* UK *(National Dock Labour Board)* HRM conseil national de la main-d'oeuvre portuaire

NDPS *abbr* UK *(National Data Processing Service)* COMMS service national de traitement des informations

NE *abbr* GEN COMM *(north east)* NE *(nord-est)*, GEN COMM *(no effects)* sans effet

NEB *abbr UK (National Environment Board)* ENVIR bureau du conseil national de l'environnement

NEC *abbr UK (National Executive Committee)* POL comité exclusif national

NEP *abbr (New Economic Policy)* ECON *Soviet Union* NPE *(nouvelle politique économique)*

NES *abbr (not elsewhere specified)* GEN COMM non-précisé par ailleurs, non-spécifié par ailleurs

NETC *abbr (no explosion of the total contents)* TRANSP contenu indivisible *m*

NF *abbr* GEN COMM *(no funds)* défaut de provision *m*, POL *UK (National Front)* ≈ FN *(Front National)*

NFA *abbr US (National Futures Association)* STOCK société nationale des opérations à terme

NFAS *abbr (National Federation of American Shipping)* TRANSP fédération nationale de la navigation américaine

NFC *abbr (National Freight Corporation)* TRANSP société internationale de fret

NFTZ *abbr (Non Free Trade Zone)* ECON, GEN COMM, IMP/EXP, POL zone de non libre-échange *f*

NGO *abbr (nongovernmental organization)* GEN COMM ONG *(organisation non-gouvernementale)*

NHP *abbr (nominal horsepower)* GEN COMM puissance nominale *f*

NHS *abbr UK (National Health Service)* HRM, WEL ≈ SS *(France)*, ≈ Sécu *(France, infrml)* *(Sécurité sociale)*

NI *abbr UK (National Insurance)* HRM, WEL sécurité sociale britannique, ≈ Assurance sociale *f (France)*

NIA *abbr (New Investment Authority)* STOCK nouvelle autorité de placement *f*

NIB *abbr (Nordic Investment Bank)* BANK BNI *(Banque nordique d'investissement)*

NIBM1 *abbr (non-interest-bearing M1)* ECON M1 non porteur d'intérêts *m*

NIC *abbr (newly industrialized country)* ECON, IND NPI *(nouveau pays industrialisé)*

NIDL *abbr (new international division of labor AmE, new international division of labour BrE)* ECON nouvelle division internationale du travail *f*

NIEO *abbr (New International Economic Order)* ECON nouvel ordre économique international *m*

NIEs *abbr (newly-industrializing economies)* ECON, IND économies de pays à industrialisation récente *f pl*, économies nouvellement industrialisées *f pl*

NIF *abbr (note issuance facility)* FIN facilité de soutien de programme d'émission d'effets *f*, facilité renouvelable à prise ferme *f*, ligne de crédit ouverte par l'émission de titres à court *f*

NIMBY *abbr (not in my backyard)* ENVIR attitude de celui qui est un faveur d'un projet à condition que celui-ci ne soit pas effectué près de chez lui

NIPA *abbr (National Income and Product Accounts)* ECON *econometrics* comptes de revenu et de produits nationaux *m pl*

NIT *abbr (negative income tax)* TAX impôt négatif sur le revenu *m*

NJ *abbr (New Jason clause)* TRANSP *shipping* clause New Jason *f*

NJC *abbr UK (National Joint Committee)* HRM commission paritaire nationale

NJIC *abbr UK (National Joint Industrial Council)* HRM conseil national paritaire industriel

NL *abbr (no liner)* TRANSP *shipping* hors conférence

NMB *abbr (National Maritime Board)* TRANSP commission maritime nationale

NMS *abbr* STOCK *(National Market System)* système de marché national *m*, système national du marché *m*, STOCK *BrE (normal market size)* quotité normale *f*, taille normale du marché *f*

n.n.p. *abbr (net national product)* ECON PNN *(produit national net)*

NNRF *abbr (non-negotiable report of findings)* GEN COMM compte-rendu non-négociable *m*

no. *abbr (number)* GEN COMM n° *(numéro)*, MATH nombre *m*

nos. *abbr (numbers)* MATH nos *(numéros)*

nop *abbr (not otherwise provided)* GEN COMM non-fourni par ailleurs, non-prévu par ailleurs

NOTO *abbr (nonofficial trade organization)* HRM organisation professionnelle non-répertoriée *f*, organisation professionnelle sans existence officielle *f*, syndicat non-officiel *m*

Nov. *abbr (November)* GEN COMM nov. *(novembre)*

NOW *abbr* BANK *(negotiable order of withdrawal)* compte-chèques rémunéré *m*, ordre de retrait de fonds négociable *m*, ordre de retrait négociable *m*, FIN *US (National Organization for Women)* Organisation nationale des femmes *f*, STOCK *(negotiable order of withdrawal)* compte-chèques rémunéré *m*, ordre de retrait de fonds négociable *m*, ordre de retrait négociable *m*

np *abbr (net proceeds)* GEN COMM, PROP produit net *m*

NPE *abbr (nonprofit enterprise)* ECON entreprise à but non-lucratif *f*

NPV *abbr* ACC *(net present value)*, ECON *(net present value)*, FIN *(net present value)* VAN *(valeur actuelle nette)*, STOCK *(no-par value)* SVN *(sans valeur nominale)*

NR *abbr* ENVIR *(nuclear reactor)* réacteur nucléaire *m*, GEN COMM *(naira)* NR *(naira)*, IND *(nuclear reactor)* réacteur nucléaire *m*, INS *(no risk until confirmed)* pas de risque avant confirmation *loc*

NRAD *abbr (no risk after discharge)* INS acquit libératoire *m*

NRT *abbr* GEN COMM *(net registered tonnage)* tonnage de jauge net *m*, GEN COMM *(net register ton)* tonne de jauge nette *f*, tonneau de jauge nette *m*

NRV *abbr (net realizable value)* ACC, ECON, FIN, S&M valeur réalisable nette *f*

NSA *abbr (non-sterling area)* ECON zone non-sterling *f*

NSB *abbr UK (National Savings Bank)* BANK ≈ CNE *(Caisse nationale d'épargne)*

n.s.f. *abbr (not sufficient funds)* BANK, GEN COMM fonds insuffisants *m pl*, insuffisance de provision *f*

nspf *abbr (not specially provided for)* GEN COMM non-expressément prévu *loc*

NSSN *abbr (national standard shipping note)* IMP/EXP, TRANSP *shipping* note de chargement nationale standard *f*

Nt *abbr* IMP/EXP *(net terms)* bord à bord, TRANSP *(night trunk)* transport de nuit *m*, TRANSP *(net terms) shipping* bord à bord

NTB *abbr (nontariff barrier)* ECON, GEN COMM, IMP/EXP, POL barrière non-douanière *f*, barrière non-tarifaire *f*

NTUC *abbr UK (national trade union council)* HRM Congrès national des syndicats *m*

NUJ *abbr UK (National Union of Journalists)* MEDIA ≈ SNJ *(Syndicat national des journalistes)*

NUM *abbr UK (National Union of Mineworkers)* HRM, IND syndicat national des mineurs *m*

NUPE *abbr UK (National Union of Public Employees)* HRM syndicat national des employés de l'État

NUS *abbr UK (National Union of Seamen)* HRM, TRANSP syndicat national des marins

NVD *abbr (no value declared)* IMP/EXP sans valeur déclarée

NVOC *abbr (non-vessel-operating carrier, non-vessel-owning carrier)* TRANSP *shipping* service de ligne maritime sans navire *m*

NVOCC *abbr (non-vessel-operating common carrier, non-vessel-owning common carrier)* TRANSP service de ligne maritime sans navire *m*

NW *abbr (north west)* GEN COMM NO *(nord-ouest)*

NWC *abbr (National Wages Council)* HRM conseil national des salaires

NYFE *abbr US (New York Futures Exchange)* STOCK Marché des transactions à terme de New York *m*, Marché à terme de New-York *m*

NYME *abbr US (New York Mercantile Exchange)* STOCK marché à terme de produits pétroliers et de platine de New York

NYMEX *abbr US (New York Mercantile Exchange)* STOCK marché à terme de produits pétroliers et de platine de New York

NYPLR *abbr US (New York prime loan rate)* BANK taux de prêt préférentiel de New York *m*, taux préférentiel de New York *m*

NYSA *abbr US (New York Shipping Association)* TRANSP association maritime de New York

NYSE *abbr US (New York Stock Exchange)* STOCK la bourse de New York

O *abbr (outboard)* TRANSP *shipping, motor* hors-bord

o/a *abbr* GEN COMM *(on account of)* en raison de *loc f*, à cause de *f*, GEN COMM *(overall)* total

OA *abbr (office automation)* ADMIN, COMP, IND bureautique *f*

OAG *abbr (official airline guide)* TRANSP *aviation* consignes officielles d'une compagnie d'aviation *f pl*

O&M *abbr (organization and methods)* GEN COMM, HRM, MGMNT organisation scientifique du travail *f*, OM *(organisation et méthodes)*

OAP *abbr BrE (old age pensioner)* GEN COMM, HRM, WEL retraité *m*

OARS *abbr (Opening Automated Report System)* STOCK système de rapport automatisé d'ouverture

OAS *abbr (Organization of American States)* ECON, WEL Organisation des états américains *f*

OASDHI *abbr US (old age, survivors, disability and health insurance)* INS ≈ ASIRGD *(Assurance santé-invalidité-retraite et garantie-décès)*

OAU *abbr (Organization of African Unity)* ECON OUA *(Organisation de l'unité africaine)*

OBE *abbr (Officer of the Order of the British Empire)* GEN COMM officier de l'ordre de l'empire britannique

OBO *abbr (order book official)* STOCK spécialiste de certains marchés d'options

OBS *abbr (off-balance-sheet)* ACC, FIN hors bilan

OBU *abbr (offshore banking unit)* BANK, FIN, TAX *investment* succursale extraterritoriale *f*, succursale offshore *f*

OC *abbr* GEN COMM *(overcharge)* majoration *f*, surcharge *f*, IND *(oil-bearing continuous liner)* pétrolier de ligne sans escales *m*, INS *(open cover)* police ouverte *f*, S&M *(overcharge)* majoration *f*, surcharge *f*, TRANSP *(open charter)* affrètement ouvert *m*, charter ouvert *m*, TRANSP *(old charter)* ancien affrètement *m*, vieux charter *m*, TRANSP *(oil-bearing continuous liner)* pétrolier de ligne sans escales *m*

OCAS *abbr (Organization of Central American States)* ECON, POL Organisation des États de l'Amérique Centrale

OCC *abbr (options clearing corporation)* STOCK société de compensation d'actions *f*, société de compensation des options *f*

OCD *abbr (other checkable deposits)* BANK autres dépôts vérifiables *m pl*

OCR *abbr (optical character recognition)* COMP ROC *(reconnaissance optique des caractères)*

Oct. *abbr (October)* GEN COMM oct. *(octobre)*

O/D *abbr* BANK *(overdraft)* découvert *m*, découvert bancaire *m*, BANK *(overdrawn)* à découvert *loc m*

ODA *abbr UK (Overseas Development Administration)* ECON, POL ≈ Organisme du développement outre-mer *m*

ODI *abbr UK (Overseas Development Institute)* ECON, POL ≈ Institut du développement outre-mer *m*

ODM *abbr (Ministry of Overseas Development)*

ECON ministère du développement outre-mer, POL ministère du développement outre-mer

OEC *abbr (overpaid entry certificate)* IMP/EXP certificat d'entrée trop perçue *m*

OECD *abbr (Organization for Economic Cooperation and Development)* ECON OCDE *(Organisation de coopération et de développement économique)*

OECF *abbr (Overseas Economic Cooperation Fund)* ECON fonds de coopération économique outre-mer

OEEC *abbr (Organization for European Economic Cooperation)* ECON OECE *(Organisation européenne de coopération économique)*

OEIC *abbr (open-end investment company)* FIN, STOCK FCP *(fonds commun de placement)*, SICAV *(société d'investissement à capital variable)*

OF *abbr (open full)* TRANSP plein ouvert

Ofgas *abbr UK (Office of Gas Supply)* ADMIN service du Gaz

OFT *abbr UK (Office of Fair Trading)* ECON ≈ Direction de la concurrence, de la consommation et de la répression de fraudes *f (Fra)*

OGIL *abbr (open general import licence BrE, open general import license AmE)* IMP/EXP licence ouverte d'importation générale *f*

OGM *abbr (ordinary general meeting)* GEN COMM, MGMNT, STOCK AGO *(assemblée générale ordinaire)*

OHMS *abbr (On Her Majesty's Service)* COMMS, GEN COMM au service de sa Majesté *loc m*

OID *abbr (original issue discount)* FIN, STOCK escompte de première émission *m*, prime d'émission *f*

OILSR *abbr US (Office of Interstate Land Sales Registration)* PROP bureau d'inscription cadastre des ventes immobilières interétat *m*

OIT *abbr (Office of International Trade)* GEN COMM Bureau de commerce international *m*

OJ *abbr (Official Journal)* ECON EU JO *(Journal officiel)*

OJT *abbr (on-the-job training)* HRM formation dans l'entreprise *f*, formation en entreprise *f*, formation sur le tas *f*, formation sur le terrain *f*, formation sur site *f*, stage en centre de formation *m*

OLB *abbr (official logbook)* TRANSP *shipping* journal réglementaire *m*, livre de bord *m*

OLG *abbr (overlapping generations model)* ECON théorème d'équivalence de Ricardo *m*

OM *abbr (options market)* STOCK marché à options *m*

OMA *abbr (orderly market agreement)* ECON, STOCK accord de régulation du marché *m*

OMB *abbr US (Office of Management and Budget)* MGMNT service du gouvernement américain en charge de la préparation du budget

on *abbr (official no., official number)* TRANSP numéro d'immatriculation *m*, numéro officiel *m*

ono *abbr (or nearest offer)* MEDIA, S&M à débattre

O/o *abbr* GEN COMM *(order of)* commande de *loc f*, l'ordre de *loc*, TRANSP *(ore-oil ship)* pétrolier-minéralier *m*

OOG *abbr (out of gage AmE, out of gauge BrE)* TRANSP engagement du gabarit *m*

OP *abbr* INS *(open policy)* police d'abonnement *f*, police flottante *f*, police maritime flottante *f*, MEDIA *(out of print)* épuisé, TRANSP *(open policy)* police d'abonnement *f*, police flottante *f*, police maritime flottante *f*

OPCS *abbr UK (Office of Population Censuses and Surveys)* WEL bureau des recensements et enquêtes de population

OPEC *abbr (Organization of Petroleum Exporting Countries)* ECON, ENVIR, POL OPEP *(Organisation des pays exportateurs de pétrole)*

OPM *abbr (other peoples' money)* FIN vente fictive d'obligations *f*, STOCK fonds empruntés *m pl*

OR *abbr* GEN COMM *(operational research)* RO *(recherche opérationnelle)*, INS *(owner's risk)* aux risques et périls du freteur *loc m*, MGMNT, S&M *(operational research)* RO *(recherche opérationnelle)*, TRANSP *(owner's risk)* shipping aux risques et périls du freteur *loc m*, TRANSP *(open registry) shipping* libre immatriculation *f*

ord. *abbr (order, order of the court)* LAW arrêt *m*, commande *f*, injonction *f*, jugement *m*, ordonnance *f*, ordre *m*

org. *abbr (organization)* ADMIN, GEN COMM ordonnance *f*, organisme *m*, LEIS organisme *m*

o.s. *abbr* COMP *(operation system)* système d'exploitation *m*, ECON *(out of stock)* épuisé, GEN COMM *(out of stock)* en rupture de stock *loc f*, épuisé, S&M *(out of stock)* en rupture de stock *loc f*, manque en magasin *m*, épuisé

OSD *abbr (open-shelter deck)* TRANSP *shipping* navire à pont-abri ouvert *m*

OSI *abbr (open-systems interconnection)* COMP ISO *(interconnexion de systèmes ouverts)*

ost *abbr (ordinary spring tide)* TRANSP marée de VE *f (marée de vive-eau)*

ot *abbr (on track)* TRANSP en voie *loc f*

OT *abbr* HRM *(overtime)* heures supp' *f pl (infrml)*, HS *(heures supplémentaires)*, TRANSP *(open-top container, open-topped container)* conteneur à toit ouvert *m*, TRANSP *(oiltight) shipping* étanche au pétrole, étanche aux hydrocarbures

OTAR *abbr (overseas tariff and regulations)* IMP/EXP tarif et réglementations extérieurs *loc m*

OTC *abbr* ECON *(Organization for Trade Cooperation) international* Organisation pour la coopération commerciale *f*, STOCK US *(over-the-counter)* hors cote, titre de hors-cote *m*, WEL *(over-the-counter)* medication sans ordonnance

OTCM *abbr US (over-the-counter market)* ECON, STOCK marché de gré à gré *m*, marché hors cote *m*

OTH *abbr (opportunities to hear)* MEDIA, S&M *advertising, radio* occasions d'entendre *f pl*

OTM *abbr (out-of-the-money)* STOCK en dehors, hors du cours, hors-jeu

OTS *abbr* ECON *UK (Overseas Trade Statistics)* Statistiques du commerce extérieur *f pl*, MEDIA *(opportunities to see) advertising, television* occasions de voir *f pl*, POL *UK (Overseas Trade Statistics)* Statistiques du commerce extérieur *f pl*, S&M *(opportunities to see) advertising, television* occasions de voir *f pl*

our: ~ **ref.** *abbr (our reference)* GEN COMM n/réf *(notre référence)*, nos rf. *(nos référence)*

over *abbr* FIN en excès *loc m*

oz *abbr (ounce)* GEN COMM once *f*

p *abbr (pence)* GEN COMM pence *m*; ~ **to p** *(port to port)* IMP/EXP, TRANSP *shipping* port à port *loc m*

p.a. *abbr* GEN COMM *(per annum)* p.a. *(par an)*, INS *(particular average) marine* avarie particulière *f*, avarie partielle *f*

PA *abbr* ADMIN *(power of attorney)* procuration *f*, HRM *(personal assistant)* assistant personnel *m*, secrétaire de direction *m*, secrétaire particulier *m*, LAW *(power of attorney)* procuration *f*, MGMNT *(personal assistant)* assistant personnel *m*, secrétaire de direction *m*, secrétaire particulier *m*

PABX *abbr UK (private automatic branch exchange)* COMMS *telephone* autocommutateur privé *m*

PAI *abbr (performance appraisal interview)* HRM entretien d'évaluation *m*, interview d'évaluation des performances *f*

PAL *abbr* FIN *(program adjustment loan AmE, programme adjustment loan BrE)* prêt-programme d'ajustement *m*, MEDIA *(phase alternation line) TV* PAL *m*

P&L *abbr (profit and loss)* ACC *annual accounts* P et P *(pertes et profits)*

p&p *abbr (postage and packing)* COMMS frais de port et d'emballage *m pl*, port et emballage *m pl*

P&R *abbr (park and ride)* TRANSP P.R. *(parc relais)*

P&S *abbr (purchase and sale statement)* STOCK état des achats et des ventes *m*

PANTRAC *abbr (Pan-American Tracing and Reservations System)* TRANSP *aviation* pan-américain système de tracement et des réservations *m*

PAR *abbr (prescribed aggregate reserve)* BANK réserve globale visée par règlement *f*, RTP

pat. *abbr (patent)* GEN COMM brevet *m*, LAW *property*, PATENTS brevet *m*, brevet d'invention *m*

pat.: ~ **pend.** *abbr (patent pending)* LAW brevet dont l'homologation est en cours *m*, brevet déposé *m*, PATENTS brevet déposé *m*, demande de brevet déposée *f*

Pat.: ~ **Off.** *abbr UK (Patent Office)* PATENTS Office des Brevets du Royaume-Uni

PAYE *abbr* ACC *AmE (Payables at Year-End)*

CAPAFE *(comptes à payer à la fin de l'exercice)*, ACC *UK (pay as you earn)*, HRM *UK (pay as you earn)*, TAX *UK (pay as you earn)* retenue de l'impôt sur le revenu à la source *f*

PB *abbr* TRANSP *(poop and bridge) shipping* château-dunette *m*, dunette et passerelle *f pl*, TRANSP *(permanent ballast) shipping* lest fixe *m*, lest permanent *m*, TRANSP *(permanent bunker) shipping* soute fixe *f*, soute permanente *f*

PBA *abbr (paid by agent)* TRANSP *shipping* réglé par l'agent

PBDS *abbr UK (Publishers and Booksellers Delivery Service)* MEDIA ≈ Service de messagerie des éditeurs et libraires *m*

PBF *abbr (poop, bridge and forecastle)* TRANSP *shipping* gaillard-château-dunette *m*

PBH *abbr (partial bulkhead)* TRANSP *shipping* cloison partielle *f*

PBR *abbr (payment by results)* HRM paiement en fonction des résultats *m*, salaire au rendement *m*, salaire basé sur le rendement *m*, salaire en fonction des résultats *m*

PBS *abbr US (Public Broadcasting System)* MEDIA services de radio-télévision publics

PBX *abbr UK (private branch exchange)* COMMS *telephone* autocommutateur privé *m*

pc *abbr* ACC *(petty cash)*, FIN *(petty cash)* menue monnaie *f*, petite caisse *f*, GEN COMM *(piece)* pièce *f*, HRM *(petty cash)* menue monnaie *f*, petite caisse *f*, MATH *(per cent)* p., p. cent *(pour cent)*, TRANSP *(platform crane)* grue plate-forme *f*

p.c. *abbr (current price)* FIN prix courant *m*, tarif *m*

PC *abbr* COMP *(personal computer)* OP *(ordinateur personnel)*, LAW *UK (Privy Council)* conseil privé, TRANSP *(passenger certificate)* certificat de transport de passagers *m*

PCC *abbr* ECON *(price consumption curve)* courbe de consommation déterminée par le prix *f*, TRANSP *(pure car carrier) shipping* transporteur d'automobiles *m*

PCT *abbr (Patent Cooperation Treaty)* LAW, PATENTS *intellectual property* traité de coopération relatif aux brevets d'invention *m*

PCTC *abbr (pure car and truck carrier)* TRANSP *shipping* transporteur d'automobiles et de camions *m*

pd *abbr* COMMS *(postdated)* postdaté, FIN *(paid) amount, dividend* acquitté, payé, versé, HRM *(paid) person, work* payé, rémunéré, IMP/EXP *(port dues)*, TRANSP *(port dues) shipping* droits de port *m pl*

PDI *abbr* ECON *(personal disposable income)* revenu disponible des particuliers *m*, revenu personnel disponible *m*, TRANSP *(predelivery inspection)* contrôle avant livraison *m*

PDM *abbr (physical distribution management)* MGMNT, TRANSP gestion de la distribution physique *f*

PDZ *abbr* (*priority development zone*) ECON, HRM, PROP ZUP (*zone à urbaniser en priorité*)

PEP *abbr UK* (*personal equity plan*) FIN, STOCK plan d'épargne en actions *m*, plan personnel de capitalisation *m*

per: ~ **pro.** *abbr frml* (*per procurationem*) GEN COMM p.p. (*par procuration*)

PER *abbr* (*price-earnings ratio*) ACC, FIN, STOCK CCR (*coefficient de capitalisation des résultats*)

PERL *abbr* (*public enterprise rationalization loan, public enterprise reform loan, public enterprise rehabilitation loan*) FIN PREP (*prêt à la rationalisation des entreprises publiques*)

PEWP *abbr UK* (*Public Expenditure White Paper*) ECON livre blanc sur les dépenses publiques

PF *abbr* (*poop and forecastle*) TRANSP *shipping* gaillard-dunette *m*

PFI *abbr* (*position-finding instrument*) TRANSP *shipping* radiogoniomètre *m*

PFP *abbr* (*policy framework paper*) ECON, STOCK DCPE (*document-cadre de politique économique*)

pg. *abbr* (*page*) COMP, GEN COMM p. (*page*)

PG *abbr* (*paying guest*) GEN COMM hôte payant *m*, pensionnaire *m*

PGCE *abbr UK* (*Postgraduate Certificate of Education*) WEL ≈ CAPES (*Certificat d'aptitude au professorat d'enseignement du second degré*)

PHA *abbr* (*port health authority*) TRANSP, WEL autorité portuaire de la santé *f*

PHC *abbr US* (*personal holding company*) TAX société individuelle de portefeuille *f*

PhD *abbr* (*Doctor of Philosophy*) WEL doctorat *m*

PHLX *abbr US* (*Philadelphia Stock Exchange*) STOCK Bourse de Philadelphie

PIBOR *abbr* (*Paris Interbank Offered Rate*) BANK TIOP (*taux interbancaire offert à Paris*)

PIBs *abbr* (*permanent income-bearing share*) STOCK obligation non-amortissable des building sociétés *f*

PIF *abbr* (*purchase issue facility*) STOCK facilité d'émission d'achat *f*

PIN *abbr* (*personal identification number*) BANK NIP (*numéro d'identification personnel*)

PIOPIC *abbr* (*Protection & Indemnity of Oil Pollution Indemnity Clause*) ENVIR protection et indemnité de la clause d'indemnité de la pollution par les hydrocarbures

PKD *abbr* (*partially knocked down*) TRANSP *consignment* partiellement déchargé

pkg *abbr* (*package*) COMMS colis *m*, paquet *m*, COMP progiciel *m*, train *m*, FIN *of grants, incentives*, MGMNT *of deals, proposals*, POL *of reforms* ensemble *m*, S&M *advertising, direct mail* paquet promotionnel *m*

pkg. *abbr* (*packaging*) GEN COMM emballage *m*, S&M conditionnement *m*, emballage *m*, *set of items sold as one* lot *m*, TRANSP conditionnement *m*, emballage *m*; ~ **instr.** (*packing instruction*) TRANSP instruction relative à l'emballage *f*

pkt. *abbr* (*packet*) GEN COMM paquet *m*

PL *abbr* INS (*partial loss*) dommages partiels *m pl*, perte partielle *f*, sinistre partiel *m*, TRANSP (*payload*) CU (*charge utile*), TRANSP (*protective location*) *of oil tanker* localisation défensive *f*

PLA *abbr* (*Port of London Authority*) GEN COMM port autonome de Londres

plc *abbr UK* (*public limited company*) GEN COMM société à responsabilité limitée *f* (*SARL*), SA

PLC *abbr* (*product life cycle*) ECON, IND, S&M marketing CVP (*cycle de vie d'un produit*)

PLR *abbr* (*public lending right*) MEDIA droits compensant un auteur sur le prêt de ses ouvrages en bibliothèque

PLTC *abbr* (*port liner terms charge*) TRANSP *shipping* frais de manutention à la charge de la marchandise *m pl*

pm *abbr* (*post meridiem*) GEN COMM après-midi

PM *abbr* (*prime minister*) POL Premier ministre *m*

PMSA *abbr US* (*primary metropolitan statistical area*) GEN COMM zone primaire de statistique métropolitaine *f*

PMTS *abbr* (*predetermined motion time system*) ECON, FIN, MGMNT PMTS (*méthode des temps prédéterminés*)

PN *abbr* (*promissory note*) BANK, FIN B/. (*billet à ordre*)

PNQ *abbr UK* (*private notice question*) POL question posée au Premier ministre dans la Chambre des Communes

PO *abbr* BANK *BrE* (*postal order*) MP (*mandat postal*), COMMS (*post office*) b. de p. (*bureau de poste*), FIN *BrE* (*postal order*) MP (*mandat postal*)

POA *abbr* (*place of acceptance*) TRANSP lieu de réception *m*

POB *abbr* (*post office box*) COMMS BP (*boîte postale*)

POD *abbr* FIN (*proof of debt*) justification de dette *f*, titre de créances *m*, GEN COMM (*proof of delivery*), TRANSP (*proof of delivery*) justification de livraison *f*, TRANSP (*place of delivery*) lieu de livraison *m*, réception *f*, TRANSP (*paid on delivery*) paiement à la livraison *loc m*

pon *abbr* (*pontoon*) TRANSP *shipping* ponton *m*

P-1 *abbr* (*prime paper*) FIN, STOCK papier commercial de premier ordre *m*

POO *abbr* (*port operations officer*) HRM, TRANSP responsable des opérations portuaires *m*

POP *abbr* (*post office preferred*) COMMS formats postaux normalisés *m pl*

POS *abbr* (*point of sale*) S&M LV (*lieu de vente*), PV (*point de vente*)

POST *abbr* (*point-of-sale terminal*) S&M TPV (*terminal point de vente*)

p.p. *abbr* COMMS (*post-paid, postage paid*) p.p. (*port payé*), GEN COMM (*per procuration*) p.p. (*par procuration*), GEN COMM (*post-paid, postage* paid) p.p. *(port payé)*, GEN COMM *(pages)* p.p. *(pages)*

pp *abbr (picked ports)* TRANSP *shipping* ports de cueillette *m pl*

pp. *abbr (prepaid)* GEN COMM payé d'avance, prépayé

PPB *abbr (planning, programming, budgeting)* POL planification, programmation, budgétisation *f pl*

PPBS *abbr (planning, programming, budgeting system)* ACC, FIN, HRM, MGMNT RCB *(rationalisation des choix budgétaires)*

PPI *abbr* ACC *(producer price index)* indice des prix à la production *m*, COMMS *(postage-paid impression)* pré-impression *f*, ECON *(producer price index) econometrics* indice des prix à la production *m*, GEN COMM *(postage-paid impression)*, IMP/EXP *(postage-paid impression)* pré-impression *f*, INS *(policy proof of interest) marine* police de justification d'intérêt *f*, police preuve de l'intérêt assuré *f*

ppm *abbr (parts per million)* GEN COMM p.p.m. *(partie par million)*

PPP *abbr* ECON *(purchasing power parity)* PPA *(parité du pouvoir d'achat)*, FIN *(profit and performance planning)*, MGMNT *(profit and performance planning)* prévision de bénéfices et de performances *f*, WEL *(Private Patients Plan)* programme hospitalier de clientèle privée

PPS *abbr* POL UK *(parliamentary private secretary)* parlementaire attaché à un ministre, TRANSP *(precise positioning service) shipping, satellite navigation* service de positionnement précis *m*

PQLI *abbr (physical quality of life index)* ECON *econometrics* qualité physique de l'indice de vie *f*

pr. *abbr (price)* ECON px *(prix)*, valeur *f*, GEN COMM px *(prix)*, STOCK cours *m*

PR *abbr* POL *(proportional representation)* RP *(représentation proportionnelle)*, S&M *(public relations) advertising* RP *(relations publiques)*

PRA *abbr (purchase and resale agreement)* STOCK accord de prise en pension *m*, faculté d'achat et de revente *f*, prise en pension *f*

pref. *abbr (preference)* GEN COMM préf. *(préférence)*

Pres. *abbr (President)* POL président *m*

PRO *abbr (public relations officer)* HRM, S&M chef du service des relations publiques *m*, directeur des relations publiques *m*, responsable des relations publiques *m*

PROBO *abbr (product/oil/bulk/ore carrier)* TRANSP *shipping* pétrolier-vraquier-minéralier-transporteur de produits *m*

Prof *abbr (Professor)* HRM prof *(professeur)*

prom: ~ dk *abbr (promenade deck)* TRANSP *shipping* pont promenade *m*

PRP *abbr* ACC *(profit-related pay)* salaire lié aux bénéfices *m*, HRM *(performance-related pay)* salaire au rendement *m*

PRT *abbr (petroleum revenue tax)* TAX impôt sur les revenus pétroliers *m*

PS *abbr* COMMS *(postscript)* PS *(post-scriptum)*, HRM *(personal secretary)*, MGMNT *(personal secretary)* assistant personnel *m*, secrétaire de direction *m*, secrétaire particulier *m*, TRANSP *(paddle steamer)* bateau à aubes *m*, propulseur de babord et de tribord *m*

PSBR *abbr* UK *(public sector borrowing requirement)* ECON, FIN besoins de financement du secteur public *m pl*

PSDR *abbr* UK *(public sector debt repayment)* ECON remboursement de la dette de l'État *m*, remboursement de la dette publique *m*

PSE *abbr (public service employment)* HRM emploi dans la fonction publique *m*

P/Sec *abbr (personal secretary)* HRM, MGMNT assistant personnel *m*, secrétaire de direction *m*, secrétaire particulier *m*

psf *abbr (per square foot)* PROP ≈ le mètre carré *m*

PSI *abbr (pounds per square inch)* TRANSP livres par pouce carré *f pl*

PSL *abbr (private sector liquidity)* ECON liquidité du secteur privé *f*

PSV *abbr (public service vehicle)* TRANSP véhicule de transport public *m*

pt *abbr (pint)* GEN COMM chopine *f (Can)*, pint *m*, pinte *f*

pta. *abbr (peseta)* GEN COMM pta. *(peseta)*

PTA *abbr (prepaid ticket advice)* TRANSP avis de billet prépayé *m*

PTL *abbr (partial/total loss)* INS perte partielle ou totale *f*

PTO *abbr (please turn over)* COMMS TSVP *(tournez s'il vous plaît)*

PUD *abbr (planned unit development)* PROP aménagement d'unité planifiée *m*

PUF *abbr (purchase underwriting facility)* FIN, INS mécanisme de garantie d'achat *m*

p.v. *abbr (par value)* STOCK parité *f*, valeur au pair *f*, valeur nominale *f*

P/V *abbr* ACC, FIN *(profit/volume ratio)* rapport profit et changement de quantités vendues *m*, rapport profit sur ventes *m*, ratio de volume de bénéfices *m*

PWB *abbr (permanent water ballast)* TRANSP *shipping* lest d'eau fixe *m*, lest liquide permanent *m*

PYO *abbr (pick-your-own)* GEN COMM *farm produce* cueillette à la ferme *f*

PYT *abbr (payment)* BANK, FIN, GEN COMM versement *m*

Q *abbr (quadruple expansion engine)* TRANSP *shipping* machine à quadruple expansion *f*

QA *abbr (quality assurance)* IND, MGMNT, S&M assurance de la qualité *f*, contrôle de la qualité *m*

QC *abbr* HRM UK *(Queen's Counsel)* avocat de la Couronne, ≈ bâtonnier de l'ordre *m*, IND *(quality* *control)* contrôle de la qualité *m*, LAW *UK (Queen's Counsel)* avocat de la Couronne, ≈ bâtonnier de l'ordre *m*, MGMNT *(quality control)*, S&M *(quality control)* contrôle de la qualité *m*

Qco *abbr (quantity at captain's option)* TRANSP *shipping* quantité à l'avantage du navire *f*

QL *abbr (query language)* COMP langage d'interrogation *m*, langage de requête *m*

qnty *abbr (quantity)* GEN COMM, MATH qté *(quantité)*

QPC *abbr (quasi-propulsive coefficient)* TRANSP *of engine* rendement propulsif *m*

QR *abbr (quantitative restriction)* ECON, IND restriction quantitative *f*

QST *abbr (Quebec sales tax)* TAX TVQ *(taxe de vente de Quebec)*

qt. *abbr* GEN COMM *(quantity)* qté *(quantité)*, GEN COMM *(quart)* quart *m*, MATH *(quantity)* qté *(quantité)*

qtr *abbr (quarter)* GEN COMM quart *m*

qv *abbr (quod vide)* GEN COMM, MEDIA *print* voir

QWL *abbr (quality of working life)* HRM qualité de la vie active *f*, qualité de la vie au travail *f*, qualité de la vie professionnelle *f*

R *abbr* GEN COMM *(riveted)* fixé, riveté, GEN COMM *(reconditioned)* remis à neuf *loc*, rénové, GEN COMM *(refrigerated)* réfrigéré, PROP *(reconditioned)* rénové, TRANSP *(refrigerated container)* conteneur frigorifique *m*, TRANSP *(refrigeration)* réfrigération *f*, TRANSP *(refrigerated)* réfrigéré, TRANSP *(reduce class rate)* air freight classification* tarif de classification avec réduction *m*

R/A *abbr (refer to acceptor)* GEN COMM voir le tiré

RAD *abbr (raised afterdeck)* TRANSP *shipping* pont arrière surélevé *m*

RAFT *abbr (revolving acceptance facility by tender)* FIN acceptation renouvelable par offre

RAM *abbr (random access memory)* COMP mémoire RAM *f*, mémoire vive *f*

RAN *abbr (revenue anticipation note)* STOCK avis fiscal anticipé *m*

R&CC *abbr (riots and civil commotions)* WEL émeutes et troubles de l'ordre public *m pl*

R&D *abbr (research and development)* IND R&D *(recherche et développement)*

RAT *abbr (ready assets trusts)* STOCK trusts d'actifs disponibles *m pl*

RATS *abbr (Restricted Articles Terminal System)* TRANSP *IATA* système de terminal pour articles réglementés *m*

RB *abbr* TRANSP *(rubber bearing)* roulement en caoutchouc *m*, TRANSP *(raised bridge)* shipping* passerelle surélevée *f*

RBT *abbr (rebuilt)* GEN COMM reconstruit

RC *abbr* TRANSP *(return cargo)* cargaison de retour *f*, TRANSP *(reversing gear clutch)* embrayage de renversement de marche *m*

RCC *abbr UK (Rural Community Council)* POL conseil intercommunal en zone rurale

RCCA *abbr (route capacity control airline)* TRANSP transporteur aérien pour le contrôle de la capacité des routes *m*

rcvd *abbr (received)* GEN COMM pour acquit *loc m*, reçu

Rd *abbr (running day)* TRANSP jour courant *m*, jours consécutifs *m pl*

Rd. *abbr (road)* TRANSP route *f (r.)*

RD *abbr* BANK *(refer to drawer)* retour au tiroir *loc m*, voir le tireur, ECON *(reserve deposit)* dépôt de couverture bancaire *m*, réserve obligatoire *f*

RDA *abbr UK (rural development area)* ECON zone d'aménagement rural *f*, zone de développement rural *f*

RDB *abbr (relational database)* COMP BDR *(base de données relationnelles)*

RDBTN *abbr (round bottom)* TRANSP *of ship* fond rond *m*

RDC *abbr (running down clause)* INS *marine* clause d'abordage *f*

RDF *abbr (radio direction finder)* TRANSP radiogoniomètre *m*

Rdk *abbr (raised deck)* TRANSP *shipping* pont surélevé *m*

RDS *abbr US (rural delivery service)* COMMS service de livraisons gratuites en zone rurale *m*

RE *abbr* ECON *(rational expectations)* anticipations rationnelles *f pl*, prévisions rationnelles *f pl*, STOCK *UK (Royal Exchange)* bourse de commerce de Londres

REART *abbr (restricted articles)* TRANSP *aviation* article réglementé *m*

recmd *abbr (recommissioned)* GEN COMM réintégré

recpt *abbr (receipt)* BANK, FIN reçu *m*, GEN COMM quittance *f*, reçu *m*, récépissé *m*, S&M reçu *m*, récépissé *m*, STOCK reçu *m*, TRANSP reçu *m*, récépissé *m*

red. *abbr (redeemable)* ACC, STOCK amortissable, rachetable, remb. *(remboursable)*

REDS *abbr UK (Registered Excise Dealers and Shippers)* IMP/EXP ≈ commissionnaires en douane et transitaires *m pl*

ref. *abbr* GEN COMM *(reference)* rf. *(référence)*, TRANSP *(reefer carrier, reefer ship)* shipping* cargo frigorifique *m*, navire polytherme *m*

regd. *abbr (registered)* COMMS *mail* r. *(recommandér)*

REIT *abbr US (real estate investment trust)* BANK fonds de placements immobiliers *m*, STOCK SCPI *(société civile de placement immobilier)*

Rentcon *abbr (Rent-a-Container)* TRANSP société de location de conteneurs

Rep. *abbr US (Representative)* POL député *mf*, représentant *m*

REP *abbr (regional employment premium)* HRM indemnité d'emploi régional *f*, prime à l'emploi régional *f*

REPO *abbr AmE (repurchase agreement)* FIN contrat de vente à réméré *m*, STOCK contrat de vente à réméré *m*, mise en pension *f*, pension livrée *f*, prise en pension *f*

rept *abbr (receipt)* BANK, FIN reçu *m*, GEN COMM quittance *f*, reçu *m*, récépissé *m*, S&M reçu *m*, récépissé *m*, STOCK reçu *m*, TRANSP reçu *m*, récépissé *m*

REV *abbr (reversing)* GEN COMM renversement *m*

rf *abbr (rise of floor)* TRANSP acculement *m*, relevé des varangues *m*

RFC *abbr (request for change)* TRANSP réaménagement *m*, *aviation* RFC *(requêt formulée par le client)*

RFD *abbr (raised foredeck)* TRANSP *shipping* demigaillard *m*

RFR *abbr (required freight rate)* TRANSP tarif marchandises demandé *m*

RHA *abbr UK (Road Haulage Association)* TRANSP association britannique des transports routiers

RHV *abbr (road haulage vehicle)* TRANSP poids lourd *m*

RIC *abbr (rehabilitation import credit)* ECON, FIN crédit à l'importation pour le redressement économique *m*

RIE *abbr* STOCK *(recognized investment exchange)* marché d'investissement agréé *m*, STOCK *UK (Registered International Exchange)* échanges internationaux autorisés *m pl*

RIF *abbr (reduction in force)* HRM réduction d'emplois secondaires *f*, suppression d'emplois *f*

RIL *abbr (rehabilitation import loan)* FIN emprunt de redressement *m*, prêt de l'importation pour le redressement économique *m*

RIN *abbr UK (Royal Institute of Navigation)* TRANSP institut britannique de la navigation

RK *abbr (rubbing keel)* TRANSP *shipping* fausse quille *f*

RN *abbr (release note)* TRANSP *cargo* bordereau de livraison *m*

RNR *abbr (rate not reported)* TRANSP tarif nonrépertorié *m*

RNS *abbr UK (Regulatory News Service)* STOCK service d'information relative à la réglementation, ≈ chronoval *m*

RO *abbr* GEN COMM *(receiving office)* bureau de messageries *m*, bureau de réception *m*, PATENTS *(receiving office)* office récepteur *m*, TRANSP *(receiving order)* ordonnance de mise sous séquestre *f*, TRANSP *(routing order) cargo* bordereau d'acheminement *m*

ROA *abbr (return on assets)* FIN rendement des fonds propres *m*

ROB *abbr (remain on board)* TRANSP *cargo* reste à bord *loc m*

ROC *abbr (return on capital)* ACC, ECON, FIN rendement du capital *m*

ROCE *abbr (return on capital employed)* ACC, ECON, FIN RCI *(rentabilité des capitaux investis)*

ROE *abbr (return on equity)* ACC, FIN, STOCK rendement de l'action *m*, rendement des capitaux propres *m*, rendement des fonds propres *m*

ROG *abbr (receipt of goods)* TRANSP *cargo* réception des marchandises *f*

ROI *abbr (return on investment)* ACC, FIN TRI *(taux de rentabilité d'un investissement)*, rendement des actifs *m*, rendement des investissements *m*, rentabilité d'investissements *f*, rentabilité des actifs *f*

ROIC *abbr (return on invested capital)* ACC, ECON, FIN rendement du capital investi *m*

ROM *abbr (read only memory)* COMP mémoire ROM *f*, mémoire fixe *f*, mémoire morte *f*

ROP *abbr (run of paper)* MEDIA *print* emplacement indéterminé *m*, importance d'un tirage moyen *f*, insertion sauvage *f*, S&M emplacement indéterminé *m*

RORCE *abbr (rate of return on capital employed)* ECON, FIN taux de rendement des capitaux investis *m*, taux de rendement sur le capital employé *m*

ro/ro *abbr (roll on/roll off)* TRANSP manutention horizontale *f*

ROT *abbr (reference our telex)* COMMS référence notre télex *loc f*

ROW *abbr (the rest of the world)* ECON le reste du monde *m*

RP *abbr* COMMS *(radiophone)* radiotéléphone *m*, FIN *(repurchase agreement)* contrat de vente à réméré *m*, STOCK *(repurchase agreement)* contrat de vente à réméré *m*, mise en pension *f*, pension livrée *f*, prise en pension *f*, TRANSP *(return to port for orders) shipping* retour au port en attendant des instructions *loc m*

RPA *abbr UK (Redundancy Payments Act)* HRM *1965* loi sur les primes de reconversions

RPB *abbr UK (recognized professional body)* FIN corps professionnel reconnu *m*, organisme professionnel *m*, organisme spécialisé accrédité *m*

R.P.Ct. *abbr UK (Restrictive Practices Court)* GEN COMM tribunal chargé de l'application des lois antitrusts *m*, tribunal statuant sur toute atteinte à la libre concurrence *m*, LAW tribunal statuant sur toute atteinte à la libre concurrence *m*,

RPI *abbr (retail price index)* ECON, GEN COMM indice des prix de détail *m*

RPM *abbr* ECON *(resale price maintenance)*, FIN *(resale price maintenance)*, S&M *(retail price maintenance) sales* maintien du prix de revente *m*, prix de vente imposé *m*

RQD *abbr (raised quarterdeck)* TRANSP *shipping* demi-dunette *f*

RR *abbr* STOCK *(rate resetting)* refixation de taux *f*, STOCK *(rate resetter)* rétablisseur de taux *m*

RRA *abbr UK (Race Relations Act)* LAW loi protégeant l'égalité des droits pour chaque race

RRIF *abbr (registered retirement income fund)* INS caisse de retraite agréée *f*

RRP *abbr (recommended retail price)* S&M *sales* prix conseillé *m*

RRR *abbr (real rate of return)* BANK taux de rendement réel *m*

RRSP *abbr (registered retirement savings plan)* INS régime enregistré d'épargne-retraite *m*

RSA *abbr* ECON *UK (regional selective assistance)* assistance régionale sélective *f*, WEL *UK (Royal Society of Arts)* Académie royale des arts *f*

RSD *abbr (raised shelter deck)* TRANSP *shipping* pont-abri surélevé *m*

RSG *abbr UK (rate support grant)* ECON subvention de l'État aux collectivités locales *f*, subvention de soutien de taux *f*

RSI *abbr (repetitive strain injury)* ADMIN atteinte due à des tensions répétées *f*

RSVP *abbr (please reply)* COMMS RSVP *(répondez s'il vous plaît)*

Rt: ~ **Hon** *abbr UK (Right Honourable)* POL très honorable

RT *abbr* COMMS *(radiotelegraphy)* radiotélégraphie *f*, COMMS *(radiotelephony)* radiotéléphonie *f*, COMMS *(radiotelephone)* radiotéléphone *m*

RTBA *abbr (rate to be agreed)* TRANSP tarif à déterminer *m*

RTh *abbr* TRANSP *(high frequency radiotelephony)* radiotéléphonie haute fréquence *f*, TRANSP *(high frequency radiotelephone)* *shipping* radiotéléphone haute fréquence *m*

RTm *abbr* TRANSP *(medium frequency radiotelephony)* radiotéléphonie moyenne fréquence *f*, TRANSP *(medium frequency radiotelephone)* *shipping* radiotéléphone moyenne fréquence *m*

RTv *abbr* TRANSP *(very high frequency radiotelephony)* radiotéléphonie très haute fréquence *f*, TRANSP *(very high frequency telephone)* *shipping* radiotéléphone très haute fréquence *m*

RUF *abbr (revolving underwriting facility)* INS *investment banking* garantie d'émission renouvelable *f*, moyen de souscription renouvelable *m*

RW *abbr (riveted and welded)* TRANSP *shipping* riveté et soudé

Rws *abbr (round the world service)* TRANSP *shipping* service tour-du-monde *m*

S *abbr* TRANSP *(station)* gare *f*, TRANSP *(South compass point)* navigation S *(quart sud)*, TRANSP *(single expansion engine)* *shipping* machine à expansion simple *f*, TRANSP *(starboard side)* *shipping* tribord *m*

s/a *abbr* TRANSP *(safe arrival)* heureuse arrivée *f*, TRANSP *(single-acting)* *machinery* à simple effet

s.a.a.r. *abbr (seasonally adjusted annual rate)* ECON taux annuel corrigé des variations saisonnières *m*

SAD *abbr (single administrative document)* ADMIN, IMP/EXP, TRANSP *EU* DAU *(document administratif unique)*

s.a.e *abbr BrE (stamped addressed envelope)*

COMMS, GEN COMM enveloppe affranchie *f*, enveloppe timbrée à vos nom et adresse *f*

SAEF *abbr UK (SEAQ Automated Execution Facility)* STOCK système international de cotation automatisé *m*

SAF *abbr (structural adjustment facility)* FIN facilité d'ajustement structurel *f*

Sallie: ~ **Mae** *abbr US (Student Loan Marketing Association)* FIN, WEL Association de gestion des prêts étudiants *f*

SAMA *abbr (Saudi Arabian Monetary Agency)* FIN Agence monétaire d'Arabie Saoudite *f*

s&c *abbr (shipper and carrier)* TRANSP chargeur et transporteur *loc m*, courtier d'affrètement maritime *m*

S&FA *abbr (shipping and forwarding agent)* HRM, IMP/EXP, TRANSP agent maritime-transitaire *m*, chargeur transitaire *m*

S&H/exct *abbr (Sundays and holidays excepted)* TRANSP *shipping* dimanches et jours fériés exceptés *loc m*

SANR *abbr (subject approval no risk)* INS risque couvert sous réserve d'acceptation *m*, sans risque sous réserve d'acceptation des conditions

SARA *abbr (salary adjustment reserve allotment)* HRM ARRT *(affectation de réserve pour le rajustement des salaires)*

s.a.s.e. *abbr AmE (self-addressed stamped envelope)* COMMS, GEN COMM enveloppe affranchie *f*, enveloppe timbrée à vos nom et adresse *f*

Sat. *abbr (Saturday)* GEN COMM samedi *m*

SAYE *abbr UK (save as you earn)* ECON, HRM plan d'épargne national par prélèvements mensuels

SB *abbr (short bill)* TRANSP traite à courte échéance *f*

SBA *abbr (small business administration)* GEN COMM administration des petites entreprises *f*, gestion d'une petite entreprise *f*

SBAC *abbr (Society of British Aerospace Companies)* TRANSP société des entreprises aérospatiales britanniques

SBDB *abbr (small business development bond)* GEN COMM ODPE *(obligation pour le développement de la petite entreprise)*

SBM *abbr (single-buoy mooring)* TRANSP *shipping* amarrage sur un seul coffre *m*

SBP *abbr (solid non-ferrous propeller)* TRANSP *shipping* hélice monobloc nonferreuse *f*

SBT *abbr (segregated ballast tank)* TRANSP *shipping* ballast séparé *m*

SC *abbr* LEIS *(Sports Council)* organisme autonome d'encouragement aux activités sportives, TRANSP *(slip coupling)* couplage extensible *m*, TRANSP *(steel covers)* couvercle d'acier *m*, panneaux de cale en acier *m pl*

SCIP *abbr (solid cast-iron propeller)* TRANSP *shipping* hélice monobloc en fonte de fer *f*

SCN *abbr (specification change notice)* TRANSP

aviation SCN *(spécification de changement notifié)*

SCP *abbr* ECON *(structure-conduct-performance model)* modèle structure-conduite-performance *m*, IMP/EXP *(simplified clearance procedure)* procédure de dédouanement simplifiée *f*, STOCK *(sterling commercial paper)* papier commercial en livres sterling *m*

SCSP *abbr (solid cast-steel propeller)* TRANSP *shipping* hélice monobloc en fonte d'acier *f*

S/D *abbr (sailing date)* TRANSP *shipping* date de départ *f*, jour de départ *m*

SD *abbr* BANK *(sight draft)*, GEN COMM *(sight draft)* traite à vue *f*, IND *(standard design)* de série, INS *(sea damage)*, TRANSP *(sea damage) shipping* fortune de mer *f*

SDA *abbr* UK *(Sex Discrimination Act)* HRM loi relative à la discrimination sexuelle

S d/k *abbr (shelter deck)* TRANSP *shipping* pont-abri *m*

SDR *abbr (special drawing rights)* BANK droits particuliers de retrait *m pl*, LAW DTS *(droits de tirage spéciaux)*

SDRIBOR *abbr* UK *(six month SDRs interbank offered rate)* BANK taux interbancaire offert pour droits de tirage spéciaux sur six mois

SDT *abbr (side tank)* TRANSP *shipping* citerne latérale *f*

SDW *abbr (side wheel)* TRANSP roue latérale *f*

SE *abbr (southeast)* GEN COMM, TRANSP *shipping* sud-est *m*

SEA *abbr (Single European Act)* LAW, POL AUE *(Acte unique européen)*

SEAQ *abbr (Stock Exchange Automated Quotation)* STOCK système de cotation automatisé *m*

SEAQI *abbr (Stock Exchange Automated Quotation International)* STOCK système international de cotation des valeurs étrangères automatisé

SEAT *abbr* UK *(Stock Exchange Alternative Trading Service)* STOCK tableau électronique de cotations *m*

SEATAG *abbr (South East Asia Trade Advisory Group)* ECON, IMP/EXP groupe consultatif commercial d'Asie du Sud-Est

SEB *abbr* STOCK US *(Specialist Electronic Book)* annuaire électronique spécialisé *m*, carnet électronique spécialisé *m*, TRANSP *(single-ended boiler) shipping* chaudière ordinaire *f*

sec. *abbr* ADMIN *(secretary)* secrétaire *mf*, GEN COMM *(second)* s. *(seconde)*, HRM *(secretary)*, MGMNT *(secretary)* secrétaire *mf*

SEC *abbr (Securities and Exchange Commission)* STOCK ≈ COB *(France) (Commission des opérations de Bourse)*

SECAL *abbr (sector adjustment loan)* FIN emprunt de redressement sectoriel *m*

2Q *abbr (second quarter)* GEN COMM deuxième trimestre *m*

SEDOL *abbr* UK *(Stock Exchange Daily Official List)* STOCK ≈ BOCB *(France) (Bulletin officiel des cours de la Bourse)*

SEM *abbr (special employment measures)* HRM mesures particulières pour l'emploi *f pl*

SEPON *abbr* UK *(Stock Exchange Pool Nominees)* STOCK société intermédiaire pour la compensation des titres *f*

Sept. *abbr (September)* GEN COMM sept. *(septembre)*

SERPS *abbr* UK *(State Earnings Related Pension Scheme)* ECON régime de retraite étatique basé sur le salaire

SF *abbr (sparring fitting)* TRANSP *shipping* vaigrage *m*

SFA *abbr* UK *(Securities and Futures Authority)* STOCK organisme de surveillance des bourses de valeurs et des marchés à terme

SFO *abbr* UK *(Serious Fraud Office)* STOCK bureau d'investigation des fraudes graves *m*

SFTC *abbr (standard freight trade classification)* TRANSP classement standard du commerce de marchandises *m*

SG *abbr (specific gravity)* GEN COMM poids spécifique *m*

sgd *abbr (signed)* COMMS s. *(signé)*

SH *abbr (superheater)* TRANSP surchauffeur *m*

SHC *abbr (super high cube)* TRANSP SHC *(conteneur spécial hors-cotes)*

SHEX *abbr (Sundays and holidays excepted)* TRANSP *shipping* dimanches et jours fériés exceptés *loc m*

SHINC *abbr (Sundays and holidays included)* TRANSP *shipping* dimanches et jours fériés compris *loc m*

shp *abbr (shaft horsepower)* TRANSP *of turbine* puissance sur l'arbre *f*

shr. *abbr (share)* STOCK act. *(action)*

SHSV *abbr (superheater safety valve)* TRANSP soupape de sûreté du surchauffeur *f*

SIB *abbr* STOCK UK *(Securities and Investments Board)* ≈ COB *(France) (Commission des opérations de Bourse)*

SIBOR *abbr (Singapore Interbank Offered Rate)* BANK TIOS *(taux interbancaire offert à Singapour)*

SIC *abbr (standard industrial classification)* IND classification industrielle standard *f*

SIL *abbr* FIN *(specific investment loan)* prêt spécial à l'investissement *m*, IMP/EXP, TRANSP *(specific individual licence BrE, specific individual license AmE)* permis spécifique individuel *m*

SILIC *abbr (severely indebted low-income country)* FIN pays au revenu bas sévèrement endetté *m*

SIM *abbr (sector investment and maintenance loan)* FIN IES *(prêt d'investissement et d'entretien sectoriel)*

SIMEX *abbr (Singapore International Monetary*

Exchange) STOCK bourse d'échange internationale de Singapour

SIMIC *abbr (severely indebted middle-income country)* FIN pays au revenu moyen sévèrement endetté *m*

SIN *abbr (social insurance number)* TAX, WEL NAS *(numéro d'assurance sociale)*

SIPROCOM *abbr (Committee for the Simplification of International Trade Procedures)* ADMIN Comité pour la simplification des procédures du commerce international *m*

SIS *abbr (special intermediate survey)* TRANSP visite spéciale intermédiaire *f*

sit. *abbr (situation)* HRM carrière *f*, emploi *m*

SITC *abbr (Standard International Trade Classification)* ECON, GEN COMM classification des normes du commerce international *f*

sitrep *abbr (situation report)* GEN COMM rapport de situation *m*

sits.: ~ vac. *abbr BrE (situations vacant)* HRM offres d'emploi *f pl*, postes à pourvoir *m pl*

SKD *abbr (semiknocked down)* TRANSP partiellement démonté

SL *abbr (surveillance licence BrE, surveillance license AmE)* IMP/EXP licence de surveillance *f*

S/LC *abbr (sue and labor clause AmE, sue and labour clause BrE)* INS clause de recours et de conservation *f*

SLM *abbr (single labor market, single labour market)* HRM marché unique du travail *m*

SLMA *abbr US (Student Loan Marketing Association)* STOCK organisme de garantie des prêts étudiants *m*

SL/NL *abbr (ship lost or not lost)* INS *marine* navire perdu ou non-perdu *loc m*

SMA *abbr* STOCK *(Secondary Market Association)* Association du marché secondaire *f*, STOCK *(special miscellaneous account)* compte de divers *m*

SME *abbr (small and medium-sized enterprises)* GEN COMM PME *(petites et moyennes entreprises)*

SMME *abbr (small and medium-sized manufacturing companies)* GEN COMM PMI *(petites et moyennes industries)*

SMMT *abbr UK (Society of Motor Manufacturers and Traders)* TRANSP société des constructeurs et négociants automobiles

SMP *abbr (special multiperil insurance)* INS assurance combinée spécifique *f*, police multirisque spéciale *f*

SMSA *abbr (standard metropolitan statistical area)* MATH *statistics* zone standard de statistique métropolitaine *f*

S/N *abbr (shipping note)* TRANSP note de chargement *f*

SNA *abbr (System of National Accounts)* ACC système de comptabilité nationale *m*

SNIF *abbr (short-term note issuance facility)* STOCK facilité de soutien de programme d'émission d'effets *f*, émission d'une obligation à court terme *f*

SNIG *abbr (sustained non-inflationary growth)* ECON croissance non-inflationniste soutenue *f*

Snr *abbr (senior)* GEN COMM *in age* aîné, *in rank* principal, supérieur, HRM principal

s.o. *abbr* BANK UK *(standing order)* ordre de paiement permanent *m*, ordre de transfert permanent *m*, ordre permanent *m*, GEN COMM *(seller's option)*, STOCK *(seller's option)* livraison au gré du vendeur *f*

SO *abbr (senior officer)* HRM officier supérieur *m*

SOFFEX *abbr (Swiss Options and Financial Futures Exchange)* STOCK bourse d'échange des options et valeurs à terme Suisse

SOL *abbr (shipowner's liability)* INS, LAW, TRANSP *shipping* responsabilité de l'armateur *f*

s.o.p. *abbr (standard operating procedure)* GEN COMM mode d'exploitation normal *m*, procédure normale à suivre *f*

sor *abbr (starboard)* TRANSP *shipping* tribord *m*

Sp *abbr (sloop)* TRANSP *shipping* sloop *m*

SPA *abbr (subject to particular average)* INS assujetti à l'avarie particulière

SPAR *abbr (Standard Portfolio Analysis of Risk)* FIN analyse des risques liés au portefeuille *f*

SPC *abbr* PATENTS *(supplementary protection certificate)* certificat de protection renforcée *m*, certificat de protection supplémentaire *m*, TRANSP *(self-polishing copolymer)* copolymère autolisseur *m*

SPGER *abbr (simplified procedure for goods carried by rail)* TRANSP procédure simplifiée pour marchandises transportées par chemin de fer *f*

SPHL *abbr (self-propelled hyperbaric lifeboat)* TRANSP *shipping* canot de sauvetage hyperbare autopropulsé *m*

SPM *abbr (single-point mooring)* TRANSP *shipping* méthode d'amarrage sur un seul point fixe *f*

sq *abbr (square)* GEN COMM c *(carré)*

SQC *abbr (statistical quality control)* MATH contrôle statistique de qualité *m*

Sr *abbr* TRANSP *(schooner)* goélette *f*, TRANSP *(single-reduction gearing)* *shipping* réducteur simple *m*

SR *abbr (short run)* IND petite série *f*

SR&CC *abbr (strikes, riots and civil commotions)* LAW grèves, émeutes et insurrections civiles *loc f*

SRCPP *abbr Canada (Special Recovery Capital Projects Program)* GEN COMM programme spécial de relance des projets d'investissement *m*

SRNA *abbr UK (Shipbuilders and Repairers National Association)* TRANSP association nationale des constructeurs et réparateurs de navires

SRO *abbr* GEN COMM UK *(self-regulatory organization)* organisation de centrales des intermédiaires financiers *f*, organisation indépendante *f*, organisme autorégulateur *m*, STOCK UK *(self-regulating organization)* organisation autonome *f*, organisme auto-réglementé *m*

SS *abbr* TRANSP *(steamship)* vap. *(vapeur)*, TRANSP *(ship's special survey, special survey)* visite spéciale *f*

SSA *abbr (standard spending assessment)* ECON évaluation standard des dépenses *f*

SSAP *abbr UK (Statement of Standard Accounting Practice)* ACC norme comptable *f*

SSC *abbr (Swiss Shippers Council)* TRANSP Conseil des affréteurs suisses *m*

SSD *abbr (single-sided disk)* COMP disque monoface *m*, disque simple face *m*

SSDD *abbr (single-sided double density)* COMP simple face-double densité

SSH *abbr (special survey of the hull)* TRANSP *shipping* visite spéciale de la coque *f*

SSIA *abbr UK (Shiprepairers and Shipbuilders Independent Association)* TRANSP association indépendante des réparateurs et constructeurs de navire

SSM *abbr (special survey of the machinery)* TRANSP *shipping* visite spéciale des machines *f*

SSP *abbr* INS *UK (statutory sick pay)* prestation maladie réglementaire *f*, TRANSP *(stainless-steel propeller) shipping* hélice en acier inoxydable *f*

SSSD *abbr (single-sided single density)* COMP simple face-simple densité

SSSI *abbr (Site of Special Scientific Interest)* ENVIR Site d'intérêt scientifique spécial *m*

SST *abbr (supplementary service tariff)* TRANSP tarif de services supplémentaires *m*

ST *abbr (side tank)* TRANSP *shipping* citerne latérale *f*

STAGs *abbr UK (sterling transferable accruing government securities)* STOCK obligation à coupon zéro basée sur des bons du Trésor

Std *abbr (standard)* GEN COMM étalon *m*

STD *abbr BrE (subscriber trunk dialling)* COMMS appel automatique longue distance *loc m*, automatique interurbain *m*, l'automatique *m*

STEP *abbr (science and technology for environmental protection programme)* ENVIR *EU* science et technologie pour la protection de l'environnement programme *f*

stg *abbr (sterling)* GEN COMM ster. *(sterling)*

STN *abbr (special traffic notice)* TRANSP affiche spéciale circulation *f*

STOL *abbr (short take-off and landing)* TRANSP *aircraft* ADAC *(avion à décollage et atterrissage courts)*

STRIPS *abbr (Separate Trading of Registered Interest and Principal Securities)* STOCK démembrement *m*

stvdr *abbr (stevedore)* HRM docker *m*, TRANSP arrimeur *m*, docker *m*

STVP *abbr (short-term vehicle park)* TRANSP parking courte durée *m*

Sun. *abbr (Sunday)* GEN COMM dim. *(dimanche)*

SV *abbr (sailing vessel)* TRANSP navire à voiles *m*

SW *abbr* GEN COMM *(southwest)* sud-ouest *m*, TRANSP *(shipper weight)* poids transitaire *m*, TRANSP *(southwest)* sud-ouest *m*

SWIFT *abbr (Society for Worldwide Interbank Financial Telecommunications)* BANK, COMMS Société internationale de télécommunications financières interbanques *f*

SWING *abbr UK (sterling warrant into gilt edged stock)* STOCK bon de souscription d'obligations d'État *m*

SWOT *abbr (strengths, weaknesses, opportunities and threats analysis)* GEN COMM, S&M analyse des forces, des faiblesses, des opportunités et des menaces *f*

SWR *abbr (steel wire rope)* TRANSP câble en fils d'acier *m*

t. *abbr* GEN COMM *(tare)* t. *(tare)*, GEN COMM *(ton, tonne)* t. *(tonne)*

T *abbr* GEN COMM *(tropical)* tropique, TRANSP *(triple expansion engine)* moteur à triple expansion *m*, TRANSP *(tug)* remorqueur *m*, TRANSP *(twin-screw)* à deux hélices

TA *abbr* ACC *(transactional analysis)*, BANK *(transactional analysis)* analyse transactionnelle *f*, COMMS *(telegraphic address)* adr. tél. *(adresse télégraphique)*, ECON *(transactional analysis)*, FIN *(transactional analysis)*, GEN COMM *(transactional analysis)* analyse transactionnelle *f*, HRM *UK (Training Agency)* ≈ AFPA *(Association pour la formation professionnelle des adultes)*, MGMNT *(transactional analysis)* analyse transactionnelle *f*

TAA *abbr (transferable account area)* TRANSP zone de comptes négociables *f*

TAB *abbr US (tax anticipation bill)* TAX obligation d'impôts anticipés *f*

TACs *abbr (total allowable catches)* ENVIR prises totales autorisées *f pl*

TAL *abbr (technical assistance loan)* FIN prêt d'assistance technique *m*

TAMS *abbr (thruster-assisted mooring system)* TRANSP *shipping* système d'amarrage à propulsion *m*

TAN *abbr (tax anticipation note)* TAX obligation d'impôts anticipés *f*

T&G *abbr (tongued and grooved)* TRANSP affourché

TAPS *abbr (turret anchored production system)* TRANSP système de production à tourelle d'ancrage *m*

TAT *abbr (transitional automated ticket)* TRANSP billet automatisé de transition *m*

TAURUS *abbr UK (Transfer & Automated Registration of Uncertified Stock)* ECON, STOCK transfert et enregistrement automatisé de titres non-certifiés

TAWB *abbr (through air waybill)* IMP/EXP, TRANSP lettre de transport aérien de bout en bout *f*

TBN *abbr* (*total base number*) ENVIR indice de base total *m*

TBR *abbr* (*Treasury bill rate*) ECON, STOCK taux de bons du Trésor *m*

T/C *abbr* GEN COMM (*until countermanded*) jusqu'à nouvel ordre *loc*, TRANSP (*time charter*) affrètement à temps *m*

TCDC *abbr* (*technical cooperation amongst developing countries*) ECON, POL coopération technique entre pays en voie de développement *f*

TDA *abbr* (*transport distribution analysis*) TRANSP analyse de la distribution de transport *f*

TDB *abbr* (*Trade Development Board*) ECON *international* conseil du développement commercial *m*

TDC *abbr* (*top dead center AmE, top dead centre BrE*) TRANSP PMH (*point mort haut*)

TDED *abbr* (*Trade Data Elements Directory*) ECON *international* annuaire de données commerciales de base *m*

TDI *abbr* (*Trade Data Interchange*) ECON *international* échange d'informations commerciales *m*

TDP *abbr* ECON (*tradable discharge permit*), ENVIR (*tradable discharge permit*) autorisation de décharge négociable *f*, autorisation négociable de décharge de polluants *f*

TDW *abbr* (*tons deadweight*) TRANSP TPL (*Tonne Port en Lourd*)

TE *abbr* (*triple-expansion*) TRANSP à triple expansion

TEC *abbr UK* (*Training and Enterprise Council*) HRM programmes de formation en entreprises

TEFRA *abbr* (*tax equity and fiscal responsibility act of 1982*) TAX loi de 1982 sur l'équité des impôts et de la responsabilité fiscale

tel. *abbr* (*telephone*) COMMS tél. (*téléphone*); **~ add.** (*telephone address*) COMMS adresse téléphonique *f*; **~ no.** *abbr* (*phone number, telephone number*) COMMS n° tél. (*numéro de téléphone*)

TESSA *abbr UK* (*tax-exempt special savings account*) BANK, ECON, TAX compte spécial d'épargne exonéré d'impôts *m*

TEU *abbr* (*twenty foot equivalent unit*) TRANSP équivalent d'un conteneur de vingt pieds, EVP (*équivalent vingt pieds*)

TF *abbr* (*tropical fresh water load line*) TRANSP TD (*ligne de charge tropicale en eau douce*)

TFR *abbr* ECON (*total fertility rate*)taux global de fertilité *m*, TRANSP (*transfer*) TFR (*transfert*)

TGWU *abbr UK* (*Transport and General Workers' Union*) HRM, IND syndicat des transports et des travailleurs confédérés *m*

THE *abbr* (*technical help to exporters*) IMP/EXP assistance technique aux exportateurs *f*

3Q *abbr* (*third quarter*) GEN COMM troisième trimestre *m*

TIBOR *abbr* (*Tokyo Interbank Offered Rate*) ECON TIOT (*taux interbancaire offert à Tokyo*)

TIC *abbr* (*take into consideration*) GEN COMM tenir compte de

TIGR *abbr* (*Treasury Investment Growth Receipt*) STOCK certificat de croissance des investissements du Trésor *m*

TINA *abbr* (*there is no alternative*) GEN COMM aucune alternative n'est possible *loc f*, il n'y a pas d'alternative *loc f*

TIP *abbr* (*tax-based incomes policy*) ECON, FIN, TAX politique d'imposition des sociétés basée sur les salaires versés

T/L *abbr* (*total loss*) INS perte totale *f*

TLC *abbr* (*transferable loan certificate*) FIN certificat d'emprunt cessible *m*

TLF *abbr* (*transferable loan facility*) FIN facilité d'emprunt cessible *f*, facilité de prêt transférable *f*

TLI *abbr* (*transferable loan instrument*) FIN instrument d'emprunt cessible *m*

TLO *abbr* (*total loss only*) INS perte totale uniquement *f*

TM *abbr* HRM (*traffic manager*) chef de la circulation *m*, *railway traffic* directeur de la circulation ferroviaire *m*, directeur des transports *m*, TRANSP (*ton mile, tonne mile*) ≈ tk (*tonnekilomètre*), TRANSP (*traffic manager*) chef de la circulation *m*, directeur des transports *m*, *railway traffic* directeur de la circulation ferroviaire *m*

TMESS *abbr* (*telemessage*) COMMS télémessage *m*

TMO *abbr* (*telegraph money order, telegraphic money order*) BANK mandat postal télégraphique *m*, FIN mandat postal télégraphe *m*, mandat postal télégraphique *m*

TNC *abbr* (*transnational corporation*) ECON, GEN COMM, POL entreprise transnationale *f*, société transnationale *f*

TO *abbr* (*telegraphic office*) COMMS service télégraphique *m*

TOB *abbr* (*takeover bid*) ACC, GEN COMM, STOCK OPA (*offre publique d'achat*)

TOPIC *abbr UK* (*Teletex Output of Price Information by Computer*) STOCK ≈ informations boursières par MINITEL *f pl*

TOVALOP *abbr* (*tanker owners' voluntary agreement concerning liability for oil pollution*) ENVIR, INS, TRANSP *shipping* engagement volontaire des propriétaires de pétroliers en cas de pollution pétrolière

TP *abbr* (*third party*) INS, LAW, PATENTS tierce personne *f*, tiers *m*

TPC *abbr* (*tonnes per centimeter AmE, tonnes per centimetre BrE*) GEN COMM tonnes au centimètre *f pl*

TPI *abbr* (*Tropical Products Institute*) ECON Institut des produits tropicaux *m*

TQC *abbr* (*total quality control*) GEN COMM, IND, MGMNT, S&M QG (*contrôle de la qualité globale*)

TQM *abbr* (*total quality management*) IND, MGMNT, S&M gestion de la QG *f* (*gestion de la qualité globale*)

tr. *abbr (transfer)* ACC virt *(virement)*, BANK transfert *m*, transfert de fonds *m*, FIN virt *(virement)*

TR *abbr (triple reduction)* GEN COMM triple réduction

TRANS *abbr (transverse)* GEN COMM transversal

trem: **~ card** *abbr (transport emergency card)* TRANSP carte d'urgence de transport *f*

TS *abbr* HRM *(traffic superintendent)* chef de la circulation *m*, responsable des transports *m*, surveillant de circulation *m*, MEDIA *(trial subscription)* abonnement à l'essai *m*, TRANSP *(traffic superintendent)* chef de la circulation *m*, responsable des transports *m*, surveillant de circulation *m*

TSA *abbr UK (The Securities Association)* STOCK ≈ CBV *(Conseil des bourses de valeurs)*

TSE *abbr Canada (the Toronto Stock Exchange)* STOCK la Bourse de Toronto *f (Canada)*

TSR *abbr (Trans-Siberian Railway)* TRANSP *rail* Transsibérien *m*

tsw *abbr (telesoftware)* COMP logiciel de télétexte *m*, télélogiciel *m*

TT *abbr* BANK *(telegraphic transfer)*, COMMS *(telegraphic transfer)* TT *(transfert télégraphique)*, TRANSP *(timetable)* horaire *m*, TRANSP *(tank top)* plafond de ballast *m*

TTC *abbr (tender to contract)* GEN COMM soumission d'offre *f*

TU *abbr UK (trade union)* HRM syndicat *m*

TUA *abbr UK (trade union act)* ECON, HRM, IND, LAW, POL loi sur les syndicats *f*

TUC *abbr UK (Trades Union Congress)* HRM confédération des syndicats britanniques, ≈ CGT *(Confédération générale du travail)*

Tues. *abbr (Tuesday)* GEN COMM mardi *m*

TULRA *abbr UK (Trade Unions and Labour Relations Act)* HRM, IND, LAW loi sur les syndicats et les relations de travail

TV *abbr (television)* COMMS, GEN COMM, MEDIA télé *(infrml)* *(télévision)*

TVA *abbr (Tennessee Valley Authority)* ECON agence fédérale de la vallée du Tennessee

TWD *abbr ('tween deck, 'tween deck space)* TRANSP *shipping* entrepont *m*

TWI *abbr (training within industry)* HRM, IND formation dans l'entreprise *f*

TWRA *abbr (Transpacific Westbound Rate Agreement)* TRANSP Accord tarifaire transpacifique en direction de l'ouest *m*

tx. *abbr (telex)* COMMS télex *m*

typo *abbr (typing error)* COMP, GEN COMM, MEDIA faute de frappe *f*

U *abbr* TRANSP *(universal container)* conteneur pour usage général *m*, TRANSP *(unit load) distribution* unité de charge *f*, unité de chargement *f*

U/a *abbr (underwriting account)* INS compte de souscripteur *m*

UAE *abbr (United Arab Emirates)* GEN COMM Émirats Arabes Unis *m pl*

UAF *abbr (European Agricultural Fund)* ECON, FIN, POL Fonds agricole européen *m*

UAW *abbr US (United Automobile Workers)* HRM TUA *(travailleurs unifié de l'automobile)*

UAWB *abbr (universal air waybill)* IMP/EXP, TRANSP LTAU *(lettre de transport aérien universelle)*

UBR *abbr (Uniform Business Rate)* FIN taux d'activité constant *m*, taux normalisé d'activités *m*

u.c. *abbr (upper case)* ADMIN, COMP, MEDIA capitale *f*, haut de casse *m*, lettre capitale *f*, lettre de haut de casse *f*, lettre majuscule *f*, majuscule *f*

UCITS *abbr (undertakings for collective investment in transferables)* FIN *EU* OPCVM *(organisme de placements collectifs en valeurs mobilières)*

UC&P *abbr (Uniform Customs and Practice for Documentary Credits)* ECON *international trade* unification des pratiques et coutumes pour les crédits documentaires *f*

UDEAC *abbr (Central African Customs and Economics Union)* IMP/EXP UDEAC *(Union douanière et économique de l'Afrique centrale)*

Udk *abbr (upper deck)* TRANSP pont supérieur *m*

UI *abbr (unemployment insurance)* HRM AC *(assurance-chômage)*

UK *abbr (United Kingdom)* GEN COMM Royaume-Uni *m*

UKAEA *abbr (United Kingdom Atomic Energy Authority)* IND agence de l'énergie atomique du Royaume-Uni

UK/Cont *abbr (United Kingdom or Continent)* TRANSP Royaume-Uni ou Continent *n pr*

UKREP *abbr (United Kingdom Permanent Representative to the European Community)* ECON, POL représentant permanent du Royaume-Uni à la Communauté Européenne *m*

ULD *abbr (unit load device)* TRANSP *aviation* unité de chargement aérienne *f*

ult. *abbr (ultimo)* GEN COMM du mois dernier *loc m*, ultimo *(frml)*, écoulé

UMA *abbr (union membership agreement)* HRM accord d'appartenance syndicale *m*

UN *abbr (United Nations)* ECON, POL ONU *(Organisation des Nations Unies)*

UNA *abbr (United Nations Association)* ADMIN ANU *(Association des Nations Unies)*

UNCED *abbr (United Nations Conference on Environment and Development)* ENVIR, GEN COMM CNUED *(Conférence des Nations Unies sur l'environnement et le développement)*

UNCITRAL *abbr (United Nations Commission of International Trade Law)* LAW Commission des Nations Unies pour le droit commercial international

UNCON *abbr (uncontainerable goods)* TRANSP marchandises non-conteneurisables *f pl*

UNCTAD *abbr (United Nations Conference on Trade and Development)* ECON CNUCED *(Conférence des Nations Unies sur le commerce et le développement)*

UNCTAD MMO *abbr (UNCTAD multimodal-transport convention)* ECON *international trade* convention de transport multimodal de la CNUCED *f*, convention sur le transport modal de la CNUCED *f*

UnDk *abbr (under deck tank)* TRANSP *shipping* citerne en cale *f*, citerne sous le pont *f*

UNITAR *abbr (United Nations Institute for Training and Research)* HRM Institut des Nations Unies pour la formation et la recherche *m*

UNO *abbr (United Nations Organization)* ECON, POL ONU *(Organisation des Nations Unies)*

UNRISD *abbr (United Nations Research Institute for Social Development)* WEL IRNUDS *(Institut de Recherche des Nations Unies pour le développement social)*

UNRWA *abbr (United Nations Relief and World Agency)* ECON, POL Office de secours et de travaux des Nations Unies pour les réfugiés *m*

UPS *abbr jarg* COMP *(uninterruptible power supply)* alimentation non-interruptible *f*, POL *(uncontested physical search) by members of intelligence services* fouille incontestée *f*

UPU *abbr (Universal Postal Union)* ACC, COMMS UPU *(Union postale universelle)*

URN *abbr (unique reference number)* ADMIN numéro de référence unique *m*

u/s *abbr (unsorted)* GEN COMM non-trié

US *abbr (United States)* GEN COMM États-Unis *m pl*

USA *abbr (United States of America)* GEN COMM États-Unis d'Amérique *m pl*

USDAW *abbr UK (Union of Shop, Distributive & Allied Workers)* HRM Syndicat des employés de la distribution et assimilés *m*

USIA *abbr (United States Information Agency)* COMMS agence d'informations des États-Unis

USM *abbr UK (Unlisted Securities Market)* STOCK marché des valeurs non-cotées *m*, second marché *m*

USMC *abbr (United States Maritime Commission)* TRANSP commission maritime des États-Unis

USP *abbr (unique selling point, unique selling proposition)* S&M promesse unique de vente *f*

USPS *abbr (United States Postal Service)* COMMS Poste des États-Unis *f*

USSR *abbr obs (Union of Soviet Socialist Republics)* GEN COMM appelé maintenant la Communauté des États Indépendants, URSS *(obs)* *(Union des Républiques Socialistes Soviétiques)*

UTC *abbr (universal time coordinated)* GEN COMM heure universelle *f*, TU *(temps universel)*

UVI *abbr (unit value index)* ECON indice des valeurs unitaires *m*

U/W *abbr (underwriter)* INS souscripteur *m*

V *abbr (volt)* GEN COMM V *(volt)*

VA *abbr (value analysis)* ACC, FIN, S&M *marketing* analyse de valeur *f*

VAN *abbr (value-added network)* COMP réseau à valeur ajoutée *f*

VAR *abbr* COMP *(value-added reseller)* revendeur de systèmes à valeur ajoutée *m*, MATH *(vector autoregression) statistics* autorégression de vecteur *f*

VAT *abbr UK (value-added tax)* TAX TVA *(taxe sur la valeur ajoutée)*

VBLT *abbr US (vee built)* TRANSP *shipping* à fond en V *loc m*

VC *abbr* GEN COMM *(variable charge)* charge variable *f*, INS *(valuation clause)* clause d'évaluation *f*

VDT *abbr (visual display terminal)* COMP terminal *m*, terminal à écran de visualisation *m*, visuel *m*

VDU *abbr (visual display unit)* COMP terminal *m*, terminal à écran de visualisation *m*, unité de visualisation *f*, visuel *m*

VEE: ~ BTM *abbr (vee bottom)* TRANSP *shipping* fond en V *m*

VER *abbr (voluntary export restraint)* IMP/EXP RVE *(restriction volontaire des exportations)*

vert. *abbr (vertical)* ECON, GEN COMM, IND, MEDIA, STOCK, TAX vertical

VGA *abbr (video graphics adaptor card, video graphics array card)* COMP carte VGA *f*

VHF *abbr (very high frequency)* GEN COMM VHF *(très haute fréquence)*

VIC *abbr (very important cargo)* TRANSP cargaison très importante *f*

VIO *abbr (very important object)* TRANSP objet très important *m*

VIP *abbr (very important person)* GEN COMM personnage de marque *m*

VLCC *abbr (very large crude carrier)* TRANSP *shipping* très gros transporteur de brut *m*

VLR *abbr (variable lending rate)* FIN taux de crédit variable *m*

VLS *abbr (very large-scale)* ECON, GEN COMM à très grande échelle *loc f*

VMP *abbr (value as marine policy)* INS *marine* évaluer en police maritime

vo *abbr (verso)* GEN COMM, MEDIA vo *(verso)*

vol. *abbr (volume)* GEN COMM vol *(volume)*

Volcoa *abbr (volume contract of affreightment)* TRANSP Volcoa *m*

VOP *abbr (value as in original policy)* INS valeur de la police d'origine *f*

VP *abbr (vice-president)* HRM V-P *(vice-président)*

VTOL *abbr (vertical takeoff and landing)* TRANSP ADAV *(avion à décollage et atterrisage vertical)*

w *abbr (wood)* TRANSP bois *m*

W *abbr (West compass point)* TRANSP *navigation* O *(quart ouest)*

W.A. *abbr (with average)* INS avec avaries *loc*

WACCC *abbr (Worldwide Air Cargo Commodity Classification)* TRANSP classification mondiale de marchandises de fret aérien *f*

WAN *abbr (wide area network)* COMP grand réseau *m*, réseau longue distance *m*, réseau étendu *m*, MGMNT grand réseau *m*

wbs *abbr (without benefit of salvage)* INS *marine* sans bénéfice du sauvetage

w.c. *abbr (without charge)* GEN COMM gratis, gratuitement, sans frais, gratis, gratuit

wccon *abbr (whether cleared customs or not)* IMP/EXP dédouané ou non *loc*

W/d *abbr (warranted)* INS garanti

Wed. *abbr (Wednesday)* GEN COMM mercredi *m*

wef *abbr (with effect from)* GEN COMM avec effet à compter du *loc m*, à partir de

WEU *abbr (Western European Union)* POL *defence* UEO *(Union de l'Europe occidentale)*

WFP *abbr (World Food Program, World Food Programme)* ECON programme alimentaire mondial *m*

WFSE *abbr (World Federation of Stock Exchanges)* STOCK FIBV *(Fédération internationale des bourses de valeurs)*

WFTU *abbr (World Federation of Trade Unions)* HRM FSM *(fédération syndicale mondiale)*

WFUNA *abbr (World Federation of United Nations Associations)* ADMIN Fédération mondiale des associations des Nations Unies *f*

wg *abbr (weight guaranteed)* TRANSP poids garanti *m*

wgt *abbr (weight)* TRANSP poids *m*

WH *abbr (workable hatch)* TRANSP panneau utilisable *m*

WHB *abbr (waste heat boiler)* TRANSP *shipping* chaudière de récupération *f*

WHO *abbr (World Health Organization)* ADMIN, WEL OMS *(Organisation mondiale de la santé)*

whse *abbr (warehouse)* IMP/EXP, TRANSP entrepôt *m*

WHWTB *abbr (waste heat water tube boiler)* TRANSP *shipping* chaudière de récupération aquatubulaire *f*, chaudière de récupération à tubes d'eau *f*

WINGS *abbr (warrant into government securities)* STOCK valeurs garanties par le gouvernement *f pl*

WIP *abbr (work in progress)* GEN COMM travail en cours *loc m*

WIPO *abbr (World Intellectual Property Organization)* LAW Organisation mondiale pour la propriété intellectuelle *f*

wk. *abbr (week)* GEN COMM semaine *f*

W/M *abbr (weight and/or measurements at ship's option)* TRANSP *shipping* poids et/ou cubage à l'avantage du navire *loc m*

WMARC *abbr (World Maritime Administrative Radio Conference)* TRANSP *shipping* Conférence mondiale administrative radio-maritime *f*

WMO *abbr (World Meteorological Organization)* TRANSP Organisation météorologique mondiale *f*

wob *abbr (washed overboard)* TRANSP *shipping* enlevé par la mer *loc*

WOL *abbr* LAW *(wharf-owner's liability)* responsabilité du propriétaire du quai *f*

WP *abbr* ADMIN *(word processor)*, COMP *(word processor)* machine à traitement de texte *f*, traitement de texte *m*, GEN COMM *(working party)* groupe de réflexion *m*, GEN COMM *(without prejudice)* sans préjudice, INS *(without prejudice)* sans constituer de précédent, sous toutes réserves, TRANSP *(working pressure)* pression de service *f*

WPA *abbr (with particular average)* INS avec avaries particulières *loc*, avec avaries simples *loc*

wpm *abbr (words per minute)* ADMIN mots à la minute *loc*

WR *abbr (warehouse receipt)* GEN COMM, IMP/EXP, LAW, S&M, TRANSP récépissé d'entrepôt *m*, récépissé-warrant *m*

wro *abbr (war risk only)* INS risque de guerre exclusivement *m*, risque de guerre uniquement *m*

WS *abbr (wood-sheathed)* TRANSP *shipping* doublé, doublé en bois

wt *abbr (weight)* GEN COMM p. *(poids)*

wtdb *abbr (water tube domestic boiler)* TRANSP *shipping* chaudière domestique aquatubulaire *f*, chaudière domestique à tubes d'eau *f*

WW *abbr (warehouse warrant)* GEN COMM, IMP/EXP, LAW, S&M, TRANSP bulletin de consigne *m*, récépissé d'entrepôt *m*, récépissé-warrant *m*, warrant *m*

WWF *abbr (World Wide Fund)* ENVIR Fonds mondial pour la nature *m*

WYSIWYG *abbr jarg (what you see is what you get)* COMP tel écran, tel écrit

X *abbr (telephone extension)* COMMS poste *m*

XC *abbr (ex-coupon)* GEN COMM, STOCK ex-c, ex-coup *(ex-coupon)*

XD *abbr* COMMS *(ex-directory, unlisted)* sur la liste rouge *loc f*, STOCK *(ex-dividend)*, STOCK *(ex dividend)* ex-d, ex-div. *(ex-dividende)*

xl: ~ & ul *abbr (exclusive of loading and unloading)* IMP/EXP, TRANSP chargement et déchargement exclus *loc m*

x pri *abbr (without privileges)* GEN COMM sans privilège

YAR *abbr (York Antwerp Rules)* INS règles d'York et d'Anvers

y/c *abbr (your cable)* TRANSP votre câble *m*

yd *abbr (yard)* GEN COMM yard *m*

YGS *abbr (year of grace survey)* TRANSP *shipping* visite annuelle *f*

Y'ld-Gr's *abbr (gross dividend yield)* ECON, STOCK rendement boursier brut *m*, rendement de dividende brut *m*, rendement des actions brut *m*

yr *abbr* COMMS *(your)* votre, GEN COMM *(year)* an *m*, année *f*; **~ ref.** *(your reference)* COMMS V/réf. *(votre référence)*

YT *abbr UK (youth training)* HRM formation des jeunes *f*

YTM *abbr (yield to maturity)* BANK rendement actualisé *m*, rendement à l'échéance *m*, taux actuariel *m*, ECON, FIN rendement à l'échéance *m*, STOCK rendement actualisé *m*, rendement à l'échéance *m*, taux actuariel *m*

YTS *abbr UK (Youth Training Scheme)* ECON ≈ TUC *(travaux d'utilité collective)*, HRM ≈ TUC *(travaux d'utilité collective)*, ≈ CES *(France) (contrat d'emploi-solidarité)*, POL, WEL ≈ TUC *(travaux d'utilité collective)*

ZBB *abbr (zero-base budgeting)* ACC, FIN budget base zéro *m*, budgétisation base zéro *f*, technique du budget base zéro *f*

ZEBRAs *abbr (zero coupon Eurosterling bearer-registered accruing securities)* STOCK obligations en Eurosterling à coupon zéro *f pl*, valeurs ZEBRA *f pl*

ZIP *abbr US (zone improvement plan)* GEN COMM plan d'aménagement d'une zone *m*

ZPG *abbr (zero population growth)* ECON, POL croissance démographique nulle *f*, croissance démographique zéro *f*

English–French appendix/
Appendice anglais–français

Contents/Table des matières

Business correspondence and situations/
Correspondance et situations commerciales

Discussing contracts/Discuter de contrats

Sales conditions

CLIENT: I'm pleased to inform you that we are prepared to include your company as one of our suppliers. Before we sign an agreement, we need to agree on terms and conditions.

SUPPLIER: We're delighted. What in particular do we need to agree?

CLIENT: Firstly, our terms of payment are 20 per cent on receipt of the goods and the remainder within 90 days.

SUPPLIER: We normally expect to be paid in full within 60 days, but if we can have a two-year agreement, we could accept your conditions.

CLIENT: Fine. We also want a 10 per cent discount for orders of over 5,000 parts. Deliveries must also be made by the specified date, with penalties for late delivery. I think you've been given some details.

SUPPLIER: Yes, and I can assure you that we are accustomed to just-in-time delivery. I'm sure that you know already that we offer good service at a good price. We're ready to sign.

CLIENT: That's good. I have the agreement here.

Conditions de vente

CLIENT: Je suis heureux de vous apprendre que nous sommes prêts à inclure votre entreprise sur la liste de nos fournisseurs. Avant de signer un contrat, nous devons nous nous mettre d'accord sur les termes et conditions.

FOURNISSEUR: Nous en sommes enchantés. Sur quels aspects particuliers devons-nous nous mettre d'accord?

CLIENT: Tout d'abord nos termes de règlement sont de 20% à la réception des marchandises et le solde sous 90 jours.

FOURNISSEUR: Normalement, nous préférons être réglés entièrement sous 60 jours, mais si nous avons un contrat de deux ans, nous pourrions accepter vos conditions.

CLIENT: Très bien. Nous voulons également une ristourne de 10% pour les commandes supérieures à 5 000 pièces. Les livraisons doivent être effectuées à des dates spécifiées et soumises à des amendes pour livraison tardive. Je crois que l'on vous a donné des détails à ce sujet, n'est-ce pas?

FOURNISSEUR: Oui, je peux vous garantir que nous avons l'habitude de livrer dans les délais. Je suis sûr que vous êtes tout à fait conscient que nous offrons un bon service. Nous sommes prêts à signer.

CLIENT: Parfait. Voici le contrat.

Contract of employment

Dear

Following recent discussions we are pleased to offer you employment at our Company as Area Manager on the following terms and conditions:

Remuneration
Your salary will be £15,000 per annum plus commission on the basis we have already discussed with you. As with all our staff your salary will be paid monthly on the last Thursday in each month, your first review being in July 199-.

Notice
As with all our staff, you will be employed for an initial trial period of six months, during which time either you or we may terminate your appointment at any time upon giving seven days' notice in writing to each other. Provided that we are satisfied with your performance during the trial period, we will thereafter immediately confirm your appointment as a permanent member of our staff and the seven days' period of notice referred to above will be increased to one month.

Sickness Pay
During any reasonable absence for illness the Company, at its discretion, will make up the amount of your National Insurance Benefit to the equivalent of your normal salary, although this will be essentially relative to your length of service.

Holidays
Your normal paid holiday entitlement will be 20 working days in a full year, the holiday year running from January 1st to December 31st.

Car
We will provide you with a suitable Company car (cost circa £14,000), which is to be mainly for your business use but also for your private use. We will meet all normal running expenses associated with the car such as road tax, insurance, repairs, servicing and petrol.

Pensions
The Company operates a Pension Plan. You can either decide to join the Company Scheme after 6 months' service at the Scheme's next anniversary date (July 199-), or alternatively choose a Personal Pension Plan to which the Company would contribute.

Hours
Normal office hours are from 9.00 a.m. to 5.15 p.m. from Monday to Friday with one hour for lunch. However, it is probable that additional calls will be made upon your time.

Grievance and Disciplinary Procedure
Should you wish to seek redress for any grievance relating to your employment, you should refer, as appropriate, either to the Company Secretary or to the Managing Director. Matters involving discipline will be dealt with in as fair and equitable a manner as possible.

Health and Safety at Work Act
A copy of the Staff Notice issued under the Health & Safety at Work etc. Act 1974 will be given to you on the first day of employment. Your acceptance of the appointment will be deemed to constitute your willingness to comply with these regulations.

Start date
The date on which your employment by the Company is to start remains to be agreed by us. We look forward to establishing a mutually acceptable date with you as soon as possible.

Will you kindly provide us with your acceptance of this offer of employment by signing and returning to us the enclosed duplicate copy of this letter.

We trust that you will have a long, happy and successful association with our Company.

Yours sincerely

B. Foster
Managing Director

Contrat de travail

Monsieur,

A la suite de nos récentes discussions, nous sommes heureux de vous offrir le poste de directeur régional au sein de notre entreprise, selon les termes et conditions suivants:

Rémunération:
Votre salaire s'élèvera à 15.000,00 livres sterling par an plus une commission relevant des points déjà discutés avec vous. Comme tout le personnel, votre salaire sera payé mensuellement le dernier jeudi de chaque mois. La première réévaluation sera en juillet 199-.

Préavis:
Comme tous nos employés, vous serez employé pendant une période initiale de six mois pendant lesquels chacune des deux parties pourra mettre un terme à son engagement en en avisant l'autre partie par écrit sept jours au préalable. Si nous sommes satisfaits de vos performances pendant le période d'essai, nous vous confirmerons, dès son échéance, votre engagement permanent et la période de préavis d'une semaine sera prolongée à un mois.

Indemnisation de maladie:
Toute absence raisonnable pour cause de maladie sera indemnisée, pour la partie non prise en charge par la sécurité sociale par nos soins à la hauteur de votre salaire normal. Toutefois, il est à noter que cette participation sera relative à votre durée de service chez nous.

Vacances:
Vous aurez droit à 20 jours ouvrables de vacances payées dans une année entière, la période normale des congés étant comprise entre le 1er janvier et le 31 décembre.

Voiture:
Nous vous fournirons une voiture d'entreprise appropriée (coût environ 14 000,00 livres sterling), qui est prévue pour un usage principalement lié à vos activités d'entreprise mais dont vous pourrez également vous servir pour votre utilisation personnelle. Nous prendrons en charge tous les coûts normaux engendrés par ce véhicule: vignette, assurance, réparations, entretien et essence.

Retraite:
L'entreprise est à même d'offrir un régime de retraite. Vous aurez ainsi la possibilité soit d'y souscrire après six mois de service lors de l'anniversaire de la mise en place de ce régime en juillet 19–, soit de choisir un régime de retraite indépendant auquel l'entreprise contribuerait.

Horaires:
Les heures de bureau normales sont de 9h00 à 17h15 du lundi au vendredi avec une heure pour le déjeuner. Il se peut cependant que vous soyez parfois amené à travailler au-delà de ces horaires.

Différends et procédures disciplinaires:
Si vous avez quelques plaintes que ce soit vous devrez les soumettre soit au Secrétaire Général, soit au Directeur Général. Les problèmes de discipline seront réglés de la manière la plus équitable et juste possible.

Santé et Sécurité sur le lieu de travail:
Un exemplaire de la "Notification au Personnel" publié suivant la loi 1974 'Santé et sécurité au Travail' vous sera donné le jour de votre prise de fonction. L'acceptation du poste vous engage également à accepter et respecter ces consignes.

Date d'entrée en fonction:
Votre date d'entrée en fonction n'a toujours pas été déterminée. Nous serions heureux de la fixer avec vous dans les plus brefs délais.

Nous vous serions reconnaissants de bien vouloir nous faire parvenir votre acceptation de cette offre d'emploi et de nous retourner un exemplaire dûment signé de cette lettre.

Nous espérons que votre association à notre entreprise sera de longue durée, heureuse et pleine de succès.

Je vous prie d'agréer, Monsieur, l'assurance de mes meilleurs sentiments.

B. Foster,
Directeur Général.

Breach of contract

CLIENT: Well, here we have the order contract that you wanted to discuss.

SUPPLIER: Yes, thanks. The paragraph I wanted to look at was this one, 9b.

CLIENT: Is there a problem?

SUPPLIER: It indicates that unless we deliver within three days of the date indicated we are in breach of contract, and the order can be cancelled.

CLIENT: That's part of our normal contract. Would you have a problem with that?

SUPPLIER: I find it a bit unusual.

CLIENT: We've had to introduce it, because in the past we had lots of problems with suppliers missing the delivery dates by weeks. We have lost customers because of that. Since we introduced this new clause we've had far fewer problems with delay.

SUPPLIER: Is it possible to vary it a little?

CLIENT: In what way?

SUPPLIER: Well, I find three days very restrictive. We'd be much happier with one week.

CLIENT: I'm sure you would! Any particular reason? Have you had difficulties meeting dates in the past?

SUPPLIER: Only rarely, but it does happen. And it's usually because a supplier has let us down. I'd like to modify that paragraph a bit, to give us a little more time.

CLIENT: Let me check it out with my manager. I'll get back to you in the next 24 hours.

SUPPLIER: Thanks.

Rupture d'un contrat

CLIENT: Bon, voici le contrat d'achat dont vous désiriez discuter.

FOURNISSEUR: Oui, merci. Le paragraphe qui m'intéresse est celui-ci, 9b.

CLIENT: Y a-t-il un problème?

FOURNISSEUR: Il est dit que si nous ne livrons pas sous les trois jours après la date indiquée, il y aura rupture de contrat et que la commande sera annulée.

CLIENT: Cela fait partie des clauses normales de nos contrats. Cela vous créera-t-il un problème?

FOURNISSEUR: J'ai rarement vu cela.

CLIENT: Il a fallu que nous prenions ce genre de mesure car il nous est arrivé d'avoir beaucoup de problèmes avec des fournisseurs qui avaient jusqu'à plusieurs semaines de retard. Nous avons perdu des clients à cause de cela. Depuis que nous avons adopté cette nouvelle clause, nous avons eu beaucoup moins de problèmes au niveau des retards.

FOURNISSEUR: Serait il possible de la modifier un petit peu?

CLIENT: Dans quel sens?

FOURNISSEUR: Eh bien, je trouve que trois jours c'est un petit peu trop restrictif. Nous serions bien plus satisfaits s'il s'agissait d'une semaine.

CLIENT: Je n'en doute pas! Avez-vous des raisons particulières? Avez-vous déjà eu des difficultés à respecter les délais imposés?

FOURNISSEUR: Rarement, mais c'est arrivé. Et c'est généralement parce qu'un fournisseur n'a pas respecté les siens. J'aimerais que ce paragraphe soit un peu modifié, pour nous donner un peu plus de temps.

CLIENT: Laissez-moi en parler avec mon directeur. Je vous contacterai d'ici vingt-quatre heures.

FOURNISSEUR: Merci.

Payment conditions

CLIENT: When will I be required to complete the payment of the instalments on the new equipment?

SUPPLIER: There are several plans under which you have maximum flexibility of conditions. Obviously, you can pay the full amount in a one-off sum, which would mean a substantial saving overall as interest costs are always high in the transport sector.

CLIENT: Suppose I could pay you 50 per cent of the total cost now, what sort of arrangements would best suit us both for the other half over a couple of years?

SUPPLIER: That would depend on how we structure our own borrowing requirement, but in principle there is no reason why payments cannot be adjusted exactly to suit your circumstances.

CLIENT: Fine. Can you give me a few days to discuss this with my accountant? If the bank is willing to lend me more money than I had first thought, I may perhaps be able to pay you outright.

SUPPLIER: Why not? With general interest rates as they are it could be worth risking a big outlay. But remember that whatever your decision, we can help as our own finances are secured by the parent company.

CLIENT: Thanks for the reassurance. I'll let you know a.s.a.p.

Conditions de paiement

CLIENT: A quelle date voulez-vous que le règlement final soit effectué pour l'installation du nouveau matériel?

FOURNISSEUR: Il y a plusieurs contrats qui offrent un maximum de souplesse au niveau des conditions. Bien sûr, vous pouvez régler la somme d'un seul coup, ce qui vous permettrait de faire pas mal d'économies car comme vous le savez, les intérêts sont toujours élevés dans le domaine du transport.

CLIENT: Supposons que je puisse vous payer 50% du montant total dès maintenant, quel genre de contrat nous conviendrait le mieux, à vous tant qu'à moi, si l'on voulait échelonner la somme restante sur deux ans?

FOURNISSEUR: Cela dépend de la façon dont nous structurerions notre propre endettement; en principe il n'y a aucune raison pour que les règlements ne puissent pas être ajustés pour convenir à vos circonstances.

CLIENT: Très bien. Pouvez-vous me donner quelques jours pour discuter de tout cela avec mon comptable? Si la banque accepte de me prêter plus que je ne le pensais au départ, je pourrais peut-être faire cet achat comptant.

FOURNISSEUR: Pourquoi pas? Avec des taux d'intérêts généraux tels qu'ils sont il vaudrait peut-être la peine de risquer une grosse dépense. Mais souvenez-vous que quelle que soit votre décision, nous pouvons vous aider car nos propres finances sont garanties par notre société-mère.

CLIENT: Je vous remercie de m'avoir rassuré. Je vous ferai connaître ma décision dès que possible.

Considering legal action

Francis Designs Ltd
114 Bestwood Park
West Hampstead
London

Cabinet Rossignol
4 rue des Glaïeuls
75009 Paris
France

24 May 199-

For the attention of Maître Patelin

Dear Maître Patelin

Your name was given to us by Robert Mackenzie of Canine Crunch Ltd for whom you acted last year.

We have a complaint against the newspaper *La Gazette du Samedi* who have in our opinion seriously defamed us in the enclosed article dealing with the closure of our plant at Roissy-en-France.

We would wish to take legal action against the said newspaper but first would like to have your professional advice about the strength of our case. Could you also let us know how long the case might run and the likely scale of our legal costs.

Yours sincerely

Lionel E Bone
Managing Director

Informer du désir d'intenter une action en justice

Francis Designs Ltd,
114 Bestwood Park,
West Hampstead,
London

Cabinet Rossignol,
4, rue des Glaïeuls,
75009 Paris,
France.

West Hampstead, le 24 mai 199-

A l'attention de Maître Patelin.

Cher Maître,

Votre nom nous a été communiqué par Robert Mackenzie de chez Canine Crunch Ltd pour qui vous avez travaillé l'année dernière.

Nous avons une plainte à formuler contre le journal *La Gazette du Samedi* qui nous a sérieusement diffamés dans l'article que nous joignons à cette lettre concernant la fermeture de notre usine de Roissy-en-France.

Nous désirons intenter une action en justice contre ledit journal mais nous aimerions tout d'abord avoir votre avis professionnel concernant la solidité de notre cas. Pourriez-vous également nous faire savoir la durée probable de cette action et nous donner une idée du montant des frais judiciaires que cette poursuite pourrait engendrer.

Vous en remerciant par avance, nous vous prions d'agréer, cher Maître, nos salutations distinguées.

Lionel E. Bone
Président Directeur Général

Contacting official agencies/Contacter des organismes publics

Chamber of Commerce

RC: How do you do? I'm Robert Cid, from Textiles United.

AC: Pleased to meet you. Arthur Collin. My staff told me you were going to call in this morning. How can we help?

RC: We are thinking of expanding the business, especially to focus on the '30s to 50s' market. We were advised to seek your views on how and where best to establish retail outlets for our fashion products.

AC: Well, Mr Cid. I hope you will join the Chamber as and when you set up in the city, but for the time being you are welcome to our assistance.

RC: Yes, I understand, but right now we are keen to obtain some information on local retail figures, the competition, some data on the local population, available premises and so on.

AC: That's no problem. We can provide you with what you request and much more. Are you likely to be creating any jobs through your new initiative?

RC: We will inevitably need new staff, both in the factory and in the local shops. Do you happen to have a good contact at the Job Centre?

AC: Yes, of course. If you'd like to come through to my office, we'll have a coffee and get down to discussing things.

La Chambre de commerce

RC: Bonjour, Monsieur. Robert Cid de chez Textiles United.

AC: Enchanté de faire votre connaissance. Arthur Collin. Ma secrétaire m'a prévenu que vous alliez venir ce matin. Que puis-je faire pour vous?

RC: Nous pensons sérieusement à agrandir notre entreprise, et nous visons principalement le marché touchant les 'trente à cinquante ans'. On m'a conseillé de venir recueillir vos conseils quant à la meilleure localisation de nos magasins pour la vente de nos produits de mode.

AC: Eh bien, M. Cid, j'espère que vous adhérerez à la Chambre de Commerce lorsque votre société sera établie dans notre ville. En attendant, je me ferai effectivement un plaisir de vous aider.

RC: Oui, je comprends. Pour le moment, nous aimerions obtenir des renseignements d'ordre général, les chiffres de ventes réalisés dans la région, des informations concernant la concurrence, la population locale, les locaux actuellement disponibles et ainsi de suite.

AC: Il n'y a aucun problème. Nous pouvons vous procurer toutes ces informations et bien plus encore. Allez-vous créer de nouveaux emplois grâce à cette nouvelle initiative?

RC: Nous aurons inévitablement besoin de personnel tant à l'usine que dans les magasins. Avez-vous de bonnes relations avec l'ANPE?

AC: Oui, bien sûr. Mais, venez plutôt dans mon bureau. Nous boirons une tasse de café et discuterons affaires plus à notre aise.

Customs and Excise

CUSTOMS AND EXCISE OFFICER: Good morning, Sir.

RETAILER: Hello, I have a query regarding the import of meat.

CUSTOMS AND EXCISE OFFICER: Certainly. Can you explain?

RETAILER: We're a meat retailer based here in Dover, and we're intending to import a range of cooked meats and sausages from a German supplier. So far we've only been supplied by British companies. I need to know what the regulations are.

CUSTOMS AND EXCISE OFFICER: It's rather difficult and complex to explain briefly. There is a range of regulations and restrictions. They're contained in our information brochures. When are you intending to import these products?

RETAILER: We'll get the first shipment in a couple of weeks.

CUSTOMS AND EXCISE OFFICER: Then you'd better move fast. I'll collect all the information for you. The best thing is for you to read it and then come back to us with any queries.

RETAILER: Fine. I'll get down to it.

La douane

DOUANIER: Bonjour, Monsieur.

DÉTAILLANT: Bonjour, j'ai besoin de quelques renseignements concernant l'importation de produits à base de viande. Pouvez-vous m'aider?

DOUANIER: Bien sûr. Que voulez-vous exactement?

DÉTAILLANT: Nous vendons de la viande ici à Douvres et nous aimerions importer une sélection de viandes cuites et de saucisses qui nous viendraient d'un fournisseur allemand. Jusqu'à présent, nous étions approvisionnés par des fournisseurs britanniques. Je dois donc connaître les réglementations.

DOUANIER: C'est relativement complexe et difficile à expliquer brièvement. J'ai ici tout un tas de réglementations et de restrictions à respecter. Elles figurent toutes dans nos brochures d'information. Quand comptiez-vous importer ces produits?

DÉTAILLANT: Nous devrions recevoir notre première commande d'ici deux semaines.

DOUANIER: Il faut donc se dépêcher. Alors. Je vais rassembler ces informations pour vous. La meilleure chose à faire est de les lire et de nous contacter si vous avez d'autres questions.

DÉTAILLANT: Très bien. Je vais étudier cela de près.

Apologizing for non-attendance/Se faire excuser de ne pas pouvoir assister

At a future meeting

NANCY RICHARDS: Nancy Richards.

BILL PERKINS: Morning, Nancy. Bill Perkins here.

NANCY RICHARDS: Hello, Bill, how are you?

BILL PERKINS: Fine thanks. Look, I've just received notice of the meeting for the Sales Department next Tuesday.

NANCY RICHARDS: Yes, is there a problem?

BILL PERKINS: Afraid so. I'll have to send my apologies. I've already committed to a trade fair trip.

NANCY RICHARDS: OK. I'll pass on your apologies. Can you send someone else?

BILL PERKINS: I've a colleague who can probably come. Her name is Susie Rogerson. She'll contact you later today.

NANCY RICHARDS: Fine. Well, have a nice trip. I'll see you when you get back.

A une réunion ultérieure

NADINE RICHARD: Allô, Nadine Richard à l'appareil.

BERNARD PÉGUY: Bonjour Nadine. C'est Bernard Péguy.

NADINE RICHARD: Bonjour Bernard, comment allez-vous?

BERNARD PÉGUY: Très bien, merci. Je viens juste d'apprendre qu'il y aura une réunion pour le service commercial mardi.

NADINE RICHARD: Oui. Y a-t-il un problème?

BERNARD PÉGUY: Oui, j'en ai peur. Il faudra que vous m'excusiez mais je me suis déjà engagé et dois me rendre à un salon professionnel.

NADINE RICHARD: D'accord. Je transmettrai. Quelqu'un d'autre pourrait-il-vous représenter?

BERNARD PÉGUY: J'ai une collègue qui pourrait probablement venir. Il s'agit de Suzanne Roger. Elle vous contactera plus tard dans la journée.

NADINE RICHARD: Très bien. Bon, faites bon voyage. Je vous verrai lors de votre retour.

At a meeting that has already been held

GEORGE PARSONS: Could you put me through to the Managing Director please.

SECRETARY: Certainly, sir. One moment please.

HENRY SACHS: Hello, George. We missed you yesterday.

GEORGE PARSONS: I am calling to apologize. I didn't write because I intended to come and was prevented at the last moment.

HENRY SACHS: I gather there's a spot of bother in the Gulf.

GEORGE PARSONS: Oh, you've heard. Bad news travels fast. Yes, we have a container ship on its way and rumours of war at its destination.

HENRY SACHS: What will you do? Send it somewhere else pro tem?

GEORGE PARSONS: Yes, but don't worry – I'll sort it out. Meanwhile how did your 'do' go?

HENRY SACHS: Very well. All the important people came. Barry Clerkenwell from the BOTB was asking for you. I said you'd give him a bell.

GEORGE PARSONS: Will do. I'm really sorry that I couldn't make it.

A une réunion qui a déjà eu lieu

GEORGE POISSON: Pourriez-vous me passer le directeur général s'il vous plaît?

SECRÉTAIRE: Bien sûr, Monsieur. Veuillez patienter quelques instants s'il vous plaît.

HENRI SACHS: Bonjour Georges. Tu nous as manqué hier.

GEORGE POISSON: Je te demande de m'excuser. Je n'ai pas écrit car je pensais vraiment pouvoir venir mais j'ai eu un empêchement de dernière minute.

HENRI SACHS: J'ai cru comprendre que le Golfe est à la source de quelques soucis.

GEORGE POISSON: Ah, tu es au courant. Les mauvaises nouvelles se répandent vite. Oui, nous avons un porte-conteneurs en route, et il y a rumeur de guerre à destination.

HENRI SACHS: Que vas-tu faire? L'envoyer ailleurs temporairement?

GEORGE POISSON: Oui mais ne t'inquiète pas. Je résoudrai ce problème. Et pour toi, comment s'est passée ta soirée?

HENRI SACHS: Très bien. Thierry Maréchal du Ministère m'a demandé de tes nouvelles. Je lui ai dit que tu lui passerais un coup de fil.

GEORGE POISSON: Je le ferai. Je suis vraiment désolé ne pas avoir pu venir.

Job titles used in commerce/Titres de fonction employés dans le domaine commercial

in the UK and US/ *au Royaume-Uni et aux États-Unis*	in France/ *en France*
account executive	*in PR company, advertising* chef de publicité *mf*
account executive	*in finance* responsable de budget *mf*
account manager	*in advertising* chef de publicité d'agence *mf*
account manager	*in finance* responsable de budget *mf*
administration officer	responsable administratif *mf*, agent administratif *m*
administrator	gestionnaire *mf*, gérant *m*, administrateur *m*
advertising director	chef de publicité *mf*
advertising manager	chef du service publicité *mf*, directeur de la publicité *m*
after-sales manager	directeur du service après-ventes *m*
agency representative	chef de publicité *mf*, chef de publicité d'agence *mf*
area manager	chef de région *mf*, chef de secteur *mf*
art manager	directeur artistique *m*
asset manager	gestionnaire de l'actif *mf*
assistant controller	contrôleur adjoint *m*
assistant director	directeur adjoint *m*
assistant director general	directeur général adjoint *m*
assistant general director	directeur général adjoint *m*
assistant general manager	directeur général adjoint *m*
assistant head of section *UK*	chef d'unité adjoint *m*, adjoint du chef de section *m*
assistant manager	directeur adjoint *m*, sous-directeur *m*, sous-chef *mf*
authorized representative	mandataire *mf*
brand manager	chef de produit *mf*, chef de marque *mf*
cash manager	trésorier *m*, responsable financier *mf*
chair	président *m*, président du conseil d'administration *m*
chairman	président *m*, président du conseil d'administration *m*
chairman and chief executive *US*	président-directeur général *m*, directeur général *m*
chairman and managing director *UK*	président-directeur général *m*
chairman and general manager	président-directeur général *m*
chairman of the administrative board	président-directeur général *m*
chairman of the board	président du conseil *m*
chairman of the board of directors	président du conseil d'administration *m*
chairman of the board of management	président du directoire *m*, président-directeur général *m*
chairman of the executive committee	président du comité exécutif *m*
chairman of the supervisory board	*in PLCs* * président du conseil de surveillance *m*
chairperson	président *m*
chairwoman	présidente *f*
charge hand	chef d'équipe *mf*
chief buyer	chef des achats *mf*, directeur des achats *m*, responsable des achats *mf*, chef d'approvisionnement *mf*, chef du service achats *mf*
chief clerk	chef de bureau *mf*, commis principal *m*
chief executive	directeur général *m*
chief executive officer *US*	directeur général *m*, président-directeur général *m*
chief financial officer	directeur financier *m*, responsable financier *m*
chief inspector	inspecteur en chef *m*, inspecteur principal *m*
chief operating officer	chef de service *mf*
circulation manager	directeur du service des ventes *m*, responsable du service de distribution *mf*
claims inspector	inspecteur des plaintes *m*
claims manager	chef du service des réclamations *mf*
co-director	codirecteur *m*
co-manager	codirecteur *m*
commercial and development manager	directeur commercial et du développement *m*

in the UK and US/ *au Royaume-Uni et aux États-Unis*	in France/ *en France*
commercial manager	cadre commercial *m*, directeur commercial *m*
commercial director	administrateur commercial *m*
company secretary *UK*	secrétaire général *m*
confidential secretary	secrétaire privé *m*
consumer relations manager	chef du service consommateurs *mf*, directeur des relations avec la clientèle *m*, directeur clientèle *m*
contracts manager	directeur chargé des contrats *m*
contracts officer	cadre chargé des contrats *m*
co-owner	co-propriétaire *mf*
credit controller	vérificateur des crédits *m*
customer relations manager	directeur des relations avec la clientèle *m*
department head	directeur de département *m*
departmental manager	chef de service *mf*
deputy chairman	vice-président *m*
deputy chairman of the supervisory board	*in PLCs** vice-président du conseil de surveillance *m*
deputy chairman of the board of management	*in PLCs** vice-président du directoire *m*
deputy chief executive	directeur général adjoint *m*
deputy director	directeur adjoint *m*, sous-directeur *m*
deputy manager	directeur adjoint *m*, sous-directeur *m*
deputy managing director	directeur général adjoint *m*
deputy member of the board of management	*in PLCs** membre suppléant du directoire *m*
development director	administrateur chargé du développement *m*
development manager	directeur du développement *m*
director	directeur *m*, administrateur *m*
director general	directeur général *m*
director of labor relations *AmE* director of labour relations *BrE*	directeur des affaires sociales *m*
director of public relations	chef du service des relations publiques *mf*, directeur des relations publiques *m*, responsable des relations publiques *mf*
district officer	responsable régional *m*
district training officer	directeur régional de la formation professionnelle *m*, responsable régional de la formation professionnelle *m*
division head	directeur de division *m*
division manager	chef de division *mf*, chef de département *mf*
engineering manager	directeur technique *m*
executive director	directeur exécutif *m*
executive manager	directeur général *m*
executive officer	cadre supérieur *m*
executive vice president	vice-président *m*, directeur général *m*
export coordinator	coordinateur des exportations *m*
export director	directeur des exportations *m*, directeur export *m*, administrateur des exportations *m*
export marketing manager	directeur marketing des exportations *m*
field sales manager	directeur des ventes-clientèle *m*, chef de terrain *mf*
financial manager	directeur financier *m*, responsable financier *m*
fleet manager	directeur du parc automobile *m*
foreman	chef d'équipe *mf*, contremaître *m*
general counsel *US* (*cf* head of legal department)	chef du service juridique *mf*
general manager *US limited companies* (*cf* managing director)	gérant *m*, directeur général *m*, président-directeur général *m*
general executive manager	*in associations* secrétaire général *m*
general partner	*in limited partnership* commandité *m*
group leader	animateur de groupe *m*, accompagnateur *m*

in the UK and US/ *au Royaume-Uni et aux États-Unis*	in France/ *en France*
head buyer	chef des achats *mf*, directeur des achats *m*, responsable des achats *mf*, chef d'approvisionnement *mf*, chef du service achats *mf*
head clerk	premier commis *m*, chef de bureau *mf*
head foreman	chef d'atelier *mf*
head of legal department *UK* (*cf* general counsel *US*)	chef du service juridique *mf*
head of personnel	chef du service personnel *mf*
head of personnel (department)	chef du service personnel *mf*
honorary chairman	président d'honneur *m*
honorary chairman of the board of directors	*in associations* président d'honneur *m*
honorary president	président d'honneur *m*
import documentation supervisor	inspecteur des documents d'importation *m*
import manager	directeur des importations *m*
import sales executive	responsable des ventes d'importation *mf*
indoor sales manager	directeur de ventes sédentaires *m*, directeur de ventes intérieures *m*
industrial relations director	directeur des relations industrielles *m*, directeur des relations professionelles *m*, directeur des relations humaines *m*
industrial relations manager	directeur des relations industrielles *m*, directeur des relations professionelles *m*, directeur des relations humaines *m*
information officer	cadre à l'information *m*, chef du service de renseignements *mf*
inspector	inspecteur *m*
investigation officer	enquêteur *m*, agent d'enquête *m*
joint director	codirecteur *m*
joint manager	codirecteur *m*, cogérant *m*
junior manager	sous-directeur *m*, jeune cadre *m*
limited partner	associé commanditaire *m*
line executive	dirigeant opérationnel *m*
line manager	cadre hiérarchique *m*, chef hiérarchique *mf*, chef direct *mf*, directeur hiérarchique *m*, responsable opérationnel *m*, chef d'atelier *mf*, surveillant de premier niveau *m*, contremaître *m*, agent de maîtrise *m*
line supervisor	surveillant de premier niveau *m*, agent de maîtrise *m*, contremaître *m*
manager	directeur *m*, manager *m*, chef *m*, dirigeant *m*, gestionnaire *m*, gérant *m*, responsable *m*
manageress	gérante *f*, directrice *f*
managing director *UK* (*cf* general manager*)	gérant *m*, directeur général *m*, président-directeur général *m*
managing partner	associé gérant *m*
marketing director	directeur du marketing *m*, directeur commercial *m*
marketing manager	directeur du marketing *m*, directeur commercial *m*
marketing officer	chargé de la mercatique *m*, chargé du marketing *m*
member of the board of management	*in PLCs** membre du directoire *m*
member of the supervisory board	*in PLCs** membre du conseil de surveillance *m*
merchandising director	directeur commercial *m*, directeur du merchandising *m*
middle manager	cadre moyen *m*
motor transport officer	responsable des transports motorisés *mf*, agent de transportation routière *m*
national accounts manager	responsable national du budget *m*
non-executive director	administrateur non dirigeant *m*, administrateur externe *m*
office manager	chef de bureau *mf*, directeur de bureau *m*
operational manager	directeur des opérations *m*
operations manager	directeur des opérations *m*
outside director	administrateur externe *m*
overseer	contremaître *m*

in the UK and US/ *au Royaume-Uni et aux États-Unis*	in France/ *en France*
owner-manager	propriétaire-gérant *m*
personal secretary	secrétaire particulier *m*, secrétaire de direction *mf*, assistant personnel *m*
personnel director	chef du service personnel *mf*, chef du personnel *mf*
personnel manager	chef du personnel *mf*, chef du service personnel *mf*
plant manager	chef d'établissement *mf*, directeur d'usine *m*
president	président-directeur général *m*
press officer	responsable du service de presse *mf*
private secretary	secrétaire particulier *m*, secrétaire privé *m*
procurement manager	chef des achats *mf*, directeur des achats *m*, responsable des achats *mf*, chef d'approvisionnement *mf*, chef du service achats *mf*
product manager	directeur de produit *m*, chef de produit *mf*
production director	directeur de fabrication *m*, chef de production *mf*, chef de fabrication *mf*, directeur technique *m*
production manager	directeur de fabrication *m*, chef de production *mf*, directeur technique *m*, chef de fabrication *mf*
project leader	chef de projet *mf*
project manager	directeur de projet *m*, chef de projet *mf*
proprietor	propriétaire exploitant *m*
publicity manager	*in advertising company* chef de publicité *mf*, chef du service publicité *mf*, directeur de la publicité *m*
public relations officer	responsable des relations publiques *mf*, chef du service des relations publiques *mf*, directeur des relations publiques *m*
purchasing manager	directeur des achats *m*, chef des achats *mf*
purchasing officer	responsable des achats *mf*
regional manager	chef de région *mf*, responsable régional *m*
registered manager	responsable de conformité aux règlements *mf*, responsable des permis de transports maritimes *mf*
research director	directeur de la recherche *m*
sales director	administrateur commercial *m*
sales engineer	ingénieur commercial *m*, technico-commercial *m*
sales executive	cadre commercial *m*
sales manager	directeur des ventes *m*, chef du service des ventes *mf*, responsable des ventes *mf*, commercial *m*, directeur commercial *m*
sales representative	voyageur de commerce *m*, représentant *m*, agent commercial *m*
senior clerk	commis principal *m*, chef de bureau *mf*
senior executive	cadre supérieur *m*
senior export clerk	chef de bureau des exportations *mf*
senior import clerk	chef de bureau des importations *mf*
senior manager	cadre supérieur *m*
senior officer	officier supérieur *m*
senior vice president *US*	responsable supérieur *mf*
shareholder, member *UK*	associé *m*
shareholder, stockholder *US*	associé *m*
site foreman	chef de chantier *mf*
staff manager	chef du service personnel *mf*, chef du personnel *mf*
stock controller	responsable des stocks *mf*
submanager	sous-directeur *m*
supervisor	surveillant *m*, agent de maîtrise *m*
team leader	chef d'équipe *mf*
technical director	directeur technique *m*
technical manager	directeur technique *m*
territory manager	chef de région *mf*
top executive	cadre supérieur *m*
traffic executive	responsable de la circulation *mf*
traffic manager	chef de la circulation *mf*, directeur des transports *m*

in the UK and US/ *au Royaume-Uni et aux États-Unis*	in France/ *en France*
traffic superintendent	chef de la circulation *mf*, directeur des transports *m*, surveillant de la circulation *m*
traffic supervisor	inspecteur de la circulation *m*
trainee manager	cadre en formation *m*
training officer	directeur de formation *m*, cadre chargé de la formation *m*, responsable de la formation professionnelle *mf*
transport controller	contrôleur des transports *m*
vice-chairman	vice-président *m*
vice-president	vice-président *m*, président adjoint *m*
works manager	chef d'établissement *mf*, directeur d'usine *m*

* US Stock corporations

Stock exchanges/Bourses des marchés et des valeurs

English name/*nom anglais*	country, city/*pays, ville*	French name/*nom français*
	UK/ **le Royaume-Uni**	
Baltic Futures Exchange	London	Marché à terme baltique *m*
Belfast Stock Exchange	Belfast	Bourse de Belfast *f*
Birmingham Stock Exchange	Birmingham	Bourse de Birmingham *f*
Glasgow Stock Exchange	Glasgow	Bourse de Glasgow *f*
International Stock Exchange (*also* London Stock Exchange)	London	Bourse de Londres *f*
Liverpool Commodity Exchange	Liverpool	Bourse de commerce de Liverpool *f*
Liverpool Stock Exchange	Liverpool	Bourse de Liverpool *f*
London Futures and Options Exchange	London	Bourse des marchés à terme et options de Londres *f*
London Trader Options Exchange	London	Bourse des options négociables de Londres *f*
London Metal Exchange	London	Bourse des métaux de Londres *f*
London Commodity Exchange	London	Bourse de matières premières de Londres *f*
London International Financial Futures Exchange	London	Bourse internationale financière à terme de Londres *f*
Manchester Commodity Exchange	Manchester	Bourse de commerce du Manchester *f*
Royal Exchange	London	Bourse de Commerce de Londres *f*
Unlisted Securities Market	London	Marché des valeurs non-cotées *m*
	USA/ **aux États-Unis**	
American Stock Exchange	New York	Amex (marché financier secondaire de New York) *m*
Amex Commodity Exchange	New York	Bourse de commerce de l'Amex *f*
Boston Stock Exchange	Boston	Bourse de Boston *f*
Chicago Stock Exchange (Midwest Stock Exchange)	Chicago	Bourse du Midwest *f*
Chicago Mercantile Exchange	Chicago	Bourse de commerce de Chicago *f*
Chicago Board Options Exchange	Chicago	Bourse d'options de Chicago *f*
Cincinnatti Stock Exchange	Cincinnatti	Bourse de Cincinnatti *f*
Mid-America Commodity Exchange	Chicago	Bourse des marchandises de Chicago *f*
Minneapolis Grain Exchange	Minneapolis	Bourse des céréales de Minnéapolis *f*
New York Coffee, Sugar and Cocoa Exchange	New York	Bourse du café, du sucre et du cacao de New York *f*
New York Curb Exchange	New York	Marché hors cote de New York *m*
New York Cotton Exchange and Petroleum and Citrus Associates	New York	Bourse du coton de New York *f*
New York Mercantile Exchange	New York	Bourse de commerce de New York *f*
New Orleans Commodity Exchange	New Orleans	Bourse de commerce de la Nouvelle Orléans *f*
New York Stock Exchange	New York	Bourse de New York *f*
Pacific Stock Exchange (Los Angeles Stock Exchange) (San Francisco Stock Exchange)	Los Angeles and San Francisco	Bourse de Los Angeles *f* Bourse de San Francisco *f*
Philadelphia Stock Exchange	Philadelphia	Bourse de Philadelphie *f*
Salt Lake City Stock Exchange	Salt Lake City	Bourse de Salt Lake City *f*
Spokane Stock Exchange	Spokane	Bourse de Spokane *f*
	Canada/ **le Canada**	
Toronto Stock Exchange	Toronto	Bourse de Toronto *f*

English name/ *nom anglais*	country, city/ *pays, ville*	French name/ *nom français*
	France/ *la France*	
Paris Financial Futures Exchange	Paris	Bourse des marchés financiers à terme de Paris *f*
Paris Stock Exchange	Paris	Bourse de Paris *f*
Paris Trader Options Exchange	Paris	Marché des options négociables de Paris *m*
	Switzerland/ *la Suisse*	
Geneva Stock Exchange	Geneva	Bourse de Genève *f*
Swiss Options and Financial Futures Exchange	Zürich	Bourse des options et valeurs à terme suisse *f*
Zürich Stock Exchange	Zürich	Bourse de Zurich *f*

Financial and economic indexes/Indices financiers et économiques

Area/Domaine	Index/*Indice*	Translation/*Traduction*	coverage/*étendue*
AC	consumer price index	indice des prix à la consommation *m*	General
AC	price index	indice des prix *m*	General
EC	balance of trade	balance commerciale *f*	General
EC	composite index	indice composé *m*, indice composite *m*	General
EC	consumer price index	indice des prix à la consommation *m*	General
EC	cost-of-living index	indice du coût de la vie *m*	General
EC	diffusion index	indice de diffusion *m*	General
EC	discomfort index	indice d'inconfort *m*	General
EC	Divisia money Index	masse monétaire *m*	International
EC	gross national income	revenu national brut *m*	General
EC	gross national product	produit national brut *m*	General
EC	growth index	indice de croissance *m*	General
EC	income per capita	salaire individuel *m*	General
EC	Laspeyre's index	indice de Laspeyre *m*	General
EC	Lerner index	indice de Lerner *m*	General
EC	national expenditure	dépenses de l'État *mpl*	General
EC	net national income	revenu national net *m*	General
EC	net national product	produit national net *m*	General
EC	Paasche index	indice de Paasche *m*	General
EC	price index	indice des prix *m*	General
EC	producer price index	indice des prix à la production *m*	General
EC	rate of inflation	taux d'inflation *m*	General
EC	retail price index	indice des prix de détail *m*	General
EC	salary grade	indice de traitement *m*	General
EC	scarcity index	indice de rareté *m*	General
EC	unemployment rate	taux de chômage *m*	General
EC	unit value index	indice des valeurs unitaires *m*	General
EC	wholesale price index	indice des prix de gros *m*	General
FI	composite index	indice composé *m*, indice composite *m*	General
FI	index of coincident indicators	indice des indicateurs simultanés *m*	General
FI	index of lagging indicators	indice des indicateurs retardés d'activité *m*	General
FI	index of leading indicators	indice des indicateurs de tête *m*	General
FI	index of longer leading indicators	indice des indicateurs à longue durée *m*	General
FI	index of shorter leading indicators	indice des indicateurs à courte durée *m*	General
FI	price index	indice des prix *m*	General
GC	retail price index	indice des prix de détail *m*	General
GC	weighted index	indice pondéré *m*	General
IND	Index of Industrial Production	indice de production industrielle *m*	UK
IND	Thirty-Share Index	indice des principales valeurs industrielles *m*	UK
ST	All Ordinaries Index	indice de toutes les actions ordinaires *m*	Australia
ST	Barclays Index	indice de la Bourse néo-zélandaise *m*	New Zealand
ST	Barron's confidence index	indice de Barron *m*	US
ST	bond index	indice des obligations *m*	General
ST	Capital International World Index	indice mondial des bourses de valeurs *m*	International
ST	CBS Tendency Index	indice des principales valeurs de la bourse d'Amsterdam *m*	Netherlands
ST	Comit index	indice Comit *m*	Italy
ST	commodities index	indice des marchandises *m*	General
ST	composite leading index	indice composite principal *m*	General
ST	construction cost index	indice du coût de la construction *m*	General
ST	Credit suisse index	indice du Crédit Suisse *m*	Switzerland
ST	Donoghue's Money Fund average	indice Donoghue des fonds monétaires *m*	International
ST	Dow-Jones index	indice Dow Jones *m*	US

Area/ *Domain*	Index/*Indice*	Translation/*Traduction*	coverage/ *étendue*
ST	Eurodollar Index	indice de l'eurodollar *m*	Europe
ST	Financial Times Index FT Index	indice du Financial Times *m*	UK
ST	Financial Times Industrial Ordinary Share Index	indice des actions industrielles ordinaires du Financial Times *m*	UK
ST	Financial Times Actuaries All Share Index All Share Index	indice du Financial Times et de l'Institut d'Actuaires *m*	UK
ST	Financial Times Stock Exchange index, FT-SE 100 Share Index	indice des FTSE 100 *m*, indice FTSE 100 valeurs *m*, indice Footsie *m*	UK
ST	FT-SE Eurotrack 100 Index	indice FTSE eurotrack des 100 valeurs *m*	Europe
ST	FT-SE Eurotrack 200 Index	indice FTSE eurotrack des 200 valeurs *m*	Europe
ST	golds index	indice des métaux précieux	General
ST	Hang Seng Index	indice Hang Seng *m*, Indice Hong Kong *m*	Hong Kong
ST	index of leading indicators	indice des grandes valeurs *m*, indice des indicateurs de tête *m*	General
ST	International monetary market Three-Month Discount Index	indice de décompte trimestriel du Marché monétaire international *m*	International
ST	International monetary market Three-Month Add-On Index	Rajout trimestriel à l'indice du Marché monétaire international *m*	International
ST	International monetary market Certificate of Deposit Index	indice des certificats de dépôt du Marché monétaire international *m*	International
ST	International monetary market Treasury-bill Index	indice des bons du trésor du Marché monétaire international *m*	International
ST	Major Market Index	indice du marché principal *m*	General
ST	market index	indice boursier *m*	General
ST	market value-weighted index	indice pondéré de valeur marchande *m*, indice pondéré par la capitalisation boursière *m*	General
ST	Morgan Stanley Capital International World Index	indice boursier mondial morgan Stanley *m*	International
ST	New York Stock Exchange Composite Index	indice composé de la bourse de New York *m*	US
ST	Nikkei average, Nikkei index	indice Nikkei *m*	Japan
ST	price-weighted index	indice pondéré des cours, indice pondéré, par les prix *m*	General
ST	share index	indice des actions *m*, indice des cours des actions *m*	General
ST	stock price index	indice boursier *m*	General
ST	stock exchange price index	indice boursier *m*, indice des actions *m*, indice des cours des actions *m*	General
ST	stock market index	indice boursier *m*	General
ST	stock indexes and averages	indices boursiers *m*	General
ST	stock market price index	indice boursier *m*	General
ST	Thirty-Share Index	indice des principales valeurs industrielles *m*	UK
ST	Unitas All Share Index	indice boursier de la Bourse de Helsinki *m*	Finland
ST	utility average	indice moyen des services publics *m*	General
ST	Value Line Composite Index	indice composite 'value line' *m*	US
ST	Value Line Stock Index	indice boursier 'value line' *m*	US
ST	weighted index	indice pondéré *m*	General

Key/Légende

AC:	Accountancy	EC:	Economics	
FI:	Finance	IND:	Industry	
ST:	Stock Market	WE:	Welfare	

Countries/Les pays

Country/ *Pays*	Capital/ *Capitale*	Inhabitant/ *Habitant*	Official language/s *langue/s officielle/s**	Currency/ *Devise*
Afghanistan	Kabul	Afghan	Pushtu/Dari	afghni
Afghanistan m	*Kaboul*	*Afghan m*	*pushtou/dari*	*afghani m*
Albania	Tirana	Albanian	Albanian	lek
Albanie f	*Tirana*	*Albanais m*	*albanais*	*lek m*
Algeria	Algiers	Algerian	Arabic/French	dinar
Algérie f	*Alger*	*Algérien m*	*arabe/français*	*dinar m*
Andorra	Andorra la Vella	Andorran	Catalan/French/Spanish	French franc peseta
Andorre f	*Andorre-la-Vieille*	*Andorran m*	*catalan/français/espagnol*	*franc français m* *peseta f*
Angola	Luanda	Angolan	Portuguese	kwanza
Angola m	*Luanda*	*Angolais m*	*portugais*	*kwanza m*
Antigua and Barbuda	St. John's	Antiguan/Barbudian	English	East Caribbean dollar
Antigua f	*Saint-Jean Saint-John's*	*d'Antigua*	*anglais*	*dollar antillais m*
Argentina	Buenos Aires	Argentinian/Argentine	Spanish	austral
Argentine f	*Buenos Aires*	*Argentin m*	*espagnol*	*austral m*
Armenia	Yerevan	Armenian	Armenian	rouble
Arménie f	*Erevan*	*Arménien m*	*arménien*	*rouble/ruble m*
Australia	Canberra	Australian	English	Australian dollar
Australie f	*Canberra*	*Australien m*	*anglais*	*dollar australien m*
Austria	Vienna	Austrian	German	schilling
Autriche f	*Vienne*	*Autrichien m*	*allemand*	*schilling m*
Azerbaijan	Baku	Azeri/Azerbaijani	Azeri/Russian	manat
Azerbaïdjan m	*Bakou*	*Azeri/Azerbaïdjanais m*	*azeri/russe*	*manat m*
Bahamas	Nassau	Bahamian	English	Bahamian dollar
Bahamas f pl	*Nassau*	*des Bahamas*	*anglais*	*dollar des Bahamas m*
Bahrain	Manama	Bahraini	Arabic	dinar
Bahreïn m	*Manama*	*Bahreïni m*	*arabe*	*dinar m*
Bangladesh	Dhaka	Bangladeshi	Bengali	taka
Bangladesh m	*Dacca*	*Bangladeshi/Bangladais m*	*bengali*	*takka m*
Barbados	Bridgetown	Barbadian	English	Barbados dollar
Barbade f	*Bridgetown*	*Barbadien m*	*anglais*	*dollar de Barbade m*
Belarus	Minsk	Belarussian	Belarussian	Belarussian rouble
Biélorussie f	*Minsk*	*Biélorusse mf*	*Biélorusse*	*rouble biélorusse m*
Belgium	Brussels	Belgian	French/Flemish	Belgian franc
Belgique f	*Bruxelles*	*Belge mf*	*français/flamand*	*franc belge m*
Belize	Belmopan	Belizean	English/Spanish/Creole	Belize dollar
Bélize m	*Belmopan*	*Bélizien m*	*anglais/espagnol/créole*	*dollar de Bélize m*
Benin	Porto Novo	Beninese	French	C.F.A. franc
Bénin m	*Porto Novo*	*Béninois m*	*français*	*franc CFA m*
Bermuda	Hamilton	Bermudan/Bermudian	English	dollar (dol.)
Bermudes f pl	*Hamilton*	*Bermudien m*	*anglais*	*dollar (dol.) m*
Bhutan	Thamphu	Bhutanese/Bhutani	Dzongka	ngultrum/Indian rupee
Bhoutan m	*Thimbu*	*Bhoutanais m*	*dzongka*	*ngultrum m* *roupie de l'Inde f*

Country/ *Pays*	Capital/ *Capitale*	Inhabitant/ *Habitant*	Official language/s *langue/s officielle/s**	Currency/ *Devise*
Bolivia	La Paz	Bolivian	Spanish, Indian languages	Bolivian peso
Bolivie f	*La Paz*	*Bolivien m*	*espagnol, langues indiennes*	*peso bolivien m*
Bosnia-Herzegovina	Sarajevo	Bosnian	Serbo-Croat	dinar
Bosnie-Herzégovine f	*Sarajevo*	*Bosniaque mf* *Bosnien m*	*serbo-croate*	*dinar m*
Botswana	Gaborone	Botswanan	English/Setswana	pula
Botswana m	*Gaborone*	*du Botswana*	*anglais, tswana*	*pula m*
Brazil	Brasilia	Brazilian	Portuguese	cruzeiro
Brésil m	*Brasilia*	*Brésilien m*	*portugais*	*cruzeiro m*
Brunei	Bandar Seri Begawan	Brunei/Bruneian	Malay/English	Brunei dollar
Brunei m	*Bandar Seri Begawan*	*du Brunei*	*malais/anglais*	*dollar du Brunei m*
Bulgaria	Sofia	Bulgarian	Bulgarian	lev
Bulgarie f	*Sofia*	*Bulgare mf*	*bulgare*	*lev m*
Burkina Faso	Ouagadougou	Burkinabe	French/Mossi	C.F.A. franc
Burkina Faso m	*Ouagadougou*	*du Burkina Faso*	*français/mossi*	*franc CFA m*
Burma	Rangoon	Burmese	Burmese	kyat
Birmanie f	*Rangoon*	*Birman m*	*birman*	*kyat m*
Burundi	Bujumbura	Burundian	Kirundi/French	Burundi franc
Burundi m	*Bujumbura*	*Burundais m*	*kirundi/français*	*franc du Burundi m*
Cambodia	Phnom Penh	Cambodian	Khmer	riel
Combodge m	*Phnom Penh*	*Cambodgien m*	*khmer*	*riel m*
Cameroon	Yaoundé	Cameroonian	French/English	C.F.A. franc
Cameroun m	*Yaoundé*	*Camerounais m*	*français/anglais*	*franc CFA m*
Canada	Ottawa	Canadian	English/French	Canadian dollar
Canada m	*Ottawa*	*Canadien m*	*anglais/français*	*dollar canadien m*
Central African Republic	Bangui	from the Central African Republic	French/Sango	C.F.A. franc
République centrafricaine f	*Bangui*	*de la République centrafricaine*	*français/sango*	*franc CFA m*
Chad	N'Djamena	Chadian	Arabic/French	C.F.A. franc
Tchad m	*N'Djamena*	*Tchadien m*	*arabe/français*	*franc CFA m*
Chile	Santiago	Chilean	Spanish	peso
Chili m	*Santiago*	*Chilien m*	*espagnol*	*peso m*
China	Beijing (Peking)	Chinese	Mandarin/Chinese	yuan
Chine f	*Beijing (Pékin)*	*Chinois m*	*mandarin/chinois*	*yuan m*
Colombia	Bogotá	Colombian	Spanish	peso
Colombie f	*Bogotá*	*Colombien m*	*espagnol*	*peso m*
Comoros	Moroni	Comorian/Comoran	French/Arabic	Comorian franc
Comores f pl	*Moroni*	*Comorien m*	*français/arabe*	*franc comorien m*
Congo	Brazzaville	Congolese	French	C.F.A. franc
Congo m	*Brazzaville*	*Congolais m*	*français*	*franc CFA m*
Costa Rica	San José	Costa Rican	Spanish	colón
Costa Rica m	*San José*	*Costaricain m*	*espagnol*	*colón m*
Côte d'Ivoire	Yamoussoukro	Ivorian	French	C.F.A. franc
Côte d'Ivoire f	*Yamoussoukro*	*Ivoirien m*	*français*	*franc CFA m*
Croatia	Zagreb	Croat/Croatian	Serbo-Croat	kuna
Croatie f	*Zagreb*	*Croate mf*	*serbo-croate*	*kuna m*
Cuba	Havana	Cuban	Spanish	Cuban peso
Cuba f	*La Havane*	*Cubain m*	*espagnol*	*peso cubain m*
Cyprus	Nicosia	Cypriot	Greek/Turkish	Cyprus pound
Chypre f	*Nicosie*	*Cypriote/Chypriote mf*	*grec/turc*	*livre chypriote f*

Country/ Pays	Capital/ Capitale	Inhabitant/ Habitant	Official language/s langue/s officielle/s*	Currency/ Devise
Czech Republic	Prague	Czech	Czech	koruna
République tchèque f	Prague	Tchèque mf	tchèque	couronne f
Denmark	Copenhagen	Dane	Danish	Danish krone
Danemark m	Copenhague	Danois m	danois	krone danoise f
Djibouti	Djibouti	Djibuti/Djibutian	Arabic/French	Djibouti franc
Djibouti m	Djibouti	Djiboutien m	arabe/français	franc de Djibouti m
Dominica	Roseau	Dominican	English	East Caribbean dollar
Dominique f	Roseau	Dominiquais m	anglais	dollar antillais m
Dominican Republic	Santo Domingo	Dominican	Spanish	Dominican peso
République dominicaine f	Santo Domingo	Dominicain m	espagnol	peso dominicain m
Ecuador	Quito	Ecuadorian/ Ecuadoran	Spanish	sucre
Équateur m	Quito	Équatorien m	espagnol	sucre m
Egypt	Cairo	Egyptian	Arabic	Egyptian pound
Égypte f	Le Caire	Égyptien m	arabe	livre égyptienne f
El Salvador	San Salvador	Salvadoran/ Salvadorean	Spanish	colón
Salvador m	San Salvador	Salvadorien m	espagnol	colón m
England	London	Englishman/-woman	English	Sterling pound
Angleterre f	Londres	Anglais m	anglais	livre sterling f
Equatorial Guinea	Malabo	Equatorial Guinean	Spanish	C.F.A. franc
Guinée équatoriale f	Malabo	Guinéen équatorial m	espagnol	franc CFA m
Estonia	Tallinn	Estonian	Estonian	kroon
Estonie f	Tallinn	Estonien m	estonien	kroon f
Ethiopia	Addis Ababa	Ethiopian	Amharic	birr
Éthiopie f	Addis-Abeba	Éthiopien m	Amharic	birr m
Fiji	Suva	Fijian	English	Fiji dollar
Fidji f pl	Suva	Fidjien m	anglais	dollar fidjien m
Finland	Helsinki	Finn	Finnish	markka
Finlande f	Helsinki	Finlandais m	finlandais	markka m
France	Paris	Frenchman/woman	French	French franc
France f	Paris	Français m	français	franc français m
Gabon	Libreville	Gabonese	French	C.F.A. franc
Gabon m	Libreville	Gabonais m	français	franc CFA m
Gambia	Banjul	Gambian	English	dalasi
Gambie f	Banjul	Gambien m	anglais	dalasi m
Georgia	Tbilisi	Georgian	Georgian	lari
Géorgie f	Tbilissi	Géorgien m	géorgien	lari m
Germany	Berlin	German	German	Deutsche Mark
Allemagne f	Berlin	Allemand m	allemand	Deutsche Mark m
Ghana	Accra	Ghanaian	English	cedi
Ghana m	Accra	Ghanéen m	anglais	cédi m
Greece	Athens	Greek	Greek	drachma
Grèce f	Athènes	Grec m	grec	drachme m
Grenada	St. George's	Grenadian	English	East Caribbean dollar
Grenade f	St. George's	Grenadin m	anglais	dollar antillais m
Guatemala	Guatemala City	Guatemalan	Spanish	quetzal
Guatemala m	Guatemala City	Guatémaltèque mf	espagnol	quetzal m

Country/ *Pays*	Capital/ *Capitale*	Inhabitant/ *Habitant*	Official language/s *langue/s officielle/s**	Currency/ *Devise*
Guinea	Conakry	Guinean	French	Guinean franc
Guinée f	*Conakry*	*Guinéen m*	*français*	*franc guinéen f*
Guinea-Bissau	Bissau	from Guinea-Bissau	Spanish	Guinea-Bissau peso
Guinée-Bissau f	*Bissau*	*de Guinée-Bissau*	*espagnol*	*peso de Guinée-Bissau m*
Guyana	Georgetown	Guyanese/Guyanan	English	Guyana dollar
Guyane f	*Georgetown*	*Guyanais m*	*anglais*	*dollar guyanais m*
Haiti	Port-au-Prince	Haitian	French	gourde
Haïti m	*Port-au-Prince*	*Haïtien m*	*français*	*gourde f*
Holland (also Netherlands, The)	Amsterdam/ The Hague	Dutchman/-woman Netherlander	Dutch	guilder
Pays Bas, Les m pl	*Amsterdam/La Haye*	*Hollandais/ Néerlandais m*	*hollandais/ néerlandais*	*florin m*
Honduras	Tegucigalpa	Honduran	Spanish	lempira
Honduras m	*Tegucigalpa*	*Hondurien m*	*espagnol*	*lempira m*
Hong Kong	Victoria	from Hong Kong	English	Hong Kong dollar
Hong Kong f	*Victoria*	*d'Hong Kong*	*anglais*	*dollar de Hong Kong m*
Hungary	Budapest	Hungarian	Hungarian	forint
Hongrie f	*Budapest*	*Hongrois m*	*hongrois*	*forint m*
Iceland	Reykjavik	Icelander	Icelandic	krona
Islande f	*Reykjavik*	*Islandais m*	*islandais*	*krona f*
India	New Delhi	Indian	Hindi/English	Indian rupee
Inde f	*New Delhi*	*Indien m*	*hindi/anglais*	*roupie indienne f*
Indonesia	Jakarta	Indonesian	Indonesia	Indonesian rupiah
Indonésie f	*Djakarta*	*Indonésien m*	*indonésien*	*roupie indonésienne f*
Iran	Tehran/Teheran	Iranian	Iranian	rial
Iran m	*Téhéran*	*Iranien m*	*iranien*	*rial m*
Iraq (also Irak)	Baghdad	Iraqi/Iraki	Arabic	Iraqi dinar/Iraki dinar
Iraq (also Irak) m	*Bagdad*	*Iraquien/Irakien m*	*arabe*	*dinar iraquien m dinar irakien m*
Israel	Jerusalem	Israeli	Hebrew/Arabic	shekel
Israël m	*Jérusalem*	*Israélien m*	*hébreu/arabe*	*shekel m*
Italy	Rome	Italian	Italian	lira
Italie f	*Rome*	*Italien m*	*italien*	*lire f*
Jamaica	Kingston	Jamaican	English	Jamica dollar
Jamaïque f	*Kingston*	*Jamaïquain/Jamaïcain m*	*anglais*	*dollar jamaïcain m*
Japan	Tokyo	Japanese	Japanese	yen
Japon m	*Tokyo*	*Japonais m*	*japonais*	*yen m*
Jordan	Amman	Jordanian	Arabic	Jordan dinar
Jordanie f	*Amman*	*Jordanien m*	*arabe*	*dinar jordanien m*
Kazakhstan	Alma-Ata	Kazakh/Kazak	Kazakh	rouble
Kazakhstan m	*Alma-Ata*	*Kazakh mf*	*Kazakh*	*rouble/ruble m*
Kenya	Nairobi	Kenyan	Swahili/English	shilling
Kenya m	*Nairobi*	*Kényen m*	*swahili/anglais*	*shilling m*
Korea, North	Pyongyang	North Korean	Korean	won
Corée du Nord f	*Pyongyang*	*Nord-Coréen m*	*coréen*	*won m*
Korea, South	Seoul	South Korean	Korean	won
Corée du Sud f	*Séoul*	*Sud-Coréen m*	*coréen*	*won m*
Kuwait	Kuwait City	Kuwaiti	Arabic	Kuwaiti dinar
Koweït m	*Koweït City*	*Koweïtien m*	*arabe*	*dinar koweïtien m*

Country/ _Pays_	Capital/ _Capitale_	Inhabitant/ _Habitant_	Official language/s _langue/s officielle/s*_	Currency/ _Devise_
Kyrgyzstan	Bishkek	Kyrgyz	Kyrgyz	som
Kyrghyzstan m	_Bichkek_	_du Kyrghyzstan_	_kyrgyz_	_som m_
Laos	Vientiane	Laotian	Lao	kip
Laos m	_Vientiane_	_Laotien m_	_laotien_	_kip m_
Latvia	Riga	Latvian	Latvian	lats
Lettonie f	_Riga_	_Letton m_	_letton_	_lats m_
Lebanon	Beirut	Lebanese	Arabic	Lebanese pound
Liban m	_Beyrouth_	_Libanais m_	_arabe_	_livre libanaise f_
Lesotho	Maseru	Mosotho/Basotho	Sotho/English	loti
Lesotho m	_Masaru_	_du Lesotho_	_sotho/anglais_	_loti m_
Liberia	Monrovia	Liberian	English	Liberian dollar
Libéria m	_Monrovia_	_Libérien m_	_anglais_	_dollar libérien m_
Libya	Tripoli	Libyan	Arabic	Libyan dinar
Libye f	_Tripoli_	_Libyen m_	_arabe_	_dinar libyen m_
Liechtenstein	Vaduz	Liechtensteiner	German	Swiss franc
Liechtenstein m	_Vaduz_	_du Liechtenstein_	_allemand_	_franc suisse m_
Lithuania	Vilnius	Lithuanian	Lithuanian	litas
Lituanie f	_Vilnius_	_Lituanien m_	_lituanien_	_litas m_
Luxembourg	Luxembourg	Luxemburger	French/German	Luxembourg franc
Luxembourg m	_Luxembourg_	_Luxembourgeois m_	_français/allemand_	_franc luxembourgeois m_
Macedonia	Skopje	Macedonian	Macedonian	dinar
Macédoine f	_Skopje_	_Macédonien m_	_macédonien_	_dinar m_
Madagascar	Antananarivo	Madagascan	Malagasy/French	Malagasy franc
Madagascar f	_Tananarive_	_Malgache mf_	_malgache/français_	_franc malgache m_
Malawi	Lilongwe	Malawian	English	kwacha
Malawi m	_Lilongwe_	_Malawien m_	_anglais_	_kwacha m_
Malaysia	Kuala Lumpur	Malaysian/Malay	Malay	Malaysian ringgit
Malaisie f	_Kuala Lumpur_	_Malaisien m_	_malais_	_ringgit malaisien m_
Maldives	Malé	Maldivian	Divehi	Maldivian rupee
Maldives f pl	_Malé_	_des Maldives_	_divehi_	_roupie des Maldives f_
Mali	Bamako	Malian	French	C.F.A. franc
Mali m	_Bamako_	_Malien m_	_français_	_franc CFA m_
Malta	Valletta	Maltese	Maltese/English	Maltese pound
Malte f	_La Valette_	_Maltais m_	_maltais/anglais_	_livre maltaise f_
Mauritania	Nouakchott	Mauritanian	Arabic/French	ouguiya
Mauritanie f	_Nouakchott_	_Mauritanien m_	_arabe/français_	_ouguija m_
Mauritius	Port Louis	Mauritian	English/French	Mauritian rupee
Île Maurice f	_Port Louis_	_Mauricien m_	_anglais/français_	_roupie mauricienne f_
Mexico	Mexico City	Mexican	Spanish	peso
Mexique m	_Mexico_	_Mexicain m_	_espagnol_	_peso m_
Moldova	Kishinev	Moldovan	Romanian Rumanian	leu
Moldavie f	_Kichinev_	_Moldave mf_	_roumain_	_leu m_
Monaco	Monaco	Monegasque	French	French franc
Monaco m	_Monaco_	_Monégasque mf_	_français_	_franc français m_
Mongolia	Ulaanbaatar (Ulan Bator)	Mongolian	Khalkha/Mongol	tugrik
Mongolie f	_Oulan Bator_	_Mongol m_	_khalkha/mongol_	_tugrik m_
Montenegro	Titograd	Montenegrin	Serbo-Croat	dinar
Monténégro m	_Titograd_	_Monténégrin m_	_serbo-croate_	_dinar m_
Morocco	Rabat	Moroccan	Arabic/French	dirham
Maroc m	_Rabat_	_Marocain m_	_arabe/français_	_dirham m_
Mozambique	Maputo	Mozambican	Portuguese	metical
Mozambique m	_Maputo_	_Mozambicain m_	_portugais_	_metical m_

Country/ Pays	Capital/ Capitale	Inhabitant/ Habitant	Official language/s langue/s officielle/s*	Currency/ Devise
Myanmar	Yangon (Rangoon)	Burmese	Burmese	kyat
Birmanie f	Yangon (Rangoon)	Birman m	birman	kyat m
Namibia	Windhoek	Namibian	English/Afrikaans	Namibian dollar
Namibie f	Windhoek	Namibien m	anglais/afrikaans	dollar namibien m
Nepal	Kathmandu	Nepalese/Nepali	Nepali	Nepali rupee
Népal m	Katmandou/ Katmandu	Népalais m	népalais	roupie népalaise f
Netherlands, The (also Holland)	Amsterdam/ The Hague	Dutchman/-woman Netherlander	Dutch	guilder
Pays Bas, Les m pl	Amsterdam/La Haye	Hollandais/ Néerlandais m	hollandais/ néerlandais	florin m
New Zealand	Wellington	New Zealander	English/Maori	New Zealand dollar
Nouvelle-Zélande f	Wellington	Néo-Zélandais m	anglais/maori	dollar néo-zélandais m
Nicaragua	Managua	Nicaraguan	Spanish	cordoba
Nicaragua m	Managua	Nicaraguayen m	espagnol	cordoba f
Niger	Niamey	Nigerian	French	C.F.A. franc
Niger m	Niamey	Nigérien m	français	franc CFA m
Nigeria	Abuja	Nigerian	English	naira
Nigéria m	Abuja	Nigérien m	anglais	naira m
Northern Ireland	Belfast	Irishman/-woman	Irish Gaelic/ English	Sterling pound
Irlande du Nord f	Belfast	Irlandais m	gaélique irlandais/ anglais	livre sterling f
Norway	Oslo	Norse (only pl)	Norwegian	Norwegian krone
Norvège f	Oslo	Norvégien m	norvégien	krone norvégienne f
Oman	Muscat	Omani	Arabic	Omani rial
Oman m	Mascate	Omanais m	arabe	rial oman m
Pakistan	Islamabad	Pakistani	Urdu/English	Pakistan rupee
Pakistan m	Islamabad	Pakistanais m	Ourdi/anglais	roupie pakistanaise f
Panama	Panama City	Panamanian	Spanish	balboa
Panama m	Panama	Panaméen m	espagnol	balboa m
Papua New Guinea	Port Moresby	from Papua New Guinea, Papuan	English	kina
Papouasie-Nouvelle Guinée f	Port Moresby	de Papouasie-Nouvelle Guinée	anglais	kina m
Paraguay	Asunción	Paraguayan	Spanish	guarani
Paraguay m	Asunción	Paraguayen m	espagnol	guarani m
Peru	Lima	Peruvian	Spanish/Quechua	nuevo sol
Pérou m	Lima	Péruvien m	espagnol/quechua	sol m
Philippines	Manila	Philippine/Filipino	Philipino/English	Philippine peso
Philippines f pl	Manille	Philippin m	philippin/anglais	peso philippin m
Poland	Warsaw	Pole	Polish	zloty
Pologne f	Varsovie	Polonais m	polonais	zloty m
Portugal	Lisbon	Portuguese	portuguese	escudo
Portugal m	Lisbonne	Portugais m	portugais	escudo m
Puerto Rico	San Juan	Puerto Rican	Spanish/English	U.S. dollar
Porto Rico m	San Juan	Portoricain m	espagnol/anglais	dollar US m
Qatar	Doha	Qatari	Arabic	riyal
Qatar m	Doha	du Qatar	arabe	riyal m

Country/ *Pays*	Capital/ *Capitale*	Inhabitant/ *Habitant*	Official language/s *langue/s officielle/s**	Currency/ *Devise*
Republic of Ireland (also Eire)	Dublin	Irishman/-woman	Irish Gaelic/ English	Irish pound (also punt)
République d'Irlande f (also Eire)	*Dublin*	*Irlandais m*	*gaélique irlandais/ anglais*	*livre irlandaise f*
Romania/ Rumania	Bucharest	Romanian/Rumanian	Romanian	Romanian leu
Roumanie f	*Bucarest*	*Roumain m*	*roumain*	*leu roumain m*
Russia	Moscow	Russian	Russian	rouble
Russie f	*Moscou*	*Russe mf*	*russe*	*rouble/ruble m*
Rwanda	Kigali	Rwandese	French/ Kinyarwanda	Rwanda franc
Ruanda/Rwanda m	*Kigali*	*Ruandais/Rwandais m*	*français/ kinyaruandais*	*franc ruandais m franc rwandais m*
Saint Lucia	Castries	Saint Lucian	English	East Caribbean dollar
Sainte-Lucie f	*Castries*	*de Sainte-Lucie*	*anglais*	*dollar antillais m*
Saint Vincent and the Grenadines	Kingstown	Vincentian	English	East Caribbean dollar
Saint-Vincent et Grenades m pl	*Kingstown*	*de Saint-Vincent*	*anglais*	*dollar antillais m*
San Marino	San Marino	San Marinese	Italian	Italian lira
Saint-Marin m	*Saint-Marin*	*de Saint-Marin*	*italien*	*lire italienne f*
Saudi Arabia	Riyadh	Saudi/Saudi Arabian	Arabic	riyal
Arabie Saoudite f	*Riyad/Riad*	*Saoudien m*	*arabe*	*riyal m*
Scotland	Edinburgh	Scot, Scotsman/-woman	English	Sterling pound
Écosse f	*Edimbourg*	*Écossais m*	*anglais*	*livre sterling f*
Senegal	Dakar	Senegalese	French	C.F.A. franc
Sénégal m	*Dakar*	*Sénégalais m*	*français*	*franc CFA m*
Seychelles	Victoria	Seychellois/Seselwa	English/French/ Creole	Seychelles rupee
Seychelles f pl	*Victoria*	*des Seychelles*	*anglais/français/ créole*	*roupie des Seychelles f*
Sierra Leone	Freetown	Sierra Leonean	English	leone
Sierra Léone m	*Freetown*	*Sierra Léonais m*	*anglais*	*leone m*
Singapore	Singapore	Singaporean	Chinese/Malay Tamil/English	Singapore dollar
Singapour m	*Singapour*	*Singapourien m*	*chinois/malais tamoul/anglais*	*dollar de Singapour m*
Slovakia	Bratislava	Slovak	Slovak	Slovak koruna
Slovaquie f	*Bratislava*	*Slovaque mf*	*slovaque*	*koruna slovaque f*
Slovenia	Ljubljana	Slovenian/Slovene	Slovene	tolar
Slovénie f	*Ljubljana*	*Slovène mf*	*slovène*	*tolar m*
Somalia	Mogadishu	Somali/Somalian	Somali/Arabic	Somali shilling
Somalie f	*Mogadiscio*	*Somalien m*	*somali/anglais*	*shilling somalien m*
South Africa	Pretoria	South African	Afrikaans/English	rand
Afrique du Sud f	*Pretoria*	*Sud-Africain m*	*afrikaans/anglais*	*rand m*
Spain	Madrid	Spaniard	Spanish	peseta
Espagne f	*Madrid*	*Espagnol m*	*espagnol*	*peseta f*
Sri Lanka	Colombo	Sri Lankan	Sinhalese/Tamil/ English	Sri Lanka rupee
Sri Lanka m	*Colombo*	*Sri-Lankais m*	*cingalais/tamoul/ anglais*	*roupie cingalaise f*
Sudan	Khartoum	Sudanese	Arabic	Sudanese pound
Soudan m	*Khartoum*	*Soudanais m*	*arabe*	*livre soudanaise f*

Country/ *Pays*	Capital/ *Capitale*	Inhabitant/ *Habitant*	Official language/s *langue/s officielle/s* *	Currency/ *Devise*
Suriname *Surinam m*	Paramaribo *Paramaribo*	Surinamese *Surinamais m*	Dutch/English *hollandais/ néerlandais/anglais*	Suriname guilder *florin du Surinam m*
Swaziland *Swaziland m*	Mbabane *Mbabane*	Swazi *Swazi m*	Swazi/English *swazi/anglais*	lilangeni *lilangeni m*
Sweden *Suède f*	Stockholm *Stockholm*	Swede *Suédois m*	Swedish *suédois*	Swedish krona *krone suédoise f*
Switzerland *Suisse f*	Bern *Berne*	Swiss *Suisse mf*	French/German/ Italian *français/allemand/ italian*	Swiss franc *franc suisse m*
Syria *Syrie f*	Damascus *Damas*	Syrian *Syrien m*	Arabic *arabe*	Syrian pound *livre syrienne f*
Taiwan *Taïwan m*	Taipei *Taipei/Taipeh*	Taiwanese *Taiwanais m*	Mandarin/Chinese *mandarin/chinois*	Taiwan dollar *dollar de Taïwan m*
Tajikistan *Tadjikistan m*	Dushanbe *Duchambe*	Tajik *Tadjik mf*	Tajik *Tadjik*	rouble *rouble/ruble m*
Tanzania *Tanzanie f*	Dar es Salaam *Dar es Salaam*	Tanzanian *Tanzanien m*	Swahili/English *swahili/anglais*	Tanzanian shilling *shilling tanzanien m*
Thailand *Thaïlande f*	Bangkok *Bangkok*	Thai *Thaïlandais m*	Thai *thaï*	baht *baht m*
Togo *Togo m*	Lomé *Lomé*	Togolese *Togolais m*	French *français*	C.F.A. franc *franc CFA m*
Trinidad and Tobago *Trinité-et-Tobago f*	Port of Spain *Port of Spain*	Trinidadian/ Tobagoan/ Tobagodian *Trinidadien m de la Trinité*	English *anglais*	Trinidad and Tobago dollar *dollar de Trinité-et-Tobago m*
Tunisia *Tunisie f*	Tunis *Tunis*	Tunisian *Tunisien m*	Arabic *arabe*	dinar *dinar m*
Turkey *Turquie f*	Ankara *Ankara*	Turk *Turc m*	Turkish *turc*	Turkish lira *lire turque f*
Turkmenistan *Turkménistan m*	Ashkhabad *Achkabad*	Turkmen *Turkmène mf*	Turkmen *turkmène*	manat *manat m*
Uganda *Ouganda m*	Kampala *Kampala*	Ugandan *Ougandais m*	Swahili/English *swahili/anglais*	Uganda shilling *shilling ougandais m*
Ukraine *Ukraine f*	Kiev *Kiev*	Ukrainian *Ukrainien m*	Ukrainian *ukrainien*	karbovanet *karbovanet m*
United Arab Emirates *Émirats Arabes Unis m pl*	Abu Dhabi *Abou-Dhabi*	from the United Arab Emirates *des Émirats Arabes Unis*	Arabic *arabe*	dirham *dirham m*
United Kingdom *Royaume Uni m*	London *Londres*	Briton *Britannique mf*	English *anglais*	Sterling pound *livre sterling f*
United States of America *États-Unis d'Amérique m pl*	Washington, D.C. *Washington, D.C.*	American *Américain m*	English *anglais*	dollar (dol.) *dollar (dol.) m*
Uruguay *Uruguay m*	Montevideo *Montevideo*	Uruguayan *Uruguayen m*	Spanish *espagnol*	peso *peso m*
Uzbekistan *Ouzbékistan m*	Tashkent *Tachkent*	Uzbek *Ouzbek m*	Uzbek *ouzbek*	rouble *rouble/ruble m*

Country/ *Pays*	Capital/ *Capitale*	Inhabitant/ *Habitant*	Official language/s *langue/s officielle/s* *	Currency/ *Devise*
Venezuela	Caracas	Venezuelan	Spanish	bolivar
Vénézuela m	*Caracas*	*Vénézuélien m*	*espagnol*	*bolivar m*
Vietnam	Hanoi	Vietnamese	Vietnamese	dong
Viêt Nam m	*Hanoï*	*Vietnamien m*	*vietnamien*	*dong m*
Wales	Cardiff	Welshman/-woman	English/Welsh	Sterling pound
Pays de Galles m	*Cardiff*	*Gallois m*	*anglais/gallois*	*livre sterling f*
Yemen	Sanaa	Yemeni	Arabic	Yemeni dinar
Yémen m	*Sanaa*	*Yéménite mf*	*arabe*	*dinar yéménite m*
Yugoslavia	Belgrade	Yugoslav	Serbo-Croat	dinar
Yougoslavie f (ex-~)	*Belgrade*	*Yougoslave mf*	*serbo-croate*	*dinar m*
Zaïre	Kinshasha	Zaïrese/Zairean	French	zaïre
Zaïre m	*Kinshasha*	*Zaïrois m*	*français*	*zaïre m*
Zambia	Lusaka	Zambian	English	kwacha
Zambie f	*Lusaka*	*Zambien m*	*anglais*	*kwacha m*
Zimbabwe	Harare	Zimbabwean	English	Zimbabwe dollar
Zimbabwe m	*Harare*	*Zimbabwéen m*	*anglais*	*dollar du Zimbabwe m*

* All languages listed in this table are masculine/Toutes les langues inclues dans ce tableau sont masculins

Cardinal and ordinal numbers/Les nombres cardinaux et ordinaux

Cardinal Cardinaux	English anglais	French français	Ordinal Ordinaux	French français	English anglais
1	one	un	1st	premier	first
2	two	deux	2nd	deuxième	second
3	three	trois	3rd	troisième	third
4	four	quatre	4th	quatrième	fourth
5	five	cinq	5th	cinquième	fifth
6	six	six	6th	sixième	sixth
7	seven	sept	7th	septième	seventh
8	eight	huit	8th	huitième	eighth
9	nine	neuf	9th	neuvième	ninth
10	ten	dix	10th	dixième	tenth
11	eleven	onze	11th	onzième	eleventh
12	twelve	douze	12th	douzième	twelfth
13	thirteen	treize	13th	treizième	thirteenth
14	fourteen	quatorze	14th	quatorzième	fourteenth
15	fifteen	quinze	15th	quinzième	fifteenth
16	sixteen	seize	16th	seizième	sixteenth
17	seventeen	dix-sept	17th	dix-septième	seventeenth
18	eighteen	dix-huit	18th	dix-huitième	eighteenth
19	nineteen	dix-neuf	19th	dix-neuvième	nineteenth
20	twenty	vingt	20th	vingtième	twentieth
21	twenty-one	vingt et un	21st	vingt et unième	twenty-first
22	twenty-two	vingt-deux	22nd	vingt-deuxième	twenty-second
23	twenty-three	vingt-trois	23th	vingt-troisième	twenty-third
24	twenty-four	vingt-quatre	24th	vingt-quatrième	twenty-fourth
25	twenty-five	vingt-cinq	25th	vingt-cinquième	twenty-fifth
30	thirty	trente	30th	trentième	thirtieth
40	forty	quarante	40th	quarantième	fortieth
50	fifty	cinquante	50th	cinquantième	fiftieth
60	sixty	soixante	60th	soixantième	sixtieth
70	seventy	soixante-dix	70th	soixante-dixième	seventieth
80	eighty	quatre-vingts	80th	quatre-vingtième	eightieth
90	ninety	quatre-vingts-dix	90th	quatre-vingt-dixième	ninetieth
100	one hundred	cent	100th	centième	one hundredth
101	one hundred and one	cent un	101st	cent et unième	one hundred and first
156	one hundred and fifty-six	cent cinquante-six	156th	cent cinquante-sixième	one hundred and fifty-sixth
200	two hundred	deux cents	200th	deux centième	two hundredth
300	three hundred	trois cents	300th	trois centième	three hundredth
400	four hundred	quatre cents	400th	quatre centième	four hundredth
1 000	one thousand	mille	1 000th	millième	one thousandth
1 001	one thousand and one	mille un	1 001st	mille et unième	one thousand and first
1 247	one thousand, two hundred and forty-seven	mille deux cent quarante-sept	1 247th	mille deux cent quarante-septième	one thousand, two hundred and forty-seventh

Cardinal *Cardinaux*	English *anglais*	French *français*	Ordinal *Ordinaux*	French *français*	English *anglais*
2 000	two thousand	deux mille	2 000th	deux millième	two thousandth
3 000	three thousand	trois mille	3 000th	trois millième	three thousandth
10 000	ten thousand	dix mille	10 000th	dix millième	ten thousandth
20 000	twenty thousand	vingt mille	20 000th	vingt millième	twenty thousandth
100 000	one hundred thousand	cent mille	100 000th	cent millième	one hundred thousandth
200 000	two hundred thousand	deux cent mille	200 000th	deux cent millième	two hundred thousandth
325 863	three hundred and twenty-five thousand, eight hundred and sixty-three	trois cent vingt-cinq mille huit cent soixante-trois	225 863rd	deux cent vingt-cinq mille huit cent soixante troisième	two hundred and twenty-five thousand, eight hundred and sixty-third
1 000 000	one million	un million	1 000 000th	millionième	one millionth
1 739 412	one million, seven hundred and thirty-nine thousand, four hundred and twelve	un million sept trente-neuf mille quatre cent douze			
10 000 000	ten million(s)	dix millions			
100 000 000	one hundred million(s)	cent millions			
1 000 000 000	one thousand million(s) *(UK)* (one billion *US*)	un milliard			
1 000 000 000 000	one billion *(UK)* (one trillion *US*)	un trillion			